The Norton Anthology of World Masterpieces

EXPANDED EDITION

VOLUME 2

D0022101

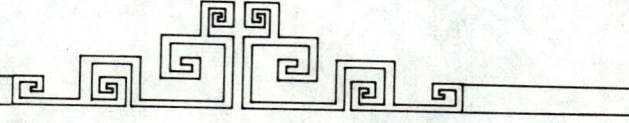

The Norton Anthology
of World Masterpieces

EXPANDED EDITION

Maynard Mack, *General Editor*
STERLING PROFESSOR OF ENGLISH EMERITUS,
YALE UNIVERSITY

VOLUME 2

1650 to the Present

W·W·NORTON & COMPANY · *New York* · *London*

The text of this book is composed in Electra, with display type set in Bernhard
Modern. Composition by Maple-Vail Book Manufacturing Group. Manufacturing by R. R.
Donnelley. Book design by Antonina Krass.

Cover painting is *Self-Portrait with Monkey* (1940) by Frida Kahlo. Private collection.
Reproduced by courtesy of Art Resource, NY.

ISBN 0-393-96348-9 Vol. II-paper

W.W. Norton & Company, Inc., 500 Fifth Avenue, New York, N.Y. 10110
W.W. Norton & Company Ltd., 10 Coptic Street, London WC1A 1PU

4 5 6 7 8 9 0

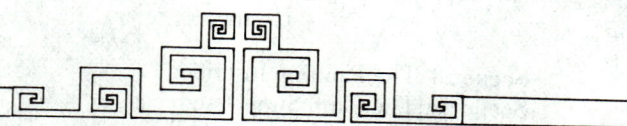

Contents

Part II   1800 to 1900

Urdu Lyric Poetry in North India   1051

Realism, Symbolism, and European Realities   1061

PART III

The Twentieth Century: Self and Other in Global Context

Preface

In 1956, the first edition of this anthology brought to college and university courses in literature the option of a more spacious experience. More spacious in content because it was not confined to English or American literature but embraced the entire literature of the West and ranged in time from the Old Testament and Homer to Joyce, Brecht, Faulkner, Lorca, and Camus. More spacious likewise in purpose because its aim was not simply, as in older books, to place the individual work in its historical and authorial contexts but to penetrate and display as far as possible the inward complexity of structure and the outward reach into the realities of our common life that empower such works to inform and please through so many generations, even centuries.

Today, guided by our own broader classroom experience, much generous counsel from our readers, and the expertise and hard work of several added editorial associates, we place before you this Expanded Edition of *The Norton Anthology of World Masterpieces*. With very few exceptions it contains all that the Sixth Edition (1992) contains; it adds, however, to the masterpieces of the Western tradition some two thousand pages of major works by major artists of Africa, the Arab countries of the Middle East, Israel, the Caribbean, China, Egypt, India, Japan, native America, and the Persia that became Iran. In its scope and presentation, the Expanded Edition is very much a new book.

It goes without saying that no anthology, however vast, can do full justice to the diversity and depth of the literatures of all places and all times. The basic principle of this anthology from its beginnings has been to offer works having recognized authority in their own languages and cultures, but also in the judgment of a larger world. We have sought to maintain that principle here, in the conviction that students of all dispositions and capacities retain more of value from an acquaintance of some depth with a few literatures than from a shrapnel burst of many. Though there is no perfect resolution of this dilemma, we believe from much trial and error that our choice is the wiser of the two.

It also goes without saying that no course in literature enrolling live students can expect them to consume without severe intellectual convulsions more than a reasonable fraction of what is now available between the covers of the original Sixth Edition, or of this its somewhat chubbier sibling. Yet those teachers seeking a wider choice among non-Western works than the regular Sixth Edition provides will meet, we think, with all or much of what they seek in this Expanded Edition: a fascinating assembly of "world masterpieces," presented not in bits and pieces but, as is the Norton custom, in complete or generous selections, chosen, edited, annotated, and explicated by a top authority in each field.

Whether to use the standard or expanded edition will be determined by the preference of the teacher, the capacity and constituency of the class, and the aims of the course. Either choice is capable of honoring equally the two-sided challenge of intelligent education: that we grow chiefly by encounters with what is Other than ourselves, the unfamiliar experience, event, or thought that unsettles our securities and clichés; but also—and it is a "but also" of large significance—that we best assimilate the unfamiliar by way of the familiar. To know what makes a mule we need some idea of a horse and a jenny.

Turning now specifically to this Expanded Edition, we want to clarify some important points about its character and contents.

Each volume consists of three parts. And since most of the terms customarily used in categorizing Western literatures—Middle Ages, Renaissance, Enlightenment, Romanticism, and the like—have little or no relevance when applied elsewhere, our parts are now temporally determined. In Volume 1 they reach from the beginnings at around 2500 B.C. to A.D. 100, from 100 to 1500, and from 1500 to 1650; in Volume 2, from 1650 to 1800, 1800 to 1900, and 1900 to the present. During some of these periods, it is important to add—notably the period that Western parlance assigns to "The Renaissance" and again during parts of the periods denoted by "The Enlightenment" and "Romanticism"—selections from the non-Western literatures diminish because in any culture the upwellings of creativity that produce works of great stature obey no time schedule.

Within the volumes themselves we follow not a strict chronological sequence but rather an order that blends time's happenstance with pedagogical common sense. As you know from your experience in the classroom and we know from ours, it is folly to subject unsuspecting students (some of them already bewildered by the controversies surrounding "multiculturalism," others dug in to defend to the death some parochial point of view) to a strictly chronological succession of unrelated works from disparate and unfamiliar civilizations. It will remind them of nothing so much as the eating machine that force-feeds Charlie Chaplin in *Modern Times*, one strange dish slapped to his mouth to be replaced by another with such velocity that he all but strangles. The effect on Chaplin is acute indigestion; on students, intellectual nausea plus a hasty retreat from the subject and possibly from all future contacts with literature.

Mindful of this problem, and of the pedagogical difficulties involved in each part save the last, we have disposed our selections within "sweeps." These are continuities from a single cultural tradition enabling students to reach at least a modest familiarity with its characteristic forms of expression before moving on to the next. Admittedly, on some occasions this practice calls for difficult decisions. The placing of Petrarch, for instance. In strict chronology, he belongs with Boccaccio and Chaucer. Yet he speaks with a distinctly new voice and new concerns that give him more affinity with Erasmus and Machiavelli, Montaigne and Shakespeare, than with Chaucer. He can be read with his contemporaries as spokesman of a new era already forming, as new eras always do, in the heart of the old. Or he can be read with his successors—in our view more intelligibly—as precentor in a choir of voices for which his powerful individualism set the tone and mode. An equal difficulty arises with Rousseau. Should he be read in company with Voltaire, whose younger contemporary he was and who said of him wryly after their first and only meeting (anticipating much that was later to be called Romantic egoism): "That man has no talent for dialogue"? Or should he be read like Petrarch—and again, as we think, more intelligibly—in the vanguard of those whom his thought and example most inspired?

In this and all such instances, we consider that our first obligation is to the needs of the students. In that interest, we have broadened introductions, headnotes, and footnotes throughout the two volumes to facilitate cross-cultural comparison and have transformed the Instructor's Guide into a treasure-house of aids and resources, both print and electronic, to that end. We have supplied for each of our sweeps a map designed to facilitate understanding of the geographical settings of the several great civilizations whose master works these volumes offer. Likewise for each sweep, we have supplemented the map with a timeline clarifying the chronological relations of major works and events within the sweep. Informed use of these resources can generate fascinating classroom explorations of the impact of particular times, climes, and topographies on the characteristics of societies, individuals, and works of art.

You will also find here, prefacing most of our selections, brief glossaries for the pronunciation of unfamiliar words and names (a list of the phonetic equivalents we use is located on page xxxiii). These make no attempt at linguistic exactitude, even if that were possible. Their much humbler aim is to supply useable English approximations—approximations that are necessarily governed sometimes by convention and long use (as, say, with *Ghent*, early naturalized in English to rhyme with *tent*); sometimes by arbitrary compromise between the actual or supposed sound of the original and the sounds available or recognizable in modern English speech (as with Beowulf's people the Geats, to whose name the closest one can come in today's English is *Yay-ahts*). No one now alive can say with certainty exactly how the author of *Sir Gawain and the Green Knight* pronounced Uriel, the name he gives to Yvain's father at line 113. We can speak the name today only as it seems to us. Conversely, though we know for certain that he and his contemporaries pronounced his name *Bed-day*, few moderns would be able to identify from those sounds the author of the single most important source for the history of England in the Middle Ages, the Benedictine monk now known everywhere as the Venerable Bede. The finding of suitable English phonetic equivalents for foreign terms and names is as far from being an exact science as negotiating a mine field, and every step requires a judgment call involving risk. Nevertheless, if our efforts help even one student to feel more comfortable about speaking up in class or discussing a passage full of hard names with a classmate, the risk is worth it.

A final note on the sweeps. Though for the most part, as earlier stated, they bring you continuities from a single culture, we have allowed three exceptions, two minor and one major, again on practical grounds. The initial sweep of Volume 1, Part I, intentionally presents works from three different cultural traditions—Babylonian, Egyptian, Judaic—each among the oldest works that have come down to us in written form, each in its origins reaching well back into a preliterate past, yet accessible and still provocative at the end of the twentieth century. They exemplify what we mean by "world-class," and they assure any student that, bizarre as some of the world's literary traditions may seem on first contact, there is always something in them that reflects our common human nature, our common hopes, lusts, ideals, and fears, our common vulnerability to time and change. This lesson must be learned early if any course drawing on unfamiliar cultures is to succeed.

A similar drawing together of three different cultures—Arabian, Persian, Turkish—has been made in the fourth sweep of Volume 1, Part II, and for the same reasons. All three have a world-view in common and feed into each other with great effectiveness when contrasted and compared. The one *major* exception is made in Volume 2, Part III. Here we meet almost uniformly with a modern sensibility that can be recognized as global, or quasi-global, no matter how variably colored it may be in the individual case by nationality, ethnicity, and history. At this point, having outlived their usefulness, sweeps disappear.

The considerations of classroom practicality that impel us to favor sweeps over unmediated chronology have also impelled us to make the next sweep after the introductory one a continuity of Greek literature featuring Homer, Sappho, and the Greek playwrights. Reading this sequence early, parts of which many students know by hearsay and some by contact, builds their confidence and can elicit lively comparisons between *Gilgamesh* and the Greek epics, Egyptian poetry and Sappho, and the Greek and Judaic inheritances. Exploring these relationships lays a foundation for further comparisons with the distinctive qualities of the Chinese and Indian sweeps that immediately follow.

On similar grounds, we preserve in this Expanded Edition most of the mainly Western literature found in the Standard Edition of *The Norton Anthology of World Masterpieces*. Whatever our individual or ethnic associations may be, if we live in the United States it is important to understand the moral and intellectual sources of the country that we inhabit and that in some inescapable sense (even more so when we exercise our right to dissent from it) inhabits us. Though as a nation of immigrants we are continually in the process of redefining our collective life, that life for three centuries was defined primarily through ideas and experiences brought with them by immigrants from Britain and the countries of western and eastern Europe. This tradition constitutes the American half of such terms as African American, Asian American, German American, Hispanic American, Irish American, Italian American, Polish American, and the rest. So far as our collective life in this country has roots, these are to be found in the Western tradition, whose influence in the fabric of our everyday existence is best discovered by immersion in its recognized masterpieces of drama, poetry, and fiction.

Still, our central objective in this Expanded Edition is to encourage exploration of other traditions as well. As in the forest world the effect of roots is the production of spreading leaves and branches and the effect of spreading leaves and branches is the invigoration of roots, so in our human world the vigor of cultural traditions thrives rather from reaching out than from closing in. All over the planet there flourish faiths, fears, arts, and aspirations; needs and markets, likes and dislikes; racial, gender, and ethnic tensions—matters that our shrinking planet of airplanes, television, computer networks, and long-range nuclear missiles has made it materially important for us to know about as well as intellectually and spiritually foolish to ignore. Hostilities at all levels are usually first generated and then exacerbated by xenophobia ("fear of the stranger") and by the ease with which the unfamiliar book, picture, person, food, custom, costume, or skin color can be demonized. For this phobia the only cure is frequent and prolonged exposure to what is different from ourselves until the unfamiliar becomes familiar, the unaccustomed perspective brings more generous ways of seeing, and we discover how much there is still to learn about ourselves.

With these thoughts in mind, we welcome you to the great menu from multiple cuisines that awaits within. Here are twelve short novels, complete, with large selections from eight more too massive to be printed in their entirety, among them *The Tale of Genji* from Japan and *Journey to the West* (more popularly known as *Monkey*) and *The Story of the Stone* (*Dream of the Red Chamber*) from China. Here also is short fiction of varying lengths, thirty stories in all, emigrating to our pages from native America, Arabia, Argentina, Austria, Canada, China, Colombia, Egypt, France, Germany, India, Israel, Japan, Nigeria, Russia, Senegal, South Africa, and the United States. And here, further, are twenty-five complete plays, including three Nō plays from Japan, Kalidasa's *Śakuntalā and the Ring of Recollection* from India, Tawfiq al-Hakim's delicious *The Sultan's Dilemma* from Egypt, Derek Walcott's *Dream on Monkey Mountain* from St. Lucia, Wole Soyinka's *Death and the King's Horseman* from Nigeria, plus a play-length section of K'ung Shang-jen's vast song-drama *The Peach Blossom Fan* from China.

As for poems long and short, we have brought you as many of the best as acceptable translations can be found for and space allows. In the long-poem genre—epic, heroic, chivalric, romantic—are four complete and eleven in selection, including the *Mahābhārata* of India and the great oral epic of Mali, the epic of *Son-Jara*. In the genre of the short poem—lyric, meditative, anecdotal—you will find more individual items than any course can use, representing African, Caribbean, Chinese, ancient Egyptian, Indian, Inuit, Israeli, Japanese, Mayan, Navajo, Persian, and Zuni poets as well as those of Europe and the United States. Nor, though we have had to be frugal in this area, have we neglected expository prose, wherever distinguished for its content or style. Major examples appear here from the Western traditions, but also from the *Analects* of Confucius, the meditations of Chuang Chou and T'ao Ch'ien, the epigrams of Bharthrhari, Ibn Ishaq's account of the prophet Muhammad, selections from the Koran itself, the diary of Sei Shōnagon (her "Pillow Book"), the essays of Yoshida Kenkō, the travels of Evliya Çelebi, the wonderfully sensitive observations of Tanizaki Jun'ichiro on "Shadows," and many more.

We cannot repeat too often that no anthology can replace the judgment of a teacher, who must appraise the makeup, ability, and possible areas of interest of the individual class together with the aims of the course and the time at her or his disposal. The opportunities in these pages for thought-provoking comparisons and contrasts of value systems, styles of living, habits of mind, lyric, narrative, and dramatic traditions and techniques are obvious and obviously inexhaustible. So are the opportunities for those fascinating but more speculative (and in the end never fully answerable) questions as to what aspects of a culture, ethnicity, race, or artistic tradition orient it toward some forms of self-expression and away from others. Why has the Chinese outlook and experience led to some of the world's finest songs and lyrics but never to an epic poem? What exactly was there in the world-view of ancient India and ancient Israel that left no room for the development of a tragic drama, yet created, in Israel, a religious literature that is among the wonders of the world and, in India, a sculpture and architecture that have few peers?

If the decision finally taken is to approach the least-known literatures through the somewhat more accessible and to allow each literature space enough and time to show its qualities before pressing on to the next, you will be well served by our sweeps. If the decision leans instead toward a program of topics, genres, themes, or parallel situations, you will discover in our Instructor's Guide many helpful considerations, as indicated above. As our arrangement of materials indicates, we ourselves tend to favor the former procedure, finding that it results in a surer grasp by students of temporal and geographical relationships and thus provides more frames of reference by which individual works are clarified and made memorable. We cheerfully agree, however, that any strategy that works is worth pursuing, since we all share the same objective: to widen our students' understanding along with our own, so that on returning home they and we may look within ourselves as well as around the globe, and then, as a poet of our day once put it in a different context, "know the place for the first time."

We want to remember in closing John C. McGalliard, gentleman, great scholar, and loyal friend, whose knowledge of medieval literature in all languages was profound and profoundly valuable to this anthology. The third of the founding editors to be taken from us, he died in the early summer of 1993. We pay tribute also to Barbara Stoler Miller, who, until her death in 1993, chaired the Department of Oriental Studies at Barnard College. A dedicated teacher, scholar, and translator, she is universally known for her masterly translations of Sanskrit poetry and drama, including *The Bhagavad-Gītā* and the plays of Kālidāsa. Her inspiration and great learning guided us in planning our selections from Indian literature, and we are deeply grateful for her wise and generous advice. We also remember here with greatest affection and admiration Barry K. Wade, former student of one of us, who quickly became a pillar of Norton publishing standards and the impresario of this anthology, most particularly this first Expanded Edition, which we dedicate to his memory. He died too young, after a long illness, in the spring of 1993.

On a far happier note, we wish to take this occasion to welcome six new colleagues in the editorship of this Expanded Edition. John Bierhorst (B.A., Cornell) is a writer, editor, and translator specializing in native American literature; Jerome Wright Clinton (Ph.D., Michigan) is Professor of Near Eastern Studies at Princeton University; Robert Lyons Danly (Ph.D., Yale) is Professor of Asian Languages and Cultures at the University of Michigan; F. Abiola Irele (Ph.D., Sorbonne) is Professor of African, French, and Comparative Literatures at The Ohio State University; Stephen Owen (Ph.D., Yale) is Professor of Chinese and Comparative Literature at Harvard University; Indira Peterson (Ph.D., Harvard) is Associate Professor and chair of the Asian Studies Program at Mount Holyoke College. Without them, this anthology would not be the flexible and innovative teaching instrument that it is.

The Editors

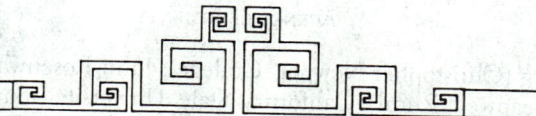

Acknowledgments

Among our many critics, advisers, and friends, the following were of special help in providing suggestions and corrections: Richard Adicks (University of Central Florida); Fawzia Afzal-Khan (Montclair State College); Ruth Albrecht (Lane Community College); Sarah Bahous Allen (North Georgia College); Tommaso Astarita (Georgetown University); Murtha Baca (Getty Art History Information Program); Donald M. Bahr (Arizona State University); Michael Beard (University of North Dakota); Paula Berggren (Bernard Baruch College—CUNY); Edith Blicksilver (Georgia Institute of Technology); Harold Boudreau (University of Massachusetts—Amherst); W. K. Buckley (Indiana University Northwest); Jerry Burns (Marian College); Victoria Carchidi (Massey University); Robert L. Casebeer (Southern Oregon State College); Thomas Cassidy (South Carolina State College); Robert W. Chambers (El Centro College); Roger Craik (Kent State University—Ashtabula); Jace Crouch (Michigan State University); Sara Cushing Smith (Piedmont Technical College); O. R. Dathorne (University of Kentucky); James Doan (Nova University); Caroline D. Eckhardt (Pennsylvania State University); Fidel Fajardo-Acosta (Creighton University); Joseph Fenley (St. Petersburg Junior College); Stephen D. Fox (Gallaudet University); Tidiane Gadio (Ohio State University); Bruce Golden (California State University—San Bernardino); Sharon L. Gravett (Valdosta State College); Cynthia A. Gravlee (University of Montevallo); Lynda Haas (Hillsborough Community College); Thomas Haberg (Northeastern Illinois University); Marjorie Hoskinson (Los Angeles Pierce College); Carolina Hospital (Miami-Dade Community College—Kendall Campus); Gail Houston (Brigham Young University); William Hutchings (University of Alabama at Birmingham); Alan Jacobs (Wheaton College); Jane Anderson Jones (Manatee Community College—South Campus); Martha A. Kallstrom (Georgia Southern University); Alan Kaufman (Bergen Community College); Andrew Knoedler (University of Colorado); Margaret Kouidis (Auburn University); Victoria Lague (Miami Dade Community College—Kendall Campus); Bernard Levine (Wayne State University); Murray Levith (Skidmore College); Sandra W. Lott (University of Montevallo); Thomas E. Luddy (Salem State College); Philip Lutgendorf (University of Iowa); Antonia MacDonald (Ohio State University); Victor Manfredi (Boston University); Iely B. Mohamed (Jackson State University); Maggie P. Monteverde (Belmont University); Michael Palencia-Roth (University of Illinois at Urbana-Champaign); Philip Pfatteicher (East Stroudsburg University); Mary Sue Ply (Southeastern Louisiana University); Michael I. Prochilo (Salem State College); Joseph Roesch (Onondaga Community College); Roberta

Rosenberg (Christopher Newport College); John Rosenwald (Beloit College); Treadwell Ruml (California State University—San Bernardino); John Paul Russo (University of Miami—Coral Gables); Francesca Santovetti (Georgetown University); Nina Scott (University of Massachusetts—Amherst); Lili Selden (University of Michigan); Jeanette Sordyl-Kibler (University of Michigan); Linda L. Strever (Pierce College); Robert H. Sykes (West Liberty State College); John S. Tanner (Brigham Young University); Dennis Tedlock (State University of New York—Buffalo); Cammy Thomas (Millsaps College); Diana E. Valdina (Cayuga County Community College); Sidney J. Vance (University of Montevallo); Janet A. Walker (Rutgers University); Benjamin R. Wiley (St. Petersburg Junior College—Clearwater Campus); Linda E. Yable (St. Petersburg Junior College—Clearwater Campus); Sape A. Zylstra (University of South Florida).

We would also like to thank the following people who contributed to the Sixth Edition of *The Norton Anthology of World Masterpieces*, which served as the core for this text: Tamara Agha-Jaffar (Kansas City Community College); Kerry Ahearn (Oregon State University); David Anderson (Texas A & M University); Denise Baker (University of North Carolina—Greensboro); William F. Belcher (University of North Texas); L. Michael Bell (University of Colorado); Ernest Bernhardt (Indiana University); Craig Bernthal (Fresno State University); Gene Blanton (Jacksonville State University); Betsy Bowden (Rutgers University—Camden); Max Braffett (Southwest Texas State University); Edythe Briggs (Santa Rosa Junior College); Gary Brodsky (Northeastern Illinois University); Byron Brown (Valdosta State College); James L. Brown (Kansas City Kansas Community College); Corbin S. Carnell (University of Florida); Michael Carson (University of Evansville); Rose-Ann Cecere (Broward Community College); John Cech (University of Florida); Howard Clarke (University of California—Santa Barbara); Stephen Cooper (Troy State University); T. A. Copeland (Youngstown State University); Walter Coppedge (Virginia Commonwealth University); Bill Crider (Alvin Community College); George Crosland (California State University—Chico); Lennet Daigle (Georgia Southwestern College); Charles Daniel (Valdosta State College); Rosemary DePaolo (Augusta State College); Joseph DeRocco (Bridgewater State College); Ronald DiLorenzo (St. Louis University); Brooks Dodson (University of North Carolina—Wilmington); Patricia Doyle (Lynchburg College); Francis X. Duggan (Santa Clara University); Seth Ellis (University of North Carolina—Charlotte); Tom Ferte (Western Oregon State College); Joyce Field; Rowena Flanagan (Kansas City Community College); Marco Fraschella (San Joaquin Delta College); Ruth Fry (Auburn University); Michael Fukuchi (Atlantic Christian College); Robert Gariepy (Eastern Washington University); Robert Garrity (St. Joseph's College); Gerald Gordon (Kirkwood Community College); Richard Guzman (North Central College); Richard Hannaford (University of Idaho); Stephen Hemenway (Hope College); Beverly Heneghan (Northern Virginia Community College—Annandale); John Hennedy (Providence College); John Hiers (Valdosta State College); Robert Hogan (Rhode Island College); Rebecca Hogan (University of Wisconsin—Whitewater); Phil Holcomb (Angelo State University); Julia Bolton Holloway (University of Colorado); Wallace Hooker (Houston Baptist University); Richard Keithley (Georgia Southern College); Steven G. Kellman (University of Texas at San Antonio); Barbara Kemps (Union County College); Eric LaGuardia (University of Washington); Marthe LaVallee (Temple University); William Levison (Valdosta State College); Christiaan Lievestro (Santa Clara University); William Lutz (Rutgers University—Camden); Kathleen Lyons (Bellarmine College); Marianne Mayo (Valdosta State College); Barry McAndrew (Mercyhurst College); Glenn McCartney; James McKusick (University of Maryland—Baltimore College); David Middleton (Trinity University); Robert Miller (North Harris Community College, South); James Misenheimer (Indiana State University); David Neff (University of Alabama—Huntsville); Kurt Olsson (University of Idaho); Robert Oxley (Embry-Riddle Aeronautical University); Richard Pacholski (Milliken University); Frank Palmeri (University of Miami); Elysee Peavy (Houston Baptist University); Larry H. Peer (Brigham Young University); John Pennington (Valdosta State College); K. J. Phillips (University of Hawaii); Ira Plybon (Marshall University); Willard Potts (Oregon State University); Victoria Poulakis (Northern Virginia Community College); Joseph Price (Northern Kentucky University); Richard Priebe (Virginia Commonwealth University); Otto Reinert (University of Washington); Janet Robinson (St. Petersburg Community College); James Rolleston (Duke University); John Rudy (Indiana University—Kokomo); Pamela Sheridan (Moorpark College); Judith P. Shoaf (University of Florida); Jack Shreve (Allegany Community College); Martha Simonsen (William Rainey Harper College); George Simson (University of Hawaii at Manoa); Melvin Storm (Emporia State University); Frank Stringfellow (University of Miami); Norman Stroh (Angelo State University); Nathaniel Teich (University of Oregon); Eric Thorn (Marshall University); Bruce Thornton (California State University—Fresno); Mason Tung (University of Idaho); Linnea Vacca (St. Mary's College); Robert Vuturo (Kansas City Community College); Sidney Wade (University of Florida); Martha Waller (Butler University); Roger Weaver (Oregon State University); Gibb Weber (Anderson University); Henry Weinfield (New Jersey Institute of Technology); Michael White (Odessa College); Gary Williams (University of Idaho); J. Wooliscroft (Edinboro University of Pennsylvania).

Phonetic Equivalents

for use with the Pronouncing Glossaries preceding
most selections in this volume

a as in *cat*
ah as in *father*
ai as in *light*
ay as in *day*
aw as in *raw*
e as in *pet*
ee as in *street*
ehr as in *air*
er as in *bird*
g as in *good*
i as in *sit*
j as in *joke*
nh as in *vin* (French)
o as in *pot*
oh as in *no*
oo as in *boot*
oy as in *toy*
or as in *bore*
ow as in *now*
s as in *mess*
ts as in *ants*
u as in *us*
zh as in *vision*

The Norton Anthology
of World Masterpieces

EXPANDED EDITION

VOLUME 2

Part I

1650 TO 1800

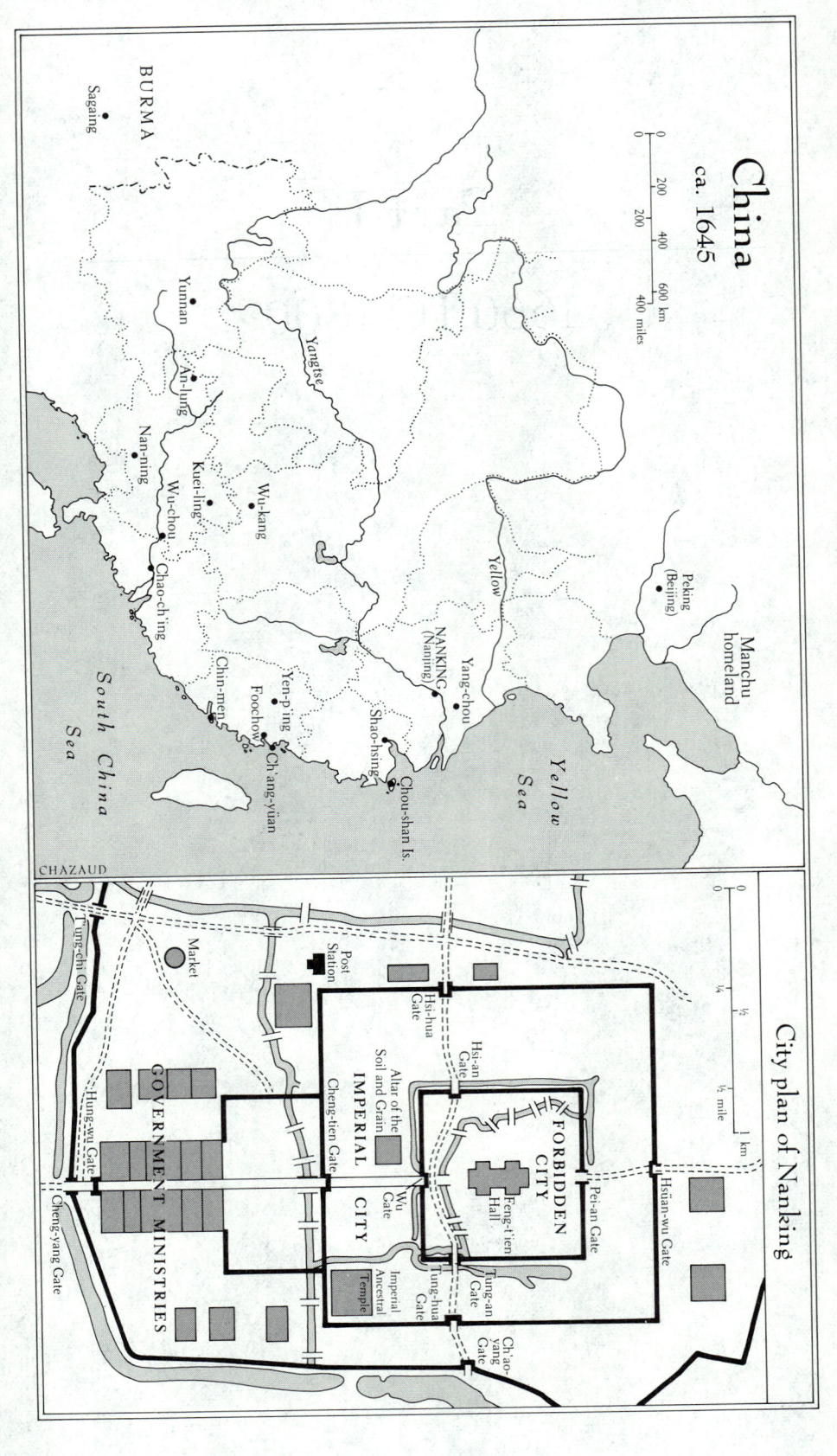

China
ca. 1645

0   200   400   600 km
0   200   400 miles

BURMA

Sagaing

Yunnan

An-lung

Nan-ning

Wu-chou

Kuei-ling

Chao-ch'ing

Wu-kang

Chin-men

Foochow

Ch'ang-yüan

Yen-p'ing

Shao-hsing

Chou-shan Is.

Yang-chou

NANKING
(Nanjing)

Peking
(Beijing)

Manchu
homeland

Yangtse

Yellow

South
China
Sea

Yellow
Sea

CHAZAUD

City plan of Nanking

0   ¼   ½   ¾   1 km
0   ½   1 mile

Tung-chi Gate

Market

Post
Station

Hsi-hua
Gate

Hsi-an
Gate

Altar of the
Soil and Grain

IMPERIAL
CITY

Cheng-tien
Gate

FORBIDDEN
CITY

Feng-t'ien
Hall

Wu
Gate

Pei-an
Gate

Hsüan-wu Gate

GOVERNMENT MINISTRIES

Hung-wu Gate

Cheng-yang Gate

Imperial
Ancestral
Temple

Tung-an
Gate

Tung-hua
Gate

Ch'ao-
yang
Gate

Vernacular Literature in China

Several decades after completing the conquest of north China, Mongol armies crossed the Yangtse River and conquered the Southern Sung Dynasty in 1279. At the time their empire stretched across all of Asia, but as a Chinese dynasty the Mongols were known as the Yüan. Although they assumed a Chinese dynastic title and some of the trappings of Chinese imperial government, the Mongols did not base their state on Confucian principles, for which they had the greatest contempt. To the everlasting shock of Chinese intellectuals, the Mongols suspended the examination system, by which members of the educated elite were recruited for government service. The long-established link between classical literature (poetry and nonfiction prose), an education in the Confucian classics, and service in the government was temporarily broken. Even after the civil service examinations were reestablished later in the dynasty, classical literature never regained its place as the core around which public, social, and private life was organized. Through the rest of the imperial period, classical literature remained an important part of the life of intellectuals, but its general role had been diminished to something like that of literature in Western civilization, an important adjunct of social life but not at its core.

As classical literature lost its importance, literature in vernacular Chinese (plays, verse romances, and prose fiction) began to be published. The steady rise of the bourgeoisie in the great cities and the spread of literacy in urban areas created a market for written versions of literary forms that already flourished in performance. In Europe and Great Britain the authority of classical drama could be used to defend the validity of Renaissance drama in the vernacular tongues. Greek and Latin prose romance, though with lesser prestige than drama, likewise informed the development of vernacular narrative prose. In China, by contrast, there was no ancient drama, and classical prose fiction was generally considered pure entertainment.

In the cities of China, however, rich traditions of theater, oral verse romance, and storytelling flourished. The thirteenth and fourteenth centuries produced the first published versions of these forms, with each written form carefully preserving the ambience of performance. Some intellectuals were fascinated by this urban popular literature, and what survives of it is the result of their efforts. Such literature grew steadily in volume and importance through the Ming Dynasty (1368–1644).

Although Yüan and Ming vernacular literature lacked the subtlety of classical literature, much that had been repressed in classical literature burst forth in the vernacular: sex, violence, satire, and humor. Plays, verse romances, and prose stories were often elaborations of some source in the classical language, spinning out a few pages into thirty or a thousand. This was a literature whose strength lay not in inventing plots but in filling in details and saying what had been omitted. In that strength, it became something different in kind from classical literature, with new virtues and new failings.

Chinese popular literature is largely a vast tissue of interrelated stories. The illiterate and semiliterate population had learned history from storytellers, who took a time period and elaborated it in the spoken tongue, including poems and songs. A dramatist might take one incident from a story cycle and develop it into a play. A fiction writer might cover an entire story cycle in a novel. A number of these historical romances survive, the most famous being *The Romance of the Three Kingdoms (San-kuo chih yen-yi)*—attributed to Lo Kuan-chung (earliest printed version 1522)—an elaboration of the official history of the period in which the Han Dynasty disintegrated, around the turn of the third century A.D. In *The Romance of the Three Kingdoms*, the somewhat dry historical account was transformed into a dazzling saga of battles and clever stratagems.

Popular literature worked with other materials as well. Murder mysteries, often based on recent cases, circulated, in which the wise magistrate, "Judge Pao," played a role equivalent to that of the modern detective. Stories of a famous group of twelfth-century bandits, like Robin Hood representing justice against corrupt authority, developed into the novel *Water Margin (Shui-hu chuan)* (early 1500s). One small incident in *Water Margin* was elaborated into the saga of a corrupt sensualist whose greed and sexual escapades give a vivid if skewed portrait of urban life in Ming China; this is *Golden Lotus (Chin P'ing Mei)* (1617). And the story of the Buddhist monk Hsuan Tsang who went west to India to get scriptures, guarded by a band of fantastic creatures headed by a wily monkey possessed of supernatural powers, became the novel *Monkey (Hsi-yu chi)* (1592).

As literature lost its role in public life, the vital link between literature and Confucian intellectual culture also gave way. High culture favored neo-Confucianism, at best prim and at worst dogmatic. Neo-Confucianism was an attempt to discover the philosophical grounds of the Confucian classics, and it developed into a system of private and social ethics that was to guide all aspects of life. Its rigid strictures on self-cultivation and ethical behavior failed in basic ways to address the complexities of human nature and the pressures of living in an increasingly complex world. Except among a very few committed thinkers, it was a philosophical position that invited gross hypocrisy. Vernacular literature, on the other hand, celebrated liberty, violent energy, and passion. Though such works often contained elements of neo-Confucian ethics and were later given pious neo-Confucian interpretations, by and large they either voiced qualities that neo-Confucianism sought to repress or savagely attacked society as a world of false appearances and secret evils.

In 1644 Manchu armies from the northeast descended into China and established a new dynasty, the Ch'ing, which would rule China until the revolution in 1911. Once again under non-Chinese rule and forced to wear the Manchu queue, a long ponytail, as a mark of submission, many Chinese harbored strong anti-Manchu sentiments. The Manchus, for their part, became very sensitive to native opposition. Censors set to survey current writings for hostility to the regime continually discovered slights, both real and imagined, against the dynasty. The late seventeenth and eighteenth centuries, known as the "literary inquisition," had a chilling effect on writing, especially in classical Chinese.

Such political realities may strongly affect, but do not entirely determine the intellectual and literary climate of an era. Ch'ing intellectual culture was a strong reaction against the radical individualism of the last part of the Ming, when personal freedom was celebrated at the expense of social responsibility. Early Ch'ing intellectuals held this late Ming ethos responsible for the decline of the Ming Dynasty. In the latter part of the seventeenth century and into the eighteenth century intellectuals turned away from Ming "subjectivism," the belief that each individual contained within himself or herself the grounds to make moral decisions and to interpret the authoritative texts of the tradition. The reaction saw not only a conservative public morality but also a new historical and philological rigor in the interpretation of early texts. This was closely analogous to the contemporary Western conflict in biblical studies between subjectivist "liberty of interpretation" and the development of historical philology—that is, the understanding of early texts by close study of how words were used at the time when the text was written. The new emphasis on historical scholarship had profound consequences for both China and the West, each of which had depended to some degree on the authority of received texts. This historical and philological approach to early texts was a form of empiricism, basing judgments on evidence and proof rather than tradition or private inclination. In China, as in the West at the same time, such empiricism in scholarship became linked to other forms of empiricism, such as interest in the natural sciences.

Ming subjectivist thought had found its strongest literary manifestation in a fascination with dreams, a world of illusion that was both a prominent theme in and a metaphor for the theater. And like Shakespeare, Chinese dramatists also observed that "all the world's a stage" and thus also a dream, as did the Spanish dramatist Calderon, whose *Life Is a Dream* is printed in Volume 1. Drama, far more than prose fiction, dominated the literary world, both in the theater and in published texts. Social rituals and ceremonies had been one of the pillars of Confucian society, and these came increasingly to be represented in terms of theatrical performance. What had been norms of behavior became "roles," strongly suggesting awareness of their unreality and the presence of an individual who was only "playing" a role.

The eighteenth century was the last period of glory and self-confidence for traditional Chinese civilization. Although China had been in continuous contact with Europe since the sixteenth century, in the early nineteenth century European colonial powers began to make major inroads on Chinese autonomy. The opium trade, dominated by British merchants, drained away silver while producing a major social problem. In their campaign to stop the drug trade, the Chinese fired on a ship flying the British flag. From this followed the Opium War (1840–42), in which Great Britain inflicted a series of humiliating defeats on Chinese forces. In the treaty that followed, Hong Kong was ceded to Great Britain and five so-called treaty ports were established, subject to British law and control. Other European powers rushed to carve out their own enclaves. Christian missionaries, protected by treaty, spread throughout the country. One consequence was the T'ai-p'ing T'ien-kuo, the "Heavenly Kingdom of Great Peace," a political movement and religious sect that mingled Christianity and native Chinese beliefs. The T'ai-p'ing T'ien-kuo rose in rebellion against the Ch'ing government, and between 1850 and 1864 carried out a war that left central China in desolation.

Humiliated and exhausted, the Ch'ing government found itself unable to adapt, either culturally or technologically, to the world that had been thrust on it. Through the latter half of the nineteenth century and first decade of the twentieth, the Ch'ing Dynasty slowly disintegrated, until it was overthrown with remarkable ease in 1911, when the Republic of China was established.

FURTHER READING

A basic survey of the history of Chinese drama can be found in William Dolby, *A History of Chinese Drama* (1976). C. T. Hsia, *The Classic Chinese Novel: A Critical Introduction* (1968), remains one of the most readable introductions to the major novels. Patrick Hanan, *The Chinese Vernacular Story* (1981), provides an insightful study of the cultural background of vernacular fiction.

TIMELINE

TEXTS	CONTEXTS
1300–1350 Earliest printed versions of vernacular drama **ca. 1350** Earliest publication of vernacular short stories	
	1368 Ming Dynasty is established with the capital at Nanking
	1405–1421 Ming admiral Cheng Ho explores southeast Asia, Sri Lanka, and the coast of Africa
	1421 The capital is moved to Peking
early 16th century Earliest edition of *Water Margin*, an episodic novel about a band of outlaws	
1522 Earliest edition of *Romance of the Three Kingdoms*, a long historical novel about the fall of the Han dynasty	
1550–1617 T'ang Hsien-tsu, a major dramatist who developed the long *ch'uan-ch'i* play into a literary form	
1574–1646 Feng Meng-lung, collector and author of vernacular stories and popular songs, important in raising the status of vernacular literature	**1580–1644** Late Ming, a period of radical subjectivism and questioning of authority of tradition
	1583–1610 Matteo Ricci, Jesuit missionary, serves in China
1592 Earliest extant edition of **Monkey** (***Journey to the West***)	
1611–1680 Li Yü, comic dramatist, story writer, and champion of vernacular literature	
1617 Earliest edition of *Chin P'ing Mei* (Golden lotus), a satirical novel of manners about a corrupt sensualist	
	1644–1645 Manchus conquer China • Ch'ing Dynasty is established • All Chinese males are forced to cut their hair and wear the queue

TIMELINE

TEXTS	CONTEXTS
1648–1718 K'ung Shang-jen, author of *The Peach Blossom Fan* (1699)	
1715–1763 Cao Xueqin, author of *The Story of the Stone* (1740–50)	
	1736–1794 "Literary inquisition": earlier works are censored and many writers imprisoned for suspected critical references to the Ch'ing Dynasty
ca. 1750 *Ju-lin wai-shih* (The scholars), a satirical novel; first extant edition 1803	
1788 The completion of the *Ssu-k'u ch'üan-shu*, a massive collection of all important earlier literature	

WU CH'ENG-EN
ca. 1506–1581

Like Malory's *Morte Darthur*, which combines Arthurian legends of the European Middle Ages, the novel or prose romance *Monkey* (properly, "Journey to the West," *Hsi-yu chi*) was not the work of a single person. First published in 1592, it represents a cumulative retelling and elaboration of materials that evolved over many centuries. Yet the final form of these stories in a vast, sprawling novel of one hundred chapters, often attributed to Wu Ch'eng-en, transformed the traditional material into a work of genius. The core of the story had a historical basis in the journey of the T'ang Buddhist monk Hsüan Tsang, or Tripitaka (596–664) from China to India in search of Buddhist scriptures. On his return, Hsüan Tsang left a short account of his experiences. The contents of this account had virtually nothing to do with the novel, but they may have served as the early basis from which the story began to be retold. Pilgrimages to India were by no means unique among Chinese monks of this era, but Tripitaka's journey somehow captured the popular imagination; it was retold in stories and plays, until it finally emerged as *Monkey*.

As Hsüan Tsang's journey was retold, the most important addition was his acquisition of a wondrous disciple Sun Wu-k'ung, Monkey Aware-of-Vacuity. Monkey had already made his appearance in a thirteenth-century version of the story and came to so dominate the full novel version that Arthur Waley named his condensation of the novel after this character.

It has long been debated whether *Monkey* is a work of exuberant play, celebrating Monkey's free spirit and turbulent ingenuity, or a serious allegory of Monkey and Tripitaka's journey toward Buddhist enlightenment. The novel is certainly something of both. An argument can be made, from a Buddhist point of view, that Tripitaka, however inept and timorous, is the novel's true hero. But for most readers, Chinese and Western, Monkey's splendid vitality and boundless humor remain the center of interest. Monkey's guardianship over Tripitaka is seconded by the ever-hungry and lustful Pigsy, who becomes increasingly unsympathetic as the journey progresses. Tripitaka's third disciple and protector is the gentle dragon Sandy, a former marshal of the hosts of Heaven who was sent to the bottom of a river to expiate the sin of having broken the Jade Emperor's (a Taoist divinity) crystal cup.

Above the four travelers is a divine machinery built of a synthesis of benign boddhisattvas (potential buddhas who linger in this world to help suffering humanity) and a Taoist pantheon of unruly and sometimes dangerous deities. On the earthly plane the pilgrims move through a landscape of strange kingdoms and monsters, stopping sometimes to help those in need or to protect themselves from harm. Some of the earthly monsters belong to the places where the pilgrims find them, but many of the demons and temptresses that the travelers encounter either are exiles and escapees from the heavenly realm or are sent on purpose to test the pilgrims.

Surrounded by three guardian disciples whose characters at the very least verge on the allegorical, Tripitaka is not only human but all too human. He is easily frightened, sometimes petulant, and never knows what to do. He is not so much driven on the pilgrimage by determined resolve as merely carried along by it. Yet he alone is the character destined for full buddhahood at the end, and his apparent lack of concern for the quest and for his disciples has been interpreted as the true manifestation of Buddhist detachment. Although Monkey grows increasingly devoted to his master through the course of the novel, Tripitaka never fully trusts him, however much he depends on him; and if there is a difficult Buddhist lesson in the novel, it is to grasp how Tripitaka, the ordinary man as saint, can be the novel's true hero. He is the empty center of the group, kept alive and carried forward by his more powerful and active disciples, both willing and unwilling. Yet he remains the master, and without him the pilgrimage would not exist.

Both Monkey and Pigsy are creatures of desire, though the nature of their desires differs greatly. Monkey, who had once lived an idyllic life with his monkey subjects in Water Curtain Cave, is, in the novel's early chapters, driven by a hunger for knowledge and immortality to search through the earth and the heavens. In the first stage of his existence, Monkey's hunger of the mind is never perfectly directed; it is a turbulence of spirit that always leads to mischief and an urge to create chaos. He acquires skills and magic tools that make him more powerful, but since he uses them unwisely, they only lead him to ever more outrageous escapades. After wreaking havoc in Heaven and being subdued by the god Erh-lang, he is imprisoned by the Buddha under a mountain for five hundred years; at last Monkey is given a chance to redeem himself by guarding Tripitaka on his pilgrimage to India.

During the course of the pilgrimage, Monkey becomes increasingly bound both to his master and to the quest itself, without ever losing his energy and humor. Despite occasional outbursts of his former mischief making, the quest becomes for Monkey a structured series of challenges by which he can focus and discipline his rambunctious intellect. The journey is driven forward by Monkey alone, with Tripitaka ever willing to give up in despair and Pigsy always ready to be seduced or return to his wife. Monkey understands the world with a comic detachment that is in some ways akin to Buddhist detachment, and this detachment makes him always more resourceful and often wiser than Tripitaka. Yet in his fierce energy and sheer joy in the use of his mind, Monkey falls short of the Buddhist ideal of true tranquility, while remaining the hero for unenlightened mortals.

Monkey is a complex character with many contradictions, as is perhaps fitting for a creature that may be seen in some sense as an allegory of the human mind. Pigsy, on the other hand, is a straightforward and predictable emblem of human sensual appetites. In his initial domestic setting, as the unwelcome son-in-law on Mr. Kao's farm, Pigsy was at least reliable and hardworking. But in the enforced celibacy of the pilgrimage, he grows increasingly slothful and undependable, always requiring Monkey's watchful prodding. Now and then on the journey he is permitted to gorge himself, but every time he finds a beautiful woman, something prevents him from satisfying his sexual appetite. Drafted into the quest, Pigsy did not freely choose it as expiation, as Monkey and Sandy did. And Pigsy wants to go home to his wife—or to take another along the way. Yet his Rabelaisian preoccupation with food and sex often makes him an endearing character.

The selections printed here treat Monkey's birth, his release by Tripitaka from imprisonment under the mountain, the gathering of the other disciples, and one of the early adventures in the kingdom of Cock-crow. Chapters II through XIII treat Monkey's acquisition of magical powers and his disruptions of Heaven and subsequent imprisonment as well as Tripitaka's commission from the T'ang emperor to go to India in search of scriptures. After leaving the kingdom of Cock-crow, the pilgrims continue on through numerous adventures, finally reaching India and acquiring the scriptures. In the last chapters all the pilgrims are whisked back to China by divine winds and are rewarded according to their merits (Pigsy, over his loud objections, is made janitor of the altars).

Like most Chinese novels, *Monkey* is very long. Arthur Waley's translation (1943) is an abridged version of thirty chapters out of the original one hundred, but Waley's gifts as a translator and the nature of his abridgement make this version a delight to read. In addition to Waley's abridgement, there is a complete and accurate four-volume translation of the novel by Anthony Yu, *Journey to the West* (1977–83), with a long introduction. There is also an excellent chapter on the novel in C. T. Hsia, *The Classic Chinese Novel: A Critical Introduction* (1968).

PRONOUNCING GLOSSARY

The following list uses common English syllables to provide rough equivalents of selected words whose pronunciation may be unfamiliar to the general reader.

Amitabha: *ah-mee-tahb-ha*

Ao-lai: *au–lai*

Chang Liang: *jahng lyahng*

Erh-lang: *ur–lahng*

Hsiao Ho: *shyau huh*

hsing: *shing*

Huang Shih Kung: *hwahng shir goong*

Hsüan Tsang: *shooahn dzahng*

Hui-yen: *hway–yen*

Jambudvīpa: *jahm-bood-vee-pah*

Kao Ts'ai: *gau tsai*

Kuan-yin: *gwahn–yin*

Lao Tzu: *lau dzuh*

Li Shih-min: *lee shir–min*

Lu Chia: *loo jyah*

Manjúsrī: *mahn-joosh-ree*

Sākyamuni: *shahk-yah-moo-nee*

śramana: *shrah-mah-nah*

Subodhi: *soo-bod-hee*

Sun Wu-k'ung: *swun woo-koong*

Trayaśimstra: *trah-ya-sheem-strah*

Wu Ch'eng-en: *woo chung-uhn*

Wu-ssu: *woo–suh*

Yü: *yoo*

Monkey[1]

CHAPTER I

There was a rock that since the creation of the world had been worked upon by the pure essences of Heaven and the fine savours of Earth, the vigour of sunshine and the grace of moonlight, till at last it became magically pregnant and one day split open, giving birth to a stone egg, about as big as a playing ball. Fructified by the wind it developed into a stone monkey, complete with every organ and limb. At once this monkey learned to climb and run; but its first act was to make a bow towards each of the four quarters. As it did so, a steely light darted from this monkey's eyes and flashed as far as the Palace of the Pole Star. This shaft of light astonished the Jade Emperor[2] as he sat in the Cloud Palace of the Golden Gates, in the Treasure Hall of the Holy Mists, surrounded by his fairy Ministers. Seeing this strange light flashing, he ordered Thousand-league Eye and Down-the-wind Ears[3] to open the gate of the Southern Heaven and look out. At his bidding these two captains went out to the gate and looked so sharply and listened so well that presently they were able to report, "This steely light comes from the borders of the small country of Ao-lai, that lies to the east of the Holy Continent, from the Mountain of Flowers and Fruit. On this mountain is a magic rock, which gave birth to an egg. This egg changed into a stone monkey, and when he made his bow to the four quarters a steely light flashed from his eyes with a beam that reached the Palace of the Pole Star. But now he is taking a drink, and the light is growing dim."

The Jade Emperor condescended to take an indulgent view. "These creatures in the world below," he said, "were compounded of the essence of heaven and earth, and nothing that goes on there should surprise us." That monkey walked, ran, leapt and bounded over the hills, feeding on grasses and shrubs, drinking from streams and springs, gathering the mountain flowers, looking for fruits. Wolf, panther and tiger were his companions, the deer and civet were his friends, gibbons and baboons his kindred. At night he lodged under cliffs of rock, by day he wandered among the peaks and caves. One very hot morning, after playing in the shade of some pine-trees, he and the other monkeys went to bathe in a mountain stream. See how those waters bounce and tumble like rolling melons!

There is an old saying, "Birds have their bird language, beasts have their beast talk." The monkeys said, "We none of us know where this stream comes from. As we have nothing to do this morning, wouldn't it be fun to follow it up to its source?" With a whoop of joy, dragging their sons and carrying their daughters, calling out to younger brother and to elder brother, the whole troupe rushed along the streamside and scrambled up the steep places, till they reached the source of the stream. They found themselves standing before the curtain of a great waterfall.

All the monkeys clapped their hands and cried aloud, "Lovely water,

---

1. Translated by and with notes adapted from Arthur Waley.   2. The chief deity in the Taoist pantheon.   3. Here and throughout *Monkey* there are fantastic deities and places invented by the author.

lovely water! To think that it starts far off in some cavern below the base
of the mountain, and flows all the way to the Great Sea! If any of us were
bold enough to pierce that curtain, get to where the water comes from
and return unharmed, we would make him our king!" Three times the
call went out, when suddenly one of them leapt from among the throng
and answered the challenge in a loud voice. It was the Stone Monkey. "I
will go," he cried, "I will go!" Look at him! He screws up his eyes and
crouches; then at one bound he jumps straight through the waterfall.
When he opened his eyes and looked about him, he found that where he
had landed there was no water. A great bridge stretched in front of him,
shining and glinting. When he looked closely at it, he saw that it was made
all of burnished iron. The water under it flowed through a hole in the
rock, filling in all the space under the arch. Monkey climbed up on to the
bridge and, spying as he went, saw something that looked just like a house.
There were stone seats and stone couches, and tables with stone bowls
and cups. He skipped back to the hum of the bridge and saw that on the
cliff there was an inscription in large square writing which said, "This cave
of the Water Curtain in the blessed land of the Mountain of Flowers and
Fruit leads to Heaven." Monkey was beside himself with delight. He
rushed back and again crouched, shut his eyes and jumped through the
curtain of water.

"A great stroke of luck," he cried, "A great stroke of luck." "What is it
like on the other side?" asked the monkeys, crowding round him. "Is the
water very deep?" "There is no water," said the Stone Monkey. "There is
an iron bridge, and at the side of it a heaven-sent place to live in." "What
made you think it would do to live in?" asked the monkeys. "The water,"
said the Stone Monkey, "flows out of a hole in the rock, filling in the
space under the bridge. At the side of the bridge are flowers and trees, and
there is a chamber of stone. Inside are stone tables, stone cups, stone
dishes, stone couches, stone seats. We could really be very comfortable
there. There is plenty of room for hundreds and thousands of us, young
and old. Let us all go and live there; we shall be splendidly sheltered in
every weather." "You go first and show us how!" cried the monkeys, in
great delight. Once more he closed his eyes and was through at one
bound. "Come along, all of you!" he cried. The bolder of them jumped
at once; the more timid stretched out their heads and then drew them
back, scratched their ears, rubbed their cheeks, and then with a great shout
the whole mob leapt forward. Soon they were all seizing dishes and
snatching cups, scrambling to the hearth or fighting for the beds, dragging
things along or shifting them about, behaving indeed as monkeys with
their mischievous nature might be expected to do, never quiet for an
instant, till at last they were thoroughly worn out. The Stone Monkey took
his seat at the head of them and said, "Gentlemen! 'With one whose word
cannot be trusted there is nothing to be done!'[4] You promised that any of
us who managed to get through the waterfall and back again, should be
your king. I have not only come and gone and come again, but also found

---

4. From Confucius's *Analects* II.22.

you a comfortable place to sleep, put you in the enviable position of being householders. Why do you not bow down to me as your king?"

Thus reminded, the monkeys all pressed together the palms of their hands and prostrated themselves, drawn up in a line according to age and standing, and bowing humbly they cried, "Great king, a thousand years!" After this the Stone Monkey discarded his old name and became king, with the title "Handsome Monkey King." He appointed various monkeys, gibbons and baboons to be his ministers and officers. By day they wandered about the Mountain of Flowers and Fruit; at night they slept in the Cave of the Water Curtain. They lived in perfect sympathy and accord, not mingling with bird or beast, in perfect independence and entire happiness.

The Monkey King had enjoyed this artless existence for several hundred years when one day, at a feast in which all the monkeys took part, the king suddenly felt very sad and burst into tears. His subjects at once ranged themselves in front of him and bowed down, saying, "Why is your Majesty so sad?" "At present," said the king, "I have no cause for unhappiness. But I have a misgiving about the future, which troubles me sorely." "Your Majesty is very hard to please," said the monkeys, laughing. "Every day we have happy meetings on fairy mountains, in blessed spots, in ancient caves, on holy islands. We are not subject to the Unicorn or Phoenix, nor to the restraints of any human king. Such freedom is an immeasurable blessing. What can it be that causes you this sad misgiving?" "It is true," said the Monkey King, "that to-day I am not answerable to the law of any human king, nor need I fear the menace of any beast or bird. But the time will come when I shall grow old and weak. Yama, King of Death, is secretly waiting to destroy me. Is there no way by which, instead of being born again on earth, I might live forever among the people of the sky?"

When the monkeys heard this they covered their faces with their hands and wept, each thinking of his own mortality. But look! From among the ranks there springs out one monkey commoner, who cries in a loud voice "If that is what troubles your Majesty, it shows that religion has taken hold upon your heart. There are indeed, among all creatures, three kinds that are not subject to Yama, King of Death." "And do you know which they are?" asked the Monkey King. "Buddhas, Immortals and Sages,"[5] he said. "These three are exempt from the Turning of the Wheel, from birth and destruction. They are eternal as Heaven and Earth, as the hills and streams." "Where are they to be found?" asked the Monkey King. "Here on the common earth," said the monkey, "in ancient caves among enchanted hills."

The king was delighted with this news. "To-morrow," he said, "I shall say good-bye to you, go down the mountain, wander like a cloud to the corners of the sea, far away to the end of the world, till I have found these three kinds of Immortal. From them I will learn how to be young forever and escape the doom of death." This determination it was that led him to leap clear of the toils of Re-incarnation and turned him at last into the

---

5. The highest stages of religious perfection in Buddhism, Taoism, and Confucianism, respectively.

Great Monkey Sage, equal of Heaven. The monkeys clapped their hands and cried aloud, "Splendid! Splendid! To-morrow we will scour the hills for fruits and berries and hold a great farewell banquet in honour of our king."

Next day they duly went to gather peaches and rare fruits, mountain herbs, yellow-sperm,[6] tubers, orchids, strange plants and flowers of every sort, and set out the stone tables and benches, laid out fairy meats and drinks. They put the Monkey King at the head of the table, and ranged themselves according to their age and rank. The pledge-cup[7] passed from hand to hand; they made their offerings to him of flowers and fruit. All day long they drank, and next day their king rose early and said, "Little ones, cut some pine-wood for me and make me a raft; then find a tall bamboo for pole, and put together a few fruits and such like. I am going to start." He got on to the raft all alone and pushed off with all his might, speeding away and away, straight out to sea, till favoured by a following wind he arrived at the borders of the Southern World. Fate indeed had favoured him; for days on end, ever since he set foot on the raft, a strong southeast wind blew and carried him at last to the north-western bank, which is indeed the frontier of the Southern World. He tested the water with his pole and found that it was shallow; so he left the raft and climbed ashore. On the beach were people fishing, shooting wild geese, scooping oysters, draining salt. He ran up to them and for fun began to perform queer antics which frightened them so much that they dropped their baskets and nets and ran for their lives. One of them, who stood his ground, Monkey caught hold of, and ripping off his clothes, found out how to wear them himself, and so dressed up went prancing through towns and cities, in market and bazaar, imitating the people's manners and talk. All the while his heart was set only on finding the Immortals and learning from them the secret of eternal youth. But he found the men of the world all engrossed in the quest of profit or fame; there was not one who had any care for the end that was in store for him. So Monkey went looking for the way of Immortality, but found no chance of meeting it. For eight or nine years he went from city to city and town to town till suddenly he came to the Western Ocean. He was sure that beyond this ocean there would certainly be Immortals, and he made for himself a raft like the one he had before. He floated on over the Western Ocean till he came to the Western Continent, where he went ashore, and when he had looked about for some time, he suddenly saw a very high and beautiful mountain, thickly wooded at the base. He had no fear of wolves, tigers or panthers, and made his way up to the very top. He was looking about him when he suddenly heard a man's voice coming from deep amid the woods. He hurried towards the spot and listened intently. It was some one singing, and these were the words that he caught:

> I hatch no plot, I scheme no scheme;
> Fame and shame are one to me,
> A simple life prolongs my days.
> Those I meet upon my way

---

6. Unidentified plant.   7. A cup used for offering toasts.

Are Immortals, one and all,
Who from their quiet seats expound
The Scriptures of the Yellow Court.[8]

When Monkey heard these words he was very pleased. "There must then be Immortals somewhere hereabouts," he said. He sprang deep into the forest and looking carefully saw that the singer was a woodman, who was cutting brushwood. "Reverend Immortal," said Monkey, coming forward, "your disciple raises his hands." The woodman was so astonished that he dropped his axe. "You have made a mistake," he said, turning and answering the salutation, "I am only a shabby, hungry woodcutter. What makes you address me as an 'Immortal'?" "If you are not an Immortal," said Monkey, "why did you talk of yourself as though you were one?" "What did I say," asked the woodcutter, "that sounded as though I were an Immortal?" "When I came to the edge of the wood," said Monkey, "I heard you singing 'Those I meet upon my way are Immortals, one and all, who from their quiet seats expound the Scriptures of the Yellow Court.' Those scriptures are secret, Taoist texts. What can you be but an Immortal?" "I won't deceive you," said the woodcutter. "That song was indeed taught to me by an Immortal, who lives not very far from my hut. He saw that I have to work hard for my living and have a lot of troubles; so he told me when I was worried by anything to say to myself the words of that song. This, he said, would comfort me and get me out of my difficulties. Just now I was upset about something and so I was singing that song. I had no idea that you were listening."

"If the Immortal lives close by," said Monkey, "how is it that you have not become his disciple? Wouldn't it have been as well to learn from him how never to grow old?" "I have a hard life of it," said the woodcutter. "When I was eight or nine I lost my father. I had no brothers and sisters, and it fell upon me alone to support my widowed mother. There was nothing for it but to work hard early and late. Now my mother is old and I dare not leave her. The garden is neglected, we have not enough either to eat or wear. The most I can do is to cut two bundles of firewood, carry them to market and with the penny or two that I get buy a few handfuls of rice which I cook myself and serve to my aged mother. I have no time to go and learn magic." "From what you tell me," said Monkey, "I can see that you are a good and devoted son, and your piety will certainly be rewarded. All I ask of you is that you will show me where the Immortal lives; for I should very much like to visit him."

"It is quite close," said the woodcutter. "This mountain is called the Holy Terrace Mountain, and on it is a cave called the Cave of the Slanting Moon and Three Stars. In that cave lives an Immortal called the Patriarch Subodhi. In his time he has had innumerable disciples, and at this moment there are some thirty or forty of them studying with him. You have only to follow that small path southwards for eight or nine leagues,[9] and you will come to his home." "Honoured brother," said Monkey, drawing the woodcutter towards him, "come with me, and if I profit by the visit

---

8. Texts of esoteric knowledge, containing secrets of immortality.   9. One league was equal to 360 steps.

I will not forget that you guided me." "It takes a lot to make some people understand," said the woodcutter. "I've just been telling you why I can't go. If I went with you, what would become of my work? Who would give my old mother her food? I must go on cutting my wood, and you must find your way alone."

When Monkey heard this, he saw nothing for it but to say good-bye. He left the wood, found the path, went uphill for some seven or eight leagues and sure enough found a cave-dwelling. But the door was locked. All was quiet, and there was no sign of anyone being about. Suddenly he turned his head and saw on top of the cliff a stone slab about thirty feet high and eight feet wide. On it was an inscription in large letters saying, "Cave of the Slanting Moon and Three Stars on the Mountain of the Holy Terrace." "People here," said Monkey, "are certainly very truthful. There really is such a mountain, and such a cave!" He looked about for a while, but did not venture to knock at the door. Instead he jumped up into a pine-tree and began eating the pine-seed and playing among the branches. After a time he heard someone call; the door of the cave opened and a fairy boy of great beauty came out, in appearance utterly unlike the common lads that he had seen till now. The boy shouted, "Who is making a disturbance out there?" Monkey leapt down from his tree, and coming forward said with a bow, "Fairy boy, I am a pupil who has come to study Immortality. I should not dream of making a disturbance." "You a pupil!" said the boy laughing. "To be sure," said Monkey. "My master is lecturing," said the boy. "But before he gave out his theme he told me to go to the door and if anyone came asking for instruction, I was to look after him. I suppose he meant you." "Of course he meant me," said Monkey. "Follow me this way," said the boy. Monkey tidied himself and followed the boy into the cave. Huge chambers opened out before them, they went on from room to room, through lofty halls and innumerable cloisters and retreats, till they came to a platform of green jade, upon which was seated the Patriarch Subodhi, with thirty lesser Immortals assembled before him. Monkey at once prostrated himself and bumped his head three times upon the ground, murmuring, "Master, master! As pupil to teacher I pay you my humble respects." "Where do you come from?" asked the Patriarch. "First tell me your country and name, and then pay your respects again." "I am from the Water Curtain Cave," said Monkey, "on the Mountain of Fruit and Flowers in the country of Ao-lai." "Go away!" shouted the Patriarch. "I know the people there. They're a tricky, humbugging set. It's no good one of them supposing he's going to achieve Enlightenment." Monkey, kowtowing violently, hastened to say, "There's no trickery about this; it's just the plain truth I'm telling you." "If you claim that you're telling the truth," said the Patriarch, "how is it that you say you came from Ao-lai? Between there and here there are two oceans and the whole of the Southern Continent. How did you get here?" "I floated over the oceans and wandered over the lands for ten years and more," said Monkey, "till at last I reached here." "Oh well," said the Patriarch, "I suppose if you came by easy stages, it's not altogether impossible. But tell me, what is your *hsing*?"[1] "I never show *hsing*," said Monkey. "If I am abused, I am

_____

1. This is a pun. *Hsing* can mean "surname" or "temper."

not at all annoyed. If I am hit, I am not angry; but on the contrary, twice
more polite than before. All my life I have never shown *hsing*."

"I don't mean that kind of *hsing*," said the Patriarch. "I mean what was
your family, what surname had they?" "I had no family," said Monkey,
"neither father nor mother." "Oh indeed!" said the Patriarch. "Perhaps
you grew on a tree!" "Not exactly," said Monkey. "I came out of a stone.
There was a magic stone on the Mountain of Flowers and Fruit. When its
time came, it burst open and I came out."

"We shall have to see about giving you a school-name,"[2] said the Patriarch. "We have twelve words that we use in these names, according to the
grade of the pupil. You are in the tenth grade." "What are the twelve
words?" asked Monkey. "They are Wide, Big, Wise, Clever, True, Con-
forming, Nature, Ocean, Lively, Aware, Perfect and Illumined. As you
belong to the tenth grade, the word Aware must come in your name. How
about Aware-of-Vacuity?" "Splendid!" said Monkey, laughing. "From now
onwards let me be called Aware-of-Vacuity."

So that was his name in religion. And if you do not know whether in
the end, equipped with this name, he managed to obtain enlightenment
or not, listen while it is explained to you in the next chapter.

✳   ✳   ✳

CHAPTER XIV

The hunter and Tripitaka were still wondering who had spoken, when
again they heard the voice saying, "The Master has come." The hunter's
servants said, "That is the voice of the old monkey who is shut up in the
stone casket of the mountain side." "Why, to be sure it is!" said the hunter.
"What old monkey is that?" asked Tripitaka. "This mountain," said the
hunter, "was once called the Mountain of the Five Elements. But after
our great T'ang Dynasty had carried out its campaigns to the West, its
name was changed to Mountain of the Two Frontiers. Years ago a very
old man told me that at the time when Wang Mang overthrew the First
Han Dynasty, Heaven dropped this mountain in order to imprison a magic
monkey under it. He has local spirits as his gaolers, who, when he is hungry give him iron pills to eat, and when he is thirsty give him copper-juice
to drink, so that despite cold and short commons[3] he is still alive. That cry
certainly comes from him. You need not be uneasy. We'll go down and
have a look."

After going downhill for some way they came to the stone box, in which
there was really a monkey. Only his head was visible, and one paw, which
he waved violently through the opening, saying, "Welcome, Master! Welcome! Get me out of here, and I will protect you on your journey to
the West." The hunter stepped boldly up, and removing the grasses from
Monkey's hair and brushing away the grit from under his chin, "What
have you got to say for yourself?" he asked. "To you, nothing," said Monkey. "But I have something to ask of that priest. Tell him to come here."
"What do you want to ask me?" said Tripitaka. "Were you sent by the
Emperor of T'ang to look for Scriptures in India?" asked Monkey. "I was,"

2. A religious name assumed by a disciple.   3. Daily provisions.

said Tripitaka. "And what of that?" "I am the Great Sage Equal of Heaven," said Monkey. "Five hundred years ago I made trouble in the Halls of Heaven, and Buddha clamped me down in this place. Not long ago the Bodhisattva Kuan-yin,[4] whom Buddha had ordered to look around for someone to fetch Scriptures from India, came here and promised me that if I would amend my ways and faithfully protect the pilgrim on his way, I was to be released, and afterwards would find salvation. Ever since then I have been waiting impatiently night and day for you to come and let me out. I will protect you while you are going to get Scriptures and follow you as your disciple."

Tripitaka was delighted. "The only trouble is," he said, "that I have no axe or chisel, so how am I to get you out?" "There is no need for axe or chisel," said Monkey. "You have only to want me to be out, and I shall be out." "How can that be?" asked Tripitaka. "On the top of the mountain," said Monkey, "is a seal stamped with golden letters by Buddha himself. Take it away, and I shall be out." Tripitaka was for doing so at once, but the hunter took him aside and said there was no telling whether one could believe the monkey or not. "It's true, it's true!" screamed Monkey from inside the casket. At last the hunter was prevailed upon to come with him and, scrambling back again to the very top, they did indeed see innumerable beams of golden light streaming from a great square slab of rock, on which was imprinted in golden letters the inscription OM MANI PADME HUM.[5]

Tripitaka knelt down and did reverence to the inscription, saying, "If this monkey is indeed worthy to be a disciple, may this imprint be removed and may the monkey be released and accompany me to the seat of Buddha. But if he is not fit to be a disciple, but an unruly monster who would discredit my undertaking, may the imprint of this seal remain where it is." At once there came a gust of fragrant wind that carried the six letters[6] of the inscription up into the air, and a voice was heard saying, "I am the Great Sage's gaoler. To-day the time of his penance is ended and I am going to ask Buddha to let him loose." Having bowed reverently in the direction from which the voice came, Tripitaka and the hunter went back to the stone casket and said to Monkey, "The inscription is removed. You can come out." "You must go to a little distance," said Monkey. "I don't want to frighten you." They withdrew a little way, but heard Monkey calling to them "Further, further!" They did as they were bid, and presently heard a tremendous crushing and rending. They were all in great consternation, expecting the mountain to come hurtling on top of them, when suddenly the noise subsided, and Monkey appeared, kneeling in front of Tripitaka's horse, crying, "Master, I am out!" Then he sprang up and called to the hunter, "Brother, I'll trouble you to dust the grass-wisps from my cheek." Then he put together the packs and hoisted them on to the horse, which on seeing him became at once completely obedient. For Monkey had been a groom in Heaven, and it was natural that an ordinary horse should hold him in great awe.

4. Associated with mercy and compassion. A bodhisattva is a potential buddha who remains in the world to help others achieve salvation.   5. A magic spell (in Sanskrit) that keeps Monkey imprisoned.
6. The inscription consists of six letters in devanagari, the script in which Sanskrit is written.

Tripitaka, seeing that he knew how to make himself useful and looked as though he would make a pretty tolerable śramana,[7] said to him, "Disciple, we must give you a name in religion." "No need for that," said Monkey, "I have one already. My name in religion is 'Aware-of-Vacuity.'" "Excellent!" said Tripitaka. "That fits in very well with the names of my other disciples. You shall be Monkey Aware-of-Vacuity."

The hunter, seeing that Monkey had got everything ready, said to Tripitaka, "I am very glad you have been fortunate enough to pick up this excellent disciple. As you are so well provided for, I will bid you good-bye and turn back." "I have brought you a long way from home," said Tripitaka, "and cannot thank you enough. Please also apologize to your mother and wife for all the trouble I gave, and tell them I will thank them in person on my return."

Tripitaka had not been long on the road with Monkey and had only just got clear of the Mountain of the Two Frontiers, when a tiger suddenly appeared, roaring savagely and lashing its tail. Tripitaka was terrified, but Monkey seemed delighted. "Don't be frightened, Master," he said. "He has only come to supply me with an apron."[8] So saying, he took a needle from behind his ear and, turning his face to the wind, made a few magic passes, and instantly it became a huge iron cudgel.[9] "It is five hundred years since I last used this precious thing," he said, "and to-day it is going to furnish me with a little much-needed clothing."

Look at him! He strides forward, crying, "Cursed creature, stand your ground!" The tiger crouched in the dust and dared not budge. Down came the cudgel on its head. The earth was spattered with its blood. Tripitaka rolled off his horse as best he could, crying with an awe-struck voice, "Heavens! When the hunter killed that stripy tiger yesterday, he struggled with it for hours on end. But this disciple of mine walked straight up to the tiger and struck it dead. True indeed is the saying 'Strong though he be, there is always a stronger.'" "Sit down a while," said Monkey, "and wait while I undress him; then when I am dressed, we'll go on." "How can you undress him?" said Tripitaka. "He hasn't got any clothes." "Don't worry about me," said Monkey. "I know what I am about." Dear Monkey! He took a hair from his tail, blew on it with magic breath, and it became a sharp little knife, with which he slit the tiger's skin straight down and ripped it off in one piece. Then he cut off the paws and head, and trimmed the skin into one big square. Holding it out, he measured it with his eye, and said, "A bit too wide. I must divide it in two." He cut it in half, put one half aside and the other round his waist, making it fast with some rattan that he pulled up from the roadside. "Now we can go," he said, "and when we get to the next house, I'll borrow a needle and thread and sew it up properly."

"What has become of your cudgel?" asked Tripitaka, when they were on their way again. "I must explain to you," said Monkey. "This cudgel is a piece of magic iron that I got in the Dragon King's palace, and it was with it that I made havoc in Heaven. I can make it as large or as small as

---

7. A Buddhist monk.   8. That is, Monkey will kill the tiger and take the tiger skin to wear around his waist.   9. A club.

I please. Just now I made it the size of an embroidery needle and put it away behind my ear, where it is always at hand in case I need it." "And why," asked Tripitaka, "did that tiger, as soon as it saw you, crouch down motionless and allow you to strike it just as you chose?" "The fact is," said Monkey, "that not only tigers but dragons too dare not do anything against me. But that is not all. I have such arts as can make rivers turn back in their course, and can raise tempests on the sea. Small wonder, then, that I can filch a tiger's skin. When we get into real difficulties you will see what I am really capable of."

"Master," said Monkey presently, "it is getting late. Over there is a clump of trees, and I think there must be a house. We had better see if we can spend the night there." Tripitaka whipped his horse, and soon they did indeed come to a farm, outside the gates of which he dismounted. Monkey cried "Open the door!" and presently there appeared a very old man, leaning on a staff. Muttering to himself, he began to push open the door, but when he saw Monkey, looking (with the tiger skin at his waist) for all the world like a thunder demon, he was terrified out of his wits and could only murmur "There's a devil at the door, sure enough there's a devil!" Tripitaka came up to him just in time to prevent him hobbling away. "Old patron," he said, "you need not be afraid. This is not a devil; it is my disciple." Seeing that Tripitaka at any rate was a clean-built, comely man, he took comfort a little and said, "I don't know what temple you come from, but you have no right to bring such an evil-looking fellow to my house." "I come from the Court of T'ang," said Tripitaka, "and I am going to India to get Scriptures. As my way brought me near your house, I have come here in the hope that you would consent to give me a night's lodging. I shall be starting off again tomorrow before daybreak." "You may be a man of T'ang," said the old man, "but I'll warrant that villainous fellow is no man of T'ang!" "Have you no eyes in your head," shouted Monkey. "The man of T'ang is my master. I am his disciple, and no man of T'ang or sugar-man[1] or honey-man either. I am the Great Sage Equal to Heaven. You people here know me well enough, and I have seen you before." "Where have you seen me?" he asked. "Didn't you when you were small cut the brushwood from in front of my face and gather the herbs that grew on my cheek?" "The stone monkey in the stone casket!" gasped the old man. "I see that you are a little like him. But how did you get out?" Monkey told the whole story, and the old man at once bowed before him, and asked them both to step inside. "Great Sage, how old are you?" the old man asked, when they were seated. "Let us first hear your age," said Monkey. "A hundred and thirty," said the old man. "Then you are young enough to be my great-great-grandson at least," said Monkey. "I have no idea when I was born. But I was under that mountain for five hundred years." "True enough," said the old man. "I remember my grand-father telling me that this mountain was dropped from Heaven in order to trap a monkey divinity, and you say that you have only just got out. When I used to see you in my childhood, there was grass growing out of your head and mud on your cheeks. I was not at all afraid of you then. Now

---

1. *T'ang* can mean "sugar."

there is no mud on your cheeks and no grass on your head. You look thinner, and with that tiger-skin at your waist, who would know that you weren't a devil?" "I don't want to give you all a lot of trouble," said Monkey presently, "but it is five hundred years since I last washed. Could you let us have a little hot water? I am sure my Master would be glad to wash too."

When they had both washed, they sat down in front of the lamp. "One more request," said Monkey. "Could you lend me a needle and thread?" "By all means, by all means," said the old man, and he told his old wife to bring them. Just then Monkey caught sight of a white shirt that Tripitaka had taken off when he washed and not put on again. He snatched it up and put it on. Then he wriggled out of the tiger-skin, sewed it up in one piece, made a "horse-face fold"[2] and put it round his waist again, fastening the rattan belt. Presenting himself to Tripitaka he said, "How do you like me in this garb? Is it an improvement?" "Splendid!" said Tripitaka. "Now you really do look like a pilgrim." "Disciple," added Tripitaka, "if you don't mind accepting an off-cast, you can have that shirt for your own."

They rose early next day, and the old man brought them washing-water and breakfast. Then they set out again on their way, lodging late and starting early for many days. One morning they suddenly heard a cry and six men rushed out at them from the roadside, all armed with pikes and swords. "Halt, priest!" they cried. "We want your horse and your packs, and quickly too, or you will not escape with your life."

Tripitaka, in great alarm, slid down from his horse and stood there speechless. "Don't worry," said Monkey. "This only means more clothes and travelling-money for us." "Monkey, are you deaf?" said Tripitaka. "They ordered us to surrender the horse and luggage, and you talk of getting clothes and money from them!" "You keep an eye on the packs and the horse," said Monkey, "while I settle matters with them! You'll soon see what I mean." "They are very strong men and there are six of them," said Tripitaka. "How can a little fellow like you hope to stand up against them single-handed?"

Monkey did not stop to argue, but strode forward and, folding his arms across his chest, bowed to the robbers and said, "Sirs, for what reason do you stop poor priests from going on their way?" "We are robber kings," they said, "mountain lords among the Benevolent.[3] Everyone knows us. How comes it that you are so ignorant? Hand over your things at once, and we will let you pass. But if half the word 'no' leaves your lips, we shall hack you to pieces and grind your bones to powder." "I, too," said Monkey, "am a great hereditary king, and lord of a mountain for hundreds of years; yet I have never heard your names." "In that case, let us tell you," they said. "The first of us is called Eye that Sees and Delights; the second, Ear that Hears and is Angry; the third, Nose that Smells and Covets; the fourth, Tongue that Tastes and Desires; the fifth, Mind that Conceives and Lusts; the sixth, Body that Supports and Suffers." "You're nothing but six hairy ruffians," said Monkey, laughing. "We priests, I would have you know, are

---

2. Unclear; the modern edition reads "sewed it into a skirt." 3. The thieves' slang for "bandit."

your lords and masters, yet you dare block our path. Bring out all the stolen goods you have about you and divide them into seven parts. Then, if you leave me one part, I will spare your lives."

The robbers were so taken aback that they did not know whether to be angry or amused. "You must be mad," they said. "You've just lost all you possess, and you talk of sharing our booty with us!" Brandishing their spears and flourishing their swords they all rushed forward and began to rain blows upon Monkey's head. But he stood stock still and betrayed not the slightest concern. "Priest, your head must be very hard!" they cried. "That's all right," said Monkey, "I'm not in a hurry. But when your arms are tired, I'll take out my needle and do my turn." "What does he mean?" they said. "Perhaps he's a doctor turned priest. But we are none of us ill, so why should he talk about using the needle?"

Monkey took his needle from behind his ear, recited a spell which changed it into a huge cudgel, and cried, "Hold your ground and let old Monkey try his hand upon you!" The robbers fled in confusion, but in an instant he was among them and striking right and left he slew them all, stripped off their clothing and seized their baggage. Then he came back to Tripitaka and said laughing, "Master, we can start now; I have killed them all." "I am very sorry to hear it," said Tripitaka. "One has no right to kill robbers, however violent and wicked they may be. The most one may do is to bring them before a magistrate. It would have been quite enough in this case if you had driven them away. Why kill them? You have behaved with a cruelty that ill becomes one of your sacred calling." "If I had not killed them," said Monkey, "they would have killed you." "A priest," said Tripitaka, "should be ready to die rather than commit acts of violence." "I don't mind telling you," said Monkey, "that five hundred years ago, when I was a king, I killed a pretty fair number of people, and if I had held your view I should certainly never have become the Great Sage Equal of Heaven." "It was because of your unfortunate performances in Heaven," said Tripitaka, "that you had to do penance for five hundred years. If now that you have repented and become a priest you go on behaving as in old days, you can't come with me to India. You've made a very bad start." The one thing Monkey had never been able to bear was to be scolded, and when Tripitaka began to lecture him like this, he flared up at once and cried, "All right! I'll give up being a priest, and won't go with you to India. You needn't go on at me any more. I'm off!" Tripitaka did not answer. His silence enraged Monkey even further. He shook himself and with a last "I'm off!" he bounded away. When Tripitaka looked up, he had completely disappeared. "It's no use trying to teach people like that," said Tripitaka to himself gloomily. "I only said a word or two, and off he goes. Very well then. Evidently it is not my fate to have a disciple; so I must get on as best I can without one."

He collected the luggage, hoisted it on to the horse's back and set out on foot, leading the horse with one hand and carrying his priest's staff with the other, in very low spirits. He had not gone far, when he saw an old woman carrying a brocaded coat and embroidered cap. As she came near, Tripitaka drew his horse to the side of the road to let her pass. "Where are you off to all alone?" she asked. "The Emperor of China has sent me to

India to fetch Scriptures," said Tripitaka. "The Temple of the Great Thunder Clap where Buddha lives," said she, "is a hundred and one thousand leagues away. You surely don't expect to get there with only one horse and no disciple to wait upon you?" "I picked up a disciple a few days ago," said Tripitaka, "but he behaved badly and I was obliged to speak rather severely to him; whereupon he went off in a huff, and I have not seen him since." "I've got a brocade coat and a cap with a metal band," said the old woman. "They belonged to my son. He entered a monastery, but when he had been a monk for three days, he died. I went and fetched them from the monastery to keep in memory of him. If you had a disciple, I should be very glad to let you have them." "That is very kind of you," said Tripitaka, "but my disciple has run away, so I cannot accept them." "Which way did he go?" asked the old woman. "The last time I heard his voice, it came from the east," said Tripitaka. "That's the way that my house lies," said the old woman. "I expect he'll turn up there. I've got a spell here which I'll let you learn, if you promise not to teach it to anybody. I'll go and look for him and send him back to you. Make him wear this cap and coat. If he disobeys you, say the spell, and he'll give no more trouble and never dare to leave you." Suddenly the old woman changed into a shaft of golden light, which disappeared towards the east. Tripitaka at once guessed that she was the Bodhisattva Kuan-yin in disguise. He bowed and burned incense towards the east. Then having stored away the cap and coat he sat at the roadside, practising the spell.

After Monkey left the Master, he somersaulted through the clouds and landed right in the palace of the Dragon King of the Eastern Ocean. "I heard recently that your penance was over," said the dragon, "and made sure you would have gone back to be king in your fairy cave." "That's what I am doing," said Monkey. "But to start with I became a priest." "A priest?" said the dragon. "How did that happen?" "Kuan-yin persuaded me to accompany a priest of T'ang," said Monkey, "who is going to India to get Scriptures; so I was admitted to the Order." "That's certainly a step in the right direction," said the dragon. "I am sure I congratulate you. But in that case, what are you doing here in the east?" "It comes of my master being so unpractical," said Monkey. "We met some brigands, and naturally I killed them. Then he started scolding me. You may imagine I wasn't going to stand that. So I left him at once, and am going back to my kingdom. But I thought I would look you up on the way, and see if you could give me a cup of tea."

When he had been given his cup of tea, he looked round the room, and saw on the wall a picture of Chang Liang[4] offering the slipper. Monkey asked what it was about. "You were in Heaven at the time," said the dragon, "and naturally would not know about it. The immortal in the picture is Huang Shih Kung, and the other figure is Chang Liang. Once when Shih Kung was sitting on a bridge, his shoe came off and fell under the bridge. He called to Chang Liang to pick it up and bring it to him. Chang Liang did so, whereupon the Immortal at once let it fall again, and Chang Liang again fetched it. This happened three times, without Chang

---

4. A general who helped found the Han Dynasty; he was supposed to have had magical skills.

Liang showing the slightest sign of impatience. Huang Shih Kung then gave him a magic treatise, by means of which he defeated all the enemies of the House of Han, and became the greatest hero of the Han dynasty. In his old age he became a disciple of the Immortal Red Pine Seed and achieved Tao.[5] Great Sage, you must learn to have a little more patience, if you hope to accompany the pilgrim to India and gain the Fruits of Illumination." Monkey looked thoughtful. "Great Sage," said the dragon, "you must learn to control yourself and submit to the will of others, if you are not to spoil all your chances." "Not another word!" said Monkey, "I'll go back at once."

On the way he met the Bodhisattva Kuan-yin. "What are you doing here?" she asked. "The seal was removed and I got out," said Monkey, "and became Tripitaka's disciple. But he said I didn't know how to behave, and I gave him the slip. But now I am going back to look after him." "Go as fast as you can," said the Bodhisattva, "and try to do better this time." "Master," said Monkey, when he came back and found Tripitaka sitting dejectedly by the roadside, "what are you doing still sitting here?" "And where have you been?" asked Tripitaka. "I hadn't the heart to go on, and was just sitting here waiting for you." "I only went to the dragon of the eastern ocean," said Monkey, "to drink a cup of tea." "Now Monkey," said Tripitaka, "priests must always be careful to tell the truth. You know quite well that the dragon king lives far away in the east, and you have only been gone an hour." "That's easily explained," said Monkey. "I have the art of somersaulting through the clouds. One bound takes me a hundred and eight thousand leagues." "It seemed to me that you went off in a huff," said Tripitaka, "because I had to speak rather sharply to you. It's all very well for you to go off and get tea like that, if you are able to. But I think you might remember that I can't go with you. Doesn't it occur to you that I may be thirsty and hungry too?" "If you are," said Monkey, "I'll take a bowl and go and beg for you." "There isn't any need to do that," said Tripitaka. "There are some dried provisions in the pack." When Monkey opened the pack, his eye was caught by something bright. "Did you bring this coat and cap with you from the east?" he asked. "I used to wear them when I was young," replied Tripitaka, saying the first thing that came into his head. "Anyone who wears this cap can recite scriptures without having to learn them. Anyone who wears this coat can perform ceremonies without having practised them." "Dear Master," said Monkey, "let me put them on." "By all means," said Tripitaka. Monkey put on the coat and cap, and Tripitaka, pretending to be eating the dried provisions, silently mumbled the spell. "My head is hurting!" screamed Monkey. Tripitaka went on reciting, and Monkey rolled over on the ground, frantically trying to break the metal fillet of the cap. Fearing that he would succeed, Tripitaka stopped for a moment. Instantly the pain stopped. Monkey felt his head. The cap seemed to have taken root upon it. He took out his needle and tried to lever it up; but all in vain. Fearing once more that he would break the band, Tripitaka began to recite again. Monkey was soon writhing and turning somersaults. He grew purple in the face and his eyes bulged

5. That is, immortality.

out of his head. Tripitaka, unable to bear the sight of such agony, stopped reciting, and at once Monkey's head stopped hurting.

"You've been putting a spell upon me," he said. "Nothing of the kind," said Tripitaka. "I've only been reciting the Scripture of the Tight Fillet."[6] "Start reciting again," said Monkey. When he did so, the pain began at once. "Stop, stop!" screamed Monkey. "Directly you begin, the pain starts; you can't pretend it's not you that are causing it." "In future, will you attend to what I say?" asked Tripitaka. "Indeed I will," said Monkey. "And never be troublesome again?" said Tripitaka. "I shouldn't dare," said Monkey. So he said, but in his heart there was still lurking a very evil intent. He took out his cudgel and rushed at Tripitaka, fully intending to strike. Much alarmed, the Master began to recite again, and Monkey fell writhing upon the ground; the cudgel dropped from his hand. "I give in, I give in!" he cried. "Is it possible," said Tripitaka, "that you were going to be so wicked as to strike me?" "I shouldn't dare, I shouldn't dare," groaned Monkey. "Master, how did you come by this spell?" "It was taught me by an old woman whom I met just now," said Tripitaka. "Not another word!" said Monkey. "I know well enough who she was. It was the Bodhisattva Kuan-yin. How dare she plot against me like that? Just wait a minute while I go to the Southern Ocean and give her a taste of my stick." "As it was she who taught me the spell," said Tripitaka, "she can presumably use it herself. What will become of you then?" Monkey saw the logic of this, and kneeling down he said contritely, "Master, this spell is too much for me. Let me go with you to India. You won't need to be always saying this spell. I will protect you faithfully to the end." "Very well then," said Tripitaka. "Help me on to my horse." Very crestfallen, Monkey put the luggage together, and they started off again towards the west.

If you do not know how the story goes on, you must listen to what is told in the next chapter.

CHAPTER XV

It was mid-winter, a fierce north wind was blowing and icicles hung everywhere. Their way took them up precipitous cliffs and across ridge after ridge of jagged mountain. Presently Tripitaka heard the roaring of a torrent and asked Monkey what this river might be. "I remember," said Monkey, "that there is a river near here called the Eagle Grief Stream." A moment later they came suddenly to the river side, and Tripitaka reined in his horse. They were looking down at the river, when suddenly there was a swirling sound and a dragon appeared in mid-stream. Churning the waters, it made straight for the shore, clambered up the bank and had almost reached them, when Monkey dragged Tripitaka down from the horse and turning his back to the river, hastily threw down the luggage and carried the Master up the bank. The dragon did not pursue them, but swallowed the horse, harness and all, and then plunged once more into the stream. Meanwhile Monkey had set down Tripitaka upon a high mound, and gone back to recover the horse and luggage. The luggage was

6. A fillet is usually a strip of cloth — but here a band of metal — worn around the head. By reciting the scripture like a spell, Tripitaka can make the fillet tighten.

there, but the horse had disappeared. He brought up the luggage to where Tripitaka was sitting. "The dragon has made off," he said. "The only trouble is that the horse has taken fright and bolted." "How are we to find it?" asked Tripitaka. "Just wait while I go and have a look," said Monkey. He sprang straight up into the sky, and shading his fiery eyes with his hand he peered down in every direction. But nowhere was the least sign of the horse. He lowered his cloud-trapeze. "I can't see it anywhere," he said. "There is only one thing that can have happened to it. It has been eaten by the dragon." "Now Monkey, what can you be thinking of?" said Tripitaka, "It would have to have a big mouth indeed to swallow a large horse, harness and all. It is much more likely that it bolted and is hidden by a fold of the hill. You had better have another look." "Master, you underrate my powers," said Monkey. "My sight is so good that in daylight I can see everything that happens a thousand leagues around. Within a thousand leagues a gnat cannot move its wings without my seeing it. How could I fail to see a horse?" "Well, suppose it has been eaten," said Tripitaka, "how am I to travel? It's a great deal too far to walk." And as he spoke his tears began to fall like rain. "Don't make such an object of yourself," shouted Monkey, infuriated by this exhibition of despair. "Just sit here, while I go and look for the wretch and make him give us back the horse." "You can't do anything unless he comes out of the water," said Tripitaka, "and if he does it will be me that he will eat this time." "You're impossible, impossible," thundered Monkey, angrier than ever. "You say you need the horse to ride, and yet you won't let me go and recover it. At this rate, you'll sit here staring at the luggage for ever."

He was still storming, when a voice spoke out of the sky, saying, "Monkey, do not be angry. Priest of T'ang, do not weep. We divinities have been sent by Kuan-yin to protect you in your quest." Tripitaka at once did obeisance.[7] "Which divinities are you?" cried Monkey. "Tell me your names, and I'll tick you off on the roll." "Here present are Lu Ting and Lu Chia," they said, "the Guardians of the Five Points, the Four Sentinels and the Eighteen Protectors of Monasteries. We attend upon you in rotation." "And which of you are on duty this morning?" asked Monkey. "Lu Chia, one Sentinel and the Protectors are on duty," they said, "and the Golden-headed Guardian is always somewhere about, night and day." "Those who aren't on duty can retire," said Monkey. "But Lu Ting, the Sentinel of the day, and all the Guardians had better stay and look after the Master, while I go to the river and look for that dragon, and see if I can get him to return the horse." Tripitaka, feeling somewhat reassured, sat down on the brink, begging Monkey to be careful. "Don't you worry about me!" said Monkey.

Dear Monkey! He tightened the belt of his brocade jacket, hitched up his tiger-skin, grasped his iron cudgel, and going straight down to the water's edge called in a loud voice, "Cursed fish, give me back my horse!" The dragon was lying quietly at the bottom of the river, digesting the white horse. But hearing some one cursing him and demanding his prey, he fell into a great rage, and leapt up through the waves crying, "Who is it that

---

7. Bowed.

dares make such a hullabaloo outside my premises?" "Stand your ground,"
hissed Monkey, "and give me back my horse." He brandished his cudgel
and struck at the dragon's head. The dragon advanced upon him with
open jaws and threatening claws. It was a valiant fight that those two had
on the banks of the river. To and fro they went, fighting for a long while,
hither and thither, round and round. At last the dragon's strength began
to fail, he could hold out no longer, and with a rapid twist of the tail he
fled from the encounter and disappeared in the river. Monkey, standing
on the bank, cursed and taunted him unceasingly, but he turned a deaf
ear. Monkey saw nothing for it but to go back and report to Tripitaka.
"Master," he said, "I taunted him till he came out and fought many bouts,
and in the end he took fright and ran away. He is now at the bottom of
the river and won't come out." "We are still not sure whether he did
swallow the horse," said Tripitaka. "How can you say such a thing?" said
Monkey. "If he hadn't eaten it, why should he have come out and
answered my challenge?" "The other day when you dealt with that tiger,"
said Tripitaka, "you mentioned that you could also subdue dragons. I don't
understand why you are having such difficulties with this dragon to-day."
To such a taunt as this no one could be more sensitive than Monkey. "Not
another word!" he cried, stung to the quick. "I'll soon show you which is
master!"

He strode to the stream-side, and used a magic which stirred up the
clear waters of the river till they became as turbulent as the waves of the
Yellow River.[8] The dragon soon became very uncomfortable as he lay at
the bottom of the stream. "Misfortunes never come singly," he thought to
himself. "Hardly a year has passed since I barely escaped with my life from
the Tribunal of Heaven and was condemned to this exile; and now I have
fallen foul of this cursed monster, who seems determined to do me
injury." The more he thought, the angrier he became. At last, determined
not to give in, he leapt up through the waves and gnashing his teeth he
snarled, "What monster are you, and where do you come from, that you
dare affront me in this fashion?" "Never mind where I come from or don't
come from," said Monkey. "Just give me back my horse, or you shall pay
for it with your life." "Your horse," said the dragon, "is inside me. How
am I to give it back to you? And anyhow, if I don't, what can you do to
me?" "Have a look at this cudgel," said Monkey. "If you don't give me
back the horse you shall pay for it with your life." Again they fought upon
the bank, and after several rounds the dragon could hold out no longer,
made one great wriggle and, changing itself into a water-snake, disappeared into the long grass. Beating the grass with his cudgel, Monkey
pranced wildly about, trying to track it down, but all in vain. At last, fuming with impatience he uttered a loud OM, as a secret summons to the
spirits of the locality. In a moment they were kneeling before him. "Hold
out your shanks," said Monkey, "and I'll give you each five strokes with
the cudgel just to relieve my feelings." "Great Sage," they besought him,
"pray give us a chance to put our case to you. We had no idea that you
had been released from your penance, or we should have come to meet

8. The largest river in north China.

you before. We humbly beg you to forgive us." "Very well then," said
Monkey. "You shan't be beaten. But answer me this. Where does this
dragon come from, who lives in the Eagle Grief River? Why did he swallow my Master's white horse?" "Great Sage," they said, "in old days you
had no Master, and indeed refused obedience to any power in Heaven or
Earth. What do you mean by your Master's horse?" "After I got into trouble
about that affair in Heaven," said Monkey, "I had to do penance for five
hundred years. But now I have been taken in hand by the Bodhisattva
Kuan-yin and put in charge of a priest who is going to India to fetch
Scriptures. I was travelling with him as his disciple, when we lost my
Master's horse." "If you want to catch this dragon, surely your best plan
would be to get the Bodhisattva to come and deal with it," they said.
"There used not to be any dragon here, and it is she who sent it." They all
went and told Tripitaka of this plan. "How long shall you be?" he asked.
"Shan't I be dead of cold or starvation before you come back?" While he
spoke, the voice of the Golden-headed Guardian was heard saying from
the sky, "None of you need move a step. I will go and ask the Bodhisattva."
"Much obliged," said Monkey. "Pray go at once." The Guardian soared
up through the clouds and made straight for the Southern Ocean. Monkey
told the local deities to look after the Master, and the Sentinels to supply
food. Then he went back to the banks of the river. "What have you come
for?" asked the Bodhisattva, when the Golden-headed Guardian was
brought to her where she sat in her bamboo-grove. "The priest of T'ang,"
said he, "has lost his horse at the Eagle Grief River. It was swallowed by a
dragon, and the Great Sage sent me for your help," "That dragon," said
Kuan-yin, "is a son of the dragon-king of the Western Ocean. By his carelessness he set fire to the magic pearls in the palace and they were
destroyed. His father accused him of subversive intents, and the Tribunal
of Heaven condemned him to death. I saw the Jade Emperor about it, and
asked that the sentence might be commuted if the dragon consented to
carry the priest of T'ang on his journey to India. I cannot understand how
he came to swallow the horse. I'll come and look into it." She got down
from her lotus seat, left her fairy cave, and riding on a beam of magic light
crossed the Southern Sea. When she came near the River of Eagle Grief,
she looked down and saw Monkey on the bank uttering ferocious curses.
She sent the Guardian to announce her arrival. Monkey at once sprang
into the air and shouted at her, "A fine 'Teacher of the Seven Buddhas,' a
fine 'Founder of the Faith of Mercy' you are, to plot in this way against
us!" "You impudent stableman, you half-witted red-bottom," said the
Bodhisattva. "After all the trouble I have taken to find someone to fetch
scriptures, and tell him to redeem you, instead of thanking me you make
a scene like this!" "You've played a fine trick on me," said Monkey. "You
might in decency, when you let me out, have allowed me to go round and
amuse myself as I pleased. But you gave me a dressing down and told me
I was to spend all my time and energy in looking after this T'ang priest.
Very well! But why did you give him a cap that he coaxed me into putting
on, and now I can't get it off, and whenever he says some spell or other I
have frightful pains in the head?" "Oh Monkey," laughed Kuan-yin, "if
you were not controlled in some such way as this, there would be no doing

anything with you. Before long we should have you at all your old tricks again." "It's no good trying to put the blame on me," said Monkey. "How comes it that you put this dragon here, after he had been condemned by the Courts, and let him eat my Master's horse? It was you who put it in his way to continue his villainies here below. You ought to be ashamed of yourself!" "I specially asked the Jade Emperor," said Kuan-yin, "to let this dragon be stationed here, so that he might be used to carry the master on his way to India. No ordinary Chinese horse would be able to carry him all that way." "Well, now he is frightened of me and is hiding," said Monkey, "so what is to be done?" Kuan-yin called the Golden-haired Guardian and said to him, "Go to the edge of the river and cry 'Third son of the Dragon King, come out! The Bodhisattva is here.' He'll come out all right." The dragon leapt up through the waves and immediately assumed human form. "Don't you know that this is the Scripture-seeker's disciple?" Kuan-yin said, pointing at Monkey. "Bodhisattva," said the young dragon, "I've been having a fight with him. I was hungry yesterday and ate his horse. He never once mentioned anything about 'Scripture-seeking.'" "You never asked my name," said Monkey, "so why should I tell you?" "Didn't I ask you what monster you were and where you came from?" asked the dragon. "And didn't you shout at me 'Never mind where I came from or didn't come from, but just give me back my horse'? You never so much as mentioned the word T'ang." "Monkey is fonder of showing off his own powers than mentioning his connexion with other people," said Kuan-yin. "But in future if anyone questions him, he must be sure to say that he is seeking Scriptures. Then there will be no more trouble."

The Bodhisattva then went to the dragon and removed the jewel of wisdom from under his chin. Then she took her willow-spray[9] and sprinkled him all over with sweet dew, and blowing upon him with magic breath cried "Change!" Whereupon the dragon immediately changed into the exact image of the lost horse. She then solemnly called upon the once-dragon to turn from his evil ways, and promised that when his task was ended he should be given a golden body and gain illumination. The young dragon humbled himself and promised faithfully to do as he was bid. Then she turned to go, but Monkey grabbed at her, crying "This is not good enough! The way to the West is very bad going, and it would be difficult enough in any case to get an earthly priest over all those precipices and crags. But if we are going to have encounters like this all the time, I shall have hard work keeping alive at all, let alone any thought of achieving salvation. I'm not going on!" "That's odd," said the Bodhisattva, "because in the old days you used to be very keen on obtaining illumination. I am surprised that, having escaped from the punishment imposed upon you by Heaven, you should be so unwilling to take a little trouble. When you get into difficulties you have only to call upon Earth, and Earth will perform its miracles. If need be, I will come myself to succour you. And, by the way, come here! I am going to endow you with one more power." She took the willow leaves from her willow-spray, and dropping them down Monkey's back cried "Change." At once they changed into

9. A handful of willow twigs with the leaves still on them.

three magic hairs. "These," she said, "will get you out of any trouble,
however menacing." Monkey thanked the Bodhisattva, who now set out
for the Southern Heaven, and taking the horse by the forelock he led it to
Tripitaka, saying, "Master, here's a horse any way!" "It's in much better
condition than the old one," said Tripitaka. "However did you manage to
find it?" "What have you been doing all the while? Dreaming?" said Monkey. "The Golden-haired Guardian sent for Kuan-yin, who changed the
dragon into the exact image of our white horse. The only thing it lacks is
harness." "Where is the Bodhisattva?" asked Tripitaka, very much surprised. "I should like to thank her." "You're too late," said Monkey. "By
this time she is already crossing the Southern Ocean." However Tripitaka
burned incense and bowed towards the south. Then he helped Monkey
to put together the luggage, and they set out. "It's not going to be easy to
ride a horse without saddle and reins," said Tripitaka. "I'd better find a
boat to get across the river, and see if I can't get some harness on the other
side." "That's not a very practical suggestion," said Monkey. "What chance
is there of finding a boat in this wild, desolate place? The horse has lived
here for some time and must know his way through the waters. Just sit
tight on his back and let him carry you across." They had got to the river
bank, Tripitaka astride the horse and Monkey carrying the luggage, when
an old fisherman appeared upstream, punting a crazy old raft. Monkey
waved to him, crying, "We have come from the east to fetch scriptures.
My Master does not know how to get across, and would like you to ferry
him." The old man punted rapidly towards them, and Monkey told Tripitaka to dismount. He then helped him on board, and embarked the horse
and luggage. The old man punted them swiftly across to the far side, where
Tripitaka told Monkey to look in the pack for some Chinese money to
give to the old fisherman. But the old man pushed off again at once, saying
he did not want money. Tripitaka felt very uncomfortable and could only
press together his palms in token of gratitude. "Don't you worry about
him," said Monkey. "Didn't you see who he really is? This is the river
divinity who failed to come and meet us. I was on the point of giving him
a good hiding, which he richly deserved. The fact that I let him off is
payment enough. No wonder he hadn't the face to take your cash." Tripitaka was not at all sure whether to believe this story or not. He got astride
the horse once more, and followed Monkey along the road to the west.
And if you do not know where they got to, you must listen to what is told
in the next chapter.

CHAPTER XVI

They had been travelling for several days through very wild country
when at last, very late in the evening, they saw a group of houses in the
far distance. "Monkey," said Tripitaka, "I think that is a farm over there.
Wouldn't it be a good plan to see if we can't sleep there to-night?" "Let
me go and have a look at it," said Monkey, "to see whether it looks lucky or
unlucky, and we can then act accordingly." "You can proceed," Monkey
reported presently. "I am certain that good people live there." Tripitaka

urged on the white horse and soon came to a gate leading into a lane
down which came a lad with a cotton wrap round his head, wearing a
blue jacket, umbrella in hand and a bundle on his back. He was striding
along, with a defiant air. "Where are you off to?" said Monkey stopping
him. "There's something I want to ask you. What place is this?" The man
tried to brush him aside, muttering, "Is there no one else on the farm, that
you must needs pester me with questions?" "Now don't be cross," said
Monkey laughing. "What harm can it do you to tell me the name of a
place? If you're obliging to us, maybe we can do something to oblige you."
Finding he could not get past, for Monkey was holding on to him tightly,
he began to dance about in a great rage. "It's enough to put anyone out,"
he cried. "I've just been insulted by the master of the house, and then I
run straight into this wretched bald-pate, and have to swallow his impudence!" "Unless you're clever enough to shake me off, which I very much
doubt," said Monkey, "here you'll stay." The man wriggled this way and
that, but all to no purpose. He was caught as though by iron pincers. In
the struggle he dropped his bundle, dropped his umbrella, and began to
rain blows on Monkey with both fists. Monkey kept one hand free to catch
on to the luggage, and with the other held the lad fast. "Monkey," said
Tripitaka, "I think there's someone coming over there. Wouldn't it do just
as well if you asked him, and let this lad go?" "Master," said Monkey, "you
don't know what you're talking about. There's no point in asking anyone
else. This is the only fellow out of whom we can get what we want."

At last, seeing that he would never get free, the lad said, "This is called
old Mr. Kao's farm. Most of the people that live and work here have the
surname Kao, so the whole place is called Kao Farm. Now let me go!"
"You look as if you were going on a journey," said Monkey. "Tell me
where you are going, and on what business, and I will let you go."

"My name," he said, "is Kao Ts'ai. Old Mr. Kao has a daughter about
twenty years old and unmarried. Three years ago she was carried off by a
monster, who since has kept her as his wife, and lived with her here on
the farm. Old Mr. Kao was not pleased. 'To have a monster as a son-in-
law in the house,' he says, 'doesn't work very well. It's definitely discreditable to the house, and unpleasant not to be able to look forward to comings and goings between the two families.' He did everything in his power
to drive away the monster, but it was no good; and in the end the creature
took the girl and locked her away in that back building, where she has
been for six months and no one in the family has seen her.

"Old Mr. Kao gave me two or three pieces of silver and told me to go
and find an exorcist, and I spent a long time chasing round all over the
countryside. I succeeded at last in getting the names of three or four practitioners, but they all turned out to be unfrocked priests or mouldy Taoists,
quite incapable of dealing with such a monster. Mr. Kao only just now
gave me a great scolding and accused me of bungling the business. Then
he gave me five pieces of silver to pay for my travelling expenses and told
me to go on looking till I found a really good exorcist, and I should be
looking for one now if I hadn't run into this little scamp who won't let me
pass. There! You have forced me to tell you how things are, and now you
can let me go." "You've thrown a lucky number," said Monkey. "This is

just my job. You needn't go a step further or spend an ounce of your silver. I'm no unfrocked priest or mouldy Taoist, I really do know how to catch monsters. You've 'got your stye cured on the way to the doctor's.' I'll trouble you to go to the master of the house, and tell him that a priest and his disciple have come, who are on their way to get scriptures in India, and that they can deal with any monster." "I hope you're telling me the truth," said the lad. "You'll get me into great trouble if you fail." "I'll positively guarantee," said Monkey, "that I'm not deceiving you. Make haste and lead us in."

The lad saw nothing for it but to pick up his bundle and go back to the house. "You half-wit," roared old Mr. Kao, "what have you come back for?" But as soon as he had heard the lad's story, he quickly changed into his best clothes and came out to greet the guests, smiling affably. Tripitaka returned his greeting, but Monkey did not bow or say a word. The old man looked him up and down, and not knowing quite what to make of him did not ask him how he did. "And how about me? Don't you want to know how I am?" said Monkey. "Isn't it enough to have a monster in the house as son-in-law," grumbled the old man, "without your bringing in this frightful creature to molest me?" "In all the years you've lived," said Monkey, "you've evidently learnt very little wisdom. If you judge people by their appearances, you'll always be going wrong. I'm not much to look at, I grant; but I have great powers, and if you are having any trouble with bogeys or monsters in the house, that's just where I come in. I'm going to get you back your daughter, so you had better stop grumbling about my appearance." Mr. Kao, trembling with fear, managed at last to pull himself together sufficiently to invite them both in. Monkey, without so much as by-your-leave, led the horse into the courtyard and tied it to a pillar. Then he drew up an old weather-beaten stool, asked Tripitaka to be seated, and taking another stool for himself calmly sat down at Tripitaka's side. "The little priest knows how to make himself at home," said Mr. Kao. "This is nothing," said Monkey. "Keep me here a few months and you'll see me really making myself at home!" "I don't quite understand," said the old man, "whether you've come for a night's lodging or to drive out the monster." "We've come for a night's lodging," said Monkey, "but if there are any monsters about I don't mind dealing with them, just to pass the time. But first, I should like to know how many of them there are?" "Heavens!" cried the old man, "isn't one monster enough to afflict the household, living here as my son-in-law?" "Just tell me about it from the beginning," said Monkey. "If I know what he's good for, I can deal with him." "We'd never had any trouble with ghosts or goblins or monsters on this farm before," said the old man. "Unfortunately I have no son, but only three daughters. The eldest is called Fragrant Orchid, the second Jade Orchid, and the third Blue Orchid. The first two were betrothed from childhood into neighbouring families. Our plan for the youngest was to marry her to someone who would come and live with her here and help look after us in our old age. About three years ago a very nice-looking young fellow turned up, saying that he came from Fu-ling, and that his surname was Hog. He said he had no parents or brothers and sisters, and was looking for a family where he would be taken as son-in-law, in return for the work that he did about the place. He sounded just the sort we wanted, and I accepted him. I must say he worked very hard. He pushed the plough himself and never asked to use a bull; he managed to do all his reaping without knife or staff. For some time we were perfectly satisfied, except for one thing—his appearance began to change in a very odd way." "In what way!" asked Monkey. "When he first came," said the old man, "he was just a dark, stoutish fellow. But afterwards his nose began to turn into a regular snout, his ears became larger and larger, and great bristles began to grow at the back of his neck. In fact, he began to look more and more like a hog. His appetite is enormous. He eats four or five pounds of rice at each meal, and as a light collation in the morning I've known him get through over a hundred pasties.[1] He's not at all averse to fruit and vegetables either, and what with this and all the wine he drinks, in the course of the last six months he's pretty well eaten and drunk us out of house and home." "No doubt," said Tripitaka, "anyone who works so hard as he does needs a lot of nourishment." "If it were only this business of food," said the old man, "it wouldn't be so bad. But he frightens everybody round by raising magic winds, suddenly vanishing and appearing again, making stones fly through the air and such like tricks. Worst of all, he has locked up Blue Orchid in the back outhouse,[2] and it is six months since we set eyes on her. We don't even know if she is dead or alive. It is evident that he's an ogre of some kind, and that is why we were trying to get hold of an exorcist." "Don't you worry," said Monkey. "This very night I'll catch him and make him sign a Deed of Relinquishment[3] and give you back your daughter." "The main thing is to catch him," said Mr. Kao. "It doesn't so much matter about documents." "Perfectly easy," said Monkey. "To-night as soon as it is dark, you'll see the whole thing settled." "What weapons do you need, and how many men to help you?" asked Mr. Kao. "We must get on with the preparations." "I'm armed already," said Monkey. "So far as I can see, all you've got between you is a priest's staff," said the old man. "That wouldn't be much use against such a fiend as this." Monkey took his embroidery needle from behind his ear and once more changed it into a great iron cudgel. "Does this satisfy you?" he asked. "I doubt if your house could provide anything tougher." "How about followers?" said the old man. "I need no followers," said Monkey. "All I ask for is some decent elderly person to sit with my master and keep him company." Several respectable friends and relatives were fetched, and having looked them up and down Monkey said to Tripitaka, "Sit here quietly and don't worry. I'm off to do this job." "Take me to the back building," he said to Mr. Kao, grasping his cudgel. "I'd like to have a look at the monster's lodging-place." "Give me the key," he said, when they came to the door. "Think what you're saying," said the old man. "Do you suppose that if a key was all that was wanted, we should be troubling you?" "What's the use of living so long in the world if you haven't learnt even to recognize a joke when you hear one?" said Monkey laughing. Then he went up to the door and with a terrific blow of his cudgel smashed it down. Within, it was pitch dark. "Call to your daughter and see if she is there," said Monkey.

1. Meat pies. *Collation:* meal.   2. That is, outbuilding.   3. Divorce papers.

The old man summoned up his courage and cried, "Miss Three!" Recognizing her father's voice, she answered with a faint "Papa, I am here." Monkey peered into the darkness with his steely eyes, and it was a pitiable sight that he saw. Unwashed cheeks, matted hair, bloodless lips, weak and trembling. She tottered towards her father, flung her arms round him and burst into tears. "Don't make that noise," said Monkey, "but tell us where your monster is." "I don't know," she said. "Nowadays he goes out at dawn and comes back at dusk, I can't keep track of him at all. He knows that you're trying to find someone to exorcize him; that's why he keeps away all day." "Not a word more!" said Monkey. "Old man, take your darling back to the house and calm her down. I'll wait here for the monster. If he doesn't come, it is not my fault, and if he comes I'll pluck up your trouble by the roots."

Left alone, Monkey used his magic arts to change himself into the exact image of Blue Orchid, and sat waiting for the monster to return. Presently there was a great gust of wind; stones and gravel hurtled through the air. When the wind subsided there appeared a monster of truly terrible appearance. He had short bristles on his swarthy cheeks, a long snout and huge ears. He wore a cotton jacket that was green but not green, blue but not blue, and had a spotted handkerchief tied round his head. "That's the article," laughed Monkey to himself.

Dear Monkey! He did not go to meet the monster or ask him how he did, but lay on the bed groaning, as though he were ill. The monster, quite taken in, came up to the bed and grabbing at Monkey tried to kiss him. "None of your lewd tricks on old Monkey!" laughed Monkey to himself, and giving the monster a great clout on the nose sent him reeling. "Dear sister," said the monster, picking himself up, "why are you cross with me to-day? Is it because I am so late?" "I'm not cross," said Monkey. "If you're not cross," said the monster, "why do you push me away?" "You've got such a clumsy way of kissing," said Monkey. "You might have known that I'm not feeling well to-day, when you saw I did not come to the door to meet you. Take off your clothes and get into bed." Still suspecting nothing the monster began to undress. Monkey meanwhile jumped up and sat on the commode. When the monster got into bed he felt everywhere but could not find his bride. "Sister," he called, "what has become of you? Take off your clothes and get into bed." "You go to sleep first," said Monkey. "I'll follow when I've done my duties." Monkey suddenly began to sigh, murmuring "Was there ever such an unhappy girl as I?" "What are you grumbling about?" said the monster. "Since I came here, I've cost you something in food and drink, that I own. But I've more than earned what I have got. Haven't I cleaned the ground and drained ditches, carried bricks and tiles, built walls, ploughed fields, planted grain, and improved the farm out of all knowing? You've good clothes to wear and all the food you need. What's all this childish nonsense about being unhappy?" "That's not it at all," said Monkey. "To-day my parents came and made a fearful scene through the partition wall." "What did they make a scene about?" said the monster. "They don't like having you here as their son-in-law." said Monkey. "They say you've got an ugly face, and they don't know who your father is and haven't seen any of your relations.

They say you come and go no one knows when or where, and it's bad for the credit of the house that we don't know your name or anything at all about you." That's what they said, and it has made me miserable." "What do looks matter?" said the monster. "It's a strong man they need about the place, and they can't say anything against me on that score. And if they think so ill of me, why did they accept me here at all? As for who I am, there's no mystery about it. I come from the Cloud-Ladder Cave at Fuling, and because I look a bit like a pig they call me Pigsy—Pigsy Bristles; next time they ask just tell them that." "Confiding monster!" thought Monkey. "It needs no tortures to get a confession from him. Now we know where he comes from and who he is. It only remains to catch him." "They are looking for an exorcist to drive you away," he said to the monster. "Go to sleep," said Pigsy, "and don't worry about them any more. Am not I strong enough, with my nine-pronged muck-rake, to frighten off any exorcist or priest or what-not? Even if your old man's prayers could bring down the master of all devils from the Ninth Heaven,[4] as a matter of fact he's an old friend of mine and wouldn't do anything against me." "He's done more than that," said Monkey. "He has called in the Great Sage, who five hundred years ago made turmoil in Heaven." "If that's so," said Pigsy, "I'm off! There'll be no more kissing to-night!" "Why are you going?" asked Monkey. "You don't know," said Pigsy. "That chap is terribly powerful, and I don't know that I could deal with him. I'm frightened of losing my reputation." He dressed hastily, opened the door and went out. But Monkey caught hold of him and making a magic pass changed himself back into his true form. "Monster, look round," he cried, "and you will see that I am he."

When Pigsy turned and saw Monkey with his sharp little teeth and grinning mouth, his fiery, steely eyes, his flat head and hairy cheeks, for all the world like a veritable thunder-demon, he was so startled that his hands fell limp beside him and his legs gave way. With a scream he tore himself free, leaving part of his coat in Monkey's hand, and was gone like a whirlwind. Monkey struck out with his cudgel; but Pigsy had already begun to make for the cave he came from. Soon Monkey was after him, crying, "Where are you off to? If you go up to Heaven I will follow you to the summit of the Pole Star, and if you go down into the earth I will follow you to the deepest pit of hell."

If you do not know how far he chased him or which of them won the fight, you must listen to what is told in the next chapter.

CHAPTER XVII

The monster fled with Monkey at his heels, till they came at last to a high mountain, and here the monster disappeared into a cave, and a moment later came back brandishing a nine-pronged muck-rake. They set to at once and battled all night long, from the second watch till dawn began to whiten in the sky. At last the monster could hold his ground no longer, and retreating into the cave bolted the door behind him. Standing outside the cave-door, Monkey saw that on a slab of rock was the inscrip-

---

4. The highest level of Heaven.

tion "Cloudladder Cave." As the monster showed no sign of coming out
again and it was now broad daylight, Monkey thought to himself, "The
Master will be wondering what has happened to me. I had better go and
see him and then come back and catch the monster." So tripping from
cloud to cloud he made his way back to the farm.

Tripitaka was still sitting with the old man, talking of this and that. He
had not slept all night. He was just wondering why Monkey did not return
when Monkey alighted in the courtyard, and suddenly stood before them.
"Master, here I am," he said. The old men all bowed down before him,
and supposing that he had accomplished his task thanked him for all his
trouble. "You must have had a long way to go, to catch the creature," said
Tripitaka. "Master," said Monkey, "the monster is not a common incubus[5]
or elf. I have recognized him as a former inhabitant of Heaven, where he
was in command of all the watery hosts. He was expelled to earth after an
escapade with the daughter of the Moon Goddess, and though he was
here re-incarnated with a pig-like form, he retains all his magic powers. I
chased him to his mountain-cave, where he fetched out a nine-pronged
muck-rake, and we fought together all night. Just at dawn he gave up the
fight, and locked himself up in his cave. I would have beaten down the
door and forced him to fight to a decision, but I was afraid the Master
might be getting anxious, so I thought I had better come back first and
report."

"Reverend Sir," said old Mr. Kao to Monkey, "I am afraid this hasn't
helped matters much. True, you have driven him away; but after you have
gone he's certain to come back again, and where shall we be then? We
shall have to trouble you to catch him for us. That is the only way to pluck
out our trouble by the root. I'll see to it that you have no cause to regret
the trouble you take. You shall have half of all that is ours, both land and
goods. If you like, my friends and relations shall sign a document to this
effect. It will be well worth their while, if only we can remove this shame
from our home."

"I think you make too much of the whole affair," said Monkey. "The
monster himself admits that his appetite is large; but he has done quite a
lot of useful work. All the recent improvements in the estate are his work.
He claims to be well worth what he costs in keep, and does not see why
you should be so anxious to get rid of him. He is a divinity from Heaven,
although condemned to live on earth, he helps to keep things going, and
so far as I can see he hasn't done any harm to your daughter." "It may be
true," said old Mr. Kao, "that he's had no influence upon her. But I stick
to it that it's very bad for our reputation. Wherever I go I hear people
saying 'Mr. Kao has taken a monster as his son-in-law.' What is one to say
to that?" "Now, Monkey," said Tripitaka, "don't you think you had better
go and have one more fight with him and see if you can't settle the business once and for all?" "As a matter of fact," said Monkey, "I was only
having a little game with him, to see how things would go. This time I
shall certainly catch him and bring him back for you to see. Don't you
worry!" "Look after my master," he cried to Mr. Kao, "I'm off!"

5. Demon.

So saying, he disappeared into the clouds and soon arrived at the cave. With one blow of his cudgel he beat the doors to bits, and standing at the entrance he cried, "You noisome lout, come out and fight with Old Monkey." Pigsy lay fast asleep within, snoring heavily. But when he heard the door being beaten down and heard himself called a noisome lout, he was so much enraged that he snatched up his rake, pulled himself together and rushed out, crying, "You wretched stableman, if ever there was a rogue, you're he! What have I to do with you, that you should come and knock down my door? Go and look at the Statute Book.[6] You'll find that 'obtaining entry to premises by forcing a main door' is a Miscellaneous Capital Offence." "You fool," said Monkey. "Haven't I a perfectly good justification at law for forcing your door? Remember that you laid violent hands on a respectable girl, and lived with her without matchmaker or testimony, tea, scarlet,[7] wine or any other ceremony. Are you aware that heads are cut off for less than that?" "Stop that nonsense, and look at Old Pig's rake," cried Pigsy. He struck out, but Monkey warded off the blow, crying, "I suppose that's the rake you used when you worked on the farm. Why should you expect me to be frightened of it?" "You are very much mistaken," said Pigsy. "This rake was given to me by the Jade Emperor himself." "A lie!" cried Monkey. "Here's my head. Hit as hard as you please, and we'll see!" Pigsy raised the rake and brought it down with such force on Monkey's head that the sparks flew. But there was not a bruise or scratch. Pigsy was so much taken aback, that his hands fell limp at his side. "What a head!" he exclaimed. "You've still something to learn about me," said Monkey. "After I made havoc in Heaven and was caught by Erhlang, all the deities of Heaven hacked me with their axes, hammered me with their mallets, slashed me with their swords, set fire to me, hurled thunderbolts at me, but not a hair of my body was hurt. Lao Tzu[8] put me in his alchemic stove and cooked me with holy fire. But all that happened was that my eyes became fiery, my head and shoulders hard as steel. If you don't believe it, try again, and see whether you can hurt me or not." "I remember," said Pigsy, "that before you made havoc in Heaven, you lived in the Cave of the Water-Curtain. Lately nothing has been heard of you. How did you get here? Perhaps my father-in-law asked you to come and deal with me." "Not at all," said Monkey, "I have been converted and am now a priest, and am going with a Chinese pilgrim called Tripitaka, who has been sent by the Emperor to fetch scriptures from India. On our way we happened to come past Mr. Kao's farm, and we asked for a night's lodging. In the course of conversation Mr. Kao asked for help about his daughter. That's why I'm after you, you noisome lout!"

No sooner did Pigsy hear these words than the rake fell from his hand. "Where is that pilgrim?" he gasped. "Take me to him." "What do you want to see him for?" asked Monkey. "I've been converted," said Pigsy. "Didn't you know? The Bodhisattva Kuan-yin converted me and put me here to prepare myself by fasting and abstention for going to India with a pilgrim to fetch scriptures; after which, I am to receive illumination. That

6. Law book.   7. Wedding gifts.   8. An ancient sage and one of the founders of Taoism. He was believed to have become immortal and occupied an important place in the Taoist pantheon.

all happened some years ago, and since then I have had no news of this pilgrim. If you are his disciple, what on earth possessed you not to mention this scripture-seeking business? Why did you prefer to pick a quarrel and knock me about in front of my own door?" "I suspect," said Monkey, "that you are just making all this up, in order to get away. If it's really true that you want to escort my Master to India, you must make a solemn vow to Heaven that you're telling the truth. Then I'll take you to him." Pigsy flung himself upon his knees and, kowtowing at the void,[9] up and down like a pestle in the mortar, he cried "I swear before the Buddha Amitabha, praised be his name, that I am telling the truth; and if I am not, may I be condemned once more by the tribunals of Heaven and sliced into ten thousand pieces."

When Monkey heard him make this solemn vow, "Very well then," he said. "First take a torch and burn down your lair, and then I will take you with me." Pigsy took some reeds and brambles, lit a fire and soon reduced the cave to the state of a burnt-out kiln. "You've nothing against me now," he said. "Take me along with you." "You'd better give your rake to me," said Monkey. When Pigsy had handed over the rake, Monkey took a hair, blew on it with magic breath, and changed it into a three-ply hemp cord. Pigsy put his hands behind his back and let himself be bound. Then Monkey caught hold of his ear and dragged him along, crying, "Hurry up! Hurry up!" "Don't be so rough," begged Pigsy. "You're hurting my ear." "Rough indeed!" said Monkey. "I shouldn't get far by being gentle with you. The proverb says, 'The better the pig, the harder to hold.' Wait till you have seen the Master and shown that you are in earnest. Then we'll let you go."

When they reached the farm, Monkey twitched Pigsy's ear, saying, "You see that old fellow sitting so solemnly up there? That's my Master." Mr. Kao and the other old men, seeing Monkey leading the monster by the ear, were delighted beyond measure, and came out into the courtyard to meet him. "Reverend Sir," they cried, "that's the creature, sure enough, that married our master's daughter." Pigsy fell upon his knees and with his hands still tied behind his back, kowtowed to Tripitaka, crying, "Master, forgive me for failing to give you a proper reception. If I had known that it was you who were staying with my father-in-law I would have come to pay my respects, and all these unpleasantnesses would never have happened." "Monkey," said Tripitaka, "how did you manage to bring him to this state of mind?" Monkey let go his ear, and giving him a knock with the handle of the rake, shouted, "Speak, fool!" Pigsy then told how he had been commissioned by Kuan-yin. "Mr. Kao," said Tripitaka, when he heard the story, "this is the occasion for a little incense." Mr. Kao then brought out the incense tray, and Tripitaka washed his hands, and burning incense he turned towards the south and said, "I am much beholden, Bodhisattva!" Then he went up into the hall and resumed his seat, bidding Monkey to release Pigsy from his bonds. Monkey shook himself; the rope became a hair again and returned to his body. Pigsy was free. He again

9. Sky.

did obeisance, and vowed that he would follow Tripitaka to the west. Then he bowed to Monkey, whom as the senior disciple he addressed as "Elder Brother and Teacher."

"Where's my wife?" said Pigsy to Mr. Kao. "I should like her to pay her respects to my Father and Brother in the Law." "Wife indeed!" laughed Monkey. "You haven't got a wife now. There are some sorts of Taoists that are family men; but who ever heard of a Buddhist priest calmly talking about his 'wife'? Sit down and eat your supper, and early to-morrow we'll all start out for India." After supper Mr. Kao brought out a red lacquer bowl full of broken pieces of silver and gold, and offered the contents to the three priests, as a contribution towards their travelling expenses. He also offered them three pieces of fine silk to make clothes. Tripitaka said, "Travelling priests must beg their way as they go. We cannot accept money or silk." But Monkey came up and plunging his hand into the dish took out a handful of gold and silver, and called to the lad Kao Ts'ai, "You were kind enough yesterday to introduce my Master into the house and we owe it to you that we have found a new disciple. I have no other way of showing my thanks but giving you these broken pieces of gold and silver, which I hope you will use to buy yourself a pair of shoes. If you come across any more monsters, please bespeak them for me, and I shall be even further obliged to you." "Reverend Sirs," said Mr. Kao, "if I can't persuade you to accept silver or gold, I hope that you will at least let me show my gratitude by giving you these few pieces of coarse stuff, to make into cassocks." "A priest who accepts so much as a thread of silk," said Tripitaka, "must do penance for a thousand aeons to expiate his crime. All I ask is a few scraps left over from the household meal, to take with us as dry provisions." "Wait a minute," cried Pigsy. "If I get my due for all I've done on this estate since I married into the family, I should carry away several tons of provisions. That's by the way. But I think my father-in-law might in decency give me a new jacket. My old one was torn by Brother Monkey in the fight last night. And my shoes are all in pieces; I should be glad of a new pair."

Mr. Kao acceded to his request, and Pigsy, delighted by his new finery, strutted up and down in front of the company, calling to Mr. Kao, "Be so kind as to inform my mother-in-law, my sisters-in-law and all my kinsmen by marriage that I have become a priest and must ask their pardon for going off without saying good-bye to them in person. And father-in-law, I'll trouble you to take good care of my bride. For if we don't bring off this scripture business, I shall turn layman again and live with you as your son-in-law." "Lout!" cried Monkey. "Don't talk rubbish." "It's not rubbish," said Pigsy. "Things may go wrong, and then I shall be in a pretty pass! No salvation, and no wife either." "Kindly stop this silly argument," said Tripitaka. "It is high time we started." So they put together the luggage, which Pigsy was told to carry, and when the white horse was saddled Tripitaka was set astride. Monkey, with his cudgel over his shoulder, led the way. And so, parting from Mr. Kao and all his relations, the three of them set out for the West. And if you do not know what befell them, you must listen to what is told in the next chapter.

CHAPTER XVIII

So the three of them travelled on towards the West, and came at last to a great plain. Summer had passed and autumn come. They heard "the cicada singing in the rotten willow," saw "the Fire-Star rolling to the west." At last they came to a huge and turbulent river, racing along with gigantic waves. "That's a very broad river," cried Tripitaka from on horseback. "There does not seem to be a ferry anywhere about. How are we to get across?" "A boat wouldn't be much use in waters as rough as that," said Pigsy. Monkey leapt up into the air, and shading his eyes with his hand gazed at the waters. "Master," he cried, "this is going to be no easy matter. For me, yes. I should only have to shake my hips, and I should be across at one bound. But for you it's not going to be such easy work." "I can't even see the other side," said Tripitaka. "How far is it, do you suppose?" "About eight hundred leagues," said Monkey. "How do you come to that reckoning?" asked Pigsy. "I'll tell you frankly," said Monkey. "My sight is so good that I can see everything, lucky or unlucky, a thousand leagues away, and when I looked down on this river from above I could see well enough that it must be a good eight hundred leagues across." Tripitaka was very much depressed, and was just turning his horse when he saw a slab of stone on which was the inscription "River of Flowing Sands." Underneath in small letters was the verse:

In the Floating Sands, eight hundred wide,
In the Dead Waters, three thousand deep,
A goose-feather will not keep afloat,
A rush-flower sinks straight to the bottom.

They were looking at this inscription when suddenly a monster of horrifying aspect came surging through the mountainous waves. His hair was flaming red, his eyes were like two lanterns; at his neck were strung nine skulls, and he carried a huge priest's-staff. Like a whirlwind he rushed straight at the pilgrims. Monkey seized Tripitaka and hurried him up the bank to a safe distance. Pigsy dropped his load and rushed at the monster with his rake. The monster fended off the blow with his priest's-staff. The fight that followed was a good one, each displaying his powers on the shores of the River of Flowing Sands. They fought twenty bouts without reaching a decision. Monkey, seeing the grand fight that was in progress, itched to go and join in it. At last he said to Tripitaka, "You sit here and don't worry. I am going off to have a bit of fun with the creature." Tripitaka did his best to dissuade him. But Monkey with a wild whoop leapt into the fray. At this moment the two of them were locked in combat, and it was hard to get between them. But Monkey managed to put in a tremendous blow of the cudgel right on the monster's head. At once the monster broke away, and rushing madly back to the water's edge leapt in and disappeared. Pigsy was furious. "Heigh, brother," he cried. "Who asked you to interfere? The monster was just beginning to tire. After another three or four rounds he would not have been able to fend off my rake, and I should have had him at my mercy. But as soon as he saw your ugly face he took to his heels. You've spoilt everything!" "I'll just tell you how it happened," said Monkey. "It's months since I had a chance to use my cudgel, and when I saw you having such a rare time with him my feet itched with longing not to miss the fun, and I couldn't hold myself back. How was I to know that the monster wouldn't play?" So hand in hand, laughing and talking, the two of them went back to Tripitaka. "Have you caught the monster?" he asked. "He gave up the fight," said Monkey, "and went back again into the water." "It wouldn't be a bad thing," said Tripitaka, "if we could persuade him to show us how to get across. He's lived here a long time, and must know this river inside out. Otherwise I don't see how we are to get across an enormous river like this without a boat." "There is something in that," said Monkey. "Does not the proverb say 'You cannot live near cinnabar[1] without becoming red, or near ink without becoming black.' If we succeed in catching him we certainly ought not to kill him, but make him take the Master across this river and then dispose of him." "You shall have your chance this time," said Pigsy to Monkey. "I'll stay here and look after the Master."

"That's all very well," said Monkey, "but this job is not at all in my line. I'm not at my best in the water. To get along here, I have to change myself into some water creature, such as a fish or crab. If it were a matter of going up into the clouds, I have tricks enough to deal with the ugliest situation. But in the water I confess I am at a disadvantage." "I used, of course," said Pigsy, "to be Marshal of the River of Heaven, and had the command of eighty thousand watery fellows, so that I certainly ought to know something about that element. My only fear is that if whole broods of water-creatures were to come to the monster's help, I might get myself into a bit of a fix." "What you must do," said Monkey, "is to lure the monster out, and not get yourself involved in more of a scrap than you can help. Once he is out, I'll come to your assistance." "That's the best plan," said Pigsy, "I'll go at once." So saying, he stripped off his blue embroidered jacket and shoes, and brandishing his rake plunged into the river. He found that he had forgotten none of his old water-magic, and lashing through the waves soon reached the bed of the stream and made his way straight ahead. After retiring from the fight, the monster lay down and had a nap. Soon however he was woken by the sound of someone coming through the water, and starting up he saw Pigsy pushing through the waves, rake in hand. Seizing his staff, he came towards him shouting, "Now then, shaven pate, just look where you're going or you'll get a nasty knock with this staff!" Pigsy struck the staff aside with his rake, crying, "What monster are you, that you dare to bar my path?" "I'm surprised that you don't recognize me,' said the monster. "I am not an ordinary spook, but a divinity with name and surname." "If that is so," said Pigsy, "what are you doing here, taking human lives? Tell me who you are, and I'll spare you!"

"So great was my skill in alchemic arts," said the monster, "that I was summoned to Heaven by the Jade Emperor and became a Marshal of the Hosts of Heaven. One day, at a celestial banquet, my hand slipped and I broke a crystal cup. The Jade Emperor was furious, and I was hurried away to the execution ground. Fortunately for me the Red-legged Immortal begged for my release, and my sentence was changed to one of banish-

---

1. A red ore of mercury.

ment to the River of Flowing Sands. When I am hungry I go ashore and eat whatever living thing comes my way. Many are the woodmen and fishermen who have fallen to me as my prey, and I don't mind telling you I am very hungry at this moment. Don't imagine that your flesh would be too coarse for me to eat. Chopped up fine and well sauced, you'll suit me nicely!" "Coarse indeed!" said Pigsy. "I'm a dainty enough morsel to make any mouth water. Mind your manners, and swallow your grandfather's rake!" The monster ducked and avoided the blow. Then both of them came up to the surface of the water, and treading the waves fought stubbornly for two hours without reaching a decision. It was a case of "the copper bowl meeting the iron broom, the jade gong confronted by the metal bell."[2]

After some thirty rounds Pigsy pretended to give in, and dragging his rake after him made for the shore, with the monster hard on his heels. "Come on!" cried Pigsy. "With firm ground under our feet we'll have a better fight than before." "I know what you're up to," cried the monster. "You've lured me up here, so that your partner may come and help you. We'll go back into the water and finish the fight there." The monster was too wily to come any further up the bank and they soon were fighting again, this time at the very edge of the water. This was too much for Monkey, who was watching them from a distance. "Wait here," he said to Tripitaka, "while I try the trick called 'The ravening eagle pouncing on its prey.' " So saying, he catapulted into the air and swooped down on the monster, who swiftly turning his head and seeing Monkey pouncing down upon him from the clouds, leapt straight into the water and was seen no more. "He's given us the slip," said Monkey. "He's not likely to come out on the bank again. What are we going to do?" "It's a tough job," said Pigsy, "I doubt if I can beat him. Even if I sweat till I burst I can't get beyond quits." "Let's go and see the Master," said Monkey.

They climbed the bank, and finding Tripitaka they told him of their predicament. Tripitaka burst into tears. "We shall never get across," he sobbed. "Don't you worry," said Monkey. "It is true that with that creature lying in wait for us, we can't get across. But Pigsy, you stay here by the Master and don't attempt to do any more fighting. I am going off to the Southern Ocean." "And what are you going to do there?" asked Pigsy. "This scripture-seeking business," said Monkey, "is an invention of the Bodhisattva, and it was she who converted us. It is surely for her to find some way of getting us over this river. I'll go and ask her. It's a better idea than fighting with the monster." "Brother," said Pigsy, "when you're there you might say a word to her for me; tell her I'm very much obliged indeed for having been put on the right way." "If you are going," said Tripitaka, "you had better start at once and get back as soon as you can."

Monkey somersaulted into the clouds, and in less than half an hour he had reached the Southern Ocean and saw Mount Potalaka[3] rise before him. After landing, he went straight to the Purple Bamboo Grove, where he was met by the Spirits of the Twenty-Four Ways. "Great Sage, what

---

2. A proverb for things different but equally matched.   3. Sacred mountain where the bodhisattva Kuan-yin lives.

brings you here?" they said. "My Master is in difficulties," said Monkey, "and I wish to have an interview with the Bodhisattva." "Sit down," they said, "and we will announce you." The Bodhisattva was leaning against the parapet of the Lotus Pool, looking at the flowers, with the Dragon King's daughter, bearer of the Magic Pearl, at her side. "Why aren't you looking after your Master?" she said to Monkey, when he was brought in. "When we came to the River of Flowing Sands," said Monkey, "we found it guarded by a monster formidable in the arts of war. My fellow-disciple Pigsy, whom we picked up on the way, did his best to subdue the creature, but was not successful. That is why I have ventured to come and ask you to take pity on us, and rescue my Master from this predicament." "You obstinate ape," said the Bodhisattva, "this is the same thing all over again. Why didn't you say that you were in charge of the priest of T'ang?" "We were both far too busy trying to catch him and make him take the Master across," said Monkey. "I put him there on purpose to help scripture-seekers," said Kuan-yin. "If only you had mentioned the fact that you had come from China to look for scriptures, you would have found him very helpful."

"At present," said Monkey, "he is skulking at the bottom of the river. How are we to get him to come out and make himself useful? And how is Tripitaka going to get across the river?" The Bodhisattva summoned her disciple Hui-yen, and taking a red gourd from her sleeve she said to him, "Take this gourd, go with Monkey to the river and shout "Sandy!" He will come out at once, and you must then bring him to the Master to make his submission. Next string together the nine skulls that he wears at his neck according to the disposition of the Magic Square, with the gourd in the middle, and you will find you have a holy ship that will carry Tripitaka across the River of Flowing Sands."

Soon Hui-yen and Monkey alighted on the river-bank. Seeing who Monkey had brought with him, Pigsy led forward the Master to meet them. After salutations had been exchanged, Hui-yen went to the edge of the water and called, "Sandy, Sandy! The scripture-seekers have been here a long time. Why do you not come out and pay your respects to them?"

The monster Sandy, knowing that this must be a messenger from Kuan-yin, hastened to the surface, and as soon as his head was above water he saw Hui-yen and Monkey. He put on a polite smile and came towards them bowing and saying to Hui-yen, "Forgive me for not coming to meet you. Where is the Bodhisattva?" "She has not come," said Hui-yen. "She sent me to tell you to put yourself at Tripitaka's disposal and become his disciple. She also told me to take the skulls that you wear at your neck and this gourd that I have brought, and make a holy ship to carry the Master across."

"Where are the pilgrims?" asked Sandy. "Sitting there on the eastern bank," said Hui-yen. "Well," said Sandy, looking at Pigsy, "that filthy creature never said a word about scriptures, though I fought with him for two days." Then seeing Monkey, "What, is that fellow there too?" he cried. "He's the other's partner. I'm not going near them." "The first is Pigsy," said Hui-yen, "and the second is Monkey. They are both Tripitaka's disciples and both were converted by the Bodhisattva. You have nothing to fear from them. I myself will introduce you to the Master." Sandy put away his staff, tidied himself and scrambled up the bank. When they reached Tripitaka, Sandy knelt before him, exclaiming, "How can I have been so blind as not to recognize you? Forgive me for all my rudeness!" "You brazen creature," said Pigsy, "why did you insist on having a row with us, instead of joining our party from the start?" "Brother," laughed Monkey, "don't scold him. It is we who are to blame, for never having told him that we were going to get scriptures." "Is it indeed your earnest desire to dedicate yourself to our religion?" asked Tripitaka. Sandy bowed his assent, and Tripitaka told Monkey to take a knife and shave his head.[4] He then once more did homage to Tripitaka, and in a less degree to Monkey and Pigsy. Tripitaka thought that Sandy shaped very well as a priest, and was thoroughly satisfied with him.

"You had better be quick and get on with your boat-building," said Hui-yen.

Sandy obediently took the skulls from his neck, and tying them in the pattern of the Magic Square he put the Bodhisattva's gourd in the middle, and called to Tripitaka to come down to the water. Tripitaka then ascended the holy ship, which he found as secure as any light craft. Pigsy supported him on the left, Sandy on the right, while Monkey in the stern held the halter of the white horse, which followed as best it could. Hui-yen floated just above them. They soon arrived in perfect safety at the other side.

And if you do not know how long it was before they got Illumination you must listen to what is told in the next chapter.

CHAPTER XIX

Tripitaka sat in the Zen Hall[5] of the Treasure Wood Temple, under the lamp; he recited the Water Litany of the Liang Emperor and read through the True Scripture of the Peacock. It was now the third watch (12 p.m.), and he put his books back into their bag, and was just going to get up and go to bed when he heard a great banging outside the gate and felt a dank blast of ghostly wind. Fearing the lamp would be blown out, he hastened to screen it with his sleeve. But the lamp continued to flicker in the strangest way, and Tripitaka began to tremble. He was, however, very tired, and presently he lay down across the reading-desk and dozed. Although his eyes were closed, he still knew what was going on about him, and in his ears still sounded the dark wind that moaned outside the window. And when the wind had passed by, he heard a voice outside the Zen Hall whispering: "Master!"

Tripitaka raised his head, and in his dream he saw a man standing there, dripping from head to foot, with tears in his eyes, and continually murmuring, "Master, Master." Tripitaka sat up and said, "What can you be but a hobgoblin, evil spirit, monster or foul bogey, that you should come to this place and molest me in the middle of the night? But I must tell you that I am no common scrambler in the greedy world of man. I am a great and illustrious priest who at the bidding of the Emperor of

---

4. A sign of leaving the secular world and taking a Buddhist vow of monkhood.   5. Meditation room.

T'ang am going to the West to worship the Buddha and seek scriptures. And I have three disciples, each of whom is adept in quelling dragons and subduing tigers, removing monsters and making away with bogeys. If these disciples were to see you, they would grind you to powder. I tell you this for your own good, in kindness and compassion. You had best hide at once, and not set foot in this place of Meditation." But the man drew nearer to the room and said, "Master, I am no hobgoblin, evil spirit, monster, nor foul bogey either." "If you are none of these things," said Tripitaka, "what are you doing here at depth of night?" "Master," said the man, "rest your eyes upon me and look at me well." Then Tripitaka looked at him with a fixed gaze and saw that there was a crown upon his head and a sceptre at his waist, and that he was dressed and shod as only a king can be.

When Tripitaka saw this he was much startled and amazed. At once he bowed down and cried out with a loud voice: "Of what court is your majesty the king? I beg of you, be seated." But the hand he stretched to help the king to his seat plunged through empty space. Yet when he was back in his seat and looked up, the man was still there. "Tell me, your majesty," he cried "of what are you emperor, of where are you king? Doubtless there were troubles in your land, wicked ministers rebelled against you and at midnight you fled for your life. What is your tale? Tell it for me to hear." "Master," he said, "my home is due west of here, only forty leagues away. At that place, there is a city moated and walled, and this city is where my kingdom was founded." "And what is its name?" asked Tripitaka. "I will not deceive you," he said. "When my dynasty was set up there, a new name was given to it, and it was called Crow-cock." "But tell me," said Tripitaka, "what brings you here in such consternation?" "Master," he said, "five years ago there was a great drought. The grass did not grow and my people were all dying of hunger. It was pitiful indeed!" Tripitaka nodded. "Your majesty," he said, "there is an ancient saying, 'Heaven favours, where virtue rules.' I fear you have no compassion for your people; for now that they are in trouble, you leave your city. Go back and open your storehouses, sustain your people, repent your misdeeds, and do present good twofold to make recompense. Release from captivity any whom you have unjustly condemned, and Heaven will see to it that rain comes and the winds are tempered." "All the granaries in my kingdom were empty," he said, "I had neither cash nor grain. My officers civil and military were unpaid, and even at my own board no relish could be served. I have shared sweet and bitter with my people no less than Yü the Great[6] when he quelled the floods; I have bathed and done penance; morning and night I have burnt incense and prayed. For three years it was like this, till the rivers were all empty, the wells dry.

"Suddenly, when things were at their worst, there came a magician from the Chung-nan mountains[7] who could call the winds and summon the rain, and make stones into gold. First he obtained audience with my many officers, civil and military, and then with me. At once I begged him to mount the altar and pray for rain. He did so, and was answered; no

6. Mythical Chinese emperor of antiquity who carved the rivers of China to drain off floods.   7. A range south of the capital Ch'ang-an.

sooner did his magic tablet resound than floods of rain fell. I told him three feet would be ample. But he said after so long a drought, it took a lot to soak the ground, and he brought down another two inches. And I, seeing him to be of such great powers, prostrated myself before him and treated him henceforth as my elder brother." "This was a great piece of luck," said Tripitaka. "Whence should my luck come?" asked he. "Why," said Tripitaka, "if your magician could make rain when you wanted it, and gold whenever you needed it, what did you lack that you must needs leave your kingdom and come to me here?"

"For two years," he said, "he was my fellow at board and bed. Then at spring time when all the fruit trees were in blossom and young men and girls from every house, gallants from every quarter, went out to enjoy the sights of spring, there came a time when my officers had all returned to their desks and the ladies of the court to their bowers. I with that magician went slowly stepping hand in hand, till we came to the flower-garden and to the eight-cornered crystal well. Here he threw down something, I do not know what, and at once there was a great golden light. He led me to the well-side, wondering what treasure was in the well. Then he conceived an evil intent, and with a great shove pushed me into the well; then took a paving-stone and covered the well-top and sealed it with clay, and planted a banana-plant on top of it. . . . Pity me! I have been dead three years; I am the phantom unavenged of one that perished at the bottom of a well."

When the man said that he was a ghost, Tripitaka was terrified; his legs grew flabby beneath him, and his hair stood on end. Controlling himself at last, he asked him saying, "Your Majesty's story is hard to reconcile with reason. You say you have been dead for three years. How is it that in all this time none of your officers civil and military, nor of your queens and concubines and chamberlains ever came to look for you?" "I have told you already," the man said, "of the magician's powers. There can be few others like him in all the world. He had but to give himself a shake, and there and then, in the flower-garden, he changed himself into the exact image of me. And now he holds my rivers and hills, and has stolen away my kingdom. All my officers, the four hundred gentlemen of my court, my queens and concubines—all, all are his."

"Your Majesty is easily daunted," said Tripitaka. "Easily daunted?" he asked. "Yes," said Tripitaka, "that magician may have strange powers, turn himself into your image, steal your lands, your officers knowing nothing, and your ladies unaware. But you that were dead at least knew that you were dead. Why did you not go to Yama, King of Death, and put in a complaint?"

"The magician's power," he said, "is very great, and he is on close terms with the clerks and officers of Death. The Spirit of Wall and Moat is forever drinking with him; all the Dragon-kings of the Sea are his kinsmen. The God of the Eastern Peak is his good friend; the ten kings of Judgment are his cousins. I should be barred in every effort to lay my plaint before the King of Death."

"If your Majesty," said Tripitaka, "is unable to lay your case before the Courts of the Dead, what makes you come to the world of the living with any hope of redress?" "Master," he said, "how should a wronged ghost dare approach your door? The Spirit that Wanders at Night caught me in a gust of magic wind and blew me along. He said my three years' water-misery was ended and that I was to present myself before you; for at your service, he said, there was a great disciple, the Monkey Sage, most able to conquer demons and subdue impostors. I beg of you to come to my kingdom, lay hands on the magician and make clear the false from the true. Then, Master, I would repay you with all that will be mine to give."

"So then," said Tripitaka, "you have come to ask that my disciple should drive out the false magician?" "Indeed, indeed," he said. "My disciple," said Tripitaka, "in other ways is not all that he should be. But subduing monsters and evil spirits just suits his powers. I fear however that the circumstances make it hard for him to deal with this evil power." "Why so?" asked the king. "Because," said Tripitaka, "the magician has used his magic powers to change himself into the image of you. All the officers of your court have gone over to him, and all your ladies have accepted him. My disciple could no doubt deal with them; but he would hesitate to do violence to them. For should he do so, would not he and I be held guilty of conspiring to destroy your kingdom? And what would this be but to paint the tiger and carve the swan?"[8]

"There is still someone of mine at Court," he said. "Excellent, excellent," said Tripitaka. "No doubt it is some personal attendant, who is guarding some fastness[9] for you." "Not at all," he said. "It is my own heir apparent." "But surely," said Tripitaka, "the false magician has driven him away." "Not at all," he said. "He is in the Palace of Golden Bells, in the Tower of the Five Phoenixes, studying with his tutor, or on the steps of the magician's throne. But all these three years he has forbidden the prince to go into the inner chambers of the Palace, and he can never see his mother." "Why is that?" asked Tripitaka. "It is the magician's scheme," he said. "He fears that if they were to meet, the queen might in the course of conversation let drop some word that would arouse the prince's suspicions. So these two never meet, and he all this long time has lived secure."

"The disaster that has befallen you, no doubt at Heaven's behest, is much like my own misfortune. My own father was killed by brigands, who seized my mother, and after three months she gave birth to me. I at length escaped from their hands and by good chance met with kindness from a priest of the Golden Mountain Temple, who brought me up. Remembering my own unhappy state, without father or mother, I can sympathize with your prince, who has lost both his parents. But tell me, granted that this prince is still at Court, how can I manage to see him?" "What difficulty in that?" he said. "Because he is kept under strict control," said Tripitaka, "and is not even allowed to see the mother who bore him. How will a stray monk get to him?" "To-morrow," the king said, "he leaves the Court at daybreak." "For what purpose?" "To-morrow, early in the morning, with three thousand followers and falcons and dogs, he will go hunting outside the city, and it will certainly be easy for you to see him. You

---

8. The full proverb is: "A poorly drawn tiger looks like a dog; an ill-carved swan looks like a duck." That is, an ambitious undertaking, if not successful, may be worse than inaction.   9. That is, guarding some secure place.

must then tell him what I have told you, and he cannot fail to believe you." "He is only a common mortal," said Tripitaka, "utterly deceived by the false magician in the palace, and at every turn calling him father and king. Why should he believe what I tell him?" "If that is what worries you," the king said, "I will give you a token to show to him." "And what can you give me?"

In his hand the king carried a tablet of white jade, bordered with gold. This he laid before Tripitaka saying, "Here is my token." "What thing is this?" asked Tripitaka. "When the magician disguised himself as me," said the king, "this treasure was the one thing he forgot about. When the queen asked what had become of it, he said that the wonder-worker who came to make rain took it away with him. If my prince sees it, his heart will be stirred towards me and he will avenge me." "That will do," said Tripitaka. "Wait for me a little, while I tell my disciple to arrange this matter for you. Where shall I find you?" "I dare not wait," he said. "I must ask the Spirit that wanders at Night to blow me to the inner chambers of the palace, where I will appear to the queen in a dream and tell her how to work with her son, and to conspire with you and your disciple." Tripitaka nodded and agreed, saying, "Go, if you will." Then the wronged ghost beat its head on the floor and turned as though to depart. Somehow it stumbled, and went sprawling with a loud noise that woke Tripitaka up. He knew that it had all been a dream, and finding himself sitting with the dying lamp in front of him, he hurriedly cried: "Disciple, disciple!" "Hey, what's that?" cried Pigsy, waking up and coming across to him. "In the old days when I was a decent chap and had my whack of human flesh whenever I wanted, and all the stinking victuals I needed, that was a happy life indeed. A very different matter from coddling an old cleric on his journey! I thought I was to be an acolyte, but this is more like being a slave. By day I hoist the luggage and lead the horse; by night I run my legs off bringing you your pot. No sleep early or late! What's the matter this time? "Disciple," said Tripitaka, "I was dozing just now at my desk, and had a strange dream."

At this point Monkey sat up, and coming across to Tripitaka said, "Master, dreams come from waking thoughts. Each time we come to a hill before we have even begun to climb it, you are in a panic about ogres and demons. And you are always brooding about what a long way it is to India, and wondering if we shall ever get there; and thinking about Ch'ang-an,[1] and wondering if you will ever see it again. All this brooding makes dreams. You should be like me. I think only about seeing Buddha in the West, and not a dream comes near me." "Disciple," said Tripitaka, "this was not a dream of home-sickness. No sooner had I closed my eyes than there came a wild gust of wind, and there at the door stood an Emperor, who said he was the King of Crow-cock. He was dripping from head to foot, and his eyes were full of tears." Then he told Monkey the whole story. "You need say no more," said Monkey. "It is clear enough that this dream came to you in order to bring a little business my way. No doubt at all that this magician is an ogre who has usurped the throne. Just let me

---

1. The capital of T'ang China, from which Tripitaka had come.

put him to the test. I don't doubt my stick will make short work of him."
"Disciple," said Tripitaka, "he said the magician was terribly powerful."
"What do I care how powerful he is?" said Monkey. "If he had any inkling
that Monkey might arrive on the scene, he would have cleared out long
ago." "Now I come to think of it," said Tripitaka, "he left a token." Pigsy
laughed. "Now, Master," he said, "you must pull yourself together. A
dream's a dream. Now it is time to talk sense again." But Sandy broke in,
" 'He who does not believe that straight is straight must guard against the
wickedness of good.' Let us light torches, open the gate, and see for ourselves whether the token has been left or not."

Monkey did indeed open the gate, and there, in the light of the stars
and moon, with no need for torches, they saw lying on the ramp of the
steps a tablet of white jade with gold edges. Pigsy stepped forward and
picked it up, saying, "Brother, what's this thing?" "This," said Monkey, "is
the treasure that the king carried in his hand. It is called a jade tablet.
Master, now that we have found this thing, there is no more doubt about
the matter. To-morrow it will be my job to catch this fiend."

Dear Monkey! He plucked a hair from his tail, blew on it with magic
breath, cried out "Change!" and it became a casket lacquered in red and
gold; he laid the tablet in it, and said, "Master, take this in your hand, and
when day comes put on your embroidered cassock, and sit reading the
scriptures in the great hall. Meanwhile I will inspect that walled city. If I
find that an ogre is indeed ruling there, I will slay him, and do a deed by
which I shall be remembered here. But if it is not an ogre, we must beware
of meddling in the business at all." "You are right," said Tripitaka. "If,"
said Monkey, "the prince does not go out hunting, then there is nothing
to be done. But if the dream comes true, I will bring him here to see you."
"And if he comes here, how am I to receive him?" "When I let you know
that he is coming, open the casket and wait while I change myself into a
little priest two inches long, and put me in the casket. When the prince
comes here, he will go and bow to the Buddha. Don't you take any notice
of the prince or kneel down before him. When he sees that you, a commoner, do not bow down to him, he will order his followers to seize you.
You will, of course, let yourself be seized, and beaten too, if they choose
to beat you, and bound if they choose to bind you. Let them kill you,
indeed, if they want to." "They will be well armed," said Tripitaka. "They
might very well kill me. That is not a good idea at all." "It would not
matter," said Monkey. "I could deal with that. I will see to it that nothing
really serious happens. If he questions you, say that you were sent by the
Emperor of China to worship Buddha and get scriptures, and that you
have brought treasures with you. When he asks what treasures, show him
your cassock and say it is the least of the three treasures, and that there are
two others. Then show him the casket and tell him that there is a treasure
within that knows what happened five hundred years ago, and what will
happen in five hundred years long hence, and five hundred years between.
One thousand five hundred years in all, of things past and present. Then
let me out of the casket and I will tell the prince what was revealed in the
dream. If he believes, I will go and seize the magician and the prince will
be avenged upon his father's murderer and we shall win renown. But if

he does not believe, I will show him the jade tablet. Only I fear he is too young, and will not recognize it." Tripitaka was delighted. "An excellent plan," he said. "But what shall we call the third treasure? The first is the embroidered cassock, the second the white jade tablet. What is your trans-formation[2] to be called?" "Call it," said Monkey, "the Baggage that makes Kings." Tripitaka agreed, and committed the name to memory.

Neither disciple nor teacher could sleep. How gladly would they have been able, by a nod, to call up the sun from the Mulberry Tree where it rests,[3] and by a puff of breath blow away the stars that filled the sky!

However, at last it began to grow white in the East, and Monkey got up and gave his orders to Pigsy and Sandy. "Do not," he said, "upset the other priests in the temple by coming out of your cell and rollicking about. Wait till I have done my work, and then we will go on again together."

As soon as he had left them he turned a somersault and leapt into the air. Looking due west with his fiery eyes he soon saw a walled and moated city. You may ask how it was that he could see it. Well, it was only forty leagues away from the temple, and being so high in the air he could see as far as that.

Going on a little way and looking closely, he saw that baleful clouds hung round the city and fumes of discontent surrounded it, and suspended in mid-air Monkey recited:

> Were he a true king seated on the throne,
> Then there would be a lucky gleam and fire-coloured clouds.
> But as it is, a false friend has seized the Dragon Seat,
> And coiling wreaths of black fume tarnish the Golden Gate.[4]

While he was gazing at this sad sight, Monkey suddenly heard a great clanging, and looking down he saw the eastern gate of the city open, and from it a great throng of men and horses come out; truly a host of hunts-men. Indeed, a brave show; look at them:

> At dawn they left the east of the Forbidden City;[5]
> They parted and rounded up in the fields of low grass,
> Their bright banners opened and caught the sun,
> Their white palfreys charged abreast the wind.
> Their skin drums clatter with a loud roll;
> The hurled spears fly each to its mark.

The hunters left the city and proceeded eastwards for twenty leagues towards a high plain. Now Monkey could see that in the midst of them was a little, little general in helmet and breast-plate, in his hand a jewelled sword, riding a bay charger, his bow at his waist. "Don't tell me!" said Monkey in the air, "that is the prince. Let me go and play a trick on him."

Dear Monkey! He lowered himself on his cloud, made his way through the ranks of the huntsmen and, when he came to the prince, changed himself into a white hare and ran in front of the prince's horse. The prince was delighted, took an arrow from his quiver, strung it and shot at the hare, which he hit. But Monkey had willed the arrow to find its aim, and

---

2. Magic trick.   3. The Fu-sang Tree, where the sun rests before it rises.   4. The gate to the palace.
Dragon Seat: the throne.   5. The palace compound.

with a swift grab, just as it was about to touch him, he caught hold of it and ran on.

The prince, seeing that he had hit his mark, broke away from his companions and set out in pursuit. When the horse galloped fast, Monkey ran like the wind; when it slowed down, Monkey slowed down. The distance between them remained always the same, and so bit by bit he enticed the prince to the gates of the Treasure Wood Temple. The hare had vanished, for Monkey went back to his own form. But in the door-post an arrow was stuck.

"Here we are, Master," said Monkey, and at once changed again into a two-inch priest and hid in the casket.

Now when the prince came to the temple-gate and found no hare, but only his own arrow sticking in the gate-post, "Very strange!" said the prince, "I am certain I hit the hare. How is it that the hare has disappeared, but the arrow is here? I think it was not a common hare, but one that had lived too long and changed at last into a sprite."

He pulled out the arrow, and looking up saw that above the gate of the temple was an inscription which said "Treasure Wood Temple, erected by Royal Command." "Why, of course!" said the prince. "I remember years ago my father the king ordered an officer to take gold and precious stuffs to the priests of this temple, so that they might repair the chapel and images. I little thought that I would come here one day like this! A couplet says:

> Chance brought me to a priest's cell
> and I listened to his holy talk;
> From the life of the troubled world I got
> Half a day's rest.

I will go in."

The prince leapt from his horse's back and was just going in when three thousand officers who were in attendance upon him came galloping up in a great throng, and were soon pouring into the courtyard. The priests of the temple, much astonished, came out to do homage to the prince, and escort him into the Buddha Hall, to worship the Buddha. The prince was admiring the cloisters, when suddenly he came upon a priest who sat there and did not budge when he came past. "Has this priest no manners?" the prince cried in a rage. "As no warning was given that I was visiting this place, I could not expect to be met at a distance. But so soon as you saw men-at-arms approaching the gate, you ought to have stood up. How comes it that you are still sitting here without budging? Seize him!"

No sooner had he uttered the command than soldiers rushed from the sides, dragged Tripitaka off with them and made ready to bind him hand and foot. But Monkey in the casket soundlessly invoked the guardian spirits, Devas that protect the Law,[6] and Lu Ting and Lu Chia: "I am now on an errand to subdue an evil spirit. But this prince, in his ignorance, has bade his servants bind my master, and you must come at once to his aid. If he is indeed bound, you will be held responsible!"

---

6. *Dharma*, the Buddhist "law." *Devas*: deities.

Thus secretly addressed by Monkey, how could they venture to disobey? They set a magic ring about Tripitaka, so that each time any one tried to lay hands on him, he could not be reached, any more than if he had been hedged in with a stout wall. "Where do you come from," the prince asked at last, "that you can cheat us like this, making yourself unapproachable?" Tripitaka now came forward and bowed. "I have no such art," he said. "I am only a priest from China, going to the West to worship Buddha and get scriptures."

"China?" said the prince. "Although it is called The Middle Land,[7] it is a most destitute place. Tell me, for example, if you have anything of value upon you." "There is the cassock on my back," said Tripitaka. "It is only a third-class treasure. But I have treasures of the first and second class, which are far superior."

"A coat like yours," said the prince, "that leaves half the body bare! It seems a queer thing to call that a treasure." "This cassock," said Tripitaka, "although it covers only half my body, is described in a poem:

Buddha's coat left one side bare,
But it hid the Absolute from the world's dust.
Its ten thousand threads and thousand stitches fulfilled the fruits of
    Meditation.
Is it a wonder that when I saw you come
                    I did not rise to greet you?
You who call yourself a man, yet have failed to avenge a father's
    death!"

"What wild nonsense this priest is talking!" said the prince in a great rage. "That half-coat, if it has done nothing else for you, has given you the courage to babble ridiculous fustian.[8] How can my father's death be unavenged, since he is not dead? Just tell me that!"

Tripitaka came one step forward, pressed the palms of his hands together and said: "Your Majesty, to how many things does man, born into the world, owe gratitude?" "To four things," said the prince. "To what four things?" "He is grateful," said the prince, "to Heaven and Earth for covering and supporting him, to the sun and moon for shining upon him, to the king for lending him water and earth, and to his father and mother for rearing him."

Tripitaka laughed. "To the other three he owes gratitude indeed," he said. "But what need has he of a father and mother to rear him?" "That's all very well for you," said the prince, "who are a shaven-headed, disloyal, food-cadging wanderer. But if a man had no father or mother, how could he come into the world?" "Your Majesty," said Tripitaka, "I do not know. But in this casket there is a treasure called 'The baggage that makes kings.' It knows everything that happened during the five hundred years long ago, the five hundred years between, and the five hundred years to come, one thousand five hundred years in all. If he can quote a case where there was no gratitude to father and mother, then let me be detained captive here."

"Show him to me," said the prince. Tripitaka took off the cover and out

---

7. So-called because it was supposed to be the middle of the world.   8. Pompous, extravagant language.

jumped monkey, and began to skip about this way and that. "A little fellow like that can't know much," said the prince. Hearing himself described as too small, Monkey used his magic power and stretched himself till he was three feet four inches high. The huntsmen were astonished, and said, "If he goes on growing like this, in a few days he will be bumping his head against the sky." But when he reached his usual height, Monkey stopped growing. At this point the prince said to him, "Baggage who Makes Kings, the old priest says you know all things good and ill, in past and present. Do you divine by the tortoise or by the milfoil?[9] Or do you decide men's fates by sentences from books?" "Not a bit of it," said Monkey; "all I rely on is my three inches of tongue, that tells about everything."

"This fellow talks great nonsense," said the prince. "It has always been by the *Book of Changes*[1] that mysteries have been elucidated and the prospects of the world decided, so that people might know what to pursue and what to avoid. Is it not said: 'The tortoise for divination, the milfoil for prognostication?'[2] But so far as I can make out you go on no principle at all. You talk at random about fate and the future, exciting and misleading people to no purpose." "Now don't be in a hurry, Your Highness," said Monkey, "but listen to me. You are the Crown Prince of Crow-cock. Five years ago there was a famine in your land. The king and his ministers prayed and fasted, but they could not get a speck of rain. Then there came a wizard from the Chung-nan mountains who could call the winds, fetch rain, and turn stone into gold. The king was deceived by his wiles and hailed him as elder brother. Is this true?"

"Yes, yes, yes," said the prince. "Go on!" "For the last three years the magician has not been seen," said Monkey. "Who is it that has been on the throne?" "It is true about the wizard," said the prince. "My father did make this wizard his brother, and ate with him and slept with him. But three years ago, when they were walking in the flower garden and admiring the view, a gust of magic wind that the magician sent blew the jade tablet that the king carried out of his hand, and the magician went off with it straight to the Chung-nan mountains. My father still misses him and has no heart to walk in the flower garden without him. Indeed, for three years it has been locked up and no one has set foot in it. If the king is not my father, who is he?"

At this Monkey began to laugh, and did not stop laughing when the prince asked him what was the matter, till the prince lost his temper. "Why don't you say something?" he said, "instead of standing there laughing." "I have quite a lot to say," said Monkey, "but I cannot say it in front of all these people." The prince thought this reasonable, and motioned to the huntsmen to retire. The leader gave his orders, and soon the three thousand men and horses were all stationed outside the gates. None of the priests of the temple were about. Monkey stopped laughing and said, "Your Highness, he who vanished was the father that begot you; he who sits on the throne is the magician that brought rain."

9. Yarrow. In ancient China prophecies were made from the cracks that formed in tortoiseshells when put in a fire. Divination was also done by casting stalks of milfoil.   1. One of the Confucian classics, also known as the *I Ching;* a book of prophecy and wisdom.   2. Actually, prognostication and divination are basically the same thing.

"Nonsense," cried the prince. "Since the magician left us, the winds have been favouring, the people have been at peace. But according to you it is not my father who is on the throne. It is all very well to say such things to me who am young and let it pass; but if my father were to hear you uttering this subversive talk, he would have you seized and torn into ten thousand pieces." He began railing at Monkey, who turned to Tripitaka and said, "What is to be done? I have told him and he does not believe me. Let's get to work. Show him your treasure, and then get your papers seen to, and go off to India." Tripitaka handed the lacquer-box to Monkey, and Monkey taking it gave himself a shake, and the box became invisible. For it was in reality one of Monkey's hairs, which he had changed into a box, but now put back again as a hair on his body. But the white jade tablet he presented to the prince.

"A fine sort of priest," the prince exclaimed. "You it was who came five years ago disguised as a magician, and stole the family treasure, and now, disguised as a priest, are offering it back again! Seize him!" This command startled Tripitaka out of his wits and pointing at Monkey, "It's you," he cried, "you wretched horse-groom, who have brought this trouble on us for no reason at all." Monkey rushed forward and checked him. "Hold your tongue," he said, "and don't let out my secrets. I am not called 'the Baggage that Makes Kings.' My real name is quite different." "I shall be glad to know your real name," said the prince, "that I may send you to the magistrate to be dealt with as you deserve."

"My name then," said Monkey, "is the Great Monkey Sage, and I am this old man's chief disciple. I was going with my Master to India to get scriptures, and last night we came to this temple and asked for shelter. My Master was reading scriptures by night, and at the third watch he had a dream. He dreamt that your father came to him and said he had been attacked by that magician, who in the flower garden pushed him into the eight-cornered crystal well. Then the wizard changed himself into your father's likeness. The court and all the officers were completely deceived; you yourself were too young to know. You were forbidden to enter the inner apartments of the Palace and the flower garden was shut up, lest the secret should get out. Tonight your father came and asked me to subdue the false magician. I was not sure that he was an evil spirit, but when I looked down from the sky I was quite certain of it. I was just going to seize him, when I met you and your huntsmen. The white hare you shot was me. It was I who led you here and brought you to my Master. This is the truth, every word of it. You have recognized the white tablet, and all that remains is for you to repay your father's care and revenge yourself on his enemy."

This upset the prince very much. "If I do not believe this story," he said to himself, "it must in any case have an unpleasant amount of truth in it. But if I believe it, how can I any longer look upon the present king as my father?" He was in great perplexity. "If you are in doubt," said Monkey, "ride home and ask your mother a question that will decide it. Ask whether she and the king, as man and wife, are on changed terms, these last three years."

"That is a good idea," said the prince. "Just wait while I go and ask my mother." He snatched up the jade tablet and was about to make off, when Monkey stopped him, saying, "If all your gentlemen follow you back to the palace, suspicions will be aroused, and how can I succeed in my task? You must go back all alone and attract no attention. Do not go in at the main gate but by the back gate. And when you get to the inner apartments and see your mother, do not speak loudly or clearly, but in a low whisper; for if the magician should hear you, so great is his power that your life and your mother's would be in danger."

The prince did as he was told, and as he left the temple he told his followers to remain there on guard and not to move. "I have some business," he said. "Wait till I have got to the city and then come on yourselves!" Look at him!

> He gives his orders to the men-at-arms,
> Flies on horseback home to the citadel.

If you do not know whether on this occasion he succeeded in seeing his mother, and if so what passed between them, you must listen to the next chapter.

CHAPTER XX

The prince was soon back at the city of Crow-cock, and as instructed he made no attempt to go in by the main gate, but without announcing himself went to the back gate, where several eunuchs were on guard. They did not dare to stop him, and (dear prince!) he rode in all alone, and soon reached the Arbour of Brocade Perfume, where he found his mother surrounded by her women, who were fanning her, while she leant weeping over a carven balustrade. Why, you will ask, was she weeping? At the fourth watch she had had a dream, half of which she could remember and half of which had faded; and she was thinking hard. Leaping from his horse, the prince knelt down before her and cried "Mother!" She forced herself to put on a happier countenance, and exclaimed, "Child, this is a joy indeed! For years past you have been so busy in the men's quarters at the Palace, studying with your father, that I have never seen you, which has been a great sorrow to me. How have you managed to find time to-day? It is an unspeakable pleasure! My child, why is your voice so mournful? Your father is growing old. Soon the time will come when the 'dragon returns to the pearl-gray sea, the phoenix to the pink mists'; you will then become king. Why should you be dispirited?"

The prince struck the floor with his forehead. "Mother, I ask you," he said, "who is it that sits upon the throne?" "He has gone mad," said the queen. "The ruler is your father and the king. Why should you ask?" "Mother," the prince said, "if you will promise me forgiveness I will speak. But if not, I dare not speak." "How can there be questions of guilt and pardon between mother and son? Of course, you are free to speak. Be quick and begin." "Mother," said the prince, "if you compare your life with my father these last three years with your life with him before, should you say that his affection was as great?" Hearing this question the queen altogether lost her presence of mind, and leaping to her feet ran down from the arbour and flung herself into his arms, saying, "Child, why, when I have not seen you for so long, should you suddenly come and ask me such a question?" "Mother," said the prince hotly, "do not evade this question. For much hangs upon the answer to it."

Then the queen sent away all the Court ladies, and with tears in her eyes said in a low voice, "Had you not asked me, I would have gone down to the Nine Springs[3] of Death without ever breathing a word about this matter. But since you have asked, hear what I have to say:

> What three years ago was warm and bland,[4]
> These last three years has been cold as ice.
> When at the pillow's side I questioned him,
> He told me age had impaired his strength
> and that things did not work."

When he heard this, the prince shook himself free, gripped the saddle and mounted his horse. His mother tried to hold him back, saying, "Child, what is it that makes you rush off before our talk is done?" The prince returned and knelt in front of her. "Mother," he said, "I dare not speak. To-day at dawn I received a command to go hunting outside the city with falcon and dog. By chance I met a priest sent by the Emperor of China to fetch scriptures. He has a chief disciple named Monkey, who is very good at subduing evil spirits. According to him my father the king was drowned in the crystal well in the flower garden, and a wizard impersonated him and seized his throne. Last night at the third watch my father appeared in a dream to this priest and asked him to come to the city and seize the impostor. I did not believe all this, and so came to question you. But what you have just told me makes me certain that it is an evil spirit."

"My child," said the queen, "why should you believe strangers, of whom you have no knowledge?" "I should not," said the prince, "have dared to accept the story as true, had not the king my father left behind a token in the hands of these people." The queen asked what it was, and the prince took out from his sleeve the white jade tablet bordered with gold, and handed it to his mother. When she saw that it was indeed a treasure that had been the king's in old days, she could not stop her tears gushing out like a water-spring. "My lord and master," she cried, "why have you been dead three years and never come to me, but went first to a priest and afterwards to the prince?" "Mother," said the prince, "what do these words mean?" "My child," she said, "at the fourth watch I too had a dream. I dreamt I saw your father stand in front of me, all dripping wet, saying that he was dead, and that his soul had visited a priest of Tʻang and asked him to defeat the false king and rescue his own body from where it had been thrown. That is all I can remember, and it is only half. The other half I cannot get clear, and I was puzzling about it when you came. It is strange that you should just at this moment come with this tale, and bring this tablet with you. I will put it away, and you must go and ask that priest to come at once and do what he promises. If he can drive away the impostor

---

3. The underworld.   4. Gentle.

and distinguish the false from the true, you will have repaid the king your father for the pains he bestowed upon your upbringing."

The prince was soon back at the gates of the Treasure Wood Temple, where he was joined by his followers. The sun's red disc was now falling. He told his followers to stay quietly where they were, went into the temple alone, arranged his hat and clothes, and paid his respects to Monkey, who came hopping and skipping from the main hall. The prince knelt down, saying, "Here I am again, Father." Monkey raised him from his knees. "Did you ask anyone anything when you were in the city?" he said. "I questioned my mother," said the prince; and he told the whole story. Monkey smiled. "If it is as cold as that," he said, "he is probably a transformation of some chilly creature. No matter! Just wait while I mop him up for you. But to-day it is growing late, and I cannot very well start doing anything. You go back now, and I will come early to-morrow."

"Master," said the prince, kneeling before him, "let me wait here till the morning, and then go along with you." "That will not do," said Monkey. "If I were to come into the city at the same time as you, the suspicions of the impostor would be aroused. He would not believe that I forced myself upon you, but would be sure you had invited me. And in this way the blame would fall on you."

"I shall get into trouble anyhow," said the prince, "if I go into the city now." "What about?" asked Monkey. "I was sent out hunting," said the prince, "and I have not got a single piece of game. How dare I face the king? If he accuses me of incompetence and casts me into prison, who will you have to look after you when you arrive to-morrow? There is not one of the officers who knows you." "What matter?" said Monkey. "You have only to mention that you need some game, and I will procure it for you." Dear Monkey! Watch him while he displays his arts before the prince. He gives himself a shake, jumps up on to the fringe of a cloud, performs a magic pass and murmurs a spell which compels the spirits of the mountain and the local deities to come before him and do obeisance. "Great Sage," they said, "what orders have you for us little divinities?" "I guarded a priest of T'ang on his way here," said Monkey. "I want to seize an evil spirit, but this prince here has nothing to show for his hunting, and does not dare return to Court. I have sent for you divinities to ask you to do me a favour. Find some musk deer, wild boar, hares and so on—any wild beasts or birds you can discover, and bring them here." The divinities dared not disobey. "How many do you require of each?" they asked. "It does not matter exactly how many," said Monkey. "Just bring some along; that is all."

Then these divinities, using the secret instruments that appertained to them, made a magic wind that drew together wild beasts. Soon there were hundreds and thousands of wild fowl, deer, foxes, hares, tigers, panthers and wolves collected in front of Monkey. "It is not I who want them!" he cried. "You must get them on the move again, and string them out on each side of the road for forty leagues. The hunters will be able to take them home without use of falcon or dog. That is all that is required of you."

The divinities obeyed, and spread out the game on each side of the road. Monkey then lowered his cloud and said to the prince, "Your Highness may now go back. There is game all along the road; you have only to collect it."

When the prince saw him floating about in the air and exercising magic powers, he was deeply impressed, and bent his head on the ground in prostration before Monkey, from whom he humbly took his leave. He then went out in front of the temple and gave orders to the huntsmen to return to Court. They were astonished to find endless wild game on each side of the road, which they took without use of falcon or dog, merely by laying hands upon it. They all believed that this blessing had been vouchsafed to the prince, and had no idea that it was Monkey's doing. Listen to the songs of triumph that they sing as they throng back to the city!

When the priests of the temple saw on what terms Tripitaka and the rest were with the prince, they began to treat them with a new deference. They invited them to refreshments, and again put the Zen Hall at Tripitaka's disposal. It was near the first watch; but Monkey had something on his mind and could not get to sleep at once. Presently he crept across to Tripitaka's bed and called, "Master!" Tripitaka was not asleep either; but knowing that Monkey liked giving people a start, he pretended to be asleep. Monkey rubbed his tonsure and shaking him violently, he said, "Master, why are you sleeping?" "The rogue!" cried Tripitaka crossly. "Why can't you go to sleep, instead of pestering me like this?" "Master," said Monkey, "there is something you must give me your advice about." "What is that?" said Tripitaka. "I talked very big to the prince," said Monkey, "giving him to understand that my powers were high as the hills and deep as the sea, and that I could catch the false wizard as easily as one takes things out of a bag—I had only to stretch out my hand and carry him off. But I cannot get to sleep, for it has occurred to me that it may not be so easy." "If you think it's too difficult, why do it?" said Tripitaka. "It's not that there's any difficulty about catching him," said Monkey. "The only question is whether it is legal." "What nonsense this monkey talks," said Tripitaka. "How can it be illegal to arrest a monster that has seized a monarch's throne?" "You only know how to read scriptures, worship Buddha and practise Zen, and have never studied the Code of Hsiao Ho.[5] But you must at least know the proverb 'Take robber, take loot.' The magician has been king for three years and not the slightest suspicion has been felt by anyone. All the late king's ladies sleep with him, and the ministers civil and military disport themselves with him. Even if I succeed in catching him, how am I to convince anyone of his guilt?" "What is the difficulty?" asked Tripitaka. "Even if he were as dumb as a calabash,[6] he would be able to talk one down. He would say boldly, 'I am the king of Crow-cock. What crime have I committed against Heaven that you should arrest me?' How would one argue with him then?" "And you," said Tripitaka, "what plan have you got?" "My plan is already made," said Monkey smiling. "The only obstacle is that you have a partiality." "A partiality for whom?"

---

5. A minister of the Han Dynasty who established laws.   6. A type of gourd.

said Tripitaka. "Pigsy," said Monkey; "you have a preference for him because he is so strong." "What makes you think that?" asked Tripitaka. "If it were not so," said Monkey, "you would pull yourself together and have the courage to stay here with Sandy to look after you, while I and Pigsy go off to the city of Crow-cock, find the flower garden, uncover the well, and bring up the Emperor's body, which we will wrap in our wrapper, and next day bring to Court. There we will get our papers put in order, confront the Magician, and I will fell him with my cudgel. If he tries to exonerate himself, I will show him the body and say, 'Here is the man you drowned.' And I will make the prince come forward and wail over his father, the queen come out and recognize her husband, the officers civil and military look upon their lord, and then I and my brother will get to work. In this way the whole thing will be on a proper footing."

Tripitaka thought this was a splendid plan, but he was not sure that Pigsy would consent. "Why not?" said Monkey. "Didn't I say you were partial to him and did not want him to go? You think he would refuse to go because you know that when I call you it is often half an hour before you take any notice. You'll see when I start, that I shall only need a turn or two of my three-inch tongue, and no matter if he is Pigsy or Wigsy I am quite capable of making him follow me." "Very well," said Tripitaka, "call him when you go."

"Pigsy, Pigsy," cried Monkey at Pigsy's bedside. That fool did most of the hard work when they were on the road, and no sooner did his head touch the pillow than he was snoring, and it took a great deal more than a shout to wake him.

Monkey pulled his ears, tweaked his bristles and dragged him from the pillow, shouting "Pigsy!" That fool pushed him away. Monkey shouted again. "Go to sleep and don't be so stupid," Pigsy said. "To-morrow we have got to be on the road again." "I am not being stupid," said Monkey, "there is a bit of business I want your help in." "What business?" asked Pigsy. "You heard what the prince said?" said Monkey. "No," said Pigsy, "I did not set eyes on him, or hear anything he said." "He told me," said Monkey, "that the magician has a treasure worth more than an army of ten thousand men. When we go to the city to-morrow, we are sure to fall foul of him, he will use it to overthrow us. Wouldn't it be much better if we got in first and stole the treasure?"

"Brother," said Pigsy, "are you asking me to commit robbery? If so, that's a business I have experience of and can really be of some help. But there is one thing we must get clear. If I steal a treasure or subdue a magician I expect more than a petty, skunking share. The treasure must be mine." "What do you want it for?" asked Monkey. "I am not so clever as you are at talking people into giving me alms. I am strong, but I have a very common way of talking, and I don't know how to recite the scriptures. When we get into a tight place, wouldn't this treasure be good to exchange for something to eat and drink?" "I only care for fame," said Monkey. "I don't want any treasures. You may have it all to yourself."

That fool, when he heard that it was all to be his, was in high glee. He rolled out of bed, hustled into his clothes and set out with Monkey.

Clear wine brings a blush to the cheeks;
Yellow gold moves even a philosophic heart.

The two of them opened the temple gate very quietly and, leaving Tripitaka, mounted a wreath of cloud and soon reached the city, where they
lowered their cloud, just as the second watch was being sounded on the
tower. "Brother! it's the second watch," said Monkey. "Couldn't be better,"
said Pigsy. "Everyone will just be deep in their first sleep."

They did not go to the main gate, but to the back gate, where they
heard the sound of the watchman's clappers and bells. "Brother," said
Monkey, "they are on the alert at all the gates. How shall we get in?"
"When did thieves ever go in by a gate?" said Pigsy. "We must scramble
over the wall." Monkey did so, and at a bound was over the rampart and
wall. Pigsy followed, and the two stealthily made their way in, soon
rejoining the road from the gate. They followed this till they came to the
flower garden.

In front of them was a gate-tower with three thatched white gables, and
high up was an inscription in shining letters, catching the light of the
moon and stars. It said "Imperial Flower Garden." When Monkey came
close, he saw that the locks were sealed up several layers deep, and he told
Pigsy to get to work. That fool wielded his iron rake, which he brought
crashing down upon the gate and smashed it to bits. Monkey stepped
over the fragments, and once inside could not stop himself jumping and
shouting for joy. "Brother," said Pigsy, "you'll be the ruin of us. Who ever
heard of a thief making all that noise? You'll wake everyone up, we shall
be arrested and taken before the judge, and if we are not condemned to
death we shall certainly be sent back to where we came from and drafted
into the army." "Why try to make me nervous?" said Monkey. "Look!

The painted and carven balustrades are scattered and strewn;
The jewel-studded arbours and trees are toppling down.
The sedgy islands and knot-weed banks are buried in dust;
The white peonies and yellow glove-flowers, all dust-destroyed.
Jasmine and rose perfume the night;
The red peony and tiger-lily bloom in vain,
The hibiscus and Syrian mallow are choked with weeds;
Strange plant and rare flower are crushed and die."

"And what does it matter if they do." said Pigsy. "Let's get on with our
business." Monkey, although deeply affected by the scene, called to mind
Tripitaka's dream, in which he was told that the well was underneath a
banana-plant, and when they had gone a little further they did indeed
discover a most singular banana-plant, which grew very thick and high.

"Now Pigsy," said Monkey. "Are you ready? The treasure is buried
under this tree." That fool lifted his rake in both hands, beat down the
banana-tree and began to nuzzle with his snout till he had made a hole
three or four feet deep. At last he came to a slab of stone. "Brother," he
cried, "here's luck. We've found the treasure. It's bound to be under this
slab. If it's not in a coffer it will be in a jar." "Hoist it up and see," said
Monkey. Pigsy went to work again with his snout and raised the slab till
they could see underneath. Something sparkled and flashed. "Didn't I say

we were in luck," said Pigsy. "That is the treasure glittering." But when they looked closer, it was the light of the stars and moon reflected in a well. "Brother," said Pigsy, "you should not think so much of the trunk that you forget the root." "Now, what does that mean?" asked Monkey. "This is a well," said Pigsy. "If you had told me before we started that the treasure was in a well, I should have brought with me the two ropes we tie up our bundles with, and you could have contrived to let me down. As it is, how are we to get at anything down there and bring it up again?" "You intend to go down?" said Monkey. "That's what I should do," said Pigsy, "if I had any rope." "Take off your clothes," said Monkey, "and I'll manage it for you." "I don't go in for much in the way of clothes," said Pigsy. "But I'll take off my jerkin, if that's any good."

Dear Monkey! He took out his metal-clasped cudgel, called to it "Stretch!" and when it was some thirty feet long he said to Pigsy, "You catch hold of one end, and I'll let you down." "Brother," said Pigsy, "let me down as far as you like, so long as you stop when I come to the water." "Just so," said Monkey. Pigsy caught hold of one end of the staff, and was very gently raised and let down into the well by Monkey. He soon reached the water. "I'm at the water," he called up. Monkey, hearing this, let him down just a little further. That fool Pigsy, when he felt the water touch him, began to beat out with his trotters, let go of the staff and flopped right into the water. "The rascal!" he cried, spluttering and blowing. "I told him to stop when I came to the water, and instead he let me down further."

Monkey only laughed, and withdrew the staff. "Brother," he said, "have you found the treasure?" "Treasure indeed!" said Pigsy. "There's nothing but well-water." "The treasure is under the water," said Monkey. "Just have a look."

Pigsy, it so happened, was thoroughly at home in the water. He took a great plunge straight down into the well. But, oh what a long way it was to the bottom! He dived again with all his might, and suddenly opening his eyes saw in front of him an entrance, above which was written "The Crystal Palace." This astonished him very much. "That finishes it," he cried. "I've come the wrong way and got into the sea! There is a Crystal Palace in the sea; but I never heard of one down a well." For he did not know that the Dragon King of the Well also has a Crystal Palace.

Pigsy was thus debating with himself when a yaksha,[7] on patrol-duty in the waters, opened the door, saw the intruder, and immediately withdrew to the interior, announcing: "Great King, a calamity! A long-snouted, long-eared priest has dropped down into our well, all naked and dripping. He is still alive, and speaks to himself rationally."

The Dragon King of the Well was, however, not at all surprised. "If I am not mistaken," he said, "this is General Pigsy. Last night the Spirit that Wanders by Night received orders to come here and fetch the soul of the king of Crow-cock and bring it to the priest of T'ang to ask the Monkey Sage to subdue the wicked magician. I imagine that Monkey has come, as well as General Pigsy. They must be treated with great consideration. Go at once and ask the General to come in." The Dragon King then

7. An Indian demigod, imported into China along with Buddhism.

tidied his clothes, adjusted his hat, and bringing with him all his watery
kinsmen he came to the gate and cried in a loud voice: "General Pigsy,
pray come inside and be seated!" Pigsy was delighted. "Fancy meeting
with an old friend!" he said. And without thinking what he was in for, that
fool went into the Crystal Palace. Caring nothing for good manners, all
dripping as he was, he sat down in the seat of honour. "General," said the
Dragon King, "I heard lately that your life was spared to you on condition
you should embrace the faith of Śākyamuni[8] and protect Tripitaka on his
journey to India. What then are you doing down here?" "It's just in that
connection that I come," said Pigsy. "My brother Monkey presents his
best compliments and sends me to fetch some treasure or other." "I am
sorry," said the Dragon King, "but what should I be doing with any treasure? You're mixing me up with the dragons of the Yangtze, the Yellow
River, the Huai and the Chi, who soar about the sky and assume many
shapes. They no doubt have treasures. But I stay down here all the time
in this wretched hole never catching a glimpse of the sky above. Where
should I get a treasure from?" "Don't make excuses," said Pigsy. "I know
you have got it; so bring it out at once." "The one treasure I have," said
the Dragon King, "can't be brought out. I suggest you should go and look
at it for yourself." "Excellent," said Pigsy. "I'll come and have a look." The
Dragon King led him through the Crystal Palace till they came to a cloister in which lay a body six feet long. Pointing at it the Dragon King said,
"General, there is your treasure." Pigsy went up to it, and oh! what did he
see before him? It was a dead Emperor, on his head a tall crown, dressed
in a red gown, on his feet upturned shoes, girded with a belt of jades, who
lay stretched full length upon the floor. Pigsy laughed. "You won't kid me
like that," he said. "Since when did this count as a treasure? Why, when I
was an ogre in the mountains I made my supper on them every day. When
one has not only seen a thing time after time, but also eaten it again and
again, can one be expected to regard it as a treasure."

"General," said the Dragon King, "you do not understand. This is the
body of the King of Crow-cock. When he fell into the well I preserved
him with a magic pearl, and he suffered no decay. If you care to take him
up with you, show him to Monkey and succeed in bringing him back to
his senses, you need worry no more about 'treasures,' you'll be able to get
anything out of him that you choose to ask for." "Very well then," said
Pigsy, "I'll remove him for you, if you'll let me know how much I shall
get as my undertaker's fee." "I haven't got any money," said the Dragon
King. "So you expect to get jobs done for nothing?" said Pigsy. "If you
haven't got any money I won't remove him." "If you won't," said the
Dragon King, "I must ask you to go away." Pigsy at once retired. The
Dragon King ordered two powerful yakshas to carry the body to the gate
of the Crystal Palace and leave it just outside. They removed from the gate
its water-fending pearls, and at once there was a sound of rushing waters!
Pigsy looked round. The gate had vanished, and while he was poking
about for it, his hand touched the dead king's body, which gave him such

8. The original name of the present buddha. Buddhas appear at intervals in the history of the universe;
thus there are past, present, and future buddhas.

a start that his legs gave way under him. He scrambled to the surface of the water, and squeezing against the well-wall, he cried, "Brother, let down your staff and get me out of this." "Did you find the treasure?" asked Monkey. "How should I?" said Pigsy. "All I found was a Dragon King at the bottom of the water, who wanted me to remove a corpse. I refused, and he had me put out at the door. Then his palace vanished, and I found myself touching the corpse. It gave me such a turn that I feel quite weak. Brother, you must get me out of this." "That was your treasure," said Monkey. "Why didn't you bring it up with you?" "I knew he had been dead a long time," said Pigsy. "What was the sense of bringing him?" "You'd better," said Monkey, "or I shall go away." "Go?" said Pigsy. "Where to?" "I shall go back to the temple," said Monkey, "and go to sleep like Tripitaka." "And I shall be left down here?" said Pigsy. "If you can climb out," said Monkey, "there is no reason why you should stay here; but if you can't there's an end of it." Pigsy was thoroughly frightened; he knew he could not possibly climb out. "Just think," he said, "even a city wall is difficult to get up. But this well-shaft has a big belly and a small mouth. Its walls slope in, and as no water has been drawn from it for several years they have become all covered with slime. It's far too slippery to climb. Brother, just to keep up a nice spirit between friends, I'll carry it up."

"That's right," said Monkey. "And be quick about it, so that we can both of us go home to bed."

That fool Pigsy dived down again, found the corpse, hoisted it on to his back, clambered up to the surface of the water, and propped himself and the body against the wall. "Brother," he called. "I've brought it." Monkey peered down, and seeing that Pigsy had indeed a burden on his back, he lowered his staff into the well.

That fool was a creature of much determination. He opened his mouth wide, bit hard on the staff, and Monkey pulled him gently up. Putting down the corpse, Pigsy pulled himself into his clothes. The Emperor, Monkey found on examining him, was indeed in the most perfect preservation. "Brother," he asked, "how comes it that a man who has been dead for three years can look so fresh?" "According to the Dragon King of the Well," said Pigsy, "he used a magic pearl which prevented the body from decaying." "That was a bit of luck," said Monkey. "But it still remains to take vengeance upon his enemy and win glory for ourselves. Make haste and carry him off." "Where to?" asked Pigsy. "To the temple," said Monkey, "to show him to Tripitaka." "What an idea!" grumbled Pigsy to himself. "A fellow was having a nice, sound sleep, and along comes this baboon with a wonderful yarn about a job that must be done, and in the end it turns out to be nothing but this silly game of carting about a corpse. Carry that stinking thing! It will dribble filthy water all over me and dirty my clothes; there's no one to wash them for me. There are patches in several places, and if the water gets through I have nothing to change into." "Don't worry about your clothes," said Monkey. "Get the body to the temple, and I will give you a change of clothes." "Impudence!" cried Pigsy. "You've none of your own. How can you give me any to change into?" "Does that twaddle mean that you won't carry it?" asked Monkey. "I'm not going to carry it," said Pigsy. "Then hold out your paw and take twenty," said Monkey. "Brother," said Pigsy, much alarmed, "that cudgel is very heavy; after twenty strokes of it there would not be much to choose between me and this Emperor." "If you don't want to be beaten," said Monkey, "make haste and carry it off."

Pigsy did indeed fear the cudgel, and sorely against his will he hoisted the corpse on to his back and began to drag himself along towards the garden gate. Dear Monkey! He performed a magic pass, recited a spell, traced a magic square on the ground, and going to it blew a breath that turned into a great gust of wind which blew Pigsy clean out of the palace grounds and clear of the city moat. The wind stopped, and alighting they set out slowly on their way. Pigsy was feeling very ill-used and thought of a plan to revenge himself. "This monkey," he said to himself "has played a dirty trick on me, but I'll get even with him all right when we get back to the temple, I will tell Tripitaka that Monkey can bring the dead to life. If he says he can't, I shall persuade Tripitaka to recite the spell that makes this monkey's head ache, and I shan't be satisfied till his brains are bursting out of his head." But thinking about it as he went along, he said to himself, "That's no good! If he is asked to bring the king to life, he won't have any difficulty; he will go straight to Yama, King of Death, ask for the soul, and so bring the king to life. I must make it clear that he is not to go to the Dark Realm, but must do his cure here in the World of Light. That's the thing to do."

They were now at the temple gate, went straight in, and put down the corpse at the door of the Zen Hall, saying, "Master, get up and look!" Tripitaka was not asleep, but was discussing with Sandy why the others were away so long. Suddenly he heard them calling, and jumping up he said, "Disciples, what is this I see?" "Monkey's father-in-law," said Pigsy; "he made me carry him." "You rotten fool," said Monkey, "where have I any father-in-law?" "Brother, if he isn't your father-in-law," said Pigsy, "why did you make me carry him? It has been tiring work for me, I can tell you that!"

When Tripitaka and Sandy examined the body, and saw that the Emperor looked just like a live man, Tripitaka suddenly burst into lamentation. "Alas, poor Emperor," he cried, "in some forgotten existence you doubtless did great wrong to one that in this incarnation has now confounded you, and brought you to destruction. You were torn from wife and child; none of your generals or counsellors knew, none of your officers were aware. Alas, for the blindness of your queen and prince that offered no incense, no tea to your soul!" Here he broke down, and his tears fell like rain. "Master," said Pigsy, "what does it matter to you that he is dead? He is not your father or grandfather, why should you wail over him?" "Disciple," said Tripitaka, "for us who are followers of Buddha compassion is the root, indulgence the gate. Why is your heart so hard?" "It isn't that my heart is hard," said Pigsy. "But Brother Monkey tells me he can bring him to life. If he fails I am certainly not going to cart him about any more."

Now Tripitaka, being by nature pliable as water, was easily moved by that fool's story. "Monkey," he said, "if you can indeed bring this Emperor back to life, you will be doing what matters more than that we should reach the Holy Mountain and worship the Buddha. They say 'To save one life is better than to build a seven-storeyed pagoda.' " "Master," said Monkey, "do you really believe this fool's wild talk? When a man is dead, in three times seven, five times seven, or at the end of seven hundred days, when he has done penance for his sins in the World of Light, his turn comes to be born again. This king has been dead for three years. How can he possibly be saved?" "I expect we had better give up the idea," said Tripitaka, when he heard this. But Pigsy was not to be cheated of his revenge. "Don't let him put you off," he said to Tripitaka. "Remember, his head is very susceptible. You have only to recite that stuff of yours, and I guarantee that he'll turn the king into a live man."

Tripitaka accordingly did recite the head-ache spell, and it gripped so tight that Monkey's eyes started out of his head, and he suffered frightful pain.

If you do not know whether in the end this king was brought to life, you must listen to what is unfolded in the next chapter.

CHAPTER XXI

The pain in that great Monkey Sage's head was so great that at last he could bear it no longer and cried piteously, "Master, stop praying, stop praying! I'll doctor him." "How will you do it?" asked Tripitaka. "The only way is to visit Yama, King of Death, in the Land of Darkness, and get him to let me have the king's soul," said Monkey. "Don't believe him, Master," said Pigsy. "He told me there was no need to go to the Land of Darkness. He said he knew how to cure him here and now, in the World of Light." Tripitaka believed this wicked lie, and began praying again; and Monkey was so harassed that he soon gave in. "All right, all right," he cried. "I'll cure him in the World of Light." "Don't stop," said Pigsy. "Go on praying as hard as you can." "You ill-begotten idiot," cursed Monkey, "I'll pay you out for making the Master put a spell upon me." Pigsy laughed till he fell over. "Ho, ho, brother," he cried, "you thought it was only on me that tricks could be played. You didn't think that I could play a trick on you." "Master, stop praying," said Monkey, "and let me cure him in the World of Light." "How can that be done?" asked Tripitaka. "I will rise on my cloud-trapeze," said Monkey, "and force my way into the southern gate of Heaven. I shall not go to the Palace of the Pole and Ox, nor to the Hall of Holy Mists, but go straight up to the thirty-third heaven, and in the Trayaśimstra Courtyard of the heavenly palace of Quit Grief I shall visit Lao Tzu[9] and ask for a grain of his Nine Times Sublimated Life Restoring Elixir, and with it I shall bring the king back to life."

This suggestion pleased Tripitaka very much. "Lose no time about it," he said. "It is only the third watch," said Monkey. "I shall be back before it is light. But it would look all wrong if the rest of you went quietly to sleep. It is only decent that someone should watch by the corpse and mourn." "You need say no more," said Pigsy. "I can see that you expect me to act as mourner." "I should like to see you refuse!" said Monkey. "If you don't act as mourner, I certainly shan't bring him to life." "Be off,

9. See n. 8, p. 39

Brother," said Pigsy, "and I'll do the mourning." "There are more ways than one of mourning," said Monkey. "Mere bellowing with dry eyes is no good. Nor is it any better just to squeeze out a few tears. What counts is a good hearty howling, with tears as well. That's what is wanted for a real, miserable mourning." "I'll give you a specimen," said Pigsy. He then from somewhere or other produced a piece of paper which he twisted into a paper-spill and thrust up his nostrils. This soon set him snivelling and his eyes running, and when he began to howl he kept up such a din that anyone would have thought he had indeed lost his dearest relative. The effect was so mournful that Tripitaka too soon began to weep bitterly. "That's what you've got to keep up the whole time I'm away," said Monkey laughing. "What I am frightened of is that this fool, the moment my back is turned, will stop wailing. I shall creep back and listen, and if he shows any sign of leaving off he will get twenty on the paw." "Be off with you," laughed Pigsy. "I could easily keep this up for two days on end."

Sandy, seeing that Pigsy had settled down to his job, went off to look for some sticks of incense to burn as an offering. "Excellent!" laughed Monkey. "The whole family is engaged in works of piety! Now's the time for Old Monkey to get to work."

Dear Monkey! Just at midnight he left his teacher and fellow-disciples, mounted his cloud-trapeze and flew in at the southern gate of Heaven. He did not indeed call at the Precious Hall of Holy Mists or go on to the Palace of the Pole and Ox, but only along a path of cloudy light went straight to the thirty-third heaven, to the Trayaśimstra Courtyard of the heavenly palace of Quit Grief. Just inside the gate he saw Lao Tzu in his alchemical studio, with a number of fairy boys holding banana-leaf fans, and fanning the fire in which the cinnabar was sublimating.[1]

As soon as Lao Tzu saw him coming, he called to the boys, "Be careful, all of you. Here's the thief who stole the elixir come back again." Monkey bowed, and said laughing, "Reverend Sir, there is no need to be in such a fret. You need take no precautions against me. I have come on quite different business." "Monkey," said Lao Tzu, "five hundred years ago you made great trouble in the Palace of Heaven, and stole a great quantity of my holy elixir; for which crime you were arrested and placed in my crucible, where you were smelted for forty-nine days, at the cost of I know not how much charcoal. Now you have been lucky enough to obtain forgiveness, enter the service of Buddha, and go with Tripitaka, the priest of T'ang, to get scriptures in India. Some while ago you quelled a demon in the Flat Topped Mountain and tricked disaster, but did not give me my share in the treasure. What brings you here to-day?" "In those old days," said Monkey, "I lost no time in returning to you those five treasures of yours. You have no reason to be suspicious of me." "But what are you doing here?" asked Lao Tzu, "creeping into my palace instead of getting on with your journey?" "On our way to the West," said Monkey, "we came to a country called Crow-cock. The king of the country employed a wizard, who had disguised himself as a Taoist, to bring rain. This wizard secretly did away with the king, whose form he assumed, and now he is ensconced in the

---

1. The boys were extracting mercury from cinnabar. Mercury was used in elixirs of immortality.

Hall of Golden Bells. My Master was reading the scriptures in the Treasure Wood Temple, when the soul of the king came to him and earnestly requested that I might be sent to subdue the wizard, and expose his imposture. I felt that I had no proof of the crime, and went with my fellow-disciple Pigsy. We broke into the flower garden by night, and looked for the crystal well into which the king had been thrown. We fished him up, and found him still sound and fresh. When we got back to the temple and saw Tripitaka, his compassion was aroused and he ordered me to bring the king to life. But I was not to go to the World of Darkness to recover his soul; I must cure him here in the World of Light. I could think of no way but to ask for your help. Would you be so kind as to lend me a thousand of your nine times sublimated life-restoring pills. Then I shall be able to set him right." "A thousand pills indeed!" exclaimed Lao Tzu. "Why not two thousand? Is he to have them at every meal instead of rice? Do you think one has only to stoop and pick them up like dirt from the ground? Shoo! Be off with you! I've nothing for you." "I'd take a hundred," said Monkey laughing. "I dare say," said Lao Tzu. "But I haven't any." "I'd take ten," said Monkey. "A curse on this Monkey!" said Lao Tzu, very angry. "Will he never stop haggling? Be off with you immediately." "If you really haven't got any," said Monkey, "I shall have to find some other way of bringing him to life." "Go, go, go!" screamed Lao Tzu. Very reluctantly Monkey turned away. But suddenly Lao Tzu thought to himself: "This monkey is very crafty. If he really went away and stayed away, it would be all right. But I am afraid he will slip back again and steal some." So he sent a fairy boy to bring Monkey back, and said to him, "If you are really so anxious to have some, I'll spare you just one pill." "Sir," said Monkey, "if you had an inkling of what I can do if I choose, you would think yourself lucky to go shares in it with me. If you hadn't given in, I should have come with my dredge and fished up the whole lot." Lao Tzu took a gourd-shaped pot and, tilting it up, emptied one grain of elixir and passed it across to Monkey, saying, "That's all you'll get, so be off with it. And if with this one grain you can bring the king back to life, you are welcome to the credit of it." "Not so fast," said Monkey. "I must taste it first. I don't want to be put off with a sham." So saying, he tossed it into his mouth. Lao Tzu rushed forward to stop him, and pressing his fists against his skull-cap he cried in despair, "If you swallow it, I shall kill you on the spot!" "Revolting meanness," said Monkey. "Keep calm; no one is eating anything of yours. And how much is it worth, anyhow? It's pretty wretched stuff, and come to that, I haven't swallowed it; it's here."

For the fact is that monkeys have a pouch under the gullet, and Monkey had stored the grain of elixir in his pouch. Lao Tzu pinched him and said, "Be off with you, be off with you, and don't let me find you hanging round here any more." So Monkey took leave of him, and quitted the Trayaśimstra Heaven. In a moment he had left by the Southern Gate, and turning eastward he saw the great globe of the sun just mounting. Lowering his cloud-seat, he soon reached the Treasure Wood Temple, where even before he entered the gate he could hear Pigsy still howling. He stepped briskly forward and cried "Master." "Is that Monkey?" said Tripitaka delightedly. "Have you got your elixir?" "Certainly," said Monkey.

"What's the use of asking?" said Pigsy. "You can count on a sneak like that to bring back some trifle that doesn't belong to him." "Brother," laughed Monkey, "you can retire. We don't need you any more. Wipe your eyes, and if you want to do more howling do it elsewhere. And you, Sandy, bring me a little water." Sandy hurried out to the well behind the temple, where there was a bucket of water ready drawn. He dipped his bowl into it and brought half a bowlful of water. Monkey filled his mouth with water, and then spat out the elixir into the Emperor's lips. Next he forced open his jaws, and pouring in some clean water, he floated the elixir down into his belly. In a few moments there was a gurgling sound inside; but the body still did not move. "Master," said Monkey, "what will become of me if my elixir fails? Shall I be beaten to death?" "I don't see how it can fail," said Tripitaka. "It's already a miracle that a corpse that has been dead so long can swallow water. After the elixir entered his belly, we heard the guts ring. When the guts ring, the veins move in harmony. It only remains to get the breath into circulation. But even a piece of iron gets a bit rusty when it has been under water for three years; it is only natural that something of the same kind should happen to a man. All that's wrong with him is that he needs a supply of breath. If someone puts a mouthful of good breath into him, he would be quite himself again."

Pigsy at once offered himself for this service, but Tripitaka held him back. "You're no use for that," he cried. "Let Monkey do it." Tripitaka knew what he was talking about. For Pigsy had in his early days eaten living things, and even monstrously devoured human flesh, so that all his stock of breath was defiled. Whereas Monkey had always lived on pine-seeds, cypress cones, peaches and the like, and his breath was pure.

So Monkey stepped forward, and putting his wide mouth against the Emperor's lips he blew hard into his throat. The breath went down to the Two-Storeyed Tower, round the Hall of Light, on to the Cinnabar Field, and from the Jetting Spring went back again into the Mud Wall Palace.[2] Whereupon there was a deep panting sound. The king's humours concentrated, his spirits returned. He rolled over, brandished his fist, and bent his legs. Then with a cry "Master!" he knelt down in the dust and said, "Little did I think, when my soul visited you last night, that to-day at dawn I should again belong to the World of Light!" Tripitaka quickly raised him from his knees and said, "Your Majesty, this is no doing of mine. You must thank my disciple." "What talk is that?" said Monkey laughing. "The proverb says 'A household cannot have two masters.' There is no harm in letting him pay his respects to you."

Tripitaka, still feeling somewhat embarrassed, raised the Emperor to his feet and brought him to the Hall of Meditation, where he and his disciples again prostrated themselves, and set him on a seat. The priests of the temple had got ready their breakfast, and invited Tripitaka and his party to join them. Imagine their astonishment when they saw an Emperor, his clothes still dripping. "Don't be surprised," said Monkey, coming forward. "This is the King of Crow-cock, your rightful lord. Three years ago he was robbed of his life by a fiend, and to-night I brought him back to life. Now

2. All elegant terms for the internal organs.

we must take him to the city and surprise the impostor. If you have any-thing for us to eat, serve it now, and we will start as soon as we have breakfasted."

The priests brought the Emperor hot water to wash in, and helped him out of his clothes. The almoner[3] brought him a cloth jacket, and instead of his jade belt tied a silk sash round his waist; took off his upturned shoes, and gave him a pair of old priest's sandals. Then they all had breakfast, and saddled the horse. "Pigsy, is your luggage very heavy?" asked Monkey. "Brother, I've carried it so many days on end that I don't know whether it's heavy or not." "Divide the pack into two," said Monkey, "take one half yourself, and give the other to this Emperor to carry. In that way we shall get quicker to the city and dispose of our business." "That's a bit of luck," said Pigsy. "It was a nuisance getting him here. But now that he's been made alive, he is coming in useful as a partner."

Pigsy then divided the luggage after his own methods. Borrowing a hod[4] from the priests of the temple he put everything light into his own load, and everything heavy into the king's. "I hope your Majesty has no objec-tion," said Monkey laughing, "to being dressed up like this, and carrying the luggage, and following us on foot." "Master," said the Emperor, instantly flinging himself upon his knees, "I can only regard you as my second progenitor, and let alone carrying luggage for you, my heartfelt desire is to go with you all the way to India, even if I were only to serve you as the lowest menial, running beside you whip in hand as you ride."

"There's no need for you to go to India," said Monkey. "That's our special concern. All you have to do is to carry the luggage forty leagues to the city and then let us seize the fiend. After which you can go on being Emperor again, and we can go on looking for scriptures."

"That's all very well," said Pigsy. "But in that case he gets off with forty leagues, while I shall be on the job all the time. "Brother," said Monkey, "don't talk nonsense, but be quick and lead the way out." Pigsy and the Emperor accordingly led the way, while Sandy supported Tripitaka on his horse and Monkey followed behind. They were accompanied to the gates by five hundred priests in gorgeous procession, blowing conches as they walked. "Don't come with us any further," said Monkey. "If some official were to notice, our plans might get out, and everything would go wrong. Go back at once, and have the Emperor's clothes well cleaned, and send them to the city to-night or early tomorrow. I will see to it that you are well paid for your pains."

They had not travelled for half a day when the walls and moat of the city of Crow-cock came into view. "Monkey," said Tripitaka, "I think this place in front of us must be the city of Crow-cock." "It certainly is," said Monkey. "Let us hurry on and do our business."

When they reached the city they found the streets and markets thronging with people, and everywhere a great stir and bustle. Soon they saw rising before them towers and gables of great magnificence. "Disci-ples," said Tripitaka, "let us go at once to Court and get our papers put in order. Then we shall have no more trouble hanging about in government

3. A court officer who dispenses alms.   4. A device for carrying heavy things on one's back.

offices." "That is a good idea," said Monkey. "We will all come with you; the more the tellers, the better the story." "Well, if you all come," said Tripitaka, "you must behave nicely, and not say anything till you have done homage as humble subjects of the throne." "But that means bowing down," said Monkey. "To be sure," said Tripitaka. "You have to bow down five times and strike your forehead on the ground three times." "Master," said Monkey, "that's not a good idea. To pay homage to a thing like that is really too silly. Let me go in first, and I will decide what we are to do. If he addresses us, let me answer him. If you see me bow, then you must bow too; if I squat, then you must squat."

Look at him, that Monkey King, maker of many troubles, how he goes straight up to the door and says to the high officer in charge: "We were sent by the Emperor of China to worship Buddha in India, and fetch scriptures. We want to have our papers put in order here, and would trouble you to announce our arrival. By doing so, you will not fail to gain religious merit." The eunuch went in and knelt on the steps of the throne, announcing the visitors and their request. "I did not think it right to let them straight in," he said. "They await your orders outside the door." The false king then summoned them in. Tripitaka entered, accompanied by the true king, who as he went could not stop the tears that coursed down his cheeks. "Alas," he sighed to himself, "for my dragon-guarded rivers and hills, my iron-girt shrines! Who would have guessed that a creature of darkness would possess you all?" "Emperor," said Monkey, "you must control your emotion, or we shall be discovered. I can feel the truncheon behind my ear twitching, and I am certain that I shall be successful. Leave it to me to slay the monster and when things are cleaned up, those rivers and hills will soon be yours again."

The true king dared not demur. He wiped away his tears, and followed as best he could. At last they reached the Hall of Golden Bells, where they saw the two rows of officials civil and military, and the four hundred Court officers, all of imposing stature and magnificently apparelled. Monkey led forward Tripitaka to the white jade steps, where they both stood motionless and erect. The officials were in consternation. "Are these priests so utterly bereft of decency and reason?" they exclaimed. "How comes it that, seeing our king, they do not bow down or greet him with any word of blessing? Not even a cry of salutation escaped their lips. Never have we seen such impudent lack of manners!" "Where do they come from?" interrupted the false king. "We were sent from the eastern land of T'ang in Southern Jambudvīpa," said Monkey haughtily, "by royal command, to go to India that is in the Western Region, and there to worship the Living Buddha in the Temple of the Great Thunder Clap, and obtain true scriptures. Having arrived here we dare not proceed without coming first to you to have our passports put in order." The false king was very angry. "What is this eastern land of yours?" he said. "Do I pay tribute to it, that you should appear before me in this rude fashion, without bowing down? I have never had any dealings with your country." "Our eastern land," said Monkey, "long ago set up a Heavenly Court and became a Great Power. Whereas yours is a Minor Power, a mere frontier land. There is an old saying, 'The king of a Great Country is father and lord; the king of a lesser country is vassal and son.' You admit that you have had no dealings with our country. How dare you contend that we ought to bow down?" "Remove that uncivil priest," the king called to his officers of war. At this all the officers sprang forward. But Monkey made a magic pass and cried "Halt!" The magic of the pass was such that these officers all suddenly remained rooted to the spot and could not stir. Well might it be said:

The captains standing round the steps became like figures of wood,
The generals on the Royal Dais were like figures of clay.

Seeing that Monkey had brought his officers civil and military to a stand-still, the false king leapt from his Dragon Couch and made as though to seize him. "Good," said Monkey to himself. "That is just what I wanted. Even if his hand is made of iron, this cudgel of mine will make some pretty dents in it!"

But just at this moment a star of rescue arrived. "Who can this have been?" you ask. It was no other than the prince of Crow-cock, who has-tened forward and clutched at the false king's sleeve, and kneeling before him cried, "Father and king, stay your anger." "Little son," asked the king, "why should you say this?" "I must inform my father and king," said the prince. "Three years ago I heard someone say that a priest had been sent from T'ang to get scriptures in India, and it is he who has now unexpect-edly arrived in our country. If my father and king, yielding to the ferocity of his noble nature, now arrests and beheads this priest, I fear that the news will one day reach the Emperor of T'ang, who will be furiously angry. You must know that after Li Shih-min had established this great dynasty of T'ang and united the whole land, his heart was still not content, and he has now begun to conquer far-away lands. If he hears that you have done harm to his favourite priest, he will raise his hosts and come to make war upon you. Our troops are few and our generals feeble. You will, when it is too late, be sorry indeed that you provoked him. If you were to follow your small son's advice, you would question these four priests, and only punish such of them as are proved not to travel at the King of China's bidding."

This was a stratagem of the prince's. For he feared that harm might come to Tripitaka, and therefore tried to check the king, not knowing that Monkey was ready to strike.

The false king believed him, and standing in front of the Dragon Couch, he cried in a loud voice: "Priest, how long ago did you leave China, and why were you sent to get scriptures?"

"My Master," said Monkey haughtily, "is called Tripitaka, and is treated by the Emperor of China as his younger brother. The Emperor in a vision went to the Realms of Death, and on his return he ordered a great Mass for all souls in torment. On this occasion my Master recited so well and showed such compassionate piety that the Goddess Kuan-yin chose him to go on a mission to the West. My Master vowed that he would faithfully perform this task in return for his sovereign's bounties, and he was fur-nished by the Emperor with credentials for the journey. He started in the thirteenth year of the Emperor's reign, in the ninth month, three days before the full moon. After leaving China, he came first to the Land of the Two Frontiers, where he picked up me, and made me his chief disciple. In the hamlet of the Kao family, on the borders of the country of Wu-ssu, he picked up a second disciple, called Pigsy; and at the river of Flowing Sands he picked up a third, whom we call Sandy. Finally a few days ago, at the Temple of the Treasure Wood, he found another recruit—the servant who is carrying the luggage."

The false king thought it unwise to ask any more questions about Tripitaka; but he turned savagely upon Monkey and addressed to him a crafty question. "I can accept," he said, "that one priest set out from China, and picked up three priests on the way. But your story about the fourth member of your party I altogether disbelieve. This servant is certainly someone whom you have kidnapped. What is his name? Has he a passport,[5] or has he none? Bring him before me to make his deposition!"

The true king shook with fright. "Master," he whispered, "what am I to depose?" "That's all right," said Monkey. "I'll make your deposition for you."

Dear Monkey! He stepped boldly forward and cried to the magician in a loud, clear voice: "Your Majesty, this old man is dumb and rather hard of hearing. But it so happens that when he was young, he travelled in India, and knows the way there. I know all about his career and origins and with your Majesty's permission I will make a deposition on his behalf." "Make haste," said the false king, "and furnish a true deposition or you will get into trouble."

Monkey then recited as follows:

> The subject of this deposition is far advanced in years; he is deaf and dumb, and has fallen upon evil days. His family for generations has lived in these parts; but five years ago disaster overtook his house. Heaven sent no rain; the people perished of drought, the lord king and all his subjects fasted and did penance. They burned incense, purified themselves and called upon the Lord of Heaven; but in all the sky not a wisp of cloud appeared. The hungry peasants dropped by the roadside, when suddenly there came a Taoist magician from the Chung-nan Mountains, a monster in human form. He called to the winds and summoned the rain, displaying godlike power; but soon after secretly destroyed this wretched man's life. In the flower-garden he pushed him down into the crystal well; then set himself on the Dragon Throne, none knowing it was he. Luckily I came and achieved a great success; I raised him from the dead and restored him to life without hurt or harm. He earnestly begged to be admitted to our faith, and act as carrier on the road, to join with us in our quest and journey to the Western Land. The false king who sits on the throne is that foul magician; he that now carries our load is Crow-cock's rightful king!

When the false king in the Palace of Golden Bells heard these words, he was so startled that his heart fluttered like the heart of a small deer. Then clouds of shame suffused his face, and leaping to his feet he was about to flee, when he remembered that he was unarmed. Looking round he saw a captain of the Guard with a dagger at his waist, standing there dumb and foolish as a result of Monkey's spell. The false king rushed at him and snatched the dagger; then leapt upon a cloud and disappeared into space.

5. Here, papers from the T'ang authorities, identifying the traveler and telling his or her mission.

Sandy burst into an exclamation of rage, and Pigsy loudly abused Monkey for his slowness. "It's a pity you didn't look sharp and stop him," he said. "Now he has sailed off on a cloud, and we shall never be able to find him." "Don't shout at me, brothers!" said Monkey laughing. "Let us call to the prince to come and do reverence to his true father, and the queen to her husband." Then undoing by a magic pass the spell that he had put upon the officers, he told them to wake up and do homage to their lord, acknowledging him as their true king. "Give me a few facts to go upon," he said, "and as soon as I have got things clear, I will go and look for him."

Dear Monkey! He instructed Pigsy and Sandy to take good care of the prince, king, ministers, queen and Tripitaka; but while he was speaking he suddenly vanished from sight. He had already jumped up into the empyrean,[6] and was peering round on every side, looking for the wizard. Presently he saw that monster flying for his life towards the north-east. Monkey caught him up and shouted, "Monster, where are you off to? Monkey has come." The wizard turned swiftly, drew his dagger and cried, "Monkey, you scamp, what has it got to do with you whether I usurp someone else's throne? Why should you come calling me to account and letting out my secrets?" "Ho, ho," laughed Monkey. "You impudent rascal! Do you think I am going to allow you to play the emperor? Knowing who I am you would have done well to keep out of my way. Why did you bully my master, demanding depositions and what not? You must admit now that the deposition was not far from the truth. Stand your ground and take old Monkey's cudgel like a man!"

The wizard dodged and parried with a thrust of his dagger at Monkey's face. It was a fine fight! After several bouts the magician could no longer stand up against Monkey, and suddenly turning he fled back the way he had come, leapt into the city and slipped in among the officers who were assembled before the steps of the throne. Then giving himself a shake, he changed into an absolute counterpart of Tripitaka and stood beside him in front of the steps. Monkey rushed up and was about to strike what he supposed to be the wizard, when this Tripitaka said, "Disciple, do not strike! It is I!" It was impossible to distinguish between them. "If I kill Tripitaka, who is a transformation of the wizard, then I shall have achieved a glorious success; but supposing, on the other hand, it turns out that I have killed the real Tripitaka, that would not be so good. . . ." There was nothing for it but to stay his hand, and calling to Pigsy and Sandy he asked, "Which really is the wizard, and which is our master? Just point for me, and I will strike the one you point at." "We were watching you going for one another up in the air," said Pigsy, "when suddenly we looked round and saw that there were two Tripitakas. We have no idea which is the real one."

When Monkey heard this, he made a single pass and recited a spell to summon the *devas* that protect the Law, the local deities and the spirits of the neighbouring hills, and told them of his predicament. The wizard thought it time to mount the clouds again, and began to make towards the door. Thinking that Tripitaka was clearing the ground for him, Monkey

6. The higher reaches of the sky.

raised his cudgel, and had it not been for the deities he had summoned he would have struck such a big blow at his master as would have made mince-meat of twenty Tripitakas. But in the nick of time the guardian deities stopped him, saying, "Great Sage, the wizard is just going to mount the clouds again." Monkey rushed after him, and was just about to cut off his retreat, when the wizard turned round, slipped back again into the crowd, and was once more indistinguishable from the real Tripitaka.

Much to Monkey's annoyance, Pigsy stood by, laughing at his discomfiture. "You've nothing to laugh at, you hulking brute," he said. "This means you've got two masters to order you about. It's not going to do you much good." "Brother," said Pigsy, "you call me a fool, but you're a worse fool than I. You can't recognize your own Master, and it's a waste of effort to go on trying. But you would at least recognize your own headache, and if you ask our Master to recite his spell, Sandy and I will stand by and listen. The one who doesn't know the spell will certainly be the wizard. Then all will be easy." "Brother," said Monkey, "I am much obliged to you. There are only three people who know that spell. It sprouted from the heart of the Lord Buddha himself; it was handed down to the Bodhisattva Kuan-yin, and was then taught to our master by the Bodhisattva herself. No one else knows it. Good, then! Master, recite!"

The real Tripitaka at once began to recite the spell; while the wizard could do nothing but mumble senseless sounds. "That's the wizard," cried Pigsy. "He's only mumbling." And at the same time he raised his rake and was about to strike when the wizard sprang into the air and ran up along the clouds. Dear Pigsy! With a loud cry he set off in pursuit, and Sandy, leaving Tripitaka, hastened to the attack with his priest's staff. Tripitaka stopped reciting, and Monkey, released from his head-ache, seized his iron cudgel and sped through the air. Heigh, what a fight! Three wild priests beleagured one foul fiend. With rake and staff Pigsy and Sandy assailed him from right and left. "If I join in," said Monkey, "and attack him in front, I fear he is so frightened of me that he will run away again. Let me get into position above him and give him a real garlic-pounding blow that will finish him off for good and all." He sprang up into the empyrean, and was about to deliver a tremendous blow when, from a many-coloured cloud in the north-east, there came a voice which said, "Monkey, stay your hand!" Monkey looked round and saw it was the Bodhisattva Mañjuśrī. He withdrew his cudgel, and coming forward did obeisance, saying "Bodhisattva, where are you going to?" "I came to take this monster off your hands," said Mañjuśrī. "I am sorry you should have the trouble," said Monkey. The Bodhisattva then drew from his sleeve a magic mirror that showed demons in their true form. Monkey called to the other two to come and look, and in the mirror they saw the wizard in his true shape. He was Mañjuśrī's lion! "Bodhisattva," said Monkey, "this is the blue-maned lion that you sit upon. How comes it that it ran away and turned into an evil spirit? Can't you keep it under control?" "It did not run away," said Mañjuśrī. "It acted under orders from Buddha himself." "You mean to tell me," said Monkey, "that it was Buddha who told this creature to turn into an evil spirit and seize the Emperor's throne? In that case all the troubles I meet with while escorting Tripitaka are very likely ordered by His Holiness. A nice thought!"

"Monkey," said Manjuśrī, "you don't understand. In the beginning this king of Crow-cock was devoted to good works and the entertaining of priests. Buddha was so pleased that he sent me to fetch him away to the Western Paradise, where he was to assume a golden body and become an Arhat.[7] As it was not proper for me to show myself in my true form I came disguised as a priest and begged for alms. Something I said gave him offence, and not knowing that I was anyone in particular he had me bound and cast into the river, where I remained under water for three nights and three days, till at last a guardian spirit rescued me and brought me back to Paradise. I complained to Buddha, who sent this creature to throw the king into the well, and let him remain there three years as a retaliation for the three days that I was in the river. You know the saying: 'Not a sip, not a sup[8] . . .' But now you have arrived on the scene, the episode is successfully closed." "That is all very well," said Monkey. "All these 'sips and sups' may have enabled you to get even with your enemy. But what about all the unfortunate people whom this fiend has ruined?" "He hasn't ruined any one," said Manjuśrī. "During the three years that he was on the throne, rain has fallen, the crops have been good, and the people at perfect peace. How can you speak of his ruining people?" "That may be," said Monkey. "But how about all the ladies of the Court who have been sleeping with him and unwittingly been led into a heinous and unnatural offence? They would hardly subscribe to the view that he had done no harm." "He isn't in a position to defile anyone," said Manjuśrī. "He's a gelded lion!" At this Pigsy came up to the wizard and felt him. "Quite true," he announced, laughing. "This is a 'blotchy nose that never sniffed wine'; 'a bad name and nothing to show for it.' "

"Very well then," said Monkey. "Take him away. If you had not come just in time, he'd have been dead by now." Manjuśrī then recited a spell and said, "Creature, back to your true shape and look sharp about it!" The wizard at once changed into his real lion form, and Manjuśrī, putting down the lotus that he carried in his hand, harnessed the lion, mounted him and rode away over the clouds.

If you do not know how Tripitaka and his disciples left the city you must listen while it is explained to you in the next chapter.

*　　　*　　　*

7. A Buddhist saint.　　8. That is, everything that happens depends on *karma. Karma* is the burden of deeds, both good and bad, that the soul carries from lifetime to lifetime.

K'UNG SHANG-JEN
1648–1718

Although there are indications of quasi-dramatic performances in China at an early period, drama grew in sophistication during the Sung Dynasty (960–1279). The earliest extant Chinese plays date from the thirteenth century.

Chinese theater has certain distinctive traits that contrast sharply with Western drama. Foremost among these is the alternation between prose dialogue and arias, which were sung in performance. Originally an act of a play was organized around a suite of arias, all in the same musical mode. In early northern plays only one character was allowed to sing in each act. The dialogue around the arias, often very lively, was given considerably less attention in early works, though when drama matured, the interplay between aria and fully developed dialogue was central to the artistic success of the play.

K'ung Shang-jen's *The Peach Blossom Fan* (1699) is a late work in a tradition of southern drama known as *ch'uan-ch'i* (the same term used for T'ang tales in the classical language). *Ch'uan-ch'i* are very long plays, most between thirty and fifty acts, and were performed either in single acts or in their entirety, spread out over a number of days. Drama also developed as a literary form with printed editions designed for reading. *The Peach Blossom Fan* is just such a play, circulating in manuscript long before it was performed. *Ch'uan-ch'i* plots are intricate and sprawling affairs, often weaving together numerous characters and multiple storylines. Although the plots have a degree of linear unity, it is clear that the primary sense of artistic coherence comes from parallel scenes and situations, in which each moment gains significance by echoes of corresponding moments in the play (and often echoes of earlier dramatic works). Drama was immensely popular in late imperial China, and audiences developed a high degree of connoisseurship and close knowledge of a wide range of plays.

K'ung Shang-jen was from the great K'ung family of Shan-tung, which claimed descent from Confucius (K'ung Ch'iu). He found favor with the K'ang-hsi emperor while visiting the great complex of Confucian temples at Ch'ü-fu, his home, and after a moderately successful official career turned to playwriting relatively late in his life.

Unlike most Chinese plays, which are set in a safely removed past, *The Peach Blossom Fan* treats one of the most politically sensitive events of recent history: the fall of the Ming and of its afterecho, the brief southern regime of the Ming prince Fu (1644–45) in Nanking. K'ung drew on a wide variety of historical sources to create a play that would function as a kind of history. It was an appropriate medium since Prince Fu's short-lived regime was itself a species of play-acting that begged comparison to the theater—though it is hard to say whether Prince Fu's inept government should be considered a tragedy or a farce. As K'ung has the master of ceremonies observe in the prologue to the second part:

> In bygone years, reality was the play;
> The play becomes reality today.
> Twice I have watched its progress: Heaven preserves
> This passive gazer with his cold clear eyes.

Versions of theatricality and performance occur throughout the play, for K'ung was much interested in the degree to which human acts and relationships involve playing roles. When we first meet the heroine, Fragrant Princess, she is a young courtesan being taught by her singing master to perform the arias sung by the heroine in another famous play *Peony Pavilion*. At the same time she is given her adult name, Fragrant Princess, by the painter Yang Wen-ts'ung. Through the course of *The Peach Blossom Fan*, Fragrant Princess does indeed become the conventional heroine of romantic drama and goes beyond it. This act is framed by the first scene, in which the hero witnesses a performance by a storyteller, and the third scene, in which a ceremony in honor of Confucius, yet another performance, is disrupted by the appearance of the villain, Juan Ta-ch'eng. Juan himself is a playwright, producing immensely popular but vapid romantic comedies in the midst of national disaster. Prince Fu is an ardent admirer of Juan's plays and joins in the performance. Everywhere true identity is shaped by or revealed in performance.

The course of the play turns on the relation between art and a historical reality in which people bleed and suffer. Emblematic of this relation is the object from which the play takes its title: the peach blossom fan. The fan, bearing a love poem by the hero, Hou Fang-yü, is his wedding gift to Fragrant Princess. Since the other, more expensive wedding gifts must finally be rejected because they come from Juan Ta-ch'eng, the fan becomes the only external thing that symbolizes their union. Later, after Hou Fang-yü has been forced to flee Nanking, the fan is spattered with Fragrant Princess's blood when she is injured as she resists being carried away and forcibly married to another. Still later, as Fragrant Princess lies asleep, the painter Yang Wen-ts'ung comes in and sees the fan. Though knowing the source of the bloodstain, the true artist cannot help admiring its shade of red, and he paints green leaves and twigs around the splotches of blood to form peach blossoms: pain is transformed into art.

After this scene Fragrant Princess sends the fan off to her beloved, Hou Fang-yü, as a token of her faith. But at this point she is forced to enter the palace to serve in the emperor's acting troop, where the emperor (Prince Fu), admiring her beauty, gives her another fan painted with peach blossoms. Later, when Hou Fang-yü finally manages to get back to Nanking, he goes to Fragrant Princess's house, which in her absence has been taken over by the painter Lan Yin, who is painting a picture of peach blossoms. This painting comes into the hands of one Chang Wei, the commander of the Imperial Guard, and proves instrumental in saving Hou Fang-yü's life. The peach blossoms themselves have a double significance: as an image of a woman's beauty and young love and also as the symbol of Peach Blossom Spring, a mountain haven from the world's violence, discovered, as T'ao Ch'ien (fourth century) wrote, by a fisherman following a trail of peach blossoms in the water. And the play does indeed conclude in just such a location.

The character of the painter Yang Wen-ts'ung is central to the action. Yang moves easily between the villains and the virtuous, friends with both. The plot belongs to Yang: he is responsible both for the lovers coming together and for their being torn apart. He brings troubles on them and saves them from those same troubles.

Like Shakespeare, K'ung Shang-jen makes use of different classes and levels of language to give perspective and sometimes to call into question the values of the main characters. In the third scene, for example, the politically upright young scholars hold a solemn ceremony in honor of Confucius. This is interrupted by the intrusion of the villain Juan Ta-ch'eng, whose very presence is seen to corrupt the solemn purity of the occasion. The scene has begun, however, with a comic exchange between the servants taking inventory of the stocks of ritual goods, as if to remind the reader of the pragmatic details beneath the sacred rite. Again in the seventh scene, Fragrant Princess, playing the romantic heroine, grandly refuses the wedding gifts because they come from Juan Ta-ch'eng (arranged, of course, by Yang Wen-ts'ung). Her mother, Li Chen-li, observes:

> All the same, it was a pity to lose those valuable gifts. [*Sings.*]
> When gold and pearls are in your hand,
> Heedless you let them slip away
> Daughter, you fail to understand
> All that your mother had to pay.

If Li Chen-li were simply a greedy, unsympathetic character, these lines would not have the ring of truth, the reminder that someone has to pay for grand romantic gestures. In fact, she has great love for Fragrant Princess and ultimately sacrifices herself to protect her daughter from forced marriage.

The story of the lovers unfolds against the backdrop of major historical events: the suicide of the last Ming emperor after the rebel Li Tzu-ch'eng took Peking, the establishment of the corrupt and inept government of Prince Fu in Nanking, the Manchu conquest of north China and the crumbling of the Ming armies, Shih K'o-fa's desperate attempt to defend Yang-chou, and finally the fall of Nanking.

The play closes with the flight of all protagonists from Nanking to live as Taoist hermits in the mountains. Much like Elizabethan romantic comedy, Chinese romantic comedy always ends with the reunion of the separated hero and heroine. There among the Taoist nuns and acolytes, Hou Fang-yü and Fragrant Princess discover one another again. There the two lovers begin to play the reunion scene:

> HOU: [*Speaking of those who had helped them to escape.*] When we are home once more as man and wife, we shall endeavor to repay their kindness.

Chang Wei, now the abbot of the Taoist temple, interrupts to remind them that there is no home any more.

> CHANG: What is all this meaningless chatter? How laughable to cling to your amorous desires when the whole world has been turned upside down.

Or as he later sings:

> Are you not ashamed to hear
> The laughter your performance brings?

In this moment the lovers are enlightened to love's illusion, and they separate.

A biography of K'ung Shang-jen may be found in Richard E. Strassberg's *The World of K'ung Shang-jen: A Man of Letters in Early Ch'ing China* (1985).

PRONOUNCING GLOSSARY

The following list uses common English syllables to provide rough equivalents of selected words whose pronunciation may be unfamiliar to the general reader.

Chang Wei: *jahng way*

Chin: *jin*

Ch'in Shih-huang-ti: *chin shir–hwahng–dee*

Ch'ü-fu: *choo–foo*

Juan Ta-ch'eng: *rwahn dah–chuhng*

K'ang-hsi: *kahng–shee*

Kuei-te: *gway–duh*

K'ung Ch'iu: *koong chyoh*

K'ung Tzu: *koong dzuh*

Li Chen-li: *lee juhn–lee*

Li Tzu-ch'eng: *lee dzuh–chuhng*

Liu Ching-t'ing: *lyoh jing–ting*

Ma Shih-ying: *mah shir–ying*

Nanking: *nahn-jing*

Shan-tung: *shahn–doong*

Shih K'o-fa: *shir kuh–fah*

Sung: *soong*

T'ao Ch'ien: *tao chyen*

Tso Liang-yü: *dzwoh lyahng–yoo*

Yang-chou: *yahng–joh*

Yang Wen-ts'ung: *yahng wuhn–tsoong*

From The Peach Blossom Fan[1]
Prologue
1684

[*Enter an old man with a long white beard. He is the former* MASTER OF CEREMONIES[2] *of the Imperial Temple. He now wears a felt cap and a broad-sleeved Taoist robe.*[3]]

MASTER OF CEREMONIES: [*Sings.*]

> Where in the world is a quainter curio
> In jade or bronze than I, my face patined with age?
> Though superannuated, lone and lost,
> Why should I shrink when striplings mock at me?
> I extirpate old sorrows from my breast,   5
> And where there's wine and song I'm apt to linger.
> When filial duty and loyalty reign, the universe will thrive
> And the fruit of longevity grow superfluous.

[*Speaks.*] The sun beams brightly on a world well governed. The flowers bloom in the first year of the cycle; the mountains are free   10
from bandits; the whole earth belongs to the blessed. Formerly an official of the Board of Rites,[4] I used to announce the ceremonies in the Imperial Temple of Nanking. Since my post was humble, I need not reveal my name. Happily I have been spared most calamities. During ninety-seven years of life I have seen the rise and   15
fall of many generations. Now another cycle has dawned. Our ruler is supremely wise and virtuous, and his ministers are loyal and efficient. The people are quiet and contented after an uninterrupted succession of good harvests. During this twenty-third year of K'ang-hsi's[5] reign, twelve kinds of auspicious omens have appeared.   20

VOICE FROM BACKSTAGE: What were the omens?

MASTER OF CEREMONIES: [*Counting on his fingers.*] The Chart of Revelation emerged from the Yellow River, and the Holy Scripture from the River Lo.[6] We have seen both the Fortunate Star and the Felicitous Cloud; the sweet dew and the fruitful rain have fallen;   25
the phoenix pair have returned and the unicorn roams at large. The bean-pods burst and the orchid flourishes; the sea is calm and the Yellow River clear. All the omens are complete. Is this not a matter for congratulation? My old body is glad to survive in so wondrous a world, and I have been enjoying innumerable excursions.   30
Last night, in the Garden of Great Serenity, I saw a new play entitled *The Peach Blossom Fan*. The events it portrays took place in Nanking not long ago, during the last years of the Ming dynasty. The rise and fall of an empire are evoked in a story of meeting and separation. Both plot and protagonists were drawn from life. Not   35

---

1. Translated by and with notes adapted from Chen Shih-hsiang and Harold Acton, with the collaboration of Cyril Birch.   2. An officer of the state who calls out the prescribed actions in a Confucian ritual.
3. His clothes signify that he has retired from public office.   4. The government bureau in charge of conducting state rituals.   5. The reign title of Emperor Sheng-tsu; he ruled from 1662 to 1723—thus it is 1684.   6. These magical events were actually legendary happenings of high antiquity.

only did I hear tell of the originals; I saw them with my own eyes.
How amusing it was to recognise my decrepit self in a minor role!
I was stirred so deeply that I laughed and wept, raged and cursed
by turns. Needless to say, the audience had no idea that I was
included in the drama.   40
VOICE FROM BACKSTAGE: Who was the author of this remarkable play?
MASTER OF CEREMONIES: Perhaps you gentlemen do not realize that
    famous playwrights never divulge their names. Suffice it that in
    distributing praise and blame he follows the tradition of his ances-
    tor, the author of the *Spring and Autumn Annals*; by melodic   45
    means he revives the lofty style of the classic Odes, and demon-
    strates the quality of his upbringing.[7]
VOICE FROM BACKSTAGE: It must be the Mountain Hermit of the
    Cloud Pavilion.[8]
MASTER OF CEREMONIES: You are not mistaken.   50
VOICE FROM BACKSTAGE: The play will be performed at today's assem-
    bly. Since you are one of the characters and a veteran familiar with
    the latest tunes, please favour us with a synopsis. We shall listen
    with rapt attention.
MASTER OF CEREMONIES: It is summarized in a song by the Taoist   55
    priest Chang Wei. [*Sings.*]

> The young scholar Hou, residing in Mo-ling,[9]
> Lost his heart to a southern beauty there.
> But love was wounded; evil slandering
> Soon forced asunder this too happy pair.   60
> Chaos was loosened; warriors ran wild;
> A worthless debauchee the Throne defiled;
> Murderous traitors sprang from civil strife.
> Forever ended was the blissful life
> Of our fond lovers; he in fetters lay,   65
> While she true heroism did display.
> Aided by Su and Liu,[1] with all their might,
> The Emperor and his Premier fled by night.
> Over the misty waves I gaze and falter:
> Who is to chant the patriot's lament?   70
> The painted fan of peach blossoms was rent,
> And true love's token shattered at an altar.
> How matters went astray, we shall disclose.

VOICE FROM BACKSTAGE: Bravo, bravo! But your masterly trills some-
    times made it difficult for us to follow the meaning. Please oblige 75
    us with a short outline of the plot.
MASTER OF CEREMONIES: [*Sings.*]

> Within and without the court, traitors Ma and Juan hide their blades;
> Liu and Su astutely plot to foil their machinations;
> Master Hou's life of rapture falls into ruin;
> Chang the Taoist tells the fates of dynasties in a song.   80

---

7. K'ung Shang-jen counted himself a descendant of Confucius in the sixty-fourth generation. Confucius (K'ung Tzu) wrote the *Spring and Autumn Annals* and compiled the *Classic Odes* (or *Book of Songs*). 8. One of K'ung Shang-jen's sobriquets. 9. Nanking. 1. Su K'un-sheng and Liu Ching-t'ing, respectively.

[*Speaks.*] Before I have finished speaking, Master Hou steps onto the stage. Your attention please!

From *Part I*

SCENE 1

The Storyteller

1643, SECOND MONTH

[*Enter* HOU FANG-YÜ *in the robes of a scholar.*]
HOU: [*Sings.*]

On Grieve-Not Lake beside the Poet's Tower,[2]
The weeping willows burgeon once again.
The sun is setting: hill and river blend
In perfect beauty, and the traveller is tempted
To drink, recalling beauties long ago,   5
Painted and powdered in the southern courts.
Sad thoughts come with twilight, while the swallows
Frolic regardless of the fall of kings.

[*Recites.*]

Hushed is the courtyard, cold the kitchen stove;
And I have risen late from heavy slumber.   10
Though flowers bloom, fatigue invades the limbs,
And while it rains at every dawn of day,
And trees around the royal tombs decay,
The river swollen with the melted snows
Washes away the palace's foundations.   15
I write new poems grieving for the past;
An exile's sorrow, dreaming dreams of home.
Where will the swallows choose to nest this year,
In my village home far west of the misty waters?

[*Speaks.*] My name is Hou Fang-yü, and I am a native of Kuei-te   20
in the heart of the empire. I am descended from a long line of
scholars and officials; my father and grandfather were Ministers of
State, and both set up their standards in the Eastern Forest. Trained
in poetry and the classics, I have won distinction in the world of
letters and allied myself with the Revival Society.[3] My early writings   25
were influenced by those master-spirits Pan Ku and Sung Yü; in
maturity I am drawing nearer to Han Yü and Su Tung-p'o.[4] I have

---

2. Built for the 4th-century poet Sun Ch'u, located just to west of the city wall of Nanking.   3. The Tung-lin, or Eastern Forest Party, was a school of intellectuals who organized opposition to the corrupt dictatorship of the eunuch Wei Chung-hsien and his secret police. The Fu-she (*Revival*) Society for the revival of ancient learning was an offshoot of the Eastern Forest Party, whose aim was to "make friends by means of literature" and help its members prepare for the civil service examination. Wu Ying-chi, who appears in this play, in historical fact recorded more than two thousand members of this influential society.   4. Or Su Shih (1036–1101), leading poet and essayist of the Sung Dynasty. Pan Ku (died A.D. 92), eminent historian. Sung Yü (3rd century B.C.), statesman and poet whose works form part of the *Elegies of Ch'u.* Han Yü (768–824), poet and essayist, leader of the influential plain style movement of the T'ang Dynasty. The plain style movement advocated a more direct prose style that was conducive to serious argument.

written in praise of wine in the Yueh-hua Palace, despite my reluctance to plant more flowers in the garden at Loyang.⁵ Since finishing my examinations last year, I have been staying on the shore of   30
Grieve-Not Lake. But the clouds of war continue to cover us, and
news from home is scarce. It is mid-spring and the green grass
stretches to the dim horizon, but where shall I find a companion
for my homeward journey? The yellow dust rises from the earth,
but here I sit in solitary exile. Oh! Grieve Not, Grieve Not! How   35
can I fail to grieve? Fortunately, my literary friends Ch'en Chen-
hui and Wu Ying-chi are staying over Ts'ai Yi-so's bookshop. We
often meet and cheer each other's solitude. Today we shall gather
at the Fair City Monastery and enjoy the splendour of the plum
blossoms. I must start immediately or I shall be late. [*He proceeds*   40
to sing.]

> New warmth invades the breeze,
> Mist 'whelms the river glade.
> We stroll through flowery leas
> With wine in jars of jade.
> Thrilled by a sudden flute   45
> The pilgrim's heart is mute.
> Don't pass by Swallow Lane:
> New owners are repainting
> The lintels of your friends
> Who will not come again. [*Exit.*]   50

    [*Enter* CH'EN CHEN-HUI *and* WU YING-CHI.]
CH'EN: [*Sings.*]

> The royal power is fading from Nanking.
> The war-flags wave, the drums of battle beat.
> One dreads to cross the river, though it flows
> So placidly through willow groves and orchards.

    [*Each announces his name.*]
CH'EN: What is the latest news of the roving bandits?   55
WU: Yesterday I saw an official report. After defeating the national
armies, the bandits are drawing near the capital. Tso Liang-yü, the
Earl of Ning-nan, has retreated to Hsiang-yang, and central China
is totally unprotected. The fate of the dynasty is sealed. We might
as well enjoy the spring while it lasts.   60
CH'EN and WU together: [*Singing.*]

> Spring floods the air, but wind and rain
> Have scattered petals of the pear,
> And so dawn seems dishevelled and in pain.

HOU: [*Reentering.*] Greetings! So the two of you came betimes.
WU: Of course. We could not bear to keep you waiting.   65
CH'EN: I sent my servant ahead to sweep the monastery courtyard and
serve refreshments.

---

5. Hou Fang-yü uses these allusions to compare himself with the poet Tsou Yang (ca. 206–129 B.C.),
guest in the Yueh-hua Palace built by Prince Hsiao of Liang, and with the poet Shih Ch'ung (died A.D.
300), owner of a famous garden outside Loyang.

SERVANT: [*Entering in haste.*] When it is cold, the wine's not warm
    enough; when flowers bloom, the trippers[6] are too many. . . . We
    arrived too late, Your Honour. Let us all go home.   70
CH'EN: What do you mean, too late?
SERVANT: Master Hsu from the Wei Palace is giving a party in honour
    of the blossoms. The whole monastery is crammed with his guests.
HOU: Let us go up the river then, and visit the beauties of the Water
    Pavilion.   75
WU: Why trouble to go so far? Do you know that brilliant minstrel Liu
    Ching-t'ing of T'ai-chou? He is highly esteemed by such connois-
    seurs as the Ministers Fan Ching-wen and Ho Ju-ch'ung, and I hear
    that he lives nearby. On this languid spring day, would it not be
    pleasant to listen to him?   80
CH'EN: That is also a good suggestion.
HOU: [*Angrily.*] Pock-marked Liu was a toady of Juan Ta-ch'eng,
    Bearded Juan, the eunuch's adopted son. I would rather avoid such
    a creature.
WU: Apparently you do not know the facts. Since the despicable Juan   85
    persisted in patronising singers and dancers and flattering the pow-
    erful at court instead of resigning, I wrote an impeachment
    exposing his crimes and demanding his punishment. When at last
    his troupe of artists discovered that he was a member of the treach-
    erous Ts'ui and Wei cliques, they all walked out on him in the   90
    middle of a performance, and pock-marked Liu was among them.
    In my opinion Liu deserves our respect.
HOU: I should never have expected to find such high principles in a
    man of that sort. Let us pay him a visit. [*They proceed together.*]
HOU, WU, and CHEN together: [*Singing.*]

        Random pipe-notes in the Courts of the Transcendents   95
        Where the secluded Alchemist
        Watches "the vast sea turn into mulberry groves."[7]

SERVANT: Here we are. I'll knock at the door. [*Shouts.*] Is pock-marked
    Liu at home?
CH'EN: Fie, fie! He is a celebrity: you should address him as *Master*   100
    Liu.
SERVANT: Master Liu, open the door!
    [*Enters* LIU—*a "ch'ou" or comedian type with a white beard, a skull
    cap, and a blue gown.*]
LIU: [*Sings.*]

        Green moss and weeds grow rank and high
        Beside my long-locked door.
        Woodsmen and fishingfolk amble nigh   105
        To praise the times of yore.

[*Seeing the visitors, he exclaims.*] Oh, Masters Ch'en and Wu! Forgive my ignorance of your arrival. Who is the gentleman you have
brought along with you?

---

6. Visitors.   7. A common Taoist (or alchemist) metaphor for the mutability of all phenomena.

CH'EN: This is our friend Hou Fang-yü of Honan, whose fame is in 110
the ascendant. He has long admired your art and hopes to hear
you.

LIU: I am overwhelmed. Pray be seated and drink some tea. [*They sit,
and* LIU *continues.*] You gentlemen are such fine scholars, so familiar with the *Records of the Historian,* the *Comprehensive Mirror,*[8] or 115
whatever; what pleasure or instruction could you hope to gain from
my vulgar discourse? [*He points at his courtyard and sings.*]

> In the forsaken garden, a withered pine leans over a broken wall;
> On the fragrant grass of the palace ruins, the silky showers fall.
> The Six Great Dynasties'[9] decay brings thoughts too sad to render; 120
> In telling tales I often weep, because my heart's too tender.

HOU: You are excessively modest. Please favour us with a sample of
your skill.

LIU: Since you honour me with your company, I dare not disappoint
you. But I fear that my crude versions of history and blind man's 125
tales are unworthy of your ears, so I shall comment on a chapter of
Confucius's *Analects* instead.

HOU: How strange! One would hardly expect you to choose such a
theme.

LIU: [*Laughing.*] You scholars discuss the *Analects,* why shouldn't I? 130
Today you will judge my slender claim to learning. [*Recites.*]

> "I dwell among green hills: you ask me why.
> My soul at ease, I smile without reply.
> The peach petals are swept along the stream
> To other lands outside this mortal dream."[1] 135

[*He claps his "wakener-board"*[2] *and continues, speaking.*] I shall
tell how the crime of three powerful clans who conspired against
their ruler was exposed. I shall also tell how wonderously Confucius
succeeded in the reform of music. The great doctrine of the Way
was on the wane. Avarice and covetousness were deeply embedded 140
in the heart of man. On returning to Lu from the state of Wei, our
great Sage began to restore the true principles of music. So profoundly were performers affected by the result that they were
ashamed to realize they had been serving the wrong masters, and
abandoned those tribes of malefactors. The theatres of the mighty, 145
which had been full of glowing colour and vibrant melody, were
deserted in a twinkling. Truly fearsome, truly marvelous was the
influence of the Sage! [*He sings to drum or ta-ku*[3] *accompaniment,
keeping rhythmic time.*]

> The great Sage of antiquity was most versatile in magic;
> He could sway the wind and rain, 150
> And turn handfuls of peas into armies of warriors.

8.. The history of China by Ssu-ma Kuang (1019–1086). The *Records of the Historian* is by Ssu-ma Ch'ien (145–ca. 90 B.C.), who after his reformation of the calendar took up and completed the monumental work begun by his father, the history of China from the earliest ages to his own time.　9. Those that from the 3rd through the 6th centuries maintained their capital at Nanking.　1. A poem by the great T'ang master Li Po (699–762).　2. A wooden clapper, used to punctuate storytelling.　3. A large drum.

When he saw that the turbulent nobles
Had lost all sense of propriety in their dancing and music,
He played a subtle trick on them.
Hence the lowest of slaves   155
Began to behave like the highest of heroes.

[LIU *claps his board and continues, speaking.*] The first player to
leave for the state of Ch'i was good Master Chih. And why did he
leave for Ch'i? I'll tell you. [*He drums and sings.*]

Alas, he exclaimed,   160
Why should I ring the bell for these three clans?
I must have been blind to wallow in such mire.
I shall leave at once,
Setting forth with long swift strides towards the northeast;
There I shall join my old comrades and win fresh laurels.   165
I shall play for the delight of Master K'ung himself,
Who forgot the flavour of meat
For three months after hearing my performance.
And the virtuous Duke Ching
Will also be moved to tears by my art.   170
Even if the usurpers have swallowed
The heart of a leopard and the gall of a bear,
I doubt if they would pursue me to Ch'i,
The land of Chiang T'ai-kung's[4] descendants!

[LIU *claps his board and continues speaking.*] The second master's   175
name was Kan. He left for the state of Ch'u. The third master, Liao,
retired to the state of Ts'ai. The fourth one was Ch'üeh, who went
to the state of Ch'in. Why did these three leave? I'll tell you. [*He
drums and sings.*]

All these musicians, who played at every banquet,
Had lost their leader now;
One by one they embarked on a new career.   180
The second master said: "See the usurper
Grasp his rice-bowl in the hall!
Why should we blow trumpets
And beat drums for his entertainment?
Our leader has left for the state of Ch'i;   185
Nobody can make him return.
As for me, I propose to play for Hsiung Yi, the King of Ch'u,
Committing myself to his powerful protection."
The third master said: "Though the state of Ts'ai,
South of the river, is not extensive,   190
It is near the capital
And in the heart of the central plain."
The fourth master gazed towards the south and said:
"I can see a new imperial spirit
Rising from the state of Ch'in,   195
Which has strong armies and fortifications;

---

4. Legendary octogenarian (12th century B.C.), who consolidated the Chou dynasty. He was said to exercise authority over the spirits of the unseen universe and hence was often depicted over doors to frighten away evil spirits.

Thither I shall take my lute."
All three of them pointed at the usurpers and said:
"We have endured your tyranny too long;   200
Henceforth we shall make you wince at the sound of our names."

[LIU *claps his board and continues speaking.*] One drummer
named Fang Shu went to the Yellow River region, and another
named Wu to the Han River region. The junior leader's name was
Yang and the gong-beater's name was Hsiang, and these repaired   205
to the seacoast. The manner of their leaving was different. I'll tell
you. [*He drums and sings.*]

> Altogether there were four drummers and gong-beaters.
> "Our theatre remains in confusion," said they,
> "And we have no desire to stay.   210
> Disgusted with our fiendish patrons,
> We shall seek employment elsewhere,
> Even though it is unlikely that we shall fare better.
> Let us sail a light boat to the Peach Blossom Spring;[5]
> At least we may win renown   215
> As fishermen of the lakes and rivers."

[LIU *claps his board and continues speaking.*] These four made the
wisest decision. Hearken to their speech! [*He drums and sings.*]

> "The trees of coral soar a hundred feet, vermilion in the sunlight;
> The crystal palace of the sea-god is built on a terrace of pearls.   220
> The Dragon King will invite us to a banquet
> Where golden boys and jade girls excel earthly mortals.
> Phoenix flutes and ivory pipes
> Will be tuned to the dragon's most exquisite melodies;
> For this time, *others* will play while *we* shall listen.   225
> Though the usurpers may try to pursue us down the rivers,
> There will be thousands of leagues[6] between us
> In which they will lose their way.
> We need not fear to be friendless
> Among the mountains and distant waters,   230
> For all men within the four seas
> And beyond the horizon are our comrades.
> We should tear the paper windowpane
> And look at the real world.
> We have saved ourselves from the abyss by divine inspiration.   235
> Even if sea becomes land, and land sea,
> The vision of our Sage endures in the Six Canons.[7]

---

5. During the Tsin Dynasty (265–420) the poet T'ao Ch'ien wrote of a fisherman of Wu-ling who, following a stream without noticing its length, suddenly came to a grove of flowering peach trees. Fascinated by
the beauty of the trees and the abundance of scented plants, he wandered on until he reached a country
of well-tilled fields, clear water, and pleasant cottages. The inhabitants were highly civilized and law
abiding. He asked where they had come from and was told that their ancestors had fled from the tyranny
of the Ch'in Dynasty in the 3rd century B.C. and had found refuge in this country cut off from the rest of
the world. After leaving them, the fisherman reported his adventure. Men went out to investigate this
unknown region, but they lost their way. Hence the expression *Peach Blossom Spring* became a metaphor
for a place of retirement, far from the noise and turmoil of the world. The allusion is anachronistic here,
coming from the lips of a contemporary of Confucius (6th century B.C.).   6. Unit of distance, roughly
equal to one-third of a mile.   7. The oldest enumeration of Chinese classics gave only five canons: the
Book of Changes, the *Book of Documents*, the *Book of Songs*, the *Record of Rites*, and the *Spring and
Autumn Annals*. The *Record of Music* was later added as the sixth canon, but it is usually classed as one
of the books of the *Record of Rites*.

[*Standing up,* LIU *speaks.*] Thank you for listening! I have shown what trifling talents I possess.

CH'EN: Superb! None of our modern pundits could express himself so well. You are indeed a consummate artist.   240

WU: Since leaving Juan, Liu has not cared to seek another patron. This last recital was autobiographical.

HOU: I perceive he has a noble character, untainted by worldliness. He is truly one of us. Story-telling is merely one of his minor accomplishments.   245

CH'EN, WU, and HOU together: [*Singing.*]

> The deep red dust is suddenly clear,
> And all shines bright as snow.
> The warm spring light is suddenly chill;
> The Sage solves all below.   250

[*They laugh, and continue.*]

> Your mocking satire, our delight,
> Each phrase at once caress and bite,
> The triple beat of Yü-yang drum[8]
> To judgment come!

LIU: [*Sings.*]

> Please come another day;   255
> And if to Peach Blossom source
> You fail to find the way,
> To this old fisherman have recourse.

WU: Which of your other colleagues left the house of Juan?

LIU: We are all dispersed. Only the master-singer Su K'un-sheng remains in this neighborhood.   260

HOU: I should like to meet him too, and hope you will both pay me a visit.

LIU: Of course we should be most honoured.

[*Each sings a line of the following quatrain.*]

LIU: After my song is sung, the sun is setting.   265

CH'EN: The fragrance of fallen petals fills the courtyard.

WU: Terraces and towers seem myriad blades of grass.

HOU: Spiritual discourse and imperial strategy melt into the void.

SCENE 2

The Singing-Master

1643, SECOND MONTH

[LI CHEN-LI, *the heroine's foster mother, enters. She is the hostess of an elegant house of pleasure.*]

---

8. Alludes to the drumming that accompanied Mi Heng when he cursed the tyrant Ts'ao Ts'ao in the time of the Three Kingdoms (3rd century A.D.).

LI: [*Sings.*]

With delicate firm strokes I paint my eyebrows.
The doors of these red chambers are seldom closed;
The drooping willows by the wooden bridge
Cause riders to dismount.
I shall embroider the bag of my reed-organ and tighten the strings of
    my lute.   5

  [*Recites a quatrain.*]

      The pear blossoms are like snow, the grass like mist;
      Spring settles on the banks of the Ch'in-huai River.
      A row of pleasure-chambers fronts on the water,
      Reflecting from each window a lovely face.

[*Speaks.*] My name is Li Chen-li. I have won fame in the world of   10
"mists and flowers," and high rank in the circles of "wind and
moon."[9] I was educated in the old tradition of my calling. Though
I have escorted countless guests along the bridge to the pleasure-
quarters, the rose of my complexion has not faded and my charms
are as fresh as ever. I have adopted a daughter of exquisite grace,   15
who has recently begun to appear at social functions. She is very
shy and utterly enchanting; so far she has had no experience behind
the hibiscus-embroidered bed-curtains. I happen to know a former
magistrate named Yang Wen-ts'ung who is the brother-in-law of Ma
Shih-ying, Governor of Feng-yang, and a sworn brother of Juan Ta-   20
ch'eng. Whenever he visits us, he lavishes praise on my adopted
daughter and promises to introduce an influential patron to "comb
her hair."[1] On such a fine spring day, I expect he will pay me a
visit. [*Calls.*] Draw the curtains, maid, and sweep the floor. See that
everything is ready for our guests.   25
VOICE FROM BACKSTAGE: Aye, aye, ma'am.
    [YANG WEN-TS'UNG *enters.*]
YANG: This magnificent view of the three mounts is like a masterpiece
of painting. The romance of the Six Dynasties is a perennial theme
of poetry. I am Yang Wen-ts'ung, a retired magistrate. Since I am
on the best of terms with Mistress Li, the famous hostess of the   30
Ch'in-huai River, I'll take advantage of the fine weather to call on
her. Here is her house. [*He enters it.*] Where is Mistress Li? [*On
seeing her.*] The plum petals have fallen and the willow floss turned
yellow. The courtyard is filled with soft harmonies of spring. How
can we extract the utmost enjoyment from it?   35

---

9. Metaphors for romantic love.   1. That is, to deflower her. In the case of a young courtesan-to-be of
exceptional beauty and talent—like Fragrant Princess—this was an honor for which young men would
eagerly vie. If the process led to a more enduring attachment, there was the possibility that the young man
might purchase the girl's freedom from her adoptive mother (the madam of the house) and install her as
his wife or secondary wife. This is what indeed happens to Hou Fang-yü and Fragrant Princess. The vows
of fidelity and plans to marry are to be taken as serious intentions. Their union, however, was not regarded
by others as totally binding.

LI: Let us climb to the upper chamber. Up there we can burn sweet
incense, sip tea, and enjoy some poetry.

YANG: That sounds delightful. [*Both climb the stairs. He recites.*]

> The bamboo screen suggests bars of a cage
> For the bird on his perch;
> Flower shadows seem like a cover   40
> For the fish in the bowl.

[*Looking round, he says.*] This must be the sitting-room of your
charming daughter. Where is she now?

LI: She has not finished dressing.   45

YANG: Please ask her to join us.

LI: [*Calls.*] Come out, my dear. His Honour Yang has arrived.

YANG: [*Examining the poems hanging on the walls.*] These are all gifts
from famous masters of calligraphy. What a choice collection! [*He
reads them out loud to himself.*]

[*The heroine, a* GIRL *of about sixteen, enters in an exquisite dress.*]

GIRL: [*Sings.*]

> Returning from the scented land of dreams,   50
> I leave the red quilt embroidered with mandarin ducks,[2]
> To redden my lips and dress my hair.
> I shall con some recent poems
> To dispel the languor of spring.

[*Says to* YANG.] Your Honour, a thousand blessings!   55

YANG: I have not seen you for several days, and you have grown much
lovelier in the meantime. What profound truth the poems on this
wall express! I see that some were written by my dearest friends.
Since they have paid you such a compliment, I must join them.

[MISTRESS LI *promptly brings him a brush and ink-slab.* YANG *holds
the brush in silence before saying.*]

I doubt if I could ever compete with these masters. To conceal my   60
failings, I shall contribute a sketch of orchids.

LI: I can assure you it will be appreciated.

YANG: Here is a fist-shaped rock by Lan T'ien-shu.[3] I'll paint some
orchids beside it. [*Sings.*]

> The white wall gleams like silk for me to paint on: 65
> Fresh leaves, sweet buds, an aura of mist and rain.
> Here a fist-rock bursts with ink-splashed energy,
> There specks of moss are elegantly scattered.

[*Standing back to survey his finished painting, he says.*] I believe it
will do. [*Sings.*]   70

> No match for the splendid vigor of the Yuan masters,
> But at least our ladies will have orchids to set them off.

---

2. Emblems of conjugal fidelity.   3. Or Lan Ying (1578–1660), one of the most accomplished painters
of his time, a last representative of the Che school; he appears later in the play.

LI: This is a genuine work of art. It vastly improves the room.

YANG: Don't mock me! [To the GIRL.] Please tell me your name so
that I can inscribe it here.   75

GIRL: I am too young to have a name.[4]

LI: We should be obliged if Your Honour would choose one for her.

YANG: According to the *Tso chuan*,[5] "the fragrance of the orchid pervades a whole nation, it captivates all mankind." Why not call her
Fragrant Princess?   80

LI: That is perfect. Fragrant Princess, come and thank His Honour.

FRAGRANT PRINCESS: [*Curtseying.*] I thank Your Honour kindly.

YANG: [*Laughing.*] It provides us with a name for the house also. [*As
he writes the inscription, he reads it aloud.*] In the springtime of
the Year of the Horse during the reign of Ch'ung-chen,[6] I painted   85
these orchids in the Abode of Entrancing Perfumes, in order to
win a smile from Fragrant Princess. Signed, Yang Wen-ts'ung of
Kweiyang.

LI: Both the calligraphy and brushwork are supreme. I can never
thank you enough. [*All sit down.*]   90

YANG: Surely Fragrant Princess is the greatest beauty in the land. What
training in the arts has she received?

LI: I brought her up so tenderly that she has only just begun to study
in earnest. The day before yesterday I found a teacher to instruct
her in the art of lyric.   85

YANG: Who is he?

LI: A certain Su K'un-sheng.

YANG: I know him well. He used to go by the name of Chou Ju-sung,
and lived in Wusi. He deserves the highest praise. What tunes has
he taught her so far?   100

LI: "The Four Dreams of the Jade Tea-House."[7]

YANG: How much has she learned?

LI: Only half "The Peony Pavilion." Dear daughter, as His Honour
Yang is an old friend of ours, do bring your music book and sing a
few tunes for him.   105

FRAGRANT PRINCESS: I dare not.

LI: Don't be silly. In our profession, sleeves and skirts are in constant
motion. Why not sing when you have the chance? [*Sings.*]

> Born amid powdered faces and painted eyebrows,
> Nurtured as one of the orioles and flowers,   110
> A tuneful voice is your only source of wealth.
> Be not too prodigal with your emotions, but learn to sing

---

4. The Chinese had a number of personal names. At birth a male received a "milk name," which was
used by relatives and neighbors. On entering school, he was given a "book name" to be used by schoolmasters, school fellows, officials, and in literary connections. At marriage he was given a "great name" for use
by acquaintances. Every writer or scholar took one or more "studio names." If he won a literary degree,
entered official life, or had official rank, he took an "official name." After death he might be given a
posthumous name. Names usually had some appropriate significance. A female received a milk name, a
marriage name, and perhaps a nickname. "Fragrant Princess" corresponds to the last.   5. An important
commentary on the *Spring and Autumn Annals*, written in the 1st century A.D.   6. The last full reign
of the Ming, from 1628 to 1644. *Year of the Horse*: 1643.   7. The studio name of T'ang Hsien-tsu
(1550–1617), outstanding dramatist of the Ming period. *Four Dreams*: his plays.

Songs of the morning breeze and broken moon.
Beat gentle time with your ivory castanets,
Bear off the singer's prize,   115
And princes will tether horses at your gate.

[SU K'UN-SHENG *enters, in everyday garb.*]

SU: On my way to the songbird in the emerald chamber, I stop to gaze
at the peonies by the porch. Since leaving the house of Juan, I have
been teaching music to the loveliest courtesans. Isn't this better
than waiting on the whims of an eunuch's foster son? [*He steps in.*] 120
Ah! Your Honour Yang, it is an age since we have met!

YANG: I congratulate you on your entrancing pupil.

LI: Master Su has arrived. Run and welcome him, dear daughter.

[FRAGRANT PRINCESS *curtseys.*]

SU: Let us avoid formalities. Have you memorized the song we practised yesterday?   125

FRAGRANT PRINCESS: I have, sir.

SU: Since His Honour Yang is present, let us hear it. We should take
advantage of his criticism.

YANG: I shall be content merely to listen.

SU and FRAGRANT PRINCESS: [*Sitting opposite each other, sing.*]

Clusters of purple, witching hues of red,   130
Now blossom from below and overhead,
Even from dried-up wells and broken walls.
How shall we spend so glorious a day?

SU: [*Stopping.*] Your rhythm is weak. The accent should fall on
"spend" and "glorious"; don't run them together. Again! [*The last*   135
line is repeated. Then they continue.]

SU and FRAGRANT PRINCESS: [*Singing.*]

Where at this hour can perfect bliss be found?
Now twilight gathers, and the day has fled.
The many-coloured clouds are drifting round
The green-tiled roofs, and gusty showers fall. . . .

SU: [*Interrupting.*] The word "showers" should be stressed, and sung   140
from deep in the throat. [*The last line is repeated. Then they con-*
tinue.]

SU and FRAGRANT PRINCESS: [*Singing.*]

Over the misty waves doth float
A fragile painted boat.
Yet by the cloistered maid these things are seen
Only as visions on a painted screen.   145

SU: Well done, well done! You have sung it without a mistake. Let us
continue.

SU and FRAGRANT PRINCESS: [*Singing.*]

The cuckoo's tears have stained the verdant hills,
The willow branches droop as drunk with wine;
New peonies reign; but when the spring is gone,   150
What will survive of their bright sovereignty?

SU: [*Interrupting.*] This line is new to you, try it again. [*They repeat the last line and then continue.*]

SU and FRAGRANT PRINCESS: [*Singing.*]

> Now feast your gaze in sheer serenity:
> Behold the twittering swallows, how they fare,
> Flashing their tails like scissors through the air,   155
> While orioles drop their notes like rounded pearls.

SU: Better and better! Now we have mastered another melody.

YANG: [*To* LI.] I'm delighted to discover that your daughter has such talent. She is certain to reach the peak of her profession. [*To* SU.] Yesterday I met Hou Fang-yü, the son of Minister Hou. He has   160
brilliant prospects as well as literary genius, and he is looking for a beautiful mate. Have you heard of him, old friend?

SU: He is a fellow countryman of mine, a youth of exceptional promise.

YANG: A match between such a couple should be very successful.   165
[*Sings.*]

> The sixteen-year-old maid, as fair as emerald jade,
> Is ripe for nuptial bliss—how ravishing her song!
> Her suitor rides with silken gifts and trinkets for
>   her hair.
> Hand in hand they will drain the cups of wine,
> While friends chant verses in congratulation;   170
> The halls are freshly garnished for the wedding.
> A couple perfectly matched,
> Year after year they will abide together,
> In a peace tree grove beside the sweet spring waters.

LI: I hope you will persuade this young gentleman to pay us a visit. It 175
would be wonderful if such a match could be arranged.

YANG: I promise to keep it in mind.

LI: [*Sings.*]

> My daughter is more precious to me than rarest pearls,
> Her voice is purer than the new-born oriole's;
> But her virgin youth is barred by many doors,   180
> Unnoticed by the passing wanderer.

[*Speaks to all.*] This day should be celebrated. Let us drink some wine below.

YANG: With the greatest pleasure.

[*Exeunt, each one singing.*]

YANG: Outside the curtain, flowers fill the courtyard.   185

LI: The oriole feels drunk, the swallow drowsy.

FRAGRANT PRINCESS: My crimson kerchief holds a heap of cherries.

SU: Waiting to fling them at P'an's chariot![8]

---

8. Poet (3rd century) renowned for his exceptional handsomeness; women would pelt his carriage with flowers and fruits when he rode in the capital.

SCENE 3

The Disrupted Ceremonies

1643, THIRD MONTH

[*Enter two* TEMPLE SERVANTS, *both clowns.*]

FIRST SERVANT: For generations, the sacrificial peas have been symbols of this rite.[9]

SECOND SERVANT: Ever since the days of my old grandad's might.

FIRST SERVANT: The sacrificial vessels at each altar are catalogued in the books.

SECOND SERVANT: Count them like stooks.

FIRST SERVANT: In the beginning and middle of each month, we light the candles and open the door.

SECOND SERVANT: Sweep the floor.

FIRST SERVANT: Kneel down and greet the Master of Ceremonies as soon as he is sighted.

SECOND SERVANT: Make sure that everything is righted. But you have bungled all the words.

FIRST SERVANT: If you can do better, go ahead.

SECOND SERVANT: Grain tribute is brought to the treasury all the year round.

FIRST SERVANT: Bragging of wealth by the pound.

SECOND SERVANT: The whole family lives under a green-tiled roof with scarlet walls.

FIRST SERVANT: Leading a wife to the stalls.

SECOND SERVANT: Dry timber is felled as soon as an axe you seize.

FIRST SERVANT: Plundering neighbours' trees.

SECOND SERVANT: Year in, year out, no vegetable need you eat.

FIRST SERVANT: Nothing but salted meat.

SECOND SERVANT: Shame on you, you have made a hash of it with your cheap rhymes. [*Both laugh.*]

FIRST and SECOND SERVANT together: We prepare the rites of the Imperial Academy in Nanking. After six months of idleness, we are back in the middle of spring, the season for sacrifice. All the ritual vessels and provisions have arrived from the Minister's office. Let us set them in proper order.

[*They set out the altar.*]

FIRST SERVANT: Chestnuts, dates, fresh water-roots.

SECOND SERVANT: Ox, sheep, pig, rabbit, and deer.

FIRST SERVANT: Fish, spinach, celery, bamboo shoots, and garlic.

SECOND SERVANT: Salt, wine, incense, silk, and candles.

FIRST SERVANT: The list is complete. Keep an eye on everything, for we shall be blamed if the stewards pilfer.

MASTER OF CEREMONIES: [*Entering.*] Fie on you! If you don't pilfer, well and good. Why cast aspersions on others?

FIRST SERVANT: [*Bows with folded hands.*] I beg your pardon. I was

---

9. In early youth, Confucius was reputed to have used peas to imitate the arrangement of a ritual altar, thereby indicating his precocious interest in the rites.

referring to those who shall be nameless since they are shameless.
Of course a respectable person like you would be blameless.

MASTER OF CEREMONIES: Let us not waste words. It is already daybreak. You should light the candles and incense.

SECOND SERVANT: Aye, aye, sir. [*Exeunt.*]   45

[LIBATIONER[1] *appears in his official robes.*]

LIBATIONER: [*Sings.*]

> The smoke of incense clouds the pillared hall
> Where scarlet candles flame beside the altar.
> And now the orchestra strikes up a prelude;
> The vessels, food and wine are all prepared.

[*His* ASSISTANT *appears in his official robes.*]

ASSISTANT: [*Sings.*]

> The ranks are drawn up   50
> For the observance of ceremonies in the Southern Academy.

LIBATIONER: I am the Libationer in the Imperial Academy of Nanking.

ASSISTANT: I am the Assistant Libationer. Today is the day of sacrifice
at the Temple of Confucius, and we are about to begin the cere-   55
mony.

[*They stand on either side of the stage.* WU YING-CHI *enters.*]

WU: [*Sings.*]

> The drum is booming; soon it will be dawn.
> The scholars file before the Almond Altar.

[*Enter* FOUR SCHOLARS *of the Imperial Academy.*]

FOUR SCHOLARS, together: [*Singing.*]

> Of yore this music and these rites inspired three thousand disciples.
> Today we shall again behold our Sage.   60

[JUAN TA-CH'ENG *enters in formal attire, his face covered with a heavy
beard.*]

JUAN: [*Sings.*] I have brazened myself to join this solemn gathering.

WU: I, Wu Ying-chi, together with my comrades Yang Wei-tou, Liu
Po-tsung, Shen K'un-t'ung, and Shen Mei-sheng, am ready to
attend the sacrifice.

FOUR SCHOLARS: Let us take our appointed places.   65

JUAN: [*Hiding his face behind his sleeve.*] Having nothing else to do
in Nanking, I came to see the ceremony. [*He takes up a position
in the front rank.*]

MASTER OF CEREMONIES: [*Enters and calls.*] Go to your places. Stand
in even ranks. Bow; kneel; prostrate yourselves; arise! [*Thrice
repeated.*]

ALL together: [*Singing.*]

> A hundred feet above the clouds, the golden tablet gleams;   70
> Behold our Sage enthroned in majesty,

---

1. The official who pours out ritual offerings.

His four supreme disciples sit beside him,
While strains of music bid his spirit welcome.
Let us prostrate ourselves below the steps,
We who have studied poetry and the classics   75
That we may come into his heritage.
Now tremble in his presence, struck with awe.

[*After burning paper offerings, all salute each other.*]
LIBATIONER and ASSISTANT: [*Singing.*]

> Facing the north, we celebrate together
> Our Sage's glory with the spring's return;
> Observing all the hallowed regulations,   80
> The time and order of each sacrifice.

WU: [*Leading the* SCHOLARS' *chorus.*]

> Let us unite in worship of the Sage,
> Like his disciples in a nobler age.

JUAN: [*Sings.*]

> What joy to stroll the capital,
> A man of pleasure,   85
> Without official duties
> To rob me of my leisure.

[*Exeunt* LIBATIONER *and* ASSISTANT. JUAN *bows to all.*]
WU: [*Startled.*] Are you not whiskered Juan? What are you doing at
the sacrifice? This is an insult to the Sage. You are a disgrace to the
world of letters. [*Shouting.*] Away with you!   90
JUAN: [*Angrily.*] I am a distinguished Doctor of Literature, descended
from a famous family. Why should I not be allowed to attend the
sacrifice? What sin have I committed?
WU: At court and outside it, your guilt is notorious. You have covered
your face with a mask and lost your conscience. How dare you set   95
foot in this temple? Did not my public impeachment say enough
about your crimes?
JUAN: That was precisely why I attended these ceremonies, to confess
what is in my heart.
WU: Let me tell you plainly who and what you are. [*Sings.*]   100

> Godson of Wei, godson of K'o,[2]
> To any family you will go.
> With Ts'ui Ch'eng-hsiu, and T'ien Erh-ching,[3]
> Consorting in stealth,
> You guzzle iniquities and gobble filth.   105
> Shooting secret arrows into the Eastern Forest,[4]
> Weaving your plots in the Western Shed,[5]
> Beware, beware — men will not be misled.

---

2. K'o-shih, Emperor Hsi-tsung's wet nurse. Wei Chung-hsien (1568–1637), one of the most powerful
eunuchs in Chinese history, whose persecution of able generals and ministers weakened the Chinese
defenses against the threatening Manchus. On the emperor's death, Wei hanged himself to escape trial
and K'o-shih was executed.   3. Leading associates of Wei's clique.   4. See n. 3, p. 83.   5. The
notorious torture chamber of the court secret police.

SCHOLARS: [*Singing in unison.*]

> Ha! behold the melting glacier,
> The baseless, toppling iron pillar!   110

JUAN: Brothers, you revile me without trying to understand my
motives. You do not realize that I am a disciple of the great Chao
Chung-i. When the Grand Eunuch Wei rose to power, I had
retired to the country to mourn the death of my parents. How could
I have harmed anyone? On what grounds do you accuse me?   115
[*Sings.*]

> To such injustice Heaven once responded
> By sending frost in midsummer.
> Hide me under no black bowl[6]
> To suffer slander
> No more substantial than a shadow.   120
> Why did I cultivate Wei Chung-hsien?
> To try to save the upright censors,
> Wei Ta-chung, Chou Ch'ao-jui!
> For their sake, my good name
> Gladly I sacrificed.   125

[*Speaks.*] Have you forgotten Master K'ang Hai of yore, who curried
favour with the eunuch Liu Chin[7] in order to save the life of an
upright man? If I associated with Wei Chung-hsien, it was to protect my noble friends of the Eastern Forest Party. How can I be
blamed for this? [*Sings.*]   130

> Every problem demands a fair solution,
> But I have been ten times wronged,
> Yet no one rises to defend me;
> I am vilified by all.
> These giddy striplings break wind in my face. . . .   135

WU: How dare you use such language here!
ALL: It is insufferable that a traitor like you should speak so foully in
the temple of Confucius.
MASTER OF CEREMONIES: It is absolutely monstrous. Old as I am, I
long to thrash the traitor! [*Beats* JUAN.]   140
WU: Pummel his face and pull out all his hair!
[*Everybody attacks* JUAN.]
ALL: [*Singing.*]

> Damned spawn of a eunuch!
> You should not even be allowed
> To worship the Sage;
> A disgrace to the world of letters!   145
> We shall wage war against you and your like
> And drive you to the farthest wilderness,
> To feed wolves and tigers with your swinish carcass.

6. An image for an impenetrable cloud of unwarranted suspicion. *Frost in midsummer:* sent down by
Heaven, in an ancient legend, to convince the emperor of the loyalty of an unjustly slandered minister.
7. A eunuch who became virtual head of the government under the Ming emperor Wu-tsung. A cabal
formed against him, and he was executed in 1510.

JUAN: Have you done with assaulting me? [*To* MASTER OF CEREMON-
IES.] Even an old gaffer like you has the nerve to strike me!   150
MASTER OF CEREMONIES: I can thrash you as vigorously as any man.
JUAN: [*Gazing ruefully at his beard.*] I have lost half my beard. How
shall I ever appear in public again? [*He runs off the stage, singing.*]

> This volley of fists has laid me low,
> I am in agony;   155
> My arms feel broken, my back as well.
> I flee from this place of torment.

WU and ALL: [*Singing.*]

> Between the virtuous and the vile
> There is always a clear distinction,
> And this man's crimes are heavy and solid as lead.   160
> Not long ago his power could reach to Heaven—
> Today how ignominious was his flight!
> His scholar's hat was beaten flat;
> It is time for him to burn his ink and brushes.

WU: This incident has avenged the Eastern Forest Party and brought   165
honour to the Academy of Nanking. We should persevere in this
resolute course, and prevent all such villains from showing them-
selves again in public.
CHORUS: Hear, Hear! We have done a righteous deed before the
Sage's gate.   170
WU: Between light and darkness we should champion light.
CHORUS:

> Alas, 'tis never easy to decide
> Which be the winning, which the losing side.

WU:

> Heaven may loosen Chaos; 'tis for Man
> To conjure Order wheresoe'er he can.   175

SCENE 4

The Play Observed

1643, THIRD MONTH

[JUAN TA-CH'ENG *enters, in obvious distress.*]
JUAN: [*Sings.*]

> The old game is played out,
> My former colleagues scattered.
> The hair grows white upon my temples,
> No spirit is left in my song.
> Insulted by these upstarts without cease,   5
> How shall I ever sleep and eat in peace?

[*Speaks.*] Until recently I enjoyed a triumphant career. Power,
fame, and rank were within my grasp. Unfortunately, I was tempted

by vanity and greed to join the eunuch Wei's party. For a time I became one of his foster sons. While his influence was spreading like fire, I was like a wolf within sight of its prey. Now that it has dwindled to cold ashes, I am more like a wretched owl in a withered forest. Everybody curses me and spits in my face; I am assaulted from every side. Alas, I am a scholar who has absorbed a whole library of books. Why did I attach myself to that evil eunuch? I was neither demented nor delirious, yet how could I have made such a blunder as to become his henchman? [*Stamps his foot.*] When I think of the past, I am filled with mortification. Luckily, this huge city affords a shelter for all sorts. I have a spacious mansion in Breeches' Bottom, which I have embellished with gardens and pavilions, and here I have trained a private troupe of singers and dancers. Should any high official deign to associate with me, I would go to any expense to gratify him. Perhaps I may still win some good man's sympathy, and the chance to amend past errors. . . . [*Whispers.*] But if Heaven allowed dead ashes to flare up again, I would waste no further thought on my reputation. I would commit every crime again to my heart's content! Yesterday I was grossly insulted by the young urchins of the Revival Club in the temple of Confucius. Though they were to blame, I was rash to expose myself. But I am anxious to find a way to propitiate them. [*He scratches his head in thought and sings.*]

> Coxcombs combined, a feather-pated crew,
> To cheat and slander my distinguished name.
> Like whirling winds they tore away the beard
> About my lips—these very lips, the same
> That uttered purest poetry; broke this wrist
> Whose calligraphic skill once brought me fame.
> Nor can I find revenge, but only hide
> Indoors in all my shame.

FIRST SERVANT: [*Entering with a letter.*] Few notabilities come this way; all the fine birds are flown, alackaday! [*To* JUAN.] Your Honour, here is a note requesting the loan of your troupe of players.

JUAN: [*Reading it aloud.*] "Your friend Ch'en Chen-hui salutes you." Aha, this comes from a great celebrity. Why would such a great man as this stoop to borrowing my troupe of players? What did his messenger have to say?

SERVANT: He says there are two other gentlemen named Fang Mi-chih and Mao P'i-chiang who are drinking with him at the Crowing Cock Inn. They are all agog to enjoy your new play, *The Swallow Letter*.

JUAN: Run upstairs, choose the best costumes, and summon the leading players. See that they brush themselves up and hasten to oblige the scholars. You go with them, take my greetings, and keep a careful eye on everything.

[*Exit* FIRST SERVANT. *Several players cross the stage, followed by another* SERVANT *carrying costumes.* JUAN *beckons to him.*]

JUAN: [*Whispers.*] When you get there, listen carefully to their remarks
while they watch the play.   55

SERVANT: As you command, sir. [*Exit.*]

JUAN: [*Chuckling to himself.*] Ha-ha, I never expected them to apply
to me. This is an encouraging sign. I'll sit in my study and wait for
the servant's report. [*Exit.*]

[YANG WEN-TS'UNG *enters.*]

YANG: In the hope of hearing the latest tunes, I have come to call on   60
my old crony. He excels in composing lyrics and plays as I do in
painting and calligraphy. Today I have a chance of hearing his
latest song for *The Swallow Letter.* Here is the Stone Nest Garden.
How exquisitely all the rocks and flowers are arranged. It must have
been designed by the famous Chang Nan-yüan.[8] [*Pointing at the*   65
rocks and flowers, he sings.]

> Flowering groves carefully spaced,
> Rocks mantled with moss,
> Create the effect of a landscape
> By Ni Tsan or Huang Kung-wang.[9]

[*Looking up, he reads from a tablet.*] "The Hall of Lyrics. Calligra-   70
phy by Wang To."[1] What vigorous characters! Red carpets strew
the ground; this is where he rehearses his plays. [*Sings.*]

> A thatched pavilion completes the picture.
> There in his high black cap he directs the players
> With silver lute and crimson clappers.   75

[*Speaks.*] Maybe I shall find him in the flower garden. [*Sings.*]

> But why closed gates, a scene forlorn?
> Is he writing new poems or revising old ones?

[*Standing still, he listens and says.*] Somebody seems to be chanting; it must be old Juan reading aloud. Brother Juan, come and   80
relax awhile. Don't give up all your time to literature!

JUAN: [*Enters, laughing.*] I was wondering who had come to see me.
So it is you! Sit down, sit down.

YANG: Why shut yourself indoors on a fine spring day?

JUAN: My four plays are being printed, so I have to scrutinize the   85
proofs for mistakes.

YANG: So that explains it. I heard you had finished rehearsing *The
Swallow Letter,* and I long to see it.

JUAN: Unfortunately my actors are away.

YANG: Where have they gone?   90

JUAN: They have gone to entertain some friends of mine.

YANG: Would you let me see a copy of the script? I should enjoy
nothing better than to read it with some wine beside me.

---

8. Or Chang Lien, a landscape architect of the late Ming and early Ch'ing periods who designed many
famous gardens in Chekiang and Kiangsu.   9. Ni Tsan (1301–1374) and Huang Kung-wang (1269–
1354), two of the most celebrated artists of the Yuan Dynasty, which was a golden age of Chinese painting.
1. An eminent poet, painter, and calligrapher (1592–1652), who attained the exalted post of president of
the Board of Rites, first under the Ming and then again under the Manchus.

JUAN: [*To* SERVANTS.] Bring the wine. His Honour Yang and I will
quench our thirst.   95
VOICES FROM BACKSTAGE: Aye, aye, sir.
  [*Wine and refreshments are brought in.* YANG *and* JUAN *drink while
  reading the play.*]
YANG: [*Sings.*]

> Column by column, new poems flow onto paper,
> Each line as gold freshly sifted from sand.
> A beautiful woman speaks her reverie,
> As mist drifts over the sea and far clouds form.   100

[*Speaks.*] While reading this passage, I feel I have fallen in love!
[*Sings.*]

> Though willow buds whiten, and hair be sprinkled with snow,
> The swallow retains a fragment of spring in its beak.

JUAN: My doggerel and commonplace tunes must strike you as absurd.
Pray drink some more wine.   105
FIRST SERVANT: [*Entering hastily.*] I bring my random words to allay
my master's concern. Your Honour, I have been watching the per-
formance at the Crowing Cock Inn. They have finished three
scenes, so I hurried back to report.
JUAN: What were the comments of the audience?   110
SERVANT: All expressed the highest admiration. [*Sings.*]

> They nodded their heads and beat time in approval.
> They forgot their wine cups to lap every line of the play.

JUAN: Their approbation seems to have been genuine. What else did
they say?   115
SERVANT: [*Sings.*]

> They exclaimed:
> "A true genius with a remarkable pen!"

JUAN: Oho! I am surprised that they were so complimentary. What
else?
SERVANT: [*Sings.*]

> They said: "His style is that of an immortal,   120
> Expressing himself in human speech.
> In modern letters his art stands supreme."

JUAN: [*Feigning embarrassment.*] This is too much; they are exaggerating. But I shall look forward to hearing their comments when
they have seen more of it. Be quick and find out, then run back   125
and tell me. [SERVANT *obeys.* JUAN *laughs aloud.*] I never guessed
those young men were so discerning! [*To* YANG.] No heel-taps!
[*Sings.*]

> Ah, I have seen
> All the landscapes of the southern school,
> Read all the old romances.   130
> I have toiled till dusk in my tower or rain pavilion,

Toiled on from nightfall under a lamp;
I have drained my heart's blood in solitary composing.
At last I have found discriminating hearers!

YANG: Who are these gentlemen?   135
JUAN: Ch'en Ting-sheng, Fang Mi-chih, and Mao P'i-chiang—all
    men of the deepest culture. They have proved their esteem for me.
YANG: These persons are seldom addicted to praise, but your *Swallow
    Letter* is so fine in versification and melody that their admiration is
    natural.   140
FIRST SERVANT: [*Returning.*] I ran out like a rabbit; I fly back like a
    raven. Your Honour, now that they have seen half the play, I have
    returned with another report.
JUAN: How did the audience respond?
SERVANT: [*Sings.*]

> They called Your Honour "Pride of the south,   145
> Chief ornament of the Eastern Forest,
> Worthy of the Han-lin Academy itself."

JUAN: Every sentence is so laudatory that I feel embarrassed. What
    else?
SERVANT: [*Sings.*]

> They added: "But why did you join the traitors Ts'ui and Wei,   150
> And turn against your old friends?

JUAN: [*Frowning angrily.*] That was only a passing misjudgment; there
    was no need to bring it up again. What else?
SERVANT: They said more in the same strain, but being your humble
    servant I dare not repeat it.   155
JUAN: Never mind, proceed.
SERVANT: [*Sings.*]

> They said: "Your Honour called a stranger his father,
> And became his foster son;
> Utterly shameless and heartless,
> Fawning on your protector like a cur."   160

JUAN: [*Furiously.*] So they starting reviling me again! I cannot endure
    it. [*Sings.*]

> What have politics to do with art?
> I lent them my latest music and poetry
> To increase their enjoyment of wine and flowers.   165
> Alas, it was in vain.
> They never tried to fathom my motives,
> But only heaped on me the vilest abuse.
> I am overwhelmed by so many insults.

YANG: Why did they attack you?   170
JUAN: I cannot imagine. Recently I went to worship at the temple of
    Confucius, where I was set upon and beaten by five young gradu-
    ates. Now I have lent them my play and private actors to propitiate

them, only to reap further calumnies. I must find a remedy, or I
shall never dare step out-of-doors.   175

YANG: Don't worry, elder brother, I have been pondering a solution.

JUAN: You give me a ray of hope. I shall be grateful for your advice.

YANG: The leaders of the graduates is Wu Tzu-wei, and the leader of
the nobles is Ch'en Ting-sheng. If these stop attacking you, your
peace will be restored.   180

JUAN: Of course; but who would venture to defend me?

YANG: I think Hou Fang-yü might be approached. He is their boon
companion in the literary club as well as at the wine table. Both
are influenced by his opinions. Only yesterday I heard that he was
feeling lonely for lack of employment. He longs for a girl compan-   185
ion, and I have found him one ideal in every respect. Her name is
Fragrant Princess. She excels in beauty as in the gentle arts; I am
sure he will be captivated by her. Now if you provide a dowry, he
would be obliged to show some gratitude. I could then ask him to
speak in your favour, which would lead to a general appeasement.   190

JUAN: [*Clapping his hands and laughing.*] Excellent! What a splendid
idea. Hou's father was my classmate, so he is almost a nephew to
me. I feel I should do whatever I can for him. But what will it cost
me?

YANG: About two hundred silver *taels*[2] should suffice for the wardrobe   195
and banquet.

JUAN: I can easily afford it. I'll send three hundred over to your house.
Spend the money as you think fit.

YANG: That is too large a sum. [*Sings.*]

> A young willow leans over the gate   200
> For the lover to climb in late.

JUAN: [*Sings.*]

> My poems and music proved inadequate;
> Only this beauteous girl may serve as bait.

YANG: [*Sings.*]

> Upon your bounty will depend their fate.

SCENE 5

A Visit to the Beauty

1643, THIRD MONTH

[HOU FANG-YÜ, *elegantly gowned, enters singing.*]

HOU: [*Sings.*]

> The golden glory has not quite departed,
> The fragrance of the southern courts still lingers;
> These misty meadows melt into my soul,

2. The *tael* was the former monetary unit; it was worth approximately one ounce of silver.

While breezes coax the budding flowers to open,
But wind and rain will pass, and likewise spring.   5

[*Speaks.*]Too long I have been roving with only my books and
sword for company, and no prospect of seeing my home. During
this third month I have been steeped in nostalgia for the bygone
Six Dynasties. As a wanderer I suffer from homesickness, nor can I
help being stirred by the spring scenery. Yesterday I met Yang Wen-   10
ts'ung, who sang the praises of Fragrant Princess Li, of her youthful
grace and exceptional beauty. He also told me that Su K'un-sheng
was giving her singing lessons, and proposed that I should buy her
trousseau. Alas, my purse is almost empty; I cannot afford what I
ardently desire. Today is the Festival of Pure Brightness.[3] I feel so   15
lonely that I shall take a stroll through the meadows. Perhaps I may
have a chance to visit the beauty's house.
          [*Sings.*]

I gaze towards the Forbidden City, where all the beauties dwell,
Their gates concealed behind the drooping willows.
Young cavaliers are riding down the highway,   20
Flourishing elegant reins of purple silk,
But where are the tender couples of young swallows?

LIU CHING-T'ING: [*Entering.*]

          An oriole awoke me from my dreams;
          My white hair kindles memory's fading gleams.

[*To* HOU.] Where are you going, Master Hou?   25
HOU: Oh, it is Ching-t'ing! What a pleasant surprise! I set out for a
walk hoping to meet a companion like yourself.
LIU: I shall be glad to keep you company. [*As they stroll,* LIU *points
and says.*] There is the Water Pavilion, beyond the Ch'in Huai
River.   30
HOU: [*Sings.*]

          Over the waves a green mist creeps,
          Brushing the windows; against the sky,
          Bright blossom of the almond peeps
          Above the house-wall high.

LIU: [*Pointing.*] Here is Long Bridge. Let us loiter on the way.   35
HOU: [*Sings.*]

          Passing the wine and tea shops
          And the noisy vendors of flowers . . .

LIU: Ha! This is the old quarter now.
HOU: [*Sings.*]

          We saunter across the wooden bridge
          To reach a labyrinth of lanes.   40

---

3. The Ch'ing-ming Festival, corresponding to the Christian Easter, was usually in early April. On this
day offerings were made to the dead, while their graves were put in good order; it was also a time for
picnics and excursions into the country.

LIU: In yonder lane the most famous beauties dwell.
HOU: It has an air of voluptuous refinement. [*Sings.*]

> Over these twin black lacquered gates,
> A tender willow droops as if with dew.

LIU: That is the house of Mistress Li Chen-li.   45
HOU: And where does Fragrant Princess live?
LIU: She is Mistress Li's daughter.
HOU: How lucky! I have been longing to meet her, and here we are!
LIU: I'll knock at her door. [*Knocks.*]
VOICE FROM BACKSTAGE: Who's there?   50
LIU: It is old Liu, a regular visitor. I have brought a distinguished
  guest.
VOICE FROM BACKSTAGE: Mistress Li and Fragrant Princess are not at
  home.
LIU: Where are they?   55
VOICE: They went to a hamper party at Mistress Pien's.
LIU: Oh, of course! I had quite forgotten about it.
HOU: Why did they have to go out today of all days?
LIU: My legs are tired. Let's sit on these stone steps and rest while I
  explain. [*Both sit down.*] Just as men become sworn brothers by   60
  burning incense together, courtesans become sworn sisters by
  exchanging kerchiefs. In due course, they hold parties in celebration at times of festival. [*Sings.*]

> These beauties become sisters
> By knotting silken kerchiefs together.   65
> On days of festival,
> They meet in friendly rivalry.

HOU: I see; but why do they call it a hamper party?
LIU: Each must bring a hamper filled with delicacies. [*Sings.*]

> Dainty dishes from the sea,   70
> Succulent rarities from the rivers,
> And the choicest of wines.

HOU: What do they do on these occasions?
LIU: Usually they hold musical contests. [*Sings.*]

> They play the lute,   75
> The reed-organ, and the bamboo flute.

HOU: How fascinating! Are men allowed to join them?
LIU: No, at such times they shun male society. They bolt their doors
  and climb to an upper storey. Men are only allowed to admire them
  from below.   80
HOU: Supposing one glimpsed his heart's desire, how could a meeting
  be arranged?
LIU: In that case, a personal trinket might be thrown up into the tower,
  and the recipient might throw down fruit. [*Sings.*]

> If the girl is gratified,   85
> She will descend to offer wine
> And make an assignation.

HOU: I am tempted to go and see for myself.

LIU: There's no harm in trying.

HOU: But I don't know where Mistress Pien lives.   90

LIU: Her place is called the Halcyon Lodge; it isn't far from here. I'll
   show the way. [*As they proceed, each recites one line of a quatrain.*]

HOU: Before the worship at the tombs, each family hangs out a willow
   branch.

LIU: Everywhere the bamboo flute celebrates this festival.   95

HOU: Three miles of streets are adorned with birds and flowers.

LIU: We cross two bridges over the misty river.
   [*Points.*] Here is the house. Let's go in.
      [YANG WEN-TS'UNG *and* SU K'UN-SHENG *enter and meet* HOU *and* LIU.]

YANG: In my leisure I search for orioles and flowers.

SU: We have come to see powdered faces and painted eyebrows. [*They* 100
   greet each other.]

YANG: How astonishing to find you in such a resort!

HOU: All the more so since I heard you had gone to visit bearded Juan.

SU: We happened to come here expressly on your account.

LIU: Let us all sit down.

HOU: [*Looking up.*] What a charming lodge! [*Sings.*]   105

> The windows glowing on the spacious courtyard
> Transport one to a gentle land of dreams.

[*Speaks.*] But where is Fragrant Princess?

YANG: She is upstairs.

SU: Can you hear the music? [*A flute and a reed-organ are played* 110
offstage.]

HOU: [*Listens and sings.*]

> The fairy organs and phoenix pipes echo among the clouds.

[*Lute and zither play.*]

> What subtle rhythm!
> What a harmony of strings!

[*A yün-lo or small gong is heard.*]

> What jade-like tinkling!
> Each note plucks at my heart.   115

[*Pan-pipes play.*]

> The phoenix pair soar fluttering through the air . . .

[*Speaks.*] These pipes have seized my soul and borne it away. I can
restrain myself no longer. I shall throw my pledge aloft. [*He*

*removes the pendant from his fan and throws it into the upper
room, singing.*]

> This treasure from the southern seas
> Is wafted high upon the breeze   120
> Into the lodge, my beauty's heart to tease.

[*A kerchief full of cherries is thrown down to him.*]

LIU: How curious! A shower of fruit.

SU: [*Opening the kerchief.*] Strange that there should be cherries at
this season!

HOU: I wonder who threw them. If it was Fragrant Princess, I shall be   125
overjoyed.

YANG: This kerchief is woven of the finest silk. I'll wager nine to one
that it is hers.

[*Enter* LI CHEN-LI *with a teapot in her hand, followed by* FRAGRANT
PRINCESS *with a vase of flowers.*]

LIU: The light grass trembles under the butterfly's wings, the beauty
now descends the Phoenix Terrace.   130

SU: Look! They advance like goddesses.

LIU: [*With palms together as in prayer.*] Amida Buddha![4]

YANG: [*Whispering to* HOU.] Observe them carefully. [ALL *rise.*] That
is Mistress Li, and that is Fragrant Princess.

HOU: [*Greeting* MISTRESS LI.] I am Hou Fang-yü of Honan. After hear-   135
ing so much about you I am delighted to have this opportunity. [*To*
FRAGRANT PRINCESS.] You are indeed a perfect beauty in the flush
of youth. My friend Yang's keen eyes have proved him a connoisseur.

LI: May I offer you gentlemen some fresh tea from Tiger Hill? [*She*   140
pours tea.]

FRAGRANT PRINCESS: [*Showing her vase.*] These green willows and
pink almond blossoms enhance the season's beauty.

ALL: [*In chorus of admiration.*] Delicious, to sip the rarest tea and
gaze upon such flowers!

YANG: On this occasion we should be drinking wine.   145

LI: I have already ordered it. Aunt Pien is occupied with guests in the
lodge, so I shall act as hostess in her stead. [*Wine is brought by a*
MAID.] Would it not be amusing to play some drinking games?

LIU: We await your orders.

MISTRESS LI: It is not for me to give orders.   150

SU: However, it is customary.

[MISTRESS LI *produces dice and a jar to throw them in.*]

LI: Fragrant Princess, you pour the wine when I ask you to, depending
on the dice. The rule of the game is that each must give a sample
of his talent after every cup of wine. Number one stands for cherry,
two for tea, three for willow, four for almond blossom, five for the   155
pendant, and six for the silk handkerchief. Your Honour Hou
comes first. [FRAGRANT PRINCESS *pours* HOU *a cup;* MISTRESS LI

---

4. An oath.

throws the dice and says.] It's the pendant. Drain your cup, Master
Hou, and let us hear your contribution.

HOU: [*Drinks and says.*] I'll improvise a verse. [*Chants.*]   160

> This came from the south for my beauty to wear;
> It should hang from her fan like a moon in midair,
> To sway and swing at her every turn,
> Catching the breeze from her fragrant hair.

YANG: How clever!   165

LIU: The pendant is a fine one, I'm only afraid it would sway once too
often and get broken!

LI: Now it is His Honour Yang's turn to drink. [FRAGRANT PRINCESS
pours and YANG *drinks.* MISTRESS LI *throws the dice and says.*] It's
the silk handkerchief.   170

YANG: I'll compose a verse about the handkerchief.

LI: Please change the metre for variety.

YANG: Then I'll make it an examination essay: "The silk that dabs off
perspiration evokes the lustrous skin of its possessor. The sweat that
moistens the kerchief is spring's hot breath on a lovely face. And   175
whose face is worthy of so fine a fabric? The rosy cheek and white
silk blend, enhancing each other's perfection."

HOU: That's excellent.

LIU: What subtle talent! For this you should pass both provincial and
metropolitan examinations at once!   180

FRAGRANT PRINCESS: [*Serving wine to* LIU.] Your turn, please, Master
Liu.

LI: [*Throwing dice.*] Number two; that stands for tea.

LIU: [*Drinks, but jokes.*] You mean I only get tea to drink, while you
drink wine?   185

LI: No, your *forfeit*[5] must be about tea.

LIU: Shall I tell the tale of Chang San-lang, drinking tea with his
paramour Yen P'o-hsi in *The Men of the Marshes?*

LI: That's too long-winded. Just tell us a joke.

LIU: All right. Su Tung-p'o and Huang T'ing-chien went to visit the   190
Buddhist monk Fo Yin.[6] Su brought a pot of fine Ting-yao porcelain, and Huang a pound of excellent Yang-hsien tea. All three sat
under a spreading pine to savour the brew. The monk said: "Master
Huang has a notorious passion for tea, but I don't know about
bearded Su's tea-drinking capacities. Why not have a competition   195
now?" Su asked: "How shall we arrange it?" The monk replied,
"You ask him a riddle. If he cannot answer at once, I'll put it on
record that the Beard[7] has beaten the Graduate. He will then ask
you a riddle, and if you fail to give a prompt reply, I'll put down
that the Graduate has beaten the Beard. In the end we shall make   200
a count. Each must drink a cup of tea on being defeated." "Very
well," said Su, and asked: "How can you run a thread through a

---

5. Drinking games like those described were common at parties. The loser had to drink a *forfeit*, usually
wine.   6. A rollicking Buddhist monk and convivial associate. For Su Tung-p'o, see n. 4, p. 83. Huang
T'ing-chien (1045–1105), a poet and disciple of Su.   7. That is, Su.

pin without a hole?" "Scratch away the pinpoint," Huang replied.[8]
"Well answered," said Fo Yin. Huang asked: "How can you hold a
gourd without a handle?" "By throwing it into the water," said Su.   205
"Another good answer," said Fo Yin. Su asked: "If there is a louse
in your breeches, will you see it or won't you?" Before Huang could
reply, Su seized a stick to beat him. At that moment Huang was
holding the teapot, and it slipped and was shattered on the ground.
Su shouted: "Remember this, you monk, the Beard has beaten the   210
Graduate." Fo Yin laughed and said: "But I only heard a crash. The
Graduate broke the pot; the Beard[9] did not break the Graduate."
[*General laughter.*] This is no laughing matter. Graduates can be
dangerous fellows. [*Fingering the teapot.*] They can break a hard-
ware pot, not to mention a soft one![1]   215

HOU: He deserves another drink for his rollicking wit and humour.

LI: Fragrant Princess, pour your teacher some wine.

> [LIU *drinks.* MISTRESS LI *throws dice and gets number four, almond
> blossom.*]

SU: [*Sings.*]

> The almond blossoms droop within the tower,
> And clothes grow thin at this cool evening hour.

FRAGRANT PRINCESS: [*Pouring wine for* MISTRESS LI.] It is your turn   220
now, Mama.

> [MISTRESS LI *drinks and throws dice, getting number one, the cherry.*]

SU: Let me sing for you.

> "Those cherry lips the pearly teeth betray,
> Before a single syllable they say."

LIU: Master Su should be fined. The cherries he sings of are not the   225
edible kind.

SU: I accept the fine. [*He pours and drinks.*]

LI: Fragrant Princess, you will have to pour your own wine.

HOU: No, allow me. [*He pours and she drinks.*]

LI: [*Throwing dice.*] Number three. Fragrant Princess must sing   230
about the willow. [*But* FRAGRANT PRINCESS *coyly declines.*] My
daughter is too shy. Would somebody else perform in her stead?
Perhaps Master Liu would oblige us?

SU: We are really making him work today!

LIU: My name means willow, and I have been afraid of that word all   235
my life. On this Festival of Pure Brightness, there are willow garlands everywhere. Might as well put one on me as a "dog-collar."[2]

> [ALL *roar with laughter.*]

SU: Oh, that's enough of your jokes!

HOU: Having finished the wine, we ought to be taking our leave.

---

8. There are many anecdotes about Su Tung-p'o and Fo Yin. These riddles are intended to be pointless,
deliberate non sequiturs to confound the logical processes and thereby liberate true understanding, in
approved Zen fashion.   9. A pun; the Chinese word *hu-tzu* means both "pot" and "beard."
1. Another pun: in Chinese, *juan hu-tzu,* which plays on "Bearded Juan."   2. It was a local custom on
this festival for children to wear willow garlands, which they called dog collars.

LIU: It is seldom that a handsome young genius is brought together   240
with such a radiant girl. [*He pulls* HOU *and* FRAGRANT PRINCESS
together.] Why don't you exchange vows over a cup of wine?
    [FRAGRANT PRINCESS *hides her face behind her sleeve and runs out
covered with confusion.*]

SU: The girl is sensitive. You shouldn't have talked like that in front
of her. What is to be done about her trousseau? Has His Excellency
Hou any suggestions to offer?   245

HOU: [*Laughing.*] Would a Graduate object to becoming a Prize Candidate? My case is similar.

LI: Since you are so favourably disposed, let us choose an auspicious
day.

YANG: The fifteenth of the third month is the best time for flowers and   250
the full moon; it is also the best time for mating.

HOU: The only drawback is that, being a traveller, I'm short of ready
cash. I'm afraid I couldn't make a suitable offer.

YANG: Never mind, you can leave that to me.

HOU: How could I put you to so much trouble?

YANG: I shall be only too pleased to assist you.   255

HOU: I am overwhelmed. [*Sings.*]

> Now fate has led me towards the magic peak.
> My passions rise like clouds, and in their tumult
> My eyes cannot discern the radiant goddess.   260
> This night of spring, these flowers, and the moon
> Lighting the silent land, are they illusions?
> Nay, for the joyful moment hurries near;
> Now for this blessed union I'll prepare.

  [HOU *bows farewell.*]

LI: I dare not detain you. Let us decide on the fifteenth provisionally.   265
I shall send out the invitations and ask several fair sisters to join us.
The finest music should be played for this occasion. [*Exit.*]

LIU: Alas, I had forgotten a previous engagement.

YANG: Couldn't you postpone it?

SU: Admiral Huang's warship is anchored west of the city, and on the   270
fifteenth he is holding a flag ceremony. We shall have to attend it.

HOU: What a pity! We shall miss you.

YANG: There are plenty of others to make up a merry party. I suggest
Ting Chi-chih, Shen Kung-hsien, and Chang Yen-chu.
  [*Exeunt, singing.*]

SU: Powdered cheeks are fragrant before the boudoir bright,   275

YANG: The grace of bygone ages returns to our delight,

LIU: Our outing of today found only hints of spring;

HOU: We think of the fair blossom tomorrow's warmth will bring.

SCENE 6

The Fragrant Couch

1643, THIRD MONTH

[*Enter* MISTRESS LI *in gorgeous attire.*]

LI: [*Sings.*]

> In short spring jacket, sleeves folded back,
> She tunes the zither in the fairy park.
> Today in expectation her curtains are raised;
> Let not the willow fronds
> Hide from view the groom's magnolia-wood boat.   5

[*Speaks.*] Since Fragrant Princess turned sixteen, I have been worrying night and day about her future. Luckily, Master Yang introduced us to Master Hou, who came to drink wine with us the other day—a distinguished young man of good family. Today is the auspicious day of their union banquet. Soon the guests will arrive, and I   10
am expecting all our fair sisters. To entertain so large a party is quite a responsibility. Where is the maid?

MAID: [*A clown, enters waving a fan.*] How I love cracking jokes at a banquet, and eavesdropping under a blanket! But mum, the mistress is calling me! [*To* MISTRESS LI.] What are your orders now,   15
ma'am? More pillows and quilts to be brought for some itching couple?

LI: Fie! The guests are due to arrive, and there you dawdle in a stupid daze. Make haste and draw the curtains, sweep the floor and arrange the chairs.   20

MAID: Always at your service, ma'am. [MISTRESS LI *directs her.*]

YANG WEN-TS'UNG: [*Entering in festive garb, singing.*]

> Like red embroidery, the peach blossoms
> Make patterns on the lady's banquet board;
> The screens are spread like golden peacocks' tails;
> Scent floats from the heraldic incense-burner.   25
> The crimson lady seated by the stove[3]
> Is the ideal mate for him to cherish.

[*Speaks.*] I have come on behalf of Juan Ta-ch'eng to deliver the wedding gifts. Where is Mistress Li?

LI: [*Coming to greet him.*] A thousand thanks for helping to arrange   30
this match. The feast is ready, but where is His Honour Hou?

YANG: I imagine he will soon be with us. I have brought a selection of dresses for Fragrant Princess's wardrobe. [*To* MAID, *who brings in chests containing hair ornaments and gowns.*] Take them into the bridal chamber and set them out neatly. [MAID *exits.*]   35

LI: Such an expense—how kind of you!

---

3. An allusion to Ssu-ma Hsiang-ju (died 117 B.C.), a Han Dynasty poet whose singing so captivated the young widow Cho Wen-chün that she eloped with him. They set up a small wine shop, where she served the customers and he washed the cups. Shamed by such bohemian conduct, her wealthy father took them back into his favor. Ssu-ma's fame as a poet reached Emperor Wu-ti, who appointed him to high office.

YANG: [*Drawing silver bars from his sleeve.*] Here are thirty *taels* of
silver, to provide the best wines and dishes for the banquet.

LI: You are far too generous! [*She calls* FRAGRANT PRINCESS, *who
enters magnificently dressed.*] His Honour Yang has showered so   40
many presents on you that you ought to thank him. [FRAGRANT
PRINCESS *curtseys.*]

YANG: These are mere trifles, no need for such ceremony. Please retire
to your boudoir. [*Exit* FRAGRANT PRINCESS.]

MAID: [*Entering breathlessly.*] The bridegroom has arrived.

HOU: [*Entering in his best clothes, followed by several* SERVANTS.]
Though I did not win the highest degree in the examinations, I   45
now belong to the realm of the Moon Goddess.[4]

YANG: Congratulations, brother! You have won the paragon of feminine beauty. In token of my regard for you, I could only bring these
paltry offerings as a contribution to your household expenses. I only
hope they will add to the evening's enjoyment.   50

HOU: I am struck speechless by your munificence.

LI: Pray sit down and have some tea. [ALL *sit down. The* MAID *waits
on them.*]

YANG: Is everything ready for the feast?

LI: Thanks to Your Honour, the arrangements are complete.

YANG: [*To* HOU.] I won't intrude on your private rejoicings. Tomorrow   55
I shall return to congratulate you again.

HOU: Why don't you join the party?

YANG: In my position that would not be proper.[5] [*He takes his leave.*]

MAID: May I remind the bridegroom that it is time for him to change?
[HOU, *onstage, is assisted in removing his gown and donning a new
one.*]

LI: I must go and help the bride to dress for the banquet. [*Exit.*]   60
[*Three male guests appear:* TING CHI-CHIH, SHEN KUNG-HSIEN, *and*
CHANG YEN-CHU.]

THREE GUESTS: [*Recite.*]

> Poet-singers are we
> Like Chang Hsien and Li Erh[6] of old.

[*Each announces his name. Then, together, they say*]:
We have come to attend the auspicious banquet for His Honour
Hou, and we are punctual to the minute.

CHANG: I wonder which of the girls I shall sit next to?   65

SHEN: I hear that there will be several queens of their profession.

CHANG: Then we should have no difficulty in winning their favours.

TING: But are you rich enough to afford such luxuries?

CHANG: Everybody can get some outside help. Look at His Honour
Hou. Has he had to spend a penny of his own on this?   70

SHEN: Stop gossiping. He is changing his clothes upstairs. Let us go
and greet him. [*Together bowing to* HOU, *who is still on stage.*]

---

4. Successful examination candidates were eulogized as having plucked the blossoms of the mythical
cassia tree tended by the goddess in the moon.   5. Yang had been the principal matchmaker.   6. A
dramatist (14th century). Chang Hsien (11th century), a song lyricist.

THREE GUESTS: Congratulations!

HOU: I thank you all for coming.

[*Enter three singing-girls:* PIEN YÜ-CHING, K'OU PAI-MEN, *and* CHENG T'O-NIANG.]

THREE GIRLS: Our passions run riot like grass, ever in a pleasant state   75
of titillation. And though we are as delicate as willow catkins, we
are kept busy night and day. [*They greet the guests.*]

CHANG: From which pavilion of delight have you ladies sprung?
Please announce your names.

FIRST GIRL: Are you the director of the conservatoire[7] to ask us such a   80
question?

HOU: [*Laughing, to* FIRST GIRL.] I should be happy to learn your honourable name.

FIRST GIRL: Your humble servant's name is Pien Yü-ching, "Jade Capital."   85

HOU: "Fairy from the Jade Capital" would be more suitable.

SECOND GIRL: And my name is K'ou Pai-men, "White Gate."

HOU: You truly deserve it.

THIRD GIRL: [*A clown.*] And I'm Cheng T'o-niang, "Lady Safety."

HOU: You certainly look quite safe.   90

CHANG: I'm afraid I don't agree.

SHEN: Why not?

CHANG: She would never be safe, from her husband's point of view.

CHENG: You should be ashamed of yourself. If I had not stuck to my
job, you would never have grown so fat on overfeeding! [*General*   95
laughter.]

PIEN: Since the bridegroom is ready, let us ask Fragrant Princess to
join him. [MISTRESS LI *leads* FRAGRANT PRINCESS *in.*]

SHEN: We should welcome the bride with music.

[CHANG, TING, *and* SHEN *play music on the right side of the stage.*
BRIDE *and* GROOM *greet each other.*]

CHENG: It isn't the custom in our houses to perform the ceremonies
of worship, so we can go straight to the celebration wine.[8]   100

[BRIDE *and* GROOM *take their seats, center; the* THREE SINGING-GIRLS
sit near, at left. The MAID *brings wine, which is served from the left.*]

HOU: [*Sings.*]

> In the company of famous flowers and willows,
> Daily I write of love in jewelled rhymes,
> Like Tu Mu[9] of Yangchow, clad in silken robes,
> Entirely given to painting my beauty's eyebrows
> And teaching her perfection on the flute.   105
> This very moment spring begins anew;
> My fevered thirst will soon be quenched.
> But oh, how slowly sinks the setting sun!
> Meantime I'll drink another cup of wine.

---

7. The state-sponsored orchestra.   8. Since Hou and Fragrant Princess have not performed the ceremonies of obeisance to Heaven and earth and the ancestors, their "marriage" is more an expression of
intention than a strict legal contract. This is why Fragrant Princess can later be urged to "marry again"—
without need of divorce from Hou.   9. T'ang poet (803–852), famous for the number and beauty of his
concubines and singing girls.

FRAGRANT PRINCESS: [*Sings.*]

> Flowers tremble on the terrace, curtains flutter.   110
> My lord, so handsome and so elegant,
> Withholds no mark of favour;
> I shall be wife, not slave-girl, in his eyes,
> And worthy must I prove;
> A random flower still lovely,   115
> A wild herb no less fragrant.
> Under the glow of many scarlet lanterns,
> Tonight I am to be the chosen bride.
> Even adepts in the art of love would quail—
> How fearful then a virgin's trepidation!   120

TING: Now that the red sun is swallowing the mountains and the crows are choosing their roosts, we should escort the young couple to their chamber.

SHEN: Why such haste? His Honour Hou is a distinguished man of letters who has won the heart of an exceptional beauty. He has   125
celebrated his happy union with wine, but poetry should not be neglected.

CHANG: You are right. I'll fetch ink and paper to wait upon his inspiration.

HOU: I need no paper, since I have a fan. I shall write a poem on it   130
for Fragrant Princess to keep as a lifelong token of my love.

CHENG: Marvelous! Let me hold the ink-slab for you.

LI: Such a freak is only fit to remove His Honour's shoes.

PIEN: Fragrant Princess should hold the ink-slab.

ALL: That is correct.   135

[FRAGRANT PRINCESS *does accordingly, while* HOU *writes on the fan.* ALL *chant the words of his poem.*]

ALL: [*Chanting.*]

> On a path between two rows of crimson towers,
> The lucky Prince advances in his chariot.
> From the magnolias he turns aside
> To gaze in rapture at the breeze-blown peach blossoms.

ALL: What an exquisite poem! Fragrant Princess, mind you keep it   140
carefully. [FRAGRANT PRINCESS *puts the fan in her sleeve.*]

CHENG: Though we may not be as pretty as peach blossoms, why should he call us magnolias?

CHANG: Don't worry; the magnolia withers, but returns to life in the spring.   145

CHENG: That's as may be, but who will water my blossom?

MAID: [*Entering with a scroll.*] His Honour Yang has sent you these verses.

HOU: [*Takes it and reads aloud.*]

> Lady Fragrance was born with a beauty to overwhelm cities,
> Yet how demurely she yields to her lord's embrace!   150
> In his arms she is like the goddess of the twelve Magic Mountains,
> Appearing in a dream to the King of Ch'u.

HOU: That old gentleman shows a profound understanding of love.
His verse is admirable.

CHANG: It is a fine evocation of Fragrant Princess's slender grace. She   155
reminds me of the jade pendant of a scented fan.

CHENG: Well, what's a jade pendant worth, anyway? At least I'm an
amber one! [ALL *laugh.*]

TING: Let us have more music to inspire the young couple to drink.

CHENG: And excite them all the more to enter the love nest.   160

[*Wine and music follow.*]

HOU *and* FRAGRANT PRINCESS: [*Singing a duet.*]

> These golden cups create a thirst for wine,
> And friendly voices urge us on to drink.
> The hour is late; we droop with drowsiness,
> Furtively clasping hands, our eager eyes
> Look forward to a night of endless bliss,   165
> Longing to loosen our hibiscus clothes.
> Burn out, oh candles! Let the feast be done
> Ere the palace water-clock[1] its course has run!

TING: The second watch is announced; it is growing late. Let the
banquet be cleared away.   170

CHANG: But we have not finished all the dishes. It would be a pity to
remove them.

CHENG: I haven't eaten enough, either. Please wait awhile.

PIEN: Stop fussing. Let us escort the young couple with music to their
chamber.   175

ALL: [*Singing.*]

> To the strains of pipes and flutes we descend the stair,
> Swaying to the lilt of songs under glowing lamplight.
> On yonder heavenly terrace the comely pair
> Will enter the 'broidered haven of scented curtains
> While others knit their brows with envy. Lo,   180
> How beautiful their wine-flushed self-abandon!
> Such love as this was certainly predestined.

[*Exeunt* HOU *and* FRAGRANT PRINCESS *hand in hand.*]

CHANG: Let us divide into couples and all go to bed together.

CHENG: Old Chang, you'd better not delude yourself. I'll take nothing
less than hard cash for favours. [CHANG *hands her ten coppers*[2] *and*   185
she counts them.]

ALL: [*Singing in chorus.*]

> The misty moon above the Ch'in-huai River
> Abides forever,
> Yet how much powder and rouge are washed away
> Day after day!
> Irrevocably love's supreme delight   190
> Is lost each night.

---

1. Used before mechanical clocks became widespread, it marked time by the slow draining of a fixed
amount of water. Here the reference is to the passing of the night.   2. Coins.

TING: South of the river grow the flowers, the current flows fast away.
K'OU: All who live on the river's banks are debonair and gay.
SHEN: Though your home be distant many a league, through clouds
    of dust and spray,   195
PIEN: Here ballads of love are sung till break of day.

SCENE 7

The Rejected Trousseau

1643, THIRD MONTH

MAID: [*A clown, entering with a chamberpot, sings.*]

> Turtle-piss, turtle-piss,
> Little turtles come of this;
> Tortoise-blood, tortoise-blood,
> Turning into tortoise brood.
> Mixing, mating, copulating,   5
> Wholly undiscriminating,
> Never know who fathered who;
> Wouldn't matter if they knew.

[*Speaks.*] Ha, ha, hee hee! Yesterday Fragrant Princess lost her
maidenhead and I lost half a night's sleep. Today I must rise early   10
to empty the chamberpot, but who knows how late the lucky lovebirds will slumber on? [*She scrubs out the pot.*]
YANG: [*Enters and sings.*]

> They sleep serene behind the willow screen.
> Flower-vendors cry outside the door, "Come buy!"
> Yet they dream on; the curtains never open.   15
> At last you hear the tinkling of jade hooks;[3]
> All spring is wrapped within those folds of silk.

[*Speaks.*] I have returned to congratulate His Honour Hou, but the
doors are closed and nobody seems to be stirring. They must be fast
asleep. [*Calls.*] Maid, please run to the young couple's window and   20
tell them that I have come to congratulate them.
MAID: They retired very late; I doubt if they have risen. Would you
    mind returning tomorrow?
YANG: [*Laughing.*] Nonsense, you do as you're bid.
LI: [*From inside.*] Maid, who is there?   25
MAID: It's His Honour Yang come to offer congratulations.
LI: [*Still inside.*] Once heads touch pillow, how short the spring night
    seems! Then comes a knock at the door, always someone to inter-
    rupt! [*Greeting* YANG.] I must thank Your Honour for arranging this
    match.   30
YANG: Don't mention it. Where are the young couple?
LI: Please sit down while I call them. They have not risen yet.
YANG: Pray don't disturb them. [*Exit* MISTRESS LI. YANG *sings.*]

---

3. Used to hold up the curtains when they were raised.

> Young love's like liquid honey fresh from flowers,
> So beautiful, so innocent and pure,   35
> Gently distilled in a dark world of dreams.

[*Says.*] Thanks to myself. [*Again singing.*]

> Pearls and emeralds glow
> And silken dresses flow,
> And every precious toy
> Is here for lover's joy.   40

LI: It was as pretty as a picture. The two of them were buttoning each
other's clothes and gazing at each other's reflection in a mirror.
They have just finished dressing. Will Your Honour step through
to call them out for a cup of wine?

YANG: I am sorry to have interrupted their sweet dreams. [*Exeunt.*]   45
[HOU *and* FRAGRANT PRINCESS *enter, dressed in their finest and singing together.*]

HOU *and* FRAGRANT PRINCESS: [*Singing.*]

> Cloud after cloud and shower after shower—
> Desire fulfilled without satiety!
> Who comes to rouse the lovebirds at this hour?
> The scarlet quilt is rolled into a billow;[4]   50
> Scent lingers on the coverlet and pillow;
> Throbbing with joy we rise as from a trance.

[*Enter* YANG *and* MISTRESS LI.]

YANG: So at last your have succeeded in rising! Congratulations! [*Sitting down.*] How did you like the poem I sent last night?

HOU: [*Bowing.*] It was a splendid composition. My only criticism is
that Fragrant Princess, slender as she is, deserves to be kept in a   55
house of pure gold.[5] How could I keep her under these sleeves of
mine?

YANG: I expect you were also inspired to write poetry last night.

HOU: I merely improvised a little stanza.

YANG: Where is it?   60

FRAGRANT PRINCESS: On this fan. [*Drawing the fan from her sleeve.*]

YANG: [*Examining it.*] White silk, and what a graceful shape, what
a subtle aroma! [*He chants the poem inscribed on it, and then
recites.*]

> Like Tso Szu, your verse
> Sends up the price of paper in Loyang;   65
> Like P'an Yueh,[6]
> Your carriage draws all eyes.
> Beauteous and fragrant are the peach and apricot blossoms;
> Their very souls are captured on this fan.

---

4. Wave; here a metaphor for the bedcovers.   5. A reference to the Han emperor Wu-ti (140–87 B.C.),
a great patron of literature and student of Taoism. When he fell in love with his future consort, he
remarked, "If I could only win A-chiao, I would build a house of gold to keep her in."   6. Tso Szu and
P'an Yueh (see n. 8, p. 94) won renown for their elegant rhapsodies in the last decades of the 3rd century.
So many people wanted copies of Tso Szu's *Rhapsody on the Three Capitals* that, according to legend,
the price of paper soared.

But of outer storms and treacherous winds beware!   70
Preserve it under your sleeve with tender care!

[*Looking at* FRAGRANT PRINCESS, *he says.*] You are even lovelier
since your nuptials. [*To* HOU.] How fortunate you are to have won
such a prize.

HOU: Fragrant Princess was destined to be the beauty of her age, but   75
today the pearls and emeralds in her hair and apparel display her
charms to perfection.

FRAGRANT PRINCESS: [*To* YANG.] Thanks entirely to your munificence!
[*Sings.*]

You gave me the fillets to weave in my hair,
And a casket of a hundred precious stones,   80
Jewelled tassels for my curtain, and silver candlesticks,
Lanterns of silk to shine all through the night,
And golden cups for the wine that flows with song.

[*Speaks.*] And then, coming so soon to greet us like this! [*Sings.*]

You have treated me as a daughter of your own,   85
Having filled my wardrobe, you come to bless my union.

[*Speaks.*] Though related to General Ma, you are a stranger in this
region. Why should you have incurred such expense for people like
us? I feel deeply embarrassed, since you have been so extravagant
without any apparent motive. Please explain, so that I may make   90
amends in future.

HOU: Fragrant Princess's question is opportune. Brother Yang and I
chanced to meet like duckweed floating on water. These lavish gifts
have made me quite uneasy.

YANG: Since you ask, I'll be candid. The dresses and banquet cost over   95
two hundred *taels* of silver, all of which came from Huai-ning.

HOU: How do you mean, "from Huai-ning"?

YANG: From the former Minister Juan Ta-ch'eng, who is from Huai-
ning.

HOU: Why should he have done this for me?   100

YANG: He is anxious to gain your friendship. [*Sings.*]

He admires your talent and reputation,
The fame of which is spreading far and wide.
Since you sought a fair companion on the banks of the Ch'in-huai
River,
Hibiscus wardrobe and mandarin duck quilts were indispensable.   105
These were presented by Master Juan,
Your good neighbour from the south.

HOU: Old Juan was a classmate of my father's, but I have always
despised and avoided him. I am puzzled why he should show me
such kindness now.   110

YANG: He has various private troubles, and thinks you may be able to
help him.

HOU: What is the matter?

YANG: Juan was originally associated with our comrades. He only

joined the eunuch Wei Chung-hsien's faction to protect his friends   115
of the Eastern Forest Party, never dreaming that these would treat
him so shockingly since Wei's downfall. The Revival Club
launched a campaign against him, and he was attacked and reviled
by all its members. It is just like a family feud. Juan's old cronies
are so suspicious that none will step forward in his defence. In his   120
utter dejection, he keeps on saying: "That old friends should fall
out like this is deplorable. Only Master Hou can save me." Hence
his anxiety to gain your goodwill.

HOU: Now I understand. If he is in such distress as to need my help, I
pity him. Although he belonged to Wei's faction, he has repented   125
of it since. I disapprove of such violent extremes. Wu and Ch'en
are both close friends of mine. If I see them tomorrow, I shall try
and explain the situation to them.

YANG: That would be doing him a great kindness, and it would benefit
all concerned.   130

FRAGRANT PRINCESS: [*Indignantly to* HOU.] How can you say such
things, my honoured lord? Juan Ta-ch'eng shamelessly supported
the traitors; even women and children would gladly spit in his face.
Yet when others justly attack him, you propose to defend him. Consider how this will affect your own position. [*Sings.*]   135

> How can you make such promises
> So thoughtlessly?
> Though you wish to save that creature from ruin,
> You must also bear in mind
> How others will judge yourself!   140

[*Speaks.*] Merely because he has done you a personal favour, you
forget the commonweal. Can't you see that I am indifferent to all
this finery? [*She removes her headdress and outer gown, singing.*]

> I care not whether I seem poor,
> Of lowly birth and station;   145
> In humble homespun I may win a virtuous reputation.

YANG: Dear me, what a fiery temper!

LI: The pity of it, the pity of it! Fancy throwing such precious things
all over the floor! [*She picks them up.*]

HOU: No! No! This is well done! Fragrant Princess has shown such   150
excellent judgment that I feel she is my superior in this. She is a
friend to be looked up to with respect and trembling! [*To* YANG.]
Please do not blame me, elder brother. Much as I should like to
oblige you, I am afraid I would be scorned by a woman if I did so.
[*Sings.*]

> Though frivolous her profession,   155
> How keen her sense of justice and propriety.
> Shame on those
> Who belong to the Academy and the Emperor's Court,
> Yet cannot distinguish between blue and yellow!

[*Speaks.*] In the past I have won the respect of my colleagues on   160
account of my firm convictions. If I compromised with a traitor, I
would become a target myself. Why should I defend such a villain?
[*Sings.*]

> One should never risk losing
> One's character and reputation.
> The serious and the trivial   165
> Must be clearly distinguished.

YANG: But old Juan has taken such pains to please you. I beg you not
to send him a flat refusal.

HOU: I may be foolish, but I won't throw myself into a well on his
behalf.   170

YANG: Then I had better say goodbye.

HOU: All those things in the wardrobe belong to old Juan. Since Fragrant Princess will not use them, please take them away.

YANG: This is a bitter disappointment. [*Exit, while* FRAGRANT PRINCESS
stares angrily after him.]

HOU: My Fragrant Princess was born a great beauty without jewelled   175
ornaments, and she is even lovelier without her satin gown.

LI: All the same, it was a pity to lose those valuable gifts. [*Sings.*]

> When gold and pearls are in your hand,
> Heedless you let them slip away
> Daughter, you fail to understand   180
> All that your mother had to pay.

HOU: Those trifles are not worth worrying about. I shall find others for
her.

LI: That will be ample compensation. [*Sings.*]

> For the cost of powder and rouge do have a care.   185

FRAGRANT PRINCESS: I do not mind what simple clothes I wear.

HOU: Only such beauty could have such wisdom rare.

FRAGRANT PRINCESS: Distinction's free from fashion's passing flare.

*   *   *

Scenes 8 to 22 Summary

Scenes 8 to 22 Summary   The plot becomes complicated, as Hou Fang-yü
is drawn into political intrigues and the ever-worsening military crisis that besets
the empire. The scene shifts to the camp of one of the Ming armies stationed near
Nanking. General Tso Liang-yü, who had once been a protégé of Hou Fang-yü's
father, is faced with the threat of mutiny because of lack of provisions. To placate
his troops Tso Liang-yü is forced to violate his orders and move the army to the
east. This move suggests rebellion and greatly worries the commandant of Nanking. Yang Wen-ts'ung reports this news to Hou Fang-yü and asks him, as the son
of Tso Liang-yü's former commanding officer, to write a letter to Tso asking him
to halt his advance. A storyteller, Liu Ching-t'ing, offers to carry the letter and
persuade the general.

The civil and military officials of Nanking, including Juan Ta-ch'eng and Yang Wen-ts'ung, meet to decide what action to take in face of the situation. Because of his grudge against Hou, Juan denounces Hou Fang-yü as plotting rebellion with Tso, but Yang protests, and General Shih K'o-fa does not believe the charge. Nevertheless the military governor, Ma Shih-ying (eventually revealed as a major villain together with Juan Ta-ch'eng), is persuaded and orders Hou Fang-yü's arrest. Yang Wen-ts'ung hurries off to warn Hou, who is forced to part from Fragrant Princess and to flee to Shih K'o-fa for protection.

Eventually grain arrives for Tso's army, but news also comes that rebels have taken Peking, the Ming emperor has hanged himself, and the crown prince has disappeared. When one clique in Nanking wishes to put Prince Fu on the throne, Hou Fang-yü presents a strong case against it to General Shih K'o-fa. Nevertheless, Ma Shih-ying, working with Juan Ta-ch'eng, succeeds in enthroning Prince Fu; for he knows Prince Fu's weaknesses and believes he can manipulate the new emperor. Among the many appointments made by the new government is a kinsman of Yang Wen-ts'ung, and Yang suggests that he purchase Fragrant Princess as his concubine. Fragrant Princess absolutely refuses, determined to keep faith with Hou Fang-yü. Meanwhile to the north, the Manchus have moved into China and ousted the Chinese rebels from Peking; the Ming armies under the command of Shih K'o-fa are torn apart by internal rivalries and will prove ineffective in blocking the Manchus' southward advance. With this ends the first part of the play.

An interlude follows, beginning with a discussion at an inn between three travelers making their way south to Nanking on the Night of All Souls Festival, when the dead walk the earth. The three will play important roles in the second half of the play. The first is Lan Ying, a painter; the second is Ts'ai Yi-so, a bookseller; and the third is Chang Wei, an officer in the Imperial Guard, who has personally buried the last Ming emperor. After they fall asleep, a storm blows up, bringing with it the ghosts of the Ming emperor and empress, along with all who died in the wars in the north. Chang Wei, who rises and sees the procession of souls, vows to carry out a proper memorial service for the dead Ming emperor in Nanking on the same day in the following year.

As the second half of the play begins, the villain Ma Shih-ying, now prime minister, and Juan Ta-ch'eng hear from Yang Wen-ts'ung of Fragrant Princess's refusal to accept the proposal. Juan Ta-ch'eng is enraged and orders that she be forced to marry Yang's kinsman. When Yang Wen-ts'ung and Li Chen-li try to drag her downstairs, Fragrant Princess bangs her head on the floor until she knocks herself out, spattering her fan with blood. Horrified, Li Chen-li offers to take Fragrant Princess's place

From *Part II*

SCENE 23

The Message on the Fan

1644, ELEVENTH MONTH

[FRAGRANT PRINCESS *enters, looking pale and wan.*]
FRAGRANT PRINCESS: [*Sings.*]

> The cold wind pierces my thin gown,
> I am too weary to burn incense.
> A streak of bright blood still glistens on my eyebrow.
> My languid soul floats over my lone shadow;

My life is spring gossamer in this frosty moonlit tower.   5
The night seems endless:
When dawn appears, the same grief lingers on.

[*Speaks.*] In a moment of despair, I tore my flesh to defend my
virtue. Alone, I peek and pine in my empty room. I have lost my
sole companion. [*Sings.*]   10

> Long Bridge is wrapped in cloud and frozen snow,
> My tower is closed and visitors are few.
> Beyond the balustrade, a line of wild geese;
> Outside the curtain, icicles are dripping.
> The brazier is burnt out, all perfume faded—   15
> I shrink and shiver in the biting wind.

[*Speaks.*] Though I live in a pleasure resort, the flowers and moon
have ceased to bring me joy. I have done with worldly vanities.
[*Sings.*]

> My 'broidered window curtain is forlorn,
> Though the parrot's foolish voice cries "Serving tea,"   20
> And the white cat sleeps serenely on its cushion.
> So loose my skirt, it flaps about my waist;
> So tired my feet, their phoenix-patterned shoes
> Feel tossed upon the crests of boisterous waves.
> Excess of grief breeds sickness. Love and joy   25
> Have fled this chamber never to return.

[*Speaks.*] I never cease thinking of my beloved lord. Since his flight
I have had no news of him, but I shall preserve my chastity for his
sake. [*Sings.*]

> In a twinkling, our song of rapture was interrupted;   30
> At midnight the passionate lovers had to part.
> Neither at Swallow Cliff nor Peach-leaf Wharf[7]
> Shall my true love be seen.
> Over the mazy clouds and windy mountains
> The solitary swan has taken flight.   35
> Each year the blossoms of the plum return,
> Each year my love is ever more remote.
> From my balcony, I gaze into the distance,
> My falling tears like pools of autumn rain
> which only the harsh wind will ever dry.   40

[*Speaks.*] The Prime Minister's sycophants would have forced me
to marry, but how could I betray my lord? [*Sings.*]

> They persecute me, feeble blossom afloat on the mist,
> Helpless before the arrogance of these ministers.
> But to preserve my purity, jade without flaw,   45
> Gladly I wound the flower-like bloom of my cheeks.

[*Speaks.*] My poor mother is most to be pitied! Suddenly she left
without a word, to take my place on that disastrous night. Her bed
remains, but when will she return? [*Sings.*]

---

7. Famous beautiful spots where lovers used to meet.

Like a peach petal adrift in a snowstorm,　　　　50
Like a willow catkin wafted by the wind,
Hiding her face behind her sleeve, she left at dead of night.
Now I am left alone,
No one to brush the dust from my coverlet,
Desolate,　　　　55
A flower that opens for none to view.

[*Speaks.*] When I think of all this, I am heartbroken. [*She weeps and sings.*]

A broken heart,
How many tears that fall!
And never a companion's cheery call,　　　　60
Only the knocking of the curtain-hooks.

[*Speaks.*] I shall take out my precious fan again and read my beloved's poem. Ah me, it is stained with blood. What shall I do? [*Sings.*]

The bloodstains spread in bright confusion,
Some thick, some thin, some heavy and some light;　　　　65
Not the cuckoo's tears of blood,
But raindrops reddened by the peachbloom of my cheeks
Spattering this silken fan.

[*Speaks.*] My lord, my lord! All this was for your sake! [*Sings.*]

I tore my cloudy hair and bruised my limbs　　　　70
Until I swooned into a world of darkness,
Like a long-buried queen beneath a hill-slope.
Dripping with blood, my body seemed to fall
As from the summit of the highest tower,
Unconscious of the voices calling me;　　　　75
My melting soul past human invocation.
The red clouds darken in the setting sun:
I wake to find my pillow drenched with tears.
Sorrow is graven on my heart and brow,
Washing the rouge from my face,　　　　80
Staining the silk of my robe.

[*Speaks.*] I'm so overwhelmed with weariness that I shall fall asleep at this table. [*She dozes off, clutching her fan.*]

YANG WEN-TS'UNG: [*Enters and recites.*]

The tower a slanting shadow throws
Over the stream, and nesting crows　　　　85
Caw in the withered willow boughs.

SU K'UN-SHENG: [*Entering.*]

This chamber where sweet music used to flow,
Is now a hermit's cell where wild winds blow.

YANG: Oh Master Su, I'm so glad to see you again.
SU: Since Mistress Li's departure, Fragrant Princess has been living　　　　90
here alone. I felt anxious about her, so I came to pay her a visit.

YANG: The night of Mistress Li's departure, I kept vigil with Fragrant
    Princess till dawn. Since then I have been so occupied with official
    business that I have not been able to see her. [*They enter the house
    together.*]

SU: Fragrant Princess will never come downstairs. Let us go up and   95
    see her. [*Both walk upstairs to find* FRAGRANT PRINCESS *asleep.*]

YANG: How ill and woebegone she looks in her sleep. We ought not
    to wake her.

SU: The fan lies open before her. But why is it splashed with red?

YANG: This was Brother Hou's gift of betrothal. She treasured it above   100
    everything in the world and was always reluctant to show it. Finding
    it stained with her blood, she must have intended to dry it. [*Exam-
    ining it.*] The stains are still very bright. I'll paint a few leaves and
    twigs around them, so that it will resemble a picture of peach blos-
    soms. Unfortunately, I lack green paint.   105

SU: If I squeeze some sap from the plant in yonder vase, perhaps you
    may use it instead.

YANG: What a clever idea. [SU *procures him some, and* YANG *proceeds
    to paint, reciting.*]

> The leaves are green with the sap of a fragrant plant
> To protect the blossoms dyed in a beauty's blood.   110

SU: This is the finest picture of peach blossoms I have seen.

YANG: It is a genuine peach blossom fan.

FRAGRANT PRINCESS: [*Waking up.*] O gentlemen, forgive my lack of
    courtesy! Pray sit down.

YANG: The wound on your forehead looks almost healed. [*Laughing.*]   115
    I have brought you a little gift—on which I have painted some
    peach blossoms. [*Hands it to her.*]

FRAGRANT PRINCESS: But this is my old fan. As it is covered with blood-
    stains, I would rather not look at it. [*Puts it in her sleeve.*]

SU: But there is an exquisite picture which you really ought to see.   120

FRAGRANT PRINCESS: When was it painted?

YANG: Forgive me for not asking permission. I fear I might have
    spoiled it.

FRAGRANT PRINCESS: [*Opening and examining it.*] Alas, peach blos-
    som is the most ill-fated of flowers, condemned to float forever on   125
    this fan. I thank Your Honour. You have almost painted a portrait
    of myself. [*Sings.*]

> Each branch a swaying sorrow in the wind,
> Each petal a lost soul swept by the rising tide.
> Only a master's hand could render thus   130
> A vivid line so natural, evoking
> The lips of beauty and the lotus cheek.
> A few bold strokes, and the tree springs to life,
> Red petals and green leaves; but evil fate
> Awaits the pictured flower and its possessor.   135

YANG: Now that you have this peach blossom fan, you need a partner
to appreciate it with you. Why turn yourself into a widow? Do you
want to be like the Moon Goddess who flew from the world?[8]

FRAGRANT PRINCESS: What is the use of discussing it? The famous
Kuan P'an-p'an[9] was also a professional singing-girl, but she lived   140
alone in her Swallow Tower until extreme old age.

SU: Supposing Master Hou returned tomorrow, would you promptly
recover your spirits and come downstairs?

FRAGRANT PRINCESS: Ah, then the whole world would be different. I
should feel as if my future were spread out like a beautiful tapestry.   145
Not only would I leave this tower, I would travel anywhere.

YANG: Such steadfast resolve is most unusual. Master Su, to prove
your devoted relationship as teacher to pupil, would you try to find
Brother Hou and bring them together again? I am sure it would be
a blessing for all concerned.   150

SU: After repeated inquiries, I finally discovered that he spent half a
year in Huai-an-fu with Minister Shih, whence he proceeded to
Yang-chou by way of Nanking. He is at present with General Kao's
army defending the Yellow River. I had intended to return to my
home, so I may search for him on the journey. But I should have a   155
letter from Fragrant Princess to take with me.

FRAGRANT PRINCESS: [*To* YANG.] Though my thoughts and emotions
are boundless, I have never been trained to express them in writing.
Would Your Honour be so kind as to write the letter for me?

YANG: How could I express what lies in the depths of your heart?   160

FRAGRANT PRINCESS: [*Pensively.*] All my fears and sorrows are associated with this fan. Perhaps it will suffice if you merely take it to
him.

SU: What an original notion, to use a fan as a letter!

FRAGRANT PRINCESS: I'll seal it now. [*She seals it, singing.*]   165

> The poem he will recognize as the fruit of his flourishing brush,
> The red blossoms he will see as a new picture.
> So small a space holds the blood of a faithful heart,
> Ten thousand longings bound with silken strands—
> It is worth a volume of characters on paper.   170

SU: I promise to deliver it safely to his hands.

FRAGRANT PRINCESS: When will you start on the journey, Master?

SU: Within the next few days.

FRAGRANT PRINCESS: I hope you will set out as soon as possible.

YANG: It is time for our departure. Fragrant Princess, take care of your-   175
self! The hardship you have suffered for purity's sake deserves the
highest credit. When Brother Hou hears of it, he will certainly hasten to see you.

SU: I may not have time to say goodbye before I leave. Truly, a new
message on the peach blossom fan.   180

---

8. According to legend, Ch'ang O, the goddess of the moon, stole the elixir of immortality and flew away
to the moon, where she lives alone for all eternity.   9. Brilliant dancer and singer who became the
favorite of Chang Chien (died 651), a great-nephew of the founder of the T'ang Dynasty. When he died,
P'an-p'an refused to marry and lived alone in the Swallow Tower for ten years.

YANG: An old constancy, locked in the Swallow Tower.
>   [*Exeunt* YANG *and* SU.]
FRAGRANT PRINCESS: [*Weeping.*] My mother has left me, and now my
>   dear teacher has gone. Alone in this room, my sorrows will seem
>   eternal. [*Sings.*]

> I have ceased to sing the ballads of north and south,   185
> My lute is silent, nor do I touch the flute:
> I have thrust aside my instruments, and left them to rot away.
> If only my fan could reach him soon, and my teacher were on his way!
> When my lord returns, upon that joyful day,
> Hand in hand we shall leave the tower together.   190
> I hope my message reaches him before the snow has melted,
> Though hills and vales seem endless on the voyage.

*   *   *

Scenes 24 to 27 Summary   At a party attended by Yang Wen-ts'ung, Juan
Ta-ch'eng and Ma Shih-ying, a group of singing girls—including Fragrant Princess—is called to perform. Fragrant Princess denounces Juan and Ma, and they
have her sent to the palace, where she will be forced to play the role of clown in
Juan Ta-ch'eng's play *Swallow Letter*, for the newly enthroned Prince Fu, who is
a devotee of the theater. Prince Fu admires her and decides to keep her as an
actress in the imperial troupe.

Meanwhile in the north Hou Fang-yü has been sent by Shih K'o-fa to serve on
the staff of one of his subordinate generals. The general is killed in a private feud,
and Hou is forced to flee. On the river, Hou chances to meet Li Chen-li, who has
been sold again by the man who bought her as a concubine. At the same time,
they encounter Su K'un-sheng, who is carrying the peach blossom fan as a token
from Fragrant Princess to show her love. Hou returns to Nanking and goes to
Fragrant Princess's lodgings only to discover that they are occupied by the painter
Lan Ying.

SCENE 28

The Painting Inscribed

1645, THIRD MONTH

[*Enter* LAN YING *in the garb of a mountain hermit.*]
LAN: [*Recites.*]

> Listless she sits, the incense cold, her embroidery neglected,
> The peach-flowers open, but the garden gate is shut.
> In the limitless mists and rain of the rising spring,
> All that's left of the Southern courts are these painted hills.

[*Speaks.*] From early youth I have won fame as a painter. I heard   5
that my old friend Yang Wen-ts'ung has recently been appointed to
a post in the Ministry of War, and I bought a boat and came to visit
him. He has persuaded me to lodge in this Tower of Enchanted
Fragrance, which used to be the home of the celebrated singing-
girl Fragrant Princess. Since her departure the house has been   10

empty, but it is quiet enough to suit me. I shall now return to my
painting. [*He washes his ink-stone and painting-brush, and mixes
the pigment.*] But where can I find pure water? Ah, I had almost
forgotten that the morning dew on leaves and flowers is the purest
for mixing colours. I'll gather some in the garden. [*Exits with a*   15
cup.]

HOU: [*Enters and sings.*]

> I have roamed between earth below and Heaven above,
> My heart ever bound by a thread of perfect love.
> Now the lanes are full of willow catkins; lo,
> They float while swallows flutter to and fro.
> Seeing the familiar house, the crimson tower,   20
> My tenderest feelings like green meadows flower,
> Fresh longings rise and fall in a misty shower.

[*Speaks.*] After meeting Su K'un-sheng on the Yellow River, I
curbed my excitement and travelled with him to Nanking. This
morning I left him at an inn, and came alone to look for Fragrant   25
Princess. How wonderful to see the Old House again! [*Sings.*]

> So little trace of human habitation,
> The birds are twittering in consternation.
> The walls are crumbling among weeds in piles,
> And green moss gathers on the lustrous tiles   30
> Beside the blossoms which should harmonize
> With her fair features. Now my spirit flies
> To meet my love and gaze into her eyes.

[*Pushing the door, he says.*] Oh, the doors are not locked! I'll walk
in and see who is there. [*Sings.*]   35

> My footsteps startle the birds and raise a squall,
> While mud from nests drops down into the hall;
> It seems this empty hall, where no man follows,
> Provides the perfect mating-place for swallows.
> I'll steal on tiptoe till I reach her room . . .   40

[*Speaks.*] Here is the Tower of Enchanted Fragrance—but oh, how
desolate! Though it is daytime, the curtains are drawn. Perhaps she
is still asleep. Instead of rousing her, I shall creep up the Tower
and stand beside her bed. When she wakes up and recognizes me,
what rapture we shall share! [*Sings.*]   45

> Clutching my gown, I part the drooping branches,
> And climb the crumbling staircase step by step,
> Among the dust and cobwebs. Out-of-doors
> The spring is all-pervading.
> Why does my love retire behind her curtains?   50

[*Seeing the bare table, he sings.*]

> Since when has she banished her lute?
> And all these pigments in boxes and jars:
> Has she become a recluse who paints for a living?

[*Speaks.*] The tower of song and dance has been turned into a studio. How strange! I wonder why. . . . Perhaps to protect her virtue, she wished to forget the arts of her vocation. Perhaps she hoped to express her lonely thoughts with her brush. Here is her bedroom. I'll open the door gently. Why is it barred? It seems to have been so for ages. This is very strange. Is there no caretaker in the house? [*Sings.*]

> The room is forlorn; my beauty's far away,
> Where has she fled beyond the myriad hills,
> Locking her door? Maybe the birds can tell.
> Light-heartedly they frolic in the air,
> Heedless of my fond question. In despair
> I turn; by yonder hedge the twigs are stirring,
> A curtain rustles: do I hear her breathe?

[LAN *enters with a jar. Seeing* HOU, *he starts with surprise.*]

LAN: Who are you, sir? And why do you come to my tower?

HOU: It belongs to my beloved Fragrant Princess. I was about to ask you the same question.

LAN: I am an artist, and my name is Lan Ying. My friend Yang Wen-ts'ung invited me to stay here.

HOU: So you are the eminent painter! I have long been your distant admirer. [LAN *asks his name, and* HAN *answers.*] I am also acquainted with Master Yang, and my name is Hou Fang-yü.

LAN: Your literary fame has even reached my ears. What good fortune has brought us together? Pray sit down.

HOU: First of all, please tell me where is my Fragrant Princess?

LAN: I have heard that she has been removed to the Inner Palace.

HOU: [*In amazement.*] But how and when did that happen?

LAN: I'm afraid I do not know.

HOU: [*Wiping away tears, sings.*]

> After searching everywhere,
> I stand alone in the east wind.
> It is clear noon,
> But she is not to be seen.

[*Looking round.*]

> The window-paper and the curtain-gauze are torn.
> No relic of her remains;
> Neither an old scarf or hairpin,
> Nor the familiar flute.
> Her mandarin-duck quilts are put away;
> The mirrors are turned face down.
> There is no beauty left for the flowers to compete with.

[*Speaks.*] The peach trees were in full blossom on our marriage day. This tower had been newly decorated; now, no sooner has she left than it looks desolate again. I return to find the peach trees again in flower. How can I check my tears at the sight of them? [*Sings.*]

Their petals flutter in the light spring breeze.
Gossamer fills the air like snowflakes,
Petals fall and scatter.

[*Speaks.*] I'll look at the peach blossoms on my fan. [*Sings.*]

Painted in blood,   100
Brighter petals are here than on the trees.

[*Speaks.*] And I was responsible for them. [*Sings.*]

Opening this fan,
Here in the desolation of her boudoir,
I realize it was this very peach bloom   105
That joined her fate with mine, to live or die.

LAN: Who painted this fan of yours?
HOU: Your distinguished patron, Master Yang.
LAN: But why does it make you weep?
HOU: This fan is the tangible token of our vow. [*Sings.*]   110

Full of tenderness she held the ink-stone;
In the candlelight she asked me for a poem.
Thus line by line, I wrote a vow of love.

[*Speaks.*] But within less than a month, I had to escape my foes.
Fragrant Princess segregated herself for my sake, and by doing so   115
she offended the ruling powers. They sent bloodhounds after her
and drove her from her tower, so that in despair she tried to destroy
her beauty. Still clutching this fan, she stained it with her blood.
LAN: Your story has moved me deeply.
HOU: Our friend Yang painted in a few leaves and converted it into a 120
peach blossom fan. It is my only keepsake of my beloved.
LAN: The brushwork is so skillful that one cannot detect the bloodstains. How did you recover it?
HOU: Fragrant Princess sent her teacher to search for me, taking it
instead of a letter. Immediately upon receiving it, I made this jour- 125
ney, never dreaming that she would have been removed to the
Imperial Palace. [*Weeps.*]
     [*Enter* YANG WEN-TS'UNG, *with attendants to clear the way for him.*]
YANG: The Beauty is long gone from her tower, but in her place is
installed a famous painter.
SERVANT: [*Comes in and announces.*] His Honour Yang has come to   130
visit Master Lan.
     [YANG *steps out of his sedan-chair.* LAN *advances to meet him and
     escorts him upstairs.*]
YANG: [*Seeing* HOU.] When did you arrive, Brother Hou?
HOU: This very day, so I have not yet had time to visit you.
YANG: I heard that you were on the staff of His Excellency Shih, and
also that you accompanied Kao Chieh to the Yellow River. This   135
morning I read an official report that Kao was murdered last month
by Hsu Ting-kuo. Where were you in the meantime?
HOU: At home in my native village. On hearing of that disaster, I had

to escape with my father into the hills, and there we stayed a
month. Then I was warned that Hsu might send soldiers in pursuit   140
of me, so I hired a boat and came south. On the way I chanced to
meet Su K'un-sheng, who was searching for me. So I hurried to
Nanking to find Fragrant Princess, or rather to find her gone.
Where is she now?[1]

YANG: She was taken to the palace on the eighth of the first month.   145

HOU: When will she be able to leave it?

YANG: I cannot tell.

HOU: Then I shall have to wait here until she is set free.

YANG: There is no sense in that. You should find some other beauty
to replace her.   150

HOU: How could I break my vow? You do not understand. If I could
only obtain a message from her I would have a grain of comfort.
[Sings.]

> Her dwelling, close at hand,
> Seems as remote as the sky.
> How can I find a fairy maiden   155
> To smuggle a letter to her?
> She has left the blossom-shaded tower,
> The wine pavilions, shrouded in mist and rain,
> And languishes unwilling in the palace;
> While I, her husband, wait at the far horizon   160
> Where each day seems a year.

YANG: Don't distress yourself unduly, Brother Hou. Let us watch
Brother Lan at his painting. [YANG and HOU sit beside LAN as he
paints. YANG asks.] Is this a picture of the Peach Blossom Fountain?[2]
    165

LAN: You are right.

YANG: For whom are you painting it?

LAN: For Chang Wei, the Commanding Officer of the Imperial
Guard. The picture is to be mounted on a screen for the Pine Wind
Pavilion he has recently finished building.   170

HOU: I congratulate you on its fine qualities. Both the color and the
composition are extremely original, quite different from the traditional school of Nanking.

LAN: Thank you for taking so much notice of it. Would you kindly
grace it with an inscription? That would increase its value consider-   175
ably.

HOU: If you are not afraid of my spoiling such a work of art, I shall
practice my lame calligraphy upon it. [He composes a quatrain for
the inscription.]

> "I dwelt in the hidden cave by Peach Blossom Fountain,
> But on my way back I could not find the road.   180
> For the fisherman had misled me over the mountain,
> To keep this sanctuary for his own abode."

---

1. Though aware of the facts, he evidently requires verbal confirmation from Yang, whose conduct has
been ambiguous.   2. See n. 5, p. 88.

[*He signs his name to it.*]

YANG: Three are several recondite[3] allusions in your poem. You
    appear to blame me somewhat.

HOU: No, there you are mistaken. [*Points to the painting and sings.*]   185

> How lovely the rippling brook,
> Where thousands of crimson petals fall,
> And streaks of cloud drift over
> Dense woods and far blue hills!
> The place remains the same,   190
> But no love is there to welcome me.
> The cave at Peach Blossom Spring is desolate;
> I turn back my boat as the sun sets.

[HOU *rises.*]

YANG: It is useless to repine, brother. Now Ma and Juan are in power,
    and you know how vindictive they are. Though intimate with both   195
    of them, I dare not appeal on behalf of either of you, especially
    since the New Year's banquet when Fragrant Princess was asked to
    sing. Instead of singing, she pointed at Ma and Juan and
    denounced them to their faces.

HOU: Alas! I fear she must have been tortured in consequence.   200

YANG: Luckily I was present. I tried my best to calm their indignation,
    so she was only cast out into the snow. No doubt she was distressed,
    but as long as she is in the Inner Court her life will be protected.
    But your connection with her is too well known, and you had better
    not remain here.   205

HOU: Thank you for the warning. [*Sings.*]

> Though my enemies use all their power against me,
> I'll clasp the peach blossom fan to my heart.

[*He turns abruptly to leave.*]

YANG: Let us bid Brother Lan farewell and leave together.

HOU: Forgive me; I had forgotten to say goodbye.   210

> [*Farewells are exchanged. Exit* LAN *first, closing the door.* HOU *and*
> YANG *walk off together, singing.*]

HOU: Bewildered by this return to the crimson tower,

YANG: Idly we watched the painter at his task.

HOU: The beauty and her lover are cast asunder,

YANG: But peach flowers are as fine this year as last.

SCENE 29

The Club Suppressed

1645, THIRD MONTH

[*Enter* TS 'AI YI-SO, *the bookseller.*]

TS'AI: [*Sings.*]

> In my shop, like the famous caves of Yu-shan,
> A myriad precious volumes are assembled;

---

3. Obscure.

My labours as a collector have won for me
Both learned reputation and hard cash.
A scholar-merchant, I, who only hope 5
To avoid any book-burning First Emperor of Ch'in!

[*Speaks.*] Nanking ranks first among cities for the wealth of its books, and most of these are in Three Mountain Street, where I keep the largest bookshop. [*Points.*] Here are the Thirteen Canons, the twenty-one Dynastic Histories,[4] all the tomes of the nine 10 schools of philosophy, of the three religions and the hundred thinkers, besides collections of eight-legged essays[5] and fashionable modern novels. They cram the shelves and innumerable boxes and rooms. I have travelled north and south to gather this collection, minutely examining old editions to make fine reprints with schol- 15 arly annotations. As well as earning a handsome profit by these transactions, I have helped to preserve and circulate the noblest thoughts of mankind. Even the doctors and masters of literature greet me with deference. I have reason to be satisfied with my reputation. [*He laughs.*] This year the general civil service examination 20 will be held again, and the finest literary talents will receive due honour. The government has endorsed a proposal by the Minister of Ceremonies, Ch'ien Ch'ien-i, advocating a new style of writing to express the spirit of the new reign. Consequently I have invited several leading critics to compile anthologies as models for compo- 25 sition. They will start work today. I'll hang up my latest advertisement. [*He hangs a couplet on each side of the door, which he reads.*]

"The style in vogue was created by men of renown,
Imitation of these models will please the chief examiner."

[*Exit.*]

[*Enter* HOU FANG-YÜ *and* SU K'UN-SHENG, *with baggage.*]
HOU: [*Sings.*]

The moonlit tower of those bygone years 30
Is far off as a dream;
And the sound of pipes is stilled,
Remote from each other as the star-lovers
Across the Milky Way,
Will no one bear a message, 35
No one aid us in our distress?

[*Speaks.*] Master Su, we have travelled hundreds of miles to answer the summons of my Fragrant Princess, but we arrived too late. She is now immured in the palace, and it is impossible even to reach her with a message. Last night I was warned to leave my lodgings. 40
I don't know where we can stay in safety until we get news of her.

---

4. The dynastic histories have by now reached a total of twenty-four. See n. 7, p. 88, for the Six Canons; later subdivisions and additions led to a corpus of thirteen works, which remain canonical to this day.
5. The examination essay of Ming and Ch'ing times was christened *eight-legged* because it developed a prescribed form in eight sections.

[*Sings.*]

> If needs be,
> I shall wait for her till my hair turns white.
> But perhaps that happy day
> Is reserved for another lifetime.   50

SU: It is clear that the political situation is going from bad to worse.
Public opinion has also changed considerably. Those in authority
are launching an offensive against the virtuous to settle old scores.
It would be wiser to keep out of their way and practise patience.

HOU: You may be right; I have hardly any friends left in this neigh-   55
bourhood. My old comrades Ch'en and Wu have retired to their
native provinces. Perhaps I should follow them. [*Sings.*]

> My friends are seagulls by the shore.
> Prouder than kings,
> They turn aside from the dusty world,   60
> And frown at the muddled chess-game in the capital.
> Why not sail to the south
> And seek them among the hills?

SU: We are near the book market in Three Mountain Street, where
there is always a large crowd. We had better avoid it. [*He quickens*   65
his pace, singing.]

> Keep away from the leopards and wolves,
> The apes who wear the robes of government.
> On Three Mountain Street the mob is like a torrent.

HOU: [*Stopping.*] Here is Ts'ai Yi-so's bookshop, where my old comrades used to stay. Let us inquire whether they are still here. [*Look-* 70
ing up.] I see two new advertisements posted on these pillars.
[*Reads.*] "The Revival Club reopened." And there's a small notice
beside it: "New selections of model examination essays by Messrs.
Ch'en Chen-hui and Wu Ying-chi. Do you think they are here
now?   75

SU: I'll ask. [*Calls.*] Is the worthy proprietor at home?

TS'AI: [*Entering.*] Welcome. Are you gentlemen looking for books?

HOU: No, sir. I come for some information. Have you seen Messrs.
Ch'en and Wu?

TS'AI: They are inside at the moment. I'll go and call them. [*Exit.*]   80

CH'EN and WU: [*Entering.*] Oh, it's Brother Hou and Master Su as
well. What a delightful surprise! [*Mutual bows.*]

CH'EN: Where have you come from?

HOU: I have been in my native village.

WU: When did you arrive in the capital?   85

HOU: Only yesterday. [*Sings.*]

> The smoke of war has covered half the land.
> I have been with the army north and south,
> One camp after another, three wasted years.
> Now I return; who pities this wasted body?   90
> I have lingered by the Ch'in-huai River,

Among the peach blossoms of my former haunt,
But the shore no longer extends its former welcome.

[*Speaks.*] So I see that you, brothers, are creating a new literary
style.   95
CH'EN and WU: You mock us. [*Sing.*]

Here in Chin-ling,[6] seat of ancient learning,
We labour side by side on compilations
To hold up T'ang and Sung as worthy models
And discourage the decadent Six Dynasties styles.   100
Studying our selections from the Eastern Forest,
All will acknowledge our classic purity.

TS'AI: [*From backstage.*] Please join me for a cup of tea.
CH'EN and WU: Thank you, we are coming.
[*They accompany* HOU *and* SU *to a room at the back. A* SERVANT *of*
JUAN TA -CH'ENG *enters with a bundle of large visiting cards.*]
SERVANT: My master, His Excellency Juan, has just been promoted to   105
Vice-Minister of War, and has received a new python robe and jade
belt as tokens of Imperial favour. He will be sent to direct the
defence of the river, so he is paying a round of farewell visits to his
friends.
[JUAN *enters in python robe and jade belt, sitting proudly in his sedan*
chair, followed by retainers with fans and official umbrellas.]
JUAN: [*Sings.*]

See my attendants, rank on rank,   110
Fans waving, parasols held high.
And who is this, in lofty state?
The man you scorned in years gone by.

SERVANT: Let Your Excellency's chair be halted. We are near the residence of His Excellency Yueh. [*Leaves a card at the latter's gate.*]   115
JUAN: You need not clear the street. Allow the public to gather round
and admire me. [*Waving his fan, brags.*] Having received this high
appointment from His Majesty, I'm paying a series of ceremonious
visits. My foes of the Eastern Forest Party will be arrested by Imperial decree. They seem to have fled, for I see no sign of them.   120
[*Sings.*]

Now I'll show them power and glory!
At last the wrinkles on my brow will vanish.

[*Noting the sign on the bookshop.*] What's this advertisement?
Revival Club? Tear it down and show it to me. [SERVANT *does so.*
JUAN *reads.*] "Reopening of the Revival Club. Ch'en Chen-hui and   125
Wu Ying-chi are editing new selections." How now! That Club is
an offshoot of the Eastern Forest Party which has been in close
collaboration with the rebels Chou and Lei. Now that a warrant is
out for their arrest, who dares invite them to make anthologies?
This book dealer is a rash fellow. Stop my chair! [*Steps out of the*   130

6. One of the ancient names of Nanking.

sedan, sits before the bookshop, and says.] Summon the local official in charge of the book trade. [*The* OFFICIAL *is summoned.*]

OFFICIAL: [*Kneeling before* JUAN.] What is Your Excellency's wish?

JUAN: [*Sings.*]

> This bookseller defies the law
> By conspiring with the Revival Club. 135
> My duty is to suppress these rebels,
> Yours, to expose them root and branch.

OFFICIAL: Don't worry, Your Excellency. I'm an expert at making
arrests. [*Exits and re-enters with* TS'AI YI-SO.] The criminal Ts'ai Yi-
so is here, Your Excellency. 140

TS'AI: [*Kneeling.*] As a loyal subject of His Majesty, I protest that I
have not violated any law.

JUAN: You have commissioned members of the Revival Club to work
for you.

TS'AI: New selections of model essays are made every year before the 145
civil service examination.

JUAN: Fie! Are you ignorant of the Imperial decree, whereby all rebels
are to be arrested? The law knows no mercy. You have harboured
these rebels in your shop, yet you refuse to admit your guilt. You
had better plead guilty at once. 150

TS'AI: I did not give them shelter. The gentlemen came of their own
accord, because they are interested in the new anthologies.

JUAN: So you admit that they are inside your shop. [*To his* ATTEN-
DANTS.] Make sure that none of them slip out.

[*Exeunt* ATTENDANTS.]

JUAN: [*Whispers to the* OFFICIAL.] Send an immediate message to the 155
City Marshal, who has the exclusive duty to deal with rebels. He
must send his guards to arrest them. [*Sings.*]

> The Scarlet Guard will see the prisons filled,
> As these new rebels are in turn suppressed.

OFFICIAL: Yes, Your Excellency. [*Exit hurriedly.* JUAN *re-enters his* 160
sedan.]

HOU, CH'EN, and WU [*Enter, shouting.*] What crime have we committed that we should be kept in custody? Whoever you are, you have
no regard for justice.

JUAN: [*Smiling.*] I have given you no offence. Why are you all so
indignant? What are your names? [*They announce them.*] Aha, so 165
it's you three gentlemen. Don't you recognize this humble official?
[*Sings.*]

> How imposing now my dignity must appear,
> How overwhelming my majestic frame!

[*To* WU.] Do you remember how you prevented me from joining
the sacrifice at the Temple of Confucius? [*To* CH'EN.] Do you 170
remember borrowing my troupe of actors? Why did you call me
ugly names while enjoying my "Swallow Letter"? [*To* HOU.] When
I bought you a valuable wardrobe, you threw it away.

HOU: So it is Bearded Juan gloating on his revenge!

CH'EN and WU: Indeed. Let us drag him to the palace and tell what   175
sort of man he is.

JUAN: [*Laughing.*] No need to hurry: you will have ample opportunity
to tell. [*Pointing.*] See who is coming to fetch you! [*Exit in sedan.*]

FOUR GUARDS: [*Enter, shouting.*] Which is Ts'ai Yi-so?

TS'AI: I am. What is the matter?   180

GUARD: We have come from the Marshal's headquarters to make certain arrests.

TS'AI: Who are you arresting?

GUARD: The three graduates Ch'en, Wu, and Hou.

HOU: We are all present. On what grounds do you arrest us?   185

GUARD: Come at once to headquarters. There you will discover. [*He
leads them out in chains.*]

TS'AI: What is behind all this? [*Calls.*] Brother Su, come quickly.

SU: [*Entering.*] What has happened?

TS'AI: It is terrible, terrible! The two scholars who were making selections for me have been arrested, and Master Hou as well.   190

SU: So it has really come to this! [*Sings.*]

> Hawks swoop down on innocent citizens;
> The Revival Club is an unprotected babe.
> Ma and Juan are now omnipotent.
> Woe to the world   195
> When the savage Prime Minister of a foolish Emperor
> Gives public pretexts for private revenge!

[*Speaks.*] Let us find out what is happening. We may yet be able to
save them.

TS'AI: We must. I'll inquire where they are being kept, so that I can   200
take them some food. [*They sing.*]

TS'AI: Court officers are furthering private feuds.

SU: Like the man of Ch'i, we fear the sky will fall.

TS'AI: Who can prevent this new Burning of Books?[7]

SU: On the Commander-in-Chief, Earl Tso, we call.   205

SCENE 30

The Return to the Hills

1645, THIRD MONTH

[CHANG WEI *enters; he wears a long white beard.*]

CHANG: [*Sings.*]

> Aged retainer of the Imperial court,
> I look back in vain towards my northern home.
> Mist and rain shroud the city of Nanking.
> Alas, the hopeful notes of restoration
> Have changed into the wail of a new tyranny,   5
> And the old court robes cannot hide the new decline.

7. The most infamous burning of books in Chinese history was the work of the first emperor, Ch'in Shih-
huang-ti (259–209 B.C.), the unifier of the country whose name became a byword for ferocious despotism.

[*Speaks.*] Formerly a Commander of the Imperial Guard in
Peking, I came south after the downfall of the old capital. Here the
new Emperor rewarded me with the same rank I held before, but
evil counsels sway the government. The condition of the country   10
deteriorates. As for me, I have built myself a house in the southern
suburbs, with a pavilion called Pine Wind Hall, where I hope to
retire and enjoy a calm old age. Unfortunately I have charge of two
state prisoners, the so-called rebels Chou and Lei. These are sworn
adversaries of Ma and Juan, who are determined to have them con-   15
victed. I am aware that this is grossly unjust, but I have not been
able to find a way to save them. This harasses me day and night, so
that I cannot decide to retire. [*Sings.*]

> The court is all intrigue and party strife:
> All honest men retire from such a life.   20
> Wherefore should I uphold the butcher's knife
> For malefactors? Quickly would I flee
> To my thatched Pine Pavilion and be free,
> Singing aloud to every passing cloud.
> But a terrible injustice haunts my breast,   25
> Until I stave it off I cannot rest.

SERVANT: [*Entering.*] Your Excellency, the City Marshal has captured
three rebels, who await your immediate judgment.
> [*Four* GUARDS *carrying instruments of torture enter and stand on
> either side of the stage.* CHANG *ascends the tribune of justice. A* GUARD
> *leads in* HOU, WU, *and* CH'EN, *and kneels before* CHANG *to hand him
> the written warrant.* CHANG *examines it.*]

CHANG: According to a report from the local official in charge of the
book trade, you are accused of organizing a secret society and plot-   30
ting to purchase the freedom of Chou and Lei with bribes. Therefore you have been arrested. What have you to say in self-defense?
CH'EN and WU: [*Sing.*]

> We plead not guilty.
> Scholars of the Revival Club,
> Our friends are none but literary men.   35
> Only the tyranny of Ch'in Shih-huang[8]
> Would convict such innocent people as ourselves.

HOU: [*Sings.*]

> Do not torture us.
> I came to Nanking to visit old friends,
> And have no part in any clandestine meeting.   40
> Why should we be destroyed
> Like fish in a pond or swallows on a beam?

CHANG: You allege that you have been arrested without cause. It is
impossible that the City Marshal should have committed such a
blunder. [*Pounding on the table with a wooden block.*] Bring out   45
the whips. Make them confess the truth.

8. See n. 7, p. 137.

CH'EN: [*Kneeling.*] Please do not take umbrage, Your Honour. I am
   Ch'en Chen-hui from I-hsing. My only crime is to have selected
   literary models at Ts'ai Yi-so's bookshop. I can think of no other
   offence.

WU: [*Kneeling.*] I am Wu Ying-chi from Juei-ch'ih, and a colleague
   of Ch'en Chen-hui. I was engaged in the same work, apart from
   which I did nothing.

CHANG: [*To* GUARD.] If these men are accused of organizing a secret
   society and plotting at Ts'ai's bookshop, Ts'ai himself should know
   the truth. Why was he not arrested? [*Throwing a warrant to the*
   GUARD.] Make haste and fetch Ts'ai Yi-so. [*Exit* GUARD.]

HOU: [*Kneeling.*] I am Hou Fang-yü from Kuei-te in Honan, and I
   travelled to Nanking with the sole purpose of visiting friends. When
   I heard that these old schoolmates of mine were in the bookshop,
   I
   called to visit them and was promptly arrested.

CHANG: [*Pondering.*] Recently the artist Lan Ying brought me a picture of the Peach Blossom Fountain for my Pine Wind Pavilion. It
   contained an inscription signed Hou Fang-yü of Kuei-te. Are you
   the same individual?

HOU: It is I, the accused, Your Honour.

CHANG: [*With a faint bow.*] This is most regrettable. I was greatly
   impressed by your calligraphy, and your verse is full of subtle
   import. I am sure you had nothing to do with this business. Please
   stand by.

HOU: I thank Your Honour for your kind expression of sympathy. [*He
   is offered a chair and sits down.*]

GUARD: [*Re-entering with warrant.*] Your Honour, Ts'ai Yi-so has
   bolted his shop and fled.

CHANG: How can this case be judged without any proof of the organization or of the alleged bribery?

GUARD: [*Entering with a letter.*] Here is a letter from Their Excellencies Wang and Ch'ien for Your Honour's perusal.

CHANG: So it comes from two highly respected Ministers of State.
   [*After reading it.*] They are absolutely right. I did not realize that
   Ch'en and Wu were leaders of the Revival Club. [*Sings.*]

> One is an essayist of renown;
> The other has won fame as a poet.
> What harm have they done to deserve arrest,
> And why should I serve as the agent of vile intrigues?
> As a judge, I hold independent authority;
> I should bring the light of the sun to the darkest hell.
> Let not the righteous be persecuted,
> Or art and literature decay in consequence.

[*Politely, to* CH'EN *and* WU.] Gentlemen, excuse my lack of courtesy. Are Their Excellencies Wang Chueh-ssu and Ch'ien Mu-chai
   old friends of yours?

CH'EN and WU: We have never had the pleasure of knowing them
   personally.

CHANG: Even so, they have written to me about your lofty characters
and literary attainments.   95
CH'EN and WU: Perhaps it was due to Their Excellencies' sense of
justice.
CHANG: Precisely. Though a member of the military profession, I am
also devoted to literature and learning. How can I sacrifice worthy
men just to please the powers that be? I understand how deeply   100
you have been wronged. Please stand by and wait until I pronounce
the verdict. You will then be released. [CH'EN *and* WU *are given
seats while he writes the verdict. A* GUARD *arrives with a court bulletin.*]
GUARD: [*To* CHANG.] Today's bulletin contains an important new
decree. Please read it, Your Honour.
CHANG: [*Reading it aloud.*] "In accordance with Prime Minister Ma's 105
memorial concerning the swift execution of rebels to pacify the
country, Chou Piao and Lei Yin-tso, who plotted with the Prince
of Lu and have been conclusively proved traitors, should promptly
be executed to vindicate justice. A decree is hereby issued to that
effect. Furthermore, a memorial has been presented by Vice-Minis-   110
ter of War Juan which runs as follows: 'Concerning the extermina-
tion of secret societies and the pacification of the country: it has
been discovered that the former members of the Eastern Forest
Party are still as numerous as locusts darkening the sun, and the
young upstarts of the Revival Club are breeding like their larvae.   115
The locusts have already become a plague and must be wiped out.
Their larvae are the calamity of the future and should be exterminated as a precaution. I, Your Majesty's servant Juan Ta-ch'eng,
possess a black list of these locusts and larvae. Mass arrests will be
effected with the guidance of the aforesaid list.' The decree is   120
hereby issued that those enumerated on the list aforesaid are to
be searched for and arrested. The urgent attention of authorities
concerned is called with regard to these matters." [CHANG, *deeply
shocked.*] Ma and Juan are growing more and more vindictive. I'm
afraid no good man will survive. [*Sings.*]   125

> While I try to serve justice and mitigate penalties,
> They impose iniquitous laws and persecutions.
> A foul torrent has invaded our clean rivers,
> Every action of theirs is a monument of infamy.
> Soon they will catch everyone of worth in their evil snare;   130
> Few dare resist their authority.
> The members of the Revival Club and Eastern Forest Party
> Will be hunted down as victims of the new tyranny.

[*To* HOU, CH'EN, *and* WU.] Sympathising with the wrongs you have
suffered, I was about to release you, but the latest decrees prevent   135
me. Not only are Masters Chou and Lei to be executed but all
members of the Eastern Forest Party and Revival Club are proscribed.
HOU, CH'EN and WU: [*Kneeling.*] We implore your Honour to save us.
CHANG: If I released you, you might be caught by others. Then you   140

would certainly be doomed. I advise you to be patient. [*Reading aloud as he writes.*] "After cross-examination, no evidence of secret organizations or bribery could be discovered. The accused should be kept in temporary custody. When Ts'ai Yi-so becomes available as a witness, the verdict will be given." [*To* HOU, CH'EN, *and* WU.]   145
Although he is mainly concerned with self-advancement, the City Marshal is not devoid of conscience. I shall send him a personal letter. [*Reading aloud as he writes.*] "Having served for many years in the Imperial Guard, I have seen more than most people of victims sacrificed to intrigue. I have reached the conclusion that the   150
good and the evil are in perpetual conflict: they rise and fall alternately. Every situation changes after a crisis. We who are responsible for preserving justice and the law should beware of favouritism. It is not our business to wield the butcher's knife for those in temporary power. There is a heaven above, and public opinion never dies.   155
Let us avoid mistakes we shall never cease to regret." [*He bows to* HOU, CH'EN, *and* WU.] Please wait patiently in confinement for the day when these wrongs will be righted. [*The prisoners are led off, and* CHANG *continues.*] I served the late Emperor throughout his reign, but now that the country is ruined and my home destroyed,   160
I have given up all hope of a future career. Why should I continue in the service of tyrants? There is an old proverb, "When you make a decision, don't wait till the day is over." I can hesitate no longer. [*Calls.*] Groom, bring my horse. I shall ride to my Pine Wind Pavilion. [GROOM *leads in horse.* CHANG *mounts it, singing.*]   165

> In the Spring, evening petals fill the sky,
> Green undulating mountains soothe the eye.
> South of the city, I waken from a dream
> As a tired traveller finds a gushing stream.

[*Speaks.*] Here I am back in my Pine Wind Pavilion. It seems as   170
far from the world as the Peach Blossom Spring. I'll go and enjoy the view. [*Sings as he goes upstairs.*]

> Few people approach this stream among the rocks.
> The wind in the pines recalls the murmur of waves.

[*Calls.*] Tell the gardener to open the windows and sweep the   175
porch.
GARDENER: [*Entering, sweeps and recites.*]

> Catkins have flown where the swallow settles,
> Cobwebs have caught the flying petals.

[*Speaks.*] The porch is swept clean, Your Honour. [*Exit.*]
CHANG: [*Gazing out from the porch.*] How the shadows of the pines   180
caress the window. My heart feels calm and rested. This would be a suitable place to put my couch. [*Wanders across to the balcony.*] Spring water fills the pond and casts a green reflection on my beard. Here I ought to set up a tea-stove. [*Laughing.*] What a hurry I was in! I am still wearing my official uniform, most unbecoming to this   185
hermitage. I must look ridiculous. [*To* SERVANT.] Open my bamboo

chest. I shall change into my loose robe, straw sandals, and bamboo
hat. [*Changes and sings.*]

> This is my compensation for old age.
> Once my three houses are roofed with plain bamboo   190
> I'll pack my uniform.

[*Enter* GUARD *with* TS'AI YI-SO.]

GUARD: Among pines he must still preside over the law, and among
  the bamboos over documents pore. I have just captured Ts'ai Yi-so.
  Though His Honour Chang has left his office, I must report that
  his order has been executed. [*Calls.*] Is anybody there?   195
SERVANT: What urgent business has brought you so far from the city?
GUARD: Please report that Ts'ai Yi-so is at His Honour's disposal.
SERVANT: [*Goes upstairs and announces.*] The guard has caught Ts'ai
  Yi-so, and he is waiting for Your Honour's instructions.
CHANG: Now that this has happened, what can I do about the others?   200
  Tell the guard to wait downstairs and listen to me. [*To* GUARD *from
  the porch.*] This is a very serious case and it must be kept secret.
  Ts'ai Yi-so is one of the chief witnesses; he will have to remain
  here. I shall question him presently.
GUARD: Yes, Your Honour. [GUARD *fastens* TS'AI *to a tree, and is about*   205
  to leave when he is recalled.]
CHANG: Come back. You may take my horse to the city as well as
  my official cap, belt, robe, and boots. I wish to meditate in peace.
  Remember not to disturb me here again. [*Exit* GUARD *with horse,
  etc.* CHANG *stamps his foot.*] What an outrage, that a guard should
  trespass in my private garden and tie a witness to my favourite pine-   210
  tree! What sort of a hermitage is this? I shall have to see the prisoner. [*Seeing* TS'AI.] So it is you, Ts'ai Yi-so.
TS'AI: Perhaps Your Honour may remember meeting me before?
CHANG: Of course I do, but that has nothing to do with the case. You
  have been accused of violating the new decree by harbouring rebels   215
  of the Revival Club.
TS'AI: [*Trying to kowtow.*] Yes, Your Honour.
CHANG: The latest books in your shop have some connection with the
  members of that club. They will be held as evidence against you.
TS'AI: [*Again trying to kowtow.*] Please be merciful, Your Honour!   220
CHANG: Your life can only be saved if you are willing to sacrifice your
  fortune.
TS'AI: I'm willing to give up everything.
CHANG: [*Delighted.*] Then everything will turn out well. [*To servant.*]
  Unbind him quickly. [TS'AI *is released.* CHANG *says to him.*] If you   225
  are willing to give up your property, why not follow me to the hills?
TS'AI: My life depends on Your Honour.
CHANG: [*Pointing.*] Look towards the northeast. How white the clouds
  are and how blue the hills. [*To* SERVANT.] Take good care of the
  house. Master Ts'ai and I are going to view the scenery. We shall   230
  soon return.

[*Exit* SERVANT. CHANG *and* TS'AI *walk along together.*]

CHANG: [*Points.*] We shall spend tonight in the green forest.

TS'AI: If Your Honour wants to enjoy mountain scenery, you should send a servant to prepare lodgings in advance. Otherwise where can you stay except in some secluded temple?   235

CHANG: You are still in the dark. Once I have surrendered my official cap, I shall become a poor Taoist priest. Any mountain cave will serve me for a dwelling.

TS'AI: What does Your Honour mean?

CHANG: Come, hesitate no longer. Ask no questions. Follow me.   240
[*Sings.*]

> My eyes are fixed upon the floating clouds,
> Regardless of the rocky distances.
> Slowly the pine woods darken, peace descends.
> Deep in the forest men are very few;
> A lonely path will wind between the peaks.   245
> Over the hills I'll walk with open heart,
> Visiting all the temples and forgetting
> Whatever dynasty may rule the land.
> In the realm of Immortals, far from the world's dust,
> A few wild peaches will be my nourishment.   250
> Now I know how easy it is to escape the turmoil.
> At dawn we shall leave our hut among the clouds;
> When we reach the summit the sun will still be high.

*   *   *

Scenes 31 to 39 Summary

Su K'un-sheng goes off to seek General Tso, the protégé of Hou Fang-yü's father, to tell him of the unjust imprisonment of Hou Fang-yü and the evils being worked by the Juan Ta-ch'eng faction. Tso, enraged, decides to move his army against Nanking but is blocked by armies sent out of the city and dies. Meanwhile Juan Ta-ch'eng and Ma Shih-ying hold a memorial service for the former Ming emperor, and their theatrical hypocrisy is a mockery of the service that Chang Wei had earlier vowed to hold.

With the Ming armies in total disarray, Shih-k'o Fa prepares for a desperate defense of the great city of Yang-chou against the advancing Manchu armies. Yang-chou falls, and the Manchu army moves down on the southern capital Nanking, from which everyone is trying to flee. Ma Shih-ying and Juan Ta-ch'eng are attacked by rioters, beaten, and stripped of their possessions. Fragrant Princess escapes from the inner palace, and Hou Fang-yü and his friends in the Revival Club are released from jail. The puppet emperor, Prince Fu, flees to one of his generals, but the general's subordinates kill the general and plan to offer the prince to the Manchus. By different routes Hou Fang-yü, his friends, and Fragrant Princess all reach refuge in two Taoist temples in the mountains.

SCENE 40

Entering the Way[9]

1645, SEVENTH MONTH

[*Enter* CHANG WEI. *He wears the broad-sleeved robe and gourd-shaped hat of a Taoist priest, and carries a whisk.*[1]]

CHANG: [*Sings.*]

> The blush of youth had faded from my cheeks
> Ere half a life-span in the dusty world.
> Too long I watched the puppet-play,
> Wept tears, and then in turn laughed loud.
> No more of folly. In these secluded haunts,   5
> Few men have ever cherished worldly sorrows.

[*Speaks.*] Ever since I retired from the official world, I have lived in seclusion in this White Cloud Temple under the name of Chang the Taoist. This is my lot, to cultivate the Way and have no more to do with the world's affairs. It was my good fortune to be   10 accompanied here by Ts'ai Yi-so, the bookseller, who brought five cartloads of classics and histories. Lan Ying the painter made the same resolution, and he has painted scrolls depicting our rustic retreat. So, since in these bare hills I can study and let my fancy roam to my heart's content, when the time comes for my Transfor-   15 mation[2] it will be no doltish ignoramus who ascends to the clouds. The one regret that persists from my former life is my failure to repay the gracious favour of His Majesty the Emperor Ch'ung-chen. Therefore today, the fifteenth day of the seventh month, I have invited many celebrants to a major memorial service for His   20 late Majesty. I have been fortunate enough also to secure the attendance of a former Master of Ceremonies from Nanking, who with some of the local elders will offer the prayers. Now let me call my disciple to make sure all is ready. Boy!

TS'AI and LAN: [*Entering in Taoist garb, recite.*]

> Farewell to dusty world;   25
> In the clouds we gather as followers of the Way.
> Greetings from Ts'ai Yi-so and Lan Ying.

CHANG: Do you both prepare the altars and lead our brethren in the ritual. I will purify myself and change my garments so that I may offer up prayer with the utmost devotion. Truly a pure repast before   30 the gods, an offering from the chaste hearts of men.

[CHANG *exits.* TS'AI *and* LAN *set up a triple altar which they furnish with incense, flowers, fruits, and tea. They set up banners and tablets, and then sing.*]

TS'AI and LAN together: [*Singing.*]

> As the sun rises from the sea, we build our high altar.
> All spirits of the sky, appear!

---

9. The life of a Taoist hermit.   1. Held as a religious sign.   2. Becoming immortal.

Lords of the stars and planets, come to audience!
Your banners float on the breeze   35
As prayers ascend for the seventh-month sacrifices.

TS'AI: The altar is raised and furnished. All is ready.
LAN: And lo, here comes a throng of village elders with gifts of wine
and incense.
    [*Enter* MASTER OF CEREMONIES *at the head of a crowd of* VILLAGERS.
    They bear wine, incense, paper money, and embroidered banners.]
VILLAGERS: [*Sing.*]

> Home-brewed wines we bear,   40
> Incense purple and yellow
> We've wrapped in broidered kerchiefs.
> Upward we gaze, to the royal Throne
> In the Jade Palace of the Purest Void,
> And ask: How came our Emperor   45
> To leave us villagers fatherless? [*They weep.*]
> Now in the seventh month, deep in the folded hills,
> Offerings we burn to His late Majesty.

[*They greet* TS'AI *and* LAN, *and say.*] Reverend Sirs, we of the laity
are all present and prepared for the service. Please ask His Rever-   50
ence the Abbot to come forth and circumambulate the altar.
TS'AI and LAN: [*Calling offstage.*] All is in readiness for Your Reverence to circumambulate the altar and perform the rites of purification.
    [*Three drumbeats. Four* TAOIST MUSICIANS *appear.* TS'AI *and* LAN *put
    on robes decorated with magic symbols, and follow behind bearing
    censers. Last comes* CHANG, *in similar robe and gold mitre. He walks
    around the altar, carrying a vial of water and a pine branch with
    which he conducts the rituals of purification.*]
ALL: [*Singing.*]

> Hands new purified   55
> Flourish branch of pine,
> Scatter healing dew
> In droplets superfine.
> Round the altar and around,
> Thrice threefold and nine: 60
> Banish dust, vanish lust,
> From this place divine.
> Incense smoke ascending,
> Cloud with cloud entwine,
> Airy palace towers   65
> For his royal line.

[*Exit* CHANG.]
TS'AI and LAN: [*Calling to* CHANG, *offstage.*] The ritual of purification
is complete. Now let Your Reverence change your robe and offer
the memorial prayer at the altar.
    [TS'AI *and* LAN *proceed to set up the tablet of the Emperor Ch'ung-
    chen on the central altar. On the left are set the tablets of the civil*

martyrs of the year 1644, and on the right the tablets of the military martyrs of the same year. Soft music plays. CHANG *enters wearing a nine-ridged hat (indicating highest rank in the bureaucracy) and a crane-embroidered robe of audience. His thick-soled boots also are such as are worn in Imperial audience. He wears a golden girdle and carries an ivory tablet.*]

CHANG: [*Kneeling.*] Let the stars of the heavens lend brightness to the   70
vision of the Land of the Immortals. Let the winds and the thunder bear word that the gates of Heaven be opened. Here in all reverence we implore the attendance of His Imperial Majesty Ch'ung-chen and of all noble martyrs, both civil and military. Let the Imperial procession now appear in all its splendour, flanked by gleaming   75
banners and followed by the attendant throng. Ride the white clouds to where we humbly await Your Imperial Presence with offerings of sacred music and hallowed wine.

[*Music sounds.* CHANG *makes a triple libation[3] and prostrates himself four times.* MASTER OF CEREMONIES *and* VILLAGERS *join in his prostrations.*]

CHANG: [*Sings.*]

> Adepts here assembled
> Implore Your Majesty to descend from the azure clouds.   80
> Leave Coal Hill,[4] the fatal tree,
> Untie the silken sash,
> Come relish pepper wine,
> Breathe incense of the pine,
> Lament no more the crimes of bandit rogues.   85
> No earthly pomp can last a thousand years,
> But in these hills your spirit lives forever.

[CHANG *exits.* TS'AI *and* LAN *make libations at either side of the stage, then prostrate themselves.* MASTER OF CEREMONIES *and* VILLAGERS *join in the prostrations.*]

TS'AI and LAN together: [*Singing.*]

> For every martyr's soul we pray
> Who died on that ill-fated day.
> All who found death by slow starvation,   90
> Knife, or well, or strangulation,
> Let no more rage your bosoms fill,
> Join us here and feast at will.

[*They speak.*] Now pour libations and burn the spirit offerings, that the spirits may be escorted to their heavenly home.   95

[*All present burn paper offerings, make libations, and wail.*]

MASTER OF CEREMONIES: Now for the first time they have been fittingly bewailed.

VILLAGERS: Having expressed our devotion, let us go to our own pure repast. [*Exeunt.*]

---

3. Pours out wine three times as an offering.   4. Where the Ming emperor Ch'ung-chen hanged himself.

TS'AI and LAN: [*Calling to* CHANG, *offstage.*] The ceremonies of invita-   100
tion are completed. Now is the time for Your Reverence to change
your robes and ascend to the altar to offer food to the wandering
souls.

> [TS'AI *and* LAN *set out the food offerings. To soft music,* CHANG *re-
> enters, now wearing a turban and a cloak trimmed with crane's down,
> and carrying his whisk. After prostrating himself, he ascends the steps
> of the altar. When* TS'AI *and* LAN *have assumed their positions behind
> him, he strikes the altar with his fist.*]

CHANG: Though endless spread the sandy battlefields, raising our eyes
we see the mansions of Heaven; lost as we are in the boundless   105
ocean of sorrows, turning our heads we see the Isles of Blessing.
We commemorate the host of those who gave their lives for their
country, whether they fought hard by the capital or in the central
plains, south of the great lakes or far in the desert northwest;
whether to them came death by water, death by fire, death by   110
sword's edge, death by arrow, death beneath trampling feet, or
death from sickness and starvation. Though your bones lie tangled
in thorny thickets, though your spirits flicker as will-o'-the-wisps,
come to our holy hill, our sacred altar. Come drink the cup that
agelong will quench your thirst. Come taste the grain that for a   115
thousand springs will be your nourishment. [*He scatters grains of
rice, sprinkles water, and burns paper offerings. Then he sings.*]

> Out on the dusty battlefield
> With wild herbs overgrown,
> Crimson stains of blood must yield
> To slowly whitening bone.   120
> In howl of wind, rage of rain,
> Homeward gazing, they gaze in vain.
> Poor ghosts who linger drear and chill:
> Come eat this once, come eat your fill.

TS'AI and LAN: Now the gifts of food have been made, it is time for   125
Your Reverence to send forth the rays of holy light which will illumine the Three Realms,[5] so that the wandering spirits may be
guided each to his proper altar.

CHANG: They have been long in Heaven, the souls of the martyrs of
last year's disaster.   130

TS'AI and LAN: But what of the victims of this year's struggle, Prince
and ministers pitted against the north? We entreat you to seek a
sign of what fates have befallen them.

CHANG: Then attend with steadfast hearts while I offer incense and
enter meditation, closing my eyes to see the more intently. [TS'AI   135
and LAN *stand with bowed heads, incense sticks held before them.
A long pause ensues.*] No, I find no manifestation of the Emperor
Hung-kuang, the two Generals Liu, T'ien Hsiung, and the rest.
They must still be among the living.

5. From Buddhism, the realms of Desire, Form, and Formlessness.

TS'AI and LAN: What of Shih K'o-fa, Tso Liang-yü, and Huang Te-
kung, who died in this year's fighting?   140
CHANG: Let me see.

> [*He closes his eyes, whereupon there enters, to soft music, a* WHITE-
> BEARDED FIGURE *wearing court headdress and crimson robe. His face
> is covered with a yellow silk cloth, and he has a retinue of* ATTEN-
> DANTS *carrying streamers of silk such as decorate shrines.*]

FIRST APPARITION: I, Shih K'o-fa, former Field Marshal and President
of the Board of War, am newly appointed Original of the Purple
Void, in the Palace of Great Purity. To this post I now ride.

> [*He mimes the act of riding, and exits. A* SECOND FIGURE, *in gold
> armour and with a red silk cloth over his face, enters to drums and
> pipes. His retinue carries banners.*]

SECOND APPARITION: I, Tso Liang-yü, former Earl of Southern Peace,   145
am newly appointed Heaven-soaring Envoy. To this post I now
ride.

> [*He exists. A* THIRD FIGURE *enters with banners, drums, and pipes.
> His armour is silver, and the cloth over his face is black.*]

THIRD APPARITION: I, Huang Te-kung, former Earl of Southern Tran-
quillity, am newly appointed Heaven-roaming Envoy. To this post
I now ride. [*Exit.*]   150
CHANG: [*Opens his eyes.*] Wonderful! I have just had visions of Their
Excellencies Shih K'o-fa, Tso Liang-yü, and Huang Te-kung, each
riding to assume a glorious new appointment in Heaven. [*Sings.*]

> Celestial steeds astride the clouds,
> In heroes' pride they go.   155
> Heavenly music sounds on every side,
> Banners and parasols wave,
> Swords, robes, and insignia befit
> The majesty of other-worldly office.
> High Heaven recognized their worth,   160
> And now they ride in glory.

TS'AI and LAN: [*Bowing with folded hands.*] Homage to Heaven's
Lord! Thus virtue reaps reward, and the justice of Heaven is displayed for all to see. [*Turning to* CHANG.] But what retribution has
befallen the traitors Ma Shih-ying and Juan Ta-ch'eng?   165
CHANG: Let me see.

> [*Enter, running, a* FOURTH FIGURE, *with dishevelled hair and
> clothes.*]

FOURTH APPARITION: After a lifetime of misdeeds, I, Ma Shih-ying,
met my end in the T'aichou Mountains. [*Following him comes
the* SPIRIT OF THE THUNDERCLAP, *who chases him around the stage.
The* APPARITION *kneels, clutching his head.*] Have mercy! Have
mercy!   170

> [*The* SPIRIT *strikes him dead, strips his body, and departs. Enter a*
> FIFTH FIGURE *in court robes and girdle.*]

FIFTH APPARITION: Done it! A superb achievement for Juan Ta-ch'eng,
to cross this Ridge of the Immortals!

[*He climbs a peak, whereupon the* MOUNTAIN SPIRIT *and* ATTENDANT
YAKSHAS[6] *enter and push him off. He falls to his death.*]

CHANG: [*Opens his eyes.*] Horror, horror! A vision of Ma Shih-ying
struck dead by a thunderbolt in the T'aichou Mountains, and Juan
Ta-ch'eng fallen to his death from the Ridge of the Immortals. 175
Each with his skull cracked open, terrible to behold. [*Sings.*]

> Bright is the image in the karmic mirror,[7]
> Close is the mesh of Heaven's all-compassing net.
> Flee where you may over a thousand hills,
> Thunder Spirit and Yakshas will hunt you down.   180
> Those who have scooped the brains from so many skulls,
> Will scarcely feed a dog with their remains.

TS'AI and LAN: [*Hands folded.*] Homage to Heaven's Lord! Thus evil
meets retribution, and the justice of Heaven is displayed for all to
see. [*Turning to* CHANG.] Your attendants still lack the fullest 185
understanding. We beseech Your Reverence to fill our ears with
truth.

[*While* CHANG *raises his whisk and sings at the top of his voice,* MAS-
TER OF CEREMONIES *and* VILLAGERS *re-enter to listen respectfully,
incense sticks held before them.*]

CHANG: [*Sings.*]

> Every mortal creature's
> Misdeeds, however small,
> However closely hidden,   190
> To his account must fall.
> And yet the karmic circle
> Each merit will recall,
> Reward and retribution
> Made visible to all.   195
> North succeeds to South,
> State gives way to state,
> Each dynastic cycle
> Predeterminate.
> Just men and the ungodly   200
> Meet their appointed fate,
> Sure of resolution,
> Whether soon or late.

[MASTER OF CEREMONIES *and* VILLAGERS *kowtow and exit. Enter* FRA-
GRANT PRINCESS *with* PIEN YÜ-CHING.]

PIEN: Happiest in all this world are those who devote themselves to
acts of piety. In the company of Taoist priestesses we have set up 205
banners before the altar to the Empress Chou, and now we come
to hear the Abbot in his sermon hall.

FRAGRANT PRINCESS: Am I permitted to accompany you?

PIEN: See, here is a throng of Taoist priests and laymen, there can be
no harm in our presence as observers.   210

[PIEN *prostrates herself before the altar, then takes up a position at*

---

6. Demon messengers from the underworld, in popular Buddhist belief.   7. A metaphor for seeing the
fate suffered by those who committed misdeeds during their lifetimes.

one side, with FRAGRANT PRINCESS. *Enter the minstrel* TING CHI-
CHIH.]

TING: Hard to ensure return in mortal form; mysterious and secret is
the Way. [*He prostrates himself before the altar, then rises and calls
offstage.*] Master Hou, come see the sermon hall.

[HOU FANG-YÜ *hastens onstage.*]

HOU: At last! Long have I suffered in the dusty world. Now to seek
bliss beyond its narrow confines. [*He follows* TING *to a position at*   215
the other side of the stage from FRAGRANT PRINCESS.]

CHANG: [*Pounds his lectern.*] You, my hearers, hearts turned to piety:
know that only the total voidance of your dusty desires can free you
to rise towards purity. One single speck of lingering mortal passion,
and you are condemned to a thousand further revolutions of the
wheel of karma.   220

[*Concealing his face with his fan,* HOU *peers at* FRAGRANT PRINCESS,
and starts in astonishment.]

HOU: That is my Fragrant Princess! How can it be that I find her
standing here? [*He hurries over to* FRAGRANT PRINCESS *and tugs at
her hand. She is equally startled to see him.*]

FRAGRANT PRINCESS: It is Master Hou! Oh, the longing for you has
almost caused my death! [*Sings.*]

> Ah, when I recall   225
> The abruptness of our parting!
> No bridge was ours, to cross the Milky Way;
> Higher than Heaven seemed the walls between us.
> No letters could we exchange,
> Dreams were a vain recourse,   230
> Longing was endless;
> And when I left the palace,
> Ever more distant wanderings seemed to face me.

HOU: [*Points to the fan.*] Gazing on the peach blossoms of this fan, I
have asked myself how I could ever requite you. [*Sings.*]   235

> The blossoms on this fan:
> Were they really formed from bloodstains?
> Or are they the petals that rained down
> When the holy Abbot preached?[8]

[HOU *and* FRAGRANT PRINCESS *look at the fan together. Then they are
dragged apart by* TING *and* PIEN.]

TING: You should not discuss private matters while the Abbot is in the   240
middle of his sermon.

[HOU *and* FRAGRANT PRINCESS *take no notice, and* CHANG *pounds his
lectern again.*]

CHANG: Tchah! What kind of fractious children are these who babble
of love before this sacred altar? [*He hastens down, tears the fan
from the hands of* HOU *and* FRAGRANT PRINCESS, *and flings it to*

---

8. According to Buddhist legend, when Abbot Kuang-ch'ang reached the climax of this exposition of the
sutras, a shower of flower petals fell from the sky.

the ground.] This a place of sanctity, not to be defiled by wanton youths.

TS'AI: Ai-ya! But Your Reverence knows this man. It is Hou Fang-yü of Honan.

CHANG: And the girl?

LAN: I know her. She is Fragrant Princess, who became Master Hou's bride.

CHANG: And what has brought them here?

TING: Master Hou is residing at my Gather Purity Temple.

PIEN: And Fragrant Princess at my Foster Purity Temple.

HOU: [*Bowing to* CHANG.] And you, sir, are Chang Wei, from whom in former days I received much favour.

CHANG: Master Hou, I am delighted to see you released from prison. Did you know it was because of you that I left the world to follow the Way?

HOU: No, I had no means of knowing that.

TS'AI: I also left the world on your account. I shall tell you the story all in good time.

LAN: And I came here as escort to Fragrant Princess in her search for you. I little dreamed that we should find you at last.

HOU: How shall Fragrant Princess and I ever repay the debts we owe to you, Ting Chi-chih and Pien Yü-ching, who gave us refuge, or to you, Ts'ai Yi-so and Lan Ying, who aided our search for each other?

FRAGRANT PRINCESS: And Su K'un-sheng also accompanied me here.

HOU: And Liu Ching-t'ing came in my company.

FRAGRANT PRINCESS: We owe so much to Su and Liu, who stayed loyally beside us in defiance of all hardships.

HOU: When we are home once more as man and wife, we shall endeavour to repay their kindness.

CHANG: What is all this meaningless chatter? How laughable to cling to your amorous desires when the world has been turned upside down!

HOU: Sir, you are mistaken. The marriage of man with maid is the source of human relationship. Sorrows of separation, joys of reunion, all these are the fruits of love. Why should you object to our discussion of them?

CHANG: [*Angrily.*] Pshaw! Two piteous passion-clinging bugs! Where now is the nation, where the home, where the prince, where the father? Can't you get rid of this miserable infatuation? [*Sings.*]

> Alas for silly youths,
> Ignorant of the changing of their world.
> A stream of lascivious chatter,
> Hand in hand they plan their marital bliss,
> Here, in the very presence of the spirits!
> Can't you divine love's final dissolution,
> Hear the flapping of wings
> As the mandarin ducks fly apart,

> See the shattered fragments
> Of the jewelled mirror of union?
> Are you not ashamed to hear
> The laughter your performance brings?   295
> Are you not ready to follow
> The broad highway of Escape?

HOU: [*Bows.*] I hear your words and wake from my dream, drenched
in a chilling sweat.
CHANG: Do you understand them?
HOU: I understand.
CHANG: Then if you do, salute Ting Chi-chih as your tutor. [HOU *does*
so.]
FRAGRANT PRINCESS: I also understand.   300
CHANG: If you also understand, salute Pien Yü-ching as your tutor.
[*She does so.*]
CHANG: [*To* TING *and* PIEN.] Help them change into Taoist robes. 305
[*They do so.*]
TING and PIEN: Ascend to your seat, Your Reverence, so that we may
present our disciples.
> [CHANG *takes his seat, and* TING *and* PIEN *lead* HOU *and* FRAGRANT
> PRINCESS *to prostrate themselves before him.*]
TING and PIEN together: [*Singing.*]

> Crop the sprouts of love
> And see them wither, the sprigs of gold and jade.
> Root out passion   310
> From these descendants of the dragon and phoenix.
> Life is brief as bubble of foam,
> Short as spark, struck from stone.
> Let them spend their remnant years
> Following our doctrine.   315

CHANG: For the male, let the south be his direction. Let Hou Fang-
yü depart for the southernmost hills, there to cultivate the Way.
HOU: I go. Understanding the Way, I perceive the depths of my folly.
[TING *leads* HOU *offstage.*]
CHANG: For the female, let her direction be the north. Let Fragrant
Princess depart for the northernmost hills, there to cultivate the 320
Way.
FRAGRANT PRINCESS: I go. All is illusion; I know not that man before
me.
> [PIEN *leads* FRAGRANT PRINCESS *offstage, the opposite side from* HOU*'s*
> *exit.* CHANG *descends from his seat and utters three great shouts of*
> *laughter.*]
CHANG: [*Sings.*]

> See them take their leave
> With never a backward glance.   325
> My task it was to shred the peach blossom fan,
> That never more the strands of folly
> Shall bind the heart of man and maid.

White bones are laid in the dust,
The southern realm concludes its span.   330
Dreams of revival fall to earth
In shreds with the peach blossom fan.

*   *   *

Summary   An epilogue follows (not printed here) in which Su K'un-sheng, Liu Ching-t'ing, and the Master of Ceremonies meet in the mountains three years later. Each recalls the events of the past, with Su K'un-sheng singing a long ballad about the ruins of Nanking, which he had recently visited. An emissary of the Ch'ing government makes an appearance and says that he is seeking virtuous men who are hiding in the mountains, so that he can bring them back to serve in the new government. When he tries to bring them in, they run off in different directions.

CAO XUEQIN (TS'AO HSÜEH-CH'IN)
1715–1763

Of all the world's novels perhaps only *Don Quixote* rivals *The Story of the Stone* as the embodiment of a nation's cultural identity in recent times, much as the epic once embodied cultural identity in the ancient world. For Chinese readers of the past two centuries *The Story of the Stone* (also known as the *Dream of the Red Chamber*) has come to represent the best and worst of traditional China in its final phase. It is the story of an extended family, centered around its women, and of the relationships within the family. Even after nearly a century of war, revolution, and social experiment, a century that has seen the dissolution of the traditional extended family, *The Story of the Stone* has retained its hold on the Chinese imagination.

As the title tells us, the novel is also, on a basic level, the story of a magical and conscious stone, the one block left over when the goddess Nü-wa repaired the damaged vault of the sky in the mythic past. Transported into the mortal world by a pair of priests, one Buddhist and one Taoist, Stone is destined to find enlightenment by suffering the pains of love, loss, and disillusion as a human being. In his incarnation, Stone is born as the sole legitimate male heir of a wealthy and powerful household, the Jias, which is about to pass from the height of prosperity into decline. Miraculously, the baby is born with an inscribed piece of jade in his mouth, from which he is given his name Bao-yu (Precious Jade) and which he wears always.

The novel itself has a peculiar genesis. The first eighty chapters are the work of Cao Xueqin, himself the scion of a once-wealthy family fallen on hard times. It is believed that he wrote the novel, in at least five drafts, between 1740 and 1750. There is another figure in the process of the novel's composition, someone who used the pseudonym "Red Inkstone" (or more properly "He of Red Inkstone Studio") and who added commentary and made corrections to the manuscript versions. He was obviously a close friend or relative of Cao Xueqin and acted the role of virtual collaborator. His comments suggest that the characters in the main portion of the novel are based on real people.

The novel was left unfinished and probably was never intended for publication, but it did circulate widely in Peking in manuscript copies, whose many variations show a complex process of revision. One version of the manuscript came into the hands of the writer Gao E (ca. 1740–ca. 1815), who completed the story by adding another 40 chapters, publishing the full 120-chapter version in 1791, about a half century after Cao Xueqin began to write. The transformations of the novel in its manuscript versions, the role of the mysterious Red Inkstone (and of another early commentator who calls himself "Odd Tablet"), and the relation of the characters to Cao's life are questions that continue to engage professional and amateur scholars.

Chinese novels are, as a rule, very long, and *The Story of the Stone* is longer than most, taking up five substantial volumes in its complete English translation. The narrative is impossible to summarize and difficult to excerpt. It has a huge cast of characters, both major and minor, who appear and disappear in intricately interwoven incidents. But, in part because of its very magnitude, the novel gradually draws its readers into the details of everyday life and the complexities of human relationships, occasionally punctuated by reminders that the intense emotions and the values given to things are all illusory. That sense of illusion is underscored by the family name Jia, a real Chinese surname that happens to be homophonous with another character meaning "false" or "feigned."

In addition to Bao-yu, the human metamorphosis of Stone, one other central character originates in the supernatural frame story and its fanciful landscape. This is Crimson Pearl Flower, a semidivine plant that grew near the Rock of Rebirth. In the opening chapter, while Stone is serving at the court of the goddess Disenchantment, he takes a fancy to this flower and waters it with sweet dew. This eventually brings the flower to life in the form of a fairy girl, who is obsessed with repaying the kindness of Stone, and for his gift of sweet dew she owes him the "debt of tears." This character is born as Bao-yu's cousin, the delicate and highstrung Lin Dai-yu (*Dai-yu* means "Black Jade").

The early chapters are devoted to the supernatural frame story and to bringing the characters together. In chapters seventeen and eighteen, Bao-yu's elder sister, an imperial concubine, has been permitted to pay a visit to her home. The women of the emperor's harem were usually confined to the palace; in permitting her to return, the emperor is displaying his favor to her and to her family. In her honor a huge garden (Prospect Garden) is constructed on the grounds of the family compound. After the imperial concubine's departure, the adolescent girls of the extended family are allowed to take up residence in the various buildings in the garden, and by special permission Bao-yu is also permitted to live there with his maids. The world of the garden is one of adolescent love in full flower, though we never forget the violent and ugly world outside, a world that often creeps into the garden world.

The adolescent love between Bao-yu and Dai-yu forms the core of the novel. Each is intensely sensitive to the other, and neither can express what he or she feels. Communication between them often depends on subtle gestures with implicit meanings, meanings that are inevitably misunderstood. Both, and particularly Dai-yu, believe in a perfect understanding of hearts, but even in the charmed world of the garden, closeness eludes them. The novel often juxtaposes brutish characters (usually male) with those possessed of a finer sensibility; but in the case of Dai-yu, sensibility is carried to the extreme. Dai-yu's relation to Bao-yu is balanced by that of another distant relation, Xue Bao-chai, whose plump good looks and gentle common sense are the very opposite of Dai-yu's frailty and histrionic morbidity. Bao-chai ("Precious Hairpin") has a golden locket with an inscription that matches Bao-yu's jade, and the marriage of "jade and gold" is a possibility seriously considered by older members of the family. Eventually, in Gao E's ending for the novel, as Dai-yu is dying of consumption, Bao-yu will be tricked into marrying Bao-chai. Bao-yu will finally carry out his obligation to continue the family line and at last renounce the world to become a Buddhist monk.

Although the triangle of Bao-yu, Dai-yu, and Bao-chai stands at the center of the novel, scores of subplots involve characters of all types. *The Story of the Stone* is, as noted, a novel about family, its internal relationships and its place in the larger social world. The reader easily becomes absorbed in the intensity of the family's internal relationships, always to be reminded how those relationships touch and are touched by the world outside. Because this family has social power, the actions taken by family members to serve its interests and loyalties can also be seen as corruption. In some cases the corruption is obvious, but in a far subtler way the reader comes to identify with the family and takes many acts of power and privilege for granted. At the same time, the outside world has the capacity to impinge on the protected space of the family, and the reader sees these forces from the point of view of the insider, as intrusions. It is a world of concentric circles of proximity, both of kinship and affinity. Petty details and private loves and hates grow larger and larger as they approach the center. And above this is the Buddhist and Taoist lesson about the illusion of care, of a world driven by blind but powerful emotions that at last cause only suffering, both to self and others.

The reader will find much unfamiliar about the Jia household, a vast establishment of close and distant family members, personal maids, and servants, each with his or her own level of status. Although the personal maids had some responsibilities, it will be obvious that the number of maids attached to each family member was primarily a mark of status. For a girl from a poor family, the position of personal maid was very desirable, providing room, board, and income to send to her own family. Bao-yu often flirts with his maids, but he has sexual relations only with his chief maid, Aroma.

The selection printed here includes part of the opening frame story and a series of chapters on Bao-yu and his female relations in Prospect Garden, with the blossoming of the love between him and Dai-yu.

There is a complete translation of *The Story of the Stone* in five volumes (1973–82), the first three volumes by David Hawkes and the last two by John Minford. Andrew Plaks, *Archetype and Allegory in the Dream of the Red Chamber* (1976), is a useful study.

PRONOUNCING GLOSSARY

The following list uses common English syllables to provide rough equivalents of selected words whose pronunciation may be unfamiliar to the general reader.

Cao Xueqin: *tsao shueh-chin*

Feng-shi: *fuhng–shir*

Feng Zi-ying: *fuhng dzuh–ying*

Gao E: *gau uh*

Jia Yu-cun: *jyah yow–tswuhn*

Jia Zheng: *jyah juhng*

Kong Mei-xi: *koong may–shee*

qiang: *chyahng*

Shi Xiang-yun: *shir shyahng–yoon*

Wang Ji-ren: *wahng jee–ruhn*

Wu Yu-feng: *woo yow–fuhng*

Xi-feng: *shee–fuhng*

Xue Bao-chai: *shooeh bau–chai*

Ying-lian: *ying–lyen*

Zhao: *jau*

Zhen Shi-yin: *juhn shir–yin*

Zhi-xiao: *juhr–shyau*

From The Story of the Stone[1]

From *Volume 1*

CHAPTER 1

Zhen Shi-yin makes the Stone's acquaintance in a dream
And Jia Yu-cun finds that poverty is not incompatible with romantic
feelings

Gentle Reader,

What, you may ask, was the origin of this book?

Though the answer to this question may at first seem to border on the absurd, reflection will show that there is a good deal more in it than meets the eye.

Long ago, when the goddess Nü-wa was repairing the sky, she melted down a great quantity of rock and, on the Incredible Crags of the Great Fable Mountains, moulded the amalgam into thirty-six thousand, five hundred and one large building blocks, each measuring seventy-two feet by a hundred and forty-four feet square. She used thirty-six thousand five hundred of these blocks in the course of her building operations, leaving a single odd block unused, which lay, all on its own, at the foot of Greensickness Peak in the aforementioned mountains.

Now this block of stone, having undergone the melting and moulding of a goddess, possessed magic powers. It could move about at will and could grow or shrink to any size it wanted. Observing that all the other blocks had been used for celestial repairs and that it was the only one to have been rejected as unworthy, it became filled with shame and resentment and passed its days in sorrow and lamentation.

One day, in the midst of its lamentings, it saw a monk and a Taoist approaching from a great distance, each of them remarkable for certain eccentricities of manner and appearance. When they arrived at the foot of Greensickness Peak, they sat down on the ground and began to talk. The monk, catching sight of a lustrous, translucent stone—it was in fact the rejected building block which had now shrunk itself to the size of a fan-pendant[2] and looked very attractive in its new shape—took it up on the palm of his hand and addressed it with a smile:

"Ha, I see you have magical properties! But nothing to recommend you. I shall have to cut a few words on you so that anyone seeing you will know at once that you are something special. After that I shall take you to a certain

brilliant
successful
poetical
cultivated
aristocratic
elegant
delectable

---

1. Translated by David Hawkes. Note that Hawkes used the pinyin system of spelling (whereas this volume usually uses the Wade-Giles system).   2. Jade decoration strung from the bottom of a fan.

> luxurious
> opulent
> locality on a little trip."

The stone was delighted.

"What words will you cut? Where is this place you will take me to? I beg to be enlightened."

"Do not ask," replied the monk with a laugh. "You will know soon enough when the time comes."

And with that he slipped the stone into his sleeve and set off at a great pace with the Taoist. But where they both went to I have no idea.

Countless aeons went by and a certain Taoist called Vanitas in quest of the secret of immortality chanced to be passing below that same Green-sickness Peak in the Incredible Crags of the Great Fable Mountains when he caught sight of a large stone standing there, on which the characters of a long inscription were clearly discernible.

Vanitas read the inscription through from beginning to end and learned that this was a once lifeless stone block which had been found unworthy to repair the sky, but which had magically transformed its shape and been taken down by the Buddhist mahāsattva[3] Impervioso and the Taoist illuminate Mysterioso into the world of mortals, where it had lived out the life of a man before finally attaining nirvana and returning to the other shore.[4] The inscription named the country where it had been born, and went into considerable detail about its domestic life, youthful amours, and even the verses, mottoes and riddles it had written. All it lacked was the authentication of a dynasty and date. On the back of the stone was inscribed the following quatrain:

> Found unfit to repair the azure sky
> Long years a foolish mortal man was I.
> My life in both worlds on this stone is writ:
> Pray who will copy out and publish it?

From his reading of the inscription Vanitas realized that this was a stone of some consequence. Accordingly he addressed himself to it in the following manner:

"Brother Stone, according to what you yourself seem to imply in these verses, this story of yours contains matter of sufficient interest to merit publication and has been carved here with that end in view. But as far as I can see (a) it has no discoverable dynastic period, and (b) it contains no examples of moral grandeur among its characters—no statesmanship, no social message of any kind. All I can find in it, in fact, are a number of females, conspicuous, if at all, only for their passion or folly or for some trifling talent or insignificant virtue. Even if I were to copy all this out, I cannot see that it would make a very remarkable book."

"Come, your reverence," said the stone (for Vanitas had been correct in assuming that it could speak) "must you be so obtuse? All the romances ever written have an artificial period setting—Han or Tang for the most part. In refusing to make use of that stale old convention and telling my

---

3. Wise man.   4. That is, achieving enlightenment and passing beyond the cycles of rebirth.

Story of the Stone exactly as it occurred, it seems to me that, far from *depriving* it of anything, I have given it a freshness these other books do not have.

"Your so-called 'historical romances,' consisting, as they do, of scandalous anecdotes about statesmen and emperors of bygone days and scabrous attacks on the reputations of long-dead gentlewomen, contain more wickedness and immorality than I care to mention. Still worse is the 'erotic novel,' by whose filthy obscenities our young folk are all too easily corrupted. And the 'boudoir romances,' those dreary stereotypes with their volume after volume all pitched on the same note and their different characters undistinguishable except by name (all those ideally beautiful young ladies and ideally eligible young bachelors)—even they seem unable to avoid descending sooner or later into indecency.

"The trouble with this last kind of romance is that it only gets written in the first place because the author requires a framework in which to show off his love-poems. He goes about constructing this framework quite mechanically, beginning with the names of his pair of young lovers and invariably adding a third character, a servant or the like, to make mischief between them, like the *chou*[5] in a comedy.

"What makes these romances even more detestable is the stilted, bombastic language—inanities dressed in pompous rhetoric, remote alike from nature and common sense and teeming with the grossest absurdities.

"Surely my 'number of females,' whom I spent half a lifetime studying with my own eyes and ears, are preferable to this kind of stuff? I do not claim that they are better people than the ones who appear in books written before my time; I am only saying that the contemplation of their actions and motives may prove a more effective antidote to boredom and melancholy. And even the inelegant verses with which my story is interlarded could serve to entertain and amuse on those convivial occasions when rhymes and riddles are in demand.

"All that my story narrates, the meetings and partings, the joys and sorrows, the ups and downs of fortune, are recorded exactly as they happened. I have not dared to add the tiniest bit of touching-up, for fear of losing the true picture.

"My only wish is that men in the world below may sometimes pick up this tale when they are recovering from sleep or drunkenness, or when they wish to escape from business worries or a fit of the dumps, and in doing so find not only mental refreshment but even perhaps, if they will heed its lesson and abandon their vain and frivolous pursuits, some small arrest in the deterioration of their vital forces. What does your reverence say to that?"

For a long time Vanitas stood lost in thought, pondering this speech. He then subjected *The Story of the Stone* to a careful second reading. He could see that its main theme was love; that it consisted quite simply of a true record of real events; and that it was entirely free from any tendency to deprave and corrupt. He therefore copied it all out from beginning to end and took it back with him to look for a publisher.

---

5. The stock role of the clown in a play.

As a consequence of all this, Vanitas, starting off in the Void (which is Truth) came to the contemplation of Form (which is Illusion); and from Form engendered Passion; and by communicating Passion, entered again into Form; and from Form awoke to the Void (which is Truth). He therefore changed his name from Vanitas to Brother Amor, or the Passionate Monk, (because he had approached Truth by way of Passion), and changed the title of the book from *The Story of the Stone* to *The Tale of Brother Amor.*

Old Kong Mei-xi from the homeland of Confucius called the book *A Mirror for the Romantic.* Wu Yu-feng called it *A Dream of Golden Days.* Cao Xueqin in his Nostalgia Studio worked on it for ten years, in the course of which he rewrote it no less than five times, dividing it into chapters, composing chapter headings, renaming it *The Twelve Beauties of Jin-ling,* and adding an introductory quatrain. Red Inkstone restored the original title when he recopied the book and added his second set of annotations to it.

This, then, is a true account of how *The Story of the Stone* came to be written.

> Pages full of idle words
> Penned with hot and bitter tears:
> All men call the author fool;
> None his secret message hears.

The origin of *The Story of the Stone* has now been made clear. The same cannot, however, be said of the characters and events which it recorded. Gentle reader, have patience! This is how the inscription began:

Long, long ago the world was tilted downwards towards the south-east; and in that lower-lying south-easterly part of the earth there is a city called Soochow; and in Soochow the district around the Chang-men Gate is reckoned one of the two or three wealthiest and most fashionable quarters in the world of men. Outside the Chang-men Gate is a wide thoroughfare called Worldly Way; and somewhere off Worldly Way is an area called Carnal Lane. There is an old temple in the Carnal Lane area which, because of the way it is bottled up inside a narrow *cul-de-sac,* is referred to locally as Bottle-gourd Temple. Next door to Bottle-gourd Temple lived a gentleman of private means called Zhen Shi-yin and his wife Feng-shi, a kind, good woman with a profound sense of decency and decorum. The household was not a particularly wealthy one, but they were nevertheless looked up to by all and sundry as the leading family in the neighbourhood.

Zhen Shi-yin himself was by nature a quiet and totally unambitious person. He devoted his time to his garden and to the pleasures of wine and poetry. Except for a single flaw, his existence could, indeed, have been described as an idyllic one. The flaw was that, although already past fifty, he had no son, only a little girl, just two years old, whose name was Ying-lian.

Once, during the tedium of a burning summer's day, Shi-yin was sitting idly in his study. The book had slipped from his nerveless grasp and his head had nodded down onto the desk in a doze. While in this drowsy state he seemed to drift off to some place he could not identify, where he became aware of a monk and a Taoist walking along and talking as they went.

"Where do you intend to take that thing you are carrying?" the Taoist was asking.

"Don't you worry about him!" replied the monk with a laugh. "There is a batch of lovesick souls awaiting incarnation in the world below whose fate is due to be decided this very day. I intend to take advantage of this opportunity to slip our little friend in amongst them and let him have a taste of human life along with the rest."

"Well, well, so another lot of these amorous wretches is about to enter the vale of tears," said the Taoist. "How did all this begin? And where are the souls to be reborn?"

"You will laugh when I tell you," said the monk. "When this stone was left unused by the goddess, he found himself at a loose end and took to wandering about all over the place for want of better to do, until one day his wanderings took him to the place where the fairy Disenchantment lives.

"Now Disenchantment could tell that there was something unusual about this stone, so she kept him there in her Sunset Glow Palace and gave him the honorary title of Divine Luminescent Stone-in-Waiting in the Court of Sunset Glow.

"But most of his time he spent west of Sunset Glow exploring the banks of the Magic River. There, by the Rock of Rebirth, he found the beautiful Crimson Pearl Flower, for which he conceived such a fancy that he took to watering her every day with sweet dew, thereby conferring on her the gift of life.

"Crimson Pearl's substance was composed of the purest cosmic essences, so she was already half-divine; and now, thanks to the vitalizing effect of the sweet dew, she was able to shed her vegetable shape and assume the form of a girl.

"This fairy girl wandered about outside the Realm of Separation, eating the Secret Passion Fruit when she was hungry and drinking from the Pool of Sadness when she was thirsty. The consciousness that she owed the stone something for his kindness in watering her began to prey on her mind and ended by becoming an obsession.

" 'I have no sweet dew here that I can repay him with,' she would say to herself. 'The only way in which I could perhaps repay him would be with the tears shed during the whole of a mortal lifetime if he and I were ever to be reborn as humans in the world below.'

"Because of this strange affair, Disenchantment has got together a group of amorous young souls, of which Crimson Pearl is one, and intends to send them down into the world to take part in the great illusion of human life. And as today happens to be the day on which this stone is fated to go into the world too, I am taking him with me to Disenchantment's tribunal for the purpose of getting him registered and sent down to earth with the rest of these romantic creatures."

"How very amusing!" said the Taoist. "I have certainly never heard of a debt of tears before. Why shouldn't the two of us take advantage of this opportunity to go down into the world ourselves and save a few souls? It would be a work of merit."

"That is exactly what I was thinking," said the monk. "Come with me to Disenchantment's palace to get this absurd creature cleared. Then, when this last batch of romantic idiots goes down, you and I can go down with them. At present about half have already been born. They await this last batch to make up the number."

"Very good, I will go with you then," said the Taoist. Shi-yin heard all this conversation quite clearly, and curiosity impelled him to go forward and greet the two reverend gentlemen. They returned his greeting and asked him what he wanted.

"It is not often that one has the opportunity of listening to a discussion of the operations of *karma*[6] such as the one I have just been privileged to overhear," said Shi-yin. "Unfortunately I am a man of very limited understanding and have not been able to derive the full benefit from your conversation. If you would have the very great kindness to enlighten my benighted understanding with a somewhat fuller account of what you were discussing, I can promise you the most devout attention. I feel sure that your teaching would have a salutary effect on me and—who knows— might save me from the pains of hell."

The reverend gentlemen laughed. "These are heavenly mysteries and may not be divulged. But if you wish to escape from the fiery pit, you have only to remember us when the time comes, and all will be well."

Shi-yin saw that it would be useless to press them. "Heavenly mysteries must not, of course, be revealed. But might one perhaps inquire what the 'absurd creature' is that you were talking about? Is it possible that I might be allowed to see it?"

"Oh, as for that," said the monk: "I think it is on the cards for you to have a look at *him*," and he took the object from his sleeve and handed it to Shi-yin.

Shi-yin took the object from him and saw that it was a clear, beautiful jade on one side of which were carved the words "Magic Jade." There were several columns of smaller characters on the back, which Shi-yin was just going to examine more closely when the monk, with a cry of "Here we are, at the frontier of Illusion," snatched the stone from him and disappeared, with the Taoist, through a big stone archway above which

THE LAND OF ILLUSION

was written in large characters. A couplet in smaller characters was inscribed vertically on either side of the arch:

> Truth becomes fiction when the fiction's true;
> Real becomes not-real where the unreal's real.

Shi-yin was on the point of following them through the archway when suddenly a great clap of thunder seemed to shake the earth to its very foundations, making him cry out in alarm.

---

6. The accumulation of good and bad deeds that determines a soul's future lives.

And there he was sitting in his study, the contents of his dream already half forgotten, with the sun still blazing on the ever-rustling plantains outside, and the wet-nurse at the door with his little daughter Ying-lian in her arms. Her delicate little pink-and-white face seemed dearer to him than ever at that moment, and he stretched out his arms to take her and hugged her to him.

✳   ✳   ✳

Chapters 1 to 25 Summary   After waking from his dream in the middle of the first chapter, Zhen Shi-yin meets the monk and the Taoist in the flesh, and they seek to take his daughter Ying-lian from him, informing him that otherwise she will be involved in misfortune. Zhen Shi-yin refuses and subsequently, in a series of misadventures, the baby is stolen from her nurse and will reappear in Chapter 4 as "Caltrop," raised by kidnappers and eventually sold to be the concubine of Xue Pan in the Jia household.

In Chapter 3 the scene shifts to the Jia household, which has made a home for the young Lin Dai-yu after her mother's death and for the Xue family, including Xue Pan and his sister Xue Bao-chai. The Xues had been a powerful family in Nanjing; but in acquiring Caltrop as his concubine, Xue Pan had another suitor beaten to death, and after Xue Pan had bribed his way out of a murder charge, the family thought it prudent to move to the capital to stay with their powerful relatives, the Jias.

The Jia household is dominated by Grandmother Jia, whose favorite is the adolescent Bao-yu, the only surviving son of Jia Zheng and his wife Lady Wang. Bao-yu, born with a piece of jade in his mouth, is the metamorphosis of Stone. Jia Zheng has another son, Jia Huan, by his concubine, known as Aunt Zhao. Note that concubinage was commonly practiced in large households, though normally only the sons of the legitimate wife could inherit.

In Chapter 17 Prospect Garden is constructed to receive the visit of the imperial concubine, one of Lady Wang's daughters and Bao-yu's sister. After the visit, all the young girls of the household are given lodgings in the various buildings in the garden; Bao-yu, who is very close to his sisters and cousins and prefers the company of girls to boys, is also allowed to take up residence in the garden.

As we pick up the story in Chapter 25, Jia Huan has spilled hot wax on his half brother Bao-yu's face in a fit of jealousy. Lady Wang rebukes Aunt Zhao for the behavior of her son, and Aunt Zhao, in a rage, pays a sorceress to cast a spell on Bao-yu. Bao-yu is ill for a while, but recovers.

CHAPTER 26

*A conversation on Wasp Waist Bridge is a cover for
communication of a different kind
And a soliloquy overhead in the Naiad's House reveals
unsuspected depths of feeling.*

By the time the thirty-three days' convalescence had ended, not only were Bao-yu's health and strength completely restored, but even the burnmarks on his face had vanished, and he was allowed to move back into the Garden.

It may be recalled that when Bao-yu's sickness was at its height, it had been found necessary to call in Jia Yun[7] with a number of pages under his command to take turns in watching over him. Crimson[8] was there too at that time, having been brought in with the other maids from his apartment. During those few days she and Jia Yun therefore had ample opportunity of seeing each other, and a certain familiarity began to grow up between them.

Crimson noticed that Jia Yun was often to be seen sporting a handkerchief very much like the one she had lost. She nearly asked him about it, but in the end was too shy. Then, after the monk's visit, the presence of the menfolk was no longer required and Jia Yun went back to his tree-planting. Though Crimson could still not dismiss the matter entirely from her mind, she did not ask anyone about it for fear of arousing their suspicions.

A day or two after their return to Green Delights,[9] Crimson was sitting in her room, still brooding over this handkerchief business, when a voice outside the window inquired whether she was in. Peeping through an eyelet in the casement she recognized Melilot,[1] a little maid who belonged to the same apartment as herself.

"Yes, I'm in," she said. "Come inside!"

Little Melilot came bounding in and sat down on the bed with a giggle.

"I'm in luck!" she said. "I was washing some things in the yard when Bao-yu asked for some tea to be taken round to Miss Lin's for him and Miss Aroma[2] gave *me* the job of taking it. When I got there, Miss Lin had just been given some money by Her Old Ladyship[3] and was sharing it out among her maids; so when she saw me she just said 'Here you are!' and gave me two big handfuls of it. I've no idea how much it is. Will you look after it for me, please?"

She undid her handkerchief and poured out a shower of coins. Crimson carefully counted them for her and put them away in a safe place.

"What's been the matter with you lately?" said Melilot. "If you ask me, I think you ought to go home for a day or two and call in a doctor. I expect you need some medicine."

"Silly!" said Crimson. "I'm perfectly all right. What should I want to go home for?"

"I know what, then," said Melilot. "Miss Lin's very weakly. She's always taking medicine. Why don't you ask her to give you some of hers? It would probably do just as well."

"Oh, nonsense!" said Crimson. "You can't take other people's medicines just like that!"

"Well, you can't go on in this way," said Melilot, "never eating or drinking properly. What will become of you?"

"Who *cares?*" said Crimson. "The sooner I'm dead the better!"

"You shouldn't say such things," said Melilot. "It isn't right."

"Why not?" said Crimson. "How do you know what is on my mind?"

Melilot shook her head sympathetically.

"I can't say I really blame you," she said. "Things *are* very difficult here at times. Take yesterday, for example. Her Old Ladyship said that as Bao-

---

7. A poor relation of the Jias employed in the household.   8. One of Bao-yu's maids.   9. Bao-yu's residence in the garden.   1. One of Bao-yu's maids.   2. Bao-yu's chief maid. Miss Lin is Lin Dai-yu.
3. Bao-yu's grandmother.

yu was better now and there was to be a thanksgiving for his recovery, all those who had the trouble of nursing him during his illness were to be rewarded according to their grades. Well now, I can understand the very young ones like me not being included, but why should they leave *you* out? I felt really sorry for you when I heard that they'd left you out. Aroma, of course, you'd expect to get more than anyone else. I don't blame *her* at all. In fact, I think it's owing to her. Let's be honest: none of us can compare with Aroma. I mean, even if she didn't always take so much trouble over everything, no one would want to quarrel about *her* having a bigger share. What makes me so angry is that people like Skybright and Mackerel should count as top grade when everyone knows they're only put there to curry favour with Bao-yu. Doesn't it make you angry?"

"I don't see much point in getting angry," said Crimson. "You know what they said about the mile-wide marquee: 'Even the longest party must have an end'? Well, none of us is here for ever, you know. Another four or five years from now when we've each gone our different ways it won't *matter* any longer what all the rest of us are doing."

Little Melilot found this talk of parting and impermanence vaguely affecting and a slight moisture was to be observed about her eyes. She thought shame to cry without good cause, however, and masked her emotion with a smile:

"That's perfectly true. Only yesterday Bao-yu was going on about all the things he's going to do to his rooms and the clothes he's going to have made and everything, just as if he had a hundred or two years ahead of him with nothing to do but kill time in."

Crimson laughed scornfully, though whether at Melilot's simplicity or at Bao-yu's improvidence is unclear, since just as she was about to comment, a little maid came running in, so young that her hair was still done up in two little girl's horns. She was carrying some patterns and sheets of paper.

"You're to copy out these two patterns."

She threw them in Crimson's direction and straightway darted out again. Crimson shouted after her:

"Who are they for, then? You might at least finish your message before rushing off. What are you in such a tearing hurry about? Is someone steaming wheatcakes for you and you're afraid they'll get cold?"

"They're for Mackerel." The little maid paused long enough to bawl an answer through the window, then picking up her heels, went pounding off, *plim-plam, plim-plam, plim-plam*, as fast as she had come.

Crimson threw the patterns crossly to one side and went to hunt in her drawer for a brush to trace them with. After rummaging for several minutes she had only succeeded in finding a few worn-out ones, too moulted for use.

"Funny!" she said. "I could have sworn I put a new one in there the other day . . ."

She thought a bit, then laughed at herself as she remembered:

"Of course. Oriole[4] took it, the evening before last." She turned to Melilot. "Would you go and get it for me, then?"

---

4. One of Bao-chai's maids.

"I'm afraid I can't," said Melilot. "Miss Aroma's waiting for me to fetch some boxes for her. You'll have to get it yourself."

"If Aroma's waiting for you, why have you been sitting here gossiping all this time?" said Crimson. "If I hadn't asked you to go and get it, she wouldn't have been waiting, would she? Lazy little beast!"

She left the room and walked out of the gate of Green Delights and in the direction of Bao-chai's courtyard. She was just passing by Drenched Blossoms Pavilion when she caught sight of Bao-yu's old wet-nurse, Nannie Li, coming from the opposite direction and stood respectfully aside to wait for her.

"Where have you been, Mrs. Li?" she asked her. "I didn't expect to see you here."

Nannie Li made a flapping gesture with her hand:

"What do you think, my dear: His Nibs has taken a fancy to the young fellow who does the tree-planting—'Yin' or 'Yun' or whatever his name is—so Nannie has to go and ask him in. Let's hope Their Ladyships don't find out about it. There'll be trouble if they do."

"Are you really going to ask him in?"

"Yes. Why?"

Crimson laughed:

"If your Mr. Yun knows what's good for him, he won't agree to come."

"He's no fool," said Nannie Li. "Why shouldn't he?"

"Any way, if he *does* come in," said Crimson, ignoring her question, "you can't just bring him in and then leave him, Mrs. Li. You'll have to take him back again yourself afterwards. You don't want him wandering off on his own. There's no knowing *who* he might bump into."

(Crimson herself, was the secret hope.)

"Gracious me! I haven't got *that* much spare time," said Nannie Li. "All I've done is just to tell him that he's got to come. I'll send someone else to fetch him in when I get back presently—one of the girls, or one of the older women, maybe."

She hobbled off on her stick, leaving Crimson standing there in a muse, her mission to fetch the tracing-brush momentarily forgotten. She was still standing there a minute or two later when a little maid came along, who, seeing that it was Crimson, asked her what she was doing there. Crimson looked up. It was Trinket, another of the maids from Green Delights.

"Where are you going?" Crimson asked her.

"I've been sent to fetch Mr. Yun," said Trinket. "I have to bring him inside to meet Master Bao."

She ran off on her way.

At the gate to Wasp Waist Bridge Crimson ran into Trinket again, this time with Jia Yun in tow. His eyes sought Crimson's; and hers, as she made pretence of conversing with Trinket, sought his. Their two pairs of eyes met and briefly skirmished; then Crimson felt herself blushing, and turning away abruptly, she made off for Allspice Court.

Our narrative now follows Jia Yun and Trinket along the winding pathway to the House of Green Delights. Soon they were at the courtyard gate and Jia Yun waited outside while she went in to announce his arrival. She returned presently to lead him inside.

There were a few scattered rocks in the courtyard and some clumps of jade-green plantain. Two storks stood in the shadow of a pine-tree, preening themselves with their long bills. The gallery surrounding the courtyard was hung with cages of unusual design in which perched or fluttered a wide variety of birds, some of them gay-plumaged exotic ones. Above the steps was a little five-frame[5] penthouse building with a glimpse of delicately-carved partitions visible through the open doorway, above which a horizontal board hung, inscribed with the words

CRIMSON JOYS AND GREEN DELIGHTS

"So that's why it's called 'The House of Green Delights,'" Jia Yun told himself. "The name is taken from the inscription."

A laughing voice addressed him from behind one of the silk gauze casements:

"Come on in! It must be two or three months since I first forgot our appointment!"

Jia Yun recognized the voice as Bao-yu's and hurried up the steps inside. He looked about him, dazzled by the brilliance of gold and semi-precious inlay-work and the richness of the ornaments and furnishings, but unable to see Bao-yu in the midst of it all. To the left of him was a full-length mirror from behind which two girls now emerged, both about fifteen or sixteen years old and of much the same build and height. They addressed him by name and asked him to come inside. Slightly overawed, he muttered something in reply and hurried after them, not daring to take more than a furtive glance at them from the corner of his eye. They ushered him into a tent-like summer "cabinet" of green net, whose principal furniture was a tiny lacquered bed with crimson hangings heavily patterned in gold. On this Bao-yu, wearing everyday clothes and a pair of bedroom slippers, was reclining, book in hand. He threw the book down as Jia Yun entered and rose to his feet with a welcoming smile. Jia Yun swiftly dropped knee and hand to floor in greeting. Bidden to sit, he modestly placed himself on a bedside chair.

"After I invited you round to my study that day," said Bao-yu, "a whole lot of things seemed to happen one after the other, and I'm afraid I quite forgot about your visit."[6]

Jia Yun returned his smile:

"Let's just say that it wasn't my luck to see you then. But you have been ill since then, Uncle Bao. Are you quite better now?"

"Quite better, thank you. I hear you've been very busy these last few days."

"That's as it should be,' said Jia Yun. "But I'm glad you are better, Uncle. That's a piece of good fortune for *all* of us."

As they chatted, a maid came in with some tea. Jia Yun was talking to Bao-yu as she approached, but his eyes were on her. She was tall and rather thin with a long oval face, and she was wearing a rose-pink dress over a closely pleated white satin skirt and a black satin sleeveless jacket over the dress.

---

5. A unit for measuring space in a building; a *five-frame* building is relatively small.　6. Earlier, Jia Yun had been invited to pay a visit on Bao-yu.

In the course of his brief sojourn among them in the early days of Bao-yu's illness, Jia Yun had got by heart the names of most of the principal females of Bao-yu's establishment. He knew at a glance that the maid now serving him tea was Aroma. He was also aware that she was in some way more important than the other maids and that to be waited on by her in the seated presence of her master was an honour. Jumping hastily to his feet he addressed her with a modest smile:

"You shouldn't pour tea for *me*, Miss! I'm not like a visitor here. You should let me pour for myself!"

"Oh *do* sit down!" said Bao-yu. "You don't have to be like that in front of the *maids!*"

"I know," said Jia Yun. "But a body-servant![7] I don't like to presume."

He sat down, nevertheless, and sipped his tea while Bao-yu made conversation on a number of unimportant topics. He told him which household kept the best troupe of players, which had the finest gardens, whose maids were the prettiest, who gave the best parties, and who had the best collection of curiosities or the strangest pets. Jia Yun did his best to keep up with him. After a while Bao-yu showed signs of flagging, and when Jia Yun, observing what appeared to be fatigue, rose to take his leave, he did not very strongly press him to stay.

"You must come again when you can spare the time," said Bao-yu, and ordered Trinket to see him out of the Garden.

Once outside the gateway of Green Delights, Jia Yun looked around him on all sides, and having ascertained that there was no one else about, slowed down to a more dawdling pace so that he could ask Trinket a few questions. Indeed, the little maid was subjected to quite a catechism: How old was she? What was her name? What did her father and mother do? How many years had she been working for his Uncle Bao? How much pay did she get a month? How many girls were there working for him altogether? Trinket seemed to have no objection, however, and answered each question as it came.

"That girl you were talking to on the way in," he said, "isn't her name 'Crimson'?"

Trinket laughed:

"Yes. Why do you ask?"

"I heard her asking you about a handkerchief. Only it just so happens that I picked one up."

Trinket showed interest.

"She's asked me about that handkerchief of hers a number of times. I told her, I've got better things to do with my time than go looking for people's handkerchiefs. But when she asked me about it again today, she said that if I could find it for her, she'd give me a reward. Come to think of it, you were there when she said that, weren't you? It was when we were outside the gate of Allspice Court. So you can bear me out. Oh Mr. Jia, please let me have it if you've picked it up and I'll be able to see what she will give me for it!"

Jia Yun had picked up a silk handkerchief a month previously at the time when his tree-planting activities had just started. He knew that it

---

7. A personal servant of higher status than maids.

must have been dropped by one or another of the female inmates of the Garden, but not knowing which, had not so far ventured to do anything about his discovery. When earlier on he had heard Crimson question Trinket about her loss, he had realized, with a thrill of pleasure, that the handkerchief he had picked up must have been hers. Trinket's request now gave him just the opening he required. He drew a handkerchief of his own from inside his sleeve and held it up in front of her with a smile:

"I'll give it to you on one condition. If she lets you have this reward you were speaking of, you've *got* to let me know. No cheating, mind!"

Trinket received the handkerchief with eager assurances that he would be informed of the outcome, and having seen him out of the Garden, went back again to look for Crimson.

Our narrative returns now to Bao-yu.

After disposing of Jia Yun, Bao-yu continued to feel extremely lethargic and lay back on the bed with every appearance of being about to doze off to sleep. Aroma hurried over to him and, sitting on the edge of the bed, roused him with a shake:

"Come on! Surely you are not going to sleep *again?* You need some fresh air. Why don't you go outside and walk around for a bit?"

Bao-yu took her by the hand and smiled at her.

"I'd like to go," he said, "but I don't want to leave you."

"Silly!" said Aroma with a laugh. "Don't say what you don't mean!"

She hoicked[8] him to his feet.

"Well, where am I going to go then?" said Bao-yu. "I just feel so *bored.*"

"Never mind where, just go out!" said Aroma. "If you stay moping indoors like this, you'll get even more bored."

Bao-yu followed her advice, albeit half-heartedly, and went out into the courtyard. After visiting the cages in the gallery and playing for a bit with the birds, he ambled out of the courtyard into the Garden and along the bank of Drenched Blossoms Stream, pausing for a while to look at the goldfish in the water. As he did so, a pair of fawns came running like the wind from the hillside opposite. Bao-yu was puzzled. There seemed to be no reason for their mysterious terror. But just then little Jia Lan came running down the same slope after them, a tiny bow clutched in his hand. Seeing his uncle ahead of him, he stood politely to attention and greeted him cheerfully:

"Hello, Uncle. I didn't know you were at home. I thought you'd gone out."

"Mischievous little blighter, aren't you?" said Bao-yu. "What do you want to go shooting them for, poor little things?"

"I've got no reading to do today," said Jia Lan, "and I don't like to hang about doing nothing, so I thought I'd practise my archery and equitation."[9]

"Goodness! You'd better not waste time jawing, then," said Bao-yu, and left the young toxophilite[1] to his pursuits.

Moving on, without much thinking where he was going, he came presently to the gate of a courtyard.

---

8. Yanked.   9. Horseback riding.   1. Archer.

Denser than feathers on the phoenix' tail
The stirred leaves murmured with a pent dragon's moan.

The multitudinous bamboos and the board above the gate confirmed that his feet had, without conscious direction, carried him to the Naiad's House. Of their own accord they now carried him through the gateway and into the courtyard.

The House seemed silent and deserted, its bamboo door-blind hanging unrolled to the ground; but as he approached the window, he detected a faint sweetness in the air, traceable to a thin curl of incense smoke which drifted out through the green gauze of the casement. He pressed his face to the gauze; but before his eyes could distinguish anything, his ear became aware of a long, languorous sigh and the sound of a voice speaking:

"Each day in a drowsy waking dream of love."

Bao-yu felt a sudden yearning for the speaker. He could see her now. It was Dai-yu, of course, lying on her bed, stretching herself and yawning luxuriously.

He laughed:

"Why 'each day in a drowsy waking dream of love'?" he asked through the window (the words were from his beloved *Western Chamber*[2]); then going to the doorway he lifted up the door-blind and walked into the room.

Dai-yu realized that she had been caught off her guard. She covered her burning face with her sleeve, and turning over towards the wall, pretended to be asleep. Bao-yu went over intending to turn her back again, but just at that moment Dai-yu's old wet-nurse came hurrying in with two other old women at her heels:

"Miss Lin's asleep, sir. Would you mind coming back again after she's woken up?"

Dai-yu at once turned over and sat up with a laugh:

"Who's asleep?"

The three old women laughed apologetically.

"Sorry, miss. We thought you were asleep. Nightingale! Come inside now! Your mistress is awake."

Having shouted for Nightingale, the three guardians of morality retired.

"What do you mean by coming into people's rooms when they're asleep?" said Dai-yu, smiling up at Bao-yu as she sat on the bed's edge patting her hair into shape.

At the sight of those soft cheeks so adorably flushed and the starry eyes a little misted with sleep a wave of emotion passed over him. He sank into a chair and smiled back at her:

"What was that you were saying just now before I came in?"

"I didn't say anything," said Dai-yu.

Bao-yu laughed and snapped his fingers at her:

"Put that on your tongue, girl! I heard you say it."

While they were talking to one another, Nightingale came in.

2. A 13th-century romantic play.

"Nightingale," said Bao-yu, "what about a cup of that excellent tea of yours?"

"Excellent tea?" said Nightingale. "There's nothing very special about the tea we drink here. If nothing but the best will do, you'd better wait for Aroma to come."

"Never mind about *him!*" said Dai-yu. "First go and get me some water!"

"He *is* our guest," said Nightingale. "I can't fetch you any water until I've given him his tea." And she went to pour him a cup.

"Good girl!" said Bao-yu.

> "If with your amorous mistress I should wed,
> 'Tis you, sweet maid, must make our bridal bed."

The words, like Dai-yu's languorous line, were from *Western Chamber*, but in somewhat dubious taste. Dai-yu was dreadfully offended by them. In an instant the smile had vanished from her face.

"*What* was that you said?"

He laughed:

"I didn't say anything."

Dai-yu began to cry.

"This is your latest amusement, I suppose. Every time you hear some coarse expression outside or read some crude, disgusting book, you have to come back here and give me the benefit of it. I am to become a source of entertainment for the *menfolk* now, it seems."

She rose, weeping, from the bed and went outside. Bao-yu followed her in alarm.

"Dearest coz, it was very wrong of me to say that, but it just slipped out without thinking. Please don't go and tell! I promise never to say anything like that again. May my mouth rot and my tongue decay if I do!"

Just at that moment Aroma came hurrying up:

"Quick!" she said. "You must come back and change. The Master[3] wants to see you."

The descent of this thunderbolt drove all else from his mind and he rushed off in a panic. As soon as he had changed, he hurried out of the Garden. Tealeaf[4] was waiting for him outside the inner gate.

"I suppose you don't know what he wants to see me about?" Bao-yu asked him.

"I should hurry up, if I were you," said Tealeaf. "All I know is that he wants to see you. You'll find out why soon enough when you get there."

He hustled him along as he spoke.

They had passed round the main hall, Bao-yu still in a state of fluttering apprehensiveness, when there was a loud guffaw from a corner of the wall. It was Xue Pan,[5] clapping his hands and stamping his feet in mirth.

"Ho! Ho! Ho! You'd never have come this quickly if you hadn't been told that Uncle wanted you!"

Tealeaf, also laughing, fell on his knees. Bao-yu stood there looking puzzled. It was some moments before it dawned on him that he had been

---

3. Jia Sheng, Bao-yu's father.   4. One of Bao-yu's male pages.   5. A troublemaker, Xue Bao-chai's brother.

hoaxed. Xue Pan was by this time being apologetic—bowing repeatedly and pumping his hands to show how sorry he was:

"Don't blame the lad!" he said. "It wasn't his fault. I talked him into it."

Bao-yu saw that he could do nothing, and might as well accept with a good grace.

"I don't mind being made a fool of," he said, "but I think it was going a bit far to bring my father into it. I think perhaps I'd better tell Aunt Xue and see what *she* thinks about it all."

"Now look here, old chap," said Xue Pan, getting agitated, "it was only because I wanted to fetch you out a bit quicker. I admit it was very wrong of me to make free with your Parent, but after all, you've only got to mention *my* father next time you want to fool *me* and we'll be quits!"

"Aiyo!" said Bao-yu. "Worse and worse!" He turned to Tealeaf: "Treacherous little beast! What are you still kneeling for?"

Tealeaf kotowed and rose to his feet.

"Look," said Xue Pan. "I wouldn't have troubled you otherwise, only it's my birthday on the third of next month and old Hu and old Cheng and a couple of the others, I don't know where they got them from but they've given me:

> a piece of fresh lotus root, ever so crisp and crunchy, as thick as that, look, and as long as that;
> a huge great melon, look, as big as that;
> a freshly-caught sturgeon as big as that;
> and a cypress-smoked Siamese sucking-pig as big as that that came in the tribute from Siam.

Don't you think it was clever of them to get me those things? Maybe not so much the sturgeon and the sucking-pig. They're just expensive. But where would you go to get a piece of lotus root or a melon like that? However did they get them to *grow* so big? I've given some of the stuff to Mother, and while I was about it I sent some round to your grandmother and Auntie Wang, but I've still got a lot left over. I can't eat it all myself: it would be unlucky. But apart from me, the only person I can think of who is *worthy* to eat a present like this is you. That's why I came over specially to invite you. And we're lucky, because we've got a little chap who sings coming round as well. So you and I will be able to sit down and make a day of it, eh? Really enjoy ourselves."

Xue Pan, still talking, conducted Bao-yu to his "study," where Zhan Guang, Cheng Ri-xing, Hu Si-lai and Dan Ping-ren (the four donors of the feast) and the young singer he had mentioned were already waiting. They rose to welcome Bao-yu as he entered. When the bowings and courtesies were over and tea had been taken, Xue Pan called for his servants to lay.[6] A tremendous bustle ensued, which seemed to go on for quite a long time before everything was finally ready and the diners were able to take their places at the table.

Bao-yu noticed sliced melon and lotus root among the dishes, both of unusual quality and size.

---

6. That is, to set the table.

"It seems wrong to be sharing your presents with you before I have given you anything myself," he said jokingly.

"Yes," said Xue Pan. "What are you planning to give me for my birthday next month? Something new and out of the ordinary, I hope."

"I haven't really *got* anything much to give you," said Bao-yu. "Things like money and food and clothing I don't want for, but they're not really mine to give. The only way I could give you something that would *really* be mine would be by doing some calligraphy or painting a picture for you."

"Talking of pictures," said Xue Pan genially, "that's reminded me. I saw a set of dirty pictures in someone's house the other day. They were real beauties. There was a lot of writing on top that I didn't pay much attention to, but I did notice the signature. I think it was 'Geng Huang,' the man who painted them. They were really good!"

Bao-yu was puzzled. His knowledge of the masters of painting and calligraphy both past and present was not inconsiderable, but he had never in all his experience come across a "Geng Huang." After racking his brains for some moments he suddenly began to chuckle and called for a writing-brush. A writing-brush having been produced by one of the servants, he wrote two characters with it in the palm of his hand.

"Are you quite *sure* the signature you saw was 'Geng Huang'?" he asked Xue Pan.

"What do you mean?" said Xue Pan. "Of course I'm sure."

Bao-yu opened his hand and held it up for Xue Pan to see:

"You sure it wasn't these two characters? They *are* quite similar."

The others crowded round to look. They all laughed when they saw what he had written:

"Yes, it must have been 'Tang Yin.'[7] Mr. Xue couldn't have been seeing straight that day. Ha! Ha! Ha!"

Xue Pan realized that he had made a fool of himself, but passed it off with an embarrassed laugh:

"Oh, Tankin' or wankin'," he said, "what difference does it make, anyway?"

Just then "Mr. Feng" was announced by one of the servants, which Bao-yu knew could only mean General Feng Tang's son, Feng Zi-ying. Xue Pan and the rest told the boy to bring him in immediately, but Feng Zi-ying was already striding in, talking and laughing as he went. The others hurriedly rose and invited him to take a seat.

"Ha!" said Feng Zi-ying. "No need to go out then. Enjoyin' yourselves at home, eh? Very nice too!"

"It's a long time since we've seen you around," said Bao-yu. "How's the General?"

"Fahver's in good health, thank you very much," said Feng Zi-ying, "but Muvver hasn't been too well lately. Caught a chill or somethin'."

Observing with glee that Feng Zi-ying was sporting a black eye, Xue Pan asked him how he had come by it:

---

7. This joke shows Xue Pan's ignorance: he has misread the Chinese characters for one of the most famous of all Ming painters.

"Been having a dust-up, then? Who was it this time? Looks as if he left his signature!"

Feng Zi-ying laughed:

"Don't use the mitts any more nowadays—not since that time I laid into Colonel Chou's son and did him an injury. That was a lesson to me. I've learned to keep my temper since then. No, this happened the other day durin' a huntin' expedition in the Iron Net Mountains. I got flicked by a goshawk's wing."

"When was this?" Bao-yu asked him.

"We left on the twenty-eighth of last month," said Feng Zi-ying. "Didn't get back till a few days ago."

"Ah, that explains why I didn't see you at Shen's party earlier this month," said Bao-yu. "I meant at the time to ask why you weren't there, but I forgot. Did you go alone on this expedition or was the General there with you?"

"Fahver most certainly *was* there," said Feng Zi-ying. "I was practically dragged along in tow. Do you think I'm mad enough to go rushin' off in pursuit of hideous hardships when I could be sittin' comfortably at home eatin' good food and drinkin' good wine and listenin' to the odd song or two? Still, some good came of it. It was a lucky accident."

As he had now finished his tea, Xue Pan urged him to join them at table and tell them his story at leisure, but Feng Zi-ying rose to his feet again and declined.

"I ought by rights to stay and drink a few cups with you," he said, "but there's somethin' very important I've got to see Fahver about now, so I'm afraid I really must refuse."

But Xue Pan, Bao-yu and the rest were by no means content to let him get away with this excuse and propelled him insistently towards the table.

"Now look here, this is too bad!" Feng Zi-ying good-humouredly protested. "All the years we've been knockin' around togevver we've never before insisted that a fellow should have to stay if he don't want to. The fact is, I really *can't*. Oh well, if I *must* have a drink, fetch some decent-sized cups and I'll just put down a couple of quick ones!"

This was clearly the most he would concede and the others perforce acquiesced. Two sconce-cups were brought and ceremoniously filled, Bao-yu holding the cups and Xue Pan pouring from the wine-kettle.[8] Feng Zi-ying drank them standing, one after the other, each in a single breath.

"Now come on," said Bao-yu, "let's hear about this 'lucky accident' before you go!"

Feng Zi-ying laughed:

"Couldn't tell it properly just now," he said. "It's somethin' that needs a special party all to itself. I'll invite you all round to my place another day and you shall have the details then. There's a favour I want to ask too, by the bye, so we'll be able to talk about that then as well."

He made a determined movement towards the door.

"Now you've got us all peeing ourselves with curiosity!" said Xue Pan.

8. Chinese wine was heated before it was drunk. *Sconce-cups:* large wine cups.

"You might at least tell us when this party is going to be, to put us out of our suspense."

"Not more than ten days' time and not less than eight," said Feng Zi-ying; and going out into the courtyard, he jumped on his horse and clattered away.

Having seen him off, the others went in again, reseated themselves at table, and resumed their potations. When the party finally broke up, Bao-yu returned to the Garden in a state of cheerful inebriation. Aroma, who had had no idea what the summons from Jia Zheng might portend and was still wondering anxiously what had become of him, at once demanded to know the cause of his condition. He gave her a full account of what had happened.

"Well really!" said Aroma. "Here were we practically beside ourselves with anxiety, and all the time you were there enjoying yourself! You might at least have sent word to let us know you were all right."

"I was going to send word," said Bao-yu. "Of course I was. But then old Feng arrived and it put it out of my mind."

At that moment Bao-chai walked in, all smiles.

"I hear you've made a start on the famous present," she said.

"But surely you and your family must have had some already?" said Bao-yu.

Bao-chai shook her head:

"Pan was very pressing that I should have some, but I refused. I told him to save it for other people. I know I'm not really the right sort of person for such superior delicacies. If *I* were to eat any, I should be afraid of some frightful nemesis overtaking me."

A maid poured tea for her as she spoke, and conversation of a desultory kind proceeded between sips.

Our narrative returns now to Dai-yu.

Having been present when Bao-yu received his summons, Dai-yu, too, was greatly worried about him—the more so as the day advanced and he had still not returned. Then in the evening, some time after dinner, she heard that he had just got back and resolved to go over and ask him exactly what had happened. She was sauntering along on the way there when she caught sight of Bao-chai some distance ahead of her, just entering Bao-yu's courtyard. Continuing to amble on, she came presently to Drenched Blossoms Bridge, from which a large number of different kinds of fish were to be seen swimming about in the water below. Dai-yu did not know what kinds of fish they were, but they were so beautiful that she had to stop and admire them, and by the time she reached the House of Green Delights, the courtyard gate had been shut for the night and she was obliged to knock for admittance.

Now it so happened that Skybright had just been having a quarrel with Emerald, and being thoroughly out of temper, was venting some of her ill-humour on the lately arrived Bao-chai, complaining *sotto voce* behind her back about "people who were always inventing excuses to come dropping in and who kept other people staying up half the night when they would like to be in bed." A knock at the gate coming in the midst of these resentful mutterings was enough to make her really angry.

"They've all gone to bed," she shouted, not even bothering to inquire who the caller was. "Come again tomorrow!"

Dai-yu was aware that Bao-yu's maids often played tricks on one another, and it occurred to her that the girl in the courtyard, not recognizing her voice, might have mistaken her for another maid and be keeping her locked out for a joke. She therefore called out again, this time somewhat louder than before:

"Come on! Open up, please! It's me."

Unfortunately Skybright had still not recognized the voice.

"I don't care who you are," she replied bad-temperedly. "Master Bao's orders are that I'm not to let *anyone* in."

Dumbfounded by her insolence, Dai-yu stood outside the gate in silence. She could not, however much she felt like it, give vent to her anger in noisy expostulation. "Although they are always telling me to treat my Uncle's house as my own," she reflected, "I am still really an outsider. And now that Mother and Father are both dead and I am on my own, to make a fuss about a thing like this when I am living in someone else's house could only lead to further unpleasantness."

A big tear coursed, unregarded, down her cheek.

She was still standing there irresolute, unable to decide whether to go or stay, when a sudden volley of talk and laughter reached her from inside. It resolved itself, as she listened attentively, into the voices of Bao-yu and Bao-chai. An even bitterer sense of chagrin took possession of her. Suddenly, as she hunted in her mind for some possible reason for her exclusion, she remembered the events of the morning and concluded that Bao-yu must think she had told on him to his parents and was punishing her for her betrayal.

"But I would never betray you!" she expostulated with him in her mind. "Why couldn't you have asked first, before letting your resentment carry you to such lengths? If you won't see me today, does that mean that from now on we are going to stop seeing each other altogether?"

The more she thought about it the more distressed she became.

> Chill was the green moss pearled with dew
> And chill was the wind in the avenue;

but Dai-yu, all unmindful of the unwholesome damp, had withdrawn into the shadow of a flowering fruit-tree by the corner of the wall, and grieving now in real earnest, began to cry as though her heart would break. And as if Nature herself were affected by the grief of so beautiful a creature, the crows who had been roosting in the trees round about flew up with a great commotion and removed themselves to another part of the Garden, unable to endure the sorrow of her weeping.

> Tears filled each flower and grief their hearts perturbed,
> And silly birds were from their nests disturbed.

The author of the preceding couplet has given us a quatrain in much the same vein:

> Few in this world fair Frowner's looks surpassed,
> None matched her store of sweetness unexpressed.

The first sob scarcely from her lips had passed
When blossoms fell and birds flew off distressed.

As Dai-yu continued weeping there alone, the courtyard door suddenly opened with a loud creak and someone came out.

But in order to find out who it was, you will have to wait for the next chapter.

From *Volume 2*

CHAPTER 27

Beauty Perspiring sports with butterflies
by the Raindrop Pavilion
And Beauty Suspiring weeps for fallen blossoms
by the Flowers' Grave

As Dai-yu stood there weeping, there was a sudden creak of the court-yard gate and Bao-chai walked out, accompanied by Bao-yu with Aroma and a bevy of other maids who had come out to see her off. Dai-yu was on the point of stepping forward to question Bao-yu, but shrank from embarrassing him in front of so many people. Instead she slipped back into the shadows to let Bao-chai pass, emerging only when Bao-yu and the rest were back inside and the gate was once more barred. She stood for a while facing it, and shed a few silent tears; then, realizing that it was pointless to remain standing there, she turned and went back to her room and began, in a listless, mechanical manner, to take off her ornaments and prepare herself for the night.

Nightingale and Snowgoose had long since become habituated to Dai-yu's moody temperament; they were used to her unaccountable fits of depression, when she would sit, the picture of misery, in gloomy silence broken only by an occasional gusty sigh, and to her mysterious, perpetual weeping, that was occasioned by no observable cause. At first they had tried to reason with her, or, imagining that she must be grieving for her parents or that she was feeling homesick or had been upset by some unkindness, they would do their best to comfort her. But as the months lengthened into years and she still continued exactly the same as before, they gradually became accustomed and no longer sought reasons for her behaviour. That was why they ignored her on this occasion and left her alone to her misery, remaining where they were in the outer room and continuing to occupy themselves with their own affairs.

She sat, motionless as a statue, leaning against the back of the bed, her hands clasped about her knees, her eyes full of tears. It had already been dark for some hours when she finally lay down to sleep.

Our story passes over the rest of that night in silence.

Next day was the twenty-sixth of the fourth month, the day on which, this year, the festival of Grain in Ear was due to fall. To be precise, the festival's official commencement was on the twenty-sixth day of the fourth month

at two o'clock in the afternoon. It has been the custom from time immemorial to make offerings to the flower fairies on this day. For Grain in Ear
marks the beginning of summer; it is about this time that the blossom
begins to fall; and tradition has it that the flowerspirits, their work now
completed, go away on this day and do not return until the following year.
The offerings are therefore thought of as a sort of farewell party for the
flowers.

This charming custom of "speeding the fairies" is a special favourite
with the fair sex, and in Prospect Garden all the girls were up betimes on
this day making little coaches and palanquins[9] out of willow-twigs and
flowers and little banners and pennants from scraps of brocade and any
other pretty material they could find, which they fastened with threads of
coloured silk to the tops of flowering trees and shrubs. Soon every plant
and tree was decorated and the whole garden had become a shimmering
sea of nodding blossoms and fluttering coloured streamers. Moving about
in the midst of it all, the girls in their brilliant summer dresses, beside
which the most vivid hues of plant and plumage became faint with envy,
added the final touch of brightness to a scene of indescribable gaiety and
colour.

All the young people—Bao-chai, Ying-chun, Tan-chun, Xi-chun, Li
Wan, Xi-feng[1] and her little girl and Caltrop, and all the maids from all
the different apartments—were outside in the Garden enjoying themselves—all, that is, except Dai-yu, whose absence, beginning to be noticed,
was first commented on by Ying-chun:

"What's happened to Cousin Lin? Lazy girl! Surely she can't *still* be in
bed at this hour?"

Bao-chai volunteered to go and fetch her:

"The rest of you wait here; I'll go and rout her out for you," she said;
and breaking away from the others, she made off in the direction of the
Naiad's House.

While she was on her way, she caught sight of Élégante and the eleven
other little actresses, evidently on their way to join in the fun. They came
up and greeted her, and for a while she stood and chatted with them. As
she was leaving them, she turned back and pointed in the direction from
which she had just come:

"You'll find the others somewhere over there," she said. "I'm on my way
to get Miss Lin. I'll join the rest of you presently."

She continued, by the circuitous route that the garden's contours
obliged her to take, on her way to the Naiad's House. Raising her eyes as
she approached it, she suddenly became aware that the figure ahead of
her just disappearing inside it was Bao-yu. She stopped and lowered her
eyes pensively again to the ground.

"Bao-yu and Dai-yu have known each other since they were little," she
reflected. "They are used to behaving uninhibitedly when they are alone
together. They don't seem to care what they say to one another; and one
is never quite sure what sort of mood one is going to find them in. And

---

9. Sedan chairs, carried on poles by bearers.   1. The wife of Bao-yu's uncle; she manages the household.

Dai-yu, at the best of times, is always so touchy and suspicious. If I go in now after him, *he* is sure to feel embarrassed and *she* is sure to start imagining things. It would be better to go back without seeing her."

Her mind made up, she turned round and began to retrace her steps, intending to go back to the other girls; but just at that moment she noticed two enormous turquoise-coloured butterflies a little way ahead of her, each as large as a child's fan, fluttering and dancing on the breeze. She watched them fascinated and thought she would like to play a game with them. Taking a fan from inside her sleeve and holding it outspread in front of her, she followed them off the path and into the grass.

To and fro fluttered the pair of butterflies, sometimes alighting for a moment, but always flying off again before she could reach them. Once they seemed on the point of flying across the little river that flowed through the midst of the garden and Bao-chai had to stalk them with bated breath for fear of startling them out on to the water. By the time she had reached the Raindrop Pavilion she was perspiring freely and her interest in the butterflies was beginning to evaporate. She was about to turn back when she became aware of a low murmur of voices coming from inside the pavilion.

Raindrop Pavilion was built in such a way that it projected into the middle of the pool into which the little watercourse widened out at this point, so that on three of its sides it looked out on to the water. It was surrounded by a verandah, whose railing followed the many angles formed by the bays and projections of the base. In each of its wooden walls there was a large paper-covered casement of elegantly patterned latticework.

Hearing voices inside the pavilion, Bao-chai halted and inclined her ear to listen.

"Are you *sure* this is your handkerchief?" one of the voices was saying. "If it is, take it; but if it isn't, I must return it to Mr. Yun."

"Of course it's mine," said the second voice. "Come on, let me have it!"

"Are you going to give me a reward? I hope I haven't taken all this trouble for nothing."

"I promised you I would give you a reward, and so I shall. Surely you don't think I was deceiving you?"

"All right, I get a reward for bringing it to you. But what about the person who picked it up? Doesn't *he* get anything?"

"Don't talk nonsense," said the second voice. "He's one of the masters. A master picking up something belonging to one of us should give it back as a matter of course. How can there be any question of *rewarding* him?"

"If you don't intend to reward him, what am I supposed to tell him when I see him? He was most insistent that I wasn't to give you the handkerchief unless you gave him a reward."

There was a long pause, after which the second voice replied:

"Oh, all right. Let him have this other handkerchief of mine then. That will have to do as his reward—But you must swear a solemn oath not to tell anyone else about this."

"May my mouth rot and may I die a horrible death if I ever tell anyone else about this, amen!" said the first voice.

"Goodness!" said the second voice again. "Here we are talking away, and all the time someone could be creeping up outside and listening to every word we say. We had better open these casements;[2] then even if anyone outside sees us, they'll think we are having an ordinary conversation; and *we* shall be able to see *them* and know in time when to stop."

Bao-chai, listening outside, gave a start.

"No wonder they say 'venery and thievery sharpen the wits,'" she thought. "If they open those windows and see me here, they are going to feel terribly embarrassed. And one of those voices sounds like that proud, peculiar girl Crimson who works in Bao-yu's room. If a girl like that knows that I have overheard her doing something she shouldn't be doing, it will be a case of 'the desperate dog will jump a wall, the desperate man will hazard all': there'll be a great deal of trouble and I shall be involved in it. There isn't time to hide. I shall have to do as the cicada does when he jumps out of his skin: give them something to put them off the scent—"

There was a loud creak as the casement yielded. Bao-chai advanced with deliberately noisy tread.

"Frowner!" she called out gaily. "*I* know where you're hiding."

Inside the pavilion Crimson and Trinket, who heard her say this and saw her advancing towards them just as they were opening the casement, were speechless with amazement; but Bao-chai ignored their confusion and addressed them genially:

"Have you two got Miss Lin hidden away in there?"

"I haven't *seen* Miss Lin," said Trinket.

"I saw her just now from the river-bank," said Bao-chai. "She was squatting down over here playing with something in the water. I was going to creep up and surprise her, but she spotted me before I could get up to her and disappeared round this corner. Are you *sure* she's not hiding in there?"

She made a point of going inside the pavilion and searching; then, coming out again, she said in a voice loud enough for them to hear:

"If she's not in the pavilion, she must have crept into that grotto. Oh well, if she's not afraid of being bitten by a snake—!"

As she walked away she laughed inwardly at the ease with which she had extricated herself from a difficult situation.

"I think I'm fairly safely out of *that* one," she thought. "I wonder what those two will make of it."

What indeed! Crimson believed every word that Bao-chai had said, and as soon as the latter was at a distance, she seized hold of Trinket in alarm:

"Oh, how terrible! If Miss Lin was squatting there, she must have heard what we said before she went away."

Her companion was silent.

"Oh dear! What do you think she'll *do*?" said Crimson.

"Well, suppose she *did* hear," said Trinket, "it's not *her* backache. If we mind our business and she minds hers, there's no reason why anything should come of it."

"If it were Miss Bao that had heard us, I don't suppose anything *would*," said Crimson; "but Miss Lin is so critical and so intolerant. If *she* heard it and it gets about—oh dear!"

But just at that moment Caltrop, Advent, Chess and Scribe were seen approaching the pavilion, and Crimson and Trinket had to drop the subject in a hurry and join in a general conversation. Crimson noticed Xi-feng standing half-way up the rockery above the little grotto, beckoning. Breaking away from the others, she bounded up to her with a smiling face:

"What can I do for you, madam?"

Xi-feng ran an appraising eye over her. A neat, pretty, pleasantly-spoken girl, she decided, and smiled at her graciously:

"I have come here without my maids and need someone to take a message back to my apartment. I wonder if you are clever enough to get it right."

"Tell me the message, madam. If I don't get it right and make a mess of it, it will be up to you to punish me."

"Which of the young ladies do you work for?" said Xi-feng. "I'd better know, so that I can explain to her if she asks for you while you are doing my errand."

"I work for Master Bao," said Crimson.

Xi-feng laughed.

"Ah ha! You work for Master Bao. No wonder. Very well, then, if he asks for you while you are away, I shall explain. I want you to go to my apartment and tell Patience that there is a roll of money under the stand of the Ru-ware dish on the table in the outside room. There are a hundred and twenty taels[3] of silver in it to pay the embroiderers with. Tell her that when Zhang Cai's wife comes for it, she is to weigh it out in front of her before handing it over. And there's one other thing. There's a little purse at the head of the bed in my inside room. I want you to bring it to me."

"Yes madam," said Crimson, and hurried off.

Returning shortly afterwards, she found that Xi-feng was no longer on the rockery; but Chess had just emerged from the little grotto beneath it and was standing there doing up her sash. Crimson ran down to speak to her:

"Excuse me, did you see where Mrs. Lian went to?"

" 'Fraid I didn't notice," said Chess.

Crimson looked around her. Bao-chai and Tan-chun were standing at the edge of the pool looking at the fish. She went up to them:

"Excuse me, does either of you young ladies happen to know where Mrs. Lian went to just now, please?"

"Try Mrs. Zhu's place," said Tan-chun.

Crimson hurried off in the direction of Sweet-rice Village. On her way she ran head-on into a party of maids consisting of Skybright, Mackerel, Emerald, Ripple, Musk, Scribe, Picture and Oriole.

"Here, what are you gadding about like this for?" said Skybright as soon

---

3. A unit of currency. *Ru-ware:* fine porcelain.

as she saw who it was. "The flowers want watering; the birds need feeding; the stove for the tea-water needs seeing to. You've no business to go wandering around outside!"

"Master Bao gave orders yesterday that the flowers were only to be watered every other day," said Crimson. "I fed the birds when you were still fast asleep in bed."

"What about the stove?" said Emerald.

"It isn't my day for the stove," said Crimson. "The tea-water today has nothing to do with me."

"Listen to Miss Pert!" said Mackerel. "I wouldn't bother about her, if I were you—just leave her to wander about as she pleases."

"I'm *not* 'wandering about,' if you really want to know," said Crimson. "If you really want to know, Mrs. Lian sent me outside to take a message and to fetch something for her."

She held up the purse for them to see; at which they were silent. But when they had passed each other, Skybright laughed sneeringly:

"You can see why she's so uppity. She's on the climb again. Look at her—all cock-a-hoop because someone's given her a little message to carry! And she probably doesn't even know who it's about. Well, one little message isn't going to get her very far. It's what happens in the long run that counts. Now if she were clever enough to climb her way right out of this Garden and stay there, that would be really something!"

These words were spoken for Crimson to hear, but in such a way that she was unable to answer them. She had to swallow her anger and hurry on to look for Xi-feng.

Xi-feng was in Li Wan's room, as Tan-chun had predicted, and Crimson found the two of them in conversation. She went up to Xi-feng and delivered her message:

"Patience says that she found the silver just after you had gone and took care of it; and she says that when Zhang Cai's wife came for it she did weigh it out in front of her before giving it to her to take away."

Crimson now produced the purse and handed it to Xi-feng.

Then she added:

"Patience told me to tell you that Brightie has just been in to inquire what your instructions were for his visit, and she said that she gave him a message to take based on the things she thought you would want him to say."

"Oh?" said Xi-feng, amused. "And what *was* this message 'based on the things she thought I would want him to say'?"

"She said he was to tell them: 'Our lady hopes your lady is well and she says that the Master is away at present and may not be back for another day or two, but your lady is not to worry; and when the lady from West Lane is better, our lady will come with their lady to see your lady. And our lady says that the lady from West Lane sent someone the other day with a message from the *elder* Lady Wang[4] saying that she hopes our lady is well and will she please see if *our* Lady Wang can let her have a few of her Golden Myriad Macrobiotic Pills; and if she can, will our lady please

---

4. Lady Wang's mother and Bao-yu's grandmother.

send someone with them to *her*, because someone will be going from there to the *elder* Lady Wang's in a few days' time and they will be able to take them for her—' "

Crimson was still in full spate when Li Wan interrupted her with a laugh:

"What an extraordinary number of 'ladies'! I hope you can understand what it's all about, Feng. I'm sure *I* can't!"

"I'm not surprised," said Xi-feng. "There are four or five different households involved in that message." She smiled graciously at Crimson. "You're a clever girl, my dear, to have got it all right—not like the simpering little ninnies I usually have to put up with. You have no idea, cousin," she said, turning to Li Wan again. "Apart from the one or two girls and one or two older women that I always keep about me, I just dread talking to servants nowadays. They take such an *interminable* time to tell you anything—so long-winded! And the airs and graces they give themselves! and the simpering! and the um-ing and ah-ing! If they only knew how it makes me *fume!* Our Patience used to be like that when she first came to me. I used to say to her, 'Do you think it makes you seem glamorous, all that affected humming?—like a little gnat!' I had to talk to her several times about it before she would mend her ways."

Li Wan laughed.

"I suppose if they were all peppercorns like you, it would be all right."

"This girl's all right," said Xi-feng. "Those two messages she gave me just now may not have been very long ones, but you could see how clear-cut her delivery of them was."

She smiled at Crimson again.

"How would you like to come and work for me and be my god-daughter? With a little grooming from me you could go far."

Crimson suppressed a giggle.

"Why do you laugh?" said Xi-feng. "I suppose you think I'm too young to be your god-mother. You're very silly if you think that. You just ask around a bit: there are plenty much older than you who'd give their ears to be my god-daughter. What I'm offering you is a very special favour."

Crimson smiled.

"I wasn't laughing because of that, madam. I was laughing because you had got the generation wrong. My mother is your god-daughter already. If you made me your god-daughter too, I should be my own mother's sister!"

"Who *is* your mother?" said Xi-feng.

"Do you mean to say that you don't know who this girl is that you've been talking to all this time?" said Li Wan. "This is Lin Zhi-xiao's daughter."

Xi-feng registered surprise:

"You mean to tell me that this is the *Lins'* daughter?" She laughed. "*That* couple of old sticks? I can never get a peep out of either of them. I've always maintained that Lin Zhi-xiao and his wife were the perfect match: one *hears* nothing and the other *says* nothing. Well! To think they should have produced a bright little thing like this between them!—How old are you?" she asked Crimson.

"Sixteen."

"And what's your name?"

" 'Crimson,' madam. I used to be called 'Jade,' but they made me change it on account of Master Bao."

Xi-feng looked away with a frown of displeasure.

"I should think so too," she muttered. "Odious people! One can hear them saying it: 'We've got a "Jade" in our family the same as you,' or some such impertinence."

She turned to Li Wan again:

"I don't think you know, Wan, but I told this girl's mother that as Lai Da's wife is so busy nowadays that she doesn't even know who half the girls in the household *are* any longer, I wanted *her* to pick out a couple of likely-looking girls to work under me. Now she promised that she would do this; but you see, not only has she not done so, but she's actually gone and sent her own daughter to work for someone else. Do you suppose she *really* thinks her girl would have had such a terrible time with me?"

"Don't be so touchy," said Li Wan. "Her mother is not to blame. The girl had already started service in the Garden before you ever spoke to her about it."

"Oh well, in that case," said Xi-feng, recovering her good humour, "I'll have a word with Bao-yu about it tomorrow. I'll tell him to find someone else and let me have this girl to work under *me*. Still—" she turned to Crimson, "perhaps we ought to ask the party most concerned if she is willing."

Crimson smiled.

"As to being willing or not, madam, I don't think it's my place to say. But I do know this: that if I was to work for you, I should get to know what's what and all the inside and outside of household management. I'm sure it would be wonderful experience."

Just then a maid arrived from Lady Wang's asking for Xi-feng, who promptly excused herself to Li Wan and left. Crimson returned to Green Delights—where our story now leaves her.

We now return to Dai-yu, who, having slept so little the night before, was very late getting up on the morning of the festival. Hearing that the other girls were all out in the garden "speeding the fairies" and fearing to be teased by them for her lazy habits, she hurried over her toilet and went out as soon as it was completed. A smiling Bao-yu appeared in the gateway as she was stepping down into the courtyard.

"Well, coz," he said, "I hope you *didn't* tell on me yesterday. You had me worrying about it all last night."

Dai-yu turned back, ignoring him, to address Nightingale inside:

"When you do the room, leave one of the casements open so that the parent swallows can get in. And put the lion doorstop on the bottom of the blind to stop it flapping. And don't forget to put the cover back on the burner after you've lighted the incense."

She made her way across the courtyard, still ignoring him.

Bao-yu, who knew nothing of the little drama that had taken place outside his gate the night before, assumed that she was still angry about his unfortunate lapse earlier on that same day, when he had offended her susceptibilities with a somewhat risqué quotation from *The Western Chamber*. He offered her now, with energetic bowing and hand-pumping, the apologies that the previous day's emergency had caused him to neglect. But Dai-yu walked straight past him and out of the gate, not deigning so much as a glance in his direction, and stalked off in search of the others.

Bao-yu was nonplussed. He began to suspect that something more than he had first imagined must be wrong.

"Surely it can't only be because of yesterday lunchtime that she's carrying on in this fashion? There must be something else. On the other hand, I didn't get back until late and I didn't see her again last night, so how *could* I have offended her?"

Preoccupied with these reflections, he followed her at some distance behind.

Not far ahead Bao-chai and Tan-chun were watching the ungainly courtship dance of some storks. When they saw Dai-yu coming, they invited her to join them, and the three girls stood together and chatted. Then Bao-yu arrived. Tan-chun greeted him with sisterly concern:

"How have you been keeping, Bao? It's three whole days since I saw you last."

Bao-yu smiled back at her.

"How have *you* been keeping, sis? I was asking Cousin Wan about you the day before yesterday."

"Come over here a minute," said Tan-chun. "I want to talk to you."

He followed her into the shade of a pomegranate tree a little way apart from the other two.

"Has Father asked to see you at all during this last day or two?" Tan-chun began.

"No."

"I thought I heard someone say yesterday that he had been asking for you."

"No," said Bao-yu, smiling at her concern. "Whoever it was was mistaken. He certainly hasn't asked for *me*."

Tan-chun smiled and changed the subject.

"During the past few months," she said, "I've managed to save up another ten strings or so of cash.[5] I'd like you to take it again like you did last time, and next time you go out, if you see a nice painting or calligraphic scroll or some amusing little thing that would do for my room, I'd like you to buy it for me."

"Well, I don't know," said Bao-yu. "In the trips I make to bazaars and temple fairs, whether it's inside the city or round about, I can't say that I ever see anything *really* nice or out of the ordinary. It's all bronzes and jades and porcelain and that sort of stuff. Apart from that it's mostly dressmaking materials and clothes and things to eat."

"Now what would I want things like that for?" said Tan-chun. "No, I mean something like that little wickerwork basket you bought me last time, or the little box carved out of bamboo root, or the little clay burner.

---

5. Chinese copper coins had holes in the center and thus could be strung together.

I thought they were sweet. Unfortunately the others took such a fancy to them that they carried them off as loot and wouldn't give them back to me again."

"Oh, if *those* are the sort of things you want," said Bao-yu laughing, "it's very simple. Just give a few strings of cash to one of the boys and he'll bring you back a whole cartload of them."

"What do the boys know about it?" said Tan-chun. "I need someone who can pick out the interesting things and the ones that are in good taste. You get me lots of nice little things, and I'll embroider a pair of slippers for you like the ones I made for you last time—only this time I'll do them more carefully."

"Talking of those slippers reminds me," said Bao-yu. "I happened to run into Father once when I was wearing them. He was Most Displeased. When he asked me who made them, I naturally didn't dare to tell him that *you* had, so I said that Aunt Wang had given them to me as a birthday present a few days before. There wasn't much he could do about it when he heard that they came from Aunt Wang; so after a very long pause he just said, 'What a pointless waste of human effort and valuable material, to produce things like that!' I told this to Aroma when I got back, and she said, 'Oh, that's nothing! You should have heard your Aunt Zhao complaining about those slippers. She was *furious* when she heard about them: "Her own natural brother so down at heel he scarcely dares show his face to people, and she spends her time making things like that!" ' "

Tan-chun's smile had vanished:

"How *can* she talk such nonsense? Why should *I* be the one to make shoes for him? Huan[6] gets a clothing allowance, doesn't he? He gets his clothing and footwear provided for the same as all the rest of us. And fancy saying a thing like that in front of a roomful of servants! For whose benefit was this remark made, I wonder? I make an occasional pair of slippers just for something to do in my spare time; and if I give a pair to someone I particularly like, that's my own affair. Surely no one else has any business to start telling me who I should give them to? Oh, she's so *petty!*"

Bao-yu shook his head:

"Perhaps you're being a bit hard on her. She's probably got her reasons."

This made Tan-chun really angry. Her chin went up defiantly:

"Now you're being as stupid as her. Of *course* she's got her reasons; but they are ignorant, stupid reasons. But she can think what she likes: as far as *I* am concerned, Sir Jia is my father and Lady Wang is my mother, and who was born in whose room doesn't interest me—the way I choose my friends inside the family has nothing to do with that. Oh, I know I shouldn't talk about her like this; but she is *so* idiotic about these things. As a matter of fact I can give you an even better example than your story of the slippers. That last time I gave you my savings to get something for me, she saw me a few days afterwards and started telling me how short of money she was and how difficult things were for her. I took no notice, of course. But later, when the maids were out of the room, she began attacking me for giving the money I'd saved to other people instead of

---

6. Jia Huan, Bao-yu's half-brother, born to his father and the concubine Aunt Zhao.

giving it to Huan. Really! I didn't know whether to laugh or get angry with her. In the end I just walked out of the room and went round to see Mother."

There was an amused interruption at this point from Bao-chai, who was still standing where they had left her a few minutes before:

"Do finish your talking and come back soon! It's easy to see that you two are brother and sister. As soon as you see each other, you get into a huddle and start talking about family secrets. Would it *really* be such a disaster if anything you are saying were to be overheard?"

Tan-chun and Bao-yu rejoined her, laughing.

Not seeing Dai-yu, Bao-yu realized that she must have slipped off elsewhere while he was talking.

"Better leave it a day or two," he told himself on reflection. "Wait until her anger has calmed down a bit."

While he was looking downwards and meditating, he noticed that the ground where they were standing was carpeted with a bright profusion of wind-blown flowers—pomegranate and balsam for the most part.

"You can see she's upset," he thought ruefully. "She's neglecting her flowers. I'll bury this lot for her and remind her about it next time I see her."

He became aware that Bao-chai was arranging for him and Tan-chun to go with her outside.

"I'll join you two presently," he said, and waited until they were a little way off before stooping down to gather the fallen blossoms into the skirt of his gown. It was quite a way from where he was to the place where Dai-yu had buried the peach-blossom on that previous occasion,[7] but he made his way towards it, over rocks and bridges and through plantations of trees and flowers. When he had almost reached his destination and there was only the spur of a miniature "mountain" between him and the burial-place of the flowers, he heard the sound of a voice, coming from the other side of the rock, whose continuous, gentle chiding was occasionally broken by the most pitiable and heart-rending sobs.

"It must be a maid from one of the apartments," thought Bao-yu. "Someone has been ill-treating her, and she has run here to cry on her own."

He stood still and endeavoured to catch what the weeping girl was saying. She appeared to be reciting something:

> The blossoms fade and falling fill the air,
> Of fragrance and bright hues bereft and bare.
> Floss drifts and flutters round the Maiden's bower,
> Or softly strikes against her curtained door.
>
> The Maid, grieved by these signs of spring's decease,
> Seeking some means her sorrow to express,
> Has rake in hand into the garden gone,
> Before the fallen flowers are trampled on.

---

7. A reference to an incident in Chap. 23. Dai-yu explains that she is burying the blossoms to return them to the earth, rather than letting them be simply swept away. Because beautiful women were commonly compared to flowers, this foreshadows her own death.

Elm-pods and willow-floss are fragrant too;
Why care, Maid, where the fallen flowers blew?
Next year, when peach and plum-tree bloom again,
Which of your sweet companions will remain?

This spring the heartless swallow built his nest
Beneath the eaves of mud with flowers compressed.
Next year the flowers will blossom as before,
But swallow, nest, and Maid will be no more.

Three hundred and three-score the year's full tale:
From swords of frost and from the slaughtering gale
How can the lovely flowers long stay intact,
Or, once loosed, from their drifting fate draw back?

Blooming so steadfast, fallen so hard to find!
Beside the flowers' grave, with sorrowing mind,
The solitary Maid sheds many a tear,
Which on the boughs as bloody drops appear.

At twilight, when the cuckoo sings no more,
The Maiden with her rake goes in at door
And lays her down between the lamplit walls,
While a chill rain against the window falls.

I know not why my heart's so strangely sad,
Half grieving for the spring and yet half glad:
Glad that it came, grieved it so soon was spent.
So soft it came, so silently it went!

Last night, outside, a mournful sound was heard:
The spirits of the flowers and of the bird.
But neither bird nor flowers would long delay,
Bird lacking speech, and flowers too shy to stay.

And then I wished that I had wings to fly
After the drifting flowers across the sky:
Across the sky to the world's farthest end,
The flowers' last fragrant resting-place to find.

But better their remains in silk to lay
And bury underneath the wholesome clay,
Pure substances the pure earth to enrich,
Than leave to soak and stink in some foul ditch.

Can I, that these flowers' obsequies attend,
Divine how soon or late *my* life will end?
Let others laugh flower-burial to see:
Another year who will be burying me?

As petals drop and spring begins to fail,
The bloom of youth, too, sickens and turns pale.
One day, when spring has gone and youth has fled.
The Maiden and the flowers will both be dead.

All this was uttered in a voice half-choked with sobs; for the words
recited seemed only to inflame the grief of the reciter—indeed, Bao-yu,

listening on the other side of the rock, was so overcome by them that he had already flung himself weeping upon the ground.

But the sequel to this painful scene will be told in the following chapter.

CHAPTER 28

A crimson cummerbund becomes a pledge of friendship
And a chaplet of medicine-beads becomes a source of
embarrassment

On the night before the festival, it may be remembered, Lin Dai-yu had mistakenly supposed Bao-yu responsible for Skybright's refusal to open the gate for her. The ceremonial farewell to the flowers of the following morning had transformed her pent-up and still smouldering resentment into a more generalized and seasonable sorrow. This had finally found its expression in a violent outburst of grief as she was burying the latest collection of fallen blossoms in her flower-grave. Meditation on the fate of flowers had led her to a contemplation of her own sad and orphaned lot; she had burst into tears, and soon after had begun a recitation of the poem whose words we recorded in the preceding chapter.

Unknown to her, Bao-yu was listening to this recitation from the slope of the near-by rockery. At first he merely nodded and sighed sympathetically; but when he heard the words

"Can I, that these flowers' obsequies attend,
Divine how soon or late *my* life will end?"

and, a little later,

"One day when spring has gone and youth has fled,
The Maiden and the flowers will both be dead."

he flung himself on the ground in a fit of weeping, scattering the earth all about him with the flowers he had been carrying in the skirt of his gown.

Lin Dai-yu dead! A world from which that delicate, flower-like countenance had irrevocably departed! It was unutterable anguish to think of it. Yet his sensitized imagination *did* now consider it—went on, indeed, to consider a world from which the others, too—Bao-chai, Caltrop, Aroma and the rest—had also irrevocably departed. Where would *he* be then? What would have become of him? And what of the Garden, the rocks, the flowers, the trees? To whom would they belong when he and the girls were no longer there to enjoy them? Passing from loss to loss in his imagination, he plunged deeper and deeper into a grief that seemed inconsolable. As the poet says:

Flowers in my eyes and bird-song in my ears
Augment my loss and mock my bitter tears.

Dai-yu, then, as she stood plunged in her own private sorrowing, suddenly heard the sound of another person crying bitterly on the rocks above her.

"The others are always telling me I'm a 'case,'" she thought. "Surely there can't be another 'case' up there?"

But on looking up she saw that it was Bao-yu.

"Pshaw!" she said crossly to herself. "I thought it was another girl, but all the time it was that cruel, hate—"

"Hateful" she had been going to say, but clapped her mouth shut before uttering it. She sighed instead and began to walk away.

By the time Bao-yu's weeping was over, Dai-yu was no longer there. He realized that she must have seen him and have gone away in order to avoid him. Feeling suddenly rather foolish, he rose to his feet and brushed the earth from his clothes. Then he descended from the rockery and began to retrace his steps in the direction of Green Delights. Quite by coincidence Dai-yu was walking along the same path a little way ahead.

"Stop a minute!" he cried, hurrying forward to catch up with her. "I know you are not taking any notice of me, but I only want to ask you one simple question, and then you need never have anything more to do with me."

Dai-yu had turned back to see who it was. When she saw that it was Bao-yu still, she was going to ignore him again; but hearing him say that he only wanted to ask her one question, she told him that he might do so.

Bao-yu could not resist teasing her a little.

"How about *two* questions? Would you wait for two?"

Dai-yu set her face forwards and began walking on again.

Bao-yu sighed.

"If it has to be like this now," he said, as if to himself, "it's a pity it was ever like it was in the beginning."

Dai-yu's curiosity got the better of her. She stopped walking and turned once more towards him.

"Like *what* in the beginning?" she asked. "And like what now?"

"Oh, the *beginning*!" said Bao-yu. "In the *beginning*, when you first came here, I was your faithful companion in all your games. Anything I had, even the thing most dear to me, was yours for the asking. If there was something to eat that I specially liked, I had only to hear that you were fond of it too and I would religiously hoard it away to share with you when you got back, not daring even to touch it until you came. We ate at the same table. We slept in the same bed. I used to think that because we were so close then, there would be something special about our relationship when we grew up—that even if we weren't particularly affectionate, we should at least have more understanding and forbearance for each other than the rest. But how wrong I was! Now that you *have* grown up, you seem only to have grown more touchy. You don't seem to care about *me* any more at all. You spend all your time brooding about outsiders like Feng and Chai. I haven't got any *real* brothers and sisters left here now. There are Huan and Tan, of course; but as you know, they're only my half-brother and half-sister: they aren't my mother's children. I'm on my own, like you. I should have thought we had so much in common—But what's the use? I try and try, but it gets me nowhere; and nobody knows or cares."

At this point—in spite of himself—he burst into tears.

The palpable evidence of her own eyes and ears had by now wrought a considerable softening on Dai-yu's heart. A sympathetic tear stole down her own cheek, and she hung her head and said nothing. Bao-yu could see that he had moved her.

"I know I'm not much use nowadays," he continued, "but however bad you may think me, I would never wittingly do anything in your presence to offend you. If I *do* ever slip up in some way, you ought to tell me off about it and warn me not to do it again, or shout at me—hit me, even, if you feel like it; I shouldn't mind. But you don't do that. You just ignore me. You leave me utterly at a loss to know what I'm supposed to have done wrong, so that I'm driven half frantic wondering what I ought to do to make up for it. If I were to die now, I should die with a grievance, and all the masses and exorcisms in the world wouldn't lay my ghost. Only when you explained what your reason was for ignoring me should I cease from haunting you and be reborn into another life."

Dai-yu's resentment for the gate incident had by now completely evaporated. She merely said:

"Oh well, in that case why did you tell your maids not to let me in when I came to call on you?"

"I honestly don't know what you are referring to," said Bao-yu in surprise. "Strike me dead if I ever did any such thing!"

"Hush!" said Dai-yu. "Talking about death at this time of the morning! You should be more careful what you say. If you did, you did. If you didn't, you didn't. There's no need for these horrible oaths."

"I really and truly didn't know you had called," said Bao-yu. "Cousin Bao came and sat with me a few minutes last night and then went away again. That's the only call I know about."

Dai-yu reflected for a moment or two, then smiled.

"Yes, it must have been the maids being lazy. Certainly they can be very disagreeable at such times."

"Yes, I'm sure that's what it was," said Bao-yu. "When I get back, I'll find out who it was and give her a good talking-to."

"I think some of your young ladies could *do* with a good talking-to," said Dai-yu, "—though it's not really for me to say so. It's a good job it was only me they were rude to. If Miss Bao or Miss Cow were to call and they behaved like that to *her*, that would be really serious."

She giggled mischievously. Bao-yu didn't know whether to laugh with her or grind his teeth. But just at that moment a maid came up to ask them both to lunch and the two of them went together out of the Garden and through into the front part of the mansion, calling in at Lady Wang's[8] on the way.

"How did you get on with that medicine of Dr. Bao's," Lady Wang asked Dai-yu as soon as she saw her, "—the Court Physician? Do you think you are any better for it?"

"It didn't seem to make very much difference," said Dai-yu. "Grandmother has put me back on Dr. Wang's prescription."

"Cousin Lin has got a naturally weak constitution, Mother," said Bao-yu. "She takes cold very easily. These strong decoctions are all very well provided she only takes one or two to dispel the cold. For regular treatment it's probably best if she sticks to pills."

8. Bao-yu's mother.

"The doctor was telling me about some pills for her the other day," said Lady Wang, "but I just can't remember the name."

"I know the names of most of those pills," said Bao-yu. "I expect he wanted her to take Ginseng Tonic Pills."[9]

"No, that wasn't it," said Lady Wang.

"Eight Gem Motherwort Pills?" said Bao-yu. "Zhang's Dextrals? Zhang's Sinistrals? If it wasn't any of them, it was probably Dr. Cui's Adenophora Kidney Pills."

"No," said Lady Wang, "it was none of those. All I can remember is that there was a 'Vajra'[1] in it."

Bao-yu gave a hoot and clapped his hands:

"I've never heard of 'Vajra Pills.' If there are 'Vajra Pills,' I suppose there must be 'Buddha Boluses'!"[2]

The others all laughed. Bao-chai looked at him mockingly.

"I should think it was probably 'The Deva-king Cardiac Elixir Pills,' " she said.

"Yes, yes, that's it!" said Lady Wang. "Of course! How stupid of me!"

"No, Mother, not stupid," said Bao-yu. "It's the strain. All those Vajra-kings and Bodhisattvas have been overworking you!"

"You're a naughty boy to make fun of your poor mother," said Lady Wang. "A good whipping from your Pa is what you need."

"Oh, Father doesn't whip me for that sort of thing nowadays," said Bao-yu.

"Now that we know the name of the pills, we must get them to buy some for your Cousin Lin," said Lady Wang.

"None of those things are any good," said Bao-yu. "You give me three hundred and sixty taels of silver and I'll make up some pills for Cousin Lin that I guarantee will have her completely cured before she has finished the first boxful."

"Stuff!" said Lady Wang. "Whoever heard of a medicine that cost so much?"

"No, honestly!" said Bao-yu. "This prescription is a very unusual one with very special ingredients. I can't remember all of them, but I know they include

the caul[3] of a first-born child;
a ginseng root shaped like a man, with the leaves still on it;
a turtle-sized polygonum[4] root;

and

lycoperdon from the stump of a thousand-year-old pine-tree.

—Actually, though, there's nothing so *very* special about those ingredients. They're all in the standard pharmacopoeia. For 'sovereign remedies' they use ingredients that would *really* make you jump. I once gave the prescription for one to Cousin Xue. He was more than a year begging me for it before I would give it to him, and it took him another two or three years

9. This passage plays on the fantastic names of Chinese medicines.   1. The thunderbolt of the Indian god Indra, a conventional image for something hard and powerful.   2. A large pill given to a horse. 3. The membrane around the newborn.   4. The translator is using the Latin names of the plants used in the prescription.

and nearly a thousand taels of silver to get all the ingredients together. Ask Bao-chai if you don't believe me, Mother."

"I know nothing about it," said Bao-chai. "I've never heard it mentioned. It's no good telling Aunt to ask *me*."

"You see! Bao-chai is a *good* girl. *She* doesn't tell lies," said Lady Wang.

Bao-yu was standing in the middle of the floor below the kang. He clapped his hands at this and turned to the others appealingly.

"But it's the *truth* I'm telling you. This is no lie."

As he turned, he happened to catch sight of Dai-yu, who was sitting behind Bao-chai, smiling mockingly and stroking her cheek with her finger—which in sign-language means, "You are a great big liar and you ought to be ashamed of yourself."

But Xi-feng, who happened to be in the inner room supervising the laying of the table and had overheard the preceding remarks, now emerged into the outer room to corroborate:

"It's quite true, what Bao says. I don't think he *is* making it up," she said. "Not so long ago Cousin Xue came to me asking for some pearls, and when I asked him what he wanted them for, he said, 'To make medicine with.' Then he started grumbling about the trouble he was having in getting the right ingredients and how he had half a mind not to make this medicine up after all. I said, 'What medicine?' and he told me that it was a prescription that Cousin Bao had given him and reeled off a lot of ingredients—I can't remember them now. 'Of course,' he said, 'I could easily enough *buy* a few pearls; only these have to be ones that have been worn. That's why I'm asking *you* for them. If you haven't got any loose ones,' he said, 'a few pearls broken off a bit of jewellery would do. I'd get you something nice to replace it with.' He was so insistent that in the end I had to break up two of my ornaments for him. Then he wanted a yard of Imperial red gauze. That was to put over the mortar to pound the pearls through. He said they had to be ground until they were as fine as flour.'

"You see!" "You see!" Bao-yu kept interjecting throughout this recital.

"Incidentally, Mother," he said, when it was ended, "even *that* was only a substitute. According to the prescription, the pearls ought really to have come from an ancient grave. They should really have been pearls taken from jewellery on the corpse of a long-buried noblewoman. But as one can't very well go digging up graves and rifling tombs every time one wants to make this medicine, the prescription allows pearls worn by the living as a second-best."

"Blessed name of the Lord!" said Lady Wang. "What a *dreadful* idea! Even if you *did* get them from a grave, I can't believe that a medicine made from pearls that had been come by so wickedly—desecrating people's bones that had been lying peacefully in the ground all those hundreds of years—could possibly do you any good."

Bao-yu turned to Dai-yu.

"Did you hear what Feng said?" he asked her. "I hope you're not going to say that *she* was lying."

Although the remark was addressed to Dai-yu, he winked at Bao-chai as he made it.

Dai-yu clung to Lady Wang.

"Listen to him, Aunt!" she wailed. "Bao-chai won't be a party to his lies, but he still expects *me* to be."

"Bao-yu, you are very unkind to your cousin," said Lady Wang.

Bao-yu only laughed.

"You don't know the reason, Mother. Bao-chai didn't know a half of what Cousin Xue got up to, even when she was living with her mother outside; and now that she's moved into the Garden, she knows even less. When she said she didn't know, she *really* didn't know: she wasn't giving me the lie. What you don't realize is that Cousin Lin was all the time sitting behind her making signs to show that she didn't believe me."

Just then a maid came from Grandmother Jia's apartment to fetch Bao-yu and Dai-yu to lunch.

Without saying a word to Bao-yu, Dai-yu got up and, taking the maid's hand, began to go. But the maid was reluctant.

"Let's wait for Master Bao and we can go together."

"He's not eating lunch today," said Dai-yu. "Come on, let's go!"

"Whether he's eating lunch or not," said the maid, "he'd better come with us, so that he can explain to Her Old Ladyship about it when she asks."

"All right, you wait for him then," said Dai-yu. "I'm going on ahead."

And off she went.

"I think I'd rather eat with *you* today, Mother," said Bao-yu.

"No, no, you can't," said Lady Wang. "Today is one of my fast-days:[5] I shall only be eating vegetables. You go and have a proper meal with your Grandma."

"I shall share your vegetables," said Bao-yu. "Go on, you can go," he said, dismissing the maid; and rushing up to the table, he sat himself down at it in readiness.

"You others had better get on with your own lunch," Lady Wang said to Bao-chai and the girls. "Let him do as he likes."

"You really ought to go," Bao-chai said to Bao-yu. "Whether you have lunch there or not, you ought to keep Cousin Lin company. She is very upset, you know. Why don't you?"

"Oh, leave her alone!" said Bao-yu. "She'll be all right presently."

Soon they had finished eating, and Bao-yu, afraid that Grandmother Jia might be worrying and at the same time anxious to rejoin Dai-yu, hurriedly demanded tea to rinse his mouth with. Tan-chun and Xi-chun were much amused.

"Why are you always in such a hurry, Bao?" they asked him. "Even your eating and drinking all seems to be done in a rush."

"You should let him finish quickly, so that he can get back to his Dai-yu," said Bao-chai blandly. "Don't make him waste time here with us."

Bao-yu left as soon as he had drunk his tea, and made straight for the west courtyard where his Grandmother Jia's apartment was. But as he was passing by the gateway of Xi-feng's courtyard, it happened that Xi-feng herself was standing in her doorway with one foot on the threshold, groom-

---

5. Days when no meat is eaten; a Buddhist practice.

ing her teeth with an ear-cleaner and keeping a watchful eye on nine or
ten pages who were moving potted plants about under her direction.

"Ah, just the person I wanted to see!" she said, as soon as she caught
sight of Bao-yu. "Come inside. I want you to write something down for
me."

Bao-yu was obliged to follow her indoors. Xi-feng called for some paper,
an inkstone and a brush, and at once began dictating:

"Crimson lining-damask forty lengths, dragonet figured satin forty
lengths, miscellaneous Imperial gauze one hundred lengths, gold necklets
four, —"

"Here, what *is* this?" said Bao-yu. "It isn't an invoice and it isn't a presentation list. How am I supposed to write it?"

"Never you mind about that," said Xi-feng. "As long as *I* know what it
is, that's all that matters. Just put it down anyhow."

Bao-yu wrote down the four items. As soon as he had done so, Xi-feng
took up the paper and folded it away.

"Now," she said, smiling pleasantly, "there's something I want to talk to
you about. I don't know whether you'll agree to this or not, but there's a
girl in your room called 'Crimson' whom I'd like to work for me. If I find
you someone to replace her with, will you let me have her?"

"There are so many girls in my room," said Bao-yu. "Please take any
you have a fancy to. You really don't need to ask me about it."

"In that case," said Xi-feng, "I'll send for her straight away."

"Please do," said Bao-yu, and started to go.

"Hey, come back!" said Xi-feng. "I haven't finished with you yet."

"I've got to see Grandma now," said Bao-yu. "If you've got anything else
to say, you can tell me on my way back."

When he got to Grandmother Jia's apartment, they had all just finished
lunch. Grandmother Jia asked him if he had had anything nice to eat with
his mother.

"There wasn't anything nice," he said. "But I had an extra bowl of rice."

Then, after the briefest pause:

"Where's Cousin Lin?"

"In the inner room," said Grandmother Jia.

In the inner room a maid stood below the kang[6] blowing on a flat-iron.
Up on the kang two maids were marking some material with a chalked
string, while Dai-yu, her head bent low over her work, was engaged in
cutting something from it with her shears.

"What are you making?" he asked her. "You'll give yourself a headache,
stooping down like that immediately after your lunch."

Dai-yu took no notice and went on cutting.

"That corner looks a bit creased still," said one of the maids. "It will
have to be ironed again."

"*Leave it alone!*" said Dai-yu, laying down her shears. "*It will be all right
presently.*"

Bao-yu found her reply puzzling.

Bao-chai, Tan-chun and the rest had now arrived in the outer room and

---

6. A brick platform, heated by a small fire underneath, that could be used for sitting on or as a bed.

were talking to Grandmother Jia. Presently Bao-chai drifted inside and asked Dai-yu what she was doing; then, when she saw that she was cutting material, she exclaimed admiringly.

"What a lot of things you can do, Dai! Fancy, even dress-making now!"

Dai-yu smiled malignantly.

"Oh, it's all lies, really. I just do it to fool people."

"I've got something to tell you that I think will amuse you, Dai," said Bao-chai pleasantly. "When our cousin was holding forth about that medicine just now and I said I didn't know about it, I believe actually he was rather wounded."

"*Oh, leave him alone!*" said Dai-yu. "*He will be all right presently.*"

"Grandma wants someone to play dominoes with," said Bao-yu to Bao-chai. "Why don't you go and play dominoes?"

"Oh, is *that* what I came for?" said Bao-chai; but she went, notwithstanding.

"Why don't *you* go?" said Dai-yu. "There's a tiger in this room. You might get eaten."

She said this still bending over her cutting, which she continued to work away at without looking up at him.

Finding himself once more ignored, Bao-yu nevertheless attempted to remain jovial.

"Why don't you come out for a bit too? You can do this cutting later."

Dai-yu continued to take no notice.

Failing to get a response from her, he tried the maids:

"Who told her to do this dress-making?"

"Whoever told her to do it," said Dai-yu, "it has nothing whatever to do with Master Bao."

Bao-yu was about to retort, but just at that moment someone came in to say that he was wanted outside, and he was obliged to hurry off.

Dai-yu leaned forward and shouted after him:

"Holy name! By the time you get back, I shall be dead."

Outside the gateway to the inner quarters Bao-yu found Tealeaf waiting.

"Mr. Feng invites you round to his house," said Tealeaf.

Bao-yu realized that this must be in connection with the matter Feng Zi-ying had spoken of on the previous day. He told Tealeaf to send for his going-out clothes, and went into his outer study to wait for them.

Tealeaf went back to the west inner gate to wait for someone who would carry a message inside to the maids. Presently an old woman came out:

"Excuse me, missus," said Tealeaf. "Master Bao is waiting in the outer study for his going-out clothes. Could you take a message inside to say that he wants them?"

"—your mother's twat!"[7] said the old woman. "Master Bao lives in the Garden now. All his maids are in the Garden. What do you want to come running round here for?"

Tealeaf laughed at his own mistake.

"You're quite right. I'm going cuckoo."

7. The casual use of vulgarity marks the woman's low class and reminds the reader of an uglier world surrounding the garden.

He ran round to the gate of the Garden. As luck would have it, the boys on that gate were playing football[8] in the open space below the terraced walk, and when Tealeaf had explained his errand, one of them ran off inside for him. He returned after a very long wait, carrying a large bundle, which he handed to Tealeaf, and which Tealeaf carried back to the outer study.

While he was changing, Bao-yu asked for his horse to be saddled, and presently set off, taking only Tealeaf, Ploughboy, Two-times and Oldie as his attendants. When they reached Feng Zi-ying's gate, someone ran in to announce his arrival, and Feng Zi-ying came out in person to greet him and led him inside to meet the company.

This comprised Xue Pan, who had evidently been waiting there for some time, a number of boy singers, a female impersonator called Jiang Yu-han and a girl called Nuageuse from the Budding Grove, a high-class establishment specializing in female entertainers. When everyone had been introduced, tea was served.

"Now come on!" said Bao-yu, as he picked up the proffered cup of tea. "What about this 'lucky accident' you mentioned yesterday? I've been waiting anxiously to hear about it ever since I saw you. That's why I came so promptly when I got your invitation."

Feng Zi-ying laughed.

"You and your cousin are such simple souls—I find it rahver touchin'! Afraid it was pure invention, what I said yesterday. I said it to make you come, because I fought that if I asked you outright to come and drink wiv me, you'd make excuses. Anyway, it worked."

The company joined in his merriment.

Wine was now brought in and everyone sat down in the places assigned to them. Feng Zi-ying first got one of the singing-boys to pour for them; then he called on Nuageuse to drink with each of the guests in turn.

Xue Pan, by the time he had three little cupfuls of wine inside him, was already beginning to be obstreperous. He seized Nuageuse by the hand and drew her towards him:

"If you'd sing me a nice new song—one of your specials, I'd drink a whole jarful for you. How about it, eh?"

Nuageuse had to oblige him by taking up her lute and singing the following song for him to her own accompaniment:

> Two lovely boys
> Are both in love with me
> And I can't get either from my mind.
> Both are so beautiful
> So wonderful
> So marvellous
> To give up either one would be unkind.
> Last night I promised I would go
> To meet one of them in the garden where the roses grow;
> The other came to see what he could find.
> And now that we three are all

---

8. Here, a game similar to soccer.

> Here in this tribunal,
> There are no words that come into my mind.

"There you are!" she said. "Now drink your jarful!"

"That one's not worth a jarful," said Xue Pan. "Sing us a better one."

"Now just a minute," said Bao-yu. "Just guzzling like this will make us drunk in no time without giving us any real enjoyment. I've got a good new drinking-game for you. Let me first drink the M.C.'s starting-cup,[9] and I'll tell you the rules. After that, anyone who doesn't toe the line will be made to drink ten sconce-cups straight off as a forfeit, give up his seat at the party, and spend the rest of the time pouring out drinks for the rest of us."

Feng Zi-ying and Jiang Yu-han agreed enthusiastically, and Bao-yu picked up one of the extra large cups that had now been provided and drained its contents at a single draught.

"Now," he said. "We're going to take four words—let's say 'upset,' 'glum,' 'blest' and 'content.' You have to begin by saying 'The girl is—,' and then you say one of the four words. That's your first line. The next line has to rhyme with the first line and it has to give the reason why the girl is whatever it says—'upset' or 'glum' or 'blest' or 'content.' When you've done all four, you're entitled to drink the wine in front of you. Only, before drinking it, you've first got to sing some new popular song; and *after* you've drunk it, you've got to choose some animal or vegetable object from the things in front of us and recite a line from a well-known poem, or an old couplet, or a quotation from the classics—"

Before he could finish, Xue Pan was on his feet, protesting vigorously:

"You can count *me* out of this. *I'm* taking no part in this. This is just to make a fool of me, isn't it?"

Nuageuse, too, stood up and attempted to push him back into his seat:

"What are you so afraid of, a practised drinker like you? You can't be any worse at this sort of thing than I am, and *I'm* going to have a go when *my* turn comes. If you do it all right, you've got nothing to worry about, and even if you can't, you'll only be made to drink a few cups of wine; whereas if you refuse to follow the rules at the very outset, you'll have to drink ten sconces straight off in a row and then be thrown out of the party and made to pour drinks for the rest of us."

"Bravo!" cried the others, clapping; and Xue Pan, seeing them united against him, subsided.

Bao-yu now began his own turn:

> "The girl's upset:
>   The years pass by, but no one's claimed her yet.
> The girl looks glum:
>   Her true-love's gone to follow ambition's drum.
> The girl feels blest:
>   The mirror shows her looks are at their best.
> The girl's content:
>   Long summer days in pleasant pastimes spent."

9. Bao-yu is going to set up the drinking games, so he drinks first.

The others all applauded, except Xue Pan, who shook his head disapprovingly:

"No good, no good!" he said. "Pay the forfeit."

"Why, what's wrong with it?" they asked him.

"I couldn't understand a word of it."

Nuageuse gave him a pinch:

"Keep quiet and try to think what *you*'re going to say," she advised him;
"otherwise you'll have nothing ready when your own turn comes and
you'll have to pay the forfeit yourself."

Thereupon she picked up her lute and accompanied Bao-yu as he sang
the following song:

> "Still weeping tears of blood about our separation:
> Little red love-beans of my desolation.
> Still blooming flowers I see outside my window growing.
> Still awake in the dark I hear the wind a-blowing.
> Still oh still I can't forget those old hopes and fears.
> Still can't swallow food and drink, 'cos I'm choked with tears.
> Mirror, mirror on the wall, tell me it's not true:
> Do I look so thin and pale, do I look so blue?
> Mirror, mirror, this long night how shall I get through?
> Oh—oh—oh!
> Blue as the mist upon the distant mountains,
> Blue as the water in the ever-flowing fountains."

General applause—except from Xue Pan, who objected that there was
"no rhythm."

Bao-yu now drank his well-earned cup—the "pass cup" as they call it—
and, picking up a slice of pear from the table, concluded his turn with the
following quotation:

> "Rain whips the pear-tree, shut fast the door."

Now it was Feng Zi-ying's turn:

> "The girl's upset:
>   Her husband's ill and she's in debt.
> The girl looks glum:
>   The gale has turned her room into a slum.
> The girl feels blest:
>   She's got twin babies at the breast.
> The girl's content:
>   Waiting a certain pleasurable event."

Next, holding up his cupful of wine in readiness to drink, he sang this
song:

> "You're so exciting,
> And so inviting;
> You're my Mary Contrary;
> You're a crazy, mad thing.
> You're my goddess, but oh! you're deaf to my praying:
> Why won't you listen to what I am saying?
> If you don't believe me, make a small investigation:
> You will soon find out the true depth of my admiration."

Then he drained his bumper and, picking up a piece of chicken from one of the dishes, ended the performance, prior to popping it into his mouth, with a line from Wen Ting-yun:[1]

> "From moonlit cot the cry of chanticleer."

Next it was the turn of Nuageuse:

> "The girl's upset:"

she began,

> "Not knowing how the future's to be met—"

Xue Pan laughed noisily.

"That's all right, my darling, don't you worry! Your Uncle Xue will take care of you."

"Shush!" said the others. "Don't confuse her."

She continued:

> "The girl looks glum:
>   Nothing but blows and hard words from her Mum—"

"I saw that Mum of yours the other day," said Xue Pan, "and I particularly told her that she wasn't to beat you."

"Another word from you," said the others, "and you'll be made to drink ten cups as a punishment."

Xue Pan gave his own face a slap.

"Sorry! I forgot. Won't do it again."

> "The girl feels blest:"

said Nuageuse,

> "Her young man's rich and beautifully dressed.
> The girl's content:
>   She's been performing in a big event."

Next Nuageuse sang her song:

> "A flower began to open in the month of May.
> Along came a honey-bee to sport and play.
> He pushed and he squeezed to get inside,
> But he couldn't get in however hard he tried.
> So on the flower's lip he just hung around,
> A-playing the see-saw up and down.
>   Oh my honey-sweet,
>   Oh my sweets of sin,
>   If I don't open up,
>   How will you get in?"

After drinking her "pass cup," she picked up a peach:

> "So bonny blooms the peach-tree-o."[2]

It was now Xue Pan's turn.

"Ah yes, now, let's see! *I* have to say something now, don't I?"

1. Poet (9th century).   2. From the *Book of Songs*.

"The girl's upset—"

But nothing followed.

"All right, what's she upset about then?" said Feng Zi-ying with a laugh. "Buck up!"

Xue Pan appeared to be engaged in a species of mental effort so frightful that his eyes seemed about to pop out of his head. After glaring fixedly for an unconscionable time, he said:

"The girl's upset—"

He coughed a couple of times. Then at last it came:

"The girl's upset:
    She's married to a marmoset."

The others greeted this with a roar of laughter.

"What are you laughing at?" said Xue Pan. "That's perfectly reasonable, isn't it? If a girl was expecting a proper husband and he turned out to be one of *them*, she'd have cause to be upset, wouldn't she?"

His audience were by now doubled up.

"That's perfectly true," they conceded. "Very good. Now what about the next bit?"

Xue Pan glared a while very concentratedly, then:

"The girl looks glum—"

But after that was silence.

"Come on!" said the others. "Why was she glum?"

"His dad's a baboon with a big red bum."

"Ho! Ho! Ho! Pay the forfeit," they cried. "The first one was bad enough. We really can't let this one go."

The more officious of them even began filling the sconce-cups for him. But Bao-yu allowed the line.

"As long as it rhymes," he said, "we'll let it pass."

"There you are!" said Xue Pan. "The M.C. says it's all right. What are the rest of you making such a fuss about?"

At this the others desisted.

"The next two are even harder," said Nuageuse. "Shall I do them for you, dear?"

"Piss off!" said Xue Pan. "D'you think I haven't got any good lines of my own? Listen to this:

The girl feels blest:
    In bridal bower she takes her rest."

The others stared at him in amazement:

"I say, old chap, that's a bit poetical for you, isn't it?"

Xue Pan continued unconcernedly:

"The girl's content:
    She's got a big prick up her vent."

The others looked away with expressions of disgust.

"Oh dear, oh dear! Hurry up and get on with the song, then."

"One little gnat went hum hum hum,"

Xue Pan began tunelessly. The others looked at him open-mouthed:
"What sort of song is that?"
Xue Pan droned on, ignoring the question:

"Two little flies went bum bum bum,
Three little—"

"Stop!" shouted the others.
"Sod you lot!" said Xue Pan. "This is the very latest new hit. It's called
the Hum-bum Song. If you can't be bothered to listen to it, you'll have to
let me off the other thing. I'll agree not to sing the rest of the song on that
condition."
"Yes, yes, we'll let you off," they said. "Just don't interfere with the rest
of us, that's all we ask."
This meant that it was now Jiang Yu-han's turn to perform. This is what
he said:

"The girl's upset:
Her man's away, she fears he will forget.
The girl looks glum:
So short of cash she can't afford a crumb.
The girl feels blest:
Her lampwick's got a lucky crest.
The girl's content:
She's married to a perfect gent."

Then he sang this song:

"A mischievous bundle of charm and love,
Or an angel come down from the skies above?
Sweet sixteen
And so very green,
Yet eager to see all there is to be seen.
Aie aie aie
The galaxy's high
In the roof of the sky,
And the drum from the tower
Sounds the midnight hour.
So trim the lamp, love, and come with me
Inside the bed-curtains, and you shall see!"

He raised the pass cup to his lips, but before drinking it, smiled round
at his auditors and made this little speech:
"I'm afraid my knowledge of poetry is strictly limited. However, I happened to see a couplet on someone's wall yesterday which has stuck in my
mind; and as one line in it is about something I can see here, I shall use
it to finish my turn with."
So saying, he drained the cup and then, picking up a spray of cassia,
recited the following line:

"The flowers' aroma breathes of hotter days."

The others all accepted this as a satisfactory conclusion of the performance. Not so Xue Pan, however, who leaped to his feet and began protesting noisily:

"Terrible! Pay the forfeit. Where's the little doll? I can't see any doll on the table."

"I didn't say anything about a doll," said Jiang Yu-han. "What are you talking about?"

"Come on, don't try to wriggle out of it!" said Xue Pan. "Say what you said just now again."

"The flowers' aroma breathes of hotter days."

"There you are!" said Xue Pan. " 'Aroma.' That's the name of a little doll.[3] Ask *him* if you don't believe me." —He pointed to Bao-yu.

Bao-yu looked embarrassed.

"Cousin Xue, this time I think you *do* have to pay the forfeit."

"All right, all right!" said Xue Pan. "I'll drink."

And he picked up the wine in front of him and drained it at a gulp.

Feng Zi-ying and Jiang Yu-han were still puzzled and asked him what this was all about. But it was Nuageuse who explained. Immediately Jiang Yu-han was on his feet apologizing. The others reassured him.

"It's not your fault. 'Ignorance excuses all,' " they said.

Shortly after this Bao-yu had to take temporary leave of the company to ease his bladder and Jiang Yu-han followed him outside. As the two of them stood side by side under the eaves, Jiang Yu-han once more offered Bao-yu his apologies. Much taken with the actor's winsome looks and gentleness of manner, Bao-yu impulsively took his hand and gave it a squeeze.

"Do come round to our place some time when you are free," he said. "There's something I want to ask you about. You have an actor in your company called 'Bijou' whom everyone is talking about lately. I should so much like to meet him, but so far I haven't had an opportunity."

"That's me!" said Jiang Yu-han. " 'Bijou' is my stage-name."

Bao-yu stamped with delight.

"But this is wonderful! I must say, you fully deserve your reputation. Oh dear! What am I going to do about a First Meeting present?"[4]

He thought for a bit, then took a fan from his sleeve and broke off its jade pendant.

"Here you are," he said, handing it to Bijou. "It's not much of a present, I'm afraid, but it will do to remind you of our meeting."

Bijou smiled and accepted it ceremoniously:

"I have done nothing to deserve this favour. It is too great an honour. Well, thank you. There's rather an unusual thing I'm wearing—I put it on today for the first time, so it's still fairly new: I wonder if you will allow me to give it to you as a token of my warm feelings towards you?"

He opened up his gown, undid the crimson cummerbund with which his trousers were fastened, and handed it to Bao-yu.

"It comes from the tribute sent by the Queen of the Madder Islands. It's for wearing in summer. It makes you smell nice and it doesn't show perspiration stains. I was given it yesterday by the Prince of Bei-jing, and today is the first time it's ever been worn. I wouldn't give a thing like this

3. Aroma is also the name of Bao-yu's chief maid.   4. Exchanged when people become friends.

to anyone else, but I'd like *you* to have it. Will you take your own sash off, please, so that I can put it on instead?"

Bao-yu received the crimson cummerbund with delight and quickly took off his own viridian-coloured sash to give to Bijou in exchange. They had just finished fastening the sashes on again when Xue Pan jumped out from behind and seized hold of them both.

"What are you two up to, leaving the party and sneaking off like this?" he said. "Come on, take 'em out again and let's have a look!"

It was useless for them to protest that the situation was not what he imagined. Xue Pan continued to force his unwelcome attentions upon them until Feng Zi-ying came out and rescued them. After that they returned to the party and continued drinking until the evening.

Back in his own apartment in the Garden, Bao-yu took off his outer clothes[5] and relaxed with a cup of tea. While he did so, Aroma noticed that the pendant of his fan was missing and asked him what had become of it. Bao-yu told her that it had come off while he was riding, and she gave the matter no more thought. But later, when he was going to bed, she saw the magnificent blood-red sash round his waist and began to put two and two together.

"Since you've got a better sash now," she said, "do you think I could have mine back, please?"

Bao-yu remembered, too late, that the viridian sash had been Aroma's and that he ought never to have given it away. He now very much regretted having done so, but instead of apologizing, attempted to pass it off with a laugh.

"I'll get you another," he told her lightly.

Aroma shook her head and sighed.

"I knew you still got up to these tricks,"[6] she said, "but at least you might refrain from giving *my* things to those disgusting creatures. I'm surprised you haven't got more sense."

She was going to say more, but checked herself for fear of provoking an explosion while he was in his cups.[7] And since there was nothing else she could do, she went to bed.

She awoke at first daylight next morning to find Bao-yu smiling down at her:

"We might have been burgled last night for all you'd have known about it—Look at your trousers!"

Looking down, Aroma saw the sash that Bao-yu had been wearing yesterday tied round her own waist, and knew that he must have exchanged it for hers during the night. She tore it off impatiently.

"*I* don't want the horrible thing. The sooner you take it away the better."

Bao-yu was anxious that she should keep it, and after a great deal of coaxing she consented, very reluctantly, to tie it on again. But she took it off once and for all as soon as he was out of the room and threw it into an empty chest, having first found another one of her own to put on in its place.

---

5. Clothes were worn in multiple layers.   6. This may suggest that Aroma suspects him of engaging in homosexual acts.   7. That is, he was drunk.

Bao-yu made no comment on the change when they were together again. He merely inquired whether anything had happened the day before, while he was out.

"Mrs. Lian sent someone round to fetch Crimson," said Aroma. "She wanted to wait for you; but it seemed to me that it wasn't all that important, so I took it on myself to send her off straight away."

"Quite right," said Bao-yu. "I already knew about it. There was no need to wait till I got back."

Aroma continued:

"Her Grace[8] sent that Mr. Xia of the Imperial Bedchamber yesterday with a hundred and twenty taels of silver to pay for a three-day *Pro Viventibus* by the Taoists of the Lunar Queen temple starting on the first of next month. There are to be plays performed as part of the Offering, and Mr. Zhen and all the other gentlemen are to go there to burn incense. Oh, and Her Grace's presents for the Double Fifth[9] have arrived."

She ordered a little maid to get out Bao-yu's share of the things sent. There were two Palace fans of exquisite workmanship, two strings of red musk-scented medicine-beads, two lengths of maidenhair chiffon and a grass-woven "lotus" mat to lie on in the hot weather.

"Did the others all get the same?" he asked.

"Her Old Ladyship's presents were the same as yours with the addition of a perfume-sceptre and an agate head-rest, and Sir Zheng's, Lady Wang's and Mrs. Xue's were the same as Her Old Ladyship's but without the head-rest; Miss Bao's were exactly the same as yours; Miss Lin, Miss Ying-chun, Miss Tan-chun and Miss Xi-chun got only the fans and the beads; and Mrs. Zhu and Mrs. Lian both got two lengths of gauze, two lengths of chiffon, two perfume sachets and two moulded medicine-cakes."

"Funny!" said Bao-yu. "I wonder why Miss Lin didn't get the same as me and why only Miss Bao's and mine were the same. There must have been some mistake, surely?"

"When they unpacked them yesterday, the separate lots were all labelled," said Aroma. "I don't see how there could have been any mistake. Your share was in Her Old Ladyship's room and I went round there to get it for you. Her Old Ladyship says she wants you to go to Court at four o'clock tomorrow morning to give thanks."

"Yes, of course," said Bao-yu inattentively, and gave Ripple instructions to take his presents round to Dai-yu:

"Tell Miss Lin that I got these things yesterday and that if there's anything there she fancies, I should like her to keep it."

Ripple went off with the presents. She was back in a very short time, however.

"Miss Lin says she got some yesterday too, and will you please keep these for yourself."

Bao-yu told her to put them away. As soon as he had washed, he left to pay his morning call on Grandmother Jia; but just as he was going out he saw Dai-yu coming towards him and hurried forward to meet her.

---

8. Bao-yu's elder sister, the imperial concubine.   9. A holiday that falls on the fifth day of the Fifth Month.

"Why didn't you choose anything from the things I sent you?"

Yesterday's resentments were now quite forgotten; today Dai-yu had fresh matter to occupy her mind.

"I'm not equal to the honour," she said. "You forget, I'm not in the gold and jade class like you and your Cousin Bao. I'm only a common little wall-flower!"

The reference to gold and jade immediately aroused Bao-yu's suspicions.

"I don't know what anyone else may have been saying on the subject," he said, "but if any such thought ever so much as crossed *my* mind, may Heaven strike me dead, and may I never be reborn as a human being!"

Seeing him genuinely bewildered, Dai-yu smiled in what was meant to be a reassuring manner.

"I wish you wouldn't make these horrible oaths. It's so disagreeable. Who *cares* about your silly old 'gold and jade,' anyway?"

"It's hard to make you *see* what is in my heart," said Bao-yu. "One day perhaps you will know. But I can tell you this. My heart has room for four people only. Grannie and my parents are three of them and Cousin Dai is the fourth. I swear to you there isn't a fifth."

"There's no need for you to swear," said Dai-yu. "I know very well that Cousin Dai has a place in your heart. The trouble is that as soon as Cousin Chai comes along, Cousin Dai gets forgotten."

"You imagine these things," said Bao-yu. "It really isn't as you say."

"Yesterday when Little Miss Bao wouldn't tell lies for you, why did you turn to *me* and expect *me* to? How would you like it if I did that sort of thing to you?"

Bao-chai happened to come along while they were still talking and the two of them moved aside to avoid her. Bao-chai saw this clearly, but pretended not to notice and hurried by with lowered eyes. She went and sat with Lady Wang for a while and from there went on to Grandmother Jia's. Bao-yu was already at his grandmother's when she got there.

Bao-chai had on more than one occasion heard her mother telling Lady Wang and other people that the golden locket she wore had been given her by a monk, who had insisted that when she grew up the person she married must be someone who had "a jade to match the gold." This was one of the reasons why she tended to keep aloof from Bao-yu. The slight embarrassment she always felt as a result of her mother's chatter had yesterday been greatly intensified when Yuan-chun singled her out as the only girl to receive the same selection of presents as Bao-yu. She was relieved to think that Bao-yu, so wrapped up in Dai-yu that his thoughts were only of her, was unaware of her embarrassment.

But now here was Bao-yu smiling at her with sudden interest.

"Cousin Bao, may I have a look at your medicine-beads?"

She happened to be wearing one of the little chaplets[1] on her left wrist and began to pull it off now in obedience to his request. But Bao-chai was inclined to plumpness and perspired easily, and for a moment or two it would not come off. While she was struggling with it, Bao-yu had ample

---

1. Strings of beads.

opportunity to observe her snow-white arm, and a feeling rather warmer than admiration was kindled inside him.

"If that arm were growing on Cousin Lin's body," he speculated, "I might hope one day to touch it. What a pity it's hers! Now I shall never have that good fortune."

Suddenly he thought of the curious coincidence of the gold and jade talismans and their matching inscriptions, which Dai-yu's remark had reminded him of. He looked again at Bao-chai—

> that face like the full moon's argent bowl;
> those eyes like sloes;
> those lips whose carmine hue no Art contrived;
> and brows by none but Nature's pencil lined.

This was beauty of quite a different order from Dai-yu's. Fascinated by it, he continued to stare at her with a somewhat dazed expression, so that when she handed him the chaplet, which she had now succeeded in getting off her wrist, he failed to take it from her.

Seeing that he had gone off into one of his trances, Bao-chai threw down the chaplet in embarrassment and turned to go. But Dai-yu was standing on the threshold, biting a corner of her handkerchief, convulsed with silent laughter.

"I thought you were so delicate," said Bao-chai. "What are you standing there in the draught for?"

"I've been in the room all the time," said Dai-yu. "I just this moment went to have a look outside because I heard the sound of something in the sky. It was a gawping goose."

"Where?" said Bao-chai. "Let *me* have a look."

"Oh," said Dai-yu, "as soon as I went outside he flew away with a *whir-r-r—*"

She flicked her long handkerchief as she said this in the direction of Bao-yu's face.

"Ow!" he exclaimed—She had flicked him in the eye.

The extent of the damage will be examined in the following chapter.

CHAPTER 29

*In which the greatly blessed pray for yet greater blessings
And the highly strung rise to new heights of passion*

We told in the last chapter how, as Bao-yu was standing lost in one of his trances, Dai-yu flicked her handkerchief at him and made him jump by inadvertently catching him in the eye with it.

"Who did that?" he asked.

Dai-yu laughingly shook her head.

"I'm sorry. I didn't mean to. Bao-chai wanted to look at a *gawping goose*, and I accidently flicked you while I was showing her how it went."

Bao-yu rubbed his eye. He appeared to be about to say something, but then thought better of it.

And so the matter passed.

Shortly after this incident Xi-feng arrived and began talking about the arrangements that had been made for the purification ceremonies, due to begin on the first of next month at the Taoist temple of the Lunar Goddess. She invited Bao-chai, Bao-yu and Dai-yu to go with her there to watch the plays.

"Oh *no!*" said Bao-chai. "It's too *hot.* Even if they were to do something we haven't seen before—which isn't likely—I think I should still not want to go."

"But it's *cool* there," said Xi-feng. "There are upstairs galleries on all three sides that you can watch from in the shade. And if we go, I shall send someone a day or two in advance to turn the Taoists out of that part of the temple and make it nice and clean for us and get them to put up blinds.[2] And I'll ask them not to let any other visitors in on that day. I've already told Lady Wang I'm going, so if you others won't come with me, I shall go by myself. I'm so bored lately. And it's such a business when we put on our own plays at home, that I can never enjoy them properly."

"All right then, *I'll* come," said Grandmother Jia, who had been listening.

"*You'll* come, Grannie? Well that's splendid, isn't it! That means it will be just as bad for me as it would be if I were watching here at home."

"Now look here," said Grandmother Jia, "I shan't want you to stand and wait on me. Let me take the gallery facing the stage and you can have one of the side galleries all to yourself; then you can sit down and enjoy yourself in comfort."

Xi-feng was touched.

"*Do* come!" Grandmother Jia said to Bao-chai. "I'll see that your mother comes too. The days are so long now, and there's nothing to do at home except go to sleep."

Bao-chai had to promise that she would go.

Grandmother Jia now sent someone to invite Aunt Xue. The messenger was to call in on the way at Lady Wang's and ask her if the girls might go as well.

Lady Wang had already made it clear that she would not be going herself, partly because she was not feeling very well, and partly because she wanted to be at home in case any further messages arrived from Yuan-chun; but when she learned of Grandmother Jia's enthusiasm, she had word carried into the Garden that not just the girls but anyone else who wanted to might go along with Grandmother Jia's party on the first.

When this exciting news had been transmitted throughout the Garden, the maids—some of whom hardly set foot outside their own courtyards from one year's end to the next—were all dying to go, and those whose mistresses showed a lethargic disinclination to accept employed a hundred different wiles to make sure that they did so. The result was that in the end *all* the Garden's inhabitants said that they would be going. Grandmother Jia was quite elated and at once issued orders for the cleaning and preparation of the temple theatre.

---

2. Although Taoist religious observances were respected, Taoist priests themselves were rarely of high status. When an important family like the Jias visited the temple, it had to be specially cleaned and a large section was set off.

But these are details with which we need not concern ourselves.

On the morning of the first sedans,[3] carriages, horses and people filled all the roadway outside Rong-guo[4] House. The stewards in charge knew that the occasion of this outing was a *Pro Viventibus* ordered by Her Grace the Imperial Concubine and that Her Old Ladyship was going in person to burn incense—quite apart from the fact that this was the first day of the month and the first day of the Summer Festival; consequently the turnout was as splendid as they could make it and far exceeded anything that had been seen on previous occasions.

Presently Grandmother Jia appeared, seated, in solitary splendour, in a large palanquin carried by eight bearers. Li Wan, Xi-feng and Aunt Xue followed, each in a palanquin with four bearers. After them came Bao-chai and Dai-yu sharing a carriage with a splendid turquoise-coloured canopy trimmed with pearls. The carriage after them, in which Ying-chun, Tan-chun and Xi-chun sat, had vermilion-painted wheels and was shaded with a large embroidered umbrella. After them rode Grandmother Jia's maids, Faithful, Parrot, Amber and Pearl; after them Lin Dai-yu's maids, Nightingale, Snowgoose and Delicate; then Bao-chai's maids, Oriole and Apricot; then Ying-chun's maids, Chess and Tangerine; then Tan-chun's maids, Scribe and Ebony; then Xi-chun's maids, Picture and Landscape; then Aunt Xue's maids, Providence and Prosper, sharing a carriage with Caltrop and Caltrop's own maid, Advent; then Li Wan's maids, Candida and Casta; then Xi-feng's own maids, Patience, Felicity and Crimson, with two of Lady Wang's maids, Golden and Suncloud, whom Xi-feng had agreed to take with her, in the carriage behind. In the carriage after them sat another couple of maids and a nurse holding Xi-feng's little girl. Yet more carriages followed carrying the nannies and old women from the various apartments and the women whose duty it was to act as duennas when the ladies of the household went out of doors. The street was packed with carriages as far as the eye could see in either direction, and Grandmother Jia's palanquin was well on the way to the temple before the last passengers in the rear had finished taking their places. A confused hubbub of laughter and chatter rose from the line of carriages while they were doing so, punctuated by an occasional louder and more distinctly audible protest, such as:

"I'm not sitting next to *you!*"

or,

"You're squashing the Mistress's bundle!"

or,

"Look, you've trodden on my spray!"

or,

"You've ruined my fan, clumsy!"

Zhou Rui's wife walked up and down calling for some order:

"Girls! Girls! You're out in the street now, where people can see you. A little behaviour, *please!*"

She had to do this several times before the clamour subsided somewhat.

The footmen and insignia-bearers at the front of the procession had

---

3. That is, sedan chairs.   4. The branch of the Jia clan to which Bao-yu belongs.

now reached the temple, and as the files of their column opened out to range themselves on either side of the gateway, the onlookers lining the sides of the street were able to see Bao-yu on a splendidly caparisoned white horse riding at the head of the procession immediately in front of his grandmother's great palanquin with its eight bearers. As Grandmother Jia and her party approached the temple, there was a crash of drums and cymbals from the roadside. It was the Taoists of the temple come out to welcome them, with old Abbot Zhang at their head, resplendent in cope and vestments and with a burning joss-stick[5] in his hand.

The palanquin passed through the gateway and into the first courtyard. From her seat inside it Grandmother Jia could see the terrifying painted images of the temple guardians, one on each side of the inner gate, flanked by that equally ferocious pair, Thousand League Eye with his blue face and Favourable Wind Ear with his green one, and farther on, the benigner forms of the City God and the little Local Gods. She ordered the bearers to halt, and Cousin Zhen[6] at the head of the younger male members of the clan came forward from the inner courtyard to meet her.

Xi-feng, whose palanquin was nearest to Grandmother Jia's, realized that Faithful and the other maids were too far back in the procession to be able to reach the old lady in time to help her out, and hurried forward to perform this service herself. Unfortunately a little eleven- or twelve-year-old acolyte, who had been going round with a pair of snuffers trimming the wicks of the numerous candles that were burning everywhere and whom the arrival of the procession had caught unawares, chose this very moment to attempt a getaway and ran head-on into her. Out flew Xi-feng's hand and dealt him a resounding smack on the face that sent him flying.

"Clumsy brat!" she shouted. "Look where you're going!"

The little acolyte picked himself up and, leaving his snuffers where they had fallen, darted off in the direction of the gate. But by now Bao-chai and the other young ladies were getting down from their carriages and a phalanx of women-servants clustered all round them, making egress impossible. Seeing a little Taoist running towards them, the women began to scream and shout:

"Catch him! Catch him! Hit him! Hit him!"

"What is it?" asked Grandmother Jia in alarm, hearing this hubbub behind her, and Cousin Zhen went forward to investigate.

"It's one of the young acolytes," said Xi-feng as she helped the old lady from her conveyance. "He was snuffing the candles and didn't get away in time and now he's rushing around trying to find a way out."

"Bring him to me, poor little thing!" said Grandmother Jia. "And don't frighten him. These children from poorer families have generally been rather spoiled. You can't expect them to stand up to great occasions like this. It would be a shame to frighten the poor little thing out of his wits. Think how upset his mother and father would be. Go on!" she said to Cousin Zhen. "Go and fetch him yourself."

Cousin Zhen was obliged to retrieve the little Taoist in person and led

---

5. A stick of incense.   6. Jia Zhen is the acting head of a branch of the Jia clan, one to which Bao-yu does not belong.

him by the hand to Grandmother Jia. The boy knelt down in front of her, the snuffers—now restored to him—clutched in one hand, trembling like a leaf. Grandmother Jia asked Cousin Zhen to raise him to his feet.

"Don't be afraid," she told the boy. "How old are you?"

But the little boy's mouth was hurting him too badly to speak.

"*Poor* little thing!" said Grandmother Jia. "You'd better take him away, Zhen. Give him some money to buy sweeties with and tell the others that they are not to grumble at him."

Cousin Zhen had to promise, and led the boy away, while the old lady led *her* party inside to begin a systematic tour of the shrines.

The pages in the outer courtyard, who had a moment before witnessed Grandmother Jia and her train trooping through the gateway that led into the inner courtyard, were surprised to see Cousin Zhen now emerging from it again with a little Taoist in tow. They heard him say that the boy was to be taken out and given a few hundred cash and that he was to be treated kindly. A few of them came forward and led the child away in obedience to his instructions.

Still standing at the top of the steps to the inner gate, Cousin Zhen inquired what had become of the stewards.

"Steward! Steward!" shouted the pages in unison, and almost immediately Lin Zhi-xiao came running out from heaven knows where, adjusting his hat with one hand as he ran.

"This is a big place," said Cousin Zhen when Lin Zhi-xiao was standing in front of him, "and we weren't expecting so many here today. I want you to take all the people you need and stay here in this courtyard with them. Those you don't need here can wait in the second courtyard. And pick some reliable boys to go on this gate and the two posterns to pass word through to those outside if those inside need anything. Do you understand? All the ladies are here today and I don't want any outsiders to get in. Is that understood?"

"Yessir!" said Lin Zhi-xiao. "Sir!"

"Well get on with it!" said Cousin Zhen. "Where's Rong got to?"

The words were scarcely out of his mouth when Jia Rong came bounding out of the bell-tower, buttoning his jacket as he ran.

"Look at him!" said Cousin Zhen irately. "Enjoying himself in the cool while I am roasting down here! Spit at him, someone."

Long familiarity with Cousin Zhen's temper had taught the boys that he would brook no opposition when roused. One of them obediently stepped forward and spat in Jia Rong's face; then, as Cousin Zhen continued to glare at him, he rebuked Jia Rong for presuming to be cool while his father was still sweating outside in the sun. Jia Rong was obliged to stand with his arms hanging submissively at his sides throughout this public humiliation, not daring to utter a word.

The other members of Jia Rong's generation who were present—Jia Yun, Jia Ping, Jia Qin and the rest—were greatly alarmed by this outburst; indeed, even the clansmen of Cousin Zhen's own generation—the Jia Bins and Jia Huangs and Jia Qiongs—were to be seen putting their hats on and slinking out, one by one, from the shadow of the walls.

"What are you standing here for?" said Cousin Zhen to Jia Rong. "Why don't you get on your horse and go back home and tell your mother and that new wife of yours that Her Old Ladyship is here with all the Rong-guo girls. Tell them they must come here at once to wait on her."

Jia Rong ran outside and began bawling impatiently for his horse. "What on earth can have got into him that he should suddenly have picked on me like that?" he muttered to himself resentfully; then, as his horse had still not arrived, he shouted angrily at the grooms:

"Come on, bring that horse, damn you! Are your hands tied or something?"

He would have liked to send a boy in his place, but was afraid that if he did, his father would find out when he went back later to report; and so, when the horse arrived, he mounted and rode off home.

Cousin Zhen was about to turn and go in again when he discovered old Abbot Zhang at his elbow, smiling somewhat unnaturally.

"Perhaps I don't come in quite the same category as the others," said the old Taoist. "Perhaps I should be allowed inside to wait on Her Old Ladyship. However. In this inclement heat, and with so many young ladies about, I shouldn't like to presume. I will do whatever you say. I *did* just wonder whether Her Old Ladyship might ask for me, or whether she might require a guide to take her round the shrines . . . However. Perhaps it would be best if I waited here."

Cousin Zhen was aware that, though Abbot Zhang had started life a poor boy and entered the Taoist church as "proxy novice" of Grandmother Jia's late husband, a former Emperor had with his own Imperial lips conferred on him the title "Doctor Mysticus," and he now held the seals of the Board of Commissioners of the Taoist Church, had been awarded the title "Doctor Serenissimus"[7] by the reigning sovereign, and was addressed as "Holiness" by princes, dukes and governors of provinces. He was therefore not a man to be trifled with. Moreover he was constantly in and out of the two mansions and on familiar terms with most of the Jia ladies. Cousin Zhen at once became affable.

"Oh, *you*'re one of the family, Papa Zhang, so let's have no more of that kind of talk, or I'll take you by that old beard of yours and give it a good pull. Come on, follow me!"

Abbot Zhang followed him inside, laughing delightedly.

Having found Grandmother Jia, Cousin Zhen ducked and smiled deferentially.

"Papa Zhang has come to pay his respects, Grannie."

"Help him, then!" said Grandmother Jia; and Cousin Zhen hurried back to where Abbot Zhang was waiting a few yards behind him and supported him by an elbow into her presence. The abbot prefaced his greeting with a good deal of jovial laughter.

"Blessed Buddha of Boundless Life! And how has Your Old Ladyship been all this while? In rude good health, I trust? And Their Ladyships, and all the younger ladies?—also flourishing? It's quite a while since I was at the mansion to call on Your Old Ladyship, but I declare you look more blooming than ever!"

7. The translator is imitating the pompous titles of the Taoist clergy.

"And how are *you*, old Holy One?" Grandmother Jia asked him with a pleased smile.

"Thank Your Old Ladyship for asking. I still keep pretty fit. But never mind about that. What *I* want to know is, how's our young hero been keeping, eh? We were celebrating the blessed Nativity of the Veiled King[8] here on the twenty-sixth. Very select little gathering. Tasteful offerings. I thought our young friend might have enjoyed it; but when I sent round to invite him, they told me he was out."

"He really *was* out," said Grandmother Jia, and turned aside to summon the "young hero"; but Bao-yu had gone to the lavatory. He came hurrying forward presently.

"Hallo, Papa Zhang! How are you?"

The old Taoist embraced him affectionately and returned his greeting.

"He's beginning to fill out," he said, addressing Grandmother Jia.

"He looks well enough on the outside," said Grandmother Jia, "but underneath he's delicate. And his Pa doesn't improve matters by forcing him to study all the time. I'm afraid he'll end up by *making* the child ill."

"Lately I've been seeing calligraphy and poems of his in all kinds of places," said Abbot Zhang, "—all quite remarkably good. I really can't understand why Sir Zheng is concerned that the boy doesn't study enough. If you ask me, I think he's all right as he is." He sighed. "Of course, you know who this young man reminds me of, don't you? Whether it's his looks or the way he talks or the way he moves, to me he's the spit and image of Old Sir Jia."

The old man's eyes grew moist, and Grandmother Jia herself showed a disposition to be tearful.

"It's quite true," she said. "None of our children or our children's children turned out like him, except my Bao. Only my little Jade Boy is like his grandfather."

"Of course, your generation wouldn't remember Old Sir Jia," Abbot Zhang said, turning to Cousin Zhen. "It's before your time. In fact, I don't suppose even Sir She and Sir Zheng can have a very clear recollection of what their father was like in his prime."

He brightened as another topic occurred to him and once more quaked with laughter.

"I saw a most attractive young lady when I was out visiting the other day. Fourteen this year. Seeing her put me in mind of our young friend here. It must be about time we started thinking about a match for him, surely? In looks, intelligence, breeding, background this girl was ideally suited. What does Your Old Ladyship feel? I didn't want to rush matters. I thought I'd better first wait and see what Your Old Ladyship thought before saying anything to the family."

"A monk who once told the boy's fortune said that he was not to marry young," said Grandmother Jia; "so I think we had better wait until he is a little older before we arrange anything definite. But do by all means go on inquiring for us. It doesn't matter whether the family is wealthy or not; as long as the girl *looks* all right, you can let me know. Even if it's a poor

---

8. The Taoist pantheon was filled with literally thousands of deities with such grandiloquent names.

family, we can always help out over the expenses. Money is no problem. It's looks and character that count."

"Now come on, Papa Zhang!" said Xi-feng when this exchange had ended. "Where's that new amulet for my little girl? You had the nerve to send someone round the other day for gosling satin, and of course, as we didn't want to embarrass the old man by refusing, we had to send you some. So now what about that amulet?"

Abbot Zhang once more quaked with laughter.

"Ho! ho! ho! You can tell how bad my eyes are getting; I didn't even see you there, dear lady, or I should have thanked you for the satin. Yes, the amulet has been ready for some time. I was going to send it to you two days ago, but then Her Grace unexpectedly asked us for this *Pro Viventibus* and I stupidly forgot all about it. It's still on the high altar being sanctified. I'll go and get it for you."

He went off, surprisingly nimbly, to the main hall of the temple and returned after a short while carrying the amulet on a little tea-tray, using a red satin book-wrap as a tray-cloth. Baby's nurse took the amulet from him, and he was just about to receive the little girl from her arms when he caught sight of Xi-feng laughing at him mockingly.

"Why didn't you bring it in your hand?" she asked him.

"The hands get so sweaty in this weather," he said. "I thought a tray would be more hygienic."

"You gave me quite a fright when I saw you coming in with that tray," said Xi-feng. "I thought for one moment you were going to take up a collection!"

There was a loud burst of laughter from the assembled company. Even Cousin Zhen was unable to restrain himself.

"Monkey! Monkey!" said Grandmother Jia. "Aren't you afraid of going to the Hell of Scoffers when you die and having your tongue cut out?"

"Oh, Papa and I say what we like to each other," said Xi-feng. *He's* always telling *me* I must 'acquire merit' and threatening me with a short life if I don't pay up quickly. That's right, isn't it Papa?"

"As a matter of fact I *did* have an ulterior motive in bringing this tray," said Abbot Zhang, laughing, "but it wasn't in order to make a collection, I assure you. I wanted to ask this young gentleman here if he would be so very kind as to lend me the famous jade for a few minutes. The tray is for carrying it outside on, so that my Taoist friends, some of whom have travelled long distances to be here, and my old students, and *their* students, all of whom are gathered here today, may have the privilege of examining it."

"My dear good man, in that case let the boy go with it round his neck and show it to them himself!" said Grandmother Jia. "No need for all this running to and fro with trays—at your age, too!"

"Most kind! Most considerate!—But Your Old Ladyship is deceived," said the abbot. "I may look my eighty years, but I'm still hale and hearty. No, the point is that with so many of them here today and the weather so hot, the smell is sure to be somewhat overpowering. Our young friend here is certainly not used to it. We shouldn't want him to be overcome by the—ah—effluvia, should we?"

Hearing this, Grandmother Jia told Bao-yu to take off the Magic Jade and put it on the tray. Abbot Zhang draped the crimson cloth over his hands, grasped the tray between satin-covered thumbs and fingers, and, holding it like a sacred relic at eye level in front of him, conveyed it reverently from the courtyard.

Grandmother Jia and the others now continued their sightseeing. They had finished with everything at ground level and were about to mount the stairs into the galleries when Cousin Zhen came up to report that Abbot Zhang had returned with the jade. He was followed by the smiling figure of the abbot, holding the tray in the same reverential manner as before.

"Well, they've all seen the jade now," he said, "—and very grateful they were. They agreed that it really is a most remarkable object, and they regretted that they had nothing of value to show their appreciation with. Here you are!—this is the best they could do. These are all little Taoist trinkets they happened to have about them. Nothing very special, I'm afraid; but they'd like our young friend to keep them, either to amuse himself with or to give away to his friends."

Grandmother Jia looked at the tray. It was covered with jewellery. There were golden crescents, jade thumb-rings and a lot of "motto" jewellery— a tiny sceptre and persimmons with the rebus-meaning "success in all things," a little quail and a vase with corn-stalks meaning "peace through-out the years,"[9] and many other designs—all in gold- or jade-work, and much of it inlaid with pearls and precious stones. Altogether there must have been about forty pieces.

"What have you been up to, you naughty old man?" she said. "Those men are all poor priests—they can't afford to give things like *this* away. You really shouldn't have done this. We can't possibly accept them."

"It was their own idea, I do assure you," said the abbot. "There was nothing I could do to stop them. If you refuse to take these things, I am afraid you will destroy my credit with these people. They will say that I cannot really have the connection with your honoured family that I have always claimed to have."

After this Grandmother Jia could no longer decline. She told one of the servants to receive the tray.

"We obviously can't refuse, Grannie, after what Papa Zhang has just said," said Bao-yu; "but I really have no use for this stuff. Why not let one of the boys carry it outside for me and I'll distribute it to the poor?"

"I think that's a very good idea," said Grandmother Jia.

But Abbot Zhang thought otherwise and hastily intervened:

"I'm sure it does our young friend credit, this charitable impulse. How-ever. Although these things are, as I said, of no especial value, they are— what shall I say—objects of *virtù*, and if you give them to the poor, in the first place the poor won't have much use for them, and in the second place the objects themselves will get spoiled. If you want to give something to the poor, a largesse of money would, I suggest, be far more appropriate."

9. The names or forms of the objects in the jewelry would take on different meanings through puns and other kinds of wordplay.

"Very well, look after this stuff for me, then," said Bao-yu to the servant, "and this evening you will distribute a largesse."

This being now settled, Abbot Zhang withdrew, and Grandmother Jia and her party went up to the galleries. Grandmother Jia sat with Bao-yu and the girls in the gallery facing the stage and Xi-feng and Li Wan sat in the east gallery. The maids all sat in the west gallery and took it in turns to go off and wait on their mistresses.

Not long after they were all seated, Cousin Zhen came upstairs to say that the gods had now chosen which plays were to be performed—by which was meant, of course, that the names had been shaken from a pot in front of the altar, since this was the only way in which the will of the gods could be known. The first play selected was *The White Serpent*.

"What's the story?" said Grandmother Jia.

Cousin Zhen explained that it was about the emperor Gao-zu, founder of the Han dynasty, who began his rise to greatness by decapitating a monstrous white snake.

The second choice was *A Heap of Honours*, which shows the sixtieth birthday party of the great Tang general Guo Zi-yi, attended by his seven sons and eight sons-in-law, all of whom held high office, the "heap of honours" of the title being a reference to the table in his reception-hall piled high with their insignia.

"It seems a bit conceited to have this second one played," said Grandmother Jia. "Still, if that's what the gods chose, I suppose we'd better have it. What's the third one going to be?"

"*The South Branch*,"[1] said Cousin Zhen.

Grandmother Jia was silent. She knew that *The South Branch* likens the world to an ant-heap and tells a tale of power and glory which turns out in the end to have been a dream.

Hearing no reply, Cousin Zhen went off downstairs again to see about the Offertory Scroll, which had to be ceremonially burnt in front of the holy images along with paper money and paper ingots before the theatrical performance could begin.

Our record omits any description of that ceremony and moves back to Bao-yu, who was sitting in the central gallery beside his grandmother, and who now called for a maid to bring the tray up so that he could put on his Magic Jade again. When he had done so, he began to pick over the other trinkets with which the tray was covered and to hand them one by one to Grandmother Jia for her inspection. Her attention was taken by a little red-gold kylin[2] with kingfisher-feather inlay. She stretched out her hand to take it.

"Now where have I seen something like this before?" she said. "I feel certain I've seen some girl wearing an ornament like this."

"Cousin Shi's got one," said Bao-chai. "It's the same as this one only a little smaller."

"Funny!" said Bao-yu. "All the times she's been to our house, I don't remember ever having seen it."

---

1. A play by T'ang Hsien-tsu (1550–1617).   2. A unicorn, considered good luck.

"Cousin Bao is observant," said Tan-chun. "No matter what it is, she remembers everything."

"Well, perhaps not quite *everything*," said Dai-yu wryly. "But she's certainly very observant where things like *this* are concerned."

Bao-chai turned her head away and pretended not to have heard.

Now that he knew the kylin on the tray was like one that Shi Xiang-yun[3] wore, Bao-yu hurriedly picked it up and thrust it inside his jacket. But no sooner had he done so than it occurred to him that his action might be misconstrued; so instead of dropping it into his inside pocket, he continued to hold it there, at the same time glancing about him furtively to see if he had been observed. None of the others seemed to have noticed except Dai-yu, who was staring at him fixedly and nodding her head in mock approval.

Bao-yu felt suddenly embarrassed. Drawing his hand out again with the ornament still in it, he returned her look and laughed sheepishly:

"It's rather nice, isn't it? I thought I'd keep it for you," he said. "When we get home we can thread it on a ribbon and you'll be able to wear it."

Dai-yu tossed her head.

"*I* don't want it!"

"If *you* don't want it, I'll keep it for myself, then," said Bao-yu, and popped it once more inside his jacket.

He was about to add something, but just at that moment Cousin Zhen's wife, You-shi, and his new daughter-in-law, Hu-shi, arrived and came upstairs to pay their respects to Grandmother Jia.

"Now why have *you* come here? You really shouldn't have bothered," said Grandmother Jia. "We only came to amuse ourselves. It isn't a formal visit."

No sooner had she said this than it was announced that representatives from General Feng's household had arrived. It appeared that Feng Zi-ying's mother, hearing that the Jia ladies were having a *Pro Viventibus* performed at the Taoist temple, had immediately prepared an offering of pork, mutton, incense, tea and cakes and sent it post-haste to the temple with her compliments. Xi-feng, hearing the announcement, came hurrying round to the central gallery. She clapped her hands and laughed.

"Dear oh dear! This is something I hadn't bargained for. My idea was a quiet little outing for us girls; but here is everyone sending offerings and behaving as if we'd come here for a high mass or something. It's all your fault, Grannie! And we haven't even got any vails[4] ready to give to the bearers."

Even as she said this, two stewardesses from the Feng household were already mounting the stairs. And before *they* had gone, other messengers arrived with offerings from Vice-president Zhao's lady. From then on it was a steady stream: friends, kinsmen, family connections, business associates—all who had heard that the Jia ladies were holding a *Pro Viventibus* sent their representatives along with offerings and complimentary messages. Grandmother Jia began to regret that she had ever come.

"It isn't as if we'd come here for the ceremony," she grumbled. "We

---

3. An orphaned great-niece of Grandmother Jia.   4. Tips.

only wanted to enjoy ourselves. But all we seem to have done is to have stirred up a lot of fuss."

Consequently, although she stayed and watched the plays for that day, she returned home fairly early in the afternoon and next day professed herself too lacking in energy to go again. Xi-feng reacted differently. "In for a penny, in for a pound" was her motto. They had already had the fuss; and since the players were there anyway, they might as well go again today and enjoy themselves in peace.

For Bao-yu the whole of the previous day had been spoilt by Abbot Zhang's proposal to Grandmother Jia to arrange a match for him. He came home in a thoroughly bad temper and kept telling everyone that he would "never see Abbot Zhang again as long as he lived." Not associating his ill-humour with the abbot's proposal, the others were mystified.

Grandmother Jia's unwillingness was further reinforced by the fact that Dai-yu, since her return home yesterday, had been suffering from mild sunstroke. What with one thing and another, the old lady declined absolutely to go again, and Xi-feng had to make up her own party and go by herself.

But Xi-feng's play-going does not concern us.

Bao-yu, believing that Dai-yu's sunstroke was serious and that she might even be in danger of her life, was so worried that he could not eat, and rushed round in the middle of the lunch-hour to see how she was. He found her neither as ill as he had feared nor as responsive as he might have hoped.

"Why don't you go and watch your plays?" she asked him. "What are you mooning about at home for?"

Abbot Zhang's recent attempt at match-making had profoundly distressed Bao-yu and he was shocked by her seeming indifference.

"I can forgive the others for not understanding what has upset me," he thought; "but that *she* should want to trifle with me at a time like this . . . !"

The sense that she had failed him made the annoyance he now felt with her a hundred times greater than it had been on any previous occasion. Never could any other person have stirred him to such depths of atrabilious[5] rage. Coming from other lips, her words would scarcely have touched him. Coming from hers, they put him in a passion. His face darkened.

"It's all along been a mistake, then," he said. "You're not what I took you for."

Dai-yu gave an unnatural little laugh.

"Not what you took me for? That's hardly surprising, is it? I haven't got that *little something* which would have made me worthy of you."

Bao-yu came right up to her and held his face close to hers:

"You do realize, don't you, that you are deliberately willing my death?"

Dai-yu could not for the moment understand what he was talking about.

"I swore an oath to you yesterday," he went on. "I said that I hoped

---

5. Literally "black bile"; here, dark mood.

Heaven might strike me dead if this 'gold and jade' business meant anything to me. Since you have now brought it up again, it's clear to me that
you *want* me to die. Though what you hope to gain by my death I find it
hard to imagine."

Dai-yu now remembered what had passed between them on the previous day. She knew that she was wrong to have spoken as she did, and felt
both ashamed and a little frightened. Her shoulders started shaking and
she began to cry.

"May Heaven strike *me* dead if I ever willed your death!" she said. "But
I don't see what you have to get so worked up about. It's only because of
what Abbot Zhang said about arranging a match for you. You're afraid he
might interfere with your precious 'gold and jade' plans; and because
you're angry about that, you have to come along and take it out on me—
That's all it is, isn't it?"

Bao-yu had from early childhood manifested a streak of morbid sensibility, which being brought up in close proximity with a nature so closely in
harmony with his own had done little to improve. Now that he had
reached an age when both his experience and the reading of forbidden
books had taught him something about "worldly matters," he had begun
to take a rather more grown-up interest in girls. But although there were
plenty of young ladies of outstanding beauty and breeding among the Jia
family's numerous acquaintance, none of them, in his view, could
remotely compare with Dai-yu. For some time now his feeling for her had
been a very special one; but precisely because of this same morbid sensibility, he had shrunk from telling her about it. Instead, whenever he was
feeling particularly happy or particularly cross, he would invent all sorts of
ways of probing her to find out if this feeling for her was reciprocated. It
was unfortunate for him that Dai-yu herself possessed a similar streak of
morbid sensibility and disguised her real feelings, as he did his, while
attempting to discover what *he* felt about *her*.

Here was a situation, then, in which both parties concealed their real
emotions and assumed counterfeit ones in an endeavour to find out what
the real feelings of the other party were. And because

> When false meets false the truth will oft-times out,

there was the constant possibility that the innumerable little frustrations
that were engendered by all this concealment would eventually erupt into
a quarrel.

Take the present instance. What Bao-yu was actually thinking at this
moment was something like this:

"In my eyes and in my thoughts there is no one else but you. I can
forgive the others for not knowing this, but surely *you* ought to realize? If
at a time like this you can't share my anxiety—if you can think of nothing
better to do than provoke me with that sort of silly talk, it shows that the
concern I feel for you every waking minute of the day is wasted: that you
just don't care about me at all."

This was what he *thought*; but of course he didn't *say* it. On her side
Dai-yu's thoughts were somewhat as follows:

"I know you must care for me a little bit, and I'm sure you don't take
this ridiculous 'gold and jade' talk seriously. But if you cared *only* for me

and had absolutely no inclination at all in another direction, then every time I mentioned 'gold and jade' you would behave quite naturally and let it pass almost as if you hadn't noticed. How is it, then, that when I do refer to it you get so excited? It shows that it must be on your mind. You *pretend* to be upset in order to allay my suspicions."

Meanwhile a quite different thought was running through Bao-yu's mind:

"I would do anything—absolutely *anything*," he was thinking, "if only you would be nice to me. If you would be nice to me, I would gladly die for you this moment. It doesn't really matter whether you know what I feel for you or not. Just be nice to me, then at least we shall be a little closer to each other, instead of so horribly far apart."

At the same time Dai-yu was thinking:

"Never mind me. Just be your own natural self. If *you* were all right, *I* should be all right too. All these manoeuvrings to try and anticipate my feelings don't bring us any closer together; they merely draw us farther apart."

The percipient reader will no doubt observe that these two young people were already of one mind, but that the complicated procedures by which they sought to draw together were in fact having precisely the opposite effect. Complacent reader! Permit us to remind you that your correct understanding of the situation is due solely to the fact that we have been revealing to you the secret, innermost thoughts of those two young persons, which neither of them had so far ever felt able to express.

Let us now return from the contemplation of inner thoughts to the recording of outward appearances.

When Dai-yu, far from saying something nice to him, once more made reference to the "gold and jade," Bao-yu became so choked with rage that for a moment he was quite literally bereft of speech. Frenziedly snatching the "Magic Jade" from his neck and holding it by the end of its silken cord he gritted his teeth and dashed it against the floor with all the strength in his body.

"*Beastly* thing!" he shouted. "I'll smash you to pieces and put an end to this once and for all."

But the jade, being exceptionally hard and resistant, was not the tiniest bit damaged. Seeing that he had not broken it, Bao-yu began to look around for something to smash it with. Dai-yu, still crying, saw what he was going to do.

"Why smash a dumb, lifeless object?" she said. "If you want to smash something, let it be me."

The sound of their quarrelling brought Nightingale and Snowgoose hurrying in to keep the peace. They found Bao-yu apparently bent on destroying his jade and tried to wrest it from him. Failing to do so, and sensing that the quarrel was of more than usual dimensions, they went off to fetch Aroma. Aroma came back with them as fast as she could run and eventually succeeded in prising the jade from his hand. He glared at her scornfully.

"It's my own thing I'm smashing," he said. "What business is it of yours to interfere?"

Aroma saw that his face was white with anger and his eyes wild and dangerous. Never had she seen him in so terrible a rage. She took him gently by the hand:

"You shouldn't smash the jade just because of a disagreement with your cousin," she said. "What do you think she would feel like and what sort of position would it put her in if you really *were* to break it?"

Dai-yu heard these words through her sobs. They struck a responsive chord in her breast, and she wept all the harder to think that even Aroma seemed to understand her better than Bao-yu did. So much emotion was too much for her weak stomach. Suddenly there was a horrible retching noise and up came the tisane of elsholtzia[6] leaves she had taken only a short while before. Nightingale quickly held out her handkerchief to receive it and, while Snowgoose rubbed and pounded her back, Dai-yu continued to retch up wave upon wave of watery vomit, until the whole handkerchief was soaked with it.

"However cross you may be, Miss, you ought to have more regard for your health," said Nightingale. "You'd only just taken that medicine and you were beginning to feel a little bit better for it, and now because of your argument with Master Bao you've gone and brought it all up again. Suppose you were to be *really* ill as a consequence. How do you think Master Bao would feel?"

When Bao-yu heard these words they struck a responsive chord in *his* breast, and he reflected bitterly that even Nightingale seemed to understand him better than Dai-yu. But then he looked again at Dai-yu, who was sobbing and panting by turns, and whose red and swollen face was wet with perspiration and tears, and seeing how pitiably frail and ill she looked, his heart misgave him.

"I shouldn't have taken her up on that 'gold and jade' business," he thought. "I've got her into this state and now there's no way in which I can relieve her by sharing what she suffers." As he thought this, he, too, began to cry.

Now that Bao-yu and Dai-yu were both crying, Aroma instinctively drew towards her master to comfort him. A pang of pity for him passed through her and she squeezed his hand sympathetically. It was as cold as ice. She would have liked to tell him not to cry but hesitated, partly from the consideration that he might be suffering from some deep-concealed hurt which crying would do something to relieve, and partly from the fear that to do so in Dai-yu's presence might seem presumptuous. Torn between a desire to speak and fear of the possible consequences of speaking, she did what girls of her type often do when faced with a difficult decision: she avoided the necessity of making one by bursting into tears.

As for Nightingale, who had disposed of the handkerchief of vomited tisane and was now gently fanning her mistress with her fan, seeing the other three all standing there as quiet as mice with the tears streaming down their faces, she was so affected by the sight that she too started crying and was obliged to have recourse to a second handkerchief.

There the four of them stood, then, facing each other; all of them crying; none of them saying a word. It was Aroma who broke the silence with a strained and nervous laugh.

---

6. Unidentified. *Tisane:* a tea or infusion.

"You ought not to quarrel with Miss Lin," she said to Bao-yu, "if only for the sake of this pretty cord she made you."

At these words Dai-yu, ill as she was, darted forward, grabbed the jade from Aroma's hand, and snatching up a pair of scissors that were lying nearby, began feverishly cutting at its silken cord with them. Before Aroma and Nightingale could stop her, she had already cut it into several pieces.

"It was a waste of time making it," she sobbed. "He doesn't really care for it. And there's someone else who'll no doubt make him a better one!"

"What a shame!" said Aroma, retrieving the jade. "It's all my silly fault. I should have kept my mouth shut."

"Go on! Cut away!" said Bao-yu. "I shan't be wearing the wretched thing again anyway, so it doesn't matter."

Preoccupied with the quarrel, the four of them had failed to notice several old women, who had been drawn by the sound of it to investigate. Apprehensive, when they saw Dai-yu hysterically weeping and vomiting and Bao-yu trying to smash his jade, of the dire consequences to be expected from a scene of such desperate passion, they had hurried off in a body to the front of the mansion to report the matter to Grandmother Jia and Lady Wang, hoping in this way to establish in advance that whatever the consequences might be, *they* were not responsible for them. From their precipitate entry and the grave tone of their announcement Grandmother Jia and Lady Wang assumed that some major catastrophe had befallen and hurried with them into the Garden to find out what it was.

Their arrival filled Aroma with alarm. "What did Nightingale want to go troubling Their Ladyships for?" she thought crossly, supposing that the talebearer had been sent to them by Nightingale; while Nightingale for her part was angry with Aroma, thinking that the talebearer must have been one of Aroma's minions.

Grandmother Jia and Lady Wang entered the room to find a silent Bao-yu and a silent Dai-yu, neither of whom, when questioned, would admit that anything at all was the matter. They therefore visited their wrath on the heads of the two unfortunate maids, insisting that it was entirely owing to their negligence that matters had got so much out of hand. Unable to defend themselves, the girls were obliged to endure a long and abusive dressing-down, after which Grandmother Jia concluded the affair by carrying Bao-yu off to her own apartment.

Next day, the third of the fifth month, was Xue Pan's birthday and there was a family party with plays, to which the Jias were all invited. Bao-yu, who had still not seen Dai-yu since his outburst—which he now deeply regretted—was feeling far too dispirited to care about seeing plays, and declined to go on the ground that he was feeling unwell.

Dai-yu, though somewhat overcome on the day previous to this by the sultry weather, had by no means been seriously ill. Arguing that if *she* was not ill, it was impossible that *he* should be, she felt sure, when she heard of Bao-yu's excuse that it must be a false one.

"He usually enjoys drinking and watching plays," she thought. "If he's not going, it must be because he is still angry about yesterday; or if it isn't that, it must be because he's heard that I'm not going and doesn't want to go without me. Oh! I should *never* have cut that cord! Now he won't ever wear his jade again—unless I make him another cord to wear it on."

So she, too, regretted the quarrel.

Grandmother Jia knew that Bao-yu and Dai-yu were angry with each other, but she had been assuming that they would see each other at the Xues' party and make it up there. When neither of them turned up at it, she became seriously upset.

"I'm a miserable old sinner," she grumbled. "It must be my punishment for something I did wrong in a past life to have to live with a pair of such obstinate, addle-headed little geese! I'm sure there isn't a day goes by without their giving me some fresh cause for anxiety. It must be fate. That's what it says in the proverb, after all:

> 'Tis Fate brings foes and lo'es[7] tegither.

I'll be glad when I've drawn my last breath and closed my old eyes for the last time; then the two of them can snap and snarl at each other to their hearts' content, for I shan't be there to see it, and 'what the eye doesn't see, the heart doesn't grieve.' The Lord knows, it's not *my* wish to drag on this wearisome life any longer!"

Amidst these muttered grumblings the old lady began to cry.

In due course her words were transmitted to Bao-yu and Dai-yu. It happened that neither of them had ever heard the saying

> 'Tis Fate brings foes and lo'es tegither,

and its impact on them, hearing it for the first time, was like that of a Zen "perception": something to be meditated on with bowed head and savoured with a gush of tears. Though they had still not made it up since their quarrel, the difference between them had now vanished completely:

> In Naiad's House one to the wind made moan,
> In Green Delights one to the moon complained,

to parody the well-known lines. Or, in homelier verses:

> Though each was in a different place,
> Their hearts in friendship beat as one.

On the second day after their quarrel Aroma deemed that the time was now ripe for urging a settlement.

"Whatever the rights and wrongs of all this may be," she said to Bao-yu, "*you* are certainly the one who is *most* to blame. Whenever in the past you've heard about a quarrel between one of the pages and one of the girls, you've always said that the boy was a brute for not understanding the girl's feelings better—yet here you are behaving in exactly the same way yourself! Tomorrow will be the Double Fifth. Her Old Ladyship will be really angry if the two of you are still at daggers drawn on the day of the festival, and that will make life difficult for *all* of us. Why not put your pride in your pocket and go and say you are sorry, so that we can all get back to normal again?"

But as to whether or not Bao-yu followed her advice, or, if he did so, what the effect of following it was—those questions will be dealt with in the following chapter.

7. Loves.

CHAPTER 30

Bao-chai speaks of a fan and castigates her deriders
Charmante scratches a "qiang" and mystifies a beholder

Dai-yu, as we have shown, regretted her quarrel with Bao-yu almost as soon as it was over; but since there were no conceivable grounds on which she could run after him and tell him so, she continued, both day and night, in a state of unrelieved depression that made her feel almost as if a part of her was lost. Nightingale had a shrewd idea how it was with her and resolved at last to tackle her:

"I think the day before yesterday you were too hasty, Miss. We ought to know what things Master Bao is touchy about, if no one else does. Look at all the quarrels we've had with him in the past on account of that jade!"

"Poh!" said Dai-yu scornfully. "You are trying to make out that it was my fault because you have taken his side against me. Of course I wasn't too hasty."

Nightingale gave her a quizzical smile.

"No? Then why did you cut that cord up? If three parts of the blame was Bao-yu's, I'm sure at least seven parts of it was yours. From what I've seen of it, he's all right with you when you allow him to be; it's because you're so prickly with him and always trying to put him in the wrong that he gets worked up."

Dai-yu was about to retort when they heard someone at the courtyard gate calling to be let in. Nightingale turned to listen:

"That's Bao-yu's voice," she said. "I expect he has come to apologize."

"I forbid you to let him in," said Dai-yu.

"There you go again!" said Nightingale. "You're going to keep him standing outside in the blazing sun on a day like this. Surely *that*'s wrong, if nothing else is?"

She was moving outside, even as she said this, regardless of her mistress's injunction. Sure enough, it *was* Bao-yu. She unfastened the gate and welcomed him in with a friendly smile.

"Master Bao! I was beginning to think you weren't coming to see us any more. I certainly didn't expect to see you here again so soon."

"Oh, you've been making a mountain out of a molehill," said Bao-yu, returning her smile. "Why ever shouldn't I come? Even if I died, my *ghost* would be round here a hundred times a day. How is my cousin? Quite better now?"

"Physically she's better," said Nightingale, "but she's still in very poor spirits."

"Ah yes—I know she's upset."

This exchange took place as they were crossing the forecourt. He now entered the room. Dai-yu was sitting on the bed crying. She had not been crying to start with, but the bittersweet pang she experienced when she heard his arrival had started the tears rolling. Bao-yu went up to the bed and smiled down at her.

"How are you, coz? Quite better now?"

As Dai-yu seemed to be too busy wiping her eyes to make a reply, he sat down close beside her on the edge of the bed:

"I know you're not *really* angry with me," he said. "It's just that if the others noticed I wasn't coming here, they would think we had been quarrelling; and if we waited for them to interfere, we should be allowing other people to come between us. It would be better to hit me and shout at me now and get it over with, if you still bear any hard feelings, than to go on ignoring me. Coz dear! Coz dear!—"

He must have repeated those same two words in the same tone of passionate entreaty upwards of twenty times. Dai-yu had been meaning to ignore him, but what he had just been saying about other people "coming between" them seemed to prove that he must in *some* way feel closer to her than the rest, and she was unable to maintain her silence.

"You don't have to treat me like a child," she blurted out tearfully. "From now on I shall make no further claims on you. You can behave exactly as if I had gone away."

"Gone away?" said Bao-yu laughingly. "Where would you go to?"

"Back home."

"I'd follow you."

"As if I were dead then."

"If you died," he said, "I should become a monk."

Dai-yu's face darkened immediately:

"What an utterly idiotic thing to say! Suppose your own sisters were to die? Just how many times can one person become a monk? I think I had better see what the others think about that remark."

Bao-yu had realized at once that she would be offended; but the words were already out of his mouth before he could stop them. He turned very red and hung his head in silence. It was a good thing that no one else was in the room at that moment to see him. Dai-yu glared at him for some seconds—evidently too enraged to speak, for she made a sound somewhere between a snort and a sigh, but said nothing—then, seeing him almost purple in the face with suppressed emotion, she clenched her teeth, pointed her finger at him, and, with an indignant "Hmn!", stabbed the air quite savagely a few inches away from his forehead:

"You—!"

But whatever it was she had been going to call him never got said. She merely gave a sigh and began wiping her eyes again with her handkerchief.

Bao-yu had been in a highly emotional state when he came to see Dai-yu and it had further upset him to have inadvertently offended her so soon after his arrival. This angry gesture and the unsuccessful struggle, ending in sighs and tears, to say what she wanted to say now affected him so deeply that he, too, began to weep. In need of a handkerchief but finding that he had come out without one, he wiped his eyes on his sleeve.

Although Dai-yu was crying, the spectacle of Bao-yu using the sleeve of his brand-new lilac-coloured summer gown as a handkerchief had not escaped her, and while continuing to wipe her own eyes with one hand, she leaned over and reached with the other for the square of silk that was draped over the head-rest at the end of the bed. She lifted it off and threw it at him—all without uttering a word—then, once more burying her face in her own handkerchief, resumed her weeping. Bao-yu picked up the handkerchief she had thrown him and hurriedly wiped his eyes with it. When he had dried them, he drew up close to her again and took one of her hands in his own, smiling at her gently.

"I don't know why you go on crying," he said. "I feel as if all my insides were shattered. Come! Let's go and see Grandmother together."

Dai-yu flung off his hand.

"Take your hands off me! We're not children any more. You really can't go on mauling me about like this all the time. Don't you understand *anything—*?"

"Bravo!"

The shouted interruption startled them both. They spun round to look just as Xi-feng, full of smiles, came bustling into the room.

"Grandmother has been grumbling away something *awful*," she said. "She insisted that I should come over and see if you were both all right. 'Oh,' I said, 'there's no need to go and look, Grannie; they'll have made it up by now without any interference from *us.*' So she told me I was lazy. Well, here I am—and of course it's *exactly* as I said it would be. *I* don't know. I don't understand you two. What is it you find to argue about? For every three days that you're friends you must spend at least two days quarrelling. You really are a couple of babies. And the older you get, the worse you get. Look at you *now*—holding hands crying! And a couple of days ago you were glaring at each other like fighting-cocks. Come on! Come with me to see Grandmother. Let's put the old lady's mind at rest."

As she said this, she seized Dai-yu's hand and began marching off with her. Dai-yu turned back and called for her maids, but there was no response.

"What do you want to call *them* for?" said Xi-feng. "You've got *me* to wait on you, haven't you?"

She continued to walk away, still holding Dai-yu by the hand. Bao-yu followed a little way behind. They went out of the Garden and through into Grandmother Jia's apartment.

"I *told* you they could be left to themselves to make it up and that there was no need for you to worry," said Xi-feng to Grandmother Jia when they were all in the old lady's presence; "but you wouldn't believe me, would you? You insisted on my going there to act the peacemaker. Well, I went there; and what did I find? I found the two of them together *apologizing* to each other. It was like the kite and the kestrel[8] holding hands: they were positively *locked in a clinch!* No need of a peacemaker that *I* could see."

There was a burst of laughter from all present. Bao-chai was among these, but Dai-yu slipped past her without speaking and took a seat next to Grandmother Jia. Bao-yu, rather at a loss for something to say, turned to Bao-chai.

"I'm afraid I wasn't very well on your brother's birthday; so apart from not giving him a present, I couldn't even make him a kotow this year. I'm afraid he may not have realized I was ill and thought that I was merely making excuses. If you can spare a moment next time you see him, I do hope you will explain to him for me."

---

8. Two types of hawks.

Bao-chai looked amused.

"That seems a trifle excessive. I am sure he would have felt uncomfortable about your kotowing[9] to him, even if you had been able to come; so I'm quite sure he wouldn't have wanted you to come when you weren't feeling well. It would be rather unfriendly, surely, if cousins who see each other all the time were to start worrying about trifles like *that*?"

Bao-yu smiled.

"Well, as long as *you* understand, that's all right—But why aren't you watching the players?"

"I can't stand the heat," said Bao-chai. "I did watch a couple of acts of something, but it was so hot that I couldn't stay any longer. Unfortunately none of the guests showed any sign of going, so I had to pretend I was ill in order to get away."

"*Touché!*" thought Bao-yu; but he hid his embarrassment in a stupid laugh.

"No wonder they compare you to Yang Gui-fei,[1] cousin. You are well-covered like her, and they always say that plump people fear the heat."

The colour flew into Bao-chai's face. An angry retort was on her lips, but she could hardly make it in front of company. Yet reflection only made her angrier. Eventually, after a scornful sniff or two, she said:

"I may be like Yang Gui-fei in some respects, but I don't think there is much danger of my cousin becoming a Prime Minister."[2]

It happened that just at that moment a very young maid called "Prettikins" jokingly accused Bao-chai of having hidden a fan she was looking for.

"I *know* Miss Bao's hidden it," she said. "Come on, Miss! *Please* let me have it."

"You be careful," said Bao-chai, pointing at the girl angrily and speaking with unwonted stridency. "When did you last see *me* playing games of this sort with anyone? If there are other young ladies who are in the habit of *romping about* with you, you had better ask *them*."

Prettikins fled.

Bao-yu realized that he had once again given offence by speaking thoughtlessly; and as this time it was in front of a lot of people, his embarrassment was correspondingly greater. He turned aside in confusion and began talking nervously to someone else.

Bao-yu's rudeness to Bao-chai had given Dai-yu secret satisfaction. When Prettikins came in looking for her fan, she had been on the point of adding some facetiousness of her own at Bao-chai's expense; but Bao-chai's brief explosion caused her to drop the prepared witticism and ask instead what play the two acts were from that Bao-chai said she had just been watching.

Bao-chai had observed the smirk on Dai-yu's face and knew very well that Bao-yu's rudeness must have pleased her. The smiling answer she gave to Dai-yu's question was therefore not without a touch of malice.

9. Bowing the head to the ground, here as congratulations.   1. The favorite consort of the Tang emperor Xuan-zong, known for her plump beauty.   2. Yang Gui-fei's cousin became a corrupt prime minister. The comparison is a pointed reference to Bao-yu's neglect of his studies.

"The play I saw was *Li Kui Abuses Song Jiang and Afterwards Has to Say He Is Sorry.*"

Bao-yu laughed.

"What a mouthful! Surely, with all your learning, cousin, you must know the proper name of that play? It's called *The Abject Apology.*"

"*The Abject Apology?*" said Bao-chai. "Well, no doubt you clever people know all there is to know about abject apology. I'm afraid it's something I wouldn't know about."

Her words touched Bao-yu and Dai-yu on a sensitive spot, and by the time she had finished, they were both blushing hotly with embarrassment.

Xi-feng was insufficiently educated to have understood all these nuances, but by studying the speakers' expressions she had formed a pretty good idea of what they were talking about.

"Rather hot weather to be eating raw ginger, isn't it?" she asked.

No one present could understand what she meant.

"No one's been eating raw ginger," they said.

Xi-feng affected great surprise and rubbed her cheek meaningfully with her hand:

"If no one's been eating raw ginger, then why are they looking so hot and bothered?"

At this Bao-yu and Dai-yu felt even more uncomfortable. Bao-chai was about to add something, but seeing the abject look on Bao-yu's face, she laughed and held her tongue. None of the others present had understood what the four of them were talking about and treated these exchanges as a joke.

Shortly after this, when Bao-chai and Xi-feng had gone out of the room, Dai-yu said to Bao-yu.

"You see? There are people even more dangerous to trifle with than I. If I weren't such a tongue-tied, slow-witted creature, you wouldn't get away with it quite so often, my friend."

Bao-yu was still smarting from Bao-chai's testiness. To be set upon now by Dai-yu as well seemed positively the last straw. But though he wanted to reply, he knew how easily she would take offence and controlled himself with an effort. Feeling in very low spirits, he left the room himself now and went off on his own.

It was the hottest part of the day. Lunch had long been over, and in every apartment mistress and maids alike had succumbed to the lassitude of the hour. As he sauntered slowly by, hands clasped behind his back, everywhere he went was hushed in the breathless silence of noon. From the back of Grandmother Jia's quarters he passed eastwards through the gallery that ended near the wall of Xi-feng's courtyard. He went up to the gate, but it was closed, and remembering that it was her invariable custom when the weather was hot to take two whole hours off in the middle of the day for her siesta, he thought he had better not go in. He continued, instead, through the corner gate that led into his parents' courtyard.

On entering his mother's apartment, he found several maids dozing over their embroidery. Lady Wang herself was lying on a summer-bed[3] in

---

3. A couch set up to catch the breeze.

the inner room, apparently fast asleep. Her maid Golden, who was sitting beside her gently pounding her legs, also seemed half asleep, for her head was nodding and her half-closed eyes were blinking drowsily. Bao-yu tip-toed up to her and tweaked an ear-ring. She opened her eyes wide and saw that it was Bao-yu.

He smiled at her and whispered.

"So sleepy?"

Golden pursed her lips up in a smile, motioned to him with her hand to go away, and then closed her eyes again. But Bao-yu lingered, fasci-nated. Silently craning forward to make sure that Lady Wang's eyes were closed, he took a Fragrant Snow "quencher"[4] from the embroidered pouch at his waist and popped it between Golden's lips. Golden nibbled it dreamily without opening her eyes.

"Shall I ask Her Ladyship to let me have you, so that we can be together?" he whispered jokingly.

Golden made no reply.

"When she wakes up, I'll talk to her about it," he said.

Golden opened her eyes wide and gave him a little push.

"What's the hurry?" she said playfully. " 'Yours is yours, wherever it be,' as they said to the lady when she dropped her gold comb in the well. Haven't you ever heard that saying?—I'll tell you something to do, if you want a bit of fun. Go into the little east courtyard and you'll be able to catch Sunset and Huan together."

"Who cares about *them?*" said Bao-yu. "Let's talk about *us.*"

At this point Lady Wang sat bolt upright and dealt Golden a slap in the face.

"Shameless little harlot!" she cried, pointing at her wrathfully. "It's you and your like who corrupt our innocent young boys."

Bao-yu had slipped silently away as soon as his mother sat up. Golden, one of whose cheeks was now burning a fiery red, was left without a word to say. The other maids, hearing that their mistress was awake, came hur-rying into the room.

"Silver!" said Lady Wang. "Go and fetch your mother. I want her to take your sister Golden away."

Golden threw herself, weeping, upon her knees:

"No, Your Ladyship, please! Beat me and revile me as much as you like, but please, for pity's sake, don't send me away. I've been with Your Ladyship nigh on ten years now. How can I ever hold up my head again if you dismiss me?"

Lady Wang was not naturally unkind. On the contrary, she was an exceptionally lenient mistress. This was, in fact, the first time in her life that she had ever struck a maid. But the kind of "shamelessness" of which—in her view—Golden had just been guilty was the one thing she had always most abhorred. It was the uncontrollable anger of the morally outraged that had caused her to strike Golden and call her names; and though Golden now begged and pleaded, she refused to retract her dis-missal. When Golden's mother, old Mrs. Bai, had eventually been

---

4. A type of candy.

fetched, the wretched girl, utterly crushed by her shame and humiliation, was led away.

But of her no more.

Embarrassed by his mother's awakening, Bao-yu had slipped hurriedly into the Garden.

The burning sun was now in the height of heaven, the contracted shadows were concentrated darkly beneath the trees, and the stillness of noon, filled with the harsh trilling of cicadas, was broken by no human voice; but as he approached the bamboo trellises of the rose-garden, a sound like a suppressed sob seemed to come from inside the pergola. Uncertain what it was that he had heard, he stopped to listen. Undoubtedly there was someone there.

This was the fifth month of the year, when the rambler roses are in fullest bloom. Peeping through the fragrant panicles[5] with which the pergola was smothered, he saw a girl crouching down on the other side of the trellis, scratching at the ground with one of those long, blunt pins that girls use for fastening their back hair with.

"Can this be some silly maid come here to bury flowers like Frowner?"[6] he wondered.

He was reminded of Zhuang-zi's story of the beautiful Xi-shi's ugly neighbour, whose endeavours to imitate the little frown that made Xi-shi captivating produced an aspect so hideous that people ran from her in terror. The recollection of it made him smile.

"This is 'imitating the Frowner' with a vengeance," he thought, "—if that is really what she is doing. Not merely unoriginal, but downright disgusting!"

"Don't imitate Miss Lin," he was about to shout; but a glimpse of the girl's face revealed to him just in time that this was no maid, but one of the twelve little actresses from Peartree Court—though which of them, since he had seen them only in their make-up on the stage, he was unable to make out. He stuck out his tongue in a grimace and clapped a hand to his mouth.

"Good job I didn't speak too soon," he thought. "I've been in trouble twice already today for doing that, once with Frowner and once with Chai. It only needs me to go and upset these twelve actresses as well and I shall be well and truly in the cart!"[7]

His efforts to identify the girl made him study her more closely. It was curious that he should have thought her an imitator of Dai-yu, for she had much of Dai-yu's ethereal grace in her looks: the same delicate face and frail, slender body; the same

> . . . brows like hills in spring,
> And eyes like autumn's limpid pools;

—even the same little frown that had often made him compare Dai-yu with Xi-shi of the legend.

It was now quite impossible for him to tear himself away. He watched

---

5. Bunches of flowers.   6. That is, Dai-yu.   7. That is, in big trouble.

her fascinated. As he watched, he began to see that what she was doing with the pin was not scratching a hole to bury flowers in, but writing. He followed the movements of her hand, and each vertical and horizontal stroke, each dot and hook that she made he copied with a finger on the palm of his hand. Altogether there were eighteen strokes. He thought for a moment. The character he had just written in his hand was QIANG. The name of the roses which covered the pergola contained the same character: "Qiang-wei."

"The sight of the roses has inspired her to write a poem," he thought. "Probably she's just thought of a good couplet and wants to write it down before she forgets it; or perhaps she has already composed several lines and wants to work on them a bit. Let's see what she writes next."

The girl went on writing, and he followed the movements of her hand as before. It was another QIANG. Again she wrote, and again he followed, and again it was a QIANG. It was as though she were under some sort of spell. As soon as she had finished writing one QIANG she began writing another.

   QIANG QIANG QIANG QIANG QIANG QIANG QIANG. . .

He must have watched her write several dozen QIANG's in succession. He seemed to be as much affected by the spell on his side of the pergola as the girl herself was on hers, for his eyeballs continued to follow her pin long after he had learned to anticipate its movements.

"This girl must have something on her mind that she cannot tell anyone about to make her behave in this way," he thought. "One can see from her outward behaviour how much she must be suffering inwardly. And she looks so frail. Too frail for suffering. I wish I could bear some of it for you, my dear!"

In the stifling dog-days of summer the transition from clear to overcast is often sudden, and a little cloudlet can sometimes be the harbinger of a heavy shower. As Bao-yu watched the girl, a sudden gust of cool wind blew by, followed, within moments, by the hissing downpour of rain. He could see the water running off her head in streams and soaking into her clothes.

"Oh, it's raining! With her delicate constitution she ought not to be outside in a downpour like this."

In his anxiety he cried out to her involuntarily:

"Don't write any more. Look! You're getting soaked."

The girl looked up, startled, when she heard the voice. She could see someone amidst the roses saying "Don't write"; but partly because of Bao-yu's almost girlishly beautiful features, and partly because she could in any case only see about half of his face, everything above and below being hidden by flowers and foliage, she took him for a maid; so instead of rushing from his presence as she would have done if she had known that it was Bao-yu, she smiled up at him gratefully:

"Thank you for reminding me. But what about you? You must be getting wet too, surely?"

"Aiyo!"—her words made him suddenly aware that the whole of his body was icy cold, and when he looked down, he saw that he was soaked.

"Oh lord!"

He rushed off in the direction of Green Delights; but all the time he was worrying about the girl, who had nowhere where she could shelter from the rain.

As this was the day before the Double Fifth festival, Élégante and the other little actresses—including the one whom Bao-yu had just been watching—had already started their holiday and had gone into the Garden to amuse themselves. Two of them, Trésor—one of the two members of the company who played Principal Boy parts—and Topaze—one of the company's two soubrettes[8]—happened to be in the House of Green Delights playing with Aroma when the rain started and prevented their leaving. They and the maids amused themselves by blocking up the gutters and letting the water collect in the courtyard. When it was nicely flooded, they rounded up a number of mallards, sheldrakes, mandarin ducks and other waterfowl, tied their wings together, and having first closed the courtyard gate, set them down in the water to swim about. Aroma and the girls were all in the outside gallery enjoying this spectacle when Bao-yu arrived at the gate. Finding it shut, he knocked on it for someone to come and open up for him. But there was little chance of a knock being heard above the excited laughter of the maids. He had to shout for some minutes and pound the gate till it shook before anyone heard him inside.

Aroma was not expecting him back so soon.

"I wonder who it can be at this time," she said. "Won't someone go and answer it?"

"It's *me!*" shouted Bao-yu.

"That's Miss Bao's voice," said Musk.

"Nonsense!" said Skybright. "What would *she* be doing visiting us at this time of day?"

"Let me just take a peep through the crack," said Aroma. "If I think it's all right, I'll let them in. We don't want to turn anyone away in the pouring rain."

Keeping under cover of the gallery, she made her way round to the gate and peered through the chink between the double doors. The sight of Bao-yu standing there like a bedraggled hen with the water running off him in streamlets was both alarming and—she could not help but feel—very funny. She opened the gate as quickly as she could, then, when she saw him fully, clapped her hands and doubled up with laughter.

"Master Bao! I *never* thought it would be you. What did you want to come running back in the pouring rain for?"

Bao-yu was by now in a thoroughly evil temper and had fully resolved to give whoever opened the gate a few kicks. As soon as it was open, therefore, he lashed out with his foot, not bothering to see who it was—for he assumed that the person answering it would be one of the younger maids—and dealt Aroma a mighty kick in the ribs that caused her to cry out in pain.

8. Young actresses, who are often cast as maids.

"Worthless lot!" he shouted. "Because I always treat you decently, you think you can get away with *anything*. I'm just your laughing-stock."

It was not until he looked down and saw Aroma crying that he realized he had kicked the wrong person.

"Aiyo! It's you! Where did I kick you?"

Up to this moment Aroma had never had so much as a harsh word from Bao-yu, and the combination of shame, anger and pain she now felt on being kicked and shouted at by him in front of so many people was well-nigh insupportable. Nevertheless she forced herself to bear it, reflecting that to have made an outcry would be like admitting that it was *her* he had meant to kick, which she knew was almost certainly not the case.

"You didn't; you missed me," she said. "Come in and get changed."

When Bao-yu had gone indoors and was changing his clothes, he said to her jokingly:

"In all these years this is the first time I've ever struck anyone in anger. Too bad that *you* should have been the one to get in the way of the blow!"

In spite of the pain, which it cost her some effort to master, Aroma was helping him with his changing. She smiled when he said this.

"I'm the person you always begin things with," she said. "Whether it's big things or little things or pleasant ones or unpleasant ones, it's only natural that you should try them out first on me. Only in this instance I hope that now you've hit me you won't from now on go around hitting other people."

"I didn't mean to kick *you*, you know," said Bao-yu.

"Who said you did?" said Aroma. "It's the younger ones who normally see to the gate; and they've grown so insolent nowadays, it's enough to put *anyone* in a rage. If you'd given one of *them* a few kicks and put the fear of God into them, it would have been a very good thing. No, it was my own silly fault. I should have made *them* open the gate and not gone to open it myself."

While they were speaking, the rain had stopped and Trésor and Topaze had left. The pain in Aroma's side was such that it was giving her a feeling of nausea and she could eat no dinner. At bedtime, when she took off her clothes, she saw a great black bruise the size of a rice-bowl spreading over the side of her chest. The extent of it frightened her, but she forbore to cry out. Nevertheless even her dreams that night were full of pain and she several times uttered an "Aiyo" in the midst of her sleep.

Although it was understood that he had not kicked her deliberately, Bao-yu had felt a little uneasy when he saw how sluggish Aroma seemed in her movements; and when, during the night, he heard her groaning in her sleep, he knew that he must have kicked her really hard. Getting out of bed, he picked up a lamp and tiptoed over to have a look. Just as he reached the foot of her bed, he heard her cough a couple of times and spit out a mouthful of something.

"Aiyo!"

She opened her eyes wide and saw Bao-yu. Startled, she asked him what he was doing there.

"You've been groaning in your sleep," he said. "I must have hurt you badly. Let me have a look."

"My head feels giddy," said Aroma, "and I've got a sweet, sickly taste in my throat. Have a look on the floor."

Bao-yu shone his lamp on the floor. Beside the bed, where she had spat, there was a mouthful of bright red blood. He was horrified.

"Oh, help!"

Aroma looked too, and felt the grip of fear on her heart.

The outcome will be told in the following chapter.

CHAPTER 31

A torn fan is the price of silver laughter
And a lost kylin is the clue to a happy marriage

A cold fear came over Aroma when she saw the fresh blood on the floor. She had often heard people say that if you spat blood when you were young, you would die early, or at the very least be an invalid all your life; and remembering this now, she felt all her bright, ambitious hopes for the future turn into dust and ashes. Tears of misery ran down her cheeks. The sight of them made Bao-yu, too, distressed.

"What is it?" he asked her.

"It's nothing." She forced herself to smile. "I'm all right."

Bao-yu was all for calling one of the maids and getting her to heat some rice wine, so that Aroma could be given hot wine and Hainan kid's[9]-blood pills; but Aroma, smiling through her tears, caught at his hand to restrain him.

"It's all right for *you* to make a fuss," she said; "but if you go involving the others, they are sure to accuse me of putting on airs. And besides, it will do neither of us any good to draw attention to ourselves—especially when so far no one seems to have noticed anything. The sensible thing would be for you to send one of the boys round tomorrow to Dr. Wang's and get me some medicine to take. I shall probably be all right again after a few doses, without a single soul knowing anything about it. Surely that's best, isn't it?"

Bao-yu knew that she was right and abandoned his intention of rousing the others. Instead he poured her a cup of tea from a pot on the table and gave it to her to rinse her mouth with. Aroma was uneasy about being waited on by her master; but fearing that if she refused his services he would insist on disturbing everybody, she lay back and allowed him to fuss over her.

As soon as it was daylight, Bao-yu threw on his clothes and, without even waiting to wash or comb, went out of the Garden to his study in the front part of the mansion, whither he summoned the doctor Wang Ji-ren for detailed questioning. When this worthy had elicited the information that the haemorrhage inquired about had been caused by a blow, he seemed less disposed to take a serious view of the case, merely naming some pills and giving perfunctory instructions for taking them internally and for applying them in solution as a poultice. Bao-yu made a note of these instructions and went back into the Garden to carry them out.

But that is no part of our story.

9. A kid is a young goat.

It was now the festival of the Double Fifth. Sprays of calamus and artemisia crowned the doorways and everyone wore tiger amulets fastened on their clothing at the back. At noon Lady Wang gave a little party at which Aunt Xue and Bao-chai were the guests.

Bao-yu, finding Bao-chai somewhat glacial in her manner and evidently unwilling to talk to him, knew that it must be because of his rudeness to her of the day before.

Lady Wang, observing Bao-yu's dejected appearance, attributed it to embarrassment about yesterday's episode with Golden and ignored him even more pointedly than Bao-chai.

Dai-yu, seeing how morose Bao-yu looked assumed that it was because Bao-chai was offended with him and, feeling resentful that he should care, at once became as morose as he was.

Xi-feng, having been told all about Bao-yu and Golden the night before by Lady Wang, could scarcely be her usual laughing and joking self when she knew of her aunt's displeasure and, taking her cue from the latter, was if anything even more glacial than the others.

And Ying-chun, Tan-chun and Xi-chun, seeing everyone else so uncomfortable, soon began to feel just as uncomfortable themselves.

The result was that after sitting for only a very short time, the party broke up.

Dai-yu had a natural aversion to gatherings, which she rationalized by saying that since the inevitable consequence of getting together was parting, and since parting made people feel lonely and feeling lonely made them unhappy, *ergo* it was better for them not to get together in the first place. In the same way she argued that since the flowers, which give us so much pleasure when they open, only cause us a lot of extra sadness when they die, it would be better if they didn't come out at all.

Bao-yu was just the opposite. He always wanted the party to go on for ever and flowers to be in perpetual bloom; and when at last the party did end and the flowers did wither—well, it was infinitely sad and distressing, but it couldn't be helped.

And so today, while everyone else left the party with feelings of gloom, Dai-yu alone was completely unaffected. Bao-yu, on the other hand, returned to his room in a mood of black despondency, sighing and muttering as he went.

Unfortunately it was the sharp-tongued Skybright who came forward to help him change his clothes. With provoking carelessness she dropped a fan while she was doing so and snapped the bone fan-sticks by accidentally treading on it.

"Clumsy!" said Bao-yu reproachfully. "You won't be so careless with things when you have a household of your own."

Skybright gave a sardonic sniff.

"You're getting quite a temper lately, Master Bao. Almost every time we move nowadays we get a nasty look from you. Yesterday even Aroma caught it. Today you're finding fault with me, so I suppose I can expect a few kicks too. Well, kick away. But I must say, I shouldn't have thought treading on a *fan* was such a very terrible thing to do. In the past any number of glass bowls and agate cups have got broken without your turn-

ing a hair. Why this fuss about a fan, then? If you're not satisfied with my
service, you ought to dismiss me and get someone better. Easy come, easy
go. No need for beating about the bush."

By the time she had finished, Bao-yu was so angry that he was shaking
all over.

"You'll go soon enough, don't you worry!" he said.

Aroma had heard all this from the adjoining room and now came hurrying in.

"Now what's all this about?" she said, addressing herself to Bao-yu.
"Didn't I tell you? As soon as I turn my back there's trouble."

"If you knew that already," said Skybright, "it's a pity you couldn't have
come in a bit sooner and saved me from provoking him. Of course, we all
know that you're the only one who knows how to serve him properly.
None of the rest of us knows how it's done. I suppose it's because you
serve him so well that he gave you a kick in the ribs yesterday. Heaven
knows what he's got in store for *me* for having served him so badly!"

Angry, and at the same time ashamed, Aroma was about to retort; but
the sight of Bao-yu's face, now white with anger, made her restrain herself.

"Be a good girl—just go away and play for a bit. It's *we* who are in the
wrong."

Skybright naturally assumed that "we" meant Aroma and Bao-yu. Her
jealousy was further inflamed.

"What do you mean, 'we'?" she said. "You two make me feel ashamed
for you, you really do—because you needn't think you deceive *me*. *I* know
what goes on between you when you think no one is looking. But when
all's said and done, in actual fact, when you come down to it, you're not
even a 'Miss' by *rights*. By *rights* you're no better than any of the rest of us.
I don't know where you get this 'we' from."

Aroma blushed and blushed with shame, until her face had become a
dusky red colour. Too late she realized her slip. By "we" she had meant
no more than "you and I"; not "Bao-yu and I" as Skybright imagined. But
the pronoun had invited misunderstanding.

It was Bao-yu who retorted, however.

"I'll make her a 'Miss' then; I'll make her my chamber-wife[1] tomorrow,
if that's all that's worrying you. You can spare your jealousy on *that*
account."

Aroma seized his hand impulsively.

"Don't argue with her, she's only a silly girl. In any case, you've put up
with much worse than this in the past; why be so touchy today?"

Skybright gave a harsh little laugh.

"Oh, yes. I'm too stupid to talk to. I'm only a slave."

"Are you arguing with me, Miss, or with Master Bao?" said Aroma. "If
it's me you've got it in for, you'd better address your remarks to me elsewhere. There's no cause to go quarrelling with me in front of Master Bao.
But if it's Master Bao you want to quarrel with, then at least you might do
it a bit more quietly and not let everyone else know about it. When I came
in just now, it was for everyone's sake, so that we could have a bit of peace

---

1. A concubine, which would raise her status.

and quiet. I don't know why you had to turn on *me* and start picking on *my* shortcomings. It seems as if you can't make up your mind whether you're angry with me or with Master Bao. Slipping in a dig here and a dig there. I don't know what you think you're up to. Anyway, I shan't say any more; I'll just leave you here to get on with it."

She walked out.

"There's no need for you to be so angry," Bao-yu said to Skybright. "I can guess what it is that's bothering you. I shall go and tell Her Ladyship that you're old enough to leave us now and ask her to send you away. That's what you really want, isn't it?"

"I don't want to go away. Why should I want to go away?" said Skybright with tears in her eyes—now more upset than ever. "You're inventing this as a means of getting rid of me, aren't you, because I'm in your way? But you won't get away with it."

"Look, I've never had to put up with scenes like *this* before," said Bao-yu. "What other reason *can* there be but that you want to leave? I really think I *had* better go and see Her Ladyship about this."

He got up and began to go; but Aroma came in again and barred his way.

"Where are you off to?" she asked him smilingly.

"To see Her Ladyship."

"Oh, that's silly," said Aroma. "I wonder you're not ashamed to. Even if Skybright really does want to leave, there will be plenty of time to tell Her Ladyship about it when everyone has cooled down a bit and you are feeling calm and collected. If you go rushing off in your present state, Her Ladyship will suspect something."

"Her Ladyship won't suspect anything," said Bao-yu. "I shall tell her quite openly that Skybright has been agitating to leave."

"When have I ever agitated to leave?" said Skybright, weeping now in earnest. "Even if you're angry with me, you ought not to twist things round in order to get the better of me. But you go and tell her! I don't care if I have to beat my own brains out, I'm not going out of that door."

"Now that's really strange," said Bao-yu. "You don't want to go, yet at the same time you won't keep quiet. It's no good; I really can't stand this quarrelling. I shall really *have* to see Her Ladyship about this and get it over with."

This time he seemed quite determined to go.

Seeing that she was unable to hold him back, Aroma went down on her knees. Emerald, Ripple, Musk and the other maids, aware that a quarrel of more than usual magnitude was going on inside, were waiting together outside in breathless silence. When word reached them that Aroma was now on her knees interceding for Skybright, they came silently trooping in to kneel down behind her. Bao-yu raised Aroma to her feet, sighed, sat down on the edge of the bed, and told the other maids to get up.

"What do you want me to do?" he asked Aroma. "My heart is destroyed inside me, but none of you knows or cares."

Tears started from his eyes and rolled down his cheeks unheeded. Seeing his tears, Aroma too began to cry. Skybright, who stood crying beside them, was about to say something; but just at that moment Dai-yu walked in and she slipped outside.

Dai-yu beamed at the weeping pair:

"Crying on a holiday? What's all this about? Have you been quarrelling over the rice-cakes?"

Bao-yu and Aroma both burst out laughing.

"Well, if Cousin Bao won't tell me," she went on, "I'm sure that *you* will. Come!" she said, slapping Aroma familiarly on the shoulder. "Tell sis all about it. It's obvious that the two of you have been having an argument. Tell me what it's all about and I'll make it up between you."

"Oh, Miss!" Aroma gave her a push. "Don't carry on so! I'm only a maid; you shouldn't say such things to me."

"Only a maid?" said Dai-yu. "I always think of you as my sister-in-law."

"Don't you see that you're simply *encouraging* people to be nasty to her?" Bao-yu protested. "Even as it is, people already gossip about her. How can she stand up to them if *you* come along and lend your weight to what they are saying?"

"You don't know what I feel, Miss," said Aroma. "If I only knew how to stop breathing, I'd gladly die."

Dai-yu smiled.

"If you were to die, I don't know about anyone else, but I know that *I* should die of grief."

"*I* should become a monk," said Bao-yu.

"Try to be a bit more serious," said Aroma. "You and Miss Lin are both laughing at me."

Dai-yu held up two fingers and looked at Bao-yu with a quizzical expression.

"That's twice you're going to become a monk. From now on I'm keeping the score."

Bao-yu recognized the allusion to what he had said to her the day before. Fortunately he was able to pass it off with a laugh. Shortly after that, Dai-yu left them.

No sooner had Dai-yu gone than someone arrived with an invitation from Xue Pan. Bao-yu thought that this time he had better go. It turned out to be only a drinking-party, but Xue Pan refused to release him and kept him there until it was over. He returned home in the evening more than a little drunk.

As he came lurching into his courtyard, he saw that someone in quest of coolness had taken a bed outside and was lying down on it asleep. Assuming that it must be Aroma, he sat down on the edge of it and gave her a push.

"Is the pain any better?"

"Can't you leave me alone?" she said, rising up wrathfully.

He looked again and saw that it was not Aroma after all but Skybright. Taking her by the hand, he drew her down on the bed beside him.

"You're getting so self-willed," he said laughingly. "When you trod on that fan this morning, I only made a harmless little remark, but look how you flew up in the air about it! And then when Aroma, out of the kindness of her heart, tried to reason with you, look how you pitched into *her!* Seriously, now, don't you think it was all a bit uncalled-for?"

"I'm so *hot*," said Skybright. "Do you *have* to maul me about like this? Suppose someone were to see us? Anyway, it's not right for me to be sitting here."

"If you know it's not right to be sitting here," he said teasingly, "what were you doing lying down?"

"Che-e-e!" Unable at once to reply, she gave a little laugh. Then she said:

"When you are not here it doesn't matter. It's *your* being here that makes it wrong. Anyway, let me get up now, because I want to have a bath. Aroma and Musk have had theirs already. I'll send *them* out to you."

"I've just had rather a lot to drink and I could do with a bath myself," said Bao-yu. "As you haven't had yours yet, bring the water out here and we'll have a bath together."

Skybright laughed and declined with a vigorous gesture of her hand.

"*Oh* no! I daren't start you off on that caper. I still remember that time you got Emerald to help you bath. You must have been two or three hours in there, so that we began to get quite worried. We didn't like to go in while you were there, but when we did go in to have a look afterwards, we found water all over the floor, pools of water round the legs of the bed, and even the mat on the bed had water splashed all over it. Heaven only knows what you'd been up to. We laughed about it for days afterwards. I haven't got time to fetch *that* amount of water. And in any case, you don't want to go taking baths with *me*. As a matter of fact it's cooler now, so I don't think I shall have a bath after all. Why don't you let me fetch you a bowl of water so that you can have a nice wash and comb your hair? Faithful just sent a lot of fruit round and we've got it soaking in iced water in the big glass bowl. I'll tell them to bring some out to you, shall I?"

"All right," said Bao-yu. "If you're not having a bath yourself, I'll just wash my hands; and you can get me some of that fruit to eat."

Skybright smiled.

"You've already told me once today how clumsy I am. I can't even drop a fan without treading on it. So I'm much too clumsy to get your fruit for you. Suppose I were to break a plate. That would be terrible!"

"If you *want* to break it, by all means break it," said Bao-yu. "These things are there for our use. What we use them *for* is a matter of individual taste. For example, fans are made for fanning with; but if you prefer to tear them up because it gives you pleasure, there's no reason why you shouldn't. What you *mustn't* do is to use them as objects to vent your anger on. It's the same with plates and cups. Plates and cups are made to put food and drink in. But if you want to smash them on purpose because you like the noise, it's perfectly all right to do so. As long as you don't get into a passion and start taking it out on *things*—that is the golden rule."

"All right then," said Skybright with a mischievous smile. "Give me your fan to tear. I love the sound of a fan being torn."

Bao-yu held it out to her. She took it eagerly and—*chah!*—promptly tore it in half. And again—*chah! chah! chah!*—she tore it several more times. Bao-yu, an appreciative onlooker, laughed and encouraged her.

"Well torn! Well torn! Now again—a really loud one!"

Just then Musk appeared. She stared at them indignantly.

"Don't do that!" she said. "It's *wicked* to waste things like that."

But Bao-yu leaped up to her, snatched the fan from her hand, and passed it to Skybright, who at once tore it into several pieces. The two of them, Bao-yu and Skybright, then burst into uproarious laughter.

"What do you think you're doing?" said Musk. "That's *my fan* you've just ruined."

"What's an old fan?" said Bao-yu. "Open up the fan box and get yourself another."

"If that's your attitude," said Musk, "we might as well carry out the whole boxful and let her tear away to her heart's content."

"All right. Go and get it," said Bao-yu.

"And be born a beggar in my next life?" said Musk. "No thank you! She hasn't broken her arm. Let her go and get it herself."

Skybright stretched back on the bed, smiling complacently.

"I'm rather tired just now. I think I shall tear some more tomorrow."

Bao-yu laughed.

"The ancients used to say that for one smile of a beautiful woman a thousand taels are well spent. For a few old fans it's cheap at the price!"

He called to Aroma, who had just finished changing into clean clothes, to come outside and join them. Little Melilot came and cleared away the broken bits of fan, and everyone sat for a while and enjoyed the cool.

But our narrative supplies no further details of that evening.

About noon next day, while Lady Wang, Bao-chai, Dai-yu and the girls were sitting in Grandmother Jia's room, someone came in to announce that "Miss Shi" had arrived. Shortly afterwards Shi Xiang-yun appeared in the courtyard, attended by a bevy of matrons and maids. Bao-chai, Dai-yu and the rest hurried out to the foot of the steps to welcome her.

For young girls like the cousins a reunion after a mere month's separation is an occasion for touching demonstrations of affection. After these initial transports, when they were all indoors and the greetings, introductions and salutations had been completed, Grandmother Jia suggested that, as the weather was so hot, Xiang-yun should remove her outer garments. Xiang-yun rose to her feet with alacrity and divested herself of one or two layers. Lady Wang was amused.

"Gracious, child! What a lot you have on! I don't think I've ever seen anyone wearing so much."

"It's my Aunt Shi who makes me wear it all," said Xiang-yun. "You wouldn't catch me wearing this stuff if I didn't have to."

"You don't know our Xiang-yun, Aunt," Bao-chai interposed. "She's really happiest in boy's clothes. That time she was here in the third or fourth month last year, I remember one day she dressed up in one of Bao-yu's gowns and put a pair of his boots on and one of his belts round her waist. At first glance she looked exactly like Cousin Bao. It was only the ear-rings that gave her away. When she stood behind that chair over there, Grandmother was completely taken in. She said, 'Bao-yu, come over here! You'll get the dust from that hanging lamp in your eyes if you're not care-

ful.' But Xiang-yun just smiled and didn't move. It was only when everyone couldn't hold it in any longer and started laughing that Grandmother
realized who it was and joined in the laugh. She told her that she made a
very good-looking boy."

"That's nothing," said Dai-yu. "What about that time last year when she
came to stay for a couple of days with us in the first month and it snowed?
Grandma and Auntie Wang had just got back from somewhere—I think
it was from visiting the ancestors' portraits[2]—and she saw Grandma's new
scarlet felt rain-cape lying there and put it on when no one was looking.
Of course, it was much too big and much too long for her, so she hitched
it up and tied it round her waist with a sash and went out like that into
the back courtyard to help the maids build a snowman. And then she
slipped over in it and got covered all over with mud—"

The others all laughed at the recollection.

Bao-chai asked Xiang-yun's nurse, Mrs. Zhou, whether Xiang-yun was
still as tomboyish as ever. Nurse Zhou laughed but said nothing.

"I don't mind her being tomboyish," said Ying-chun, "but I do wish she
wasn't such a chatterbox. You wouldn't believe it—even when she's in bed
at night it still goes on. Jabber-jabber, jabber-jabber. Then she laughs.
Then she talks a bit more. Then she laughs again. And you never heard
such a lot of rubbish in your life. I don't know where she gets it all from."

"Well, perhaps she'll have got over that by now," said Lady Wang. "I
hear that someone was round the other day to talk about a betrothal. Now
that there's a future mother-in-law to think about, she can't be *quite* as
tomboyish as she used to be."

"Are you staying this time, or do you have to go back tonight?" asked
Grandmother Jia.

"Your Old Ladyship hasn't seen all the clothes she's brought," said
Nurse Zhou. "She'll be staying two days here at the very least."

"Isn't Bao at home?" said Xiang-yun.

"Listen to her!" said Bao-chai. "Cousin Bao is the only one she thinks
about. He and she get on well together because they are both fond of
mischief. You can see she hasn't really changed."

"Perhaps now that you're getting older you had better stop using baby-
names," said Grandmother Jia, reminded by the talk of betrothal that her
babies were rapidly turning into grown-ups.

Just then Bao-yu came in.

"Ah! Hallo, Yun! Why didn't you come when we sent for you the other
day?"

"Grandmother has just this moment been saying that it is time you all
stopped using baby-names," said Lady Wang. "I must say, this isn't a very
good beginning."

"Our cousin has got something nice to give you," said Dai-yu to Xiang-
yun.

"Oh? What is it?" said Xiang-yun.

"Don't believe her," said Bao-yu. "Goodness! It's no time since you were
here last, but you seem to have grown taller already."

2. Kept in shrines and honored as part of Chinese ancestor worship.

Xiang-yun laughed.

"How's Aroma?"

"She's fine. Thank you for asking."

"I've brought something for her," said Xiang-yun. She produced a knotted-up silk handkerchief.

"What treasure have you got wrapped up in there?" said Bao-yu. "The best present you could have brought Aroma would have been a couple of those cheap agate rings like the ones you sent us the other day."

"What are these, then?"

With a triumphant smile she opened her little bundle and revealed four rings, each inset with the veined red agate they had so much admired on a previous occasion.

"What a girl!" said Dai-yu. "These are exactly the same as the ones you sent us the other day by messenger. Why didn't you get him to bring these too and save yourself some trouble? I thought you must have got some wonderful rarity tied up in that handkerchief, seeing that you'd gone to all the trouble of bringing it here yourself—and all the time it was only a few more of *those*! You really are rather a silly."

"Thilly yourthelf!" said Xiang-yun. "The others can decide which of us is the silly one when I have explained my reason. If I send things for you and the girls, it's assumed that they are for you without the messenger even needing to say anything; but if I send things for any of the maids, I have to explain very carefully to the messenger which ones I mean. Now if the messenger is someone intelligent, that's all right; but if it's someone not so bright who has difficulty in remembering names, they'll probably make such a mess of it that they'll get not only the maids' presents mixed up, but yours as well. Then again, if the messenger is a woman, it's not so bad; but the other day it was one of the boys—and you know how hopeless *they* are over girls' names. So you see, I thought it would be simpler if I delivered the maids' ones myself. There!"—she laid the rings down one after another on the table—"One for Aroma; one for Faithful; one for Golden; and one for Patience. Can you imagine one of the boys getting those four names right?"

The others laughed.

"Clever! Clever!" they said.

"You're always so eloquent," said Bao-yu. "No one else gets a chance."

"If she weren't so eloquent, she wouldn't be worthy of the gold kylin," said Dai-yu huffily, rising from her seat and walking off as she spoke.

Fortunately no one heard her but Bao-chai, who made a laughing grimace, and Bao-yu, who immediately regretted having once more spoken out of turn, but who, suddenly catching sight of Bao-chai's expression, could not help laughing himself. Seeing him laugh, Bao-chai at once rose from her seat and hurried off to joke with Dai-yu.

"When you've finished your tea and rested a bit," said Grandmother Jia to Xiang-yun, "you can go and see your married cousins. After that, you can amuse yourself in the Garden with the girls. It's nice and cool there."

Xiang-yun thanked her grandmother. She wrapped up three of the rings again, and after sitting a little longer, went off, attended by her nannies and maids, to call on Wang Xi-feng. After chatting a while with her, she went into the Garden and called on Li Wan. Then, after sitting a short while with Li Wan, she went off in the direction of Green Delights in quest of Aroma. Before doing so, however, she turned to dismiss her escort.

"You needn't stay with me any longer," she said. "You can go off now and visit your relations. I'll just keep Fishy to wait on me."

The others thanked her and went off to look for various kith and kin, leaving Xiang-yun alone with Kingfisher.

"Why aren't these water-lilies out yet?" said Kingfisher.

"It isn't time for them yet," said Xiang-yun.

"Look, they're going to be 'double-decker' ones, like the ones in our lily-pond at home," said Kingfisher.

"Our ones are better," said Xiang-yun.

"They've got a pomegranate-tree here which has four or five lots of flowers growing one above the other on each branch," said Kingfisher. "That's a double-double-double-decker. I wonder what makes them grow like that."

"Plants are the same as people," said Xiang-yun. "The healthier their constitution is, the better they grow."

"I don't believe that," said Kingfisher with a toss of her head. "If that were so, why don't we see people walking around with one head growing on top of the other?"

Xiang-yun was unable to avoid laughing at the girl's simplicity.

"I've told you before, you talk too much," she said. "Let's see: how can one answer a question like that? Everything in the world is moulded by the forces of Yin and Yang. That means that, besides the normal, the abnormal, the peculiar, the freakish—in fact all the thousands and thousands of different variations we find in things—are caused by different combinations of Yin and Yang. Even if something appears that is so rare that no one has ever seen it before, the principle is still the same."

"So according to what you say," said Kingfisher, "all the things that have ever existed, from the time the world began right up to the present moment, have just been a lot of Yins and Yangs."

"No, stupid!" said Xiang-yun. "The more you say, the sillier you get. 'Just a lot of Yins and Yangs' indeed! In any case, strictly speaking Yin and Yang are not two things but one and the same thing. By the time the Yang has become exhausted, it *is* Yin; and by the time the Yin has become exhausted, it *is* Yang. It isn't a case of one of them coming to an end and then the other one growing out of nothing."

"That's too deep for me," said Kingfisher. "What sort of thing is a Yin-yang, I'd like to know? No one's ever seen one. You just answer that, Miss. What does a Yin-yang look like?"

"Yin-yang is a sort of *force*," said Xiang-yun. "It's the force in things that gives them their distinctive forms. For example, the sky is Yang and the earth is Yin; water is Yin and fire is Yang; the sun is Yang and the moon is Yin."

"Ah yes! *Now* I understand," said Kingfisher happily. "That's why astrologers call the sun the 'Yang star' and the moon the 'Yin star.'"

"Holy name!" said Xiang-yun. "She understands."

"That's not so difficult," said Kingfisher. "But what about things like mosquitoes and fleas and midges and plants and flowers and bricks and tiles? Surely you are not going to say that they are all Yin-yang too?"

"Certainly they are!" said Xiang-yun. "Take the leaf of a tree, for example. That's divided into Yin and Yang. The side facing upwards towards the sky is Yang; the underside, facing towards the ground, is Yin."

Kingfisher nodded.

"I see. Yes. I can understand that. But take these fans we are holding. Surely *they* don't have Yin and Yang?"

"Yes they do. The front of the fan is Yang; the back of the fan is Yin."

Kingfisher nodded, satisfied. She tried to think of some other object to ask about, but being for the moment unable to, she began looking around her for inspiration. As she did so, her eye chanced to light on the gold kylin fastened in the intricate loopings of her mistress's girdle.

"Well, Miss," she said, pointing triumphantly to the kylin, "you're not going to say that *that's* got Yin and Yang?"

"Certainly. In the case of birds and beasts and males are Yang and the females are Yin."

"Is this a daddy one or a mummy one?" said Kingfisher.

" 'A daddy one or a mummy one'! Silly girl!"

"All right, then," said Kingfisher. "But why is it that everything else has Yin and Yang but we haven't?"

"Get along with you, naughty girl! What subject will you get on to next?"

"Why? Why can't you tell me?" said Kingfisher. "Anyway, I know; so there's no need for you to be so nasty to me."

Xiang-yun suppressed a giggle.

"You're Yang and I'm Yin," said Kingfisher.

Xiang-yun held her handkerchief to her mouth and laughed.

"Well, that's right, isn't it?" said Kingfisher. "What are you laughing at?"

"Yes, yes," said Xiang-yun. "That's quite right."

"That's what they always say," said Kingfisher: "the master is Yang and the servant is Yin. Even I can understand that principle."

"I'm sure you can," said Xiang-yun. "Very good."

While they were talking, a glittering golden object at the foot of the rose pergola caught Xiang-yun's eye. She pointed it out to Kingfisher.

"Go and see what it is."

Kingfisher bounded over and picked it up.

"Ah ha!" she said, examining the object in her hand. "Now we shall be able to see whether it's Yin or Yang."

She took hold of the kylin fastened to Xiang-yun's girdle and held it up to look at it more closely. Xiang-yun wanted to see what it was that she held in her hand, but Kingfisher wouldn't let her.

"It's *my* treasure," she said with a laugh. "I won't let you see it, Miss. Funny, though. I wonder where it came from. I've never seen anyone here wearing it."

"Come on! Let me look," said Xiang-yun.

"There you are, Miss!" Kingfisher opened her hand.

Xiang-yun looked. It was a beautiful, shining gold kylin, both larger and more ornate than the one she was wearing. Reaching out and taking it from Kingfisher, she held it on the palm of her hand and contemplated it for some moments in silence.

Whatever reverie the contemplation inspired was broken by the sudden arrival of Bao-yu.

"What are you doing, standing out here in the blazing sun?" he asked her. "Why don't you go and see Aroma?"

"We were on our way," said Xiang-yun, hurriedly concealing the gold kylin.

The three of them entered the courtyard of Green Delights together.

Aroma had gone outside to take the air and was leaning on the verandah railings at the foot of the front door steps. As soon as she caught sight of Xiang-yun, she hurried down into the courtyard to welcome her, and taking her by the hand, led her into the house, animatedly exchanging news with her as they went.

"You should have come sooner," said Bao-yu when they were indoors and Aroma had made Xiang-yun take a seat. "I've got something nice for you here and I've been waiting for you to come so that I could give it to you."

He had been hunting through his pockets as he said this. Not finding what he was searching for, he exclaimed in surprise.

"Aiyo!" He turned to Aroma. "Have you put it away somewhere?"

"Put what away?"

"That little kylin I got the other day."

"You've been carrying it around with you everywhere," said Aroma. "Why ask *me* about it?"

Bao-yu clapped his hands together in vexation.

"Oh, I've lost it! Wherever am I going to look for it?"

He got up to begin searching.

Xiang-yun now realized that it must have been Bao-yu who dropped the kylin she had only a few minutes earlier discovered outside.

"Since when have *you* had a kylin?" she asked him.

"Oh, several days now," said Bao-yu. "What a shame! I'll never get another one like that. And the trouble is, I don't know when I can have lost it. Oh dear! How stupid of me!"

"It's only an ornament you're getting so upset about," said Xiang-yun. "What a good job it wasn't something more serious!"

She opened her hand:

"Look! Is that it?"

Bao-yu looked and saw, with extravagant delight, that it was.

The remainder of this episode will be told in the following chapter.

CHAPTER 32

*Bao-yu demonstrates confusion of mind by making
his declaration to the wrong person
And Golden shows an unconquerable spirit by ending
her humiliation in death*

Our last chapter told of Bao-yu's delight at seeing the gold kylin again. He reached out eagerly and took it from Xiang-yun's hand.

"Fancy *your* finding it!" he said. "How did you come to pick it up?"

"It's a good job it was only this you lost," she said. "One of these days it will be your seal of office—and then it won't be quite so funny."[3]

"Oh, losing one's seal of office is nothing," said Bao-yu. "Losing a thing like this is much more serious."

Aroma meanwhile was pouring tea.

"I heard your good news the other day," she said, handing Xiang-yun a cup. "Congratulations!"

Xiang-yun bent low over the cup to hide her blushes and made no reply.

"Why so bashful, Miss?" said Aroma. "Have you forgotten the things you used to tell me at night all those years ago, when we used to sleep together in the little closet-bed[4] at Her Old Ladyship's? You weren't very bashful then. What makes you so bashful with me now, all of a sudden?"

Xiang-yun's face became even redder. She gave a forced little laugh.

"Who's talking? That was a time when you and I were very close to each other. Then I had to go back home when my uncle's first wife died and you were given Cousin Bao to look after, and I don't know why, but whenever I came back here after that, you seemed somehow changed towards me."

It was now Aroma's turn to blush and protest.

"When you first came to live here it was 'Pearl dear this' and 'Pearl dear that' all the time. You were always coaxing me to do things for you—do your hair, wash your face, or I don't know what. But now that's all changed. Now you're the young lady, aren't you? You can't act the young lady with me and expect me to stay on the same familiar terms as before."

"Holy name!" said Xiang-yun, now genuinely indignant. "That's *tho* unfair. I wish I may die if I ever 'acted the young lady' with you, as you put it. I come here in this frightful heat, and the very first person I want to see when I get here is you. Ask Fishy if you don't believe me. *She* can tell you. At home I'm *always* going on about you."

Aroma and Bao-yu both laughed.

"Don't take it to heart so, it was only a joke. You shouldn't be so excitable."

"Don't, whatever you do, admit that what *you* said was wounding," said Xiang-yun. "Say I'm 'excitable' and put *me* in the wrong!"

While she said this, she was undoing the knotted silk handkerchief and extracting one of the three rings from it. She handed it to Aroma. Aroma was greatly touched.

"I've got one like this already," she said. "It was given to me when you sent those ones the other day to the young ladies. But fancy your bringing this one here specially! Now I *know* you haven't forgotten me. It's little things like this that show you what a person really is. The ring itself isn't worth much, I know. It's the thought behind it."

"Who gave you the one you've already got?" said Xiang-yun.

"Miss Bao," said Aroma.

"Ah," said Xiang-yun, "Miss Bao. And I was thinking it must have been Miss Lin. Often when I'm at home I think to myself that of all my cousins

---

3. The assumption is that Bao-yu will some day become a government official. All officials had seals with which to stamp documents, and such stamps had authorizing power, like a signature. Hence the loss of a seal was a serious matter.   **4.** A small temporary bed, like a cot.

Bao-chai is the one I like best. It's a pity we couldn't have been born of the same mother. With her for an elder sister it wouldn't matter so much being an orphan."

Her eyelids reddened as she said this and she seemed to be on the verge of tears.

"Now, now, now!" said Bao-yu. "Don't say things like that."

"And why not?" said Xiang-yun. "Oh, I know your trouble. You're afraid that Cousin Lin might hear and get angry with me again for praising Cousin Bao. That's what's worrying you, isn't it?"

Aroma giggled.

"Oh Miss Yun! You're just as outspoken as you used to be."

"Well, I've said that you lot are difficult to talk to," said Bao-yu, "and I was certainly right!"

"Don't make me sick," said Xiang-yun. "You say what you like to us. It's with your Cousin Lin that you have to be so careful."

"Never mind about that," said Aroma. "Joking apart, now: I want to ask you a favour."

"What is it?" said Xiang-yun.

"I've got a pair of slipper-tops here that I've already cut the openwork pattern in, but as I haven't been very well this last day or two, I haven't been able to sew them on to the backing material. Do you think you'd have time to do them for me?"

"That's rather a strange request," said Xiang-yun. "Quite apart from all the clever maids this household employs you have your own full-time tailors and embroiderers. Why ask *me* to do your sewing? You could give it to anyone here you liked. They could hardly refuse you."

"You can't be serious," said Aroma. "None of the sewing in this room is allowed to go outside.[5] Surely you knew that?"

Xiang-yun inferred from this that the slippers in question were for Bao-yu.

"Oh well," she said, "in that case I suppose I'd better do them for you. On one condition, though: I'll do them if they are for *you* to wear, but if they are for anyone else, I'm afraid I can't."

"Get along with you!" said Aroma. "Ask you to make slippers for *me*? I wouldn't have the nerve. No, I'll be honest with you, they're not for me. Never mind who they're for. Just tell yourself that I'm the one you'll be doing the favour."

"It isn't *that*," said Xiang-yun. "In the past I've done lots of things for you. Surely you must *know* what makes me unwilling now?"

"I'm sorry, I don't," said Aroma.

"What about the person who got in a temper the other day when that fan-case I made for you was compared with hers and cut it up with a pair of scissors? I heard all about that, so don't start protesting. If you expect me to do sewing for you after *that*, you're just treating me as your drudge."

"I didn't know at the time it was you who made it," Bao-yu put in hurriedly.

"He really didn't," said Aroma. "I pretended there was someone outside

---

5. Bao-yu wants all his sewing done by only those who are close to him.

we'd just discovered who could do very fine and original needlework. I told him I'd got them to do that fan-case for him as a sample. He believed what I said and went around showing it to everyone. Unfortunately while he was doing this he upset you know who and she took a pair of scissors and cut it in pieces. Afterwards he was very anxious to have some more work done by the same person, so I had to tell him who it really was. He was very upset when he heard that it was you."

"I still think this is a very strange request," said Xiang-yun. "If Miss Lin can cut things up, she can sew them for him, too. Why not ask *her* to do them for you?"

"Oh, *she* wouldn't want to do them," said Aroma. "And even if she did, Her Old Ladyship wouldn't let her, for fear of her tiring herself. The doctors say she needs rest and quiet. I wouldn't want to trouble *her* with them. Last year she took practically the whole year embroidering one little purse, and this last six months I don't think she's picked up a needle."

Their conversation was interrupted by a servant with a message:

"Mr. Jia of Rich Street is here. The Master says will Master Bao receive him, please?"

Recognizing the "Mr. Jia" of the message as Jia Yu-cun, Bao-yu was more than a little vexed. While Aroma hurried off for his going-out clothes, he sat pulling his boots on and grumbling.

"He's got Father to talk to, surely that's enough for him? Why does he always have to see me?"

Xiang-yun laughed at his disgruntlement:

"I'm sure you're very good at entertaining people," she said. "That's why Sir Zheng asks you to see him."

"That message didn't come from Father," said Bao-yu. "He'll have made it up himself."

" 'When the host is refined, the callers are frequent,' " said Xiang-yun. "There must be something about you that has impressed him, otherwise he wouldn't want to see you."

"I make no claim to being refined, thanks all the same," said Bao-yu. "I'm as common as dirt. And furthermore I have no wish to mix with people of his sort."

"You're incorrigible," said Xiang-yun. "Now that you're older, you ought to be mixing with these officials and administrators as much as you can. Even if you don't want to take the Civil Service examinations and become an administrator yourself, you can learn a lot from talking to these people about the way the Empire is governed and the people who govern it that will stand you in good stead later on, when you come to manage your own affairs and take your place in society. You might even pick up one or two decent, respectable friends that way. You'll certainly never get anywhere if you spend all your time with us girls."

Bao-yu found such talk highly displeasing.

"I think perhaps you'd better go and sit in someone else's room," he said. "I wouldn't want a *decent, respectable* young lady like you to get contaminated."

"Don't try reasoning with him, Miss," Aroma put in hurriedly. "Last time Miss Bao tried it, he was just as rude to her. No consideration for her

feelings whatever. He just said 'Hai!', picked up his heels, and walked out
of the room, leaving her still half-way through her sentence. Poor Miss
Bao! She was so embarrassed she turned bright red. She didn't know *what*
to say. A good job it was her, though, and not Miss Lin. If it had been
Miss Lin, there'd have been weeping and carrying on and I don't know
what. I really admire the way Miss Bao behaved on that occasion. She just
stood there a while collecting herself and then walked quietly out of the
room. Myself, I was quite upset, thinking she must be offended. But not a
bit of it. Next time she came round, it was just as if nothing had happened.
A real little lady, Miss Bao—and generous-hearted, too. And yet the funny
thing is that his lordship seems to have fallen out with her, whereas Miss
Lin, who is always getting on her high horse and ignoring him, has him
running round and apologizing to her all the time."

"Have you ever heard Miss Lin talking that sort of stupid rubbish?" said
Bao-yu. "I'd long since have fallen out with *her* if she did."

Aroma and Xiang-yun shook their heads pityingly.

"So that's 'stupid rubbish,' is it?" they said, laughing.

Dai-yu rightly surmised that now Xiang-yun had arrived, Bao-yu would
lose no time in telling her about his newly-acquired kylin.

Now Dai-yu had observed that in the romances which Bao-yu smuggled
in to her and of which she was nowadays an avid consumer, it was always
some trinket or small object of clothing or jewellery—a pair of lovebirds,
a male and female phoenix, a jade ring, a gold buckle, a silken handkerchief, an embroidered belt or what not—that brought the heroes and heroines together. And since the fate and future happiness of those fortunate
beings seemed to depend wholly on the instrumentality of such trifling
objects, it was natural for her to suppose that Bao-yu's acquisition of the
gold kylin would become the occasion of a dramatic rupture with *her* and
the beginning of an association with Xiang-yun in which he and Xiang-
yun would do together all those delightful things that she had read about
in the romances.

It was with such apprehensions that she made her way stealthily towards
Green Delights, her intention being to observe how the two of them were
behaving and shape her own actions accordingly. Imagine her surprise
when, just as she was about to enter, she heard Xiang-yun lecturing Bao-
yu on his social obligations and Bao-yu telling Xiang-yun that "Cousin Lin
never talked that sort of rubbish" and that if she did he would have "fallen
out with her long ago." Mingled emotions of happiness, alarm, sorrow and
regret assailed her.

Happiness:

Because after all (she thought) I wasn't mistaken in my judgement of
you. I always thought of you as a true friend, and I was right.

Alarm:

Because if you praise me so unreservedly in front of other people, your
warmth and affection are sure, sooner or later, to excite suspicion and be
misunderstood.

Regret:

Because if you are my true friend, then I am yours and the two of us are a perfect match. But in that case why did there have to be all this talk of "the gold and the jade"? Alternatively, if there had to be all this talk of gold and jade, why weren't we the two to have them? Why did there have to be a Bao-chai with her golden locket?

Sorrow:

Because though there are things of burning importance to be said, without a father or a mother I have no one to say them for me. And besides, I feel so muzzy lately and I know that my illness is gradually gaining a hold on me. (The doctors say that the weakness and anaemia I suffer from may be the beginnings of a consumption.) So even if I *am* your true-love, I fear I may not be able to wait for you. And even though you are mine, you can do nothing to alter my fate.

At that point in her reflections she began to weep; and feeling in no fit state to be seen, she turned away from the door and began to make her way back again.

Bao-yu had finished his hasty dressing and now came out of the house. He saw Dai-yu slowly walking on ahead of him and, judging by her appearance from behind, wiping her eyes. He hurried forward to catch up with her.

"Where are you off to, coz? Are you crying again? Who has upset you this time?"

Dai-yu turned and saw that it was Bao-yu.

"I'm perfectly all right," she said, forcing a smile. "What would I be crying for?"

"Look at you! The tears are still wet on your face. How can you tell such fibs?"

Impulsively he stretched out his hand to wipe them. Dai-yu recoiled several paces:

"You'll get your head chopped off!" she said. "You really *must* keep your hands to yourself."

"I'm sorry. My feelings got the better of me. I'm afraid I wasn't thinking about my head."

"No, I forgot," said Dai-yu. "Losing your head is nothing, is it? It's losing your kylin—the famous *gold* kylin—that is really serious!"

Her words immediately put Bao-yu in a passion. He came up to her and held his face close to hers.

"Do you say these things to put a curse on me? or is it merely to make me angry that you say them?"

Remembering their recent quarrel, Dai-yu regretted her careless reintroduction of its theme and hastened to make amends:

"Now don't get excited. I shouldn't have said that—oh come now, it really isn't *that* important! Look at you! The veins are standing out on your forehead and your face is all covered with sweat."

She moved forward and wiped the perspiration from his brow. For some moments he stood there motionless, staring at her. Then he said:

"*Don't worry!*"

Hearing this, Dai-yu herself was silent for some moments.

"Why *should* I worry?" she said eventually. "I don't understand you. Would you mind telling me what you are talking about?"

Bao-yu sighed.

"Do you really not understand? Can I really have been all this time mistaken in my feelings towards you? If you don't even know your *own* mind, it's small wonder that you're always getting angry on *my* account."

"I really don't understand what you mean about not worrying," said Dai-yu.

Bao-yu sighed again and shook his head.

"My dear coz, don't think you can fool me. If you don't understand what I've just said, then not only have *my* feelings towards *you* been all along mistaken, but all that *you* have ever felt for *me* has been wasted, too. It's because you worry so much that you've made yourself ill. If only you could take things a bit easier, your illness wouldn't go on getting more and more serious all the time."

Dai-yu was thunderstruck. He had read her mind—had seen inside her more clearly than if she had plucked out her entrails and held them out for his inspection. And now there were a thousand things that she wanted to tell him; yet though she was dying to speak, she was unable to utter a single syllable and stood there like a simpleton, gazing at him in silence.

Bao-yu, too, had a thousand things to say, but he, too, stood mutely gazing at her, not knowing where to begin.

After the two of them had stared at each other for some considerable time in silence, Dai-yu heaved a deep sigh. The tears gushed from her eyes and she turned and walked away. Bao-yu hurried after her and caught at her dress.

"Coz dear, stop a moment! Just let me say one word."

As she wiped her eyes with one hand, Dai-yu pushed him away from her with the other.

"There's nothing to say. I already know what you want to tell me."

She said this without turning back her head, and having said it, passed swiftly on her way. Bao-yu remained where he was standing, gazing after her in silent stupefaction.

Now Bao-yu had left the apartment in such haste that he had forgotten to take his fan with him. Fearing that he would be very hot without it, Aroma hurried outside to give it to him, but when she noticed him standing some way ahead of her talking to Dai-yu, she halted. After a little while she saw Dai-yu walk away and Bao-yu continue standing motionless where he was. She chose this moment to go up and speak to him.

"You've gone out without your fan," she said. "It's a good job I noticed. Here you are. I ran out to give it to you."

Bao-yu, still in a muse, saw Aroma there talking to him, yet without clearly perceiving who it was. With the same glazed look in his eyes, he began to speak.

"Dearest coz! I've never before dared to tell you what I felt for you. Now at last I'm going to pluck up courage and tell you, and after that I don't care what becomes of me. Because of you I, too, have made myself ill—only I haven't dared tell anyone about it and have had to bear it all in silence. And the day that your illness is cured, I do believe that mine, too, will get better. Night and day, coz, sleeping and dreaming, you are never out of my mind."

Aroma listened to this declaration aghast.

"Holy saints preserve us!" she exclaimed. "He'll be the death of me."
She gave him a shake.

"What are you talking about? Are you bewitched? You'd better hurry."

Bao-yu seemed suddenly to waken from his trance and recognized the
person he had been speaking to as Aroma. His face turned a deep red with
embarrassment and he snatched the fan from her and fled.

After he had gone, Aroma began thinking about the words he had just said
and realized that they must have been intended for Dai-yu. She reflected
with some alarm that if things between them were as his words seemed to
indicate, there was every likelihood of an ugly scandal developing, and
wondered how she could arrange matters to prevent it. Preoccupied with
these reflections, she stood as motionless and unseeing as her master had
done a few moments before. Bao-chai found her in this state on her way
back from the house.

"What are you brooding on, out in the burning sun?" she asked her,
laughing.

Aroma laughed back.

"There were two little sparrows here having a fight. They were so funny,
I had to stand and watch them."

"Where was Cousin Bao rushing off to just now, all dressed up for going
out?" said Bao-chai. "I was going to call out and ask him, but he is getting
so crotchety lately that I thought I had better not."

"The Master sent for him," said Aroma.

"Oh dear!" said Bao-chai. "I wonder why he should send for him in
heat like this? I hope he hasn't thought of something to be angry about and
called him over to be punished."

"No, it isn't that," said Aroma. "I think it's to receive a visitor."

"It must be a very tiresome visitor," said Bao-chai, "to go around bothering people on a boiling day like this instead of staying at home and
trying to keep cool."

"You can say that again!" said Aroma.

"What's young Xiang-yun been doing at your place?" said Bao-chai,
changing the subject.

"We were having a chat," said Aroma, "and after that she had a look at
some slipper-tops that I've got ready pasted and have asked her to sew for
me."

"You're an intelligent young woman," said Bao-chai, having first looked
to right and left of her to make sure that no one else was about, "I should
have thought you'd have sense enough to leave her a few moments in
peace. I've been watching our Yun lately, and from what I've observed of
her and various stray remarks I've heard, I get the impression that back at
home she can barely call her soul her own. I know for a fact that they are
too mean to pay for professional seamstresses and that nearly all the sewing
has to be done by the women of the household, and I'm pretty sure that's
why, whenever she's found herself alone with me on these last few visits,
she's told me how tired she gets at home. When I press her for details, her
eyes fill with tears and she answers evasively, as though she'd like to tell
me but daren't. It must be very hard for her, losing both her parents when
she was so young. It quite wrings my heart to see her so exploited."

Aroma smote her hands together as understanding dawned.

"Yes, I *see*. I see now why she was so slow with those ten butterfly bows I asked her to sew for me last month. It was ages before she sent them, and even then there was a message to say that she'd only been able to do them roughly. She told me I'd better use them on something else. 'If you want nice, even ones,' she said, 'you'll have to wait until next time I come to stay with you.' Now I can see why. She didn't like to refuse when I asked her, but I suppose she had to sit up till midnight doing them, poor thing. Oh, how stupid of me! I'd never have asked her if I'd realized."

"Last time she was here, she told me that it's quite normal for her to sit up sewing until midnight," said Bao-chai; "and if her aunt or the other women catch her doing the slightest bit of work for anyone else, they are angry with her."

"It's all the fault of that pig-headed young master of mine," said Aroma. "He refuses to let any of his sewing be done by the seamstresses outside. Every bit of work, large or small, has to be done in his room—and I just can't manage it all on my own."

Bao-chai laughed.

"Why do you take any notice of him? Why not simply give it to the seamstresses without telling him?"

"He's not so easy to fool," said Aroma. "He can tell the difference. I'm afraid there's nothing for it. I shall just have to work through it all gradually on my own."

"Now just a minute!" said Bao-chai. "We'll think of a way round this. Suppose *I* were to do some of it for you?"

"Would you really?" said Aroma. "I'd be so grateful if you would. I'll come over with some this evening then."

She had barely finished saying this when an old woman came rushing up to them in a state of great agitation.

"Isn't it dreadful? Miss Golden has drowned herself in the well."

"Which Golden?" said Aroma, startled.

"Which Golden?" said the old woman. "There aren't two Goldens that I know of. Golden from Her Ladyship's room, of course, that was dismissed the day before yesterday. She'd been crying and carrying on at home ever since, but nobody paid much attention to her. Then suddenly, when they went to look for her, she wasn't there, and just now someone going to fetch water from the well by the south-east corner found a body in it and rushed inside for help, and when they fished it out, they found that it was Golden. They did all they could to revive her, but it was too late. She was dead."

"How strange!" said Bao-chai.

Aroma shook her head wonderingly and a tear or two stole down her cheek. She and Golden had been like sisters to each other.

Bao-chai hurried off to Lady Wang's to offer her sympathy. Aroma went back to Green Delights.

When Bao-chai arrived at Lady Wang's apartment she found the whole place hushed and still and Lady Wang sitting in the inner room on her own, crying. Deeming it an unsuitable moment to raise the subject of her visit, Bao-chai sat down beside her in silence.

"Where have you just come from?" Lady Wang asked her.

"The Garden."

"The Garden," Lady Wang echoed. "Did you by any chance see your cousin Bao-yu there?"

"I saw him going out just now wearing his outdoor clothes, but I don't know where he was going to."

Lady Wang nodded and gave a sigh.

"I don't know if you've heard. Something very strange has happened. Golden has drowned herself in a well."

"That *is* strange," said Bao-chai. "Why ever did she do that?"

"The day before yesterday she broke something of mine," said Lady Wang, "and in a moment of anger I struck her a couple of times and sent her back to her mother's. I had only been meaning to leave her there a day or two to punish her. After that I would have had her back again. I never dreamed that she would be so angry with me as to drown herself. Now that she has, I feel that it is all my fault."

"It's only natural that a kind person like you should see it in that way," said Bao-chai, "but in my opinion Golden would never have drowned herself in anger. It's much more likely that she was playing about beside the well and slipped in accidentally. While she was in service her movements were restricted and it would be natural for her to go running around everywhere during her first day or two outside. There's no earthly reason why she should have felt angry enough with you to drown herself. If she did, all I can say is that she was a stupid person and not worth feeling sorry for!"

Lady Wang sighed and shook her head doubtfully.

"Well, it may be as you say, but I still feel very uneasy in my mind."

"I'm sure you have no cause, Aunt," said Bao-chai, "but if you feel *very* much distressed, I suggest that you simply give her family a little extra for the funeral. In that way you will more than fulfil any moral obligation you may have towards her as a mistress."

"I have just given her mother fifty taels," said Lady Wang. "I wanted to give her two new outfits as well from one of the girls' wardrobes, but it just so happens that at the moment none of them apart from your Cousin Lin has got anything new that would do. Your Cousin Lin has got two sets that we had made for her next birthday, but she is such a sensitive child and has had so much sickness and misfortune in her life that I'm afraid she would almost certainly feel superstitious about the clothes made for her birthday being used for dressing a corpse with, so I've had to ask the tailors to make up a couple in a hurry. Of course, if it were any other maid, I should have given the mother a few taels and that would have been the end of the matter. But though Golden was only a servant, she had been with me so long that she had become almost like a daughter to me."

She began to cry again as she said this.

"There's no need to hurry the tailors about this," said Bao-chai. "I've got two new outfits that I recently finished making for myself. Why not let her mother have *them* and save them the trouble? Golden once or twice wore old dresses of mine in the past, so I know they will fit her."

"That's very kind of you, but aren't you superstitious?" said Lady Wang.

Bao-chai laughed.

"Don't worry about *that*, Aunt. That sort of thing has never bothered me."

At that she rose and went off to fetch them. Lady Wang hurriedly ordered two of the servants to go after her.

When Bao-chai returned with the clothes, she found Bao-yu sitting beside his mother in tears. Lady Wang was evidently in the midst of rebuking him about something, but as soon as she caught sight of Bao-chai, she closed her mouth and fell silent. From the scene before her eyes and the word or two she had overheard, Bao-chai was able to form a pretty good idea of what had been happening. She handed the clothes over to Lady Wang and Lady Wang summoned Golden's mother to come and fetch them.

What happened after that will be told in the following chapter.

CHAPTER 33

An envious younger brother puts in a malicious word or two
And a scapegrace elder brother receives a terrible chastisement

Our story last told how Golden's mother was summoned to take away the clothing that Bao-chai had brought for Golden's laying-out. When she arrived, Lady Wang called her inside, and after making her an additional present of some jewellery, advised her to procure the services of some Buddhist monks to recite a *sūtra*[6] for the salvation of the dead girl's soul. Golden's mother kotowed her thanks and departed with the clothes and jewellery.

The news that Golden's disgrace had driven her to take her own life had reached Bao-yu as he was returning from his interview with Jia Yu-cun, and he was already in a state of shock when he went in to see his mother, only to be subjected by her to a string of accusations and reproaches, to which he was unable to reply. He availed himself of the opportunity presented by Bao-chai's arrival to slip quietly out again, and wandered along, scarcely knowing where he was going, still in a state of shock, hands clasped behind him, head down low, and sighing as he went.

Without realizing it he was drifting towards the main reception hall, and was in fact just emerging from behind the screen-wall that masked the gateway leading from the inner to the outer part of the mansion, when he walked head-on into someone coming from the opposite direction.

"Stand where you are!" said this person in a harsh voice.

Bao-yu looked up with a start and saw that it was his father. He gave an involuntary gasp of fear and, dropping his hands to his sides, hastily assumed a more deferential posture.

"Now," said Jia Zheng, "will you kindly explain the meaning of these sighs and of this moping, hang-dog appearance? You took your time coming when Yu-cun called for you just now, and I gather that when you did eventually vouchsafe your presence, he found you dull and listless and without a lively word to say for yourself. And look at you now—sullenness

6. A Buddhist scripture.

and secret depravity written all over your face! What are these sighings and groanings supposed to indicate? What have *you* got to be discontented or displeased about? Come, sir! What is the meaning of this?"

Bao-yu was normally ready enough with his tongue, but on this occasion grief for Golden so occupied his mind (at that moment he would very willingly have changed places with her) that though he heard the words addressed to him by his father, he failed to take in their meaning and merely stared back at him stupidly.

Seeing him too hypnotized by fear—or so it appeared—to answer with his usual promptness, Jia Zheng, who had not been angry to start with, was now well on the way to becoming so; but the irate comment he was about to make was checked when a servant from the outer gate announced that a representative of "His Highness the Prince of Zhong-shun" had arrived.

Jia Zheng was puzzled.

"The Prince of Zhong-shun?" he thought. "I have never had any dealings with the Prince of Zhong-shun. I wonder why *he* should suddenly send someone to see me . . . ?"

He told the man to invite the prince's messenger to sit in the hall, while he himself hurried inside and changed into court dress. On entering the hall to receive his visitor, he found that it was the Prince of Zhong-shun's chamberlain who had come to see him. After an exchange of bows and verbal salutations, the two men sat down and tea was served. The chamberlain cut short the customary civilities by coming straight to the point.

"It would have been temerity on my part to have intruded on the leisure of an illustrious scholar in the privacy of his home, but in fact it is not for the purpose of paying a social call that I am here, but on orders from His Highness. His Highness has a small request to make of you. If you will be so good as to oblige him, not only will His Highness be extremely grateful himself, but I and my colleagues will also be very much beholden to you."

Jia Zheng was totally at a loss to imagine what the purpose of the man's visit might be; nevertheless he rose to his feet out of respect for the prince and smiled politely.

"You have orders from His Highness for me? I shall be happy to perform them if you will have the goodness to instruct me."

"I don't think any *performing* will be necessary," said the chamberlain drily. "All we want from you is a few words. A young actor called Bijou—a female impersonator—has gone missing from the palace. He hasn't been back now for four or five days; and though we have looked everywhere we can think of, we can't make out where he can have got to. However, in the course of the very extensive inquiries we have made both inside and outside the city, eight out of ten of the people we have spoken to say that he has recently been very thick with the young gentleman who was born with the jade in his mouth. Well, obviously we couldn't come inside here and search as we would have done if this had been anyone else's house, so we had to go back and report the matter to His Highness; and His Highness says that though he could view the loss of a hundred ordinary actors with equanimity, this Bijou is so skilled in anticipating his wishes and so essential to his peace of mind that it would be utterly impossible for him to dispense with his services. I have therefore come here to request you to ask your son if he will be good enough to let Bijou come back again. By doing so he will not only earn the undying gratitude of the Prince, but will also save me and my colleagues a great deal of tiring and disagreeable searching."

The chamberlain concluded with a sweeping bow.

Surprised and angered by what he had heard, Jia Zheng immediately sent for Bao-yu, who presently came hurrying in, ignorant of what the reason for his summons might be.

"Miserable scum!" said Jia Zheng. "It is not enough, apparently, that you should neglect your studies when you are at home. It seems that you must needs go perpetrating enormities outside. This Bijou I have been hearing about is under the patronage of His Royal Highness the Prince of Zhong-shun. How could you have the unspeakable effrontery to commit an act of enticement on his person—involving *me*, incidentally, in the consequences of your wrong-doing?"

The question made Bao-yu start.

"I honestly know nothing about this," he said. "I don't even know who or what 'Bijou' is, let alone what you mean by 'enticement.'"

Jia Zheng was about to exclaim, but the chamberlain forestalled him.

"There is really no point in concealment, young gentleman," he said coldly. "Even if you are not hiding him here, we are sure that you know where he is. In either case you had much better say straight out and save us a lot of trouble. I'd be greatly obliged if you would."

"I really don't know," said Bao-yu. "You must have been misinformed."

The chamberlain gave a sardonic laugh.

"I have, of course, got evidence for what I am saying and I'm afraid you are doing yourself little good by forcing me to mention it in front of your father. You say you don't know who Bijou is. Very well. Then will you kindly explain how his red cummerbund came to find its way around your waist?"

Bao-yu stared at him open-mouthed, too stunned to reply.

"If he knows even a private thing like that," he thought, "there's little likelihood of my being able to hoodwink him about anything else. I'd better get rid of him as quickly as possible, before he can say any more."

"Since you have managed to find out so much about him," he said, finding his tongue at last, "I'm surprised that so important a thing as buying a house should have escaped you. From what I've heard, he recently acquired a little villa and an acre or so of land at Fort Redwood, seven miles east of the walls. I suppose he could be there."

The chamberlain smiled.

"If you say so, then no doubt that is where we shall find him. I shall go and look there immediately. If I do find him there, you will hear no more from me; if not, I shall be back again for further instructions."

So saying, he hurriedly took his leave.

Jia Zheng, his eyes glaring and his mouth contorted with rage, went after the chamberlain to see him out. He turned briefly towards Bao-yu as he was leaving the hall.

"You stay where you are. I shall deal with you when I get back."

As he was on his way in again after seeing the chamberlain off the premises, Jia Huan with two or three pages at his heels came stampeding across the courtyard.

"Hit that boy!" Jia Zheng shouted, outraged. But Jia Huan, reduced to a quivering jelly of fear by the sight of his father, had already jolted to a halt and was standing with bowed head in front of him.

"And what is the meaning of this?" said Jia Zheng. "What has become of the people who are supposed to look after you? Why do they allow you to gallop around in this extraordinary fashion?" His voice rose to a shout: "Where are the people responsible for taking this boy to school?"

Jia Huan saw in his father's anger an opportunity of exercising his malice.

"I didn't mean to run, Father, but just as I was going by the well back there I saw the body of a maid who had drowned herself—all swollen up with water, and her head all swollen. It was *horrible*. I just couldn't help myself."

Jia Zheng heard him with incredulous horror.

"*What* are you saying? *Who* has drowned herself? Such a thing has never before happened in our family. Our family has always been lenient and considerate in its treatment of inferiors. It is one of our traditions. I suppose it is because I have been too neglectful of household matters during these last few years. Those in charge have felt encouraged to abuse their authority, until finally an appalling thing like this can happen—an innocent young life cut off by violence. What a terrible disgrace to our ancestors if this should get about!" He turned and shouted a command.

"Fetch Jia Lian and Lai Da!"

"Sir!" chorused the pages, and were on the point of doing so when Jia Huan impulsively stepped forward, threw himself on his knees and clung to his father's skirts.

"Don't be angry with me, Father, but apart from the servants in Lady Wang's room, no one else knows anything about this. I heard my mother say—"

He broke off and glanced around behind him. Jia Zheng understood and signalled with his eyes to the pages, who obediently withdrew some distance back to either side of the courtyard. Jia Huan continued in a voice lowered almost to a whisper.

"My mother told me that the day before yesterday, in Lady Wang's room, my brother Bao-yu tried to rape one of Her Ladyship's maids called Golden, and when she wouldn't let him, he gave her a beating; and Golden was so upset that she threw herself in the well and was drowned—"

Jia Zheng, whose face had now turned to a ghastly gold-leaf colour, interrupted him with a dreadful cry.

"Fetch Bao-yu!"

He began to stride towards his study, shouting to all and sundry as he went.

"If anyone tries to stop me *this* time, I shall make over my house and property and my post at the Ministry and everything else I have to him and Bao-yu. I absolutely refuse to be responsible for the boy any longer. I

shall cut off my few remaining hairs (those that worry and wretchedness
have left me) and look for some clean and decent spot to end my days in.
Perhaps in that way I shall escape the charge of having disgraced my
ancestors by rearing this unnatural monster as my son."

When they saw the state he was in, the literary gentlemen and senior
menservants who were waiting for him in the study, guessed that Bao-yu
must be the cause of it and, looking at each other with various grimaces,
biting their thumbs or sticking their tongues out, hastily retreated from the
room. Jia Zheng entered it alone and sat down, stiffly upright, in a chair.
He was breathing heavily and his face was bathed in tears. Presently, when
he had regained his breath, he barked out a rapid series of commands:

"Bring Bao-yu here. Get a heavy bamboo. Get some rope to tie him
with. Close the courtyard gates. If anyone tries to take word through inside,
kill him!"

"Sir!—Sir!—Sir!" the terrified pages chorused in unison at each of his
commands, and some of them went off to look for Bao-yu.

Jia Zheng's ominous "Stay where you are" as he went out with the
chamberlain had warned Bao-yu that something dire was imminent—
though just how much more dire as a result of Jia Huan's malicious intervention he could not have foreseen and as he stood where his father had
left him, he twisted and turned himself about, anxiously looking for some
passer-by who could take a message through to the womenfolk inside. But
no one came. Even the omnipresent Tealeaf was on this occasion
nowhere to be seen. Then suddenly, in answer to his prayers, an old
woman appeared—a darling, precious treasure of an old woman (or so
she seemed at that moment)—and he dashed forward and clung to her
beseechingly.

"Quickly!" he said. "Go and tell them that Sir Zheng is going to beat
me. Quickly! Quickly! Go and tell. GO AND TELL."

Partly because agitation had made him incoherent and partly because,
as ill luck would have it, the old woman was deaf, almost everything he
said had escaped her—except for the "Go and tell," which she misheard
as "in the well." She smiled at him reassuringly.

"Let her jump in the well then, young master. Don't you worry your
pretty head about it!"

Realizing that he had deafness, too, to contend with, he now became
quite frantic.

"GO AND TELL MY PAGES."

"Her wages?" the old woman asked in some surprise. "Bless you, of
course they paid her wages! Her Ladyship gave a whole lot of money
towards the funeral as well. And clothes. Paid her wages, indeed!"

Bao-yu stamped his feet in a frenzy of impatience. He was still wondering despairingly how to make her understand when Jia Zheng's pages
arrived and forced him to go with them to the study.

Jia Zheng turned a pair of wild and bloodshot eyes on him as he
entered. Forgetting the "riotous and dissipated conduct abroad leading to
the unseemly bestowal of impudicities on a theatrical performer" and the
"neglect of proper pursuits and studies at home culminating in the
attempted violation of a parent's maidservant" and all the other high-

sounding charges he had been preparing to hurl against him, he shouted two brief orders to the pages.

"Gag his mouth. Beat him to death."

The pages were too frightened not to comply. Two held Bao-yu face downwards on a bench while a third lifted up the flattened bamboo sweep and began to strike him with it across the hams. After about a dozen blows Jia Zheng, not satisfied that his executioner was hitting hard enough, kicked him impatiently aside, wrested the bamboo from his grasp, and, gritting his teeth, brought it down with the utmost savagery on the places that had already been beaten.

At this point the literary gentlemen, sensing that Bao-yu was in serious danger of life and limb, came in again to remonstrate; but Jia Zheng refused to hear them.

"Ask him what he has done and then tell me if you think I should spare him," he said. "It is the encouragement of people like you that has corrupted him; and now, when things have come to this pass, you intercede for him. I suppose you would like me to wait until he commits parricide, or worse. Would you still intercede for him then?"

They could see from this reply that he was beside himself. Wasting no further time on words, they quickly withdrew and looked for someone to take a message through inside.

Lady Wang did not stop to tell Grandmother Jia when she received it. She snatched up an outer garment, pulled it about her, and, supported by a single maid, rushed off, not caring what menfolk might see her, to the outer study, bursting into it with such suddenness that the literary gentlemen and other males present were unable to avoid her.

Her entry provoked Jia Zheng to fresh transports of fury. Faster and harder fell the bamboo on the prostrate form of Bao-yu, which by now appeared to be unconscious, for when the boys holding it down relaxed their hold and fled from their Mistress's presence, it had long since ceased even to twitch. Even so Jia Zheng would have continued beating it had not Lady Wang clasped the bamboo to her bosom and prevented him.

"Enough!" said Jia Zheng. "Today you are determined, all of you, to drive me insane."

"No doubt Bao-yu deserved to be beaten," said Lady Wang tearfully, "but it is bad for you to get over-excited. Besides, you ought to have some consideration for Lady Jia. She is not at all well in this frightful heat. It may not seem to you of much consequence to kill Bao-yu, but think what the effect would be on *her*."

"Don't try that sort of talk with me!" said Jia Zheng bitterly. "Merely by fathering a monster like this I have proved myself an unfilial son; yet whenever in the past I have tried to discipline him, the rest of you have all conspired against me to protect him. Now that I have the opportunity at last, I may as well finish off what I have begun and put him down, like the vermin he is, before he can do any more damage."

So saying, he took up a rope and would have put his threat into execution, had not Lady Wang held her arms around him to prevent it.

"Of course you should discipline your son," she said, weeping, "but you have a wife too, Sir Zheng, don't forget. I am nearly fifty now and this wretched boy is the only son I have. If you insist on making an example of him, I dare not do much to dissuade you. But to kill him outright— that is deliberately to make me childless. Better strangle me first, if you are going to strangle him. Let the two of us die together. At least I shall have some support then in the world to come, if all support in this world is to be denied me!"

With these words she threw herself upon Bao-yu's body and, lifting up her voice, began weeping with noisy abandon. Jia Zheng, who had heard her with a sigh, sank into a chair and himself broke down in a fit of weeping.

Presently Lady Wang began to examine the body she was clasping. Bao-yu's face was ashen, his breathing was scarcely perceptible, and the trou-sers of thin green silk which clothed the lower part of his body were so soaked with blood that their colour was no longer recognizable. Feverishly she unfastened his waistband and drew them back. Everywhere, from the upper part of his buttocks down to his calves, was either raw and bloody or purplish black with bruises. Not an inch of sound flesh was to be seen. The sight made her cry out involuntarily.

"Oh my son! My unfortunate son!"

Once more she broke down into uncontrollable weeping.

Her own words reminded her of the son she had already lost, and now, with added bitterness, she began to call out his name.

"Oh, Zhu! Zhu! If only you had lived, I shouldn't have minded losing a *hundred* other sons!"

By this time news of Lady Wang's *démarche*[7] had circulated to the other members of the inner mansion and Li Wan, Xi-feng, Ying-chun, Tan-chun and Xi-chun had come to join her. The invocation of her dead husband's name, painful to all of them, was altogether too much for Li Wan, who broke into loud sobs on hearing it. Jia Zheng himself was deeply affected, and tears as round as pumpkins rolled down both his cheeks. It was beginning to look as if they might all go on weeping there indefinitely, since no one would make a move; but just then there was a cry of "Her Old Ladyship—!" from one of the maids, interrupted by a quavering voice outside the window.

"Kill me first! You may as well kill both of us while you are about it!"

As much distressed by his mother's words as he was alarmed by her arrival, Jia Zheng hurried out to meet her. She was leaning on the shoul-der of a little maid, her old head swaying from side to side with the effort of running, and panting as she ran.

Jia Zheng bowed down before her and his face assumed the semblance of a smile.

"Surely, Mother, in such hot weather as this there is no need for you to come here? If you have any instructions, you should call for me and let *me* come to *you*."

Grandmother Jia had stopped when she heard this voice and now stood panting for some moments while she regained her breath. When she spoke, her voice had an unnatural shrillness in it.

---

7. A strategically chosen course of action.

"Oh! Are you speaking to *me*?"—Yes, as a matter of fact I *have* got 'instructions,' as you put it; but as unfortunately I've never had a good son who cares for me, there's no one I can give them to."

Wounded in his most sensitive spot, Jia Zheng fell on his knees before her. The voice in which he replied to her was broken with tears.

"How can I bear it, Mother, if you speak to me like that? What I did to the boy I did for the honour of the family."

Grandmother Jia spat contemptuously.

"A single harsh word from me and you start whining that you can't bear it. How do you think Bao-yu could bear your cruel rod? And you say you've been punishing him for the honour of the family, but you just tell me this: did your own father ever punish *you* in such a way?—I think not."

She was weeping now herself.

"Don't upset yourself, Mother," said Jia Zheng, with the same forced smile. "I acted too hastily. From now on I'll never beat him again, if that's what you wish."

"Hoity-toity, keep your temper!" said Grandmother Jia. "He's your son. If you want to beat him, that's up to you. If we women are in your way, we'll leave you alone to get on with it." She turned to her attendants. "Call my carriage. Your Mistress and I and Bao-yu are going back to Nanking. We shall be leaving immediately."

The servants made a show of compliance.

"No need for you to cry," she said, turning to Lady Wang. "You love Bao-yu now that he's young, but when he's grown up and become an important official, he'll like enough forget that you're his mother. Much better force yourself not to love him now and save yourself some anguish later on."

Jia Zheng threw himself forward on his face.

"Don't say that, Mother! Don't reject your own son!"

"On the contrary," said Grandmother Jia, "it is *you* who have rejected *me*. But don't worry. When I have gone back to Nanking, there will be no one here to stop you. You can beat away to your heart's content." She turned to the servants.

"Come on, hurry up with that packing! And get the carriage and horses ready so that we can be on our way."

Jia Zheng's kotows were by now describing the whole quarter-circle from perpendicular to ground. But the old lady walked on inside, ignoring him.

From the sight that met her eyes she could tell that this had been no ordinary beating. It filled her with anguish for the sufferer and fresh anger for the man who had inflicted it, and for a long time she clung to the inert form and wept, only gradually calming down under the combined coaxing of Lady Wang, Xi-feng and Li Wan.

At this point several of the maids and womenservants came forward and attempted to raise Bao-yu to his feet.

"Idiots!" said Xi-feng. "Haven't you got eyes in your heads? Can't you *see* that he's in no fit state to walk? Go and get that wicker summer-bed from inside and carry him in on that."

The servants rushed out and presently reappeared carrying a long, nar-

row couch of woven rattan between them, on to which they lifted Bao-yu.
Then, with Grandmother Jia, Lady Wang and the rest of the womenfolk
leading the way, they carried him to Grandmother Jia's apartment and set
him down inside it.

Jia Zheng, conscious that his mother's wrath against him had not abated
and unwilling to leave things where they stood, had followed the little
procession inside. His eyes travelled from Bao-yu, who, he now saw, really
had been beaten very badly, to Lady Wang. She was sobbing bitterly, interspersing her sobs with cries of "My child!" and "My son!." Presently she
broke off and began railing at the object of her sorrow: "Why couldn't you
have died instead of Zhu? Zhu wouldn't have made his father angry the
way you do and I should have been spared this constant anxiety. What is
to become of me if *you* go away and leave me, too?" Then, with a cry of
"Poor, worthless boy!," she fell once more to weeping. When Jia Zheng
heard this, his own heart was softened and he began to wish that he had
not beaten the boy quite so savagely. He tried to find words of comfort for
his old mother, but she answered him tearfully.

"A father *ought* to punish his son if he's done wrong, but not like *that!* —
Why don't you go now? Won't you be content until you've seen the boy
die under your own eyes?"

Jia Zheng, with flustered deference, withdrew.

By now Aunt Xue, Bao-chai, Caltrop, Aroma and Shi Xiang-yun were
there too. Aroma was deeply distressed, but could not show the extent of
her feelings in the presence of so many others. Indeed, Bao-yu was so
ringed around with people fanning him or forcing water through his lips
that there was nothing she could have done for him if she had tried. Feeling somewhat superfluous, she left the apartment and went out to the
inner gate, where she asked the pages to look for Tealeaf, so that she could
find out what had happened.

"Why did the Master suddenly beat him like that?" she asked Tealeaf
when he arrived. "He hadn't been doing anything. And why couldn't you
have warned us in time?"

Tealeaf was indignant.

"I couldn't help it, I wasn't *there*. He was half-way through beating him
before I even got to hear about it. I did my best to find out the reason,
though. It seems that there were two things the Master was upset about:
one was to do with Bijou and the other was to do with Golden."

"How did the Master get to know about them?" said Aroma.

"Well, the Bijou business he probably knew about indirectly through
Mr. Xue," said Tealeaf. "Mr. Xue had been feeling very jealous, and it
looks as though he may have put someone else up to telling the Master
about it out of spite. And Golden he probably heard about from Master
Huan—leastways, that's what the Master's own people told me."

The two reasons Tealeaf had given corresponded well enough with
Aroma's own observations, and she was more than half inclined to believe
them. Fairly confident, therefore, that she now knew the cause of what
had happened, she returned once more to the apartment. The ministrations of those surrounding Bao-yu had by now restored him to full consciousness, and Grandmother Jia was instructing the servants to carry him

back to his own room. There was an answering cry and something of a
scramble as many willing hands lifted up the cane bed. Then, preceded
as before by Grandmother Jia, Lady Wang and the rest, they carried him
through into the Garden and back to Green Delights, where they finally
got him on to his own bed. After a good deal more bustle they gradually
all drifted away and Aroma at last had Bao-yu alone to herself.

But in order to know what happened then, you must refer to the following chapter.

CHAPTER 34

A wordless message meets with silent understanding
And a groundless imputation leads to undeserved rebukes

When she saw that Grandmother Jia, Lady Wang and the rest had all
gone, Aroma went and sat down at Bao-yu's bedside and asked him, with
tears in her eyes, the reason why he had been beaten so severely.

Bao-yu sighed.

"Oh, the usual things. Need you ask? I wish you'd take a look down
below, though, and tell me if anything's broken. It's hurting so dreadfully
down there."

Very gently Aroma inserted her fingers into the top of his trousers and
began to draw them off. She had barely started when he gritted his teeth
and let out a cry, and she had to stop immediately. This happened three
or four times before she finally succeeded in getting them off. The sight
revealed made her grit her own teeth.

"Mother of mine!" she gasped, "he must have hit you savagely. If only
you'd listened to me a bit in the past, it would never have come to *this*.
Why, you might have been crippled for life. It doesn't bear thinking of."

Just then Bao-chai's arrival was announced by one of the maids. Since
putting his trousers on again was out of the question, Aroma snatched up
a lightweight coverlet and hurriedly threw it over him. Bao-chai came in
carrying a large tablet of some sort of solid medicine which she instructed
Aroma to pound up in wine and apply to Bao-yu's injuries in the evening.

"This is a decongestant," she said, handing it to her. "It will take away
the inflammation by dispersing the bad blood in his bruises. After that, he
should heal quite quickly."

She turned to Bao-yu.

"Are you feeling any better now?"

Bao-yu thanked her. "Yes," he said, he was feeling a little better, and
invited her to sit down beside him. Bao-chai was relieved to see him with
his eyes open and talking again. She shook her head sadly.

"If you had listened to what one said, this would never have happened.
Everyone is so upset now. It isn't only Grandmother and Lady Wang, you
know. Even—"

She checked herself abruptly, regretting that she had allowed her feelings to run away with her, and lowered her head, blushing. Bao-yu had
sensed hidden depths of feeling in the passionate earnestness of her tone,
and when she suddenly faltered and turned red, there was something so

touching about the pretty air of confusion with which she dropped her head and played with the ends of her girdle, that his spirits soared and his pain was momentarily forgotten.

"What have I undergone but a few whacks of the bamboo?" he thought, "—yet already they are so sad and concerned about me! What dear, adorable, sweet, noble girls they are! Heaven knows how they would grieve for me if I were actually to die! It would be almost worth dying, just to find out. The loss of a life's ambitions would be a small price to pay, and I should be a peevish, ungrateful ghost if I did not feel proud and happy when such darling creatures were grieving for me."

He was roused from this reverie by the sound of Bao-chai's voice asking Aroma what it was that had moved his father to such violent anger against him. Aroma's low reply, in which she merely repeated what Tealeaf had told her, was his first inkling of the part that Jia Huan had played in his misfortune. Her mention of Xue Pan's involvement, however, made him apprehensive that Bao-chai might feel embarrassed, and he hastily interrupted Aroma to prevent her from saying more.

"Old Xue would never do a thing like that," he said. "It's silly to make these wild assertions."

Bao-chai knew that it was out of respect for her feelings that he was silencing Aroma, and she wondered at his considerateness.

"What delicacy of feeling!" she thought, "—after so terrible a beating and in spite of all the pain, to be still able to worry about the possibility of someone else's being offended! If only you could apply some of that thoughtfulness to the more important things of life, my friend, you would make my Uncle so happy; and then perhaps these awful things would never happen. And when all's said and done, this sensibility on my behalf is rather wasted. Do you *really* think I know my own brother so little that I am unaware of his unruly nature? Nothing has ever been allowed to stand in the way of Pan's desires. Look at the terrible trouble he made for you that time over Qin Zhong. That was a long time ago, and I am sure he has got much worse since then."

Those were her thoughts, but what she said was:

"There's really no need to look around for someone to blame. If you ask me, the mere fact that Cousin Bao has been willing to keep such company was in itself quite enough to make Uncle angry. And though my brother can be very tactless and may well have let something out about Cousin Bao in the course of conversation, I'm sure it wouldn't have been deliberate trouble-making on his part. In the first place, it is, after all, true, what he is supposed to have said: Cousin Bao *has* been going around with that actor. And in the second place, my brother simply hasn't got it in him to be discreet. You have lived all your life with sensitive, considerate people like Cousin Bao, my dear Aroma. You have never had to deal with a crude, forthright person like my brother—someone who says whatever comes into his head with complete disregard for the consequences."

When Bao-yu cut short her remarks about Xue Pan, Aroma had realized at once that she was being tactless and inwardly prayed that Bao-chai had not taken exception to them. To her, therefore, these words of Bao-chai's were a source of tongue-tied embarrassment. Bao-yu, on the other hand, could see in them only the refusal of a frank and generous nature to admit deviousness in others and a sensibility capable of matching and responding to his own. As a consequence his spirits soared yet higher. He was about to say something, but Bao-chai rose to her feet and anticipated him.

"I'll come and see you again tomorrow. You must rest now and give yourself a chance to get well. I've given Aroma something to make a lotion with. Get her to put it on for you in the evening. I can guarantee that it will hasten your recovery."

She was moving towards the door as she said this. When she was outside, Aroma hurried after her to see her off and to thank her for her trouble.

"As soon as he's better," she said, "Master Bao will come over and thank you himself, Miss."

"It's nothing at all," said Bao-chai, turning back to her with a smile. "Do tell him to rest properly, though, and not to brood. And if there's anything at all he wants, just quietly come round to my place for it. Don't go bothering Lady Jia or Lady Wang or any of the others, in case my uncle gets to hear of it. It probably wouldn't matter at the time, but it might do later on, next time there is any trouble."

With that she left, and Aroma turned back into the courtyard, her heart full of gratitude for Bao-chai's kindness. Re-entering Bao-yu's room, she found him lying back quietly, plunged in thought. From the look of it, he was already half asleep. Tiptoeing out again, she went off to wash her hair.

But it was difficult for Bao-yu to lie quietly for very long. The pain in his buttocks was like the stabbing and pricking of knives and needles and there was a burning sensation in them as if he were being grilled over a fire, so that the slightest movement made him cry out. Already it was growing late. Aroma appeared to have gone away, but two or three maids were still in attendance. As there was nothing that they could do for him, he told them that they might go off and prepare themselves for the night, provided that they remained within call. The maids accordingly withdrew, leaving him on his own.

He had dozed off. The shadowy form of Jiang Yu-han had come in to tell him of his capture by the Prince of Zhong-shun's men, followed, shortly after, by Golden, who gave him a tearful account of how she had drowned herself. In his half-dreaming, half-awake state he was having the greatest difficulty in attending to what they were saying, when suddenly he felt someone pushing him and became dimly aware of a sound of weeping in his ear. He gave a start. Fully awake now, he opened his eyes. It was Lin Dai-yu. Suspecting this, too, to be a dream, he raised his head to look. A pair of eyes swollen like peaches met his own, and a face that was glistening with tears. It was Dai-yu all right, no doubt about that. He would have looked longer, but the strain of raising himself was causing such excruciating pain in his nether parts, that he fell back again with a groan. The groan was followed by a sigh.

"Now what have *you* come for?" he said. "The sun's not long set and the ground must still be very hot underfoot. You could still get a heatstroke at this time of day, and that would be a fine how-do-you-do. Actually, in spite of the beating, I don't feel very much pain. This fuss I make is put on to fool the others. I'm hoping they'll spread the word around outside how badly I've been hurt, so that Father gets to hear of it. It's all shamming, really. You mustn't be taken in by it."

Dai-yu's sobbing had by this time ceased to be audible; but somehow her strangled, silent weeping was infinitely more pathetic than the most clamorous grief. At that moment volumes would have been inadequate to contain the things she wanted to say to him; yet all she could get out, after struggling for some time with her choking sobs, was:

"I suppose you'll change now."

Bao-yu gave a long sigh.

"Don't worry, I shan't change. People like that are worth dying for. I wouldn't change if he killed me."

The words were scarcely out of his mouth when they heard someone outside in the courtyard saying:

"Mrs. Lian has come."

Dai-yu had no wish to see Xi-feng, and rose to her feet hurriedly.

Bao-yu seized hold of her hand.

"Now that's funny. Why should you start being afraid of *her* all of a sudden?"

She stamped with impatience.

"Look at the state my eyes are in!" she said. "I don't want them all making fun of me again."

At that Bao-yu released her hand and she bounded round to the back of the bed, slipping into the rear courtyard just as Xi-feng was entering the room from the front.

"A bit better now?" said Xi-feng. "Is there anything you feel like eating yet? If there is, tell them to come round to my place and get it."

As soon as Xi-feng had gone, Bao-yu was visited by Aunt Xue, and shortly after that by someone whom his grandmother had sent to see how he was getting on. At lighting-up time, after taking a few mouthfuls of soup, he settled down into a fitful sleep.

Just then a new group of visitors arrived, consisting of Zhou Rui's wife, Wu Xin-deng's wife, Zheng Hao-shi's wife, and those other members of the mansion's female staff who had had most to do with Bao-yu in the past and who, having heard of his beating, were anxious to see how he was. Aroma came out smiling on to the verandah to welcome them.

"You're just too late to see him, ladies," she told them in a low voice. "He's just this minute dropped off."

She ushered them into the outer room, invited them to be seated, and served them with tea. After sitting there very quietly for several minutes, they got up to take their leave, requesting Aroma as they did so that she would inform Bao-yu when he waked that they had been round to ask about him. Aroma promised to do so and showed them out. Just as she was about to go in again, an old woman arrived from Lady Wang's to say that "Her Ladyship would like to see one of Master Bao's people." After reflecting for a moment, Aroma turned to the house and called softly to Skybright, Musk and Ripple inside.

"Her Ladyship wants to see someone, so I'm going over. Stay indoors and keep an eye on things while I'm away. I shan't be long."

Then she followed the old woman out of the Garden and round to Lady Wang's apartment in the central courtyard. She found Lady Wang sitting on a cane summer-bed and fanning herself with a palm-leaf fan. She appeared not entirely pleased when she saw that it was Aroma.

"You could have sent one of the others," she said. "There was no need for *you* to come and leave him unattended."

Aroma smiled reassuringly.

"Master Bao has just settled down for the night, Madam. If he *should* want anything, the others are nowadays quite capable of looking after him on their own. Your Ladyship has no need to worry. I thought I had better come myself and not send one of the others, in case Your Ladyship had something important to tell us. I was afraid that if I sent one of the others, they might not understand what you wanted."

"I have nothing in particular to tell you," said Lady Wang. "I merely wanted to ask about my son. How is the pain now?"

"Much better since I put on some of the lotion that Miss Bao brought for him," said Aroma. "It was so bad before that he couldn't lie still, but now he's sleeping quite soundly, so you can tell it must be better than it was."

"Has he had anything to eat yet?" said Lady Wang.

"He had a few sips of some soup Her Old Ladyship sent," said Aroma, "but that's all he would take. He kept complaining that he felt dry. He wanted me to give him plum bitters to drink, but of course that's an astringent, and I thought to myself that as he'd just had a beating and not been allowed to cry out during it, a lot of hot blood and hot poison must have been driven inwards and still be collected round his heart, and if he were to drink some of that stuff, it might stir them up and bring on a serious illness, so I talked him out of it. After a lot of persuading, I got him to take some rose syrup instead, that I mixed up in water for him; but after only half a cup of it he said it tasted sickly and he couldn't get it down."

"Oh dear, I wish you'd told me sooner," said Lady Wang. "We were sent some bottles of flavouring the other day that I could have let you have. As a matter of fact I *was* going to send him some of them, but then I thought that if I did they would probably only get wasted, so I didn't. If he can't manage the rose syrup, I can easily give you a few of them to take back with you. You need only mix a teaspoonful of essence in a cupful of water. The flavours are quite delicious." She called Suncloud to her. "Fetch me a few of those bottles of flavouring essence that were sent us the other day."

"Two will be enough," said Aroma, "otherwise it will only get wasted. If we run out, I can always come back for more later."

Suncloud was gone for a considerable time. Eventually she returned with two little glass bottles, each about three inches high, which she handed to Aroma. They had screw-on silver tops and yellow labels. One of them was labelled "Essence of Cassia Flower" and the other one "Essence of Roses."

"What tiny little bottles!" said Aroma. "They can't hold very much. I suppose the stuff inside them must be very precious."

"It was made specially for the Emperor," said Lady Wang. "That's what the yellow labels mean. Haven't you seen labels like that before? Mind you look after them and don't let the stuff in them get wasted."

Aroma promised to be careful and began to go.

"Just a minute!" said Lady Wang. "I've thought of something else that I wanted to ask you."

Aroma returned. Lady Wang first glanced about her to make sure that no one else was in the room, then she said:

"I think I heard someone say that Bao-yu's beating today was because of something that Huan had said to Sir Zheng. I suppose *you* don't happen to have heard anything about that?"

"No. I haven't heard anything about *that*," said Aroma. "What *I* heard was that it was because Master Bao had been going around with one of Prince Somebody-or-other's players and the Master was told about it by someone who called."

Lady Wang nodded her head mysteriously.

"Yes, that was one of the reasons. But there was another reason as well."

"I really know nothing about any other reason, Your Ladyship," said Aroma. She dropped her head and hesitated a moment before going on. "I wonder if I might be rather bold and say something very outspoken to Your Ladyship? Really and truly—" She faltered.

"Please go on."

"I will if Your Ladyship will promise not to be angry with me."

"That's all right," said Lady Wang. "Just tell me what you have to say."

"Well, really and truly," said Aroma, "Master Bao *needed* punishing. If the Master didn't keep an eye on him, there's no knowing *what* he mightn't get up to."

"My child," said Lady Wang with a warmth rarely seen in her, "those are exactly my own sentiments. How clever of you to have understood! Of course, I know perfectly well that Bao-yu is in need of discipline; and anyone who saw how strict I used to be with Mr. Zhu would realize that I am capable of exercising it. But I have my reasons. A woman of fifty cannot expect to bear any more children and Bao-yu is now the only son I have. He is not a very strong boy; and his Grannie dotes on him. I daren't *risk* being strict. I daren't risk losing another son. I daren't risk angering Her Old Ladyship and upsetting the whole household. I do once in a while have it out with him: but though I have argued and pleaded and wept, it doesn't do any good. He *seems* all right at the time, but he'll be just the same again a short while afterwards and I always know that I have failed to reach him. I am afraid he *has* to suffer before he can learn—but suppose it's too much for him?—suppose he doesn't get over *this* beating? What will become of *me*?"

She began to cry.

Seeing her mistress so distressed, Aroma herself was affected and began to cry too.

"I can understand Your Ladyship being so upset," she said, "when he's your own son. Even we servants that have been with him for a few years get worried about him. The most that *we* can ever hope for is to do our duty and get by without too much trouble—but even *that* won't be possible if he goes on the way he has been doing. I'm always telling him to change his ways. Every day—every hour—I tell him. But it's no use; he won't listen. Of course, if these people *will* make so much fuss of him, you can hardly blame him for going round with them—though it does make our job more difficult. But now that Your Ladyship has spoken like this, it puts me in mind of something that's been worrying me which I should like to have asked Your Ladyship's advice about, only I was afraid you might take it amiss, and then not only should I have spoken to no purpose, but I should leave myself without even a grave to lie in . . ."

It was evident to Lady Wang that what she was struggling to get out was a matter of some consequence.

"What is it you want to tell me, my child?" she said kindly. "I've heard a lot of people praising you recently, and I confess that I assumed it must be because you took special pains in serving Bao-yu or in making yourself agreeable to other people—little things of that sort. But I see that I was wrong. These are not at all little things that you have been talking about. What you have said so far makes very good sense and entirely accords with my own opinion of the matter. So if you have anything to tell me, I should like to hear it. But I must ask you not to discuss it with anyone else."

"All I really wanted to ask," said Aroma, "was if Your Ladyship could advise me how later on we can somehow or other contrive to get Master Bao moved back outside the Garden."

Lady Wang looked startled and clutched Aroma's hand in some alarm.

"I hope Bao-yu hasn't been doing something dreadful with one of the girls?"

"Oh no, Your Ladyship, please don't suspect that!" said Aroma hurriedly. "That wasn't my meaning at all. It's just that—if you'll allow me to say so—Master Bao and the young ladies are beginning to grow up now, and though they are all cousins, there *is* the difference of sex between them, which makes it very awkward sometimes when they are all living together, especially in the case of Miss Lin and Miss Bao, who aren't even of the same clan. One can't help feeling uneasy. Even to outsiders it looks like a very strange sort of family. They say 'where nothing happens, imagination is busiest,' and I'm sure lots of unaccountable misfortunes begin when some innocent little thing we did unthinkingly gets misconstrued in someone else's imagination and reported as something terrible. We just have to be on our guard against that sort of thing happening—especially when Master Bao has such a peculiar character, as Your Ladyship knows, and spends all his time with girls. He only has to make the tiniest slip in an unguarded moment, and whether he really did anything or not, with so many people about—and some of them no better than they should be—there is sure to be scandal. For you know what some of these people are like, Your Ladyship. If they feel well-disposed towards you, they'll make you out to be a saint; but if they're not, then Heaven help you! If Master Bao lives to be spoken well of, we can count ourselves lucky; but the way things are, it only needs someone to breathe a word of scandal and—I say nothing of what will happen to us servants—it's of no consequence if *we're* all chopped up for mincemeat—but what's more important, Master Bao's reputation will be destroyed for life and all the care and worry Your Ladyship and Sir Zheng have had on his account will have been wasted. I know Your Ladyship is very busy and can't be expected to think of everything, and I probably shouldn't have thought of this myself, but once I *had* thought of it, it seemed to me that it would be wrong of me not to tell Your Ladyship, and it's been preying on my mind ever since. The only reason I haven't mentioned it before is because I was afraid Your Ladyship might be angry with me."

What Aroma had just been saying about misconstructions and scandals so exactly fitted what had in fact happened in the case of Golden that for a moment Lady Wang was quite taken aback. But on reflection she felt nothing but love and gratitude for this humble servant-girl who had shown so much solicitude on her behalf.

"It is very perceptive of you, my dear, to have thought it all out so carefully," she said. "I have, of course, thought about this matter myself, but other things have put it from my mind, and what you have just said has reminded me. It is most thoughtful of you. You are a very, very good girl—Well, you may go now. I think I now know what to do. There is just one thing before you go, though. Now that you have spoken to me like this, I am going to place Bao-yu entirely in your hands. Be very careful with him, won't you? Remember that anything you do for him you will be doing also for me. You will find that I am not ungrateful."

Aroma stood for a moment with bowed head, weighing the import of these words. Then she said:

"I will do what Your Ladyship has asked me to the utmost of my ability."

She left the apartment slowly and made her way back to Green Delights, pondering as she went. When she arrived, Bao-yu had just woken up, so she told him about the flavourings. He was pleased and made her mix some for him straight away. It was quite delicious. He kept thinking about Dai-yu and wanted to send someone over to see her, but he was afraid that Aroma would disapprove, so, as a means of getting her out of the way, he sent her over to Bao-chai's place to borrow a book. As soon as she had gone, he summoned Skybright.

"I want you to go to Miss Lin's for me," he said. "Just see what she's doing, and if she asks about me, tell her I'm all right."

"I can't go rushing in there bald-headed without a reason," said Skybright. "You'd better give me *some* kind of a message, just to give me an excuse for going there."

"I have none to give," said Bao-yu.

"Well, give me something to take, then," said Skybright, "or think of something I can ask her for. Otherwise it will look so silly."

Bao-yu thought for a bit and then, reaching out and picking up two of his old handkerchiefs, he tossed them towards her with a smile.

"All right. Tell her I said you were to give her these."

"That's an odd sort of present!" said Skybright. "What's she going to do with a pair of your old handkerchiefs? Most likely she'll think you're making fun of her and get upset again."

"No she won't," said Bao-yu. "She'll understand."

Skybright deemed it pointless to argue, so she picked up the handkerchiefs and went off to the Naiad's House. Little Delicate, who was hanging some towels out to dry on the verandah railings, saw her enter the courtyard and attempted to wave her away.

"She's gone to bed."

Skybright ignored her and went on inside. The lamps had not been lit and the room was in almost total darkness. The voice of Dai-yu, lying awake in bed, spoke to her out of the shadows.

"Who is it?"

"Skybright."

"What do you want?"

"Master Bao has sent me with some handkerchiefs, Miss."

Dai-yu seemed to hesitate. She found the gift puzzling and was wondering what it could mean.

"I suppose they must be very good ones," she said. "Probably someone gave them to him. Tell him to keep them and give them to somebody else. I have no use for them just now myself."

Skybright laughed.

"They're not new ones, Miss. They're two of his old, everyday ones."

This was even more puzzling. Dai-yu thought very hard for some moments. Then suddenly, in a flash, she understood.

"Put them down. You may go now."

Skybright did as she was bid and withdrew. All the way back to Green Delights she tried to make sense of what had happened, but it continued to mystify her.

Meanwhile the message that eluded Skybright had thrown Dai-yu into a turmoil of conflicting emotions.

"I feel so happy," she thought, "that in the midst of his own affliction he has been able to grasp the cause of all *my* trouble.

"And yet at the same time I am sad," she thought; "because how do I know that my trouble will end in the way I want it to?

"Actually, I feel rather amused," she thought. "Fancy his sending a pair of old handkerchiefs like that! Suppose I hadn't understood what he was getting at?

"But I feel alarmed that he should be sending presents to me in secret.

"Oh, and I feel so ashamed when I think how I am forever crying and quarrelling," she thought, "and all the time he has understood! . . ."

And her thoughts carried her this way and that, until the ferment of excitement within her cried out to be expressed. Careless of what the maids might think, she called for a lamp, sat herself down at her desk, ground some ink, softened her brush, and proceeded to compose the following quatrains, using the handkerchiefs themselves to write on:

1

> Seeing my idle tears, you ask me why
> These foolish drops fall from my teeming eye:
> Then know, your gift, being by the merfolk[8] made,
> In merman's currency must be repaid.

---

8. Mythical beings who live in the sea. They were famous for the fine fabric they wove, and when they wept, their tears formed pearls.

2

Jewelled drops by day in secret sorrow shed
Or, in the night-time, in my wakeful bed,
Lest sleeve or pillow they should spot or stain,
Shall on these gifts shower down their salty rain.

3

Yet silk preserves but ill the Naiad's tears:
Each salty trace of them fast disappears.
Only the speckled bamboo[9] stems that grow
Outside the window still her tear-marks show.

She had only half-filled the second handkerchief and was preparing to
write another quatrain, when she became aware that her whole body was
burning hot all over and her cheeks were afire. Going over to the dressing-
table, she removed the brocade cover from the mirror and peered into it.

"Hmn! 'Brighter than the peach-flower's hue,' " she murmured complacently to the flushed face that stared out at her from the glass, and, little
imagining that what she had been witnessing was the first symptom of a
serious illness, went back to bed, her mind full of handkerchiefs.

                         ✳   ✳   ✳

---

9. This bamboo was supposed to have gotten its spots by the tears once shed on it by the two goddesses of
the Hsiang River, who were lamenting the death of their husband, the sage-king Shun.

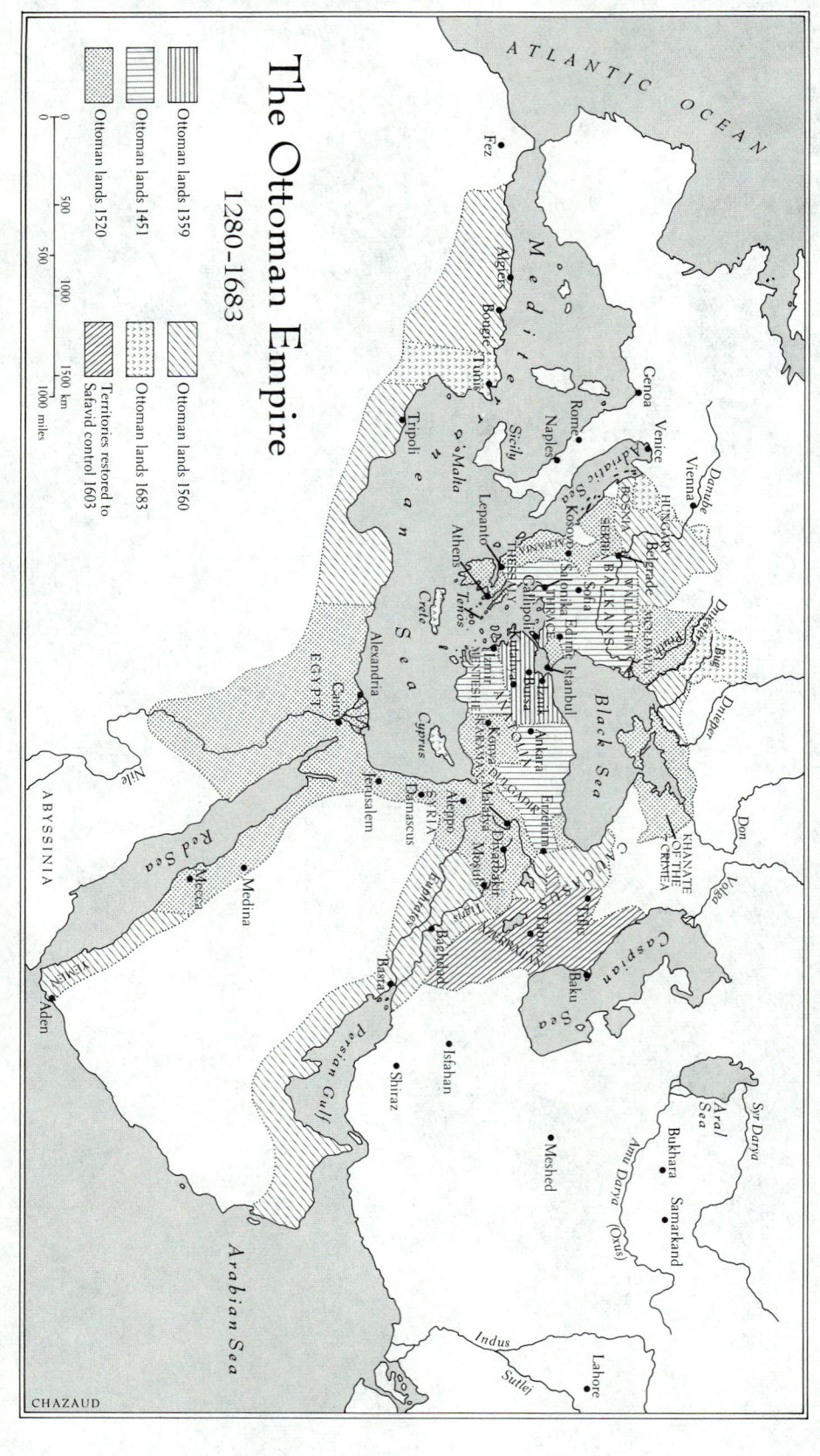

The Ottoman Empire
1280-1683

Legend:

- Ottoman lands 1359
- Ottoman lands 1451
- Ottoman lands 1520
- Ottoman lands 1560
- Ottoman lands 1683
- Territories restored to Safavid control 1603

Scale: 0 — 500 — 500 — 1000 — 1500 — 1000 km / 1000 miles

Labels on map:

ATLANTIC OCEAN

Fez
Algiers
Bougie
Tunis
Tripoli
Genoa
Venice
Vienna
Danube
Rome
Naples
Sicily
Malta
Lepanto
Athens
Tenos
Crete
Mediterranean Sea
Adriatic Sea
BOSNIA
SERBIA
Kosovo
HUNGARY
Belgrade
WALLACHIA
MOLDAVIA
Prut
Dniester
Bug
Dnieper
Don
Volga
KHANATE OF THE CRIMEA
Black Sea
Salonika
Sofia
BALKANS
THRACE
Gallipoli
Istanbul
Bursa
İzmir
Ankara
Edirne
Vidin
Janina
THESSALY
Konya
KARAMAN
Erzurum
CAUCASUS
Tiflis
Baku
Caspian Sea
Tabriz
Erzurum
Diyarbakir
Mosul
SYRIA
Aleppo
Damascus
Jerusalem
Alexandria
Cairo
EGYPT
Nile
Red Sea
Medina
Mecca
ABYSSINIA
YEMEN
Aden
Arabian Sea
Persian Gulf
Basra
Baghdad
Tigris
Euphrates
Isfahan
Shiraz
Meshed
Bukhara
Samarkand
Aral Sea
Syr Darya
Amu Darya (Oxus)
Lahore
Indus
Sutlej
Cyprus

CHAZAUD

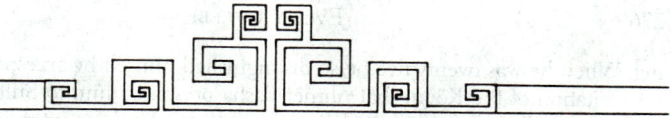

The Ottoman Empire: Çelebi's Book of Travels

EVLIYA ÇELEBI
1611–1684

On the tenth night of the Muslim month of Muharram in the year 1040 of the Prophet's flight to Madina (August 19, 1630) and the twentieth year of his life, Evliya Çelebi had a dream in which the Prophet Muhammad appeared to him and encouraged him to pursue the life of a wanderer. The dream occurred at an opportune moment for the young Evliya. His family wished him to choose the settled life of an official in the imperial Ottoman administration at Istanbul, but his own inclination was to follow his wanderlust. The Prophet's encouragement both strengthened his resolve and silenced his family's objections, and for the next forty-odd years he journeyed throughout the Ottoman Empire. Sometimes he traveled in the retinue of a high officer of the state (*pasha*), sometimes he went as an official himself, and sometimes he traveled as a private individual. But always he was an acute observer of the life around him, and he recorded what he saw in a vivid, anecdotal style. These observations, collected in ten volumes as the *Book of Travels* (*Seyâhatnâme*), provide us with a detailed, panoramic view of the Ottoman Empire in the mid-seventeenth century, when its geographic extent was greatest and its power had declined only a little from its apogee. There is no comparable record for any other Islamic state.

Evliya Çelebi, the son of Dervish Mehmet Zilli, was born in Istanbul on March 25, 1611, and died in the same city late in 1684. (Mehmet is Turkish for Muhammad.) His father's family was originally from the city of Kutahya in northwestern Anatolia, but had moved to Istanbul sometime after the Ottoman conquest of that city in 1453. Evliya's father was the chief jeweler of the court, a position of considerable distinction. He was a wealthy man as well, with houses and estates in several cities and four shops in Istanbul itself. These easy circumstances made it possible for his son to indulge his passion for travel. Evliya's mother was from the Caucasus and came to the royal household in the time of Sultan Ahmet I (1603–1617), where she married. She was related through her mother to the imperial son-in-law and high-ranking official of the court Melek Ahmet Pasha. This connection was a fortunate one for Evliya since it allowed him to join the retinue of the pasha during his embassies to Tabriz and his stints as governor of one or another of the Ottoman Empire's far-flung provinces: Bosnia, Diyarbakir, Baghdad, and Damascus among them. Ahmet Pasha's assistance to his younger relative served his ends as well since Evliya wrote glowingly of his patron's character and abilities in his journals.

As a boy, Evliya attended an elementary school for seven years and then, for another eleven years, a school where he was trained in the art of reciting the Koran. His father also taught him the manual skills associated with jewelry mak-

ing. When he was twenty-five he so distinguished himself by an especially beautiful recitation of the Koran that Ahmet Pasha presented him to Sultan Murat IV,
and as a result, he was accepted into the palace school for extensive training in
music, calligraphy, Arabic grammar, and advanced Koranic recitation.

Evliya began his travels at about this time, although initially his journeys did
not take him far from home. The first volume of his *Book of Travels* is devoted to
extensive descriptions of Istanbul and its environs. The plan of the remaining nine
volumes is not systematic but dictated by the accidents of opportunity. A single
volume may take him from Bosnia to Azerbaijan (Volume ii) or be devoted to
travels in a single region. In Volume viii, from which the selection anthologized
here is taken, Evliya travels exclusively in the Balkan peninsula, and Volume x is
devoted to Cairo, upper Egypt, the Sudan, and Abyssinia. Inevitably, there are
cities and regions he visited more than once. Egypt is the region he most enjoyed,
or at least, it is the one where he lived longest, staying there for eight or nine years.

Although Evliya often traveled in an official capacity and was concerned about
giving detailed and accurate descriptions of the places he visited, he was not a
historian, and he had a penchant for the legendary and the miraculous. He exaggerates his adventures, sometimes to comic effect, and recounts journeys that he
cannot possibly have taken. At times he seems to include anecdotes and stories
merely to leaven the more pedestrian descriptions of forts and cities. His audience
was the literate members of the Ottoman community, who wished to be amused
as well as instructed. He suits his style to their taste in that he writes in a language
that approximates the colloquial usage of the seventeenth century but also draws
on the more formal style of the court and chancery. The hero of a travel journal
is inevitably the author, and the man who emerges from the *Book of Travels* is
one who must have made an appealing travel companion—lively, imaginative,
inquisitive, and sensible.

THE OTTOMAN EMPIRE

The Ottoman state was the last of the great Muslim empires and the one whose
impact on the history of both modern Europe and the modern Middle East has
been the most consequential. The Ottomans were originally leaders of an Oghuz
(Turkomen) tribal confederation that came to Anatolia (Turkey) from central Asia
as part of the Saljuqid army sometime in the eleventh or twelfth century. After the
destruction of the Saljuqid state in the thirteenth century, they established themselves as an independent dynasty in northwestern Anatolia. From there they
expanded into Europe, crossing the strait to Gallipoli in 1354 and rapidly
extending their rule into northern Greece, Macedonia, and Bulgaria. In 1389 they
defeated the Serbs at Kosovo (in Serbia) and so gained mastery of the western
Balkans as well. In their rapid conquest of the region, the Ottomans were aided by
their ready access to numbers of Turkomen warriors in Anatolia, by the deep
dissension among the Balkan Slavs, and by the religious enmity between the Eastern Orthodox and Catholic Churches. From their secure base in the Balkans
(which they called Rumelia), the Ottomans launched an aggressive campaign to
extend their rule over their Turkomen neighbors to the east. Tamurlaine's invasion
of Anatolia in 1402 checked their advance, but only briefly. They soon retook their
former possessions. In 1453 Ottoman armies under Mehmed II the Conqueror
(1444–1446, 1451–1481) vanquished Constantinople (which they pronounce
Istanbul), the city that had defeated every Muslim army since the time of
Muhammad.

Mehmed was the first of the Ottoman sultans to see himself as the successor to
both the Muslim caliphs and the Byzantine emperors. His ambition was to found,
like them, a universal empire. He adopted a style in architecture that symbolized

that imperial ambition, constructing magnificent palaces and great congregational mosques that rivaled the finest monuments of Byzantine art. He also established a new legal code, and most important, he initiated the policy of imperial expansion that ultimately gave the Ottoman state dominance over a region almost as vast as that of the Abbasid state, which ruled Islam in its golden age (eighth to thirteenth centuries). At its peak, the Ottoman empire extended from the Crimea in the north to Aden on the Indian Ocean and from the borders of Iran to Morocco. Throughout the sixteenth and seventeenth centuries the Ottoman state waged war successfully against its European rivals to the west and north as well as against the Iranian Safavid state to the east. Ottoman ships controlled the eastern Mediterranean and provided the sole successful challenge to the Portuguese expansion into the Indian Ocean.

Although they were descended from the leaders of an Oghuz tribal confederation and spoke a Turkish language, the Ottomans saw themselves primarily not as Turkomans but as heirs to Abbasid imperial culture. They continued and enriched the Arabic and Persian tradition in literature, science, and the arts and established a rich and cosmopolitan court society in which learned and accomplished men of many origins were welcome. Ottoman literature was linguistically Turkish but drew heavily on both Arabic and Persian vocabulary, themes, and literary forms. Ottoman poets were often masters of all three languages. At its height, the poetry and prose of Ottoman Turkish achieved a richness and complexity that made it the third great literature of the Islamic tradition, after the Arabic and Persian.

The Ottoman Empire reached its apogee in the mid-seventeenth century and then began a slow process of decline. By the eighteenth century Europe had developed the military and economic strength to check further Ottoman advances and, probably, to defeat the empire outright, but rivalries between the various European states helped to preserve the ailing Ottoman Empire through its gradual dissolution over the next two centuries. Under the Albanian governor Muhammad Ali, Egypt became effectively autonomous in 1829. In the Balkans, powerful nationalist ambitions engendered by the French Revolution inspired the Balkan communities to rebel against Ottoman rule throughout the nineteenth century. Greece won its independence in 1829, and one by one the other states did as well until at the end of the Second Balkan War (1912–13) Turkey retained control of only one small province of Greece (eastern Thrace) from all its former vast empire in Europe. After World War I the victorious Allies stripped Turkey of its Arab provinces by reason of its support for the Central Powers. Within the remaining fragment of the Ottoman state itself, the nationalist leader Mustafa Kemal (later Atatürk) led a movement to establish a Turkish national state, repudiating the Ottoman heritage and distancing the Turkish people from the humiliations of the previous two centuries. In 1924 the caliphate was ended and the last Ottoman Sultan, Abd al-Majid, was deposed.

THE CITY OF BOUDONÍTZA

The selection from the *Book of Travels* printed here displays, if not the full range, at least the polar extremes of Evliya's style. It begins with a factual account of the state of Boudonítza's fortifications, with the helpful suggestion that they could be repaired easily should the need or desire arise. Evliya then moves quickly to a vivid and detailed account of a pirate raid and to a somewhat despairing description of this remote and unpromising outpost of the empire where Muslims are outnumbered by Christians, the economy is depressed, and the community is at the mercy of the European pirates who ravage the coast. One can see the mind of the imperial official at work in his emphasizing that the raid originated as much in the cruelty and injustice of the chief judge as it did in the rapacity of the pirates.

Following immediately on the heels of these shrewd and careful observations we have one of his most extraordinary flights of fantasy—the description of how Saint Veliüllah was miraculously saved from a horrible death and, as a result, converted an entire community to Islam.

Accounts of how a community was converted to Islam were of continuing interest to Muslims generally, and to the Ottomans in particular, since their proximity to the Christian world and the presence of large Christian communities within their borders gave them a sense of being in competition with Christians for the loyalties of their subjects and the control of their western provinces. Finally, this wonderful story is brought home by visiting God's curse on both the pirates and those greedy members of the community who wished either to despoil the saint's tomb or to carry away the property of the dervishes (pious mendicants). Although Evliya recounts this story as though he had viewed it with his own eyes, he frequently includes hearsay materials, and what we have here may simply be a wonderful anecdote he picked up in the local tea house. That is not to say that he is himself skeptical of the tale. Belief in the miraculous powers of saints was as widespread in Islam as it was in the Christian world to the west and not at all incongruous even in a man of Evliya's learning and sophistication. Saint Veliüllah was a Shi'ite who, like the Imams of Shi'ism, claimed descent from the Prophet Muhammad through his daughter Fatima and son-in-law Ali. By reciting the names of the saint's illustrious ancestors, Evliya invokes the divine authority of that lineage and lends a note of probability to this miraculous occurrence.

It is striking that he should celebrate this poor, small and depressed community with one of his richest imaginative flights. Although Evliya himself lived comfortably, he had a romantic and quite genuine admiration for the simple, hard-bitten residents of remote and impoverished outposts like Boudonítza. It would be completely in character for him to compose this heroic fantasy as a gesture of gratitude for the hospitality he received.

The Book of Travels circulated in manuscript during Evliya's lifetime; the first printed editions appeared in the nineteenth century. Though the bulk of the *Book of Travels* is still unavailable in English, Robert Dankoff has translated extensive selections from Volumes i to viii in *The Intimate Life of an Ottoman Statesman* (1991). The focus of his selections is Evliya's relative and long-time patron Melek Ahmet Pasha. There is a sketch of Evliya's life, a listing of the contents of the *Book of Travels*, and a guide to translations of his work into English and other European languages in the *Encyclopedia of Islam* (1954–   ), where his name is transliterated as Ewliyā Čelebī. The selection printed here is excerpted from a fuller translation being prepared by Pierre A. MacKay.

PRONOUNCING GLOSSARY

The following list uses common English syllables and stress accents to provide rough equivalents of selected words whose pronunciation may be unfamiliar to the general reader.

Boudonítza: *boo'-doe-nitz'-uh*

Diyarbakir: *dee-ar'-buh-keer'*

Esed: *e-said'*

Evliya Çelebi: *ev-lee'-uh che'-luh-bee*

Fatiha: *fa'-ti-huh*

Haji: *haw'-jee*

Ibrahim: *eeb-ruh-heem'*

Kutahya: *koo-tah'-yuh*

Mehmed Bektash Veli: *me'-met bek'-tash ve'-lee*

Mehmet Zilli: *me'-met zil'-lee*

Melek Ahmet Pasha: *me'-lek ah'-met pa'-shuh*

Muharram: *mu-har-ram'*

Safavids: *sa'-fuh-vids*
Saljuqids: *sal-joo'-kids*
Seyâhatnâme: *say-ah-hat'-nah-may*
Sheyh: *shay*
Suleyman Dede: *sue-lay-mahn' de'-de*

Umayyad: *oo-my'-yad*
Veliüllah: *ve-lee'-uh-lah'*
Yezid: *ye-zeed'*
Zeyn al-Abidin: *zay'-n ol–ah'-bi-deen'*
Zitúni: *zee-too'-nee*

TIMELINE

TEXTS	CONTEXTS
16th century The leading poets of the time leave Iran for the more hospitable courts of India and central Asia	**1502** Shah Ismâ'il founds the Safavid Dynasty, which rules Iran until 1732. The Safavids make Shi'ism the official faith of Iran and defend Iran's borders against the Ottomans to the west and the Özbegs to the northeast
	1520–1566 During Sultan Suleymân's reign, the Ottomans add Hungary to their empire, besiege Vienna, and engage the Portuguese navy in the Indian Ocean
	1589–1629 Shah Abbâs creates the splendid architectural monuments that still survive in Isfahan and establishes diplomatic contacts with Europe
1611–1684 Evliya Çelebi, who decides at about age 25 to devote his life to travel and begins to work on the *Book of Travels*	
	1683 The second unsuccessful siege of Vienna marks the limits of Ottoman power and heralds its decline
1720–1730 The Ottomans make their first attempts at Westernization, importing a printing press	**1726** The Safavids are defeated by the Turkoman, Nader Shah, founder of the Afshar Dynasty, which rules Iran until 1795
	1729 Nader Shah sacks Delhi, further weakening the Mughals
	1750 Karim Khân takes control of Iran from the last Afshar and establishes a dynasty that rules Iran until 1779
1757–1790 Sheyh Galip, the last great master of Ottoman court poetry	
	1779–1924 The Qajars under Agha Muhammad Khan gradually take control of Iran from the Zands; they will rule into the modern period
	1798 Napoleon invades Egypt, marking the beginning of the modern period in the Middle East

From The Book of Travels[1]

The City of Boudonítza

The castle is less than two hours distance westward from the seashore. It is a strongly built circular castle, with four subdivisions, on a high place in the mountains, and it is altogether four thousand paces round in circumference. The two lower divisions of the castle, however, were destroyed after the conquest, and since that event the walls have stood in ruins in several places. But it would be an easy matter, if there were money and interest enough, to restore them. As for the third subdivision and the inner keep, they are very strong indeed.

By the will of the Lord, before arriving at this castle, your poor servant heard the noise of cannonfire and musketry on the road in front of us. Since we also heard the shouting of the Muhammedan war-cry,[3] however, we were not frightened off, but as we came up, slowly slowly, towards the city, we encountered several thousand of Muhammad's people, together with their entire households, who had fled from the place, with rags bound around their heads and feet. It appeared that the infidel[4] fleet had disembarked an army which came up from the sea-shore into the residential section of the castle. Together with a certain infidel named Captain Giorgio,[5] who had come from the landward side, they attacked the city; sacked and plundered it; and after throwing everything into confusion, set fire to it and departed with two hundred prisoners, thousands of groats[6] worth of commercial goods and supplies, and the chief judge himself, whom they had taken prisoner along with his entire household.

CAUSE OF THE ASSAULT ON THE CASTLE OF BOUDONÍTZA.

The judge is alleged to have been a tyrant so manifestly oppressive in his infringement of the rights of both the tributary and the exempt populace that the tributary subjects,[7] because of the judge's oppression, went off in boats to Captain Giorgio, whom they found cruising near the Venetian island of Tenos. When they got there, they complained of the judge, saying, "He has taken all our property from us so, in the name of our Lord Jesus, restore our rights to us." So saying, they gave this Captain Giorgio the pretext by which he came by land and sea, and for the sake of a single oppressive judge, the infidels destroyed and devastated this charming city, looted it, and took all those many prisoners.

We made so bold as to come into the city in the midst of this turmoil, and saw that the infidels were still busy binding and chaining their captives, poor creatures of the Lord, and sending them off. Those of Muhammad's people who were shut up in the castle opened the castle gate as soon as they saw us, and cried out to us, "Hey Heroes, what shall we do,

---

1. Translated by and with notes adapted from Pierre MacKay.   2. A small city on the coast of the island of Morea in southern Greece.   3. Probably the phrase *Allahu akbar!* ("God is great!").   4. Christian. 5. A known pirate of the region.   6. An English silver coin widely used in commerce.   7. Christians. *Exempt populace:* Muslims.

when so many of our families, our wives and our children, are taken prisoner, and now, see, they are taking them away."

Then, making up a party together with my servants and the men of the town, we extinguished such fires as we could in some of the neighborhoods, and while we were doing so, we saw the warlike hero warriors from Zitúni,[8] horse and foot, coming to help. Then all the people of the city gathered together and attacked the low-born infidels where they had assembled their forces near the sea shore, and rescued much wealth and property and many prisoners, elderly men and women of Muhammad's people. There were also forty-five infidels whose strength was exhausted from running and from carrying their heavy load of loot. These remained behind, and thanks be to the Lord, we took them prisoner. But as we went further on and arrived close to the infidels' boats at the sea-shore, the accursed infidels let loose at us from their galleons and six gunnery barges, with their large cannon, and we were forced to take all our prisoners and retire once again. Having liberated so many of Muhammad's people, and repossessed so much material and heavy baggage, we made them very happy when we went back to the city with our infidel prisoners and in keeping with our exploits they gave your humble servant one of the infidel prisoners. Praise be to God, we found ourselves thus in a purely fortuitous battle, but what good was there in it, since all those people of Muhammad had been taken captive? There came news too that there were infidels lying in ambush in the mountains, so all the men from Boudonítza, from Zitúni and from Molo[9] came in, several thousands of them, and gathering together they patrolled through the hills and valleys around the city, and remained on watch there.

CONCLUDING DESCRIPTION OF THE CITY.

One ruinous old mosque in the lower residential quarter escaped the fire, and one inn. One dirty bath, ten shops, a hundred Muslim houses and a hundred and fifty infidel houses remained, all with tile roofs, and gardens and orchards. The rest were all set afire and burned.

Later on, the warriors from Boudonítza and Zitúni who had gone out into the mountains and valleys came back with the news that there was no trace or sign of infidels to be found, but we were still too fearful to sleep in the outer city, and so went into the middle redoubt,[1] where we were hospitably entertained. It is indeed a castle which rises level with the very sky, but the hills along the road that leads to Molo give artillery command over it. In the inner redoubt there are fifty dwellings for the poor wretches of garrison personnel, supplies of produce, and stores and depositories for weapons. But the arsenal is a small one, containing only five long brass falconets.[2] There is only the one small mosque, and no other public edifices. Here and there outside the castle there are gardens and orchards.

---

8. A town just to the north of Boudonítza.   9. A coastal village to the north of Boudonítza.   1. Fortification   2. Small cannon.

DESCRIPTION OF PLACES OF PILGRIMAGE TO THE GREAT SAINTS OF
GOD IN THE CASTLE OF BOUDONÍTZA.

Outside the city, in the high lands to the east, there is an elevated park-
land of cypresses and tall trees. Here, in a meadow from which the entire
world may be observed, under a huge lead-roofed cupola, is buried that
source of sacred knowledge, who is sprung from an illustrious stock, the
seed of Musa Reza, the venerated offspring of Kâzim, who is buried in the
heavenly paradise of Baghdad, that recourse of the righteous, entranced
by the uniqueness of God, and annihilated in his power, that guide
through the stations of sanctity and mirror of illustrious generosity, that
son of the noblest of princes, the chosen servant of God, the Sheyh[3] Sultan
Veliüllah, son of the Imam Ali Musa Reza, son of the Imam Kâzim, son
of the Imam Ja'fer Sadik, son of the Imam Bâkir, son of the Imam Zeyn
al-Abidin, son of the Imam Hüseyin, son of the Imam Ali Murteza and his
wife, the glorious Lady Fatima, daughter of the excellent Muḥammad,
who is Ahmed, Mahmud, and Mustafa, may God exalt him, and be
pleased with all of them.[4]

This excellent sultan Veliüllah, being of such an illustrious line, found
a final repose in this city of Boudonítza, and lies here in tranquillity, buried with all his dependents, children and friends in a brilliant shrine
beneath a luminous dome.

THE EMINENT GLORIES OF THE SAINT, VELIÜLLAH.

Because of the abuse and persecution which the family of Yezid the
Umayyad visited on the Imam Hüseyin after the disaster on the plains of
Kerbela,[5] this sultan Veliüllah departed from his homeland and, desiring
to become a member of the spiritual brethren in Greece, he wandered
and traveled over the earth. When he came to this city of Boudonítza,
which was at that time in the hands of the great King of Spain,[6] he performed the Sultani celebration of God's unity for this perverted and evil-
doing king. When they had all gathered together before him to the beat
of the great kettledrums, the king asked about their condition and circumstances, their origins and their quality. Once made cognizant of their
secrets, this cursed king was inflamed with poisonous rage and said, "What
business have you in my country? For what reason have you set your foot
in this land, making your call to prayer and performing the celebration of
the unity of God? Is it not because of you that the Turkish race will march
into this land after you, and that you have come to show them the way?"
So saying, he thrust sultan Veliüllah into a huge cannon, but just as he
was on the point of firing it, the saint, in perfect conviction and belief,
began the continuous recitation of the sacred verse from the Sura "The

3. Or sheikh.   4. This somewhat eccentric genealogy traces the descent of the Shi'ite Imam from
Muhammad. *Ahmed* ("most praiseworthy"), *Mahmud* ("praised"), and *Mustafa* ("chosen [by God]") are
attributes of *Muhammad* ("praised").   5. A reference to the disastrous uprising of the Shi'a under the
leadership of Hüseyin (Hussein), the grandson of the prophet Muhammad. Hüseyin was defeated and
beheaded near Kerbela, southwest of Baghdad. The shrine built there in memory of his martyrdom is the
most sacred of all the special Shi'a places of worship. Shi'as believed that the son-in-law of Muhammad
should have been the first caliph and that the caliphate should have stayed in his family.   6. The
Spanish Catalans took over east-central Greece and ruled both Athens and Thebes during the first half of
the 14th century.

Prophets" of the Glorious Koran, "We said, Oh fire, be cold and harmless to Ibrahim."[7] While he was reciting this verse, at the very moment when the great crowd of followers at his side was totally absorbed in the celebration of the unity of God, the decision of the infidels who are consigned to Hell was no longer stayed, and the cannon was fired. By the will of God, the Imam Veliüllah blew higher and higher into the air, and as he appeared out of the sky, his voice could be heard crying, "O God, O my protector." And so, by the will of God, he floated down to land standing upright on the earth, having suffered not the slightest injury to his delicate body at impact. As soon as he had busied himself with an act of thanksgiving to All-glorious God, all the infidels ran to see the condition of the saint, and on that occasion seven thousand unbelieving infidels produced the words of witness and, having become believers and followers of the saint, stood to be led in worship. Even the king, on seeing this, produced the forefinger of attestation and on his recalling the verse that speaks the unity of God, he was honored with the welcome into Islam.[8] All his children and household too became faithful believers in God's unity, and so the first beginnings of Islam in Greece took place among those people of Boudonítza who were thus converted.

Afterwards they built a great shrine, which is still in use, on the place where the saint came down after being fired from the cannon, and gave the rations of food and drink which he established. Infidels from all the seven regions of the world used to come here and visit the saint but, for his own part, this same saint did not survive for long after he had made manifest his blessedness, but soon made the transition to the ultimate world. When he had gone to his pardon, his many thousands of followers buried him here at this palatial edifice, which is still a place of pilgrimage for men of all conditions, an immense hall full of ascetic followers and a cloister for the devotees of Haji Mehmed Bektash Veli.[9]

There are seventy Bektashis here. Wealthy in their want and poverty, rich in the skills of self-annihilation into God, brethren in the arts of self-abandonment and contemplative abstraction, they are all wonderfully kind, cultivated and wholesome spirits. Each of them is appointed to a specific task as they perform all services for the horses of every wayfarer. No matter how many horses a person may have, they do not leave it to him to deal with the blankets and nose-bags, but they bring the horses into the cloister stables and, after they have watered them, they hang a nosebag of feed on them. Then they make coffee for the traveler, and from their kitchens they offer the good things of their hospitable dining halls: soups, stewed meats, pilavs and saffron rice, to rich and poor, old and young, yea even to Jew and heathen, for theirs is an immense bequest, from which they distribute their goods to all wandering travelers in accordance with the holy Sura, "There is no creature on the earth, but God has given it sustenance."[1]

All the kings of infideldom, and other infidels as well, are believers in

---

7. Sura 21:68. A sura is a section of the Koran, similar to a chapter.   8. One of the ways a Muslim may express the unity of God is to raise the right-hand forefinger while saying "God is One." The gesture has particular resonance in Greek Orthodox lands, where it contrasts directly and intentionally with the ritual Christian attestation of the Trinity, which is to raise three fingers side by side in blessing.   9. Founder of a major and still-flourishing Sufi order. A sufi is a Muslim mystic.   1. Sura 11:6.

this important sultan (Veliüllah), and every year old women come from infideldom, and traveling at the time of the new year, after the sounding of the festival kettledrum, under sacred Muhammadan sanctions, they make collections of money and provisions to provide for the sustenance of travelers.

This is a convent with a world-wide prospect which must be visited. All the buildings are roofed over with pure lead, which is one of the good works and benefactions of . . .[2] Pasha. On all sides of the sarcophagus of Saint Veliüllah, where he lies at rest under the luminous cupola, there are any number of glorious phrases written in a beautiful hand, and any number of precious incense burners, rosewater flasks, candle-holders and suspended lamps of every sort. There are rare and precious hangings too, and beautifully written inscriptions where each devout traveler by sea has left his mark. And there are articles from the apparatus of mendicant dervishes,[3] such as staffs, begging bowls, halters and gourd flasks. Besides these, there are all sorts of drums, pennants, iron clappers, banners, tambourines, kettledrums, trumpets, cymbals, . . . and whips. The Bektashis sprinkle rosewater over each pilgrim as he arrives. Beside Sultan Veliüllah is buried . . . sultan, one of his venerable sons, and beside him, . . . sultan, is buried. In the outer court also, there are great numbers of blessed saints buried. May God have mercy on them all.

AN ACCOUNT OF THE VERIFICATION OF THE SAINT'S BLESSED EFFICACY

Your lowly servitor himself and with his own eyes witnessed it, and we have ventured to recount it here that during the previous day's raid and pillaging by the many thousands of despicable and accursed infidels, there was a dull-witted, obstinate and impious detachment of several hundred infidels which came up to the sacred tomb chapel, where they saw a detachment of dervishes standing with hands clasped before them. Since all infidels are believers in this saint, they did not take his followers captive, but many of them fell upon the raw foodstuffs and set their minds to looting various articles from the cellars of the kitchen building and the dervish quarters, and stuffing them in their sacks to carry them off as booty. Now the infidels imagined that mere looting posed no danger of harm to those who were carrying off goods and possessions, so a large number of them went in and seized the dishes, stew-pots, kettles and ladles from the kitchen, and some came out wearing the black stew-pots on their heads, on top of their black hats. On seeing this another lot of vicious infidels ventured to enter the blessed shrine itself, where they stole some items of dervish apparatus and some beautiful copies of sacred writ.[4] One infidel, however, made a particular show of defiance by laying his hands on the sacred headdress set up over the blessed head of the saint. At this moment, an aged follower named Suleyman Dede cried out distractedly, "O Saint, why do you lie there? If only you would see what is happening! Where now is the honor of Muhammad."

2. Evliya left lacunae in his writings to be filled in later. He died before completing the task.   3. Muslim religious mendicants, usually sufis.   4. The Koran.

Glory be to God, as soon as he spoke, there came seven separate flashes and bright tongues of fire which struck each of the seven enemy infidels who were outside the luminous dome. All seven of those wretched unbelievers, condemned to eternal fire, were then destroyed within that brilliant shrine, set burning on the spot, like blackest coals. As for your humble servant, when I arrived to make my pilgrimage to the shrine, the seven human carcasses of those infidels who had been set afire, looking like skins full of black pitch, were lying like refuse under foot in the shade of the cypress trees. Your humble servant, together with my retinue and the dervishes themselves, got ropes around the feet of these stinking infidel carcases and dragged them off away from the shrine into the open, where we left them, and when the infidels from the city saw these burned infidel cadavers they acquired the most absolute and complete belief in the sultan Veliüllah.

Many of the other infidels, seeing that these were being burnt black as pitch, dropped the things they had just picked up and ran to tell the others, those who had earlier looted the kitchen of its dishes and pots, about these extremely depressing events. Some of the looters then dropped their booty but others dared to hold on to it and, while the latter were carrying it off, it happened by the will of God that the stew-pots on the heads of those infidels who were wearing them like black hats became suddenly hot. At once their black hair and their black heads began to ignite under their black hats from the red heat of the cooking pots. At this they dropped the pots and ran, but some remained stubbornly determined and carried their booty until their strength was at an end. They passed on their loads to other infidels, but these in turn as their bodies became powerless left the load to be taken up by others and, in the end, whatever they had taken from the shrine of Veliüllah they left strewn around the plain while they rushed onto the ships for dear life, crying out, "Let's be done with it!"

At the same time or just previously we had prevailed against the infidels . . . with what army we had and had made them drop much of their spoils, had freed many prisoners, and had captured forty-five infidel prisoners. And now, glory be to God, all the apparatus and paraphernalia came back to where it belonged. Not a single thing was lost and the worthy dervishes were recently still engaged in the task of putting all the various sorts of dervish apparatus back in their proper places. The significant inference to be drawn from all these noteworthy events is that all the blessed efficacy of the saint as written about in various books of belief is absolutely true. For the soul of the eminent Sheyh Veliüllah and for the souls of his family and his sons, that God may be pleased with them, a recitation of the Fatiha.[5]

Your humble servant spent an evening being entertained by these mendicants at the gates of God and engaging in uplifting conversation. Truly these are an orthodox people here, a community of the purest law and a congregation of poor followers of the truest belief. Their spiritual leader most particularly, that Hafız Arslan Dede who is their leader in the true way of religious adoration, is the very essence of a dervish who keeps the

---

5. The first sura of the Koran, often recited independently as a prayer.

fast assiduously, in David's manner,[6] and utters an invocation to God in his every breath. . . . He gave us a few dervishes to take along as companions and all of our party bade farewell, but just as we were leaving, there occurred a most extraordinary spectacle as several hundred people of Boudonítza arrived with the judge from Zitúni and began to lay claim to the wealth, the apparatus and the apparel of the dervishes from this chapel.

It would seem that this lot of people from Boudonítza were all of the Greek race, a company of stubborn recusant doubters, and it was alleged that since they did not believe in Sultan Veliüllah or in any other great saints they had appropriated for their own use and enjoyment any number of gardens, orchards and cultivable fields which they treated as their own property. These doubters stated in the judge's presence that the infidel raiders had come and had robbed them and made prisoners of their entire families and households at the same time as they, the infidels, were assaulting the dervishes. They alleged further that, "As the infidels were carrying off your property, they dropped it because it was too heavy a load, but they also dropped our property as well and you, on the pretext that it was all the saint's property, gathered up all our things from the fields and brought them all to this chapel." When they made this claim, the dervishes answered, "Misguided men, the infidels went off with our dervish apparel and the pots and dishes from our kitchen, except that the infidels who came into the shrine and were taking the lamps and candle-holders and the copies of holy writ—those infidels caught fire and are left behind here burned black as cinders."

Now just as they were saying this, one man announced that, "Those Korans are mine, and just such an amount of my belongings was taken," and with that he went straight into the sacred sepulchre and in the presence of the judge and of my humble self, he took three large copies of the Koran from off the reading stand saying, "These are mine."

But just as he was going out the door he was struck down into a neat little heap, and his soul was burned black as hell-fire. The dervishes picked up the holy writings from the spot and put them back where they belonged. Your humble servant was left in a state of rapturous ecstasy, unable to draw breath, but then, together with my servants, we got this doubter's corpse by head and feet, and dragged it out among the above-mentioned infidels' carcasses and left it there. All the people from Boudonítza, on seeing this occurrence, took to their heels.

The poor judge was very distressed to have come from Zitúni, and he too, saying, "Glory be to God," remounted his horse and traced his steps back to Zitúni. There are any number of trustworthy witnesses to the outcome of this matter.

We ourselves, at that very time, mounted our own horses and set out once again from Boudonítza in a southeasterly direction. Taking God as our refuge, we crossed through difficult rocky hills and gulleys and over mountains and valleys and came in 4 hours to Esed Abad.

---

6. King David is exemplary for his piety in Muslim tradition.

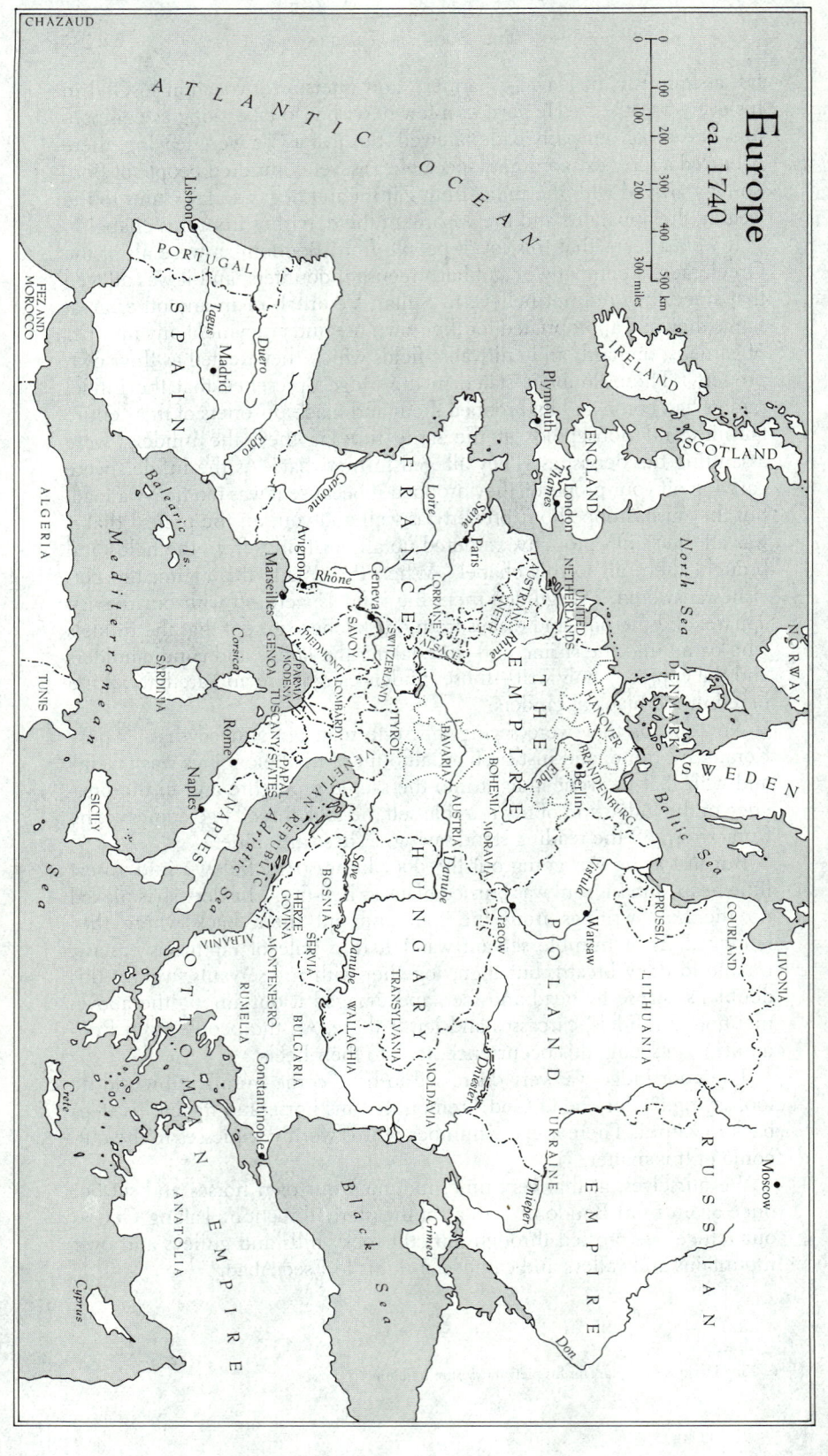

CHAZAUD

Europe
ca. 1740

0
100
100
200
200 300
300
400
300 500 km
500 miles

ATLANTIC OCEAN

FEZ AND
MOROCCO

PORTUGAL

Lisbon

SPAIN

Tagus
Madrid
Duero

Ebro

ALGERIA

Balearic Is.

Mediterranean Sea

TUNIS

SARDINIA

Corsica

SICILY

Garonne

FRANCE

Loire
Seine

Paris

Avignon
Rhône

Marseilles

Geneva
SWITZERLAND
SAVOY
PIEDMONT
GENOA
PARMA
MODENA
TUSCANY
PAPAL
STATES
Rome

Naples

NAPLES

Adriatic Sea

LORRAINE
ALSACE

Rhine

AUSTRIAN
NETHERLANDS
UNITED
NETHERLANDS

TYROL
LOMBARDY
VENETIAN
REPUBLIC
VENETIA

Rhône

THE
EMPIRE

BAVARIA
Danube

BOHEMIA

MORAVIA

AUSTRIA

HUNGARY

Save
Danube

BOSNIA
HERZE-
GOVINA
SERVIA
MONTENEGRO
RUMELIA
ALBANIA

BULGARIA
WALLACHIA
TRANSYLVANIA
MOLDAVIA

Constantinople

Black Sea

OTTOMAN EMPIRE

ANATOLIA

Crete

Cyprus

IRELAND

Plymouth
ENGLAND
Thames
London

SCOTLAND

North Sea

DENMARK

HANOVER
BRANDENBURG
Berlin
Elbe

SWEDEN

Baltic Sea

Vistula

Cracow
Warsaw

POLAND

PRUSSIA

COURLAND

LITHUANIA

Dniester

UKRAINE
Dnieper

Don

RUSSIAN EMPIRE

Moscow

NORWAY

LIVONIA

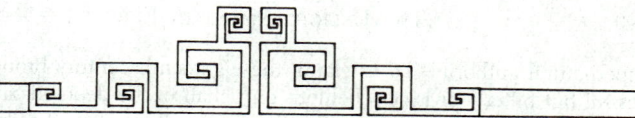

The Enlightenment in Europe

"I wonder if it is not better to try to correct and moderate men's passions than to try to suppress them altogether." The sentence, from Jean-Baptiste Molière's 1669 preface to his biting comedy about religious hypocrisy, *Tartuffe*, captures something of the anxiety and the optimism of a period for which subsequent generations have found no adequate single designation. "The Neo-Classic Period," "The Age of Reason," "The Enlightenment": such labels suggest, accurately enough, that thinkers between (roughly) 1660 and 1770 emphasized the powers of the mind and turned to the Roman past for models. But these terms do not convey the awareness of limitation expressed in Molière's sentence, an awareness as typical of the historical period to which the sentence belongs as is the expressed aspiration toward correctness and moderation. The effort to correct and moderate the passions might prove less foolhardy than the effort to suppress them, but both endeavors would involve human nature's struggle with itself, a struggle necessarily perpetual. "On life's vast ocean diversely we sail, / Reason the card, but Passion is the gale," Alexander Pope's *Essay on Man* (1733) pointed out. One could hope to steer with reason as guide only by remembering the omnipresence of passion as impetus. Eighteenth-century thinkers analyzed and eighteenth-century imaginative writers dramatized intricate interchanges and conflicts between these aspects of our selves.

The drama of reason and passion played itself out in society, the system of association human beings had devised partly to control passion and institutionalize reason. Structured on the basis of a rigid class system, the traditional social order began to face incipient challenges in the eighteenth century as new commerce generated new wealth, whose possessors felt entitled to claim their own share of social power. The threat to established hierarchies extended even to kings. Thomas Hobbes, in *Leviathan* (1651), had argued for the secular origins of the social contract. Kings arise, he said, not by divine ordinance but out of human need; they exist to prevent what would otherwise be a war of all on all. Monarchs still presided over European nations in the eighteenth century, but with less security than before. The English had executed their ruler in 1642; the French would perform another royal decapitation before the end of the eighteenth century. The mortality of kings had become a political fact, a fact implying the conceivable instability of the social order over which kings presided.

A sense of the contingencies of the human condition impinged on many minds in a world where men and women no longer automatically assumed God's benign supervision of human affairs or the primacy of their own Christian obligations. The fierce strife between Protestants and Catholics lapsed into relative quiescence by the end of the seventeenth century, but the Protestant English deposed their king in 1688 because of his marriage to a Catholic princess and their fear of a Catholic dynasty; and in France Louis XIV in 1685 revoked the Edict of Nantes, which had granted religious toleration to Protestants. The overt English struggle of Cavaliers and Puritans ended with the restoration of Charles II to the throne in 1660. Religious differences now became translated into divisions of social class and of political conviction—divisions no less powerful for lacking the claim of supernatural authority. To England, the eighteenth century brought two unsuccessful but bitterly divisive rebellions on behalf of the deposed Stuart succession as well as the cataclysmic American Revolution. In France, the century ended in revolution. Throughout the eighteenth century, wars erupted over succession to European thrones and over nationalistic claims, although no fighting took place on such a scale as that of the devastating Thirty Years' War (1618–48). On the whole, divisions *within* nations (in France and England) assumed greater importance than those between nations.

Philosophers now turned their attention to defining the possibilities and limitations of the human position in the material universe. "I think, therefore I am," René Descartes pronounced, declaring the mind the source of individual being. But this idea proved less reassuring than it initially seemed. Subsequent philosophers, exploring the concept's implications, realized the possibility of the mind's isolation in its own constructions. Perhaps, Wilhelm Leibnitz suggested, no real communication can take place between one consciousness and another. Possibly, according to David Hume, the idea of individual identity itself derives from the mind's efforts to manufacture continuity out of discontinuous memories. Philosophers pointed out the impossibility of knowing for sure even the reality of the external world: the only certainty is that we think it exists. If contemplating the nature of human reason thus led philosophic skeptics to restrict severely the area of what we can know with certainty, other contemplations induced other thinkers to insist on the existence, beyond ourselves, of an entirely rational physical and moral universe. Isaac Newton's demonstrations of the order of natural law greatly encouraged this line of thought. The fullness and complexity of the perceived physical world testified, as many wrote, to the sublime rationality of a divine plan. The Planner, however, did not necessarily supervise the day-to-day operations of His arrangements; He might rather, as a popular analogy had it, resemble the watchmaker who winds the watch and leaves it running.

Deism, evoking a depersonalized deity, insisted on the logicality of the universe and encouraged the separation of ethics from religion. Ethics, too, could be understood as a matter of reason. "He that thinks reasonably must think morally," Samuel Johnson observed, echoing the noble horses Jonathan Swift had imagined in the fourth book of *Gulliver's Travels*. But such statements expressed wish more than perception. Awareness of the passions continued to haunt thinkers yearning for rationality. Swift's Houyhnhnms, creatures of his imagination, might achieve flawless rationality—with accompanying wisdom and benevolence—but actual human beings could only dream of such an ideal, while experiencing—as men and women have always experienced—the confusion of conflicting impulses often at war with the dictates of reason.

Although the social, economic, and political organizations in which the thinkers of this period participated hardly resemble our own, the questions they raised about the human condition have plagued the Western mind ever since. Though we no longer locate the solution to all problems in an unattainable ideal of "reason," we too struggle to find the limits of certainty, have problems of identity and isolation, and recognize the impossibility of altogether controlling internal forces now identified as "the unconscious" rather than "the passions." But we confront such issues largely from the position of isolated individuals. In the late seventeenth and early eighteenth centuries, in England and on the Continent, the sense of obligation to society had far more power than it possesses today. Society provided the standards and the instruments of control that might help to counter the tumult of individual impulse.

SOCIETY

Society, in this period, designates both a powerful idea and an omnipresent fact of experience. Prerevolutionary French society, like English society in the same period, depended on clear hierarchical structures. The literature of both countries issued from a small cultural elite, writing for others of their kind and assuming the rightness of their own knowledge of how people should feel and behave.

For the English and French upper classes, as for the ancient Romans they admired, public life mattered more than private. At one level, the *public* designated the realms of government and diplomacy: occupations allowing and encouraging oratory, frequent travel, negotiation, the exercise of political and economic power. In this sense, the public world belonged entirely to men, who determined the course of government, defined the limits of the important, enforced their sense of the fitness of things. By another definition, *public* might refer to the life of formal social intercourse. In France, such social life took place often in "salons," gatherings to engage in intellectual as well as frivolous conversation. Women typically presided over these salons, thus declaring both their intellectual authority and their capacity to combine high thought with high style. Until rather late in the eighteenth century, on the other hand, England allowed women no such commanding position; there, men controlled intellectual as well as political discourse. The male voice, accordingly, dominated English literature until the development of the novel provided new opportunities for women writers and for the articulation of domestic values.

Both the larger and the more limited "public" spheres depended on well-defined codes of behavior. The discrepancy between the forms of self-presentation dictated by these codes and the operations such forms might disguise—a specific form of the reason-passion conflict—provides one of the insistent themes of French and English literature in the century beginning around 1660. Molière, examining religious sham; Swift, lashing the English for institutionalized hypocrisy; Pope, calling attention to ambiguities inherent in sexual mores; Voltaire, sending a naive fictional protagonist to encounter the world's inconsistencies of profession and practice—such writers call attention to the deceptiveness and the possible misuses of social norms as well as to their necessity. None suggests that the codes themselves are at fault. If people lived up to what they profess, the world would be a better place; ideally, they would modify not their standards of behavior but their tendency to hide behind them.

We in the twentieth century have become accustomed to the notion of the sacredness of the individual, encouraged to believe in the high value of expressiveness, originality, specialness. Eighteenth-century writers, on the other hand, assumed the superior importance of the social group and of shared opinion. "Expressiveness," in their view, should provide an instrument for articulating the will of the community, not the eccentric desires of individuals. The mad astronomer in Johnson's *Rasselas*, who as a result of isolation develops an exaggerated sense of his own power, epitomizes the danger of allowing oneself to believe too readily in the self's specialness. Society implies subordination: not only class hierarchy but individual submission to the good of the group.

French writers of imaginative literature often used domestic situations as ways to examine larger problems. Marriage, an institution at once social and personal, provides a useful image for human relationship as social and emotional fact. The developing eighteenth-century novel, in England and France alike, would assume marriage as the normal goal for men and women; Molière and Racine, writing before the turn of the century, examine economic, psychological, moral, and social implications of specific imagined marriages. The sexual alliances of rulers, Racine's subject in *Phaedra*, have literal consequences far beyond the individuals involved. Molière evokes a private family to suggest how professed sentiment can obscure the operations of ambition. Both understand marriage as social micro-cosm, a society in miniature, not merely as a structure for fulfillment of personal desire.

In England, writers in genres other than the novel typically focus their attention on a broader panorama. Pope and Swift, like Voltaire satirists of the human scene, consider varied operations of social law and pressure. In *The Rape of the Lock*, Pope uses a card party to epitomize social structures. Swift imagines idealized forms of social institutions ranging from marriage to parliament, contrasting the ideals with evocations of their actual English counterparts; or he fantasizes the horrifying consequences of venture capitalism in the processing of infants for food. Voltaire's world tourists witness and participate in a vast range of sobering experi-ence. In general, women fill subordinate roles in the harsh social environments evoked by these satiric works. Johnson praised Shakespeare because he did not make love the only spring of action; other passions, Johnson suggested, more pow-erfully motivate human activity. As the evoked social scene widens, erotic love plays a less important part and the position of women becomes increasingly insig-nificant: women's sphere is the home, and home life matters less than does public life. It is perhaps not irrelevant to note that no work in this section (with the horrifying exception of *A Modest Proposal*) describes or evokes children. Only in adulthood do people assume social responsibility; only then do they provide inter-esting substance for social commentary.

NATURE

Society establishes one locus of reality for eighteenth-century thinkers, although they understand it as a human construct. Nature comprises another assumed mea-sure of the real. The meanings of the word *nature* vary greatly in eighteenth-century usage, but two large senses are most relevant to the works here included: nature as the inherent order of things, including the physical universe, hence evidence of the deity's plan, and nature meaning specifically *human* nature.

Despite their pervasive awareness of natural contingency (vividly dramatized by Voltaire among others, in his account of the disastrous Lisbon earthquake), writers of this period locate their sense of permanence particularly in the idea of nature. Pope's *Essay on Man* is one of the most extensive—as well as intensive—examina-tions of the concept of natural order and its implications. Emphasizing the inade-quacy of human reason, the poem insistently reminds the reader of limitation. We cannot hope to grasp the arrangement of the universe, Pope tells us: how can a part comprehend the whole? Human pride in reason only obscures from its pos-sessors the great truths of a universal structure as flawlessly articulated in every detail as the stellar systems Newton and others had revealed. Contemplation of nature can both humble and exalt its practitioner, teaching the insufficiency of human powers in comparison with divine but also reminding human beings that they inhabit a wondrous universe in which all functions precisely as it should.

The notion of a permanent, divinely ordained natural order offers a good deal of comfort to those aware of flaws in actual social arrangements. It embodies an ideal of harmony, of order in variety, which, although it cannot be fully grasped by human intelligence, can yet provide a model for social complexities. It posits a *system*, a structure of relationships that at some theoretical level necessarily makes sense; thus it provides an assumed substructure of rationality for all experience of irrationality. It supplies a means of valuing all appearances of the natural world: every flower, every minnow, has meaning beyond itself, as part of the great pattern. The ardency with which the period's thinkers cling to belief in such a pattern suggests once more a pervasive anxiety about what human reason could not do. Human beings create a vision of something at once sublimely reasonable and beyond reason's grasp to reassure themselves that the limits of the rational need not coincide with the limits of the human.

The permanence of the conceptual natural order corresponds to that of human nature, as conceived in the eighteenth century. Human nature, it was generally believed, remains in all times and places the same. Thus Racine could re-present a fable from Greek tragedy, using classical setting and characters, with complete assurance that his imagining of Phaedra's conflict and suffering would speak to his contemporaries without falsifying the classical original. Despite social divergencies, fundamental aspects of personality do in fact remain constant: all people hope and fear, feel envy and lust, possess the capacity to reason. All suffer loss, all face death. Thinkers of the Enlightenment emphasized these common aspects of humanity far more than they considered cultural divergencies. Readers and writers alike could draw on this conviction about universality. It provided a test of excellence: if an author's imagining of character failed to conform to what eighteenth-century readers understood as human nature, a work might be securely judged inadequate. Conversely, the idea of a constant human nature held out the hope of longevity for writers who successfully evoked it. Moral philosophers could define human obligation and possibility in the conviction that they too wrote for all time; ethical standards would never change. Like the vision of order in the physical universe, the notion of constancy in human nature provided bedrock for an increasingly secularized society.

CONVENTION AND AUTHORITY

Eighteenth-century society, like all societies, operated, and its literary figures wrote, on the basis of established conventions. Manners are social conventions: agreed-on systems of behavior declared appropriate for specific situations. Guides to manners proliferated in the eighteenth century, expressing a widespread sense that commitment to decorum helped to preserve society's important standards. Literary conventions—agreed-on systems of verbal behavior—served comparable purposes in another sphere. Like established codes of manners, such conventions declare continuity between present and past.

The literary conventions of the past, like outmoded manners or styles of dress, may strike the twentieth-century reader as antiquated and artificial. A woman who curtsied in a modern living room, a man who appeared in a wig, would seem to us ridiculous, even insane; but of course a young woman in jeans would affect our predecessors as equally perverse. The plaintive lyrics of current country music, say, are governed by highly restrictive conventions that affect their hearers as "natural" only because they are so familiar. Eighteenth-century writers had at their disposal an established set of conventions for every traditional literary genre. As the repetitive rhythms of the country ballad tell listeners what to expect, these literary conventions provided readers with clues about the kind of experience they could anticipate in a given poem or play.

Underlying all specific conventions was the classical assumption that literature existed to delight and to instruct its readers. The various genres represented in this period embody such belief in literature's dual function. Stage comedy and tragedy, the early novel, satire in prose and verse, didactic poetry, the philosophic tale: each form developed its own set of devices for involving audiences and readers in situations requiring moral choice as well as for creating pleasure. The insistence in drama on unity of time and place (stage action occupying no more time than its representation, with no change of scene) exemplifies one such set, intended to facilitate in audiences the kind of belief encouraging maximum emotional and moral effect. The elevated diction of the *Essay on Man* ("Mark how it mounts, to Man's imperial race, / From the green myriads in the peopled grass"), like the mannered but less dignified language of *The Rape of the Lock* ("Here thou, great

Anna! whom three realms obey, / Dost sometimes counsel take—and sometimes tea"), and the two-dimensional characters of Voltaire's tales: such (to us) unfamiliar aspects of these texts provide signals about authorial intention and about anticipated reader response.

One dominant convention of twentieth-century poetry and prose is something we call "realism." In fiction, verse, and drama, writers often attempt to convey the literal feel of experience, the shape in which events actually occur in the world, the way people really talk. Racine, Pope, and Voltaire pursued no such goal. Despite their concern with permanent patterns of thought and feeling, they employed deliberate and obvious forms of artifice as modes of emphasis and of indirection. The sonorous verse in which Racine's characters reflect on their passions, for example ("I hate my life, abominate my lust; / Longing by death to rescue my good name / And hide my black love from the light of day"), embodies a form of stylization. Artistic transformation of life, the period's writers believed, involves the imposition of formal order on the endless flux of event and feeling. The formalities of this literature constitute part of its meaning: its statement that what experience shows as unstable, art makes stable.

Reliance on convention as a mode of control expressed an aspect of the period's constant effort toward elusive stability. The classical past, for many, provided an emblem of that stability, a standard of permanence. But some felt a problem inherent in the high valuing of the past, a problem dramatized by the so-called quarrel of Ancients and Moderns in England and in France. At stake in this controversy was the value of permanence as against the value of change. Proponents of the Ancients believed that the giants of Greece and Rome had not only established standards applicable to all subsequent accomplishment but provided models of achievement never to be excelled. Homer wrote the first great epics; subsequent endeavors in the same genre could only imitate him. Innovation came when it came by making the old new, as Pope makes a woman's dressing for conquest new by comparing it to the arming of Achilles. Moderns who valued originality for its own sake, who multiplied worthless publications, who claimed significance for what time had not tested thereby testified to their own inadequacies and their foolish pride.

Those proud to be Moderns, on the other hand, held that men (possibly even women) standing on the shoulders of the Ancients could see farther than their predecessors. The new conceivably exceeded in value the old; one might discover flaws even in revered figures of the classic past. Not everything had yet been accomplished; fresh possibilities remained always possible. This view, of course, corresponds to one widely current since the eighteenth century, but it did not triumph easily: many powerful thinkers of the late seventeenth and early eighteenth century adhered to the more conservative position.

Also at issue in this debate was the question of authority. What position should one assume who hoped to write and be read? Did authority reside only in tradition? If so, one must write in classical forms, rely on classical allusions. Until late in the eighteenth century, virtually all important writers attempted to ally themselves with the authority of tradition, declaring themselves part of a community extending through time as well as space. The problems of authority became particularly important in connection with satire, a popular Enlightenment form. Satire involves criticism of vice and folly; Molière, Pope, Swift, and Voltaire at least on occasion wrote in the satiric mode. To establish the right to criticize fellow men and women, the satirist must establish a rhetorical ascendancy such as the pulpit gives the priest—an ascendancy most readily obtained by at least implicit alliance with literary and moral tradition. The satirist, like the moral philosopher, cannot afford to seem idiosyncratic when prescribing and condemning the behavior of others. The fact that satire flourished so richly in this period suggests another version of the central conflict between reason and passion, the forces of stability and of instability. In its heightened description of the world (people eating babies, young women initiating epic battles over the loss of a lock of hair), satire calls attention to the powerful presence of the irrational, opposing to that presence the clarity of the satirist's own claim to reason and tradition. As it chastises human beings for their eruptions of passion, urging resistance and control, satire reminds its readers of the universality of the irrational as well as of opposition to it. The effort "to correct and moderate men's [and women's] passions," that great theme of the Enlightenment, can equally generate hope or despair: opposed moods richly expressed throughout this period.

FURTHER READING

Useful books on the Enlightenment include, for English background, H. Nicolson, *The Age of Reason: The Eighteenth Century* (1960); and for an opposed view, D. Greene, *The Age of Exuberance: Backgrounds to Eighteenth-Century English Literature* (1970). For the intellectual and social situation in France, see L. Crocker, *An Age of Crisis: Man and World in Eighteenth-Century French Thought* (1959); L. Gossman, *French Society and Culture: Background for Eighteenth-Century Literature* (1972); and A. Adam, *Grandeur and Illusion: French Literature and Society, 1600–1715* (1972). An excellent treatment of the period's literature in England is M. Price, *To the Palace of Wisdom: Studies in Order and Energy from Dryden to Blake* (1964). M. Williamson, *Raising Their Voices, 1650–1750* (1990), discusses women's contributions to the English Enlightenment. A good introduction to the intellectual situation of eighteenth-century England is J. Sambrook, *The Eighteenth Century: The Intellectual and Cultural Context of English Literature, 1700–1789* (1986).

TIMELINE

TEXTS	CONTEXTS
	1660 Civil War in England ends with Charles II's ascension to the throne (the "Restoration")
1664 Jean-Baptiste Poquelin Molière, **Tartuffe**	
1665 François de La Rochefoucauld, *Reflections*	
	1666 Isaac Newton uncovers laws of gravitation • London, already stricken by plague, is destroyed in the Great Fire and subsequently rebuilt in more orderly fashion
1667 Publication of John Milton's **Paradise Lost**	
1677 Jean Racine, **Phaedra**	
1678 Marie de la Vergne de La Fayette, *The Princess of Clèves*	
1690 John Locke, *Essay Concerning Human Understanding*, establishes psychological and philosophic principles of British philosophical empiricism	
1691 Sor Juana Inés de la Cruz, **Reply to Sor Filotea de la Cruz**	
	1694 Bank of England is chartered, forerunner of modern national banks and treasury systems; London stock exchange follows in 1698
	1697 Russian czar Peter the Great visits Western Europe and England, resolves to Westernize Russia
	1707 United Kingdom of Great Britain formed by union of England and Scotland
	1709 Up to 100,000 slaves a year cross the Atlantic, 20,000 to Britain's Caribbean colonies alone
1710 First British copyright law, transferring rights of property in a published work from publisher to author	
1717 Alexander Pope, **The Rape of the Lock**	
1719 Daniel Defoe publishes *Robinson Crusoe*, often called the first true novel in English	
	1721 J. S. Bach, *The Brandenburg Concertos*

TIMELINE

TEXTS	CONTEXTS
1726 Jonathan Swift, *Gulliver's Travels* 1729 Swift, *A Modest Proposal* 1733–1734 Alexander Pope, *An Essay on Man* 1740 Samuel Richardson, *Pamela*, arguably the first fully developed English novel 1751 First edition of French *Encyclopédie*, edited by Denis Diderot 1755 Samuel Johnson publishes the *Dictionary of the English Language*, the first comprehensive English dictionary on historical principles 1759 François-Marie Arouet de Voltaire, *Candide*	
	1753 British Museum founded 1756–1763 Seven Years' War, involving nine European powers; Britain acquires Canada and Florida, Spain gets Cuba and the Philippines, France wins colonies in India and Africa as well as Guadeloupe and Martinique 1764 New British tax laws create American unrest • W. A. Mozart, eight years old, writes his first symphony 1765 James Watt, a Scott, invents the steam engine, first in a series of mechanical innovations ushering in the Industrial Revolution
1771 First publication of *Encyclopedia Britannica* and complete French *Encyclopédie* testify to characteristic "Enlightenment" impulse to organize knowledge	1775–1783 American War of Independence; Declaration of Independence, 1776 • Constitution of the United States, 1787, the year of Mozart's opera *Don Giovanni*
1792 Mary Wollstonecraft, *Vindication of the Rights of Woman*, makes feminist case for female equality	1789 French Revolution begins; French National Assembly adopts the Declaration of the Rights of Man 1793 Captured by revolutionaries, Louis XVI and his queen, Marie Antoinette, are guillotined in Paris 1799 After successful conquests throughout Europe, Napoleon Bonaparte becomes first consul—in effect, dictator—of France • Ludwig van Beethoven writes first symphony (1799–1800)

JEAN-BAPTISTE POQUELIN MOLIÈRE
1622–1673

Son of a prosperous Paris merchant, Jean-Baptiste Molière (originally named Poquelin) devoted his entire adult life to the creation of stage illusion, as playwright and as actor. At about the age of twenty-five, he joined a company of traveling players established by the Béjart family; with them he toured the provinces for about twelve years. In 1658 the company was ordered to perform for Louis XIV in Paris; a year later, Molière's first great success, *The High-Brow Ladies* (*Les Précieuses ridicules*), was produced. The theatrical company to which he belonged, patronized by the king, became increasingly successful, developing finally (1680) into the Comédie Française. In 1662, Molière married Armande Béjart. He died a few hours after performing in the lead role of his own play *The Imaginary Invalid*.

Molière wrote both broad farce and comedies of character, in which he caricatured some form of vice or folly by embodying it in a single figure. His targets included the miser, the aspiring but vulgar middle class, female would-be intellectuals, the hypochondriac, and in *Tartuffe*, the religious hypocrite.

In *Tartuffe* (1664), as in his other plays, Molière employs classic comic devices of plot and character—here, a foolish, stubborn father blocking the course of young love; an impudent servant commenting on her superiors' actions; a happy ending involving a marriage facilitated by implausible means. He often uses such devices, however, to comment on his own immediate social scene, imagining how universal patterns play themselves out in a specific historical context. *Tartuffe* had contemporary relevance so transparent that the Catholic Church forced the king to ban it, although Molière managed to have it published and produced once more by 1669.

The play's emotional energy derives not from the simple discrepancy of man and mask in Tartuffe ("Is not a face quite different from a mask?" inquires the normative character Cléante, who has no trouble making such distinctions) but from the struggle for erotic, psychic, and economic power in which people employ their masks. One can readily imagine modern equivalents for the stresses and strains within Orgon's family. Orgon, an aging man with grown children, seeks ways to preserve control. His mother, Madame Pernelle, encourages his efforts, thus fostering her illusion that *she* still runs things. Orgon identifies his own interests with those of the hypocritical Tartuffe, toward whom he plays a benevolent role. Because Tartuffe fulsomely hails him as benefactor, Orgon feels utterly powerful in relation to his fawning dependent. When he orders his passive daughter Mariane to marry Tartuffe, he reveals his vision of complete domestic autocracy. Tartuffe's lust, one of those passions forever eluding human mastery, disturbs Orgon's arrangements; in the end, the will of the offstage king orders everything, as though a benevolent god had intervened.

To make Tartuffe a specifically religious hypocrite is an act of inventive daring. Orgon, like his mother, conceals from himself his will to power by verbally subordinating himself to that divinity which Tartuffe too invokes. Although one may readily accept Molière's defense of his intentions (not to mock faith but to attack its misuse), it is not hard to see why the play might trouble religious authorities. Molière suggests how readily religious faith lends itself to misuse, how high-sounding pieties allow men and women to evade self-examination and immediate responsibilities. Tartuffe deceives others by his grandiosities of mortification ("Hang up my hair shirt") and charity; he encourages his victims in their own grandiosities. Orgon can indulge a fantasy of self-subordination (remarking of Tartuffe, "He guides our lives") at the same time that he furthers his more hidden desire for power. Religion offers ready justification for a course manifestly destructive as well as self-seeking.

Cléante, before he meets Tartuffe, claims (accurately) to understand him by his effects on others. Throughout the play, Cléante speaks in the voice of wisdom, counseling moderation, common sense, and self-control, calling attention to folly. More important, he emphasizes how the issues Molière examines in this comedy relate to dominant late seventeenth-century themes:

> Ah, Brother, man's a strangely fashioned creature
> Who seldom is content to follow Nature,
> But recklessly pursues his inclination
> Beyond the narrow bounds of moderation,
> And often, by transgressing Reason's laws,
> Perverts a lofty aim or noble cause.

To follow Nature means to act appropriately to the human situation in the created universe. Humankind occupies a middle position, between beasts and angels; such aspirations as Orgon's desire to control his daughter completely, or his apparent wish to submit himself absolutely to Tartuffe's claim of heavenly wisdom, imply a hope to surpass limitations inherent in the human condition. As Cléante's observations suggest, "to follow Nature," given the rationality of the universe, implies adherence to "Reason's laws." All transgression involves failure to submit to reason's dictates. Molière, with his stylized comic plot, makes that point as insistently as does Racine, who depicts grand passions and cataclysmic effects from them.

Although Cléante understands and can enunciate the principles of proper conduct, his wisdom has no direct effect on the play's action. In spite of the fact that the comedy suggests a social world in which women exist in utter subordination to fathers and husbands, in the plot, two women bring about the clarifications that unmask the villain. The virtuous wife Elmire, object of Tartuffe's lust, and the articulate servant girl Dorine confront the immediate situation with pragmatic inventiveness. Dorine goads others to response; Elmire encourages Tartuffe to play out his sexual fantasies before a hidden audience. Both women have a clear sense of right and wrong, although they express it in less resounding terms than does Cléante. Their concrete insistence on facing what is really going on, cutting through all obfuscation, rescues the men from entanglement in their own abstract formulations.

The women's clarifications, however, do not resolve the comedy's dilemmas. Suddenly the context shifts: economic terms replace erotic ones. It is as though Tartuffe were only playing in his attempt to seduce Elmire; now we get to what really matters: money. For all his claims of disinterestedness, Tartuffe has managed to get control of his dupe's property. Control of property, the action gradually reveals, amounts to power over life itself: prison threatens Orgon, and the prospect of expulsion from their home menaces him and his family alike. Only the convenient and ostentatious artifice of royal intervention rescues the victims and punishes their betrayer.

Comedies conventionally end in the restoration of order, declaring that good inevitably triumphs; rationality renews itself despite the temporary deviations of the foolish and the vicious. At the end of *Tartuffe*, Orgon and his mother have been chastened by revelation of their favorite's depravity; Mariane has been allowed to marry her lover; Tartuffe has been judged; the king's power and justice have reasserted themselves and been acknowledged. In the organization of family and nation (metaphorically a larger family), order reassumes dominion. Yet the arbitrary intervention of the king leaves a disturbing emotional residue. The play has demonstrated that Tartuffe's corrupt will to power (as opposed to Orgon's merely foolish will) can ruthlessly aggrandize itself. Money speaks, in Orgon's society as in ours; possession of wealth implies total control over others. Only a kind of miracle can save Orgon. The miracle occurs, given the benign world of comedy, but the play reminds its readers of the extreme precariousness with which reason finally triumphs, even given the presence of such reasonable people as Cléante and Elmire. Tartuffe's monstrous lust, for women, money, power, genuinely endangers the social structure. *Tartuffe* enforces recognition of the constant threats to rationality, of how much we have at stake in trying to use reason as principle of action.

K. Mantzius, *Molière* (1908), provides a good biographical introduction to Molière. Useful critical studies include J. D. Hubert, *Molière and the Comedy of Intellect* (1962); L. Gossman, *Men and Masks: A Study of Molière* (1963); Jacques Guicharnaud, ed., *Molière: A Collection of Critical Essays* (1964); and N. Gross, *From Gesture to Idea: Esthetics and Ethics in Molière's Comedy* (1982). An excellent treatment of Molière in his historical context is W. D. Howarth, *Molière: A Playwright and His Audience* (1984). Harold C. Knutson, *The Triumph of Wit* (1988), examines Molière in relation to Shakespeare and Ben Jonson.

PRONOUNCING GLOSSARY

The following list uses common English syllables and stress accents to provide rough equivalents of selected words whose pronunciation may be unfamiliar to the general reader.

Cléante: *clay-ahnt'*	Molière: *moh-lyar'*
Damis: *dah-mee'*	Orante: *oh-rahnt'*
Dorine: *do-reen'*	Orgon: *or-gohnh'*
Elmire: *el-meer'*	Pernelle: *payr-nel'*
Flipote: *flee'-pot*	Tartuffe: *tahr-toof'*
Laurent: *lor'-awn*	Valère: *vah-layr'*
Loyal: *lwah-al'*	Vincennes: *vanh-s*

Tartuffe[1]

Preface

Here is a comedy that has excited a good deal of discussion and that has been under attack for a long time; and the persons who are mocked by it have made it plain that they are more powerful in France than all whom my plays have satirized up to this time. Noblemen, ladies of fashion, cuckolds, and doctors all kindly consented to their presentation, which they themselves seemed to enjoy along with everyone else; but hypocrites do not understand banter: they became angry at once, and found it strange that I was bold enough to represent their actions and to care to describe a profession shared by so many good men. This is a crime for which they cannot forgive me, and they have taken up arms against my comedy in a terrible rage. They were careful not to attack it at the point that had wounded them: they are too crafty for that and too clever to reveal their true character. In keeping with their lofty custom, they have used the cause of God to mask their

---

1. Translated by Richard Wilbur. The first version of *Tartuffe* was performed in 1664 and the second in 1667. When a 2nd edition of the third version was printed in June 1669, Molière added his three petitions to Louis XIV; they follow the preface.

private interests; and *Tartuffe*, they say, is a play that offends piety: it is filled with abominations from beginning to end, and nowhere is there a line that does not deserve to be burned. Every syllable is wicked, the very gestures are criminal, and the slightest glance, turn of the head, or step from right to left conceals mysteries that they are able to explain to my disadvantage. In vain did I submit the play to the criticism of my friends and the scrutiny of the public: all the corrections I could make, the judgment of the king and queen[2] who saw the play, the approval of great princes and ministers of state who honored it with their presence, the opinion of good men who found it worthwhile, all this did not help. They will not let go of their prey, and every day of the week they have pious zealots abusing me in public and damning me out of charity.

I would care very little about all they might say except that their devices make enemies of men whom I respect and gain the support of genuinely good men, whose faith they know and who, because of the warmth of their piety, readily accept the impressions that others present to them. And it is this which forces me to defend myself. Especially to the truly devout do I wish to vindicate my play, and I beg of them with all my heart not to condemn it before seeing it, to rid themselves of preconceptions, and not aid the cause of men dishonored by their actions.

If one takes the trouble to examine my comedy in good faith, he will surely see that my intentions are innocent throughout, and tend in no way to make fun of what men revere; that I have presented the subject with all the precautions that its delicacy imposes; and that I have used all the art and skill that I could to distinguish clearly the character of the hypocrite from that of the truly devout man. For that purpose I used two whole acts to prepare the appearance of my scoundrel. Never is there a moment's doubt about his character; he is known at once from the qualities I have given him; and from one end of the play to the other, he does not say a word, he does not perform an action which does not depict to the audience the character of a wicked man, and which does not bring out in sharp relief the character of the truly good man which I oppose to it.

I know full well that by way of reply, these gentlemen try to insinuate that it is not the role of the theater to speak of these matters; but with their permission, I ask them on what do they base this fine doctrine. It is a proposition they advance as no more than a supposition, for which they offer not a shred of proof; and surely it would not be difficult to show them that comedy, for the ancients, had its origin in religion and constituted a part of its ceremonies; that our neighbors, the Spaniards, have hardly a single holiday celebration in which a comedy is not a part; and that even here in France, it owes its birth to the efforts of a religious brotherhood who still own the Hôtel de Bourgogne, where the most important mystery plays of our faith were presented;[3] that you can still find comedies printed in gothic letters under the name of a learned doctor[4] of the Sorbonne; and without going so far, in our own day the religious dramas of Pierre Corneille[5] have been performed to the admiration of all France.

If the function of comedy is to correct men's vices, I do not see why any should be exempt. Such a condition in our society would be much more dangerous than the thing itself; and we have seen that the theater is admirably suited to provide correction. The most forceful lines of a serious moral statement are usually less powerful than those of satire; and nothing will reform most men better than the depiction of their faults. It is a vigorous blow to vices to expose them to public

---

2. Louis XIV was married to Marie Thérèse of Austria.   3. A reference to the *Confrérie de la Passion et Résurrection de Notre-Seigneur* (Fraternity of the passion and resurrection of our Savior), founded in 1402. The Hôtel de Bourgogne was a theater in rivalry with Molière's.   4. Probably Maître Jéhan Michel, a medical doctor who wrote mystery plays.   5. Pierre Corneille (1606–1684) and Racine were France's two greatest writers of classic tragedy. The two dramas Molière doubtlessly had in mind were *Polyeucte* (1643) and *Théodore, vierge et martyre* (1645).

laughter. Criticism is taken lightly, but men will not tolerate satire. They are quite willing to be mean, but they never like to be ridiculed.

I have been attacked for having placed words of piety in the mouth of my impostor. Could I avoid doing so in order to represent properly the character of a hypocrite? It seemed to me sufficient to reveal the criminal motives which make him speak as he does, and I have eliminated all ceremonial phrases, which nonetheless he would not have been found using incorrectly. Yet some say that in the fourth act he sets forth a vicious morality; but is not this a morality which everyone has heard again and again? Does my comedy say anything new here? And is there any fear that ideas so thoroughly detested by everyone can make an impression on men's minds; that I make them dangerous by presenting them in the theater; that they acquire authority from the lips of a scoundrel? There is not the slightest suggestion of any of this; and one must either approve the comedy of *Tartuffe* or condemn all comedies in general.

This has indeed been done in a furious way for some time now, and never was the theater so much abused.[6] I cannot deny that there were Church Fathers who condemned comedy; but neither will it be denied me that there were some who looked on it somewhat more favorably. Thus authority, on which censure is supposed to depend, is destroyed by this disagreement; and the only conclusion that can be drawn from this difference of opinion among men enlightened by the same wisdom is that they viewed comedy in different ways, and that some considered it in its purity, while others regarded it in its corruption and confused it with all those wretched performances which have been rightly called performances of filth.

And in fact, since we should talk about things rather than words, and since most misunderstanding comes from including contrary notions in the same word, we need only to remove the veil of ambiguity and look at comedy in itself to see if it warrants condemnation. It will surely be recognized that as it is nothing more than a clever poem which corrects men's faults by means of agreeable lessons, it cannot be condemned without injustice. And if we listened to the voice of ancient times on this matter, it would tell us that its most famous philosophers have praised comedy—they who professed so austere a wisdom and who ceaselessly denounced the vices of their times. It would tell us that Aristotle spent his evenings at the theater[7] and took the trouble to reduce the art of making comedies to rules. It would tell us that some of its greatest and most honored men took pride in writing comedies themselves;[8] and that others did not disdain to recite them in public; that Greece expressed its admiration for this art by means of handsome prizes and magnificent theaters to honor it; and finally, that in Rome this same art also received extraordinary honors; I do not speak of Rome run riot under the license of the emperors, but of disciplined Rome, governed by the wisdom of the consuls, and in the age of the full vigor of Roman dignity.

I admit that there have been times when comedy became corrupt. And what do men not corrupt every day? There is nothing so innocent that men cannot turn it to crime; nothing so beneficial that its values cannot be reversed; nothing so good in itself that it cannot be put to bad uses. Medical knowledge benefits mankind and is revered as one of our most wonderful possessions; and yet there was a time when it fell into discredit, and was often used to poison men. Philosophy is a gift of Heaven; it has been given to us to bring us to the knowledge of a God by contemplating the wonders of nature; and yet we know that often it has been

6. Molière had in mind Nicole's two attacks on the theater: *Visionnaires* (1666) and *Traité de la Comédie* (1667) as well as the prince de Conti's *Traité de la Comédie* (1666).   7. A reference to Aristotle's *Poetics* (composed between 335 and 322 B.C., the year of his death).   8. Scipio Africanus Minor (ca. 185–129 B.C.), the Roman consul and general responsible for the final destruction of Carthage in 146 B.C., collaborated with Terence (Publius Terentius Afer, ca. 195 or 185–ca. 159 B.C.), a writer of comedies.

turned away from its function and has been used openly in support of impiety. Even the holiest of things are not immune from human corruption, and every day we see scoundrels who use and abuse piety, and wickedly make it serve the greatest of crimes. But this does not prevent one from making the necessary distinctions. We do not confuse in the same false inference the goodness of things that are corrupted with the wickedness of the corrupt. The function of an art is always distinguished from its misuse; and as medicine is not forbidden because it was banned in Rome,[9] nor philosophy because it was publicly condemned in Athens,[1] we should not suppress comedy simply because it has been condemned at certain times. This censure was justified then for reasons which no longer apply today; it was limited to what was then seen; and we should not seize on these limits, apply them more rigidly than is necessary, and include in our condemnation the innocent along with the guilty. The comedy that this censure attacked is in no way the comedy that we want to defend. We must be careful not to confuse the one with the other. There may be two persons whose morals may be completely different. They may have no resemblance to one another except in their names, and it would be a terrible injustice to want to condemn Olympia, who is a good woman, because there is also an Olympia who is lewd. Such procedures would make for great confusion everywhere. Everything under the sun would be condemned; now since this rigor is not applied to the countless instances of abuse we see every day, the same should hold for comedy, and those plays should be approved in which instruction and virtue reign supreme.

I know there are some so delicate that they cannot tolerate a comedy, who say that the most decent are the most dangerous, that the passions they present are all the more moving because they are virtuous, and that men's feelings are stirred by these presentations. I do not see what great crime it is to be affected by the sight of a generous passion; and this utter insensitivity to which they would lead us is indeed a high degree of virtue! I wonder if so great a perfection resides within the strength of human nature, and I wonder if it is not better to try to correct and moderate men's passions than to try to suppress them altogether. I grant that there are places better to visit than the theater; and if we want to condemn every single thing that does not bear directly on God and our salvation, it is right that comedy be included, and I should willingly grant that it be condemned along with everything else. But if we admit, as is in fact true, that the exercise of piety will permit interruptions, and that men need amusement, I maintain that there is none more innocent than comedy. I have dwelled too long on this matter. Let me finish with the words of a great prince on the comedy, *Tartuffe*.[2]

Eight days after it had been banned, a play called *Scaramouche the Hermit*[3] was performed before the court; and the king, on his way out, said to this great prince: "I should really like to know why the persons who make so much noise about Molière's comedy do not say a word about *Scaramouche*." To which the prince replied, "It is because the comedy of *Scaramouche* makes fun of Heaven and religion, which these gentlemen do not care about at all, but that of Molière makes fun of *them*, and that is what they cannot bear."

THE AUTHOR

---

9. Pliny the Elder says that the Romans expelled their doctors at the same time that the Greeks did theirs. 1. An allusion to Socrates' condemnation to death.   2. One of Molière's benefactors who liked the play was the prince de Condé; de Condé had *Tartuffe* read to him and also privately performed for him. 3. A troupe of Italian comedians had just performed the licentious farce, in which a hermit dressed as a monk makes love to a married woman, announcing that *questo e per mortificar la carne* ("this is to mortify the flesh").

FIRST PETITION[4]

(Presented to the King on the Comedy of Tartuffe)

Sire,

✝ As the duty of comedy is to correct men by amusing them, I believed that in my occupation I could do nothing better than attack the vices of my age by making them ridiculous; and as hypocrisy is undoubtedly one of the most common, most improper, and most dangerous, I thought, Sire, that I would perform a service for all good men of your kingdom if I wrote a comedy which denounced hypocrites and placed in proper view all of the contrived poses of these incredibly virtuous men, all of the concealed villainies of these counterfeit believers who would trap others with a fraudulent piety and a pretended virtue.

I have written this comedy, Sire, with all the care and caution that the delicacy of the subject demands; and so as to maintain all the more properly the admiration and respect due to truly devout men, I have delineated my character as sharply as I could; I have left no room for doubt; I have removed all that might confuse good with evil, and have used for this painting only the specific colors and essential lines that make one instantly recognize a true and brazen hypocrite.

Nevertheless, all my precautions have been to no avail. Others have taken advantage of the delicacy of your feelings on religious matters, and they have been able to deceive you on the only side of your character which lies open to deception: your respect for holy things. By underhanded means, the Tartuffes have skillfully gained Your Majesty's favor, and the models have succeeded in eliminating the copy, no matter how innocent it may have been and no matter what resemblance was found between them.

Although the suppression of this work was a serious blow for me, my misfortune was nonetheless softened by the way in which Your Majesty explained his attitude on the matter; and I believed, Sire, that Your Majesty removed any cause I had for complaint, as you were kind enough to declare that you found nothing in this comedy that you would forbid me to present in public.

Yet, despite this glorious declaration of the greatest and most enlightened king in the world, despite the approval of the Papal Legate[5] and of most of our churchmen, all of whom, at private readings of my work, agreed with the views of Your Majesty, despite all this, a book has appeared by a certain priest[6] which boldly contradicts all of these noble judgments. Your Majesty expressed himself in vain, and the Papal Legate and churchmen gave their opinion to no avail: sight unseen, my comedy is diabolical, and so is my brain; I am a devil garbed in flesh and disguised

---

4. The first of the three *petitions* or *placets* to Louis XIV concerning the play. On May 12, 1664, *Tartuffe*—or at least the first three acts roughly as they now stand—was performed at Versailles. A cabal unfavorable to Molière, including the archbishop of Paris, Hardouin de Péréfixe, Queen Mother Anne of Austria, certain influential courtiers, and the Brotherhood or Company of the Holy Sacrament (formed in 1627 to enforce morality), arranged that the play be banned and Molière censured.   **5.** Cardinal Legate Chigi, nephew to Pope Alexander VII, heard a reading of *Tartuffe* at Fontainebleau on August 4, 1664.   **6.** Pierre Roullé, the curate of St. Barthélémy, who wrote a scathing attack on the play and sent his book to the king.

as a man,[7] a libertine, a disbeliever who deserves a punishment that will set an example. It is not enough that fire expiate my crime in public, for that would be letting me off too easily: the generous piety of this good man will not stop there; he will not allow me to find any mercy in the sight of God; he demands that I be damned, and that will settle the matter.

This book, Sire, was presented to Your Majesty; and I am sure that you see for yourself how unpleasant it is for me to be exposed daily to the insults of these gentlemen, what harm these abuses will do my reputation if they must be tolerated, and finally, how important it is for me to clear myself of these false charges and let the public know that my comedy is nothing more than what they want it to be. I will not ask, Sire, for what I need for the sake of my reputation and the innocence of my work: enlightened kings such as you do not need to be told what is wished of them; like God, they see what we need and know better than we what they should give us. It is enough for me to place my interests in Your Majesty's hands, and I respectfully await whatever you may care to command.

(*August, 1664*)

SECOND PETITION[8]

(*Presented to the King in His Camp Before the City of Lille, in Flanders*)

Sire,

It is bold indeed for me to ask a favor of a great monarch in the midst of his glorious victories; but in my present situation, Sire, where will I find protection anywhere but where I seek it, and to whom can I appeal against the authority of the power that crushes me,[9] if not to the source of power and authority, the just dispenser of absolute law, the sovereign judge and master of all?

My comedy, Sire, has not enjoyed the kindnesses of Your Majesty. All to no avail, I produced it under the title of *The Hypocrite* and disguised the principal character as a man of the world; in vain I gave him a little hat, long hair, a wide collar, a sword, and lace clothing,[1] softened the action and carefully eliminated all that I thought might provide even the shadow of grounds for discontent on the part of the famous models of the portrait I wished to present; nothing did any good. The conspiracy of opposition revived even at mere conjecture of what the play would be like. They found a way of persuading those who in all other matters plainly insist that they are not to be deceived. No sooner did my comedy appear than it was struck down by the very power which should impose respect; and all that I could do to save myself from the fury of this tempest was to say that Your Majesty had given me permission to present the play and I

---

7. Molière took some of these phrases from Roullé. 8. On August 5, 1667, *Tartuffe* was performed at the Palais-Royal. The opposition—headed by the first president of parliament—brought in the police, and the play was stopped. Since Louis was campaigning in Flanders, friends of Molière brought the second *placet* to Lille. Louis had always been favorable toward the playwright; in August 1665 Molière's company, the *Troupe de Monsieur* (nominally sponsored by Louis's brother Philippe, duc d'Orléans), had become the *Troupe du Roi*. 9. President de Lanvignon, in charge of the Paris police. 1. There is evidence that in 1664 Tartuffe played his role dressed in a cassock, thus allying him more directly to the clergy.

did not think it was necessary to ask this permission of others, since only Your Majesty could have refused it.

I have no doubt, Sire, that the men whom I depict in my comedy will employ every means possible to influence Your Majesty, and will use, as they have used already, those truly good men who are all the more easily deceived because they judge of others by themselves.[2] They know how to display all of their aims in the most favorable light; yet, no matter how pious they may seem, it is surely not the interests of God which stir them; they have proven this often enough in the comedies they have allowed to be performed hundreds of times without making the least objection. Those plays attacked only piety and religion, for which they care very little; but this play attacks and makes fun of them, and that is what they cannot bear. They will never forgive me for unmasking their hypocrisy in the eyes of everyone. And I am sure that they will not neglect to tell Your Majesty that people are shocked by my comedy. But the simple truth, Sire, is that all Paris is shocked only by its ban, that the most scrupulous persons have found its presentation worthwhile, and men are astounded that individuals of such known integrity should show so great a deference to people whom everyone should abominate and who are so clearly opposed to the true piety which they profess.

I respectfully await the judgment that Your Majesty will deign to pronounce: but it's certain, Sire, that I need not think of writing comedies if the Tartuffes are triumphant, if they thereby seize the right to persecute me more than ever, and find fault with even the most innocent lines that flow from my pen.

Let your goodness, Sire, give me protection against their envenomed rage, and allow me, at your return from so glorious a campaign, to relieve Your Majesty from the fatigue of his conquests, give him innocent pleasures after such noble accomplishments, and make the monarch laugh who makes all Europe tremble!

(*August*, 1667)

THIRD PETITION

(*Presented to the King*)

Sire,

A very honest doctor[3] whose patient I have the honor to be, promises and will legally contract to make me live another thirty years if I can obtain a favor for him from Your Majesty. I told him of his promise that I do not deserve so much, and that I should be glad to help him if he will merely agree not to kill me. This favor, Sire, is a post of canon at your royal chapel of Vincennes, made vacant by death.

May I dare to ask for this favor from Your Majesty on the very day of the glorious resurrection of *Tartuffe*, brought back to life by your goodness? By this first favor I have been reconciled with the devout, and the second will

---

2. Molière apparently did not know that de Lanvignon had been affiliated with the Company of the Holy Sacrament for the previous ten years.   3. A physician friend, M. de Mauvillain, who helped Molière with some of the medical details of *Le Malade imaginaire*.

reconcile me with the doctors.[4] Undoubtedly this would be too much grace for me at one time, but perhaps it would not be too much for Your Majesty, and I await your answer to my petition with respectful hope.

(*February*, 1669)

CHARACTERS[5]

MADAME PERNELLE, *Orgon's mother*
ORGON, *Elmire's husband*
ELMIRE, *Orgon's wife*
DAMIS, *Orgon's son, Elmire's stepson*
MARIANE, *Orgon's daughter, Elmire's stepdaughter, in love with Valère*

VALÈRE, *in love with Mariane*
CLÉANTE, *Orgon's brother-in-law*
TARTUFFE, *a hypocrite*
DORINE, *Mariane's lady's-maid*
M. LOYAL, *a bailiff*
A POLICE OFFICER
FLIPOTE, *Mme Pernelle's maid*

The SCENE *throughout: Orgon's house in Paris*

Act I

SCENE 1[6]

MADAME PERNELLE *and* FLIPOTE, *her maid,* ELMIRE,
MARIANE, DORINE, DAMIS, CLÉANTE

MADAME PERNELLE: Come, come, Flipote; it's time I left this place.
ELMIRE: I can't keep up, you walk at such a pace.
MADAME PERNELLE: Don't trouble, child; no need to show me out.
  It's not your manners I'm concerned about.
ELMIRE: We merely pay you the respect we owe.   5
  But, Mother, why this hurry? Must you go?
MADAME PERNELLE: I must. This house appals me. No one in it
  Will pay attention for a single minute.
  I offer good advice, but you won't hear it.
  Children, I take my leave much vexed in spirit.   10
  You all break in and chatter on and on.
  It's like a madhouse with the keeper gone.
DORINE: If . . .
MADAME PERNELLE:
        Girl, you talk too much, and I'm afraid
  You're far too saucy for a lady's-maid.
  You push in everywhere and have your say.   15
DAMIS: But . . .

4. Doctors are ridiculed to varying degrees in earlier plays of Molière: *Dom Juan, L'Amour médecin,* and *Le Médecin malgré lui.*   5. The name Tartuffe has been traced back to an older word associated with liar or charlatan: *truffer,* "to deceive" or "to cheat." Then there was also the Italian actor Tartufo, physically deformed and truffle shaped. Most of the other names are typical of this genre of court comedy and possess rather elegant connotations of pastoral and *bergerie.* Dorine would be a *demoiselle de compagne* and not a mere maid, that is, a female companion to Mariane of roughly the same social status. This in part accounts for the liberties she takes in conversation with Orgon, Madame Pernelle, and others. Her name is short for Théodorine.   6. In French drama, the scene changes every time a character enters or exits.

MADAME PERNELLE:
              You, boy, grow more foolish every day.
To think my grandson should be such a dunce!
I've said a hundred times, if I've said it once,
That if you keep the course on which you've started,
You'll leave your worthy father broken-hearted.   20
MARIANE: I think . . .
MADAME PERNELLE: And you, his sister, seem so pure,
So shy, so innocent, and so demure.
But you know what they say about still waters.
I pity parents with secretive daughters.
ELMIRE: Now, Mother . . .
MADAME PERNELLE: And as for you, child, let me add   25
That your behavior is extremely bad,
And a poor example for these children, too.
Their dear, dead mother did far better than you.
You're much too free with money, and I'm distressed
To see you so elaborately dressed.   30
When it's one's husband that one aims to please,
One has no need of costly fripperies.
CLÉANTE: Oh, Madam, really . . .
MADAME PERNELLE: You are her brother, Sir,
And I respect and love you; yet if I were
My son, this lady's good and pious spouse,   35
I wouldn't make you welcome in my house.
You're full of worldly counsels which, I fear,
Aren't suitable for decent folk to hear.
I've spoken bluntly, Sir; but it behooves us
Not to mince words when righteous fervor moves us.   40
DAMIS: Your man Tartuffe is full of holy speeches . . .
MADAME PERNELLE: And practises precisely what he preaches.
He's a fine man, and should be listened to.
I will not hear him mocked by fools like you.
DAMIS: Good God! Do you expect me to submit   45
To the tyranny of that carping hypocrite?
Must we forgo all joys and satisfactions
Because that bigot censures all our actions?
DORINE: To hear him talk—and he talks all the time—
There's nothing one can do that's not a crime.   50
He rails at everything, your dear Tartuffe.
MADAME PERNELLE: Whatever he reproves deserves reproof.
He's out to save your souls, and all of you
Must love him, as my son would have you do.
DAMIS: Ah no, Grandmother, I could never take   55
To such a rascal, even for my father's sake.
That's how I feel, and I shall not dissemble.
His every action makes me seethe and tremble
With helpless anger, and I have no doubt
That he and I will shortly have it out.   60

DORINE: Surely it is a shame and a disgrace
  To see this man usurp the master's place—
  To see this beggar who, when first he came,
  Had not a shoe or shoestring to his name
  So far forget himself that he behaves
  As if the house were his, and we his slaves.   65
MADAME PERNELLE: Well, mark my words, your souls would fare far better
  If you obeyed his precepts to the letter.
DORINE: You see him as a saint. I'm far less awed;
  In fact, I see right through him. He's a fraud.   70
MADAME PERNELLE: Nonsense!
DORINE: His man Laurent's the same, or worse;
  I'd not trust either with a penny purse.
MADAME PERNELLE: I can't say what his servant's morals may be;
  His own great goodness I can guarantee.
  You all regard him with distaste and fear   75
  Because he tells you what you're loath to hear,
  Condemns your sins, points out your moral flaws,
  And humbly strives to further Heaven's cause.
DORINE: If sin is all that bothers him, why is it
  He's so upset when folk drop in to visit?   80
  Is Heaven so outraged by a social call
  That he must prophesy against us all?
  I'll tell you what I think: if you ask me,
  He's jealous of my mistress' company.
MADAME PERNELLE: Rubbish!
  [*To* ELMIRE.]   He's not alone, child, in complaining   85
  Of all of your promiscuous entertaining.
  Why, the whole neighborhood's upset, I know,
  By all these carriages that come and go,
  With crowds of guests parading in and out
  And noisy servants loitering about.   90
  In all of this, I'm sure there's nothing vicious;
  But why give people cause to be suspicious?
✗ CLÉANTE: They need no cause; they'll talk in any case.
  Madam, this world would be a joyless place
  If, fearing what malicious tongues might say,   95
  We locked our doors and turned our friends away.
  And even if one did so dreary a thing,
  D' you think those tongues would cease their chattering?
  One can't fight slander; it's a losing battle;
  Let us instead ignore their tittle-tattle.   100
  Let's strive to live by conscience' clear decrees,
  And let the gossips gossip as they please.
DORINE: If there is talk against us, I know the source:
  It's Daphne and her little husband, of course.
  Those who have greatest cause for guilt and shame   105
  Are quickest to besmirch a neighbor's name.
  When there's a chance for libel, they never miss it;

When something can be made to seem illicit
They're off at once to spread the joyous news,
Adding to fact what fantasies they choose.   110
By talking up their neighbor's indiscretions
They seek to camouflage their own transgressions,
Hoping that others' innocent affairs
Will lend a hue of innocence to theirs,
Or that their own black guilt will come to seem   115
Part of a general shady color-scheme.
MADAME PERNELLE: All this is quite irrelevant. I doubt
    That anyone's more virtuous and devout
    Than dear Orante; and I'm informed that she
    Condemns your mode of life most vehemently.   120
DORINE: Oh, yes, she's strict, devout, and has no taint
    Of worldliness; in short, she seems a saint.
    But it was time which taught her that disguise;
    She's thus because she can't be otherwise.
    So long as her attractions could enthrall,   125
    She flounced and flirted and enjoyed it all,
    But now that they're no longer what they were
    She quits a world which fast is quitting her,
    And wears a veil of virtue to conceal
    Her bankrupt beauty and her lost appeal.   130
    That's what becomes of old coquettes today:
    Distressed when all their lovers fall away,
    They see no recourse but to play the prude,
    And so confer a style on solitude.
    Thereafter, they're severe with everyone,   135
    Condemning all our actions, pardoning none,
    And claiming to be pure, austere, and zealous
    When, if the truth were known, they're merely jealous,
    And cannot bear to see another know
    The pleasures time has forced them to forgo.   140
MADAME PERNELLE: [*Initially to* ELMIRE.]
    That sort of talk[7] is what you like to hear;
    Therefore you'd have us all keep still, my dear,
    While Madam rattles on the livelong day.
    Nevertheless, I mean to have my say.
    I tell you that you're blest to have Tartuffe   145
    Dwelling, as my son's guest, beneath this roof;
    That Heaven has sent him to forestall its wrath
    By leading you, once more, to the true path;
    That all he reprehends is reprehensible,
    And that you'd better heed him, and be sensible.   150
    These visits, balls, and parties in which you revel
    Are nothing but inventions of the Devil.

7. In the original, a reference to a collection of novels about chivalry found in *La Bibliothèque bleue*
(The blue library), written for children.

One never hears a word that's edifying:
Nothing but chaff and foolishness and lying,
As well as vicious gossip in which one's neighbor   155
Is cut to bits with épée, foil, and saber.
People of sense are driven half-insane
At such affairs, where noise and folly reign
And reputations perish thick and fast.
As a wise preacher said on Sunday last,   160
Parties are Towers of Babylon,[8] because
The guests all babble on with never a pause;
And then he told a story which, I think . . .
[*To* CLÉANTE.] I heard that laugh, Sir, and I saw that wink!
Go find your silly friends and laugh some more!   165
Enough; I'm going; don't show me to the door.
I leave this household much dismayed and vexed;
I cannot say when I shall see you next.
          [*Slapping* FLIPOTE.]
Wake up, don't stand there gaping into space!
I'll slap some sense into that stupid face.   170
Move, move, you slut.

SCENE 2

CLÉANTE, DORINE

CLÉANTE: I think I'll stay behind;
I want no further pieces of her mind.
How that old lady . . .
DORINE: Oh, what wouldn't she say
If she could hear you speak of her that way!
She'd thank you for the *lady,* but I'm sure   5
She'd find the *old* a little premature.
CLÉANTE: My, what a scene she made, and what a din!
And how this man Tartuffe has taken her in!
DORINE: Yes, but her son is even worse deceived;
His folly must be seen to be believed.   10
In the late troubles,[9] he played an able part
And served his king with wise and loyal heart,
But he's quite lost his senses since he fell
Beneath Tartuffe's infatuating spell.
He calls him brother, and loves him as his life,   15
Preferring him to mother, child, or wife.
In him and him alone will he confide;
He's made him his confessor and his guide;
He pets and pampers him with love more tender
Than any pretty maiden could engender,   20

---

8. Tower of Babel. Madame Pernelle's malapropism is the cause of Cléante's laughter. **9.** A series of
political disturbances during the minority of Louis XIV. Specifically these consisted of the *Fronde* ("opposition") of the Parlement (1648–49) and the *Fronde* of the Princes (1650–53). Orgon is depicted as supporting Louis XIV in these outbreaks and their resolution.

Gives him the place of honor when they dine,
Delights to see him gorging like a swine,
Stuffs him with dainties till his guts distend,
And when he belches, cries "God bless you, friend!"
In short, he's mad; he worships him; he dotes;   25
His deeds he marvels at, his words, he quotes,
Thinking each act a miracle, each word
Oracular as those that Moses heard.
Tartuffe, much pleased to find so easy a victim,
Has in a hundred ways beguiled and tricked him,   30
Milked him of money, and with his permission
Established here a sort of Inquisition.
Even Laurent, his lackey, dares to give
Us arrogant advice on how to live;
He sermonizes us in thundering tones   35
And confiscates our ribbons and colognes.
Last week he tore a kerchief into pieces
Because he found it pressed in a *Life of Jesus:*
He said it was a sin to juxtapose
Unholy vanities and holy prose.   40

SCENE 3

ELMIRE, MARIANE, DAMIS, CLÉANTE, DORINE

ELMIRE: [*To* CLÉANTE.] You did well not to follow; she stood in the door
   And said *verbatim* all she'd said before.
   I saw my husband coming. I think I'd best
   Go upstairs now, and take a little rest.
CLÉANTE: I'll wait and greet him here; then I must go.   5
   I've really only time to say hello.
DAMIS: Sound him about my sister's wedding, please.
   I think Tartuffe's against it, and that he's
   Been urging Father to withdraw his blessing.
   As you well know, I'd find that most distressing.   10
   Unless my sister and Valère can marry,
   My hopes to wed *his* sister will miscarry.
   And I'm determined . . .
DORINE: He's coming.

SCENE 4

ORGON, CLÉANTE, DORINE

ORGON: Ah, Brother, good-day.
CLÉANTE: Well, welcome back, I'm sorry I can't stay.
   How was the country? Blooming, I trust, and green?
ORGON: Excuse me, Brother; just one moment.
   [*To* DORINE.]   Dorine . . .
   [*To* CLÉANTE.] To put my mind at rest, I always learn   5
   The household news the moment I return.

[*To* DORINE.] Has all been well, these two days I've been gone?
  How are the family? What's been going on?
DORINE: Your wife, two days ago, had a bad fever,
  And a fierce headache which refused to leave her.   10
ORGON: Ah. And Tartuffe?
DORINE: Tartuffe? Why, he's round and red.
  Bursting with health, and excellently fed.
ORGON: Poor fellow!
DORINE: That night, the mistress was unable
  To take a single bite at the dinner-table.
  Her headache-pains, she said, were simply hellish.   15
ORGON: Ah. And Tartuffe?
DORINE: He ate his meal with relish,
  And zealously devoured in her presence
  A leg of mutton and a brace of pheasants.
ORGON: Poor fellow!
DORINE: Well, the pains continued strong,
  And so she tossed and tossed the whole night long,   20
  Now icy-cold, now burning like a flame.
  We sat beside her bed till morning came.
ORGON: Ah. And Tartuffe?
DORINE: Why, having eaten, he rose
  And sought his room, already in a doze,
  Got into his warm bed, and snored away   25
  In perfect peace until the break of day.
ORGON: Poor fellow!
DORINE: After much ado, we talked her
  Into dispatching someone for the doctor.
  He bled her, and the fever quickly fell.
ORGON: Ah. And Tartuffe?
DORINE: He bore it very well.   30
  To keep his cheerfulness at any cost,
  And make up for the blood Madame had lost,
  He drank, at lunch, four beakers full of port.
ORGON: Poor fellow.
DORINE: Both are doing well, in short.
  I'll go and tell Madame that you've expressed   35
  Keen sympathy and anxious interest.

SCENE 5

ORGON, CLÉANTE

CLÉANTE: That girl was laughing in your face, and though
  I've no wish to offend you, even so
  I'm bound to say that she had some excuse.
  How can you possibly be such a goose?
  Are you so dazed by this man's hocus-pocus   5
  That all the world, save him, is out of focus?
  You've given him clothing, shelter, food, and care;

Why must you also . . .

ORGON: Brother, stop right there.
   You do not know the man of whom you speak.

CLÉANTE: I grant you that. But my judgment's not so weak   10
   That I can't tell, by his effect on others . . .

ORGON: Ah, when you meet him, you two will be like brothers!
   There's been no loftier soul since time began.
   He is a man who . . . a man who . . . an excellent man.
   To keep his precepts is to be reborn,   15
   And view this dunghill of a world with scorn.
   Yes, thanks to him I'm a changed man indeed.
   Under his tutelage my soul's been freed
   From earthly loves, and every human tie:
   My mother, children, brother, and wife could die,   20
   And I'd not feel a single moment's pain.

CLÉANTE: That's a fine sentiment, Brother; most humane.

ORGON: Oh, had you seen Tartuffe as I first knew him,
   Your heart, like mine, would have surrendered to him.
   He used to come into our church each day   25
   And humbly kneel nearby, and start to pray.
   He'd draw the eyes of everybody there
   By the deep fervor of his heartfelt prayer;
   He'd sigh and weep, and sometimes with a sound
   Of rapture he would bend and kiss the ground;   30
   And when I rose to go, he'd run before
   To offer me holy-water at the door.
   His serving-man, no less devout than he,
   Informed me of his master's poverty;
   I gave him gifts, but in his humbleness   35
   He'd beg me every time to give him less.
   "Oh, that's too much," he'd cry, "too much by twice!
   I don't deserve it. The half, Sir, would suffice."
   And when I wouldn't take it back, he'd share
   Half of it with the poor, right then and there.   40
   At length, Heaven prompted me to take him in
   To dwell with us, and free our souls from sin.
   He guides our lives, and to protect my honor
   Stays by my wife, and keeps an eye upon her;
   He tells me whom she sees, and all she does,   45
   And seems more jealous than I ever was!
   And how austere he is! Why, he can detect
   A moral sin where you would least suspect;
   In smallest trifles, he's extremely strict.
   Last week, his conscience was severely pricked   50
   Because, while praying, he had caught a flea
   And killed it, so he felt, too wrathfully.[1]

---

1. In the *Golden Legend* (*Legenda sanctorum*), a popular collection of the lives of the saints written in the 13th century, it is said of St. Marcarius the Elder (died 390) that he dwelt naked in the desert for six months, a penance he felt appropriate for having killed a flea.

CLÉANTE: Good God, man! Have you lost your common sense —
   Or is this all some joke at my expense?
   How can you stand there and in all sobriety . . .   55
ORGON: Brother, your language savors of impiety.
   Too much free-thinking's made your faith unsteady,
   And as I've warned you many times already,
   'Twill get you into trouble before you're through.
CLÉANTE: So I've been told before by dupes like you: 60
   Being blind, you'd have all others blind as well;
   The clear-eyed man you call an infidel,
   And he who sees through humbug and pretense
   Is charged, by you, with want of reverence.
   Spare me your warnings, Brother; I have no fear   65
   Of speaking out, for you and Heaven to hear,
   Against affected zeal and pious knavery.
   There's true and false in piety, as in bravery,
   And just as those whose courage shines the most
   In battle, are the least inclined to boast,   70
   So those whose hearts are truly pure and lowly
   Don't make a flashy show of being holy.
   There's a vast difference, so it seems to me,
   Between true piety and hypocrisy:
   How do you fail to see it, may I ask?   75
   Is not a face quite different from a mask?
   Cannot sincerity and cunning art,
   Reality and semblance, be told apart?
   Are scarecrows just like men, and do you hold
   That a false coin is just as good as gold?   80
   Ah, Brother, man's a strangely fashioned creature
   Who seldom is content to follow Nature,
   But recklessly pursues his inclination
   Beyond the narrow bounds of moderation,
   And often, by transgressing Reason's laws,   85
   Perverts a lofty aim or noble cause.
   A passing observation, but it applies.
ORGON: I see, dear Brother, that you're profoundly wise;
   You harbor all the insight of the age.
   You are our one clear mind, our only sage,   90
   The era's oracle, its Cato[2] too,
   And all mankind are fools compared to you.
CLÉANTE: Brother, I don't pretend to be a sage,
   Nor have I all the wisdom of the age.
   There's just one insight I would dare to claim: 95
   I know that true and false are not the same;
   And just as there is nothing I more revere
   Than a soul whose faith is steadfast and sincere,
   Nothing that I more cherish and admire

---

2. Roman statesman (95–46 B.C.) with an enduring reputation for honesty and incorruptibility.

Than honest zeal and true religious fire,   100
So there is nothing that I find more base
Than specious piety's dishonest face —
Than these bold mountebanks, these histrios
Whose impious mummeries and hollow shows
Exploit our love of Heaven, and make a jest   105
Of all that men think holiest and best;
These calculating souls who offer prayers
Not to their Maker, but as public wares,
And seek to buy respect and reputation
With lifted eyes and sighs of exaltation;   110
These charlatans, I say, whose pilgrim souls
Proceed, by way of Heaven, toward earthly goals,
Who weep and pray and swindle and extort,
Who preach the monkish life, but haunt the court,
Who make their zeal the partner of their vice —   115
Such men are vengeful, sly, and cold as ice,
And when there is an enemy to defame
They cloak their spite in fair religion's name,
Their private spleen and malice being made
To seem a high and virtuous crusade,   120
Until, to mankind's reverent applause,
They crucify their foe in Heaven's cause.
Such knaves are all too common; yet, for the wise,
True piety isn't hard to recognize,
And, happily, these present times provide us   125
With bright examples to instruct and guide us.
Consider Ariston and Périandre;
Look at Oronte, Alcidamas, Clitandre;[3]
Their virtue is acknowledged; who could doubt it?
But you won't hear them beat the drum about it.   130
They're never ostentatious, never vain,
And their religion's moderate and humane;
It's not their way to criticize and chide:
They think censoriousness a mark of pride,
And therefore, letting others preach and rave,   135
They show, by deeds, how Christians should behave.
They think no evil of their fellow man,
But judge of him as kindly as they can.
They don't intrigue and wangle and conspire;
To lead a good life is their one desire;   140
The sinner wakes no rancorous hate in them;
It is the sin alone which they condemn;
Nor do they try to show a fiercer zeal
For Heaven's cause than Heaven itself could feel.
These men I honor, these men I advocate   145
As models for us all to emulate.

---

3. Vaguely Greek and Roman names derived from the elegant literature of the day.

Your man is not their sort at all, I fear:
And, while your praise of him is quite sincere,
I think that you've been dreadfully deluded.
ORGON: Now then, dear Brother, is your speech concluded?   150
CLÉANTE: Why, yes.
ORGON: Your servant, Sir.
    [*He turns to go.*]
CLÉANTE: No, Brother; wait.
    There's one more matter. You agreed of late
    That young Valère might have your daughter's hand.
ORGON: I did.
CLÉANTE: And set the date, I understand.
ORGON: Quite so.
CLÉANTE: You've now postponed it; is that true?   155
ORGON: No doubt.
CLÉANTE: The match no longer pleases you?
ORGON: Who knows?
CLÉANTE: D'you mean to go back on your word?
ORGON: I won't say that.
CLÉANTE: Has anything occurred
    Which might entitle you to break your pledge?
ORGON: Perhaps.
CLÉANTE: Why must you hem, and haw, and hedge?   160
    The boy asked me to sound you in this affair . . .
ORGON: It's been a pleasure.
CLÉANTE: But what shall I tell Valère?
ORGON. Whatever you like.
CLÉANTE: But what have you decided?
    What are your plans?
ORGON: I plan, Sir, to be guided
    By Heaven's will.
CLÉANTE: Come, Brother, don't talk rot.   165
    You've given Valère your word; will you keep it, or not?
ORGON: Good day.
CLÉANTE: This looks like poor Valère's undoing;
    I'll go and warn him that there's trouble brewing.

Act II

SCENE 1

ORGON, MARIANE

ORGON: Mariane.
MARIANE: Yes, Father?
ORGON: A word with you; come here.
MARIANE: What are you looking for?
ORGON: [*Peering into a small closet.*] Eavesdroppers, dear.
    I'm making sure we shan't be overheard.

Someone in there could catch our every word.
Ah, good, we're safe. Now, Mariane, my child,   5
You're a sweet girl who's tractable and mild,
Whom I hold dear, and think most highly of.
MARIANE: I'm deeply grateful, Father, for your love.
ORGON: That's well said, Daughter; and you can repay me
If, in all things, you'll cheerfully obey me.   10
MARIANE: To please you, Sir, is what delights me best.
ORGON: Good, good. Now, what d'you think of Tartuffe, our guest?
MARIANE: I, Sir?
ORGON: Yes. Weigh your answer; think it through.
MARIANE: Oh, dear. I'll say whatever you wish me to.
ORGON: That's wisely said, my Daughter. Say of him, then,   15
That he's the very worthiest of men,
And that you're fond of him, and would rejoice
In being his wife, if that should be my choice.
Well?
MARIANE: What?
ORGON: What's that?
MARIANE: I . . .
ORGON: Well?
MARIANE: Forgive me, pray.
ORGON: Did you not hear me?
MARIANE: Of *whom*, Sir, must I say   20
That I am fond of him, and would rejoice
In being his wife, if that should be your choice?
ORGON: Why, of Tartuffe.
MARIANE: But, Father, that's false, you know.
Why would you have me say what isn't so?
ORGON: Because I am resolved it shall be true.   25
That it's my wish should be enough for you.
MARIANE: You can't mean, Father . . .
ORGON: Yes, Tartuffe shall be
Allied by marriage[4] to this family,
And he's to be your husband, is that clear?
It's a father's privilege . . .   30

SCENE 2

DORINE, ORGON, MARIANE

ORGON: [*To* DORINE.]   What are you doing in here?
Is curiosity so fierce a passion
With you, that you must eavesdrop in this fashion?
DORINE: There's lately been a rumor going about—

---

4. This assertion is important and more than a mere device in the plot of the day. The second *placet* or petition insists that Tartuffe be costumed as a layman, and Orgon's plan for him to marry again asserts Tartuffe's position in the laity. In the 1664 version of the play Tartuffe had been dressed in a cassock suggestive of the priesthood, and Molière was now anxious to avoid any suggestion of this kind.

Based on some hunch or chance remark, no doubt—   5
That you mean Mariane to wed Tartuffe.
  I've laughed it off, of course, as just a spoof.
ORGON: You find it so incredible?
DORINE: Yes, I do.
  I won't accept that story, even from you.
ORGON: Well, you'll believe it when the thing is done.   10
DORINE: Yes, yes, of course. Go on and have your fun.
ORGON: I've never been more serious in my life.
DORINE: Ha!
ORGON: Daughter, I mean it; you're to be his wife.
DORINE: No, don't believe your father; it's all a hoax.
ORGON: See here, young woman . . .
DORINE: Come, Sir, no more jokes;   15
  You can't fool us.
ORGON: How dare you talk that way?
DORINE: All right, then: we believe you, sad to say.
  But how a man like you, who looks so wise
  And wears a moustache of such splendid size,
  Can be so foolish as to . . .
ORGON: Silence, please!   20
  My girl, you take too many liberties.
  I'm master here, as you must not forget.
DORINE: Do let's discuss this calmly; don't be upset.
  You can't be serious, Sir, about this plan.
  What should that bigot want with Mariane?   25
  Praying and fasting ought to keep him busy.
  And then, in terms of wealth and rank, what is he?
  Why should a man of property like you
  Pick out a beggar son-in-law?
ORGON: That will do.
  Speak of his poverty with reverence.   30
  His is a pure and saintly indigence
  Which far transcends all worldly pride and pelf.
  He lost his fortune, as he says himself,
  Because he cared for Heaven alone, and so
  Was careless of his interests here below.   35
  I mean to get him out of his present straits
  And help him to recover his estates—
  Which, in his part of the world, have no small fame.
  Poor though he is, he's a gentleman just the same.
DORINE: Yes, so he tells us; and, Sir, it seems to me   40
  Such pride goes very ill with piety.
  A man whose spirit spurns this dungy earth
  Ought not to brag of lands and noble birth;
  Such worldly arrogance will hardly square
  With meek devotion and the life of prayer.   45
  . . . But this approach, I see, has drawn a blank;

Let's speak, then, of his person, not his rank.
Doesn't it seem to you a trifle grim
To give a girl like her to a man like him?
When two are so ill-suited, can't you see   50
What the sad consequence is bound to be?
A young girl's virtue is imperilled, Sir,
When such a marriage is imposed on her;
For if one's bridegroom isn't to one's taste,
It's hardly an inducement to be chaste,   55
And many a man with horns upon his brow
Has made his wife the thing that she is now.
It's hard to be a faithful wife, in short,
To certain husbands of a certain sort,
And he who gives his daughter to a man she hates   60
Must answer for her sins at Heaven's gates.
Think, Sir, before you play so risky a role.
ORGON: This servant-girl presumes to save my soul!
DORINE: You would do well to ponder what I've said.
ORGON: Daughter, we'll disregard this dunderhead.   65
Just trust your father's judgment. Oh, I'm aware
That I once promised you to young Valère;
But now I hear he gambles, which greatly shocks me;
What's more, I've doubts about his orthodoxy.
His visits to church, I note, are very few.   70
DORINE: Would you have him go at the same hours as you,
And kneel nearby, to be sure of being seen?
ORGON: I can dispense with such remarks, Dorine.
[*To* MARIANE.] Tartuffe, however, is sure of Heaven's blessing.
And that's the only treasure worth possessing.   75
This match will bring you joys beyond all measure;
Your cup will overflow with every pleasure;
You two will interchange your faithful loves
Like two sweet cherubs, or two turtle-doves.
No harsh word shall be heard, no frown be seen,   80
And he shall make you happy as a queen.
DORINE: And she'll make him a cuckold, just wait and see.
ORGON: What language!
DORINE: Oh, he's a man of destiny;
He's *made* for horns, and what the stars demand
Your daughter's virtue surely can't withstand.   85
ORGON: Don't interrupt me further. Why can't you learn
That certain things are none of your concern?
DORINE: It's for your own sake that I interfere.
[*She repeatedly interrupts* ORGON *just as he is turning to speak to his
daughter.*]
ORGON: Most kind of you. Now, hold your tongue, d'you hear?
DORINE: If I didn't love you . . .
ORGON: Spare me your affection.   90
DORINE: I'll love you, Sir, in spite of your objection.

ORGON: Blast!

DORINE: I can't bear, Sir, for your honor's sake,
　To let you make this ludicrous mistake.

ORGON: You mean to go on talking?

DORINE: If I didn't protest
　This sinful marriage, my conscience couldn't rest.   95

ORGON: If you don't hold your tongue, you little shrew . . .

DORINE: What, lost your temper? A pious man like you?

ORGON: Yes! Yes! You talk and talk. I'm maddened by it.
　Once and for all, I tell you to be quiet.

DORINE: Well, I'll be quiet. But I'll be thinking hard.   100

ORGON: Think all you like, but you had better guard
　That saucy tongue of yours, or I'll . . .
　[*Turning back to* MARIANE.]   Now, child,
　I've weighed this matter fully.

DORINE: [*Aside.*]   It drives me wild
　That I can't speak.
　　[ORGON *turns his head, and she is silent.*]

ORGON: Tartuffe is no young dandy,
　But, still, his person . . .

DORINE: [*Aside.*]   Is as sweet as candy.   105

ORGON: Is such that, even if you shouldn't care
　For his other merits . . .
　[*He turns and stands facing* DORINE, *arms crossed.*]

DORINE: [*Aside.*]   They'll make a lovely pair.
　If I were she, no man would marry me
　Against my inclination, and go scot-free.
　He'd learn, before the wedding-day was over,   110
　How readily a wife can find a lover.

ORGON: [*To* DORINE.] It seems you treat my orders as a joke.

DORINE: Why, what's the matter? 'Twas not to you I spoke.

ORGON: What *were* you doing?

DORINE: Talking to myself, that's all.

ORGON: Ah! [*Aside.*] One more bit of impudence and gall,   115
　And I shall give her a good slap in the face.
　[*He puts himself in position to slap her;* DORINE, *whenever he glances
　at her, stands immobile and silent.*]
　Daughter, you shall accept, and with good grace,
　The husband I've selected . . . Your wedding-day . . .
　[*To* DORINE.] Why don't you talk to yourself?

DORINE: I've nothing to say.

ORGON. Come, just one word.

DORINE: No thank you, Sir. I pass.   120

ORGON: Come, speak; I'm waiting.

DORINE: I'd not be such an ass.

ORGON. [*Turning to* MARIANE.]
　In short, dear Daughter, I mean to be obeyed,
　And you must bow to the sound choice I've made.

DORINE: [*Moving away.*] I'd not wed such a monster, even in jest.

[ORGON *attempts to slap her, but misses.*]

ORGON: Daughter, that maid of yours is a thorough pest;   125
  She makes me sinfully annoyed and nettled.
  I can't speak further; my nerves are too unsettled.
  She's so upset me by her insolent talk,
  I'll calm myself by going for a walk.

SCENE 3

DORINE, MARIANE

DORINE: [*Returning.*] Well, have you lost your tongue, girl? Must I play
  Your part, and say the lines you ought to say?
  Faced with a fate so hideous and absurd,
  Can you not utter one dissenting word?
MARIANE: What good would it do? A father's power is great.   5
DORINE: Resist him now, or it will be too late.
MARIANE: But . . .
DORINE: Tell him one cannot love at a father's whim;
  That you shall marry for yourself, not him;
  That since it's you who are to be the bride,
  It's you, not he, who must be satisfied;   10
  And that if his Tartuffe is so sublime,
  He's free to marry him at any time.
MARIANE: I've bowed so long to Father's strict control,
  I couldn't oppose him now, to save my soul.
DORINE: Come, come, Mariane. Do listen to reason, won't you?   15
  Valère has asked your hand. Do you love him, or don't you?
MARIANE: Oh, how unjust of you! What can you mean
  By asking such a question, dear Dorine?
  You know the depth of my affection for him;
  I've told you a hundred times how I adore him.   20
DORINE: I don't believe in everything I hear;
  Who knows if your professions were sincere?
MARIANE: They were, Dorine, and you do me wrong to doubt it;
  Heaven knows that I've been all too frank about it.
DORINE: You love him, then?
MARIANE: Oh, more than I can express.   25
DORINE: And he, I take it, cares for you no less?
MARIANE: I think so.
DORINE: And you both, with equal fire,
  Burn to be married?
MARIANE: That is our one desire.
DORINE: What of Tartuffe, then? What of your father's plan?
MARIANE: I'll kill myself, if I'm forced to wed that man.   30
DORINE: I hadn't thought of that recourse. How splendid!
  Just die, and all your troubles will be ended!
  A fine solution. Oh, it maddens me
  To hear you talk in that self-pitying key.
MARIANE: Dorine, how harsh you are! It's most unfair.   35

You have no sympathy for my despair.
DORINE: I've none at all for people who talk drivel
   And, faced with difficulties, whine and snivel.
MARIANE: No doubt I'm timid, but it would be wrong . . .
DORINE: True love requires a heart that's firm and strong.   40
MARIANE: I'm strong in my affection for Valère,
   But coping with my father is his affair.
DORINE: But if your father's brain has grown so cracked
   Over his dear Tartuffe that he can retract
   His blessing, though your wedding-day was named,   45
   It's surely not Valère who's to be blamed.
MARIANE: If I defied my father, as you suggest,
   Would it not seem unmaidenly, at best?
   Shall I defend my love at the expense
   Of brazenness and disobedience?   50
   Shall I parade my heart's desires, and flaunt . . .
DORINE: No, I ask nothing of you. Clearly you want
   To be Madame Tartuffe, and I feel bound
   Not to oppose a wish so very sound.
   What right have I to criticize the match?   55
   Indeed, my dear, the man's a brilliant catch.
   Monsieur Tartuffe! Now, there's a man of weight!
   Yes, yes, Monsieur Tartuffe, I'm bound to state,
   Is quite a person; that's not to be denied;
   'Twill be no little thing to be his bride.   60
   The world already rings with his renown;
   He's a great noble—in his native town;
   His ears are red, he has a pink complexion,
   And all in all, he'll suit you to perfection.
MARIANE: Dear God!
DORINE: Oh, how triumphant you will feel   65
   At having caught a husband so ideal!
MARIANE: Oh, do stop teasing, and use your cleverness
   To get me out of this appalling mess.
   Advise me, and I'll do whatever you say.
DORINE: Ah, no, a dutiful daughter must obey   70
   Her father, even if he weds her to an ape.
   You've a bright future; why struggle to escape?
   Tartuffe will take you back where his family lives,
   To a small town aswarm with relatives—
   Uncles and cousins whom you'll be charmed to meet.   75
   You'll be received at once by the elite,
   Calling upon the bailiff's[5] wife, no less—
   Even, perhaps, upon the mayoress,[6]
   Who'll sit you down in the *best* kitchen chair.[7]

---

5. A high-ranking official in the judiciary, not simply a sheriff's deputy as today.   6. The wife of a tax collector (*élue*), an important official controlling imports, elected by the Estates General.   7. In elegant society of Molière's day, there was a hierarchy of seats, and the use of each was determined by rank. The

Then, once a year, you'll dance at the village fair   80
To the drone of bagpipes—two of them, in fact—
And see a puppet-show, or an animal act.[8]
Your husband . . .
MARIANE: Oh, you turn my blood to ice!
Stop torturing me, and give me your advice.
DORINE: [*Threatening to go.*]
Your servant, Madam.
MARIANE.   Dorine, I beg of you . . .   85
DORINE: No, you deserve it; this marriage must go through.
MARIANE: Dorine!
DORINE: No.
MARIANE: Not Tartuffe! You know I think him . . .
DORINE: Tartuffe's your cup of tea, and you shall drink him.
MARIANE: I've always told you everything, and relied . . .
DORINE: No. You deserve to be tartuffified.   90
MARIANE: Well, since you mock me and refuse to care,
I'll henceforth seek my solace in despair:
Despair shall be my counsellor and friend,
And help me bring my sorrows to an end. [*She starts to leave.*]
DORINE: There now, come back; my anger has subsided.   95
You do deserve some pity, I've decided.
MARIANE: Dorine, if Father makes me undergo
This dreadful martyrdom, I'll die, I know.
DORINE: Don't fret; it won't be difficult to discover
Some plan of action . . . But here's Valère, your lover.   100

SCENE 4

VALÈRE, MARIANE, DORINE

VALÈRE: Madam, I've just received some wondrous news
Regarding which I'd like to hear your views.
MARIANE: What news?
VALÈRE: You're marrying Tartuffe.
MARIANE: I find
That Father does have such a match in mind.
VALÈRE: Your father, Madam . . .
MARIANE: . . . has just this minute said   5
That it's Tartuffe he wishes me to wed.
VALÈRE: Can he be serious?
MARIANE: Oh, indeed he can;
He's clearly set his heart upon the plan.
VALÈRE: And what position do you propose to take,
Madam?

---

seats descended from *fauteuils* to *chaises, perroquets, tabourets,* and *pliants.* Thus Mariane would get
the lowest seat in the room.   8. In the original, *fagotin,* literally "a monkey dressed up in a man's
clothing."

MARIANE: Why—I don't know.
VALÈRE: For heaven's sake—   10
  You don't know?
MARIANE: No.
VALÈRE: Well, well!
MARIANE: Advise me, do.
VALÈRE: Marry the man. That's my advice to you.
MARIANE: That's your advice?
VALÈRE: Yes.
MARIANE: Truly?
VALÈRE: Oh, absolutely.
  You couldn't choose more wisely, more astutely.
MARIANE: Thanks for this counsel; I'll follow it, of course.   15
VALÈRE: Do, do; I'm sure 'twill cost you no remorse.
MARIANE: To give it didn't cause your heart to break.
VALÈRE: I gave it, Madam, only for your sake.
MARIANE: And it's for your sake that I take it, Sir.
DORINE: [*Withdrawing to the rear of the stage.*]
  Let's see which fool will prove the stubborner.   20
VALÈRE: So! I am nothing to you, and it was flat
  Deception when you . . .
MARIANE: Please, enough of that.
  You've told me plainly that I should agree
  To wed the man my father's chosen for me,
  And since you've deigned to counsel me so wisely,   25
  I promise, Sir, to do as you advise me.
VALÈRE: Ah, no, 'twas not by me that you were swayed.
  No, your decision was already made;
  Though now, to save appearances, you protest
  That you're betraying me at my behest.   30
MARIANE: Just as you say.
VALÈRE: Quite so. And I now see
  That you were never truly in love with me.
MARIANE: Alas, you're free to think so if you choose.
VALÈRE: I choose to think so, and here's a bit of news:
  You've spurned my hand, but I know where to turn   35
  For kinder treatment, as you shall quickly learn.
MARIANE: I'm sure you do. Your noble qualities
  Inspire affection . . .
VALÈRE: Forget my qualities, please.
  They don't inspire you overmuch, I find.
  But there's another lady I have in mind   40
  Whose sweet and generous nature will not scorn
  To compensate me for the loss I've borne.
MARIANE: I'm no great loss, and I'm sure that you'll transfer
  Your heart quite painlessly from me to her.
VALÈRE: I'll do my best to take it in my stride.   45
  The pain I feel at being cast aside

Time and forgetfulness may put an end to.
Or if I can't forget, I shall pretend to.
No self-respecting person is expected
To go on loving once he's been rejected.   50
MARIANE: Now, that's a fine, high-minded sentiment.
VALÈRE: One to which any sane man would assent.
  Would you prefer it if I pined away
  In hopeless passion till my dying day?
  Am I to yield you to a rival's arms   55
  And not console myself with other charms?
MARIANE: Go then; console yourself; don't hesitate.
  I wish you to; indeed, I cannot wait.
VALÈRE: You wish me to?
MARIANE: Yes.
VALÈRE: That's the final straw.
  Madam, farewell. Your wish shall be my law.   60
    [*He starts to leave, and then returns: this repeatedly.*]
MARIANE: Splendid.
VALÈRE: [*Coming back again.*] This breach, remember, is of your making;
  It's you who've driven me to the step I'm taking.
MARIANE: Of course.
VALÈRE: [*Coming back again.*] Remember, too, that I am merely
  Following your example.
MARIANE: I see that clearly.
VALÈRE. Enough. I'll go and do your bidding, then.   65
MARIANE: Good.
VALÈRE: [*Coming back again.*] You shall never see my face again.
MARIANE: Excellent.
VALÈRE: [*Walking to the door, then turning about.*]
                Yes?
MARIANE: What?
VALÈRE: What's that? What did you say?
MARIANE: Nothing. You're dreaming.
VALÈRE: Ah. Well, I'm on my way.
  Farewell, Madame.
    [*He moves slowly away.*]
MARIANE: Farewell.
DORINE: [*To MARIANE.*]   If you ask me,
  Both of you are as mad as mad can be.   70
  Do stop this nonsense, now. I've only let you
  Squabble so long to see where it would get you.
  Whoa there, Monsieur Valère!
    [*She goes and seizes VALÈRE by the arm; he makes a great show of
    resistance.*]
VALÈRE: What's this, Dorine?
DORINE: Come here.
VALÈRE: No, no, my heart's too full of spleen.
  Don't hold me back; her wish must be obeyed.   75

DORINE: Stop!

VALÈRE: It's too late now; my decision's made.

DORINE. Oh, pooh!

MARIANE: [*Aside.*] He hates the sight of me, that's plain.
   I'll go, and so deliver him from pain.

DORINE: [*Leaving* VALÈRE, *running after* MARIANE.]
   And now *you* run away! Come back.

MARIANE: No, no
   Nothing you say will keep me here. Let go!   80

VALÈRE: [*Aside.*] She cannot bear my presence, I perceive.
   To spare her further torment, I shall leave.

DORINE: [*Leaving* MARIANE, *running after* VALÈRE.]
   Again! You'll not escape, Sir; don't you try it.
   Come here, you two. Stop fussing and be quiet.
      [*She takes* VALÈRE *by the hand, then* MARIANE, *and draws them
      together.*]

VALÈRE: [*To* DORINE.] What do you want of me?   85

MARIANE: [*To* DORINE.] What is the point of this?

DORINE. We're going to have a little armistice.
   [*To* VALÈRE.] Now, weren't you silly to get so overheated?

VALÈRE: Didn't you see how badly I was treated?

DORINE: [*To* MARIANE.] Aren't you a simpleton, to have lost your head? 90

MARIANE: Didn't you hear the hateful things he said?

DORINE: [*To* VALÈRE.] You're both great fools. Her sole desire, Valère,
   Is to be yours in marriage. To that I'll swear.
   [*To* MARIANE.] He loves you only, and he wants no wife
   But you, Mariane. On that I'll stake my life.   95

MARIANE. [*To* VALÈRE.] Then why you advised me so, I cannot see.

VALÈRE: [*To* MARIANE.] On such a question, why ask advice of *me*?

DORINE: Oh, you're impossible. Give me your hands, you two.
   [*To* VALÈRE.] Yours first.

VALÈRE: [*Giving* DORINE *his hand.*] But why?

DORINE: [*To* MARIANE.]   And now a hand from you. 100

MARIANE: [*Also giving* DORINE *her hand.*]
   What are you doing?

DORINE: There: a perfect fit.
   You suit each other better than you'll admit.
      [VALÈRE *and* MARIANE *hold hands for some time without looking at
      each other.*]

VALÈRE: [*Turning toward* MARIANE.]
   Ah, come, don't be so haughty. Give a man
   A look of kindness, won't you, Mariane?
      [MARIANE *turns toward* VALÈRE *and smiles.*]

DORINE: I tell you, lovers are completely mad!   105

VALÈRE: [*To* MARIANE.] Now come, confess that you were very bad
   To hurt my feelings as you did just now.
   I have a just complaint, you must allow.

MARIANE: *You* must allow that you were most unpleasant ....

DORINE: Let's table that discussion for the present;   110
 Your father has a plan which must be stopped.
MARIANE: Advise us, then; what means must we adopt?
DORINE: We'll use all manner of means, and all at once.
 [*To* MARIANE.] Your father's addled; he's acting like a dunce.
 Therefore you'd better humor the old fossil.   115
 Pretend to yield to him, be sweet and docile,
 And then postpone, as often as necessary,
 The day on which you have agreed to marry.
 You'll thus gain time, and time will turn the trick.
 Sometimes, for instance, you'll be taken sick,   120
 And that will seem good reason for delay;
 Or some bad omen will make you change the day—
 You'll dream of muddy water, or you'll pass
 A dead man's hearse, or break a looking-glass.
 If all else fails, no man can marry you   125
 Unless you take his ring and say "I do."
 But now, let's separate. If they should find
 Us talking here, our plot might be divined.
 [*To* VALÈRE.] Go to your friends, and tell them what's occurred,
 And have them urge her father to keep his word.   130
 Meanwhile, we'll stir her brother into action,
 And get Elmire,[9] as well, to join our faction.
 Good-bye.
VALÈRE: [*To* MARIANE.] Though each of us will do his best,
 It's your true heart on which my hopes shall rest.   135
MARIANE: [*To* VALÈRE.] Regardless of what Father may decide,
 None but Valère shall claim me as his bride.
VALÈRE: Oh, how those words content me! Come what will . . .
DORINE: Oh, lovers, lovers! Their tongues are never still.
 Be off, now.
VALÈRE: [*Turning to go, then turning back.*]
    One last word . . .
DORINE: No time to chat: 140
 You leave by this door; and *you* leave by that.
 [DORINE *pushes them, by the shoulders, toward opposing doors.*]

Act III

SCENE 1

DAMIS, DORINE

DAMIS: May lightning strike me even as I speak,
 May all men call me cowardly and weak,

---

9. Orgon's second wife.

If any fear or scruple holds me back
From settling things, at once, with that great quack!
DORINE: Now, don't give way to violent emotion.   5
   Your father's merely talked about this notion,
   And words and deeds are far from being one.
   Much that is talked about is never done.
DAMIS: No, I must stop that scoundrel's machinations;
   I'll go and tell him off; I'm out of patience.   10
DORINE: Do calm down and be practical. I had rather
   My mistress dealt with him—and with your father.
   She has some influence with Tartuffe, I've noted.
   He hangs upon her words, seems most devoted,
   And may, indeed, be smitten by her charm.   15
   Pray Heaven it's true! 'Twould do our cause no harm.
   She sent for him, just now, to sound him out
   On this affair you're so incensed about;
   She'll find out where he stands, and tell him, too,
   What dreadful strife and trouble will ensue   20
   If he lends countenance to your father's plan.
   I couldn't get in to see him, but his man
   Says that he's almost finished with his prayers.
   Go, now. I'll catch him when he comes downstairs.
DAMIS: I want to hear this conference, and I will.   25
DORINE: No, they must be alone.
DAMIS: Oh, I'll keep still.
DORINE: Not you. I know your temper. You'd start a brawl,
   And shout and stamp your foot and spoil it all.
   Go on.
DAMIS: I won't; I have a perfect right . . .
DORINE: Lord, you're a nuisance! He's coming; get out of sight.   30
   [DAMIS *conceals himself in a closet at the rear of the stage.*]

SCENE 2

TARTUFFE, DORINE

TARTUFFE: [*Observing* DORINE, *and calling to his manservant off-stage.*]
   Hang up my hair-shirt, put my scourge in place,
   And pray, Laurent, for Heaven's perpetual grace.
   I'm going to the prison now, to share
   My last few coins with the poor wretches there.
DORINE: [*Aside.*] Dear God, what affectation! What a fake!   5
TARTUFFE: You wished to see me?
DORINE: Yes . . .
TARTUFFE. [*Taking a handkerchief from his pocket.*]
                                  For mercy's sake,
   Please take this handkerchief, before you speak.
DORINE: What?

TARTUFFE: Cover that bosom,[1] girl. The flesh is weak.
  And unclean thoughts are difficult to control.
  Such sights as that can undermine the soul.   10
DORINE: Your soul, it seems, has very poor defenses,
  And flesh makes quite an impact on your senses.
  It's strange that you're so easily excited;
  My own desires are not so soon ignited,
  And if I saw you naked as a beast,   15
  Not all your hide would tempt me in the least.
TARTUFFE: Girl, speak more modestly; unless you do,
  I shall be forced to take my leave of you.
DORINE: Oh, no, it's I who must be on my way;
  I've just one little message to convey.   20
  Madame is coming down, and begs you, Sir,
  To wait and have a word or two with her.
TARTUFFE: Gladly.
DORINE: [*Aside.*] *That* had a softening effect!
  I think my guess about him was correct.
TARTUFFE: Will she be long?
DORINE: No: that's her step I hear.   25
  Ah, here she is, and I shall disappear.

SCENE 3

ELMIRE, TARTUFFE

TARTUFFE: May Heaven, whose infinite goodness we adore,
  Preserve your body and soul forevermore,
  And bless your days, and answer thus the plea
  Of one who is its humblest votary.
ELMIRE: I thank you for that pious wish. But please,   5
  Do take a chair and let's be more at ease.
  [*They sit down.*]
TARTUFFE: I trust that you are once more well and strong?
ELMIRE: Oh, yes: the fever didn't last for long.
TARTUFFE: My prayers are too unworthy, I am sure,
  To have gained from Heaven this most gracious cure;   10
  But lately, Madam, my every supplication
  Has had for object your recuperation.
ELMIRE: You shouldn't have troubled so. I don't deserve it.
TARTUFFE: Your health is priceless, Madam, and to preserve it
  I'd gladly give my own, in all sincerity.   15
ELMIRE: Sir, you outdo us all in Christian charity.
  You've been most kind. I count myself your debtor.
TARTUFFE: 'Twas nothing, Madam. I long to serve you better.
ELMIRE: There's a private matter I'm anxious to discuss.

---

1. The Brotherhood of the Holy Sacrament practiced alms giving to prisoners and kept a careful, censorious check on women's clothing if they deemed it lascivious. Thus Molière's audience would have identified Tartuffe as sympathetic—hypocritically—to the aims of the organization.

I'm glad there's no one here to hinder us.   20
TARTUFFE: I too am glad; it floods my heart with bliss
  To find myself alone with you like this.
  For just this chance I've prayed with all my power—
  But prayed in vain, until this happy hour.
ELMIRE: This won't take long, Sir, and I hope you'll be   25
  Entirely frank and unconstrained with me.
TARTUFFE: Indeed, there's nothing I had rather do
  Than bare my inmost heart and soul to you.
  First, let me say that what remarks I've made
  About the constant visits you are paid   30
  Were prompted not by any mean emotion,
  But rather by a pure and deep devotion,
  A fervent zeal . . .
ELMIRE: No need for explanation.
  Your sole concern, I'm sure, was my salvation.
TARTUFFE: [*Taking* ELMIRE'S *hand and pressing her fingertips.*]
  Quite so; and such great fervor do I feel . . .   35
ELMIRE: Ooh! Please! You're pinching!
TARTUFFE: 'Twas from excess of zeal.
  I never meant to cause you pain, I swear.
  I'd rather . . .
      [*He places his hand on* ELMIRE'S *knee.*]
ELMIRE: What can your hand be doing there?
TARTUFFE: Feeling your gown: what soft, fine-woven stuff!
ELMIRE: Please, I'm extremely ticklish. That's enough.   40
      [*She draws her chair away;* TARTUFFE *pulls his after her.*]
TARTUFFE: [*Fondling the lace collar of her gown.*]
  My, my, what lovely lacework on your dress!
  The workmanship's miraculous, no less.
  I've not seen anything to equal it.
ELMIRE: Yes, quite. But let's talk business for a bit.
  They say my husband means to break his word   45
  And give his daughter to you, Sir. Had you heard?
TARTUFFE: He did once mention it. But I confess
  I dream of quite a different happiness.
  It's elsewhere, Madam, that my eyes discern
  The promise of that bliss for which I yearn.   50
ELMIRE: I see: you care for nothing here below.
TARTUFFE: Ah, well—my heart's not made of stone, you know.
ELMIRE: All your desires mount heavenward, I'm sure,
  In scorn of all that's earthly and impure.
TARTUFFE: A love of heavenly beauty does not preclude   55
  A proper love for earthly pulchritude;
  Our senses are quite rightly captivated
  By perfect works our Maker has created.
  Some glory clings to all that Heaven has made;
  In you, all Heaven's marvels are displayed.   60

On that fair face, such beauties have been lavished,
The eyes are dazzled and the heart is ravished;
How could I look on you, O flawless creature,
And not adore the Author of all Nature,
Feeling a love both passionate and pure   65
For you, his triumph of self-portraiture?
At first, I trembled lest that love should be
A subtle snare that Hell had laid for me;
I vowed to flee the sight of you, eschewing
A rapture that might prove my soul's undoing;   70
But soon, fair being, I became aware
That my deep passion could be made to square
With rectitude, and with my bounden duty,
I thereupon surrendered to your beauty.
It is, I know, presumptuous on my part   75
To bring you this poor offering of my heart,
And it is not my merit, Heaven knows,
But your compassion on which my hopes repose.
You are my peace, my solace, my salvation;
On you depends my bliss—or desolation;   80
I bide your judgment and, as you think best,
I shall be either miserable or blest.
ELMIRE: Your declaration is most gallant, Sir,
But don't you think it's out of character?
You'd have done better to restrain your passion   85
And think before you spoke in such a fashion.
It ill becomes a pious man like you . . .
TARTUFFE: I may be pious, but I'm human too:
With your celestial charms before his eyes,
A man has not the power to be wise.   90
I know such words sound strangely, coming from me,
But I'm no angel, nor was meant to be,
And if you blame my passion, you must needs
Reproach as well the charms on which it feeds.
Your loveliness I had no sooner seen   95
Than you became my soul's unrivalled queen;
Before your seraph glance, divinely sweet,
My heart's defenses crumbled in defeat,
And nothing fasting, prayer, or tears might do
Could stay my spirit from adoring you.   100
My eyes, my sighs have told you in the past
What now my lips make bold to say at last,
And if, in your great goodness, you will deign
To look upon your slave, and ease his pain,—
If, in compassion for my soul's distress,   105
You'll stoop to comfort my unworthiness,
I'll raise to you, in thanks for that sweet manna,
An endless hymn, an infinite hosanna.

With me, of course, there need be no anxiety,
No fear of scandal or of notoriety.   110
These young court gallants, whom all the ladies fancy,
Are vain in speech, in action rash and chancy;
When they succeed in love, the world soon knows it;
No favor's granted them but they disclose it
And by the looseness of their tongues profane   115
The very altar where their hearts have lain.
Men of my sort, however, love discreetly,
And one may trust our reticence completely.
My keen concern for my good name insures
The absolute security of yours;   120
In short, I offer you, my dear Elmire,
Love without scandal, pleasure without fear.
ELMIRE: I've heard your well-turned speeches to the end,
And what you urge I clearly apprehend.
Aren't you afraid that I may take a notion   125
To tell my husband of your warm devotion,
And that, supposing he were duly told,
His feelings toward you might grow rather cold?
TARTUFFE: I know, dear lady, that your exceeding charity
Will lead your heart to pardon my temerity;   130
That you'll excuse my violent affection
As human weakness, human imperfection;
And that—O fairest!— you will bear in mind
That I'm but flesh and blood, and am not blind.
ELMIRE: Some women might do otherwise, perhaps,   135
But I shall be discreet about your lapse;
I'll tell my husband nothing of what's occurred
If, in return, you'll give your solemn word
To advocate as forcefully as you can
The marriage of Valère and Mariane,   140
Renouncing all desire to dispossess
Another of his rightful happiness,
And . . .

SCENE 4

DAMIS, ELMIRE, TARTUFFE

DAMIS: [*Emerging from the closet where he has been hiding.*]
            No! We'll not hush up this vile affair;
I heard it all inside that closet there,
Where Heaven, in order to confound the pride
Of this great rascal, prompted me to hide.
Ah, now I have my long-awaited chance   5
To punish his deceit and arrogance,
And give my father clear and shocking proof
Of the black character of his dear Tartuffe.

ELMIRE: Ah no, Damis; I'll be content if he
   Will study to deserve my leniency.   10
   I've promised silence—don't make me break my word;
   To make a scandal would be too absurd.
   Good wives laugh off such trifles, and forget them;
   Why should they tell their husbands, and upset them?
DAMIS: You have your reasons for taking such a course,   15
   And I have reasons, too, of equal force.
   To spare him now would be insanely wrong.
   I've swallowed my just wrath for far too long
   And watched this insolent bigot bringing strife
   And bitterness into our family life.   20
   Too long he's meddled in my father's affairs,
   Thwarting my marriage-hopes, and poor Valère's.
   It's high time that my father was undeceived,
   And now I've proof that can't be disbelieved—
   Proof that was furnished me by Heaven above.   25
   It's too good not to take advantage of.
   This is my chance, and I deserve to lose it
   If, for one moment, I hesitate to use it.
ELMIRE: Damis . . .
DAMIS: No, I must do what I think right.
   Madam, my heart is bursting with delight,   30
   And, say whatever you will, I'll not consent
   To lose the sweet revenge on which I'm bent.
   I'll settle matters without more ado;
   And here, most opportunely, is my cue.[2]

SCENE 5

ORGON, DAMIS, TARTUFFE, ELMIRE

DAMIS: Father, I'm glad you've joined us. Let us advise you
   Of some fresh news which doubtless will surprise you.
   You've just now been repaid with interest
   For all your loving-kindness to our guest.
   He's proved his warm and grateful feelings toward you;   5
   It's with a pair of horns he would reward you.
   Yes, I surprised him with your wife, and heard
   His whole adulterous offer, every word.
   She, with her all too gentle disposition,
   Would not have told you of his proposition;   10
   But I shall not make terms with brazen lechery,
   And feel that not to tell you would be treachery.
ELMIRE: And I hold that one's husband's peace of mind
   Should not be spoilt by tattle of this kind.
   One's honor doesn't require it: to be proficient   15

---

2. In the original stage directions, Tartuffe now reads silently from his breviary—in the Roman Catholic Church, the book containing the Divine Office for each day, which those in holy orders are required to recite.

In keeping men at bay is quite sufficient.
These are my sentiments, and I wish, Damis,
That you had heeded me and held your peace.

SCENE 6

ORGON, DAMIS, TARTUFFE

ORGON: Can it be true, this dreadful thing I hear?
TARTUFFE: Yes, Brother, I'm a wicked man, I fear:
  A wretched sinner, all depraved and twisted,
  The greatest villain that has ever existed.
  My life's one heap of crimes, which grows each minute;   5
  There's naught but foulness and corruption in it;
  And I perceive that Heaven, outraged by me,
  Has chosen this occasion to mortify me.
  Charge me with any deed you wish to name;
  I'll not defend myself, but take the blame.   10
  Believe what you are told, and drive Tartuffe
  Like some base criminal from beneath your roof;
  Yes, drive me hence, and with a parting curse:
  I shan't protest, for I deserve far worse.
ORGON: [To DAMIS.] Ah, you deceitful boy, how dare you try   15
  To stain his purity with so foul a lie?
DAMIS: What! Are you taken in by such a fluff?
  Did you not hear . . . ?
ORGON: Enough, you rogue, enough!
TARTUFFE: Ah, Brother, let him speak: you're being unjust.
  Believe his story; the boy deserves your trust.   20
  Why, after all, should you have faith in me?
  How can you know what I might do, or be?
  Is it on my good actions that you base
  Your favor? Do you trust my pious face?
  Ah, no, don't be deceived by hollow shows;   25
  I'm far, alas, from being what men suppose;
  Though the world takes me for a man of worth,
  I'm truly the most worthless man on earth.
  [To DAMIS.] Yes, my dear son, speak out now: call me the chief
  Of sinners, a wretch, a murderer, a thief;   30
  Load me with all the names men most abhor;
  I'll not complain; I've earned them all, and more;
  I'll kneel here while you pour them on my head
  As a just punishment for the life I've led.
ORGON: [To TARTUFFE.]
  This is too much, dear Brother.
  [To DAMIS.]   Have you no heart?   35
DAMIS: Are you so hoodwinked by this rascal's art . . . ?
ORGON: Be still, you monster.
  [To TARTUFFE.]   Brother, I pray you, rise.
  [To DAMIS.] Villain!

DAMIS: But . . .

ORGON: Silence!

DAMIS: Can't you realize . . . ?

ORGON: Just one word more, and I'll tear you limb from limb.

TARTUFFE: In God's name, Brother, don't be harsh with him.   40
  I'd rather far be tortured at the stake
  Than see him bear one scratch for my poor sake.

ORGON: [*To* DAMIS.] Ingrate!

TARTUFFE: If I must beg you, on bended knee,
  To pardon him . . .

ORGON: [*Falling to his knees, addressing* TARTUFFE.]
  Such goodness cannot be!
  [*To* DAMIS.] Now, *there's* true charity!

DAMIS: What, you . . . ?

ORGON: Villain, be still!   45
  I know your motives; I know you wish him ill:
  Yes, all of you—wife, children, servants, all—
  Conspire against him and desire his fall,
  Employing every shameful trick you can
  To alienate me from this saintly man.   50
  Ah, but the more you seek to drive him away,
  The more I'll do to keep him. Without delay,
  I'll spite this household and confound its pride
  By giving him my daughter as his bride.

DAMIS: You're going to force her to accept his hand?   55

ORGON: Yes, and this very night, d'you understand?
  I shall defy you all, and make it clear
  That I'm the one who gives the orders here.
  Come, wretch, kneel down and clasp his blessed feet,
  And ask his pardon for your black deceit.   60

DAMIS: I ask that swindler's pardon? Why, I'd rather . . .

ORGON: So! You insult him, and defy your father!
  A stick! A stick! [*To* TARTUFFE.] No, no—release me, do.
  [*To* DAMIS.] Out of my house this minute! Be off with you,
  And never dare set foot in it again.   65

DAMIS: Well, I shall go, but . . .

ORGON: Well, go quickly, then.
  I disinherit you; an empty purse
  Is all you'll get from me—except my curse!

SCENE 7

ORGON, TARTUFFE

ORGON: How he blasphemed your goodness! What a son!

TARTUFFE: Forgive him, Lord, as I've already done.
  [*To* ORGON.] You can't know how it hurts when someone tries
  To blacken me in my dear brother's eyes.

ORGON: Ahh!

TARTUFFE: The mere thought of such ingratitude   5
    Plunges my soul into so dark a mood . . .
    Such horror grips my heart . . . I gasp for breath,
    And cannot speak, and feel myself near death.
ORGON: [*He runs, in tears, to the door through which he has just driven*
    his son.]
    You blackguard! Why did I spare you? Why did I not
    Break you in little pieces on the spot?   10
    Compose yourself, and don't be hurt, dear friend.
TARTUFFE: These scenes, these dreadful quarrels, have got to end.
    I've much upset your household, and I perceive
    That the best thing will be for me to leave.
ORGON: What are you saying!
TARTUFFE: They're all against me here;   15
    They'd have you think me false and insincere.
ORGON: Ah, what of that? Have I ceased believing in you?
TARTUFFE: Their adverse talk will certainly continue,
    And charges which you now repudiate
    You may find credible at a later date.   20
ORGON: No, Brother, never.
TARTUFFE: Brother, a wife can sway
    Her husband's mind in many a subtle way.
ORGON: No, no.
TARTUFFE: To leave at once is the solution;
    Thus only can I end their persecution.
ORGON: No, no, I'll not allow it; you shall remain.   25
TARTUFFE: Ah, well; 'twill mean much martyrdom and pain,
    But if you wish it . . .
ORGON: Ah!
TARTUFFE: Enough; so be it.
    But one thing must be settled, as I see it.
    For your dear honor, and for our friendship's sake,
    There's one precaution I feel bound to take.   30
    I shall avoid your wife, and keep away . . .
ORGON: No, you shall not, whatever they may say.
    It pleases me to vex them, and for spite
    I'd have them see you with her day and night.
    What's more, I'm going to drive them to despair   35
    By making you my only son and heir;
    This very day, I'll give to you alone
    Clear deed and title to everything I own.
    A dear, good friend and son-in-law-to-be
    Is more than wife, or child, or kin to me.   40
    Will you accept my offer, dearest son?
TARTUFFE: In all things, let the will of Heaven be done.
ORGON: Poor fellow! Come, we'll go draw up the deed.
    Then let them burst with disappointed greed!

Act IV

SCENE 1

CLÉANTE, TARTUFFE

CLÉANTE: Yes, all the town's discussing it, and truly,
　　Their comments do not flatter you unduly.
　　I'm glad we've met, Sir, and I'll give my view
　　Of this sad matter in a word or two.
　　As for who's guilty, that I shan't discuss;   5
　　Let's say it was Damis who caused the fuss;
　　Assuming, then, that you have been ill-used
　　By young Damis, and groundlessly accused,
　　Ought not a Christian to forgive, and ought
　　He not to stifle every vengeful thought?   10
　　Should you stand by and watch a father make
　　His only son an exile for your sake?
　　Again I tell you frankly, be advised:
　　The whole town, high and low, is scandalized;
　　This quarrel must be mended, and my advice is   15
　　Not to push matters to a further crisis.
　　No, sacrifice your wrath to God above,
　　And help Damis regain his father's love.
TARTUFFE: Alas, for my part I should take great joy
　　In doing so. I've nothing against the boy.   20
　　I pardon all, I harbor no resentment;
　　To serve him would afford me much contentment.
　　But Heaven's interest will not have it so:
　　If he comes back, then I shall have to go.
　　After his conduct—so extreme, so vicious—   25
　　Our further intercourse would look suspicious.
　　God knows what people would think! Why, they'd describe
　　My goodness to him as a sort of bribe;
　　They'd say that out of guilt I made pretense
　　Of loving-kindness and benevolence—   30
　　That, fearing my accuser's tongue, I strove
　　To buy his silence with a show of love.
CLÉANTE: Your reasoning is badly warped and stretched,
　　And these excuses, Sir, are most far-fetched.
　　Why put yourself in charge of Heaven's cause?   35
　　Does Heaven need our help to enforce its laws?
　　Leave vengeance to the Lord, Sir; while we live,
　　Our duty's not to punish, but forgive;
　　And what the Lord commands, we should obey
　　Without regard to what the world may say.   40
　　What! Shall the fear of being misunderstood
　　Prevent our doing what is right and good?
　　No, no: let's simply do what Heaven ordains,
　　And let no other thoughts perplex our brains.

TARTUFFE: Again, Sir, let me say that I've forgiven   45
   Damis, and thus obeyed the laws of Heaven;
   But I am not commanded by the Bible
   To live with one who smears my name with libel.
CLÉANTE: Were you commanded, Sir, to indulge the whim
   Of poor Orgon, and to encourage him   50
   In suddenly transferring to your name
   A large estate to which you have no claim?
TARTUFFE: 'Twould never occur to those who know me best
   To think I acted from self-interest.
   The treasures of this world I quite despise;   55
   Their specious glitter does not charm my eyes;
   And if I have resigned myself to taking
   The gift which my dear Brother insists on making,
   I do so only, as he well understands,
   Lest so much wealth fall into wicked hands,   60
   Lest those to whom it might descend in time
   Turn it to purposes of sin and crime,
   And not, as I shall do, make use of it
   For Heaven's glory and mankind's benefit.
CLÉANTE: Forget these trumped-up fears. Your argument   65
   Is one the rightful heir might well resent;
   It *is* a moral burden to inherit
   Such wealth, but give Damis a chance to bear it.
   And would it not be worse to be accused
   Of swindling, than to see that wealth misused?   70
   I'm shocked that you allowed Orgon to broach
   This matter, and that you feel no self-reproach;
   Does true religion teach that lawful heirs
   May freely be deprived of what is theirs?
   And if the Lord has told you in your heart   75
   That you and young Damis must dwell apart,
   Would it not be the decent thing to beat
   A generous and honorable retreat,
   Rather than let the son of the house be sent,
   For your convenience, into banishment?   80
   Sir, if you wish to prove the honesty
   Of your intentions . . .
TARTUFFE: Sir, it is a half past three.
   I've certain pious duties to attend to,
   And hope my prompt departure won't offend you.
CLÉANTE: [*Alone.*] Damn.

SCENE 2

ELMIRE, MARIANE, CLÉANTE, DORINE

DORINE: Stay, Sir, and help Mariane, for Heaven's sake!
   She's suffering so, I fear her heart will break.
   Her father's plan to marry her off tonight

Has put the poor child in a desperate plight.
I hear him coming. Let's stand together, now,   5
And see if we can't change his mind, somehow,
About this match we all deplore and fear.

SCENE 3

ORGON, ELMIRE, MARIANE, CLÉANTE, DORINE

ORGON: Hah! Glad to find you all assembled here.
   [*To* MARIANE.] This contract, child, contains your happiness,
   And what it says I think your heart can guess.
MARIANE: [*Falling to her knees.*]
   Sir, by that Heaven which sees me here distressed,
   And by whatever else can move your breast,   5
   Do not employ a father's power, I pray you,
   To crush my heart and force it to obey you,
   Nor by your harsh commands oppress me so
   That I'll begrudge the duty which I owe—
   And do not so embitter and enslave me   10
   That I shall hate the very life you gave me.
   If my sweet hopes must perish, if you refuse
   To give me to the one I've dared to choose,
   Spare me at least—I beg you, I implore—
   The pain of wedding one whom I abhor;   15
   And do not, by a heartless use of force,
   Drive me to contemplate some desperate course.
ORGON: [*Feeling himself touched by her.*]
   Be firm, my soul. No human weakness, now.
MARIANE: I don't resent your love for him. Allow
   Your heart free rein, Sir; give him your property,   20
   And if that's not enough, take mine from me;
   He's welcome to my money; take it, do,
   But don't, I pray, include my person too.
   Spare me, I beg you; and let me end the tale
   Of my sad days behind a convent veil.   25
ORGON: A convent! Hah! When crossed in their amours,
   All lovesick girls have the same thought as yours.
   Get up! The more you loathe the man, and dread him,
   The more ennobling it will be to wed him.
   Marry Tartuffe, and mortify your flesh!   30
   Enough; don't start that whimpering afresh.
DORINE: But why . . . ?
ORGON: Be still, there. Speak when you're spoken to.
   Not one more bit of impudence out of you.
CLÉANTE: If I may offer a word of counsel here . . .
ORGON: Brother, in counselling you have no peer;   35
   All your advice is forceful, sound, and clever;
   I don't propose to follow it, however.

ELMIRE: [*To* ORGON.] I am amazed, and don't know what to say;
    Your blindness simply takes my breath away.
    You are indeed bewitched, to take no warning   40
    From our account of what occurred this morning.
ORGON: Madam, I know a few plain facts, and one
    Is that you're partial to my rascal son;
    Hence, when he sought to make Tartuffe the victim
    Of a base lie, you dared not contradict him.   45
    Ah, but you underplayed your part, my pet;
    You should have looked more angry, more upset.
ELMIRE: When men make overtures, must we reply
    With righteous anger and a battle-cry?
    Must we turn back their amorous advances   50
    With sharp reproaches and with fiery glances?
    Myself, I find such offers merely amusing,
    And make no scenes and fusses in refusing;
    My taste is for good-natured rectitude,
    And I dislike the savage sort of prude   55
    Who guards her virtue with her teeth and claws,
    And tears men's eyes out for the slightest cause:
    The Lord preserve me from such honor as that,
    Which bites and scratches like an alley-cat!
    I've found that a polite and cool rebuff   60
    Discourages a lover quite enough.
ORGON: I know the facts, and I shall not be shaken.
ELMIRE: I marvel at your power to be mistaken.
    Would it, I wonder, carry weight with you
    If I could *show* you that our tale was true?   65
ORGON: Show me?
ELMIRE: Yes.
ORGON: Rot.
ELMIRE: Come, what if I found a way
    To make you see the facts as plain as day?
ORGON: Nonsense.
ELMIRE: Do answer me; don't be absurd.
    I'm not now asking you to trust our word.
    Suppose that from some hiding-place in here   70
    You learned the whole sad truth by eye and ear—
    What would you say of your good friend, after that?
ORGON: Why, I'd say . . . nothing, by Jehoshaphat!
    It can't be true.
ELMIRE: You've been too long deceived,
    I'm quite tired of being disbelieved.   75
    Come now: let's put my statements to the test,
    And you shall see the truth made manifest.
ORGON: I'll take that challenge. Now do your uttermost.
    We'll see how you make good your empty boast.
ELMIRE: [*To* DORINE.] Send him to me.

DORINE: He's crafty; it may be hard   80
   To catch the cunning scoundrel off his guard.
ELMIRE: No, amorous men are gullible. Their conceit
   So blinds them that they're never hard to cheat.
   Have him come down.
   [*To* CLÉANTE *and* MARIANE.] Please leave us, for a bit.

SCENE 4

ELMIRE, ORGON

ELMIRE: Pull up this table, and get under it.
ORGON: What?
ELMIRE.   It's essential that you be well-hidden.
ORGON: Why there?
ELMIRE: Oh, Heavens! Just do as you are bidden.
   I have my plans; we'll soon see how they fare.
   Under the table, now; and once you're there,   5
   Take care that you are neither seen nor heard.
ORGON: Well, I'll indulge you, since I gave my word
   To see you through this infantile charade.
ELMIRE: Once it is over, you'll be glad we played.
   [*To her husband, who is now under the table.*]
   I'm going to act quite strangely, now, and you   10
   Must not be shocked at anything I do.
   Whatever I may say, you must excuse
   As part of that deceit I'm forced to use.
   I shall employ sweet speeches in the task
   Of making that impostor drop his mask;   15
   I'll give encouragement to his bold desires,
   And furnish fuel to his amorous fires.
   Since it's for your sake, and for his destruction,
   That I shall seem to yield to his seduction,
   I'll gladly stop whenever you decide   20
   That all your doubts are fully satisfied.
   I'll count on you, as soon as you have seen
   What sort of man he is, to intervene,
   And not expose me to his odious lust
   One moment longer than you feel you must.   25
   Remember: you're to save me from my plight
   Whenever . . . He's coming! Hush! Keep out of sight!

SCENE 5

TARTUFFE, ELMIRE, ORGON

TARTUFFE: You wish to have a word with me, I'm told.
ELMIRE: Yes, I've a little secret to unfold.
   Before I speak, however, it would be wise
   To close that door, and look about for spies.

[TARTUFFE *goes to the door, closes it, and returns.*]
The very last thing that must happen now   5
Is a repetition of this morning's row.
I've never been so badly caught off guard.
Oh, how I feared for you! You saw how hard
I tried to make that troublesome Damis
Control his dreadful temper, and hold his peace.   10
In my confusion, I didn't have the sense
Simply to contradict his evidence;
But as it happened, that was for the best,
And all has worked out in our interest.
This storm has only bettered your position;   15
My husband doesn't have the least suspicion,
And now, in mockery of those who do,
He bids me be continually with you.
And that is why, quite fearless of reproof,
I now can be alone with my Tartuffe,   20
And why my heart—perhaps too quick to yield—
Feels free to let its passion be revealed.
TARTUFFE: Madam, your words confuse me. Not long ago,
   You spoke in quite a different style, you know.
ELMIRE: Ah, Sir, if that refusal made you smart,   25
   It's little that you know of woman's heart,
   Or what that heart is trying to convey
   When it resists in such a feeble way!
   Always, at first, our modesty prevents
   The frank avowal of tender sentiments: 30
   However high the passion which inflames us,
   Still, to confess its power somehow shames us.
   Thus we reluct, at first, yet in a tone
   Which tells you that our heart is overthrown,
   That what our lips deny, our pulse confesses,   35
   And that, in time, all noes will turn to yesses.
   I fear my words are all too frank and free,
   And a poor proof of woman's modesty;
   But since I'm started, tell me, if you will—
   Would I have tried to make Damis be still,   40
   Would I have listened, calm and unoffended,
   Until your lengthy offer of love was ended,
   And been so very mild in my reaction,
   Had your sweet words not given me satisfaction?
   And when I tried to force you to undo   45
   The marriage-plans my husband has in view,
   What did my urgent pleading signify
   If not that I admired you, and that I
   Deplored the thought that someone else might own
   Part of a heart I wished for mine alone?   50
TARTUFFE: Madam, no happiness is so complete

As when, from lips we love, come words so sweet;
Their nectar floods my every sense, and drains
In honeyed rivulets through all my veins.
To please you is my joy, my only goal;   55
Your love is the restorer of my soul;
And yet I must beg leave, now, to confess
Some lingering doubts as to my happiness.
Might this not be a trick? Might not the catch
Be that you wish me to break off the match   60
With Mariane, and so have feigned to love me?
I shan't quite trust your fond opinion of me
Until the feelings you've expressed so sweetly
Are demonstrated somewhat more concretely,
And you have shown, by certain kind concessions,   65
That I may put my faith in your professions
ELMIRE: [*She coughs, to warn her husband.*]
  Why be in such a hurry? Must my heart
  Exhaust its bounty at the very start?
  To make that sweet admission cost me dear,
  But you'll not be content, it would appear,   70
  Unless my store of favors is disbursed
  To the last farthing, and at the very first.
TARTUFFE: The less we merit, the less we dare to hope,
  And with our doubts, mere words can never cope.
  We trust no promised bliss till we receive it;   75
  Not till a joy is ours can we believe it.
  I, who so little merit your esteem,
  Can't credit this fulfillment of my dream,
  And shan't believe it, Madam, until I savor
  Some palpable assurance of your favor.   80
ELMIRE: My, how tyrannical your love can be,
  And how it flusters and perplexes me!
  How furiously you take one's heart in hand,
  And make your every wish a fierce command!
  Come, must you hound and harry me to death?   85
  Will you not give me time to catch my breath?
  Can it be right to press me with such force,
  Give me no quarter, show me no remorse,
  And take advantage, by your stern insistence,
  Of the fond feelings which weaken my resistance?   90
TARTUFFE: Well, if you look with favor upon my love,
  Why, then, begrudge me some clear proof thereof?
ELMIRE: But how can I consent without offense
  To Heaven, toward which you feel such reverence?
TARTUFFE: If Heaven is all that holds you back, don't worry.   95
  I can remove that hindrance in a hurry.
  Nothing of that sort need obstruct our path.
ELMIRE: Must one not be afraid of Heaven's wrath?

TARTUFFE: Madam, forget such fears, and be my pupil,
    And I shall teach you how to conquer scruple.   100
    Some joys, it's true, are wrong in Heaven's eyes;
    Yet Heaven is not averse to compromise;
    There is a science, lately formulated,
    Whereby one's conscience may be liberated,[3]
    And any wrongful act you care to mention   105
    May be redeemed by purity of intention.
    I'll teach you, Madam, the secrets of that science;
    Meanwhile, just place on me your full reliance.
    Assuage my keen desires, and feel no dread:
    The sin, if any, shall be on my head.   110
       [ELMIRE *coughs, this time more loudly.*]
    You've a bad cough.
ELMIRE: Yes, yes, It's bad indeed.
TARTUFFE: [*Producing a little paper bag.*]
    A bit of licorice may be what you need.
ELMIRE: No, I've a stubborn cold, it seems. I'm sure it
    Will take much more than licorice to cure it.
TARTUFFE: How aggravating.
ELMIRE: Oh, more than I can say.   115
TARTUFFE: If you're still troubled, think of things this way:
    No one shall know our joys, save us alone,
    And there's no evil till the act is known;
    It's scandal, Madam, which makes it an offense,
    And it's no sin to sin in confidence.   120
ELMIRE: [*Having coughed once more.*]
    Well, clearly I must do as you require,
    And yield to your importunate desire.
    It is apparent, now, that nothing less
    Will satisfy you, and so I acquiesce.
    To go so far is much against my will;   125
    I'm vexed that it should come to this; but still,
    Since you are so determined on it, since you
    Will not allow mere language to convince you,
    And since you ask for concrete evidence, I
    See nothing for it, now, but to comply.   130
    If this is sinful, if I'm wrong to do it,
    So much the worse for him who drove me to it.
    The fault can surely not be charged to me.
TARTUFFE: Madam, the fault is mine, if fault there be,
    And . . .
ELMIRE: Open the door a little, and peek out;   135
    I wouldn't want my husband poking about.
TARTUFFE: Why worry about the man? Each day he grows
    More gullible; one can lead him by the nose.

---

3. Molière created his own footnote to this line: "It is a scoundrel who speaks."

To find us here would fill him with delight,
And if he saw the worst, he'd doubt his sight.   140
ELMIRE: Nevertheless, do step out for a minute
Into the hall, and see that no one's in it.

SCENE 6

ORGON, ELMIRE

ORGON: [Coming out from under the table.]
That man's a perfect monster, I must admit!
I'm simply stunned. I can't get over it.
ELMIRE: What, coming out so soon? How premature!
Get back in hiding, and wait until you're sure.
Stay till the end, and be convinced completely;   5
We mustn't stop till things are proved concretely.
ORGON: Hell never harbored anything so vicious!
ELMIRE: Tut, don't be hasty. Try to be judicious.
Wait, and be certain that there's no mistake.
No jumping to conclusions, for Heaven's sake!   10
[She places ORGON behind her, as TARTUFFE re-enters.]

SCENE 7

TARTUFFE, ELMIRE, ORGON

TARTUFFE: [Not seeing ORGON.]
Madam, all things have worked out to perfection;
I've given the neighboring rooms a full inspection;
No one's about; and now I may at last . . .
ORGON: [Intercepting him.] Hold on, my passionate fellow, not so fast!
I should advise a little more restraint.   5
Well, so you thought you'd fool me, my dear saint!
How soon you wearied of the saintly life—
Wedding my daughter, and coveting my wife!
I've long suspected you, and had a feeling
That soon I'd catch you at your double-dealing.   10
Just now, you've given me evidence galore;
It's quite enough; I have no wish for more.
ELMIRE: [To TARTUFFE.] I'm sorry to have treated you so slyly,
But circumstances forced me to be wily.
TARTUFFE: Brother, you can't think . . .
ORGON: No more talk from you;   15
Just leave this household, without more ado.
TARTUFFE: What I intended . . .
ORGON: That seems fairly clear.
Spare me your falsehoods and get out of here.
TARTUFFE: No, I'm the master, and you're the one to go!
This house belongs to me, I'll have you know,   20
And I shall show you that you can't hurt me

By this contemptible conspiracy,
That those who cross me know not what they do,
And that I've means to expose and punish you,
Avenge offended Heaven, and make you grieve   25
That ever you dared order me to leave.

SCENE 8

ELMIRE, ORGON

ELMIRE: What was the point of all that angry chatter?
ORGON: Dear God, I'm worried. This is no laughing matter.
ELMIRE: How so?
ORGON: I fear I understood his drift.
  I'm much disturbed about that deed of gift.
ELMIRE: You gave him . . . ?
ORGON: Yes, it's all been drawn and signed.   5
  But one thing more is weighing on my mind.
ELMIRE: What's that?
ORGON: I'll tell you; but first let's see if there's
  A certain strong-box in his room upstairs.

Act V

SCENE 1

ORGON, CLÉANTE

CLÉANTE: Where are you going so fast?
ORGON: God knows!
CLÉANTE: Then wait;
  Let's have a conference, and deliberate
  On how this situation's to be met.
ORGON: That strong-box has me utterly upset;
  This is the worst of many, many shocks.   5
CLÉANTE: Is there some fearful mystery in that box?
ORGON: My poor friend Argas brought that box to me
  With his own hands, in utmost secrecy;
  'Twas on the very morning of his flight.
  It's full of papers which, if they came to light,   10
  Would ruin him—or such is my impression.
CLÉANTE: Then why did you let it out of your possession?
ORGON: Those papers vexed my conscience, and it seemed best
  To ask the counsel of my pious guest.
  The cunning scoundrel got me to agree   15
  To leave the strong-box in his custody,
  So that, in case of an investigation,
  I could employ a slight equivocation
  And swear I didn't have it, and thereby,
  At no expense to conscience, tell a lie.   20

CLÉANTE: It looks to me as if you're out on a limb.
   Trusting him with that box, and offering him
   That deed of gift, were actions of a kind
   Which scarcely indicate a prudent mind.
   With two such weapons, he has the upper hand,   25
   And since you're vulnerable, as matters stand,
   You erred once more in bringing him to bay.
   You should have acted in some subtler way.
ORGON: Just think of it: behind that fervent face,
   A heart so wicked, and a soul so base!   30
   I took him in, a hungry beggar, and then . . .
   Enough, by God! I'm through with pious men:
   Henceforth I'll hate the whole false brotherhood,
   And persecute them worse than Satan could.
CLÉANTE: Ah, there you go—extravagant as ever!   35
   Why can you not be rational? You never
   Manage to take the middle course, it seems,
   But jump, instead, between absurd extremes.
   You've recognized your recent grave mistake
   In falling victim to a pious fake;   40
   Now, to correct that error, must you embrace
   An even greater error in its place,
   And judge our worthy neighbors as a whole
   By what you've learned of one corrupted soul?
   Come, just because one rascal made you swallow   45
   A show of zeal which turned out to be hollow,
   Shall you conclude that all men are deceivers,
   And that, today, there are no true believers?
   Let atheists make that foolish inference;
   Learn to distinguish virtue from pretense,   50
   Be cautious in bestowing admiration,
   And cultivate a sober moderation.
   Don't humor fraud, but also don't asperse
   True piety; the latter fault is worse,
   And it is best to err, if err one must,   55
   As you have done, upon the side of trust.

SCENE 2

DAMIS, ORGON, CLÉANTE

DAMIS: Father, I hear that scoundrel's uttered threats
   Against you; that he pridefully forgets
   How, in his need, he was befriended by you,
   And means to use your gifts to crucify you.
ORGON: It's true, my boy. I'm too distressed for tears.   5
DAMIS: Leave it to me, Sir; let me trim his ears.
   Faced with such insolence, we must not waver.
   I shall rejoice in doing you the favor

Of cutting short his life, and your distress.
CLÉANTE: What a display of young hotheadedness!   10
Do learn to moderate your fits of rage.
In this just kingdom, this enlightened age,
One does not settle things by violence.

SCENE 3

MADAME PERNELLE, MARIANE, ELMIRE, DORINE, DAMIS,
ORGON, CLÉANTE

MADAME PERNELLE: I hear strange tales of very strange events.
ORGON: Yes, strange events which these two eyes beheld.
The man's ingratitude is unparalleled.
I save a wretched pauper from starvation,
House him, and treat him like a blood relation,   5
Shower him every day with my largesse,
Give him my daughter, and all that I possess;
And meanwhile the unconscionable knave
Tries to induce my wife to misbehave;
And not content with such extreme rascality,   10
Now threatens me with my own liberality,
And aims, by taking base advantage of
The gifts I gave him out of Christian love,
To drive me from my house, a ruined man,
And make me end a pauper, as he began.   15
DORINE: Poor fellow!
MADAME PERNELLE: No, my son, I'll never bring
Myself to think him guilty of such a thing.
ORGON: How's that?
MADAME PERNELLE. The righteous always were maligned.
ORGON: Speak clearly, Mother. Say what's on your mind.
MADAME PERNELLE: I mean that I can smell a rat, my dear.   20
You know how everybody hates him, here.
ORGON: That has no bearing on the case at all.
MADAME PERNELLE: I told you a hundred times, when you were small,
That virtue in this world is hated ever;
Malicious men may die, but malice never.   25
ORGON: No doubt that's true, but how does it apply?
MADAME PERNELLE: They've turned you against him by a clever lie.
ORGON: I've told you, I was there and saw it done.
MADAME PERNELLE: Ah, slanderers will stop at nothing, Son.
ORGON: Mother, I'll lose my temper . . . For the last time,   30
I tell you I was witness to the crime.
MADAME PERNELLE: The tongues of spite are busy night and noon,
And to their venom no man is immune.
ORGON: You're talking nonsense. Can't you realize
I saw it; saw it; saw it with my eyes?   35
Saw, do you understand me? Must I shout it

Into your ears before you'll cease to doubt it?
MADAME PERNELLE: Appearances can deceive, my son. Dear me,
　　We cannot always judge by what we see.
ORGON: Drat! Drat!
MADAME PERNELLE: One often interprets things awry;   40
　　Good can seem evil to a suspicious eye.
ORGON: Was I to see his pawing at Elmire
　　As an act of charity?
MADAME PERNELLE:　　Till his guilt is clear,
　　A man deserves the benefit of the doubt.
　　You should have waited, to see how things turned out.   45
ORGON: Great God in Heaven, what more proof did I need?
　　Was I to sit there, watching, until he'd . . .
　　You drive me to the brink of impropriety.
MADAME PERNELLE: No, no, a man of such surpassing piety
　　Could not do such a thing. You cannot shake me.   50
　　I don't believe it, and you shall not make me.
ORGON: You vex me so that, if you weren't my mother,
　　I'd say to you . . . some dreadful thing or other.
DORINE: It's your turn now, Sir, not to be listened to;
　　You'd not trust us, and now she won't trust you.   55
CLÉANTE: My friends, we're wasting time which should be spent
　　In facing up to our predicament.
　　I fear that scoundrel's threats weren't made in sport.
DAMIS: Do you think he'd have the nerve to go to court?
ELMIRE: I'm sure he won't: they'd find it all too crude   60
　　A case of swindling and ingratitude.
CLÉANTE: Don't be too sure. He won't be at a loss
　　To give his claims a high and righteous gloss;
　　And clever rogues with far less valid cause
　　Have trapped their victims in a web of laws.   65
　　I say again that to antagonize
　　A man so strongly armed was most unwise.
ORGON: I know it; but the man's appalling cheek
　　Outraged me so, I couldn't control my pique.
CLÉANTE: I wish to Heaven that we could devise   70
　　Some truce between you, or some compromise.
ELMIRE: If I had known what cards he held, I'd not
　　Have roused his anger by my little plot.
ORGON: [*To* DORINE, *as* M. LOYAL *enters.*]
　　What is that fellow looking for? Who is he?
　　Go talk to him—and tell him that I'm busy.   75

SCENE 4

MONSIEUR LOYAL, MADAME PERNELLE, ORGON, DAMIS, MARIANE, DORINE,
ELMIRE, CLÉANTE

MONSIEUR LOYAL: Good day, dear sister. Kindly let me see
　　Your master.

DORINE: He's involved with company,
   And cannot be disturbed just now, I fear.
MONSIEUR LOYAL: I hate to intrude; but what has brought me here
   Will not disturb your master, in any event.   5
   Indeed, my news will make him most content.
DORINE: Your name?
MONSIEUR LOYAL: Just say that I bring greetings from
   Monsieur Tartuffe, on whose behalf I've come.
DORINE: [*To* ORGON.] Sir, he's a very gracious man, and bears
   A message from Tartuffe, which, he declares,   10
   Will make you most content.
CLÉANTE: Upon my word,
   I think this man had best be seen, and heard.
ORGON: Perhaps he has some settlement to suggest.
   How shall I treat him? What manner would be best?
CLÉANTE: Control your anger, and if he should mention   15
   Some fair adjustment, give him your full attention.
MONSIEUR LOYAL: Good health to you, good Sir. May Heaven confound
   Your enemies, and may your joys abound.
ORGON: [*Aside, to* CLÉANTE.] A gentle salutation: it confirms
   My guess that he is here to offer terms.   20
MONSIEUR LOYAL: I've always held your family most dear;
   I served your father, Sir, for many a year.
ORGON: Sir, I must ask your pardon; to my shame,
   I cannot now recall your face or name.
MONSIEUR LOYAL: Loyal's my name; I come from Normandy,   25
   And I'm a bailiff, in all modesty.
   For forty years, praise God, it's been my boast
   To serve with honor in that vital post,
   And I am here, Sir, if you will permit
   The liberty, to serve you with this writ . . .   30
ORGON: To—*what?*
MONSIEUR LOYAL: Now, please, Sir, let us have no friction:
   It's nothing but an order of eviction.
   You are to move your goods and family out
   And make way for new occupants, without
   Deferment or delay, and give the keys . . .   35
ORGON: I? Leave this house?
MONSIEUR LOYAL: Why yes, Sir, if you please.
   This house, Sir, from the cellar to the roof,
   Belongs now to the good Monsieur Tartuffe,
   And he is lord and master of your estate
   By virtue of a deed of present date,   40
   Drawn in due form, with clearest legal phrasing . . .
DAMIS: Your insolence is utterly amazing!
MONSIEUR LOYAL: Young man, my business here is not with you
   But with your wise and temperate father, who,
   Like every worthy citizen, stands in awe   45
   Of justice, and would never obstruct the law.

ORGON: But . . .

MONSIEUR LOYAL: Not for a million, Sir, would you rebel
　Against authority; I know that well.
　You'll not make trouble, Sir, or interfere
　With the execution of my duties here.   50

DAMIS: Someone may execute a smart tattoo
　On that black jacket[4] of yours, before you're through.

MONSIEUR LOYAL: Sir, bid your son be silent. I'd much regret
　Having to mention such a nasty threat
　Of violence, in writing my report.   55

DORINE: [*Aside.*] This man Loyal's a most disloyal sort!

MONSIEUR LOYAL: I love all men of upright character,
　And when I agreed to serve these papers, Sir,
　It was your feelings that I had in mind.
　I couldn't bear to see the case assigned   60
　To someone else, who might esteem you less
　And so subject you to unpleasantness.

ORGON: What's more unpleasant than telling a man to leave
　His house and home?

MONSIEUR LOYAL:　　　You'd like a short reprieve?
　If you desire it, Sir, I shall not press you,   65
　But wait until tomorrow to dispossess you.
　Splendid. I'll come and spend the night here, then,
　Most quietly, with half a score of men.
　For form's sake, you might bring me, just before
　You go to bed, the keys to the front door.   70
　My men, I promise, will be on their best
　Behavior, and will not disturb your rest.
　But bright and early, Sir, you must be quick
　And move out all your furniture, every stick:
　The men I've chosen are both young and strong,   75
　And with their help it shouldn't take you long.
　In short, I'll make things pleasant and convenient,
　And since I'm being so extremely lenient,
　Please show me, Sir, a like consideration,
　And give me your entire cooperation.   80

ORGON: [*Aside.*] I may be all but bankrupt, but I vow
　I'd give a hundred louis, here and now,
　Just for the pleasure of landing one good clout
　Right on the end of that complacent snout.

CLÉANTE: Careful; don't make things worse.

DAMIS:　　　　　　　　　　　　My bootsole itches   85
　To give that beggar a good kick in the breeches.

DORINE: Monsieur Loyal, I'd love to hear the whack
　Of a stout stick across your fine broad back.

---

4. In the original, *justaucorps à longues basques*, a close-fitting, long black coat with skirts, the customary dress of a bailiff.

MONSIEUR LOYAL: Take care: a woman too may go to jail if
  She uses threatening language to a bailiff.   90
CLÉANTE: Enough, enough, Sir. This must not go on.
  Give me that paper, please, and then begone.
MONSIEUR LOYAL: Well, *au revoir.* God give you all good cheer!
ORGON: May God confound you, and him who sent you here!

SCENE 5

ORGON, CLÉANTE, MARIANE, ELMIRE, MADAME PERNELLE, DORINE, DAMIS

ORGON: Now, Mother, was I right or not? This writ
  Should change your notion of Tartuffe a bit.
  Do you perceive his villainy at last?
MADAME PERNELLE: I'm thunderstruck. I'm utterly aghast.
DORINE: Oh, come, be fair. You mustn't take offense   5
  At this new proof of his benevolence.
  He's acting out of selfless love, I know.
  Material things enslave the soul, and so
  He kindly has arranged your liberation
  From all that might endanger your salvation.   10
ORGON: Will you not ever hold your tongue, you dunce?
CLÉANTE: Come, you must take some action, and at once.
ELMIRE: Go tell the world of the low trick he's tried.
  The deed of gift is surely nullified
  By such behavior, and public rage will not   15
  Permit the wretch to carry out his plot.

SCENE 6

VALÈRE, ORGON, CLÉPANTE, ELMIRE, MARIANE, MADAME PERNELLE,
            DAMIS, DORINE

VALÈRE: Sir, though I hate to bring you more bad news,
  Such is the danger that I cannot choose.
  A friend who is extremely close to me
  And knows my interest in your family
  Has, for my sake, presumed to violate   5
  The secrecy that's due to things of state,
  And sends me word that you are in a plight
  From which your one salvation lies in flight.
  That scoundrel who's imposed upon you so
  Denounced you to the King an hour ago   10
  And, as supporting evidence, displayed
  The strong-box of a certain renegade
  Whose secret papers, so he testified,
  You had disloyally agreed to hide.
  I don't know just what charges may be pressed,   15

But there's a warrant out for your arrest;
Tartuffe has been instructed, furthermore,
To guide the arresting officer to your door.
CLÉANTE: He's clearly done this to facilitate
His seizure of your house and your estate.   20
ORGON: That man, I must say, is a vicious beast!
VALÈRE: You can't afford to delay, Sir, in the least.
My carriage is outside, to take you hence;
This thousand louis should cover all expense.
Let's lose no time, or you shall be undone;   25
The sole defense, in this case, is to run.
I shall go with you all the way, and place you
In a safe refuge to which they'll never trace you.
ORGON: Alas, dear boy, I wish that I could show you
My gratitude for everything I owe you.   30
But now is not the time; I pray the Lord
That I may live to give you your reward.
Farewell, my dears; be careful . . .
CLÉANTE.   Brother, hurry.
We shall take care of things; you needn't worry.

SCENE 7

The OFFICER, TARTUFFE, VALÈRE, ORGON, ELMIRE, MARIANE,
MADAME PERNELLE, DORINE, CLÉANTE, DAMIS

TARTUFFE: Gently, Sir, gently; stay right where you are.
No need for haste; your lodging isn't far.
You're off to prison, by order of the Prince.
ORGON: This is the crowning blow, you wretch; and since
It means my total ruin and defeat,   5
Your villainy is now at last complete.
TARTUFFE: You needn't try to provoke me; it's no use.
Those who serve Heaven must expect abuse.
CLÉANTE: You are indeed most patient, sweet, and blameless.
DORINE: How he exploits the name of Heaven! It's shameless.   10
TARTUFFE: Your taunts and mockeries are all for naught;
To do my duty is my only thought.
MARIANE: Your love of duty is most meritorious,
And what you've done is little short of glorious.
TARTUFFE: All deeds are glorious, Madam, which obey   15
The sovereign prince who sent me here today.
ORGON: I rescued you when you were destitute;
Have you forgotten that, you thankless brute?
TARTUFFE: No, no, I well remember everything;
But my first duty is to serve my King.   20
That obligation is so paramount
That other claims, beside it, do not count;
And for it I would sacrifice my wife,
My family, my friend, or my own life.

ELMIRE: Hypocrite!
DORINE: All that we most revere, he uses   25
  To cloak his plots and camouflage his ruses.
CLÉANTE: If it is true that you are animated
  By pure and loyal zeal, as you have stated,
  Why was this zeal not roused until you'd sought
  To make Orgon a cuckold, and been caught?   30
  Why weren't you moved to give your evidence
  Until your outraged host had driven you hence?
  I shan't say that the gift of all his treasure
  Ought to have damped your zeal in any measure;
  But if he is a traitor, as you declare,   35
  How could you condescend to be his heir?
TARTUFFE: [*To the* OFFICER.]
  Sir, spare me all this clamor; it's growing shrill.
  Please carry out your orders, if you will.
OFFICER:[5] Yes, I've delayed too long, Sir. Thank you kindly.
  You're just the proper person to remind me.   40
  Come, you are off to join the other boarders
  In the King's prison, according to his orders.
TARTUFFE: Who? I, Sir?
OFFICER: Yes.
TARTUFFE: To prison? This can't be true!
OFFICER: I owe an explanation, but not to you.
  [*To* ORGON.] Sir, all is well; rest easy, and be grateful.   45
  We serve a Prince to whom all sham is hateful,
  A Prince who sees into our inmost hearts,
  And can't be fooled by any trickster's arts.
  His royal soul, though generous and human,
  Views all things with discernment and acumen;   50
  His sovereign reason is not lightly swayed,
  And all his judgments are discreetly weighed.
  He honors righteous men of every kind,
  And yet his zeal for virtue is not blind,
  Nor does his love of piety numb his wits   55
  And make him tolerant of hypocrites.
  'Twas hardly likely that this man could cozen
  A King who's foiled such liars by the dozen.
  With one keen glance, the King perceived the whole
  Perverseness and corruption of his soul,   60
  And thus high Heaven's justice was displayed:
  Betraying you, the rogue stood self-betrayed.
  The King soon recognized Tartuffe as one
  Notorious by another name, who'd done
  So many vicious crimes that one could fill   65
  Ten volumes with them, and be writing still.
  But to be brief: our sovereign was appalled

---

5. In the original, *un exempt*. He would actually have been a gentleman from the king's personal bodyguard with the rank of lieutenant colonel or "master of the camp."

By this man's treachery toward you, which he called
The last, worst villainy of a vile career,
And bade me follow the impostor here   70
To see how gross his impudence could be,
And force him to restore your property.
Your private papers, by the King's command,
I hereby seize and give into your hand.
The King, by royal order, invalidates   75
The deed which gave this rascal your estates,
And pardons, furthermore, your grave offense
In harboring an exile's documents.
By these decrees, our Prince rewards you for
Your loyal deeds in the late civil war,[6]   80
And shows how heartfelt is his satisfaction
In recompensing any worthy action,
How much he prizes merit, and how he makes
More of men's virtues than of their mistakes.
DORINE: Heaven be praised!
MADAME PERNELLE.   I breathe again, at last.   85
ELMIRE: We're safe.
MARIANE: I can't believe the danger's past.
ORGON: [*To* TARTUFFE.] Well, traitor, now you see . . .
CLÉANTE.   Ah, brother, please
Let's not descend to such indignities.
Leave the poor wretch to his unhappy fate,
And don't say anything to aggravate   90
His present woes; but rather hope that he
Will soon embrace an honest piety,
And mend his ways, and by a true repentance
Move our just King to moderate his sentence.
Meanwhile, go kneel before your sovereign's throne   95
And thank him for the mercies he has shown.
ORGON: Well said: let's go at once and, gladly kneeling,
Express the gratitude which all are feeling.
Then, when that first great duty has been done,
We'll turn with pleasure to a second one,   100
And give Valère, whose love has proven so true,
The wedded happiness which is his due.

6. A reference to Orgon's role in supporting the king during the *Frondes*.

JEAN RACINE
1639–1699

Jean Racine's capacity to communicate the full intensity of passion in tragedies marked by their formal decorum and their elevated tone gave him immediate and lasting fame among French dramatists. He brings to material adapted from classic texts an immediacy of psychological insight to which twentieth-century audiences readily respond.

Born into the family of a government official in the Valois district, eighty miles from Paris, Racine attended the College de Beauvais. Later (1655–59) he studied in the Jansenist center of Port-Royal. (Jansenism, a strict Catholic movement emphasizing moral self-examination and severely controlled conduct, exercised a profound influence on Racine.) In 1660, encouraged by the poet Jean de la Fontaine, Racine came to Paris, where his early plays failed, driving him to a period of seclusion in Provence. When he returned to Paris in 1663, however, the court and the nobility patronized him, and he rapidly developed a reputation as a major playwright. In 1677 he left Paris and returned to Port-Royal, an environment appropriate to his increasing interest in religious thought. He married Catherine de Romanet, with whom he had seven children, most of whom became nuns or priests. Remaining in the country, he wrote history, made short trips to Paris, and traveled as historiographer with Louis XIV's campaigns. Buried at Port-Royal, his body was exhumed in 1711 and reburied next to Pascal at the church of St. Étienne-du-Mont in Paris.

Only one of Racine's twelve plays, an early comedy, deviated from the tragic mode. His first tragedies imitated the work of his contemporary Pierre Corneille; later he chose biblical and classical models. *Phaedra* (1677) adapts, with new emphasis, the action of Euripides' *Hippolytus*, making the guilty woman rather than the relatively passive man the protagonist and using the highly charged sexual situation between the two to generate intense psychological drama. To twentieth-century readers, the play's most immediately obvious aspect may be its conventional formalities: long declamatory speeches, stylized exchanges in compressed half lines, the artificiality of conveying such complicated relationships and histories through the action of a single day. Such devices, however—which would have seemed as artificial to seventeenth-century audiences as they do to us, although more familiar—intensify the impact of the central characters' anguish and their desperate attempts to deal with it. If the play's surface is formal, its depths seethe with passion.

Passion, of course, is the subject of *Phaedra*. The conflict between reason and passion that preoccupied many thinkers in the late seventeenth and early eighteenth centuries—that conflict resolved on the side of reason at such great cost for the Princess of Clèves—here plays itself out with stark urgency. Passion triumphs, in *Phaedra*, over all principles of control, bringing death to the two central characters and misery to their survivors. As in Greek tragedy, although by rather different means, the reader feels not only the self-destructiveness of the human psyche but the pathos and the heroism of the doomed effort to transcend the limits of the given.

The play opens not with Phaedra herself but with Hippolytus, meditating about his heroic father, Theseus. Like Molière, Racine uses the family as microcosm of larger social orders, but the intense conflicts that throb beneath the surface in many real-life families here undergo no comic transformation. Hippolytus has his own problems, quite apart from Phaedra. Blessed and burdened with a larger-than-life father, he must choose whether to try to imitate that father or to seek other ways of being a man. "I sucked that pride which seems so strange to you / From an Amazonian mother," he tells his friend Theramenes, alluding to the "austere and proud / Persuasions" that have prevented him from feeling interest in any woman. But matters cannot remain so simple. Theseus has distinguished himself in two ways: by heroic womanizing (he leaves a trail of women behind him wherever he goes) and by heroic action, the conquering and destruction of monsters human and inhuman. As the play opens, Hippolytus acknowledges in himself the first incursions of love. No longer can his adolescent defense, his refusal of any resemblance to his father, serve him. When Theseus returns, Hippolytus will beg permission to seek his own heroism:

> Before you'd lived as long as I have done,
> More than one tyrant, monsters more than one
> Had felt your strength of arm, your sword's keen blade . . .
> Let me at long last show my courage.

He wants, he says, even by death to "prove to all the world I was your son." By the time he makes this plea, however, his innocent desire to prove his manhood, to declare his separateness from and worthiness of his father, has been overwhelmed by darker forces.

Phaedra's impulses are less innocent—less "natural," she suggests. In a poignant passage, she imagines Hippolytus and his youthful beloved, Aricia, expressing their love in a natural setting, themselves a part of the natural world. She understands her own sin as an internal revolution of feeling against control; she speaks of desperately seeking her "lost reason" in the entrails of sacrifices she makes to Venus, trying to avert her fate. Never does she excuse herself, never does she believe herself justified in loving the son of the man who kidnapped her into marriage. When Theseus is thought dead, Phaedra declares herself unworthy to rule a nation because she cannot rule herself. Yet such moral awareness fails to help her: knowing her sin, she continues to enact it, at least in feeling. The play evokes the full torment of such experience.

As for powerful Theseus, conqueror of women, defier of the supernatural, ally of Neptune—this kingly figure returns to find himself powerless at home. The son and wife who by social convention exist in utter subordination to him turn into enemies he has no capacity to master. First his wife's nurse tells him that his son has attempted to seduce Phaedra. The rivalry of sons and fathers lies deep: if sons fear they can never equal their fathers, fathers fear that the young necessarily overcome the old. Theseus believes the nurse's bare assertion, unsupported by substantial evidence. He banishes his son and invokes Neptune's power to destroy him. Then Aricia's hints lead him to suspect his wife, who confesses her own emotional sin while already on the verge of self-inflicted death. Theseus remains alone, bereft, his tyrannical impulse now devoid of domestic object. His own passions, too quickly fired—jealous possessiveness of his wife, jealous rivalry with his son—have deprived him of two beings he loved.

The play provides no villains. Phaedra, in some versions of the story a monster of lust, here becomes a woman struggling against her nature, as profoundly committed to standards of control as to the violent feelings that overthrow them. Hippolytus, in the process of self-discovery, at a delicate balance point between youth and maturity, cannot protect himself against the alternations of closely linked love and hate in a woman whose passions, and whose self-awareness, far exceed his. Theseus, in the ignorance of success, fails in comprehension, not understanding himself, his wife, or his son. All three exemplify the pathos and the dignity of the human struggle to be human.

Phaedra dies with the word *purity* on her lips, seeking self-purification in death, the only course now possible to her. Hippolytus dies in the beauty of his youth, deprived of age's suffering and fulfillment. Theseus lives to try once more to rule adequately, perhaps chastened by suffering into greater awareness. The names of the Greek gods survive in this drama: Aphrodite torments Phaedra, Neptune serves Theseus's impetuous will. But the gods now function as projections of human passion: Phaedra's sexual lust, Theseus's lust for power. Phaedra's torment suggests a Christian effort at purification, a Christian ideal of self-denial. The drama, in Racine's handling of the ancient story, projects on a giant screen conflicts all men and women undergo, the surge of feeling warring with the ideal of self-restraint.

By concentrating the play of passions within a small family group and a confined space of time, while recalling connections between the characters' feelings and historical events that lie behind them; by giving Theseus and Phaedra heroic dignity and stature; by linking this family with the fate of nations, Racine forces his readers to feel the intensity and the large significance of feelings and happenings that might in other treatments seem merely sordid. He gives his characters timeless reality—speaking to his time, and to ours.

To translate Racine into English involves particularly difficult problems, since the French Alexandrine couplet, composed of twelve-syllable lines, does not adapt naturally to English verse. Richard Wilbur's version uses the common English pentameter, the ten-syllable line, to construct fluent, pointed, and dignified verse. His couplets by their formal elegance remind the reader steadily of the discipline that the play embodies and celebrates.

A useful biography of Racine is G. Brereton, *Jean Racine: A Critical Biography* (1951), which combines biography with literary criticism. Valuable critical insight is provided by O. de Mourgues, *Racine: Or, The Triumph of Relevance* (1967), and P. J. Yarrow, *Racine* (1978). A treatment of French tragic drama that includes extensive and valuable material on Racine is Albert Cook, *French Tragedy: The Power of Enactment* (1981). For an interpretation that includes stage history of Racine's plays, see D. Maskell, *Racine: A Theatrical Reading* (1991).

PRONOUNCING GLOSSARY

The following list uses common English syllables and stress accents to provide rough equivalents of selected words whose pronunciation may be unfamiliar to the general reader.

Acheron: *ah-ker-awn'*

Ariadne: *ah-ree-ahd'-ne*

Aricia: *ah-ree'-sha*

Cocytus: *cohs-i'-tuhs*

Euripides: *yoo-rip'-uh-deez*

Hippolytus: *hip-pol'-i-tuhs*

Ismene: *is-mee'-ne*

Medea: *me-dee'-a*

Mycenae: *mai-see'-nee*

Oenone: *ee-noh'-ne*

Panope: *pah'-no-pe*

Pasiphaë: *pa-si'-fa-ee*

Peirithous: *pay-rith'-oo-uhs*

Peloponnesus: *pel-luh-puh-nee'-suhs*

Phaedra: *fee'-drah*

Scythia: *sai'-thee-uh*

Taenarus: *ten'-a-ruhs*

Theramenes: *thee-ram'-uh-neez*

Theseus: *thee'-see-uhs*

Troezen: *troh'-zen*

Phaedra[1]

CHARACTERS

THESEUS, *son of Aegeus, King of Athens*

PHAEDRA, *wife of Theseus, daughter of Minos and Pasiphaë*

HIPPOLYTUS, *son of Theseus and Antiope, Queen of the Amazons*

ARICIA, *princess of the blood royal of Athens*

THERAMENES, *Hippolytus' tutor*

OENONE, *Phaedra's nurse and confidante*

ISMENE, *Aricia's confidante*

PANOPE, *lady-in-waiting to Phaedra*

GUARDS

---

1. Translated by Richard Wilbur.

The action takes place within and without a palace at Troezen, a town in the Peloponnesus.

Act I

SCENE 1

HIPPOLYTUS, THERAMENES

HIPPOLYTUS: No, dear Theramenes, I've too long delayed
In pleasant Troezen; my decision's made.
I'm off; in my anxiety, I commence
To tax myself with shameful indolence.
My father has been gone six months and more,   5
And yet I do not know what distant shore
Now hides him, or what trials he now may bear.
THERAMENES: You'll go in search of him, my lord? But where?
Already, to appease your fears, I've plied
The seas which lie on Corinth's either side;   10
I've asked for Theseus among tribes who dwell
Where Acheron[2] goes plunging into Hell;
Elis I've searched and, from Taenarus[3] bound,
Reached even that sea where Icarus[4] was drowned.
In what fresh hope, in what unthought-of places,   15
Do you set out to find your father's traces?
Who knows, indeed, if he wants the truth about
His long, mysterious absence to come out,
And whether, while we tremble for him, he's
Not fondling some new conquest at his ease   20
And planning to deceive her like the rest? . . .
HIPPOLYTUS: Enough, Theramenes. In King Theseus' breast,
The foolish fires of youth have ceased to burn;
No tawdry dalliance hinders his return.
Phaedra need fear no rivals now; the King   25
Long since, for her sake, ceased philandering.
I go then, out of duty—and as a way
To flee a place in which I dare not stay.
THERAMENES: Since when, my lord, have you begun to fear
This peaceful place your childhood held so dear,   30
And which I've often known you to prefer
To Athens' court, with all its pomp and stir?
What danger or affliction drives you hence?
HIPPOLYTUS: Those happy times are gone. All's altered since
The Gods dispatched to us across the sea   35
The child of Minos and Pasiphaë.[5]

---

2. A river that flows into Hades; across it Charon ferried the dead.   3. A point of land in southern Greece, near Sparta. Elis is a district of Greece on the west coast of the Peloponnesus.   4. Son of Daedalus. Escaping from Crete by means of wings made by his father, Icarus flew so high that the sun melted the wax holding his wings together, and he fell to his death.   5. Phaedra was the daughter of King Minos of Crete and of Pasiphaë, sister to Circe. Enamored of a white bull sent by Poseidon, Pasiphaë

THERAMENES: Ah. Then it's Phaedra's presence in this place
  That weighs on you. She'd hardly seen your face
  When, as the King's new consort, she required
  Your banishment, and got what she desired.   40
  But now her hatred for you, once so great,
  Has vanished, or has cooled, at any rate.
  And why, my lord, should you feel threatened by
  A dying woman who desires to die?
  Sick unto death—with what, she will not say,   45
  Weary of life and of the light of day,
  Could Phaedra plot to do you any harm?
HIPPOLYTUS: Her vain hostility gives me no alarm.
  It is, I own, another enemy.
  The young Aricia, from whom I flee,   50
  Last of a line which sought to overthrow
  Our house.
THERAMENES: What! Will you also be her foe?
  That gentle maiden, though of Pallas' line,
  Had no part in her brothers' base design.[6]
  If she is guiltless, why should you hate her, Sir?   55
HIPPOLYTUS: I would not flee her if I hated her.
THERAMENES: Dare I surmise, then, why you're leaving us?
  Are you no longer that Hippolytus
  Who spurned love's dictates and refused with scorn
  The yoke which Theseus has so often borne?   60
  Has Venus, long offended by your pride,
  Contrived to see her Theseus justified
  By making you confess her power divine
  And bow, like other men, before her shrine?
  Are you in love, Sir?
HIPPOLYTUS: What do you mean, dear man   65
  You who have known me since my life began?
  How can you wish that my austere and proud
  Persuasions be so basely disvowed?
  I sucked that pride which seems so strange to you
  From an Amazonian mother,[7] and when I grew   70
  To riper years, and knew myself, I thought
  My given nature to be nobly wrought.
  You then, devoted friend, instructed me
  In all my father's brilliant history,
  And you recall how glowingly I heard   75
  His exploits, how I hung on every word
  As you portrayed a sire whose deeds appease
  Men's longing for another Hercules—
  Those monsters slain, those brigands all undone,

---

consequently gave birth to the Minotaur, the Cretan monster later killed by Theseus. Phaedra was thus half-sister to the Minotaur.   6. Theseus killed all fifty sons of Pallas because they threatened his kingdom of Athens. Aricia is Pallas's daughter.   7. Hippolytus's mother was Antiope, sister of Hippolyta, queen of the Amazons.

Procrustes, Sciron, Sinis, Cercyon,—   80
The Epidaurian giant's scattered bones,
The Minotaur's foul blood on Cretan stones!
But when you told me of less glorious feats,
His far-flung chain of amorous deceits,
Helen of Sparta[8] kidnapped as a maid;   85
Sad Periboea[9] in Salamis betrayed;
Others, whose very names escape him now,
Too-trusting hearts, deceived by sigh and vow;
Wronged Ariadne,[1] telling the rocks her moan,
Phaedra abducted, though to grace a throne,—   90
You know how, loathing stories of that sort,
I begged you oftentimes to cut them short,
And wished posterity might never hear
The worser half of Theseus' great career.
Shall I, in my turn, be subjected so   95
To passion, by the Gods be brought so low—
The more disgraced because I cannot claim
Such honors as redeem King Theseus' name,
And have not, by the blood of monsters, won
The right to trespass as my sire has done?   100
And even if my pride laid down its arms,
Could I surrender to Aricia's charms?
Would not my wayward passions heed the ban
Forbidding her to me, or any man?
The King's no friend to her, and has decreed   105
That she not keep alive her brothers' seed;
Fearing some new shoot from their guilty stem,
He wants her death to be the end of them;
For her, the nuptial torch shall never blaze;
He's doomed her to be single all her days.   110
Shall I take up her cause then, brave his rage,
Set a rebellious pattern for the age,
Commit my youth to love's delirium . . . ?
THERAMENES: Ah, Sir, if love's appointed hour has come,
It's vain to reason; Heaven will not hear.   115
What Theseus bans, he makes you hold more dear.
His hate for her but stirs your flames the more,
And lends new grace to her whom you adore.
Why fear, my lord, a love that's true and chaste?
Of what's so sweet, will you not dare to taste?   120
Shall timid scruples make your blood congeal?
What Hercules once felt, may you not feel?
What hearts has Venus' power failed to sway?

---

8. Daughter of Zeus and Leda, later the wife of Menelaus of Sparta (and the cause of the Trojan War). In her girlhood she was abducted by Theseus and Peirithoüs; her brothers rescued her and brought her back home.   9. The mother of Ajax, one of the women Theseus seduced and abandoned.   1. Phaedra's sister, who was abandoned by Theseus on the island of Naxos after she rescued him from the Minotaur.

Where would you be, who strive with her today,
If fierce Antiope had not grown tame[2]   125
And loved king Theseus with a virtuous flame?
But come, my lord, why posture and debate?
Admit that you have changed, and that of late
You're seen less often, in your lonely pride,
Racing your chariot by the oceanside,   130
Or deftly using Neptune's[3] art to train
Some charger to obey the curb and rein.
The woods less often echo to our cries.
A secret fire burns in your heavy eyes.
No question of it: you're sick with love, you feel   135
A wasting passion which you would conceal.
Has fair Aricia wakened your desire?
HIPPOLYTUS: I'm off, Theramenes, to find my sire.
THERAMENES: Will you not see the Queen before you go,
My lord?
HIPPOLYTUS:
I mean to. You may tell her so.   140
Duty requires it of me. Ah, but here's
Her dear Oenone; what new grief prompts her tears?

SCENE 2

HIPPOLYTUS, OENONE, THERAMENES

OENONE: Alas, my lord, what grief could equal mine?
The Queen has gone into a swift decline.
I nurse her, tend her day and night, but she
Is dying of some nameless malady.
Disorder rules within her heart and head.   5
A restless pain has dragged her from her bed;
She longs to see the light; but in her keen
Distress she is unwilling to be seen. . . .
She's coming.
HIPPOLYTUS: I understand, and I shall go.
My hated face would but increase her woe.   10

SCENE 3

PHAEDRA, OENONE

PHAEDRA: Let's go no farther; stay, Oenone dear.
I'm faint; my strength abandons me, I fear.
My eyes are blinded by the glare of day,
And now I feel my trembling knees give way.
Alas!
[She sits.]

---

2. As an Amazon, Hippolytus's mother, Antiope, was committed to chastity.   3. Or Poseidon, god of
the sea, who was also identified with Hippios, god of horses.

OENONE: O Gods, abate our misery!   5
PHAEDRA: These veils, these baubles, how they burden me!
   What meddling hand has twined my hair, and made
   Upon my brow so intricate a braid?
   All things oppress me, vex me, do me ill.
OENONE: Her wishes war against each other still.   10
   'Twas you who, full of self-reproach, just now
   Insisted that our hands adorn your brow;
   You who called back your strength so that you might
   Come forth again and once more see the light.
   Yet, seeing it, you all but turn and flee,   15
   Hating the light which you came forth to see.
PHAEDRA: Founder of our sad race, bright god of fire,
   You whom my mother dared to boast her sire,[4]
   Who blush perhaps to see my wretched case,
   For the last time, O Sun, I see your face.   20
OENONE: Can't you shake off that morbid wish? Must I
   Forever hear you laying plans to die?
   What is this pact with death which you have made?
PHAEDRA: Oh, to be sitting in the woods' deep shade!
   When shall I witness, through a golden wrack   25
   Of dust, a chariot flying down the track?
OENONE: What, Madam?
PHAEDRA: Where am I? Madness! What did I say?
   Where have I let my hankering senses stray?
   The Gods have robbed me of my wits. A rush
   Of shame, Oenone, causes me to blush.   30
   I make my guilty torments all too plain.
   My eyes, despite me, fill with tears of pain.
OENONE: If you must blush, then blush for your perverse
   Silence, which only makes your sickness worse.
   Spurning our care, and deaf to all we say—   35
   Is it your cruel design to die this way?
   What madness dooms your life in middle course?
   What spell, what poison has dried up its source?
   Three times the night has overrun the skies
   Since sleep last visited your hollow eyes,   40
   And thrice the day has made dim night retreat
   Since you, though starving, have refused to eat.
   What frightful evil does your heart intend?
   What right have you to plot your own life's end?
   You thereby wrong the Gods who authored you;   45
   Betray the spouse to whom your faith is due;
   Betray your children by the selfsame stroke,
   And thrust their necks beneath a heavy yoke.
   Yes, on the day their mother's life is done,
   Proud hopes will stir in someone else's son—   50

---

4. Helios, the sun god, was the father of Phaedra's mother, Pasiphaë.

Your foe, the foe of all your lineage, whom
An Amazon once carried in her womb:
Hippolytus . . .
PHAEDRA: Gods!
OENONE: My words strike home at last.
PHAEDRA: Oh, wretched woman, what was that name which passed
    Your lips?
OENONE: Ah, now you're roused to anger. Good.   55
    That name has made you shudder, as it should.
    Live, then. Let love and duty fire your spirit.
    Live, lest a Scythian's[5] son should disinherit
    Your children, lest he crush the noblest fruit
    Of Greece and of the Gods beneath his boot.   60
    But lose no time; each moment now could cost
    Your life; retrieve the strength that you have lost,
    While still your feeble fires, which sink so low,
    Smoulder and may be fanned into a glow.
PHAEDRA: Alas, my guilty flame has burnt too long.   65
OENONE: Come, what remorse can flay you so? What wrong
    Can you have done to be so crushed with guilt?
    There is no innocent blood your hands have spilt.
PHAEDRA: My hands, thank Heaven, are guiltless, as you say.
    Gods! That my heart were innocent as they!   70
OENONE: What fearful notion can your thoughts have bred
    So that your heart still shrinks from it in dread?
PHAEDRA: I've said enough, Oenone. Spare me the rest.
    I die, to keep that horror unconfessed.
OENONE: Then die, and keep your heartless silence, do;   75
    But someone else must close your eyes for you.
    Although your flickering life has all but fled,
    I shall go down before you to the dead.
    There are a thousand roads that travel there;
    I'll choose the shortest, in my just despair.   80
    O cruel mistress! When have I failed or grieved you?
    Remember: at your birth, these arms received you.
    For you I left my country, children, kin:
    Is this the prize my faithfulness should win?
PHAEDRA: What can you gain by this? Why rant and scold?   85
    You'd shake with terror if the truth were told.
OENONE: Great Gods! What words could match the terror I
    Must daily suffer as I watch you die?
PHAEDRA: When you have learnt my crime, my fate, my shame,
    I'll die no less, but with a guiltier name.   90
OENONE: My lady, by the tears which stain my face,
    And by your trembling knees which I embrace,
    Enlighten me; deliver me from doubt.
PHAEDRA: You've asked it. Rise.

---

5. Scythia, home of the Amazons, was for the Greeks associated with barbarians.

OENONE: I'm listening. Come, speak out.
PHAEDRA: O Gods! What shall I say to her? Where shall I start?   95
OENONE: Speak, speak. Your hesitations wound my heart.
PHAEDRA: Alas, how Venus hates us! As Love's thrall,
  Into what vileness did my mother fall!
OENONE: Dear Queen, forget it; to the end of time
  Let silence shroud the memory of that crime.   100
PHAEDRA: O sister Ariadne! Through love, once more,
  You died abandoned on a barren shore![6]
OENONE: Madame, what's this? What anguish makes you trace
  So bitterly the tale of all your race?
PHAEDRA: And now, since Venus wills it, I must pine   105
  And die, the last of our accursèd line.
OENONE: You are in love?
PHAEDRA: I feel love's raging thirst.
OENONE: For whom?
PHAEDRA: Of all dire things, now hear the worst.
  I love . . . From that dread name I shrink, undone;
  I love . . .
OENONE: Whom?
PHAEDRA: Think of a Scythian woman's son,   110
  A prince I long ill-used and heaped with blame.
OENONE: Hippolytus? Gods!
PHAEDRA: 'Twas you who spoke his name.
OENONE: Just Heaven! All my blood begins to freeze.
  O crime, despair, most curst of families!
  Why did we voyage to this ill-starred land   115
  And set our feet upon its treacherous strand?
PHAEDRA: My ills began far earlier. Scarcely had I
  Pledged with Aegeus' son our marriage-tie,
  Secure in that sweet joy a bride should know,
  When I, in Athens, met my haughty foe.   120
  I stared, I blushed, I paled, beholding him;
  A sudden turmoil set my mind aswim;
  My eyes no longer saw, my lips were dumb;
  My body burned, and yet was cold and numb.
  I knew myself possessed by Venus, whose   125
  Fierce flames torment the quarry she pursues.
  I thought to appease her then by constant prayer,
  And built for her a temple, decked with care.
  I made continual sacrifice, and sought
  In entrails[7] for a spirit less distraught—   130
  But what could cure a lovesick soul like mine?
  In vain my hands burnt incense at her shrine:
  Though I invoked the Goddess' name, 'twas he
  I worshipped; I saw his image constantly,
  And even as I fed the altar's flame   135

---

6. Ariadne died on Naxos after Theseus's desertion of her.   7. Examining the entrails of an animal
sacrifice was a means of prophecy.

Made offering to a god I dared not name.
I shunned him; but—O horror and disgrace!—
My eyes beheld him in his father's face.
At last I knew that I must act, must urge
Myself, despite myself, to be his scourge.   140
To rid me of the foe I loved, I feigned
A harsh stepmother's malice, and obtained
By ceaseless cries my wish that he be sent
From home and father into banishment.
I breathed once more, Oenone; once he was gone,   145
My blameless days could flow more smoothly on.
I hid my grief, was faithful to my spouse,
And reared the offspring of our luckless vows.
Ah, mocking Fate! What use was all my care?
Brought by my spouse himself to Troezen, there   150
I yet again beheld my exiled foe:
My unhealed wound began once more to flow.
Love hides no longer in these veins, at bay:
Great Venus fastens on her helpless prey.
I look with horror on my crime; I hate   155
My life; my passion I abominate.
I hoped by death to keep my honor bright,
And hide so dark a flame from day's pure light;
Yet, yielding to your tearful argument,
I've told you all; of that I'll not repent   160
Provided you do not, as death draws near,
Pour more unjust reproaches in my ear,
Or seek once more in vain to fan a fire
Which flickers and is ready to expire.

SCENE 4

PHAEDRA, OENONE, PANOPE

PANOPE: Madam, there's grievous news which I'd withhold
If I were able; but it must be told.
Death's claimed your lord, who feared no other foe—
Of which great loss you are the last to know.
OENONE: You tell us, Panope . . . ?
PANOPE: That the Queen in vain   5
Prays for her Theseus to return again;
That mariners have come to port, from whom
Hippolytus has learned his father's doom.
PHAEDRA: Gods!
PANOPE: Who'll succeed him, Athens can't agree.
The Prince your son commands much loyalty,   10
My lady; yet, despite their country's laws,[8]
Some make the alien woman's son their cause;

---

8. Athenian law made the son of an Athenian and a non-Greek woman illegitimate. Hippolytus's mother was Antiope the Amazon. It is not clear why Phaedra's children are not similarly classified.

Some plot, they say, to put in Theseus' place
Aricia, the last of Pallas' race.
Of both these threats I thought that you should know.   15
Hippolytus has rigged his ship to go,
And if, in Athens' ferment, he appeared,
The fickle mob might back him, it is feared.
OENONE: Enough. The Queen has heard you. She'll give thought
To these momentous tidings you have brought.   20

SCENE 5

PHAEDRA, OENONE

OENONE: Mistress, I'd ceased to urge you not to die;
I thought to follow you to the grave, since my
Dissuasions had no longer any force:
But this dark news prescribes a change of course.
Your destiny now wears a different face: 5
The King is dead, and you must take his place.
He leaves a son who needs your sheltering wing—
A slave without you; if you live, a king.
Who else will soothe his orphan sorrows, pray?
If you are dead, who'll wipe his tears away?   10
His innocent cries, borne up to Heaven, will make
The Gods, his forebears, curse you for his sake.
Live, then: there's nothing now you're guilty of.
Your love's become like any other love.
With Theseus' death, those bonds exist no more   15
Which made your passion something to abhor.
Hippolytus need no longer cause you fear;
Seeing him now, your conscience can be clear.
Perhaps, convinced that you're his bitter foe,
He means to lead the rebels. Make him know   20
His error; win him over; stay his hand.
He's king, by right, of Troezen's pleasant land;
But as for bright Minerva's[9] citadel,
It is your son's by law, as he knows well.
You should, indeed, join forces, you and he: 25
Aricia is your common enemy.
PHAEDRA: So be it. By your advice I shall be led;
I'll live, if I can come back from the dead,
And if my mother-love still has the power
To rouse my weakened spirits in this hour.   30

---

9. The Greek goddess Athene, protector of Athens.

Act II

SCENE 1

ARICIA, ISMENE

ARICIA: Hippolytus asks to see me? Can this be?
　He seeks me out to take his leave of me?
　There's no mistake, Ismene?
ISMENE:　　　　　　　　　Indeed, there's not.
　This shows how Theseus' death has changed your lot.
　Expect now to receive from every side　　　　　　　5
　The homage which, through him, you've been denied.
　At last, Aricia rules her destiny;
　Soon, at her feet, all Greece shall bend the knee.
ARICIA: This is no doubtful rumor, then? I've shed
　The bonds of slavery? My oppressor's dead?　　　　10
ISMENE: The Gods relent, my lady. It is so.
　Theseus has joined your brothers' shades below.
ARICIA: And by what mishap did he come to grief?
ISMENE: The tales are many, and they strain belief.
　Some say that he, abducting from her home　　　　15
　A new beloved, was swallowed by the foam.
　It's even thought, as many tongues now tell,
　That, faring with Pirithoüs down to Hell,[1]
　He walked alive amid the dusky ranks
　Of souls, and saw Cocytus'[2] dismal banks,　　　　20
　But found himself a prisoner in that stern
　Domain from which no mortal can return.
ARICIA: Shall I believe that, while he still draws breath,
　A man can penetrate the realms of death?
　What spell could lure him to that fearsome tract?　25
ISMENE: Theseus is dead. You, only, doubt the fact.
　All Athens grieves; the news was scarcely known
　When Troezen raised Hippolytus to its throne.
　Here in this palace, trembling for her son,
　Phaedra confers on what must now be done.　　　　30
ARICIA: You think Hippolytus will be more kind
　Than Theseus was to me, that he'll unbind
　My chains, and show me pity?
ISMENE:　　　　　　　Madam, I do.
ARICIA: Isn't the man's cold nature known to you?
　What makes you think that, scorning women, he　　35
　Will yet show pity and respect to me?
　He long has shunned us, and as you well know
　Haunts just those places where we do not go.
ISMENE: He's called, I know, the most austere of men,

---

1. Theseus went to Hades with Pentithoüs, king of the Lapiths—with whom he had earlier abducted Helen—to help his friend steal Persephone. Hercules freed Theseus, whom the god Hades had imprisoned, but could not free Pentithoüs, who was later killed.　　2. River in Hades, tributary to Acheron.

But I have seen him in your presence, when,   40
Intrigued by his repute, I thought to observe
His celebrated pride and cold reserve.
His manner contradicted all I'd heard:
At your first glance, I saw him flushed and stirred.
His eyes, already full of languor, tried   45
To leave your face, but could not turn aside.
He has, though love's a thing he may despise,
If not a lover's tongue, a lover's eyes.
ARICIA: Ismene, how your words delight my ear!
Even if baseless, they are sweet to hear.   50
O you who know me, can you believe of me,
Sad plaything of a ruthless destiny,
Forever fed on tears and bitterness,
That love could touch me, and its dear distress?
Last offspring of that king whom Earth once bore,[3]   55
I only have escaped the rage of war.
I lost six brothers, young and fresh as May,
In whom the hopes of our great lineage lay:
The sharp sword reaped them all; Earth, soaked and red,
Drank sadly what Erectheus' heirs had shed.   60
You know that, since their death, a harsh decree
Forbids all Greeks to pay their court to me,
Lest, through my progeny, I should revive
My brothers' ashes, and keep their cause alive.
But you know too with what disdain I bore   65
The ban of our suspicious conqueror.
You know how I, a lifelong enemy
Of love, gave thanks for Theseus' tyranny,
Since he forbade what I was glad to shun.
But then . . . but then I had not seen his son.   70
Not that my eyes alone, charmed by his grace,
Have made me love him for his form or face,
Mere natural gifts for which he seems to care
But little, or of which he's unaware.
I find in him far nobler gifts than these—   75
His father's strengths, without his frailties.
I love, I own, a heart that's never bowed
Beneath Love's yoke, but stayed aloof and proud.
Small glory Phaedra gained from Theseus' sighs!
More proud than she, I spurn the easy prize   80
Of love-words said a thousand times before,
And of a heart that's like an open door.
Ah, but to move a heart that's firm as stone,
To teach it pangs which it has never known,
To bind my baffled captive in a chain   85
Against whose sweet constraint he strives in vain:

---

3. Erectheus, their ancestor, son of Earth and reared by Athene.

There's what excites me in Hippolytus; he's
A harder conquest than was Hercules,
Whose heart, so often vanquished and inflamed,
Less honored those by whom he had been tamed.　90
But, dear Ismene, how rashly I have talked!
My hopes may all too easily be balked,
And I may humbly grieve in future days
Because of that same pride which now I praise.
Of fortune can it be . . . ?

ISMENE: You'll shortly learn;　95
He's coming.

SCENE 2

HIPPOLYTUS, ARICIA, ISMENE

HIPPOLYTUS: Madam, I felt, ere leaving here,
That I should make your altered fortunes clear.
My sire is dead. My fears divined, alas,
By his long absence, what had come to pass.
Death only, ending all his feats and frays,　5
Could hide him from the world so many days.
The Gods have yielded to destroying Fate
Hercules' heir[4] and friend and battle-mate.
Although you hated him, I trust that you
Do not begrudge such praise as was his due.　10
One thought, however, soothes my mortal grief:
I now may offer you a just relief,
Revoking the most cruel of decrees.
Your heart, your hand, bestow them as you please;
For here in Troezen, where I now shall reign,　15
Which was my grandsire Pittheus' domain,
And which with one voice gives its throne to me,
I make you free as I; indeed, more free.

ARICIA: Your goodness stuns me, Sir. By this excess
Of noble sympathy for my distress,　20
You leave me, more than you could dream, still yoked
By those strict laws which you have just revoked.

HIPPOLYTUS: Athens, unsure of who should rule, divides
'Twixt you and me, and the Queen's son besides.

ARICIA: They speak of me?

HIPPOLYTUS: Their laws, I'm well aware,　25
Would seem to void my claim as Theseus' heir,
Because an alien bore me. But if my one
Opponent were my brother, Phaedra's son,
I would, my lady, have the better cause,
And would contest those smug and foolish laws.　30
What checks me is a truer claim, your own;

---

4. *Heir* in the sense of being, like Hercules, a destroyer of monsters.

I yield, or, rather, give you back, a throne
And scepter which your sires inherited
From that great mortal whom the Earth once bred.
Aegeus,[5] though adopted, took their crown.   35
Theseus, his son, enlarged the state, cast down
Her foes, and was the choice of everyone,
Leaving your brothers in oblivion.
Now Athens calls you back within her walls.
Too long she's grieved for these dynastic brawls;   40
Too long your kinsmen's blood has drenched her earth,
Rising in steam from fields which gave it birth.
Troezen is mine, then. The domain of Crete
Offers to Phaedra's son a rich retreat.
Athens is yours. I go now to combine   45
In your cause all your partisans and mine.

ARICIA: These words so daze me that I almost fear
Some dream, some fancy has deceived my ear.
Am I awake? This plan which you have wrought—
What god, what god inspired you with the thought?   50
How just that, everywhere, men praise your name!
And how the truth, my lord, exceeds your fame!
You'll press my claims, against your interest?
'Twas kind enough that you should not detest
My house and me, should not be governed by   55
Old hatreds. . . .

HIPPOLYTUS: Hate you, Princess? No, not I.
I'm counted rough and proud, but don't assume
That I'm the issue of some monster's womb.
What hate-filled heart, what brute however wild
Could look upon your face and not grow mild?   60
Could I withstand your sweet, beguiling spell?

ARICIA: What's this, my lord?

HIPPOLYTUS: I've said too much. Ah, well.
My reason can't rein in my heart, I see.
Since I have spoken thus impetuously,
I must go on, my lady, and make plain   65
A secret I no longer can contain.
You see before you a most sorry prince,
A signal case of blind conceit. I wince
To think how I, Love's enemy, long disdained
Its bonds, and all whom passion had enchained;   70
How, pitying poor storm-tossed fools, I swore
Ever to view such tempests from the shore;
And now, like common men, for all my pride,
Am lost to reason in a raging tide.
One moment saw my vain defenses fall: 75
My haughty spirit is at last in thrall.
For six months now, ashamed and in despair,

---

5. Pandion's son by adoption, and Theseus's father.

I've borne Love's piercing arrow everywhere;
I've striven with you, and with myself, and though
I shun you, you are everywhere I go;   80
In the deep woods, your image haunts my sight;
The light of day, the shadows of the night,
All things call up your charms before my eyes
And vie to make my rebel heart your prize.
What use to struggle? I am not as before: 85
I seek myself, and find myself no more.
My bow, my javelins and my chariot pall;
What Neptune taught me once, I can't recall;
My idle steeds forget the voice they've known,
And the woods echo to my plaints alone.   90
You blush, perhaps, for so uncouth a love
As you have caused, and which I tell you of.
What a rude offer of my heart I make!
How strange a captive does your beauty take!
Yet that should make my offering seem more rich.   95
Remember, it's an unknown tongue in which
I speak; don't scorn these words, so poorly turned,
Which, but for you, my lips had never learned.

SCENE 3

HIPPOLYTUS, ARICIA, THERAMENES, ISMENE

THERAMENES: My lord: the Queen, they tell me, comes this way.
  It's you she seeks.
HIPPOLYTUS: Me?
THERAMENES: Why, I cannot say.
  But Phaedra's sent ahead to let you know
  That she must speak with you before you go.
HIPPOLYTUS: I, talk with Phaedra? What should we talk about?   5
ARICIA: My lord, you can't refuse to hear her out.
  Malignant toward you as the Queen appears,
  You owe some pity to her widow's tears.
HIPPOLYTUS: But now you'll leave me! And I shall sail before
  I learn my fate from her whom I adore,   10
  And in whose hands I leave this heart of mine. . . .
ARICIA: Go, Prince; pursue your generous design.
  Make Athens subject to my royal sway.
  All of your gifts I gladly take this day.
  But that great empire, glorious though it be,   15
  Is not the offering most dear to me.

SCENE 4

HIPPOLYTUS, THERAMENES

HIPPOLYTUS: Are we ready, friend? But the Queen's coming: hark.
  Go, bid them trim our vessel; we soon embark.

Quick, give the order and return, that you
May free me from a vexing interview.

SCENE 5

PHAEDRA, HIPPOLYTUS, OENONE

PHAEDRA: [*To* OENONE, *at stage rear.*]
   He's here. Blood rushes to my heart: I'm weak,
   And can't recall the words I meant to speak.
OENONE: Think of your son, whose one hope rests with you.
PHAEDRA: My lord, they say you leave us. Before you do,
   I've come to join your sorrows and my tears,   5
   And tell you also of a mother's fears.
   My son now lacks a father; and he will learn
   Ere long that death has claimed me in my turn.
   A thousand foes already seek to end
   His hopes, which you, you only, can defend.   10
   Yet I've a guilty fear that I have made
   Your ears indifferent to his cries for aid.
   I tremble lest you visit on my son
   Your righteous wrath at what his mother's done.
HIPPOLYTUS: So base a thought I could not entertain.   15
PHAEDRA: Were you to hate me, I could not complain,
   My lord. You've seen me bent on hurting you,
   Though what was in my heart you never knew.
   I sought your enmity. I would not stand
   Your dwelling with me in the selfsame land.   20
   I vilified you, and did not feel free
   Till oceans separated you and me.
   I went so far, indeed, as to proclaim
   That none should, in my hearing, speak your name.
   Yet if the crime prescribes the culprit's fate,   25
   If I must hate you to have earned your hate,
   Never did woman more deserve, my lord,
   Your pity, or less deserve to be abhorred.
HIPPOLYTUS: It's common, Madam, that a mother spites
   The stepson who might claim her children's rights.   30
   I know that in a second marriage-bed
   Anxiety and mistrust are often bred.
   Another woman would have wished me ill
   As you have, and perhaps been harsher still.
PHAEDRA: Ah, Prince! The Gods, by whom I swear it, saw   35
   Fit to except me from that general law.
   By what a different care am I beset!
HIPPOLYTUS: My lady, don't give way to anguish yet.
   Your husband still may see the light of day;
   Heaven may hear us, and guide his sail this way.   40
   Neptune protects him, and that deity
   Will never fail to heed my father's plea.

PHAEDRA: No one goes twice among the dead; and since
   Theseus has seen those gloomy regions, Prince,
   No god will bring him back, hope though you may,   45
   Nor greedy Acheron yield up his prey.
   But no! He is not dead; he breathes in you.
   My husband still seems present to my view.
   I see him, speak with him . . . Ah, my lord, I feel
   Crazed with a passion which I can't conceal.   50
HIPPOLYTUS: In your strong love, what wondrous power lies!
   Theseus, though dead, appears before your eyes.
   For love of him your soul is still on fire.
PHAEDRA: Yes, Prince, I burn for him with starved desire,
   Though not as he was seen among the shades,   55
   The fickle worshiper of a thousand maids,
   Intent on cuckolding the King of Hell;
   But constant, proud, a little shy as well,
   Young, charming, irresistible, much as we
   Depict our Gods, or as you look to me.   60
   He had your eyes, your voice, your virile grace,
   It was your noble blush that tinged his face
   When, crossing on the waves, he came to Crete
   And made the hearts of Minos' daughters[6] beat.
   Where were you then? Why no Hippolytus   65
   Among the flower of Greece he chose for us?
   Why were you yet too young to join that band
   Of heroes whom he brought to Minos' land?
   You would have slain the Cretan monster then,
   Despite the endless windings of his den.[7]   70
   My sister would have armed you with a skein
   Of thread, to lead you from that dark domain.
   But no: I'd first have thought of that design,
   Inspired by love; the plan would have been mine.
   It's I who would have helped you solve the maze,   75
   My Prince, and taught you all its twisting ways.
   What I'd have done to save that charming head!
   My love would not have trusted to a thread.
   No, Phaedra would have wished to share with you
   Your perils, would have wished to lead you through   80
   The Labyrinth, and thence have side by side
   Returned with you; or else, with you, have died.
HIPPOLYTUS: Gods! What are you saying, Madam? Is Theseus not
   Your husband, and my sire? Have you forgot?
PHAEDRA: You think that I forget those things? For shame,   85
   My lord. Have I no care for my good name?
HIPPOLYTUS: Forgive me, Madam. I blush to have misread
   The innocent intent of what you said.

---

6. Phaedra and Ariadne.   7. The Minotaur inhabited the heart of a maze. Ariadne provided Theseus
with a ball of thread by which he left a trail behind him and could retrace his steps after killing the
monster.

I'm too abashed to face you; I shall take
My leave. . . .
PHAEDRA: Ah, cruel Prince, 'twas no mistake.   90
You understood; my words were all too plain.
Behold then Phaedra as she is, insane
With love for you. Don't think that I'm content
To be so, that I think it innocent,
Or that by weak compliance I have fed   95
The baneful love that clouds my heart and head.
Poor victim that I am of Heaven's curse,[8]
I loathe myself; you could not hate me worse.
The Gods could tell how in this breast of mine
They lit the flame that's tortured all my line,   100
Those cruel Gods for whom it is but play
To lead a feeble woman's heart astray.
You too could bear me out; remember, do,
How I not only shunned but banished you.
I wanted to be odious in your sight;   105
To balk my love, I sought to earn your spite.
But what was gained by all of that distress?
You hated me the more; I loved no less,
And what you suffered made you still more dear.
I pined, I withered, scorched by many a tear.   110
That what I say is true, your eyes could see
If for a moment they could look at me.
What have I said? Do you suppose I came
To tell, of my free will, this tale of shame?
No, anxious for a son I dared not fail,   115
I came to beg you not to hate him. Frail
Indeed the heart is that's consumed by love!
Alas, it's only you I've spoken of.
Avenge yourself, now; punish my foul desire.
Come, rid the world, like your heroic sire,   120
Of one more monster; do as he'd have done.
Shall Theseus' widow dare to love his son?
No, such a monster is too vile to spare.
Here is my heart. Your blade must pierce me there.
In haste to expiate its wicked lust,   125
My heart already leaps to meet your thrust.
Strike, then. Or if your hatred and disdain
Refuse me such a blow, so sweet a pain,
If you'll not stain your hand with my abhorred
And tainted blood, lend me at least your sword.   130
Give it to me!
OENONE: Just Gods! What's this, my Queen?
Someone is coming. You must not be seen.
Quick! Flee! You'll be disgraced if you delay.

---

8. Phaedra feels herself a victim of Venus, the goddess of love; she loves Hippolytus against her will.

SCENE 6

HIPPOLYTUS, THERAMENES

THERAMENES: Did I see Phaedra vanish, dragged away?
  Why do I find you pale and overcome?
  Where is your sword, Sir? Why are you stricken dumb?
HIPPOLYTUS: Theramenes, I'm staggered. Let's go in haste.
  I view myself with horror and distaste.   5
  Phaedra . . . but no, great Gods! This thing must not
  Be told, but ever buried and forgot.
THERAMENES: Sir, if you wish to sail, our ship's prepared.
  But Athens' choice already is declared.
  Her clans have all conferred; their leaders name   10
  Your brother; Phaedra has achieved her aim.
HIPPOLYTUS: Phaedra?
THERAMENES: A herald's come at their command
  To give the reins of state into her hand.
  Her son is king.
HIPPOLYTUS: Gods, what she is you know;
  Is it her virtue you've rewarded so?   15
THERAMENES: Meanwhile, it's rumored that the King's not dead,
  That in Epirus he has shown his head.
  But I, who searched that land, know well, my lord . . .
HIPPOLYTUS: No, let all clues be weighed, and none ignored.
  We'll track this rumor down. Should it appear   20
  Too insubstantial to detain us here,
  We'll sail, and at whatever cost obtain
  Great Athens' crown for one who's fit to reign.

Act III

SCENE 1

PHAEDRA, OENONE

PHAEDRA: Ah, let their honors deck some other brow.
  Why urge me? How can I let them see me now?
  D'you think to soothe my anguished heart with such
  Vain solace? Hide me, rather. I've said too much.
  My frenzied love's burst forth in act and word.   5
  I've spoken what should never have been heard.
  And how he heard me! How, with many a shift,
  The brute pretended not to catch my drift!
  How ardently he longed to turn and go!
  And how his blushes caused my shame to grow!   10
  Why did you come between my death and me?
  Ah, when his sword-point neared my breast, did he
  Turn pale with horror, and snatch back the blade?
  No. I had touched it, and that touch had made

Him see it as a thing defiled and stained,   15
By which his pure hand must not be profaned.
OENONE: Dwelling like this on all you're grieved about,
You feed a flame which best were beaten out.
Would it not suit King Minos' child to find
In loftier concerns her peace of mind,   20
To flee an ingrate whom you love in vain,
Assume the conduct of the State, and reign?
PHAEDRA: I, reign? You'd trust the State to my control,
When reason rules no longer in my soul?
When passion's overthrown me? When, from the weight   25
Of shame I bear, I almost suffocate?
When I am dying?
OENONE: Flee him.
PHAEDRA: How could I? How?
OENONE: You once could banish him; can't you shun him now?
PHAEDRA: Too late. He knows what frenzy burns in me.
I've gone beyond the bounds of modesty.   30
My conqueror has heard my shame confessed,
And hope, despite me, has crept into my breast.
'Twas you who, when my life was near eclipse
And my last breath was fluttering on my lips,
Revived me with sweet lies that took me in.   35
You said that now my love was free of sin.
OENONE: Ah, whether or not your woes are on my head,
To save you, what would I not have done or said?
But if an insult ever roused your spleen,
How can you pardon his disdainful mien?   40
How stonily, and with what cold conceit
He saw you all but grovel at his feet!
Oh, but his arrogance was rude and raw!
Why did not Phaedra see the man I saw?
PHAEDRA: This arrogance which irks you may grow less.   45
Bred in the forests, he has their ruggedness,
And, trained in harsh pursuits since he was young,
Has never heard, till now, love's gentle tongue.
No doubt it was surprise which made him mute,
And we do wrong to take him for a brute.   50
OENONE: Remember that an Amazon gave him life.
PHAEDRA: True: yet she learned to love like any wife.
OENONE: He has a savage hate for womankind.
PHAEDRA: No fear of rivals, then, need plague my mind.
Enough. Your counsels now are out of season.   55
Oenone, serve my madness, not my reason.
His heart is armored against love; let's seek
Some point where his defenses may be weak.
Imperial rule was in his thoughts, I feel;
He wanted Athens; that he could not conceal;   60
His vessels' prows already pointed there,

With sails all set and flapping in the air.
Go in my name, then; find this ambitious boy;
Dangle the crown before him like a toy.
His be the sacred diadem; in its stead   65
I ask no honor but to crown his head,
And yield a power I cannot hold. He'll school
My son in princely arts, teach him to rule,
And play for him, perhaps, a father's role.
Both mother and son I yield to his control.   70
Sway him, Oenone, by every wile that's known:
Your words will please him better than my own.
Sigh, groan, harangue him; picture me as dying;
Make use of supplication and of crying;
I'll sanction all you say. Go. I shall find,   75
When you return, what fate I am assigned.

SCENE 2

PHAEDRA, *alone*

PHAEDRA: O you who see to what I have descended,
Implacable Venus, is your vengeance ended?
Your shafts have all struck home; your victory's
Complete; what need for further cruelties?
If you would prove your pitiless force anew,   5
Attack a foe who's more averse to you.
Hippolytus flouts you; braving your divine
Wrath, he has never knelt before your shrine.
His proud ears seem offended by your name.
Take vengeance, Goddess; our causes are the same.   10
Force him to love . . . Oenone! You've returned
So soon? He hates me, then; your words were spurned.

SCENE 3

PHAEDRA, OENONE

OENONE: Madam, your hopeless love must be suppressed.
Call back the virtue which you once possessed.
The King, whom all thought dead, will soon be here;
Theseus has landed; Theseus is drawing near.
His people rush to see him, rapturous.   5
I'd just gone out to seek Hippolytus
When a great cry went up on every hand. . . .
PHAEDRA: My husband lives, Oenone; I understand.
I have confessed a love he will abhor.
He lives, and I have wronged him. Say no more.   10
OENONE: What?
PHAEDRA: I foresaw this, but you changed my course.
Your tears won out over my just remorse.
I might have died this morning, mourned and chaste;

I took your counsels, and I die disgraced.
OENONE: You die?
PHAEDRA: Just Heaven! Think what I have done!   15
My husband's coming; with him will be his son.
I'll see the witness of my vile desire
Watch with what countenance I can greet his sire,
My heart still heavy with rejected sighs,
And tears which could not move him in my eyes.   20
Mindful of Theseus' honor, will he conceal
The scandal of my passion, do you feel,
Deceiving both his sire and king? Will he
Contain the horror that he feels for me?
His silence would be vain. What ill I've done   25
I know, Oenone, and I am not one
Of those bold women who, at ease in crime,
Are never seen to blush at any time.
I know my mad deeds, I recall them all.
I think that in this place each vault, each wall   30
Can speak, and that, impatient to accuse,
They wait to give my trusting spouse their news.
I'll die, then; from these horrors I'll be free.
It is so sad a thing to cease to be?
Death is not fearful to a suffering mind.   35
My only fear's the name I leave behind.
For my poor children, what a dire bequest!
Each has the blood of Jove within his breast,
But whatsoever pride of blood they share,
A mother's crime's a heavy thing to bear.   40
I tremble lest—alas, too truly!—they
Be chided for their mother's guilt some day.
I tremble lest, befouled by such a stain,
Neither should dare to lift his head again.
OENONE: I pity both of them; you could not be   45
More justified in your anxiety.
But why expose them to such insult? Why
Witness against yourself? You've but to die,
And folk will say that Phaedra, having strayed
From virtue, flees the husband she betrayed.   50
Hippolytus will rejoice that, cutting short
Your days, you lend his charges your support.
How shall I answer your accuser? He
Will have no trouble in refuting me.
I'll watch him gloating hatefully, and hear   55
Him pour your shame in every listening ear.
Let Heaven's fire consume me ere I do!
But come, speak frankly; is he still dear to you?
How do you see this prince so full of pride?
PHAEDRA: I see a monster, of whom I'm terrified.   60
OENONE: Then why should he triumph, when all can be reversed?

You fear the man. Dare to accuse him first
Of that which he might charge you with today.
What could belie you? The facts all point his way:
The sword which by good chance he left behind,   65
Your past mistrust, your present anguished mind,
His sire long cautioned by your warning voice,
And he sent into exile by your choice.
PHAEDRA: I, charge an innocent man with doing ill?
OENONE: Trust to my zeal. You've only to be still.   70
Like you I tremble, and feel a sharp regret.
I'd sooner face a thousand deaths. And yet
Since, lacking this sad remedy, you'll perish;
Since, above all, it is your life I cherish,
I'll speak to Theseus. He will do no more   75
Than doom his son to exile, as before.
A sire, when he must punish, is still a sire;
A lenient sentence will appease his ire.
But even if guiltless blood must flow, the cost
Were less than if your honor should be lost.   80
That honor is too dear to risk; its cause
Is priceless, and its dictates are your laws.
You must give up, since honor is at stake,
Everything, even virtue, for its sake.
Ah! Here comes Theseus.
PHAEDRA: And Hippolytus, he   85
In whose cold eyes I read the end of me.
Do what you will; I yield myself to you.
In my confusion, I know not what to do.

SCENE 4

THESEUS, HIPPOLYTUS, PHAEDRA, OENONE, THERAMENES

THESEUS: Fortune has blessed me after long delay,
And in your arms, my lady . . .
PHAEDRA: Theseus, stay,
And don't profane the love those words express.
I am not worthy of your tenderness.
You have been wronged. Fortune or bitter fate   5
Did not, while you were absent, spare your mate.
Unfit to please you, or to be at your side,
Henceforth my only thought must be to hide.

SCENE 5

THESEUS, HIPPOLYTUS, THERAMENES

THESEUS: Why am I welcomed in this curious vein?
HIPPOLYTUS: That, Father, only Phaedra can explain.
But if my prayers can move you, grant me, Sir,
Never again to set my eyes on her.

Allow Hippolytus to say farewell   5
To any region where your wife may dwell.
THESEUS: Then you, my son, would leave me?
HIPPOLYTUS: I never sought her:
When to this land she came, 'twas you who brought her.
Yes, you, my lord, when last you left us, bore
Aricia and the Queen to Troezen's shore.   10
You bade me be their guardian then; but how
Should any duties here detain me now?
Too long my youthful skill's been thrown away
Amidst these woods, upon ignoble prey.
May I not flee my idle pastimes here   15
To stain with worthier blood my sword or spear?
Before you'd lived as long as I have done,
More than one tyrant, monsters more than one
Had felt your strength of arm, your sword's keen blade;
Already, scourging such as sack and raid,   20
You had made safe the coasts of either sea.
The traveler lost his fears of banditry,
And Hercules, to whom your fame was known,
Welcomed your toils, and rested from his own.
But I, the unknown son of such a sire,   25
Lack even the fame my mother's deeds inspire.[9]
Let me at long last show my courage, and,
If any monster has escaped your hand,
Bring back its pelt and lay it at your feet,
Or let me by a glorious death complete   30
A life that will defy oblivion
And prove to all the world I was your son.
THESEUS: What have I found? What horror fills this place,
And makes my family flee before my face?
If my unwished return makes all grow pale,   35
Why, Heaven, did you free me from my jail?
I'd one dear friend. He had a hankering
To steal the consort of Epirus'[1] king.
I joined his amorous plot, though somewhat loath;
But outraged Fate brought blindness on us both.   40
The tyrant caught me, unarmed and by surprise.
I saw Pirithoüs with my weeping eyes
Flung by the barbarous king to monsters then,
Fierce beasts who drink the blood of luckless men.
Me he confined where never light invades,   45
In caverns near the empire of the shades.
After six months, Heaven pitied my mischance.
Escaping from my guardians' vigilance,
I cleansed the world of one more fiend, and threw

---

9. Hippolytus's mother, an Amazon, also performed brave deeds.   1. A district in western Greece, on
the Ionian Sea.

To his own beasts the bloody corpse to chew.   50
But now when, joyful, I return to see
The dearest whom the Gods have left to me;
Now, when my spirits, glad once more and light,
Would feast again upon that cherished sight,
I'm met with shudders and with frightened faces;   55
All flee me, all deny me their embraces.
Touched by the very terror I beget,
I wish I were Epirus' prisoner yet.
Speak! Phaedra says that I've been wronged. By whom?
Why has the culprit not yet met his doom?   60
Has Greece, so often sheltered by my arm,
Chosen to shield this criminal from harm?
You're silent. Is my own son, if you please,
In some alliance with my enemies?
I shall go in, and end this maddening doubt.   65
Both crime and culprit must be rooted out,
And Phaedra tell why she is so distraught.

SCENE 6

HIPPOLYTUS, THERAMENES

HIPPOLYTUS: How her words chilled me! What was in her thought?
Will Phaedra, who is still her frenzy's prey,
Accuse herself, and throw her life away?
What will the King say? Gods! What love has done
To poison all this house while he was gone!   5
And I, who burn for one who bears his curse,
Am altered in his sight, and for the worse!
I've dark forebodings; something ill draws near.
Yet surely innocence need never fear.
Come, let's consider now how I may best   10
Revive the kindness in my father's breast,
And tell him of a love which he may take
Amiss, but all his power cannot shake.

Act IV

SCENE 1

THESEUS, OENONE

THESEUS: What do I hear? How bold and treacherous
To plot against his father's honor thus!
How sternly you pursue me, Destiny!
Where shall I turn? I know not. Where can I be?
O love and kindness not repaid in kind!   5
Outrageous scheme of a degenerate mind!
To seek his lustful end he had recourse,

Like any blackguard, to the use of force.
I recognize the sword his passion drew—
My gift, bestowed with nobler deeds in view.   10
Why did our ties of blood prove no restraint?
Why too did Phaedra make no prompt complaint?
Was it to spare the culprit?
OENONE: It was rather
That she, in pity, wished to spare his father.
Ashamed because her beauty had begot   15
So foul a passion, and so fierce a plot,
By her own hand, my lord, she sought to die,
And darken thus the pure light of her eye.
I saw her raise her arm; to me you owe
Her life, because I ran and stayed the blow.   20
Now, pitying both her torment and your fears,
I have, against my will, spelled out her tears.
THESEUS: The traitor! Ah, no wonder he turned pale.
When first he sighted me, I saw him quail.
'Twas strange to see no greeting in his face.   25
My heart was frozen by his cold embrace.
But did he, even in Athens, manifest
This guilty love by which he is possessed?
OENONE: The Queen, remember, could not tolerate him.
It was his infamous love which made her hate him.   30
THESEUS: That love, I take it, was rekindled here
In Troezen?
OENONE: I've told you all, my lord. I fear
I've left the Queen too long in mortal grief.
Let me now haste to bring her some relief.

SCENE 2

THESEUS, HIPPOLYTUS

THESEUS: Ah, here he comes. Gods! By that noble mien
What eye would not be duped, as mine has been!
Why must the brow of an adulterer
Be stamped with virtue's sacred character?
Should there not be clear signs by which one can   5
Divine the heart of a perfidious man?
HIPPOLYTUS: May I enquire what louring cloud obscures,
My lord, that royal countenance of yours?
Dare you entrust the secret to your son?
THESEUS: Dare you appear before me, treacherous one?   10
Monster, at whom Jove's thunder should be hurled!
Foul brigand, like those of whom I cleaned the world!
Now that your vile, unnatural love has led
You even to attempt your father's bed,
How dare you show your hated self to me   15
Here in the precincts of your infamy,

Rather than seek some unknown land where fame
Has never brought the tidings of my name?
Fly, wretch. Don't brave the hate which fills my soul,
Or tempt a wrath it pains me to control.   20
I've earned, forevermore, enough disgrace
By fathering one who'd do a deed so base,
Without your death upon my hands, to soil
A noble history of heroic toil.
Fly, and unless you wish to join the band   25
Of knaves who've met quick justice at my hand,
Take care lest by the sun's eye you be found
Setting an insolent foot upon this ground.
Now, never to return, be off; take flight;
Cleanse all my realms of your abhorrent sight.   30
And you, O Neptune, if by courage I
Once cleared your shores of murderers, hear my cry.
Recall that, as reward for that great task,
You swore to grant the first thing I should ask.
Pent in a cruel jail for endless hours,   35
I never called on your immortal powers.
I've hoarded up the aid you promised me
Till greater need should justify my plea.
I make it now. Avenge a father's wrong.
Seize on this traitor, and let your rage be strong.   40
Drown in his blood his brazen lust. I'll know
Your favor by the fury that you show.
HIPPOLYTUS: Phaedra accuses me of lust? I'm weak
With horror at the thought, and cannot speak;
By all these sudden blows I'm overcome;   45
They leave me stupefied, and stricken dumb.
THESEUS: Scoundrel, you thought that Phaedra'd be afraid
To tell of the depraved assault you made.
You should have wrested from her hands the hilt
Of the sharp sword that points now to your guilt;   50
Or, better, crowned your outrage of my wife
By robbing her at once of speech and life.
HIPPOLYTUS: In just resentment of so black a lie,
I might well let the truth be known, but I
Suppress what comes too near your heart. Approve,   55
My lord, a silence which bespeaks my love.
Restrain, as well, your mounting rage and woe:
Review my life; recall the son you know.
Great crimes grow out of small ones. If today
A man first oversteps the bounds, he may   60
Abuse in time all laws and sanctities;
For crime, like virtue, ripens by degrees;
But when has one seen innocence, in a trice,
So change as to embrace the ways of vice?
Not in a single day could time transmute   65

A virtuous man to an incestuous brute.
I had an Amazon mother, brave and chaste,
Whose noble blood my life has not debased.
And when I left her hands, 'twas Pitteus,[2] thought
Earth's wisest man, by whom my youth was taught.   70
I shall not vaunt such merits as I've got,
But if one virtue's fallen to my lot,
It is, my lord, a fierce antipathy
To just that vice imputed now to me.
It is for that Hippolytus is known   75
In Greece—for virtue cold and hard as stone.
By harsh austerity I am set apart.
The daylight is not purer than my heart.
Yet I, it's charged, consumed by lechery . . .
THESEUS: This very boast betrays your guilt. I see   80
What all your vaunted coldness signifies:
Phaedra alone could please your lustful eyes;
No other woman moved you, or could inspire
Your scornful heart with innocent desire.
HIPPOLYTUS: No Father: hear what it's time I told you of;   85
I have not scorned to feel a blameless love.
I here confess my only true misdeed:
I am in love, despite what you decreed.
Aricia has enslaved me; my heart is won,
And Pallas' daughter has subdued your son.   90
I worship her against your orders, Sir,
Nor could I burn or sigh except for her.
THESEUS: You love her? Gods! But no, I see your game.
You play the criminal to clear your name.
HIPPOLYTUS: Six months I've shunned her whom my heart adored.   95
I came in fear to tell you this, my lord.
Why must you be so stubbornly mistaken?
To win your trust, what great oath must be taken?
By Earth, and Heaven, and all the things that be . . .
THESEUS: A rascal never shrinks from perjury.   100
Cease now to weary me with sly discourse,
If your false virtue has but that resource.
HIPPOLYTUS: My virtue may seem false and sly to you,
But Phaedra has good cause to know it true.
THESEUS: Ah, how your impudence makes my temper boil!   105
HIPPOLYTUS: How long shall I be banished? On what soil?
THESEUS: Were you beyond Alcides' pillars,[3] I
Would think yet that a rogue was too nearby.
HIPPOLYTUS: Who will befriend me now—a man suspected
Of such a crime, by such a sire rejected?   110

---

2. The most learned man of his age, Theseus's guardian. After marrying Phaedra, Theseus sent Hippolytus to Pitteus (or Pitheus), who had adopted him as heir to the throne of Troezen.   3. The Pillars of
Hercules, the two points of land on either side of the Strait of Gibraltar, at the western end of the Mediterranean and thus representing one edge of the known world.

THESEUS: Go look for friends who think adultery cause
  For accolades, and incest for applause,
  Yes, ingrates, traitors, to law and honor blind,
  Fit to protect a blackguard of your kind.
HIPPOLYTUS: Incest! Adultery! Are these still your themes?   115
  I'll say no more. Yet Phaedra's mother, it seems,
  And, as you know, Sir, all of Phaedra's line
  Knew more about such horrors than did mine.
THESEUS: So! You dare storm and rage before my face?
  I tell you for the last time: leave this place.   120
  Be off, before I'm roused to violence
  And have you, in dishonor, driven hence.

SCENE 3

THESEUS, *alone*

THESEUS: Poor wretch, the path you take will end in blood.
  What Neptune swore by Styx, that darkest flood
  Which frights the Gods themselves, he'll surely do.
  And none escapes when vengeful Gods' pursue.
  I loved you; and in spite of what you've done,   5
  I mourn your coming agonies, my son.
  But you have all too well deserved my curse.
  When was a father ever outraged worse?
  Just Gods, who see this grief which drives me wild,
  How could I father such a wicked child?   10

SCENE 4

PHAEDRA, THESEUS

PHAEDRA: My lord, I hasten to you, full of dread.
  I heard your threatening voice, and what it said.
  Pray Heaven no deed has followed on your threat.
  I beg you, if there is time to save him yet,
  To spare your son; spare me the dreadful sound   5
  Of blood, your own blood, crying from the ground.
  Do not impose on me the endless woe
  Of having caused your hand to make it flow.
THESEUS: No, Madam, my blood's not on my hands. But he,
  The thankless knave, has not escaped from me.   10
  A God's great hand will be his nemesis
  And your avenger. Neptune owes me this.
PHAEDRA: Neptune! And will your angry prayers be heard?
THESEUS: What! Are you fearful lest he keep his word?
  No, rather join me in my righteous pleas.   15
  Recount to me my son's black treacheries;
  Stir up my sluggish wrath, that's still too cold.
  He has done crimes of which you've not been told:
  Enraged at you, he slanders your good name:

Your mouth is full of lies, he dares to claim;   20
  He states that heart and soul, his love is pledged
  To Aricia.
PHAEDRA: What, my lord!
THESEUS: So he alleged;
  But I saw through so obvious a trick.
  Let's hope that Neptune's justice will be quick.
  I go now to his altars, to implore   25
  A prompt fulfillment of the oath he swore.

SCENE 5

PHAEDRA, *alone*

PHAEDRA: He's gone. What news assails my ear? What ill-
  Extinguished fire flares in my bosom still?
  By what a thunderbolt I am undone!
  I'd flown here with one thought, to save his son.
  Escaping from Oenone's arms by force,   5
  I'd yielded to my torturing remorse.
  How far I might have gone, I cannot guess.
  Guilt might perhaps have driven me to confess.
  Perhaps, had shock not caused my voice to fail,
  I might have blurted out my hideous tale.   10
  Hippolytus can feel, but not for me!
  Aricia has his love, his loyalty!
  Gods! When he steeled himself against my sighs
  With that forbidding brow, those scornful eyes,
  I thought his heart, which love-darts could not strike,   15
  Was armed against all womankind alike.
  And yet another's made his pride surrender;
  Another's made his cruel eyes grow tender.
  Perhaps his heart is easy to ensnare.
  It's me, alone of women, he cannot bear!   20
  Shall I defend a man by whom I'm spurned?

SCENE 6

PHAEDRA, OENONE

PHAEDRA: Oenone dear, do you know what I have learned?
OENONE: No, but in truth I'm quaking still with fear
  Of the wild urge that sent you rushing here:
  I feared some blunder fatally adverse.
PHAEDRA: I had a rival. Who would have thought it, Nurse?   5
OENONE: What?
PHAEDRA: Yes, Hippolytus is in love; it's true.
  That savage creature no one could subdue,
  Who scorned regard, who heard no lovers' pleas,
  That tiger whom I viewed with trembling knees,

Is tame now, broken by a woman's art: 10
Aricia's found the way into his heart.
OENONE: Aricia?
PHAEDRA: O pain I never felt before!
  What new, sharp torments have I kept in store!
  All that I've suffered—frenzies, fears, the dire
  Oppression of remorse, my heart on fire,   15
  The merciless rebuff he gave to me—
  All were but foretastes of this agony.
  They love each other! By what magic, then,
  Did they beguile me? Where did they meet, and when?
  You knew. Why did you keep me unaware,   20
  Deceived as to their furtive love-affair?
  Were they much seen together? Were they known
  To haunt the deep woods, so as to be alone?
  Alas, they'd perfect liberty to meet.
  Heaven smiled on hearts so innocent and sweet;   25
  Without remorse, they savored love's delight;
  For them, each dawn arose serene and bright—
  While I, creation's outcast, hid away
  From the Sun's eye, and fled the light of day.
  Death was the only God I dared implore.   30
  I longed for him; I prayed to be no more.
  Quenching my thirst with tears, and fed on gall,
  Yet in my woe too closely watched by all,
  I dared not weep and grieve in fullest measure;
  I sipped in secret at that bitter pleasure;   35
  And often, wearing a serene disguise,
  I kept my pain from welling in my eyes.
OENONE: What will their love avail them? They will never
  Meet again.
PHAEDRA: But they will love forever.
  Even as I speak—ah, deadly thought!—they dare   40
  To mock my crazed desire and my despair.
  Despite this exile which will make them part,
  They swear forever to be joined in heart.
  No, no, their bliss I cannot tolerate,
  Oenone. Take pity on my jealous hate.   45
  Aricia must die. Her odious house
  Must once more feel the anger of my spouse.
  Nor can the penalty be light, for her
  Misdeeds are darker than her brothers' were.
  In my wild jealousy I will plead with him.   50
  I'll what? Has my poor reason grown so dim?
  I, jealous! And it's with Theseus I would plead!
  My husband lives, and still my passions feed
  On whom? Toward whom do all my wishes tend?
  At every word, my hair stands up on end.   55
  The measure of my crimes is now replete.

I foul the air with incest and deceit.
My murderous hands are itching to be stained
With innocent blood, that vengeance be obtained.
Wretch that I am, how can I live, how face   60
That sacred Sun, great elder of my race?
My grandsire was, of all the Gods, most high;
My forebears fill the world, and all the sky.
Where can I hide? For Hades' night I yearn.
No, there my father holds the dreadful urn   65
Entrusted to his hands by Fate, it's said:
There Minos judges all the ashen dead.
Ah, how his shade will tremble with surprise
To see his daughter brought before his eyes —
Forced to confess a throng of sins, to tell   70
Of crimes perhaps unheard of yet in Hell!
What will you say then, Father? As in a dream,
I see you drop the fearful urn;[4] you seem
To ponder some new torment fit for her,
Yourself become your own child's torturer.   75
Forgive me. A cruel God destroys your line;
Behold her hand in these mad deeds of mine.
My heart, alas! not once enjoyed the fruit
Of its dark, shameful crime. In fierce pursuit,
Misfortune dogs me till, with my last breath,   80
My sad life shall, in torments, yield to death.
OENONE: My lady, don't give in to needless terror.
Look freshly at your pardonable error.
You love. But who can conquer Destiny?
Lured by a fatal spell, you were not free.   85
Is that a marvel hitherto unknown?
Has Love entrapped no heart but yours alone?
Weakness is natural to us, is it not?
You are a mortal; accept your mortal lot.
To chafe against our frail estate is vain.   90
Even the Gods who on Olympus reign,
And with their thunders chasten men for crime,
Have felt illicit passions many a time.
PHAEDRA: Ah, what corrupting counsels do I hear?
Wretch! Will you pour such poison in my ear   95
Right to the end? Look how you've ruined me.
You dragged me back to all I sought to flee.
You blinded me to duty; called it no wrong
To see Hippolytus, whom I'd shunned so long.
Ah, meddling creature, why did your sinful tongue   100
Falsely accuse a soul so pure and young?

---

4. After his death, Minos of Crete became, along with his brother Rhadamanthus, one of the judges of
souls in the underworld. The urn held the lots determining to what abode in the underworld the souls of
the dead were to be sent.

He'll die, it may be, if the Gods can bear
To grant his maddened father's impious prayer.
No, say no more. Go, monster whom I hate.
Go, let me face at last my own sad fate. 105
May Heaven reward you for your deeds! And may
Your punishment forever give dismay
To all who, like yourself, by servile arts
Nourish the weaknesses of princes' hearts,
Incline them to pursue the baser path, 110
And smooth for them the way to sin and wrath —
Accursèd flatterers, the worst of things
That Heaven's anger can bestow on kings!
OENONE: I've given my life to her. Ah, Gods! It hurts
To be thus thanked. Yet I have my just deserts. 115

Act V

SCENE 1

HIPPOLYTUS, ARICIA

ARICIA: Come, in this mortal danger, will you not make
Your loving sire aware of his mistake?
If, scorning all my tears, you can consent
To parting and an endless banishment,
Go, leave Aricia in her life alone. 5
But first assure the safety of your own.
Defend your honor against a foul attack,
And force your sire to call his prayers back.
There yet is time. What moves you, if you please,
Not to contest Queen Phaedra's calumnies? 10
Tell Theseus the truth.
HIPPOLYTUS: What more should I
Have told him? How she smirched their marriage-tie?
How could I, by disclosing everything,
Humiliate my father and my king?
It's you alone I've told these horrors to. 15
I've bared my heart but to the Gods and you.
Judge of my love, which forced me to confide
What even from myself I wished to hide.
But, mind you, keep this secret ever sealed.
Forget, if possible, all that I've revealed, 20
And never let those pure lips part to bear
Witness, my lady, to this vile affair.
Let us rely upon the Gods' high laws:
Their honor binds them to defend my cause;
And Phaedra, sooner or later brought to book, 25
Will blush for crimes their justice cannot brook.

To that restraint I ask you to agree.
In all things else, just anger makes me free.
Come, break away from this, your slavish plight;
Dare follow me, dare join me in my flight;   30
Be quit of an accursèd country where
Virtue must breathe a foul and poisoned air.
Under the cover of this turbulence
Which my disfavor brings, slip quickly hence.
I can assure a safe escape for you.   35
Your only guards are of my retinue.
Strong states will champion us; upon our side
Is Sparta; Argos' arms are open wide:
Let's plead then to these friends our righteous case,
Lest Phaedra, profiting by our disgrace,   40
Deny our lineal claims to either throne,
And pledge her son my birthright and your own.
Come, let us seize the moment; we mustn't wait.
What holds you back? You seem to hesitate.
It's zeal for you that moves me to be bold.   45
When I am all on fire, what makes you cold?
Are you afraid to join a banished man?

ARICIA: Alas, my lord, how sweet to share that ban!
What deep delight, as partner of your lot,
To live with you, by all the world forgot!   50
But since no blessèd tie unites us two,
Can I, in honor, flee this land with you?
The sternest code, I know, would not deny
My right to break your father's bonds and fly;
I'd grieve no loving parents thus; I'm free,   55
As all are, to escape from tyranny.
But, Sir, you love me, and my fear of shame . . .

HIPPOLYTUS: Ah, never doubt my care for your good name.
It is a nobler plan that I propose:
Flee with your husband from our common foes.   60
Freed my mischance, since Heaven so commands,
We need no man's consent to join our hands.
Not every nuptial needs the torch's light.
At Troezen's gate, amidst that burial site
Where stand our princes' ancient sepulchers,   65
There is a temple feared by perjurers.
No man there dares to break his faith, on pain
Of instant doom, or swear an oath in vain;
There all deceivers, lest they surely die,
Bridle their tongues and are afraid to lie.   70
There, if you trust me, we will go, and of
Our own accord shall pledge eternal love;
The temple's God will witness to our oath;
We'll pray that he be father to us both.
I shall invoke all deities pure and just.   75

The chaste Diana, Juno[5] the august,
And all the Gods who know my faithfulness
Will guarantee the vows I shall profess.
ARICIA: The king is coming. Go, Prince, make no delay.
To cloak my own departure, I'll briefly stay.   80
Go, go; but leave with me some faithful guide
Who'll lead my timid footsteps to your side.

SCENE 2

THESEUS, ARICIA, ISMENE

THESEUS: O Gods, bring light into my troubled mind;
Show me the truth which I've come here to find.
ARICIA: Make ready for our flight, Ismene dear.

SCENE 3

THESEUS, ARICIA

THESEUS: Your color changes, Madame, and you appear
Confused. Why was Hippolytus here with you?
ARICIA: He came, my lord, to say a last adieu.
THESEUS: Ah, yes. You've tamed his heart, which none could capture.
And taught his stubborn lips to sigh with rapture.   5
ARICIA: I shan't deny the truth, my lord. No, he
Did not inherit your malignity,
Nor treat me as a criminal, in your fashion.
THESEUS: I see. He's sworn, no doubt, eternal passion.
Put no reliance on the vows of such   10
A fickle lover. He's promised others as much.
ARICIA: He, Sir?
THESEUS: You should have taught him not to stray.
How could you share his love in that base way?
ARICIA: How could you let a shameful lie besmear
The stainless honor of his young career?   15
Have you so little knowledge of his heart?
Can't you tell sin and innocence apart?
Must some black cloud bedim your eyes alone
To the bright virtue for which your son is known?
Shall slander ruin him? That were too much to bear.   20
Turn back: repent now of your murderous prayer.
Fear, my lord, fear lest the stern deities
So hate you as to grant your wrathful pleas.
Our sacrifices anger Heaven at times;
Its gifts are often sent to scourge our crimes.   25
THESEUS: Your words can't cover up that sin of his:
Love's blinded you to what the scoundrel is.

---

5. The wife of Jupiter and queen of the gods. Diana was goddess of the moon and of chastity.

But I've sure proofs on which I may rely:
I have seen tears—yes, tears which could not lie.
ARICIA: Take care, my lord. You have, in many lands,   30
Slain countless monsters with your conquering hands;
But all are not destroyed; there still lives one
Who . . . No, I am sworn to silence by your son.
Knowing his wish to shield your honor, I'd
Afflict him if I further testified.   35
I'll imitate his reticence, and flee
Your presence, lest the truth should burst from me.

SCENE 4

THESEUS, *alone*

THESEUS: What does she mean? These speeches which begin
And then break off—what are they keeping in?
Is this some sham those two have figured out?
Have they conspired to torture me with doubt?
But I myself, despite my stern control—   5
What plaintive voice cries from my inmost soul?
I feel a secret pity, a surge of pain.
Oenone must be questioned once again.
I'll have more light on this. Not all is known.
Guards, go and bring Oenone here, alone.   10

SCENE 5

THESEUS, PANOPE

PANOPE: I don't know what the Queen may contemplate,
My lord, but she is in a frightening state.
Mortal despair is what her looks bespeak;
Death's pallor is already on her cheek.
Oenone, driven from her in disgrace,   5
Has thrown herself into the sea's embrace.
None knows what madness caused the thing she did;
Beneath the waves she lies forever hid.
THESEUS: What do you tell me?
PANOPE: This death has left the Queen
No calmer; her distraction grows more keen.   10
At moments, to allay her dark unrest,
She clasps her children, weeping, to her breast;
Then, with a sudden horror, she will shove
Them both away, and starve her mother-love.
She wanders aimlessly about the floor;   15
Her blank eye does not know us any more.
Thrice she has written; and thrice, before she'd done,
Torn up the letter which she had begun.
We cannot help her. I beg you, Sire, to try.

THESEUS: Oenone's dead? And Phaedra wants to die?   20
  O bring me back my son, and let him clear
  His name! If he'll but speak, I now will hear.
  O Neptune, let your gifts not be conferred
  Too swiftly; let my prayers go unheard.
  Too much I've trusted what may not be true,   25
  Too quickly raised my cruel hands to you.
  How I'd despair if what I asked were done!

SCENE 6

THESEUS, THERAMENES

THESEUS: Is it you, Theramenes? Where have you left my son?
  You've been his mentor since his tenderest years.
  But why do I behold you drenched in tears?
  Where's my dear son?
THERAMENES: Too late, Sire, you restore
  Your love to him. Hippolytus is no more.   5
THESEUS: Gods!
THERAMENES: I have seen the best of mortals slain,
  My lord, and the least guilty, I maintain.
THESEUS: My son is dead? What! Just when I extend
  My arms to him, Heaven's haste has caused his end?
  What thunderbolt bereaved me? What was his fate?   10
THERAMENES: Scarcely had we emerged from Troezen's gate:
  He drove his chariot, and his soldiery
  Were ranged about him, mute and grave as he.
  Brooding, he headed toward Mycenae. Lax
  In his hands, the reins lay on his horses' backs.   15
  His haughty chargers, quick once to obey
  His voice, and give their noble spirits play,
  Now, with hung head and mournful eye, seemed part
  Of the sad thoughts that filled their master's heart.
  Out of the sea-deeps then a frightful cry   20
  Arose, to tear the quiet of the sky,
  And a dread voice from far beneath the ground
  Replies in groans to that appalling sound.
  Our hearts congeal; blood freezes in our veins.
  The horses, hearing, bristle up their manes.   25
  And now there rises from the sea's calm breast
  A liquid mountain with a seething crest.
  The wave approaches, breaks, and spews before
  Our eyes a raging monster on the shore.
  His huge brow's armed with horns; the spray unveils   30
  A body covered all with yellow scales;
  Half bull he is, half dragon; fiery, bold;
  His thrashing tail contorts in fold on fold.
  With echoing bellows now he shakes the strand.

The sky, aghast, beholds him; he makes the land   35
Shudder; his foul breath chokes the atmosphere;
The wave which brought him in recoils in fear.
All flee, and in a nearby temple save
Their lives, since it is hopeless to be brave.
Hippolytus alone dares make a stand.   40
He checks his chargers, javelins in hand,
Has at the monster and, with a sure-aimed throw,
Pierces his flank: a great wound starts to flow.
In rage and pain the beast makes one dread spring,
Falls near the horses' feet, still bellowing,   45
Rolls over toward them, with fiery throat takes aim
And covers them with smoke and blood and flame.
Sheer panic takes them; deaf now, they pay no heed
To voice or curb, but bolt in full stampede;
Their master strives to hold them back, in vain.   50
A bloody slaver drips from bit and rein.
It's said that, in that tumult, some caught sight
Of a God who spurred those dusty flanks to flight.
Fear drives them over rocks; the axletree
Screeches and breaks. The intrepid Prince must see   55
His chariot dashed to bits, for all his pains;
He falls at last, entangled in the reins.
Forgive my grief. That cruel sight will be
An everlasting source of tears for me.
I've seen, my lord, the heroic son you bred   60
Dragged by the horses which his hand had fed.
His shouts to them but make their fear more strong.
His body seems but one great wound, ere long.
The plain re-echoes to our cries of woe.
At last, their headlong fury starts to slow: 65
They stop, then, near that graveyard which contains,
In royal tombs, his forebears' cold remains.
I run to him in tears; his guards are led
By the bright trail of noble blood he shed;
The rocks are red with it; the briars bear   70
Their red and dripping trophies of his hair.
I reach him; speak his name; his hand seeks mine;
His eyelids lift a moment, then decline.
"Heaven takes," he says, "my innocent life away.
Protect my sad Aricia, I pray.   75
If ever, friend, my sire is disabused,
And mourns his son who falsely was accused,
Bid him appease my blood and plaintive shade
By dealing gently with that captive maid.
Let him restore . . ." His voice then died away,   80
And in my arms a mangled body lay
Which the God's wrath had claimed, a sorry prize

Which even his father would not recognize.
THESEUS: My son, dear hope whom folly made me kill!
   O ruthless Gods, too well you did my will!   85
   I'll henceforth be the brokenest of men.
THERAMENES: Upon this scene came shy Aricia then,
   Fleeing your wrath, and ready to espouse
   Your son before the Gods by holy vows.
   She comes, and sees the red and steaming grass;   90
   She sees—no sight for loving eyes, alas!—
   Hippolytus sprawled there, lacking form or hue.
   At first, she won't believe her loss is true.
   Not recognizing her beloved, she
   Both looks at him and asks where he may be.   95
   At last she knows too well what's lying there;
   She lifts to the Gods a sad, accusing stare;
   Then, moaning, cold, and all but dead, the sweet
   Maid drops unconscious at her lover's feet.
   Ismene, weeping, kneels and seeks to bring   100
   Her back to life—a life of suffering.
   And I, my lord, have come, who now detest
   This world, to bring a hero's last request,
   And so perform the bitter embassy
   Which, with his dying breath, he asked of me.   105
   But look: his mortal enemy comes this way.

SCENE 7

THESEUS, PHAEDRA, THERAMENES, PANOPE, GUARDS

THESEUS: Well, Madam, my son's no more; you've won the day!
   Ah, but what qualms I feel! What doubts torment
   My heart, and plead that he was innocent!
   But, madam, claim your victim. He is dead.
   Enjoy his death, unjust or merited.   5
   I'm willing to be evermore deceived.
   You've called him guilty; let it be believed.
   His death is grief enough for me to bear
   Without my further probing this affair,
   Which could not bring his dear life back again   10
   And might perhaps but aggravate my pain.
   No, far from you and Troezen, I shall flee
   My dead son's torn and bloody memory.
   It will pursue me ever, like a curse:
   Would I were banished from the universe!   15
   All seems to chide my wicked wrathfulness.
   My very fame now adds to my distress.
   How shall I hide, who have a name so great?
   Even the Gods' high patronage I hate.
   I go to mourn this murderous gift of theirs,   20

Nor trouble them again with useless prayers.
Do for me what they might, it could not pay
For what their deadly favor took away.
PHAEDRA: Theseus, my wrongful silence must be ended.
  Your guiltless son must be at last defended.   25
  He did no ill.
THESEUS: How curst a father am I!
  I doomed him, trusting in your heartless lie!
  Do you think to be excused for such a crime?
PHAEDRA: Hear me, my lord. I have but little time.
  I was the lustful and incestuous one   30
  Who dared desire your chaste and loyal son.
  Heaven lit a fatal blaze within my breast.
  Detestable Oenone did the rest.
  She, fearing lest Hippolytus, who knew
  Of my vile passion, might make it known to you,   35
  Abused my weakness and, by a vicious ruse,
  Made haste to be the first one to accuse.
  For that she's paid; fleeing my wrath, she found
  Too mild a death, and in the waves is drowned.
  Much though I wished to die then by the sword,   40
  Your son's pure name cried out to be restored.
  That my remorse be told, I chose instead
  A slower road that leads down to the dead.
  I drank, to give my burning veins some peace,
  A poison which Medea[6] brought to Greece.   45
  Already, to my heart, the venom gives
  An alien coldness, so that it scarcely lives;
  Already, to my sight, all clouds and fades—
  The sky, my spouse, the world my life degrades;
  Death dims my eyes, which soiled what they could see, 50
  Restoring to the light its purity.
PANOPE: She's dead, my lord!
THESEUS: Would that I could inter
  The memory of her black misdeeds with her!
  Let's go, since now my error's all too clear,
  And mix my poor son's blood with many a tear,   55
  Embrace his dear remains, and expiate
  The fury of a prayer which now I hate.
  To his great worth all honor shall be paid,
  And, further to appease his angry shade,
  Aricia, despite her brother's offense,   60
  Shall be my daughter from this moment hence.

---

6. A sorceress who helped Jason get the Golden Fleece and later, deserted by him, killed her rival and her own children and burned her palace before fleeing to Athens. According to one legend, she tried to poison Theseus.

SOR JUANA INÉS DE LA CRUZ
1648–1695

One hardly expects to find a spirited defense of women's intellectual rights issuing from the pen of a seventeenth-century Mexican nun, but *Reply to Sor Filotea de la Cruz,* by Sister Juana Inés de la Cruz, is exactly that. In the guise of declaring her humility and her religious subordination, this nun manages to advance claims for her sex more far-reaching and profound than any previously offered.

Born into an upper-class family, Sister Juana in her teens served as lady-in-waiting at the Viceregal court. She soon took the veil, however; her *Reply* suggests a reason in her desire for a safe environment in which to pursue her intellectual interests. Religious vocation did not prevent her from writing in secular forms: lyric poetry and drama. Indeed, she achieved an important literary reputation, later coming to be known throughout the Spanish-speaking world as the "Tenth Muse." Since her religious superiors intermittently rebuked her for her worldly interests, however, she appears to have developed a powerful sense of guilt. It is said that the natural disasters—a solar eclipse, storms, and famine—plaguing Mexico City in the 1690s intensified her guilt; in 1694, she reaffirmed her faith, signing the statement in her own blood with the words, "I, Sister Juana Inés de la Cruz, the worst in the world." She died after nursing the sick in an epidemic.

The *Reply* stems directly from Sister Juana's venture into theological polemic. In 1690 she wrote a commentary on a sermon delivered forty years earlier by the Portuguese Jesuit Antonio de Vieyra, a sermon in which he disputed with St. Augustine and St. Thomas about the nature of Christ's greatest expression of love at His life's end. Her commentary, in the form of a letter, was published, without her consent, by the bishop of Puebla. The bishop provided the title, *Athenagoric Letter,* or "letter worthy of the wisdom of Athena," but he also prefixed his own letter to Sister Juana, signed with the pseudonym "Filotea de la Cruz." Here he advised the nun to focus her attention and her talents more on religious matters. In her *Reply* (1691), she nominally accepted the bishop's rebuke; the smooth surface of her elegant prose, however, conceals both rage and determination to assert her right—and that of other women—to a fully realized life of the mind.

The artistry of this piece of self-defense demonstrates Sister Juana's powers and thus constitutes part of her justification. Systematically refusing to make any overt claims for herself, she declares her desire to do whatever her associates wish or demand of her. While asserting her own unimportance, she illustrates the range of her knowledge and of her rhetorical skill. The sheer abundance of her biblical allusions and of her quotations from theological texts, for instance, proves that she has mastered a large body of religious material and that she has not sacrificed religious to secular study. Her elaborate protestations of deference, her vocabulary of insignificance, her narrative of subservience: all show the verbal dexterity that enables her to achieve her own rhetorical ends even as she denies her commitment to purely personal goals.

If she acknowledges no self-seeking, she nevertheless declares and demonstrates her ungovernable passion for the life of the mind. She tells of how she joined the convent despite fears that the community "would intrude upon the peaceful silence of my books." "Certain learned persons," however, explained to her that her desire for solitary intellectual experience constituted "temptation." She therefore entered the religious life, believing, she says, "that I was fleeing from myself, but—wretch that I am!—I brought with me my worst enemy, my inclination, which I do not know whether to consider a gift or a punishment from Heaven; for once dimmed and encumbered by the many activities common to Religion, that inclination exploded in me like gunpowder." Although this sentence explicitly labels her intellectual inclinations her worst enemy and suggests that they might be considered divine punishment, the same sentence dramatizes the uncontrollable, explosive force of those inclinations and hints at the negative potential of religious experience, which dims and encumbers the mind. No matter how often Sister Juana admits that her longings amount to a form of "vice," she embodies in her prose the energy and the vividness they generate and makes her audience feel their positive weight.

The autobiographical aspects of Sister Juana's self-defense give it special immediacy for modern readers, who may recognize versions of their own dilemmas in her narrative of difficulties. Of course, girls no longer have to trick their way into learning or plead for permission to dress in boy's clothes to go to a university. But even twentieth-century young women have been known to experience the kind of hostility Sister Juana reports as the response to her remarkable achievement. Yet more recognizable as a frequent form of female anxiety is the nun's concern to proclaim her responsiveness to others, her "tender and affable nature," which causes the other nuns, she says, to hold her "in great affection." She insists that she fills all the responsibilities of a woman as well as displays the kinds of capacity more generally associated with men, and she performs her womanly and her religious duties *first*, reserving her scholarly pursuits for leisure hours.

But of course her larger argument depends on her utter denial that intelligence or a thirst for knowledge should be considered a sex-linked characteristic. She draws on history for evidence of female intellectual power; one may feel the irony of the fact that her list of female worthies requires so much annotation today. The names of these notable women have hardly become household words. Still, these names, these histories, do exist, providing powerful support for Sister Juana's position. Even more forceful is the testimony of her own experience: her account of how, deprived of books, she finds matter for intellectual inquiry everywhere—in the yolk of an egg, the spinning of a top, the reading of the Bible. This is, the reader comes to believe, a woman born to think. If she arouses uneasiness when she implicitly equates herself, as object of persecution, with Christ, she also makes one feel directly the horror of women's official exclusion, in the past, from intellectual pursuits.

Little has been written in English about Sister Juana. A volume in the Twayne series by Gerard Flynn, *Sor Juana Inés de la Cruz* (1971), provides a biographical, critical, and bibliographical introduction. She is also treated in histories of Latin American literature: for example, J. Franco, *An Introduction to Spanish-American Literature* (1969). This first English-language translation of the *Reply*, by Margaret Sayers Peden, was commissioned in 1981 by a small independent publisher in Salisbury, Connecticut (Lime Rock Press). An important critical work, belatedly translated into English, is Octavio Paz, *Sor Juana; Or, The Traps of Faith* (1988).

Reply to Sor Filotea de la Cruz[1]

My most illustrious *señora*, dear lady. It has not been my will, my poor health, or my justifiable apprehension that for so many days delayed my response. How could I write, considering that at my very first step my clumsy pen encountered two obstructions in its path? The first (and, for me, the most uncompromising) is to know how to reply to your most learned, most prudent, most holy, and most loving letter. For I recall that

1. Translated by Margaret Sayers Peden.

when Saint Thomas, the Angelic Doctor of Scholasticism, was asked about his silence regarding his teacher Albertus Magnus,[2] he replied that he had not spoken because he knew no words worthy of Albertus. With so much greater reason, must not I too be silent? Not, like the Saint, out of humility, but because in reality I know nothing I can say that is worthy of you. The second obstruction is to know how to express my appreciation for a favor as unexpected as extreme, for having my scribblings printed, a gift so immeasurable as to surpass my most ambitious aspiration, my most fervent desire, which even as an entity of reason never entered my thoughts. Yours was a kindness, finally, of such magnitude that words cannot express my gratitude, a kindness exceeding the bounds of appreciation, as great as it was unexpected—which is as Quintilian[3] said: *aspirations engender minor glory; benefices,[4] major.* To such a degree as to impose silence on the receiver.

When the blessedly sterile—that she might miraculously become fecund—Mother of John the Baptist saw in her house such an extraordinary visitor as the Mother of the Word, her reason became clouded and her speech deserted her; and thus, in the place of thanks, she burst out with doubts and questions: *And whence is to me [that the mother of my Lord should come to me?]*[5] And whence cometh such a thing to *me?* And so also it fell to Saul when he found himself the chosen, the anointed, King of Israel: *Am I not a son of Jemini, of the least tribe of Israel, and my kindred the last among all the families of the tribe of Benjamin? Why then hast thou spoken this word to me?*[6] And thus say I, most honorable lady. Why do I receive such favor? By chance, am I other than an humble nun, the lowliest creature of the world, the most unworthy to occupy your attention? "Wherefore then speakest thou so to me?" "And whence is this to me?" Nor to the first obstruction do I have any response other than I am little worthy of your eyes; nor to the second, other than wonder, in the stead of thanks, saying that I am not capable of thanking you for the smallest part of that which I owe you. This is not pretended modesty, lady, but the simplest truth issuing from the depths of my heart, that when the letter which with propriety you called *Atenagórica*[7] reached my hands, in print, I burst into tears of confusion (withal, that tears do not come easily to me) because it seemed to me that your favor was but a remonstrance God made against the wrong I have committed, and that in the same way He corrects others with punishment He wishes to subject me with benefices, with this special favor for which I know myself to be myself to be His debtor, as for an infinitude of others from His boundless kindness. I looked upon this favor as a particular way to shame and confound me, it being the most exquisite means of castigation, that of causing me, by my own intellect, to be the judge who pronounces sentence and who denounces my ingratitude. And thus, when here in my solitude I think on these things, I am wont to say: Blessed art Thou, oh Lord, for Thou hast not

---

2. St. Albert the Great (1193?–1280), scholastic philosopher, called the Universal Doctor; he exercised great influence on his student Thomas Aquinas.   3. Marcus Fabius Quintilianus (ca. A.D. 35–100), born in Spain, became a famous Roman orator and wrote on rhetoric.   4. This word would be better understood as "good works."   5. Luke 1:43.   6. 1 Samuel 9:21.   7. Sister Juana's letter criticizing Father Vieyra's sermon was retitled by the bishop *Carta Atenagórica* (Letter worthy of Athena). Athena was the Greek goddess of wisdom.

chosen to place in the hands of others my judgment, nor yet in mine, but hast reserved that to Thy own, and freed me from myself, and from the necessity to sit in judgment on myself, which judgment, forced from my own intellect, could be no less than condemnation, but Thou hast reserved me to Thy mercy, because Thou lovest me more than I can love myself.

I beg you, lady, to forgive this digression to which I was drawn by the power of truth, and, if I am to confess all the truth, I shall confess that I cast about for some manner by which I might flee the difficulty of a reply, and was sorely tempted to take refuge in silence. But as silence is a negative thing, though it explains a great deal through the very stress of not explaining, we must assign some meaning to it that we may understand what the silence is intended to say, for if not, silence will say nothing, as that is its very office: *to say nothing.* The holy Chosen Vessel, Saint Paul, having been caught up into paradise, and having heard the arcane secrets of God, *heard secret words, which it is not granted to man to utter.*[8] He does not say what he heard; he says that he cannot say it. So that of things one cannot say, it is needful to say at least that they cannot be said, so that it may be understood that not speaking is not the same as having nothing to say, but rather being unable to express the many things there are to say. Saint John says that if all the marvels our Redeemer wrought "were written every one, the world itself, I think, would not be able to contain the books that should be written."[9] And Vieyra[1] says on this point that in this single phrase the Evangelist said more than in all else he wrote; and this same Lusitanian[2] Phoenix speaks well (but when does he not speak well, even when he does not speak well of others?) because in those words Saint John said everything left unsaid and expressed all that was left to be expressed. And thus I, lady, shall respond only that I do not know how to respond; I shall thank you in saying only that I am incapable of thanking you; and I shall say, through the indication of what I leave to silence, that it is only with the confidence of one who is favored and with the protection of one who is honorable that I presume to address your magnificence, and if this be folly, be forgiving of it, for folly may be good fortune, and in this manner I shall provide further occasion for your benignity and you will better shape my intellect.

Because he was halting of speech, Moses thought himself unworthy to speak with Pharaoh, but after he found himself highly favored of God, and thus inspired, he not only spoke with God Almighty but dared ask the impossible: *shew me thy face.*[3] In this same manner, lady, and in view of how you favor me, I no longer see as impossible the obstructions I posed in the beginning: for who was it who had my letter printed unbeknownst to me? Who entitled it, who bore the cost, who honored it, it being so unworthy in itself, and in its author? What will such a person not do, not pardon? What would he fail to do, or fail to pardon? And thus, based on the supposition that I speak under the safe-conduct of your favor, and with the assurance of your benignity, and with the knowledge that like a second

---

8. 2 Corinthians 12:4.   9. John 21:25.   1. Antonio Vieira (1608–1697), author of the sermon that Sister Juana had earlier criticized, was a Portuguese ecclesiastic whose most important work was converting the Indians of Brazil.   2. Roman name for Portugal.   3. Exodus 33:13.

Ahasuerus[4] you have offered to me to kiss the top of the golden scepter of your affection as a sign of conceding to me your benevolent license to speak and offer judgments in your exalted presence, I say to you that I have taken to heart your most holy admonition that I apply myself to the study of the Sacred Books, which, though it comes in the guise of counsel, will have for me the authority of a precept, but with the not insignificant consolation that even before your counsel I was disposed to obey your pastoral suggestion as your direction, which may be inferred from the premise and argument of my Letter. For I know well that your most sensible warning is not directed against it, but rather against those worldly matters of which I have written.[5] And thus I had hoped with the Letter to make amends for any lack of application you may (with great reason) have inferred from others of my writings; and, speaking more particularly, I confess to you with all the candor of which you are deserving, and with the truth and clarity which are the natural custom in me, that my not having written often of sacred matters was not caused by disaffection or by want of application, but by the abundant fear and reverence due those Sacred Letters, knowing myself incapable of their comprehension and unworthy of their employment. Always resounding in my ears, with no little horror, I hear God's threat and prohibition to sinners like myself. *Why dost thou declare my justices, and take my covenant in thy mouth?*[6] This question, as well as the knowledge that even learned men are forbidden to read the Canticle of Canticles[7] until they have passed thirty years of age, or even Genesis—the latter for its obscurity; the former in order that the sweetness of those epithalamia not serve as occasion for imprudent youth to transmute their meaning into carnal emotion, as borne out by my exalted Father Saint Jerome,[8] who ordered that these be the last verses to be studied, and for the same reason: *And finally, one may read without peril the Song of Songs, for if it is read one may suffer harm through not understanding those Epithalamia of the spiritual wedding which is expressed in carnal terms.* And Seneca[9] says: *In the early years the faith is dim.* For how then would I have dared take in my unworthy hands these verses, defying gender, age, and, above all, custom? And thus I confess that many times this fear has plucked my pen from my hand and has turned my thoughts back toward the very same reason from which they had wished to be born: which obstacle did not impinge upon profane matters, for a heresy against art is not punished by the Holy Office but by the judicious with derision, and by critics with censure, and censure, *just or unjust, is not to be feared,* as it does not forbid the taking of communion or hearing of mass, and offers me little or no cause for anxiety, because in the opinion of those who defame my art, I have neither the obligation to know nor the aptitude to triumph. If, then, I err, I suffer neither blame nor discredit: I suffer no blame, as I have no obligation; no discredit, as I

---

4. King of Persia, who stretched out his gold scepter to his queen, Esther, and said he would grant her whatever she wished (Esther 5:2–3).   5. Sister Juana had published secular poetry and drama.
6. Psalm 50:16.   7. Song of Songs (that is, Song of Solomon), which employs erotic imagery.
8. Eusebius Sophronius Hieronymus (ca. 342–420), ascetic and scholar, most learned of the Latin Church fathers, a prolific author of treaties and commentaries. Sister Juana belonged to a Jeronymite convent; Jerome had founded the order.   9. Lucius Annaeus Seneca (ca. 3 B.C.–A.D. 63), Roman philosopher and orator.

have no possibility of triumphing—*and no one is obliged to do the impossible*. And, in truth, I have written nothing except when compelled and constrained, and then only to give pleasure to others; not alone without pleasure of my own, but with absolute repugnance, for I have never deemed myself one who has any worth in letters or the wit necessity demands of one who would write; and thus my customary response to those who press me, above all in sacred matters, is, what capacity of reason have I? what application? what resources? what rudimentary knowledge of such matters beyond that of the most superficial scholarly degrees? Leave these matters to those who understand them; I wish no quarrel with the Holy Office, for I am ignorant, and I tremble that I may express some proposition that will cause offense or twist the true meaning of some scripture. I do not study to write, even less to teach—which in one like myself were unseemly pride—but only to the end that if I study, I will be ignorant of less. This is my response, and these are my feelings.

I have never written of my own choice, but at the urging of others, to whom with reason I might say, *You have compelled me.*[1] But one truth I shall not deny (first, because it is well-known to all, and second, because although it has not worked in my favor, God has granted me the mercy of loving truth above all else), which is that from the moment I was first illuminated by the light of reason, my inclination toward letters has been so vehement, so overpowering, that not even the admonitions of others—and I have suffered many—nor my own meditations—and they have not been few—have been sufficient to cause me to forswear this natural impulse that God placed in me: the Lord God knows why, and for what purpose. And He knows that I have prayed that He dim the light of my reason, leaving only that which is needed to keep His Law, for there are those who would say that all else is unwanted in a woman, and there are even those who would hold that such knowledge does injury. And my Holy Father knows too that as I have been unable to achieve this (my prayer has not been answered), I have sought to veil the light of my reason—along with my name—and to offer it up only to Him who bestowed it upon me, and He knows that none other was the cause of my entering into Religion, notwithstanding that the spiritual exercises and company of a community were repugnant to the freedom and quiet I desired for my studious endeavors. And later, in that community, the Lord God knows—and, in the world, only the one who must know[2]—how diligently I sought to obscure my name, and how this was not permitted, saying it was temptation: and so it would have been. If it were in my power, lady, to repay you in some part what I owe you, it might be done by telling you this thing which has never before passed my lips, except to be spoken to the one who should hear it. It is my hope that by having opened wide to you the doors of my heart, by having made patent to you its most deeply-hidden secrets, you will deem my confidence not unworthy of the debt I owe to your most august person and to your most uncommon favors.

Continuing the narrations of my inclinations, of which I wish to give you a thorough account, I will tell you that I was not yet three years old

---

1. 2 Corinthians 12:11.   2. Presumably her confessor, Father Antonio Núñez.

when my mother determined to send one of my elder sisters to learn to read at a school for girls we call the *Amigas*. Affection, and mischief, caused me to follow her, and when I observed how she was being taught her lessons I was so inflamed with the desire to know how to read, that deceiving—for so I knew it to be—the mistress, I told her that my mother had meant for me to have lessons too. She did not believe it, as it was little to be believed, but, to humour me, she acceded. I continued to go there, and she continued to teach me, but now, as experience had disabused her, with all seriousness; and I learned so quickly that before my mother knew of it I could already read, for my teacher had kept it from her in order to reveal the surprise and reap the reward at one and the same time. And I, you may be sure, kept the secret, fearing that I would be whipped for having acted without permission. The woman who taught me, may God bless and keep her, is still alive and can bear witness to all I say. I also remember that in those days, my tastes being those common to that age, I abstained from eating cheese because I had heard that it made one slow of wits, for in me the desire for learning was stronger than the desire for eating—as powerful as that is in children. When later, being six or seven, and having learned how to read and write, along with all the other skills of needlework and household arts that girls learn, it came to my attention that in Mexico City there were Schools, and a University, in which one studied the sciences. The moment I heard this, I began to plague my mother with insistent and importunate pleas: she should dress me in boy's clothing and send me to Mexico City to live with relatives, to study and be tutored at the University. She would not permit it, and she was wise, but I assuaged my disappointment by reading the many and varied books belonging to my grandfather, and there were not enough punishments, nor reprimands, to prevent me from reading: so that when I came to the city many marveled, not so much at my natural wit, as at my memory, and at the amount of learning I had mastered at an age when many have scarcely learned to speak well.

I began to study Latin grammar—in all, I believe, I had no more than twenty lessons—and so intense was my concern that though among women (especially a woman in the flower of her youth) the natural adornment of one's hair is held in such high esteem, I cut off mine to the breadth of some four to six fingers, measuring the place it had reached, and imposing upon myself the condition that if by the time it had again grown to that length I had not learned such and such a thing I had set for myself to learn while my hair was growing, I would again cut it off as punishment for being so slow-witted. And it did happen that my hair grew out and still I had not learned what I had set for myself—because my hair grew quickly and I learned slowly—and in fact I did cut it in punishment for such stupidity: for there seemed to me no cause for a head to be adorned with hair and naked of learning—which was the more desired embellishment. And so I entered the religious order, knowing that life there entailed certain conditions (I refer to superficial, and not fundamental, regards) most repugnant to my nature; but given the total antipathy I felt for marriage, I deemed convent life the least unsuitable and the most honorable I could elect if I were to insure my salvation. Working against that end, first (as, finally, the most important) was the matter of all the trivial aspects of my nature which nourished my pride, such as wishing to live alone, and wishing to have no obligatory occupation that would inhibit the freedom of my studies, nor the sounds of a community that would intrude upon the peaceful silence of my books. These desires caused me to falter some while in my decision, until certain learned persons enlightened me, explaining that they were temptation, and, with divine favor, I overcame them, and took upon myself the state which now so unworthily I hold. I believed that I was fleeing from myself, but— wretch that I am!—I brought with me my worst enemy, my inclination, which I do not know whether to consider a gift or a punishment from Heaven, for once dimmed and encumbered by the many activities common to Religion, that inclination exploded in me like gunpowder, proving how *privation is the source of appetite.*

I turned again (which is badly put, for I never ceased), I continued, then, in my studious endeavour (which for me was respite during those moments not occupied by my duties) of reading and more reading, of study and more study, with no teachers but my books. Thus I learned how difficult it is to study those soulless letters, lacking a human voice or the explication of a teacher. But I suffered this labor happily for my love of learning. Oh, had it only been for love of God, which were proper, how worthwhile it would have been! I strove mightily to elevate these studies, to dedicate them to His service, as the goal to which I aspired was to study Theology—it seeming to me debilitating for a Catholic not to know everything in this life of the Divine Mysteries that can be learned through natural means—and, being a nun and not a layperson, it was seemly that I profess my vows to learning through ecclesiastical channels; and especially, being a daughter of a Saint Jerome and a Saint Paula,[3] it was essential that such erudite parents not be shamed by a witless daughter. This is the argument I proposed to myself, and it seemed to me well-reasoned. It was, however (and this cannot be denied) merely glorification and approbation of my inclination, and enjoyment of it offered as justification. And so I continued, as I have said, directing the course of my studies toward the peak of Sacred Theology, it seeming necessary to me, in order to scale those heights, to climb the steps of the human sciences and arts; for how could one undertake the study of the Queen of Sciences if first one had not come to know her servants?

How, without Logic, could I be apprised of the general and specific way in which the Holy Scripture is written? How, without Rhetoric, could I understand its figures, its tropes, its locutions? How, without Physics,[4] so many innate questions concerning the nature of animals, their sacrifices, wherein exist so many symbols, many already declared, many still to be discovered? How should I know whether Saul's being refreshed by the sound of David's harp was due to the virtue and natural power of Music, or to a transcendent power God wished to place in David? How, without

3. A Roman woman (died 404), converted to Christianity after her daughter's death, who founded a nunnery next to St. Jerome's monastery at Bethlehem and helped Jerome in his studies.   4. That is, physic, or medicine.

Arithmetic, could one understand the computations of the years, days, months, hours, those mysterious weeks communicated by Gabriel to Daniel,[5] and others for whose understanding one must know the nature, concordance, and properties of numbers? How, without Geometry, could one measure the Holy Arc of the Covenant and the Holy City of Jerusalem, whose mysterious measures are foursquare in their dimensions, as well as the miraculous proportions of all their parts? How, without Architecture, could one know the great Temple of Solomon, of which God Himself was the Author who conceived the disposition and the design, and the Wise King but the overseer who executed it, of which temple there was no foundation without mystery, no column without symbolism, no cornice without allusion, no architrave without significance; and similarly others of its parts, of which the least fillet was never intended solely for the service and complement of Art, but as symbol of greater things? How, without great knowledge of the laws and parts of which History is comprised, could one understand historical Books? Or those recapitulations in which many times what happened first is seen in the narrated account to have happened later? How, without great learning in Canon and Civil Law, could one understand Legal Books? How, without great erudition, could one apprehend the secular histories of which the Holy Scripture makes mention, such as the many customs of the Gentiles, their many rites, their many ways of speaking? How without the abundant laws and lessons of the Holy Fathers could one understand the obscure lesson of the Prophets? And without being expert in Music, how could one understand the exquisite precision of the musical proportions that grace so many Scriptures, particularly those in which Abraham beseeches God in defense of the Cities,[6] asking whether He would spare the place were there but fifty just men therein; and then Abraham reduced that number to five less than fifty, forty-five, which is a ninth, and is as Mi to Re; then to forty, which is a tone, and is as Re to Mi; from forty to thirty, which is a diatessaron, the interval of the perfect fourth; from thirty to twenty, which is the perfect fifth; and from twenty to ten, which is the octave, the diapason; and as there are no further harmonic proportions, made no further reductions. How might one understand this without Music? And there in the Book of Job, God says to Job: *Shalt thou be able to join together the shining stars the Pleiades, or canst thou stop the turning about of Arcturus? Canst thou bring forth the day star in its time, and make the evening star to rise upon the children of the earth?*[7] Which message, without knowledge of Astrology, would be impossible to apprehend. And not only these noble sciences; there is no applied art that is not mentioned. And, finally, in consideration of the Book that comprises all books, and the Science in which all sciences are embraced, and for whose comprehension all sciences serve, and even after knowing them all (which we now see is not easy, nor even possible), there is one condition that takes precedence over all the rest, which is uninterrupted prayer and purity of life, that one may

---

5. While Daniel was praying, Gabriel came to him to interpret, in great chronological detail, a vision Daniel had previously had (Daniel 9:21–27).   6. Abraham beseeches God to save Sodom for the sake of its just inhabitants (Genesis 18:23–33).   7. Job 38:31–32.

entreat of God that purgation of spirit and illumination of mind necessary for the understanding of such elevated matters: and if that be lacking, none of the aforesaid will have been of any purpose.

Of the Angelic Doctor Saint Thomas[8] the Church affirms: *When reading the most difficult passages of the Holy Scripture, he joined fast with prayer. And he was wont to say to his companion Brother Reginald that all he knew derived not so much from study or his own labor as from the grace of God.* How then should I—so lacking in virtue and so poorly read— find courage to write? But as I had acquired the rudiments of learning, I continued to study ceaselessly divers subjects, having for none any particular inclination, but for all in general; and having studied some more than others was not owing to preference, but to the chance that more books on certain subjects had fallen into my hands, causing the election of them through no discretion of my own. And as I was not directed by preference, nor, forced by the need to fulfill certain scholarly requirements, constrained by time in the pursuit of any subject, I found myself free to study numerous topics at the same time, or to leave some for others; although in this scheme some order was observed, for some I deigned[9] study and others diversion, and in the latter I found respite from the former. From which it follows that though I have studied many things I know nothing, as some have inhibited the learning of others. I speak specifically of the practical aspect of those arts that allow practice, because it is clear that when the pen moves the compass must lie idle, and while the harp is played the organ is stilled, *et sic de caeteris.*[1] And because much practice is required of one who would acquire facility, none who divides his interest among various exercises may reach perfection. Whereas in the formal and theoretical arts the contrary is true, and I would hope to persuade all with my experience, which is that one need not inhibit the other, but, in fact, each may illuminate and open the way to others, by nature of their variations and their hidden links, which were placed in this universal chain by the wisdom of their Author in such a way that they conform and are joined together with admirable unity and harmony. This is the very chain the ancients believed did issue from the mouth of Jupiter, from which were suspended all things linked one with another, as is demonstrated by the Reverend Father Athanasius Kircher[2] in his curious book, *De Magnate.* All things issue from God, Who is at once the center and the circumference from which and in which all lines begin and end.

I myself can affirm that what I have not understood in an author in one branch of knowledge I may understand in a second in a branch that seems remote from the first. And authors, in their elucidation, may suggest metaphorical examples in other arts: as when logicians say that to prove whether parts are equal, the means is to the extremes as a determined measure to two equidistant bodies; or in stating how the argument of the logician moves, in the manner of a straight line, along the shortest route, while that of the rhetorician moves as a curve, by the longest, but that

---

8. Thomas Aquinas (ca. 1225–1274), Dominican theologian, author of *Summa Theologica* (ca. 1266), and for centuries the most important authority on Church doctrine. 9. Deemed, considered. 1. And so for other things (Latin). 2. German Jesuit scientist (1601?–1680), author of *Magnes sive de arte magnetica* (The Magnet: or, of the magnetic science).

both finally arrive at the same point. And similarly, as it is when they say that the Exegetes are like an open hand, and the Scholastics like a closed fist.[3] And thus it is no apology, nor do I offer it as such, to say that I have studied many subjects, seeing that each augments the other; but that I have not profited is the fault of my own ineptitude and the inadequacy of my intelligence, not the fault of the variety. But what may be offered as exoneration is that I undertook this great task without benefit of teacher, or fellow students with whom to confer and discuss, having for a master no other than a mute book, and for a colleague, an insentient inkwell; and in the stead of explication and exercise, many obstructions, not merely those of my religious obligations (for it is already known how useful and advantageous is the time employed in them), rather, all the attendant details of living in a community: how I might be reading, and those in the adjoining cell would wish to play their instruments, and sing; how I might be studying, and two servants who had quarreled would select me to judge their dispute; or how I might be writing, and a friend come to visit me, doing me no favor but with the best of will, at which time one must not only accept the inconvenience, but be grateful for the hurt. And such occurrences are the normal state of affairs, for as the times I set apart for study are those remaining after the ordinary duties of the community are fulfilled, they are the same moments available to my sisters, in which they may come to interrupt my labor; and only those who have experience of such a community will know how true this is, and how it is only the strength of my vocation that allows me happiness; that, and the great love existing between me and my beloved sisters, for as love is union, it knows no extremes of distance.

With this I confess how interminable has been my labor; and how I am unable to say what I have with envy heard others state—that they have not been plagued by the thirst for knowledge: blessed are they. For me, not the knowing (for still I do not know), merely the desiring to know, has been such torment that I can say, as has my Father Saint Jerome (although not with his accomplishment) . . . *my conscience is witness to what effort I have expended, what difficulties I have suffered, how many times I have despaired, how often I have ceased my labors and turned to them again, driven by the hunger for knowledge; my conscience is witness, and that of those who have lived beside me.* With the exception of the companions and witnesses (for I have been denied even this consolation), I can attest to the truth of these words. And to the fact that even so, my black inclination has been so great that it has conquered all else!

It has been my fortune that, among other benefices,[4] I owe to God a most tender and affable nature, and because of it my sisters (who being good women do not take note of my faults) hold me in great affection, and take pleasure in my company; and knowing this, and moved by the great love I hold for them—having greater reason than they—I enjoy even more *their* company. Thus I was wont in our rare idle moments to visit among them, offering them consolation and entertaining myself in their conversation. I could not help but note, however, that in these times I was

---

3. The Exegetes emphasized interpretation; the Scholastics, logic.   **4.** Benefits or kindnesses.

neglecting my study, and I made a vow not to enter any cell unless obliged by obedience or charity; for without such a compelling constraint—the constraint of mere intention not being sufficient—my love would be more powerful than my will. I would (knowing well my frailty) make this vow for the period of a few weeks, or a month; and when that time had expired, I would allow myself a brief respite of a day or two before renewing it, using that time not so much for rest (for *not* studying has never been restful for me) as to assure that I not be deemed cold, remote, or ungrateful in the little-deserved affection of my dearest sisters.

In this practice one may recognize the strength of my inclination. I give thanks to God, Who willed that such an ungovernable force be turned toward letters and not to some other vice. From this it may also be inferred how obdurately against the current my poor studies have sailed (more accurately, have foundered). For still to be related is the most arduous of my difficulties—those mentioned until now, either compulsory or fortuitous, being merely tangential—and still unreported the more directly aimed slings and arrows that have acted to impede and prevent the exercise of my study. Who would have doubted, having witnessed such general approbation, that I sailed before the wind across calm seas, amid the laurels of widespread acclaim. But our Lord God knows that it has not been so; He knows how from amongst the blossoms of this very acclaim emerged such a number of aroused vipers, hissing their emulation and their persecution, that one could not count them. But the most noxious, those who most deeply wounded me, have not been those who persecuted me with open loathing and malice, but rather those who in loving me and desiring my well-being (and who are deserving of God's blessing for their good intent) have mortified and tormented me more than those others with their abhorrence. "Such studies are not in conformity with sacred innocence; surely she will be lost; surely she will, by cause of her very perspicacity and acuity, grow heady at such exalted heights." How was I to endure? An uncommon sort of martyrdom in which I was both martyr and executioner. And for my (in me, twice hapless) facility in making verses, even though they be sacred verses, what sorrows have I not suffered? What sorrows not ceased to suffer? Be assured, lady, it is often that I have meditated on how one who distinguishes himself—or one on whom God chooses to confer distinction, for it is only He who may do so—is received as a common enemy, because it seems to some that he usurps the applause they deserve, or that he dams up the admiration to which they aspired, and so they persecute that person.

That politically barbaric law of Athens by which any person who excelled by cause of his natural gifts and virtues was exiled from his Republic in order that he not threaten the public freedom still endures, is still observed in our day, although not for the reasons held by the Athenians. Those reasons have been replaced by another, no less efficient though not as well founded, seeming, rather, a maxim more appropriate to that impious Machiavelli[5]—which is to abhor one who excels, because he

---

5. Niccolò Machiavelli (1469–1527), Italian statesman whose writings (notably *The Prince*) advocated political unscrupulousness.

deprives others of regard. And thus it happens, and thus it has always happened.

For if not, what was the cause of the rage and loathing the Pharisees[6] directed against Christ, there being so many reasons to love Him? If we behold His presence, what is more to be loved than that Divine beauty? What more powerful to stir one's heart? For if ordinary human beauty holds sway over strength of will, and is able to subdue it with tender and enticing vehemence, what power would Divine beauty exert, with all its prerogatives and sovereign endowments? What might move, what effect, what not move and not effect, such incomprehensible beauty, that beauteous face through which, as through a polished crystal, were diffused the rays of Divinity? What would not be moved by that semblance which beyond incomparable human perfections revealed Divine illuminations? If the visage of Moses, merely from conversation with God, caused men to fear to come near him,[7] how much finer must be the face of God-made-flesh? And among other virtues, what more to be loved than that celestial modesty? That sweetness and kindness disseminating mercy in every movement? That profound humility and gentleness? Those words of eternal life and eternal wisdom? How therefore is it possible that such beauty did not stir their souls, that they did not follow after Him, enamored and enlightened?

The Holy Mother, my Mother Teresa,[8] says that when she beheld the beauty of Christ never again was she inclined toward any human creature, for she saw nothing that was not ugliness compared to such beauty. How was it then that in men it engendered such contrary reactions? For although they were uncouth and vile and had no knowledge or appreciation of His perfections, not even as they might profit from them, how was it they were not moved by the many advantages of such benefices as He performed for them, healing the sick, resurrecting the dead, restoring those possessed of the devil? How was it they did not love Him? But God is witness that it was for these very acts they did not love Him, that they despised Him. As they themselves testified.

They gather together in their council and say: *What do we? for this man doth many miracles.*[9] Can this be cause? If they had said: here is an evil-doer, a transgressor of the law, a rabble-rouser who with deceit stirs up the populace, they would have lied—as they did indeed lie when they spoke these things. But there were more opposite reasons for effecting what they desired, which was to take His life; and to give as reason that he had performed wondrous deeds seems not befitting learned men, for such were the Pharisees. Thus it is that in the heat of passion learned men erupt with such irrelevancies; for we know it as truth that only for this reason was it determined that Christ should die. Oh, men, if men you may be called, being so like to brutes, what is the cause of so cruel a determination? Their only response is that "this man doth many miracles." May God forgive them. Then is performing signal deeds cause enough that one

6. The Pharisees, members of a strict Jewish sect that emphasized conformity to the law, were according to the New Testament of the Bible prominent in plotting the death of Jesus (Mark 3:6, John 11:47–57).   7. Exodus 34:30.   8. St. Teresa de Ávila (1515–1582), a mystical writer, responsible for a great awakening of religious fervor.   9. John 11:47.

should die? This "he doth many miracles" evokes *the root of Jesse, who standeth for an ensign of the people,*[1] and that *and for a sign which shall be contradicted.*[2] He is a sign? Then He shall die. He excels? Then He shall suffer, for that is the reward for one who excels.

Often on the crest of temples are placed as adornment figures of the winds and of fame, and to defend them from the birds, they are covered with iron barbs; this appears to be in defense, but is in truth obligatory propriety: the figure thus elevated cannot survive without the very barbs that prick it; there on high is found the animosity of the air, on high the ferocity of the elements, on high is unleashed the anger of the thunderbolt, on high stands the target for slings and arrows. Oh unhappy eminence, exposed to such uncounted perils. Oh sign, become the target of envy and the butt of contradiction. Whatever eminence, whether that of dignity, nobility, riches, beauty, or science, must suffer this burden; but the eminence that undergoes the most severe attack is that of reason. First, because it is the most defenseless, for riches and power strike out against those who dare attack them; but not so reason, for while it is the greater it is more modest and long-suffering, and defends itself less. Second, as Gracian[3] stated so eruditely, *favors in man's reason are favors in his nature.*

For no other cause except that the angel is superior in reason is the angel above man; for no other cause does man stand above the beast but by his reason; and thus, as no one wishes to be lower than another, neither does he confess that another is superior in reason, as reason is a consequence of being superior. One will abide, and will confess that another is nobler than he, that another is richer, more handsome, and even that he is more learned, but that another is richer in reason scarcely any will confess: *Rare is he who will concede genius.* That is why the assault against this virtue works to such profit.

When the soldiers mocked, made entertainment and diversion of our Lord Jesus Christ, they brought Him a worn purple garment and a hollow reed, and a crown of thorns to crown Him King of Fools.[4] But though the reed and the purple were an affront, they did not cause suffering. Why does only the crown give pain? Is it not enough that like the other emblems the crown was a symbol of ridicule and ignominy, as that was its intent? No. Because the sacred head of Christ and His divine intellect were the depository of wisdom, and the world is not satisfied for wisdom to be the object of mere ridicule, it must also be done injury and harm. A head that is a storehouse of wisdom can expect nothing but a crown of thorns. What garland may human wisdom expect when it is known what was bestowed on that divine wisdom? Roman pride crowned the many achievements of their Captains with many crowns: he who defended the city received the civic crown; he who fought his way into the hostile camp received the camp crown; he who scaled the wall, the mural;[5] he who liberated a beseiged city, or any army besieged either in the field or in the enemy camp, received the obsidional, the siege, crown; other feats were crowned with naval, ovation, or triumphal crowns, as described by Pliny

---

1. Isaiah 11:10.   2. Luke 2:34.   3. Baltasar Gracián (1601–1658), Spanish Jesuit philosopher. 4. Matthew 27:28–31.   5. Pertaining to walls; the word *crown* is understood.

and Aulus Gellius.[6] Observing so many and varied crowns, I debated as to which Christ's crown must have been, and determined that it was the siege crown, for (as well you know, lady) that was the most honored crown and was called obsidional after *obsidio*, which means siege; which crown was made not from gold, or silver, but from the leaves and grasses flourishing on the field where the feat was achieved. And as the heroic feat of Christ was to break the siege of the Prince of Darkness, who had laid siege to all the earth, as is told in the Book of Job, quoting Satan: *I have gone round about the earth, and walked through it,*[7] and as St. Peter says: *As a roaring lion, goeth about seeking whom he may devour.*[8] And our Master came and caused him to lift the siege: *Now shall the prince of this world be cast out.*[9] So the soldiers crowned Him not with gold or silver but with the natural fruit of the world, which was the field of battle—and which, after the curse *Thorns also and thistles shall it bring forth to thee,*[1] produced only thorns—and thus it was a most fitting crown for the courageous and wise Conqueror, with which His mother Synagogue crowned Him. And the daughters of Zion, weeping, came out to witness the sorrowful triumph,[2] as they had come rejoicing for the triumph of Solomon,[3] because the triumph of the wise is earned with sorrow and celebrated with weeping, which is the manner of the triumph of wisdom; and as Christ is the King of wisdom, He was the first to wear that crown; and as it was sanctified on His brow, it removed all fear and dread from those who are wise, for they know they need aspire to no other honor.

The Living Word, Life, wished to restore life to Lazarus, who was dead. His disciples did not know His purpose and they said to Him: *Rabbi, the Jews but now sought to stone thee; and goest thou thither again?* And the Redeemer calmed their fear: *Are there not twelve hours of the day?*[4] It seems they feared because there had been those who wished to stone Him when He rebuked them, calling them thieves and not shepherds of sheep.[5] And thus the disciples feared that if He returned to the same place—for even though rebukes be just, they are often badly received—He would be risking his life. But once having been disabused and having realized that He was setting forth to raise up Lazarus from the dead, what was it that caused Thomas, like Peter in the Garden, to say *Let us also go, that we may die with him?*[6] What say you, Sainted Apostle? The Lord does not go out to die; whence your misgiving? For Christ goes not to rebuke, but to work an act of mercy, and therefore they will do Him no harm. These same Jews could have assured you, for when He reproved those who wished to stone Him, *Many good works I have shewed you from my Father; for which of those works do you stone me?* they replied: *For a good work we stone thee not; but for blasphemy.*[7] And as they say they will not stone Him for doing good works, and now He goes to do a work so great as to raise up Lazarus from the dead, whence your misgiving? Why do you fear? Were it not better to say: let us go to gather the fruits of appreciation for

---

6. Latin writer (2nd century A.D.), author of *Noctes Atticae*, valuable for its quotations from lost works. Pliny the Younger (62?–ca. 113) was a Roman orator and statesman and author of well-known letters about Roman life.   7. Job 1:7.   8. 1 Peter 5:8.   9. John 12:31.   1. The curse on Adam and Eve after the Fall (Genesis 3:18).   2. Luke 23:27–28.   3. Song of Solomon 3:11.   4. John 11:8–9.
5. John 10:1–31.   6. John 11:16.   7. John 10:32–33.

the good work our Master is about to do; to see him lauded and applauded for His benefice; to see men marvel at His miracle. Why speak words seemingly so alien to the circumstance as *Let us also go?* Ah, woe, the Saint feared as a prudent man and spoke as an Apostle. Does Christ not go to work a miracle? Why, what *greater* peril? It is less to be suffered that pride endure rebukes than envy witness miracles. In all the above, most honored lady, I do not wish to say (nor is such folly to be found in me) that I have been persecuted for my wisdom, but merely for my love of wisdom and letters, having achieved neither one nor the other.

At one time even the Prince of the Apostles was very far from wisdom, as is emphasized in that *But Peter followed afar off.*[8] Very distant from the laurels of a learned man is one so little in his judgment that he was *Not knowing what he said.*[9] And being questioned on his mastery of wisdom, he himself was witness that he had not achieved the first measure: *But he denied him, saying: Woman, I know him not.*[1] And what becomes of him? We find that having this reputation of ignorance, he did not enjoy its good fortune, but, rather, the affliction of being taken for wise. And why? There was no other motive but: *This man also was with him*[2] He was fond of wisdom, it filled His heart, He followed after it, He prided himself as a pursuer and lover of wisdom; and although He followed from so *afar off* that He neither understood nor achieved it, His love for it was sufficient that He incur its torments. And there was present that soldier to cause Him distress, and a certain maid-servant to cause Him grief. I confess that I find myself very distant from the goals of wisdom, for all that I have desired to follow it, even from *afar off.* But in this I have been brought closer to the fire of persecution, to the crucible of torment, and to such lengths that they have asked that study be forbidden to me.

At one time this was achieved through the offices of a very saintly and ingenuous Abbess who believed that study was a thing of the Inquisition, who commanded me not to study. I obeyed her (the three some[3] months her power to command endured) in that I did not take up a book; but that I study not at all is not within my power to achieve, and this I could not obey, for though I did not study in books, I studied all the things that God had wrought, reading in them, as in writing and in books, all the workings of the universe. I looked on nothing without reflection; I heard nothing without meditation, even in the most minute and imperfect things; because as there is no creature, however lowly, in which one cannot recognize that *God made me,* there is none that does not astound reason, if properly meditated on. Thus, I reiterate, I saw and admired all things; so that even the very persons with whom I spoke, and the things they said, were cause for a thousand meditations. Whence the variety of genius and wit, being all of a single species? Which the temperaments and hidden qualities that occasioned such variety? If I saw a figure, I was forever combining the proportion of its lines and measuring it with my reason and reducing it to new proportions. Occasionally as I walked along the far wall of one of our dormitories (which is a most capacious room) I observed

---

8. Luke 22:54.   9. Refers to Peter (Luke 9:33).   1. Luke 22:57.   2. A serving maid says this of Peter, who thereupon denies knowing Jesus (Luke 22:56).   3. That is, "the three or so."

that though the lines of the two sides were parallel and the ceiling perfectly level, in my sight they were distorted, the lines seeming to incline toward one another, the ceiling seeming lower in the distance than in proximity: from which I inferred that *visual* lines run straight but not parallel, forming a pyramidal figure. I pondered whether this might not be the reason that caused the ancients to question whether the world were spherical. Because, although it so seems, this could be a deception of vision, suggesting concavities where possibly none existed.

This manner of reflection has always been my habit, and is quite beyond my will to control; on the contrary, I am wont to become vexed that my intellect makes me weary; and I believed that it was so with everyone, as well as making verses, until experience taught me otherwise; and it is so strong in me this nature, or custom, that I look at nothing without giving it further examination. Once in my presence two young girls were spinning a top and scarcely had I seen the motion and the figure described, when I began, out of this madness of mine, to meditate on the effortless *motus*[4] of the spherical form, and how the impulse persisted even when free and independent of its cause—for the top continued to dance even at some distance from the child's hand, which was the causal force. And not content with this, I had flour brought and sprinkled about, so that as the top danced one might learn whether these were perfect circles it described with its movement; and I found that they were not, but, rather, spiral lines that lost their circularity as the impetus declined. Other girls sat playing at spillikins[5] (surely the most frivolous game that children play); I walked closer to observe the figures they formed, and seeing that by chance three lay in a triangle, I set to joining one with another, recalling that this was said to be the form of the mysterious ring of Solomon,[6] in which he was able to see the distant splendor and images of the Holy Trinity, by virtue of which the ring worked such prodigies and marvels. And the same shape was said to form David's harp, and that is why Saul was refreshed at its sound; and harps today largely conserve that shape.

And what shall I tell you, lady, of the natural secrets I have discovered while cooking? I see that an egg holds together and fries in butter or in oil, but, on the contrary, in syrup shrivels into shreds; observe that to keep sugar in a liquid state one need only add a drop or two of water in which a quince or other bitter fruit has been soaked; observe that the yolk and the white of one egg are so dissimilar that each with sugar produces a result not obtainable with both together. I do not wish to weary you with such inconsequential matters, and make mention of them only to give you full notice of my nature, for I believe they will be occasion for laughter. But, lady, as women, what wisdom may be ours if not the philosophies of the kitchen? Lupercio Leonardo[7] spoke well when he said: how well one may philosophize when preparing dinner. And I often say, when observing these trivial details: had Aristotle prepared victuals, he would have written more. And pursuing the manner of my cogitations, I tell you that this process is so continuous in me that I have no need for books. And on one

4. Motion.   5. Jackstraws, or pick-up sticks.   6. It may, like Solomon's seal, have contained the image of the star of David, composed of triangles.   7. Lupercio Leonardo de Argensola (1559–1639), poet, playwright, and historian.

occasion, when because of a grave upset of the stomach the physicians forbade me to study, I passed thus some days, but then I proposed that it would be less harmful if they allowed me books, because so vigorous and vehement were my cogitations that my spirit was consumed more greatly in a quarter of an hour than in four days' studying books. And thus they were persuaded to allow me to read. And moreover, lady, not even have my dreams been excluded from this ceaseless agitation of my imagination; indeed, in dreams it is wont to work more freely and less encumbered, collating with greater clarity and calm the gleanings of the day, arguing and making verses, of which I could offer you an extended catalogue, as well as of some arguments and inventions that I have better achieved sleeping than awake. I relinquish this subject in order not to tire you, for the above is sufficient to allow your discretion and acuity to penetrate perfectly and perceive my nature, as well as the beginnings, the methods, and the present state of my studies.

Even, lady, were these merits (and I see them celebrated as such in men), they would not have been so in me, for I cannot but study. If they are faults, then, for the same reasons, I believe I have none. Nevertheless, I live always with so little confidence in myself that neither in my study, nor in any other thing, do I trust my judgment; and thus I remit the decision to your sovereign genius, submitting myself to whatever sentence you may bestow, without controversy, without reluctance, for I have wished here only to present you with a simple narration of my inclination toward letters.

I confess, too, that though it is true, as I have stated, that I had no need of books, it is nonetheless also true that they have been no little inspiration, in divine as in human letters. Because I find a Debbora[8] administering the law, both military and political, and governing a people among whom there were many learned men. I find a most wise Queen of Saba,[9] so learned that she dares to challenge with hard questions the wisdom of the greatest of all wise men, without being reprimanded for doing so, but, rather, as a consequence, to judge unbelievers. I see many and illustrious women; some blessed with the gift of prophecy, like Abigail,[1] others of persuasion, like Esther;[2] others with pity, like Rehab;[3] others with perseverance, like Anna,[4] the mother of Samuel; and an infinite number of others, with divers gifts and virtues.

If I again turn to the Gentiles, the first I encounter are the Sibyls,[5] those women chosen by God to prophesy the principal mysteries of our Faith, and with learned and elegant verses that surpass admiration. I see adored as a goddess of the sciences a woman like Minerva,[6] the daughter of the first Jupiter and mistress over all the wisdom of Athens. I see a Polla Argentaria, who helped Lucan, her husband, write his epic *Pharsalia*.[7] I

8. Or Deborah, a prophetess who judged the Israelites (Judges 4:4–14).   9. Or Sheba, who tested King Solomon with questions (1 Kings 10:1–3).   1. Wife of a surly husband, Nabal. After Nabal insulted King David, she went to the king with presents and prophesied his future triumphs, thus saving her husband's life (1 Samuel 25:2–35).   2. She persuaded her husband, King Ahasuerus, to protect the Jews (Esther 5–9).   3. Or Rahab, a harlot who protected two Israelites from the King of Jericho (Joshua 2:1–7).   4. Or Hannah, who after years of childlessness received the answer to her prayers in the birth of Samuel (1 Samuel 1:1–20).   5. Female prophets of the ancient world.   6. Or Athena, goddess of wisdom.   7. Epic poem on the civil war between Caesar and Pompey, properly called *Bellum Civile* (ca. A.D. 62–65).

see the daughter of the divine Tiresias,[8] more learned than her father. I see a Zenobia, Queen of the Palmyrans,[9] as wise as she was valiant. An Arete, most learned daughter of Aristippus.[1] A Nicostrate,[2] framer of Latin verses and most erudite in Greek. An Aspasia Milesia, who taught philosophy and rhetoric, and who was a teacher of the philosopher Pericles. An Hypatia, who taught astrology, and studied many years in Alexandria. A Leontium, a Greek woman, who questioned the philosopher Theophrastus, and convinced him. A Julia, a Corinna, a Cornelia;[3] and, finally, a great throng of women deserving to be named, some as Greeks, some as muses, some as seers; for all were nothing more than learned women, held, and celebrated—and venerated as well—as such by antiquity. Without mentioning an infinity of other women whose names fill books. For example, I find the Egyptian Catherine,[4] studying and influencing the wisdom of all the wise men of Egypt. I see a Gertrudis[5] studying, writing, and teaching. And not to overlook examples close to home, I see my most holy mother Paula, learned in Hebrew, Greek, and Latin, and most able in interpreting the Scriptures. And what greater praise than, having as her chronicler a Jeronimus Maximus,[6] that Saint scarcely found himself competent for his task, and says, with that weighty deliberation and energetic precision with which he so well expressed himself: "If all the members of my body were tongues, they still would not be sufficient to proclaim the wisdom and virtue of Paula." Similarly praiseworthy was the widow Blesilla; also, the illustrious virgin Eustochium,[7] both daughters of this same saint; especially the second, who, for her knowledge, was called the Prodigy of the World. The Roman Fabiola[8] was most well-versed in the Holy Scripture. Proba Falconia, a Roman woman, wrote elegant centos,[9] containing verses from Virgil, about the mysteries of Our Holy Faith. It is well-known by all that Queen Isabel,[1] wife of the tenth Alfonso, wrote about astrology. Many others I do not list, out of the desire not merely to transcribe what others have said (a vice I have always abominated); and many are flourishing today, as witness Christina Alexandra,[2] Queen of Sweden, as learned as she is valiant and magnanimous, and the Most Honorable Ladies, the Duquesa of Abeyro and the Condesa of Villaumbrosa.

The venerable Doctor Arce[3] (by his virtue and learning a worthy teacher of the Scriptures) in his scholarly *Bibliorum* raises this question: *Is it permissible for women to dedicate themselves to the study of the Holy Scriptures, and to their interpretation?* and he offers as negative arguments

---

8. Legendary blind Theban seer. His daughter was Manto, known for her skill in divination by fire.   9. Learned widow of Odenathus, she declared her independence from Rome and expanded the Middle-Eastern territory under her rule, naming herself Augusta, empress of Rome. She was finally defeated and captured in 272.   1. Greek philosopher (ca. 435–ca. 360 B.C.).   2. Or Carmentis, legendary daughter of Pallas, king of Arcadia, and (in legend) inventor of the Roman alphabet.   3. Noted for her devotion to her children's education after her husband's death (2nd century B.C.); she was the second daughter of Scipio Africanus and wife of Tiberius Sempronius Gracchus. Julia Domna (2nd century A.D.), wife of the Roman emperor Septimius Severus, known for her learning as Julia the Philosopher. Corinna (ca. 500? B.C.) was a lyric poet of Tanagra who wrote for a group of women.   4. St. Catherine (4th century?), allegedly so wise she could refute fifty philosophers at once.   5. St. Gertrude (died 1302), Benedictine nun and visionary, an important mystic.   6. St. Jerome.   7. Blesilla and Eustochium were daughters of St. Paula, and, like her, were taught by St. Jerome.   8. One of Jerome's disciples.   9. Compositions made up of verses from other authors.   1. Of Spain, wife of Alfonso X, Alfonso the Wise (1221–1284).   2. She attracted many scholars and artists to her court (1626–1689).   3. Juan Díaz de Arce (1594–1653), author of theological books.

the opinions of many saints, especially that of the Apostle: *Let women keep silence in the churches; for it is not permitted them to speak,* etc.[4] He later cites other opinions and, from the same Apostle, verses from his letter to Titus: *The aged women in like manner, in holy attire . . . teaching well,*[5] with interpretations by the Holy Fathers. Finally he resolves, with all prudence, that teaching publicly from a University chair, or preaching from the pulpit, is not permissible for women; but that to study, write, and teach privately not only is permissible, but most advantageous and useful. It is evident that this is not to be the case with all women, but with those to whom God may have granted special virtue and prudence, and who may be well advanced in learning, and having the essential talent and requisites for such a sacred calling. This view is indeed just, so much so that not only women, who are held to be so inept, but also men, who merely for being men believe they are wise, should be prohibited from interpreting the Sacred Word if they are not learned and virtuous and of gentle and well-inclined natures; that this is not so has been, I believe, at the root of so much sectarianism and so many heresies. For there are many who study but are ignorant, especially those who are in spirit arrogant, troubled, and proud, so eager for new interpretations of the Word (which itself rejects new interpretations) that merely for the sake of saying what no one else has said they speak a heresy, and even then are not content. Of these the Holy Spirit says: *For wisdom will not enter into a malicious soul.*[6] To such as these more harm results from knowing than from ignorance. A wise man has said: he who does not know Latin is not a complete fool; but he who knows it is well qualified to be.[7] And I would add that a fool may reach perfection (if ignorance may tolerate perfection) by having studied his tittle of philosophy and theology and by having some learning of tongues, by which he may be a fool in many sciences and languages: a great fool cannot be contained solely in his mother tongue.

For such as these, I reiterate, study is harmful, because it is as if to place a sword in the hands of a madman; which, though a most noble instrument for defense, is in his hands his own death and that of many others. So were the Divine Scriptures in the possession of the evil Pelagius[8] and the intractable Arius,[9] of the evil Luther,[1] and the other heresiarchs like our own Doctor (who was neither ours nor a doctor) Cazalla.[2] To these men, wisdom was harmful, although it is the greatest nourishment and the life of the soul; in the same way that in a stomach of sickly constitution and adulterated complexion, the finer the nourishment it receives, the more arid, fermented, and perverse are the humors it produces; thus these evil men: the more they study, the worse opinions they engender, their reason being obstructed with the very substance meant to nourish it, and they study much and digest little, exceeding the limits of the vessel of their reason. Of which the Apostle says: *For I say, by the grace that is given me,*

4. 1 Corinthians 14:34.   5. Titus 2:3–5.   6. Book of Wisdom 1:4 (in the Apocrypha).   7. Alludes to the Spanish proverb "A fool, unless he knows Latin, is never a great fool."   8. Heretical monk (ca. 355–ca. 425) who taught that people do not need divine grace, since they have a natural tendency to seek the good.   9. Libyan theologian (ca. 256–336), founder of the Arian heresy that declared that Christ was neither eternal nor equal with God.   1. Martin Luther (1483–1546), German leader of the Protestant Reformation and, from Sister Juana's point of view, another heretic.   2. Augustino Cazallo (1510–1559), Spanish Protestant executed by the Inquisition for promulgating Lutheran doctrine.

to all that are among you, not to be more wise than it behoveth to be wise, but to be wise unto sobriety, and according as God hath divided to every one the measure of faith.[3] And in truth, the Apostle did not direct these words to women, but to men; and that *keep silence* is intended not only for women, but for *all* incompetents. If I desire to know as much, or more, than Aristotle or Saint Augustine, and if I have not the aptitude of Saint Augustine or Aristotle, though I study more than either, not only will I not achieve learning, but I will weaken and dull the workings of my feeble reason with the disproportionateness of the goal.

Oh, that each of us—I, being ignorant, the first—should take the measure of our talents before we study, or, more importantly, write, with the covetous ambition to equal and even surpass others, how little spirit we should have for it, and how many errors we should avoid, and how many tortured intellects of which we have experience, we should have had no experience! And I place my own ignorance in the forefront of all these, for if I knew all I should, I would not write. And I protest that I do so only to obey you; and with such apprehension that you owe me more that I have taken up my pen in fear than you would have owed had I presented you more perfect works. But it is well that they go to your correction. Cross them out, tear them up, reprove me, and I shall appreciate that more than all the vain applause others may offer. *That just men shall correct me in mercy, and shall reprove me; but let not the oil of the sinner fatten my head.*[4] And returning again to our Arce, I say that in affirmation of his opinion he cites the words of my father, Saint Jerome: *To Leta, Upon the Education of Her Daughter.* Where he says: *Accustom her tongue, still young, to the sweetness of the Psalms. Even the names through which little by little she will become accustomed to form her phrases should not be chosen by chance, but selected and repeated with care; the prophets must be included, of course, and the apostles, as well, and all the Patriarchs beginning with Adam and down to Matthew and Luke, so that as she practices other things she will be readying her memory for the future. Let your daily task be taken from the flower of the Scriptures.* And if this Saint desired that a young girl scarcely beginning to talk be educated in this fashion, what would he desire for his nuns and his spiritual daughters? These beliefs are illustrated in the examples of the previously mentioned Eustochium and Fabiola, and Marcella, her sister, and Pacatula, and others whom the Saint honors in his epistles, exhorting them to this sacred exercise, as they are recognized in the epistle I cited, *Let your daily task . . .* , which is affirmation of and agreement with the *aged women . . . teaching well* of Saint Paul. My illustrious Father's *Let your daily task . . .* makes clear that the teacher of the child is to be Leta herself, the child's mother.

Oh, how much injury might have been avoided in our land if our aged women had been learned, as was Leta, and had they known how to instruct as directed by Saint Paul and by my Father, Saint Jerome. And failing this, and because of the considerable idleness to which our poor women have been relegated, if a father desires to provide his daughters with more than ordinary learning, he is forced by necessity, and by the

---

3. Romans 12:3.   4. Psalm 141:5.

absence of wise elder women, to bring men to teach the skills of reading, writing, counting, the playing of musical instruments, and other accomplishments, from which no little harm results, as is experienced every day in doleful examples of perilous association, because through the immediacy of contact and the intimacy born from the passage of time, what one may never have thought possible is easily accomplished. For which reason many prefer to leave their daughters unpolished and uncultured rather than to expose them to such notorious peril as that of familiarity with men, which quandary could be prevented if there were learned elder women, as Saint Paul wished to see, and if the teaching were handed down from one to another, as is the custom with domestic crafts and all other traditional skills.

For what objection can there be that an older woman, learned in letters and in sacred conversation and customs, have in her charge the education of young girls? This would prevent these girls being lost either for lack of instruction or for hesitating to offer instruction through such dangerous means as male teachers, for even when there is no greater risk of indecency than to seat beside a modest woman (who still may blush when her own father looks directly at her) a strange man who treats her as if he were a member of the household and with the authority of an intimate, the modesty demanded in interchange with men, and in conversation with them, is sufficient reason that such an arrangement not be permitted. For I do not find that the custom of men teaching women is without its peril, lest it be in the severe tribunal of the confessional, or from the remote decency of the pulpit, or in the distant learning of books—never in the personal contact of immediacy. And the world knows this is true; and, notwithstanding, it is permitted solely from the want of learned elder women. Then is it not detrimental, the lack of such women? This question should be addressed by those who, bound to that *Let women keep silence in the church,* say that it is blasphemy for women to learn and teach, as if it were not the Apostle himself who said: *The aged women . . . teaching well.* As well as the fact that this prohibition touches upon historical fact as reported by Eusebium:[5] which is that in the early Church, women were charged with teaching the doctrine to one another in the temples and the sound of this teaching caused confusion as the Apostles were preaching and this is the reason they were ordered to be silent; and even today, while the homilist is preaching, one does not pray aloud.

Who will argue that for the comprehension of many Scriptures one must be familiar with the history, customs, ceremonies, proverbs, and even the manners of speaking of those times in which they were written, if one is to apprehend the references and allusions of more than a few passages of the Holy Word. *And rend your heart and not your garments.*[6] Is this not a reference to the ceremony in which Hebrews rent their garments as a sign of grief, as did the evil pontiff when he said that Christ had blasphemed? In many scriptures the Apostle writes of succour for widows; did they not refer to the customs of those times? Does not the example of the

5. Probably Eusebius of Caesaria (ca. 263–339?), an early Church historian.   6. Joel 2:13.

valiant woman, *Her husband is honourable in the gates*,[7] allude to the fact that the tribunals of the judges were at the gates of the cities? That *Dare terram Deo*, give of your land to God, did that not mean to make some votive offering? And did they not call the public sinners *hiemantes*, those who endure the winter, because they made their penance in the open air instead of at a town gate as others did? And Christ's plaint to that Pharisee who had neither kissed him nor given him water for his feet,[8] was that not because it was the Jews' usual custom to offer these acts of hospitality? And we find an infinite number of additional instances not only in the Divine Letters, but human, as well, such as *adorate purpuram*, venerate the purple, which meant obey the King; *manumittere eum*, manumit them, alluding to the custom and ceremony of striking the slave with one's hand to signify his freedom. That *intonuit coelum*, heaven thundered, in Virgil, which alludes to the augury of thunder from the west, which was held to be good.[9] Martial's *tu nunquam leporem edisti*,[1] you never ate hare, has not only the wit of ambiguity in its *leporem*,[2] but, as well, the allusion to the reputed propensity of hares [to bless with beauty those who dine on them]. That proverb, *maleam legens, que sunt domi obliviscere*, to sail along the shore of Malia is to forget what one has at home, alludes to the great peril of the promontory of Laconia.[3] That chaste matron's response to the unwanted suit of her pretender: "the hinge-pins shall not be oiled for my sake, nor shall the torches blaze," meaning that she did not want to marry, alluded to the ceremony of anointing the doorways with oils and lighting the nuptial torches in the wedding ceremony, as if now we would say, they shall not prepare the thirteen coins for my dowry, nor shall the priest invoke the blessing. And thus it is with many comments of Virgil and Homer and all the poets and orators. In addition, how many are the difficulties found even in the grammar of the Holy Scripture, such as writing a plural for a singular, or changing from the second to third persons, as in the Psalms, *Let him kiss me with the kiss of his mouth, for thy breasts are better than wine*.[4] Or placing adjectives in the genitive instead of the accusative, as in *Calicem salutaris accipiam*, I will take the chalice of salvation.[5] Or to replace the feminine with the masculine, and, in contrast, to call any sin adultery.

All this demands more investigation than some believe, who strictly as grammarians, or, at most, employing the four principles of applied logic, attempt to interpret the Scriptures while clinging to that *Let the women keep silence in the church*, not knowing how it is to be interpreted. As well as that other verse, *Let the women learn in silence*.[6] For this latter scripture works more to women's favor than their disfavor, as it commands them to learn; and it is only natural that they must maintain silence while they learn. And it is also written, *Hear, oh Israel, and be silent*.[7] Which addresses the entire congregation of men and women, commanding all to silence, because if one is to hear and learn, it is with good reason that he

---

7. Proverbs 31:23.   8. Luke 7:44–45.   9. Sister Juana possibly misremembers *Aeneid* 2.693: "thunder on the left."   1. Marcus Valerius Martialis (ca. 40–ca. 104), Roman epigrammatic poet; "Edisti numquam, Gellia, tu leporem" (*Epigrams* 5:29).   2. This word can also mean charm, grace, attractiveness.   3. The site of ancient Sparta, conquered by Macedonia in the 4th century B.C.   4. Song of Solomon 1:2.   5. Psalm 116:13.   6. 1 Timothy 2:11.   7. Not a biblical quotation.

attend and be silent. And if it is not so, I would want these interpreters and expositors of Saint Paul to explain to me how they interpret that scripture, *Let the women keep silence in the church*. For either they must understand it to refer to the material church, that is the church of pulpits and cathedras,[8] or to the spiritual, the community of the faithful, which is the Church. If they understand it to be the former, which, in my opinion, is its true interpretation, then we see that if in fact it is not permitted of women to read publicly in church, nor preach, why do they censure those who study privately? And if they understand the latter, and wish that the prohibition of the Apostle be applied transcendentally—that not even in private are women to be permitted to write or study—how are we to view the fact that the Church permitted a Gertrudis, a Santa Teresa, a Saint Birgitta,[9] the Nun of Agreda,[1] and so many others, to write? And if they say to me that these women were saints, they speak the truth; but this poses no obstacle to my argument. First, because Saint Paul's proposition is absolute, and encompasses all women not excepting saints, as Martha and Mary,[2] Marcella,[3] Mary, mother of Jacob, and Salome,[4] all were in their time, and many other zealous women of the early church. But we see, too, that the Church allows women who are not saints to write, for the Nun of Agreda and Sor María de la Antigua[5] are not canonized, yet their writings are circulated. And when Santa Teresa and the others were writing, they were not as yet canonized. In which case, Saint Paul's prohibition was directed solely to the public office of the pulpit, for if the Apostle had forbidden women to write, the Church would not have allowed it. Now I do not make so bold as to teach—which in me would be excessively presumptuous—and as for writing, that requires a greater talent than mine, and serious reflection. As Saint Cyprian[6] says: *The things we write require most conscientious consideration.* I have desired to study that I might be ignorant of less; for (according to Saint Augustine[7]) some things are learned to be enacted and others only to be known: *We learn some things to know them, others, to do them.* Then, where is the offense to be found if even what is licit to women—which is to teach by writing—I do not perform, as I know that I am lacking in means, following the counsel of Quintilian: *Let each person learn not only from the precepts of others, but also let him reap counsel from his own nature.*

If the offense is to be found in the *Atenagórica* letter, was that letter anything other than the simple expression of my feeling, written with the implicit permission of our Holy Mother Church? For if the Church, in her most sacred authority, does not forbid it, why must others do so? That I proffered an opinion contrary to that of de Vieyra was audacious, but, as a Father, was it not audacious that he speak against the three Holy Fathers of the Church? My reason, such as it is, is it not as unfettered as his, as

---

8. The cathedra is the throne of the bishop in his church.   9. Or Bridget (1303–1373), of Sweden. 1. Maria de Agreda (1602–1635), Spanish Franciscan nun, author of *The Mystic City of God* (1670), a work allegedly divinely inspired.   2. Sisters. Mary anointed Jesus' feet (John 12:3). Martha was preoccupied with household tasks (Luke 10:40–42).   3. One of the women taught by Jerome.   4. In the King James Bible she is the mother of James and Salome, who came to the empty sepulcher to anoint Jesus' body (Mark 16:1).   5. Spanish nun (1544–1617).   6. Thascius Caecilius Cyprianus (ca. 200–258), one of the Church fathers, known for his efforts to enforce Church discipline.   7. Aurelius Augustinus (354–430), baptized by St. Ambrose in 387, author of *De Civitate Dei*, a vindication of the Church that long possessed great authority.

both issue from the same source? Is his opinion to be considered as a revelation, as a principle of the Holy Faith, that we must accept blindly? Furthermore, I maintained at all times the respect due such a virtuous man, a respect in which his defender was sadly wanting, ignoring the phrase of Titus Lucius:[8] *Respect is companion to the arts.* I did not touch a thread of the robes of the Society of Jesus; nor did I write for other than the consideration of the person who suggested that I write. And, according to Pliny, *how different the condition of one who writes from that of one who merely speaks.* Had I believed the letter was to be published I would not have been so inattentive. If, as the censor says, the letter is heretical, why does he not denounce it? And with that he would be avenged, and I content, for, which is only seemly, I esteem more highly my reputation as a Catholic and obedient daughter of the Holy Mother Church than all the approbation due a learned woman. If the letter is rash, and he does well to criticize it, then laugh, even if with the laugh of the rabbit, for I have not asked that he approve; as I was free to dissent from de Vieyra, so will anyone be free to oppose my opinion.

But how I have strayed, lady. None of this pertains here, nor is it intended for your ears, but as I was discussing my accusers I remembered the words of one that recently have appeared, and, though my intent was to speak in general, my pen, unbidden, slipped, and began to respond in particular. And so, returning to our Arce, he says that he knew in this city two nuns: one in the Convent of the Regina, who had so thoroughly committed the Breviary to memory that with the greatest promptitude and propriety she applied in her conversation its verses, psalms, and maxims of saintly homilies. The other, in the Convent of the Conception, was so accustomed to reading the Epistles of my Father Saint Jerome, and the Locutions of this Saint, that Arce says, *It seemed I was listening to Saint Jerome himself, speaking in Spanish.* And of this latter woman he says that after her death he learned that she had translated these Epistles into the Spanish language. What pity that such talents could not have been employed in major studies with scientific principles. He does not give the name of either, although he offers these women as confirmation of his opinion, which is that not only is it licit, but most useful and essential for women to study the Holy Word, and even more essential for nuns; and that study is the very thing to which your wisdom exhorts me, and in which so many arguments concur.

Then if I turn my eyes to the oft-chastized faculty of making verses— which is in me so natural that I must discipline myself that even this letter not be written in that form—I might cite those lines, *All I wished to express took the form of verse.*[9] And seeing that so many condemn and criticize this ability, I have conscientiously sought to find what harm may be in it, and I have not found it, but, rather, I see verse acclaimed in the mouths of the Sibyls; sanctified in the pens of the Prophets, especially King David, of whom the exalted Expositor my beloved Father[1] says (explicating the measure of his meters): *in the manner of Horace and Pindar, now it hurries*

8. Better known as Saturantius Apuleius, greatly celebrated in his time (2d century A.D.) for eloquence.
9. Ovid's *Tristia* 4.10.25ff.   1. Jerome.

along in iambs, now it rings in alcaic, now swells in sapphic, then arrives in broken feet. The greater part of the Holy Books are in meter, as is the Book of Moses; and those of Job (as Saint Isidore[2] states in his *Etymologiae*) are in heroic verse. Solomon wrote the Canticle of Canticles in verse; and Jeremias, his *Lamentations.* And so, says Cassiodorus:[3] *All poetic expression had as its source the Holy Scriptures.* For not only does our Catholic Church not disdain verse, it employs verse in its hymns, and recites the lines of Saint Ambrose,[4] Saint Thomas, Saint Isidore, and others. Saint Bonaventure[5] was so taken with verse that he writes scarcely a page where it does not appear. It is readily apparent that Saint Paul had studied verse, for he quotes and translates verses of Aratus: *For in him we live, and move, and are.*[6] And he quotes also that verse of Parmenides: *The Cretians are always liars, evil beasts, slothful bellies.*[7] Saint Gregory Nazianzen[8] argues in elegant verses the questions of matrimony and virginity. And, how should I tire? The Queen of Wisdom, Our Lady, with Her sacred lips, intoned the Canticle of the Magnificat;[9] and having brought forth this example, it would be offensive to add others that were profane, even those of the most serious and learned men, for this alone is more than sufficient confirmation; and even though Hebrew elegance could not be compressed into Latin measure, for which reason, although the sacred translator, more attentive to the importance of the meaning, omitted the verse, the Psalms retain the number and divisions of verses, and what harm is to be found in them? For misuse is not the blame of art, but rather of the evil teacher who perverts the arts, making of them the snare of the devil; and this occurs in all the arts and sciences.

And if the evil is attributed to the fact that a woman employs them, we have seen how many have done so in praiseworthy fashion; what then is the evil in my being a woman? I confess openly my own baseness and meanness; but I judge that no couplet of mine has been deemed indecent. Furthermore, I have never written of my own will, but under the pleas and injunctions of others; to such a degree that the only piece I remember having written for my own pleasure was a little trifle they called *El sueño.*[1] That letter, lady, which you so greatly honored, I wrote more with repugnance than any other emotion; both by reason of the fact that it treated sacred matters, for which (as I have stated) I hold such reverent awe, and because it seems to wish to impugn, a practice for which I have natural aversion; and I believe that had I foreseen the blessed destiny to which it was fated—for like a second Moses I had set it adrift, naked, on the waters of the Nile of silence, where you, a princess, found and cherished it[2]—I believe, I reiterate, that had I known, the very hands of which it was born would have drowned it, out of the fear that these clumsy scribblings from my ignorance appear before the light of your great wisdom; by which one

2. Spanish archbishop (ca. 560–636), who helped organize the Church in Spain.   3. Flavius Magnus Aurelius Cassiodorus (ca. 485–ca.580), Roman monk and author of *Institutiones*, a course of studies for monks.   4. Bishop of Milan (339–397), who had an important share in the conversion of St. Augustine.   5. Franciscan bishop and cardinal (1221–1274), who preached the importance of study.   6. Acts 17:28.   7. Titus 1:12.   8. Gregorius Nazianzenus, bishop of Constantinople and associate of Jerome. The allusion is to the first of his forty moral poems, 732 lines eulogizing virginity.   9. Luke 1:46–55.   1. *The Dream*, one of Sister Juana's best-known poems, which tells of the flight of her soul toward learning.   2. Because Pharaoh had ordered all male Hebrew infants killed, Moses' mother placed him in a basket by the Nile, where he was found and rescued by Pharaoh's daughter (Exodus 2:1–10).

knows the munificence of your kindness, for your goodwill applauds precisely what your reason must wish to reject. For as fate cast it before your doors, so exposed, so orphaned, that it fell to you even to give it a name, I must lament that among other deformities it also bears the blemish of haste; both because of the unrelenting ill-health I suffer, and for the profusion of duties imposed on me by obedience, as well as the want of anyone to guide me in my writing and the need that it all come from my hand, and, finally, because the writing went against my nature and I wished only to keep my promise to one whom I could not disobey, I could not find the time to finish properly, and thus I failed to include whole treatises and many arguments that presented themselves to me, but which I omitted in order to put an end to the writing—many, that had I known the letter was to be printed, I would not have excluded, even if merely to satisfy some objections that have since arisen and which could have been refuted. But I shall not be so ill-mannered as to place such indecent objects before the purity of your eyes, for it is enough that my ignorance be an offense in your sight, without need of entrusting to it the effronteries of others. If they should wing your way (and they are of such little weight that this will happen), then you will command what I am to do; for, if it does not run contrary to your will, my defense shall be not to take up my pen, for I deem that one affront need not occasion another, if one recognizes the error in the very place it lies concealed. As my Father Saint Jerome says, *good discourse seeks not things*, and Saint Ambrose, *it is the nature of a guilty conscience to lie concealed.* Nor do I consider that I have been impugned, for one statute of the Law states: *An accusation will not endure unless nurtured by the person who brought it forth.* What is a matter to be weighed is the effort spent in copying the accusation. A strange madness, to expend more effort in denying acclaim than in earning it! I, lady, have chosen not to respond (although others did so without my knowledge); it suffices that I have seen certain treatises, among them one so learned I send it to you so that reading it will compensate in part for the time you squandered on my writing. If, lady, you wish that I act contrary to what I have proposed here for your judgment and opinion, the merest indication of your desire will, as is seemly, countermand my inclination, which, as I have told you, is to be silent, for although Saint John Chrysostom[3] says, *those who slander must be refuted, and those who question, taught,* I know also that Saint Gregory[4] says, *It is no less a victory to tolerate enemies than to overcome them.* And that patience conquers by tolerating and triumphs by suffering. And if among the Roman Gentiles it was the custom when their captains were at the highest peak of glory—when returning triumphant from other nations, robed in purple and wreathed with laurel, crowned-but-conquered kings pulling their carriages in the stead of beasts, accompanied by the spoils of the riches of all the world, the conquering troops adorned with the insignia of their heroic feats, hearing the plaudits of the people who showered them with titles of honor and renown such as Fathers of the Nation, Columns of the Empire, Walls of Rome, Shelter

---

3. Syrian prelate (ca. 347–407), known as the greatest orator of the Church, author of many homilies and treatises.   4. Gregory the Great (ca. 540–604), pope from 590, deeply concerned with the reformation of the Church.

of the Republic, and other glorious names—a soldier went before these captains in this moment of the supreme apogee of glory and human happiness crying out in a loud voice to the conqueror (by his consent and order of the Senate): Behold how you are mortal; behold how you have this or that defect, not excepting the most shameful, as happened in the triumph of Caesar, when the vilest soldiers clamored in his ear: *Beware, Romans, for we bring you the bald adulterer.* Which was done so that in the midst of such honor the conquerers not be swelled up with pride, and that the ballast of these insults act as counterweight to the bellying sails of such approbation, and that the ship of good judgment not founder amidst the winds of acclamation. If this, I say, was the practice among Gentiles, who knew only the light of Natural Law, how much might we Catholics, under the injunction to love our enemies, achieve by tolerating them? And in my own behalf I can attest that calumny has often mortified me, but never harmed me, being that I hold as a great fool one who having occasion to receive credit suffers the difficulty and loses the credit, as it is with those who do not resign themselves to death, but, in the end, die anyway, their resistance not having prevented death, but merely deprived them of the credit of resignation and caused them to die badly when they might have died well. And thus, lady, I believe these experiences do more good than harm, and I hold as greater the jeopardy of applause to human weakness, as we are wont to appropriate praise that is not our own, and must be ever watchful, and carry graven on our hearts those words of the Apostle: *Or what hast thou that thou hast not received? And if thou hast received, why doest thou glory as if thou hadst not received it?*[5] so that these words serve as a shield to fend off the sharp barbs of commendations, which are as spears which when not attributed to God (whose they are), claim our lives and cause us to be thieves of God's honor and usurpers of the talents He bestowed on us and the gifts that He lent to us, for which we must give the most strict accounting. And thus, lady, I fear applause more than calumny, because the latter, with but the simple act of patience becomes gain, while the former requires many acts of reflection and humility and proper recognition so that it not become harm. And I know and recognize that it is by special favor of God that I know this, as it enables me in either instance to act in accord with the words of Saint Augustine: *One must believe neither the friend who praises nor the enemy who detracts.* Although most often I squander God's favor, or vitiate with such defects and imperfections that I spoil what, being His, was good. And thus in what little of mine that has been printed, neither the use of my name, nor even consent for the printing, was given by my own counsel, but by the license of another who lies outside my domain, as was also true with the printing of the *Atenagórica* letter, and only a few *Exercises of the Incarnation* and *Offerings of the Sorrow* were printed for public devotions with my pleasure, but without my name; of which I am sending some few copies that (if you so desire) you may distribute them among our sisters, the nuns of that holy community, as well as in that city. I send but one copy of the *Sorrows* because the others have been exhausted and I could find no other copy. I wrote them

---

5. 2 Corinthians 11:4.

long ago, solely for the devotions of my sisters, and later they were spread abroad; and their contents are disproportionate as regards my unworthiness and my ignorance, and they profited that they touched on matters of our exalted Queen; for I cannot explain what it is that inflames the coldest heart when one refers to the Most Holy Mary. It is my only desire, esteemed lady, to remit to you works worthy of your virtue and wisdom; as the poet said: *Though strength may falter, good will must be praised. In this, I believe, the gods will be content.*

If ever I write again, my scribbling will always find its way to the haven of your holy feet and the certainty of your correction, for I have no other jewel with which to pay you, and, in the lament of Seneca, he who has once bestowed benefices has committed himself to continue; and so you must be repaid out of your own munificence, for only in this way shall I with dignity be freed from debt and avoid that the words of that same Seneca come to pass: *It is contemptible to be surpassed in benefices.*[6] For in his gallantry the generous creditor gives to the poor debtor the means to satisfy his debt. So God gave his gift to a world unable to repay Him: He gave his son that He be offered a recompense worthy of Him.

If, most venerable lady, the tone of this letter may not have seemed right and proper, I ask forgiveness for its homely familiarity, and the less than seemly respect in which by treating you as a nun, one of my sisters, I have lost sight of the remoteness of your most illustrious person; which, had I seen you without your veil, would never have occurred; but you in all your prudence and mercy will supplement or amend the language, and if you find unsuitable the *Vos* of the address I have employed, believing that for the reverence I owe you, Your Reverence seemed little reverent, modify it in whatever manner seems appropriate to your due, for I have not dared exceed the limits of your custom, nor transgress the boundary of your modesty.

And hold me in your grace, and entreat for me divine grace, of which the Lord God grant you large measure, and keep you, as I pray Him, and am needful. From this convent of our Father Saint Jerome in Mexico City, the first day of the month of March of sixteen hundred and ninety-one. Allow me to kiss your hand, your most favored

Juana Inés de la Cruz

---

6. *On Benefits* 5.2.1.

JONATHAN SWIFT
1667–1745

In virtually all his writing, Jonathan Swift displays his gift for making other people uncomfortable. He makes us uneasy by making us aware of our own moral inadequacies, and by his wit, energy, and inventiveness, he actually compels us to enjoy the process of being brought to such awareness.

Born in Dublin to English parents, Swift was educated at Trinity College, Dublin. In 1689, the young man went to England, where he served as secretary to the statesman Sir William Temple. During his residence at Moor Park, Sir William's estate, Swift became friendly with Esther Johnson, daughter of the steward there; he remained on close terms with her for the rest of his life. (His playful, intimate letters to her—he used the name "Stella"—were published in a collection called *Journal to Stella.*) In 1692, Swift received an M.A. from Oxford University; three years later, he took orders, becoming a clergyman in the Anglican Church but continuing in Sir William's employ, although with intermittent stays in Ireland. Early in the eighteenth century, he began his career of political journalism; he also published brilliant satiric works, including *A Tale of a Tub* (1704), of which he is supposed to have said, late in his life, "What a genius I had when I composed that book!" Although he had hoped for church advancement in England, as a reward for his writings in the Tory cause, in 1713 he was instead named dean of St. Patrick's Cathedral, Dublin. He spent the rest of his life in Ireland (save for two brief visits to friends in England) writing passionately on behalf of the oppressed Irish people. In his final years, he was declared mentally incompetent, suffering, presumably, from senility. As he had prophesied in his verses *On the Death of Dr. Swift*, "He gave what little wealth he had / To build a house for fools and mad"; the mental hospital founded by his legacy still exists in Dublin.

For *Gulliver's Travels* (1726) Swift used the travel book, a form hovering between fact and fiction, as his model. Lemuel Gulliver, ship's surgeon, travels into four imagined nations. The first book takes him to Lilliput, where he duly observes the customs and traditions of a race of people six inches high. The narrative of their preoccupations and procedures mocks the pettiness of the English, although Gulliver, himself involved in the intrigues of his tiny hosts, fails to note the resemblance between Lilliput and his native land. His simple patriotism survives through the second book, where Gulliver encounters the giants of Brobdingnag, whose benevolent king, after hearing Gulliver's patriotic account of England, comments, "I cannot but conclude the bulk of your natives, to be the most pernicious race of little odious vermin that nature ever suffered to crawl upon the surface of the earth." The third book is more various, and Gulliver on the whole seems less gullible in his encounters with the ludicrous or dangerous results of abstract speculation divorced from practical concerns (philosophers, for instance, so deep in ratiocination that they have to be attended by "flappers," servants who "flap" them into awareness of immediate actuality), with the ghosts of great men from the past who stress the lies of historians and the moral and physical decline of their descendants, and with the terrifying Struldbrugs, who grow old but live forever in horrible senility.

Book Four, printed here, has always presented problems to critics. More directly than any other imaginative work of its period, it confronts problems inherent in the idealization of reason as sufficient guide to human conduct. It is easy enough to see that Swift has here imagined an absolute separation between the animal and the rational aspects of human nature. As Gulliver gradually and with horror realizes (the reader undergoing a comparable process), the disgusting Yahoos manifest degraded human form and embody characteristics of human beings deprived of all rational capacity. They act on the basis of pure—and ugly—passion: lust, envy, avarice, greed, rage. The Houyhnhnms, the governing class of horses, treat them as beasts, but consider them more ungovernable than other creatures; Gulliver, looking at them, sees a horrifying version of the human, become (by the absence of reason) subhuman.

As for the Houyhnhnms, those noble horses exemplify pure rationality. They lead monotonous, orderly lives, with no need for disagreement (the truth being self-evident to rational creatures) or excitement. Under their influence, Gulliver wants to stay forever in this land without literal or metaphorical salt. After the

Houyhnhnms expel him, Gulliver can make no distinction among human beings: he condemns the benevolent Pedro Mendez as a Yahoo, resents his connection with his own wife and children, and spends as much time as possible in his stable. Life with the Houyhnhnms has driven him mad: he cannot adjust to English actuality.

The question is, Why? By one interpretation, Gulliver judges rightly in perceiving his fellow human beings as essentially Yahoos. His Houyhnhnm master concludes, Gulliver says, that humans are "a sort of animals to whose share . . . some small pittance of reason had fallen, whereof we made no other use than by its assistance to aggravate our natural corruptions, and to acquire new ones which nature had not given us." Perhaps he is right. The Houyhnhnms exemplify an ideal to which human beings should aspire, although they can never reach it; to call attention to the monotony of their lives or the failure of their curiosity only reveals the reader's participation in human depravity. Pedro Mendez is a good man, as men go, but the gulf between the best of humans and a Houyhnhnm gapes so hugely that Gulliver sees correctly in detesting all humans. If he implicitly excepts himself, he thus acknowledges the difference his education by Houyhnhnms has made: at least he knows the gulf's existence.

Another view has it that the Houyhnhnms exemplify a way of being utterly irrelevant to humankind, as well as deeply boring. To hate the animal and glorify the rational denies the inextricable mixture of our nature. Gulliver's pride leads him to aspire to an essentially inhuman state; he wishes, sinfully, to exceed ordained natural limits. Moreover, he ignores the Christian virtue of charity, the command to love one's neighbors. Captain Mendez demonstrates that virtue; Gulliver cannot perceive the moral distinction between the generous captain and the bloodthirsty natives who shoot the Englishman with an arrow shortly after he leaves the Houyhnhnms, producing a lasting scar. Gulliver's condemnation of pride in others emphasizes his blindness to his own flaws.

A compromise position might remind us that to declare the Houyhnhnms irrelevant perhaps leaves the reader in rather too comfortable a position, considering Swift's declared intention "to vex the world rather than divert it." *Gulliver's Travels*, this comment implies, involves serious attack. We can perhaps dismiss the Houyhnhnms as boring (they have virtually nothing to talk about) or heartless (they make no distinctions of parentage; they expel Gulliver despite his ardent desire to remain) because our natures include more than reason and we appropriately value principles of conduct beyond the rational. Gulliver becomes crazy when he returns to England, unable to accept his full human nature and to make necessary distinctions; given the limits of the human condition, men and women must find the way to operate within them. Gulliver fails and, failing, reminds us of necessities to which we must adapt. The Houyhnhnms provide no solution to human problems: their extirpation of passion, their narrow commitment to reason, prove "inhumane." (They are, after all, horses!) Humankind, as Swift suggested in a letter, is only capable of reason, not fully reasonable; perhaps the spontaneous generosity of the Portuguese captain exemplifies the greatest good to which human beings should aspire.

On the other hand, we claim to value reason; Gulliver has seen in pure form an ideal to which we pay lip service. His realization of the terrible discrepancy between ideal and actual has made it impossible for him to function in his own society. It has given him a harsh perspective by which he sees how morally intolerable social arrangements in fact are. The readiness of most people to compromise, given social necessity, shows how far they are from taking seriously the values they profess. Swift calls our attention to the divergences in our own lives between what we say we believe and how we actually behave. The reality of reason exceeds human capacities; *Gulliver's Travels* reminds us that we live by hypocrisies. The Houyhnhnms thus tell us something about ourselves despite their lack of humanity.

The problems in interpretation that *Gulliver's Travels* has always generated come partly from the fact that we receive all information about Gulliver's experience from the traveler himself, an untrustworthy source. In reading his narrative, we must assess his understanding—a slippery process, since we lack a point of reference. *Gulliver's Travels* abounds in allusions to such phenomena as corrupt lawyers and politicians, avaricious doctors, mass slaughter in wars over trivial pretexts—aspects of our experience as well as of Gulliver's, and reminders that this narrative has something to do with us. The necessity of arriving at a coherent judgment of Gulliver and his experiences implicates the reader in the moral problem of how to judge—and perhaps how to change—society.

Such implication of the reader in often uncomfortable processes of judgment typifies an important aspect of satire. *A Modest Proposal* (1729), Swift's attack on the economic oppression of the Irish by the English, keeps the reader constantly off balance, trying to understand exactly who is being criticized and why. Swift is writing out of his firsthand awareness of the suffering caused by English policies in Ireland. Absentee landlords who never saw the actual situation of their tenants, British politicians who made policy at a distance, presumably did not know that Ireland had become a land of the starving. In Swift's view, however, the Irish people collaborated by their apathy with the oppressors. In *A Modest Proposal*, he attacks English and Irish alike.

Even more emphatically than Gulliver, the nameless speaker in *A Modest Proposal* proves an undependable guide, tempting us to identify with his tone of rationality and compassion, only to reveal that his plausible economic orientation leads to advocacy of cannibalism. He offers a series of morally sound and economically feasible suggestions for solutions to Ireland's problems, but draws back immediately, declaring them impossible, since no one will put them in practice. The satire indicts the English for inhumanity, the Irish for passivity, and the economically oriented proposer of remedies for moral blindness. But it also reaches out to criticize the reader as representative of all who endure calmly the intolerable actuality in the world (but not, perhaps, where we have to see it ourselves) of our own inhumanity to our fellow human beings. Swift's self-chosen epitaph, on his tomb, may be translated, "Where fierce indignation no longer tears the heart." *A Modest Proposal* exemplifies the lacerating power of that indignation.

A good introduction to Swift's life and character is I. Ehrenpreis, *The Personality of Jonathan Swift* (1958). An interpretation of the writer in his intellectual context is K. Williams, *Jonathan Swift and the Age of Compromise* (1959). E. Zimmerman, *Swift's Narrative Satires: Author and Authority* (1983), provides acute interpretation of the prose satires. Useful and varied collections of essays about Swift include C. Probyn, ed., *Jonathan Swift: The Contemporary Background* (1978); C. Rawson, ed., *The Art of Swift's Satire: A Revised Focus* (1983); C. Rawson, ed., *Swift: A Collection of Critical Essays* (1994); and Harold Bloom, ed., *Jonathan Swift's Gulliver's Travels* (1986). R. A. Greenberg, ed., *Gulliver's Travels* (1970), is annotated and includes critical essays.

From Gulliver's Travels[1]

A *Letter from Captain Gulliver to His Cousin Sympson*[2]

I hope you will be ready to own publicly, whenever you shall be called to it, that by your great and frequent urgency you prevailed on me to publish a very loose and uncorrect account of my travels; with direction to hire some young gentlemen of either University to put them in order, and correct the style, as my Cousin Dampier[3] did by my advice, in his book called A *Voyage round the World*. But I do not remember I gave you power to consent that anything should be omitted, and much less that anything should be inserted: therefore, as to the latter, I do here renounce everything of that kind; particularly a paragraph about her Majesty the late Queen Anne, of most pious and glorious memory; although I did reverence and esteem her more than any of human species. But you, or your interpolator, ought to have considered that as it was not my inclination, so was it not decent to praise any animal of our composition before my master Houyhnhnm; and besides, the fact was altogether false; for to my knowledge, being in England during some part of her Majesty's reign, she did govern by a chief Minister; nay, even by two successively; the first whereof was the Lord of Godolphin, and the second the Lord of Oxford; so that you have made me *say the thing that was not*. Likewise, in the account of the Academy of Projectors, and several passages of my discourse to my master Houyhnhnm, you have either omitted some material circumstances, or minced or changed them in such a manner, that I do hardly know mine own work. When I formerly hinted to you something of this in a letter, you were pleased to answer that you were afraid of giving offense; that people in power were very watchful over the press; and apt not only to interpret, but to punish everything which looked like an *inuendo* (as I think you called it). But pray, how could that which I spoke so many years ago, and at above five thousand leagues distance, in another reign, be applied to any of the Yahoos, who now are said to govern the herd; especially, at a time when I little thought on or feared the unhappiness of living under them. Have not I the most reason to complain, when I see these very Yahoos carried by Houyhnhnms in a vehicle, as if these were brutes, and those the rational creatures? And, indeed, to avoid so monstrous and detestable a sight was one principal motive of my retirement hither.[4]

Thus much I thought proper to tell you in relation to yourself, and to the trust I reposed in you.

I do in the next place complain of my own great want of judgment, in being prevailed upon by the intreaties and false reasonings of you and some others, very much against mine own opinion, to suffer my travels to be published. Pray bring to your mind how often I desired you to consider, when you insisted on the motive of public good, that the Yahoos were a

1. Swift's full title for this work was *Travels into Several Remote Nations of the World. In Four Parts. By Lemuel Gulliver, First a Surgeon, and then a Captain of several Ships*. The text is based on the Dublin edition of Swift's work (1735).   2. In this letter, first published in 1735, Swift complains, among other matters, of the alterations in his original text made by the publisher, Benjamin Motte, in the interest of what he considered political discretion.   3. William Dampier (1652–1715), the explorer, whose account of his circumnavigation of the globe Swift had read.   4. To Nottinghamshire in central England.

species of animals utterly incapable of amendment by precepts or examples; and so it hath proved; for instead of seeing a full stop put to all abuses and corruptions, at least in this little island, as I had reason to expect, behold, after above six months warning. I cannot learn that my book hath produced one single effect according to mine intentions; I desired you would let me know by a letter, when party and faction were extinguished; judges learned and upright; pleaders honest and modest, with some tincture of common sense; and Smithfield[5] blazing with pyramids of law books; the young nobility's education entirely changed; the physicians banished; the female Yahoos abounding in virtue, honor, truth, and good sense; courts and levees of great ministers thoroughly weeded and swept; wit, merit, and learning rewarded; all disgracers of the press in prose and verse, condemned to eat nothing but their own cotton,[6] and quench their thirst with their own ink. These, and a thousand other reformations, I firmly counted upon by your encouragement; as indeed they were plainly deducible from the precepts delivered in my book. And, it must be owned that seven months were a sufficient time to correct every vice and folly to which Yahoos are subject; if their natures had been capable of the least disposition to virtue or wisdom; yet so far have you been from answering mine expectation in any of your letters, that on the contrary, you are loading our carrier every week with libels, and keys, and reflections, and memoirs, and second parts; wherein I see myself accused of reflecting upon great statesfolk; of degrading human nature (for so they have still the confidence to style it) and of abusing the female sex. I find likewise, that the writers of those bundles are not agreed among themselves; for some of them will not allow me to be author of mine own travels; and others make me author of books to which I am wholly a stranger.

I find likewise that your printer hath been so careless as to confound the times, and mistake the dates of my several voyages and returns; neither assigning the true year, or the true month, or day of the month; and I hear the original manuscript is all destroyed, since the publication of my book. Neither have I any copy left; however, I have sent you some corrections, which you may insert, if ever there should be a second edition; and yet I cannot stand to them, but shall leave that matter to my judicious and candid readers, to adjust it as they please.

I hear some of our sea Yahoos find fault with my sea language, as not proper in many parts, nor now in use. I cannot help it. In my first voyages, while I was young, I was instructed by the oldest mariners, and learned to speak as they did. But I have since found that the sea Yahoos are apt, like the land ones, to become new fangled in their words; which the latter change every year; insomuch, as I remember upon each return to mine own country, their old dialect was so altered, that I could hardly understand the new. And I observe, when any Yahoo comes from London out of curiosity to visit me at mine own house, we neither of us are able to deliver our conceptions in a manner intelligible to the other.

If the censure of Yahoos could any way affect me, I should have great

---

5. An area of London, used in the 16th century for burning heretics, that should now be used (Swift implies) to burn the incentives to litigation.   6. The fiber favored for paper making.

reason to complain that some of them are so bold as to think my book of travels a mere fiction out of mine own brain; and have gone so far as to drop hints that the Houyhnhnms and Yahoos have no more existence than the inhabitants of Utopia.

Indeed I must confess that as to the people of Lilliput, Brobdingrag (for so the word should have been spelled, and not erroneously Brobdingnag) and Laputa, I have never yet heard of any Yahoo so presumptuous as to dispute their being, or the facts I have related concerning them; because the truth immediately strikes every reader with conviction. And, is there less probability in my account of the Houyhnhnms or Yahoos, when it is manifest as to the latter, there are so many thousands even in this city, who only differ from their brother brutes in Houyhnhnmland, because they use a sort of a jabber, and do not go naked. I wrote for their amendment, and not their approbation. The united praise of the whole race would be of less consequence to me, than the neighing of those two degenerate Houyhnhnms I keep in my stable; because, from these, degenerate as they are, I still improve in some virtues, without any mixture of vice.

Do these miserable animals presume to think that I am so far degenerated as to defend my veracity; Yahoo as I am, it is well known through all Houyhnhnmland, that by the instructions and example of my illustrious master, I was able in the compass of two years (although I confess with the utmost difficulty) to remove that infernal habit of lying, shuffling, deceiving, and equivocating, so deeply rooted in the very souls of all my species; especially the Europeans.

I have other complaints to make upon this vexatious occasion; but I forbear troubling myself or you any further. I must freely confess that since my last return, some corruptions of my Yahoo nature have revived in me by conversing with a few of your species, and particularly those of mine own family, by an unavoidable necessity; else I should never have attempted so absurd a project as that of reforming the Yahoo race in this kingdom; but I have now done with all such visionary schemes for ever.

The Publisher to the Reader

The author of these travels, Mr. Lemuel Gulliver, is my ancient and intimate friend; there is likewise some relation between us by the mother's side. About three years ago Mr. Gulliver, growing weary of the concourse of curious people coming to him at his house in Redriff,[7] made a small purchase of land, with a convenient house, near Newark, in Nottinghamshire, his native country; where he now lives retired, yet in good esteem among his neighbors.

Although Mr. Gulliver were born in Nottinghamshire, where his father dwelt, yet I have heard him say his family came from Oxfordshire; to confirm which, I have observed in the churchyard at Banbury, in that county, several tombs and monuments of the Gullivers.

Before he quitted Redriff, he left the custody of the following papers in

---

7. Rotherhithe, a district in south London then frequented by sailors.

my hands, with the liberty to dispose of them as I should think fit. I have carefully perused them three times; the style is very plain and simple; and the only fault I find is that the author, after the manner of travelers, is a little too circumstantial. There is an air of truth apparent through the whole; and indeed the author was so distinguished for his veracity, that it became a sort of proverb among his neighbors at Redriff, when anyone affirmed a thing, to say, it was as true as if Mr. Gulliver had spoke it.

By the advice of several worthy persons, to whom, with the author's permission, I communicated these papers, I now venture to send them into the world; hoping they may be, at least for some time, a better entertainment to our young noblemen, than the common scribbles of politics and party.

This volume would have been at least twice as large, if I had not made bold to strike out innumerable passages relating to the winds and tides, as well as to the variations and bearings in the several voyages; together with the minute descriptions of the management of the ship in storms, in the style of sailors; likewise the account of the longitudes and latitudes, wherein I have reason to apprehend that Mr. Gulliver may be a little dissatisfied; but I was resolved to fit the work as much as possible to the general capacity of readers. However, if my own ignorance in sea affairs shall have led me to commit some mistakes, I alone am answerable for them; and if any traveler hath a curiosity to see the whole work at large, as it came from the hand of the author, I will be ready to gratify him.

As for any further particulars relating to the author, the reader will receive satisfaction from the first pages of the book.

RICHARD SYMPSON

Part IV

A Voyage to the Country of the Houyhnhnms[8]

CHAPTER I

The Author sets out as Captain of a ship. His men conspire against him, confine him a long time to his cabin, set him on shore in an unknown land. He travels up into the country. The Yahoos, a strange sort of animal, described. The Author meets two Houyhnhnms.

I continued at home with my wife and children about five months in a very happy condition, if I could have learned the lesson of knowing when I was well. I left my poor wife big with child, and accepted an advantageous offer made me to be Captain of the *Adventure*, a stout merchantman of 350 tons; for I understood navigation well, and being grown weary of a surgeon's employment at sea, which however I could exercise upon occasion, I took a skillful young man of that calling, one Robert Purefoy, into my ship. We set sail from Portsmouth upon the 7th day of September, 1710; on the 14th we met with Captain Pocock of Bristol, at Tenariff, who

---

8. The word suggests the sound of a horse neighing.

was going to the Bay of Campeachy[9] to cut logwood. On the 16th he was parted from us by a storm; I heard since my return that his ship foundered and none escaped, but one cabin boy. He was an honest man and a good sailor, but a little too positive in his own opinions, which was the cause of his destruction, as it hath been of several others. For if he had followed my advice, he might at this time have been safe at home with his family as well as myself.

I had several men died in my ship of calentures,[1] so that I was forced to get recruits out of Barbadoes and the Leeward Islands,[2] where I touched by the direction of the merchants who employed me; which I had soon too much cause to repent, for I found afterwards that most of them had been buccaneers. I had fifty hands on board; and my orders were that I should trade with the Indians in the South Sea, and make what discoveries I could. These rogues whom I had picked up debauched my other men, and they all formed a conspiracy to seize the ship and secure me; which they did one morning, rushing into my cabin, and binding me hand and foot, threatening to throw me overboard, if I offered to stir. I told them I was their prisoner, and would submit. This they made me swear to do, and then unbound me, only fastening one of my legs with a chair near my bed, and placed a sentry at my door with his piece charged, who was commanded to shoot me dead if I attempted my liberty. They sent me down victuals and drink, and took the government of the ship to themselves. Their design was to turn pirates and plunder the Spaniards, which they could not do, till they got more men. But first they resolved to sell the goods in the ship, and then go to Madagascar for recruits, several among them having died since my confinement. They sailed many weeks, and traded with the Indians; but I knew not what course they took, being kept close prisoner in my cabin, and expecting nothing less than to be murdered, as they often threatened me.

Upon the 9th day of May, 1711, one James Welch came down to my cabin; and said he had orders from the Captain to set me ashore. I expostulated with him, but in vain; neither would he so much as tell me who their new Captain was. They forced me into the longboat, letting me put on my best suit of clothes, which were as good as new, and a small bundle of linen, but no arms except my hanger;[3] and they were so civil as not to search my pockets, into which I conveyed what money I had, with some other little necessaries. They rowed about a league, and then set me down on a strand. I desired them to tell me what country it was; they all swore, they knew no more than myself, but said that the Captain (as they called him) was resolved, after they had sold the lading, to get rid of me in the first place where they discovered land. They pushed off immediately, advising me to make haste, for fear of being overtaken by the tide, and bade me farewell.

In this desolate condition I advanced forward, and soon got upon firm ground, where I sat down on a bank to rest myself, and consider what I

---

9. Probably Campeche, in southeast Mexico, on the western side of the Yucatan peninsula. Tenariff is the largest of the Canary Islands, off northwest Africa in the Atlantic.   1. Tropical fever.   2. The northern group of the Lesser Antilles in the West Indies, extending southeast from Puerto Rico. Barbados is the easternmost of the West Indies.   3. A small sword.

had best to do. When I was a little refreshed, I went up into the country, resolving to deliver myself to the first savages I should meet, and purchase my life from them by some bracelets, glass rings, and other toys, which sailors usually provide themselves with in those voyages, and whereof I had some about me. The land was divided by long rows of trees, not regularly planted, but naturally growing; there was great plenty of grass, and several fields of oats. I walked very circumspectly for fear of being surprised, or suddenly shot with an arrow from behind, or on either side. I fell into a beaten road, where I saw many tracks of human feet, and some of cows, but most of horses. At last I beheld several animals in a field, and one or two of the same kind sitting in trees. Their shape was very singular, and deformed, which a little discomposed me, so that I lay down behind a thicket to observe them better. Some of them coming forward near the place where I lay, gave me an opportunity of distinctly marking their form. Their heads and breasts were covered with a thick hair, some frizzled and others lank; they had beards like goats, and a long ridge of hair down their backs, and the fore parts of their legs and feet; but the rest of their bodies were bare, so that I might see their skins, which were of a brown buff color. They had no tails, nor any hair at all on their buttocks, except about the anus; which, I presume Nature had placed there to defend them as they sat on the ground; for this posture they used, as well as lying down, and often stood on their hind feet. They climbed high trees, as nimbly as a squirrel, for they had strong extended claws before and behind, terminating in sharp points, and hooded.[4] They would often spring, and bound, and leap with prodigious agility. The females were not so large as the males; they had long lank hair on their heads, and only a sort of down on the rest of their bodies, except about the anus, and pudenda. Their dugs hung between their forefeet, and often reached almost to the ground as they walked. The hair of both sexes was of several colors, brown, red, black, and yellow. Upon the whole, I never beheld in all my travels so disagreeable an animal, or one against which I naturally conceived so strong an antipathy. So that thinking I had seen enough, full of contempt and aversion, I got up and pursued the beaten road, hoping it might direct me to the cabin of some Indian: I had not gone far when I met one of these creatures full in my way, and coming up directly to me. The ugly monster, when he saw me, distorted several ways every feature of his visage, and stared as at an object he had never seen before; then approaching nearer, lifted up his forepaw, whether out of curiosity or mischief, I could not tell; but I drew my hanger, and gave him a good blow with the flat side of it; for I durst not strike him with the edge, fearing the inhabitants might be provoked against me, if they should come to know that I had killed or maimed any of their cattle. When the beast felt the smart, he drew back, and roared so loud, that a herd of at least forty came flocking about me from the next field, howling and making odious faces; but I ran to the body of a tree, and leaning my back against it, kept them off, by waving my hanger. Several of this cursed brood getting hold of the

---

4. Concealed, or sheathed by flesh.

branches behind, leaped up into the tree, from whence they began to discharge their excrements on my head; however, I escaped pretty well, by sticking close to the stem of the tree, but was almost stifled with the filth, which fell about me on every side.

In the midst of this distress, I observed them all to run away on a sudden as fast as they could; at which I ventured to leave the tree, and pursue the road, wondering what it was that could put them into this fright. But looking on my left hand, I saw a horse walking softly in the field; which my persecutors having sooner discovered, was the cause of their flight. The horse started a little when he came near me, but soon recovering himself, looked full in my face with manifest tokens of wonder; he viewed my hands and feet, walking round me several times. I would have pursued my journey, but he placed himself directly in the way, yet looking with a very mild aspect, never offering the least violence. We stood gazing at each other for some time; at last I took the boldness, to reach my hand towards his neck, with a design to stroke it; using the common style and whistle of jockies when they are going to handle a strange horse. But, this animal seeming to receive my civilities with disdain, shook his head, and bent his brows, softly raising up his left forefoot to remove my hand. Then he neighed three or four times, but in so different a cadence, that I almost began to think he was speaking to himself in some language of his own.

While he and I were thus employed, another horse came up; who applying himself to the first in a very formal manner, they gently struck each other's right hoof before, neighing several times by turns, and varying the sound, which seemed to be almost articulate. They went some paces off, as if it were to confer together, walking side by side, backward and forward, like persons deliberating upon some affair of weight; but often turning their eyes towards me, as it were to watch that I might not escape. I was amazed to see such actions and behavior in brute beasts; and concluded with myself that if the inhabitants of this country were endued with a proportionable degree of reason, they must needs be the wisest people upon earth. This thought gave me so much comfort, that I resolved to go forward until I could discover some house or village, or meet with any of the natives, leaving the two horses to discourse together as they pleased. But the first, who was a dapple grey, observing me to steal off, neighed after me in so expressive a tone that I fancied myself to understand what he meant; whereupon I turned back, and came near him, to expect his farther commands; but concealing my fear as much as I could; for I began to be in some pain, how this adventure might terminate; and the reader will easily believe I did not much like my present situation.

The two horses came up close to me, looking with great earnestness upon my face and hands. The grey steed rubbed my hat all round with his right fore hoof, and discomposed it so much that I was forced to adjust it better, by taking it off, and settling it again; whereat both he and his companion (who was a brown bay) appeared to be much surprised; the latter felt the lappet of my coat, and finding it to hang loose about me, they both looked with new signs of wonder. He stroked my right hand, seeming to admire the softness, and color; but he squeezed it so hard between his hoof and his pastern,[5] that I was forced to roar; after which they both touched me with all possible tenderness. They were under great perplexity about my shoes and stockings, which they felt very often, neighing to each other, and using various gestures, not unlike those of a philosopher, when he would attempt to solve some new and difficult phenomenon.

Upon the whole, the behavior of these animals was so orderly and rational, so acute and judicious, that I at last concluded, they must needs be magicians, who had thus metamorphosed themselves upon some design; and seeing a stranger in the way, were resolved to divert themselves with him; or perhaps were really amazed at the sight of a man so very different in habit, feature, and complexion from those who might probably live in so remote a climate. Upon the strength of this reasoning, I ventured to address them in the following manner: "Gentlemen, if you be conjurers, as I have good cause to believe, you can understand any language; therefore I make bold to let your worships know that I am a poor distressed Englishman, driven by his misfortunes upon your coast; and I entreat one of you, to let me ride upon his back, as if he were a real horse, to some house or village, where I can be relieved. In return of which favor, I will make you a present of this knife and bracelet" (taking them out of my pocket). The two creatures stood silent while I spoke, seeming to listen with great attention; and when I had ended, they neighed frequently towards each other, as if they were engaged in serious conversation. I plainly observed, that their language expressed the passions very well, and the words might with little pains be resolved into an alphabet more easily than the Chinese.

I could frequently distinguish the word *Yahoo*, which was repeated by each of them several times; and although it were impossible for me to conjecture what it meant, yet while the two horses were busy in conversation, I endeavored to practice this word upon my tongue; and as soon as they were silent, I boldly pronounced "Yahoo" in a loud voice, imitating, at the same time, as near as I could, the neighing of a horse; at which they were both visibly surprised, and the grey repeated the same word twice, as if he meant to teach me the right accent, wherein I spoke after him as well as I could, and found myself perceivably to improve every time, although very far from any degree of perfection. Then the bay tried me with a second word, much harder to be pronounced; but reducing it to the English orthography, may be spelt thus *Houyhnhnm*. I did not succeed in this so well as the former, but after two or three farther trials, I had better fortune; and they both appeared amazed at my capacity.

After some farther discourse, which I then conjectured might relate to me, the two friends took their leaves, with the same compliment of striking each other's hoof; and the grey made me signs that I should walk before him; wherein I thought it prudent to comply, till I could find a better director. When I offered to slacken my pace, he would cry, "Hhuun, Hhuun"; I guessed his meaning, and gave him to understand, as well as I could that I was weary, and not able to walk faster; upon which, he would stand a while to let me rest.

---

5. The part of a horse's foot between the joint at the rear and the hoof.

CHAPTER II

*The Author conducted by a Houyhnhnm to his house. The house
described. The Author's reception. The food of the Houyhnhnms. The
Author in distress for want of meat is at last relieved. His manner of
feeding in that country.*

Having traveled about three miles, we came to a long kind of building,
made of timber, stuck in the ground, and wattled across; the roof was low,
and covered with straw. I now began to be a little comforted, and took out
some toys, which travelers usually carry for presents to the savage Indians
of America and other parts, in hopes the people of the house would be
thereby encouraged to receive me kindly. The horse made me a sign to
go in first; it was a large room with a smooth clay floor, and a rack and
manger extending the whole length on one side. There were three nags,
and two mares, not eating, but some of them sitting down upon their
hams, which I very much wondered at; but wondered more to see the rest
employed in domestic business; the last seemed but ordinary cattle; however this confirmed my first opinion, that a people who could so far civilize
brute animals must needs excel in wisdom all the nations of the world.
The grey came in just after, and thereby prevented any ill treatment,
which the others might have given me. He neighed to them several times
in a style of authority, and received answers.

Beyond this room there were three others, reaching the length of the
house, to which you passed through three doors, opposite to each other,
in the manner of a vista; we went through the second room towards the
third; here the grey walked in first, beckoning me to attend; I waited in
the second room, and got ready my presents, for the master and mistress
of the house; they were two knives, three bracelets of false pearl, a small
looking glass and a bead necklace. The horse neighed three or four times,
and I waited to hear some answers in a human voice, but I heard no other
returns than in the same dialect, only one or two a little shriller than his.
I began to think that this house must belong to some person of great note
among them, because there appeared so much ceremony before I could
gain admittance. But, that a man of quality should be served all by horses,
was beyond my comprehension. I feared my brain was disturbed by my
sufferings and misfortunes; I roused myself, and looked about me in the
room where I was left alone; this was furnished as the first, only after a
more elegant manner. I rubbed my eyes often, but the same objects still
occurred. I pinched my arms and sides, to awake myself, hoping I might
be in a dream. I then absolutely concluded that all these appearances
could be nothing else but necromancy and magic. But I had no time to
pursue these reflections; for the grey horse came to the door, and made
me a sign to follow him into the third room; where I saw a very comely
mare, together with a colt and foal, sitting on their haunches, upon mats
of straw, not unartfully made, and perfectly neat and clean.

The mare soon after my entrance, rose from her mat, and coming up
close, after having nicely observed my hands and face, gave me a most
contemptuous look; then turning to the horse, I heard the word Yahoo
often repeated betwixt them; the meaning of which word I could not then

comprehend, although it were the first I had learned to pronounce; but I
was soon better informed, to my everlasting mortification: for the horse
beckoning to me with his head, and repeating the word, "Hhuun,
Hhuun," as he did upon the road, which I understood was to attend him,
led me out into a kind of court, where was another building at some distance from the house. Here we entered, and I saw three of those detestable
creatures, which I first met after my landing, feeding upon roots, and the
flesh of some animals, which I afterwards found to be that of asses and
dogs, and now and then a cow dead by accident or disease. They were all
tied by the neck with strong withes,[6] fastened to a beam; they held their
food between the claws of their forefeet, and tore it with their teeth.

The master horse ordered a sorrel nag, one of his servants, to untie the
largest of these animals, and take him into a yard. The beast and I were
brought close together; and our countenances diligently compared, both
by master and servant, who thereupon repeated several times the word
"Yahoo." My horror and astonishment are not to be described, when I
observed, in this abominable animal, a perfect human figure; the face of
it indeed was flat and broad, the nose depressed, the lips large, and the
mouth wide; but these differences are common to all savage nations,
where the lineaments of the countenance are distorted by the natives suffering their infants to lie groveling on the earth, or by carrying them on
their backs, nuzzling with their face against the mother's shoulders. The
forefeet of the Yahoo differed from my hands in nothing else but the
length of the nails, the coarseness and brownness of the palms, and the
hairiness on the backs. There was the same resemblance between our feet,
with the same differences, which I knew very well, although the horses
did not, because of my shoes and stockings; the same in every part of our
bodies, except as to hairiness and color, which I have already described.

The great difficulty that seemed to stick with the two horses was to see
the rest of my body so very different from that of a Yahoo, for which I was
obliged to my clothes, whereof they had no conception; the sorrel nag
offered me a root, which he held (after their manner, as we shall describe
in its proper place) between his hoof and pastern; I took it in my hand,
and having smelled it, returned it to him again as civilly as I could. He
brought out of the Yahoo's kennel a piece of ass's flesh, but it smelled so
offensively that I turned from it with loathing; he then threw it to the
Yahoo, by whom it was greedily devoured. He afterwards showed me a
wisp of hay, and a fetlock[7] full of oats; but I shook my head, to signify that
neither of these were food for me. And indeed, I now apprehended that I
must absolutely starve, if I did not get to some of my own species; for as to
those filthy Yahoos, although there were few greater lovers of mankind, at
that time, than myself, yet I confess I never saw any sensitive being so
detestable on all accounts; and the more I came near them, the more
hateful they grew, while I stayed in that country. This the master horse
observed by my behavior, and therefore sent the Yahoo back to his kennel.
He then put his forehoof to his mouth, at which I was much surprised,

---

6. Fibers braided into rope.   7. The joint at the back of a horse's foot, just above the hoof, in which
the Houyhnhnm holds the oats.

although he did it with ease, and with a motion that appeared perfectly natural; and made other signs to know what I would eat; but I could not return him such an answer as he was able to apprehend; and if he had understood me, I did not see how it was possible to contrive any way for finding myself nourishment. While we were thus engaged, I observed a cow passing by; whereupon I pointed to her, and expressed a desire to let me go and milk her. This had its effect; for he led me back into the house, and ordered a mare-servant to open a room, where a good store of milk lay in earthen and wooden vessels, after a very orderly and cleanly manner. She gave me a large bowl full, of which I drank very heartily, and found myself well refreshed.

About noon I saw coming towards the house a kind of vehicle, drawn like a sledge by four Yahoos. There was in it an old steed, who seemed to be of quality; he alighted with his hind feet forward, having by accident got a hurt in his left forefoot. He came to dine with our horse, who received him with great civility. They dined in the best room, and had oats boiled in milk for the second course, which the old horse eat warm, but the rest cold. Their mangers were placed circular in the middle of the room, and divided into several partitions, round which they sat on their haunches upon bosses of straw. In the middle was a large rack with angles answering to every partition of the manger. So that each horse and mare eat their own hay, and their own mash of oats and milk, with much decency and regularity. The behavior of the young colt and foal appeared very modest; and that of the master and mistress extremely cheerful and complaisant to their guest. The grey ordered me to stand by him; and much discourse passed between him and his friend concerning me, as I found by the stranger's often looking on me, and the frequent repetition of the word Yahoo.

I happened to wear my gloves; which the master grey observing, seemed perplexed; discovering signs of wonder what I had done to my forefeet; he put his hoof three or four times to them, as if he would signify, that I should reduce them to their former shape, which I presently did, pulling off both my gloves, and putting them into my pocket. This occasioned farther talk, and I saw the company was pleased with my behavior, whereof I soon found the good effects. I was ordered to speak the few words I understood; and while they were at dinner, the master taught me the names for oats, milk, fire, water, and some others which I could readily pronounce after him, having from my youth a great facility in learning languages.

When dinner was done, the master horse took me aside, and by signs and words made me understand the concern he was in that I had nothing to eat. Oats in their tongue are called *hlunnh.* This word I pronounced two or three times; for although I had refused them at first, yet upon second thoughts, I considered that I could contrive to make a kind of bread, which might be sufficient with milk to keep me alive, till I could make my escape to some other country, and to creatures of my own species. The horse immediately ordered a white mare-servant of his family to bring me a good quantity of oats in a sort of wooden tray. These I heated before the fire as well as I could, and rubbed them till the husks came off, which I made a shift to winnow from the grain; I ground and beat them between two stones, then took water, and made them into a paste or cake, which I toasted at the fire, and eat warm with milk. It was at first a very insipid diet, although common enough in many parts of Europe, but grew tolerable by time; and having been often reduced to hard fare in my life, this was not the first experiment I had made how easily nature is satisfied. And I cannot but observe that I never had one hour's sickness, while I staid in this island. It is true, I sometimes made a shift to catch a rabbit, or bird, by springes made of Yahoos' hairs; and I often gathered wholesome herbs, which I boiled, or ate as salads with my bread; and now and then, for a rarity, I made a little butter, and drank the whey. I was at first at a great loss for salt; but custom soon reconciled the want of it; and I am confident that the frequent use of salt among us is an effect of luxury, and was first introduced only as a provocative to drink; except where it is necessary for preserving of flesh in long voyages, or in places remote from great markets. For we observe no animal to be fond of it but man;[8] and as to myself, when I left this country, it was a great while before I could endure the taste of it in anything that I eat.

This is enough to say upon the subject of my diet, wherewith other travelers fill their books, as if the readers were personally concerned whether we fare well or ill. However, it was necessary to mention this matter, lest the world should think it impossible that I could find sustenance for three years in such a country, and among such inhabitants.

When it grew towards evening, the master horse ordered a place for me to lodge in; it was but six yards from the house, and separated from the stable of the Yahoos. Here I got some straw, and covering myself with my own clothes, slept very sound. But I was in a short time better accommodated, as the reader shall know hereafter, when I come to treat more particularly about my way of living.

CHAPTER III

The Author studious to learn the language, the Houyhnhnm his master
assists in teaching him. The language described. Several Houyhnhnms of
quality come out of curiosity to see the Author. He gives his master a
short account of his voyage.

My principal endeavor was to learn the language, which my master (for so I shall henceforth call him) and his children, and every servant of his house were desirous to teach me. For they looked upon it as a prodigy, that a brute animal should discover such marks of a rational creature. I pointed to everything, and enquired the name of it, which I wrote down in my journal book when I was alone, and corrected my bad accent, by desiring those of the family to pronounce it often. In this employment, a sorrel nag, one of the under servants, was very ready to assist me.

In speaking, they pronounce through the nose and throat, and their language approaches nearest to the High Dutch or German, of any I know in Europe; but is much more graceful and significant. The Emperor

---

8. Gulliver's error; many animals are very fond of salt.

Charles V made almost the same observation, when he said, that if he were to speak to his horse, it should be in High Dutch.[9]

The curiosity and impatience of my master were so great, that he spent many hours of his leisure to instruct me. He was convinced (as he afterwards told me) that I must be a Yahoo, but my teachableness, civility, and cleanliness astonished him; which were qualities altogether so opposite to those animals. He was most perplexed about my clothes, reasoning sometimes with himself whether they were a part of my body; for I never pulled them off till the family were asleep, and got them on before they waked in the morning. My master was eager to learn from whence I came; how I acquired those appearances of reason, which I discovered in all my actions; and to know my story from my own mouth, which he hoped he should soon do by the great proficiency I made in learning and pronouncing their words and sentences. To help my memory, I formed all I learned into the English alphabet, and writ the words down with the translations. This last, after some time, I ventured to do in my master's presence. It cost me much trouble to explain to him what I was doing; for the inhabitants have not the least idea of books or literature.

In about ten weeks time I was able to understand most of his questions; and in three months could give him some tolerable answers. He was extremely curious to know from what part of the country I came, and how I was taught to imitate a rational creature; because the Yahoos (whom he saw I exactly resembled in my head, hands, and face, that were only visible) with some appearance of cunning, and the strongest disposition to mischief, were observed to be the most unteachable of all brutes. I answered that I came over the sea, from a far place, with many others of my own kind, in a great hollow vessel made of the bodies of trees; that my companions forced me to land on this coast, and then left me to shift for myself. It was with some difficulty, and by the help of many signs, that I brought him to understand me. He replied that I must needs be mistaken, or that I *said the thing which was not.* (For they have no word in their language to express lying or falsehood.) He knew it was impossible that there could be a country beyond the sea, or that a parcel of brutes could move a wooden vessel whither they pleased upon water. He was sure no Houyhnhnm alive could make such a vessel, or would trust Yahoos to manage it.

The word Houyhnhnm, in their tongue, signifies a Horse; and in its etymology, the Perfection of Nature. I told my master that I was at a loss for expression, but would improve as fast as I could; and hoped in a short time I should be able to tell him wonders; he was pleased to direct his own mare, his colt, and foal, and the servants of the family to take all opportunities of instructing me; and every day for two or three hours, he was at the same pains himself; several horses and mares of quality in the neighborhood came often to our house, upon the report spread of a wonderful Yahoo, that could speak like a Houyhnhnm, and seemed in his words and actions to discover some glimmerings of reason. These

---

9. Charles was reputed to have said he would address his God in Spanish, his mistress in Italian, and his horse in German.

delighted to converse with me; they put many questions, and received such answers as I was able to return. By all which advantages, I made so great a progress, that in five months from my arrival, I understood whatever was spoke, and could express myself tolerably well.

The Houyhnhnms who came to visit my master, out of a design of seeing and talking with me, could hardly believe me to be a right Yahoo, because my body had a different covering from others of my kind. They were astonished to observe me without the usual hair or skin, except on my head, face, and hands; but I discovered that secret to my master, upon an accident, which happened about a fortnight before.

I have already told the reader, that every night when the family were gone to bed, it was my custom to strip and cover myself with my clothes; it happened one morning early, that my master sent for me, by the sorrel nag, who was his valet; when he came, I was fast asleep, my clothes fallen off on one side, and my shirt above my waist. I awaked at the noise he made, and observed him to deliver his message in some disorder; after which he went to my master, and in a great fright gave him a very confused account of what he had seen; this I presently discovered; for going as soon as I was dressed, to pay my attendance upon his honor, he asked me the meaning of what his servant had reported; that I was not the same thing when I slept as I appeared to be at other times; that his valet assured him, some part of me was white, some yellow, at least not so white, and some brown.

I had hitherto concealed the secret of my dress, in order to distinguish myself as much as possible, from that cursed race of Yahoos; but now I found it in vain to do so any longer. Besides, I considered that my clothes and shoes would soon wear out, which already were in a declining condition, and must be supplied by some contrivance from the hides of Yahoos, or other brutes; whereby the whole secret would be known. I therefore told my master, that in the country from whence I came, those of my kind always covered their bodies with the hairs of certain animals prepared by art, as well for decency, as to avoid inclemencies of air both hot and cold; of which, as to my own person I would give him immediate conviction, if he pleased to command me; only desiring this excuse, if I did not expose those parts that nature taught us to conceal. He said, my discourse was all very strange, but especially the last part; for he could not understand why Nature should teach us to conceal what Nature had given. That neither himself nor family were ashamed of any parts of their bodies; but however I might do as I pleased. Whereupon, I first unbuttoned my coat, and pulled it off. I did the same with my waistcoat; I drew off my shoes, stockings, and breeches. I let my shirt down to my waist, and drew up the bottom, fastening it like a girdle about my middle to hide my nakedness.

My master observed the whole performance with great signs of curiosity and admiration. He took up all my clothes in his pastern, one piece after another, and examined them diligently; he then stroked my body very gently, and looked round me several times; after which he said, it was plain I must be a perfect Yahoo; but that I differed very much from the rest of my species, in the whiteness and smoothness of my skin, my want of hair in several parts of my body, the shape and shortness of my claws

behind and before, and my affectation of walking continually on my two
hinder feet. He desired to see no more; and gave me leave to put on my
clothes again, for I was shuddering with cold.

I expressed my uneasiness at his giving me so often the appellation of
Yahoo, an odious animal, for which I had so utter an hatred and contempt.
I begged he would forbear applying that word to me, and take the same
order in his family, and among his friends whom he suffered to see me. I
requested likewise, that the secret of my having a false covering to my
body might be known to none but himself, at least as long as my present
clothing should last; for as to what the sorrel nag his valet had observed,
his honor might command him to conceal it.

All this my master very graciously consented to; and thus the secret was
kept till my clothes began to wear out, which I was forced to supply by
several contrivances, that shall hereafter be mentioned. In the meantime,
he desired I would go on with my utmost diligence to learn their language,
because he was more astonished at my capacity for speech and reason,
than at the figure of my body, whether it were covered or no; adding that
he waited with some impatience to hear the wonders which I promised to
tell him.

From thenceforward he doubled the pains he had been at to instruct
me; he brought me into all company, and made them treat me with civility, because, as he told them privately, this would put me into good
humor, and make me more diverting.

Every day when I waited on him, beside the trouble he was at in teaching, he would ask me several questions concerning myself, which I
answered as well as I could; and by those means he had already received
some general ideas, although very imperfect. It would be tedious to relate
the several steps, by which I advanced to a more regular conversation,
but the first account I gave of myself in any order and length was to this
purpose:

That, I came from a very far country, as I already had attempted to tell
him, with about fifty more of my own species; that we traveled upon the
seas, in a great hollow vessel made of wood, and larger than his honor's
house. I described the ship to him in the best terms I could; and explained
by the help of my handkerchief displayed, how it was driven forward by
the wind. That, upon a quarrel among us, I was set on shore on this coast,
where I walked forward without knowing whither, till he delivered me
from the persecution of those execrable Yahoos. He asked me who made
the ship, and how it was possible that the Houyhnhnms of my country
would leave it to the management of brutes? My answer was that I durst
proceed no farther in my relation, unless he would give me his word and
honor that he would not be offended; and then I would tell him the wonders I had so often promised. He agreed; and I went on by assuring him,
that the ship was made by creatures like myself, who in all the countries I
had traveled, as well as in my own, were the only governing, rational animals; and that upon my arrival hither, I was as much astonished to see the
Houyhnhnms act like rational begins, as he or his friends could be in
finding some marks of reason in a creature he was pleased to call a Yahoo;
to which I owned my resemblance in every part, but could not account

for their degenerate and brutal nature. I said farther, that if good fortune ever restored me to my native country, to relate my travels hither, as I resolved to do; everybody would believe that I *said the thing which was not;* that I invented the story out of my own head; and with all possible respect to himself, his family, and friends, and under his promise of not being offended, our countrymen would hardly think it probable, that a Houyhnhnm should be the presiding creature of a nation, and a Yahoo the brute.

CHAPTER IV

The Houyhnhnms' notion of truth and falsehood. The author's discourse disapproved by his master. The author gives a more particular account of himself, and the accidents of his voyages.

My master heard me with great appearances of uneasiness in his countenance; because *doubting* or *not believing* are so little known in this country, that the inhabitants cannot tell how to behave themselves under such circumstances. And I remember in frequent discourses with my master concerning the nature of manhood, in other parts of the world, having occasion to talk of *lying* and *false representation,* it was with much difficulty that he comprehended what I meant; although he had otherwise a most acute judgment. For he argued thus: that the use of speech was to make us understand one another, and to receive information of facts; now if anyone *said the thing which was not,* these ends were defeated; because I cannot properly be said to understand him; and I am so far from receiving information, that he leaves me worse than in ignorance; for I am led to believe a thing *black* when it is *white,* and *short* when it is *long.* And these were all the notions he had concerning that faculty of *lying,* so perfectly well understood, and so universally practiced among human creatures.

To return from this digression; when I asserted that the Yahoos were the only governing animals in my country, which my master said was altogether past his conception, he desired to know, whether we had Houyhnhnms among us, and what was their employment; I told him we had great numbers; that in summer they grazed in the fields, and in winter were kept in houses, with hay and oats, where Yahoo servants were employed to rub their skins smooth, comb their manes, pick their feet, serve them with food, and make their beds. "I understand you well," said my master; "it is now very plain from all you have spoken, that whatever share of reason the Yahoos pretend to, the Houyhnhnms are your masters; I heartily wish our Yahoos would be so tractable." I begged his honor would please to excuse me from proceeding any farther, because I was very certain that the account he expected from me would be highly displeasing. But he insisted in commanding me to let him know the best and the worst; I told him he should be obeyed. I owned that the Houyhnhnms among us, whom we called Horses, were the most generous[1] and comely animal we had; that they excelled in strength and swiftness; and when they belonged to persons of quality, employed in traveling, racing, and

1. Noble.

drawing chariots, they were treated with much kindness and care, till they fell into diseases, or became foundered in the feet; but then they were sold, and used to all kind of drudgery till they died; after which their skins were stripped and sold for what they were worth, and their bodies left to be devoured by dogs and birds of prey. But the common race of horses had not so good fortune, being kept by farmers and carriers, and other mean people, who put them to greater labor, and fed them worse. I described as well as I could, our way of riding; the shape and use of a bridle, a saddle, a spur, and a whip; of harness and wheels. I added, that we fastened plates of a certain hard substance called iron at the bottom of their feet, to preserve their hoofs from being broken by the stony ways on which we often traveled.

My master, after some expressions of great indignation, wondered how we dared to venture upon a Houyhnhnm's back; for he was sure, that the weakest servant in his house would be able to shake off the strongest Yahoo; or by lying down, and rolling upon his back, squeeze the brute to death. I answered that our horses were trained up from three or four years old to the several uses we intended them for; that if any of them proved intolerably vicious, they were employed for carriages; that they were severely beaten while they were young for any mischievous tricks; that the males, designed for the common use of riding or draught, were generally castrated about two years after their birth, to take down their spirits, and make them more tame and gentle; that they were indeed sensible of rewards and punishments; but his honor would please to consider that they had not the least tincture of reason any more than the Yahoos in this country.

It put me to the pains of many circumlocutions to give my master a right idea of what I spoke; for their language doth not abound in variety of words, because their wants and passions are fewer than among us. But it is impossible to express his noble resentment at our savage treatment of the Houyhnhnm race; particularly after I had explained the manner and use of castrating horses among us, to hinder them from propagating their kind, and to render them more servile. He said, if it were possible there could be any country where Yahoos alone were endued with reason, they certainly must be the governing animal, because reason will in time always prevail against brutal strength. But, considering the frame of our bodies, and especially of mine, he thought no creature of equal bulk was so ill-contrived for employing that reason in the common offices of life; where-upon he desired to know whether those among whom I lived resembled me or the Yahoos of his country. I assured him that I was as well shaped as most of my age; but the younger and the females were much more soft and tender, and the skins of the latter generally as white as milk. He said I differed indeed from other Yahoos, being much more cleanly, and not altogether so deformed; but in point of real advantage, he thought I differed for the worse. That my nails were of no use either to my fore or hinder feet; as to my forefeet, he could not properly call them by that name, for he never observed me to walk upon them; that they were too soft to bear the ground; that I generally went with them uncovered, neither was the covering I sometimes wore on them of the same shape, or so strong as that on my feet behind. That I could not walk with any security; for if either of my hinder feet slipped, I must inevitably fall. He then began to find fault with other parts of my body; the flatness of my face, the prominence of my nose, my eyes placed directly in front, so that I could not look on either side without turning my head; that I was not able to feed myself without lifting one of my forefeet to my mouth; and therefore nature had placed those joints to answer that necessity. He knew not what could be the use of those several clefts and divisions in my feet behind; that these were too soft to bear the hardness and sharpness of stones without a covering made from the skin of some other brute; that my whole body wanted a fence against heat and cold, which I was forced to put on and off every day with tediousness and trouble. And lastly, that he observed every animal in his country naturally to abhor the Yahoos, whom the weaker avoided, and the stronger drove from them. So that supposing us to have the gift of reason, he could not see how it were possible to cure that natural antipathy which every creature discovered against us; nor consequently, how we could tame and render them serviceable. However, he would (as he said) debate the matter no farther, because he was more desirous to know my own story, the country where I was born, and the several actions and events of my life before I came hither.

I assured him how extremely desirous I was that he should be satisfied in every point; but I doubted much whether it would be possible for me to explain myself on several subjects whereof his honor could have no conception, because I saw nothing in his country to which I could resemble them. That however, I would do my best, and strive to express myself by similitudes, humbly desiring his assistance when I wanted proper words; which he was pleased to promise me.

I said, my birth was of honest parents, in an island called England, which was remote from this country, as many days journey as the strongest of his honor's servants could travel in the annual course of the sun. That I was bred a surgeon, whose trade it is to cure wounds and hurts in the body, got by accident or violence. That my country was governed by a female man, whom we called a queen.[2] That I left it to get riches, whereby I might maintain myself and family when I should return. That in my last voyage, I was Commander of the ship and had about fifty Yahoos under me, many of which died at sea, and I was forced to supply them by others picked out from several nations. That our ship was twice in danger of being sunk; the first time by a great storm, and the second, by striking against a rock. Here my master interposed, by asking me, how I could persuade strangers out of different countries to venture with me, after the losses I had sustained, and the hazards I had run. I said, they were fellows of desperate fortunes, forced to fly from the places of their birth, on account of their poverty or their crimes. Some were undone by lawsuits; others spent all they had in drinking, whoring, and gaming; others fled for treason; many for murder, theft, poisoning, robbery, perjury, forgery, coining false money; for committing rapes or sodomy; for flying from their

---

2. Queen Anne (1665–1714), the last Stuart ruler.

colors, or deserting to the enemy; and most of them had broken prison. None of these durst return to their native countries for fear of being hanged, or of starving in a jail; and therefore were under a necessity of seeking livelihood in other places.

During this discourse, my master was pleased often to interrupt me. I had made use of many circumlocutions in describing to him the nature of the several crimes, for which most of our crew had been forced to fly their country. This labor took up several days conversation before he was able to comprehend me. He was wholly at a loss to know what could be the use or necessity of practicing those vices. To clear up which I endeavored to give him some ideas of the desire of power and riches; of the terrible effects of lust, intemperance, malice, and envy. All this I was forced to define and describe by putting of cases, and making suppositions. After which, like one whose imagination was struck with something never seen or heard of before, he would lift up his eyes with amazement and indignation. Power, government, war, law, punishment, and a thousand other things had no terms, wherein that language could express them; which made the difficulty almost insuperable to give my master any conception of what I meant; but being of an excellent understanding, much improved by contemplation and converse, he at last arrived at a competent knowledge of what human nature in our parts of the world is capable to perform; and desired I would give him some particular account of that land, which we call Europe, especially, of my own country.

CHAPTER V

The Author, at his master's commands, informs him of the state of England. The causes of war among the princes of Europe. The Author begins to explain the English Constitution.

The reader may please to observe that the following extract of many conversations I had with my master contains a summary of the most material points, which were discoursed at several times for above two years; his honor often desiring fuller satisfaction as I farther improved in the Houyhnhnm tongue. I laid before him, as well as I could, the whole state of Europe; I discoursed of trade and manufactures, of arts and sciences; and the answers I gave to all the questions he made, as they arose upon several subjects, were a fund of conversation not to be exhausted. But I shall here only set down the substance of what passed between us concerning my own country, reducing it into order as well as I can, without any regard to time or other circumstances, while I strictly adhere to truth. My only concern is that I shall hardly be able to do justice to my master's arguments and expressions; which must needs suffer by my want of capacity, as well as by a translation into our barbarous English.

In obedience therefore to his honor's commands, I related to him the Revolution under the Prince of Orange; the long war with France entered into by the said Prince, and renewed by his successor the present queen; wherein the greatest powers of Christendom were engaged, and which still continued. I computed at his request, that about a million of Yahoos might have been killed in the whole progress of it; and perhaps a hundred or more cities taken, and five times as many ships burned or sunk.[3]

He asked me what were the usual causes or motives that made one country to go to war with another. I answered, they were innumerable; but I should only mention a few of the chief. Sometimes the ambition of princes, who never think they have land or people enough to govern; sometimes the corruption of ministers, who engage their master in a war in order to stifle or divert the clamor of the subjects against their evil administration. Difference in opinions hath cost many millions of lives; for instance, whether flesh be bread, or bread be flesh; whether the juice of a certain berry be blood or wine; whether whistling be a vice or a virtue; whether it be better to kiss a post, or throw it into the fire; what is the best color for a coat, whether black, white, red, or grey; and whether it should be long or short, narrow or wide, dirty or clean;[4] with many more. Neither are any wars so furious and bloody, or of so long continuance, as those occasioned by difference in opinion, especially if it be in things indifferent.

Sometimes the quarrel between two princes is to decide which of them shall dispossess a third of his dominions, where neither of them pretend to any right. Sometimes one prince quarreleth with another, for fear the other should quarrel with him. Sometimes a war is entered upon, because the enemy is too strong, and sometimes because he is too weak. Sometimes our neighbors want the things which we have, or have the things which we want; and we both fight, till they take ours or give us theirs. It is a very justifiable cause of war to invade a country after the people have been wasted by famine, destroyed by pestilence, or embroiled by factions amongst themselves. It is justifiable to enter into a war against our nearest ally, when one of his towns lies convenient for us, or a territory of land, that would render our dominions round and compact. If a prince send forces into a nation, where the people are poor and ignorant, he may lawfully put half of them to death, and make slaves of the rest, in order to civilize and reduce them from their barbarous way of living. It is a very kingly, honorable, and frequent practice, when one prince desires the assistance of another to secure him against an invasion, that the assistant, when he hath driven out the invader, should seize on the dominions himself, and kill, imprison, or banish the prince he came to relieve. Alliance by blood or marriage is a sufficient cause of war between princes; and the nearer the kindred is, the greater is their disposition to quarrel; poor nations are hungry, and rich nations are proud; and pride and hunger will ever be at variance. For these reasons, the trade of a soldier is held the most honorable of all others: because a soldier is a Yahoo hired to kill in cold blood as many of his own species, who have never offended him, as possibly he can.

There is likewise a kind of beggarly princes in Europe, not able to make war by themselves, who hire out their troops to richer nations for so much

---

3. Gulliver relates recent English history: the Glorious Revolution of 1688 and the War of the Spanish Succession (1703–13). He greatly exaggerates the casualties in the war.   **4.** Gulliver refers to the religious controversies of the Reformation and Counter Reformation: the doctrine of transubstantiation, the use of music in church services, the veneration of the Crucifix, and the wearing of priestly vestments.

a day to each man; of which they keep three fourths to themselves, and it is the best part of their maintenance; such are those in many northern parts of Europe.

"What you have told me," said my master, "upon the subject of war, doth indeed discover most admirably the effects of that reason you pretend to; however, it is happy that the shame is greater than the danger; and that Nature hath left you utterly uncapable of doing much mischief; for your mouths lying flat with your faces, you can hardly bite each other to any purpose, unless by consent. Then, as to the claws upon your feet before and behind, they are so short and tender, that one of our Yahoos would drive a dozen of yours before him. And therefore in recounting the numbers of those who have been killed in battle, I cannot but think that you have *said the thing which is not.*"

I could not forebear shaking my head and smiling a little at his ignorance. And, being no stranger to the art of war, I gave him a description of cannons, culverins, muskets, carabines, pistols, bullets, powder, swords, bayonets, battles, sieges, retreats, attacks, undermines, countermines, bombardments, sea fights; ships sunk with a thousand men; twenty thousand killed on each side; dying groans, limbs flying in the air; smoke, noise, confusion, trampling to death under horses' feet; flight, pursuit, victory; fields strewed with carcasses left for food to dogs, and wolves, and birds of prey; plundering, stripping, ravishing, burning, and destroying. And, to set forth the valor of my own dear countrymen, I assured him that I had seen them blow up a hundred enemies at once in a siege, and as many in a ship; and beheld the dead bodies drop down in pieces from the clouds, to the great diversion of all the spectators.

I was going on to more particulars, when my master commanded me silence. He said, whoever understood the nature of Yahoos might easily believe it possible for so vile an animal, to be capable of every action I had named, if their strength and cunning equaled their malice. But, as my discourse had increased his abhorrence of the whole species, so he found it gave him a disturbance in his mind, to which he was wholly a stranger before. He thought his ears being used to such abominable words, might by degrees admit them with less detestation. That, although he hated the Yahoos of this country, yet he no more blamed them for their odious qualities, than he did a *gnnayh* (a bird of prey) for its cruelty, or a sharp stone for cutting his hoof. But, when a creature pretending to reason could be capable of such enormities, he dreaded lest the corruption of that faculty might be worse than brutality itself. He seemed therefore confident, that instead of reason, we were only possessed of some quality fitted to increase our natural vices; as the reflection from a troubled stream returns the image of an ill-shapen body, not only larger, but more distorted.

He added that he had heard too much upon the subject of war, both in this and some former discourses. There was another point which a little perplexed him at present. I had said that some of our crew left their country on account of being ruined by law: that I had already explained the meaning of the word; but he was at a loss how it should come to pass, that the law which was intended for every man's preservation, should be any man's ruin. Therefore he desired to be farther satisfied what I meant by law, and the dispensers thereof, according to the present practice in my own country; because he thought nature and reason were sufficient guides for a reasonable animal, as we pretended to be, in showing us what we ought to do, and what to avoid.

I assured his honor that law was a science wherein I had not much conversed, further than by employing advocates, in vain, upon some injustices that had been done me. However, I would give him all the satisfaction I was able.

I said there was a society of men among us, bred up from their youth in the art of proving by words multiplied for the purpose, that white is black, and black is white, according as they are paid. To this society all the rest of the people are slaves.

"For example. If my neighbor hath a mind to my cow, he hires a lawyer to prove that he ought to have my cow from me. I must then hire another to defend my right; it being against all rules of law that any man should be allowed to speak for himself. Now in this case, I who am the true owner lie under two great disadvantages. First, my lawyer being practiced almost from his cradle in defending falsehood is quite out of his element when he would be an advocate for justice, which as an office unnatural, he always attempts with great awkwardness, if not with ill-will. The second disadvantage is that my lawyer must proceed with great caution, or else he will be reprimanded by the judges, and abhorred by his breathren, as one who would lessen the practice of the law. And therefore I have but two methods to preserve my cow. The first is to gain over my adversary's lwayer with a double fee; who will then betray his client, by insinuating that he hath justice on his side. The second way is for my lawyer to make my cause appear as unjust as he can; by allowing the cow to belong to my adversary; and this if it be skillfully done, will certainly bespeak the favor of the bench.

"Now, your honor is to know that these judges are persons appointed to decide all controversies of property, as well as for the trial of criminals; and picked out from the most dextrous lawyers who are grown old or lazy; and having been biased all their lives against truth and equity, lie under such a fatal necessity of favoring fraud, perjury, and oppression, that I have known some of them to have refused a large bribe from the side where justice lay, rather than injure the faculty,[5] by doing anything unbecoming their nature or their office.

"It is a maxim among these lawyers, that whatever hath been done before may legally be done again; and therefore they take special care to record all the decisions formerly made against common justice and the general reason of mankind. These, under the name of *precedents*, they produce as authorities to justify the most iniquitous opinions; and the judges never fail of directing accordingly.

"In pleading, they studiously avoid entering into the merits of the cause; but are loud, violent, and tedious in dwelling upon all circumstances which are not to the purpose. For instance, in the case already mentioned, they never desire to know what claim or title my adversary hath to my cow;

5. Profession.

but whether the said cow were red or black; her horns long or short; whether the field I graze her in be round or square; whether she were milked at home or abroad; what diseases she is subject to, and the like. After which they consult precedents, adjourn the cause, from time to time, and in ten, twenty, or thirty years come to an issue.

"It is likewise to be observed, that this society hath a peculiar cant and jargon of their own, that no other mortal can understand, and wherein all their laws are written, which they take special care to multiply; whereby they have wholly confounded the very essence of truth and falsehood, of right and wrong; so that it will take thirty years to decide whether the field, left me by my ancestors for six generations, belong to me, or to a stranger three hundred miles off.

"In the trial of persons accused for crimes against the state, the method is much more short and commendable: the judge first sends to sound the disposition of those in power; after which he can easily hang or save the criminal, strictly preserving all the forms of law."

Here my master interposing said it was a pity that creatures endowed with such prodigious abilities of mind as these lawyers, by the description I gave of them must certainly be, were not rather encouraged to be instructors of others in wisdom and knowledge. In answer to which, I assured his honor that in all points out of their own trade, they were usually the most ignorant and stupid generation among us, the most despicable in common conversation, avowed enemies to all knowledge and learning; and equally disposed to pervert the general reason of mankind, in every other subject of discourse as in that of their own profession.

CHAPTER VI

A continuation of the state of England, under Queen Anne. The character of a first minister in the courts of Europe.

My master was yet wholly at a loss to understand what motives could incite this race of lawyers to perplex, disquiet, and weary themselves by engaging in a confederacy of injustice, merely for the sake of injuring their fellow animals; neither could he comprehend what I meant in saying they did it for hire. Whereupon I was at much pains to describe to him the use of money, the materials it was made of, and the value of the metals; that when a Yahoo had got a great store of this precious substance, he was able to purchase whatever he had a mind to; the finest clothing, the noblest houses, great tracts of land, the most costly meats and drinks; and have his choice of the most beautiful females. Therefore since money alone was able to perform all these feats, our Yahoos thought they could never have enough of it to spend or to save, as they found themselves inclined from their natural bent either to profusion or avarice. That the rich man enjoyed the fruit of the poor man's labor, and the latter were a thousand to one in proportion to the former. That the bulk of our people was forced to live miserably, by laboring every day for small wages to make a few live plentifully. I enlarged myself much on these and many other particulars to the same purpose, but his honor was still to seek, for he went upon a supposition that all animals had a title to their share in the productions of the earth; and especially those who presided over the rest. Therefore he desired I would let him know what these costly meats were, and how any of us happened to want[6] them. Whereupon I enumerated as many sorts as came into my head, with the various methods of dressing them, which could not be done without sending vessels by sea to every part of the world, as well for liquors to drink, as for sauces, and innumerable other conveniencies. I assured him, that this whole globe of earth must be at least three times gone round, before one of our better female Yahoos could get her breakfast, or a cup to put it in. He said, "That must needs be a miserable country which cannot furnish food for its own inhabitants." But what he chiefly wondered at, was how such vast tracts of ground as I described, should be wholly without fresh water, and the people put to the necessity of sending over the sea for drink. I replied that England (the dear place of my nativity) was computed to produce three times the quantity of food, more than its inhabitants are able to consume, as well as liquors extracted from grain, or pressed out of the fruit of certain trees, which made excellent drink; and the same proportion in every other convenience of life. But, in order to feed the luxury and intemperance of the males, and the vanity of the females, we sent away the greatest part of our necessary things to other countries, from whence in return we brought the materials of diseases, folly, and vice, to spend among ourselves. Hence it follows of necessity, that vast numbers of our people are compelled to seek their livelihood by begging, robbing, stealing, cheating, pimping, foreswearing, flattering, suborning, forging, gaming, lying, fawning, hectoring, voting, scribbling, star gazing, poisoning, whoring, canting, libeling, freethinking, and the like occupations; every one of which terms, I was at much pains to make him understand.

That, wine was not imported among us from foreign countries, to supply the want of water or other drinks, but because it was a sort of liquid which made us merry, by putting us out of our senses; diverted all melancholy thoughts, begat wild extravagant imaginations in the brain, raised our hopes, and banished our fears; suspended every office of reason for a time, and deprived us of the use of our limbs, until we fell into a profound sleep; although it must be confessed, that we always awaked sick and dispirited; and that the use of this liquor filled us with diseases, which made our lives uncomfortable and short.

But beside all this, the bulk of our people supported themselves by furnishing the necessities or conveniencies of life to the rich, and to each other. For instance, when I am at home and dressed as I ought to be, I carry on my body the workmanship of an hundred tradesmen; the building and furniture of my house employ as many more; and five times the number to adorn my wife.

I was going on to tell him of another sort of people, who get their livelihood by attending the sick; having upon some occasions informed his honor that many of my crew had died of diseases. But here it was with the utmost difficulty that I brought him to apprehend what I meant. He could

6. Lack.

easily conceive that a Houyhnhnm grew weak and heavy a few days before his death; or by some accident might hurt a limb. But that nature, who worketh all things to perfection, should suffer any pains to breed in our bodies, he thought impossible; and desired to know the reason of so unaccountable an evil. I told him, we fed on a thousand things which operated contrary to each other; that we eat when we were not hungry, and drank without the provocation of thirst; that we sat whole nights drinking strong liquors without eating a bit, which disposed us to sloth, inflamed our bodies, and precipitated or prevented digestion. That, prostitute female Yahoos acquired a certain malady, which bred rottenness in the bones of those who fell into their embraces; that this and many other diseases were propagated from father to son; so that great numbers come into the world with complicated maladies upon them; that it would be endless to give him a catalogue of all diseases incident to human bodies; for they could not be fewer than five or six hundred, spread over every limb, and joint; in short, every part, external and intestine, having diseases appropriated to each. To remedy which, there was a sort of people bred up among us, in the profession or pretense of curing the sick. And because I had some skill in the faculty, I would in gratitude to his honor let him know the whole mystery and method by which they proceed.

Their fundamental is that all diseases arise from repletion; from whence they conclude, that a great evacuation of the body is necessary, either through the natural passage, or upwards at the mouth. Their next business is, from herbs, minerals, gums, oils, shells, salts, juices, seaweed, excrements, barks of trees, serpents, toads, frogs, spiders, dead men's flesh and bones, birds, beasts and fishes, to form a composition for smell and taste the most abominable, nauseous, and detestable, that they can possibly contrive, which the stomach immediately rejects with loathing, and this they call a vomit. Or else from the same storehouse, with some other poisonous additions, they command us to take in at the orifice above or below (just as the physician then happens to be disposed) a medicine equally annoying and disgustful to the bowels; which relaxing the belly, drives down all before it; and this they call a purge, or a clyster. For nature (as the physicians allege) having intended the superior anterior orifice only for the intromission of solids and liquids, and the inferior posterior for ejection, these artists ingeniously considering that in all diseases nature is forced out of her seat; therefore to replace her in it, the body must be treated in a manner directly contrary, but interchanging the use of each orifice; forcing solids and liquids in at the anus, and making evacuations at the mouth.

But, besides real diseases, we are subject to many that are only imaginary, for which the physicians have invented imaginary cures; these have their several names, and so have the drugs that are proper for them; and with these our female Yahoos are always infested.

One great excellency in this tribe is their skill at prognostics, wherein they seldom fail; their predictions in real diseases, when they rise to any degree of malignity, generally portending death, which is always in their power, when recovery is not, and therefore, upon any unexpected signs of amendment, after they have pronounced their sentence, rather than be accused as false prophets, they know how to approve[7] their sagacity to the world by a seasonable dose.

They are likewise of special use to husbands and wives, who are grown weary of their mates; to eldest sons, to great ministers of state, and often to princes.

I had formerly upon occasion discoursed with my master upon the nature of government in general, and particularly of our own excellent constitution, deservedly the wonder and envy of the whole world. But having here accidentally mentioned a minister of state, he commanded me some time after to inform him what species of Yahoo I particularly meant by that appellation.

I told him that a first or chief minister of state, whom I intended to describe, was a creature wholly exempt from joy and grief, love and hatred, pity and anger; at least makes use of no other passions but a violent desire of wealth, power, and titles; that he applies his words to all uses, except to the indication of his mind; that he never tells a truth, but with an intent that you should take it for a lie; nor a lie, but with a design that you should take it for a truth; that those he speaks worst of behind their backs are in the surest way to preferment; and whenever he begins to praise you to others or to yourself, you are from that day forlorn. The worst mark you can receive is a promise, especially when it is confirmed with an oath; after which every wise man retires, and gives over all hopes.

There are three methods by which a man may rise to be chief minister: the first is by knowing how with prudence to dispose of a wife, a daughter, or a sister; the second, by betraying or undermining his predecessor; and the third is by a furious zeal in public assemblies against the corruptions of the court. But a wise prince would rather choose to employ those who practice the last of these methods; because such zealots prove always the most obsequious and subservient to the will and passions of their master. That, these ministers having all employments at their disposal, preserve themselves in power by bribing the majority of a senate or great council; and at last by an expedient called an Act of Indemnity (whereof I described the nature to him) they secure themselves from after-reckonings, and retire from the public, laden with the spoils of the nation.

The palace of a chief minister is a seminary to breed up others in his own trade; the pages, lackies, and porter, by imitating their master, become ministers of state in their several districts, and learn to excel in the three principal ingredients, of insolence, lying, and bribery. Accordingly, they have a subaltern court paid to them by persons of the best rank; and sometimes by the force of dexterity and impudence, arrive through several gradations to be successors to their lord.

He is usually governed by a decayed wench, or favorite footman, who are the tunnels through which all graces are conveyed, and may properly be called, in the last resort, the governors of the kingdom.

One day, my master, having heard me mention the nobility of my country, was pleased to make me a compliment which I could not pretend to

---

7. Prove.

deserve: that, he was sure, I must have been born of some noble family, because I far exceeded in shape, color, and cleanliness, all the Yahoos of his nation, although I seemed to fail in strength, and agility, which must be imputed to my different way of living from those other brutes; and besides, I was not only endowed with the faculty of speech, but likewise with some rudiments of reason, to a degree, that with all his acquaintance I passed for a prodigy.

He made me observe, that among the Houyhnhnms, the white, the sorrel, and the iron grey were not so exactly shaped as the bay, the dapple grey, and the black; nor born with equal talents of mind, or a capacity to improve them; and therefore continued always in the condition of servants, without ever aspiring to match out of their own race, which in that country would be reckoned monstrous and unnatural.

I made his honor my most humble acknowledgements for the good opinion he was pleased to conceive of me; but assured him at the same time, that my birth was of the lower sort, having been born of plain, honest parents, who were just able to give me a tolerable education; that, nobility among us was altogether a different thing from the idea he had of it; that, our young noblemen are bred from their childhood in idleness and luxury; that, as soon as years will permit, they consume their vigor, and contract odious diseases among lewd females; and when their fortunes are almost ruined, they marry some woman of mean birth, disagreeable person, and unsound constitution, merely for the sake of money, whom they hate and despise. That, the productions of such marriages are generally scrofulous, rickety or deformed children; by which means the family seldom continues above three generations, unless the wife take care to provide a healthy father among her neighbors, or domestics, in order to improve and continue the breed. That a weak diseased body, a meager countenance, and sallow complexion are the true marks of noble blood; and a healthy robust appearance is so disgraceful in a man of quality, that the world concludes his real father to have been a groom or a coachman. The imperfections of his mind run parallel with those of his body; being a composition of spleen, dullness, ignorance, caprice, sensuality, and pride.

Without the consent of this illustrious body, no law can be enacted, repealed, or altered, and these nobles have likewise the decision of all our possessions without appeal.

CHAPTER VII

The Author's great love of his native country. His master's observations upon the constitution and administration of England, as described by the Author, with parallel cases and comparisons. His master's observations upon human nature.

The reader may be disposed to wonder how I could prevail on myself to give so free a representation of my own species, among a race of mortals who were already too apt to conceive the vilest opinion of humankind, from that entire congruity betwixt me and their Yahoos. But I must freely confess that the many virtues of those excellent quadrupeds placed in opposite view to human corruptions had so far opened my eyes, and enlarged my understanding, that I began to view the actions and passions of man in a very different light; and to think the honor of my own kind not worth managing; which, besides, it was impossible for me to do before a person of so acute a judgment as my master, who daily convinced me of a thousand faults in myself, whereof I had not the least perception before, and which with us would never be numbered even among human infirmities. I had likewise learned from his example an utter detestation of all falsehood or disguise; and truth appeared so amiable to me, that I determined upon sacrificing everything to it.

Let me deal so candidly with the reader as to confess that there was yet a much stronger motive for the freedom I took in my representation of things. I had not been a year in this country, before I contracted such a love and veneration for the inhabitants, that I entered on a firm resolution never to return to humankind, but to pass the rest of my life among these admirable Houyhnhnms in the contemplation and practice of every virtue; where I could have no example or incitement to vice. But it was decreed by fortune, my perpetual enemy, that so great a felicity should not fall to my share. However, it is now some comfort to reflect that in what I said of my countrymen, I extenuated their faults as much as I durst before so strict an examiner; and upon every article, gave as favorable a turn as the matter would bear. For, indeed, who is there alive that will not be swayed by his bias and partiality to the place of his birth?

I have related the substance of several conversations I had with my master, during the greatest part of the time I had the honor to be in his service; but have indeed for brevity sake omitted much more than is here set down.

When I had answered all his questions, and his curiosity seemed to be fully satisfied; he sent for me one morning early, and commanding me to sit down at some distance (an honor which he had never before conferred upon me), he said he had been very seriously considering my whole story, as far as it related both to myself and my country; that, he looked upon us as a sort of animal to whose share, by what accident he could not conjecture, some small pittance of reason had fallen, whereof we made no other use than by its assistance to aggravate our natural corruptions, and to acquire new ones which nature had not given us. That we disarmed ourselves of the few abilities she had bestowed; had been very successful in multiplying our original wants, and seemed to spend our whole lives in vain endeavors to supply them by our own inventions. That, as to myself, it was manifest I had neither the strength or agility of a common Yahoo; that I walked infirmly on my hinder feet; had found out a contrivance to make my claws of no use or defense, and to remove the hair from my chin, which was intended as a shelter from the sun and the weather. Lastly, that I could neither run with speed, nor climb trees like my brethren (as he called them) the Yahoos in this country.

That our institutions of government and law were plainly owing to our gross defects in reason, and by consequence, in virtue; because reason alone is sufficient to govern a rational creature; which was therefore a character we had no pretense to challenge, even from the account I had given of my own people; although he manifestly perceived, that in order to favor them, I had concealed many particulars, and often *said the thing which was not.*

He was the more confirmed in this opinion, because he observed that I agreed in every feature of my body with other Yahoos, except where it was to my real disadvantage in point of strength, speed, and activity, the short- ness of my claws, and some other particulars where nature had no part; so, from the representation I had given him of our lives, our manners, and our actions, he found as near a resemblance in the disposition of our minds. He said the Yahoos were known to hate one another more than they did any different species of animals; and the reason usually assigned was the odiousness of their own shapes, which all could see in the rest, but not in themselves. He had therefore begun to think it not unwise in us to cover our bodies, and by that invention, conceal many of our deform- ities from each other, which would else be hardly supportable. But he now found he had been mistaken; and that the dissentions of those brutes in his country were owing to the same cause with ours, as I had described them. For, if (said he) you throw among five Yahoos as much food as would be sufficient for fifty, they will, instead of eating peaceably, fall together by the ears, each single one impatient to have all to itself; and therefore a servant was usually employed to stand by while they were feed- ing abroad, and those kept at home were tied at a distance from each other. That, if a cow died of age or accident, before a Houyhnhnm could secure it for his own Yahoos, those in the neighborhood would come in herds to seize it, and then would ensue such a battle as I had described, with terrible wounds made by their claws on both sides, although they seldom were able to kill one another, for want of such convenient instru- ments of death as we had invented. At other times the like battles have been fought between the Yahoos of several neighborhoods without any visible cause; those of one district watching all opportunities to surprise the next before they are prepared. But if they find their project hath mis- carried, they return home, and for want of enemies, engage in what I call a civil war among themselves.

That, in some fields of his country, there are certain shining stones of several colors, whereof the Yahoos are violently fond; and when part of these stones are fixed in the earth, as it sometimes happeneth, they will dig with their claws for whole days to get them out, and carry them away, and hide them by heaps in their kennels; but still looking round with great caution, for fear their comrades should find out their treasure. My master said he could never discover the reason of this unnatural appetite, or how these stones could be of any use to a Yahoo; but now he believed it might proceed from the same principle of avarice, which I had ascribed to man- kind. That he had once, by way of experiment, privately removed a heap of these stones from the place where one of his Yahoos had buried it, whereupon, the sordid animal missing his treasure, by his loud lamenting brought the whole herd to the place, there miserably howled, then fell to biting and tearing the rest; began to pine away, would neither eat nor sleep, nor work, till he ordered a servant privately to convey the stones into the same hole, and hide them as before; which when his Yahoo had found, he presently recovered his spirits and good humor; but took care to remove them to a better hiding place; and hath ever since been a very serviceable brute.

My master farther assured me, which I also observed myself; that in the fields where these shining stones abound, the fiercest and most frequent battles are fought, occasioned by perpetual inroads of the neighboring Yahoos.

He said it was common when two Yahoos discovered such a stone in a field, and were contending which of them should be the proprietor, a third would take the advantage, and carry it away from them both; which my master would needs contend to have some resemblance with our suits at law; wherein I thought it for our credit not to undeceive him; since the decision he mentioned was much more equitable than many decrees among us; because the plaintiff and defendant there lost nothing beside the stone they contended for; whereas our courts of equity would never have dismissed the cause while either of them had anything left.

My master continuing his discourse said there was nothing that rendered the Yahoos more odious, than their undistinguished appetite to devour everything that came in their way, whether herbs, roots, berries, corrupted flesh of animals, or all mingled together; and it was peculiar in their temper, that they were fonder of what they could get by rapine or stealth at a greater distance, than much better food provided for them at home. If their prey held out, they would eat till they were ready to burst, after which nature had pointed out to them a certain root that gave them a general evacuation.

There was also another kind of root very juicy, but something rare and difficult to be found, which the Yahoos fought for with much eagerness, and would suck it with great delight; it produced the same effects that wine hath upon us. It would make them sometimes hug, and sometimes tear one another; they would howl and grin, and chatter, and reel, and tumble, and then fall asleep in the mud.

I did indeed observe that the Yahoos were the only animals in this country subject to any diseases; which however, were much fewer than horses have among us, and contracted not by any ill treatment they meet with, but by the nastiness and greediness of that sordid brute. Neither has their language any more than a general appellation for those maladies; which is borrowed from the name of the beast, and called *Hnea Yahoo*, or the Yahoo's Evil; and the cure prescribed is a mixture of their own dung and urine, forcibly put down the Yahoo's throat. This I have since often known to have been taken with success, and do here freely recommend it to my countrymen, for the public good, as an admirable specific against all diseases produced by repletion.

As to learning, government, arts, manufactures, and the like, my master confessed he could find little or no resemblance between the Yahoos of that country and those in ours. For he only meant to observe what parity there was in our natures. He had heard indeed some curious Houyhnhnms observe that in most herds there was a sort of ruling Yahoo (as among us there is generally some leading or principal stag in a park) who was always more deformed in body, and mischievous in disposition, than any of the rest. That this leader had usually a favorite as like himself as he could get, whose employment was to lick his master's feet and posteriors, and drive the female Yahoos to his kennel; for which he was now and then rewarded with a piece of ass's flesh. This favorite is hated by the whole herd; and therefore to protect himself, keeps always near the person of his leader. He usually continues in office till a worse can be found; but the very moment he is discarded, his successor, at the head of all the Yahoos in that district, young and old, male and female, come in a body, and discharge their excrements upon him from head to foot. But how far this might be applicable to our courts and favorites, and ministers of state, my master said I could best determine.

I durst make no return to this malicious insinuation, which debased human understanding below the sagacity of a common hound, who hath judgment enough to distinguish and follow the cry of the ablest dog in the pack, without being ever mistaken.

My master told me there were some qualities remarkable in the Yahoos, which he had not observed me to mention, or at least very slightly, in the accounts I had given him of humankind. He said, those animals, like other brutes, had their females in common; but in this differed, that the she-Yahoo would admit the male while she was pregnant; and that the hes would quarrel and fight with the females as fiercely as with each other. Both which practices were such degrees of infamous brutality, that no other sensitive creature ever arrived at.

Another thing he wondered at in the Yahoos was their strange disposition to nastiness and dirt; whereas there appears to be a natural love of cleanliness in all other animals. As to the two former accusations, I was glad to let them pass without any reply, because I had not a word to offer upon them in defense of my species, which otherwise I certainly had done from my own inclinations. But I could have easily vindicated humankind from the imputation of singularity upon the last article, if there had been any swine in that country (as unluckily for me there were not) which although it may be a sweeter quadruped than a Yahoo, cannot I humbly conceive in justice pretend to more cleanliness; and so his honor himself must have owned, if he had seen their filthy way of feeding, and their custom of wallowing and sleeping in the mud.

My master likewise mentioned another quality, which his servants had discovered in several Yahoos, and to him was wholly unaccountable. He said, a fancy would sometimes take a Yahoo, to retire into a corner, to lie down and howl, and groan, and spurn away all that came near him, although he were young and fat, and wanted neither food nor water; nor did the servants imagine what could possibly ail him. And the only remedy they found was to set him to hard work, after which he would infallibly come to himself. To this I was silent out of partiality to my own kind; yet here I could plainly discover the true seeds of spleen,[8] which only seizeth on the lazy, the luxurious, and the rich; who, if they were forced to undergo the same regimen, I would undertake for the cure.

His Honor had farther observed, that a female Yahoo would often stand

8. Hypochondria.

behind a bank or a bush, to gaze on the young males passing by, and then appear, and hide, using many antic gestures and grimaces; at which time it was observed, that she had a most offensive smell; and when any of the males advanced, would slowly retire, looking back, and with a counterfeit show of fear, run off into some convenient place where she knew the male would follow her.

At other times, if a female stranger came among them, three or four of her own sex would get about her, and stare and chatter, and grin, and smell her all over; and then turn off with gestures that seemed to express contempt and disdain.

Perhaps my master might refine a little in these speculations, which he had drawn from what he observed himself, or had been told by others; however, I could not reflect without some amazement, and much sorrow, that the rudiments of lewdness, coquetry, censure, and scandal, should have place by instinct in womankind.

I expected every moment that my master would accuse the Yahoos of those unnatural appetites in both sexes, so common among us. But nature it seems hath not been so expert a school-mistress; and these politer pleasures are entirely the productions of art and reason, on our side of the globe.

CHAPTER VIII

The Author relateth several particulars of the Yahoos. The great virtues of the Houyhnhnms. The education and exercises of their youth. Their general assembly.

As I ought to have understood human nature much better than I supposed it possible for my master to do, so it was easy to apply the character he gave of the Yahoos to myself and my countrymen; and I believed I could yet make farther discoveries from my own observation. I therefore often begged his honor to let me go among the herds of Yahoos in the neighborhood; to which he always very graciously consented, being perfectly convinced that the hatred I bore those brutes would never suffer me to be corrupted by them; and his honor ordered one of his servants, a strong sorrel nag, very honest and good-natured, to be my guard; without whose protection I durst not undertake such adventures. For I have already told the reader how much I was pestered by those odious animals upon my first arrival. I afterwards failed very narrowly three or four times of falling into their clutches, when I happened to stray at any distance without my hanger. And I have reason to believe, they had some imagination that I was of their own species, which I often assisted myself, by stripping up my sleeves, and shewing my naked arms and breast in their sight, when my protector was with me; at which times they would approach as near as they durst, and imitate my actions after the manner of monkeys, but ever with great signs of hatred; as a tame jackdaw with cap and stockings is always persecuted by the wild ones, when he happens to be got among them.

They are prodigiously nimble from their infancy; however, I once caught a young male of three years old, and endeavored by all marks of tenderness to make it quiet; but the little imp fell a squalling, scratching, and biting with such violence, that I was forced to let it go; and it was high time, for a whole troop of old ones came about us at the noise; but finding the cub was safe (for away it ran) and my sorrel nag being by, they durst not venture near us. I observed the young animal's flesh to smell very rank, and the stink was somewhat between a weasel and a fox, but much more disagreeable. I forgot another circumstance (and perhaps I might have the reader's pardon, if it were wholly omitted) that while I held the odious vermin in my hands, it voided its filthy excrements of a yellow liquid substance, all over my clothes; but by good fortune there was a small brook hard by, where I washed myself as clean as I could; although I durst not come into my master's presence until I were sufficiently aired.

By what I could discover, the Yahoos appear to be the most unteachable of all animals, their capacities never reaching higher than to draw or carry burdens. Yet I am of opinion, this defect ariseth chiefly from a perverse, restive disposition. For they are cunning, malicious, treacherous and revengeful. They are strong and hardy, but of a cowardly spirit, and by consequence insolent, abject, and cruel. It is observed that the red-haired of both sexes are more libidinous and mischievous than the rest, whom yet they much exceed in strength and activity.

The Houyhnhnms keep the Yahoos for present use in huts not far from the house; but the rest are sent abroad to certain fields, where they dig up roots, eat several kinds of herbs, and search about for carrion, or sometimes catch weasels and *luhimuhs* (a sort of wild rat) which they greedily devour. Nature hath taught them to dig deep holes with their nails on the side of a rising ground, wherein they lie by themselves; only the kennels of the females are larger, sufficient to hold two or three cubs.

They swim from their infancy like frogs, and are able to continue long under water, where they often take fish, which the females carry home to their young. And upon this occasion, I hope the reader will pardon my relating an odd adventure.

Being one day abroad with my protector the sorrel nag, and the weather exceeding hot, I entreated him to let me bathe in a river that was near. He consented, and I immediately stripped myself stark naked, and went down softly into the stream. It happened that a young female Yahoo standing behind a bank, saw the whole proceeding; and inflamed by desire, as the nag and I conjectured, came running with all speed, and leaped into the water within five yards of the place where I bathed. I was never in my life so terribly frighted; the nag was grazing at some distance, not suspecting any harm; she embraced me after a most fulsome manner; I roared as loud as I could, and the nag came galloping towards me, whereupon she quitted her grasp, with the utmost reluctancy, and leaped upon the opposite bank, where she stood gazing and howling all the time I was putting on my clothes.

This was matter of diversion to my master and his family, as well as of mortification to myself. For now I could no longer deny that I was a real Yahoo, in every limb and feature, since the females had a natural propensity to me as one of their own species; neither was the hair of this brute of a red color (which might have been some excuse for an appetite a little irregular) but black as a sole, and her countenance did not make an appearance altogether so hideous as the rest of the kind; for I think, she could not be above eleven years old.

Having already lived three years in this country, the reader I suppose will expect that I should, like other travelers, give him some account of the manners and customs of its inhabitants, which it was indeed my principal study to learn.

As these noble Houyhnhnms are endowed by Nature with a general disposition to all virtues, and have no conceptions or ideas of what is evil in a rational creature; so their grand maxim is to cultivate reason, and to be wholly governed by it. Neither is reason among them a point problematical as with us, where men can argue with plausibility on both sides of a question; but strikes you with immediate conviction; as it must needs do where it is not mingled, obscured, or discolored by passion and interest. I remember it was with extreme difficulty that I could bring my master to understand the meaning of the word "opinion," or how a point could be disputable; because reason taught us to affirm or deny only where we are certain; and beyond our knowledge we cannot do either. So that controversies, wranglings, disputes, and positiveness in false or dubious propositions are evils unknown among the Houyhnhnms. In the like manner when I used to explain to him our several systems of natural philosophy, he would laugh that a creature pretending to reason should value itself upon the knowledge of other people's conjectures, and in things, where that knowledge, if it were certain, could be of no use. Wherein he agreed entirely with the sentiments of Socrates, as Plato delivers them, which I mention as the highest honor I can do that prince of philosophers. I have often since reflected what destruction such a doctrine would make in the libraries of Europe; and how many paths to fame would be then shut up in the learned world.

Friendship and benevolence are the two principal virtues among the Houyhnhnms; and these not confined to particular objects, but universal to the whole race. For a stranger from the remotest part is equally treated with the nearest neighbor, and wherever he goes, looks upon himself as at home. They preserve decency and civility in the highest degrees, but are altogether ignorant of ceremony. They have no fondness for[9] their colts or foals; but the care they take in educating them proceedeth entirely from the dictates of reason. And I observed my master to show the same affection to his neighbor's issue that he had for his own. They will have it that nature teaches them to love the whole species, and it is reason only that maketh a distinction of persons, where there is a superior degree of virtue.

When the matron Houyhnhnms have produced one of each sex, they no longer accompany with their consorts, except they lose one of their issue by some casualty, which very seldom happens; but in such a case they meet again; or when the like accident befalls a person whose wife is past bearing, some other couple bestows on him one of their own colts, and then go together a second time, until the mother be pregnant. This

---

9. Attachment to.

caution is necessary to prevent the country from being overburdened with numbers. But the race of inferior Houyhnhnms bred up to be servants is not so strictly limited upon this article; these are allowed to produce three of each sex, to be domestics in the noble families.

In their marriages they are exactly careful to choose such colors as will not make any disagreeable mixture in the breed. Strength is chiefly valued in the male, and comeliness in the female; not upon the account of love, but to preserve the race from degenerating; for, where a female happens to excel in strength, a consort is chosen with regard to comeliness. Courtship, love, presents, jointures, settlements, have no place in their thoughts, or terms whereby to express them in their language. The young couple meet and are joined, merely because it is the determination of their parents and friends; it is what they see done every day; and they look upon it as one of the necessary actions in a reasonable being. But the violation of marriage, or any other unchastity, was never heard of; and the married pair pass their lives with the same friendship and mutual benevolence that they bear to all others of the same species who come in their way, without jealousy, fondness, quarreling, or discontent.

In educating the youth of both sexes, their method is admirable, and highly deserveth our imitation. These are not suffered to taste a grain of oats, except upon certain days, till eighteen years old; nor milk, but very rarely; and in summer they graze two hours in the morning, and as many in the evening, which their parents likewise observe; but the servants are not allowed above half that time; and a great part of the grass is brought home, which they eat at the most convenient hours, when they can be best spared from work.

Temperance, industry, exercise, and cleanliness are the lessons equally enjoined to the young ones of both sexes; and my master thought it monstrous in us to give the females a different kind of education from the males, except in some articles of domestic management; whereby, as he truly observed, one half of our natives were good for nothing but bringing children into the world; and to trust the care of their children to such useless animals, he said was yet a greater instance of brutality.

But the Houyhnhnms train up their youth to strength, speed, and hardiness, by exercising them in running races up and down steep hills, or over hard stony grounds; and when they are all in a sweat, they are ordered to leap over head and ears into a pond or a river. Four times a year the youth of certain districts meet to show their proficiency in running, and leaping, and other feats of strength or agility; where the victor is rewarded with a song made in his or her praise. On this festival the servants drive a herd of Yahoos into the field, laden with hay, and oats, and milk for a repast to the Houyhnhnms; after which these brutes are immediately driven back again, for fear of being noisome to the assembly.

Every fourth year, at the vernal equinox, there is a representative council of the whole nation, which meets in a plain about twenty miles from our house, and continueth about five or six days. Here they inquire into the state and condition of the several districts; whether they abound or be deficient in hay or oats, or cows or Yahoos? And wherever there is any want (which is but seldom) it is immediately supplied by unanimous consent and contribution. Here likewise the regulation of children is settled: as for instance, if a Houyhnhnm hath two males, he changeth one of them with another who hath two females, and when a child hath been lost by any casualty, where the mother is past breeding, it is determined what family in the district shall breed another to supply the loss.

CHAPTER IX

A grand debate at the general assembly of the Houyhnhnms, and how it was determined. The learning of the Houyhnhnms. Their buildings. Their manner of burials. The defectiveness of their language.

One of these grand assemblies was held in my time, about three months before my departure, whither my master went as the representative of our district. In this council was resumed their old debate, and indeed, the only debate that ever happened in their country; whereof my master after his return gave me a very particular account.

The question to be debated was whether the Yahoos should be exterminated from the face of the earth. One of the members for the affirmative offered several arguments of great strength and weight, alleging that, as the Yahoos were the most filthy, noisome, and deformed animal which nature ever produced, so they were the most restive and indocile, mischievous, and malicious; they would privately suck the teats of the Houyhnhnms' cows; kill and devour their cats, trample down their oats and grass, if they were not continually watched; and commit a thousand other extravagancies. He took notice of a general tradition, that Yahoos had not been always in their country, but that many ages ago, two of these brutes appeared together upon a mountain; whether produced by the heat of the sun upon corrupted mud and slime, or from the ooze and froth of the sea, was never known. That these Yahoos engendered, and their brood in a short time grew so numerous as to overrun and infest the whole nation. That the Houyhnhnms to get rid of this evil, made a general hunting, and at last enclosed the whole herd; and destroying the older, every Houyhnhnm kept two young ones in a kennel, and brought them to such a degree of tameness as an animal so savage by nature can be capable of acquiring, using them for draft and carriage. That there seemed to be much truth in this tradition, and that those creatures could not be *ylnhniamshy* (or aborigines of the land) because of the violent hatred the Houyhnhnms as well as all other animals bore them; which although their evil disposition sufficiently deserved, could never have arrived at so high a degree, if they had been aborigines, or else they would have long since been rooted out. That the inhabitants taking a fancy to use the service of the Yahoos, had very imprudently neglected to cultivate the breed of asses, which were a comely animal, easily kept, more tame and orderly, without any offensive smell, strong enough for labor, although they yield to the other in agility of body; and if their braying be no agreeable sound, it is far preferable to the horrible howlings of the Yahoos.

Several others declared their sentiments to the same purpose, when my master proposed an expedient to the assembly, whereof he had indeed borrowed the hint from me. He approved of the tradition, mentioned by the honorable member, who spoke before; and affirmed, that the two Yahoos said to be first seen among them, had been driven thither over the sea; that coming to land, and being forsaken by their companions, they retired to the mountains, and degenerating by degrees, became in process of time much more savage than those of their own species in the country from whence these two originals came. The reason of his assertion was that he had now in his possession a certain wonderful Yahoo (meaning myself) which most of them had heard of, and many of them had seen. He then related to them how he first found me; that my body was all covered with an artificial composure of the skins and hairs of other animals; that I spoke in a language of my own, and had thoroughly learned theirs; that I had related to him the accidents which brought me thither; that when he saw me without my covering, I was an exact Yahoo in every part, only of a whiter color, less hairy and with shorter claws. He added how I had endeavored to persuade him that in my own and other countries the Yahoos acted as the governing, rational animal, and held the Houyhnhnms in servitude; that he observed in me all the qualities of a Yahoo, only a little more civilized by some tincture of reason, which however was in a degree as far inferior to the Houyhnhnm race as the Yahoos of their country were to me; that among other things, I mentioned a custom we had of castrating Houyhnhnms when they were young, in order to render them tame; that the operation was easy and safe; that it was no shame to learn wisdom from brutes, as industry is taught by the ant, and building by the swallow (for so I translate the world *lyhannh*, although it be a much larger fowl). That this invention might be practiced upon the younger Yahoos here, which, besides rendering them tractable and fitter for use, would in an age put an end to the whole species without destroying life. That in the meantime the Houyhnhnms should be exhorted to cultivate the breed of asses, which, as they are in all respects more valuable brutes, so they have this advantage, to be fit for service at five years old, which the others are not till twelve.

This was all my master thought fit to tell me at that time, of what passed in the grand council. But he was pleased to conceal one particular, which related personally to myself, whereof I soon felt the unhappy effect, as the reader will know in its proper place, and from whence I date all the succeeding misfortunes of my life.

The Houyhnhnms have no letters, and consequently, their knowledge is all traditional. But there happening few events of any moment among a people so well united, naturally disposed to every virtue, wholly governed by reason, and cut off from all commerce with other nations, the historical part is easily preserved without burdening their memories. I have already observed that they are subject to no diseases, and therefore can have no need of physicians. However, they have excellent medicines composed of herbs, to cure accidental bruises and cuts in the pastern or frog of the foot by sharp stones, as well as other maims and hurts in the several parts of the body.

They calculate the year by the revolution of the sun and the moon, but use no subdivisions into weeks. They are well enough acquainted with the motions of those two luminaries, and understand the nature of eclipses; and this is the utmost progress of their astronomy.

In poetry they must be allowed to excel all other mortals; wherein the justness of their similes, and the minuteness, as well as exactness of their descriptions, are indeed inimitable. Their verses abound very much in both of these, and usually contain either some exalted notions of friendship and benevolence, or the praises of those who were victors in races and other bodily exercises. Their buildings, although very rude and simple, are not inconvenient, but well contrived to defend them from all injuries of cold and heat. They have a kind of tree, which at forty years old loosens in the root, and falls with the first storm; it grows very straight, and being pointed like stakes with a sharp stone (for the Houyhnhnms know not the use of iron), they stick them erect in the ground about ten inches asunder, and then weave in oat straw, or sometimes wattles, betwixt them. The roof is made after the same manner, and so are the doors.

The Houyhnhnms use the hollow part between the pastern and the hoof of their forefeet as we do our hands, and this with greater dexterity than I could at first imagine. I have seen a white mare of our family thread a needle (which I lent her on purpose) with that joint. They milk their cows, reap their oats, and do all the work which requires hands in the same manner. They have a kind of hard flints, which by grinding against other stones they form into instruments that serve instead of wedges, axes, and hammers. With tools made of these flints, they likewise cut their hay, and reap their oats, which there groweth naturally in several fields; the Yahoos draw home the sheaves in carriages, and the servants tread them in certain covered huts, to get out the grain, which is kept in stores. They make a rude kind of earthen and wooden vessels, and bake the former in the sun.

If they can avoid casualties, they die only of old age, and are buried in the obscurest places that can be found, their friends and relations expressing neither joy nor grief at their departure; nor does the dying person discover the least regret that he is leaving the world, any more than if he were upon returning home from a visit to one of his neighbors; I remember my master having once made an appointment with a friend and his family to come to his house upon some affair of importance; on the day fixed, the mistress and her two children came very late; she made two excuses, first for her husband, who, as she said, happened that very morning to *lhnuwnh*. The word is strongly expressive in their language, but not easily rendered into English; it signifies, *to retire to his first Mother*. Her excuse for not coming sooner was that her husband dying late in the morning, she was a good while consulting her servants about a convenient place where his body should be laid; and I observed she behaved herself at our house, as cheerfully as the rest; she died about three months after.

They live generally to seventy or seventy-five years, very seldom to fourscore; some weeks before their death they feel a gradual decay, but without pain. During this time they are much visited by their friends, because they cannot go abroad with their usual ease and satisfaction. However, about ten days before their death, which they seldom fail in computing, they return the visits that have been made by those who are nearest in the neighborhood, being carried in a convenient sledge drawn by Yahoos; which vehicle they use, not only upon this occasion, but when they grow old, upon long journeys, or when they are lamed by any accident. And therefore when the dying Houyhnhnms return those visits, they take a solemn leave of their friends, as if they were going to some remote part of the country, where they designed to pass the rest of their lives.

I know not whether it may be worth observing, that the Houyhnhnms have no word in their language to express anything that is evil, except what they borrow from the deformities or ill qualities of the Yahoos. Thus they denote the folly of a servant, an omission of a child, a stone that cuts their feet, a continuance of foul or unseasonable weather, and the like, by adding to each the epithet of Yahoo. For instance, *hhnm Yahoo, whnaholm Yahoo, ynlhmndwihlma Yahoo,* and an ill-contrived house, *ynholmhnmrohlnw Yahoo.*

I could with great pleasure enlarge farther upon the manners and virtues of this excellent people; but intending in a short time to publish a volume by itself expressly upon that subject, I refer the reader thither. And in the meantime, proceed to relate my own sad catastrophe.

CHAPTER X

The Author's economy, and happy life among the Houyhnhnms. His great improvement in virtue, by conversing with them. Their conversations. The Author hath notice given him by his master that he must depart from the country. He falls into a swoon for grief, but submits. He contrives and finishes a canoe, by the help of a fellow servant, and puts to sea at a venture.

I had settled my little economy to my own heart's content. My master had ordered a room to be made for me after their manner, about six yards from the house; the sides and floors of which I plastered with clay, and covered with rush mats of my own contriving; I had beaten hemp, which there grows wild, and made of it a sort of ticking; this I filled with the feathers of several birds I had taken with springes made of Yahoos' hairs, and were excellent food. I had worked two chairs with my knife, the sorrel nag helping me in the grosser and more laborious part. When my clothes were worn to rags, I made myself others with the skins of rabbits, and of a certain beautiful animal about the same size, called *nnuhnoh,* the skin of which is covered with a fine down. Of these I likewise made very tolerable stockings. I soled my shoes with wood which I cut from a tree, and fitted to the upper leather, and when this was worn out, I supplied it with the skins of Yahoos, dried in the sun. I often got honey out of hollow trees, which I mingled with water, or eat it with my bread. No man could more verify the truth of these two maxims, that *Nature is very easily satisfied;* and, that *Necessity is the mother of invention.* I enjoyed perfect health of body, and tranquility of mind; I did not feel the treachery or inconstancy of a friend, nor the inquiries of a secret or open enemy. I had no occasion of bribing, flattering, or pimping to procure the favor of any great man, or of his minion. I wanted no fence against fraud or oppression; here was neither physician to destroy my body, nor lawyer to ruin my fortune; no informer to watch my words and actions, or forge accusations against me for hire; here were no gibers, censurers, backbiters, pickpockets, highwaymen, housebreakers, attorneys, bawds, buffoons, gamesters, politicians, wits, splenetics, tedious talkers, controvertists, ravishers, murderers, robbers, virtuosos; no leaders or followers of party and faction; no encouragers to vice, by seducement or examples; no dungeons, axes, gibbets, whipping posts, or pillories; no cheating shopkeepers or mechanics; no pride, vanity or affectation; no fops, bullies, drunkards, strolling whores, or poxes; no ranting, lewd, expensive wives; no stupid, proud pedants; no importunate, overbearing, quarrelsome, noisy, roaring, empty, conceited, swearing companions; no scoundrels raised from the dust upon the merit of their vices; or nobility thrown into it on account of their virtues; no lords, fiddlers, judges, or dancing masters.

I had the favor of being admitted to several Houyhnhnms, who came to visit or dine with my master; where his honor graciously suffered me to wait in the room, and listen to their discourse. Both he and his company would often descend to ask me questions, and receive my answers. I had also sometimes the honor of attending my master in his visits to others. I never presumed to speak, except in answer to a question; and then I did it with inward regret, because it was a loss of so much time for improving myself; but I was infinitely delighted with the station of an humble auditor in such conversations, where nothing passed but what was useful, expressed in the fewest and most significant words; where (as I have already said) the greatest decency was observed, without the least degree of ceremony; where no person spoke without being pleased himself, and pleasing his companions; where there was no interruption, tediousness, heat, or difference of sentiments. They have a notion, that when people are met together, a short silence doth much improve conversation; this I found to be true; for during those little intermissions of talk, new ideas would arise in their minds, which very much enlivened the discourse. Their subjects are generally on friendship and benevolence; on order and economy; sometimes upon the visible operations of nature, or ancient traditions; upon the bounds and limits of virtue; upon the unerring rules of reason; or upon some determinations, to be taken at the next great assembly; and often upon the various excellencies of poetry. I may add, without vanity, that my presence often gave them sufficient matter for discourse, because it afforded my master an occasion of letting his friends into the history of me and my country, upon which they were all pleased to discant in a manner not very advantageous to human kind; and for that reason I shall not repeat what they said; only I may be allowed to observe that his honor, to my great admiration, appeared to understand the nature of Yahoos much better than myself. He went through all our vices and follies, and discovered many which I had never mentioned to him; by only supposing what qualities a Yahoo of their country, with a small proportion of reason, might be capable of exerting; and concluded, with too much probability, how vile as well as miserable such a creature must be.

I freely confess, that all the little knowledge I have of any value was acquired by the lectures I received from my master, and from hearing the discourses of him and his friends; to which I should be prouder to listen, than to dictate to the greatest and wisest assembly in Europe. I admired the strength, comeliness, and speed of the inhabitants; and such a constellation of virtues in such amiable persons produced in me the highest veneration. At first, indeed, I did not feel that natural awe which the Yahoos and all other animals bear towards them; but it grew upon me by degrees, much sooner than I imagined, and was mingled with a respectful love and gratitude, that they would condescend to distinguish me from the rest of my species.

When I thought of my family, my friends, my countrymen, or human race in general, I considered them as they really were, Yahoos in shape and disposition, perhaps a little more civilized, and qualified with the gift of speech; but making no other use of reason than to improve and mutiply those vices, whereof their brethren in this country had only the share that nature allotted them. When I happened to behold the reflection of my own form in a lake or fountain, I turned away my face in horror and detestation of myself, and could better endure the sight of a common Yahoo than of my own person. By conversing with the Houyhnhnms, and looking upon them with delight, I fell to imitate their gait and gesture, which is now grown into a habit; and my friends often tell me in a blunt way, that I trot like a horse; which, however, I take for a great compliment; neither shall I disown, that in speaking I am apt to fall into the voice and manner of the Houyhnhnms, and hear myself ridiculed on that account without the least mortification.

In the midst of this happiness, when I looked upon myself to be fully settled for life, my master sent for me one morning a little earlier than his usual hour. I observed by his countenance that he was in some perplexity, and at a loss how to begin what he had to speak. After a short silence, he told me, he did not know how I would take what he was going to say; that, in the last general assembly, when the affair of the Yahoos was entered upon, the representatives had taken offense at his keeping a Yahoo (meaning myself) in his family more like a Houyhnhnm than a brute animal. That he was known frequently to converse with me, as if he could receive some advantage of pleasure in my company; that such a practice was not agreeable to reason or nature, or a thing ever heard of before among them. The assembly did therefore exhort him, either to employ me like the rest of my species, or command me to swim back to the place from whence I came. That the first of these expedients was utterly rejected by all the Houyhnhnms who had ever seen me at his house or their own; for, they alleged, that because I had some rudiments of reason, added to the natural pravity of those animals, it was to be feared, I might be able to seduce them into the woody and mountainous parts of the country, and bring them in troops by night to destroy the Houyhnhnms' cattle, as being naturally of the ravenous kind, and averse from labor.

My master added that he was daily pressed by the Houyhnhnms of the neighborhood to have the assembly's exhortation executed, which he could not put off much longer. He doubted[1] it would be impossible for

---

1. Suspected.

me to swim to another country; and therefore wished I would contrive some sort of vehicle resembling those I had described to him, that might carry me on the sea; in which work I should have the assistance of his own servants, as well as those of his neighbors. He concluded that for his own part he could have been content to keep me in his service as long as I lived; because he found I had cured myself of some bad habits and dispositions, by endeavoring, as far as my inferior nature was capable, to imitate the Houyhnhnms.

I should here observe to the reader, that a decree of the general assembly in this country is expressed by the word *hnhloayn*, which signifies an exhortation, as near as I can render it; for they have no conception how a rational creature can be compelled, but only advised, or exhorted; because no person can disobey reason without giving up his claim to be a rational creature.

I was struck with the utmost grief and despair at my master's discourse; and being unable to support the agonies I was under, I fell into a swoon at his feet; when I came to myself, he told me that he concluded I had been dead (for these people are subject to no such imbecilities of nature). I answered, in a faint voice, that death would have been too great an happiness; that although I could not blame the assembly's exhortation, or the urgency of his friends; yet in my weak and corrupt judgment, I thought it might consist with reason to have been less rigorous. That I could not swim a league, and probably the nearest land to theirs might be distant above an hundred; that many materials, necessary for making a small vessel to carry me off, were wholly wanting in this country, which, however, I would attempt in obedience and gratitude to his honor, although I concluded the thing to be impossible, and therefore looked on myself as already devoted[2] to destruction. That the certain prospect of an unnatural death was the least of my evils; for, supposing I should escape with life by some strange adventure, how could I think with temper[3] of passing my days among Yahoos, and relapsing into my old corruptions, for want of examples to lead and keep me within the paths of virtue. That I knew too well upon what solid reasons all the determinations of the wise Houyhnhnms were founded, not to be shaken by arguments of mine, a miserable Yahoo; and therefore after presenting him with my humble thanks for the offer of his servants' assistance in making a vessel, and desiring a reasonable time for so difficult a work, I told him I would endeavor to preserve a wretched being; and, if ever I returned to England, was not without hopes of being useful to my own species by celebrating the praises of the renowned Houyhnhnms, and proposing their virtues to the imitation of mankind.

My master in a few words made me a very gracious reply, allowed me the space of two months to finish my boat, and ordered the sorrel nag, my fellow servant (for so at this distance I may presume to call him), to follow my instructions, because I told my master that his help would be sufficient, and I knew he had a tenderness for me.

2. Doomed.   3. Equanimity.

In his company my first business was to go to that part of the coast where my rebellious crew had ordered me to be set on shore. I got upon a height, and looking on every side into the sea, fancied I saw a small island towards the northeast; I took out my pocket glass, and could then clearly distinguish it about five leagues off, as I computed; but it appeared to the sorrel nag to be only a blue cloud; for, as he had no conception of any country besides his own, so he could not be as expert in distinguishing remote objects at sea, as we who so much converse in that element.

After I had discovered this island, I considered no farther; but resolved, it should, if possible, be the first place of my banishment, leaving the consequence to fortune.

I returned home, and consulting with the sorrel nag, we went into a copse at some distance, where I with my knife, and he with a sharp flint fastened very artificially,[4] after their manner, to a wooden handle, cut down several oak wattles about the thickness of a walking staff, and some larger pieces. But I shall not trouble the reader with a particular description of my own mechanics; let it suffice to say, that in six weeks time, with the help of the sorrel nag, who performed the parts that required most labor, I finished a sort of Indian canoe; but much larger, covering it with the skins of Yahoos, well stitched together, with hempen threads of my own making. My sail was likewise composed of the skins of the same animal; but I made use of the youngest I could get, the older being too tough and thick; and I likewise provided myself with four paddles. I laid in a stock of boiled flesh, of rabbits and fowls; and took with me two vessels, one filled with milk, and the other with water.

I tried my canoe in a large pond near my master's house, and then corrected in it what was amiss, stopping all the chinks with Yahoo's tallow, till I found it staunch, and able to bear me and my freight. And when it was as complete as I could possibly make it, I had it drawn on a carriage very gently by Yahoos, to the seaside, under the conduct of the sorrel nag and another servant.

When all was ready, and the day came for my departure, I took leave of my master and lady, and the whole family, my eyes flowing with tears and my heart quite sunk with grief. But his honor, out of curiosity, and perhaps (if I may speak it without vanity) partly out of kindness, was determined to see me in my canoe; and got several of his neighboring friends to accompany him. I was forced to wait above an hour for the tide, and then observing the wind very fortunately bearing towards the island to which I intended to steer my course, I took a second leave of my master; but as I was going to prostrate myself to kiss his hoof, he did me the honor to raise it gently to my mouth. I am not ignorant how much I have been censured for mentioning this last particular. Detractors are pleased to think it improbable that so illustrious a person should descend to give so great a mark of distinction to a creature so inferior as I. Neither have I forgot how apt some travelers are to boast of extraordinary favors they have received. But, if these censurers were better acquainted with the noble and courte-

4. Adroitly.

ous disposition of the Houyhnhnms, they would soon change their opinion. I paid my respects to the rest of the Houyhnhnms in his honor's company; then getting into my canoe, I pushed off from shore.

CHAPTER XI

The Author's dangerous voyage. He arrives at New Holland, hoping to settle there. Is wounded with an arrow by one of the natives. Is seized and carried by force into a Portuguese ship. The great civilities of the Captain. The Author arrives at England.

I began this desperate voyage on February 15, 1714/5,[5] at 9 o'clock in the morning. The wind was very favorable; however, I made use at first only of my paddles; but considering I should soon be weary, and that the wind might probably chop about, I ventured to set up my little sail; and thus, with the help of the tide, I went at the rate of a league and a half an hour, as near as I could guess. My master and his friends continued on the shore, till I was almost out of sight; and I often heard the sorrel nag (who always loved me) crying out, *"Hnuy illa nyha maiah Yahoo"* ("Take care of thyself, gentle Yahoo").

My design was, if possible, to discover some small island uninhabited, yet sufficient by my labor to furnish me with necessaries of life, which I would have thought a greater happiness than to be first minister in the politest court of Europe, so horrible was the idea I conceived of returning to live in the society and under the government of Yahoos. For in such a solitude as I desired, I could at least enjoy my own thoughts, and reflect with delight on the virtues of those inimitable Houyhnhnms, without any opportunity of degenerating into the vices and corruptions of my own species.

The reader may remember what I related when my crew conspired against me, and confined me to my cabin, how I continued there several weeks, without knowing what course we took; and when I was put ashore in the longboat, how the sailors told me with oaths, whether true or false, that they knew not in what part of the world we were. However, I did then believe us to be about 10 degrees southward of the Cape of Good Hope, or about 45 degrees southern latitude, as I gathered from some general words I overheard among them, being I supposed to the southeast in their intended voyage to Madagascar. And although this were but little better than conjecture, yet I resolved to steer my course eastward, hoping to reach the southwest coast of New Holland, and perhaps some such island as I desired, lying westward of it. The wind was full west, and by six in the evening I computed I had gone eastward at least eighteen leagues; when I spied a very small island about half a league off, which I soon reached. It was nothing but a rock with one creek,[6] naturally arched by the force of tempests. Here I put in my canoe, and climbing a part of the rock, I could plainly discover land to the east, extending from south to north. I lay all night in my canoe; and repeating my voyage early in the morning, I

5. That is, 1714. The year began on March 25.   6. A bay.

arrived in seven hours to the southeast point of New Holland.[7] This confirmed me in the opinion I have long entertained, that the maps and charts place this country at least three degrees more to the east than it really is; which thought I communicated many years ago to my worthy friend Mr. Herman Moll,[8] and gave him my reasons for it, although he hath rather chosen to follow other authors.

I saw no inhabitants in the place where I landed; and being unarmed, I was afraid of venturing far into the country. I found some shellfish on the shore, and eat them raw, not daring to kindle a fire, for fear of being discovered by the natives. I continued three days feeding on oysters and limpets, to save my own provisions; and I fortunately found a brook of excellent water, which gave me great relief.

On the fourth day, venturing out early a little too far, I saw twenty or thirty natives upon a height, not above five hundred yards from me. They were stark naked, men, women, and children round a fire, as I could discover by the smoke. One of them spied me, and gave notice to the rest; five of them advanced towards me, leaving the women and children at the fire. I made what haste I could to the shore, and getting into my canoe, shoved off; the savages observing me retreat, ran after me; and before I could get far enough into the sea, discharged an arrow, which wounded me deeply on the inside of my left knee. (I shall carry the mark to my grave.) I apprehended the arrow might be poisoned; and paddling out of the reach of their darts (being a calm day) I made a shift to suck the wound, and dress it as well as I could.

I was at a loss what to do, for I durst not return to the same landing place, but stood to the north, and was forced to paddle; for the wind, although very gentle, was against me, blowing northwest. As I was looking about for a secure landing place, I saw a sail to the north northeast, which appearing every minute more visible, I was in some doubt whether I should wait for them or no; but at last my detestation of the Yahoo race prevailed; and turning my canoe, I sailed and paddled together to the south, and got into the same creek from whence I set out in the morning, choosing rather to trust myself among these barbarians than live with European Yahoos. I drew up my canoe as close as I could to the shore, and hid myself behind a stone by the little brook, which, as I have already said, was excellent water.

The ship came within half a league of this creek, and sent out her longboat with vessels to take in fresh water (for the place it seems was very well known), but I did not observe it until the boat was almost on shore; and it was too late to seek another hiding place. The seamen at their landing observed my canoe, and rummaging it all over, easily conjectured that the owner could not be far off. Four of them well armed searched every cranny and lurking hole, till at last they found me flat on my face behind the stone. They gazed a while in admiration at my strange uncouth dress; my coat made of skins, my wooden-soled shoes, and my furred stockings; from whence, however, they concluded I was not a native of the place, who all go naked. One of the seamen in Portuguese bid me rise,

7. Present-day Republic of South Africa.   8. A famous contemporary mapmaker.

and asked who I was. I understood that language very well, and getting upon my feet, said I was a poor Yahoo, banished from the Houyhnhnms, and desired they would please to let me depart. They admired to hear me answer them in their own tongue, and saw by my complexion I must be an European; but were at a loss to know what I meant by Yahoos and Houyhnhnms, and at the same time fell a laughing at my strange tone in speaking, which resembled the neighing of a horse. I trembled all the while betwixt fear and hatred; I again desired leave to depart, and was gently moving to my canoe; but they laid hold on me, desiring to know what country I was of? whence I came? with many other questions. I told them I was born in England, from whence I came about five years ago, and then their country and ours was at peace. I therefore hoped they would not treat me as an enemy, since I meant them no harm, but was a poor Yahoo, seeking some desolate place where to pass the remainder of his unfortunate life.

When they began to talk, I thought I never heard or saw any thing so unnatural; for it appeared to me as monstrous as if a dog or a cow should speak in England, or a Yahoo in Houyhnhnmland. The honest Portuguese were equally amazed at my strange dress, and the odd manner of delivering my words, which however they understood very well. They spoke to me with great humanity, and said they were sure their Captain would carry me *gratis* to Lisbon, from whence I might return to my own country; that two of the seamen would go back to the ship, to inform the Captain of what they had seen, and receive his orders; in the meantime, unless I would give my solemn oath not to fly, they would secure me by force. I thought it best to comply with their proposal. They were very curious to know my story, but I gave them very little satisfaction; and they all conjectured, that my misfortunes had impaired my reason. In two hours the boat, which went laden with vessels of water, returned with the Captain's commands to fetch me on board. I fell on my knees to preserve my liberty; but all was in vain, and the men having tied me with cords, heaved me into the boat, from whence I was taken into the ship, and from thence into the Captain's cabin.

His name was Pedro de Mendez; he was a very courteous and generous person; he entreated me to give some account of myself, and desired to know what I would eat or drink; said I should be used as well as himself, and spoke so many obliging things, that I wondered to find such civilities from a Yahoo. However, I remained silent and sullen; I was ready to faint at the very smell of him and his men. At last I desired something to eat out of my own canoe; but he ordered me a chicken and some excellent wine, and then directed that I should be put to bed in a very clean cabin. I would not undress myself, but lay on the bedclothes; and in half an hour stole out, when I thought the crew was at dinner; and getting to the side of the ship, was going to leap into the sea, and swim for my life, rather than continue among Yahoos. But one of the seamen prevented me, and having informed the Captain, I was chained to my cabin.

After dinner Don Pedro came to me, and desired to know my reason for so desperate an attempt; assured me he only meant to do me all the service he was able; and spoke so very movingly, that at last I descended to treat him like an animal which had some little portion of reason. I gave him a very short relation of my voyage; of the conspiracy against me by my own men; of the country where they set me on shore, and of my five years residence there. All which he looked upon as if it were a dream or a vision; whereat I took great offense; for I had quite forgot the faculty of lying, so peculiar to Yahoos in all countries where they preside, and consequently the disposition of suspecting truth in others of their own species. I asked him whether it were the custom of his country to *say the thing that was not?* I assured him I had almost forgot what he meant by falsehood; and if I had lived a thousand years in Houyhnhnmland, I should never have heard a lie from the meanest servant. That I was altogether indifferent whether he believed me or no; but however, in return for his favors, I would give so much allowance to the corruption of his nature, as to answer any objection he would please to make; and he might easily discover the truth.

The Captain, a wise man, after many endeavors to catch me tripping in some part of my story, at last began to have a better opinion of my veracity. But he added that since I professed so inviolable an attachment to truth, I must give him my word of honor to bear him company in this voyage without attempting anything against my life; or else he would continue me a prisoner till we arrived at Lisbon. I gave him the promise he required; but at the same time protested that I would suffer the greatest hardships rather than return to live among Yahoos.

Our voyage passed without any considerable accident. In gratitude to the Captain I sometimes sat with him at his earnest request, and strove to conceal my antipathy against humankind, although it often broke out; which he suffered to pass without observation. But the greatest part of the day, I confined myself to my cabin, to avoid seeing any of the crew. The Captain had often entreated me to strip myself of my savage dress, and offered to lend me the best suit of clothes he had. This I would not be prevailed on to accept, abhorring to cover myself with anything that had been on the back of a Yahoo. I only desired he would lend me two clean shirts, which having been washed since he wore them, I believed would not so much defile me. These I changed every second day, and washed them myself.

We arrived at Lisbon, Nov. 5, 1715. At our landing, the Captain forced me to cover myself with his cloak, to prevent the rabble from crowding about me. I was conveyed to his own house; and at my earnest request, he led me up to the highest room backwards.[9] I conjured him to conceal from all persons what I had told him of the Houyhnhnms; because the least hint of such a story would not only draw numbers of people to see me, but probably put me in danger of being imprisoned, or burned by the Inquisition. The Captain persuaded me to accept a suit of clothes newly made; but I would not suffer the tailor to take my measure; however, Don Pedro being almost of my size, they fitted me well enough. He accoutred

---

9. At the rear.

me with other necessaries, all new, which I aired for twenty-four hours before I would use them.

The Captain had no wife, nor above three servants, none of which were suffered to attend at meals; and his whole deportment was so obliging, added to very good human understanding, that I really began to tolerate his company. He gained so far upon me, that I ventured to look out of the back window. By degrees I was brought into another room, from whence I peeped into the street, but drew my head back in a fright. In a week's time he seduced me down to the door. I found my terror gradually lessened, but my hatred and contempt seemed to increase. I was at last bold enough to walk the street in his company, but kept my nose well stopped with rue, or sometimes with tobacco.

In ten days, Don Pedro, to whom I had given some account of my domestic affairs, put it upon me as a point of honor and conscience that I ought to return to my native country, and live at home with my wife and children. He told me there was an English ship in the port just ready to sail, and he would furnish me with all things necessary. It would be tedious to repeat his arguments, and my contradictions. He said it was altogether impossible to find such a solitary island as I had desired to live in; but I might command in my own house, and pass my time in a manner as recluse as I pleased.

I complied at last, finding I could not do better. I left Lisbon the 24th day of November, in an English merchantman, but who was the Master I never inquired. Don Pedro accompanied me to the ship, and lent me twenty pounds. He took kind leave of me, and embraced me at parting; which I bore as well as I could. During this last voyage I had no commerce with the Master, or any of his men; but pretending I was sick kept close in my cabin. On the fifth of December, 1715, we cast anchor in the Downs about nine in the morning, and at three in the afternoon I got safe to my house at Redriff.

My wife and family received me with great surprise and joy, because they concluded me certainly dead; but I must freely confess, the sight of them filled me only with hatred, disgust, and contempt; and the more, by reflecting on the near alliance I had to them. For, although since my unfortunate exile from the Houyhnhnm country, I had compelled myself to tolerate the sight of Yahoos, and to converse with Don Pedro de Mendez; yet my memory and imaginations were perpetually filled with the virtues and ideas of those exalted Houyhnhnms. And when I began to consider that by copulating with one of the Yahoo species, I had become a parent of more, it struck me with the utmost shame, confusion, and horror.

As soon as I entered the house, my wife took me in her arms, and kissed me; at which, having not been used to the touch of that odious animal for so many years, I fell in a swoon for almost an hour. At the time I am writing, it is five years since my last return to England; during the first year I could not endure my wife or children in my presence, the very smell of them was intolerable; much less could I suffer them to eat in the same room. To this hour they dare not presume to touch my bread, or drink out of the same cup; neither was I ever able to let one of them take me by the hand. The first money I laid out was to buy two young stone-horses,[1] which I keep in a good stable, and next to them the groom is my greatest favorite; for I feel my spirits revived by the smell he contracts in the stable. My horses understand me tolerably well; I converse with them at least four hours every day. They are strangers to bridle or saddle; they live in great amity with me, and friendship to each other.

CHAPTER XII

The Author's veracity. His design in publishing this work. His censure of those travelers who swerve from the truth. The Author clears himself from any sinister ends in writing. An objection answered. The method of planting colonies. His native country commended. The right of the crown to those countries described by the Author is justified. The difficulty of conquering them. The Author takes his last leave of the reader; proposeth his manner of living for the future; gives good advice, and concludeth.

Thus, gentle reader, I have given thee a faithful history of my travels for sixteen years, and above seven months; wherein I have not been so studious of ornament as of truth. I could perhaps like others have astonished thee with strange improbable tales; but I rather chose to relate plain matter of fact in the simplest manner and style; because my principal design was to inform, and not to amuse thee.

It is easy for us who travel into remote countries, which are seldom visited by Englishmen or other Europeans, to form descriptions of wonderful animals both at sea and land. Whereas a traveler's chief aim should be to make men wiser and better, and to improve their minds by the bad as well as good example of what they deliver concerning foreign places.

I could heartily wish a law were enacted, that every traveler, before he were permitted to publish his voyages, should be obliged to make oath before the Lord High Chancellor that all he intended to print was absolutely true to the best of his knowledge; for then the world would no longer be deceived as it usually is, while some writers, to make their works pass the better upon the public, impose the grossest falsities on the unwary reader. I have perused several books of travels with great delight in my younger days; but, having since gone over most parts of the globe, and been able to contradict many fabulous accounts from my own observation, it hath given me a great disgust against this part of reading, and some indignation to see the credulity of mankind so impudently abused. Therefore, since my acquaintance were pleased to think my poor endeavors might not be unacceptable to my country; I imposed on myself as a maxim, never to be swerved from, that I would *strictly adhere to truth*; neither indeed can I be ever under the least temptation to vary from it, while I retain in my mind the lectures and example of my noble master, and the other illustrious Houyhnhnms, of whom I had so long the honor to be an humble hearer.

1. Stallions.

——*Nec si miserum Fortuna Sinonem*
Finxit, vanum etiam, mendacemque improba finget.[2]

I know very well how little reputation is to be got by writings which require neither genius nor learning, nor indeed any other talent, except a good memory, or an exact *Journal*. I know likewise, that writers of travels, like dictionary-makers, are sunk into oblivion by the weight and bulk of those who come last, and therefore lie uppermost. And it is highly probable that such travelers who shall hereafter visit the countries described in this work of mine, may be detecting my errors (if there be any) and adding many new discoveries of their own, jostle me out of vogue, and stand in my place, making the world forget that ever I was an author. This indeed would be too great a mortification if I wrote for fame; but, as my sole intention was the PUBLIC GOOD, I cannot be altogether disappointed. For, who can read the virtues I have mentioned in the glorious Houyhnhnms, without being ashamed of his own vices, when he considers himself as the reasoning, governing animal of his country? I shall say nothing of those remote nations where Yahoos preside; amongst which the least corrupted are the Brobdingnagians, whose wise maxims in morality and government it would be our happiness to observe. But I forbear descanting further, and rather leave the judicious reader to his own remarks and applications.

I am not a little pleased that this work of mine can possibly meet with no censurers; for what objections can be made against a writer who relates only plain facts that happened in such distant countries, where we have not the least interest with respect either to trade or negotiations? I have carefully avoided every fault with which common writers of travels are often too justly charged. Besides, I meddle not the least with any party, but write without passion, prejudice, or ill-will against any man or number of men whatsoever. I write for the noblest end, to inform and instruct mankind, over whom I may, without breach of modesty, pretend to some superiority, from the advantages I received by conversing so long among the most accomplished Houyhnhnms. I write without any view towards profit or praise. I never suffer a word to pass that may look like reflection, or possibly give the least offense even to those who are most ready to take it. So that, I hope, I may with justice pronounce myself an Author perfectly blameless; against whom the tribes of answerers, considerers, observers, reflectors, detecters, remarkers will never be able to find matter for exercising their talents.

I confess it was whispered to me that I was bound in duty as a subject of England, to have given in a memorial to a secretary of state, at my first coming over; because, whatever lands are discovered by a subject, belong to the Crown. But I doubt whether our conquests in the countries I treat of would be as easy as those of Ferdinando Cortez[3] over the naked Americans. The Lilliputians, I think, are hardly worth the charge of a fleet and army to reduce them; and I question whether it might be prudent or safe to attempt the Brobdingnagians; or, whether an English army would be much at their ease with the Flying Island over their heads. The Houy-

---

2. Fortune has made a derelict of Sinon / but the bitch won't make an empty liar of him, too (Latin; Virgil's *Aeneid* 2.79–80).   3. Hernando Cortez (1485–1547), who destroyed the Aztec Empire.

hnhnms, indeed, appear not to be so well prepared for war, a science to which they are perfect strangers, and especially against missive weapons. However, supposing myself to be a minister of state, I could never give my advice for invading them. Their prudence, unanimity, unacquaintedness with fear, and their love of their country would amply supply all defects in the military art. Imagine twenty thousand of them breaking into the midst of an European army, confounding the ranks, overturning the carriages, battering the warriors' faces into mummy, by terrible yerks[4] from their hinder hoofs: for they would well deserve the character given to Augustus, *Recalcitrat undique tutus*.[5] But instead of proposals for conquering that magnanimous nation, I rather wish they were in a capacity or disposition to send a sufficient number of their inhabitants for civilizing Europe; by teaching us the first principles of Honor, Justice, Truth, Temperance, Public Spirit, Fortitude, Chastity, Friendship, Benevolence, and Fidelity. The names of all which Virtues are still retained among us in most languages, and are to be met with in modern as well as ancient authors, which I am able to assert from my own small reading.

But I had another reason which made me less forward to enlarge his majesty's dominions by my discoveries: to say the truth, I had conceived a few scruples with relation to the distributive justice of princes upon those occasions. For instance, a crew of pirates are driven by a storm they know not whither; at length a boy discovers land from the topmast; they go on shore to rob and plunder; they see an harmless people, are entertained with kindness, they give the country a new name, they take formal possession of it for the king, they set up a rotten plank or a stone for a memorial, they murder two or three dozen of the natives, bring away a couple more by force for a sample, return home, and get their pardon. Here commences a new dominion acquired with a title by Divine Right. Ships are sent with the first opportunity; the natives driven out or destroyed, their princes tortured to discover their gold; a free license given to all acts of inhumanity and lust; the earth reeking with the blood of its inhabitants: and this execrable crew of butchers employed in so pious an expedition is a *modern colony* sent to convert and civilize an idolatrous and barbarous people.

But this description, I confess, doth by no means affect the British nation, who may be an example to the whole world for their wisdom, care, and justice in planting colonies; their liberal endowments for the advancement of religion and learning; their choice of devout and able pastors to propagate Christianity; their caution in stocking their provinces with people of sober lives and conversations from this the Mother Kingdom; their strict regard to the distribution of justice, in supplying the civil administration through all their colonies with officers of the greatest abilities, utter strangers to corruption: and to crown all, by sending the most vigilant and virtuous governors, who have no other views than the happiness of the people over whom they preside, and the honor of the king their master.

---

4. Kicks. *Mummy:* pulp.   5. He kicks backward, at every point on his guard (Latin; Horace's *Satires* 2.20).

But, as those countries which I have described do not appear to have any desire of being conquered, and enslaved, murdered, or driven out by colonies, nor abound either in gold, silver, sugar, or tobacco, I did humbly conceive they were by no means proper objects of our zeal, our valor, or our interest. However, if those whom it may concern, think fit to be of another opinion, I am ready to depose, when I shall be lawfully called, that no European did ever visit these countries before me. I mean, if the inhabitants ought to be believed.

But, as to the formality of taking possession in my sovereign's name, it never came once into my thoughts; and if it had, yet as my affairs then stood, I should perhaps in point of prudence and self-preservation have put it off to a better opportunity.

Having thus answered the only objection that can be raised against me as a traveler, I here take a final leave of my courteous readers, and return to enjoy my own speculations in my little garden at Redriff; to apply those excellent lessons of virtue which I learned among the Houyhnhnms; to instruct the Yahoos of my own family as far as I shall find them docible animals; to behold my figure often in a glass, and thus if possible habituate myself by time to tolerate the sight of a human creature; to lament the brutality of Houyhnhnms in my own country, but always treat their persons with respect, for the sake of my noble master, his family, his friends, and the whole Houyhnhnm race, whom these of ours have the honor to resemble in all their lineaments, however their intellectuals came to degenerate.

I began last week to permit my wife to sit at dinner with me, at the farthest end of a long table; and to answer (but with the utmost brevity) the few questions I ask her. Yet the smell of a Yahoo continuing very offensive, I always keep my nose well stopped with rue, lavender, or tobacco leaves. And although it be hard for a man late in life to remove old habits, I am not altogether out of hopes in some time to suffer a neighbor Yahoo in my company, without the apprehensions I am yet under of his teeth or his claws.

My reconcilement to the Yahoo kind in general might not be so difficult, if they would be content with those vices and follies only which nature hath entitled them to. I am not in the least provoked at the sight of a lawyer, a pickpocket, a colonel, a fool, a lord, a gamester, politician, a whoremonger, a physician, an evidence, a suborner, an attorney, a traitor, or the like: this is all according to the due course of things. But when I behold a lump of deformity, and diseases both in body and mind, smitten with pride, it immediately breaks all the measures of my patience; neither shall I be ever able to comprehend how such an animal and such a vice could tally together. The wise and virtuous Houyhnhnms, who abound in all excellencies that can adorn a rational creature, have no name for this vice in their language, which hath no terms to express anything that is evil, except those whereby they describe the detestable qualities of their Yahoos, among which they were not able to distinguish this of pride, for want of thoroughly understanding human nature, as it showeth itself in other countries, where that animal presides. But I, who had more experience, could plainly observe some rudiments of it among the wild Yahoos.

But the Houyhnhnms, who live under the government of reason, are no more proud of the good qualities they possess, than I should be for not wanting a leg or an arm, which no man in his wits would boast of, although he must be miserable without them. I dwell the longer upon this subject from the desire I have to make the society of an English Yahoo by any means not insupportable; and therefore I here entreat those who have any tincture of this absurd vice, that they will not presume to appear in my sight.

A Modest Proposal[1]

for Preventing the Children of poor People in Ireland, *from being a Burden to their Parents or Country; and for making them beneficial to the Publick.*

Written in the year 1729

It is a melancholy object to those who walk through this great town,[2] or travel in the country, when they see the streets, the roads, and cabin-doors crowded with beggars of the female sex, followed by three, four, or six children, all in rags, and importuning every passenger for an alms. These mothers, instead of being able to work for their honest livelihood, are forced to employ all their time in strolling to beg sustenance for their helpless infants: who, as they grow up, either turn thieves for want of work, or leave their dear native country to fight for the Pretender in Spain, or sell themselves to the Barbadoes.[3]

I think it is agreed by all parties, that this prodigious number of children in the arms, or on the backs, or at the heels of their mothers, and frequently of their fathers, is, in the present deplorable state of the kingdom, a very great additional grievance; and, therefore, whoever could find out a fair, cheap, and easy method of making these children sound and useful members of the commonwealth, would deserve so well of the public, as to have his statue set up for a preserver of the nation.

But my intention is very far from being confined to provide only for the children of professed beggars; it is of a much greater extent, and shall take in the whole number of infants at a certain age, who are born of parents in effect as little able to support them as those who demand our charity in the streets.

As to my own part, having turned my thoughts for many years upon this important subject, and maturely weighed the several schemes of other projectors,[4] I have always found them grossly mistaken in their computation. It is true, a child, just dropped from its dam, may be supported by her milk for a solar year with little other nourishment; at most, not above the value of two shillings, which the mother may certainly get, or the value

---

1. The complete text edited by Herbert Davis. 2. Dublin. 3. At this time a British possession, with a prosperous sugar industry. Workers were needed in the sugar plantations. *The Pretender:* James Edward (1688–1766), son of the Catholic King James II of England, called the "Old Pretender" (in distinction to his son Charles, nine years old at the time of this work, called the "Young Pretender"). Many thought him a legitimate claimant to the throne. 4. Planners.

in scraps, by her lawful occupation of begging; and it is exactly at one year old that I propose to provide for them in such a manner, as, instead of being a charge upon their parents or the parish, or wanting food and raiment for the rest of their lives, they shall, on the contrary, contribute to the feeding, and partly to the clothing, of many thousands.

There is likewise another advantage in my scheme, that it will prevent those voluntary abortions, and that horrid practice of women murdering their bastard children, alas, too frequent among us, sacrificing the poor innocent babes, I doubt more to avoid the expense than the shame, which would move tears and pity in the most savage and inhuman breast.

The number of souls in this kingdom being usually reckoned one million and a half, of these I calculate there may be about two hundred thousand couple whose wives are breeders; from which number I subtract thirty thousand couple, who are able to maintain their own children (although I apprehend there cannot be so many, under the present distresses of the kingdom); but this being granted, there will remain an hundred and seventy thousand breeders. I again subtract fifty thousand for those women who miscarry, or whose children die by accident or disease within the year. There only remain a hundred and twenty thousand children of poor parents annually born. The question therefore is how this number shall be reared and provided for? which, as I have already said, under the present situation of affairs, is utterly impossible by all the methods hitherto proposed. For we can neither employ them in handicraft or agriculture; we neither build houses (I mean in the country) nor cultivate land: they can very seldom pick up a livelihood by stealing until they arrive at six years old, except where they are of towardly parts;[5] although I confess they learn the rudiments much earlier; during which time they can, however, be properly looked upon only as probationers; as I have been informed by a principal gentleman in the county of Cavan, who protested to me, that he never knew above one or two instances under the age of six, even in a part of the kingdom so renowned for the quickest proficiency in that art.

I am assured by our merchants that a boy or a girl before twelve years old is no saleable commodity; and even when they come to this age they will not yield above three pounds or three pounds and half-a-crown at most, on the exchange; which cannot turn to account either to the parents or kingdom, the charge of nutriment and rags having been at least four times that value.

I shall now, therefore, humbly propose my own thoughts, which I hope will not be liable to the least objection.

I have been assured by a very knowing American of my acquaintance in London, that a young healthy child, well nursed, is, at a year old, a most delicious, nourishing, and wholesome food, whether stewed, roasted, baked, or boiled; and I make no doubt that it will equally serve in a fricassee or a ragout.

I do therefore humbly offer it to public consideration, that of the hundred and twenty thousand children already computed, twenty thousand

5. Particularly talented, unusually gifted.

may be reserved for breed, whereof only one-fourth part to be males; which is more than we allow to sheep, black cattle, or swine; and my reason is, that these children are seldom the fruits of marriage, a circumstance not much regarded by our savages, therefore one male will be sufficient to serve four females. That the remaining hundred thousand may, at a year old, be offered in sale to the persons of quality and fortune through the kingdom; always advising the mother to let them suck plentifully in the last month, so as to render them plump and fat for a good table. A child will make two dishes at an entertainment for friends; and when the family dines alone, the fore or hind quarter will make a reasonable dish, and, seasoned with a little pepper or salt, will be very good boiled on the fourth day, especially in winter.

I have reckoned, upon a medium,[6] that a child just born will weigh twelve pounds, and in a solar year, if tolerably nursed, increaseth to twenty-eight pounds.

I grant this food will be somewhat dear,[7] and therefore very proper for landlords, who, as they have already devoured most of the parents, seem to have the best title to the children.

Infants' flesh will be in season throughout the year, but more plentifully in March, and a little before and after: for we are told by a grave author, an eminent French physician,[8] that fish being a prolific diet, there are more children born in Roman Catholic countries about nine months after Lent than at any other season; therefore, reckoning a year after Lent, the markets will be more glutted than usual, because the number of popish infants is at least three to one in this kingdom; and therefore it will have one other collateral advantage, by lessening the number of papists among us.

I have already computed the charge of nursing a beggar's child (in which list I reckon all cottagers, labourers, and four-fifths of the farmers) to be about two shillings per annum,[9] rags included; and I believe no gentleman would repine to give ten shillings for the carcass of a good fat child, which, as I have said, will make four dishes of excellent nutritive meat, when he has only some particular friend, or his own family, to dine with him. Thus the squire will learn to be a good landlord, and grow popular among his tenants; the mother will have eight shillings net profit, and be fit for work till she produces another child.

Those who are more thrifty (as I must confess the times require) may flay the carcass; the skin of which, artificially dressed, will make admirable gloves for ladies, and summer-boots for fine gentlemen.

As to our city of Dublin, shambles[1] may be appointed for this purpose in the most convenient parts of it, and butchers we may be assured will not be wanting; although I rather recommend buying the children alive, and dressing them hot from the knife, as we do roasting pigs.

A very worthy person, a true lover of his country, and whose virtues I highly esteem, was lately pleased, in discoursing on this matter, to offer a refinement upon my scheme. He said, that many gentlemen of this king-

6. Average.   7. Expensive.   8. François Rabelais (1494?–1553), French satirist and author of *Gargantua and Pantagruel* (1532–52).   9. Per year.   1. Slaughterhouses.

dom, having of late destroyed their deer, he conceived that the want of venison might be well supplied by the bodies of young lads and maidens, not exceeding fourteen years of age, nor under twelve; so great a number of both sexes in every country being now ready to starve for want of work and service; and these to be disposed of by their parents, if alive, or otherwise by their nearest relations. But, with due deference to so excellent a friend, and so deserving a patriot, I cannot be altogether in his sentiments; for as to the males, my American acquaintance assured me from frequent experience, that their flesh was generally tough and lean, like that of our schoolboys, by continual exercise, and their taste disagreeable; and to fatten them would not answer the charge. Then as to the females, it would, I think, with humble submission, be a loss to the public, because they soon would become breeders themselves: and besides, it is not improbable that some scrupulous people might be apt to censure such a practice (although indeed very unjustly) as a little bordering upon cruelty; which, I confess hath always been with me the strongest objection against any project, how well soever intended.

But in order to justify my friend, he confessed that this expedient was put into his head by the famous Psalmanazar,[2] a native of the island Formosa, who came from thence to London above twenty years ago; and in conversation told my friend, that in his country, when any young person happened to be put to death, the executioner sold the carcass to persons of quality as a prime dainty; and that in his time the body of a plump girl of fifteen, who was crucified for an attempt to poison the emperor, was sold to his Imperial Majesty's prime minister of state, and other great mandarins of the court, in joints from the gibbet,[3] at four hundred crowns. Neither indeed can I deny, that if the same use were made of several plump young girls in this town, who, without one single groat to their fortunes, cannot stir abroad without a chair,[4] and appear at playhouse and assemblies in foreign fineries which they never will pay for, the kingdom would not be the worse.

Some persons of a desponding spirit are in great concern about the vast number of poor people who are aged, diseased, or maimed; and I have been desired to employ my thoughts what course may be taken to ease the nation of so grievous an encumbrance. But I am not in the least pain upon that matter, because it is very well known, that they are every day dying, and rotting, by cold and famine, and filth and vermin, as fast as can be reasonably expected. And as to the younger labourers, they are now in almost as hopeful a condition: they cannot get work, and consequently pine away for want of nourishment, to a degree, that if at any time they are accidentally hired to common labour, they have not strength to perform it; and thus the country and themselves are happily delivered from the evils to come.

---

2. George Psalmanazar (1679?–1763), a literary impostor born in southern France who claimed to be a native of Formosa and a recent Christian convert. He published a catechism in an invented language that he called Formosan as well as a description of Formosa with an introductory autobiography.   3. The post from which the bodies of criminals were hung in chains after execution. *Joints:* portions of a carcass carved up by a butcher.   4. That is, a sedan chair, an enclosed seat carried on poles by men.

I have too long digressed, and therefore shall return to my subject. I think the advantages by the proposal which I have made are obvious and many, as well as of the highest importance.

For first, as I have already observed, it would greatly lessen the number of papists, with whom we are yearly overrun, being the principal breeders of the nation as well as our most dangerous enemies; and who stay at home on purpose with a design to deliver the kingdom to the Pretender, hoping to take their advantage by the absence of so many good Protestants, who have chosen rather to leave their country than stay at home and pay tithes against their conscience to an idolatrous Episcopal curate.

Secondly, the poorer tenants will have something valuable of their own, which by law may be made liable to distress,[5] and help to pay their land-lord's rent; their corn and cattle being already seized, and money a thing unknown.

Thirdly, whereas the maintenance of an hundred thousand children, from two years old and upwards, cannot be computed at less than ten shillings a piece per annum, the nation's stock will be thereby increased fifty thousand pounds per annum; besides the profit of a new dish intro-duced to the tables of all gentlemen of fortune in the kingdom who have any refinement in taste. And the money will circulate among ourselves, the goods being entirely of our own growth and manufacture.

Fourthly, the constant breeders, besides the gain of eight shillings ster-ling per annum by the sale of their children, will be rid of the charge of maintaining them after the first year.

Fifthly, this food would likewise bring great custom to taverns; where the vinters will certainly be so prudent as to procure the best receipts[6] for dressing it to perfection, and, consequently, have their houses frequented by all the fine gentlemen, who justly value themselves upon their knowl-edge in good eating: and a skilful cook, who understands how to oblige his guests, will contrive to make it as expensive as they please.

Sixthly, this would be a great inducement to marriage, which all wise nations have either encouraged by rewards, or enforced by laws and penal-ties. It would increase the care and tenderness of mothers towards their children, when they were sure of a settlement for life to the poor babes, provided in some sort by the public, to their annual profit instead of expense. We should soon see an honest emulation among the married women, which of them could bring the fattest child to the market. Men would become as fond of their wives during the time of their pregnancy, as they are now of their mares in foal, their cows in calf, or sows when they are ready to farrow; nor offer to beat or kick them (as is too frequent a practice) for fear of a miscarriage.

Many other advantages might be enumerated. For instance, the addi-tion of some thousand carcasses in our exportation of barrelled beef; the propagation of swine's flesh, and improvement in the art of making good bacon, so much wanted among us by the great destruction of pigs, too frequent at our tables, which are no way comparable in taste or magnifi-

5. The legal seizing of goods to satisfy a debt, particularly for unpaid rent. 6. Recipes.

cence to a well-grown, fat yearling child, which, roasted whole, will make a considerable figure at a Lord Mayor's feast, or any other public entertainment. But this, and many others, I omit, being studious of brevity.

Supposing that one thousand families in this city would be constant customers for infants' flesh, besides others who might have it at merry meetings, particularly weddings and christenings. I compute that Dublin would take off annually about twenty thousand carcasses; and the rest of the kingdom (where probably they will be sold somewhat cheaper) the remaining eighty thousand.

I can think of no one objection that will possibly be raised against this proposal, unless it should be urged, that the number of people will be thereby much lessened in the kingdom. This I freely own, and it was indeed one principal design in offering it to the world. I desire the reader will observe that I calculate my remedy *for this one individual kingdom of Ireland, and for no other that ever was, is, or I think ever can be, upon earth.* Therefore let no man talk to me of other expedients: *of taxing our absentees at five shillings a pound: of using neither clothes nor household-furniture except what is of our own growth and manufacture: of utterly rejecting the materials and instruments that promote foreign luxury: of curing the expensiveness of pride, vanity, idleness, and gaming in our women; of introducing a vein of parsimony, prudence, and temperance: of learning to love our country, wherein we differ even from Laplanders, and the inhabitants of Topinamboo:*[7] *of quitting our animosities and factions, nor act any longer like the Jews,*[8] *who were murdering one another at the very moment their city was taken: of being a little cautious not to sell our country and consciences for nothing: of teaching landlords to have at least one degree of mercy towards their tenants: lastly, of putting a spirit of honesty, industry, and skill into our shopkeepers; who, if a resolution could now be taken to buy only our native goods, would immediately unite to cheat and exact upon us in the price, the measure, and the goodness, nor could ever yet be brought to make one fair proposal of just dealing, though often and earnestly invited to it.*[9]

Therefore I repeat, let no man talk to me of these and the like expedients, till he hath at least some glimpse of hope that there will ever be some hearty and sincere attempts to put them in practice.

But, as to myself, having been wearied out for many years with offering vain, idle, visionary thoughts, and at length utterly despairing of success, I fortunately fell upon this proposal; which, as it is wholly new, so it hath something solid and real, of no expense and little trouble, full in our own power, and whereby we can incur no danger in disobliging England. For this kind of commodity will not bear exportation, the flesh being of too tender a consistence to admit a long continuance in salt, although perhaps I could name a country[1] which would be glad to eat up our whole nation without it.

After all, I am not so violently bent upon my own opinion as to reject any offer proposed by wise men which shall be found equally innocent,

7. In Brazil.   8. Referring to the factionalism under Herod Agrippa II at the time of the destruction of Jerusalem by the Roman emperor Titus.   9. The italicized proposals are Swift's serious suggestions for remedying the situation of Ireland.   1. England.

cheap, easy, and effectual. But before something of that kind shall be advanced in contradiction to my scheme, and offering a better, I desire the author, or authors, will be pleased maturely to consider two points. First, as things now stand, how they will be able to find food and raiment for a hundred thousand useless mouths and backs? And, secondly, there being a round million of creatures in human figure throughout this kingdom, whose whole subsistence put into a common stock would leave them in debt two millions of pounds sterling, adding those who are beggars by profession, to the bulk of farmers, cottagers, and labourers, with the wives and children who are beggars in effect; I desire those politicians who dislike my overture, and may perhaps be so bold as to attempt an answer, that they will first ask the parents of these mortals, whether they would not at this day think it a great happiness to have been sold for food at a year old, in the manner I prescribe, and thereby have avoided such a perpetual scene of misfortunes as they have since gone through, by the oppression of landlords, the impossibility of paying rent without money or trade, the want of common sustenance, with neither house nor clothes to cover them from the inclemencies of weather, and the most inevitable prospect of entailing the like, or greater miseries, upon their breed for ever.

I profess, in the sincerity of my heart, that I have not the least personal interest in endeavouring to promote this necessary work, having no other motive than the public good of my country, by advancing our trade, providing for infants, relieving the poor, and giving some pleasure to the rich. I have no children by which I can propose to get a single penny; the youngest being nine years old, and my wife past child-bearing.

ALEXANDER POPE
1688–1744

"If Pope be not a poet, where is poetry to be found?" Samuel Johnson inquired. Transmuting the commonplace, claiming as subject matter everything from the minutiae of social existence to speculation about the nature of universal order, Alexander Pope made unlikely raw material into brilliant poetry.

Born to Roman Catholic parents in the year of the Glorious Revolution that deposed Catholic James II in favor of Protestant William and Mary, Pope lived when repressive legislation against Catholics restricted his financial, educational, professional, and residential possibilities. He could not attend a university or hold public employment; he had to live ten miles outside London. Sickly and undersized (he probably suffered a tubercular infection in infancy), he was educated largely at home. He also educated himself by literary friendships beginning in his youth; throughout his life, he enjoyed close associations with other men and with a few women, in particular his neighbor and intimate friend Martha Blount, to whom he left his estate. Increasingly, he won wealth and reputation by his writing, notably his translations of Homer. Following Candide's course of cultivating his garden, he perfected his grounds and grotto at Twickenham, living in retirement from the city. He died of asthma and edema.

Pope's work ranged through most of the poetic genres of his period. Beginning, as Virgil had done, with pastorals, he later produced An Essay on Criticism, versi-

fied advice about proper literary and critical procedure, and went on to publish a
great philosophic poem, *An Essay on Man*, and to edit Shakespeare's plays. The
bulk of his verse, however, was satiric. In *The Dunciad* (1743), he provided a satiric
epic for his age, a history of the progress of dullness.

Writing to a woman friend, Pope described *The Rape of the Lock* (1717) as "at
once the most a satire, and the most inoffensive, of anything of mine. . . . 'Tis a
sort of writing very like tickling." He thus suggests the tonal complexity of a work
that conveys serious social criticism through a fanciful and playful fable narrated
in verse of surpassing grace and elegance. The joke of the poem, as well as its
serious point, derives from the cataclysmic disturbance a young woman makes
over her loss of a lock of hair. Pope adapts epic conventions to his narrative of
trivia, including even a supernatural species—the sylphs—parodying the functions
of the Greek gods. These reminders of the epic, a genre by definition concerned
with important matters, emphasize the poet's consciousness of the relative triviality
of eighteenth-century high-society preoccupations. The world Belinda inhabits
confuses small things with great; "Puffs, powders, patches, Bibles, billet-doux"
occupy her dressing table in indiscriminate assembly. Members of this society take
their own pleasure more seriously than anything else: "wretches hang that jurymen
may dine." Men and women coexist in fascinated tension, tension that, given even
slight provocation, explodes in hostilities. Sexual issues govern the conflict: women
guard their "honor," the reputation of chastity, more intently than they preserve
their physical purity; men seek to violate both. The ideals of good sense and good
humor, expressed in the poem by Clarissa, govern no one in action. Instead, both
sexes value beauty (which, as Clarissa points out, fades) and accept it as an excuse
for emotional self-indulgence (the theme of Umbriel's excursion to the Cave of
Spleen). In its accounts of moral and psychological confusion, of hysterical fits
and battles, the poem employs the familiar satiric techniques of exaggeration and
distortion intended to reveal the truth and to inspire reform.

But *The Rape of the Lock* celebrates as well as criticizes. The delicacy and grace
of the verse, the ethereal beauty of the sylphs, recapitulate Belinda's genuine grace
and beauty: "If to her share some female errors fall, / Look on her face, and you'll
forget 'em all." Belinda's world operates mainly on the basis of style. In its separation of style from moral substance, the society demands criticism; but the beauty
it values—elegant conversation, boat trips on the Thames, magnificent women—
like the beauty the poet creates, has meaning in itself. When the disputed lock of
hair ascends to the constellations, when the poet calls attention to his own preservation of Belinda's beauty and fame, *The Rape of the Lock* reminds us that praise
and blame sometimes appropriately attach to the same objects. Its mixture of playfulness and seriousness, of beauty and harshness, mark the poem's unique achievement.

In *An Essay on Man* (1733–34), a very different work, Pope set out to consider,
in successive epistles, humanity in relation to the universe, to itself, to society, and
to happiness: an enterprise of ambition almost comparable to Milton's in *Paradise
Lost*. Indeed, in the first section of the poem Pope alludes specifically to his predecessor, describing the world as a "Garden, tempting with forbidden fruit" and
declaring his own intention to "vindicate [Milton had used *justify*] the ways of
God to man." Unlike Milton, Pope pursues this goal not through a dramatic fable
but by an extended versified meditation on the philosophic issues involved. That
meditation, however, generates its own drama.

Pope draws on a number of intellectual traditions to define the human condition in both cosmic and social terms. The breadth of his reference—to Catholic
and Protestant theology, to Platonic and Stoic philosophy, to his period's notions
of plenitude and natural order—itself reinforces the underlying assumption of universal, unchanging human nature. The poet evokes a timeless vision of humanity

in the universe, poised at the middle of the Great Chain of Being that extends from God to the most minute forms of life, with the fullest possible range of being above and below humankind. Complaints that the poem's philosophy is shallow ignore the complexity of its synthesis and the seriousness of its ideas. The resounding assertion that concludes the first epistle, for instance ("One truth is clear, WHATEVER IS, IS RIGHT"), implies no unawareness of human misery or evil. Abundant examples of both have been presented in the text. The point is, rather, that the nature of God's plan—by definition not fully comprehensible to human reason—must allow evil for the sake of larger good. And human beings, to possess free will, must have available to them the choice of evil. Such assumptions belong to the intellectual position called "philosophical optimism"—by no means equivalent to what we usually think of as optimism, the faith that everything will turn out well in the long run. The belief expounded in *An Essay on Man*, on the contrary, allows the possibility that matters may turn out badly for individual men and women but assumes that personal misfortune takes its place in a larger, essentially benign, pattern.

The first epistle of the poem, printed here, progresses through ten logically connected sections. It begins by insisting on the necessary limitation of human judgment: we see only parts, not the whole. Nonetheless, this fact does not imply the imperfection of humankind; it means, rather, that we are adapted to our position in the general order of things. Our ignorance of future events and our hope for eternal life give us the possibility of happiness. The poem then indicts human beings for pride and impiety (we claim more power of judgment and more knowledge than we can have), for the absurdity of assuming themselves the center of the created universe, and for the unreasonableness of complaints against the providential order (we demand, the poet suggests, both the perfection of angels and the physical sensitivities of animals, although increase in our capacities would bring misery). Turning to the nature of the universal order, the argument insists on the gradations of faculties from the lower animals to humankind, then suggests that this order extends farther than we can know: any interference with it would destroy the whole. Even the speculative possibility of such interference suggests the insanity of human pride. Our only proper course is absolute submission to Providence.

This logical sequence structures the *Essay on Man*, but we should not read the poem only as a versified handbook of eighteenth-century philosophy. Here, as in *The Rape of the Lock*, Pope displays his poetic brilliance, converting philosophic argument into a rich emotional and intellectual texture. He draws us into the poem by addressing us directly, reminding us of our own tendencies to presumption, our own inevitable desire to understand the universe as revolving around us. "In Pride, in reas'ning Pride, our error lies": we all share bewilderment at our situation, we all need to interpret it, we all face, every day, our necessary limitations. The poet rapidly shifts tone, sometimes berating his readers, sometimes reminding us (and himself) of his own participation in the universal dilemma, sometimes assuming a godlike perspective and suggesting his superior knowledge. By his changing voice, his changing forms of address, he makes dramatic the futile, yet noble, effort to understand what only the deity can fully comprehend.

At its best, *An Essay on Man* transforms philosophy into emotional experience. It generates drama out of shifting, intersecting perspectives: the lamb licking the hand of its butcher, the Indian looking forward to a Heaven his dog will share, the scientist trying to interpret the physical universe. It also makes the abstract vividly specific and concrete, as when reflection on the necessary limitation of human faculties produces the penetrating image of someone dying "of a rose in aromatic pain." Pope's imagination summons up a vast range of concrete reference, and it does not avoid the disturbing: we are invited to think of the human condition in the universe as comparable to that of the ox, which tills the fields, goes to slaughter, or finds itself worshiped as a god, according to accidents of situation. The fly's "microscopic eye" excels our powers; we resemble weeds more than oaks. Yet the poet, ranging from the conversational ease of his opening lines to the ringing certainties of his conclusion, incorporates perceptions of human inadequacy into assertions of a grand scheme, which he makes not only rational but exciting.

Pope has been the subject of a great deal of writing. Biographies include G. Sherburn, *The Early Career of Alexander Pope* (1934), and M. Mack, *Alexander Pope* (1985). A range of responses is represented in M. Mack and J. A. Winn, eds., *Pope: Recent Essays by Several Hands* (1980); H. Bloom, ed., *Alexander Pope* (1985); and W. Jackson and R. P. Yoder, eds., *Critical Essays on Alexander Pope* (1993). Perceptive critical books include R. A. Brower, *Alexander Pope: The Poetry of Allusion* (1959), and T. R. Edwards, *This Dark Estate: A Reading of Pope* (1963). Other useful studies include D. B. Morris, *The Genius of Sense* (1984); L. Damrosch Jr., *The Imaginative World of Alexander Pope* (1987); and R. Ferguson, *The Unbalanced Mind: Pope and the Rule of Passion* (1985).

The Rape of the Lock[1]

An Heroi-Comical Poem

> *Nolueram, Belinda, tuos violare capillos;*
> *sed juvat hoc precibus me tribuisse tuis.*[2]
> —MARTIAL

TO MRS. ARABELLA FERMOR

MADAM,

It will be in vain to deny that I have some regard for this piece, since I dedicate it to you. Yet you may bear me witness, it was intended only to divert a few young ladies, who have good sense and good humor enough to laugh not only at their sex's little unguarded follies, but at their own. But as it was communicated with the air of a secret, it soon found its way into the world. An imperfect copy having been offered to a bookseller, you had the good nature for my sake to consent to the publication of one more correct; this I was forced to, before I had executed half my design, for the machinery was entirely wanting to complete it.

The machinery, Madam, is a term invented by the critics, to signify that part which the deities, angels, or demons are made to act in a poem; for the ancient poets are in one respect like many modern ladies: let an action be never so trivial in itself, they always make it appear of the utmost importance. These machines I determined to raise on a very new and odd foundation, the Rosicrucian[3] doctrine of spirits.

I know how disagreeable it is to make use of hard words before a lady; but 'tis so much the concern of a poet to have his works understood, and particularly by your sex, that you must give me leave to explain two or three difficult terms.

---

1. Text and notes by Samuel Holt Monk.   2. "I was unwilling, Belinda, to ravish your locks; but I rejoice to have conceded this to your prayers" (Martial, *Epigrams* XII. lxxxiv. 1–2). Pope substituted his heroine for Martial's Polytimus. The epigraph is intended to suggest that the poem was published at Miss Fermor's request.   3. A system of arcane philosophy introduced into England from Germany in the seventeenth century.

The Rosicrucians are a people I must bring you acquainted with. The best account I know of them is in a French book called *Le Comte de Gabalis*,[4] which both in its title and size is so like a novel, that many of the fair sex have read it for one by mistake. According to these gentlemen, the four elements are inhabited by spirits, which they call Sylphs, Gnomes, Nymphs, and Salamanders. The Gnomes or Demons of earth delight in mischief; but the Sylphs, whose habitation is in the air, are the best-conditioned creatures imaginable. For they say, any mortals may enjoy the most intimate familiarities with these gentle spirits, upon a condition very easy to all true adepts, an inviolate preservation of chastity.

As to the following cantos, all the passages of them are as fabulous as the vision at the beginning, or the transformation at the end; (except the loss of your hair, which I always mention with reverence). The human persons are as fictitious as the airy ones; and the character of Belinda, as it is now managed, resembles you in nothing but in beauty.

If this poem had as many graces as there are in your person, or in your mind, yet I could never hope it should pass through the world half so uncensured as you have done. But let its fortune be what it will, mine is happy enough, to have given me this occasion of assuring you that I am, with the truest esteem,

MADAM,
Your most obedient, humble servant,
A. POPE

CANTO I

What dire offense from amorous causes springs,
What mighty contests rise from trivial things,
I sing—This verse to Caryll,[5] Muse! is due:
This, even Belinda may vouchsafe to view:
Slight is the subject, but not so the praise,   5
If she inspire, and he approve my lays.
Say what strange motive, Goddess! could compel
A well-bred lord t' assault a gentle belle?
Oh, say what stranger cause, yet unexplored,
Could make a gentle belle reject a lord?   10
In tasks so bold can little men engage,
And in soft bosoms dwells such mighty rage?
Sol through white curtains shot a timorous ray,
And oped those eyes that must eclipse the day.
Now lapdogs give themselves the rousing shake,   15
And sleepless lovers just at twelve awake:
Thrice rung the bell, the slipper knocked the ground,
And the pressed watch[6] returned a silver sound.
Belinda still her downy pillow pressed,
Her guardian Sylph prolonged the balmy rest: 20
'Twas he had summoned to her silent bed

---

4. By the Abbé de Montfaucon de Villars, published in 1670.   **5.** John Caryll (1666?–1736), a close friend of Pope's who suggested that he write this poem.   **6.** A watch that chimes the hour and the quarter hour when the stem is pressed down. *Thrice rung the bell*: Belinda thus summons her maid.

The morning dream that hovered o'er her head.
A youth more glittering than a birthnight beau[7]
(That even in slumber caused her cheek to glow)
Seemed to her ear his winning lips to lay,   25
And thus in whispers said, or seemed to say:
    "Fairest of mortals, thou distinguished care
Of thousand bright inhabitants of air!
If e'er one vision touched thy infant thought,
Of all the nurse and all the priest have taught,   30
Of airy elves by moonlight shadows seen,
The silver token, and the circled green,[8]
Or virgins visited by angel powers,
With golden crowns and wreaths of heavenly flowers,
Hear and believe! thy own importance know,   35
Nor bound thy narrow views to things below.
Some secret truths, from learned pride concealed,
To maids alone and children are revealed:
What though no credit doubting wits may give?
The fair and innocent shall still believe.   40
Know, then, unnumbered spirits round thee fly,
The light militia of the lower sky:
These, though unseen, are ever on the wing,
Hang o'er the box,[9] and hover round the Ring.
Think what an equipage thou hast in air,   45
And view with scorn two pages and a chair.[1]
As now your own, our beings were of old,
And once enclosed in woman's beauteous mold;
Thence, by a soft transition, we repair
From earthly vehicles to these of air.   50
Think not, when woman's transient breath is fled,
That all her vanities at once are dead:
Succeeding vanities she still regards,
And though she plays no more o'erlooks the cards.
Her joy in gilded chariots, when alive,   55
And love of ombre,[2] after death survive.
For when the Fair in all their pride expire,
To their first elements[3] their souls retire:
The sprites of fiery termagants in flame
Mount up, and take a Salamander's name.[4]   60
Soft yielding minds to water glide away,
And sip, with Nymphs, their elemental tea.[5]

---

7. Courtiers wore especially fine clothes on the sovereign's birthday.   8. According to popular belief, fairies skim off the cream from jugs of milk left standing overnight and leave a coin in payment. *The circled green*: rings of bright green grass, which are common in England even in winter, were held to be due to the round dances of fairies.   9. *Box* in the theater and the fashionable circular drive *(Ring)* in Hyde Park.   1. Sedan chair.   2. The popular card game. See III.27ff. and note.   3. The four elements out of which all things were believed to have been made were fire, water, earth, and air. One or another of these elements was supposed to be predominant in both the physical and psychological makeup of each human being. In this context they are spoken of as "humors."   4. Pope borrowed his supernatural beings from Rosicrucian mythology. Each element was inhabited by a spirit, as the following lines explain. The salamander is a lizardlike animal, in antiquity believed to live in fire.   5. Pronounced *tay*.

The graver prude sinks downward to a Gnome,
In search of mischief still on earth to roam.
The light coquettes in Sylphs aloft repair,   65
And sport and flutter in the fields of air.
    "Know further yet; whoever fair and chaste
Rejects mankind, is by some Sylph embraced:
For spirits, freed from mortal laws, with ease
Assume what sexes and what shapes they please.   70
What guards the purity of melting maids,
In courtly balls, and midnight masquerades,
Safe from the treacherous friend, the daring spark,
The glance by day, the whisper in the dark,
When kind occasion prompts their warm desires,   75
When music softens, and when dancing fires?
'Tis but their Sylph, the wise Celestials know,
Though Honor is the word with men below.
    "Some nymphs there are, too conscious of their face,
For life predestined to the Gnomes' embrace.   80
These swell their prospects and exalt their pride,
When offers are disdained, and love denied:
Then gay ideas⁶ crowd the vacant brain,
While peers, and dukes, and all their sweeping train,
And garters, stars, and coronets appear,   85
And in soft sounds, 'your Grace' salutes their ear.
'Tis these that early taint the female soul,
Instruct the eyes of young coquettes to roll,
Teach infant cheeks a bidden blush to know,
And little hearts to flutter at a beau.   90
    "Oft, when the world imagine women stray,
The Sylphs through mystic mazes guide their way,
Through all the giddy circle they pursue,
And old impertinence expel by new.
What tender maid but must a victim fall   95
To one man's treat, but for another's ball?
When Florio speaks what virgin could withstand,
If gentle Damon did not squeeze her hand?
With varying vanities, from every part,
They shift the moving toyshop⁷ of their heart;   100
Where wigs with wigs, with sword-knots sword-knots strive,
Beaux banish beaux, and coaches coaches drive.
This erring mortals levity may call;
Oh, blind to truth! the Sylphs contrive it all.
    "Of these am I, who thy protection claim,   105
A watchful sprite, and Ariel is my name.
Late, as I ranged the crystal wilds of air,
In the clear mirror of thy ruling star
I saw, alas! some dread event impend,

---

6. Images.   7. A shop stocked with baubles and trifles.

Ere to the main this morning sun descend,   110
But Heaven reveals not what, or how, or where:
Warned by thy Sylph, O pious maid, beware!
This to disclose is all thy guardian can:
Beware of all, but most beware of Man!"
He said; when Shock,[8] who thought she slept too long,   115
Leaped up, and waked his mistress with his tongue.
'Twas then, Belinda, if report say true,
Thy eyes first opened on a billet-doux;
Wounds, charms, and ardors were no sooner read,
But all the vision vanished from thy head.   120
And now, unveiled, the toilet stands displayed,
Each silver vase in mystic order laid.
First, robed in white, the nymph intent adores,
With head uncovered, the cosmetic powers.
A heavenly image in the glass appears;   125
To that she bends, to that her eyes she rears.
The inferior priestess, at her altar's side,
Trembling begins the sacred rites of Pride.
Unnumbered treasures ope at once, and here
The various offerings of the world appear;   130
From each she nicely culls with curious toil,
And decks the goddess with the glittering spoil.
This casket India's glowing gems unlocks,
And all Arabia breathes from yonder box.
The tortoise here and elephant unite,   135
Transformed to combs, the speckled and the white.
Here files of pins extend their shining rows,
Puffs, powders, patches, Bibles, billet-doux.
Now awful Beauty puts on all its arms;
The fair each moment rises in her charms,   140
Repairs her smiles, awakens every grace,
And calls forth all the wonders of her face;
Sees by degrees a purer blush arise,
And keener lightnings quicken in her eyes.
The busy Sylphs surround their darling care,   145
These set the head, and those divide the hair,
Some fold the sleeve, whilst others plait the gown;
And Betty's[9] praised for labors not her own.

CANTO II

Not with more glories, in the ethereal plain,
The sun first rises o'er the purpled main,
Than, issuing forth, the rival of his beams
Launched on the bosom of the silver Thames.
Fair nymphs and well-dressed youths around her shone,   5

---

8. Belinda's lapdog.   9. Belinda's maid, the "inferior priestess" mentioned in line 127.

But every eye was fixed on her alone.
On her white breast a sparkling cross she wore,
Which Jews might kiss, and infidels adore.
Her lively looks a sprightly mind disclose,
Quick as her eyes, and as unfixed as those: 10
Favors to none, to all she smiles extends;
Oft she rejects, but never once offends.
Bright as the sun, her eyes the gazers strike,
And, like the sun, they shine on all alike.
Yet graceful ease, and sweetness void of pride,   15
Might hide her faults, if belles had faults to hide:
If to her share some female errors fall,
Look on her face, and you'll forget 'em all.
　　This nymph, to the destruction of mankind,
Nourished two locks which graceful hung behind   20
In equal curls, and well conspired to deck
With shining ringlets the smooth ivory neck.
Love in these labyrinths his slaves detains,
And mighty hearts are held in slender chains.
With hairy springes we the birds betray,   25
Slight lines of hair surprise the finny prey,
Fair tresses man's imperial race ensnare,
And beauty draws us with a single hair.
　　The adventurous Baron the bright locks admired,
He saw, he wished, and to the prize aspired.   30
Resolved to win, he meditates the way,
By force to ravish, or by fraud betray;
For when success a lover's toil attends,
Few ask if fraud or force attained his ends.
　　For this, ere Phoebus rose, he had implored   35
Propitious Heaven, and every power adored,
But chiefly Love—to Love an altar built,
Of twelve vast French romances, neatly gilt.
There lay three garters, half a pair of gloves,
And all the trophies of his former loves.   40
With tender billet-doux he lights the pyre,
And breathes three amorous sighs to raise the fire.
Then prostrate falls, and begs with ardent eyes
Soon to obtain, and long possess the prize:
The powers gave ear, and granted half his prayer,   45
The rest the winds dispersed in empty air.
　　But now secure the painted vessel glides,
The sunbeams trembling on the floating tides,
While melting music steals upon the sky,
And softened sounds along the waters die.   50
Smooth flow the waves, the zephyrs gently play,
Belinda smiled, and all the world was gay.
All but the Sylph—with careful thoughts oppressed,
The impending woe sat heavy on his breast.

He summons straight his denizens of air;   55
The lucid squadrons round the sails repair:
Soft o'er the shrouds aërial whispers breathe
That seemed but zephyrs to the train beneath.
Some to the sun their insect-wings unfold,
Waft on the breeze, or sink in clouds of gold.   60
Transparent forms too fine for mortal sight,
Their fluid bodies half dissolved in light,
Loose to the wind their airy garments flew,
Thin glittering textures of the filmy dew,
Dipped in the richest tincture of the skies,   65
Where light disports in ever-mingling dyes,
While every beam new transient colors flings,
Colors that change whene'er they wave their wings.
Amid the circle, on the gilded mast,
Superior by the head was Ariel placed;   70
His purple[1] pinions opening to the sun,
He raised his azure wand, and thus begun:
    "Ye Sylphs and Sylphids, to your chief give ear!
Fays, Fairies, Genii, Elves, and Daemons, hear!
Ye know the spheres and various tasks assigned   75
By laws eternal to the aërial kind.
Some in the fields of purest ether play,
And bask and whiten in the blaze of day.
Some guide the course of wandering orbs on high,
Or roll the planets through the boundless sky.   80
Some less refined, beneath the moon's pale light
Pursue the stars that shoot athwart the night,
Or suck the mists in grosser air below,
Or dip their pinions in the painted bow,
Or brew fierce tempests on the wintry main,   85
Or o'er the glebe distill the kindly rain.
Others on earth o'er human race preside,
Watch all their ways, and all their actions guide:
Of these the chief the care of nations own,
And guard with arms divine the British Throne.   90
    "Our humbler province is to tend the Fair,
Not a less pleasing, though less glorious care:
To save the powder from too rude a gale,
Nor let the imprisoned essences exhale;
To draw fresh colors from the vernal flowers   95
To steal from rainbows e'er they drop in showers
A brighter wash;[2] to curl their waving hairs,
Assist their blushes, and inspire their airs;
Nay oft, in dreams invention we bestow,

---

1. In eighteenth-century poetic diction, the word might mean "blood-red," "purple," or simply (as is likely here) "brightly colored." The word derives from Virgil, *Eclogue* IX.40, *pupureus*.   2. Cosmetic lotion.

To change a flounce, or add a furbelow.   100
  "This day black omens threat the brightest fair,
That e'er deserved a watchful spirit's care;
Some dire disaster, or by force or slight,
But what, or where, the Fates have wrapped in night:
Whether the nymph shall break Diana's[3] law,   105
Or some frail china jar receive a flaw,
Or stain her honor or her new brocade,
Forget her prayers, or miss a masquerade,
Or lose her heart, or necklace, at a ball;
Or whether Heaven has doomed that Shock must fall.   110
Haste, then, ye spirits! to your charge repair:
The fluttering fan be Zephyretta's care;
The drops[4] to thee, Brillante, we consign;
And, Momentilla, let the watch be thine;
Do thou, Crispissa,[5] tend her favorite Lock;   115
Ariel himself shall be the guard of Shock.
  "To fifty chosen Sylphs, of special note,
We trust the important charge, the petticoat;
Oft have we known that sevenfold fence to fail,
Though stiff with hoops, and armed with ribs of whale.   120
Form a strong line about the silver bound,
And guard the wide circumference around.
  "Whatever spirit, careless of his charge,
His post neglects, or leaves the fair at large,
Shall feel sharp vengeance soon o'ertake his sins,   125
Be stopped in vials, or transfixed with pins,
Or plunged in lakes of bitter washes lie,
Or wedged whole ages in a bodkin's eye;[6]
Gums and pomatums shall his flight restrain,
While clogged he beats his silken wings in vain,   130
Or alum styptics with contracting power
Shrink his thin essence like a riveled[7] flower:
Or, as Ixion fixed,[8] the wretch shall feel
The giddy motion of the whirling mill,
In fumes of burning chocolate shall glow,   135
And tremble at the sea that froths below!"
  He spoke; the spirits from the sails descend;
Some, orb in orb, around the nymph extend;
Some thread the mazy ringlets of her hair;
Some hang upon the pendants of her ear: 140
With beating hearts the dire event they wait,
Anxious, and trembling for the birth of Fate.

---

3. Diana was the goddess of chastity.   4. Diamond earrings.   5. From Latin *crispere*, to curl.   6. A
blunt needle with a large eye, used for drawing ribbon through eyelets in the edging of women's garments.
7. To "rivel" is to "contract into wrinkles and corrugations" (Johnson's *Dictionary*).   8. In the Greek
myth Ixion was punished in the underworld by being bound on an ever-turning wheel.

CANTO III

Close by those meads, forever crowned with flowers,
Where Thames with pride surveys his rising towers,
There stands a structure of majestic frame,
Which from the neighboring Hampton⁹ takes its name.
Here Britain's statesmen oft the fall foredoom   5
Of foreign tyrants and of nymphs at home;
Here thou, great Anna! whom three realms obey,
Dost sometimes counsel take—and sometimes tea.
    Hither the heroes and the nymphs resort,
To taste awhile the pleasures of a court;   10
In various talk the instructive hours they passed,
Who gave the ball, or paid the visit last;
One speaks the glory of the British Queen,
And one describes a charming Indian screen;
A third interprets motions, looks, and eyes;   15
At every word a reputation dies.
Snuff, or the fan, supply each pause of chat,
With singing, laughing, ogling, and all that.
    Meanwhile, declining from the noon of day,
The sun obliquely shoots his burning ray;   20
The hungry judges soon the sentence sign,
And wretches hang that jurymen may dine;
The merchant from the Exchange returns in peace,
And the long labors of the toilet cease.
Belinda now, whom thirst of fame invites,   25
Burns to encounter two adventurous knights,
At ombre¹ singly to decide their doom
And swells her breast with conquests yet to come.
Straight the three bands prepare in arms to join,
Each band the number of the sacred nine.   30
Soon as she spreads her hand, the aërial guard
Descend, and sit on each important card:
First Ariel perched upon a Matadore,
Then each according to the rank they bore;
For Sylphs, yet mindful of their ancient race,   35
Are, as when women, wondrous fond of place.
    Behold, four Kings in majesty revered,
With hoary whiskers and a forky beard;
And four fair Queens whose hands sustain a flower,
The expressive emblem of their softer power;   40
Four Knaves in garbs succinct,² a trusty band,

---

9. Hampton Court, the royal palace, about fifteen miles up the Thames from London.   1. The game that Belinda plays against the baron and another young man is too complicated for complete explication here. Pope has carefully arranged the cards so that Belinda wins. The baron's hand is strong enough to be a threat, but the third player's is of little account. The hand is played exactly according to the rules of ombre, and Pope's description of the cards is equally accurate. Each player holds nine cards (line 30). The "Matadores" (line 33), when spades are trumps, are "Spadillio" (line 49), the ace of spades; "Manillio" (line 51), the two of spades; "Basto" (line 53), the ace of clubs; Belinda holds all three of these. 2. Girded up.

Caps on their heads, and halberts in their hand;
And parti-colored troops, a shining train,
Draw forth to combat on the velvet plain.
The skillful nymph reviews her force with care;   45
"Let Spades be trumps!" she said, and trumps they were.
   Now move to war her sable Matadores,
In show like leaders of the swarthy Moors.
Spadillio first, unconquerable lord!
Led off two captive trumps, and swept the board.   50
As many more Manillio forced to yield,
And marched a victor from the verdant field.
Him Basto followed, but his fate more hard
Gained but one trump and one plebeian card.
With his broad saber next, a chief in years,   55
The hoary Majesty of Spades appears,
Puts forth one manly leg, to sight revealed,
The rest his many-colored robe concealed.
The rebel Knave, who dares his prince engage,
Proves the just victim of his royal rage.   60
Even mighty Pam,[3] that kings and queens o'erthrew
And mowed down armies in the fights of loo,
Sad chance of war! now destitute of aid,
Falls undistinguished by the victor Spade.
   Thus far both armies to Belinda yield;   65
Now to the Baron fate inclines the field.
His warlike amazon her host invades,
The imperial consort of the crown of Spades.
The Club's black tyrant first her victim died,
Spite of his haughty mien and barbarous pride.   70
What boots the regal circle on his head,
His giant limbs, in state unwieldy spread?
That long behind he trails his pompous robe,
And of all monarchs only grasps the globe?
   The Baron now his Diamonds pours apace;   75
The embroidered King who shows but half his face,
And his refulgent Queen, with powers combined
Of broken troops an easy conquest find.
Clubs, Diamonds, Hearts, in wild disorder seen,
With throngs promiscuous strew the level green.   80
Thus when dispersed a routed army runs,
Of Asia's troops, and Afric's sable sons,
With like confusion different nations fly,
Of various habit, and of various dye,
The pierced battalions disunited fall   85
In heaps on heaps; one fate o'erwhelms them all.
   The Knave of Diamonds tries his wily arts,
And wins (oh, shameful chance!) the Queen of Hearts.

---

3. The knave of clubs, the highest trump in the game of loo.

At this, the blood the virgin's cheek forsook,
A livid paleness spreads o'er all her look;   90
She sees, and trembles at the approaching ill,
Just in the jaws of ruin, and Codille,[4]
And now (as oft in some distempered state)
On one nice trick depends the general fate.
An Ace of Hearts steps forth: the King unseen   95
Lurked in her hand, and mourned his captive Queen.
He springs to vengeance with an eager pace,
And falls like thunder on the prostrate Ace.
The nymph exulting fills with shouts the sky,
The walls, the woods, and long canals reply.   100
    O thoughtless mortals! ever blind to fate,
Too soon dejected, and too soon elate:
Sudden these honors shall be snatched away,
And cursed forever this victorious day.
    For lo! the board with cups and spoons is crowned,   105
The berries crackle, and the mill turns round;[5]
On shining altars of Japan[6] they raise
The silver lamp; the fiery spirits blaze:
From silver spouts the grateful liquors glide,
While China's earth receives the smoking tide.   110
At once they gratify their scent and taste,
And frequent cups prolong the rich repast.
Straight hover round the fair her airy band;
Some, as she sipped, the fuming liquor fanned,
Some o'er her lap their careful plumes displayed,   115
Trembling, and conscious of the rich brocade.
Coffee (which makes the politician wise,
And see through all things with his half-shut eyes)
Sent up in vapors to the Baron's brain
New stratagems, the radiant Lock to gain.   120
Ah, cease, rash youth! desist ere 'tis too late,
Fear the just Gods, and think of Scylla's fate![7]
Changed to a bird, and sent to flit in air,
She dearly pays for Nisus' injured hair!
    But when to mischief mortals bend their will,   125
How soon they find fit instruments of ill!
Just then, Clarissa drew with tempting grace
A two-edged weapon from her shining case:
So ladies in romance assist their knight,
Present the spear, and arm him for the fight.   130
He takes the gift with reverence, and extends
The little engine on his fingers' ends;

---

4. The term applied to losing a hand at cards.   5. That is, coffee is roasted and ground.   6. That is,
small, lacquered tables. The word "altars" suggests the ritualistic character of coffee drinking in Belinda's
world.   7. Scylla, daughter of Nisus, was turned into a sea bird because, for the sake of her love for
Minos of Crete, who was besieging her father's city of Megara, she cut from her father's head the purple
lock on which his safety depended. She is not the Scylla of the "Scylla and Charybdis" episode in the
Odyssey.

This just behind Belinda's neck he spread,
As o'er the fragrant steams she bends her head.
Swift to the Lock a thousand sprites repair,   135
A thousand wings, by turns, blow back the hair,
And thrice they twitched the diamond in her ear,
Thrice she looked back, and thrice the foe drew near.
Just in that instant, anxious Ariel sought
The close recesses of the virgin's thought;   140
As on the nosegay in her breast reclined,
He watched the ideas rising in her mind,
Sudden he viewed, in spite of all her art,
An earthly lover lurking at her heart.
Amazed, confused, he found his power expired,   145
Resigned to fate, and with a sigh retired.
    The Peer now spreads the glittering forfex[8] wide,
T' enclose the Lock; now joins it, to divide.
Even then, before the fatal engine closed,
A wretched Sylph too fondly interposed;   150
Fate urged the shears, and cut the Sylph in twain
(But airy substance soon unites again):
The meeting points the sacred hair dissever
From the fair head, forever, and forever!
    Then flashed the living lightning from her eyes,   155
And screams of horror rend the affrighted skies.
Not louder shrieks to pitying heaven are cast,
When husbands, or when lapdogs breathe their last;
Or when rich china vessels fallen from high,
In glittering dust and painted fragments lie!   160
"Let wreaths of triumph now my temples twine,"
The victor cried, "the glorious prize is mine!
While fish in streams, or birds delight in air,
Or in a coach and six the British Fair,
As long as *Atalantis*[9] shall be read,   165
Or the small pillow grace a lady's bed,
While visits shall be paid on solemn days,
When numerous wax-lights in bright order blaze,
While nymphs take treats, or assignations give,
So long my honor, name, and praise shall live!   170
What Time would spare, from Steel receives its date,
And monuments, like men, submit to fate!
Steel could the labor of the Gods destroy,
And strike to dust the imperial towers of Troy;
Steel could the works of mortal pride confound,   175
And hew triumphal arches to the ground.
What wonder then, fair nymph! thy hairs should feel,
The conquering force of unresisted Steel?"

8. Scissors.   9. Mrs. Manley's *New Atalantis* (1709) was notorious for its thinly concealed allusions to contemporary scandals.

CANTO IV

But anxious cares the pensive nymph oppressed,
And secret passions labored in her breast.
Not youthful kings in battle seized alive,
Not scornful virgins who their charms survive,
Not ardent lovers robbed of all their bliss,   5
Not ancient ladies when refused a kiss,
Not tyrants fierce that unrepenting die,
Not Cynthia when her manteau's[1] pinned awry,
E'er felt such rage, resentment, and despair,
As thou, sad virgin! for thy ravished hair.   10
   For, that sad moment, when the Sylphs withdrew
And Ariel weeping from Belinda flew,
Umbriel,[2] a dusky, melancholy sprite
As ever sullied the fair face of light,
Down to the central earth, his proper scene,   15
Repaired to search the gloomy Cave of Spleen.[3]
   Swift on his sooty pinions flits the Gnome,
And in a vapor[4] reached the dismal dome.
No cheerful breeze this sullen region knows,
The dreaded east is all the wind that blows.   20
Here in a grotto, sheltered close from air,
And screened in shades from day's detested glare,
She sighs forever on her pensive bed,
Pain at her side, and Megrim[5] at her head.
   Two handmaids wait the throne: alike in place,   25
But differing far in figure and in face.
Here stood Ill-Nature like an ancient maid,
Her wrinkled form in black and white arrayed;
With store of prayers for mornings, nights, and noons,
Her hand is filled; her bosom with lampoons.   30
   There Affectation, with a sickly mien,
Shows in her cheek the roses of eighteen,
Practiced to lisp, and hang the head aside,
Faints into airs, and languishes with pride,
On the rich quilt sinks with becoming woe,   35
Wrapped in a gown, for sickness and for show.
The fair ones feel such maladies as these,
When each new nightdress gives a new disease.
   A constant vapor[6] o'er the palace flies,
Strange phantoms rising as the mists arise;   40
Dreadful as hermit's dreams in haunted shades,
Or bright as visions of expiring maids.
Now glaring fiends, and snakes on rolling spires,[7]
Pale specters, gaping tombs, and purple fires;

---

1. Negligee, or loose robe.   2. The name suggests shade and darkness.   3. Ill humor.   4. Punning on *vapor* as (1) mist and (2) an excessively emotional (even peevish) state of mind, appropriate to the realm of "spleen."   5. Headache.   6. Emblematic of "the vapors"—hypochondria, melancholy, peevishness, often affected by fashionable women.   7. Coils.

Now lakes of liquid gold, Elysian scenes,   45
And crystal domes, and angels in machines.[8]
    Unnumbered throngs on every side are seen
Of bodies changed to various forms by Spleen.
Here living teapots stand, one arm held out,
One bent; the handle this, and that the spout: 50
A pipkin[9] there, like Homer's tripod, walks;
Here sighs a jar, and there a goose pie talks;
Men prove with child, as powerful fancy works,
And maids, turned bottles, call aloud for corks.
    Safe passed the Gnome through this fantastic band,   55
A branch of healing spleenwort[1] in his hand.
Then thus addressed the Power: "Hail, wayward Queen!
Who rule the sex to fifty from fifteen:
Parent of vapors and of female wit,
Who give the hysteric or poetic fit,   60
On various tempers act by various ways,
Make some take physic, others scribble plays;
Who cause the proud their visits to delay,
And send the godly in a pet to pray.
A nymph there is that all your power disdains,   65
And thousands more in equal mirth maintains.
But oh! if e'er thy Gnome could spoil a grace,
Or raise a pimple on a beauteous face,
Like citron-waters[2] matrons' cheeks inflame,
Or change complexions at a losing game;   70
If e'er with airy horns[3] I planted heads,
Or rumpled petticoats, or tumbled beds,
Or caused suspicion when no soul was rude,
Or discomposed the headdress of a prude,
Or e'er to costive lapdog gave disease,   75
Which not the tears of brightest eyes could ease,
Hear me, and touch Belinda with chagrin:[4]
That single act gives half the world the spleen."
    The Goddess with a discontented air
Seems to reject him though she grants his prayer.   80
A wondrous bag with both her hands she binds,
Like that where once Ulysses held the winds;[5]
There she collects the force of female lungs,
Sighs, sobs, and passions, and the war of tongues.
A vial next she fills with fainting fears,   85

---

8. Mechanical devices used in the theaters for spectacular effects. The fantasies of neurotic women here merge with the sensational stage effects popular with contemporary audiences.   9. An earthen pot. In *Iliad* XVIII.434–40, Vulcan furnishes the gods with self-propelling "tripods" (three-legged stools). 1. An herb, efficacious against the spleen. Pope alludes to the golden bough that Aeneas and the Cumaean sybil carry with them for protection into the underworld in *Aeneid* VI.   2. Brandy flavored with orange or lemon peel.   3. The symbol of the cuckold; here "airy," because they exist only in the jealous suspicions of the husband, the victim of the mischievous Umbriel.   4. Ill humor.   5. Acolus (later conceived of as god of the winds) gave Ulysses a bag containing all the winds adverse to his voyage home. When his ship was in sight of Ithaca, his companions opened the bag and the storms that ensued drove Ulysses far away (*Odyssey* X.19ff.).

Soft sorrows, melting griefs, and flowing tears.
The Gnome rejoicing bears her gifts away,
Spreads his black wings, and slowly mounts to day.
    Sunk in Thalestris'[6] arms the nymph he found,
Her eyes dejected and her hair unbound.   90
Full o'er their heads the swelling bag he rent,
And all the Furies issued at the vent.
Belinda burns with more than mortal ire,
And fierce Thalestris fans the rising fire.
"O wretched maid!" she spread her hands, and cried   95
(While Hampton's echoes, "Wretched maid!" replied),
"Was it for this you took such constant care
The bodkin, comb, and essence to prepare?
For this your locks in paper durance bound,
For this with torturing irons wreathed around?   100
For this with fillets strained your tender head,
And bravely bore the double loads of lead?[7]
Gods! shall the ravisher display your hair,
While the fops envy, and the ladies stare!
Honor forbid! at whose unrivaled shrine   105
Ease, pleasure, virtue, all, our sex resign.
Methinks already I your tears survey,
Already hear the horrid things they say,
Already see you a degraded toast,
And all your honor in a whisper lost!   110
How shall I, then, your helpless fame defend?
'Twill then be infamy to seem your friend!
And shall this prize, the inestimable prize,
Exposed through crystal to the gazing eyes,
And heightened by the diamond's circling rays,   115
On that rapacious hand forever blaze?
Sooner shall grass in Hyde Park Circus grow,
And wits take lodgings in the sound of Bow;[8]
Sooner let earth, air, sea, to chaos fall,
Men, monkeys, lapdogs, parrots, perish all!"   120
    She said; then raging to Sir Plume repairs,
And bids her beau demand the precious hairs
(Sir Plume of amber snuffbox justly vain,
And the nice conduct of a clouded cane).
With earnest eyes, and round unthinking face,   125
He first the snuffbox opened, then the case,
And thus broke out—"My Lord, why, what the devil!
Z——ds! damn the lock! 'fore Gad, you must be civil!

---

6. The name is borrowed from a queen of the Amazons, hence a fierce and warlike woman. Thalestris, according to legend, traveled thirty days in order to have a child by Alexander the Great. Plutarch denies the story.   7. The frame on which the elaborate coiffures of the day were arranged.   8. A person born within sound of the bells of St. Mary-le-Bow in Cheapside is said to be a cockney. No fashionable wit would have so vulgar an address.

Plague on't! 'tis past a jest—nay prithee, pox!
Give her the hair"—he spoke, and rapped his box.   130
    "It grieves me much," replied the Peer again,
"Who speaks so well should ever speak in vain.
But by this Lock, this sacred Lock I swear
(Which never more shall join its parted hair;
Which never more its honors shall renew,   135
Clipped from the lovely head where late it grew),
That while my nostrils draw the vital air,
This hand, which won it, shall forever wear."
He spoke, and speaking, in proud triumph spread
The long-contended honors[9] of her head.   140
    But Umbriel, hateful Gnome, forbears not so;
He breaks the vial whence the sorrows flow.
Then see! the nymph in beauteous grief appears,
Her eyes half languishing, half drowned in tears;
On her heaved bosom hung her drooping head,   145
Which with a sigh she raised, and thus she said:
    "Forever cursed be this detested day,
Which snatched my best, my favorite curl away!
Happy! ah, ten times happy had I been,
If Hampton Court these eyes had never seen!   150
Yet am not I the first mistaken maid,
By love of courts to numerous ills betrayed.
Oh, had I rather unadmired remained
In some lone isle, or distant northern land;
Where the gilt chariot never marks the way,   155
Where none learn ombre, none e'er taste bohea![1]
There kept my charms concealed from mortal eye,
Like roses that in deserts bloom and die.
What moved my mind with youthful lords to roam?
Oh, had I stayed, and said my prayers at home!   160
'Twas this the morning omens seemed to tell,
Thrice from my trembling hand the patch box[2] fell;
The tottering china shook without a wind,
Nay, Poll sat mute, and Shock was most unkind!
A Sylph too warned me of the threats of fate,   165
In mystic visions, now believed too late!
See the poor remnants of these slighted hairs!
My hands shall rend what e'en thy rapine spares.
These in two sable ringlets taught to break,
Once gave new beauties to the snowy neck;   170
The sister lock now sits uncouth, alone,
And in its fellow's fate foresees its own;
Uncurled it hangs, the fatal shears demands,

---

9. Ornaments, hence locks; a Latinism.   1. A costly sort of tea.   2. A box to hold the ornamental patches of court plaster worn on the face by both sexes. Cf. *Spectator* 81.

And tempts once more thy sacrilegious hands.
Oh, hadst thou, cruel! been content to seize   175
Hairs less in sight, or any hairs but these!"

CANTO V

She said: the pitying audience melt in tears.
But Fate and Jove had stopped the Baron's ears.
In vain Thalestris with reproach assails,
For who can move when fair Belinda fails?
Not half so fixed the Trojan[3] could remain,   5
While Anna begged and Dido raged in vain.
Then grave Clarissa graceful waved her fan;
Silence ensued, and thus the nymph began:
    "Say why are beauties praised and honored most,
The wise man's passion, and the vain man's toast?   10
Why decked with all that land and sea afford,
Why angels called, and angel-like adored?
Why round our coaches crowd the white-gloved beaux,
Why bows the side box from its inmost rows?
How vain are all these glories, all our pains,   15
Unless good sense preserve what beauty gains;
That men may say when we the front box grace,
'Behold the first in virtue as in face!'
Oh! if to dance all night, and dress all day,
Charmed the smallpox, or chased old age away,   20
Who would not scorn what housewife's cares produce,
Or who would learn one earthly thing of use?
To patch, nay ogle, might become a saint,
Nor could it sure be such a sin to paint.
But since, alas! frail beauty must decay,   25
Curled or uncurled, since locks will turn to gray;
Since painted, or not painted, all shall fade,
And she who scorns a man must die a maid;
What then remains but well our power to use,
And keep good humor still whate'er we lose?   30
And trust me, dear, good humor can prevail
When airs, and flights, and screams, and scolding fail.
Beauties in vain their pretty eyes may roll;
Charms strike the sight, but merit wins the soul."[4]
    So spoke the dame, but no applause ensued;   35
Belinda frowned, Thalestris called her prude.
"To arms, to arms!" the fierce virago cries,
And swift as lightning to the combat flies.
All side in parties, and begin the attack;

---

3. Aeneas, who forsook Dido at the bidding of the gods, despite her reproaches and the supplications of her sister Anna. Virgil compares him to a steadfast oak that withstands a storm (*Aeneid* IV.437–43).
4. The speech is a close parody of Pope's own translation of the speech of Sarpedon to Glaucus, first published in 1709 and slightly revised in his version of the *Iliad* (XII.371–96).

Fans clap, silks rustle, and tough whalebones crack;   40
Heroes' and heroines' shouts confusedly rise,
And bass and treble voices strike the skies.
No common weapons in their hands are found,
Like Gods they fight, nor dread a mortal wound.
　　So when bold Homer makes the Gods engage,   45
And heavenly breasts with human passions rage;
'Gainst Pallas, Mars; Latona, Hermes arms;
And all Olympus rings with loud alarms:
Jove's thunder roars, heaven trembles all around,
Blue Neptune storms, the bellowing deeps resound: 50
Earth shakes her nodding towers, the ground gives way,
And the pale ghosts start at the flash of day!
　　Triumphant Umbriel on a sconce's height
Clapped his glad wings, and sat to view the fight:
Propped on their bodkin spears, the sprites survey   55
The growing combat, or assist the fray.
　　While through the press enraged Thalestris flies,
And scatters death around from both her eyes,
A beau and witling perished in the throng,
One died in metaphor, and one in song.   60
"O cruel nymph! a living death I bear,"
Cried Dapperwit, and sunk beside his chair.
A mournful glance Sir Fopling upwards cast,
"Those eyes are made so killing"—was his last.
Thus on Maeander's flowery margin lies   65
The expiring swan, and as he sings he dies.
　　When bold Sir Plume had drawn Clarissa down,
Chloe stepped in, and killed him with a frown;
She smiled to see the doughty hero slain,
But, at her smile, the beau revived again.   70
Now Jove suspends his golden scales in air,
Weighs the men's wits against the lady's hair;
The doubtful beam long nods from side to side;
At length the wits mount up, the hairs subside.
　　See, fierce Belinda on the Baron flies,   75
With more than usual lightning in her eyes;
Nor feared the chief the unequal fight to try,
Who sought no more than on his foe to die.
But this bold lord with manly strength endued,
She with one finger and a thumb subdued: 80
Just where the breath of life his nostrils drew,
A charge of snuff the wily virgin threw;
The Gnomes direct, to every atom just,
The pungent grains of titillating dust.
Sudden, with starting tears each eye o'erflows,   85
And the high dome re-echoes to his nose.
　　"Now meet thy fate," incensed Belinda cried,

And drew a deadly bodkin[5] from her side.
(The same, his ancient personage to deck,
Her great-great-grandsire wore about his neck,   90
In three seal rings; which after, melted down,
Formed a vast buckle for his widow's gown:
Her infant grandame's whistle next it grew,
The bells she jingled, and the whistle blew;
Then in a bodkin graced her mother's hairs,   95
Which long she wore, and now Belinda wears.)
    "Boast not my fall," he cried, "insulting foe!
Thou by some other shalt be laid as low.
Nor think to die dejects my lofty mind:
All that I dread is leaving you behind!   100
Rather than so, ah, let me still survive,
And burn in Cupid's flames—but burn alive."
    "Restore the Lock!" she cries; and all around
"Restore the Lock!" the vaulted roofs rebound.
Not fierce Othello in so loud a strain   105
Roared for the handkerchief that caused his pain.[6]
But see how oft ambitious aims are crossed,
And chiefs contend till all the prize is lost!
The lock, obtained with guilt, and kept with pain,
In every place is sought, but sought in vain: 110
With such a prize no mortal must be blessed,
So Heaven decrees! with Heaven who can contest?
    Some thought it mounted to the lunar sphere,
Since all things lost on earth are treasured there.
There heroes' wits are kept in ponderous vases,   115
And beaux' in snuffboxes and tweezer cases.
There broken vows and deathbed alms are found,
And lovers' hearts with ends of riband bound,
The courtier's promises, and sick man's prayers,
The smiles of harlots, and the tears of heirs,   120
Cages for gnats, and chains to yoke a flea,
Dried butterflies, and tomes of casuistry.
    But trust the Muse—she saw it upward rise,
Though marked by none but quick, poetic eyes
(So Rome's great founder[7] to the heavens withdrew,   125
To Proculus alone confessed in view);
A sudden star, it shot through liquid air,
And drew behind a radiant trail of hair.
Not Berenice's[8] locks first rose so bright,
The heavens bespangling with disheveled light.   130
The Sylphs behold it kindling as it flies,
And pleased pursue its progress through the skies.

---

5. An ornamental pin shaped like a dagger, to be worn in the hair.   **6.** *Othello* III.4.   **7.** Romulus, the "founder" and first king of Rome, was snatched to heaven in a storm cloud while reviewing his army in the Campus Martius (Livy I.16).   **8.** Berenice, the wife of Ptolemy III, dedicated a lock of her hair to the gods to ensure her husband's safe return from war. It was turned into a constellation.

  This the beau monde shall from the Mall[9] survey,
  And hail with music its propitious ray.
  This the blest lover shall for Venus take,   135
  And send up vows from Rosamonda's Lake.[1]
  This Partridge soon shall view in cloudless skies,
  When next he looks through Galileo's eyes;[2]
  And hence the egregious wizard shall foredoom
  The fate of Louis, and the fall of Rome.   140
    Then cease, bright nymph! to mourn thy ravished hair,
  Which adds new glory to the shining sphere!
  Not all the tresses that fair head can boast,
  Shall draw such envy as the Lock you lost.
  For, after all the murders of your eye,   145
  When, after millions slain, yourself shall die:
  When those fair suns shall set, as set they must,
  And all those tresses shall be laid in dust,
  This Lock the Muse shall consecrate to fame,
  And 'midst the stars inscribe Belinda's name.   150

An Essay on Man

To Henry St. John, Lord Bolingbroke

EPISTLE I

ARGUMENT OF THE NATURE AND STATE OF MAN, WITH RESPECT TO THE UNIVERSE. Of man in the abstract—I. That we can judge only with regard to our own system, being ignorant of the relations of systems and things, ver. 17, &c.—II. That man is not to be deemed imperfect, but a being suited to his place and rank in the creation, agreeable to the general order of things, and conformable to ends and relations to him unknown, ver. 35, &c.—III. That it is partly upon his ignorance of future events, and partly upon the hope of a future state, that all his happiness in the present depends, ver. 77, &c.—IV. The pride of aiming at more knowledge, and pretending to more perfection, the cause of man's error and misery. The impiety of putting himself in the place of God, and judging of the fitness or unfitness, perfection or imperfection, justice or injustice of his dispensations, ver. 113, &c.—V. The absurdity of conceiving himself the final cause of the creation, or expecting that perfection in the moral world which is not in the natural, ver. 131, &c.—VI. The unreasonableness of his complaints against Providence, while on the one hand he demands the perfections of the angels, and on the other the bodily qualifications of the brutes; though, to possess any of the sensitive faculties in a higher degree, would render him miserable, ver. 173, &c.—VII. That throughout the whole visible world, an universal order and gradation in the sensual and mental faculties is observed, which causes a subordination of creature

---

9. A walk laid out by Charles II in St. James's Park, a resort for strollers of all sorts. 1. In St. James's Park; associated with unhappy lovers. 2. A telescope. John Partridge was an astrologer whose annually published predictions had been amusingly satirized by Swift and other wits in 1708.

to creature, and of all creatures to man. The gradations of sense, instinct, thought, reflection, reason: that reason alone countervails all the other faculties, ver. 207.—VIII. How much further this order and subordination of living creatures may extend, above and below us; were any part of which broken, not that part only, but the whole connected creation must be destroyed, ver. 233—IX. The extravagance, madness, and pride of such a desire, ver. 259.—X. The consequence of all, the absolute submission due to Providence, both as to our present and future state, ver. 281, &c., to the end.

Awake, my St. John![1] leave all meaner things
To low ambition, and the pride of Kings.
Let us (since Life can little more supply
Than just to look about us and to die)
Expatiate free o'er all this scene of Man;   5
A mighty maze! but not without a plan;
A Wild, where weeds and flowers promiscuous shoot;
Or Garden, tempting with forbidden fruit.
Together let us beat this ample field,
Try what the open, what the covert yield;   10
The latent tracts, the giddy heights, explore
Of all who blindly creep, or sightless soar;
Eye Nature's walks, shoot Folly as it flies,
And catch the Manners living as they rise;
Laugh where we must, be candid where we can;   15
But vindicate the ways of God to man.[2]

   I. Say first, of God above, or Man below,
What can we reason, but from what we know?
Of Man, what see we but his station here,
From which to reason, or to which refer?   20
Through worlds unnumbered though the God be known,
'Tis ours to trace him only in our own.
He, who through vast immensity can pierce,
See worlds on worlds compose one universe,
Observe how system into system runs,   25
What other planets circle other suns,
What varied Being peoples every star,
May tell why Heaven has made us as we are.
But of this frame the bearings, and the ties,
The strong connections, nice dependencies,   30
Gradations just, has thy pervading soul
Looked through? or can a part contain the whole?
   Is the great chain,[3] that draws all to agree,
And drawn supports, upheld by God, or thee?

---

1. Pope's friend, who had thus far neglected to keep his part of their friendly bargain: Pope was to write his philosophical speculations in verse, Bolingbroke was to write his in prose.   2. Compare Milton's *Paradise Lost* I.26. Pope's theme is essentially the same as Milton's, and even the opening image of the garden reminds us of the earlier poet's Paradise.   3. A reference to the popular eighteenth-century notion of the Great Chain of Being, in which elements of the universe took their places in a hierarchy ranging from the lowest matter to God.

II. Presumptuous Man! the reason wouldst thou find,   35
Why formed so weak, so little, and so blind?
First, if thou canst, the harder reason guess,
Why formed no weaker, blinder, and no less?
Ask of thy mother earth, why oaks are made
Taller or stronger than the weeds they shade?   40
Or ask of yonder argent fields above,
Why Jove's satellites[4] are less than JOVE?
  Of Systems possible, if 'tis confest.
That Wisdom infinite must form the best,
Where all must full[5] or not coherent be,   45
And all that rises, rise in due degree;
Then, in the scale of reasoning life, 'tis plain,
There must be, somewhere, such a rank as Man:
And all the question (wrangle e'er so long)
Is only this, if God has placed him wrong?   50
  Respecting Man, whatever wrong we call,
May, must be right, as relative to all.
In human works, though laboured on with pain,
A thousand movements scarce one purpose gain;
In God's, one single can its end produce;   55
Yet serves to second too some other use.
So Man, who here seems principal alone,
Perhaps acts second to some sphere unknown,
Touches some wheel, or verges to some goal;
'Tis but a part we see, and not a whole.   60
  When the proud steed shall know why Man restrains
His fiery course, or drives him o'er the plains;
When the dull Ox, why now he breaks the clod,
Is now a victim, and now Egypt's God:
Then shall Man's pride and dullness comprehend   65
His actions', passions', being's use and end;
Why doing, suffering, checked, impelled; and why
This hour a slave, the next a deity.
  Then say not Man's imperfect, Heaven in fault;
Say rather, Man's as perfect as he ought: 70
His knowledge measured to his state and place;
His time a moment, and a point his space.
If to be perfect in a certain sphere,
What matter, soon or late, or here or there?
The blest to-day is as completely so,   75
As who began a thousand years ago.

  III. Heaven from all creatures hides the book of Fate,
All but the page prescribed, their present state:
From brutes what men, from men what spirits know:
Or who could suffer Being here below?   80
The lamb thy riot dooms to bleed to-day,

---

4. Here pronounced satéllités.   5. According to the principle of plenitude, there can be no gaps in the Chain.

Had he thy Reason, would he skip and play?
Pleased to the last, he crops the flowery food,
And licks the hand just raised to shed his blood.
Oh blindness to the future! kindly given,   85
That each may fill the circle marked by Heaven:
Who sees with equal eye, as God of all,
A hero perish, or a sparrow fall,
Atoms or systems into ruin hurled,
And now a bubble burst, and now a world.   90
    Hope humbly then; with trembling pinions soar;
Wait the great teacher Death; and God adore.
What future bliss, he gives not thee to know,
But gives that Hope to be thy blessing now.
Hope springs eternal in the human breast: 95
Man never Is, but always To be blest:
The soul, uneasy and confined from home,
Rests and expatiates in a life to come.
    Lo, the poor Indian! whose untutored mind
Sees God in clouds, or hears him in the wind;   100
His soul, proud Science never taught to stray
Far as the solar walk, or milky way;
Yet simple Nature to his hope has given,
Behind the cloud-topt hill, an humbler heaven;
Some safer world in depth of woods embraced,   105
Some happier island in the watery waste,
Where slaves once more their native land behold,
No fiends torment, no Christians thirst for gold.
To Be, contents his natural desire,
He asks no Angel's wing, no Seraph's fire;   110
But thinks, admitted to that equal sky,
His faithful dog shall bear him company.

    IV. Go, wiser thou! and, in thy scale of sense,
Weigh thy Opinion against Providence;
Call imperfection what thou fanciest such,   115
Say, here he gives too little, there too much:
Destroy all Creatures for thy sport or gust,
Yet cry, If Man's unhappy, God's unjust;
If Man alone engross not Heaven's high care,
Alone made perfect here, immortal there: 120
Snatch from his hand the balance and the rod,
Re-judge his justice, be the GOD of GOD.
In Pride, in reasoning Pride, our error lies;
All quit their sphere, and rush into the skies.
Pride still is aiming at the blest abodes,   125
Men would be Angels, Angels would be Gods.
Aspiring to be Gods, if Angels fell,
Aspiring to be Angels, Men rebel:
And who but wishes to invert the laws
Of ORDER, sins against the Eternal Cause.   130

V. Ask for what end the heavenly bodies shine,
Earth for whose use? Pride answers, "'Tis for mine:
For me kind Nature wakes her genial Power,
Suckles each herb, and spreads out ev'ry flower;
Annual for me, the grape, the rose, renew,   135
The juice nectareous, and the balmy dew;
For me, the mine a thousand treasures brings;
For me, health gushes from a thousand springs;
Seas roll to waft me, suns to light me rise;
My footstool earth, my canopy the skies."   140
        But errs not Nature from this gracious end,
From burning suns when livid deaths descend,
When earthquakes swallow, or when tempests sweep
Towns to one grave, whole nations to the deep?
"No," 'tis replied, "the first Almighty Cause   145
Acts not by partial, but by general laws;
The exceptions few; some change since all began:
And what created perfect?"—Why then Man?
If the great end be human happiness,
Then Nature deviates; and can man do less?   150
As much that end a constant course requires
Of showers and sunshine, as of man's desires;
As much eternal springs and cloudless skies,
As Men forever temperate, calm, and wise.
If plagues or earthquakes break not Heaven's design,   155
Why then a Borgia, or a Catiline?[6]
Who knows but He whose hand the lightning forms,
Who heaves old Ocean, and who wings the storms;
Pours fierce Ambition in a Caesar's mind,
Or turns young Ammon[7] loose to scourge mankind?   160
From pride, from pride, our very reasoning springs;
Account for moral, as for natural things:
Why charge we Heaven in those, in these acquit?
In both, to reason right is to submit.
        Better for Us, perhaps, it might appear,   165
Where there all harmony, all virtue here;
That never air or ocean felt the wind;
That never passion discomposed the mind.
But ALL subsists by elemental strife;
And Passions are the elements of Life.   170
The general ORDER, since the whole began,
Is kept in Nature, and is kept in Man.

        VI. What would this Man? Now upward will he soar,
And little less than Angel, would be more;

6. Roman who conspired against the state in 63 B.C. Cesare Borgia (1476–1507) was an Italian prince notorious for his crimes.   7. Alexander the Great, who when he visited the oracle of Zeus Ammon in Egypt was hailed by the priest there as son of the god.

Now looking downwards, just as grieved appears   175
To want the strength of bulls, the fur of bears.
Made for his use all creatures if he call,
Say what their use, had he the powers of all?
Nature to these, without profusion, kind,
The proper organs, proper powers assigned;   180
Each seeming want compénsated of course,
Here with degrees of swiftness, there of force;
All in exact proportion to the state;
Nothing to add, and nothing to abate.
Each beast, each insect, happy in its own: 185
Is Heaven unkind to Man, and Man alone?
Shall he alone, whom rational we call,
Be pleased with nothing, if not blessed with all?
    The bliss of Man (could Pride that blessing find)
Is not to act or think beyond mankind;   190
No powers of body or of soul to share,
But what his nature and his state can bear.
Why has not Man a microscopic eye?
For this plain reason, Man is not a Fly.
Say what the use, were finer optics[8] given,   195
T' inspect a mite, not comprehend the heaven?
Or touch, if tremblingly alive all o'er,
To smart and agonize at every pore?
Or quick effluvia[9] darting through the brain,
Die of a rose in aromatic pain?   200
If nature thundered in his opening ears,
And stunned him with the music of the spheres,[1]
How would he wish that Heaven had left him still
The whispering Zephyr, and the purling rill?
Who finds not Providence all good and wise,   205
Alike in what it gives, and what denies?

    VII. Far as Creation's ample range extends,
The scale of sensual, mental powers ascends:
Mark how it mounts, to Man's imperial race,
From the green myriads in the peopled grass: 210
What modes of sight betwixt each wide extreme,
The mole's dim curtain, and the lynx's[2] beam:
Of smell, the headlong lioness between,
And hound sagacious[3] on the tainted green:
Of hearing, from the life that fills the Flood,   215
To that which warbles through the vernal wood:
The spider's touch, how exquisítely fine!
Feels at each thread, and lives along the line:
In the nice bee, what sense so subtly true

---

8. Eyes.   9. Stream of minute particles.   1. The old notion that the movement of the planets created
a "higher" music.   2. Legend made this animal one of the keenest sighted. *Dim curtain*: the mole's
poor vision.   3. Here meaning "exceptionally quick of scent."

From poisonous herbs extracts the healing dew?   220
How Instinct varies in the grovelling swine,
Compared, half-reasoning elephant, with thine!
'Twixt that, and Reason, what a nice barriér,
For ever separate, yet for ever near!
Remembrance and Reflection how allied;   225
What thin partitions Sense from Thought divide:
And Middle natures,[4] how they long to join,
Yet never pass the insuperable line!
Without this just gradation, could they be
Subjected, these to those, or all to thee?   230
The powers of all subdued by thee alone,
Is not thy Reason all these powers in one?

    VIII. See, through this air, this ocean, and this earth,
All matter quick, and bursting into birth.
Above, how high, progressive life may go!   235
Around, how wide! how deep extend below!
Vast chain of Being! which from God began,
Natures ethereal, human, angel, man,
Beast, bird, fish, insect, what no eye can see,
No glass can reach; from Infinite to thee,   240
From thee to Nothing.—On superior powers
Were we to press, inferior might on ours:
Or in the full creation leave a void,
Where, one step broken, the great scale's destroyed:
From Nature's chain whatever link you strike,   245
Tenth or ten thousandth, breaks the chain alike.
    And, if each system in gradation roll
Alike essential to the amazing Whole,
The least confusion but in one, not all
That system only, but the Whole must fall.   250
Let Earth unbalanced from her orbit fly,
Planets and Suns run lawless through the sky;
Let ruling angels from their spheres be hurled,
Being on Being wrecked, and world on world;
Heaven's whole foundations to their center nod,   255
And Nature tremble to the throne of God.
All this dread ORDER break—for whom? for thee?
Vile worm!—oh Madness! Pride! Impiety!

    IX. What if the foot, ordained the dust to tread,
Or hand, to toil, aspired to be the head?   260
What if the head, the eye, or ear repined
To serve mere engines to the ruling Mind?
Just as absurd for any part to claim
To be another, in this general frame:

---

4. Animals that seem to share the characteristics of several different classes, for example, the duck-billed platypus.

Just as absurd, to mourn the tasks or pains,   265
The great directing MIND of ALL ordains.
  All are but parts of one stupendous whole,
Whose body Nature is, and God the soul;
That, changed through all, and yet in all the same;
Great in the earth, as in the ethereal frame;   270
Warms in the sun, refreshes in the breeze,
Glows in the stars, and blossoms in the trees,
Lives through all life, extends through all extent,
Spreads undivided, operates unspent;
Breathes in our soul, informs our mortal part,   275
As full, as perfect, in a hair as heart;
As full, as perfect, in vile Man that mourns,
As the rapt Seraph that adores and burns:
To him no high, no low, no great, no small;
He fills, he bounds, connects, and equals all.   280

  X. Cease then, nor ORDER imperfection name:
Our proper bliss depends on what we blame.
Know thy own point: this kind, this due degree
Of blindness, weakness, Heaven bestows on thee.
Submit.—In this, or any other sphere,   285
Secure to be as blest as thou canst bear:
Safe in the hand of one disposing Power,
Or in the natal, or the mortal hour.
All Nature is but Art, unknown to thee;
All Chance, Direction, which thou canst not see;   290
All Discord, Harmony not understood;
All partial Evil, universal Good:
And, spite of Pride, in erring Reason's spite,
One truth is clear, WHATEVER IS, IS RIGHT.[5]

FRANÇOIS-MARIE AROUET DE VOLTAIRE
1694–1778

Voltaire's *Candide* (1759) brings to near perfection the art of black comedy. It subjects its characters to an accumulation of horrors so bizarre that they provoke a bewildered response of laughter as self-protection—even while they demand that the reader pay attention to the serious implications of such extravagance.

  Voltaire had prepared himself to write such a work by varied experience—including that of political imprisonment. He was born François-Marie Arouet, son of a minor treasury official in Paris. After attending a Jesuit school, he took up the study of law, which, however, he soon abandoned. In his early twenties (1717–18), he spent eleven months in the Bastille for writing satiric verses about the

---

5. Epistle II deals with "the Nature and State of Man with respect to himself, as an Individual"; Epistle III examines "the Nature and State of Man with respect to Society"; and the last epistle concerns "the Nature and State of Man with Respect to Happiness."

aristocracy. His incarceration did not dissuade him from a literary career; by 1718 he was using the name *Voltaire* and beginning to acquire literary and social reputation—as well as some wealth (his speculations in the Compagnie des Indes made him rich by 1726). Money, however, did not protect him from spending more time in the Bastille during that year; after his release, he passed three years in exile, mainly in England. From 1734 to 1749, he studied widely, living with Madame du Châtelet on her estate at Cirey. For the next three years he stayed with Frederick the Great of Prussia at his Potsdam court; after that arrangement collapsed, Voltaire bought property in Switzerland and in adjacent France, settling first at his own château, Les Delices, outside Geneva, and later at nearby Ferney, in France. His international reputation as writer and social critic steadily increased; in the year of his death, he returned triumphantly to Paris.

Like his English contemporary Samuel Johnson, Voltaire wrote in many important genres: tragedy, epic, history, philosophy, fiction. His *Philosophical Dictionary* (1764), with its witty and penetrating definitions, typifies his range and acumen and his participation in his period's effort to take control of experience by intellect. While still a young man, Voltaire wrote a *History of Charles XII* of Sweden, a work unusual for its time in its novelistic technique and its assumption that "history" includes the personal lives of powerful individuals and has nothing to do with divine intervention. Before *Candide* he had published another philosophic tale, *Zadig* (1748), following the pattern of Oriental narrative. Like Candide, Zadig goes through an experiential education; it teaches him inconclusive lessons about life's unforeseeable contingencies.

Candide mocks both the artificial order of fiction (through its ludicrously multiplied recognition scenes and its symmetrical division of the protagonist's travels into three equal parts) and what Voltaire suggests is the equally artificial order posited by philosophic optimists. The view of the universe suggested by Pope's *Essay on Man*, for instance, insists on the rationality of a pattern ungraspable by human reason. *Candide* implicitly argues, however, that it does so only by attending to the abstract and undemonstrable and ignoring the omnipresent pain of immediate experience. Gottfried Leibniz, the German philosopher, provides Voltaire's most specific target in *Candide*, with the complexities of his version of optimism reduced for satiric purposes to the facile formula "Everything is for the best in this best of all possible worlds." The formulation is of course unfair to Leibniz, whose philosophic optimism, like Pope's, implies belief in an unknowable universal order—roughly equivalent to Christian Providence—but no lack of awareness about the actual misery and depravity human beings experience.

The exuberance and extravagance of Voltaire's imagination force us to laugh at what we may feel embarrassed to laugh at: the plight of the woman whose buttock has been cut off to make rump steak for her hungry companions, the weeping of two girls whose monkey-lovers have been killed, the situation of six exiled, poverty-stricken kings. Like Swift, Voltaire keeps his readers off balance. Raped, cut to pieces, hanged, stabbed in the belly, the central characters of *Candide* keep coming back to life at opportune moments, as though no disaster could have permanent or ultimately destructive effects. Such reassuring fantasy suggests that we don't need to worry, it is all a joke, an outpouring of fertile fancy designed to ridicule an outmoded philosophic system with no particular relevance to us. On the other hand, historical reality keeps intruding. Those six hungry kings are real, actual figures, actually dispossessed. Candide sees Admiral Byng executed: an admiral who really lived and really died by firing squad for not engaging an enemy with sufficient ferocity. The Lisbon earthquake actually occurred; thirty to forty thousand people lost their lives in it. The extravagances of reality equal those of the storyteller; Voltaire demands that the reader imaginatively confront and somehow come to terms with horrors that surround us still.

✕ The real problem, *Candide* suggests, is not natural or human disaster so much as human complacency. When Candide sees Admiral Byng shot, he comments on the injustice of the execution. "That's perfectly true, came the answer; but in this country it is useful from time to time to kill one admiral in order to encourage the others." Early in the nineteenth century, William Wordsworth wrote, "much it grieved my heart to think / What man has made of man." His tone and perspective differ dramatically from Voltaire's, but his point is the same: human beings use their faculties to increase corruption. Failure to take seriously any human death is a form of moral corruption; failure to acknowledge the intolerability of war, in all its concrete detail of rape and butchery, epitomizes such corruption at its worst.

In a late chapter of *Candide*, the central character, less naïve than he once was, inquires about whether people have always massacred one another. Have they, he asks, "always been liars, traitors, ingrates, thieves, weaklings, sneaks, cowards, backbiters, gluttons, drunkards, misers, climbers, killers, calumniators, sensualists, fanatics, hypocrites, and fools?" His interlocutor, Martin, responds that, just as hawks have always devoured pigeons, human beings have always manifested the same vices. This ironic variation on the period's conviction of the universality and continuity of human nature epitomizes Voltaire's sense of outrage, which in some respects parallels Swift's in the fourth part of *Gulliver's Travels*. Swift demonstrates the implications of "reason" considered as an ideal and shows its irrelevance to actual human behavior; Voltaire shows how the claim of a rational universal order avoids the hard problems of living in a world where human beings have become liars, traitors, and so on. His Swiftian catalog of vice and folly expresses the moral insufficiency and perversity of humankind. Martin's cynical assumption that people are naturally corrupt, as hawks naturally eat smaller birds, constitutes another form of avoidance. The assumed inevitability of vice, like belief that all is for the best, justifies passivity. Nothing *can* be done, nothing *should* be done, or nothing *matters* (the view of Lord Pococurante, another figure Candide encounters). So the characters of this fiction, including Candide himself, mainly pursue self-gratification. Even this course they do not follow judiciously: when Candide and Cacambo find themselves in the earthly paradise of Eldorado, "the two happy men resolved to be so no longer," driven by fantasies of improving their condition. Yet, unlike Gulliver, they acquire wisdom at last, learning to withstand "three great evils, boredom, vice, and poverty," by working hard at what comes to hand and avoiding futile theorizing about the nature of the universe.

Although Voltaire's picture of the human condition reveals the same indignation that marks Swift's, he allows at least conditional hope for moderate satisfaction in this life. Candide's beloved Cunégonde loses all her beauty, but she becomes an accomplished pastry cook; Candide possesses a garden he can cultivate. Greed, malice, and lust do not comprise the total possibility for humankind. If Voltaire's tone sometimes expresses outrage, at other times it verges on the playful. When, for example, he mocks the improbabilities of romance by his characters' miraculous resuscitations or parodies the restrictions of classical form by sending Candide and his friends on an epic journey, one can feel his amused awareness of our human need to make order and our human desire to comfort ourselves by fictions. But as he insists that much of the order we claim to perceive itself comprises a comforting fiction, as he uses satire's fierce energies to challenge our complacencies, he reveals once more the underside of the Enlightenment ideal of reason. That we human beings have reason, Voltaire tells us, is no ground on which to flatter ourselves; rightly used, it exposes our insufficiencies.

Biographies and critical studies of Voltaire include R. Aldington, *Voltaire* (1934); G. Brandes, *The Life of Voltaire* (undated); I. O. Wade, *Voltaire and "Candide"* (1959); and T. Besterman, *Voltaire* (1969). A good general introduction is

P. E. Richter and Ilona Ricardo, *Voltaire* (1980). A work placing Voltaire in a broad context is F. M. Keener, *The Chain of Becoming* (1983), on Voltaire and his English contemporaries. For a collection of essays by various writers, see M. Culler, ed., *Voltaire: The Enlightenment and the Comic Mode* (1990).

PRONOUNCING GLOSSARY

The following list uses common English syllables and stress accents to provide rough equivalents of selected words whose pronunciation may be unfamiliar to the general reader.

Abare: *a-bahr'*	Pangloss: *pan-gloos'*
Cacambo: *ka-kahm'-bo*	Paquette: *pah-ket'*
Candide: *kahn-deed'*	Pococurante: *poh-koh-ku-rahn'-te*
Cunégonde: *koon-e-gond'*	Thunder-Ten-Tronckh: *tun-dayr'–ten– trawnk*
Giroflée: *jee-roh-flay'*	
Issachar: *ee-sahk-ahr'*	

Candide, or Optimism[1]

translated from the German of Doctor Ralph with the additions which were found in the Doctor's pocket when he died at Minden in the Year of Our Lord 1759

CHAPTER 1

How Candide Was Brought up in a Fine Castle and How He Was Driven Therefrom

There lived in Westphalia,[2] in the castle of the Baron of Thunder-Ten-Tronckh, a young man on whom nature had bestowed the perfection of gentle manners. His features admirably expressed his soul; he combined an honest mind with great simplicity of heart; and I think it was for this reason that they called him Candide. The old servants of the house suspected that he was the son of the Baron's sister by a respectable, honest gentleman of the neighborhood, whom she had refused to marry because he could prove only seventy-one quarterings,[3] the rest of his family tree having been lost in the passage of time.

The Baron was one of the most mighty lords of Westphalia, for his castle had a door and windows. His great hall was even hung with a tapestry. The dogs of his courtyard made up a hunting pack on occasion, with the stableboys as huntsmen; the village priest was his grand almoner. They all called him "My Lord," and laughed at his stories.

The Baroness, who weighed in the neighborhood of three hundred and fifty pounds, was greatly respected for that reason, and did the honors of the house with a dignity which rendered her even more imposing. Her

---

1. Translated and with notes by Robert M. Adams.   **2.** A province of western Germany, near Holland and the lower Rhineland. Flat, boggy, and drab, it is noted chiefly for its excellent ham. In a letter to his niece, written during his German expedition of 1750, Voltaire described the "vast, sad, sterile, detestable countryside of Westphalia."   **3.** Genealogical divisions of one's family-tree. Seventy-one of them is a grotesque number to have, representing something over 2,000 years of uninterrupted nobility.

daughter Cunégonde,[4] aged seventeen, was a ruddy-cheeked girl, fresh, plump, and desirable. The Baron's son seemed in every way worthy of his father. The tutor Pangloss was the oracle of the household, and little Candide listened to his lectures with all the good faith of his age and character.

Pangloss gave instruction in metaphysico-theologico-cosmoloonigology.[5] He proved admirably that there cannot possibly be an effect without a cause and that in this best of all possible worlds the Baron's castle was the best of all castles and his wife the best of all possible Baronesses.

—It is clear, said he, that things cannot be otherwise than they are, for since everything is made to serve an end, everything necessarily serves the best end. Observe: noses were made to support spectacles, hence we have spectacles. Legs, as anyone can plainly see, were made to be breeched, and so we have breeches. Stones were made to be shaped and to build castles with; thus My Lord has a fine castle, for the greatest Baron in the province should have the finest house; and since pigs were made to be eaten, we eat pork all year round.[6] Consequently, those who say everything is well are uttering mere stupidities; they should say everything is for the best.

Candide listened attentively and believed implicitly; for he found Miss Cunégonde exceedingly pretty, though he never had the courage to tell her so. He decided that after the happiness of being born Baron of Thunder-Ten-Tronckh, the second order of happiness was to be Miss Cunégonde; the third was seeing her every day, and the fourth was listening to Master Pangloss, the greatest philosopher in the province and consequently in the entire world.

One day, while Cunégonde was walking near the castle in the little woods that they called a park, she saw Dr. Pangloss in the underbrush; he was giving a lesson in experimental physics to her mother's maid, a very attractive and obedient brunette. As Miss Cunégonde had a natural bent for the sciences, she watched breathlessly the repeated experiments which were going on; she saw clearly the doctor's sufficient reason, observed both cause and effect, and returned to the house in a distracted and pensive frame of mind, yearning for knowledge and dreaming that she might be the sufficient reason of young Candide—who might also be hers.

As she was returning to the castle, she met Candide, and blushed; Candide blushed too. She greeted him in a faltering tone of voice; and Candide talked to her without knowing what he was saying. Next day, as everyone was rising from the dinner table, Cunégonde and Candide found themselves behind a screen; Cunégonde dropped her handkerchief, Candide picked it up; she held his hand quite innocently, he kissed her hand quite innocently with remarkable vivacity and emotion; their lips met, their eyes lit up, their knees trembled, their hands wandered. The Baron

---

4. Cunégonde gets her odd name from Kunigunda (wife to Emperor Henry II) who walked barefoot and blindfolded on red-hot irons to prove her chastity; Pangloss gets his name from Greek words meaning all-tongue.   5. The "looney" buried in this burlesque word corresponds to a buried *nigaud*—"booby" in the French. Christian Wolff, disciple of Leibniz, invented and popularized the word "cosmology." The catch phrases in the following sentence, echoed by popularizers of Leibniz, make reference to the determinism of his system, its linking of cause with effect, and its optimism.   6. The argument from design supposes that everything in this world exists for a specific reason; Voltaire objects not to the argument as a whole, but to the abuse of it.

of Thunder-Ten-Tronckh passed by the screen and, taking note of this cause and this effect, drove Candide out of the castle by kicking him vigorously on the backside. Cunégonde fainted; as soon as she recovered, the Baroness slapped her face; and everything was confusion in the most beautiful and agreeable of all possible castles.

CHAPTER 2

What Happened to Candide Among the Bulgars[7]

Candide, ejected from the earthly paradise, wandered for a long time without knowing where he was going, weeping, raising his eyes to heaven, and gazing back frequently on the most beautiful of castles which contained the most beautiful of Baron's daughters. He slept without eating, in a furrow of a plowed field, while the snow drifted over him; next morning, numb with cold, he dragged himself into the neighboring village, which was called Waldberghoff-trarbk-dikdorff; he was penniless, famished, and exhausted. At the door of a tavern he paused forlornly. Two men dressed in blue[8] took note of him:

—Look, chum, said one of them, there's a likely young fellow of just about the right size.

They approached Candide and invited him very politely to dine with them.

—Gentlemen, Candide replied with charming modesty, I'm honored by your invitation, but I really don't have enough money to pay my share.

—My dear sir, said one of the blues, people of your appearance and your merit don't have to pay; aren't you five feet five inches tall?

—Yes, gentlemen, that is indeed my stature, said he, making a bow.

—Then, sir, you must be seated at once; not only will we pay your bill this time, we will never allow a man like you to be short of money; for men were made only to render one another mutual aid.

—You are quite right, said Candide; it is just as Dr. Pangloss always told me, and I see clearly that everything is for the best.

They beg him to accept a couple of crowns, he takes them, and offers an I.O.U.; they won't hear of it, and all sit down at table together.

—Don't you love dearly . . . ?

—I do indeed, says he, I dearly love Miss Cunégonde.

—No, no, says one of the gentlemen, we are asking if you don't love dearly the King of the Bulgars.

—Not in the least, says he, I never laid eyes on him.

—What's that you say? He's the most charming of kings, and we must drink his health.

—Oh, gladly, gentlemen; and he drinks.

—That will do, they tell him; you are now the bulwark, the support, the defender, the hero of the Bulgars; your fortune is made and your future assured.

7. Voltaire chose this name to represent the Prussian troops of Frederick the Great because he wanted to make an insinuation of pederasty against both the soldiers and their master. Cf. French *bougre*, English "bugger."   8. The recruiting officers of Frederick the Great, much feared in eighteenth-century Europe, wore blue uniforms. Frederick had a passion for sorting out his soldiers by size; several of his regiments would accept only six-footers.

Promptly they slip irons on his legs and lead him to the regiment. There they cause him to right face, left face, present arms, order arms, aim, fire, doubletime, and they give him thirty strokes of the rod. Next day he does the drill a little less awkwardly and gets only twenty strokes; the third day, they give him only ten, and he is regarded by his comrades as a prodigy.

Candide, quite thunderstruck, did not yet understand very clearly how he was a hero. One fine spring morning he took it into his head to go for a walk, stepping straight out as if it were a privilege of the human race, as of animals in general, to use his legs as he chose.[9] He had scarcely covered two leagues when four other heroes, each six feet tall, overtook him, bound him, and threw him into a dungeon. At the court-martial they asked which he preferred, to be flogged thirty-six times by the entire regiment or to receive summarily a dozen bullets in the brain. In vain did he argue that the human will is free and insist that he preferred neither alternative; he had to choose; by virtue of the divine gift called "liberty" he decided to run the gauntlet thirty-six times, and actually endured two floggings. The regiment was composed of two thousand men. That made four thousand strokes, which laid open every muscle and nerve from his nape to his butt. As they were preparing for the third beating, Candide, who could endure no more, begged as a special favor that they would have the goodness to smash his head. His plea was granted; they bandaged his eyes and made him kneel down. The King of the Bulgars, passing by at this moment, was told of the culprit's crime; and as this king had a rare genius, he understood, from everything they told him of Candide, that this was a young metaphysician, extremely ignorant of the ways of the world, so he granted his royal pardon, with a generosity which will be praised in every newspaper in every age. A worthy surgeon cured Candide in three weeks with the ointments described by Dioscorides.[1] He already had a bit of skin back and was able to walk when the King of the Bulgars went to war with the King of the Abares.[2]

CHAPTER 3

How Candide Escaped from the Bulgars, and What Became of Him

Nothing could have been so fine, so brisk, so brilliant, so well-drilled as the two armies. The trumpets, the fifes, the oboes, the drums, and the cannon produced such a harmony as was never heard in hell. First the cannons battered down about six thousand men on each side; then volleys of musket fire removed from the best of worlds about nine or ten thousand rascals who were cluttering up its surface. The bayonet was a sufficient reason for the demise of several thousand others. Total casualties might well amount to thirty thousand men or so. Candide, who was trembling

---

9. This episode was suggested by the experience of a Frenchman named Courtilz, who had deserted from the Prussian army and been bastinadoed for it. Voltaire intervened with Frederick to gain his release. But it also reflects the story that Wolff, Leibniz's disciple, got into trouble with Frederick's father when someone reported that his doctrine denying free will had encouraged several soldiers to desert. "The argument of the grenadier," who was said to have pleaded preestablished harmony to justify his desertion, so infuriated the king that he had Wolff expelled from the country.   1. Dioscorides' treatise on *materia medica*, dating from the first century A.D., was not the most up to date.   2. A tribe of semicivilized Scythians, who might be supposed at war with the Bulgars; allegorically, the Abares are the French, who opposed the Prussians in the Seven Years' War (1756–63). According to the title page of 1761, "Doctor Ralph," the dummy author of *Candide*, himself perished at the battle of Minden (Westphalia) in 1759.

like a philosopher, hid himself as best he could while this heroic butchery was going on.

Finally, while the two kings in their respective camps celebrated the victory by having *Te Deums* sung, Candide undertook to do his reasoning of cause and effect somewhere else. Passing by mounds of the dead and dying, he came to a nearby village which had been burnt to the ground. It was an Abare village, which the Bulgars had burned, in strict accordance with the laws of war. Here old men, stunned from beatings, watched the last agonies of their butchered wives, who still clutched their infants to their bleeding breasts; there, disemboweled girls, who had first satisfied the natural needs of various heroes, breathed their last; others, half-scorched in the flames, begged for their death stroke. Scattered brains and severed limbs littered the ground.

Candide fled as fast as he could to another village; this one belonged to the Bulgars, and the heroes of the Abare cause had given it the same treatment. Climbing over ruins and stumbling over corpses, Candide finally made his way out of the war area, carrying a little food in his knapsack and never ceasing to dream of Miss Cunégonde. His supplies gave out when he reached Holland; but having heard that everyone in that country was rich and a Christian, he felt confident of being treated as well as he had been in the castle of the Baron before he was kicked out for the love of Miss Cunégonde.

He asked alms of several grave personages, who all told him that if he continued to beg, he would be shut up in a house of correction and set to hard labor.

Finally he approached a man who had just been talking to a large crowd for an hour on end; the topic was charity. Looking doubtfully at him, the orator demanded:

—What are you doing here? Are you here to serve the good cause?

—There is no effect without a cause, said Candide modestly; all events are linked by the chain of necessity and arranged for the best. I had to be driven away from Miss Cunégonde, I had to run the gauntlet, I have to beg my bread until I can earn it; none of this could have happened otherwise.

—Look here, friend, said the orator, do you think the Pope is Antichrist?[3]

—I haven't considered the matter, said Candide; but whether he is or not, I'm in need of bread.

—You don't deserve any, said the other; away with you, you rascal, you rogue, never come near me as long as you live.

Meanwhile, the orator's wife had put her head out of the window, and, seeing a man who was not sure the Pope was Antichrist, emptied over his head a pot full of—— Scandalous! The excesses into which women are led by religious zeal!

A man who had never been baptized, a good Anabaptist[4] named Jacques, saw this cruel and heartless treatment being inflicted on one of

---

3. Voltaire is satirizing extreme Protestant sects that have sometimes seemed to make hatred of Rome the sum and substance of their creed.   4. Holland, as the home of religious liberty, had offered asylum to the Anabaptists, whose radical views on property and religious discipline had made them unpopular during the sixteenth century. Granted tolerance, they settled down into respectable burghers. Since this behavior confirmed some of Voltaire's major theses, he had a high opinion of contemporary Anabaptists.

his fellow creatures, a featherless biped possessing a soul;[5] he took Candide home with him, washed him off, gave him bread and beer, presented him with two florins, and even undertook to give him a job in his Persian-rug factory—for these items are widely manufactured in Holland. Candide, in an ecstasy of gratitude, cried out:

—Master Pangloss was right indeed when he told me everything is for the best in this world; for I am touched by your kindness far more than by the harshness of that black-coated gentleman and his wife.

Next day, while taking a stroll about town, he met a beggar who was covered with pustules, his eyes were sunken, the end of his nose rotted off, his mouth twisted, his teeth black, he had a croaking voice and a hacking cough, and spat a tooth every time he tried to speak.

CHAPTER 4

How Candide Met His Old Philosophy Tutor, Doctor Pangloss, and What Came of It

Candide, more touched by compassion even than by horror, gave this ghastly beggar the two florins that he himself had received from his honest Anabaptist friend Jacques. The phantom stared at him, burst into tears, and fell on his neck. Candide drew back in terror.

—Alas, said one wretch to the other, don't you recognize your dear Pangloss any more?

—What are you saying? You, my dear master! you, in this horrible condition? What misfortune has befallen you? Why are you no longer in the most beautiful of castles? What has happened to Miss Cunégonde, that pearl among young ladies, that masterpiece of Nature?

—I am perishing, said Pangloss.

Candide promptly led him into the Anabaptist's stable, where he gave him a crust of bread, and when he had recovered:—Well, said he, Cunégonde?

—Dead, said the other.

Candide fainted. His friend brought him around with a bit of sour vinegar which happened to be in the stable. Candide opened his eyes.

—Cunégonde, dead! Ah, best of worlds, what's become of you now? But how did she die? It wasn't of grief at seeing me kicked out of her noble father's elegant castle?

—Not at all, said Pangloss; she was disemboweled by the Bulgar soldiers, after having been raped to the absolute limit of human endurance; they smashed the Baron's head when he tried to defend her, cut the Baroness to bits, and treated my poor pupil exactly like his sister. As for the castle, not one stone was left on another, not a shed, not a sheep, not a duck, not a tree; but we had the satisfaction of revenge, for the Abares did exactly the same thing to a nearby barony belonging to a Bulgar nobleman.

At this tale Candide fainted again; but having returned to his senses and

---

5. Plato's famous minimal definition of man, which he corrected by the addition of a soul to distinguish man from a plucked chicken.

said everything appropriate to the occasion, he asked about the cause and effect, the sufficient reason, which had reduced Pangloss to his present pitiful state.

—Alas, said he, it was love; love, the consolation of the human race, the preservative of the universe, the soul of all sensitive beings, love, gentle love.

—Unhappy man, said Candide, I too have had some experience of this love, the sovereign of hearts, the soul of our souls; and it never got me anything but a single kiss and twenty kicks in the rear. How could this lovely cause produce in you such a disgusting effect?

Pangloss replied as follows: —My dear Candide! you knew Paquette, that pretty maidservant to our august Baroness. In her arms I tasted the delights of paradise, which directly caused these torments of hell, from which I am now suffering. She was infected with the disease, and has perhaps died of it. Paquette received this present from an erudite Franciscan, who took the pains to trace it back to its source; for he had it from an elderly countess, who picked it up from a captain of cavalry, who acquired it from a marquise, who caught it from a page, who had received it from a Jesuit, who during his novitiate got it directly from one of the companions of Christopher Columbus. As for me, I shall not give it to anyone, for I am a dying man.

—Oh, Pangloss, cried Candide, that's a very strange genealogy. Isn't the devil at the root of the whole thing?

—Not at all, replied that great man; it's an indispensable part of the best of worlds, a necessary ingredient; if Columbus had not caught, on an American island, this sickness which attacks the source of generation and sometimes prevents generation entirely—which thus strikes at and defeats the greatest end of Nature herself—we should have neither chocolate nor cochineal. It must also be noted that until the present time this malady, like religious controversy, has been wholly confined to the continent of Europe. Turks, Indians, Persians, Chinese, Siamese, and Japanese know nothing of it as yet; but there is a sufficient reason for which they in turn will make its acquaintance in a couple of centuries. Meanwhile, it has made splendid progress among us, especially among those big armies of honest, well-trained mercenaries who decide the destinies of nations. You can be sure that when thirty thousand men fight a pitched battle against the same number of the enemy, there will be about twenty thousand with the pox on either side.

—Remarkable indeed, said Candide, but we must see about curing you.

—And how can I do that, said Pangloss, seeing I don't have a cent to my name? There's not a doctor in the whole world who will let your blood or give you an enema without demanding a fee. If you can't pay yourself, you must find someone to pay for you.

These last words decided Candide; he hastened to implore the help of his charitable Anabaptist, Jacques, and painted such a moving picture of his friend's wretched state that the good man did not hesitate to take in Pangloss and have him cured at his own expense. In the course of the cure, Pangloss lost only an eye and an ear. Since he wrote a fine hand and knew arithmetic, the Anabaptist made him his bookkeeper. At the end of two months, being obliged to go to Lisbon on business, he took his two philosophers on the boat with him. Pangloss still maintained that everything was for the best, but Jacques didn't agree with him.

—It must be, said he, that men have corrupted Nature, for they are not born wolves, yet that is what they become. God gave them neither twenty-four-pound cannon nor bayonets, yet they have manufactured both in order to destroy themselves. Bankruptcies have the same effect, and so does the justice which seizes the goods of bankrupts in order to prevent the creditors from getting them.[6]

—It was all indispensable, replied the one-eyed doctor, since private misfortunes make for public welfare, and therefore the more private misfortunes there are, the better everything is.

While he was reasoning, the air grew dark, the winds blew from all directions, and the vessel was attacked by a horrible tempest within sight of Lisbon harbor.

CHAPTER 5

Tempest, Shipwreck, Earthquake, and What Happened to Doctor Pangloss, Candide, and the Anabaptist, Jacques

Half of the passengers, weakened by the frightful anguish of seasickness and the distress of tossing about on stormy waters, were incapable of noticing their danger. The other half shrieked aloud and fell to their prayers, the sails were ripped to shreds, the masts snapped, the vessel opened at the seams. Everyone worked who could stir, nobody listened for orders or issued them. The Anabaptist was lending a hand in the after part of the ship when a frantic sailor struck him and knocked him to the deck; but just at that moment, the sailor lurched so violently that he fell head first over the side, where he hung, clutching a fragment of the broken mast. The good Jacques ran to his aid, and helped him to climb back on board, but in the process was himself thrown into the sea under the very eyes of the sailor, who allowed him to drown without even glancing at him. Candide rushed to the rail, and saw his benefactor rise for a moment to the surface, then sink forever. He wanted to dive to his rescue; but the philosopher Pangloss prevented him by proving that the bay of Lisbon had been formed expressly for this Anabaptist to drown in. While he was proving the point *a priori*, the vessel opened up and everyone perished except for Pangloss, Candide, and the brutal sailor who had caused the virtuous Anabaptist to drown; this rascal swam easily to shore, while Pangloss and Candide drifted there on a plank.

When they had recovered a bit of energy, they set out for Lisbon; they still had a little money with which they hoped to stave off hunger after escaping the storm.

Scarcely had they set foot in the town, still bewailing the loss of their benefactor, when they felt the earth quake underfoot; the sea was lashed to a froth, burst into the port, and smashed all the vessels lying at anchor there. Whirlwinds of fire and ash swirled through the streets and public

---

6. Voltaire had suffered losses from various bankruptcy proceedings.

squares; houses crumbled, roofs came crashing down on foundations, foundations split; thirty thousand inhabitants of every age and either sex were crushed in the ruins.[7] The sailor whistled through his teeth, and said with an oath: —There'll be something to pick up here.

—What can be the sufficient reason of this phenomenon? asked Pangloss.

—The Last Judgment is here, cried Candide.

But the sailor ran directly into the middle of the ruins, heedless of danger in his eagerness for gain; he found some money, laid violent hands on it, got drunk, and, having slept off his wine, bought the favors of the first streetwalker he could find amid the ruins of smashed houses, amid corpses and suffering victims on every hand. Pangloss however tugged at his sleeve.

—My friend, said he, this is not good form at all; your behavior falls short of that required by the universal reason; it's untimely, to say the least.

—Bloody hell, said the other, I'm a sailor, born in Batavia; I've been four times to Japan and stamped four times on the crucifix;[8] get out of here with your universal reason.

Some falling stonework had struck Candide; he lay prostrate in the street, covered with rubble, and calling to Pangloss: —For pity's sake bring me a little wine and oil; I'm dying.

—This earthquake is nothing novel, Pangloss replied; the city of Lima, in South America, underwent much the same sort of tremor, last year; same causes, same effects; there is surely a vein of sulphur under the earth's surface reaching from Lima to Lisbon.

—Nothing is more probable, said Candide; but, for God's sake, a little oil and wine.

—What do you mean, probable? replied the philosopher; I regard the case as proved.

Candide fainted and Pangloss brought him some water from a nearby fountain.

Next day, as they wandered amid the ruins, they found a little food which restored some of their strength. Then they fell to work like the others, bringing relief to those of the inhabitants who had escaped death. Some of the citizens whom they rescued gave them a dinner as good as was possible under the circumstances; it is true that the meal was a melancholy one, and the guests watered their bread with tears; but Pangloss consoled them by proving that things could not possibly be otherwise.

—For, said he, all this is for the best, since if there is a volcano at Lisbon, it cannot be somewhere else, since it is unthinkable that things should not be where they are, since everything is well.

A little man in black, an officer of the Inquisition,[9] who was sitting beside him, politely took up the question, and said: —It would seem that

---

7. The great Lisbon earthquake and fire occurred on November 1, 1755; between thirty and forty thousand deaths resulted.   8. The Japanese, originally receptive to foreign visitors, grew fearful that priests and proselytizers were merely advance agents of empire and expelled both the Portuguese and Spanish early in the seventeenth century. Only the Dutch were allowed to retain a small foothold, under humiliating conditions, of which the notion of stamping on the crucifix is symbolic. It was never what Voltaire suggests here, an actual requirement for entering the country.   9. Specifically, a *familier* or *poursuivant*, an undercover agent with powers of arrest.

the gentleman does not believe in original sin, since if everything is for the best, man has not fallen and is not liable to eternal punishment.

—I most humbly beg pardon of your excellency, Pangloss answered, even more politely, but the fall of man and the curse of original sin entered necessarily into the best of all possible worlds.

—Then you do not believe in free will? said the officer.

—Your excellency must excuse me, said Pangloss; free will agrees very well with absolute necessity, for it was necessary that we should be free, since a will which is determined . . .

Pangloss was in the middle of his sentence, when the officer nodded significantly to the attendant who was pouring him a glass of port, or Oporto, wine.

CHAPTER 6

How They Made a Fine Auto-da-Fé to Prevent Earthquakes, and How Candide Was Whipped

After the earthquake had wiped out three quarters of Lisbon, the learned men of the land could find no more effective way of averting total destruction than to give the people a fine auto-da-fé;[1] the University of Coimbra had established that the spectacle of several persons being roasted over a slow fire with full ceremonial rites is an infallible specific against earthquakes.

In consequence, the authorities had rounded up a Biscayan convicted of marrying a woman who had stood godmother to his child, and two Portuguese who while eating a chicken had set aside a bit of bacon used for seasoning.[2] After dinner, men came with ropes to tie up Doctor Pangloss and his disciple Candide, one for talking and the other for listening with an air of approval; both were taken separately to a set of remarkably cool apartments, where the glare of the sun is never bothersome; eight days later they were both dressed in *san-benitos* and crowned with paper mitres;[3] Candide's mitre and *san-benito* were decorated with inverted flames and with devils who had neither tails nor claws; but Pangloss's devils had both tails and claws, and his flames stood upright. Wearing these costumes, they marched in a procession, and listened to a very touching sermon, followed by a beautiful concert of plainsong. Candide was flogged in cadence to the music; the Biscayan and the two men who had avoided bacon were burned, and Pangloss was hanged, though hanging is not customary. On the same day there was another earthquake, causing frightful damage.[4]

Candide, stunned, stupefied, despairing, bleeding, trembling, said to himself: —If this is the best of all possible worlds, what are the others like? The flogging is not so bad, I was flogged by the Bulgars. But oh my dear

---

1. Literally, "act of faith," a public ceremony of repentance and humiliation. Such an auto-da-fé was actually held in Lisbon, June 20, 1756.   2. The Biscayan's fault lay in marrying someone within the forbidden bounds of relationship, an act of spiritual incest. The men who declined pork or bacon were understood to be crypto-Jews.   3. The cone-shaped paper cap (intended to resemble a bishop's mitre) and flowing yellow cape were customary garb for those pleading before the Inquisition.   4. In fact, the second quake occurred December 21, 1755.

Pangloss, greatest of philosophers, was it necessary for me to watch you being hanged, for no reason that I can see? Oh my dear Anabaptist, best of men, was it necessary that you should be drowned in the port? Oh Miss Cunégonde, pearl of young ladies, was it necessary that you should have your belly slit open?

He was being led away, barely able to stand, lectured, lashed, absolved, and blessed, when an old woman approached and said, — My son, be of good cheer and follow me.

CHAPTER 7

How an Old Woman Took Care of Candide, and How He Regained What He Loved

Candide was of very bad cheer, but he followed the old woman to a shanty; she gave him a jar of ointment to rub himself, left him food and drink; she showed him a tidy little bed; next to it was a suit of clothing.

—Eat, drink, sleep, she said; and may Our Lady of Atocha, Our Lord St. Anthony of Padua, and Our Lord St. James of Compostela watch over you. I will be back tomorrow.

Candide, still completely astonished by everything he had seen and suffered, and even more by the old woman's kindness, offered to kiss her hand.

—It's not *my* hand you should be kissing, said she. I'll be back tomorrow; rub yourself with the ointment, eat and sleep.

In spite of his many sufferings, Candide ate and slept. Next day the old woman returned bringing breakfast; she looked at his back and rubbed it herself with another ointment; she came back with lunch; and then she returned in the evening, bringing supper. Next day she repeated the same routine.

—Who are you? Candide asked continually. Who told you to be so kind to me? How can I ever repay you?

The good woman answered not a word; she returned in the evening, and without food.

—Come with me, says she, and don't speak a word.

Taking him by the hand, she walks out into the countryside with him for about a quarter of a mile; they reach an isolated house, quite surrounded by gardens and ditches. The old woman knocks at a little gate, it opens. She takes Candide up a secret stairway to a gilded room furnished with a fine brocaded sofa; there she leaves him, closes the door, disappears. Candide stood as if entranced; his life, which had seemed like a nightmare so far, was now starting to look like a delightful dream.

Soon the old woman returned; on her feeble shoulder leaned a trembling woman, of a splendid figure, glittering in diamonds, and veiled.

—Remove the veil, said the old woman to Candide.

The young man stepped timidly forward, and lifted the veil. What an event! What a surprise! Could it be Miss Cunégonde? Yes, it really was! She herself! His knees give way, speech fails him, he falls at her feet, Cunégonde collapses on the sofa. The old woman plies them with brandy, they return to their senses, they exchange words. At first they could utter only broken phrases, questions and answers at cross purposes, sighs, tears, exclamations. The old woman warned them not to make too much noise, and left them alone.

—Then it's really you, said Candide, you're alive, I've found you again in Portugal. Then you never were raped? You never had your belly ripped open, as the philosopher Pangloss assured me?

—Oh yes, said the lovely Cunégonde, but one doesn't always die of these two accidents.

—But your father and mother were murdered then?

—All too true, said Cunégonde, in tears.

—And your brother?

—Killed too.

—And why are you in Portugal? and how did you know I was here? and by what device did you have me brought to this house?

—I shall tell you everything, the lady replied; but first you must tell me what has happened to you since that first innocent kiss we exchanged and the kicking you got because of it.

Candide obeyed her with profound respect; and though he was overcome, though his voice was weak and hesitant, though he still had twinges of pain from his beating, he described as simply as possible everything that had happened to him since the time of their separation. Cunégonde lifted her eyes to heaven; she wept at the death of the good Anabaptist and at that of Pangloss; after which she told the following story to Candide, who listened to every word while he gazed on her with hungry eyes.

CHAPTER 8

Cunégonde's Story

—I was in my bed and fast asleep when heaven chose to send the Bulgars into our castle of Thunder-Ten-Tronckh. They butchered my father and brother, and hacked my mother to bits. An enormous Bulgar, six feet tall, seeing that I had swooned from horror at the scene, set about raping me; at that I recovered my senses, I screamed and scratched, bit and fought, I tried to tear the eyes out of that big Bulgar—not realizing that everything which had happened in my father's castle was a mere matter of routine. The brute then stabbed me with a knife on my left thigh, where I still bear the scar.

—What a pity! I should very much like to see it, said the simple Candide.

—You shall, said Cunégonde; but shall I go on?

—Please do, said Candide.

So she took up the thread of her tale: —A Bulgar captain appeared, he saw me covered with blood and the soldier too intent to get up. Shocked by the monster's failure to come to attention, the captain killed him on my body. He then had my wound dressed, and took me off to his quarters, as a prisoner of war. I laundered his few shirts and did his cooking; he found me attractive, I confess it, and I won't deny that he was a handsome fellow, with a smooth, white skin; apart from that, however, little wit, little philosophical training; it was evident that he had not been brought up by

Doctor Pangloss. After three months, he had lost all his money and grown sick of me; so he sold me to a Jew named Don Issachar, who traded in Holland and Portugal, and who was mad after women. This Jew developed a mighty passion for my person, but he got nowhere with it; I held him off better than I had done with the Bulgar soldier; for though a person of honor may be raped once, her virtue is only strengthened by the experience. In order to keep me hidden, the Jew brought me to his country house, which you see here. Till then I had thought there was nothing on earth so beautiful as the castle of Thunder-Ten-Tronckh; I was now undeceived.

— One day the Grand Inquisitor took notice of me at mass; he ogled me a good deal, and made known that he must talk to me on a matter of secret business. I was taken to his palace; I told him of my rank; he pointed out that it was beneath my dignity to belong to an Israelite. A suggestion was then conveyed to Don Issachar that he should turn me over to My Lord the Inquisitor. Don Issachar, who is court banker and a man of standing, refused out of hand. The inquisitor threatened him with an auto-da-fé. Finally my Jew, fearing for his life, struck a bargain by which the house and I would belong to both of them as joint tenants; the Jew would get Mondays, Wednesdays, and the Sabbath, the inquisitor would get the other days of the week. That has been the arrangement for six months now. There have been quarrels; sometimes it has not been clear whether the night from Saturday to Sunday belonged to the old or the new dispensation. For my part, I have so far been able to hold both of them off; and that, I think, is why they are both still in love with me.

— Finally, in order to avert further divine punishment by earthquake, and to terrify Don Issachar, My Lord the Inquisitor chose to celebrate an auto-da-fé. He did me the honor of inviting me to attend. I had an excellent seat; the ladies were served with refreshments between the mass and the execution. To tell you the truth, I was horrified to see them burn alive those two Jews and that decent Biscayan who had married his child's godmother; but what was my surprise, my terror, my grief, when I saw, huddled in a *san-benito* and wearing a mitre, someone who looked like Pangloss! I rubbed my eyes, I watched his every move, I saw him hanged; and I fell back in a swoon. Scarcely had I come to my senses again, when I saw you stripped for the lash; that was the peak of my horror, consternation, grief, and despair. I may tell you, by the way, that your skin is even whiter and more delicate than that of my Bulgar captain. Seeing you, then, redoubled the torments which were already overwhelming me. I shrieked aloud, I wanted to call out, 'Let him go, you brutes!' but my voice died within me, and my cries would have been useless. When you had been thoroughly thrashed: 'How can it be,' I asked myself, 'that agreeable Candide and wise Pangloss have come to Lisbon, one to receive a hundred whiplashes, the other to be hanged by order of My Lord the Inquisitor, whose mistress I am? Pangloss must have deceived me cruelly when he told me that all is for the best in this world.'

— Frantic, exhausted, half out of my senses, and ready to die of weakness, I felt as if my mind were choked with the massacre of my father, my mother, my brother, with the arrogance of that ugly Bulgar soldier, with the knife slash he inflicted on me, my slavery, my cookery, my Bulgar captain, my nasty Don Issachar, my abominable inquisitor, with the hanging of Doctor Pangloss, with that great plainsong *miserere* which they sang while they flogged you—and above all, my mind was full of the kiss which I gave you behind the screen, on the day I saw you for the last time. I praised God, who had brought you back to me after so many trials. I asked my old woman to look out for you, and to bring you here as soon as she could. She did just as I asked; I have had the indescribable joy of seeing you again, hearing you and talking with you once more. But you must be frightfully hungry; I am, myself; let us begin with a dinner.

So then and there they sat down to table; and after dinner, they adjourned to that fine brocaded sofa, which has already been mentioned; and there they were when the eminent Don Issachar, one of the masters of the house, appeared. It was the day of the Sabbath; he was arriving to assert his rights and express his tender passion.

CHAPTER 9

What Happened to Cunégonde, Candide, the Grand Inquisitor, and a Jew

This Issachar was the most choleric Hebrew seen in Israel since the Babylonian captivity.

—What's this, says he, you bitch of a Christian, you're not satisfied with the Grand Inquisitor? Do I have to share you with this rascal, too?

So saying, he drew a long dagger, with which he always went armed, and, supposing his opponent defenceless, flung himself on Candide. But our good Westphalian had received from the old woman, along with his suit of clothes, a fine sword. Out it came, and though his manners were of the gentlest, in short order he laid the Israelite stiff and cold on the floor, at the feet of the lovely Cunégonde.

—Holy Virgin! she cried. What will become of me now? A man killed in my house! If the police find out, we're done for.

—If Pangloss had not been hanged, said Candide, he would give us good advice in this hour of need, for he was a great philosopher. Lacking him, let's ask the old woman.

She was a sensible body, and was just starting to give her opinion of the situation, when another little door opened. It was just one o'clock in the morning, Sunday morning. This day belonged to the inquisitor. In he came, and found the whipped Candide with a sword in his hand, a corpse at his feet, Cunégonde in terror, and an old woman giving them both good advice.

Here now is what passed through Candide's mind in this instant of time; this is how he reasoned: —If this holy man calls for help, he will certainly have me burned, and perhaps Cunégonde as well; he has already had me whipped without mercy; he is my rival; I have already killed once; why hesitate?

It was a quick, clear chain of reasoning; without giving the inquisitor time to recover from his surprise, he ran him through, and laid him beside the Jew.

—Here you've done it again, said Cunégonde; there's no hope for us now. We'll be excommunicated, our last hour has come. How is it that you, who were born so gentle, could kill in two minutes a Jew and a prelate?

—My dear girl, replied Candide, when a man is in love, jealous, and just whipped by the Inquisition, he is no longer himself.

The old woman now spoke up and said:—There are three Andalusian steeds in the stable, with their saddles and bridles; our brave Candide must get them ready: my lady has some gold coin and diamonds; let's take to horse at once, though I can only ride on one buttock; we will go to Cadiz. The weather is as fine as can be, and it is pleasant to travel in the cool of the evening.

Promptly, Candide saddled the three horses. Cunégonde, the old woman, and he covered thirty miles without a stop. While they were fleeing, the Holy Brotherhood[5] came to investigate the house; they buried the inquisitor in a fine church, and threw Issachar on the dunghill.

Candide, Cunégonde, and the old woman were already in the little town of Avacena, in the middle of the Sierra Morena; and there, as they sat in a country inn, they had this conversation.

CHAPTER 10

In Deep Distress, Candide, Cunégonde, and the Old Woman Reach Cadiz; They Put to Sea

—Who then could have robbed me of my gold and diamonds? said Cunégonde, in tears. How shall we live? what shall we do? where shall I find other inquisitors and Jews to give me some more?

—Ah, said the old woman, I strongly suspect that reverend Franciscan friar who shared the inn with us yesterday at Badajoz. God save me from judging him unfairly! But he came into our room twice, and he left long before us.

—Alas, said Candide, the good Pangloss often proved to me that the fruits of the earth are a common heritage of all, to which each man has equal right. On these principles, the Franciscan should at least have left us enough to finish our journey. You have nothing at all, my dear Cunégonde?

—Not a maravedi, said she.

—What to do? said Candide.

—We'll sell one of the horses, said the old woman; I'll ride on the croup behind my mistress, though only on one buttock, and so we will get to Cadiz.

There was in the same inn a Benedictine prior; he bought the horse cheap. Candide, Cunégonde, and the old woman passed through Lucena, Chillas, and Lebrixa, and finally reached Cadiz. There a fleet was being fitted out and an army assembled, to reason with the Jesuit fathers in Paraguay, who were accused of fomenting among their flock a revolt against

5. A semireligious order with police powers, very active in eighteenth-century Spain.

the kings of Spain and Portugal near the town of St. Sacrement.[6] Candide, having served in the Bulgar army, performed the Bulgar manual of arms before the general of the little army with such grace, swiftness, dexterity, fire, and agility, that they gave him a company of infantry to command. So here he is, a captain; and off he sails with Miss Cunégonde, the old woman, two valets, and the two Andalusian steeds which had belonged to My Lord the Grand Inquisitor of Portugal.

Throughout the crossing, they spent a great deal of time reasoning about the philosophy of poor Pangloss.

—We are destined, in the end, for another universe, said Candide; no doubt that is the one where everything is well. For in this one, it must be admitted, there is some reason to grieve over our physical and moral state.

—I love you with all my heart, said Cunégonde; but my soul is still harrowed by thoughts of what I have seen and suffered.

—All will be well, replied Candide; the sea of this new world is already better than those of Europe, calmer and with steadier winds. Surely it is the New World which is the best of all possible worlds.

—God grant it, said Cunégonde; but I have been so horribly unhappy in the world so far, that my heart is almost dead to hope.

—You pity yourselves, the old woman told them; but you have had no such misfortunes as mine.

Cunégonde nearly broke out laughing; she found the old woman comic in pretending to be more unhappy than she.

—Ah, you poor old thing, said she, unless you've been raped by two Bulgars, been stabbed twice in the belly, seen two of your castles destroyed, witnessed the murder of two of your mothers and two of your fathers, and watched two of your lovers being whipped in an auto-da-fé, I do not see how you can have had it worse than me. Besides, I was born a baroness, with seventy-two quarterings, and I have worked in a scullery.

—My lady, replied the old woman, you do not know my birth and rank; and if I showed you my rear end, you would not talk as you do, you might even speak with less assurance.

These words inspired great curiosity in Candide and Cunégonde, which the old woman satisfied with this story.

CHAPTER 11

The Old Woman's Story

—My eyes were not always bloodshot and red-rimmed, my nose did not always touch my chin, and I was not born a servant. I am in fact the daughter of Pope Urban the Tenth and the Princess of Palestrina.[7] Till the age of fourteen, I lived in a palace so splendid that all the castles of all your German barons would not have served it as a stable; a single one

6. Actually, Colonia del Sacramento. Voltaire took great interest in the Jesuit role in Paraguay, which he has much oversimplified and largely misrepresented here in the interests of his satire. In 1750 they did, however, offer armed resistance to an agreement made between Spain and Portugal. They were subdued and expelled in 1769.   7. Voltaire left behind a comment on this passage, a note first published in 1829: "Note the extreme discretion of the author; hitherto there has never been a pope named Urban X; he avoided attributing a bastard to a known pope. What circumspection! what an exquisite conscience!"

of my dresses was worth more than all the assembled magnificence of Westphalia. I grew in beauty, in charm, in talent, surrounded by pleasures, dignities, and glowing visions of the future. Already I was inspiring the young men to love; my breast was formed—and what a breast! white, firm, with the shape of the Venus de Medici; and what eyes! what lashes, what black brows! What fire flashed from my glances and outshone the glitter of the stars, as the local poets used to tell me! The women who helped me dress and undress fell into ecstasies, whether they looked at me from in front or behind; and all the men wanted to be in their place.

—I was engaged to the ruling prince of Massa-Carrara; and what a prince he was! as handsome as I, softness and charm compounded, brilliantly witty, and madly in love with me. I loved him in return as one loves for the first time, with a devotion approaching idolatry. The wedding preparations had been made, with a splendor and magnificence never heard of before; nothing but celebrations, masks, and comic operas, uninterruptedly; and all Italy composed in my honor sonnets of which not one was even passable. I had almost attained the very peak of bliss, when an old marquise who had been the mistress of my prince invited him to her house for a cup of chocolate. He died in less than two hours, amid horrifying convulsions. But that was only a trifle. My mother, in complete despair (though less afflicted than I), wished to escape for a while the oppressive atmosphere of grief. She owned a handsome property near Gaeta.[8] We embarked on a papal galley gilded like the altar of St. Peter's in Rome. Suddenly a pirate ship from Salé swept down and boarded us. Our soldiers defended themselves as papal troops usually do; falling on their knees and throwing down their arms, they begged of the corsair absolution *in articulo mortis*.[9]

—They were promptly stripped as naked as monkeys, and so was my mother, and so were our maids of honor, and so was I too. It's a very remarkable thing, the energy these gentlemen put into stripping people. But what surprised me even more was that they stuck their fingers in a place where we women usually admit only a syringe. This ceremony seemed a bit odd to me, as foreign usages always do when one hasn't traveled. They only wanted to see if we didn't have some diamonds hidden there; and I soon learned that it's a custom of long standing among the genteel folk who swarm the seas. I learned that my lords the very religious knights of Malta never overlook this ceremony when they capture Turks, whether male or female; it's one of those international laws which have never been questioned.

—I won't try to explain how painful it is for a young princess to be carried off into slavery in Morocco with her mother. You can imagine everything we had to suffer on the pirate ship. My mother was still very beautiful; our maids of honor, our mere chambermaids, were more charming than anything one could find in all Africa. As for myself, I was ravishing, I was loveliness and grace supreme, and I was a virgin. I did not remain so for long; the flower which had been kept for the handsome

---

8. About halfway between Rome and Naples.   9. Literally, when at the point of death. Absolution from a corsair in the act of murdering one is of very dubious validity.

prince of Massa-Carrara was plucked by the corsair captain; he was an abominable negro, who thought he was doing me a great favor. My Lady the Princess of Palestrina and I must have been strong indeed to bear what we did during our journey to Morocco. But on with my story; these are such common matters that they are not worth describing.

— Morocco was knee deep in blood when we arrived. Of the fifty sons of the emperor Muley-Ismael,[1] each had his faction, which produced in effect fifty civil wars, of blacks against blacks, of blacks against browns, halfbreeds against halfbreeds; throughout the length and breadth of the empire, nothing but one continual carnage.

— Scarcely had we stepped ashore, when some negroes of a faction hostile to my captor arrived to take charge of his plunder. After the diamonds and gold, we women were the most prized possessions. I was now witness of a struggle such as you never see in the temperate climate of Europe. Northern people don't have hot blood; they don't feel the absolute fury for women which is common in Africa. Europeans seem to have milk in their veins; it is vitriol or liquid fire which pulses through these people around Mount Atlas. The fight for possession of us raged with the fury of the lions, tigers, and poisonous vipers of that land. A Moor snatched my mother by the right arm, the first mate held her by the left; a Moorish soldier grabbed one leg, one of our pirates the other. In a moment's time almost all our girls were being dragged four different ways. My captain held me behind him while with his scimitar he killed everyone who braved his fury. At last I saw all our Italian women, including my mother, torn to pieces, cut to bits, murdered by the monsters who were fighting over them. My captive companions, their captors, soldiers, sailors, blacks, browns, whites, mulattoes, and at last my captain, all were killed, and I remained half dead on a mountain of corpses. Similar scenes were occurring, as is well known, for more than three hundred leagues around, without anyone skimping on the five prayers a day decreed by Mohammed.

— With great pain, I untangled myself from this vast heap of bleeding bodies, and dragged myself under a great orange tree by a neighboring brook, where I collapsed, from terror, exhaustion, horror, despair, and hunger. Shortly, my weary mind surrendered to a sleep which was more of a swoon than a rest. I was in this state of weakness and languor, between life and death, when I felt myself touched by something which moved over my body. Opening my eyes, I saw a white man, rather attractive, who was groaning and saying under his breath: 'O *che sciagura d'essere senza coglioni!*'[2]

CHAPTER 12

The Old Woman's Story Continued

— Amazed and delighted to hear my native tongue, and no less surprised by what this man was saying, I told him that there were worse evils

---

1. Having reigned for more than fifty years, a potent and ruthless sultan of Morocco, he died in 1727 and left his kingdom in much the condition described.   2. "Oh what a misfortune to have no testicles!"

than those he was complaining of. In a few words, I described to him the horrors I had undergone, and then fainted again. He carried me to a nearby house, put me to bed, gave me something to eat, served me, flattered me, comforted me, told me he had never seen anyone so lovely, and added that he had never before regretted so much the loss of what nobody could give him back.

'I was born at Naples, he told me, where they caponize two or three thousand children every year; some die of it, others acquire a voice more beautiful than any woman's, still others go on to become governors of kingdoms.[3] The operation was a great success with me, and I became court musician to the Princess of Palestrina . . .'

'Of my mother,' I exclaimed.

'Of your mother,' cried he, bursting into tears; 'then you must be the princess whom I raised till she was six, and who already gave promise of becoming as beautiful as you are now!'

'I am that very princess; my mother lies dead, not a hundred yards from here, buried under a pile of corpses.'

—I told him my adventures, he told me his: that he had been sent by a Christian power to the King of Morocco, to conclude a treaty granting him gunpowder, cannon, and ships with which to liquidate the traders of the other Christian powers.

'My mission is concluded,' said this honest eunuch; 'I shall take ship at Ceuta and bring you back to Italy. *Ma che sciagura d'essere senza coglioni!*'

—I thanked him with tears of gratitude, and instead of returning me to Italy, he took me to Algiers and sold me to the dey of that country. Hardly had the sale taken place, when that plague which has made the rounds of Africa, Asia, and Europe broke out in full fury at Algiers. You have seen earthquakes; but tell me, young lady, have you ever had the plague?

—Never, replied the baroness.

—If you had had it, said the old woman, you would agree that it is far worse than an earthquake. It is very frequent in Africa, and I had it. Imagine, if you will, the situation of a pope's daughter, fifteen years old, who in three months' time had experienced poverty, slavery, had been raped almost every day, had seen her mother quartered, had suffered from famine and war, and who now was dying of pestilence in Algiers. As a matter of fact, I did not die; but the eunuch and the dey and nearly the entire seraglio of Algiers perished.

—When the first horrors of this ghastly plague had passed, the slaves of the dey were sold. A merchant bought me and took me to Tunis; there he sold me to another merchant, who resold me at Tripoli; from Tripoli I was sold to Alexandria, from Alexandria resold to Smyrna, from Smyrna to Constantinople. I ended by belonging to an aga of janizaries, who was shortly ordered to defend Azov against the besieging Russians.[4]

—The aga, who was a gallant soldier, took his whole seraglio with him, and established us in a little fort amid the Maeotian marshes,[5] guarded by

---

3. The castrato Farinelli (1705–1782), originally a singer, came to exercise considerable political influence on the kings of Spain, Philip V and Ferdinand VI.   4. Azov, near the mouth of the Don, was besieged by the Russians under Peter the Great in 1695–96. *Janizaries:* an elite corps of the Ottoman armies.   5. The Roman name of the so-called Sea of Azov, a shallow swampy lake near the town.

two black eunuchs and twenty soldiers. Our side killed a prodigious number of Russians, but they paid us back nicely. Azov was put to fire and sword without respect for age or sex; only our little fort continued to resist, and the enemy determined to starve us out. The twenty janizaries had sworn never to surrender. Reduced to the last extremities of hunger, they were forced to eat our two eunuchs, lest they violate their oaths. After several more days, they decided to eat the women too.

—We had an imam,[6] very pious and sympathetic, who delivered an excellent sermon, persuading them not to kill us altogether.

'Just cut off a single rumpsteak from each of these ladies,' he said, 'and you'll have a fine meal. Then if you should need another, you can come back in a few days and have as much again; heaven will bless your charitable action, and you will be saved.'

—His eloquence was splendid, and he persuaded them. We underwent this horrible operation. The imam treated us all with the ointment that they use on newly circumcised children. We were at the point of death.

—Scarcely had the janizaries finished the meal for which we furnished the materials, when the Russians appeared in flat-bottomed boats; not a janizary escaped. The Russians paid no attention to the state we were in; but there are French physicians everywhere, and one of them, who knew his trade, took care of us. He cured us, and I shall remember all my life that when my wounds were healed, he made me a proposition. For the rest, he counselled us simply to have patience, assuring us that the same thing had happened in several other sieges, and that it was according to the laws of war.

—As soon as my companions could walk, we were herded off to Moscow. In the division of booty, I fell to a boyar who made me work in his garden, and gave me twenty whiplashes a day; but when he was broken on the wheel after about two years, with thirty other boyars, over some little court intrigue,[7] I seized the occasion; I ran away; I crossed all Russia; I was for a long time a chambermaid in Riga, then at Rostock, Vismara, Leipzig, Cassel, Utrecht, Leyden, The Hague, Rotterdam; I grew old in misery and shame, having only half a backside and remembering always that I was the daughter of a Pope; a hundred times I wanted to kill myself, but always I loved life more. This ridiculous weakness is perhaps one of our worst instincts; is anything more stupid than choosing to carry a burden that really one wants to cast on the ground? to hold existence in horror, and yet to cling to it? to fondle the serpent which devours us till it has eaten out our heart?

—In the countries through which I have been forced to wander, in the taverns where I have had to work, I have seen a vast number of people who hated their existence; but I never saw more than a dozen who deliberately put an end to their own misery: three negroes, four Englishmen, four Genevans, and a German professor named Robeck.[8] My last post was as

---

6. In effect, a chaplain. 7. Voltaire had in mind an ineffectual conspiracy against Peter the Great known as the "revolt of the streltsy" or musketeers, which took place in 1698. Though easily put down, it provoked from the emperor a massive and atrocious program of reprisals. 8. Johann Robeck (1672–1739) published a treatise advocating suicide and showed his conviction by drowning himself at the age of sixty-seven.

servant to the Jew Don Issachar; he attached me to your service, my lovely one; and I attached myself to your destiny, till I have become more concerned with your fate than with my own. I would not even have mentioned my own misfortunes, if you had not irked me a bit, and if it weren't the custom, on shipboard, to pass the time with stories. In a word, my lady, I have had some experience of the world, I know it; why not try this diversion? Ask every passenger on this ship to tell you his story, and if you find a single one who has not often cursed the day of his birth, who has not often told himself that he is the most miserable of men, then you may throw me overboard head first.

CHAPTER 13

How Candide Was Forced to Leave the Lovely Cunégonde and the Old Woman

Having heard out the old woman's story, the lovely Cunégonde paid her the respects which were appropriate to a person of her rank and merit. She took up the wager as well, and got all the passengers, one after another, to tell her their adventures. She and Candide had to agree that the old woman had been right.

—It's certainly too bad, said Candide, that the wise Pangloss was hanged, contrary to the custom of autos-da-fé; he would have admirable things to say of the physical evil and moral evil which cover land and sea, and I might feel within me the impulse to dare to raise several polite objections.

As the passengers recited their stories, the boat made steady progress, and presently landed at Buenos Aires. Cunégonde, Captain Candide, and the old woman went to call on the governor, Don Fernando d'Ibaraa y Figueroa y Mascarenes y Lampourdos y Souza. This nobleman had the pride appropriate to a man with so many names. He addressed everyone with the most aristocratic disdain, pointing his nose so loftily, raising his voice so mercilessly, lording it so splendidly, and assuming so arrogant a pose, that everyone who met him wanted to kick him. He loved women to the point of fury; and Cunégonde seemed to him the most beautiful creature he had ever seen. The first thing he did was to ask directly if she were the captain's wife. His manner of asking this question disturbed Candide; he did not dare say she was his wife, because in fact she was not; he did not dare say she was his sister, because she wasn't that either; and though this polite lie was once common enough among the ancients,[9] and sometimes serves moderns very well, he was too pure of heart to tell a lie.

—Miss Cunégonde, said he, is betrothed to me, and we humbly beg your excellency to perform the ceremony for us.

Don Fernando d'Ibaraa y Figueroa y Mascarenes y Lampourdos y Souza twirled his moustache, smiled sardonically, and ordered Captain Candide to go drill his company. Candide obeyed. Left alone with My

---

9. Voltaire has in mind Abraham's adventures with Sarah (Genesis 12) and Isaac's with Rebecca (Genesis 26).

Lady Cunégonde, the governor declared his passion, and protested that he would marry her tomorrow, in church or in any other manner, as it pleased her charming self. Cunégonde asked for a quarter-hour to collect herself, consult the old woman, and make up her mind.

The old woman said to Cunégonde: —My lady, you have seventy-two quarterings and not one penny; if you wish, you may be the wife of the greatest lord in South America, who has a really handsome moustache; are you going to insist on your absolute fidelity? You have already been raped by the Bulgars; a Jew and an inquisitor have enjoyed your favors; miseries entitle one to privileges. I assure you that in your position I would make no scruple of marrying My Lord the Governor, and making the fortune of Captain Candide.

While the old woman was talking with all the prudence of age and experience, there came into the harbor a small ship bearing an alcalde and some alguazils.[1] This is what had happened.

As the old woman had very shrewdly guessed, it was a long-sleeved Franciscan who stole Cunégonde's gold and jewels in the town of Badajoz, when she and Candide were in flight. The monk tried to sell some of the gems to a jeweler, who recognized them as belonging to the Grand Inquisitor. Before he was hanged, the Franciscan confessed that he had stolen them, indicating who his victims were and where they were going. The flight of Cunégonde and Candide was already known. They were traced to Cadiz, and a vessel was hastily dispatched in pursuit of them. This vessel was now in the port of Buenos Aires. The rumor spread that an alcalde was aboard, in pursuit of the murderers of My Lord the Grand Inquisitor. The shrewd old woman saw at once what was to be done.

—You cannot escape, she told Cunégonde, and you have nothing to fear. You are not the one who killed my lord, and, besides, the governor, who is in love with you, won't let you be mistreated. Sit tight.

And then she ran straight to Candide: —Get out of town, she said, or you'll be burned within the hour.

There was not a moment to lose; but how to leave Cunégonde, and where to go?

CHAPTER 14

How Candide and Cacambo Were Received by the Jesuits of Paraguay

Candide had brought from Cadiz a valet of the type one often finds in the provinces of Spain and in the colonies. He was one quarter Spanish, son of a halfbreed in the Tucuman;[2] he had been choirboy, sacristan, sailor, monk, merchant, soldier, and lackey. His name was Cacambo, and he was very fond of his master because his master was a very good man. In hot haste he saddled the two Andalusian steeds.

—Hurry, master, do as the old woman says; let's get going and leave this town without a backward look.

Candide wept: —O my beloved Cunégonde! must I leave you now, just

---

1. Police officers.   2. A province of Argentina, to the northwest of Buenos Aires.

when the governor is about to marry us! Cunégonde, brought from so far, what will ever become of you?

—She'll become what she can, said Cacambo; women can always find something to do with themselves; God sees to it; let's get going.

—Where are you taking me? where are we going? what will we do without Cunégonde? said Candide.

—By Saint James of Compostela, said Cacambo, you were going to make war against the Jesuits, now we'll go make war for them. I know the roads pretty well, I'll bring you to their country, they will be delighted to have a captain who knows the Bulgar drill; you'll make a prodigious fortune. If you don't get your rights in one world, you will find them in another. And isn't it pleasant to see new things and do new things?

—Then you've already been in Paraguay? said Candide.

—Indeed I have, replied Cacambo; I was cook in the College of the Assumption, and I know the government of Los Padres[3] as I know the streets of Cadiz. It's an admirable thing, this government. The kingdom is more than three hundred leagues across; it is divided into thirty provinces. Los Padres own everything in it, and the people nothing; it's a masterpiece of reason and justice. I myself know nothing so wonderful as Los Padres, who in this hemisphere make war on the kings of Spain and Portugal, but in Europe hear their confessions; who kill Spaniards here, and in Madrid send them to heaven; that really tickles me; let's get moving, you're going to be the happiest of men. Won't Los Padres be delighted when they learn they have a captain who knows the Bulgar drill!

As soon as they reached the first barricade, Cacambo told the frontier guard that a captain wished to speak with My Lord the Commander. A Paraguayan officer ran to inform headquarters by laying the news at the feet of the commander. Candide and Cacambo were first disarmed and deprived of their Andalusian horses. They were then placed between two files of soldiers; the commander was at the end, his three-cornered hat on his head, his cassock drawn up, a sword at his side, and a pike in his hand. He nods, and twenty-four soldiers surround the newcomers. A sergeant then informs them that they must wait, that the commander cannot talk to them, since the reverend father provincial has forbidden all Spaniards from speaking, except in his presence, and from remaining more than three hours in the country.

—And where is the reverend father provincial? says Cacambo.

—He is reviewing his troops after having said mass, the sergeant replies, and you'll only be able to kiss his spurs in three hours.

—But, says Cacambo, my master the captain, who, like me, is dying from hunger, is not Spanish at all, he is German; can't we have some breakfast while waiting for his reverence?

The sergeant promptly went off to report this speech to the commander.

—God be praised, said this worthy; since he is German, I can talk to him; bring him into my bower.

Candide was immediately led into a leafy nook surrounded by a hand-

3. The Jesuit fathers.

some colonnade of green and gold marble and trellises amid which sported parrots, birds of paradise,[4] hummingbirds, guinea fowl, and all the rarest species of birds. An excellent breakfast was prepared in golden vessels; and while the Paraguayans ate corn out of wooden bowls in the open fields under the glare of the sun, the reverend father commander entered into his bower.

He was a very handsome young man, with an open face, rather blonde in coloring, with ruddy complexion, arched eyebrows, liquid eyes, pink ears, bright red lips, and an air of pride, but a pride somehow different from that of a Spaniard or a Jesuit. Their confiscated weapons were restored to Candide and Cacambo, as well as their Andalusian horses; Cacambo fed them oats alongside the bower, always keeping an eye on them for fear of an ambush.

First Candide kissed the hem of the commander's cassock, then they sat down at the table.

—So you are German? said the Jesuit, speaking in that language.

—Yes, your reverence, said Candide.

As they spoke these words, both men looked at one another with great surprise, and another emotion which they could not control.

—From what part of Germany do you come? said the Jesuit.

—From the nasty province of Westphalia, said Candide; I was born in the castle of Thunder-Ten-Tronckh.

—Merciful heavens! cries the commander. Is it possible?

—What a miracle! exclaims Candide.

—Can it be you? asks the commander.

—It's impossible, says Candide.

They both fall back in their chairs, they embrace, they shed streams of tears.

—What, can it be you, reverend father! you, the brother of the lovely Cunégonde! you, who were killed by the Bulgars! you, the son of My Lord the Baron! you, a Jesuit in Paraguay! It's a mad world, indeed it is. Oh, Pangloss! Pangloss! how happy you would be, if you hadn't been hanged.

The commander dismissed his negro slaves and the Paraguayans who served his drink in crystal goblets. He thanked God and Saint Ignatius a thousand times, he clasped Candide in his arms, their faces were bathed in tears.

—You would be even more astonished, even more delighted, even more beside yourself, said Candide, if I told you that My Lady Cunégonde, your sister, who you thought was disemboweled, is enjoying good health.

—Where?

—Not far from here, in the house of the governor of Buenos Aires; and to think that I came to make war on you!

Each word they spoke in this long conversation added another miracle.

---

4. In this passage and several later ones, Voltaire uses in conjunction two words, both of which mean hummingbird. The French system of classifying hummingbirds, based on the work of the celebrated Buffon, distinguishes *oiseaux-mouches* with straight bills from *colibris* with curved bills. This distinction is wholly fallacious. Hummingbirds have all manner of shaped bills, and the division of species must be made on other grounds entirely. At the expense of ornithological accuracy, I have therefore introduced birds of paradise to get the requisite sense of glitter and sheen.

Their souls danced on their tongues, hung eagerly at their ears, glittered in their eyes. As they were Germans, they sat a long time at table, waiting for the reverend father provincial; and the commander spoke in these terms to his dear Candide.

CHAPTER 15

How Candide Killed the Brother of His Dear Cunégonde

—All my life long I shall remember the horrible day when I saw my father and mother murdered and my sister raped. When the Bulgars left, that adorable sister of mine was nowhere to be found; so they loaded a cart with my mother, my father, myself, two serving girls, and three little murdered boys, to carry us all off for burial in a Jesuit chapel some two leagues from our ancestral castle. A Jesuit sprinkled us with holy water; it was horribly salty, and a few drops got into my eyes; the father noticed that my lid made a little tremor; putting his hand on my heart, he felt it beat; I was rescued, and at the end of three weeks was as good as new. You know, my dear Candide, that I was a very pretty boy; I became even more so; the reverend father Croust,[5] superior of the abbey, conceived a most tender friendship for me; he accepted me as a novice, and shortly after, I was sent to Rome. The Father General had need of a resupply of young German Jesuits. The rulers of Paraguay accept as few Spanish Jesuits as they can; they prefer foreigners, whom they think they can control better. I was judged fit, by the Father General, to labor in this vineyard. So we set off, a Pole, a Tyrolean, and myself. Upon our arrival, I was honored with the posts of subdeacon and lieutenant; today I am a colonel and a priest. We are giving a vigorous reception to the King of Spain's men; I assure you they will be excommunicated as well as trounced on the battle-field. Providence has sent you to help us. But is it really true that my dear sister, Cunégonde, is in the neighborhood, with the governor of Buenos Aires?

Candide reassured him with a solemn oath that nothing could be more true. Their tears began to flow again.

The baron could not weary of embracing Candide; he called him his brother, his savior.

—Ah, my dear Candide, said he, maybe together we will be able to enter the town as conquerors, and be united with my sister Cunégonde.

—That is all I desire, said Candide; I was expecting to marry her, and I still hope to.

—You insolent dog, replied the baron, you would have the effrontery to marry my sister, who has seventy-two quarterings! It's a piece of pre-sumption for you even to mention such a crazy project in my presence.

Candide, terrified by this speech, answered: —Most reverend father, all the quarterings in the world don't affect this case; I have rescued your sister out of the arms of a Jew and an inquisitor; she has many obligations to me, she wants to marry me. Master Pangloss always taught me that men are equal; and I shall certainly marry her.

5. A Jesuit rector at Colmar with whom Voltaire had quarreled in 1754.

—We'll see about that, you scoundrel, said the Jesuit baron of Thunder-Ten-Tronckh; and so saying, he gave him a blow across the face with the flat of his sword. Candide immediately drew his own sword and thrust it up to the hilt in the baron's belly; but as he drew it forth all dripping, he began to weep.

—Alas, dear God! said he, I have killed my old master, my friend, my brother-in-law; I am the best man in the world, and here are three men I've killed already, and two of the three were priests.

Cacambo, who was standing guard at the entry of the bower, came running.

—We can do nothing but sell our lives dearly, said his master; someone will certainly come; we must die fighting.

Cacambo, who had been in similar scrapes before, did not lose his head; he took the Jesuit's cassock, which the commander had been wearing, and put it on Candide; he stuck the dead man's square hat on Candide's head, and forced him onto horseback. Everything was done in the wink of an eye.

—Let's ride, master; everyone will take you for a Jesuit on his way to deliver orders; and we will have passed the frontier before anyone can come after us.

Even as he was pronouncing these words, he charged off, crying in Spanish: —Way, make way for the reverend father colonel!

CHAPTER 16

What Happened to the Two Travelers with Two Girls, Two Monkeys, and the Savages Named Biglugs

Candide and his valet were over the frontier before anyone in the camp knew of the death of the German Jesuit. Foresighted Cacambo had taken care to fill his satchel with bread, chocolate, ham, fruit, and several bottles of wine. They pushed their Andalusian horses forward into unknown country, where there were no roads. Finally a broad prairie divided by several streams opened before them. Our two travelers turned their horses loose to graze; Cacambo suggested that they eat too, and promptly set the example. But Candide said: —How can you expect me to eat ham when I have killed the son of My Lord the Baron, and am now condemned never to see the lovely Cunégonde for the rest of my life? Why should I drag out my miserable days, since I must exist far from her in the depths of despair and remorse? And what will the *Journal de Trévoux*[6] say of all this?

Though he talked this way, he did not neglect the food. Night fell. The two wanderers heard a few weak cries which seemed to be voiced by women. They could not tell whether the cries expressed grief or joy; but they leaped at once to their feet, with that uneasy suspicion which one always feels in an unknown country. The outcry arose from two girls, completely naked, who were running swiftly along the edge of the meadow, pursued by two monkeys who snapped at their buttocks. Candide was

6. A newspaper published by the Jesuit order, founded in 1701 and consistently hostile to Voltaire.

moved to pity; he had learned marksmanship with the Bulgars, and could have knocked a nut off a bush without touching the leaves. He raised his Spanish rifle, fired twice, and killed the two monkeys.

—God be praised, my dear Cacambo! I've saved these two poor creatures from great danger. Though I committed a sin in killing an inquisitor and a Jesuit, I've redeemed myself by saving the lives of two girls. Perhaps they are two ladies of rank, and this good deed may gain us special advantages in the country.

He had more to say, but his mouth shut suddenly when he saw the girls embracing the monkeys tenderly, weeping over their bodies, and filling the air with lamentations.

—I wasn't looking for quite so much generosity of spirit, said he to Cacambo; the latter replied: —You've really fixed things this time, master; you've killed the two lovers of these young ladies.

—Their lovers! Impossible! You must be joking, Cacambo; how can I believe you?

—My dear master, Cacambo replied, you're always astonished by everything. Why do you think it so strange that in some countries monkeys succeed in obtaining the good graces of women? They are one quarter human, just as I am one quarter Spanish.

—Alas, Candide replied, I do remember now hearing Master Pangloss say that such things used to happen, and that from these mixtures there arose pans, fauns, and satyrs, and that these creatures had appeared to various grand figures of antiquity; but I took all that for fables.

—You should be convinced now, said Cacambo; it's true, and you see how people make mistakes who haven't received a measure of education. But what I fear is that these girls may get us into real trouble.

These sensible reflections led Candide to leave the field and to hide in a wood. There he dined with Cacambo; and there both of them, having duly cursed the inquisitor of Portugal, the governor of Buenos Aires, and the baron, went to sleep on a bed of moss. When they woke up, they found themselves unable to move; the reason was that during the night the Biglugs,[7] natives of the country, to whom the girls had complained of them, had tied them down with cords of bark. They were surrounded by fifty naked Biglugs, armed with arrows, clubs, and stone axes. Some were boiling a caldron of water, others were preparing spits, and all cried out: — It's a Jesuit, a Jesuit! We'll be revenged and have a good meal; let's eat some Jesuit, eat some Jesuit!

—I told you, my dear master, said Cacambo sadly, I said those two girls would play us a dirty trick.

Candide, noting the caldron and spits, cried out: —We are surely going to be roasted or boiled. Ah, what would Master Pangloss say if he could see these men in a state of nature? All is for the best, I agree; but I must say it seems hard to have lost Miss Cunégonde and to be stuck on a spit by the Biglugs.

Cacambo did not lose his head.

---

7. Voltaire's name is "Oreillons" from Spanish "Orejones," a name mentioned in Garcilaso de Vega's *Historia General del Perú* (1609), on which Voltaire drew for many of the details in his picture of South America.

—Don't give up hope, said he to the disconsolate Candide; I understand a little of the jargon these people speak, and I'm going to talk to them.

—Don't forget to remind them, said Candide, of the frightful inhumanity of eating their fellow men, and that Christian ethics forbid it.

—Gentlemen, said Cacambo, you have a mind to eat a Jesuit today? An excellent idea; nothing is more proper than to treat one's enemies so. Indeed, the law of nature teaches us to kill our neighbor, and that's how men behave the whole world over. Though we Europeans don't exercise our right to eat our neighbors, the reason is simply that we find it easy to get a good meal elsewhere; but you don't have our resources, and we certainly agree that it's better to eat your enemies than to let the crows and vultures have the fruit of your victory. But, gentlemen, you wouldn't want to eat your friends. You think you will be spitting a Jesuit, and it's your defender, the enemy of your enemies, whom you will be roasting. For my part, I was born in your country; the gentleman whom you see is my master, and far from being a Jesuit, he has just killed a Jesuit, the robe he is wearing was stripped from him; that's why you have taken a dislike to him. To prove that I am telling the truth, take his robe and bring it to the nearest frontier of the kingdom of Los Padres; find out for yourselves if my master didn't kill a Jesuit officer. It won't take long; if you find that I have lied, you can still eat us. But if I've told the truth, you know too well the principles of public justice, customs, and laws, not to spare our lives.

The Biglugs found this discourse perfectly reasonable; they appointed chiefs to go posthaste and find out the truth; the two messengers performed their task like men of sense, and quickly returned bringing good news. The Biglugs untied their two prisoners, treated them with great politeness, offered them girls, gave them refreshments, and led them back to the border of their state, crying joyously: —He isn't a Jesuit, he isn't a Jesuit!

Candide could not weary of exclaiming over his preservation.

—What a people! he said. What men! what customs! If I had not had the good luck to run a sword through the body of Miss Cunégonde's brother, I would have been eaten on the spot! But, after all, it seems that uncorrupted nature is good, since these folk, instead of eating me, showed me a thousand kindnesses as soon as they knew I was not a Jesuit.

CHAPTER 17

*Arrival of Candide and His Servant at the Country of Eldorado,
and What They Saw There*

When they were out of the land of the Biglugs, Cacambo said to Candide: —You see that this hemisphere is no better than the other; take my advice, and let's get back to Europe as soon as possible.

—How to get back, asked Candide, and where to go? If I go to my own land, the Bulgars and Abares are murdering everyone in sight; if I go to Portugal, they'll burn me alive; if we stay here, we risk being skewered any

day. But how can I ever leave that part of the world where Miss Cunégonde lives?

—Let's go toward Cayenne, said Cacambo, we shall find some
Frenchmen there, for they go all over the world; they can help us; perhaps
God will take pity on us.

To get to Cayenne was not easy; they knew more or less which way to
go, but mountains, rivers, cliffs, robbers, and savages obstructed the way
everywhere. Their horses died of weariness; their food was eaten; they
subsisted for one whole month on wild fruits, and at last they found themselves by a little river fringed with coconut trees, which gave them both
life and hope.

Cacambo, who was as full of good advice as the old woman, said to
Candide: —We can go no further, we've walked ourselves out; I see an
abandoned canoe on the bank, let's fill it with coconuts, get into the boat,
and float with the current; a river always leads to some inhabited spot or
other. If we don't find anything pleasant, at least we may find something
new.

—Let's go, said Candide, and let Providence be our guide.

They floated some leagues between banks sometimes flowery, sometimes sandy, now steep, now level. The river widened steadily; finally it
disappeared into a chasm of frightful rocks that rose high into the heavens.
The two travelers had the audacity to float with the current into this
chasm. The river, narrowly confined, drove them onward with horrible
speed and a fearful roar. After twenty-four hours, they saw daylight once
more; but their canoe was smashed on the snags. They had to drag themselves from rock to rock for an entire league; at last they emerged to an
immense horizon, ringed with remote mountains. The countryside was
tended for pleasure as well as profit; everywhere the useful was joined to
the agreeable. The roads were covered, or rather decorated, with elegantly
shaped carriages made of a glittering material, carrying men and women
of singular beauty, and drawn by great red sheep which were faster than
the finest horses of Andalusia, Tetuan, and Mequinez.

—Here now, said Candide, is a country that's better than Westphalia.

Along with Cacambo, he climbed out of the river at the first village he
could see. Some children of the town, dressed in rags of gold brocade,
were playing quoits at the village gate; our two men from the other world
paused to watch them; their quoits were rather large, yellow, red, and
green, and they glittered with a singular luster. On a whim, the travelers
picked up several; they were of gold, emeralds, and rubies, and the least
of them would have been the greatest ornament of the Great Mogul's
throne.

—Surely, said Cacambo, these quoit players are the children of the king
of the country.

The village schoolmaster appeared at that moment, to call them back
to school.

—And there, said Candide, is the tutor of the royal household.

The little rascals quickly gave up their game, leaving on the ground
their quoits and playthings. Candide picked them up, ran to the school-

master, and presented them to him humbly, giving him to understand by sign language that their royal highnesses had forgotten their gold and jewels. With a smile, the schoolmaster tossed them to the ground, glanced quickly but with great surprise at Candide's face, and went his way.

The travelers did not fail to pick up the gold, rubies, and emeralds.

—Where in the world are we? cried Candide. The children of this land must be well trained, since they are taught contempt for gold and jewels.

Cacambo was as much surprised as Candide. At last they came to the finest house of the village; it was built like a European palace. A crowd of people surrounded the door, and even more were in the entry; delightful music was heard, and a delicious aroma of cooking filled the air. Cacambo went up to the door, listened, and reported that they were talking Peruvian; that was his native language, for every reader must know that Cacambo was born in Tucuman, in a village where they talk that language exclusively.

—I'll act as interpreter, he told Candide; it's an hotel, let's go in.

Promptly two boys and two girls of the staff, dressed in cloth of gold, and wearing ribbons in their hair, invited them to sit at the host's table. The meal consisted of four soups, each one garnished with a brace of parakeets, a boiled condor which weighed two hundred pounds, two roast monkeys of an excellent flavor, three hundred birds of paradise in one dish and six hundred hummingbirds in another, exquisite stews, delicious pastries, the whole thing served up in plates of what looked like rock crystal. The boys and girls of the staff poured them various beverages made from sugar cane.

The diners were for the most part merchants and travelers, all extremely polite, who questioned Cacambo with the most discreet circumspection, and answered his questions very directly.

When the meal was over, Cacambo as well as Candide supposed he could settle his bill handsomely by tossing onto the table two of those big pieces of gold which they had picked up; but the host and hostess burst out laughing, and for a long time nearly split their sides. Finally they subsided.

—Gentlemen, said the host, we see clearly that you're foreigners; we don't meet many of you here. Please excuse our laughing when you offered us in payment a couple of pebbles from the roadside. No doubt you don't have any of our local currency, but you don't need it to eat here. All the hotels established for the promotion of commerce are maintained by the state. You have had meager entertainment here, for we are only a poor town; but everywhere else you will be given the sort of welcome you deserve.

Cacambo translated for Candide all the host's explanations, and Candide listened to them with the same admiration and astonishment that his friend Cacambo showed in reporting them.

—What is this country, then, said they to one another, unknown to the rest of the world, and where nature itself is so different from our own? This probably is the country where everything is for the best; for it's absolutely necessary that such a country should exist somewhere. And whatever Master Pangloss said of the matter, I have often had occasion to notice that things went badly in Westphalia.

CHAPTER 18

What They Saw in the Land of Eldorado

Cacambo revealed his curiosity to the host, and the host told him: —I am an ignorant man and content to remain so; but we have here an old man, retired from the court, who is the most knowing person in the kingdom, and the most talkative.

Thereupon he brought Cacambo to the old man's house. Candide now played second fiddle, and acted as servant to his own valet. They entered an austere little house, for the door was merely of silver and the paneling of the rooms was only gold, though so tastefully wrought that the finest paneling would not surpass it. If the truth must be told, the lobby was only decorated with rubies and emeralds; but the patterns in which they were arranged atoned for the extreme simplicity.

The old man received the two strangers on a sofa stuffed with bird-of-paradise feathers, and offered them several drinks in diamond carafes; then he satisfied their curiosity in these terms.

—I am a hundred and seventy-two years old, and I heard from my late father, who was liveryman to the king, about the astonishing revolutions in Peru which he had seen. Our land here was formerly part of the kingdom of the Incas, who rashly left it in order to conquer another part of the world, and who were ultimately destroyed by the Spaniards. The wisest princes of their house were those who had never left their native valley; they decreed, with the consent of the nation, that henceforth no inhabitant of our little kingdom should ever leave it; and this rule is what has preserved our innocence and our happiness. The Spaniards heard vague rumors about this land, they called it El Dorado;[8] and an English knight named Raleigh even came somewhere close to it about a hundred years ago; but as we are surrounded by unscalable mountains and precipices, we have managed so far to remain hidden from the rapacity of the European nations, who have an inconceivable rage for the pebbles and mud of our land, and who, in order to get some, would butcher us all to the last man.

The conversation was a long one; it turned on the form of the government, the national customs, on women, public shows, the arts. At last Candide, whose taste always ran to metaphysics, told Cacambo to ask if the country had any religion.

The old man grew a bit red.

—How's that? he said. Can you have any doubt of it? Do you suppose we are altogether thankless scoundrels?

Cacambo asked meekly what was the religion of Eldorado. The old man flushed again.

8. The myth of this land of gold somewhere in Central or South America had been widespread since the sixteenth century. *The Discovery of Guiana*, published in 1595, described Sir Walter Ralegh's infatuation with the myth of Eldorado and served to spread the story still further.

—Can there be two religions? he asked. I suppose our religion is the same as everyone's, we worship God from morning to evening.

—Then you worship a single deity? said Cacambo, who acted throughout as interpreter of the questions of Candide.

—It's obvious, said the old man, that there aren't two or three or four of them. I must say the people of your world ask very remarkable questions.

Candide could not weary of putting questions to this good old man; he wanted to know how the people of Eldorado prayed to God.

—We don't pray to him at all, said the good and respectable sage; we have nothing to ask him for, since everything we need has already been granted; we thank God continually.

Candide was interested in seeing the priests; he had Cacambo ask where they were. The old gentleman smiled.

—My friends, said he, we are all priests; the king and all the heads of household sing formal psalms of thanksgiving every morning, and five or six thousand voices accompany them.

—What! you have no monks to teach, argue, govern, intrigue, and burn at the stake everyone who disagrees with them?

—We should have to be mad, said the old man; here we are all of the same mind, and we don't understand what you're up to with your monks.

Candide was overjoyed at all these speeches, and said to himself: — This is very different from Westphalia and the castle of My Lord the Baron; if our friend Pangloss had seen Eldorado, he wouldn't have called the castle of Thunder-Ten-Tronckh the finest thing on earth; to know the world one must travel.

After this long conversation, the old gentleman ordered a carriage with six sheep made ready, and gave the two travelers twelve of his servants for their journey to the court.

—Excuse me, said he, if old age deprives me of the honor of accompanying you. The king will receive you after a style which will not altogether displease you, and you will doubtless make allowance for the customs of the country if there are any you do not like.

Candide and Cacambo climbed into the coach; the six sheep flew like the wind, and in less than four hours they reached the king's palace at the edge of the capital. The entryway was two hundred and twenty feet high and a hundred wide; it is impossible to describe all the materials of which it was made. But you can imagine how much finer it was than those pebbles and sand which we call gold and jewels.

Twenty beautiful girls of the guard detail welcomed Candide and Cacambo as they stepped from the carriage, took them to the baths, and dressed them in robes woven of hummingbird feathers; then the high officials of the crown, both male and female, led them to the royal chamber between two long lines, each of a thousand musicians, as is customary. As they approached the throne room, Cacambo asked an officer what was the proper method of greeting his majesty: if one fell to one's knees or on one's belly; if one put one's hands on one's head or on one's rear; if one licked up the dust of the earth—in a word, what was the proper form?[9]

9. Candide's questions are probably derived from those of Gulliver on a similar occasion, in the third part of *Gulliver's Travels*.

—The ceremony, said the officer, is to embrace the king and kiss him on both cheeks.

Candide and Cacambo fell on the neck of his majesty, who received them with all the dignity imaginable, and asked them politely to dine.

In the interim, they were taken about to see the city, the public buildings rising to the clouds, the public markets and arcades, the fountains of pure water and of rose water, those of sugar cane liquors which flowed perpetually in the great plazas paved with a sort of stone which gave off odors of gillyflower and rose petals. Candide asked to see the supreme court and the hall of parliament; they told him there was no such thing, that lawsuits were unknown. He asked if there were prisons, and was told there were not. What surprised him more, and gave him most pleasure, was the palace of sciences, in which he saw a gallery two thousand paces long, entirely filled with mathematical and physical instruments.

Having passed the whole afternoon seeing only a thousandth part of the city, they returned to the king's palace. Candide sat down to dinner with his majesty, his own valet Cacambo, and several ladies. Never was better food served, and never did a host preside more jovially than his majesty. Cacambo explained the king's witty sayings to Candide, and even when translated they still seemed witty. Of all the things which astonished Candide, this was not, in his eyes, the least astonishing.

They passed a month in this refuge. Candide never tired of saying to Cacambo: —It's true, my friend, I'll say it again, the castle where I was born does not compare with the land where we now are; but Miss Cunégonde is not here, and you doubtless have a mistress somewhere in Europe. If we stay here, we shall be just like everybody else, whereas if we go back to our own world, taking with us just a dozen sheep loaded with Eldorado pebbles, we shall be richer than all the kings put together, we shall have no more inquisitors to fear, and we shall easily be able to retake Miss Cunégonde.

This harangue pleased Cacambo; wandering is such pleasure, it gives a man such prestige at home to be able to talk of what he has seen abroad, that the two happy men resolved to be so no longer, but to take their leave of his majesty.

—You are making a foolish mistake, the king told them; I know very well that my kingdom is nothing much; but when you are pretty comfortable somewhere, you had better stay there. Of course I have no right to keep strangers against their will, that sort of tyranny is not in keeping with our laws or our customs; all men are free; depart when you will, but the way out is very difficult. You cannot possibly go up the river by which you miraculously came; it runs too swiftly through its underground caves. The mountains which surround my land are ten thousand feet high, and steep as walls; each one is more than ten leagues across; the only way down is over precipices. But since you really must go, I shall order my engineers to make a machine which can carry you conveniently. When we take you over the mountains, nobody will be able to go with you, for my subjects have sworn never to leave their refuge, and they are too sensible to break their vows. Other than that, ask of me what you please.

—We only request of your majesty, Cacambo said, a few sheep loaded with provisions, some pebbles, and some of the mud of your country.

The king laughed.

—I simply can't understand, said he, the passion you Europeans have for our yellow mud; but take all you want, and much good may it do you.

He promptly gave orders to his technicians to make a machine for lifting these two extraordinary men out of his kingdom. Three thousand good physicists worked at the problem; the machine was ready in two weeks' time, and cost no more than twenty million pounds sterling, in the money of the country. Cacambo and Candide were placed in the machine; there were two great sheep, saddled and bridled to serve them as steeds when they had cleared the mountains, twenty pack sheep with provisions, thirty which carried presents consisting of the rarities of the country, and fifty loaded with gold, jewels, and diamonds. The king bade tender farewell to the two vagabonds.

It made a fine spectacle, their departure, and the ingenious way in which they were hoisted with their sheep up to the top of the mountains. The technicians bade them good-bye after bringing them to safety, and Candide had now no other desire and no other object than to go and present his sheep to Miss Cunégonde.

—We have, said he, enough to pay off the governor of Buenos Aires— if, indeed, a price can be placed on Miss Cunégonde. Let us go to Cayenne, take ship there, and then see what kingdom we can find to buy up.

CHAPTER 19

What Happened to Them at Surinam, and How Candide
Got to Know Martin

The first day was pleasant enough for our travelers. They were encouraged by the idea of possessing more treasures than Asia, Europe, and Africa could bring together. Candide, in transports, carved the name of Cunégonde on the trees. On the second day two of their sheep bogged down in a swamp and were lost with their loads; two other sheep died of fatigue a few days later; seven or eight others starved to death in a desert; still others fell, a little after, from precipices. Finally, after a hundred days' march, they had only two sheep left. Candide told Cacambo: —My friend, you see how the riches of this world are fleeting; the only solid things are virtue and the joy of seeing Miss Cunégonde again.

—I agree, said Cacambo, but we still have two sheep, laden with more treasure than the king of Spain will ever have; and I see in the distance a town which I suspect is Surinam; it belongs to the Dutch. We are at the end of our trials and on the threshold of our happiness.

As they drew near the town, they discovered a negro stretched on the ground with only half his clothes left, that is, a pair of blue drawers; the poor fellow was also missing his left leg and his right hand.

—Good Lord, said Candide in Dutch, what are you doing in that horrible condition, my friend?

—I am waiting for my master, Mr. Vanderdendur,[1] the famous merchant, answered the negro.

—Is Mr. Vanderdendur, Candide asked, the man who treated you this way?

—Yes, sir, said the negro, that's how things are around here. Twice a year we get a pair of linen drawers to wear. If we catch a finger in the sugar mill where we work, they cut off our hand; if we try to run away, they cut off our leg: I have undergone both these experiences. This is the price of the sugar you eat in Europe. And yet, when my mother sold me for ten Patagonian crowns on the coast of Guinea, she said to me: 'My dear child, bless our witch doctors, reverence them always, they will make your life happy; you have the honor of being a slave to our white masters, and in this way you are making the fortune of your father and mother.' Alas! I don't know if I made their fortunes, but they certainly did not make mine. The dogs, monkeys, and parrots are a thousand times less unhappy than we are. The Dutch witch doctors who converted me tell me every Sunday that we are all sons of Adam, black and white alike. I am no genealogist; but if these preachers are right, we must all be remote cousins; and you must admit no one could treat his own flesh and blood in a more horrible fashion.

—Oh Pangloss! cried Candide, you had no notion of these abominations! I'm through, I must give up your optimism after all.

—What's optimism? said Cacambo.

—Alas, said Candide, it is a mania for saying things are well when one is in hell.

And he shed bitter tears as he looked at this negro, and he was still weeping as he entered Surinam.

The first thing they asked was if there was not some vessel in port which could be sent to Buenos Aires. The man they asked was a Spanish merchant who undertook to make an honest bargain with them. They arranged to meet in a café; Candide and the faithful Cacambo, with their two sheep, went there to meet with him.

Candide, who always said exactly what was in his heart, told the Spaniard of his adventures, and confessed that he wanted to recapture Miss Cunégonde.

—I shall take good care *not* to send you to Buenos Aires, said the merchant; I should be hanged, and so would you. The lovely Cunégonde is his lordship's favorite mistress.

This was a thunderstroke for Candide; he wept for a long time; finally he drew Cacambo aside.

—Here, my friend, said he, is what you must do. Each one of us has in his pockets five or six millions' worth of diamonds; you are cleverer than I; go get Miss Cunégonde in Buenos Aires. If the governor makes a fuss, give him a million; if that doesn't convince him, give him two millions; you never killed an inquisitor, nobody will suspect you. I'll fit out another

---

1. A name perhaps intended to suggest VanDuren, a Dutch bookseller with whom Voltaire had quarreled. In particular, the incident of gradually raising one's price recalls VanDuren, to whom Voltaire had successively offered 1,000, 1,500, 2,000, and 3,000 florins for the return of the manuscript of Frederick the Great's *Anti-Machiavel*.

boat and go wait for you in Venice. That is a free country, where one need have no fear either of Bulgars or Abares or Jews or inquisitors.

Cacambo approved of this wise decision. He was in despair at leaving a good master who had become a bosom friend; but the pleasure of serving him overcame the grief of leaving him. They embraced, and shed a few tears; Candide urged him not to forget the good old woman. Cacambo departed that very same day; he was a very good fellow, that Cacambo.

Candide remained for some time in Surinam, waiting for another merchant to take him to Italy, along with the two sheep which were left him. He hired servants and bought everything necessary for the long voyage; finally Mr. Vanderdendur, master of a big ship, came calling.

—How much will you charge, Candide asked this man, to take me to Venice—myself, my servants, my luggage, and those two sheep over there?

The merchant set a price of ten thousand piastres; Candide did not blink an eye.

—Oh, ho, said the prudent Vanderdendur to himself, this stranger pays out ten thousand piastres at once, he must be pretty well fixed.

Then, returning a moment later, he made known that he could not set sail under twenty thousand.

—All right, you shall have them, said Candide.

—Whew, said the merchant softly to himself, this man gives twenty thousand piastres as easily as ten.

He came back again to say he could not go to Venice for less than thirty thousand piastres.

—All right, thirty then, said Candide.

—Ah ha, said the Dutch merchant, again speaking to himself; so thirty thousand piastres mean nothing to this man; no doubt the two sheep are loaded with immense treasures; let's say no more; we'll pick up the thirty thousand piastres first, and then we'll see.

Candide sold two little diamonds, the least of which was worth more than all the money demanded by the merchant. He paid him in advance. The two sheep were taken aboard. Candide followed in a little boat, to board the vessel at its anchorage. The merchant bides his time, sets sail, and makes his escape with a favoring wind. Candide, aghast and stupefied, soon loses him from view.

—Alas, he cries, now there is a trick worthy of the old world!

He returns to shore sunk in misery; for he had lost riches enough to make the fortunes of twenty monarchs.

Now he rushes to the house of the Dutch magistrate, and, being a bit disturbed, he knocks loudly at the door; goes in, tells the story of what happened, and shouts a bit louder than is customary. The judge begins by fining him ten thousand piastres for making such a racket; then he listens patiently to the story, promises to look into the matter as soon as the merchant comes back, and charges another ten thousand piastres as the costs of the hearing.

This legal proceeding completed the despair of Candide. In fact he had experienced miseries a thousand times more painful, but the coldness of the judge, and that of the merchant who had robbed him, roused his bile and plunged him into a black melancholy. The malice of men rose up before his spirit in all its ugliness, and his mind dwelt only on gloomy thoughts. Finally, when a French vessel was ready to leave for Bordeaux, since he had no more diamond-laden sheep to transport, he took a cabin at a fair price, and made it known in the town that he would pay passage and keep, plus two thousand piastres, to any honest man who wanted to make the journey with him, on condition that this man must be the most disgusted with his own condition and the most unhappy man in the province.

This drew such a crowd of applicants as a fleet could not have held. Candide wanted to choose among the leading candidates, so he picked out about twenty who seemed companionable enough, and of whom each pretended to be more miserable than all the others. He brought them together at his inn and gave them a dinner, on condition that each would swear to tell truthfully his entire history. He would select as his companion the most truly miserable and rightly discontented man, and among the others he would distribute various gifts.

The meeting lasted till four in the morning. Candide, as he listened to all the stories, remembered what the old woman had told him on the trip to Buenos Aires, and of the wager she had made, that there was nobody on the boat who had not undergone great misfortunes. At every story that was told him, he thought of Pangloss.

—That Pangloss, he said, would be hard put to prove his system. I wish he was here. Certainly if everything goes well, it is in Eldorado and not in the rest of the world.

At last he decided in favor of a poor scholar who had worked ten years for the booksellers of Amsterdam. He decided that there was no trade in the world with which one should be more disgusted.

This scholar, who was in fact a good man, had been robbed by his wife, beaten by his son, and deserted by his daughter, who had got herself abducted by a Portuguese. He had just been fired from the little job on which he existed; and the preachers of Surinam were persecuting him because they took him for a Socinian.[2] The others, it is true, were at least as unhappy as he, but Candide hoped the scholar would prove more amusing on the voyage. All his rivals declared that Candide was doing them a great injustice, but he pacified them with a hundred piastres apiece.

CHAPTER 20

What Happened to Candide and Martin at Sea

The old scholar, whose name was Martin, now set sail with Candide for Bordeaux. Both men had seen and suffered much; and even if the vessel had been sailing from Surinam to Japan via the Cape of Good Hope, they would have been able to keep themselves amused with instances of moral evil and physical evil during the entire trip.

However, Candide had one great advantage over Martin, that he still hoped to see Miss Cunégonde again, and Martin had nothing to hope for; besides, he had gold and diamonds, and though he had lost a hundred big red sheep loaded with the greatest treasures of the earth, though he had

2. A follower of Faustus and Laelius Socinus, sixteenth-century Polish theologians, who proposed a form of "rational" Christianity which exalted the rational conscience and minimized such mysteries as the trinity. The Socinians, by a special irony, were vigorous optimists.

always at his heart a memory of the Dutch merchant's villainy, yet, when he thought of the wealth that remained in his hands, and when he talked of Cunégonde, especially just after a good dinner, he still inclined to the system of Pangloss.

—But what about you, Monsieur Martin, he asked the scholar, what do you think of all that? What is your idea of moral evil and physical evil?

—Sir, answered Martin, those priests accused me of being a Socinian, but the truth is that I am a Manichee.[3]

—You're joking, said Candide; there aren't any more Manichees in the world.

—There's me, said Martin; I don't know what to do about it, but I can't think otherwise.

—You must be possessed of the devil, said Candide.

—He's mixed up with so many things of this world, said Martin, that he may be in me as well as elsewhere; but I assure you, as I survey this globe, or globule, I think that God has abandoned it to some evil spirit—all of it except Eldorado. I have scarcely seen one town which did not wish to destroy its neighboring town, no family which did not wish to exterminate some other family. Everywhere the weak loathe the powerful, before whom they cringe, and the powerful treat them like brute cattle, to be sold for their meat and fleece. A million regimented assassins roam Europe from one end to the other, plying the trades of murder and robbery in an organized way for a living, because there is no more honest form of work for them; and in the cities which seem to enjoy peace and where the arts are flourishing, men are devoured by more envy, cares, and anxieties than a whole town experiences when it's under siege. Private griefs are worse even than public trials. In a word, I have seen so much and suffered so much, that I am a Manichee.

—Still there is some good, said Candide.

—That may be, said Martin, but I don't know it.

In the middle of this discussion, the rumble of cannon was heard. From minute to minute the noise grew louder. Everyone reached for his spyglass. At a distance of some three miles they saw two vessels fighting; the wind brought both of them so close to the French vessel that they had a pleasantly comfortable seat to watch the fight. Presently one of the vessels caught the other with a broadside so low and so square as to send it to the bottom. Candide and Martin saw clearly a hundred men on the deck of the sinking ship; they all raised their hands to heaven, uttering fearful shrieks; and in a moment everything was swallowed up.

—Well, said Martin, that is how men treat one another.

—It is true, said Candide, there's something devilish in this business.

As they chatted, he noticed something of a striking red color floating near the sunken vessel. They sent out a boat to investigate; it was one of his sheep. Candide was more joyful to recover this one sheep than he had been afflicted to lose a hundred of them, all loaded with big Eldorado diamonds.

---

3. Mani, a Persian sage and philosopher of the third century A.D., taught (probably under the influence of traditions stemming from Zoroaster and the worshipers of the sun god Mithra) that the earth is a field of dispute between two almost equal powers, one of light and one of darkness, both of which must be propitiated.

The French captain soon learned that the captain of the victorious vessel was Spanish and that of the sunken vessel was a Dutch pirate. It was the same man who had robbed Candide. The enormous riches which this rascal had stolen were sunk beside him in the sea, and nothing was saved but a single sheep.

—You see, said Candide to Martin, crime is punished sometimes; this scoundrel of a Dutch merchant has met the fate he deserved.

—Yes, said Martin; but did the passengers aboard his ship have to perish too? God punished the scoundrel, and the devil drowned the others.

Meanwhile the French and Spanish vessels continued on their journey, and Candide continued his talks with Martin. They disputed for fifteen days in a row, and at the end of that time were just as much in agreement as at the beginning. But at least they were talking, they exchanged their ideas, they consoled one another. Candide caressed his sheep.

—Since I have found you again, said he, I may well rediscover Miss Cunégonde.

CHAPTER 21

Candide and Martin Approach the Coast of France: They Reason Together

At last the coast of France came in view.

—Have you ever been in France, Monsieur Martin? asked Candide.

—Yes, said Martin, I have visited several provinces. There are some where half the inhabitants are crazy, others where they are too sly, still others where they are quite gentle and stupid, some where they venture on wit; in all of them the principal occupation is love-making, the second is slander, and the third stupid talk.

—But, Monsieur Martin, were you ever in Paris?

—Yes, I've been in Paris; it contains specimens of all these types; it is a chaos, a mob, in which everyone is seeking pleasure and where hardly anyone finds it, at least from what I have seen. I did not live there for long; as I arrived, I was robbed of everything I possessed by thieves at the fair of St. Germain; I myself was taken for a thief, and spent eight days in jail, after which I took a proofreader's job to earn enough money to return on foot to Holland. I knew the writing gang, the intriguing gang, the gang with fits and convulsions.[4] They say there are some very civilized people in that town; I'd like to think so.

—I myself have no desire to visit France, said Candide; you no doubt realize that when one has spent a month in Eldorado, there is nothing else on earth one wants to see, except Miss Cunégonde. I am going to wait for her at Venice; we will cross France simply to get to Italy; wouldn't you like to come with me?

—Gladly, said Martin; they say Venice is good only for the Venetian nobles, but that on the other hand they treat foreigners very well when they have plenty of money. I don't have any; you do, so I'll follow you anywhere.

---

4. The Jansenists, a sect of strict Catholics, became notorious for spiritual ecstasies. Their public displays reached a height during the 1720s, and Voltaire described them in *Le Siècle de Louis XIV* (chap. 37), as well as in the article "Convulsions" in the *Philosophical Dictionary*.

—By the way, said Candide, do you believe the earth was originally all ocean, as they assure us in that big book belonging to the ship's captain?[5]

—I don't believe that stuff, said Martin, nor any of the dreams which people have been peddling for some time now.

—But why, then, was this world formed at all? asked Candide.

—To drive us mad, answered Martin.

—Aren't you astonished, Candide went on, at the love which those two girls showed for the monkeys in the land of the Biglugs that I told you about?

—Not at all, said Martin, I see nothing strange in these sentiments; I have seen so many extraordinary things that nothing seems extraordinary any more.

—Do you believe, asked Candide, that men have always massacred one another as they do today? That they have always been liars, traitors, ingrates, thieves, weaklings, sneaks, cowards, backbiters, gluttons, drunkards, misers, climbers, killers, calumniators, sensualists, fanatics, hypocrites, and fools?

—Do you believe, said Martin, that hawks have always eaten pigeons when they could get them?

—Of course, said Candide.

—Well, said Martin, if hawks have always had the same character, why do you suppose that men have changed?

—Oh, said Candide, there's a great deal of difference, because freedom of the will . . .

As they were disputing in this manner, they reached Bordeaux.

CHAPTER 22

What Happened in France to Candide and Martin

Candide paused in Bordeaux only long enough to sell a couple of Dorado pebbles and to fit himself out with a fine two-seater carriage, for he could no longer do without his philosopher Martin; only he was very unhappy to part with his sheep, which he left to the academy of science in Bordeaux. They proposed, as the theme of that year's prize contest, the discovery of why the wool of the sheep was red; and the prize was awarded to a northern scholar[6] who demonstrated by A plus B minus C divided by Z that the sheep ought to be red and die of sheep rot.

But all the travelers with whom Candide talked in the roadside inns told him: —We are going to Paris.

This general consensus finally inspired in him too a desire to see the capital; it was not much out of his road to Venice.

He entered through the Faubourg Saint-Marceau,[7] and thought he was in the meanest village of Westphalia.

---

5. The Bible: Genesis 1.   6. Maupertuis Le Lapon, philosopher and mathematician, whom Voltaire had accused of trying to adduce mathematical proofs of the existence of God.   7. A district on the left bank, notably grubby in the eighteenth century. "As I entered [Paris] through the Faubourg Saint-Marceau, I saw nothing but dirty stinking little streets, ugly black houses, a general air of squalor and poverty, beggars, carters, menders of clothes, sellers of herb-drinks and old hats." Jean-Jacques Rousseau, *Confessions*, Book IV.

Scarcely was Candide in his hotel, when he came down with a mild illness caused by exhaustion. As he was wearing an enormous diamond ring, and people had noticed among his luggage a tremendously heavy safe, he soon found at his bedside two doctors whom he had not called, several intimate friends who never left him alone, and two pious ladies who helped to warm his broth. Martin said: —I remember that I too was ill on my first trip to Paris; I was very poor; and as I had neither friends, pious ladies, nor doctors, I got well.

However, as a result of medicines and bleedings, Candide's illness became serious. A resident of the neighborhood came to ask him politely to fill out a ticket, to be delivered to the porter of the other world.[8] Candide wanted nothing to do with it. The pious ladies assured him it was a new fashion; Candide replied that he wasn't a man of fashion. Martin wanted to throw the resident out the window. The cleric swore that without the ticket they wouldn't bury Candide. Martin swore that he would bury the cleric if he continued to be a nuisance. The quarrel grew heated; Martin took him by the shoulders and threw him bodily out the door; all of which caused a great scandal, from which developed a legal case.

Candide got better; and during his convalescence he had very good company in to dine. They played cards for money; and Candide was quite surprised that none of the aces were ever dealt to him, and Martin was not surprised at all.

Among those who did the honors of the town for Candide there was a little abbé from Perigord, one of those busy fellows, always bright, always useful, assured, obsequious, and obliging, who waylay passing strangers, tell them the scandal of the town, and offer them pleasures at any price they want to pay. This fellow first took Candide and Martin to the theatre. A new tragedy was being played. Candide found himself seated next to a group of wits. That did not keep him from shedding a few tears in the course of some perfectly played scenes. One of the commentators beside him remarked during the intermission: —You are quite mistaken to weep, this actress is very bad indeed; the actor who plays with her is even worse; and the play is even worse than the actors in it. The author knows not a word of Arabic, though the action takes place in Arabia; and besides, he is a man who doesn't believe in innate ideas. Tomorrow I will show you twenty pamphlets written against him.

—Tell me, sir, said Candide to the abbé, how many plays are there for performance in France?

—Five or six thousand, replied the other.

—That's a lot, said Candide; how many of them are any good?

—Fifteen or sixteen, was the answer.

—That's a lot, said Martin.

Candide was very pleased with an actress who took the part of Queen Elizabeth in a rather dull tragedy[9] that still gets played from time to time.

---

8. In the middle of the eighteenth century, it became customary to require persons who were grievously ill to sign *billets de confession*, without which they could not be given absolution, admitted to the last sacraments, or buried in consecrated ground.   9. *Le Comte d'Essex* by Thomas Corneille.

—I like this actress very much, he said to Martin, she bears a slight resemblance to Miss Cunégonde; I should like to meet her.

The abbé from Perigord offered to introduce him. Candide, raised in Germany, asked what was the protocol, how one behaved in France with queens of England.

—You must distinguish, said the abbé; in the provinces, you take them to an inn; at Paris they are respected while still attractive, and thrown on the dunghill when they are dead.[1]

—Queens on the dunghill! said Candide.

—Yes indeed, said Martin, the abbé is right; I was in Paris when Miss Monime herself[2] passed, as they say, from this life to the other; she was refused what these folk call 'the honors of burial,' that is, the right to rot with all the beggars of the district in a dirty cemetery; she was buried all alone by her troupe at the corner of the Rue de Bourgogne; this must have been very disagreeable to her, for she had a noble character.

—That was extremely rude, said Candide.

—What do you expect? said Martin; that is how these folk are. Imagine all the contradictions, all the incompatibilities you can, and you will see them in the government, the courts, the churches, and the plays of this crazy nation.

—Is it true that they are always laughing in Paris? asked Candide.

—Yes, said the abbé, but with a kind of rage too; when people complain of things, they do so amid explosions of laughter; they even laugh as they perform the most detestable actions.

—Who was that fat swine, said Candide, who spoke so nastily about the play over which I was weeping, and the actors who gave me so much pleasure?

—He is a living illness, answered the abbé, who makes a business of slandering all the plays and books; he hates the successful ones, as eunuchs hate successful lovers; he's one of those literary snakes who live on filth and venom; he's a folliculator . . .

—What's this word *folliculator*? asked Candide.

—It's a folio filler, said the abbé, a Fréron.[3]

It was after this fashion that Candide, Martin, and the abbé from Perigord chatted on the stairway as they watched the crowd leaving the theatre.

—Although I'm in a great hurry to see Miss Cunégonde again, said Candide, I would very much like to dine with Miss Clairon,[4] for she seemed to me admirable.

The abbé was not the man to approach Miss Clairon, who saw only good company.

—She has an engagement tonight, he said; but I shall have the honor of introducing you to a lady of quality, and there you will get to know Paris as if you had lived here for years.

---

1. Voltaire engaged in a long and vigorous campaign against the rule that actors and actresses could not be buried in consecrated ground. The superstition probably arose from a feeling that by assuming false identities they drained their own souls.   2. Adrienne Lecouvreur (1690–1730), so called because she made her debut as Monime in Racine's *Mithridate*. Voltaire had assisted at her secret midnight funeral and wrote an indignant poem about it.   3. A successful and popular journalist, who had attacked several of Voltaire's plays, including *Tancrède*.   4. Actually Claire Leris (1723–1803). She had played the lead role in *Tancrède* and was for many years a leading figure on the Paris stage.

Candide, who was curious by nature, allowed himself to be brought to the lady's house, in the depths of the Faubourg St.-Honoré; they were playing faro;[5] twelve melancholy punters held in their hands a little sheaf of cards, blank summaries of their bad luck. Silence reigned supreme, the punters were pallid, the banker uneasy; and the lady of the house, seated beside the pitiless banker, watched with the eyes of a lynx for the various illegal redoublings and bets at long odds which the players tried to signal by folding the corners of their cards; she had them unfolded with a determination which was severe but polite, and concealed her anger lest she lose her customers. The lady caused herself to be known as the Marquise of Parolignac.[6] Her daughter, fifteen years old, sat among the punters and tipped off her mother with a wink to the sharp practices of these unhappy players when they tried to recoup their losses. The abbé from Perigord, Candide, and Martin came in; nobody arose or greeted them or looked at them; all were lost in the study of their cards.

— My Lady the Baroness of Thunder-Ten-Tronckh was more civil, thought Candide.

However, the abbé whispered in the ear of the marquise, who, half rising, honored Candide with a gracious smile and Martin with a truly noble nod; she gave a seat and dealt a hand of cards to Candide, who lost fifty thousand francs in two turns; after which they had a very merry supper. Everyone was amazed that Candide was not upset over his losses; the lackeys, talking together in their usual lackey language, said: — He must be some English milord.

The supper was like most Parisian suppers: first silence, then an indistinguishable rush of words; then jokes, mostly insipid, false news, bad logic, a little politics, a great deal of malice. They even talked of new books.

— Have you seen the new novel by Dr. Gauchat, the theologian?[7] asked the abbé from Perigord.

— Oh yes, answered one of the guests; but I couldn't finish it. We have a horde of impudent scribblers nowadays, but all of them put together don't match the impudence of this Gauchat, this doctor of theology. I have been so struck by the enormous number of detestable books which are swamping us that I have taken up punting at faro.

— And the *Collected Essays* of Archdeacon T——[8] asked the abbé, what do you think of them?

— Ah, said Madame de Parolignac, what a frightful bore he is! He takes such pains to tell you what everyone knows; he discourses so learnedly on matters which aren't worth a casual remark! He plunders, and not even wittily, the wit of other people! He spoils what he plunders, he's disgusting! But he'll never disgust me again; a couple of pages of the archdeacon have been enough for me.

---

5. A game of cards, about which it is necessary to know only that a number of punters play against a banker or dealer. The pack is dealt out two cards at a time, and each player may bet on any card as much as he pleases. The sharp practices of the punters consist essentially of tricks for increasing their winnings without corresponding risks.   6. A *paroli* is an illegal redoubling of one's bet; her name therefore implies a title grounded in cardsharping.   7. He had written against Voltaire, and Voltaire suspected him (wrongly) of having written the novel *L'Oracle des nouveaux philosophes.*   8. His name was Trublet, and he had said, among other disagreeable things, that Voltaire's epic poem, the *Henriade*, made him yawn and that Voltaire's genius was "the perfection of mediocrity."

There was at table a man of learning and taste, who supported the marquise on this point. They talked next of tragedies; the lady asked why there were tragedies which played well enough but which were wholly unreadable. The man of taste explained very clearly how a play could have a certain interest and yet little merit otherwise; he showed succinctly that it was not enough to conduct a couple of intrigues, such as one can find in any novel, and which never fail to excite the spectator's interest; but that one must be new without being grotesque, frequently touch the sublime but never depart from the natural; that one must know the human heart and give it words; that one must be a great poet without allowing any character in the play to sound like a poet; and that one must know the language perfectly, speak it purely, and maintain a continual harmony without ever sacrificing sense to mere sound.

—Whoever, he added, does not observe all these rules may write one or two tragedies which succeed in the theatre, but he will never be ranked among the good writers; there are very few good tragedies; some are idylls in well-written, well-rhymed dialogue, others are political arguments which put the audience to sleep, or revolting pomposities; still others are the fantasies of enthusiasts, barbarous in style, incoherent in logic, full of long speeches to the gods because the author does not know how to address men, full of false maxims and emphatic commonplaces.

Candide listened attentively to this speech and conceived a high opinion of the speaker; and as the marquise had placed him by her side, he turned to ask her who was this man who spoke so well.

—He is a scholar, said the lady, who never plays cards and whom the abbé sometimes brings to my house for supper; he knows all about tragedies and books, and has himself written a tragedy that was hissed from the stage and a book, the only copy of which ever seen outside his publisher's office was dedicated to me.

—What a great man, said Candide, he's Pangloss all over.

Then, turning to him, he said: —Sir, you doubtless think everything is for the best in the physical as well as the moral universe, and that nothing could be otherwise than as it is?

—Not at all, sir, replied the scholar, I believe nothing of the sort. I find that everything goes wrong in our world; that nobody knows his place in society or his duty, what he's doing or what he ought to be doing, and that outside of mealtimes, which are cheerful and congenial enough, all the rest of the day is spent in useless quarrels, as of Jansenists against Molinists,[9] parliament-men against churchmen, literary men against literary men, courtiers against courtiers, financiers against the plebs, wives against husbands, relatives against relatives—it's one unending warfare.

Candide answered: —I have seen worse; but a wise man, who has since had the misfortune to be hanged, taught me that everything was marvelously well arranged. Troubles are just the shadows in a beautiful picture.

—Your hanged philosopher was joking, said Martin; the shadows are horrible ugly blots.

---

9. The Jansenists (from Corneille Jansen, 1585–1638) were a relatively strict party of religious reform; the Molinists (from Luis Molina) were the party of the Jesuits. Their central issue of controversy was the relative importance of divine grace and human will to the salvation of man.

—It is human beings who make the blots, said Candide, and they can't
do otherwise.

—Then it isn't their fault, said Martin.

Most of the faro players, who understood this sort of talk not at all, kept
on drinking; Martin disputed with the scholar, and Candide told part of
his story to the lady of the house.

After supper, the marquise brought Candide into her room and sat him
down on a divan.

—Well, she said to him, are you still madly in love with Miss Cunégonde of Thunder-Ten-Tronckh?

—Yes, ma'am, replied Candide. The marquise turned upon him a
tender smile.

—You answer like a young man of Westphalia, said she; a Frenchman
would have told me: 'It is true that I have been in love with Miss Cunégonde; but since seeing you, madame, I fear that I love her no longer.'

—Alas, ma'am, said Candide, I will answer any way you want.

—Your passion for her, said the marquise, began when you picked up
her handkerchief; I prefer that you should pick up my garter.

—Gladly, said Candide, and picked it up.

—But I also want you to put it back on, said the lady; and Candide put
it on again.

—Look you now, said the lady, you are a foreigner; my Paris lovers I
sometimes cause to languish for two weeks or so, but to you I surrender
the very first night, because we must render the honors of the country to
a young man from Westphalia.

The beauty, who had seen two enormous diamonds on the two hands
of her young friend, praised them so sincerely that from the fingers of
Candide they passed over to the fingers of the marquise.

As he returned home with his Perigord abbé, Candide felt some
remorse at having been unfaithful to Miss Cunégonde; the abbé sympathized with his grief; he had only a small share in the fifty thousand francs
which Candide lost at cards, and in the proceeds of the two diamonds
which had been half-given, half-extorted. His scheme was to profit, as
much as he could, from the advantage of knowing Candide. He spoke at
length of Cunégonde, and Candide told him that he would beg forgiveness for his beloved for his infidelity when he met her at Venice.

The Perigordian overflowed with politeness and unction, taking a
tender interest in everything Candide said, everything he did, and everything he wanted to do.

—Well, sir, said he, so you have an assignation at Venice?

—Yes indeed, sir, I do, said Candide; it is absolutely imperative that I
go there to find Miss Cunégonde.

And then, carried away by the pleasure of talking about his love, he
recounted, as he often did, a part of his adventures with that illustrious
lady of Westphalia.

—I suppose, said the abbé, that Miss Cunégonde has a fine wit and
writes charming letters.

—I never received a single letter from her, said Candide; for, as you
can imagine, after being driven out of the castle for love of her, I couldn't

write; shortly I learned that she was dead; then I rediscovered her; then I lost her again, and I have now sent, to a place more than twenty-five hundred leagues from here, a special agent whose return I am expecting.

The abbé listened carefully, and looked a bit dreamy. He soon took his leave of the two strangers, after embracing them tenderly. Next day Candide, when he woke up, received a letter, to the following effect:

—Dear sir, my very dear lover, I have been lying sick in this town for a week, I have just learned that you are here. I would fly to your arms if I could move. I heard that you had passed through Bordeaux; that was where I left the faithful Cacambo and the old woman, who are soon to follow me here. The governor of Buenos Aires took everything, but left me your heart. Come; your presence will either return me to life or cause me to die of joy.

This charming letter, coming so unexpectedly, filled Candide with inexpressible delight, while the illness of his dear Cunégonde covered him with grief. Torn between these two feelings, he took gold and diamonds, and had himself brought, with Martin, to the hotel where Miss Cunégonde was lodging. Trembling with emotion, he enters the room; his heart thumps, his voice breaks. He tries to open the curtains of the bed, he asks to have some lights.

—Absolutely forbidden, says the serving girl; light will be the death of her.

And abruptly she pulls shut the curtain.

—My dear Cunégonde, says Candide in tears, how are you feeling? If you can't see me, won't you at least speak to me?

—She can't talk, says the servant.

But then she draws forth from the bed a plump hand, over which Candide weeps a long time, and which he fills with diamonds, meanwhile leaving a bag of gold on the chair.

Amid his transports, there arrives a bailiff followed by the abbé from Perigord and a strong-arm squad.

—These here are the suspicious foreigners? says the officer; and he has them seized and orders his bullies to drag them off to jail.

—They don't treat visitors like this in Eldorado, says Candide.

—I am more a Manichee than ever, says Martin.

—But, please sir, where are you taking us? says Candide.

—To the lowest hole in the dungeons, says the bailiff.

Martin, having regained his self-possession, decided that the lady who pretended to be Cunégonde was a cheat, the abbé from Perigord was another cheat who had imposed on Candide's innocence, and the bailiff still another cheat, of whom it would be easy to get rid.

Rather than submit to the forms of justice, Candide, enlightened by Martin's advice and eager for his own part to see the real Cunégonde again, offered the bailiff three little diamonds worth about three thousand pistoles apiece.

—Ah, my dear sir! cried the man with the ivory staff, even if you have committed every crime imaginable, you are the most honest man in the world. Three diamonds! each one worth three thousand pistoles! My dear sir! I would gladly die for you, rather than take you to jail. All foreigners get arrested here; but let me manage it; I have a brother at Dieppe in Normandy; I'll take you to him; and if you have a bit of a diamond to give him, he'll take care of you, just like me.

—And why do they arrest all foreigners? asked Candide.

The abbé from Perigord spoke up and said: —It's because a beggar from Atrebatum[1] listened to some stupidities; that made him commit a parricide, not like the one of May, 1610, but like the one of December, 1594, much on the order of several other crimes committed in other years and other months by other beggars who had listened to stupidities.

The bailiff then explained what it was all about.[2]

—Foh! what beasts! cried Candide. What! monstrous behavior of this sort from a people who sing and dance? As soon as I can, let me get out of this country, where the monkeys provoke the tigers. In my own country I've lived with bears; only in Eldorado are there proper men. In the name of God, sir bailiff, get me to Venice where I can wait for Miss Cunégonde.

—I can only get you to Lower Normandy, said the guardsman.

He had the irons removed at once, said there had been a mistake, dismissed his gang, and took Candide and Martin to Dieppe, where he left them with his brother. There was a little Dutch ship at anchor. The Norman, changed by three more diamonds into the most helpful of men, put Candide and his people aboard the vessel, which was bound for Portsmouth in England. It wasn't on the way to Venice, but Candide felt like a man just let out of hell; and he hoped to get back on the road to Venice at the first possible occasion.

CHAPTER 23

Candide and Martin Pass the Shores of England; What They See There

—Ah, Pangloss! Pangloss! Ah, Martin! Martin! Ah, my darling Cunégonde! What is this world of ours? sighed Candide on the Dutch vessel.

—Something crazy, something abominable, Martin replied.

—You have been in England; are people as crazy there as in France?

—It's a different sort of crazy, said Martin. You know that these two nations have been at war over a few acres of snow near Canada, and that they are spending on this fine struggle more than Canada itself is worth.[3] As for telling you if there are more people in one country or the other who need a strait jacket, that is a judgment too fine for my understanding; I know only that the people we are going to visit are eaten up with melancholy.

As they chatted thus, the vessel touched at Portsmouth. A multitude of

1. The Latin name for the district of Artois, from which came Robert-François Damiens, who tried to stab Louis XV in 1757. The assassination failed, like that of Châtel, who tried to kill Henri IV in 1594, but unlike that of Ravaillac, who succeeded in killing him in 1610.   2. The point, in fact, is not too clear since arresting foreigners is an indirect way at best to guard against homegrown fanatics, and the position of the abbé from Perigord in the whole transaction remains confused. Has he called in the officer just to get rid of Candide? If so, why is he sardonic about the very suspicions he is trying to foster? Candide's reaction is to the notion that Frenchmen should be capable of political assassination at all; it seems excessive.   3. The wars of the French and English over Canada dragged intermittently through the eighteenth century till the peace of Paris sealed England's conquest (1763). Voltaire thought the French should concentrate on developing Louisiana, where the Jesuit influence was less marked.

people covered the shore, watching closely a rather bulky man who was kneeling, his eyes blindfolded, on the deck of a man-of-war. Four soldiers, stationed directly in front of this man, fired three bullets apiece into his brain, as peaceably as you would want; and the whole assemblage went home, in great satisfaction.[4]

—What's all this about? asked Candide. What devil is everywhere at work?

He asked who was that big man who had just been killed with so much ceremony.

—It was an admiral, they told him.

—And why kill this admiral?

—The reason, they told him, is that he didn't kill enough people; he gave battle to a French admiral, and it was found that he didn't get close enough to him.

—But, said Candide, the French admiral was just as far from the English admiral as the English admiral was from the French admiral.

—That's perfectly true, came the answer; but in this country it is useful from time to time to kill one admiral in order to encourage the others.

Candide was so stunned and shocked at what he saw and heard, that he would not even set foot ashore; he arranged with the Dutch merchant (without even caring if he was robbed, as at Surinam) to be taken forthwith to Venice.

The merchant was ready in two days; they coasted along France, they passed within sight of Lisbon, and Candide quivered. They entered the straits, crossed the Mediterranean, and finally landed at Venice.

—God be praised, said Candide, embracing Martin; here I shall recover the lovely Cunégonde. I trust Cacambo as I would myself. All is well, all goes well, all goes as well as possible.

CHAPTER 24

About Paquette and Brother Giroflée

As soon as he was in Venice, he had a search made for Cacambo in all the inns, all the cafés, all the stews—and found no trace of him. Every day he sent to investigate the vessels and coastal traders; no news of Cacambo.

—How's this? said he to Martin. I have had time to go from Surinam to Bordeaux, from Bordeaux to Paris, from Paris to Dieppe, from Dieppe to Portsmouth, to skirt Portugal and Spain, cross the Mediterranean, and spend several months at Venice—and the lovely Cunégonde has not come yet! In her place, I have met only that impersonator and that abbé from Perigord. Cunégonde is dead, without a doubt; and nothing remains for me too but death. Oh, it would have been better to stay in the earthly paradise of Eldorado than to return to this accursed Europe. How right you are, my dear Martin; all is but illusion and disaster.

He fell into a black melancholy, and refused to attend the fashionable operas or take part in the other diversions of the carnival season; not a

---

4. Candide has witnessed the execution of Admiral John Byng, defeated off Minorca by the French fleet under Galisonnière and executed by firing squad on March 14, 1757. Voltaire had intervened to avert the execution.

single lady tempted him in the slightest. Martin told him: —You're a real simpleton if you think a half-breed valet with five or six millions in his pockets will go to the end of the world to get your mistress and bring her to Venice for you. If he finds her, he'll take her for himself; if he doesn't, he'll take another. I advise you to forget about your servant Cacambo and your mistress Cunégonde.

Martin was not very comforting. Candide's melancholy increased, and Martin never wearied of showing him that there is little virtue and little happiness on this earth, except perhaps in Eldorado, where nobody can go.

While they were discussing this important matter and still waiting for Cunégonde, Candide noticed in St. Mark's Square a young Theatine[5] monk who had given his arm to a girl. The Theatine seemed fresh, plump, and flourishing; his eyes were bright, his manner cocky, his glance brilliant, his step proud. The girl was very pretty, and singing aloud; she glanced lovingly at her Theatine, and from time to time pinched his plump cheeks.

—At least you must admit, said Candide to Martin, that these people are happy. Until now I have not found in the whole inhabited earth, except Eldorado, anything but miserable people. But this girl and this monk, I'd be willing to bet, are very happy creatures.

—I'll bet they aren't, said Martin.

—We have only to ask them to dinner, said Candide, and we'll find out if I'm wrong.

Promptly he approached them, made his compliments, and invited them to his inn for a meal of macaroni, Lombardy partridges, and caviar, washed down with wine from Montepulciano, Cyprus, and Samos, and some Lacrima Christi. The girl blushed but the Theatine accepted gladly, and the girl followed him, watching Candide with an expression of surprise and confusion, darkened by several tears. Scarcely had she entered the room when she said to Candide: —What, can it be that Master Candide no longer knows Paquette?

At these words Candide, who had not yet looked carefully at her because he was preoccupied with Cunégonde, said to her: —Ah, my poor child! so you are the one who put Doctor Pangloss in the fine fix where I last saw him.

—Alas, sir, I was the one, said Paquette; I see you know all about it. I heard of the horrible misfortunes which befell the whole household of My Lady the Baroness and the lovely Cunégonde. I swear to you that my own fate has been just as unhappy. I was perfectly innocent when you knew me. A Franciscan, who was my confessor, easily seduced me. The consequences were frightful; shortly after My Lord the Baron had driven you out with great kicks on the backside, I too was forced to leave the castle. If a famous doctor had not taken pity on me, I would have died. Out of gratitude, I became for some time the mistress of this doctor. His wife, who was jealous to the point of frenzy, beat me mercilessly every day; she was a gorgon. The doctor was the ugliest of men, and I the most miserable

---

5. A Catholic order founded in 1524 by Cardinal Cajetan and G. P. Caraffa, later Pope Paul IV.

creature on earth, being continually beaten for a man I did not love. You will understand, sir, how dangerous it is for a nagging woman to be married to a doctor. This man, enraged by his wife's ways, one day gave her as a cold cure a medicine so potent that in two hours' time she died amid horrible convulsions. Her relatives brought suit against the bereaved husband; he fled the country, and I was put in prison. My innocence would never have saved me if I had not been rather pretty. The judge set me free on condition that he should become the doctor's successor. I was shortly replaced in this post by another girl, dismissed without any payment, and obliged to continue this abominable trade which you men find so pleasant and which for us is nothing but a bottomless pit of misery. I went to ply the trade in Venice. Ah, my dear sir, if you could imagine what it is like to have to caress indiscriminately an old merchant, a lawyer, a monk, a gondolier, an abbé; to be subjected to every sort of insult and outrage; to be reduced, time and again, to borrowing a skirt in order to go have it lifted by some disgusting man; to be robbed by this fellow of what one has gained from that; to be shaken down by the police, and to have before one only the prospect of a hideous old age, a hospital, and a dunghill, you will conclude that I am one of the most miserable creatures in the world.

Thus Paquette poured forth her heart to the good Candide in a hotel room, while Martin sat listening nearby. At last he said to Candide: —You see, I've already won half my bet.

Brother Giroflée[6] had remained in the dining room, and was having a drink before dinner.

—But how's this? said Candide to Paquette. You looked so happy, so joyous, when I met you; you were singing, you caressed the Theatine with such a natural air of delight; you seemed to me just as happy as you now say you are miserable.

—Ah, sir, replied Paquette, that's another one of the miseries of this business; yesterday I was robbed and beaten by an officer, and today I have to seem in good humor in order to please a monk.

Candide wanted no more; he conceded that Martin was right. They sat down to table with Paquette and the Theatine; the meal was amusing enough, and when it was over, the company spoke out among themselves with some frankness.

—Father, said Candide to the monk, you seem to me a man whom all the world might envy; the flower of health glows in your cheek, your features radiate pleasure; you have a pretty girl for your diversion, and you seem very happy with your life as a Theatine.

—Upon my word, sir, said Brother Giroflée, I wish that all the Theatines were at the bottom of the sea. A hundred times I have been tempted to set fire to my convent, and go turn Turk. My parents forced me, when I was fifteen years old, to put on this detestable robe, so they could leave more money to a cursed older brother of mine, may God confound him! Jealousy, faction, and fury spring up, by natural law, within the walls of convents. It is true, I have preached a few bad sermons which earned me a little money, half of which the prior stole from me; the remainder serves

6. His name means "carnation" and Paquette means "daisy."

to keep me in girls. But when I have to go back to the monastery at night, I'm ready to smash my head against the walls of my cell; and all my fellow monks are in the same fix.

Martin turned to Candide and said with his customary coolness:

—Well, haven't I won the whole bet?

Candide gave two thousand piastres to Paquette and a thousand to Brother Giroflée.

—I assure you, said he, that with that they will be happy.

—I don't believe so, said Martin; your piastres may make them even more unhappy than they were before.

—That may be, said Candide; but one thing comforts me, I note that people often turn up whom one never expected to see again; it may well be that, having rediscovered my red sheep and Paquette, I will also rediscover Cunégonde.

—I hope, said Martin, that she will some day make you happy; but I very much doubt it.

—You're a hard man, said Candide.

—I've lived, said Martin.

—But look at these gondoliers, said Candide; aren't they always singing?

—You don't see them at home, said Martin, with their wives and squalling children. The doge has his troubles, the gondoliers theirs. It's true that on the whole one is better off as a gondolier than as a doge; but the difference is so slight, I don't suppose it's worth the trouble of discussing.

—There's a lot of talk here, said Candide, of this Senator Pococurante,[7] who has a fine palace on the Brenta and is hospitable to foreigners. They say he is a man who has never known a moment's grief.

—I'd like to see such a rare specimen, said Martin.

Candide promptly sent to Lord Pococurante, asking permission to call on him tomorrow.

CHAPTER 25

Visit to Lord Pococurante, Venetian Nobleman

Candide and Martin took a gondola on the Brenta, and soon reached the palace of the noble Pococurante. The gardens were large and filled with beautiful marble statues; the palace was handsomely designed. The master of the house, sixty years old and very rich, received his two inquisitive visitors perfectly politely, but with very little warmth; Candide was disconcerted and Martin not at all displeased.

First two pretty and neatly dressed girls served chocolate, which they whipped to a froth. Candide could not forbear praising their beauty, their grace, their skill.

—They are pretty good creatures, said Pococurante; I sometimes have them into my bed, for I'm tired of the ladies of the town, with their stupid tricks, quarrels, jealousies, fits of ill humor and petty pride, and all the sonnets one has to make or order for them; but, after all, these two girls are starting to bore me too.

---

7. His name means "small care."

After lunch, Candide strolled through a long gallery, and was amazed at the beauty of the pictures. He asked who was the painter of the two finest.

—They are by Raphael, said the senator; I bought them for a lot of money, out of vanity, some years ago; people say they're the finest in Italy, but they don't please me at all; the colors have all turned brown, the figures aren't well modeled and don't stand out enough, the draperies bear no resemblance to real cloth. In a word, whatever people may say, I don't find in them a real imitation of nature. I like a picture only when I can see in it a touch of nature itself, and there are none of this sort. I have many paintings, but I no longer look at them.

As they waited for dinner, Pococurante ordered a concerto performed. Candide found the music delightful.

—That noise? said Pococurante. It may amuse you for half an hour, but if it goes on any longer, it tires everybody though no one dares to admit it. Music today is only the art of performing difficult pieces, and what is merely difficult cannot please for long. Perhaps I should prefer the opera, if they had not found ways to make it revolting and monstrous. Anyone who likes bad tragedies set to music is welcome to them; in these performances the scenes serve only to introduce, inappropriately, two or three ridiculous songs designed to show off the actress's sound box. Anyone who wants to, or who can, is welcome to swoon with pleasure at the sight of a castrate wriggling through the role of Caesar or Cato, and strutting awkwardly about the stage. For my part, I have long since given up these paltry trifles which are called the glory of modern Italy, and for which monarchs pay such ruinous prices.

Candide argued a bit, but timidly; Martin was entirely of a mind with the senator.

They sat down to dinner, and after an excellent meal adjourned to the library. Candide, seeing a copy of Homer in a splendid binding, complimented the noble lord on his good taste.

—That is an author, said he, who was the special delight of great Pangloss, the best philosopher in all Germany.

—He's no special delight of mine, said Pococurante coldly. I was once made to believe that I took pleasure in reading him; but that constant recital of fights which are all alike, those gods who are always interfering but never decisively, that Helen who is the cause of the war and then scarcely takes any part in the story, that Troy which is always under siege and never taken—all that bores me to tears. I have sometimes asked scholars if reading it bored them as much as it bores me; everyone who answered frankly told me the book dropped from his hands like lead, but that they had to have it in their libraries as a monument of antiquity, like those old rusty coins which can't be used in real trade.

Your Excellence doesn't hold the same opinion of Virgil? said Candide.

—I concede, said Pococurante, that the second, fourth, and sixth books of his *Aeneid* are fine; but as for his pious Aeneas, and strong Cloanthes, and faithful Achates, and little Ascanius, and that imbecile King Latinus, and middle-class Amata, and insipid Lavinia, I don't suppose there was ever anything so cold and unpleasant. I prefer Tasso and those sleepwalkers' stories of Ariosto.

—Dare I ask, sir, said Candide, if you don't get great enjoyment from reading Horace?

—There are some maxims there, said Pococurante, from which a man of the world can profit, and which, because they are formed into vigorous couplets, are more easily remembered; but I care very little for his trip to Brindisi, his description of a bad dinner, or his account of a quibblers' squabble between some fellow Pupilus, whose words he says *were full of pus*, and another whose words *were full of vinegar*.[8] I feel nothing but extreme disgust at his verses against old women and witches; and I can't see what's so great in his telling his friend Maecenas that if he is raised by him to the ranks of lyric poets, he will strike the stars with his lofty forehead. Fools admire everything in a well-known author. I read only for my own pleasure; I like only what is in my style.

Candide, who had been trained never to judge for himself, was much astonished by what he heard; and Martin found Pococurante's way of thinking quite rational.

—Oh, here is a copy of Cicero, said Candide. Now this great man I suppose you're never tired of reading.

—I never read him at all, replied the Venetian. What do I care whether he pleaded for Rabirius or Cluentius? As a judge, I have my hands full of lawsuits. I might like his philosophical works better, but when I saw that he had doubts about everything, I concluded that I knew as much as he did, and that I needed no help to be ignorant.

—Ah, here are eighty volumes of collected papers from a scientific academy, cried Martin; maybe there is something good in them.

—There would be indeed, said Pococurante, if one of these silly authors had merely discovered a new way of making pins; but in all those volumes there is nothing but empty systems, not a single useful discovery.

—What a lot of stage plays I see over there, said Candide, some in Italian, some in Spanish and French.

—Yes, said the senator, three thousand of them, and not three dozen good ones. As for those collections of sermons, which all together are not worth a page of Seneca, and all these heavy volumes of theology, you may be sure I never open them, nor does anybody else.

Martin noticed some shelves full of English books.

—I suppose, said he, that a republican must delight in most of these books written in the land of liberty.

—Yes, replied Pococurante, it's a fine thing to write as you think; it is mankind's privilege. In all our Italy, people write only what they do not think; men who inhabit the land of the Caesars and Antonines dare not have an idea without the permission of a Dominican. I would rejoice in the freedom that breathes through English genius, if partisan passions did not corrupt all that is good in that precious freedom.

---

8. *Satires* I.vii; Pococurante, with gentlemanly negligence, has corrupted Rupilius to Pupilus. Horace's poems against witches are *Epodes* V, VIII, XII; the one about striking the stars with his lofty forehead is *Odes* I.i.

Candide, noting a Milton, asked if he did not consider this author a great man.

—Who? said Pococurante. That barbarian who made a long commentary on the first chapter of Genesis in ten books of crabbed verse?[9] That clumsy imitator of the Greeks, who disfigures creation itself, and while Moses represents the eternal being as creating the world with a word, has the messiah take a big compass out of a heavenly cupboard in order to design his work? You expect me to admire the man who spoiled Tasso's hell and devil? who disguises Lucifer now as a toad, now as a pigmy? who makes him rehash the same arguments a hundred times over? who makes him argue theology? and who, taking seriously Ariosto's comic story of the invention of firearms, has the devils shooting off cannon in heaven? Neither I nor anyone else in Italy has been able to enjoy these gloomy extravagances. The marriage of Sin and Death, and the monster that Sin gives birth to, will nauseate any man whose taste is at all refined; and his long description of a hospital is good only for a gravedigger. This obscure, extravagant, and disgusting poem was despised at its birth; I treat it today as it was treated in its own country by its contemporaries. Anyhow, I say what I think, and care very little whether other people agree with me.

Candide was a little cast down by this speech; he respected Homer, and had a little affection for Milton.

—Alas, he said under his breath to Martin, I'm afraid this man will have a supreme contempt for our German poets.

—No harm in that, said Martin.

—Oh what a superior man, said Candide, still speaking softly, what a great genius this Pococurante must be! Nothing can please him.

Having thus looked over all the books, they went down into the garden. Candide praised its many beauties.

—I know nothing in such bad taste, said the master of the house; we have nothing but trifles here; tomorrow I am going to have one set out on a nobler design.

When the two visitors had taken leave of his excellency: —Well now, said Candide to Martin, you must agree that this was the happiest of all men, for he is superior to everything he possesses.

—Don't you see, said Martin, that he is disgusted with everything he possesses? Plato said, a long time ago, that the best stomachs are not those which refuse all food.

—But, said Candide, isn't there pleasure in criticizing everything, in seeing faults where other people think they see beauties?

—That is to say, Martin replied, that there's pleasure in having no pleasure?

—Oh well, said Candide, then I am the only happy man . . . or will be, when I see Miss Cunégonde again.

—It's always a good thing to have hope, said Martin.

But the days and the weeks slipped past; Cacambo did not come back, and Candide was so buried in his grief, that he did not even notice that Paquette and Brother Giroflée had neglected to come and thank him.

9. The first edition of *Paradise Lost* had ten books, which Milton later expanded to twelve.

CHAPTER 26

About a Supper that Candide and Martin Had with Six Strangers, and Who They Were

One evening when Candide, accompanied by Martin, was about to sit down for dinner with the strangers staying in his hotel, a man with a soot-colored face came up behind him, took him by the arm, and said: —Be ready to leave with us, don't miss out.

He turned and saw Cacambo. Only the sight of Cunégonde could have astonished and pleased him more. He nearly went mad with joy. He embraced his dear friend.

—Cunégonde is here, no doubt? Where is she? Bring me to her, let me die of joy in her presence.

—Cunégonde is not here at all, said Cacambo, she is at Constantinople.

—Good Heavens, at Constantinople! but if she were in China, I must fly there, let's go.

—We will leave after supper, said Cacambo; I can tell you no more; I am a slave, my owner is looking for me, I must go wait on him at table; mum's the word; eat your supper and be prepared.

Candide, torn between joy and grief, delighted to have seen his faithful agent again, astonished to find him a slave, full of the idea of recovering his mistress, his heart in a turmoil, his mind in a whirl, sat down to eat with Martin, who was watching all these events coolly, and with six strangers who had come to pass the carnival season at Venice.

Cacambo, who was pouring wine for one of the strangers, leaned respectfully over his master at the end of the meal, and said to him: — Sire, Your Majesty may leave when he pleases, the vessel is ready.

Having said these words, he exited. The diners looked at one another in silent amazement, when another servant, approaching his master, said to him: —Sire, Your Majesty's litter is at Padua, and the bark awaits you.

The master nodded, and the servant vanished. All the diners looked at one another again, and the general amazement redoubled. A third servant, approaching a third stranger, said to him: —Sire, take my word for it, Your Majesty must stay here no longer; I shall get everything ready.

Then he too disappeared.

Candide and Martin had no doubt, now, that it was a carnival masquerade. A fourth servant spoke to a fourth master: —Your Majesty will leave when he pleases—and went out like the others. A fifth followed suit. But the sixth servant spoke differently to the sixth stranger, who sat next to Candide. He said: —My word, sire, they'll give no more credit to Your Majesty, nor to me either; we could very well spend the night in the lockup, you and I. I've got to look out for myself, so good-bye to you.

When all the servants had left, the six strangers, Candide, and Martin remained under a pall of silence. Finally Candide broke it.

—Gentlemen, said he, here's a funny kind of joke. Why are you all royalty? I assure you that Martin and I aren't.

Cacambo's master spoke up gravely then, and said in Italian: —This is no joke, my name is Achmet the Third.[1] I was grand sultan for several years; then, as I had dethroned my brother, my nephew dethroned me. My viziers had their throats cut; I was allowed to end my days in the old seraglio. My nephew, the Grand Sultan Mahmoud, sometimes lets me travel for my health; and I have come to spend the carnival season at Venice.

A young man who sat next to Achmet spoke after him, and said: —My name is Ivan; I was once emperor of all the Russias.[2] I was dethroned while still in my cradle; my father and mother were locked up, and I was raised in prison; I sometimes have permission to travel, though always under guard, and I have come to spend the carnival season at Venice.

The third said: —I am Charles Edward, king of England;[3] my father yielded me his rights to the kingdom, and I fought to uphold them; but they tore out the hearts of eight hundred of my partisans, and flung them in their faces. I have been in prison; now I am going to Rome, to visit the king, my father, dethroned like me and my grandfather; and I have come to pass the carnival season at Venice.

The fourth king then spoke up, and said: —I am a king of the Poles;[4] the luck of war has deprived me of my hereditary estates; my father suffered the same losses; I submit to Providence like Sultan Achmet, Emperor Ivan, and King Charles Edward, to whom I hope heaven grants long lives; and I have come to pass the carnival season at Venice.

The fifth said: —I too am a king of the Poles;[5] I lost my kingdom twice, but Providence gave me another state, in which I have been able to do more good than all the Sarmatian kings ever managed to do on the banks of the Vistula. I too have submitted to Providence, and I have come to pass the carnival season at Venice.

It remained for the sixth monarch to speak.

—Gentlemen, said he, I am no such great lord as you, but I have in fact been a king like any other. I am Theodore; I was elected king of Corsica.[6] People used to call me *Your Majesty*, and now they barely call me *Sir*; I used to coin currency, and now I don't have a cent; I used to have two secretaries of state, and now I scarcely have a valet; I have sat on a throne, and for a long time in London I was in jail, on the straw; and I may well be treated the same way here, though I have come, like your majesties, to pass the carnival season at Venice.

The five other kings listened to his story with noble compassion. Each one of them gave twenty sequins to King Theodore, so that he might buy a suit and some shirts; Candide gave him a diamond worth two thousand sequins.

—Who in the world, said the five kings, is this private citizen who is in

1. Ottoman ruler (1673–1736); he was deposed in 1730.   2. Ivan VI reigned from his birth in 1740 until 1756, then was confined in the Schlusselberg, and executed in 1764.   3. This is the Young Pretender (1720–1788), known to his supporters as Bonnie Prince Charlie. The defeat so theatrically described took place at Culloden, April 16, 1746.   4. Augustus III (1696–1763), Elector of Saxony and King of Poland, dethroned by Frederick the Great in 1756.   5. Stanislas Leczinski (1677–1766), father-in-law of Louis XV, who abdicated the throne of Poland in 1736, was made Duke of Lorraine and in that capacity befriended Voltaire.   6. Theodore von Neuhof (1690–1756), an authentic Westphalian, an adventurer and a soldier of fortune, who in 1736 was (for about eight months) the elected king of Corsica. He spent time in an Amsterdam as well as a London debtor's prison.

a position to give a hundred times as much as any of us, and who actually gives it?[7]

Just as they were rising from dinner, there arrived at the same establishment four most serene highnesses, who had also lost their kingdoms through the luck of war, and who came to spend the rest of the carnival season at Venice. But Candide never bothered even to look at these newcomers because he was only concerned to go find his dear Cunégonde at Constantinople.

CHAPTER 27

Candide's Trip to Constantinople

Faithful Cacambo had already arranged with the Turkish captain who was returning Sultan Achmet to Constantinople to make room for Candide and Martin on board. Both men boarded ship after prostrating themselves before his miserable highness. On the way, Candide said to Martin: —Six dethroned kings that we had dinner with! and yet among those six there was one on whom I had to bestow charity! Perhaps there are other princes even more unfortunate. I myself have only lost a hundred sheep, and now I am flying to the arms of Cunégonde. My dear Martin, once again Pangloss is proved right, all is for the best.

—I hope so, said Martin.

—But, said Candide, that was a most unlikely experience we had at Venice. Nobody ever saw, or heard tell of, six dethroned kings eating together at an inn.

—It is no more extraordinary, said Martin, than most of the things that have happened to us. Kings are frequently dethroned; and as for the honor we had from dining with them, that's a trifle which doesn't deserve our notice.[8]

Scarcely was Candide on board than he fell on the neck of his former servant, his friend Cacambo.

—Well! said he, what is Cunégonde doing? Is she still a marvel of beauty? Does she still love me? How is her health? No doubt you have bought her a palace at Constantinople.

—My dear master, answered Cacambo, Cunégonde is washing dishes on the shores of the Propontis, in the house of a prince who has very few dishes to wash; she is a slave in the house of a onetime king named Ragotski,[9] to whom the Great Turk allows three crowns a day in his exile;

---

7. A late correction of Voltaire's makes this passage read:
—Who is this man who is in a position to give a hundred times as much as any of us, and who actually gives it? Are you a king too, sir?
—No, gentlemen, and I have no desire to be.
But this reading, though Voltaire's on good authority, produces a conflict with Candide's previous remark: —Why are you all royalty? I assure you that Martin and I aren't.
Thus, it has seemed better for literary reasons to follow an earlier reading. Voltaire was very conscious of his situation as a man richer than many princes; in 1758 he had money on loan to no fewer than three highnesses, Charles Eugene, Duke of Wurtemburg; Charles Theodore, Elector Palatine; and the Duke of Saxe-Gotha.   8. Another late change adds the following question: —*What does it matter whom you dine with as long as you fare well at table?* I have omitted it, again on literary grounds.   9. Francis Leopold Rakoczy (1676–1735), who was briefly king of Transylvania in the early eighteenth century. After 1720 he was interned in Turkey.

but, what is worse than all this, she has lost all her beauty and become horribly ugly.

—Ah, beautiful or ugly, said Candide, I am an honest man, and my duty is to love her forever. But how can she be reduced to this wretched state with the five or six millions that you had?

—All right, said Cacambo, didn't I have to give two millions to Señor don Fernando d'Ibaraa y Figueroa y Mascarenes y Lampourdos y Souza, governor of Buenos Aires, for his permission to carry off Miss Cunégonde? And didn't a pirate cleverly strip us of the rest? And didn't this pirate carry us off to Cape Matapan, to Melos, Nicaria, Samos, Petra, to the Dardanelles, Marmora, Scutari? Cunégonde and the old woman are working for the prince I told you about, and I am the slave of the dethroned sultan.

—What a lot of fearful calamities linked one to the other, said Candide. But after all, I still have a few diamonds, I shall easily deliver Cunégonde. What a pity that she's become so ugly!

Then, turning toward Martin, he asked: —Who in your opinion is more to be pitied, the Emperor Achmet, the Emperor Ivan, King Charles Edward, or myself?

—I have no idea, said Martin; I would have to enter your hearts in order to tell.

—Ah, said Candide, if Pangloss were here, he would know and he would tell us.

—I can't imagine, said Martin, what scales your Pangloss would use to weigh out the miseries of men and value their griefs. All I will venture is that the earth holds millions of men who deserve our pity a hundred times more than King Charles Edward, Emperor Ivan, or Sultan Achmet.

—You may well be right, said Candide.

In a few days they arrived at the Black Sea canal. Candide began by repurchasing Cacambo at an exorbitant price; then, without losing an instant, he flung himself and his companions into a galley to go search out Cunégonde on the shores of Propontis, however ugly she might be.

There were in the chain gang two convicts who bent clumsily to the oar, and on whose bare shoulders the Levantine[1] captain delivered from time to time a few lashes with a bullwhip. Candide naturally noticed them more than the other galley slaves, and out of pity came closer to them. Certain features of their disfigured faces seemed to him to bear a slight resemblance to Pangloss and to that wretched Jesuit, that baron, that brother of Miss Cunégonde. The notion stirred and saddened him. He looked at them more closely.

—To tell you the truth, he said to Cacambo, if I hadn't seen Master Pangloss hanged, and if I hadn't been so miserable as to murder the baron, I should think they were rowing in this very galley.

At the names of 'baron' and 'Pangloss' the two convicts gave a great cry, sat still on their bench, and dropped their oars. The Levantine captain came running, and the bullwhip lashes redoubled.

—Stop, stop, captain, cried Candide. I'll give you as much money as you want.

_____
1. From the eastern Mediterranean.

—What, can it be Candide? cried one of the convicts.

—What, can it be Candide? cried the other.

—Is this a dream? said Candide. Am I awake or asleep? Am I in this galley? Is that My Lord the Baron, whom I killed? Is that Master Pangloss, whom I saw hanged?

—It is indeed, they replied.

—What, is that the great philosopher? said Martin.

—Now, sir, Mr. Levantine Captain, said Candide, how much money do you want for the ransom of My Lord Thunder-Ten-Tronckh, one of the first barons of the empire, and Master Pangloss, the deepest metaphysician in all Germany?

—Dog of a Christian, replied the Levantine captain, since these two dogs of Christian convicts are barons and metaphysicians, which is no doubt a great honor in their country, you will give me fifty thousand sequins for them.

—You shall have them, sir, take me back to Constantinople and you shall be paid on the spot. Or no, take me to Miss Cunégonde.

The Levantine captain, at Candide's first word, had turned his bow toward the town, and he had them rowed there as swiftly as a bird cleaves the air.

A hundred times Candide embraced the baron and Pangloss.

—And how does it happen I didn't kill you, my dear baron? and my dear Pangloss, how can you be alive after being hanged? and why are you both rowing in the galleys of Turkey?

—Is it really true that my dear sister is in this country? asked the baron.

—Yes, answered Cacambo.

—And do I really see again my dear Candide? cried Pangloss.

Candide introduced Martin and Cacambo. They all embraced; they all talked at once. The galley flew, already they were back in port. A Jew was called, and Candide sold him for fifty thousand sequins a diamond worth a hundred thousand, while he protested by Abraham that he could not possibly give more for it. Candide immediately ransomed the baron and Pangloss. The latter threw himself at the feet of his liberator, and bathed them with tears; the former thanked him with a nod, and promised to repay this bit of money at the first opportunity.

—But is it really possible that my sister is in Turkey? said he.

—Nothing is more possible, replied Cacambo, since she is a dishwasher in the house of a prince of Transylvania.

At once two more Jews were called; Candide sold some more diamonds; and they all departed in another galley to the rescue of Cunégonde.

CHAPTER 28

What Happened to Candide, Cunégonde, Pangloss, Martin, &c.

—Let me beg your pardon once more, said Candide to the baron, pardon me, reverend father, for having run you through the body with my sword.

—Don't mention it, replied the baron. I was a little too hasty myself, I confess it; but since you want to know the misfortune which brought me to the galleys, I'll tell you. After being cured of my wound by the brother who was apothecary to the college, I was attacked and abducted by a Spanish raiding party; they jailed me in Buenos Aires at the time when my sister had just left. I asked to be sent to Rome, to the father general. Instead, I was named to serve as almoner in Constantinople, under the French ambassador. I had not been a week on this job when I chanced one evening on a very handsome young ichoglan.[2] The evening was hot; the young man wanted to take a swim; I seized the occasion, and went with him. I did not know that it is a capital offense for a Christian to be found naked with a young Moslem. A cadi sentenced me to receive a hundred blows with a cane on the soles of my feet, and then to be sent to the galleys. I don't suppose there was ever such a horrible miscarriage of justice. But I would like to know why my sister is in the kitchen of a Transylvanian king exiled among Turks.

—But how about you, my dear Pangloss, said Candide; how is it possible that we have met again?

—It is true, said Pangloss, that you saw me hanged; in the normal course of things, I should have been burned, but you recall that a cloudburst occurred just as they were about to roast me. So much rain fell that they despaired of lighting the fire; thus I was hanged, for lack of anything better to do with me. A surgeon bought my body, carried me off to his house, and dissected me. First he made a cross-shaped incision in me, from the navel to the clavicle. No one could have been worse hanged than I was. In fact, the executioner of the high ceremonials of the Holy Inquisition, who was a subdeacon, burned people marvelously well, but he was not in the way of hanging them. The rope was wet, and tightened badly; it caught on a knot; in short, I was still breathing. The cross-shaped incision made me scream so loudly that the surgeon fell over backwards; he thought he was dissecting the devil, fled in an agony of fear, and fell downstairs in his flight. His wife ran in, at the noise, from a nearby room; she found me stretched out on the table with my cross-shaped incision, was even more frightened than her husband, fled, and fell over him. When they had recovered a little, I heard her say to him: 'My dear, what were you thinking of, trying to dissect a heretic? Don't you know those people are always possessed of the devil? I'm going to get the priest and have him exorcised.' At these words, I shuddered, and collected my last remaining energies to cry: 'Have mercy on me!' At last the Portuguese barber[3] took courage; he sewed me up again; his wife even nursed me; in two weeks I was up and about. The barber found me a job and made me lackey to a Knight of Malta who was going to Venice; and when this master could no longer pay me, I took service under a Venetian merchant, whom I followed to Constantinople.

—One day it occurred to me to enter a mosque; no one was there but an old imam and a very attractive young worshipper who was saying her prayers. Her bosom was completely bare; and between her two breasts she had a lovely bouquet of tulips, roses, anemones, buttercups, hyacinths,

---

2. A page to the sultan.   3. The two callings of barber and surgeon, since they both involved sharp instruments, were interchangeable in the early days of medicine.

and primroses. She dropped her bouquet, I picked it up, and returned it to her with the most respectful attentions. I was so long getting it back in place that the imam grew angry, and, seeing that I was a Christian, he called the guard. They took me before the cadi, who sentenced me to receive a hundred blows with a cane on the soles of my feet, and then to be sent to the galleys. I was chained to the same galley and precisely the same bench as My Lord the Baron. There were in this galley four young fellows from Marseilles, five Neapolitan priests, and two Corfu monks, who assured us that these things happen every day. My Lord the Baron asserted that he had suffered a greater injustice than I; I, on the other hand, proposed that it was much more permissible to replace a bouquet in a bosom than to be found naked with an ichoglan. We were arguing the point continually, and getting twenty lashes a day with the bullwhip, when the chain of events within this universe brought you to our galley, and you ransomed us.

—Well, my dear Pangloss, Candide said to him, now that you have been hanged, dissected, beaten to a pulp, and sentenced to the galleys, do you still think everything is for the best in this world?

—I am still of my first opinion, replied Pangloss; for after all I am a philosopher, and it would not be right for me to recant since Leibniz could not possibly be wrong, and besides pre-established harmony is the finest notion in the world, like the plenum and subtle matter.[4]

CHAPTER 29

How Candide Found Cunégonde and the Old Woman Again

While Candide, the baron, Pangloss, Martin, and Cacambo were telling one another their stories, while they were disputing over the contingent or non-contingent events of this universe, while they were arguing over effects and causes, over moral evil and physical evil, over liberty and necessity, and over the consolations available to one in a Turkish galley, they arrived at the shores of Propontis and the house of the prince of Transylvania. The first sight to meet their eyes was Cunégonde and the old woman, who were hanging out towels on lines to dry.

The baron paled at what he saw. The tender lover Candide, seeing his lovely Cunégonde with her skin weathered, her eyes bloodshot, her breasts fallen, her cheeks seamed, her arms red and scaly, recoiled three steps in horror, and then advanced only out of politeness. She embraced Candide and her brother; everyone embraced the old woman; Candide ransomed them both.

There was a little farm in the neighborhood; the old woman suggested that Candide occupy it until some better fate should befall the group. Cunégonde did not know she was ugly, no one had told her; she reminded

---

4. Rigorous determinism requires that there be no empty spaces in the universe, so wherever it seems empty, one posits the existence of the "plenum." "Subtle matter" describes the soul, the mind, and all spiritual agencies—which can, therefore, be supposed subject to the influence and control of the great world machine, which is, of course, visibly material. Both are concepts needed to round out the system of optimistic determinism.

Candide of his promises in so firm a tone that the good Candide did not dare to refuse her. So he went to tell the baron that he was going to marry his sister.

—Never will I endure, said the baron, such baseness on her part, such insolence on yours; this shame at least I will not put up with; why, my sister's children would not be able to enter the Chapters in Germany.[5] No, my sister will never marry anyone but a baron of the empire.

Cunégonde threw herself at his feet, and bathed them with her tears; he was inflexible.

—You absolute idiot, Candide told him, I rescued you from the galleys, I paid your ransom, I paid your sister's; she was washing dishes, she is ugly, I am good enough to make her my wife, and you still presume to oppose it! If I followed my impulses, I would kill you all over again.

—You may kill me again, said the baron, but you will not marry my sister while I am alive.

CHAPTER 30

Conclusion

At heart, Candide had no real wish to marry Cunégonde; but the baron's extreme impertinence decided him in favor of the marriage, and Cunégonde was so eager for it that he could not back out. He consulted Pangloss, Martin, and the faithful Cacambo. Pangloss drew up a fine treatise, in which he proved that the baron had no right over his sister and that she could, according to all the laws of the empire, marry Candide morganatically.[6] Martin said they should throw the baron into the sea. Cacambo thought they should send him back to the Levantine captain to finish his time in the galleys, and then send him to the father general in Rome by the first vessel. This seemed the best idea; the old woman approved, and nothing was said to his sister; the plan was executed, at modest expense, and they had the double pleasure of snaring a Jesuit and punishing the pride of a German baron.

It is quite natural to suppose that after so many misfortunes, Candide, married to his mistress, and living with the philosopher Pangloss, the philosopher Martin, the prudent Cacambo, and the old woman—having, besides, brought back so many diamonds from the land of the ancient Incas—must have led the most agreeable life in the world. But he was so cheated by the Jews[7] that nothing was left but his little farm; his wife, growing every day more ugly, became sour-tempered and insupportable; the old woman was ailing and even more ill-humored than Cunégonde. Cacambo, who worked in the garden and went into Constantinople to sell vegetables, was worn out with toil, and cursed his fate. Pangloss was in despair at being unable to shine in some German university. As for Martin, he was firmly persuaded that things are just as bad wherever you are; he endured in patience. Candide, Martin, and Pangloss sometimes argued over metaphysics and morals. Before the windows of the farmhouse they

5. Knightly assemblies.   6. A morganatic marriage confers no rights on the partner of lower rank or on the offspring.   7. Voltaire's anti-Semitism, derived from various unhappy experiences with Jewish financiers, is not the most attractive aspect of his personality.

often watched the passage of boats bearing effendis, pashas, and cadis into exile on Lemnos, Mytilene, and Erzeroum; they saw other cadis, other pashas, other effendis coming, to take the place of the exiles and to be exiled in their turn. They saw various heads, neatly impaled, to be set up at the Sublime Porte.[8] These sights gave fresh impetus to their discussions; and when they were not arguing, the boredom was so fierce that one day the old woman ventured to say: —I should like to know which is worse, being raped a hundred times by negro pirates, having a buttock cut off, running the gauntlet in the Bulgar army, being flogged and hanged in an auto-da-fé, being dissected and rowing in the galleys—experiencing, in a word, all the miseries through which we have passed—or else just sitting here and doing nothing?

—It's a hard question, said Candide.

These words gave rise to new reflections, and Martin in particular concluded that man was bound to live either in convulsions of misery or in the lethargy of boredom. Candide did not agree, but expressed no positive opinion. Pangloss asserted that he had always suffered horribly; but having once declared that everything was marvelously well, he continued to repeat the opinion and didn't believe a word of it.

One thing served to confirm Martin in his detestable opinions, to make Candide hesitate more than ever, and to embarrass Pangloss. It was the arrival one day at their farm of Paquette and Brother Giroflée, who were in the last stages of misery. They had quickly run through their three thousand piastres, had split up, made up, quarreled, been jailed, escaped, and finally Brother Giroflée had turned Turk. Paquette continued to ply her trade everywhere, and no longer made any money at it.

—I told you, said Martin to Candide, that your gifts would soon be squandered and would only render them more unhappy. You have spent millions of piastres, you and Cacambo, and you are no more happy than Brother Giroflée and Paquette.

—Ah ha, said Pangloss to Paquette, so destiny has brought you back in our midst, my poor girl! Do you realize you cost me the end of my nose, one eye, and an ear? And look at you now! eh! what a world it is, after all!

This new adventure caused them to philosophize more than ever.

There was in the neighborhood a very famous dervish, who was said to be the best philosopher in Turkey; they went to ask his advice. Pangloss was spokesman, and he said: —Master, we have come to ask you to tell us why such a strange animal as man was created.

—What are you getting into? answered the dervish. Is it any of your business?

—But, reverend father, said Candide, there's a horrible lot of evil on the face of the earth.

—What does it matter, said the dervish, whether there's good or evil? When his highness sends a ship to Egypt, does he worry whether the mice on board are comfortable or not?

—What shall we do then? asked Pangloss.

8. The gate of the sultan's palace is often used by extension to describe his government as a whole. But it was in fact a real gate where the heads of traitors and public enemies were gruesomely exposed.

—Hold your tongue, said the dervish.

—I had hoped, said Pangloss, to reason a while with you concerning effects and causes, the best of possible worlds, the origin of evil, the nature of the soul, and pre-established harmony.

At these words, the dervish slammed the door in their faces.

During this interview, word was spreading that at Constantinople they had just strangled two viziers of the divan,[9] as well as the mufti, and impaled several of their friends. This catastrophe made a great and general sensation for several hours. Pangloss, Candide, and Martin, as they returned to their little farm, passed a good old man who was enjoying the cool of the day at his doorstep under a grove of orange trees. Pangloss, who was as inquisitive as he was explanatory, asked the name of the mufti who had been strangled.

—I know nothing of it, said the good man, and I have never cared to know the name of a single mufti or vizier. I am completely ignorant of the episode you are discussing. I presume that in general those who meddle in public business sometimes perish miserably, and that they deserve their fate; but I never listen to the news from Constantinople; I am satisfied with sending the fruits of my garden to be sold there.

Having spoken these words, he asked the strangers into his house; his two daughters and two sons offered them various sherbets which they had made themselves, Turkish cream flavored with candied citron, orange, lemon, lime, pineapple, pistachio, and mocha coffee uncontaminated by the inferior coffee of Batavia and the East Indies. After which the two daughters of this good Moslem perfumed the beards of Candide, Pangloss, and Martin.

—You must possess, Candide said to the Turk, an enormous and splendid property?

I have only twenty acres, replied the Turk; I cultivate them with my children, and the work keeps us from three great evils, boredom, vice, and poverty.

Candide, as he walked back to his farm, meditated deeply over the words of the Turk. He said to Pangloss and Martin: —This good old man seems to have found himself a fate preferable to that of the six kings with whom we had the honor of dining.

—Great place, said Pangloss, is very perilous in the judgment of all the philosophers; for, after all, Eglon, king of the Moabites, was murdered by Ehud; Absalom was hung up by the hair and pierced with three darts; King Nadab, son of Jeroboam, was killed by Baasha; King Elah by Zimri; Ahaziah by Jehu; Athaliah by Jehoiada; and Kings Jehoiakim, Jeconiah, and Zedekiah were enslaved. You know how death came to Croesus, Astyages, Darius, Dionysius of Syracuse, Pyrrhus, Perseus, Hannibal, Jugurtha, Ariovistus, Caesar, Pompey, Nero, Otho, Vitellius, Domitian, Richard II of England, Edward II, Henry VI, Richard III, Mary Stuart, Charles I, the three Henrys of France, and the Emperor Henry IV? You know . . .

—I know also, said Candide, that we must cultivate our garden.

—You are perfectly right, said Pangloss; for when man was put into the

9. Intimate advisers of the sultan.

garden of Eden, he was put there *ut operaretur eum*, so that he should work it; this proves that man was not born to take his ease.

—Let's work without speculating, said Martin; it's the only way of rendering life bearable.

The whole little group entered into this laudable scheme; each one began to exercise his talents. The little plot yielded fine crops. Cunégonde was, to tell the truth, remarkably ugly; but she became an excellent pastry cook. Paquette took up embroidery; the old woman did the laundry. Everyone, down even to Brother Giroflée, did something useful; he became a very adequate carpenter, and even an honest man; and Pangloss sometimes used to say to Candide: —All events are linked together in the best of possible worlds; for, after all, if you had not been driven from a fine castle by being kicked in the backside for love of Miss Cunégonde, if you hadn't been sent before the Inquisition, if you hadn't traveled across America on foot, if you hadn't given a good sword thrust to the baron, if you hadn't lost all your sheep from the good land of Eldorado, you wouldn't be sitting here eating candied citron and pistachios.

—That is very well put, said Candide, but we must cultivate our garden.

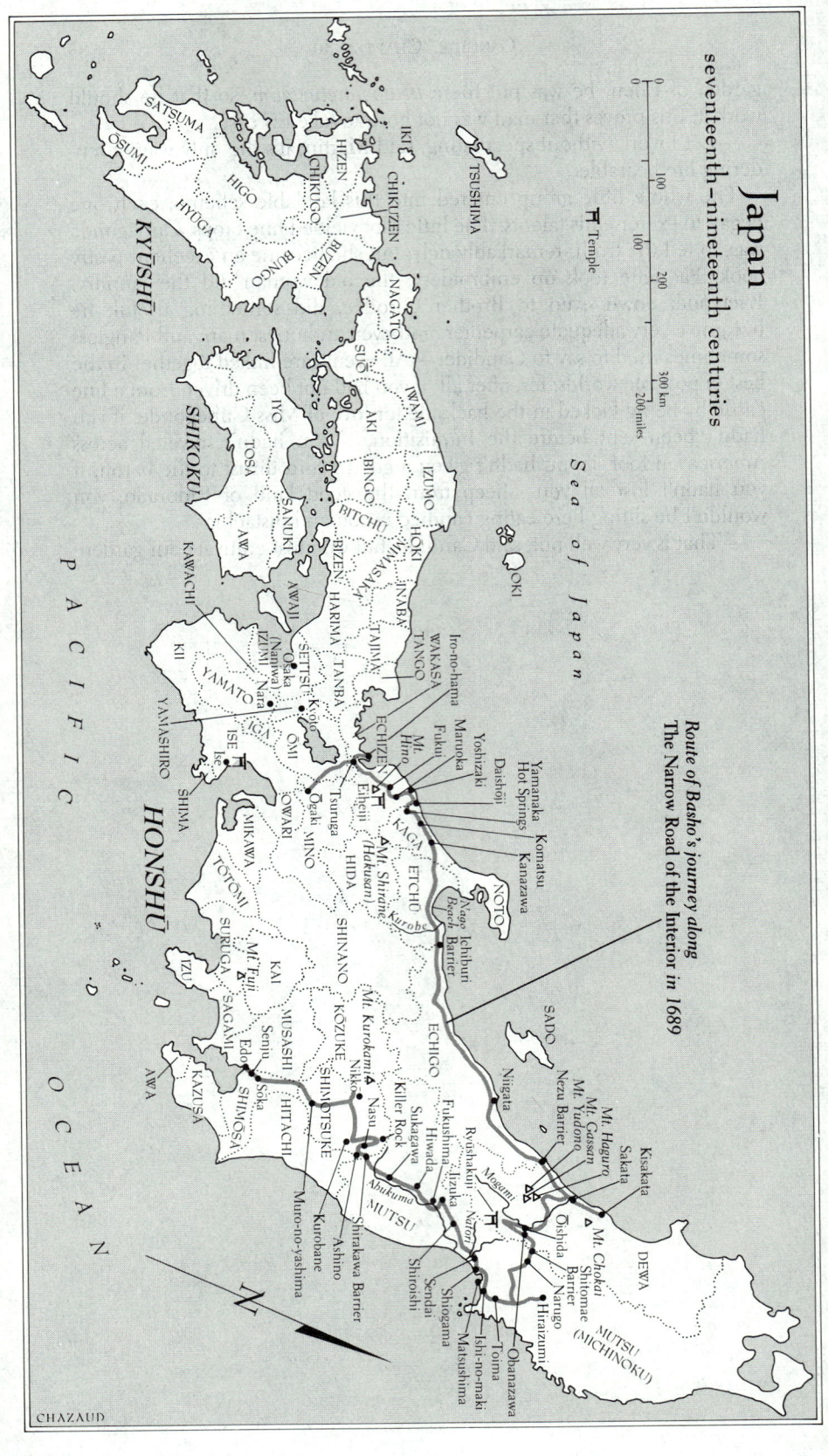

Japan

seventeenth–nineteenth centuries

Route of Basho's journey along
The Narrow Road of the Interior in 1689

⛩ Temple

0
100
100
200
300 km
200 miles

KYŪSHŪ

SHIKOKU

HONSHŪ

Sea of Japan

PACIFIC OCEAN

SATSUMA
OSUMI
HYŪGA
HIGO
CHIKUGO
HIZEN
CHIKUZEN
BUZEN
BINGO
NAGATO
SUŌ
IKI
TSUSHIMA
AKI
IWAMI
IZUMO
HŌKI
BINGO
BITCHŪ
BIZEN
MIMASAKA
INABA
TAJIMA
HARIMA
TANBA
TANGO
WAKASA
TOSA
IYO
SANUKI
AWA
KAWACHI
AWAJI
SETTSU
IZUMI
Naniwa
Osaka
YAMATO
Nara
Kyoto
ŌMI
IGA
ISE
SHIMA
YAMASHIRO
KII
OKI
SADO
NOTO
ECHIZEN
KAGA
ETCHŪ
HIDA
MINO
OWARI
MIKAWA
TOTOMI
SURUGA
IZU
KAI
SHINANO
ECHIGO
KŌZUKE
MUSASHI
SAGAMI
AWA
KAZUSA
SHIMOSA
HITACHI
SHIMOTSUKE
MUTSU
(MICHINOKU)
DEWA

Iro-no-hama
Maruoka
Mt. Hino
Fukui
Yoshizaki
Daishoji
Yamanaka Hot Springs
Komatsu
Kanazawa
Ōsaki
Tsuruga
Eiheiji
Mt. Shirane (Hakusan)
Kurobe
Naga Ichiburi Beach Barrier
Niigata
Ryūshaku
Mogami
Sakata
Kisakata
Mt. Haguro
Mt. Gassan
Mt. Yudono
Nezu Barrier
Mt. Chokai
Ōishida
Shitomae Barrier
Narugo
Obanazawa
Hiraizumi
Ishi-no-maki
Toima
Matsushima
Shiogama
Sendai
Shiroishi
Shirakawa Barrier
Ashino
Kurobane
Muro-no-yashima
Nikkō
Killer Rock
Nasu
Sukagawa
Hiwada
Fukushima
Iizaka
Abukuma
Nitori
Mt. Kurokami
Senju
Sōka
Edo

N

CHAZAUD

The Rise of Popular Arts in Premodern Japan

In one of the grand ironies of history, Japan—a country whose prosperity now depends on intense cultivation of foreign markets—began its so-called early modern era as a world recluse. Its leaders chose to seal Japan from foreign influence, fearful that the toehold European traders and Christian missionaries had been gaining in Japan from the mid-sixteenth century through the early seventeenth would end up undermining their political control.

Since the late twelfth century, in the wake of the civil war chronicled in *The Tale of the Heike* (see Volume 1), Japan had been governed by a series of military clans who held de facto power as peacekeepers and national administrators on behalf of the emperor, the formal if politically emasculated sovereign. In some periods the reigning military house succeeded as peacekeeper. In others, the country lapsed into disorder as rival clans jousted for supremacy. Gradually, the country splintered until chaos and bloodshed descended on Japan during 150 unruly years lasting from 1467 until the opening of the seventeenth century, when one clan, the Tokugawa, managed to dominate its rivals and thereby reunify the nation under strict but peaceful rule.

The Tokugawa shoguns quickly decided that the foreigners must go. They had seen the Portuguese missionaries play one feudal baron against another and, worse, claim to represent a higher authority to which the converted ranks must ultimately submit. In 1639, therefore, the government of Japan announced a policy of national seclusion. European traders and Christian missionaries were given a choice of expulsion or execution. The building of ocean-going vessels was prohibited, and any Japanese intrepid enough to venture abroad faced certain death if he got homesick. The country closed in on itself for two and a half centuries and, far from withering from a lack of outside stimulation, experienced one of its headiest periods of cultural ferment.

In sum, the shogunal authorities tried to stop time by freezing political, social, and economic conditions in a status quo that favored their predominance. For a remarkably long interval they did succeed in eradicating foreign influence. But they never succeeded in stopping time. When peace and stability returned to Japan, a new class quickly rose in economic and cultural significance. It was a bourgeois, mercantile class, and it came into being as the inevitable consequence of the new political administration. The shogun's vast bureaucracy was staffed by *samurai* retainers. With no more wars to fight, these former soldiers became bureaucrats, and with a government to run they clustered in the cities. Removed from the land and their previous military and agricultural pursuits, the urban *samurai* developed new needs, which were promptly met by enterprising merchants, artisans, and laborers whose numbers swelled in response to economic opportunity. City life and long-distance transport eventually made rice an unwieldy medium of exchange. Coin took its place in business transactions, and the growth of a money economy had a slow but irreversible effect on every aspect of Japanese life. Although the new commercial class was denied access to the political system, as the nation's bankers and suppliers it increasingly held the real power, which was financial.

These aggressive, upstart merchants were not hidebound by the traditions of another age, as could be said of both the *samurai* and their political predecessors, the sadly attenuated aristocrats, who barely kept the flame of classical Japanese convention from sputtering and dying out. Now and then the new merchant princes played dress-up with the trappings of high culture, but most of the time they were absorbed in a culture completely of their own making. As a reflection of their world, it was an urban culture. Woodblock prints, short stories, novels, poetry, and plays depicted city life—fast, varied, crowded, and competitive—where people lived by their wits and appreciated wit. Puns and parody took pride of place in the new popular literature, which itself became big business. Publishing proved yet another way of making money in this commercial age, so that for the first time books circulated in printed form rather than in manuscript. Literature came to the masses, or at least the urban masses.

To succeed, it had to meet their tastes. Like metropolitans the world over, Japanese townspeople of the seventeenth and eighteenth centuries moved to a faster beat. They were impatient, and it showed in their fiction. The stately pace of courtly prose yielded to narratives moving at a rapid clip, where action is compressed and any fine-grained analysis of character is likely to be jettisoned as a drag on the reader's fractured attention. The townspeople were also intensely rivalrous. By day they sweat to best the competition; by night they dressed to trump their neighbors in the social contest. Style was an essential component of success, and the new class demanded no less of its writers and artists, who were expected to capture the city scene with acuity and a sense of humor and to execute their work with verbal and visual panache.

Naturally, as tradesmen, the townspeople were nothing if not pragmatic, and naturally too their practical bent affected the literature they supported. The bourgeois audience had little use for tales of noble romance or martial prowess. Like the audience for whom Molière wrote *Tartuffe* (p. 300) and Pope his *Rape of the Lock* (p. 492), the members of this new middle class demanded realism. What was real to them were other people like themselves, the gossip of their own tight world, the perils and the thrills of the marketplace, and the pleasures to be had from prosperity. For the first time, in other words, ordinary people became standard literary characters, and the material and sexual aspects of life were deemed worthy subjects of literature.

Inevitably, at times, there was a certain excess to this exuberant young culture, giddy and energized by the excitement of its own self-creation. It could be, for example, startlingly graphic: every artist of repute enjoyed a lucrative sideline producing erotic woodblock prints. It could also be vulgar, for the nouveaux riches of the merchant class were sometimes prone to a particularly mindless form of conspicuous consumption. A man dallies upstairs at a teahouse with his favorite courtesan. His friend sends over a giant dumpling, so enormous that it cannot be carried up the stairway. Instead of coming down to enjoy the dumpling, he hires six carpenters to widen the stairs. With events like this in the historical record, it is not surprising that caricature and lampoon compose the other side of popular "realism."

For the most part ignored by the *samurai* authorities and removed from foreign influence, the new urban culture developed organically. Actors, courtesans, adventurers, shopkeepers, rice brokers, moneylenders, fashion-plate wives, and precocious sons and daughters created their own cosmopolitan customs. *Kabuki* playwrights, *haiku* poets, woodblock artists, and best-selling novelists all captured in their own genres an intimate glimpse of kinetic bourgeois life—blunt, expansive, iconoclastic, irrepressibly playful. Few here ever heard of the Enlightenment or the scientific revolution. The walled garden of Japan in the seventeenth and eighteenth centuries bloomed nicely without the irrigation of European currents.

A note on the Japanese calendar and time-keeping practices will be helpful in reading the following selections. Until 1873, when Japan adopted the Gregorian calendar of the West, the official calendar was derived from China and was divided into twelve lunations (months) of twenty-nine or thirty days. The resulting lunar year was approximately eleven days shorter than the solar year, which required the insertion of a thirteenth intercalary month every third year or thereabout to align the calendrical year with the solar. In addition, by custom the Japanese year began slightly later than the Western, so that New Year's Day fell anywhere from January 15 to February 15. The beginning of the new year also marked an increase in one's age, in contrast to the Western practice of reckoning age by birthdays. A child born in the twelfth month, for instance, would turn two with the new year.

Years were numbered serially from the year when a reigning emperor ascended the throne. In the modern period (beginning in 1868) the reign of an emperor has one name for its duration. For example, the reign of Emperor Hirohito is called the Shōwa ("enlightened peace") era, which lasted from his ascension in 1926 until his death in 1989. In addition to following the Western practice of number-ing years by the Gregorian calendar, the year 1930, say, is reckoned as Shōwa 5. In the premodern period, rather than having one name throughout, an emperor's reign was usually divided into various eras, each with its own name.

Both the months and the hours of the day were designated by the signs of the Chinese zodiac. The day was divided into twelve units, each equivalent to 120 minutes:

Hour		Modern Equivalent
1	Rat	11 P.M.–1 A.M.
2	Ox	1 A.M.–3 A.M.
3	Tiger	3 A.M.–5 A.M.
4	Rabbit	5 A.M.–7 A.M.
5	Dragon	7 A.M.–9 A.M.
6	Snake	9 A.M.–11 A.M.
7	Horse	11 A.M.–1 P.M.
8	Ram	1 P.M.–3 P.M.
9	Monkey	3 P.M.–5 P.M.
10	Rooster	5 P.M.–7 P.M.
11	Dog	7 P.M.–9 P.M.
12	Boar	9 P.M.–11 P.M.

PRONOUNCING GLOSSARY

The following list uses common English syllables to provide rough equivalents of selected words whose pronunciation may be unfamiliar to the general reader.

haiku: *hai-koo*

Heike: *hay-kay*

kabuki: *kah-boo-kee*

nō: *noh*

Tokugawa: *toh-koo-gah-wah*

Zeami: *ze-ah-mee*

TIMELINE

TEXTS	CONTEXTS
	1600–1868 Edo period: Tokugawa family establishes dynasty of shoguns who rule from Edo (present-day Tokyo)
1609 Commercial publishing begins in Japan	
	1616–1660 Imperial family commissions Katsura Detached Palace (icon of modernism for 20th-century architects)
	1620 The *Mayflower* carries Pilgrims to America
	ca. 1620–1716 Sōtatsu and Kōrin create masterpieces of Japanese screen painting
	1627 Korea becomes tributary state of China
1639 Aesop's *Fables* translated into Japanese	**1639** Shogun proclaims policy of national isolation, expelling Portuguese and banning Christianity and foreign travel
1682 *The Life of a Sensuous Man* (Ihara Saikaku) launches comic realism and popular fiction	
1686 *The Barrelmaker Brimful of Love* published in Ihara Saikaku's collection *Five Women Who Loved Love*	
1690–1694 *The Narrow Road of the Interior* (Matsuo Bashō), verse inset in travel memoir by the foremost *haiku* poet	
1721 *The Love Suicides at Amijima* (Chikamatsu Monzaemon), masterpiece among tragedies of fatal love written for the puppet theater	
1745 *Haiku* poet Yosa Buson anticipates modern free verse with innovative poems in his *Elegy to Hokuju Rōsen*	

TIMELINE

TEXTS	CONTEXTS
1748 *The Treasury of Loyal Retainers* (Takeda Izumo II), popular play immortalizing fealty of *samurai* who avenge their master's death	
1758–1801 Studies by Motoori Norinaga revive interest in *The Ten Thousand Leaves*, *The Tale of Genji*, and other Japanese classics	
	1760s Harunobu inaugurates heyday of color woodblock print
	1769–1800 James Watt's refinements of the steam engine fuel Industrial Revolution
1770–1790 Center of literary activity shifts from Kyoto-Osaka area eastward to Edo (present-day Tokyo)	**1770–1790** Glory days of *kabuki* with actor Ichikawa Danjūrō V
ca. 1776 *Tales of Moonlight and Rain* (Ueda Akinari), a collection of supernatural stories, including **Bewitched**	**1776** American colonies adopt the Declaration of Independence
	1790 Utamaro's portraits of women add psychological depth to woodblock print tradition
	1810–1880 Landscapes by Hokusai and Hiroshige take art of woodblock print to its zenith

IHARA SAIKAKU
1642–1693

No writer caught the substance of seventeenth-century Japanese city life as completely as Ihara Saikaku. He knew the foibles of the merchant class inside out, because he was one of them. Born in Osaka in 1642, when the city was the commercial epicenter of Japan, Saikaku's real name was Hirayama Tōgo. Ihara is thought to have been his mother's surname, and Saikaku* is the pen name he took when he became a writer.

It appears that Saikaku's people were tradesmen of substantial means and that at a young age he inherited the family business, though the nature of that business is uncertain. Evidence suggests that the family may have been swordsmiths. In any case, Saikaku had years of economic experience under his belt when, after his young wife died in 1675, he left the business in the hands of trusted clerks, shaved his head in the monastic style, and embarked on the life of a retired gentleman, dabbling in poetry, traveling, and scribbling for his own amusement. Actually, he ended up working as hard as ever, for his talent and drive soon made Saikaku one of Japan's first professional writers.

By the time of his "retirement," Saikaku was already a well-known amateur poet. A prime mover in refashioning traditional Japanese verse to the tastes of the new metropolitan class, he had gained notoriety as a poetic radical. In Saikaku's day a form of extended, linked verse had all but supplanted the short classical five-line poem known as the *tanka* (see *The Man'yōshū* and *The Kokinshū*, in Volume 1). The new poetry was usually composed by several people, who took turns penning alternating units of two and three lines, so that each new link, when yoked to its antecedent, momentarily completed a verse resembling the traditional five-line poem, before, in turn, becoming the beginning of another verse, on and on into a sequence that suggested a kind of poetic stream of consciousness. This ingenious form existed well before Saikaku, but it was in large measure his audacity that brought the genre of linked poetry completely into the profane world.

Impatient with technical correctness and orthodox poetic conceits, Saikaku turned "chain poetry" in a new direction. An exhibitionist at heart, he rejected the input of other poets. His solo sequences gave the illusion of maintaining the linked-verse ideal of overlapping voices and shifting points of view while concentrating on single-minded descriptions of the world actually observed. Until now linked poetry had been, essentially, a protracted and often pedantic form of word-play, but Saikaku used the medium to fashion a series of fleeting genre scenes of seventeenth-century life. Freewheeling and down-to-earth, the Saikaku string of slice-of-life vignettes moved with the speed and vividness of film flying through a projector:

> A thief!
> I thought,
> and feigned sleep.
>
> Between mother and child
> a man crawls in.
>
> His heart aflame,
> he hesitates
> to lift the quilt.

* Note that names are given in the Japanese order, with surname first. In the case of writers like Saikaku, who replace their given names with pen names, Japanese convention designates them by the pen name rather than the surname—hence Saikaku, not Ihara.

Stage fright:
the first visit to a brothel.

"Hey!
Anything offbeat
for sale?"

"Yesterday again two fools
committed double suicide."*

On a single move
he staked the game† —
and lost.

Already we can see a storyteller in the making, a novelist in search of his medium. Frustrated with the narrative and descriptive limitations of poetry and confident in the colloquial freedom he had carved for himself, Saikaku finally discarded prosodic constraints and tried his hand at fiction. He wrote his first novel in 1682, at the age of forty. *The Life of a Sensuous Man* was a brilliant beginning: a picaresque tale of the amorous exploits of a sexually precocious and ultimately insatiable hero. At seven the young lad falls in love with a maidservant; by nine he is commissioning love letters. A mere youth, he has already found his calling, and by the time the book ends, the sixty-year-old hero has racked up over four thousand conquests.

In his first novel Saikaku managed to preserve both the formal balance and the kaleidoscopic sweep of a linked verse sequence, along with the irreverence that had become his trademark. Structurally, *The Life of a Sensuous Man* is clearly the offspring of linked poetry. The loosely connected chapters are anecdotal, each introduced with a rhetorical flourish in the poetic mode, followed by the "story," a brief episode frequently interrupted when the author pauses to sketch little genre scenes depicting the various mores encountered by the hero as he wends his randy way through life. After a few pages the chapter ends, often abruptly, and the next chapter—another link in the narrative chain—takes the hero in a new direction. The novel's structure in fifty-four chapters also parodies *The Tale of Genji* (in Volume 1), the classic work of Japanese prose fiction, and the hero's methodic quest for love renders him an updated, if burlesque, version of the romantic noble. It is altogether a more spirited and vulgar world. Merchants replace aristocrats; the customs of the red-light district supersede the rituals of court life. In Saikaku the denizens of this new world had a novelist who spoke their language, and they quickly made the book a best-seller.

Perhaps unintentionally he had launched a new career. In the remaining eleven years of his life Saikaku produced at least twenty-six books (not counting several works considered spurious). He shared with his first hero, the sensuous man, a voracious appetite for life, and in his fiction Saikaku's stamina and curiosity took him everywhere: temples, shrines, teahouses, *nō* and *kabuki* theaters, Chinese trading posts, *samurai* barracks, riverboats, pawnshops, law courts, breweries, and brothels. It is hard to imagine a writer more cosmopolitan than Saikaku. The combination of business experience, ample leisure, and a nose for human mischief made him a shrewd observer of almost every level of Japanese society.

His choice of subject was also wide ranging. He wrote parodies of Confucian ethics, crime stories, lampoons of famous people, and accounts of martial valor. A penchant for travel led him to publish a collection of regional folktales and the first geographical guide to the whole of Japan. But his richest material by far was

---

* Also known as "love suicide." Occasionally, a prostitute and a client would fall in love; the frequent visits could ruin a man financially. The most impassioned lovers escaped their difficulties by committing suicide together. In this verse, the brothel owner mentions the latest case to discourage the young customer from nursing any romantic illusions.
† Saikaku switches from the game of love to *go*: like chess, a game of strategy.

the daily life of townspeople. In some works he focused on their love lives, in others on their pocketbooks. Both money and sex were radically new topics for Japanese literature. The subject matter alone would probably have guaranteed Saikaku a certain popularity. What made him an icon was the wit he brought to his material.

Saikaku has been called a realist, but, like Petronius (in Volume 1), his art is closer to caricature. The people crowding the pages of his novels and short stories are never fully drawn. Instead, their flaws or idiosyncrasies are exaggerated in a few bold strokes. This representation is realistic not because it paints the whole picture but because the quirks it captures have the immediate ring of truth. No doubt, from the first, readers found Saikaku realistic in comparison with the output of his direct predecessors: fairy tales and sentimental novelettes, juvenile parodies of classical literature, dreary didactic tales, how-to books with a thin veneer of fiction.

As the founder of a new popular "realistic" literature, which cut to the bone of bourgeois experience (more often than not, the funny bone), Saikaku caught both the substance and the spirit of his frenzied age. The immediacy of his subject and his virtuoso style not only won him a full complement of contemporary admirers but a place among the greatest writers of Japan.

The Barrelmaker Brimful of Love is a worthy introduction. The novella is part of a collection of stories, *Five Women Who Loved Love*, written in 1686 when Saikaku had reached his full stride. It should be remembered, though, that this is a writer for whom language is always a bravura performance. Translation, inevitably obscuring linguistic aspects of a text, cannot display the stylist's forte to best advantage. Saikaku's many other strengths, however, do emerge.

For other stories from the same collection, see William Theodore de Bary, *Five Women Who Loved Love* (1956). Numerous translations of Saikaku's fiction are available, of which the following can be recommended: G. W. Sargent, *The Japanese Family Storehouse* (1959); Ivan Morris, *The Life of an Amorous Woman and Other Writings* (1963); Peter Nosco, *Some Final Words of Advice* (1980); Paul Gordon Schalow, *The Great Mirror of Male Love* (1990). For an introduction to Saikaku and his times see Howard Hibbett, *The Floating World in Japanese Fiction* (1959), and for a history of Japanese literature in the seventeenth and eighteenth centuries see Donald Keene, *World within Walls* (1976).

PRONOUNCING GLOSSARY

The following list uses common English syllables to provide rough equivalents of selected words whose pronunciation may be unfamiliar to the general reader.

Chozaemon: *choh-zah-e-mohn*

Dotom-bori: *doh-tohm–boh-ree*

Genji: *gen-jee*

Gion-machi: *gee-ohn–mah-chee*

Heike: *hay-kay*

Hirayama Tōgo: *hee-rah-yah-mah toh-goh*

Hokkeji: *hohk-ke-jee*

Ihara Saikaku: *ee-hah-rah sai-kah-koo*

Ise: *ee-say*

Jokyo: *joh-kyoh*

Kawara-machi: *kah-wah-rah–mah-chee*

Kinoe-ne: *kee-noh-e–ne*

Kyushichi: *kyoo-shee-chee*

momme: *mohm-me*

Nabeshima: *nah-be-shee-mah*

Nihei: *nee-hay*

Nokaze: *noh-kah-ze*

Shimmei: *sheem-may*

Shimabara: *shee-mah-bah-rah*

Sumiyoshi: *soo-mee-yoh-shee*

The Barrelmaker Brimful of Love[1]

1

The Cleaning of a Well by a Man Unhappy in Love

Life is short; love is long.

There once was a cooper who, from the coffins he built with his own hands, realized how impermanent the world is. Although he worked his saw and gimlet assiduously for a living, he made very little money and could rent only a thatched hut in Osaka. He lived in a manner befitting the poorer section of Temma.[2]

There was also a girl who surpassed all the others who lived in her remote village. Her complexion was white even to the ears and her feet were not stained by contact with the soil. On New Year's Eve of her thirteenth year her parents were short the sum of silver required as a village tax, which amounted to one-third of their income, and so the girl was sent to serve as a lady's maid in an imposing city-house near Temma.

As time went on her natural disposition and ready wit came to be appreciated. She was solicitous toward the old couple, pleased the lady of the house, and was well thought of by all the others. Later she was allowed free access to the inner storeroom where all the fine things were kept. Everyone thought so highly of her that it was said: "What would happen to this house if Osen were not around?" This was all because of her intelligence.

Osen knew nothing of the ways of love. She had spent all of her nights in a manner which some might think unworthy of her—alone. Once when a lighthearted fellow pulled her dress she responded with a full-throated shriek, leaving the man to bewail this unfortunate turn of events. After that no man would ever speak flirtingly to her. People may criticize Osen for such behavior, but it would probably be a good thing if all men's daughters acted as she did.

Our story begins on the seventh day of autumn, the Tanabata Festival[3] day, when silk clothes—guaranteed never to have been worn before—are piled up seven high, right sleeve over left, to be rented to celebrants. It is amusing to see how the upper-class ladies celebrate by tying familiar poems to juniper twigs while the poor people decorate their houses with gourds and persimmons on the branch.

This particular day was a special occasion for the people of the neighborhood because the common well was being cleaned. The people living in rented houses on the side lanes participated in this cleaning and kept water on the boil for tea to be served to the workmen. After most of the dirty water had been scooped out, the bottom of the well was scraped and up came a variety of things mixed in with pebbles. A kitchen knife, the disappearance of which had puzzled people, came to light, and so did a

---

1. Translated by and with notes adapted from William Theodore de Bary. 2. A section near the outskirts of Osaka, which was still fairly rustic. A number of coopers, or barrelmakers, located their shops there. 3. Celebrated on the seventh night of the Seventh Month to commemorate the annual meeting of the stars Vega (the weaver maiden) and Altair (the herd boy). According to what was originally Chinese legend, the stars were lovers separated by the Milky Way and could meet only one night a year.

bunch of seaweed into which a needle had been thrust.[4] I wonder why that was done. Then, on further search, more things came up including some old pony-design coppers,[5] a naked doll without a face, a one-sided sword-handle peg of crude workmanship, and a patched-over baby's bib. You can never tell just what you will find at the bottom of an uncovered, outside well.

Then, when the well cleaners got down to the barrel planking close to the spring, an old two-headed nail came loose and the planking came apart. They sent for the cooper we have mentioned to make a new hoop for the barrel. When he had succeeded in stopping up the slowly flowing water, the cooper noticed an old woman with a crooked back who was fondling a live lizard.

He asked her what it was, and she answered: "This is a newt which just now was brought up from the well. Don't you recognize one when you see it? If you put this lizard in a bamboo tube and burn it, and then sprinkle its ashes in the hair of the person you love, that person will love you in turn." She spoke with a great deal of conviction.

This woman was formerly an abortionist known as Kosan from Myoto Pond, but when this profession was prohibited she gave up her cruel practice and worked at making noodle-flour with a mortar. Because of the hand-to-mouth nature of such an occupation, she had to work so hard that she did not even hear the temple bell sounding the end of the day. However, as she sank lower and lower in the social scale she learned the lesson of karma[6] and she thought more about the future life.

When she told the cooper about the terrible things that would happen to people who did wrong in this world, he paid no attention to her. Rather, he questioned her the more intently about the efficacy of burning a newt to help in one's love affairs.

Naturally, she became more sympathetic as he talked to her with such earnestness, and she finally asked: "Who is it that you love? I won't tell another soul."

The cooper forgot himself, so much was he thinking of the one he loved, and as he beat on the bottom of the cask he let himself be carried away by his own words, pouring out all of his story to the old woman. "The one I love does not live far away. I love Osen, the maid of the house here. I have sent her a hundred letters without getting a word in reply."

The old woman nodded and said: "You don't need any newts to win her. I can bridge the stream of love for you. I will disperse the clouds and make your love successful in no time at all."

The cooper was surprised to hear her undertake the matter so lightly. "If this will involve a great deal of money, I am afraid I won't be able to supply it, no matter how much I would like to, for this has been a bad season for me. Naturally, if I had the money I wouldn't begrudge it. All I can promise you is a cotton kimono dyed to your liking at New Year's and a set of Nara-hemp[7] clothes of second quality for the mid-summer festival of O-Bon. Is it a bargain?"

---

4. To put a curse or cast a spell on someone, an effigy of seaweed with a needle through it was stuck to a tree or cast into a well.   5. Coins minted by the private sector, engraved with the image of a pony. They were carried as magic charms to increase one's wealth.   6. The force generated by a person's thoughts, words, and actions believed in Buddhism to determine one's specific destiny in the next existence. 7. Bleached hemp made in Nara (the old capital, south of Kyoto) was used for summer clothing.

"Love that can talk that way must be based on selfishness. I am not looking for that sort of thing at all. You know there is a great art in getting a person to feel love for you. In my lifetime I've helped thousands of people, and always with success. I'll see to it that you meet her before the Chrysanthemum Festival[8] in September."

This set the flames of love burning more fiercely in the cooper's heart and he cried: "My lady, I will supply you with all the firewood you will need to make tea the rest of your life."

In this world no one knows how long a person may live, and it is amusing to think that love should have made him promise so much.

2

After the Dance: A Witch in the Night

There are seven mysterious things in the Temma section of Osaka: the umbrella-shaped flame before the Daikyo Temple; the boy without hands at Shimmei Shrine; the topsy-turvy lady at Sonezaki;[9] the phantom noose of Eleventh Avenue; the crying monk of Kawasaki; the laughing cat of Ikeda-machi; and the smouldering Chinese mortar at the Bush-Warbler's Mound.[1] But these are just the magical tricks of old foxes and badgers. Much more to be feared are those demons in human form who play havoc with the lives of ignorant men.

Our souls are dark indeed. And it was so dark the twenty-eighth night of July[2] that hanging lanterns threw no light under the eaves of houseroofs. Street dancers, hoping to sustain their revels till dawn, shouted, "Just one more day to dance till the month is over," but they too reluctantly broke up and returned to their homes. Even the vigilant dog of Four Corners[3] fell fast asleep.

At this late hour old Nanny, the mischievous crone in whom the cooper had put his trust, noticed that the entrance to the great landlord's house was still open. She burst in, slammed the door, and tumbled down onto the kitchen floor, crying: "Oh, oh, it's terrible. Give me a drink of water!"

To those within the house she appeared on the brink of death, but her continued breathing encouraged them to call her back to consciousness, and without more ado she came to life.

"What can you have seen that was so terrifying?" asked the landlord's wife and her aged mother-in-law.

"Well, it's a shameful thing for an old woman to admit, but I went out walking the streets tonight. I went to bed early and couldn't get to sleep, so I decided to go see the dancing. My, it was wonderful! I couldn't get enough of it, especially the Kudoki[4] songs with rhymes made up using *yama* and *matsu*.[5] There was one fellow down in front of the Nabe-

---

8. Celebrated on the ninth day of the Ninth Month, according to the Chinese calendar. It was one of five major seasonal festivals, as was the Tanabata festival (see n. 3, p. 595).　9. A quarter known for its female prostitutes. *Shimmei Shrine:* a Shinto shrine frequented by homosexual prostitutes.　1. None of these mysteries has been identified.　2. The translation is misleading. In Chapter 1 we are told that it is autumn but here it is July. The lunar calendar followed in Japan at this time was about a month ahead of the Western calendar. Autumn was considered to begin on the seventh day of the Seventh Month, which would normally have corresponded to August in the Western calendar.　3. That is, on the street corner.　4. A long ballad in which one tune was repeated over and over.　5. A word frequently used in poetry for its pun on "pine" and "wait." *Yama:* mountain.

shima mansion who sang exactly like Nihei, the great Donen[6] singer of Kyoto.

"I pushed my way through a crowd of men and watched the show with my fan as an eye-shade so that people couldn't see what an old woman I was. But the men knew what was what, even in the dark. I wiggled my old hips in a most flirtatious way and was really quite sexy in this white gown and black sash. But no one so much as pinched my bottom. 'A woman is a sometime thing.'[7]

"So I started home again, my mind recollecting the old days of my youth, and suddenly near your gate I was hailed by a handsome young fellow of twenty-four or twenty-five. He was desperately in love, so tortured by his fatal passion that he had only a day or two to live in this Fleeting World.[8] It was the cruel Osen, he said, upon whom his heart had fixed itself so hopelessly.[9] He swore that within a week after his death his ghost would come to kill every member of this household. Oh, he was so frightsome! He had a great nose, his face was flushed with fever, and his eyes gleamed, just as if he were possessed by the *tengu*[1] whose figure is paraded before the Sumiyoshi festival procession. I was so frightened that I had to run in here."

Everyone who had crowded around to hear her story was aghast, and the householder's aged father wept a little.

"To be unhappy in love," he said, "is not unheard of. Osen is old enough to get married now, and we should keep this man in mind if he has a suitable livelihood. Providing he is not a gambler or widow chaser, and is thrifty and frugal, he might make a good choice. Of course, I do not know the man at all, but I can sympathize with him."

By the long silence which followed, it was plain that the others sympathized with him too. The shrewd old hen certainly knew her business when it came to promoting a love affair.

It was now past midnight and, after she had been helped to her feet, old Nanny returned to her hovel. While she lay there plotting her next move, dawn broke through the east window. Nearby she could hear the sound of flint on steel, as a neighbor started up his fire. Somewhere an infant began to cry. Sleepily the tenants of that squalid quarter chased out the mosquitoes which had slipped through the breaks in their paper nets and plagued them throughout the night. One minute the women's fingers were pinching at the fleas in their underclothes, the next pinching for some odd coins on the sanctuary shelf[2] with which to buy a few green vegetables. Still, amidst the bitter struggle for existence, pleasure could yet be found by those who, through wedlock, had won partners for their beds. In what delights may they not have indulged, with pillows to the south and mattresses in utter disarray, violating the vigil of Kinoe-ne?[3]

---

6. *Donen-bushi* was a type of ballad made popular by Donen Ganzaburo of Kyoto around the time this story was written.   7. Literal trans.: a woman is something only as long as she is young.   8. Sometimes translated as "Floating World," refers to the transitory nature of life in Buddhist teaching and, by extension, to the sensual aspects of human existence.   9. The language used is that associated with a Buddhist belief concerning human passions, according to which obsessions of the soul will, if unsatisfied or unrelieved during a person's lifetime, return after death to wreak vengeance on the object of that passion.   1. A fabulous being with wings and an extremely long nose.   2. A shelf where statues of Buddha were to be kept.   3. On this night a vigil was kept in honor of the god of plenty, and continence was to be observed until midnight. Children conceived at this time were thought to become

At last the sun rose to shine upon a brisk, breezy autumn day. The old woman tied her head up in a towel and treated herself for a headache, calling upon the services of Dr. Okajima without worrying how the bill would be paid. She had just served herself some broth of fresh herbs, when Osen came in from the back alley to visit her.

"How are you today?" Osen inquired sweetly, as from her left sleeve she brought forth half a melon pickled in the Nara style and wrapped in a lotus leaf, which she set down on a bundle of firewood. "Perhaps you would like it with some soy sauce," she said modestly and made to go get it without waiting for the other's thanks.

"Wait," the old woman insisted. "It is because of you that I am about to die before my time, and since I have no daughter of my own, you must pray for me when I am gone." Then, reaching into a hemp basket, she brought out a pair of purple socks with red ribbons and a patched-up rosary bag,[4] from which she removed her divorce papers. The socks and bag she gave to Osen, saying they would be keepsakes.

Impressionable, as most women are, Osen believed the story and wept. "If there is truly someone in love with me, why didn't he come for help from a love-wise person like yourself? If I had known his intentions, I should not have spurned him lightly."

Old Nanny saw that this was as good a time as any to come out with the whole story. "There is no reason to hide anything from you now. He did come to me many times, and the deep sincerity of his love for you was more touching and pitiful than I can say. If you should reject him now, my resentment will fall upon no one but you." She spoke with all the cleverness that years of wide experience had given her, and, as was only to have been expected, Osen soon yielded.

"I shall be glad to meet him anytime," she cried, dizzy with emotion.

Thereupon the old crone, delighted to have obtained such a promise, whispered: "It just occurred to me how you might best meet him. On the eleventh day of August you must make a secret pilgrimage to Ise.[5] Traveling alone together, you would become fast friends and could spend your bedtime hours sweetly, heart murmuring to heart of undying love. And you know," she added casually, "he is not at all bad looking."

Without further persuasion and before she had even seen him, Osen was consumed with love for this man. "Can he write letters himself? Does his hair fall long and pretty behind his head? I suppose, since he is a craftsman, his back may be a little stooped. Well, when we set out from here, I should like to stop at noon in Moriguchi or Hirakata, so we can get a room and go to bed early."

She was babbling on like this when the chief maid-servant was heard calling outside: "Miss Osen, you're wanted!"

Osen quickly took her leave: "It's all set for the eleventh then. . . ."

---

criminals. *Pillows to the south:* husbands and wives slept with their pillows at the southern end of the bed. Widows and widowers placed their pillows to the north, as a sign of mourning.   4. To carry beads used for prayer in Buddhism.   5. It was a popular custom to make a pilgrimage to Ise without the knowledge of one's parents or master. When the pilgrim returned, he or she was supposed to be forgiven for absconding.

3

As Delicious as the Water of Kyoto:
The Intimacy of Lovers Meeting in Secret

"The morning-glories are in bloom and it would be nice to have a look at them tomorrow early—nice and cool, too," the lady of the house added as she began her instructions to the servants that evening. "I want you to arrange some seats out near the back hedge, away from the house. Spread out the flower-mats, put baked rice and toothpicks in the different compartments of the picnic box, and don't forget the tea bottle. I shall take a bath just before six in the morning and then I want my hair done up simply in three plain rolls. As for a gown, let me have the hempen one with open sleeves and a pink lining. I shall wear my gray-satin sash with circle designs on it, the informal, two-piece one dotted with our family crest. I want you to take the utmost care in everything because we may be seen by people in the adjacent streets. So each of you must dress in decent-looking clothes. A litter should be sent at the usual rising time to my sister's house in Tenjinbashi."

She put all the arrangements in the charge of Osen, who attended the lady upon her retirement into an ample mosquito net, at the four corners of which little bells jingled while Osen gently fanned her to sleep. Imagine so much fuss over nothing but some flowers in your back yard!

But perhaps such vanity is not the weakness of women alone. At this time the master of the house was probably wasting himself and his money on Miss Nokaze of Shimabara and Miss Ogino of Shimmachi,[6] buying both of them the same day, one for each end of his carrying-pole.[7] Though he spoke of visiting Tsumura Temple each morning, and carried a shoulder pad[8] for that purpose, it is much more likely that he went straight to the licensed quarter for a morning of sport and pleasure.

Just before dawn on the eleventh of August old Nanny heard a light tapping on the door of her shanty.

"It is Osen," the girl outside whispered as she threw in a bundle which had been hastily wrapped in a large kerchief. Returning immediately to her master's house, Osen did not realize that the old crone would lose no time in searching through the bundle to see what was there: five strings of cash worth about one farthing of silver each, and perhaps eighteen *momme* of pony-engraved silver pieces;[9] nearly a peck of polished rice; a dried bonito;[1] two combs in a charm bag; a one-piece sash of many colors; a silver and brown garment for cooler weather; a lighter gown, well worn, with a fan pattern; cotton socks, the soles of which were unfinished; sandals with loose straps; and a parasol on which Osen had naïvely written her address! The old woman quickly set about erasing the telltale characters in

---

6. Names of expensive prostitutes in the licensed pleasure quarters of Kyoto and Osaka, respectively. 7. A pole balanced on the shoulders, with items hung at each end for transporting; hence *carrying-pole* is slang for the hiring of two prostitutes at the same time. 8. An item of priestly vestments sometimes worn by lay devotees. 9. Three kinds of currency circulated at the time. In Edo (Tokyo), seat of the shogunal government, gold was the primary currency. In the Kyoto-Osaka region silver prevailed. Copper coins, with a value approximate to pennies, were in use throughout Japan. Gold currency was denominated, but silver had to be measured by weight in *momme*. The silver pieces here are *komagane* ("small silver") coins that weighed one to five *momme* each, the equivalent of several dollars. The homonym *koma* means "pony," thus the translator's *pony-engraved silver pieces*. 1. A favorite fish among townspeople.

such a way as to leave no unsightly smear upon the parasol. As she did so, someone greeted her from the entranceway.

"Old Nanny, I shall go on ahead now," the cooper called in on his way past.

Later Osen appeared, trembling a little. "Sorry to be late. I was detained at the house."

The old woman then took up the bundle of personal belongings and hastened with Osen down an unfamiliar byway. "It would be a great effort for me, but perhaps for the sake of the pilgrimage I should accompany you to Ise," old Nanny suggested.

Osen was plainly upset. "It's a long trip for an elderly woman and you would find it hard going. Why don't you take the night boat down from Fushimi after you have taken me to meet this man?" she replied tactlessly, for she had now no patience with anything that might upset the headlong progress of her affair.

Just as they were crossing the Capital Bridge, along came Kyushichi, a manservant in the same household as Osen. He had come this way to watch the morning change of guard at Osaka Castle, but, his curiosity aroused when the two women came by, Kyushichi inevitably became a further obstacle in the path of the lovers.

"Why, I have been thinking for some time of making the same pilgrimage and there could be no better companions for the journey than yourselves. Just leave your baggage for me to carry. Fortunately, I have plenty of spending money and can see to it that you suffer no inconvenience on that score." From his excessive politeness one could guess that Kyushichi was inspired by some secret design on Osen, and old Nanny's hostility was immediately aroused.

"A young lady traveling in the company of a man! Now wouldn't that seem most extraordinary to the people who saw us! Besides, the gods of Ise frown on that sort of thing. I have heard and seen enough of people who willfully disgrace themselves before society. Please don't follow us."

"Well, I hardly expected to run into objections of this sort. Believe me, I have no designs on Miss Osen; faith alone moves me to this. In love, the gods will assure my success, without my having to solicit their protection, for my heart is true, true as the road we shall travel together. If the sun and moon favor us and Miss Osen so inclines, we can travel anywhere— to the capital perhaps. This would be just the time to spend four or five days there, seeing the maples of Takao in their bright fall colors and the blooming mushrooms of Saga. The master generally stops at a hotel in Kawara-machi, but I think we would find it awkward there. We could do better," Kyushichi continued as if he would have everything his own way, "by taking some cozy rooms at the western end of Third Avenue. Then the old lady here could visit the Temple of the Original Vow,[2] on Sixth Avenue.

By this time the autumn sun was up over the mountainside, and the travelers were halfway past the pine-shaded banks of the Yodo River when they ran upon a man who looked very conspicuous, seated beneath a cat's-

---

2. Honganji, a Buddhist temple, whose name translates as "Temple of the Original (or True) Vow."

paw willow as if waiting for someone. On closer examination the old crone recognized him as the cooper. From the look in her eyes he could tell that something had gone wrong; it had not worked out as planned after he went on ahead of them.

"You look as if you were going to Ise too," old Nanny addressed him. "But why go alone? You seem to be an agreeable fellow and we'd like to have you spend the night with us somewhere."

The cooper was delighted, of course. "It's so true: 'The kindness of others always brightens a journey.' I am certainly grateful for the invitation."

Kyushichi, on the other hand, looked bewildered. "It seems a little odd, especially with this young lady along, to have someone join us when you don't even know where he's going."

"Oh," the old woman replied, "God watches over everything. And with a stout fellow like you along, what can possibly happen?"

Thereafter the four of them slept in the same inn each night. Kyushichi, watching carefully for any opportunity to satisfy his secret desires, removed one of the sliding doors which separated him from the ladies and would peek in at them on his way to the bath. At night, when the four of them slept in a row, he stretched out his hand and tipped up the oil lamp so as to smother the light.

Then, just as it was about to fail, the cooper exclaimed, "It's awfully warm for fall," and opened the window near him so that bright moonlight shone through upon the four sleeping figures.

Again, when Osen made a pretense of snoring and Kyushichi moved his right leg over upon her, he was quickly detected by the cooper, who promptly started up a song about the Soga brothers,[3] "Love plays mischief with all . . ." while beating time with the end of his fan. Osen then abandoned the pretense of sleeping and started to talk with old Nanny.

"There is nothing so calamitous as to bring a girl-child into the world. I have been thinking that it would be a good idea to become a novice at the Fudo Chapel of Kitano[4] next New Year's and eventually become a nun."

"Very good idea," the crone answered sleepily. "Better than to live on in a world full of disappointments."

Thus the two men stood in each other's way the whole night through. The upshot of their bedtime activities was only this: that Kyushichi, who started the evening with his pillow to the west, wriggled around and wound up with his head to the south and his underclothing missing—a shocking piece of carelessness for a pilgrim with money in his waistband; while the cooper slept with a resentful scowl on his face, a wad of tissue paper in his hand, and a clamshell full of clove oil[5] beside him.

The next morning at Mt. Osaka they hired an Otsu man's horse and proceeded on their journey with Osen riding in the middle and the men mounted on either side of her. Funny though an onlooker would have found this arrangement, there was something, whether fatigue or simply pleasure, which made the riders oblivious to their absurdity. On one side

---

3. Warriors famous for their daring.   4. A buddhist convent in Osaka. Fudo was a deity who destroys evil.   5. Used as cologne.

Kyushichi fondled Osen's toes; on the other the cooper reached up and put his arm around her waist; and each playfully indulged his secret desires as best he could in a manner that seems somewhat amusing to anyone who knows what each was after.

None of the group had any real interest in the pilgrimage itself. At Ise they failed to visit the Inner Shrine or the sacred beach at which homage is paid to the Sun,[6] stopping only at the Outer Shrine for a few minutes and purchasing as their only souvenirs a purification brooch and some seaweed.

On the way back the two men kept their eyes on each other, so nothing of consequence happened. When they reached the capital, Kyoto, and Kyushichi had guided them to the hotel he knew, the cooper reckoned in his head what he owed Kyushichi for bills the latter had paid, thanked him for his trouble, and took his leave with a bow. Thinking that he would henceforth have Osen to himself, Kyushichi went out and bought many presents and souvenirs for her. He could hardly wait for night to fall, but decided to while away the time visiting someone he knew in the neighborhood of Karasumaru.

In the meantime old Nanny left the hotel with Osen, ostensibly to visit Kiyomizu Temple. They went directly to Gion-machi, to a little shop which sold box lunches, and there found a card upon which was written "Gimlet and Saw." Recognizing this as the cooper's way of identifying himself, Osen slipped inside almost unnoticeably. Upstairs she found her lover, and together they drank the cup of betrothal,[7] pledging themselves to each other forever.

Thereupon old Nanny retired downstairs. "The water here is simply delicious," she exclaimed as she guzzled cups of tea one after another.

Having won from Osen the first installment on their marriage, the cooper left early for Osaka by day boat. Old Nanny and Osen, upon their return to the hotel, gave notice of immediate departure. Kyushichi pleaded with them to stay for a few more days of sight-seeing, but the old woman was determined.

"No, no. What would your mistress say if she thought Osen was chasing around with men?" So off they started.

"I know it's a lot to ask, but this bundle is so heavy. Won't you help us with it, Kyushichi?"

"My back aches. Sorry," he replied.

And when they stopped to rest in a wisteria grove before the Great Buddha of Inari, the women had to pay for their own tea.

4

Shingles Kindle a Fire in the Heart, and so in the Hearth

"If you had told us you wanted to go on a pilgrimage, we would have sent you in a litter or on hired horseback. But to make a secret pilgrimage in the fantastic way you did, and come back with all these presents bought by lord knows whom—why, it's—it's just the sort of thing one never does,

6. The sun goddess, mythical ancestor of the imperial family, who is enshrined at Ise.   7. Or fidelity.

not even married couples. And traveling to the capital together, drinking and sleeping together—who would dare go that far?

"Osen is just a woman, and it may be too much to expect that she could resist the urgings of Kyushichi. But Kyushichi, the smart aleck, thinks he must teach the innocent gods what manliness is, and teach this innocent girl . . ."

Their mistress was in a frightful rage. Kyushichi's explanations had no effect on her at all, and the poor, guiltless fellow was finally discharged, without waiting for the regular biannual replacement time of September fifth. Later he worked several terms in a wholesale house called Bizen-ya in Kitano and married a drifter[8] named Longie of Eighthbridge. Now he earns a living as a *sushi*[9] vendor on Willow Lane and has simply forgotten about Osen.

Osen went back to the uneventful routine of household duties, but she was unable to forget her brief romance with the cooper or get him out of her mind. She began to neglect herself, becoming shabby in appearance, careless in conduct, and little by little more gaunt and pale. Finally, losing control of herself, Osen started to wail throughout the night like a sick hen.

About the same time a series of further misfortunes overtook the household. The great cauldron rusted so that its bottom fell out; there was a sudden change between breakfast and supper in the taste of the prepared bean-paste; and lightning struck the roof of the storehouse, setting fire to the shingles. All of these things had a perfectly natural explanation, but people felt that in this case they had some special significance. Someone said: "It is the implacable spirit of the man who is madly in love with Osen—the cooper."

When her master and mistress heard this, they decided to do everything in their power to bring Osen and the cooper together in wedlock. Nanny was called in for a consultation.

"Osen," the old crone said craftily, "has told me several times that she would not have a hand laborer for a husband, and she isn't sure whether or not the cooper will do. But it seems to me that she is being unnecessarily choosy. If, in spite of all, they can just get along in life together, she should be satisfied."

Having heard old Nanny's ideas on the subject, Osen's employers sent for the cooper and concluded a marriage contract with him. Soon afterward, Osen had her sleeves sewn up and her teeth blackened[1] in preparation for the marriage, an auspicious date for which had already been chosen. Her dowry consisted of twenty-three items, including a second-grade chest with a natural finish, a wicker hamper for her trousseau, a folding pasteboard box, two castoff gowns from her mistress, quilted bedclothes, a mosquito net with red lining, and a scarf of classic colors. With all of these, more than a pound of silver was sent to the cooper's house.

---

8. Literal trans.: "lotus-leaf woman"; a prostitute hired by a business to entertain traveling merchants. She floated, like a lotus leaf on the water, from one man to another.   9. Small servings of vinegared rice topped, rolled, or mixed with raw seafood, seaweed, or other ingredients.   1. Both are in the adult fashion and are signs that a woman is nubile.

The newlyweds proved quite compatible and their luck was good. Honest and industrious, the husband kept his head bent assiduously over the work of his craft, while his good wife took up weaving striped cloth of dark-dyed Fushikane[2] thread. Night and day they worked and never failed to meet their debts on the last day of the year or the day before the Bon Festival.[3] Osen took especially good care of the cooper. In winter, on windy days or when it snowed, she carefully covered his rice to keep it warm when he took it out. In summer she kept a fan close to her pillow to cool him with. When he was out of the house she locked the gate and never looked at another man. If she had occasion to speak of anything, it was always "my husband this, my husband that." Even when, after several years and months, she bore two children, Osen did not forsake her husband for them.

✦ Alas, however, most women are fickle creatures. Captivated by some delicious love story, or deluded by the latest dramatic productions of Dotom-bori[4] their souls are caught up in giddy corruption. Amidst the falling cherry blossoms of the Temple of the Heavenly Kings[5] or under a blooming wisteria trellis, they fall head over heels in love with some handsome fellow. And so, upon returning home, they find loathsome the man who has supported them for many long years.

There is no greater folly than this. From the moment of their seduction such women abandon all prudence and frugality, light great fires in their ovens and leave them untended, burn lamps thoughtlessly where no lamp is needed, and while their family fortunes dwindle, wait impatiently for leisure hours to spend away from home. Such marriages are dreadful indeed.

And should their husbands die, in seven days these women are out looking for other husbands. Divorced once, they marry and divorce again, six or seven times. That, unfortunately, is what the morals of the lower classes have sunk to, but this sort of thing, of course, never ever happens among the upper classes. A woman should give herself to only one man during her lifetime. If trouble arises or misfortune strikes, even when she is young, it is quite possible for her to become a nun in the Convent of Kaga or in the Hokkeji Nunnery of the Southern Capital, for this has been done many times before.

There are many others in the Fleeting World[6] who live in sin with secret lovers, but when they are discovered, either their husbands send them home without taking the matter to court, for fear of creating a sensation, or, in the case of husbands greedy for gold, some kind of deal is made and the matter dropped. Thus sinful women are spared through laxity in punishment, and for this reason adultery cannot be stamped out.

But there are gods and there is retribution. Every secret will be made known. How much to be dreaded—this ruinous road!

---

2. A dye process that uses gall (swollen plant tissue caused by an invasion of fungus or other parasites).
3. In honor of the dead; accounts were to be settled the day before.   4. The theater district of Osaka.
5. Tenjōji, a Buddhist temple in Osaka known for its cherry trees.   6. See n. 8, p. 598.

5

Life Is Shorter Than a Toothpick Made from Woodshavings

This is to announce an informal supper party to be held at my home on the sixteenth next. I should greatly appreciate having the honor of your company.

P.S. Guests not listed in order of local prominence.[7]

Chozaemon, the yeast maker, found the years and months passing as if life were only a dream. Already it was fifty years since his father died, and he had reason to congratulate himself on living long enough to celebrate such an anniversary. According to the ancients: "When one goes into mourning on the fiftieth anniversary of his father's death, it is customary to abstain from meat in the morning, but eat fish for supper and drink and sing throughout the evening, having thereafter no further obligations to perform." Since these were to be the last services, Chozaemon did not begrudge a little expense in conducting them properly. The wives of the neighborhood joined in the preparations. They got out the wooden bowls, trays, crockery, and different kinds of wooden plates used only on special occasions, dusted them, and set them on the sideboard.

It happened that the cooper's wife was on friendly terms with these people, so she too dropped in to offer her services. "Isn't there some work to be done in the kitchen?"

Osen was known as an intelligent and capable person, and they gave her a delicate job. "There are some sweets in the bedroom. Set them out on the deep trays."

Osen began her job of arranging the imperial persimmons, Chinese walnuts, falling-goose candies, and toothpicks of kaya and cryptomeria wood.[8] When she was almost finished, Master Chozaemon came in to fetch a nest of bowls from the shelf, but in doing so he clumsily dropped one on Osen's head so that her hairdo came apart all at once. He apologized profusely.

"Oh, it didn't hurt at all," Osen assured him as she hastily tied up her hair and went into the kitchen.

When the lady of the house saw her, however, she was immediately aroused. "Until a few minutes ago your hair was done up most beautifully. How could it become disarranged so suddenly?"

Osen, with a clear conscience, replied calmly: "The master was taking some bowls down from the shelf and one fell on me. That's how it happened."

But the lady would not believe her at all. "Indeed! A bowl falling off the shelf in broad daylight! What a playful bowl that must be. If you ask me, somebody fell into bed without going to sleep and her hair came undone. Of all things for an older man to be doing, when he is supposed to be mourning for his father!"

---

7. This is the text of the invitation sent out by Chozaemon.   8. Japanese cedar. *Falling-goose candies*: confections made from a flour of glutinous rice, barley, chestnuts, or adzuki beans, which are sweetened with sugar, kneaded, shaped in a decorative mold, and toasted. *Kaya:* Japanese nutmeg, or plum yew, an evergreen with edible seeds.

In a violent rage, she picked up some slices of fresh fish, which had been cut and arranged with much care, and began throwing them about the kitchen. No matter what anyone else talked of during the day, vinegar or flour or anything, she would drag in the subject of Osen and not let it drop, to the complete disgust of all who heard about the incident later. Truly it is the greatest of misfortunes for a man to have a wife of such fierce jealousy.

At first Osen put up patiently with the lady's ranting, though she could not help being annoyed by it. Later, the more she thought about it the more bitter and depressed Osen became. "My sleeve is already wet with tears. Having suffered the shame, there is nothing left to lose. I shall make love to Chozaemon and teach that woman a lesson." And, dwelling upon this idea, she aroused in herself a passion for Chozaemon which soon resulted in a secret exchange of promises between the two. They waited only for a suitable occasion to fulfill their desires.

The evening of January twenty-second, in the second year of Jokyo[9] (1685), seemed a propitious one for lovers since the women and children of the neighborhood were amusing themselves at the traditional spring pastime of drawing strings for prizes.[1] On into the night they played, completely absorbed in the game. Some lost and quit, others won and kept on with insatiable enthusiasm. Still others dozed off and started to snore. The cooper turned down his lamp and went to bed early, apparently so tired from the day's toil that he would not have awakened even if someone had pinched his nose.

Chozaemon followed Osen home from the party. "Now is the time to fulfill our mutual promise," he urged, and Osen, unable to refuse him, took Chozaemon into her house.

Then began what was to be their first and last attempt at love-making.

No sooner had they removed their underclothes than the cooper awoke. "Hold on! If I catch you, I'll never let you go!" he shouted.

Chozaemon quickly threw off the bedcovers. Naked and terrified, he dashed out and ran a great distance to the house of a close relative, barely escaping with his life.

Osen, realizing that it was a hopeless situation for her, plunged the blade of a carpenter's plane into her heart and died. Her corpse was exposed in the Shame Field[2] with that of the scoundrel Chozaemon when he was at last executed. Their names, known in countless ballads and songs, spread to distant provinces with the warning: This is a stern world and sin never goes unpunished.[3]

---

9. The reign name of the current emperor. *January:* better translated as "First Month." **1.** A game played during the New Year holidays. Contestants each selected a string, or cord, hoping to draw the one with the winning token attached. **2.** The execution grounds. **3.** Saikaku based this story on an actual event of the year before.

MATSUO BASHŌ
1644–1694

Until the seventeenth century, Japanese literature was privileged property. Court aristocrats and provincial warlords (and the occasional member of the Buddhist clergy) had exclusive access to "books": a narrow supply of manuscript copies. Even when the first printed books began to appear at the beginning of the seventeenth century, they were still luxury items. Connoisseurs underwrote lavishly illustrated printings of the Japanese classics available in limited editions, usually of no more than one hundred copies and intended not for sale but for presentation. Like the manuscripts they replaced, the first printed books were an indulgence. But when printing and publishing became commercial endeavors around the second decade of the new century, books changed from being rare works of art, whose mysteries were known only to the chosen few, into tools and pastimes for the multitude.

The diffusion of literacy, and thus education, was both a cause and an effect of the diffusion of the printed word. Print not only provided new channels of communication, a new medium for artists, and new commercial opportunities, it created for the first time in Japan the conditions necessary for that peculiarly modern phenomenon, celebrity.

The *haiku* poet Matsuo Bashō was an odd candidate for the new renown. Born in 1644 as the second son of a low-ranking provincial *samurai* who cobbled a living by teaching calligraphy, he had little in his background or early years that augured celebrity. Adult life commenced in the most ordinary way, when Bashō entered the service of a cadet branch of the local ruling military house. But he became close to his employer, the young heir, who was a devotee of linked verse, and Bashō too developed a taste for the popular poetry. Together they studied with Kitamura Kigin, one of the leading poets of the day, and they shared the excitement of seeing their compositions—two by Bashō and one by his patron—published in a poetry anthology in 1664. The easygoing days of poetastering and unchallenging service must have been very pleasant for Bashō and must have seemed the shape his days would take for the rest of his life.

But everything changed suddenly with the premature death in 1666 of his master. Bashō lost not only a friend and poetry companion but the protector who would have guaranteed him security and advancement in the ranks of the *samurai*. In 1672 Bashō left for Edo (now Tokyo), the expanding military capital of the shogun's new government, where he decided to make his career as a professional poet. To do so he had to build a following. With some thirty of his verses now in anthologies and his first book recently published, the twenty-eight-year-old Bashō must have conjectured that he had a better chance of establishing himself in a new city, where the competition for income as a teacher and corrector of poetry (an expert paid to correct other people's poetry) would be less intense than in the old capital of Kyoto or the seasoned commercial town of Osaka. This departure for the east was in its own quiet way daring. By leaving his home district and the employ of the local clan, he was forfeiting his status as a *samurai*, a member (however lowly) of the elite ruling class. In relocating to the boomtown of Edo, with a population already over six hundred thousand and growing, Bashō was in fact courting fame.

Not surprisingly, the first years in Edo were not easy. "Sometimes," he would later recall, "I grew weary of poetry and thought I would abandon it. Other times, I vowed to establish my name as the foremost poet. The two alternatives battled within, making me utterly restless." For a while, Bashō was forced to supplement his income with a post in the city's department of waterworks.

But ultimately he succeeded. Linked-verse anthologies sold well in the late seventeenth century, and Bashō's poems appeared in them with increasing frequency. Within eight years he had made a name for himself. He was asked to judge linked-verse competitions, and his published commentaries on these contests found a ready audience. Over time, he had gathered a stable of students large enough by 1680 for him to publish their best poems in an anthology. And Bashō's followers were so devoted that in the same year the more prosperous ones built a cottage for him in a quiet, still rural part of the city.

In front of this cottage, his students planted a banana tree. Its rare flowers were so small as to be unobtrusive, and the large, delicate leaves were easily torn when the wind blew in from the sea. The whole thing looked somehow lonesome. In a climate too cool for it to bear fruit, the tree was deprived of its purpose. Alone inside his hut, Bashō professed an affinity for his banana tree:

> Banana tree in autumn winds:
> a night passed hearing
> raindrops in a basin.

His persona was now complete: the lonely wayfarer who had traveled far from home, the man of simple tastes who had consecrated his life to poetry, the delicate sensibility as fragile as the leaves of a banana tree. It was only fitting that he took the word *banana*—Bashō—for his pen name.

One might well smile at Bashō's canniness. In the choice of his personal metaphor, he managed to join self-image and apparent, actual attributes with a public stance edited seamlessly into his literary product: like an actor so indistinguishable from his interchangeable roles that we think we know the "real" person. Bashō cast himself as a pilgrim, but the purpose of his frequent travels was a poetic devotion to nature—the beauty and truth it alone could reveal—not religious piety. Like a Zen monk, he shaved his head and donned the dark, drab garb of a cleric, setting off, as in *The Narrow Road of the Interior*, on paths by no means always certain, into wilderness not entirely safe. Whether home alone in his rustic cottage or enduring the ardors of the open road, Bashō sought an austere existence, as though he had taken a vow of poverty. *Economy* could have been his watchword.

In person and in art, he was the antithesis of Ihara Saikaku, that prosperous chronicler of rich, material life, and in fact Bashō appears to have disdained Saikaku's prolific literary output. To him, it was vulgar and excessive. (Not surprisingly, Bashō-the-perfectionist's entire oeuvre, about 1,000 *haiku*, is an afternoon's work for Saikaku, whose most frenzied single sitting of solo linked-verse composition yielded 23,500 poems in twenty-four hours!) Perhaps Saikaku in turn disdained Bashō's fastidiousness, endlessly revising a mere seventeen syllables. In the world of poetry, however, the tortoise won the race. Bashō's lapidary style perfected a kind of epigram that indeed seems to capture the universe in a grain of sand. His sympathy with nature, and particularly with its frailest elements, which speak of the transience and vulnerability of living things, was permanently accepted as the essence of Japanese poetic feeling.

The *haiku* was the perfect form for Bashō's art: a flash of lyric verse as fleeting as the momentary impression it encapsulates—a scene from nature or a natural object that evokes a truth larger than itself—expressed in cryptic, unrhymed lines of five, seven, and five syllables:

> Upon a bare branch
> a crow has descended—
> autumn in evening.

It is a form of poetry that looks effortless. Anyone can string together seventeen syllables and make them sound ponderous or picturesque, which is probably why *haiku* have become so popular (though syntactic differences between Japanese and English can sometimes defeat translation attempts that hold to the exact syllable count). Only a true poet can work within the slender margins of this constricted form and create something beyond aphorism. It was Bashō's gift to fuse the transitory and the eternal, both the moment observed and its greater significance. The crow landing on the branch of a withered tree is the "now" of the poem; time's passing and loneliness are the universals.

Actually, *haiku* began as part of linked verse, and in this respect too its apparent simplicity is deceptive. In the composition of linked poetry, resulting normally in sequences of thirty-six or one hundred verses (although they could stretch into one thousand verses or more), several poets worked in tandem. They took turns composing alternating links, or verses, in three lines with syllable counts of five, seven, and five (identical in form to *haiku*) and in two lines with syllable counts of seven each. Eventually, anthologies of linked poetry began to appear, excerpting the opening verses from various sequences. Thus these short poems in three lines of seventeen syllables, originally intended as the base to which subsequent lines of verse would be added, came to stand on their own. Poets began to write *haiku* as self-contained lyrics. But however independent they became, for a long time *haiku* retained a vestigial sense that they were somehow part of a larger matrix, or ought to be. This is one reason that poems in *The Narrow Road of the Interior* are embedded in a travel narrative, the prose equivalent of a linked sequence. By subtly following some of the structural principles of linked verse, Bashō's narrative achieves a kind of covert unity. And by including an occasional poem by his traveling companion, Sora, it retains something of the feel of linked verse. Once again poets were collaborating.

The Narrow Road of the Interior was written, or begun, in 1689, when Bashō embarked on his most ambitious journey. It would cover fifteen hundred miles of hinterland and take Bashō and Sora to the far corners of northern Japan. Although he is first thought of as a *haiku* poet, many of Bashō's best poems originally appeared in the five travel memoirs that he wrote in the final decade of his life. *The Narrow Road* is the last of these travel diaries, the longest, and the most esteemed. It also represents the climax of a venerable tradition in Japan, where the travel diary as poetic memoir enjoyed a distinguished eight-hundred-year history.

This fact too is an indication that Bashō's poetry involves more than meets the eye. The journey depicted in *The Narrow Road* is another pilgrimage through nature, but it is also a very conscious emulation of the conventions of the past. "Bewitched by the god of restlessness" Bashō describes himself as the trip gets under way. "Seduced by the call of history" would be just as accurate. Bashō, or his literary persona, sets off as the hero on a quest. His goal is to seek inspiration from remote places made famous by literature and history. Reputation, celebrity, tradition intertwine.

In 1943, some 250 years later, a second diary was published. This was Sora's account of their trip together, and it came like a thunderclap. The man who represented himself as a frail pilgrim at the mercy of nature and fate, and who was later deified by the Shinto religion, is described by Sora as a much more practical and wily figure, who altered the facts of his trip, abridged, and deleted to maintain the ascetic tone appropriate for a poetic saint, a man who saw himself as the successor to all poet-travelers of the past and was not about to reveal that among the motives for his trip were cultivating patrons and recruiting new students.

But *The Narrow Road of the Interior* is a literary creation. Its spare, supple prose anchors wise poetic insights. Its *haiku* transcend entertainment. The material has been shaped only by taking great pains, and that is the nature of artistry.

For another, more colloquial rendering of *The Narrow Road of the Interior*, translated by the poet Cid Corman in collaboration with Kamaike Susumu, see *Back Roads to Far Towns* (1986). All five of Bashō's travel journals are found in *The Narrow Road to the Deep North and Other Travel Sketches* (1966), translated by Nobuyuki Yuasa, whose re-creation of *haiku* as four-line poems seems less successful. For additional *haiku* by Bashō see Lucien Stryk, trans., *On Love and Barley* (1985). For examples of Bashō's linked poetry see Earl Miner and Hiroko Odagiri, trans., *The Monkey's Straw Raincoat* (1981). For more poems by Bashō and his followers see Steven D. Carter, *Traditional Japanese Poetry: An Anthology* (1991). Two excellent book-length introductions to Bashō, both by Makoto Ueda, are *Matsuo Bashō* (1982) and *Bashō and His Interpreters* (1991). Shorter introductions are found in two literary histories by Donald Keene: *World within Walls* (1976) and *Travelers of a Hundred Ages* (1989). For a general study of *haiku* see Kenneth Yasuda, *The Japanese Haiku* (1957), and for an anthology of *haiku* from Bashō to modern times see Harold G. Henderson, *An Introduction to Haiku* (1958).

PRONOUNCING GLOSSARY

The following list uses common English syllables to provide rough equivalents of selected words whose pronunciation may be unfamiliar to the general reader.

Atsumi: *ah-tsoo-mee*

Benkei: *ben-kay*

Butchō: *boot-choh*

Date: *dah-tay*

Echigo: *e-chee-goh*

Edo: *e-doh*

Fukuura: *foo-koo-oo-rah*

Genji: *gen-jee*

Genroku: *gen-roh-koo*

haikai: *hai-kai*

Heike: *hay-kay*

hototogisu: *hoh-toh-toh-gee-soo*

Ihara Saikaku: *ee-hah-rah sai-kah-koo*

Iizuka: *ee-ee-zoo-kah*

Ji: *jee*

Kanemori: *kah-ne-moh-ree*

Kawai: *kah-wai*

Kisakata: *kee-sah-kah-tah*

Kokinshū: *koh-keen-shoo*

konoshiro: *koh-noh-shee-roh*

koromogae: *koh-roh-moh-gah-e*

Kūkai: *koo-kai*

Kurokamiyama: *koo-roh-kah-mee-yah-mah*

Kyohaku: *kyoh-hah-koo*

Matsuo Bashō: *mah-tsoo-oh bah-shoh*

Minamidani: *mee-nah-mee-dah-nee*

Nikkō: *neek-koh*

Nōin: *noh-een*

Satō Shōji: *sah-toh shoh-jee*

Shinto: *sheen-toh*

Shiogoshi: *shee-oh-goh-shee*

Shirakawa: *shee-rah-kah-wah*

Sōgorō: *soh-goh-roh*

Tsuruga: *tsoo-roo-gah*

Yasuhira: *yah-soo-hee-rah*

Yoichi: *yoh-ee-chee*

Yudono: *yoo-doh-noh*

The Narrow Road of the Interior[1]

The sun and the moon are eternal voyagers; the years that come and go are travelers too. For those whose lives float away on boats, for those who greet old age with hands clasping the lead ropes of horses, travel is life, travel is home. And many are the men of old who have perished as they journeyed.

I myself fell prey to wanderlust some years ago, desiring nothing better than to be a vagrant cloud scudding before the wind. Only last autumn, after having drifted along the seashore for a time, had I swept away the old cobwebs from my dilapidated riverside hermitage. But the year ended before I knew it, and I found myself looking at hazy spring skies and thinking of crossing Shirakawa Barrier.[2] Bewitched by the god of restlessness, I lost my peace of mind; summoned by the spirits of the road, I felt unable to settle down to anything. By the time I had mended my torn trousers, put a new cord on my hat, and cauterized my legs with moxa,[3] I was thinking only of the moon at Matsushima. I turned over my dwelling to others, moved to a house belonging to Sanpū,[4] and affixed the initial page of a linked-verse sequence to one of the pillars at my cottage.

> Even my grass-thatched hut
> will have new occupants now:
> a display of dolls.[5]

It was the Twenty-seventh Day, almost the end of the Third Month. The wan morning moon retained little of its brilliance, but the silhouette of Mount Fuji was dimly visible in the first pale light of dawn. With a twinge of sadness, I wondered when I might see the flowering branches at Ueno and Yanaka again. My intimate friends, who had all assembled the night before, got on the boat to see me off.

We disembarked at Senju.[6] Transitory though I know this world to be, I shed tears when I came to the parting of the ways, overwhelmed by the prospect of the long journey ahead.

> Departing springtime:
> birds lament and fishes too
> have tears in their eyes.

With that as the initial entry in my journal, we started off, hard though it was to stride out in earnest. The others lined up part way along the road, apparently wanting to watch us out of sight.

That year was, I believe, the second of the Genroku[7] era [1689]. I had taken a sudden fancy to make the long pilgrimage on foot to Mutsu and Dewa[8]—to view places I had heard about but never seen, even at the cost of hardships severe enough to "whiten a man's hair under the skies of

---

1. Translated by Helen Craig McCullough and Steven D. Carter, with notes adapted from McCullough.
2. An old official checkpoint where travelers entered Mutsu Province.   3. A combustible substance used in traditional East Asian medicine. Moxa cones, made from pulverized plant leaves, were burned at specific therapeutic points on the skin, depending on the symptoms. The resulting heat was thought to adjust physical disorders by releasing energy obstructed at a crucial point and returning it to smooth circulation.   4. A disciple and patron.   5. It is the time of the Doll Festival, in the Third Month, when dolls representing the emperor, the empress, and their attendants are displayed in every household.
6. Near Edo (Tokyo). The path of Bashō's journey is traced on the map on p. 586.   7. The era name. For information on the Japanese calendar, see the introduction "The Rise of Popular Arts in Premodern Japan" (p. 589).   8. Two northern provinces.

Wu."[9] The outlook was not reassuring, but I resolved to hope for the best and be content merely to return alive.

We barely managed to reach Sōka Post Station that night. My greatest trial was the pack I bore on my thin, bony shoulders. I had planned to set out with no baggage at all, but had ended by taking along a paper coat for cold nights, a cotton bath garment, rain gear, and ink and brushes, as well as certain farewell presents, impossible to discard, which simply had to be accepted as burdens on the way.

We went to pay our respects at Muro-no-yashima. Sora, my fellow pilgrim, said, "This shrine honors Ko-no-hana-sakuya-hime, the goddess worshipped at Mount Fuji. The name Muro-no-yashima is an allusion to the birth of Hohodemi-no-mikoto inside the sealed chamber the goddess entered and set ablaze in fulfillment of her vow. It is because of that same incident that poems about the shrine usually mention smoke. The passage in the shrine history telling of the prohibition against *konoshiro* fish[1] is also well known."

On the Thirtieth, we lodged at the foot of the Nikkō Mountains. "I am called Buddha Gozaemon," the master of the house informed us. "People have given me that title because I make it a point to be honest in all my dealings. You may rest here tonight with your minds at ease."

"What kind of Buddha is it who has manifested himself in this impure world to help humble travelers like us—mendicant monks, as it were, on a pious pilgrimage?" I wondered. By paying close attention to his behavior, I satisfied myself that he was indeed a man of stubborn integrity, devoid of shrewdness and calculation. He was one of those, "firm, resolute, simple, and modest, who are near virtue,"[2] and I found his honorable, unassuming nature wholly admirable.

On the First of the Fourth Month, we went to worship at the shrine. In antiquity, the name of that holy mountain was written Nikōsan [Two-Storm Mountain], but the Great Teacher Kūkai changed it to Nikkō [Sunlight] when he founded the temple. It is almost as though the Great Teacher had been able to see 1,000 years into the future, for today the shrine's radiance extends throughout the realm, its beneficence overflows in the eight directions, and the four classes[3] of people dwell in security and peace. This is an awesome subject of which I shall write no more.

> Ah, awesome sight!
> on summer leaves and spring leaves,
> the radiance of the sun!

Kurokamiyama was veiled in haze, dotted with lingering patches of white snow. Sora composed this poem:

> Black hair shaved off,
> at Kurokamiyama[4]
> I change to new robes.

9. An allusion to a Chinese poem written by someone seeing off a monk on his travels: "Your hat will be heavy with the snows of Wu; / Your boots will be fragrant with the fallen blossoms of Chu." Snow on a traveler's hat was associated with hardships and with whitening hair.   1. Gizzard shad. It was taboo to eat the fish because, when broiled, it gave off a smell like flesh burning.   2. From Confucius's *Analects*. 3. Samurai, farmer, artisan, and merchant. The shrine held the mausoleum of the founder of the Tokugawa shogunate.   4. Or Mount Kurokami, homonymous with "black hair."

Sora is of the Kawai family; he was formerly called Sōgorō. He lived in a house adjoining mine, almost under the leaves of the banana plant, and used to help me with the chores of hauling wood and drawing water. Delighted by the thought of seeing Matsushima and Kisakata with me on this trip, and eager also to spare me some of the hardships of the road, he shaved his head at dawn on the day of our departure, put on a monk's black robe, and changed his name to Sōgo. That is why he composed the Kurokamiyama poem. The word *koromogae* ["I change to new robes"][5] was most effective.

There is a waterfall half a league or so up the mountain. The stream leaps with tremendous force over outthrust rocks at the top and descends 100 feet into a dark green pool strewn with 1,000 rocks. Visitors squeeze into the space between the rocks and the cascade to view it from the rear, which is why it is called Urami-no-take [Rearview Falls].

> In brief seclusion
> at a waterfall—the start
> of a summer retreat.

I knew someone at Kurobane in Nasu, so we decided to head straight across the plain from there. It began to rain as we walked along, taking our bearings on a distant village, and the sun soon sank below the horizon. After borrowing accommodations for the night at a farmhouse, we started out across the plain again in the morning. A horse was grazing nearby. We appealed for help to a man who was cutting grass and found him by no means incapable of understanding other people's feelings, rustic though he was.

"What's the best thing to do, I wonder?" he said. "I can't leave my work. Still, inexperienced travelers are bound to get lost on this plain, what with all the trails branching off in every direction. Rather than see you go on alone, I'll let you take the horse. Send him back when he won't go any farther." With that, he lent us the animal.

Two small children came running behind the horse. One of them, a little girl, was called Kasane. Sora composed this poem:

> Kasane must be
> a name for a wild pink
> with double petals![6]

Before long, we arrived at a hamlet and turned the horse back with some money tied to the saddle.

We called on Jōbōji, the warden at Kurobane. Surprised and delighted to see us, he kept us in conversation day and night; and his younger brother, Tōsui, came morning and evening. We went with Tōsui to his own house and were also invited to the homes of various other relatives. So the time passed.

One day, we strolled into the outskirts of the town for a brief visit to the site of the old dog shoots, then pressed through the Nasu bamboo fields

---

5. The first day of the Fourth Month was the date for changing from winter to summer clothing.
6. This poem uses wordplay. The name *Kasane* can mean "double." The word for "wild pink" (a flower) can also mean "beloved child."

to Lady Tamamo's tumulus,[7] and went on to pay our respects at Hachiman Shrine. Someone told me that when Yoichi shot down the fan target, it was to this very shrine that he prayed, "and especially Shōhachiman, the tutelary deity of my province."[8] The thought of the divine response evoked deep emotion. We returned to Tōsui's house as darkness fell.

There was a mountain-cult temple, Kōmyōji, in the vicinity. We visited it by invitation and worshipped at the Ascetic's Hall.[9]

> Toward summer mountains
> we set off after prayers
> before the master's clogs.

The site of the Venerable Butchō's[1] hermitage was behind Unganji Temple in that province. Butchō once told me that he had used pine charcoal to inscribe a poem on a rock there:

> Ah, how I detest
> building any shelter at all,
> even a grass-thatched
> hovel less than five feet square!
> Were it not for the rainstorms . . .

Staff in hand, I prepared to set out for the temple to see what was left of the hermitage. A number of people encouraged one another to accompany me, and I acquired a group of young companions who kept up a lively chatter along the way. We reached the lower limits of the temple grounds in no time. The mountains created an impression of great depth. The valley road stretched far into the distance, pines and cryptomerias rose in dark masses, the moss dripped with moisture, and there was a bite to the air, even though it was the Fourth Month. We viewed all of the Ten Sights[2] and entered the main gate by way of a bridge.

Eager to locate the hermitage, I scrambled up the hill behind the temple to a tiny thatched structure on a rock, a lean-to built against a cave. It was like seeing the holy Yuanmiao's Death Gate or the monk Fayun's[3] rock chamber. I left an impromptu verse on a pillar:

> Even woodpeckers
> seem to spare the hermitage
> in the summer grove.

From Kurobane, I headed toward Killer Rock astride a horse lent us by the warden. When the groom asked if I would write a poem for him, I

---

7. According to legend, Lady Tamamo was a fox-woman with whom an emperor fell in love. After having been unmasked by a diviner, she fled to Nasu, where local warriors shot her down. Her vindictive spirit survived as Killer Rock, a large boulder that releases poisonous fumes, which Bashō will soon visit on his journey. *Dog shoots:* for a brief time in the 13th century dog shooting had been a sport.   8. Refers to an episode in *The Tale of the Heike* (in Volume 1). Yoichi is a minor *samurai* in the service of the Minamoto/Genji. An expert archer, he succeeds in shooting a fan suspended off the prow of an enemy ship, put there to taunt the Genji. Hachiman Shrine was dedicated to the god of war.   9. Dedicated to a miracle-working mountain ascetic of the 8th century, whose enshrined image is believed to have shown a holy man wearing high clogs (referred to in the following poem) and clothes made from leaves, holding a staff, and leaning against a rock.   1. A Zen master with whom Bashō had studied.   2. Various rocks, peaks, buildings, etc., within the temple precincts.   3. A Chinese priest; he lived in a hut perched atop a high rock. Yuanmiao was a Chinese priest who confined himself for fifteen years to a cave he called Death's Gate.

gave him this, surprised and impressed that he should exhibit such cultivated taste:

> A cuckoo[4] song:
> please make the horse angle off
> across the field.

Killer Rock stands in the shadow of a mountain near a hot spring. It still
emits poisonous vapors: dead bees, butterflies, and other insects lie in
heaps near it, hiding the color of the sand.

The willow "where fresh spring water flowed"[5] survives on a ridge
between two ricefields in Ashino Village. The district officer there, a man
called Kohō, had often expressed a desire to show me the tree, and I had
wondered each time about its exact location—but on this day I rested in
its shade.

> Ah, the willow tree:
> a whole rice paddy planted
> before I set out.

So the days of impatient travel had accumulated, until at last I had
reached Shirakawa Barrier. It was there, for the first time, that I felt truly
on the way. I could understand why Kanemori had been moved to say,
"Would that there were a means somehow to send people word in the
capital!"[6]

As one of the Three Barriers, Shirakawa has always attracted the notice
of poets and other writers. An autumn wind seemed to sound in my ears,
colored leaves seemed to appear before my eyes—but even the leafy summer branches were delightful in their own way. Wild roses bloomed alongside the whiteness of the deutzia, making us feel as though we were
crossing snow. I believe one of Kiyosuke's writings preserves a story about
a man of the past who straightened his hat and adjusted his dress there.[7]
Sora composed this poem:

> With deutzia[8] flowers
> we adorn our hats—formal garb
> for the barrier.

We passed beyond the barrier and crossed the Abukuma River. To the
left, the peak of Aizu soared; to the right, the districts of Iwaki, Sōma,
and Mihara lay extended; to the rear, mountains formed boundaries with
Hitachi and Shimotsuke provinces. We passed Kagenuma Pond, but the
sky happened to be overcast that day, so there were no reflections.[9]

---

4. In Japanese *hototogisu*; the name is an onomatopoeia derived from the bird's call: *ho-to-to*. Its song was
deemed the quintessence of summer and is so beautiful that Bashō would like his horse to follow after it.
5. Refers to a verse by the famed poet-priest Saigyō (1118–1190): "On the wayside / where a clear spring
flowed / in a willow's shade: / 'Just for a moment,' I thought, / but then I lingered there." Saigyō was an
inveterate traveler and an important influence on Bashō.   6. Alludes to a poem by Kanemori (died
990): "Would there were means / to let them know, somehow, / the people of the capital: / 'Today I have
crossed / Shirakawa Barrier.'"   7. Fujiwara Kiyosuke (1104–1177) was a court noble and a poet-scholar.
The man's actions show respect to Nōin (998–1050?), a monk and early poet-traveler who established
Shirakawa Barrier as a place with poetic associations. In earlier times, travelers approaching checkpoints
between provinces adjusted their clothes before crossing the barrier.   8. A shrub of the saxifrage family,
an ornamental bush with white or pink flowers. It blooms in the Fourth Month.   9. The name of the
pond is literally "Shadow Swamp"; with the sun obscured, it does not fulfill its reputation.

At the post town of Sukagawa, we visited a man called Tōkyū, who persuaded us to stay four or five days. His first act was to inquire, "How did you feel when you crossed Shirakawa Barrier?"

"What with the fatigue of the long, hard trip, the distractions of the scenery, and the stress of so many nostalgic associations, I couldn't manage to think of a decent poem," I said. "Still, it seemed a pity to cross with nothing to show for it . . .":

> A start for connoisseurs
> of poetry—rice-planting song
> of Michinoku.

We added a second verse and then a third, and continued until we had completed three sequences.

Under a great chestnut tree in the corner of the town, there lived a hermit monk. It seemed to me that his cottage, with its aura of lonely tranquility, must resemble that other place deep in the mountains where someone had gathered horse chestnuts.[1] I set down a few words:

To form the character "chestnut," we write "tree of the west."[2] I have heard, I believe, that the bodhisattva Gyōgi perceived an affinity between this tree and the Western Paradise,[3] and that he used its wood for staffs and pillars throughout his life:

> Chestnut at the eaves—
> here are blossoms unremarked
> by ordinary folk.

Asakayama is just beyond Hiwada Post Station, about five leagues from Tōkyū's house. It is close to the road, and there are numerous marshes in the vicinity. It was almost the season for reaping *katsumi*.[4] We kept asking, "Which plant is the flowering *katsumi*?" But nobody knew. We wandered about, scrutinizing marshes, questioning people, and seeking *"katsumi, katsumi"* until the sun sank to the rim of the hills.

We turned off to the right at Nihonmatsu, took a brief look at Kurozuka Cave,[5] and stopped for the night at Fukushima.

On the following day, we went to Shinobu in search of the Fern-print Rock,[6] which proved to be half buried under the soil of a remote hamlet in the shadow of a mountain. Some village urchins came up and told us, "In the old days, the rock used to be on top of that mountain, but the farmers got upset because the people who passed would destroy the young grain so they could test it. They shoved it off into this valley; that's why it's lying upside down." A likely story, perhaps.

---

1. Refers to Saigyō (see n. 5, p. 616) and one of his poems: "In these remote hills, / I try to trap water / dripping onto the rocks; / I gather horse chestnuts / dropping to the ground." 2. The character for "chestnut" consists of the character for "tree" surmounted by an element resembling the character for "west." 3. One of the various "Buddha worlds" (Buddhist equivalents of Heaven); this one is located in the western sector of the universe and is presided over by Amida, the most popular Buddhist deity of the time. *Bodhisattva:* a person who attains enlightenment but compassionately refrains from entering paradise to save others, a future Buddha. Gyōgi (668–749) was a Buddhist monk known for his asceticism and charisma. 4. Wild rice. 5. Rich in folklore. A witch was said to be interred beneath Kurozuka, a hillock whose name means "black mound," and the nearby rocky cave was thought a goblins' lair. 6. Said to have been used to imprint cloth with a moss-fern design, a specialty of the area.

Hands planting seedlings
evoke Shinobu patterns
of the distant past.

We crossed the river at Tsukinowa Ford and emerged at Senoue Post Station. Satō Shōji's[7] old home was about a league and a half away, near the mountains to the left. Told that we would find the site at Sabano in Iizuka Village, we went along, asking directions, until we came upon it at a place called Maruyama. That was where Shōji had had his house. I wept as someone explained that the front gate had been at the foot of the hill. Still standing at an old temple nearby were a number of stone monuments erected in memory of the family. It was especially moving to see the memorials to the two young wives.[8] "Women though they were, all the world knows of their bravery." The thought made me drench my sleeve. The Tablet of Tears[9] was not far to seek!

We entered the temple to ask for tea, and there we saw Yoshitsune's sword and Benkei's pannier,[1] preserved as treasures.

Paper carp flying!
Display pannier and sword, too,
in the Fifth Month.

It was the First Day of the Fifth Month.

We lodged that night at Iizuka, taking advantage of the hot springs in the town to bathe before engaging a room. The hostelry turned out to be a wretched hovel, its straw mats spread over dirt floors. In the absence of a lamp, we prepared our beds and stretched out by the light from a fire-pit. Thunder rumbled during the night, and rain fell in torrents. What with the roof leaking right over my head and the fleas and mosquitoes biting, I got no sleep at all. To make matters worse, my old complaint[2] flared up, causing me such agony that I almost fainted.

At long last, the short night ended and we set out again. Still feeling the effects of the night, I rode a rented horse to Kōri Post Station. It was unsettling to fall prey to an infirmity while so great a distance remained ahead. But I told myself that I had deliberately planned this long pilgrimage to remote areas, a decision that meant renouncing worldly concerns and facing the fact of life's uncertainty. If I were to die on the road—very well, that would be Heaven's decree. Such reflections helped to restore my spirits a bit, and it was with a jaunty step that I passed through the Great Gate into the Date[3] domain.

We entered Kasajima District by way of Abumizuri and Shiraishi Castle. I asked someone about the Fujiwara Middle Captain Sanekata's[4] grave and was told, "Those two villages far off to the right at the edge of the hills are Minowa and Kasajima. The Road Goddess's shrine and the 'memento

---

7. A brave warrior and supporter of the Genji chieftain Yoshitsune (in *The Tale of the Heike*).   8. Of Satō Shōji's two sons, who died in battle. The young widows were said to have worn their husbands' suits of armor as a way of consoling their grieving mother-in-law, who still hoped to see her sons riding home victorious.   9. A memorial erected in China in honor of a virtuous official. All who saw it were said to weep.   1. A large basket. Yoshitsune is the great hero who leads his clan to victory in the war recounted in *The Tale of the Heike*. Benkei is his faithful lieutenant.   2. Bashō was troubled with stomachaches and hemorrhoids.   3. A clan that included some of the richest and most powerful provincial barons.   4. Fujiwara Sanekata (died 998) was a court poet whose quarrel with a clansman led to his exile in the northern provinces.

miscanthus' are still there."[5] The road was in a dreadful state from the recent early-summer rains, and I was exhausted, so we contented ourselves with looking in that direction as we trudged on. Because the names Minowa and Kasajima suggested the rainy season,[6] I composed this verse.

> Where is Rain Hat Isle?
> Somewhere down the muddy roads
> of the Fifth Month!

We lodged at Iwanuma. It was exciting to see the Takekuma Pine. The trunk forks a bit above the ground, and one knows instantly that this is just how the old tree must have looked. My first thought was of Nōin.[7] Did he compose the poem, "Not a trace this time of the pine" because a certain man, appointed long ago to serve as Governor of Mutsu, had felled the tree to get pilings for a bridge to span the Natori River? Someone told me that generations of people have been alternately cutting down the existing tree and planting a replacement. The present one is a magnificent specimen—quite capable, I should imagine, of living 1,000 years.

Kyohaku[8] had given me a poem as a farewell present:

> Late cherry blossoms:
> please show my friend the pine tree
> at Takekuma.

Thus:

> After three months:
> the twin-trunked pine awaited
> since the cherry trees bloomed.

We crossed the Natori River into Sendai on the day when people thatch their roofs with sweet-flag leaves.[9] We sought out a lodging and stayed four or five days.

I made the acquaintance of a local painter, Kaemon by name, who had been described to me as a man of cultivated taste. He told us he had devoted several years to locating famous old places that had become hard to identify, and took us to see some of them one day. The bush clover grew thick at Miyagino; I could imagine the sight in autumn. It was the season when the pieris[1] bloomed at Tamada, Yokono, and Tsutsuji-gaoka. We entered a pine grove where no sunlight penetrated—a place called Konoshita, according to Kaemon—and I thought it must have been the same kind of heavy moisture, dripping from those very trees long ago, that inspired the poem, "Suggest to your lord, attendants, that he wear his hat."[2] We paid our respects at the Yakushidō Hall and at Tenjin Shrine before the day ended.

---

5. Someone had planted a clump of miscanthus, a variety of ornamental grass, at Sanekata's grave in allusion to a memorial poem by Saigyō: "Only his name, / eternally unwithered, / has escaped decay: / we see, as a memento, / miscanthus on a dry plain."   6. *Mino* can mean "straw raincoat," and *kasa* can mean "rain hat."   7. See n. 7, p. 616.   8. A disciple.   9. On Boys' Day, a holiday on the fifth day of the Fifth Month, it was the custom for families with sons to fly carp streamers, a symbol of vigor and success. On the day before, irises *(sweet-flag)*, because they were thought to ward off evil, were hung from the eaves. The holiday was also known as the Iris Festival.   1. Japanese andromeda *(Pieris japonica)*, a broad-leafed evergreen with drooping clusters of white flowers.   2. A poem in the *Kokinshū* (Collection of ancient and modern times; in Volume 1), the first of twenty-one imperially commissioned anthologies of classical Japanese poetry; it was completed around 905 and contains 1,111 poems. The poem referred

Kaemon sent us off with a map on which he had drawn famous scenes of Shiogama and Matsushima. He also gave us two pairs of straw sandals, bound with dark blue cords, as a farewell present. The gifts showed him to be quite as cultivated as I had surmised.

> Let us bind sweet-flags
> to our feet, making of them
> cords for straw sandals.

Continuing on our way with the help of the map, we came to the *tofu* [ten-strand] sedge, growing at the base of the mountains where the "narrow road of the interior"[3] runs. I am told that the local people still make ten-strand mats every year for presentation to the provincial Governor.

We saw the Courtyard Monument Stone at Tagajō in Ichikawa Village. It was a little more than six feet tall and perhaps three feet wide. Some characters, faintly visible as depressions in the moss, listed distances to the provincial boundaries in the four directions. There was also an inscription: "This castle was erected in the first year of Jinki [724] by the Inspector-Garrison Commander Ōno no Ason Azumabito. It was rebuilt in the sixth year of Tenpyō Hōji [762] by the Consultant-Garrison Commander Emi no Ason Asakari. First Day, Twelfth Month." That was in the reign of Emperor Shōmu.

Although we hear about many places celebrated in verse since antiquity, most of them have vanished with the passing of time. Mountains have crumbled, rivers have entered unaccustomed channels, roads have followed new routes, stones have been buried and hidden underground, aged trees have given way to saplings. But this monument was a genuine souvenir from 1,000 years ago, and to see it before my eyes was to feel that I could understand the sentiments of the old poets. "This is a traveler's reward," I thought. "This is the joy of having survived into old age." Moved to tears, I forgot the hardships of the road.

From there, we went to see Noda-no-tamagawa and Oki-no-ishi. A temple, Masshōzan, had been built at Sue-no-matsuyama, and there were graves everywhere among the pine trees, saddening reminders that such must be the end of all vows to "interchange wings and link branches."[4] The evening bell was tolling as we entered Shiogama.

The perpetual overcast of the rainy season had lifted enough to reveal Magaki Island close at hand, faintly illuminated by the evening moon. A line of small fishing boats came rowing in. As I listened to the voices of the men dividing the catch, I felt that I understood the poet who sang, "There is deep pathos in a boat pulled by a rope," and my own emotion deepened.[5] That night, a blind singer recited a Michinoku ballad[6] to the accompaniment of his lute. He performed not far from where I was trying

---

to here is: "Suggest to your lord, / attendants, / that he wear his hat, / for beneath the trees of Miyagino / the dew comes down harder than the rain."   **3.** This road, the source of Bashō's title, extended from what is now northeastern Sendai to Tagajō City (see the map on p. 586).   **4.** An allusion to the pledge exchanged by the Chinese emperor and his beloved in the *Song of Everlasting Sorrow* by Po Chü-i: "In heaven, may we be birds with shared wings; / On earth, may we be trees with linked branches." The places mentioned here are in the vicinity of Sendai.   **5.** Reference to a poem in the *Kokinshū*: "However it may be elsewhere / in Michinoku, / there is deep pathos / in a boat pulled by a rope / along Shiogama shore."   **6.** A local ballad; Bashō is now in the province of Michinoku.

to sleep, and I found his loud, countrified falsetto rather noisy—a chanting style quite different from either *Heike* recitation or the *kōwaka-mai*[7] ballad drama. But then I realized how admirable it was that the fine old customs were still preserved in that distant land.

Early the next day, we visited Shiogama Shrine, which had been restored by the provincial Governor. Its pillars stood firm and majestic, its painted rafters sparkled, its stone steps rose in flight after flight, and its sacred red fences gleamed in the morning sunlight. With profound reverence, I reflected that it is the way of our land for the miraculous powers of the gods to manifest themselves even in such remote, out-of-the-way places as this.

In front of the sanctuary, there was a splendid old lantern with an inscription on its iron door: "Presented as an offering by Izumi no Saburō in the third year of Bunji [1187]." It was rare, indeed, to see before one's eyes an object that had remained unchanged for 500 years. Izumi no Saburō was a brave, honorable, loyal, and filial warrior. His fame endures even today; there is no one who does not admire him. How true it is that men must strive to walk in the Way and uphold the right! "Fame will follow of itself."

Noon was already approaching when we engaged a boat for the crossing to Matsushima, a distance of a little more than two leagues. We landed at Ojima Beach.

Trite though it may seem to say so, Matsushima is the most beautiful spot in Japan, by no means inferior to Dongting Lake or West Lake.[8] The sea enters from the southeast into a bay extending for three leagues, its waters as ample as the flow of the Zhejiang Bore.[9] There are more islands than anyone could count. The tall ones rear up as though straining toward the sky; the flat ones crawl on their bellies over the waves. Some seem made of two layers, others of three folds. To the left, they appear separate; to the right, linked. Here and there, one carries another on its back or cradles it in its arms, as though caring for a beloved child or grandchild. The pines are deep green in color, and their branches, twisted by the salt gales, have assumed natural shapes so dramatic that they seem the work of human hands. The tranquil charm of the scene suggests a beautiful woman who has just completed her toilette. Truly, Matsushima might have been made by Ōyamazumi[1] in the ancient age of the mighty gods! What painter can reproduce, what author can describe the wonder of the creator's divine handiwork?

Ojima Island projects into the sea just offshore from the mainland. It is the site of the Venerable Ungo's[2] dwelling, and of the rock on which that holy man used to practice meditation. There also seemed to be a few recluses living among the pine trees. Upon seeing smoke rising from a fire of twigs and pine cones at one peaceful thatched hut, we could not help approaching the spot, even though we had no way of knowing what kind

---

7. Dramatic ballad-dances recounting military episodes from *The Tale of the Heike* (originally performed as an oral narrative) and other warrior stories. *Kōwaka-mai* were one of the precursors of *nō* plays.   8. Chinese sites (which Bashō had never seen) famed for their beauty.   9. In China.   1. A mountain god who was son of the gods who created the Japanese islands.   2. A monk who rebuilt a temple at Matsushima. He was the teacher of Butchō, Bashō's Zen master.

of man the occupant might be. Meanwhile, the moon began to shine on the water, transforming the scene from its daytime appearance.

We returned to the Matsushima shore to engage lodgings—a second-story room with a window on the sea. What marvelous exhilaration to spend the night so close to the winds and clouds! Sora recited this:

> Ah, Matsushima!
> Cuckoo, you ought to borrow
> the guise of the crane.[3]

I remained silent, trying without success to compose myself for sleep. At the time of my departure from the old hermitage, Sodō and Hara Anteki[4] had given me poems about Matsushima and Matsu-ga-urashima (the one in Chinese and the other in Japanese), and I got them out of my bag now to serve as companions for the evening. I also had some *hokku*, compositions by Sanpū and Jokushi.[5]

On the Eleventh, we visited Zuiganji.[6] Thirty-two generations ago, Makabe no Heishirō entered holy orders, went to China, and returned to found that temple. Later, through the virtuous influence of the Venerable Ungo, the seven old structures were transformed into a great religious center, a veritable earthly paradise, with dazzling golden walls and resplendent furnishings. I thought with respectful admiration of the holy Kenbutsu[7] and wondered where his place of worship might have been.

On the Twelfth, we left for Hiraizumi, choosing a little-frequented track used by hunters, grass-cutters, and woodchoppers, which was supposed to take us past the Aneha Pine and Odae Bridge. Blundering along, we lost our way and finally emerged at the port town of Ishino-maki. Kinkazan, the mountain of which the poet wrote, "Golden flowers have blossomed," was visible across the water.[8] Hundreds of coastal vessels rode together in the harbor, and smoke ascended everywhere from the cooking fires of houses jostling for space. Astonished to have stumbled on such a place, we looked for lodgings, but nobody seemed to have a room for rent, and we spent the night in a wretched shack.

The next morning, we set out again on an uncertain journey over strange roads, plodding along an interminable dike from which we could see Sode-no-watari, Obuchi-no-maki, and Mano-no-kayahara[9] in the distance. We walked beside a long, dismal marsh to a place called Toima, where we stopped overnight, and finally arrived in Hiraizumi. I think the distance was something over twenty leagues.

The glory of three generations[1] was but a dozing dream. Paddies and

---

3. The gist of the poem is: "Your song is appealing, cuckoo, but the stately white crane is the bird we expect to see at Matsushima [Pine Isles]." Pines and cranes were a conventional pair, both symbols of longevity. Sora's poem alludes to an old poem of uncertain provenance and unstable wording, one version of which reads in part: "[When snow falls] does the plover borrow / the crane's [white] plumage?"   4. Two friends of Bashō, both amateur poets. Hara was also a physician.   5. Bashō's disciples. *Hokku*: the first three lines of a linked-verse sequence, from which *haiku* evolved.   6. The temple restored by Ungo (see n. 2, p. 621).   7. A monk who lived approximately six hundred years earlier and who confined himself to a small temple at Matsushima.   8. Refers to a poem in the *Man'yōshū* (The collection of ten thousand leaves; in Volume 1), which was completed around 759 and is the earliest compilation of Japanese poetry, containing more than forty-five hundred poems. The poem referred to here was written when gold was discovered in the area: "For our sovereign's reign, / an auspicious augury: / among the mountains of Michinoku / in the east, / golden flowers have blossomed."   9. All are located between Ishi-no-maki and Toima and had associations with earlier poetry.   1. That is, of the powerful Fujiwara family—Kiyohira, Motohira, and Hidehira—who created the so-called golden age of the north in the 12th century.

wild fields have claimed the land where Hidehira's mansion stood, a league beyond the site of the great gate, and only Mount Kinkeizan looks as it did in the past. My first act was to ascend to Takadachi. From there, I could see both the mighty Kitakami River, which flows down from Nanbu, and the Koromo River, which skirts Izumi Castle and empties into the larger stream below Takadachi. Yasuhira's[2] castle, on the near side of Koromo Barrier, seems to have guarded the Nanbu entrance against barbarian encroachments. There at Takadachi, Yoshitsune[3] shut himself up with a chosen band of loyal men—yet their heroic deeds lasted only a moment, and nothing remains but evanescent clumps of grass.

> The nation is destroyed; the mountains and rivers remain.
> Spring comes to the castle; the grasses are green.[4]

Sitting on my sedge hat with those lines running through my head, I wept for a long time.

> A dream of warriors,
> and after dreaming is done,
> the summer grasses.

> Ah, the white hair:
> vision of Kanefusa[5]
> in deutzia flowers.
> —Sora

The two halls of which we had heard so many impressive tales were open to visitors. The images of the three chieftains are preserved in the Sutra Hall, and in the Golden Hall there are the three coffins and the three sacred images.[6] In the past, the Golden Hall's seven precious substances were scattered and lost; gales ravaged the magnificent jewel-studded doors, and the golden pillars rotted in the frosts and snows. But just as it seemed that the whole building must collapse, leaving nothing but clumps of grass, new walls were put around it, and a roof was erected against the winds and rains. So it survives for a time, a memento of events that took place 1,000 years ago.

> Do the Fifth-Month rains
> stay away when they fall,
> sparing that Hall of Gold?

After journeying on with the Nanbu Road visible in the distance, we spent the night at Iwade-no-sato. From there, we passed Ogurazaki and Mizu-no-ojima and arrived at Shitomae Barrier by way of Narugo Hot Springs, intending to cross into Dewa Province. The road was so little frequented by travelers that we excited the guards' suspicions, and we barely managed to get through the checkpoint. The sun had already begun to set as we toiled upward through the mountains, so we asked for

2. Son of Fujiwara Hidehira, whose fight with his brother destroyed the clan's prosperity in the region. After killing his brother, Yasuhira was in turn killed by the Minamoto/Genji chieftain Yoritomo. 3. See n. 1, p. 618. 4. A quote from the Chinese poet Tu Fu, lamenting the devastation caused by a rebellion in 755, from which the T'ang dynasty never fully recovered. 5. A loyal retainer of Yoshitsune. 6. Of Amida Buddha and his attendants Kannon and Seishi. The coffins contained the mummified remains of Hidehira, his father, and his grandfather.

shelter when we saw a border guard's house. Then the wind howled and the rain poured for three days, trapping us in those miserable hills.

> The fleas and the lice—
> and next to my pillow,
> a pissing horse.

The master of the house told us that our route into Dewa was an ill-marked trail through high mountains; we would be wise to engage a guide to help us with the crossing. I took his advice and hired a fine, stalwart young fellow, who strode ahead with a short, curved sword tucked into his belt and an oak staff in his hand. As we followed him, I felt an uncomfortable presentiment that this would be the day on which we would come face to face with danger at last. Just as our host had said, the mountains were high and thickly wooded, their silence unbroken even by the chirp of a bird. It was like traveling at night to walk in the dim light under the dense canopy. Feeling as though dust must be blowing down from the edge of the clouds,[7] we pushed through bamboo, forded streams, and stumbled over rocks, all the time in a cold sweat, until we finally emerged at Mogami-no-shō. Our guide took his leave in high spirits, after having informed us that the path we had followed was one on which unpleasant things were always happening, and that it had been a great stroke of luck to bring us through safely. Even though the danger was past, his words made my heart pound.

At Obanazawa, we called on Seifū, a man whose tastes were not vulgar despite his wealth. As a frequent visitor to the capital, he understood what it meant to be a traveler, and he kept us for several days, trying in many kind ways to make us forget the hardships of the long journey.

> I sit at ease,
> taking this coolness
> as my lodging place.

> Come on, show yourself!
> Under the silkworm nursery
> the croak of a toad.

> In my mind's eye,
> a brush for someone's brows:
> the safflower blossom.

> The silkworm nurses—
> figures reminiscent
> of a distant past.[8]
>
> —Sora

In the Yamagata domain, there is a mountain temple called Ryū-sha-kuji, a serene, quiet seat of religion founded by the Great Teacher Jikaku.[9] Urged by others to see it, we retraced our steps some seven leagues from

---

7. To emphasize the murkiness of the atmosphere, Bashō borrows from a poem in which Tu Fu compliments a princess by implying that she lives in the sky: "When I begin to ascend the breezy stone steps, / a dust storm blows down from the edge of the clouds."   8. The silkworm tenders (nurses) dress in an old style. Here, as Bashō does elsewhere, Sora expresses nostalgia for a way of life that had disappeared from the cities to the west.   9. Better known as Ennin (794–864), a famous priest who helped establish Buddhism in Japan. *Yamagata domain:* from the early 17th century until 1868, Japan was divided into domains, or fiefdoms, held directly by the shogun and his family or by the feudal barons who, to one degree or another, supported him. Yamagata was in the province of Dewa.

Obanazawa. We arrived before sundown, reserved accommodations in the pilgrims' hostel at the foot of the hill, and climbed to the halls above. The mountain consists of piles of massive rocks. Its pines and other evergreens bear the marks of many long years; its moss lies like velvet on the ancient rocks and soil. Not a sound emanated from the temple buildings at the summit, which all proved to be closed, but we skirted the cliffs and clambered over the rocks to view the halls. The quiet, lonely beauty of the environs purified the heart.

> Ah, tranquility!
> Penetrating the very rock,
> a cicada's voice.

At Ōishida, we awaited fair weather with a view to descending the Mogami River by boat. In that spot where the seeds of the old *haikai*[1] had fallen, some people still cherished the memory of the flowers. With hearts softened by poetry's civilizing touch, those onetime blowers of shrill reed flutes[2] had been groping for the correct way of practicing the art, so they told me, but had found it difficult to choose between the old styles and the new with no one to guide them. I felt myself under an obligation to leave them a sequence. Such was one result of this journey in pursuit of my art.

The Mogami River has its source deep in the northern mountains and its upper reaches in Yamagata. After presenting formidable hazards like Goten and Hayabusa,[3] it skirts Mount Itajiki on the north and finally empties into the sea at Sakata. Our boat descended amid luxuriant foliage, the mountains pressing overhead from the left and the right. It was probably similar craft, loaded with sheaves, that the old song meant when it spoke of rice boats.[4] Travelers can see the cascading waters of Shiraito Falls through gaps in the green leaves. The Sennindō Hall is there too, facing the bank.

The swollen waters made the journey hazardous:

> Bringing together
> the summer rains in swiftness:
> Mogami River!

On the Third of the Sixth Month, we climbed Mount Haguro. We called on Zushi Sakichi[5] and then were received by the Holy Teacher Egaku, the Abbot's deputy, who lodged us at the Minamidani Annex and treated us with great consideration.

On the Fourth, there was a *haikai* gathering at the Abbot's residence:

> Ah, what a delight!
> Cooled as by snow, the south wind
> at Minamidani.

On the Fifth, we went to worship at Haguro Shrine. Nobody knows when the founder, the Great Teacher Nōjo, lived. The *Engi Canon*[6] men-

---

1. Nonstandard, or eccentric, linked verse. Masters from two older *haikai* schools had spent time in the area.   2. That is, untutored country people.   3. Two treacherous spots in the river, one with rocks and the other with swift currents.   4. Refers to a folk song whose chief interest lies in its puns on the word *rice*.   5. A dyer by trade and an amateur poet.   6. An early collection of governmental regulations (compiled 905–927), designed to flesh out the broad administrative structure that was then being adapted from China.

tions a shrine called "Satoyama in Dewa Province," which leads one to
wonder if *sato* might be a copyist's error for *kuro*. Perhaps "Haguroyama"
is a contraction of "Dewa no Kuroyama" [Kuroyama in Dewa Province].
I understand that the official gazetteer says Dewa acquired its name
because the province used to present birds' feathers to the throne as
tribute.[7]

Hagurosan, Gassan, and Yudono are known collectively as the Three
Mountains. At Haguro, a subsidiary of Tōeizan Kan'eiji Temple in Edo,
the moon of Tendai[8] enlightenment shines bright, and the lamp of the
Law of perfect understanding and all-permeating vision burns high. The
temple buildings stand roof to roof; the ascetics vie in the practice of rituals. We can but feel awe and trepidation before the miraculous powers of
so holy a place, which may with justice be called a magnificent mountain,
destined to flourish forever.

On the Eighth, we made the ascent of Gassan. Donning paper garlands,
and with our heads wrapped in white turbans, we toiled upward for eight
leagues, led by a porter guide through misty mountains with ice and snow
underfoot. We could almost have believed ourselves to be entering the
cloud barrier beyond which the sun and the moon traverse the heavens.
The sun was setting and the moon had risen when we finally reached the
summit, gasping for breath and numb with cold. We stretched out on beds
of bamboo grass until dawn, and descended toward Yudono after the rising
sun had dispersed the clouds.

Near a valley, we saw a swordsmith's cottage. The Dewa smiths,
attracted by the miraculous waters, had purified themselves there before
forging their famous blades, which they had identified by the carved signature, "Gassan."[9] I was reminded of the weapons tempered at Dragon
Spring.[1] It also seemed to me that I could understand the dedication with
which those men had striven to master their art, inspired by the ancient
example of Gan Jiang and Moye.[2]

While seated on a rock for a brief rest, I noticed some half-opened buds
on a cherry tree about three feet high. How admirable that those late
blooms had remembered spring, despite the snowdrifts under which they
had lain buried! They were like "plum blossoms in summer heat"[3] per-
fuming the air. The memory of Archbishop Gyōson's touching poem[4]
added to the little tree's charm.

It is a rule among ascetics not to give outsiders details about Mount
Yudono, so I shall lay aside my brush and write no more.

When we returned to our lodgings, Egaku asked us to inscribe poem
cards with verses suggested by our pilgrimage to the Three Mountains:

---

7. The characters representing *sato* and *kuro* are similar in appearance, especially when written in cursive
script. The *ha* of "Haguroyama" and the *wa* of "Dewa" can be written with the same phonetic symbol
and were once the same sound. The connection between Dewa and birds' feathers is in the orthography:
wa is written with the character for "feathers."   8. A Buddhist sect.   9. A famous swordsmith in the
late 12th century.   1. A spring in China whose waters were used for tempering sword blades.   2. Gan
Jiang was a Chinese swordsmith. He and his wife, Moye, forged two famous swords.   3. A Zen metaphor for the rare and unusual and, by extension, for passing beyond this world to enlightenment.   4. A
reference to a poem that Gyōson (1055–1135), an ascetic, composed when he discovered cherries blooming out of season: "Let us sympathize / with one another, / cherry tree on the mountain: / were it not for
your blossoms, / I would have no friend at all."

Ah, what coolness!
Under a crescent moon,
Mount Haguro glimpsed.

Mountain of the Moon:
after how many cloud peaks
had formed and crumbled?

My sleeve was drenched
at Yudono, the mountain
of which none may speak.

Yudonoyama:
tears fall as I walk the path
where feet tread on coins.[5]
                                                —Sora

After our departure from Haguro, we were invited to the warrior Naga-yama Shigeyuki's home, where we composed a sequence. (Sakichi accompanied us that far.) Then we boarded a river boat and traveled downstream to Sakata Harbor. We stayed with a physician, En'an Fugyoku.

Evening cool!
A view from Mount Atsumi
to Fukuura.

Mogami River—
it has plunged the hot sun
into the sea.

I had already enjoyed innumerable splendid views of rivers and mountains, ocean and land; now I set my heart on seeing Kisakata. It was a journey of ten leagues northeast from Sakata, across mountains and along sandy beaches. A wind from the sea stirred the white sand early in the afternoon, and Mount Chōkai disappeared behind misting rain. "Groping in the dark," we found "the view in the rain exceptional too."[6] The surroundings promised to be beautiful once the skies had cleared. We crawled into a fisherman's thatched shanty to await the end of the rain.

The next day was fine, and we launched forth onto the bay in a boat as the bright morning sun rose. First of all, we went to Nōinjima to visit the spot where Saigyō had lived in seclusion for three years. Then we disembarked on the opposite shore and saw a memento of the poet, the old cherry tree that had suggested the verse, "rowing over flowers."[7] Near the water's edge, we noticed a tomb that was said to be the grave of Empress Jingū,[8] together with a temple, Kanmanjuji. I had never heard that the Empress had gone to that place. I wonder how her grave happened to be there.

---

5. The coins have been strewn by pilgrims, but unlike the secular world, no one scrambles to pick them up. Sora sheds tears at this miraculous behavior, which he can only attribute to the power of the gods. 6. Bashō compares Kisakata to the famous West Lake in China, of which Su Tongbo (1037–1101) wrote: "The sparkling, brimming waters are beautiful in sunshine; / The view when a misty rain veils the mountains is exceptional too." "*Groping in the dark*": probably an allusion to a poem composed at the lake by a visiting Japanese monk, Sakugen (1501–1579): "The sun is setting beyond Yuhangmen; / All sights are indistinct, there is no view. / But I recall the poem, 'Exceptional in rain, beautiful in sunshine'; / Groping in the dark, I feel West Lake's charm."   7. From a poem attributed to Saigyō: "The cherry blossoms / at Kisakata / lie buried under waves: / seafolk in their fishing boat / go rowing over flowers."   8. Legendary empress said to have ruled in the second half of the 4th century.

Seated in the temple's front apartment with the blinds raised, we commanded a panoramic view. To the south, Mount Chōkai propped up the sky, its image reflected in the bay; to the west, Muyamuya Barrier blocked the road; to the east, the Akita Road stretched far into the distance on an embankment; to the north, there loomed the majestic bulk of the sea, its waves entering the bay at a place called Shiogoshi.

The bay measures about a league in length and breadth. It resembles Matsushima in appearance but has a quality of its own: where Matsushima seems to smile, Kisakata droops in dejection. The lonely, melancholy scene suggests a troubled human spirit.

> Xi Shi's[9] drooping eyelids:
> mimosa in falling rain
> at Kisakata.

> At Shiogoshi
> crane legs drenched by high tide—
> and how cool the sea!

A festival:

> A shrine festival:
> what foods do worshippers eat
> at Kisakata?
> —Sora

> At fishers' houses,
> people lay down rain shutters,
> seeking evening cool.[1]
> —Teiji, a Mino merchant

Seeing an osprey nest on a rock:

> Might they have vowed,
> "Never shall waves cross here"[2]—
> those nesting ospreys?
> —Sora

After several days of reluctant farewells to friends in Sakata, we set out under the clouds of the Northern Land Road, quailing before the prospect of the long journey ahead. It was reported to be 130 leagues to the castle town of the Kaga domain. Once past Nezu Barrier, we made our way on foot through Echigo Province to Ichiburi Barrier in Etchū Province, a tiring journey of nine miserably hot, rainy days. I felt too ill to write anything.

> In the Seventh Month,
> even the Sixth Day differs
> from ordinary nights.[3]

9. A Chinese beauty of the 5th century B.C. Originally the consort of the king of Yue, she was later forced to wed his conqueror, the king of Wu.　　1. That is, they remove the rain shutters from their houses and put them on the beach, where they sit, enjoying the evening cool.　　2. This phrase constitutes a vow of eternal fidelity, derived from a poem in the Kokinshū: "Would I be the sort / to cast you aside / and turn to someone new? / Sooner would the waves traverse / Sue-no-matsu Mountain."　　3. Because people were preparing for the Tanabata Festival, which was held on the seventh day of the Seventh Month in honor of the stars Altair (the herd boy) and Vega (the weaver maiden). Legend held that the two lovers were separated by the Milky Way, except for this one night, when they would meet for their annual rendezvous.

Tumultuous seas:
spanning the sky to Sado Isle,
the Milky Way.

That night I drew up a pillow and lay down to sleep, exhausted after
having traversed the most difficult stretches of road in all the north country—places with names like "Children Forget Parents," "Parents Forget
Children," "Dogs Go Back," and "Horses Sent Back." The voices of young
women drifted in from the adjoining room in front—two of them, it
appeared, talking to an elderly man, whose voice was also audible. As I
listened, I realized that they were prostitutes from Niigata in Echigo,
bound on a pilgrimage to the Grand Shrines of Ise. The old man was to
be sent home to Niigata in the morning, after having escorted them as
far as this barrier, and they seemed to be writing letters and giving him
inconsequential messages to take back. Adrift on "the shore where white
breakers roll in," these "fishermen's daughters" had fallen low indeed,
exchanging fleeting vows with every passerby.[4] How wretched the karma
that had doomed them to such an existence! I fell asleep with their voices
in my ears.

The next morning, the same two girls spoke to us as we were about to
leave. "We're feeling terribly nervous and discouraged about going off on
this hard trip over strange roads. Won't you let us join your party, even if
we only stay close enough to catch a glimpse of you now and then? You
wear the robes of mercy: please let us share the Buddha's compassion and
form a bond with the Way," they said, weeping.

"I sympathize with you, but we'll be making frequent stops. Just follow
others going to the same place; I'm sure the gods will see you there safely."
We walked off without waiting for an answer, but it was some time before
I could stop feeling sorry for them.

Ladies of pleasure
sleeping in the same hostel:
bush clover and moon.[5]

I recited those lines to Sora, who wrote them down.

After crossing the "forty-eight channels" of the Kurobe River and
innumerable other streams, we reached the coast at Nago. Even though
the season was not spring, it seemed a shame to miss the wisteria at Tako
in early autumn. We asked someone how to get there, but the answer
frightened us off. "Tako is five leagues along the beach from here, in the
hollow of those mountains. The only houses are a few ramshackle
thatched huts belonging to fishermen; you probably wouldn't find anyone
to put you up for the night." Thus we went on into Kaga Province.

Scent of ripening ears:[6]
to the right as I push through,
surf crashing onto rocks.

---

4. Alludes to a classical poem: "I have no abode, / for I am but the daughter of a fisherman, / spending
my life / on the shore / where white waves roll in." Prostitutes went out in small boats to greet in-coming
vessels.   5. In this much-discussed poem Bashō is probably not making an invidious comparison
between the prostitutes (showy, ephemeral flowers) and himself (the pure remote moon) but simply using
aspects of the scene at the inn to comment in amusement on a chance encounter between two very
different types of people. It has often been suggested that he may have recorded the meeting at the
barrier—or possibly invented it—as a means of including a reference to love, a standard topic in linked
verse.   6. That is, of the maturing rice crop.

We arrived at Kanazawa on the Fifteenth of the Seventh Month, after crossing Unohana Mountain and Kurikara Valley. There we met the merchant Kasho,[7] who had come up from Ōsaka, and joined him in his lodgings. A certain Isshō had been living in Kanazawa—a man who had gradually come to be known as a serious student of poetry, and who had gained a reputation among the general public as well. I now learned that he had died last winter, still in the prime of life. At the Buddhist service arranged by his older brother:

> Stir, burial mound!
> The voice I raise in lament
> is the autumn wind.

On being invited to a thatched cottage:

> The cool of autumn:
> let's each of us peel his own
> melons and eggplant.

Composed on the way:

> Despite the red blaze
> of the pitiless sun—
> an autumn breeze.

At Komatsu [Young Pines]:

> An appealing name:
> The wind in Young Pines ruffles
> bush clover and miscanthus.

At Komatsu we visited Tada Shrine, which numbers among its treasures a helmet and a piece of brocade that once belonged to Sanemori.[8] We were told that the helmet was a gift from Lord Yoshitomo[9] in the old days when Sanemori served the Genji—and indeed it was no ordinary warrior's headgear. From visor to earflaps, it was decorated with a gold-filled chrysanthemum arabesque in the Chinese style, and the front was surmounted by a dragon's head and a pair of horns. The shrine history tells in vivid language of how Kiso no Yoshinaka[1] presented a petition there after Sanemori's death in battle, and of how Higuchi no Jirō served as a messenger.

> A heartrending sound!
> Underneath the helmet,
> the cricket.

We could see Shirane's peaks behind us as we trudged toward Yamanaka Hot Springs. The Kannon Hall[2] stood at the base of the mountains to the left. Someone said the hall was founded by Retired Emperor Kazan, who enshrined an image of the bodhisattva there and named the spot Nata after completing a pious round of the Thirty-three Places. (The name Nata

---

7. Like others Bashō calls on during his journey, Kasho is an amateur poet.   8. Saitō Sanemori (1111–1183), a *samurai* in the service of the Minamoto/Genji who defects to the Taira/Heike.   9. See n. 1, p. 618   1. Leader of the northern Genji forces in the war against the Heike.   2. In honor of Kannon, the bodhisattva of compassion and an attendant of the Buddha known as Amida.

was explained to us as having been coined from Nachi and Tanigumi.[3])
It was a beautiful, impressive site, with many unusual rocks, rows of
ancient pine trees, and a small thatched chapel, built on a rock against
the cliff.

> Even whiter
> than the Ishiyama rocks—
> the wind of autumn.

We bathed in the hot springs, which were said to be second only to
Ariake in efficacy.

> At Yamanaka,
> no need to pluck chrysanthemums:[4]
> the scent of the springs.

The master was a youth called Kumenosuke. His father, an amateur of
haikai, had embarrassed Teishitsu[5] with his knowledge when the master
visited Yamanaka from the capital as a young man. Teishitsu returned to
the city, joined Teitoku's[6] school, and built up a reputation, but it is said
that he never accepted money for reviewing the work of anyone from this
village after he became famous. The story is an old one now.

Sora was suffering from a stomach complaint. Because he had relatives
at Nagashima in Ise Province, he set off ahead of me. He wrote a poem as
he was about to leave:

> Journeying onward:
> fall prostrate though I may—
> a bush-clover field!

The sorrow of the one who departed and the unhappiness of the one
who remained resembled the feelings of a lapwing wandering lost in the
clouds, separated from its friend.

> From this day forward,
> the legend will be erased:
> dewdrops on the hat.[7]

Still in Kaga, I lodged at Zenshōji, a temple outside the castle town of
Daishōji. Sora had stayed there the night before and left this poem:

> All through the night,
> listening to the autumn wind—
> the mountain in back.

One night's separation is the same as 1,000 leagues. I too listened to the
autumn wind as I lay in the guest dormitory. Toward dawn, I heard clear
voices chanting a sutra, and then the sound of a gong beckoned me into
the dining hall. I left the hall as quickly as possible, eager to reach Echizen
Province that day, but a group of young monks pursued me to the foot of
the stairs with paper and inkstone. Observing that some willow leaves had

---

3. Two towns in different provinces; they were the beginning and ending points on an eleven-province
tour of thirty-three places sacred to Kannon.   4. These flowers were associated with longevity.   5. An
adept of *haikai*.   6. Matsunaga Teitoku (1571–1653), one of the leading practitioners of linked verse.
7. A reference to a common practice when people traveled in pairs. They would write on their hats the
phrase "Two persons following the same path."

scattered in the courtyard, I stood there in my sandals and dashed off these lines:

> To sweep your courtyard
> of willow leaves, and then depart:
> that would be my wish!

At the Echizen border, I crossed Lake Yoshizaki by boat for a visit to the Shiogoshi pines.

> Inviting the gale
> to carry the waves ashore
> all through the night,
> they drip moonlight from their boughs—
> the pines of Shiogoshi!
>
> —Saigyō

In that single verse, the poet captures the essence of the scene at Shiozaki. For anyone to say more would be like "sprouting a useless digit."

In Maruoka, I called on the Tenryūji Abbot, an old friend.

A certain Hokushi from Kanazawa had planned to see me off a short distance, but had finally come all the way to Maruoka, reluctant to say good-bye. Always intent on conveying the effect of beautiful scenery in verse, he had produced some excellent poems from time to time. Now that we were parting, I composed this:

> Hard to say good-bye—
> to tear apart the old fan
> covered with scribbles.

I journeyed about a league and a half into the mountains to worship at Eiheiji, Dōgen's[8] temple. I believe I have heard that Dōgen had an admirable reason for avoiding the vicinity of the capital and founding his temple in those remote mountains.

After the evening meal, I set out for Fukui, three leagues away. It was a tedious, uncertain journey in the twilight.

A man named Tōsai had been living in Fukui as a recluse for a long time. He had come to Edo and visited me once—I was not sure just when, but certainly more than ten years earlier. I thought he must be very old and feeble by now, or perhaps even dead, but someone assured me that he was very much alive. Following my informant's directions into a quiet corner of the town, I came upon a poor cottage, its walls covered with moonflower and snake-gourd vines, and its door hidden by cockscomb and goosefoot.[9] That would be it, I thought. A woman of humble appearance emerged when I rapped on the gate.

"Where are you from, Reverend Sir? The master has gone to see someone in the neighborhood. Please look for him there if you have business with him." She was apparently the housewife.

I hurried off to find Tōsai, feeling as though I had strayed into an old romance, and spent two nights at his house. Then I prepared to leave,

---

8. Founder of one of the main sects of Zen Buddhism.   9. A plant with small greenish blossoms. *Cockscomb:* a plant with fan-shaped clusters of red or yellow blossoms.

hopeful of seeing the full moon at Tsuruga Harbor on the Fifteenth of the Eighth Month. Having volunteered to keep me company, Tōsai set out in high spirits as my guide, his skirts tucked jauntily into his sash.

The peaks of Shirane disappeared as Hina-ga-take came into view. We crossed Azamuzu Bridge, saw ears[1] on the reeds at Taema, journeyed beyond Uguisu Barrier and Yunoo Pass, heard the first wild geese of the season at Hiuchi Stronghold and Mount Kaeru, and took lodgings in Tsuruga at dusk on the Fourteenth. The sky was clear, the moon remarkably fine. When I asked if we might hope for the same weather on the following night, the landlord offered us wine, replying, "In the northern provinces, who knows whether the next night will be cloudy or fair?"

That night, I paid a visit to Kehi Shrine, the place where Emperor Chūai[2] is worshipped. An atmosphere of holiness pervaded the surroundings. Moonlight filtered in between the pine trees, and the white sand in front of the sanctuary glittered like frost. "Long ago, in pursuance of a great vow, the Second Pilgrim[3] himself cut grass and carried dirt and rock to fill a marsh that was a trial to worshippers going back and forth. The precedent is still observed; every new Pilgrim takes sand to the area in front of the shrine. The ceremony is called 'the Pilgrim's Carrying of the Sand,'" my landlord said.

> Shining on sand
> transported by pilgrims—
> pure light of the moon.

It rained on the Fifteenth, just as the landlord had warned it might.

> Night of the full moon:
> no predicting the weather
> in the northern lands.

The weather was fine on the Sixteenth, so we went in a boat to Ironohama Beach to gather red shells. It was seven leagues by sea. A man named Ten'ya provided us with all kinds of refreshments—compartmented lunch boxes, wine flasks, and the like—and also ordered a number of servants to go along in the boat. A fair wind delivered us to our destination in no time. The beach was deserted except for a few fishermen's shacks and a forlorn Nichiren[4] temple. As we drank tea and warmed wine at the temple, I struggled to control feelings evoked by the loneliness of the evening.

> Ah, what loneliness!
> More desolate than Suma,[5]
> this beach in autumn.

> Between wave and wave:
> mixed with small shells, the remains
> of bush-clover bloom.

---

1. The spikes on a plant that contain the seeds.   2. According to tradition, the fourteenth emperor, married to Empress Jingū (see n. 8, p. 627).   3. Taa Shōnin (1237–1319). *Pilgrim* was a title given to the patriarch of the Ji sect of Buddhism.   4. Buddhist monk (1222–1282) and founder of a sect that bore his name.   5. A coastal town made famous as the hero's place of exile in *The Tale of Genji* (in Volume 1).

I persuaded Tōsai to write a description of the day's outing to be left at the temple.

Rōtsu came to meet me at Tsuruga and accompanied me to Mino Province. Thus I arrived at Ōgaki, my journey eased by a horse. Sora came from Ise, Etsujin galloped in on horseback, and we all gathered at Jokō's house. Zensenji, Keikō, Keikō's sons, and other close friends called day and night, rejoicing and pampering me as though I had returned from the dead.

Despite my travel fatigue, I set out again by boat on the Sixth of the Ninth Month to witness the relocation of the Ise sanctuaries.[6]

> Off to Futami,
> loath to part as clam from shell
> in waning autumn.

6. The two sanctuaries at the Grand Shrines of Ise, dedicated to the ancestral gods of the imperial family, are rebuilt every twenty years as a kind of repurification.

UEDA AKINARI
1734–1809

In the two hundred years since they were first published, the supernatural stories of Ueda Akinari have intrigued generations of Japanese readers. The ghost story has a long history in Japan, but no writer has so successfully insinuated the supernatural into the everyday or better understood the irrational implications of erotic attachment. Akinari's cooly objective mix of realism and the fantastic asserts, long before Freud, that fantasy is part of reality and that our "real" lives embrace much that is "unreal."

Tales of Moonlight and Rain, published in 1776, is a collection of nine short stories that explore the discontinuity between routine life and the abrupt intrusion of the inexplicable. In one story, a money-loving *samurai* receives a visit from the spirit of wealth. In another, a grieving priest, unhinged by the death of his lover, consumes the corpse and thus develops a taste for decomposing flesh. In a work in a very different key, fish depicted by an eccentric artist spring to life, detach themselves from their paintings, and swim to freedom in a lake nearby. Two of the most popular stories recount the misadventures of husbands who abandon their wives. In one, the man finally returns; after a happy reunion he awakens to discover that he has spent the night with the ghost of his dead wife. In the other, the abandoned wife's vengeful spirit haunts her unfaithful husband:

> Taken completely by surprise, he saw that it was the wife he had deserted. She looked pale. Her eyes were dull and ghastly. As she stretched out a bony, emaciated hand and pointed at him, he cried out and fainted in sheer terror. After a while he regained his senses. He opened his eyes and looked around. What had seemed like a house a moment ago was in fact the funeral hut of a graveyard.

The stories range, then, from whimsical to chilling, but each is articulated in a rhythmic poetic prose suffused with eerie beauty and abundant acknowledgment of the authority of Japan's literary past. A product of the merchant milieu, Ueda Akinari was a physician and scholar as well as a writer, and he would probably have been surprised to find that posterity remembers him for his ghost stories rather than his scholarship. His learning, however, permeates this fiction. Its presence is subtle and sometimes veiled in translation, but it is one of the components that raise his supernatural tales above escapist fiction.

As a student of the Japanese classics and the linguistic origins of his native culture, Akinari crafted an agreeable combination of vernacular and literary language. His scholarly command of *The Man'yōshū* (in Volume 1), Japan's earliest poetry anthology, inspired both subject and style. The collection served as a sourcebook for stories and geographical settings and also for an archaic diction that seemed, by virtue of its distance, well suited to the spectral. Akinari exploited some of the technical devices of classical poetry and drew on the long-standing Japanese tradition of implanting poetry within a prose context. He was also steeped in *The Tale of the Heike* (in Volume 1) and other military chronicles, to which he frequently alludes as part of the realistic fabric he weaves for his tales, made credible in part by recurring references to actual people, places, and events of the historic past. A voracious reader, Akinari appropriated some of his ideas from medieval Japanese folktales (which abound in the sort of miracles that appealed to his imagination) and others from Chinese literature, both classical and current. In fact, Akinari composed his tales during a craze in Japan for Chinese stories of the supernatural, and some of his own stories were elaborate adaptations reworked into the contemporary Japanese idiom.

Of all the various influences he received, however, the legacy of *nō* drama was one of the most important. Like the *nō* playwrights, in some stories Akinari takes a famous poem as the kernel for his narrative. In others he employs a formal device borrowed from the *nō*. Action is set in motion by a journey, and dramatic tension derives from an encounter between the traveler and a ghost. The ghost, of course, as in the *nō*, is the physical manifestation of some gnawing emotion, a restless spirit in the grip of an obsession—hatred, revenge, or jealousy, for example.

In *Bewitched*, Akinari goes further. He incorporates specific myth-making elements from the *nō* play *Dōjōji* (in Volume 1). In the play, itself derived from folklore and eleventh-century miracle stories, rejection (or, in the Buddhist scheme of things, passion) transforms a lovesick girl into a serpent. Sexual heat takes a new and deadly form when the venomous snake destroys the man who jilted her: she coils her scaly flesh around his hiding place and roasts him alive. Manago, the heroine of *Bewitched*, is just as lethal. The original title, *A Serpent's Lust*, would have suggested to eighteenth-century readers, if only subliminally, the danger of dragon ladies, a threat already embedded in Japanese literature.

But Akinari reverses the usual narrative. If jealousy can transform a woman into a serpent, he says, then love can turn a serpent into a woman. Drawing on his reading across two cultures and deep into Japan's ancient mythology, he creates one of the great demon-goddesses of Japanese literature. His hypnotic, ethereally beautiful Manago is as weird, mesmerizing, and frightening as the wild serpent-girl in *Dōjōji*. And because *Bewitched* is not a stylized *nō* play but a fairly long short story, Akinari can fashion a vivid image of a woman hell-bent on love, a creature whose passion transcends the ordinary realities of this world.

Like an Alfred Hitchcock of the supernatural, he sets up the story in such a way that the reader has ominous feelings from the very beginning. From the outset we sense that the hero, the handsome, spoiled Toyo-o, a young man with no head for practical matters and no real discipline, is about to get himself caught in something far beyond his ability to control. From the first time he hears Manago's voice, "rich as the sound of rolling jewels," and lays eyes on her "bewitchingly voluptuous" beauty, we know that this is not going to be any ordinary encounter. In due course, both reader and hero discover that Toyo-o is locked in a fatal attraction with a possessive and fiendish apparition.

What is most impressive in *Bewitched* is the way that Akinari controls our descent into the uncanny. Every time Toyo-o's known world is about to rupture, the phantom-woman offers him a plausible excuse for her strange maneuvers, and indeed it is this very plausibility that makes her so frightening. Even after he should know better, Toyo-o hovers on the verge of believing, holding the reader with him. Suspended in uncertainty, we begin to question whether or not the real and the unreal are irreversible opposites, and this is the fantastic's golden opportunity. The tension between logic and fable stretches like a tightrope. As Akinari leads us gingerly across, even modern readers may wonder if rationality's eradication of ghouls and angels is not just another of our own contemporary illusions.

Akinari strives to make the supernatural world credible by finding rational explanations for the fantastic. One could say that in the process *Bewitched* becomes a text that continually denies itself. But one could also say that for Akinari and his readers no denial was necessary. In the spiritual and psychological cosmology of eighteenth-century Japan, the extraordinary was in a certain sense the ordinary. The spirit world had impinged on Japanese life from the country's earliest days, when Shinto, the indigenous religion, taught a kind of nature worship based on the assumption that the boundaries between animate and inanimate, or the living and the dead, are exceedingly permeable. A tree, or river, or mountain, a single rock even, could be the manifestation of a god. The dead could also be gods, and the spirits of ancestors loomed over the living as more than shadowy presences. By the time of *The Tale of Genji* (eleventh century; in Volume 1), the supernatural was construed as a normal part of daily life. Directional taboos, for example, often governed one's activities, so that a person could not proceed down a path where diviners sensed a naughty spirit prowling.

Even Buddhism, a much more sophisticated religion than Shinto, helped buttress the Japanese belief in the supernatural. The doctrine of transmigration, for example, taught that the dead are reborn after a brief, uncertain existence in an in-between world. Those who had failed to reconcile their passions could come back to life as ghosts. The most frightening were the "hungry ghosts," whose greed and moral depravity had turned them into the grotesque physical embodiment of their former appetites: skeletal fiends lurking in cesspools, trying futilely to fill their empty though enormous stomachs, bloated not with food but with hunger. When organized religion held that ghosts commingle with human beings, it is not surprising that a whole panoply of spirit-creatures—devils, mountain goblins, magic monkeys, lusty serpents, foxes who transform themselves into temptresses—should be given credence in premodern Japan, or that Akinari, a student of traditional Japanese culture, should take the supernatural for his theme.

One should read a story like *Bewitched* with an understanding that its "unreal" aspects may have seemed a good deal more "real" to its original audience and with an awareness that the presence of ghosts in such fiction is not to be identified with the play of the unconscious. We need to imagine, or reimagine, a mental life that addresses at the conscious level things that we would call the irrational, which modern psychology relegates to the unconscious. Akinari helps us in our reimagining. His ability to paint such a bold picture of desire incarnate and to give his tales the most stunning and delicate atmospherics, thick with fog and mist and midnight apparitions, places him among the forefront of the world's great gothic writers.

For the other stories in Akinari's collection see Kengi Hamada, trans., *Tales of Moonlight and Rain* (1972), and Leon M. Zolbrod, trans., *Ugetsu Monogatari: Tales of Moonlight and Rain* (1974), which contains an extensive introduction. A second collection of Akinari's fiction published posthumously, which contains several more supernatural stories, has been translated by Barry Jackman, *Tales of the Spring Rain* (1975). For biographical and critical studies see Blake Morgan Young,

Ueda Akinari (1982), and the chapter on Akinari in Donald Keene, *World within Walls* (1976). An interesting art historical introduction to the supernatural in Japan is found in Stephen Addiss, *Japanese Ghosts and Demons* (1985).

PRONOUNCING GLOSSARY

The following list uses common English syllables to provide rough equivalents of selected words whose pronunciation may be unfamiliar to the general reader.

Abe no Yumimaro: *ah-bay noh yoo-mee-mah-roh*

Bunya no Hiroyuki: *boon-yah noh hee-roh-yoo-kee*

Dōjōji: *doh-joh-jee*

Gongen: *gohn-gen*

Hokai Oshō: *hoh-kai oh-shoh*

Kanetada: *kah-ne-tah-dah*

Kii: *kee-ee*

Komatsubara: *koh-mah-tsoo-bah-rah*

Manago: *mah-nah-goh*

Man'yōshū: *mahn-yoh-shoo*

Maroya: *mah-roh-yah*

Miwagasaki: *mee-wah-gah-sah-kee*

Naniwa: *nah-nee-wah*

Suguri: *soo-goo-ree*

Tanabe: *tah-nah-bay*

Toyo-o: *toh-yoh–oh*

Tsubaichi: *tsoo-bah-ee-chee*

Ueda Akinari: *oo-e-dah ah-kee-nah-ree*

Ugetsu: *oo-ge-tsoo*

Yunomine: *yoo-noh-mee-ne*

yū-ō: *yoo–oh*

Bewitched[1]

1

Some time in the remote past, in the coastal village of Miwagasaki, in the province of Kii, there lived a man called Ōya no Takesuke, who was blessed by the sea. He had a good many fishermen working for him, and he caught a great deal of fish every day, both big and small. He was very prosperous indeed.

Ōya no Takesuke had two sons and a daughter. Taro, the elder son, was honest and rugged, devoted to his work, and he carried on the family business. The daughter was married to a man in neighboring Yamato province. Toyo-o, the third child, was a handsome youth with a predilection for learning and cultural pursuits typical of life in Kyoto, the nation's capital. He had no desire or inclination to devote his time and efforts to the family occupation.

Because of this, Toyo-o was something of a problem to his father. Pondering his wayward son's future welfare, Ōya no Takesuke thought of dividing the family wealth and settling upon Toyo-o his portion so that he could live serenely the kind of life that suited him. But then Toyo-o was the sort who, once he came into possession of money, would soon be deceived and robbed of all he owned. If, on the other hand, he were given away for adoption to another family, there might be endless complaints

---

1. Translated by Kengi Hamada.

from that family that he was shiftless and irresponsible; that too would be
inadvisable.

In the end, Toyo-o's father decided to let him become a scholar or a
priest, or whatever his own whims dictated, and thus to allow him to be a
burden on his older brother for the rest of his life. Therefore he did not
object when Toyo-o went daily to study with his tutor, Abe no Yumimaro,
the chief priest of the Kumano Shrine.

On this particular day, toward the end of September, the sky was clear
and the sea calm. Suddenly, clouds began to gather over the sea from the
southeast and light rain soon began to fall. Toyo-o borrowed an umbrella
from his tutor on his way home. As he reached the spot where he could
see the depository of sacred treasures of the Asuka Shrine, the rain became
a real downpour. He therefore sought shelter at a nearby fisherman's
hut.

An old man emerged to greet him: "Welcome, young master, to this
shabby house. Pardon me," he said, dusting off a cushion, "let me offer
this for you to sit on."

"Oh, don't bother, please," said Toyo-o. "I just came in from the rain
to stay awhile," and he sat down on the raised *tatami*.[2]

At that moment a voice called from outside, rich as the sound of rolling
jewels, "May we take shelter in this house for a short while?"

No sooner said than, to Toyo-o's utter amazement, in stepped a beautiful woman less than twenty years of age. Her features, the way she wore
her hair, her colorful robe, the perfume she exuded—all this, Toyo-o
noted, made her bewitchingly voluptuous. With her was a pretty little
maid of fourteen or fifteen carrying a bundle. Both were soaking wet.

2

Toyo-o felt sorry for the woman. And she seemed surprised to see him.
Her face lighted up, blushing modestly. There was refinement in her look,
and Toyo-o felt instantly attracted to her.

At the same time, it occurred to him that he had never heard of such a
beautiful, refined-looking woman living in this neighborhood. She must
be a woman from Kyoto, he surmised, who had come on a pilgrimage to
the three famous Kumano shrines[3] and had perhaps been strolling on the
beach to view the charming scenery when it began to rain. Even so, he
felt it was rather unseemly that she was not accompanied by a male escort.

"Come sit here," he invited, making room for her. "The weather will
soon clear up, I'm sure."

"Just for a while then, thank you," the woman said.

The house was small and there was barely enough room for her to sit
beside him. At such close range, she seemed to Toyo-o more beautiful
than ever, almost otherworldly, and his heart leaped with excitement.

"You seem to be a lady of high station in life," he said. "Did you come

---

2. Woven straw mats. These mats are still used in Japan as floor coverings.   3. Among the most popular
Shinto shrines, located south of Kyoto and Nara in a mountainous region overlooking the sea. The native
deities worshiped there were viewed as manifestations of Buddhist divinities who could prolong life and
help the faithful attain rebirth in paradise.

here on a pilgrimage to the three Kumano shrines? Or to visit the Yuno-mine Hotspring?[4] But why have you been strolling at such a bare, unat-tractive beach as this? An ancient poet once commented:

> Oh, how bothersome indeed
> The rain, falling suddenly
> At Sano in Miwagasaki,
> Where there's no shelter for me.

"He probably got caught by just the kind of miserable weather we are having today. This is only a shabby hut, but the owner is a man employed by my father. So please be at ease and rest here. Where, by the way, are you lodging in the village? I should accompany you there—but perhaps that would be too personal and impolite. Why don't you take this umbrella with you?"

"Thank you for your hospitality," the woman replied. "I shall dry my clothes with the warmth of your kindness and then leave. I am not a visitor from Kyoto. I have lived near this village at Shingū for a long time. Today started out to be a clear day, so I went to offer prayers at the Nachi Shrine. But the downpour forced me to seek shelter here without knowing that you had done the same thing. My lodging is not far from here."

Rising, she continued, "The sky is already clearing, so I shall take my leave while there is still a light rain falling."

Toyo-o delayed her, saying, "The rain has not really stopped yet. Please use this umbrella. You may return it to me whenever it is convenient for you. Better still, where do you live? I can send someone for the umbrella later."

"Ask for Agata no Manago's house in Shingū. It will soon be sundown so I shall have to go now. I will take the umbrella you so graciously offered."

And so Toyo-o saw her off as she spread the umbrella and left, watching until she vanished from his sight. He himself borrowed a straw umbrella from the old man of the hut and went home.

3

That night Toyo-o could not sleep, disturbed by the image of the woman which flittered ceaselessly before his mind's eye. Toward morning, however, fitfully hovering on the edge of sleep, he dreamed that he went calling at Manago's house.

It was a huge structure, as was the front gate. The shutters and the bamboo blinds indicated that Manago lived in elegant style.

Manago herself came to greet him at the door, saying, "I cannot forget your kindness, and I love you. Please come in."

Showing him into an inner chamber, she laid out a feast before him, wine and all kinds of fruit. Made cheerfully drunk by the excesses of her hospitality, he yielded to her caresses and lay down beside her, talking intimately.

Came the dawn, however, and the end of his dream.

Toyo-o thought, if only what had happened were real and not just a

---

4. Where pilgrims to Kumano often rested.

dream, how happy he would be! He felt so restless that he even forgot to eat his breakfast, and he literally leaped out of the house, so eager was he to see her. But when he asked around for the house of Agata no Manago, no one seemed to know about it. He kept on searching until late in the afternoon, when he saw Manago's maid coming toward him from the east. Quickly he went to speak to her. "Say," he called, "where is the house of your mistress? I came to get the umbrella."

The maid smiled pleasantly. "I am glad you came. This way, please," and she led the way. Soon she pointed and said, "This is it."

Toyo-o saw that the front gate and the house were huge indeed. The shutters and bamboo blinds were just as impressive as he had imagined in his dream. Strange, he thought, as he walked through the gate. The maid preceded him into the house, announcing, "The man who loaned you the umbrella yesterday was coming this way, so I invited him in."

"Where is he? Bring him here quickly." There was no doubt about it. It was Manago herself who came out to greet Toyo-o.

"I happened to be returning from my studies at the house of my tutor, the Shinto priest Abe no Yumimaro, so I dropped in to get the umbrella. I shall look around your house today and perhaps come again another day."

Manago pressed him to stay. "Maroya," she called to her maid, "don't let Toyo-o leave the house."

Maroya blocked his way. "You forced us to accept your umbrella. It is only right that we force you to stay here now." She pushed him into a room with wooden flooring and a southern exposure, and spread a tatami mat for him to sit on.

It was a splendidly decorated room. The panels on the wall, the shelves, the screens—all seemed to be of valuable classical vintage. This, thought Toyo-o, must be the home, not of an ordinary person, but of someone wealthy and of high station in life.

4

Manago entered. "For certain reasons," she said, "this house no longer has a master. I cannot therefore offer you anything in the way of lavish entertainment. I have brought you some poor wine." So saying, she placed before him a small table and dishes piled high with seafood delicacies, and wine jars. Maroya, the maid, offered to pour the wine.

But Toyo-o was racked with doubts and suspicion. Can I still be dreaming, and will it soon come to an end? All this, however, seemed to be real enough. Still, it was all so mysterious that he could not fathom it.

Guest and hostess drank together immoderately, feeling a pleasant sensation. Manago lifted her wine cup and spoke coquettishly, with an expression reminiscent of a blooming cherry reflected in the water below while a spring zephyr brushed its face. In a bewitching voice like that of a nightingale flitting from branch to branch, she said, "Perhaps I should not tell you this, for it makes me feel ashamed. But if I should die without confessing, people might say something preposterous—that I had been put to death by some angry, vengeful god. So listen to what I have to say without doubting it—trust me that I am not blurting it out on the spur of the moment.

"I was born in Kyoto but my parents died soon afterward and I was brought up by my nurse. Due to family ties, a minor official named Agata in the governor's office of this district brought me here as his wife. My husband died of illness before his term of office expired, and I was left alone and uncared for. My former nurse in Kyoto had meanwhile become a nun and departed on a devotional journey without a fixed destination. And so, Kyoto, my birthplace, has become a strange, distant land to me. I have nowhere else to go.

"Yesterday, while seeking shelter from the rain, I enjoyed the blessings of your hospitality and friendship. I felt certain that you were a sincere man, and that I should devote the rest of my life to you. If you do not dislike me and are willing to accept my love, please drink the wine in this cup to seal our eternal pledge as husband and wife."

Toyo-o hesitated. He himself had felt in his heart the same intention— to marry her, for he was in love with her. And so her proposal caused his heart to leap with joy, like a bird taking flight from its roost. Still, dependent on his father and older brother for his livelihood, he realized he was in no position to make a hasty promise on his own initiative alone—without consulting them and obtaining their consent. Glad though he was, therefore, he told her he could not give her an immediate reply.

Manago, angry and looking miserable, said, "I am afraid I have spoken rather rashly, like a woman crying out from the depths of her heart, and I regret I cannot take back what I said. A woman in my miserable situation should perhaps drown herself in the sea. But if I did, it would weigh heavily on your heart and that, too, would be a serious crime. What I have said is the truth, but please dismiss it as the foolish talk of a drunken woman and forget about it."

Toyo-o relented: "From the beginning I realized you were a cultured woman of Kyoto and I feel now that I have not been mistaken. Brought up as I have been in this rugged region where whales offshore spout seawater, I could not even have dreamed of such a fine proposal, bringing me so much happiness. I cannot, however, accept it immediately because I am still dependent on my parents. I have no property of my own except the hair on my head and the nails on my fingers. I have no power to earn my own living. How could I support you? I feel wretched in my present situation. But, if you are willing to accept these conditions, I shall willingly be of service to you. Confucius said, 'Even a mountain of love crumbles.' And as for myself, how can I help but overlook my obligations of filial piety and sacrifice myself for your sake?"

Manago responded gaily: "Now that you have given me such happy assurances, come and see me from time to time in this poor abode. Here is a sword which was a precious possession of my late husband. Wear it constantly," and she presented it to Toyo-o.

Toyo-o on examining it saw that it was a magnificent long sword with gold and silver trimmings on the scabbard. The blade was a sharp and fearsome thing. He realized it would be inauspicious to reject an engagement gift, so he inserted the sword in his hip sash.

He was repeatedly asked to spend the night there, but he rejected the offer, saying, "I would be chided by my father and older brother if I spent the night here without their permission. I promise you I will invent some kind of excuse to put them at their ease and come tomorrow night."

Thereupon he left without further ado. But at home, the next day dawned before he could sleep soundly.

5

His older brother Taro got up early to supervise the day's work for the fishermen in the family's employ. He peeped into Toyo-o's room through a crack in the door, and in the feeble light of the still-sputtering oil lamp he saw the glittering sword lying beside Toyo-o's pillow.

Strange, Taro thought. Where in the world could he have gotten such a sword?[5] He slid the door open noisily, awakening Toyo-o. Surprised to see Taro in the room, Toyo-o stammered, "Did you call me, Brother?"

"What is that thing glittering beside your pillow?" Taro demanded. "Such a thing is hardly appropriate in a fisherman's house. If Father hears about it, he will surely give you a sound scolding."

"But I didn't buy it. Someone gave it to me yesterday, so I brought it here."

"There is no one in this village who has such a precious thing to give away. I have always felt it was a waste of money for you to buy books written in Chinese characters,[6] but still I have not interfered because Father has been lenient about it . . ." He added derisively, "Are you going to wear that sword to march and show off in the festival parade here? There is a limit to making a fool of yourself."

Their father heard the loud quarrelsome voice. "What is that good-for-nothing son up to now? Bring him in here."

Taro shouted back, "I don't know where he bought this thing. It is a glittering sword such as a general wears on his hip. To buy such a thing is unseemly, I think. Talk to him about it. I must go now to oversee the fishermen's work; otherwise they would idle their time away."

After Taro left, his mother summoned Toyo-o. "Why have you bought such a thing?" she demanded. "Everything in this house—food, money, goods—belongs to Taro. There is nothing you can claim as your own. We have usually let you do as you pleased. But if you were to incur Taro's displeasure, I am afraid you would have no place in the whole world to go and live. Why can't you, with all your learning, understand this simple truth?"

"I truly did not buy the sword," Toyo-o insisted. "It was given to me for a good reason. Yet Brother has scolded me so roughly just on seeing it."

His father roared, "What have you done to deserve such a precious prize? I cannot imagine! Tell us frankly, without holding back any detail."

"I am ashamed to tell you about it. Let me tell it through another person."

5. The possession of swords was a privilege of the *samurai* class.   6. Only the well educated could read Chinese. The brother perhaps makes fun of Toyo-o, because the term *Chinese characters* was also slang for "secret code," suggesting the uselessness of such knowledge.

"To whom do you intend to reveal something you are ashamed of telling your own parents or your older brother?"

Taro's wife, who had been listening patiently, could no longer endure the violence of the family quarrel, so she interceded. "Let me hear it from him in his room," she said, pushing Toyo-o there, "though this may be presumptuous on my part."

So Toyo-o told the story to his brother's wife: "Before being found out and scolded by my brother, I had planned to discuss this matter quietly with you. I had not expected things to turn out in this explosive way. The truth is that there is a young widow called Agata no Manago living a lonely life near here, and she asked me to help her, giving me this sword at the same time. As you know, I am inexperienced in the ways of the world and have no means of making an independent living. If, because of this incident, I am driven out of this house, it cannot be helped. I do regret what I have done. But please, Sister, take pity upon me and intercede for me."

His sister-in-law laughed out loud. "I have always felt sorry that a fine young man like you should remain single so long. I think you have done the normal thing. Yes, I will do whatever I can for you."

6

That night she explained the situation to her husband, Taro. "I think it's about time Toyo-o became involved with a woman, don't you? Will you speak to Father about it, so he will approve?"

Taro knit his brows. "This is strange," he said. "I have never heard of a minor official called Agata who served as assistant to the governor of this district. Since our family serves as village headman, we should have been informed if and when any such official died. Anyway, let me see the sword."

When the sword was brought in, Taro examined it thoroughly and seemed to be troubled.

"This is no trifling matter," he said. "Recently ministers of state from the capital arrived at the Kumano Gongen Shrine for special prayers invoking the blessings of the gods and presented numerous precious gifts to the shrine. Then all the valuable gifts were stolen from the shrine depository. The chief priest reported the robbery to the governor's office. And in order to apprehend the robber, the vice governor, Bunya no Hiroyuki, is now conferring with the priest at the priest's house. I have a feeling this sword was not something worn by a minor official here. I shall show it to Father and see what he has to say."

When his father saw the sword and was told about the recent robbery of the precious gifts from the shrine, he turned pale.

"What a terrible thing to happen to us! That good-for-nothing son is the sort who can't even pluck a single hair from another person's head. How such an evil thought as committing this irreverent crime should have entered his head, I cannot understand. If news of this affair leaks out, our family is sure to come to ruin because it is a serious crime, a violation of the code governing shrines. We cannot afford to spare or protect a single member of the family from his misdeed. We must consider our obligations to our ancestors and to our descendants. Tomorrow let us make a clean confession to the authorities."

7

"Yes, indeed," said the surprised chief priest on examining the sword, "this is one of the precious gifts presented to this shrine by the state ministers."

The vice governor, Bunya no Hiroyuki, on receiving the report on the case, said, "Now let us go into the robbery of all the other precious gifts." He gave orders that Toyo-o be arrested immediately for questioning.

A group of some ten samurai, with Taro leading the way, thus went to the Ōya house. Toyo-o, ignorant of what had happened in the meantime, was reading a book in his room. The samurai stamped in unceremoniously, knocked him down, and bound him like a prisoner without even explaining the crime for which he was being arrested. His parents and his brother and his wife wept, saying it was all so sad.

"You have been summoned to the government office," the samurai said. "Now walk quickly."

Bound like a common criminal and surrounded by his captors, Toyo-o was taken to the government office.

Bunya, the vice governor, glared at the prisoner. "You must understand," he roared, "that to steal the offering to the gods of the shrine is a serious, unprecedented crime. Where have you hidden the other precious things you have stolen? Confess the truth without hedging."

At last Toyo-o began to understand that he had been accused of the theft of the sword. With tears flowing, he said, "I swear before the gods that I did not steal anything." He explained how he had been given the sword as a gift by the woman called Manago, who claimed to be the widow of a certain minor official named Agata who had worn the sword while he was still living.

"To prove my innocence," Toyo-o urged, "why don't you arrest that woman at once?"

Bunya, the vice governor, became even more furious. "There has been no one in my employ here by the name of Agata. If you keep on evading the truth, I am warning you that the crime for which you have been arrested will become progressively more serious."

"Why should I keep on lying to you after being arrested for a crime I did not commit?" Toyo-o insisted. "Please, for the sake of the truth, bring the woman here for questioning."

Bunya thereupon said to the samurai, "Where is the house of this Agata no Manago? Go and arrest her."

The samurai, acknowledging the command, pushed Toyo-o ahead of them to lead them to Manago's house.

8

But what had appeared to Toyo-o as imposing pillars on the front gate of Manago's house were sagging with rot; the roof tiles were mostly broken, fallen to the ground. The yard was overgrown with weeds. There were no signs of anyone living in the house. Toyo-o was amazed, to say the least.

The ten samurai searched the neighborhood and rounded up several men, including an aged woodcutter and a rice thrasher. These men squatted in fear before the samurai, one of whom demanded, "Tell me, what manner of people lived here? Is it true that a man called Agata lived in this house?"

An old blacksmith edged forward on his knees and said, "I have not heard of any person by that name. About three years ago a certain man called Suguri lived prosperously in this house. But after his ship loaded with goods bound for Tsukushi was lost at sea, those remaining in the house left for places unknown. It has been unoccupied since then. But I heard from this old dyer that yesterday that young man," he pointed at Toyo-o, "entered the house and left it after a while, which he thought very mysterious indeed."

"Very well," said the samurai. "We shall go into the house and examine it thoroughly to report to the governor." The rest of the samurai, along with Toyo-o, followed the leader through the front gate and into the house itself.

The inside of the building was in a greater state of ruin and desolation than the outside. As they approached the inner courtyard they found what must once have been a lavishly built garden. The pond had dried up, the flowering plants were dead. Wild bushes and weeds flourished everywhere. A lone pine tree, broken by strong winds, looked ghastly.

Opening the latticed door leading to the main hall, they felt a raw-smelling spectral gust of wind and fell back in fearful excitement. Toyo-o, struck with amazement at the change, could not utter a word.

One of the samurai, a big, burly, daring man called Kose no Kumagashi, shouted, "Follow me in!" and stamped his way roughly into the wooden-floored room. A carpet of dust about an inch thick covered the floor, with rat droppings strewn everywhere. And in this filthy room, beside a screen, sat a woman, pretty as a flower.

"In the name of the governor, I arrest you," shouted Kumagashi. "Come with me."

But the woman made no answer. As Kumagashi approached to seize her, there was a sudden clap of thunder, so loud that it seemed as though the earth itself had been split apart. Stunned by the impact, everyone fell to the floor before they could flee the room. When the rumbling ceased they looked around. The woman had disappeared. Nor was there any indication where she might have gone.

But scattered on the floor they saw a great many glittering articles— rolls of imported Korean cotton, Chinese figured silk, colorful linen, *katori*[7] cloth, metal hoes, as well as valuable weapons such as spears, shields, and quivers, the offerings that had been made to the shrine by the ministers of state and were stolen from the shrine depository.

The samurai gathered up the goods and reported back to the vice governor, giving him a detailed description of what had happened at the mysterious, dilapidated house. Both the vice governor and the chief priest of the

---

7. A thin silk used for summer kimonos.

Kumano Gongen Shrine were convinced that the robbery must have been the work of a spectral monster. The charge against Toyo-o was therefore reduced, but the fact that he had been in possession of the stolen sword could not be officially overlooked. He was thrown into jail and chained to the wall. However, the Ōya family bribed the officials with costly gifts, and Toyo-o was released after serving only a hundred days.

9

But Toyo-o felt that his family could never endure the unpleasant notoriety when his involvement in the affair became the subject of neighborhood gossip. He asked that he be allowed to go to his married sister's house in Nara and live there for a while. The family agreed, fearing that otherwise, after that dreadful experience, he might become seriously ill. And so they sent him off with a traveling companion to look after him.

Toyo-o's sister lived at a place called Tsubaichi in Nara province, married to a merchant called Tanabe no Kanetada. The couple greeted him warmly and, feeling sorry for him after his harrowing experience of the last few months, told him he could stay with them as long as he wanted.

That year passed without further incident. Soon it was February of the following year. The town of Tsubaichi, noted for its many temples and shrines, was near the Hasedera, a temple famous for the blessings of the Goddess of Mercy and known far and wide, even in China. Many were the worshipers from cities and distant villages who went on pilgrimages there each spring. The pilgrims usually lodged at Tsubaichi, and merchants competed for their trade.

Since the Tanabe store dealt in candles, lampwicks, and other lighting goods for religious ceremonies, it enjoyed a lucrative trade. So many customers crowded the shop that movement inside it was almost impossible.

10

One day in the middle of this prosperous season a woman, seemingly from the city and dazzlingly beautiful, squeezed herself into the Tanabe store, accompanied by a maid, to purchase incense.

The maid, recognizing Toyo-o, shouted, "Here is our master!"

Toyo-o, taken completely by surprise, saw it was Maroya, the maid, and her mistress Manago. "Oh, how dreadful," he cried, and ran into the interior of the shop to hide.

"What is the matter?" asked his sister and her husband, Kanetada.

"That devil has come after me here. Keep away from her!"

The crowd in the shop began screaming: "Where is the devil?"

At this point Manago herself spoke up. "People, you need not fear me. And you, my husband, need not tremble so. I am sorry that I pushed you rashly into committing a crime. I searched for you after that in order to tell you the truth and put you at ease. Fortunately I have found out where you now live.

"I also ask the people of this house to listen carefully to me. If I were really a devil, would I be walking around carelessly in broad daylight, in dense crowds? The garments I am wearing have seams. When I walk against the sun my shadow shows clearly. Consider these things as logical proof and you will be convinced that I am not a devil. So be relieved of your doubts and suspicion."

Toyo-o at last regained his senses, emerged from his hiding place, and said, "I discovered that you are not a human being when I was arrested by the samurai and went back with them to your house. It was in an amazingly wretched state, completely different from the day before. And in that house inhabited only by devils I saw you again, and when the samurai tried to seize you there was a clap of thunder on that sunny day and you disappeared in a flash. I tell you I saw it all with my own eyes. And here you have the effrontery to come chasing after me again. Get out of here, you devil! At once!"

Manago clung to him with tears in her eyes. "I cannot blame you entirely for denouncing me. But please listen to what I have to say. I felt very sorry for you when I heard you were arrested and taken to the government office. So I discussed the matter with an old man in the neighborhood whom I had befriended and had him quickly reduce the house to its hideous state. The thunder that seemed to have rolled when I was about to be seized was a trick played by Maroya. I fled by ship toward Naniwa, but I wanted to find out what had happened to you after that and I prayed to the Goddess of Mercy of the Hasedera.[8] It was revealed to me during my prayer that I should come to the temple here, where the three cryptomeria trees[9] of sacred origin stand. I was thus able to trace you here to Tsubaichi, thanks to the infinite mercy of the goddess Kannon.

"Furthermore, how could a mere woman like me steal and carry away all those precious offerings from the Gongen Shrine depository? The robbery must have been the work of the spirit of my late husband. Please think all this over carefully, trusting the sincerity of my love for you."

Toyo-o, teetering in an ambivalent state of lingering doubt and pity, could find no words to alienate her further. His sister and her husband, however, were so moved by Manago's seemingly straightforward, singularly feminine pleadings that they had no doubt whatever that she had spoken the truth. And although Toyo-o claimed that Manago was a spectral monster, there could be no such thing in this world, they reasoned. They were impressed by her zeal—and her pitiful state—having come all the way here to search for him. Even though Toyo-o was not convinced, they themselves welcomed her into their household and provided her with a room.

In a day or so Manago, ingratiating herself to her host and hostess, pleaded with them tearfully to win back Toyo-o for her. Completely overcome by her tender pleas, they succeeded in urging Toyo-o to go through with formal wedding rites. Toyo-o, who, in any event, had first been attracted to Manago's physical beauty, daily became less and less intransigent and more attached to her than ever, and finally he pledged eternal love. Now nothing could separate them even for a day, for such was the intensity of their tender love for each other.

---

8. Famous Buddhist temple south of Nara, established in the 8th century and dedicated to Kannon, goddess of mercy, who was revered for her vow to save all beings.   9. Japanese cedars.

11

Then came the month of March, and Kanetada proposed that the whole family go on a picnic to the famed Yoshino.

"This province of Kii," he said, "naturally cannot compare with Kyoto in beauty and elegance, but we have our unrivaled scenic beauties, too. Yoshino[1] is especially beautiful in the spring. You will never tire of seeing Mount Mifune and the Natsumi River, no matter how often you visit there. At this time of year the cherries are in bloom, which makes it all the more beautiful." He urged Toyo-o and Manago, saying "Let us all go on a picnic together."

Manago smiled and said, "There is a saying, Yoshino is a good place which good people look upon as good," quoting the famous verse by Emperor Tenmu which paraphrases the literal implications of the word *yoshi* [good] in Yoshino. "It is the envy of the people of Kyoto, I hear. Yes, it must surely be glorious when the cherries are in bloom. But since childhood I have suffered from a congenital illness which makes me dizzy when I find myself in the midst of a huge throng, or when I have to walk a long distance on the highway. I am sorry to say I cannot accompany you on the picnic. But I shall expect a lot of souvenirs of your trip when you return."

"You need not worry about that," Kanetada replied. "We would never let you walk to the picnic grounds. We do not own a private palanquin[2] but we can always hire one for you. Besides, if you do not come along with us, Toyo-o will be worried and may refuse to go."

Toyo-o added his encouragement: "Since he has made this offer out of kindness, I don't see how we can refuse, even though you might collapse on the wayside."

Thus Manago reluctantly agreed to go along.

12

Many people along the picnic route were dressed in colorful finery but none could compare with Manago's dazzling beauty.

The family first went calling at a certain temple on Mount Yoshino, where the chief priest was a friend of long standing. In welcoming them the priest said, "You are rather late this spring. The petals of the cherry blossoms are already scattering, and the warbling of the nightingale is waning. But I will escort you to some places where cherry trees are still in bloom."

But first he had a rather tidy supper prepared for them.

At dawn the area was thickly covered with mist. But as the mist cleared they could appreciate the view in all directions, for the temple was situated at a high elevation. Priests' quarters scattered here and there in the lower regions could be seen clearly. The warbling of mountain birds could be heard from hither and yon. Flowers and trees thrived in a riot of colors. The area was so beautiful as to dazzle one's eyes.

For those who were visiting this spot for the first time, the view at a

---

1. Famous for its cherry blossoms.   2. An enclosed seat, mounted on poles, that was designed to carry a single passenger.

waterfall below was said to be the best, so they were sent in that direction with a guide. As they descended the slope along a circuitous route, they came upon a site where an ancient imperial detached palace was said to have once stood. Nearby was the waterfall. The water below formed a foaming, bubbling whirlpool, in which some small fish were leaping, presenting a pleasing sight.

They sat down to eat their picnic lunch while enjoying the scenery. Presently a man was seen coming from downstream, stepping from boulder to boulder. His hair was as white as newly spun linen. But his legs seemed to be still vigorous with health and vitality. As he approached the waterfall, he stood looking at the picnicking group sitting on the bank. He seemed mystified.

Manago and Maroya deliberately turned their backs on him and pretended not to have seen him standing there. But the old man had already recognized them.

"You devils!" he grumbled. "Again you are bewitching and deceiving human beings. How can you dare assume that shape and form before my very eyes!"

Manago and Maroya stood up in a frenzy of confusion and plunged into the waterfall. The swirling waters suddenly shot up into the air and the two vanished from sight. At the same time a jet black cloud appeared over the spot like a splash of ink, and rain fell in a torrent, rattling noisily like thin bamboo slats.

13

The old man, seeing that the other picnickers in the group had been thrown into excited confusion, calmed them and led them down to a village. "You have been bewitched by that devil who attached itself to you," he told Toyo-o, fixing him with a steady gaze. "If I had not been there to save you, it might have taken your life. Beware of it in the future."

Toyo-o, kneeling on the ground with head bowed in profound thankfulness, revealed to the old man the entire history of his affair with Manago and pleaded earnestly for future protection from the devil.

"I thought so," the old man said. "That devil is really a huge old serpent—a lecherous monster. It mates with a bull and begets a freak calf; it mates with a stallion and begets a freak colt. It has bewitched you because it was fascinated by your good looks. Its evil attachment to its victims is so tenacious that you must be constantly on your guard. Otherwise you will lose your life."

All heard the venerable man with fear in their hearts and prayed to him, saying, "You must be the incarnation of a god."

He laughed. "I am not a god. My name is Tagima no Kibito, and I serve at the Yamato Shrine. I will escort you to your lodging now, so come along." They rose and followed him.

The next day the family returned to Tsubaichi, where the Yamato Shrine was situated. By way of expressing their gratitude to the old man, Tagima no Kibito, they presented him with three rolls of Mino silk and bundles of Tsukushi cotton. They pleaded with him to perform *misogi*[3]

---

3. Purification.

rites to ward off future visitations of the devil. He accepted the gifts on behalf of the shrine and distributed them among the priests there, without keeping any for his own use.

"That devil has put you under its spell because you are good looking," he told Toyo-o. "You have been bewitched by the beauty of the temporary abode of that serpent. You must develop a more manly, a more determined spirit, which you now lack, in order to repulse it. By so doing you will not need to rely on my powers to cast off the devil. You must never yield to temptations of passion and lust."

Toyo-o felt as though he had just emerged from a dream, and he thanked the old man profusely for his counsel. To Kanetada, his brother-in-law, he said, "It was due to my wrong thinking that I was subjected to the spell of that serpent for a whole year. I have been remiss in my duties to my parents and my older brother. I can no longer complacently place myself under your roof and favor. I thank you kindly for all you have done for me, and I hope to see you again sometime."

So saying, he left Tsubaichi for his parents' home in Miwagasaki.

14

His parents and his older brother, Taro, on hearing from him about his dreadful experience in Tsubaichi, realized at last that he was in no way to blame for the affair involving Manago and the stolen sword. Pitying him on the one hand, and dreading the evil tenacity of that devil on the other, they decided that they should not let him remain a bachelor any longer and discussed plans to get a wife for him.

At a place called Shiba there lived a petty official named Shōji. Shōji had an only daughter, who was then serving as a lady-in-waiting at the imperial palace in Kyoto. It was said that she would soon be resigning from her work there to return to her father's home in Shiba. Her father thus asked a go-between to call at the Ōya home in Miwagasaki with the proposal that Toyo-o become his son-in-law and live in Shiba. The proposal was immediately accepted as a desirable match.

Tomiko, for such was the girl's name, was sent for. She gladly returned from Kyoto to become Toyo-o's bride. As she was accustomed to the refined manners of court life, there was a glamorous quality in her appearance and behavior; she looked quite beautiful among provincial girls.

Toyo-o, on taking her as his wife, saw that she had pretty eyes and that she was alert, perspicacious, and assiduous about everything. He recalled how he had been bewitched by Manago and remembered one thing and another about their affair. Teasing Tomiko, he told her, "Since you have been accustomed for years to glamorous court life, surely you must find a provincial like me wanting in many respects. One day a general, the next day a minister of state must have made romantic love to you. I feel envious indeed."

Tomiko looked steadily up at him, saying, "In pampering a woman of no distinction like me and forgetting your own glamorous affair, you force me to be even more envious than you."

Though her appearance was different, her words were spoken precisely as Manago, the devil, would have spoken them. It was her voice!

Toyo-o's hair bristled with terror. He was amazed by the tenacity of that devil.

She laughed. "My dear husband, there is nothing strange about all this. Even if you have forgotten your pledge to me, made across the seas and over the mountains, we meet again because it has been predestined. If you continue to believe in the lies of other people and try to avoid me, vengeance is sure to overtake you. No matter how tall the mountains of Kii may be, it is easy for me to spatter your blood from the highest peak to the valley below. And I warn you, don't ever try to do away with yourself."

Toyo-o, shivering from head to toe, felt as though he were about to die. In fact, he was feeling more dead than alive when someone spoke from behind the screen: "Master, how cross you are tonight on this happy occasion!" It was Maroya, the devil's maid.

Again Toyo-o felt his stomach turn. He closed his eyes and dropped face down on the floor. Manago and her maid tried to mollify and threaten him by turns, but he remained deathlike in this prone position out of sheer terror throughout the night.

15

As the day dawned he leaped out of the bedroom and told his father-in-law about the terrible thing that had happened during the night. "Tell me how I can escape from the wrath of that devil," he said. Even while he spoke, he feared the devil might be listening behind him, so he lowered his voice.

Shōji and his wife turned pale. But Shōji said, "There is a priest here from the Kurama Temple in Kyoto, who comes to perform austerities[4] every year. Since yesterday he has been staying at the temple on the hill across from here. He is particularly effective in invoking divine help against such visitations as the plague, specters, and swarms of crop-destroying locusts. He is held in high esteem by the people of this community. Let us ask him to come and help us."

The priest was sent for in a flurry of excitement, and at length he arrived. When the frightful circumstances were explained to him, the priest said with a condescending air, "Don't worry. It is easy to catch such a devil." Thus placated, the people felt less uneasy.

He concocted a magic potion consisting of a plant called yū-ō and water, put the mixture in a pot, and proceeded to the bedroom which had now become the devil's den. As the people excitedly sought hiding places, the priest grinned, saying, "Old people and children, you need not hide yourselves out of fear. Stay where you are. I shall seize this serpent and show it to you."

No sooner had he opened the door of the bedroom than the serpent thrust out its head toward the priest. It filled the entire space as the door opened. Glittering whiter than the whitest snowdrift, its eyes like mirrors, its horns like branches of a huge tree, it opened its three-foot-wide mouth, spat out its crimson-colored tongue, and looked as though it would swallow the priest in a mouthful.

---

4. Renunciations of food and material comforts as forms of self-discipline and religious devotion.

"Oh, how terrible!" cried the priest. He dropped the pot of magical potion then and there and fell to the floor. Unable to rise, he barely succeeded in crawling back. "Frightful! Frightful! This is indeed a profound curse of evil gods," he cried. "How can a stupid priest like me destroy the spell with incantations? Without my hands and feet I could never have come back alive." Then he fainted away.

When the people lifted him up, they found his body red, hot, and blackened, as though they were clutching burning wood, perhaps because of the poison spat out by the serpent. His eyes were blinking, as if he wanted to say something, but his voice failed him. The people dashed cold water on his head to revive him, but he finally died. And the people wept over him as though they themselves had been bewitched.

Thereupon Toyo-o seemed to have regained some control of himself. "If the devil is so tenacious as to be impervious to the incantations of such an exalted priest, then it will continue to pursue me as long as I live," he said. "It is not right that so many people should suffer on my account. I will not rely on the help of others any more. I am prepared to die. So please be at ease."

He then walked toward the bedroom. All the members of the household cried, "Are you mad?" and tried to stop him. But he pretended not to have heard them and, walking serenely to the devil's den, opened the door. There was no sign of disturbance. He found Tomiko seated silently opposite Maroya, the devil's maid.

Tomiko asked in the devil's voice, "What manner of grudge are you holding against me, asking others to put me out of the way? If you persist in trying to eliminate me, I shall be forced to be cruel not only to you but also to all the people of this community. Be happy over my undeviating love for you. And never, never transfer your affection to another woman."

She said this last in a coquettish fashion that was intolerable to Toyo-o.

He replied, "There is a saying that human beings have no intention of hurting the tiger. The tiger, on the other hand, is predisposed to hurt human beings. Just so, with an inhuman spirit you have bewitched me cruelly so many times. What is more, over a trifling matter you have threatened me with dire things. There is the worst kind of evil in you. To pursue me out of love may be normally human, but to inflict cruelty on other people in this household is abominable. I beg of you to spare the life of this Tomiko. Then you may take me wherever you wish."

She nodded happily.

16

Toyo-o went out of the bedroom and told Tomiko's father, Shōji, "Since I am being pursued so relentlessly, it is wrong for me to remain in this house and thereby to bring trouble upon others. With your permission, I shall leave forever. That way Tomiko will be free from further molestation."

Shōji would not hear of it. "I have the blood of samurai in my veins," he said. "It would be shameful on my part to submit to such cowardice, and unfair to your family, the Ōyas. Let us plan a better scheme. . . . Oh yes, in Komatsubara, at the Dōjō Temple, there is a priest called Hokai Oshō who is exalted in the performance of incantations. He is an aged person and rarely goes out of his study, but I am sure he will not forsake us in this crisis."

No sooner had he said this than he leaped upon his horse and galloped away. The venerable priest's temple was situated some distance away, so it was late that night when he reached it. Hokai Oshō came out from the back room to greet Shōji. When the priest heard Shōji's story and appeal for help, he said, "It must be a wretched state of affairs indeed. I am an old man now, so I doubt if there would be any effectiveness in my prayers. But I cannot remain idle when your household is faced with such a calamity. Return to your house quickly. I will follow you directly."

He fetched a priest's surplice[5] stained with burned poppy incense and gave it to Shōji, saying, "Try to beguile the monster and coax it into submission, then cover its head with this sacred surplice, pressing down with all your might. If you don't press it hard enough, the monster might escape. Say your prayers as you do it."

Shōji leaped upon his horse again, and galloped homeward with joy in his heart.

He called Toyo-o aside and gave him the surplice, instructing him, as Hokai Oshō had explained, on how to subdue the devil. Toyo-o hid the surplice in the folds of his robe and entered the bedroom. He told the devil, "Shōji has agreed to let me go, so let us depart together."

Tomiko's body responded by rising, very happily, it seemed. Immediately Toyo-o took out the surplice and covered her head with it, pressing it down with all his might, and she fell to the floor.

"Oh, how painful," she cried out, in a muffled voice. "Why are you tormenting me like this? Please quit pressing me here . . . and here." But Toyo-o kept on pressing her down and covering her with all his strength.

Then Hokai Oshō arrived in a palanquin. Escorted into Shōji's house, he kept mumbling an incantation. He went into the bedroom and, shoving Toyo-o aside, lifted the surplice. A serpent lay coiled atop Tomiko's prone, unconscious body. There was no movement. The priest seized the dead snake and put it into an iron pot carried by the acolyte who had accompanied him. He was still mumbling some incantations when another snake, only a foot long, came slithering up from behind the standing screen. This, too, the priest caught and put into the pot, which he covered tightly with the surplice.

And then he got on his palanquin and returned to his temple. He had a grave dug deep in the temple yard and buried the pot, together with its contents. In this way he sealed forever the chances of the serpent reemerging to bedevil and bewitch human beings. Even now, it is said, the serpent's grave mound may be seen in the temple yard.

The people at the Shōji household meanwhile prayerfully shed tears of gratitude. But Tomiko, as a consequence of her horrible experience, became seriously ill and died. Toyo-o, on the other hand, suffered no ill effects but lived a long and healthy life, it is recorded.

---

5. A loose outer robe, extending to the knees, worn by priests.

Part II

1800 TO 1900

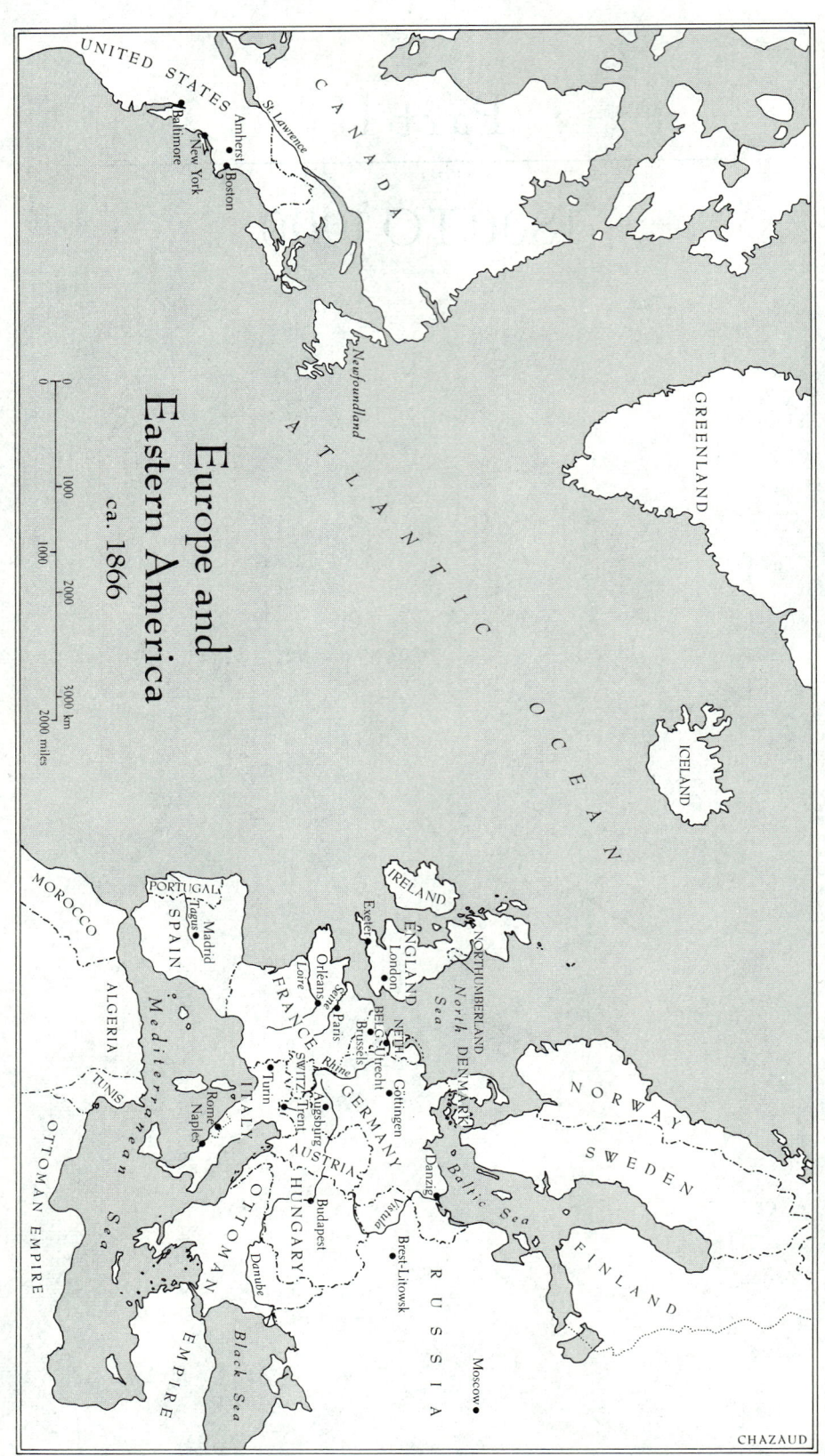

Europe and
Eastern America

ca. 1866

CHAZAUD

Revolution and Romanticism in Europe and America

"Bliss was it in that dawn to be alive, / But to be young was very heaven." William Wordsworth alludes here to his experience, at the age of seventeen, of the French Revolution. The possibility of referring to a national cataclysm in such terms suggests the remarkable shift in sensibility, in dominant assumptions, in intellectual preoccupations, that occurred late in the eighteenth century. We call the evidence of that shift "Romanticism"—a designation so grandly inclusive as to defy definition. If our terms for the late seventeenth and early eighteenth centuries ("Enlightenment," "Age of Reason") emphasize one aspect of the prevailing intellectual culture to the exclusion of others equally important, the label of "Romanticism" refers to so many cultural manifestations that one can hardly pin it down. In general, it implies new emphases on imagination, on feeling, on the value of the primitive and untrammeled, and particularly a narrowing of outlook from the universal to the particular, from humankind or "man" (the subject of Pope's *Essay*) to nation or ethnic group and from the stability of community to the "fulfillment" of the individual. Such shifts have important political and philosophic as well as literary implications.

In the writings of individuals, one finds lines of continuity between the late and early parts of the eighteenth century; but when it comes to generalizations, all the important truths appear to have reversed themselves. In the middle of the century, reason was the guide to certainty; at the century's end, *feeling* tested authenticity. Earlier, tradition still anchored experience; now, the ideal of joyous liberation implied rejection of traditional authority. Wisdom had long associated itself with maturity, even with old age; by the 1790s, William Blake hinted at the child's superior insight, and Wordsworth openly claimed for the infant holy wisdom inevitably lost in the process of aging. Johnson had valued experience as a vital path to knowledge; at the beginning of the nineteenth century, innocence—in its nature evanescent—provided a more generally treasured resource.

Cause and effect, in such massive shifts of perspective, can never be ascertained. The French Revolution derived from new ideas about the sacredness of the individual; it also helped to generate such ideas. Without trying to distinguish causes from effects—indeed, with a strong suspicion that the period's striking phenomena constitute simultaneous causes and effects—one can specify a number of ways that the world appeared to change, as the eighteenth century approached the nineteenth, as well as ways that these changes both solidified themselves and evoked challenges later in the nineteenth century.

NEW AND OLD

The embattled farmers of Concord, Massachusetts, fired the shot heard round the world in 1775; fourteen years later, the Bastille fell. Both the American and the French revolutions developed out of strong convictions about the innate rights of individual human beings—in other words, Protestantism in political form. Those who developed revolutionary theory glimpsed new human possibility. The hope of salvation lay in the overturning of established institutions. Swift, in *Gulliver's Travels*, had made a clear distinction between institutions as ideal constructions of human reason and their corruption in practice. Lawyers might be a money-grubbing, hypocritical lot, but the idea of law, of a social structure designed to ensure the provision of justice, has its own inherent power. The theory of revolution implied radical assault on virtually all social institutions. Fundamental hierarchies of government, notions of sovereignty and of aristocracy, inherited systems of distinction—all fell. Old conventions, once emblems of social and of literary stability, now exemplified the dead hand of the past. Only a few years before, the old, the inherited, and the traditional embodied truth, its power attested by its survival. But the revolutionaries felt themselves to be originators; the newness of what they proposed gave it the almost religious authority suggested by Wordsworth's allusions to "bliss" and "Heaven."

The blessed state evoked by the new political thinkers embodied a sense of infinite possibility. Pope had written, in the *Essay on Man*, "The bliss of Man (could Pride that blessing find) / Is not to act or think beyond mankind." By the century's end, people were doing their best to "think beyond mankind"—or, at any rate, beyond what had been considered normal limitations. Evidence of this abounds, in revolutionary sermons preached from pulpits even in England, in writings by such flamboyant defenders of human rights as Thomas Paine, in the development, even, of a political theory about women's social position. Mary Wollstonecraft was not the first to note the oppression of women; a century before her, Mary Astell had suggested the need for broader female education, and outcries on the subject emerged sporadically even earlier in the seventeenth century. But Wollstonecraft's *Vindication of the Rights of Women* (1792) offered the first detailed argument that the ideal of fulfilled human possibility for men and for women demanded political acknowledgment of women's equality.

The very existence of such a work (which achieved a second edition in the year of its first publication) testifies to the atmosphere of political expectancy in which men and women could rethink "self-evident" principles. Replacing the ideal of hierarchy, for example, was the revolutionary notion of human brotherhood. Liberty, equality, and fraternity, the French proclaimed; the new American nation celebrated essentially the same ideals. In practice, though, "fraternity" turned out to involve the citizens specifically of France or of the new United States. The emphasis on individual uniqueness extended itself to national uniqueness. In America particularly, ideas of national character and of national destiny developed almost talismanic force. Although peace generally prevailed among nations in the early nineteenth century, the developing distinctions dividing one country imaginatively from another foretold future danger.

New ideas with massive practical consequences included more than the political. In 1776, Adam Smith published *The Wealth of Nations*, a theory of laissez-faire economics presaging the enormous importance of money in subsequent history. Matters of exchange and acquisition, Smith argued, could be left to regulate themselves—a doctrine behind which still lurked unobtrusively the confidence, expressed in market terms, that Pope had expressed in religious ones: "All Chance, Direction, which thou canst not see, / All Discord, Harmony, not understood." As manufacturing and trade developed increasing financial vitality, however, their importance as financial resources in fact heightened discord, through growing nationalism. Early in the century, at the end of *Windsor Forest* (1713), Pope had recognized in Britain's trade a form of power. A century later, the acceleration of this power would have astonished Pope. No longer did agriculture provide England's central economic resource. New forms of manufacture provided new substance for trade, generated new fortunes, produced a new social class—a "mid-

dle class" with the influence of wealth and without the inherited system of responsibilities, restrictions, decorums that had helped to control aristocratic possessors
of wealth in preceding generations. Aristocrats had used their money, on the
whole, to enlarge and beautify their estates. The new money-holders developed
new ideas about what money might do. Reinvested, it could support innovation in
manufacture and trade. It could educate the children of the uneducated; it could
buy them (as it had been doing for a century) husbands and wives from the aristocracy; it could help to obviate ancient class distinctions. England's increasing economic ascendancy in the nineteenth century derived not only from new money
but from the development of men and women willing and able to employ money
ingeniously as power.

The enlarged possibilities of manufacture testified to practical applications of
scientific research, another area of activity in which the new overwhelmingly
replaced the old. In England and America especially, inventions multiplied: the
steam engine, the spinning jenny, the cotton gin. Increasingly often, and in
increasing numbers, men and women left their native rural environments to con-
gregate in cities, where opportunities for relatively unskilled workers abounded—
and where more and more people lived in congestion, poverty, and misery.

More vividly, perhaps, than ever before in history, the world was changing—
was becoming, in fact, the world we ourselves assume, in which "mankind" as an
ideal wanes, nations define themselves in psychic as well as military opposition to
one another, money constitutes immediate power, science serves manufacture,
hence commerce. From the beginning of these crucial changes, certain thinkers
and writers realized the destructive possibilities inherent in every form of "progress." Blake, for example, glimpsed London's economic brutality and human
wastefulness; his "revolutionary" impulses expressed themselves partly in resistance
to the consequences of the new. That is to say, the new gave way to the newer, as
it had not previously done on such a scale. No longer did the impulse to conserve
past values express itself with the authority and power that Swift and Johnson had
brought to the theme. As M. H. Abrams has written, "the Romantic period was
eminently an age obsessed with the fact of violent change." Such change might
provide ground for fear; it also supplied the substance for hope.

INDIVIDUALISM

Immanuel Kant (1724–1804), a German philosopher whose work influenced virtually all philosophers after him, questioned the power of reason to provide the
most significant forms of knowledge—knowledge of the ultimately real. Feeling,
on the other hand, might offer a guide. The individual will must engage itself in
ethical struggle to locate and experience the good. Such followers of Kant as
Johann Fichte (1762–1814) more clearly suggested an identification between will
and what we call "ego." The idea of the self took on ever greater importance, for
philosophers and for poets, for political thinkers, autobiographers, and novelists.

To locate authority in the self rather than in society implies yet another radical
break with the assumptions of the previous period. The idea of the self's importance is so familiar to us that it may be difficult to imagine the startling implications of the new focus. "I know the feelings of my heart, and I know men,"
Jean-Jacques Rousseau writes, at the beginning of his *Confessions*. "I am not made
like any of those I have seen; I venture to believe that I am not made like any of
those who are in existence." Earlier thinkers would have felt certain that a man
who could write such words must be mad. Yet faith in the absolute uniqueness of
every consciousness became increasingly prevalent. Rousseau's significance for his
period derives partly from the fact that his stress on the feelings of his heart and
on his own specialness aroused recognition in his audience. No longer did the
universality of human nature supply comfort to individuals; now they might seek

reassurance instead in their uniqueness. It was the ultimate development of Protestantism—to everyone his or her own Church.

Not only could individuals now see themselves as unique, they could also understand themselves as *good*. In its earlier forms, Christianity had emphasized the fallen nature of the human soul. Every self, according to this view, contains the potential for violence and destructiveness. One must rely on God's grace for salvation, which cannot depend on human worth. At the secular level, human beings need institutions to provide the controls that save us from anarchy—from the evil latent in ourselves. Rousseau and his successors articulated the opposite position, stressing the essential goodness of human nature and the corresponding danger of institutional restraint. Repressiveness now became the fearful enemy, uniformity the menace. We may recognize the fear of external control today in the slogans of those celebrating the importance of "individual rights," and we still hear the older faith in institutions in the proponents of "law and order."

The new stress on and interest in the individual implied revaluation of inner as opposed to outer experience. Previously, life in the public arena had been assumed to test human capacities and to provide meaningful forms of experience. After Rousseau, however, psychic experience could provide the proper measure of an individual's emotional capacity. To place value *there* opened the possibility of taking women as seriously as men, children as seriously as adults, "savages" as seriously as civilized beings. Indeed, women, children, and "primitive" peoples were often thought to exceed cultivated adult males in their capacity both to feel and to express their feelings spontaneously—although the social subordination of such groups continued unchanged.

Even before Rousseau, the novel of sensibility in England and on the Continent revealed interest in highly developed emotional responsiveness. Johann Wolfgang von Goethe's *The Sorrows of Young Werther* (1774) made its author famous and inspired a cult of introverted, melancholy young people. In England, Henry Mackenzie's *The Man of Feeling* (1771) associated intense emotion with benevolent action. By the latter part of the century, the Gothic novel had become an important form—a novelistic mode, often practiced by women, that typically placed a young woman at the center of the action. The heroines of such novels confront a kind of experience (usually involving at least apparent supernatural elements) for which their social training, that important resource of earlier heroines, provided no help; instead, quick intuitions and subtle feelings ensure their triumph over apparently insurmountable obstacles with no loss of feminine delicacy.

Given the view of feeling's centrality that replaced the earlier stress on passion's fruitful tension with reason, new kinds of feeling drew literary attention. From its beginnings (*The Princess of Clèves* is an early example), the novel had tended to emphasize (usually in decorous terms) love between the sexes. Now romantic love became a central subject of poetry and drama as well. More surprising kinds of emotion also attracted literary attention. William Blake imagined a chimney sweep's emotional relation to the idea of heaven; Samuel Taylor Coleridge and Percy Bysshe Shelley made poetry of dejection; Alfred, Lord Tennyson, at the midpoint of the nineteenth century, wove his anxieties about the revelations of recent scientific inquiry into the texture of an elegiac poem. As these examples indicate, painful as well as pleasurable emotion interested readers and writers. The poet, Wordsworth said, is a man speaking to other men; poetry originates in recollected emotion and recapitulates lost feeling. Lyric, not epic, typifies poetry for Wordsworth, who understands his genre as a form of emotional communication.

Wordsworth's definition ignores the fact that women, too (including his own sister, Dorothy), wrote poetry. Emily Brontë, Christina Rossetti, Elizabeth Barrett

Browning, Emily Dickinson—all evoked intense passion in verse. In the Romantic novel, too, women excelled in the rendering of powerful feeling. The Brontë sisters, like George Eliot after them in England, like the equally passionate George Sand in France, wrote under male pseudonyms but established distinctively female visions of the struggle not only for love but also for freedom and power within a context of social restriction. Mary Shelley (daughter of Mary Wollstonecraft and married to the poet Shelley) in her eloquent fable of creativity, *Frankenstein* (1818), epitomizes the peculiar intensity of much women's writing in this period.

As the nineteenth century wore on, hope for a new terrestrial Eden faded. The efflorescence of commerce and the innovations of science turned out to have negative as well as positive consequences. As the novels of Charles Dickens and of William Thackeray insist, the new middle class frequently became the repository of moral mediocrity. The autocracy of money had effects more brutal than those of inherited privilege. Science, once the emblem of progress, began to generate theological confusion. Charles Darwin's *Origin of Species* (1859) stated clearly humanity's mean rather than transcendent origins: animal and plant species had evolved over the centuries, adapting themselves to their environment by the process of natural selection. Fossils found in rocks provided supporting evidence for this theory—an assertion troubling to many Christians because it contradicted the biblical account of Creation. Five years after Darwin's revolutionary work, Karl Marx published *Das Kapital*, with its dialectical theory of history and its vision of capitalism's eventual decay and of the working class inevitably triumphant. In the United States civil war raged from 1860 to 1865, its central issue the morality of slavery—that by-product of agricultural capitalism. Neither the making of money nor the effort to fathom natural law seemed merely reassuring.

In the face of history's threats—the menace of Marx's prophecy and of Darwin's biology, the chaos of civil war—to insist on the importance of private experience offered tentative security, a standing place, a temporary source of authority. The voices of blacks as well as, in increasing numbers, of women could now be heard: placing high value on the personal implied respecting all persons. The American Civil War made African-Americans for the first time truly visible to the society that both contained and denied them. Slave narratives—sometimes wholly or partly fictionized, sometimes entirely authentic renditions of often horrifying experience—provided useful propaganda for the abolitionist cause, the ideology opposed to the institution of slavery. They also opened a new emotional universe. In their typical emphasis, for instance, on the salvationary force of reading and writing (for most slaves officially forbidden knowledge), these narratives illuminated a new area of the taken-for-granted, thus extending the enterprise of Romantic poetry.

The capacity for revelatory illumination belonged, according to the dominant nineteenth-century view, to imagination, a mysterious and virtually sacred power of individual consciousness. When Samuel Johnson, in *Rasselas*, suggested that all predominance of imagination over reason constituted a degree of insanity, he intended, to put it crudely, an antithesis of true and false. Imagination, the faculty of generating images, had no necessary anchor in the communal, historical experience that tested truth. For Wordsworth and Coleridge and those who came after them, imagination was a visionary and unifying force (a new incarnation of the seventeenth century's inner light or candle of the Lord) through which the gifted person discovered and communicated new truth. As Coleridge wrote,

> from the soul itself must issue forth
> A light, a glory, a fair luminous cloud
> Enveloping the Earth—

Imagination derives from the soul, the aspect of human being that links the human with the eternal. Through it, men and women can transcend earthly limitations, can express high aspiration, can escape, and help one another escape, the dreariness of mortality without necessarily positing a life beyond the present one.

A corollary of the high value attached to creative imagination was a new concern with originality. The notion of "the genius," the man or woman so gifted as to operate by principles unknown to ordinary mortals, developed only in the late eighteenth century. Previously, a person *had* rather than *was* a genius: the term designated a particular tendency or gift (a genius for cooking, say) rather than a human being with vast creative power. Now the genius was revered for his or her extraordinary difference from others, idealized as a being set apart; and the literary or artistic products of genius, it could be assumed, would correspondingly differ from everything previously produced. Newness itself became as never before a measure of value. The language, the themes, the forms of the preceding century would no longer suffice. In the early eighteenth century, literary figures wishing to congratulate themselves and their contemporaries would compare their artistic situation to that of Rome under the benevolent patronage of Augustus Caesar. A hundred years later, the note of self-congratulation would express itself in the claim of an unprecedented situation, unprecedented kinds of accomplishment. John Keats, in a letter, characterized Wordsworth as representing "the egotistical sublime." Such sublimity—authority and grandeur emanating from a unique self still in touch with something beyond itself—was the nineteenth century's special achievement.

NATURE

Nature and nature's laws, the rationally ordered universe, provided the foundation for much early eighteenth-century thought. In the nineteenth century, nature's importance possibly increased—but *nature* now meant something new. *Wuthering Heights* (1847) creates a setting of windswept moors for its romantic lovers—both environment and metaphor of their love. Wordsworth could value a host of daffodils or fog-enveloped hills or an icy lake. The physical reality of the natural world, in its varied abundance, became a matter of absorbing interest for poets and novelists. Nature provided an alternative to the human, a possibility for imaginative as well as literal escape. Its imagery—flowers, clouds, ocean—became the common poetic stock. Workers still hastened from the country to the city, because the city housed possibilities of wealth; yet educated men and women increasingly declared their nostalgia for rural or sylvan landscapes embodying peace and beauty.

Nature, in the nineteenth-century mind, however, did not consist only in physical details. It also implied a totality, an enveloping whole greater than the sum of its parts, a vast unifying spirit. Wordsworth evokes

> a sense sublime
> Of something far more deeply interfused,
> Whose dwelling is the light of setting suns,
> And the round ocean and the living air,
> And the blue sky, and in the mind of man:
> A motion and a spirit, that impels
> All thinking things, all objects of all thought,
> And rolls through all things.

Coleridge and Shelley hint similar visions, vague yet comforting. The unifying whole, as Wordsworth's language suggests, depends less on rational system than on emotional association. Human beings link themselves with the infinite by what Wordsworth elsewhere terms "wise passiveness," the capacity to submit to feeling and be led by it to transcendence. Natural detail, too, acquires value by evoking and symbolizing emotion. Nature belongs to the realm of the nonrational, the superrational.

The idea of the natural can also imply the uncivilized, or precivilized. Philosophers have differed dramatically in their hypotheses about what humankind was like in its "natural" state. Thomas Hobbes, in the seventeenth century, argued that the natural human condition was one of conflict. Society developed to curb the violent impulses human beings would manifest without its restraint. The prevailing nineteenth-century view, on the other hand, made civilization the agent of corruption. Rousseau expounded the crippling effect of institutions. The child raised with the greatest possible freedom, he maintained, would develop in more admirable ways than one subjected to system. By the second half of the eighteenth century, a French novelist could contrast the decadent life of Europe unfavorably with existence on an unspoiled island (Bernardin de Saint-Pierre, *Paul and Virginia*, 1788); Thomas Chatterton, before committing suicide in 1770 at the age of eighteen, wrote poems rich in nostalgia for a more primitive stage of social development which he tried to pass off as medieval works; the forged Ossian poems (1760–63) of James Macpherson, purportedly ancient texts, attracted a large and enthusiastic audience. New interest manifested itself in ballads, poetic survivals of the primitive; Romantic poets imitated the form. The interest in a simpler past, a simpler life, continued throughout the nineteenth century: in Victorian England, Tennyson recast Arthurian legend in modern verse; the Pre-Raphaelites evoked the medieval in visual and verbal arts.

The revolutionary fervor of the late eighteenth century had generated a vision of infinite human possibility, political and personal. The escapist implications of the increasing emphasis on nature, the primitive, the uncomplicated past, suggest, however, a sense of alienation. Blake, Wordsworth, Shelley, all wrote poems of social protest. "Society" would not help the individual work out his or her salvation; on the contrary, it embodied forces opposed to individual development. Indeed, the word *society* had come to embody the impulses that desecrated nature and oppressed the poor in the interests of industry and "progress." Melancholy marked the Romantic hero (Lord Byron in his poetic self-manifestations; Heathcliff in fiction, for example) and tinged nineteenth-century poetry and fiction. The satiric spirit—that spirit of social reform—was in abeyance. Hope lay in the individual's separation from, not participation in, society. In the woods and mountains, one might feel free.

The Waste Land (1922), T. S. Eliot's twentieth-century epic, contains the line, "In the mountains, there you feel free," a line given complex ironic overtones by its context. Its occurrence, however, may remind us how powerfully ideas that came into currency in the late eighteenth and early nineteenth centuries survive into our own time. The world of the Romantic period specifically prefigures our own, despite all the differences dividing the two cultures. We have developed more fully important Romantic tendencies: stress on the sacredness of the individual, suspicion of social institutions, belief in expressed feeling as the sign of authenticity, nostalgia for simpler ways of being, faith in genius, valuing of originality and imagination, an ambivalent relation to science. Although Wordsworth and Dickinson and Melville employ vocabularies and use references partly strange to us, they speak directly to the preoccupations of our time. By attending closely to them, we may learn more about ourselves: not only in the common humanity that we share with all our predecessors but in our special historical situation as both direct heirs of nineteenth-century assumptions and rebels against them.

FURTHER READING

Useful introductions to the Romantic period include L. Furst, *Romanticism in Perspective: A Comparative Study of Aspects of the Romantic Movements in*

England, France, and Germany (1979); R. F. Gleckner and G. E. Enscoe, eds., *Romanticism: Points of View* (1962), a collection of essays by various contributors; R. W. Harris, *Romanticism and the Social Order, 1780–1830* (1969); and M. Butler, *Romantics, Rebels, and Reactionaries: English Literature and Its Background, 1760–1830* (1982). On French Romanticism, see P. T. Comeau, *Diehards and Innovators: The French Romantic Struggle, 1800–1830* (1988); on Germany, T. Ziolkowski, *German Romanticism and Its Institutions* (1990); on English and American developments, B. Taylor, R. Bain, and M. H. Abrams, *The Cast of Consciousness: Concepts of the Mind in British and American Romanticism* (1987); on the English and German situation, C. Jacobs, *Uncontainable Romanticism* (1989).

TIMELINE

TEXTS	CONTEXTS
1781–1788 Jean-Jacques Rousseau, ***Confessions***	
1794 William Blake, ***Songs of Innocence and Experience***	
1798 William Wordsworth and Samuel Taylor Coleridge, ***Lyrical Ballads***	
	1801 United Kingdom of Great Britain (England and Scotland) and Ireland established
1802 Coleridge, ***Dejection: An Ode*** • François René, Vicomte de Chateaubriand, *René*	
	1803 President Thomas Jefferson purchases French "Louisiana"
	1804 Napoleon crowned emperor of France
1808 Johann Wolfgang von Goethe, ***Faust, Part I*** (*Part II*, 1832)	
1812–1870 Charles Dickens, English novelist	
	1815 Battle of Waterloo, ending Napoleon's career
1816 Coleridge, ***Kubla Khan*** • John Keats, ***On First Looking into Chapman's Homer***	
1818–1820 Lyrics by Percy Bysshe Shelley and John Keats	
1827 Heinrich Heine, ***Book of Songs***	
1828 Victor Hugo, ***Odes and Ballads***	
	1831 Invention of chloroform inaugurates a new medical era
1834 Alexander Sergeyevich Pushkin, ***The Queen of Spades***	
1837 Giacomo Leopardi, ***The Broom***	**1837** Victoria crowned queen of the United Kingdom

TIMELINE

TEXTS	CONTEXTS
1842 Alfred, Lord Tennyson, *Ulysses*	
1845 Frederick Douglass, *Narrative of the Life of Frederick Douglass, An American Slave*	
1847 Charlotte Brontë, *Jane Eyre* • Emily Brontë, *Wuthering Heights*	
	1848 Karl Marx and Friedrich Engels, *Communist Manifesto* • Revolutions in France, Italy, Austria, Prague • Gold discovered in California
1850 Alfred, Lord Tennyson, *In Memoriam A. H. H.*	
1842–1855 Robert Browning writes poems, including *"Childe Roland to the Dark Tower Came"*	
1855 Walt Whitman, *Song of Myself*	
	1859 Charles Darwin's *Origin of Species*, presenting his theory of evolution
	1861 Serfs emancipated in Russia • Beginning of American Civil War
	1863 Universal emancipation of slaves in the United States
	1864 Louis Pasteur, who formulated germ theory of infection, invents pasteurization
	1865 American Civil War ends • President Abraham Lincoln assassinated
	1867 Karl Marx, *Capital*
	1876 Alexander Graham Bell invents the telephone
1890 Emily Dickinson, *Poems,* published posthumously	
1891 Herman Melville leaves manuscript of *Billy Budd, Sailor* at his death; not published until 1924	
	1894 X-rays discovered by Bavarian physicist Wilhelm Röentgen

JEAN-JACQUES ROUSSEAU
1712–1778

It would be difficult to overstate the historical importance of Jean-Jacques Rousseau's *Confessions* (composed between 1765 and 1770, published 1781–88), which inaugurated a new form of autobiography and suggested new ways of thinking about the self and its relation to other selves. Even for readers two centuries after its first publication, the book's sheer audacity compels attention, demanding that we rethink easy assumptions about important and trivial, right and wrong.

The facts of Rousseau's life are not altogether clear, partly because the *Confessions*, despite its claim of absolute truthfulness, sometimes appears more concerned to create a self-justifying story than to confine itself strictly to actuality. The son of a Geneva watchmaker, Rousseau left home in his teens and lived for some time with Françoise-Louise de Warens, his protector and eventually his mistress, the "mamma" of the *Confessions*. He worked at many occupations, from secretary to government official (under the king of Sardinia). In Paris, where he settled in 1745, he lived with Thérèse le Vasseur; he claims she bore him five children, all consigned to an orphanage, but the claim has never been substantiated (or, for that matter, disproved). At various times his controversial writing forced Rousseau to leave France, usually for Switzerland; in 1766 he went to England as the guest of the philosopher David Hume. He was allowed to return to Paris in 1770 only on condition that he write nothing against the government or the Church.

Rousseau's social ideas, elaborated in his didactic novels *Julie, or the New Heloise* (1761) and *Émile* (1762) as well as in his autobiographical writings and political treatises (for example, *The Social Contract*, 1762), stirred much contemporary discussion. He believed in the destructiveness of institutions, the gradual corruption of humankind throughout history, the importance of nature and of feeling in individual development and consequently in society. Also knowledgeable about music (he worked for a time as music teacher), he published several works on the subject, including a musical dictionary as well as a comic opera, *The Village Soothsayer* (1752).

The *Confessions* presents its subject as a man (and boy) striving always to express natural impulses and recurrently frustrated by society's demands and assumptions. The central figure described here rather resembles Candide in his naïveté and good feeling. Experience chastens him less than it does Candide, however, although he reports many psychic hard knocks. For Voltaire's didactic purposes, his character's experience was more important than his personality; for Rousseau, his own nature has much more significance than anything that happens to him.

To read even a few pages of the work reveals how completely Rousseau exemplifies several of his period's dominant values. He describes himself as a being of powerful passions but confused ideas, he makes feeling the guide of conduct, he glorifies imagination and romantic love, he believes the common people morally superior to the upper classes. The emphasis on imagination and passion for him seems not a matter of ideology but of experience: life presents itself to him in this way. The fact emphasizes the degree to which the movement we call Romanticism involved genuine re-vision. Everything looked different in the late eighteenth century, everything demanded categories changed from those previously accepted without question. The new way of looking at the world that characterizes the Romantic movement, inasmuch as it implies valuing the inner life of emotion and fancy for its own sake (not for the sake of any insight it might provide), always includes the danger of narcissism, a kind of concentration on the self that shuts out awareness of the reality and integrity of others. Rousseau, in the *Confessions*, vividly expresses the narcissistic side of Romanticism.

Implicit in Rousseau's ways of understanding himself and his life are new moral assumptions as well. Honesty of a particular kind becomes the highest value; however disreputable his behavior, Rousseau can feel comfortable about it because he reports it accurately. What Johnson or Pope would see as self-indulgence, care exclusively for one's own pleasure, seems acceptable to Rousseau because of the minute, exacting attention devoted to it. The autobiographer examines each nuance of his own happiness, as if to know it fully constituted moral achievement. To take the self this seriously as subject—not in relation to a progress of education or of salvation, merely in its moment-to-moment being—implies belief in self-knowledge (knowledge of feeling, thought, action) as a high moral achievement. This is not the slowly achieved, arduous discipline recommended by Socrates but a somewhat more indulgent form of self-contemplation. To connect it, as Rousseau does, with morality conveys the view that self-absorption without self-judgment provides valuable and sufficient insight.

In his presentation of self, Rousseau contrasts vividly with his great predecessor, Montaigne. Rousseau insists on his uniqueness: "I am not made like any of those I have seen; I venture to believe that I am not made like any of those who are in existence." He presents himself for the reader's contemplation as a remarkable phenomenon. Montaigne, on the other hand, reminds us constantly of what author and reader (and humankind in general) have in common. "Not only does the wind of accidents stir me according to its blowing, but I am also stirred and troubled by the instability of my attitude; and he who examines himself closely will seldom find himself twice in the same state." The movement within the sentence from *I* to the universalizing *he* characterizes a more outward-looking mode.

It must be said, however, that the intensity of Rousseau's self-concentration makes his subject compelling for others as well. However distasteful one might find his obsessive focus, it is difficult to stop reading. The writer hints—makes us believe—that he will reveal all secrets about himself; and learning such secrets, despite Rousseau's insistence on his own uniqueness, tells us of human weakness, inconsistency, power, scope—tells us, therefore, something of ourselves.

F. C. Green, *Jean-Jacques Rousseau: A Critical Study of His Life and Writings* (1955), provides biography and criticism. I. Babbitt, *Rousseau and Romanticism* (1919), examines the relation of Rousseau's assumptions to those of the Romantic movement. A thorough modern evaluation of Rousseau's achievement is L. G. Crocker, *Jean-Jacques Rousseau: A New Interpretative Analysis of His Works* (1973). More directly focused on the *Confessions* is H. Williams, *Rousseau and Romantic Autobiography* (1983). Recent studies include T. M. Kavanagh, *Writing the Truth: Authority and Desire in the Works of Rousseau* (1987), and C. Kelly, *Rousseau's Exemplary Life: The Confessions as Political Philosophy* (1987). A collection of essays by various authors is H. Bloom, ed., *Jean-Jacques Rousseau* (1988).

PRONOUNCING GLOSSARY

The following list uses common English syllables and stress accents to provide rough equivalents of selected words whose pronunciation may be unfamiliar to the general reader.

de Vulson: *du vyu-saw'*

de Warens: *du vah-rahnh'*

Jean-Jacques Rousseau: *jahnh-jahk roo-soh'*

Lausanne: *loh-zahn'*

Montaigne: *mon-tenh'*

Nyon: *nee-yawnh'*

Saone: *sohn*

St. Marceau: *sanh mahr-soh'*   Vaud: *voh*

Turin: *too-ranh'*   Vévay: *vay-vay'*

From Confessions

Part I

BOOK I

[*The Years 1712–1719*]

I am commencing an undertaking, hitherto without precedent, and
which will never find an imitator. I desire to set before my fellows the
likeness of a man in all the truth of nature, and that man myself.

Myself alone! I know the feelings of my heart, and I know men. I am
not made like any of those I have seen; I venture to believe that I am not
made like any of those who are in existence. If I am not better, at least I
am different. Whether Nature has acted rightly or wrongly in destroying
the mould in which she cast me, can only be decided after I have been
read.

Let the trumpet of the Day of Judgment sound when it will, I will
present myself before the Sovereign Judge with this book in my hand. I
will say boldly: "This is what I have done, what I have thought, what I was.
I have told the good and the bad with equal frankness. I have neither
omitted anything bad, nor interpolated anything good. If I have occasionally made use of some immaterial embellishments, this has only been in
order to fill a gap caused by lack of memory. I may have assumed the truth
of that which I knew might have been true, never of that which I knew to
be false. I have shown myself as I was: mean and contemptible, good,
high-minded and sublime, according as I was one or the other. I have
unveiled my inmost self even as Thou hast seen it, O Eternal Being.
Gather round me the countless host of my fellow-men; let them hear my
confessions, lament for my unworthiness, and blush for my imperfections.
Then let each of them in turn reveal, with the same frankness, the secrets
of his heart at the foot of the Throne, and say, if he dare, '*I was better than
that man!*' " * * *

I felt before I thought: this is the common lot of humanity. I experienced it more than others. I do not know what I did until I was five or six
years old. I do not know how I learned to read; I only remember my
earliest reading, and the effect it had upon me; from that time I date
my uninterrupted self-consciousness. My mother had left some romances
behind her, which my father and I began to read after supper. At first it
was only a question of practising me in reading by the aid of amusing
books; but soon the interest became so lively, that we used to read in turns
without stopping, and spent whole nights in this occupation. We were
unable to leave off until the volume was finished. Sometimes, my father,
hearing the swallows begin to twitter in the early morning, would say,
quite ashamed, "Let us go to bed; I am more of a child than yourself."

In a short time I acquired, by this dangerous method, not only extreme facility in reading and understanding what I read, but a knowledge of the passions that was unique in a child of my age. I had no idea of things in themselves, although all the feelings of actual life were already known to me. I had conceived nothing, but felt everything. These confused emotions which I felt one after the other, certainly did not warp the reasoning powers which I did not as yet possess; but they shaped them in me of a peculiar stamp, and gave me odd and romantic notions of human life, of which experience and reflection have never been able wholly to cure me. * * *

How could I become wicked, when I had nothing but examples of gentleness before my eyes, and none around me but the best people in the world? My father, my aunt, my nurse, my relations, our friends, our neighbours, all who surrounded me, did not, it is true, obey me, but they loved me; and I loved them in return. My wishes were so little excited and so little opposed, that it did not occur to me to have any. I can swear that, until I served under a master, I never knew what a fancy was. Except during the time I spent in reading or writing in my father's company, or when my nurse took me for a walk, I was always with my aunt, sitting or standing by her side, watching her at her embroidery or listening to her singing; and I was content. Her cheerfulness, her gentleness and her pleasant face have stamped so deep and lively an impression on my mind that I can still see her manner, look, and attitude; I remember her affectionate language: I could describe what clothes she wore and how her head was dressed, not forgetting the two little curls of black hair on her temples, which she wore in accordance with the fashion of the time.

I am convinced that it is to her I owe the taste, or rather passion, for music, which only became fully developed in me a long time afterwards. She knew a prodigious number of tunes and songs which she used to sing in a very thin, gentle voice. This excellent woman's cheerfulness of soul banished dreaminess and melancholy from herself and all around her. The attraction which her singing possessed for me was so great, that not only have several of her songs always remained in my memory, but even now, when I have lost her, and as I grow older, many of them, totally forgotten since the days of my childhood, return to my mind with inexpressible charm. Would anyone believe that I, an old dotard, eaten up by cares and troubles, sometimes find myself weeping like a child, when I mumble one of those little airs in a voice already broken and trembling?

* * * I have spent my life in idle longing, without saying a word, in the presence of those whom I loved most. Too bashful to declare my taste, I at least satisfied it in situations which had reference to it and kept up the idea of it. To lie at the feet of an imperious mistress, to obey her commands, to ask her forgiveness—this was for me a sweet enjoyment; and, the more my lively imagination heated my blood, the more I presented the appearance of a bashful lover. It may be easily imagined that this manner of making love does not lead to very speedy results, and is not very dangerous to the virtue of those who are its object. For this reason I have rarely possessed, but have none the less enjoyed myself in my own way— that is to say, in imagination. Thus it has happened that my senses, in harmony with my timid disposition and my romantic spirit, have kept my

sentiments pure and my morals blameless, owing to the very tastes which, combined with a little more impudence, might have plunged me into the most brutal sensuality. * * *

I am a man of very strong passions, and, while I am stirred by them, nothing can equal my impetuosity; I forget all discretion, all feelings of respect, fear and decency; I am cynical, impudent, violent and fearless; no feeling of shame keeps me back, no danger frightens me; with the exception of the single object which occupies my thoughts, the universe is nothing to me. But all this lasts only for a moment, and the following moment plunges me into complete annihilation. In my calmer moments I am indolence and timidity itself; everything frightens and discourages me; a fly, buzzing past, alarms me; a word which I have to say, a gesture which I have to make, terrifies my idleness; fear and shame overpower me to such an extent that I would gladly hide myself from the sight of my fellow-creatures. If I have to act, I do not know what to do; if I have to speak, I do not know what to say; if anyone looks at me, I am put out of countenance. When I am strongly moved I sometimes know how to find the right words, but in ordinary conversation I can find absolutely nothing, and my condition is unbearable for the simple reason that I am obliged to speak.

Add to this, that none of my prevailing tastes centre in things that can be bought. I want nothing but unadulterated pleasures, and money poisons all. For instance, I am fond of the pleasures of the table; but, as I cannot endure either the constraint of good society or the drunkenness of the tavern, I can only enjoy them with a friend; alone, I cannot do so, for my imagination then occupies itself with other things, and eating affords me no pleasure. If my heated blood longs for women, my excited heart longs still more for affection. Women who could be bought for money would lose for me all their charms; I even doubt whether it would be in me to make use of them. I find it the same with all pleasures within my reach; unless they cost me nothing, I find them insipid. I only love those enjoyments which belong to no one but the first man who knows how to enjoy them.

* * * I worship freedom; I abhor restraint, trouble, dependence. As long as the money in my purse lasts, it assures my independence; it relieves me of the trouble of finding expedients to replenish it, a necessity which always inspired me with dread; but the fear of seeing it exhausted makes me hoard it carefully. The money which a man possesses is the instrument of freedom; that which we eagerly pursue is the instrument of slavery. Therefore I hold fast to that which I have, and desire nothing.

My disinterestedness is, therefore, nothing but idleness; the pleasure of possession is not worth the trouble of acquisition. In like manner, my extravagance is nothing but idleness; when the opportunity of spending agreeably presents itself, it cannot be too profitably employed. Money tempts me less than things, because between money and the possession of the desired object there is always an intermediary, whereas between the thing itself and the enjoyment of it there is none. If I see the thing, it tempts me; if I only see the means of gaining possession of it, it does not. For this reason I have committed thefts, and even now I sometimes pilfer trifles which tempt me, and which I prefer to take rather than to ask for;

but neither when a child nor a grown-up man do I ever remember to have robbed anyone of a farthing, except on one occasion, fifteen years ago, when I stole seven *livres* ten *sous.*

*   *   *

BOOK II

[*The Years 1728–1731*]

* * * I have drawn the great moral lesson, perhaps the only one of any practical value, to avoid those situations of life which bring our duties into conflict with our interests, and which show us our own advantage in the misfortunes of others; for it is certain that, in such situations, however sincere our love of virtue, we must, sooner or later, inevitably grow weak without perceiving it, and become unjust and wicked in act, without having ceased to be just and good in our hearts.

This principle, deeply imprinted on the bottom of my heart, which, although somewhat late, in practice guided my whole conduct, is one of those which have caused me to appear a very strange and foolish creature in the eyes of the world, and, above all, amongst my acquaintances. I have been reproached with wanting to pose as an original, and different from others. In reality, I have never troubled about acting like other people or differently from them. I sincerely desired to do what was right. I withdrew, as far as it lay in my power, from situations which opposed my interests to those of others, and might, consequently, inspire me with a secret, though involuntary, desire of injuring them.

* * * I loved too sincerely, too completely, I venture to say, to be able to be happy easily. Never have passions been at once more lively and purer than mine; never has love been tenderer, truer, more disinterested. I would have sacrificed my happiness a thousand times for that of the person whom I loved; her reputation was dearer to me than my life, and I would never have wished to endanger her repose for a single moment for all the pleasures of enjoyment. This feeling has made me employ such carefulness, such secrecy, and such precaution in my undertakings, that none of them have ever been successful. My want of success with women has always been caused by my excessive love for them.

*   *   *

BOOK III

[*The Years 1731–1732*]

* * * I only felt the full strength of my attachment when I no longer saw her.[1] When I saw her, I was only content; but, during her absence, my restlessness became painful. The need of living with her caused me outbreaks of tenderness which often ended in tears. I shall never forget how, on the day of a great festival, while she was at vespers, I went for a walk outside the town, my heart full of her image and a burning desire to spend my life with her. I had sense enough to see that at present this was

---

1. Rousseau refers here to Françoise-Louise de Warens, whom he also calls "mamma."

impossible, and that the happiness which I enjoyed so deeply could only be short. This gave to my reflections a tinge of melancholy, about which, however, there was nothing gloomy, and which was tempered by flattering hopes. The sound of the bells, which always singularly affects me, the song of the birds, the beauty of the daylight, the enchanting landscape, the scattered country dwellings in which my fancy placed our common home—all these produced upon me an impression so vivid, tender, melancholy and touching, that I saw myself transported, as it were, in ecstasy, into that happy time and place, wherein my heart, possessing all the happiness it could desire, tasted it with inexpressible rapture, without even a thought of sensual pleasure. I never remember to have plunged into the future with greater force and illusion than on that occasion; and what has struck me most in the recollection of this dream after it had been realised, is that I have found things again exactly as I had imagined them. If ever the dream of a man awake resembled a prophetic vision, it was assuredly that dream of mine. I was only deceived in the imaginary duration; for the days, the years, and our whole life were spent in serene and undisturbed tranquillity, whereas in reality it lasted only for a moment. Alas! my most lasting happiness belongs to a dream, the fulfilment of which was almost immediately followed by the awakening. * * *

Two things, almost incompatible, are united in me in a manner which I am unable to understand: a very ardent temperament, lively and tumultuous passions, and, at the same time, slowly developed and confused ideas, which never present themselves until it is too late. One might say that my heart and my mind do not belong to the same person. Feeling takes possession of my soul more rapidly than a flash of lightning; but, instead of illuminating, inflames and dazzles me. I feel everything and see nothing. I am carried away by my passions, but stupid; in order to think, I must be cool. The astonishing thing is that, notwithstanding, I exhibit tolerably sound judgment, penetration, even finesse, if I am not hurried; with sufficient leisure I can compose excellent impromptus; but I have never said or done anything worthy of notice on the spur of the moment. I could carry on a very clever conversation through the post, as the Spaniards are said to carry on a game of chess. When I read of that Duke of Savoy, who turned round on his journey, in order to cry, "At your throat, Parisian huckster," I said, "There you have myself!"

This sluggishness of thought, combined with such liveliness of feeling, not only enters into my conversation, but I feel it even when alone and at work. My ideas arrange themselves in my head with almost incredible difficulty; they circulate in it with uncertain sound, and ferment till they excite and heat me, and make my heart beat fast; and, in the midst of this excitement, I see nothing clearly and am unable to write a single word—I am obliged to wait. Imperceptibly this great agitation subsides, the confusion clears up, everything takes its proper place, but slowly, and only after a period of long and confused agitation.

*   *   *

BOOK IV

[The Years 1731–1732]

* * * I returned, not to Nyon, but to Lausanne. I wanted to sate myself with the sight of this beautiful lake, which is there seen in its greatest extent. Few of the secret motives which have determined me to act have been more rational. Things seen at a distance are rarely powerful enough to make me act. The uncertainty of the future has always made me look upon plans, which need considerable time to carry them out, as decoys for fools. I indulge in hopes like others, provided it costs me nothing to support them; but if they require continued attention, I have done with it. The least trifling pleasure which is within my reach tempts me more than the joys of Paradise. However, I make an exception of the pleasure which is followed by pain; this has no temptation for me, because I love only pure enjoyments, and these a man never has when he knows that he is preparing for himself repentance and regret. * * *

Why is it that, having found so many good people in my youth, I find so few in my later years? Is their race extinct? No; but the class in which I am obliged to look for them now, is no longer the same as that in which I found them. Among the people, where great passions only speak at intervals, the sentiments of nature make themselves more frequently heard; in the higher ranks they are absolutely stifled, and, under the mask of sentiment, it is only interest or vanity that speaks.

* * * Whenever I approach the Canton of Vaud, I am conscious of an impression in which the remembrance of Madame de Warens, who was born there, of my father who lived there, of Mademoiselle de Vulson who enjoyed the first fruits of my youthful love, of several pleasure trips which I made there when a child and, I believe, some other exciting cause, more mysterious and more powerful than all this, is combined. When the burning desire of this happy and peaceful life, which flees from me and for which I was born, inflames my imagination, it is always the Canton of Vaud, near the lake, in the midst of enchanting scenery, to which it draws me. I feel that I must have an orchard on the shore of this lake and no other, that I must have a loyal friend, a loving wife, a cow, and a little boat. I shall never enjoy perfect happiness on earth until I have all that. I laugh at the simplicity with which I have several times visited this country merely in search of this imaginary happiness. I was always surprised to find its inhabitants, especially the women, of quite a different character from that which I expected. How contradictory it appeared to me! The country and its inhabitants have never seemed to me made for each other.

During this journey to Vévay, walking along the beautiful shore, I abandoned myself to the sweetest melancholy. My heart eagerly flung itself into a thousand innocent raptures; I was filled with emotion, I sighed and wept like a child. How often have I stopped to weep to my heart's content, and, sitting on a large stone, amused myself with looking at my tears falling into the water! * * *

How greatly did the entrance into Paris belie the idea I had formed of it! The external decorations of Turin, the beauty of its streets, the symmetry and regularity of the houses, had made me look for something quite different in Paris. I had imagined to myself a city of most imposing aspect, as beautiful as it was large, where nothing was to be seen but splendid streets and palaces of gold and marble. Entering by the suburb of St. Marceau, I saw nothing but dirty and stinking little streets, ugly black houses, a general air of slovenliness and poverty, beggars, carters, menders of old clothes, criers of decoctions and old hats. All this, from the outset, struck me so forcibly, that all the real magnificence I have since seen in Paris has been unable to destroy this first impression, and I have always retained a secret dislike against residence in this capital. I may say that the whole time, during which I afterwards lived there, was employed solely in trying to find means to enable me to live away from it.

Such is the fruit of a too lively imagination, which exaggerates beyond human exaggeration, and is always ready to see more than it has been told to expect. I had heard Paris so much praised, that I had represented it to myself as the ancient Babylon, where, if I had ever visited it, I should, perhaps, have found as much to take off from the picture which I had drawn of it. The same thing happened to me at the Opera, whither I hastened to go the day after my arrival. The same thing happened to me later at Versailles; and again, when I saw the sea for the first time; and the same thing will always happen to me, when I see anything which has been too loudly announced; for it is impossible for men, and difficult for Nature herself, to surpass the exuberance of my imagination.

* * * The sight of the country, a succession of pleasant views, the open air, a good appetite, the sound health which walking gives me, the free life of the inns, the absence of all that makes me conscious of my dependent position, of all that reminds me of my condition—all this sets my soul free, gives me greater boldness of thought, throws me, so to speak, into the immensity of things, so that I can combine, select, and appropriate them at pleasure, without fear or restraint. I dispose of Nature in its entirety as its lord and master; my heart, roaming from object to object, mingles and identifies itself with those which soothe it, wraps itself up in charming fancies, and is intoxicated with delicious sensations. If, in order to render them permanent, I amuse myself by describing them by myself, what vigorous outlines, what fresh colouring, what power of expression I give them!

* * * At night I lay in the open air, and, stretched on the ground or on a bench, slept as calmly as upon a bed of roses. I remember, especially, that I spent a delightful night outside the city, on a road which ran by the side of the Rhône or Saône, I do not remember which. Raised gardens, with terraces, bordered the other side of the road. It had been very hot during the day; the evening was delightful; the dew moistened the parched grass; the night was calm, without a breath of wind; the air was fresh, without being cold; the sun, having gone down, had left in the sky red vapours, the reflection of which cast a rose-red tint upon the water; the trees on the terraces were full of nightingales answering one another. I walked on in a kind of ecstasy, abandoning my heart and senses to the enjoyment of all, only regretting, with a sigh, that I was obliged to enjoy it alone. Absorbed in my delightful reverie, I continued my walk late into

the night, without noticing that I was tired. At last, I noticed it. I threw myself with a feeling of delight upon the shelf of a sort of niche or false door let into a terrace wall; the canopy of my bed was formed by the tops of trees; a nightingale was perched just over my head, and lulled me to sleep with his song; my slumbers were sweet, my awaking was still sweeter. * * *

In relating my journeys, as in making them, I do not know how to stop. My heart beat with joy when I drew near to my dear mamma, but I walked no faster. I like to walk at my ease, and to stop when I like. A wandering life is what I want. To walk through a beautiful country in fine weather, without being obliged to hurry, and with a pleasant prospect at the end, is of all kinds of life the one most suited to my taste. My idea of a beautiful country is already known. No flat country, however beautiful, has ever seemed so to my eyes. I must have mountain torrents, rocks, firs, dark forests, mountains, steep roads to climb or descend, precipices at my side to frighten me.

✻   ✻   ✻

BOOK V

[The Years 1732–1736]

* * * It is sometimes said that the sword wears out the scabbard. That is my history. My passions have made me live, and my passions have killed me. What passions? will be asked. Trifles, the most childish things in the world, which, however, excited me as much as if the possession of Helen or the throne of the universe had been at stake. In the first place—women. When I possessed one, my senses were calm; my heart, never. The needs of love devoured me in the midst of enjoyment; I had a tender mother, a dear friend; but I needed a mistress. I imagined one in her place; I represented her to myself in a thousand forms, in order to deceive myself. If I had thought that I held mamma in my arms when I embraced her, these embraces would have been no less lively, but all my desires would have been extinguished; I should have sobbed from affection, but I should never have felt any enjoyment. Enjoyment! Does this ever fall to the lot of man? If I had ever, a single time in my life, tasted all the delights of love in their fulness, I do not believe that my frail existence could have endured it; I should have died on the spot.

Thus I was burning with love, without an object; and it is this state, perhaps, that is most exhausting. I was restless, tormented by the hopeless condition of poor mamma's affairs, and her imprudent conduct, which were bound to ruin her completely at no distant date. My cruel imagination, which always anticipates misfortunes, exhibited this particular one to me continually, in all its extent and in all its results. I already saw myself compelled by want to separate from her to whom I had devoted my life, and without whom I could not enjoy it. Thus my soul was ever in a state of agitation; I was devoured alternately by desires and fears.

✻   ✻   ✻

BOOK VI

[The Year 1736]

* * * At this period commences the brief happiness of my life; here approach the peaceful, but rapid moments which have given me the right to say, *I have lived.* Precious and regretted moments! Begin again for me your delightful course; and, if it be possible, pass more slowly in succession through my memory, than you did in your fugitive reality. What can I do, to prolong, as I should like, this touching and simple narrative, to repeat the same things over and over again, without wearying my readers by such repetition, any more than I was wearied of them myself, when I recommenced the life again and again? If all this consisted of facts, actions, and words, I could describe, and in a manner, give an idea of them; but how is it possible to describe what was neither said nor done, nor even thought, but enjoyed and felt, without being able to assign any other reason for my happiness than this simple feeling? I got up at sunrise, and was happy; I walked, and was happy; I saw mamma, and was happy; I left her, and was happy; I roamed the forests and hills, I wandered in the valleys, I read, I did nothing, I worked in the garden, I picked the fruit, I helped in the work of the house, and happiness followed me everywhere—happiness, which could not be referred to any definite object, but dwelt entirely within myself, and which never left me for a single instant. * * *

I should much like to know, whether the same childish ideas ever enter the hearts of other men as sometimes enter mine. In the midst of my studies, in the course of a life as blameless as a man could have led, the fear of hell still frequently troubled me. I asked myself: "In what state am I? If I were to die this moment, should I be damned?" According to my Jansenists,[2] there was no doubt about the matter; but, according to my conscience, I thought differently. Always fearful, and a prey to cruel uncertainty, I had recourse to the most laughable expedients to escape from it, for which I would unhesitatingly have anyone locked up as a madman if I saw him doing as I did. One day, while musing upon this melancholy subject, I mechanically amused myself by throwing stones against the trunks of trees with my usual good aim, that is to say, without hardly hitting one. While engaged in this useful exercise, it occurred to me to draw a prognostic from it to calm my anxiety. I said to myself: "I will throw this stone at the tree opposite; if I hit it, I am saved; if I miss it, I am damned." While speaking, I threw my stone with a trembling hand and a terrible palpitation of the heart, but with so successful an aim that it hit the tree right in the middle, which, to tell the truth, was no very difficult feat, for I had been careful to choose a tree with a thick trunk close at hand. From that time I have never had any doubt about my salvation! When I recall this characteristic incident, I do not know whether to laugh or cry at myself. You great men, who are most certainly laughing, may congratulate yourselves; but do not mock my wretchedness, for I swear to you that I feel it deeply. * * *

---

2. A sect of strict Catholics, named for Corneille Jansen (1585–1638). Voltaire mentions them in *Candide*, chaps. 21 and 22.

JOHANN WOLFGANG VON GOETHE

1749–1832

Recasting the ancient legend of Faust, Johann Wolfgang von Goethe created a powerful symbol of the Romantic imagination in all its aspiration and anxiety. Faust himself, central character of the epic drama, emerges as a Romantic hero, ever testing the limits of possibility. Yet to achieve his ends he must make a contract with the Devil: as if to say that giving full scope to imagination necessarily partakes of sin.

Goethe's *Faust* (Part I, 1808; Part II, 1832) constituted the crowning masterpiece of a life rich in achievement. Goethe exemplifies the nineteenth-century meaning of *genius*. Accomplished as poet, dramatist, novelist, and autobiographer, he also practiced law, served as a diplomat, and pursued scientific research. He had a happy childhood in Frankfurt, after which he studied law at Leipzig and then at Strasbourg, where in 1770–71 he met Gottfried Herder, leader of a new literary movement called the Sturm und Drang (Storm and Stress) movement. Participants in this movement emphasized the importance of revolt against established standards; they interested Goethe in such newly discovered forms as the folk song and in the literary vitality of Shakespeare, as opposed to more formally constricted writers.

During the brief period when he practiced law, after an unhappy love affair, Goethe wrote *The Sorrows of Young Werther* (1774), a novel of immense influence in establishing the image of the introspective, self-pitying, melancholy Romantic hero. In 1775 he accepted an invitation to the court of Charles Augustus, duke of Saxe-Weimar. He remained in Weimar for the rest of his life, for ten years serving the duke as chief minister. A trip to Italy from 1786 to 1788 aroused his interest in classic sources. He wrote dramas based on classic texts, most notably *Iphigenia* (1787); novels (for example, *Elective Affinities*, 1809) that pointed the way to the psychological novel; lyric poetry; and an important autobiography, *Poetry and Truth* (1811–33). He also did significant work in botany and physiology. Increasingly famous, he became in his own lifetime a legendary figure; all Europe flocked to Weimar to visit him.

The legend of Dr. Faustus (the real Johannes Faustus, a scholar, lived from 1480 to 1540), in most versions a seeker after forbidden knowledge, had attracted other writers before Goethe. The most important previous literary embodiment of the tale was Christopher Marlowe's *Doctor Faustus* (ca. 1588), a drama ending in its protagonist's damnation as a result of his search for illegitimate power through learning. Goethe's Faust meets no such fate. Pursuing not knowledge but experience, he embodies the ideal of limitless aspiration in all its glamour and danger. His contract with Mephistopheles provides that he will die at the moment he declares himself satisfied, content to rest in the present; he stakes his life and his salvation on his capacity ever to yearn for something beyond.

In Part I of Goethe's play, the protagonist's vision of the impossible locates itself specifically in the figure of Margaret (in German, *Margarete* or its diminutive, *Gretchen*), the simple, innocent girl whom he possesses physically but with whom he can never attain total union. In a speech epitomizing Romantic attitudes toward nature and toward emotion (especially the emotion of romantic love), Faust responds to his beloved's question, "Do you believe in God?"

> Does not the heaven vault above?
> Is the earth not firmly based down here?
> And do not, friendly,

Eternal stars arise?
Do we not look into each other's eyes,
And all in you is surging
To your head and heart,
And weaves in timeless mystery,
Unseeable, yet seen, around you?
Then let it fill your heart entirely,
And when your rapture in this feeling is complete,
Call it then as you will,
Call it bliss! heart! love! God!
I do not have a name
For this. Feeling is all.

The notion of *bliss*, for Pope associated with respect for limitation, for Wordsworth connected with revolutionary vision, here designates an unnameable feeling, derived from experience of nature and of romantic love, possibly identical with God, but valued partly for its very vagueness.

Modern readers may feel that Faust bullies Margaret, allowing her no reality except as instrument for his desires. In a poignant moment early in the play, interrupting Faust's rhapsody about her "meekness" and "humility," Margaret suggests, "If you should think of me one moment only . . ." Faust seems incapable of any such awareness, too busy inventing his loved one to see her as she is. He dramatically represents the "egotistical sublime," with a kind of imaginative grandeur inseparable from his utter absorption in the wonder of his own being, his own experience.

Yet the action of Part I turns on Faust's development of just that consciousness of another's reality which seemed impossible for him, and Margaret is the agent of his development. In the great final scene—Margaret in prison, intermittently mad, condemned to death for murdering her illegitimate child by Faust—the woman again appeals to the man to think about her, to *know* her: "Do you know, my love, *whom* you are setting free?" Her anguish, his responsibility for it, force themselves on Faust. He wishes he had never been born: his lust for experience has resulted in this terrible culpability, this agonizing loss. At the final moment of separation, with Margaret's spiritual redemption proclaimed from above, Faust implicitly acknowledges the full reality of the woman he has lost and thus, even though he departs with Mephistopheles, distinguishes himself from his Satanic mentor. Mephistopheles in his nature cannot grasp a reality utterly apart from his own; he can only recognize what belongs to him. Faust, at least fleetingly, realizes the otherness of the woman and the value of what he has lost.

Mephistopheles, at the outset witty and powerful in his own imagination, gradually reveals his limitations. In the *Prologue in Heaven*, the Devil seems energetic, perceptive, enterprising, fearless: as the Lord says, a "joker," apparently more playful than malign. His bargain with the Lord turns on his belief in the essentially "beastly" nature of humankind: like Gulliver's Houyhnhnm master, he emphasizes the human misuse of reason. Although the scene is modeled on the interchange between God and Satan in the Book of Job, it differs significantly in that the Lord gives an explicit reason for allowing the Tempter to function. "Man errs as long as he will," He says, but He adds that Mephistopheles's value is in prodding humanity into action. The introductory scene thus suggests that Mephistopheles will function as an agent of salvation rather than damnation. The Devil's subsequent exchanges with Faust, in Mephistopheles's mind predicated on his own superior knowledge and comprehension, gradually make one realize that the man in significant respects knows more than does the Devil. Mephistopheles, for example, can understand Faust's desire for Margaret only in sexual terms. His witty cynicism seems more and more inadequate to the actual situation. By the end of Part I, Faust's suffering has enlarged him; but from the beginning, his capacity for sympathy marks his potential superiority to the Devil.

The *Walpurgis Night* section, with the *Walpurgis Night's Dream*, marks a stage in Faust's education and an extreme moment in the play's dramatic structure. Goethe here allows himself to indulge in unrestrained fantasy—grotesque, obscene, comic, with an explosion of satiric energy in the dream. The shifting tone and reference of these passages embody ways in which the diabolic might be thought to operate in human terms. While Margaret suffers the consequences of her sin, Faust experiences the ambiguous freedom of the imagination, always at the edge of horror.

The pattern of Faust's moral development in Part I prepares the reader for a nontragic denouement to the drama as a whole. In Part II, which he worked on for some thirty years, completing it only the year before his death, Goethe moves from the individual to the social. Faust marries Helen of Troy, who gives birth to Euphorion, symbol of new humanity. He turns soldier to save a kingdom; he reclaims land from the sea; finally he rests contented in a vision of happy community generated by the industry of humankind. Mephistopheles thinks this his moment of victory: now Faust has declared himself satisfied. But since his satisfaction depends still on aspiration, on a dream of the future, the Angels rescue him at last and take him to Heaven.

One cannot read *Faust* with twentieth-century expectations of what a play should be like. This is above all *poetic* drama, to be read with pleasure in the richness of its language, the fertility and daring of its imagination. Although its cast of characters natural and supernatural and its sequence of supernaturally generated events are far from "realistic," it addresses problems still very much with us. How can individual ambition and desire be reconciled with responsibility to others? Does a powerful imagination—an artist's, say, or a scientist's—justify its possessor in ignoring social obligations? Goethe investigates such perplexing issues in symbolic terms, drawing his readers into personal involvement by playing on their emotions even as he questions the proper functions and limitations of commitment to desire—that form of emotional energy that leads to the greatest human achievements, but involves the constant danger of debilitating narcissism.

E. Ludwig, *Goethe, The History of a Man, 1749–1832* (1928), is a solid biography. Also useful are V. Lange, ed., *Goethe: A Collection of Critical Essays* (1960); and the essays contained in the critical edition of W. Arndt and C. Hamlin, eds., *Faust* (1976). See also H. Hatfield, *Goethe: A Critical Introduction* (1963), M. Bidney, *Blake and Goethe* (1988); and specifically for *Faust*, L. Dieckmann, *Goethe's Faust: A Critical Reading* (1972). A study relating Goethe's play to other versions of the Faust legend is A. Hoelzel, *The Paradoxical Quest: A Study of Faustian Vicissitudes* (1988). A varied group of essays appears in Reinhold Grimm and Jost Hermand, eds., *Our Faust? Roots and Ramifications of a Modern German Myth* (1987).

PRONOUNCING GLOSSARY

The following list uses common English syllables and stress accents to provide rough equivalents of selected words whose pronunciation may be unfamiliar to the general reader.

Altmayer: *ahlt'-maier*

Auerbach: *aw'-er-bahk*

Elend: *ay'-lend*

encheirisis naturae: *en-kai-ree'-sis nah-tyu'-ree*

Euphorion: *yoo-foh'-ree-on*

Faust: *fowst*

Goethe: *gur'te*

Leipzig: *laip'-zig*

Proktophantasmist: *prohk-toh-fan-tas'-*

   mist

Schierke: *sheer'ke*

Sturm und Drang: *shturm unt drahng*

Te Deum: *tay day'-um*

Wagner: *vahg'-ner*

Walpurgis: *vahl-poor'-gis*

Werther: *vayr'-ter*

Zenien: *tsay'-nee-en*

Faust[1]

Prologue in Heaven[2]

[*The* LORD, *the* HEAVENLY HOSTS. *Later,* MEPHISTOPHELES.[3] *The three* ARCHANGELS *step forward.*]

RAPHAEL: The sun intones, in ancient tourney
   With brother spheres, a rival air;
   And his predestinated journey,
   He closes with a thundrous blare.
   His sight, as none can comprehend it,   5
   Gives strength to angels; the array
   Of works, unfathomably splendid,
   Is glorious as on the first day.
GABRIEL: Unfathomably swiftly speeded,
   Earth's pomp revolves in whirling flight,   10
   As Eden's brightness is succeeded
   By deep and dread-inspiring night;
   In mighty torrents foams the ocean
   Against the rocks with roaring song—
   In ever-speeding spheric motion,   15
   Both rock and sea are swept along.
MICHAEL: And rival tempests roar and ravage
   From sea to land, from land to sea,
   And, raging, form a chain of savage,
   Deeply destructive energy.   20
   There flames a flashing devastation
   To clear the thunder's crashing way;
   Yet, Lord, thy herald's admiration
   Is for the mildness of thy day.
THE THREE: The sight, as none can comprehend it,   25
   Gives strength to angels; thy array
   Of works, unfathomably splendid
   Is glorious as on the first day.
MEPHISTOPHELES: Since you, oh Lord, have once again drawn near,
   And ask how we have been, and are so genial,   30

---

1. Translated by Walter Kaufman.   2. The scene is patterned on Job 1:6–12 and 2:1–6.   3. The origin of the name remains debatable. It may come from Hebrew, Persian, or Greek, with such meanings as "destroyer-liar," "no friend of Faust," and "no friend of light."

And since you used to like to see me here,
You see me, too, as if I were a menial.
I cannot speak as nobly as your staff,
Though by this circle here I shall be spurned:
My pathos would be sure to make you laugh,   35
Were laughing not a habit you've unlearned.
Of suns and worlds I know nothing to say;
I only see how men live in dismay.
The small god of the world will never change his ways
And is as whimsical—as on the first of days.   40
His life might be a bit more fun,
Had you not given him that spark of heaven's sun;
He calls it reason and employs it, resolute
To be more brutish than is any brute.
He seems to me, if you don't mind, Your Grace,   45
Like a cicada of the long-legged race,
That always flies, and, flying, springs,
And in the grass the same old ditty sings;
If only it were grass he could repose in!
There is no trash he will not poke his nose in.   50
THE LORD: Can you not speak but to abuse?
 Do you come only to accuse?
 Does nothing on the earth seem to you right?
MEPHISTOPHELES: No, Lord. I find it still a rather sorry sight.
 Man moves me to compassion, so wretched is his plight.   55
 I have no wish to cause him further woe.
THE LORD: Do you know Faust?
MEPHISTOPHELES: The doctor?[4]
THE LORD: Aye, my servant.
MEPHISTOPHELES: Lo!
 He serves you[5] most peculiarly, I think.
 Not earthly are the poor fool's meat and drink.
 His spirit's ferment drives him far,   60
 And he half knows how foolish is his quest:
 From heaven he demands the fairest star,
 And from the earth all joys that he thinks best;
 And all that's near and all that's far
 Cannot soothe the upheaval in his breast.   65
THE LORD: Though now he serves me but confusedly,
 I shall soon lead him where the vapor clears.
 The gardener knows, however small the tree,
 That bloom and fruit adorn its later years.
MEPHISTOPHELES: What will you bet? You'll lose him yet to me, 70
 If you will graciously connive
 That I may lead him carefully.
THE LORD: As long as he may be alive,

---

4. Of philosophy.   5. In the German text, Mephistopheles shifts from *du* to *ihr*, indicating his lack of respect for God.

So long you shall not be prevented.
Man errs as long as he will strive.   75
MEPHISTOPHELES: Be thanked for that; I've never been contented
    To waste my time upon the dead.
    I far prefer full cheeks, a youthful curly-head.
    When corpses come, I have just left the house—
    I feel as does the cat about the mouse.   80
THE LORD: Enough—I grant that you may try to clasp him,
    Withdraw this spirit from his primal source
    And lead him down, if you can grasp him,
    Upon your own abysmal course—
    And stand abashed when you have to attest: 85
    A good man in his darkling aspiration
    Remembers the right road throughout his quest.
MEPHISTOPHELES: Enough—he will soon reach his station;
    About my bet I have no hesitation,
    And when I win, concede your stake   90
    And let me triumph with a swelling breast:
    Dust he shall eat, and that with zest,
    As my relation does, the famous snake.
THE LORD: Appear quite free on that day, too;
    I never hated those who were like you: 95
    Of all the spirits that negate,
    The knavish jester gives me least to do.
    For man's activity can easily abate,
    He soon prefers uninterrupted rest;
    To give him this companion hence seems best   100
    Who roils and must as Devil help create.
    But you, God's rightful sons, give voice
    To all the beauty in which you rejoice;
    And that which ever works and lives and grows
    Enfold you with fair bonds that love has wrought,   105
    And what in wavering apparition flows
    That fortify with everlasting thought.
    [*The heavens close, the* ARCHANGELS *disperse.*]
MEPHISTOPHELES: [*Alone.*] I like to see the Old Man now and then
    And try to be not too uncivil.
    It's charming in a noble squire when   110
    He speaks humanely with the very Devil.

The First Part of the Tragedy

NIGHT

[*In a high-vaulted, narrow Gothic den,* FAUST, *restless in his armchair
    at the desk.*]
FAUST: I have, alas, studied philosophy,
    Jurisprudence and medicine, too,
    And, worst of all, theology

With keen endeavor, through and through—
And here I am, for all my lore,   5
The wretched fool I was before.
Called Master of Arts, and Doctor to boot,
For ten years almost I confute
And up and down, wherever it goes,
I drag my students by the nose—   10
And see that for all our science and art
We can know nothing. It burns my heart.
Of course, I am smarter than all the shysters,
The doctors, and teachers, and scribes, and Christers;
No scruple nor doubt could make me ill,   15
I am not afraid of the Devil or hell—
But therefore I also lack all delight,
Do not fancy that I know anything right,
Do not fancy that I could teach or assert
What would better mankind or what might convert.   20
I also have neither money nor treasures,
Nor worldly honors or earthly pleasures;
No dog would want to live longer this way!
Hence I have yielded to magic to see
Whether the spirit's mouth and might   25
Would bring some mysteries to light,
That I need not with work and woe
Go on to say what I don't know;
That I might see what secret force
Hides in the world and rules its course.   30
Envisage the creative blazes
Instead of rummaging in phrases.

Full lunar light, that you might stare
The last time now on my despair!
How often I've been waking here   35
At my old desk till you appeared,
And over papers, notes, and books
I caught, my gloomy friend, your looks.
Oh, that up on a mountain height
I could walk in your lovely light   40
And float with spirits round caves and trees,
Weave in your twilight through the leas,
Cast dusty knowledge overboard,
And bathe in dew until restored.

Still this old dungeon, still a mole!   45
Cursed be this moldy walled-in hole
Where heaven's lovely light must pass,
And lose its luster, through stained glass.
Confined with books, and every tome
Is gnawed by worms, covered with dust,   50
And on the walls, up to the dome,
A smoky paper, spots of rust;

Enclosed by tubes and jars that breed
More dust, by instruments and soot,
Ancestral furniture to boot—
That is your world! A world indeed!   55

And need you ask why in your breast
Your cramped heart throbs so anxiously?
Life's every stirring is oppressed
By an unfathomed agony?   60
Instead of living nature which
God made man for with holy breath,
Must[6] stifles you, and every niche
Holds skulls and skeletons and death.

Flee! Out into the open land!   65
And this book full of mystery,
Written in Nostradamus'[7] hand—
Is it not ample company?
Stars' orbits you will know; and bold,
You learn what nature has to teach;   70
Your soul is freed, and you behold
The spirits' words, the spirits' speech.
Though dry reflection might expound
These holy symbols, it is dreary:
You float, oh spirits, all around;   75
Respond to me, if you can hear me.
    [*He opens the book and sees the symbol of the macrocosm.*[8]]
What jubilation bursts out of this sight
Into my senses—now I feel it flowing,
Youthful, a sacred fountain of delight,
Through every nerve, my veins are glowing.   80
Was it a god that made these symbols be
That soothe my feverish unrest,
Filling with joy my anxious breast,
And with mysterious potency
Make nature's hidden powers around me, manifest?   85

Am I a god? Light grows this page—
In these pure lines my eye can see
Creative nature spread in front of me.
But now I grasp the meaning of the sage:
"The realm of spirits is not far away;   90
Your mind is closed, your heart is dead.
Rise, student, bathe without dismay
In heaven's dawn your mortal head."
    [*He contemplates the symbol.*]
All weaves itself into the whole,

---

6. Mustiness, mold.   7. Latin name of the French astrologer and physician Michel de Notredame
(1503–1566). His collection of rhymed prophecies, *The Centuries*, appeared in 1555.   8. Literally, "the
great world"; the universe as a whole.

Each living in the other's soul.   95
How heaven's powers climb up and descend.
Passing the golden pails from hand to hand!
Bliss-scented, they are winging
Through the sky and earth—their singing
Is ringing through the world.   100

What play! Yet but a play, however vast!
Where, boundless nature, can I hold you fast?
And where you breasts? Wells that sustain
All life—the heaven and the earth are nursed.
The wilted breast craves you in thirst—   105
You well, you still—and I languish in vain?
   [*In disgust, he turns some pages and beholds the symbol of the earth*
   SPIRIT.[9]]
How different is the power of this sign!
You, spirit of the earth, seem close to mine:
I look and feel my powers growing,
As if I'd drunk new wine I'm glowing,   110
I feel a sudden courage, and should dare
To plunge into the world, to bear
All earthly grief, all earthly joy—compare
With gales my strength, face shipwreck without care.
Now there are clouds above—   115
The moon conceals her light—
The lamp dies down.
It steams. Red light rays dash
About my head—a chill
Blows from the vaulting dome   120
And seizes me.
I feel you near me, spirit I implored.
Reveal yourself!
Oh, how my heart is gored
By never felt urges,   125
And my whole body surges—
My heart is yours; yours, too, am I.
You must. You must. Though I should have to die.
   [*He seizes the book and mysteriously pronounces the symbol of the*
   spirit. A reddish flame flashes, and the SPIRIT *appears in the flame.*]
SPIRIT: Who calls me?
FAUST: [*Turning away.*] Vision of fright!   130
SPIRIT: With all your might you drew me near
   You have been sucking at my sphere,
   And now—
FAUST: I cannot bear your sight!
SPIRIT: You have implored me to appear,
   Make known my voice, reveal my face;   135

---

9. The macrocosm represented the ordered, harmonious universe in its totality; this figure seems to be a symbol for the energy of terrestrial nature—neither good nor bad, merely powerful.

Your soul's entreaty won my grace:
Here I am! What abject fear
Grasps you, oh superman! Where is the soul's impassioned
Call? And where the breast that even now had fashioned
A world to bear and nurse within—that trembled thus,   140
Swollen with joy that it resembled us?
Where are you, Faust, whose voice pierced my domain,
Who surged against me with his might and main?
Could it be you who at my breath's slight shiver
Are to the depths of life aquiver,   145
A miserably writhing worm?
FAUST: Should I, phantom of fire, fly?
 It's I, it's Faust; your peer am I!
SPIRIT: In the floods of life and creative storm
 To and fro I wave.   150
 Weave eternally.
 And birth and grave,
 An eternal sea,
 A changeful strife,
 A glowing life: 155
 At the roaring loom of the ages I plod
 And fashion the life-giving garment of God.
FAUST: You that traverse worlds without end,
 Sedulous spirit, I feel close to you.
SPIRIT: Peer of the spirit that you comprehend   160
 Not mine! [*Vanishes.*]
FAUST: [*Collapsing.*] Not yours?
 Whose then?
 I, image of the godhead!
 And not even yours!   165
  [*A knock.*]
 O death! My famulus[1]—I know it well.
 My fairest happiness destroyed!
 This wealth of visions I enjoyed
 The dreary creeper must dispel!
  [WAGNER *enters in a dressing gown and night cap, a light in his hand.*
   FAUST *turns away in disgust.*]
WAGNER: Forgive! I hear your declamation;   170
 Surely, you read a Grecian tragedy?
 I'd profit from some work in this vocation,
 These days it can be used effectively.
 I have been told three times at least
 That a comedian could instruct a priest.   175
FAUST: Yes, when the priest is a comedian for all his Te Deum.[2]
 As happens more often than one would own.
WAGNER: Ah, when one is confined to one's museum
 And sees, the world on holidays alone,

---

1. Assistant to a medieval scholar.   2. A chant of praise to God.

But from a distance, only on occasion,   180
How can one guide it by persuasion?
FAUST: What you don't feel, you will not grasp by art,
Unless it wells out of your soul
And with sheer pleasure takes control,
Compelling every listener's heart.   185
But sit—and sit, and patch and knead,
Cook a ragout, reheat your hashes,
Blow at the sparks and try to breed
A fire out of piles of ashes!
Children and apes may think it great,   190
If that should titillate your gum,
But from heart to heart you will never create.
If from your heart it does not come.
WAGNER: Yet much depends on the delivery;
I still lack much; don't you agree?   195
FAUST: Oh, let him look for honest gain!
Let him not be a noisy fool!
All that makes sense you can explain
Without the tricks of any school.
If you have anything to say,   200
Why juggle words for a display?
Your glittering rhet'ric, subtly disciplined,
Which for mankind thin paper garlands weaves,
Is as unwholesome as the foggy wind
That blows in autumn through the wilted leaves.   205
WAGNER: Oh God, art is forever
And our life is brief.
I fear that with my critical endeavor
My head and heart may come to grief.
How hard the scholars' means are to array   210
With which one works up to the source;
Before we have traversed but half the course,
We wretched devils pass away.
FAUST: Parchment—is that the sacred fount
From which you drink to still your thirst forever?   215
If your refreshment does not mount.
From your own soul, you gain it never.
WAGNER: Forgive! It does seem so sublime,
Entering into the spirit of the time
To see what wise men, who lived long ago, believed,   220
Till we at last have all the highest aims achieved.
FAUST: Up to the stars—achieved indeed!
My friend, the times that antecede
Our own are books safely protected
By seven seals.[3] What spirit of the time you call,   225
Is but the scholars' spirit, after all,

3. Revelation 5:1.

In which times past are now reflected.
In truth, it often is pathetic,
And when one sees it, one would run away:
A garbage pail, perhaps a storage attic,　　　　230
At best a pompous moralistic play
With wonderfully edifying quips,
Most suitable to come from puppets' lips.
WAGNER: And yet the world! Man's heart and spirit! Oh,
That everybody knew part of the same!　　　　235
FAUST: The things that people claim to know!
Who dares to call the child by its true name?
The few that saw something like this and, starry-eyed
But foolishly, with glowing hearts averred
Their feelings and their visions before the common herd　　　240
Have at all times been burned and crucified.
I beg you, friend, it is deep in the night;
We must break off this interview.
WAGNER: Our conversation was so erudite,
I should have liked to stay awake with you.　　　　245
Yet Easter comes tomorrow; then permit
That I may question you a bit.
Most zealously I've studied matters great and small;
Though I know much, I should like to know all.
　　[Exit.]
FAUST: [Alone.] Hope never seems to leave those who affirm,　　　250
The shallow minds that stick to must and mold—
They dig with greedy hands for gold
And yet are happy if they find a worm.
Dare such a human voice be sounded
Where I was even now surrounded　　　　255
By spirits' might? And yet I thank you just this once,
You, of all creatures the most wretched dunce.
You tore me from despair that had surpassed
My mind and threatened to destroy my sense.
Alas, the apparition was so vast　　　　260
That I felt dwarfed in impotence.

I, image of the godhead, that began
To dream eternal truth was within reach,
Exulting on the heavens' brilliant beach
As if I had stripped off the mortal man;　　　　265
I, more than cherub, whose unbounded might
Seemed even then to flow through nature's veins,
Shared the creative joys of God's domains—
Presumptuous hope for which I pay in pains:
One word of thunder swept me from my height.　　　270

I may no longer claim to be your peer:
I had the power to attract you here,
But to retain you lacked the might.

In that moment of bliss, alack,
In which I felt so small, so great,   275
You, cruel one, have pushed me back
Into uncertain human fate.
Who teaches me? What should I shun?
Should I give in to that obsession?
Not our sufferings only, the deeds that we have done   280
Inhibit our life's progression.

Whatever noblest things the mind received,
More and more foreign matter spoils the theme;
And when the good of this world is achieved,
What's better seems an idle dream.   285
That gave us our life, the noblest urges
Are petrified in the earth's vulgar surges.

Where fantasy once rose in glorious flight,
Hopeful and bold to capture the sublime,
It is content now with a narrow site,   290
Since joy on joy crashed on the rocks of time.
Deep in the heart there dwells relentless care
And secretly infects us with despair;
Restless, she sways and poisons peace and joy
She always finds new masks she can employ: 295
She may appear as house and home, as child and wife,
As fire, water, poison, knife—
What does not strike, still makes you quail,
And what you never lose, for that you always wail.

I am not like the gods! That was a painful thrust;   300
I'm like the worm that burrows in the dust,
Who, as he makes of dust his meager meal,
Is crushed and buried by a wanderer's heel.
Is it not dust that stares from every rack
And narrows down this vaulting den?   305
This moths' world full of bric-a-brac
In which I live as in a pen?
Here I should find for what I care?
Should I read in a thousand books, maybe,
That men have always suffered everywhere,   310
Though now and then some man lived happily?—
Why, hollow skull, do you grin like a faun?
Save that your brain, like mine, once in dismay
Searched for light day, but foundered in the heavy dawn
And, craving truth, went wretchedly astray.   315
You instruments, of course, can scorn and tease
With rollers, handles, cogs, and wheels:
I found the gate, you were to be the keys;
Although your webs are subtle, you cannot break the seals.
Mysterious in the light of day,   320

Nature, in veils, will not let us perceive her,
And what she is unwilling to betray,
You cannot wrest from her with thumbscrews, wheel, or lever.
You ancient tools that rest upon the rack,
Unused by me, but used once by my sire,[4]   325
You ancient scroll that slowly has turned black
As my lamp on this desk gave off its smoky fire—

Far better had I squandered all of my wretched share
Than groan under this wretched load and thus address it!
What from your fathers you received as heir,   330
Acquire if you would possess it.
What is not used is but a load to bear;
But if today creates it, we can use and bless it.

Yet why does this place over there attract my sight?
Why is that bottle as a magnet to my eyes?   335
Why does the world seem suddenly so bright,
As when in nightly woods one sees the moon arise?
I welcome you, incomparable potion,
Which from your place I fetch now with devotion:
In you I honor human wit and art.   340
You essence from all slumber-bringing flowers,
You extract of all subtly fatal powers,
Bare to your master your enticing heart!
I look upon you, soothed are all my pains,
I seize you now, and all my striving wanes,   345
The spirit's tidal wave now ebbs away.
Slowly I float into the open sea,
The waves beneath me now seem gay and free,
To other shores beckons another day.
A fiery chariot floats on airy pinions   350
Cleaving the ether—tarry and descend!
Uncharted orbits call me, new dominions
Of sheer creation, active without end.
This higher life, joys that no mortal won!
You merit this—but now a worm, despairing?   355
Upon the mild light of the earthly sun
Turn, bold, your back! And with undaunted daring
Tear open the eternal portals
Past which all creatures slink in silent dread.
The time has come to prove by deeds that mortals   360
Have as much dignity as any god,
And not to tremble at that murky cave
Where fantasy condemns itself to dwell
In agony. The passage brave
Whose narrow mouth is lit by all the flames of hell;   365
And take this step with cheerful resolution,
Though it involve the risk of utter dissolution.

---

4. Later we find that Faust's father was a doctor of medicine.

Now you come down to me, pure crystal vase,
Emerge again out of your ancient case
Of which for many years I did not think. 370
You glistened at my father's joyous feasts
And cheered the solemn-looking guests,
When you were passed around for all to drink.
The many pictures, glistening in the light,
The drinker's duty rhyming to explain them,[5] 375
To scan your depths and in one draught to drain them,
Bring back to mind many a youthful night.
There is no friend now to fulfill this duty,
Nor shall I exercise my wit upon your beauty.
Here is a juice that fast makes drunk and mute; 380
With its brown flood it fills this crystal bowl,
I brewed it and shall drink it whole
And offer this last drink with all my soul
Unto the morning as a festive high salute. [*He puts the bowl to his lips.*]
    [*Chime of bells and choral song.*]
CHOIR OF ANGELS: Christ is arisen. 385
        Hail the meek-spirited
        Whom the ill-merited,
        Creeping, inherited
        Faults held in prison.
FAUST: What deeply humming strokes, what brilliant tone 390
    Draws from my lips the crystal bowl with power?
    Has the time come, deep bells, when you make known
    The Easter holiday's first holy hour?
    Is this already, choirs, the sweet consoling hymn
    That was first sung around his tomb by cherubim, 395
    Confirming the new covenant?
CHOIR OF WOMEN: With myrrh, when bereaved,
        We had adorned him;
        We that believed
        Laid down and mourned him. 400
        Linen we twined
        Round the adored—
        Returning, we cannot find
        Christ, our Lord.
CHOIR OF ANGELS: Christ is arisen. 405
        Blessed be the glorious
        One who victorious
        Over laborious
        Trials has risen.
FAUST: Why would you, heaven's tones, compel 410
    Me gently to rise from my dust?
    Resound where tenderhearted people dwell:
    Although I hear the message, I lack all faith or trust;

---

5. Faust here alludes to the drinking of toasts. The maker of a toast often produced impromptu rhymes.

And faith's favorite child is miracle.
For those far spheres I should not dare to strive,   415
From which these tidings come to me;
And yet these chords, which I have known since infancy:
Call me now, too, back into life.
Once heaven's love rushed at me as a kiss
In the grave silence of the Sabbath day,   420
The rich tones of the bells, it seemed, had much to say,
And every prayer brought impassioned bliss.
An unbelievably sweet yearning
Drove me to roam through wood and lea,
Crying, and as my eyes were burning,   425
I felt a new world grow in me.
This song proclaimed the spring feast's free delight, appealing
To the gay games of youth—they plead:
Now memory entices me with childlike feeling
Back from the last, most solemn deed.   430
Sound on, oh hymns of heaven, sweet and mild!
My tears are flowing; earth, take back your child!

CHOIR OF DISCIPLES: Has the o'ervaulted one
    Burst from his prison,
    The living-exalted one   435
    Gloriously risen,
    Is in this joyous birth
    Zest for creation near—
    Oh, on the breast of earth
    We are to suffer here.   440
    He left his own
    Pining in sadness;
    Alas, we bemoan,
    Master, your gladness.

CHOIR OF ANGELS: Christ is arisen   445
    Out of corruption's womb.
    Leave behind prison,
    Fetters and gloom!
    Those who proceed for him,
    Lovingly bleed for him,   450
    Brotherly feed for him,
    Travel and plead for him,
    And to bliss lead for him,
    For you the Master is near,
    For you he is here.   455

BEFORE THE CITY GATE

[*People of all kinds are walking out.*]
SOME APPRENTICES: Why do you go that way?
OTHERS: We are going to Hunter's Lodge today.
THE FIRST: But we would rather go to the mill.

AN APPRENTICE: Go to the River Inn, that's my advice.
ANOTHER: I think, the way there isn't nice.   5
THE OTHERS: Where are you going?
A THIRD ONE: Up the hill.
A FOURTH ONE: Burgdorf would be much better. Let's go there with the
    rest:
    The girls there are stunning, their beer is the best,
    And it's first-class, too, for a fight.
A FIFTH ONE: You are indeed a peppy bird,   10
    Twice spanked, you're itching for the third.
    Let's not, the place is really a fright.
SERVANT GIRL: No, no! I'll go back to the town again.
ANOTHER: We'll find him at the poplars, I'm certain it is true.
THE FIRST: What's that to me? Is it not plain,   15
    He'll walk and dance only with you?
    He thinks, you are the only one.
    And why should I care for your fun?
THE OTHER ONE: He will not be alone. He said,
    Today he'd bring the curly-head.   20
STUDENT: Just see those wenches over there!
    Come, brother, let us help the pair.
    A good strong beer, a smarting pipe,
    And a maid, nicely dressed—that is my type!
CITIZEN'S DAUGHTER: Look there and see those handsome blades!   25
    I think it is a crying shame:
    They could have any girl that meets with their acclaim,
    And chase after these silly maids.
SECOND STUDENT: [*To the* FIRST.] Don't go so fast; behind us are two
    more,
    And they are dressed at least as neatly.   30
    I know one girl, she lives next door,
    And she bewitches me completely.
    The way they walk, they seem demure,
    But won't mind company, I'm sure.
THE FIRST: No, brother, I don't like those coy addresses.   35
    Come on, before we lose the wilder prey.
    The hand that wields the broom on Saturday
    Will, comes the Sunday, give the best caresses.
CITIZEN: No, the new mayor is no good, that's what I say.
    Since he's in, he's fresher by the day.   40
    What has he done for our city?
    Things just get worse; it is a pity!
    We must obey, he thinks he's clever,
    And we pay taxes more than ever.
BEGGAR: [*Sings.*] Good gentlemen and ladies fair,   45
        So red of cheek, so rich in dress,
        Be pleased to look on my despair,
        To see and lighten my distress.
        Let me not grind here, vainly waiting!

    For only those who give are gay,   50
    And when all men are celebrating,
    Then I should have my harvest day.
ANOTHER CITIZEN: On Sun- and holidays, there is no better fun,
    Than chattering of wars and warlike fray,
    When off in Turkey, far away,   55
    One people beats the other one.
    We stand at the window, drink a wine that is light,
    Watch the boats glide down the river, see the foam,
    And cheerfully go back at night,
    Grateful that we have peace at home.   60
THIRD CITIZEN: Yes, neighbor, that is nicely said.
    Let them crack skulls, and wound, and maim,
    Let all the world stand on its head;
    But here, at home, all should remain the same.
OLD WOMAN: [*To the* CITIZEN'S DAUGHTERS.]
    Ah, how dressed up! So pretty and so young!   65
    Who would not stop to stare at you?
    Don't be puffed up, I'll hold my tongue.
    I know your wish, and how to get it, too.
CITIZEN'S DAUGHTER: Come quickly, Agatha! I take good heed
    Not to be seen with witches; it's unwise. —   70
    Though on St. Andrew's Night[6] she brought indeed
    My future lover right before my eyes.
THE OTHER ONE: She showed me mine, but in a crystal ball
    With other soldiers, bold and tall;
    I have been looking ever since,   75
    But so far haven't found my prince.
SOLDIERS: Castles with lofty
    Towers and banners,
    Maidens with haughty,
    Disdainful manners   80
    I want to capture.
    Fair is the dare,
    Splendid the pay.
    And we let trumpets
    Do our wooing,   85
    For our pleasures
    And our undoing.
    Life is all storming,
    Life is all splendor,
    Maidens and castles   90
    Have to surrender.
    Fair is the dare,
    Splendid the pay.
    And then the soldiers

---

6. St. Andrew's Eve, November 29, the traditional time for young girls to consult fortune-tellers about their future lovers or husbands.

March on away.   95
[FAUST *and* WAGNER.]
FAUST: Released from the ice are river and creek,
    Warmed by the spring's fair quickening eye;
    The valley is green with hope and joy;
    The hoary winter has grown so weak
    He has withdrawn to the rugged mountains.   100
    From there he sends, but only in flight,
    Impotent showers of icy hail
    That streak across the greening vale;
    But the sun will not suffer the white;
    Everywhere stirs what develops and grows,   105
    All he would quicken with color that glows;
    Flowers are lacking, blue, yellow, and red,
    But he takes dressed-up people instead.
    Turn around now and look down
    From the heights back to the town.   110
    Out of the hollow gloomy gate
    Surges and scatters a motley horde.
    All seek sunshine. They celebrate
    The resurrection of the Lord.
    For they themselves are resurrected   115
    From lowly houses, musty as stables,
    From trades to which they are subjected,
    From the pressure of roofs and gables,
    From the stifling and narrow alleys,
    From the churches' reverent night   120
    They have emerged into the light.
    Look there! Look, how the crowd now sallies
    Gracefully into the gardens and leas,
    How on the river, all through the valley,
    Frolicsome floating boats one sees,   125
    And, overloaded beyond its fill,
    This last barge now is swimming away.
    From the far pathways of the hill
    We can still see how their clothes are gay.
    I hear the village uproar rise;   130
    Here is the people's paradise,
    And great and small shout joyously:
    Here I am human, may enjoy humanity.
WAGNER: To take a walk with you, good sir,
    Is a great honor and reward,   135
    But I myself should never so far err,
    For the uncouth I always have abhorred.
    This fiddling, bowling, loud delight—
    I hate these noises of the throng;
    They rage as if plagued by an evil sprite   140
    And call it joy and call it song.

[peasants *under the linden tree. Dance and Song.*]
     The shepherd wished to dance and dressed
     With ribbons, wreath, and motley vest,
     He was a dandy beau.
     Around the linden, lass and lad.   145
     Were crowding, dancing round like mad.
     Hurrah! Hurrah!
     Hurrah! Hi-diddle-dee!
     Thus went the fiddle bow.

     He pressed into the dancing whirl   150
     His elbow bumped a pretty girl,
     And he stepped on her toe.
     The lively wench, she turned and said:
     "You seem to be a dunderhead!"
     Hurrah! Hurrah!   155
     Hurrah! Hi-diddle-dee!
     Don't treat a poor girl so.

     The circle whirled in dancing flight,
     Now they danced left, now they danced right,
     The skirts flow high and low.   160
     Their cheeks were flushed and they grew warm
     And rested, panting, arm in arm.
     Hurrah! Hurrah!
     Hurrah! Hi-diddle-dee!
     With waists and elbows so.   165

     Please do not make so free with me!
     For many fool their bride-to-be
     And lie, as you well know.
     And yet he coaxed the girl aside,
     And from the linden, far and wide: 170
     Hurrah! Hurrah!
     Hurrah! Hi-diddle-dee!
     Clamor and fiddle bow.
old peasant: Dear doctor, it is good of you
     That you don't spurn us on this day   175
     But find into this swarming throng,
     Though a great scholar, still your way.
     So please accept the finest mug;
     With a good drink it has been filled,
     I offer it and wish aloud: 180
     Not only may your thirst be stilled;
     As many drops as it conveys
     Ought to be added to your days.
faust: I take the bumper and I, too,
     Thank and wish health to all of you.   185
     [*The people gather around in a circle.*]
old peasant: Indeed, it is most kind of you
     That you appear this happy day;

When evil days came in the past,
You always helped in every way.
And many stand here, still alive,   190
Whom your good father toiled to wrest
From the hot fever's burning rage
When he prevailed over the pest.[7]
And you, a young man at that time,
Made to the sick your daily round.   195
While many corpses were brought out,
You always emerged safe and sound,
And took these trials in your stride:
The Helper helped the helper here.
ALL: Health to the man so often tried!   200
   May he yet help for many a year!
FAUST: Bow down before Him, all of you,
   Who teaches help and sends help, too. [*He walks on with* WAGNER.]
WAGNER: Oh, what a feeling you must have, great man,
   When crowds revere you like a mighty lord.   205
Oh, blessed are all those who can
Employ their gifts for such reward.
The father shows you to his son,
They ask what gives and come and run,
The fiddle stops, the dance is done.   210
You walk, they stand in rows to see,
Into the air their caps will fly—
A little more, and they would bend their knee
As if the Holy Host[8] went by.
FAUST: Now just a few more steps uphill to the big stone,   215
   From our wandering we can rest up there.
I often sat there, thoughtful and alone,
And vexed myself with fasting and with prayer.
In hope still rich, with faith still blessed,
I thought entreaties, tears, and sighs   220
Would force the Master of the Skies
To put an end to the long pest.
The crowd's applause now sounds like caustic fun.
I only wish you could read in my heart
How little father and son   225
Deserve such fame for their poor art.
My father was obscure, if quite genteel,
And pondered over nature and every sacred sphere
In his own cranky way, though quite sincere,
With ardent, though with wayward, zeal.   230
And with proficient devotees,
In his black kitchen he would fuse
After unending recipes,
Locked in, the most contrary brews.

---

7. Pestilence or plague.   8. The Eucharist, the consecrated bread and wine of the Sacrament.

They made red lions, a bold wooer came,   235
In tepid baths was mated to a lily;
And then the pair was vexed with a wide-open flame
From one bride chamber to another, willy-nilly.
And when the queen appeared, all pied,
Within the glass after a spell,   240
The medicine was there, and though the patients died,
Nobody questioned: who got well?[9]
And thus we raged fanatically
In these same mountains, in this valley,
With hellish juice worse than the pest.   245
Though thousands died from poison that I myself would give,
Yes, though they perished, I must live
To hear the shameless killers blessed.
WAGNER: I cannot see why you are grieved.
What more can honest people do   250
Than be conscientious and pursue
With diligence the art that they received?
If you respect your father as a youth,
You'll learn from him what you desire;
If as a man you add your share of truth   255
To ancient lore, your son can go still higher.
FAUST: Oh, happy who still hopes to rise
Out of this sea of errors and false views!
What one does *not* know, one could utilize,
And what one knows one cannot use.   260
But let the beauty offered by this hour
Not be destroyed by our spleen!
See how, touched by the sunset's parting power,
The huts are glowing in the green.
The sun moves on, the day has had its round;   265
He hastens on, new life greets his salute.
Oh,[1] that no wings lift me above the ground
To strive and strive in his pursuit!
In the eternal evening light
The quiet world would lie below   270
With every valley tranquil, on fire every height,
The silver stream to golden rivers flow.
Nor could the mountain with its savage guise
And all its gorges check my godlike ways;
Already ocean with its glistening bays   275
Spreads out before astonished eyes.
At last the god sinks down, I seem forsaken;
But I feel new unrest awaken
And hurry hence to drink his deathless light,
The day before me, and behind me night,   280

9. This confusing sequence evokes a kind of medicine closely allied to magic and inappropriate to the needs of the ill people seeking help.   1. Alas.

The billows under me, and over me the sky.
A lovely dream, while he makes his escape.
The spirit's wings will not change our shape:
Our body grows no wings and cannot fly.
Yet it is innate in our race   285
That our feelings surge in us and long
When over us, lost in the azure space
The lark trills out her glorious song;
When over crags where fir trees quake
In icy winds, the eagle soars,   290
And over plains and over lakes
The crane returns to homeward shores.
WAGNER: I, too, have spells of eccentricity,
But such unrest has never come to me.
One soon grows sick of forest, field, and brook,   295
And I shall never envy birds their wings.
Far greater are the joys the spirit brings—
From page to page, from book to book.
Thus winter nights grow fair and warm the soul;
Yes, blissful life suffuses every limb,   300
And when one opens up an ancient parchment scroll,
The very heavens will descend on him.
FAUST: You are aware of only one unrest;
Oh, never learn to know the other!
Two souls, alas, are dwelling in my breast,   305
And one is striving to forsake its brother.
Unto the world in grossly loving zest,
With clinging tendrils, one adheres;
The other rises forcibly in quest
Of rarefied ancestral spheres.   310
If there be spirits in the air
That hold their sway between the earth and sky,
Descend out of the golden vapors there
And sweep me into iridescent life.
Oh, came a magic cloak into my hands   315
To carry me to distant lands,
I should not trade it for the choicest gown,
Nor for the cloak and garments of the crown.
WAGNER: Do not invoke the well-known throng that flow
Through mists above and spread out in the haze,   320
Concocting danger in a thousand ways
For man wherever he may go.
From the far north the spirits' deadly fangs
Bear down on you with arrow-pointed tongues;
And from the east they come with withering pangs   325
And nourish themselves from your lungs.
The midday sends out of the desert those
Who pile heat upon heat upon your crown,
While evening brings the throng that spells repose—

And then lets you, and fields and meadows, drown.　　　　330
They gladly listen, but are skilled in harm,
Gladly obey, because they like deceit;
As if from heaven sent, they please and charm,
Whispering like angels when they cheat.
But let us go! The air has cooled, the world　　　　335
Turned gray, mists are unfurled.
When evening comes one values home,
Why do you stand amazed? What holds your eyes?
What in the twilight merits such surprise?
FAUST: See that black dog through grain and stubble roam?　　　　340
WAGNER: I noticed him way back, but cared not in the least.
FAUST: Look well! For what would *you* take this strange beast?
WAGNER: Why, for a poodle fretting doggedly
　　As it pursues the tracks left by its master.
FAUST: It spirals all around us, as you see,　　　　345
　　And it approaches, fast and faster.
　　And if I do not err, a fiery eddy
　　Whirls after it and marks the trail.
WAGNER: I see the poodle, as I said already;
　　As for the rest, your eyesight seems to fail.　　　　350
FAUST: It seems to me that he winds magic snares
　　Around our feet, a bond of future dangers.
WAGNER: He jumps around, unsure, and our presence scares
　　The dog who seeks his master, and finds instead two strangers.
FAUST: The spiral narrows, he is near!　　　　355
WAGNER: You see, a dog and not a ghost is here.
　　He growls, lies on his belly, thus he waits,
　　He wags his tail: all canine traits.
FAUST: Come here and walk along with us!
WAGNER: He's poodlishly ridiculous.　　　　360
　　You stand and rest, and he waits, too;
　　You speak to him, and he would climb on you;
　　Lose something, he will bring it back again,
　　Jump in the lake to get your cane.
FAUST: You seem quite right, I find, for all his skill,　　　　365
　　No trace of any spirit: all is drill.
WAGNER: By dogs that are expertly trained
　　The wisest man is entertained.
　　He quite deserves your favor: it is prudent
　　To cultivate the students' noble student.　　　　370
　　[*They pass through the City Gate.*]

STUDY

FAUST: [*Entering with the poodle.*] The fields and meadows I have fled
　　　　As night enshrouds them and the lakes;
　　　　With apprehensive, holy dread
　　　　The better soul in us awakes.

Wild passions have succumbed to sleep,   5
All vehement exertions bow;
The love of man stirs in us deep,
The love of God is stirring now.

Be quiet, poodle! Stop running around!
Why do you snuffle at the sill like that?   10
Lie down behind the stove—not on the ground:
Take my best cushion for a mat.
As you amused us on our way
With running and jumping and did your best,
Let me look after you and say: 15
Be quiet, please, and be my guest.

When in our narrow den
The friendly lamp glows on the shelf,
Then light pervades our breast again
And fills the heart that knows itself.   20
Reason again begins to speak,
Hope blooms again with ancient force,
One longs for life and one would seek
Its rivers and, alas, its source.

Stop snarling poodle! For the sacred strain   25
To which my soul is now submitting
Beastly sounds are hardly fitting.
We are accustomed to see *men* disdain
What they don't grasp;
When it gives trouble, they profane   30
Even the beautiful and the good.
Do dogs, too, snarl at what's not understood?

Even now, however, though I tried my best,
Contentment flows no longer through my breast.
Why does the river rest so soon, and dry up, and   35
Leave us to languish in the sand?
How well I know frustration!
This want, however, we can overwhelm:
We turn to the supernatural realm,
We long for the light of revelation   40
Which is nowhere more magnificent
Than in our New Testament.
I would for once like to determine—
Because I am sincerely perplexed—
How the sacred original text[2]   45
Could be translated into my beloved German.

[*He opens a tome and begins.*]
It says: "In the beginning was the *Word*."[3]

---

2. That is, the Greek.   3. John 1:1.

Already I am stopped. It seems absurd.
The *Word* does not deserve the highest prize,
I must translate it otherwise 50
If I am well inspired and not blind.
It says: In the beginning was the *Mind*.
Ponder that first line, wait and see,
Lest you should write too hastily.
Is mind the all-creating source? 55
It ought to say: In the beginning there was *Force*.
Yet something warns me as I grasp the pen,
That my translation must be changed again.
The spirit helps me. Now it is exact.
I write: In the beginning was the *Act*. 60

If I am to share my room with you,
Poodle, stop moaning so!
And stop your bellow,
For such a noisy, whiny fellow
I do not like to have around. 65
One of us, black hound,
Will have to give ground.
With reluctance I change my mind:
The door is open, you are not confined.
But what must I see! 70
Can that happen naturally?
Is it a shadow? Am I open-eyed?
How grows my poodle long and wide!
He reaches up like rising fog—
This is no longer the shape of a dog! 75
Oh, what a specter I brought home!
A hippopotamus of foam,
With fiery eyes; how his teeth shine!
You are as good as mine:
For such a semi-hellish brow 80
The Key of Solomon[4] will do.

SPIRITS: [*In the corridor.*] One has been caught inside.
Do not follow him! Abide!
As a fox in a snare,
Hell's old lynx is caught in there. 85
But give heed!
Float up high, float down low,
To and fro,
And he tries, and he is freed.
Can you avail him? 90
Then do not fail him!
For you must not forget,
We are in his debt.

---

4. The *Clavicula Salomonis*, a standard work used by magicians for conjuring; in many medieval legends, Solomon was noted as a great magician.

FAUST: Countering the beast, I might well
  First use the fourfold spell: 95

    Salamander shall broil,
    Undene shall grieve,
    Sylphe shall leave,
    Kobold⁵ shall toil.

Whoever ignores 100
The elements' cores,
Their energy
And quality,
Cannot command
In the spirits' land. 105

    Disappear flashing,
    Salamander!
    Flow together, splashing,
    Undene!
    Glow in meteoric beauty, 110
    Sylphe!
    Do your domestic duty,
    Incubus! Incubus!
    Step forward and finish thus.

None of the four 115
Is this beast's core.
It lies quite calmly there and beams;
I have not hurt it yet, it seems.
Now listen well
To a stronger spell. 120

    If you should be
    Hell's progeny,
    Then see this symbol
    Before which tremble
    The cohorts of Hell! 125

Already it bristles and starts to swell.

    Spirit of shame,
    Can you read the name
    Of the Uncreated,
    Defying expression, 130
    With whom the heavens are sated,
    Who was pierced in transgression?

Behind the stove it swells
As an elephant under my spells;
It fills the whole room and quakes, 135

5. A spirit of the earth. The *salamander* was a spirit of the fire. An undine (*undene*) was a water nymph. A sylph (*sylphe*) was a spirit of the air.

It would turn into mist and fleet.
Stop now before the ceiling breaks!
Lie down at your master's feet!

You see, I do not threaten in vain:
With holy flames I cause you pain.   140
Do not require
The threefold glowing fire![6]
Do not require
My art in its full measure!

MEPHISTOPHELES: [*Steps forward from behind the stove, dressed as a traveling scholar, while the mist clears away.*]
Why all the noise? Good sir, what is your pleasure?   145
FAUST: Then this was our poodle's core!
Simply a traveling scholar? The *casus*[7] makes me laugh.
MEPHISTOPHELES: Profound respects to you and to your lore:
You made me sweat with all your chaff.
FAUST: What is your name?
MEPHISTOPHELES: This question seems minute   150
For one who thinks the word so beggarly,
Who holds what seems in disrepute,
And craves only reality.[8]
FAUST: Your real being no less than your fame
Is often shown, sirs, by your name,   155
Which is not hard to analyze
When one calls you the Liar, Destroyer, God of Flies.[9]
Enough, who are you then?
MEPHISTOPHELES: Part of that force which would
Do evil evermore, and yet creates the good.
FAUST: What is it that this puzzle indicates?   160
MEPHISTOPHELES: I am the spirit that negates.
And rightly so, for all that comes to be
Deserves to perish wretchedly;
'Twere better nothing would begin.
Thus everything that your terms, sin,   165
Destruction, evil represent—
That is my proper element.
FAUST: You call yourself a part, yet whole make your debut?
MEPHISTOPHELES: The modest truth I speak to you.
While man, this tiny world of fools, is droll   170
Enough to think himself a whole,
I am part of the part that once was everything,
Part of the darkness which gave birth to light,
That haughty light which envies mother night
Her ancient rank and place and would be king—   175
Yet it does not succeed: however it contend,

---

6. Perhaps the Trinity or a triangle with divergent rays.   7. Occurrence.   8. Mephistopheles refers to Faust's substitution of *Act* for *Word* in the passage from John (see line 60).   9. An almost literal translation of the name of the Philistine deity Beelzebub.

It sticks to bodies in the end.
It streams from bodies, it lends bodies beauty,
A body won't let it progress;
So it will not take long, I guess,   180
And with the bodies it will perish, too.
FAUST: I understand your noble duty:
Too weak for great destruction, you
Attempt it on a minor scale.
MEPHISTOPHELES: And I admit it is of slight avail.   185
What stands opposed to our Nought,
The some, your wretched world—for aught
That I have so far undertaken,
It stands unruffled and unshaken:
With billows, fires, storms, commotion,   190
Calm, after all, remain both land and ocean.
And that accursed lot, the brood of beasts and men,
One cannot hurt them anyhow.
How many have I buried now!
Yet always fresh new blood will circulate again.   195
Thus it goes on—I could rage in despair!
From water, earth, and even air,
A thousand seeds have ever grown
In warmth and cold and drought and mire!
If I had not reserved myself the fire,   200
I should have nothing of my own.
FAUST: And thus, I see, you would resist
The ever-live creative power
By clenching your cold devil's fist
Resentfully—in vain you glower.   205
Try something new and unrelated,
Oh you peculiar son of chaos!
MEPHISTOPHELES: Perchance your reasoning might sway us—
The next few times we may debate it.
But for the present, may I go?   210
FAUST: I cannot see why you inquire.
Now that we met, you ought to know
That you may call as you desire.
Here is the window, here the door,
A chimney there, if that's preferred.   215
MEPHISTOPHELES: I cannot leave you that way, I deplore:
By a small obstacle I am deterred:
The witch's foot on your threshold, see—
FAUST: The pentagram[1] distresses you?
Then, son of hell, explain to me: 220
How could you enter here without ado?
And how was such a spirit cheated?
MEPHISTOPHELES: Behold it well: It is not quite completed;

---

1. A magic five-pointed star designed to keep away evil spirits.

One angle—that which points outside—
Is open just a little bit.   225
FAUST: That was indeed a lucky hit.
I caught you and you must abide.
How wonderful, and yet how queer!
MEPHISTOPHELES: The poodle never noticed, when he first jumped in here,
But now it is a different case;   230
The Devil cannot leave this place.
FAUST: The window's there. Are you in awe?
MEPHISTOPHELES: The devils and the demons have a law:
Where they slipped in, they always must withdraw.
The first time we are free, the second time constrained.   235
FAUST: For hell, too, laws have been ordained?
Superb! Then one should surely make a pact,
And one of you might enter my employ.
MEPHISTOPHELES: What we would promise you, you would enjoy,
And none of it we would subtract.   240
But that we should not hurry so,
And we shall talk about it soon;
For now I ask the single boon
That you permit me now to go.
FAUST: For just a moment stay with me   245
And let me have some happy news.
MEPHISTOPHELES: Not now. I'll come back presently,
Then you may ask me what you choose.
FAUST: You were not caught by my device
When you were snared like this tonight.   250
Who holds the Devil, hold him tight!
He can't expect to catch him twice.
MEPHISTOPHELES: If you prefer it, I shall stay
With you, and I shall not depart,
Upon condition that I may   255
Amuse you with some samples of my art.
FAUST: Go right ahead, you are quite free—
Provided it is nice to see.
MEPHISTOPHELES: Right in this hour you will obtain
More for your senses than you gain   260
In a whole year's monotony.
What tender spirits now will sing,
The lovely pictures that they bring
Are not mere magic for the eye:
They will delight your sense of smell,   265
Be pleasing to your taste as well,
Excite your touch, and give you joy.
No preparation needs my art,
We are together, let us start.
SPIRITS: Vanish, you darkling   270
Arches above him.
Friendlier beaming,

Sky should be gleaming
Down upon us.
Ah, that the darkling   275
Clouds had departed!
Stars now are sparkling,
More tenderhearted
Suns shine on us.
Spirits aerial,   280
Fair and ethereal,
Wavering and bending,
Sail by like swallows.
Yearning unending
Sees them and follows,   285
Garments are flowing,
Ribbons are blowing,
Covering the glowing
Land and the bower
Where, in the hedges,   290
Thinking and dreaming,
Lovers make pledges.
Bower on bower.
Tendrils are streaming;
Heavy grapes shower   295
Their sweet excesses
Into the presses;
In streams are flowing
Wines that are glowing,
Foam, effervescent,   300
Through iridescent
Gems; they are storming
Down from the mountains;
Lakes they are forming,
Beautiful fountains   305
Where hills are ending,
Birds are descending,
Drink and fly onward,
Fly ever sunward,
Fly from the highlands   310
Toward the ocean
Where brilliant islands
Sway in soft motion.
Jubilant choirs
Soothe all desires,   315
And are entrancing
Those who are dancing
Like whirling satyrs,
But the throng scatters.
Some now are scaling   320
Over the mountains,

Others are sailing
Toward the fountains,
Others are soaring,
All life adoring,   325
All crave the far-off
Love-spending star of
Rapturous bliss.

MEPHISTOPHELES: He sleeps. I thank you, airy, tender throng.
    You made him slumber with your song.   330
    A splendid concert. I appreciate this.
    You are not yet the man to hold the Devil fast.
    Go, dazzle him with dream shapes, sweet and vast,
    Plunge him into an ocean of untruth.
    But now, to break the threshold's spell at last,   335
    I have to get a rat's sharp tooth.
    I need no conjuring today,
    One's rustling over there and will come right away.
    The lord of rats, the lord of mice,
    Of flies and frogs, bedbugs and lice,   340
    Bids you to dare now to appear
    To gnaw upon this threshold here,
    Where he is dabbing it with oil.
    Ah, there you come. Begin your toil.
    The point that stopped me like a magic hedge   345
    Is way up front, right on the edge.
    Just one more bite, and that will do.
    Now, Faustus, sleep and dream, till I come back to you.
FAUST: [*Awakening.*] Betrayed again? Fooled by a scheme?
    Should spirits' wealth so suddenly decay   350
    That I behold the Devil in a dream,
    And that a poodle jumps away?

STUDY

[FAUST, MEPHISTOPHELES.]

FAUST: A knock? Come in! Who comes to plague me now?
MEPHISTOPHELES: It's I.
FAUST: Come in!
MEPHISTOPHELES: You have to say it thrice.
FAUST: Come in, then.
MEPHISTOPHELES: Now you're nice.
    We should get along well, I vow.
    To chase your spleen away, allow   5
    That I appear a noble squire:[2]
    Look at my red and gold attire,
    A little cloak of silk brocade,
    The rooster's feather in my hat,

---

2. In the popular plays based on the Faust legend, the Devil often appeared as a monk when the play
catered to a Protestant audience and as a noble squire when the audience was predominantly Catholic.

And the long, nicely pointed blade— 10
And now it is my counsel that
You, too, should be like this arrayed;
Then you would feel released and free,
And you would find what life can be.
FAUST: I shall not cease to feel in all attires, 15
The pains of our narrow earthly day.
I am too old to be content to play,
Too young to be without desire.
What wonders could the world reveal?
You must renounce! You ought to yield! 20
That is the never-ending drone
Which we must, our life long, hear,
Which, hoarsely, all our hours intone
And grind into our weary ears.
Frightened I waken to the dismal dawn, 25
Wish I had tears to drown the sun
And check the day that soon will scorn
My every wish—fulfill not one.
If I but think of any pleasure,
Bright critic day is sure to chide it, 30
And if my heart creates itself a treasure,
A thousand mocking masks deride it.
When night descends at last, I shall recline
But anxiously upon my bed;
Though all is still, no rest is mine 35
As dreams enmesh my mind in dread.
The god that dwells within my heart
Can stir my depths, I cannot hide—
Rules all my powers with relentless art,
But cannot move the world outside; 40
And thus existence is for me a weight,
Death is desirable, and life I hate.
MEPHISTOPHELES: And yet when death approaches, the welcome is not
    great.
FAUST: Oh, blessed whom, as victory advances,
He lends the blood-drenched laurel's grace, 45
Who, after wildly whirling dances,
Receives him in a girl's embrace!
Oh, that before the lofty spirit's power
I might have fallen to the ground, unsouled!
MEPHISTOPHELES: And yet someone, in that same nightly hour 50
Refused to drain a certain bowl.
FAUST: You seem to eavesdrop quite proficiently.
MEPHISTOPHELES: Omniscient I am not, but there is much I see.
FAUST: As in that terrifying reeling
I heard the sweet familiar chimes 55
That duped the traces of my childhood feeling
With echoes of more joyous times,

I now curse all that would enamor
The human soul with lures and lies,
Enticing it with flattering glamour   60
To live on in this cave of sighs.
Cursed above all our high esteem,
The spirit's smug self-confidence,
Cursed be illusion, fraud, and dream
That flatter our guileless sense!   65
Cursed be the pleasing make-believe
Of fame and long posthumous life!
Cursed be possessions that deceive,
As slave and plough, and child and wife!
Cursed, too, be Mammon[3] when with treasures   70
He spurs us on to daring feats,
Or lures us into slothful pleasures
With sumptuous cushions and smooth sheets!
A curse on wine that mocks our thirst!
A curse on love's last consummations!   75
A curse on hope! Faith, too, be cursed!
And cursed above all else be patience!
CHOIR OF SPIRITS: [*Invisible.*] Alas!
          You have shattered
          The beautiful world   80
          With brazen fist;
          It falls, it is scattered—
          By a demigod destroyed.
          We are trailing
          The ruins into the void   85
          And wailing
          Over beauty undone
          And ended.
          Earth's mighty son,
          More splendid   90
          Rebuild it, you that are strong,
          Build it again within!
          And begin
          A new life, a new way,
          Lucid and gay,   95
          And play
          New songs.
MEPHISTOPHELES: These are the small
          Ones of my thralls.
          Hear how precociously they plead   100
          For pleasure and deed!
          To worldly strife
          From your lonely life

---

3. The Aramaic word for "riches," used in the New Testament of the Bible. Medieval writers interpreted the word as a proper noun, the name of the Devil, as representing covetousness or avarice.

Which dries up sap and sense,
They would lure you hence. 105

Stop playing with your melancholy
That, like a vulture, ravages your breast;
The worst of company still cures this folly,
For you are human with the rest.
Yet that is surely not to say 110
That you should join the herd you hate.
I'm not one of the great,
But if you want to make your way
Through the world with me united,
I should surely be delighted 115
To be yours, as of now,
Your companion, if you allow;
And if you like the way I behave,
I shall be your servant, or your slave.
FAUST: And in return, what do you hope to take? 120
MEPHISTOPHELES: There's so much time—so why insist?
FAUST: No, no! The Devil is an egoist
And would not just for heaven's sake
Turn into a philanthropist.
Make your conditions very clear; 125
Where such a servant lives, danger is near.
MEPHISTOPHELES: *Here* you shall be the master, I be bond,
And at your nod I'll work incessantly;
But when we meet again *beyond,*
Then you shall do the same for me. 130
FAUST: Of the beyond I have no thought;
When you reduce this world to nought,
The other one may have its turn.
My joys come from this earth, and there,
That sun has burnt on my despair: 135
Once I have left those, I don't care:
    What happens is of no concern.
I do not even wish to hear
Whether beyond they hate and love,
And whether in that other sphere 140
One realm's below and one above.
MEPHISTOPHELES: So minded, dare it cheerfully.
Commit yourself and you shall see
My arts with joy. I'll give you more
Than any man has seen before. 145
FAUST: What would you, wretched Devil, offer?
Was ever a man's spirit in its noble striving
Grasped by your like, devilish scoffer?
But have you food that is not satisfying,
Red gold that rolls off without rest, 150
Quicksilver-like, over your skin—

A game in which no man can win—
A girl who, lying at my breast,
Ogles already to entice my neighbor,
And honor—that perhaps seems best—   155
Though like a comet it will turn to vapor?
Show me fruit that, before we pluck them, rot,
And trees whose foliage every day makes new!

MEPHISTOPHELES: Such a commission scares me not,
With such things I can wait on you.   160
But, worthy friend, the time comes when we would
Recline in peace and feast on something good.

FAUST: If ever I recline, calmed, on a bed of sloth,
You may destroy me then and there.
If ever flattering you should wile me   165
That in myself I find delight,
If with enjoyment you beguile me,
Then break on me, eternal night!
This bet I offer.

MEPHISTOPHELES: I accept it.

FAUST: Right.
If to the moment I should say: 170
Abide, you are so fair—
Put me in fetters on that day,
I *wish* to perish then, I swear.
Then let the death bell ever toll,
Your service done, you shall be free,   175
The clock may stop, the hand may fall,
As time comes to an end for me.

MEPHISTOPHELES: Consider it, for we shall not forget it.

FAUST: That is a right you need not waive.
I did not boast, and I shall not regret it.   180
As I grow stagnant I shall be a slave,
Whether or not to anyone indebted.

MEPHISTOPHELES: At the doctor's banquet[4] tonight I shall do
My duties as a servant without fail.
But for life's sake, or death's—just one detail: 185
Could you give me a line or two?

FAUST: You pedant need it black on white?
Are man and a man's word indeed new to your sight?
Is not my spoken word sufficient warrant
When it commits my life eternally?   190
Does not the world rush on in every torrent,
And a mere promise should hold me?
Yet this illusion our heart inherits,
And who would want to shirk his debt?
Blessed who counts loyalty among his merits.   195
No sacrifice will he regret.

---

4. The dinner given by a successful candidate for a Ph.D. degree.

And yet a parchment, signed and sealed, is an abhorrent
Specter that haunts us, and it makes us fret.
The word dies when we seize the pen,
And wax and leather lord it then.   200
What, evil spirit, do you ask?
Paper or parchment, stone or brass?
Should I use chisel, style, or quill?
It is completely up to you.
MEPHISTOPHELES: Why get so hot and overdo   205
Your rhetoric? Why must you shrill?
Use any sheet, it is the same;
And with a drop of blood you sign your name.
FAUST: If you are sure you like this game,
Let it be done to humor you.   210
MEPHISTOPHELES: Blood is a very special juice.
FAUST: You need not fear that someday I retract.
That all my striving I unloose
Is the whole purpose of the pact.
Oh, I was puffed up all too boldly,   215
At your rank only is my place.
The lofty spirit spurned me coldly,
And nature hides from me her face.
Torn is the subtle thread of thought,
I loathe the knowledge I once sought.   220
In sensuality's abysmal land
Let our passions drink their fill!
In magic veils, not pierced by skill,
Let every wonder be at hand!
Plunge into time's whirl that dazes my sense,   225
Into the torrent of events!
And let enjoyment, distress,
Annoyance and success
Succeed each other as best they can;
For restless activity proves a man.   230
MEPHISTOPHELES: You are not bound by goal or measure.
If you would nibble everything
Or snatch up something on the wing,
You're welcome to what gives you pleasure.
But help yourself and don't be coy!   235
FAUST: Do you not hear, I have no thought of joy!
The reeling whirl I seek, the most painful excess,
Enamored hate and quickening distress.
Cured from the craving to know all, my mind
Shall not henceforth be closed to any pain,   240
And what is portioned out to all mankind,
I shall enjoy deep in my self, contain
Within my spirit summit and abyss,
Pile on my breast their agony and bliss,
And thus let my own self grow into theirs, unfettered,   245

Till as they are, at last I, too, am shattered.
MEPHISTOPHELES: Believe me who for many a thousand year
　　Has chewed this cud and never rested,
　　That from the cradle to the bier
　　The ancient leaven cannot be digested.　　　　　250
　　Trust one like me, this whole array
　　Is for a God—there's no contender:
　　He dwells in his eternal splendor,
　　To darkness we had to surrender,
　　And you need night as well as day.　　　　　255
FAUST: And yet it is my will.
MEPHISTOPHELES:　　　　　It does sound bold.
　　But I'm afraid, though you are clever,
　　Time is too brief, though art's forever.
　　Perhaps you're willing to be told.
　　Why don't you find yourself a poet,　　　　　260
　　And let the gentleman ransack his dreams:
　　And when he finds a noble trait, let him bestow it
　　Upon your worthy head in reams and reams:
　　The lion's daring,
　　The swiftness of the hind,　　　　　265
　　The northerner's forbearing
　　And the Italian's fiery mind,
　　Let him resolve the mystery
　　How craft can be combined with magnanimity,
　　Or how a passion-crazed young man　　　　　270
　　Might fall in love after a plan.
　　If there were such a man, I'd like to meet him,
　　As Mr. Microcosm I would greet him.
FAUST: Alas, what am I, if I can
　　Not reach for mankind's crown which merely mocks　　　　　275
　　Our senses' craving like a star?
MEPHISTOPHELES: You're in the end—just what you are!
　　Put wigs on with a million locks
　　And put your foot on ell-high socks,
　　You still remain just what you are.　　　　　280
FAUST: I feel, I gathered up and piled up high
　　In vain the treasures of the human mind:
　　When I sit down at last, I cannot find
　　New strength within—it is all dry.
　　My stature has not grown a whit,　　　　　285
　　No closer to the Infinite.
MEPHISTOPHELES: Well, my good sir, to put it crudely,
　　You see matters just as they lie;
　　We have to look at them more shrewdly,
　　Or all life's pleasures pass us by.　　　　　290
　　Your hands and feet—indeed that's trite—
　　And head and seat are yours alone;
　　Yet all in which I find delight,

Should they be less my own?
Suppose I buy myself six steeds: 295
I buy their strength; while I recline
I dash along at whirlwind speeds,
For their two dozen legs are mine.
Come on! Let your reflections rest
And plunge into the world with zest! 300
I say, the man that speculates
Is like a beast that in the sand,
Led by an evil spirit, round and round gyrates,
And all about lies gorgeous pasture land.

FAUST: How shall we set about it?

MEPHISTOPHELES: Simply leave. 305
What torture room is this? What site of grief?
Is this the noble life of prudence—
You bore yourself and bore your students?
Oh, let your neighbor, Mr. Paunch, live so!
Why work hard threshing straw, when it annoys? 310
The best that you could ever know
You may not tell the little boys.
Right now I hear one in the aisle.

FAUST: I simply cannot face the lad.

MEPHISTOPHELES: The poor chap waited quite a while, 315
I do not want him to leave sad.
Give me your cap and gown. Not bad! [*He dresses himself up.*]
This mask ought to look exquisite!
Now you can leave things to my wit.
Some fifteen minutes should be all I need; 320
Meanwhile get ready for our trip, and speed!
[*Exit* FAUST.]

MEPHISTOPHELES: [*In* FAUST*'s long robe.*]
Have but contempt for reason and for science,
Man's noblest force spurn with defiance,
Subscribe to magic and illusion,
The Lord of Lies aids your confusion, 325
And, pact or no, I hold you tight.—
The spirit which he has received from fate
Sweeps ever onward with unbridled might,
Its hasty striving is so great
It leaps over the earth's delights. 330
Through life I'll drag him at a rate,
Through shallow triviality,
That he shall writhe and suffocate;
And his insatiability,
With greedy lips, shall see the choicest plate 335
And ask in vain for all that he would cherish—
And were he not the Devil's mate
And had not signed, he still must perish.
[*A* STUDENT *enters.*]

STUDENT: I have arrived quite recently
  And come, full of humility,   340
  To meet that giant intellect
  Whom all refer to with respect.
MEPHISTOPHELES: This is a charming pleasantry.
  A man as others are, you see.—
  Have you already called elsewhere?   345
STUDENT: I pray you, take me in your care.
  I am, believe me, quite sincere,
  Have some odd cash and lots of cheer;
  My mother scarcely let me go,
  But there is much I hope to know.   350
MEPHISTOPHELES: This is just the place for you to stay.
STUDENT: To be frank, I should like to run away.
  I cannot say I like these walls,
  These gloomy rooms and somber halls.
  It seems so narrow, and I see   355
  No patch of green, no single tree;
  And in the auditorium
  My hearing, sight, and thought grow numb.
MEPHISTOPHELES: That is a question of mere habit.
  The child, offered the mother's breast,   360
  Will not in the beginning grab it;
  But soon it clings to it with zest.
  And thus at wisdom's copious breasts
  You'll drink each day with greater zest.
STUDENT: I'll hang around her neck, enraptured;   365
  But tell me first: how is she captured?
MEPHISTOPHELES: Before we get into my views—
  What Department do you choose?
STUDENT: I should like to be erudite,
  And from the earth to heaven's height   370
  Know every law and every action:
  Nature and science is what I need.
MEPHISTOPHELES: That is the way; you just proceed
  And scrupulously shun distraction.
STUDENT: Body and soul, I am a devotee;   375
  Though, naturally, everybody prays
  For some free time and liberty
  On pleasant summer holidays.
MEPHISTOPHELES: Use well your time, so swiftly it runs on!
  Be orderly, and time is won!   380
  My friend, I shall be pedagogic,
  And say you ought to start with Logic.
  For thus your mind is trained and braced,
  In Spanish boots it will be laced,
  That on the road of thought maybe   385
  It henceforth creep more thoughtfully,
  And does not crisscross here and there,

Will-o'-the-wisping through the air.
Days will be spent to let you know
That what you once did at one blow,   390
Like eating and drinking so easy and free,
Can only be done with One, Two, Three.
Yet the web of thought has no such creases
And is more like a weaver's masterpieces:
One step, a thousand threads arise,   395
Hither and thither shoots each shuttle,
The threads flow on, unseen and subtle,
Each blow effects a thousand ties.
The philosopher comes with analysis
And proves it had to be like this: 400
The first was so, the second so,
And hence the third and fourth was so,
And were not the first and the second here,
Then the third and fourth could never appear.
That is what all the students believe,   405
But they have never learned to weave.
Who would study and describe the living, starts
By driving the spirit out of the parts:
In the palm of his hand he holds all the sections,
Lacks nothing, except the spirit's connections.   410
Encheirisis naturae[5] the chemists baptize it,
Mock themselves and don't realize it.
STUDENT: I did not quite get everything.
MEPHISTOPHELES: That will improve with studying:
You will reduce things by and by   415
And also learn to classify.
STUDENT: I feel so dazed by all you said
As if a mill went around in my head.
MEPHISTOPHELES: Then, without further circumvention,
Give metaphysics your attention.   420
There seek profoundly to attain
What does not fit the human brain;
Whether you do or do not understand,
An impressive word is always at hand.
But now during your first half-year,   425
Keep above all our order here.
Five hours a day, you understand,
And when the bell peals, be on hand.
Before you come, you must prepare,
Read every paragraph with care,   430
Lest you, forbid, should overlook
That all he says is in the book.
But write down everything, engrossed

5. The natural process by which substances are united into a living organism—a name for an action no one understands.

As if you took dictation from the Holy Ghost.
STUDENT: Don't say that twice—I understood: 435
    I see how useful it's to write,
    For what we possess black on white
    We can take home and keep for good.
MEPHISTOPHELES: But choose a field of concentration!
STUDENT: I have no hankering for jurisprudence.   440
MEPHISTOPHELES: For that I cannot blame the students,
    I know this science is a blight.
    The laws and statutes of a nation
    Are an inherited disease,
    From generation unto generation   445
    And place to place they drag on by degrees.
    Wisdom becomes nonsense; kindness, oppression:
    To be a grandson is a curse.
    The right that is innate in us
    Is not discussed by the profession.   450
STUDENT: My scorn is heightened by your speech.
    Happy the man that you would teach!
    I almost think theology would pay.
MEPHISTOPHELES: I should not wish to lead you astray.
    When it comes to this discipline,   455
    The way is hard to find, wrong roads abound,
    And lots of hidden poison lies around
    Which one can scarcely tell from medicine.
    Here, too, it would be best you heard
    One only and staked all upon your master's word.   460
    Yes, stick to words at any rate;
    There never was a surer gate
    Into the temple, Certainty.
STUDENT: Yet some idea there must be.
MEPHISTOPHELES: All right. But do not plague yourself too anxiously;   465
    For just where no ideas are
    The proper word is never far.
    With words a dispute can be won,
    With words a system can be spun,
    In words one can believe unshaken,   470
    And from a word no tittle can be taken.
STUDENT: Forgive, I hold you up with many questions,
    But there is one more thing I'd like to see.
    Regarding medicine, maybe,
    You have some powerful suggestions?   475
    Three years go by so very fast,
    And, God, the field is all too vast.
    If but a little hint is shown,
    One can attempt to find one's way.
MEPHISTOPHELES: [*Aside.*] I'm sick of this pedantic tone.   480
    The Devil now again I'll play.
    [*Aloud.*] The spirit of medicine is easy to know:

Through the macro-and microcosm you breeze,
And in the end you let it go
As God may please.   485
In vain you roam about to study science,
For each learns only what he can;
Who places on the moment his reliance,
He is the proper man.
You are quite handsome, have good sense,   490
And no doubt, you have courage, too,
And if you have self-confidence,
Then others will confide in you.
And give the women special care;
Their everlasting sighs and groans   495
In thousand tones
Are cured at *one* point everywhere.
And if you seem halfway discreet,
They will be lying at your feet.
First your degree inspires trust,   500
As if your art had scarcely any peers;
Right at the start, remove her clothes and touch her bust,
Things for which others wait for years and years.
Learn well the little pulse to squeeze,
And with a knowing, fiery glance you seize   505
Her freely round her slender waist
To see how tightly she is laced.
STUDENT: That looks much better, sir. For one sees how and where.
MEPHISTOPHELES: Gray, my dear friend, is every theory,
And green alone life's golden tree.   510
STUDENT: All this seems like a dream, I swear.
Could I impose on you sometime again
And drink more words of wisdom then?
MEPHISTOPHELES: What I can give you, you shall get.
STUDENT: Alas, I cannot go quite yet: 515
My album I must give to you;
Please, sir, show me this favor, too.
MEPHISTOPHELES: All right. [*He writes and returns it.*]
STUDENT: [*Reads.*] Eritis sicut Deus, scientes bonum et malum.[6] [*Closes
the book reverently and takes his leave.*]
MEPHISTOPHELES: Follow the ancient text and my relation, the snake;   520
Your very likeness to God will yet make you quiver and quake.
[FAUST *enters.*]
FAUST: Where are we heading now?
MEPHISTOPHELES: Wherever you may please.
We'll see the small world, then the larger one.
You will reap profit and have fun
As you sweep through this course with ease.   525

6. A slight alteration of the serpent's words to Eve in Genesis: "Ye shall be as God, knowing good and evil" (Latin).

FAUST: With my long beard I hardly may
  Live in this free and easy way.
  The whole endeavor seems so futile;
  I always felt the world was strange and brutal.
  With others, I feel small and harassed,   530
  And I shall always be embarrassed.
MEPHISTOPHELES: Good friend, you will become less sensitive:
  Self-confidence will teach you how to live.
FAUST: How shall we get away from here?
  Where are your carriage, groom and steed?   535
MEPHISTOPHELES: I rather travel through the air:
  We spread this cloak—that's all we need.
  But on this somewhat daring flight,
  Be sure to keep your luggage light.
  A little fiery air, which I plan to prepare,   540
  Will raise us swiftly off the earth;
  Without ballast we'll go up fast—
  Congratulations, friend, on your rebirth!

AUERBACH'S KELLER IN LEIPZIG

[Jolly fellows' drinking bout.]

FROSCH: Will no one drink and no one laugh?
  I'll teach you not to look so wry.
  Today you look like sodden chaff
  And usually blaze to the sky
BRANDER: It's all your fault; you make me sick: 5
  No joke, and not a single dirty trick.
FROSCH: [*Pours a glass of wine over* BRANDER'*s head.*]
  There you have both.
BRANDER: You filthy pig!
FROSCH: You said I shouldn't be a prig.
SIEBEL: Let those who fight, stop or get out!
  With all your lungs sing chorus, swill, and shout!   10
  Come! Holla-ho!
ALTMAYER: Now this is where I quit.
  Get me some cotton or my ears will split.
SIEBEL: When the vault echoes and the place
  Is quaking, then you can enjoy a bass.
FROSCH: Quite right! Throw out who fusses because he is lampooned! 15
  A! tara lara da!
ALTMAYER: A! tara lara da!
FROSCH: The throats seem to be tuned.
    [*Sings.*] Dear Holy Roman Empire,
    What holds you still together?   20
BRANDER: A nasty song! It reeks of politics!
  A wretched song! Thank God in daily prayer,
  That the old Empire isn't your affair!
  At least I think it is much to be grateful for

That I'm not Emperor nor Chancellor.   25
And yet we, too, need someone to respect—
I say, a Pope let us elect.
You know the part that elevates
And thereby proves the man who rates.
FROSCH: [*Sings.*] Oh, Dame Nightingale, arise!   30
    Bring my sweet love ten thousand sighs!
SIEBEL: No sighs for your sweet love! I will not have such mush.
FROSCH: A sigh and kiss for her! You cannot make me blush.
    [*Sings*] Ope the latch in silent night!
    Ope the latch, your love invite!   35
    Shut the latch, there is the dawn!
SIEBEL: Go, sing and sing and sing, pay compliments and fawn!
    The time will come when I shall laugh:
    She led me by the nose, and you are the next calf.
    Her lover should be some mischievous gnome!   40
    He'd meet her at a crossroads and make light,
    And an old billy goat that's racing home
    From Blocksberg could still bleat to her "Good night!"
    A decent lad of real flesh and blood
    Is far too good to be her stud.   45
    I'll stand no sighs, you silly ass,
    But throw rocks through her window glass.
BRANDER: [*Pounding on the table.*]
    Look here! Look here! Listen to me!
    My friends, confess I know what's right;
    There are lovers here, and you'll agree   50
    That it's only civility
    That I should try to honor them tonight.
    Watch out! This song's the latest fashion.
    And join in the refrain with passion!
    [*Sings.*] A cellar once contained a rat   55
        That couldn't have been uncouther,
        Lived on grease and butter and grew fat—
        Just like old Doctor Luther.[7]
        The cook put poison in his food,
        Then he felt cramped and just as stewed,   60
        As if love gnawed his vitals.
CHORUS: [*Jubilant.*] As if love gnawed his vitals.
BRANDER: He dashed around, he dashed outdoors,
        Sought puddles and swilled rain,
        He clawed and scratched up walls and floors,   65
        But his frenzy was in vain;
        He jumped up in a frightful huff,
        But soon the poor beast had enough,
        As if love gnawed his vitals.

---

7. Martin Luther (1483–1546), German leader of the Protestant reformation, hence an object of distaste for Catholics.

CHORUS: As if love gnawed his vitals.   70
BRANDER: At last he rushed in open day
    Into the kitchen, crazed with fear,
    Dropped near the stove and writhed and lay,
    And puffed out his career.
    The poisoner only laughed: I hope   75
    He's at the end now of his rope,
    As if love gnawed his vitals.
CHORUS: As if love gnawed his vitals.
SIEBEL: How pleased these stupid chaps are! That's,
    I think, indeed a proper art   80
    To put out poison for poor rats.
BRANDER: I see, you'd like to take their part.
ALTMAYER: Potbelly with his shiny top!
    His ill luck makes him mild and tame.
    He sees the bloated rat go flop—   85
    And sees himself: they look the same.
    [FAUST *and* MEPHISTOPHELES *enter.*]
MEPHISTOPHELES: Above all else, it seems to me,
    You need some jolly company
    To see life can be fun—to say the least:
    The people here make every day a feast.   90
    With little wit and boisterous noise,
    They dance and circle in their narrow trails
    Like kittens playing with their tails.
    When hangovers don't vex these boys,
    And while their credit's holding out,   95
    They have no cares and drink and shout.
BRANDER: Those two are travelers, I swear.
    I tell it right off by the way they stare.
    They have been here at most an hour.
FROSCH: No doubt about it. Leipzig is a flower,   100
    It is a little Paris and educates its people.
SIEBEL: What may they be? Who knows the truth?
FROSCH: Leave it to me! A drink that interposes—
    And I'll pull like a baby tooth
    The worms they hide, out of these fellows' noses.   105
    They seem to be of noble ancestry,
    For they look proud and act disdainfully.
BRANDER: They are mere quacks and born in squalor.
ALTMAYER: Maybe.
FROSCH: Watch out! We shall commence.
MEPHISTOPHELES: [*To* FAUST.] The Devil people never sense,   110
    Though he may hold them by the collar.
FAUST: Good evening, gentlemen.
SIEBEL: Thank you, to you the same.
    [*Softly, looking at* MEPHISTOPHELES *from the side.*]
    Look at his foot. Why is it lame?[8]

---

8. By tradition, the Devil had a cloven foot, split like a sheep's hoof.

MEPHISTOPHELES: We'll join you, if you grant the liberty.
  The drinks they have are poor, their wine not very mellow,   115
  So we'll enjoy your company.
ALTMAYER: You seem a most fastidious fellow.
FROSCH: Did you leave Rippach rather late and walk?
  And did you first have dinner with Master Jackass there?
MEPHISTOPHELES: Tonight we had no time to spare.   120
  Last time, however, we had quite a talk.
  He had a lot to say of his relations
  And asked us to send each his warmest salutations. [*He bows to* FROSCH.]
ALTMAYER: [*Softly.*] You got it! He's all right.
SIEBEL: A pretty repartee!
FROSCH: I'll get him yet. Just wait and see.   125
MEPHISTOPHELES: Just now we heard, if I'm not wrong,
  Some voices singing without fault.
  Indeed this seems a place for song;
  No doubt, it echoes from the vault.
FROSCH: Are you perchance a virtuoso?   130
MEPHISTOPHELES: Oh no, the will is great, the power only so-so.
ALTMAYER: Give us a song!
MEPHISTOPHELES: As many as you please.
SIEBEL: But let us have a brand-new strain!
MEPHISTOPHELES: We have just recently returned from Spain,
  The beauteous land of wine and melodies.   135
    [*Sings.*] A king lived long ago
    Who had a giant flea—
FROSCH: Hear, hear! A flea! That's what I call a jest.
  A flea's a mighty pretty guest.
MEPHISTOPHELES: [*Sings.*] A king lived long ago   140
    Who had a giant flea,
    He loved him just as though
    He were his son and heir.
    He sent his tailor a note
    And offered the tailor riches   145
    If he would measure a coat
    And also take measure for breeches.
BRANDER: Be sure to tell the tailor, if he twinkles,
    That he must take fastidious measure;
    He'll lose his head, not just the treasure,   150
    If in the breeches there are wrinkles.
MEPHISTOPHELES: He was in silk arrayed,
    In velvet he was dressed,
    Had ribbons and brocade,
    A cross upon his chest   155
    A fancy star, great fame—
    A minister, in short;
    And all his kin became
    Lords at the royal court.
    The other lords grew lean   160

And suffered with their wives,
The royal maid and the queen
Were all but eaten alive,
But weren't allowed to swat them
And could not even scratch,   165
While we can swat and blot them
And kill the ones we catch.
CHORUS: [*Jubilant.*] While we can swat and blot them
    And kill the ones we catch.
FROSCH: Bravo! Bravo! That was a treat!   170
SIEBEL: That is the end all fleas should meet.
BRANDER: Point your fingers and catch 'em fine!
ALTMAYER: Long live our freedom! And long live wine!
MEPHISTOPHELES: When freedom is the toast, my own voice I should
    add,
    Were your forsaken wines only not quite so bad.[9]   175
SIEBEL: You better mind your language, lad.
MEPHISTOPHELES: I only fear the landlord might protest,
    Else I should give each honored guest
    From our cellar a good glass.
SIEBEL: Let's go! The landlord is an ass.   180
FROSCH: If you provide good drinks, you shall be eulogized;
    But let your samples be good-sized.
    When I'm to judge, I'm telling him,
    I want my snout full to the brim.
ALTMAYER: [*Softly.*] They're from the Rhineland, I presume.   185
MEPHISTOPHELES: Bring me a gimlet.
BRANDER: What could that be for?
    You couldn't have the casks in the next room?
ALTMAYER: The landlord keeps his tools right there behind the door.
MEPHISTOPHELES: [*Takes the gimlet. To* FROSCH.]
    What would you like? Something that's cool?
FROSCH: What do you mean? You got a lot of booze?   190
MEPHISTOPHELES: I let each have what he may choose.
ALTMAYER: [*To* FROSCH.] Oho! You lick your chops and start to drool.
FROSCH: If it is up to me, I'll have a Rhenish brand:
    There's nothing that competes with our fatherland.
MEPHISTOPHELES: [*Boring a hole near the edge of the table where* FROSCH
    sits.] Now let us have some wax to make a cork that sticks.   195
ALTMAYER: Oh, is it merely parlor tricks?
MEPHISTOPHELES: [*To* BRANDER.] And you?
BRANDER: I want a good champagne—
    Heady; I do not like it plain.
    [MEPHISTOPHELES *bores; meanwhile someone else has made the wax
    stoppers and plugged the holes.*]
BRANDER: Not all that's foreign can be banned,
    For what is far is often fine.   200

---

9. Cursed.

A Frenchman is a thing no German man can stand,
  And yet we like to drink their wine.
SIEBEL: [As MEPHISTOPHELES *approaches his place*.]
  I must confess, I think the dry tastes bad,
  The sweet alone is exquisite.
MEPHISTOPHELES: [*Boring*.] Tokay[1] will flow for you, my lad.   205
ALTMAYER: I think, you might as well admit,
  Good gentlemen, that these are simply jests.
MEPHISTOPHELES: Tut, tut! With such distinguished guests
  That would be quite a lot to dare.
  So don't be modest, and declare   210
  What kind of wine you would prefer.
ALTMAYER: I like them all, so I don't care.
  [*After all the holes have been bored and plugged*.]
MEPHISTOPHELES: [*With strange gestures*.] The grape the vine adorns,
  The billy goat sports horns;
  The wine is juicy, vines are wood,   215
  The wooden table gives wine as good,
  Profound insight! Now you perceive
  A miracle; only believe!
Now pull the stoppers and have fun!
ALL: [*As they pull out the stoppers and the wine each asked for flows into
  his glass*.] A gorgeous well for everyone!   220
MEPHISTOPHELES: Be very careful lest it overrun!
  [*They drink several times*.]
ALL: [*Sing*.] We feel gigantically well,
  Just like five hundred sows.
MEPHISTOPHELES: Look there how well men are when they are free.
FAUST: I should like to get out of here.   225
MEPHISTOPHELES: First watch how their bestiality
  Will in full splendor soon appear.
SIEBEL: [*Drinks carelessly and spills his wine on the floor where it turns
  into a flame*.] Help! Fire! Help! Hell blew a vent!
MEPHISTOPHELES: [*Conjuring the flame*.] Be quiet, friendly element!
  [*To the fellow*.] For this time it was only a drop of purgatory.   230
SIEBEL: You'll pay for it, and you can save your story!
  What do you think we are, my friend?
FROSCH: Don't dare do that a second time, you hear!
ALTMAYER: Just let him leave in silence; that is what I say, gents!
SIEBEL: You have the brazen impudence   235
  To do your hocus-pocus here?
MEPHISTOPHELES: Be still, old barrel!
SIEBEL: Broomstick, you!
  Will you insult us? Mind your prose!
BRANDER: Just wait and see, there will be blows.
ALTMAYER: [*Pulls a stopper out of the table and fire leaps at him*.]
  I burn! I burn!

---

1. A sweet Hungarian wine.

SIEBEL: It's magic, as I said.   240
  He is an outlaw. Strike him dead!
    [*They draw their knives and advance on* MEPHISTOPHELES.]
MEPHISTOPHELES: [*With solemn gestures.*]
    False images prepare
    Mirages in the air.
    Be here and there!
    [*They stand amazed and stare at each other.*]
ALTMAYER: Where am I? What a gorgeous land!   245
FROSCH: And vineyards! Am I mad?
SIEBEL: And grapes right by my hand!
BRANDER: See in the leaves that purple shape?
  I never saw that big a grape!
    [*Grabs* SIEBEL's *nose. They all do it to each other and raise their
    knives.*]
MEPHISTOPHELES: [*As above.*] Fall from their eyes, illusion's band!
  Remember how the Devil joked.   250
    [*He disappears with* FAUST, *the revelers separate.*]
SIEBEL: What's that?
ALTMAYER: Hah?
FROSCH: Your nose I stroked?
BRANDER: [*To* SIEBEL.] And yours is in my hand!
ALTMAYER: The shock is more than I can bear.
  I think I'll faint. Get me a chair!
FROSCH: What was all this? Who understands?   255
SIEBEL: Where is the scoundrel? I'm so sore,
  If I could only get my hands—
ALTMAYER: I saw him whiz right through the cellar door,
  Riding a flying barrel. Zounds,
  The fright weighs on me like a thousand pounds.   260
    [*Turning toward the table.*] Do you suppose the wine still flows?
SIEBEL: That was a fraud! You're asinine!
FROSCH: I surely thought that I drank wine.
BRANDER: But what about the grapes, I say.
ALTMAYER: Who says there are no miracles today!   265

WITCH'S KITCHEN

[*On a low stove, a large caldron stands over the fire. In the steam that
rises from it, one can see several shapes. A longtailed* FEMALE MONKEY
*sits near the caldron, skims it, and sees to it that it does not overflow.
The* MALE MONKEY *with the little ones sits next to her and warms
himself. Walls and ceiling are decorated with the queerest imple-
ments of witchcraft.* FAUST *and* MEPHISTOPHELES *enter.*]
FAUST: How I detest this crazy sorcery!
  I should get well, you promise me,
  In this mad frenzy of a mess?
  Do I need the advice of hag fakirs?
  And should this quackish sordidness   5

Reduce my age by thirty years?
I'm lost if that's all you could find.
My hope is drowned in sudden qualm.
Has neither nature nor some noble mind
Invented or contrived a wholesome balm?   10
MEPHISTOPHELES: My friend, that was nice oratory!
Indeed, to make you young there is one way that's apter;
But, I regret, that is another story
And forms quite an amazing chapter.
FAUST: I want to know it.
MEPHISTOPHELES: All right, you need no sorcery   15
And no physician and no dough.
Just go into the fields and see
What fun it is to dig and hoe;
Live simply and keep all your thoughts
On a few simple objects glued;   20
Restrict yourself and eat the plainest food;
Live with the beasts, a beast: it is no thievery
To dress the fields you work, with your own dung.
That is the surest remedy:
At eighty, you would still be young.   25
FAUST: I am not used to that and can't, I am afraid,
Start now to work with hoe and spade.
For me a narrow life like that's too small.
MEPHISTOPHELES: We need the witch then after all.
FAUST: Why just the hag with all her grime!   30
Could you not brew it—with *your* head!
MEPHISTOPHELES: A splendid way to waste my time!
A thousand bridges I could build instead.[2]
Science is not enough, nor art;
In this work patience plays a part.   35
A quiet spirit plods and plods at length;
Nothing but time can give the brew its strength.
With all the things that go into it,
It's sickening just to *see* them do it.
The Devil taught them, true enough   40
But he himself can't make the stuff.
    [*He sees the* ANIMALS.]
Just see how delicate they look!
This is the maid, and that the cook.
[*To the* ANIMALS.] It seems the lady isn't home?
ANIMALS: She went to roam   45
        Away from home,
        Right through the chimney in the dome.
MEPHISTOPHELES: And how long will she walk the street?
ANIMALS: As long as we warm our feet.

---

2. According to folk legend, the Devil built bridges at the request of human beings. As a reward, he caught either the first or the thirteenth soul to cross each new bridge.

MEPHISTOPHELES: [*To* FAUST.] How do you like this dainty pair?   50
FAUST: They are inane beyond comparison.
MEPHISTOPHELES: A conversation like this one
    Is just the sort of thing for which I care.
    [*To the* ANIMALS.] Now tell me, you accursed group,
    Why do you stir that steaming mess?   55
ANIMALS: We cook a watery beggars' soup.
MEPHISTOPHELES: You should do a brisk business.
MALE MONKEY: [*Approaches* MEPHISTOPHELES *and fawns.*]
      Oh please throw the dice
      And lose, and be nice
      And let me get wealthy!   60
      We are in the ditch,
      And if I were rich,
      Then I might be healthy.
MEPHISTOPHELES: How happy every monkey thinks he'd be,
    If he could play the lottery.   65
    [*Meanwhile the monkey youngsters have been playing with a large*
    ball, and now they roll it forward.]
MALE MONKEY: The world and ball
      Both rise and fall
      And roll and wallow;
      It sounds like glass,
      It bursts, alas,   70
      The inside's hollow.
      Here it is light,
      There still more bright,
      Life's mine to swallow!
      Dear son, I say,   75
      Please keep away!
      You'll die first.
      It's made of clay
      It will burst.
MEPHISTOPHELES: The sieve there, chief—?   80
MALE MONKEY: [*Gets it down.*] If you were a thief,
      I'd be wise to you.
    [*He runs to the* FEMALE MONKEY *and lets her see through it.*]
      Look through, be brief!
      You know the thief,
      But may not say *who?*   85
MEPHISTOPHELES: [*Approaching the fire.*] And here this pot?
BOTH BIG MONKEYS: The half-witted sot!
      Does not know the pot,
      Does not know the kettle!
MEPHISTOPHELES: You impolite beast!   90
MALE MONKEY: Take this brush at least
      And sit down and settle!
    [*He makes* MEPHISTOPHELES *sit down.*]
FAUST: [*Who has been standing before a mirror all this time, now stepping*

close to it, now back.] What blissful image is revealed
To me behind this magic glass!
Lend me your swiftest pinions, love, that I might pass   95
From here to her transfigured field!
When I don't stay right on this spot, but, pining,
Dare to step forward and go near
Mists cloud her shape and let it disappear.
The fairest image of a woman!   100
Indeed, could woman be so fair?
Or is this body which I see reclining
Heaven's quintessence from another sphere?
Is so much beauty found on earth?
MEPHISTOPHELES: Well, if a god works hard for six whole days, my
        friend,   105
And then says bravo in the end,
It ought to have a little worth.
For now, stare to your heart's content!
I could track down for you just such a sweet—
What bliss it would be to get her consent,   110
To marry her and be replete.
    [FAUST *gazes into the mirror all the time.* MEPHISTOPHELES, *stretch-*
    ing in the armchair and playing with the brush, goes on speaking.]
I sit here like the king upon his throne:
The scepter I hold here, I lack the crown alone.
ANIMALS: [*Who have so far moved around in quaint confusion, bring a*
    crown to MEPHISTOPHELES, *clamoring loudly.*] Oh, please be so good.
        With sweat and with blood   115
        This crown here to lime!
    [*They handle the crown clumsily and break it into two pieces with*
    which they jump around.]
        It's done, let it be!
        We chatter and see,
        We listen and rhyme—
FAUST: [*At the mirror.*] Alas, I think I'll lose my wits.   120
MEPHISTOPHELES: [*Pointing toward the* ANIMALS.]
    I fear that my head, too, begins to reel.
ANIMALS: And if we score hits
        And everything fits,
        It's thoughts that we feel.
FAUST: [*As above.*] My heart and soul are catching fire.   125
Please let us go away from here!
MEPHISTOPHELES: [*In the same position as above.*]
    The one thing one has to admire
    Is that their poetry is quite sincere.
    [*The caldron which the* FEMALE MONKEY *has neglected begins to run*
    over, and a huge flame blazes up through the chimney. The WITCH
    scoots down through the flame with a dreadful clamor.]
WITCH: Ow! Ow! Ow! Ow!
You damned old beast! You cursed old sow!   130

You leave the kettle and singe the frau.
You cursed old beast! [*Sees* FAUST *and* MEPHISTOPHELES.]
    What goes on here?
    Why are you here?
    Who are you two?   135
    Who sneaked inside?
    Come, fiery tide!
    Their bones be fried!
[*She plunges the skimming spoon into the caldron and spatters flames at* FAUST, MEPHISTOPHELES, *and the* ANIMALS. *The* ANIMALS *whine.*]
MEPHISTOPHELES: [*Reversing the brush he holds in his hand, and striking into the glasses and pots.*]
    In two! In two!
    There lies the brew.   140
    There lies the glass.
    A joke, my lass,
    The beat, you ass,
    For melodies from you.
[*As the* WITCH *retreats in wrath and horror.*]
You know me now? You skeleton! You shrew!   145
You know your master and your lord?
What holds me? I could strike at you
And shatter you and your foul monkey horde.
Does not the scarlet coat reveal His Grace?
Do you not know the rooster's feather, ma'am?   150
Did I perchance conceal my face?
Or must I tell you who I am?
WITCH: Forgive the uncouth greeting, though
  You have no cloven feet, you know.
  And your two ravens, where are they?   155
MEPHISTOPHELES: For just this once you may get by,
  For it has been some time, I don't deny,
  Since I have come your way,
  And culture which licks out at every stew
  Extends now to the Devil, too: 160
  Gone is the Nordic phantom that former ages saw;
  You see no horns, no tail or claw.
  And as regards the foot with which I can't dispense,
  That does not look the least bit suave;
  Like other young men nowadays, I hence   165
  Prefer to pad my calves.
WITCH: [*Dancing.*] I'll lose my wits, I'll lose my brain
  Since Squire Satan has come back again.
MEPHISTOPHELES: That name is out, hag! Is that plain?
WITCH: But why? It never gave you pain!   170
MEPHISTOPHELES: It's dated, called a fable; men are clever,
  But they are just as badly off as ever:
  The Evil One is gone, the evil ones remain.

You call me baron, hag, and you look out:
I am a cavalier with cavalierly charms, 175
And my nobility don't dare to doubt!
Look here and you will see my coat of arms!
[*He makes an indecent gesture.*]
WITCH: [*Laughs immoderately.*] Ha! Ha! That is your manner, sir!
You are a jester as you always were.
MEPHISTOPHELES: [*To* FAUST.] My friend, mark this, but don't repeat it: 180
This is the way a witch likes to be treated.
WITCH: Now tell me why you came in here.
MEPHISTOPHELES: A good glass of the famous juice, my dear!
But I must have the oldest kind:
Its strength increases with each year. 185
WITCH: I got a bottle on this shelf
From which I like to nip myself;
By now it doesn't even stink.
I'll give you some, it has the power.
[*Softly.*] But if, quite unprepared, this man should have a drink, 190
He could, as you know well, not live another hour.
MEPHISTOPHELES: He is a friend of mine, and he will take it well
The best you have is not too good for him.
Now draw your circle, say your spell,
And fill a bumper to the brim. 195
[WITCH *draws a circle with curious gestures and puts quaint objects
into it, while the glasses begin to tinkle, the caldrons begin to resound
and they make music. In the end, she gets a big book and puts the*
MONKEYS *into the circle, and they serve her as a desk and have to
hold a torch for her. She motions* FAUST *to step up.*]
FAUST: [*To* MEPHISTOPHELES.] No, tell me why these crazy antics?
The mad ado, the gestures that are frantic,
The most insipid cheat—this stuff
I've known and hated long enough.
MEPHISTOPHELES: Relax! It's fun—a little play; 200
Don't be so serious, so sedate!
Such hocus-pocus is a doctor's way,
Of making sure the juice will operate.
[*He makes* FAUST *step into the circle.*]
WITCH: [*Begins to recite from the book with great emphasis.*]
This you must know!
From one make ten, 205
And two let go,
Take three again,
Then you'll be rich.
The four you fix.
From five and six, 210
Thus says the witch,
Make seven and eight,
That does the trick;
And nine is one,

      And ten is none.   215
      That is the witch's arithmetic.
FAUST: It seems to me the old hag runs a fever.
MEPHISTOPHELES: You'll hear much more before we leave her.
    I know, it sounds like that for many pages.
    I lost much time on this accursed affliction   220
    Because a perfect contradiction
    Intrigues not only fools but also sages.
    This art is old and new, forsooth:
    It was the custom in all ages
    To spread illusion and not truth   225
    With Three in One and One in Three.[3]
    They teach it twittering like birds;
    With fools there is no intervening.
    Men usually believe, if only they hear words,
    That there must also be some sort of meaning.   230
WITCH: [*Continues.*] The lofty prize
      Of science lies
      Concealed today as ever.
      Who has no thought,
      To him it's brought   235
      To own without endeavor.
FAUST: What nonsense does she put before us?
    My head aches from her stupidness.
    It seems as if I heard a chorus
    Of many thousand fools, no less.   240
MEPHISTOPHELES: Excellent sybil, that is quite enough!
    Now pour the drink—just put the stuff
    Into this bowl here. Fill it, sybil, pour;
    My friend is safe from any injuries:
    He has a number of degrees   245
    And has had many drinks before.
      [WITCH *pours the drink into a bowl with many ceremonies; as* FAUST
      puts it to his lips, a small flame spurts up.]
MEPHISTOPHELES: What is the matter? Hold it level!
    Drink fast and it will warm you up.
    You are familiar with the Devil,
    And shudder at a fiery cup?   250
      [*The* WITCH *breaks the circle.* FAUST *steps out.*]
MEPHISTOPHELES: Come on! Let's go! You must not rest.
WITCH: And may this gulp give great delight!
MEPHISTOPHELES: [*To the* WITCH.] If there is anything that you request,
    Just let me know the next Walpurgis Night.[4]
WITCH: Here is a song; just sing it now and then,   255
    And you will feel a queer effect indeed.
MEPHISTOPHELES: [*To* FAUST.] Come quickly now before you tire,

---

3. The Christian doctrine of the Trinity.   4. The eve of May Day (May 1), when witches are supposed
to assemble on the Brocken, a peak in the Hartz Mountains, which are in central Germany.

And let me lead while you perspire
So that the force can work out through your skin.
I'll teach you later on to value noble leisure,   260
And soon you will perceive the most delightful pleasure,
As Cupid starts to stir and dance like jumping jinn.[5]
FAUST: One last look at the mirror where I stood!
So beauteous was that woman's form!
MEPHISTOPHELES: No! No! The paragon of womanhood   265
You shall soon see alive and warm.
[*Softly.*] You'll soon find with this potion's aid,
Helen of Troy in every maid.

STREET

[FAUST. MARGARET *passing by.*]
FAUST: Fair lady, may I be so free
To offer my arm and company?
MARGARET: I'm neither a lady nor am I fair,
And can go home without your care.
[*She frees herself and exits.*]
FAUST: By heaven, this young girl is fair!   5
Her like I don't know anywhere.
She is so virtuous and pure,
But somewhat pert and not demure.
The glow of her cheeks and her lips so red
I shall not forget until I am dead.   10
Her downcast eyes, shy and yet smart,
Are stamped forever on my heart;
Her curtness and her brevity
Was sheer enchanting ecstasy!
[MEPHISTOPHELES *enters.*]
FAUST: Get me that girl, and don't ask why!   15
MEPHISTOPHELES: Which one?
FAUST: She only just went by.
MEPHISTOPHELES: That one! She saw her priest just now,
And he pronounced her free of sin.
I stood right there and listened in.
She's so completely blemishless   20
That there was nothing to confess.
Over her I don't have any power.
FAUST: She is well past her fourteenth year.
MEPHISTOPHELES: Look at the gay Lothario[6] here!
He would like to have every flower,   25
And thinks each prize or pretty trick
Just waits around for him to pick;
But sometimes that just doesn't go.

---

5. A supernatural being that can take human or animal form.   6. The seducer in Nicholas Rowe's play *The Fair Penitent* (1703); hence, figuratively, any seducer. The German reads *Hans Liederlich*, meaning a profligate, since *liederlich* means "careless" or "dissolute."

FAUST: My Very Reverend Holy Joe,
    Leave me in peace with law and right!   30
    I tell you, if you don't comply,
    And this sweet young blood doesn't lie
    Between my arms this very night,
    At midnight we'll have parted ways.
MEPHISTOPHELES: Think of the limits of my might.   35
    I need at least some fourteen days
    To find a handy evening.
FAUST: If I had peace for seven hours,
    I should not need the Devil's powers
    To seduce such a little thing.   40
MEPHISTOPHELES: You speak just like a Frenchman. Wait
    I beg you, and don't be annoyed:
    What have you got when it's enjoyed?
    The fun is not nearly so great
    As when you bit by bit imbibe it,   45
    And first resort to playful folly
    To knead and to prepare your dolly,
    The way some Gallic tales describe it.
FAUST: I've appetite without all that.
MEPHISTOPHELES: Now without jokes or tit-for-tat: 50
    I tell you, with this fair young child
    We simply can't be fast or wild.
    We'd waste our time storming and running;
    We have to have recourse to cunning.
FAUST: Get something from the angel's nest!   55
    Or lead me to her place of rest!
    Get me a kerchief from her breast,
    A garter from my darling's knee.
MEPHISTOPHELES: Just so you see, it touches me
    And I would soothe your agony,   60
    Let us not linger here and thus delay:
    I'll take you to her room today.
FAUST: And shall I see her? Have her?
MEPHISTOPHELES: No.
    To one of her neighbors she has to go.
    But meanwhile you may at your leisure   65
    Relish the hopes of future pleasure,
    Till you are sated with her atmosphere.
FAUST: Can we go now?
MEPHISTOPHELES: It's early yet, I fear.
FAUST: Get me a present for the dear!
    [Exit.]
MEPHISTOPHELES: A present right away? Good! He will be a hit.   70
    There's many a nice place I know
    With treasures buried long ago;
    I better look around a bit.
    [Exit.]

EVENING

[*A small neat room.*]
MARGARET: [*Braiding and binding her hair.*]
I should give much if I could say
Who was that gentleman today.
He looked quite gallant, certainly,
And is of noble family;
That much even his forehead told—   5
How else could he have been so bold?
[*Exit. Enter* MEPHISTOPHELES, FAUST.]
MEPHISTOPHELES: Come in, but very quietly!
FAUST: [*After a short silence.*] I beg you, leave and let me be!
MEPHISTOPHELES: [*Sniffing around.*] She's neater than a lot of girls I see.
[*Exit.*]
FAUST: [*Looking up and around.*] Sweet light of dusk, guest from above 10
That fills this shrine, be welcome you!
Seize now my heart, sweet agony of love
That languishes and feeds on hope's clear dew!
What sense of calm embraces me,
Of order and complete content!   15
What bounty in this poverty!
And in this prison, ah, what ravishment!
[*He throws himself into the leather armchair by the bed.*]
Welcome me now, as former ages rested
Within your open arms in grief and joy!
How often was this fathers' throne contested   20
By eager children, prized by girl and boy!
And here, perhaps, her full cheeks flushed with bliss,
My darling, grateful for a Christmas toy,
Pressed on her grandsire's withered hand a kiss.
I feel your spirit, lovely maid,   25
Of ordered bounty breathing here
Which, motherly, comes daily to your aid
To teach you how a rug is best on tables laid
And how the sand should on the floor appear.[7]
Oh godlike hand, to you it's given   30
To make a cottage, a kingdom of heaven.
And here!
[*He lifts a bed curtain.*]
          What raptured shudder makes me stir?
How I should love to be immured
Where in light dreams nature matured
The angel that's innate in her,   35
Here lay the child, developed slowly,
Her tender breast with warm life fraught,
And here, through weaving pure and holy,
The image of the gods was wrought.

---

7. Floors were sprinkled with sand after cleaning.

And you! Alas, what brought you here?   40
I feel so deeply moved, so queer!
What do you seek? Why is your heart so sore?
Poor Faust! I do not know you any more.

Do magic smells surround me here?
Immediate pleasure was my bent,   45
But now—in dreams of love I'm all but spent.
Are we mere puppets of the atmosphere?

If she returned this instant from her call,
How for your mean transgression you would pay!
The haughty lad would be so small,   50
Lie at her feet and melt away.

MEPHISTOPHELES: [*Entering.*] Let's go! I see her in the lane!
FAUST: Away! I'll never come again.
MEPHISTOPHELES: Here is a fairly decent case,
   I picked it up some other place.   55
   Just leave it in the chest up there.
   She'll go out of her mind, I swear;
   For I put things in it, good sir,
   To win a better one than her.
   But child is child and play is play.   60
FAUST: I don't know—should I?
MEPHISTOPHELES: Why delay?
   You do not hope to save your jewel?
   Or I'll give your lust this advice:
   Don't waste fair daytime like this twice,
   Nor my exertions: it is cruel.   65
   It is not simple greed, I hope!
   I scratch my head, I fret and mope—
     [*He puts the case into the chest and locks it again.*]
   Away! Let's go!—
   It's just to make the child fulfill
   Your heart's desire and your will;   70
   And you stand and frown
   As if you had to lecture in cap and gown—
   As if in gray there stood in front of you
   Physics and Metaphysics, too.
   Away!   75
     [*Exeunt.*]
MARGARET: [*With a lamp.*] It seems so close, so sultry now,
     [*She opens the window.*]
   And yet outside it's not so warm.
   I feel so strange, I don't know how—
   I wish my mother would come home.
   A shudder grips my body, I feel chilly—   80
   How fearful I am and how silly!
     [*She begins to sing as she undresses.*]

In Thule[8] there was a king,
Faithful unto the grave,
To whom his mistress, dying,
A golden goblet gave.   85

Nothing he held more dear.
At every meal he used it;
His eyes would fill with tears
As often as he mused it.

And when he came to dying,   90
The towns in his realm he told.
Naught to his heir denying,
Except the goblet of gold.

He dined at evenfall
With all his chivalry   95
In the ancestral hall
In the castle by the sea.

The old man rose at last
And drank life's sunset glow.
And the sacred goblet he cast   100
Into the flood below.

He saw it plunging, drinking.
And sinking into the sea;
His eyes were also sinking,
And nevermore drank he.   105

[*She opens the chest to put away her clothes and sees the case.*]
How did this lovely case get in my chest?
I locked it after I got dressed.
It certainly seems strange. And what might be in there?
It might be a security
Left for a loan in Mother's care.   110
There is a ribbon with a key;
I think I'll open it and see.
What is that? God in heaven! There—
I never saw such fine array!
These jewels! Why a lord's lady could wear   115
These on the highest holiday.
How would this necklace look on me?
Who owns all this? It is so fine.
[*She adorns herself and steps before the mirror.*]
If those earrings were only mine!
One looks quite different right away.   120
What good is beauty, even youth?

---

8. The fabled *ultima Thule* of Latin literature—those distant lands just beyond the reach of every explorer. Goethe wrote the ballad in 1774; it was published and set to music in 1782 and later inspired the
slow movement of Mendelssohn's *Italian Symphony*.

All that may be quite good and fair,
But does it get you anywhere?
Their praise is half pity, you can be sure.
For gold contend,   125
On gold depend
All things. Woe to us poor!

PROMENADE

[FAUST *walking up and down, lost in thought.* MEPHISTOPHELES
enters.]
MEPHISTOPHELES: By the pangs of despised love! By the elements of hell!
I wish I knew something worse to curse by it as well!
FAUST: What ails you? Steady now, keep level!
I never saw a face like yours today.
MEPHISTOPHELES: I'd wish the Devil took me straightaway,   5
If I myself were not a devil.
FAUST: Has something in your head gone bad?
It sure becomes you raving like one mad.
MEPHISTOPHELES: Just think, the jewels got for Margaret—
A dirty priest took the whole set.   10
The mother gets to see the stuff
And starts to shudder, sure enough:
She has a nose to smell things out—
In prayerbooks she keeps her snout—
A whiff of anything makes plain   15
Whether it's holy or profane.
She sniffed the jewelry like a rat
And knew no blessings came with that.
My child, she cried, ill-gotten wealth
Will soil your soul and spoil your health.   20
We'll give it to the Mother of the Lord
And later get a heavenly reward.
Poor Margaret went into a pout;
She thought: a gift horse![9] and, no doubt,
Who[1] brought it here so carefully   25
Could not be godless, certainly.
The mother called a priest at once,
He saw the gems and was no dunce;
He drooled and then said: Without question,
Your instinct is quite genuine,   30
Who overcomes himself will win.
The Church has a superb digestion,
Whole countries she has gobbled up,
But never is too full to sup;
The Church alone has the good health   35
For stomaching ill-gotten wealth.

---

9. Like the wooden horse in which Greek soldiers entered Troy to capture it; an emblem of treachery.
1. Whoever.

FAUST: Why, everybody does: a Jew
   And any king can do it, too.
MEPHISTOPHELES: So he picked up a clasp, necklace, and rings,
   Like toadstools or some worthless things,   40
   And did not thank them more nor less
   Than as if it were nuts or some such mess,
   And he promised them plenty after they died—
   And they were duly edified.
FAUST: And Gretchen?[2]
MEPHISTOPHELES: She, of course, feels blue,   45
   She sits and doesn't know what to do,
   Thinks day and night of every gem—
   Still more of him who furnished them.
FAUST: My darling's grief distresses me.
   Go, get her some new jewelry.   50
   The first one was a trifling loss.
MEPHISTOPHELES: Oh sure, it's child's play for you, boss.
FAUST: Just fix it all to suit my will;
   Try on the neighbor, too, your skill.
   Don't, Devil, act like sluggish paste!   55
   Get some new jewels and make haste!
MEPHISTOPHELES: Yes, gracious lord, it is a pleasure.
   [FAUST exits.]
MEPHISTOPHELES: A fool in love just doesn't care
   And, just to sweeten darling's leisure,
   He'd make sun, moon, and stars into thin air.   60
   [Exit.]

THE NEIGHBOR'S HOUSE

MARTHA: [Alone.] May God forgive my husband! He
   Was certainly not good to me.
   He went into the world to roam
   And left me on the straw at home.
   God knows that I have never crossed him,   5
   And loved him dearly; yet I lost him.
   [She cries.] Perhaps—the thought kills me—he died!—
   If it were only certified!
      [MARGARET enters.]
MARGARET: Dame Martha!
MARTHA: Gretchen, what could it be?
MARGARET: My legs feel faint, though not with pain: 10
   I found another case, again
   Right in my press,[3] of ebony,
   With things more precious all around
   Than was the first case that I found.
MARTHA: You must not show them to your mother,   15

---

2. Diminutive of the German *Margarete*. She is given this name through much of the play.   **3.** A type of cupboard in which pressed linens were stored.

She'd tell the priest as with the other.
MARGARET: Oh look at it! Oh see! Please do!
MARTHA: [*Adorns her.*] You lucky, lucky creature, you!
MARGARET: Unfortunately, it's not meet
    To wear them in the church or street.   20
MARTHA: Just come here often to see me,
    Put on the jewels secretly,
    Walk up and down an hour before the mirror here,
    And we shall have a good time, dear.
    Then chances come, perhaps a holiday,   25
    When we can bit by bit, gem after gem display,
    A necklace first, than a pearl in your ear;
    Your mother—we can fool her, or she may never hear.
MARGARET: Who brought the cases and has not appeared?
    It certainly seems very weird.   30
    [*A knock.*]
    Oh God, my mother—is it her?
MARTHA: [*Peeping through the curtain.*] It is a stranger—come in, sir!
    [MEPHISTOPHELES *enters.*]
MEPHISTOPHELES: I'll come right in and be so free,
    If the ladies will grant me the liberty.
    [*Steps back respectfully as he sees* MARGARET.]
    To Martha Schwerdtlein I wished to speak.   35
MARTHA: It's I. What does your honor seek?
MEPHISTOPHELES: [*Softly to her.*] I know you now, that satisfies me,
    You have very elegant company;
    Forgive my intrusion; I shall come back soon—
    If you don't mind, this afternoon.   40
MARTHA: [*Loud.*] Oh goodness gracious! Did you hear?
    He thinks you are a lady, dear!
MARGARET: I'm nothing but a poor young maid;
    You are much too kind, I am afraid;
    The gems and jewels are not my own.   45
MEPHISTOPHELES: It is not the jewelry alone!
    Your noble eyes—indeed, it is your whole way!
    How glad I am that I may stay!
MARTHA: What is your errand? Please, good sir—
MEPHISTOPHELES: I wish I had better news for her!   50
    And don't get cross with your poor guest:
    Your husband is dead and sends his best.
MARTHA: Is dead? The faithful heart! Oh dear!
    My husband is dead! I shall faint right here.
MARGARET: Oh my dear woman! Don't despair!   55
MEPHISTOPHELES: Let me relate the sad affair.
MARGARET: I should sooner never be a bride:
    The grief would kill me if he died.
MEPHISTOPHELES: Joy needs woe, woe requires joy.
MARTHA: Tell me of the end of my sweet boy.   60
MEPHISTOPHELES: In Padua, in Italy,

He is buried in St. Anthony
In ground that has been duly blessed
For such cool, everlasting rest.
MARTHA: Surely, there is something more you bring.   65
MEPHISTOPHELES: One solemn and sincere request:
For his poor soul they should three hundred masses sing.
That's all, my purse is empty, though not of course my breast.
MARTHA: What? Not a gem? No work of art?
I am sure, deep in his bag the poorest wanderer   70
Keeps some remembrance that gives pleasure,
And sooner starves than yields this treasure.
MEPHISTOPHELES: Madam, don't doubt it breaks my heart.
And you may rest assured, he was no squanderer.
He knew his errors well, and he repented,   75
Though his ill fortune was the thing he most lamented.
MARGARET: That men are so unfortunate and poor!
I'll say some Requiems, and for his soul I'll pray.
MEPHISTOPHELES: You would deserve a marriage right away,
For you are charming, I am sure.   80
MARGARET: Oh no! I must wait to be wed.
MEPHISTOPHELES: If not a husband, have a lover instead.
It is one of heaven's greatest charms
To hold such a sweetheart in one's arms.
MARGARET: That is not the custom around here.   85
MEPHISTOPHELES: Custom or not, it's done, my dear.
MARTHA: Please tell me more!
MEPHISTOPHELES: I stood beside the bed he died on;
It was superior to manure,
Of rotted straw, and yet he died a Christian, pure,
And found that there was more on his unsettled score.   90
"I'm hateful," he cried; "wicked was my life,
As I forsook my trade and also left my wife.
To think of it now makes me die.
If only she forgave me even so!"
MARTHA: [*Weeping.*] The darling! I forgave him long ago.   95
MEPHISTOPHELES: "And yet, God knows, she was far worse than I."
MARTHA: He lied—alas, lied at the brink of death!
MEPHISTOPHELES: Surely, he made up things with dying breath,
If ever I saw death before.
"To pass the time, I could not look around," he said;   100
"First she got children, then they needed bread—
When I say bread, I mean much more—
And she never gave peace for me to eat my share."
MARTHA: Did he forget my love, my faithfulness and care
And how I slaved both day and night?   105
MEPHISTOPHELES: Oh no, he thought of that with all his might;
He said: "When we left Malta for another trip,
I prayed for wife and children fervently,
So heaven showed good grace to me.

And our boat soon caught a Turkish ship 110
That had the mighty sultan's gold on it.
Then fortitude got its reward,
And I myself was given, as was fit,
My share of the great sultan's hoard."
MARTHA: Oh how? Oh where? Might it be buried now? 115
MEPHISTOPHELES: The winds have scattered it, and who knows how?
  A pretty girl in Naples, sweet and slim,
  Cared for him when he was without a friend
  And did so many deeds of love for him
  That he could feel it till his blessed end. 120
MARTHA: The rogue! He robbed children and wife!
  No misery, no lack of bread
  Could keep him from his shameful life!
MEPHISTOPHELES: You see! For that he now is dead.
  If I were in your place, I'd pause 125
  To mourn him for a year, as meet,
  And meanwhile I would try to find another sweet.
MARTHA: Oh God, the way my first one was
  I'll hardly find another to be mine!
  How could there be a little fool that's fonder? 130
  Only he liked so very much to wander,
  And foreign women, and foreign wine,
  And that damned shooting of the dice.
MEPHISTOPHELES: Well, well! It could have been quite nice,
  Had he been willing to ignore 135
  As many faults in you, or more.
  On such terms, I myself would woo
  And willingly change rings with you.
MARTHA: The gentleman is pleased to jest.
MEPHISTOPHELES: [*Aside.*] I better get away from here; 140
  She'd keep the Devil to his word, I fear.
  [*To* GRETCHEN.] And how is your heart? Still at rest?
MARGARET: What do you mean, good sir?
MEPHISTOPHELES: [*Aside.*]   You good, innocent child!
  [*Aloud.*] Good-by, fair ladies!
MARGARET: Good-by.
MARTHA: Oh, not so fast and wild! 145
  I'd like to have it certified
  That my sweetheart was buried, and when and where he died.
  I always hate to see things done obliquely
  And want to read his death in our weekly.
MEPHISTOPHELES: Yes, lady, what is testified by two 150
  Is everywhere known to be true;
  And I happen to have a splendid mate
  Whom I'll take along to the magistrate.
  I'll bring him here.
MARTHA: Indeed, please do!
MEPHISTOPHELES: And will this maiden be here, too? 155

A gallant lad! Has traveled much with me
And shows young ladies all courtesy.
MARGARET: I would have to blush before him, poor thing.[4]
MEPHISTOPHELES: Not even before a king!
MARTHA: Behind the house, in my garden, then,   160
Tonight we shall expect the gentlemen.

STREET

[FAUST. MEPHISTOPHELES.]
FAUST: How is it? Well? Can it be soon?
MEPHISTOPHELES: Oh bravo! Now you are on fire?
Soon Gretchen will still your desire.
At Martha's you may see her later this afternoon:
That woman seems expressly made   5
To ply the pimps' and gypsies' trade.
FAUST: Oh good!
MEPHISTOPHELES: But something's wanted from us, too.
FAUST: One good turn makes another due.
MEPHISTOPHELES: We merely have to go and testify   10
That the remains of her dear husband lie
In Padua where Anthony once sat.
FAUST: Now we shall have to go there. Now that was smart of you!
MEPHISTOPHELES: Sancta simplicitas![5] Who ever thought of that?
Just testify, and hang whether it's true!   15
FAUST: If you know nothing better, this plan has fallen through.
MEPHISTOPHELES: Oh, holy man! You are no less!
Is this the first time in your life that you
Have testified what is not true?
Of God and all the world, and every single part,   20
Of man and all that stirs inside his head and heart
You gave your definitions with power and finesse.
With brazen cheek and haughty breath.
And if you stop to think, I guess,
You know as much of that, you must confess,   25
As you know now of Mr. Schwerdtlein's death.
FAUST: You are and you remain a sophist and a liar.
MEPHISTOPHELES: Yes, if one's knowledge were not just a little higher.
Tomorrow, won't you, pure as air,
Deceive poor Gretchen and declare   30
Your soul's profoundest love, and swear?
FAUST: With all my heart.
MEPHISTOPHELES: Good and fair!
Then faithfulness and love eternal
And the super-almighty urge supernal—
Will that come from your heart as well?   35
FAUST: Leave off! It will.—When, lost in feeling,
For this urge, for this surge

---

4. Referring to herself, not to Faust.   5. Holy simplicity (Latin).

I seek a name, find none, and, reeling
All through the world with all my senses gasping,
At all the noblest words I'm grasping   40
And call this blaze in which I flame,
Infinite, eternal eternally—
Is that a game or devilish jugglery?
MEPHISTOPHELES: I am still right.
FAUST: Listen to me,
I beg of you, and don't wear out my lung: 45
Whoever would be right and only has a tongue,
Always will be.
Come on! I'm sick of prating, spare your voice,
For you are right because I have no choice.

GARDEN

[MARGARET on FAUST's arm, MARTHA with MEPHISTOPHELES, walking
    up and down.]
MARGARET: I feel it well, good sir, you're only kind to me:
You condescend—and you abash.
It is the traveler's courtesy
To put up graciously with trash.
I know too well, my poor talk never can   5
Give pleasure to a traveled gentleman.
FAUST: One glance from you, one word gives far more pleasure
Than all the wisdom of this world. [He kisses her hand.]
MARGARET: Don't incommode yourself! How could you kiss it? You?
It is so ugly, is so rough.   10
But all the things that I have had to do!
For Mother I can't do enough.
    [They pass.]
MARTHA: And you, sir, travel all the time, you say?
MEPHISTOPHELES: Alas, our trade and duty keeps us going!
Though when one leaves the tears may well be flowing,   15
One never is allowed to stay.
MARTHA: While it may do in younger years
To sweep around the world, feel free and suave,
There is the time when old age nears,
And then to creep alone, a bachelor, to one's grave.   20
That's something everybody fears.
MEPHISTOPHELES: With dread I see it far away.
MARTHA: Then, my dear sir, consider while you may.
    [They pass.]
MARGARET: Yes, out of sight is out of mind.
You are polite, you can't deny,   25
And often you have friends and find
That they are cleverer than I.
FAUST: Oh dearest, trust me, what's called clever on this earth
Is often vain and rash rather than clever.

MARGARET: What?

FAUST: Oh, that the innocent and simple never 30
Appreciate themselves and their own worth!
That meekness and humility, supreme
Among the gifts of loving, lavish nature—

MARGARET: If you should think of me one moment only,
I shall have time enough to think of you and dream. 35

FAUST: Are you so often lonely?

MARGARET: Yes; while our household is quite small,
You see, I have to do it all.
We have no maid, so I must cook, and sweep, and knit.
And sew, and run early and late; 40
And mother is in all of it
So accurate!
Not that it's necessary; our need is not so great.
We could afford much more than many another:
My father left a tidy sum to mother, 45
A house and garden near the city gate.
But now my days are rather plain:
A soldier is my brother,
My little sister dead.
Sore was, while she was living, the troubled life I led; 50
But I would gladly go through all of it again:
She was so dear to me.

FAUST: An angel, if like you.

MARGARET: I brought her up, and she adored me, too.
She was born only after father's death;
Mother seemed near her dying breath, 55
As stricken as she then would lie,
Though she got well again quite slowly, by and by.
She was so sickly and so slight,
She could not nurse the little mite;
So I would tend her all alone, 60
With milk and water; she became my own.
Upon my arms and in my lap
She first grew friendly, tumbled, and grew up.

FAUST: You must have felt the purest happiness.

MARGARET: But also many hours of distress. 65
The baby's cradle stood at night
Beside my bed, and if she stirred I'd wake,
I slept so light.
Now I would have to feed her, now I'd take
Her into my bed, now I'd rise 70
And dandling pace the room to calm the baby's cries.
And I would wash before the sun would rise,
Fret in the market and over the kitchen flame,
Tomorrow as today, always the same.
One's spirits, sir, are not always the best, 75
But one can relish meals and relish rest.

[*They pass.*]

MARTHA: Poor woman has indeed a wretched fate:
　A bachelor is not easy to convert.
MEPHISTOPHELES: For one like you the job is not too great;　　　　　80
　You might convince me if you are alert.
MARTHA: Be frank, dear sir, so far you have not found?
　Has not your heart in some way yet been bound?
MEPHISTOPHELES: A hearth one owns and a good wife, we're told,
　Are worth as much as pearls and gold.
MARTHA: I mean, have you not ever had a passion?　　　　　85
MEPHISTOPHELES: I always was received in the most friendly fashion.
MARTHA: Would say: weren't you ever in earnest in your breast?
MEPHISTOPHELES: With women one should never presume to speak in
　jest.
MARTHA: Oh, you don't understand.
MEPHISTOPHELES:　　　　　　　　　I'm sorry I'm so blind!
　But I do understand—that you are very kind.　　　　　90
　　　[*They pass.*]
FAUST: Oh little angel, you did recognize
　Me as I came into the garden?
MARGARET: Did you not notice? I cast down my eyes.
FAUST: My liberty you're then prepared to pardon?
　What insolence presumed to say　　　　　95
　As you left church the other day?
MARGARET: I was upset, I did not know such daring
　And no one could have spoken ill of me.
　I thought that something in my bearing
　Must have seemed shameless and unmaidenly.　　　　　100
　He seemed to have the sudden feeling
　That this wench could be had without much dealing.
　Let me confess, I didn't know that there
　Were other feelings stirring in me, and they grew;
　But I was angry with myself, I swear,　　　　　105
　That I could not get angrier with you.
FAUST: Sweet darling!
MARGARET:　　　　　　　Let me do this! [*She plucks a daisy and pulls out the
　petals one by one.*]
FAUST:　　　　　　　　　　　　　A nosegay? Or what shall it be?
MARGARET:
　No, it is just a game.
FAUST:　　　　　　　What?
MARGARET:　　　　　　　　　Go, you will laugh at me. [*She pulls out pet-
　als and murmurs.*]
FAUST: What do you murmur?
MARGARET: [*Half aloud.*]　　He loves me—loves me not.
FAUST: You gentle countenance of heaven!　　　　　110
MARGARET: [*Continues.*] Loves me—not—loves me—not—
　[*Tearing out the last leaf, in utter joy.*]
　He loves me.

FAUST: Yes, my child. Let this sweet flower's word
  Be as a god's word to you. He loves you.
  Do you know what this means? He loves you. [*He takes both her hands.*]
MARGARET: My skin creeps.   115
FAUST: Oh, shudder not! But let this glance,
  And let this clasp of hands tell you
  What is unspeakable:
  To yield oneself entirely and feel
  A rapture which must be eternal.   120
  Eternal! For its end would be despair.
  No, no end! No end!
    [MARGARET *clasps his hands, frees herself, and runs away. He stands
    for a moment, lost in thought; then he follows her.*]
MARTHA: [*Entering.*] The night draws near.
MEPHISTOPHELES: Yes, and we want to go.
MARTHA: I should ask you to tarry even so,
  But this place simply is too bad: 125
  It is as if nobody had
  Work or labor
  Except to spy all day long on his neighbor,
  And one gets talked about, whatever life one leads.
  And our couple?
MEPHISTOPHELES: Up that path I heard them whirr—   130
  Frolicking butterflies.
MARTHA: He is taking to her.
MEPHISTOPHELES: And she to him. That's how the world proceeds.

A GARDEN BOWER

  [MARGARET *leaps into it, hides behind the door, puts the tip of one
  finger to her lips, and peeks through the crack.*]
MARGARET: He comes.
FAUST: [*Entering.*]   Oh rogue, you're teasing me.
  Now I see. [*He kisses her.*]
MARGARET: [*Seizing him and returning the kiss.*]
  Dearest man! I love you from my heart.
    [MEPHISTOPHELES *knocks.*]
FAUST: [*Stamping his foot.*]
  Who's there?
MEPHISTOPHELES:
    A friend.
FAUST: A beast!
MEPHISTOPHELES: The time has come to part.
MARTHA: [*Entering.*]
  Yes, it is late, good sir.
FAUST: May I not take you home?   5
MARGARET: My mother would—Farewell!
FAUST: Must I leave then?
  Farewell.

MARTHA: Adieu.

MARGARET: Come soon again!

    [FAUST *and* MEPHISTOPHELES *exeunt.*]

MARGARET: Dear God, the things he thought and said!
  How much goes on in a man's head!
  Abashed, I merely acquiesce   10
  And cannot answer, except Yes!
  I am a poor, dumb child and cannot see
  What such a man could find in me.
    [*Exit.*]

WOOD AND CAVE

FAUST: [*Alone.*] Exalted spirit, all you gave me, all
  That I have asked. And it was not in vain
  That amid flames you turned your face toward me.
  You gave me royal nature as my own dominion,
  Strength to experience her, enjoy her. Not   5
  The cold amazement of a visit only
  You granted me, but let me penetrate
  Into her heart as into a close friend's.
  You lead the hosts of all that is alive
  Before my eyes, teach me to know my brothers   10
  In quiet bushes and in air and water.
  And when the storm roars in the wood and creaks,
  The giant fir tree, falling, hits and smashes
  The neighbor branches and the neighbor trunks,
  And from its hollow thud the mountain thunders,   15
  Then you lead me to this safe cave and show
  Me to myself, and all the most profound
  And secret wonders of my breast are opened.
  And when before my eyes the pure moon rises
  And passes soothingly, there float to me   20
  From rocky cliffs and out of dewy bushes
  The silver shapes of a forgotten age,
  And soften meditation's somber joy.
  Alas, that man is granted nothing perfect
  I now experience. With this happiness   25
  Which brings me close and closer to the gods,
  You gave me the companion whom I can
  Forego no more, though with cold impudence
  He makes me small in my own eyes and changes
  Your gifts to nothing with a few words' breath.   30
  He kindles in my breast a savage fire
  And keeps me thirsting after that fair image.
  Thus I reel from desire to enjoyment,
  And in enjoyment languish for desire.

MEPHISTOPHELES: [*Enters.*] Have you not led this life quite long enough? 35
  How can it keep amusing you?

It may be well for once to try such stuff
But then one turns to something new.
FAUST: I wish that you had more to do
And would not come to pester me.   40
MEPHISTOPHELES: All right. I gladly say adieu—
You should not say that seriously.
A chap like you, unpleasant, mad, and cross,
Would hardly be a serious loss.
All day long one can work and slave away.   45
And what he likes and what might cause dismay,
It simply isn't possible to say.
FAUST: That is indeed the proper tone!
He wants my thanks for being such a pest.
MEPHISTOPHELES: If I had left you wretch alone,   50
Would you then live with greater zest?
Was it not I that helped you to disown,
And partly cured, your feverish unrest
Yes, but[6] for me, the earthly zone
Would long be minus one poor guest.   55
And now, why must you sit like an old owl
In caves and rocky clefts, and scowl?
From soggy moss and dripping stones you lap your food
Just like a toad, and sit and brood.
A fair, sweet way to pass the time!   60
Still steeped in your doctoral slime!
FAUST: How this sojourn in the wilderness
Renews my vital force, you cannot guess.
And if you apprehended this,
You would be Devil enough, to envy me my bliss.   65
MEPHISTOPHELES: A supernatural delight!
To lie on mountains in the dew and night,
Embracing earth and sky in raptured reeling,
To swell into a god—in one's own feeling—
To probe earth's marrow with vague divination,   70
Sense in your breast the whole work of creation,
With haughty strength enjoy, I know not what,
Then overflow into all things with love so hot,
Gone is all earthly inhibition,
And then the noble intuition— [*With a gesture.*]   75
Of—need I say of what emission?
FAUST: Shame!
MEPHISTOPHELES:
          That does not meet with your acclaim;
You have the right to cry indignant: shame!
One may not tell chaste ears what, beyond doubt,
The chastest heart could never do without.   80
And, once for all, I don't grudge you the pleasure

6. Were it not.

Of little self-deceptions at your leisure;
But it can't last indefinitely.
Already you are spent again,
And soon you will be rent again,   85
By madness and anxiety.
Enough of that. Your darling is distraught,
Sits inside, glum and in despair,
She can't put you out of her mind and thought
And loves you more than she can bear.   90
At first your raging love was past control,
As brooks that overflow when filled with melted snow;
You poured it out into her soul,
But now your little brook is low.
Instead of posing in the wood,   95
It seems to me it might be good
If for her love our noble lord
Gave the poor monkey some reward.
Time seems to her intolerably long;
She stands at her window and sees the clouds in the sky   100
Drift over the city wall and go by.
Were I a little bird! thus goes her song
For days and half the night long.
Once she may be cheerful, most of the time sad,
Once she has spent her tears,   105
Then she is calm, it appears,
And always loves you like mad.
FAUST: Serpent! Snake!
MEPHISTOPHELES: [*Aside.*] If only I catch the rake!
FAUST: Damnable fiend! Get yourself hence,   110
    And do not name the beautiful maid!
    Let not the lust for her sweet limbs invade
    And ravish once again my frenzied sense!
MEPHISTOPHELES: What do you mean? She thinks you've run away;
    And it is half-true, I must say.   115
FAUST: I am near her, however far I be,
    She'll never be forgotten and ignored;
    Indeed, I am consumed with jealousy
    That her lips touch the body of the Lord.[7]
MEPHISTOPHELES: I'm jealous of my friend when she exposes   120
    The pair of twins that feed among the roses.[8]
FAUST: Begone, pander!
MEPHISTOPHELES: Fine! Your wrath amuses me.
    The God who fashioned man and maid
    Was quick to recognize the noblest trade,   125
    And procured opportunity.
    Go on! It is a woeful pain!
    You're to embrace your love again,

---

7. When the bread of Communion miraculously turns to the body of Christ.   8. Compare Song of Solomon 4:5: "Thy two breasts are like two young roes that are twins, which feed among the lilies."

Not sink into the tomb.
FAUST: What are the joys of heaven in her arms? 130
Let me embrace her, feel her charms —
Do I not always sense her doom?
Am I not fugitive? without a home?
Inhuman, without aim or rest,
As, like the cataract, from rock to rock I foam, 135
Raging with passion, toward the abyss?
And nearby, she — with childlike blunt desires
Inside her cottage on the Alpine leas,
And everything that she requires
Was in her own small world at ease. 140
And I, whom the gods hate and mock,
Was not satisfied
That I seized the rock
And smashed the mountainside.
Her — her peace I had to undermine. 145
You, hell, desired this sacrifice upon your shrine.
Help, Devil, shorten this time of dread.
What must be done, come let it be.
Let then her fate come shattering on my head,
And let her perish now with me. 150
MEPHISTOPHELES: How now it boils again and how you shout.
Go in and comfort her, you dunce.
Where such a little head sees no way out,
He thinks the end must come at once.
Long live who holds out undeterred! 155
At other times you have the Devil's airs.
In all the world there's nothing more absurd
Than is a Devil who despairs.

GRETCHEN'S ROOM

GRETCHEN: [*At the spinning wheel, alone.*]
My peace is gone,
My heart is sore;
I find it never
And nevermore.

Where him I not have 5
There is my grave.
This world is all
Turned into gall.

And my poor head
Is quite insane, 10
And my poor mind
Is rent with pain.

My peace is gone,
My heart is sore;

I find it never   15
And nevermore.

For him only I look
From my window seat,
For him only I go
Out into the street.   20

His lofty gait,
His noble guise,
The smile of his mouth,
The force of his eyes,

And his words' flow—   25
Enchanting bliss—
The touch of his hand,
And, oh, his kiss.

My peace is gone,
My heart is sore;   30
I find it never
And nevermore.

My bosom surges
For him alone,
Oh that I could clasp him   35
And hold him so,

And kiss him
To my heart's content,
Till in his kisses
I were spent.   40

MARTHA'S GARDEN

[MARGARET. FAUST.]

MARGARET: Promise me, Heinrich.[9]

FAUST: Whatever I can.

MARGARET: How is it with your religion, please admit—
    You certainly are a very good man,
    But I believe you don't think much of it.

FAUST: Leave that, my child. I love you, do not fear   5
    And would give all for those whom I hold dear,
    Would not rob anyone of church or creed.

MARGARET: That is not enough, it is faith we need.

FAUST: Do we?

MARGARET: Oh that I had some influence!
    You don't respect the holy sacraments.   10

FAUST: I do respect them.

MARGARET: But without desire.

9. Faust. In the legend, Faust's name was generally Johann (John). Goethe changed it to Heinrich (Henry).

The mass and confession you do not require.
Do you believe in God?

FAUST: My darling who may say
I believe in God?
Ask priests and sages, their reply   15
Looks like sneers that mock and prod
The one who asked the question.

MARGARET: Then you deny him there?

FAUST: Do not mistake me, you who are so fair.
Him—who may name?
And who proclaim: 20
I believe in him?
Who may feel,
Who dare reveal
In words: I believe him not?
The All-Embracing,   25
The All-Sustaining,
Does he not embrace and sustain
You, me, himself?
Does not the heaven vault above?
Is the earth not firmly based down here?   30
And do not, friendly,
Eternal stars rise?
Do we not look into each other's eyes,
And all in you is surging
To your head and heart,   35
And weaves in timeless mystery,
Unseeable, yet seen, around you?
Then let it fill your heart entirely,
And when your rapture in this feeling is complete,
Call it then as you will,   40
Call it bliss! heart! love! God!
I do not have a name
For this. Feeling is all;
Names are but sound and smoke
Befogging heaven's blazes.   45

MARGARET: Those are very fair and noble phrases;
The priest says something, too, like what you spoke—
Only his words are not quite so—

FAUST: Wherever you go,
All hearts under the heavenly day   50
Say it, each in its own way;
Why not I in mine?

MARGARET: When one listens to you, one might incline
To let it pass—but I can't agree,
For you have no Christianity.   55

FAUST: Dear child!

MARGARET: It has long been a grief to me
To see you in such company.

FAUST: Why?

MARGARET: The man that goes around with you
    Seems hateful to me through and through: 60
    In all my life there's not a thing
    That gave my heart as sharp a sting
    As his repulsive eyes.

FAUST: Sweet doll, don't fear him anywise.

MARGARET: His presence makes me feel quite ill.   65
    I bear all other men good will;
    But just as to see you I languish,
    This man fills me with secret anguish;
    He seems a knave one should not trust.
    May God forgive me if I am unjust.   70

FAUST: There must be queer birds, too, you know.

MARGARET: But why live with them even so?
    Whenever he comes in,
    He always wears a mocking grin
    And looks half threatening: 75
    One sees, he has no sympathy for anything;
    It is written on his very face
    That he thinks love is a disgrace.
    In your arm I feel good and free,
    Warm and abandoned as can be;   80
    Alas, my heart and feelings are choked when he comes, too.

FAUST: Oh, you foreboding angel, you.

MARGARET: It makes my heart so sore
    That, when he only comes our way,
    I feel I do not love you any more;   85
    And where he is, I cannot pray.
    It eats into my heart. Oh you,
    Dear Heinrich, must feel that way, too.

FAUST: That is just your antipathy.

MARGARET: I must go.

FAUST: Will there never be   90
    At your sweet bosom one hour of rest
    When soul touches on soul and breast on breast?

MARGARET: Had I my own room when I sleep,
    I should not bolt the door tonight;
    But Mother's slumber is not deep,   95
    And if she found us thus—oh fright,
    Right then and there I should drop dead.

FAUST: My angel, if that's what you dread,
    Here is a bottle. Merely shake
    Three drops into her cup,   100
    And she won't easily wake up.

MARGARET: What should I not do for your sake?
    It will not harm her if one tries it?

FAUST: Dear, if it would, would I advise it?

MARGARET: When I but look at you, I thrill,   105

I don't know why, my dear, to do your will;
I have already done so much for you
That hardly anything seems left to do.
   [*Exit. Enter* MEPHISTOPHELES.]
MEPHISTOPHELES: The monkey! Is she gone?
FAUST: You spied?
MEPHISTOPHELES: Are you surprised?
   I listened and I understood   110
   Our learned doctor just was catechized.
   I hope that it may do you good.
   The girls are quite concerned to be apprised
   If one is pious and obeys tradition.
   If yes, they trust they can rely on his submission.   115
FAUST: You monster will not see nor own
   That this sweet soul, in loyalty,
   Full of her own creed
   Which alone,
   She trusts, can bring salvation, lives in agony   120
   To think her lover lost, however she may plead.
MEPHISTOPHELES: You supersensual, sensual wooer,
   A maiden leads you by the nose.
FAUST: You freak of filth and fire! Evildoer!
MEPHISTOPHELES: And what a knowledge of physiognomy she shows.   125
   She feels, she knows not what, whenever I'm about;
   She finds a hidden meaning in my eyes:
   I am a demon, beyond doubt,
   Perhaps the Devil, that is her surmise.
   Well, tonight—?
FAUST: What's that to you?   130
MEPHISTOPHELES: I have my pleasure in it, too.

AT THE WELL

   [GRETCHEN *and* LIESCHEN *with jugs.*]
LIESCHEN: Of Barbara you haven't heard?
GRETCHEN: I rarely see people—no, not a word.
LIESCHEN: Well, Sibyl just told me in front of the school:
   That girl has at last been made a fool.
   That comes from having airs.
GRETCHEN: How so?
LIESCHEN: It stinks!   5
   She is feeding two when she eats and drinks.
GRETCHEN: Oh!
LIESCHEN: At last she has got what was coming to her.
   She stuck to that fellow like a burr.
   That was some prancing,
   In the village, and dancing,   10
   She was always the first in line;
   And he flirted with her over pastries and wine;

And she thought that she looked divine—
But had no honor, no thought of her name,   15
And took his presents without any shame.
The way they slobbered and carried on;
But now the little flower is gone.
GRETCHEN: Poor thing!
LIESCHEN: That you don't say!
When girls like us would be spinning away,   20
And mother kept us at home every night,
She was with her lover in sweet delight
On the bench by the door, in dark alleys they were,
And the time was never too long for her.
Now let her crouch and let her bend down   25
And do penance in a sinner's gown!
GRETCHEN: He will surely take her to be his wife.
LIESCHEN: He would be a fool! A handsome boy
Will elsewhere find more air and joy.
He's already gone.
GRETCHEN: That is not fair!   30
LIESCHEN: And if she gets him, let her beware:
Her veil the boys will throw to the floor,
And we shall strew chaff in front of her door.[1]
[Exit.]
GRETCHEN: [Going home.] How I once used to scold along
When some poor woman had done wrong.   35
How for another person's shame
I found not words enough of blame.
How black it seemed—I made it blacker still,
And yet not black enough to suit my will.
I blessed myself, would boast and grin—   40
And now myself am caught in sin.
Yet—everything that brought me here,
God, was so good, oh, was so dear.

CITY WALL

[In a niche in the wall, an image of the Mater Dolorosa.[2] Ewers with
flowers in front of it.]
GRETCHEN: [Puts fresh flowers into the ewers.]
Incline,
Mother of pain,
Your face in grace to my despair.

A sword in your heart,
With pain rent apart,   5
Up to your son's dread death you stare.

1. In Germany this treatment was reserved for young women who had sexual relations before marriage.
2. Sorrowful mother (Latin, literal trans.); that is, the Virgin Mary.

On the Father your eyes,
You send up sighs
For your and your son's despair.

Who knows   10
My woes—
Despair in every bone!

How my heart is full of anguish,
How I tremble, how I languish,
Know but you, and you alone.   15

Wherever I may go,
What woe, what woe, what woe
Is in my bosom aching!

Scarcely alone am I,
I cry, I cry, I cry;   20
My heart in me is breaking.

The pots in front of my window
I watered with tears as the dew,
When early in the morning
I broke these flowers for you.   25

When bright into my room
The sun his first rays shed,
I sat in utter gloom
Already on my bed.

Help! Rescue me from shame and death!   30
Incline,
Mother of pain,
Your face in grace to my despair.

NIGHT

[*Street in front of* GRETCHEN'S *door.*]
VALENTINE: [*Soldier,* GRETCHEN'*s brother.*]
When I would sit at a drinking bout
Where all had much to brag about,
And many fellows raised their voice
To praise the maidens of their choice,
Glass after glass was drained with toasting,   5
I listened smugly to their boasting,
My elbow propped up on the table,
And sneered at fable after fable.
I'd stroke my beard and smile and say,
Holding my bumper in my hand: 10
Each may be nice in her own way,
But is there one in the whole land
Like sister Gretchen to outdo her,
Hear, hear! Clink! Clink! it went around;

And some would cry: It's true, yes sir,   15
There is no other girl like her!
The braggarts sat without a sound.
And *now*—I could tear out my hair
And dash my brain out in despair!
His nose turned up, a scamp can face me,   20
With taunts and sneers he can disgrace me;
And I should I sit, like one in debt,
Each chance remark should make me sweat!
I'd like to grab them all and maul them,
But liars I could never call them.   25

What's coming there? What sneaks in view?
If I mistake not, there are two.
If it is he, I'll spare him not,
He shall not living leave this spot.
      [FAUST *and* MEPHISTOPHELES *enter.*]
FAUST: How from the window of that sacristy   30
The light of the eternal lamp is glimmering,
And weak and weaker sideward shimmering,
As night engulfs it like the sea.
My heart feels like this nightly street.
MEPHISTOPHELES: And I feel like a cat in heat,   35
That creeps around a fire escape
Pressing against the wall its shape.
I feel quite virtuous, I confess,
A little thievish lust, a little rammishness.
Thus I feel spooking through each vein   40
The wonderful Walpurgis Night.
In two days it will come again,
And waking then is pure delight.
FAUST: And will the treasure that gleams over there
Rise in the meantime up into the air?   45
MEPHISTOPHELES: Quite soon you may enjoy the pleasure
Of taking from the pot the treasure.
The other day I took a squint
And saw fine lion dollars in't.
FAUST: Not any jewelry, not a ring   50
To adorn my beloved girl?
MEPHISTOPHELES: I did see something like a string,
Or something like it, made of pearl.
FAUST: Oh, that is fine, for it's unpleasant
To visit her without a present.   55
MEPHISTOPHELES: It should not cause you such distress
When you have gratis such success.
Now that the sky gleams with its starry throng,
Prepare to hear a work of art:
I shall sing her a moral song   60
To take no chance we fool her heart.

[*Sings to the cither.*³]
  It's scarcely day,
  Oh, Katie, say,
  Why do you stay
  Before your lover's door?   65
  Leave now, leave now!
  For in you'll go
  A maid, I know,
  Come out a maid no more.

  You ought to shun   70
  That kind of fun;
  Once it is done,
  Good night, you poor, poor thing.
  For your own sake
  You should not make   75
  Love to a rake
  Unless you have the ring.⁴

VALENTINE: [*Comes forward.*] Whom would you lure? God's element!
 Rat-catching piper! Oh, perdition!
 The Devil take your instrument!   80
 The Devil then take the musician!
MEPHISTOPHELES: The cither is all smashed. It is beyond repair.
VALENTINE: Now let's try splitting skulls. Beware!
MEPHISTOPHELES: [*To* FAUST.] Don't withdraw, doctor! Quick, don't
 tarry!
 Stick close to me, I'll lead the way.   85
 Unsheathe your toothpick, don't delay;
 Thrust out at him, and I shall parry.
VALENTINE: Then parry that!
MEPHISTOPHELES: Of course.
VALENTINE: And that.
MEPHISTOPHELES: All right.
VALENTINE: I think the Devil must be in this fight.
 What could that be? My hand is getting lame.   90
MEPHISTOPHELES: [*To* FAUST.] Thrust home!
VALENTINE: [*Falls.*] Oh God!
MEPHISTOPHELES: The rogue is tame.
 Now hurry hence, for we must disappear:
 A murderous clamor rises instantly,
 And while the police does not trouble me,   95
 The blood ban is a thing I fear.
MARTHA: [*At a window.*] Come out! Come out!
GRETCHEN: [*At a window.*] Quick! Bring a light.
MARTHA: [*As above.*] They swear and scuffle, yell and fight.
PEOPLE: There is one dead already, see.   100
MARTHA: [*Coming out.*] The murderers—where did they run?

---

3. Or zither, a stringed instrument. 4. Lines 63–78 are adapted by Goethe from Shakespeare's *Hamlet*
IV.5.

GRETCHEN: [*Coming out.*] Who lies there?

PEOPLE: Your own mother's son.

GRETCHEN: Almighty God! What misery!

VALENTINE: I'm dying. That is quickly said,

    And still more quickly done.   105

    Why do you women wail in dread?

    Come here, listen to me.

       [*All gather around him.*]

    My Gretchen, you are still quite green,

    Not nearly smart enough or keen,

    You do not do things right.   110

    In confidence, I should say more:

    Since after all you are a whore,

    Be one with all your might.

GRETCHEN: My brother! God! What frightful shame!

VALENTINE: Leave the Lord God out of this game.   115

    What has been done, alas, is done,

    And as it must, it now will run.

    You started secretly with one,

    Soon more will come to join the fun,

    And once a dozen lays you down,   120

You might as well invite the town.

    When shame is born and first appears,

    It is an underhand delight,

    And one drags the veil of night

    Over her head and ears;   125

    One is tempted to put her away.

    But as she grows, she gets more bold,

    Walks naked even in the day,

    Though hardly fairer to behold.

    The more repulsive grows her sight,   130

    The more she seeks day's brilliant light.

    The time I even now discern

    When honest citizens will turn,

    Harlot, away from you and freeze

    As from a corpse that breeds disease.   135

    Your heart will flinch, your heart will falter

    When they will look you in the face.

    You'll wear no gold, you'll wear no lace,

    Nor in the church come near the altar.

    You will no longer show your skill   140

    At dances, donning bow and frill,

    But in dark corners on the side

    With beggars and cripples you'll seek to hide;

    And even if God should at last forgive,

    Be cursed as long as you may live!   145

MARTHA: Ask God to show your own soul grace.

    Don't make it with blasphemies still more base.

VALENTINE: That I could lay my hands on you,
  You shriveled, pimping bugaboo,
  Then, I hope, I might truly win   150
  Forgiveness for my every sin.
GRETCHEN: My brother! This is agony!
VALENTINE: I tell you, do not bawl at me.
  When you threw honor overboard,
  You pierced my heart more than the sword.   155
  Now I shall cross death's sleeping span
  To God, a soldier and an honest man.
    [*Dies.*]

CATHEDRAL

[*Service, Organ, and Singing.* GRETCHEN *among many people.* EVIL
SPIRIT *behind* GRETCHEN.]
EVIL SPIRIT: How different you felt, Gretchen,
  When in innocence
  You came before this altar;
  And from the well-worn little book
  You prattled prayers,   5
  Half childish games,
  Half God in your heart!
  Gretchen!
  Where are your thoughts?
  And in your heart   10
  What misdeed?
  Do you pray for your mother's soul that went
  Because of you from sleep to lasting, lasting pain?
  Upon your threshold, whose blood?
  And underneath your heart,   15
  Does it not stir and swell,
  Frightened and frightening you
  With its foreboding presence?
GRETCHEN: Oh! Oh!
  That I were rid of all the thoughts   20
  Which waver in me to and fro
  Against me!
CHOIR: Dies irae, dies illa
      Solvet saeclum in favilla.[5]
    [*Sound of the organ.*]
EVIL SPIRIT: Wrath grips you.   25
  The great trumpet sounds.
  The graves are quaking.
  And your heart,
  Resurrected
  From ashen calm   30

___

5. Day of wrath, that day that dissolves the world into ashes (Latin). This is a famous 13th-century hymn by Thomas Celano.

To flaming tortures,
Flares up.
GRETCHEN: Would I were far!
I feel as if the organ had
Taken my breath,   35
As if the song
Dissolved my heart!
CHOIR: Judex ergo cum sedebit,
    Quidquid latet adparebit,
    Nil inultum remanebit.[6]   40
GRETCHEN: I feel so close.
The stony pillars
Imprison me.
The vault above
Presses on me.—Air!   45
EVIL SPIRIT: Hide yourself. Sin and shame
Do not stay hidden.
Air? Light?
Woe unto you!
CHOIR: Quid sum miser tunc dicturus?   50
    Quem patronum rogaturus?
    Cum vix justus sit securus.[7]
EVIL SPIRIT: The transfigured turn
Their countenance from you.
To hold out their hands to you   55
Makes the pure shudder.
Woe!
CHOIR: Quid sum miser tunc dicturus?
GRETCHEN: Neighbor! Your smelling salts! [She faints.]

WALPURGIS NIGHT

[Harz Mountains. Region of Schierke and Elend. FAUST and MEPHI-
STOPHELES.]
MEPHISTOPHELES: How would you like a broomstick now to fly?
I wish I had a billy goat that's tough.
For on this road we still have to climb high.
FAUST: As long as I feel fresh, and while my legs are spry,
This knotted staff seems good enough.   5
Why should we shun each stumbling block?
To creep first through the valleys' lovely maze,
And then to scale this wall of rock
From which the torrent foams in silver haze—
There is the zest that spices our ways.   10
Around the birches weaves the spring,
Even the fir tree feels its spell:

---

6. When the judge shall be seated, what is hidden shall appear, nothing shall remain unavenged (Latin).
7. What shall I say in my wretchedness? To whom shall I appeal when scarcely the righteous man is safe?
(Latin).

Should it not stir in our limbs as well?
MEPHISTOPHELES: Of all that I don't feel a thing.
  In me the winter is still brisk,   15
  I wish my path were graced with frost and snow.
  How wretchedly the moon's imperfect disk
  Arises now with its red, tardy glow,
  And is so dim that one could bump one's head
  At every step against a rock or tree!   20
  Let's use a will-o'-the-wisp[8] instead!
  I see one there that burns quite merrily.
  Hello there! Would you come and join us, friend?
  Why blaze away to no good end?
  Please be so kind and show us up the hill!   25
WILL-O'-THE-WISP: I hope my deep respect will help me force
  My generally flighty will;
  For zigzag is the rule in our course.
MEPHISTOPHELES: Hear! Hear! It's man you like to imitate!
  Now, in the Devil's name, go straight—   30
  Or I shall blow your flickering life span out.
WILL-O'-THE-WISP: You are the master of the house, no doubt,
  And I shall try to serve you nicely.
  But don't forget, the mountain is magic-mad today,
  And if Will-o'-the-wisp must guide you on your way,   35
  You must not take things too precisely.
FAUST, MEPHISTOPHELES, *and* WILL-O'-THE-WISP: [*In alternating song.*]
    In the sphere of dream and spell
    We have entered now indeed.
    Have some pride and guide us well
    That we get ahead with speed   40
    In the vast deserted spaces!

    See the trees behind the trees,
    See how swiftly they change places,
    And the cliffs that bow with ease,
    Craggy noses, long and short,   45
    How they snore and how they snort!

    Through the stones and through the leas
    Tumble brooks of every sort.
    Is it splash or melodies?
    Is it love that wails and prays,   50
    Voices of those heavenly days?
    What we hope and what we love!
    Echoes and dim memories
    Of forgotten times come back.

    Oo-hoo! Shoo-hoo! Thus they squawk,   55
    Screech owl, plover, and the hawk;

---

8. *Ignis fatuus,* a wavering light formed by marsh gas. In German folklore it was thought to lead travelers to their destruction.

Did they all stay up above?
Are those salamanders crawling?
Bellies bloated, long legs sprawling!
And the roots, as serpents, coil   60
From the rocks through sandy soil,
With their eerie bonds would scare us,
Block our path and then ensnare us;
Hungry as a starving leech,
Their strong polyp's tendrils reach   65
For the wanderer. And in swarms
Mice of myriad hues and forms
Storm through moss and heath and lea.
And a host of fireflies
Throng about and improvise   70
The most maddening company.

Tell me: do we now stand still,
Or do we go up the hill?
Everything now seems to mill,
Rocks and trees and faces blend,   75
Will-o'-the-wisps grow and extend
And inflate themselves at will.

MEPHISTOPHELES: Grip my coat and hold on tight!
    Here is such a central height
    Where one sees, and it amazes,   80
    In the mountain, Mammon's blazes.[9]
FAUST: How queer glimmers a dawnlike sheen
    Faintly beneath this precipice,
    And plays into the dark ravine
    Of the near bottomless abyss.   85
    Here mists arise, there vapors spread,
    And here it gleams deep in the mountain,
    Then creeps along, a tender thread,
    And gushes up, a glistening fountain.

    Here it is winding in a tangle,   90
    With myriad veins the gorges blaze,
    And here in this congested angle
    A single stream shines through the haze.
    There sparks are flying at our right,
    As plentiful as golden sand.   95
    But look! In its entire height
    The rock becomes a firebrand.
MEPHISTOPHELES: Sir Mammon never spares the light
    To hold the feast in proper fashion.
    How lucky that you saw this sight!   100
    I hear the guests approach in wanton passion.

---

9. Mammon is imagined as leading a group of fallen angels in digging out gold and gems from the
ground of Hell, presumably for Satan's palace, as described in Milton's *Paradise Lost* I.678ff.

FAUST: The tempests lash the air and rave,
   And with gigantic blows they hit my shoulders.
MEPHISTOPHELES: You have to clutch the ribs of those big hoary boulders,
   Or they will hurtle you to that abysmal grave.   105
   A fog blinds the night with its hood.
   Do you hear the crashes in the wood?
   Frightened, the owls are scattered.
   Hear how the pillars
   Of ever green castles are shattered.   110
   Quaking and breaking of branches!
   The trunks' overpowering groaning!
   The roots' creaking and moaning!
   In a frightfully tangled fall
   They crash over each other, one and all,   115
   And through the ruin-covered abysses
   The frenzied air howls and hisses.
   Do you hear voices up high?
   In the distance and nearby?
   The whole mountain is afire   120
   With a furious magic choir.
WITCHES' CHORUS: The witches ride to Blocksberg's top,
   The stubble is yellow, and green the crop.
   They gather on the mountainside,
   Sir Urian[1] comes to preside.   125
   We are riding over crag and brink,
   The witches fart, the billy goats stink.
VOICE: Old Baubo[2] comes alone right now,
   She is riding on a mother sow.
CHORUS: Give honor to whom honor's due!   130
   Dame Baubo, lead our retinue!
   A real swine and mother, too,
   The witches' crew will follow you.
VOICE: Which way did you come?
VOICE: By the Ilsenstone.
   I peeped at the owl who was roosting alone.   135
   Did she ever make eyes!
VOICE: Oh, go to hell!
   Why ride so pell-mell?
VOICE: See how she has flayed me!
   The wounds she made me!
WITCHES' CHORUS: The way is wide, the way is long;   140
     Just see the frantic pushing throng!
     The broomstick pokes, the pitchfork thrusts
     The infant chokes, the mother bursts.
WIZARDS' HALF CHORUS: Slow as the snail's is our pace,
     The women are ahead and race;   145

---

1. A name for the Devil.   2. In Greek mythology, the nurse of Demeter, noted for her obscenity and bestiality.

When it goes to the Devil's place,
By a thousand steps they win the race.
OTHER HALF: If that is so, we do not mind it:
    With a thousand steps the women find it;
    But though they rush, we do not care: 150
    With one big jump the men get there.
VOICE: [*Above.*] Come on, come on from Rocky Lake!
VOICES: [*From below.*] We'd like to join you and partake.
  We wash, but though we are quite clean,
  We're barren as we've always been. 155
BOTH CHORUSES: The wind is hushed, the star takes flight,
    The dreary moon conceals her light.
    As it whirls by, the wizards' choir
    Scatters a myriad sparks of fire.
VOICE: [*From below.*] Halt, please! Halt, ho! 160
VOICE: [*From above.*] Who calls out of the cleft below?
VOICE: [*Below.*] Take me along! Take me along!
  I've been climbing for three hundred years,
  And yet the peak I cannot find.
  But I would like to join my kind. 165
BOTH CHORUSES: The stick and broom can make you float,
    So can pitchfork and billy goat;
    Who cannot rise today to soar,
    That man is doomed for evermore.
HALF-WITCH: [*Below.*] I move and move and try and try; 170
  How did the others get so high?
  At home I'm restless through and through,
  And now shall miss my chance here, too.
WITCHES' CHORUS: The salve gives courage to the witch,
    For sails we use a rag and switch, 175
    A tub's a ship, if you know how;
    If you would ever fly, fly now!
BOTH CHORUSES: We near the peak, we fly around,
    Now sweep down low over the ground,
    And cover up the heath's vast regions 180
    With witches' swarms and wizards' legions.
    [*They alight.*]
MEPHISTOPHELES: They throng and push, they rush and clatter.
  They hiss and whirl, they pull and chatter.
  It glistens, sparks, and stinks and flares;
  Those are indeed the witches' airs! 185
  Stay close to me, or we'll be solitaires!
  Where are you?
FAUST: [*Far away.*] Here.
MEPHISTOPHELES: So far? Almost a loss!
  Then I must show them who is boss.
  Back! Squire Nick is coming! Back, sweet rabble! Slump!
  Here, Doctor, take a hold! And now in one big jump 190
  Let's leave behind this noisy crowd;

Even for me it's much too loud.
On that side is a light with quite a special flare,
Let's penetrate the bushes' shroud;
Come, come! Now let us slink in there!   195
FAUST: Spirit of Contradiction! Go on! I'll follow him.
I must say, it's exceptionally bright
To wander to the Blocksberg in the Walpurgis Night,
To isolate ourselves to follow out some whim.
MEPHISTOPHELES: You see that multicolored flare?   200
A cheerful club is meeting there:
In small groups one is not alone.
FAUST: I'd rather be up there: around that stone
The fires blaze, they have begun;
The crowds throng to the Evil One   205
Where many riddles must be solved.
MEPHISTOPHELES: But many new ones are evolved.
Leave the great world, let it run riot,
And let us stay where it is quiet.
It's something that has long been done,   210
To fashion little worlds within the bigger one.
I see young witches there, completely nude,
And old ones who are veiled as shrewdly.
Just for my sake, don't treat them rudely;
It's little effort and great fun!   215
There are some instruments that grind and grit.
Damnable noise! One must get used to it.
Come on! Come on! Please do not fret!
I'll lead the way and take you to this place,
And you will be quite grateful yet!   220
What do you say? There isn't enough space?
Just look! You barely see the other end.
A hundred fires in a row, my friend!
They dance, they chat, they cook, they drink, they court;
Now you just tell me where there's better sport!   225
FAUST: When you will introduce us at this revel,
Will you appear a sorcerer or devil?
MEPHISTOPHELES: I generally travel, without showing my station,
But on a gala day one shows one's decoration.
I have no garter[3] I could show,   230
But here the cloven foot is honored, as you know.
Do you perceive that snail? It comes, though it seems stiff;
For with its eager, groping face
It knows me with a single whiff.
Though I'd conceal myself, they'd know me in this place.   235
Come on! From flame to flame we'll make our tour,
I am the go-between, and you the wooer.
    [*To some who sit around dying embers.*]

---

3. That is, he has no decoration of nobility, such as the Order of the Garter.

Old gentlemen, why tarry outside? Enter!
I'd praise you if I found you in the center,
Engulfed by youthful waves and foam;   240
You are alone enough when you are home.
GENERAL: Who ever thought nations were true,
   Though you have served them with your hands and tongue;
   For people will, as women do,
   Reserve their greatest favors for the young.   245
STATESMAN: Now they are far from what is sage;
   The old ones should be kept in awe;
   For, truly, when our word was law,
   Then was indeed the golden age.
PARVENU: We, too, had surely ample wits,   250
   And often did things that we shouldn't;
   But now things are reversed and go to bits,
   Just when we changed our mind and wished they wouldn't.
AUTHOR: Today, who even looks at any book
   That makes some sense and is mature?   255
   And our younger generation—look,
   You never saw one that was so cocksure.
MEPHISTOPHELES: [*Who suddenly appears very old.*]
   I think the Judgment Day must soon draw nigh,
   For this is the last time I can attend this shrine;
   And as my little cask runs dry,   260
   The world is certain to decline.
HUCKSTER-WITCH: Please, gentlemen, don't pass like that!
   Don't miss this opportunity!
   Look at my goods attentively:
   There is a lot to marvel at.   265
   And my shop has a special charm—
   You will not find its peer on earth:
   All that I sell has once done harm
   To man and world and what has worth.
   There is no dagger here which has not gored;   270
   No golden cup from which, to end a youthful life,
   A fatal poison was not poured;
   No gems that did not help to win another's wife;
   No sword but broke the peace with sly attack,
   By stabbing, for example, a rival in the back.   275
MEPHISTOPHELES: Dear cousin, that's no good in times like these!
   What's done is done; what's done is trite.
   You better switch to novelties,
   For novelties alone excite.
FAUST: I must not lose my head, I swear;   280
   For this is what I call a fair.
MEPHISTOPHELES: This eddy whirls to get above,
   And you are shoved, though you may think you shove.
FAUST: And who is that?
MEPHISTOPHELES: That little madam?

    That's Lilith.[4]
FAUST: Lilith?
MEPHISTOPHELES: The first wife of Adam.   285
    Watch out and shun her captivating tresses:
    She likes to use her never-equaled hair
    To lure a youth into her luscious lair,
    And he won't lightly leave her lewd caresses.
FAUST: There two sit, one is young, one old;   290
    They certainly have jumped and trolled!
MEPHISTOPHELES: They did not come here for a rest.
    There is another dance. Come, let us do our best.
FAUST: [*Dancing with the young one.*]
        A pretty dream once came to me
        In which I saw an apple tree;
        Two pretty apples gleamed on it,   295
        They lured me, and I climbed a bit.
THE FAIR ONE: You find the little apples nice
        Since first they grew in Paradise.
        And I am happy telling you   300
        That they grow in my garden, too.
MEPHISTOPHELES: [*With the old one.*]
        A wanton dream once came to me
        In which I saw a cloven tree.
        It had the most tremendous hole;
        Though it was big, it pleased my soul.   305
THE OLD ONE: I greet you with profound delight,
        My gentle, cloven-footed knight!
        Provide the proper grafting-twig,
        If you don't mind the hole so big.
PROKTOPHANTASMIST:[5] Damnable folk! How dare you make such fuss! 310
    Have we not often proved to you
    That tales of walking ghosts cannot be true?
    And now you dance just like the rest of us!
THE FAIR ONE: [*Dancing.*] What does he want at our fair?
FAUST: [*Dancing.*] Oh, he! You find him everywhere.   315
    What others dance, he must assess;
    No step has really occurred, unless
    His chatter has been duly said.
    And what annoys him most, is when we get ahead.
    If you would turn in circles, in endless repetition,   320
    As he does all the time in his old mill,
    Perhaps he would not take it ill,
    Especially if you would first get his permission.
PROKTOPHANTASMIST: You still are there! Oh no! That's without precedent.

---

4. According to rabbinical legend, Adam's first wife; the *female* mentioned in Genesis 1:27: "So God created man in his own image, in the image of God created he him; male and female created he them." After Eve was created, Lilith became a ghost who seduced men and inflicted evil on children.   5. A German coinage meaning "Rump-ghostler." The figure caricatures Friedrich Nicolai (1733–1811), who opposed modern movements in German thought and literature and had parodied Goethe's *The Sorrows of Young Werther* (1774).

Please go! Have we not brought enlightenment?   325
By our rules these devils are not daunted;
We are so smart, but Tegel[6] is still haunted.
To sweep illusion out, my energies were spent,
But things never get clean; that's without precedent.
THE FAIR ONE: Why don't you stop annoying us and quit!   330
PROKTOPHANTASMIST: I tell you spirits to your face,
  The spirit's despotism's a disgrace:
  My spirit can't make rules for it.
      [*The dancing goes on.*]
  Today there's nothing I can do;
  But traveling is always fun,   335
  And I still hope, before my final step is done,
  I'll ban the devils, and the poets, too.
MEPHISTOPHELES: He'll sit down in a puddle and unbend:
  That is how his condition is improved;
  For when the leeches prosper on his fat rear end,[7]   340
  The spirits and his spirit are removed.
      [*To* FAUST, *who has left the dance.*]
  Why did you let that pretty woman go
  Who sang so nicely while you danced?
FAUST: She sang, and suddenly there pranced
  Out of her mouth a little mouse, all red.   345
MEPHISTOPHELES: That is a trifle and no cause for dread!
  Who cares? At least it was not gray.
  Why bother on this glorious lovers' day?
FAUST: Then I saw—
MEPHISTOPHELES: What?
FAUST: Mephisto, do you see
  That pale, beautiful child, alone there on the heather?   350
  She moves slowly but steadily,
  She seems to walk with her feet chained together.
  I must confess that she, forbid,
  Looks much as my good Gretchen did.
MEPHISTOPHELES: That does nobody good; leave it alone!   355
  It is a magic image, a lifeless apparition.
  Encounters are fraught with perdition;
  Its icy stare turns human blood to stone
  In truth, it almost petrifies;
  You know the story of Medusa's[8] eyes.   360
FAUST: Those are the eyes of one that's dead I see,
  No loving hand closed them to rest.
  That is the breast that Gretchen offered me,
  And that is the sweet body I possessed.
MEPHISTOPHELES: That is just sorcery; you're easily deceived!   365
  All think she is their sweetheart and are grieved.

6. A town near Berlin, where ghosts had been reported.   7. Nicolai claimed that he had been bothered by ghosts but had repelled them by applying leeches to his rump.   8. The Gorgon with hair of serpents whose glance turned people to stone.

FAUST: What rapture! Oh, what agony!
　I cannot leave her, cannot flee.
　How strange, a narrow ruby band should deck,
　The sole adornment, her sweet neck,   370
　No wider than a knife's thin blade.
MEPHISTOPHELES: I see it, too; it is quite so.
　Her head under her arm she can parade,
　Since Perseus lopped it off, you know. —
　Illusion holds you captive still.   375
　Come, let us climb that little hill,
　The Prater's⁹ not so full of glee;
　And if they're not bewitching me,
　There is a theatre I see.
　What will it be?
SERVIBILIS:　　　　They'll resume instantly.   380
　We'll have the seventh play, a brand-new hit;
　We do not think, so many are exacting.
　An amateur has written it,
　And amateurs do all the acting.
　Forgive, good sirs, if now I leave you;   385
　It amateurs me to draw up the curtain.
MEPHISTOPHELES: When it's on Blocksberg I perceive you,
　I'm glad; for that's where you belong for certain.

WALPURGIS NIGHT'S DREAM
OR THE GOLDEN WEDDING OF OBERON AND TITANIA

*Intermezzo*¹

STAGE MANAGER: This time we can keep quite still,
　Mieding's² progeny;
　Misty vale and hoary hill,
　That's our scenery.
HERALD: To make a golden wedding day   5
　Takes fifty years to the letter;
　But when their quarrels pass away,
　That gold I like much better.
OBERON: If you spirits can be seen,
　Show yourselves tonight;   10
　Fairy king and fairy queen
　Now will reunite.
PUCK: Puck is coming, turns about,
　And drags his feet to dance;
　Hundreds come behind and shout   15
　And join with him and prance.
ARIEL:³ Ariel stirs up a song,
　A heavenly pure air;

---

9. A famous park in Vienna.　　1. Brief interlude. Oberon and Titania are the king and queen of the
fairies.　　2. Johann Martin Mieding (died 1782), a master carpenter and scene builder in the Weimar
theater.　　3. A helpful sprite, unlike Puck, who is a mischievous spirit.

Many gargoyles come along,
    And many who are fair.   20
OBERON: You would get along, dear couple?
    Learn from us the art;
    If you want to keep love supple,
    You only have to part.
TITANIA: He is sulky, sullen she,   25
    Grab them, upon my soul;
    Take her to the Southern Sea,
    And him up to the pole.
ORCHESTRA TUTTI: [*Fortissimo.*] Snout of Fly, Mosquito Nose,
    With family additions,   30
    Frog O'Leaves and Crick't O'Grass,
    Those are the musicians.
SOLO: Now the bagpipe's joining in,
    A soap bubble it blows;
    Hear the snicker-snacking din   35
    Come through his blunted nose.
SPIRIT IN PROCESS OF FORMATION: Spider feet, belly of toad,
    And little wings, he'll grow 'em;
    There is no animal like that,
    But it's a little poem.   40
A LITTLE COUPLE: Mighty leaps and nimble feet,
    Through honey scent up high;
    While you bounce enough, my sweet,
    Still you cannot fly.
INQUISITIVE TRAVELER: Is that not mummery right there?   45
    Can that be what I see?
    Oberon who is so fair
    Amid this company!
ORTHODOX: No claws or tail or satyr's fleece!
    And yet you cannot cavil: 50
    Just like the gods of ancient Greece,
    He, too, must be a devil.
NORDIC ARTIST: What I do in the local clime,
    Are sketches of this tourney;
    But I prepare, while it is time,   55
    For my Italian journey.
PURIST: Bad luck brought me to these regions:
    They could not be much louder;
    And in the bawdy witches' legions
    Two only have used powder.   60
YOUNG WITCH: White powder, just like dresses, serves
    Old hags who are out of luck;
    I want to show my luscious curves,
    Ride naked on my buck.
MATRON: Our manners, dear, are far too neat   65
    To argue and to scold;
    I only hope that young and sweet,

Just as you are, you mold.
CONDUCTOR: Snout of Fly, Mosquito Nose,
    Leave off the naked sweet;   70
    Frog O'Leaves and Crick't O'Grass
    Get back into the beat!
WEATHERCOCK: [*To one side.*] The most exquisite company!
    Each girl should be a bride;
    The bachelors, grooms; for one can see   75
    How well they are allied.
WEATHERCOCK: [*To the other side.*] The earth should open up and gape
    To swallow this young revel,
    Or I will make a swift escape
    To hell to see the Devil.   80
XENIEN:[4] We appear as insects here,
    Each with a little stinger,
    That we may fittingly revere
    Satan, our sire and singer.
HENNINGS:[5] Look at their thronging legions play,   85
    Naïve, with little art;
    The next thing they will dare to say
    Is that they're good at heart.
MUSAGET:[6] To dwell among the witches' folk
    Seems quite a lot of fun;   90
    They are the ones I should invoke,
    Not Muses, as I've done.
CI-DEVANT GENIUS OF THE AGE:[7]
    Choose your friends well and you will zoom,
    Join in and do not pass us!
    Blocksberg has almost as much room   95
    As Germany's Parnassus.[8]
INQUISITIVE TRAVELER: Say, who is that haughty man
    Who walks as if he sits?
    He sniffs and snuffles as best he can:
    "He smells out Jesuits."   100
CRANE: I like to fish where it is clear,
    Also in muddy brew;
    That's why the pious man is here
    To mix with devils, too.
CHILD OF THE WORLD: The pious need no fancy prop,   105
    All vehicles seem sound:
    Even up here on Blocksberg's top
    Conventicles abound.
DANCERS: It seems, another choir succeeds,
    I hear the drums resuming.   110

---

4. Literally, polemical verses written by Goethe and Friedrich von Schiller (1739–1805). The characters here are versions of Goethe himself.   5. August Adolf von Hennings (1746–1826), publisher of a journal called *Genius of the Age* that had attacked Schiller.   6. The title of a collection of Hennings's poetry.   7. That is, "Former Genius of the Age"; probably alludes to the journal's change of title in 1800 to *Genius of the 19th Century*.   8. A mountain sacred to Apollo and the muses; hence figuratively the locale of poetic excellence.

"That dull sound comes out of the reeds,
    It is the bitterns' booming."
BALLET MASTER: How each picks up his legs and toddles,
    And comes by hook or crook!
    The stooped one jumps, the plump one waddles: 115
    They don't know how they look!
FIDDLER: They hate each other, wretched rabble,
    And each would kill the choir;
    They're harmonized by bagpipe babble,
    As beasts by Orpheus' lyre.[9]   120
DOGMATIST: I am undaunted and resist
    Both skeptic and critique;
    The Devil simply must exist,
    Else *what* would he be? Speak!
IDEALIST: Imagination is in me   125
    Today far too despotic;
    If I am everything I see,
    Then I must be idiotic.
REALIST: The spirits' element is vexing,
    I wish it weren't there;   130
    I never saw what's so perplexing,
    It drives me to despair.
SUPERNATURALIST: I am delighted by this whir,
    And glad that they persist;
    For from the devils I infer,   135
    Good spirits, too, exist.
SKEPTIC: They follow little flames about,
    And think they're near the treasure;
    Devil alliterates with doubt
    So I am here with pleasure.   140
CONDUCTOR: Snout of Fly, Mosquito Nose,
    Damnable amateurs!
    Frog O'Leaves and Crick't O'Grass
    You are musicians, sirs!
ADEPTS: Sansouci,[1] that is the name   145
    Of our whole caboodle;
    Walking meets with ill acclaim,
    So we move on our noodle.
NE'ER-DO-WELLS: We used to be good hangers-on
    And sponged good wine and meat;   150
    We danced till our shoes were gone,
    And now walk on bare feet.
WILL-O'-THE-WISPS: We come out of the swamps where we
    Were born without a penny;
    But now we join the revelry,   155
    As elegant as any.

---

9. In Greek mythology, Orpheus's music was said to have the power to quiet wild animals.   1. Without care or unhappiness (French).

SHOOTING STAR: I shot down from starry height
     With brilliant, fiery charm;
     But I lie in the grass tonight:
     Who'll proffer me his arm?   160
MASSIVE MOB: All around, give way! Give way!
     Trample down the grass!
     Spirits come, and sometimes they
     Form a heavy mass.
PUCK: Please don't walk like elephants,   165
     And do not be so rough;
     Let no one be as plump as Puck,
     For he is plump enough.
ARIEL: If nature gave with lavish grace,
     Or Spirit, wings and will,   170
     Follow in my airy trace
     Up to the roses' hill!
ORCHESTRA: [*Pianissimo.*] Floating clouds and wreaths of fog
     Dawn has quickly banished;
     Breeze in leaves, wind in the bog,   175
     And everything has vanished.

DISMAL DAY

[*Field.* FAUST. MEPHISTOPHELES.]

FAUST: In misery! Despairing! Long lost wretchedly on the earth, and
now imprisoned! As a felon locked up in a dungeon with horrible
torments, the fair ill-fated creature! It's come to that! To that!—
Treacherous, despicable Spirit—and that you have kept from
me!—Keep standing there, stand! Roll your devilish eyes wrathfully   5
in your face! Stand and defy me with your intolerable presence!
Imprisoned! In irreparable misery! Handed over to evil spirits and
judging, unfeeling mankind! And meanwhile you soothe me with
insipid diversions; hide her growing grief from me, and let her perish helplessly!   10
MEPHISTOPHELES: She's not the first one.
FAUST: Dog! Abominable monster!—Change him, oh infinite spirit!
Change back this worm into his dogshape, as he used to amuse himself in the night when he trotted along before me, rolled in front
of the feet of the harmless wanderer and, when he stumbled, clung   15
to his shoulders. Change him again to his favorite form that he may
crawl on his belly in the sand before me and I may trample on him
with my feet, the caitiff!—Not the first one!—Grief! Grief! past
what a human soul can grasp, that more than one creature has sunk
into the depth of this misery, that the first one did not enough for 20
the guilt of all the others, writhing in the agony of death before the
eyes of the everforgiving one! The misery of this one woman surges
through my heart and marrow, and you grin imperturbed over the
fate of thousands!
MEPHISTOPHELES: Now we're once again at our wit's end where your   25

human minds snap. Why do you seek fellowship with us if you
can't go through with it? You would fly, but get dizzy? Did we
impose on you, or you on us?

FAUST: Don't bare your greedy teeth at me like that! It sickens me!—
Great, magnificent spirit that deigned to appear to me, that know   30
my heart and soul—why forge me to this monster who gorges himself on harm, and on corruption—feasts.

MEPHISTOPHELES: Have you finished?

FAUST: Save her! or woe unto you! The most hideous curse upon you
for millenniums!   35

MEPHISTOPHELES: I cannot loosen the avenger's bonds, nor open his
bolts.—Save her!—Who was it that plunged her into ruin? I or you?
[FAUST *looks around furiously.*] Are you reaching for thunder? Well
that it was not given to you wretched mortals! Shattering those who
answer innocently, is the tyrant's way of easing his embarrassment.   40

FAUST: Take me there! She shall be freed!

MEPHISTOPHELES: And the dangers you risk? Know that blood-guilt
from your hand still lies on the town. Over the slain man's site
avenging spirits hover, waiting for the returning murderer.

FAUST: That, too, from you? A world's murder and death upon you,   45
monster! Guide me to her, I say, and free her!

MEPHISTOPHELES: I shall guide you; hear what I can do. Do I have all
the power in the heaven and on the earth? I shall make the jailer's
senses foggy, and you may get the keys and lead her out with
human hands. I shall stand guard, magic horses shall be prepared,   50
and I shall carry you away. That I can do.

FAUST: Up and away!

NIGHT, OPEN FIELD

[FAUST *and* MEPHISTOPHELES, *storming along on black horses.*]

FAUST: What are they weaving around the Ravenstone?

MEPHISTOPHELES: I do not know what they do and brew.

FAUST: Floating to, floating fro, bowing and bending.

MEPHISTOPHELES: A witches' guild.

FAUST: They strew and dedicate.   5

MEPHISTOPHELES: Go by! Go by!

DUNGEON

FAUST: [*With a bunch of keys and a lamp before a small iron gate.*]
A long unwonted shudder grips,
Mankind's entire grief grips me.
She's here, behind this wall that drips,
And all her crime was a fond fantasy.
You hesitate to go in?   5
You dread to see her again?
On! Your wavering waves on death's decree. [*He seizes the lock.*]
[*Song from within.*]

GRETCHEN: My mother, the whore,

Who has murdered me —
My father, the rogue,   10
Who has eaten me —
My little sister alone
Picked up every bone,
In a cool place she put them away;
Into a fair bird I now have grown;   15
Fly away, fly away!

FAUST: [*Unlocking.*] She does not dream how her lover at the door
  Hears the clanking chains and the rustling straw. [*Enters.*]
MARGARET: [*Hiding on her pallet.*] Oh! Oh! They come. Death's bitter-
  ness!
FAUST: [*Softly.*] Still! Still! I come to set you free.   20
MARGARET: [*Groveling toward his feet.*] If you are human, pity my distress.
FAUST: You'll awaken the guards. Speak quietly.
  [*He seizes the chains to unlock them.*]
MARGARET: [*On her knees.*] Who, hangman, could give
  You over me this might?
  You come for me in the middle of the night.   25
  Have pity on me, let me live!
  Is it not time when the morning chimes have rung?
    [*She gets up.*]
  I am still so young, so very young.
  And must already die.
  I was beautiful, too, and that was why.   30
  Near was the friend, now he is away.
  Torn lies the wreath, the flowers decay.
  Do not grip me so brutally. What shall I do?
  Spare me. What have I done to you?
  Let me not in vain implore.   35
  After all, I have never seen you before.
FAUST: After such grief, can I live any more?
MARGARET: Now I am entirely in your might.
  Only let me nurse the baby again.
  I fondled it all through the night;   40
  They took it from me to give me pain,
  And now they say I put it away.
  And I shall never again be gay.
  They sing songs about me. The people are wicked.
  An ancient fairy tale ends that way,   45
  Who made them pick it?
FAUST: [*Casts himself down.*] One loving you lies at your feet
  To end your bondage. Listen, sweet!
MARGARET: [*Casts herself down beside him.*]
  Ah, let us kneel, send to the saints our prayers!
  See, underneath these stairs,   50
  Underneath the sill
  There seethes hell.
  The Devil

Makes a thundering noise
With his angry revel.   55
FAUST: [*Loud.*] Gretchen! Gretchen!
MARGARET: [*Attentively.*] That was my lover's voice!
    [*She jumps up. The chains drop off.*]
Where is he? I heard him call. I am free.
No one shall hinder me.
To his neck I shall fly,   60
On his bosom lie.
He called Gretchen. He stood on the sill.
Amid the wailing and howling of hell,
Through the angry and devilish jeers
The sweet and loving tone touched my ears.   65
FAUST: It is I.
MARGARET: It is you. Oh, do say it again. [*She seizes him.*]
It is he. It is he. Where, then, is all my pain?
Where the fear of the dungeon? the chain?
It is you. Come to save me.   70
I am saved!
Now I see the road again, too,
Where, for the first time, I laid eyes on you—
And the garden and the gate
Where I and Martha stand and wait.   75
FAUST: [*Striving away.*] Come on! Come on!
MARGARET: O Stay!
Because I am so happy where you are staying. [*Caresses him.*]
FAUST: Do not delay.
If you keep on delaying,   80
We shall have to pay dearly therefor.
MARGARET: What? You cannot kiss any more?
My friend, you were not gone longer than this—
And forgot how to kiss?
Why, at your neck, do I feel such dread,   85
When once from your eyes and from what you said
A whole heaven surged down to fill me,
And you would kiss me as if you wanted to kill me?
Kiss me!
Else I'll kiss you. [*She embraces him.*]   90
Oh, grief! Your lips are cold,
Are mute.
Where
Is your loving air?
Who took it from me? [*She turns away from him.*]   95
FAUST: Come, follow me, dearest, and be bold!
I shall caress you a thousandfold;
Only follow me! That is all I plead.
MARGARET: [*Turning toward him.*] And is it you? Is it you indeed?
FAUST: It is I. Come along!   100
MARGARET: You take off the chain,

And take me into your lap again.
How is it that you do not shrink from me?—
Do you know at all, my friend, whom you make free?
FAUST: Come! Come! Soon dawns the light of day.   105
MARGARET: I've put my mother away,
I've drowned my child, don't you see?
Was it not given to you and to me?
You, too—it is you! Could it merely seem?
Give me your hand! It is no dream.   110
Your dear hand!—But alas, it is wet.
Wipe it off! There is yet
Blood on this one.
Oh God! What have you done!
Sheathe your sword;   115
I am begging you.
FAUST: Let the past be forever past—oh Lord,
You will kill me, too.
MARGARET: Oh no, you must outlive us!
I'll describe the graves you should give us.   120
Care for them and sorrow
Tomorrow:
Give the best place to my mother,
And next to her lay my brother;
Me, a little aside,   125
Only don't make the space too wide!
And the little one at my right breast.
Nobody else will lie by my side.—
Oh, to lie with you and to hide
In your arms, what happiness!   130
Now it is more than I can do;
I feel, I must force myself on you,
And you, it seems, push back my caress;
And yet it is you, and look so pure, so devout.
FAUST: If you feel, it is I, come out!   135
MARGARET: Out where?
FAUST: Into the open.
MARGARET: If the grave is there,
If death awaits us, then come!
From here to the bed of eternal rest,   140
And not a step beyond—no!
You are leaving now? Oh, Heinrich, that I could go!
FAUST: You can! If only you would! Open stands the door.
MARGARET: I may not go; for me there is no hope any more.
What good to flee? They lie in wait for me.   145
To have to go begging is misery,
And to have a bad conscience, too.
It is misery to stray far and forsaken,
And, anyhow, I would be taken.
FAUST: I shall stay with you.   150

MARGARET: Quick! Quick! I pray.
  Save your poor child.
  On! Follow the way
  Along the brook,
  Over the bridge,   155
  Into the wood,
  To the left where the planks stick
  Out of the pond.
  Seize it—oh, quick!
  It wants to rise,   160
  It is still struggling.
  Save! Save!
FAUST: Can you not see,
  It takes *one* step, and you are free.
MARGARET: If only we were past the hill!   165
  My mother sits there on a stone,
  My scalp is creeping with dread!
  My mother sits there on a stone
  And wags and wags her head;
  She becks not, she nods not, her head is heavy and sore,   170
  She has slept so long, she awakes no more.
  She slept that we might embrace.
  Those were the days of grace.
FAUST: In vain is my pleading, in vain what I say;
  What can I do but bear you away?   175
MARGARET: Leave me! No, I shall suffer no force!
  Do not grip me so murderously!
  After all, I did everything else you asked.
FAUST: The day dawns. Dearest! Dearest!
MARGARET: Day. Yes, day is coming. The last day breaks;   180
  It was to be my wedding day.
  Tell no one that you have already been with Gretchen.
  My veil! Oh pain!
  It just happened that way.
  We shall meet again,   185
  But not dance that day.
  The crowd is pushing, no word is spoken.
  The alleys below
  And the streets overflow.
  The bell is tolling, the wand is broken.   190
  How they tie and grab me, now one delivers
  Me to the block and gives the sign,
  And for every neck quivers
  The blade that quivers for mine.
  Mute lies the world as a grave.   195
FAUST: That I had never been born!
MEPHISTOPHELES: [*Appears outside.*] Up! Or you are lost.
  Prating and waiting and pointless wavering.
  My horses are quavering,

Over the sky creeps the dawn. 200
MARGARET: What did the darkness spawn?
He! He! Send him away!
What does he want in this holy place?
He wants me!
FAUST: You shall live.
MARGARET: Judgment of God! I give 205
Myself to you.
MEPHISTOPHELES: [*To* FAUST.]
Come! Come! I shall abandon you with her.
MARGARET: Thine I am, father. Save me!
You angels, hosts of heaven, stir,
Encamp about me, be my guard. 210
Heinrich! I quail at thee.
MEPHISTOPHELES: She is judged.
VOICE: [*From above.*] Is saved.
MEPHISTOPHELES: [*To* FAUST.] Hither to me! [*Disappears with
FAUST.*]
VOICE: [*From within, fading away.*] Heinrich! Heinrich!

WILLIAM BLAKE

1757–1827

Few works so ostentatiously "simple" as William Blake's *Songs of Innocence and of Experience* (1794) can ever have aroused such critical perplexity. Employing uncomplicated vocabulary and, often, variants of traditional ballad structure; describing the experience usually of naive subjects; supplying no obvious intellectual substance, these short lyrics have long fascinated and baffled their readers.

With no formal education, Blake, son of a London hosier, was at the age of fourteen apprenticed to the engraver James Basire. He developed both as painter and as engraver, partly influenced by the painter Henry Fuseli and the sculptor John Flaxman, both his friends, but remaining always highly individual in style and technique. An acknowledged mystic, he saw visions from the age of four: trees filled with Angels, God looking at him through the window. His highly personal view of a world penetrated by the divine helped to form both his visual and verbal art. In 1800, Blake moved from London to Felpham, where the poet William Hayley was his patron. He returned to London in 1803 and remained there for the rest of his life, married but childless, engaged in writing, printing, and engraving.

Blake felt a close relation between the visual and the verbal; he illustrated the works of many poets, notably Milton and Dante. His first book, *Poetical Sketches* (1783), was conventionally published, but he produced all his subsequent books himself, combining pictorial engravings with lettering, striking off only a few copies of each work by hand. Gradually, in increasingly long poems, he developed an elaborate private mythology, with important figures appearing in one work after another. His major mythic poems include *The Marriage of Heaven and Hell* (1793), *America* (1793), *The Book of Los* (1795), *Milton* (1804), *Jerusalem* (1804), and *The Four Zoas* (which he never completed).

As his short poem *Mock On, Mock On, Voltaire, Rousseau* testifies, Blake was bitterly opposed to what he thought the destructive and repressive rationalism of the eighteenth century. Voltaire and Rousseau might have been surprised to find themselves thus associated; they belong together, in Blake's view, because both implicitly oppose not only orthodox Christianity but the more private variety of revealed religion so vital to Blake himself. Although, like his contemporaries, Blake idealizes imagination and emotion and believes in the sacredness of the individual, he entirely avoids the "egotistical sublime," neither speaking directly of himself in his poetry, as Wordsworth did, nor, like Goethe, creating self-absorbed characters. In his short lyrics he adopts many different voices; the difficulties of interpretation stem partly from this fact. He insistently deals with metaphysical questions about our place in the universe and with social questions about the nature of human responsibility.

In *Songs of Innocence*, the speaker is often a child: asking questions of a lamb, meditating on his own blackness, describing the experience of a chimney sweep. Ostensibly these children in their innocence feel no anger or bitterness at the realities of the world in which they find themselves. The "little black boy" assures himself of a future when the "little English boy" will resemble him and love him; the child addressing the lamb evokes a realm of pure delight; the chimney sweep comforts himself with conventional morality and with a companion's dream. When an adult observer watches children, as in *Holy Thursday*, he too sees a benign arrangement, in which children are "flowers of London town," supervised by "agèd men, wise guardians of the poor." In the *Introduction* to the volume, the adult speaker receives empowering advice from a child, who instructs him to write. Everything is for the best in this best of all possible worlds.

But not quite. Disturbing undertones reverberate through even the most "innocent" of these songs. Innocence is, after all, by definition a state automatically lost through experience and never possible to regain. If the children evoked by the text still possess their innocence, the adult reader does not. *The Little Black Boy* suggests the kind of ambiguity evoked by the conjunction between innocent speaker and experienced reader. The poem opens with a situation that the speaker does not entirely understand—but one likely to be painfully familiar to the reader. "White as an angel is the English child: / But I am black as if bereaved of light": the child's similes indicate how completely he has incorporated the value judgments of his society, in which white suggests everything good and black means deficiency and deprivation. In this context, the mother's teaching, a comforting myth, becomes comprehensible as a way of dealing with her child's bewilderment and anxiety about his difference. At the end of the poem, the boy extends his mother's story into a prophetic vision in which black means protective power ("I'll shade him from the heat till he can bear / To lean in joy upon our father's knee"), and difference disappears into likeness, hostility into love. The vision evokes an ideal situation located in an imagined afterlife; it has only an antithetical connection to present actuality. Its emphatic divergence from real social conditions creates the subterranean disturbance characteristic of Blake's lyrics, the disturbance that calls attention to the serious social criticism implicit even in lyrics that may appear sweet to the point of blandness.

For all Blake's dislike of the earlier eighteenth century, he shares with his forebears one important assumption: his poetry, too, instructs as well as pleases. The innocent chimney sweep evokes parental death and betrayal, horrifying working conditions (soot and nakedness, darkness and shaved heads), and compensatory dreams. He never complains, but when he ends with the tag, "So if all do their duty, they need not fear harm," it generates moral shock. The discrepancy between the child's purity and his brutal exploitation indicts the society that allows such things. Innocence may be its own protection, these poems suggest, but that fact does not obviate social guilt.

If the *Songs of Innocence,* for all their atmosphere of brightness, cheer, and peace, convey outrage at the ways that social institutions harm those they should protect, the *Songs of Experience* more directly evoke a world worn, constricted, burdened with misery created by human beings. Now a new version of *The Chimney Sweeper* openly states what the earlier poem suggested:

> "And because I am happy, & dance & sing,
> They think they have done me no injury,
> And are gone to praise God & his Priest & King,
> Who make up a heaven of our misery."

The child understands the protective self-blinding of adults.

London in its sixteen lines sums up many of the collection's implications. Like most of the *Songs of Experience, London* presents an adult speaker, a wanderer through the city, who finds wherever he goes, in every face, "Marks of weakness, marks of woe." The city is the repository of suffering: men and infants and chimney sweepers cry; soldiers sigh; harlots curse. All are victims of corrupt institutions: blackening Church, bloody palace. Marriage and death interpenetrate; the curses of illness and corruption pass through the generations. The speaker reports only what he sees and hears, without commentary. He evokes a society in dreadful decay, and he conveys his despairing rage at a situation he cannot remedy.

Blake's lyrics, in their mixture of the visionary and the observational, strike notes far different from those of satire. Like the visionary observations of Swift and Voltaire, though, they insist on the connection between literature and life. Literature has transformative capacity, but it works with the raw material of actual experience. And its visions have the power to insist on the necessity of change.

Blake has provided material for an enormous outpouring of critical work. Particularly useful for the student are the collections of critical essays, N. Frye, ed., *Blake* (1966), and H. Adams, ed., *Critical Essays on William Blake* (1991). Valuable longer studies include M. Schorer, *William Blake: The Politics of Vision* (1946); H. Adams, *William Blake: A Reading of the Shorter Poems* (1963); E. D. Hirsch, *Innocence and Experience* (1969); D. G. Gilham, *William Blake* (1973); and S. Gardner, *Blake's Innocence and Experience Retraced* (1986). H. Bloom, ed., *William Blake* (1985), provides a useful compendium of mostly recent criticism; N. Hilton, ed., *Essential Articles for the Study of William Blake* (1986), is more wide ranging. A valuable recent general study is E. Larrissy, *William Blake* (1985).

Songs of Innocence and of Experience

SHEWING THE TWO CONTRARY STATES OF THE HUMAN SOUL

Songs of Innocence[1]

Introduction

Piping down the valleys wild
Piping songs of pleasant glee

---

1. The text for all of Blake's works is edited by David V. Erdman and Harold Bloom. *Songs of Innocence* (1789) was later combined with *Songs of Experience* (1794), and the poems were etched and accompanied by Blake's illustrations, the process accomplished by copper engravings stamped on paper, then colored by hand.

On a cloud I saw a child,
And he laughing said to me,

"Pipe a song about a Lamb"; 5
So I piped with merry chear;
"Piper pipe that song again"—
So I piped, he wept to hear.

"Drop thy pipe thy happy pipe
Sing thy songs of happy chear"; 10
So I sung the same again
While he wept with joy to hear.

"Piper sit thee down and write
In a book that all may read"—
So he vanished from my sight. 15
And I plucked a hollow reed,

And I made a rural pen,
And I stained the water clear,
And I wrote my happy songs
Every child may joy to hear. 20

The Lamb

Little Lamb, who made thee?
  Dost thou know who made thee?
Gave thee life & bid thee feed,
By the stream & o'er the mead;
Gave thee clothing of delight, 5
Softest clothing wooly bright;
Gave thee such a tender voice,
Making all the vales rejoice!
  Little Lamb who made thee?
  Dost thou know who made thee? 10

Little Lamb I'll tell thee,
  Little Lamb I'll tell thee!
He is callèd by thy name,
For he calls himself a Lamb:
He is meek & he is mild, 15
He became a little child:
I a child & thou a lamb,
We are callèd by his name.[1]
  Little Lamb God bless thee.
  Little Lamb God bless thee. 20

The Little Black Boy

My mother bore me in the southern wild,
And I am black, but O! my soul is white;

1. Christians use the name of Christ to designate themselves.

White as an angel is the English child:
But I am black as if bereaved of light.

My mother taught me underneath a tree,   5
And sitting down before the heat of day,
She took me on her lap and kissèd me,
And pointing to the east, began to say:

"Look on the rising sun: there God does live,
And gives his light, and gives his heat away;   10
And flowers and trees and beasts and men receive
Comfort in morning, joy in the noon day.

"And we are put on earth a little space,
That we may learn to bear the beams of love,
And these black bodies and this sun-burnt face   15
Is but a cloud, and like a shady grove.

"For when our souls have learned the heat to bear,
The cloud will vanish; we shall hear his voice,
Saying: 'Come out from the grove, my love & care,
And round my golden tent like lambs rejoice.' "   20

Thus did my mother say, and kissèd me;
And thus I say to little English boy:
When I from black and he from white cloud free,
And round the tent of God like lambs we joy,

I'll shade him from the heat till he can bear   25
To lean in joy upon our father's knee;
And then I'll stand and stroke his silver hair,
And be like him, and he will then love me.

Holy Thursday[1]

'Twas on a Holy Thursday, their innocent faces clean,
The children walking two & two, in red & blue & green,[2]
Grey headed beadles[3] walked before with wands as white as snow,
Till into the high dome of Paul's they like Thames' waters flow.

O what a multitude they seemed, these flowers of London town!   5
Seated in companies they sit with radiance all their own.
The hum of multitudes was there, but multitudes of lambs,
Thousands of little boys & girls raising their innocent hands.

Now like a mighty wind they raise to heaven the voice of song,
Or like harmonious thunderings the seats of heaven among.   10
Beneath them sit the agèd men, wise guardians[4] of the poor;
Then cherish pity, lest you drive an angel from your door.[5]

---

1. Ascension Day, forty days after Easter, when children from charity schools were marched to St. Paul's
Cathedral.   2. Each school had its own distinctive uniform.   3. Ushers and minor functionaries,
whose job was to maintain order.   4. The governors of the charity schools.   5. See Hebrews 13:2:
"Be not forgetful to entertain strangers: for thereby some have entertained angels unawares."

The Chimney Sweeper

When my mother died I was very young,
And my father sold me[1] while yet my tongue
Could scarcely cry " 'weep![2] 'weep! 'weep! 'weep!"
So your chimneys I sweep & in soot I sleep.

There's little Tom Dacre, who cried when his head   5
That curled like a lamb's back, was shaved, so I said,
"Hush, Tom! never mind it, for when your head's bare,
You know that the soot cannot spoil your white hair."

And so he was quiet, & that very night,
As Tom was a-sleeping he had such a sight!   10
That thousands of sweepers, Dick, Joe, Ned, & Jack,
Were all of them locked up in coffins of black;

And by came an Angel who had a bright key,
And he opened the coffins & set them all free;
Then down a green plain, leaping, laughing they run,   15
And wash in a river and shine in the Sun;

Then naked[3] & white, all their bags left behind,
They rise upon clouds, and sport in the wind.
And the Angel told Tom, if he'd be a good boy,
He'd have God for his father & never want joy.   20

And so Tom awoke; and we rose in the dark
And got with our bags & our brushes to work.
Tho' the morning was cold, Tom was happy & warm;
So if all do their duty, they need not fear harm.

Songs of Experience

Introduction

Hear the voice of the Bard!
Who Present, Past, & Future sees;
Whose ears have heard
The Holy Word
That walked among the ancient trees;[1]   5

Calling the lapsèd Soul
And weeping in the evening dew;[2]
That might control
The starry pole,
And fallen, fallen light renew!   10

---

1. It was common practice in Blake's day for fathers to sell, or indenture, their children to become chimney sweeps. The average age at which such children began working was six or seven; they were generally employed for seven years, until they were too big to ascend the chimneys.   2. The child's lisping effort to say "sweep," as he walks the streets looking for work.   3. They climbed up the chimneys naked.   1. Genesis 3:8: "And [Adam and Eve] heard the voice of the Lord God walking in the garden in the cool of the day."   2. Blake's ambiguous use of pronouns makes for interpretive difficulties. It would seem that *The Holy Word* (Jehovah, a name for God in the Old Testament of the Bible) calls *the lapsèd Soul*, and weeps—not the Bard.

"O Earth, O Earth, return!
Arise from out the dewy grass;
Night is worn,
And the morn
Rises from the slumberous mass.   15

"Turn away no more;
Why wilt thou turn away?
The starry floor
The watery shore
Is given thee till the break of day."   20

Earth's Answer

Earth raised up her head,
From the darkness dread & drear.
Her light fled:
Stony dread!
And her locks covered with grey despair.   5

"Prisoned on watery shore
Starry Jealousy does keep my den,
Cold and hoar
Weeping o'er
I hear the Father[1] of the ancient men.   10

"Selfish father of men,
Cruel, jealous, selfish fear!
Can delight
Chained in night
The virgins of youth and morning bear?   15

"Does spring hide its joy
When buds and blossoms grow?
Does the sower
Sow by night,
Or the plowman in darkness plow?   20

"Break this heavy chain
That does freeze my bones around;
Selfish! vain!
Eternal bane!
That free Love with bondage bound."   25

The Tyger

Tyger! Tyger! burning bright
In the forests of the night,

1. In Blake's later prophetic works, one of the four Zoas, representing the four chief faculties of humankind, is Urizen. In general, he stands for the orthodox conception of the Divine Creator, sometimes Jehovah in the Old Testament, often the God conceived by Newton and Locke—in all instances a tyrant associated with excessive rationalism, sexual repression, and the opponent of the imagination and creativity. This may be "the Holy Word" in *Introduction* (see p. 788, line 4).

What immortal hand or eye
Could frame thy fearful symmetry?

In what distant deeps or skies   5
Burnt the fire of thine eyes?
On what wings dare he aspire?
What the hand dare seize the fire?

And what shoulder, & what art,
Could twist the sinews of thy heart?   10
And when thy heart began to beat,
What dread hand? & what dread feet?

What the hammer? what the chain?
In what furnace was thy brain?
What the anvil? what dread grasp   15
Dare its deadly terrors clasp?

When the stars threw down their spears,
And watered heaven with their tears,
Did he smile his work to see?
Did he who made the Lamb make thee?   20

Tyger! Tyger! burning bright
In the forests of the night,
What immortal hand or eye
Dare frame thy fearful symmetry?

The Sick Rose

O Rose, thou art sick.
The invisible worm
That flies in the night
In the howling storm

Has found out thy bed   5
Of crimson joy,
And his dark secret love
Does thy life destroy.

London

I wander thro' each chartered[1] street,
Near where the chartered Thames does flow,
And mark in every face I meet
Marks of weakness, marks of woe.

In every cry of every Man,   5
In every Infant's cry of fear,
In every voice, in every ban,
The mind-forged manacles I hear:

---

1. Literally, hired. Blake implies that the streets and the river are controlled by commercial interests.

How the Chimney-sweeper's cry
Every blackening Church appalls;[2]
And the hapless Soldier's sigh
Runs in blood down Palace walls.   10

But most thro' midnight streets I hear
How the youthful Harlot's curse
Blasts the new-born Infant's tear,[3]
And blights with plagues the Marriage hearse.   15

The Chimney Sweeper

A little black thing among the snow
Crying "'weep, 'weep," in notes of woe!
"Where are thy father & mother? say?"
"They are both gone up to the church to pray.

"Because I was happy upon the heath,   5
And smiled among the winter's snow;
They clothèd me in the clothes of death,
And taught me to sing the notes of woe.

"And because I am happy, & dance & sing,
They think they have done me no injury,   10
And are gone to praise God & his Priest & King,
Who make up a heaven of our misery."

Mock On, Mock On, Voltaire, Rousseau

Mock on, Mock on, Voltaire, Rousseau;
Mock on, Mock on, 'tis all in vain.
You throw the sand against the wind,
And the wind blows it back again.

And every sand becomes a Gem   5
Reflected in the beams divine;
Blown back, they blind the mocking Eye,
But still in Israel's paths they shine.

The Atoms of Democritus[1]
And Newton's Particles of light[2]   10
Are sands upon the Red sea shore,
Where Israel's tents do shine so bright.

---

2. Literally, "makes white," punning also on *appall* (to dismay) and *pall* (the cloth covering a corpse or bier). 3. The harlot infects the parents with venereal disease, and thus the infant is inflicted with neonatal blindness. 1. Greek philosopher (460?–362? B.C.), who advanced a theory that all things are merely patterns of atoms. 2. Sir Isaac Newton's (1642–1727) corpuscular theory of light. For Blake, both men were condemned as materialists.

And Did Those Feet

And did those feet[1] in ancient time
Walk upon England's mountains green?
And was the holy Lamb of God
On England's pleasant pastures seen?

And did the Countenance Divine   5
Shine forth upon our clouded hills?
And was Jerusalem builded here,
Among those dark Satanic Mills?[2]

Bring me my Bow of burning gold:
Bring me my Arrows of desire: 10
Bring me my Spear: O clouds unfold!
Bring me my Chariot of fire!

I will not cease from Mental Fight,
Nor shall my Sword sleep in my hand,
Till we have built Jerusalem   15
In England's green & pleasant Land.

1. A reference to an ancient legend that Jesus came to England with Joseph of Arimathea.   2. Possibly industrial England, but "mills" also meant for Blake 18th-century arid, mechanistic philosophy.

WILLIAM WORDSWORTH
1770–1850

William Wordsworth both proclaimed and embodied the *newness* of the Romantic movement. In his preface to the second edition of *Lyrical Ballads* (1800), a collection of poems by him and his friend Samuel Taylor Coleridge, he announced the advent of a poetic revolution. Like other revolutionaries, Wordsworth and Coleridge created their identities by rebelling against and travestying their predecessors. Now no longer would poets write in "dead" forms; now they had discovered a "new" direction, "new" subject matter; now poetry could at last serve as an important form of human communication. Reading Wordsworth's poems with the excitement of that revolution long past, we can still feel the power of his desire to communicate. The human heart is his subject; he writes, in particular, of growth and of memory and of the perplexities inherent in the human condition.

Born at Cockermouth, Cumberland, to the family of an attorney, Wordsworth attended St. John's College, Cambridge, from 1787 to 1791. The next year, early in the French Revolution, he spent in France, where he met Annette Vallon and had a daughter by her. In 1795, Wordsworth met Coleridge; two years later, Wordsworth and his sister, Dorothy, moved to Alfoxden, near Coleridge's home in Nether Stowey, in the county of Somerset. There the two men conceived the idea of collaboration; in 1798, the first edition of their *Lyrical Ballads* appeared, anonymously. The next year, Wordsworth and his sister settled in the Lake District of northwest England. In 1802, the poet married Mary Hutchinson, with whom he had five children. He received the sinecure of stamp distributor in 1813 and in 1843 succeeded Robert Southey as England's poet laureate, having long since abandoned the political radicalism of his youth.

Wordsworth wrote little prose, except for the famous preface of 1800 and another preface in 1815; his accomplishment was almost entirely poetic. His early work employed conventional eighteenth-century techniques, but *Lyrical Ballads* marked a new direction: an effort to employ simple language and to reveal the high significance of simple themes, the transcendent importance of the everyday. Between 1798 and 1805, he composed his nineteenth-century version of an epic, *The Prelude*, an account of the development of a poet's mind—his own. His subsequent work included odes, sonnets, and many poems written to mark specific occasions.

It would be difficult to overestimate the extent of Wordsworth's historical and poetic importance. In *The Prelude*, not published until 1850, he not only made powerful poetry out of his own experience but also specified a way of valuing experience:

> There are in our existence spots of time,
> That with distinct pre-eminence retain
> A renovating virtue, whence, depressed
> By false opinion and contentious thought,
> Or aught of heavier or more deadly weight,
> In trivial occupations, and the round
> Of ordinary intercourse, our minds
> Are nourished and invisibly repaired;
> A virtue, by which pleasure is enhanced,
> That penetrates, enables us to mount
> When high, more high, and lifts us up when fallen.

To take seriously the moment, this passage suggests, enables us to resist the dulling force of everyday life ("trivial occupations") and provides the means of personal salvation.

Wordsworth often uses religious language (a religious reference is hinted in the idea of being lifted up when fallen) to insist on the importance of his doctrine. He inaugurated an attempt—lasting far into the century—to establish and sustain a secular religion to substitute for Christian faith. The attempt was, even for Wordsworth, only intermittently successful. *The Prelude* records experiences of persuasive visionary intensity, as when the poet speaks of seeing a shepherd in the distance:

> Or him have I descried in distant sky,
> A solitary object and sublime,
> Above all height! like an aerial cross
> Stationed alone upon a spiry rock
> Of the Chartreuse, for worship.

But such "spots of time" exist in isolation; it is difficult to maintain a saving faith on their basis.

The two long poems printed here treat the problem of discovering and sustaining faith. *Lines Composed a Few Miles Above Tintern Abbey*, first published in *Lyrical Ballads*, and *Ode on Intimations of Immortality*, published in 1807 but written between 1802 and 1806, share a preoccupation with loss and with the saving power of memory. Both speak of personal experience, although the ode, a more formal poem, also generalizes to a hypothetical "we." Both insist that nature—the external world experienced through the senses and the containing pattern assumed beyond that world—offers the possibility of wisdom to combat the pain inherent in human growth.

But it would be a mistake to assume that the poems exist to promulgate a doctrine of natural salvation, although some readers have considered their "pantheism" (the belief that God pervades every part of His created universe) their most important aspect. Both poems evoke an intellectual and emotional process, not a conclusion; they sketch dramas of human development.

In *Tintern Abbey*, the speaker conveys his relief at returning to a sylvan scene that has been important to him in memory. His recollections of this natural beauty, he says, have helped sustain him in the confusion and weariness of city life; he thinks they may also have encouraged him toward goodness and serenity. But this second suggestion, that memories of nature have a moral effect, is only hypothetical, qualified in the text by such words and phrases as "I trust" and "perhaps." Indeed, the poem's next section opens with explicit statement that this may "Be but a vain belief." True or false, though, the belief comforts the speaker, who then recalls his more direct relation with nature in the past, when "The sounding cataract / Haunted me like a passion." He hopes, but cannot quite be sure, that his present awareness of "the still, sad music of humanity" and of the great "presence" that infuses nature compensates for what he has sacrificed in losing the immediacy of youthful experience.

The last section of *Tintern Abbey* emphasizes still more that the speaker is struggling with depression over his sense of loss; he observes that the presence of his "dearest Friend," his sister, would protect his "genial spirits" from decay even without his faith in what he has learned. That sister now becomes the focus for his thoughts about nature; he imagines her growth as like his own, but perfected, and her power of memory as able to contain not only the beauties of the landscape but his presence as part of that landscape. The poem thus resolves itself with emphasis on a human relationship, between the man and his sister, as well as on the importance of nature. Its emotional power derives partly from its evocation of the *need* to believe in nature as a form of salvation and of the process of development through which that need manifests itself.

At about the same time that he wrote the *Ode on Intimations of Immortality*, Wordsworth composed his sonnet *The World Is Too Much with Us*:

> . . . we lay waste our powers
> Little we see in Nature that is ours;
> . . . we are out of tune.

Despite the rhapsodic tone that dominates the ode, it too reveals itself as a hard-won act of faith, an effort to combat the view of the present world conveyed in the sonnet.

The ode opens with insistence on loss: "The things which I have seen I now can see no more." The speaker feels grief; he tries to deny it, because it seems at odds with the harmony and joy of the natural world. Yet the effort fails: even natural beauty speaks to him of what he no longer possesses. Stanzas V through VIII emphasize the association of infancy with natural communion and the inevitable deprivation attending growth. In stanza IX, the speaker attempts to value what still remains to him: it's all he has, he's grateful for it. In the concluding stanzas, however, he arrives at a new revelation: now nature acquires value not as a form of unmixed ecstasy, but in connection with the experience of human suffering:

> Though nothing can bring back the hour
> Of splendour in the grass, of glory in the flower;
> We will grieve not, rather find
> Strength in what remains behind; . . .
> In the soothing thoughts that spring
> Out of human suffering . . .

It is "the human heart by which we live" that finally enables the poet to experience the wonder of a flower, now become the source of "Thoughts that do often lie too deep for tears."

The view that the processes of maturing involve giving up a kind of wisdom accessible only to children belongs particularly to the Romantic period, but most people at least occasionally feel that in growing up they have left behind something they would rather keep. Wordsworth's poetic expression of the effort to come to terms with such feelings may remind his readers of barely noticed aspects of their own experience.

G. M. Harper, *Wordsworth* (1916–1929), remains the standard biography. A more recent biographical study is S. C. Gill, *William Wordsworth* (1989). Other important works (critical in emphasis) include R. D. Havens, *The Mind of a Poet* (1950); G. Hartman, *Wordsworth's Poetry* (1964); and J. H. Alexander, *Reading Wordsworth* (1987). A useful collection of critical essays is G. Gilpin, ed., *Critical Essays on William Wordsworth* (1990).

Lines Composed a Few Miles Above Tintern Abbey

On Revisiting the Banks of the Wye During a Tour, July 13, 1798

Five years have past; five summers, with the length
Of five long winters! and again I hear
These waters, rolling from their mountain-springs
With a soft inland murmur.—Once again
Do I behold these steep and lofty cliffs,   5
That on a wild secluded scene impress
Thoughts of more deep seclusion; and connect
The landscape with the quiet of the sky.
The day is come when I again repose
Here, under this dark sycamore, and view   10
These plots of cottage-ground, these orchard-tufts,
Which at this season, with their unripe fruits,
Are clad in one green hue, and lose themselves
'Mid groves and copses. Once again I see
These hedge-rows, hardly hedge-rows, little lines   15
Of sportive wood run wild: these pastoral farms,
Green to the very door; and wreaths of smoke
Sent up, in silence, from among the trees!
With some uncertain notice, as might seem
Of vagrant dwellers in the houseless woods,   20
Or of some Hermit's cave, where by his fire
The Hermit sits alone.

           These beauteous forms,
Through a long absence, have not been to me
As is a landscape to a blind man's eye:
But oft, in lonely rooms, and 'mid the din   25
Of towns and cities, I have owed to them,
In hours of weariness, sensations sweet,
Felt in the blood, and felt along the heart;
And passing even into my purer mind,
With tranquil restoration:—feelings too   30

Of unremembered pleasure: such, perhaps,
As have no slight or trivial influence
On that best portion of a good man's life,
His little, nameless, unremembered, acts
Of kindness and of love. Nor less, I trust,   35
To them I may have owed another gift,
Of aspect more sublime; that blessèd mood,
In which the burthen of the mystery,
In which the heavy and the weary weight
Of all this unintelligible world,   40
Is lightened: — that serene and blessèd mood,
In which the affections gently lead us on, —
Until, the breath of this corporeal frame
And even the motion of our human blood
Almost suspended, we are laid asleep   45
In body, and become a living soul:
While with an eye made quiet by the power
Of harmony, and the deep power of joy,
We see into the life of things.

                        If this
Be but a vain belief, yet, oh! how oft—   50
In darkness and amid the many shapes
Of joyless daylight; when the fretful stir
Unprofitable, and the fever of the world,
Have hung upon the beatings of my heart—
How oft, in spirit, have I turned to thee,   55
O sylvan Wye! thou wanderer thro' the woods,
How often has my spirit turned to thee!

    And now, with gleams of half-extinguished thought,
With many recognitions dim and faint,
And somewhat of a sad perplexity,   60
The picture of the mind revives again:
While here I stand, not only with the sense
Of present pleasure, but with pleasing thoughts
That in this moment there is life and food
For future years. And so I dare to hope,   65
Though changed, no doubt, from what I was when first
I came among these hills; when like a roe
I bounded o'er the mountains, by the sides
Of the deep rivers, and the lonely streams,
Wherever nature led: more like a man   70
Flying from something that he dreads, than one
Who sought the thing he loved. For nature then
(The coarser pleasures of my boyish days,
And their glad animal movements all gone by)
To me was all in all. — I cannot paint   75
What then I was. The sounding cataract
Haunted me like a passion: the tall rock,
The mountain, and the deep and gloomy wood,
Their colours and their forms, were then to me
An appetite; a feeling and a love,   80
That had no need of a remoter charm,

By thought supplied, nor any interest
Unborrowed from the eye.—That time is past,
And all its aching joys are now no more,
And all its dizzy raptures. Not for this   85
Faint I, nor mourn nor murmur; other gifts
Have followed; for such loss, I would believe,
Abundant recompense. For I have learned
To look on nature, not as in the hour
Of thoughtless youth; but hearing oftentimes   90
The still, sad music of humanity,
Nor harsh nor grating, though of ample power
To chasten and subdue. And I have felt
A presence that disturbs me with the joy
Of elevated thoughts; a sense sublime   95
Of something far more deeply interfused,
Whose dwelling is the light of setting suns,
And the round ocean and the living air,
And the blue sky, and in the mind of man:
A motion and a spirit, that impels   100
All thinking things, all objects of all thought,
And rolls through all things. Therefore am I still
A lover of the meadows and the woods,
And mountains; and of all that we behold
From this green earth; of all the mighty world   105
Of eye, and ear,—both what they half create,
And what perceive; well pleased to recognise
In nature and the language of the sense,
The anchor of my purest thoughts, the nurse,
The guide, the guardian of my heart, and soul   110
Of all my moral being.

                  Nor perchance,
If I were not thus taught, should I the more
Suffer my genial[1] spirits to decay:
For thou art with me here upon the banks
Of this fair river; thou my dearest Friend,   115
My dear, dear Friend; and in thy voice I catch
The language of my former heart, and read
My former pleasures in the shooting lights
Of thy wild eyes. Oh! yet a little while
May I behold in thee what I was once,   120
My dear, dear Sister! and this prayer I make,
Knowing that Nature never did betray
The heart that loved her; 'tis her privilege,
Through all the years of this our life, to lead
From joy to joy: for she can so inform   125
The mind that is within us, so impress
With quietness and beauty, and so feed
With lofty thoughts, that neither evil tongues,
Rash judgments, nor the sneers of selfish men,
Nor greetings where no kindness is, nor all   130
The dreary intercourse of daily life,

1. Generative, creative.

Shall e'er prevail against us, or disturb
Our cheerful faith, that all which we behold
Is full of blessings. Therefore let the moon
Shine on thee in thy solitary walk;   135
And let the misty mountain-winds be free
To blow against thee: and, in after years,
When these wild ecstasies shall be matured
Into a sober pleasure; when thy mind
Shall be a mansion for all lovely forms,   140
Thy memory be as a dwelling-place
For all sweet sounds and harmonies; oh! then,
If solitude, or fear, or pain, or grief
Should be thy portion, with what healing thoughts
Of tender joy wilt thou remember me,   145
And these my exhortations! Nor, perchance—
If I should be where I no more can hear
Thy voice, nor catch from thy wild eyes these gleams
Of past existence—wilt thou then forget
That on the banks of this delightful stream   150
We stood together; and that I, so long
A worshipper of Nature, hither came
Unwearied in that service; rather say
With warmer love—oh! with far deeper zeal
Of holier love. Nor wilt thou then forget   155
That after many wanderings, many years
Of absence, these steep woods and lofty cliffs,
And this green pastoral landscape, were to me
More dear, both for themselves and for thy sake!

Ode on Intimations of Immortality

From Recollections of Early Childhood

> The Child is father of the Man;
> And I could wish my days to be
> Bound each to each by natural piety.

I

There was a time when meadow, grove, and stream,
The earth, and every common sight,
    To me did seem
    Apparelled in celestial light,
The glory and the freshness of a dream.   5
It is not now as it hath been of yore;—
    Turn wheresoe'er I may,
      By night or day,
The things which I have seen I now can see no more.

II

The Rainbow comes and goes,   10
And lovely is the Rose;

The Moon doth with delight
Look round her when the heavens are bare,
   Waters on a starry night
    Are beautiful and fair;   15
  The sunshine is a glorious birth;
   But yet I know, where'er I go,
That there hath past away a glory from the earth.

III

Now, while the birds thus sing a joyous song,
   And while the young lambs bound   20
    As to the tabor's sound,
To me alone there came a thought of grief:
A timely utterance gave that thought relief,
   And I again am strong:
The cataracts blow their trumpets from the steep;   25
No more shall grief of mine the season wrong;
I hear the Echoes through the mountains throng,
The Winds come to me from the fields of sleep,
   And all the earth is gay;
    Land and sea   30
  Give themselves up to jollity,
   And with the heart of May
Doth every Beast keep holiday;—
   Thou Child of Joy,
Shout round me, let me hear thy shouts, thou happy   35
  Shepherd-boy!

IV

Ye blessèd Creatures, I have heard the call
  Ye to each other make; I see
The heavens laugh with you in your jubilee;
   My heart is at your festival,   40
    My head hath its coronal,
The fulness of your bliss, I feel—I feel it all.
   Oh evil day! if I were sullen
   While Earth herself is adorning,
    This sweet May-morning,   45
   And the Children are culling
    On every side,
  In a thousand valleys far and wide,
  Fresh flowers; while the sun shines warm,
And the Babe leaps up on his Mother's arm:—   50
   I hear, I hear, with joy I hear!
   —But there's a Tree, of many, one,
A single Field which I have looked upon,
Both of them speak of something that is gone:
   The Pansy at my feet   55
   Doth the same tale repeat:
Whither is fled the visionary gleam?
Where is it now, the glory and the dream?

V

Our birth is but a sleep and a forgetting:
The Soul that rises with us, our life's Star,   60
    Hath had elsewhere its setting,
      And cometh from afar:
    Not in entire forgetfulness,
    And not in utter nakedness,
But trailing clouds of glory do we come   65
    From God, who is our home:
Heaven lies about us in our infancy!
Shades of the prison-house begin to close
    Upon the growing Boy,
But He beholds the light, and whence it flows,   70
    He sees it in his joy;
The Youth, who daily farther from the east
    Must travel, still is Nature's Priest,
    And by the vision splendid
    Is on his way attended;   75
At length the Man perceives it die away,
And fade into the light of common day.

VI

Earth fills her lap with pleasures of her own;
Yearnings she hath in her own natural kind,
And, even with something of a Mother's mind,   80
    And no unworthy aim,
    The homely Nurse doth all she can
To make her Foster-child, her Inmate, Man,
    Forget the glories he hath known,
And that imperial palace whence he came.   85

VII

Behold the Child among his new-born blisses,
A six years' Darling of a pigmy size!
See, where 'mid work of his own hand he lies,
Fretted by sallies of his mother's kisses,
With light upon him from his father's eyes!   90
See, at his feet, some little plan or chart,
Some fragment from his dream of human life,
Shaped by himself with newly-learnèd art;
    A wedding or a festival,
    A mourning or a funeral;   95
    And this hath now his heart,
    And unto this he frames his song:
    Then will he fit his tongue
To dialogues of business, love, or strife;
    But it will not be long   100
    Ere this be thrown aside,
    And with new joy and pride
The little Actor cons another part;
Filling from time to time his "humorous stage"

With all the Persons, down to palsied Age,   105
That Life brings with her in her equipage;
    As if his whole vocation
    Were endless imitation.

VIII

Thou, whose exterior semblance doth belie
    Thy Soul's immensity;   110
Thou best Philosopher, who yet dost keep
Thy heritage, thou Eye among the blind,
That, deaf and silent, read'st the eternal deep,
Haunted for ever by the eternal mind,—
    Mighty Prophet! Seer blest!   115
    On whom those truths do rest,
Which we are toiling all our lives to find,
In darkness lost, the darkness of the grave;
Thou, over whom thy Immortality
Broods like the Day, a Master o'er a Slave,   120
A Presence which is not to be put by;
    [To whom the grave
Is but a lonely bed without the sense or sight
    Of day or the warm light,
A place of thought where we in waiting lie;]¹   125
Thou little Child, yet glorious in the might
Of heaven-born freedom on thy being's height,
Why with such earnest pains dost thou provoke
The years to bring the inevitable yoke,
Thus blindly with thy blessedness at strife?   130
Full soon thy Soul shall have her earthly freight,
And custom lie upon thee with a weight,
Heavy as frost, and deep almost as life!

IX

    O joy! that in our embers
    Is something that doth live,   135
    That nature yet remembers
    What was so fugitive!
The thought of our past years in me doth breed
Perpetual benediction: not indeed
For that which is most worthy to be blest;   140
Delight and liberty, the simple creed
Of Childhood, whether busy or at rest,
With new-fledged hope still fluttering in his breast—
    Not for these I raise
    The song of thanks and praise;   145
But for those obstinate questionings
Of sense and outward things,
Fallings from us, vanishings;
Blank misgivings of a Creature

---

1. The lines within brackets were included in the *Ode* in the 1807 and 1815 editions of Wordsworth's poems but were omitted in the 1820 and subsequent editions, as a result of Coleridge's severe censure of them.

Moving about in worlds not realized,   150
High instincts before which our mortal Nature
Did tremble like a guilty Thing surprised:
    But for those first affections,
    Those shadowy recollections,
  Which, be they what they may,   155
Are yet the fountain-light of all our day,
Are yet a master-light of all our seeing;
  Uphold us, cherish, and have power to make
Our noisy years seem moments in the being
Of the eternal Silence: truths that wake,   160
    To perish never;
Which neither listlessness, nor mad endeavour,
    Nor Man nor Boy,
Nor all that is at enmity with joy,
Can utterly abolish or destroy!   165
  Hence in a season of calm weather
    Though inland far we be,
Our Souls have sight of that immortal sea
    Which brought us hither,
    Can in a moment travel thither,   170
And see the Children sport upon the shore,
And hear the mighty waters rolling evermore.

X

Then sing, ye Birds, sing, sing a joyous song!
    And let the young Lambs bound
    As to the tabor's sound!   175
We in thought will join your throng,
    Ye that pipe and ye that play,
    Ye that through your hearts to-day
    Feel the gladness of the May!
What though the radiance which was once so bright   180
Be now for ever taken from my sight,
  Though nothing can bring back the hour
Of splendour in the grass, of glory in the flower;
    We will grieve not, rather find
    Strength in what remains behind;   185
    In the primal sympathy
    Which having been must ever be;
    In the soothing thoughts that spring
    Out of human suffering;
    In the faith that looks through death,   190
In years that bring the philosophic mind.

XI

And O, ye Fountains, Meadows, Hills, and Groves,
Forebode not any severing of our loves!
Yet in my heart of hearts I feel your might;
I only have relinquished one delight   195
To live beneath your more habitual sway.
I love the Brooks which down their channels fret,

Even more than when I tripped lightly as they;
The innocent brightness of a new-born Day
          Is lovely yet;
The Clouds that gather round the setting sun   200
Do take a sober colouring from an eye
That hath kept watch o'er man's mortality;
Another race hath been, and other palms are won.
Thanks to the human heart by which we live,   205
Thanks to its tenderness, its joys, and fears,
To me the meanest flower that blows can give
Thoughts that do often lie too deep for tears.

Composed upon Westminster Bridge,
September 3, 1802

Earth has not anything to show more fair:
Dull would he be of soul who could pass by
A sight so touching in its majesty;
This City now doth, like a garment, wear
The beauty of the morning; silent, bare,   5
Ships, towers, domes, theatres, and temples lie
Open unto the fields, and to the sky;
All bright and glittering in the smokeless air.
Never did sun more beautifully steep
In his first splendour, valley, rock, or hill;   10
Ne'er saw I, never felt, a calm so deep!
The river glideth at his own sweet will:
Dear God! the very houses seem asleep;
And all that mighty heart is lying still!

The World Is Too Much with Us

The world is too much with us; late and soon,
Getting and spending, we lay waste our powers:
Little we see in Nature that is ours;
We have given our hearts away, a sordid boon![1]
This Sea that bares her bosom to the moon,   5
The winds that will be howling at all hours,
And are up-gathered now like sleeping flowers;
For this, for everything, we are out of tune;
It moves us not.—Great God! I'd rather be
A Pagan suckled in a creed outworn;   10
So might I, standing on this pleasant lea,
Have glimpses that would make me less forlorn;
Have sight of Proteus[2] rising from the sea;
Or hear old Triton[3] blow his wreathèd horn.

1. Gift. *Sordid:* refers to the act of giving the heart away.   2. An old man of the sea who, in the *Odyssey,* could assume a variety of shapes.   3. A sea deity, usually represented as blowing on a conch shell.

SAMUEL TAYLOR COLERIDGE
1772–1834

For Samuel Taylor Coleridge, the mystery of the imagination provided the most compelling and perplexing of subjects. In prose and in verse, by reasoned discussion and by poetic symbol making, he explored the subject, affirming imagination's virtually divine status as a creative power and suggesting his own emotional dependence on it.

Son of an English clergyman, Coleridge attended Jesus College, Cambridge, from 1791 to 1793. In 1795, he married Sara Fricker; the same year he met Wordsworth and began the fruitful collaboration leading to *Lyrical Ballads*. In 1810, his period of greatest poetic creativity already over, he separated from his wife; subsequently, he became increasingly addicted to opium. Known for his brilliant conversation, he spent much time talking and lecturing as well as writing.

The most intellectual of the English Romantics, Coleridge, after an early trip to Germany, was strongly influenced by the German Idealist philosophers, notably Immanuel Kant and Johann Fichte. His best-known critical work, *Biographia Literaria* (1817), in which he develops most fully and explicitly his theory of imagination, contains many borrowings from German sources. His output of poetry was relatively small. In some of his most important poems (such as *The Rime of the Ancient Mariner*), he tries to incorporate the supernatural into essentially psychological narrative. He was also much interested in the native English ballad tradition, which on occasion influenced his choice of stanzaic form and meter.

Like other Romantic poets, Coleridge was fascinated by the Aeolian harp (it figures in the first stanza of *Dejection: An Ode*), an instrument that makes music without human intervention, by the action of wind on its strings. *Kubla Khan*, a poem recording what the writer remembered of a dream stimulated by opium, comprises a kind of poetic equivalent for the Aeolian harp: a work for which its author disclaims conscious responsibility. It simply came to his mind, he says, to be broken off when he was interrupted by a person from Porlock. The poem therefore makes no claim to rational coherence, but it has always invited exegesis. Evoking a lush and splendid setting, it yet contains ominous suggestions: the ruler who presides over the magnificence of landscape ("deep romantic chasm," river, caves, incense-bearing trees) and building, hears "Ancestral voices prophesying war." The theme of mingled beauty and danger intensifies as the poem focuses on the figure of a singer, a "damsel with a dulcimer," whose power the poem's speaker wishes to "revive" within himself. Then he could re-create the vision of Kubla Khan's domain, and people would respond to him with "holy dread," recognizing his association with the magic, the sacred, the dangerous, the unpredictable and uncontrollable power of imagination. Thus the singer becomes an image for the poet, and we are reminded that the uncannily evocative scene of the poem's opening section itself issues from the poetic imagination, which creates for its possessor and for his readers a new version of reality, closer to the heart's desire than our workaday world, but not without danger—including the danger of becoming lost in it.

In *Dejection: An Ode*, Coleridge concerns himself with the same theme in more extended personal terms. Paradoxically, this poem—mourning his loss of creative imagination—demonstrates the active presence of that quality whose absence it deplores, as it creates out of the dullness of depression a rich emotional and psychological texture. Like Wordsworth's *Ode on Intimations of Immortality, Dejec-*

tion confronts the speaker's sense of diminishing power. He has lost the "joy" that he considers associated with the spontaneity of youth. More emphatically than Wordsworth, Coleridge attributes even the beauty of nature to the human imagination:

> O Lady! we receive but what we give,
> And in our life alone does Nature live: . . .
> Ah! from the soul itself must issue forth
> A light, a glory, a fair luminous cloud
> Enveloping the Earth —

One cannot hope for inspiration from nature, cannot expect to receive from without that reassurance and pleasure whose sources are within. As the poem develops, it demonstrates the operation of imagination on the external world by hearing meaning — meaning related to human action and suffering — in the sound of wind and storm. The imaginative activity provides its own solace; although the speaker never ceases to assert his dejection, he, like Wordsworth, is enabled finally to displace his vision of joy, harmony, and peace onto the figure of a woman who will embody all that he now feels impossible for himself.

In its emphasis on the "shaping spirit of Imagination," that presiding power of Romantic poetry, *Dejection* makes a strong statement of Coleridge's central concern. By its capacity to evoke emotional complexity — longing for what is lost, resentment at its passing, struggle to repossess what is mourned — and to demonstrate the patterns in which the mind deals with its own problems, it exemplifies the subtlety and the force of his poetic achievement.

E. K. Chambers, *Samuel Taylor Coleridge* (1938), is a solid biography. More recently, R. Holmes has published the first part of a projected two-part biography: *Coleridge: Early Visions* (1989). W. J. Bate, *Coleridge* (1968), combines biographical insight with critical commentary. J. L. Lowes, *The Road to Xanadu* (1927), provides a fascinating study of the sources of *Kubla Khan*. For criticism, see also J. Cornwell, *Coleridge* (1973); J. Beer, *Coleridge's Poetic Intelligence* (1975); G. Davidson, *Coleridge's Career* (1990); and P. Campbell, ed., *Wordsworth and Coleridge: Lyrical Ballads: Critical Perspectives* (1991), a collection of essays. Two useful works that treat Coleridge in conjunction with Wordsworth are G. W. Ruoff, *Wordsworth and Coleridge* (1989), and P. Magnuson, *Coleridge and Wordsworth* (1988).

Kubla Khan

Or, a Vision in a Dream. A Fragment

The following fragment is here published at the request of a poet of great and deserved celebrity [Lord Byron], and, as far as the Author's own opinions are concerned, rather as a psychological curiosity, than on the ground of any supposed *poetic* merits.

In the summer of the year 1797, the Author, then in ill health, had retired to a lonely farm-house between Porlock and Linton, on the Exmoor confines of Somerset and Devonshire.[1] In consequence of a slight indisposition, an anodyne had been prescribed, from the effects of which he fell asleep in his chair at the moment that he was reading the following

---

1. A high moorland shared by the two southwestern counties in England.

sentence, or words of the same substance, in "Purchas's Pilgrimage":[2] "Here the Khan Kubla commanded a palace to be built, and a stately garden thereunto. And thus ten miles of fertile ground were inclosed with a wall." The Author continued for about three hours in a profound sleep, at least of the external senses, during which time he has the most vivid confidence, that he could not have composed less than from two to three hundred lines; if that indeed can be called composition in which all the images rose up before him as *things*, with a parallel production of the correspondent expressions, without any sensation or consciousness of effort.[3] On awaking he appeared to himself to have a distinct recollection of the whole, and taking his pen, ink, and paper, instantly and eagerly wrote down the lines that are here preserved. At this moment he was unfortunately called out by a person on business from Porlock, and detained by him above an hour, and on his return to his room, found, to his no small surprise and mortification, that though he still retained some vague and dim recollection of the general purport of the vision, yet, with the exception of some eight or ten scattered lines and images, all the rest had passed away like the images on the surface of a stream into which a stone has been cast, but, alas! without the after restoration of the latter!

> Then all the charm
> Is broken—all that phantom-world so fair
> Vanishes, and a thousand circlets spread,
> And each mis-shape[s] the other. Stay awhile,
> Poor youth! who scarcely dar'st lift up thine eyes—
> The stream will soon renew its smoothness, soon
> The visions will return! And lo, he stays,
> And soon the fragments dim of lovely forms
> Come trembling back, unite, and now once more
> The pool becomes a mirror.[4]

Yet from the still surviving recollections in his mind, the Author has frequently purposed to finish for himself what had been originally, as it were, given to him. Σαμερον αδιον ασω:[5] but the to-morrow is yet to come. . . .

> In Xanadu did Kubla Khan[6]
> A stately pleasure-dome decree:
> Where Alph,[7] the sacred river, ran
> Through caverns measureless to man
> Down to a sunless sea.   5

2. Samuel Purchas (1575?–1626) published *Purchas his Pilgrimage, or Relations of the World and the Religions observed in all Ages* in 1613. The passage in Purchas is slightly different: "In Xamdu did Cublai Can build a stately Palace, encompassing sixteene miles of plaine ground with a wall, wherein are fertile meddowes, pleasant Springs, delightfull Streames, and all sorts of beasts of chase and game, and in the middest thereof a sumptuous house of pleasure, which may be removed from place to place" (book IV, chap. 13).   3. Coleridge's statement that he dreamed the poem and wrote down what he could later remember verbatim has been queried, most recently by medical opinion. The belief that opium produces special dreams, or even any dreams at all, seems to lack confirmation.   4. From Coleridge's poem *The Picture; or, the Lover's Resolution*, lines 91–100.   5. From Theocritus's *Idylls* I.145: "I'll sing a sweeter song tomorrow" (Greek).   6. Mongol emperor (1215?–1294), visited by Marco Polo.   7. J. L. Lowes, in *The Road to Xanadu* (1927), thinks that Coleridge may have had in mind the river Alpheus—linked with the Nile—mentioned by Virgil.

So twice five miles of fertile ground
With walls and towers were girdled round:
And there were gardens bright with sinuous rills,
Where blossomed many an incense-bearing tree;
And here were forests ancient as the hills,   10
Enfolding sunny spots of greenery.

But oh! that deep romantic chasm which slanted
Down the green hill athwart a cedarn cover!
A savage place! as holy and enchanted
As e'er beneath a waning moon was haunted   15
By woman wailing for her demon-lover!
And from this chasm, with ceaseless turmoil seething,
As if this earth in fast thick pants were breathing,
A mighty fountain momently was forced:
Amid whose swift half-intermitted burst   20
Huge fragments vaulted like rebounding hail,
Or chaffy grain beneath the thresher's flail:
And 'mid these dancing rocks at once and ever
It flung up momently the sacred river.
Five miles meandering with a mazy motion   25
Through wood and dale the sacred river ran,
Then reached the caverns measureless to man,
And sank in tumult to a lifeless ocean:
And 'mid this tumult Kubla heard from far
Ancestral voices prophesying war!   30
    The shadow of the dome of pleasure
    Floated midway on the waves;
    Where was heard the mingled measure
    From the fountain and the caves.
It was a miracle of rare device,   35
A sunny pleasure-dome with caves of ice!
    A damsel with a dulcimer
    In a vision once I saw:
    It was an Abyssinian maid,
    And on her dulcimer she played,   40
    Singing of Mount Abora.[8]
    Could I revive within me
    Her symphony and song,
    To such a deep delight 'twould win me,
That with music loud and long,   45
I would build that dome in air,
That sunny dome! those caves of ice!
And all who heard should see them there,
And all should cry, Beware! Beware!
His flashing eyes, his floating hair!   50
Weave a circle round him thrice,
And close your eyes with holy dread,
For he on honey-dew hath fed,
And drunk the milk of Paradise.

---

8. Lowes argues that this may have been "Mt. Amara," mentioned by Milton in *Paradise Lost* (IV.28), or Amhara in Samuel Johnson's *Rasselas*.

Dejection: An Ode

Late, late yestreen I saw the new Moon,
With the old Moon in her arms;
And I fear, I fear, my Master dear!
We shall have a deadly storm.
                    Ballad of Sir Patrick Spence

I

Well! If the Bard was weather-wise, who made
　The grand old ballad of Sir Patrick Spence,
　This night, so tranquil now, will not go hence
Unroused by winds, that ply a busier trade
Than those which mould yon cloud in lazy flakes,   5
Or the dull sobbing draft, that moans and rakes
Upon the strings of this Aeolian lute,[1]
　　Which better far were mute.
　For lo! the New-moon winter-bright!
　And overspread with phantom light,   10
　(With swimming phantom light o'erspread
　But rimmed and circled by a silver thread)
I see the old Moon in her lap, foretelling
　The coming-on of rain and squally blast.
And oh! that even now the gust were swelling,   15
　And the slant night-shower driving loud and fast!
Those sounds which oft have raised me, whilst they awed,
　And sent my soul abroad,
Might now perhaps their wonted impulse give,
Might startle this dull pain, and make it move and live!   20

II

A grief without a pang, void, dark, and drear,
　A stifled, drowsy, unimpassioned grief,
　Which finds no natural outlet, no relief,
　　In word, or sigh, or tear—
O Lady! in this wan and heartless mood,   25
To other thoughts by yonder throstle[2] woo'd,
　All this long eve, so balmy and serene,
Have I been gazing on the western sky,
　And its peculiar tint of yellow green:
And still I gaze—and with how blank an eye!   30
And those thin clouds above, in flakes and bars,
That give away their motion to the stars;
Those stars, that glide behind them or between,
Now sparkling, now bedimmed, but always seen:
Yon crescent Moon, as fixed as if it grew   35
In its own cloudless, starless lake of blue;
I see them all so excellently fair,
I see, not feel, how beautiful they are!

---

1. A frame fitted with strings or wires that produce musical tones when the wind hits them. Named after Aeolus, god of the winds.   2. The song thrush.

III

My genial spirits[3] fail;
    And what can these avail 40
To lift the smothering weight from off my breast?
    It were a vain endeavour,
    Though I should gaze forever
On that green light that lingers in the west:
I may not hope from outward forms to win 45
The passion and the life, whose fountains are within.

IV

O Lady! we receive but what we give,
And in our life alone does Nature live:
Ours is her wedding garment, ours her shroud!
    And would we aught behold of higher worth, 50
Than that inanimate cold world allowed
To the poor loveless ever-anxious crowd,
    Ah! from the soul itself must issue forth
A light, a glory, a fair luminous cloud
    Enveloping the Earth— 55
And from the soul itself must there be sent
    A sweet and potent voice, of its own birth,
Of all sweet sounds the life and element!

V

O pure of heart! thou need'st not ask of me
What this strong music in the soul may be! 60
What, and wherein it doth exist,
This light, this glory, this fair luminous mist,
This beautiful and beauty-making power.
    Joy, virtuous Lady! Joy that ne'er was given,
Save to the pure, and in their purest hour, 65
Life, and Life's effluence, cloud at once and shower,
Joy, Lady! is the spirit and the power,
Which wedding Nature to us gives in dower
    A new Earth and new Heaven,
Undreamt of by the sensual and the proud— 70
Joy is the sweet voice, Joy the luminous cloud—
    We in ourselves rejoice!
And thence flows all that charms or ear or sight,
    All melodies the echoes of that voice,
All colours a suffusion from that light. 75

VI

There was a time when, though my path was rough,
    This joy within me dallied with distress,
And all misfortunes were but as the stuff

---

3. Generative spirits; in short, creativity. This poem was written soon after Wordsworth had composed the first four stanzas of the *Ode on Intimations of Immortality*, and the themes are similar.

Whence Fancy made me dreams of happiness:
For hope grew round me, like the twining vine,   80
And fruits, and foliage, not my own, seemed mine.
But now afflictions bow me down to earth:
Nor care I that they rob me of my mirth;
    But oh! each visitation[4]
Suspends what nature gave me at my birth,   85
    My shaping spirit of Imagination.[5]
For not to think of what I needs must feel,
    But to be still and patient, all I can;
And haply by abstruse research to steal
    From my own nature all the natural man—   90
    This was my sole resource, my only plan:
Till that which suits a part infects the whole,
And now is almost grown the habit of my soul.

VII

Hence, viper thoughts, that coil around my mind,
    Reality's dark dream!   95
I turn from you, and listen to the wind,
    Which long has raved unnoticed. What a scream
Of agony by torture lengthened out
That lute sent forth! Thou Wind that rav'st without,
    Bare crag, or mountain-tairn,[6] or blasted tree,   100
Or pine-grove whither woodman never clomb,
Or lonely house, long held the witches' home,
    Methinks were fitter instruments for thee,
Mad Lutanist![7] who in this month of showers,
Of dark-brown gardens, and of peeping flowers,   105
Mak'st Devils' yule[8] with worse than wintry song,
The blossoms, buds, and timorous leaves among.
    Thou Actor, perfect in all tragic sounds!
Thou mighty Poet, e'en to frenzy bold!
    What tell'st thou now about?   110
    'Tis of the rushing of an host in rout,
With groans, of trampled men, with smarting wounds—
At once they groan with pain, and shudder with the cold!
But hush! there is a pause of deepest silence!
    And all that noise, as of a rushing crowd,   115
With groans, and tremulous shudderings—all is over—
    It tells another tale,[9] with sounds less deep and loud!
    A tale of less affright,
    And tempered with delight,
As Otway's self[1] had framed the tender lay,—   120
    'Tis of a little child
    Upon a lonesome wild,
Not far from home, but she hath lost her way:

---

4. Of the *misfortunes* (line 78) and *afflictions* (line 82).   5. Coleridge made much of the distinction between *Fancy* (line 79) and *Imagination*. Fancy makes pleasant combinations of images; Imagination is a higher faculty of the mind that combines images in such a way that they create a higher reality, a poetic "truth" more valid than that which is perceived by the ordinary senses.   6. Tarn or small mountain lake.   7. The storm wind in line 99.   8. Originally, a heathen feast.   9. The story of Wordsworth's *Lucy Gray*.   1. Originally "William" (Wordsworth). Thomas Otway (1652–1685) was a tragic dramatist, admired for his mastery of pathos.

And now moans low in bitter grief and fear,
And now screams loud, and hopes to make her mother hear.   125

VIII

'Tis midnight, but small thoughts have I of sleep.
Full seldom may my friend such vigils keep!
Visit her, gentle Sleep! with wings of healing,
    And may this storm be but a mountain birth,
May all the stars hang bright above her dwelling,   130
    Silent as though they watched the sleeping Earth!
        With light heart may she rise,
        Gay fancy, cheerful eyes,
    Joy lift her spirit, joy attune her voice;
To her may all things live, from pole to pole,   135
Their life the eddying of her living soul!
    O simple spirit, guided from above,
Dear Lady! friend devoutest of my choice,
Thus mayest thou ever, evermore rejoice.

PERCY BYSSHE SHELLEY
1792–1822

A longing for alternatives to things as they are dominates much of Shelley's poetry. Whether he writes of his own dejection, of the energizing force of the west wind, or of the political situation of England, he writes often from conviction that matters could and should be better.

Son of a country squire in Sussex, Shelley led a privileged early life, attending Eton and Oxford. He was, however, expelled from Oxford after a single year, for writing a work called *The Necessity of Atheism*: already he had begun to defy convention. He dramatized his defiance yet more forcefully in 1814, when, after three years of marriage (and two children) with Harriet Westbrook, he eloped with Mary Wollstonecraft Godwin, daughter of two advanced social thinkers. Harriet committed suicide; the lovers married and had several children. Shelley was on friendly terms with other important Romantic writers; in Italy, where he moved in 1818, he associated closely with Byron. He was drowned while sailing off the Italian coast.

Productive as a poet, Shelley mastered tones ranging from the satiric to the prophetic. His most important works include *Prometheus Unbound* (1820), a philosophic-visionary-revolutionary expansion of a classical theme; *Epipsychidon* (1821), a defense of free love; and the elegy *Adonais* (1821), for the death of Keats. He also wrote a verse play having to do with the incest of a father and daughter, *The Cenci* (1819).

At the end of his essay *A Defence of Poetry*, posthumously published in 1840, Shelley insists on poetry's necessary connection with the future. Poets, he says, are "the mirrors of the gigantic shadows which futurity casts upon the present . . . : the influence which is moved not but moves. Poets are the unacknowledged legislators of the World." His own lyrics corroborate such grandiose claims by insistently establishing images of the possible. The sonnet *England in 1819*, for example, after twelve lines of nouns and noun clauses about the political and social horrors of the current English situation, concludes that all these phenomena "Are graves from which a glorious Phantom may / Burst, to illumine our tempestuous day." The possibility—never the certainty—of good coming from evil always exists.

Like Coleridge, Shelley writes about his own dejection, interspersing penetrating images of natural beauty with detailed presentation of his painful psychic state. In the poem called *Stanzas Written in Dejection*, the speaker dreams of death as a kind of mild fulfillment, a reabsorption into nature. The ending of the poem, however, has less dismal implications. Finally, the speaker compares himself with the dying day as a presence in memory. Men do not love him, but would regret his passing; the day, which he has enjoyed, will linger "like joy in Memory." The comparison, which at first appears to sustain the mood of self-pity, also transcends that self-perpetuating emotion: it reminds the speaker of the capacity for enjoyment that he retains even in his bleakest mood. While he fancies his own easeful death, he still takes pleasure in the scene around him; that pleasure remains a lasting element in memory.

Ode to the West Wind makes a particularly emphatic statement of the good-from-evil theme. Images of violence and sinister power ("Thou, from whose unseen presence the leaves dead / Are driven, like ghosts from an enchanter fleeing") dominate the early part of the poem. The third section creates an atmosphere of luxurious beauty but ends with the depths of the sea growing suddenly "grey with fear" at the wind's advent. In the next section, however, the speaker places himself in relation with the natural force he has described, begging to be lifted, to "share / The impulse of thy strength." Finally, in imagination, the poet becomes the "lyre" (in effect, Coleridge's Aeolian harp) of the wind, now revealed as a force of inspiration and change, which enables him to function as "The trumpet of a prophecy!" *Defence of Poetry* describes poets as "the trumpets which sing to battle"; in *Ode to the West Wind*, Shelley suggests that they acquire such inspirational capacity by imaginative union with nature and, particularly, as in the west wind blowing away the remnants of the past year, with the forces of regeneration and reform.

E. Blunden, *Shelley: A Life Story* (1946), provides a useful biography. For criticism, see C. Baker, *Shelley's Major Poetry: The Fabric of a Vision* (1948); E. Wasserman, *Shelley* (1971); R. L. Holmes, *Shelley: The Pursuit* (1974); J. Hall, *The Transforming Image: A Study of Shelley's Major Poetry* (1980); S. M. Sperry, *Shelley's Major Verse* (1989); and M. O'Neill, *The Human Mind's Imaginings* (1989).

Stanzas Written in Dejection— December 1818, Near Naples

The Sun is warm, the sky is clear,
The waves are dancing fast and bright,
Blue isles and snowy mountains wear
The purple noon's transparent might,
The breath of the moist earth is light   5
Around its unexpanded buds;
Like many a voice of one delight,
The winds, the birds, the Ocean-floods,
The City's voice, itself is soft like Solitude's.

I see the Deep's untrampled floor   10
With green and purple seaweeds strown;
I see the waves upon the shore

Like light dissolved in star-showers, thrown;
 I sit upon the sands alone;
The lightning of the noontide Ocean   15
 Is flashing round me, and a tone
 Arises from its measured motion,
How sweet! did any heart now share in my emotion.

Alas, I have nor hope nor health
 Nor peace within nor calm around,   20
Nor that content surpassing wealth
 The sage in meditation found,
 And walked with inward glory crowned;
Nor fame nor power nor love nor leisure—
 Others I see whom these surround,   25
 Smiling they live and call life pleasure:
To me that cup has been dealt in another measure.

Yet now despair itself is mild,
 Even as the winds and waters are;
I could lie down like a tired child   30
 And weep away the life of care
Which I have borne and yet must bear
 Till Death like Sleep might steal on me,
 And I might feel in the warm air
My cheek grow cold, and hear the Sea   35
Breathe o'er my dying brain its last monotony.

Some might lament that I were cold,
 As I, when this sweet day is gone,
Which my lost heart, too soon grown old,
 Insults with this untimely moan—   40
They might lament,—for I am one
 Whom men love not, and yet regret;
 Unlike this day, which, when the Sun
Shall on its stainless glory set,
Will linger though enjoyed, like joy in Memory yet.   45

England in 1819

An old, mad, blind, despised, and dying King;[1]
Princes,[2] the dregs of their dull race, who flow
Through public scorn,—mud from a muddy spring;
Rulers who neither see nor feel nor know,
But leechlike to their fainting country cling   5
Till they drop, blind in blood, without a blow.
A people starved and stabbed in th' untilled field;
An army, whom liberticide and prey
Makes as a two-edged sword to all who wield;
Golden and sanguine[3] laws which tempt and slay;   10
Religion Christless, Godless—a book sealed;

---

1. George III (1738–1820).   2. The king's sons, including the prince regent, whose dissolute behavior gave rise to public scandals.   3. Bloody, causing bloodshed. *Golden:* bought; the laws favor the rich and powerful.

A senate, Time's worst statute,[4] unrepealed—
Are graves from which a glorious Phantom may
Burst, to illumine our tempestuous day.

Ode to the West Wind

I

O wild West Wind, thou breath of Autumn's being,
Thou, from whose unseen presence the leaves dead
Are driven, like ghosts from an enchanter fleeing,

Yellow, and black, and pale, and hectic red,
Pestilence-stricken multitudes: O Thou,   5
Who chariotest to their dark wintry bed

The winged seeds, where they lie cold and low,
Each like a corpse within its grave, until
Thine azure sister of the Spring shall blow

Her clarion o'er the dreaming earth, and fill   10
(Driving sweet buds like flocks to feed in air)
With living hues and odours plain and hill:

Wild Spirit, which art moving everywhere;
Destroyer and Preserver; hear, O hear!

II

Thou on whose stream, 'mid the steep sky's commotion,   15
Loose clouds like Earth's decaying leaves are shed,
Shook from the tangled boughs of Heaven and Ocean,

Angels of rain and lightning; there are spread
On the blue surface of thine aery surge,
Like the bright hair uplifted from the head   20

Of some fierce Mænad,[1] even from the dim verge
Of the horizon to the zenith's height,
The locks of the approaching storm. Thou Dirge

Of the dying year, to which this closing night
Will be the dome of a vast sepulchre,   25
Vaulted with all thy congregated might

Of vapors, from whose solid atmosphere
Black rain and fire and hail will burst: O hear!

III

Thou who didst waken from his summer dreams
The blue Mediterranean, where he lay,   30
Lulled by the coil of his crystalline streams,

---

4. The law by which the civil liberties of Roman Catholics and dissenters from the state religion (Anglicanism) were restricted.   1. Ecstatic female worshiper of Bacchus, Greek god of wine.

Beside a pumice isle in Baiæ's bay,[2]
And saw in sleep old palaces and towers
Quivering within the wave's intenser day,

All overgrown with azure moss and flowers 35
So sweet, the sense faints picturing them! Thou
For whose path the Atlantic's level powers

Cleave themselves into chasms, while far below
The sea-blooms and the oozy woods which wear
The sapless foliage of the ocean, know 40

Thy voice, and suddenly grow grey with fear,
And tremble and despoil themselves: O hear!

IV

If I were a dead leaf thou mightest bear;
If I were a swift cloud to fly with thee;
A wave to pant beneath thy power, and share 45

The impulse of thy strength, only less free
Than thou, O Uncontrollable! If even
I were as in my boyhood, and could be

The comrade of thy wanderings over Heaven,
As then, when to outstrip thy skiey speed 50
Scarce seemed a vision; I would ne'er have striven

As thus with thee in prayer in my sore need.
Oh! lift me as a wave, a leaf, a cloud!
I fall upon the thorns of life! I bleed!

A heavy weight of hours has chained and bowed 55
One too like thee: tameless, and swift, and proud.

V

Make me thy lyre,[3] even as the forest is:
What if my leaves are falling like its own!
The tumult of thy mighty harmonies

Will take from both a deep, autumnal tone, 60
Sweet though in sadness. Be thou, Spirit fierce,
My spirit! Be thou me, impetuous one!

Drive my dead thoughts over the universe
Like withered leaves to quicken a new birth!
And, by the incantation of this verse, 65

Scatter, as from an unextinguished hearth
Ashes and sparks, my words among mankind!
Be through my lips to unawakened Earth

The trumpet of a prophecy! O Wind,
If Winter comes, can Spring be far behind? 70

---

2. West of Naples; the Roman emperors built villas there.   3. Ancient harp. The allusion is also to the
Aeolian harp, an instrument played by the wind and a frequent image for the poet played by inspiration.

A Defence of Poetry

[*Conclusion*]

* * * Poetry is the record of the best and happiest moments of the happiest and best minds. We are aware of evanescent visitations of thought and feeling sometimes associated with place or person, sometimes regarding our own mind alone, and always arising unforeseen and departing unbidden, but elevating and delightful beyond all expression: so that even in the desire and the regret they leave, there cannot but be pleasure, participating as it does in the nature of its object. It is as it were the interpenetration of a diviner nature through our own; but its footsteps are like those of a wind over a sea, which the coming calm erases, and whose traces remain only as on the wrinkled sand which paves it. These and corresponding conditions of being are experienced principally by those of the most delicate sensibility and the most enlarged imagination; and the state of mind produced by them is at war with every base desire. The enthusiasm of virtue, love, patriotism, and friendship is essentially linked with these emotions, and whilst they last, self appears as what it is, an atom to a Universe. Poets are not only subject to these experiences as spirits of the most refined organization, but they can colour all that they combine with the evanescent hues of this ethereal world; a word, or a trait in the representation of a scene or a passion, will touch the enchanted chord, and reanimate, in those who have ever experienced these emotions, the sleeping, the cold, the buried image of the past. Poetry thus makes immortal all that is best and most beautiful in the world; it arrests the vanishing apparitions which haunt the interlunations[1] of life, and veiling them or[2] in language or in form sends them forth among mankind, bearing sweet news of kindred joy to those with whom their sisters abide—abide, because there is no portal of expression from the caverns of the spirit which they inhabit into the universe of things. Poetry redeems from decay the visitations of the divinity in man.

*   *   *

The first part of these remarks has related to Poetry in its elements and principles; and it has been shown, as well as the narrow limits assigned them would permit, that what is called poetry, in a restricted sense, has a common source with all other forms of order and of beauty according to which the materials of human life are susceptible of being arranged, and which is poetry in an universal sense.

The second part[3] will have for its object an application of these principles to the present state of the cultivation of Poetry, and a defence of the attempt to idealize the modern forms of manners and opinion, and compel them into a subordination to the imaginative and creative faculty. For the literature of England, an energetic development of which has ever preceded or accompanied a great and free development of the national will, has arisen as it were from a new birth. In spite of the low-thoughted envy which would undervalue contemporary merit, our own will be a

---

1. Dark periods between the old and new moon.   2. Either.   3. The second part was never written.

memorable age in intellectual achievements, and we live among such philosophers and poets as surpass beyond comparison any who have appeared since the last national struggle for civil and religious liberty.[4] The most unfailing herald, companion, and follower of the awakening of a great people to work a beneficial change in opinion or institution, is Poetry. At such periods there is an accumulation of the power of communicating and receiving intense and impassioned conceptions respecting man and nature. The persons in whom this power resides, may often, as far as regards many portions of their nature, have little apparent correspondence with that spirit of good of which they are the ministers. But even whilst they deny and abjure, they are yet compelled to serve, the Power which is seated upon the throne of their own soul. It is impossible to read the compositions of the most celebrated writers of the present day without being startled with the electric life which burns within their words. They measure the circumference and sound the depths of human nature with a comprehensive and all-penetrating spirit, and they are themselves perhaps the most sincerely astonished at its manifestations, for it is less their spirit than the spirit of the age. Poets are the hierophants[5] of an unapprehended inspiration, the mirrors of the gigantic shadows which futurity casts upon the present, the words which express what they understand not; the trumpets which sing to battle, and feel not what they inspire: the influence which is moved not, but moves. Poets are the unacknowledged legislators of the World.

4. The English Civil War. The great poet of that age was Milton.   5. Interpreters, as priests who interpret sacred mysteries.

JOHN KEATS
1795–1821

A poet "half in love with easeful Death," to quote a line from his *Ode to a Nightingale,* John Keats expressed with compelling intensity the Romantic longing for the unattainable, a concept that he defined in ways very different from Goethe's. In a series of brilliant lyrics, he explored subtle links between the passion for absolute beauty, which provides an imagined alternative to the everyday world's sordidness and disappointment, and the desire to melt into extinction, another form of that alternative.

At the age of sixteen, Keats was apprenticed to a druggist and surgeon; in 1816, he was licensed as an apothecary—but almost immediately abandoned medicine for poetry. Son of a hostler (a groom for horses) at a London inn, he had earlier attended school at Enfield, where he manifested an interest in literature encouraged by his friend Charles Cowden Clarke, the headmaster's son. Through Leigh Hunt, a leading political radical, poet, and critic, whose literary circle he joined in 1816, Keats came to know Shelley, William Hazlitt, and Charles Lamb, important members of the Romantic movement. He had a brief love affair with Fanny Brawne, to whom he became engaged in 1819; the next year he went to Italy, seeking a cure for his tuberculosis, only to die in Rome.

Although his first book, *Poems* (1817), met with some critical success, the long mythological poem *Endymion* which he published a year later became an object of attack by conservative literary reviews (*Blackwood's* and the *Quarterly*). Shelley, in his elegy for Keats (*Adonais*, 1821), encouraged the myth that the harsh reviews caused the poet's death. In fact, Keats lived long enough to publish his most important volume—written scarcely five years after he first tried his hand at poetry—*Lamia, Isabella, The Eve of St. Agnes, and Other Poems* (1820), which won critical applause and contained most of the poems for which he is remembered today.

Some of Keats's greatest works return to a form popular in the eighteenth century: the ode addressed to an abstraction (for example, melancholy) or another nonhuman object (for example, a nightingale or an urn). Although the basic literary device seems highly artificial, Keats uses it powerfully to express his characteristic sense of beauty so intensely experienced that it almost corresponds to pain.

> My heart aches, and a drowsy numbness pains
>   My sense, as though of hemlock I had drunk . . .
> 'Tis not through envy of thy happy lot,
>   But being too happy in thy happiness. . . .

Ode on Melancholy, in its sharp contrast to Coleridge's and Shelley's poems on dejection as well as to seventeenth- and eighteenth-century evocations of melancholy, illustrates particularly well Keats's special exemplification of the Romantic sensibility. In the first stanza, the speaker explicitly rejects traditional concomitants of melancholy—yew, the death-moth, the owl—because such associations suggest a kind of passivity or inertia that might "drown the wakeful anguish of the soul," interfering with the immediate and intense experience of melancholy that he actively seeks. Instead, he advocates trying to live as completely as possible in the immediacy of emotion. Melancholy, he continues, dwells with beauty and joy and pleasure, all in their nature evanescent. To fully feel the wonder of beauty or happiness implies awareness that it will soon vanish. Only those capable of active participation in their own positive emotions can hope to know melancholy; paradoxically, the result of energetic commitment to the life of feeling is the utter submission to melancholy's power: one can hope to "be among her cloudy trophies hung."

Prose summary of such an argument risks sounding ridiculous or incomprehensible, for Keats's emotional logic inheres in the imagery and the music of his poems, which exert their own compelling force. Without any previous belief in the desirability of melancholy as an emotion, the reader, absorbed into a rich sequence of images, feels swept into an experience comparable to that which the poem endorses. The ode generates its own sense of beauty and of melancholy and of the close relation between the two. Its brilliantly evocative specificity of physical reference always suggests more than is directly said, more than paraphrase can encompass:

> Aye, in the very temple of Delight
>   Veiled Melancholy has her sovereign shrine,
>   Though seen of none save him whose strenuous tongue
>   Can burst Joy's grape against his palate fine . . .

Everyone can recall the sensuous pleasure of a grape releasing its juice into the mouth, but it would be difficult to elucidate the full implications of the "strenuous tongue" or of "Joy's grape." Keat's great poetic gift manifests itself most unmistakably in his extraordinary power of suggestion—not only in the odes, but in the ballad-imitation, *La Belle Dame sans Merci*, with its haunting, half-told story, and in the understated sonnets, asserting the speaker's feeling but always hinting more emotion than they directly affirm.

A first-rate critical biography is A. Ward, *John Keats: The Making of a Poet* (1963). Also useful are W. J. Bate, *John Keats* (1963); C. Ricks, *Keats and Embarrassment* (1974); C. T. Watts, *A Preface to Keats* (1985); J. Barnard, *John Keats* (1987); H. Bloom, ed., *The Odes of Keats* (1987), a collection of essays; and H. De Almeida, *Critical Essays on John Keats* (1990).

On First Looking into Chapman's Homer[1]

Much have I traveled in the realms of gold,
    And many goodly states and kingdoms seen;
    Round many western islands have I been
Which bards in fealty to Apollo[2] hold.
Oft of one wide expanse had I been told   5
    That deep-browed Homer ruled as his demesne;[3]
    Yet did I never breathe its pure serene
Till I heard Chapman speak out loud and bold:
Then felt I like some watcher of the skies
    When a new planet swims into his ken;   10
Or like stout Cortez[4] when with eagle eyes
    He stared at the Pacific—and all his men
Looked at each other with a wild surmise—
    Silent, upon a peak in Darien.

Bright Star

Bright star, would I were steadfast as thou art—
    Not in lone splendor hung aloft the night,
And watching, with eternal lids apart,
    Like nature's patient, sleepless Eremite,[1]
The moving waters at their priestlike task   5
    Of pure ablution round earth's human shores,
Or gazing on the new soft fallen mask
    Of snow upon the mountains and the moors—
No—yet still steadfast, still unchangeable,
    Pillowed upon my fair love's ripening breast,   10
To feel forever its soft fall and swell,
    Awake forever in a sweet unrest,
Still, still to hear her tender-taken breath,
And so live ever—or else swoon to death.

La Belle Dame sans Merci[1]

I

O what can ail thee, knight at arms,
    Alone and palely loitering?

1. Keats's friend and former teacher Charles Cowden Clarke had introduced Keats to George Chapman's translations of the *Iliad* (1611) and the *Odyssey* (1616) the night before this poem was written.   2. God of poetic inspiration.   3. Realm, kingdom.   4. In fact, Vasco Núñez de Balboa (c. 1475–1519), Spanish conquistador, not Hernando Cortez (1485–1547), another Spaniard, was the European explorer who first saw the Pacific from Darien, Panama.   1. Hermit.   1. The title, in French, is from a medieval poem by Alain Chartier: "The Beautiful Lady without Pity."

The sedge has withered from the lake
   And no birds sing!

II

O what can ail thee, knight at arms,
   So haggard, and so woebegone?
The squirrel's granary is full
   And the harvest's done.

III

I see a lily on thy brow
   With anguish moist and fever dew,
And on thy cheeks a fading rose
   Fast withereth too.

IV

I met a lady in the meads,[2]
   Full beautiful, a faery's child,
Her hair was long, her foot was light
   And her eyes were wild.

V

I made a garland for her head,
   And bracelets too, and fragrant zone;[3]
She looked at me as she did love
   And made sweet moan.

VI

I set her on my pacing steed
   And nothing else saw all day long,
For sidelong would she bend and sing
   A faery's song.

VII

She found me roots of relish sweet,
   And honey wild, and manna[4] dew,
And sure in language strange she said
   "I love thee true."

VIII

She took me to her elfin grot[5]
   And there she wept and sighed full sore,[6]
And there I shut her wild wild eyes
   With kisses four.

2. Meadows. Here the knight answers the question asked in lines 5–6.   3. Girdle.   4. The supernatural substance with which God fed the Hebrews in the Wilderness (Exodus 16 and Joshua 5:12).   5. Cavern.   6. With great grief.

IX

And there she lullèd me asleep,
   And there I dreamed, ah woe betide!
The latest[7] dream I ever dreamt   35
   On the cold hill's side.

X

I saw pale kings, and princes too,
   Pale warriors, death-pale were they all;
They cried, "La belle dame sans merci
   Thee hath in thrall!"[8]   40

XI

I saw their starved lips in the gloam[9]
   With horrid warning gapèd wide,
And I awoke, and found me here
   On the cold hill's side.

XII

And this is why I sojourn here,   45
   Alone and palely loitering;
Though the sedge withered from the lake
   And no birds sing.

Ode on a Grecian Urn

I

Thou still unravished bride of quietness,
   Thou foster-child of silence and slow time,
Sylvan historian, who canst thus express
   A flowery tale more sweetly than our rhyme:
What leaf-fringed legend haunts about thy shape   5
   Of deities or mortals, or of both,
      In Tempe or the dales of Arcady?[1]
What men or gods are these? What maidens loth?
What mad pursuit? What struggle to escape?
      What pipes and timbrels? What wild ecstasy?   10

II

Heard melodies are sweet, but those unheard
   Are sweeter; therefore, ye soft pipes, play on;
Not to the sensual ear, but, more endeared,
   Pipe to the spirit ditties of no tone:
Fair youth, beneath the trees, thou canst not leave   15
   Thy song, nor ever can those trees be bare;

---

7. Last.   8. Bondage.   9. Twilight.   1. A mountainous region in the Peloponnese, traditionally regarded as the place of ideal rustic, bucolic contentment. *Tempe:* a valley in Thessaly between Mount Olympus and Mount Ossa.

Bold lover, never, never canst thou kiss,
Though winning near the goal—yet, do not grieve;
   She cannot fade, though thou hast not thy bliss,
For ever wilt thou love, and she be fair!   20

III

Ah, happy, happy boughs! that cannot shed
   Your leaves, nor ever bid the Spring adieu;
And, happy melodist, unwearièd,
   For ever piping songs for ever new;
More happy love! more happy, happy love!   25
   For ever warm and still to be enjoyed,
     For ever panting, and for ever young;
All breathing human passion far above,
   That leaves a heart high-sorrowful and cloyed,
     A burning forehead, and a parching tongue.   30

IV

Who are these coming to the sacrifice?
   To what green altar, O mysterious priest,
Lead'st thou that heifer lowing at the skies,
   And all her silken flanks with garlands drest?
What little town by river or sea shore,   35
   Or mountain-built with peaceful citadel,
     Is emptied of this folk, this pious morn?
And, little town, thy streets for evermore
   Will silent be; and not a soul to tell
     Why thou art desolate, can e'er return.   40

V

O Attic shape! Fair attitude! with brede[2]
   Of marble men and maidens overwrought,
With forest branches and the trodden weed;
   Thou, silent form, dost tease us out of thought
As doth eternity: Cold Pastoral!   45
   When old age shall this generation waste,
     Thou shalt remain, in midst of other woe
Than ours, a friend to man, to whom thou say'st,
   "Beauty is truth, truth beauty,"—that is all
     Ye know on earth, and all ye need to know.   50

Ode to a Nightingale

I

My heart aches, and a drowsy numbness pains
   My sense, as though of hemlock I had drunk,
Or emptied some dull opiate to the drains
   One minute past, and Lethe-wards[1] had sunk:

---

2. Pattern. *Attic:* classical (literally, Athenian).   1. That is, toward Lethe, the river of forgetfulness in
Greek mythology.

'Tis not through envy of thy happy lot, 5
But being too happy in thy happiness,
  That thou, light-winged Dryad[2] of the trees,
    In some melodious plot
Of beechen green, and shadows numberless,
  Singest of summer in full-throated ease. 10

II

O for a draught of vintage! that hath been
  Cooled a long age in the deep-delvèd earth,
Tasting of Flora[3] and the country green,
  Dance, and Provençal[4] song, and sunburnt mirth!
O for a beaker full of the warm South! 15
  Full of the true, the blushful Hippocrene,[5]
    With beaded bubbles winking at the brim,
      And purple-stainèd mouth;
That I might drink, and leave the world unseen,
  And with thee fade away into the forest dim: 20

III

Fade far away, dissolve, and quite forget
  What thou among the leaves hast never known,
The weariness, the fever, and the fret
  Here, where men sit and hear each other groan;
Where palsy shakes a few, sad, last gray hairs, 25
  Where youth grows pale, and spectre-thin, and dies;
    Where but to think is to be full of sorrow
      And leaden-eyed despairs;
Where beauty cannot keep her lustrous eyes,
  Or new love pine at them beyond tomorrow. 30

IV

Away! away! for I will fly to thee,
  Not charioted by Bacchus and his pards,[6]
But on the viewless wings of Poesy,
  Though the dull brain perplexes and retards:
Already with thee! tender is the night, 35
  And haply[7] the Queen-Moon is on her throne,
    Clustered around by all her starry Fays;[8]
      But here there is no light,
Save what from heaven is with the breezes blown
  Through verdurous glooms and winding mossy ways. 40

V

I cannot see what flowers are at my feet,
  Nor what soft incense hangs upon the boughs,
But, in embalmèd darkness, guess each sweet

2. Wood nymph. 3. Flowers. Flora was the goddess of flowers and spring. 4. From Provence, the district in France associated with the troubadours. 5. The fountain on Mount Helicon, in Greece, sacred to the Muse of poetry. 6. Leopards. Bacchus (Dionysus) was traditionally supposed to be accompanied by leopards, lions, goats, and so on. 7. Perhaps. 8. Fairies.

Wherewith the seasonable month endows
  The grass, the thicket, and the fruit-tree wild;   45
    White hawthorn, and the pastoral eglantine;
      Fast-fading violets covered up in leaves;
        And mid-May's eldest child,
    The coming musk-rose, full of dewy wine,
      The murmurous haunt of flies on summer eves.   50

VI

Darkling[9] I listen; and for many a time
  I have been half in love with easeful Death,
Called him soft names in many a musèd rhyme,
  To take into the air my quiet breath;
Now more than ever seems it rich to die,   55
  To cease upon the midnight with no pain,
    While thou art pouring forth thy soul abroad
      In such an ecstasy!
Still wouldst thou sing, and I have ears in vain—
  To thy high requiem become a sod.[1]   60

VII

Thou wast not born for death, immortal Bird!
  No hungry generations tread thee down;
The voice I hear this passing night was heard
  In ancient days by emperor and clown:
Perhaps the self-same song that found a path   65
  Through the sad heart of Ruth, when, sick for home,
    She stood in tears amid the alien corn;[2]
      The same that ofttimes hath
Charmed magic casements, opening on the foam
  Of perilous seas, in faery lands forlorn.   70

VIII

Forlorn! the very word is like a bell
  To toll me back from thee to my sole self!
Adieu! the fancy cannot cheat so well
  As she is famed to do, deceiving elf.
Adieu! adieu! thy plaintive anthem fades   75
  Past the near meadows, over the still stream,
    Up the hill-side; and now 'tis buried deep
      In the next valley-glades:
Was it a vision, or a waking dream?
  Fled is that music:—do I wake or sleep?   80

Ode on Melancholy

I

No, no, go not to Lethe,[1] neither twist
  Wolfsbane, tight-rooted, for its poisonous wine;

---

9. In the dark.   1. That is, like dirt, unable to hear.   2. See the Book of Ruth. After her Ephrathite husband died, she returned to his native land with her mother-in-law.   1. The river of forgetfulness in Hades.

Nor suffer thy pale forehead to be kissed
    By nightshade, ruby grape of Proserpine;[2]
Make not your rosary of yew-berries,[3]   5
    Nor let the beetle, nor the death-moth[4] be
        Your mournful Psyche,[5] nor the downy owl
A partner in your sorrow's mysteries;
    For shade to shade will come too drowsily,
    And drown the wakeful anguish of the soul.   10

II

But when the melancholy fit shall fall
    Sudden from heaven like a weeping cloud,
That fosters the droop-headed flowers all,
    And hides the green hill in an April shroud;
Then glut thy sorrow on a morning rose,   15
    Or on the rainbow of the salt sand-wave,
    Or on the wealth of globèd peonies;
Or if thy mistress some rich anger shows,
    Imprison her soft hand, and let her rave,
    And feed deep, deep upon her peerless eyes.   20

III

She[6] dwells with Beauty—Beauty that must die;
    And Joy, whose hand is ever at his lips
Bidding adieu; and aching Pleasure nigh,
    Turning to Poison while the bee-mouth sips:
Aye, in the very temple of Delight   25
    Veiled Melancholy has her sovereign shrine,
        Though seen of none save him whose strenuous tongue
    Can burst Joy's grape against his palate fine;
His soul shall taste the sadness of her might,
    And be among her cloudy trophies hung.[7]   30

To Autumn

I

Season of mists and mellow fruitfulness,
    Close bosom-friend of the maturing sun;
Conspiring with him how to load and bless
    With fruit the vines that round the thatch-eaves run;
To bend with apples the mossed cottage-trees,   5
    And fill all fruit with ripeness to the core;
    To swell the gourd, and plump the hazel shells
With a sweet kernel; to set budding more,
    And still more, later flowers for the bees,
    Until they think warm days will never cease,   10
    For Summer has o'er-brimmed their clammy cells.

2. Wife of Pluto, queen of the underworld.   **3.** Wolfsbane, nightshade, and yew berries are all poisonous.   **4.** The death's-head moth has markings that resemble a skull. The scarab beetle, depicted in Egyptian tombs, was an emblem of death.   **5.** The soul, portrayed by the Greeks as a butterfly.   **6.** Melancholy.   **7.** The Greeks placed war trophies in their temples to commemorate victories.

II

Who hath not seen thee oft amid thy store?
   Sometimes whoever seeks abroad may find
Thee sitting careless on a granary floor,
   Thy hair soft-lifted by the winnowing wind;   15
Or on a half-reaped furrow sound asleep,
   Drowsed with the fume of poppies, while thy hook
      Spares the next swath and all its twinèd flowers:
And sometimes like a gleaner thou dost keep
   Steady thy laden head across a brook;   20
Or by a cyder-press, with patient look,
   Thou watchest the last oozings hours by hours.

III

Where are the songs of Spring? Ay, where are they?
   Think not of them, thou hast thy music too, —
While barrèd clouds bloom the soft-dying day,   25
   And touch the stubble-plains with rosy hue;
Then in a wailful choir the small gnats mourn
   Among the river sallows,[8] borne aloft
      Or sinking as the light wind lives or dies;
And full-grown lambs loud bleat from hilly bourn;   30
   Hedge-crickets sing; and now with treble soft
   The red-breast whistles from a garden-croft;
      And gathering swallows twitter in the skies.

8. Willows.

HEINRICH HEINE
1797–1856

In his haunting lyrics of love and longing, Heinrich Heine brought to near-perfection a poetic mode based importantly on the power of the unstated. Born to German parents in Düsseldorf, at the time occupied by the French, Heine was from early adulthood largely dependent on his rich banker uncle Salomon, who lived in Hamburg. He proposed to and was rejected by two of Salomon's daughters; he failed in the business that Salomon financed for him. After studying law at Salomon's expense (and receiving a degree in 1825), he found it impossible to make a career as a lawyer. His university studies, at Bonn, Göttingen, and Berlin, had interested him in literature, and in the late 1820s he decided to pursue a career as a writer. Disillusionment with German nationalism and enthusiasm for the July Revolution of 1830 in France caused him to move to Paris (1831), where he worked as correspondent for German newspapers. Beginning in 1834, he lived with Eugenie Mirat (referred to in his poetry as "Mathilde"), an uneducated Frenchwoman whom he married in 1841. His uncle died in 1844, leaving him a small pension on condition that Heine suppress a large portion of his memoirs. After 1848, he remained bedridden as a result of spinal paralysis, but he continued to write until the very end of his life.

Most famous as a lyric poet, Heine also wrote drama, narrative poetry, political commentary, and literary criticism. Many of his lyrics were set to music and have become famous as songs. Typically, these lyrics adopt simple diction and metrical patterns often taken from traditional ballads. They do not announce grandly important themes, doing their work largely by the power of suggestion. Frequently, they reiterate the characteristic Romantic desire for an unattainable Other: the northern spruce tree's dream of a tropical palm; the young man's love for a maiden who, more or less at random, marries someone else; the bondsman pining toward death as he gazes at the Sultan's daughter; the boatman lured to destruction by "turbulent love" for the "wondrous fair" Loreley. The poet conveys the emotional ambiguity of love: physical union duplicates the snake's embrace of the *Aeneid*'s Laocoön; delight in a maiden implies rejection of all else—"The rose, the lily, the sun and the dove."

Dark undertones thus echo in even the most deceptively naive of Heine's poems, and his later work is increasingly somber. He takes up directly the actual and potential political upheavals of nineteenth-century Europe, envisioning a horde of hungry rats that sweeps over bourgeois society or creating a myth of supernatural weavers crafting Germany's doom. He writes of death—of the longing for death as ultimate escape, of the horror of death conceived as the end to all life's possibilities. He expresses his sense of alienation as an exile in France, imagining the pain of leaving his wife to make her way in a corrupt society more dreadful than anything nature's violence has to offer. Always, whether he writes of politics or of his personal situation or of imagined happenings, Heine conveys, like so many of his European and English contemporaries, the high importance of the emotional life. Although his political awareness reminds him—and he reminds his readers—that actions have consequences, he insists always that feelings provide the richest mode of insight into the meanings of action. His fable of the rats exemplifies his capacity to generate complicated emotional responses in his readers (the hungry rats are frightening, the well-fed rats contemptible in their obtuseness; we are left with no easy target for sympathy), a capacity equally manifest in the love lyrics.

Heine has been the subject of a good deal of criticism in English, notably including S. S. Prawer, *Heine the Tragic Satirist* (1961); Jeffrey L. Sammons, *Heinrich Heine, The Elusive Poet* (1969); Ursula Franklin, *Exiles and Ironists* (1988); and Jost Hermand, *The Romantic School and Other Essays* (1985). Biographies include Louis Untermeyer, *Heine* (1937); H. Spencer, *Heinrich Heine* (1982); and Philip Kossoff, *Valiant Heart* (1983).

PRONOUNCING GLOSSARY

The following list uses common English syllables and stress accents to provide rough equivalents of selected words whose pronunciation may be unfamiliar to the general reader.

Göttingen: *gurt'-in-gen*   Mirabeau: *mee-rah-boh'*

Heinrich Heine: *hain'-rik hai'-ne*   Pelides: *pay'-li-deez*

Laocoön: *lay-ok'-oh-on*   Silesian: *sai-lee'-zhahn*

Loreley: *lor'-e-lai*

The Rose, the Lily, the Sun and the Dove[1]

The rose, the lily, the sun and the dove,
I loved them all once in the rapture of love.
I love them no more, for my sole delight
Is a maiden so slight, so bright and so white,
Who, being herself the source of love,   5
Is rose and lily and sun and dove.

A Spruce Is Standing Lonely[2]

A spruce is standing lonely
in the North on a barren height.
He drowses; ice and snowflakes
wrap him in a blanket of white.

He dreams about a palm tree   5
in a distant, eastern land,
that languishes lonely and silent
upon the scorching sand.

A Young Man Loves a Maiden[3]

A young man loves a maiden
Whose heart for another sighed;
This other loves another
Who then becomes his bride.

The maiden takes the first man   5
Who happens to come her way
Just out of spite and anger;
The youth is left in dismay.

It is an old old story
And yet it's always new;   10
And to whomever it happens
't will break his heart in two.

Loreley[4]

I do not know what haunts me,
What saddened my mind all day;
An age-old tale confounds me,
A spell I cannot allay.

The air is cool and in twilight   5
The Rhine's dark waters flow;
The peak of the mountain in highlight
Reflects the evening glow.

1. Translated by P. G. L. Webb.   2. Translated by Max Knight and Joseph Fabry.   3. Translated by Ernst Feise.   4. Translated by Ernst Feise. The Loreley was a siren of the river Rhine who was believed to have lured many boatsmen to their destruction. As set to music by Silcher in 1837, this has become one of the most popular of German songs.

There sits a lovely maiden
Above, so wondrous fair,   10
With shining jewels laden,
She combs her golden hair.

It falls through her comb in a shower,
And over the valley rings
A song of mysterious power   15
That lovely maiden sings.

The boatman in his small skiff is
Seized by turbulent love,
No longer he marks where the cliff is,
He looks to the mountain above.   20

I think the waves must fling him
Against the reefs nearby,
And that did with her singing
The lovely Loreley.

My Beauty, My Love, You Have Bound Me[1]

My beauty, my love, you have bound me
As only you can do.
Wrap your arms and legs around me,
And your agile body too.

And now in mighty embraces   5
Entwining and holding on
The most beautiful serpent faces
The happiest Laocoön.[2]

The Silesian Weavers[3]

In gloomy eyes there wells no tear.
Grinding their teeth, they are sitting here:
"Germany, your shroud's on our loom;
And in it we weave the threefold doom.
    We weave; we weave.   5

"Doomed be the God who was deaf to our prayer
In Winter's cold and hunger's despair.
All in vain we hoped and bided;
He only mocked us, hoaxed, derided—
    We weave; we weave.   10

"Doomed be the king, the rich man's king,[4]
Who would not be moved by our suffering,

---

1. Translated by Meno Spann.   2. A Greek mythological figure, best known through an ancient statue that shows him entangled in a desperate struggle with two monstrous serpents.   3. Translated by Aaron Kramer. Silesia was a province of the kingdom of Prussia in northeast Germany. This poem was occasioned by violent uprisings of weavers protesting intolerable working conditions during June 1844.
4. Friedrich Wilhelm IV (1795–1861). Heine's poem is prophetic: in 1848 the king, though not deposed, was forced by revolution to grant a constitution to Prussia.

Who tore the last coin out of our hands,
And let us be shot by his blood-thirsty bands—
　　We weave; we weave.　　　　　　　　　　15

"Doomed be the fatherland, false name,
Where nothing thrives but disgrace and shame,
Where flowers are crushed before they unfold,
Where the worm is quickened by rot and mold—
　　We weave; we weave.　　　　　　　　　　20

"The loom is creaking, the shuttle flies;
Nor night nor day do we close our eyes.
Old Germany, your shroud's on our loom,
And in it we weave the threefold doom;
　　We weave; we weave!"　　　　　　　　　25

The Asra[1]

Daily went the Sultan's beauteous
Daughter walking for her pleasure
In the evening at the fountain
Where the splashing waters whiten.

Daily stood the youthful bondsman　　　　　5
In the evening at the fountain
Where the splashing waters whiten,
Daily he grew pale and paler.

Then one evening stepped the princess
Up to him with sudden questions:　　　　　10
"You must tell me what your name is,
What your country is, your kinfolk."

And the bondsman said: "Mohamet
Is my name, I am from Yemen,
And my kinsmen are the Asra,　　　　　　15
They who die when love befalls them."

Babylonian Sorrows[2]

Death calls me—Sweet, it might be good
If I could leave you in some wood,
Some forest where the firs are high,
Where vultures nest, and wild wolves cry,
And the savage sow, with dreadful roar,　　　5
Calls to her mate, the great blonde boar.

Death calls—still better would it be
To leave you on the open sea,
My wife—my child—it would be kind,
Although the maniac Northpole wind　　　　10
Lashes the waves there, and out of the deep

1. Translated by Ernst Feise.　　2. Translated by Aaron Kramer. The title alludes to the Babylonian captivity of the Old Testament Israelites. Paris is implicitly compared with the corrupt city of Babylon.

The monstrous things that lay asleep,
The shark and crocodile, arise
With open jaws and murderous eyes—
Believe me, Mathild, my wife, my child,   15
Not half so fearful is the wild,
Avenging sea, or the sulking wood,
As this our present neighborhood!
Fierce though the wolf and the vulture be,
The shark, and other beasts of the sea: 20
There are monsters of far less virtue and pity
In Paris, the world's bright capital-city,
City of Loveliness, laughter and revels,
The Hell of angels, Paradise of devils—
To think that you'll be left behind   25
In Paris, is driving me out of my mind!
Black flies are buzzing around my bed;
They seat themselves on top of my head,
On my nose and brow. That pesky race—
There's more than one with a human face,   30
But some of them are especially odd:
They've elephant-trunks like the Hindu god . . .
Inside my brain there's a tumult and cracking;
I think it is a box they're packing,
And my reason journeys off—ah woe!—   35
Before it is time for me to go.

How Slowly Time, the Loathsome Snail[1]

How slowly Time, the loathsome snail,
Keeps crawling in its slimy trace!
But I, meanwhile, quite motionless,
Must bide here in this selfsame place.

No ray of sun, no gleam of hope   5
Will fall into my darkened room;
I know I'll trade this baneful cell
For nothing but the churchyard tomb.

Perhaps I have died long ago;
And only spooks may be those vain   10
Phantasms, pageants, which at night
In wild array storm through my brain.

Or afterwalkers they could be,
Old pagan gods, an ilk of Hell;
They love to choose their rousting place   15
In a dead poet's empty skull.—

Then sometimes would seek to record
At dawn the poet's mummied hand
Those awesome lurid orgia[2]
Of specters in nocturnal band.   20

1. Translated by Ernst Feise.   2. Orgies.

The Migratory Rats[1]

There are two kinds of rat,
The hungry and the fat;
The fat ones happily stay at home,
But the hungry ones set out to roam.

They wander thousands of miles,   5
They have no domiciles;
Straight on they move in a furious run,
They cannot be stopped by rain or sun.

No mountains they cannot skim,
No lakes too broad for their swim!   10
Many get drowned or break their necks,
But those who survive pass over the wrecks.

These queer peculiar louts
Grow whiskers above their snouts;
As radical egalitarians they wear   15
In ratty fashion close-cropped their hair.

This fierce and radical squad
Knows no eternal God;
Unbaptized they leave their numerous broods,
They keep their women as common goods.   20

A sensuous mob, they think
Only of food and drink;
They ignore, since food is their only goal,
The immortality of the soul.

For such a brutal rat   25
Fears neither hell nor cat;
No goods, nor money they ever acquire,
To redivide the world they desire.

Approaching I see the foe
Of wandering rats, oh woe!   30
They come, already they are at our heels,
Their number is legion, I hear their squeals.

O woe! now we are lost!
At our portal their awful host!
The council and mayor shake their heads,   35
They despair of warding off those reds.

The burghers take up arms,
The blackfrocks ring the alarms;
The palladium of public morality,
Property, is in jeopardy.   40

No ringing of bells, no priestly pleas,
No wise and august council decrees,
Not even cannons of wildest gage
Will help you, my children, against their rage.

1. Translated by Ernst Feise.

No help you will find in verbal trick   45
Of worn political rhetoric;
You can't catch rats with syllogisms,
They nimbly jump your finest sophisms.

Soup-logic only and reason-dumplings
Will silence their hungry stomach rumblings,   50
Or arguments of soup donations
Together with Göttingen[2] sausage quotations.

A silent codfish in butter fat
Will satisfy such a radical rat
Much better than any Mirabeau[3]   55
And all the orations since Cicero.[4]

At Parting[1]

Vain worldly yearnings in my breast
Are dead and leave me unobsessed.
Hatred of evils, stilled, no more
Perturbs me — no, nor sorrow for
My own or others' pain-drawn breath.   5
Within me lives yet only death.
The curtain falls, the play now ends;
And, yawning, my dear German friends,
My public, wend their homeward way.
They're far from stupid, I must say.   10
They're dining gaily, quaffing beer,
With songs and laughter, pleasant cheer.
Right was Pelides,[2] famous prince,
Who said in Homer's book[3] long since:
A Philistine, the silliest bore   15
In Stuttgart[4] on the Neckar shore,
Alive, has happiness far more
Than I, dead hero, in the host
Of Hades now the foremost ghost.

Morphine[1]

Great is the likeness of those beauteous two,
The youthful brothers, though the one appears
Much paler than the other, also much
More stern, yes, I might almost say much more
Aristocratic than that one who clasped me   5
Tenderly in his arm — How sweetly gentle
Was then his smile, his glance so full of bliss!
Thus it would happen that his wreath of poppies,

2. Prussian university city, also a center of commerce.   3. Honoré Gabriel Riqueti Mirabeau (1749–1791), French statesman and famous orator.   4. Roman orator (died 43 B.C.). For centuries his writings on rhetoric and his collected speeches were guides for public speakers.   1. Translated by Dwight Durling.   2. Achilles, son of Peleus.   3. The *Odyssey*.   4. The capital of the kingdom of Baden-Württemberg, whose denizens remain stock figures of fun in Germany today as dull and materialistic.   1. Translated by Ernst Feise.

His head encircling, grazed my forehead also
And with strange fragrance banished all the pain   10
Out of my soul—Yet such a kind reprieve
It lasts but a short while, because completely
Restored can I be only when his brother,
The stern and pallid one, inverts his torch.[2]—
Oh, sleep is good, death better—to be sure,   15
The best of all were not to have been born.

2. That is, snuffs it out.

GIACOMO LEOPARDI
1798–1837

In his lyric *The Broom*, written in the final year of his short and tragic life, Giacomo Leopardi, the greatest Italian poet of his time, expressed definitively his sense of despair over what, in the early nineteenth century, civilization had made of itself as well as his belief in the possibility of a world governed by more humane values. A beautiful and enormously gifted child, Leopardi had grown to adulthood with his health destroyed as a result of his upbringing by pathologically rigid parents—or so he believed. His father, Count Monaldo Leopardi, the last nobleman in Italy to wear a sword, had brought himself by his extravagances to the verge of bankruptcy and had turned over the management of his affairs to an agent of his wife, Adelaide. Determined to restore the family fortunes, the countess instituted a severe regime. Her children, for instance, never received any spending money: she could not imagine how they might want to use it. Nor were they allowed to spend a night away from home until well into their adult years.

From the beginning, Giacomo Leopardi was intended for the Church, dressed always in black (like his father) from the age of six. When he began to display his remarkable intellectual powers, his parents encouraged him to spend all his time in study, forbidding him to associate with other children. By the time he was seventeen or eighteen, he had developed into a hunchback, plagued by many ailments, with failing eyesight. (A few years later, he spent some months of total blindness.) Proud of his intellectual accomplishment, his parents, although warned of danger to his health, refused to allow him to leave home. Not until he was twenty-four did he escape the family mansion.

Leopardi had early begun writing poetry; after he left his family (to which he was forced, for reasons of economy or health, periodically to return), he soon developed a high reputation as scholar, poet, and translator. But his life remained unhappy. Cursed, as he sometimes felt, with great emotional capacity, yearning for love, he found himself unable, because of his physical deformities, to attract women. He did, however, find devoted friends. For the last four years of his life, he survived only by the care of Antonio Ranieri, who dedicated himself completely to the poet. Leopardi died of edema, a few weeks short of his thirty-ninth birthday.

In mid-April 1836, Leopardi and Ranieri moved into the villa Ferrigni on the slopes of Vesuvius, about fifteen miles from Naples near Torre del Greco. The doctors thought country air might benefit Leopardi. Bushes of broom, a plant with yellow flowers that grows in waste places, surrounded the villa; here the poet composed his poem *The Broom*, in which he meditates on the setting (Vesuvius had erupted only the year before) and on humankind's position in the natural world. He wrote in a kind of free verse, which he had slowly perfected (the translation here approximates it), with occasional rhymes, internal or at the ends of lines. Believing in organic form—form evolved in response to the demands of subject and of feeling—Leopardi had long before rejected regular stanzaic organization; he maintained that regular forms had evolved only because of the ancient association between poetry and music and that they were far too likely to become mechanical. The freedom of the poem's lyrical movement embodies the imaginative openness that the text advocates as the means to secular salvation.

The theme of humanity's insignificance in the natural scheme attracted many nineteenth-century poets. Leopardi's mode of handling it avoids complete pessimism, although *The Broom* acknowledges the possibility of total destruction for humankind—annihilation not by nuclear weapons, the late twentieth-century terror, but by earthquake, flood, eruption. The third of the poem's long irregular stanzas, though, announces another possibility: that of a kind of human dignity to be gained by full recognition and acceptance of common vulnerability. Rejecting "the higher flights / Of faith in the greatness of man," the poet outlines a more specific faith in the moral grandeur of "One [who] reveals his strength / And greatness in suffering, refusing to add to / The angers and hates of his brothers." Such a person, believing in "the brotherhood of men," in effect reclaims the human condition. No such belief, no fineness of action or feeling, lessens the human susceptibility to mortal shocks, yet it can redeem, the poem suggests, our piteous condition.

In its emotional range—from anger at human self-delusion to exaltation over the vision of imaginatively conceived human unity—this remarkable poem exemplifies the intensity and the power of the nineteenth-century lyric at its best.

A useful biographical study is Iris Origo, *Leopardi: A Biography* (1935). The Cambridge edition of Geoffrey L. Bickersteth, ed., *The Poems of Leopardi* (1973), contains a long and valuable introductory essay on the poet's life, art, and thought. Bickersteth is also the author of a separately published and suggestive lecture: *Leopardi and Wordsworth* (1927). More recent studies include Jean Pierre Barricelli, *Giacomo Leopardi* (1986), and Daniela Bini, *A Fragrance from the Desert: Poetry and Philosophy in Giacomo Leopardi* (1983).

The Broom[1]

Or the Desert Flower

> And men loved darkness rather than light.
> John 3:19

Here on the barren spine
Of the stupendous mountain,
That destructor, Vesuvius,
Which takes joy from no other tree or flower,
You scatter tufts of loneliness around,   5
Sweet-smelling broom,
Patient in the wastelands. As indeed I saw you
Where your stems added beauty to the solitude
Of the dead tracts that brood
Round Rome:[2] that she was queen of cities once,   10

---

1. Translated by Edwin Morgan.   2. The Roman Campagna, in the early 19th century a desolate tract, although it had once been thickly populated. Leopardi had traveled through this region in 1833.

Set in an empire gone,
Your stalks with their grave silent presence seemed
To witness to the traveller, out of oblivion.
Now I see you again upon this ground,
Lover of sad unpeopled places, unfailing   15
Comforter of fortunes overthrown.
These fields that are strewn
With unbreeding ashes, sealed down with lava
Turned hard as stone
And echoing to each visiting foot: 20
Where the snake hides and wriggles, snug in the sun,
And where the rabbit returns
To its well-trodden warren underground:
The plough, and villas, and laughter
Were here once, and the yellowing grain, and music   25
Of the deep lowing herds;
And gardens and great mansions,
Retreats, establishments
For stately leisure; and those famous cities[3]
Which the insolent mountain from its mouth of fire   30
Roared down on, struck like lightning, crushed
With all their people. Now one desolation
Transfixes everything,
And in it you sit, gentle flower, as if
Commiserating others' grief, and send   35
Upwards a breath so very dearly sweet
It must console the desert wastes. These slopes
Should be seen by any man who loves to praise
And exalt our human state: let him see here
How much of human kind   40
Stands in the care of loving nature. Here also
He can exactly find
The measure of man's living power, a force
In instant jeopardy to his hard nurse,
The earth that with the lightest tremor cancels   45
A part of it, and with
Others hardly less light can suddenly always
Annihilate it all.
These are excellent slopes
For viewing the human soul   50
With its "grand destinies and progressive hopes."[4]

Here, here see your face,
Century of empty pride,
Abandoner of the path
Renascence thought marked forward to our days,   55
Turning your steps into the past again,
Giving the retreat your praise,
Calling your failure advance!
Your prattling voice has drawn the brilliant, born
Under your bad star, to flatter you   60

---

3. Pompeii and Herculaneum, both destroyed by the eruption of Vesuvius in A.D. 79.   **4.** A quotation
from a letter of dedication by Leopardi's cousin, Count Terenzio Mamiani della Roveri, that envisioned
a glorious future for Italy and for humanity in general.

As father, though they mock
You sometimes as they talk
Behind your back. But I
Shall not go down to the grave with shame like theirs;
I hope I can still release the scorn that flares   65
For you in my heart, and try
To make it felt—or some of it although
I know how history
Crowds out those who over-offend their age.[5]
Well, that is an evil   70
I must share with you; I have laughed at it before.
Liberty is your great dream, yet you'd make thought
An era's slave again[6] —
Thought, which was our only
Tentative step out of chaos, which alone   75
Moves us to culture and manners, best, sole
Guide of our general fate!
It seems that the lot of men
Was harsh, the truth displeased you, the narrow place
Which nature gave us. Therefore you miserably   80
Turned your back upon the light that made
It clear: and you run from that light, calling
Its followers cowards, and only
Those who are foolish or clever
In mocking themselves or others and can extol   85
The human condition above the stars have "soul"!

A man who lives poor and in poor health
Yet is well-thinking and generous of spirit
Will call and count himself
Neither wealthy nor hardy,   90
Nor does he put on a ridiculous show
Of setting up as beau
Or being a prince of men,
But rather lets his state appear, not shamed
By penury of strength or savings, speaks   95
Openly of what he is, rates what he has
At its unflattered price.
And so the higher flights
Of faith in the greatness of man I decline as witless:
A creature born to perish, schooled by hardships,   100
Saying "I was made for happiness,"
Filling volume on volume
With the stench of his boasting, his earthly promises
Of new high destinies and pleasures known
Neither on this globe nor in the whole of heaven—   105
And this to people whom
A wave of the disturbed sea,
A puff of malignant wind, a shift of the crust
Destroys so thoroughly
The later ages wonder where they lie!   110

---

5. That is, the speaker expects that he and his age will be alike forgotten.   6. Leopardi felt that his
contemporaries overvalued scientific thought, at the expense of imagination.

It is a noble nature
That ventures to look up
Through mortal eyes upon
Our common fate, and tell with a frank tongue
That hides no grain of truth   115
How frailties, evils, low estate are ours
By reason of being born:
One reveals his strength
And greatness in suffering, refusing to add to
The angers and hates of his brothers   120
(Worst harm of all within
Our human miseries!) but rather transferring
The blame of grief from man and placing it
In the true seat of guilt, the mother of men[7]
With the stepmother heart. She is the one   125
He calls his enemy! And since he believes
The brotherhood of men
To be, as indeed they are, united and set
Against this enemy yet,
He takes all men to be confederates   130
Among themselves, embraces
Them all with a true love,
Extends and expects a ready, meaningful help
As agonies and hazards strike and pass
In the common war of man. And to be armed   135
Offensively against one's kind, to strew
A neighbor's path with spike
And block he sees as utter madness—like
A man hard pressed upon the battlefield
Who at the crucial assault   140
Forgets his enemies and begins a sharp
Contest with his own friends,
Spreading the panic of a whistling blade
That cuts its own troops down.
When thoughts like these are known   145
To ordinary folk, as once they were,
And when that terror which first
Drew mortal men so close
In social links against unpitying nature
Has been won back in part   150
By true recognition, then will justice, mercy,
Fair and honorable dealing
In the dialogue of cities, find another root
Than the presumptuous idle fables which
Have had to prop the common probity   155
Of men—if one can call
Error a prop of what is bound to fall.

I often sit at night
Upon these desolate slopes:
Draped in the dark and solid fall of lava   160
They seem rippling still; and above the joyless

---

7. Nature, here alleged to be an unfriendly rather than a maternal force.

Waste, in purest blue,
I watch the far-off flashing of the stars
Whose fires are mirrored in
The sea, and the whole world is shimmering   165
With sparks that circle through the empty spaces.
And when I fix my eyes upon these lights,
Mere points to human sight
Yet truly so immense
That all this land and sea in fact is but   170
A point to them: to them
Not only man but this globe
Where man himself is nothing
Is utterly unknown; and when I see
Still farther off in boundless distances   175
What looks like knots of stars
Shining to us like mist,[8] and think that to them
Not only man, not only earth, but the whole
System of our stars infinite in number
And mass, together with our own gold sun,   180
Is either unknown or must appear as they do
To the earth, a point, a node
Of nebular light: how then do you appear
As I sit thinking there,
O seed of man? And recalling   185
Your poor and worldly state which the mere soil
I press on testifies: and then again
Your own belief that you crown
All things with mastery, finality,
And what a favorite tale you cherish still,   190
How the creators of the cosmic scene
Came down onto this murky grain of sand
Called earth, on your behalf, and often held
Sweet talk with you:[9] and when I see these myths
In their absurdity refurbished to insult   195
Wise men even today, in an epoch
That seems ahead of all
In knowledge and in culture: what feeling then,
O luckless seed of man, what thought for you
Knocks on my heart when all is said? Laughter?   200
Pity? Which comes first and which comes after?

A little apple drops down from its tree,
Pulled to the natural earth
By simple ripeness in late autumn days,
And crushes at a single stroke, lays waste   205
And buries the trim colony
Of ants whose homes were hollowed
Out of that yielding clay
With such hard labor to them, their works and wealth
Amassed with long exertions all that summer,   210

---

8. The Milky Way.   9. Alludes to stories current in many religions about the direct intervention of
deities in human affairs. God's conversations with Adam in the Garden of Eden are a Judeo-Christian
example.

Trials of diligence followed
By a provident folk: so also, plummeting down,
Hurled from a thundering womb
Up to the fathomless sky,
A night and ruin of rocks   215
And ash and pumice mingled
With boiling streams, or the vast
Torrent of metals and molten
Boulders and sizzling sand
Falling along the hill-flank,   220
Raging down unrepulsed
Through the grass, smashed and convulsed
And covered over in a few moments of time
These cities which the sea
Washed at the edge of the shore: 225
And now above the cities the goat browses,
And on the other slope
New cities rise, they stand upon the stool
Of the entombed ones and the prostrate walls
The bitter mountain seems to tramp to dust.   230
Nature has no more care
Or praise for human souls
Than for the ants: and if she slaughters men
Less terribly than them,
This is no great wonder,   235
For man's fecundity and ants' are worlds asunder.

Eighteen hundred years
And more have passed since those great populated
Places vanished, crushed by the power of fire,
And still the peasant's fears,   240
As he watches his vines struggle in these fields
To nourish life on sterile cindery clods,
Cause him to keep one eye
Warily on the fatal peak
Which never yet was moved to become gentle   245
But still sits awe-inspiring there, still threatens
Destruction to him and his children and their
Pitiful handful of possessions.
And often the wretched man
Stretched on the rustic roof   250
Of his home, lying there all night sleepless
In the wandering breeze, and time and again
Jumping to his feet, gazes along the course
Of the dreaded flux which waits to boil and pour
From unimpoverished cells   255
Along that gritty crest and raise its glow
On Margellina and
The port of Naples, on Capri and its sand.
And if he sees it coming down, or if
He ever hears a gurgling ferment in   260
The depths of his garden well, he hurriedly
Wakens his children, rouses his wife, and runs
With them, taking what things they can, far off

Till looking back he sees
His nest and home, his field—   265
His tiny, only shield against starvation—
Caught by the red-hot flood
Which crackles as it comes and over these
Victims settles, relentless, without appeal.
After long forgetfulness   270
Extinct Pompeii returns to daylight like
A buried skeleton
Brought out into the air
By worldly greed or pity;[1] and the traveller,
Paused in the empty forum,   275
Looks through the stricken rows
Of colonnades and gazes with intentness
Up to the mass of the divided summit[2]
With its smoking crater-ridge
Still menacing the ruins scattered there.   280
And in the secrecy and horror of the dark
Through vacant theatres,
Through mutilated temples and through stark
Shells of houses where bats hide their young,
The glow of the deadly lava   285
Like terror wandering with a sinister
Torch through empty palaces, runs on
And reddens in the shadows
Of the distance and paints every place it meets.
So nature, unaware of man and eras   290
Man calls ancient, unaware of links
From ancestors to sons,
Stands always green, or rather sets her feet
On such a lengthy road
She seems to stand. Meanwhile kingdoms decay,   295
Peoples and tongues die out: she does not see it:
And man presumes on his eternity.

And you, yielding broom,
Decking these ravaged fields
With your sweet-smelling groves, you too   300
Will soon go down before the cruel fires
Of that great subterranean dominion:
They will return to their station
As before, their hungry hems will crawl
Over your soft thickets. And you will bend   305
Your innocent head with unreluctant nod
Under that deadly load:
But not a head you bent till then in vain
With cowardly entreaty praying for
Your future killer's grace: not lifted up   310
In frantic vanity towards the stars,
Or over this wasteland where
Your birth and growing-place

---

1. Greed for buried treasure; pity for the dead denied Christian burial.   2. At this time, Vesuvius had
two cones at its summit; subsequent eruptions have eliminated one of them.

Were yours not by your choice but that of fate:
But wiser and less weak,   315
So much less weak than man, since you could rate
Your truly fragile race
With no self-won, no destined deathless state.[3]

3. The broom, unlike humanity, has no illusions about its own mortality.

ALEXANDER SERGEYEVICH PUSHKIN
1799–1837

In his best-known story, *The Queen of Spades*, Alexander Pushkin combines familiar elements of Romantic fiction—the penniless young woman; the ambitious,
passionate young man; the decayed beauty; the ghost—in a tale with intense ironic
overtones, a tale later a favorite of the great Russian novelist Fyodor Dostoevsky.
Pushkin's own life story sounds like a Romantic novel. Born into an aristocratic
Russian family, neglected by his parents, he early began an extensive amatory and
poetic career, publishing his first poem at the age of fifteen and becoming notorious about the same time for his many erotic involvements. At eighteen he graduated from a distinguished boarding school and accepted appointment in the
Foreign Service; six years later, the various instances of his defiance of authority
resulted in expulsion from the service and confinement, under police surveillance,
on a paternal estate. After the assassination of Tsar Alexander I and the abortive
military uprising that followed (an uprising involving several of Pushkin's friends,
five of whom were subsequently hanged), Pushkin—by then a well-known poet—
was befriended (1826) by the new tsar Nicholas. He moved back to Moscow, then
to Petersburg, leading a moneyed and relatively carefree life. In 1831, however, he
married a nineteen-year-old woman, whose apparently flirtatious behavior embittered his subsequent life. He died after a duel with his wife's putative lover.

Producing short lyrics, narrative poems, a great novel in verse (*Eugene Onegin*),
lyrical drama (notably *Boris Gudonov*), versified folk tales, and prose fiction, Pushkin established himself as one of Russia's greatest writers. His interest in his
nation's past, his tendency to challenge authority, his fascination with the character and situation of strong individuals: such obsessive concerns link his work with
that of his Romantic contemporaries elsewhere in Europe. Goethe, Byron, and
early nineteenth-century French novelists had marked influence on him. He
retained also, however, the kind of clarity, discipline, and ironic distance more
often associated with the literature of the preceding century.

The treatment of love and sexuality in *The Queen of Spades* exemplifies the
complexity of Pushkin's approach. First of all we hear the story of the "Muscovite
Venus," the beautiful young gambler who pays her debts by learning the secret of
three infallible cards. Then we encounter a young woman suffering in her dependent position and longing for a "deliverer." Hermann, the immediate object of
Lisaveta's dreams, has his own sexual fantasies: a young man himself, he imagines
becoming the lover of the eighty-seven-year-old countess. At this point, if not
before, the reader begins to realize that something's wrong here: this is not the
kind of romantic tale we're used to. Describing Hermann's first glimpse of Lisaveta, Pushkin writes, "Hermann saw a small, fresh face and a pair of dark eyes.
That moment decided his fate." A Romantic cliché—except that the young man

sees Lisaveta not as an object of devotion but as a means to an end. He sends her a love letter, copied word for word from a German novel. His rapidly developing passion focuses on financial, not erotic, gain.

Lisaveta's character remains somewhat more ambiguous. The narrator invokes sympathy for her plight, at the mercy of a tyrannical employer who makes endless irrational demands and who never pays her. Her situation prohibits her from enjoying the kinds of amorous gratification other young women can expect. We can understand, therefore, why her dreams should concentrate specifically on a deliverer. Like Hermann, although far less unscrupulous, she may indulge in intrigues as a means to an end—in her case, not money but liberty.

The Queen of Spades contains no completely attractive characters. If Lisaveta's victimization arouses compassion, her lack of moral force or determination may also provoke irritation. Hermann's will to succeed, on the other hand, makes him a potential protagonist, but his obsession with money and his mean-spirited expediency alienate most readers. The countess, old and approaching death, uses the power of her money and rank with utter disregard for the needs or feelings of others. Even such a minor figure as the countess's grandson, Tomsky, playing with Lisaveta's feelings, going through his ritualized flirtation with Princess Polina, seems thoroughly contaminated by the values of the world he inhabits.

Indeed, those values provide the central subject of this tale. Pushkin employs conventions of the kind of ghost story common in folk tales to convey serious criticism of a social structure corrupted by universal concentration on money. Gambling provides not only the chief male activity but also the central metaphor of the story. Everyone is out for what he or she can get. The countess, whose days at the card table are past, uses her money to buy subservience; Lisaveta is willing to risk her reputation, maybe even her chastity, for the possibility of escaping servitude; Hermann frightens someone to death in an effort to make his fortune; Tomsky plays elaborate social games of advance and retreat, trying to get his princess. The queen of spades is a conventional symbol of death; the kind of death most important in Pushkin's story is not literal—not the countess's demise—but figurative: it is the spiritual death suffered by the other characters, over whose world the countess/queen of spades metaphorically presides.

The "Conclusion" of The Queen of Spades, a deadpan summary of the characters' future careers, epitomizes the story's central concerns. Hermann's madness dramatizes the financial obsession he has displayed from the beginning; Lisaveta's marriage, to an anonymous "very agreeable young man" with a good position "somewhere," emphasizes the degree to which she has always wished for marriage as rescue, not as attachment to a particular beloved other. In her married state, Lisaveta, ironically, "is bringing up a poor relative," recapitulating the structure of exploitation from which she herself suffered. Tomsky, relatively unimportant to the plot line, supplies the subject for the story's concluding sentence: his promotion and his "good" marriage remind us that everyone in the society here described seeks personal advantage at all costs. Hermann has simply paid the cost in the most dramatic way.

Henri Troyat, Pushkin (1971), is an excellent biography. For biography and criticism, the student might also consult Walter Arndt, Pushkin Threefold: Narrative, Lyric, Polemic and Ribald Verse (1972); John Bayley, Pushkin: A Comparative Commentary (1971); P. Debreczeny, The Other Pushkin: A Study of Alexander Pushkin's Prose (1983); John Oliver Killens, Great Black Russian (1989); and D. M. Bethea, ed., Pushkin Today (1993), an ambitious collection of essays. A useful biography is Stephanie Sandler, Distant Pleasures (1989).

PRONOUNCING GLOSSARY

The following list uses common English syllables and stress accents to provide rough equivalents of selected words whose pronunciation may be unfamiliar to the general reader.

Chekalinsky: *chek-a-lin'-skee*

Eletskaya: *el-et-skai'-yah*

Fedotovna: *fed-ot'-ohv-nah*

Ilyitch: *il'-yich*

Lisaveta Ivanovna: *lee-zah-vet'-ah ee-vahn'-ohv-nah*

Richelieu: *ree'-sha-lyu*

St-Germain: *sanh-zher-manh'*

The Queen of Spades[1]

CHAPTER ONE

> *And on rainy days*
> *They gathered*
> *Often;*
> *Their stakes—God help them!—*
> *Wavered from fifty*
> *To a hundred,*
> *And they won*
> *And marked up their winnings*
> *With chalk.*
> *Thus on rainy days*
> *Were they*
> *Busy.*[2]

There was a card party one day in the rooms of Narumov, an officer of the Horse Guards. The long winter evening slipped by unnoticed; it was five o'clock in the morning before the assembly sat down to supper. Those who had won ate with a big appetite; the others sat distractedly before their empty plates. But champagne was brought in, the conversation became more lively, and everyone took a part in it.

"And how did you get on, Surin?" asked the host.

"As usual, I lost. I must confess, I have no luck: I never vary my stake, never get heated, never lose my head, and yet I always lose!"

"And weren't you tempted even once to back[3] on a series . . . ? Your strength of mind astonishes me."

"What about Hermann then," said one of the guests, pointing at the young Engineer.[4] "He's never held a card in his hand, never doubled a single stake in his life, and yet he sits up until five in the morning watching us play."

"The game fascinates me," said Hermann, "but I am not in the position to sacrifice the essentials of life in the hope of acquiring the luxuries."

"Hermann's a German: he's cautious—that's all," Tomsky observed.

---

1. Translated by Gillon R. Aitken.   2. Like most of the chapter epigraphs, this was presumably written by Pushkin himself.   3. Bet.   4. A member of the Corps of Engineers, concerned with fortifications.

"But if there's one person I can't understand, it's my grandmother, the Countess Anna Fedotovna."

"How? Why?" the guests inquired noisily.

"I can't understand why it is," Tomsky continued, "that my grandmother doesn't gamble."

"But what's so astonishing about an old lady of eighty not gambling?" asked Narumov.

"Then you don't know . . . ?"

"No, indeed; I know nothing."

"Oh well, listen then:

"You must know that about sixty years ago my grandmother went to Paris, where she made something of a hit. People used to chase after her to catch a glimpse of *la vénus moscovite*; Richelieu[5] paid court to her, and my grandmother vouches that he almost shot himself on account of her cruelty. At that time ladies used to play faro.[6] On one occasion at the Court, my grandmother lost a very great deal of money on credit to the Duke of Orleans. Returning home, she removed the patches[7] from her face, took off her hooped petticoat, announced her loss to my grandfather and ordered him to pay back the money. My late grandfather, as far as I can remember, was a sort of lackey to my grandmother. He feared her like fire; on hearing of such a disgraceful loss, however, he completely lost his temper; he produced his accounts, showed her that she had spent half a million francs in six months, pointed out that neither their Moscow nor their Saratov estates were in Paris, and refused point-blank to pay the debt. My grandmother gave him a box on the ear and went off to sleep on her own as an indication of her displeasure. In the hope that this domestic infliction would have had some effect on him, she sent for her husband the next day; she found him unshakeable. For the first time in her life she approached him with argument and explanation, thinking that she could bring him to reason by pointing out that there are debts and debts, that there is a big difference between a Prince and a coachmaker. But my grandfather remained adamant, and flatly refused to discuss the subject any further. My grandmother did not know what to do. A little while before, she had become acquainted with a very remarkable man. You have heard of Count St-Germain,[8] about whom so many marvellous stories are related. You know that he held himself out to be the Wandering Jew, and the inventor of the elixir of life, the philosopher's stone and so forth. Some ridiculed him as a charlatan and in his memoirs Casanova declares that he was a spy. However, St-Germain, in spite of the mystery which surrounded him, was a person of venerable appearance and much in demand in society. My grandmother is still quite infatuated with him and becomes quite angry if anyone speaks of him with disrespect. My grandmother knew that he had large sums of money at his disposal. She decided to have

---

5. Louis-Francois-Arnand De Vignerod Du Plessis, Duc de Richelieu (1696–1788), French aristocrat renowned throughout the 18th century for both his military and his sexual exploits. *La vénus moscovite:* the Venus of Moscow (French). Venus was the goddess of love.　6. A card game much used for gambling.　7. That is, beauty patches, artificial "beauty marks" made of black silk or court plaster and worn on the face or neck.　8. Celebrated adventurer (ca. 1710–1784?) who frequented the French, German, and Russian courts.

recourse to him, and wrote asking him to visit her without delay. The eccentric old man at once called on her and found her in a state of terrible grief. She depicted her husband's barbarity in the blackest light, and ended by saying that she pinned all her hopes on his friendship and kindness.

"St-Germain reflected. 'I could let you have this sum,' he said, 'but I know that you would not be at peace while in my debt, and I have no wish to bring fresh troubles upon your head. There is another solution—you can win back the money.'

" 'But, my dear Count,' my grandmother replied, 'I tell you—we have no money at all.'

" 'In this case money is not essential,' St-Germain replied. 'Be good enough to hear me out.'

"And at this point he revealed to her the secret for which any one of us here would give a very great deal . . ."

The young gamblers listened with still great attention. Tomsky lit his pipe, drew on it and continued:

"That same evening my grandmother went to Versailles, *au jeu de la Reine*.[9] The Duke of Orleans kept the bank; inventing some small tale, my grandmother lightly excused herself for not having brought her debt, and began to play against him. She chose three cards and played them one after the other: all three won and my grandmother recouped herself completely."

"Pure luck!" said one of the guests.

"A fairy-tale," observed Hermann.

"Perhaps the cards were marked!" said a third.

"I don't think so," Tomsky replied gravely.

"What!" cried Narumov. "You have a grandmother who can guess three cards in succession, and you haven't yet contrived to learn her secret."

"No, not much hope of that!" replied Tomsky. "She had four sons, including my father; all four were desperate gamblers, and yet she did not reveal her secret to a single one of them, although it would have been a good thing if she had told them—told me, even. But this is what I heard from my uncle, Count Ivan Ilyitch, and he gave me his word for its truth. The late Chaplitsky—the same who died a pauper after squandering millions—in his youth once lost nearly 300,000 roubles—to Zoritch, if I remember rightly. He was in despair. My grandmother, who was most strict in her attitude towards the extravagances of young men, for some reason took pity on Chaplitsky. She told him the three cards on condition that he played them in order; and at the same time she exacted his solemn promise that he would never play again as long as he lived. Chaplitsky appeared before his victor; they sat down to play. On the first card Chaplitsky staked 50,000 roubles and won straight off; he doubled his stake, redoubled—and won back more than he had lost. . . .

"But it's time to go to bed; it's already a quarter to six."

Indeed, the day was already beginning to break. The young men drained their glasses and dispersed.

---

9. To the queen's game (French).

CHAPTER TWO

"Il paraît que monsieur est décidément
pour les suivantes."
"Que voulez-vous, madame? Elles sont
plus fraîches."
FASHIONABLE CONVERSATION

The old Countess ***[1] was seated before the looking-glass in her dressing-room. Three lady's maids stood by her. One held a jar of rouge, another a box of hairpins, and the third a tall bonnet with flame-coloured ribbons. The Countess no longer had the slightest pretensions to beauty, which had long since faded from her face, but she still preserved all the habits of her youth, paid strict regard to the fashions of the seventies, and devoted to her dress the same time and attention as she had done sixty years before. At an embroidery frame by the window sat a young lady, her ward.

"Good morning, *grand'maman!*" said a young officer as he entered the room. "*Bonjour, mademoiselle Lise. Grand'maman,*[2] I have a request to make of you."

"What is it, Paul?"

"I want you to let me introduce one of my friends to you, and to allow me to bring him to the ball on Friday."

"Bring him straight to the ball and introduce him to me there. Were you at ***'s yesterday?"

"Of course. It was very gay; we danced until five in the morning. How charming Eletskaya was!"

"But, my dear, what's charming about her? Isn't she like her grandmother, the Princess Darya Petrovna . . . ? By the way, I dare say she's grown very old now, the Princess Darya Petrovna?"

"What do you mean, 'grown old'?" asked Tomsky thoughtlessly. "She's been dead for seven years."

The young lady raised her head and made a sign to the young man. He remembered then that the death of any of her contemporaries was kept secret from the old Countess, and he bit his lip. But the Countess heard the news, previously unknown to her, with the greatest indifference.

"Dead!" she said. "And I didn't know it. We were maids of honour together, and when we were presented, the Empress . . ."

And for the hundredth time the Countess related the anecdote to her grandson.

"Come, Paul," she said when she had finished her story, "help me to stand up. Lisanka, where's my snuff-box?"

And with her three maids the Countess went behind a screen to complete her dress. Tomsky was left alone with the young lady.

"Whom do you wish to introduce?" Lisaveta Ivanovna asked softly.

"Narumov. Do you know him?"

---

1. Asterisks in this selection are the author's and are intended to suggest that the proper name of an actual person has been omitted. The epigram can be translated as: "It appears that the gentleman is decidedly in favor of servant girls." "What would you have me do, Madam? They are fresher [than upper-class women]" (French). 2. Russian aristocrats often spoke French. Lisaveta is here called by the French name Lise, and Pavel, Paul.

"No. Is he a soldier or a civilian?"

"A soldier."

"An Engineer?"

"No, he's in the Cavalry. What made you think he was an Engineer?"

The young lady smiled but made no reply.

"Paul!" cried the Countess from behind the screen. "Bring along a new novel with you some time, will you, only please not one of those modern ones."

"What do you mean, *grand'maman?*"

"I mean not the sort of novel in which the hero strangles either of his parents or in which someone is drowned.[3] I have a great horror of drowned people."

"Such novels don't exist nowadays. Wouldn't you like a Russian one?"

"Are there such things? Send me one, my dear, please send me one."

"Will you excuse me now, *grand'maman*, I'm in a hurry. Good-bye, Lisaveta Ivanovna. What made you think that Narumov was in the Engineers?"

And Tomsky left the dressing-room.

Lisaveta Ivanovna was left on her own; she put aside her work and began to look out of the window. Presently a young officer appeared from behind the corner house on the other side of the street. A flush spread over her cheeks; she took up her work again and lowered her head over the frame. At this moment, the Countess returned, fully dressed.

"Order the carriage, Lisanka," she said, "and we'll go for a drive."

Lisanka got up from behind her frame and began to put away her work.

"What's the matter with you, my child? Are you deaf?" shouted the Countess. "Order the carriage this minute."

"I'll do so at once," the young lady replied softly and hastened into the ante-room.

A servant entered the room and handed the Countess some books from the Prince Pavel Alexandrovitch.

"Good, thank him," said the Countess. "Lisanka, Lisanka, where are you running to?"

"To get dressed."

"Plenty of time for that, my dear. Sit down. Open the first volume and read to me."

The young lady took up the book and read a few lines.

"Louder!" said the Countess. "What's the matter with you, my child? Have you lost your voice, or what . . . ? Wait . . . move that footstool up to me . . . nearer . . . that's right!"

Lisaveta Ivanovna read a further two pages. The Countess yawned.

"Put the book down," she said; "what rubbish! Have it returned to Prince Pavel with my thanks. . . . But where is the carriage?"

"The carriage is ready," said Lisaveta Ivanovna, looking out into the street.

---

3. Novels of the sort the countess does not wish to read were typical of the then current decadent movement in French literature.

"Then why aren't you dressed?" asked the Countess. "I'm always having to wait for you—it's intolerable, my dear!"

Lisa ran up to her room. Not two minutes elapsed before the Countess began to ring with all her might. The three lady's maids came running in through one door and the valet through another.

"Why don't you come when you're called?" the Countess asked them. "Tell Lisaveta Ivanovna that I'm waiting for her."

Lisaveta Ivanovna entered the room wearing her hat and cloak.

"At last, my child!" said the Countess. "But what clothes you're wearing . . . ! Whom are you hoping to catch? What's the weather like? It seems windy."

"There's not a breath of wind, your Ladyship," replied the valet.

"You never know what you're talking about! Open that small window. There; as I thought: windy and bitterly cold. Unharness the horses. Lisaveta, we're not going out—there was no need to dress up like that."

"And this is my life," thought Lisaveta Ivanovna.

And indeed Lisaveta Ivanovna was a most unfortunate creature. As Dante says: "You shall learn the salt taste of another's bread, and the hard path up and down his stairs";[4] and who better to know the bitterness of dependence than the poor ward of a well-born old lady? The Countess *** was far from being wicked, but she had the capriciousness of a woman who has been spoiled by the world, and the miserliness and cold-hearted egotism of all old people who have done with loving and whose thoughts lie with the past. She took part in all the vanities of the *haut-monde;*[5] she dragged herself to balls, where she sat in a corner, rouged and dressed in old-fashioned style, like some misshapen but essential ornament of the ball-room; on arrival, the guests would approach her with low bows, as if in accordance with an established rite, but after that, they would pay no further attention to her. She received the whole town at her house, and although no longer able to recognise the faces of her guests, she observed the strictest etiquette. Her numerous servants, grown fat and grey in her hall and servants' room, did exactly as they pleased, vying with one another in stealing from the dying old lady. Lisaveta Ivanovna was the household martyr. She poured out the tea, and was reprimanded for putting in too much sugar; she read novels aloud, and was held guilty of all the faults of the authors; she accompanied the Countess on her walks, and was made responsible for the state of the weather and the pavement. There was a salary attached to her position, but it was never paid; meanwhile, it was demanded of her to be dressed like everybody else—that is, like the very few who could afford to dress well. In society she played the most pitiable role. Everybody knew her, but nobody took any notice of her; at balls she danced only when there was a partner short, and ladies only took her arm when they needed to go to the dressing-room to make some adjustment to their dress. She was proud and felt her position keenly, and looked around her in impatient expectation of a deliverer; but the young men, calculating in their flightiness, did not honour her

4. *Paradiso* 17.59.   5. High society (French).

with their attention, despite the fact that Lisaveta Ivanovna was a hundred times prettier than the cold, arrogant but more eligible young ladies on whom they danced attendance. Many a time did she creep softly away from the bright but wearisome drawing-room to go and cry in her own poor room, where stood a papered screen, a chest of drawers, a small looking-glass and a painted bedstead, and where a tallow candle burned dimly in its copper candle-stick.

One day—two days after the evening described at the beginning of this story, and about a week previous to the events just recorded—Lisaveta Ivanovna was sitting at her embroidery frame by the window, when, happening to glance out into the street, she saw a young Engineer, standing motionless with his eyes fixed upon her window. She lowered her head and continued with her work; five minutes later she looked out again—the young officer was still standing in the same place. Not being in the habit of flirting with passing officers, she ceased to look out of the window, and sewed for about two hours without raising her head. Dinner was announced. She got up and began to put away her frame, and, glancing casually out into the street, she saw the officer again. She was considerably puzzled by this. After dinner, she approached the window with a feeling of some disquiet, but the officer was no longer outside, and she thought no more of him.

Two days later, while preparing to enter the carriage with the Countess, she saw him again. He was standing just by the front-door, his face concealed by a beaver collar; his dark eyes shone from beneath his cap. Without knowing why, Lisaveta Ivanovna felt afraid, and an unaccountable trembling came over her as she sat down in the carriage.

On her return home, she hastened to the window—the officer was standing in the same place as before, his eyes fixed upon her; she drew back, tormented by curiosity and agitated by a feeling that was quite new to her.

Since then, not a day had passed without the young man appearing at the customary hour beneath the windows of their house. A sort of mute acquaintance grew up between them. At work in her seat, she used to feel him approaching, and would raise her head to look at him—for longer and longer each day. The young man seemed to be grateful to her for this: she saw, with the sharp eye of youth, how a sudden flush would spread across his pale cheeks on each occasion that their glances met. After a week she smiled at him. . . .

When Tomsky asked leave of the Countess to introduce one of his friends to her; the poor girl's heart beat fast. But on learning that Narumov was in the Horse Guards, and not in the Engineers, she was sorry that, by an indiscreet question, she had betrayed her secret to the light-hearted Tomsky.

Hermann was the son of a Russianised German, from whom he had inherited a small amount of money. Being firmly convinced of the necessity of ensuring his independence, Hermann did not draw on the income that this yielded, but lived on his pay, forbidding himself the slightest extravagance. Moreover, he was secretive and ambitious, and his companions rarely had occasion to laugh at his excessive thrift. He had strong passions and a fiery imagination, but his tenacity of spirit saved him from the usual errors of youth. Thus, for example, although at heart a gambler, he never took a card in his hand, for he reckoned that his position did not allow him (as he put it) "to sacrifice the essentials of life in the hope of acquiring the luxuries" — and meanwhile, he would sit up at the card table for whole nights at a time, and follow the different turns of the game with feverish anxiety.

The story of the three cards had made a strong impression on his imagination, and he could think of nothing else all night.

"What if the old Countess should reveal her secret to me?" he thought the following evening as he wandered through the streets of Petersburg. "What if she should tell me the names of those three winning cards? Why not try my luck . . . ? Become introduced to her, try to win her favour, perhaps become her lover . . . ? But all that demands time, and she's eighty-seven; she might die in a week, in two days . . . ! And the story itself . . . ? Can one really believe it . . . ? No! Economy, moderation and industry; these are my three winning cards, these will treble my capital, increase it sevenfold, and earn for me ease and independence!"

Reasoning thus, he found himself in one of the principal streets of Petersburg, before a house of old-fashioned architecture. The street was crowded with vehicles; one after another, carriages rolled up to the lighted entrance. From them there emerged, now the shapely little foot of some beautiful young woman, now a rattling jack-boot, now the striped stocking and elegant shoe of a diplomat. Furs and capes flitted past the majestic hall-porter. Hermann stopped.

"Whose house is this?" he asked the watchman at the corner.

"The Countess ***'s," the watchman replied.

Hermann started. His imagination was again fired by the amazing story of the three cards. He began to walk around near the house, thinking of its owner and her mysterious faculty. It was late when he returned to his humble rooms; for a long time he could not sleep; and when at last he did drop off, cards, a green table,[6] heaps of banknotes and piles of golden coins appeared to him in his dreams. He played one card after the other, doubled his stake decisively, won unceasingly, and raked in the golden coins and stuffed his pockets with the banknotes. Waking up late, he sighed at the loss of his imaginary fortune, again went out to wander about the town and again found himself outside the house of the Countess ***. Some unknown power seemed to have attracted him to it. He stopped and began to look at the windows. At one he saw a head with long black hair, probably bent down over a book or a piece of work. The head was raised. Hermann saw a small, fresh face and a pair of dark eyes. That moment decided his fate.

---

6. Tables on which gambling took place were typically covered with green baize.

CHAPTER THREE

*Vous m'écrivez, mon ange, des lettres de
quatre pages plus vite que je ne puis
les lire.*[7]

CORRESPONDENCE

Scarcely had Lisaveta Ivanovna taken off her hat and cloak when the Countess sent for her and again ordered her to have the horses harnessed. They went out to take their seats in the carriage. At the same moment as the old lady was being helped through the carriage doors by two footmen, Lisaveta Ivanovna saw her Engineer standing close by the wheel; he seized her hand; before she could recover from her fright, the young man had disappeared—leaving a letter in her hand. She hid it in her glove and throughout the whole of the drive neither heard nor saw a thing. As was her custom when riding in her carriage, the Countess kept up a ceaseless flow of questions: "Who was it who met us just now? What's this bridge called? What's written on that signboard?" This time Lisaveta Ivanovna's answers were so vague and inappropriate that the Countess became angry.

"What's the matter with you, my child? Are you in a trance or something? Don't you hear me or understand what I'm saying . . . ? Heaven be thanked that I'm still sane enough to speak clearly."

Lisaveta Ivanovna did not listen to her. On returning home, she ran up to her room and drew the letter out of her glove; it was unsealed. Lisaveta Ivanovna read it through. The letter contained a confession of love; it was tender, respectful and taken word for word from a German novel. But Lisaveta Ivanovna had no knowledge of German and was most pleased by it.

Nevertheless, the letter made her feel extremely uneasy. For the first time in her life she was entering into a secret and confidential relationship with a young man. His audacity shocked her. She reproached herself for her imprudent behaviour, and did not know what to do. Should she stop sitting at the window and by a show of indifference cool off the young man's desire for further acquaintance? Should she send the letter back to him? Or answer it with cold-hearted finality? There was nobody to whom she could turn for advice: she had no friend or preceptress. Lisaveta Ivanovna resolved to answer the letter.

She sat down at her small writing-table, took a pen and some paper, and lost herself in thought. Several times she began her letter—and then tore it up; her manner of expression seemed to her to be either too condescending or too heartless. At last she succeeded in writing a few lines that satisfied her:

> I am sure that your intentions are honourable, and that you did not wish to offend me by your rash behaviour, but our acquaintance must not begin in this way. I return your letter to you and hope that in the future I shall have no cause to complain of undeserved disrespect.

The next day, as soon as she saw Hermann approach, Lisaveta Ivanovna rose from behind her frame, went into the ante-room, opened a small

---

7. My angel, you write me four-page-long letters faster than I can read them (French).

window, and threw her letter into the street, trusting to the agility of the young officer to pick it up. Hermann ran forward, took hold of the letter and went into a confectioner's shop. Breaking the seal of the envelope, he found his own letter and Lisaveta Ivanovna's answer. It was as he had expected, and he returned home, deeply preoccupied with his intrigue.

Three days afterwards, a bright-eyed young girl brought Lisaveta Ivanovna a letter from a milliner's shop. Lisaveta Ivanovna opened it uneasily, envisaging a demand for money, but she suddenly recognised Hermann's handwriting.

"You have made a mistake, my dear," she said; "this letter is not for me."

"Oh, but it is!" the girl answered cheekily and without concealing a sly smile. "Read it."

Lisaveta Ivanovna ran her eyes over the note. Hermann demanded a meeting.

"It cannot be," said Lisaveta Ivanovna, frightened at the haste of his demand and the way in which it was made: "this is certainly not for me." And she tore the letter up into tiny pieces.

"If the letter wasn't for you, why did you tear it up?" asked the girl. "I would have returned it to the person who sent it."

"Please, my dear," Lisaveta Ivanovna said, flushing at the remark, "don't bring me any more letters in the future. And tell the person who sent you that he should be ashamed of . . ."

But Hermann was not put off. By some means or other, he sent a letter to Lisaveta Ivanovna every day. The letters were no longer translated from the German. Hermann wrote them inspired by passion, and used a language true to his character; these letters were the expression of his obsessive desires and the disorder of his unfettered imagination. Lisaveta Ivanovna no longer thought of returning them to him: she revelled in them, began to answer them, and with each day, her replies became longer and more tender. Finally, she threw out of the window the following letter:

> This evening there is a ball at the *** Embassy. The Countess will be there. We will stay until about two o'clock. Here is your chance to see me alone. As soon as the Countess has left the house, the servants will probably go to their quarters—with the exception of the hall-porter, who normally goes out to his closet anyway. Come at half-past eleven. Walk straight upstairs. If you meet anybody in the ante-room, ask whether the Countess is at home. You will be told 'No'—and there will be nothing you can do but go away. But it is unlikely that you will meet anybody. The lady's maids sit by themselves, all in the one room. On leaving the hall, turn to the left and walk straight on until you come to the Countess' bedroom. In the bedroom, behind a screen, you will see two small doors: the one on the right leads into the study, which the Countess never goes into; the one on the left leads into a corridor and thence to a narrow winding staircase: this staircase leads to my bedroom.

Hermann quivered like a tiger as he awaited the appointed hour. He was already outside the Countess' house at ten o'clock. The weather was terrible; the wind howled, and a wet snow fell in large flakes upon the deserted streets, where the lamps shone dimly. Occasionally a passing cab-driver leaned forward over his scrawny nag, on the look-out for a late passenger. Feeling neither wind nor snow, Hermann waited, dressed only in his frock-coat. At last the Countess' carriage was brought round. Hermann saw two footmen carry out in their arms the bent old lady, wrapped in a sable fur, and immediately following her, the figure of Lisaveta Ivanovna, clad in a light cloak, and with her head adorned with fresh flowers. The doors were slammed and the carriage rolled heavily away along the soft snow. The hall-porter closed the front door. The windows became dark. Hermann began to walk about near the deserted house; he went up to a lamp and looked at his watch; it was twenty minutes past eleven. He remained beneath the lamp; his eyes fixed upon the hands of his watch, waiting for the remaining minutes to pass. At exactly half-past eleven, Hermann ascended the steps of the Countess' house and reached the brightly-lit porch. The hall-porter was not there. Hermann ran up the stairs, opened the door into the ante-room and saw a servant asleep by the lamp in a soiled antique armchair. With a light, firm tread Hermann stepped past him. The drawing-room and reception-room were in darkness, but the lamp in the ante-room sent through a feeble light. Hermann passed through into the bedroom. Before an icon-case, filled with old-fashioned images,[8] glowed a gold sanctuary lamp. Faded brocade armchairs and dull gilt divans with soft cushions were ranged in sad symmetry around the room, the walls of which were hung with Chinese silk. Two portraits, painted in Paris by Madame Lebrun,[9] were hung from one of the walls. One of these featured a plump, red-faced man of about forty, in a light-green uniform and with a star pinned to his breast; the other—a beautiful young woman with an aquiline nose and powdered hair, brushed back at the temples and adorned with a rose. In the corners of the room stood porcelain shepherdesses, table clocks from the workshop of the celebrated Leroy, little boxes, roulettes,[1] fans and the various lady's playthings which had been popular at the end of the last century, when the Montgolfiers' balloon and Mesmer's magnetism[2] were invented. Hermann went behind the screen, where stood a small iron bedstead; on the right was the door leading to the study; on the left the one which led to the corridor. Hermann opened the latter, and saw the narrow, winding staircase which led to the poor ward's room. . . . But he turned back and stepped into the dark study.

The time passed slowly. Everything was quiet. The clock in the drawing-room struck twelve; one by one the clocks in all the other rooms sounded the same hour, and then all was quiet again. Hermann stood leaning against the cold stove. He was calm; his heart beat evenly, like that of a man who has decided upon some dangerous but necessary action. One o'clock sounded; two o'clock; he heard the distant rattle of the carriage. He was seized by an involuntary agitation. The carriage drew near and stopped. He heard the sound of the carriage-steps being let down. The house suddenly came alive. Servants ran here and there, voices echoed

---

8. That is, religious images.   9. Marie Anne Elizabeth Vigée-Lebrun (1755–1842), French portrait painter, particularly of the aristocracy and royalty.   1. Little balls; or possibly portable devices for playing the gambling game of roulette. Julien Leroy (1686–1759), famous French clockmaker.   2. Franz Anton Mesmer (1734–1815) argued that a person can transmit personal force to others in the form of "animal magnetism." Joseph-Michel (1740–1810) and Jacques-Etienne (1745–1799) Montgolfier, French brothers, helped to develop the hot-air balloon and conducted the first untethered flights.

through the house and the rooms were lit. Three old maid-servants hastened into the bedroom, followed by the Countess, who, tired to death,
lowered herself into a Voltairean armchair.[3] Hermann peeped through a
crack. Lisaveta Ivanovna went past him. Hermann heard her hurried steps
as she went up the narrow staircase. In his heart there echoed something
like the voice of conscience, but it grew silent, and his heart once more
turned to stone.

The Countess began to undress before the looking-glass. Her rose-
bedecked cap was unfastened; her powdered wig was removed from her
grey, closely-cropped hair. Pins fell in showers around her. Her yellow
dress, embroidered with silver, fell at her swollen feet. Hermann witnessed
all the loathsome mysteries of her dress; at last the Countess stood in her
dressing-gown and night-cap; in this attire, more suitable to her age, she
seemed less hideous and revolting.

Like most old people, the Countess suffered from insomnia. Having
undressed, she sat down by the window in the Voltairean armchair and
dismissed her maidservants. The candles were carried out; once again the
room was lit by a single sanctuary lamp. Looking quite yellow, the Countess sat rocking to and fro in her chair, her flabby lips moving. Her dim
eyes reflected a complete absence of thought and, looking at her, one
would have thought that the awful old woman's rocking came not of her
own volition, but by the action of some hidden galvanism.

Suddenly, an indescribable change came over her death-like face. Her
lips ceased to move, her eyes came to life: before the Countess stood an
unknown man.

"Don't be alarmed, for God's sake, don't be alarmed," he said in a clear,
low voice. "I have no intention of harming you; I have come to beseech a
favour of you."

The old woman looked at him in silence, as if she had not heard him.
Hermann imagined that she was deaf, and bending right down over her
ear, he repeated what he had said. The old woman kept silent as before.

"You can ensure the happiness of my life," Hermann continued, "and
it will cost you nothing: I know that you can guess three cards in succession. . . ."

Hermann stopped. The Countess appeared to understand what was
demanded of her; she seemed to be seeking words for her reply.

"It was a joke," she said at last. "I swear to you, it was a joke."

"There's no joking about it," Hermann retorted angrily. "Remember
Chaplitsky whom you helped to win."

The Countess was visibly disconcerted, and her features expressed
strong emotion; but she quickly resumed her former impassivity.

"Can you name these three winning cards?" Hermann continued.

The Countess was silent. Hermann went on:

"For whom do you keep your secret? For your grandsons? They are rich
and they can do without it; they don't know the value of money. Your
three cards will not help a spendthrift. He who cannot keep his paternal
inheritance will die in want, even if he has the devil at his side. I am not

_____

3. A large armchair with a high back.

a spendthrift; I know the value of money. Your three cards will not be lost on me. Come . . . !"

He stopped and awaited her answer with trepidation. The Countess was silent. Hermann fell upon his knees.

"If your heart has ever known the feeling of love," he said, "if you remember its ecstasies, if you ever smiled at the wailing of your new-born son, if ever any human feeling has run through your breast, I entreat you by the feelings of a wife, a lover, a mother, by everything that is sacred in life, not to deny my request! Reveal your secret to me! What is it to you . . . ? Perhaps it is bound up with some dreadful sin, with the loss of eternal bliss, with some contract made with the devil . . . Consider: you are old; you have not long to live—I am prepared to take your sins on my own soul. Only reveal to me your secret. Realise that the happiness of a man is in your hands, that not only I, but my children, my grandchildren, my great-grandchildren will bless your memory and will revere it as something sacred. . . ."

The old woman answered not a word.

Hermann stood up.

"You old witch!" he said, clenching his teeth. "I'll force you to answer. . . ."

With these words he drew a pistol from his pocket. At the sight of the pistol, the Countess, for the second time, exhibited signs of strong emotion. She shook her head and raising her hand as though to shield herself from the shot, she rolled over on her back and remained motionless.

"Stop this childish behaviour now," Hermann said, taking her hand. "I ask you for the last time: will you name your three cards or won't you?"

The Countess made no reply. Hermann saw that she was dead.

CHAPTER FOUR

7 Mai 18**
Homme sans moeurs et sans religion![4]
CORRESPONDENCE

Still in her ball dress, Lisaveta Ivanovna sat in her room, lost in thought. On her arrival home, she had quickly dismissed the sleepy maid who had reluctantly offered her services, had said that she would undress herself, and with a tremulous heart had gone up to her room, expecting to find Hermann there and yet hoping not to find him. Her first glance assured her of his absence and she thanked her fate for the obstacle that had prevented their meeting. She sat down, without undressing, and began to recall all the circumstances which had lured her so far in so short a time. It was not three weeks since she had first seen the young man from the window—and yet she was already in correspondence with him, and already he had managed to persuade her to grant him a nocturnal meeting! She knew his name only because some of his letters had been signed; she had never spoken to him, nor heard his voice, nor heard anything about him . . . until that very evening. Strange thing! That very evening,

---

4. A man without morals and without religion! (French).

Tomsky, vexed with the Princess Polina *** for not flirting with him as she usually did, had wished to revenge himself by a show of indifference: he had therefore summoned Lisaveta Ivanovna and together they had danced an endless mazurka. All the time they were dancing, he had teased her about her partiality to officers of the Engineers, had assured her that he knew far more than she would have supposed possible, and indeed, some of his jests were so successfully aimed that on several occasions Lisaveta Ivanovna had thought that her secret was known to him.

"From whom have you discovered all this?" she asked, laughing.

"From a friend of the person whom you know so well," Tomsky answered; "from a most remarkable man!"

"Who is this remarkable man?"

"He is called Hermann."

Lisaveta made no reply, but her hands and feet turned quite numb.

"This Hermann," Tomsky continued, "is a truly romantic figure: he has the profile of a Napoleon, and the soul of a Mephistopheles. I should think that he has at least three crimes on his conscience. . . . How pale you have turned. . . . !"

"I have a headache. . . . What did this Hermann—or whatever his name is—tell you?"

"Hermann is most displeased with his friend: he says that he would act quite differently in his place . . . I even think that Hermann himself has designs on you; at any rate he listens to the exclamations of his enamoured friend with anything but indifference."

"But where has he seen me?"

"At church, perhaps; on a walk—God only knows! Perhaps in your room, whilst you were asleep: he's quite capable of it . . ."

Three ladies approaching him with the question: *"oublie ou regret?"*[5] interrupted the conversation which had become so agonisingly interesting to Lisaveta Ivanovna.

The lady chosen by Tomsky was the Princess Polina *** herself. She succeeded in clearing up the misunderstanding between them during the many turns and movements of the dance, after which he conducted her to her chair. Tomsky returned to his own place. He no longer had any thoughts for Hermann or Lisaveta Ivanovna, who desperately wanted to renew her interrupted conversation; but the mazurka came to an end and shortly afterwards the old Countess left.

Tomsky's words were nothing but ball-room chatter, but they made a deep impression upon the mind of the young dreamer. The portrait, sketched by Tomsky, resembled the image she herself had formed of Hermann, and thanks to the latest romantic novels, Hermann's quite commonplace face took on attributes that both frightened and captivated her imagination. Now she sat, her uncovered arms crossed, her head, still adorned with flowers, bent over her bare shoulders. . . . Suddenly the door opened, and Hermann entered. She shuddered.

"Where have you been?" she asked in a frightened whisper.

---

5. The ladies cut in, offering the man a choice: *oublie* (forgetting) or *regret*. He does not know which lady is which. He chooses correctly the one with whom he wants to dance.

"In the old Countess' bedroom," Hermann answered: "I have just left it. The Countess is dead."

"Good God! What are you saying?"

"And it seems," Hermann continued, "that I am the cause of her death."

Lisaveta Ivanovna looked at him, and the words of Tomsky echoed in her mind: "he has at least three crimes on his conscience"! Hermann sat down beside her on the window sill and told her everything.

Lisaveta Ivanovna listened to him with horror. So those passionate letters, those ardent demands, the whole impertinent and obstinate pursuit—all that was not love! Money—that was what his soul craved for! It was not she who could satisfy his desire and make him happy! The poor ward had been nothing but the unknowing assistant of a brigand, of the murderer of her aged benefactress! ... She wept bitterly, in an agony of belated repentance. Hermann looked at her in silence; his heart was also tormented; but neither the tears of the poor girl nor the astounding charm of her grief disturbed his hardened soul. He felt no remorse at the thought of the dead old lady. He felt dismay for only one thing: the irretrievable loss of the secret upon which he had relied for enrichment.

"You are a monster!" Lisaveta Ivanovna said at last.

"I did not wish for her death," Hermann answered. "My pistol wasn't loaded."

They were silent.

The day began to break. Lisaveta Ivanovna extinguished the flickering candle. A pale light lit up her room. She wiped her tear-stained eyes and raised them to Hermann: he sat by the window, his arms folded and with a grim frown on his face. In this position he bore an astonishing resemblance to a portrait of Napoleon. Even Lisaveta Ivanovna was struck by the likeness.

"How am I going to get you out of the house?" Lisaveta Ivanovna said at last. "I had thought of leading you along the secret staircase, but that would mean going past the Countess' bedroom, and I am afraid."

"Tell me how to find this secret staircase; I'll go on my own."

Lisaveta Ivanovna stood up, took a key from her chest of drawers, handed it to Hermann, and gave him detailed instructions. Hermann pressed her cold, unresponsive hand, kissed her bowed head and left.

He descended the winding staircase and once more entered the Countess' bedroom. The dead old lady sat as if turned to stone; her face expressed a deep calm. Hermann stopped before her and gazed at her for a long time, as if wishing to assure himself of the dreadful truth; finally, he went into the study, felt for the door behind the silk wall hangings, and, agitated by strange feelings, he began to descend the dark staircase.

"Along this very staircase," he thought, "perhaps at this same hour sixty years ago, in an embroidered coat, his hair dressed à l'oiseau royal,[6] his three-cornered hat pressed to his heart, there may have crept into this very bedroom a young and happy man now long since turned to dust in his grave—and to-day the aged heart of his mistress ceased to beat."

---

6. In the style of the royal bird (French, literal trans.); an antiquated and elaborate hairstyle.

At the bottom of the staircase Hermann found a door, which he opened with the key Lisaveta Ivanovna had given him, and he found himself in a corridor which led into the street.

CHAPTER FIVE

That evening there appeared before me
the figure of the late Baroness von V**.
She was all in white and she said to me:
"How are you, Mr. Councillor!"
                                        SWEDENBORG[7]

Three days after the fateful night, at nine o'clock in the morning, Hermann set out for the *** monastery, where a funeral service for the dead Countess was going to be held. Although unrepentant, he could not altogether silence the voice of conscience, which kept on repeating: "You are the murderer of the old woman!" Having little true religious belief, he was extremely superstitious. He believed that the dead Countess could exercise a harmful influence on his life, and he had therefore resolved to be present at the funeral, in order to ask her forgiveness.

The church was full. Hermann could scarcely make his way through the crowd of people. The coffin stood on a rich catafalque beneath a velvet canopy. Within it lay the dead woman, her arms folded upon her chest, and dressed in a white satin robe, with a lace cap on her head. Around her stood the members of her household: servants in black coats, with armorial ribbons upon their shoulders and candles in their hands; the relatives—children, grandchildren, great-grandchildren—in deep mourning. Nobody cried; tears would have been *une affectation*. The Countess was so old that her death could have surprised nobody, and her relatives had long considered her as having outlived herself. A young bishop pronounced the funeral sermon. In simple, moving words, he described the peaceful end of the righteous woman, who for many years had been in quiet and touching preparation for a Christian end. "The angel of death found her," the speaker said, "waiting for the midnight bridegroom, vigilant in godly meditation." The service was completed with sad decorum. The relatives were the first to take leave of the body. Then the numerous guests went up to pay final homage to her who had so long participated in their frivolous amusements. They were followed by all the members of the Countess' household, the last of whom was an old housekeeper of the same age as the Countess. She was supported by two young girls who led her up to the coffin. She had not the strength to bow down to the ground—and merely shed a few tears as she kissed the cold hand of her mistress. After that, Hermann decided to approach the coffin. He knelt down and for several minutes lay on the cold floor, which was strewn with fir branches; at last he got up, as pale as the dead woman herself; he went up the steps of the catafalque and bent his head over the body of the Countess. . . . At that very moment it seemed to him that the dead woman

---

7. Emmanuel Swedenborg (1688–1772), Swedish theologian, believed that he had several experiences of divine revelation, some involving appearances to him of the dead.

gave him a mocking glance, and winked at him. Hermann, hurriedly stepping back, missed his footing, and crashed on his back against the ground. He was helped to his feet. At the same moment, Lisaveta Ivanovna was carried out in a faint to the porch of the church. These events disturbed the solemnity of the gloomy ceremony for a few moments. A subdued murmur rose among the congregation, and a tall, thin chamberlain, a near relative of the dead woman, whispered in the ear of an Englishman standing by him that the young officer was the Countess' illegitimate son, to which the Englishman replied coldly: "Oh?"

For the whole of that day Hermann was exceedingly troubled. He went to a secluded inn for dinner and, contrary to his usual custom and in the hope of silencing his inward agitation, he drank heavily. But the wine fired his imagination still more. Returning home, he threw himself on to his bed without undressing, and fell into a heavy sleep.

It was already night when he awoke: the moon lit up his room. He glanced at his watch; it was a quarter to three. He found he could not go back to sleep; he sat down on his bed and thought about the funeral of the old Countess.

At that moment somebody in the street glanced in at his window, and immediately went away again. Hermann paid no attention to the incident. A minute or so later, he heard the door into the front room being opened. Hermann imagined that it was his orderly, drunk as usual, returning from some nocturnal outing. But he heard unfamiliar footsteps and the soft shuffling of slippers. The door opened: a woman in a white dress entered. Hermann mistook her for his old wet-nurse and wondered what could have brought her out at that time of the night. But the woman in white glided across the room and suddenly appeared before him—and Hermann recognised the Countess!

"I have come to you against my will," she said in a firm voice, "but I have been ordered to fulfill your request. Three, seven, ace, played in that order, will win for you, but only on condition that you play not more than one card in twenty-four hours, and that you never play again for the rest of your life. I'll forgive you my death if you marry my ward, Lisaveta Ivanovna. . . ."

With these words, she turned round quietly, walked towards the door and disappeared, her slippers shuffling. Herman heard the door in the hall bang, and again saw somebody look in at him through the window.

For a long time Hermann could not collect his senses. He went out into the next room. His orderly was lying asleep on the floor; Hermann could scarcely wake him. The orderly was, as usual, drunk, and it was impossible to get any sense out of him. The door into the hall was locked. Hermann returned to his room, lit a candle, and recorded the details of his vision.

CHAPTER SIX

"Attendez!"[8]
"How dare you say to me: 'Attendez'?"
"Your Excellency, I said: 'Attendez, sir'!"

Two fixed ideas can no more exist in one mind than, in the physical sense, two bodies can occupy one and the same place. "Three, seven, ace" soon eclipsed from Hermann's mind the form of the dead old lady. "Three, seven, ace" never left his thoughts, were constantly on his lips. At the sight of a young girl, he would say: "How shapely she is! Just like the three of hearts." When asked the time, he would reply: "About seven." Every pot-bellied man he saw reminded him of an ace. "Three, seven, ace," assuming all possible shapes, persecuted him in his sleep: the three bloomed before him in the shape of some luxuriant flower, the seven took on the appearance of a Gothic gateway, the ace—of an enormous spider. To the exclusion of all others, one thought alone occupied his mind—making use of the secret which had cost him so much. He began to think of retirement and of travel. He wanted to try his luck in the public gaming-houses of Paris. Chance spared him the trouble.

There was in Moscow a society of rich gamblers, presided over by the celebrated Chekalinsky, a man whose whole life had been spent at the card-table, and who had amassed millions long ago, accepting his winnings in the form of promissory notes and paying his losses with ready money. His long experience had earned him the confidence of his companions, and his open house, his famous cook and his friendliness and gaiety had won him great public respect. He arrived in Petersburg. The younger generation flocked to his house, forgetting balls for cards, and preferring the enticements of faro to the fascinations of courtship. Narumov took Hermann to meet him.

They passed through a succession of magnificent rooms, full of polite and attentive waiters. Several generals and privy councillors were playing whist; young men, sprawled out on brocade divans, were eating ices and smoking their pipes. In the drawing-room, seated at the head of a long table, around which were crowded about twenty players, the host kept bank. He was a most respectable-looking man of about sixty; his head was covered with silvery grey hair, and his full, fresh face expressed good nature; his eyes, enlivened by a perpetual smile, shone brightly. Narumov introduced Hermann to him. Chekalinsky shook his hand warmly, requested him not to stand on ceremony, and went on dealing.

The game lasted a long time. More than thirty cards lay on the table. Chekalinsky paused after each round in order to give the players time to arrange their cards, wrote down their losses, listened politely to their demands, and more politely still allowed them to retract any stake accidentally left on the table. At last the game finished. Chekalinsky shuffled the cards and prepared to deal again.

"Allow me to place a stake," Hermann said, stretching out his hand from behind a fat gentleman who was punting[9] there.

---

8. Wait! (French). Attendants at the gaming table called *Attendez* to indicate the end of the period to place bets.   9. Betting against the dealer.

Chekalinsky smiled and nodded silently, as a sign of his consent. Narumov laughingly congratulated Hermann on forswearing a longstanding principle and wished him a lucky beginning.

"I've staked," Hermann said, as he chalked up the amount, which was very considerable, on the back of his card.

"How much is it?" asked the banker, screwing up his eyes. "Forgive me, but I can't make it out."

"47,000 roubles," Hermann replied.

At these words every head in the room turned, and all eyes were fixed on Hermann.

"He's gone out of his mind!" Narumov thought.

"Allow me to observe to you," Chekalinsky said with his invariable smile, "that your stake is extremely high: nobody here has ever put more than 275 roubles on any single card."

"What of it?" retorted Hermann. "Do you take me or not?"

Chekalinsky, bowing, humbly accepted the stake.

"However, I would like to say," he said, "that, being judged worthy of the confidence of my friends, I can only bank against ready money. For my own part, of course, I am sure that your word is enough, but for the sake of the order of the game and of the accounts, I must ask you to place your money on the card."

Hermann drew a banknote from his pocket and handed it to Chekalinsky who, giving it a cursory glance, put it on Hermann's card.

He began to deal. On the right a nine turned up, on the left a three.[1]

"The three wins," said Hermann, showing his card.

A murmur arose among the players. Chekalinsky frowned, but instantly the smile returned to his face.

"Do you wish to take the money now?" he asked Hermann.

"If you would be so kind."

Chekalinsky drew a number of banknotes from his pocket and settled up immediately. Hermann took up his money and left the table. Narumov was too astounded even to think. Hermann drank a glass of lemonade and went home.

The next evening he again appeared at Chekalinsky's. The host was dealing. Hermann walked up to the table; the players already there immediately gave way to him. Chekalinsky bowed graciously.

Hermann waited for the next deal, took a card and placed on it his 47,000 roubles together with the winnings of the previous evening.

Chekalinsky began to deal. A knave turned up on the right, a seven on the left.

Hermann showed his seven.

There was a general cry of surprise, and Chekalinsky was clearly disconcerted. He counted out 94,000 roubles and handed them to Hermann, who pocketed them coolly and immediately withdrew.

The following evening Hermann again appeared at the table. Everyone was expecting him; the generals and privy councillors abandoned their

---

1. Bets in faro are made on the positions of cards. A player selects a card and places it facedown in front of him or her; if the card turns up on the dealer's left, the player wins; if on the right, the dealer wins.

whist in order to watch such unusual play. The young officers jumped up from their divans; all the waiters gathered in the drawing-room. Hermann was surrounded by a crowd of people. The other players held back their cards, impatient to see how Hermann would get on. Hermann stood at the table and prepared to play alone against the pale but still smiling Chekalinsky. Each unsealed a pack of cards. Chekalinsky shuffled. Hermann drew and placed his card, covering it with a heap of banknotes. It was like a duel. A deep silence reigned all around.

His hands shaking, Chekalinsky began to deal. On the right lay a queen, on the left an ace.

"The ace wins," said Hermann and showed his card.

"Your queen has lost," Chekalinsky said kindly.

Hermann started: indeed, instead of an ace, before him lay the queen of spades. He could not believe his eyes, could not understand how he could have slipped up.

At that moment it seemed to him that the queen of spades winked at him and smiled. He was struck by an unusual likeness . . .

"The old woman!" he shouted in terror.

Chekalinsky gathered up his winnings. Hermann stood motionless. When he left the table, people began to converse noisily.

"Famously punted!" the players said.

Chekalinsky shuffled the cards afresh; play went on as usual.

CONCLUSION

Hermann went mad. He is now installed in Room 17 at the Obukhov Hospital; he answers no questions, but merely mutters with unusual rapidity: "Three, seven, ace! Three, seven, queen!"

Lisaveta Ivanovna has married a very agreeable young man, who has a good position in the service somewhere; he is the son of the former steward of the old Countess. Lisaveta Ivanovna is bringing up a poor relative.

Tomsky has been promoted to the rank of Captain, and is going to marry Princess Polina.

VICTOR HUGO
1802–1885

Combining a vivid sense of the value of the concrete particular with his period's faith in the transformative force of imagination, Victor Hugo was fully aware of his role as his generation's most powerful representative of French Romanticism. Born in Besançon, to parents at odds with each other in politics as in other respects (his mother was a royalist, his father a Napoleonic army officer), the child moved with his family to Paris at the age of two. He began in early adolescence to write poetry and verse tragedies, and he then defined his literary purpose: "I want to be Chateaubriand or nothing." By the time he was twenty, he had received a royal pension as a reward for a book of poetry. He continued to write in virtually every available genre: poetry, literary criticism, essays on religion and on politics, novels (best known among them, at least to American audiences, *Les Misérables* and *The*

Hunchback of Notre Dame). Over some of these genres, he indeed exercised transformative power: his preface to *Cromwell* (1827) provided a manifesto for a new Romantic drama; three years later *Hernani* provoked battles on opening night between "classicists" and "Romantics."

Hugo felt different kinds of political allegiance at different times of his life. His father had taught him to admire Napoléon as a hero; he later became a royalist and was made a peer in 1845. On the other hand, after the 1848 revolution he was elected to the Constitutional Assembly. In 1851, however, after President Louis Napoléon seized power, Hugo, believing his life to be in danger, exiled himself to the British island of Guernsey in the English Channel, where he wrote voluminously for the next twenty years. Returning to Paris in 1871, he spent most of his time there for the rest of his life, increasingly honored as a national figure, finally buried in the Pantheon after a splendid state funeral.

The poetry here printed, including pieces as diverse as the lyrical *Reverie* and the epic *Et nox facta est*, conveys some sense of Hugo's enormous range of subject and of feeling. He writes in the role of poet (*Reverie*), begging for enlivening force in the landscape, demonstrating his own imaginative energy in the act of conjuring up on the page images that might inspire him in the world outside; or he writes as grieving father, poignantly evoking the psychic desolation that prevents him from responding to natural beauty; or as helpless onlooker to the human misery caused by the arbitrary destructiveness of a despot. He imagines the emotion of a Satan (*Et nox facta est*) as he imagines the human meaning of an old man sowing grain (*Sowing Season. Evening*). He can conjure for the reader both the exact color of woods in autumn and the relation between that color and the movement toward winter's bleakness: "You might say in these days of autumn's decline / The sun and rain turned the forest to rust." With equal precision and clarity, he evokes the "boxwood spinning-top" in a dead child's pocket and the gesture of a grandmother bending to remove the corpse's stockings.

Most obviously ambitious of the pieces in this selection is the study of Satan's fall, which exemplifies Hugo's psychological acuity as well as his imaginative involvement with the figure of a supernatural rebel. If Milton was, as Blake maintained, a true poet and hence of the devil's party without knowing it, Hugo obviously knows quite well what it means to take the devil's side. He does not do so in any simple way: he evokes the full horror of Satan as God's defier, "Opening his atrocious wing far from the heavens, / This bat flying from his eternal prison!" But if he makes us feel the terror and the ugliness of Satan's nay-saying, he also suggests the splendor of that refusal. The last star, the star on which Satan blows in a vain effort to prevent its expiration, becomes a kind of image for Satan himself, as it "refused to die without insulting the night," spitting out lava and sulfur. Like God's Word, Satan's word has creative potential—dark potential, to be sure, but still, a power of making. "Death!" he cries: "Later this word was man and was named Cain."

Hugo generates excitement in his verse—the excitement of narrative, or that of imagery, or the thrill of his imaginative intensity. Precisely as he had hoped to do, he led France—indeed, all Europe—toward richer and fuller commitment to the values of Romanticism.

Hugo's long life has attracted considerable biographical attention. Of special interest are Matthew Josephson, *Victor Hugo, a Realistic Biography* (1942), and André Maurois, *Victor Hugo and His World* (translated by Oliver Bernard, 1966). Other useful studies include John P. Houston, *Victor Hugo* (1975); Joanna Richardson, *Victor Hugo* (1976); W. N. Greenberg, *The Power of Rhetoric: Hugo's Metaphor and Poetics* (1985); J. P. Houston, *Victor Hugo* (1988), a general critical and biographical introduction; Suzanne Guerlac, *The Impersonal Sublime* (1990); and Harold Bloom, ed., *Victor Hugo* (1988), a collection of essays.

Reverie[1]

Lo giorno se n' andava, e l'aer bruno
Toglieva gli animai che sono 'n terra,
Dalle fatiche loro.[2]

DANTE

Oh, leave me! It's time for the horizon to
Hide in smoke a rough forehead under a circle of mist,
Time for the giant star[3] to grow red and fade away.
Alone the great yellowing wood makes gold the hill:
You might say in these days of autumn's decline   5
The sun and rain turned the forest to rust.

Oh! Who will suddenly bring to life,
Appearing over there—while I alone dream at the window
And the shadow darkens in the corridor deep—
Some Moorish village, in its dazzle unique   10
Like the rocket splayed out in a sheaf
Piercing this fog with arrows of gold.

Oh spirits, let it come to inspire and to quicken,
My songs darkened again like an autumn sky,
Its magic reflection cast in my eyes,   15
Lengthily, subsiding in stifled sounds,
Notching the thousand towers of its fairy palaces
In the horizon of violet, in haze and in mist.

Tomorrow, At Daybreak[1]

Tomorrow, at daybreak, when the countryside whitens
I shall set out. You wait for me, I know.
I shall go through the forest, shall go by the mountain:
I cannot stay far from you any more.

I shall walk, eyes fixed upon my thoughts,   5
Seeing nothing outside me, hearing no sound,
Alone, unrecognized, my back bent, hands clasped,
Sorrowing, and day for me will be as night.

I shall not look on the gold of evening falling
Nor on the sails descending distant towards Harfleur,[2] 10
And when I come, shall lay upon your grave
A bouquet of green holly and of flowering briar.[3]

Memory of the Night of the Fourth[1]

The child had been struck by two bullets in the head.
The dwelling was clean and modest, peaceful and good.

1. All selections translated by Mary Ann Caws.   2. "The light was departing. The brown air drew
down / all the earth's creatures, calling them to rest / from their day-roving" (*Inferno* II.1–3), the end of
Dante's first day in Hell.   3. The sun.   1. Written on September 4, 1847, the fourth anniversary of
the death by drowning of Hugo's beloved daughter Léopoldine.   2. City near the north coast of France,
where Léopoldine was buried.   3. Evergreen plants (symbols of immortality), one growing in the woods
and the other in the mountains.   1. On December 4, 1851, soldiers of Louis Napoléon Bonaparte (who
had overthrown the French Republic two days before) marched through Paris shooting at will to discourage any opposition from the populace.

Above a picture, a blessed branch,[2] and in the room
An old grandmother—weeping.
We undressed him in silence. His pale mouth open.   5
Death was clouding over his vivid eye
His arms hanging down seemed a cry for help.
In his pocket, a boxwood spinning-top.
You could have put your fingers in the slash of his wounds.
Have you ever seen blackberries bleeding in the hedges?   10
His skull was split open like a log.
The old woman watched them undress him.
Saying: "How white he is! bring the lamp closer.
Oh God! How his poor hair sticks to his forehead!"
And when it was over, took him on her knees.   15
The night was mournful; you could hear shots
In the street where others were being killed.
"We have to bury the child," some of us said.
And we took a white sheet from the walnut chest.
Then the grandmother carried him to the hearth   20
As if to warm his stiffened limbs.
Alas! what death touches with its cold hands
Can no longer be warmed at the hearths of this world.
She bent her head over and removed his stockings
And her old hands clasped the dead child's feet.   25
"Isn't this enough to break your heart,"
She cried. "Sir, he was scarcely eight!
His teachers—for he went to school—were pleased with him.
If I had a letter to send, Sir,
It was he who wrote it. Are they going   30
To start killing children now? Oh then
They are really villains! Look,
This morning he was playing right here by the window!
Can you imagine their killing my little one, can you?
Just walking in the street, and they shot at him.   35
He was gentle and kind, Sir, just like little Jesus.
As for me, I'm old and it would be easy for me to go;
How could it have hurt Mr. Bonaparte
To have killed me instead of my child!"
She stopped speaking, sobs stifling her,   40
Then said, and everyone was weeping around her:
"What will become of me now I'm all alone?
Why don't you tell me that?
Alas! I had nothing else left from his mother.
Why did they kill him! Someone has to explain.   45
The child didn't shout 'Long live the Republic!'"
We kept quiet, standing there solemn, hats off,
Trembling before this inconsolable grief.
Ah mother, you don't understand politics.
Monsieur Napoleon, that's his real name,[3]   50
Is poor and a prince; loves palaces;
Likes to have horses, valets, money

---

2. A palm branch hung above a religious picture.   3. Louis Napoléon rose to power by emphasizing his relationship to Emperor Napoléon I (the "great" Napoléon). He crowned himself Napoléon III and did not wish to be called by the family name of Bonaparte.

For his gaming, his table, his bedroom,
His hunts, and he maintains
Family, church and society,   55
He wants Saint-Cloud,[4] rose-carpeted in summer,
So prefects and mayors can respect him.
That's why it has to be this way: old grandmothers
With their poor gray fingers shaking with age
Must sew in winding-sheets children of seven.   60

Et nox facta est[1]

I

He[2] had been falling in the abyss some four thousand years.

Never had he yet managed to grasp a peak,
Nor lift even once his towering forehead.
He sank deeper in the dark and the mist, aghast,
Alone, and behind him, in the eternal nights,   5
His wing feathers fell more slowly still.
He fell dumbfounded, grim, and silent,
Sad, his mouth open and his feet towards the heavens,
The horror of the chasm imprinted on his livid face.
He cried: "Death!" his fists stretched out in the empty dark.   10
Later this word was man and was named Cain.[3]

He was falling. A rock struck his hand quite suddenly;
He held on to it, as a dead man holds on to his tomb,
And stopped. Someone, from on high, cried out to him: "Fall!
The suns will go out around you, accursed!"   15
And the voice was lost in the immensity of horror.
And pale, he looked toward the eternal dawn.
The suns were far off, but shone still.
Satan raised his head and spoke, his arms in the air:
"You lie!" This word was later the soul of Judas.[4]   20

Like the gods of bronze erect upon their pilasters,
He waited a thousand years, eyes fixed upon the stars.
The suns were far off, but were still shining.
The thunder then rumbled in the skies unhearing, cold.
Satan laughed, and spat towards the thunder.   25
Filled by the visionary shadow, the immensity
Shivered. This spitting out was later Barabbas.[5]

A passing breath made him fall lower still.

II

The fall of the damned one began once again. — Terrible,
Somber, and pierced with holes luminous as a sieve,   30

---

4. The summer residence of French rulers.   **1.** Written as part of *The End of Satan,* an epic poem never completed. The Latin title ("And There Was Night") suggests the biblical "And there was light" (Genesis 1:3).   **2.** Satan, formerly the rebellious Archangel Lucifer, thrown out of Heaven by God (Revelation 12:7–9 and Isaiah 14:12).   **3.** The first murderer, son of Adam and brother of Abel, the victim (Genesis 4:1–15).   **4.** Judas Iscariot, the apostle who betrayed Jesus (Matthew 26:47–50, 27:3–5).   **5.** The condemned criminal who was freed instead of Jesus (Mark 15:6–15).

The sky full of suns withdrew, brightness
Trembled, and in the night the great fallen one,
Naked, sinister, and pulled by the weight of his crime,
Fell, and his head wedging the abyss apart.
Lower! Lower, and still lower! Everything presently   35
Fled from him; no obstacle to seize in passing,
No mountain, no crumbling rock, no stone,
Nothing, shadow! and from fright he closed his eyes.

And when they opened, three suns only
Shone, and shadow had eaten away the firmament.   40
All the other suns had perished.

III

A rock
Emerged from blackest mist like some arm approaching.
He grasped it, and his feet touched summits.

Then the dreadful being called Never
Dreamed. His forehead sank between his guilty hands.   45
The three suns, far off, like three great eyes,
Watched him, and he watched them not.
Space resembled our earthly plains,
At evening, when the horizon sinking, retreating,
Blackens under the white eyes of the ghostly twilight.   50
Long rays entwined the feet of the great exile.
Behind him his shadow filled the infinite.
The peaks of chaos mingled in themselves.
In an instant he felt some horrendous growth of wings;
He felt himself become a monster, and that the angel in him 55
Was dying, and the rebel then knew regret.
He felt his shoulder, so bright before,
Quiver in the hideous cold of membraned wing,
And folding his arms with his head lifted high,
This bandit, as if grown greater through affront,   60
Alone in these depths that only ruin inhabits,
Looked steadily at the shadow's cave.
The noiseless darkness grew in the nothingness.
Obscure opacity closed off the gaping sky;
And making beyond the last promontory   65
A triple crack in the black pane,
The three suns mingled their three lights.
You would have thought them three wheels of a chariot of fire,
Broken after some battle in the high firmament.
Like prows, the mountains from the mist emerged.   70
"So," cried Satan, "so be it! still I can see!
He shall have the blue sky, the black sky is mine.
Does he think I will come weeping to his door?
I hate him. Three suns suffice. What do I care?
I hate the day, the blueness, fragrance and the light."   75

Suddenly he shivered; there remained only one.

IV

The abyss was fading. Nothing kept its shape.
Darkness seemed to swell its giant wave.
Something nameless and submerged, something
That is no longer, takes its leave, falls silent; 80
And no one could have said, in this deep horror,
If this frightful remnant of a mystery or a world,
Like the vague mist where the dream takes flight,
Was called shipwreck or was called night;
And the archangel felt himself become a phantom. 85
He shouted: "Hell!" This word later made Sodom.[6]

And the voice repeated slowly on his forehead:
"Accursed! all about you the stars will go dark."

And already the sun was only a star.

V

And all disappeared slowly under a veil. 90
Then the archangel quaked; Satan learned to shiver.
Toward the star trembling livid on the horizon
He hurled himself, leaping from peak to peak.
Then, although with horror at the wings of a beast,
Although it was the clothing of emprisonment, 95
Like a bird going from bush to bush,
Horrendous he took his flight from mount to mount,
And this convict began running in his cell.

He ran, he flew, he shouted: "Star of gold! Brother![7]
Wait for me! I'm running! Don't go out yet! 100
Don't leave me alone!"

           Thus the monster
Crossed the first lakes of the dead immensity,
Former chaos, emptied and already stagnant,
And into the lugubrious depths he plunged.

Now the star was only a spark. 105

He went down further in universal shadow,
Sank further, cast himself wallowing in the night,
Climbed the filthy mountains, their damp gleaming front,
Whose base is unsteady in the cesspool deeps,
And trembling stared before him.

           The spark 110
Was only a red dot in the depth of the dark abyss.

VI

As between two battlements the archer leans
On the wall, when twilight has reached his keep,
Wild he leaned from the mountain top,

---

6. Biblical city, with Gomorrah a symbol of corruption and decadence. Both were destroyed by God (Genesis 18:20–19:28).   7. Lucifer means "Light Bearer."

And upon the star, hoping to arouse its flame,   115
He started to blow as upon some ember.
And anguish caused his fierce nostrils to swell.
The breath rushing from his chest
Is now upon earth and called hurricane.

With his breath a great noise stirred the shadow, an ocean   120
No being dwells in and no fires illumine.
The mountains found nearby took their flight,
The monstrous chaos full of fright arose
And began to shriek: Jehovah Jehovah!
The infinite opened, rent apart like a cloth,   125
But nothing moved in the lugubrious star;
And the damned one, crying: "Don't go out yet! I'll go on!
I'll get there!" resumed again his desperate flight.
And the glaciers mingled with the nights resembling them
Turned on their backs like frightened beasts,   130
And the black tornadoes and the hideous chasms
Bent in terror, while above them,
Flying toward the star like some arrow to the goal,
There passed, wild and haggard, this terrible supplicant.

And ever since it has seen this frightening flight,   135
This bitter abyss, aghast like a fleeing man
Retains forever the horror and the craze,
So monstrous was it to see, in the shadow immense,
Opening his atrocious wing far from the heavens,
This bat flying from his eternal prison!   140

VII

He flew for ten thousand years.

For ten thousand years,
Stretching forth his livid neck and his frenzied hands,
He flew without finding a peak on which to rest.
The star seemed sometimes to fade and to go out,   145
And the horror of the tomb caused the angel to shiver;
Then a pale brightness, vague, strange, uncertain,
Reappeared: and in joy, he cried: "Onward!"
Around him hovered the north wind birds.
He was flying. The infinite never ceases to start again.   150
His flight circled immense in that sea.
The night watched his horrible talons fleeing.
As a cloud feels its whirlwinds fall,
He felt his strength crumble in the chasm.
The winter murmured: tremble! and the shadow said: suffer!   155

Finally he perceived a black peak far off
Which a fearsome reflection in the shadow inflamed.
Satan, like a swimmer in his effort supreme,
Stretched out his wing, with claws and bald, and specter-pale,
Panting, broken, tired, and smoking with sweat,   160
He sank down on the edge of the abrupt descent.[8]

8. Literally, escarpment, the steep wall before a fortification or cliff.

VIII

There was the sun dying in the abyss.
The star, in the deepest fog had no air to revive it,
Grew cold, dim, and was slowly destroyed.
Its sinister round was seen in the night;   165
And in this somber silence its fiery ulcers were seen
Subsiding under a leprosy of dark.
Coal of a world put out! torch blown out by God!
Its crevices still showed a trace of fire,
As if the soul could be seen through holes in the skull.   170
At the center there quivered and flickered a flame
Now and then licking the outermost edge,
And from each crater flashes came
Shivering like flaming swords,
And fading noiselessly as dreams.   175
The star was almost black. The archangel was tired
Beyond voice or breath, a pity to see.
And the star in death throes under his savage glance,
Was dying, doing battle. With its somber apertures
Into the cold darkness it spewed now and again   180
Burning streams, crimson lumps, and smoking hills,
Rocks foaming with initial brightness:
As if this giant of life and light
Engulfed by the mist where all is fading,
Had refused to die without insulting the night   185
And spitting its lava in the shadow's face.
About it time and space and number,
Form, and noise expired, making
The forbidding and black oneness of void.
Then the specter Nothing[9] raised its head from the abyss.   190

Suddenly, from the heart of the star, a jet of sulphur
Sharp, clamorous like one dying in delirium,
Burst sudden, shining, splendid with surprise,
And lighting from far a thousand deathly forms,
Massive, pierced to the shadow's depths   195
The monstrous porches of endless deep.
Night and immensity formed
Their angels. Satan, wild and out of breath,
His vision dazzled and full of this flashing,
Beat with his wing, opened his hands and then shivered   200
And cried: "Despair! see it growing pale!"

The archangel understood, as does the mast in its sinking,
That he was the drowned man of the shadows' flood;
He furled once more his wing with its granite nails,
And wrung his hands. And the star went out.   205

IX

Now, near the skies, at chasm's edge where nothing changes,
One feather escaped from the archangel's wing

9. Satan.

Remained and quivered, pure and white.
The angel on whose forehead the dazzling dawn is born
Saw and grasped it, observing the sublime sky: 210
"Lord, must it too fall into the abyss?"
God turned about, absorbed in being and in Life,
And said "Do not discard what has not fallen."[1]

                    ✳   ✳   ✳

    Black caves of the past, porches of time passed
With no date and no radiance, somber, unmeasured,   215
Cycles previous to man, chaos, heavens,
World terrible and rich in prodigious beings,
Oh fearful fog where the preadamites
Appeared, standing in limitless shadow.
Who could fathom you, oh chasms, oh unknown times.   220
The thinker barefoot like the poor,
Through respect for the One unseen, the sage,
Digs in the depths of origin and age,
Fathoms and seeks beyond the colossi,[2] further
Than the facts witnessed by the present sky,   225
Reaches with pale visage suspected things,
And finds, lifting the darkness of years
And the layers of days, worlds, voids,
Gigantic centuries dead beneath giants of centuries.
And thus the wise man dreams in the deep of the night   230
His face illumined by glints of the abyss.

Sowing Season. Evening

            It is the moment of twilight.
            Seated under a portal, I admire
            This end of day illuminating
            The last hours of labor.

            In the fields bathed by night,   5
            Deeply moved, I gaze on the rags
            Of an old man scattering fistfuls
            Of future harvest in the furrows.

            Tall, his dark silhouette
            Towers above the deep ploughing.   10
            The fruitfulness of fleeing days
            Forms visibly his belief.

            He walks along the endless plain,
            Going, coming, casting seeds afar,
            Opens his hand once more and begins afresh,   15
            And, a hidden witness, I meditate

---

1. In the second part of *The End of Satan*, "Satan's Feather," the feather is brought to life by a divine glance and becomes the female spirit Liberty. She wins God's permission to plunge into Hell in an attempt to redeem her father (Part III), and in Part IV the repentant Archangel is released and recreated as Lucifer.   2. Giants of preadamic time.

> While unfolding its veils
> The shadow where sound mixes in
> Seems to stretch up to the very stars
> The august gesture of his sowing.   20

ALFRED, LORD TENNYSON
1809–1892

Tennyson's poetry expresses a conflict—characteristic of his historical period but also of human experience generally—between the tendency to despair and the desire to hope. Hope locates itself, for Tennyson, in the human capacity to struggle toward future goals as well as, on occasion, in religious faith. Mortality causes despair: the death of others, the inevitable sense of increasing weakness as one ages, the scientific discovery that whole species have disappeared in the world's history. It is Tennyson's ability to remind us of both contradictory emotions, and of the degree to which they inevitably coexist and alternate, that makes his poetry compelling.

The poet's pervasive melancholy came partly from experience. Son of an Anglican clergyman, he spent four unhappy years in school before his father consented to allow him to be tutored at home. He attended Trinity College, Cambridge, where, with his friend Arthur Hallam, he belonged to an undergraduate society called The Apostles, whose members discussed contemporary social, religious, scientific, and literary issues. The friendship with Hallam retained its intensity after his undergraduate years; by 1830, Hallam had become engaged to Tennyson's sister. Three years later, however, at the age of twenty-two, Hallam died suddenly in Vienna. The loss acutely affected Tennyson, who during the next seventeen years gradually composed the long elegiac poem *In Memoriam* to record the profound emotional and intellectual effects on him of his friend's death.

In 1836, Tennyson became engaged to Emily Sellwood, but largely because of financial difficulties, he did not marry her until 1850, the year in which, after the publication of *In Memoriam*, he was made poet laureate. Five years earlier, he had received a pension. He lived quietly for the rest of his life, increasingly famous; in 1884, he was created first Baron Tennyson.

Tennyson's earliest independent collections of poems (1830 and 1833; he had published a collaborative volume with his brother in 1827) were the target of fierce critical attack, another cause for melancholy. He published nothing more until 1842, when a collection called simply *Poems* met great critical success. Subsequently revered as a kind of national spokesman, Tennyson won popularity particularly with *The Princess* (1847, revised 1855), *Maud* (1855), and *The Idylls of the King* (1859, 1885), a retelling of the legends of King Arthur.

In *Ulysses* (1842), Tennyson, imagining the situation of the Greek hero after his return to domestic peace, evokes the excitement and moral grandeur of the human capacity for aspiration.

> that which we are, we are;
> One equal temper of heroic hearts,
> Made weak by time and fate, but strong in will
> To strive, to seek, to find, and not to yield.

In another meditation on classic themes, *Tithonus* (published in 1860, written in 1833), he puts the other side of the case. "The woods decay, the woods decay and fall," the poem begins; its imagined speaker, a man who has been granted immortality at his own request, wishes to return the gift. "Why should a man desire in any way / To vary from the kindly race of men . . . ?" Ulysses insists on the specialness of his sort of man; Tithonus knows the burden of specialness. In conjunction, the two poems call attention to the fact that neither the Enlightenment nor the early Romantic view of experience seems entirely adequate to this poet. Tithonus's desire to share the common fate of humankind throbs with melancholy; he feels that fate as doom, although he equally experiences his exemption from it as doom. Ulysses' condescension to his prudent son ("Most blameless is he. . . . / He works his work, I mine") underlines the sense of desperation in his insistent striving. No alternative form of action or commitment satisfies the imagination.

In Memoriam (1850), Tennyson's most ambitious work, suggests reasons for the poet's inability to imagine fulfillment. The problem is not merely temperament, but the impact on his consciousness of intellectual and social actuality as well as the loss and the possibility of loss made palpable to him by Hallam's death.

> Are God and Nature then at strife,
>   That Nature lends such evil dreams?
>   So careful of the type she seems,
> So careless of the single life.

That stanza comes from number 55 of the 125 linked poems that make up the whole. The next in the series begins,

> "So careful of the type?" but no, . . .
>   She [Nature] cries, "A thousand types are gone;
>   I care for nothing, all shall go."

Reality offers not the slightest assurance of survival; contemporary scientists, studying fossils, had revealed the extinction of entire species. "Man, [Nature's] last work, who seemed so fair, / Such splendid purpose in his eyes"—with a Ulysses' capacity for fine imaginings—even man, humankind in general, may face extinction—a possibility that today looks ever more compelling. The poem concludes with the faintest possible religious hope:

> O life as futile, then, as frail!
>   O for thy voice to soothe and bless!
>   What hope of answer, or redress?
> Behind the veil, behind the veil.

By the end of the entire sequence, the poet has arrived at a more affirmative vision; he claims to have discovered God through his own pain and through the processes of feeling, which he asserts as more revelatory than those of logic. Indeed, *In Memoriam* persuasively evokes the slow reconciliation of mourning, giving its readers vicarious experience of the despair, the false starts, the inconsistencies of grief. The poem's power, however, derives not only from its record of personal emotional experience but from its demonstration, its embodiment, of how the intellectual and the emotional intertwine. The private loss of a friend assimilates itself to a more general loss of faith and certainty characteristic of the Victorian period. The determination to strive, to seek, to find, and not to yield generated scientific discovery, industrial and mercantile development. As early as 1850, though, such achievements threatened established social and theological orders. Tennyson re-creates for us what such threats felt like to those actually experiencing them. He writes an elegy not only for Arthur Hallam but for the larger losses of his moment in history.

For useful biography, see H. Nicholson, *Tennyson* (1925). Important criticism includes J. Buckley, *Tennyson: The Growth of a Poet* (1961); C. Ricks, *Tennyson* (1972); M. Shaw, *Alfred, Lord Tennyson* (1988); H. F. Tucker, *Tennyson and the Doom of Romanticism* (1988); and H. Tucker, ed., *Critical Essays on Alfred, Lord Tennyson* (1993).

Ulysses

It little profits that an idle king,
By this still hearth, among these barren crags,
Matched with an agèd wife, I mete and dole
Unequal laws unto a savage race,
That hoard, and sleep, and feed, and know not me.   5
      I cannot rest from travel; I will drink
Life to the lees. All times I have enjoyed
Greatly, have suffered greatly, both with those
That loved me, and alone; on shore, and when
Through scudding drifts the rainy Hyades[1]   10
Vexed the dim sea. I am become a name;
For always roaming with a hungry heart
Much have I seen and known, — cities of men
And manners, climates, councils, governments,
Myself not least, but honored of them all, —   15
And drunk delight of battle with my peers,
Far on the ringing plains of windy Troy.
I am a part of all that I have met;
Yet all experience is an arch where-through
Gleams that untravelled world whose margin fades   20
Forever and forever when I move.
How dull it is to pause, to make an end,
To rust unburnished, not to shine in use!
As though to breathe were life! Life piled on life
Were all too little, and of one to me   25
Little remains; but every hour is saved
From that eternal silence, something more,
A bringer of new things; and vile it were
For some three suns to store and hoard myself,
And this gray spirit yearning in desire   30
To follow knowledge like a sinking star,
Beyond the utmost bound of human thought.
      This is my son, mine own Telemachus,
To whom I leave the scepter and the isle[2] —
Well-loved of me, discerning to fulfill   35
This labor, by slow prudence to make mild
A rugged people, and through soft degrees
Subdue them to the useful and the good.
Most blameless is he, centered in the sphere
Of common duties, decent not to fail   40
In offices of tenderness, and pay

---

1. A cluster of seven stars in the constellation of Taurus. The ancients supposed that when Hyades rose with the sun, rainy weather would follow.   2. Ithaca.

Meet adoration to my household gods,
When I am gone. He works his work, I mine.
　There lies the port; the vessel puffs her sail;
There gloom the dark, broad seas. My mariners,   45
Souls that have toiled, and wrought, and thought with me—
That ever with a frolic welcome took
The thunder and the sunshine, and opposed
Free hearts, free foreheads—you and I are old;
Old age hath yet his honor and his toil;   50
Death closes all. But something ere the end,
Some work of noble note, may yet be done,
Not unbecoming men that strove with gods.
The lights begin to twinkle from the rocks;
The long day wanes; the slow moon climbs; the deep   55
Moans round with many voices. Come, my friends,
'Tis not too late to seek a newer world.
Push off, and sitting well in order smite
The sounding furrows; for my purpose holds
To sail beyond the sunset, and the baths   60
Of all the western stars, until I die.
It may be that the gulfs will wash us down;
It may be we shall touch the Happy Isles,[3]
And see the great Achilles,[4] whom we knew.
Though much is taken, much abides; and though   65
We are not now that strength which in old days
Moved earth and heaven, that which we are, we are;
One equal temper of heroic hearts,
Made weak by time and fate, but strong in will
To strive, to seek, to find, and not to yield.   70

Tithonus[1]

　The woods decay, the woods decay and fall,
The vapors weep their burthen to the ground,
Man comes and tills the field and lies beneath,
And after many a summer dies the swan.
Me only cruel immortality[2]   5
Consumes; I wither slowly in thine arms,
Here at the quiet limit of the world,
A white-haired shadow roaming like a dream
The ever-silent spaces of the East,
Far-folded mists, and gleaming halls of morn.   10
　Alas! for this gray shadow, once a man—
So glorious in his beauty and thy choice,
Who madest him thy chosen, that he seemed
To his great heart none other than a God!
I asked thee, "Give me immortality."   15
Then didst thou grant mine asking with a smile,
Like wealthy men who care not how they give.

---

3. In Greek myth, the abode of the warriors after death.   **4.** Comrade-in-arms of Ulysses at Troy.
1. A prince of Troy loved by Aurora, goddess of dawn, in whose palace he is depicted as living.   **2.** Aurora obtained for Tithonus from Zeus the gift of immortality but not of eternal youth.

But thy strong Hours[3] indignant worked their wills,
And beat me down and marred and wasted me,
And though they could not end me, left me maimed   20
To dwell in presence of immortal youth,
Immortal age beside immortal youth,
And all I was in ashes. Can thy love,
Thy beauty, make amends, though even now,
Close over us, the silver star,[4] thy guide,   25
Shines in those tremulous eyes that fill with tears
To hear me? Let me go; take back thy gift.
Why should a man desire in any way
To vary from the kindly race of men,
Or pass beyond the goal of ordinance   30
Where all should pause, as is most meet[5] for all?
     A soft air fans the cloud apart; there comes
A glimpse of that dark world where I was born.
Once more the old mysterious glimmer steals
From thy pure brows, and from thy shoulders pure,   35
And bosom beating with a heart renewed.
Thy cheek begins to redden through the gloom,
Thy sweet eyes brighten slowly close to mine,
Ere yet they blind the stars, and the wild team[6]
Which love thee, yearning for thy yoke, arise,   40
And shake the darkness from their loosened manes,
And beat the twilight into flakes of fire.
     Lo! ever thus thou growest beautiful
In silence, then before thine answer given
Departest, and thy tears are on my cheek.   45
     Why wilt thou ever scare me with thy tears,
And make me tremble lest a saying learnt,
In days far-off, on that dark earth, be true?
"The Gods themselves cannot recall their gifts."
     Ay me! ay me! with what another heart   50
In days far-off, and with what other eyes
I used to watch—if I be he that watched—
The lucid outline forming round thee; saw
The dim curls kindle into sunny rings;
Changed with thy mystic change, and felt my blood   55
Glow with the glow that slowly crimsoned all
Thy presence and thy portals, while I lay,
Mouth, forehead, eyelids, growing dewy-warm
With kisses balmier than half-opening buds
Of April, and could hear the lips that kissed   60
Whispering I knew not what of wild and sweet,
Like that strange song I heard Apollo[7] sing,
While Ilion like a mist rose into towers.[8]
     Yet hold me not forever in thine East;
How can my nature longer mix with thine?   65
Coldly thy rosy shadows bathe me, cold

---

3. Or Horae, goddesses of the seasons and of growth and decay.   **4.** The morning star that precedes
the dawn.   **5.** Suitable.   **6.** Of supernatural horses; they draw Aurora's chariot into the sky at dawn.
7. God of music and patron of Troy.   **8.** According to legend, the walls of Troy (Ilion) were raised by
the sound of Apollo's song.

Are all thy lights, and cold my wrinkled feet
Upon thy glimmering thresholds, when the steam
Floats up from those dim fields about the homes
Of happy men that have the power to die,   70
And grassy barrows[9] of the happier dead.
Release me, and restore me to the ground.
Thou seest all things, thou wilt see my grave;
Thou wilt renew thy beauty morn by morn,
I earth in earth forget these empty courts,   75
And thee returning on thy silver wheels.

From In Memoriam A. H. H.

Obit. MDCCCXXXIII

[*Prologue*]

Strong Son of God, immortal Love,[1]
    Whom we, that have not seen thy face,
    By faith, and faith alone, embrace,
Believing where we cannot prove;

Thine are these orbs of light and shade;[2]   5
    Thou madest Life in man and brute;
    Thou madest Death; and lo, thy foot
Is on the skull which thou hast made.[3]

Thou wilt not leave us in the dust:
    Thou madest man, he knows not why,   10
    He thinks he was not made to die;
And thou hast made him: thou art just.

Thou seemest human and divine,
    The highest, holiest manhood, thou.
    Our wills are ours, we know not how;   15
Our wills are ours, to make them thine.

Our little systems have their day;
    They have their day and cease to be;[4]
    They are but broken lights of thee,[5]
And thou, O Lord, art more than they.   20

We have but faith: we cannot know,
    For knowledge is of things we see;
    And yet we trust it comes from thee,
A beam in darkness: let it grow.

Let knowledge grow from more to more,   25
    But more of reverence in us dwell;
    That mind and soul, according well,
May make one music as before,

---

9. Burial mounds.   1. 1 John 4:8: "He that loveth not knoweth not God; for God is love." 1 John 4:15: "Whosoever shall confess that Jesus is the Son of God, God dwelleth in him, and he in God."   2. That is, the earth and the planets, part of each of which is sunlit, the rest in shadow.   3. That is, Jesus crushes Death underfoot, a common motif in painting and sculpture.   4. Transient theological and philosophical systems, contrasted with the enduring systems of the stars.   5. Refracted, as by a prism.

But vaster. We are fools and slight;
   We mock thee when we do not fear:
   But help thy foolish ones to bear;
Help thy vain worlds to bear thy light.

Forgive what seemed my sin in me,
   What seemed my worth since I began;
   For merit lives from man to man,
And not from man, O Lord, to thee.

Forgive my grief for one removed,
   Thy creature, whom I found so fair.
   I trust he lives in thee, and there
I find him worthier to be loved.

Forgive these wild and wandering cries,
   Confusions of a wasted[6] youth;
   Forgive them where they fail in truth,
And in thy wisdom make me wise.

1

I held it truth, with him[7] who sings
   To one clear harp in divers[8] tones,
   That men may rise on stepping-stones
Of their dead selves to higher things.

But who shall so forecast the years
   And find in loss a gain to match?
   Or reach a hand through time to catch
The far-off interest of tears?

Let Love clasp Grief lest both be drowned,
   Let darkness keep her raven gloss.
   Ah, sweeter to be drunk with loss,
To dance with Death, to beat the ground,

Than that the victor Hours[9] should scorn
   The long result of love, and boast,
   "Behold the man that loved and lost,
But all he was is overworn."[1]

2

Old yew,[2] which graspest at the stones
   That name the underlying dead,
   Thy fibers net the dreamless head,
Thy roots are wrapped about the bones.

The seasons bring the flower again,
   And bring the firstling[3] to the flock;
   And in the dusk of thee the clock
Beats out the little lives of men.

---

6. Laid waste (by Hallam's loss). 7. Goethe, who in the second part of *Faust* and elsewhere voices his conception of spiritual progress through the outgrowing of one's former selves. 8. Various. 9. Or Horae, goddesses of the seasons and of growth and decay. 1. Worn out, exhausted. 2. Evergreen capable of reaching great age. It is often planted in graveyards as symbol of immortality. 3. Firstborn.

O, not for thee the glow, the bloom,
   Who changest not in any gale,   10
   Nor branding summer suns avail
To touch thy thousand years of gloom;

And gazing on thee, sullen tree,
   Sick for thy stubborn hardihood,
   I seem to fail from out my blood   15
And grow incorporate into thee.

3

O Sorrow, cruel fellowship,
   O Priestess in the vaults of Death,
   O sweet and bitter in a breath,
What whispers from thy lying lip?

"The stars," she whispers, "blindly run;   5
   A web is woven across the sky;
   From out waste places comes a cry,
And murmurs from the dying sun;

"And all the phantom, Nature, stands—
   With all the music in her tone,
   A hollow echo of my own,—   10
A hollow form with empty hands."

And shall I take a thing so blind,
   Embrace her as my natural good;
   Or crush her, like a vice of blood,   15
Upon the threshold of the mind?

*   *   *

5

I sometimes hold it half a sin
   To put in words the grief I feel;
   For words, like Nature, half reveal
And half conceal the Soul within.

But, for the unquiet heart and brain,   5
   A use in measured language lies;
   The sad mechanic exercise,
Like dull narcotics, numbing pain.

In words, like weeds,[4] I'll wrap me o'er,
   Like coarsest clothes against the cold;   10
   But that large grief which these enfold
Is given in outline and no more.

*   *   *

7

Dark house,[5] by which once more I stand
   Here in the long unlovely street,

---

4. Garments (with allusion to mourning garments).   5. The Hallam family residence.

Doors, where my heart was used to beat
So quickly, waiting for a hand,

A hand that can be clasped no more — 5
Behold me, for I cannot sleep,
And like a guilty thing I creep
At earliest morning to the door.

He is not here; but far away
The noise of life begins again, 10
And ghastly through the drizzling rain
On the bald street breaks the blank day.

*   *   *

10

I hear the noise about thy keel;[6]
I hear the bell struck in the night;
I see the cabin-window bright;
I see the sailor at the wheel.

Thou bring'st the sailor to his wife, 5
And traveled men from foreign lands;
And letters unto trembling hands;
And, thy dark freight, a vanished life.

So bring him; we have idle dreams;
This look of quiet flatters thus 10
Our home-bred fancies. O, to us,
The fools of habit, sweeter seems

To rest beneath the clover sod,
That takes the sunshine and the rains,
Or where the kneeling hamlet drains 15
The chalice of the grapes of God;[7]

Than if with thee the roaring wells
Should gulf him fathom-deep in brine,
And hands so often clasped in mine,
Should toss with tangle[8] and with shells. 20

11

Calm is the morn without a sound,
Calm as to suit a calmer grief,
And only through the faded leaf
The chestnut pattering to the ground;[9]

Calm and deep peace on this high wold,[1] 5
And on these dews that drench the furze,
And all the silvery gossamers
That twinkle into green and gold;

6. Of the ship bringing Hallam's body back from Vienna.   7. This stanza mentions alternate modes of burial: in the churchyard or under the chancel where worshipers kneel for the Sacrament.   8. Seaweed.
9. The time is September, when Hallam's body is still en route.   1. Open uplands. That is, Tennyson is at his home in Somersby, Lincolnshire.

Calm and still light on yon great plain
    That sweeps with all its autumn bowers,   10
    And crowded farms and lessening towers,
To mingle with the bounding main;

Calm and deep peace in this wide air,
    These leaves that redden to the fall,
    And in my heart, if calm at all,   15
If any calm, a calm despair;

Calm on the seas, and silver sleep,
    And waves that sway themselves in rest,
    And dead calm in that noble breast
Which heaves but with the heaving deep.   20

      *   *   *

15

Tonight the winds begin to rise
    And roar from yonder dropping day;
    The last red leaf is whirled away,
The rooks[2] are blown about the skies;

The forest cracked, the waters curled,   5
    The cattle huddled on the lea;[3]
    And wildly dashed on tower and tree
The sunbeam strikes along the world:

And but for fancies, which aver
    That all thy motions gently pass   10
    Athwart a plane of molten glass,
I scarce could brook the strain and stir

That makes the barren branches loud;
    And but for fear it is not so,
    The wild unrest that lives in woe   15
Would dote and pore on yonder cloud[4]

That rises upward always higher,
    And onward drags a laboring breast,
    And topples round the dreary west,
A looming bastion fringed with fire.   20

16

What words are these have fall'n from me?
    Can calm despair and wild unrest
    Be tenants of a single breast,
Or Sorrow such a changeling be?

Or doth she only seem to take   5
    The touch of change in calm or storm,
    But knows no more of transient form
In her deep self, than some dead lake

That holds the shadow of a lark
   Hung in the shadow of a heaven?   10
   Or has the shock, so harshly given,
Confused me like the unhappy bark[5]

That strikes by night a craggy shelf,
   And staggers blindly ere she sink?
   And stunned me from my power to think   15
And all my knowledge of myself;

And made me that delirious man
   Whose fancy fuses old and new,
   And flashes into false and true,
And mingles all without a plan?   20

*   *   *

19

The Danube to the Severn[6] gave
   The darkened heart that beat no more;
   They laid him by the pleasant shore,
And in the hearing of the wave.[7]

There twice a day the Severn fills;   5
   The salt sea-water passes by,
   And hushes half the babbling Wye,[8]
And makes a silence in the hills.

The Wye is hushed nor moved along,
   And hushed my deepest grief of all,   10
   When filled with tears that cannot fall,
I brim with sorrow drowning song.

The tide flows down, the wave again
   Is vocal in its wooded walls;
   My deeper anguish also falls,   15
And I can speak a little then.

*   *   *

21

I sing to him that rests below,
   And, since the grasses round me wave,
   I take the grasses of the grave,
And make them pipes[9] whereon to blow.

The traveler hears me now and then,   5
   And sometimes harshly will he speak:
   "This fellow would make weakness weak,
And melt the waxen hearts of men."

Another answers: "Let him be,
   He loves to make parade of pain,   10

---

5. Ship.   6. Vienna, where Hallam died, is on the Danube; the church at Clevedon, Somerset, where he was buried, is on the Severn.   7. Tennyson was not present at the funeral and did not learn until years later that Hallam had been buried in the church, not in the graveyard by the river.   8. The tides reach far up the Bristol Channel into the Severn and the Wye, its tributary.   9. Alluding to the pipes of mourning shepherds in pastoral elegy, the genre to which *In Memoriam* in part belongs.

That with his piping he may gain
The praise that comes to constancy."

A third is wroth:[1] "Is this an hour
    For private sorrow's barren song,
    When more and more the people throng   15
The chairs and thrones of civil power?

"A time to sicken and to swoon,
    When Science reaches forth her arms
    To feel from world to world, and charms
Her secret from the latest moon?"[2]   20

Behold, ye speak an idle thing;
    Ye never knew the sacred dust.
    I do but sing because I must,
And pipe but as the linnets sing;

And one is glad; her note is gay,   25
    For now her little ones have ranged;
    And one is sad; her note is changed,
Because her brood is stolen away.

22

The path by which we twain did go,
    Which led by tracts that pleased us well,
    Through four sweet years arose and fell,
From flower to flower, from snow to snow;

And we with singing cheered the way,   5
    And, crowned with all the season lent,
    From April on to April went,
And glad at heart from May to May.

But where the path we walked began
    To slant the fifth autumnal slope,   10
    As we descended following Hope,
There sat the Shadow feared of man;

Who broke our fair companionship,
    And spread his mantle dark and cold,
    And wrapt thee formless in the fold,   15
And dulled the murmur on thy lip,

And bore thee where I could not see
    Nor follow, though I walk in haste,
    And think that somewhere in the waste[3]
The Shadow sits and waits for me.   20

23

Now, sometimes in my sorrow shut,
    Or breaking into song by fits,
    Alone, alone, to where he sits,
The Shadow cloaked from head to foot,

---

1. Very angry.   2. From 1846 to 1848, astronomers discovered the planet Neptune and its moon, the satellites of Uranus, and the eighth moon of Saturn.   3. Wasteland.

Who keeps the keys of all the creeds,   5
    I wander, often falling lame,
    And looking back to whence I came,
Or on to where the pathway leads;

And crying, How changed from where it ran
    Through lands where not a leaf was dumb,   10
    But all the lavish hills would hum
The murmur of a happy Pan;[4]

When each by turns was guide to each,
    And Fancy light from Fancy caught,
    And Thought leapt out to wed with Thought   15
Ere Thought could wed itself with Speech;

And all we met was fair and good,
    And all was good that Time could bring,
    And all the secret of the Spring
Moved in the chambers of the blood;   20

And many an old philosophy
    On Argive heights divinely sang,
    And round us all the thicket rang
To many a flute of Arcady.[5]

                    *   *   *

                    27

    I envy not in any moods
        The captive void of noble rage,
        The linnet born within the cage,
    That never knew the summer woods;

    I envy not the beast that takes   5
        His license in the field of time,
        Unfettered by the sense of crime,
    To whom a conscience never wakes;

    Nor, what may count itself as blest,
        The heart that never plighted troth[6]   10
        But stagnates in the weeds of sloth;
    Nor any want-begotten rest.[7]

    I hold it true, whate'er befall;
        I feel it, when I sorrow most;
        'Tis better to have loved and lost   15
    Than never to have loved at all.

                    28

    The time draws near the birth of Christ.
    The moon is hid, the night is still;

---

4. God of flocks and shepherds, and hence of pastoral poetry.   5. That is, they were like shepherds on the hills of Greece when what is now "old philosophy" was brand new or on the plains of Arcady (home of pastoral poetry) when pastoral poetry was young.   6. Became engaged to be married.   7. That is, any rest that comes from a lack or deficiency—specifically, from a failure to be fully human, a state that would entail vulnerability.

The Christmas bells from hill to hill
Answer each other in the mist.

Four voices of four hamlets round,   5
  From far and near, on mead and moor,
  Swell out and fail, as if a door
Were shut between me and the sound;

Each voice four changes on the wind,
  That now dilate, and now decrease,   10
  Peace and goodwill, goodwill and peace,
Peace and goodwill, to all mankind.

This year I slept and woke with pain,
  I almost wished no more to wake,
  And that my hold on life would break   15
Before I heard those bells again;

But they my troubled spirit rule,
  For they controlled me when a boy;
  They bring me sorrow touched with joy,
The merry, merry bells of Yule.   20

                *   *   *

50

Be near me when my light is low,
  When the blood creeps, and the nerves prick
  And tingle; and the heart is sick,
And all the wheels of being slow.

Be near me when the sensuous frame   5
  Is racked with pangs that conquer trust;
  And Time, a maniac scattering dust,[8]
And Life, a Fury slinging flame.[9]

Be near me when my faith is dry,
  And men the flies of latter spring,   10
  That lay their eggs, and sting and sing
And weave their petty cells and die.

Be near me when I fade away,
  To point the term of human strife,
  And on the low dark verge of life   15
The twilight of eternal day.

                *   *   *

54

O, yet we trust that somehow good
  Will be the final goal of ill,
  To pangs of nature, sins of will,
Defects of doubt, and taints of blood;

That nothing walks with aimless feet;   5
  That not one life shall be destroyed,

---

8. That is, the dust from which life comes and to which it returns.   9. The Furies, avenging deities of Greek myth, carry torches.

Or cast as rubbish to the void,
  When God hath made the pile complete;

That not a worm is cloven in vain;
  That not a moth with vain desire   10
  Is shriveled in a fruitless fire,
Or but subserves another's gain.

Behold, we know not anything;
  I can but trust that good shall fall
  At last—far off—at last, to all,   15
And every winter change to spring.

So runs my dream; but what am I?
  An infant crying in the night;
  An infant crying for the light,
And with no language but a cry.   20

55

The wish, that of the living whole
  No life may fail beyond the grave,
  Derives it not from what we have
The likest God within the soul?

Are God and Nature then at strife,   5
  That Nature lends such evil dreams?
  So careful of the type[1] she seems,
So careless of the single life,[2]

That I, considering everywhere
  Her secret meaning in her deeds   10
  And finding that of fifty seeds
She often brings but one to bear,

I falter where I firmly trod,
  And falling with my weight of cares
  Upon the great world's altar-stairs   15
That slope through darkness up to God,

I stretch lame hands of faith, and grope,
  And gather dust and chaff, and call
  To what I feel is Lord of all,
And faintly trust the larger hope.   20

56

"So careful of the type?" but no.
  From scarpèd[3] cliff and quarried stone
  She cries, "A thousand types are gone;[4]
I care for nothing, all shall go.

"Thou makest thine appeal to me: 5
  I bring to life, I bring to death;

---

1. Species.   2. The significance of Nature's prodigality and destructiveness was widely debated during Tennyson's lifetime.   3. Shorn away vertically to expose the rock strata of different ages.   4. That whole species had disappeared, not merely individuals, had become evident from Charles Lyell's researches, published in his *Principles of Geology* (1830–33) and *Elements of Geology* (1838).

The spirit does but mean the breath:
I know no more." And he, shall he,

Man, her last work, who seemed so fair,
    Such splendid purpose in his eyes,   10
    Who rolled the psalm to wintry skies,
Who built him fanes[5] of fruitless prayer,

Who trusted God was love indeed
    And love Creation's final law—
    Though Nature, red in tooth and claw   15
With ravin,[6] shrieked against his creed—

Who loved, who suffered countless ills,
    Who battled for the True, the Just,
    Be blown about the desert dust,
Or sealed within the iron hills?   20

No more? A monster then, a dream,
    A discord. Dragons of the prime,[7]
    That tear each other in their slime,
Were mellow music matched with him.

O life as futile, then, as frail!   25
    O for thy[8] voice to soothe and bless!
    What hope of answer, or redress?
Behind the veil,[9] behind the veil.

                *   *   *

                        78

Again at Christmas did we weave
    The holly round the Christmas hearth;
    The silent snow possessed the earth,
And calmly fell our Christmas-eve:

The yule-clog[1] sparkled keen with frost,   5
    No wing of wind the region swept,
    But over all things brooding slept
The quiet sense of something lost.

As in the winters left behind,
    Again our ancient games had place,   10
    The mimic picture's[2] breathing grace,
And dance and song and hoodman-blind.[3]

Who showed a token of distress?
    No single tear, no mark of pain:
    O sorrow, then can sorrow wane?   15
O grief, can grief be changed to less?

O last regret, regret can die!
    No—mixed with all this mystic frame,
    Her deep relations are the same,
But with long use her tears are dry.   20

                *   *   *

5. Temples.   6. Prey.   7. Prehistoric creatures.   8. Hallam's.   9. Death.   1. Yule log.
2. The game may be charades.   3. Blindman's buff.

95

By night we lingered on the lawn,
  For underfoot the herb was dry;
  And genial warmth; and o'er the sky
The silvery haze of summer drawn;

And calm that let the tapers burn
  Unwavering; not a cricket chirred;
  The brook alone far-off was heard,
And on the board the fluttering urn.[4]

And bats went round in fragrant skies,
  And wheeled or lit the filmy shapes
  That haunt the dusk, with ermine capes
And woolly breasts and beaded eyes;

While now we sang old songs that pealed
  From knoll to knoll, where, couched at ease,
  The white kine[5] glimmered, and the trees
Laid their dark arms about the field.

But when those others, one by one,
  Withdrew themselves from me and night,
  And in the house light after light
Went out, and I was all alone,

A hunger seized my heart; I read
  Of that glad year which once had been,
  In those fall'n leaves which kept their green,
The noble letters of the dead.

And strangely on the silence broke
  The silent-speaking words, and strange
  Was love's dumb cry defying change
To test his worth; and strangely spoke

The faith, the vigor, bold to dwell
  On doubts that drive the coward back,
  And keen through wordy snares to track
Suggestion to her inmost cell.

So word by word, and line by line,
  The dead man touched me from the past,
  And all at once it seemed at last
The living soul was flashed on mine,

And mine in this was wound, and whirled
  About empyreal[6] heights of thought,
  And came on that which is, and caught
The deep pulsations of the world,

Æonian[7] music measuring out
  The steps of Time—the shocks of Chance—
  The blows of Death. At length my trance
Was canceled, stricken through with doubt.

5

10

15

20

25

30

35

40

---

4. Boiling tea urn. *Board:* table.   5. Cattle.   6. Sublime.   7. Age-old.

Vague words! but ah, how hard to frame   45
   In matter-molded forms of speech,
   Or even for intellect to reach
Through memory that which I became;

Till now the doubtful dusk revealed
   The knolls once more where, couched at ease,   50
   The white kine glimmered, and the trees
Laid their dark arms about the field;

And sucked from out the distant gloom
   A breeze began to tremble o'er
   The large leaves of the sycamore,   55
And fluctuate all the still perfume,

And gathering freshlier overhead,
   Rocked the full-foliaged elms, and swung
   The heavy-folded rose, and flung
The lilies to and fro, and said,   60

"The dawn, the dawn," and died away;
   And East and West, without a breath,
   Mixt their dim lights, like life and death,
To broaden into boundless day.

*   *   *

106

Ring out, wild bells, to the wild sky,
   The flying cloud, the frosty light:
   The year is dying in the night;
Ring out, wild bells, and let him die.

Ring out the old, ring in the new,   5
   Ring, happy bells, across the snow:
   The year is going, let him go;
Ring out the false, ring in the true.

Ring out the grief that saps the mind,
   For those that here we see no more;   10
   Ring out the feud of rich and poor,
Ring in redress to all mankind.

Ring out a slowly dying cause,
   And ancient forms of party strife;
   Ring in the nobler modes of life,   15
With sweeter manners, purer laws.

Ring out the want, the care, the sin,
   The faithless coldness of the times;
   Ring out, ring out my mournful rhymes,
But ring the fuller minstrel in.   20

Ring out false pride in place and blood,
   The civic slander and the spite;
   Ring in the love of truth and right,
Ring in the common love of good.

Ring out old shapes of foul disease;   25
    Ring out the narrowing lust of gold;
    Ring out the thousand wars of old,
Ring in the thousand years of peace.[8]

Ring in the valiant man and free,
    The larger heart, the kindlier hand;   30
    Ring out the darkness of the land,
Ring in the Christ that is to be.

*   *   *

118

Contèmplate all this work of Time,
    The giant laboring in his youth;
    Nor dream of human love and truth,
As dying Nature's earth and lime;[9]

But trust that those we call the dead   5
    Are breathers of an ampler day
    For ever nobler ends. They say,
The solid earth whereon we tread

In tracts of fluent heat began,
    And grew to seeming-random forms,   10
    The seeming prey of cyclic storms,
Till at the last arose the man;

Who throve and branched from clime to clime,
    The herald of a higher race,
    And of himself in higher place,   15
If so he type[1] this work of time

Within himself, from more to more;
    Or, crowned with attributes of woe
    Like glories, move his course, and show
That life is not as idle ore,   20

But iron dug from central gloom,
    And heated hot with burning fears,
    And dipped in baths of hissing tears,
And battered with the shocks of doom

To shape and use. Arise and fly   25
    The reeling Faun, the sensual feast;
    Move upward, working out the beast,
And let the ape and tiger die.

*   *   *

124

That which we dare invoke to bless;
    Our dearest faith; our ghastliest doubt;

---

8. The poet has in mind Revelation 20, where it is said that Satan will be bound in chains for a thousand years, during which time the martyrs will be "priests of God and of Christ, and shall reign with him." 9. The products of the decay of flesh and bone.   1. Copy, emulate.

He, They, One, All;[2] within, without;
The Power in darkness whom we guess, —

I found Him not in world or sun,
   Or eagle's wing, or insect's eye,   5
   Nor through the questions men may try,
The petty cobwebs we have spun.

If e'er when faith had fallen asleep,
   I heard a voice, "believe no more,"   10
   And heard an ever-breaking shore
That tumbled in the Godless deep,

A warmth within the breast would melt
   The freezing reason's colder part,
   And like a man in wrath the heart   15
Stood up and answered, "I have felt."

No, like a child in doubt and fear:
   But that blind clamor made me wise;
   Then was I as a child that cries,
But, crying, knows his father near;   20

And what I am beheld again
   What is, and no man understands;
   And out of darkness came the hands
That reach through nature, molding men.

[*Epilogue*][3]

*   *   *

Today the grave is bright for me,
   For them[4] the light of life increased,
   Who stay to share the morning feast,
Who rest tonight beside the sea.

Let all my genial spirits advance   5
   To meet and greet a whiter[5] sun;
   My drooping memory will not shun
The foaming grape[6] of eastern France.

It circles round, and fancy plays,
   And hearts are warmed and faces bloom,   10
   As drinking health to bride and groom
We wish them store of happy days.

Nor count me all to blame if I
   Conjecture of a stiller guest,
   Perchance, perchance, among the rest,   15
And, though in silence, wishing joy.

But they must go, the time draws on,
   And those white-favored[7] horses wait;

---

2. Christ, as part of the Trinity, seen as three elements and as indivisible.   3. The Epilogue celebrates
the wedding of Tennyson's sister Cecilia to his friend Edmund Lushington (October 10, 1842) and brings
the poem of mourning full circle to its conclusion in a marriage and in the prospect of a new birth.
4. The new husband and wife.   5. More joyous and hopeful because of the marriage.   6. Champagne.   7. Wearing white ribbons for the wedding.

They rise, but linger; it is late;
   Farewell, we kiss, and they are gone.   20

A shade falls on us like the dark
   From little cloudlets on the grass,
   But sweeps away as out we pass
To range the woods, to roam the park,

Discussing how their courtship grew,   25
   And talk of others that are wed,
   And how she looked, and what he said,
And back we come at fall of dew.

Again the feast, the speech, the glee,
   The shade of passing thought, the wealth   30
   Of words and wit, the double health,
The crowning cup, the three-times-three,[8]

And last the dance;—till I retire.
   Dumb is that tower[9] which spake so loud,
   And high in heaven the streaming cloud,   35
And on the downs a rising fire:

And rise, O moon, from yonder down,
   Till over down and over dale
   All night the shining vapor sail
And pass the silent-lighted town,   40

The white-faced halls, the glancing rills,
   And catch at every mountain head,
   And o'er the friths[1] that branch and spread
Their sleeping silver through the hills;

And touch with shade the bridal doors,   45
   With tender gloom the roof, the wall;
   And breaking let the splendor fall
To spangle all the happy shores

By which they rest, and ocean sounds,
   And, star and system rolling past,   50
   A soul shall draw from out the vast
And strike his being into bounds,

And, moved through life of lower phase,
   Result in man, be born and think,
   And act and love, a closer link   55
Betwixt us and the crowning race

Of those that, eye to eye, shall look
   On knowledge; under whose command
   Is Earth and Earth's, and in their hand
Is Nature like an open book;   60

No longer half-akin to brute,
   For all we thought and loved and did,
   And hoped, and suffered, is but seed
Of what in them is flower and fruit;

8. Rousing cheers.   9. The church tower where wedding bells recently rang.   1. Narrow bays of the
sea.

Whereof the man that with me trod   65
   This planet was a noble type
   Appearing ere the times were ripe,
That friend of mine who lives in God,

That God, which ever lives and loves,
   One God, one law, one element,   70
   And one far-off divine event,
To which the whole creation moves.

ROBERT BROWNING
1812–1889

The pleasure of reading Robert Browning's dramatic monologues—the poems for which he is best known—involves the delight of encountering a vividly realized personality but is also, often, the kind of enjoyment one gets from detective fiction. An imaginary speaker utters words designed to generate a specific effect; from these words, typically, one can deduce a story never actually told. The poet allows us the enjoyment of figuring out what has really happened as well as more familiar poetic pleasures.

Browning was the son of a bank clerk who later became a prosperous banker. After attending the University of London, he traveled on the Continent. Back in England, he became friendly with other important Victorian literary figures: Charles Dickens, Thomas Carlyle, and Leigh Hunt, for example. His romance with the semi-invalid Elizabeth Barrett, also a poet, eventuated in marriage in 1846; the two lived mainly in Italy for the remaining fifteen years of her life. Although Browning returned to England after his wife's death, he made frequent visits to the Continent and died in Venice.

Browning wrote verse plays and introspective Shelleyan lyrics, but his most popular poems have always been the dramatic monologues, originally included in such volumes as *Bells and Pomegranates* (1841–46), *Men and Women* (1855), and *Dramatis Personae* (1864). His most ambitious work was *The Ring and the Book* (1868–1869), a linked series of blank verse dramatic monologues based on a Renaissance murder trial. In this long poem, in the course of which several people report the same events from very different points of view, Browning most clearly concentrates on the problem implicit in all his monologues, that of perspective. The nature of a story depends on who tells it: Browning's verse insistently reminds us of this fact.

My Last Duchess (1842), probably Browning's best-known and most popular monologue, in 56 lines exemplifies the characteristic technique. The speaker, a duke, prefers his wife's portrait to her corporeal existence, having put an end to her life because he found her gaiety and spiritual generosity offensive to his aristocratic pride. He explains his attitude to an envoy with whom he is negotiating for a new bride, with no awareness that his story reflects badly on himself. The pleasure of reading the poem derives largely from experiencing simultaneous communications: the story the duke thinks he tells, of offended dignity, and the story he really tells, of narcissistic self-indulgence.

The Bishop Orders His Tomb at Saint Praxed's Church (1845) invites more complicated responses to the personality it evokes. The imagined sixteenth-century bishop reveals his lack of real allegiance to the Church he nominally serves. He has violated his vows of celibacy, having had at least one mistress and several children. He feels powerful competitive impulses, as well as rage and envy, toward his predecessor as bishop. Even on his deathbed, he remains utterly absorbed in the things of this world: the lump of lapis lazuli he has buried, the splendor of the marble he imagines for his tomb. The Mass itself exists in his memory and imagination only as a sensuous experience:

> And then how I shall lie through centuries,
> And hear the blessed mutter of the mass,
> And see God made and eaten all day long,
> And feel the steady candle-flame, and taste
> Good strong thick stupefying incense-smoke!

If one wished to summarize this bishop in abstract terms, one might allude to "the corruption of the Church." Indeed, he exemplifies such corruption in many different ways, by what he fails to say as well as by what he says. "And thence ye may perceive the world's a dream": occasionally such tag lines erupt in his speech, but his lack of real religious feeling is all too apparent. He imagines himself lying in his tomb in his church through eternity; he does not think of an afterlife in Heaven—or, for that matter, in Hell, perhaps his more likely destination. Browning, however, implicitly insists on the difference between people and abstractions. To sum up this bishop in terms of ecclesiastical corruption would leave out the fact of his enormous vitality, a vitality that informs the entire poem. The dramatic monologue makes the bishop's feeling come alive, makes the reader sympathetically understand his reluctance to leave behind beauty he has valued all his life.

Browning uses the superficially remote situation he has evoked to reiterate the great Romantic theme—we have encountered it most vividly in Wordsworth and in Keats—of the poignance and the inevitability of loss. Instead of considering the problem of loss in autobiographical terms, he enters imaginatively into the experience of an invented character.

> She, men would have to be your mother once,
> Old Gandolf envied me, so fair she was!
> What's done is done, and she is dead beside,
> Dead long ago, and I am Bishop since,
> And as she died so must we die ourselves.

The dying man's emotions recapitulate a feeling we have all had: the sadness of memory, even memory of happy experiences (in this case, love of a woman and triumph over an enemy), when it tells us of what is irretrievably gone. The bishop holds on still to what he knows he must lose. His speech, as Browning captures it, expresses in its rhythms and its idiom the enduring vigor of his personality, even on the edge of death.

> Ah, ye hope
> To revel down my villas while I gasp
> Bricked o'er with beggar's mouldy travertine
> Which Gandolf from his tomb-top chuckles at!

This is not a man who has given up: he insists on the preoccupations of his life as he faces his death. The poem, demanding no judgment of the bishop, suggests, rather, the inadequacy of judgment as a reaction to the multiplicity of any single human being.

Browning's greatest gift as a poet is his capacity to convey an energetic sense of pleasure in the reality of experience. "Grow old along with me, / The best is yet to be," urges a character in one of his poems. But he also recognizes the cost of such intense living as that the bishop enjoys, since all human existence involves loss. The tonal complexity of *The Bishop Orders His Tomb* suggests the kind of richness typical of the Victorian period, with its faith and hope in the possibilities of human accomplishment mingled with doubt about what it all means after all.

"*Childe Roland to the Dark Tower Came*" (1855), on the other hand, supplies little faith or hope. A nightmare vision that lends itself to no ready rational explanation, the poem narrates, in the first person, the experience of a quester who understands neither the purpose nor the meaning of his quest. (Nor can the reader deduce purpose or meaning.) The speaker finds himself in a landscape of despair; he remembers the failures of those who have preceded him. Increasingly conscious of loss and failure, he yet finally blows on his horn a call of challenge, not knowing what he challenges or why. The affirmation implicit in that final challenge promises no cheerful outcome. It constitutes a kind of existential defiance of impossibility. The poem's peculiar appeal for twentieth-century readers depends on its acknowledgment of the kind of dark consciousness that can afflict anyone. Browning here explains nothing away. Indeed, he explains nothing at all.

A useful biography of Browning is B. Miller, *Robert Browning: A Portrait* (1952). W. C. De Vane, *A Browning Handbook* (1935), provides indispensable guidance. Valuable criticism includes I. Jack, *Browning's Major Poetry* (1973); L. Erickson, *Robert Browning: His Poetry and His Audiences* (1984); J. Woolford, *Browning, the Revisionary* (1988); and H. Bloom, ed., *Robert Browning* (1985), a collection of essays.

My Last Duchess

Ferrara

That's my last Duchess painted on the wall,
Looking as if she were alive. I call
That piece a wonder, now: Frà Pandolf's hands
Worked busily a day, and there she stands.
Will't please you sit and look at her? I said   5
'Frà Pandolf' by design, for never read
Strangers like you that pictured countenance,
The depth and passion of its earnest glance,
But to myself they turned (since none puts by
The curtain I have drawn for you, but I)   10
And seemed as they would ask me, if they durst,
How such a glance came there; so, not the first
Are you to turn and ask thus. Sir, 'twas not
Her husband's presence only, called that spot
Of joy into the Duchess' cheek: perhaps   15
Frà Pandolf chanced to say 'Her mantle laps
Over my lady's wrist too much,' or 'Paint
Must never hope to reproduce the faint
Half-flush that dies along her throat:' such stuff
Was courtesy, she thought, and cause enough   20
For calling up that spot of joy. She had
A heart—how shall I say?—too soon made glad,
Too easily impressed; she liked whate'er
She looked on, and her looks went everywhere.

Sir, 'twas all one! My favour at her breast,   25
The dropping of the daylight in the West,
The bough of cherries some officious fool
Broke in the orchard for her, the white mule
She rode with round the terrace—all and each
Would draw from her alike the approving speech,   30
Or blush, at least. She thanked men,—good! but thanked
Somehow—I know not how—as if she ranked
My gift of a nine-hundred-years-old name
With anybody's gift. Who'd stoop to blame
This sort of trifling? Even had you skill   35
In speech—(which I have not)—to make your will
Quite clear to such an one, and say, 'Just this
Or that in you disgusts me; here you miss,
Or there exceed the mark'—and if she let
Herself be lessoned so, nor plainly set   40
Her wits to yours, forsooth, and make excuse,
—E'en then would be some stooping; and I choose
Never to stoop. Oh sir, she smiled, no doubt,
Whene'er I passed her; but who passed without
Much the same smile? This grew; I gave commands;   45
Then all smiles stopped together. There she stands
As if alive. Will't please you rise? We'll meet
The company below, then. I repeat,
The Count your master's known munificence
Is ample warrant that no just pretence   50
Of mine for dowry will be disallowed;
Though his fair daughter's self, as I avowed
At starting, is my object. Nay, we'll go
Together down, sir. Notice Neptune, though,
Taming a sea-horse, thought a rarity,   55
Which Clause of Innsbruck cast in bronze for me!

The Bishop Orders His Tomb at Saint Praxed's Church[1]

Rome, 15—

Vanity, saith the preacher, vanity![2]
Draw round my bed: is Anselm keeping back?
Nephews—sons mine . . . ah God, I know not! Well—
She, men would have to be your mother once,
Old Gandolf[3] envied me, so fair she was!   5
What's done is done, and she is dead beside,
Dead long ago, and I am Bishop since,
And as she died so must we die ourselves,
And thence ye may perceive the world's a dream.
Life, how and what is it? As here I lie   10
In this state-chamber, dying by degrees,
Hours and long hours in the dead night, I ask

---

1. The bishop, his tomb, and the character Gandolf are all fictional. Saint Praxed's church, seen by Browning in 1844, is named after a 2nd-century Roman virgin.   2. Ecclesiastes 1:2.   3. The bishop's predecessor.

"Do I live, am I dead?" Peace, peace seems all.
Saint Praxed's ever was the church for peace;
And so, about this tomb of mine. I fought   15
With tooth and nail to save my niche, ye know:
—Old Gandolf cozened me, despite my care;
Shrewd was that snatch from out the corner south
He graced his carrion with, God curse the same!
Yet still my niche is not so cramped but thence   20
One sees the pulpit o' the epistle-side,[4]
And somewhat of the choir, those silent seats,
And up into the aery dome where live
The angels, and a sunbeam's sure to lurk:
And I shall fill my slab of basalt there,   25
And 'neath my tabernacle[5] take my rest,
With those nine columns round me, two and two,
The odd one at my feet where Anselm stands:
Peach-blossom marble all, the rare, the ripe
As fresh-poured red wine of a mighty pulse.   30
—Old Gandolf with his paltry onion-stone,[6]
Put me where I may look at him! True peach,
Rosy and flawless: how I earned the prize!
Draw close: that conflagration of my church
—What then? So much was saved if aught were missed!   35
My sons, ye would not be my death? Go dig
The white-grape vineyard where the oil-press stood,
Drop water gently till the surface sink,
And if ye find . . . Ah God, I know not, I! . . .
Bedded in store of rotten fig-leaves soft,   40
And corded up in a tight olive-frail,[7]
Some lump, ah God, of lapis lazuli,[8]
Big as a Jew's head cut off at the nape,
Blue as a vein o'er the Madonna's breast . . .
Sons, all have I bequeathed you, villas, all,   45
That brave Frascati[9] villa with its bath,
So, let the blue lump poise between my knees,
Like God the Father's globe on both his hands
Ye worship in the Jesu Church[1] so gay,
For Gandolf shall not choose but see and burst!   50
Swift as a weaver's shuttle[2] fleet our years:
Man goeth to the grave, and where is he?
Did I say basalt for my slab, sons? Black—
'Twas ever antique-black[3] I meant! How else
Shall ye contrast my frieze to come beneath?   55
The bas-relief in bronze ye promised me,
Those Pans and Nymphs ye wot[4] of, and perchance
Some tripod, thyrsus,[5] with a vase or so,
The Saviour at his sermon on the mount,
Saint Praxed in a glory, and one Pan   60

---

4. That is, the right side as the congregation faces the altar, from which during the service some portion of St. Paul's Epistles is read.   5. Here, the canopy over his tomb.   6. A lesser grade of green marble.
7. Basket made of rushes, for figs, raisins, olives, and so on.   8. A bright blue semiprecious stone.
9. A wealthy Roman suburb.   1. The principal Jesuit church in Rome.   2. Job 7:6.   3. A grade of good marble.   4. Know. *Pans and Nymphs:* Greek nature deities.   5. A staff tipped with a pinecone, associated with the Greek god Bacchus.

Ready to twitch the Nymph's last garment off,
And Moses with the tables[6] . . . but I know
Ye mark me not! What do they whisper thee,
Child of my bowels, Anselm? Ah, ye hope
To revel down my villas while I gasp   65
Bricked o'er with beggar's mouldy travertine[7]
Which Gandolf from his tomb-top chuckles at!
Nay, boys, ye love me—all of jasper,[8] then!
'Tis jasper ye stand pledged to, lest I grieve.
My bath must needs be left behind, alas!   70
One block, pure green as a pistachio-nut,
There's plenty jasper somewhere in the world—
And have I not Saint Praxed's ear to pray
Horses for ye, and brown Greek manuscripts,
And mistresses with great smooth marbly limbs?   75
—That's if ye carve my epitaph aright,
Choice Latin, picked phrase, Tully's[9] every word,
No gaudy ware like Gandolf's second line—
Tully, my masters? Ulpian[1] serves his need!
And then how I shall lie through centuries,   80
And hear the blessed mutter of the mass,
And see God made and eaten[2] all day long,
And feel the steady candle-flame, and taste
Good strong thick stupefying incense-smoke!
For as I lie here, hours of the dead night,   85
Dying in state and by such slow degrees,
I fold my arms as if they clasped a crook,[3]
And stretch my feet forth straight as stone can point,
And let the bedclothes, for a mortcloth,[4] drop
Into great laps and folds of sculptor's-work: 90
And as yon tapers dwindle, and strange thoughts
Grow, with a certain humming in my ears,
About the life before I lived this life,
And this life too, popes, cardinals, and priests,
Saint Praxed at his[5] sermon on the mount,   95
Your tall pale mother with her talking eyes,
And new-found agate urns as fresh as day,
And marble's language, Latin pure, discreet,
—Aha, Elucescebat[6] quoth our friend?
No Tully, said I, Ulpian at the best!   100
Evil and brief hath been my pilgrimage.
All lapis, all, sons! Else I give the Pope
My villas! Will ye ever eat my heart?
Ever your eyes were as a lizard's quick,
They glitter like your mother's for my soul,   105
Or ye would heighten my impoverished frieze,
Piece out its starved design, and fill my vase

6. The stone tablets on which the Ten Commandments were inscribed.   7. A cheap, flaky Italian building stone.   8. Reddish quartz.   9. Marcus Tullius Cicero (106–43 B.C.), Roman writer and master of Latin prose style.   1. Ulpianus Domitius (A.D. 170–228), lawyer, secretary to Emperor Alexander Severus, writer of nonclassical Latin.   2. A reference to the Sacrament of Communion.   3. The bishop's crosier.   4. Funeral pall or winding sheet.   5. Roger Cruik presents the interpretation that the drowsy bishop conflates the two allusions of lines 59 to 60, to Christ's Sermon on the Mount and to the (female) St. Prassede.   6. "He was illustrious," or "famous." In classical Latin the word would be *elucebat*. *Elucescebat* is an example of the less elegant Latin associated with Ulpian's era.

With grapes, and add a vizor and a Term,[7]
And to the tripod ye would tie a lynx
That in his struggle throws the thyrsus down,   110
To comfort me on my entablature
Whereon I am to lie till I must ask
'Do I live, am I dead?' There, leave me, there!
For ye have stabbed me with ingratitude
To death—ye wish it—God, ye wish it! Stone—   115
Gritstone,[8] a-crumble! Clammy squares which sweat
As if the corpse they keep were oozing through—
And no more lapis to delight the world!
Well go! I bless ye. Fewer tapers there,
But in a row: and, going, turn your backs   120
—Ay, like departing altar-ministrants,
And leave me in my church, the church for peace,
That I may watch at leisure if he leers—
Old Gandolf, at me, from his onion-stone,
As still he envied me, so fair she was!   125

"Childe Roland to the Dark Tower Came"

(*See Edgar's Song in* Lear)[1]

I

My first thought was, he lied in every word,
    That hoary cripple, with malicious eye
    Askance to watch the working of his lie
On mine, and mouth scarce able to afford
Suppression of the glee, that pursed and scored   5
    Its edge, at one more victim gained thereby.

II

What else should he be set for, with his staff?
    What, save to waylay with his lies, ensnare
    All travellers who might find him posted there,
And ask the road? I guessed what skull-like laugh   10
Would break, what crutch 'gin[2] write my epitaph
    For pastime in the dusty thoroughfare,

III

If at his counsel I should turn aside
    Into that ominous tract which, all agree,
    Hides the Dark Tower. Yet acquiescingly   15
I did turn as he pointed: neither pride
Nor hope rekindling at the end descried,
    So much as gladness that some end might be.

---

7. A pillar bearing a statue or a bust. *Vizor:* a masked figure.   8. Sandstone, a cheap substitute for marble.   1. Shakespeare's *King Lear* 3.4.173.   2. Begin to.

IV

For, what with my whole world-wide wandering,
   What with my search drawn out through years, my hope   20
   Dwindled into a ghost not fit to cope
With that obstreperous joy success would bring,—
I hardly tried now to rebuke the spring
   My heart made, finding failure in its scope.

V

As when a sick man very near to death   25
   Seems dead indeed, and feels begin and end
   The tears and takes the farewell of each friend,
And hears one bid the other go, draw breath
Freelier outside, ("since all is o'er," he saith,
   "And the blow fallen no grieving can amend");   30

VI

While some discuss if near the other graves
   Be room enough for this, and when a day
   Suits best for carrying the corpse away,
With care about the banners, scarves and staves:
And still the man hears all, and only craves   35
   He may not shame such tender love and stay.

VII

Thus, I had so long suffered in this quest,
   Heard failure prophesied so oft, been writ
   So many times among "The Band"—to wit,
The knights who to the Dark Tower's search addressed   40
Their steps—that just to fail as they, seemed best,
   And all the doubt was now—should I be fit?

VIII

So, quiet as despair, I turned from him,
   That hateful cripple, out of his highway
   Into the path he pointed. All the day   45
Had been a dreary one at best, and dim
Was settling to its close, yet shot one grim
   Red leer to see the plain catch its estray.[3]

IX

For mark! no sooner was I fairly found
   Pledged to the plain, after a pace or two,   50
   Than, pausing to throw backward a last view
O'er the safe road, 'twas gone; grey plain all round:
Nothing but plain to the horizon's bound.
   I might go on; nought else remained to do.

---

3. In law, a stray and unclaimed domestic animal.

X

So, on I went. I think I never saw   55
   Such starved ignoble nature; nothing throve:
   For flowers—as well expect a cedar grove!
But cockle, spurge, according to their law
Might propagate their kind, with none to awe,
   You'd think; a burr had been a treasure-trove.   60

XI

No! penury, inertness and grimace,
   In some strange sort, were the land's portion. "See
   Or shut your eyes," said Nature peevishly,
"It nothing skills: I cannot help my case:
'Tis the Last Judgment's fire must cure this place,   65
   Calcine its clods and set my prisoners free."

XII

If there pushed any ragged thistle-stalk
   Above its mates, the head was chopped; the bents[4]
   Were jealous else. What made those holes and rents
In the dock's[5] harsh swarth leaves, bruised as to baulk   70
All hope of greenness? 'tis a brute must walk
   Pashing their life out, with a brute's intents.

XIII

As for the grass, it grew as scant as hair
   In leprosy; thin dry blades pricked the mud
   Which underneath looked kneaded up with blood.   75
One stiff blind horse, his every bone a-stare,
Stood stupefied, however he came there:
   Thrust out past service from the devil's stud!

XIV

Alive? he might be dead for aught I know,
   With that red gaunt and colloped[6] neck a-strain,   80
   And shut eyes underneath the rusty mane;
Seldom went such grotesqueness with such woe;
I never saw a brute I hated so;
   He must be wicked to deserve such pain.

XV

I shut my eyes and turned them on my heart.   85
   As a man calls for wine before he fights,
   I asked one draught of earlier, happier sights,
Ere fitly I could hope to play my part.
Think first, fight afterwards—the soldier's art:
   One taste of the old time sets all to rights.   90

---

4. Coarse grasses.   5. Any of several coarse weeds of the buckwheat family.   6. Ridged.

XVI

Not it! I fancied Cuthbert's reddening face
   Beneath its garniture of curly gold,
   Dear fellow, till I almost felt him fold
An arm in mine to fix me to the place,
That way he used. Alas, one night's disgrace!   95
   Out went my heart's new fire and left it cold.

XVII

Giles then, the soul of honour—there he stands
   Frank as ten years ago when knighted first.
   What honest men should dare (he said) he durst.
Good—but the scene shifts—faugh! what hangman-hands   100
Pin to his breast a parchment?[7] his own bands
   Read it. Poor traitor, spit upon and curst!

XVIII

Better this present than a past like that;
   Back therefore to my darkening path again!
   No sound, no sight as far as eye could strain.   105
Will the night send a howlet[8] or a bat?
I asked: when something on the dismal flat
   Came to arrest my thoughts and change their train.

XIX

A sudden little river crossed my path
   As unexpected as a serpent comes.   110
   No sluggish tide congenial to the glooms;
This, as it frothed by, might have been a bath
For the fiend's glowing hoof—to see the wrath
   Of its black eddy bespate[9] with flakes and spumes.

XX

So petty yet so spiteful! All along,   115
   Low scrubby alders kneeled down over it;
   Drenched willows flung them headlong in a fit
Of mute despair, a suicidal throng:
The river which had done them all the wrong,
   Whate'er that was, rolled by, deterred no whit.   120

XXI

Which, while I forded,—good saints, how I feared
   To set my foot upon a dead man's cheek,
   Each step, or feel the spear I thrust to seek
For hollows, tangled in his hair or beard!
—It may have been a water-rat I speared,   125
   But, ugh! it sounded like a baby's shriek.

---

7. Containing an account of the crime for which he is condemned.   8. Owl.   9. Spattered.

XXII

Glad was I when I reached the other bank.
   Now for a better country. Vain presage!
   Who were the strugglers, what war did they wage,
Whose savage trample thus could pad the dank   130
Soil to a plash? Toads in a poisoned tank,
   Or wild cats in a red-hot iron cage—

XXIII

The fight must so have seemed in that fell[1] cirque.
   What penned them there, with all the plain to choose?
   No foot-print leading to the horrid mews,   135
None out of it. Mad brewage set to work
Their brains, no doubt, like galley-slaves the Turk
   Pits for his pastime, Christians against Jews.

XXIV

And more than that—a furlong on—why, there!
   What bad use was that engine for, that wheel,   140
   Or brake, not wheel—that harrow fit to reel
Men's bodies out like silk? with all the air
Of Tophet's[2] tool, on earth left unaware,
   Or brought to sharpen its rusty teeth of steel.

XXV

Then came a bit of stubbed ground, once a wood,   145
   Next a marsh, it would seem, and now mere earth
   Desperate and done with; (so a fool finds mirth,
Makes a thing and then mars it, till his mood
Changes and off he goes!) within a rood[3]—
   Bog, clay and rubble, sand and stark black dearth.   150

XXVI

Now blotches rankling, coloured gray and grim,
   Now patches where some leanness of the soul's
   Broke into moss or substances like boils;
Then came some palsied oak, a cleft in him
Like a distorted mouth that splits its rim   155
   Gaping at death, and dies while it recoils.

XXVII

And just as far as ever from the end!
   Nought in the distance but the evening, nought
   To point my footstep further! At the thought,
A great black bird. Apollyon's[4] bosom-friend,   160
Sailed past, nor beat his wide wing dragon-penned[5]
   That brushed my cap—perchance the guide I sought.

---

1. Cruel, terrible.   2. Hebrew for hell.   3. Quarter-acre (forty square rods).   4. "The angel of the bottomless pit" (Revelation 9:11).   5. Dragon-winged.

XXVIII

For, looking up, aware I somehow grew,
　'Spite of the dusk, the plain had given place
　All round to mountains—with such name to grace　　　165
Mere ugly heights and heaps now stolen in view
How thus they had surprised me,—solve it, you![6]
　How to get from them was no clearer case.

XXIX

Yet half I seemed to recognize some trick
　Of mischief happened to me, God knows when—　　　170
　In a bad dream perhaps. Here ended, then,
Progress this way. When, in the very nick
Of giving up, one time more, came a click
　As when a trap shuts—you're inside the den!

XXX

Burningly it came on me all at once,　　　175
　This was the place! those two hills on the right,
　Crouched like two bulls locked horn in horn in fight;
While to the left, a tall scalped mountain . . . Dunce,
Dotard, a-dozing at the very nonce,[7]
　After a life spent training for the sight!　　　180

XXXI

What in the midst lay but the Tower itself?
　The round squat turret, blind as the fool's heart,
　Built of brown stone, without a counterpart
In the whole world. The tempest's mocking elf
Points[8] to the shipman thus the unseen shelf　　　185
　He strikes on, only when the timbers start.

XXXII

Not see? because of night perhaps?—why, day
　Came back again for that! before it left,
　The dying sunset kindled through a cleft:
The hills, like giants at a hunting, lay,　　　190
Chin upon hand, to see the game at bay,—
　"Now stab and end the creature—to the heft!"

XXXIII

Not hear? when noise was everywhere! it tolled
　Increasing like a bell. Names in my ears
　Of all the lost adventurers my peers,—　　　195
How such a one was strong, and such was bold,
And such was fortunate, yet each of old
　Lost, lost! one moment knelled the woe of years.

6. The speaker addresses an imaginary listener—or the reader of the poem.　7. Occasion.　8. Points out.

XXXIV

There they stood, ranged along the hill-sides, met
  To view the last of me, a living frame					200
  For one more picture! in a sheet of flame
I saw them and I knew them all. And yet
Dauntless the slug-horn[9] to my lips I set,
  And blew. *"Childe Roland to the Dark Tower came."*

9. A word meaning "trumpet," apparently invented by the poet Thomas Chatterton (1752–1770).

FREDERICK DOUGLASS
1818?–1895

The *Narrative of the Life of Frederick Douglass, An American Slave* (1845) powerfully details the struggle for identity of a black man who, in the mid-nineteenth century, came to realize his own exclusion from the American myth of liberty and justice for all. His autobiographical record epitomizes the experience of many pre–Civil War slaves, but in its narrative skill it also suggests how the writer's effort to achieve selfhood and freedom partakes of a more nearly universal pattern, incident to men and women of whatever color.

Virtually everything that is known of Douglass's early life comes from the *Narrative* itself, which ends half a century before his death. The book became an immediate best-seller but also a subject of controversy when accusations of fraud (promptly refuted) were made against it by a man who claimed to have known Douglass as a slave and to know him incapable of writing such a book. Because the autobiography's publication endangered its author, who might have been returned to slavery, Douglass subsequently went to Great Britain for two years of highly successful lecture appearances. At the end of 1846, two Englishwomen purchased his freedom from his old master, Hugh Auld, and Douglass returned to the United States in March 1847. He then began a journalistic career, writing and publishing a series of newspapers and making himself a leader of his people who continued to locate and to proclaim the injustices to which blacks were subject. Late in his life, he held a number of diplomatic posts, including minister resident and consul general to the Republic of Haiti and chargé d'affaires for Santo Domingo. He died in Washington, D.C., and was buried in Rochester, New York.

Douglass gradually enlarged and elaborated his *Narrative*, which exists in three subsequent versions: *My Bondage and My Freedom* (1855) and two different editions of *Life and Times of Frederick Douglass* (1881, 1892). The earliest, shortest form has the greatest narrative integrity and clarity. For literary as well as historical reasons (its status as an important document in the abolitionist crusade), it merits reprinting. It belongs to a genre familiar in its time: thousands of slave narratives were published in America—and in many cases translated into European languages—between the end of the eighteenth century and the beginning of the American Civil War. They won a large, enthusiastic readership; by making the horrors of slavery emotionally immediate, they intensified abolitionist sentiment. From the first publication of Douglass's work, it was acknowledged as unusually forceful by virtue of its rhetorical control and its narrative skill.

Douglass casts his autobiography as an account of self-discovery. The contrast between the openings of the *Narrative* and of Rousseau's *Confessions* is instructive. Rousseau begins by proclaiming that he differs importantly from everyone else in his unique and early established personality and character. Douglass, on the other hand, starts by reporting what he does *not* know of himself. He must guess his own age, he doesn't know his birthday, he has only rumor to tell him his father's identity. Although he knows his mother, he spends virtually no time with her; she comes to him and leaves him in the dark. Most children develop their sense of who they are by precisely the clues missing in Douglass's experience: age, parentage, such ritual occasions as birthdays. Douglass has only a generic identity: slave. Like other slave children, he wears nothing but a shirt—not the trousers that would symbolize his maleness, not shoes to protect his feet, nothing to differentiate him from others of his kind. Like the other children, he eats cornmeal mush from a trough on the floor, thus, as he notes, treated like a pig and reduced to animality. Everything in Douglass's experience denies his individuality and declares his lack of particularized identity.

The narrative constructed by a man who has finally, arduously, discovered his selfhood recapitulates the process of that discovery: a process with language at its heart. The book ends with its author claiming his name: "I subscribe myself, FREDERICK DOUGLASS." The name itself is a triumph, not his father's or his mother's but the freshly bestowed name of his freedom. The author has won with difficulty the power to subscribe himself, to sign his name, for it involves the capacity to read and write as well as the claim to a name. Each step of the winning—learning to read, learning to write, acquiring a name—involves painful self-testing, but the *word* proves for Douglass literally a means to salvation.

Douglass believes his arrival in Baltimore, to serve the Aulds, a sign of Providential intervention: in Baltimore he learns to read. Mrs. Auld, wife of his master, begins to teach the boy the alphabet; her husband warns her to desist. Reading, he says, "would forever unfit him to be a slave." Douglass comments: "It was a new and special revelation, explaining dark and mysterious things, with which my youthful understanding had struggled, but struggled in vain." The word *revelation* has almost religious force: the child's vision of reading as the key to freedom saves his soul. From this point on in his story—and he is only about eight years old at the time—*words* lead Douglass to succeeding revelations. He defies all efforts to shut him up "in mental darkness." From little white street urchins, he acquires the sustaining "bread of knowledge." At the age of twelve or thereabouts, he reads a book called *The Columbian Orator*, which contains forceful antislavery arguments, and is thus enabled for the first time to utter his thoughts. Without the authority of the written word, the contact through it with other minds, he could not know how to articulate what he thinks, could hardly know what it is he thinks. He puzzles over the word *abolitionist*, hearing but not understanding it. When he figures out its meaning, he has passed another milestone. A slave's thoughts must be free, this account suggests, before he can hope for meaningful freedom of body; and freedom of thought comes only through knowledge of the word.

We know that the writer successfully achieves freedom, but he makes gripping drama out of the gradual reporting of *how* he does so. First he must painfully learn to write, another step toward taking possession of language. For his first, agonizingly abortive attempt at escape, he writes passes for himself and his friends, briefly preempting the glory of being his own master. Subjected subsequently to more brutalized conditions, he sustains himself by making an imaginary speech, in what he remembers as elaborate literary language, to the fleet of ships he sees on Chesapeake Bay, images of freedom. He defies his brutal overseer, claims his manhood, teaches fellow slaves to read; finally, as though by magic, he escapes. (He withholds details of the escape to protect others; the effect of this suppression on the narrative is to suggest that the escape occurs almost as the inevitable, natural culmination of the process of self-discovery.) A friendly white man gives him a new name. And finally Douglass discovers his own voice as well as his own words: the

Narrative concludes with his assuming the role of orator on behalf of his people.

Despite its emphasis on the power of language, the autobiography reminds us also that language cannot express everything. Rousseau exhaustively explores his own feelings; Douglass recurrently comments on the inexpressibility of his deepest feelings. At the end of Chapter I, Frederick, a small child, watches his aunt whipped until she is covered with blood. "It was a most terrible spectacle. I wish I could commit to paper the feelings with which I beheld it." His feelings exceed the possibility of verbal representation. Other episodes of comparable brutality elicit the same response: the narrator feels more than he can say. The reader is recurrently reminded that the horrible reality to which Douglass's words refer is in fact a reality beyond words.

Douglass's development of identity, his ultimate subscription of his new name as the sign of his self, leads to no claim of uniqueness. On the contrary, the identity he claims is partly *communal*. "Sincerely and earnestly hoping that this little book may do something toward throwing light on the American slave system, and hastening the glad day of deliverance to the millions of my brethren in bonds— faithfully relying upon the power of truth, love, and justice, for success in my humble efforts—and solemnly pledging my self anew to the sacred cause,—I subscribe myself, FREDERICK DOUGLASS." The "little book" exists not to establish Douglass's difference but to declare his unity. Now he possesses his own name, his own differentiating clothes, his own wife, his own self-defined occupation; but as much as when he was a half-naked child gobbling mush with the others, he feels part of a group. His love for fellow slaves, a recurrent theme of his story, provides the foundation for his identity—not, like Rousseau, emotionally isolated, but part of a sustaining community.

His language, both in the final paragraph just quoted and elsewhere, suggests that he partakes also of an even wider community. He evokes "truth" and "justice," proclaimed ideals of the American nation. He quotes John Greenleaf Whittier, "the slaves' poet," to express feelings he finds it hard to state for himself. Everywhere his prose rings with biblical rhythms and allusions. Frederick Douglass is not only a slave, not only an ex-slave; he is a literary man, an American, a Christian, claiming, relying on, and valuing these larger forms of communion as well as his union with his race—and implicitly demanding that others who call themselves Americans or Christians acknowledge his participation with them and accept the responsibility such acknowledgment implies.

An illuminating biography of Douglass, which elaborates on the information of the *Narrative,* is N. Huggins, *Slave and Citizen: The Life of Frederick Douglass* (1980). D. J. Preston, *Young Frederick Douglass: The Maryland Years* (1980), concentrates on the earlier period. A biography placing Douglass in the context of the nineteenth-century antislavery movement is W. S. McFeely, *Frederick Douglass* (1991). For critical approaches, see W. E. Martin, *The Mind of Frederick Douglass* (1984), and W. L. Andrews, ed., *Critical Essays on Frederick Douglass* (1991).

Narrative of the Life of Frederick Douglass, An American Slave[1]

CHAPTER I

I was born in Tuckahoe, near Hillsborough, and about twelve miles from Easton, in Talbot county, Maryland. I have no accurate knowledge

---

1. The text, printed in its entirety, is that of the first American edition, published by the Massachusetts Anti-Slavery Society in Boston in 1845.

of my age, never having seen any authentic record containing it. By far the larger part of the slaves know as little of their ages as horses know of theirs, and it is the wish of most masters within my knowledge to keep their slaves thus ignorant. I do not remember to have ever met a slave who could tell of his birthday. They seldom come nearer to it than planting-time, harvest-time, cherry-time, spring-time, or fall-time. A want of information concerning my own was a source of unhappiness to me even during childhood. The white children could tell their ages. I could not tell why I ought to be deprived of the same privilege. I was not allowed to make any inquiries of my master concerning it. He deemed all such inquiries on the part of a slave improper and impertinent, and evidence of a restless spirit. The nearest estimate I can give makes me now between twenty-seven and twenty-eight years of age. I come to this, from hearing my master say, some time during 1835, I was about seventeen years old.

My mother was named Harriet Bailey. She was the daughter of Isaac and Betsey Bailey, both colored, and quite dark. My mother was of a darker complexion than either my grandmother or grandfather.

My father was a white man. He was admitted to be such by all I ever heard speak of my parentage. The opinion was also whispered that my master was my father; but of the correctness of this opinion, I know nothing; the means of knowing was withheld from me. My mother and I were separated when I was but an infant—before I knew her as my mother. It is a common custom, in the part of Maryland from which I ran away, to part children from their mothers at a very early age. Frequently, before the child has reached its twelfth month, its mother is taken from it, and hired out on some farm a considerable distance off, and the child is placed under the care of an old woman, too old for field labor. For what this separation is done, I do not know, unless it be to hinder the development of the child's affection toward its mother, and to blunt and destroy the natural affection of the mother for the child. This is the inevitable result.

I never saw my mother, to know her as such, more than four or five times in my life; and each of those times was very short in duration, and at night. She was hired by a Mr. Stewart, who lived about twelve miles from my home. She made her journeys to see me in the night, travelling the whole distance on foot, after the performance of her day's work. She was a field hand, and a whipping is the penalty of not being in the field at sunrise, unless a slave has special permission from his or her master to the contrary—a permission which they seldom get, and one that gives to him that gives it the proud name of being a kind master. I do not recollect of ever seeing my mother by the light of day. She was with me in the night. She would lie down with me, and get me to sleep, but long before I waked she was gone. Very little communication ever took place between us. Death soon ended what little we could have while she lived, and with it her hardships and suffering. She died when I was about seven years old, on one of my master's farms, near Lee's Mill. I was not allowed to be present during her illness, at her death, or burial. She was gone long before I knew anything about it. Never having enjoyed, to any considerable extent, her soothing presence, her tender and watchful care, I received the tidings of her death with much the same emotions I should have probably felt at the death of a stranger.

Called thus suddenly away, she left me without the slightest intimation of who my father was. The whisper that my master was my father, may or may not be true; and, true or false, it is of but little consequence to my purpose whilst the fact remains, in all its glaring odiousness, that slaveholders have ordained, and by law established, that the children of slave women shall in all cases follow the condition of their mothers; and this is done too obviously to administer to their own lusts, and make a gratification of their wicked desires profitable as well as pleasurable; for by this cunning arrangement, the slaveholder, in cases not a few, sustains to his slaves the double relation of master and father.

I know of such cases; and it is worthy of remark that such slaves invariably suffer greater hardships, and have more to contend with, than others. They are, in the first place, a constant offence to their mistress. She is ever disposed to find fault with them; they can seldom do any thing to please her; she is never better pleased than when she sees them under the lash, especially when she suspects her husband of showing to his mulatto children favors which he withholds from his black slaves. The master is frequently compelled to sell this class of his slaves, out of deference to the feelings of his white wife; and, cruel as the deed may strike any one to be, for a man to sell his own children to human flesh-mongers, it is often the dictate of humanity for him to do so; for, unless he does this, he must not only whip them himself, but must stand by and see one white son tie up his brother, of but few shades darker complexion than himself, and ply the gory lash to his naked back; and if he lisp one word of disapproval, it is set down to his parental partiality, and only makes a bad matter worse, both for himself and the slave whom he would protect and defend.

Every year brings with it multitudes of this class of slaves. It was doubtless in consequence of a knowledge of this fact, that one great statesman of the south predicted the downfall of slavery by the inevitable laws of population. Whether this prophecy is ever fulfilled or not, it is nevertheless plain that a very different-looking class of people are springing up at the south, and are now held in slavery, from those originally brought to this country from Africa; and if their increase will do no other good, it will do away the force of the argument, that God cursed Ham,[2] and therefore American slavery is right. If the lineal descendants of Ham are alone to be scripturally enslaved, it is certain that slavery at the south must soon become unscriptural; for thousands are ushered into the world, annually, who, like myself, owe their existence to white fathers, and those fathers most frequently their own masters.

I have had two masters. My first master's name was Anthony. I do not remember his first name. He was generally called Captain Anthony—a title which, I presume, he acquired by sailing a craft on the Chesapeake Bay. He was not considered a rich slaveholder. He owned two or three farms, and about thirty slaves. His farms and slaves were under the care of an overseer. The overseer's name was Plummer. Mr. Plummer was a miserable drunkard, a profane swearer, and a savage monster. He always went

2. Noah cursed his second son, Ham, for mocking him; it was thought that a black skin resulted from the curse and that all black people descended from Ham.

armed with a cowskin and a heavy cudgel. I have known him to cut and slash the women's heads so horribly, that even master would be enraged at his cruelty, and would threaten to whip him if he did not mind himself. Master, however, was not a humane slaveholder. It required extraordinary barbarity on the part of an overseer to affect him. He was a cruel man, hardened by a long life of slaveholding. He would at times seem to take great pleasure in whipping a slave. I have often been awakened at the dawn of day by the most heartrending shrieks of an own aunt of mine, whom he used to tie up to a joist, and whip upon her naked back till she was literally covered with blood. No words, no tears, no prayers, from his gory victim, seemed to move his iron heart from its bloody purpose. The louder she screamed, the harder he whipped; and where the blood ran fastest, there he whipped longest. He would whip her to make her scream, and whip her to make her hush; and not until overcome by fatigue, would he cease to swing the blood-clotted cowskin. I remember the first time I ever witnessed this horrible exhibition. I was quite a child, but I well remember it. I never shall forget it whilst I remember any thing. It was the first of a long series of such outrages, of which I was doomed to be a witness and a participant. It struck me with awful force. It was the blood-stained gate, the entrance to the hell of slavery, through which I was about to pass. It was a most terrible spectacle. I wish I could commit to paper the feelings with which I beheld it.

This occurrence took place very soon after I went to live with my old master, and under the following circumstances. Aunt Hester went out one night,—where or for what I do not know,—and happened to be absent when my master desired her presence. He had ordered her not to go out evenings, and warned her that she must never let him catch her in company with a young man, who was paying attention to her, belonging to Colonel Lloyd. The young man's name was Ned Roberts, generally called Lloyd's Ned. Why master was so careful of her, may be safely left to conjecture. She was a woman of noble form, and of graceful proportions, having very few equals, and fewer superiors, in personal appearance, among the colored or white women of our neighborhood.

Aunt Hester had not only disobeyed his orders in going out, but had been found in company with Lloyd's Ned; which circumstance, I found, from what he said while whipping her, was the chief offence. Had he been a man of pure morals himself, he might have been thought interested in protecting the innocence of my aunt; but those who knew him will not suspect him of any such virtue. Before he commenced whipping Aunt Hester, he took her into the kitchen, and stripped her from neck to waist, leaving her neck, shoulders, and back, entirely naked. He then told her to cross her hands, calling her at the same time a d——d b——h. After crossing her hands, he tied them with a strong rope, and led her to a stool under a large hook in the joist, put in for the purpose. He made her get upon the stool, and tied her hands to the hook. She now stood fair for his infernal purpose. Her arms were stretched up at their full length, so that she stood upon the ends of her toes. He then said to her, "Now, you d——d b——h, I'll learn you how to disobey my orders!" and after rolling up his sleeves, he commenced to lay on the heavy cowskin, and soon the warm, red blood (amid heart-rending shrieks from her, and horrid oaths from him) came dripping to the floor. I was so terrified and horror-stricken at the sight, that I hid myself in a closet, and dared not venture out till long after the bloody transaction was over. I expected it would be my turn next. It was all new to me. I had never seen any thing like it before. I had always lived with my grandmother on the outskirts of the plantation, where she was put to raise the children of the younger women. I had therefore been, until now, out of the way of the bloody scenes that often occurred on the plantation.

CHAPTER II

My master's family consisted of two sons, Andrew and Richard; one daughter, Lucretia, and her husband, Captain Thomas Auld. They lived in one house, upon the home plantation of Colonel Edward Lloyd. My master was Colonel Lloyd's clerk and superintendent. He was what might be called the overseer of the overseers. I spent two years of childhood on this plantation in my old master's family. It was here that I witnessed the bloody transaction recorded in the first chapter; and as I received my first impressions of slavery on this plantation, I will give some description of it, and of slavery as it there existed. The plantation is about twelve miles north of Easton, in Talbot county, and is situated on the border of Miles River. The principal products raised upon it were tobacco, corn, and wheat. These were raised in great abundance; so that, with the products of this and the other farms belonging to him, he was able to keep in almost constant employment a large sloop, in carrying them to market at Baltimore. This sloop was named *Sally Lloyd*, in honor of one of the colonel's daughters. My master's son-in-law, Captain Auld, was master of the vessel; she was otherwise manned by the colonel's own slaves. Their names were Peter, Isaac, Rich, and Jake. These were esteemed very highly by the other slaves, and looked upon as the privileged ones of the planta-tion; for it was no small affair, in the eyes of the slaves, to be allowed to see Baltimore.

Colonel Lloyd kept from three to four hundred slaves on his home plantation, and owned a large number more on the neighboring farms belonging to him. The names of the farms nearest to the home plantation were Wye Town and New Design. "Wye Town" was under the overseer-ship of a man named Noah Willis. New Design was under the overseer-ship of a Mr. Townsend. The overseers of these, and all the rest of the farms, numbering over twenty, received advice and direction from the managers of the home plantation. This was the great business place. It was the seat of government for the whole twenty farms. All disputes among the overseers were settled here. If a slave was convicted of any high misde-meanor, became unmanageable, or evinced a determination to run away, he was brought immediately here, severely whipped, put on board the sloop, carried to Baltimore, and sold to Austin Woolfolk, or some other slave-trader, as a warning to the slaves remaining.

Here, too, the slaves of all the other farms received their monthly allow-ance of food, and their yearly clothing. The men and women slaves received, as their monthly allowance of food, eight pounds of pork, or its equivalent in fish, and one bushel of corn meal. Their yearly clothing consisted of two coarse linen shirts, one pair of linen trousers, like the shirts, one jacket, one pair of trousers for winter, made of coarse negro cloth, one pair of stockings, and one pair of shoes; the whole of which could not have cost more than seven dollars. The allowance of the slave children was given to their mothers, or the old women having the care of them. The children unable to work in the field had neither shoes, stockings, jackets, nor trousers, given to them; their clothing consisted of two coarse linen shirts per year. When these failed them, they went naked until the next allowance-day. Children from seven to ten years old, of both sexes, almost naked, might be seen at all seasons of the year.

There were no beds given the slaves, unless one coarse blanket be considered such, and none but the men and women had these. This, however, is not considered a very great privation. They find less difficulty from the want of beds, than from the want of time to sleep; for when their day's work in the field is done, the most of them having their washing, mending, and cooking to do, and having few or none of the ordinary facilities for doing either of these, very many of their sleeping hours are consumed in preparing for the field the coming day; and when this is done, old and young, male and female, married and single, drop down side by side, on one common bed,—the cold, damp floor,—each covering himself or herself with their miserable blankets; and here they sleep till they are summoned to the field by the driver's horn. At the sound of this, all must rise, and be off to the field. There must be no halting; every one must be at his or her post; and woe betides them who hear not this morning summons to the field; for if they are not awakened by the sense of hearing, they are by the sense of feeling: no age nor sex finds any favor. Mr. Severe, the overseer, used to stand by the door of the quarter, armed with a large hickory stick and heavy cowskin, ready to whip any one who was so unfortunate as not to hear, or, from any other cause, was prevented from being ready to start for the field at the sound of the horn.

Mr. Severe was rightly named: he was a cruel man. I have seen him whip a woman, causing the blood to run half an hour at the time; and this, too, in the midst of her crying children, pleading for their mother's release. He seemed to take pleasure in manifesting his fiendish barbarity. Added to his cruelty, he was a profane swearer. It was enough to chill the blood and stiffen the hair of an ordinary man to hear him talk. Scarce a sentence escaped him but that was commenced or concluded by some horrid oath. The field was the place to witness his cruelty and profanity. His presence made it both the field of blood and of blasphemy. From the rising till the going down of the sun, he was cursing, raving, cutting, and slashing among the slaves of the field, in the most frightful manner. His career was short. He died very soon after I went to Colonel Lloyd's; and he died as he lived, uttering, with his dying groans, bitter curses and horrid oaths. His death was regarded by the slaves as the result of a merciful providence.

Mr. Severe's place was filled by a Mr. Hopkins. He was a very different man. He was less cruel, less profane, and made less noise, than Mr.

Severe. His course was characterized by no extraordinary demonstrations of cruelty. He whipped, but seemed to take no pleasure in it. He was called by the slaves a good overseer.

The home plantation of Colonel Lloyd wore the appearance of a country village. All the mechanical operations for all the farms were performed here. The shoemaking and mending, the blacksmithing, cartwrighting, coopering, weaving, and grain-grinding, were all performed by the slaves on the home plantation. The whole place wore a business-like aspect very unlike the neighboring farms. The number of houses, too, conspired to give it advantage over the neighboring farms. It was called by the slaves the *Great House Farm.* Few privileges were esteemed higher, by the slaves of the out-farms, than that of being selected to do errands at the Great House Farm. It was associated in their minds with greatness. A representative could not be prouder of his election to a seat in the American Congress, than a slave on one of the out-farms would be of his election to do errands at the Great House Farm. They regarded it as evidence of great confidence reposed in them by their overseers; and it was on this account, as well as a constant desire to be out of the field from under the driver's lash, that they esteemed it a high privilege, one worth careful living for. He was called the smartest and most trusty fellow, who had this honor conferred upon him the most frequently. The competitors for this office sought as diligently to please their overseers, as the office-seekers in the political parties seek to please and deceive the people. The same traits of character might be seen in Colonel Lloyd's slaves, as are seen in the slaves of the political parties.

The slaves selected to go to the Great House Farm, for the monthly allowance for themselves and their fellow-slaves, were peculiarly enthusiastic. While on their way, they would make the dense old woods, for miles around, reverberate with their wild songs, revealing at once the highest joy and the deepest sadness. They would compose and sing as they went along, consulting neither time nor tune. The thought that came up, came out—if not in the word, in the sound;—and as frequently in the one as in the other. They would sometimes sing the most pathetic sentiment in the most rapturous tone, and the most rapturous sentiment in the most pathetic tone. Into all of their songs they would manage to weave something of the Great House Farm. Especially would they do this, when leaving home. They would then sing most exultingly the following words:—

> "I am going away to the Great House Farm!
> O, yea! O, yea! O!"

This they would sing, as a chorus, to words which to many would seem unmeaning jargon, but which, nevertheless, were full of meaning to themselves. I have sometimes thought that the mere hearing of those songs would do more to impress some minds with the horrible character of slavery, than the reading of whole volumes of philosophy on the subject could do.

I did not, when a slave, understand the deep meaning of those rude and apparently incoherent songs. I was myself within the circle; so that I neither saw nor heard as those without might see and hear. They told a tale of woe which was then altogether beyond my feeble comprehension; they were tones loud, long, and deep; they breathed the prayer and complaint of souls boiling over with the bitterest anguish. Every tone was a testimony against slavery, and a prayer to God for deliverance from chains. The hearing of those wild notes always depressed my spirit, and filled me with ineffable sadness. I have frequently found myself in tears while hearing them. The mere recurrence to those songs, even now, afflicts me; and while I am writing these lines, an expression of feeling has already found its way down my cheek. To those songs I trace my first glimmering conception of the dehumanizing character of slavery. I can never get rid of that conception. Those songs still follow me, to deepen my hatred of slavery, and quicken my sympathies for my brethren in bonds. If any one wishes to be impressed with the soul-killing effects of slavery, let him go to Colonel Lloyd's plantation, and, on allowance-day, place himself in the deep pine woods, and there let him, in silence, analyze the sounds that shall pass through the chambers of his soul,—and if he is not thus impressed, it will only be because "there is no flesh in his obdurate heart."

I have often been utterly astonished, since I came to the north, to find persons who could speak of the singing, among slaves, as evidence of their contentment and happiness. It is impossible to conceive of a greater mistake. Slaves sing most when they are most unhappy. The songs of the slave represent the sorrows of his heart; and he is relieved by them, only as an aching heart is relieved by its tears. At least, such is my experience. I have often sung to drown my sorrow, but seldom to express my happiness. Crying for joy, and singing for joy, were alike uncommon to me while in the jaws of slavery. The singing of a man cast away upon a desolate island might be as appropriately considered as evidence of contentment and happiness, as the singing of a slave; the songs of the one and of the other are prompted by the same emotion.

CHAPTER III

Colonel Lloyd kept a large and finely cultivated garden, which afforded almost constant employment for four men, besides the chief gardener, (Mr. M'Durmond). This garden was probably the greatest attraction of the place. During the summer months, people came from far and near—from Baltimore, Easton, and Annapolis—to see it. It abounded in fruits of almost every description, from the hardy apple of the north to the delicate orange of the south. This garden was not the least source of trouble on the plantation. Its excellent fruit was quite a temptation to the hungry swarms of boys, as well as the older slaves, belonging to the colonel, few of whom had the virtue or the vice to resist it. Scarcely a day passed, during the summer, but that some slave had to take the lash for stealing fruit. The colonel had to resort to all kinds of stratagems to keep his slaves out of the garden. The last and most successful one was that of tarring his fence all around; after which, if a slave was caught with tar upon his person, it was deemed sufficient proof that he had either been into the garden, or had tried to get in. In either case, he was severely whipped by the chief gardener. This plan worked well; the slaves became as fearful of tar as of the lash. They seemed to realize the impossibility of touching *tar* without being defiled.[3]

The colonel also kept a splendid riding equipage. His stable and carriage-house presented the appearance of some of our large city livery establishments. His horses were of the finest form and noblest blood. His carriage-house contained three splendid coaches, three or four gigs, besides dearborns and barouches[4] of the most fashionable style.

This establishment was under the care of two slaves—old Barney and young Barney—father and son. To attend to this establishment was their sole work. But it was by no means an easy employment; for in nothing was Colonel Lloyd more particular than in the management of his horses. The slightest inattention to these was unpardonable, and was visited upon those, under whose care they were placed, with the severest punishment; no excuse could shield them, if the colonel only suspected any want of attention to his horses—a supposition which he frequently indulged, and one which, of course, made the office of old and young Barney a very trying one. They never knew when they were safe from punishment. They were frequently whipped when least deserving, and escaped whipping when most deserving it. Every thing depended upon the looks of the horses, and the state of Colonel Lloyd's own mind when his horses were brought to him for use. If a horse did not move fast enough, or hold his head high enough, it was owing to some fault of his keepers. It was painful to stand near the stable-door, and hear the various complaints against the keepers when a horse was taken out for use. "This horse has not had proper attention. He has not been sufficiently rubbed and curried, or he has not been properly fed; his food was too wet or too dry; he got it too soon or too late; he was too hot or too cold; he had too much hay, and not enough of grain; or he had too much grain, and not enough of hay; instead of old Barney's attending to the horse, he had very improperly left it to his son." To all these complaints, no matter how unjust, the slave must answer never a word. Colonel Lloyd could not brook any contradiction from a slave. When he spoke, a slave must stand, listen, and tremble; and such was literally the case. I have seen Colonel Lloyd make old Barney, a man between fifty and sixty years of age, uncover his bald head, kneel down upon the cold, damp ground, and receive upon his naked and toil-worn shoulders more than thirty lashes at the time. Colonel Lloyd had three sons—Edward, Murray, and Daniel,—and three sons-in-law, Mr. Winder, Mr. Nicholson, and Mr. Lowndes. All of these lived at the Great House Farm, and enjoyed the luxury of whipping the servants when they pleased, from old Barney down to William Wilkes, the coach-driver. I have seen Winder make one of the house-servants stand off from him a suitable distance to be touched with the end of his whip, and at every stroke raise great ridges upon his back.

To describe the wealth of Colonel Lloyd would be almost equal to describing the riches of Job.[5] He kept from ten to fifteen house-servants.

---

3. Compare the proverb, "He who touches pitch shall be defiled."   4. Light four-wheeled carriages (*dearborns*) and carriages with a front seat for the driver and two facing back seats for couples (*barouches*). 5. Job 1:3: "His substance also was seven thousand sheep, and three thousand camels, and five hundred yoke of oxen, and five hundred she asses, and a very great household; so that this man was the greatest of all the men of the east."

He was said to own a thousand slaves, and I think this estimate quite within the truth. Colonel Lloyd owned so many that he did not know them when he saw them; nor did all the slaves of the out-farms know him. It is reported of him, that, while riding along the road one day, he met a colored man, and addressed him in the usual manner of speaking to colored people on the public highways of the south: "Well, boy, whom do you belong to?" "To Colonel Lloyd," replied the slave. "Well, does the colonel treat you well?" "No, sir," was the ready reply. "What, does he work you too hard?" "Yes, sir." "Well, don't he give you enough to eat?" "Yes, sir, he gives me enough, such as it is."

The colonel, after ascertaining where the slave belonged, rode on; the man also went on about his business, not dreaming that he had been conversing with his master. He thought, said, and heard nothing more of the matter, until two or three weeks afterwards. The poor man was then informed by his overseer that, for having found fault with his master, he was now to be sold to a Georgia trader. He was immediately chained and handcuffed; and thus, without a moment's warning, he was snatched away, and forever sundered, from his family and friends, by a hand more unrelenting than death. This is the penalty of telling the truth, of telling the simple truth, in answer to a series of plain questions.

It is partly in consequence of such facts, that slaves, when inquired of as to their condition and the character of their masters, almost universally say they are contented, and that their masters are kind. The slaveholders have been known to send in spies among their slaves, to ascertain their views and feelings in regard to their condition. The frequency of this has had the effect to establish among the slaves the maxim, that a still tongue makes a wise head. They suppress the truth rather than take the consequences of telling it, and in so doing prove themselves a part of the human family. If they have any thing to say of their masters, it is generally in their masters' favor, especially when speaking to an untried man. I have been frequently asked, when a slave, if I had a kind master, and do not remember ever to have given a negative answer; nor did I, in pursuing this course, consider myself as uttering what was absolutely false; for I always measured the kindness of my master by the standard of kindness set up among slaveholders around us. Moreover, slaves are like other people, and imbibe prejudices quite common to others. They think their own better than that of others. Many, under the influence of this prejudice, think their own masters are better than the masters of other slaves; and this, too, in some cases, when the very reverse is true. Indeed, it is not uncommon for slaves even to fall out and quarrel among themselves about the relative goodness of their masters, each contending for the superior goodness of his own over that of the others. At the very same time, they mutually execrate their masters when viewed separately. It was so on our plantation. When Colonel Lloyd's slaves met the slaves of Jacob Jepson, they seldom parted without a quarrel about their masters; Colonel Lloyd's slaves contending that he was the richest, and Mr. Jepson's slaves that he was the smartest, and most of a man. Colonel Lloyd's slaves would boast his ability to buy and sell Jacob Jepson. Mr. Jepson's slaves would boast his ability to whip Colonel Lloyd. These quarrels would almost always end in a fight between the parties, and those that whipped were supposed to have gained the point at issue. They seemed to think that the greatness of their masters was transferable to themselves. It was considered as being bad enough to be a slave; but to be a poor man's slave was deemed a disgrace indeed!

CHAPTER IV

Mr. Hopkins remained but a short time in the office of overseer. Why his career was so short, I do not know, but suppose he lacked the necessary severity to suit Colonel Lloyd. Mr. Hopkins was succeeded by Mr. Austin Gore, a man possessing, in an eminent degree, all those traits of character indispensable to what is called a first-rate overseer. Mr. Gore had served Colonel Lloyd, in the capacity of overseer, upon one of the out-farms, and had shown himself worthy of the high station of overseer upon the home or Great House Farm.

Mr. Gore was proud, ambitious, and persevering. He was artful, cruel, and obdurate. He was just the man for such a place, and it was just the place for such a man. It afforded scope for the full exercise of all his powers, and he seemed to be perfectly at home in it. He was one of those who could torture the slightest look, word, or gesture, on the part of the slave, into impudence, and would treat it accordingly. There must be no answering back to him; no explanation was allowed a slave, showing himself to have been wrongfully accused. Mr. Gore acted fully up to the maxim laid down by slaveholders, — "It is better that a dozen slaves suffer under the lash, than that the overseer should be convicted, in the presence of the slaves, of having been at fault." No matter how innocent a slave might be—it availed him nothing, when accused by Mr. Gore of any misdemeanor. To be accused was to be convicted, and to be convicted was to be punished; the one always following the other with immutable certainty. To escape punishment was to escape accusation; and few slaves had the fortune to do either, under the overseership of Mr. Gore. He was just proud enough to demand the most debasing homage of the slave, and quite servile enough to crouch, himself, at the feet of the master. He was ambitious enough to be contented with nothing short of the highest rank of overseers, and persevering enough to reach the height of his ambition. He was cruel enough to inflict the severest punishment, artful enough to descend to the lowest trickery, and obdurate enough to be insensible to the voice of a reproving conscience. He was, of all the overseers, the most dreaded by the slaves. His presence was painful; his eye flashed confusion; and seldom was his sharp, shrill voice heard, without producing horror and trembling in their ranks.

Mr. Gore was a grave man, and, though a young man, he indulged in no jokes, said no funny words, seldom smiled. His words were in perfect keeping with his looks, and his looks were in perfect keeping with his words. Overseers will sometimes indulge in a witty word, even with the slaves; not so with Mr. Gore. He spoke but to command, and commanded but to be obeyed; he dealt sparingly with his words, and bountifully with his whip, never using the former where the latter would answer as well. When he whipped, he seemed to do so from a sense of duty, and feared no consequences. He did nothing reluctantly, no matter how disagreeable;

always at his post, never inconsistent. He never promised but to fulfil. He was, in a word, a man of the most inflexible firmness and stone-like coolness.

His savage barbarity was equalled only by the consummate coolness with which he committed the grossest and most savage deeds upon the slaves under his charge. Mr. Gore once undertook to whip one of Colonel Lloyd's slaves, by the name of Demby. He had given Demby but few stripes, when, to get rid of the scourging, he ran and plunged himself into a creek, and stood there at the depth of his shoulders, refusing to come out. Mr. Gore told him that he would give him three calls, and that, if he did not come out at the third call, he would shoot him. The first call was given. Demby made no response, but stood his ground. The second and third calls were given with the same result. Mr. Gore then, without consultation or deliberation with any one, not even giving Demby an additional call, raised his musket to his face, taking deadly aim at his standing victim, and in an instant poor Demby was no more. His mangled body sank out of sight, and blood and brains marked the water where he had stood.

A thrill of horror flashed through every soul upon the plantation, excepting Mr. Gore. He alone seemed cool and collected. He was asked by Colonel Lloyd and my old master, why he resorted to this extraordinary expedient. His reply was, (as well as I can remember,) that Demby had become unmanageable. He was setting a dangerous example to the other slaves,—one which, if suffered to pass without some such demonstration on his part, would finally lead to the total subversion of all rule and order upon the plantation. He argued that if one slave refused to be corrected, and escaped with his life, the other slaves would soon copy the example; the result of which would be, the freedom of the slaves, and the enslavement of the whites. Mr. Gore's defence was satisfactory. He was continued in his station as overseer upon the home plantation. His fame as an overseer went abroad. His horrid crime was not even submitted to judicial investigation. It was committed in the presence of slaves, and they of course could neither institute a suit, nor testify against him; and thus the guilty perpetrator of one of the bloodiest and most foul murders goes unwhipped of justice, and uncensured by the community in which he lives. Mr. Gore lived in St. Michael's, Talbot county, Maryland, when I left there; and if he is still alive, he very probably lives there now; and if so, he is now, as he was then, as highly esteemed and as much respected as though his guilty soul had not been stained with his brother's blood.

I speak advisedly when I say this,—that killing a slave, or any colored person, in Talbot county, Maryland, is not treated as a crime, either by the courts or the community. Mr. Thomas Lanman, of St. Michael's, killed two slaves, one of whom he killed with a hatchet, by knocking his brains out. He used to boast of the commission of the awful and bloody deed. I have heard him do so laughingly, saying, among other things, that he was the only benefactor of his country in the company, and that when others would do as much as he had done, we should be relieved of "the d——d niggers."

The wife of Mr. Giles Hicks, living but a short distance from where I used to live, murdered my wife's cousin, a young girl between fifteen and sixteen years of age, mangling her person in the most horrible manner, breaking her nose and breastbone with a stick, so that the poor girl expired in a few hours afterward. She was immediately buried, but had not been in her untimely grave but a few hours before she was taken up and examined by the coroner, who decided that she had come to her death by severe beating. The offence for which this girl was thus murdered was this:—She had been set that night to mind Mrs. Hicks's baby, and during the night she fell asleep, and the baby cried. She, having lost her rest for several nights previous, did not hear the crying. They were both in the room with Mrs. Hicks. Mrs. Hicks, finding the girl slow to move, jumped from her bed, seized an oak stick of wood by the fireplace, and with it broke the girl's nose and breastbone, and thus ended her life. I will not say that this most horrid murder produced no sensation in the community. It did produce sensation, but not enough to bring the murderess to punishment. There was a warrant issued for her arrest, but it was never served. Thus she escaped not only punishment, but even the pain of being arraigned before a court for her horrid crime.

Whilst I am detailing bloody deeds which took place during my stay on Colonel Lloyd's plantation, I will briefly narrate another, which occurred about the same time as the murder of Demby by Mr. Gore.

Colonel Lloyd's slaves were in the habit of spending a part of their nights and Sundays in fishing for oysters, and in this way made up the deficiency of their scanty allowance. An old man belonging to Colonel Lloyd, while thus engaged, happened to get beyond the limits of Colonel Lloyd's, and on the premises of Mr. Beal Bondly. At this trespass, Mr. Bondly took offence, and with his musket came down to the shore, and blew its deadly contents into the poor old man.

Mr. Bondly came over to see Colonel Lloyd the next day, whether to pay him for his property, or to justify himself in what he had done, I know not. At any rate, this whole fiendish transaction was soon hushed up. There was very little said about it at all, and nothing done. It was a common saying, even among little white boys, that it was worth a half-cent to kill a "nigger," and a half-cent to bury one.

CHAPTER V

As to my own treatment while I lived on Colonel Lloyd's plantation, it was very similar to that of the other slave children. I was not old enough to work in the field, and there being little else than field work to do, I had a great deal of leisure time. The most I had to do was to drive up the cows at evening, keep the fowls out of the garden, keep the front yard clean, and run off errands for my old master's daughter, Mrs. Lucretia Auld. The most of my leisure time I spent in helping Master Daniel Lloyd in finding his birds, after he had shot them. My connection with Master Daniel was of some advantage to me. He became quite attached to me, and was a sort of protector of me. He would not allow the older boys to impose upon me, and would divide his cakes with me.

I was seldom whipped by my old master, and suffered little from any thing else than hunger and cold. I suffered much from hunger, but much more from cold. In hottest summer and coldest winter, I was kept almost naked—no shoes, no stockings, no jacket, no trousers, nothing on but a coarse tow linen shirt, reaching only to my knees. I had no bed. I must have perished with cold, but that, the coldest nights, I used to steal a bag which was used for carrying corn to the mill. I would crawl into this bag, and there sleep on the cold, damp, clay floor, with my head in and feet out. My feet had been so cracked with the frost, that the pen with which I am writing might be laid in the gashes.

We were not regularly allowanced. Our food was coarse corn meal boiled. This was called *mush*. It was put into a large wooden tray or trough, and set down upon the ground. The children were then called, like so many pigs, and like so many pigs they would come and devour the mush; some with oystershells, others with pieces of shingle, some with naked hands, and none with spoons. He that ate fastest got most; he that was strongest secured the best place; and few left the trough satisfied.

I was probably between seven and eight years old when I left Colonel Lloyd's plantation. I left it with joy. I shall never forget the ecstasy with which I received the intelligence that my old master (Anthony) had determined to let me go to Baltimore, to live with Mr. Hugh Auld, brother to my old master's son-in-law, Captain Thomas Auld. I received this information about three days before my departure. They were three of the happiest days I ever enjoyed. I spent the most part of all these three days in the creek, washing off the plantation scurf, and preparing myself for my departure.

The pride of appearance which this would indicate was not my own. I spent the time in washing, not so much because I wished to, but because Mrs. Lucretia had told me I must get all the dead skin off my feet and knees before I could go to Baltimore; for the people in Baltimore were very cleanly, and would laugh at me if I looked dirty. Besides, she was going to give me a pair of trousers, which I should not put on unless I got all the dirt off me. The thought of owning a pair of trousers was great indeed! It was almost a sufficient motive, not only to make me take off what would be called by pig-drovers the mange, but the skin itself. I went at it in good earnest, working for the first time with the hope of reward.

The ties that ordinarily bind children to their homes were all suspended in my case. I found no severe trial in my departure. My home was charmless; it was not home to me; on parting from it, I could not feel that I was leaving any thing which I could have enjoyed by staying. My mother was dead, my grandmother lived far off, so that I seldom saw her. I had two sisters and one brother, that lived in the same house with me; but the early separation of us from our mother had well nigh blotted the fact of our relationship from our memories. I looked for home elsewhere, and was confident of finding none which I should relish less than the one which I was leaving. If, however, I found in my new home hardship, hunger, whipping, and nakedness, I had the consolation that I should not have escaped any one of them by staying. Having already had more than a taste of them in the house of my old master, and having endured them there, I very naturally inferred my ability to endure them elsewhere, and especially at Baltimore; for I had something of the feeling about Baltimore that is expressed in the proverb, that "being hanged in England is preferable to dying a natural death in Ireland." I had the strongest desire to see Baltimore. Cousin Tom, though not fluent in speech, had inspired me with that desire by his eloquent description of the place. I could never point out any thing at the Great House, no matter how beautiful or powerful, but that he had seen something at Baltimore far exceeding, both in beauty and strength, the object which I pointed out to him. Even the Great House itself, with all its pictures, was far inferior to many buildings in Baltimore. So strong was my desire, that I thought a gratification of it would fully compensate for whatever loss of comforts I should sustain by the exchange. I left without a regret, and with the highest hopes of future happiness.

We sailed out of Miles River for Baltimore on a Saturday morning. I remember only the day of the week, for at that time I had no knowledge of the days of the month, nor the months of the year. On setting sail, I walked aft, and gave to Colonel Lloyd's plantation what I hoped would be the last look. I then placed myself in the bows of the sloop, and there spent the remainder of the day in looking ahead, interesting myself in what was in the distance rather than in things near by or behind.

In the afternoon of that day, we reached Annapolis, the capital of the State. We stopped but a few moments, so that I had no time to go on shore. It was the first large town that I had ever seen, and though it would look small compared with some of our New England factory villages, I thought it a wonderful place for its size—more imposing even than the Great House Farm!

We arrived at Baltimore early on Sunday morning, landing at Smith's Wharf, not far from Bowley's Wharf. We had on board the sloop a large flock of sheep; and after aiding in driving them to the slaughterhouse of Mr. Curtis on Louden Slater's Hill, I was conducted by Rich, one of the hands belonging on board of the sloop, to my new home in Alliciana Street, near Mr. Gardner's ship-yard, on Fells Point.

Mr. and Mrs. Auld were both at home, and met me at the door with their little son Thomas, to take care of whom I had been given. And here I saw what I had never seen before; it was a white face beaming with the most kindly emotions; it was the face of my new mistress, Sophia Auld. I wish I could describe the rapture that flashed through my soul as I beheld it. It was a new and strange sight to me, brightening up my pathway with the light of happiness. Little Thomas was told, there was his Freddy,—and I was told to take care of little Thomas; and thus I entered upon the duties of my new home with the most cheering prospect ahead.

I look upon my departure from Colonel Lloyd's plantation as one of the most interesting events of my life. It is possible, and even quite probable, that but for the mere circumstance of being removed from that plantation to Baltimore, I should have to-day, instead of being here seated by my own table, in the enjoyment of freedom and the happiness of home, writing this Narrative, been confined in the galling chains of slavery. Going to live at Baltimore laid the foundation, and opened the gateway, to all my subsequent prosperity. I have ever regarded it as the first plain manifestation of that kind providence which has ever since attended me, and marked my life with so many favors. I regarded the selection of myself as being somewhat remarkable. There were a number of slave children that might have been sent from the plantation to Baltimore. There were those younger, those older, and those of the same age. I was chosen from among them all, and was the first, last, and only choice.

I may be deemed superstitious, and even egotistical, in regarding this event as a special interposition of divine Providence in my favor. But I should be false to the earliest sentiments of my soul, if I suppressed the opinion. I prefer to be true to myself, even at the hazard of incurring the ridicule of others, rather than to be false, and incur my own abhorrence. From my earliest recollection, I date the entertainment of a deep conviction that slavery would not always be able to hold me within its foul embrace; and in the darkest hours of my career in slavery, this living word of faith and spirit of hope departed not from me, but remained like ministering angels to cheer me through the gloom. This good spirit was from God, and to him I offer thanksgiving and praise.

CHAPTER VI

My new mistress proved to be all she appeared when I first met her at the door,—a woman of the kindest heart and finest feelings. She had never had a slave under her control previously to myself, and prior to her marriage she had been dependent upon her own industry for a living. She was by trade a weaver; and by constant application to her business, she had been in a good degree preserved from the blighting and dehumanizing effects of slavery. I was utterly astonished at her goodness. I scarcely knew how to behave towards her. She was entirely unlike any other white woman I had ever seen. I could not approach her as I was accustomed to approach other white ladies. My early instruction was all out of place. The crouching servility, usually so acceptable a quality in a slave, did not answer when manifested toward her. Her favor was not gained by it; she seemed to be disturbed by it. She did not deem it impudent or unmannerly for a slave to look her in the face. The meanest slave was put fully at ease in her presence, and none left without feeling better for having seen her. Her face was made of heavenly smiles, and her voice of tranquil music.

But, alas! this kind heart had but a short time to remain such. The fatal poison of irresponsible power was already in her hands, and soon commenced its infernal work. That cheerful eye, under the influence of slavery, soon became red with rage; that voice, made all of sweet accord, changed to one of harsh and horrid discord; and that angelic face gave place to that of a demon.

Very soon after I went to live with Mr. and Mrs. Auld, she very kindly commenced to teach me the A, B, C. After I had learned this, she assisted me in learning to spell words of three or four letters. Just at this point of my progress, Mr. Auld found out what was going on, and at once forbade Mrs. Auld to instruct me further, telling her, among other things, that it was unlawful, as well as unsafe, to teach a slave to read. To use his own words, further, he said, "If you give a nigger an inch, he will take an ell.

A nigger should know nothing but to obey his master—to do as he is told to do. Learning would *spoil* the best nigger in the world. Now," said he, "if you teach that nigger (speaking of myself) how to read, there would be no keeping him. It would forever unfit him to be a slave. He would at once become unmanageable, and of no value to his master. As to himself, it could do him no good, but a great deal of harm. It would make him discontented and unhappy." These words sank deep into my heart, stirred up sentiments within that lay slumbering, and called into existence an entirely new train of thought. It was a new and special revelation, explaining dark and mysterious things, with which my youthful under-standing had struggled, but struggled in vain. I now understood what had been to me a most perplexing difficulty—to wit, the white man's power to enslave the black man. It was a grand achievement, and I prized it highly. From that moment, I understood the pathway from slavery to freedom. It was just what I wanted, and I got it at a time when I the least expected it. Whilst I was saddened by the thought of losing the aid of my kind mistress, I was gladdened by the invaluable instruction which, by the merest acci-dent, I had gained from my master. Though conscious of the difficulty of learning without a teacher, I set out with high hope, and a fixed purpose, at whatever cost of trouble, to learn how to read. The very decided manner with which he spoke, and strove to impress his wife with the evil conse-quences of giving me instruction, served to convince me that he was deeply sensible of the truths he was uttering. It gave me the best assurance that I might rely with the utmost confidence on the results which, he said, would flow from teaching me to read. What he most dreaded, that I most desired. What he most loved, that I most hated. That which to him was a great evil, to be carefully shunned, was to me a great good, to be diligently sought; and the argument which he so warmly urged, against my learning to read, only served to inspire me with a desire and determination to learn. In learning to read, I owe almost as much to the bitter opposition of my master, as to the kindly aid of my mistress. I acknowledge the benefit of both.

I had resided but a short time in Baltimore before I observed a marked difference, in the treatment of slaves, from that which I had witnessed in the country. A city slave is almost a freeman, compared with a slave on the plantation. He is much better fed and clothed, and enjoys privileges altogether unknown to the slave on the plantation. There is a vestige of decency, a sense of shame, that does much to curb and check those out-breaks of atrocious cruelty so commonly enacted upon the plantation. He is a desperate slaveholder, who will shock the humanity of his nonslave-holding neighbors with the cries of his lacerated slave. Few are willing to incur the odium attaching to the reputation of being a cruel master; and above all things, they would not be known as not giving a slave enough to eat. Every city slaveholder is anxious to have it known of him, that he feeds his slaves well; and it is due to them to say, that most of them do give their slaves enough to eat. There are, however, some painful exceptions to this rule. Directly opposite to us, on Philpot Street, lived Mr. Thomas Hamilton. He owned two slaves. Their names were Henrietta and Mary. Henrietta was about twenty-two years of age, Mary was about fourteen;

and of all the mangled and emaciated creatures I ever looked upon, these two were the most so. His heart must be harder than stone, that could look upon these unmoved. The head, neck, and shoulders of Mary were literally cut to pieces. I have frequently felt her head, and found it nearly covered with festering sores, caused by the lash of her cruel mistress. I do not know that her master ever whipped her, but I have been an eye-witness to the cruelty of Mrs. Hamilton. I used to be in Mr. Hamilton's house nearly every day. Mrs. Hamilton used to sit in a large chair in the middle of the room, with a heavy cowskin always by her side, and scarce an hour passed during the day but was marked by the blood of one of these slaves. The girls seldom passed her without her saying, "Move faster, you *black gip!*"[6] at the same time giving them a blow with the cowskin over the head or shoulders, often drawing the blood. She would then say, "Take that, you *black gip!*"—continuing, "If you don't move faster, I'll move you!" Added to the cruel lashings to which these slaves were subjected, they were kept nearly half-starved. They seldom knew what it was to eat a full meal. I have seen Mary contending with the pigs for the offal thrown into the street. So much was Mary kicked and cut to pieces, that she was oftener called "*pecked*" than by her name.

CHAPTER VII

I lived in Master Hugh's family about seven years. During this time, I succeeded in learning to read and write. In accomplishing this, I was compelled to resort to various stratagems. I had no regular teacher. My mistress, who had kindly commenced to instruct me, had, in compliance with the advice and direction of her husband, not only ceased to instruct, but had set her face against my being instructed by any one else. It is due, however, to my mistress to say of her, that she did not adopt this course of treatment immediately. She at first lacked the depravity indispensable to shutting me up in mental darkness. It was at least necessary for her to have some training in the exercise of irresponsible power, to make her equal to the task of treating me as though I were a brute.

My mistress was, as I have said, a kind and tender-hearted woman; and in the simplicity of her soul she commenced, when I first went to live with her, to treat me as she supposed one human being ought to treat another. In entering upon the duties of a slaveholder, she did not seem to perceive that I sustained to her the relation of a mere chattel, and that for her to treat me as a human being was not only wrong, but dangerously so. Slavery proved as injurious to her as it did to me. When I went there, she was a pious, warm, and tender-hearted woman. There was no sorrow or suffering for which she had not a tear. She had bread for the hungry, clothes for the naked, and comfort for every mourner that came within her reach. Slavery soon proved its ability to divest her of these heavenly qualities. Under its influence, the tender heart became stone, and the lamblike disposition gave way to one of tiger-like fierceness. The first step in her downward course was in her ceasing to instruct me. She now commenced to practise her husband's precepts. She finally became even more violent in her

6. Cheat, swindler.

opposition than her husband himself. She was not satisfied with simply doing as well as he had commanded; she seemed anxious to do better. Nothing seemed to make her more angry than to see me with a newspaper. She seemed to think that here lay the danger. I have had her rush at me with a face made all up of fury, and snatch from me a newspaper, in a manner that fully revealed her apprehension. She was an apt woman; and a little experience soon demonstrated, to her satisfaction, that education and slavery were incompatible with each other.

From this time I was most narrowly watched. If I was in a separate room any considerable length of time, I was sure to be suspected of having a book, and was at once called to give an account of myself. All this, however, was too late. The first step had been taken. Mistress, in teaching me the alphabet, had given me the *inch*, and no precaution could prevent me from taking the *ell*.

The plan which I adopted, and the one by which I was most successful, was that of making friends of all the little white boys whom I met in the street. As many of these as I could, I converted into teachers. With their kindly aid, obtained at different times and in different places, I finally succeeded in learning to read. When I was sent of errands, I always took my book with me, and by going one part of my errand quickly, I found time to get a lesson before my return. I used also to carry bread with me, enough of which was always in the house, and to which I was always welcome; for I was much better off in this regard than many of the poor white children in our neighborhood. This bread I used to bestow upon the hungry little urchins, who, in return, would give me that more valuable bread of knowledge. I am strongly tempted to give the names of two or three of those little boys, as a testimonial of the gratitude and affection I bear them; but prudence forbids;—not that it would injure me, but it might embarrass them; for it is almost an unpardonable offence to teach slaves to read in this Christian country. It is enough to say of the dear little fellows, that they lived on Philpot Street, very near Durgin and Bailey's ship-yard. I used to talk this matter of slavery over with them. I would sometimes say to them, I wished I could be as free as they would be when they got to be men. "You will be free as soon as you are twenty-one, *but I am a slave for life!* Have not I as good a right to be free as you have?" These words used to trouble them; they would express for me the liveliest sympathy, and console me with the hope that something would occur by which I might be free.

I was now about twelve years old, and the thought of being *a slave for life* began to bear heavily upon my heart. Just about this time, I got hold of a book entitled "The Columbian Orator."[7] Every opportunity I got, I used to read this book. Among much of other interesting matter, I found in it a dialogue between a master and his slave. The slave was represented as having run away from his master three times. The dialogue represented the conversation which took place between them, when the slave was retaken the third time. In this dialogue, the whole argument in behalf of

7. Caleb Bingham, *The Columbian Orator: Containing a Variety of Original and Selected Pieces: Together with Rules, Calculated to Improve Youth and Others in the Ornamental and Useful Art of Eloquence* (1807).

slavery was brought forward by the master, all of which was disposed of by the slave. The slave was made to say some very smart as well as impressive things in reply to his master—things which had the desired though unexpected effect; for the conversation resulted in the voluntary emancipation of the slave on the part of the master.

In the same book, I met with one of Sheridan's[8] mighty speeches on and in behalf of Catholic emancipation. These were choice documents to me. I read them over and over again with unabated interest. They gave tongue to interesting thoughts of my own soul, which had frequently flashed through my mind, and died away for want of utterance. The moral which I gained from the dialogue was the power of truth over the conscience of even a slaveholder. What I got from Sheridan was a bold denunciation of slavery, and a powerful vindication of human rights. The reading of these documents enabled me to utter my thoughts, and to meet the arguments brought forward to sustain slavery; but while they relieved me of one difficulty, they brought on another even more painful than the one of which I was relieved. The more I read, the more I was led to abhor and detest my enslavers. I could regard them in no other light than a band of successful robbers, who had left their homes, and gone to Africa, and stolen us from our homes, and in a strange land reduced us to slavery. I loathed them as being the meanest as well as the most wicked of men. As I read and contemplated the subject, behold! that very discontentment which Master Hugh had predicted would follow my learning to read had already come, to torment and sting my soul to unutterable anguish. As I writhed under it, I would at times feel that learning to read had been a curse rather than a blessing. It had given me a view of my wretched condition, without the remedy. It opened my eyes to the horrible pit, but to no ladder upon which to get out. In moments of agony, I envied my fellow-slaves for their stupidity. I have often wished myself a beast. I preferred the condition of the meanest reptile to my own. Any thing, no matter what, to get rid of thinking! It was this everlasting thinking of my condition that tormented me. There was no getting rid of it. It was pressed upon me by every object within sight or hearing, animate or inanimate. The silver trump of freedom had roused my soul to eternal wakefulness. Freedom now appeared, to disappear no more forever. It was heard in every sound, and seen in every thing. It was ever present to torment me with a sense of my wretched condition. I saw nothing without seeing it, I heard nothing without hearing it, and felt nothing without feeling it. It looked from every star, it smiled in every calm, breathed in every wind, and moved in every storm.

I often found myself regretting my own existence, and wishing myself dead; and but for the hope of being free, I have no doubt but that I should have killed myself, or done something for which I should have been killed. While in this state of mind, I was eager to hear any one speak of slavery. I was a ready listener. Every little while, I could hear something about the abolitionists. It was some time before I found what the word meant. It was always used in such connections as to make it an interesting word to me.

8. Thomas Sheridan (1719–1788), lecturer and writer on elocution.

If a slave ran away and succeeded in getting clear, or if a slave killed his master, set fire to a barn, or did any thing very wrong in the mind of a slaveholder, it was spoken of as the fruit of *abolition*. Hearing the word in this connection very often, I set about learning what it meant. The dictionary afforded me little or no help. I found it was "the act of abolishing;" but then I did not know what was to be abolished. Here I was perplexed. I did not dare to ask any one about its meaning, for I was satisfied that it was something they wanted me to know very little about. After a patient waiting, I got one of our city papers, containing an account of the number of petitions from the north, praying for the abolition of slavery in the District of Columbia, and of the slave trade between the States. From this time I understood the words *abolition* and *abolitionist*, and always drew near when that word was spoken, expecting to hear something of importance to myself and fellow-slaves. The light broke in upon me by degrees. I went one day down on the wharf of Mr. Waters; and seeing two Irishmen unloading a scow of stone, I went, unasked, and helped them. When we had finished, one of them came to me and asked me if I were a slave. I told him I was. He asked, "Are ye a slave for life?" I told him that I was. The good Irishman seemed to be deeply affected by the statement. He said to the other that it was a pity so fine a little fellow as myself should be a slave for life. He said it was a shame to hold me. They both advised me to run away to the north; that I should find friends there, and that I should be free. I pretended not to be interested in what they said, and treated them as if I did not understand them; for I feared they might be treacherous. White men have been known to encourage slaves to escape, and then, to get the reward, catch them and return them to their masters. I was afraid that these seemingly good men might use me so; but I nevertheless remembered their advice, and from that time I resolved to run away. I looked forward to a time at which it would be safe for me to escape. I was too young to think of doing so immediately; besides, I wished to learn how to write, as I might have occasion to write my own pass. I consoled myself with the hope that I should one day find a good chance. Meanwhile, I would learn to write.

The idea as to how I might learn to write was suggested to me by being in Durgin and Bailey's ship-yard, and frequently seeing the ship carpenters, after hewing, and getting a piece of timber ready for use, write on the timber the name of that part of the ship for which it was intended. When a piece of timber was intended for the larboard side, it would be marked thus—"L." When a piece was for the starboard side, it would be marked thus—"S." A piece for the larboard forward, would be marked thus—"L.F." When a piece was for starboard side forward, it would be marked thus—"S.F." For larboard aft, it would be marked thus—"L.A." For starboard aft, it would be marked thus—"S.A." I soon learned the names of these letters, and for what they were intended when placed upon a piece of timber in the ship-yard. I immediately commenced copying them, and in a short time was able to make the four letters named. After that, when I met with any boy who I knew could write, I would tell him I could write as well as he. The next word would be, "I don't believe you. Let me see you try it." I would then make the letters which I had been so fortunate as to learn, and ask him to beat that. In this way I got a good many lessons in writing, which it is quite possible I should never have gotten in any other way. During this time, my copy-book was the board fence, brick wall, and pavement; my pen and ink was a lump of chalk. With these, I learned mainly how to write. I then commenced and continued copying the Italics in Webster's Spelling Book, until I could make them all without looking on the book. By this time, my little Master Thomas had gone to school, and learned how to write, and had written over a number of copy-books. These had been brought home, and shown to some of our near neighbors, and then laid aside. My mistress used to go to class meeting at the Wilk Street meetinghouse every Monday afternoon, and leave me to take care of the house. When left thus, I used to spend the time in writing in the spaces left in Master Thomas's copy-book, copying what he had written. I continued to do this until I could write a hand very similar to that of Master Thomas. Thus, after a long, tedious effort for years, I finally succeeded in learning how to write.

CHAPTER VIII

In a very short time after I went to live at Baltimore, my old master's youngest son Richard died; and in about three years and six months after his death, my old master, Captain Anthony, died, leaving only his son, Andrew, and daughter, Lucretia, to share his estate. He died while on a visit to see his daughter at Hillsborough. Cut off thus unexpectedly, he left no will as to the disposal of his property. It was therefore necessary to have a valuation of the property, that it might be equally divided between Mrs. Lucretia and Master Andrew. I was immediately sent for, to be valued with the other property. Here again my feelings rose up in detestation of slavery. I had now a new conception of my degraded condition. Prior to this, I had become, if not insensible to my lot, at least partly so. I left Baltimore with a young heart overborne with sadness, and a soul full of apprehension. I took passage with Captain Rowe, in the schooner *Wild Cat*, and, after a sail of about twenty-four hours, I found myself near the place of my birth. I had now been absent from it almost, if not quite, five years. I, however, remembered the place very well. I was only about five years old when I left it, to go and live with my old master on Colonel Lloyd's plantation; so that I was now between ten and eleven years old.

We were all ranked together at the valuation. Men and women, old and young, married and single, were ranked with horses, sheep, and swine. There were horses and men, cattle and women, pigs and children, all holding the same rank in the scale of being, and all were subjected to the same narrow examination. Silvery-headed age and sprightly youth, maids and matrons, had to undergo the same indelicate inspection. At this moment, I saw more clearly than ever the brutalizing effects of slavery upon both slave and slaveholder.

After the valuation, then came the division. I have no language to express the high excitement and deep anxiety which were felt among us poor slaves during this time. Our fate for life was now to be decided. We had no more voice in that decision than the brutes among whom we were ranked. A single word from the white men was enough—against all our wishes, prayers, and entreaties—to sunder forever the dearest friends, dearest kindred, and strongest ties known to human beings. In addition to the pain of separation, there was the horrid dread of falling into the hands of Master Andrew. He was known to us all as being a most cruel wretch,— a common drunkard, who had, by his reckless mismanagement and profligate dissipation, already wasted a large portion of his father's property. We all felt that we might as well be sold at once to the Georgia traders, as to pass into his hands; for we knew that that would be our inevitable condition,—a condition held by us all in the utmost horror and dread.

I suffered more anxiety than most of my fellow-slaves. I had known what it was to be kindly treated; they had known nothing of the kind. They had seen little or nothing of the world. They were in very deed men and women of sorrow, and acquainted with grief.[9] Their backs had been made familiar with the bloody lash, so that they had become callous; mine was yet tender; for while at Baltimore I got few whippings, and few slaves could boast of a kinder master and mistress than myself; and the thought of passing out of their hands into those of Master Andrew—a man who, but a few days before, to give me a sample of his bloody disposition, took my little brother by the throat, threw him on the ground, and with the heel of his boot stamped upon his head till the blood gushed from his nose and ears—was well calculated to make me anxious as to my fate. After he had committed this savage outrage upon my brother, he turned to me, and said that was the way he meant to serve me one of these days,—meaning, I suppose, when I came into his possession.

Thanks to a kind Providence, I fell to the portion of Mrs. Lucretia, and was sent immediately back to Baltimore, to live again in the family of Master Hugh. Their joy at my return equalled their sorrow at my departure. It was a glad day to me. I had escaped a [fate] worse than lion's jaws. I was absent from Baltimore, for the purpose of valuation and division, just about one month, and it seemed to have been six.

Very soon after my return to Baltimore, my mistress, Lucretia, died, leaving her husband and one child, Amanda; and in a very short time after her death, Master Andrew died. Now all the property of my old master, slaves included, was in the hands of strangers,—strangers who had had nothing to do with accumulating it. Not a slave was left free. All remained slaves, from the youngest to the oldest. If any one thing in my experience, more than another, served to deepen my conviction of the infernal character of slavery, and to fill me with unutterable loathing of slaveholders, it was their base ingratitude to my poor old grandmother. She had served my old master faithfully from youth to old age. She had been the source of all his wealth; she had peopled his plantation with slaves; she had become a great grandmother in his service. She had rocked him in infancy, attended him in childhood, served him through life, and at his death wiped from his icy brow the cold death-sweat, and closed his eyes forever. She was nevertheless left a slave—a slave for life—a slave in the

---

9. In Isaiah 53:3, the Lord's servant is described as "a man of sorrows, and acquainted with grief."

hands of strangers; and in their hands she saw her children, her grandchildren, and her great-grandchildren, divided, like so many sheep, without being gratified with the small privilege of a single word, as to their or her own destiny. And, to cap the climax of their base ingratitude and fiendish barbarity, my grandmother, who was now very old, having outlived my old master and all his children, having seen the beginning and end of all of them, and her present owners finding she was of but little value, her frame already racked with the pains of old age, and complete helplessness fast stealing over her once active limbs, they took her to the woods, built her a little hut, put up a little mud-chimney, and then made her welcome to the privilege of supporting herself there in perfect loneliness; thus virtually turning her out to die! If my poor old grandmother now lives, she lives to suffer in utter loneliness; she lives to remember and mourn over the loss of children, the loss of grandchildren, and the loss of great-grandchildren. They are, in the language of the slave's poet, Whittier,—

> "Gone, gone, sold and gone
> To the rice swamp dank and lone,
> Where the slave-whip ceaseless swings,
> Where the noisome insect stings,
> Where the fever-demon strews
> Poison with the falling dews,
> Where the sickly sunbeams glare
> Through the hot and misty air:—
> Gone, gone, sold and gone
> To the rice swamp dank and lone,
> From Virginia hills and waters—
> Woe is me, my stolen daughters!"[1]

The hearth is desolate. The children, the unconscious children, who once sang and danced in her presence, are gone. She gropes her way, in the darkness of age, for a drink of water. Instead of the voices of her children, she hears by day the moans of the dove, and by night the screams of the hideous owl. All is gloom. The grave is at the door. And now, when weighed down by the pains and aches of old age, when the head inclines to the feet, when the beginning and ending of human existence meet, and helpless infancy and painful old age combine together—at this time, this most needful time, the time for the exercise of that tenderness and affection which children only can exercise towards a declining parent— my poor old grandmother, the devoted mother of twelve children, is left all alone, in yonder little hut, before a few dim embers. She stands—she sits—she staggers—she falls—she groans—she dies—and there are none of her children or grandchildren present, to wipe from her wrinkled brow the cold sweat of death, or to place beneath the sod her fallen remains. Will not a righteous God visit[2] for these things?

In about two years after the death of Mrs. Lucretia, Master Thomas married his second wife. Her name was Rowena Hamilton. She was the

---

1. John Greenleaf Whittier, American poet (1807–1892), wrote a large group of antislavery poems. This one is *The Farewell of a Virginia Slave Mother to her Daughters Sold into Southern Bondage.*   2. That is, visit vengeance. Compare Exodus 32:34: "Nevertheless, in the day when I visit I will visit their sin upon them."

eldest daughter of Mr. William Hamilton. Master now lived in St. Michael's. Not long after his marriage, a misunderstanding took place between himself and Master Hugh; and as a means of punishing his brother, he took me from him to live with himself at St. Michael's. Here I underwent another most painful separation. It, however, was not so severe as the one I dreaded at the division of property; for, during this interval, a great change had taken place in Master Hugh and his once kind and affectionate wife. The influence of brandy upon him, and of slavery upon her, had effected a disastrous change in the characters of both; so that, as far as they were concerned, I thought I had little to lose by the change. But it was not to them that I was attached. It was to those little Baltimore boys that I felt the strongest attachment. I had received many good lessons from them, and was still receiving them, and the thought of leaving them was painful indeed. I was leaving, too, without the hope of ever being allowed to return. Master Thomas had said he would never let me return again. The barrier betwixt himself and brother he considered impassable.

I then had to regret that I did not at least make the attempt to carry out my resolution to run away; for the chances of success are tenfold greater from the city than from the country.

I sailed from Baltimore for St. Michael's in the sloop *Amanda*, Captain Edward Dodson. On my passage, I paid particular attention to the direction which the steamboats took to go to Philadelphia. I found, instead of going down, on reaching North Point they went up the bay, in a north-easterly direction. I deemed this knowledge of the utmost importance. My determination to run away was again revived. I resolved to wait only so long as the offering of a favorable opportunity. When that came, I was determined to be off.

CHAPTER IX

I have now reached a period of my life when I can give dates. I left Baltimore, and went to live with Master Thomas Auld, at St. Michael's, in March, 1832. It was now more than seven years since I lived with him in the family of my old master, on Colonel Lloyd's plantation. We of course were now almost entire strangers to each other. He was to me a new master, and I to him a new slave. I was ignorant of his temper and disposition; he was equally so of mine. A very short time, however, brought us into full acquaintance with each other. I was made acquainted with his wife not less than with himself. They were well matched, being equally mean and cruel. I was now, for the first time during a space of more than seven years, made to feel the painful gnawings of hunger—a something which I had not experienced before since I left Colonel Lloyd's plantation. It went hard enough with me then, when I could look back to no period at which I had enjoyed a sufficiency. It was tenfold harder after living in Master Hugh's family, where I had always had enough to eat, and of that which was good. I have said Master Thomas was a mean man. He was so. Not to give a slave enough to eat, is regarded as the most aggravated development of meanness even among slaveholders. The rule is, no matter how coarse the food, only let there be enough of it. This is the theory; and in the part of Maryland from which I came, it is the general practice,— though there are many exceptions. Master Thomas gave us enough of neither coarse nor fine food. There were four of us slaves in the kitchen— my sister Eliza, my aunt Priscilla, Henny, and myself; and we were allowed less than a half of a bushel of corn-meal per week, and very little else, either in the shape of meat or vegetables. It was not enough for us to subsist upon. We were therefore reduced to the wretched necessity of living at the expense of our neighbors. This we did by begging and stealing, whichever came handy in the time of need, the one being considered as legitimate as the other. A great many times have we poor creatures been nearly perishing with hunger, when food in abundance lay mouldering in the safe and smoke-house, and our pious mistress was aware of the fact; and yet that mistress and her husband would kneel every morning, and pray that God would bless them in basket and store!

Bad as all slaveholders are, we seldom meet one destitute of every element of character commanding respect. My master was one of this rare sort. I do not know of one single noble act ever performed by him. The leading trait in his character was meanness; and if there were any other element in his nature, it was made subject to this. He was mean; and, like most other mean men, he lacked the ability to conceal his meanness. Captain Auld was not born a slaveholder. He had been a poor man, master only of a Bay craft. He came into possession of all his slaves by marriage; and of all men, adopted slaveholders are the worst. He was cruel, but cowardly. He commanded without firmness. In the enforcement of his rules, he was at times rigid, and at times lax. At times, he spoke to his slaves with the firmness of Napoleon and the fury of a demon; at other times, he might well be mistaken for an inquirer who had lost his way. He did nothing of himself. He might have passed for a lion, but for his ears.[3] In all things noble which he attempted, his own meanness shone most conspicuous. His airs, words, and actions, were the airs, words, and actions of born slaveholders, and, being assumed, were awkward enough. He was not even a good imitator. He possessed all the disposition to deceive, but wanted the power. Having no resources within himself, he was compelled to be the copyist of many, and being such, he was forever the victim of inconsistency; and of consequence he was an object of contempt, and was held as such even by his slaves. The luxury of having slaves of his own to wait upon him was something new and unprepared for. He was a slaveholder without the ability to hold slaves. He found himself incapable of managing his slaves either by force, fear, or fraud. We seldom called him "master;" we generally called him "Captain Auld," and were hardly disposed to title him at all. I doubt not that our conduct had much to do with making him appear awkward, and of consequence fretful. Our want of reverence for him must have perplexed him greatly. He wished to have us call him master, but lacked the firmness necessary to command us to do so. His wife used to insist upon our calling him so, but to no purpose.

---

3. A variation on Aesop's fable of the ass in the lion's skin, in which the fox says, "I should have been frightened too, if I had not heard you bray."

In August, 1832, my master attended a Methodist camp-meeting held in the Bay-side, Talbot county, and there experienced religion. I indulged a faint hope that his conversion would lead him to emancipate his slaves, and that, if he did not do this, it would, at any rate, make him more kind and humane. I was disappointed in both these respects. It neither made him to be humane to his slaves, nor to emancipate them. If it had any effect on his character, it made him more cruel and hateful in all his ways; for I believe him to have been a much worse man after his conversion than before. Prior to his conversion, he relied upon his own depravity to shield and sustain him in his savage barbarity; but after his conversion, he found religious sanction and support for his slaveholding cruelty. He made the greatest pretensions to piety. His house was the house of prayer. He prayed morning, noon, and night. He very soon distinguished himself among his brethren, and was soon made a class-leader and exhorter. His activity in revivals was great, and he proved himself an instrument in the hands of the church in converting many souls. His house was the preach-ers' home. They used to take great pleasure in coming there to put up; for while he starved us, he stuffed them. We have had three or four preachers there at a time. The names of those who used to come most frequently while I lived there, were Mr. Storks, Mr. Ewery, Mr. Humphry, and Mr. Hickey. I have also seen Mr. George Cookman at our house. We slaves loved Mr. Cookman. We believed him to be a good man. We thought him instrumental in getting Mr. Samuel Harrison, a very rich slaveholder, to emancipate his slaves; and by some means got the impression that he was laboring to effect the emancipation of all the slaves. When he was at our house, we were sure to be called in to prayers. When the others were there, we were sometimes called in and sometimes not. Mr. Cookman took more notice of us than either of the other ministers. He could not come among us without betraying his sympathy for us, and, stupid as we were, we had the sagacity to see it.

While I lived with my master in St. Michael's, there was a white young man, a Mr. Wilson, who proposed to keep a Sabbath school for the instruction of such slaves as might be disposed to learn to read the New Testament. We met but three times, when Mr. West and Mr. Fairbanks, both class-leaders, with many others, came upon us with sticks and other missiles, drove us off, and forbade us to meet again. Thus ended our little Sabbath school in the pious town of St. Michael's.

I have said my master found religious sanction for his cruelty. As an example, I will state one of many facts going to prove the charge. I have seen him tie up a lame young woman, and whip her with a heavy cowskin upon her naked shoulders, causing the warm red blood to drip; and, in justification of the bloody deed, he would quote this passage of Scrip-ture—"He that knoweth his master's will, and doeth it not, shall be beaten with many stripes."

Master would keep this lacerated young woman tied up in this horrid situation four or five hours at a time. I have known him to tie her up early in the morning, and whip her before breakfast; leave her, go to his store, return to dinner, and whip her again, cutting her in the places already made raw with his cruel lash. The secret of master's cruelty toward

"Henny" is found in the fact of her being almost helpless. When quite a child, she fell into the fire, and burned herself horribly. Her hands were so burnt that she never got the use of them. She could do very little but bear heavy burdens. She was to master a bill of expense; and as he was a mean man, she was a constant offence to him. He seemed desirous of getting the poor girl out of existence. He gave her away once to his sister; but, being a poor gift, she was not disposed to keep her. Finally, my benevolent master, to use his own words, "set her adrift to take care of herself." Here was a recently-converted man, holding on upon the mother, and at the same time turning out her helpless child, to starve and die! Master Thomas was one of the many pious slaveholders who hold slaves for the very charitable purpose of taking care of them.

My master and myself had quite a number of differences. He found me unsuitable to his purpose. My city life, he said, had had a very pernicious effect upon me. It had almost ruined me for every good purpose, and fitted me for every thing which was bad. One of my greatest faults was that of letting his horse run away, and go down to his father-in-law's farm, which was about five miles from St. Michael's. I would then have to go after it. My reason for this kind of carelessness, or carefulness, was, that I could always get something to eat when I went there. Master William Hamilton, my master's father-in-law, always gave his slaves enough to eat. I never left there hungry, no matter how great the need of my speedy return. Master Thomas at length said he would stand it no longer. I had lived with him nine months, during which time he had given me a number of severe whippings, all to no good purpose. He resolved to put me out, as he said, to be broken; and, for this purpose, he let me for one year to a man named Edward Covey. Mr. Covey was a poor man, a farm-renter. He rented the place upon which he lived, as also the hands with which he tilled it. Mr. Covey had acquired a very high reputation for breaking young slaves, and this reputation was of immense value to him. It enabled him to get his farm tilled with much less expense to himself than he could have had it done without such a reputation. Some slaveholders thought it not much loss to allow Mr. Covey to have their slaves one year, for the sake of the training to which they were subjected, without any other compensation. He could hire young help with great ease, in consequence of this reputation. Added to the natural good qualities of Mr. Covey, he was a professor of religion—a pious soul—a member and a class-leader in the Methodist church. All of this added weight to his reputation as a "nigger-breaker." I was aware of all the facts, having been made acquainted with them by a young man who had lived there. I nevertheless made the change gladly; for I was sure of getting enough to eat, which is not the smallest consideration to a hungry man.

CHAPTER X

I left Master Thomas's house, and went to live with Mr. Covey, on the 1st of January, 1833. I was now, for the first time in my life, a field hand. In my new employment, I found myself even more awkward than a country boy appeared to be in a large city. I had been at my new home but one week before Mr. Covey gave me a very severe whipping, cutting my back, causing the blood to run, and raising ridges on my flesh as large as my little finger. The details of this affair are as follows: Mr. Covey sent me, very early in the morning of one of our coldest days in the month of January, to the woods, to get a load of wood. He gave me a team of unbroken oxen. He told me which was the in-hand ox, and which the off-hand ox. He then tied the end of a large rope around the horns of the in-hand ox, and gave me the other end of it, and told me, if the oxen started to run, that I must hold on upon the rope. I had never driven oxen before, and of course I was very awkward. I, however, succeeded in getting to the edge of the woods with little difficulty; but I had got a very few rods into the woods, when the oxen took fright, and started full tilt, carrying the cart against trees, and over stumps, in the most frightful manner. I expected every moment that my brains would be dashed out against the trees. After running thus for a considerable distance, they finally upset the cart, dashing it with great force against a tree, and threw themselves into a dense thicket. How I escaped death, I do not know. There I was, entirely alone, in a thick wood, in a place new to me. My cart was upset and shattered, my oxen were entangled among the young trees, and there was none to help me. After a long spell of effort, I succeeded in getting my cart righted, my oxen disentangled, and again yoked to the cart. I now proceeded with my team to the place where I had, the day before, been chopping wood, and loaded my cart pretty heavily, thinking in this way to tame my oxen. I then proceeded on my way home. I had now consumed one half of the day. I got out of the woods safely, and now felt out of danger. I stopped my oxen to open the woods gate; and just as I did so, before I could get hold of my ox-rope, the oxen again started, rushed through the gate, catching it between the wheel and the body of the cart, tearing it to pieces, and coming within a few inches of crushing me against the gate-post. Thus twice, in one short day, I escaped death by the merest chance. On my return, I told Mr. Covey what had happened, and how it happened. He ordered me to return to the woods again immediately. I did so, and he followed on after me. Just as I got into the woods, he came up and told me to stop my cart, and that he would teach me how to trifle away my time, and break gates. He then went to a large gum-tree, and with his axe cut three large switches, and, after trimming them up neatly with his pocket-knife, he ordered me to take off my clothes. I made him no answer, but stood with my clothes on. He repeated his order. I still made him no answer, nor did I move to strip myself. Upon this he rushed at me with the fierceness of a tiger, tore off my clothes, and lashed me till he had worn out his switches, cutting me so savagely as to leave the marks visible for a long time after. This whipping was the first of a number just like it, and for similar offences.

I lived with Mr. Covey one year. During the first six months, of that year, scarce a week passed without his whipping me. I was seldom free from a sore back. My awkwardness was almost always his excuse for whipping me. We were worked fully up to the point of endurance. Long before day we were up, our horses fed, and by the first approach of day we were off to the field with our hoes and ploughing teams. Mr. Covey gave us enough to eat, but scarce time to eat it. We were often less than five minutes taking our meals. We were often in the field from the first approach of day till its last lingering ray had left us; and at saving-fodder time, midnight often caught us in the field binding blades.[4]

Covey would be out with us. The way he used to stand it was this. He would spend the most of his afternoons in bed. He would then come out fresh in the evening, ready to urge us on with his words, example, and frequently with the whip. Mr. Covey was one of the few slaveholders who could and did work with his hands. He was a hard-working man. He knew by himself just what a man or a boy could do. There was no deceiving him. His work went on in his absence almost as well as in his presence; and he had the faculty of making us feel that he was ever present with us. This he did by surprising us. He seldom approached the spot where we were at work openly, if he could do it secretly. He always aimed at taking us by surprise. Such was his cunning, that we used to call him, among ourselves, "the snake." When we were at work in the cornfield, he would sometimes crawl on his hands and knees to avoid detection, and all at once he would rise nearly in our midst, and scream out, "Ha, ha! Come, come! Dash on, dash on!" This being his mode of attack, it was never safe to stop a single minute. His comings were like a thief in the night. He appeared to us as being ever at hand. He was under every tree, behind every stump, in every bush, and at every window, on the plantation. He would sometimes mount his horse, as if bound to St. Michael's, a distance of seven miles, and in half an hour afterwards you would see him coiled up in the corner of the wood-fence, watching every motion of the slaves. He would, for this purpose, leave his horse tied up in the woods. Again, he would sometimes walk up to us, and give us orders as though he was upon the point of starting on a long journey, turn his back upon us, and make as though he was going to the house to get ready; and, before he would get half way thither, he would turn short and crawl into a fence-corner, or behind some tree, and there watch us till the going down of the sun.

Mr. Covey's *forte* consisted in his power to deceive. His life was devoted to planning and perpetrating the grossest deceptions. Every thing he possessed in the shape of learning or religion, he made conform to his disposition to deceive. He seemed to think himself equal to deceiving the Almighty. He would make a short prayer in the morning, and a long prayer at night; and, strange as it may seem, few men would at times appear more devotional than he. The exercises of his family devotions were always commenced with singing; and, as he was a very poor singer himself, the duty of raising the hymn generally came upon me. He would read his hymn, and nod at me to commence. I would at times do so; at others, I would not. My non-compliance would almost always produce much confusion. To show himself independent of me, he would start and stagger through with his hymn in the most discordant manner. In this state of

4. Gathering cut grain into bundles or sheaves.

mind, he prayed with more than ordinary spirit. Poor man! such was his disposition, and success at deceiving, I do verily believe that he sometimes deceived himself into the solemn belief, that he was a sincere worshipper of the most high God; and this, too, at a time when he may be said to have been guilty of compelling his woman slave to commit the sin of adultery. The facts in the case are these: Mr. Covey was a poor man; he was just commencing in life; he was only able to buy one slave; and, shocking as is the fact, he bought her, as he said, for a *breeder.* This woman was named Caroline. Mr. Covey bought her from Mr. Thomas Lowe, about six miles from St. Michael's. She was a large, able-bodied woman, about twenty years old. She had already given birth to one child, which proved her to be just what he wanted. After buying her, he hired a married man of Mr. Samuel Harrison, to live with him one year; and him he used to fasten up with her every night! The result was, that, at the end of the year, the miserable woman gave birth to twins. At this result Mr. Covey seemed to be highly pleased, both with the man and the wretched woman. Such was his joy, and that of his wife, that nothing they could do for Caroline during her confinement was too good, or too hard, to be done. The children were regarded as being quite an addition to his wealth.

If at any one time of my life more than another, I was made to drink the bitterest dregs of slavery, that time was during the first six months of my stay with Mr. Covey. We were worked in all weathers. It was never too hot or too cold; it could never rain, blow, hail, or snow, too hard for us to work in the field. Work, work, work, was scarcely more the order of the day than of the night. The longest days were too short for him, and the shortest nights too long for him. I was somewhat unmanageable when I first went there, but a few months of this discipline tamed me. Mr. Covey succeeded in breaking me. I was broken in body, soul, and spirit. My natural elasticity was crushed, my intellect languished, the disposition to read departed, the cheerful spark that lingered about my eye died; the dark night of slavery closed in upon me; and behold a man transformed into a brute!

Sunday was my only leisure time. I spent this in a sort of beast-like stupor, between sleep and wake, under some large tree. At times I would rise up, a flash of energetic freedom would dart through my soul, accompanied with a faint beam of hope, that flickered for a moment, and then vanished. I sank down again, mourning over my wretched condition. I was sometimes prompted to take my life, and that of Covey, but was prevented by a combination of hope and fear. My sufferings on this plantation seem now like a dream rather than a stern reality.

Our house stood within a few rods of the Chesapeake Bay, whose broad bosom was ever white with sails from every quarter of the habitable globe. Those beautiful vessels, robed in purest white, so delightful to the eye of freemen, were to me so many shrouded ghosts, to terrify and torment me with thoughts of my wretched condition. I have often, in the deep stillness of a summer's Sabbath, stood all alone upon the lofty banks of that noble bay, and traced, with saddened heart and tearful eye, the countless number of sails moving off to the mighty ocean. The sight of these always affected me powerfully. My thoughts would compel utterance; and there, with no audience but the Almighty, I would pour out my soul's complaint, in my rude way, with an apostrophe[5] to the moving multitude of ships: —

"You are loosed from your moorings, and are free; I am fast in my chains, and am a slave! You move merrily before the gentle gale, and I sadly before the bloody whip! You are freedom's swift-winged angels, that fly round the world; I am confined in bands of iron! O that I were free! O, that I were on one of your gallant decks, and under your protecting wing! Alas! betwixt me and you, the turbid waters roll. Go on, go on. O that I could also go! Could I but swim! If I could fly! O, why was I born a man, of whom to make a brute! The glad ship is gone; she hides in the dim distance. I am left in the hottest hell of unending slavery. O God, save me! God, deliver me! Let me be free! Is there any God? Why am I a slave? I will run away. I will not stand it. Get caught, or get clear, I'll try it. I had as well die with ague as the fever. I have only one life to lose. I had as well be killed running as die standing. Only think of it; one hundred miles straight north, and I am free! Try it? Yes! God helping me, I will. It cannot be that I shall live and die a slave. I will take to the water. This very bay shall bear me into freedom. The steam boats steered in a north-east course from North Point. I will do the same; and when I get to the head of the bay, I will turn my canoe adrift, and walk straight through Delaware into Pennsylvania. When I get there, I shall not be required to have a pass; I can travel without being disturbed. Let but the first opportunity offer, and, come what will, I am off. Meanwhile, I will try to bear up under the yoke. I am not the only slave in the world. Why should I fret? I can bear as much as any of them. Besides, I am but a boy, and all boys are bound to some one. It may be that my misery in slavery will only increase my happiness when I get free. There is a better day coming."

Thus I used to think, and thus I used to speak to myself; goaded almost to madness at one moment, and at the next reconciling myself to my wretched lot.

I have already intimated that my condition was much worse, during the first six months of my stay at Mr. Covey's, than in the last six. The circumstances leading to the change in Mr. Covey's course toward me form an epoch in my humble history. You have seen how a man was made a slave; you shall see how a slave was made a man. On one of the hottest days of the month of August, 1833, Bill Smith, William Hughes, a slave named Eli, and myself, were engaged in fanning wheat.[6] Hughes was clearing the fanned wheat from before the fan, Eli was turning, Smith was feeding, and I was carrying wheat to the fan. The work was simple, requiring strength rather than intellect; yet, to one entirely unused to such work, it came very hard. About three o'clock of that day, I broke down; my strength failed me; I was seized with a violent aching of the head, attended with extreme dizziness; I trembled in every limb. Finding what was coming, I nerved myself up, feeling it would never do to stop work. I stood as long as I could stagger to the hopper with grain. When I could stand no

5. An exclamatory form of address.   6. Separating the grain from the chaff.

longer, I fell, and felt as if held down by an immense weight. The fan of course stopped; every one had his own work to do; and no one could do the work of the other, and have his own go on at the same time.

Mr. Covey was at the house, about one hundred yards from the tread-ing-yard where we were fanning. On hearing the fan stop, he left immediately, and came to the spot where we were. He hastily inquired what the matter was. Bill answered that I was sick, and there was no one to bring wheat to the fan. I had by this time crawled away under the side of the post and rail-fence by which the yard was enclosed, hoping to find relief by getting out of the sun. He then asked where I was. He was told by one of the hands. He came to the spot, and, after looking at me awhile, asked me what was the matter. I told him as well as I could, for I scarce had strength to speak. He then gave me a savage kick in the side, and told me to get up. I tried to do so, but fell back in the attempt. He gave me another kick, and again told me to rise. I again tried, and succeeded in gaining my feet; but, stooping to get the tub with which I was feeding the fan, I again staggered and fell. While down in this situation, Mr. Covey took up the hickory slat with which Hughes had been striking off the half-bushel measure, and with it gave me a heavy blow upon the head, making a large wound, and the blood ran freely; and with this again told me to get up. I made no effort to comply, having now made up my mind to let him do his worst. In a short time after receiving this blow, my head grew better. Mr. Covey had now left me to my fate. At this moment I resolved, for the first time, to go to my master, enter a complaint, and ask his protection. In order to [do] this, I must that afternoon walk seven miles; and this, under the circumstances, was truly a severe undertaking. I was exceedingly feeble; made so as much by the kicks and blows which I received, as by the severe fit of sickness to which I had been subjected. I, however, watched my chance, while Covey was looking in an opposite direction, and started for St. Michael's. I succeeded in getting a considerable distance on my way to the woods, when Covey discovered me, and called after me to come back, threatening what he would do if I did not come. I disregarded both his calls and his threats, and made my way to the woods as fast as my feeble state would allow; and thinking I might be overhauled by him if I kept the road, I walked through the woods, keeping far enough from the road to avoid detection, and near enough to prevent losing my way. I had not gone far before my little strength again failed me. I could go no farther. I fell down, and lay for a considerable time. The blood was yet oozing from the wound on my head. For a time I thought I should bleed to death; and think now that I should have done so, but that the blood so matted my hair as to stop the wound. After lying there about three quarters of an hour, I nerved myself up again, and started on my way, through bogs and briers, barefooted and bareheaded, tearing my feet sometimes at nearly every step; and after a journey of about seven miles, occupying some five hours to perform it, I arrived at master's store. I then presented an appearance enough to affect any but a heart of iron. From the crown of my head to my feet, I was covered with blood. My hair was all clotted with dust and blood; my shirt was stiff with blood. My legs and feet were torn in sundry places with briers and thorns, and were also cov-

ered with blood. I suppose I looked like a man who had escaped a den of
wild beasts, and barely escaped them. In this state I appeared before my
master, humbly entreating him to interpose his authority for my protection. I told him all the circumstances as well as I could, and it seemed, as
I spoke, at times to affect him. He would then walk the floor, and seek to
justify Covey by saying he expected I deserved it. He asked me what I
wanted. I told him, to let me get a new home; that as sure as I lived with
Mr. Covey again, I should live with but to die with him; that Covey would
surely kill me; he was in a fair way for it. Master Thomas ridiculed the
idea that there was any danger of Mr. Covey's killing me, and said that he
knew Mr. Covey; that he was a good man, and that he could not think of
taking me from him; that, should he do so, he would lose the whole year's
wages; that I belonged to Mr. Covey for one year, and that I must go back
to him, come what might; and that I must not trouble him with any more
stories, or that he would himself *get hold of me*. After threatening me thus,
he gave me a very large dose of salts, telling me that I might remain in St.
Michael's that night, (it being quite late) but that I must be off back to
Mr. Covey's early in the morning; and that if I did not, he would *get hold
of me*, which meant that he would whip me. I remained all night, and,
according to his orders, I started off to Covey's in the morning, (Saturday
morning), wearied in body and broken in spirit. I got no supper that night,
or breakfast that morning. I reached Covey's about nine o'clock; and just
as I was getting over the fence that divided Mrs. Kemp's fields from ours,
out ran Covey with his cowskin, to give me another whipping. Before he
could reach me, I succeeded in getting to the cornfield; and as the corn
was very high, it afforded me the means of hiding. He seemed very angry,
and searched for me a long time. My behavior was altogether unaccountable. He finally gave up the chase, thinking, I suppose, that I must come
home for something to eat; he would give himself no further trouble in
looking for me. I spent that day mostly in the woods, having the alternative
before me,—to go home and be whipped to death, or stay in the woods
and be starved to death. That night, I fell in with Sandy Jenkins, a slave
with whom I was somewhat acquainted. Sandy had a free wife who lived
about four miles from Mr. Covey's; and it being Saturday, he was on his
way to see her. I told him my circumstances, and he very kindly invited
me to go home with him. I went home with him, and talked this whole
matter over, and got his advice as to what course it was best for me to
pursue. I found Sandy an old adviser. He told me, with great solemnity, I
must go back to Covey; but that before I went, I must go with him into
another part of the woods, where there was a certain *root*, which, if I would
take some of it with me, carrying it *always on my right side*, would render
it impossible for Mr. Covey, or any other white man, to whip me. He said
he had carried it for years; and since he had done so, he had never
received a blow, and never expected to while he carried it. I at first rejected
the idea, that the simple carrying of a root in my pocket would have any
such effect as he had said, and was not disposed to take it; but Sandy
impressed the necessity with much earnestness, telling me it could do no
harm, if it did no good. To please him, I at length took the root, and,
according to his direction, carried it upon my right side. This was Sunday

morning. I immediately started for home; and upon entering the yard gate, out came Mr. Covey on his way to meeting. He spoke to me very kindly, bade me drive the pigs from a lot near by, and passed on towards the church. Now, this singular conduct of Mr. Covey really made me begin to think that there was something in the *root* which Sandy had given me; and had it been on any other day than Sunday, I could have attributed the conduct to no other cause than the influence of that root; and as it was, I was half inclined to think the *root* to be something more than I at first had taken it to be. All went well till Monday morning. On this morning, the virtue of the *root* was fully tested. Long before daylight, I was called to go and rub, curry, and feed, the horses. I obeyed, and was glad to obey. But whilst thus engaged, whilst in the act of throwing down some blades from the loft, Mr. Covey entered the stable with a long rope; and just as I was half out of the loft, he caught hold of my legs, and was about tying me. As soon as I found what he was up to, I gave a sudden spring, and as I did so, he holding to my legs, I was brought sprawling on the stable floor. Mr. Covey seemed now to think he had me, and could do what he pleased; but at this moment—from whence came the spirit I don't know—I resolved to fight; and, suiting my action to the resolution, I seized Covey hard by the throat; and as I did so, I rose. He held on to me, and I to him. My resistance was so entirely unexpected, that Covey seemed taken all aback. He trembled like a leaf. This gave me assurance, and I held him uneasy, causing the blood to run where I touched him with the ends of my fingers. Mr. Covey soon called out to Hughes for help. Hughes came, and, while Covey held me, attempted to tie my right hand. While he was in the act of doing so, I watched my chance, and gave him a heavy kick close under the ribs. This kick fairly sickened Hughes, so that he left me in the hands of Mr. Covey. This kick had the effect of not only weakening Hughes, but Covey also. When he saw Hughes bending over with pain, his courage quailed. He asked me if I meant to persist in my resistance. I told him I did, come what might; that he had used me like a brute for six months, and that I was determined to be used so no longer. With that, he strove to drag me to a stick that was lying just out of the stable door. He meant to knock me down. But just as he was leaning over to get the stick, I seized him with both hands by his collar, and brought him by a sudden snatch to the ground. By this time, Bill came. Covey called upon him for assistance. Bill wanted to know what he could do. Covey said, "Take hold of him, take hold of him!" Bill said his master hired him out to work, and not to help to whip me; so he left Covey and myself to fight our own battle out. We were at it for nearly two hours. Covey at length let me go, puffing and blowing at a great rate, saying that if I had not resisted, he would not have whipped me half so much. The truth was, that he had not whipped me at all. I considered him as getting entirely the worst end of the bargain; for he had drawn no blood from me, but I had from him. The whole six months afterwards, that I spent with Mr. Covey, he never laid the weight of his finger upon me in anger. He would occasionally say, he didn't want to get hold of me again. "No," thought I, "you need not; for you will come off worse than you did before."

This battle with Mr. Covey was the turning-point in my career as a slave. It rekindled the few expiring embers of freedom, and revived within me a sense of my own manhood. It recalled the departed self-confidence, and inspired me again with a determination to be free. The gratification afforded by the triumph was a full compensation for whatever else might follow, even death itself. He only can understand the deep satisfaction which I experienced, who has himself repelled by force the bloody arm of slavery. I felt as I never felt before. It was a glorious resurrection, from the tomb of slavery, to the heaven of freedom. My long-crushed spirit rose, cowardice departed, bold defiance took its place; and I now resolved that, however long I might remain a slave in form, the day had passed forever when I could be a slave in fact. I did not hesitate to let it be known of me, that the white man who expected to succeed in whipping, must also succeed in killing me.

From this time I was never again what might be called fairly whipped, though I remained a slave four years afterwards. I had several fights, but was never whipped.

It was for a long time a matter of surprise to me why Mr. Covey did not immediately have me taken by the constable to the whipping-post, and there regularly whipped for the crime of raising my hand against a white man in defence of myself. And the only explanation I can now think of does not entirely satisfy me; but such as it is, I will give it. Mr. Covey enjoyed the most unbounded reputation for being a first-rate overseer and negro-breaker. It was of considerable importance to him. That reputation was at stake; and had he sent me—a boy about sixteen years old—to the public whipping-post, his reputation would have been lost; so, to save his reputation, he suffered me to go unpunished.

My term of actual service to Mr. Edward Covey ended on Christmas day, 1833. The days between Christmas and New Year's day are allowed as holidays; and, accordingly, we were not required to perform any labor, more than to feed and take care of the stock. This time we regarded as our own, by the grace of our masters; and we therefore used or abused it nearly as we pleased. Those of us who had families at a distance, were generally allowed to spend the whole six days in their society. This time, however, was spent in various ways. The staid, sober, thinking and industrious ones of our number would employ themselves in making corn-brooms, mats, horse-collars, and baskets; and another class of us would spend the time in hunting opossums, hares, and coons. But by far the larger part engaged in such sports and merriments as playing ball, wrestling, running footraces, fiddling, dancing, and drinking whisky; and this latter mode of spending the time was by far the most agreeable to the feelings of our masters. A slave who would work during the holidays was considered by our masters as scarcely deserving them. He was regarded as one who rejected the favor of his master. It was deemed a disgrace not to get drunk at Christmas; and he was regarded as lazy indeed, who had not provided himself with the necessary means, during the year, to get whisky enough to last him through Christmas.

From what I know of the effect of these holidays upon the slave, I believe them to be among the most effective means in the hands of the slaveholder in keeping down the spirit of insurrection. Were the slaveholders at once to abandon this practice, I have not the slightest doubt it would lead to an immediate insurrection among the slaves. These holidays serve as conductors, or safety-valves, to carry off the rebellious spirit of enslaved humanity. But for these, the slave would be forced up to the wildest desperation; and woe betide the slaveholder, the day he ventures to remove or hinder the operation of those conductors! I warn him that, in such an event, a spirit will go forth in their midst, more to be dreaded than the most appalling earthquake.

The holidays are part and parcel of the gross fraud, wrong, and inhumanity of slavery. They are professedly a custom established by the benevolence of the slaveholders; but I undertake to say, it is the result of selfishness, and one of the grossest frauds committed upon the down-trodden slave. They do not give the slaves this time because they would not like to have their work during its continuance, but because they know it would be unsafe to deprive them of it. This will be seen by the fact, that the slaveholders like to have their slaves spend those days just in such a manner as to make them as glad of their ending as of their beginning. Their object seems to be, to disgust their slaves with freedom, by plunging them into the lowest depths of dissipation. For instance, the slaveholders not only like to see the slave drink of his own accord, but will adopt various plans to make him drunk. One plan is, to make bets on their slaves, as to who can drink the most whisky without getting drunk; and in this way they succeed in getting whole multitudes to drink to excess. Thus, when the slave asks for virtuous freedom, the cunning slaveholder, knowing his ignorance, cheats him with a dose of vicious dissipation, artfully labelled with the name of liberty. The most of us used to drink it down, and the result was just what might be supposed: many of us were led to think that there was little to choose between liberty and slavery. We felt, and very properly too, that we had almost as well be slaves to man as to rum. So, when the holidays ended, we staggered up from the filth of our wallowing, took a long breath, and marched to the field,—feeling, upon the whole, rather glad to go, from what our master had deceived us into a belief was freedom, back to the arms of slavery.

I have said that this mode of treatment is a part of the whole system of fraud and inhumanity of slavery. It is so. The mode here adopted to disgust the slave with freedom, by allowing him to see only the abuse of it, is carried out in other things. For instance, a slave loves molasses; he steals some. His master, in many cases, goes off to town, and buys a large quantity; he returns, takes his whip, and commands the slave to eat the molasses, until the poor fellow is made sick at the very mention of it. The same mode is sometimes adopted to make the slaves refrain from asking for more food than their regular allowance. A slave runs through his allowance, and applies for more. His master is enraged at him; but, not willing to send him off without food, gives him more than is necessary, and compels him to eat it within a given time. Then, if he complains that he cannot eat it, he is said to be satisfied neither full nor fasting, and is whipped for being hard to please! I have an abundance of such illustrations of the same principle, drawn from my own observation, but think the cases I have cited sufficient. The practice is a very common one.

On the first of January, 1834, I left Mr. Covey, and went to live with Mr. William Freeland, who lived about three miles from St. Michael's. I soon found Mr. Freeland a very different man from Mr. Covey. Though not rich, he was what would be called an educated southern gentleman. Mr. Covey, as I have shown, was a well-trained negro-breaker and slave-driver. The former (slaveholder though he was) seemed to possess some regard for honor, some reverence for justice, and some respect for human-ity. The latter seemed totally insensible to all such sentiments. Mr. Free-land had many of the faults peculiar to slaveholders, such as being very passionate and fretful; but I must do him the justice to say, that he was exceedingly free from those degrading vices to which Mr. Covey was con-stantly addicted. The one was open and frank, and we always knew where to find him. The other was a most artful deceiver, and could be under-stood only by such as were skilful enough to detect his cunningly-devised frauds. Another advantage I gained in my new master was, he made no pretensions to, or profession of, religion; and this, in my opinion, was truly a great advantage. I assert most unhesitatingly, that the religion of the south is a mere covering for the most horrid crimes,—a justifier of the most appalling barbarity,—a sanctifier of the most hateful frauds,—and a dark shelter under which the darkest, foulest, grossest, and most infernal deeds of slaveholders find the strongest protection. Were I to be again reduced to the chains of slavery, next to that enslavement, I should regard being the slave of a religious master the greatest calamity that could befall me. For of all slaveholders with whom I have ever met, religious slavehold-ers are the worst. I have ever found them the meanest and basest, the most cruel and cowardly, of all others. It was my unhappy lot not only to belong to a religious slaveholder, but to live in a community of such religionists. Very near Mr. Freeland lived the Rev. Daniel Weeden, and in the same neighborhood lived the Rev. Rigby Hopkins. These were members and ministers in the Reformed Methodist Church. Mr. Weeden owned, among others, a woman slave, whose name I have forgotten. This woman's back, for weeks, was kept literally raw, made so by the lash of this merci-less, *religious* wretch. He used to hire hands. His maxim was, Behave well or behave ill, it is the duty of a master occasionally to whip a slave, to remind him of his master's authority. Such was his theory, and such his practice.

Mr. Hopkins was even worse than Mr. Weeden. His chief boast was his ability to manage slaves. The peculiar feature of his government was that of whipping slaves in advance of deserving it. He always managed to have one or more of his slaves to whip every Monday morning. He did this to alarm their fears, and strike terror into those who escaped. His plan was to whip for the smallest offences, to prevent the commission of large ones. Mr. Hopkins could always find some excuse for whipping a slave. It would astonish one, unaccustomed to a slaveholding life, to see with what won-derful ease a slaveholder can find things, of which to make occasion to whip a slave. A mere look, word, or motion,—a mistake, accident, or want of power,—are all matters for which a slave may be whipped at any time. Does a slave look dissatisfied? It is said, he has the devil in him, and it must be whipped out. Does he speak loudly when spoken to by his master?

Then he is getting high-minded, and should be taken down a button-hole lower. Does he forget to pull off his hat at the approach of a white person? Then he is wanting in reverence, and should be whipped for it. Does he ever venture to vindicate his conduct, when censured for it? Then he is guilty of impudence,—one of the greatest crimes of which a slave can be guilty. Does he ever venture to suggest a different mode of doing things from that pointed out by his master? He is indeed presumptuous, and getting above himself; and nothing less than a flogging will do for him. Does he, while ploughing, break a plough,—or, while hoeing, break a hoe? It is owing to his carelessness, and for it a slave must always be whipped. Mr. Hopkins could always find something of this sort to justify the use of the lash, and he seldom failed to embrace such opportunities. There was not a man in the whole county, with whom the slaves who had the getting their own home, would not prefer to live, rather than with this Rev. Mr. Hopkins. And yet there was not a man any where round, who made higher professions of religion, or was more active in revivals,—more attentive to the class, love-feast, prayer and preaching meetings, or more devotional in his family,—that prayed earlier, later, louder, and longer,— than this same reverend slave-driver, Rigby Hopkins.

But to return to Mr. Freeland, and to my experience while in his employment. He, like Mr. Covey, gave us enough to eat; but, unlike Mr. Covey, he also gave us sufficient time to take our meals. He worked us hard, but always between sunrise and sunset. He required a good deal of work to be done, but gave us good tools with which to work. His farm was large, but he employed hands enough to work it, and with ease, compared with many of his neighbors. My treatment, while in his employment, was heavenly, compared with what I experienced at the hands of Mr. Edward Covey.

Mr. Freeland was himself the owner of but two slaves. Their names were Henry Harris and John Harris. The rest of his hands he hired. These consisted of myself, Sandy Jenkins,[7] and Handy Caldwell. Henry and John were quite intelligent, and in a very little while after I went there, I succeeded in creating in them a strong desire to learn how to read. This desire soon sprang up in the others also. They very soon mustered up some old spelling-books, and nothing would do but that I must keep a Sabbath school. I agreed to do so, and accordingly devoted my Sundays to teaching these my loved fellow-slaves how to read. Neither of them knew his letters when I went there. Some of the slaves of the neighboring farms found what was going on, and also availed themselves of this little opportunity to learn to read. It was understood, among all who came, that there must be as little display about it as possible. It was necessary to keep our religious masters at St. Michael's unacquainted with the fact, that, instead of spending the Sabbath in wrestling, boxing, and drinking whiskey, we were trying to learn how to read the will of God; for they had much rather see us engaged in those degrading sports, than to see us behaving like intellec-

---

7. This is the same man who gave me the roots to prevent my being whipped by Mr. Covey. He was "a clever soul." We used frequently to talk about the fight with Covey, and as often as we did so, he would claim my success as the result of the roots which he gave me. This superstition is very common among the more ignorant slaves. A slave seldom dies but that his death is attributed to trickery [Douglass's note].

tual, moral, and accountable beings. My blood boils as I think of the bloody manner in which Messrs. Wright Fairbanks and Garrison West, both class-leaders, in connection with many others, rushed in upon us with sticks and stones, and broke up our virtuous little Sabbath school, at St. Michael's—all calling themselves Christians! humble followers of the Lord Jesus Christ! But I am again digressing.

I held my Sabbath school at the house of a free colored man, whose name I deem it imprudent to mention; for should it be known, it might embarrass him greatly, though the crime of holding the school was committed ten years ago. I had at one time over forty scholars, and those of the right sort, ardently desiring to learn. They were of all ages, though mostly men and women. I look back to those Sundays with an amount of pleasure not to be expressed. They were great days to my soul. The work of instructing my dear fellow-slaves was the sweetest engagement with which I was ever blessed. We loved each other, and to leave them at the close of the Sabbath was a severe cross indeed. When I think that those precious souls are to-day shut up in the prison-house of slavery, my feelings overcome me, and I am almost ready to ask, "Does a righteous God govern the universe? and for what does he hold the thunders in his right hand, if not to smite the oppressor, and deliver the spoiled out of the hand of the spoiler?" These dear souls came not to Sabbath school because it was popular to do so, nor did I teach them because it was reputable to be thus engaged. Every moment they spent in that school, they were liable to be taken up, and given thirty-nine lashes. They came because they wished to learn. Their minds had been starved by their cruel masters. They had been shut up in mental darkness. I taught them, because it was the delight of my soul to be doing something that looked like bettering the condition of my race. I kept up my school nearly the whole year I lived with Mr. Freeland; and, beside my Sabbath school, I devoted three evenings in the week, during the winter, to teaching the slaves at home. And I have the happiness to know, that several of those who came to Sabbath school learned how to read; and that one, at least, is now free through my agency.

The year passed off smoothly. It seemed only about half as long as the year which preceded it. I went through it without receiving a single blow. I will give Mr. Freeland the credit of being the best master I ever had, *till I became my own master.* For the ease with which I passed the year, I was, however, somewhat indebted to the society of my fellow-slaves. They were noble souls; they not only possessed loving hearts, but brave ones. We were linked and interlinked with each other. I loved them with a love stronger than any thing I have experienced since. It is sometimes said that we slaves do not love and confide in each other. In answer to this assertion, I can say, I never loved any or confided in any people more than my fellow-slaves, and especially those with whom I lived at Mr. Freeland's. I believe we would have died for each other. We never undertook to do any thing, of any importance, without a mutual consultation. We never moved separately. We were one; and as much so by our tempers and dispositions, as by the mutual hardships to which we were necessarily subjected by our condition as slaves.

At the close of the year 1834, Mr. Freeland again hired me of my master, for the year 1835. But, by this time, I began to want to live *upon free land* as well as *with Freeland*; and I was no longer content, therefore, to live with him or any other slaveholder. I began, with the commencement of the year, to prepare myself for a final struggle, which should decide my fate one way or the other. My tendency was upward. I was fast approaching manhood, and year after year had passed, and I was still a slave. These thoughts roused me—I must do something. I therefore resolved that 1835 should not pass without witnessing an attempt, on my part, to secure my liberty. But I was not willing to cherish this determination alone. My fellow-slaves were dear to me. I was anxious to have them participate with me in this, my life-giving determination. I therefore, though with great prudence, commenced early to ascertain their views and feelings in regard to their condition, and to imbue their minds with thoughts of freedom. I bent myself to devising ways and means for our escape, and meanwhile strove, on all fitting occasions, to impress them with the gross fraud and inhumanity of slavery. I went first to Henry, next to John, then to the others. I found, in them all, warm hearts and noble spirits. They were ready to hear, and ready to act when a feasible plan should be proposed. This was what I wanted. I talked to them of our want of manhood, if we submitted to our enslavement without at least one noble effort to be free. We met often, and consulted frequently, and told our hopes and fears, recounted the difficulties, real and imagined, which we should be called on to meet. At times we were almost disposed to give up, and try to content ourselves with our wretched lot; at others, we were firm and unbending in our determination to go. Whenever we suggested any plan, there was shrinking—the odds were fearful. Our path was beset with the greatest obstacles; and if we succeeded in gaining the end of it, our right to be free was yet questionable—we were yet liable to be returned to bondage. We could see no spot, this side of the ocean, where we could be free. We knew nothing about Canada. Our knowledge of the north did not extend farther than New York; and to go there, and be forever harassed with the frightful liability of being returned to slavery—with the certainty of being treated tenfold worse than before—the thought was truly a horrible one, and one which it was not easy to overcome. The case sometimes stood thus: At every gate through which we were to pass, we saw a watchman—at every ferry a guard—on every bridge a sentinel—and in every wood a patrol. We were hemmed in upon every side. Here were the difficulties, real or imagined—the good to be sought, and the evil to be shunned. On the one hand, there stood slavery, a stern reality, glaring frightfully upon us,—its robes already crimsoned with the blood of millions, and even now feasting itself greedily upon our own flesh. On the other hand, away back in the dim distance, under the flickering light of the north star, behind some craggy hill or snow-covered mountain, stood a doubtful freedom—half frozen—beckoning us to come and share its hospitality. This in itself was sometimes enough to stagger us; but when we permitted ourselves to survey the road, we were frequently appalled. Upon either side we saw grim death, assuming the most horrid shapes. Now it was starvation, causing us to eat our own flesh;—now we were contending with the waves, and were drowned;—now we were overtaken, and torn to pieces by the

fangs of the terrible bloodhound. We were stung by scorpions, chased by
wild beasts, bitten by snakes, and finally, after having nearly reached the
desired spot,—after swimming rivers, encountering wild beasts, sleeping
in the woods, suffering hunger and nakedness,—we were overtaken by our
pursuers, and, in our resistance, we were shot dead upon the spot! I say,
this picture sometimes appalled us, and made us

> "rather bear those ills we had,
> Than fly to others, that we knew not of."[8]

In coming to a fixed determination to run away, we did more than
Patrick Henry,[9] when he resolved upon liberty or death. With us it was a
doubtful liberty at most, and almost certain death if we failed. For my part,
I should prefer death to hopeless bondage.

Sandy, one of our number, gave up the notion, but still encouraged us.
Our company then consisted of Henry Harris, John Harris, Henry Bailey,
Charles Roberts, and myself. Henry Bailey was my uncle, and belonged
to my master. Charles married my aunt: he belonged to my master's father-
in-law, Mr. William Hamilton.

The plan we finally concluded upon was, to get a large canoe belonging
to Mr. Hamilton, and upon the Saturday night previous to Easter holidays,
paddle directly up the Chesapeake Bay. On our arrival at the head of the
bay, a distance of seventy or eighty miles from where we lived, it was our
purpose to turn our canoe adrift, and follow the guidance of the north star
till we got beyond the limits of Maryland. Our reason for taking the water
route was, that we were less liable to be suspected as runaways; we hoped
to be regarded as fishermen; whereas, if we should take the land route, we
should be subjected to interruptions of almost every kind. Any one having
a white face, and being so disposed, could stop us, and subject us to examination.

The week before our intended start, I wrote several protections, one for
each of us. As well as I can remember, they were in the following words,
to wit:—

> "This is to certify that I, the undersigned, have given the bearer, my
> servant, full liberty to go to Baltimore, and spend the Easter holidays.
> Written with mine own hand, &c., 1835.
>   "WILLIAM HAMILTON,
>   "Near St. Michael's, in Talbot county, Maryland."

We were not going to Baltimore; but, in going up the bay, we went toward
Baltimore, and these protections were only intended to protect us while
on the bay.

As the time drew near for our departure, our anxiety became more and
more intense. It was truly a matter of life and death with us. The strength
of our determination was about to be fully tested. At this time, I was very
active in explaining every difficulty, removing every doubt, dispelling
every fear, and inspiring all with the firmness indispensable to success in

---

8. Shakespeare's *Hamlet* 3.1.81–82: "rather bear those ills we have, / Than fly to others, that we know not
of."   9. American statesman and orator (1736–1799) whose most famous utterance was "Give me liberty or give me death."

our undertaking; assuring them that half was gained the instant we made the move; we had talked long enough; we were now ready to move; if not now, we never should be; and if we did not intend to move now, we had as well fold our arms, sit down, and acknowledge ourselves fit only to be slaves. This, none of us were prepared to acknowledge. Every man stood firm; and at our last meeting, we pledged ourselves afresh, in the most solemn manner, that, at the time appointed, we would certainly start in pursuit of freedom. This was in the middle of the week, at the end of which we were to be off. We went, as usual, to our several fields of labor, but with bosoms highly agitated with thoughts of our truly hazardous undertaking. We tried to conceal our feelings as much as possible; and I think we succeeded very well.

After a painful waiting, the Saturday morning, whose night was to witness our departure, came. I hailed it with joy, bring what of sadness it might. Friday night was a sleepless one for me. I was, by common consent, at the head of the whole affair. The responsibility of success or failure lay heavily upon me. The glory of the one, and the confusion of the other, were alike mine. The first two hours of that morning were such as I never experienced before, and hope never to again. Early in the morning, we went, as usual, to the field. We were spreading manure; and all at once, while thus engaged, I was overwhelmed with an indescribable feeling, in the fulness of which I turned to Sandy, who was near by, and said, "We are betrayed!" "Well," said he, "that thought has this moment struck me." We said no more. I was never more certain of any thing.

The horn was blown as usual, and we went up from the field to the house for breakfast. I went for the form, more than for want of any thing to eat that morning. Just as I got to the house, in looking out at the lane gate, I saw four white men, with two colored men. The white men were on horseback, and the colored ones were walking behind, as if tied. I watched them a few moments till they got up to our lane gate. Here they halted, and tied the colored men to the gate-post. I was not yet certain as to what the matter was. In a few moments, in rode Mr. Hamilton, with a speed betokening great excitement. He came to the door, and inquired if Master William was in. He was told he was at the barn. Mr. Hamilton, without dismounting, rode up to the barn with extraordinary speed. In a few moments, he and Mr. Freeland returned to the house. By this time, the three constables rode up, and in great haste dismounted, tied their horses, and met Master William and Mr. Hamilton returning from the barn; and after talking awhile, they all walked up to the kitchen door. There was no one in the kitchen but myself and John. Henry and Sandy were up at the barn. Mr. Freeland put his head in at the door, and called me by name, saying, there were some gentlemen at the door who wished to see me. I stepped to the door, and inquired what they wanted. They at once seized me, and, without giving me any satisfaction, tied me—lashing my hands closely together. I insisted upon knowing what the matter was. They at length said, that they had learned I had been in a "scrape," and that I was to be examined before my master; and if their information proved false, I should not be hurt.

In a few moments, they succeeded in tying John. They then turned to

Henry, who had by this time returned, and commanded him to cross his hands. "I won't!" said Henry, in a firm tone, indicating his readiness to meet the consequences of his refusal. "Won't you?" said Tom Graham, the constable. "No, I won't!" said Henry, in a still stronger tone. With this, two of the constables pulled out their shining pistols, and swore, by their Creator, that they would make him cross his hands or kill him. Each cocked his pistol, and, with fingers on the trigger, walked up to Henry, saying, at the same time, if he did not cross his hands, they would blow his damned heart out. "Shoot me, shoot me!" said Henry; "you can't kill me but once. Shoot, shoot,—and be damned! *I won't be tied!*" This he said in a tone of loud defiance; and at the same time, with a motion as quick as lightning, he with one single stroke dashed the pistols from the hand of each constable. As he did this, all hands fell upon him, and, after beating him some time, they finally overpowered him, and got him tied.

During the scuffle, I managed, I know not how, to get my pass out, and, without being discovered, put it into the fire. We were all now tied; and just as we were to leave for Easton jail, Betsy Freeland, mother of William Freeland, came to the door with her hands full of biscuits, and divided them between Henry and John. She then delivered herself of a speech, to the following effect:—addressing herself to me, she said, "*You devil! You yellow devil!* it was you that put it into the heads of Henry and John to run away. But for you, you long-legged mulatto devil! Henry nor John would never have thought of such a thing." I made no reply, and was immediately hurried off towards St. Michael's. Just a moment previous to the scuffle with Henry, Mr. Hamilton suggested the propriety of making a search for the protections which he had understood Frederick had written for himself and the rest. But, just at the moment he was about carrying his proposal into effect, his aid was needed in helping to tie Henry; and the excitement attending the scuffle caused them either to forget, or to deem it unsafe, under the circumstances, to search. So we were not yet convicted of the intention to run away.

When we got about half way to St. Michael's, while the constables having us in charge were looking ahead, Henry inquired of me what he should do with his pass. I told him to eat it with his biscuit, and own nothing; and we passed the word around, "*Own nothing*"; and "*Own nothing!*" said we all. Our confidence in each other was unshaken. We were resolved to succeed or fail together, after the calamity had befallen us as much as before. We were now prepared for any thing. We were to be dragged that morning fifteen miles behind horses, and then to be placed in the Easton jail. When we reached St. Michael's, we underwent a sort of examination. We all denied that we ever intended to run away. We did this more to bring out the evidence against us, than from any hope of getting clear of being sold; for, as I have said, we were ready for that. The fact was, we cared but little where we went, so we went together. Our greatest concern was about separation. We dreaded that more than any thing this side of death. We found the evidence against us to be the testimony of one person; our master would not tell who it was; but we came to a unanimous decision among ourselves as to who their informant was. We were sent off to the jail at Easton. When we got there, we were delivered up to the sheriff, Mr. Joseph Graham, and by him placed in jail. Henry, John, and myself, were placed in one room together—Charles, and Henry Bailey, in another. Their object in separating us was to hinder concert.

We had been in jail scarcely twenty minutes, when a swarm of slave traders, and agents for slave traders, flocked into jail to look at us, and to ascertain if we were for sale. Such a set of beings I never saw before! I felt myself surrounded by so many fiends from perdition. A band of pirates never looked more like their father, the devil. They laughed and grinned over us, saying, "Ah, my boys! we have got you, haven't we?" And after taunting us in various ways, they one by one went into an examination of us, with intent to ascertain our value. They would impudently ask us if we would not like to have them for our masters. We would make them no answer, and leave them to find out as best they could. Then they would curse and swear at us, telling us that they could take the devil out of us in a very little while, if we were only in their hands.

While in jail, we found ourselves in much more comfortable quarters than we expected when we went there. We did not get much to eat, nor that which was very good; but we had a good clean room, from the windows of which we could see what was going on in the street, which was very much better than though we had been placed in one of the dark, damp cells. Upon the whole, we got along very well, so far as the jail and its keeper were concerned. Immediately after the holidays were over, contrary to all our expectations, Mr. Hamilton and Mr. Freeland came up to Easton, and took Charles, the two Henrys, and John, out of jail, and carried them home, leaving me alone. I regarded this separation as a final one. It caused me more pain than any thing else in the whole transaction. I was ready for any thing rather than separation. I supposed that they had consulted together, and had decided that, as I was the whole cause of the intention of the others to run away, it was hard to make the innocent suffer with the guilty; and that they had, therefore, concluded to take the others home, and sell me, as a warning to the others that remained. It is due to the noble Henry to say, he seemed almost as reluctant at leaving the prison as at leaving home to come to the prison. But we knew we should, in all probability, be separated, if we were sold; and since he was in their hands, he concluded to go peaceably home.

I was now left to my fate. I was all alone, and within the walls of a stone prison. But a few days before, and I was full of hope. I expected to have been safe in a land of freedom; but now I was covered with gloom, sunk down to the utmost despair. I thought the possibility of freedom was gone. I was kept in this way about one week, at the end of which, Captain Auld, my master, to my surprise and utter astonishment, came up, and took me out, with the intention of sending me, with a gentleman of his acquaintance, into Alabama. But, from some cause or other, he did not send me to Alabama, but concluded to send me back to Baltimore, to live again with his brother Hugh, and to learn a trade.

Thus, after an absence of three years and one month, I was once more permitted to return to my old home at Baltimore. My master sent me away, because there existed against me a very great prejudice in the community, and he feared I might be killed.

In a few weeks after I went to Baltimore, Master Hugh hired me to Mr. William Gardner, an extensive ship-builder, on Fell's Point. I was put there to learn how to calk. It, however, proved a very unfavorable place for the accomplishment of this object. Mr. Gardner was engaged that spring in building two large man-of-war brigs, professedly for the Mexican government. The vessels were to be launched in the July of that year, and in failure thereof, Mr. Gardner was to lose a considerable sum; so that when I entered, all was hurry. There was no time to learn any thing. Every man had to do that which he knew how to do. In entering the shipyard, my orders from Mr. Gardner were, to do whatever the carpenters commanded me to do. This was placing me at the beck and call of about seventy-five men. I was to regard all these as masters. Their word was to be my law. My situation was a most trying one. At times I needed a dozen pair of hands. I was called a dozen ways in the space of a single minute. Three or four voices would strike my ear at the same moment. It was— "Fred., come help me to cant this timber here."—"Fred., come carry this timber yonder."—"Fred., bring that roller here."—"Fred., go get a fresh can of water."—"Fred., come help saw off the end of this timber."— "Fred., go quick, and get the crowbar."—"Fred., hold on the end of this fall."—"Fred., go to the blacksmith's shop, and get a new punch."— "Hurra,[1] Fred.! run and bring me a cold chisel."—"I say, Fred., bear a hand, and get up a fire as quick as lightning under that steam-box."— "Halloo, nigger! come, turn this grindstone."—"Come, come! move, move! and *bowse*[2] this timber forward."—"I say, darky, blast your eyes, why don't you heat up some pitch?"—"Halloo! halloo! halloo!" (Three voices at the same time.) "Come here!—Go there!—Hold on where you are! Damn you, if you move, I'll knock your brains out!"

This was my school for eight months, and I might have remained there longer, but for a most horrid fight I had with four of the white apprentices, in which my left eye was nearly knocked out, and I was horribly mangled in other respects. The facts in the case were these: Until a very little while after I went there, white and black ship-carpenters worked side by side, and no one seemed to see any impropriety in it. All hands seemed to be very well satisfied. Many of the black carpenters were freemen. Things seemed to be going on very well. All at once, the white carpenters knocked off, and said they would not work with free colored workmen. Their reason for this, as alleged, was, that if free colored carpenters were encouraged, they would soon take the trade into their own hands, and poor white men would be thrown out of employment. They therefore felt called upon at once to put a stop to it. And, taking advantage of Mr. Gardner's necessities, they broke off, swearing they would work no longer, unless he would discharge his black carpenters. Now, though this did not extend to me in form, it did reach me in fact. My fellow-apprentices very soon began to feel it degrading to them to work with me. They began to put on airs, and

---

1. Hurry.   2. Lift or haul (usually with the help of block and tackle).

talk about the "niggers" taking the country, saying we all ought to be
killed; and, being encouraged by the journeymen, they commenced making my condition as hard as they could, by hectoring me around, and
sometimes striking me. I, of course, kept the vow I made after the fight
with Mr. Covey, and struck back again, regardless of consequences; and
while I kept them from combining, I succeeded very well; for I could
whip the whole of them, taking them separately. They, however, at length
combined, and came upon me, armed with sticks, stones, and heavy hand-
spikes. One came in front with a half brick. There was one at each side of
me, and one behind me. While I was attending to those in front, and on
either side, the one behind ran up with the handspike, and struck me a
heavy blow upon the head. It stunned me. I fell, and with this they all ran
upon me, and fell to beating me with their fists. I let them lay on for a
while, gathering strength. In an instant, I gave a sudden surge, and rose to
my hands and knees. Just as I did that, one of their number gave me, with
his heavy boot, a powerful kick in the left eye. My eyeball seemed to have
burst. When they saw my eye closed, and badly swollen, they left me.
With this I seized the handspike, and for a time pursued them. But here
the carpenters interfered, and I thought I might as well give it up. It was
impossible to stand my hand against so many. All this took place in sight
of not less than fifty white ship-carpenters, and not one interposed a
friendly word; but some cried, "Kill the damned nigger! Kill him! kill him!
He struck a white person." I found my only chance for life was in flight. I
succeeded in getting away without an additional blow, and barely so; for
to strike a white man is death by Lynch law,—and that was the law in Mr.
Gardner's ship-yard; nor is there much of any other out of Mr. Gardner's
ship-yard.

I went directly home, and told the story of my wrongs to Master Hugh;
and I am happy to say of him, irreligious as he was, his conduct was heavenly, compared with that of his brother Thomas under similar circumstances. He listened attentively to my narration of the circumstances
leading to the savage outrage, and gave many proofs of his strong indignation of it. The heart of my once overkind mistress was again melted into
pity. My puffed-out eye and blood-covered face moved her to tears. She
took a chair by me, washed the blood from my face, and, with a mother's
tenderness, bound up my head, covering the wounded eye with a lean
piece of fresh beef. It was almost compensation for my suffering to witness,
once more, a manifestation of kindness from this, my once affectionate
old mistress. Master Hugh was very much enraged. He gave expression to
his feelings by pouring out curses upon the heads of those who did the
deed. As soon as I got a little the better of my bruises, he took me with
him to Esquire Watson's, on Bond Street, to see what could be done about
the matter. Mr. Watson inquired who saw the assault committed. Master
Hugh told him it was done in Mr. Gardner's ship-yard, at midday, where
there were a large company of men at work. "As to that," he said, "the
deed was done, and there was no question as to who did it." His answer
was, he could do nothing in the case, unless some white man would come
forward and testify. He could issue no warrant on my word. If I had been

killed in the presence of a thousand colored people, their testimony combined would have been insufficient to have arrested one of the murderers.
Master Hugh, for once, was compelled to say this state of things was too
bad. Of course, it was impossible to get any white man to volunteer his
testimony in my behalf, and against the white young men. Even those who
may have sympathized with me were not prepared to do this. It required a
degree of courage unknown to them to do so; for just at that time, the
slightest manifestation of humanity toward a colored person was
denounced as abolitionism, and that name subjected its bearer to frightful
liabilities. The watchwords of the bloody-minded in that region, and in
those days, were, "Damn the abolitionists!" and "Damn the niggers!"
There was nothing done, and probably nothing would have been done if
I had been killed. Such was, and such remains, the state of things in the
Christian city of Baltimore.

Master Hugh, finding he could get no redress, refused to let me go back
again to Mr. Gardner. He kept me himself, and his wife dressed my wound
till I was again restored to health. He then took me into the ship-yard of
which he was foreman, in the employment of Mr. Walter Price. There I
was immediately set to calking, and very soon learned the art of using my
mallet and irons. In the course of one year from the time I left Mr. Gardner's, I was able to command the highest wages given to the most experienced calkers. I was now of some importance to my master. I was bringing
him from six to seven dollars per week. I sometimes brought him nine
dollars per week: my wages were a dollar and a half a day. After learning
how to calk, I sought my own employment, made my own contracts, and
collected the money which I earned. My pathway became much more
smooth than before; my condition was now much more comfortable.
When I could get no calking to do, I did nothing. During these leisure
times, those old notions about freedom would steal over me again. When
in Mr. Gardner's employment, I was kept in such a perpetual whirl of
excitement, I could think of nothing, scarcely, but my life; and in thinking
of my life, I almost forgot my liberty. I have observed this in my experience
of slavery,—that whenever my condition was improved, instead of its
increasing my contentment, it only increased my desire to be free, and set
me to thinking of plans to gain my freedom. I have found that, to make a
contented slave, it is necessary to make a thoughtless one. It is necessary
to darken his moral and mental vision, and, as far as possible, to annihilate
the power of reason. He must be made to feel that slavery is right; and he
can be brought to that only when he ceases to be a man.

I was now getting, as I have said, one dollar and fifty cents per day. I
contracted for it; I earned it; it was paid to me; it was rightfully my own;
yet, upon each returning Saturday night, I was compelled to deliver every
cent of that money to Master Hugh. And why? Not because he earned
it,—not because he had any hand in earning it,—not because I owed it to
him,—nor because he possessed the slightest shadow of a right to it; but
solely because he had the power to compel me to give it up. The right of
the grim-visaged pirate upon the high seas is exactly the same.

CHAPTER XI

I now come to that part of my life during which I planned, and finally succeeded in making, my escape from slavery. But before narrating any of the peculiar circumstances, I deem it proper to make known my intention not to state all the facts connected with the transaction. My reasons for pursuing this course may be understood from the following: First, were I to give a minute statement of all the facts, it is not only possible, but quite probable, that others would thereby be involved in the most embarrassing difficulties. Secondly, such a statement would most undoubtedly induce greater vigilance on the part of slaveholders than has existed heretofore among them; which would, of course, be the means of guarding a door whereby some dear brother bondman might escape his galling chains. I deeply regret the necessity that impels me to suppress any thing of importance connected with my experience in slavery. It would afford me great pleasure indeed, as well as materially add to the interest of my narrative, were I at liberty to gratify a curiosity, which I know exists in the minds of many, by an accurate statement of all the facts pertaining to my most fortunate escape. But I must deprive myself of this pleasure, and the curious of the gratification which such a statement would afford. I would allow myself to suffer under the greatest imputations which evil-minded men might suggest, rather than exculpate myself, and thereby run the hazard of closing the slightest avenue by which a brother slave might clear himself of the chains and fetters of slavery.

I have never approved of the very public manner in which some of our western friends have conducted what they call the *underground railroad*,[3] but which, I think, by their open declarations, has been made most emphatically the *upperground railroad*. I honor those good men and women for their noble daring, and applaud them for willingly subjecting themselves to bloody persecution, by openly avowing their participation in the escape of slaves. I, however, can see very little good resulting from such a course, either to themselves or the slaves escaping; while, upon the other hand, I see and feel assured that those open declarations are a positive evil to the slaves remaining, who are seeking to escape. They do nothing towards enlightening the slave, whilst they do much towards enlightening the master. They stimulate him to greater watchfulness, and enhance his power to capture his slave. We owe something to the slaves south of the line[4] as well as to those north of it; and in aiding the latter on their way to freedom, we should be careful to do nothing which would be likely to hinder the former from escaping from slavery. I would keep the merciless slaveholder profoundly ignorant of the means of flight adopted by the slave. I would leave him to imagine himself surrounded by myriads of invisible tormentors, ever ready to snatch from his infernal grasp his trembling prey. Let him be left to feel his way in the dark; let darkness commensurate with his crime hover over him; and let him feel that at every step he takes, in pursuit of the flying bondman, he is running the

---

3. A system set up by opponents of slavery to help fugitive slaves from the South escape to free states and to Canada.   4. The Mason-Dixon line, the boundary between Pennsylvania and Maryland and between slave and free states.

frightful risk of having his hot brains dashed out by an invisible agency. Let us render the tyrant no aid; let us not hold the light by which he can trace the footprints of our flying brother. But enough of this. I will now proceed to the statement of those facts, connected with my escape, for which I am alone responsible, and for which no one can be made to suffer but myself.

In the early part of the year 1838, I became quite restless. I could see no reason why I should, at the end of each week, pour the reward of my toil into the purse of my master. When I carried to him my weekly wages, he would, after counting the money, look me in the face with a robber-like fierceness, and ask, "Is this all?" He was satisfied with nothing less than the last cent. He would, however, when I made him six dollars, some-times give me six cents, to encourage me. It had the opposite effect. I regarded it as a sort of admission of my right to the whole. The fact that he gave me any part of my wages was proof, to my mind, that he believed me entitled to the whole of them. I always felt worse for having received any thing; for I feared that the giving me a few cents would ease his con-science, and make him feel himself to be a pretty honorable sort of robber. My discontent grew upon me. I was ever on the look-out for means of escape; and, finding no direct means, I determined to try to hire my time, with a view of getting money with which to make my escape. In the spring of 1838, when Master Thomas came to Baltimore to purchase his spring goods, I got an opportunity, and applied to him to allow me to hire my time. He unhesitatingly refused my request, and told me this was another stratagem by which to escape. He told me I could go nowhere but that he could get me; and that, in the event of my running away, he should spare no pains in his efforts to catch me. He exhorted me to content myself, and be obedient. He told me, if I would be happy, I must lay out no plans for the future. He said, if I behaved myself properly, he would take care of me. Indeed, he advised me to complete thoughtlessness of the future, and taught me to depend solely upon him for happiness. He seemed to see fully the pressing necessity of setting aside my intellectual nature, in order to [insure] contentment in slavery. But in spite of him, and even in spite of myself, I continued to think, and to think about the injustice of my enslavement, and the means of escape.

About two months after this, I applied to Master Hugh for the privilege of hiring my time. He was not acquainted with the fact that I had applied to Master Thomas, and had been refused. He too, at first, seemed disposed to refuse; but, after some reflection, he granted me the privilege, and pro-posed the following terms: I was to be allowed all my time, make all con-tracts with those for whom I worked, and find my own employment; and, in return for this liberty, I was to pay him three dollars at the end of each week; find myself in calking tools, and in board and clothing. My board was two dollars and a half per week. This, with the wear and tear of cloth-ing and calking tools, made my regular expenses about six dollars per week. This amount I was compelled to make up, or relinquish the privi-lege of hiring my time. Rain or shine, work or no work, at the end of each week the money must be forthcoming, or I must give up my privilege. This arrangement, it will be perceived, was decidedly in my master's favor.

It relieved him of all need of looking after me. His money was sure. He received all the benefits of slaveholding without its evils; while I endured all the evils of a slave, and suffered all the care and anxiety of a freeman. I found it a hard bargain. But, hard as it was, I thought it better than the old mode of getting along. It was a step towards freedom to be allowed to bear the responsibilities of a freeman, and I was determined to hold on upon it. I bent myself to the work of making money. I was ready to work at night as well as day, and by the most untiring perseverance and industry, I made enough to meet my expenses, and lay up a little money every week. I went on thus from May till August. Master Hugh then refused to allow me to hire my time longer. The ground for his refusal was a failure on my part, one Saturday night, to pay him for my week's time. This failure was occasioned by my attending a camp meeting about ten miles from Balti-more. During the week, I had entered into an engagement with a number of young friends to start from Baltimore to the camp ground early Saturday evening; and being detained by my employer, I was unable to get down to Master Hugh's without disappointing the company. I knew that Master Hugh was in no special need of the money that night. I therefore decided to go to camp meeting, and upon my return pay him the three dollars. I staid at the camp meeting one day longer than I intended when I left. But as soon as I returned, I called upon him to pay him what he considered his due. I found him very angry; he could scarce restrain his wrath. He said he had a great mind to give me a severe whipping. He wished to know how I dared go out of the city without asking his permission. I told him I hired my time, and while I paid him the price which he asked for it, I did not know that I was bound to ask him when and where I should go. This reply troubled him; and, after reflecting a few moments, he turned to me, and said I should hire my time no longer; that the next thing he should know of, I would be running away. Upon the same plea, he told me to bring my tools and clothing home forthwith. I did so; but instead of seek-ing work, as I had been accustomed to do previously to hiring my time, I spent the whole week without the performance of a single stroke of work. I did this in retaliation. Saturday night, he called upon me as usual for my week's wages. I told him I had no wages; I had done no work that week. Here we were upon the point of coming to blows. He raved, and swore his determination to get hold of me. I did not allow myself a single word; but was resolved, if he laid the weight of his hand upon me, it should be blow for blow. He did not strike me, but told me that he would find me in constant employment in future. I thought the matter over during the next day, Sunday, and finally resolved upon the third day of September, as the day upon which I would make a second attempt to secure my free-dom. I now had three weeks during which to prepare for my journey. Early on Monday morning, before Master Hugh had time to make any engagement for me, I went out and got employment of Mr. Butler, at his ship-yard near the draw-bridge, upon what is called the City Block, thus making it unnecessary for him to seek employment for me. At the end of the week, I brought him between eight and nine dollars. He seemed very well pleased, and asked me why I did not do the same the week before. He little knew what my plans were. My object in working steadily was to remove any suspicion he might entertain of my intent to run away; and in this I succeeded admirably. I suppose he thought I was never better satisfied with my condition than at the very time during which I was planning my escape. The second week passed, and again I carried him my full wages; and so well pleased was he, that he gave me twenty-five cents, (quite a large sum for a slaveholder to give a slave,) and bade me to make a good use of it. I told him I would.

Things went on without very smoothly indeed, but within there was trouble. It is impossible for me to describe my feelings as the time of my contemplated start drew near. I had a number of warm-hearted friends in Baltimore,—friends that I loved almost as I did my life,—and the thought of being separated from them forever was painful beyond expression. It is my opinion that thousands would escape from slavery, who now remain, but for the strong cords of affection that bind them to their friends. The thought of leaving my friends was decidedly the most painful thought with which I had to contend. The love of them was my tender point, and shook my decision more than all things else. Besides the pain of separation, the dread and apprehension of a failure exceeded what I had experienced at my first attempt. The appalling defeat I then sustained returned to torment me. I felt assured that, if I failed in this attempt, my case would be a hopeless one—it would seal my fate as a slave forever. I could not hope to get off with any thing less than the severest punishment, and being placed beyond the means of escape. It required no very vivid imagination to depict the most frightful scenes through which I should have to pass, in case I failed. The wretchedness of slavery, and the blessedness of freedom, were perpetually before me. It was life and death with me. But I remained firm, and, according to my resolution, on the third day of September, 1838, I left my chains, and succeeded in reaching New York without the slightest interruption of any kind. How I did so,—what means I adopted,—what direction I travelled, and by what mode of conveyance,—I must leave unexplained, for the reasons before mentioned.

I have been frequently asked how I felt when I found myself in a free State. I have never been able to answer the question with any satisfaction to myself. It was a moment of the highest excitement I ever experienced. I suppose I felt as one may imagine the unarmed mariner to feel when he is rescued by a friendly man-of-war from the pursuit of a pirate. In writing to a dear friend, immediately after my arrival at New York, I said I felt like one who had escaped a den of hungry lions. This state of mind, however, very soon subsided; and I was again seized with a feeling of great insecurity and loneliness. I was yet liable to be taken back, and subjected to all the tortures of slavery. This in itself was enough to damp the ardor of my enthusiasm. But the loneliness overcame me. There I was in the midst of thousands, and yet a perfect stranger; without home and without friends, in the midst of thousands of my own brethren—children of a common Father, and yet I dared not to unfold to any one of them my sad condition. I was afraid to speak to any one for fear of speaking to the wrong one, and thereby falling into the hands of money-loving kidnappers, whose business it was to lie in wait for the panting fugitive, as the ferocious beasts of the forest lie in wait for their prey. The motto which I adopted when I started from slavery was this—"Trust no man!" I saw in every white man an enemy, and in almost every colored man cause for distrust. It was a most painful situation; and, to understand it, one must needs experience it, or imagine himself in similar circumstances. Let him be a fugitive slave in a strange land—a land given up to be the hunting-ground for slaveholders— whose inhabitants are legalized kidnappers—where he is every moment subjected to the terrible liability of being seized upon by his fellow-men, as the hideous crocodile seizes upon his prey!—I say, let him place himself in my situation—without home or friends—without money or credit—wanting shelter, and no one to give it—wanting bread, and no money to buy it,—and at the same time let him feel that he is pursued by merciless men-hunters, and in total darkness as to what to do, where to go, or where to stay,—perfectly helpless both as to the means of defence and means of escape,—in the midst of plenty, yet suffering the terrible gnawings of hunger,—in the midst of houses, yet having no home,— among fellow-men, yet feeling as if in the midst of wild beasts, whose greediness to swallow up the trembling and half-famished fugitive is only equalled by that with which the monsters of the deep swallow up the helpless fish upon which they subsist,—I say, let him be placed in this most trying situation,—the situation in which I was placed,—then, and not till then, will he fully appreciate the hardships of, and know how to sympathize with, the toil-worn and whip-scarred fugitive slave.

Thank Heaven, I remained but a short time in this distressed situation. I was relieved from it by the humane hand of Mr. DAVID RUGGLES,[5] whose vigilance, kindness, and perseverance, I shall never forget. I am glad of an opportunity to express, as far as words can, the love and gratitude I bear him. Mr. Ruggles is now afflicted with blindness, and is himself in need of the same kind offices which he was once so forward in the performance of toward others. I had been in New York but a few days, when Mr. Ruggles sought me out, and very kindly took me to his boarding-house at the corner of Church and Lespenard Streets. Mr. Ruggles was then very deeply engaged in the memorable *Darg* case, as well as attending to a number of other fugitive slaves, devising ways and means for their successful escape; and, though watched and hemmed in on almost every side, he seemed to be more than a match for his enemies. Very soon after I went to Mr. Ruggles, he wished to know of me where I wanted to go; as he deemed it unsafe for me to remain in New York. I told him I was a calker, and should like to go where I could get work. I thought of going to Canada; but he decided against it, and in favor of my going to New Bedford, thinking I should be able to get work there at my trade. At this time, Anna,[6] my intended wife, came on; for I wrote to her immediately after my arrival at New York, (notwithstanding my homeless, houseless, and helpless condition,) informing her of my successful flight, and wishing her to come on forthwith. In a few days after her arrival, Mr. Ruggles called in the Rev. J. W. C. Pennington, who, in the presence of Mr. Ruggles,

---

5. A black abolitionist (1810–1849), at this time living in New York, helped many slaves to escape.
6. She was free [Douglass's note].

Mrs. Michaels, and two or three others, performed the marriage ceremony, and gave us a certificate, of which the following is an exact copy:—

"THIS may certify, that I joined together in holy matrimony Freder-
ick Johnson[7] and Anna Murray, as man and wife, in the presence of
Mr. David Ruggles and Mrs. Michaels.
                                                "JAMES W. C. PENNINGTON.
"New York, Sept. 15, 1838."

Upon receiving this certificate, and a five-dollar bill from Mr. Ruggles, I
shouldered one part of our baggage, and Anna took up the other, and we
set out forthwith to take passage on board of the steamboat John W. Richmond for Newport, on our way to New Bedford. Mr. Ruggles gave me a
letter to a Mr. Shaw in Newport, and told me, in case my money did not
serve me to New Bedford, to stop in Newport and obtain further assistance;
but upon our arrival at Newport, we were so anxious to get to a place of
safety, that, notwithstanding we lacked the necessary money to pay our
fare, we decided to take seats in the stage, and promise to pay when we
got to New Bedford. We were encouraged to do this by two excellent
gentlemen, residents of New Bedford, whose names I afterward ascertained to be Joseph Ricketson and William C. Taber. They seemed at
once to understand our circumstances, and gave us such assurance of their
friendliness as put us fully at ease in their presence. It was good indeed to
meet with such friends, at such a time. Upon reaching New Bedford, we
were directed to the house of Mr. Nathan Johnson, by whom we were
kindly received, and hospitably provided for. Both Mr. and Mrs. Johnson
took a deep and lively interest in our welfare. They proved themselves
quite worthy of the name of abolitionists. When the stage-driver found us
unable to pay our fare, he held on upon our baggage as security for the
debt. I had but to mention the fact to Mr. Johnson, and he forthwith
advanced the money.

    We now began to feel a degree of safety, and to prepare ourselves for
the duties and responsibilities of a life of freedom. On the morning after
our arrival at New Bedford, while at the breakfast-table, the question arose
as to what name I should be called by. The name given me by my mother
was, "Frederick Augustus Washington Bailey." I, however, had dispensed
with the two middle names long before I left Maryland so that I was generally known by the name of "Frederick Bailey." I started from Baltimore
bearing the name of "Stanley." When I got to New York, I again changed
my name to "Frederick Johnson," and thought that would be the last
change. But when I got to New Bedford, I found it necessary again to
change my name. The reason of this necessity was, that there were so
many Johnsons in New Bedford, it was already quite difficult to distinguish
between them. I gave Mr. Johnson the privilege of choosing me a name,
but told him he must not take from me the name of "Frederick." I must
hold on to that, to preserve a sense of my identity. Mr. Johnson had just
been reading the "Lady of the Lake,"[8] and at once suggested that my name

7. I had changed my name from Frederick *Bailey* to that of *Johnson* [Douglass's note].   8. A narrative
poem by Sir Walter Scott (1810) about the fortunes of the Douglas clan in Scotland.

be "Douglass." From that time until now I have been called "Frederick Douglass;" and as I am more widely known by that name than by either of the others, I shall continue to use it as my own.

I was quite disappointed at the general appearance of things in New Bedford. The impression which I had received respecting the character and condition of the people of the north, I found to be singularly erroneous. I had very strangely supposed, while in slavery, that few of the comforts, and scarcely any of the luxuries, of life were enjoyed at the north, compared with what were enjoyed by the slaveholders of the south. I probably came to this conclusion from the fact that northern people owned no slaves. I supposed that they were about upon a level with the non-slaveholding population of the south. I knew *they* were exceedingly poor, and I had been accustomed to regard their poverty as the necessary consequence of their being non-slaveholders. I had somehow imbibed the opinion that, in the absence of slaves, there could be no wealth, and very little refinement. And upon coming to the north, I expected to meet with a rough, hard-handed, and uncultivated population, living in the most Spartan-like simplicity, knowing nothing of the ease, luxury, pomp, and grandeur of southern slaveholders. Such being my conjectures, any one acquainted with the appearance of New Bedford may very readily infer how palpably I must have seen my mistake.

In the afternoon of the day when I reached New Bedford, I visited the wharves, to take a view of the shipping. Here I found myself surrounded with the strongest proofs of wealth. Lying at the wharves, and riding in the stream, I saw many ships of the finest model, in the best order, and of the largest size. Upon the right and left, I was walled in by granite warehouses of the widest dimensions, stowed to their utmost capacity with the necessaries and comforts of life. Added to this, almost every body seemed to be at work, but noiselessly so, compared with what I had been accustomed to in Baltimore. There were no loud songs heard from those engaged in loading and unloading ships. I heard no deep oaths or horrid curses on the laborer. I saw no whipping of men; but all seemed to go smoothly on. Every man appeared to understand his work, and went at it with a sober, yet cheerful earnestness, which betokened the deep interest which he felt in what he was doing, as well as a sense of his own dignity as a man. To me this looked exceedingly strange. From the wharves I strolled around and over the town, gazing with wonder and admiration at the splendid churches, beautiful dwellings, and finely-cultivated gardens; evincing an amount of wealth, comfort, taste, and refinement, such as I had never seen in any part of slaveholding Maryland.

Every thing looked clean, new, and beautiful. I saw few or no dilapidated houses, with poverty-stricken inmates; no half-naked children and barefooted women, such as I had been accustomed to see in Hillsborough, Easton, St. Michael's, and Baltimore. The people looked more able, stronger, healthier, and happier, than those of Maryland. I was for once made glad by a view of extreme wealth, without being saddened by seeing extreme poverty. But the most astonishing as well as the most interesting thing to me was the condition of the colored people, a great many of whom, like myself, had escaped thither as a refuge from the hunters of men. I found many, who had not been seven years out of their chains, living in finer houses, and evidently enjoying more of the comforts of life, than the average of slave-holders in Maryland. I will venture to assert that my friend Mr. Nathan Johnson (of whom I can say with a grateful heart, "I was hungry, and he gave me meat; I was thirsty, and he gave me drink; I was a stranger, and he took me in")[9] lived in a neater house; dined at a better table; took, paid for, and read, more newspapers; better understood the moral, religious, and political character of the nation,—than nine tenths of the slaveholders in Talbot county Maryland. Yet Mr. Johnson was a working man. His hands were hardened by toil, and not his alone, but those also of Mrs. Johnson. I found the colored people much more spirited than I had supposed they would be. I found among them a determination to protect each other from the blood-thirsty kidnapper, at all hazards. Soon after my arrival, I was told of a circumstance which illustrated their spirit. A colored man and a fugitive slave were on unfriendly terms. The former was heard to threaten the latter with informing his master of his whereabouts. Straightway a meeting was called among the colored people, under the stereotyped notice, "Business of importance!" The betrayer was invited to attend. The people came at the appointed hour, and organized the meeting by appointing a very religious old gentleman as president, who, I believe, made a prayer, after which he addressed the meeting as follows: *Friends, we have got him here, and I would recommend that you young men just take him outside the door, and kill him!*" With this, a number of them bolted at him; but they were intercepted by some more timid than themselves, and the betrayer escaped their vengeance, and has not been seen in New Bedford since. I believe there have been no more such threats, and should there be hereafter, I doubt not that death would be the consequence.

I found employment, the third day after my arrival, in stowing a sloop with a load of oil. It was new, dirty, and hard work for me; but I went at it with a glad heart and a willing hand. I was now my own master. It was a happy moment, the rapture of which can be understood only by those who have been slaves. It was the first work, the reward of which was to be entirely my own. There was no Master Hugh standing ready, the moment I earned the money, to rob me of it. I worked that day with a pleasure I had never before experienced. I was at work for myself and newly-married wife. It was to me the starting-point of a new existence. When I got through with that job, I went in pursuit of a job of calking; but such was the strength of prejudice against color, among the white calkers, that they refused to work with me, and of course I could get no employment.[1] Finding my trade of no immediate benefit, I threw off my calking habiliments, and prepared myself to do any kind of work I could get to do. Mr. Johnson kindly let me have his wood-horse and saw, and I very soon found myself a plenty of work. There was no work too hard—none too dirty. I was ready

9. Matthew 25:35: "For I was an hungered, and ye gave me meat: I was thirsty, and ye gave me drink: I was a stranger, and ye took me in."   1. I am told that colored persons can now get employment at calking in New Bedford—a result of antislavery effort [Douglass's note].

to saw wood, shovel coal, carry the hod, sweep the chimney, or roll oil casks,—all of which I did for nearly three years in New Bedford, before I became known to the anti-slavery world.

In about four months after I went to New Bedford there came a young man to me, and inquired if I did not wish to take the "Liberator."[2] I told him I did; but, just having made my escape from slavery, I remarked that I was unable to pay for it then. I, however, finally became a subscriber to it. The paper came, and I read it from week to week with such feelings as it would be quite idle for me to attempt to describe. The paper became my meat and my drink. My soul was set all on fire. Its sympathy for my brethren in bonds—its scathing denunciations of slaveholders—its faithful exposures of slavery—and its powerful attacks upon the upholders of the institution—sent a thrill of joy through my soul, such as I had never felt before!

I had not long been a reader of the "Liberator," before I got a pretty correct idea of the principles, measures and spirit of the anti-slavery reform. I took right hold of the cause. I could do but little; but what I could, I did with a joyful heart, and never felt happier than when in an anti-slavery meeting. I seldom had much to say at the meetings, because what I wanted to say was said so much better by others. But, while attending an anti-slavery convention at Nantucket, on the 11th of August, 1841, I felt strongly moved to speak, and was at the same time much urged to do so by Mr. William C. Coffin, a gentleman who had heard me speak in the colored people's meeting at New Bedford. It was a severe cross, and I took it up reluctantly. The truth was, I felt myself a slave, and the idea of speaking to white people weighed me down. I spoke but a few moments, when I felt a degree of freedom, and said what I desired with considerable ease. From that time until now, I have been engaged in pleading the cause of my brethren—with what success, and with what devotion, I leave those acquainted with my labors to decide.

APPENDIX

I find, since reading over the foregoing Narrative, that I have, in several instances, spoken in such a tone and manner, respecting religion, as may possibly lead those unacquainted with my religious views to suppose me an opponent of all religion. To remove the liability of such misapprehension, I deem it proper to append the following brief explanation. What I have said respecting and against religion, I mean strictly to apply to the *slaveholding religion* of this land, and with no possible reference to Christianity proper; for, between the Christianity of this land, and the Christianity of Christ, I recognize the widest possible difference—so wide, that to receive the one as good, pure, and holy, is of necessity to reject the other as bad, corrupt, and wicked. To be the friend of the one, is of necessity to be the enemy of the other. I love the pure, peaceable, and impartial Christianity of Christ: I therefore hate the corrupt, slaveholding, women-whipping, cradle-plundering, partial and hypocritical Christianity of this land.

---

2. William Lloyd Garrison's antislavery newspaper, which began publication in 1831.

Indeed, I can see no reason, but the most deceitful one, for calling the religion of this land Christianity. I look upon it as the climax of all misnomers, the boldest of all frauds, and the grossest of all libels. Never was there a clearer case of "stealing the livery of the court of heaven to serve the devil in." I am filled with unutterable loathing when I contemplate the religious pomp and show, together with the horrible inconsistencies, which every where surround me. We have men-stealers for ministers, women-whippers for missionaries, and cradle-plunderers for church members. The man who wields the blood-clotted cowskin during the week fills the pulpit on Sunday, and claims to be a minister of the meek and lowly Jesus. The man who robs me of my earnings at the end of each week meets me as a class-leader on Sunday morning, to show me the way of life, and the path of salvation. He who sells my sister, for purposes of prostitution, stands forth as the pious advocate of purity. He who proclaims it a religious duty to read the Bible denies me the right of learning to read the name of the God who made me. He who is the religious advocate of marriage robs whole millions of its sacred influence, and leaves them to the ravages of wholesale pollution. The warm defender of the sacredness of the family relation is the same that scatters whole families,—sundering husbands and wives, parents and children, sisters and brothers,—leaving the hut vacant, and the hearth desolate. We see the thief preaching against theft, and the adulterer against adultery. We have men sold to build churches, women sold to support the gospel, and babes sold to purchase Bibles for the *poor heathen! all for the glory of God and the good of souls!* The slave auctioneer's bell and the church-going bell chime in with each other, and the bitter cries of the heart-broken slave are drowned in the religious shouts of his pious master. Revivals of religion and revivals in the slave-trade go hand in hand together. The slave prison and the church stand near each other. The clanking of fetters and the rattling of chains in the prison, and the pious psalm and solemn prayer in the church, may be heard at the same time. The dealers in the bodies and souls of men erect their stand in the presence of the pulpit, and they mutually help each other. The dealer gives his blood-stained gold to support the pulpit, and the pulpit, in return, covers his infernal business with the garb of Christianity. Here we have religion and robbery the allies of each other—devils dressed in angels' robes, and hell presenting the semblance of paradise.

> "Just God! and these are they,
> Who minister at thine altar, God of right!
> Men who their hands, with prayer and blessing, lay
> On Israel's ark of light.
>
> "What! preach, and kidnap men?
> Give thanks, and rob thy own afflicted poor?
> Talk of thy glorious liberty, and then
> Bolt hard the captive's door?
>
> "What! servants of thy own
> Merciful Son, who came to seek and save
> The homeless and the outcast, fettering down
> The tasked and plundered slave!

> "Pilate and Herod friends!
>   Chief priests and rulers, as of old, combine!
> Just God and holy! is that church which lends
>   Strength to the spoiler thine?"

The Christianity of America is a Christianity, of whose votaries it may be as truly said, as it was of the ancient scribes and Pharisees, "They bind heavy burdens, and grievous to be borne, and lay them on men's shoulders, but they themselves will not move them with one of their fingers. All their works they do for to be seen of men. —— They love the uppermost rooms at feasts, and the chief seats in the synagogues, ... and to be called of men, Rabbi, Rabbi. —— But woe unto you, scribes and Pharisees, hypocrites! for ye neither go in yourselves, neither suffer ye them that are entering to go in. Ye devour widows' houses, and for a pretence make long prayers; therefore ye shall receive the greater damnation. Ye compass sea and land to make one proselyte, and when he is made, ye make him twofold more the child of hell than yourselves. —— Woe unto you, scribes and Pharisees, hypocrites! for ye pay tithe of mint, and anise, and cumin, and have omitted the weightier matters of the law, judgment, mercy, and faith; these ought ye to have done, and not to leave the other undone. Ye blind guides! which strain at a gnat, and swallow a camel. Woe unto you, scribes and Pharisees, hypocrites! for ye make clean the outside of the cup and of the platter; but within, they are full of extortion and excess. —— Woe unto you, scribes and Pharisees, hypocrites! for ye are like unto whited sepulchres, which indeed appear beautiful outward, but are within full of dead men's bones, and of all uncleanness. Even so ye also outwardly appear righteous unto men, but within ye are full of hypocrisy and iniquity."[3]

Dark and terrible as is this picture, I hold it to be strictly true of the overwhelming mass of professed Christians in America. They strain at a gnat, and swallow a camel. Could any thing be more true of our churches? They would be shocked at the proposition of fellowshipping a *sheep*-stealer; and at the same time they hug to their communion a *man*-stealer, and brand me with being an infidel, if I find fault with them for it. They attend with Pharisaical strictness to the outward forms of religion, and at the same time neglect the weightier matters of the law, judgment, mercy, and faith. They are always ready to sacrifice, but seldom to show mercy. They are they who are represented as professing to love God whom they have not seen, whilst they hate their brother whom they have seen. They love the heathen on the other side of the globe. They can pray for him, pay money to have the Bible put into his hand, and missionaries to instruct him; while they despise and totally neglect the heathen at their own doors.

Such is, very briefly, my view of the religion of this land; and to avoid any misunderstanding, growing out of the use of general terms, I mean, by the religion of this land, that which is revealed in the words, deeds, and actions, of those bodies, north and south, calling themselves Christian churches, and yet in union with slaveholders. It is against religion, as presented by these bodies, that I have felt it my duty to testify.

---

3. Matthew 23.

I conclude these remarks by copying the following portrait of the religion of the south, (which is, by communion and fellowship, the religion of the north) which I soberly affirm is "true to the life," and without caricature or the slightest exaggeration. It is said to have been drawn, several years before the present anti-slavery agitation began, by a northern Methodist preacher, who, while residing at the south, had an opportunity to see slaveholding morals, manners, and piety, with his own eyes. "Shall I not visit for these things? saith the Lord. Shall not my soul be avenged on such a nation as this?"[4]

"A Parody.

"Come, saints and sinners, hear me tell
How pious priests whip Jack and Nell,
And women buy and children sell,
And preach all sinners down to hell,
    And sing of heavenly union.

"They'll bleat and baa, dona[5] like goats,
Gorge down black sheep, and strain at motes,
Array their backs in fine black coats,
Then seize their negroes by their throats,
    And choke, for heavenly union.

"They'll church you if you sip a dram,
And damn you if you steal a lamb;
Yet rob old Tony, Doll, and Sam,
Of human rights, and bread and ham;
    Kidnapper's heavenly union.

"They'll loudly talk of Christ's reward,
And bind his image with a cord,
And scold, and swing the lash abhorred,
And sell their brother in the Lord
    To handcuffed heavenly union.

"They'll read and sing a sacred song,
And make a prayer both loud and long,
And teach the right and do the wrong,
Hailing the brother, sister throng,
    With words of heavenly union.

"We wonder how such saints can sing,
Or praise the Lord upon the wing,
Who roar, and scold, and whip, and sting,
And to their slaves and mammon cling,
    In guilty conscience union.

"They'll raise tobacco, corn, and rye,
And drive, and thieve, and cheat, and lie,
And lay up treasures in the sky,
By making switch and cowskin fly,
    In hope of heavenly union.

---

4. Jeremiah 5:9.   5. Believed to be a printer's error in the original edition for "go on" or "go n-a-a-ah."

"They'll crack old Tony on the skull,
And preach and roar like Bashan bull,
Or braying ass, of mischief full,
Then seize old Jacob by the wool,
   And pull for heavenly union.

"A roaring, ranting, sleek man-thief,
Who lived on mutton, veal, and beef,
Yet never would afford relief
To needy, sable sons of grief,
   Was big with heavenly union.

" 'Love not the world,' the preacher said,
And winked his eye, and shook his head;
He seized on Tom, and Dick, and Ned,
Cut short their meat, and clothes, and bread,
   Yet still loved heavenly union.

"Another preacher whining spoke
Of One whose heart for sinners broke:
He tied old Nanny to an oak,
And drew the blood at every stroke,
   And prayed for heavenly union.

"Two others oped their iron jaws,
And waved their children-stealing paws;
There sat their children in gewgaws;
By stinting negroes' backs and maws,
   They kept up heavenly union.

"All good from Jack another takes,
And entertains their flirts and rakes,
Who dress as sleek as glossy snakes,
And cram their mouths with sweetened cakes;
   And this goes down for union."

   Sincerely and earnestly hoping that this little book may do something toward throwing light on the American slave system, and hastening the glad day of deliverance to the millions of my brethren in bonds—faithfully relying upon the power of truth, love, and justice, for success in my humble efforts—and solemnly pledging my self anew to the sacred cause,—I subscribe myself,

                            FREDERICK DOUGLASS.

Lynn, Mass., April 28, 1845.

WALT WHITMAN
1819–1892

As insistently as Rousseau, but with a far richer sense of the nature and the importance of his social context, Walt Whitman in his poetry makes himself the center of the universe. He brings to his emphatic self-presentation a detailed, partly ironic, partly celebratory sense of what it means to be an American; his poetry suggests something of what life in the United States must have felt like in the middle of the nineteenth century.

Born in Long Island, Whitman in his childhood moved with his family to Brooklyn. He was christened Walter, but shortened his first name to distinguish himself from his father. As a young man, he worked as schoolteacher, builder, bookstore owner, journalist, and poet, before moving to Washington to work as a government clerk. There he also served as a volunteer nurse, helping to care for the Civil War wounded. In 1873 he settled in Camden, New Jersey, where he remained for the rest of his life.

Whitman began writing in his youth, producing a good deal of bad poetry and a novel, a fictionalized temperance tract. He first published *Leaves of Grass* in 1855, after having become an admirer of Emerson and a Jeffersonian Democrat; he continued enlarging and revising the book for the rest of his life. In 1865, he published *Drum Taps*, poems derived from his Civil War experiences; in 1871, *Democratic Vistas*, a collection of political and philosophical essays.

Whitman's shifting diction—familiar, even slangy, to formal and rhetorical— makes possible a large range of tones in *Song of Myself*. In a single section (21), for example, these two sequences occur in close conjunction:

> I chant the chant of dilation or pride,
> We have had ducking and deprecating about enough,
> I show that size is only development.
>
> Smile O voluptuous cool-breathed earth!
> Earth of the slumbering and liquid trees!
> Earth of departed sunset—earth of the mountains misty-topt!
> Earth of the vitreous pour of the full moon just tinged with blue!

The first three-line passage, after its formal opening, falls into a pattern like that of colloquial speech. "About enough" belongs to an informal vocabulary; the final line, turning on the word *only*, makes the kind of joke one might make in conversation. ("Size doesn't matter, really, it only comes from growing.") The speaker's claim that he does not endorse conventional judgments, by which bigger is better, and his slightly mocking tone declare his independence and his willingness not to take himself with undue seriousness. Only a few lines later, when he turns to the "voluptuous cool-breathed earth," he sounds like a different person, entirely serious, almost grandiose, about his personal perceptions. Now his rhapsodic tone unites him with the Romantic poets, though his vocabulary still insists on his individuality. The conjunction of "voluptuous" with "cool-breathed," the use of "vitreous" (glasslike) to modify "pour" used as a noun, the idea of "liquid trees": such choices demand the reader's close attention to figure out exactly what the poem is saying, and they emphasize a fresh way of seeing, a precise attention to the look of things. But they also sound like poetry, in a sense familiar to readers of earlier nineteenth-century works—unlike the lines quoted just before, which resemble colloquial prose.

The range of tones here exemplified helps to communicate an important theme of Whitman's poem: the tension and exchange between desire for individuality and for community. *Narrative of the Life of Frederick Douglass* directly and without apparent conflict expresses a sense of community as part of a sense of personal identity. *Song of Myself*, on the other hand, alternates between assertions of specialness and of identification with others.

I am of old and young, of the foolish as much as the wise, . . .
One of the Nation of many nations, the smallest the same and the largest the same,

A Southerner soon as a Northerner, a planter nonchalant and hospitable down by
  the Oconee I live, . . .
At home on Kanadian snow-shoes or up in the bush, or with fishermen off New-
  foundland,
At home in the fleet of ice-boats, sailing with the rest and tacking.

Declaring his union not, like Wordsworth, with the natural universe, but with the
society of his compatriots, Whitman identifies himself with the enormous variety
he perceives and celebrates in his country. But his poem opens, "I celebrate
myself, and sing myself, / And what I assume you shall assume," insisting on his
uniqueness and dominance. Toward the end, these two lines occur: "I too am not
a bit tamed, I too am untranslatable, / I sound my barbaric yawp over the roofs of
the world." One hears the note of defiant specialness: another characteristic aspect
of *Song of Myself*. The poem's power derives partly from its capacity to embody
both feelings, the feeling of uniqueness and the sense of shared humanity, feelings
that most people experience, sometimes in confusing conjunction. Like his
Romantic predecessors, Whitman values emotion, every kind of emotion, for its
own sake. He suggests the irrelevance of the notion of contradiction to any understanding of inner life. In the realm of emotion, everything coexists. *Song of Myself*
attempts to include all of it.

The poetic daring of *Song of Myself* expresses itself not only in choice of subject
matter but in poetic technique. Whitman's unrhymed lines, avoiding the blank
verse that had been the norm, establish a new sort of rhythm—one that proved of
crucial importance to twentieth-century American poets, who adapted it to their
own purposes. Not metrical in any familiar sense, the verse establishes its own
hypnotic rhythms, evoking an individual speaking voice, an individual idiom. It
even risks the prosaic in its insistence that poetry implies, above all, personal perception and personal voice: "everything" can be included in technique as well as
in material.

Out of the Cradle Endlessly Rocking, another of Whitman's best-known pre–
Civil War poems, develops a child's imaginative relation with nature in a way that
Wordsworth might have approved. A man hears a bird song that evokes for him a
past experience—just as, at the beginning of *Remembrance of Things Past*, Proust's
narrator finds his childhood returning to his memory at the taste of a madeleine.
Reduced to tears by the song and the memory, the speaker, "chanter of pains and
joys, uniter of here and hereafter," records and explores his youthful revelation of
lyric power, achieved by identification with the bird mourning the loss of its mate.

Now in a moment I know what I am for, I awake,
And already a thousand singers, a thousand songs, clearer, louder, and more
  sorrowful than yours,
A thousand warbling echoes have started to life within me, never to die.

The poem concludes with the adult speaker meditating on the nature of his creative force in terms recalling Keats's in *Ode to a Nightingale*. Whitman, too, muses
about the attraction of death, feels the demonic and the beautiful united in the
song that inspires him. His own songs merge in his imagination with the "strong
and delicious word" spoken by the sea, another aspect of nature, and one traditionally associated with death (as well as with birth). In poetry marked, like *Song of
Myself*, by his powerfully individual rhythm and meter, Whitman reminds us once
more of a great Romantic theme: the mystery of creativity.

G. W. Allen, *The Solitary Singer: A Critical Biography of Walt Whitman* (1959),
provides both biography and criticism. M. Hindus, ed., *Walt Whitman: The Critical Heritage* (1971), contains nineteenth- and twentieth-century essays; J. E. Miller
Jr., *A Critical Guide to Leaves of Grass* (1957), is helpful. Also valuable are

R. Chase, *Walt Whitman Reconsidered* (1955); M. J. Killingsworth, *Whitman's Poetry of the Body* (1989); B. Erkkila, *Whitman the Political Poet* (1989); M. W. Thomas, *The Lunar Light of Whitman's Poetry* (1987); and J. E. Miller, *Leaves of Grass: America's Lyric-Epic of Self and Democracy* (1992).

From Song of Myself[1]

1

I celebrate myself, and sing myself,
And what I assume you shall assume,
For every atom belonging to me as good belongs to you.

I loafe and invite my soul,
I lean and loafe at my ease observing a spear of summer grass.   5

My tongue, every atom of my blood, formed from this soil, this air,
Born here of parents born here from parents the same, and their parents
    the same,
I, now thirty-seven years old in perfect health begin,
Hoping to cease not till death.

Creeds and schools in abeyance,   10
Retiring back a while sufficed at what they are, but never forgotten,
I harbor for good or bad, I permit to speak at every hazard,
Nature without check with original energy.

*   *   *

4

Trippers and askers surround me,
People I meet, the effect upon me of my early life or the ward and city I
    live in, or the nation,
The latest dates, discoveries, inventions, societies, authors old and new,
My dinner, dress, associates, looks, compliments, dues,
The real or fancied indifference of some man or woman I love,   5
The sickness of one of my folks or of myself, or ill-doing or loss or lack
    of money, or depressions or exaltations,
Battles, the horrors of fratricidal war, the fever of doubtful news, the
    fitful events;
These come to me days and nights and go from me again,
But they are not the Me myself.

Apart from the pulling and hauling stands what I am,   10
Stands amused, complacent, compassionating, idle, unitary,
Looks down, is erect, or bends an arm on an impalpable certain rest,
Looking with side-curved head curious what will come next,
Both in and out of the game and watching and wondering at it.

Backward I see in my own days where I sweated through fog with
    linguists and contenders,   15
I have no mockings or arguments, I witness and wait.

1. First published in 1855. This text is from the 1891–92 edition of *Leaves of Grass*, the so-called Deathbed Edition.

* * *

7

Has any one supposed it lucky to be born?
I hasten to inform him or her it is just as lucky to die, and I know it.

I pass death with the dying and birth with the new-washed babe, and am
    not contained between my hat and boots,
And peruse manifold objects, no two alike and every one good,
The earth good and the stars good, and their adjuncts all good.   5

I am not an earth nor an adjunct of an earth,
I am the mate and companion of people, all just as immortal and
    fathomless as myself,
(They do not know how immortal, but I know.)

Every kind for itself and its own, for me mine male and female,
For me those that have been boys and that love women,   10
For me the man that is proud and feels how it stings to be slighted,
For me the sweet-heart and the old maid, for me mothers and the
    mothers of mothers,
For me lips that have smiled, eyes that have shed tears,
For me children and the begetters of children.

Undrape! you are not guilty to me, nor stale nor discarded,   15
I see through the broadcloth and gingham whether or no,
And am around, tenacious, acquisitive, tireless, and cannot be shaken
    away.

* * *

16

I am of old and young, of the foolish as much as the wise,
Regardless of others, ever regardful of others,
Maternal as well as paternal, a child as well as a man,
Stuffed with the stuff that is coarse and stuffed with the stuff that is fine,
One of the Nation of many nations, the smallest the same and the
    largest the same,   5
A Southerner soon as a Northerner, a planter nonchalant and hospitable
    down by the Oconee[2] I live,
A Yankee bound my own was ready for trade, my joints the limberest
    joints on earth and the sternest joints on earth,
A Kentuckian walking the vale of the Elkhorn in my deer-skin leggings,
    a Louisianian or Georgian,
A boatman over lakes or bays or along coasts, a Hoosier, Badger,
    Buckeye;
At home on Kanadian snow-shoes or up in the bush, or with fishermen
    off Newfoundland,   10
At home in the fleet of ice-boats, sailing with the rest and tacking,
At home on the hills of Vermont or in the woods of Maine, or the
    Texan ranch,
Comrade of Californians, comrade of free North-Westerners, (loving
    their big proportions,)
Comrade of raftsmen and coalmen, comrade of all who shake hands
    and welcome to drink and meat,

2. River in Georgia.

A learner with the simplest, a teacher of the thoughtfullest,   15
A novice beginning yet experient of myriads of seasons,
Of every hue and caste am I, of every rank and religion,
A farmer, mechanic, artist, gentleman, sailor, quaker,
Prisoner, fancy-man, rowdy, lawyer, physician, priest.

I resist any thing better than my own diversity,   20
Breathe the air but leave plenty after me,
And am not stuck up, and am in my place.

(The moth and the fish-eggs are in their place,
The bright suns I see and the dark suns I cannot see are in their place,
The palpable is in its place and the impalpable is in its place.)   25

   * * *

21

I am the poet of the Body and I am the poet of the Soul,
The pleasures of heaven are with me and the pains of hell are with me,
The first I graft and increase upon myself, the latter I translate into a
  new tongue.

I am the poet of the woman the same as the man,
And I say it is as great to be a woman as to be a man,   5
And I say there is nothing greater than the mother of men.

I chant the chant of dilation or pride,
We have had ducking and deprecating about enough,
I show that size is only development.

Have you outstript the rest? are you the President?   10
It is a trifle, they will more than arrive there every one, and still pass on.

I am he that walks with the tender and growing night,
I call to the earth and sea half-held by the night.

Press close bare-bosomed night—press close magnetic nourishing night!
Night of south winds—night of the large few stars!   15
Still nodding night—mad naked summer night.

Smile O voluptuous cool-breathed earth!
Earth of the slumbering and liquid trees!
Earth of departed sunset—earth of the mountains misty-topt!
Earth of the vitreous pour of the full moon just tinged with blue!   20
Earth of shine and dark mottling the tide of the river!
Earth of the limpid gray of clouds brighter and clearer for my sake!
Far-swooping elbowed earth—rich apple-blossomed earth!
Smile, for your lover comes.

Prodigal, you have given me love—therefore I to you give love!   25
O unspeakable passionate love.

   * * *

24

Walt Whitman, a kosmos, of Manhattan the son,
Turbulent, fleshy, sensual, eating, drinking and breeding,
No sentimentalist, no stander above men and women or apart from
  them,
No more modest than immodest.

Unscrew the locks from the doors!   5
Unscrew the doors themselves from their jambs!

Whoever degrades another degrades me,
And whatever is done or said returns at last to me.

Through me the afflatus surging and surging, through me the current
    and index.

I speak the pass-word primeval, I give the sign of democracy,   10
By God! I will accept nothing which all cannot have their counterpart
    of on the same terms.

           *   *   *

32

I think I could turn and live with animals, they are so placid and self-con-
    tained,
I stand and look at them long and long.

They do not sweat and whine about their condition,
They do not lie awake in the dark and weep for their sins,
They do not make me sick discussing their duty to God,   5
Not one is dissatisfied, not one is demented with the mania of owning
    things,
Not one kneels to another, nor to his kind that lived thousands of years
    ago,
Not one is respectable or unhappy over the whole earth.

So they show their relations to me and I accept them,
They bring me tokens of myself, they evince them plainly in their
    possession.   10

I wonder where they get those tokens,
Did I pass that way huge times ago and negligently drop them?

Myself moving forward then and now and forever,
Gathering and showing more always and with velocity,
Infinite and omnigenous,[3] and the like of these among them,   15
Not too exclusive toward the reachers of my remembrancers,
Picking out here one that I love, and now go with him on brotherly
    terms.

A gigantic beauty of a stallion, fresh and responsive to my caresses,
Head high in the forehead, wide between the ears,
Limbs glossy and supple, tail dusting the ground,   20
Eyes full of sparkling wickedness, ears finely cut, flexibly moving.

His nostrils dilate as my heels embrace him,
His well-built limbs tremble with pleasure as we race around and return.

I but use you a minute, then I resign you, stallion,
Why do I need your paces when I myself out-gallop them?   25
Even as I stand or sit passing faster than you.

           *   *   *

3. Belonging to all races.

46

I know I have the best of time and space, and was never measured and
    never will be measured.

I tramp a perpetual journey, (come listen all!)
My signs are a rain-proof coat, good shoes, and a staff cut from the
    woods,
No friend of mine takes his ease in my chair,
I have no chair, no church, no philosophy,   5
I lead no man to a dinner-table, library, exchange,
But each man and each woman of you I lead upon a knoll,
My left hand hooking you round the waist,
My right hand pointing to landscapes of continents and the public road.

Not I, not any one else can travel that road for you,   10
You must travel it for yourself.

It is not far, it is within reach,
Perhaps you have been on it since you were born and did not know,
Perhaps it is everywhere on water and on land.

Shoulder your duds dear son, and I will mine, and let us hasten forth, 15
Wonderful cities and free nations we shall fetch as we go.

          *   *   *

51

The past and present wilt—I have filled them, emptied them,
And proceed to fill my next fold of the future.

Listener up there! what have you to confide to me?
Look in my face while I snuff the sidle of evening,[4]
(Talk honestly, no one else hears you, and I stay only a minute longer.) 5

Do I contradict myself?
Very well then I contradict myself,
(I am large, I contain multitudes.)

I concentrate toward them that are nigh, I wait on the door-slab.

Who has done his day's work? who will soonest be through with his
    supper?
Who wishes to walk with me?   10

Will you speak before I am gone? will you prove already too late?

52

The spotted hawk swoops by and accuses me, he complains of my gab
    and my loitering.

I too am not a bit tamed, I too am untranslatable,
I sound my barbaric yawp over the roofs of the world.

The last scud of day holds back for me,
It flings my likeness after the rest and true as any on the shadowed
    wilds,   5

---

4. That is, smell the fragrance of the slowly descending evening.

It coaxes me to the vapor and the dusk.

I depart as air, I shake my white locks at the runaway sun,
I effuse my flesh in eddies, and drift it in lacy jags.

I bequeath myself to the dirt to grow from the grass I love,
If you want me again look for me under your boot-soles.   10

You will hardly know who I am or what I mean,
But I shall be good health to you nevertheless,
And filter and fibre your blood.

Failing to fetch me at first keep encouraged,
Missing me one place search another,   15
I stop somewhere waiting for you.

Out of the Cradle Endlessly Rocking

Out of the cradle endlessly rocking,
Out of the mocking-bird's throat, the musical shuttle,
Out of the Ninth-month[1] midnight,
Over the sterile sands and the fields beyond, where the child leaving
    his bed wandered alone, bareheaded, barefoot,
Down from the showered halo,   5
Up from the mystic play of shadows twining and twisting as if they
    were alive,
Out from the patches of briers and blackberries,
From the memories of the bird that chanted to me,
From your memories sad brother, from the fitful risings and fallings I
    heard,
From under that yellow half-moon late-risen and swollen as if with
    tears,   10
From those beginning notes of yearning and love there in the mist,
From the thousand responses of my heart never to cease,
From the myriad thence-aroused words,
From the word stronger and more delicious than any,
From such as now they start the scene revisiting,   15
As a flock, twittering, rising, or overhead passing,
Borne hither, ere all eludes me, hurriedly,
A man, yet by these tears a little boy again,
Throwing myself on the sand, confronting the waves,
I, chanter of pains and joys, uniter of here and hereafter,   20
Taking all hints to use them, but swiftly leaping beyond them,
A reminiscence sing.

Once Paumanok,[2]
When the lilac-scent was in the air and Fifth-month[3] grass was growing,
Up this seashore in some briers,   25
Two feathered guests from Alabama, two together,
And their nest, and four light-green eggs spotted with brown,
And every day the he-bird to and fro near at hand,
And every day the she-bird crouched on her nest, silent, with bright eyes,

1. September, in Quaker usage.   2. The native American name for Long Island, where Whitman grew up.   3. May.

And every day I, a curious boy, never too close, never disturbing them, 30
Cautiously peering, absorbing, translating.

Shine! shine! shine!
Pour down your warmth, great sun!
While we bask, we two together.

Two together!   35
Winds blow south, or winds blow north,
Day come white, or night come black,
Home, or rivers and mountains from home,
Singing all time, minding no time,
While we two keep together.   40

Till of a sudden,
Maybe killed, unknown to her mate,
One forenoon the she-bird crouched not on the nest,
Nor returned that afternoon, nor the next,
Nor ever appeared again.   45

And thenceforward all summer in the sound of the sea,
And at night under the full of the moon in calmer weather,
Over the hoarse surging of the sea,
Or flitting from brier to brier by day,
I saw, I heard at intervals the remaining one, the he-bird,   50
The solitary guest from Alabama.

Blow! blow! blow!
Blow up sea-winds along Paumanok's shore;
I wait and I wait till you blow my mate to me.

Yes, when the stars glistened,   55
All night long on the prong of a moss-scalloped stake,
Down almost amid the slapping waves,
Sat the lone singer wonderful causing tears.

He called on his mate,
He poured forth the meanings which I of all men know.   60

Yes my brother I know,
The rest might not, but I have treasured every note,
For more than once dimly down to the beach gliding,
Silent, avoiding the moonbeams, blending myself with the shadows,
Recalling now the obscure shapes, the echoes, the sounds and sights
    after their sorts,   65
The white arms out in the breakers tirelessly tossing,
I, with bare feet, a child, the wind wafting my hair,
Listened long and long.

Listened to keep, to sing, now translating the notes,
Following you my brother.   70

Soothe! soothe! soothe!
Close on its wave soothes the wave behind,
And again another behind embracing and lapping, every one close,
But my love soothes not me, not me.

Low hangs the moon, it rose late,   75
It is lagging—O I think it is heavy with love, with love.

O madly the sea pushes upon the land,
With love, with love.

O night! do I not see my love fluttering out among the breakers?
What is that little black thing I see there in the white?   80

Loud! loud! loud!
Loud I call to you, my love!
High and clear I shoot my voice over the waves,
Surely you must know who is here, is here,
You must know who I am, my love.   85

Low-hanging moon!
What is that dusky spot in your brown yellow?
O it is the shape, the shape of my mate!
O moon do not keep her from me any longer.

Land! land! O land!   90
Whichever way I turn, O I think you could give me my mate back again
*   if you only would,*
For I am almost sure I see her dimly whichever way I look.

O rising stars!
Perhaps the one I want so much will rise, will rise with some of you.

O throat! O trembling throat!   95
Sound clearer through the atmosphere!
Pierce the woods, the earth,
Somewhere listening to catch you must be the one I want.

Shake out carols!
Solitary here, the night's carols!   100
Carols of lonesome love! death's carols!
Carols under that lagging, yellow, waning moon!
O under that moon where she droops almost down into the sea!
O reckless despairing carols.

But soft! sink low!   105
Soft! let me just murmur,
And do you wait a moment you husky-noised sea,
For somewhere I believe I heard my mate responding to me,
So faint, I must be still, be still to listen,
But not altogether still, for then she might not come immediately to me. 110

Hither my love!
Here I am! here!
With this just-sustained note I announce myself to you,
This gentle call is for you my love, for you.

Do not be decoyed elsewhere,   115
That is the whistle of the wind, it is not my voice,
That is the fluttering, the fluttering of the spray,
Those are the shadows of leaves.

O darkness! O in vain!
O I am very sick and sorrowful.   120

O brown halo in the sky near the moon, drooping upon the sea!
O troubled reflection in the sea!

O throat! O throbbing heart!
And I singing uselessly, uselessly all the night.

O past! O happy life! O songs of joy! 125
In the air, in the woods, over fields,
Loved! loved! loved! loved! loved!
But my mate no more, no more with me!
We two together no more.

The aria sinking, 130
All else continuing, the stars shining,
The winds blowing, the notes of the bird continuous echoing,
With angry moans the fierce old mother incessantly moaning,
On the sands of Paumanok's shore gray and rustling,
The yellow half-moon enlarged, sagging down, drooping, the face of
　　the sea almost touching, 135
The boy ecstatic, with his bare feet the waves, with his hair the atmo-
　　sphere dallying,
The love in the heart long pent, now loose, now at last tumultuously
　　bursting,
The aria's meaning, the ears, the soul, swiftly depositing,
The strange tears down the cheeks coursing,
The colloquy there, the trio, each uttering, 140
The undertone, the savage old mother incessantly crying,
To the boy's soul's questions sullenly timing, some drowned secret
　　hissing,
To the outsetting bard.

Demon or bird! (said the boy's soul,)
Is it indeed toward your mate you sing? or is it really to me? 145
For I, that was a child, my tongue's use sleeping, now I have heard you,
Now in a moment I know what I am for, I awake,
And already a thousand singers, a thousand songs, clearer, louder and
　　more sorrowful than yours,
A thousand warbling echoes have started to life within me, never to die.

O you singer solitary, singing by yourself, projecting me, 150
O solitary me listening, never more shall I cease perpetuating you,
Never more shall I escape, never more the reverberations,
Never more the cries of unsatisfied love be absent from me,
Never again leave me to be the peaceful child I was before what there
　　in the night,
By the sea under the yellow and sagging moon, 155
The messenger there aroused, the fire, the sweet hell within,
The unknown want, the destiny of me.

O give me the clue! (it lurks in the night here somewhere,)
O if I am to have so much, let me have more!

A word then, (for I will conquer it,) 160
The word final, superior to all,
Subtle, sent up—what is it?—I listen;
Are you whispering it, and have been all the time, you sea-waves?
Is that it from your liquid rims and wet sands?

Whereto answering, the sea, 165
Delaying not, hurrying not,

Whispered me through the night, and very plainly before daybreak,
Lisped to me the low and delicious word death,
And again death, death, death, death,
Hissing melodious, neither like the bird nor like my aroused child's
　　　heart,　　　　　　　　　　　　　　　　　　　　　　　　　　　　170
But edging near as privately for me rustling at my feet,
Creeping thence steadily up to my ears and laving me softly all over.
Death, death, death, death, death.

Which I do not forget,
But fuse the song of my dusky demon and brother,　　　　　　　　175
That he sang to me in the moonlight on Paumanok's gray beach,
With the thousand responsive songs at random,
My own songs awaked from that hour,
And with them the key, the word up from the waves,
The word of the sweetest song and all songs,　　　　　　　　　180
That strong and delicious word which, creeping to my feet,
(Or like some old crone rocking the cradle, swathed in sweet garments,
　　　bending aside,)
The sea whispered me.

HERMAN MELVILLE
1819–1891

Herman Melville's *Billy Budd, Sailor* has always absorbed and puzzled its readers. Its story appears to deal with the eternal struggle of good and evil as manifested in mortal affairs, but critics disagree about who or what the author considered "good." It has something to say about the nature of justice and of the individual's relation to society—but what? Commentators have asserted that the book affirms Melville's final serene acceptance of life as it is but also that it documents his ironic defiance. We don't know whether Melville had completed the work before he died, or what he intended its title to be. The challenging experience of becoming implicated in the novel's dilemmas, of confronting its perplexing characters, of trying to follow its moral logic, may lead to no firm conclusions, but it can hardly fail to generate imaginative excitement.

Melville's father died when the boy was thirteen, leaving the family in near poverty. This fact helps to account for young Melville's varied moneymaking enterprises. He taught school, kept a store, and clerked in a bank; at the age of twenty, he for the first time shipped out as a sailor. Subsequent ventures at sea included several whaling expeditions. On one of these, he jumped ship in the South Pacific, living for a month on an island in the Marquesas; on another whaling trip, he participated in a mutiny. In 1847, Melville married Elizabeth Shaw. The couple settled in Pittsfield, Massachusetts, where Melville spent his time writing. He attempted in vain to get an appointment to a foreign consulate as a means of support; his lecture tours, also intended to make money, were unsuccessful. Finally, with his wife and four children, he moved to New York City, where in 1867 he obtained a position at the Custom House, which he held for the next eighteen years.

Melville's first novels, including *Typee* (1846) and *Omoo* (1847), seafaring adventure stories based on his own experience, won popular success. His masterpiece, *Moby-Dick* (1851), however, puzzled readers by its allegorical obscurity, its apparent shapelessness, and its highly elaborate language. Melville thought it his best work and felt disappointed and somewhat embittered by its critical failure. Although he continued writing and publishing short stories, novels, and poems, none of his later work achieved popularity.

Billy Budd, Sailor existed only in a heavily revised and at some points barely comprehensible manuscript at the time of the novelist's death. It was printed for the first time, in an imperfect version (*Billy Budd, Foretopman*), in a 1924 edition of Melville's works. In 1948, Frederick Barron Freeman reedited the novel as *Billy Budd*; his text was supplemented in 1956 by emendations from the manuscript by Elizabeth Treeman. In 1962, *Billy Budd, Sailor*, source of the text printed here, was produced by Harrison Hayford and Morton M. Sealts Jr., who returned to the original manuscript, distinguished Elizabeth Melville's handwriting in it from her husband's, and generated a version substantially different from its predecessors. Although the nature of Melville's intention must remain finally impossible to ascertain, this careful effort to recapture what the novelist actually wrote at least has clear authority for every editorial choice.

The issues raised by the French Revolution, so vivid a part of literary consciousness at the beginning of the nineteenth century, once more provide a novelistic theme at the century's end—but with a new perspective. The events reported in *Billy Budd, Sailor* are said to occur in 1797. The narrator speaks of "those invading waters of novel opinion social, political, and otherwise, which carried away as in a torrent no few minds in those days." His metaphor suggests disapproval of the "novel opinion" that so greatly excited the early Romantics. Captain Vere, an important character whose name associates him with truth ("verity"), utterly resists the "invading waters." The only direct evidence, within the novel, of the actual effects of revolution is the reported mutinies, of which the narrator also appears to disapprove. Such evidence suggests a negative view of the French Revolution in its moral and political effects.

On the other hand, the narrator provides evidence of abundant cause for mutiny, particularly in the brutal practice of impressment, by which men were removed forcibly from nonnaval ships (or from their hometown streets, or their farms) and pressed into navy service, with no legal or practical recourse. When Billy Budd says good-bye to his ship, *Rights-of-Man*, he intends no irony, but others hear irony, as well they may: the concept of human rights is violated in every instance of impressment. Captain Vere's absolute devotion to legality and rule, his lack of openness to new possibility, arguably amount to extreme rigidity, even, possibly, to insanity. The narrator's wariness about "invading waters" may, like Billy's good-bye, be heard as ironic.

The conflicting claims of this series of statements, all supportable, need not be resolved; the important point is that by the end of the nineteenth century, everything that seemed true and exciting at the beginning had been called into question—not refuted, only made dubious. One can readily multiply examples from *Billy Budd, Sailor*. Billy, powerfully associated with images of innocence, resembles a child; a baby, even; a friendly dog; a big horse; Adam before the Fall. A hundred years earlier, Blake had suggested the perceptive power of the innocent, the child who points out that the emperor wears no clothes (or that chimney sweepers must rely on dreams and a black child on his mother's wishful stories to compensate for social injustice). Billy's innocence, on the other hand, has ambiguous implications. What does it mean to be an unfallen man in a fallen world? Billy can neither acquire from experience nor learn from others the knowledge that might make him capable of self-protective suspicion. His utter helplessness indicts his society but also raises troubling questions about the desirability of innocence.

Of course, one might argue that we in the twentieth century, "cynical" in the same sense as the old Dansker in the novel, are suspicious of such figures as Billy and Captain Vere in ways that our forebears would not be. Perhaps so; yet virtually all the questions suggested in the last two paragraphs appear more or less directly in the novelistic text. The narrator reflects about troubling aspects of Billy's innocence; the surgeon raises the possibility that Captain Vere is "unhinged." At many points, the narrative's symbolic language calls insistent attention to itself. It too, however, typically leaves one poised between interpretive alternatives. Here, for instance, is the description of Billy's hanging. "At the same moment it chanced that the vapory fleece hanging low in the East was shot through with a soft glory as of the fleece of the Lamb of God seen in mystical vision, and simultaneously therewith, watched by the wedged mass of upturned faces, Billy ascended; and, ascending, took the full rose of dawn." Are we to take seriously the implicit identification of Billy with Christ? Billy has willingly taken guilt upon himself, has forgiven his condemner, dies in his innocence, and "ascends." On the other hand, he ascends not to Heaven but to the yardarm, not in resurrection but in death. Is this a form of transcendence? Or is it irony again, at the expense of those who comfort themselves for social injustice by religious sentimentality?

Possibilities for interpretation depend, the novel tells us, on who formulates the story and who receives it. The book's subtitle, "An Inside Narrative," proves as ambiguous as everything else about it. This account, it suggests, will tell what really happened, as opposed to the newspaper report quoted late in the narrative that makes Billy into a suspicious foreigner who nefariously stabs the noble English Claggart. The storyteller returns intermittently to his insistence that he deals with facts; hence he draws back from the climactic scene between Billy and Captain Vere. Because no one else was present, the narrator can only speculate; in this instance, we will never know what really happened. The dialogue between the purser and the surgeon about the physical peculiarities of the hanging exemplifies the universal difficulty of interpretation. The storyteller is only one more interpreter, with his own biases. Educating us in mistrust by the nature of his story, he leaves us no certainties. The last word on Billy is presented in the sailor's ballad at the end, in which Billy's execution becomes a matter of pathos, not of moral speculation. Perhaps this story does not after all involve the conflict of good and evil; maybe it only provides a record of social contingency. This final possibility explains events as adequately—and as inadequately—as any other hypothesis.

In its questioning of the Romantic verities, revolution and innocence, as in its possibly ironic use of nature ("a soft glory as of the fleece of the Lamb of God"), Melville's novel reminds us how much can happen in a century. It may also remind us how insistently the nineteenth century foretells the twentieth. We are accustomed to feeling that we never get enough dependable information to make accurate judgments in matters of morality; we often distrust, if we think about it, the reliability of the "news" we are lavishly offered. *Billy Budd, Sailor* evokes a world that feels in many troubling respects like our own.

N. Arvin's *Herman Melville* (1950) is an excellent biographical study. Important critical works include L. Thompson, *Melville's Quarrel with God* (1952); W. Berthoff, *The Example of Melville* (1962); and H. Parker, *Reading Billy Budd* (1990). Useful collections of critical essays include R. A. Lee, ed., *Herman Melville: Reassessments* (1984), and R. Milder, ed., *Critical Essays on Melville's Billy Budd, Sailor* (1989).

Billy Budd, Sailor[1]

(*An Inside Narrative*)

1

In the time before steamships, or then more frequently than now, a stroller along the docks of any considerable seaport would occasionally have his attention arrested by a group of bronzed mariners, man-of-war's men or merchant sailors in holiday attire, ashore on liberty. In certain instances they would flank, or like a bodyguard quite surround, some superior figure of their own class, moving along with them like Aldebaran[2] among the lesser lights of his constellation. That signal object was the 'Handsome Sailor' of the less prosaic time alike of the military and merchant navies. With no perceptible trace of the vainglorious about him, rather with the offhand unaffectedness of natural regality, he seemed to accept the spontaneous homage of his shipmates.

A somewhat remarkable instance recurs to me. In Liverpool, now half a century ago, I saw under the shadow of the great dingy street-wall of Prince's Dock (an obstruction long since removed) a common sailor so intensely black that he must needs have been a native African of the unadulterate blood of Ham[3]—a symmetric figure much above the average height. The two ends of a gay silk handkerchief thrown loose about the neck danced upon the displayed ebony of his chest, in his ears were big hoops of gold, and a Highland bonnet with a tartan band set off his shapely head. It was a hot noon in July; and his face, lustrous with perspiration, beamed with barbaric good humor. In jovial sallies right and left, his white teeth flashing into view, he rollicked along, the center of a company of his shipmates. These were made up of such an assortment of tribes and complexions as would have well fitted them to be marched up by Anacharsis Cloots[4] before the bar of the first French Assembly as Representatives of the Human Race. At each spontaneous tribute rendered by the wayfarers to this black pagod[5] of a fellow—the tribute of a pause and stare, and less frequently an exclamation—the motley retinue showed that they took that sort of pride in the evoker of it which the Assyrian priests doubtless showed for their grand sculptured Bull when the faithful prostrated themselves.

To return. If in some cases a bit of a nautical Murat[6] in setting forth his person ashore, the Handsome Sailor of the period in question evinced nothing of the dandified Billy-be-Dam, an amusing character all but extinct now, but occasionally to be encountered, and in a form yet more amusing than the original, at the tiller of the boats on the tempestuous Erie Canal or, more likely, vaporing in the groggeries[7] along the towpath.

---

1. Edited by Harrison Hayford and Merton M. Sealts Jr.   2. A star of the first magnitude in the constellation of Taurus, the Bull, frequently used in navigation.   3. Ham, Noah's second son, was cursed by his father for mocking him. It was thought that a black skin was the result of the curse and that all black people descended from Ham.   4. Jean Baptiste du Val-de-Grace, Baron de Cloots, or Clootz (1755–1794), assembled a crowd of assorted nationalities and introduced them at the French National Assembly during the Revolution; he was popularly called "Anacharsis."   5. Meaning not only a pagoda but "an image of a deity, an idol" (*Oxford English Dictionary*).   6. Joachim Murat (1767–1815), marshall of France and king of Naples, Napoléon's brother-in-law, famous as a dandy.   7. Taverns. *Vaporing*: boasting or blustering.

Invariably a proficient in his perilous calling, he was also more or less of a mighty boxer or wrestler. It was strength and beauty. Tales of his prowess were recited. Ashore he was the champion; afloat the spokesman; on every suitable occasion always foremost. Close-reefing topsails in a gale, there he was, astride the weather yardarm-end, foot in the Flemish horse[8] as stirrup, both hands tugging at the earing as at a bridle, in very much the attitude of young Alexander curbing the fiery Bucephalus.[9] A superb figure, tossed up as by the horns of Taurus against the thunderous sky, cheerily hallooing to the strenuous file along the spar.

The moral nature was seldom out of keeping with the physical make. Indeed, except as toned by the former, the comeliness and power, always attractive in masculine conjunction, hardly could have drawn the sort of honest homage the Handsome Sailor in some examples received from his less gifted associates.

Such a cynosure, at least in aspect, and something such too in nature, though with important variations made apparent as the story proceeds, was welkin-eyed[1] Billy Budd—or Baby Budd, as more familiarly, under circumstances hereafter to be given, he at last came to be called—aged twenty-one, a foretopman[2] of the British fleet toward the close of the last decade of the eighteenth century. It was not very long prior to the time of the narration that follows that he had entered the King's service, having been impressed on the Narrow Seas from a homeward-bound English merchantman into a seventy-four[3] outward bound, H.M.S. *Bellipotent*; which ship, as was not unusual in those hurried days, having been obliged to put to sea short of her proper complement of men. Plump upon Billy at first sight in the gangway the boarding officer, Lieutenant Ratcliffe, pounced, even before the merchantman's crew was formally mustered on the quarter-deck for his deliberate inspection. And him only he elected. For whether it was because the other men when ranged before him showed to ill advantage after Billy, or whether he had some scruples in view of the merchantman's being rather short-handed, however it might be, the officer contented himself with his first spontaneous choice. To the surprise of the ship's company, though much to the lieutenant's satisfaction, Billy made no demur. But, indeed, any demur would have been as idle as the protest of a goldfinch popped into a cage.

Noting this uncomplaining acquiescence, all but cheerful, one might say, the shipmaster turned a surprised glance of silent reproach at the sailor. The shipmaster was one of those worthy mortals found in every vocation, even the humbler ones—the sort of person whom everybody agrees in calling 'a respectable man.' And—nor so strange to report as it may appear to be—though a ploughman of the troubled waters, lifelong contending with the intractable elements, there was nothing this honest soul at heart loved better than simple peace and quiet. For the rest, he was fifty or thereabouts, a little inclined to corpulence, a prepossessing

---

8. A hazardous activity: sailors go out on a yardarm (a spar supporting a sail) by means of foot ropes, one of which is called the *Flemish horse*.   9. Alexander the Great's warhorse.   1. Blue-eyed (*welkin*: sky).
2. Junior to a maintopman like Jack Chase, to whom the book is dedicated.   3. A third-rate ship of the line, equivalent to a light cruiser today. The designation refers to the number of guns the ship carried. *Narrow Seas*: the English Channel and the waters between England and Ireland.

face, unwhiskered, and of an agreeable color—a rather full face, humanely intelligent in expression. On a fair day with a fair wind and all going well, a certain musical chime in his voice seemed to be the veritable unobstructed outcome of the innermost man. He had much prudence, much conscientiousness, and there were occasions when these virtues were the cause of overmuch disquietude in him. On a passage, so long as his craft was in any proximity to land, no sleep for Captain Graveling. He took to heart those serious responsibilities not so heavily borne by some shipmasters.

Now while Billy Budd was down in the forecastle getting his kit together, the *Bellipotent's* lieutenant, burly and bluff, nowise disconcerted by Captain Graveling's omitting to proffer the customary hospitalities on an occasion so unwelcome to him, an omission simply caused by preoccupation of thought, unceremoniously invited himself into the cabin, and also to a flask from the spirit locker, a receptacle which his experienced eye instantly discovered. In fact he was one of those sea dogs in whom all the hardship and peril of naval life in the great prolonged wars of his time never impaired the natural instinct for sensuous enjoyment. His duty he always faithfully did; but duty is sometimes a dry obligation, and he was for irrigating its aridity, whensoever possible, with a fertilizing decoction of strong waters. For the cabin's proprietor there was nothing left but to play the part of the enforced host with whatever grace and alacrity were practicable. As necessary adjuncts to the flask, he silently placed tumbler and water jug before the irrepressible guest. But excusing himself from partaking just then, he dismally watched the unembarrassed officer deliberately diluting his grog[4] a little, then tossing it off in three swallows, pushing the empty tumbler away, yet not so far as to be beyond easy reach, at the same time settling himself in his seat and smacking his lips with high satisfaction, looking straight at the host.

These proceedings over, the master broke the silence; and there lurked a rueful reproach in the tone of his voice: 'Lieutenant, you are going to take my best man from me, the jewel of 'em.'

'Yes, I know,' rejoined the other, immediately drawing back the tumbler preliminary to a replenishing. 'Yes, I know. Sorry.'

'Beg pardon, but you don't understand, Lieutenant. See here, now. Before I shipped that young fellow, my forecastle was a rat-pit of quarrels. It was black times, I tell you, aboard the *Rights* here. I was worried to that degree my pipe had no comfort for me. But Billy came; and it was like a Catholic priest striking peace in an Irish shindy.[5] Not that he preached to them or said or did anything in particular; but a virtue went out of him, sugaring the sour ones. They took to him like hornets to treacle; all but the buffer[6] of the gang, the big shaggy chap with the fire-red whiskers. He indeed, out of envy, perhaps, of the newcomer, and thinking such a "sweet and pleasant fellow," as he mockingly designated him to the others, could hardly have the spirit of a gamecock, must needs bestir himself in trying to get up an ugly row with him. Billy forebore with him and reasoned with him in a pleasant way—he is something like myself, Lieutenant, to whom

---

4. A mixture of rum and water.   5. Free-for-all fight.   6. Big fellow.

aught like a quarrel is hateful—but nothing served. So, in the second
dogwatch[7] one day, the Red Whiskers in presence of the others, under
pretense of showing Billy just whence a sirloin steak was cut—for the
fellow had once been a butcher—insultingly gave him a dig under the
ribs. Quick as lightning Billy let fly his arm. I dare say he never meant to
do quite so much as he did, but anyhow he gave the burly fool a terrible
drubbing. It took about half a minute, I should think. And lord bless you,
the lubber was astonished at the celerity. And will you believe it, Lieutenant, the Red Whiskers now really loves Billy—loves him, or is the biggest
hypocrite that ever I heard of. But they all love him. Some of 'em do his
washing, darn his old trousers for him; the carpenter is at odd times making a pretty little chest of drawers for him. Anybody will do anything for
Billy Budd; and it's the happy family here. But now, Lieutenant, if that
young fellow goes—I know how it will be aboard the *Rights*. Not again
very soon shall I, coming up from dinner, lean over the capstan smoking
a quiet pipe—no, not very soon again, I think. Ay, Lieutenant, you are
going to take away the jewel of 'em; you are going to take away my peacemaker!' And with that the good soul had really some ado in checking a
rising sob.

'Well,' said the lieutenant, who had listened with amused interest to
all this and now was waxing merry with his tipple: 'well, blessed are the
peacemakers, especially the fighting peacemakers. And such are the seventy-four beauties some of which you see poking their noses out of the
portholes of yonder warship lying to for me,' pointing through the cabin
window at the *Bellipotent.* 'But courage! Don't look so downhearted, man.
Why, I pledge you in advance the royal approbation. Rest assured that His
Majesty will be delighted to know that in a time when his hardtack is not
sought for by sailors with such avidity as should be, a time also when some
shipmasters privily resent the borrowing from them a tar[8] or two for the
service; His Majesty, I say, will be delighted to learn that *one* shipmaster
at least cheerfully surrenders to the King the flower of his flock, a sailor
who with equal loyalty makes no dissent.—But where's my beauty? Ah,'
looking through the cabin's open door, 'here he comes; and, by Jove, lugging along his chest—Apollo with his portmanteau!—My man,' stepping
out to him, 'you can't take that big box aboard a warship. The boxes there
are mostly shot boxes. Put your duds in a bag, lad. Boot and saddle for the
cavalryman, bag and hammock for the man-of-war's man.'

The transfer from chest to bag was made. And, after seeing his man into
the cutter and then following him down, the lieutenant pushed off from
the *Rights-of-Man.* That was the merchant ship's name, though by
her master and crew abbreviated in sailor fashion into the *Rights.* The
hardheaded Dundee owner was a staunch admirer of Thomas Paine,[9]
whose book in rejoinder to Burke's arraignment of the French Revolution had then been published for some time and had gone everywhere.
In christening his vessel after the title of Paine's volume the man of
Dundee was something like his contemporary ship-owner, Stephen

---

7. From 6:00 to 8:00 P.M.   8. Sailor.   9. American Revolutionary patriot (1737–1809), born in England, published *The Rights of Man* in 1791 as a response to Edmund Burke's *Reflections on the Revolution in France* (1790). Dundee is a seaport in Scotland.

Girard[1] of Philadelphia, whose sympathies, alike with his native land and its liberal philosophers, he evinced by naming his ships after Voltaire, Diderot, and so forth.

But now, when the boat swept under the merchantman's stern, and officer and oarsmen were noting—some bitterly and others with a grin—the name emblazoned there; just then it was that the new recruit jumped up from the bow where the coxswain had directed him to sit, and waving hat to his silent shipmates sorrowfully looking over at him from the taffrail, bade the lads a genial good-bye. Then, making a salutation as to the ship herself, 'And good-bye to you too, old *Rights-of-Man.*'

'Down, sir!' roared the lieutenant, instantly assuming all the rigor of his rank, though with difficulty repressing a smile.

To be sure, Billy's action was a terrible breach of naval decorum. But in that decorum he had never been instructed; in consideration of which the lieutenant would hardly have been so energetic in reproof but for the concluding farewell to the ship. This he rather took as meant to convey a covert sally on the new recruit's part, a sly slur at impressment in general, and that of himself in especial. And yet, more likely, if satire it was in effect, it was hardly so by intention, for Billy, though happily endowed with the gaiety of high health, youth, and a free heart, was yet by no means of a satirical turn. The will to it and the sinister dexterity were alike wanting. To deal in double meanings and insinuations of any sort was quite foreign to his nature.

As to his enforced enlistment, that he seemed to take pretty much as he was wont to take any vicissitude of weather. Like the animals, though no philosopher, he was, without knowing it, practically a fatalist. And it may be that he rather liked this adventurous turn in his affairs, which promised an opening into novel scenes and martial excitements.

Aboard the *Bellipotent* our merchant sailor was forthwith rated as an able seaman and assigned to the starboard watch of the foretop. He was soon at home in the service, not at all disliked for his unpretentious good looks and a sort of genial happy-go-lucky air. No merrier man in his mess: in marked contrast to certain other individuals included like himself among the impressed portion of the ship's company; for these when not actively employed were sometimes, and more particularly in the last dog-watch when the drawing near of twilight induced revery, apt to fall into a saddish mood which in some partook of sullenness. But they were not so young as our foretopman, and no few of them must have known a hearth of some sort, others may have had wives and children left, too probably, in uncertain circumstances, and hardly any but must have had acknowledged kith and kin, while for Billy, as will shortly be seen, his entire family was practically invested in himself.

2

Though our new-made foretopman was well received in the top and on the gun decks, hardly here was he that cynosure he had previously been

1. Merchant, banker, and philanthropist (1750–1831), a native of France who emigrated at the age of twenty-seven.

among those minor ship's companies of the merchant marine, with which companies only had he hitherto consorted.

He was young; and despite his all but fully developed frame, in aspect looked even younger than he really was, owing to a lingering adolescent expression in the as yet smooth face all but feminine in purity of natural complexion but where, thanks to his seagoing, the lily was quite suppressed and the rose had some ado visibly to flush through the tan.

To one essentially such a novice in the complexities of factitious life, the abrupt transition from his former and simpler sphere to the ampler and more knowing world of a great warship; this might well have abashed him had there been any conceit or vanity in his composition. Among her miscellaneous multitude, the *Bellipotent* mustered several individuals who however inferior in grade were of no common natural stamp, sailors more signally susceptive of that air which continuous martial discipline and repeated presence in battle can in some degree impart even to the average man. As the Handsome Sailor, Billy Budd's position aboard the seventy-four was something analogous to that of a rustic beauty transplanted from the provinces and brought into competition with the highborn dames of the court. But this change of circumstances he scarce noted. As little did he observe that something about him provoked an ambiguous smile in one or two harder faces among the bluejackets. Nor less unaware was he of the peculiar favorable effect his person and demeanor had upon the more intelligent gentlemen of the quarter-deck. Nor could this well have been otherwise. Cast in a mold peculiar to the finest physical examples of those Englishmen in whom the Saxon strain would seem not at all to partake of any Norman or other admixture, he showed in face that humane look of reposeful good nature which the Greek sculptor in some instances gave to his heroic strong man, Hercules. But this again was subtly modified by another and pervasive quality. The ear, small and shapely, the arch of the foot, the curve in mouth and nostril, even the indurated hand dyed to the orange-tawny of the toucan's bill, a hand telling alike of the halyards and tar bucket; but, above all, something in the mobile expression, and every chance attitude and movement, something suggestive of a mother eminently favored by Love and the Graces; all this strangely indicated a lineage in direct contradiction to his lot. The mysteriousness here became less mysterious through a matter of fact elicited when Billy at the capstan was being formally mustered into the service. Asked by the officer, a small, brisk little gentleman as it chanced, among other questions, his place of birth, he replied, 'Please, sir, I don't know.'

'Don't know where you were born? Who was your father?'

'God knows, sir.'

Struck by the straightforward simplicity of these replies, the officer next asked, 'Do you know anything about your beginning?'

'No, sir. But I have heard that I was found in a pretty silk-lined basket hanging one morning from the knocker of a good man's door in Bristol.'

'*Found*, say you? Well,' throwing back his head and looking up and down the new recruit; 'well, it turns out to have been a pretty good find. Hope they'll find some more like you, my man; the fleet sadly needs them.'

Yes, Billy Budd was a foundling, a presumable by-blow, and, evidently, no ignoble one. Noble descent was as evident in him as in a blood horse.

For the rest, with little or no sharpness of faculty or any trace of the wisdom of the serpent, nor yet quite a dove, he possessed that kind and degree of intelligence going along with the unconventional rectitude of a sound human creature, one to whom not yet has been proffered the questionable apple of knowledge. He was illiterate; he could not read, but he could sing, and like the illiterate nightingale was sometimes the composer of his own song.

Of self-consciousness he seemed to have little or none, or about as much as we may reasonably impute to a dog of Saint Bernard's breed.

Habitually living with the elements and knowing little more of the land than as a beach, or, rather, that portion of the terraqueous globe providentially set apart for dance-houses, doxies, and tapsters, in short what sailors call a 'fiddler's green,'[2] his simple nature remained unsophisticated by those moral obliquities which are not in every case incompatible with that manufacturable thing known as respectability. But are sailors, frequenters of fiddler's greens, without vices? No; but less often than with landsmen do their vices, so called, partake of crookedness of heart, seeming less to proceed from viciousness than exuberance of vitality after long constraint: frank manifestations in accordance with natural law. By his original constitution aided by the co-operating influences of his lot, Billy in many respects was little more than a sort of upright barbarian, much such perhaps as Adam presumably might have been ere the urbane Serpent wriggled himself into his company.

And here be it submitted that apparently going to corroborate the doctrine of man's Fall, a doctrine now popularly ignored, it is observable that where certain virtues pristine and unadulterate peculiarly characterize anybody in the external uniform of civilization, they will upon scrutiny seem not to be derived from custom or convention, but rather to be out of keeping with these, as if indeed exceptionally transmitted from a period prior to Cain's city[3] and citified man. The character marked by such qualities has to an unvitiated taste an untampered-with flavor like that of berries, while the man thoroughly civilized, even in a fair specimen of the breed, has to the same moral palate a questionable smack as of a compounded wine. To any stray inheritor of these primitive qualities found, like Caspar Hauser,[4] wandering dazed in any Christian capital of our time, the good-natured poet's famous invocation, near two thousand years ago, of the good rustic out of his latitude in the Rome of the Caesars, still appropriately holds:

> Honest and poor, faithful in word and thought,
> What hath thee, Fabian, to the city brought?[5]

Though our Handsome Sailor had as much of masculine beauty as one can expect anywhere to see; nevertheless, like the beautiful woman in one of Hawthorne's minor tales, there was just one thing amiss in him. No visible blemish[6] indeed, as with the lady; no, but an occasional liability to

---

2. A sailor's utopia.   3. That is, in the time of the Garden of Eden. Cain "builded a city" in Genesis 4:16–17.   4. A German foundling (1812?–1833) who claimed to have been brought up in a primitive wilderness.   5. Martial, *Epigrams* I.iv.1–2, from Cowley's translation in the Bohn edition.   6. *The Birthmark*, in which the *blemish* is on the lady's cheek.

a vocal defect. Though in the hour of elemental uproar or peril he was everything that a sailor should be, yet under sudden provocation of strong heart-feeling his voice, otherwise singularly musical, as if expressive of the harmony within, was apt to develop an organic hesitancy, in fact more or less of a stutter or even worse. In this particular Billy was a striking instance that the arch interferer, the envious marplot of Eden, still has more or less to do with every human consignment to this planet of Earth. In every case, one way or another he is sure to slip in his little card, as much as to remind us—I too have a hand here.

The avowal of such an imperfection in the Handsome Sailor should be evidence not alone that he is not presented as a conventional hero, but also that the story in which he is the main figure is no romance.

3

At the time of Billy Budd's arbitrary enlistment into the *Bellipotent* that ship was on her way to join the Mediterranean fleet. No long time elapsed before the junction was effected. As one of that fleet the seventy-four participated in its movements, though at times on account of her superior sailing qualities, in the absence of frigates, dispatched on separate duty as a scout and at times on less temporary service. But with all this the story has little concernment, restricted as it is to the inner life of one particular ship and the career of an individual sailor.

It was the summer of 1797. In the April of that year had occurred the commotion at Spithead followed in May by a second and yet more serious outbreak in the fleet at the Nore. The latter is known, and without exaggeration in the epithet, as 'the Great Mutiny.' It was indeed a demonstration more menacing to England than the contemporary manifestoes and conquering and proselyting armies of the French Directory.[7] To the British Empire the Nore Mutiny was what a strike in the fire brigade would be to London threatened by general arson. In a crisis when the kingdom might well have anticipated the famous signal that some years later published along the naval line of battle what it was that upon occasion England expected of Englishmen;[8] *that* was the time when at the mastheads of the three-deckers and seventy-fours moored in her own roadstead—a fleet the right arm of a Power then all but the sole free conservative one of the Old World—the bluejackets, to be numbered by thousands, ran up with huzzas the British colors with the union and cross[9] wiped out; by that cancellation transmuting the flag of founded law and freedom defined, into the enemy's red meteor of unbridled and unbounded revolt. Reasonable discontent growing out of practical grievances in the fleet had been ignited into irrational combustion as by live cinders blown across the Channel from France in flames.

The event converted into irony for a time those spirited strains of Dibdin[1]—as a song-writer no mean auxiliary to the English government at

---

7. The five directors who governed France from 1795 to 1799, during the Revolution.   8. "England expects every man to do his duty!": Lord Nelson, before the battle at Trafalgar, October 21, 1805. 9. The British Union Jack, or national flag, carries the crosses of St. Andrew, St. George, and St. Patrick, patron saints of Scotland, England, and Ireland.   1. Charles Dibdin (1745–1814), English dramatist, chiefly remembered for his sea chanteys. The ballad quoted is "Poor Jack."

that European conjuncture—strains celebrating, among other things, the patriotic devotion of the British tar: 'And as for my life, 'tis the King's!'

Such an episode in the Island's grand naval story her naval historians naturally abridge, one of them (William James)[2] candidly acknowledging that fain would he pass it over did not 'impartiality forbid fastidiousness.' And yet his mention is less a narration than a reference, having to do hardly at all with details. Nor are these readily to be found in the libraries. Like some other events in every age befalling states everywhere, including America, the Great Mutiny was of such character that national pride along with views of policy would fain shade it off into the historical background. Such events cannot be ignored, but there is a considerate way of historically treating them. If a well-constituted individual refrains from blazoning aught amiss or calamitous in his family, a nation in the like circumstance may without reproach be equally discreet.

Though after parleyings between government and the ringleaders, and concessions by the former as to some glaring abuses, the first uprising— that at Spithead—with difficulty was put down, or matters for the time pacified; yet at the Nore the unforeseen renewal of insurrection on a yet larger scale, and emphasized in the conferences that ensued by demands deemed by the authorities not only inadmissible but aggressively insolent, indicated—if the Red Flag did not sufficiently do so—what was the spirit animating the men. Final suppression, however, there was; but only made possible perhaps by the unswerving loyalty of the marine corps and a voluntary resumption of loyalty among influential sections of the crews.

To some extent the Nore Mutiny may be regarded as analogous to the distempering irruption of contagious fever in a frame constitutionally sound, and which anon throws it off.

At all events, of these thousands of mutineers were some of the tars who not so very long afterwards—whether wholly prompted thereto by patriotism, or pugnacious instinct, or by both—helped to win a coronet for Nelson at the Nile, and the naval crown of crowns for him at Trafalgar.[3] To the mutineers, those battles and especially Trafalgar were a plenary absolution and a grand one. For all that goes to make up scenic naval display and heroic magnificance in arms, those battles, especially Trafalgar, stand unmatched in human annals.

4

In this matter of writing, resolve as one may to keep to the main road, some bypaths have an enticement not readily to be withstood. I am going to err into such a bypath. If the reader will keep me company I shall be glad. At the least, we can promise ourselves that pleasure which is wickedly said to be in sinning, for a literary sin the divergence will be.

Very likely it is no new remark that the inventions of our time have at last brought about a change in sea warfare in degree corresponding to the revolution in all warfare effected by the original introduction from China

---

2. *The Naval History of Great Britain* (1860). Melville mistakenly wrote "G. P. R. James."   3. Nelson was made a baronet for his victory over the French at Aboukir in 1798; his 1805 victory at Trafalgar is considered one of the greatest in naval history.

into Europe of gunpowder. The first European firearm, a clumsy contrivance, was, as is well known, scouted[4] by no few of the knights as a base implement, good enough peradventure for weavers too craven to stand up crossing steel with steel in frank fight. But as ashore knightly valor, though shorn of its blazonry, did not cease with the knights, neither on the sea — though nowadays in encounters there a certain kind of displayed gallantry be fallen out of date as hardly applicable under changed circumstances — did the nobler qualities of such naval magnates as Don John of Austria, Doria, Van Tromp, Jean Bart, the long line of British admirals, and the American Decaturs of 1812 become obsolete with their wooden walls.[5]

Nevertheless, to anybody who can hold the Present at its worth without being inappreciative of the Past, it may be forgiven, if to such an one the solitary old hulk at Portsmouth, Nelson's *Victory*, seems to float there, not alone as the decaying monument of a fame incorruptible, but also as a poetic reproach, softened by its picturesqueness, to the *Monitors*[6] and yet mightier hulls of the European ironclads. And this not altogether because such craft are unsightly, unavoidably lacking the symmetry and grand lines of the old battleships, but equally for other reasons.

There are some, perhaps, who while not altogether inaccessible to that poetic reproach just alluded to, may yet on behalf of the new order be disposed to parry it; and this to the extent of iconoclasm, if need be. For example, prompted by the sight of the star inserted in the *Victory*'s quarterdeck designating the spot where the Great Sailor fell, these martial utilitarians may suggest considerations implying that Nelson's ornate publication of his person in battle was not only unnecessary, but not military, nay, savored of foolhardiness and vanity. They may add, too, that at Trafalgar it was in effect nothing less than a challenge to death; and death came; and that but for his bravado the victorious admiral might possibly have survived the battle, and so, instead of having his sagacious dying injunctions overruled by his immediate successor in command, he himself when the contest was decided might have brought his shattered fleet to anchor, a proceeding which might have averted the deplorable loss of life by shipwreck in the elemental tempest that followed the martial one.

Well, should we set aside the more than disputable point whether for various reasons it was possible to anchor the fleet, then plausibly enough the Benthamites[7] of war may urge the above. But the *might-have-been* is but boggy ground to build on. And, certainly, in foresight as to the larger issue of an encounter, and anxious preparations for it — buoying the deadly way and mapping it out, as at Copenhagen[8] — few commanders have been so painstakingly circumspect as this same reckless declarer of his person in fight.

---

4. Scoffed at.   5. A reference to the wooden ships made obsolete by ironclads. Don Juan of Austria (1547–1578) commanded a fleet against the Turks at Lepanto in 1571, the last major sea battle in which oared ships predominated. Andrea Doria (1468–1560) liberated Genoa from the Turks. Maarten Van Tromp (1596–1653), Dutch admiral, fought successfully against the English under Charles II. Jean Bart (1651?–1702), a French captain, battled the Dutch. Stephen Decatur (1779–1820) won victories over the Barbary Coast pirates at Tripoli and over the British in the War of 1812.   6. The *Monitor* was an ironclad launched in 1862 to fight the Confederate *Merrimac* in a battle effectively ending the era of wooden ships.   7. Utilitarian thinkers and followers of Jeremy Bentham (1748–1832), who believed in the greatest good for the greatest number.   8. Where Nelson's careful planning defeated the Danish on April 2, 1801.

Personal prudence, even when dictated by quite other than selfish considerations, surely is no special virtue in a military man; while an excessive love of glory, impassioning a less burning impulse, the honest sense of duty, is the first. If the name *Wellington* is not so much of a trumpet to the blood as the simpler name *Nelson*, the reason for this may perhaps be inferred from the above. Alfred in his funeral ode on the victory of Waterloo ventures not to call him the greatest soldier of all time, though in the same ode he invokes Nelson as 'the greatest sailor since our world began.'[9]

At Trafalgar Nelson on the brink of opening the fight sat down and wrote his last brief will and testament. If under the presentiment of the most magnificent of all victories to be crowned by his own glorious death, a sort of priestly motive led him to dress his person in the jewelled vouchers of his own shining deeds; if thus to have adorned himself for the altar and the sacrifice were indeed vainglory, then affectation and fustian is each more heroic line in the great epics and dramas, since in such lines the poet but embodies in verse those exaltations of sentiment that a nature like Nelson, the opportunity being given, vitalizes into acts.

5

Yes, the outbreak at the Nore was put down. But not every grievance was redressed. If the contractors, for example, were no longer permitted to ply some practices peculiar to their tribe everywhere, such as providing shoddy cloth, rations not sound, or false in the measure; not the less impressment, for one thing, went on. By custom sanctioned for centuries, and judicially maintained by a Lord Chancellor as late as Mansfield,[1] that mode of manning the fleet, a mode now fallen into a sort of abeyance but never formally renounced, it was not practicable to give up in those years. Its abrogation would have crippled the indispensable fleet, one wholly under canvas, no steam power, its innumerable sails and thousands of cannon, everything in short, worked by muscle alone; a fleet the more insatiate in demand for men, because then multiplying its ships of all grades against contingencies present and to come of the convulsed Continent.

Discontent foreran the Two Mutinies, and more or less it lurkingly survived them. Hence it was not unreasonable to apprehend some return of trouble sporadic or general. One instance of such apprehensions: In the same year with this story, Nelson, then Rear Admiral Sir Horatio, being with the fleet off the Spanish coast, was directed by the admiral in command to shift his pennant from the *Captain* to the *Theseus*; and for this reason: that the latter ship having newly arrived on the station from home, where it had taken part in the Great Mutiny, danger was apprehended from the temper of the men; and it was thought that an officer like Nelson was the one, not indeed to terrorize the crew into base subjection, but to win them, by force of his mere presence and heroic personality, back to an allegiance if not as enthusiastic as his own yet as true.

So it was that for a time, on more than one quarter-deck, anxiety did

9. The quotation comes from Tennyson's *Ode on the Death of the Duke of Wellington* (1852), line 7.
1. William Murray, Baron Mansfield (1705–1793), lord chief justice of Great Britain from 1756 to 1788.

exist. At sea, precautionary vigilance was strained against relapse. At short notice an engagement might come on. When it did, the lieutenants assigned to batteries felt it incumbent on them, in some instances, to stand with drawn swords behind the men working the guns.

6

But on board the seventy-four in which Billy now swung his hammock, very little in the manner of the men and nothing obvious in the demeanor of the officers would have suggested to an ordinary observer that the Great Mutiny was a recent event. In their general bearing and conduct the commissioned officers of a warship naturally take their tone from the commander, that is if he have that ascendancy of character that ought to be his.

Captain the Honorable Edward Fairfax Vere, to give his full title, was a bachelor of forty or thereabouts, a sailor of distinction even in a time prolific of renowned seamen. Though allied to the higher nobility, his advancement had not been altogether owing to influences connected with that circumstance. He had seen much service, been in various engagements, always acquitting himself as an officer mindful of the welfare of his men, but never tolerating an infraction of discipline; thoroughly versed in the science of his profession, and intrepid to the verge of temerity, though never injudiciously so. For his gallantry in the West Indian waters as flag lietutenant under Rodney in that admiral's crowning victory over De Grasse,[2] he was made a post captain.

Ashore, in the garb of a civilian, scarce anyone would have taken him for a sailor, more especially that he never garnished unprofessional talk with nautical terms, and grave in his bearing, evinced little appreciation of mere humor. It was not out of keeping with these traits that on a passage when nothing demanded his paramount action, he was the most undemonstrative of men. Any landsman observing this gentleman not conspicuous by his stature and wearing no pronounced insignia, emerging from his cabin to the open deck, and noting the silent deference of the officers retiring to leeward, might have taken him for the King's guest, a civilian aboard the King's ship, some highly honorable discreet envoy on his way to an important post. But in fact this unobtrusiveness of demeanor may have proceeded from a certain unaffected modesty of manhood sometimes accompanying a resolute nature, a modesty evinced at all times not calling for pronounced action, which shown in any rank of life suggests a virtue aristocratic in kind. As with some others engaged in various departments of the world's more heroic activities, Captain Vere though practical enough upon occasion would at times betray a certain dreaminess of mood. Standing alone on the weather side of the quarter-deck, one hand holding by the rigging, he would absently gaze off at the blank sea. At the presentation to him then of some minor matter interrupting the current of his thoughts, he would show more or less irascibility; but instantly he would control it.

2. The British admiral George Brydges, Baron Rodney (1719–1792), defeated the French Admiral De Grasse off Dominica, in the Leeward Islands, in 1782.

In the navy he was popularly known by the appellation 'Starry Vere.' How such a designation happened to fall upon one who whatever his sterling qualities was without any brilliant ones, was in this wise: A favorite kinsman, Lord Denton, a freehearted fellow, had been the first to meet and congratulate him upon his return to England from his West Indian cruise; and but the day previous turning over a copy of Andrew Marvell's[3] poems had lighted, not for the first time, however, upon the lines entitled 'Appleton House,' the name of one of the seats of their common ancestor, a hero in the German wars of the seventeenth century, in which poem occur the lines:

> This 'tis to have been from the first
> In a domestic heaven nursed,
> Under the discipline severe
> Of Fairfax and the starry Vere.

And so, upon embracing his cousin fresh from Rodney's great victory wherein he had played so gallant a part, brimming over with just family pride in the sailor of their house, he exuberantly exclaimed, 'Give ye joy, Ed; give ye joy, my starry Vere!' This got currency, and the novel prefix serving in familiar parlance readily to distinguish the *Bellipotent*'s captain from another Vere his senior, a distant relative, an officer of like rank in the navy, it remained permanently attached to the surname.

7

In view of the part that the commander of the *Bellipotent* plays in scenes shortly to follow, it may be well to fill out that sketch of him outlined in the previous chapter.

Aside from his qualities as a sea officer Captain Vere was an exceptional character. Unlike no few of England's renowned sailors, long and arduous service with signal devotion to it had not resulted in absorbing and *salting* the entire man. He had a marked leaning toward everything intellectual. He loved books, never going to sea without a newly replenished library, compact but of the best. The isolated leisure, in some cases so wearisome, falling at intervals to commanders even during a war cruise, never was tedious to Captain Vere. With nothing of that literary taste which less heeds the thing conveyed than the vehicle, his bias was toward those books to which every serious mind of superior order occupying any active post of authority in the world naturally inclines: books treating of actual men and events no matter of what era—history, biography, and unconventional writers like Montaigne,[4] who, free from cant and convention, honestly and in the spirit of common sense philosophize upon realities. In this line of reading he found confirmation of his own more reserved thoughts— confirmation which he had vainly sought in social converse, so that as touching most fundamental topics, there had got to be established in him some positive convictions which he forefelt would abide in him essentially unmodified so long as his intelligent part remained unimpaired. In view of the troubled period in which his lot was cast, this was well for him. His

---

3. English lyric poet (1621–1678).   4. Michel Eyquem de Montaigne (1533–1592), French essayist.

settled convictions were as a dike against those invading waters of novel opinion social, political, and otherwise, which carried away as in a torrent no few minds in those days, minds by nature not inferior to his own. While other members of that aristocracy to which by birth he belonged were incensed at the innovators mainly because their theories were inimical to the privileged classes, Captain Vere disinterestedly opposed them not alone because they seemed to him insusceptible of embodiment in lasting institutions, but at war with the peace of the world and the true welfare of mankind.

With minds less stored than his and less earnest, some officers of his rank, with whom at times he would necessarily consort, found him lacking in the companionable quality, a dry and bookish gentleman, as they deemed. Upon any chance withdrawal from their company one would be apt to say to another something like this: 'Vere is a noble fellow, Starry Vere. 'Spite the gazettes,[5] Sir Horatio' (meaning him who became Lord Nelson) 'is at bottom scarce a better seaman or fighter. But between you and me now, don't you think there is a queer streak of the pedantic running through him? Yes, like the King's yarn in a coil of navy rope?'[6]

Some apparent ground there was for this sort of confidential criticism; since not only did the captain's discourse never fall into the jocosely familiar, but in illustrating of any point touching the stirring personages and events of the time he would be as apt to cite some historic character or incident of antiquity as he would be to cite from the moderns. He seemed unmindful of the circumstance that to his bluff company such remote allusions, however pertinent they might really be, were altogether alien to men whose reading was mainly confined to the journals. But considerateness in such matters is not easy to natures constituted like Captain Vere's. Their honesty prescribes to them directness, sometimes far-reaching like that of a migratory fowl that in its flight never heeds when it crosses a frontier.

8

The lieutenants and other commissioned gentlemen forming Captain Vere's staff it is not necessary here to particularize, nor needs it to make any mention of any of the warrant officers. But among the petty officers[7] was one who, having much to do with the story, may as well be forthwith introduced. His portrait I essay, but shall never hit it. This was John Claggart, the master-at-arms. But that sea title may to landsmen seem somewhat equivocal. Originally, doubtless, that petty officer's function was the instruction of the men in the use of arms, sword or cutlass. But very long ago, owing to the advance in gunnery making hand-to-hand encounters less frequent and giving to niter and sulphur the pre-eminence over steel, that function ceased; the master-at-arms of a great warship becoming a sort of chief of police charged among other matters with the duty of preserving order on the populous lower gun decks.

5. Official gazettes that printed accounts of naval careers and honors.   6. A thread was worked into hempen cable to mark it as belonging to the Royal Navy.   7. Enlisted men corresponding in rank to noncommissioned officers in the army. *Warrant officers:* ranked above petty and just below commissioned officers.

Claggart was a man about five-and-thirty, somewhat spare and tall, yet of no ill figure upon the whole. His hand was too small and shapely to have been accustomed to hard toil. The face was a notable one, the features all except the chin cleanly cut as those on a Greek medallion; yet the chin, beardless as Tecumseh's,[8] had something of strange protuberant broadness in its make that recalled the prints of the Reverend Dr Titus Oates,[9] the historic deponent with the clerical drawl in the time of Charles II and the fraud of the alleged Popish Plot. It served Claggart in his office that his eye could cast a tutoring glance. His brow was of the sort phrenologically associated with more than average intellect; silken jet curls partly clustering over it, making a foil to the pallor below, a pallor tinged with a faint shade of amber akin to the hue of time-tinted marbles of old. This complexion, singularly contrasting with the red or deeply bronzed visages of the sailors, and in part the result of his official seclusion from the sunlight, though it was not exactly displeasing, nevertheless seemed to hint of something defective or abnormal in the constitution and blood. But his general aspect and manner were so suggestive of an education and career incongruous with his naval function that when not actively engaged in it he looked like a man of high quality, social and moral, who for reasons of his own was keeping incog.[1] Nothing was known of his former life. It might be that he was an Englishman; and yet there lurked a bit of accent in his speech suggesting that possibly he was not such by birth, but through naturalization in early childhood. Among certain grizzled sea gossips of the gun decks and forecastle went a rumor perdue[2] that the master-at-arms was a *chevalier*[3] who had volunteered into the King's navy by way of compounding for some mysterious swindle whereof he had been arraigned at the King's Bench.[4] The fact that nobody could substantiate this report was, of course, nothing against its secret currency. Such a rumor once started on the gun decks in reference to almost anyone below the rank of a commissioned officer would, during the period assigned to this narrative, have seemed not altogether wanting in credibility to the tarry old wiseacres of a man-of-war crew. And indeed a man of Claggart's accomplishments, without prior nautical experience entering the navy at mature life, as he did, and necessarily allotted at the start to the lowest grade in it; a man too who never made allusion to his previous life ashore; these were circumstances which in the dearth of exact knowledge as to his true antecedents opened to the invidious a vague field for unfavorable surmise.

But the sailors' dogwatch gossip concerning him derived a vague plausibility from the fact that now for some period the British navy could so little afford to be squeamish in the matter of keeping up the muster rolls, that not only were press gangs notoriously abroad both afloat and ashore, but there was little or no secret about another matter, namely, that the London police were at liberty to capture any able-bodied suspect, any questionable fellow at large, and summarily ship him to the dockyard or

---

8. Shawnee chief (1768?–1813) who attempted to unite the American Indians against the United States.
9. In 1678 Oates (1649–1705) invented a plot accusing Jesuits of planning to assassinate Charles II, burn London, and slaughter English Protestants.   1. Incognito, unrecognized.   2. Surreptitious.   3. A man of high rank.   4. Formerly the supreme court of common law in Great Britain.

fleet. Furthermore, even among voluntary enlistments there were instances where the motive thereto partook neither of patriotic impulse nor yet of a random desire to experience a bit of sea life and martial adventure. Insolvent debtors of minor grade, together with the promiscuous lame ducks of morality, found in the navy a convenient and secure refuge, secure because, once enlisted aboard a King's ship, they were as much in sanctuary as the transgressor of the Middle Ages harboring himself under the shadow of the altar. Such sanctioned irregularities, which for obvious reasons the government would hardly think to parade at the time and which consequently, and as affecting the least influential class of mankind, have all but dropped into oblivion, lend color[5] to something for the truth whereof I do not vouch, and hence have some scruple in stating; something I remember having seen in print though the book I cannot recall; but the same thing was personally communicated to me now more than forty years ago by an old pensioner in a cocked hat with whom I had a most interesting talk on the terrace at Greenwich, a Baltimore Negro, a Trafalgar man.[6] It was to this effect: In the case of a warship short of hands whose speedy sailing was imperative, the deficient quota, in lack of any other way of making it good, would be eked out by drafts culled direct from the jails. For reasons previously suggested it would not perhaps be easy at the present day directly to prove or disprove the allegation. But allowed as a verity, how significant would it be of England's straits at the time confronted by those wars which like a flight of harpies rose shrieking from the din and dust of the fallen Bastille.[7] That era appears measurably clear to us who look back at it, and but read of it. But to the grandfathers of us graybeards, the more thoughtful of them, the genius of it presented an aspect like that of Camoëns' Spirit of the Cape,[8] an eclipsing menace mysterious and prodigious. Not America was exempt from apprehension. At the height of Napoleon's unexampled conquests, there were Americans who had fought at Bunker Hill who looked forward to the possibility that the Atlantic might prove no barrier against the ultimate schemes of this French portentous upstart from the revolutionary chaos who seemed in act of fulfilling judgment prefigured in the Apocalypse.

But the less credence was to be given to the gun-deck talk touching Claggart, seeing that no man holding his office in a man-of-war can ever hope to be popular with the crew. Besides, in derogatory comments upon anyone against whom they have a grudge, or for any reason or no reason mislike, sailors are much like landsmen: they are apt to exaggerate or romance it.

About as much was really known to the *Bellipotent's* tars of the master-at-arms' career before entering the service as an astronomer knows about a comet's travels prior to its first observable appearance in the sky. The verdict of the sea quidnuncs[9] has been cited only by way of showing what sort of moral impression the man made upon rude uncultivated natures

---

5. Appearance of truth.   6. A veteran of the Battle of Trafalgar. *Greenwich*: a hospital near London, a home for retired personnel.   7. The fall of the Bastille (July 14, 1789) signaled the beginning of the French Revolution.   8. The Portuguese poet Luiz Vaz de Camoëns (1524–1580) describes in his epic poem, the *Lusiads*, a monster named Adamastor who attempts to destroy Vasco da Gama and his crew. 9. What now (Latin, literal trans.); a busybody.

whose conceptions of human wickedness were necessarily of the narrowest, limited to ideas of vulgar rascality—a thief among the swinging hammocks during a night watch, or the man-brokers and land-sharks of the seaports.

It was no gossip, however, but fact that though, as before hinted, Claggart upon his entrance into the navy was, as a novice, assigned to the least honorable section of a man-of-war's crew, embracing the drudgery, he did not long remain there. The superior capacity he immediately evinced, his constitutional sobriety, an ingratiating deference to superiors, together with a peculiar ferreting genius manifested on a singular occasion; all this, capped by a certain austere patriotism, abruptly advanced him to the position of master-at-arms.

Of this maritime chief of police the ship's corporals, so called, were the immediate subordinates, and compliant ones; and this, as is to be noted in some business departments ashore, almost to a degree inconsistent with entire moral volition. His place put various converging wires of underground influence under the chief's control, capable when astutely worked through his understrappers of operating to the mysterious discomfort, if nothing worse, of any of the sea commonalty.

9

Life in the foretop well agreed with Billy Budd. There, when not actually engaged on the yards yet higher aloft, the topmen, who as such had been picked out for youth and activity, constituted an aerial club lounging at ease against the smaller stun'sails[1] rolled up into cushions, spinning yarns like the lazy gods, and frequently amused with what was going on in the busy world of the decks below. No wonder then that a young fellow of Billy's disposition was well content in such society. Giving no cause of offense to anybody, he was always alert at a call. So in the merchant service it had been with him. But now such a punctiliousness in duty was shown that his topmates would sometimes good-naturedly laugh at him for it. This heightened alacrity had its cause, namely, the impression made upon him by the first formal gangway-punishment he had ever witnessed, which befell the day following his impressment. It had been incurred by a little fellow, young, a novice afterguardsman absent from his assigned post when the ship was being put about; a dereliction resulting in a rather serious hitch to that maneuver, one demanding instantaneous promptitude in letting go and making fast. When Billy saw the culprit's naked back under the scourge, gridironed with red welts and worse, when he marked the dire expression in the liberated man's face as with his woolen shirt flung over him by the executioner he rushed forward from the spot to bury himself in the crowd, Billy was horrified. He resolved that never through remissness would he make himself liable to such a visitation or do or omit aught that might merit even verbal reproof. What then was his surprise and concern when ultimately he found himself getting into petty trouble occasionally about such matters as the stowage of his bag or some-

---

1. Studding sails (small auxiliaries to the mainsails).

thing amiss in his hammock, matters under the police oversight of the ship's corporals of the lower decks, and which brought down on him a vague threat from one of them.

So heedful in all things as he was, how could this be? He could not understand it, and it more than vexed him. When he spoke to his young topmates about it they were either lightly incredulous or found something comical in his unconcealed anxiety. 'Is it your bag, Billy?' said one. 'Well, sew yourself up in it, bully boy, and then you'll be sure to know if anybody meddles with it.'

Now there was a veteran aboard who because his years began to disqual-ify him for more active work had been recently assigned duty as main-mastman in his watch, looking to the gear belayed[2] at the rail roundabout that great spar near the deck. At off-times the foretopman had picked up some acquaintance with him, and now in his trouble it occurred to him that he might be the sort of person to go to for wise counsel. He was an old Dansker[3] long anglicized in the service, of few words, many wrinkles, and some honorable scars. His wizened face, time-tinted and weather-stained to the complexion of an antique parchment, was here and there peppered blue by the chance explosion of a gun cartridge in action.

He was an *Agamemnon* man, some two years prior to the time of this story having served under Nelson when still captain in that ship immortal in naval memory, which dismantled and in part broken up to her bare ribs is seen a grand skeleton in Haden's etching.[4] As one of a boarding party from the *Agamemnon* he had received a cut slantwise along one temple and cheek leaving a long pale scar like a streak of dawn's light falling athwart the dark visage. It was on account of that scar and the affair in which it was known that he had received it, as well as from his blue-peppered complexion, that the Dansker went among the *Bellipotent*'s crew by the name of 'Board-Her-in-the-Smoke.'

Now the first time that his small weasel eyes happened to light on Billy Budd, a certain grim internal merriment set all his ancient wrinkles into antic play. Was it that his eccentric unsentimental old sapience, primitive in its kind, saw or thought it saw something which in contrast with the warship's environment looked oddly incongruous in the Handsome Sailor? But after slyly studying him at intervals, the old Merlin's[5] equivocal merriment was modified; for now when the twain would meet, it would start in his face a quizzing[6] sort of look, but it would be but momentary and sometimes replaced by an expression of speculative query as to what might eventually befall a nature like that, dropped into a world not with-out some mantraps and against whose subtleties simple courage lacking experience and address,[7] and without any touch of defensive ugliness, is of little avail; and where such innocence as man is capable of does yet in a moral emergency not always sharpen the faculties or enlighten the will.

However it was, the Dansker in his ascetic way rather took to Billy. Nor was this only because of a certain philosophic interest in such a character. There was another cause. While the old man's eccentricities, sometimes

---

2. Stowed.   3. Dane.   4. *Breaking up of the Agamemnon,* the masterpiece of Sir Francis Seymour Haden (1818–1910).   5. King Arthur's court magician.   6. Mocking.   7. Skill and tact in han-dling situations.

bordering on the ursine, repelled the juniors, Billy, undeterred thereby, revering him as a salt hero, would make advances, never passing the old *Agamemnon* man without a salutation marked by that respect which is seldom lost on the aged, however crabbed at times or whatever their station in life.

There was a vein of dry humor, or what not, in the mastman; and, whether in freak of patriarchal irony touching Billy's youth and athletic frame, or for some other and more recondite reason, from the first in addressing him he always substituted *Baby* for Billy, the Dansker in fact being the originator of the name by which the foretopman eventually became known aboard ship.

Well then, in his mysterious little difficulty going in quest of the wrinkled one, Billy found him off duty in a dogwatch ruminating by himself, seated on a shot box of the upper gun deck, now and then surveying with a somewhat cynical regard certain of the more swaggering promenaders there. Billy recounted his trouble, again wondering how it all happened. The salt seer attentively listened, accompanying the foretopman's recital with queer twitchings of his wrinkles and problematical little sparkles of his small ferret eyes. Making an end of his story, the foretopman asked, 'And now, Dansker, do tell me what you think of it.'

The old man, shoving up the front of his tarpaulin and deliberately rubbing the long slant scar at the point where it entered the thin hair, laconically said, 'Baby Budd, *Jemmy Legs*'[8] (meaning the master-at-arms) 'is down on you.'

'*Jemmy Legs!*' ejaculated Billy, his welkin eyes expanding.

'What for? Why, he calls me "the sweet and pleasant young fellow," they tell me.'

'Does he so?' grinned the grizzled one; then said, 'Ay, Baby lad, a sweet voice has Jemmy Legs.'

'No, not always. But to me he has. I seldom pass him but there comes a pleasant word.'

'And that's because he's down upon you, Baby Budd.'

Such reiteration, along with the manner of it, incomprehensible to a novice, disturbed Billy almost as much as the mystery for which he had sought explanation. Something less unpleasingly oracular he tried to extract; but the old sea Chiron,[9] thinking perhaps that for the nonce he had sufficiently instructed his young Achilles, pursed his lips, gathered all his wrinkles together, and would commit himself to nothing further.

Years, and those experiences which befall certain shrewder men subordinated lifelong to the will of superiors, all this had developed in the Dansker the pithy guarded cynicism that was his leading characteristic.

10

The next day an incident served to confirm Billy Budd in his incredulity as to the Dansker's strange summing up of the case submitted. The ship

---

8. A disparaging nickname for the master-at-arms, still used in the American navy.   9. A Centaur, half man and half horse, skilled in healing and the wisest of his species; he taught the Greek heroes Achilles, Hercules, and Aesculapius.

at noon, going large before the wind, was rolling on her course, and he below at dinner and engaged in some sportful talk with the members of his mess, chanced in a sudden lurch to spill the entire contents of his soup pan upon the new-scrubbed deck. Claggart, the master-at-arms, official rattan[1] in hand, happened to be passing along the battery in a bay of which the mess was lodged, and the greasy liquid streamed just across his path. Stepping over it, he was proceeding on his way without comment, since the matter was nothing to take notice of under the circumstances, when he happened to observe who it was that had done the spilling. His countenance changed. Pausing, he was about to ejaculate something hasty at the sailor, but checked himself, and pointing down to the streaming soup, playfully tapped him from behind with his rattan, saying in a low musical voice peculiar to him at times, 'Handsomely done, my lad! And handsome is as handsome did it, too!' And with that passed on. Not noted by Billy as not coming within his view was the involuntary smile, or rather grimace, that accompanied Claggart's equivocal words. Aridly it drew down the thin corners of his shapely mouth. But everybody taking his remark as meant for humorous, and at which therefore as coming from a superior they were bound to laugh 'with counterfeited glee,'[2] acted accordingly; and Billy, tickled, it may be, by the allusion to his being the Handsome Sailor, merrily joined in; then addressing his messmates exclaimed, 'There now, who says that Jemmy Legs is down on me!'

'And who said he was, Beauty?' demanded one Donald with some surprise. Whereat the foretopman looked a little foolish, recalling that it was only one person, Board-Her-in-the-Smoke, who had suggested what to him was the smoky idea that his master-at-arms was in any peculiar way hostile to him. Meantime that functionary, resuming his path, must have momentarily worn some expression less guarded than that of the bitter smile, usurping the face from the heart—some distorting expression perhaps, for a drummer-boy heedlessly frolicking along from the opposite direction and chancing to come into light collision with his person was strangely disconcerted by his aspect. Nor was the impression lessened when the official, impetuously giving him a sharp cut with the rattan, vehemently exclaimed, 'Look where you go!'

11

What was the matter with the master-at-arms? And, be the matter what it might, how could it have direct relation to Billy Budd, with whom prior to the affair of the spilled soup he had never come into any special contact official or otherwise? What indeed could the trouble have to do with one so little inclined to give offense as the merchantship's 'peacemaker,' even him who in Claggart's own phrase was 'the sweet and pleasant young fellow'? Yes, why should Jemmy Legs, to borrow the Dansker's expression, be 'down' on the Handsome Sailor? But, at heart and not for nothing, as the late chance encounter may indicate to the discerning, down on him, secretly down on him, he assuredly was.

---

1. Swagger stick, light whip.   2. Oliver Goldsmith (1730–1774), *The Deserted Village*, line 201, alluding to the response of students to a severe schoolmaster.

Now to invent something touching the more private career of Claggart, something involving Billy Budd, of which something the latter should be wholly ignorant, some romantic incident implying that Claggart's knowledge of the young bluejacket began at some period anterior to catching sight of him on board the seventy-four—all this, not so difficult to do, might avail in a way more or less interesting to account for whatever of enigma may appear to lurk in the case. But in fact there was nothing of the sort. And yet the cause necessarily to be assumed as the sole one assignable is in its very realism as much charged with that prime element of Radcliffian romance, the mysterious, as any that the ingenuity of the author of *The Mysteries of Udolpho*[3] could devise. For what can more partake of the mysterious than an antipathy spontaneous and profound such as is evoked in certain exceptional mortals by the mere aspect of some other mortal, however harmless he may be, if not called forth by this very harmlessness itself?

Now there can exist no irritating juxtaposition of dissimilar personalities comparable to that which is possible aboard a great warship fully manned and at sea. There, every day among all ranks, almost every man comes into more or less of contact with almost every other man. Wholly there to avoid even the sight of an aggravating object one must needs give it Jonah's toss[4] or jump overboard himself. Imagine how all this might eventually operate on some peculiar human creature the direct reverse of a saint!

But for the adequate comprehending of Claggart by a normal nature these hints are insufficient. To pass from a normal nature to him one must cross 'the deadly space between.' And this is best done by indirection.

Long ago an honest scholar, my senior, said to me in reference to one who like himself is now no more, a man so unimpeachably respectable that against him nothing was ever openly said though among the few something was whispered, 'Yes, X—— is a nut not to be cracked by the tap of a lady's fan. You are aware that I am the adherent of no organized religion, much less of any philosophy built into a system. Well, for all that, I think that to try and get into X——, enter his labyrinth and get out again, without a clue derived from some source other than what is known as "knowledge of the world"—that were hardly possible, at least for me.'

'Why,' said I, 'X——, however singular a study to some, is yet human, and knowledge of the world assuredly implies the knowledge of human nature, and in most of its varieties.'

'Yes, but a superficial knowledge of it, serving ordinary purposes. But for anything deeper, I am not certain whether to know the world and to know human nature be not two distinct branches of knowledge, which while they may co-exist in the same heart, yet either may exist with little or nothing of the other. Nay, in an average man of the world, his constant rubbing with it blunts that finer spiritual insight indispensable to the understanding of the essential in certain exceptional characters, whether evil ones or good. In a matter of some importance I have seen a girl wind an old lawyer about her little finger. Nor was it the dotage of senile love.

---

3. An immensely popular Gothic novel by Ann Radcliffe (1764–1823).   4. Jonah 1:15: "So they took up Jonah, and cast him forth into the sea." A nautical expression when an unlucky object or person is put overboard.

Nothing of the sort. But he knew law better than he knew the girl's heart. Coke and Blackstone[5] hardly shed so much light into obscure spiritual places as the Hebrew prophets. And who were they? Mostly recluses.'

At the time, my inexperience was such that I did not quite see the drift of all this. It may be that I see it now. And, indeed, if that lexicon which is based on Holy Writ were any longer popular, one might with less difficulty define and denominate certain phenomenal men. As it is, one must turn to some authority not liable to the charge of being tinctured with the biblical element.

In a list of definitions included in the authentic translation of Plato, a list attributed to him, occurs this: 'Natural Depravity: a depravity according to nature,' a definition which, though savoring of Calvinism,[6] by no means involves Calvin's dogma as to total mankind. Evidently its intent makes it applicable but to individuals. Not many are the examples of this depravity which the gallows and jail supply. At any rate, for notable instances, since these have no vulgar alloy of the brute in them, but invariably are dominated by intellectuality, one must go elsewhere. Civilization, especially if of the austerer sort, is auspicious to it. It folds itself in the mantle of respectability. It has certain negative virtues serving as silent auxiliaries. It never allows wine to get within its guard. It is not going too far to say that it is without vices or small sins. There is a phenomenal pride in it that excludes them. It is never mercenary or avaricious. In short, the depravity here meant partakes nothing of the sordid or sensual. It is serious, but free from acerbity. Though no flatterer of mankind it never speaks ill of it.

But the thing which in eminent instances signalizes so exceptional a nature is this: Though the man's even temper and discreet bearing would seem to intimate a mind peculiarly subject to the law of reason, not the less in heart he would seem to riot in complete exemption from that law, having apparently little to do with reason further than to employ it as an ambidexter[7] implement for effecting the irrational. That is to say: Toward the accomplishment of an aim which in wantonness of atrocity would seem to partake of the insane, he will direct a cool judgment sagacious and sound. These men are madmen, and of the most dangerous sort, for their lunacy is not continuous, but occasional, evoked by some special object; it is protectively secretive, which is as much as to say it is self-contained, so that when, moreover, most active it is to the average mind not distinguishable from sanity, and for the reason above suggested: that whatever its aims may be—and the aim is never declared—the method and the outward proceeding are always perfectly rational.

Now something such an one was Claggart, in whom was the mania of an evil nature, not engendered by vicious training or corrupting books or licentious living, but born with him and innate, in short 'a depravity according to nature.'

Dark sayings are these, some will say. But why? Is it because they somewhat savor of Holy Writ in its phrase 'mystery of iniquity'?[8] If they do, such

---

5. Sir Edward Coke (1552–1634) and Sir William Blackstone (1723–1780), noted British jurists and writers on the law.   6. The religious system founded by John Calvin (1509–1564), which emphasizes predestination.   7. Two-handed.   8. 2 Thessalonians 2:7.

savor was far enough from being intended, for little will it commend these pages to many a reader of today.

The point of the present story turning on the hidden nature of the master-at-arms has necessitated this chapter. With an added hint or two in connection with the incident at the mess, the resumed narrative must be left to vindicate, as it may, its own credibility.

12

That Claggart's figure was not amiss, and his face, save the chin, well molded, has already been said. Of these favorable points he seemed not insensible, for he was not only neat but careful in his dress. But the form of Billy Budd was heroic; and if his face was without the intellectual look of the pallid Claggart's, not the less was it lit, like his, from within, though from a different source. The bonfire in his heart made luminous the rose-tan in his cheek.

In view of the marked contrast between the persons of the twain, it is more than probable that when the master-at-arms in the scene last given applied to the sailor the proverb 'Handsome is as handsome does,' he there let escape an ironic inkling, not caught by the young sailors who heard it, as to what it was that had first moved him against Billy, namely, his significant personal beauty.

Now envy and antipathy, passions irreconcilable in reason, nevertheless in fact may spring conjoined like Chang and Eng[9] in one birth. Is Envy then such a monster? Well, though many an arraigned mortal has in hopes of mitigated penalty pleaded guilty to horrible actions, did ever anybody seriously confess to envy? Something there is in it universally felt to be more shameful than even felonious crime. And not only does everybody disown it, but the better sort are inclined to incredulity when it is in earnest imputed to an intelligent man. But since its lodgment is in the heart not the brain, no degree of intellect supplies a guarantee against it. But Claggart's was no vulgar form of the passion. Nor, as directed toward Billy Budd, did it partake of that streak of apprehensive jealousy that marred Saul's visage perturbedly brooding on the comely young David.[1] Claggart's envy struck deeper. If askance he eyed the good looks, cheery health, and frank enjoyment of young life in Billy Budd, it was because these went along with a nature that, as Claggart magnetically felt, had in its simplicity never willed malice or experienced the reactionary bite of that serpent. To him, the spirit lodged within Billy, and looking out from his welkin eyes as from windows, that ineffability it was which made the dimple in his dyed cheek, suppled his joints, and dancing in his yellow curls made him pre-eminently the Handsome Sailor. One person excepted, the master-at-arms was perhaps the only man in the ship intellectually capable of adequately appreciating the moral phenomenon presented in Billy Budd. And the insight but intensified his passion, which assuming various secret forms within him, at times assumed that of cynic disdain, disdain of innocence—to be nothing more than innocent! Yet in an aesthetic way

9. Famous Siamese twins (1811–1874) who toured the United States. 1. David's comeliness and Saul's jealousy are described in 1 Samuel 16:18, 18:8ff.

he saw the charm of it, the courageous free-and-easy temper of it, and fain would have shared it, but he despaired of it.

With no power to annul the elemental evil in him, though readily enough he could hide it; apprehending the good, but powerless to be it; a nature like Claggart's, surcharged with energy as such natures almost invariably are, what recourse is left to it but to recoil upon itself and, like the scorpion for which the Creator alone is responsible, act out to the end the part allotted it.

13

Passion, and passion in its profoundest, is not a thing demanding a palatial stage whereon to play its part. Down among the groundlings,[2] among the beggars and rakers of the garbage, profound passion is enacted. And the circumstances that provoke it, however trivial or mean, are no measure of its power. In the present instance the stage is a scrubbed gun deck, and one of the external provocations a man-of-war's man's spilled soup.

Now when the master-at-arms noticed whence came that greasy fluid streaming before his feet, he must have taken it—to some extent wilfully, perhaps—not for the mere accident it assuredly was, but for the sly escape of a spontaneous feeling on Billy's part more or less answering to the antipathy on his own. In effect a foolish demonstration, he must have thought, and very harmless, like the futile kick of a heifer, which yet were the heifer a shod stallion would not be so harmless. Even so was it that into the gall of Claggart's envy he infused the vitriol of his contempt. But the incident confirmed to him certain telltale reports purveyed to his ear by 'Squeak,' one of his more cunning corporals, a grizzled little man, so nicknamed by the sailors on account of his squeaky voice and sharp visage ferreting about the dark corners of the lower decks after interlopers, satirically suggesting to them the idea of a rat in a cellar.

From his chief's employing him as an implicit tool in laying little traps for the worriment of the foretopman—for it was from the master-at-arms that the petty persecutions heretofore adverted to had proceeded—the corporal, having naturally enough concluded that his master could have no love for the sailor, made it his business, faithful understrapper that he was, to foment the ill blood by perverting to his chief certain innocent frolics of the good-natured foretopman, besides inventing for his mouth sundry contumelious epithets he claimed to have overheard him let fall. The master-at-arms never suspected the veracity of these reports, more especially as to the epithets, for he well knew how secretly unpopular may become a master-at-arms, at least a master-at-arms of those days, zealous in his function, and how the bluejackets shoot at him in private their raillery and wit; the nickname by which he goes among them (Jemmy Legs) implying under the form of merriment their cherished disrespect and dislike. But in view of the greediness of hate for pabulum[3] it hardly needed a purveyor to feed Claggart's passion.

---

2. The part of the audience that stood on the ground in an Elizabethan theater; the poorest spectators.
3. Sustenance.

An uncommon prudence is habitual with the subtler depravity, for it has everything to hide. And in case of an injury but suspected, its secretiveness voluntarily cuts it off from enlightenment or disillusion; and, not unreluctantly, action is taken upon surmise as upon certainty. And the retaliation is apt to be in monstrous disproportion to the supposed offense; for when in anybody was revenge in its exactions aught else but an inordinate usurer? But how with Claggart's conscience? For though consciences are unlike as foreheads, every intelligence, not excluding the scriptural devils who 'believe and tremble,'[4] has one. But Claggart's conscience being but the lawyer to his will, made ogres of trifles, probably arguing that the motive imputed to Billy in spilling the soup just when he did, together with the epithets alleged, these, if nothing more, made a strong case against him; nay, justified animosity into a sort of retributive righteousness. The Pharisee is the Guy Fawkes[5] prowling in the hid chambers underlying some natures like Claggart's. And they can really form no conception of an unreciprocated malice. Probably the master-at-arms' clandestine persecution of Billy was started to try the temper of the man; but it had not developed any quality in him that enmity could make official use of or even pervert into plausible self-justification; so that the occurrence at the mess, petty if it were, was a welcome one to that peculiar conscience assigned to be the private mentor of Claggart; and, for the rest, not improbably it put him upon new experiments.

14

Not many days after the last incident narrated, something befell Billy Budd that more graveled him than aught that had previously occurred.

It was a warm night for the latitude; and the foretopman, whose watch at the time was properly below, was dozing on the uppermost deck whither he had ascended from his hot hammock, one of hundreds suspended so closely wedged together over a lower gun deck that there was little or no swing to them. He lay as in the shadow of a hillside, stretched under the lee of the booms, a piled ridge of spare spars amidships between foremast and mainmast among which the ship's largest boat, the launch, was stowed. Alongside of three other slumberers from below, he lay near that end of the booms which approaches the foremast; his station aloft on duty as a foretopman being just over the deckstation of the forecastlemen, entitling him according to usage to make himself more or less at home in that neighborhood.

Presently he was stirred into semiconsciousness by somebody, who must have previously sounded the sleep of the others, touching his shoulder, and then, as the foretopman raised his head, breathing into his ear in a quick whisper, 'Slip into the lee forechains, Billy; there is something in the wind. Don't speak. Quick, I will meet you there,' and disappearing.

Now Billy, like sundry other essentially good-natured ones, had some of the weaknesses inseparable from essential good nature; and among these

---

4. James 2:19: "The devils also believe, and tremble."   5. Instigator of the Gunpowder Plot, the plan to blow up the Houses of Parliament and King James I on November 5, 1605. *Pharisee:* follower of a Jewish sect known for its strict observance of the Torah; hence anyone extremely rigid and dogmatic.

was a reluctance, almost an incapacity of plumply[6] saying *no* to an abrupt proposition not obviously absurd on the face of it, nor obviously unfriendly, nor iniquitous. And being of warm blood, he had not the phlegm[7] tacitly to negative any proposition by unresponsive inaction. Like his sense of fear, his apprehension as to aught outside of the honest and natural was seldom very quick. Besides, upon the present occasion, the drowse from his sleep still hung upon him.

However it was, he mechanically rose and, sleepily wondering what could be in the wind, betook himself to the designated place, a narrow platform, one of six, outside of the high bulwarks and screened by the great deadeyes and multiple columned lanyards of the shrouds and back-stays; and, in a great warship of that time, of dimensions commensurate to the hull's magnitude; a tarry balcony in short, overhanging the sea, and so secluded that one mariner of the *Bellipotent*, a Nonconformist[8] old tar of a serious turn, made it even in daytime his private oratory.[9]

In this retired nook the stranger soon joined Billy Budd. There was no moon as yet; a haze obscured the starlight. He could not distinctly see the stranger's face. Yet from something in the outline and carriage, Billy took him, and correctly, for one of the afterguard.

'Hist! Billy,' said the man, in the same quick cautionary whisper as before. 'You were impressed, weren't you? Well, so was I'; and he paused, as to mark the effect. But Billy, not knowing exactly what to make of this, said nothing. Then the other: 'We are not the only impressed ones, Billy. There's a gang of us.—Couldn't you—help—at a pinch?'

'What do you mean?' demanded Billy, here thoroughly shaking off his drowse.

'Hist, hist!' the hurried whisper now growing husky. 'See here,' and the man held up two small objects faintly twinkling in the night-light; 'see, they are yours, Billy, if you'll only—'

But Billy broke in, and in his resentful eagerness to deliver himself his vocal infirmity somewhat intruded. 'D—d—damme, I don't know what you are d—d—driving at, or what you mean, but you had better g—g—go where you belong!' For the moment the fellow, as confounded, did not stir; and Billy, springing to his feet, said, 'If you d—don't start, I'll t—t—toss you back over the r—rail!' There was no mistaking this, and the mysterious emissary decamped, disappearing in the direction of the main-mast in the shadow of the booms.

'Hallo, what's the matter?' here came growling from a forecastleman awakened from his deck-doze by Billy's raised voice. And as the foretop-man reappeared and was recognized by him: 'Ah, Beauty, is it you? Well, something must have been the matter, for you st—st—stuttered.'

'Oh,' rejoined Billy, now mastering the impediment, 'I found an after-guardsman in our part of the ship here, and I bid him be off where he belongs.'

'And is that all you did about it, Foretopman?' gruffly demanded another, an irascible old fellow of brick-colored visage and hair who was

---

6. Bluntly.   7. Sluggishness, apathy.   8. A Protestant dissenter from the Church of England.
9. A small chapel, especially for private prayer.

known to his associate forecastlemen as 'Red Pepper.' 'Such sneaks I should like to marry to the gunner's daughter!'—by that expression meaning that he would like to subject them to disciplinary castigation over a gun.

However, Billy's rendering of the matter satisfactorily accounted to these inquirers for the brief commotion, since of all the sections of a ship's company the forecastlemen, veterans for the most part and bigoted in their sea prejudices, are the most jealous in resenting territorial encroachments, especially on the part of any of the afterguard, of whom they have but a sorry opinion—chiefly landsmen, never going aloft except to reef or furl the mainsail, and in no wise competent to handle a marlinspike or turn in a deadeye, say.

15

This incident sorely puzzled Billy Budd. It was an entirely new experience, the first time in his life that he had ever been personally approached in underhand intriguing fashion. Prior to this encounter he had known nothing of the afterguardsman, the two men being stationed wide apart, one forward and aloft during his watch, the other on deck and aft.

What could it mean? And could they really be guineas,[1] those two glittering objects the interloper had held up to his (Billy's) eyes? Where could the fellow get guineas? Why, even spare buttons are not so plentiful at sea. The more he turned the matter over, the more he was nonplussed, and made uneasy and discomfited. In his disgustful recoil from an overture which, though he but ill comprehended, he instinctively knew must involve evil of some sort, Billy Budd was like a young horse fresh from the pasture suddenly inhaling a vile whiff from some chemical factory, and by repeated snortings trying to get it out of his nostrils and lungs. This frame of mind barred all desire of holding further parley with the fellow, even were it but for the purpose of gaining some enlightenment as to his design in approaching him. And yet he was not without natural curiosity to see how such a visitor in the dark would look in broad day.

He espied him the following afternoon in his first dogwatch below, one of the smokers on that forward part of the upper gun deck allotted to the pipe. He recognized him by his general cut and build more than by his round freckled face and glassy eyes of pale blue, veiled with lashes all but white. And yet Billy was a bit uncertain whether indeed it were he— yonder chap about his own age chatting and laughing in freehearted way, leaning against a gun; a genial young fellow enough to look at, and something of a rattlebrain, to all appearance. Rather chubby too for a sailor, even an afterguardsman. In short, the last man in the world, one would think, to be overburdened with thoughts, especially those perilous thoughts that must needs belong to a conspirator in any serious project, or even to the underling of such a conspirator.

Although Billy was not aware of it, the fellow, with a sidelong watchful glance, had perceived Billy first, and then noting that Billy was looking at

---

1. English gold coins, not minted after 1813, worth twenty-one shillings.

him, thereupon nodded a familiar sort of friendly recognition as to an old acquaintance, without interrupting the talk he was engaged in with the group of smokers. A day or two afterwards, chancing in the evening promenade on a gun deck to pass Billy, he offered a flying word of good-fellowship, as it were, which by its unexpectedness, and equivocalness under the circumstances, so embarrassed Billy that he knew not how to respond to it, and let it go unnoticed.

Billy was now left more at a loss than before. The ineffectual speculations into which he was led were so disturbingly alien to him that he did his best to smother them. It never entered his mind that here was a matter which, from its extreme questionableness, it was his duty as a loyal bluejacket to report in the proper quarter. And, probably, had such a step been suggested to him, he would have been deterred from taking it by the thought, one of novice magnanimity, that it would savor overmuch of the dirty work of a telltale. He kept the thing to himself. Yet upon one occasion he could not forebear a little disburdening himself to the old Dansker, tempted thereto perhaps by the influence of a balmy night when the ship lay becalmed; the twain, silent for the most part, sitting together on deck, their heads propped against the bulwarks. But it was only a partial and anonymous account that Billy gave, the unfounded scruples above referred to preventing full disclosure to anybody. Upon hearing Billy's version, the sage Dansker seemed to divine more than he was told; and after a little meditation, during which his wrinkles were pursed as into a point, quite effacing for the time that quizzing expression his face sometimes wore: 'Didn't I say so, Baby Budd?'

'Say what?' demanded Billy.

'Why, *Jemmy Legs* is *down* on you.'

'And what,' rejoined Billy in amazement, 'has *Jemmy Legs* to do with that cracked afterguardsman?'

'Ho, it was an afterguardsman, then. A cat's-paw,[2] a cat's-paw!' And with that exclamation, whether it had reference to a light puff of air just then coming over the calm sea, or a subtler relation to the afterguardsman, there is no telling, the old Merlin gave a twisting wrench with his black teeth at his plug of tobacco, vouchsafing no reply to Billy's impetuous question, though now repeated, for it was his wont to relapse into grim silence when interrogated in skeptical sort as to any of his sententious oracles, not always very clear ones, rather partaking of that obscurity which invests most Delphic[3] deliverances from any quarter.

Long experience had very likely brought this old man to that bitter prudence which never interferes in aught and never gives advice.

16

Yes, despite the Dansker's pithy insistence as to the master-at-arms being at the bottom of these strange experiences of Billy on board the *Bellipotent*, the young sailor was ready to ascribe them to almost anybody but the

---

2. Either a light wind perceived by its impressions on the sea or a seaman employed to entice volunteers.
3. Literally, issuing from the ancient Greek oracle of Apollo at Delphi, which made ambiguous prophecies; hence, obscure in meaning, ambiguous.

man who, to use Billy's own expression, 'always had a pleasant word for him.' This is to be wondered at. Yet not so much to be wondered at. In certain matters, some sailors even in mature life remain unsophisticated enough. But a young seafarer of the disposition of our athletic foretopman is much of a child-man. And yet a child's utter innocence is but its blank ignorance, and the innocence more or less wanes as intelligence waxes. But in Billy Budd intelligence, such as it was, had advanced while yet his simple-mindedness remained for the most part unaffected. Experience is a teacher indeed; yet did Billy's years make his experience small. Besides, he had none of that intuitive knowledge of the bad which in natures not good or incompletely so foreruns experience, and therefore may pertain, as in some instances it too clearly does pertain, even to youth.

And what could Billy know of man except of man as a mere sailor? And the old-fashioned sailor, the veritable man before the mast, the sailor from boyhood up, he, though indeed of the same species as a landsman, is in some respects singularly distinct from him. The sailor is frankness, the landsman is finesse. Life is not a game with the sailor, demanding the long head—no intricate game of chess where few moves are made in straightforwardness and ends are attained by indirection, an oblique, tedious, barren game hardly worth that poor candle burnt out in playing it.

Yes, as a class, sailors are in character a juvenile race. Even their deviations are marked by juvenility, this more especially holding true with the sailors of Billy's time. Then too, certain things which apply to all sailors do more pointedly operate here and there upon the junior one. Every sailor, too, is accustomed to obey orders without debating them; his life afloat is externally ruled for him; he is not brought into that promiscuous[4] commerce with mankind where unobstructed free agency on equal terms—equal superficially, at least—soon teaches one that unless upon occasion he exercise a distrust keen in proportion to the fairness of the appearance, some foul turn may be served him. A ruled undemonstrative distrustfulness is so habitual, not with businessmen so much as with men who know their kind in less shallow relations than business, namely, certain men of the world, that they come at last to employ it all but unconsciously; and some of them would very likely feel real surprise at being charged with it as one of their general characteristics.

17

But after the little matter at the mess Billy Budd no more found himself in strange trouble at times about his hammock or his clothes bag or what not. As to that smile that occasionally sunned him, and the pleasant passing word, these were, if not more frequent, yet if anything more pronounced than before.

But for all that, there were certain other demonstrations now. When Claggart's unobserved glance happened to light on belted Billy rolling along the upper gun deck in the leisure of the second dogwatch, exchang-

4. Indiscriminate.

ing passing broadsides of fun with other young promenaders in the crowd, that glance would follow the cheerful sea Hyperion[5] with a settled meditative and melancholy expression, his eyes strangely suffused with incipient feverish tears. Then would Claggart look like the man of sorrows.[6] Yes, and sometimes the melancholy expression would have in it a touch of soft yearning, as if Claggart could even have loved Billy but for fate and ban. But this was an evanescence, and quickly repented of, as it were, by an immitigable look, pinching and shriveling the visage into the momentary semblance of a wrinkled walnut. But sometimes catching sight in advance of the foretopman coming in his direction, he would, upon their nearing, step aside a little to let him pass, dwelling upon Billy for the moment with the glittering dental satire of a Guise.[7] But upon any abrupt unforeseen encounter a red light would flash forth from his eye like a spark from an anvil in a dusk smithy. That quick, fierce light was a strange one, darted from orbs which in repose were of a color nearest approaching a deeper violet, the softest of shades.

Though some of these caprices of the pit[8] could not but be observed by their object, yet were they beyond the construing of such a nature. And the thews of Billy were hardly compatible with that sort of sensitive spiritual organization which in some cases instinctively conveys to ignorant innocence an admonition of the proximity of the malign. He thought the master-at-arms acted in a manner rather queer at times. That was all. But the occasional frank air and pleasant word went for what they purported to be, the young sailor never having heard as yet of the 'too fair-spoken man.'

Had the foretopman been conscious of having done or said anything to provoke the ill will of the official, it would have been different with him, and his sight might have been purged if not sharpened. As it was, innocence was his blinder.

So was it with him in yet another matter. Two minor officers, the armorer and captain of the hold, with whom he had never exchanged a word, his position in the ship not bringing him into contact with them, these men now for the first began to cast upon Billy, when they chanced to encounter him, that peculiar glance which evidences that the man from whom it comes has been some way tampered with, and to the prejudice of him upon whom the glance lights. Never did it occur to Billy as a thing to be noted or a thing suspicious, though he well knew the fact, that the armorer and captain of the hold, with the ship's yeoman, apothecary, and others of that grade, were by naval usage messmates of the master-at-arms, men with ears convenient to his confidential tongue.

But the general popularity that came from our Handsome Sailor's manly forwardness upon occasion and irresistible good nature, indicating no mental superiority tending to excite an invidious feeling, this good will on the part of most of his shipmates made him the less to concern himself about such mute aspects toward him as those whereto allusion has just been made, aspects he could not so fathom as to infer their whole import.

---

5. In Greek mythology, the Titan god who came to be identified with Apollo, god of youth and beauty.
6. In Isaiah 53:3, the Lord's servant is described as "despised and rejected of men; a man of sorrows, and acquainted with grief."   7. Henri de Guise (1550–1588), a famed conspirator who could smile throughout his villainy.   8. Of hell.

As to the afterguardsman, though Billy for reasons already given necessarily saw little of him, yet when the two did happen to meet, invariably came the fellow's offhand cheerful recognition, sometimes accompanied by a passing pleasant word or two. Whatever that equivocal young person's original design may really have been, or the design of which he might have been the deputy, certain it was from his manner upon these occasions that he had wholly dropped it.

It was as if his precocity of crookedness (and every vulgar villain is precocious) had for once deceived him, and the man he had sought to entrap as a simpleton had through his very simplicity ignominiously baffled him.

But shrewd ones may opine that it was hardly possible for Billy to refrain from going up to the afterguardsman and bluntly demanding to know his purpose in the initial interview so abruptly closed in the forechains. Shrewd ones may also think it but natural in Billy to set about sounding some of the other impressed men of the ship in order to discover what basis, if any, there was for the emissary's obscure suggestions as to plotting disaffection aboard. Yes, shrewd ones may so think. But something more, or rather something else than mere shrewdness is perhaps needful for the due understanding of such a character as Billy Budd's.

As to Claggart, the monomania in the man—if that indeed it were—as involuntarily disclosed by starts in the manifestations detailed, yet in general covered over by his self-contained and rational demeanor; this, like a subterranean fire, was eating its way deeper and deeper in him. Something decisive must come of it.

18

After the mysterious interview in the forechains, the one so abruptly ended there by Billy, nothing especially germane to the story occurred until the events now about to be narrated.

Elsewhere it has been said that in the lack of frigates (of course better sailers than line-of-battle ships) in the English squadron up the Straits at that period, the *Bellipotent 74* was occasionally employed not only as an available substitute for a scout, but at times on detached service of more important kind. This was not alone because of her sailing qualities, not common in a ship of her rate,[9] but quite as much, probably, that the character of her commander, it was thought, specially adapted him for any duty where under unforeseen difficulties a prompt initiative might have to be taken in some matter demanding knowledge and ability in addition to those qualities implied in good seamanship. It was on an expedition of the latter sort, a somewhat distant one, and when the *Bellipotent* was almost at her furthest remove from the fleet, that in the latter part of an afternoon watch she unexpectedly came in sight of a ship of the enemy. It proved to be a frigate. The latter, perceiving through the glass that the weight of men and metal would be heavily against her, invoking her light heels crowded sail to get away. After a chase urged almost against hope and lasting until about the middle of the first dogwatch, she signally succeeded in effecting her escape.

9. Classification.

Not long after the pursuit had been given up, and ere the excitement incident thereto had altogether waned away, the master-at-arms, ascending from his cavernous sphere, made his appearance cap in hand by the main-mast respectfully waiting the notice of Captain Vere, then solitary walking the weather side of the quarter-deck, doubtless somewhat chafed at the failure of the pursuit. The spot where Claggart stood was the place allotted to men of lesser grades seeking some more particular interview either with the officer of the deck or the captain himself. But from the latter it was not often that a sailor or petty officer of those days would seek a hearing; only some exceptional cause would, according to established custom, have warranted that.

Presently, just as the commander, absorbed in his reflections, was on the point of turning aft in his promenade, he became sensible of Claggart's presence, and saw the doffed cap held in deferential expectancy. Here be it said that Captain Vere's personal knowledge of his petty officer had only begun at the time of the ship's last sailing from home, Claggart then for the first, in transfer from a ship detained for repairs, supplying on board the *Bellipotent* the place of a previous master-at-arms disabled and ashore.

No sooner did the commander observe who it was that now deferentially stood awaiting his notice than a peculiar expression came over him. It was not unlike that which uncontrollably will flit across the countenance of one at unawares encountering a person who, though known to him indeed, has hardly been long enough known for thorough knowledge, but something in whose aspect nevertheless now for the first provokes a vaguely repellent distaste. But coming to a stand and resuming much of his wonted official manner, save that a sort of impatience lurked in the intonation of the opening word, he said, 'Well? What is it, Master-at-arms?'

With the air of a subordinate grieved at the necessity of being a messenger of ill tidings, and while conscientiously determined to be frank yet equally resolved upon shunning overstatement, Claggart at this invitation, or rather summons to disburden, spoke up. What he said, conveyed in the language of no uneducated man, was to the effect following, if not altogether in these words, namely, that during the chase and preparations for the possible encounter he had seen enough to convince him that at least one sailor aboard was a dangerous character in a ship mustering some who not only had taken a guilty part in the late serious troubles, but others also who, like the man in question, had entered His Majesty's service under another form than enlistment.

At this point Captain Vere with some impatience interrupted him: 'Be direct, man; say *impressed men.*'

Claggart made a gesture of subservience, and proceeded. Quite lately he (Claggart) had begun to suspect that on the gun decks some sort of movement prompted by the sailor in question was covertly going on, but he had not thought himself warranted in reporting the suspicion so long as it remained indistinct. But from what he had that afternoon observed in the man referred to, the suspicion of something clandestine going on had advanced to a point less removed from certainty. He deeply felt, he added, the serious responsibility assumed in making a report involving such possible consequences to the individual mainly concerned, besides tending to augment those natural anxieties which every naval commander must feel in view of extraordinary outbreaks so recent as those which, he sorrowfully said it, it needed not to name.

Now at the first broaching of the matter Captain Vere, taken by surprise, could not wholly dissemble his disquietude. But as Claggart went on, the former's aspect changed into restiveness under something in the testifier's manner in giving his testimony. However, he refrained from interrupting him. And Claggart, continuing, concluded with this: 'God forbid, your honor, that the *Bellipotent's* should be the experience of the—'

'Never mind that!' here peremptorily broke in the superior, his face altering with anger, instinctively divining the ship that the other was about to name, one in which the Nore Mutiny had assumed a singularly tragical character that for a time jeopardized the life of its commander. Under the circumstances he was indignant at the purposed allusion. When the commissioned officers themselves were on all occasions very heedful how they referred to the recent events in the fleet, for a petty officer unnecessarily to allude to them in the presence of his captain, this struck him as a most immodest presumption. Besides, to his quick sense of self-respect it even looked under the circumstances something like an attempt to alarm him. Nor at first was he without some surprise that one who so far as he had hitherto come under his notice had shown considerable tact in his function should in this particular evince such lack of it.

But these thoughts and kindred dubious ones flitting across his mind were suddenly replaced by an intuitional surmise which, though as yet obscure in form, served practically to affect his reception of the ill tidings. Certain it is that, long versed in everything pertaining to the complicated gun-deck life, which like every other form of life has its secret mines and dubious side, the side popularly disclaimed, Captain Vere did not permit himself to be unduly disturbed by the general tenor of his subordinate's report.

Furthermore, if in view of recent events prompt action should be taken at the first palpable sign of recurring insubordination, for all that, not judicious would it be, he thought, to keep the idea of lingering disaffection alive by undue forwardness in crediting an informer, even if his own subordinate and charged among other things with police surveillance of the crew. This feeling would not perhaps have so prevailed with him were it not that upon a prior occasion the patriotic zeal officially evinced by Claggart had somewhat irritated him as appearing rather supersensible and strained. Furthermore something even in the official's self-possessed and somewhat ostentatious manner in making his specifications strangely reminded him of a bandsman,[1] a perjurous witness in a capital case before a courtmartial ashore of which when a lieutenant he (Captain Vere) had been a member.

Now the peremptory check given to Claggart in the matter of the arrested allusion was quickly followed up by this: 'You say that there is at least one dangerous man aboard. Name him.'

'William Budd, a foretopman, your honor.'

---

1. Crewman charged with the task of stitching bands of canvas into sails to strengthen them.

'William Budd!' repeated Captain Vere with unfeigned astonishment. 'And mean you the man that Lieutenant Ratcliffe took from the merchantman not very long ago, the young fellow who seems to be so popular with the men—Billy the Handsome Sailor, as they call him?'

'The same, your honor; but for all his youth and good looks, a deep one. Not for nothing does he insinuate himself into the good will of his shipmates, since at the least they will at a pinch say—all hands will—a good word for him, and at all hazards. Did Lieutenant Ratcliffe happen to tell your honor of that adroit fling of Budd's, jumping up in the cutter's bow under the merchantman's stern when he was being taken off? It is even masked by that sort of good-humored air that at heart he resents his impressment. You have but noted his fair cheek. A mantrap may be under the ruddy-tipped daisies.'

Now the Handsome Sailor as a signal figure among the crew had naturally enough attracted the captain's attention from the first. Though in general not very demonstrative to his officers, he had congratulated Lieutenant Ratcliffe upon his good fortune in lighting on such a fine specimen of the *genus homo*, who in the nude might have posed for a statue of a young Adam before the Fall. As to Billy's adieu to the ship *Rights-of-Man*, which the boarding lieutenant had indeed reported to him, but, in a deferential way, more as a good story than aught else, Captain Vere, though mistakenly understanding it as a satiric sally, had but thought so much the better of the impressed man for it; as a military sailor, admiring the spirit that could take an arbitrary enlistment so merrily and sensibly. The foretopman's conduct, too, so far as it had fallen under the captain's notice, had confirmed the first happy augury, while the new recruit's qualities as a 'sailor-man' seemed to be such that he had thought of recommending him to the executive officer for promotion to a place that would more frequently bring him under his own observation, namely, the captaincy of the mizzentop, replacing there in the starboard watch a man not so young whom partly for that reason he deemed less fitted for the post. Be it parenthesized here that since the mizzentopmen have not to handle such breadths of heavy canvas as the lower sails on the mainmast and foremast, a young man if of the right stuff not only seems best adapted to duty there, but in fact is generally selected for the captaincy of that top, and the company under him are light hands and often but striplings. In sum, Captain Vere had from the beginning deemed Billy Budd to be what in the naval parlance of the time was called a 'King's bargain': that is to say, for His Britannic Majesty's navy a capital investment at small outlay or none at all.

After a brief pause, during which the reminiscences above mentioned passed vividly through his mind and he weighed the import of Claggart's last suggestion conveyed in the phrase 'mantrap under the daisies,' and the more he weighed it the less reliance he felt in the informer's good faith, suddenly he turned upon him and in a low voice demanded: 'Do you come to me, Master-at-arms, with so foggy a tale? As to Budd, cite me an act or spoken word of his confirmatory of what you in general charge against him. Stay,' drawing nearer to him; 'heed what you speak. Just now, and in a case like this, there is a yardarm-end for the false witness.'

'Ah, your honor!' sighed Claggart, mildly shaking his shapely head as in sad deprecation of such unmerited severity of tone. Then, bridling—erecting himself as in virtuous self-assertion—he circumstantially alleged certain words and acts which collectively, if credited, led to presumptions morally inculpating Budd. And for some of these averments, he added, substantiating proof was not far.

With gray eyes impatient and distrustful essaying to fathom to the bottom Claggart's calm violet ones, Captain Vere again heard him out; then for the moment stood ruminating. The mood he evinced, Claggart—himself for the time liberated from the other's scrutiny—steadily regarded with a look difficult to render: a look curious of the operation of his tactics, a look such as might have been that of the spokesman of the envious children of Jacob deceptively imposing upon the troubled patriarch the blood-dyed coat of young Joseph.[2]

Though something exceptional in the moral quality of Captain Vere made him, in earnest encounter with a fellow man, a veritable touchstone of that man's essential nature, yet now as to Claggart and what was really going on in him his feeling partook less of intuitional conviction than of strong suspicion clogged by strange dubieties. The perplexity he evinced proceeded less from aught touching the man informed against—as Claggart doubtless opined—than from considerations how best to act in regard to the informer. At first, indeed, he was naturally for summoning that substantiation of his allegations which Claggart said was at hand. But such a proceeding would result in the matter at once getting abroad, which in the present stage of it, he thought, might undesirably affect the ship's company. If Claggart was a false witness—that closed the affair. And therefore, before trying the accusation, he would first practically test the accuser; and he thought this could be done in a quiet, undemonstrative way.

The measure he determined upon involved a shifting of the scene, a transfer to a place less exposed to observation than the broad quarter-deck. For although the few gunroom officers there at the time had, in due observance of naval etiquette, withdrawn to leeward the moment Captain Vere had begun his promenade on the deck's weather side; and though during the colloquy with Claggart they of course ventured not to diminish the distance; and though throughout the interview Captain Vere's voice was far from him, and Claggart's silvery and low; and the wind in the cordage and the wash of the sea helped the more to put them beyond earshot; nevertheless, the interview's continuance already had attracted observation from some topmen aloft and other sailors in the waist or further forward.

Having determined upon his measures, Captain Vere forthwith took action. Abruptly turning to Claggart, he asked, 'Master-at-arms, is it now Budd's watch aloft?'

'No, your honor.'

Whereupon, 'Mr Wilkes!' summoning the nearest midshipman. 'Tell Albert to come to me.' Albert was the captain's hammock-boy, a sort of sea

2. Genesis 37:31–32: "And they took Joseph's coat, and killed a kid of the goats, and dipped the coat in the blood; and they sent the coat of many colours, and they brought it to their father; and said, This have we found: know now whether it be thy son's coat or no."

valet in whose discretion and fidelity his master had much confidence. The lad appeared.

'You know Budd, the foretopman?'

'I do, sir.'

'Go find him. It is his watch off. Manage to tell him out of earshot that he is wanted aft. Contrive it that he speaks to nobody. Keep him in talk yourself. And not till you get well aft here, not till then let him know that the place where he is wanted is my cabin. You understand. Go. — Master-at-arms, show yourself on the decks below, and when you think it time for Albert to be coming with his man, stand by quietly to follow the sailor in.'

19

Now when the foretopman found himself in the cabin, closeted there, as it were, with the captain and Claggart, he was surprised enough. But it was a surprise unaccompanied by apprehension or distrust. To an immature nature essentially honest and humane, forewarning intimations of subtler danger from one's kind come tardily if at all. The only thing that took shape in the young sailor's mind was this: Yes, the captain, I have always thought, looks kindly upon me. Wonder if he's going to make me his coxswain. I should like that. And may be now he is going to ask the master-at-arms about me.

'Shut the door there, sentry,' said the commander; 'stand without, and let nobody come in. — Now, Master-at-arms, tell this man to his face what you told of him to me,' and stood prepared to scrutinize the mutually confronting visages.

With the measured step and calm collected air of an asylum physician approaching in the public hall some patient beginning to show indications of a coming paroxysm, Claggart deliberately advanced within short range of Billy and, mesmerically looking him in the eye, briefly recapitulated the accusation.

Not at first did Billy take it in. When he did, the rose-tan of his cheek looked struck as by white leprosy. He stood like one impaled and gagged. Meanwhile the accuser's eyes, removing not as yet from the blue dilated ones, underwent a phenomenal change, their wonted rich violet color blurring into a muddy purple. Those lights of human intelligence, losing human expression, were gelidly protruding like the alien eyes of certain uncatalogued creatures of the deep. The first mesmeristic glance was one of serpent fascination; the last was as the paralyzing lurch of the torpedo fish.

'Speak, man!' said Captain Vere to the transfixed one, struck by his aspect even more than by Claggart's. 'Speak! Defend yourself!' Which appeal caused but a strange dumb gesturing and gurgling in Billy; amazement at such an accusation so suddenly sprung on inexperienced nonage; this, and, it may be, horror of the accuser's eyes, serving to bring out his lurking defect and in this instance for the time intensifying it into a convulsed tongue-tie; while the intent head and entire form straining forward in an agony of ineffectual eagerness to obey the injunction to speak and defend himself, gave an expression to the face like that of a condemned

vestal priestess in the moment of being buried alive, and in the first struggle against suffocation.[3]

Though at the time Captain Vere was quite ignorant of Billy's liability
to vocal impediment, he now immediately divined it, since vividly Billy's
aspect recalled to him that of a bright young schoolmate of his whom he
had once seen struck by much the same startling impotence in the act of
eagerly rising in the class to be foremost in response to a testing question
put to it by the master. Going close up to the young sailor, and laying a
soothing hand on his shoulder, he said, 'There is no hurry, my boy. Take
your time, take your time.' Contrary to the effect intended, these words so
fatherly in tone, doubtless touching Billy's heart to the quick, prompted
yet more violent efforts at utterance — efforts soon ending for the time in
confirming the paralysis, and bringing to his face an expression which was
as a crucifixion to behold. The next instant, quick as the flame from a
discharged cannon at night, his right arm shot out, and Claggart dropped
to the deck. Whether intentionally or but owing to the young athlete's
superior height, the blow had taken effect full upon the forehead, so
shapely and intellectual-looking a feature in the master-at-arms; so that the
body fell over lengthwise, like a heavy plank tilted from erectness. A gasp
or two, and he lay motionless.

'Fated boy,' breathed Captain Vere in tone so low as to be almost a
whisper, 'what have you done! But here, help me.'

The twain raised the felled one from the loins up into a sitting position.
The spare form flexibly acquiesced, but inertly. It was like handling a dead
snake. They lowered it back. Regaining erectness, Captain Vere with one
hand covering his face stood to all appearance as impassive as the object
at his feet. Was he absorbed in taking in all the bearings of the event and
what was best not only now at once to be done, but also in the sequel?
Slowly he uncovered his face; and the effect was as if the moon emerging
from eclipse should reappear with quite another aspect than that which
had gone into hiding. The father in him, manifested towards Billy thus far
in the scene, was replaced by the military disciplinarian. In his official
tone he bade the foretopman retire to a stateroom aft (pointing it out), and
there remain till thence summoned. This order Billy in silence mechanically obeyed. Then going to the cabin door where it opened on the quarter-deck, Captain Vere said to the sentry without, 'Tell somebody to send
Albert here.' When the lad appeared, his master so contrived it that he
should not catch sight of the prone one. 'Albert,' he said to him, 'tell the
surgeon I wish to see him. You need not come back till called.'

When the surgeon entered — a self-poised character of that grave sense
and experience that hardly anything could take him aback — Captain Vere
advanced to meet him, thus unconsciously intercepting his view of Claggart, and interrupting the other's wonted ceremonious salutation, said,
'Nay. Tell me how it is with yonder man,' directing his attention to the
prostrate one.

The surgeon looked, and for all his self-command somewhat started at
the abrupt revelation. On Claggart's always pallid complexion, thick black

---

3. Vestal virgins in Rome were buried alive if they violated their vows.

blood was now oozing from nostril and ear. To the gazer's professional eye it was unmistakably no living man that he saw.

'Is it so, then?' said Captain Vere, intently watching him. 'I thought it. But verify it.' Whereupon the customary tests confirmed the surgeon's first glance, who now, looking up in unfeigned concern, cast a look of intense inquisitiveness upon his superior. But Captain Vere, with one hand to his brow, was standing motionless. Suddenly, catching the surgeon's arm convulsively, he exclaimed, pointing down to the body, 'It is the divine judgment on Ananias![4] Look!'

Disturbed by the excited manner he had never before observed in the *Bellipotent*'s captain, and as yet wholly ignorant of the affair, the prudent surgeon nevertheless held his peace, only again looking an earnest interrogatory as to what it was that had resulted in such a tragedy.

But Captain Vere was now again motionless, standing absorbed in thought. Again starting, he vehemently exclaimed, 'Struck dead by an angel of God! Yet the angel must hang!'

At these passionate interjections, mere incoherences to the listener as yet unapprised of the antecedents, the surgeon was profoundly discomposed. But now, as recollecting himself, Captain Vere in less passionate tone briefly related the circumstances leading up to the event. 'But come, we must dispatch,' he added. 'Help me to remove him' (meaning the body) 'to yonder compartment,' designating one opposite that where the foretopman remained immured. Anew disturbed by a request that, as implying a desire for secrecy, seemed unaccountably strange to him, there was nothing for the subordinate to do but comply.

'Go now,' said Captain Vere with something of his wonted manner. 'Go now. I presently shall call a drumhead court.[5] Tell the lieutenants what has happened, and tell Mr Mordant' (meaning the captain of marines), 'and charge them to keep the matter to themselves.'

20

Full of disquietude and misgiving, the surgeon left the cabin. Was Captain Vere suddenly affected in his mind, or was it but a transient excitement, brought about by so strange and extraordinary a tragedy? As to the drumhead court, it struck the surgeon as impolitic, if nothing more. The thing to do, he thought, was to place Billy Budd in confinement, and in a way dictated by usage, and postpone further action in so extraordinary a case to such time as they should rejoin the squadron, and then refer it to the admiral. He recalled the unwonted agitation of Captain Vere and his excited exclamations, so at variance with his normal manner. Was he unhinged?

But assuming that he is, it is not so susceptible of proof. What then can the surgeon do? No more trying situation is conceivable than that of an officer subordinate under a captain whom he suspects to be not mad,

4. Acts 5:3–5: "Peter said, Ananias . . . thou hast not lied unto men, but unto God. And Ananias hearing these words fell down, and gave up the ghost."   5. A court-martial, originally held around an upturned drum, to try offences committed during military operations.

indeed, but yet not quite unaffected in his intellects. To argue his order to him would be insolence. To resist him would be mutiny.

In obedience to Captain Vere, he communicated what had happened to the lieutenants and captain of marines, saying nothing as to the captain's state. They fully shared his own surprise and concern. Like him too, they seemed to think that such a matter should be referred to the admiral.

21

Who in the rainbow can draw the line where the violet tint ends and the orange tint begins? Distinctly we see the difference of the colors, but where exactly does the one first blendingly enter into the other? So with sanity and insanity. In pronounced cases there is no question about them. But in some supposed cases, in various degrees supposedly less pronounced, to draw the exact line of demarcation few will undertake, though for a fee becoming considerate some professional experts will. There is nothing nameable but that some men will, or undertake to, do it for pay.

Whether Captain Vere, as the surgeon professionally and privately surmised, was really the sudden victim of any degree of aberration, every one must determine for himself by such light as this narrative may afford.

That the unhappy event which has been narrated could not have happened at a worse juncture was but too true. For it was close on the heel of the suppressed insurrections, an aftertime very critical to naval authority, demanding from every English sea commander two qualities not readily interfusable—prudence and rigor. Moreover, there was something crucial in the case.

In the jugglery of circumstances preceding and attending the event on board the *Bellipotent*, and in the light of that martial code whereby it was formally to be judged, innocence and guilt personified in Claggart and Budd in effect changed places. In a legal view the apparent victim of the tragedy was he who had sought to victimize a man blameless; and the indisputable deed of the latter, navally regarded, constituted the most heinous of military crimes. Yet more. The essential right and wrong involved in the matter, the clearer that might be, so much the worse for the responsibility of a loyal sea commander, inasmuch as he was not authorized to determine the matter on that primitive basis.

Small wonder then that the *Bellipotent*'s captain, though in general a man of rapid decision, felt that circumspectness not less than promptitude was necessary. Until he could decide upon his course, and in each detail; and not only so, but until the concluding measure was upon the point of being enacted, he deemed it advisable, in view of all the circumstances, to guard as much as possible against publicity. Here he may or may not have erred. Certain it is, however, that subsequently in the confidential talk of more than one or two gun rooms and cabins he was not a little criticized by some officers, a fact imputed by his friends and vehemently by his cousin Jack Denton to professional jealousy of Starry Vere. Some imaginative ground for invidious comment there was. The maintenance of secrecy in the matter, the confining all knowledge of it for a time to the place where the homicide occurred, the quarter-deck cabin; in these

particulars lurked some resemblance to the policy adopted in those tragedies of the palace which have occurred more than once in the capital
founded by Peter the Barbarian.[6]

The case indeed was such that fain would the *Bellipotent's* captain have
deferred taking any action whatever respecting it further than to keep the
foretopman a close prisoner till the ship rejoined the squadron and then
submitting the matter to the judgment of his admiral.

But a true military officer is in one particular like a true monk. Not with
more of self-abnegation will the latter keep his vows of monastic obedience
than the former his vows of allegiance to martial duty.

Feeling that unless quick action was taken on it, the deed of the foretopman, so soon as it should be known on the gun decks, would tend to
awaken any slumbering embers of the Nore among the crew, a sense of
the urgency of the case overruled in Captain Vere every other consideration. But though a conscientious disciplinarian, he was no lover of
authority for mere authority's sake. Very far was he from embracing opportunities for monopolizing to himself the perils of moral responsibility,
none at least that could properly be referred to an official superior or
shared with him by his official equals or even subordinates. So thinking,
he was glad it would not be at variance with usage to turn the matter over
to a summary court of his own officers, reserving to himself, as the one on
whom the ultimate accountability would rest, the right of maintaining a
supervision of it, or formally or informally interposing at need. Accordingly a drum-head court was summarily convened, he electing the individuals composing it: the first lieutenant, the captain of marines, and the
sailing master.

In associating an officer of marines with the sea lieutenant and the
sailing master in a case having to do with a sailor, the commander perhaps
deviated from general custom. He was prompted thereto by the circumstance that he took that soldier to be a judicious person, thoughtful, and
not altogether incapable of grappling with a difficult case unprecedented
in his prior experience. Yet even as to him he was not without some latent
misgiving, for withal he was an extremely good-natured man, an enjoyer
of his dinner, a sound sleeper, and inclined to obesity—a man who though
he would always maintain his manhood in battle might not prove altogether reliable in a moral dilemma involving aught of the tragic. As to the
first lieutenant and the sailing master, Captain Vere could not but be
aware that though honest natures, of approved gallantry upon occasion,
their intelligence was mostly confined to the matter of active seamanship
and the fighting demands of their profession.

The court was held in the same cabin where the unfortunate affair had
taken place. This cabin, the commander's, embraced the entire area
under the poop deck. Aft, and on either side, was a small stateroom, the
one now temporarily a jail and the other a dead-house, and a yet smaller
compartment, leaving a space between expanding forward into a goodly
oblong of length coinciding with the ship's beam. A skylight of moderate

6. St. Petersburg, founded by Peter the Great (1672–1725) in 1703.

dimension was overhead, and at each end of the oblong space were two sashed porthole windows easily convertible back into embrasures for short carronades.[7]

All being quickly in readiness, Billy Budd was arraigned, Captain Vere necessarily appearing as the sole witness in the case, and as such temporarily sinking his rank, though singularly maintaining it in a matter apparently trivial, namely, that he testified from the ship's weather side, with that object having caused the court to sit on the lee side. Concisely he narrated all that had led up to the catastrophe, omitting nothing in Claggart's accusation and deposing as to the manner in which the prisoner had received it. At this testimony the three officers glanced with no little surprise at Billy Budd, the last man they would have suspected either of the mutinous design alleged by Claggart or the undeniable deed he himself had done. The first lieutenant, taking judicial primacy and turning toward the prisoner, said, 'Captain Vere has spoken. Is it or is it not as Captain Vere says?'

In response came syllables not so much impeded in the utterance as might have been anticipated. They were these: 'Captain Vere tells the truth. It is just as Captain Vere says, but it is not as the master-at-arms said. I have eaten the King's bread and I am true to the King.'

'I believe you, my man,' said the witness, his voice indicating a suppressed emotion not otherwise betrayed.

'God will bless you for that, your honor!' not without stammering said Billy, and all but broke down. But immediately he was recalled to self-control by another question, to which with the same emotional difficulty of utterance he said, 'No, there was no malice between us. I never bore malice against the master-at-arms. I am sorry that he is dead. I did not mean to kill him. Could I have used my tongue I would not have struck him. But he foully lied to my face and in presence of my captain, and I had to say something, and I could only say it with a blow, God help me!'

In the impulsive aboveboard manner of the frank one the court saw confirmed all that was implied in words that just previously had perplexed them, coming as they did from the testifier to the tragedy and promptly following Billy's impassioned disclaimer of mutinous intent—Captain Vere's words, 'I believe you, my man.'

Next it was asked of him whether he knew of or suspected aught savoring of incipient trouble (meaning mutiny, though the explicit term was avoided) going on in any section of the ship's company.

The reply lingered. This was naturally imputed by the court to the same vocal embarrassment which had retarded or obstructed previous answers. But in main it was otherwise here, the question immediately recalling to Billy's mind the interview with the afterguardsman in the forechains. But an innate repugnance to playing a part at all approaching that of an informer against one's own shipmates—the same erring sense of uninstructed honor which had stood in the way of his reporting the matter at the time, though as a loyal man-of-war's man it was incumbent on him,

7. Large pieces of artillery.

and failure so to do, if charged against him and proven, would have subjected him to the heaviest of penalties; this, with the blind feeling now his that nothing really was being hatched, prevailed with him. When the answer came it was a negative.

'One question more,' said the officer of marines, now first speaking and with a troubled earnestness. 'You tell us that what the master-at-arms said against you was a lie. Now why should he have so lied, so maliciously lied, since you declare there was no malice between you?'

At that question, unintentionally touching on a spiritual sphere wholly obscure to Billy's thoughts, he was nonplussed, evincing a confusion indeed that some observers, such as can readily be imagined, would have construed into involuntary evidence of hidden guilt. Nevertheless, he strove some way to answer, but all at once relinquished the vain endeavor, at the same time turning an appealing glance towards Captain Vere as deeming him his best helper and friend. Captain Vere, who had been seated for a time, rose to his feet, addressing the interrogator. 'The question you put to him comes naturally enough. But how can he rightly answer it?—or anybody else, unless indeed it be he who lies within there,' designating the compartment where lay the corpse. 'But the prone one there will not rise to our summons. In effect, though, as it seems to me, the point you make is hardly material. Quite aside from any conceivable motive actuating the master-at-arms, and irrespective of the provocation to the blow, a martial court must needs in the present case confine its attention to the blow's consequence, which consequence justly is to be deemed not otherwise than as the striker's deed.'

This utterance, the full significance of which it was not at all likely that Billy took in, nevertheless caused him to turn a wistful interrogative look toward the speaker, a look in its dumb expressiveness not unlike that which a dog of generous breed might turn upon his master, seeking in his face some elucidation of a previous gesture ambiguous to the canine intelligence. Nor was the same utterance without marked effect upon the three officers, more especially the soldier. Couched in it seemed to them a meaning unanticipated, involving a prejudgment on the speaker's part. It served to augment a mental disturbance previously evident enough.

The soldier once more spoke, in a tone of suggestive dubiety addressing at once his associates and Captain Vere: 'Nobody is present—none of the ship's company, I mean—who might shed lateral light, if any is to be had, upon what remains mysterious in this matter.'

'That is thoughtfully put,' said Captain Vere; 'I see your drift. Ay, there is a mystery; but, to use a scriptural phrase, it is a "mystery of iniquity," a matter for psychologic theologians to discuss. But what has a military court to do with it? Not to add that for us any possible investigation of it is cut off by the lasting tongue-tie of—him—in yonder,' again designating the mortuary stateroom. 'The prisoner's deed—with that alone we have to do.'

To this, and particularly the closing reiteration, the marine soldier, knowing not how aptly to reply, sadly abstained from saying aught. The first lieutenant, who at the outset had not unnaturally assumed primacy in the court, now overrulingly instructed by a glance from Captain Vere, a glance more effective than words, resumed that primacy. Turning to the prisoner, 'Budd,' he said, and scarce in equable tones, 'Budd, if you have aught further to say for yourself, say it now.'

Upon this the young sailor turned another quick glance toward Captain Vere; then, as taking a hint from that aspect, a hint confirming his own instinct that silence was now best, replied to the lieutenant, 'I have said all, sir.'

The marine—the same who had been the sentinel without the cabin door at the time that the foretopman, followed by the master-at-arms, entered it—he, standing by the sailor throughout these judicial proceedings was now directed to take him back to the after compartment originally assigned to the prisoner and his custodian. As the twain disappeared from view, the three officers, as partially liberated from some inward constraint associated with Billy's mere presence, simultaneously stirred in their seats. They exchanged looks of troubled indecision, yet feeling that decide they must and without long delay. For Captain Vere, he for the time stood—unconsciously with his back toward them, apparently in one of his absent fits—gazing out from a sashed porthole to windward upon the monotonous blank of the twilight sea. But the court's silence continuing, broken only at moments by brief consultations, in low earnest tones, this served to arouse him and energize him. Turning, he to-and-fro paced the cabin athwart; in the returning ascent to windward climbing the slant deck in the ship's lee roll, without knowing it symbolizing thus in his action a mind resolute to surmount difficulties even if against primitive instincts strong as the wind and the sea. Presently he came to a stand before the three. After scanning their faces he stood less as mustering his thoughts for expression than as one inly deliberating how best to put them to well-meaning men not intellectually mature, men with whom it was necessary to demonstrate certain principles that were axioms to himself. Similar impatience as to talking is perhaps one reason that deters some minds from addressing any popular assemblies.

When speak he did, something, both in the substance of what he said and his manner of saying it, showed the influence of unshared studies modifying and tempering the practical training of an active career. This, along with his phraseology, now and then was suggestive of the grounds whereon rested that imputation of a certain pedantry socially alleged against him by certain naval men of wholly practical cast, captains who nevertheless would frankly concede that His Majesty's navy mustered no more efficient officer of their grade than Starry Vere.

What he said was to this effect: 'Hitherto I have been but the witness, little more; and I should hardly think now to take another tone, that of your coadjutor for the time, did I not perceive in you—at the crisis too—a troubled hesitancy, proceeding, I doubt not, from the clash of military duty with moral scruple—scruple vitalized by compassion. For the compassion, how can I otherwise than share it? But, mindful of paramount obligations, I strive against scruples that may tend to enervate decision. Not, gentlemen, that I hide from myself that the case is an exceptional one. Speculatively regarded, it well might be referred to a jury of casuists. But for us here, acting not as casuists or moralists, it is a case practical, and under martial law practically to be dealt with.

'But your scruples: do they move as in a dusk? Challenge them. Make them advance and declare themselves. Come now; do they import something like this: If, mindless of palliating circumstances, we are bound to regard the death of the master-at-arms as the prisoner's deed, then does that deed constitute a capital crime whereof the penalty is a mortal one. But in natural justice is nothing but the prisoner's overt act to be considered? How can we adjudge to summary and shameful death a fellow creature innocent before God, and whom we feel to be so?—Does that state it aright? You sign sad assent. Well, I too feel that, the full force of that. It is Nature. But do these buttons that we wear attest that our allegiance is to Nature? No, to the King. Though the ocean, which is inviolate Nature primeval, though this be the element where we move and have our being as sailors, yet as the King's officers lies our duty in a sphere correspondingly natural? So little is that true, that in receiving our commissions we in the most important regards ceased to be natural free agents. When war is declared are we the commissioned fighters previously consulted? We fight at command. If our judgments approve the war, that is but coincidence. So in other particulars. So now. For suppose condemnation to follow these present proceedings. Would it be so much we ourselves that would condemn as it would be martial law operating through us? For that law and the rigor of it, we are not responsibile. Our vowed responsibility is in this: That however pitilessly that law may operate in any instances, we nevertheless adhere to it and administer it.

'But the exceptional in the matter moves the hearts within you. Even so too is mine moved. But let not warm hearts betray heads that should be cool. Ashore in a criminal case, will an upright judge allow himself off the bench to be waylaid by some tender kinswoman of the accused seeking to touch him with her tearful plea? Well, the heart here, sometimes the feminine in man, is as that piteous woman, and hard though it be, she must here be ruled out.'

He paused, earnestly studying them for a moment; then resumed.

'But something in your aspect seems to urge that it is not solely the heart that moves in you, but also the conscience, the private conscience. But tell me whether or not, occupying the position we do, private conscience should not yield to that imperial one formulated in the code under which alone we officially proceed?'

Here the three men moved in their seats, less convinced than agitated by the course of an argument troubling but the more the spontaneous conflict within.

Perceiving which, the speaker paused for a moment; then abruptly changing his tone, went on.

'To steady us a bit, let us recur to the facts.—In wartime at sea a man-of-war's man strikes his superior in grade, and the blow kills. Apart from its effect the blow itself is, according to the Articles of War, a capital crime. Furthermore—'

'Ay, sir,' emotionally broke in the officer of marines, 'in one sense it was. But surely Budd proposed neither mutiny nor homicide.'

'Surely not, my good man. And before a court less arbitrary and more merciful than a martial one, that plea would largely extenuate. At the Last

Assizes[8] it shall acquit. But how here? We proceed under the law of the Mutiny Act.[9] In feature no child can resemble his father more than that Act resembles in spirit the thing from which it derives—War. In His Majesty's service—in this ship, indeed—there are Englishmen forced to fight for the King against their will. Against their conscience, for aught we know. Though as their fellow creatures some of us may appreciate their position, yet as navy officers what reck we of it? Still less recks the enemy. Our impressed men he would fain cut down in the same swath with our volunteers. As regards the enemy's naval conscripts, some of whom may even share our own abhorrence of the regicidal French Directory, it is the same on our side. War looks but to the frontage, the appearance. And the Mutiny Act, War's child, takes after the father. Budd's intent or non-intent is nothing to the purpose.

'But while, put to it by those anxieties in you which I cannot but respect, I only repeat myself—while thus strangely we prolong proceedings that should be summary—the enemy may be sighted and an engagement result. We must do; and one of two things must we do—condemn or let go.'

'Can we not convict and yet mitigate the penalty?' asked the sailing master, here speaking, and falteringly, for the first.

'Gentlemen, were that clearly lawful for us under the circumstances, consider the consequences of such clemency. The people' (meaning the ship's company) 'have native sense; most of them are familiar with our naval usage and tradition; and how would they take it? Even could you explain to them—which our official position forbids—they, long molded by arbitrary discipline, have not that kind of intelligent responsiveness that might qualify them to comprehend and discriminate. No, to the people the foretopman's deed, however it be worded in the announcement, will be plain homicide committed in a flagrant act of mutiny. What penalty for that should follow, they know. But it does not follow. Why? they will ruminate. You know what sailors are. Will they not revert to the recent outbreak at the Nore? Ay. They know the well-founded alarm—the panic it struck throughout England. Your clement sentence they would account pusillanimous. They would think that we flinch, that we are afraid of them—afraid of practicing a lawful rigor singularly demanded at this juncture, lest it should provoke new troubles. What shame to us such a conjecture on their part, and how deadly to discipline. You see then, whither, prompted by duty and the law, I steadfastly drive. But I beseech you, my friends, do not take me amiss. I feel as you do for this unfortunate boy. But did he know our hearts, I take him to be of that generous nature that he would feel even for us on whom in this military necessity so heavy a compulsion is laid.'

With that, crossing the deck he resumed his place by the sashed porthole, tacitly leaving the three to come to a decision. On the cabin's opposite side the troubled court sat silent. Loyal lieges, plain and practical, though at bottom they dissented from some points Captain Vere had put

8. The highest courts of appeal in Great Britain. Melville refers here to the Last Judgment. 9. First passed in 1689; the act and its successors applied only to the army; the navy followed the King's Regulations and Admiralty Instructions of 1772.

to them, they were without the faculty, hardly had the inclination, to gainsay one whom they felt to be an earnest man, one too not less their superior in mind than in naval rank. But it is not improbable that even such of his words as were not without influence over them, less came home to them than his closing appeal to their instinct as sea officers: in the forethought he threw out as to the practical consequences to discipline, considering the unconfirmed tone of the fleet at the time, should a man-of-war's man's violent killing at sea of a superior in grade be allowed to pass for aught else than a capital crime demanding prompt infliction of the penalty.

Not unlikely they were brought to something more or less akin to that harassed frame of mind which in the year 1842 actuated the commander of the U.S. brig-of-war *Somers* to resolve, under the so-called Articles of War, Articles modeled upon the English Mutiny Act, to resolve upon the execution at sea of a midshipman and two sailors as mutineers designing the seizure of the brig.[1] Which resolution was carried out though in a time of peace and within not many days' sail of home. An act vindicated by a naval court of inquiry subsequently convened ashore. History, and here cited without comment. True, the circumstances on board the *Somers* were different from those on board the *Bellipotent*. But the urgency felt, well-warranted or otherwise, was much the same.

Says a writer whom few know,[2] 'Forty years after a battle it is easy for a noncombatant to reason about how it ought to have been fought. It is another thing personally and under fire to have to direct the fighting while involved in the obscuring smoke of it. Much so with respect to other emergencies involving considerations both practical and moral, and when it is imperative promptly to act. The greater the fog the more it imperils the steamer, and speed is put on though at the hazard of running somebody down. Little ween the snug card players in the cabin of the responsibilities of the sleepless man on the bridge.'

In brief, Billy Budd was formally convicted and sentenced to be hung at the yardarm in the early morning watch, it being now night. Otherwise, as is customary in such cases, the sentence would forthwith have been carried out. In wartime on the field or in the fleet, a mortal punishment decreed by a drumhead court—on the field sometimes decreed by but a nod from the general—follows without delay on the heel of conviction, without appeal.

22

It was Captain Vere himself who of his own motion communicated the finding of the court to the prisoner, for that purpose going to the compartment where he was in custody and bidding the marine there to withdraw for the time.

Beyond the communication of the sentence, what took place at this interview was never known. But in view of the character of the twain briefly closeted in that stateroom, each radically sharing in the rarer quali-

1. Melville's cousin, Guert Gansevoort, was first lieutenant of the *Somers* at the time of a mutiny. The incident may have been in the back of Melville's mind when he wrote *Billy Budd*.　2. Melville himself.

ties of our nature—so rare indeed as to be all but incredible to average minds however much cultivated—some conjectures may be ventured.

It would have been in consonance with the spirit of Captain Vere should he on this occasion have concealed nothing from the condemned one—should he indeed have frankly disclosed to him the part he himself had played in bringing about the decision, at the same time revealing his actuating motives. On Billy's side it is not improbable that such a confession would have been received in much the same spirit that prompted it. Not without a sort of joy, indeed, he might have appreciated the brave[3] opinion of him implied in his captain's making such a confidant of him. Nor, as to the sentence itself, could he have been insensible that it was imparted to him as to one not afraid to die. Even more may have been. Captain Vere in end may have developed the passion sometimes latent under an exterior stoical or indifferent. He was old enough to have been Billy's father. The austere devotee of military duty, letting himself melt back into what remains primeval in our formalized humanity, may in end have caught Billy to his heart, even as Abraham may have caught young Isaac on the brink of resolutely offering him up in obedience to the exacting behest.[4] But there is no telling the sacrament, seldom if in any case revealed to the gadding world, wherever under circumstances at all akin to those here attempted to be set forth two of great Nature's nobler order embrace. There is privacy at the time, inviolable to the survivor; and holy oblivion, the sequel to each diviner magnanimity, providentially covers all at last.

The first to encounter Captain Vere in act of leaving the compartment was the senior lieutenant. The face he beheld, for the moment one expressive of the agony of the strong, was to that officer, though a man of fifty, a startling revelation. That the condemned one suffered less than he who mainly had effected the condemnation was apparently indicated by the former's exclamation in the scene soon perforce to be touched upon.

23

Of a series of incidents within a brief term rapidly following each other, the adequate narration may take up a term less brief, especially if explanation or comment here and there seem requisite to the better understanding of such incidents. Between the entrance into the cabin of him who never left it alive, and him who when he did leave it left it as one condemned to die; between this and the closeted interview just given, less than an hour and a half had elapsed. It was an interval long enough, however, to awaken speculations among no few of the ship's company as to what it was that could be detaining in the cabin the master-at-arms and the sailor; for a rumor that both of them had been seen to enter it and neither of them had been seen to emerge, this rumor had got abroad upon

---

3. Fine, superior.   4. Genesis 22:1–18: "God did tempt Abraham, and said . . . Take now thy son, thine only son Isaac, whom thou lovest . . . and offer him . . . for a burnt offering. . . . And Abraham . . . bound Isaac his son, and laid him on the altar upon the wood. And Abraham stretched forth his hand, and took the knife to slay his son. And the angel of the Lord . . . said, Lay not thine hand upon the lad, neither do thou anything unto him: for now I know that thou fearest God. . . . And the angel of the Lord . . . said, . . . I will bless thee . . . because thou hast obeyed my voice."

the gun decks and in the tops, the people of a great warship being in one respect like villagers, taking microscopic note of every outward movement or non-movement going on. When therefore, in weather not at all tempestuous, all hands were called in the second dogwatch, a summons under such circumstances not usual in those hours, the crew were not wholly unprepared for some announcement extraordinary, one having connection too with the continued absence of the two men from their wonted haunts.

There was a moderate sea at the time; and the moon, newly risen and near to being at its full, silvered the white spar deck wherever not blotted by the clear-cut shadows horizontally thrown of fixtures and moving men. On either side the quarter-deck the marine guard under arms was drawn up; and Captain Vere, standing in his place surrounded by all the wardroom officers, addressed his men. In so doing, his manner showed neither more nor less than that properly pertaining to his supreme position aboard his own ship. In clear terms and concise he told them what had taken place in the cabin: that the master-at-arms was dead, that he who had killed him had been already tried by a summary court and condemned to death, and that the execution would take place in the early morning watch. The word *mutiny* was not named in what he said. He refrained too from making the occasion an opportunity for any preachment as to the maintenance of discipline, thinking perhaps that under existing circumstances in the navy the consequence of violating discipline shoud be made to speak for itself.

Their captain's announcement was listened to by the throng of standing sailors in a dumbness like that of a seated congregation of believers in hell listening to the clergyman's announcement of his Calvinistic text.

At the close, however, a confused murmur went up. It began to wax. All but instantly, then, at a sign, it was pierced and suppressed by shrill whistles of the boatswain and his mates. The word was given to about ship.

To be prepared for burial Claggart's body was delivered to certain petty officers of his mess. And here, not to clog the sequel with lateral matters, it may be added that at a suitable hour, the master-at-arms was committed to the sea with every funeral honor properly belonging to his naval grade.

In this proceeding as in every public one growing out of the tragedy strict adherence to usage was observed. Nor in any point could it have been at all deviated from, either with respect to Claggart or Billy Budd, without begetting undersirable speculations in the ship's company, sailors, and more particularly men-of-war's men, being of all men the greatest sticklers for usage. For similar cause, all communication between Captain Vere and the condemned one ended with the closeted interview already given, the latter being now surrendered to the ordinary routine preliminary to the end. His transfer under guard from the captain's quarters was effected without unusual precautions—at least no visible ones. If possible, not to let the men so much as surmise that their officers anticipate aught amiss from them is the tacit rule in a military ship. And the more that some sort of trouble should really be apprehended, the more do the officers keep that apprehension to themselves, though not the less unostentatious vigilance may be augmented. In the present instance, the sentry placed over the prisoner had strict orders to let no one have communication with him but the chaplain. And certain unobtrusive measures were taken absolutely to insure this point.

24

In a seventy-four of the old order the deck known as the upper gun deck was the one covered over by the spar deck, which last, though not without its armament, was for the most part exposed to the weather. In general it was at all hours free from hammocks; those of the crew swinging on the lower gun deck and berth deck, the latter being not only a dormitory but also the place for the stowing of the sailors' bags, and on both sides lined with the large chests or movable pantries of the many messes of the men.

On the starboard side of the *Bellipotent's* upper gun deck, behold Billy Budd under sentry lying prone in irons in one of the bays formed by the regular spacing of the guns comprising the batteries on either side. All these pieces were of the heavier caliber of that period. Mounted on lumbering wooden carriages, they were hampered with cumbersome harness of breeching and strong side-tackles for running them out. Guns and carriages, together with the long rammers and shorter linstocks lodged in loops overhead—all these, as customary, were painted black; and the heavy hempen breechings, tarred to the same tint, wore the like livery of the undertakers. In contrast with the funereal hue of these surroundings, the prone sailor's exterior apparel, white jumper and white duck trousers, each more or less soiled, dimly glimmered in the obscure light of the bay like a patch of discolored snow in early April lingering at some upland cave's black mouth. In effect he is already in his shroud, or the garments that shall serve him in lieu of one. Over him but scarce illuminating him, two battle lanterns swing from two massive beams of the deck above. Fed with the oil supplied by the war contractors (whose gains, honest or otherwise, are in every land an anticipated portion of the harvest of death), with flickering splashes of dirty yellow light they pollute the pale moonshine all but ineffectually struggling in obstructed flecks through the open ports from which the tampioned[5] cannon protrude. Other lanterns at intervals serve but to bring out somewhat the obscurer bays which, like small confessionals or side-chapels in a cathedral, branch from the long dim-vistaed broad aisle between the two batteries of that covered tier.

Such was the deck where now lay the Handsome Sailor. Through the rose-tan of his complexion no pallor could have shown. It would have taken days of sequestration from the winds and the sun to have brought about the effacement of that. But the skeleton in the cheekbone at the point of its angle was just beginning delicately to be defined under the warm-tinted skin. In fervid hearts self-contained, some brief experiences devour our human tissue as secret fire in a ship's hold consumes cotton in the bale.

But now lying between the two guns, as nipped in the vice of fate, Billy's agony, mainly proceeding from a generous young heart's virgin experience

---

5. Plugged with a tampion, which fits into the muzzle of a gun not in use.

of the diabolical incarnate and effective in some men—the tension of that agony was over now. It survived not the something healing in the closeted interview with Captain Vere. Without movement, he lay as in a trance, that adolescent expression previously noted as his taking on something akin to the look of a slumbering child in the cradle when the warm hearthglow of the still chamber at night plays on the dimples that at whiles mysteriously form in the cheek, silently coming and going there. For now and then in the gyved[6] one's trance a serene happy light born of some wandering reminiscence or dream would diffuse itself over his face, and then wane away only anew to return.

The chaplain, coming to see him and finding him thus, and perceiving no sign that he was conscious of his presence, attentively regarded him for a space, then slipping aside, withdrew for the time, peradventure feeling that even he, the minister of Christ though receiving his stipend from Mars,[7] had no consolation to proffer which could result in a peace transcending that which he beheld. But in the small hours he came again. And the prisoner, now awake to his surroundings, noticed his approach, and civilly, all but cheerfully, welcomed him. But it was to little purpose that in the interview following, the good man sought to bring Billy Budd to some godly understanding that he must die, and at dawn. True, Billy himself freely referred to his death as a thing close at hand; but it was something in the way that children will refer to death in general, who yet among their other sports will play a funeral with hearse and mourners.

Not that like children Billy was incapable of conceiving what death really is. No, but he was wholly without irrational fear of it, a fear more prevalent in highly civilized communities than those so-called barbarous ones which in all respects stand nearer to unadulterate Nature. And, as elsewhere said, a barbarian Billy radically was—as much so, for all the costume, as his countrymen the British captives, living trophies, made to march in the Roman triumph of Germanicus.[8] Quite as much so as those later barbarians, young men probably, and picked specimens among the earlier British converts to Christianity, at least nominally such, taken to Rome (as today converts from lesser isles of the sea may be taken to London), of whom the Pope at that time, admiring the strangeness of their personal beauty so unlike the Italian stamp, their clear ruddy complexion and curled flaxen locks, exclaimed, 'Angles' (meaning *English*, the modern derivative), 'Angles, do you call them? And is it because they look so like angels?'[9] Had it been later in time, one would think that the Pope had in mind Fra Angelico's seraphs, some of whom, plucking apples in gardens of the Hesperides,[1] have the faint rosebud complexion of the more beautiful English girls.

If in vain the good chaplain sought to impress the young barbarian with ideas of death akin to those conveyed in the skull, dial, and crossbones on old tombstones, equally futile to all appearance were his efforts to bring

---

6. Shackled, chained.   7. The god of war. That is, paid by the navy.   8. Germanicus Caesar (15 B.C.–A.D. 19), granted a triumph in Rome in A.D. 17.   9. Bede's *Ecclesiastical History of the English People* tells this anecdote about Pope Gregory the Great (540?–604).   1. Daughters of Atlas who guarded a tree bearing golden apples on an enchanted island in the western sea. Fra Angelico (1387–1455), the Florentine painter Giovanni da Fiesole.

home to him the thought of salvation and a Savior. Billy listened, but less out of awe or reverence, perhaps, than from a certain natural politeness, doubtless at bottom regarding all that in much the same way that most mariners of his class take any discourse abstract or out of the common tone of the workaday world. And this sailor way of taking clerical discourse is not wholly unlike the way in which the primer of Christianity, full of transcendent miracles, was received long ago on tropic isles by any superior *savage*, so called—a Tahitian, say, of Captain Cook's time or shortly after that time.[2] Out of a natural courtesy he received, but did not appropriate. It was like a gift placed in the palm of an outreached hand upon which the fingers do not close.

But the *Bellipotent*'s chaplain was a discreet man possessing the good sense of a good heart. So he insisted not in his vocation here. At the instance of Captain Vere, a lieutenant had apprised him of pretty much everything as to Billy; and since he felt that innocence was even a better thing than religion wherewith to go to Judgment, he reluctantly withdrew; but in his emotion not without first performing an act strange enough in an Englishman, and under the circumstances yet more so in any regular priest. Stooping over, he kissed on the fair cheek his fellow man, a felon in martial law, one whom though on the confines of death he felt he could never convert to a dogma; nor for all that did he fear for his future.

Marvel not that having been made acquainted with the young sailor's essential innocence the worthy man lifted not a finger to avert the doom of such a martyr to martial discipline. So to do would not only have been as idle as invoking the desert, but would also have been an audacious transgression of the bounds of his function, one as exactly prescribed to him by military law as that of the boatswain or any other naval officer. Bluntly put, a chaplain is the minister of the Prince of Peace serving in the host of the God of War—Mars. As such, he is as incongruous as a musket would be on the altar at Christmas. Why, then, is he there? Because he indirectly subserves the purpose attested by the cannon; because too he lends the sanction of the religion of the meek to that which practically is the abrogation of everything but brute Force.

25

The night so luminous on the spar deck, but otherwise on the cavernous ones below, levels so like the tiered galleries in a coal mine—the luminous night passed away. But like the prophet in the chariot disappearing in heaven and dropping his mantle to Elisha,[3] the withdrawing night transferred its pale robe to the breaking day. A meek, shy light appeared in the East, where stretched a diaphanous fleece of white furrowed vapor. That light slowly waxed. Suddenly *eight bells* was struck aft, responded to by one louder metallic stroke from forward. It was four o'clock in the morning. Instantly the silver whistles were heard summoning all hands to witness punishment. Up through the great hatchways rimmed with racks of

2. James Cook (1728–1779) was in Tahiti in 1769 and from 1772 to 1775.   3. 2 Kings 2:11–13: "There appeared a chariot of fire, and horses of fire, and parted them both asunder; and Elijah went up by a whirlwind into heaven. And Elisha . . . took up . . . the mantle of Elijah that fell from him."

heavy shot the watch below came pouring, overspreading with the watch already on deck the space between the mainmast and foremast including that occupied by the capacious launch and the black booms tiered on either side of it, boat and booms making a summit of observation for the powder-boys and younger tars. A different group comprising one watch of topmen leaned over the rail of that sea balcony, no small one in a seventy-four, looking down on the crowd below. Man or boy, none spake but in whisper, and few spake at all. Captain Vere—as before, the central figure among the assembled commissioned officers—stood nigh the break of the poop deck facing forward. Just below him on the quarter-deck the marines in full equipment were drawn up much as at the scene of the promulgated sentence.

At sea in the old time, the execution by halter of a military sailor was generally from the foreyard. In the present instance, for special reasons[4] the mainyard was assigned. Under an arm of that yard the prisoner was presently brought up, the chaplain attending him. It was noted at the time, and remarked upon afterwards, that in this final scene the good man evinced little or nothing of the perfunctory. Brief speech indeed he had with the condemned one, but the genuine Gospel was less on his tongue than in his aspect and manner towards him. The final preparations personal to the latter being speedily brought to an end by two boatswain's mates, the consummation impended. Billy stood facing aft. At the penultimate moment, his words, his only ones, words wholly unobstructed in the utterance, were these: 'God bless Captain Vere!' Syllables so unanticipated coming from one with the ignominious hemp about his neck—a conventional felon's benediction[5] directed aft towards the quarters of honor; syllables too delivered in the clear melody of a singing bird on the point of launching from the twig—had a phenomenal effect, not unenhanced by the rare personal beauty of the young sailor, spiritualized now through late experiences so poignantly profound.

Without volition, as it were, as if indeed the ship's populace were but the vehicles of some vocal current electric, with one voice from alow and aloft came a resonant sympathetic echo: 'God bless Captain Vere!' And yet at that instant Billy alone must have been in their hearts, even as in their eyes.

At the pronounced words and the spontaneous echo that voluminously rebounded them, Captain Vere, either through stoic self-control or a sort of momentary paralysis induced by emotional shock, stood erectly rigid as a musket in the ship-armorer's rack.

The hull, deliberately recovering from the periodic roll to leeward, was just regaining an even keel when the last signal, a preconcerted dumb one, was given. At the same moment it chanced that the vapory fleece hanging low in the East was shot through with a soft glory as of the fleece of the Lamb of God seen in mystical vision, and simultaneously therewith, watched by the wedged mass of upturned faces, Billy ascended; and, ascending, took the full rose of the dawn.

4. The *special reasons* remain obscure. The text editors suggest that the captain's motives were precautionary; the phrase, an insertion, previously read, "for strategic reasons."   5. It is a traditional ritual for the condemned man to forgive the official compelled by duty to order his death.

In the pinioned figure arrived at the yard-end, to the wonder of all no motion was apparent, none save that created by the slow roll of the hull in moderate weather, so majestic in a great ship ponderously cannoned.

26

When some days afterwards, in reference to the singularity just mentioned, the purser, a rather ruddy, rotund person more accurate as an accountant than profound as a philosopher, said at mess to the surgeon, "What testimony to the force lodged in will power,' the latter, saturnine, spare, and tall, one in whom a discreet causticity went along with a manner less genial than polite, replied. 'Your pardon, Mr Purser. In a hanging scientifically conducted—and under special orders I myself directed how Budd's was to be effected—any movement following the completed suspension and originating in the body suspended, such movement indicates mechanical spasm in the muscular system. Hence the absence of that is no more attributable to will power, as you call it, than to horsepower—begging your pardon.'

'But this muscular spasm you speak of, is not that in a degree more or less invariable in these cases?'

'Assuredly so, Mr Purser.'

'How then, my good sir, do you account for its absence in this instance?'

'Mr Purser, it is clear that your sense of the singularity in this matter equals not mine. You account for it by what you call will power—a term not yet included in the lexicon of science. For me, I do not, with my present knowledge, pretend to account for it at all. Even should we assume the hypothesis that at the first touch of the halyards the action of Budd's heart, intensified by extraordinary emotion at its climax, abruptly stopped—much like a watch when in carelessly winding it up you strain at the finish, thus snapping the chain—even under that hypothesis how account for the phenomenon that followed?'

'You admit, then, that the absence of spasmodic movement was phenomenal.'

'It was phenomenal, Mr Purser, in the sense that it was an appearance the cause of which is not immediately to be assigned.'

'But tell me, my dear sir,' pertinaciously continued the other, 'was the man's death effected by the halter, or was it a species of euthanasia?'[6]

'Euthanasia, Mr Purser, is something like your will power: I doubt its authenticity as a scientific term—begging your pardon again. It is at once imaginative and metaphysical—in short, Greek.—But,' abruptly changing his tone, 'there is a case in the sick bay that I do not care to leave to my assistants. Beg your pardon, but excuse me.' And rising from the mess he formally withdrew.

27

The silence at the moment of execution and for a moment or two continuing thereafter, a silence but emphasized by the regular wash of the sea

6. A quiet and easy death.

against the hull or the flutter of a sail caused by the helmsman's eyes being tempted astray, this emphasized silence was gradually disturbed by a sound not easily to be verbally rendered. Whoever has heard the freshet-wave of a torrent suddenly swelled by pouring showers in tropical mountains, showers not shared by the plain; whoever has heard the first muffled murmur of its sloping advance through precipitous woods may form some conception of the sound now heard. The seeming remoteness of its source was because of its murmurous indistinctness, since it came from close by, even from the men massed on the ship's open deck. Being inarticulate, it was dubious in significance further than it seemed to indicate some capricious revulsion of thought or feeling such as mobs ashore are liable to, in the present instance possibly implying a sullen revocation on the men's part of their involuntary echoing of Billy's benediction. But ere the murmur had time to wax into clamor it was met by a strategic command, the more telling that it came with abrupt unexpectedness: 'Pipe down the starboard watch, Boatswain, and see that they go.'

Shrill as the shriek of the sea hawk, the silver whistles of the boatswain and his mates pierced that ominous low sound, dissipating it; and yielding to the mechanism of discipline the throng was thinned by one-half. For the remainder, most of them were set to temporary employments connected with trimming the yards and so forth, business readily to be got up to serve occasion by any officer of the deck.

Now each proceeding that follows a mortal sentence pronounced at sea by a drumhead court is characterized by promptitude not perceptibly merging into hurry, though bordering that. The hammock, the one which had been Billy's bed when alive, having already been ballasted with shot and otherwise prepared to serve for his canvas coffin, the last offices of the sea undertakers, the sailmakers' mates, were now speedily completed. When everything was in readiness a second call for all hands, made necessary by the strategic movement before mentioned, was sounded, now to witness burial.

The details of this closing formality it needs not to give. But when the tilted plank let slide its freight into the sea, a second strange human murmur was heard, blended now with another inarticulate sound proceeding from certain larger seafowl who, their attention having been attracted by the peculiar commotion in the water resulting from the heavy sloped dive of the shotted hammock into the sea, flew screaming to the spot. So near the hull did they come, that the stridor or bony creak of their gaunt double-jointed pinions was audible. As the ship under light airs passed on, leaving the burial spot astern, they still kept circling it low down with the moving shadow of their outstretched wings and the croaked requiem of their cries.

Upon sailors as superstitious as those of the age preceding ours, men-of-war's men too who had just beheld the prodigy of repose in the form suspended in air, and now foundering in the deeps; to such mariners the action of the seafowl, though dictated by mere animal greed for prey, was big with no prosaic significance. An uncertain movement began among them, in which some encroachment was made. It was tolerated but for a moment. For suddenly the drum beat to quarters,[7] which familiar sound happening at least twice every day, had upon the present occasion a signal peremptoriness in it. True martial discipline long continued superinduces in average man a sort of impulse whose operation at the official word of command much resembles in its promptitude the effect of an instinct.

The drumbeat dissolved the multitude, distributing most of them along the batteries of the two covered gun decks. There, as wonted, the guns' crew stood by their respective cannon erect and silent. In due course the first officer, sword under arm and standing in his place on the quarter-deck, formally received the successive reports of the sworded lieutenants commanding the sections of batteries below; the last of which reports being made, the summed report he delivered with the customary salute to the commander. All this occupied time, which in the present case was the object in beating to quarters at an hour prior to the customary one. That such variance from usage was authorized by an officer like Captain Vere, a martinet as some deemed him, was evidence of the necessity for unusual action implied in what he deemed to be temporarily the mood of his men. 'With mankind,' he would say, 'forms, measured forms, are everything; and this is the import couched in the story of Orpheus with his lyre spell-binding the wild denizens of the wood.'[8] And this he once applied to the disruption of forms going on across the Channel and the consequences thereof.

At this unwonted muster at quarters, all proceeded as at the regular hour. The band on the quarter-deck played a sacred air, after which the chaplain went through the customary morning service. That done, the drum beat the retreat; and toned by music and religious rites subserving the discipline and purposes of war, the men in their wonted orderly manner dispersed to the places allotted them when not at the guns.

And now it was full day. The fleece of low-hanging vapor had vanished, licked up by the sun that late had so glorified it. And the circumambient air in the clearness of its serenity was like smooth white marble in the polished block not yet removed from the marble-dealer's yard.

28

The symmetry of form attainable in pure fiction cannot so readily be achieved in a narration essentially having less to do with fable than with fact. Truth uncompromisingly told will always have its ragged edges; hence the conclusion of such a narration is apt to be less finished than an architectural finial.

How it fared with the Handsome Sailor during the year of the Great Mutiny has been faithfully given. But though properly the story ends with his life, something in way of sequel will not be amiss. Three brief chapters will suffice.

In the general rechristening under the Directory of the craft originally

7. The signal for the sailors to return to their assigned stations.   8. When Orpheus, in Greek mythology, played his lyre and sang, wild animals were charmed, trees and stones followed him, fish left the water in which they swam, and birds flew about his head.

forming the navy of the French monarchy, the *St. Louis* line-of-battle ship was named the *Athée* (the *Atheist*). Such a name, like some other substituted ones in the Revolutionary fleet, while proclaiming the infidel audacity of the ruling power, was yet, though not so intended to be, the aptest name, if one consider it, ever given to a warship; far more so indeed than the *Devastation*, the *Erebus* (the *Hell*), and similar names bestowed upon fighting ships.

On the return passage to the English fleet from the detached cruise during which occurred the events already recorded, the *Bellipotent* fell in with the *Athée*. An engagement ensued, during which Captain Vere, in the act of putting his ship alongside the enemy with a view of throwing his boarders across her bulwarks, was hit by a musket ball from a porthole of the enemy's main cabin. More than disabled, he dropped to the deck and was carried below to the same cockpit where some of his men already lay. The senior lieutenant took command. Under him the enemy was finally captured, and though much crippled was by rare good fortune successfully taken into Gibraltar, an English port not very distant from the scene of the fight. There, Captain Vere with the rest of the wounded was put ashore. He lingered for some days, but the end came. Unhappily he was cut off too early for the Nile and Trafalgar. The spirit that 'spite its philosophic austerity may yet have indulged in the most secret of all passions, ambition, never attained to the fulness of fame.

Not long before death, while lying under the influence of that magical drug[9] which, soothing the physical frame, mysteriously operates on the subtler element in man, he was heard to murmur words inexplicable to his attendant: 'Billy Budd, Billy Budd.' That these were not the accents of remorse would seem clear from what the attendant said to the *Bellipotent*'s senior officer of marines, who, as the most reluctant to condemn of the members of the drumhead court, too well knew, though here he kept the knowledge to himself, who Billy Budd was.

29

Some few weeks after the execution, among other matters under the head of 'News from the Mediterranean,' there appeared in a naval chronicle of the time, an authorized weekly publication, an account of the affair. It was doubtless for the most part written in good faith, though the medium, partly rumor, through which the facts must have reached the writer served to deflect and in part falsify them. The account was as follows:

'On the tenth of the last month a deplorable occurrence took place on board H.M.S. *Bellipotent*. John Claggart, the ship's master-at-arms, discovering that some sort of plot was incipient among an inferior section of the ship's company, and that the ringleader was one William Budd; he, Claggart, in the act of arraigning the man before the captain, was vindictively stabbed to the heart by the suddenly drawn sheath knife of Budd.

'The deed and the implement employed sufficiently suggest that though mustered into the service under an English name the assassin was no Englishman, but one of those aliens adopting English cognomens whom

9. Opium.

the present extraordinary necessities of the service have caused to be admitted into it in considerable number.

'The enormity of the crime and the extreme depravity of the criminal appear the greater in view of the character of the victim, a middle-aged man respectable and discreet, belonging to that minor official grade, the petty officers, upon whom, as none know better than the commissioned gentlemen, the efficiency of His Majesty's navy so largely depends. His function was a responsible one, at once onerous and thankless; and his fidelity in it the greater because of his strong patriotic impulse. In this instance as in so many other instances in these days, the character of this unfortunate man signally refutes, if refutation were needed, that peevish saying attributed to the late Dr Johnson, that patriotism is the last refuge of a scoundrel.[1]

'The criminal paid the penalty of his crime. The promptitude of the punishment has proved salutary. Nothing amiss is now apprehended aboard H.M.S. *Bellipotent*.'

The above, appearing in a publication now long ago superannuated and forgotten, is all that hitherto has stood in human record to attest what manner of men respectively were John Claggart and Billy Budd.

30

Everything is for a term venerated in navies. Any tangible object associated with some striking incident of the service is converted into a monument. The spar from which the foretopman was suspended was for some few years kept trace of by the bluejackets. Their knowledges followed it from ship to dockyard and again from dockyard to ship, still pursuing it even when at last reduced to a mere dockyard boom. To them a chip of it was as a piece of the Cross. Ignorant though they were of the secret facts of the tragedy, and not thinking but that the penalty was somehow unavoidably inflicted from the naval point of view, for all that, they instinctively felt that Billy was a sort of man as incapable of mutiny as of wilful murder. They recalled the fresh young image of the Handsome Sailor, that face never deformed by a sneer or subtler vile freak of the heart within. This impression of him was doubtless deepened by the fact that he was gone, and in a measure mysteriously gone. On the gun decks of the *Bellipotent* the general estimate of his nature and its unconscious simplicity eventually found rude utterance from another foretopman, one of his own watch, gifted, as some sailors are, with an artless *poetic* temperament. The tarry hand made some lines which, after circulating among the shipboard crews for a while, finally got rudely printed at Portsmouth as a ballad. The title given to it was the sailor's.

Billy in the Darbies[2]

> Good of the chaplain to enter Lone Bay
> And down on his marrowbones here and pray
> For the likes just o' me, Billy Budd. —But, look:

1. The saying is quoted in James Boswell's *Life of Samuel Johnson, Ll. D.* (1791).   2. Handcuffs or fetters.

Through the port comes the moonshine astray!
It tips the guard's cutlass and silvers this nook;   5
But 'twill die in the dawning of Billy's last day.
A jewel-block[3] they'll make of me tomorrow,
Pendant pearl from the yardarm-end
Like the eardrop I gave to Bristol Molly—
O, 'tis me, not the sentence they'll suspend.   10
Ay, ay, all is up; and I must up too,
Early in the morning, aloft from alow.
On an empty stomach now never it would do.
They'll give me a nibble—bit o' biscuit ere I go.
Sure, a messmate will reach me the last parting cup;   15
But, turning heads away from the hoist and the belay,
Heaven knows who will have the running of me up!
No pipe to those halyards.—But aren't it all sham?
A blur's in my eyes; it is dreaming that I am.
A hatchet to my hawser? All adrift to go?   20
The drum roll to grog, and Billy never know?
But Donald he has promised to stand by the plank;
So I'll shake a friendly hand ere I sink.
But—no! It is dead then I'll be, come to think.
I remember Taff the Welshman when he sank.   25
And his cheek it was like the budding pink.
But me they'll lash in hammock, drop me deep.
Fathoms down, fathoms down, how I'll dream fast asleep.
I feel it stealing now. Sentry, are you there?
Just ease these darbies at the wrist,   30
And roll me over fair!
I am sleepy, and the oozy weeds about me twist.

3. Carries a studding-sail to the very end of the yard where it is hoisted.

EMILY DICKINSON
1830–1886

Emily Dickinson forces her readers to acknowledge the startling aspects of ordinary life. "Ordinary life" includes the mysterious actuality of death, but it also includes birds and woods and oceans, arguments between people, the weight of depression. In small facts and large, Dickinson perceives enormous meaning.

The poet's life, like her verse, was somewhat mysterious. Born to a prosperous and prominent Amherst, Massachusetts, family (her father, a lawyer, was also treasurer of Amherst College), Dickinson attended Amherst Academy and later, for a year, the Mount Holyoke Female Seminary. Thereafter, however, she remained almost entirely in her father's house, leading the life of a recluse. She had close family attachments and a few close friendships, pursued mainly through correspondence. The most important of these relationships, from a literary point of view, was with the Boston writer and critic Thomas Wentworth Higginson, who eventually published her poems. She had begun writing verse in the late 1850s; in 1862, after seeing an essay of Higginson's in the *Atlantic Monthly*, Dickinson wrote him to ask his opinion of her poems, about 300 of them in existence by this time. The correspondence thus begun continued to the end of Dickinson's life; Higginson also visited her in Amherst.

At Dickinson's death, 1,775 poems survived; only 7 had been published, anonymously. With the help of another friend, Mabel Todd Loomis, Higginson selected poems for a volume, published in 1890, which proved extremely popular. Further selections continued to appear, but not until 1955 did Dickinson's entire body of work reach print.

By 1843, the English poet Elizabeth Barrett Browning had written in verse an exhortation to social reform (*The Cry of the Children*); in 1857, she published a long poem, *Aurora Leigh*, commenting on the oppressed situation of women. Christina Rossetti, born the same year as Dickinson and like her unmarried, in poems like *Goblin Market* (1862) found indirect ways to meditate on female predicaments. Dickinson, on the other hand, seems only peripherally aware of social facts. She alludes to church services, locomotives, female costume; very occasionally (for example, "My Life had stood—a Loaded Gun—") she refers to the way a woman's life is defined in relation to a man's. More centrally, she finds brilliant and provocative formulations of the emotional import of universal phenomena. We may feel already that death amounts to an incomprehensible and indigestible fact, but we are unlikely to have imagined conversations within a tomb or a personified version of death as carriage driver. By using such images, Dickinson disarmingly suggests a kind of playful innocence. Only gradually does one realize that the naive, childlike perception, devoid of obviously ominous suggestion, conceals a complex, disturbing sense of human self-deception and reluctance to face the truth of experience.

Truth is an important word in Dickinson's poetry. "Tell all the Truth but tell it slant," she advises, pointing out that "The Truth must dazzle gradually / Or every man be blind—." She tells of a man who preaches about " 'Truth' until it proclaimed him a Liar—": truth remains an absolute, both challenging and judging us all. In one of her most haunting poems, she claims the identity of Beauty and Truth (an identity tellingly asserted earlier in Keats's *Ode on a Grecian Urn*) through the fiction of two dead people discussing their profound commitments:

> I died for Beauty—but was scarce
> Adjusted in the Tomb
> When One who died for Truth, was lain
> In an adjoining Room—

Her neighbor asks her why she "failed"; when she explains, he says that beauty and truth "are One":

> And so, as Kinsmen, met a Night—
> We talked between the Rooms—
> Until the Moss had reached our lips—
> And covered up—our names—

Until the last two lines, about the moss, the poem appears to evoke a rather cozy vision of death: neighbors amiably conversing from one room to another, as though at a slumber party ("met a Night"), two "Kinsmen" dedicated to noble abstractions and comforted by the companionship of their dedication. Only the word *failed* (meaning "died") disturbs the comfortable atmosphere, by suggesting a view of death as defeat.

The Keats poem that ends by asserting the identity of truth and beauty implies the permanence of both, as embodied in the work of art, the Grecian urn that stimulates the poet's reflections. Dickinson's poem concludes with troubling suggestions of impermanence. Talk of beauty and truth may reassure the talkers, but death necessarily implies forgetfulness: the dead forget and are forgotten, their very identities ("names") lost, their capacity for communication eliminated. Death *is* defeat; the high Romanticism of Keats's ode, on which this poem implicitly comments, blurs that fact. Despite Dickinson's fanciful images and allegories, her poems insist on their own kind of uncompromising realism. They speak of the universal human effort to imagine experience in reassuring terms, but they do not suggest that reality offers much in the way of reassurance: only brief experiences of natural beauty; and even those challenge human constructions. "I started Early—Took my dog—" a poem about visiting the sea begins; but it ends with the sea encountering "the Solid Town— / No One He seemed to know—" and withdrawing.

Dickinson's eccentric punctuation, with dashes as the chief mark of emphasis and interruption, emphasizes the movements of consciousness in her lyrics. In their early publication, the poems were typically given conventional punctuation; only in 1955 did the body of work appear as Dickinson wrote it. The highly personal mode of punctuation emphasizes the fact that this verse contains also a personal and demanding vision.

Emily Dickinson: An Interpretive Biography (1955), by T. H. Johnson, Dickinson's editor, is indispensable. Useful critical sources include C. Blake, ed., *The Recognition of Emily Dickinson* (1964), a collection of criticism since 1890; Albert Gelpi, *Emily Dickinson: The Mind of the Poet* (1966); S. Juhasz, ed., *Feminist Critics Read Emily Dickinson* (1983), a collection with a specifically feminist orientation; and J. Dobson, *Dickinson and the Strategies of Reticence* (1989). Other critical studies are K. Stocks, *Emily Dickinson and the Modern Consciousness* (1988), and M. N. Smith, *Rowing in Eden: Rereading Emily Dickinson* (1992).

216

Safe in their Alabaster Chambers—
Untouched by Morning
And untouched by Noon—
Sleep the meek members of the Resurrection—
Rafter of satin,   5
And Roof of stone.

Light laughs the breeze
In her Castle above them—
Babbles the Bee in a stolid Ear,
Pipe the Sweet Birds in ignorant cadence—   10
Ah, what sagacity perished here!

258

There's a certain Slant of light,
Winter Afternoons—
That oppresses, like the Heft
Of Cathedral Tunes—

Heavenly Hurt, it gives us—   5
We can find no scar,
But internal difference,

Where the Meanings, are—

None may teach it—Any—
'Tis the Seal Despair—   10
An imperial affliction
Sent us of the Air—

When it comes, the Landscape listens—
Shadows—hold their breath—
When it goes, 'tis like the Distance   15
On the look of Death—

303

The Soul selects her own Society—
Then—shuts the Door—
To her divine Majority—
Present no more—

Unmoved—she notes the Chariots—pausing   5
At her low Gate—
Unmoved—an Emperor be kneeling
Upon her Mat—

I've known her—from an ample nation—
Choose One—   10
Then—close the Valves of her attention—
Like Stone—

328

A Bird came down the Walk—
He did not know I saw—
He bit an Angleworm in halves
And ate the fellow, raw,

And then he drank a Dew   5
From a convenient Grass—
And then hopped sidewise to the Wall
To let a Beetle pass—

He glanced with rapid eyes
That hurried all around—   10
They looked like frightened Beads, I thought—
He stirred his Velvet Head

Like one in danger, Cautious,
I offered him a Crumb
And he unrolled his feathers   15
And rowed him softer home—

Than Oars divide the Ocean,
Too silver for a seam—
Or Butterflies, off Banks of Noon
Leap, plashless as they swim.   20

341

After great pain, a formal feeling comes—
The Nerves sit ceremonious, like Tombs—
The stiff Heart questions was it He, that bore,
And Yesterday, or Centuries before?

The Feet, mechanical, go round—   5
Of Ground, or Air, or Ought[1]—
A Wooden way
Regardless grown,
A Quartz contentment, like a stone—

This is the Hour of Lead—   10
Remembered, if outlived,
As Freezing persons, recollect the Snow—
First—Chill—then Stupor—then the letting go—

435

Much Madness is divinest Sense—
To a discerning Eye—
Much Sense—the starkest Madness—
'Tis the Majority
In this, as All, prevail—   5
Assent—and you are sane—
Demur—you're straightway dangerous—
And handled with a Chain—

449

I died for Beauty—but was scarce
Adjusted in the Tomb
When One who died for Truth, was lain
In an adjoining Room—

He questioned softly "Why I failed"?   5
"For Beauty", I replied—
"And I—for Truth—Themself are One—
We Brethren, are", He said—

And so, as Kinsmen, met a Night—
We talked between the Rooms—   10
Until the Moss had reached our lips—
And covered up—our names—

465

I heard a Fly buzz—when I died—
The Stillness in the Room

1. Zero

Was like the Stillness in the Air—
Between the Heaves of Storm—

The Eyes around—had wrung them dry—   5
And Breaths were gathering firm
For that last Onset—when the King
Be witnessed—in the Room—

I willed my Keepsakes—Signed away
What portion of me be   10
Assignable—and then it was
There interposed a Fly—

With Blue—uncertain stumbling Buzz—
Between the light—and me—
And then the Windows failed—and then   15
I could not see to see—

519

'Twas warm—at first—like Us—
Until there crept upon
A Chill—like frost upon a Glass—
Till all the scene—be gone.

The Forehead copied Stone—   5
The Fingers grew too cold
To ache—and like a Skater's Brook—
The busy eyes—congealed—

It straightened—that was all—
It crowded Cold to Cold   10
It multiplied indifference—
As[1] Pride were all it could—

And even when with Cords—
'Twas lowered, like a Weight—
It made no Signal, nor demurred,   15
But dropped like Adamant.

585

I like to see it lap the Miles—
And lick the Valleys up—
And stop to feed itself at Tanks—
And then—prodigious step

Around a Pile of Mountains—   5
And supercilious peer
In Shanties—by the sides of Roads—
And then a Quarry pare

To fit its Ribs
And crawl between   10

1. As if.

Complaining all the while
In horrid—hooting stanza—
Then chase itself down Hill—

And neigh like Boanerges[1]—
Then—punctual as a Star   15
Stop—docile and omnipotent
At its own stable door—

632

The Brain—is wider than the Sky—
For—put them side by side—
The one the other will contain
With ease—and You—beside—

The Brain is deeper than the sea—   5
For—hold them—Blue to Blue—
The one the other will absorb—
As Sponges—Buckets—do—

The Brain is just the weight of God—
For—Heft them—Pound for Pound—   10
And they will differ—if they do—
As Syllable from Sound—

657

I dwell in Possibility—
A fairer House than Prose—
More numerous of Windows—
Superior—for Doors—

Of Chambers as the Cedars—   5
Impregnable of Eye—
And for an Everlasting Roof
The Gambrels[2] of the Sky—

Of Visitors—the fairest—
For Occupation—This—   10
The spreading wide my narrow Hands
To gather Paradise—

712

Because I could not stop for Death—
He kindly stopped for me—
The Carriage held but just Ourselves—
And Immortality.

---

1. "Sons of thunder," name given by Jesus to the brothers and disciples James and John, presumably because they were thunderous preachers.   2. Slopes, as in the large, arched roofs often seen on barns.

We slowly drove—He knew no haste   5
And I had put away
My labor and my leisure too,
For His Civility—

We passed the School, where Children strove
At Recess—in the Ring—   10
We passed the Fields of Gazing Grain—
We passed the Setting Sun—

Or rather—He passed Us—
The Dews drew quivering and chill—
For only Gossamer, my Gown—   15
My Tippet—only Tulle[1]—

We paused before a House that seemed
A Swelling of the Ground—
The Roof was scarcely visible—
The Cornice—in the Ground—   20

Since then—'tis Centuries—and yet
Feels shorter than the Day
I first surmised the Horses' Heads
Were toward Eternity—

754

My Life had stood—a Loaded Gun—
In Corners—till a Day
The Owner passed—identified—
And carried Me away—

And now We roam in Sovereign Woods—   5
And now We hunt the Doe—
And every time I speak for Him—
The Mountains straight reply—

And do I smile, such cordial light
Upon the Valley glow—   10
It is as a Vesuvian face[2]
Had let its pleasure through—

And when at Night—Our good Day done—
I guard My Master's Head—
'Tis better than the Eider-Duck's   15
Deep Pillow—to have shared—

To foe of His—I'm deadly foe—
None stir the second time—
On whom I lay a Yellow Eye—
Or an emphatic Thumb—   20

Though I than He—may longer live
He longer must—than I—

1. Fine, silken netting. *Tippet:* a scarf.   2. A face glowing with light like that from an erupting volcano.

For I have but the power to kill,
Without—the power to die—

1084

At Half past Three, a single Bird
Unto a silent Sky
Propounded but a single term
Of cautious melody.

At Half past Four, Experiment   5
Had subjugated test
And lo, Her silver Principle
Supplanted all the rest.

At Half past Seven, Element
Nor Implement, be seen—   10
And Place was where the Presence was
Circumference between.

1129

Tell all the Truth but tell it slant—
Success in Circuit lies
Too bright for our infirm Delight
The Truth's superb surprise

As Lightning to the Children eased   5
With explanation kind
The Truth must dazzle gradually
Or every man be blind—

1207

He preached upon "Breadth" till it argued him narrow—
The Broad are too broad to define
And of "Truth" until it proclaimed him a Liar—
The Truth never flaunted a Sign—

Simplicity fled from his counterfeit presence   5
As Gold the Pyrites[1] would shun—
What confusion would cover the innocent Jesus
To meet so enabled[2] a Man!

---

1. Iron bisulphide, sometimes called fool's gold.   2. Competent.

1564

Pass to thy Rendezvous of Light,
Pangless except for us—
Who slowly ford the Mystery
Which thou hast leaped across!

1593

There came a Wind like a Bugle—
It quivered through the Grass
And a Green Chill upon the Heat
So ominous did pass
We barred the Windows and the Doors   5
As from an Emerald Ghost—
The Doom's electric Moccasin[1]
That very instant passed—
On a strange Mob of panting Trees
And Fences fled away   10
And Rivers where the Houses ran
Those looked that lived—that Day—
The Bell within the steeple wild
The flying tidings told—
How much can come   15
And much can go,
And yet abide the World!

1. That is, water moccasin, a poisonous snake.

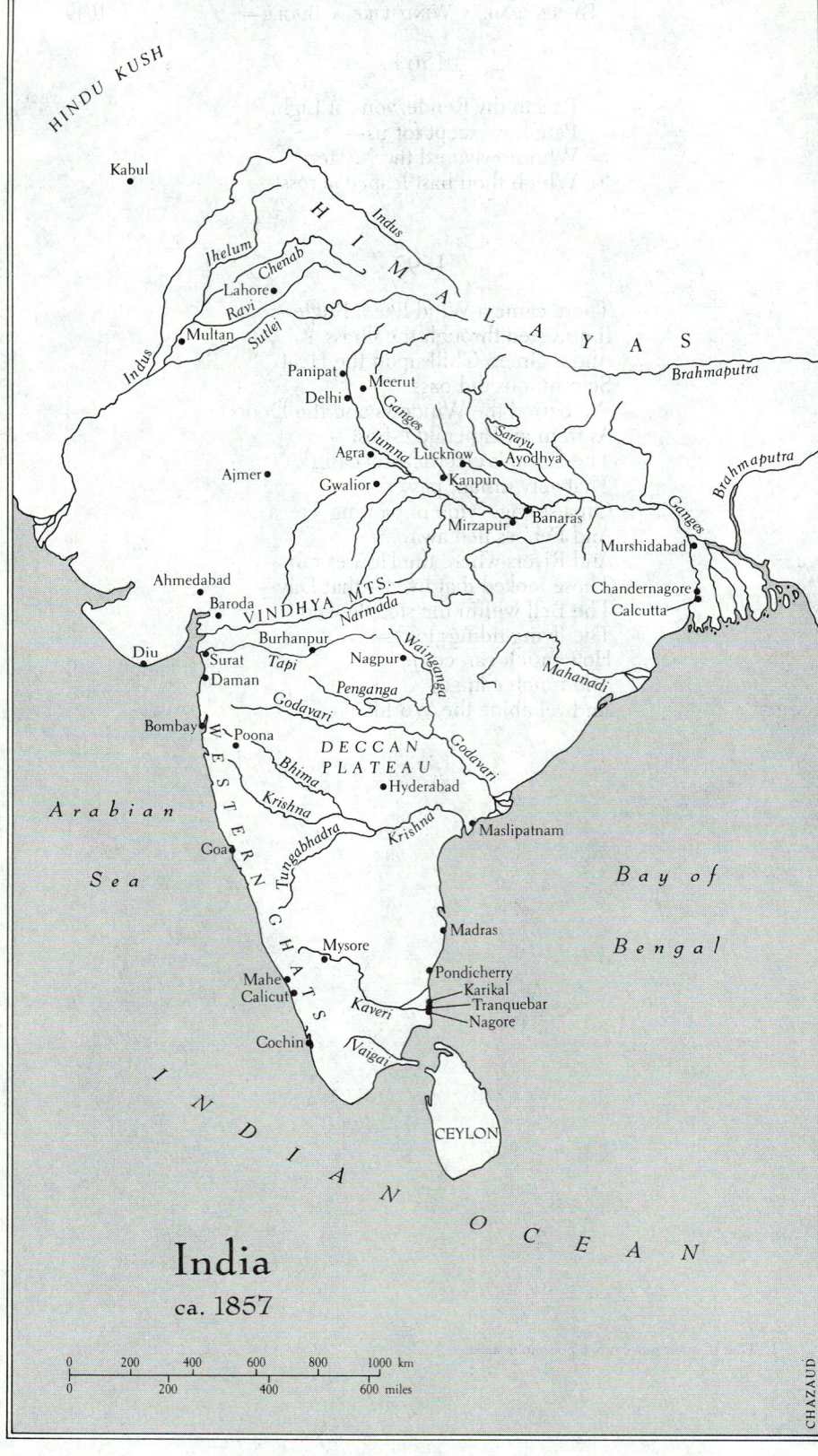

HINDU KUSH

Kabul

HIMALAYAS

Indus

Jhelum

Chenab

Lahore

Ravi

Multan

Sutlej

Indus

Brahmaputra

Panipat

Delhi

Meerut

Ganges

Jumna

Lucknow

Sarayu

Ayodhya

Agra

Ajmer

Gwalior

Kanpur

Mirzapur

Banaras

Ganges

Brahmaputra

Murshidabad

Chandernagore

Calcutta

Ahmedabad

Baroda

VINDHYA MTS.

Narmada

Burhanpur

Diu

Surat

Daman

Tapi

Nagpur

Wainganga

Mahanadi

Pengang

Godavari

Bombay

Poona

DECCAN
PLATEAU

Godavari

Bhima

Krishna

Hyderabad

Arabian

Krishna

Goa

Tungabhadra

Maslipatnam

Sea

Bay of

Bengal

Mysore

Madras

Mahe

Calicut

Pondicherry

Karikal

Tranquebar

Nagore

Kaveri

Cochin

Vaigai

INDIAN

CEYLON

OCEAN

India

ca. 1857

| 0 | 200 | 400 | 600 | 800 | 1000 km |
| 0 | | 200 | | 400 | 600 miles |

CHAZAUD

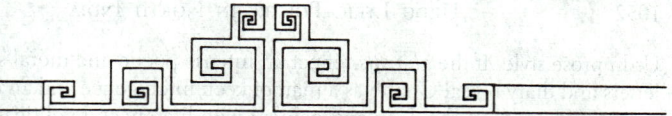

Urdu Lyric Poetry in North India

GHALIB
1797–1869

Mirza Asadullah Khan, known by his pen name Ghalib ("Conqueror"), is the preeminent poet of Urdu, a north Indian language that evolved out of the interaction between dialects of Hindi and Persian, the language used by the Muslim dynasties who ruled various parts of India from the eleventh century onward. Ghalib's fame rests on his outstanding achievement in the *ghazal*, the most important form of Urdu poetry. Born in the north Indian city of Agra to an aristocratic Muslim family of Turkish origin, the poet was educated in Agra and in Delhi. In 1812 he settled permanently in Delhi, devoting his time to writing poetry, mainly in Persian, the principal language of literature and administration in the age of the Moghals, Muslim rulers who commanded an extensive Indian empire from the mid-sixteenth century onward. By Ghalib's time, although Delhi continued to be the seat of the Moghals, the Moghal king was subservient to the British East India Company, who ruled India on behalf of the British Crown.

Financial support was a major problem for Ghalib throughout his life. After the death of his uncle, who was also his guardian, the poet spent many years negotiating with the British colonial government for his share of the uncle's military pension. It was not until 1847 that he secured a major patron. In that year Bahadur Shah, the last Moghal "emperor," accepted Ghalib at his court. Three years later, the king commissioned from the poet a Persian prose history of the Moghals, tracing their lineage back to the central Asian conqueror Timur. In 1855, a year after the death of his rival, the court poet Zauq (also a pen name, a tradition in Persian and Urdu poetry), Ghalib was appointed as Bahadur Shah's tutor in versification.

Ghalib's good fortune was short lived. When Indian princes and soldiers (*sepoys*) rose in revolt against the British regime in 1857, Delhi was besieged and looted. The British suppressed the revolt, and Bahadur Shah was deposed and exiled to Burma. Earlier events, such as the Persian king Nadir Shah's sack of Delhi in 1739, had forced poets and artists to flee from the capital city and had led to the rise of Lucknow, the capital of the north Indian state of Oudh, as a major center for Urdu literature. The chaos that surrounded the Revolt of 1857 resulted in a new exodus of poets and artists from Delhi to lesser provincial towns. Ghalib, however, remained in Delhi until his death in 1869. In addition to Persian poetry the poet left a sizable collection *(divan)* of *ghazals*, two volumes of letters, and a diary in Urdu, the spoken tongue that was progressively gaining popularity as a literary language in the north Indian courts. While the Urdu *ghazal* lyrics are unquestionably Ghalib's masterpieces, his letters and *Dastamboh* (Bouquet of flowers), the diary he wrote during the revolt of 1857, are exemplars of elegant

Urdu prose style. If the *ghazals* reflect an intense poetic and moral sensibility, the letters and diary reveal Ghalib as a man of keen intelligence and an observant eye, a sense of humor, and a deep engagement with literary and political issues.

Ghalib's bilingualism is representative of north Indian culture in the eighteenth and nineteenth centuries. While modern Hindi and Urdu are variants of a single language, literary Urdu, primarily associated with Muslim culture, is written in the Persian script and is rich in Persian vocabulary. The poets of the late Moghal age, who felt an increasing need to express Indian sensibilities and experiences in an Indian idiom, turned more and more to Urdu, and by the eighteenth century the *ghazal*, an import from Persian poetry, emerged as a mature and productive form in Urdu. Indeed, in the hands of Mir (died 1781) and other celebrated Indian poets the *ghazal* form acquired a quintessentially Indian flavor. But there is universal agreement among Urdu readers and critics that Ghalib perfected the art of the Urdu *ghazal*.

The *ghazal* is a lyric poem made up of anywhere between three and seven couplets *(she'r)*, each focusing on a separate thought, image, or mood but connected by a common meter and a rhyme scheme in the pattern *aa, ba, ca, da*, and so on. The *qāfiyah*, the compulsory rhyming element in the *ghazal*, is a syllable or sequence of sounds that appears in both lines of the first couplet and the second line of the following ones. The *qāfiyah* may optionally be followed by a refrain *(radīf)*, a word or phrase repeated without change at the end of the couplet. The final couplet usually contains the *takhallus*, the poet's pen name or signature. The concentration of images, the highly condensed form of expression, and the juxtaposition of brief sentences and phrases in each couplet require the reader or listener to respond to the couplet as a self-contained unit. However, while each of the *she'rs* in a *ghazal* may be enjoyed by itself, the appreciation of the *ghazal* as a whole involves the cumulative effect of several couplets linked by verbal and emotional associations as well as by the litany-like repeated elements.

The typical *ghazal* is a poem of reflections on love in all its aspects. Originally a part of the Arabic praise-poem genre known as *qasīdah*, in its independent form the *ghazal* became the favored vehicle for Persian and Indian mystical poets writing about the soul's yearning for God as well as for secular poets whose theme was human love. Ideally, however, secular and sacred concerns merge in the *ghazal's* philosophical tenor and its deliberately ambiguous vocabulary and imagery. Important among these built-in ambiguities is the use of masculine grammatical forms for the beloved person. Although the convention has its origins in the context of homosexual love, the Urdu poets use it to suggest both an idealized Beloved, usually a woman, and God Himself. Thus the *ghazal* is not a poem about a specific love affair, or even about a particular mood of love, but a lyrical contemplation of love as a metaphor for the relations that exist between human beings, God, and the world. Vast as these themes are, however, it is the individual poet's unique imagination that unifies and reveals these relations and is thus central to conception of the *ghazal*. Equally important is the *ghazal* repertoire of conventions and images from Persian and Arabic poetry—the garden, the fellowship of men drinking wine, the lover in the desert, the nightingale, and the rose—each capable of evoking a web of associations, all contributing to the *ghazal's* pervasive mood of sadness and unfulfilled love.

A poetry of introspection and reflection, the *ghazal* is at the same time a public, performative genre, traditionally cultivated in great "poets' gatherings" *(mus-hā'irah)*, at which poets meet to recite their poems and to compose couplets extemporaneously before enthusiastic audiences. The Urdu *ghazal* is an essential element of south Asian culture, and in the twentieth century *ghazal* recitation continues to be the focal point of gatherings of intellectuals in India, Pakistan, and Bangladesh. It is also an important model for songs in the popular Hindi cinema.

Although other Urdu *ghazal* poets—such as Mir, Sauda, and Momin (the latter two were Ghalib's contemporaries)—are celebrated for particular effects, Ghalib's couplets have become an integral part of the consciousness of Urdu speakers, who will quote them freely in the course of everyday conversation to illustrate a point or express a mood. Among the Urdu poets Ghalib achieves to perfection the *ghazal* poet's goal of balancing subjectivity with a universalizing philosophical vision. Like other forms of classical Indian and Persian poetry, the *ghazal* is a highly conventional genre. In his poems Ghalib molds the very conventions of the *ghazal* into a personal, even private, poetic language that perfectly expresses his sensibility. In the couplet "Because of you the goblet had a thousand faces; / Because of me it was mirrored in a single eye" (Ghazal XIX) the stock images of the wine goblet and mirror fuse to place the relationship between subject and object in an entirely new light. In "The dove is a clutch of ashes, nightingale a clench of color" (Ghazal XXI) the blurring of sense-experience images the intensity of feeling. Other couplets reveal the reflective, personal aspect of the *ghazal*: "Fire doesn't do it; lust for fire does it. / The heart hurts for the spirit's fading" (Ghazal XXI). The range of style and interpretation represented in the translations given here, authored by several eminent American poets, testifies to the combination of complex, brilliant images and ambiguities of language that renders Ghalib's couplets at once direct and elusive, precise and enigmatic, in much the same manner as the poems of the German poet Rilke.

Ghalib's poems are startlingly intense. Here, more than in the verse of any other Urdu poet, the *ghazal's* characteristic melancholy deepens into a profound loneliness, an overwhelming sense of loss. Some have seen in these traits a reflection of the uncertain age in which Ghalib lived, when Indian rulers were being ousted by British colonial agencies and English was beginning to take the place of Persian and Urdu language and literature among the Indian elites. The poet survived the revolt of 1857, a cataclysmic event that effectively ended Indian political power on the subcontinent. His letters and diary reveal a life constantly troubled by financial instability as well as by the decay of civilization as he knew it. Yet the voice that speaks to us most compellingly in Ghalib's *ghazals* is the private, personal one, testifying to the poet's visceral response to the enduring pain of the human condition, a darkness far more unsettling than "this time's great shadow."

A NOTE ON THE METERS OF GHALIB'S *GHAZALS*

The *ghazal* poets use a number of Persian quantitative meters. Stress patterns may vary from line to line, but the lines must be of equal length. Here is the first couplet of Ghazal XIX, in a meter with thirteen syllables per line:

> har kadam duri-e-manzil   numayan mujh se
> $=-=$ $==-$ $==$ $-==$ $=$ $=$
> With every step, my goal seems farther away from me.

> meri raftar se bhage hai   biyaban mujh se
> $=-$ $==$ $=$ $==$ $=$ $-==$ $=$ $=$
> As fast as I run, the desert runs away from me.

The $-$ and $=$ represent short and long syllables, respectively; *an* in numay*an* and biyab*an* is the rhyme (*qāfiyah*), and the fixed phrase *mujh se*, which is repeated at the end of each of the couplets that follow, is the end refrain or end rhyme (*radīf*).

FURTHER READING

Aijaz Ahmad, *Ghazals of Ghalib* (1971), presents a selection of Ghalib's *ghazals*, each one translated by several eminent American poets, among whom are Adrienne Rich and W. S. Merwin. The texts of the poems are given in Urdu script, and the poets' translations are preceded by a literal translation of each *ghazal* with explanatory notes by the editor. Ralph Russell and Khurshidul Islam, *Ghalib: Life and Letters* (1969), provide an excellent account of Ghalib's life and a translation of his letters. For further discussion of the Urdu *ghazal* and selections from the major poets, see Ralph Russell and Khurshidul Islam, *Three Mughal Poets* (1968), and Ahmed Ali, *The Golden Tradition: An Anthology of Urdu Poetry* (1973).

PRONOUNCING GLOSSARY

The following list uses common English syllables and stress accents to provide rough equivalents of selected words whose pronunciation may be unfamiliar to the general reader.

Ghalib: *ghah'-leeb*

ghazal: *ghuh-zuhl'*

Mirza Asadulla Khan: *meer-zah' uh-suhd-ool'-lah khahn*

musha'irah: *moos-shai'-rah*

qāfiyah: *quah'-fee-yah*

qasīdah: *quh-seeh'-dah*

radīf: *ruh-deehf'*

she'r: *shayr*

takhallus: *tuhk-huhl'-loos*

Urdu: *oor'-dooh*

TIMELINE

TEXTS	CONTEXTS
	1816 A group of Bengali and English men found the Hindu College in Calcutta "for the education of native youths in European literature and science"
	1817 James Mill writes a *History of India*, justifying British rule in India
ca. 1820–1865 Mirza Asadulla Khan Ghalib, preeminent poet in the Urdu language, writes ***ghazal* lyric poems** expressing the aesthetic of Islamic culture in India	
	1828 Bengali reformer Ram Mohun Roy founds the Brahmo Samaj, an organization dedicated to Hindu religious and social reform
	1835 British politician Thomas Macaulay publishes his *Minute on Education on India*, arguing for English education for Indians
ca. 1837–1841 Henry David Thoreau reads and is influenced by the *Bhaga-vad-Gītā*	
ca. 1855 Walt Whitman's *Passage to India* is published in *Leaves of Grass*	
1861 Michael Madhusudan Datta, Indian Christian convert in Calcutta, publishes *Meghanadvadh*, a Bengali version of the *Rāmāyana* epic in blank verse, modeled after Homer and Milton	
1882 Bankim Chandra Chatterjee writes the novel *Ananda Math*, an allegory of resistance to colonial rule	**1885** A group of Indian and English intellectuals found the Indian National Congress, an organization devoted to Indian representation in the British colonial government of India
1894 Rudyard Kipling publishes *The Jungle Book*	

V[1]

Waterbead ecstasy: dying in a stream;
Too strong a pain brings its own balm.

So weak now we weep sighs only;
Learn surely how water turns to air.

Spring cloud thinning after rain: 5
Dying into its own weeping.

Would you riddle the miracle of the wind's shaping?
Watch how a mirror greens in spring.[2]

Rose, Ghalib, the rose changes give us our joy in seeing.
All colors and kinds, what is should and be open always.[3]   10

VIII[4]

Here in the splendid court the great verses flow:
may such treasure tumble open for us always.

Night has arrived; again the stars tumble forth,
a stream rich as wealth from a temple.

Ignorant as I am, foreign to the Beauty's mystery,   5
yet I could rejoice that the fair[5] face begins to commune with me.

Why in this night do I find grief? Why the storm of remembered affliction?
Will the stars always avert their gaze? Choose others?

Exiled, how can I rejoice, forced here from home,
and even my letters torn open?   10

X[6]

Why didn't I shrink in the blaze of that face?
I flare up, apprehending the gaze that returned that vision unblinded.[7]

Out in the world they call me a disciple of fire
because the words of my grief fall like a shower of sparks.[8]

Many have fallen in love with the slim neck of the decanter;   5
seeing you walk, the wave of the wine trembles with envy.

We and the poems we make get bought and sold together;
but we knew all along for whom they were intended.

The lightning-stroke of the vision was meant for us, not for Sinai;
the wine should be poured for him who possesses the goblet.   10

---

1. Translated by Thomas Fitzsimmons.   2. The face of the mirror turns green with mildew, thus rival-
ing its metallic back, which is normally kept green with a kind of polish. In *ghazal* poetry the mirror is a
mystical image of perfect truth and clarity.   3. Ahmad's literal rendering of this couplet reads: "The
appearance of the rose has vouchsafed us the desire to witness (and enjoy), Ghalib! / Whatever the color
and condition of things, the eyes should always be open."   4. Translated by William Stafford.   5. Angelic.   6. Translated by Adrienne Rich.   7. The verse alludes to the Muslim myth of Moses in which
God revealed Himself to Moses on Mount Sinai in a dazzling flash, rendering him unconscious; the
mountain was burned to ashes.   8. Possibly a reference to the Parsis or Zoroastrians of India, who
worship fire.

XII[9]

I'm neither the loosening of song nor the close-drawn tent of music;
I'm the sound, simply, of my own breaking.[1]

You were meant to sit in the shade of your rippling hair;
I was made to look further, into a blacker tangle.[2]

All my self-possession is self-delusion;   5
what violent effort, to maintain this nonchalance!

Now that you've come, let me touch you in greeting
as the forehead of the beggar touches the ground.

No wonder you came looking for me, you
who care for the grieving, and I the sound of grief.[3]   10

XIII[4]

No more those meetings, partings, tears!
No more those days, nights, months, and years!

Who has time for love, its lore?
Delight in beauty?—now no more.

All that was from the thought of someone,   5
a grace that's taken, now long gone.

Tears now hurt more; they flow deep.
Heartsick these days, it's blood we weep.[5]

Oh, Ghalib!—weak limbs, no hope, disgust:
no balance now, even in this dust.   10

XIV[6]

Wings are like dust, weightless; the wind may steal them;
otherwise they would have neither power nor endurance.[7]

What beauty now is bringing nearer the face of heaven
So that the path bears not dust but flower visions?

At the mere thought of the flower's face, some are drunk.   5
There is nothing else in the cellar, in the wineskins.[8]

I have been shamed by my love's power to destroy.
In this house the wish to build lives alone.

Now Ghalib, these verses are idle amusements.
Clearly nothing is gained by such a performance.   10

---

9. Translated by Adrienne Rich.   1. *Gul-e-naghmā*, literally, "blossoming of song." *Tent:* or *pardah*, which can suggest web, curtain, tapestry, screen, veil, and note of music.   2. The beloved's dark curls are a stock image.   3. Ahmad's literal rendering of this couplet reads: "Now that you ask for me, it is no wonder; / I am helpless / poor / afflicted / miserable, and you who look after the afflicted."   4. Translated by William Stafford.   5. Ahmad's literal rendering of this couplet reads: "Weeping tears of blood is not so easy; / No more is strength in the heart, stability in our condition!"   6. Translated by W. S. Merwin.   7. Dust *(khāk)* is the leitmotif of this *ghazal*, appearing in the refrain phrase *khāk nahīñ*, which conveys a different meaning in each couplet.   8. Here *khāk nahīñ* means "There is nothing."

XIX[9]

With every step I took, my goal seemed farther away.
I ran my fastest, but the desert ran faster.

That lonely night fire inhabited my heart
And my shadow drifted from me in a thin cloud of smoke.

Because my feet were blistered in the desert   5
Of my madness, my wake shone like a chain of pearls.[1]

Because of you the goblet had a thousand faces;
Because of me it was mirrored in a single eye.

Fire runs from my burning eyes, Asad![2]
I light up the soil and the dead leaves in the garden.   10

XXI[3]

Dew on a flower[4]—tears, or something:
hidden spots mark the heart of a cruel woman.

The dove is a clutch of ashes, nightingale a clench of color:[5]
a cry in a scarred, burnt heart, to that, is nothing.

Fire doesn't do it; lust for fire does it.   5
The heart hurts for the spirit's fading.

To cry like Love's prisoner is forced by Love's prison:[6]
hand under a stone, pinned there, faithful.

Sun that bathes our world! Hold us all here!
This time's great shadow estranges us all.   10

---

9. Translated by Mark Strand.   1. Possibly an allusion to the Arabian legend of Majnoon, who wandered in the desert, mad with passion for his beloved Laila.   2. Ghalib's first name, which he used as a pen name until he adopted "Ghalib."   3. Translated by William Stafford.   4. The *lala*, tulip, or Indian red poppy.   5. *Qafas-e-rang*, literally, "prison of color."   6. Ahmad's literal rendering of this line reads: "To claim to be love's prisoner is itself a consequence of constraint (compulsion)."

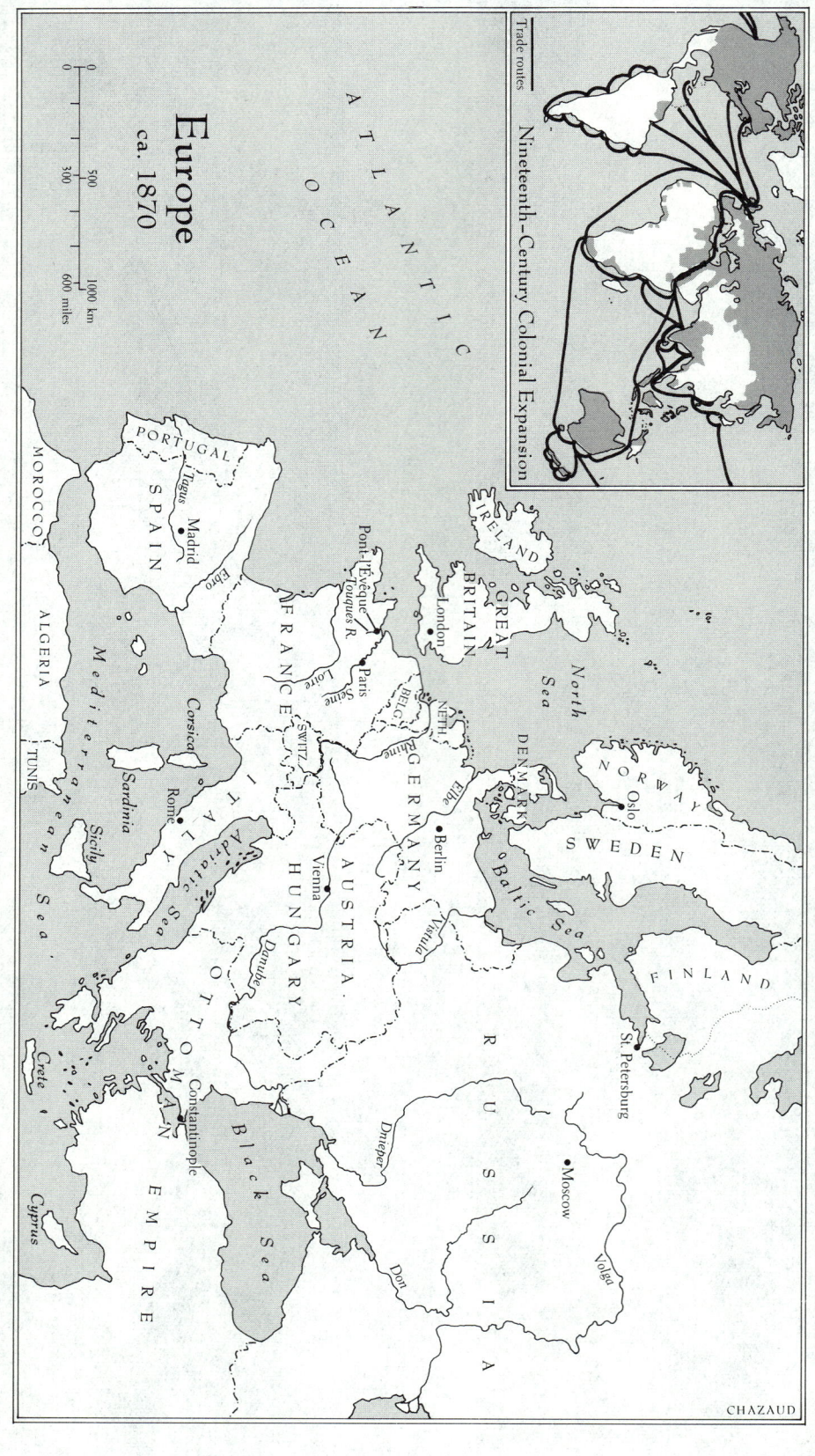

Europe
ca. 1870

0
300
500
1000 km
600 miles

ATLANTIC
OCEAN

MOROCCO

PORTUGAL

SPAIN

Madrid

Tagus

Ebro

ALGERIA

TUNIS

Mediterranean Sea

Corsica

Sardinia

Sicily

IRELAND

GREAT
BRITAIN

London

FRANCE

Pont-l'Évêque
Touques R.
Seine
Paris
Loire

SWITZ.

BELG.

NETH.

Rhine

Elbe

GERMANY

Berlin

DENMARK

North
Sea

NORWAY

Oslo

SWEDEN

Baltic Sea

FINLAND

St. Petersburg

ITALY

Rome

Adriatic Sea

HUNGARY

Vienna
Vistula

AUSTRIA

Danube

OTTOMAN

EMPIRE

Constantinople

Black
Sea

Dnieper

Don

R
U
S
S
I
A

Moscow

Volga

Crete

Cyprus

CHAZAUD

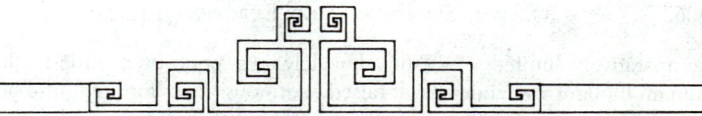

Realism, Symbolism, and European Realities

The nineteenth century is (apart from our own) the century of greatest change in the history of Western civilization. The upheavals following the French Revolution broke up the old order of Europe. The Holy Roman Empire and the Papal States were dissolved. Nationalism, nourished by the political and social aspirations of the middle classes, grew by leaps and bounds. Colonial empires were created and vast sections of the globe opened up forcibly to Western trade. "Liberty" became the dominant political slogan of the century, although the various calls for liberty focused on Western society and not on the colonies. In different countries and different decades liberty meant different things: here liberation from the rule of the foreigner, there the emancipation of the serf; here the removal of economic restrictions on trade and manufacturing, there the introduction of a constitution, free speech, parliamentary institutions, and agitation for the rights of women. Almost everywhere in Europe, the middle classes established their effective rule, though revolutions in 1830 and 1848 were crushed across Europe and monarchs remained in more or less nominal power. Two large European countries, Germany and Italy, achieved their centuries-old dreams of political unification. The predominance of France, still marked at the beginning of the century, was broken, and England—or rather Great Britain—ruled the seas throughout the century. The smaller European nations, especially in the Balkans, began to emancipate themselves from foreign rule. India, China, and Japan, in contrast, yielded in various ways to European economic and political expansion.

These major political changes were caused by, and in their turn caused, great social and economic changes. The Industrial Revolution, which had begun in England in the eighteenth century, spread over the Continent and transformed living conditions radically. The enormous increase in the speed and availability of transportation due to the development of railroads and steamships and the rapid urbanization following from the establishment of industries changed the whole pattern of human life in most countries and made possible, within a century, an unprecedented increase in population (as much as threefold in most European countries), which was also fostered by the advances of medicine and hygiene. The development of transportation and communication systems brought areas of the world into closer contact and prepared the way for global economic and political systems. The existence of widespread wealth and prosperity is undeniable, although it coexisted with wretched living conditions and other hardships of the early factory workers, many of them women. As the social and political power of the aristocracy declined, the barriers between the social classes diminished appreciably almost everywhere. Middle-class values dominated, and the industrial laborer began to be felt as a political force.

These social and economic changes were closely bound up with shifts in prevailing outlooks and philosophies. Technological innovation is impossible without the discoveries of science. The scientific outlook, hitherto dominant only in a comparatively limited area, spread widely and permeated almost all fields of human thought and endeavor. It raised enormous hopes for the future betterment of our condition on earth, especially when Darwin's evolutionary theories fortified the earlier, vaguer faith in unlimited progress. "Liberty," "science," "progress," and "evolution" are the concepts that define the mental atmosphere of the nineteenth century in Europe.

But tendencies hostile to these were by no means absent. Feudal or Catholic conservatism succeeded, especially in Austria-Hungary, in Russia, and in much of southern Europe, in preserving old regimes, and the philosophies of a conservative and religious society were reformulated in modern terms. At the same time, in England the very assumptions of the new industrial middle-class society were powerfully attacked by writers such as Carlyle and Ruskin who recommended a return to medieval forms of social cooperation and handicraft. The industrial civilization of the nineteenth century was also opposed by the fierce individualism of many artists and thinkers who were unhappy in the ugly, commercial, and "Philistine" society of the age. The writings of Nietzsche, toward the end of the century, and the whole movement of "art for art's sake," which asserted the independence of the artist from society, are the most obvious symptoms of this revolt. The free-enterprise system and the liberalism of the ruling middle classes also early clashed with the rising proletariat; diverse forms of socialism developed, preaching a new collectivism with the stress on equality. Socialism could have Christian or romantic motivations, or it could become "scientific" and revolutionary, as Marx's brand of socialism (a certain stage of which he called "communism") claimed to be.

While up through the eighteenth century religion was, at least in name, a major force in European civilization, in the nineteenth century there was a marked decrease in its influence on both intellectual leaders and ordinary people. Local, intense revivals of religious consciousness, such as the Oxford movement in England, did occur, and the traditional religious institutions were preserved everywhere, but the impact of science on religion was such that many tenets of the old faiths crumbled or were severely weakened. The discoveries of astronomy, geology, evolutionary biology, and archaeology as well as biblical criticism forced, almost everywhere, a restatement of the old creeds. Religion, especially in the Protestant countries, was frequently confined to an inner feeling of religiosity or to a system of morality that preserved the ancient Christian virtues. In Germany during the early nineteenth century, Hegel and his predecessors and followers tried to interpret the world in spiritual terms, outside the bounds of traditional religion. There were many attempts even late in the century to restate this view, but the methods and discoveries of science seemed to invalidate it, and various formulas that took science as their base in building new lay religions of hope in humanity gained popularity. French positivism, English utilitarianism, the evolutionism of Herbert Spencer are some of the best-known examples. Meanwhile, for the first time in history, at least in Europe, profoundly pessimistic and atheistic philosophies arose, of which Schopenhauer's was the most subtle, while extreme materialism was the most widespread. Thus the whole gamut of views of the universe was represented during the century in new and impressive formulations.

The plastic arts did not show a similar vitality. For a long time, in most countries, painting and architecture floundered in a sterile eclecticism — in a bewildering variety of historical masquerades in which the neo-Gothic style was replaced by the neo-Renaissance and that by the neo-Baroque and other decorative revivals of past forms. Only in France, painting (with the impressionists) found a new style that was genuinely original. In music the highly Romantic art of Richard Wagner attracted the most attention. Wagner's concept of the *Gesamtkunstwerk* — the "total work" combining music, drama, poetry, and spectacle — influenced Symbolist writers and encouraged the tendency to break down distinctions between genres.

Otherwise, the individual national schools either continued in their tradition, like Italian opera (Verdi) or founded an idiom of their own, often based on a revival of folklore, as in Russia (Tchaikovsky), Poland (Chopin), Bohemia (Dvořák), and Norway (Grieg).

But literature was the most representative and the most widely influential art of nineteenth-century Europe. It found new forms and methods and expressed the social and intellectual situation of the time most fully and memorably. It was this literature, moreover, that served as a model for many non-Western writers seeking to modernize their own literary traditions on the basis of European masterworks. Nowadays, the cultural assumptions of such literary emulation are criticized by some, and many writers seek to rediscover an earlier, precolonial tradition. The literature of nineteenth-century Europe continues nonetheless to be read and admired in its own right.

REALISM AND NATURALISM

After the great wave of the international Romantic movement had spent its force in the fourth decade of the nineteenth century, European literature moved in the direction of what is usually called *realism*. Realism was not a coherent general movement that established itself unchallenged for a long period of time, as classicism had succeeded in doing during the eighteenth century. Exceptions and reservations there were, but still in retrospect the nineteenth century appears as the period of the great realistic writers: Flaubert in France, Dostoevsky and Tolstoy in Russia, Charles Dickens in England, Henry James in America, Ibsen in Norway.

What is meant by *realism*? The term, in literary use (there is a much older philosophical use), apparently dates back to the Germans at the turn of the century—to Friedrich Schiller and August and Friedrich Schlegel. It cropped up in France as early as 1826 but became a commonly accepted literary and artistic slogan only in the 1850s. When Gustave Courbet's paintings were rejected by the Paris World's Fair of 1855, the artist exhibited them separately as "realist" art and wrote a preface to the exhibit catalog that became an unofficial manifesto for realist art. In the following year, a review called *Réalisme* began publication, and in 1857 a novelist and critic, Champfleury (the pseudonym of Jules-François-Félix Husson), published a volume of critical articles with the title *Le Réalisme*. Since then the word has been bandied about, discussed, analyzed, and abused as all slogans are. It is frequently confused with naturalism, an ancient philosophical term for materialism, epicureanism, or any secularism. As a specifically literary term, it crystallized only in France. In French, as in English, naturalist means, of course, simply student of nature, and the analogy between the writer and the naturalist, specifically the botanist and zoologist, was ready at hand. Émile Zola, in the preface to a new edition of his early novel *Thérèse Raquin* (1866), proclaimed the naturalist creed most boldly. His book, he claims, is "an analytical labor on two living bodies like that of a surgeon on corpses." He proudly counts himself among the group of "naturalist writers."

The program of the groups of writers and critics who used these terms can be easily summarized. The realists wanted a truthful representation in literature of reality—that is, of contemporary life and manners. They thought of their method as inductive, observational, and hence "objective." The personality of the author was to be suppressed or was at least to recede into the background, since reality was to be seen "as it is." The naturalistic program, as formulated by Zola, was substantially the same, except that Zola put greater stress on the analogies to science, considering the procedure of the novelist as identical with that of the experimenting scientist. He also more definitely and exclusively embraced the philosophy of scientific materialism, with its deterministic implications and its stress on heredity and environment, while the older realists were not always so clear in drawing the philosophical consequences. These French theories were anticipated, paralleled, or imitated all over the world of Western literature. In Germany, the movement called Young Germany, with which Heine was associated, had propounded a substantially anti-Romantic realistic program as early as the 1830s, but versions of the French theories definitely triumphed there only in the 1880s. In Russia, as early as the 1840s, the most prominent critic of the time, Vissarion Belinsky, praised the "natural" school of Russian fiction, which described contemporary Russia with fidelity. Italy also, from the late 1870s on, produced an analogous movement, which called itself *verismo*. The English-speaking countries were the last to adopt the critical programs and slogans of the Continent: George Moore and George Gissing brought the French theories to England in the late 1880s, and in the United States William Dean Howells began his campaign for realism in 1886, when he became editor of *Harper's Magazine*. Realistic and naturalistic theories of literature have since been widely accepted, either as the basis of literary production or as a standard against which later generations rebel. The once officially promoted doctrine in Russia is called "Socialist Realism," a combination of factual observation and implied socialist message; the novel in the United States is usually considered naturalistic and judged by the standards of nature and truth. Yet twentieth-century novelists in Europe and America have also pushed realism to an extreme in the "literature of fact," in documentary novels, and (rebelling against traditional realism's coherent arrangement of reality) in often-bewildering attempts to describe experience objectively as a series of undifferentiated perceptions given no apparent interpretation by the narrator.

The slogans "realism" and "naturalism" were thus new to the nineteenth century and served as effective formulas directed against the Romantic creed. Truth, contemporaneity, and objectivity were the obvious counterparts of Romantic imagination, of Romantic historicism and its glorification of the past, and of Romantic subjectivity, the exaltation of the ego and the individual. But, of course, the emphasis on truth and objectivity was not really new: these qualities had been demanded by many older, classical theories of imitation, and in the eighteenth century there were great writers such as Denis Diderot who wanted a literal "imitation of life" even on the stage.

The practice of realism, it could be argued, is very old indeed. There are realistic scenes in the *Iliad* and *Odyssey*, and there is plenty of realism in ancient comedy and satire, in medieval stories (fabliaux) like some of Chaucer's and Boccaccio's, in many Elizabethan plays, in the Spanish rogue novels, in the English eighteenth-century novel beginning with Daniel Defoe, and so on almost ad infinitum. But while it would be easy to find in early literature anticipations of almost every single element of modern realism, still the systematic description of contemporary society, with a serious purpose, often even with a tragic tone as well, and with sympathy for heroes drawn from the middle and lower classes, was a real innovation of the nineteenth century.

It is usually rash to explain a literary movement in social and political terms. But the new realistic art surely had something to do with the triumph of the middle classes in France after the July revolution in 1830, and in England after the passage of the Reform Bill in 1832, and with the increasing influence of the middle classes in almost every country. Russia is somewhat of an exception as no large middle class could develop there during the nineteenth century. An absolute feudal regime continued in power and the special character of most of Russian literature must be the result of this distinction, but even in Russia there emerged an "intelligentsia" (the term comes from Russia) that was open to Western ideas and was highly critical of the czarist regime and its official "ideology."

But while much nineteenth-century literature reflects the triumph of the middle classes, it would be an error to think of the great realistic writers as spokespeople or mouthpieces of the society they described. Honoré de Balzac was politically a Catholic monarchist who applauded the Bourbon restoration after the fall of Napoléon, but he had an extraordinary imaginative insight into the processes leading to the victory of the middle classes. Flaubert despised the middle-class society of the Third Empire with an intense hatred and the pride of a self-conscious artist. Dickens became increasingly critical of the middle classes and the assumptions of industrial civilization. Dostoevsky, though he took part in a conspiracy against the Russian government early in his life and spent ten years in exile in Siberia, became the propounder of an extremely conservative nationalistic and religious creed that was definitely directed against the revolutionary forces in Russia. Tolstoy, himself a count and a landowner, was violent in his criticism of the czarist regime, especially later in his life, but he cannot be described as friendly to the middle classes, to the aims of the democratic movements in Western Europe, or to the science of the time. Ibsen's political attitude was that of a proud individualist who condemns the "compact majority" and its tyranny. Possibly all art is critical of its society, but in the nineteenth century this criticism became much more explicit, as social and political issues became much more urgent or, at least, were regarded as more urgent by those writing about or within them. To a far greater degree than in earlier centuries, writers felt their isolation from society, viewed the structure and problems of the prevailing order as debatable and reformable, and in spite of all demands for objectivity became, in many cases, social propagandists and reformers in their own right.

The program of realism, while defensible enough as a reaction against Romanticism, raises critical questions that were not answered theoretically by its defenders. What is meant by "truth" of representation? Photographic copying? This seems the implication of many famous pronouncements: "A novel is a mirror walking along the road," said Stendhal (the pseudonym of Marie-Henri Beyle) as early as 1830. But such statements can hardly be taken literally. All art must select and represent; it cannot be and has never been a simple transcript of reality. What such analogies are intended to convey is rather a claim for an all-inclusiveness of subject matter, a protest against the exclusion of themes that before were considered "low," "sordid," or "trivial" (like the puddles along the road the mirror walks). Chekhov formulated this protest with the usual parallel between the scientist and the writer: "To a chemist nothing on earth is unclean. A writer must be as objective as a chemist; he must abandon the subjective line: he must know that dung heaps play a very respectable part in a landscape, and that evil passions are as inherent in life as good ones." Thus the "truth" of realistic art includes the sordid, the low, the disgusting, and the evil; and the implication is that the subject is treated objectively, without interference and falsification by the artist's personality and his own desires.

But in practice, while realistic art succeeded in expanding the themes of art, it could not fulfill the demand for total objectivity. Works of art are written by human beings and inevitably express their personalities and their points of view. As Joseph Conrad admitted, "even the most artful of writers will give himself (and his morality) away in about every third sentence." Objectivity, in the sense that Zola had in mind when he proposed a scientific method in the writing of novels and conceived of the novelist as a sociologist collecting human documents, is impossible in practice. When it has been attempted, it has led only to bad art, to dullness and the display of inert materials, to the confusion between the art of the novel and reporting, "documentation." The demand for "objectivity" can be understood only as a demand for a specific method of narration, in which the author does not interfere explicitly, in his or her own name, and as a rejection of personal themes of introspection and reverie.

The realistic program, while it has made innumerable new subjects available to art, also implies a narrowing of its themes and methods—a condemnation of the fantastic, the historical, the remote, the idealized, the "unsullied," the idyllic. Realism professes to present us with a "slice of life." But one should recognize that it is an artistic method and convention like any other. Romantic art could, without offending its readers, use coincidences, improbabilities, and even impossibilities that were not, theoretically at least, tolerated in realistic art. Ibsen, for instance, avoided many older conventions of the stage: asides, soliloquies, eavesdropping, sudden unmotivated appearances of new characters, and so on; but his dramas have their own marked conventions, which seem today almost as "unnatural" as those of the Romantics. Realistic theories of literature cannot be upheld in their literal sense; objective and impersonal truth is unobtainable, at least in art, since all art is a "making," a creating of a world of symbols that differs radically from the world that we call reality. The value of realism lies in its negation of the conventions of Romanticism, its expansion of the themes of art, and its new demonstration (never forgotten by artists) that literature has to deal also with its time and society and has, at its best, an insight into reality (not only social reality) that is not necessarily identical with that of science. Many of the great writers make us "realize" the world of their time, evoke an imaginative picture of it that seems truer and will last longer than that of historians and sociologists. But this achievement is due to their imagination and their art, or craft, two requisites that realistic theory tended to forget or minimize.

When we observe the actual practice of the great realistic writers of the nineteenth century, we notice a sharp contradiction between theory and practice, and an independent evolution of the art of the novel that is obscured for us if we pay too much attention to the theories and slogans of the time, even those that the authors themselves propounded. Flaubert, the high priest of a cult of "art for art's sake," the most consistent advocate of absolute objectivity, was actually, at least in a good half of his work, a writer of Romantic fantasies of blood and gold, flesh and jewels. There is some truth in his saying that Madame Bovary is himself, for in the drab story of a provincial adulteress he castigated his own Romanticism and Romantic dreams.

So too with Dostoevsky. Although some of his settings resemble those of the "crime novel," he is actually a writer of high tragedy, of a drama of ideas in which ordinary reality is transformed into a symbol of the spiritual world. His technique is closely associated with Balzac's (it is significant that his first publication was a translation of Balzac's *Eugénie Grandet*) and thus with many devices of the sensational melodramatic novel of French Romanticism. Tolstoy's art is more concretely real than that of any of the other great masters mentioned, yet he is, at the same time, the most personal and even literally autobiographical author in the history of the novel—a writer, besides, who knows nothing of detachment toward social and religious problems but frankly preaches his own very personal religion. And if we turn to Ibsen, we find essentially the same situation. Ibsen began as a writer of historical and fantastic dramas and slowly returned to a style that is fundamentally symbolist. All his later plays are organized by symbols, from the duck of *The Wild Duck* (1884) to the white horses in *Rosmersholm* (1886), the burned manuscript in *Hedda Gabler* (1890), and the tower in *The Master Builder* (1892). Even Zola, the propounder of the most scientific theory, was in practice a novelist who used the most extreme devices of melodrama and Symbolism. In *Germinal* (1885), his novel of mining, the mine is the central symbol, alive as an animal, heaving, breathing. It would be an odd reader who could find literal truth in the final catastrophe of the cave-in or even in such "naturalistic" scenes as a dance where the beer oozes from the nostrils of the drinkers.

One could assert, in short, that all the great realists were at bottom Romanticists, but it is probably wiser to conclude that they were simply artists who created worlds of imagination and knew (at least instinctively) that in art one can say something about reality only through symbols. The attempts at documentary art, at mere reporting and transcribing, are today forgotten.

SYMBOLISM

The later nineteenth century cannot, however, be considered simply an age of realism and naturalism. Poetry addressed in its own way the same questions of truth and reality. By the middle of the century, it was embarked on an exploration of language that would influence all forms of twentieth-century literature. Where prose fiction and drama faced outward, aiming to mirror the real world, poetry turned its attention to the mirror itself: the instrument that reflects and represents reality. Preserving the Romantic notion of the poet as seer or visionary, emphasizing a heightened self-consciousness and an inquiry into the techniques of poetic language, the innovators of nineteenth-century poetry explored both the concept of creativity and philosophic questions of human identity. They examined the perceiving subject's awareness of his or her perceptions and illustrated this awareness in allusive poetry that played with multiple and shifting perspectives and in sensuous evocations of a reality that remained ultimately beyond apprehension. Traditional verse forms exploded in the drive to find new ways of depicting experience, and the new forms heralded not only modern free verse, prose poems, and spatial poetry but also the innovative language of novelists such as James Joyce, William Faulkner, Alain Robbe-Grillet and Marguerite Duras.

The evolution was gradual until the middle of the century. Some poets continued to practice a substantially Romantic art: Tennyson, for instance, and Victor Hugo. In England, the Pre-Raphaelite movement—painters and writers such as J. E. Millais (1829–1896), W. H. Hunt (1827–1910), and D. G. Rossetti (1828–1882)—drew their inspiration from the sensuous detail of Italian medieval art in opposition to the honored Renaissance painter Raphael (1483–1520); they upheld a Romantic, escapist, and antirealist program. In France, a large and diverse group of Parnassian poets stemming from Leconte de Lisle (1818–1894) retained Romantic themes while focusing on a precise and delicate use of detail. The most important writer of this period is Charles Baudelaire (1821–1867), whose poetry and writings on art deeply influenced the course of European poetry. Baudelaire's major collection of poems, *The Flowers of Evil*, was published in the same year that Flaubert was brought to trial for *Madame Bovary* (1857). He inspired a poetic movement that would later be called Symbolism, and he remains today the French poet most widely read outside France.

Symbolism as *symbolic representation* is a philosophical concept, and the use of symbols is not restricted to the nineteenth and twentieth centuries. Using one thing to suggest another, or an image to suggest an idea, is as old as art and language. The Neolithic paintings in the caves at Lascaux, France, are symbolic pictures of the hunt. Medieval Christian literature used a shared set of symbols to signify religious concepts through earthly images: the rose symbolized love, the dove the Holy Spirit, and the serpent Satan. As a literary movement, however, Symbolism is a nineteenth-century French phenomenon with affinities to the visionary writings of eighteenth-century German Romanticism, to the Parnassian cult of artistic form and "art for art's sake," and to the poetic theories of Edgar Allan Poe. Symbolist poetry tries to manipulate language in an almost magical way to evoke hidden meanings behind the appearances of this world. A symbol in this sense is an image or cluster of images created to suggest another plane of reality that cannot be expressed in more direct and rational terms. Each poem transforms reality in its own manner, leading the reader to its own version of truth.

The aim is to touch a primitive level of being where, for example, in Baudelaire's poem *Correspondences*, the five senses fuse: colors have taste, sights have physical texture, sounds have odors, and so on. (This fusion is called *synesthesia*.) Symbolist poetry may lead to abstract or visionary conclusions, but it is firmly based in images as realistic as a rotting carcass, logs falling on the pavement, and a mangy cat trying to find a comfortable spot in rainy weather (Baudelaire's *A Carcass*, *Song of Autumn I*, and *Spleen LXXVIII*). It is not, therefore, an escape from natural reality so much as a transformation of it, the creation of a new world reassembled in the mind from pieces of the old.

After Symbolic allusion, the second great theme of Symbolist poetry is language: language as a means of communication, and language as the necessary but flawed tool of poetic creation. Like Flaubert seeking *le mot juste* (the exact word), Symbolist poets are haunted by the difficulty of writing: Baudelaire described his exhausted brain as a graveyard, and Stéphane Mallarmé felt paralyzed by "the empty paper whose whiteness defends it." The difficulty for the Symbolists is that their ideal poetic language must be distilled out of ordinary language through a totally controlled arrangement of all possible levels of form. Sound patterns, image clusters, and intertwined systems of logical and psychological associations act to create a complex architecture of inner reference. It is the relationship of words that counts, not just their dictionary definitions; the artist is, in a sense, a technician. The extraordinary self-consciousness of the Symbolist poet soon became an accepted element of the poem itself. Some poems focused on difficulties of communication (a characteristic Romantic theme); others, like Baudelaire's *Windows*, asserted joy in using language to imagine other existences and to sense, in return, their own reality. The Symbolists' acute awareness of the possibilities and limitations of language has influenced both philosophers of language and literary theorists in the twentieth century.

Symbolist writers frequently compared their poetry to music, whose characteristics they tried to reproduce; Paul Verlaine, a contemporary of Mallarmé and Rimbaud, is especially known for the musicality of his verse. Both poetry and music they felt to be "pure" arts, in which line and harmony (including calculated dissonance) meant more than separate notes or the definitions of individual words. They saw analogies, too, between their art and painting, where distinctive new methods of depicting reality were being developed in the same period. Symbolist poetry and impressionist art both represented moves away from the conventional realistic representation of reality and, in the poetic as in the art world, they both outraged the average citizen by their apparent betrayal of common sense.

Baudelaire's two most important successors were very different figures: an English teacher, Stéphane Mallarmé (1842–1898) and the adolescent prodigy Arthur Rimbaud (1854–1891). In a short and violent literary career between the ages of fifteen and twenty, Rimbaud attempted to become a seer or *voyant* through hallucinatory writing expressing the "disorder of all the senses." The visionary image sequences of his first major poem (a symbolic voyage titled *The Drunken Boat*), the agonized and mocking autobiographical prose of *A Season in Hell*, and finally the transfigured scenes from real life called *Illuminations* together represent stages in this endeavor to discover—or create—a state of natural innocence and harmony. Rimbaud's rebellion against home and authority, his experiments with drugs and alcohol, his love affair with the poet Paul Verlaine, and his search for a transfigured condition *au-delà* (beyond) all provide themes for this poetic quest. For a while, Rimbaud believed that he could manipulate language to create the vision of an ideal world: "I have strung ropes from steeple to steeple; garlands from window to window; golden chains from star to star, and I dance" (*Sentences*). His *Illuminations* offer a series of transformations that leave only traces of their varied points of departure: bridges in London, plowed fields, a park statue, dawn. They parade illusions and free association, and they cut short logical sequences to develop an almost musical organization of themes and images. Ultimately, Rimbaud became disenchanted with the efficacy of his magical or "alchemical" art, and he abruptly stopped writing. He left for Africa, where he spent the last eighteen years of his life trying to make a living. A good deal of Rimbaud's legend comes from this extraordinary example of a great poet who simply did not find what he sought in literature and, therefore, ceased to write. Rimbaud's work and the integrity of his spiritual commitment had enormous influence on later writers, especially the surrealists.

Stéphane Mallarmé, conversely, was a quiet and somewhat scholarly poet who spent his life in a search for absolute poetry *in language*. Mallarmé loved words and distrusted the sloppiness of everyday speech. (He wrote a somewhat eccentric treatise called *English Words* for the French school system.) He envisaged a special poetic language that would be built out of the precisely planned interaction of ordinary words, in poems that would "give a purer sense to the words of the crowd." Mallarmé's long poem *Dice Thrown*, with its startling arrangement of different type sizes and words scattered to create patterns on the page, heralded concrete poetry and other modern attempts to use the silence of blank space as part of poetry. Toward the end of his life, he considered everything he produced to be a fragment of an ultimate Work that he feared he would never be able to write: a massively interrelated composition of pure poetry whose function would be to assert the dignity of human imagination in the face of universal nothingness. The creative process itself is the central topic of Mallarmé's poetry, whether in the earlier autobiographical poems or in later impersonal scenes from which the narrator is excluded. Mallarmé uses Symbolist tactics, too, in preferring allusion and suggestion to direct speech, or—a specifically Mallarméan theme—potentiality and absence to a fixed and limited reality. Material objects like a bracelet, a fan, a lace curtain, or a mandolin are described so as to evoke other elements in another realm of being. A carved angel's wing gilded by the sun evokes a harp; the "harp" exists only in the imagination, however, and its implied music is doubly unreal because the source is merely suggested, not represented. This music is even more ambiguous than Keats's "melodies . . . unheard," for it is a musical *silence*. Mallarmé points rather than names; he suggests possibilities by keeping several levels of meaning alive at the same time, and he complicates his syntax and even misleads the reader to prolong the pleasure of discovery.

It is paradoxical that none of these poets—Baudelaire, Mallarmé, Rimbaud, or Verlaine—was a member of the Symbolist movement. Symbolist doctrine as such dates to a manifesto issued in 1886 by a minor poet, Jean Moréas (Joannes Papadiamantopoulous, 1856–1910). In many ways the movement is a systematization and popularization of ideas gleaned from Baudelaire, Rimbaud, Mallarmé, and Verlaine; especially influential were Verlaine's essays in 1884 describing Rimbaud, Mallarmé, and Tristan Corbière (1845–1875) as outcast or "accursed poets." A number of young poets (often called "decadents") were attracted to Symbolist ideas, and their publication and literary reviews flourished around the turn of the century. Symbolism as a movement, however, had less impact than the major poets from whom it sprang, and it was the example of these earlier poets that especially influenced writers such as W. B. Yeats, T. S. Eliot, Marcel Proust, Rainer Maria Rilke, Wallace Stevens, Rabindranath Tagore, and others around the world for whom Symbolist poetry became the model for contemporary poetry and poetics.

A NOTE ON FRENCH POETRY

English poetry receives its rhythm from the accent or stress in words, and the most common English line is iambic pentameter ("Whatever is begotten, born, and dies"). In contrast, the rhythm of French poetry is based on *quantity*—on the number and pattern of syllables in a line. The most common French line is the twelve-syllable or "alexandrine" verse, usually divided into balanced segments of six or four syllables. Baudelaire's *Correspondances* (given in French on page 1187) is a sonnet written in alexandrines that displays many of the conventions of French poetry.

Syllables are divided to reflect the sound of the line when read aloud; thus every syllable should begin with a consonant whenever possible. ("Na / tu / re . . . con / fu / ses / pa / roles.") In traditional French poetry, the unaccented or mute *e* counts as a syllable and is pronounced when it occurs before a sounded consonant (but not otherwise): thus "Com / *me* / les / prai / ries" (line 10) sound the mute *e* but "La / Na / tu / *re est* / un / tem / *ple où* /" (line 1) does not. The subtle use of the mute *e* provides rich sonorous effects that are only evident in reading aloud.

French rhymes are categorized as rich, sufficient, or weak, and also as masculine or feminine. Weak rhymes have only one accented vowel in common: prair*ies* / infin*ies* (the *ee* sound). Sufficient rhymes have two elements in common: en*fants* / triom*phants*. A rich rhyme has three or more elements in common: p*iliers* / fami*liers* (*i*, *e*, and the diphthong *ier*). A variety of rhymes is desirable. Feminine rhymes end in the sound of a mute *e*: *paroles / symboles* or *rose / chose*. All other rhymes are masculine. After the sixteenth century most poets alternated masculine and feminine rhymes. In *Correspondances*, Baudelaire uses the Petrarchan sonnet form (two quatrains, two tercets) with a rhyme scheme alternating masculine and feminine rhymes as follows: *mffm fmmf mfm fmm*. The intricacy of these and other poetic effects makes clear why later poets revered Baudelaire as a master of classical form as well as a visionary.

FURTHER READING

E. Auerbach, *Mimesis: The Representation of Reality in Western Literature* (1953), is a wide-ranging book (from Homer to Proust), with chapters on nineteenth-century realism. G. J. Becker, ed., *Documents of Modern Literary Realism* (1973), surveys the development of modern realism and offers documents and essays from 1835 to 1955. H. Levin, *The Gates of Horn: A Study of Five French Realists* (1963), contains much on realism in general, including Stendhal, Balzac, Flaubert, Zola, and Proust. Linda Nochlin, *Realism* (1971), discusses realism in the visual arts. Marcel Raymond, *From Baudelaire to Surrealism* (1933), is a fundamental study of the evolution of the new poetry. Naomi Schor, *Breaking the Chain: Women, Theory, and French Realist Fiction* (1985), discusses the realist fiction of Flaubert, Zola, Balzac, and others in terms of feminist and psychoanalytic theory. Also helpful is R. Wellek, "The Concept of Realism in Literary Scholarship," in *Concepts of Criticism* (1963). Nicholas Boyle and Martin Swales, eds., *Realism in European Literature: Essays in Honour of J. P. Stern* (1986), is a varied and useful collection that includes a discussion of realism related to modernism and language consciousness. Elise Boulding, *The Underside of History: A View of Women through Time* (1992,), arranged by periods and sociological categories, contains much pertinent information about the role of women that is omitted from traditional histories. John Rignall, *Realist Fiction and the Strolling Spectator* (1992), indebted to Nietzsche and Walter Benjamin, analyzes realism's distanced point of view in eight nineteenth-century and three twentieth-century novelists. Martin Anderson, *The Limits of Realism: Chinese Fiction in the Revolutionary Period* (1990), uses contemporary theoretical perspectives to analyze the development of Chinese realist fiction in the 1920s and 1930s as a new mode based on but different from European predecessors. Laurence M. Porter, *The Crisis of French Symbolism* (1990), offers a good discussion of Symbolist aims and practice from a contemporary theoretical perspective. An influential and still valuable presentation is found in *The Symbolist Movement in Literature* (1980, orig. 1899), by the English Symbolist Arthur Symons.

The following list uses common English syllables and stress accents to provide rough equivalents of selected words whose pronunciation may be unfamiliar to the general reader.

Balzac: *ball-zak'*

Baudelaire: *boh-d'lair'*

Champfleury: *shom-fler-ee'*

Chekhov: *chek'-off*

Chopin: *sho-panh*

Corbière: *core-bee-air'*

Courbet: *coor-bay'*

Dostoevsky: *dos-toy-eff'-skee*

Dvořák: *dvor'-zhak*

fabliaux: *fah-blee-oh'*

Gesamtkunstwerk: *ge-zamt-koonst'-varck*

Grieg: *greeg*

Mallarmé: *mall-are-may'*

Nietzsche: *neech'-uh*

Réalisme: *ray-al-eezm'*

Rimbaud: *ram-boh'*

Schlegel: *shlay'-gel*

Stendahl: *ston-dall'*

Tchaikovsky: *chai-kof'-skee*

Wagner: *vag'-ner*

Zola: *soh-lah'*

TIMELINE

TEXTS	CONTEXTS
1857 Charles Baudelaire, *The Flowers of Evil* • Gustave Flaubert, *Madame Bovary*	
	1859 Charles Darwin, *Origin of Species*
	1861 Serfs emancipated in Russia
	1861–1865 Civil War in the United States
1864 Fyodor Dostoevsky, *Notes from Underground*	
1866 Dostoevsky, *Crime and Punishment*	
1866 Emile Zola's preface to his novel *Thérèse Raquin* argues for a "naturalist" style analogous to methods in experimental science	
1869 Leo Tolstoy, *War and Peace*	1869 Suez Canal completed
	1870 Ernest Renan's *Life of Jesus* offers a historical approach to the New Testament
1871 George Eliot (Mary Ann Evans), *Middlemarch*	
	1874 Claude Monet's painting *Impression: Rising Sun* launches Impressionism as a style
	1876 Invention of the telephone
1877 Gustave Flaubert, *A Simple Heart*	
	1884–1885 Berlin Conference agrees on procedures for European acquisition of African territory; by 1914, all Africa except Ethiopia and Liberia succumbs to European rule

TIMELINE

TEXTS	CONTEXTS
1886 Arthur Rimbaud's *Illumina-tions* • Tolstoy, **The Death of Iván Ilyich**	1886 Friedrich Nietzsche's *Beyond Good and Evil* proclaims a "life force," a "will to power," and a "super-man" who embodies these qualities
	1887 Eiffel Tower built for the 1889 Paris World's Fair • Gottlieb Daim-ler's internal combustion engine for the automobile
1890 Henrik Ibsen, **Hedda Gabler** • **Poems** of Emily Dickinson (1830–1886) published posthumously	
	1894 X-rays discovered
	1894–1906 In the Dreyfus Affair, anti-Semitic sentiment polarizes France
	1898 Radium discovered by Marie and Pierre Curie • Spanish-American War breaks out
1904 Anton Chekhov, **The Cherry Orchard** performed	

GUSTAVE FLAUBERT
1821–1880

Gustave Flaubert is rightly considered the exemplary realist novelist. He displays the objectivity, the detachment from his characters demanded by the theory, and is a great virtuoso of the art of composition and of style while giving a clear picture of the society of his time. It is likewise a picture in which we can see much of ourselves.

Flaubert was born in Rouen, Normandy, on December 12, 1821, to the chief surgeon of the Hôtel Dieu. He was extremely precocious; by the age of sixteen he was writing stories in the Romantic taste, which were published only after his death. In 1840 he went to Paris to study law (he had received his baccalaureate from the local *lycée*), but he failed in his examinations and in 1843 suffered a sudden nervous breakdown that kept him at home. In 1846 he moved to Croisset, just outside of Rouen on the Seine, where he made his home for the rest of his life, devoting himself to writing. The same year, in Paris, Flaubert met Louise Colet, a minor poet and lady about town, who became his mistress. In 1849–51 he visited the Levant, traveling extensively in Greece, Syria, and Egypt. After his return he settled down to the writing of *Madame Bovary*, which took him five full years and which was a great popular success. The remainder of his life was uneventful. He made occasional trips to Paris, and one trip, in 1860, to Tunisia to see the ruins of Carthage in preparation for the writing of his novel *Salammbô*. Three more novels followed: *The Sentimental Education* (1869), *The Temptation of St. Anthony* (1874), and the unfinished *Bouvard and Pecuchet* (1881), as well as *Three Tales* (1877), consisting of *A Simple Heart, The Legend of St. Julian the Hospitaler*, and *Herodias*. Flaubert died at Croisset on May 8, 1880.

Flaubert's novel *Madame Bovary* (1856) is deservedly considered the showpiece of French realism. It would be impossible to find a novel, certainly before Flaubert, in which humble persons in a humble setting (the story concerns the adulteries and final suicide of the wife of a simple country doctor) are treated with such seriousness, restraint, verisimilitude, and imaginative clarity. There is nothing of Balzac's lurid melodrama, high-pitched tone, and passionate eloquence in Flaubert's masterpiece. At first sight, *Madame Bovary* is the prosaic description of a prosaic life, set in its daily surroundings, the French province of Normandy about the middle of the nineteenth century. Everything is told soberly, objectively. The author hides his feelings completely behind his personages. All the light falls on Emma Bovary, as we follow the story of her romantic dreams, disillusionment, despair. Every scene is superbly realized, with an extraordinary accuracy of observation, and details, which at times are based on scientific information. The topography of the two villages, the interior of the houses, great scenes—such as those of the ball, the cattle show, the operation of clubfoot, the opera in Rouen, the arsenic poisoning—imprint themselves vividly on our memory. Early readers were puzzled by Flaubert's attitude toward Emma Bovary, so accustomed were they to the usual commentary of an author, approving or condemning every action of his characters. But today, when we know the early unpublished writings of Flaubert and his revealing correspondence, there cannot be any doubt about the tone of the book. Behind all the detachment there is a victory of art over temperament, a self-imposed discipline and restraint. It is, in part, the result of a theory of the objectivity, the complete impersonality of art. According to this view, the artist has to disappear behind his or her creation as God does behind His. Future ages should hardly believe that the artist lived.

If we listen more carefully, however, we become aware of the author's savage satiric attitude toward the romantic illusions of poor Emma, his hatred for the complacent freethinking apothecary Homais, his contempt for the stupid husband and the callous, weak lovers. The pity of it all comes through only because the author lets the facts speak for themselves.

The story of the composition of *Madame Bovary*, which we know from Flaubert's letters, is one of self-inflicted martyrdom, of an artist perversely clinging to an uncongenial and even repulsive subject because he believes that the subject itself is of no importance and that the artist should, by his art, purge himself of personal indulgences and preferences. It is also the story of a struggle for style, for the "right word" (*mot juste*), for which Flaubert worked with the suppressed fury of a galley slave.

A Simple Heart, a late story published in the collection *Three Tales*, is clearly related to *Madame Bovary*. It has the same setting of the Norman countryside, the same houses and farms, some of the same kind of people. And it has the same theme of disillusionment. Félicité is anticipated in *Madame Bovary* by the figure of Catherine Leroux, who at the great agricultural show receives a silver medal, worth twenty-five francs, for fifty-four years of service at one farm. The little old woman, with the "monastic rigidity" of her face, the dumbness and calm of her animal look, has to be almost pushed by the audience to receive her prize. When she walks away with the medal, she is heard muttering, "I'll give it to our *curé* up home, to say some masses for me."

A Simple Heart, like *Madame Bovary*, treats the life of a humble person with complete objectivity, with vivid concrete imagination, clear in every detail. We see and smell the interiors of the houses and farms and can visualize the scenes of almost Dutch simplicity. But the story is also connected with the two other stories in the collection, *The Legend of St. Julian the Hospitaler* and *Hérodias*. Like these it is a saint's legend: like a saint, Félicité undergoes a Calvary of suffering—the betrayal of her lover, the death of the little girl Virginie, the loss of her nephew, the loss of the parrot. Like a saint, too, she meets savage beasts (a bull in the fields), is lashed by a whip on the road, tends the running ulcer of a dying old man, and finally sees a beatific vision, during the Corpus Christi procession, in which the Holy Ghost and the parrot fuse into one.

But one would miss the implications of Flaubert's sophisticated art if one thought of the story merely as a realistic picture of a servant girl's plight or even as a traditional saint's legend in modern times. It is no doubt a combination of these two apparently very different types: we can see a social purpose in the picture of the poor oppressed woman, her devotion to a selfish mistress, her frustration, resignation, and final dying happiness; and we can sense the author's restraint as a device of simplicity to make the tone of the tale approach that of a legend. But such a reading would not capture all the undertones of Flaubert's style. There are disturbing elements in the story, which show that a simple interpretation is insufficient. We have glimpses, for instance, of Flaubert's predilection for the exotic and strange, for the deliberately decorative mosaic: the exotic pictures that constitute "the whole of [Félicité's] literary education," the curious color combinations of the scene at Virginie's deathbed (the spots of red of the candles, the white mist, the yellow face, the blue lips), and the gorgeous Corpus Christi wayside altar—all these clash with the otherwise sober and gray tone of the narrative. More disturbing, there is an undertone of satire and contemptuous mockery of this humble world. In a letter to a correspondent (Madame Roger de Genettes; June 19, 1876) Flaubert denied that "there is anything ironical as you suppose," and went on to declare that "on the contrary, it is very serious and very sad. I want to excite pity, I want to make sensitive souls weep, as I am one of them myself." But surely this professed intention is hard to reconcile with the passages about the parrot, who is shown as grotesque and absurd, an icon of the Holy Ghost (traditionally represented as a dove) but also a moth-eaten relic with a broken wing and stuffing protruding from its stomach. There is "something of the parrot" in the church window's image of the Holy Ghost, a likeness that is confirmed by the highly colored religious print that gives the dove purple wings and an emerald body. Some readers would find not only satire but blasphemy in the description of Félicité swerving toward the parrot from time to time as she says her prayers or glimpsing, on her deathbed, "an opening in the heavens, and a gigantic parrot hovering above her head." Yet there is also imaginative power in this grotesque deathbed vision. The parrot is not absurd in itself but only when seen from an external perspective that measures spiritual insight by traditional religious iconography. Viewed from a different angle, this subversive distortion is part of a creative process by which Félicité re-creates the world around her in the image of her own intense feelings. She enters passionately into the priest's stories of sacred history, trying to understand the various images of divinity in terms of her own experience. After learning that God is "not merely a bird, but a flame as well, and a breath of other times," she interprets these images through her own narration: "It may be His light, she thought, which flits at night about the edge of the marshes, His breathing which drives on the clouds, His voice which gives harmony to the bells." Flaubert insists on Félicité's capacity for reimagining the world: she *becomes* Virginie during the latter's first communion, and she expects to see Victor's house on the map, "so stunted was her mind!" A logic of personal need governs her imaginings; by linking the religious print to the parrot, Félicité both "consecrates" her beloved Loulou and makes the Holy Ghost "more vivid to her eye and more intelligible." Seeking intelligibility (to *know* God, in the tradition of the mystics), she decides that the bird who expresses God's meaning must be one who can speak: therefore, a parrot. If the gigantic parrot of the conclusion seems to mock traditional religious imagery, which it clearly does, it also presides over a world of will and imagination that Félicité—a secular saint—has made her own.

Victor Brombert, *The Novels of Flaubert* (1966), is still a good general work. Jonathan Culler, *Flaubert: The Uses of Uncertainty* (1974), is a clear and carefully argued study that emphasizes the modernity of Flaubert's style. Aimée Israel-Pelletier, *Flaubert's Straight and Suspect Saints: The Unity of Trois Contes* (1991), contains a valuable chapter on *A Simple Heart* and also a bibliography.

PRONOUNCING GLOSSARY

The following list uses common English syllables and stress accents to provide rough equivalents of selected words whose pronunciation may be unfamiliar to the general reader.

Aubain: *oh-banh'*
Félicité: *fay-lee-see-tay'*
Flaubert: *floh-bair'*
Pont l'Evêque: *pohnh lay-veck'*
Virginie: *veer-zheen-ee'*

A Simple Heart[1]

Madame Aubain's servant Félicité was the envy of the ladies of Pont-l'Évêque[2] for half a century.

She received a hundred francs a year. For that she was cook and general servant, and did the sewing, washing, and ironing; she could bridle a horse, fatten poultry, and churn butter—and she remained faithful to her mistress, unamiable as the latter was.

Mme. Aubain had married a gay bachelor without money who died at the beginning of 1809, leaving her with two small children and a quantity of debts. She then sold all her property except the farms of Toucques and Geffosses, which brought in five thousand francs a year at most, and left her house in Saint-Melaine for a less expensive one that had belonged to her family and was situated behind the market.

This house had a slate roof and stood between an alley and a lane that went down to the river. There was an unevenness in the levels of the rooms which made you stumble. A narrow hall divided the kitchen from the "parlour" where Mme. Aubain spent her day, sitting in a wicker easy chair by the window. Against the panels, which were painted white, was a row of eight mahogany chairs. On an old piano under the barometer a heap of wooden and cardboard boxes rose like a pyramid. A stuffed arm-chair stood on either side of the Louis-Quinze chimney-piece, which was in yellow marble with a clock in the middle of it modelled like a temple of Vesta.[3] The whole room was a little musty, as the floor was lower than the garden.

The first floor began with "Madame's" room: very large, with a pale-flowered wall-paper and a portrait of "Monsieur" as a dandy of the period. It led to a smaller room, where there were two children's cots without mattresses. Next came the drawing-room, which was always shut up and full of furniture covered with sheets. Then there was a corridor leading to a study. The shelves of a large bookcase were respectably lined with books and papers, and its three wings surrounded a broad writing-table in dark-wood. The two panels at the end of the room were covered with pen-drawings, water-colour landscapes, and engravings by Audran,[4] all relics of better days and vanished splendour. Félicité's room on the top floor got its light from a dormer-window, which looked over the meadows.

She rose at daybreak to be in time for Mass, and worked till evening without stopping. Then, when dinner was over, the plates and dishes in order, and the door shut fast, she thrust the log under the ashes and went to sleep in front of the hearth with her rosary in her hand. Félicité was the stubbornest of all bargainers; and as for cleanness, the polish on her sauce-pans was the despair of other servants. Thrifty in all things, she ate slowly, gathering off the table in her fingers the crumbs of her loaf—a twelve-pound loaf expressly baked for her, which lasted for three weeks.

At all times of year she wore a print handkerchief fastened with a pin

1. Translated by Arthur MacDowall.   2. A village in Normandy on the Toucques River, twenty-five miles from Caen.   3. Temple of the Roman goddess of the hearth; it was round and enclosed by columns.   4. Gérard Audran (1640–1703) made engravings of many paintings by Poussin, Mignard, and others.

behind, a bonnet that covered her hair, grey stockings, a red skirt, and a bibbed apron—such as hospital nurses wear—over her jacket.

Her face was thin and her voice sharp. At twenty-five she looked like forty. From fifty onwards she seemed of no particular age; and with her silence, straight figure, and precise movements she was like a woman made of wood, and going by clockwork.

II

She had had her love-story like another.

Her father, a mason, had been killed by falling off some scaffolding. Then her mother died, her sisters scattered, and a farmer took her in and employed her, while she was still quite little, to herd the cows at pasture. She shivered in rags and would lie flat on the ground to drink water from the ponds; she was beaten for nothing, and finally turned out for the theft of thirty sous which she did not steal. She went to another farm, where she became dairy-maid; and as she was liked by her employers her companions were jealous of her.

One evening in August (she was then eighteen) they took her to the assembly at Colleville. She was dazed and stupefied in an instant by the noise of the fiddlers, the lights in the trees, the gay medley of dresses, the lace, the gold crosses, and the throng of people jigging all together. While she kept shyly apart a young man with a well-to-do air, who was leaning on the shaft of a cart and smoking his pipe, came up to ask her to dance. He treated her to cider, coffee, and cake, and bought her a silk handkerchief; and then, imagining she had guessed his meaning, offered to see her home. At the edge of a field of oats he pushed her roughly down. She was frightened and began to cry out; and he went off.

One evening later she was on the Beaumont road. A big haywagon was moving slowly along; she wanted to get in front of it, and as she brushed past the wheels she recognized Theodore. He greeted her quite calmly, saying she must excuse it all because it was "the fault of the drink." She could not think of any answer and wanted to run away.

He began at once to talk about the harvest and the worthies of the commune, for his father had left Colleville for the farm at Les Écots, so that now he and she were neighbours. "Ah!" she said. He added that they thought of settling him in life. Well, he was in no hurry; he was waiting for a wife to his fancy. She dropped her head; and then he asked her if she thought of marrying. She answered with a smile that it was mean to make fun of her.

"But I am not, I swear!"—and he passed his left hand round her waist. She walked in the support of his embrace; their steps grew slower. The wind was soft, the stars glittered, the huge wagon-load of hay swayed in front of them, and dust rose from the dragging steps of the four horses. Then, without a word of command, they turned to the right. He clasped her once more in his arms, and she disappeared into the shadow.

The week after Theodore secured some assignations with her.

They met at the end of farmyards, behind a wall, or under a solitary tree. She was not innocent as young ladies are—she had learned knowledge from the animals—but her reason and the instinct of her honour would not let her fall. Her resistance exasperated Theodore's passion; so much so that to satisfy it—or perhaps quite artlessly—he made her an offer of marriage. She was in doubt whether to trust him, but he swore great oaths of fidelity.

Soon he confessed to something troublesome; the year before his parents had bought him a substitute for the army, but any day he might be taken again, and the idea of serving was a terror to him. Félicité took this cowardice of his as a sign of affection, and it redoubled hers. She stole away at night to see him, and when she reached their meeting-place Theodore racked her with his anxieties and urgings.

At last he declared that he would go himself to the prefecture for information, and would tell her the result on the following Sunday, between eleven and midnight.

When the moment came she sped towards her lover. Instead of him she found one of his friends.

He told her that she would not see Theodore any more. To ensure himself against conscription he had married an old woman, Madame Lehoussais, of Toucques, who was very rich.

There was an uncontrollable burst of grief. She threw herself on the ground, screamed, called to the God of mercy, and moaned by herself in the fields till daylight came. Then she came back to the farm and announced that she was going to leave; and at the end of the month she received her wages, tied all her small belongings with a handkerchief, and went to Pont-l'Évêque.

In front of the inn there she made inquiries of a woman in a widow's cap, who, as it happened, was just looking for a cook. The girl did not know much, but her willingness seemed so great and her demands so small that Mme. Aubain ended by saying:

"Very well, then, I will take you."

A quarter of an hour afterwards Félicité was installed in her house.

She lived there at first in a tremble, as it were, at "the style of the house" and the memory of "Monsieur" floating over it all. Paul and Virginie, the first aged seven and the other hardly four, seemed to her beings of a precious substance; she carried them on her back like a horse; it was a sorrow to her that Mme. Aubain would not let her kiss them every minute. And yet she was happy there. Her grief had melted in the pleasantness of things all round.

Every Thursday regular visitors came in for a game of boston, and Félicité got the cards and foot-warmers ready beforehand. They arrived punctually at eight and left before the stroke of eleven.

On Monday mornings the dealer who lodged in the covered passage spread out all his old iron on the ground. Then a hum of voices began to fill the town, mingled with the neighing of horses, bleating of lambs, grunting of pigs, and the sharp rattle of carts along the street. About noon, when the market was at its height, you might see a tall, hook-nosed old countryman with his cap pushed back making his appearance at the door. It was Robelin, the farmer of Geffosses. A little later came Liébard, the farmer from Toucques—short, red, and corpulent—in a grey jacket and gaiters shod with spurs.

Both had poultry or cheese to offer their landlord. Félicité was invariably a match for their cunning, and they went away filled with respect for her.

At vague intervals Mme. Aubain had a visit from the Marquis de Gremanville, one of her uncles, who had ruined himself by debauchery and now lived at Falaise on his last remaining morsel of land. He invariably came at the luncheon hour, with a dreadful poodle whose paws left all the furniture in a mess. In spite of efforts to show his breeding, which he carried to the point of raising his hat every time he mentioned "my late father," habit was too strong for him; he poured himself out glass after glass and fired off improper remarks. Félicité edged him politely out of the house—"You have had enough, Monsieur de Gremanville! Another time!"—and she shut the door on him.

She opened it with pleasure to M. Bourais, who had been a lawyer. His baldness, his white stock, frilled shirt, and roomy brown coat, his way of rounding the arm as he took snuff—his whole person, in fact, created that disturbance of mind which overtakes us at the sight of extraordinary men.

As he looked after the property of "Madame" he remained shut up with her for hours in "Monsieur's" study, though all the time he was afraid of compromising himself. He respected the magistracy immensely, and had some pretensions to Latin.

To combine instruction and amusement he gave the children a geography book made up of a series of prints. They represented scenes in different parts of the world: cannibals with feathers on their heads, a monkey carrying off a young lady, Bedouins in the desert, the harpooning of a whale, and so on. Paul explained these engravings to Félicité; and that, in fact, was the whole of her literary education. The children's education was undertaken by Guyot, a poor creature employed at the town hall, who was famous for his beautiful hand and sharpened his penknife on his boots.

When the weather was bright the household set off early for a day at Geffosses Farm.

Its courtyard is on a slope, with the farmhouse in the middle, and the sea looks like a grey streak in the distance.

Félicité brought slices of cold meat out of her basket, and they breakfasted in a room adjoining the dairy. It was the only surviving fragment of a country house which was now no more. The wallpaper hung in tatters, and quivered in the draughts. Mme. Aubain sat with bowed head, overcome by her memories; the children became afraid to speak. "Why don't you play, then?" she would say, and off they went.

Paul climbed into the barn, caught birds, played at ducks and drakes over the pond, or hammered with his stick on the big casks which boomed like drums. Virginie fed the rabbits or dashed off to pick cornflowers, her quick legs showing their embroidered little drawers.

One autumn evening they went home by the fields. The moon was in its first quarter, lighting part of the sky; and mist floated like a scarf over the windings of the Toucques. Cattle, lying out in the middle of the grass, looked quietly at the four people as they passed. In the third meadow some of them got up and made a half-circle in front of the walkers. "There's nothing to be afraid of," said Félicité, as she stroked the nearest on the

back with a kind of crooning song; he wheeled round and the others did
the same. But when they crossed the next pasture there was a formidable
bellow. It was a bull, hidden by the mist. Mme. Aubain was about to run.
"No! no! don't go so fast!" They mended their pace, however, and heard
a loud breathing behind them which came nearer. His hoofs thudded on
the meadow grass like hammers; why, he was galloping now! Félicité
turned round, and tore up clods of earth with both hands and threw them
in his eyes. He lowered his muzzle, waved his horns, and quivered with
fury, bellowing terribly. Mme. Aubain, now at the end of the pasture with
her two little ones, was looking wildly for a place to get over the high bank.
Félicité was retreating, still with her face to the bull, keeping up a shower
of clods which blinded him, and crying all the time, "Be quick! be quick!"

Mme. Aubain went down into the ditch, pushed Virginie first and then
Paul, fell several times as she tried to climb the bank, and managed it at
last by dint of courage.

The bull had driven Félicité to bay against a rail-fence; his slaver was
streaming into her face; another second, and he would have gored her.
She had just time to slip between two of the rails, and the big animal
stopped short in amazement.

This adventure was talked of at Pont-l'Évêque for many a year. Félicité
did not pride herself on it in the least, not having the barest suspicion that
she had done anything heroic.

Virginie was the sole object of her thoughts, for the child developed a
nervous complaint as a result of her fright, and M. Poupart, the doctor,
advised sea-bathing at Trouville.[5] It was not a frequented place then.
Mme. Aubain collected information, consulted Bourais, and made preparations as though for a long journey.

Her luggage started a day in advance, in Liébard's cart. The next day he
brought round two horses, one of which had a lady's saddle with a velvet
back to it, while a cloak was rolled up to make a kind of seat on the
crupper of the other. Mme. Aubain rode on that, behind the farmer. Félicité took charge of Virginie, and Paul mounted M. Lechaptois' donkey,
lent on condition that great care was taken of it.

The road was so bad that its five miles took two hours. The horses sank
in the mud up to their pasterns, and their haunches jerked abruptly in the
effort to get out; or else they stumbled in the ruts, and at other moments
had to jump. In some places Liébard's mare came suddenly to a halt. He
waited patiently until she went on again, talking about the people who had
properties along the road, and adding moral reflections to their history. So
it was that as they were in the middle of Toucques, and passed under
some windows bowered with nasturtiums, he shrugged his shoulders and
said: "There's a Mme. Lehoussais lives there; instead of taking a young
man she . . ." Félicité did not hear the rest; the horses were trotting and
the donkey galloping. They all turned down a bypath; a gate swung open
and two boys appeared; and the party dismounted in front of a manure-
heap at the very threshold of the farmhouse door.

When Mme. Liébard saw her mistress she gave lavish signs of joy. She

5. A town on the English Channel, now a popular resort, some five miles from Pont-l'Évêque.

served her a luncheon with a sirloin of beef, tripe, black-pudding, a fricasse of chicken, sparkling cider, a fruit tart, and brandied plums; seasoning it all with compliments to Madame, who seemed in better health; Mademoiselle, who was "splendid" now; and Monsieur Paul, who had "filled out" wonderfully. Nor did she forget their deceased grandparents, whom the Liébards had known, as they had been in the service of the family for several generations. The farm, like them, had the stamp of antiquity. The beams on the ceiling were worm-eaten, the walls blackened with smoke, and the window-panes grey with dust. There was an oak dresser laden with every sort of useful article—jugs, plates, pewter bowls, wolf-traps, and sheep-shears; and a huge syringe made the children laugh. There was not a tree in the three courtyards without mushrooms growing at the bottom of it or a tuft of mistletoe on its boughs. Several of them had been thrown down by the wind. They had taken root again at the middle; and all were bending under their wealth of apples. The thatched roofs, like brown velvet and of varying thickness, withstood the heaviest squalls. The cart-shed, however, was falling into ruin. Mme. Aubain said she would see about it, and ordered the animals to be saddled again.

It was another half-hour before they reached Trouville. The little caravan dismounted to pass Écores—it was an overhanging cliff with boats below it—and three minutes later they were at the end of the quay and entered the courtyard of the Golden Lamb, kept by good Mme. David.

From the first days of their stay Virginie began to feel less weak, thanks to the change of air and the effect of the sea-baths. These, for want of a bathing-dress, she took in her chemise; and her nurse dressed her afterwards in a coastguard's cabin which was used by the bathers.

In the afternoons they took the donkey and went off beyond the Black Rocks, in the direction of Hennequeville. The path climbed at first through ground with dells in it like the green sward of a park, and then reached a plateau where grass fields and arable lay side by side. Hollies rose stiffly out of the briary tangle at the edge of the road; and here and there a great withered tree made zigzags in the blue air with its branches.

They nearly always rested in a meadow, with Deauville on their left, Havre on their right, and the open sea in front. It glittered in the sunshine, smooth as a mirror and so quiet that its murmur was scarcely to be heard; sparrows chirped in hiding and the immense sky arched over it all. Mme. Aubain sat doing her needlework; Virginie plaited rushes by her side; Félicité pulled up lavender, and Paul was bored and anxious to start home.

Other days they crossed the Toucques in a boat and looked for shells. When the tide went out sea-urchins, starfish, and jelly-fish were left exposed; and the children ran in pursuit of the foam-flakes which scudded in the wind. The sleepy waves broke on the sand and unrolled all along the beach; it stretched away out of sight, bounded on the land-side by the dunes which parted it from the Marsh, a wide meadow shaped like an arena. As they came home that way, Trouville, on the hill-slope in the background, grew bigger at every step, and its miscellaneous throng of houses seemed to break into a gay disorder.

On days when it was too hot they did not leave their room. From the dazzling brilliance outside light fell in streaks between the laths of the blinds. There were no sounds in the village; and on the pavement below not a soul. This silence round them deepened the quietness of things. In the distance, where men were caulking, there was a tap of hammers as they plugged the hulls, and a sluggish breeze wafted up the smell of tar.

The chief amusement was the return of the fishing-boats. They began to tack as soon as they had passed the buoys. The sails came down on two of the three masts; and they drew on with the foresail swelling like a balloon, gliding through the splash of the waves, and when they had reached the middle of the harbour suddenly dropped anchor. Then the boats drew up against the quay. The sailors threw quivering fish over the side; a row of carts was waiting, and women in cotton bonnets darted out to take the baskets and give their men a kiss.

One of them came up to Félicité one day, and she entered the lodgings a little later in a state of delight. She had found a sister again—and then Nastasie Barette, "wife of Leroux," appeared, holding an infant at her breast and another child with her right hand, while on her left was a little cabin boy with his hands on his hips and a cap over his ear.

After a quarter of an hour Mme. Aubain sent them off; but they were always to be found hanging about the kitchen, or encountered in the course of a walk. The husband never appeared.

Félicité was seized with affection for them. She bought them a blanket, some shirts, and a stove; it was clear that they were making a good thing out of her. Mme. Aubain was annoyed by this weakness of hers, and she did not like the liberties taken by the nephew, who said "thee" and "thou"[6] to Paul. So as Virginie was coughing and the fine weather gone, she returned to Pont-l'Évêque.

There M. Bourais enlightened her on the choice of a boys' school. The one at Caen was reputed to be the best, and Paul was sent to it. He said his good-byes bravely, content enough at going to live in a house where he would have companions.

Mme. Aubain resigned herself to her son's absence as a thing that had to be. Virginie thought about it less and less. Félicité missed the noise he made. But she found an occupation to distract her; from Christmas onward she took the little girl to catechism every day.

III

After making a genuflexion at the door she walked up between the double rows of chairs under the lofty nave, opened Mme. Aubain's pew, sat down, and began to look about her. The choir stalls were filled with the boys on the right and the girls on the left, and the curé stood by the lectern. On a painted window in the apse the Holy Ghost looked down upon the Virgin. Another window showed her on her knees before the child Jesus, and a group carved in wood behind the altar-shrine represented St. Michael overthrowing the dragon.

The priest began with a sketch of sacred history. The Garden, the Flood, the Tower of Babel, cities in flames, dying nations, and overturned

---

6. That is, used the familiar *tu* and *toi* rather than the more respectful *vous*.

idols passed like a dream before her eyes; and the dizzying vision left her with reverence for the Most High and fear of his wrath. Then she wept at the story of the Passion. Why had they crucified Him, when He loved the children, fed the multitudes, healed the blind, and had willed, in His meekness, to be born among the poor, on the dung-heap of a stable? The sowings, harvests, wine-presses, all the familiar things that the Gospel speaks of, were a part of her life. They had been made holy by God's passing; and she loved the lambs more tenderly for her love of the Lamb, and the doves because of the Holy Ghost.

She found it hard to imagine Him in person, for He was not merely a bird, but a flame as well, and a breath at other times. It may be His light, she thought, which flits at night about the edge of the marshes, His breathing which drives on the clouds, His voice which gives harmony to the bells; and she would sit rapt in adoration, enjoying the cool walls and the quiet of the church.

Of doctrines she understood nothing—did not even try to understand. The curé discoursed, the children repeated their lesson, and finally she went to sleep, waking up with a start when their wooden shoes clattered on the flagstones as they went away.

It was thus that Félicité, whose religious education had been neglected in her youth, learned the catechism by dint of hearing it; and from that time she copied all Virginie's observances, fasting as she did and confessing with her. On Corpus Christi Day[7] they made a festal altar together.

The first communion loomed distractingly ahead. She fussed over the shoes, the rosary, the book and gloves; and how she trembled as she helped Virginie's mother to dress her!

All through the mass she was racked with anxiety. She could not see one side of the choir because of M. Bourais but straight in front of her was the flock of maidens, with white crowns above their hanging veils, making the impression of a field of snow; and she knew her dear child at a distance by her dainty neck and thoughtful air. The bell tinkled. The heads bowed, and there was silence. As the organ pealed, singers and congregation took up the "Agnus Dei"[8]; then the procession of the boys began, and after them the girls rose. Step by step, with their hands joined in prayer, they went towards the lighted altar, knelt on the first step, received the sacrament in turn, and came back in the same order to their places. When Virginie's turn came Félicité leaned forward to see her; and with the imaginativeness of deep and tender feeling it seemed to her that she actually was the child; Virginie's face became hers, she was dressed in her clothes, it was her heart beating in her breast. As the moment came to open her mouth she closed her eyes and nearly fainted.

She appeared early in the sacristy next morning for Monsieur the curé to give her the communion. She took it with devotion, but it did not give her the same exquisite delight.

Mme. Aubain wanted to make her daughter into an accomplished person; and as Guyot could not teach her music or English she decided to place her in the Ursuline Convent at Honfleur[9] as a boarder. The child

7. Feast day commemorating the founding of the Sacrament of the Eucharist (Corpus Christi is Latin for body of Christ).   8. "Lamb of God" (Latin)—that is, Jesus; a part of the Roman Catholic Mass.   9. At the mouth of the Seine River, twelve miles from Pont-l'Évêque.

made no objection. Félicité sighed and thought that Madame lacked feeling. Then she reflected that her mistress might be right; matters of this kind were beyond her.

So one day an old spring-van drew up at the door, and out of it stepped a nun to fetch the young lady. Félicité hoisted the luggage on to the top, admonished the driver, and put six pots of preserves, a dozen pears, and a bunch of violets under the seat.

At the last moment Virginie broke into a fit of sobbing; she threw her arms round her mother, who kissed her on the forehead, saying over and over "Come be brave! be brave!" The step was raised, and the carriage drove off.

Then Mme. Aubain's strength gave way; and in the evening all her friends—the Lormeau family, Mme. Lechaptois, the Rochefeuille ladies, M. de Houppeville, and Bourais—came in to console her.

To be without her daughter was very painful for her at first. But she heard from Virginie three times a week, wrote to her on the other days, walked in the garden, and so filled up the empty hours.

From sheer habit Félicité went into Virginie's room in the mornings and gazed at the walls. It was boredom to her not to have to comb the child's hair now, lace up her boots, tuck her into bed—and not to see her charming face perpetually and hold her hand when they went out together. In this idle condition she tried making lace. But her fingers were too heavy and broke the threads; she could not attend to anything, she had lost her sleep, and was, in her own words, "destroyed."

To "divert herself" she asked leave to have visits from her nephew Victor.

He arrived on Sundays after mass, rosy-cheeked, bare-chested, with the scent of the country he had walked through still about him. She laid her table promptly and they had lunch, sitting opposite each other. She ate as little as possible herself to save expense, but stuffed him with food so generous that at last he went to sleep. At the first stroke of vespers she woke him up, brushed his trousers, fastened his tie, and went to church, leaning on his arm with maternal pride.

Victor was always instructed by his parents to get something out of her—a packet of moist sugar, it might be, a cake of soap, spirits, or even money at times. He brought his things for her to mend and she took over the task, only too glad to have a reason for making him come back.

In August his father took him off on a coasting voyage. It was holiday time, and she was consoled by the arrival of the children. Paul, however, was getting selfish, and Virginie was too old to be called "thou" any longer; this put a constraint and barrier between them.

Victor went to Morlaix, Dunkirk, and Brighton[1] in succession and made Félicité a present on his return from each voyage. It was a box made of shells the first time, a coffee cup the next, and on the third occasion a large gingerbread man. Victor was growing handsome. He was well made, had a hint of a moustache, good honest eyes, and a small leather hat pushed backwards like a pilot's. He entertained her by telling stories embroidered with nautical terms.

---

1. In England, across the channel. Morlaix and Dunkirk are in Brittany and Flanders, respectively.

On a Monday, July 14, 1819 (she never forgot the date), he told her that he had signed on for the big voyage and next night but one he would take the Honfleur boat and join his schooner, which was to weigh anchor from Havre before long. Perhaps he would be gone two years.

The prospect of this long absence threw Félicité into deep distress; one more good-bye she must have, and on the Wednesday evening, when Madame's dinner was finished, she put on her clogs and made short work of the twelve miles between Pont-l'Évêque and Honfleur.

When she arrived in front of the Calvary she took the turn to the right instead of the left, got lost in the timber-yards, and retraced her steps; some people to whom she spoke advised her to be quick. She went all round the harbour basin, full of ships, and knocked against hawsers; then the ground fell away, lights flashed across each other, and she thought her wits had left her, for she saw horses up in the sky.

Others were neighing by the quay-side, frightened at the sea. They were lifted by a tackle and deposited in a boat, where passengers jostled each other among cider casks, cheese baskets, and sacks of grain; fowls could be heard clucking, the captain swore; and a cabin-boy stood leaning over the bows, indifferent to it all. Félicité, who had not recognized him, called "Victor!" and he raised his head; all at once, as she was darting forwards, the gangway was drawn back.

The Honfleur packet, women singing as they hauled it, passed out of harbour. Its framework creaked and the heavy waves whipped its bows. The canvas had swung round, no one could be seen on board now; and on the moon-silvered sea the boat made a black speck which paled gradually, dipped, and vanished.

As Félicité passed by the Calvary she had a wish to commend to God what she cherished most, and she stood there praying a long time with her face bathed in tears and her eyes towards the clouds. The town was asleep, coastguards were walking to and fro; and water poured without cessation through the holes in the sluice, with the noise of a torrent. The clocks struck two.

The convent parlour would not be open before day. If Félicité were late Madame would most certainly be annoyed; and in spite of her desire to kiss the other child she turned home. The maids at the inn were waking up as she came in to Pont-l'Évêque.

So the poor slip of a boy was going to toss for months and months at sea! She had not been frightened by his previous voyages. From England or Brittany you came back safe enough; but America, the colonies, the islands—these were lost in a dim region at the other end of the world.

Félicité's thoughts from that moment ran entirely on her nephew. On sunny days she was harassed by the idea of thirst; when there was a storm she was afraid of the lightning on his account. As she listened to the wind growling in the chimney or carrying off the slates she pictured him lashed by that same tempest, at the top of a shattered mast, with his body thrown backwards under a sheet of foam; or else (with a reminiscence of the illustrated geography) he was being eaten by savages, captured in a wood by monkeys, or dying on a desert shore. And never did she mention her anxieties.

Mme. Aubain had anxieties of her own, about her daughter. The good sisters found her an affectionate but delicate child. The slightest emotion unnerved her. She had to give up the piano.

Her mother stipulated for regular letters from the convent. She lost patience one morning when the postman did not come, and walked to and fro in the parlour from her armchair to the window. It was really amazing; not a word for four days!

To console Mme. Aubain by her own example Félicité remarked:

"As for me, Madame, it's six months since I heard . . ."

"From whom, pray?"

"Why . . . from my nephew," the servant answered gently.

"Oh! your nephew!" And Mme. Aubain resumed her walk with a shrug of the shoulders, as much as to say: "I was not thinking of him! And what is more, it's absurd! A scamp of a cabin-boy—what does he matter? . . . whereas my daughter . . . why, just think!"

Félicité, though she had been brought up on harshness, felt indignant with Madame—and then forgot. It seemed the simplest thing in the world to her to lose one's head over the little girl. For her the two children were equally important; a bond in her heart made them one, and their destinies must be the same.

She heard from the chemist that Victor's ship had arrived at Havana. He had read this piece of news in a gazette.

Cigars—they made her imagine Havana as a place where no one does anything but smoke, and there was Victor moving among the negroes in a cloud of tobacco. Could you, she wondered, "in case you needed," return by land? What was the distance from Pont-l'Évêque? She questioned M. Bourais to find out.

He reached for his atlas and began explaining the longitudes; Félicité's consternation provoked a fine pedantic smile. Finally, he marked with his pencil a black, imperceptible point in the indentations of an oval spot, and said as he did so, "Here it is." She bent over the map; the maze of coloured lines wearied her eyes without conveying anything; and on an invitation from Bourais to tell him her difficulty she begged him to show her the house where Victor was living. Bourais threw up his arms, sneezed, and laughed immensely: a simplicity like hers was a positive joy. And Félicité did not understand the reason; how could she when she expected, very likely to see the actual image of her nephew—so stunted was her mind!

A fortnight afterwards Liébard came into the kitchen at market-time as usual and handed her a letter from her brother-in-law. As neither of them could read she took it to her mistress.

Mme. Aubain, who was counting the stitches in her knitting, put the work down by her side, broke the seal of the letter, started, and said in a low voice, with a look of meaning:

"It is bad news . . . that they have to tell you. Your nephew . . ."

He was dead. The letter said no more.

Félicité fell on to a chair, leaning her head against the wainscot; and she closed her eyelids, which suddenly flushed pink. Then with bent forehead, hands hanging, and fixed eyes, she said at intervals:

"Poor little lad! poor little lad!"

Liébard watched her and heaved sighs. Mme. Aubain trembled a little.

She suggested that Félicité should go to see her sister at Trouville. Félicité answered by a gesture that she had no need.

There was a silence. The worthy Liébard thought it was time for them to withdraw.

Then Félicité said:

"They don't care, not they!"

Her head dropped again; and she took up mechanically, from time to time, the long needles on her work-table.

Women passed in the yard with a barrow of dripping linen.

As she saw them through the window-panes, she remembered her washing; she had put it to soak the day before, to-day she must wring it out; and she left the room.

Her plank and tub were at the edge of the Toucques. She threw a pile of linen on the bank, rolled up her sleeves, and taking her wooden beater dealt lusty blows whose sound carried to the neighbouring gardens. The meadows were empty, the river stirred in the wind; and down below long grasses wavered, like the hair of corpses floating in the water. She kept her grief down and was very brave until the evening; but once in her room she surrendered to it utterly, lying stretched on the mattress with her face in the pillow and her hands clenched against her temples.

Much later she heard, from the captain himself, the circumstances of Victor's end. They had bled him too much at the hospital for yellow fever. Four doctors held him at once. He had died instantly, and the chief had said:

"Bah! there goes another!"

His parents had always been brutal to him. She preferred not to see them again; and they made no advances, either because they forgot her or from the callousness of the wretchedly poor.

Virginie began to grow weaker.

Tightness in her chest, coughing, continual fever, and veinings on her cheek-bones betrayed some deep-seated complaint. M. Poupart had advised a stay in Provence.[2] Mme. Aubain determined on it, would have brought her daughter home at once but for the climate of Pont-l'Évêque.

She made an arrangement with a job-master, and he drove her to the convent every Tuesday. There is a terrace in the garden, with a view over the Seine. Virginie took walks there over the fallen vine-leaves, on her mother's arm. A shaft of sunlight through the clouds made her blink sometimes, as she gazed at the sails in the distance and the whole horizon from the castle of Tancarville to the lighthouses at Havre. Afterwards they rested in the arbour. Her mother had secured a little cask of excellent Malaga;[3] and Virginie, laughing at the idea of getting tipsy, drank a thimble-full of it, no more.

Her strength came back visibly. The autumn glided gently away. Félicité reassured Mme. Aubain. But one evening, when she had been out on

2. In southern France.   3. A sweet wine.

a commission in the neighbourhood, she found M. Poupart's gig at the door. He was in the hall, and Mme. Aubain was tying her bonnet.

"Give me my foot-warmer, purse, gloves. Quicker, come!"

Virginie had inflammation of the lungs; perhaps it was hopeless.

"Not yet!" said the doctor, and they both got into the carriage under whirling flakes of snow. Night was coming on and it was very cold.

Félicité rushed into the church to light a taper. Then she ran after the gig, came up with it in an hour, and jumped lightly in behind. As she hung on by the fringes a thought came into her mind: "The courtyard has not been shut up; supposing burglars got in!" And she jumped down.

At dawn next day she presented herself at the doctor's. He had come in and started for the country again. Then she waited in the inn, thinking that a letter would come by some hand or other. Finally, when it was twilight, she took the Lisieux coach.

The convent was at the end of a steep lane. When she was about half-way up it she heard strange sounds—a death-bell tolling. "It is for someone else," thought Félicité, and she pulled the knocker violently.

After some minutes there was a sound of trailing slippers, the door opened ajar, and a nun appeared.

The good sister, with an air of compunction, said that "she had just passed away." On the instant the bell of St. Leonard's tolled twice as fast.

Félicité went up to the second floor.

From the doorway she saw Virginie stretched on her back, with her hands joined, her mouth open, and head thrown back under a black crucifix that leaned towards her, between curtains that hung stiffly, less pale than was her face. Mme. Aubain, at the foot of the bed which she clasped with her arms, was choking with sobs of agony. The mother superior stood on the right. Three candlesticks on the chest of drawers made spots of red, and the mist came whitely through the windows. Nuns came and took Mme. Aubain away.

For two nights Félicité never left the dead child. She repeated the same prayers, sprinkled holy water over the sheets, came and sat down again, and watched her. At the end of the first vigil she noticed that the face had grown yellow, the lips turned blue, the nose was sharper, and the eyes sunk in. She kissed them several times, and would not have been immensely surprised if Virginie had opened them again; to minds like hers the supernatural is quite simple. She made the girl's toilette, wrapped her in her shroud, lifted her down into her bier, put a garland on her head, and spread out her hair. It was fair, and extraordinarily long for her age. Félicité cut off a big lock and slipped half of it into her bosom, determined that she should never part with it.

The body was brought back to Pont-l'Évêque, as Mme. Aubain intended; she followed the hearse in a closed carriage.

It took another three-quarters of an hour after the mass to reach the cemetery. Paul walked in front, sobbing. M. Bourais was behind, and then came the chief residents, the women shrouded in black mantles, and Félicité. She thought of her nephew; and because she had not been able to pay these honours to him her grief was doubled, as though the one were being buried with the other.

Mme. Aubain's despair was boundless. It was against God that she first rebelled, thinking it unjust of Him to have taken her daughter from her—she had never done evil and her conscience was so clear! Ah, no!—she ought to have taken Virginie off to the south. Other doctors would have saved her. She accused herself now, wanted to join her child, and broke into cries of distress in the middle of her dreams. One dream haunted her above all. Her husband, dressed as a sailor, was returning from a long voyage, and shedding tears he told her that he had been ordered to take Virginie away. Then they consulted how to hide her somewhere.

She came in once from the garden quite upset. A moment ago—and she pointed out the place—the father and daughter had appeared to her, standing side by side, and they did nothing, but they looked at her.

For several months after this she stayed inertly in her room. Félicité lectured her gently; she must live for her son's sake, and for the other, in remembrance of "her."

"Her?" answered Mme. Aubain, as though she were just waking up. "Ah, yes! . . . yes! . . . You do not forget her!" This was an allusion to the cemetery, where she was strictly forbidden to go.

Félicité went there every day.

Precisely at four she skirted the houses, climbed the hill, opened the gate, and came to Virginie's grave. It was a little column of pink marble with a stone underneath and a garden plot enclosed by chains. The beds were hidden under a coverlet of flowers. She watered their leaves, freshened the gravel, and knelt down to break up the earth better. When Mme. Aubain was able to come there she felt a relief and a sort of consolation.

Then years slipped away, one like another, and their only episodes were the great festivals as they recurred—Easter, the Assumption, All Saints' Day. Household occurrences marked dates that were referred to afterwards. In 1825, for instance, two glaziers white-washed the hall; in 1827 a piece of the roof fell into the courtyard and nearly killed a man. In the summer of 1828 it was Madame's turn to offer the consecrated bread; Bourais, about this time, mysteriously absented himself; and one by one the old acquaintances passed away: Guyot, Liébard, Mme. Lechaptois, Robelin, and Uncle Gremanville, who had been paralysed for a long time.

One night the driver of the mail-coach announced the Revolution of July[4] in Pont-l'Évêque. A new sub-prefect was appointed a few days later—Baron de Larsonnière, who had been consul in America, and brought with him, besides his wife, a sister-in-law and three young ladies, already growing up. They were to be seen about on their lawn, in loose blouses, and they had a negro and a parrot. They paid a call on Mme. Aubain which she did not fail to return. The moment they were seen in the distance Félicité ran to let her mistress know. But only one thing could really move her feelings—the letters from her son.

He was swallowed up in a tavern life and could follow no career. She paid his debts, he made new ones; and the sighs that Mme. Aubain uttered as she sat knitting by the window reached Félicité at her spinning-wheel in the kitchen.

4. In 1830 the Bourbons were driven out, and Louis-Philippe became king of France.

They took walks together along the espaliered wall, always talking of Virginie and wondering if such and such a thing would have pleased her and what, on some occasion, she would have been likely to say.

All her small belongings filled a cupboard in the two-bedded room. Mme. Aubain inspected them as seldom as she could. One summer day she made up her mind to it—and some moths flew out of the wardrobe.

Virginie's dresses were in a row underneath a shelf, on which there were three dolls, some hoops, a set of toy pots and pans, and the basin that she used. They took out her petticoats as well, and the stockings and handkerchiefs, and laid them out on the two beds before folding them up again. The sunshine lit up these poor things, bringing out their stains and the creases made by the body's movements. The air was warm and blue, a blackbird warbled, life seemed bathed in a deep sweetness. They found a little plush hat with thick, chestnut-coloured pile; but it was eaten all over by moth. Félicité begged it for her own. Their eyes met fixedly and filled with tears; at last the mistress opened her arms, the servant threw herself into them, and they embraced each other, satisfying their grief in a kiss that made them equal.

It was the first time in their lives, Mme. Aubain's nature not being expansive. Félicité was as grateful as though she had received a favour; and cherished her mistress from that moment with the devotion of an animal and a religious worship.

The kindness of her heart unfolded.

When she heard the drums of a marching regiment in the street she posted herself at the door with a pitcher of cider and asked the soldiers to drink. She nursed cholera patients and protected the Polish refugees;[5] one of these even declared that he wished to marry her. They quarrelled, however; for when she came back from the Angelus one morning she found that he had got into her kitchen and made himself a vinegar salad which he was quietly eating.

After the Poles came father Colmiche, an old man who was supposed to have committed atrocities in '93.[6] He lived by the side of the river in the ruins of a pigsty. The little boys watched him through the cracks in the wall, and threw pebbles at him which fell on the pallet where he lay constantly shaken by a catarrh; his hair was very long, his eyes inflamed, and there was a tumour on his arm bigger than his head. She got him some linen and tried to clean up his miserable hole; her dream was to establish him in the bake-house without letting him annoy Madame. When the tumour burst she dressed it every day; sometimes she brought him cake, and would put him in the sunshine on a truss of straw. The poor old man, slobbering and trembling, thanked her in his worn-out voice, was terrified that he might lose her, and stretched out his hands when he saw her go away. He died; and she had a mass said for the repose of his soul.

That very day a great happiness befell her; just at dinner-time appeared Mme. de Larsonnière's negro, carrying the parrot in its cage, with perch, chain, and padlock. A note from the baroness informed Mme. Aubain that

---

5. After the Polish uprising against Russia in 1831 was suppressed, many Poles came to France.   6. In 1793 the Reign of Terror during the French Revolution began.

her husband had been raised to a prefecture and they were starting that evening; she begged her to accept the bird as a memento and mark of her regard.

For a long time he had absorbed Félicité's imagination, because he came from America; and that name reminded her of Victor, so much so that she made inquiries of the negro. She had once gone so far as to say "How Madame would enjoy having him!"

The negro repeated the remark to his mistress; and as she could not take the bird away with her she chose this way of getting rid of him.

IV

His name was Loulou. His body was green and the tips of his wings rose-pink; his forehead was blue and his throat golden.

But he had the tiresome habits of biting his perch, tearing out his feathers, sprinkling his dirt about, and spattering the water of his tub. He annoyed Mme. Aubain, and she gave him to Félicité for good.

She endeavoured to train him; soon he could repeat "Nice boy! Your servant, sir! Good morning, Marie!" He was placed by the side of the door, and astonished several people by not answering to the name Jacquot, for all parrots are called Jacquot. People compared him to a turkey and a log of wood, and stabbed Félicité to the heart each time. Strange obstinacy on Loulou's part!—directly you looked at him he refused to speak.

None the less he was eager for society; for on Sundays, while the Rochefeuille ladies, M. de Houppeville, and new familiars—Onfroy the apothecary, Monsieur Varin, and Captain Mathieu—were playing their game of cards, he beat the windows with his wings and threw himself about so frantically that they could not hear each other speak.

Bourais' face, undoubtedly, struck him as extremely droll. Directly he saw it he began to laugh—and laugh with all his might. His peals rang through the courtyard and were repeated by the echo; the neighbours came to their windows and laughed too; while M. Bourais, gliding along under the wall to escape the parrot's eye, and hiding his profile with his hat, got to the river and then entered by the garden gate. There was a lack of tenderness in the looks which he darted at the bird.

Loulou had been slapped by the butcher-boy for making so free as to plunge his head into his basket; and since then he was always trying to nip him through his shirt. Fabu threatened to wring his neck, although he was not cruel, for all his tattooed arms and large whiskers. Far from it; he really rather liked the parrot, and in a jovial humour even wanted to teach him to swear. Félicité, who was alarmed by such proceedings, put the bird in the kitchen. His little chain was taken off and he roamed about the house.

His way of going downstairs was to lean on each step with the curve of his beak, raise the right foot, and then the left; and Félicité was afraid that these gymnastics brought on fits of giddiness. He fell ill and could not talk or eat any longer. There was a growth under his tongue, such as fowls have sometimes. She cured him by tearing the pellicle off with her fingernails. Mr. Paul was thoughtless enough one day to blow some cigar smoke into his nostrils, and another time when Mme. Lormcau was teasing him with the end of her umbrella he snapped at the ferrule. Finally he got lost.

Félicité had put him on the grass to refresh him, and gone away for a minute, and when she came back—no sign of the parrot! She began by looking for him in the shrubs, by the waterside, and over the roofs, without listening to her mistress's cries of "Take care, do! You are out of your wits!" Then she investigated all the gardens in Pont-l'Évêque, and stopped the passers-by. "You don't ever happen to have seen my parrot, by any chance, do you?" And she gave a description of the parrot to those who did not know him. Suddenly, behind the mills at the foot of the hill she thought she could make out something green that fluttered. But on the top of the hill there was nothing. A hawker assured her that he had come across the parrot just before, at Saint-Melaine, in Mère Simon's shop. She rushed there; they had no idea of what she meant. At last she came home exhausted, with her slippers in shreds and despair in her soul; and as she was sitting in the middle of the garden-seat at Madame's side, telling the whole story of her efforts, a light weight dropped on to her shoulder—it was Loulou! What on earth had he been doing? Taking a walk in the neighbourhood, perhaps!

She had some trouble in recovering from this, or rather never did recover. As the result of a chill she had an attack of quinsy, and soon afterwards an earache. Three years later she was deaf; and she spoke very loud, even in church. Though Félicité's sins might have been published in every corner of the diocese without dishonour to her or scandal to anybody, his Reverence the priest thought it right now to hear her confession in the sacristy only.

Imaginary noises in the head completed her upset. Her mistress often said to her, "Heavens! how stupid you are!" "Yes, Madame," she replied, and looked about for something.

Her little circle of ideas grew still narrower; the peal of churchbells and the lowing of cattle ceased to exist for her. All living beings moved as silently as ghosts. One sound only reached her ears now—the parrot's voice.

Loulou, as though to amuse her, reproduced the click-clack of the turn-spit, the shrill call of a man selling fish, and the noise of the saw in the joiner's house opposite; when the bell rang he imitated Mme. Aubain's "Félicité! the door! the door!"

They carried on conversations, he endlessly reciting the three phrases in his repertory, to which she replied with words that were just as disconnected but uttered what was in her heart. Loulou was almost a son and a lover to her in her isolated state. He climbed up her fingers, nibbled at her lips, and clung to her kerchief; and when she bent her forehead and shook her head gently to and fro, as nurses do, the great wings of her bonnet and the bird's wings quivered together.

When the clouds massed and the thunder rumbled Loulou broke into cries, perhaps remembering the downpours in his native forests. The streaming rain made him absolutely mad; he fluttered wildly about, dashed up to the ceiling, upset everything, and went out through the window to dabble in the garden; but he was back quickly to perch on one of the fire-dogs and hopped about to dry himself, exhibiting his tail and his beak in turn.

One morning in the terrible winter of 1837 she had put him in front of the fireplace because of the cold. She found him dead, in the middle of his cage: head downwards, with his claws in the wires. He had died from congestion, no doubt. But Félicité thought he had been poisoned with parsley, and though there was no proof of any kind her suspicions inclined to Fabu.

She wept so piteously that her mistress said to her, "Well, then, have him stuffed!"

She asked advice from the chemist, who had always been kind to the parrot. He wrote to Havre, and a person called Fellacher undertook the business. But as parcels sometimes got lost in the coach she decided to take the parrot as far as Honfleur herself.

Along the sides of the road were leafless apple-trees, one after the other. Ice covered the ditches. Dogs barked about the farms; and Félicité, with her hands under her cloak, her little black sabots and her basket, walked briskly in the middle of the road.

She crossed the forest, passed High Oak, and reached St. Gatien.

A cloud of dust rose behind her, and in it a mail-coach, carried away by the steep hill, rushed down at full gallop like a hurricane. Seeing this woman who would not get out of the way, the driver stood up in front and the postilion shouted too. He could not hold in his four horses, which increased their pace, and the two leaders were grazing her when he threw them to one side with a jerk of the reins. But he was wild with rage, and lifting his arm as he passed at full speed, gave her such a lash from waist to neck with his big whip that she fell on her back.

Her first act, when she recovered consciousness, was to open her basket. Loulou was happily none the worse. She felt a burn in her right cheek, and when she put her hands against it they were red; the blood was flowing.

She sat down on a heap of stones and bound up her face with her handkerchief. Then she ate a crust of bread which she had put in the basket as a precaution, and found a consolation for her wound in gazing at the bird.

When she reached the crest of Ecquemauville she saw the Honfleur lights sparkling in the night sky like a company of stars; beyond, the sea stretched dimly. Then a faintness overtook her and she stopped; her wretched childhood, the disillusion of her first love, her nephew's going away, and Virginie's death all came back to her at once like the waves of an oncoming tide, rose to her throat, and choked her.

Afterwards, at the boat, she made a point of speaking to the captain, begging him to take care of the parcel, though she did not tell him what was in it.

Fellacher kept the parrot a long time. He was always promising it for the following week. After six months he announced that a packing-case had started, and then nothing more was heard of it. It really seemed as though Loulou was never coming back. "Ah, they have stolen him!" she thought.

He arrived at last, and looked superb. There he was, erect upon a branch which screwed into a mahogany socket, with a foot in the air and his head on one side, biting a nut which the bird-stuffer—with a taste for impressiveness-had gilded.

Félicité shut him up in her room. It was a place to which few people were admitted, and held so many religious objects and miscellaneous things that it looked like a chapel and bazaar in one.

A big cupboard impeded you as you opened the door. Opposite the window commanding the garden a little round one looked into the court; there was a table by the folding-bed with a water-jug, two combs, and a cube of blue soap in a chipped plate. On the walls hung rosaries, medals, several benign Virgins, and a holy water vessel made out of cocoa-nut; on the chest of drawers, which was covered with a cloth like an altar, was the shell box that Victor had given her, and after that a watering-can, a toy-balloon, exercise-books, the illustrated geography, and a pair of young lady's boots; and, fastened by its ribbons to the nail of the looking-glass, hung the little plush hat! Félicité carried observances of this kind so far as to keep one of Monsieur's frock-coats. All the old rubbish which Mme. Aubain did not want any longer she laid hands on for her room. That was why there were artificial flowers along the edge of the chest of drawers and a portrait of the Comte d'Artois[7] in the little window recess.

With the aid of a bracket Loulou was established over the chimney, which jutted into the room. Every morning when she woke up she saw him there in the dawning light, and recalled old days and the smallest details of insignificant acts in a deep quietness which knew no pain.

Holding, as she did, no communication with anyone, Félicité lived as insensibly as if she were walking in her sleep. The Corpus Christi processions roused her to life again. Then she went round begging mats and candlesticks from the neighbours to decorate the altar they put up in the street.

In church she was always gazing at the Holy Ghost in the window, and observed that there was something of the parrot in him. The likeness was still clearer, she thought, on a crude colour-print representing the baptism of Our Lord. With his purple wings and emerald body he was the very image of Loulou.

She bought him, and hung him up instead of the Comte d'Artois, so that she could see them both together in one glance. They were linked in her thoughts; and the parrot was consecrated by his association with the Holy Ghost, which became more vivid to her eye and more intelligible. The Father could not have chosen to express Himself through a dove, for such creatures cannot speak; it must have been one of Loulou's ancestors, surely. And though Félicité looked at the picture while she said her prayers she swerved a little from time to time towards the parrot.

---

7. Title of Charles X, the last of the Bourbons, the youngest brother of Louis XVI and Louis XVIII. He was king between 1824 and 1830 and died in exile in 1836.

She wanted to join the Ladies of the Virgin, but Mme. Aubain dissuaded her.

And then a great event loomed up before them—Paul's marriage.

He had been a solicitor's clerk to begin with, and then tried business, the Customs, the Inland Revenue, and made efforts, even, to get into the Rivers and Forests. By an inspiration from heaven he had suddenly, at thirty-six, discovered his real line—the Registrar's Office. And there he showed such marked capacity that an inspector had offered him his daughter's hand and promised him his influence.

So Paul, grown serious, brought the lady to see his mother.

She sniffed at the ways of Pont-l'Évêque, gave herself great airs, and wounded Félicité's feelings. Mme. Aubain was relieved at her departure.

The week after came news of M. Bourais' death in an inn in Lower Brittany. The rumour of suicide was confirmed, and doubts arose as to his honesty. Mme. Aubain studied his accounts, and soon found out the whole tale of his misdoings—embezzled arrears, secret sales of wood, forged receipts, etc. Besides that he had an illegitimate child, and "relations with a person at Dozulé."

These shameful facts distressed her greatly. In March 1853 she was seized with a pain in the chest; her tongue seemed to be covered with film, and leeches did not ease the difficult breathing. On the ninth evening of her illness she died, just at seventy-two.

She passed as being younger, owing to the bands of brown hair which framed her pale, pock-marked face. There were few friends to regret her, for she had a stiffness of manner which kept people at a distance.

But Félicité mourned for her as one seldom mourns for a master. It upset her ideas and seemed contrary to the order of things, impossible and monstrous, that Madame should die before her.

Ten days afterwards, which was the time it took to hurry there from Besançon,[8] the heirs arrived. The daughter-in-law ransacked the drawers, chose some furniture, and sold the rest; and then they went back to their registering.

Madame's armchair, her small round table, her foot-warmer, and the eight chairs were gone! Yellow patches in the middle of the panels showed where the engravings had hung. They had carried off the two little beds and the mattresses, and all Virginie's belongings had disappeared from the cupboard. Félicité went from floor to floor dazed with sorrow.

The next day there was a notice on the door, and the apothecary shouted in her ear that the house was for sale.

She tottered, and was obliged to sit down. What distressed her most of all was to give up her room, so suitable as it was for poor Loulou. She enveloped him with a look of anguish when she was imploring the Holy Ghost, and formed the idolatrous habit of kneeling in front of the parrot to say her prayers. Sometimes the sun shone in at the attic window and caught his glass eye, and a great luminous ray shot out of it and put her in an ecstasy.

---

8. In eastern France, near the Swiss border.

She had a pension of three hundred and eighty francs a year which her mistress had left her. The garden gave her a supply of vegetables. As for clothes, she had enough to last her to the end of her days, and she economized in candles by going to bed at dusk.

She hardly ever went out, as she did not like passing the dealer's shop, where some of the old furniture was exposed for sale. Since her fit of giddiness she dragged one leg; and as her strength was failing Mère Simon, whose grocery business had collapsed, came every morning to split the wood and pump water for her.

Her eyes grew feeble. The shutters ceased to be thrown open. Years and years passed, and the house was neither let nor sold.

Félicité never asked for repairs because she was afraid of being sent away. The boards on the roof rotted; her bolster was wet for a whole winter. After Easter she spat blood.

Then Mère Simon called in a doctor. Félicité wanted to know what was the matter with her. But she was too deaf to hear, and the only word which reached her was "pneumonia." It was a word she knew, and she answered softly "Ah! like Madame," thinking it natural that she should follow her mistress.

The time for the festal shrines was coming near. The first one was always at the bottom of the hill, the second in front of the post-office, and the third towards the middle of the street. There was some rivalry in the matter of this one, and the women of the parish ended by choosing Mme. Aubain's courtyard.

The hard breathing and fever increased. Félicité was vexed at doing nothing for the altar. If only she could at least have put something there! Then she thought of the parrot. The neighbours objected that it would not be decent. But the priest gave her permission, which so intensely delighted her that she begged him to accept Loulou, her sole possession, when she died.

From Tuesday to Saturday, the eve of the festival, she coughed more often. By the evening her face had shrivelled, her lips stuck to her gums, and she had vomitings; and at twilight next morning, feeling herself very low, she sent for a priest.

Three kindly women were round her during the extreme unction. Then she announced that she must speak to Fabu. He arrived in his Sunday clothes, by no means at his ease in the funereal atmosphere.

"Forgive me," she said, with an effort to stretch out her arm; "I thought it was you who had killed him."

What did she mean by such stories? She suspected him of murder—a man like him! He waxed indignant, and was on the point of making a row. "There," said the women, "she is no longer in her senses, you can see it well enough!"

Félicité spoke to shadows of her own from time to time. The women went away, and Mère Simon had breakfast. A little later she took Loulou and brought him close to Félicité with the words:

"Come, now, say good-bye to him!"

Loulou was not a corpse, but the worms devoured him; one of his wings was broken, and the tow was coming out of his stomach. But she was blind now; she kissed him on the forehead and kept him close against her cheek. Mère Simon took him back from her to put him on the altar.

V

Summer scents came up from the meadows; flies buzzed; the sun made the river glitter and heated the slates. Mère Simon came back into the room and fell softly asleep.

She woke at the noise of bells; the people were coming out from vespers. Félicité's delirium subsided. She thought of the procession and saw it as if she had been there.

All the school children, the church-singers, and the firemen walked on the pavement, while in the middle of the road the verger armed with his hallebard and the beadle with a large cross advanced in front. Then came the schoolmaster, with an eye on the boys, and the sister, anxious about her little girls; three of the daintiest, with angelic curls, scattered rose-petals in the air; the deacon controlled the band with outstretched arms; and two censer-bearers turned back at every step towards the Holy Sacrament, which was borne by Monsieur the curé, wearing his beautiful chasuble, under a canopy of dark-red velvet held by four churchwardens. A crowd of people pressed behind, between the white cloths covering the house walls, and they reached the bottom of the hill.

A cold sweat moistened Félicité's temples. Mère Simon sponged her with a piece of linen, saying to herself that one day she would have to go that way.

The hum of the crowd increased, was very loud for an instant and then went further away.

A fusillade shook the window-panes. It was the postilions saluting the monstrance. Félicité rolled her eyes and said as audibly as she could: "Does he look well?" The parrot was weighing on her mind.

Her agony began. A death-rattle that grew more and more convulsed made her sides heave. Bubbles of froth came at the corners of her mouth and her whole body trembled.

Soon the booming of the ophicleides,[9] the high voices of the children, and the deep voices of the men were distinguishable. At intervals all was silent, and the tread of feet, deadened by the flowers they walked on, sounded like a flock pattering on grass.

The clergy appeared in the courtyard. Mère Simon clambered on to a chair to reach the attic window, and so looked down straight upon the shrine. Green garlands hung over the altar, which was decked with a flounce of English lace. In the middle was a small frame with relics in it; there were two orange-trees at the corners, and all along stood silver candlesticks and china vases, with sunflowers, lilies, peonies, foxgloves, and tufts of hortensia. This heap of blazing colour slanted from the level of the altar to the carpet which went on over the pavement; and some rare objects caught the eye. There was a silver-gilt sugar-basin with a crown of violets; pendants of Alençon stone glittered on the moss, and two Chinese

9. An old large brass-wind instrument now replaced by the tuba.

screens displayed their landscapes. Loulou was hidden under roses, and showed nothing but his blue forehead, like a plaque of lapis lazuli.

The churchwardens, singers, and children took their places round the three sides of the court. The priest went slowly up the steps, and placed his great, radiant golden sun[1] upon the lace. Everyone knelt down. There was a deep silence; and the censers glided to and fro on the full swing of their chains.

An azure vapour rose up into Félicité's room. Her nostrils met it; she inhaled it sensuously, mystically; and then closed her eyes. Her lips smiled. The beats of her heart lessened one by one, vaguer each time and softer, as a fountain sinks, an echo disappears; and when she sighed her last breath she thought she saw an opening in the heavens, and a gigantic parrot hovering above her head.

1. The monstrance containing the consecrated Host.

FYODOR DOSTOEVSKY
1821–1881

Fyodor Dostoevsky has been a central figure in the formation of the modern sensibility. His works are fundamental to the Western tradition of the novel and a strong influence on modern literature in China and Japan. Dostoevsky formulated in fictional terms, in dramatic and even sensational scenes, some of the central predicaments of our time: the choices between God and atheism, good and evil, freedom and tyranny; the recognition of the limits and even of the fall of humanity against the belief in progress, revolution, and utopia. Most important, he captured unforgettably the enormous contradictions of which our common human nature is capable and by which it is torn.

Fyodor Mikhailovich Dostoevsky was born in Moscow on October 30, 1821. His father was a staff doctor at the Hospital for the Poor. Later he acquired an estate and serfs. In 1839 he was killed by one of his peasants in a quarrel. Dostoevsky was sent to the Military Engineering Academy in St. Petersburg, from which he graduated in 1843. He became a civil servant, a draftsman in the St. Petersburg Engineering Corps, but resigned soon because he feared that he would be transferred to the provinces when his writing was discovered. His first novel, *Poor People* (1846), proved a great success with the critics; his second, *The Double* (1846), which followed immediately, was a failure.

Subsequently, Dostoevsky became involved in the Petrashevsky circle, a secret society of antigovernment and socialist tendencies. He was arrested on April 23, 1849, and condemned to be shot. On December 22 he was led to public execution, but he was reprieved at the last moment and sent to penal servitude in Siberia (near Omsk), where he worked for four years in a stockade, wearing fetters, completely cut off from communications with Russia. On his release in February 1854, he was assigned as a common soldier to Semipalatinsk, a small town near the Mongolian frontier. There he received several promotions (eventually becoming an ensign); his rank of nobility, forfeited by his sentence, was restored; and he married the widow of a customs official. In July 1859, Dostoevsky was permitted to return to Russia, and finally, in December 1859, to St. Petersburg—after ten years of his life had been spent in Siberia.

In the last year of his exile, Dostoevsky had resumed writing, and in 1861, shortly after his return, he founded a review, *Time* (*Vremya*). This was suppressed in 1863, though Dostoevsky had changed his political opinions and was now strongly nationalistic and conservative in outlook. He made his first trip to France and England in 1862, and traveled in Europe again in 1863 and 1865, to follow a young woman friend, Apollinaria Suslova, and to indulge in gambling. After his wife's death in 1864, and another unsuccessful journalistic venture, *The Epoch* (*Epokha*, 1864–65), Dostoevsky was for a time almost crushed by gambling debts, emotional entanglements, and frequent epileptic seizures. He barely managed to return from Germany in 1865. In the winter of 1866 he wrote *Crime and Punishment* and, before he had finished it, dictated a shorter novel, *The Gambler*, to meet a deadline. He married his secretary, Anna Grigoryevna Snitkina, early in 1867 and left Russia with her to avoid his creditors. For years they wandered over Germany, Italy, and Switzerland, frequently in abject poverty. Their first child died. In 1871, when the initial chapters of *The Possessed* proved a popular success, Dostoevsky returned to St. Petersburg. He became the editor of a weekly, *The Citizen* (*Grazhdanin*), for a short time and then published a periodical written by himself, *The Diary of a Writer* (1876–81), which won great acclaim. His last novel, *The Brothers Karamazov* (1880), was an immense success, and honors and some prosperity came to him at last. At a Pushkin anniversary celebrated in Moscow in 1880 he gave the main speech. But soon after his return to St. Petersburg he died, on January 28, 1881, not yet sixty years old.

Dostoevsky, like every great writer, can be approached in different ways and read on different levels. We can try to understand him as a religious philosopher, a political commentator, a psychologist, and a novelist, and if we know much about his fascinating and varied life, we might also interpret his works as biographical.

The biographical interpretation is the one that has been pushed furthest. The lurid crimes of Dostoevsky's characters (such as the rape of a young girl) have been ascribed to him, and all his novels have been studied as if they constituted a great personal confession. Dostoevsky certainly did draw from his experiences in his books, as every writer does: he several times described the feelings of a man facing a firing squad as he himself faced it on December 22, 1849, only to be reprieved at the last moment. His writings also reflect his years in Siberia: four years working in a loghouse, in chains, as he describes it in an oddly impersonal book, *Memoirs from the House of the Dead* (1862), and six more years as a common soldier on the borders of Mongolia, in a small, remote provincial town. Similarly, he used the experience of his disease (epilepsy), ascribing great spiritual significance to the ecstatic rapture preceding the actual seizure. He assigned his disease to both his most angelic "good" man, the "Idiot," Prince Myshkin, and his most diabolical, inhuman figure, the cold-blooded unsexed murderer of the old Karamazov, the flunky Smerdyakov. Dostoevsky also used something of his experiences in Germany, where in the 1860s he succumbed to a passion for gambling, which he overcame only much later, during his second marriage. The short novel *The Gambler* (1866) gives an especially vivid account of this life and its moods.

There are other autobiographical elements in Dostoevsky's works, but it seems a gross misunderstanding of his methods and the procedures of art in general to conclude from his writings (as Thomas Mann has done) that he was a "saint and criminal" in one. Dostoevsky, after all, was an extremely hard worker who wrote and rewrote some twenty volumes. He was a novelist who employed the methods of the French sensational novel; he was constantly on the lookout for the most striking occurrences—the most shocking crimes and the most horrible disasters and scandals—because only in such fictional situations could he exalt his characters to their highest pitch, bringing out the clash of ideas and temperaments, revealing the deepest layers of their souls. But these fictions cannot be taken as literal transcriptions of reality and actual experience.

Whole books have been written to explain Dostoevsky's religious philosophy and conception of human nature. The Russian philosopher Berdyayev concludes his excellent study by saying, "So great is the value of Dostoevsky that to have produced him is by itself sufficient justification for the existence of the Russian people in the world." But there is no need for such extravagance. Dostoevsky's philosophy of religion is rather a personal version of extreme mystical Christianity, and assumes flesh and blood only in the context of the novels. Reduced to the bare bones of abstract propositions, it amounts to saying that humanity is fallen but is free to choose between evil and Christ. And choosing Christ means taking on oneself the burden of humanity in love and pity, since "everybody is guilty for all and before all." Hence in Dostoevsky there is tremendous stress on personal freedom of choice, and his affirmation of the worth of every individual is combined, paradoxically, with an equal insistence on the substantial identity of all human beings, their equality before God, the bond of love that unites them.

Dostoevsky also develops a philosophy of history, with practical political implications, based on this point of view. According to him, the West is in complete decay; only Russia has preserved Christianity in its original form. The West is either Catholic (and Catholicism is condemned by Dostoevsky as an attempt to force salvation by magic and authority) or bourgeois, and hence materialistic and fallen away from Christ, or socialist, and socialism is to Dostoevsky identical with atheism, as it dreams of a utopia in which human beings would not be free to choose even at the expense of suffering. Dostoevsky—who himself had belonged to a revolutionary group and come into contact with Russian revolutionaries abroad—had an extraordinary insight into the mentality of the Russian underground. In *The Possessed* (1871–72) he gives a lurid satiric picture of these would-be saviors of Russia and humankind. But while he was afraid of the revolution, Dostoevsky himself hoped and prophesied that Russia would save Europe from the dangers of communism, as Russia alone was the uncorrupted Christian land. Put in terms of political propositions (as Dostoevsky himself preaches them in his journal, *The Diary of a Writer*, 1876–81), what he propounds is a conservative Russian nationalism with messianic hopes for Russian Christianity.

When translated into abstractions, Dostoevsky's psychology is as unimpressive as his political theory. It is merely a derivative of theories propounded by German writers about the unconscious, the role of dreams, the ambivalence of human feelings. What makes it electric in the novels is his ability to dramatize it in scenes of sudden revelation, in characters who in today's terminology would be called split personalities, in people twisted by isolation, lust, humiliation, and resentment. The dreams of Raskolnikov may be interpreted according to Freudian psychology, but to the reader without any knowledge of science they are comprehensible in their place in the novel and function as warnings and anticipations.

Dostoevsky was first of all an artist—a novelist who succeeded in using his ideas (many old and venerable, many new and fantastic) and psychological insights for the writing of stories of absorbing interest. As an artist, Dostoevsky treated the novel like a drama, constructing it in large, vivid scenes that end with a scandal or a crime or some act of violence, filling it with unforgettable "stagelike" figures torn by great passions and swayed by great ideas. Then he set this world in an environment of St. Petersburg slums or of towns, monasteries, and country houses, all so vividly realized that we forget how the setting, the figures, and the ideas blend together into one cosmos of the imagination only remotely and obliquely related to any reality of nineteenth-century Russia. We take part in a great drama of pride and humility, good and evil, in a huge allegory of humanity's search for God and itself. We understand and share in this world because it is not merely Russia in the nineteenth century, where people could hardly have talked and behaved as Dostoevsky's people do, but a myth of humanity, universalized as all art is.

Notes from Underground (1864) precedes the four great novels: *Crime and Punishment* (1866), *The Idiot* (1868), *The Possessed*, and *The Brothers Karamazov* (1880). The *Notes* can be viewed as a prologue, an important introduction to the cycle of the four great novels, an anticipation of the mature Dostoevsky's method and thought. Though it cannot compare in dramatic power and scope with these, the story has its own peculiar and original artistry. It is made up of two parts, at first glance seemingly independent: the monologue of the Underground man and the confession that he makes about himself, called *Apropos of Wet Snow*. The monologue, though it includes no action, is dramatic—a long address to an imaginary hostile reader, whom the Underground man ridicules, defies, jeers at, but also flatters. The confession is an autobiographical reminiscence of the Underground man. It describes events that occurred long before the delivery of the monologue, but it functions as a confirmation in concrete terms of the self-portrait drawn in the monologue and as an explanation of the isolation of the hero.

The narrative of the confession is a comic variation on the old theme of the rescue of a fallen woman from vice, a seesaw series of humiliations permitting Dostoevsky to display all the cruelty of his probing psychology. The hero, out of spite and craving for human company, forces himself into the company of former schoolfellows and is shamefully humiliated by them. He reasserts his ego (as he cannot revenge himself on them) in the company of a humble prostitute by impressing her with florid and moving speeches, which he knows to be insincere, about her horrible future. Ironically, he converts her, but when she comes to him and surprises him in a degrading scene with his servant, he humiliates her again. When, even then, she understands and forgives and thus shows her moral superiority, he crowns his spite by deliberately misunderstanding her and forcing money on her. She is the moral victor and the Underground man returns to his hideout to jeer at humanity. It is hard not to feel that we are shown a tortured and twisted soul almost too despicable to elicit our compassion.

Still it would be a complete misunderstanding of Dostoevsky's story to take the philosophy expounded jeeringly in the long monologue of the first part merely as the irrational railings of a sick personality. The Underground man, though abject and spiteful, represents not only a specific Russian type of the time—the intellectual divorced from the soil and his nation—but also modern humanity, even Everyman, and strangely enough, even the author, who through the mouth of this despicable character, as through a mask, expresses his boldest and most intimate convictions. In spite of all the exaggerated pathos, wild paradox, and jeering irony used by the speaker, his self-criticism and his criticism of society and history must be taken seriously and interpreted patiently if we are to extract the meaning accepted by Dostoevsky.

The Underground man is also the hyperconscious man who examines himself as if in a mirror, and sees himself with pitiless candor. His very self-consciousness cripples his will and poisons his feelings. He cannot escape from his ego; he knows that he has acted badly toward the woman but at the same time he cannot help acting as he does. He knows that he is alone, that there is no bridge from him to humanity, that the world is hostile to him, and that he is humiliated by everyone he meets. But though he resents the humiliation, he cannot help courting it, provoking it, and even enjoying it in his perverse manner. He understands (and knows from his own experience) that something within us all enjoys evil and destruction.

His self-criticism widens, then, into a criticism of the assumptions of modern civilization, of nineteenth-century optimism about human nature and progress, of utilitarianism, and of all kinds of utopias. It is possible to identify specific allusions to a contemporary novel by a radical socialist and revolutionary, Chernyshevsky, titled *What Shall We Do?* (1863), but we do not need to know the exact target of Dostoevsky's satire to recognize what he attacks: the view that human nature is good, that we generally seek our enlightened self-interest, that science propounds immutable truths, and that a paradise on earth will be just around the corner once society is reformed along scientific lines. In a series of vivid symbols these assumptions are represented, parodied, exposed. Science says that "twice two makes four" but the Underground man laughs that "twice two makes five is sometimes a very charming thing too." Science means to him (and to Dostoevsky) the victory of the doctrine of fatality, of iron necessity, of determinism, and thus finally of death. Humanity would become an "organ stop," a "piano key," if deterministic science were valid.

Equally disastrous are the implications of the social philosophy of liberalism and of socialism (which Dostoevsky considers its necessary consequence). In this view, we need only follow our enlightened self-interest, need only be rational, and we will become noble and good and the earth will be a place of prosperity and peace. But the Underground man knows that this conception of human nature is entirely false. What if humankind does not follow, and never will follow, its own enlightened self-interest, is consciously and purposely irrational, even bloodthirsty and evil? History seems to the Underground man to speak a clear language: "civilization has made mankind if not more bloodthirsty, at least more vilely, more loathsomely bloodthirsty." Humanity wills the irrational and evil because it does not want to become an organ stop, a piano key, because it wants to be left with the freedom to choose between good and evil. This freedom of choice, even at the expense of chaos and destruction, is what makes us human.

Actually, we love something other than our own well-being and happiness, love even suffering and pain, because we are human and not animals inhabiting some great organized rational "ant heap." The ant heap, the hen house, the block of tenements, and finally the Crystal Palace (then the newest wonder of architecture, a great hall of iron and glass erected for the Universal Exhibition in London) are the images used by the Underground man to represent his hated utopia. The heroine of *What Shall We Do?* had dreamed of a building, made of cast iron and glass and placed in the middle of a beautiful garden where there would be eternal spring and summer, eternal joy. Dostoevsky had recognized there the utopian dream of Charles Fourier, the French socialist whom he had admired in his youth and whose ideals he had come to hate with a fierce revulsion. But we must realize that the Underground man, and Dostoevsky, despise this "ant heap," this perfectly organized society of automatons, in the name of something higher, in the name of freedom. Dostoevsky does not believe that humanity can achieve freedom and happiness at the same time; happiness can be bought only at the expense of freedom, and all utopian schemes seem to him devices to lure us into the yoke of slavery. This freedom is, of course, not political freedom but freedom of choice, indeterminism, even caprice and willfulness, in the paradoxical formulation of the Underground man.

There are hints at a positive solution only in the one chapter (Part I, Chapter X) that was mutilated by the censor. A letter by Dostoevsky to his brother about the "swine of a censor who let through the passages where I jeered at everything and blasphemed ostensibly" refers to the fact that he "suppressed everything where I drew the conclusion that faith in Christ is needed." In Part I, Chapter XI, of the present text (and Dostoevsky never restored the suppressed passages) the Underground man says merely, "I am lying because I know myself that it is not underground that is better, but something different, quite different, for which I am thirsting, but which I cannot find!" This "something . . . quite different" all the other writings of Dostoevsky show to be the voluntary following of the Christian savior even at the expense of suffering and pain.

In a paradoxical form, through the mouth of one of his vilest characters, Dostoevsky reveals in the story his view of humanity and history—of the evil in human nature and of the blood and tragedy in history—and his criticism of the optimistic, utilitarian, utopian, progressive view of humanity that was spreading to Russia from the West during the nineteenth century and that found its most devoted adherents in the Russian revolutionaries. Preoccupied with criticism, Dostoevsky does not here suggest any positive remedy. But if we understand the *Notes* we can understand how Raskolnikov, the murderer out of intellect in *Crime and Punishment*, can find salvation at last, and how Dmitri, the guilty-guiltless parricide of *The Brothers Karamazov*, can sing his hymn to joy in the Siberian mines. We can even understand the legend of the Grand Inquisitor told by Ivan Karamazov, in which we meet the same criticism of a utopia (this time that of Catholicism) and the same exaltation of human freedom even at the price of suffering.

Monroe C. Beardsley, "Dostoevsky's Metaphor of the 'Underground,' " *Journal of the History of Ideas*, 3 (June 1942): 265–90, is a subtle interpretation of the central metaphor of the *Notes*. Joseph Frank, "Nihilism and *Notes from Underground*," *Sewanee Review*, 69 (1961), interprets the *Notes* in the context of the history of the times. Robert L. Jackson, *The Underground Man in Russian Literature* (1981), traces the impact of the *Notes* on Russian literature. Konstantin Mochulsky, *Dostoevsky: Life and Work* (1967), is the best general work translated from Russian, the work of an emigré in Paris. René Wellek, ed., *Dostoevsky: A Collection of Critical Essays* (1962), contains an essay by the editor on the history of Dostoevsky criticism. Alba della Fazia Amoia, *Feodor Dostoevsky* (1993), is a general introduction to Dostoevsky's work, aimed at a student audience. Joseph Frank, *Dostoevsky* (1976–1986), is an impressive though still unfinished biographical study in three volumes. Frank's *Through the Russian Prism* (1990) includes review essays that examine various approaches to Dostoevsky. Louis Breger, *Dostoevsky: The Author as Psychoanalyst* (1989), takes a psychoanalytic approach in analyzing levels of meaning in Dostoevsky's work as a new sensibility that anticipates the modern novel; he includes a chapter on *Notes*. Malcolm V. Jones, *Dostoyevsky after Bakhtin: Readings in Dostoyevsky's Fantastic Realism* (1990), examines Dostoevsky's "higher realism" in various perspectives and includes a chapter on *Notes*.

PRONOUNCING GLOSSARY

The following list uses common English syllables and stress accents to provide rough equivalents of selected words whose pronunciation may be unfamiliar to the general reader.

Anton Antonych: *an'-tonn an'-tonych*

Apollon: *ah-poll-on'*

Ferfichkin: *fair-fich'-kin*

Fyodor Dostoevsky: *fyo'dor dos-toy-eff'-skee*

Karamazov: *kah-rah-mah'-zoff*

Kolya: *kol'-ya*

Podkharzhevsky: *pod-har-zheff'-skee*

Simonov: *see-mon'-off*

Trudolyubov: *troo-doll-yoo'-boff*

Zverkov: *zvyer-koff'*

Notes from Underground[1]

I

Underground[2]

I

I am a sick man. . . .[3] I am a spiteful man. I am a most unpleasant man. I think my liver is diseased. Then again, I don't know a thing about my illness; I'm not even sure what hurts. I'm not being treated and never have been, though I respect both medicine and doctors. Besides, I'm extremely superstitious—well at least enough to respect medicine. (I'm sufficiently educated not to be superstitious; but I am, anyway.) No, gentlemen, it's out of spite that I don't wish to be treated. Now then, that's something you probably won't understand. Well, I do. Of course, I won't really be able to explain to you precisely who will be hurt by my spite in this case; I know perfectly well that I can't possibly "get even" with doctors by refusing their treatment; I know better than anyone that all this is going to hurt me alone, and no one else. Even so, if I refuse to be treated, it's out of spite. My liver hurts? Good, let it hurt even more!

I've been living this way for some time—about twenty years. I'm forty now. I used to be in the civil service. But no more. I was a nasty official. I was rude and took pleasure in it. After all, since I didn't accept bribes, at least I had to reward myself in some way. (That's a poor joke, but I won't cross it out. I wrote it thinking that it would be very witty; but now, having realized that I merely wanted to show off disgracefully, I'll make a point of not crossing it out!) When petitioners used to approach my desk for information, I'd gnash my teeth and feel unending pleasure if I succeeded in causing someone distress. I almost always succeeded. For the most part they were all timid people: naturally, since they were petitioners. But among the dandies there was a certain officer whom I particularly couldn't bear. He simply refused to be humble, and he clanged his saber in a loathsome manner. I waged war with him over that saber for about a year and a half. At last I prevailed. He stopped clanging. All this, however, happened a long time ago, during my youth. But do you know, gentlemen, what the main component of my spite really was? Why, the whole point, the most disgusting thing, was the fact that I was shamefully aware at every moment, even at the moment of my greatest bitterness, that not only was I not a spiteful man, I was not even an embittered one, and that I was merely scaring sparrows to no effect and consoling myself by doing so. I was foaming at the mouth—but just bring me some trinket to play with, just serve me a nice cup of tea with sugar, and I'd probably have calmed

---

1. Translated by Michael Katz. 2. Both the author of these notes and the *Notes* themselves are fictitious, of course. Nevertheless, people like the author of these notes not only may, but actually must exist in our society, considering the general circumstances under which our society was formed. I wanted to bring before the public with more prominence than usual one of the characters of the recent past. He's a representative of the current generation. In the excerpt entitled "Underground" this person introduces himself and his views, and, as it were, wants to explain the reasons why he appeared and why he had to appear in our midst. The following excerpt ["Apropos of Wet Snow"] contains the actual "notes" of this person about several events in his life [Author's note].   3. The ellipses are the author's and do not indicate omissions from this text.

down. My heart might even have been touched, although I'd probably have gnashed my teeth out of shame and then suffered from insomnia for several months afterward. That's just my usual way.

I was lying about myself just now when I said that I was a nasty official. I lied out of spite. I was merely having some fun at the expense of both the petitioners and that officer, but I could never really become spiteful. At all times I was aware of a great many elements in me that were just the opposite of that. I felt how they swarmed inside me, these contradictory elements. I knew that they had been swarming inside me my whole life and were begging to be let out; but I wouldn't let them out, I wouldn't, I deliberately wouldn't let them out. They tormented me to the point of shame; they drove me to convulsions and—and finally I got fed up with them, oh how fed up! Perhaps it seems to you, gentlemen, that I'm repenting about something, that I'm asking your forgiveness for something? I'm sure that's how it seems to you. . . . But really, I can assure you, I don't care if that's how it seems. . . .

Not only couldn't I become spiteful, I couldn't become anything at all: neither spiteful nor good, neither a scoundrel nor an honest man, neither a hero nor an insect. Now I live out my days in my corner, taunting myself with the spiteful and entirely useless consolation that an intelligent man cannot seriously become anything and that only a fool can become something. Yes, sir, an intelligent man in the nineteenth century must be, is morally obliged to be, principally a characterless creature; a man possessing character, a man of action, is fundamentally a limited creature. That's my conviction at the age of forty. I'm forty now; and, after all, forty is an entire lifetime; why it's extreme old age. It's rude to live past forty, it's indecent, immoral! Who lives more than forty years? Answer sincerely, honestly. I'll tell you who: only fools and rascals. I'll tell those old men that right to their faces, all those venerable old men, all those silver-haired and sweet-smelling old men! I'll say it to the whole world right to its face! I have a right to say it because I myself will live to sixty. I'll make it to seventy! Even to eighty! . . . Wait! Let me catch my breath. . . .

You probably think, gentlemen, that I want to amuse you. You're wrong about that, too. I'm not at all the cheerful fellow I seem to be, or that I may seem to be; however, if you're irritated by all this talk (and I can already sense that you are irritated), and if you decide to ask me just who I really am, then I'll tell you: I'm a collegiate assessor. I worked in order to have something to eat (but only for that reason); and last year, when a distant relative of mine left me six thousand rubles in his will, I retired immediately and settled down in this corner. I used to live in this corner before, but now I've settled down in it. My room is nasty, squalid, on the outskirts of town. My servant is an old peasant woman, spiteful out of stupidity; besides, she has a foul smell. I'm told that the Petersburg climate is becoming bad for my health, and that it's very expensive to live in Petersburg with my meager resources. I know all that; I know it better than all those wise and experienced advisers and admonishers. But I shall remain in Petersburg; I shall not leave Petersburg! I shall not leave here because . . . Oh, what difference does it really make whether I leave Petersburg or not?

Now, then, what can a decent man talk about with the greatest pleasure?

Answer: about himself.

Well, then, I too will talk about myself.

II

Now I would like to tell you, gentlemen, whether or not you want to hear it, why it is that I couldn't even become an insect. I'll tell you solemnly that I wished to become an insect many times. But not even that wish was granted. I swear to you, gentlemen, that being overly conscious is a disease, a genuine, full-fledged disease. Ordinary human consciousness would be more than sufficient for everyday human needs—that is, even half or a quarter of the amount of consciousness that's available to a cultured man in our unfortunate nineteenth century, especially to one who has the particular misfortune of living in St. Petersburg, the most abstract and premeditated city in the whole world.[4] (Cities can be either premeditated or unpremeditated.) It would have been entirely sufficient, for example, to have the consciousness with which all so-called spontaneous people and men of action are endowed. I'll bet that you think I'm writing all this to show off, to make fun of these men of action, that I'm clanging my saber just like that officer did to show off in bad taste. But, gentlemen, who could possibly be proud of his illnesses and want to show them off?

But what am I saying? Everyone does that; people do take pride in their illnesses, and I, perhaps, more than anyone else. Let's not argue; my objection is absurd. Nevertheless, I remain firmly convinced that not only is being overly conscious a disease, but so is being conscious at all. I insist on it. But let's leave that alone for a moment. Tell me this: why was it, as if on purpose, at the very moment, indeed, at the precise moment that I was most capable of becoming conscious of the subtleties of everything that was "beautiful and sublime,"[5] as we used to say at one time, that I didn't become conscious, and instead did such unseemly things, things that . . . well, in short, probably everyone does, but it seemed as if they occurred to me deliberately at the precise moment when I was most conscious that they shouldn't be done at all? The more conscious I was of what was good, of everything "beautiful and sublime," the more deeply I sank into the morass and the more capable I was of becoming entirely bogged down in it. But the main thing is that all this didn't seem to be occurring accidentally; rather, it was as if it all had to be so. It was as if this were my most normal condition, not an illness or an affliction at all, so that finally I even lost the desire to struggle against it. It ended when I almost came to believe (perhaps I really did believe) that this might really have been my normal condition. But at first, in the beginning, what agonies I suffered during that struggle! I didn't believe that others were experiencing the same thing; therefore, I kept it a secret about myself all my life.

4. Petersburg was conceived as an imposing city; plans called for regular streets, broad avenues, and spacious squares.   5. This phrase originated in Edmund Burke's (1729–1797) *Philosophical Inquiry into the Origin of Our Ideas of the Sublime and Beautiful* (1756) and was repeated in Immanuel Kant's (1724–1804) *Observations on the Feeling of the Beautiful and the Sublime* (1756). It became a cliché in the writings of Russian critics during the 1830s.

I was ashamed (perhaps I still am even now); I reached the point where I felt some secret, abnormal, despicable little pleasure in returning home to my little corner on some disgusting Petersburg night, acutely aware that once again I'd committed some revolting act that day, that what had been done could not be undone, and I used to gnaw and gnaw at myself inwardly, secretly, nagging away, consuming myself until finally the bitterness turned into some kind of shameful, accursed sweetness and at last into genuine, earnest pleasure! Yes, into pleasure, real pleasure! I absolutely mean that. . . . That's why I first began to speak out, because I want to know for certain whether other people share this same pleasure. Let me explain: the pleasure resulted precisely from the overly acute consciousness of one's own humiliation; from the feeling that one had reached the limit; that it was disgusting, but couldn't be otherwise; you had no other choice—you could never become a different person; and that even if there were still time and faith enough for you to change into something else, most likely you wouldn't even want to change, and if you did, you wouldn't have done anything, perhaps because there really was nothing for you to change into. But the main thing and the final point is that all of this was taking place according to normal and fundamental laws of overly acute consciousness and of the inertia which results directly from these laws; consequently, not only couldn't one change, one simply couldn't do anything at all. Hence it follows, for example, as a result of this overly acute consciousness, that one is absolutely right in being a scoundrel, as if this were some consolation to the scoundrel. But enough of this. . . . Oh, my, I've gone on rather a long time, but have I really explained anything? How can I explain this pleasure? But I will explain it! I shall see it through to the end! That's why I've taken up my pen. . . .

For example, I'm terribly proud. I'm as mistrustful and as sensitive as a hunchback or a dwarf; but, in truth, I've experienced some moments when, if someone had slapped my face, I might even have been grateful for it. I'm being serious. I probably would have been able to derive a peculiar sort of pleasure from it—the pleasure of despair, naturally, but the most intense pleasures occur in despair, especially when you're very acutely aware of the hopelessness of your own predicament. As for a slap in the face—why, here the consciousness of being beaten to a pulp would overwhelm you. The main thing is, no matter how I try, it still turns out that I'm always the first to be blamed for everything and, what's even worse, I'm always the innocent victim, so to speak, according to the laws of nature. Therefore, in the first place, I'm guilty inasmuch as I'm smarter than everyone around me. (I've always considered myself smarter than everyone around me, and sometimes, believe me, I've been ashamed of it. At the least, all my life I've looked away and never could look people straight in the eye.) Finally, I'm to blame because even if there were any magnanimity in me, it would only have caused more suffering as a result of my being aware of its utter uselessness. After all, I probably wouldn't have been able to make use of that magnanimity: neither to forgive, as the offender, perhaps, had slapped me in accordance with the laws of nature, and there's no way to forgive the laws of nature; nor to forget, because even if there were any laws of nature, it's offensive nonetheless. Finally, even if I wanted to be entirely unmagnanimous, and had wanted to take revenge on the offender, I couldn't be revenged on anyone for anything because, most likely, I would never have decided to do anything, even if I could have. Why not? I'd like to say a few words about that separately.

III

Let's consider people who know how to take revenge and how to stand up for themselves in general. How, for example, do they do it? Let's suppose that they're seized by an impulse to take revenge—then for a while nothing else remains in their entire being except for that impulse. Such an individual simply rushes toward his goal like an enraged bull with lowered horns; only a wall can stop him. (By the way, when actually faced with a wall such individuals, that is, spontaneous people and men of action, genuinely give up. For them a wall doesn't constitute the evasion that it does for those of us who think and consequently do nothing; it's not an excuse to turn aside from the path, a pretext in which a person like me usually doesn't believe, but one for which he's always extremely grateful. No, they give up in all sincerity. For them the wall possesses some kind of soothing, morally decisive and definitive meaning, perhaps even something mystical . . . But more about the wall later.) Well, then, I consider such a spontaneous individual to be a genuine, normal person, just as tender mother nature wished to see him when she lovingly gave birth to him on earth. I'm green with envy at such a man. He's stupid, I won't argue with you about that; but perhaps a normal man is supposed to be stupid—how do we know? Perhaps it's even very beautiful. And I'm all the more convinced of the suspicion, so to speak, that if, for example, one were to take the antithesis of a normal man—that is, a man of overly acute consciousness, who emerged, of course, not from the bosom of nature, but from a laboratory test tube (this is almost mysticism, gentlemen, but I suspect that it's the case), then this test tube man sometimes gives up so completely in the face of his antithesis that he himself, with his overly acute consciousness, honestly considers himself not as a person, but a mouse. It may be an acutely conscious mouse, but a mouse nonetheless, while the other one is a person and consequently, . . . and so on and so forth. But the main thing is that he, he himself, considers himself to be a mouse; nobody asks him to do so, and that's the important point. Now let's take a look at this mouse in action. Let's assume, for instance, that it feels offended (it almost always feels offended), and that it also wishes to be revenged. It may even contain more accumulated malice than *l'homme de la nature et de la vérité*.[6] The mean, nasty, little desire to pay the offender back with evil may indeed rankle in it even more despicably than in *l'homme de la nature et de la vérité*, because *l'homme de la nature et de la vérité*, with his innate stupidity, considers his revenge nothing more than justice, pure and simple; but the mouse, as a result of its overly acute consciousness, rejects the idea of justice. Finally, we come to the act itself,

---

6. The man of nature and truth (French). The basic idea is borrowed from Jean-Jacques Rousseau's *Confessions* (1782–89), namely, that human beings in a state of nature are honest and direct and that they are only corrupted by civilization.

to the very act of revenge. In addition to its original nastiness, the mouse has already managed to pile up all sorts of other nastiness around itself in the form of hesitations and doubts; so many unresolved questions have emerged from that one single question, that some kind of fatal blow is concocted unwillingly, some kind of stinking mess consisting of doubts, anxieties and, finally, spittle showered upon it by the spontaneous men of action who stand by solemnly as judges and arbiters, roaring with laughter until their sides split. Of course, the only thing left to do is dismiss it with a wave of its paw and a smile of assumed contempt which it doesn't even believe in, and creep ignominiously back into its mousehole. There, in its disgusting, stinking underground, our offended, crushed, and ridiculed mouse immediately plunges into cold, malicious, and, above all, everlasting spitefulness. For forty years on end it will recall its insult down to the last, most shameful detail; and each time it will add more shameful details of its own, spitefully teasing and irritating itself with its own fantasy. It will become ashamed of that fantasy, but it will still remember it, rehearse it again and again, fabricating all sorts of incredible stories about itself under the pretext that they too could have happened; it won't forgive a thing. Perhaps it will even begin to take revenge, but only in little bits and pieces, in trivial ways, from behind the stove, incognito, not believing in its right to be revenged, nor in the success of its own revenge, and knowing in advance that from all its attempts to take revenge, it will suffer a hundred times more than the object of its vengeance, who might not even feel a thing. On its deathbed it will recall everything all over again, with interest compounded over all those years and. . . . But it's precisely in that cold, abominable state of half-despair and half-belief, in that conscious burial of itself alive in the underground for forty years because of its pain, in that powerfully created, yet partly dubious hopelessness of its own predicament, in all that venom of unfulfilled desire turned inward, in all that fever of vacillation, of resolutions adopted once and for all and followed a moment later by repentance—herein precisely lies the essence of that strange enjoyment I was talking about earlier. It's so subtle, sometimes so difficult to analyze, that even slightly limited people, or those who simply have strong nerves, won't understand anything about it. "Perhaps," you'll add with a smirk, "even those who've never received a slap in the face won't understand," and by so doing you'll be hinting to me ever so politely that perhaps during my life I too have received such a slap in the face and that therefore I'm speaking as an expert. I'll bet that's what you're thinking. Well, rest assured, gentlemen, I've never received such a slap, although it's really all the same to me what you think about it. Perhaps I may even regret the fact that I've given so few slaps during my lifetime. But that's enough, not another word about this subject which you find so extremely interesting.

I'll proceed calmly about people with strong nerves who don't understand certain refinements of pleasure. For example, although under particular circumstances these gentlemen may bellow like bulls as loudly as possible, and although, let's suppose, this behavior bestows on them the greatest honor, yet, as I've already said, when confronted with impossibility, they submit immediately. Impossibility—does that mean a stone wall?

What kind of stone wall? Why, of course, the laws of nature, the conclusions of natural science and mathematics. As soon as they prove to you,
for example, that it's from a monkey you're descended,[7] there's no reason
to make faces; just accept it as it is. As soon as they prove to you that in
truth one drop of your own fat is dearer to you than the lives of one hundred thousand of your fellow creatures and that this will finally put an end
to all the so-called virtues, obligations, and other such similar ravings and
prejudices, just accept that too; there's nothing more to do, since two times
two is a fact of mathematics. Just you try to object.

"For goodness sake," they'll shout at you, "it's impossible to protest: it's
two times two makes four! Nature doesn't ask for your opinion; it doesn't
care about your desires or whether you like or dislike its laws. You're
obliged to accept it as it is, and consequently, all its conclusions. A wall,
you see, is a wall . . . etc. etc." Good Lord, what do I care about the laws
of nature and arithmetic when for some reason I dislike all these laws and
I dislike the fact that two times two makes four? Of course, I won't break
through that wall with my head if I really don't have the strength to do so,
nor will I reconcile myself to it just because I'm faced with such a stone
wall and lack the strength.

As though such a stone wall actually offered some consolation and contained some real word of conciliation, for the sole reason that it means
two times two makes four. Oh, absurdity of absurdities! How much better
it is to understand it all, to be aware of everything, all the impossibilities
and stone walls; not to be reconciled with any of those impossibilities or
stone walls if it so disgusts you; to reach, by using the most inevitable
logical combinations, the most revolting conclusions on the eternal theme
that you are somehow or other to blame even for that stone wall, even
though it's absolutely clear once again that you're in no way to blame,
and, as a result of all this, while silently and impotently gnashing your
teeth, you sink voluptuously into inertia, musing on the fact that, as it
turns out, there's no one to be angry with; that an object cannot be found,
and perhaps never will be; that there's been a substitution, some sleight of
hand, a bit of cheating, and that it's all a mess—you can't tell who's who
or what's what; but in spite of all these uncertainties and sleights-of-hand,
it hurts you just the same, and the more you don't know, the more it hurts!

IV

"Ha, ha, ha! Why, you'll be finding enjoyment in a toothache next!"
you cry out with a laugh.

"Well, what of it? There is some enjoyment even in a toothache," I
reply. "I've had a toothache for a whole month; I know what's what. In
this instance, of course, people don't rage in silence; they moan. But these
moans are insincere; they're malicious, and malice is the whole point.
These moans express the sufferer's enjoyment; if he didn't enjoy it, he
would never have begun to moan. This is a good example, gentlemen, and
I'll develop it. In the first place, these moans express all the aimlessness of

---

7. A reference to the theory of evolution by natural selection developed by Charles Darwin (1809–1882).
A book on the subject was translated into Russian in 1864.

the pain which consciousness finds so humiliating, the whole system of natural laws about which you really don't give a damn, but as a result of which you're suffering nonetheless, while nature isn't. They express the consciousness that while there's no real enemy to be identified, the pain exists nonetheless; the awareness that, in spite of all possible Wagen-heims,[8] you're still a complete slave to your teeth; that if someone so wishes, your teeth will stop aching, but that if he doesn't so wish, they'll go on aching for three more months; and finally, that if you still disagree and protest, all there's left to do for consolation is flagellate yourself or beat your fist against the wall as hard as you can, and absolutely nothing else. Well, then, it's these bloody insults, these jeers coming from nowhere, that finally generate enjoyment that can sometimes reach the highest degree of voluptuousness. I beseech you, gentlemen, to listen to the moans of an educated man of the nineteenth century who's suffering from a toothache, especially on the second or third day of his distress, when he begins to moan in a very different way than he did on the first day, that is, not simply because his tooth aches; not the way some coarse peasant moans, but as a man affected by progress and European civiliza-tion, a man "who's renounced both the soil and the common people," as they say nowadays. His moans become somehow nasty, despicably spiteful, and they go on for days and nights. Yet he himself knows that his moans do him no good; he knows better than anyone else that he's merely irritat-ing himself and others in vain; he knows that the audience for whom he's trying so hard, and his whole family, have now begun to listen to him with loathing; they don't believe him for a second, and they realize full well that he could moan in a different, much simpler way, without all the flourishes and affectation, and that he's only indulging himself out of spite and malice. Well, it's precisely in this awareness and shame that the volup-tuousness resides. "It seems I'm disturbing you, tearing at your heart, pre-venting anyone in the house from getting any sleep. Well, then, you won't sleep; you too must be aware at all times that I have a toothache. I'm no longer the hero I wanted to pass for earlier, but simply a nasty little man, a rogue. So be it! I'm delighted that you've seen through me. Does it make you feel bad to hear my wretched little moans? Well, then, feel bad. Now let me add an even nastier flourish. . . ." You still don't understand, gentle-men? No, it's clear that one has to develop further and become even more conscious in order to understand all the nuances of this voluptuousness! Are you laughing? I'm delighted. Of course my jokes are in bad taste, gentlemen; they're uneven, contradictory, and lacking in self-assurance. But that's because I have no respect for myself. Can a man possessing consciousness ever really respect himself?

V

Well, and is it possible, is it really possible for a man to respect himself if he even presumes to find enjoyment in the feeling of his own humilia-tion? I'm not saying this out of any feigned repentance. In general I could

---

8. The *General Address Book of St. Petersburg* listed eight dentists named Wagenheim; contemporary readers would have recognized the name from signs throughout the city.

never bear to say: "I'm sorry, Daddy, and I won't do it again," not because I was incapable of saying it, but, on the contrary, perhaps precisely because I was all too capable, and how! As if on purpose it would happen that I'd get myself into some sort of mess for which I was not to blame in any way whatsoever. That was the most repulsive part of it. What's more, I'd feel touched deep in my soul; I'd repent and shed tears, deceiving even myself of course, though not feigning in the least. It seemed that my heart was somehow playing dirty tricks on me. . . . Here one couldn't even blame the laws of nature, although it was these very laws that continually hurt me during my entire life. It's disgusting to recall all this, and it was disgusting even then. Of course, a moment or so later I would realize in anger that it was all lies, lies, revolting, made-up lies, that is, all that repentance, all that tenderness, all those vows to mend my ways. But you'll ask why I mauled and tortured myself in that way? The answer is because it was so very boring to sit idly by with my arms folded; so I'd get into trouble. That's the way it was. Observe yourselves better, gentlemen; then you'll understand that it's true. I used to think up adventures for myself, inventing a life so that at least I could live. How many times did it happen, well, let's say, for example, that I took offense, deliberately, for no reason at all? All the while I knew there was no reason for it; I put on airs nonetheless, and would take it so far that finally I really did feel offended. I've been drawn into such silly tricks all my life, so that finally I lost control over myself. Another time, even twice, I tried hard to fall in love. I even suffered, gentlemen, I can assure you. In the depths of my soul I really didn't believe that I was suffering; there was a stir of mockery, but suffer I did, and in a genuine, normal way at that; I was jealous, I was beside myself with anger. . . . And all as a result of boredom, gentlemen, sheer boredom; I was overcome by inertia. You see, the direct, legitimate, immediate result of consciousness is inertia, that is, the conscious sitting idly by with one's arms folded. I've referred to this before. I repeat, I repeat emphatically: all spontaneous men and men of action are so active precisely because they're stupid and limited. How can one explain this? Here's how: as a result of their limitations they mistake immediate and secondary causes for primary ones, and thus they're convinced more quickly and easily than other people that they've located an indisputable basis for action, and this puts them at ease; that's the main point. For, in order to begin to act, one must first be absolutely at ease, with no lingering doubts whatsoever. Well, how can I, for example, ever feel at ease? Where are the primary causes I can rely upon, where's the foundation? Where shall I find it? I exercise myself in thinking, and consequently, with me every primary cause drags in another, an even more primary one, and so on to infinity. This is precisely the essence of all consciousness and thought. And here again, it must be the laws of nature. What's the final result? Why, the very same thing. Remember: I was talking about revenge before. (You probably didn't follow.) I said: a man takes revenge because he finds justice in it. That means, he's found a primary cause, a foundation: namely, justice. Therefore, he's completely at ease, and, as a result, he takes revenge peacefully and successfully, convinced that he's performing an honest and just deed. But I don't see any justice here at all, nor do I find any virtue in it whatever; consequently, if I begin to take revenge, it's only out of spite. Of course, spite could overcome everything, all my doubts, and therefore could successfully serve instead of a primary cause precisely because it's not a cause at all. But what do I do if I don't even feel spite (that's where I began before)? After all, as a result of those damned laws of consciousness, my spite is subject to chemical disintegration. You look—and the object vanishes, the arguments evaporate, a guilty party can't be identified, the offense ceases to be one and becomes a matter of fate, something like a toothache for which no one's to blame, and, as a consequence, there remains only the same recourse: that is, to bash the wall even harder. So you throw up your hands because you haven't found a primary cause. Just try to let yourself be carried away blindly by your feelings, without reflection, without a primary cause, suppressing consciousness even for a moment; hate or love, anything, just in order not to sit idly by with your arms folded. The day after tomorrow at the very latest, you'll begin to despise yourself for having deceived yourself knowingly. The result: a soap bubble and inertia. Oh, gentlemen, perhaps I consider myself to be an intelligent man simply because for my whole life I haven't been able to begin or finish anything. All right, suppose I am a babbler, a harmless, annoying babbler, like the rest of us. But then what is to be done[9] if the direct and single vocation of every intelligent man consists in babbling, that is, in deliberately talking in endless circles?

VI

Oh, if only I did nothing simply as a result of laziness. Lord, how I'd respect myself then. I'd respect myself precisely because at least I'd be capable of being lazy; at least I'd possess one more or less positive trait of which I could be certain. Question: who am I? Answer: a sluggard. Why, it would have been very pleasant to hear that said about oneself. It would mean that I'd been positively identified; it would mean that there was something to be said about me. "A sluggard!" Why, that's a calling and a vocation, a whole career! Don't joke, it's true. Then, by rights I'd be a member of the very best club and would occupy myself exclusively by being able to respect myself continually. I knew a gentleman who prided himself all his life on being a connoisseur of Lafite.[1] He considered it his positive virtue and never doubted himself. He died not merely with a clean conscience, but with a triumphant one, and he was absolutely correct. I should have chosen a career for myself too: I would have been a sluggard and a glutton, not an ordinary one, but one who, for example, sympathized with everything beautiful and sublime. How do you like that? I've dreamt about it for a long time. The "beautiful and sublime" have been a real pain in the neck during my forty years, but then it's been *my* forty years, whereas then—oh, then it would have been otherwise! I would've found myself a suitable activity at once—namely, drinking to everything beautiful and sublime. I would have seized upon every oppor-

---

9. An oblique reference to the controversial novel by Nikolai Chernyshevsky (1828–1889) titled *What Is to Be Done?* (1863). *Notes from Underground* is in part Dostoevsky's polemical response to it.   1. A variety of red wine from Médoc in France.

tunity first to shed a tear into my glass and then drink to everything beautiful and sublime. Then I would have turned everything into the beautiful
and sublime; I would have sought out the beautiful and sublime in the
nastiest, most indisputable trash. I would have become as tearful as a wet
sponge. An artist, for example, has painted a portrait of Ge.[2] At once I
drink to the artist who painted that portrait of Ge because I love everything
beautiful and sublime. An author has written the words, "Just as you
please,"[3] at once I drink to "Just as you please," because I love everything
"beautiful and sublime." I'd demand respect for myself in doing this, I'd
persecute anyone who didn't pay me any respect. I'd live peacefully and
die triumphantly—why, it's charming, perfectly charming! And what a
belly I'd have grown by then, what a triple chin I'd have acquired, what a
red nose I'd have developed—so that just looking at me any passerby
would have said, "Now that's a real plus! That's something really positive!"
Say what you like, gentlemen, it's extremely pleasant to hear such comments in our negative age.

VII

But these are all golden dreams. Oh, tell me who was first to announce,
first to proclaim that man does nasty things simply because he doesn't
know his own true interest; and that if he were to be enlightened, if his
eyes were to be opened to his true, normal interests, he would stop doing
nasty things at once and would immediately become good and noble,
because, being so enlightened and understanding his real advantage, he
would realize that his own advantage really did lie in the good; and that
it's well known that there's not a single man capable of acting knowingly
against his own interest; consequently, he would, so to speak, begin to do
good out of necessity. Oh, the child! Oh, the pure, innocent babe! Well,
in the first place, when was it during all these millennia, that man has ever
acted only in his own self interest? What does one do with the millions of
facts bearing witness to the one fact that people knowingly, that is, possessing full knowledge of their own true interests, have relegated them to
the background and have rushed down a different path, that of risk and
chance, compelled by no one and nothing, but merely as if they didn't
want to follow the beaten track, and so they stubbornly, willfully forged
another way, a difficult and absurd one, searching for it almost in the
darkness? Why, then, this means that stubbornness and willfulness were
really more pleasing to them than any kind of advantage. . . . Advantage!
What is advantage? Will you take it upon yourself to define with absolute
precision what constitutes man's advantage? And what if it turns out that
man's advantage sometimes not only may, but even must in certain circumstances, consist precisely in his desiring something harmful to himself
instead of something advantageous? And if this is so, if this can ever occur,
then the whole theory falls to pieces. What do you think, can such a thing
happen? You're laughing; laugh, gentlemen, but answer me: have man's

2. N. N. Ge (1831–1894), Russian artist, whose painting "The Last Supper" was displayed in Petersburg during the spring of 1863 and provoked considerable controversy.   3. An attack on the writer M. E. Saltykov-Shchedrin, who published a sympathetic review of Ge's painting titled "Just As You Please."

advantages ever been calculated with absolute certainty? Aren't there some
which don't fit, can't be made to fit into any classification? Why, as far as
I know, you gentlemen have derived your list of human advantages from
averages of statistical data and from scientific-economic formulas. But
your advantages are prosperity, wealth, freedom, peace, and so on and so
forth; so that a man who, for example, expressly and knowingly acts in
opposition to this whole list, would be, in you opinion, and in mine, too,
of course, either an obscurantist or a complete madman, wouldn't he? But
now here's what's astonishing: why is it that when all these statisticians,
sages, and lovers of humanity enumerate man's advantages, they invariably
leave one out? They don't even take it into consideration in the form in
which it should be considered, although the entire calculation depends
upon it. There would be no great harm in considering it, this advantage,
and adding it to the list. But the whole point is that this particular advantage doesn't fit into any classification and can't be found on any list. I have
a friend, for instance. . . . But gentlemen! Why, he's your friend, too! In
fact, he's everyone's friend! When he's preparing to do something, this
gentleman straight away explains to you eloquently and clearly just how
he must act according to the laws of nature and truth. And that's not all:
with excitement and passion he'll tell you all about genuine, normal
human interests; with scorn he'll reproach the shortsighted fools who
understand neither their own advantage nor the real meaning of virtue;
and then— exactly a quarter of an hour later, without any sudden outside
cause, but precisely because of something internal that's stronger than all
his interests—he does a complete about-face; that is, he does something
which clearly contradicts what he's been saying: it goes against the laws of
reason and his own advantage, in a word, against everything. . . . I warn
you that my friend is a collective personage; therefore it's rather difficult
to blame only him. That's just it, gentlemen; in fact, isn't there something
dearer to every man than his own best advantage, or (so as not to violate
the rules of logic) isn't there one more advantageous advantage (exactly
the one omitted, the one we mentioned before), which is more important
and more advantageous than all others and, on behalf of which, a man
will, if necessary, go against all laws, that is, against reason, honor, peace,
and prosperity—in a word, against all those splendid and useful things,
merely in order to attain this fundamental, most advantageous advantage
which is dearer to him than everything else?

"Well, it's advantage all the same," you say, interrupting me. Be so kind
as to allow me to explain further; besides, the point is not my pun, but the
fact that this advantage is remarkable precisely because it destroys all our
classifications and constantly demolishes all systems devised by lovers of
humanity for the happiness of mankind. In a word, it interferes with everything. But, before I name this advantage, I want to compromise myself
personally; therefore I boldly declare that all these splendid systems, all
these theories to explain to mankind its real, normal interests so that, by
necessarily striving to achieve them, it would immediately become good
and noble—are, for the time being, in my opinion, nothing more than
logical exercises! Yes, sir, logical exercises! Why, even to maintain a theory
of mankind's regeneration through a system of its own advantages, why, in

my opinion, that's almost the same as . . . well, claiming, for instance, following Buckle,[4] that man has become kinder as a result of civilization; consequently, he's becoming less bloodthirsty and less inclined to war. Why, logically it all even seems to follow. But man is so partial to systems and abstract conclusions that he's ready to distort the truth intentionally, ready to deny everything that he himself has ever seen and heard, merely in order to justify his own logic. That's why I take this example, because it's such a glaring one. Just look around: rivers of blood are being spilt, and in the most cheerful way, as if it were champagne. Take this entire nineteenth century of ours during which even Buckle lived. Take Napoleon—both the great and the present one.[5] Take North America—that eternal union.[6] Take, finally, that ridiculous Schleswig-Holstein[7]. . . . What is it that civilization makes kinder in us? Civilization merely promotes a wider variety of sensations in man and . . . absolutely nothing else. And through the development of this variety man may even reach the point where he takes pleasure in spilling blood. Why, that's even happened to him already. Haven't you noticed that the most refined bloodshedders are almost always the most civilized gentlemen to whom all these Attila the Huns and Stenka Razins[8] are scarcely fit to hold a candle; and if they're not as conspicuous as Attila and Stenka Razin, it's precisely because they're too common and have become too familiar to us. At least if man hasn't become more bloodthirsty as a result of civilization, surely he's become bloodthirsty in a nastier, more repulsive way than before. Previously man saw justice in bloodshed and exterminated whomever he wished with a clear conscience; whereas now, though we consider bloodshed to be abominable, we nevertheless engage in this abomination even more than before. Which is worse? Decide for yourselves. They say that Cleopatra (forgive an example from Roman history) loved to stick gold pins into the breasts of her slave girls and take pleasure in their screams and writhing. You'll say that this took place, relatively speaking, in barbaric times; that these are barbaric times too, because (also comparatively speaking), gold pins are used even now; that even now, although man has learned on occasion to see more clearly than in barbaric times, *he's still far from having learned* how to act in accordance with the dictates of reason and science. Nevertheless, you're still absolutely convinced that he will learn how to do so, as soon as he gets rid of some bad, old habits and as soon as common sense and science have completely re-educated human nature and have turned it in the proper direction. You're convinced that then man will voluntarily stop committing blunders, and that he will, so to speak, never willingly set his own will in opposition to his own normal interests. More than that: then, you say, science itself will teach man (though, in my opinion, that's already a luxury) that in fact he

---

4. In his *History of Civilization in England* (1857–61), Henry Thomas Buckle (1821–1862) argued that the development of civilization necessarily leads to the cessation of war. Russia had recently been involved in fierce fighting in the Crimea (1853–56).   **5.** The French emperors Napoléon I (1769–1821) and his nephew Napoléon III (1808–1873), both of whom engaged in numerous wars, though on vastly different scales.   **6.** The United States was in the middle of its Civil War (1861–65).   **7.** The German duchies of Schleswig and Holstein, held by Denmark since 1773, were reunited with Prussia after a brief war in 1864.   **8.** Cossack leader (died 1671) who organized a peasant rebellion in Russia. Attila (406?–453 A.D.), king of the Huns, who conducted devastating wars against the Roman emperors.

possesses neither a will nor any whim of his own, that he never did, and that he himself is nothing more than a kind of piano key or an organ stop;[9] that, moreover, there still exist laws of nature, so that everything he's done has been not in accordance with his own desire, but in and of itself, according to the laws of nature. Consequently, we need only discover these laws of nature, and man will no longer have to answer for his own actions and will find it extremely easy to live. All human actions, it goes without saying, will then be tabulated according to these laws, mathematically, like tables of logarithms up to 108,000, and will be entered on a schedule; or even better, certain edifying works will be published, like our contemporary encyclopedic dictionaries, in which everything will be accurately calculated and specified so that there'll be no more actions or adventures left on earth.

At that time, it's still you speaking, new economic relations will be established, all ready-made, also calculated with mathematical precision, so that all possible questions will disappear in a single instant, simply because all possible answers will have been provided. Then the crystal palace[1] will be built. And then . . . Well, in a word, those will be our halcyon days. Of course, there's no way to guarantee (now this is me talking) that it won't be, for instance, terribly boring then (because there won't be anything left to do, once everything has been calculated according to tables); on the other hand, everything will be extremely rational. Of course, what don't people think up out of boredom! Why, even gold pins get stuck into other people out of boredom, but that wouldn't matter. What's really bad (this is me talking again) is that for all I know, people might even be grateful for those gold pins. For man is stupid, phenomenally stupid. That is, although he's not really stupid at all, he's really so ungrateful that it's hard to find another being quite like him. Why, I, for example, wouldn't be surprised in the least, if, suddenly, for no reason at all, in the midst of this future, universal rationalism, some gentleman with an offensive, rather, a retrograde and derisive expression on his face were to stand up, put his hands on his hips, and declare to us all: "How about it, gentlemen, what if we knock over all this rationalism with one swift kick for the sole purpose of sending all these logarithms to hell, so that once again we can live according to our own stupid will!" But that wouldn't matter either; what's so annoying is that he would undoubtedly find some followers; such is the way man is made. And all because of the most foolish reason, which, it seems, is hardly worth mentioning: namely, that man, always and everywhere, whoever he is, has preferred to act as he wished, and not at all as reason and advantage have dictated; one might even desire something opposed to one's own advantage, and sometimes (this is now my idea) one *positively must do so.* One's very own free, unfettered desire, one's own whim, no matter how wild, one's own fantasy, even though sometimes roused to the point of madness—all this constitutes precisely that pre-

9. A reference to the last discourse of the French philosopher Denis Diderot (1713–1784) in the *Conversation of D'Alembert and Diderot* (1769).   1. An allusion to the crystal palace described in Vera Pavlovna's fourth dream in Chernyshevsky's *What Is to Be Done?* as well as to the actual building designed by Sir Joseph Paxton, erected for the Great Exhibition in London in 1851 and at that time admired as the newest wonder of architecture; Dostoevsky described it in *Winter Notes on Summer Impressions* (1863).

viously omitted, most advantageous advantage which isn't included under any classification and because of which all systems and theories are constantly smashed to smithereens. Where did these sages ever get the idea that man needs any normal, virtuous desire? How did they ever imagine that man needs any kind of rational, advantageous desire? Man needs only one thing—his own *independent* desire, whatever that independence might cost and wherever it might lead. And as far as desire goes, the devil only knows. . . .

VIII

"Ha, ha, ha! But in reality even this desire, if I may say so, doesn't exist!" you interrupt me with a laugh. "Why science has already managed to dissect man so now we know that desire and so-called free choice are nothing more than . . ."

"Wait, gentlemen, I myself wanted to begin like that. I must confess that even I got frightened. I was just about to declare that the devil only knows what desire depends on and perhaps we should be grateful for that, but then I remembered about science and I . . . . stopped short. But now you've gone and brought it up. Well, after all, what if someday they really do discover the formula for all our desires and whims, that is, the thing that governs them, precise laws that produce them, how exactly they're applied, where they lead in each and every case, and so on and so forth, that is, the genuine mathematical formula—why, then all at once man might stop desiring, yes, indeed, he probably would. Who would want to desire according to some table? And that's not all: he would immediately be transformed from a person into an organ stop or something of that sort; because what is man without desire, without will, and without wishes if not a stop in an organ pipe? What do you think? Let's consider the probabilities— can this really happen or not?"

"Hmmm . . .," you decide, "our desires are mistaken for the most part because of an erroneous view of our own advantage. Consequently, we sometimes desire pure rubbish because, in our own stupidity, we consider it the easiest way to achieve some previously assumed advantage. Well, and when all this has been analyzed, calculated on paper (that's entirely possible, since it's repugnant and senseless to assume in advance that man will never come to understand the laws of nature) then, of course, all so-called desires will no longer exist. For if someday desires are completely reconciled with reason, we'll follow reason instead of desire simply because it would be impossible, for example, while retaining one's reason, to *desire* rubbish, and thus knowingly oppose one's reason, and desire something harmful to oneself. . . . And, since all desires and reasons can really be tabulated, since someday the laws of our so-called free choice are sure to be discovered, then, all joking aside, it may be possible to establish something like a table, so that we could actually desire according to it. If, for example, someday they calculate and demonstrate to me that I made a rude gesture because I couldn't possibly refrain from it, that I had to make precisely that gesture, well, in that case, what sort of *free choice* would there be, especially if I'm a learned man and have completed a course of study somewhere? Why, then I'd be able to calculate in advance my entire life for the next thirty years; in a word, if such a table were to be drawn up, there'd be nothing left for us to do; we'd simply have to accept it. In general, we should be repeating endlessly to ourselves that at such a time and in such circumstances nature certainly won't ask our opinion; that we must accept it as is, and not as we fantasize it, and that if we really aspire to prepare a table, a schedule, and, well . . . well, even a laboratory test tube, there's nothing to be done—one must even accept the test tube! If not, it'll be accepted even without you. . . .

"Yes, but that's just where I hit a snag! Gentlemen, you'll excuse me for all this philosophizing; it's a result of my forty years in the underground! Allow me to fantasize. Don't you see: reason is a fine thing, gentlemen, there's no doubt about it, but it's only reason, and it satisfies only man's rational faculty, whereas desire is a manifestation of all life, that is, of all human life, which includes both reason, as well as all of life's itches and scratches. And although in this manifestation life often turns out to be fairly worthless, it's life all the same, and not merely the extraction of square roots. Why, take me, for instance; I quite naturally want to live in order to satisfy all my faculties of life, not merely my rational faculty, that is, some one-twentieth of all my faculties. What does reason know? Reason knows only what it's managed to learn. (Some things it may never learn; while this offers no comfort, why not admit it openly?) But human nature acts as a whole, with all that it contains, consciously and unconsciously; and although it may tell lies, it's still alive. I suspect, gentlemen, that you're looking at me with compassion; you repeat that an enlightened and cultured man, in a word, man as he will be in the future, cannot knowingly desire something disadvantageous to himself, and that this is pure mathematics. I agree with you: it really is mathematics. But I repeat for the one-hundredth time, there is one case, only one, when a man may intentionally, consciously desire even something harmful to himself, something stupid, even very stupid, namely: in order *to have the right* to desire something even very stupid and not be bound by an obligation to desire only what's smart. After all, this very stupid thing, one's own whim, gentlemen, may in fact be the most advantageous thing on earth for people like me, especially in certain cases. In particular, it may be more advantageous than any other advantage, even in a case where it causes obvious harm and contradicts the most sensible conclusions of reason about advantage—because in any case it preserves for us what's most important and precious, that is, our personality and our individuality. There are some people who maintain that in fact this is more precious to man than anything else; of course, desire can, if it so chooses, coincide with reason, especially if it doesn't abuse this option, and chooses to coincide in moderation; this is useful and sometimes even commendable. But very often, even most of the time, desire absolutely and stubbornly disagrees with reason and . . . and . . . and, do you know, sometimes this is also useful and even very commendable? Let's assume, gentlemen, that man isn't stupid. (And really, this can't possibly be said about him at all, if only because if he's stupid, then who on earth is smart?) But even if he's not stupid, he is, nevertheless, monstrously ungrateful. Phenomenally ungrateful. I even believe that the best definition of man is this: a creature who walks on two legs and is ungrateful. But that's still not all; that's still not his main defect. His main defect is his perpetual misbehavior, perpetual from the time of the Great Flood to the Schleswig-Holstein period of human destiny. Misbehavior, and consequently, imprudence; for it's long been known that imprudence results from nothing else but misbehavior. Just cast a glance at the history of mankind; well, what do you see? Is it majestic? Well, perhaps it's majestic; why, the Colossus of Rhodes,[2] for example—that alone is worth something! Not without reason did Mr Anaevsky[3] report that some people consider it to be the product of human hands, while others maintain that it was created by nature itself. Is it colorful? Well, perhaps it's also colorful; just consider the dress uniforms, both military and civilian, of all nations at all times—why, that alone is worth something, and if you include everyday uniforms, it'll make your eyes bulge; not one historian will be able to sort it all out. Is it monotonous? Well, perhaps it's monotonous, too: men fight and fight; now they're fighting; they fought first and they fought last—you'll agree that it's really much too monotonous. In short, anything can be said about world history, anything that might occur to the most disordered imagination. There's only one thing that can't possibly be said about it—that it's rational. You'll choke on the word. Yet here's just the sort of thing you'll encounter all the time: why, in life you're constantly running up against people who are so well-behaved and so rational, such wise men and lovers of humanity who set themselves the lifelong goal of behaving as morally and rationally as possible, so to speak, to be a beacon for their nearest and dearest, simply in order to prove that it's really possible to live one's life in a moral and rational way. And so what? It's a well-known fact that many of these lovers of humanity, sooner or later, by the end of their lives, have betrayed themselves: they've pulled off some caper, sometimes even quite an indecent one. Now I ask you: what can one expect from man as a creature endowed with such strange qualities? Why, shower him with all sorts of earthly blessings, submerge him in happiness over his head so that only little bubbles appear on the surface of this happiness, as if on water, give him such economic prosperity that he'll have absolutely nothing left to do except sleep, eat gingerbread, and worry about the continuation of world history—even then, out of pure ingratitude, sheer perversity, he'll commit some repulsive act. He'll even risk losing his gingerbread, and will intentionally desire the most wicked rubbish, the most uneconomical absurdity, simply in order to inject his own pernicious fantastic element into all this positive rationality. He wants to hold onto those most fantastic dreams, his own indecent stupidity solely for the purpose of assuring himself (as if it were necessary) that men are still men and not piano keys, and that even if the laws of nature play upon them with their own hands, they're still threatened by being overplayed until they won't possibly desire anything more than a schedule. But that's not all: even if man really turned out to be a piano key, even if this could be demonstrated to him by natural

---

2. A large bronze statue of the sun god, Helios, built between 292 and 280 B.C. in the harbor of Rhodes (an island in the Aegean Sea) and considered one of the Seven Wonders of the Ancient World.   3. A. E. Anaevsky was a critic whose articles were frequently ridiculed in literary polemics of the period.

science and pure mathematics, even then he still won't become reasonable; he'll intentionally do something to the contrary, simply out of ingratitude, merely to have his own way. If he lacks the means, he'll cause
destruction and chaos, he'll devise all kinds of suffering and have his own
way! He'll leash a curse upon the world; and, since man alone can do so
(it's his privilege and the thing that most distinguishes him from other
animals), perhaps only through this curse will he achieve his goal, that is,
become really convinced that he's a man and not a piano key! If you say
that one can also calculate all this according to a table, this chaos and
darkness, these curses, so that the mere possibility of calculating it all in
advance would stop everything and that reason alone would prevail—in
that case man would go insane deliberately in order not to have reason,
but to have his own way! I believe this, I vouch for it, because, after all,
the whole of man's work seems to consist only in proving to himself constantly that he's a man and not an organ stop! Even if he has to lose his
own skin, he'll prove it; even if he has to become a troglodyte, he'll prove
it. And after that, how can one not sin, how can one not praise the fact
that all this hasn't yet come to pass and that desire still depends on the
devil knows what . . . ?"

You'll shout at me (if you still choose to favor me with your shouts) that
no one's really depriving me of my will; that they're merely attempting to
arrange things so that my will, by its own free choice, will coincide with
my normal interests, with the laws of nature, and with arithmetic.

"But gentlemen, what sort of free choice will there be when it comes
down to tables and arithmetic, when all that's left is two times two makes
four? Two times two makes four even without my will. Is that what you
call free choice?"

IX

Gentlemen, I'm joking of course, and I myself know that it's not a very
good joke; but, after all, you can't take everything as a joke. Perhaps I'm
gnashing my teeth while I joke. I'm tormented by questions, gentlemen;
answer them for me. Now, for example, you want to cure man of his
old habits and improve his will according to the demands of science and
common sense. But how do you know not only whether it's possible, but
even if it's *necessary* to remake him in this way? Why do you conclude
that human desire *must* undoubtedly be improved? In short, how do you
know that such improvement will really be to man's advantage? And, to
be perfectly frank, why are you so *absolutely* convinced that not to oppose
man's real, normal advantage guaranteed by the conclusions of reason and
arithmetic is really always to man's advantage and constitutes a law for all
humanity? After all, this is still only an assumption of yours. Let's suppose
that it's a law of logic, but perhaps not a law of humanity. Perhaps, gentlemen, you're wondering if I'm insane? Allow me to explain. I agree that
man is primarily a creative animal, destined to strive consciously toward a
goal and to engage in the art of engineering, that, is, externally and incessantly building new roads for himself *wherever they lead*. But sometimes
he may want to swerve aside precisely because he's *compelled* to build

these roads, and perhaps also because, no matter how stupid the spontaneous man of action may generally be, nevertheless it sometimes occurs to
him that the road, as it turns out, almost always leads *somewhere or other*,
and that the main thing isn't so much where it goes, but the fact that it
does, and that the well-behaved child, disregarding the art of engineering,
shouldn't yield to pernicious idleness which, as is well known, constitutes
the mother of all vices. Man loves to create and build roads; that's indisputable. But why is he also so passionately fond of destruction and chaos?
Now, then, tell me. But I myself want to say a few words about this separately. Perhaps the reason that he's so fond of destruction and chaos (after
all, it's indisputable that he sometimes really loves it, and that's a fact) is
that he himself has an instinctive fear of achieving his goal and completing
the project under construction? How do you know if perhaps he loves his
building only from afar, but not from close up; perhaps he only likes building it, but not living in it, leaving it afterward *aux animaux domestiques*,[4]
such as ants or sheep, or so on and so forth. Now ants have altogether
different tastes. They have one astonishing structure of a similar type, forever indestructible—the anthill.

The worthy ants began with the anthill, and most likely, they will end
with the anthill, which does great credit to their perseverance and steadfastness. But man is a frivolous and unseemly creature and perhaps, like a
chess player, he loves only the process of achieving his goal, and not the
goal itself. And, who knows (one can't vouch for it), perhaps the only goal
on earth toward which mankind is striving consists merely in this incessant
process of achieving or to put it another way, in life itself, and not particularly in the goal which, of course, must always be none other than two
times two makes four, that is, a formula; after all, two times two makes
four is no longer life, gentlemen, but the beginning of death. At least man
has always been somewhat afraid of this two times two makes four, and
I'm afraid of it now, too. Let's suppose that the only thing man does is
search for this two times two makes four; he sails across oceans, sacrifices
his own life in the quest; but to seek it out and find it—really and truly,
he's very frightened. After all, he feels that as soon as he finds it, there'll
be nothing left to search for. Workers, after finishing work, at least receive
their wages, go off to a tavern, and then wind up at a police station—now
that's a full week's occupation. But where will man go? At any rate a certain awkwardness can be observed each time he approaches the achievement of similar goals. He loves the process, but he's not so fond of the
achievement, and that, of course is terribly amusing. In short, man is made
in a comical way; obviously there's some sort of catch in all this. But two
times two makes four is an insufferable thing, nevertheless. Two times two
makes four—why, in my opinion, it's mere insolence. Two times two
makes four stands there brazenly with its hands on its hips, blocking your
path and spitting at you. I agree that two times two makes four is a splendid
thing; but if we're going to lavish praise, then two times two makes five is
sometimes also a very charming little thing.

And why are you so firmly, so triumphantly convinced that only the

---

4. To domestic animals (French).

normal and positive—in short, only well-being is advantageous to man? Doesn't reason ever make mistakes about advantage? After all, perhaps man likes something other than well-being? Perhaps he loves suffering just as much? Perhaps suffering is just as advantageous to him as well-being? Man sometimes loves suffering terribly, to the point of passion, and that's a fact. There's no reason to study world history on this point; if indeed you're a man and have lived at all, just ask yourself. As far as my own personal opinion is concerned, to love only well-being is somehow even indecent. Whether good or bad, it's sometimes also very pleasant to demolish something. After all, I'm not standing up for suffering here, nor for well-being, either. I'm standing up for . . . my own whim and for its being guaranteed to me whenever necessary. For instance, suffering is not permitted in vaudevilles,[5] that I know. It's also inconceivable in the crystal palace; suffering is doubt and negation. What sort of crystal palace would it be if any doubt were allowed? Yet, I'm convinced that man will never renounce real suffering, that is, destruction and chaos. After all, suffering is the sole cause of consciousness. Although I stated earlier that in my opinion consciousness is man's greatest misfortune, still I know that man loves it and would not exchange it for any other sort of satisfaction. Consciousness, for example, is infinitely higher than two times two. Of course, after two times two, there's nothing left, not merely nothing to do, but nothing to learn. Then the only thing possible will be to plug up your five senses and plunge into contemplation. Well, even if you reach the same result with consciousness, that is, having nothing left to do, at least you'll be able to flog yourself from time to time, and that will liven things up a bit. Although it may be reactionary, it's still better than nothing.

X[6]

You believe in the crystal palace, eternally indestructible, that is, one at which you can never stick out your tongue furtively nor make a rude gesture, even with your fist hidden away. Well, perhaps I'm so afraid of this building precisely because it's made of crystal and it's eternally indestructible, and because it won't be possible to stick one's tongue out even furtively.

Don't you see: if it were a chicken coop instead of a palace, and if it should rain, then perhaps I could crawl into it so as not to get drenched; but I would still not mistake a chicken coop for a palace out of gratitude, just because it sheltered me from the rain. You're laughing, you're even saying that in this case there's no difference between a chicken coop and a mansion. Yes, I reply, if the only reason for living is to keep from getting drenched.

But what if I've taken it into my head that this is not the only reason for living, and, that if one is to live at all, one might as well live in a mansion? Such is my wish, my desire. You'll expunge it from me only when you've changed my desires. Well, then, change them, tempt me with something

5. A dramatic genre, popular on the Russian stage, consisting of scenes from contemporary life acted with a satirical twist, often in racy dialogue.   6. This chapter was badly mutilated by the censor, as Dostoevsky makes clear in the letter to his brother Mikhail, dated March 26, 1864 (see the headnote).

else, give me some other ideal. In the meantime, I still won't mistake a chicken coop for a palace. But let's say that the crystal palace is a hoax, that according to the laws of nature it shouldn't exist, and that I've invented it only out of my own stupidity, as a result of certain antiquated, irrational habits of my generation. But what do I care if it doesn't exist? What difference does it make if it exists only in my own desires, or, to be more precise, if it exists as long as my desires exist? Perhaps you're laughing again? Laugh, if you wish; I'll resist all your laughter and I still won't say I'm satiated if I'm really hungry; I know all the same that I won't accept a compromise, an infinitely recurring zero, just because it exists according to the laws of nature and it *really* does exist. I won't accept as the crown of my desires a large building with tenements for poor tenants to be rented for a thousand years and, just in case, with the name of the dentist Wagenheim on the sign. Destroy my desires, eradicate my ideals, show me something better and I'll follow you. You may say, perhaps, that it's not worth getting involved; but, in that case, I'll say the same thing in reply. We're having a serious discussion; if you don't grant me your attention, I won't grovel for it. I still have my underground.

And, as long as I'm still alive and feel desire—may my arm wither away before it contributes even one little brick to that building! Never mind that I myself have just rejected the crystal palace for the sole reason that it won't be possible to tease it by sticking out one's tongue at it. I didn't say that because I'm so fond of sticking out my tongue. Perhaps the only reason I got angry is that among all your buildings there's still not a single one where you don't feel compelled to stick out your tongue. On the contrary, I'd let my tongue be cut off out of sheer gratitude, if only things could be so arranged that I'd no longer want to stick it out. What do I care if things can't be so arranged and if I must settle for some tenements? Why was I made with such desires? Can it be that I was made this way only in order to reach the conclusion that my entire way of being is merely a fraud? Can this be the whole purpose? I don't believe it.

By the way, do you know what? I'm convinced that we underground men should be kept in check. Although capable of sitting around quietly in the underground for some forty years, once he emerges into the light of day and bursts into speech, he talks on and on and on. . . .

XI

The final result, gentlemen, is that it's better to do nothing! Conscious inertia is better! And so, long live the underground! Even though I said that I envy the normal man to the point of exasperation, I still wouldn't want to be him under the circumstances in which I see him (although I still won't keep from envying him. No, no, in any case the underground is more advantageous!) At least there one can . . . Hey, but I'm lying once again! I'm lying because I know myself as surely as two times two, that it isn't really the underground that's better, but something different, altogether different, something that I long for, but I'll never be able to find! To hell with the underground! Why, here's what would be better: if I myself were to believe even a fraction of everything I've written. I swear to you, gentlemen, that I don't believe one word, not one little word of all that I've scribbled. That is, I do believe it, perhaps, but at the very same time, I don't know why, I feel and suspect that I'm lying like a trooper.

"Then why did you write all this?" you ask me.

"What if I'd shut you up in the underground for forty years with nothing to do and then came back forty years later to see what had become of you? Can a man really be left alone for forty years with nothing to do?"

"Isn't it disgraceful, isn't it humiliating!" you might say, shaking your head in contempt. "You long for life, but you try to solve life's problems by means of a logical tangle. How importunate, how insolent your outbursts, and how frightened you are at the same time! You talk rubbish, but you're constantly afraid of them and make apologies. You maintain that you fear nothing, but at the same time you try to ingratiate yourself with us. You assure us that you're gnashing your teeth, yet at the same time you try to be witty and amuse us. You know that your witticisms are not very clever, but apparently you're pleased by their literary merit. Perhaps you really have suffered, but you don't even respect your own suffering. There's some truth in you, too, but no chastity; out of the pettiest vanity you bring your truth out into the open, into the marketplace, and you shame it. . . . You really want to say something, but you conceal your final word out of fear because you lack the resolve to utter it; you have only cowardly impudence. You boast about your consciousness, but you merely vacillate, because even though your mind is working, your heart has been blackened by depravity, and without a pure heart, there can be no full, genuine consciousness. And how importunate you are; how you force yourself upon others; you behave in such an affected manner. Lies, lies, lies!"

Of course, it was I who just invented all these words for you. That, too, comes from the underground. For forty years in a row I've been listening to all your words through a crack. I've invented them myself, since that's all that's occurred to me. It's no wonder that I've learned it all by heart and that it's taken on such a literary form. . . .

But can you really be so gullible as to imagine that I'll print all this and give it to you to read? And here's another problem I have: why do I keep calling you "gentlemen"? Why do I address you as if you really were my readers? Confessions such as the one I plan to set forth here aren't published and given to other people to read. Anyway, I don't possess sufficient fortitude, nor do I consider it necessary to do so. But don't you see, a certain notion has come into my mind, and I wish to realize it at any cost. Here's the point.

Every man has within his own reminiscences certain things he doesn't reveal to anyone, except, perhaps, to his friends. There are also some that he won't reveal even to his friends, only to himself perhaps, and even then, in secret. Finally, there are some which a man is afraid to reveal even to himself; every decent man has accumulated a fair number of such things. In fact, it can even be said that the more decent the man, the more of these things he's accumulated. Anyway, only recently I myself decided to recall some of my earlier adventures; up to now I've always avoided them, even with a certain anxiety. But having decided not only to recall them, but even to write them down, now is when I wish to try an experiment: is it possible to be absolutely honest even with one's own self and not to fear the whole truth? Incidentally, I'll mention that Heine maintains that faithful autobiographies are almost impossible, and that a man is sure to lie about himself.[7] In Heine's opinion, Rousseau, for example, undoubtedly told untruths about himself in his confession and even lied intentionally, out of vanity. I'm convinced that Heine is correct; I understand perfectly well that sometimes it's possible out of vanity alone to impute all sorts of crimes to oneself, and I can even understand what sort of vanity that might be. But Heine was making judgments about a person who confessed to the public. I, however, am writing for myself alone and declare once and for all that if I write as if I were addressing readers, that's only for show, because it's easier for me to write that way. It's a form, simply a form; I shall never have any readers. I've already stated that. . . . I don't want to be restricted in any way by editing my notes. I won't attempt to introduce any order or system. I'll write down whatever comes to mind.

Well, now, for example, someone might seize upon my words and ask me, if you really aren't counting on any readers, why do you make such compacts with yourself, and on paper no less; that is, if you're not going to introduce any order or system, if you're going to write down whatever comes to mind, etc., etc.? Why do you go on explaining? Why do you keep apologizing?

"Well, imagine that," I reply.

This, by the way, contains an entire psychology. Perhaps it's just that I'm a coward. Or perhaps it's that I imagine an audience before me on purpose, so that I behave more decently when I'm writing things down. There may be a thousand reasons.

But here's something else: why is it that I want to write? If it's not for the public, then why can't I simply recall it all in my own mind and not commit it to paper?

Quite so; but somehow it appears more dignified on paper. There's something more impressive about it; I'll be a better judge of myself; the style will be improved. Besides, perhaps I'll actually experience some relief from the process of writing it all down. Today, for example, I'm particularly oppressed by one very old memory from my distant past. It came to me vividly several days ago and since then it's stayed with me, like an annoying musical motif that doesn't want to leave you alone. And yet you must get rid of it. I have hundreds of such memories; but at times a single one emerges from those hundreds and oppresses me. For some reason I believe that if I write it down I can get rid of it. Why not try?

Lastly, I'm bored, and I never do anything. Writing things down actually seems like work. They say that work makes a man become good and honest. Well, at least there's a chance.

It's snowing today, an almost wet, yellow, dull snow. It was snowing

---

7. A reference to the work *On Germany* (1853–54) by the German poet Heinrich Heine (1797–1856), in which on the very first page Heine speaks of Rousseau as lying and inventing disgraceful incidents about himself for his *Confessions*.

yesterday too, a few days ago as well. I think it was apropos of the wet snow that I recalled this episode and now it doesn't want to leave me alone. And so, let it be a tale apropos of wet snow.

II

Apropos of Wet Snow

> When from the darkness of delusion
> I saved your fallen soul
> With ardent words of conviction,
> And, full of profound torment,
> Wringing your hands, you cursed
> The vice that had ensnared you;
> When, punishing by recollection
> Your forgetful conscience,
> You told me the tale
> Of all that had happened before,
> And, suddenly, covering your face,
> Full of shame and horror,
> You tearfully resolved,
> Indignant, shaken . . .
> Etc., etc., etc.
>   From the poetry of N. A. Nekrasov[8]

I

At that time I was only twenty-four years old. Even then my life was gloomy, disordered, and solitary to the point of savagery. I didn't associate with anyone; I even avoided talking, and I retreated further and further into my corner. At work in the office I even tried not to look at anyone; I was aware not only that my colleagues considered me eccentric, but that they always seemed to regard me with a kind of loathing. Sometimes I wondered why it was that no one else thinks that others regard him with loathing. One of our office-workers had a repulsive pock-marked face which even appeared somewhat villainous. It seemed to me that with such a disreputable face I'd never have dared look at anyone. Another man had a uniform so worn that there was a foul smell emanating from him. Yet, neither of these two gentlemen was embarrassed—neither because of his clothes, nor his face, nor in any moral way. Neither one imagined that other people regarded him with loathing; and if either had so imagined, it wouldn't have mattered at all, as long as their supervisor chose not to view him that way. It's perfectly clear to me now, because of my unlimited vanity and the great demands I accordingly made on myself, that I frequently regarded myself with a furious dissatisfaction verging on loathing; as a result, I intentionally ascribed my own view to everyone else. For example, I despised my own face; I considered it hideous, and I even suspected that there was something repulsive in its expression. Therefore, every time I arrived at work, I took pains to behave as independently as

---

8. Nikolay A. Nekrasov (1821–1878) was a famous Russian poet and editor of radical sympathies. The poem quoted dates from 1845, and is without title. It ends with the lines, "And enter my house bold and free / To become its full mistress!"

possible, so that I couldn't be suspected of any malice, and I tried to assume as noble an expression as possible. "It may not be a handsome face," I thought, "but let it be noble, expressive, and above all, extremely *intelligent*." But I was agonizingly certain that my face couldn't possibly express all these virtues. Worst of all, I considered it positively stupid. I'd have been reconciled if it had looked intelligent. In fact, I'd even have agreed to have it appear repulsive, on the condition that at the same time people would find my face terribly intelligent.

Of course, I hated all my fellow office-workers from the first to the last and despised every one of them; yet, at the same time it was as if I were afraid of them. Sometimes it happened that I would even regard them as superior to me. At this time these changes would suddenly occur: first I would despise them, then I would regard them as superior to me. A cultured and decent man cannot be vain without making unlimited demands on himself and without hating himself, at times to the point of contempt. But, whether hating them or regarding them as superior, I almost always lowered my eyes when meeting anyone. I even conducted experiments: could I endure someone's gaze? I'd always be the first to lower my eyes. This infuriated me to the point of madness. I slavishly worshipped the conventional in everything external. I embraced the common practice and feared any eccentricity with all my soul. But how could I sustain it? I was morbidly refined, as befits any cultured man of our time. All others resembled one another as sheep in a flock. Perhaps I was the only one in the whole office who constantly thought of himself as a coward and a slave; and I thought so precisely because I was so cultured. But not only did I think so, it actually was so: I was a coward and a slave. I say this without any embarrassment. Every decent man of our time is and must be a coward and a slave. This is his normal condition. I'm deeply convinced of it. This is how he's made and what he's meant to be. And not only at the present time, as the result of some accidental circumstance, but in general at all times, a decent man must be a coward and a slave. This is a law of nature for all decent men on earth. If one of them should happen to be brave about something or other, we shouldn't be comforted or distracted: he'll still lose his nerve about something else. That's the single and eternal way out. Only asses and their mongrels are brave, and even then, only until they come up against a wall. It's not worthwhile paying them any attention because they really don't mean anything at all.

There was one more circumstance tormenting me at that time: no one was like me, and I wasn't like anyone else. "I'm alone," I mused, "and they are *everyone*"; and I sank deep into thought.

From all this it's clear that I was still just a boy.

The exact opposite would also occur. Sometimes I would find it repulsive to go to the office: it reached the point where I would often return home from work ill. Then suddenly, for no good reason at all, a flash of skepticism and indifference would set in (everything came to me in flashes); I would laugh at my own intolerance and fastidiousness, and reproach myself for my *romanticism*. Sometimes I didn't even want to talk to anyone; at other times it reached a point where I not only started talking, but I even thought about striking up a friendship with others. All my fastidiousness would suddenly disappear for no good reason at all. Who knows? Perhaps I never really had any, and it was all affected, borrowed from books. I still haven't answered this question, even up to now. And once I really did become friends with others; I began to visit their houses, play préférance,[9] drink vodka, talk about promotions. . . . But allow me to digress.

We Russians, generally speaking, have never had any of those stupid, transcendent German romantics, or even worse, French romantics, on whom nothing produces any effect whatever: the earth might tremble beneath them, all of France might perish on the barricades, but they remain the same, not even changing for decency's sake; they go on singing their transcendent songs, so to speak, to their dying day, because they're such fools. We here on Russian soil have no fools. It's a well-know fact; that's precisely what distinguishes us from foreigners. Consequently, transcendent natures cannot be found among us in their pure form. That's the result of our "positive" publicists and critics of that period, who hunted for the Kostanzhonglo and the Uncle Pyotr Ivanoviches,[1] foolishly mistaking them for our ideal and slandering our own romantics, considering them to be the same kind of transcendents as one finds in Germany or France. On the contrary, the characteristics of our romantics are absolutely and directly opposed to the transcendent Europeans; not one of those European standards can apply here. (Allow me to use the word "romantic"—it's an old-fashioned little word, well-respected and deserving, familiar to everyone.) The characteristics of our romantics are to understand everything, *to see everything, often to see it much more clearly than our most positive minds*; not to be reconciled with anyone or anything, but, at the same time, not to balk at anything; to circumvent everything, to yield on every point, to treat everyone diplomatically; never to lose sight of some useful, practical goal (an apartment at government expense, a nice pension, a decoration)—to keep an eye on that goal through all his excesses and his volumes of lyrical verse, and, at the same time, to preserve intact the "beautiful and sublime" to the end of their lives; and, incidentally, to preserve themselves as well, wrapped up in cotton like precious jewelry, if only, for example, for the sake of that same "beautiful and sublime." Our romantic has a very broad nature and is the biggest rogue of all, I can assure you of that . . . even by my own experience. Of course, all this is true if the romantic is smart. But what am I saying? A romantic is always smart; I merely wanted to observe that although we've had some romantic fools, they really don't count at all, simply because while still in their prime they would degenerate completely into Germans, and, in order to preserve their precious jewels more comfortably, they'd settle over there, either in Weimar or in the Black Forest. For instance, I genuinely despised my official position and refrained from throwing it over merely out of necessity, because I myself sat there working and received good money for doing it. And, as a result, please note, I still refrained from

9. A card game for three players.   1. A character in Ivan Goncharov's novel *A Common Story* (1847); a high bureaucrat, a factory owner who teaches lessons of sobriety and good sense to the romantic hero, Alexander Aduyev. Konstanzhonglo is the ideal efficient landowner in the second part of Nikolai Gogol's novel *Dead Souls* (1852).

throwing it over. Our romantic would sooner lose his mind (which, by the way, very rarely occurs) than give it up, if he didn't have another job in mind; nor is he ever kicked out, unless he's hauled off to the insane asylum as the "King of Spain,"[2] and only if he's gone completely mad. Then again, it's really only the weaklings and towheads who go mad in our country. An enormous number of romantics later rise to significant rank. What extraordinary versatility! And what a capacity for the most contradictory sensations! I used to be consoled by these thoughts back then, and still am even nowadays. That's why there are so many "broad natures" among us, people who never lose their ideals, no matter how low they fall; even though they never lift a finger for the sake of their ideals, even though they're outrageous villains and thieves, nevertheless they respect their original ideals to the point of tears and are extremely honest men at heart. Yes, only among us Russians can the most outrageous scoundrel be absolutely, even sublimely honest at heart, while at the same time never ceasing to be a scoundrel. I repeat, nearly always do our romantics turn out to be very efficient rascals (I use the word "rascal" affectionately); they suddenly manifest such a sense of reality and positive knowledge that their astonished superiors and the general public can only click their tongues at them in amazement.

Their versatility is really astounding; God only knows what it will turn into, how it will develop under subsequent conditions, and what it holds for us in the future. The material is not all that bad! I'm not saying this out of some ridiculous patriotism or jingoism. However, I'm sure that once again you think I'm joking. But who knows? Perhaps it's quite the contrary, that is, you're convinced that this is what I really think. In any case, gentlemen, I'll consider that both of these opinions constitute an honor and a particular pleasure. And do forgive me for this digression.

Naturally, I didn't sustain any friendships with my colleagues, and soon I severed all relations after quarreling with them; and, because of my youthful inexperience at the same time, I even stopped greeting them, as if I'd cut them off entirely. That, however, happened to me only once. On the whole, I was always alone.

At home I spent most of my time reading. I tried to stifle all that was constantly seething within me with external sensations. And of all external sensations available, only reading was possible for me. Of course, reading helped a great deal—it agitated, delighted, and tormented me. But at times it was terribly boring. I still longed to be active; and suddenly I sank into dark, subterranean, loathsome depravity—more precisely, petty vice. My nasty little passions were sharp and painful as a result of my constant, morbid irritability. I experienced hysterical fits accompanied by tears and convulsions. Besides reading, I had nowhere else to go—that is, there was nothing to respect in my surroundings, nothing to attract me. In addition, I was overwhelmed by depression; I possessed a hysterical craving for contradictions and contrasts; and, as a result, I plunged into depravity. I haven't said all this to justify myself. . . . But, no, I'm lying. I did want to

2. An allusion to the hero of Gogol's short story *Diary of a Madman* (1835). Poprishchin, a low-ranking civil servant, sees his aspirations crushed by the enormous bureaucracy. He ends by going insane and imagining himself to be king of Spain.

justify myself. It's for myself, gentlemen, that I include this little observation. I don't want to lie. I've given my word.

I indulged in depravity all alone, at night, furtively, timidly, sordidly, with a feeling of shame that never left me even in my most loathsome moments and drove me at such times to the point of profanity. Even then I was carrying around the underground in my soul. I was terribly afraid of being seen, met, recognized. I visited all sorts of dismal places.

Once, passing by some wretched little tavern late at night, I saw through a lighted window some gentlemen fighting with billiard cues; one of them was thrown out the window. At some other time I would have been disgusted; but just then I was overcome by such a mood that I envied the gentleman who'd been tossed out; I envied him so much that I even walked into the tavern and entered the billiard room. "Perhaps," I thought, "I'll get into a fight, and they'll throw me out the window, too."

I wasn't drunk, but what could I do—after all, depression can drive a man to this kind of hysteria. But nothing came of it. It turned out that I was incapable of being tossed out the window; I left without getting into a fight.

As soon as I set foot inside, some officer put me in my place.

I was standing next to the billiard table inadvertently blocking his way as he wanted to get by; he took hold of me by the shoulders and without a word of warning or explanation, moved me from where I was standing to another place, and he went past as if he hadn't even noticed me. I could have forgiven even a beating, but I could never forgive his moving me out of the way and entirely failing to notice me.

The devil knows what I would have given for a genuine, ordinary quarrel, a decent one, a more *literary* one, so to speak. But I'd been treated as if I were a fly. The officer was about six feet tall, while I'm small and scrawny. The quarrel, however, was in my hands; all I had to do was protest, and of course they would've thrown me out the window. But I reconsidered and preferred . . . to withdraw resentfully.

I left the tavern confused and upset and went straight home; the next night I continued my petty vice more timidly, more furtively, more gloomily than before, as if I had tears in my eyes—but I continued nonetheless. Don't conclude, however, that I retreated from that officer as a result of any cowardice; I've never been a coward at heart, although I've constantly acted like one in deed, but—wait before you laugh—I can explain this. I can explain anything, you may rest assured.

Oh, if only this officer had been the kind who'd have agreed to fight a duel! But no, he was precisely one of those types (alas, long gone) who preferred to act with their billiard cues or, like Gogol's Lieutenant Pirogov,[3] by appealing to the authorities. They didn't fight duels; in any case, they'd have considered fighting a duel with someone like me, a lowly civilian, to be indecent. In general, they considered duels to be somehow

---

3. One of two main characters in Gogol's short story *Nevsky Prospect* (1835). A shallow and self-satisfied officer, he mistakes the wife of a German artisan for a woman of easy virtue and receives a sound thrashing. He decides to lodge an official complaint, but after consuming a cream-filled pastry, thinks better of it.

inconceivable, free-thinking, French, while they themselves, especially if they happened to be six feet tall, offended other people rather frequently.

In this case I retreated not out of any cowardice, but because of my unlimited vanity. I wasn't afraid of his height, nor did I think I'd receive a painful beating and get thrown out the window. In fact, I'd have had sufficient physical courage; it was moral fortitude I lacked. I was afraid that everyone present—from the insolent billiard marker to the foul-smelling, pimply little clerks with greasy collars who used to hang about—wouldn't understand and would laugh when I started to protest and speak to them in literary Russian. Because, to this very day, it's still impossible for us to speak about a point of honor, that is, not about honor itself, but a point of honor (*point d'honneur*), except in literary language. One can't even refer to a "point of honor" in everyday language. I was fully convinced (a sense of reality, in spite of all my romanticism!) that they would all simply split their sides laughing, and that the officer, instead of giving me a simple beating, that is, an inoffensive one, would certainly apply his knee to my back and drive me around the billiard table; only then perhaps would he have the mercy to throw me out the window. Naturally, this wretched story of mine couldn't possibly end with this alone. Afterward I used to meet this officer frequently on the street and I observed him very carefully. I don't know whether he ever recognized me. Probably not; I reached that conclusion from various observations. As for me, I stared at him with malice and hatred, and continued to do so for several years! My malice increased and became stronger over time. At first I began to make discreet inquiries about him. This was difficult for me to do, since I had so few acquaintances. But once, as I was following him at a distance as though tied to him, someone called to him on the street: that's how I learned his name. Another time I followed him back to his own apartment and for a ten-kopeck piece learned from the doorman where and how he lived, on what floor, with whom, etc.—in a word, all that could be learned from a doorman. One morning, although I never engaged in literary activities, it suddenly occurred to me to draft a description of this officer as a kind of exposé, a caricature, in the form of a tale. I wrote it with great pleasure. I exposed him; I even slandered him. At first I altered his name only slightly, so that it could be easily recognized; but then, upon careful reflection, I changed it. Then I sent the tale off to *Notes of the Fatherland*.[4] But such exposés were no longer in fashion, and they didn't publish my tale. I was very annoyed by that. At times I simply choked on my spite. Finally, I resolved to challenge my opponent to a duel. I composed a beautiful, charming letter to him, imploring him to apologize to me; in case he refused, I hinted rather strongly at a duel. The letter was composed in such a way that if that officer had possessed even the smallest understanding of the "beautiful and sublime," he would have come running, thrown his arms around me, and offered his friendship. That would have been splendid! We would have led such a wonderful life! Such a life! He would have shielded me with his rank; I would have ennobled him with my culture,

---

4. A radical literary and political journal published in Petersburg from 1839 to 1867.

and, well, with my ideas. Who knows what might have come of it! Imagine it, two years had already passed since he'd insulted me; my challenge was the most ridiculous anachronism, in spite of all the cleverness of my letter in explaining and disguising that fact. But, thank God (to this day I thank the Almighty with tears in my eyes), I didn't send that letter. A shiver runs up and down my spine when I think what might have happened if I had. Then suddenly . . . suddenly, I got my revenge in the simplest manner, a stroke of genius! A brilliant idea suddenly occurred to me. Sometimes on holidays I used to stroll along Nevsky Prospect at about four o'clock in the afternoon, usually on the sunny side. That is, I didn't really stroll; rather, I experienced innumerable torments, humiliations, and bilious attacks. But that's undoubtedly just what I needed. I darted in and out like a fish among the strollers, constantly stepping aside before generals, cavalry officers, hussars, and young ladies. At those moments I used to experience painful spasms in my heart and a burning sensation in my back merely at the thought of my dismal apparel as well as the wretchedness and vulgarity of my darting little figure. This was sheer torture, uninterrupted and unbearable humiliation at the thought, which soon became an incessant and immediate sensation, that I was a fly in the eyes of society, a disgusting, obscene fly—smarter than the rest, more cultured, even nobler—all that goes without saying, but a fly, nonetheless, who incessantly steps aside, insulted and injured by everyone. For what reason did I inflict this torment on myself? Why did I stroll along Nevsky Prospect? I don't know. But something simply *drew* me there at every opportunity.

Then I began to experience surges of that pleasure about which I've already spoken in the first chapter. After the incident with the officer I was drawn there even more strongly; I used to encounter him along Nevsky most often, and it was there that I could admire him. He would also go there, mostly on holidays. He, too, would give way before generals and individuals of superior rank; he, too, would spin like a top among them. But he would simply trample people like me, or even those slightly superior; he would walk directly toward them, as if there were empty space ahead of him; and under no circumstance would he ever step aside. I revelled in my malice as I observed him, and . . . bitterly stepped aside before him every time. I was tortured by the fact that even on the street I found it impossible to stand on an equal footing with him. "Why is it you're always first to step aside?" I badgered myself in insane hysteria, at times waking up at three in the morning. "Why always you and not he? After all, there's no law about it; it isn't written down anywhere. Let it be equal, as it usually is when people of breeding meet: he steps aside halfway and you halfway, and you pass by showing each other mutual respect." But that was never the case, and I continued to step aside, while he didn't even notice that I was yielding to him. Then a most astounding idea suddenly dawned on me. "What if," I thought, "what if I were to meet him and . . . not step aside? Deliberately not step aside, even if it meant bumping into him: how would that be?" This bold idea gradually took such a hold that it afforded me no peace. I dreamt about it incessantly, horribly, and even went to Nevsky more frequently so that I could imagine more clearly how I would do it. I was in ecstasy. The scheme was becoming more and more possible and even probable to me. "Of course, I wouldn't really collide with him," I thought, already feeling more generous toward him in my joy, "but I simply won't turn aside. I'll bump into him, not very painfully, but just so, shoulder to shoulder, as much as decency allows. I'll bump into him the same amount as he bumps into me." At last I made up my mind completely. But the preparations took a very long time. First, in order to look as presentable as possible during the execution of my scheme, I had to worry about my clothes. "In any case, what if, for example, it should occasion a public scandal? (And the public there was superflu:[5] a countess, Princess D., and the entire literary world.) It was essential to be well-dressed; that inspires respect and in a certain sense will place us immediately on an equal footing in the eyes of high society." With that goal in mind I requested my salary in advance, and I purchased a pair of black gloves and a decent hat at Churkin's store. Black gloves seemed to me more dignified, more *bon ton*[6] than the lemon-colored ones I'd considered at first. "That would be too glaring, as if the person wanted to be noticed"; so I didn't buy the lemon-colored ones. I'd already procured a fine shirt with white bone cufflinks; but my overcoat constituted a major obstacle. In and of itself it was not too bad at all; it kept me warm; but it was quilted and had a raccoon collar, the epitome of bad taste. At all costs I had to replace the collar with a beaver one, just like on an officer's coat. For this purpose I began to frequent the Shopping Arcade; and, after several attempts, I turned up some cheap German beaver. Although these German beavers wear out very quickly and soon begin to look shabby, at first, when they're brand new, they look very fine indeed; after all, I only needed it for a single occasion. I asked the price: it was still expensive. After considerable reflection I resolved to sell my raccoon collar. I decided to request a loan for the remaining amount—a rather significant sum for me—from Anton Antonych Setochkin, my office chief, a modest man, but a serious and solid one, who never lent money to anyone, but to whom, upon entering the civil service, I'd once been specially recommended by an important person who'd secured the position for me. I suffered terribly. It seemed monstrous and shameful to ask Anton Antonych for money. I didn't sleep for two or three nights in a row; in general I wasn't getting much sleep those days, and I always had a fever. I would have either a vague sinking feeling in my heart, or else my heart would suddenly begin to thump, thump, thump! . . . At first Anton Antonych was surprised, then he frowned, thought it over, and finally gave me the loan, after securing from me a note authorizing him to deduct the sum from my salary two weeks later. In this way everything was finally ready; the splendid beaver reigned in place of the mangy raccoon, and I gradually began to get down to business. It was impossible to set about it all at once, in a foolhardy way; one had to proceed in this matter very carefully, step by step. But I confess that after many attempts I was ready to despair: we didn't bump into each other, no matter what! No matter how I prepared, no matter how determined I was—it seems that we're just about to bump, when I look up—and once again I've stepped aside while he's gone by

5. Excessively refined (French).   6. In good taste (French).

without even noticing me. I even used to pray as I approached him that God would grant me determination. One time I'd fully resolved to do it, but the result was that I merely stumbled and fell at his feet because, at the very last moment, only a few inches away from him, I lost my nerve. He stepped over me very calmly, and I bounced to one side like a rubber ball. That night I lay ill with a fever once again and was delirious. Then, everything suddenly ended in the best possible way. The night before I decided once and for all not to go through with my pernicious scheme and to give it all up without success; with that in mind I went to Nevsky Prospect for one last time simply in order to see how I'd abandon the whole thing. Suddenly, three paces away from my enemy, I made up my mind unexpectedly; I closed my eyes and—we bumped into each other forcefully, shoulder to shoulder! I didn't yield an inch and walked by him on a completely equal footing! He didn't even turn around to look at me and pretended that he hadn't even noticed; but he was merely pretending, I'm convinced of that. To this very day I'm convinced of that! Naturally, I got the worst of it; he was stronger, but that wasn't the point. The point was that I'd achieved my goal, I'd maintained my dignity, I hadn't yielded one step, and I'd publicly placed myself on an equal social footing with him. I returned home feeling completely avenged for everything. I was ecstatic. I rejoiced and sang Italian arias. Of course, I won't describe what happened to me three days later; if you've read the first part entitled "Underground," you can guess for yourself. The officer was later transferred somewhere else; I haven't seen him for some fourteen years. I wonder what he's doing nowadays, that dear friend of mine! Whom is he trampling underfoot?

II

But when this phase of my nice, little dissipation ended I felt terribly nauseated. Remorse set in; I tried to drive it away because it was too disgusting. Little by little, however, I got used to that, too. I got used to it all; that is, it wasn't that I got used to it, rather, I somehow voluntarily consented to endure it. But I had a way out that reconciled everything—to escape into "all that was beautiful and sublime," in my dreams, of course. I was a terrible dreamer; I dreamt for three months in a row, tucked away in my little corner. And well you may believe that in those moments I was not at all like the gentlemen who, in his faint-hearted anxiety, had sewn a German beaver onto the collar of his old overcoat. I suddenly became a hero. If my six-foot tall lieutenant had come to see me then, I'd never have admitted him. I couldn't even conceive of him at that time. It's hard to describe now what my dreams consisted of then, and how I could've been so satisfied with them, but I was. Besides, even now I can take pride in them at certain times. My dreams were particularly sweet and vivid after my little debauchery; they were filled with remorse and tears, curses and ecstasy. There were moments of such positive intoxication, such happiness, that I felt not even the slightest trace of mockery within me, really and truly. It was all faith, hope and love. That's just it: at the time I believed blindly that by some kind of miracle, some external circumstance, everything would suddenly open up and expand; a vista of appropriate activity would suddenly appear—beneficent, beautiful, and most of all, *ready-made* (what precisely, I never knew, but, most of all, it had to be ready-made), and that I would suddenly step forth into God's world, almost riding on a white horse and wearing a laurel wreath. I couldn't conceive of a secondary role; and that's precisely why in reality I very quietly took on the lowest one. Either a hero or dirt—there was no middle ground. That was my ruin because in the dirt I consoled myself knowing that at other times I was a hero, and that the hero covered himself with dirt; that is to say, an ordinary man would be ashamed to wallow in filth, but a hero is too noble to become defiled; consequently, he can wallow. It's remarkable that these surges of everything "beautiful and sublime" occurred even during my petty depravity, and precisely when I'd sunk to the lowest depths. They occurred in separate spurts, as if to remind me of themselves; however, they failed to banish my depravity by their appearance. On the contrary, they seemed to add spice to it by means of contrast; they came in just the right amount to serve as a tasty sauce. This sauce consisted of contradictions, suffering, and agonizing internal analysis; all of these torments and trifles lent a certain piquancy, even some meaning to my depravity—in a word, they completely fulfilled the function of a tasty sauce. Nor was all this even lacking in a measure of profundity. Besides, I would never have consented to the simple, tasteless, spontaneous little debauchery of an ordinary clerk and have endured all that filth! How could it have attracted me then and lured me into the street late at night? No, sir, I had a noble loophole for everything. . . .

But how much love, oh Lord, how much love I experienced at times in those dreams of mine, in those "escapes into everything beautiful and sublime." Even though it was fantastic love, even though it was never directed at anything human, there was still so much love that afterward, in reality, I no longer felt any impulse to direct it: that would have been an unnecessary luxury. However, everything always ended in a most satisfactory way by a lazy and intoxicating transition into art, that is, into beautiful forms of being, ready-made, largely borrowed from poets and novelists, and adapted to serve every possible need. For instance, I would triumph over everyone; naturally, everyone else grovelled in the dust and was voluntarily impelled to acknowledge my superiority, while I would forgive them all for everything. Or else, being a famous poet and chamberlain, I would fall in love; I'd receive an enormous fortune and would immediately sacrifice it all for the benefit of humanity, at the same time confessing before all peoples my own infamies, which, needless to say, were not simple infamies, but contained a great amount of "the beautiful and sublime," something in the style of Manfred.[7] Everyone would weep and kiss me (otherwise what idiots they would have been), while I went about barefoot and hungry preaching new ideas and defeating all the reactionaries of Austerlitz.[8] Then a march would be played, a general amnesty

---

7. The romantic hero of Byron's poetic tragedy *Manfred* (1817), a lonely, defiant figure whose past conceals some mysterious crime.   8. The site of Napoleon's great victory in December 1805 over the combined armies of the Russian czar Alexander I and the Austrian emperor Francis II.

declared, and the Pope would agree to leave Rome and go to Brazil;[9] a ball would be hosted for all of Italy at the Villa Borghese on the shores of Lake Como,[1] since Lake Como would have been moved to Rome for this very occasion; then there would be a scene in the bushes, etc., etc.—as if you didn't know. You'll say that it's tasteless and repugnant to drag all this out into the open after all the raptures and tears to which I've confessed. But why is it so repugnant? Do you really think I'm ashamed of all this or that it's any more stupid than anything in your own lives, gentlemen? Besides, you can rest assured that some of it was not at all badly composed. . . . Not everything occurred on the shores of Lake Como. But you're right; in fact, it is tasteless and repugnant. And the most repugnant thing of all is that now I've begun to justify myself before you. And even more repugnant is that now I've made that observation. But enough, otherwise there'll be no end to it: each thing will be more repugnant than the last. . . .

I was never able to dream for more than three months in a row, and I began to feel an irresistible urge to plunge into society. To me plunging into society meant paying a visit to my office chief, Anton Antonych Setochkin. He's the only lasting acquaintance I've made during my lifetime; I too now marvel at this circumstance. But even then I would visit him only when my dreams had reached such a degree of happiness that it was absolutely essential for me to embrace people and all humanity at once; for that reason I needed to have at least one person on hand who actually existed. However, one could only call upon Anton Antonych on Tuesdays (his receiving day); consequently, I always had to adjust the urge to embrace all humanity so that it occurred on Tuesday. This Anton Antonych lived near Five Corners,[2] on the fourth floor, in four small, low-ceilinged rooms, each smaller than the last, all very frugal and yellowish in appearance. He lived with his two daughters and an aunt who used to serve tea. The daughters, one thirteen, the other fourteen, had little snub noses. I was very embarrassed by them because they used to whisper all the time and giggle to each other. The host usually sat in his study on a leather couch in front of a table together with some gray-haired guest, a civil servant either from our office or another one. I never saw more than two or three guests there, and they were always the same ones. They talked about excise taxes, debates in the Senate, salaries, promotions, His Excellency and how to please him, and so on and so forth. I had the patience to sit there like a fool next to these people for four hours or so; I listened without daring to say a word to them or even knowing what to talk about. I sat there in a stupor; several times I broke into a sweat; I felt numbed by paralysis; but it was good and useful. Upon returning home I would postpone for some time my desire to embrace all humanity.

I had one other sort of acquaintance, however, named Simonov, a former schoolmate of mine. In fact, I had a number of schoolmates in Petersburg, but I didn't associate with them, and I'd even stopped greeting them

---

9. Napoleon announced his annexation of the Papal States to France in 1809 and was promptly excommunicated by Pope Pius VII. The pope was imprisoned and forced to sign a new concordat, but in 1814 returned to Rome in triumph.   1. Located in the foothills of the Italian Alps in Lombardy. Villa Borghese was the elegant summer palace built by Scipione Cardinal Borghese outside the Porta del Popolo in Rome.   2. A well-known landmark in Petersburg.

along the street. I might even have transferred into a different department at the office so as not to be with them and to cut myself off from my hated childhood once and for all. Curses on that school and those horrible years of penal servitude. In short, I broke with my schoolmates as soon as I was released. There remained only two or three people whom I would greet upon encountering them. One was Simonov, who hadn't distinguished himself in school in any way; he was even-tempered and quiet, but I detected in him a certain independence of character, even honesty. I don't even think that he was all that limited. At one time he and I experienced some rather bright moments, but they didn't last very long and somehow were suddenly clouded over. Evidently he was burdened by these recollections, and seemed in constant fear that I would lapse into that former mode. I suspect that he found me repulsive, but not being absolutely sure, I used to visit him nonetheless.

So once, on a Thursday, unable to endure my solitude, and knowing that on that day Anton Antonych's door was locked, I remembered Simonov. As I climbed the stairs to his apartment on the fourth floor, I was thinking how burdensome this man found my presence and that my going to see him was rather useless. But since it always turned out, as if on purpose, that such reflections would impel me to put myself even further into an ambiguous situation, I went right in. It had been almost a year since I'd last seen Simonov.

III

I found two more of my former schoolmates there with him. Apparently they were discussing some important matter. None of them paid any attention to me when I entered, which was strange since I hadn't seen them for several years. Evidently they considered me some sort of ordinary house fly. They hadn't even treated me like that when we were in school together, although they'd all hated me. Of course, I understood that they must despise me now for my failure in the service and for the fact that I'd sunk so low, was badly dressed, and so on, which, in their eyes, constituted proof of my ineptitude and insignificance. But I still hadn't expected such a degree of contempt. Simonov was even surprised by my visits. All this disconcerted me; I sat down in some distress and began to listen to what they were saying.

The discussion was serious, even heated, and concerned a farewell dinner which these gentlemen wanted to organize jointly as early as the following day for their friend Zverkov, an army officer who was heading for a distant province. Monsieur Zverkov had also been my schoolmate all along. I'd begun to hate him especially in the upper grades. In the lower grades he was merely an attractive, lively lad whom everyone liked. However, I'd hated him in the lower grades, too, precisely because he was such an attractive, lively lad. He was perpetually a poor student and had gotten worse as time went on; he managed to graduate, however, because he had influential connections. During his last year at school he'd come into an inheritance of some two hundred serfs, and, since almost all the rest of us were poor, he'd even begun to brag. He was an extremely uncouth fellow, but a nice lad nonetheless, even when he was bragging. In spite of our superficial, fantastic, and high-flown notions of honor and pride, all of us, except for a very few, would fawn upon Zverkov, the more so the more he bragged. They didn't fawn for any advantage; they fawned simply because he was a man endowed by nature with gifts. Moreover, we'd somehow come to regard Zverkov as a cunning fellow and an expert on good manners. This latter point particularly infuriated me. I hated the shrill, self-confident tone of his voice, his adoration for his own witticisms, which were terribly stupid in spite of his bold tongue; I hated his handsome, stupid face (for which, however, I'd gladly have exchanged my own intelligent one), and the impudent bearing typical of officers during the 1840s. I hated the way he talked about his future successes with women. (He'd decided not to get involved with them yet, since he still hadn't received his officer's epaulettes; he awaited those epaulettes impatiently.) And he talked about all the duels he'd have to fight. I remember how once, although I was usually very taciturn, I suddenly clashed with Zverkov when, during our free time, he was discussing future exploits with his friends; getting a bit carried away with the game like a little puppy playing in the sun, he suddenly declared that not a single girl in his village would escape his attention—that it was his *droit de seigneur*,[3] and that if the peasants even dared protest, he'd have them all flogged, those bearded rascals; and he'd double their quit-rent.[4] Our louts applauded, but I attacked him—not out of any pity for the poor girls or their fathers, but simply because everyone else was applauding such a little insect. I got the better of him that time, but Zverkov, although stupid, was also cheerful and impudent. Therefore he laughed it off to such an extent that, in fact, I really didn't get the better of him. The laugh remained on his side. Later he got the better of me several times, but without malice, just so, in jest, in passing, in fun. I was filled with spite and hatred, but I didn't respond. After graduation he took a few steps toward me; I didn't object strongly because I found it flattering; but soon we came to a natural parting of the ways. Afterward I heard about his barrack-room successes as a lieutenant and about his *binges*. Then there were other rumors—about his *successes* in the service. He no longer bowed to me on the street; I suspected that he was afraid to compromise himself by acknowledging such an insignificant person as myself. I also saw him in the theater once, in the third tier, already sporting an officer's gold braids. He was fawning and grovelling before the daughters of some aged general. In those three years he'd let himself go, although he was still as handsome and agile as before; he sagged somehow and had begun to put on weight; it was clear that by the age of thirty he'd be totally flabby. So it was for this Zverkov, who was finally ready to depart, that our schoolmates were organizing a farewell dinner. They'd kept up during these three years, although I'm sure that inwardly they didn't consider themselves on an equal footing with him.

One of Simonov's two guests was Ferfichkin, a Russified German, a short man with a face like a monkey, a fool who made fun of everybody,

---

3. Lord's privilege (French); the feudal lord's right to spend the first night with the bride of a newly married serf.   4. The annual sum paid in cash or produce by serfs to landowners for the right to farm their land in feudal Russia, as opposed to the *corvée*, a certain amount of labor owed.

my bitterest enemy from the lower grades—a despicable, impudent show-off who affected the most ticklish sense of ambition, although, of course, he was a coward at heart. He was one of Zverkov's admirers and played up to him for his own reasons, frequently borrowing money from him. Simonov's other guest, Trudolyubov, was insignificant, a military man, tall, with a cold demeanor, rather honest, who worshipped success of any kind and was capable of talking only about promotions. He was a distant relative of Zverkov's, and that, silly to say, lent him some importance among us. He'd always regarded me as a nonentity; he treated me not altogether politely, but tolerably.

"Well, if each of us contributes seven rubles," said Trudolyubov, "with three of us that makes twenty-one altogether—we can have a good dinner. Of course, Zverkov won't have to pay."

"Naturally," Simonov agreed, "since we're inviting him."

"Do you really think," Ferfichkin broke in arrogantly and excitedly, just like an insolent lackey bragging about his master-the-general's medals, "do you really think Zverkov will let us pay for everything? He'll accept out of decency, but then he'll order *half a dozen bottles* on his own."

"What will the four of us do with half a dozen bottles?" asked Trudolyubov, only taking note of the number.

"So then, three of us plus Zverkov makes four, twenty-one rubles, in the Hôtel de Paris, tomorrow at five o'clock," concluded Simonov definitively, since he'd been chosen to make the arrangements.

"Why only twenty-one?" I asked in trepidation, even, apparently, somewhat offended. "If you count me in, you'll have twenty-eight rubles instead of twenty-one."

It seemed to me that to include myself so suddenly and unexpectedly would appear as quite a splendid gesture and that they'd all be smitten at once and regard me with respect.

"Do you really want to come, too?" Simonov inquired with displeasure, managing somehow to avoid looking at me. He knew me inside out.

It was infuriating that he knew me inside out.

"And why not? After all, I was his schoolmate, too, and I must admit that I even feel a bit offended that you've left me out," I continued, just about to boil over again.

"And how were we supposed to find you?" Ferfichkin interjected rudely.

"You never got along very well with Zverkov," added Trudolyubov frowning. But I'd already latched on and wouldn't let go.

"I think no one has a right to judge that," I objected in a trembling voice, as if God knows what had happened. "Perhaps that's precisely why I want to take part now, since we didn't get along so well before."

"Well, who can figure you out . . . such lofty sentiments . . . ," Trudolyubov said with an ironic smile.

"We'll put your name down," Simonov decided, turning to me. "Tomorrow at five o'clock at the Hôtel de Paris. Don't make any mistakes."

"What about the money?" Ferfichkin started to say in an undertone to Simonov while nodding at me, but he broke off because Simonov looked embarrassed.

"That'll do," Trudolyubov said getting up. "If he really wants to come so much, let him."

"But this is our own circle of friends," Ferfichkin grumbled, also picking up his hat. "It's not an official gathering. Perhaps we really don't want you at all. . . ."

They left. Ferfichkin didn't even say goodbye to me as he went out; Trudolyubov barely nodded without looking at me. Simonov, with whom I was left alone, was irritated and perplexed, and he regarded me in a strange way. He neither sat down nor invited me to.

"Hmmm . . . yes . . . , so, tomorrow. Will you contribute your share of the money now? I'm asking just to know for sure," he muttered in embarrassment.

I flared up; but in doing so, I remembered that I'd owed Simonov fifteen rubles for a very long time, which debt, moreover, I'd forgotten, but had also never repaid.

"You must agree, Simonov, that I couldn't have known when I came here . . . oh, what a nuisance, but I've forgotten. . . ."

He broke off and began to pace around the room in even greater irritation. As he paced, he began to walk on his heels and stomp more loudly.

"I'm not detaining you, am I?" I asked after a few moments of silence.

"Oh, no!" he replied with a start. "That is, in fact, yes. You see, I still have to stop by at . . . It's not very far from here . . . ," he added in an apologetic way with some embarrassment.

"Oh, good heavens! Why didn't you say so?" I exclaimed, seizing my cap; moreover I did so with a surprisingly familiar air, coming from God knows where.

"But it's really not far . . . only a few steps away . . . ," Simonov repeated, accompanying me into the hallway with a bustling air which didn't suit him well at all. "So, then, tomorrow at five o'clock sharp!" he shouted to me on the stairs. He was very pleased that I was leaving. However, I was furious.

"What possessed me, what on earth possessed me to interfere?" I gnashed my teeth as I walked along the street. "And for such a scoundrel, a pig like Zverkov! Naturally, I shouldn't go. Of course, to hell with them. Am I bound to go, or what? Tomorrow I'll inform Simonov by post. . . ."

But the real reason I was so furious was that I was sure I'd go. I'd go on purpose. The more tactless, the more indecent it was for me to go, the more certain I'd be to do it.

There was even a definite impediment to my going: I didn't have any money. All I had was nine rubles. But of those, I had to hand over seven the next day to my servant Apollon for his monthly wages; he lived in and received seven rubles for his meals.

Considering Apollon's character it was impossible not to pay him. But more about that rascal, that plague of mine, later.

In any case, I knew that I wouldn't pay him his wages and that I'd definitely go.

That night I had the most hideous dreams. No wonder: all evening I was burdened with recollections of my years of penal servitude at school and I couldn't get rid of them. I'd been sent off to that school by distant relatives on whom I was dependent and about whom I've heard nothing since. They dispatched me, a lonely boy, crushed by their reproaches, already introspective, taciturn, and regarding everything around him savagely. My schoolmates received me with spiteful and pitiless jibes because I wasn't like any of them. But I couldn't tolerate their jibes; I couldn't possibly get along with them as easily as they got along with each other. I hated them all at once and took refuge from everyone in fearful, wounded and excessive pride. Their crudeness irritated me. Cynically they mocked my face and my awkward build; yet, what stupid faces they all had! Facial expressions at our school somehow degenerated and became particularly stupid. Many attractive lads had come to us, but in a few years they too were repulsive to look at. When I was only sixteen I wondered about them gloomily; even then I was astounded by the pettiness of their thoughts and the stupidity of their studies, games and conversations. They failed to understand essential things and took no interest in important, weighty subjects, so that I couldn't help considering them beneath me. It wasn't my wounded vanity that drove me to it; and, for God's sake, don't repeat any of those nauseating and hackneyed clichés, such as, "I was merely a dreamer, whereas they already understood life." They didn't understand a thing, not one thing about life, and I swear, that's what annoyed me most about them. On the contrary, they accepted the most obvious, glaring reality in a fantastically stupid way, and even then they'd begun to worship nothing but success. Everything that was just, but oppressed and humiliated, they ridiculed hard-heartedly and shamelessly. They mistook rank for intelligence; at the age of sixteen they were already talking about occupying comfortable little niches. Of course, much of this was due to their stupidity and the poor examples that had constantly surrounded them in their childhood and youth. They were monstrously depraved. Naturally, even this was more superficial, more affected cynicism; of course, their youth and a certain freshness shone through their depravity; but even this freshness was unattractive and manifested itself in a kind of rakishness. I hated them terribly, although, perhaps, I was even worse than they were. They returned the feeling and didn't conceal their loathing for me. But I no longer wanted their affection; on the contrary, I constantly longed for their humiliation. In order to avoid their jibes, I began to study as hard as I could on purpose and made my way to the top of the class. That impressed them. In addition, they all began to realize that I'd read certain books which they could never read and that I understood certain things (not included in our special course) about which they'd never even heard. They regarded this with savagery and sarcasm, but they submitted morally, all the more since even the teachers paid me some attention on this account. Their jibes ceased, but their hostility remained, and relations between us became cold and strained. In the end I myself couldn't stand it: as the years went by, my need for people, for friends, increased. I made several attempts to get closer to some of them; but these attempts always turned out to be unnatural and ended of their own accord. Once I even had a friend of sorts. But I was already a despot at heart; I wanted to exercise unlimited power over his soul; I wanted to instill in him contempt for his surroundings; and I demanded from him a disdainful and definitive break with those surroundings. I frightened him with my passionate friendship, and I reduced him to tears and convulsions. He was a naive and giving soul, but as soon as he'd surrendered himself to me totally, I began to despise him and reject him immediately—as if I only needed to achieve a victory over him, merely to subjugate him. But I was unable to conquer them all; my one friend was not at all like them, but rather a rare exception. The first thing I did upon leaving school was abandon the special job in the civil service for which I'd been trained, in order to sever all ties, break with my past, cover it over with dust. . . . The devil only knows why, after all that, I'd dragged myself over to see this Simonov! . . .

Early the next morning I roused myself from bed, jumped up in anxiety, just as if everything was about to start happening all at once. But I believed that some radical change in my life was imminent and was sure to occur that very day. Perhaps because I wasn't used to it, but all my life, at any external event, albeit a trivial one, it always seemed that some sort of radical change would occur. I went off to work as usual, but returned home two hours earlier in order to prepare. The most important thing, I thought, was not to arrive there first, or else they'd all think I was too eager. But there were thousands of most important things, and they all reduced me to the point of impotence. I polished my boots once again with my own hands. Apollon wouldn't polish them twice in one day for anything in the world; he considered it indecent. So I polished them myself, after stealing the brushes from the hallway so that he wouldn't notice and then despise me for it afterward. Next I carefully examined my clothes and found that everything was old, shabby, and worn out. I'd become too slovenly. My uniform was in better shape, but I couldn't go to dinner in a uniform. Worst of all, there was an enormous yellow stain on the knee of my trousers. I had an inkling that the spot alone would rob me of nine-tenths of my dignity. I also knew that it was unseemly for me to think that. "But this isn't the time for thinking. Reality is now looming," I thought, and my heart sank. I also knew perfectly well at that time, that I was monstrously exaggerating all these facts. But what could be done? I was no longer able to control myself, and was shaking with fever. In despair I imagined how haughtily and coldly that "scoundrel" Zverkov would greet me; with what dull and totally relentless contempt that dullard Trudolyubov would regard me; how nastily and impudently that insect Ferfichkin would giggle at me in order to win Zverkov's approval; how well Simonov would understand all this and how he'd despise me for my wretched vanity and cowardice; and worst of all, how petty all this would be, not *literary*, but commonplace. Of course, it would have been better not to go at all. But that was no longer possible; once I began to feel drawn to something, I plunged right in, head first. I'd have reproached myself for the rest of my life: "So, you retreated, you retreated before reality, you retreated!" On the contrary, I desperately wanted to prove to all this "rabble" that I really wasn't the coward I imagined myself to be. But that's not all: in the strongest paroxysm of cowardly fever I dreamt of gaining the upper hand, of conquering them, of carrying them away, compelling them to love me— if only "for the nobility of my thought and my indisputable wit." They would abandon Zverkov; he'd sit by in silence and embarassment, and I'd crush him. Afterward, perhaps, I'd be reconciled with Zverkov and drink to our *friendship*, but what was most spiteful and insulting for me was that I knew even then, I knew completely and for sure, that I didn't need any of this at all; that in fact I really didn't want to crush them, conquer them, or attract them, and that if I could have ever achieved all that, I'd be the first to say that it wasn't worth a damn. Oh, how I prayed to God that this day would pass quickly! With inexpressible anxiety I approached the window, opened the transom,[5] and peered out into the murky mist of the thickly falling wet snow. . . .

At last my worthless old wall clock sputtered out five o'clock. I grabbed my hat, and, trying not to look at Apollon—who'd been waiting since early morning to receive his wages, but didn't want to be the first one to mention it out of pride—I slipped out the door past him and intentionally hired a smart cab with my last half-ruble in order to arrive at the Hôtel de Paris in style.

IV

I knew since the day before that I'd be the first one to arrive. But it was no longer a question of who was first.

Not only was no one else there, but I even had difficulty finding our room. The table hadn't even been set. What did it all mean? After many inquiries I finally learned from the waiters that dinner had been ordered for closer to six o'clock, instead of five. This was also confirmed in the buffet. It was too embarrassing to ask any more questions. It was still only twenty-five minutes past five. If they'd changed the time, they should have let me know; that's what the city mail was for. They shouldn't have subjected me to such "shame" in my own eyes and . . . and, at least not in front of the waiters. I sat down. A waiter began to set the table. I felt even more ashamed in his presence. Toward six o'clock candles were brought into the room in addition to the lighted lamps already there, yet it hadn't occurred to the waiters to bring them in as soon as I'd arrived. In the next room two gloomy customers, angry-looking and silent, were dining at separate tables. In one of the distant rooms there was a great deal of noise, even shouting. One could hear the laughter of a whole crowd of people, including nasty little squeals in French—there were ladies present at that dinner. In short, it was disgusting. Rarely had I passed a more unpleasant hour, so that when they all arrived together precisely at six o'clock, I was initially overjoyed to see them, as if they were my liberators, and I almost forgot that I was supposed to appear offended.

Zverkov, obviously the leader, entered ahead of the rest. Both he and they were laughing; but, upon seeing me, Zverkov drew himself up, approached me unhurriedly, bowed slightly from the waist almost coquettishly, and extended his hand politely, but not too, with a kind of careful civility, almost as if he were a general both offering his hand, but also guarding against something. I'd imagined, on the contrary, that as soon as

5. A small hinged pane in the window of a Russian house, used for ventilation especially during the winter when the main part of the window is sealed.

he entered he'd burst into his former, shrill laughter with occasional squeals, and that he'd immediately launch into his stale jokes and witticisms. I'd been preparing for them since the previous evening; but in no way did I expect such condescension, such courtesy characteristic of a general. Could it be that he now considered himself so immeasurably superior to me in all respects? If he'd merely wanted to offend me by this superior attitude, it wouldn't have been so bad, I thought; I'd manage to pay him back somehow. But what if, without any desire to offend, the notion had crept into his dumb sheep's brain that he really was immeasurably superior to me and that he could only treat me in a patronizing way? From this possibility alone I began to gasp for air.

"Have you been waiting long?" Trudolyubov asked.

"I arrived at five o'clock sharp, just as I was told yesterday," I answered loudly and with irritation presaging an imminent explosion.

"Didn't you let him know that we changed the time?" Trudolyubov asked, turning to Simonov.

"No, I didn't. I forgot," he replied, but without any regret; then, not even apologizing to me, he went off to order the hors d'oeuvres.

"So you've been here for a whole hour, you poor fellow!" Zverkov cried sarcastically, because according to his notions, this must really have been terribly amusing. That scoundrel Ferfichkin chimed in after him with nasty, ringing laughter that sounded like a dog's yapping. My situation seemed very amusing and awkward to him, too.

"It's not the least bit funny!" I shouted at Ferfichkin, getting more and more irritated. "The others are to blame, not me. They neglected to inform me. It's, it's, it's . . . simply preposterous."

"It's not only preposterous, it's more than that," muttered Trudolyubov, naively interceding on my behalf. "You're being too kind. It's pure rudeness. Of course, it wasn't intentional. And how could Simonov have . . . hmm!"

"If a trick like that had been played on me," said Ferfichkin, "I'd . . ."

"Oh, you'd have ordered yourself something to eat," interrupted Zverkov, "or simply asked to have dinner served without waiting for the rest of us."

"You'll agree that I could've done that without asking anyone's permission," I snapped. "If I did wait, it was only because . . ."

"Let's be seated, gentlemen," cried Simonov upon entering. "Everything's ready. I can vouch for the champagne; it's excellently chilled. . . . Moreover, I didn't know where your apartment was, so how could I find you?" he said turning to me suddenly, but once again not looking directly at me. Obviously he was holding something against me. I suspect he got to thinking after what had happened yesterday.

Everyone sat down; I did, too. The table was round. Trudolyubov sat on my left, Simonov, on my right. Zverkov sat across; Ferfichkin, next to him, between Trudolyubov and him.

"Tell-l-l me now, are you . . . in a government department?" Zverkov continued to attend to me. Seeing that I was embarrassed, he imagined in earnest that he had to be nice to me, encouraging me to speak. "Does he want me to throw a bottle at his head, or what?" I thought in a rage. Unaccustomed as I was to all this, I was unnaturally quick to take offense.

"In such and such an office," I replied abruptly, looking at my plate.

"And . . . is it p-p-profitable? Tell-l-l me, what ma-a-de you decide to leave your previous position?"

"What ma-a-a-de me leave my previous position was simply that I wanted to," I dragged my words out three times longer than he did, hardly able to control myself. Ferfichkin snorted. Simonov looked at me ironically; Trudolyubov stopped eating and began to stare at me with curiosity.

Zverkov was jarred, but didn't want to show it.

"Well-l, and how is the support?"

"What support?"

"I mean, the s-salary?"

"Why are you cross-examining me?"

However, I told him right away what my salary was. I blushed terribly.

"That's not very much," Zverkov observed pompously.

"No, sir, it's not enough to dine in café-restaurants!" added Ferfichkin insolently.

"In my opinion, it's really very little," Trudolyubov observed in earnest.

"And how thin you've grown, how you've changed . . . since . . . ," Zverkov added, with a touch of venom now, and with a kind of impudent sympathy, examining me and my apparel.

"Stop embarrassing him," Ferfichkin cried with a giggle.

"My dear sir, I'll have you know that I'm not embarrassed," I broke in at last. "Listen! I'm dining in this 'café-restaurant' at my own expense, my own, not anyone else's; note that, Monsieur Ferfichkin."

"Wha-at? And who isn't dining at his own expense? You seem to be . . ." Ferfichkin seized hold of my words, turned as red as a lobster, and looked me straight in the eye with fury.

"Just so-o," I replied, feeling that I'd gone a bit too far, "and I suggest that it would be much better if we engaged in more intelligent conversation."

"It seems that you're determined to display your intelligence."

"Don't worry, that would be quite unnecessary here."

"What's all this cackling, my dear sir? Huh? Have you taken leave of your senses in that *duh*-partment of yours?"

"Enough, gentlemen, enough," cried Zverkov authoritatively.

"How stupid this is!" muttered Simonov.

"Really, it is stupid. We're gathered here in a congenial group to have a farewell dinner for our good friend, while you're still settling old scores," Trudolyubov said, rudely addressing only me. "You forced yourself upon us yesterday; don't disturb the general harmony now. . . ."

"Enough, enough," cried Zverkov. "Stop it, gentlemen, this'll never do. Let me tell you instead how I very nearly got married a few days ago . . ."

There followed some scandalous, libelous anecdote about how this gentleman very nearly got married a few days ago. There wasn't one word about marriage, however; instead, generals, colonels, and even gentlemen of the bed chamber figured prominently in the story, while Zverkov played the leading role among them all. Approving laughter followed; Ferfichkin even squealed.

Everyone had abandoned me by now, and I sat there completely crushed and humiliated.

"Good Lord, what kind of company is this for me?" I wondered. "And what a fool I've made of myself in front of them all! But I let Ferfichkin go too far. These numbskulls think they're doing me an honor by allowing me to sit with them at their table, when they don't understand that it's I who's done them the honor, and not the reverse. 'How thin I've grown! What clothes!' Oh, these damned trousers! Zverkov's already noticed the yellow spot on my knee. . . . What's the use? Right now, this very moment, I should stand up, take my hat, and simply leave without saying a single word. . . . Out of contempt! And tomorrow—I'll even be ready for a duel. Scoundrels! It's not the seven rubles I care about. But they may think that . . . To hell with it! I don't care about the seven rubles. I'm leaving at once! . . ."

Of course, I stayed.

In my misery I drank Lafite and sherry by the glassful. Being unaccustomed to it, I got drunk very quickly; the more intoxicated I became, the greater my annoyance. Suddenly I felt like offending them all in the most impudent manner—and then I'd leave. To seize the moment and show them all who I really was—let them say: even though he's ridiculous, he's clever . . . and . . . and . . . in short, to hell with them!

I surveyed them all arrogantly with my dazed eyes. But they seemed to have forgotten all about me. *They* were noisy, boisterous and merry. Zverkov kept on talking. I began to listen. He was talking about some magnificent lady whom he'd finally driven to make a declaration of love. (Of course, he was lying like a trooper.) He said that he'd been assisted in this matter particularly by a certain princeling, the hussar Kolya, who possessed some three thousand serfs.

"And yet, this same Kolya who has three thousand serfs hasn't even come to see you off," I said, breaking into the conversation suddenly. For a moment silence fell.

"You're drunk already," Trudolyubov said, finally deigning to notice me, and glancing contemptuously in my direction. Zverkov examined me in silence as if I were an insect. I lowered my eyes. Simonov quickly began to pour champagne.

Trudolyubov raised his glass, followed by everyone but me.

"To your health and to a good journey!" he cried to Zverkov. "To old times, gentlemen, and to our future, hurrah!"

Everyone drank up and pressed around to exchange kisses with Zverkov. I didn't budge; my full glass stood before me untouched.

"Aren't you going to drink?" Trudolyubov roared at me, having lost his patience and turning to me menacingly.

"I wish to make my own speech, all by myself . . . and then I'll drink, Mr. Trudolyubov."

"Nasty shrew!" Simonov muttered.

I sat up in my chair, feverishly seized hold of my glass, and prepared for something extraordinary, although I didn't know quite what I'd say.

"*Silence!*" cried Ferfichkin. "And now for some real intelligence!" Zverkov waited very gravely, aware of what was coming.

"Mr. Lieutenant Zverkov," I began, "you must know that I detest phrases, phrasemongers, and corsetted waists. . . . That's the first point; the second will follow."

Everyone stirred uncomfortably.

"The second point: I hate obscene stories and the men who tell them.[6] I especially hate the men who tell them!"

"The third point: I love truth, sincerity and honesty," I continued almost automatically, because I was beginning to become numb with horror, not knowing how I could be speaking this way. . . . "I love thought, Monsieur Zverkov. I love genuine comradery, on an equal footing, but not . . . hmmm . . . I love . . . But, after all, why not? I too will drink to your health, Monsieur Zverkov. Seduce those Circassian[7] maidens, shoot the enemies of the fatherland, and . . . and . . . To your health, Monsieur Zverkov!"

Zverkov rose from his chair, bowed, and said: "I'm most grateful."

He was terribly offended and had even turned pale.

"To hell with him," Trudolyubov roared, banging his fist down on the table.

"No, sir, people should be whacked in the face for saying such things!" squealed Ferfichkin.

"We ought to throw him out!" muttered Simonov.

"Not a word, gentlemen, not a move!" Zverkov cried triumphantly, putting a stop to this universal indignation. "I'm grateful to you all, but I can show him myself how much I value his words."

"Mr. Ferfichkin, tomorrow you'll give me satisfaction for the words you've just uttered!" I said loudly, turning to Ferfichkin with dignity.

"Do you mean a duel? Very well," he replied, but I must have looked so ridiculous as I issued my challenge, it must have seemed so out of keeping with my entire appearance, that everyone, including Ferfichkin, collapsed into laughter.

"Yes, of course, throw him out! Why, he's quite drunk already," Trudolyubov declared in disgust.

"I shall never forgive myself for letting him join us," Simonov muttered again.

"Now's the time to throw a bottle at the lot of them," I thought. So I grabbed a bottle and . . . poured myself another full glass.

". . . No, it's better to sit it out to the very end!" I went on thinking. "You'd be glad, gentlemen, if I left. But nothing doing! I'll stay here deliberately and keep on drinking to the very end, as a sign that I accord you no importance whatsoever. I'll sit here and drink because this is a tavern, and I've paid good money to get in. I'll sit here and drink because I consider you to be so many pawns, nonexistent pawns. I'll sit here and drink . . . and sing too, if I want to, yes, sir, I'll sing because I have the right to . . . sing . . . hmm."

But I didn't sing. I just tried not to look at any of them; I assumed the most carefree poses and waited impatiently until they would be the first to speak to me. But, alas, they did not. How much, how very much I longed to be reconciled with them at that moment! The clock struck eight, then nine. They moved from the table to the sofa. Zverkov sprawled on the couch, placing one foot on the round table. They brought the wine over,

---

6. A phrase borrowed from the inveterate liar Nozdryov, one of the provincial landowners in the first volume of Gogol's *Dead Souls* (1842).   7. A Muslim people inhabiting a region in the northern Caucasus.

too. He really had ordered three bottles at his own expense. Naturally, he didn't invite me to join them. Everyone surrounded him on the sofa. They listened to him almost with reverence. It was obvious they liked him. "What for? What for?" I wondered to myself. From time to time they were moved to drunken ecstasy and exchanged kisses. They talked about the Caucasus, the nature of true passion, card games, profitable positions in the service; they talked about the income of a certain hussar Podkharzhev-sky, whom none of them knew personally, and they rejoiced that his income was so large; they talked about the unusual beauty and charm of Princess D., whom none of them had ever seen; finally, they arrived at the question of Shakespeare's immortality.

I smiled contemptuously and paced up and down the other side of the room, directly behind the sofa, along the wall from the table to the stove and back again. I wanted to show them with all my might that I could get along without them; meanwhile, I deliberately stomped my boots, thumping my heels. But all this was in vain. *They* paid me no attention. I had the forbearance to pace like that, right in front of them, from eight o'clock until eleven, in the very same place, from the table to the stove and from the stove back to the table. "I'm pacing just as I please, and no one can stop me." A waiter who came into the room paused several times to look at me; my head was spinning from all those turns; there were moments when it seemed that I was delirious. During those three hours I broke out in a sweat three times and then dried out. At times I was pierced to the heart with a most profound, venomous thought: ten years would pass, twenty, forty; and still, even after forty years, I'd remember with loathing and humiliation these filthiest, most absurd, and horrendous moments of my entire life. It was impossible to humiliate myself more shamelessly or more willingly, and I fully understood that, fully; nevertheless, I continued to pace from the table to the stove and back again. "Oh, if you only knew what thoughts and feelings I'm capable of, and how cultured I really am!" I thought at moments, mentally addressing the sofa where my enemies were seated. But my enemies behaved as if I weren't even in the room. Once, and only once, they turned to me, precisely when Zverkov started in about Shakespeare, and I suddenly burst into contemptuous laughter. I snorted so affectedly and repulsively that they broke off their conversation immediately and stared at me in silence for about two minutes, in earnest, without laughing, as I paced up and down, from the table to the stove, while *I paid not the slightest bit of attention to them.* But nothing came of it; they didn't speak to me. A few moments later they abandoned me again. The clock struck eleven.

"Gentlemen," exclaimed Zverkov, getting up from the sofa, "Now let's all go *to that place.*"[8]

"Of course, of course!" the others replied.

I turned abruptly to Zverkov. I was so exhausted, so broken, that I'd have slit my own throat to be done with all this! I was feverish; my hair, which had been soaked through with sweat, had dried and now stuck to my forehead and temples.

"Zverkov, I ask your forgiveness," I said harshly and decisively. "Fer-

---

8. That is, a brothel.

fichkin, yours too, and everyone's, everyone's. I've insulted you all!" "Aha!
So a duel isn't really your sort of thing!" hissed Ferfichkin venomously.

His remark was like a painful stab to my heart.

"No, I'm not afraid of a duel, Ferfichkin! I'm ready to fight with you
tomorrow, even after we're reconciled. I even insist upon it, and you can't
refuse me. I want to prove that I'm not afraid of a duel. You'll shoot first,
and I'll fire into the air."

"He's amusing himself," Simonov observed.

"He's simply taken leave of his senses!" Trudolyubov added.

"Allow us to pass; why are you blocking our way? . . . Well, what is it
you want?" Zverkov asked contemptuously. They were all flushed, their
eyes glazed. They'd drunk a great deal.

"I ask for your friendship, Zverkov, I've insulted you, but . . ."

"Insulted me? You? In-sul-ted me? My dear sir, I want you to know that
never, under any circumstances, could you possibly insult *me*!"

"And that's enough from you. Out of the way!" Trudolyubov added.
"Let's go."

"Olympia is mine, gentlemen, that's agreed!" cried Zverkov.

"We won't argue, we won't," they replied, laughing.

I stood there as if spat on. The party left the room noisily, and Trudolyubov struck up a stupid song. Simonov remained behind for a brief moment
to tip the waiters. All of a sudden I went up to him.

"Simonov! Give me six rubles," I said decisively and desperately.

He looked at me in extreme amazement with his dulled eyes. He was
drunk, too.

"Are you really going *to that place* with us?"

"Yes!"

"I have no money!" he snapped; then he laughed contemptuously and
headed out of the room.

I grabbed hold of his overcoat. It was a nightmare.

"Simonov! I know that you have some money. Why do you refuse me?
Am I really such a scoundrel? Beware of refusing me: if you only knew, if
you only knew why I'm asking. Everything depends on it, my entire future,
all my plans. . . ."

Simonov took out the money and almost threw it at me.

"Take it, if you have no shame!" he said mercilessly, then ran out to
catch up with the others.

I remained behind for a minute. The disorder, the leftovers, a broken
glass on the floor, spilled wine, cigarette butts, drunkenness and delirium
in my head, agonizing torment in my heart; and finally, a waiter who'd
seen and heard everything and who was now looking at me with curiosity.

"*To that place!*" I cried. "Either they'll all fall on their knees, embracing
me, begging for my friendship, or . . . or else, I'll give Zverkov a slap in
the face."

V

"So here it is, here it is at last, a confrontation with reality," I muttered,
rushing headlong down the stairs. "This is no longer the Pope leaving
Rome and going to Brazil; this is no ball on the shores of Lake Como!"

"You're a scoundrel," the thought flashed through my mind, "if you laugh at that now."

"So what!" I cried in reply. "Everything is lost now, anyway!"

There was no sign of them, but it didn't matter. I knew where they were going.

At the entrance stood a solitary, late-night cabby in a coarse peasant coat powdered with wet, seemingly warm snow that was still falling. It was steamy and stuffy outside. The little shaggy piebald nag was also dusted with snow and was coughing; I remember that very well. I headed for the rough-hewn sledge; but as soon as I raised one foot to get in, the recollection of how Simonov had just given me six rubles hit me with such force that I tumbled into the sledge like a sack.

"No! There's a lot I have to do to make up for that!" I cried. "But make up for it I will or else I'll perish on the spot this very night. Let's go!" We set off. There was an entire whirlwind spinning around inside my head.

"They won't fall on their knees to beg for my friendship. That's a mirage, an indecent mirage, disgusting, romantic, and fantastic; it's just like the ball on the shores of Lake Como. Consequently, I *must* give Zverkov a slap in the face! I am obligated to do it. And so, it's all decided; I'm rushing there to give him a slap in the face."

"Hurry up!"

The cabby tugged at the reins.

"As soon as I go in, I'll slap him. Should I say a few words first before I slap him in the face? No! I'll simply go in and slap him. They'll all be sitting there in the drawing room; he'll be on the sofa with Olympia. That damned Olympia! She once ridiculed my face and refused me. I'll drag Olympia around by the hair and Zverkov by the ears. No, better grab one ear and lead him around the room like that. Perhaps they'll begin to beat me, and then they'll throw me out. That's even likely. So what? I'll still have slapped him first; the initiative will be mine. According to the laws of honor, that's all that matters. He'll be branded, and nothing can wipe away that slap except a duel.[9] He'll have to fight. So just let them beat me now! Let them, the ingrates! Trudolyubov will hit me hardest, he's so strong. Ferfichkin will sneak up alongside and will undoubtedly grab my hair, I'm sure he will. But let them, let them. That's why I've come. At last these blockheads will be forced to grasp the tragedy in all this! As they drag me to the door, I'll tell them that they really aren't even worth the tip of my little finger!"

"Hurry up, driver, hurry up!" I shouted to the cabby.

He was rather startled and cracked his whip. I'd shouted very savagely.

"We'll fight at daybreak, and that's settled. I'm through with the department. Ferfichkin recently said duh-partment, instead of department. But where will I get pistols? What nonsense! I'll take my salary in advance and buy them. And powder? Bullets? That's what the second will attend to. And how will I manage to do all this by daybreak? And where will I find a second? I have no acquaintances. . . ."

---

9. Duels as a means of resolving points of honor were officially discouraged but still fairly common.

"Nonsense!" I shouted, whipping myself up into even more of a frenzy, "Nonsense!"

"The first person I meet on the street will have to act as my second, just as he would pull a drowning man from the water. The most extraordinary possibilities have to be allowed for. Even if tomorrow I were to ask the director himself to act as my second, he too would have to agree merely out of a sense of chivalry, and he would keep it a secret! Anton Antonych . . ."

The fact of the matter was that at that very moment I was more clearly and vividly aware than anyone else on earth of the disgusting absurdity of my intentions and the whole opposite side of the coin, but . . .

"Hurry up, driver, hurry, you rascal, hurry up!"

"Hey, sir!" that son of the earth replied.

A sudden chill came over me.

"Wouldn't it be better . . . wouldn't it be better . . . to go straight home right now? Oh, my God! Why, why did I invite myself to that dinner yesterday? But no, it's impossible. And my pacing for three hours from the table to the stove? No, they, and no one else will have to pay me back for that pacing! They must wipe out that disgrace!"

"Hurry up!"

"What if they turn me over to the police? They wouldn't dare! They'd be afraid of a scandal. And what if Zverkov refuses the duel out of contempt? That's even likely; but I'll show them. . . . I'll rush to the posting station when he's supposed to leave tomorrow; I'll grab hold of his leg, tear off his overcoat just as he's about to climb into the carriage. I'll fasten my teeth on his arm and bite him. 'Look, everyone, see what a desperate man can be driven to!' Let him hit me on the head while others hit me from behind. I'll shout to the whole crowd, 'Behold, here's a young puppy who's going off to charm Circassian maidens with my spit on his face!' "

"Naturally, it'll all be over after that. The department will banish me from the face of the earth. They'll arrest me, try me, drive me out of the service, send me to prison; ship me off to Siberia for resettlement. Never mind! Fifteen years later when they let me out of jail, a beggar in rags, I'll drag myself off to see him. I'll find him in some provincial town. He'll be married and happy. He'll have a grown daughter. . . . I'll say, 'Look, you monster, look at my sunken cheeks and my rags. I've lost everything—career, happiness, art, science, a *beloved woman*—all because of you. Here are the pistols. I came here to load my pistol, and . . . and I forgive you.' Then I'll fire into the air, and he'll never hear another word from me again. . . ."

I was actually about to cry, even though I knew for a fact at that very moment that all this was straight out of Silvio and Lermontov's *Masquerade*.[1] Suddenly I felt terribly ashamed, so ashamed that I stopped the horse, climbed out of the sledge, and stood there amidst the snow in the middle of the street. The driver looked at me in amazement and sighed.

What was I to do? I couldn't go there—that was absurd; and I couldn't

---

1. A drama by Mikhail Lermontov (1835) about romantic conventions of love and honor. Silvio is the protagonist of Alexander Pushkin's short story *The Shot* (1830), about a man dedicated to revenge. Both works conclude with bizarre twists.

drop the whole thing, because then it would seem like . . . Oh, Lord! How could I drop it? After such insults!

"No!" I cried, throwing myself back into the sledge. "It's predestined; it's fate! Drive on, hurry up, *to that place!*"

In my impatience, I struck the driver on the neck with my fist.

"What's the matter with you? Why are you hitting me?" cried the poor little peasant, whipping his nag so that she began to kick up her hind legs.

Wet snow was falling in big flakes; I unbuttoned my coat, not caring about the snow. I forgot about everything else because now, having finally resolved on the slap, *I felt with horror that it was imminent* and that *nothing on earth could possibly stop it.* Lonely street lamps shone gloomily in the snowy mist like torches at a funeral. Snow got in under my overcoat, my jacket, and my necktie, and melted there. I didn't button up; after all, everything was lost, anyway. At last we arrived. I jumped out, almost beside myself, ran up the stairs, and began to pound at the door with my hands and feet. My legs, especially my knees, felt terribly weak. The door opened rather quickly; it was as if they knew I was coming. (In fact, Simonov had warned them that there might be someone else, since at this place one had to give notice and in general take precautions. It was one of those "fashionable shops" of the period that have now been eliminated by the police. During the day it really was a shop; but in the evening men with recommendations were able to visit as guests.) I walked rapidly through the darkened shop into a familiar drawing-room where there was only one small lit candle, and I stopped in dismay: there was no one there.

"Where are they?" I asked.

Naturally, by now they'd all dispersed. . . .

Before me stood a person with a stupid smile, the madam herself, who knew me slightly. In a moment a door opened, and another person came in.

Without paying much attention to anything, I walked around the room, and, apparently, was talking to myself. It was as if I'd been delivered from death, and I felt it joyously in my whole being. I'd have given him the slap, certainly, I'd certainly have given him the slap. But now they weren't here and . . . everything had vanished, everything had changed! . . . I looked around. I still couldn't take it all in. I glanced up mechanically at the girl who'd come in: before me there flashed a fresh, young, slightly pale face with straight dark brows and a serious, seemingly astonished look. I liked that immediately; I would have hated her if she'd been smiling. I began to look at her more carefully, as though with some effort: I'd still not managed to collect my thoughts. There was something simple and kind in her face, but somehow it was strangely serious. I was sure that she was at a disadvantage as a result, and that none of those fools had even noticed her. She couldn't be called a beauty, however, even though she was tall, strong, and well built. She was dressed very simply. Something despicable took hold of me; I went up to her. . . .

I happened to glance into a mirror. My overwrought face appeared extremely repulsive: it was pale, spiteful and mean; and my hair was dishevelled. "It doesn't matter. I'm glad," I thought. "In fact, I'm even delighted that I'll seem so repulsive to her; that pleases me. . . ."

VI

Somewhere behind a partition a clock was wheezing as if under some strong pressure, as though someone were strangling it. After this unnaturally prolonged wheezing there followed a thin, nasty, somehow unexpectedly hurried chime, as if someone had suddenly leapt forward. It struck two. I recovered, although I really hadn't been asleep, only lying there half-conscious.

It was almost totally dark in the narrow, cramped, low-ceilinged room, which was crammed with an enormous wardrobe and cluttered with cartons, rags, and all sorts of old clothes. The candle burning on the table at one end of the room flickered faintly from time to time, and almost went out completely. In a few moments total darkness would set in.

It didn't take long for me to come to my senses; all at once, without any effort, everything returned to me, as though it had been lying in ambush ready to pounce on me again. Even in my unconscious state some point had constantly remained in my memory, never to be forgotten, around which my sleepy visions had gloomily revolved. But it was a strange thing: everything that had happened to me that day now seemed, upon awakening, to have occurred in the distant past, as if I'd long since left it all behind.

My mind was in a daze. It was as though something were hanging over me, provoking, agitating, and disturbing me. Misery and bile were welling inside me, seeking an outlet. Suddenly I noticed beside me two wide-open eyes, examining me curiously and persistently. The gaze was coldly detached, sullen, as if belonging to a total stranger. I found it oppressive.

A dismal thought was conceived in my brain and spread throughout my whole body like a nasty sensation, such as one feels upon entering a damp, mouldy underground cellar. It was somehow unnatural that only now these two eyes had decided to examine me. I also recalled that during the course of the last two hours I hadn't said one word to this creature, and that I had considered it quite unnecessary; that had even given me pleasure for some reason. Now I'd suddenly realized starkly how absurd, how revolting as a spider, was the idea of debauchery, which, without love, crudely and shamelessly begins precisely at the point where genuine love is consummated. We looked at each other in this way for some time, but she didn't lower her gaze before mine, nor did she alter her stare, so that finally, for some reason, I felt very uneasy.

"What's your name?" I asked abruptly, to put an end to it quickly.

"Liza," she replied, almost in a whisper, but somehow in a very unfriendly way; and she turned her eyes away.

I remained silent.

"The weather today . . . snow . . . foul!" I observed, almost to myself, drearily placing one arm behind my head and staring at the ceiling.

She didn't answer. The whole thing was obscene.

"Are you from around here?" I asked her a moment later, almost angrily, turning my head slightly toward her.

"No."

"Where are you from?"

"Riga," she answered unwillingly.

"German?"

"No, Russian."

"Have you been here long?"

"Where?"

"In this house."

"Two weeks." She spoke more and more curtly. The candle had gone out completely; I could no longer see her face.

"Are your mother and father still living?"

"Yes . . . no . . . they are."

"Where are they?"

"There . . . in Riga."

"Who are they?"

"Just . . ."

"Just what? What do they do?"

"Tradespeople."

"Have you always lived with them?"

"Yes."

"How old are you?"

"Twenty."

"Why did you leave them?"

"Just because . . . "

That "just because" meant: leave me alone, it makes me sick. We fell silent.

Only God knows why, but I didn't leave. I too started to feel sick and more depressed. Images of the previous day began to come to mind all on their own, without my willing it, in a disordered way. I suddenly recalled a scene that I'd witnessed on the street that morning as I was anxiously hurrying to work. "Today some people were carrying a coffin and nearly dropped it," I suddenly said aloud, having no desire whatever to begin a conversation, but just so, almost accidentally.

"A coffin?"

"Yes, in the Haymarket; they were carrying it up from an underground cellar."

"From a cellar?"

"Not a cellar, but from a basement . . . well, you know . . . from down-stairs . . . from a house of ill repute . . . There was such filth all around. . . . Eggshells, garbage . . . it smelled foul . . . it was disgusting."

Silence.

"A nasty day to be buried!" I began again to break the silence.

"Why nasty?"

"Snow, slush . . ." (I yawned.)

"It doesn't matter," she said suddenly after a brief silence.

"No, it's foul. . . ." (I yawned again.) "The grave diggers must have been cursing because they were getting wet out there in the snow. And there must have been water in the grave."

"Why water in the grave?" she asked with some curiosity, but she spoke even more rudely and curtly than before. Something suddenly began to goad me on.

"Naturally, water on the bottom, six inches or so. You can't ever dig a dry grave at Volkovo cemetery."

"Why not?"

"What do you mean, why not? The place is waterlogged. It's all swamp. So they bury them right in the water. I've seen it myself . . . many times. . . ."

(I'd never seen it, and I'd never been to Volkovo cemetery, but I'd heard about it from other people.)

"Doesn't it matter to you if you die?"

"Why should I die?" she replied, as though defending herself.

"Well, someday you'll die; you'll die just like that woman did this morning. She was a . . . she was also a young girl . . . she died of consumption."

"The wench should have died in the hospital. . . ." (She knows all about it, I thought, and she even said "wench" instead of "girl.")

"She owed money to her madam," I retorted, more and more goaded on by the argument. "She worked right up to the end, even though she had consumption. The cabbies standing around were chatting with the soldiers, telling them all about it. Her former acquaintances, most likely. They were all laughing. They were planning to drink to her memory at the tavern." (I invented a great deal of this.)

Silence, deep silence. She didn't even stir.

"Do you think it would be better to die in a hospital?"

"Isn't it just the same? . . . Besides, why should I die?" she added irritably.

"If not now, then later?"

"Well, then later . . ."

"That's what you think! Now you're young and pretty and fresh—that's your value. But after a year of this life, you won't be like that any more; you'll fade."

"In a year?"

"In any case, after a year your price will be lower," I continued, gloating. "You'll move out of here into a worse place, into some other house. And a year later, into a third, each worse and worse, and seven years from now you'll end up in a cellar on the Haymarket. Even that won't be so bad. The real trouble will come when you get some disease, let's say a weakness in the chest . . . or you catch cold or something. In this kind of life it's no laughing matter to get sick. It takes hold of you and may never let go. And so, you die."

"Well, then, I'll die," she answered now quite angrily and stirred quickly.

"That'll be a pity."

"For what?"

"A pity to lose a life."

Silence.

"Did you have a sweetheart? Huh?"

"What's it to you?"

"Oh, I'm not interrogating you. What do I care? Why are you angry? Of course, you may have had your own troubles. What's it to me? Just the same, I'm sorry."

"For whom?"

"I'm sorry for you."

"No need . . . ," she whispered barely audibly and stirred once again.

That provoked me at once. What! I was being so gentle with her, while she . . .

"Well, and what do you think? Are you on the right path then?"

"I don't think anything."

"That's just the trouble—you don't think. Wake up, while there's still time. And there is time. You're still young and pretty; you could fall in love, get married, be happy.[2] . . ."

"Not all married women are happy," she snapped in her former, rude manner.

"Not all, of course, but it's still better than this. A lot better. You can even live without happiness as long as there's love. Even in sorrow life can be good; it's good to be alive, no matter how you live. But what's there besides . . . stench? Phew!"

I turned away in disgust; I was no longer coldly philosophizing. I began to feel what I was saying and grew excited. I'd been longing to expound these cherished *little ideas* that I'd been nurturing in my corner. Something had suddenly caught fire in me, some kind of goal had "manifested itself" before me.

"Pay no attention to the fact that I'm here. I'm no model for you. I may be even worse than you are. Moreover, I was drunk when I came here." I hastened nonetheless to justify myself. "Besides, a man is no example to a woman. It's a different thing altogether; even though I degrade and defile myself, I'm still no one's slave; if I want to leave, I just get up and go. I shake it all off and I'm a different man. But you must realize right from the start that you're a slave. Yes, a slave! You give away everything, all your freedom. Later, if you want to break this chain, you won't be able to; it'll bind you ever more tightly. That's the kind of evil chain it is. I know. I won't say anything else; you might not even understand me. But tell me this, aren't you already in debt to your madam? There, you see!" I added, even though she hadn't answered, but had merely remained silent; but she was listening with all her might. "There's your chain! You'll never buy yourself out. That's the way it's done. It's just like selling your soul to the devil. . . .

"And besides . . . I may be just as unfortunate, how do you know, and I may be wallowing in mud on purpose, also out of misery. After all, people drink out of misery. Well, I came here out of misery. Now, tell me, what's so good about this place? Here you and I were . . . intimate . . . just a little while ago, and all that time we didn't say one word to each other; afterward you began to examine me like a wild creature, and I did the same. Is that the way people love? Is that how one person is supposed to encounter another? It's a disgrace, that's what it is!"

"Yes!" she agreed with me sharply and hastily. The haste of her answer surprised even me. It meant that perhaps the very same idea was flitting through her head while she'd been examining me earlier. It meant that

---

2. A popular theme treated by Gogol, Chernyshevsky, and Nekrasov, among others. Typically, an innocent and idealistic young man attempts to rehabilitate a prostitute or "fallen woman."

she too was capable of some thought. . . . "Devil take it; this is odd, this *kinship*," I thought, almost rubbing my hands together. "Surely I can handle such a young soul."

It was the sport that attracted me most of all.

She turned her face closer to mine, and in the darkness it seemed that she propped her head up on her arm. Perhaps she was examining me. I felt sorry that I couldn't see her eyes. I heard her breathing deeply.

"Why did you come here?" I began with some authority.

"Just so . . ."

"But think how nice it would be living in your father's house! There you'd be warm and free; you'd have a nest of your own."

"And what if it's worse than that?"

"I must establish the right tone," flashed through my mind. "I won't get far with sentimentality."

However, that merely flashed through my mind. I swear that she really did interest me. Besides, I was somewhat exhausted and provoked. After all, artifice goes along so easily with feeling.

"Who can say?" I hastened to reply. "All sorts of things can happen. Why, I was sure that someone had wronged you and was more to blame than you are. After all, I know nothing of your life story, but a girl like you doesn't wind up in this sort of place on her own accord. . . ."

"What kind of a girl am I?" she whispered hardly audibly; but I heard it.

"What the hell! Now I'm flattering her. That's disgusting! But, perhaps it's a good thing. . . ." She remained silent.

"You see, Liza, I'll tell you about myself. If I'd had a family when I was growing up, I wouldn't be the person I am now. I think about this often. After all, no matter how bad it is in your own family—it's still your own father and mother, and not enemies or strangers. Even if they show you their love only once a year, you still know that you're at home. I grew up without a family; that must be why I turned out the way I did—so unfeeling."

I waited again.

"She might not understand," I thought. "Besides, it's absurd—all this moralizing."

"If I were a father and had a daughter, I think that I'd have loved her more than my sons, really," I began indirectly, talking about something else in order to distract her. I confess that I was blushing.

"Why's that?"

Ah, so she's listening!

"Just because. I don't know why, Liza. You see, I knew a father who was a stern, strict man, but he would kneel before his daughter and kiss her hands and feet; he couldn't get enough of her, really. She'd go dancing at a party, and he'd stand in one spot for five hours, never taking his eyes off her. He was crazy about her; I can understand that. At night she'd be tired and fall asleep, but he'd wake up, go in to kiss her, and make the sign of the cross over her while she slept. He used to wear a dirty old jacket and was stingy with everyone else, but would spend his last kopeck on her, buying her expensive presents; it afforded him great joy if she liked his presents. A father always loves his daughters more than their mother does. Some girls have a very nice time living at home. I think that I wouldn't even have let my daughter get married."

"Why not?" she asked with a barely perceptible smile.

"I'd be jealous, so help me God. Why, how could she kiss someone else? How could she love a stranger more than her own father? It's even painful to think about it. Of course, it's all nonsense; naturally, everyone finally comes to his senses. But I think that before I'd let her marry, I'd have tortured myself with worry. I'd have found fault with all her suitors. Nevertheless, I'd have ended up by allowing her to marry whomever she loved. After all, the one she loves always seems the worst of all to the father. That's how it is. That causes a lot of trouble in many families."

"Some are glad to sell their daughters, rather than let them marry honorably," she said suddenly.

Aha, so that's it!

"That happens, Liza, in those wretched families where there's neither God nor love," I retorted heatedly. "And where there's no love, there's also no good sense. There are such families, it's true, but I'm not talking about them. Obviously, from the way you talk, you didn't see much kindness in your own family. You must be very unfortunate. Hmm . . . But all this results primarily from poverty."

"And is it any better among the gentry? Honest folk live decently even in poverty."

"Hmmm . . . Yes. Perhaps. There's something else, Liza. Man only likes to count his troubles; he doesn't calculate his happiness. If he figured as he should, he'd see that everyone gets his share. So, let's say that all goes well in a particular family; it enjoys God's blessing, the husband turns out to be a good man, he loves you, cherishes you, and never leaves you. Life is good in that family. Sometimes, even though there's a measure of sorrow, life's still good. Where isn't there sorrow? If you choose to get married, *you'll find out for yourself*. Consider even the first years of a marriage to the one you love: what happiness, what pure bliss there can be sometimes! Almost without exception. At first even quarrels with your husband turn out well. For some women, the more they love their husbands, the more they pick fights with them. It's true; I once knew a woman like that. 'That's how it is,' she'd say. 'I love you very much and I'm tormenting you out of love, so that you'll feel it.' Did you know that one can torment a person intentionally out of love? It's mostly women who do that. Then she thinks to herself, 'I'll love him so much afterward, I'll be so affectionate, it's no sin to torment him a little now.' At home everyone would rejoice over you, and it would be so pleasant, cheerful, serene, and honorable. . . . Some other women are very jealous. If her husband goes away, I knew one like that, she can't stand it; she jumps up at night and goes off on the sly to see. Is he there? Is he in that house? Is he with that one? Now that's bad. Even she herself knows that it's bad; her heart sinks and she suffers because she really loves him. It's all out of love. And how nice it is to make up after a quarrel, to admit one's guilt or forgive him! How nice it is for both of them, how good they both feel at once, just as if they'd met again, married again, and begun their love all over again. No one, no one at all has to know what goes on between a husband and wife, if they love each other. However their quarrel ends, they should never call in either one of their mothers to act as judge or to hear complaints about the other one. They must act as their own judges. Love is God's mystery and should be hidden from other people's eyes, no matter what happens. This makes it holier, much better. They respect each other more, and a great deal is based on this respect. And, if there's been love, if they got married out of love, why should love disappear? Can't it be sustained? It rarely happens that it can't be sustained. If the husband turns out to be a kind and honest man, how can the love disappear? The first phase of married love will pass, that's true, but it's followed by an even better kind of love. Souls are joined together and all their concerns are managed in common; there'll be no secrets from one another. When children arrive, each and every stage, even a very difficult one, will seem happy, as long as there's both love and courage. Even work is cheerful; even when you deny yourself bread for your children's sake, you're still happy. After all, they'll love you for it afterward; you're really saving for your own future. Your children will grow up, and you'll feel that you're a model for them, a support. Even after you die, they'll carry your thoughts and feelings all during their life. They'll take on your image and likeness, since they received it from you. Consequently, it's a great obligation. How can a mother and father keep from growing closer? They say it's difficult to raise children. Who says that? It's heavenly joy! Do you love little children, Liza? I love them dearly. You know—a rosy little boy, suckling at your breast; what husband's heart could turn against his wife seeing her sitting there holding his child? The chubby, rosy little baby sprawls and snuggles; his little hands and feet are plump; his little nails are clean and tiny, so tiny it's even funny to see them; his little eyes look as if he already understood everything. As he suckles, he tugs at your breast playfully with his little hand. When the father approaches, the child lets go of the breast, bends way back, looks at his father, and laughs—as if God only knows how funny it is—and then takes to suckling again. Afterward, when he starts cutting teeth, he'll sometimes bite his mother's breast; looking at her sideways his little eyes seem to say, 'See, I bit you!' Isn't this pure bliss—the three of them, husband, wife, and child, all together? You can forgive a great deal for such moments. No, Liza, I think you must first learn how to live by yourself, and only afterward blame others."

"It's by means of images," I thought to myself, "just such images that I can get to you," although I was speaking with considerable feeling, I swear it; and all at once I blushed. "And what if she suddenly bursts out laughing—where will I hide then?" That thought drove me into a rage. By the end of my speech I'd really become excited, and now my pride was suffering somehow. The silence lasted for a while. I even considered shaking her.

"Somehow you . . ." she began suddenly and then stopped.

But I understood everything already: something was trembling in her voice now, not shrill, rude or unyielding as before, but something soft and timid, so timid that I suddenly was rather ashamed to watch her and felt guilty.

"What?" I asked with tender curiosity.

"Well, you . . ."

"What?"

"You somehow . . . it sounds just like a book," she said, and once again something which was noticeably sarcastic was suddenly heard in her voice.

Her remark wounded me dreadfully. That's not what I'd expected.

Yet, I didn't understand that she was intentionally disguising her feelings with sarcasm; that was usually the last resort of people who are timid and chaste of heart, whose souls have been coarsely and impudently invaded; and who, until the last moment, refuse to yield out of pride and are afraid to express their own feelings to you. I should've guessed it from the timidity with which on several occasions she tried to be sarcastic, until she finally managed to express it. But I hadn't guessed, and a malicious impulse took hold of me.

"Just you wait," I thought.

VII

"That's enough, Liza. What do books have to do with it, when this disgusts me as an outsider? And not only as an outsider. All this has awakened in my heart . . . Can it be, can it really be that you don't find it repulsive here? No, clearly habit means a great deal. The devil only knows what habit can do to a person. But do you seriously think that you'll never grow old, that you'll always be pretty, and that they'll keep you on here forever and ever? I'm not even talking about the filth. . . . Besides, I want to say this about your present life: even though you're still young, good-looking, nice, with soul and feelings, do you know, that when I came to a little while ago, I was immediately disgusted to be here with you! Why, a man has to be drunk to wind up here. But if you were in a different place, living as nice people do, I might not only chase after you, I might actually fall in love with you. I'd rejoice at a look from you, let alone a word; I'd wait for you at the gate and kneel down before you; I'd think of you as my betrothed and even consider that an honor. I wouldn't dare have any impure thoughts about you. But here, I know that I need only whistle, and you, whether you want to or not, will come to me, and that I don't have to do your bidding, whereas you have to do mine. The lowliest peasant may hire himself out as a laborer, but he doesn't make a complete slave of himself; he knows that it's only for a limited term. But what's your term? Just think about it. What are you giving up here? What are you enslaving? Why, you're enslaving your soul, something you don't really own, together with your body! You're giving away your love to be defiled by any drunkard! Love! After all, that's all there is! It's a precious jewel, a maiden's treasure, that's what it is! Why, to earn that love a man might be ready to offer up his own soul, to face death. But what's your love worth now? You've been bought, all of you; and why should anyone strive for your love, when you offer everything even without it? Why, there's no greater insult for a girl, don't you understand? Now, I've heard that they console you foolish girls, they allow you to see your own lovers here. But that's merely child's play, deception, making fun of you, while you believe it.

And do you really think he loves you, that lover of yours? I don't believe it. How can he, if he knows that you can be called away from him at any moment? He'd have to be depraved after all that. Does he possess even one drop of respect for you? What do you have in common with him? He's laughing at you and stealing from you at the same time—so much for his love. It's not too bad, as long as he doesn't beat you. But perhaps he does. Go on, ask him, if you have such a lover, whether he'll ever marry you. Why, he'll burst out laughing right in your face, if he doesn't spit at you or smack you. He himself may be worth no more than a few lousy kopecks. And for what, do you think, did you ruin your whole life here? For the coffee they give you to drink, or for the plentiful supply of food? Why do you think they feed you so well? Another girl, an honest one, would choke on every bite, because she'd know why she was being fed so well. You're in debt here, you'll be in debt, and will remain so until the end, until such time comes as the customers begin to spurn you. And that time will come very soon; don't count on your youth. Why, here youth flies by like a stagecoach. They'll kick you out. And they'll not merely kick you out, but for a long time before that they'll pester you, reproach you, and abuse you—as if you hadn't ruined your health for the madam, hadn't given up your youth and your soul for her in vain, but rather, as if you'd ruined her, ravaged her, and robbed her. And don't expect any support. Your friends will also attack you to curry her favor, because they're all in bondage here and have long since lost both conscience and pity. They've become despicable, and there's nothing on earth more despicable, more repulsive, or more insulting than their abuse. You'll lose everything here, everything, without exception—your health, youth, beauty, and hope— and at the age of twenty-two you'll look as if you were thirty-five, and even that won't be too awful if you're not ill. Thank God for that. Why, you probably think that you're not even working, that it's all play! But there's no harder work or more onerous task than this one in the whole world and there never has been. I'd think that one's heart alone would be worn out by crying. Yet you dare not utter one word, not one syllable; when they drive you out, you leave as if you were the guilty one. You'll move to another place, then to a third, then somewhere else, and finally you'll wind up in the Haymarket. And there they'll start beating you for no good reason at all; it's a local custom; the clients there don't know how to be nice without beating you. You don't think it's so disgusting there? Maybe you should go and have a look sometime, and see it with your own eyes. Once, at New Year's, I saw a woman in a doorway. Her own kind had pushed her outside as a joke, to freeze her for a little while because she was wailing too much; they shut the door behind her. At nine o'clock in the morning she was already dead drunk, dishevelled, half-naked, and all beaten up. Her face was powdered, but her eyes were bruised; blood was streaming from her nose and mouth; a certain cabby had just fixed her up. She was sitting on a stone step, holding a piece of salted fish in her hand; she was howling, wailing something about her 'fate,' and slapping the fish against the stone step. Cabbies and drunken soldiers had gathered around the steps and were taunting her. Don't you think you'll wind up the same way? I wouldn't want to believe it myself, but how do you know, perhaps eight or ten years ago this same girl, the one with the salted fish, arrived here from somewhere or other, all fresh like a little cherub, innocent, and pure; she knew no evil and blushed at every word. Perhaps she was just like you—proud, easily offended, unlike all the rest; she looked like a queen and knew that total happiness awaited the man who would love her and whom she would also love. Do you see how it all ended? What if at the very moment she was slapping the fish against that filthy step, dead drunk and dishevelled, what if, even at that very moment she'd recalled her earlier, chaste years in her father's house when she was still going to school, and when her neighbor's son used to wait for her along the path and assure her that he'd love her all his life and devote himself entirely to her, and when they vowed to love one another forever and get married as soon as they grew up! No, Liza, you'd be lucky, very lucky, if you died quickly from consumption somewhere in a corner, in a cellar, like that other girl. In a hospital, you say? All right—they'll take you off, but what if the madam still requires your services? Consumption is quite a disease—it's not like dying from a fever. A person continues to hope right up until the last minute and declares that he's in good health. He consoles himself. Now that's useful for your madam. Don't worry, that's the way it is. You've sold your soul; besides, you owe her money—that means you don't dare say a thing. And while you're dying, they'll all abandon you, turn away from you—because there's nothing left to get from you. They'll even reproach you for taking up space for no good reason and for taking so long to die. You won't even be able to ask for something to drink, without their hurling abuse at you: 'When will you croak, you old bitch? You keep on moaning and don't let us get any sleep—and you drive our customers away.' That's for sure; I've overheard such words myself. And as you're breathing your last, they'll shove you into the filthiest corner of the cellar—into darkness and dampness; lying there alone, what will you think about then? After you die, some stranger will lay you out hurriedly, grumbling all the while, impatiently—no one will bless you, no one will sigh over you; they'll merely want to get rid of you as quickly as possible. They'll buy you a wooden trough and carry you out as they did that poor woman I saw today; then they'll go off to a tavern and drink to your memory. There'll be slush, filth, and wet snow in your grave—why bother for the likes of you? 'Let her down, Vanyukha; after all, it's her fate to go down with her legs up, that's the sort of girl she was. Pull up on that rope, you rascal!' 'It's okay like that.' 'How's it okay? See, it's lying on its side. Was she a human being or not? Oh, never mind, cover it up.' They won't want to spend much time arguing over you. They'll cover your coffin quickly with wet, blue clay and then go off to the tavern. . . . That'll be the end of your memory on earth; for other women, children will visit their graves, fathers, husbands—but for you—no tears, no sighs; no remembrances. No one, absolutely no one in the whole world, will ever come to visit you; your name will disappear from the face of the earth, just as if you'd never been born and had never existed. Mud and filth, no matter how you pound on the lid of your coffin at night when other corpses arise: 'Let me out, kind people, let me live on earth for a little while! I lived, but I didn't really see life; my life went down the drain; they drank it away in a tavern at the Haymarket; let me out, kind people, let me live in the world once again!' "

I was so carried away by my own pathos that I began to feel a lump forming in my throat, and . . . I suddenly stopped, rose up in fright, and, leaning over apprehensively, I began to listen carefully as my own heart pounded. There was cause for dismay.

For a while I felt that I'd turned her soul inside out and had broken her heart; the more I became convinced of this, the more I strived to reach my goal as quickly and forcefully as possible. It was the sport, the sport that attracted me; but it wasn't only the sport. . . .

I knew that I was speaking clumsily, artificially, even bookishly; in short, I didn't know how to speak except "like a book." But that didn't bother me, for I knew, I had a premonition, that I would be understood and that this bookishness itself might even help things along. But now, having achieved this effect, I suddenly lost all my nerve. No, never, never before had I witnessed such despair! She was lying there, her face pressed deep into a pillow she was clutching with her hands. Her heart was bursting. Her young body was shuddering as if she were having convulsions. Suppressed sobs shook her breast, tore her apart, and suddenly burst forth in cries and moans. Then she pressed her face even deeper into the pillow: she didn't want anyone, not one living soul, to hear her anguish and her tears. She bit the pillow; she bit her hand until it bled (I noticed that afterward); or else, thrusting her fingers into her dishevelled hair, she became rigid with the strain, holding her breath and clenching her teeth. I was about to say something, to ask her to calm down; but I felt that I didn't dare. Suddenly, all in a kind of chill, almost in a panic, I groped hurriedly to get out of there as quickly as possible. It was dark: no matter how I tried, I couldn't end it quickly. Suddenly I felt a box of matches and a candlestick with a whole unused candle. As soon as the room was lit up, Liza started suddenly, sat up, and looked at me almost senselessly, with a distorted face and a half-crazy smile. I sat down next to her and took her hands; she came to and threw herself at me, wanting to embrace me, yet not daring to. Then she quietly lowered her head before me.

"Liza, my friend, I shouldn't have . . . you must forgive me," I began, but she squeezed my hands so tightly in her fingers that I realized I was saying the wrong thing and stopped.

"Here's my address, Liza. Come to see me."

"I will," she whispered resolutely, still not lifting her head.

"I'm going now, good-bye . . . until we meet again."

I stood up; she did, too, and suddenly blushed all over, shuddered, seized a shawl lying on a chair, threw it over her shoulders, and wrapped herself up to her chin. After doing this, she smiled again somewhat painfully, blushed, and looked at me strangely. I felt awful. I hastened to leave, to get away.

"Wait," she said suddenly as we were standing in the hallway near the door, and she stopped me by putting her hand on my overcoat. She quickly put the candle down and ran off; obviously she'd remembered something or wanted to show me something. As she left she was blushing all over, her eyes were gleaming, and a smile had appeared on her lips—what on earth did it all mean? I waited against my own will; she returned a moment later with a glance that seemed to beg forgiveness for something. All in all it was no longer the same face or the same glance as before—sullen, distrustful, obstinate. Now her glance was imploring, soft, and, at the same time, trusting, affectionate, and timid. That's how children look at people whom they love very much, or when they're asking for something. Her eyes were light hazel, lovely, full of life, as capable of expressing love as brooding hatred.

Without any explanation, as if I were some kind of higher being who was supposed to know everything, she held a piece of paper out toward me. At that moment her whole face was shining with a most naive, almost childlike triumph. I unfolded the paper. It was a letter to her from some medical student containing a high-flown, flowery, but very respectful declaration of love. I don't remember the exact words now, but I can well recall the genuine emotion that can't be feigned shining through that high style. When I'd finished reading the letter, I met her ardent, curious, and childishly impatient gaze. She'd fixed her eyes on my face and was waiting eagerly to see what I'd say. In a few words, hurriedly, but with some joy and pride, she explained that she'd once been at a dance somewhere, in a private house, at the home of some "very, very good people, *family people*, where they *knew nothing*, nothing at all," because she'd arrived at this place only recently and was just . . . well, she hadn't quite decided whether she'd stay here and she'd certainly leave as soon as she'd paid off her debt. . . . Well, and this student was there; he danced with her all evening and talked to her. It turned out he was from Riga; he'd known her as a child, they'd played together, but that had been a long time ago; he was acquainted with her parents—but he knew nothing, absolutely nothing *about this place* and he didn't even suspect it! And so, the very next day, after the dance, (only some three days ago), he'd sent her this letter through the friend with whom she'd gone to the party . . . and . . . well, that's the whole story."

She lowered her sparkling eyes somewhat bashfully after she finished speaking.

The poor little thing, she'd saved this student's letter as a treasure and had run to fetch this one treasure of hers, not wanting me to leave without knowing that she too was the object of sincere, honest love, and that someone exists who had spoken to her respectfully. Probably that letter was fated to lie in her box without results. But that didn't matter; I'm sure that she'll guard it as a treasure her whole life, as her pride and vindication; and now, at a moment like this, she remembered it and brought it out to exult naively before me, to raise herself in my eyes, so that I could see it for myself and could also think well of her. I didn't say a thing; I shook her hand and left. I really wanted to get away. . . . I walked all the way home in spite of the fact that wet snow was still falling in large flakes. I was exhausted, oppressed, and perplexed. But the truth was already glimmering behind that perplexity. The ugly truth!

VIII

It was some time, however, before I agreed to acknowledge that truth. I awoke the next morning after a few hours of deep, leaden sleep. Instantly recalling the events of the previous day, even I was astonished at my *sentimentality* with Liza last night, at all of yesterday's "horror and pity." "Why, it's an attack of old woman's nervous hysteria, phew!" I decided. "And why on earth did I force my address on her? What if she comes? Then again, let her come, it doesn't make any difference. . . ." But *obviously* that was not the main, most important matter: I had to make haste and rescue at all costs my reputation in the eyes of Zverkov and Simonov. That was my main task. I even forgot all about Liza in the concerns of that morning.

First of all I had to repay last night's debt to Simonov immediately. I resolved on desperate means: I would borrow the sum of fifteen rubles from Anton Antonych. As luck would have it, he was in a splendid mood that morning and gave me the money at once, at my first request. I was so delighted that I signed a promissory note with a somewhat dashing air, and told him *casually* that on the previous evening "I'd been living it up with some friends at the Hôtel de Paris. We were holding a farewell dinner for a comrade, one might even say, a childhood friend, and, you know— he's a great carouser, very spoiled—well, naturally; he comes from a good family, has considerable wealth and a brilliant career; he's witty and charming, and has affairs with certain ladies, you understand. We drank up an extra 'half-dozen bottles' and . . ." There was nothing to it; I said all this very easily, casually, and complacently.

Upon arriving home I wrote to Simonov at once.

To this very day I recall with admiration the truly gentlemanly, good-natured, candid tone of my letter. Cleverly and nobly, and, above all, without unnecessary words, I blamed myself for everything. I justified myself, "if only I could be allowed to justify myself," by saying that, being so totally unaccustomed to wine, I'd gotten drunk with the first glass, which (supposedly) I'd consumed even before their arrival, as I waited for them in the Hôtel de Paris between the hours of five and six o'clock. In particular, I begged for Simonov's pardon; I asked him to convey my apology to all the others, especially to Zverkov, whom, "I recall, as if in a dream," it seems, I'd insulted. I added that I'd have called upon each of them, but was suffering from a bad headache, and, worst of all, I was ashamed. I was particularly satisfied by the "certain lightness," almost casualness (though, still very proper), unexpectedly reflected in my style; better than all possible arguments, it conveyed to them at once that I regarded "all of last night's unpleasantness" in a rather detached way, and that I was not at all, not in the least struck down on the spot as you, gentlemen, probably suspect. On the contrary, I regard this all serenely, as any self-respecting gentleman would. The true story, as they say, is no reproach to an honest young man.

"Why, there's even a hint of aristocratic playfulness in it," I thought admiringly as I reread my note. "And it's all because I'm such a cultured and educated man! Others in my place wouldn't know how to extricate themselves, but I've gotten out of it, and I'm having a good time once again, all because I'm an 'educated and cultured man of our time.' It may even be true that the whole thing occurred as a result of that wine yesterday. Hmmm ... well, no, it wasn't really the wine. And I didn't have anything to drink between five and six o'clock when I was waiting for them. I lied to Simonov; it was a bold-faced lie—yet I'm not ashamed of it even now. . . ."

But, to hell with it, anyway! The main thing is, I got out of it.

I put six rubles in the letter, sealed it up, and asked Apollon to take it to Simonov. When he heard that there was money in it, Apollon became more respectful and agreed to deliver it. Toward evening I went out for a stroll. My head was still aching and spinning from the events of the day before. But as evening approached and twilight deepened, my impressions changed and became more confused, as did my thoughts. Something hadn't yet died within me, deep within my heart and conscience; it didn't want to die, and it expressed itself as burning anguish. I jostled my way along the more populous, commercial streets, along Meshchanskaya, Sadovaya, near the Yusupov Garden. I particularly liked to stroll along these streets at twilight, just as they became most crowded with all sorts of pedestrians, merchants, and tradesmen, with faces preoccupied to the point of hostility, on their way home from a hard day's work. It was precisely the cheap bustle that I liked, the crass prosaic quality. But this time all that street bustle irritated me even more. I couldn't get a hold of myself or puzzle out what was wrong. Something was rising, rising up in my soul continually, painfully, and didn't want to settle down. I returned home completely distraught. It was just as if some crime were weighing on my soul.

I was constantly tormented by the thought that Liza might come to see me. It was strange, but from all of yesterday's recollections, the one of her tormented me most, somehow separately from all the others. I'd managed to forget the rest by evening, to shrug everything off, and I still remained completely satisfied with my letter to Simonov. But in regard to Liza, I was not at all satisfied. It was as though I were tormented by her alone. "What if she comes?" I thought continually. "Well, so what? It doesn't matter. Let her come. Hmm. The only unpleasant thing is that she'll see, for instance, how I live. Yesterday I appeared before her such a ... hero ... but now, hmm! Besides, it's revolting that I've sunk so low. The squalor of my apartment. And I dared go to dinner last night wearing such clothes! And that oilcloth sofa of mine with its stuffing hanging out! And my dressing gown that doesn't quite cover me! What rags! ... She'll see it all—and she'll see Apollon. That swine will surely insult her. He'll pick on her, just to be rude to me. Of course, I'll be frightened, as usual. I'll begin to fawn before her, wrap myself up in my dressing gown. I'll start to smile and tell lies. Ugh, the indecency! And that's not even the worst part! There's something even more important, nastier, meaner! Yes, meaner! Once again, I'll put on that dishonest, deceitful mask! . . ."

When I reached this thought, I simply flared up.

"Why deceitful? How deceitful? Yesterday I spoke sincerely. I recall that there was genuine feeling in me, too. I was trying no less than to arouse noble feelings in her . . . and if she wept, that's a good thing; it will have a beneficial effect. . . ."

But I still couldn't calm down.

All that evening, even after I returned home, even after nine o'clock, when by my calculations Liza could no longer have come, her image continued to haunt me, and, what's most important, she always appeared in one and the same form. Of all that had occurred yesterday, it was one moment in particular which stood out most vividly: that was when I lit up the room with a match and saw her pale, distorted face with its tormented gaze. What a pitiful, unnatural, distorted smile she'd had at that moment! But little did I know then that even fifteen years later I'd still picture Liza to myself with that same pitiful, distorted, and unnecessary smile which she'd had at that moment.

The next day I was once again prepared to dismiss all this business as nonsense, as the result of overstimulated nerves; but most of all, as exaggeration. I was well aware of this weakness of mine and sometimes was even afraid of it; "I exaggerate everything, that's my problem," I kept repeating to myself hour after hour. And yet, "yet, Liza may still come, all the same"; that was the refrain which concluded my reflections. I was so distressed that I sometimes became furious. "She'll come! She'll definitely come!" If not today, then tomorrow, she'll seek me out! That's just like the damned romanticism of all these *pure hearts*! Oh, the squalor, the stupidity, the narrowness of these 'filthy, sentimental souls!' How could all this be understood, how on earth could it not be understood?. . ." But at this point I would stop myself, even in the midst of great confusion.

"And how few, how very few words were needed," I thought in passing, "how little idyllic sentiment (what's more, the sentiment was artificial, bookish, composed) was necessary to turn a whole human soul according to my wishes at once. That's innocence for you! That's virgin soil!"

At times the thought occurred that I might go to her myself "to tell her everything," and to beg her not to come to me. But at this thought such venom arose in me that it seemed I'd have crushed that "damned" Liza if she'd suddenly turned up next to me. I'd have insulted her, spat at her, struck her, and chased her away!

One day passed, however, then a second, and a third; she still hadn't come, and I began to calm down. I felt particularly reassured and relaxed after nine o'clock in the evening, and even began to daydream sweetly at times. For instance, I'd save Liza, precisely because she'd come to me, and I'd talk to her. . . . I'd develop her mind, educate her. At last I'd notice that she loved me, loved me passionately. I'd pretend I didn't understand. (For that matter, I didn't know why I'd pretend; most likely just for the effect.) At last, all embarrassed, beautiful, trembling, and sobbing, she'd throw herself at my feet and declare that I was her saviour and she loved me more than anything in the world. I'd be surprised, but . . . "Liza," I'd say, "Do you really think that I haven't noticed your love? I've seen every-thing. I guessed, but dared not be first to make a claim on your heart because I had such influence over you, and because I was afraid you might deliberately force yourself to respond to my love out of gratitude, that you might forcibly evoke within yourself a feeling that didn't really exist. No, I didn't want that because it would be . . . despotism. . . . It would be indelicate (well, in short, here I launched on some European, George Sandian,[3] inexplicably lofty subtleties . . .). But now, now—you're mine, you're my creation, you're pure and lovely, you're my beautiful wife."

> And enter my house bold and free,
> To become its full mistress![4]

"Then we'd begin to live happily together, travel abroad, etc., etc." In short, it began to seem crude even to me, and I ended it all by sticking my tongue out at myself.

"Besides, they won't let her out of there, the 'bitch,' " I thought. "After all, it seems unlikely that they'd release them for strolls, especially in the evening (for some reason I was convinced that she had to report there every evening, precisely at seven o'clock). Moreover, she said that she'd yet to become completely enslaved there, and that she still had certain rights; that means, hmm. Devil take it, she'll come, she's bound to come!"

It was a good thing I was distracted at the time by Apollon's rudeness. He made me lose all patience. He was the bane of my existence, a punishment inflicted on me by Providence. We'd been squabbling constantly for several years now and I hated him. My God, how I hated him! I think that I never hated anyone in my whole life as much as I hated him, especially at those times. He was an elderly, dignified man who worked part-time as a tailor. But for some unknown reason he despised me, even beyond all measure, and looked down upon me intolerably. However, he looked down on everyone. You need only glance at that flaxen, slicked-down hair, at that single lock brushed over his forehead and greased with vegetable oil, at his strong mouth, always drawn up in the shape of the letter V,[5] and you felt that you were standing before a creature who never doubted himself. He was a pedant of the highest order, the greatest one I'd ever met on earth; in addition he possessed a sense of self-esteem appropriate perhaps only to Alexander the Great, King of Macedonia. He was in love with every one of his buttons, every one of his fingernails—absolutely in love, and he looked it! He treated me quite despotically, spoke to me exceedingly little, and, if he happened to look at me, cast a steady, majestically self-assured, and constantly mocking glance that sometimes infuriated me. He carried out his tasks as if he were doing me the greatest of favors. Moreover, he did almost nothing at all for me; nor did he assume that he was obliged to do anything. There could be no doubt that he considered me the greatest fool on earth, and, that if he "kept me on," it was only because he could receive his wages from me every month. He agreed to "do nothing" for seven rubles a month. I'll be forgiven many of my sins because of him. Sometimes my hatred reached such a point that his gait alone would throw me into convulsions. But the most repulsive thing about him was his lisping. His tongue was a bit larger than normal or something of the sort; as a result, he constantly lisped and hissed. Appar-

---

3. George Sand was the pseudonym of the French woman novelist Aurore Dudevant (1804–1876), famous also as a promoter of feminism.   4. The last lines of the poem by Nekrasov used as the epigraph of Part II of this story (see p. 1128).   5. The last letter of the old Russian alphabet, triangular in shape.

ently, he was terribly proud of it, imagining that it endowed him with enormous dignity. He spoke slowly, in measured tones, with his hands behind his back and his eyes fixed on the ground. It particularly infuriated me when he used to read the Psalter to himself behind his partition. I endured many battles on account of it. He was terribly fond of reading during the evening in a slow, even singsong voice, as if chanting over the dead. It's curious, but that's how he ended up: now he hires himself out to recite the Psalter over the dead; in addition, he exterminates rats and makes shoe polish. But at that time I couldn't get rid of him; it was as if he were chemically linked to my own existence. Besides, he'd never have agreed to leave for anything. It was impossible for me to live in a furnished room: my own apartment was my private residence, my shell, my case, where I hid from all humanity. Apollon, the devil only knows why, seemed to belong to this apartment, and for seven long years I couldn't get rid of him.

It was impossible, for example, to delay paying him his wages for even two or three days. He'd make such a fuss that I wouldn't know where to hide. But in those days I was so embittered by everyone that I decided, heaven knows why or for what reason, to *punish* Apollon by not paying him his wages for two whole weeks. I'd been planning to do this for some time now, about two years, simply in order to teach him that he had no right to put on such airs around me, and that if I chose to, I could always withhold his wages. I resolved to say nothing to him about it and even remain silent on purpose, to conquer his pride and force him to be the first one to mention it. Then I would pull all seven rubles out of a drawer and show him that I actually had the money and had intentionally set it aside, but that "I didn't want to, didn't want to, simply didn't want to pay him his wages, and that I didn't want to simply because *that's what I wanted*," because such was "my will as his master," because he was disrespectful and because he was rude. But, if he were to ask respectfully, then I might relent and pay him; if not, he might have to wait another two weeks, or three, or even a whole month. . . .

But, no matter how angry I was, he still won. I couldn't even hold out for four days. He began as he always did, because there had already been several such cases (and, let me add, I knew all this beforehand; I knew his vile tactics by heart), to wit: he would begin by fixing an extremely severe gaze on me. He would keep it up for several minutes in a row, especially when meeting me or accompanying me outside of the house. If, for example, I held out and pretended not to notice these stares, then he, maintaining his silence as before, would proceed to further tortures. Suddenly, for no reason at all, he'd enter my room quietly and slowly, while I was pacing or reading; he'd stop at the door, place one hand behind his back, thrust one foot forward, and fix his gaze on me, no longer merely severe, but now utterly contemptuous. If I were suddenly to ask him what he wanted, he wouldn't answer at all. He'd continue to stare at me reproachfully for several more seconds; then, compressing his lips in a particular way and assuming a very meaningful air, he'd turn slowly on the spot and slowly withdraw to his own room. Two hours later he'd emerge again and suddenly appear before me in the same way. It's happened sometimes that in my fury I hadn't even asked what he wanted, but simply raised my head sharply and imperiously, and begun to stare reproachfully back at him. We would stare at each other thus for some two minutes or more; at last he'd turn slowly and self-importantly, and withdraw for another few hours.

If all this failed to bring me back to my senses and I continued to rebel, he'd suddenly begin to sigh while staring at me. He'd sigh heavily and deeply, as if trying to measure with each sigh the depth of my moral decline. Naturally, it would end with his complete victory: I'd rage and shout, but I was always forced to do just as he wished on the main point of dispute.

This time his usual maneuvers of "severe stares" had scarcely begun when I lost my temper at once and lashed out at him in a rage. I was irritated enough even without that.

"Wait!" I shouted in a frenzy, as he was slowly and silently turning with one hand behind his back, about to withdraw to his own room. "Wait! Come back, come back, I tell you!" I must have bellowed so unnaturally that he turned around and even began to scrutinize me with a certain amazement. He continued, however, not to utter one word, and that was what infuriated me most of all.

"How dare you come in here without asking permission and stare at me? Answer me!"

But after regarding me serenely for half a minute, he started to turn around again.

"Wait!" I roared, rushing up to him. "Don't move! There! Now answer me: why do you come in here to stare?"

"If you've got any orders for me now, it's my job to do 'em," he replied after another pause, lisping softly and deliberately, raising his eyebrows, and calmly shifting his head from one side to the other—what's more, he did all this with horrifying composure.

"That's not it! That's not what I'm asking you about, you executioner!" I shouted, shaking with rage. "I'll tell you myself, you executioner, why you came in here. You know that I haven't paid you your wages, but you're so proud that you don't want to bow down and ask me for them. That's why you came in here to punish me and torment me with your stupid stares, and you don't even sus-s-pect, you torturer, how stupid it all is, how stupid, stupid, stupid, stupid!"

He would have turned around silently once again, but I grabbed hold of him.

"Listen," I shouted to him. "Here's the money, you see! Here it is! (I pulled it out of a drawer.) All seven rubles. But you won't get it, you won't until you come to me respectfully, with your head bowed, to ask my forgiveness. Do you hear?"

"That can't be!" he replied with some kind of unnatural self-confidence.

"It will be!" I shrieked. "I give you my word of honor, it will be!"

"I have nothing to ask your forgiveness for," he said as if he hadn't even noticed my shrieks, "because it was you who called me an 'executioner,' and I can always go lodge a complaint against you at the police station."

"Go! Lodge a complaint!" I roared. " Go at once, this minute, this very second! You're still an executioner! Executioner! Executioner!" But he only looked at me, then turned and, no longer heeding my shouts, calmly withdrew to his own room without looking back.

"If it hadn't been for Liza, none of this would have happened!" I thought to myself. Then, after waiting a minute, pompously and solemnly, but with my heart pounding heavily and forcefully, I went in to see him behind the screen.

"Apollon!" I said softly and deliberately, though gasping for breath, "go at once, without delay to fetch the police supervisor!"

He'd already seated himself at his table, put on his eyeglasses, and picked up something to sew. But, upon hearing my order, he suddenly snorted with laughter.

"At once! Go this very moment! Go, go, or you can't imagine what will happen to you!"

"You're really not in your right mind," he replied, not even lifting his head, lisping just as slowly, and continuing to thread his needle. "Who's ever heard of a man being sent to fetch a policeman against himself? And as for trying to frighten me, you're only wasting your time, because nothing will happen to me."

"Go," I screeched, seizing him by the shoulder. I felt that I might strike him at any moment.

I never even heard the door from the hallway suddenly open at that very moment, quietly and slowly, and that someone walked in, stopped, and began to examine us in bewilderment. I glanced up, almost died from shame, and ran back into my own room. There, clutching my hair with both hands, I leaned my head against the wall and froze in that position.

Two minutes later I heard Apollon's deliberate footsteps.

"There's *some woman* asking for you," he said, staring at me with particular severity; then he stood aside and let her in—it was Liza. He didn't want to leave, and he scrutinized us mockingly.

"Get out, get out!" I commanded him all flustered. At that moment my clock strained, wheezed, and struck seven.

IX

> And enter my house bold and free,
> To become its full mistress!
> From the same poem.[6]

I stood before her, crushed, humiliated, abominably ashamed; I think I was smiling as I tried with all my might to wrap myself up in my tattered, quilted dressing gown—exactly as I'd imagined this scene the other day during a fit of depression. Apollon, after standing over us for a few minutes, left, but that didn't make things any easier for me. Worst of all was that she suddenly became embarrassed too, more than I'd ever expected. At the sight of me, of course.

"Sit down," I said mechanically and moved a chair up to the table for her, while I sat on the sofa. She immediately and obediently sat down,

6. See n. 4, p. 1170.

staring at me wide-eyed, and, obviously, expecting something from me at once. This naive expectation infuriated me, but I restrained myself.

She should have tried not to notice anything, as if everything were just as it should be, but she . . . And I vaguely felt that she'd have to pay dearly *for everything*.

"You've found me in an awkward situation, Liza," I began, stammering and realizing that this was precisely the wrong way to begin.

"No, no, don't imagine anything!" I cried, seeing that she'd suddenly blushed. "I'm not ashamed of my poverty. . . . On the contrary, I regard it with pride. I'm poor, but noble. . . . One can be poor and noble," I muttered. "But . . . would you like some tea?"

"No . . . ," she started to say.

"Wait!"

I jumped up and ran to Apollon. I had to get away somehow.

"Apollon," I whispered in feverish haste, tossing down the seven rubles which had been in my fist the whole time, "here are your wages. There, you see, I've given them to you. But now you must rescue me: bring us some tea and a dozen rusks from the tavern at once. If you don't go, you'll make me a very miserable man. You have no idea who this woman is. . . . This means—everything! You may think she's . . . But you've no idea at all who this woman really is!"

Apollon, who'd already sat down to work and had put his glasses on again, at first glanced sideways in silence at the money without abandoning his needle; then, paying no attention to me and making no reply, he continued to fuss with the needle he was still trying to thread. I waited there for about three minutes standing before him with my arms folded *à la Napoleon*.[7] My temples were soaked in sweat. I was pale, I felt that myself. But, thank God, he must have taken pity just looking at me. After finishing with the thread, he stood up slowly from his place, slowly pushed back his chair, slowly took off his glasses, slowly counted the money and finally, after inquiring over his shoulder whether he should get a whole pot, slowly walked out of the room. As I was returning to Liza, it occurred to me: shouldn't I run away just as I was, in my shabby dressing gown, no matter where, and let come what may.

I sat down again. She looked at me uneasily. We sat in silence for several minutes.

"I'll kill him." I shouted suddenly, striking the table so hard with my fist that ink splashed out of the inkwell.

"Oh, what are you saying?" she exclaimed, startled.

"I'll kill him, I'll kill him!" I shrieked, striking the table in an absolute frenzy, but understanding full well at the same time how stupid it was to be in such a frenzy.

"You don't understand, Liza, what this executioner is doing to me. He's my executioner. . . . He's just gone out for some rusks; he . . ."

And suddenly I burst into tears. It was a nervous attack. I felt so ashamed amidst my sobs, but I couldn't help it. She got frightened.

"What's the matter? What's wrong with you?" she cried, fussing around me.

---

7. In the style of Napoleon.

"Water, give me some water, over there!" I muttered in a faint voice, realizing full well, however, that I could've done both without the water and without the faint voice. But I was *putting on an act*, as it's called, in order to maintain decorum, although my nervous attack was genuine.

She gave me some water while looking at me like a lost soul. At that very moment Apollon brought in the tea. It suddenly seemed that this ordinary and prosaic tea was horribly inappropriate and trivial after everything that had happened, and I blushed. Liza stared at Apollon with considerable alarm. He left without looking at us.

"Liza, do you despise me?" I asked, looking her straight in the eye, trembling with impatience to find out what she thought.

She was embarrassed and didn't know what to say.

"Have some tea," I said angrily. I was angry at myself, but she was the one who'd have to pay, naturally. A terrible anger against her suddenly welled up in my heart; I think I could've killed her. To take revenge I swore inwardly not to say one more word to her during the rest of her visit. "She's the cause of it all," I thought.

Our silence continued for about five minutes. The tea stood on the table; we didn't touch it. It reached the point of my not wanting to drink on purpose, to make it even more difficult for her; it would be awkward for her to begin alone. Several times she glanced at me in sad perplexity. I stubbornly remained silent. I was the main sufferer, of course, because I was fully aware of the despicable meanness of my own spiteful stupidity; yet, at the same time, I couldn't restrain myself.

"I want to . . . get away from . . . that place . . . once and for all," she began just to break the silence somehow; but, poor girl, that was just the thing she shouldn't have said at that moment, stupid enough as it was to such a person as me, stupid as I was. My own heart even ached with pity for her tactlessness and unnecessary straightforwardness. But something hideous immediately suppressed all my pity; it provoked me even further. Let the whole world go to hell. Another five minutes passed.

"Have I disturbed you?" she began timidly, barely audibly, and started to get up.

But as soon as I saw this first glimpse of injured dignity, I began to shake with rage and immediately exploded.

"Why did you come here? Tell me why, please," I began, gasping and neglecting the logical order of my words. I wanted to say it all at once, without pausing for breath; I didn't even worry about how to begin.

"Why did you come here? Answer me! Answer!" I cried, hardly aware of what I was saying. "I'll tell you, my dear woman, why you came here. You came here because I spoke some *words of pity* to you that time. Now you've softened, and want to hear more 'words of pity.' Well, you should know that I was laughing at you then. And I'm laughing at you now. Why are you trembling? Yes, I was laughing at you! I'd been insulted, just prior to that, at dinner, by those men who arrived just before me that evening. I came intending to thrash one of them, the officer; but I didn't succeed; I couldn't find him; I had to avenge my insult on someone, to get my own back; you turned up and I took my anger out at you, and I laughed at you. I'd been humiliated, and I wanted to humiliate someone else; I'd been treated like a rag, and I wanted to exert some power. . . . That's what it was; you thought that I'd come there on purpose to save you, right? Is that what you thought? Is that it?"

I knew that she might get confused and might not grasp all the details, but I also knew that she'd understand the essence of it very well. That's just what happened. She turned white as a sheet; she wanted to say something. Her lips were painfully twisted, but she collapsed onto a chair just as if she'd been struck down with an ax. Subsequently she listened to me with her mouth gaping, her eyes wide open, shaking with awful fear. It was the cynicism, the cynicism of my words that crushed her. . . .

"To save you!" I continued, jumping up from my chair and rushing up and down the room in front of her, "to save you from what? Why, I may be even worse than you are. When I recited that sermon to you, why didn't you throw it back in my face? You should have said to me, 'Why did you come here? To preach morality or what?' Power, it was the power I needed then, I craved the sport, I wanted to reduce you to tears, humiliation, hysteria—that's what I needed then! But I couldn't have endured it myself, because I'm such a wretch. I got scared. The devil only knows why I foolishly gave you my address. Afterward, even before I got home, I cursed you like nothing on earth on account of that address. I hated you already because I'd lied to you then, because it was all playing with words, dreaming in my own mind. But, do you know what I really want now? For you to get lost, that's what! I need some peace. Why, I'd sell the whole world for a kopeck if people would only stop bothering me. Should the world go to hell, or should I go without my tea? I say, let the world go to hell as long as I can always have my tea. Did you know that or not? And I know perfectly well that I'm a scoundrel, a bastard, an egotist, and a sluggard. I've been shaking from fear for the last three days wondering whether you'd ever come. Do you know what disturbed me most of all these last three days? The fact that I'd appeared to you then as such a hero, and that now you'd suddenly see me in this torn dressing gown, dilapidated and revolting. I said before that I wasn't ashamed of my poverty; well, you should know that I am ashamed, I'm ashamed of it more than anything, more afraid of it than anything, more than if I were a thief, because I'm so vain; it's as if the skin's been stripped away from my body so that even wafts of air cause pain. By now surely even you've guessed that I'll never forgive you for having come upon me in this dressing gown as I was attacking Apollon like a vicious dog. Your saviour, your former hero, behaving like a mangy, shaggy mongrel, attacking his own lackey, while that lackey stood there laughing at me! Nor will I ever forgive you for those tears which, like an embarrassed old woman, I couldn't hold back before you. And I'll never forgive *you* for all that I'm confessing now. Yes— you, you alone must pay for everything because you turned up like this, because I'm a scoundrel, because I'm the nastiest, most ridiculous, pettiest, stupidest, most envious worm of all those living on earth who're no better than me in any way, but who, the devil knows why, never get embarrassed, while all my life I have to endure insults from every louse—that's my fate. What do I care that you don't understand any of this? What do I care, what do I care about you and whether or not you perish there? Why, don't you realize how much I'll hate you now after having said all this with your being here listening to me? After all, a man can only talk like this once in his whole life, and then only in hysteria! . . . What more do you want? Why, after all this, are you still hanging around here tormenting me? Why don't you leave?"

But at this point a very strange thing suddenly occurred.

I'd become so accustomed to inventing and imagining everything according to books, and picturing everything on earth to myself just as I'd conceived of it in my dreams, that at first I couldn't even comprehend the meaning of this strange occurrence. But here's what happened: Liza, insulted and crushed by me, understood much more than I'd imagined. She understood out of all this what a woman always understands first of all, if she sincerely loves—namely, that I myself was unhappy.

The frightened and insulted expression on her face was replaced at first by grieved amazement. When I began to call myself a scoundrel and a bastard, and my tears had begun to flow (I'd pronounced this whole tirade in tears), her whole face was convulsed by a spasm. She wanted to get up and stop me; when I'd finished, she paid no attention to my shouting, "Why are you here? Why don't you leave?" She only noticed that it must have been very painful for me to utter all this. Besides, she was so defenseless, the poor girl. She considered herself immeasurably beneath me. How could she get angry or take offense? Suddenly she jumped up from the chair with a kind of uncontrollable impulse, and yearning toward me, but being too timid and not daring to stir from her place, she extended her arms in my direction. . . . At this moment my heart leapt inside me, too. Then suddenly she threw herself at me, put her arms around my neck, and burst into tears. I, too, couldn't restrain myself and sobbed as I'd never done before.

"They won't let me . . . I can't be . . . good!"[8] I barely managed to say; then I went over to the sofa, fell upon it face down, and sobbed in genuine hysterics for a quarter of an hour. She knelt down, embraced me, and remained motionless in that position.

But the trouble was that my hysterics had to end sometime. And so (after all, I'm writing the whole loathsome truth), lying there on the sofa and pressing my face firmly into that nasty leather cushion of mine, I began to sense gradually, distantly, involuntarily, but irresistibly, that it would be awkward for me to raise my head and look Liza straight in the eye. What was I ashamed of? I don't know, but I was ashamed. It also occurred to my overwrought brain that now our roles were completely reversed; now she was the heroine, and I was the same sort of humiliated and oppressed creature she'd been in front of me that evening—only four days ago. . . . And all this came to me during those few minutes as I lay face down on the sofa!

My God! Was it possible that I envied her?

I don't know; to this very day I still can't decide. But then, of course, I was even less able to understand it. After all, I couldn't live without exercising power and tyrannizing over another person. . . . But . . . but, then, you really can't explain a thing by reason; consequently, it's useless to try.

However, I regained control of myself and raised my head; I had to

---

8. This epithet *dobryi* ("good") must be read in combination with that in the second sentence of the work, where the hero describes himself as *zloi*—not only "spiteful" but also "evil."

sooner or later. . . . And so, I'm convinced to this day that it was precisely because I felt too ashamed to look at her, that another feeling was suddenly kindled and burst into flame in my heart—the feeling of domination and possession. My eyes gleamed with passion; I pressed her hands tightly. How I hated her and felt drawn to her simultaneously! One feeling intensified the other. It was almost like revenge! . . . At first there was a look of something resembling bewilderment, or even fear, on her face, but only for a brief moment. She embraced me warmly and rapturously.

X

A quarter of an hour later I was rushing back and forth across the room in furious impatience, constantly approaching the screen to peer at Liza through the crack. She was sitting on the floor, her head leaning against the bed, and she must have been crying. But she didn't leave, and that's what irritated me. By this time she knew absolutely everything. I'd insulted her once and for all, but . . . there's nothing more to be said. She guessed that my outburst of passion was merely revenge, a new humiliation for her, and that to my former, almost aimless, hatred there was added now a *personal, envious* hatred of her. . . . However, I don't think that she understood all this explicitly; on the other hand, she fully understood that I was a despicable man, and, most important, that I was incapable of loving her.

I know that I'll be told this is incredible—that it's impossible to be as spiteful and stupid as I am; you may even add that it was impossible not to return, or at least to appreciate, this love. But why is this so incredible? In the first place, I could no longer love because, I repeat, for me love meant tyrannizing and demonstrating my moral superiority. All my life I could never even conceive of any other kind of love, and I've now reached the point that I sometimes think that love consists precisely in a voluntary gift by the beloved person of the right to tyrannize over him. Even in my underground dreams I couldn't conceive of love in any way other than a struggle. It always began with hatred and ended with moral subjugation; afterward, I could never imagine what to do with the subjugated object. And what's so incredible about that, since I'd previously managed to corrupt myself morally; I'd already become unaccustomed to "real life," and only a short while ago had taken it into my head to reproach her and shame her for having come to hear "words of pity" from me. But I never could've guessed that she'd come not to hear words of pity at all, but to love me, because it's in that kind of love that a woman finds her resurrection, all her salvation from whatever kind of ruin, and her rebirth, as it can't appear in any other form. However, I didn't hate her so much as I rushed around the room and peered through the crack behind the screen. I merely found it unbearably painful that she was still there. I wanted her to disappear. I longed for "peace and quiet"; I wanted to remain alone in my underground. "Real life" oppressed me—so unfamiliar was it—that I even found it hard to breathe.

But several minutes passed, and she still didn't stir, as if she were oblivious. I was shameless enough to tap gently on the screen to remind her. . . . She started suddenly, jumped up, and hurried to find her shawl, hat, and coat, as if she wanted to escape from me. . . . Two minutes later she slowly emerged from behind the screen and looked at me sadly. I smiled spitefully; it was forced, however, for *appearance's sake only*; and I turned away from her look.

"Good-bye," she said, going toward the door.

Suddenly I ran up to her, grabbed her hand, opened it, put something in . . . and closed it again. Then I turned away at once and bolted to the other corner, so that at least I wouldn't be able to see. . . .

I was just about to lie—to write that I'd done all this accidentally, without knowing what I was doing, in complete confusion, out of foolishness. But I don't want to lie; therefore I'll say straight out, that I opened her hand and placed something in it . . . out of spite. It occurred to me to do this while I was rushing back and forth across the room and she was sitting there behind the screen. But here's what I can say for sure: although I did this cruel thing deliberately, it was not from my heart, but from my stupid head. This cruelty of mine was so artificial, cerebral, intentionally invented, *bookish*, that I couldn't stand it myself even for one minute—at first I bolted to the corner so as not to see, and then, out of shame and in despair, I rushed out after Liza. I opened the door into the hallway and listened. "Liza! Liza!" I called down the stairs, but timidly, in a soft voice.

There was no answer; I thought I could hear her footsteps at the bottom of the stairs.

"Liza!" I cried more loudly.

No answer. But at that moment I heard down below the sound of the tight outer glass door opening heavily with a creak and then closing again tightly. The sound rose up the stairs.

She'd gone. I returned to my room deep in thought. I felt horribly oppressed.

I stood by the table near the chair where she'd been sitting and stared senselessly into space. A minute or so passed, then I suddenly started: right before me on the chair I saw . . . in a word, I saw the crumpled blue five-ruble note, the very one I'd thrust into her hand a few moments before. It was the same one; it couldn't be any other; I had none other in my apartment. So she'd managed to toss it down on the table when I'd bolted to the other corner.

So what? I might have expected her to do that. Might have expected it? No. I was such an egotist, in fact, I so lacked respect for other people, that I couldn't even conceive that she'd ever do that. I couldn't stand it. A moment later, like a madman, I hurried to get dressed. I threw on whatever I happened to find, and rushed headlong after her. She couldn't have gone more than two hundred paces when I ran out on the street.

It was quiet; it was snowing heavily, and the snow was falling almost perpendicularly, blanketing the sidewalk and the deserted street. There were no passers-by; no sound could be heard. The street lights were flickering dismally and vainly. I ran about two hundred paces to the crossroads and stopped.

"Where did she go? And why am I running after her? Why? To fall down before her, sob with remorse, kiss her feet, and beg her forgiveness! That's just what I wanted. My heart was being torn apart; never, never will

I recall that moment with indifference. But—why?" I wondered. "Won't I grow to hate her, perhaps as soon as tomorrow, precisely because I'm kissing her feet today? Will I ever be able to make her happy? Haven't I found out once again today, for the hundredth time, what I'm really worth? Won't I torment her?"

I stood in the snow, peering into the murky mist, and thought about all this.

"And wouldn't it be better, wouldn't it," I fantasized once I was home again, stifling the stabbing pain in my heart with such fantasies, "wouldn't it be better if she were to carry away the insult with her forever? Such an insult—after all, is purification; it's the most caustic and painful form of consciousness. Tomorrow I would have defiled her soul and wearied her heart. But now that insult will never die within her; no matter how abominable the filth that awaits her, that insult will elevate and purify her . . . by hatred . . . hmm . . . perhaps by forgiveness as well. But will that make it any easier for her?"

And now, in fact, I'll pose an idle question of my own. Which is better: cheap happiness or sublime suffering? Well, come on, which is better?

These were my thoughts as I sat home that evening, barely alive with the anguish in my soul. I'd never before endured so much suffering and remorse; but could there exist even the slightest doubt that when I went rushing out of my apartment, I'd turn back again after going only halfway? I never met Liza afterward, and I never heard anything more about her. I'll also add that for a long time I remained satisfied with my theory about the use of insults and hatred, in spite of the fact that I myself almost fell ill from anguish at the time.

Even now, after so many years, all this comes back to me as *very unpleasant*. A great deal that comes back to me now is very unpleasant, but . . . perhaps I should end these *Notes* here? I think that I made a mistake in beginning to write them. At least, I was ashamed all the time I was writing this *tale*: consequently, it's not really literature, but corrective punishment. After all, to tell you long stories about how, for example, I ruined my life through moral decay in my corner, by the lack of appropriate surroundings, by isolation from any living beings, and by futile malice in the underground—so help me God, that's not very interesting. A novel needs a hero, whereas here all the traits of an anti-hero have been assembled *deliberately*; but the most important thing is that all this produces an extremely unpleasant impression because we've all become estranged from life, we're all cripples, every one of us, more or less. We've become so estranged that at times we feel some kind of revulsion for genuine "real life," and therefore we can't bear to be reminded of it. Why, we've reached a point where we almost regard "real life" as hard work, as a job, and we've all agreed in private that it's really better in books. And why do we sometimes fuss, indulge in whims, and make demands? We don't know ourselves. It'd be even worse if all our whimsical desires were fulfilled. Go on, try it. Give us, for example, a little more independence; untie the hands of any one of us, broaden our sphere of activity, relax the controls, and . . . I can assure you, we'll immediately ask to have the controls reinstated. I know that you may get angry at me for saying this, you may shout and stamp your feet: "Speak for yourself," you'll say, "and for your own miseries in the underground, but don't you dare say *'all of us.'* " If you'll allow me, gentlemen; after all, I'm not trying to justify myself by saying *all of us*. What concerns me in particular, is that in my life I've only taken to an extreme that which you haven't even dared to take half-way; what's more, you've mistaken your cowardice for good sense; and, in so deceiving yourself, you've consoled yourself. So, in fact, I may even be "more alive" than you are. Just take a closer look! Why, we don't even know where this "real life" lives nowadays, what it really is, and what it's called. Leave us alone without books and we'll get confused and lose our way at once—we won't know what to join, what to hold on to, what to love or what to hate, what to respect or what to despise. We're even oppressed by being men—men with real bodies and blood of *our very own*. We're ashamed of it; we consider it a disgrace and we strive to become some kind of impossible "general-human-beings." We're stillborn; for some time now we haven't been conceived by living fathers; we like it more and more. We're developing a taste for it. Soon we'll conceive of a way to be born from ideas. But enough; I don't want to write any more "from Underground. . . ."

However, the "notes" of this paradoxalist don't end here. He couldn't resist and kept on writing. But it also seems to us that we might as well stop here.

CHARLES BAUDELAIRE
1821–1867

Few writers have had such impact on succeeding generations as Charles Baude-laire, called both the "first modern poet" and the "father of modern criticism." Nor is his reputation confined to the West, for Baudelaire is the most widely read French poet around the globe. Yet for a long time Baudelaire's literary image was dominated by his reputation as a scandalous writer whose blatant eroticism and open fascination with evil outraged all right-thinking people. Both he and Flaubert were brought to trial in 1857 for "offenses against public and religious morals"— Flaubert for *Madame Bovary* and Baudelaire for his just-published book of poetry *Les Fleurs de Mal* (The flowers of evil). Some of this reputation is justified; the poet did intend to shock, and he displayed in painfully vivid scenes his own spiritual and sensual torment. Haunted by a religiously framed vision of human nature as fallen and corrupt, he lucidly analyzed his own weaknesses as well as the hypoc-risy and sins he found in society. Lust, hatred, laziness, a disabling self-awareness that ironized all emotions, a horror of death and decay, and finally an apathy that swallowed up all other vices—all contrasted bitterly with the poet's dreams of a lost Eden, an ideal harmony of being. Perfection existed only in the distance: in scenes of erotic love, faraway voyages, or artistic beauty created often out of ugli-ness and crude reality. Baudelaire's ability to present realistic detail inside larger symbolic horizons, his constant use of imagery and suggestion, his consummate craftsmanship and the intense musicality of his verse made him a precursor of Symbolism and, in the words of T. S. Eliot, "the greatest exemplar in *modern* poetry in any language."

Baudelaire was born in Paris on April 9, 1821. His father died when he was six, and his widowed mother married Captain (later General) Jacques Aupick a year later. In 1832 the family moved to Lyons, and young Charles was placed in boarding school; in 1836, Aupick and his family were reassigned to Paris. Throughout his life Baudelaire remained greatly attached to his mother and detested his disciplinarian stepfather. He was a rebellious and difficult youth whom his parents sent on a long voyage to the Indies in 1841 to remove him from bad influences; but he cut short the trip at Reunion Island and insisted on returning home after ten months. Baudelaire's unconventional behavior and extravagant lifestyle continued to worry his family, especially after he turned twenty-one and received his father's inheritance. In 1844, they obtained a court order to supervise his finances, and from then on the poet subsisted on allowances paid by a notary.

In contrast to the Romantics with their love of nature and pastoral scenes, Baudelaire was a city poet fascinated by the variety and excitement of modern urban life. Living in Paris, he collaborated with other writers, published poems, translations, and criticism in different journals, and in 1842 began a lifelong liaison with Jeanne Duval, the "black Venus" of many poems. When he read Edgar Allan Poe for the first time, he was struck by the similarity of their ideas: by Poe's dedication to beauty, his fascination with bizarre images and death, and above all by his emphasis on craftsmanship and perfectly controlled art. The French poet recognized in Poe "not only subjects I had dreamed of, but SENTENCES that I had thought and he had written twenty years earlier." Baudelaire's translations of Poe, collected in five volumes published from 1856 to 1865, were immensely popular and introduced the American writer to a broad European audience.

Public scandal greeted the appearance in 1857 of Baudelaire's major work, *The Flowers of Evil*. French authorities, already annoyed at Flaubert's acquittal, seized the book immediately. Less than two months later, the poet and his publisher were condemned to pay a fine and to delete six poems. A second edition with more poems appeared in 1861, and new lyrics were added to later printings. By now the poet was also well known as a critic. He championed the modern art of his time, interpreting and upholding the spirit of modernity in the art criticism of his 1845, 1846, and 1859 *Salons*, in remarkable studies of the painters Eugène Delacroix and Constantin Guys, and in a spirited defense of the German composer Richard Wagner. His literary criticism, although it included studies of *Madame Bovary*, Victor Hugo, and Théophile Gautier, was in general limited to brief journal reviews. Baudelaire started publishing prose poetry at the beginning of the 1860s, experimenting with a form that was almost unknown in France and in which he hoped to achieve "the miracle of a poetic prose, musical without rhythm or rhyme, able . . . to adapt itself to the soul's lyric movements, to the undulations of reverie, to the sudden starts of consciousness." A slim book of twenty prose poems appeared in 1862; the complete *Prose Poems* (also called *Paris Spleen*) would contain fifty poems in all. Baudelaire's health was precarious during these years. In 1862, he had what was apparently a minor stroke, which he called a "warning" and described with characteristically vivid imagery: "I felt pass over me a draft of wind from imbecility's wing." Four years later, in Belgium, he was stricken with aphasia and hemiplegia; unable to speak, he was brought back to Paris where he died on August 31, 1867.

His audience was never far from Baudelaire's mind. He wished to shock, to startle, to make the reader rethink cherished ideas and values. In the prefatory poem to *The Flowers of Evil*, *To the Reader*, Baudelaire ends a catalogue of human vices by insisting that both he and the reader are caught in a common guilt: "You—hypocrite Reader—my double—my brother!" The poet's insistent theme of *ennui* (pathological boredom or apathy) occurs here at the beginning of the book: it is the melancholy inertia that keeps human beings from acting either for good or for evil, placing them outside the realm of choice much as Dante relegated to Limbo those who were unwilling to take a moral stand. (In Catholic theology, such spiritual inertia is termed *acedia*.) This *spleen*, as it is also called (from the part of the body governing a splenetic or bilious humor), appears throughout *The Flowers of Evil* as an insidious, debilitating force. In *To the Reader* Baudelaire argues that the Devil's most terrifying weapon against humankind is not the litany of sins so colorfully described, but rather his ability to diminish the possibility of action: to evaporate—like a chemist in a laboratory—the precious metal of human will.

The Voyage, placed by Baudelaire at the end of the collection, describes the opposite of inertia: an active search for goals always out of reach. Written in a consciously Byronic tone and intended, according to the poet, to upset current faith in human progress, *The Voyage* describes "progress" as a series of temporary advances that end in disappointment and disgust. These smaller achievements— discovering new lands, inventing new luxuries, gaining fame and fortune, seeking ecstasy in sadism and sensuality—are all bound to deceive because they are merely symbols of a larger unending voyage: the quest for the infinite. Since human beings contain an "inner [spiritual] infinite" they cannot be satisfied with any limits and must constantly travel toward the unknown and the new. The "country" of earthly experience is not adequate for travelers impelled by an inner fire; their voyage ends, therefore, with a final plunge—for answers—into the unfathomable obscurity of death. The last line, "In the depths of the Unknown, we'll discover the New!" became a famous rallying cry for generations who sought new insights by exploring such unmapped frontiers.

Baudelaire alternates between acid melancholy and glimpses of happiness. Not all voyages are unhappy; one of his rare contented and even tender poems is the lyrical *Invitation to the Voyage*, a lover's invitation to an exotic land of peace, beauty, and sensuous harmony. The voyage is imaginary, of course, implying two forms of escape from reality: an escape out of real time into a primeval accord of the senses, and an escape into another artistic vision—the glowing interiors painted by such Dutch masters as Jan Vermeer. A similar but more cynical voyage of escape occurs in *Her Hair*. Here the poet, abandoning himself to passion, buries his face in the dark tide of his mistress's hair as if to submerge himself in the dark ocean of dream. This escape is available only on a temporary basis, however; the woman remains his "oasis" only so long as he adorns her hair with jewels. In both poems, and probably in Baudelaire's poetry in general, we must admit that women do not exist as separate personalities even if there are specific historical figures behind the poems. They are foils for poetic inspiration, conventional images of beauty, coldness, vision, or vice given one or another form. The woman in *The Carcass* exists only as an appropriate listener in a poem that mocks Petrarchan ideals of feminine beauty. Even if male subjectivity governs the descriptions, men are absent, in a different way; they exist only generically, as brothers (or doubles) of the poet himself. What emerges is that Baudelaire is even more clamped in his own solitude, registering repeatedly a personal experience from which he builds an amazingly complex imaginative universe.

Baudelaire was convinced that "every good poet has always been a realist," and he himself was a master of realistic details used for effects that go beyond conventional or photographic realism. The rhythmic thump of firewood being delivered is repeated throughout *Song of Autumn I*, where it coordinates ascending images of death. Imagery in *The Carcass* is more brutal. Even if the contrast between the language of courtly love ("star of my eyes") and crude and obscene descriptions no longer shocks in quite the same way, there remains the striking feat of imagination in which Baudelaire superimposes a swarming, vibrating new life onto the blurred outlines of a decaying animal carcass. The poem's ostensible theme is familiar—*carpe diem*, "seize the day" or "think of the future and love me now," since only a poet can preserve beauty—but one has only to compare Yeats's poem, *When You Are Old*, to recognize the harshness of this address to the beloved. The mixture of tones is more subtle in the *Spleen* poems, celebrated for their evocation of gray misery. Here Baudelaire inserts mundane items like bats, spiders, old-fashioned clothes, uncorked perfume bottles, and noisy rainspouts. Such down-to-earth details give substance to concurrent mythical or allegorical scenes. A chill revelation of mortality emerges from the sequence of thoroughly practical references to water in *Spleen LXXVIII*, beginning with the rain and fog in the city and including a cat twisting and turning uncomfortably on clammy tiles, the whine of a rainspout, the wheeze of wet wood and a damp clock pendulum, and finally a deck of cards left by an old woman who died of dropsy. If the sequence is interesting as a tour de force of linked images, it also serves cumulatively to evoke an atmosphere of lethargy and decay climaxing in a tiny, altogether unrealistic final scene in which two face cards talk sinisterly of their past loves.

Similar themes are to be found in the prose poems (published as *Little Poems in Prose* or *Paris Spleen*), although with a more openly autobiographical tone and a more homely setting. This prose must also find its own way to be musical "without rhyme." Stanzas become paragraphs; rhythm is created through variations in sentence length, syntax, and sound patterns, and the juxtaposition of scenes and tones. Rhythm is undeniably present, however changed: it is audible in the triple cadence ending *Windows* (helping him "to live, to feel that I am, and what I am") or in the contrasting dialogue leading up to the soul's explosion at the end of *Anywhere out of the World*.

The realism that is often buried in the lyrics of *The Flowers of Evil* appears on the surface in the prose poems. Baudelaire reviews an irritating day in *One O'Clock in the Morning*, recasts the topics of *The Voyage* as an imaginary dialogue in *Anywhere out of the World*, and ponders his solitude and the nature of creative genius in *Crowds* and *Windows*. In *Windows*, after having deduced the life story of an old woman seen across the roofs, he ends by saying that her story is only a "legend"—or, at least, that he does not care whether it is true so long as it provides a point of departure for his own imagination. Correspondingly, the poet relishes crowds because, moving among so many people, he is able to imagine himself in their place: "to be himself or someone else, as he chooses." In each case the artist is visibly alone, experiencing either the melancholy of *spleen* or the joy of an artistic imagination that creates and populates its own world. In verse or in prose, the alternation between dream and reality continues.

Baudelaire is a complex and ironic poet, an inheritor of that Romantic irony that wishes to embrace all the opposites of human existence: good and evil, love and hate, self and other, dream and reality. His is a universe of relationships, of echoes and correspondences. His best-known poem, in fact, is the sonnet *Correspondences*. This poem describes a vision of the mystic unity of all nature, which is demonstrated by the reciprocity of our five senses *(synesthesia)*. Nature, says the poet, is a system of perpetual analogies in which one thing always corresponds to another—physical objects to each other (colonnades in a temple, for example, to trees in the forest), spiritual reality to physical reality, and the five senses (taste, smell, touch, sight, and hearing) among themselves—to produce such combinations as "bitter green," a "soft look," or "a harsh sound." Human beings are not usually aware of the "universal analogy"—the forest of the first stanza watches us without our knowing it—but it is the role of the poet to act as seer and guide, urging us toward a state of awareness where both mind and senses fuse in another dimension. *Correspondences* is no vaguely intuitive poem, however. Even though it describes a state of ecstatic awareness, it works through the stages of a logical argument. The thesis is set out in the first stanza, explained in the second, and illustrated with cumulative examples in the third and fourth. Baudelaire's yearning for mystic harmony does not make him neglect either a base in reality or a rigorous application of intellect. His fusion of idealist vision, realistic detail, and artistic discipline made him the most influential poet of the nineteenth century, and the first poet of the modern age.

The selections printed here, from a range of Baudelaire's most influential lyric and prose poems, are translated by different modern poets. While remaining faithful to the original text, each translation necessarily stresses different aspects (for example, images, meter and rhyme, word order, tone, a particular set of associations when more than one is possible) to create a genuine English poem. The footnotes occasionally point out elements that are especially significant in the French text.

Lois Boe Hyslop, *Charles Baudelaire Revisited* (1992), is a useful introductory survey. Enid Starkie, *Baudelaire* (1953), is the fullest biography in English. Henri Peyre, ed., *Baudelaire: A Collection of Critical Essays* (1962), contains eleven essays on *The Flowers of Evil*, with selections by major writers including Proust, Valéry, Mauriac, Auerbach, and Georges Poulet. Harold Bloom, ed., *Charles Baudelaire* (1987), presents ten contemporary critics on Baudelaire's themes, literary and artistic criticism, selected texts, and relation to Poe. Patricia Clements, *Baudelaire and the English Tradition* (1985), is a penetrating analysis of Baudelaire's influence on English literature from Swinburne to T. S. Eliot; it includes comparisons and contrasts with late symbolist tradition. Edward Kaplan, *Baudelaire's Prose Poems* (1990), studies the prose poems as a many-sided but coherent ensemble of "fables of modern life," and Margery A. Evans, *Baudelaire and Intertextuality: Poetry at the Crossroads* (1993), analyzes the literary conventions manipulated in the prose poems. Rosemary Lloyd, *Baudelaire's Literary Criticism* (1981), offers a useful discussion of Baudelaire's criticism, arranged chronologically, by author, and in historical context. Lloyd's *Selected Letters of Charles Baudelaire: The Conquest of Solitude* (1986) contains a range of personal and literary letters. Laurence M. Porter, *The Crisis of French Symbolism* (1990), has a interesting chapter on Baudelaire's relation to his imagined audience. F. W. Leakey, *Baudelaire, Les Fleurs du Mal* (1992), is a short guide to the poet's major work.

PRONOUNCING GLOSSARY

The following list uses common English syllables and stress accents to provide rough equivalents of selected words whose pronunciation may be unfamiliar to the general reader.

Baudelaire: *boh-d'lair'*

ennui: *on-wee'*

Pylades: *pill'-ah-deez*

Venustre: *ven-yew'-struh*

THE FLOWERS OF EVIL

To the Reader[1]

Infatuation, sadism, lust, avarice
possess our souls and drain the body's force;

---

1. Translated by Robert Lowell. The translation pays primary attention to the insistent rhythm of the original poetic language and keeps the *abba* rhyme scheme.

we spoonfeed our adorable remorse,
like whores or beggars nourishing their lice.

Our sins are mulish, our confessions lies;　　5
we play to the grandstand with our promises,
we pray for tears to wash our filthiness,
importantly pissing hogwash through our styes.

The devil, watching by our sickbeds, hissed
old smut and folk-songs to our soul, until　　10
the soft and precious metal of our will
boiled off in vapor for this scientist.

Each day his flattery[2] makes us eat a toad,
and each step forward is a step to hell,
unmoved, though previous corpses and their smell　　15
asphyxiate our progress on this road.

Like the poor lush who cannot satisfy,
we try to force our sex with counterfeits,
die drooling on the deliquescent tits,
mouthing the rotten orange we suck dry.　　20

Gangs of demons are boozing in our brain—
ranked, swarming, like a million warrior-ants,[3]
they drown and choke the cistern of our wants;
each time we breathe, we tear our lungs with pain.

If poison, arson, sex, narcotics, knives　　25
have not yet ruined us and stitched their quick,
loud patterns on the canvas of our lives,
it is because our souls are still too sick.[4]

Among the vermin, jackals, panthers, lice,
gorillas and tarantulas that suck　　30
and snatch and scratch and defecate and fuck
in the disorderly circus of our vice,

there's one more ugly and abortive birth.
It makes no gestures, never beats its breast,
yet it would murder for a moment's rest,[5]　　35
and willingly annihilate the earth.

It's BOREDOM. Tears have glued its eyes together.
You know it well, my Reader. This obscene
beast chain-smokes yawning for the guillotine—
you—hypocrite Reader—my double—my brother!　　40

Correspondences[1]

Nature is a temple whose living colonnades
Breathe forth a mystic speech in fitful sighs;
Man wanders among symbols in those glades
Where all things watch him with familiar eyes.

---

2. The Devil is literally described as a puppet master controlling our strings.　3. Literally, intestinal worms.　4. Literally, not bold enough.　5. Literally, swallow the world in a yawn.　1. Translated by Richard Wilbur. The translation keeps the intricate melody of the sonnet's original rhyme scheme.

Like dwindling echoes gathered far away 5
Into a deep and thronging unison
Huge as the night or as the light of day,
All scents and sounds and colors meet as one.

Perfumes there are as sweet as the oboe's sound,
Green as the prairies, fresh as a child's caress,[2] 10
—And there are others, rich, corrupt, profound[3]

And of an infinite pervasiveness,
Like myrrh, or musk, or amber,[4] that excite
The ecstasies of sense, the soul's delight.

Correspondances

La Nature est un temple où de vivants piliers
Laissent parfois sortir de confuses paroles;
L'homme y passe à travers des forêts de symboles
Qui l'observent avec des regards familiers.

Comme de longs échos qui de loin se confondent 5
Dans une ténébreuse et profonde unité,
Vaste comme la nuit et comme la clarté,
Les parfums, les couleurs et les sons se répondent.

Il est des parfums frais comme des chairs d'enfants,
Doux comme les hautbois, verts comme les prairies, 10
—Et d'autres, corrompus, riches et triomphants,

Ayant l'expansion des choses infinies,
Comme l'ambre, le musc, le benjoin et l'encens,
Qui chantent les transports de l'esprit et des sens.

Her Hair[1]

O fleece, that down the neck waves to the nape!
O curls! O perfume nonchalant and rare!
O ecstacy! To fill this alcove[2] shape
With memories that in these tresses sleep,
I would shake them like pennons in the air! 5

Languorous Asia, burning Africa,
And a far world, defunct almost, absent,
Within your aromatic forest stay!
As other souls on music drift away,
Mine, o my love! still floats upon your scent. 10

I shall go there where, full of sap, both tree
And man swoon in the heat of southern climes;

2. Literally, flesh. 3. Literally, triumphant. 4. Or ambergris, a substance secreted by whales. Ambergris and musk (a secretion of the male musk deer) are used in making perfume. 1. Translated by Doreen Bell. The translation emulates the French original's challenging *abaab* rhyme pattern. 2. Bedroom.

Strong tresses, be the swell that carries me!
I dream upon your sea of ebony
Of dazzling sails, of oarsmen, masts and flames: 15

A sun-drenched and reverberating port,
Where I imbibe color and sound and scent;
Where vessels, gliding through the gold and moire,
Open their vast arms as they leave the shore
To clasp the pure and shimmering firmament.   20

I'll plunge my head, enamored of its pleasure,
In this black ocean where the other hides;
My subtle spirit then will know a measure
Of fertile idleness and fragrant leisure,
Lulled by the infinite rhythm of its tides!   25

Pavilion, of blue-shadowed tresses spun,
You give me back the azure from afar;
And where the twisted locks are fringed with down
Lurk mingled odors I grow drunk upon
Of oil of coconut, of musk and tar.   30

A long time! always! my hand in your hair
Will sow the stars of sapphire, pearl, ruby,
That you be never deaf to my desire,
My oasis and gourd whence I aspire
To drink deep of the wine of memory![3]   35

A Carcass[1]

Remember, my love, the item you saw
　　That beautiful morning in June:
By a bend in the path a carcass reclined
　　On a bed sown with pebbles and stones;

Her legs were spread out like a lecherous whore,   5
　　Sweating out poisonous fumes,
Who opened in slick invitational style
　　Her stinking and festering womb.

The sun on this rottenness focused its rays
　　To cook the cadaver till done,   10
And render to Nature a hundredfold gift
　　Of all she'd united in one.

And the sky cast an eye on this marvelous meat
　　As over the flowers in bloom.
The stench was so wretched that there on the grass   15
　　You nearly collapsed in a swoon.

The flies buzzed and droned on these bowels of filth
　　Where an army of maggots arose,

---

3. The last two lines are a question: "Are you not. . . ?"   1. Translated by James McGowan with special attention to imagery. The alternation of long and short lines in English emulates the French meter's rhythmic swing between twelve-syllable and eight-syllable lines in an *abab* rhyme scheme.

Which flowed like a liquid and thickening stream
    On the animate rags of her clothes.[2]   20

And it rose and it fell, and pulsed like a wave,
    Rushing and bubbling with health.
One could say that this carcass, blown with vague breath,
    Lived in increasing itself.

And this whole teeming world made a musical sound   25
    Like babbling brooks and the breeze,
Or the grain that a man with a winnowing-fan
    Turns with a rhythmical ease.

The shapes wore away as if only a dream
    Like a sketch that is left on the page   30
Which the artist forgot and can only complete
    On the canvas, with memory's aid.

From back in the rocks, a pitiful bitch
    Eyed us with angry distaste,
Awaiting the moment to snatch from the bones   35
    The morsel she'd dropped in her haste.

—And you, in your turn, will be rotten as this:
    Horrible, filthy, undone,
Oh sun of my nature and star of my eyes,
    My passion, my angel[3] in one!   40

Yes, such will you be, oh regent of grace,
    After the rites have been read,
Under the weeds, under blossoming grass
    As you molder with bones of the dead.

Ah then, oh my beauty, explain to the worms   45
    Who cherish your body so fine,
That I am the keeper for corpses of love
    Of the form, and the essence divine![4]

Invitation to the Voyage[1]

    My child, my sister, dream
    How sweet all things would seem
Were we in that kind land to live together,
    And there love slow and long,
    There love and die among   5
Those scenes that image you, that sumptuous weather.
    Drowned suns that glimmer there
    Through cloud-disheveled air
Move me with such a mystery as appears
    Within those other skies   10

2. By extension. The torn flesh is described as "living rags."   3. Series of conventional Petrarchan images that idealize the beloved.   4. "Any form created by man is immortal. For form is independent of matter. . ." from Baudelaire's journal *My Heart Laid Bare*, LXXX.   1. Translated by Richard Wilbur. The translation maintains both the rhyme scheme and the rocking motion of the original meter, which follows an unusual pattern of two five-syllable lines followed by one seven-syllable line, and a seven-syllable couplet as refrain.

Of your treacherous eyes
When I behold them shining through their tears.

There, there is nothing else but grace and measure,
Richness, quietness, and pleasure.

   Furniture that wears   15
   The lustre of the years
Softly would glow within our glowing chamber,
   Flowers of rarest bloom
   Proffering their perfume
Mixed with the vague fragrances of amber;   20
   Gold ceilings would there be,
   Mirrors deep as the sea,
The walls all in an Eastern splendor hung—
   Nothing but should address
   The soul's loneliness,   25
Speaking her sweet and secret native tongue.

There, there is nothing else but grace and measure,
Richness, quietness, and pleasure.

   See, sheltered from the swells
   There in the still canals   30
Those drowsy ships that dream of sailing forth;
   It is to satisfy
   Your least desire, they ply
Hither through all the waters of the earth.
   The sun at close of day   35
   Clothes the fields of hay,
Then the canals, at last the town entire
   In hyacinth and gold:
   Slowly the land is rolled
Sleepward under a sea of gentle fire.   40

There, there is nothing else but grace and measure,
Richness, quietness, and pleasure.

Song of Autumn I[1]

Soon we shall plunge into the chilly fogs;
Farewell, swift light! our summers are too short!
I hear already the mournful fall of logs
Re-echoing from the pavement of the court.

All of winter will gather in my soul: 5
Hate, anger, horror, chills, the hard forced work;
And, like the sun in his hell by the north pole,
My heart will be only a red and frozen block.

I shudder, hearing every log that falls;
No scaffold could be built with hollower sounds.   10

1. Translated by C. F. MacIntyre to follow the original rhyme pattern.

My spirit is like a tower whose crumbling walls
The tireless battering-ram brings to the ground.

It seems to me, lulled by monotonous shocks,
As if they were hastily nailing a coffin today.
For whom?—Yesterday was summer. Now autumn knocks.   15
That mysterious sound is like someone's going away.

Spleen LXXVIII[1]

Old Pluvius,[2] month of rains, in peevish mood
Pours from his urn chill winter's sodden gloom
On corpses fading in the near graveyard,
On foggy suburbs pours life's tedium.

My cat seeks out a litter on the stones,   5
Her mangy body turning without rest.
An ancient poet's soul in monotones
Whines in the rain-spouts like a chilblained ghost.

A great bell mourns, a wet log wrapped in smoke
Sings in falsetto to the wheezing clock,   10
While from a rankly perfumed deck of cards
(A dropsical old crone's fatal bequest)
The Queen of Spades, the dapper Jack of Hearts
Speak darkly of dead loves, how they were lost.

Spleen LXXIX[1]

I have more memories than if I had lived a thousand years.

Even a bureau crammed with souvenirs,
Old bills, love letters, photographs, receipts,
Court depositions, locks of hair in plaits,
Hides fewer secrets than my brain could yield.   5
It's like a tomb, a corpse-filled Potter's Field,[2]
A pyramid where the dead lie down by scores.
I am a graveyard that the moon abhors:
Like guilty qualms, the worms burrow and nest
Thickly in bodies that I loved the best.   10
I'm a stale boudoir where old-fashioned clothes
Lie scattered among wilted fern and rose,
Where only the Boucher girls[3] in pale pastels
Can breathe the uncorked scents and faded smells.

1. Translated by Kenneth O. Hanson, with emphasis on the imagery. The French original uses identical *abab* rhymes in the two quatrains and shifts to *ccd, eed* in the tercets.   2. Pluvius is literally "the rainy time" (Latin), a period extending from January 20 to February 18 as the fifth month of the French Revolutionary calendar.   1. Translated by Anthony Hecht. The translation follows the original rhymed couplets except for one technical impossibility: Baudelaire's repetition (in a poem about monotony) of an identical rhyme for eight lines (lines 11–18, the sound of long *a*).   2. A general term describing the common cemetery for those buried at public expense.   3. François Boucher (1703–1770), court painter for Louis XV of France, drew many pictures of young women clothed and nude.

Nothing can equal those days for endlessness   15
When in the winter's blizzardy caress
Indifference expanding to Ennui[4]
Takes on the feel of Immortality.
O living matter, henceforth you're no more
Than a cold stone encompassed by vague fear   20
And by the desert, and the mist and sun;
An ancient Sphinx ignored by everyone,
Left off the map, whose bitter irony
Is to sing as the sun sets in that dry sea.[5]

Spleen LXXXI[1]

When the low heavy sky weighs like a lid
Upon the spirit aching for the light
And all the wide horizon's line is hid
By a black day sadder than any night;

When the changed earth is but a dungeon dank   5
Where batlike Hope goes blindly fluttering
And, striking wall and roof and mouldered plank,
Bruises his tender head and timid wing;

When like grim prison bars stretch down the thin,
Straight, rigid pillars of the endless rain,   10
And the dumb throngs of infamous spiders spin
Their meshes in the caverns of the brain,

Suddenly, bells leap forth into the air,
Hurling a hideous uproar to the sky
As 'twere a band of homeless spirits who fare   15
Through the strange heavens, wailing stubbornly.

And hearses, without drum or instrument,
File slowly through my soul; crushed, sorrowful,
Weeps Hope, and Grief, fierce and omnipotent,
Plants his black banner on my drooping skull.   20

The Voyage[1]

To Maxime du Camp[2]

I

The child, in love with prints and maps,
Holds the whole world in his vast appetite.
How large the earth is under the lamplight!
But in the eyes of memory, how the world is cramped!

---

4. Melancholy, paralyzing boredom.   5. Baudelaire combines two references to ancient Egypt, the sphinx and the legendary statue of Memnon at Thebes, which was supposed to sing at sunset.   1. Translated by Sir John Squire in accord with the original rhyme scheme.   1. Translated by Charles Henri Ford. The French poem is written in the traditional twelve-syllable (alexandrine) line with an *abab* rhyme scheme.   2. A wry dedication to the progress-oriented author of *Modern Songs* (1855), which began "I was born a traveler."

We set out one morning, brain afire,   5
Hearts fat with rancor and bitter desires,
Moving along to the rhythm of wind and waves,
Lull the inner infinite on the finite of seas:

Some are glad, glad to leave a degraded home;
Others, happy to shake off the horror of their hearts,   10
Still others, astrologers drowned in the eyes of woman—
Oh the perfumes of Circe,[3] the power and the pig!—

To escape conversion to the Beast, get drunk
On space and light and the flames of skies;
The tongue of the sun and the ice that bites   15
Slowly erase the mark of the Kiss.

But the true voyagers are those who leave
Only to be going; hearts nimble as balloons,
They never diverge from luck's black sun,
And with or without reason, cry, Let's be gone!   20

Desire to them is nothing but clouds,
They dream, as a draftee dreams of the cannon,
Of vast sensualities, changing, unknown,
Whose name the spirit has never pronounced!

                              II

We imitate—horrible!—the top and ball   25
In their waltz and bounce; even in sleep
We're turned and tormented by Curiosity,
Who, like a mad Angel, lashes the stars.

Peculiar fortune that changes its goal,
And being nowhere, is anywhere at all!   30
And Man, who is never untwisted from hope,
Scrambling like a madman to get some rest!

The soul's a three-master seeking Icaria;[4]
A voice on deck calls: "Wake up there!"
A voice from the mast-head, vehement, wild: 35
"Love . . . fame . . . happiness!" We're on the rocks!

Every island that the lookout hails
Becomes the Eldorado[5] foretold by Fortune;
Then Imagination embarks on its orgy
But runs aground in the brightness of morning.   40

Poor little lover of visionary fields!
Should he be put in irons, dumped in the sea,
This drunken sailor, discoverer of Americas,
Mirage that makes the gulf more bitter?

---

3. In Homer's *Odyssey*, an island sorceress who changed visitors into beasts; Odysseus's men were transformed into pigs.   **4.** Greek island in the Aegean Sea, named after the mythological Icarus, who, escaping from prison on self-made wings, plunged into nearby waters and drowned when they gave way. His name was associated with utopian flights, as in Etienne Cabet's novel about a utopian community, *Voyage to Icaria* (1840). *Three-master:* a ship.   **5.** Fabled country of gold and abundance.

So the old vagabond, shuffling in mud,   45
Dreams, nose hoisted, of a shining paradise,
His charmed eye lighting on Capua's[6] coast
At every candle aglow in a hovel.

III

Astounding voyagers! what noble stories
We read in your eyes, deeper than seas;   50
Show us those caskets, filled with rich memories,
Marvelous jewels, hewn from stars and aether.

Yes, we would travel, without sail or steam!
Gladden a little our jail's desolation,
Sail over our minds, stretched like a canvas,   55
All your memories, framed with gold horizons.

Tell us, what have you seen?

IV

                              "We have seen stars
And tides; we have seen sands, too,
And, despite shocks and unforeseen disasters,
We were often bored, just as we are here.   60

The glory of sun on a violet sea,
The glory of cities in the setting sun,
Kindled our hearts with torment and longing
To plunge into the sky's magnetic reflections.

Neither the rich cities nor sublime landscapes,   65
Ever possessed that mysterious attraction
Of Change and Chance having fun with the clouds.
And always Desire kept us anxious!

—Enjoyment adds force to Appetite!
Desire, old tree nurtured by pleasure,   70
Although your dear bark thicken and harden,
Your branches throb to hold the sun closer!

Great tree, will you outgrow the cypress?
Still we have gathered carefully
Some sketches for your hungry album,   75
Brothers, for whom all things from far away

Are precious! We've bowed down to idols;
To thrones encrusted with luminous rocks;
To figured palaces whose magic pomp
Would ruin your bankers with a ruinous dream;   80

To costumes that intoxicate the eye,
To women whose teeth and nails are dyed,
To clever jugglers, fondled by the snake."[7]

---

6. City on the Volturno River in southern Italy, famous for its luxury and sensuality.   7. Snake charmers. The images in this stanza evoke India.

V

And then, and what more?

VI

"O childish minds!

Not to forget the principal thing,   85
We saw everywhere, without looking for it,
From top to toe of the deadly scale,
The tedious drama of undying sin:

Woman, low slave, vain and stupid,
Without laughter self-loving, and without disgust,   90
Man, greedy despot, lewd, hard and covetous,
Slave of the slave, rivulet in the sewer;

The hangman exulting, the martyr sobbing;
Festivals that season and perfume the blood;[8]
The poison of power unnerving the tyrant,   95
The masses in love with the brutalizing whip;

Many religions, very like our own,
All climbing to heaven; and Holiness,
Like a delicate wallower in a feather bed,
Seeking sensation from hair shirts and nails.   100

Jabbering humanity, drunk with its genius,
As crazy now as it was in the past,
Crying to God in its raging agony:
'O master, fellow creature, I curse thee forever!'

And then the least stupid, brave lovers of Lunacy,   105
Fleeing the gross herd that Destiny pens in,
Finding release in the vast dreams of opium!
—Such is the story, the whole world over."

VII

Bitter knowledge that traveling brings!
The globe, monotonous and small, today,   110
Yesterday, tomorrow, always, throws us our image:
An oasis of horror in a desert of boredom!

Should we go? Or stay? If you can stay, stay;
But go if you must. Some run, some hide
To outwit Time, the enemy so vigilant and   115
Baleful. And many, alas, must run forever

Like the wandering Jew[9] and the twelve apostles,
Who could not escape his relentless net[1]
By ship or by wheel; while others knew how
To destroy him without leaving home.   120

---

8. Literally, "Festivals seasoned and perfumed by blood."   9. According to medieval legend, a Jew who mocked Christ on his way to the cross and was condemned to wander unceasingly until Judgment Day. 1. These three stanzas describe Time (ultimately Death) as a Roman gladiator, the *retiarius*, who used a net to trap his opponent.

When finally he places his foot on our spine,
May we be able to hope and cry, Forward!
As in days gone by when we left for China,
Eyes fixed on the distance, hair in the wind,

With heart as light as a young libertine's   125
We'll embark on the sea of deepening shadows.
Do you hear those mournful, enchanting voices[2]
That sing: "Come this way, if you would taste

The perfumed Lotus. Here you may pick
Miraculous fruits for which the heart hungers.   130
Come and drink deep of this strange,
Soft afternoon that never ends?"

Knowing his voice, we visualize the phantom—
It is our Pylades there, his arms outstretched.
While she whose knees we used to kiss cries out,   135
"For strength of heart, swim back to your Electra!"[3]

                              VIII

O Death, old captain, it is time! weigh anchor!
This country confounds us; hoist sail and away!
If the sky and sea are black as ink,
Our hearts, as you know them, burst with blinding rays.   140

Pour us your poison, that last consoling draft!
For we long, so the fire burns in the brain,
To sound the abyss, Hell or Heaven, what matter?
In the depths of the Unknown, we'll discover the New!

Paris Spleen[1]

One O'Clock in the Morning

At last! I am alone! Nothing can be heard but the rumbling of a few belated and weary cabs. For a few hours at least silence will be ours, if not sleep. At last! The tyranny of the human face has disappeared, and now there will be no one but myself to make me suffer.

At last! I am allowed to relax in a bath of darkness! First a double turn of the key in the lock. This turn of the key will, it seems to me, increase my solitude and strengthen the barricades that, for the moment, separate me from the world.

Horrible life! Horrible city! Let us glance back over the events of the day: saw several writers, one of them asking me if you could go to Russia by land (he thought Russia was an island, I suppose); disagreed liberally with the editor of a review who to all my objections kept saying: "Here we

2. The voices of the dead, luring the sailor to the Lotus-land of ease and forgetfulness.   3. In Greek mythology, Orestes and Pylades were close friends ready to sacrifice their lives for each other. Electra was Orestes' faithful sister, who saved him from the Furies.   1. Translated by Louise Varèse.

are on the side of respectability," implying that all the other periodicals were run by rascals; bowed to twenty or more persons of whom fifteen were unknown to me; distributed hand shakes in about the same proportion without having first taken the precaution of buying gloves; to kill time during a shower, dropped in on a dancer who asked me to design her a costume of *Venustre;*[2] went to pay court to a theatrical director who in dismissing me said: "Perhaps you would do well to see Z. . . . ; he is the dullest, stupidest and most celebrated of our authors; with him you might get somewhere. Consult him and then we'll see": boasted (why?) of several ugly things I never did, and cravenly denied some other misdeeds that I had accomplished with the greatest delight; offense of fanfaronnade,[3] crime against human dignity; refused a slight favor to a friend and gave a written recommendation to a perfect rogue; Lord! let's hope that's all!

Dissatisfied with everything, dissatisfied with myself, I long to redeem myself and to restore my pride in the silence and solitude of the night. Souls of those whom I have loved, souls of those whom I have sung, strengthen me, sustain me, keep me from the vanities of the world and its contaminating fumes; and You, dear God! grant me grace to produce a few beautiful verses to prove to myself that I am not the lowest of men, that I am not inferior to those whom I despise.

Crowds

It is not given to every man to take a bath of multitude; enjoying a crowd is an art; and only he can relish a debauch of vitality at the expense of the human species, on whom, in his cradle, a fairy has bestowed the love of masks and masquerading, the hate of home, and the passion for roaming.

Multitude, solitude: identical terms, and interchangeable by the active and fertile poet. The man who is unable to people his solitude is equally unable to be alone in a bustling crowd.

The poet enjoys the incomparable privilege of being able to be himself or someone else, as he chooses. Like those wandering souls who go looking for a body, he enters as he likes into each man's personality. For him alone everything is vacant; and if certain places seem closed to him, it is only because in his eyes they are not worth visiting.

The solitary and thoughtful stroller finds a singular intoxication in this universal communion. The man who loves to lose himself in a crowd enjoys feverish delights that the egoist locked up in himself as in a box, and the slothful man like a mollusk in his shell, will be eternally deprived of. He adopts as his own all the occupations, all the joys and all the sorrows that chance offers.

What men call love is a very small, restricted, feeble thing compared with this ineffable orgy, this divine prostitution of the soul giving itself entire, all its poetry and all its charity, to the unexpected as it comes along, to the stranger as he passes.

---

2. Venus. Baudelaire ironically reproduces the dancer's mispronunciation.   3. Boasting.

It is a good thing sometimes to teach the fortunate of this world, if only to humble for an instant their foolish pride, that there are higher joys than theirs, finer and more uncircumscribed. The founders of colonies, shepherds of peoples, missionary priests exiled to the ends of the earth, doubtlessly know something of this mysterious drunkenness; and in the midst of the vast family created by their genius, they must often laugh at those who pity them because of their troubled fortunes and chaste lives.

Windows

Looking from outside into an open window one never sees as much as when one looks through a closed window. There is nothing more profound, more mysterious, more pregnant, more insidious, more dazzling than a window lighted by a single candle. What one can see out in the sunlight is always less interesting than what goes on behind a windowpane. In that black or luminous square life lives, life dreams, life suffers.

Across the ocean of roofs I can see a middle-aged woman, her face already lined, who is forever bending over something and who never goes out. Out of her face, her dress, and her gestures, out of practically nothing at all, I have made up this woman's story, or rather legend, and sometimes I tell it to myself and weep.

If it had been an old man I could have made up his just as well.

And I go to bed proud to have lived and to have suffered in some one besides myself.

Perhaps you will say "Are you sure that your story is the real one?" But what does it matter what reality is outside myself, so long as it has helped me to live, to feel that I am, and what I am?

Anywhere out of the World[1]

Life is a hospital where every patient is obsessed by the desire of changing beds. One would like to suffer opposite the stove, another is sure he would get well beside the window.

It always seems to me that I should be happy anywhere but where I am, and this question of moving is one that I am eternally discussing with my soul.

"Tell me, my soul, poor chilly soul, how would you like to live in Lisbon? It must be warm there, and you would be as blissful as a lizard in the sun. It is a city by the sea; they say that it is built of marble, and that its inhabitants have such a horror of the vegetable kingdom that they tear up all the trees. You see it is a country after my own heart; a country entirely made of mineral and light, and with liquid to reflect them."

My soul does not reply.

"Since you are so fond of being motionless and watching the pageantry of movement, would you like to live in the beatific land of Holland? Per-

---

1. The title (given in English by Baudelaire) is based on a line from Thomas Hood's poem *Bridge of Sighs*: "Anywhere, anywhere—out of the world." Baudelaire probably found the reference in Poe's *Poetic Principle*.

haps you could enjoy yourself in that country which you have so long admired in paintings on museum walls. What do you say to Rotterdam,[2] you who love forests of masts, and ships that are moored on the doorsteps of houses?"

My soul remains silent.

"Perhaps you would like Batavia[3] better? There, moreover, we should find the wit of Europe wedded to the beauty of the tropics."

Not a word. Can my soul be dead?

"Have you sunk into so deep a stupor that you are happy only in your unhappiness? If that is the case, let us fly to countries that are the counterfeits of Death. I know just the place for us, poor soul. We will pack up our trunks for Torneo.[4] We will go still farther, to the farthest end of the Baltic Sea; still farther from life if possible; we will settle at the Pole. There the sun only obliquely grazes the earth, and the slow alternations of daylight and night abolish variety and increase that other half of nothingness, monotony. There we can take deep baths of darkness, while sometimes for our entertainment, the Aurora Borealis will shoot up its rose-red sheafs like the reflections of the fireworks of hell!"

At last my soul explodes! "Anywhere! Just so it is out of the world!"

2. Large Dutch seaport.   3. Former name of Djakarta, capital of the Dutch East Indies and now the
capital city of Indonesia.   4. A city in Finland.

LEO TOLSTOY
1828–1910

Count Leo Tolstoy excited the interest of Europe mainly as a public figure: a count owning large estates who decided to give up his wealth and live like a simple Russian peasant—to dress in a blouse, to eat peasant food, and even to plow the fields and make shoes with his own hands. By the time of his death he had become the leader of a religious cult, the propounder of a new religion. It was, in substance, a highly simplified primitive Christianity that he reduced to a few moral commands (such as, "Do not resist evil") and from which he drew, with radical consistency, a complete condemnation of modern civilization: the state, courts and law, war, patriotism, marriage, modern art and literature, science and medicine. In debating this Christian anarchism people have tended to forget that Tolstoy established his command of the public ear as a novelist, or they have exaggerated the contrast between the early worldly novelist and the later prophet who repudiated all his early, great novelistic work: *War and Peace*, the enormous epic of the 1812 invasion of Russia, and *Anna Karenina*, the story of an adulterous love, superbly realized in accurately imagined detail.

Tolstoy was born at Yásnaya Polyána, his mother's estate near Tula (about 130 miles south of Moscow), on August 28, 1828. His father was a retired lieutenant colonel; one of his ancestors, the first count, had served Peter the Great as an ambassador. His mother's father was a Russian general-in-chief. Tolstoy lost both parents early in his life and was brought up by aunts. He went to the University of Kazan between 1844 and 1847, drifted along aimlessly for a few years more, and in 1851 became a cadet in the Caucasus. As an artillery officer he saw action in the wars with the mountain tribes and again, in 1854–55, during the Crimean War against the French and English. Tolstoy had written fictional reminiscences of his childhood while he was in the Caucasus, and during the Crimean War he wrote war stories, which established his literary reputation. For some years he lived on his estate, where he founded and himself taught an extremely "progressive" school for peasant children. He made two trips to western Europe, in 1857 and in 1860–61. In 1862 he married the daughter of a physician, Sonya Bers, with whom he had thirteen children.

In the first years of his married life, between 1863 and 1869, he wrote his enormous novel *War and Peace.* The book made him famous in Russia but was not translated into English until long afterward. Superficially, *War and Peace* is an historical novel about the Napoléonic invasion of Russia in 1812, a huge swarming epic of a nation's resistance to the foreigner. Tolstoy himself interprets history in general as a struggle of anonymous collective forces that are moved by unknown irrational impulses, waves of communal feeling. Heroes, great men and women, are actually not heroes but merely insignificant puppets; the best general is the one who does nothing to prevent the unknown course of Providence. But *War and Peace* is not only an impressive and vivid panorama of historical events but also the profound story—centered in two main characters, Pierre Bezukhov and Prince Andrey Bolkonsky—of a search for meaning in life. Andrey finds meaning in love and forgiveness of his enemies. Pierre, at the end of a long groping struggle, an education by suffering, finds it in an acceptance of ordinary existence, its duties and pleasures, the family, the continuity of the race.

Tolstoy's next long novel, *Anna Karenina* (1875–77), resumes this second thread of *War and Peace.* It is a novel of contemporary manners, a narrative of adultery and suicide. But this vivid story, told with incomparable concrete imagination, is counterpointed and framed by a second story, that of Levin, another seeker after the meaning of life, a figure who represents the author as Pierre did in the earlier book; the work ends with a promise of salvation, with the ideal of a life in which we should "remember God." Thus *Anna Karenina* also anticipates the approaching crisis in Tolstoy's life. When it came, with the sudden revulsion he describes in *A Confession* (1879), he condemned his earlier books and spent the next years in writing pamphlets and tracts expounding his religion.

Only slowly did Tolstoy return to the writing of fiction, now regarded entirely as a means of presenting his creed. The earlier novels seemed to him unclear in their message, overdetailed in their method. Hence Tolstoy tried to simplify his art; he wrote plays with a thesis, stories that are like fables or parables, and one long, rather inferior novel, *The Resurrection* (1899), his most savage satire on Russian and modern institutions.

In 1901 Tolstoy was excommunicated. A disagreement with his wife about the nature of the good life and about financial matters sharpened into a conflict over his last will, which finally led to a complete break: he left home in the company of a doctor friend. He caught cold on the train journey south and died in the house of the stationmaster of Astápovo, on November 20, 1910.

If we look back on Tolstoy's work as a whole, we must recognize its continuity. From the very beginning he was a Rousseauist. As early as 1851, when he was in the Caucasus, his diary announced his intention of founding a new, simplified religion. Even as a young man on his estate he had lived quite simply, like a peasant, except for occasional sprees and debauches. He had been horrified by war from the very beginning, though he admired the heroism of the individual soldier and had remnants of patriotic feeling. All his books concern the same theme, the good life, and they all say that the good life lies outside of civilization, near to the soil, in simplicity and humility, in love of one's neighbor. Power, the lust for power, luxury, are always evil.

Tolstoy's roots as a novelist are part of another, older realistic tradition. He read and knew the English writers of the eighteenth century—and also William Make-peace Thackeray and Anthony Trollope—though he did not care for the recent French writers (he was strong in his disapproval of Gustave Flaubert) except for Guy de Maupassant, who struck him as truthful and useful in his struggle against hypocrisy. Tolstoy's long novels are loosely plotted, though they have large over-all designs. They work by little scenes vividly visualized, by an accumulation of exact detail. Each character is drawn by means of repeated emphasis on certain physical traits, like Pierre's shortsightedness and his hairy, clumsy hands, or Prin-cess Marya's luminous eyes, the red patches on her face, and her shuffling gait. This concretely realized surface, however, everywhere recedes into depths: to the depiction of disease, delirium, and death and to glimpses into eternity. In *War and Peace* the blue sky is the recurrent symbol for the metaphysical spirit within us. Tolstoy is so robust, has his feet so firmly on the ground, presents what he sees with such clarity and objectivity, that one can be easily deluded into considering his dominating quality to be physical, sensual, antithetical to Dostoevsky's spiritu-ality. The contrasts between the two greatest Russian novelists are indeed obvious. While Tolstoy's method can be called epic, Dostoevsky's is dramatic; while Tol-stoy's view of humanity is Rousseauistic, Dostoevsky stresses the Fall; while Tolstoy rejects history and status, Dostoevsky appeals to the past and desires a hierarchical society, and so on. But these profound differences should not obscure one basic similarity: the deep spirituality of both writers, their rejection of the basic material-ism and the conception of truth propounded by modern science and theorists of realism.

The Death of Iván Ilyich (1886) belongs to the period after Tolstoy's religious conversion when he slowly returned to fiction writing. It represents a happy medium between his early and late manner. Its story and moral are simple and obvious, as always with Tolstoy (in contrast to Dostoevsky). And it expresses what almost all of his works are intended to convey—that humanity is leading the wrong kind of life, that we should return to essentials, to "nature." In *The Death of Iván Ilyich* Tolstoy combines a savage satire on the futility and hypocrisy of conven-tional life with a powerful symbolic presentation of isolation in the struggle with death and of hope for a final resurrection. Iván Ilyich is a Russian judge, an official, but he is also the average man of the prosperous middle classes of his time and ours, and he is also Everyman confronted with disease and dying and death. He is an ordinary person, neither virtuous nor particularly vicious, a "go-getter" in his profession, a "family man," as marriages go, who has children but has drifted apart from his wife. Through his disease, which comes about by a trivial accident in the trivial business of fixing a curtain, Iván Ilyich is slowly awakened to self-conscious-ness and a realization of the falsity of his life and ambitions. The isolation that disease imposes on him, the wall of hypocrisy erected around him by his family and his doctors, his suffering and pain, drive him slowly to the recognition of It: to a knowledge, not merely theoretical but proved on his pulses, of his own mortal-ity. At first he would like simply to return to his former pleasant and normal life— even in the last days of his illness, knowing he must die, he screams in his agony, "I won't!"—but at the end, struggling in the black sack into which he is being pushed, he sees the light at the bottom. " 'Death is finished,' he said to himself. 'It is no more!' "

The people around him are egotists and hypocrites: his wife, who can remember only how she suffered during his agony; his daughter, who thinks only of the delay in her marriage; his colleagues, who speculate only about the room his death will make for promotions in the court; the doctors, who think only of the name of the disease and not of the patient; all except his shy and frightened son, Vásya, and the servant Gerásim. Because he is young, near to "nature," and free from hypoc-risy, Gerásim is able to make his master more comfortable, and even to mention death, while all the others conceal the truth from him. The doctors, especially, are shown as mere specialists, inhuman and selfish. The first doctor is like a judge—like Iván himself when he sat in court—summing up and cutting off further questions of the patient. The satire at points appears ineffectively harsh in its violence, but it will not seem exceptional to those who know the older Tolstoy's general attitude toward courts, medicine, marriage, and even modern literature. The cult of art is jeered at, in small touches, only incidentally; it belongs, according to Tolstoy, to the falsities of modern civilization, alongside marriage (which merely hides bestial sensuality), and science (which merely hides rapacity and ignorance).

The story is deliberately deprived of any element of suspense, not only by the announcement contained in the title but by the technique of the cutback. We first hear of Iván Ilyich's death and see the reaction of the widow and friends, and only then listen to the story of his life. The detail, as always in Tolstoy, is superbly concrete and realistic: he does not shy away from the smell of disease, the physical necessity of using a chamber pot, or the sound of screaming. He can employ the creaking of a hassock as a recurrent motif to point out the comedy of hypocrisy played by the widow and her visitor. He can seriously and tragically use the humble image of a black sack or the illusion of the movement of a train.

But all this naturalistic detail serves the one purpose of making us come to realize, as Iván Ilyich realizes, that not only Caius is mortal but you and I also, and that the life of "civilized" people is a great lie simply because it disguises and ignores its dark background, the metaphysical abyss, the reality of Death. While the presentation of *The Death of Iván Ilyich* approaches, at moments, the tone of a legend or fable ("Iván Ilyich's life had been most simple and most ordinary and therefore most terrible"), Tolstoy in this story manages to stay within the concrete situation of his society and to combine the aesthetic method of realism with the universalizing power of symbolic art.

R. F. Christian, *Tolstoy: A Critical Introduction* (1969), is clear, instructive, and informative. E. B. Greenwood, *Tolstoy: The Comprehensive Vision* (1975), is helpful in placing *The Death of Iván Ilyich* in the perspective of Tolstoy's work as a whole. Some good analysis is found in H. Gifford, ed., *Leo Tolstoy: A Critical Anthology* (1971). Ralph E. Matlaw, *Tolstoy: A Collection of Critical Essays* (1967), and Philip Rahv, *Image and Idea* (1949), both present essays on *The Death of Iván Ilyich*. Theodore Redpath, *Tolstoy* (1960), provides a brief introduction with good criticism of ideas. Ernest J. Simmons, *Leo Tolstoy* (1946), and A. N. Wilson, *Tolstoy* (1988), are both excellent biographies. Rimvydas Silbajons, *Tolstoy's Aesthetics and His Art* (1991), includes accounts of reactions to the author at home and abroad as well as many substantial quotations.

PRONOUNCING GLOSSARY

The following list uses common English syllables and stress accents to provide rough equivalents of selected words whose pronunciation may be unfamiliar to the general reader.

Fëdor Petróvich: *fyo'-dor pet-ro'vich*

Fëdor Vasílievich: *fyo'-dor vas-eel'-ye-vich*

Gerásim: *jair-ah'-seem*

Golovín: *go-lo-veen'*

Iván Ilyich: *ee-van' il'-yich*

Ivánovich: *ee-van'-oh-vich*

Karenina: *kah-ren'-yina*

The Death of Iván Ilyich[1]

I

During an interval in the Melvínski trial in the large building of the Law Courts the members and public prosecutor met in Iván Egórovich Shébek's private room, where the conversation turned on the celebrated Krasóvski case. Fëdor Vasílievich warmly maintained that it was not subject to their jurisdiction, Iván Egórovich maintained the contrary, while Peter Ivánovich, not having entered into the discussion at the start, took no part in it but looked through the *Gazette* which had just been handed in.

"Gentlemen," he said, "Iván Ilyich has died!"

"You don't say!"

"Here read it yourself," replied Peter Ivánovich, handing Fëdor Vasílievich the paper still damp from the press. Surrounded by a black border were the words: "Praskóvya Fëdorovna Goloviná, with profound sorrow, informs relatives and friends of the demise of her beloved husband Iván Ilyich Golovín, Member of the Court of Justice, which occurred on February the 4th of this year 1882. The funeral will take place on Friday at one o'clock in the afternoon."

Iván Ilyich had been a colleague of the gentlemen present and was liked by them all. He had been ill for some weeks with an illness said to be incurable. His post had been kept open for him, but there had been conjectures that in case of his death Alexéev might receive his appointment, and that either Vínnikov or Shtábel would succeed Alexéev. So on receiving the news of Iván Ilyich's death the first thought of each of the gentlemen in that private room was of the changes and promotions it might occasion among themselves or their acquaintances.

"I shall be sure to get Shtábel's place or Vínnikov's," thought Fëdor Vasílievich. "I was promised that long ago, and the promotion means an extra eight hundred rubles a year for me besides the allowance."

"Now I must apply for my brother-in-law's transfer from Kalúga," thought Peter Ivánovich. "My wife will be very glad, and then she won't be able to say that I never do anything for her relations."

"I thought he would never leave his bed again," said Peter Ivánovich aloud. "It's very sad."

"But what really was the matter with him?"

"The doctors couldn't say—at least they could, but each of them said something different. When last I saw him I thought he was getting better."

"And I haven't been to see him since the holidays. I always meant to go."

"Had he any property?"

"I think his wife had a little—but something quite trifling."

"We shall have to go to see her, but they live so terribly far away."

"Far away from you, you mean. Everything's far away from your place."

"You see, he never can forgive my living on the other side of the river,"

1. Translated by Louise Maude and Aylmer Maude.

said Peter Ivánovich, smiling at Shébek. Then, still talking of the distances between different parts of the city, they returned to the Court.

Besides considerations as to the possible transfers and promotions likely to result from Iván Ilyich's death, the mere fact of the death of a near acquaintance aroused, as usual, in all who heard of it the complacent feeling that, "it is he who is dead and not I."

Each one thought or felt, "Well, he's dead but I'm alive!" But the more intimate of Iván Ilyich's acquaintances, his so-called friends, could not help thinking also that they would now have to fulfil the very tiresome demands of propriety by attending the funeral service and paying a visit of condolence to the widow.

Fëdor Vasílievich and Peter Ivánovich had been his nearest acquaintances. Peter Ivánovich had studied law with Iván Ilyich and had considered himself to be under obligations to him.

Having told his wife at dinner-time of Iván Ilyich's death, and of his conjecture that it might be possible to get her brother transferred to their circuit, Peter Ivánovich sacrificed his usual nap, put on his evening clothes, and drove to Iván Ilyich's house.

At the entrance stood a carriage and two cabs. Leaning against the wall in the hall downstairs near the cloak-stand was a coffin-lid covered with cloth of gold, ornamented with gold cord and tassels, that had been polished up with metal powder. Two ladies in black were taking off their fur cloaks. Peter Ivánovich recognized one of them as Iván Ilyich's sister, but the other was a stranger to him. His colleague Schwartz was just coming downstairs, but on seeing Peter Ivánovich enter he stopped and winked at him, as if to say: "Iván Ilyich has made a mess of things—not like you and me."

Schwartz's face with his Piccadilly whiskers, and his slim figure in evening dress, had as usual an air of elegant solemnity which contrasted with the playfulness of his character and had a special piquancy here, or so it seemed to Peter Ivánovich.

Peter Ivánovich allowed the ladies to precede him and slowly followed them upstairs. Schwartz did not come down but remained where he was, and Peter Ivánovich understood that he wanted to arrange where they should play bridge that evening. The ladies went upstairs to the widow's room, and Schwartz with seriously compressed lips but a playful look in his eyes, indicated by a twist of his eyebrows the room to the right where the body lay.

Peter Ivánovich, like everyone else on such occasions, entered feeling uncertain what he would have to do. All he knew was that at such times it is always safe to cross oneself. But he was not quite sure whether one should make obeisances while doing so. He therefore adopted a middle course. On entering the room he began crossing himself and made a slight movement resembling a bow. At the same time, as far as the motion of his head and arm allowed, he surveyed the room. Two young men—apparently nephews, one of whom was a high-school pupil—were leaving the room, crossing themselves as they did so. An old woman was standing motionless, and a lady with strangely arched eyebrows was saying something to her in a whisper. A vigorous, resolute Church Reader, in a frock-coat, was reading something in a loud voice with an expression that precluded any contradiction. The butler's assistant, Gerásim, stepping lightly in front of Peter Ivánovich, was strewing something on the floor. Noticing this, Peter Ivánovich was immediately aware of a faint odour of a decomposing body.

The last time he had called on Iván Ilyich, Peter Ivánovich had seen Gerásim in the study. Iván Ilyich had been particularly fond of him and he was performing the duty of a sick nurse.

Peter Ivánovich continued to make the sign of the cross slightly inclining his head in an intermediate direction between the coffin, the Reader, and the icons on the table in a corner of the room. Afterwards, when it seemed to him that this movement of his arm in crossing himself had gone on too long, he stopped and began to look at the corpse.

The dead man lay, as dead men always lie, in a specially heavy way, his rigid limbs sunk in the soft cushions of the coffin, with the head forever bowed on the pillow. His yellow waxen brow with bald patches over his sunken temples was thrust up in the way peculiar to the dead, the protruding nose seeming to press on the upper lip. He was much changed and had grown even thinner since Peter Ivánovich had last seen him, but, as is always the case with the dead, his face was handsomer and above all more dignified than when he was alive. The expression on the face said that what was necessary had been accomplished, and accomplished rightly. Besides this there was in that expression a reproach and a warning to the living. This warning seemed to Peter Ivánovich out of place, or at least not applicable to him. He felt a certain discomfort and so he hurriedly crossed himself once more and turned and went out of the door—too hurriedly and too regardless of propriety, as he himself was aware.

Schwartz was waiting for him in the adjoining room with legs spread wide apart and both hands toying with his top-hat behind his back. The mere sight of that playful, well-groomed, and elegant figure refreshed Peter Ivánovich. He felt that Schwartz was above all these happenings and could not surrender to any depressing influences. His very look said that this incident of a church service for Iván Ilyich could not be a sufficient reason for infringing the order of the session—in other words, that it would certainly not prevent his unwrapping a new pack of cards and shuffling them that evening while a footman placed four fresh candles on the table: in fact, that there was no reason for supposing that this incident would hinder their spending the evening agreeably. Indeed he said this in a whisper as Peter Ivánovich passed him, proposing that they should meet for a game at Fëdor Vasílievich's. But apparently Peter Ivánovich was not destined to play bridge that evening. Praskóvya Fëdorovna (a short, fat woman who despite all efforts to the contrary had continued to broaden steadily from her shoulders downwards and who had the same extraordinary arched eyebrows as the lady who had been standing by the coffin), dressed all in black, her head covered with lace, came out of her own room with some other ladies, conducted them to the room where the dead body lay, and said: "The service will begin immediately. Please go in."

Schwartz, making an indefinite bow, stood still, evidently neither accepting nor declining this invitation. Praskóvya Fëdorovna recognizing

Peter Ivánovich, sighed, went close up to him, took his hand, and said: "I know you were a true friend to Iván Ilyich . . ." and looked at him awaiting some suitable response. And Peter Ivánovich knew that, just as it had been the right thing to cross himself in that room, so what he had to do here was to press her hand, sigh, and say, "Believe me . . ." So he did all this and as he did it felt that the desired result had been achieved: that both he and she were touched.

"Come with me. I want to speak to you before it begins," said the widow. "Give me your arm."

Peter Ivánovich gave her his arm and they went to the inner rooms, passing Schwartz who winked at Peter Ivánovich compassionately.

"That does for our bridge! Don't object if we find another player. Perhaps you can cut in when you do escape," said his playful look.

Peter Ivánovich sighed still more deeply and despondently, and Praskó-vya Fëdorovna pressed his arm gratefully. When they reached the drawing-room, upholstered in pink cretonne and lighted by a dim lamp, they sat down at the table—she on a sofa and Peter Ivánovich on a low hassock, the springs of which yielded spasmodically under his weight. Praskóvya Fëdorovna had been on the point of warning him to take another seat, but felt that such a warning was out of keeping with her present condition and so changed her mind. As he sat down on the hassock Peter Ivánovich recalled how Iván Ilyich had arranged this room and had consulted him regarding this pink cretonne with green leaves. The whole room was full of furniture and knick-knacks, and on her way to the sofa the lace of the widow's black shawl caught on the carved edge of the table. Peter Ivánovich rose to detach it, and the springs of the hassock, relieved of his weight, rose also and gave him a push. The widow began detaching her shawl herself, and Peter Ivánovich again sat down, suppressing the rebellious springs of the hassock under him. But the widow had not quite freed herself and Peter Ivánovich got up again, and again the hassock rebelled and even creaked. When this was all over she took out a clean cambric handkerchief and began to weep. The episode with the shawl and the struggle with the hassock had cooled Peter Ivánovich's emotions and he sat there with a sullen look on his face. This awkward situation was interrupted by Sokolóv, Iván Ilyich's butler, who came to report that the plot in the cemetery that Praskóvya Fëdorovna had chosen would cost two hundred rubles. She stopped weeping and, looking at Peter Ivánovich with the air of a victim, remarked in French that it was very hard for her. Peter Ivánovich made a silent gesture signifying his full conviction that it must indeed be so.

"Please smoke," she said in a magnanimous yet crushed voice, and turned to discuss with Sokolóv the price of the plot for the grave.

Peter Ivánovich while lighting his cigarette heard her inquiring very circumstantially into the prices of different plots in the cemetery and finally decide which she would take. When that was done she gave instructions about engaging the choir. Sokolóv then left the room.

"I look after everything myself," she told Peter Ivánovich, shifting the albums that lay on the table; and noticing that the table was endangered by his cigarette-ash, she immediately passed him an ashtray, saying as she did so: "I consider it an affectation to say that my grief prevents my attending to practical affairs. On the contrary, if anything can—I won't say console me, but—distract me, it is seeing to everything concerning him." She again took out her handkerchief as if preparing to cry, but suddenly, as if mastering her feeling, she shook herself and began to speak calmly. "But there is something I want to talk to you about."

Peter Ivánovich bowed, keeping control of the springs of the hassock, which immediately began quivering under him.

"He suffered terribly the last few days."

"Did he?" said Peter Ivánovich.

"Oh, terribly! He screamed unceasingly, not for minutes but for hours. For the last three days he screamed incessantly. It was unendurable. I cannot understand how I bore it; you could hear him three rooms off. Oh, what I have suffered!"

"Is it possible that he was conscious all that time?" asked Peter Ivánovich.

"Yes," she whispered. "To the last moment. He took leave of us a quarter of an hour before he died, and asked us to take Vásya away."

The thought of the sufferings of this man he had known so intimately, first as a merry little boy, then as a school-mate, and later as a grown-up colleague, suddenly struck Peter Ivánovich with horror, despite an unpleasant consciousness of his own and this woman's dissimulation. He again saw that brow, and that nose pressing down on the lip, and felt afraid for himself.

"Three days of frightful suffering and then death! Why, that might suddenly, at any time, happen to me," he thought, and for a moment felt terrified. But—he did not himself know how—the customary reflection at once occurred to him that this had happened to Iván Ilyich and not to him, and that it should not and could not happen to him, and that to think that it could would be yielding to depression which he ought not to do, as Schwartz's expression plainly showed. After which reflection Peter Ivánovich felt reassured, and began to ask with interest about the details of Iván Ilyich's death, as though death was an accident natural to Iván Ilyich but certainly not to himself.

After many details of the really dreadful physical sufferings Iván Ilyich had endured (which details he learnt only from the effect those sufferings had produced on Praskóvya Fëdorovna's nerves) the widow apparently found it necessary to get to business.

"Oh, Peter Ivánovich, how hard it is! How terribly, terribly hard!" and she again began to weep.

Peter Ivánovich sighed and waited for her to finish blowing her nose. When she had done so he said, "Believe me . . ." and she again began talking and brought out what was evidently her chief concern with him—namely, to question him as to how she could obtain a grant of money from the government on the occasion of her husband's death. She made it appear that she was asking Peter Ivánovich's advice about her pension, but he soon saw that she already knew about that to the minutest detail, more even than he did himself. She knew how much could be got out of the government in consequence of her husband's death, but wanted to find out whether she could possibly extract something more. Peter Ivánovich tried to think of some means of doing so, but after reflecting for a while and, out of propriety, condemning the government for its niggardliness, he said he thought that nothing more could be got. Then she sighed and evidently began to devise means of getting rid of her visitor. Noticing this, he put out his cigarette, rose, pressed her hand, and went out into the anteroom.

In the dining-room where the clock stood that Iván Ilyich had liked so much and had bought at an antique shop, Peter Ivánovich met a priest and a few acquaintances who had come to attend the service, and he recognized Iván Ilyich's daughter, a handsome young woman. She was in black and her slim figure appeared slimmer than ever. She had a gloomy, determined, almost angry expression, and bowed to Peter Ivánovich as though he were in some way to blame. Behind her, with the same offended look, stood a wealthy young man, an examining magistrate, whom Peter Ivánovich also knew and who was her fiancé, as he had heard. He bowed mournfully to them and was about to pass into the death-chamber, when from under the stairs appeared the figure of Iván Ilyich's schoolboy son, who was extremely like this father. He seemed a little Iván Ilyich, such as Peter Ivánovich remembered when they studied law together. His tear-stained eyes had in them the look that is seen in the eyes of boys of thirteen or fourteen who are not pure-minded.

When he saw Peter Ivánovich he scowled morosely and shamefacedly. Peter Ivánovich nodded to him and entered the death-chamber. The service began: candles, groans, incense, tears, and sobs. Peter Ivánovich stood looking gloomily down at his feet. He did not look once at the dead man, did not yield to any depressing influence, and was one of the first to leave the room. There was no one in the anteroom, but Gerásim darted out of the dead man's room, rummaged with his strong hands among the fur coats to find Peter Ivánovich's and helped him on with it.

"Well, friend Gerásim," said Peter Ivánovich, so as to say something. "It's a sad affair, isn't it?"

"It's God's will. We shall all come to it some day," said Gerásim, displaying his teeth—the even, white teeth of a healthy peasant—and, like a man in the thick of urgent work, he briskly opened the front door, called the coachman, helped Peter Ivánovich into the sledge, and sprang back to the porch as if in readiness for what he had to do next.

Peter Ivánovich found the fresh air particularly pleasant after the smell of incense, the dead body, and carbolic acid.

"Where to, sir?" asked the coachman.

"It's not too late even now. . . . I'll call round on Fëdor Vasílievich."

He accordingly drove there and found them just finishing the first rubber, so that it was quite convenient for him to cut in.

II

Iván Ilyich's life had been most simple and most ordinary and therefore most terrible.

He had been a member of the Court of Justice, and died at the age of

forty-five. His father had been an official who after serving in various ministries and departments in Petersburg had made the sort of career which
brings men to positions from which by reason of their long service they
cannot be dismissed, though they are obviously unfit to hold any responsible position, and for whom therefore posts are specially created, which
though fictitious, carry salaries of from six to ten thousand rubles that are
not fictitious, and in receipt of which they live on to a great age.

Such was the Privy Councillor and superfluous member of various
superfluous institutions, Ilya Efímovich Golovín.

He had three sons, of whom Iván Ilyich was the second. The eldest son
was following in his father's footsteps only in another department, and was
already approaching that stage in the service at which a similar sinecure
would be reached. The third son was a failure. He had ruined his prospects in a number of positions and was now serving in the railway department. His father and brothers, and still more their wives, not merely
disliked meeting him, but avoided remembering his existence unless compelled to do so. His sister had married Baron Greff, a Petersburg official
of her father's type. Iván Ilyich was *le phénix de la famille*[2] as people said.
He was neither as cold and formal as his elder brother nor as wild as the
younger, but was a happy mean between them—an intelligent, polished,
lively and agreeable man. He had studied with his younger brother at the
School of Law, but the latter had failed to complete the course and was
expelled when he was in the fifth class. Iván Ilyich finished the course
well. Even when he was at the School of Law he was just what he
remained for the rest of his life: a capable, cheerful, good-natured, and
sociable man, though strict in the fulfilment of what he considered to be
his duty: and he considered his duty to be what was so considered by those
in authority. Neither as a boy nor as a man was he a toady, but from early
youth was by nature attracted to people of high station as a fly is drawn to
the light, assimilating their ways and views of life and establishing friendly
relations with them. All the enthusiasms of childhood and youth passed
without leaving much trace on him; he succumbed to sensuality, to vanity,
and latterly among the highest classes to liberalism, but always within limits which his instinct unfailingly indicated to him as correct.

At school he had done things which had formerly seemed to him very
horrid and made him feel disgusted with himself when he did them; but
when later on he saw that such actions were done by people of good
position and that they did not regard them as wrong, he was able not
exactly to regard them as right, but to forget about them entirely or not be
at all troubled at remembering them.

Having graduated from the School of Law and qualified for the tenth
rank of the civil service, and having received money from his father for
his equipment, Iván Ilyich ordered himself clothes at Scharmer's, the fashionable tailor, hung a medallion inscribed *respice finem*[3] on his watch-
chain, took leave of his professor and the prince who was patron of the
school, had a farewell dinner with his comrades at Donon's first-class res-

---

2. The phoenix of the family (French). The word *phoenix* is used here to mean "rare bird," "prodigy."
3. Regard the end (a Latin motto).

taurant, and with his new and fashionable portmanteau, linen, clothes, shaving and other toilet appliances, and a travelling rug, all purchased at the best shops, he set off for one of the provinces where, through his father's influence, he had been attached to the governor as an official for special service.

In the province Iván Ilyich soon arranged as easy and agreeable a position for himself as he had at the School of Law. He performed his official tasks, made his career, and at the same time amused himself pleasantly and decorously. Occasionally he paid official visits to country districts, where he behaved with dignity both to his superiors and inferiors, and performed the duties entrusted to him, which related chiefly to the sectarians,[4] with an exactness and incorruptible honesty of which he could not but feel proud.

In official matters, despite his youth and taste for frivolous gaiety, he was exceedingly reserved, punctilious, and even severe; but in society he was often amusing and witty, and always good-natured, correct in his manner, and *bon enfant*, as the governor and his wife—with whom he was like one of the family—used to say of him.

In the province he had an affair with a lady who made advances to the elegant young lawyer, and there was also a milliner; and there were carousals with aides-de-camp who visited the district, and after-supper visits to a certain outlying street of doubtful reputation; and there was too some obsequiousness to his chief and even to his chief's wife, but all this was done with such a tone of good breeding that no hard names could be applied to it. It all came under the heading of the French saying: *"Il faut que jeunesse se passe."*[5] It was all done with clean hands, in clean linen, with French phrases, and above all among people of the best society and consequently with the approval of people of rank.

So Iván Ilyich served for five years and then came a change in his official life. The new and reformed judicial institutions were introduced, and new men were needed. Iván Ilyich became such a new man. He was offered the post of Examining Magistrate, and he accepted it though the post was in another province and obliged him to give up the connexions he had formed and to make new ones. His friends met to give him a send-off; they had a group-photograph taken and presented him with a silver cigarette-case, and he set off to his new post.

As examining magistrate Iván Ilyich was just as *comme il faut* and decorous a man, inspiring general respect and capable of separating his official duties from his private life, as he had been when acting as an official on special service. His duties now as examining magistrate were far more interesting and attractive than before. In his former position it had been pleasant to wear an undress uniform made by Scharmer, and to pass through the crowd of petitioners and officials who were timorously awaiting an audience with the governor, and who envied him as with free and easy gait he went straight into his chief's private room to have a cup of tea and a cigarette with him. But not many people had then been directly

4. The Old Believers, a large group of Russians (about twenty-five million in 1900), members of a sect that originated in a break with the Orthodox Church in the 17th century; they were subject to many legal restrictions.   5. Youth must have its fling [Translator's note].

dependent on him—only police officials and the sectarians when he went on special missions—and he liked to treat them politely, almost as comrades, as if he were letting them feel that he who had the power to crush them was treating them in this simple, friendly way. There were then but few such people. But now, as an examining magistrate, Iván Ilyich felt that everyone without exception, even the most important and self-satisfied, was in his power, and that he need only write a few words on a sheet of paper with a certain heading, and this or that important, self-satisfied person would be brought before him in the role of an accused person or a witness, and if he did not choose to allow him to sit down, would have to stand before him and answer his questions. Iván Ilyich never abused his power; he tried on the contrary to soften its expression, but the consciousness of it and of the possibility of softening its effect, supplied the chief interest and attraction of his office. In his work itself, especially in his examinations, he very soon acquired a method of eliminating all considerations irrelevant to the legal aspect of the case, and reducing even the most complicated case to a form in which it would be presented on paper only in its externals, completely excluding his personal opinion of the matter, while above all observing every prescribed formality. The work was new and Iván Ilyich was one of the first men to apply the new Code of 1864.[6]

On taking up the post of examining magistrate in a new town, he made new acquaintances and connexions, placed himself on a new footing, and assumed a somewhat different tone. He took up an attitude of rather dignified aloofness towards the provincial authorities, but picked out the best circle of legal gentlemen and wealthy gentry living in the town and assumed a tone of slight dissatisfaction with the government, of moderate liberalism, and of enlightened citizenship. At the same time, without at all altering the elegance of his toilet, he ceased shaving his chin and allowed his beard to grow as it pleased.

Iván Ilyich settled down very pleasantly in this new town. The society there, which inclined towards opposition to the governor, was friendly, his salary was larger, and he began to play *vint* [a form of bridge], which he found added not a little to the pleasure of life, for he had a capacity for cards, played good-humouredly, and calculated rapidly and astutely, so that he usually won.

After living there for two years he met his future wife, Praskóvya Fëdorovna Míkhel, who was the most attractive, clever, and brilliant girl of the set in which he moved, and among other amusements and relaxations from his labours as examining magistrate, Iván Ilyich established light and playful relations with her.

While he had been an official on special service he had been accustomed to dance, but now as an examining magistrate it was exceptional for him to do so. If he danced now, he did it as if to show that though he served under the reformed order of things, and had reached the fifth official rank, yet when it came to dancing he could do it better than most

6. The emancipation of the serfs in 1861 was followed by a thorough all-round reform of judicial proceedings [Translator's note].

people. So at the end of an evening he sometimes danced with Praskóvya Fëdorovna, and it was chiefly during these dances that he captivated her. She fell in love with him. Iván Ilyich had at first no definite intention of marrying, but when the girl fell in love with him he said to himself: "Really, why shouldn't I marry?"

Praskóvya Fëdorovna came of a good family, was not bad looking, and had some little property. Iván Ilyich might have aspired to a more brilliant match, but even this was good. He had his salary, and she, he hoped, would have an equal income. She was well connected, and was a sweet, pretty, and thoroughly correct young woman. To say that Iván Ilyich married because he fell in love with Praskóvya Fëdorovna and found that she sympathized with his views of life would be as incorrect as to say that he married because his social circle approved of the match. He was swayed by both these considerations: the marriage gave him personal satisfaction, and at the same time it was considered the right thing by the most highly placed of his associates.

So Iván Ilyich got married.

The preparations for marriage and the beginning of married life, with its conjugal caresses, the new furniture, new crockery, and new linen, were very pleasant until his wife became pregnant—so that Iván Ilyich had begun to think that marriage would not impair the easy, agreeable, gay, and always decorous character of his life, approved of by society and regarded by himself as natural, but would even improve it. But from the first months of his wife's pregnancy, something new, unpleasant, depressing, and unseemly, and from which there was no way of escape, unexpectedly showed itself.

His wife, without any reason—*de gaieté de coeur*[7] as Iván Ilyich expressed it to himself—began to disturb the pleasure and propriety of their life. She began to be jealous without any cause, expected him to devote his whole attention to her, found fault with everything, and made coarse and ill-mannered scenes.

At first Iván Ilyich hoped to escape from the unpleasantness of this state of affairs by the same easy and decorous relation to life that had served him heretofore: he tried to ignore his wife's disagreeable moods, continued to live in his usual easy and pleasant way, invited friends to his house for a game of cards, and also tried going out to his club or spending his evenings with friends. But one day his wife began upbraiding him so vigorously, using such coarse words, and continued to abuse him every time he did not fulfil her demands, so resolutely and with such evident determination not to give way till he submitted—that is, till he stayed at home and was bored just as she was—that he became alarmed. He now realized that matrimony—at any rate with Praskóvya Fëdorovna—was not always conducive to the pleasures and amenities of life, but on the contrary often infringed both comfort and propriety, and that he must therefore entrench himself against such infringement. And Iván Ilyich began to seek for means of doing so. His official duties were the one thing that imposed upon Praskóvya Fëdorovna, and by means of his official work and the

---

7. From sheer animal spirits (French).

duties attached to it he began struggling with his wife to secure his own independence.

With the birth of their child, the attempts to feed it and the various failures in doing so, and with the real and imaginary illnesses of mother and child, in which Iván Ilyich's sympathy was demanded but about which he understood nothing, the need of securing for himself an existence outside his family life became still more imperative.

As his wife grew more irritable and exacting and Iván Ilyich transferred the centre of gravity of his life more and more to his official work, so did he grow to like his work better and became more ambitious than before.

Very soon, within a year of his wedding, Iván Ilyich had realized that marriage, though it may add some comforts to life, is in fact a very intricate and difficult affair towards which in order to perform one's duty, that is, to lead a decorous life approved of by society, one must adopt a definite attitude just as towards one's official duties.

And Iván Ilyich evolved such an attitude towards married life. He only required of it those conveniences—dinner at home, housewife, and bed—which it could give him, and above all that propriety of external forms required by public opinion. For the rest he looked for light-hearted pleasure and propriety, and was very thankful when he found them, but if he met with antagonism and querulousness he at once retired into his separate fenced-off world of official duties, where he found satisfaction.

Iván Ilyich was esteemed a good official, and after three years was made Assistant Public Prosecutor. His new duties, their importance, the possibility of indicting and imprisoning anyone he chose, the publicity his speeches received, and the success he had in all these things, made his work still more attractive.

More children came. His wife became more and more querulous and ill-tempered, but the attitude Iván Ilyich had adopted towards his home life rendered him almost impervious to her grumbling.

After seven years' service in that town he was transferred to another province as Public Prosecutor. They moved, but were short of money and his wife did not like the place they moved to. Though the salary was higher the cost of living was greater, besides which two of their children died and family life became still more unpleasant for him.

Praskóvya Fëdorovna blamed her husband for every inconvenience they encountered in their new home. Most of the conversations between husband and wife, especially as to the children's education, led to topics which recalled former disputes, and those disputes were apt to flare up again at any moment. There remained only those rare periods of amorousness which still came to them at times but did not last long. These were islets at which they anchored for a while and then again set out upon that ocean of veiled hostility which showed itself in their aloofness from one another. This aloofness might have grieved Iván Ilyich had he considered that it ought not to exist, but he now regarded the position as normal, and even made it the goal at which he aimed in family life. His aim was to free himself more and more from those unpleasantnesses and to give them a semblance of harmlessness and propriety. He attained this by spending less and less time with his family, and when obliged to be at home he tried to safeguard his position by the presence of outsiders. The chief thing however was that he had his official duties. The whole interest of his life now centered in the official world and that interest absorbed him. The consciousness of his power, being able to ruin anybody he wished to ruin, the importance, even the external dignity of his entry into court, or meetings with his subordinates, his success with superiors and inferiors, and above all his masterly handling of cases, of which he was conscious—all this gave him pleasure and filled his life, together with chats with his colleagues, dinners, and bridge. So that on the whole Iván Ilyich's life continued to flow as he considered it should do—pleasantly and properly.

So things continued for another seven years. His eldest daughter was already sixteen, another child had died, and only one son was left, a schoolboy and a subject of dissensions. Iván Ilyich wanted to put him in the School of Law, but to spite him Praskóvya Fëdorovna entered him at the High School. The daughter had been educated at home and had turned out well: the boy did not learn badly either.

III

So Iván Ilyich lived for seventeen years after his marriage. He was already a Public Prosecutor of long standing, and had declined several proposed transfers while awaiting a more desirable post, when an unanticipated and unpleasant occurrence quite upset the peaceful course of his life. He was expecting to be offered the post of presiding judge in a University town, but Hoppe somehow came to the front and obtained the appointment instead. Iván Ilyich became irritable, reproached Hoppe, and quarrelled both with him and with his immediate superiors—who became colder to him and again passed him over when other appointments were made.

This was in 1880, the hardest year of Iván Ilyich's life. It was then that it became evident on the one hand that his salary was insufficient for them to live on, and on the other that he had been forgotten, and not only this, but that what was for him the greatest and most cruel injustice appeared to others a quite ordinary occurrence. Even his father did not consider it his duty to help him. Iván Ilyich felt himself abandoned by everyone, and that they regarded his position with a salary of 3,500 rubles as quite normal and even fortunate. He alone knew that with the consciousness of the injustices done him, with his wife's incessant nagging, and with the debts he had contracted by living beyond his means his position was far from normal.

In order to save money that summer he obtained leave of absence and went with his wife to live in the country at her brother's place.

In the country, without his work, he experienced *ennui* for the first time in his life, and not only *ennui* but intolerable depression, and he decided that it was impossible to go on living like that, and that it was necessary to take energetic measures.

Having passed a sleepless night pacing up and down the veranda, he decided to go to Petersburg and bestir himself, in order to punish those who had failed to appreciate him and to get transferred to another ministry.

Next day, despite many protests from his wife and her brother, he started for Petersburg with the sole object of obtaining a post with a salary of five thousand rubles a year. He was no longer bent on any particular department, or tendency, or kind of activity. All he now wanted was an appointment to another post with a salary of five thousand rubles, either in the administration, in the banks, with the railways, in one of the Empress Márya's Institutions,[8] or even in the customs—but it had to carry with it a salary of five thousand rubles and be in a ministry other than that in which they had failed to appreciate him.

And this quest of Iván Ilyich's was crowned with remarkable and unexpected success. At Kursk an acquaintance of his, F. I. Ilyín, got into the first-class carriage, sat down beside Iván Ilyich, and told him of a telegram just received by the governor of Kursk announcing that a change was about to take place in the ministry: Peter Ivánovich was to be superseded by Iván Semënovich.

The proposed change, apart from its significance for Russia, had a special significance for Iván Ilyich, because by bringing forward a new man, Peter Petróvich, and consequently his friend Zachár Ivánovich, it was highly favourable for Iván Ilyich, since Zachár Ivánovich was a friend and colleague of his.

In Moscow his news was confirmed, and on reaching Petersburg Iván Ilyich found Zachár Ivánovich and received a definite promise of an appointment in his former department of Justice.

A week later he telegraphed to his wife: "Zachár in Miller's place. I shall receive appointment on presentation of report."

Thanks to this change of personnel, Iván Ilyich had unexpectedly obtained an appointment in his former ministry which placed him two stages above his former colleagues besides giving him five thousand rubles salary and three thousand five hundred rubles for expenses connected with his removal. All his ill humour towards his former enemies and the whole department vanished, and Iván Ilyich was completely happy.

He returned to the country more cheerful and contented than he had been for a long time. Praskóvya Fëdorovna also cheered up and a truce was arranged between them. Iván Ilyich told of how he had been fêted by everybody in Petersburg, how all those who had been his enemies were put to shame and now fawned on him, how envious they were of his appointment, and how much everybody in Petersburg had liked him.

Praskóvya Fëdorovna listened to all this and appeared to believe it. She did not contradict anything, but only made plans for their life in the town to which they were going. Iván Ilyich saw with delight that these plans were his plans, that he and his wife agreed, and that, after a stumble, his life was regaining its due and natural character of pleasant lightheartedness and decorum.

8. Reference to the charitable organization founded by the Empress Márya, wife of Paul I, late in the 18th century.

Iván Ilyich had come back for a short time only, for he had to take up his new duties on the 10th of September. Moreover, he needed time to settle into the new place, to move all his belongings from the province, and to buy and order many additional things: in a word, to make such arrangements as he had resolved on, which were almost exactly what Praskóvya Fëdorovna too had decided on.

Now that everything had happened so fortunately, and that he and his wife were at one in their aims and moreover saw so little of one another they got on together better than they had done since the first years of marriage. Iván Ilyich had thought of taking his family away with him at once, but the insistence of his wife's brother and her sister-in-law, who had suddenly become particularly amiable and friendly to him and his family, induced him to depart alone.

So he departed, and the cheerful state of mind induced by his success and by the harmony between his wife and himself, the one intensifying the other, did not leave him. He found a delightful house, just the thing both he and his wife had dreamt of. Spacious, lofty reception rooms in the old style, a convenient and dignified study, rooms for his wife and daughter, a study for his son—it might have been specially built for them. Iván Ilyich himself superintended the arrangements, chose the wallpapers, supplemented the furniture (preferably with antiques which he considered particularly *comme il faut*), and supervised the upholstering. Everything progressed and progressed and approached the ideal he had set himself: even when things were only half completed they exceeded his expectations. He saw what a refined and elegant character, free from vulgarity, it would all have when it was ready. On falling asleep he pictured to himself how the reception-room would look. Looking at the yet unfinished drawing-room he could see the fireplace, the screen, the what-not, the little chairs dotted here and there, the dishes and plates on the walls, and the bronzes, as they would be when everything was in place. He was pleased by the thought of how his wife and daughter, who shared his taste in this matter, would be impressed by it. They were certainly not expecting as much. He had been particularly successful in finding, and buying cheaply, antiques which gave a particularly aristocratic character to the whole place. But in his letters he intentionally understated everything in order to be able to surprise them. All this so absorbed him that his new duties—though he liked his official work—interested him less than he had expected. Sometimes he even had moments of absent-mindedness during the Court Sessions, and would consider whether he should have straight or curved cornices for his curtains. He was so interested in it all that he often did things himself, rearranging the furniture, or rehanging the curtains. Once when mounting a step-ladder to show the upholsterer, who did not understand, how he wanted the hangings draped, he made a false step and slipped, but being a strong and agile man he clung on and only knocked his side against the knob of the window frame. The bruised place was painful but the pain soon passed, and he felt particularly bright and well just then. He wrote: "I feel fifteen years younger." He thought he would have everything ready by September, but it dragged on till mid-

October. But the result was charming not only in his eyes but to everyone who saw it.

In reality it was just what is usually seen in the houses of people of moderate means who want to appear rich, and therefore succeed only in resembling others like themselves: there were damasks, dark wood, plants, rugs, and dull and polished bronzes—all the things people of a certain class have in order to resemble other people of that class. His house was so like the others that it would never have been noticed, but to him it all seemed to be quite exceptional. He was very happy when he met his family at the station and brought them to the newly furnished house all lit up, where a footman in a white tie opened the door into the hall decorated with plants, and when they went on into the drawing room and the study uttering exclamations of delight. He conducted them everywhere, drank in their praises eagerly, and beamed with pleasure. At tea that evening, when Praskóvya Fëdorovna among other things asked him about his fall, he laughed, and showed them how he had gone flying and had frightened the upholsterer.

"It's a good thing I'm a bit of an athlete. Another man might have been killed, but I merely knocked myself, just here; it hurts when it's touched, but it's passing off already—it's only a bruise."

So they began living in their new home—in which, as always happens, when they got thoroughly settled in they found they were just one room short—and with the increased income, which as always was just a little (some five hundred rubles) too little, but it was all very nice.

Things went particularly well at first, before everything was finally arranged and while something had still to be done: this thing bought, that thing ordered, another thing moved, and something else adjusted. Though there were some disputes between husband and wife, they were both so well satisfied and had so much to do that it all passed off without any serious quarrels. When nothing was left to arrange it became rather dull and something seemed to be lacking, but they were then making acquaintances, forming habits, and life was growing fuller.

Iván Ilyich spent his mornings at the law court and came home to dinner, and at first he was generally in a good humour, though he occasionally became irritable just on account of his house. (Every spot on the tablecloth or the upholstery, and every broken window-blind string, irritated him. He had devoted so much trouble to arranging it all that every disturbance of it distressed him.) But on the whole his life ran its course as he believed life should do: easily, pleasantly, and decorously.

He got up at nine, drank his coffee, read the paper, and then put on his undress uniform and went to the law courts. There the harness in which he worked had already been stretched to fit him and he donned it without a hitch: petitioners, inquiries at the chancery, the chancery itself, and the sittings public and administrative. In all this the thing was to exclude everything fresh and vital, which always disturbs the regular course of official business, and to admit only official relations with people, and then only on official grounds. A man would come, for instance, wanting some information. Iván Ilyich, as one in whose sphere the matter did not lie, would have nothing to do with him: but if the man had some business with him in his official capacity, something that could be expressed on officially stamped paper, he would do everything, positively everything he could within the limits of such relations, and in doing so would maintain the semblance of friendly human relations, that is, would observe the courtesies of life. As soon as the official relations ended, so did everything else. Iván Ilyich possessed this capacity to separate his real life from the official side of affairs and not mix the two, in the highest degree, and by long practice and natural aptitude had brought it to such a pitch that sometimes, in the manner of a virtuoso, he would even allow himself to let the human and official relations mingle. He let himself do this just because he felt that he could at any time he chose resume the strictly official attitude again and drop the human relation. And he did it all easily, pleasantly, correctly, and even artistically. In the intervals between the sessions he smoked, drank tea, chatted a little about politics, a little about general topics, a little about cards, but most of all about official appointments. Tired, but with the feelings of a virtuoso—one of the first violins who has played his part in an orchestra with precision—he would return home to find that his wife and daughter had been out paying calls, or had a visitor, and that his son had been to school, had done his homework with his tutor, and was duly learning what is taught at High Schools. Everything was as it should be. After dinner, if they had no visitors, Iván Ilyich sometimes read a book that was being much discussed at the time, and in the evening settled down to work, that is, read official papers, compared the depositions of witnesses, and noted paragraphs of the Code applying to them. This was neither dull nor amusing. It was dull when he might have been playing bridge, but if no bridge was available it was at any rate better than doing nothing or sitting with his wife. Iván Ilyich's chief pleasure was giving little dinners to which he invited men and women of good social position, and just as his drawing-room resembled all other drawing-rooms so did his enjoyable little parties resemble all other such parties.

Once they even gave a dance. Iván Ilyich enjoyed it and everything went off well, except that it led to a violent quarrel with his wife about the cakes and sweets. Praskóvya Fëdorovna had made her own plans, but Iván Ilyich insisted on getting everything from an expensive confectioner and ordered too many cakes, and the quarrel occurred because some of those cakes were left over and the confectioner's bill came to forty-five rubles. It was a great and disagreeable quarrel. Praskóvya Fëdorovna called him "a fool and an imbecile," and he clutched at his head and made angry allusions to divorce.

But the dance itself had been enjoyable. The best people were there, and Iván Ilyich had danced with Princess Trúfonova, a sister of the distinguished founder of the Society "Bear my Burden."

The pleasures connected with his work were pleasures of ambition; his social pleasures were those of vanity; but Iván Ilyich's greatest pleasure was playing bridge. He acknowledged that whatever disagreeable incident happened in his life, the pleasure that beamed like a ray of light above everything else was to sit down to bridge with good players, not noisy partners, and of course to four-handed bridge (with five players it was annoying to have to stand out, though one pretended not to mind), to play a clever and serious game (when the cards allowed it) and then to have supper and drink a glass of wine. After a game of bridge, especially if he had won a little (to win a large sum was unpleasant), Iván Ilyich went to bed in specially good humour.

So they lived. They formed a circle of acquaintances among the best people and were visited by people of importance and by young folk. In their views as to their acquaintances, husband, wife, and daughter were entirely agreed, and tacitly and unanimously kept at arm's length and shook off the various shabby friends and relations who, with much show of affection, gushed into the drawing-room with its Japanese plates on the walls. Soon these shabby friends ceased to obtrude themselves and only the best people remained in the Golovíns' set.

Young men made up to Lisa, and Petríshchev, an examining magistrate and Dmítri Ivánovich Petríshchchev's son and sole heir, began to be so attentive to her that Iván Ilyich had already spoken to Praskóvya Fëdorovna about it, and considered whether they should not arrange a party for them, or get up some private theatricals.

So they lived, and all went well, without change, and life flowed pleasantly.

IV

They were all in good health. It could not be called ill health if Iván Ilyich sometimes said that he had a queer taste in his mouth and felt some discomfort in his left side.

But this discomfort increased and, though not exactly painful, grew into a sense of pressure in his side accompanied by ill humour. And his irritability became worse and worse and began to mar the agreeable, easy, and correct life that had established itself in the Golovín family. Quarrels between husband and wife became more and more frequent, and soon the ease and amenity disappeared and even the decorum was barely maintained. Scenes again became frequent, and very few of those islets remained on which husband and wife could meet without an explosion. Praskóvya Fëdorovna now had good reason to say that her husband's temper was trying. With characteristic exaggeration she said he had always had a dreadful temper, and that it had needed all her good nature to put up with it for twenty years. It was true that now the quarrels were started by him. His bursts of temper always came just before dinner, often just as he began to eat his soup. Sometimes he noticed that a plate or dish was chipped, or the food was not right, or his son put his elbow on the table, or his daughter's hair was not done as he liked it, and for all this he blamed Praskóvya Fëdorovna. At first she retorted and said disagreeable things to him, but once or twice he fell into such a rage at the beginning of dinner that she realized it was due to some physical derangement brought on by taking food, and so she restrained herself and did not answer, but only hurried to get the dinner over. She regarded this self-restraint as highly praiseworthy. Having come to the conclusion that her husband had a dreadful temper and made her life miserable, she began to feel sorry for herself, and the more she pitied herself the more she hated her husband. She began to wish he would die; yet she did not want him to die because then his salary would cease. And this irritated her against him still more. She considered herself dreadfully unhappy just because not even his death could save her, and though she concealed her exasperation, that hidden exasperation of hers increased his irritation also.

After one scene in which Iván Ilyich had been particularly unfair and after which he had said in explanation that he certainly was irritable but that it was due to his not being well, she said that if he was ill it should be attended to, and insisted on his going to see a celebrated doctor.

He went. Everything took place as he had expected and as it always does. There was the usual waiting and the important air assumed by the doctor, with which he was so familiar (resembling that which he himself assumed in court), and the sounding and listening, and the questions which called for answers that were foregone conclusions and were evidently unnecessary, and the look of importance which implied that "if only you put yourself in our hands we will arrange everything—we know indubitably how it has to be done, always in the same way for everybody alike." It was all just as it was in the law courts. The doctor put on just the same air towards him as he himself put on towards an accused person.

The doctor said that so-and-so indicated that there was so-and-so inside the patient, but if the investigation of so-and-so did not confirm this, then he must assume that and that. If he assumed that and that, then . . . and so on. To Iván Ilyich only one question was important: was his case serious or not? But the doctor ignored that inappropriate question. From his point of view it was not the one under consideration, the real question was to decide between a floating kidney, chronic catarrh, or appendicitis. It was not a question of Iván Ilyich's life or death, but one between a floating kidney and appendicitis. And that question the doctor solved brilliantly, as it seemed to Iván Ilyich, in favour of the appendix, with the reservation that should an examination of the urine give fresh indications the matter would be reconsidered. All this was just what Iván Ilyich had himself brilliantly accomplished a thousand times in dealing with men on trial. The doctor summed up just as brilliantly, looking over his spectacles triumphantly and even gaily at the accused. From the doctor's summing up Iván Ilyich concluded that things were bad, but that for the doctor, and perhaps for everybody else, it was a matter of indifference, though for him it was bad. And this conclusion struck him painfully, arousing in him a great feeling of pity for himself and of bitterness towards the doctor's indifference to a matter of such importance.

He said nothing of this, but rose, placed the doctor's fee on the table, and remarked with a sigh: "We sick people probably often put inappropriate questions. But tell me, in general, is this complaint dangerous or not? . . ."

The doctor looked at him sternly over his spectacles with one eye, as if to say: "Prisoner, if you will not keep to the questions put to you, I shall be obliged to have you removed from the court."

"I have already told you what I consider necessary and proper. The analysis may show something more." And the doctor bowed.

Iván Ilyich went out slowly, seated himself disconsolately in his sledge, and drove home. All the way home he was going over what the doctor had said, trying to translate those complicated, obscure, scientific phrases into plain language and find in them an answer to the question: "Is my condition bad? Is it very bad? Or is there as yet nothing much wrong?" And it seemed to him that the meaning of what the doctor had said was it was very bad. Everything in the streets seemed depressing. The cabmen, the houses, the passers-by, and the shops, were dismal. His ache, this dull gnawing ache that never ceased for a moment, seemed to have acquired a new and more serious significance from the doctor's dubious remarks. Iván Ilyich now watched it with a new and oppressive feeling.

He reached home and began to tell his wife about it. She listened, but in the middle of his account his daughter came in with her hat on, ready to go out with her mother. She sat down reluctantly to listen to this tedious story, but could not stand it long, and her mother too did not hear him to the end.

"Well, I am very glad," she said. "Mind now to take your medicine regularly. Give me the prescription and I'll send Gerásim to the chemist's." And she went to get ready to go out.

While she was in the room Iván Ilyich had hardly taken time to breathe, but he sighed deeply when she left it.

"Well," he thought, "perhaps it isn't so bad after all."

He began taking his medicine and following the doctor's directions, which had been altered after the examination of the urine. But then it happened that there was a contradiction between the indications drawn from the examination of the urine and the symptoms that showed themselves. It turned out that what was happening differed from what the doctor had told him, and that he had either forgotten, or blundered, or hidden something from him. He could not, however, be blamed for that, and Iván Ilyich still obeyed his orders implicitly and at first derived some comfort from doing so.

From the time of his visit to the doctor, Iván Ilyich's chief occupation was the exact fulfilment of the doctor's instructions regarding hygiene and the taking of medicine, and the observation of his pain and his excretions. His chief interests came to be people's ailments and people's health. When sickness, deaths, or recoveries were mentioned in his presence, especially when the illness resembled his own, he listened with agitation which he tried to hide, asked questions, and applied what he heard to his own case.

The pain did not grow less, but Iván Ilyich made efforts to force himself to think that he was better. And he could do this so long as nothing agitated him. But as soon as he had any unpleasantness with his wife, any lack of success in his official work, or held bad cards at bridge, he was at once acutely sensible of his disease. He had formerly borne such mischances, hoping soon to adjust what was wrong, to master it and attain success, or make a grand slam. But now every mischance upset him and plunged him into despair. He would say to himself. "There now, just as I was beginning to get better and the medicine had begun to take effect, comes this accursed misfortune, or unpleasantness . . ." And he was furious with the mishap, or with the people who were causing the unpleasantness and killing him, for he felt that this fury was killing him but could not restrain it. One would have thought that it should have been clear to him that this exasperation with circumstances and people aggravated his illness, and that he ought therefore to ignore unpleasant occurrences. But he drew the very opposite conclusion: he said that he needed peace, and he watched for everything that might disturb it and became irritable at the slightest infringement of it. His condition was rendered worse by the fact that he read medical books and consulted doctors. The progress of his disease was so gradual that he could deceive himself when comparing one day with another—the difference was so slight. But when he consulted the doctors it seemed to him that he was getting worse, and even very rapidly. Yet despite this he was continually consulting them.

That month he went to see another celebrity, who told him almost the same as the first had done but put his questions rather differently, and the interview with this celebrity only increased Iván Ilyich's doubts and fears. A friend of a friend of his, a very good doctor, diagnosed his illness again quite differently from the others, and though he predicted recovery, his questions and suppositions bewildered Iván Ilyich still more and increased his doubts. A homeopathist diagnosed the disease in yet another way, and prescribed medicine which Iván Ilyich took secretly for a week. But after a week, not feeling any improvement and having lost confidence both in the former doctor's treatment and in this one's, he became still more despondent. One day a lady acquaintance mentioned a cure effected by a wonder-working icon. Iván Ilyich caught himself listening attentively and beginning to believe that it had occurred. This incident alarmed him. "Has my mind really weakened to such an extent?" he asked himself. "Nonsense! It's all rubbish. I mustn't give way to nervous fears but having chosen a doctor must keep strictly to his treatment. That is what I will do. Now it's all settled. I won't think about it, but will follow the treatment seriously till summer, and then we shall see. From now there must be no more of this wavering!" This was easy to say but impossible to carry out. The pain in his side oppressed him and seemed to grow worse and more incessant, while the taste in his mouth grew stranger and stranger. It seemed to him that his breath had a disgusting smell, and he was conscious of a loss of appetite and strength. There was no deceiving himself: something terrible, new, and more important than anything before in his life, was taking place within him of which he alone was aware. Those about him did not understand or would not understand it, but thought everything in the world was going on as usual. That tormented Iván Ilyich more than anything. He saw that his household, especially his wife and daughter who were in a perfect whirl of visiting, did not understand anything of it and were annoyed that he was so depressed and so exacting, as if he were to blame for it. Though they tried to disguise it he saw that he was an obstacle in their path, and that his wife had adopted a definite line in regard to his illness and kept to it regardless of anything he said or did. Her attitude was this: "You know," she would say to her friends, "Iván Ilyich can't do as other people do, and keep to the treatment prescribed for him. One day he'll take his drops and keep strictly to his diet and go to bed in good time, but the next day unless I watch him he'll suddenly forget his medicine, eat sturgeon—which is forbidden—and sit up playing cards till one o'clock in the morning."

"Oh, come, when was that?" Iván Ilyich would ask in vexation. "Only once at Peter Ivánovich's."

"And yesterday with Shébek."

"Well, even if I hadn't stayed up, this pain would have kept me awake."

"Be that as it may you'll never get well like that, but will always make us wretched."

Praskóvya Fédorovna's attitude to Iván Ilyich's illness, as she expressed it both to others and to him, was that it was his own fault and was another of the annoyances he caused her. Iván Ilyich felt that this opinion escaped her involuntarily—but that did not make it easier for him.

At the law courts too, Iván Ilyich noticed, or thought he noticed, a strange attitude towards himself. It sometimes seemed to him that people were watching him inquisitively as a man whose place might soon be vacant. Then again, his friends would suddenly begin to chaff him in a friendly way about his low spirits, as if the awful, horrible, and unheard-of thing that was going on within him, incessantly gnawing at him and irresistibly drawing him away, was a very agreeable subject for jests. Schwartz in particular irritated him by his jocularity, vivacity, and *savoir-faire*, which reminded him of what he himself had been ten years ago.

Friends came to make up a set and they sat down to cards. They dealt, bending the new cards to soften them, and he sorted the diamonds in his hand and found he had seven. His partner said "No trumps" and supported him with two diamonds. What more could be wished for? It ought to be jolly and lively. They would make a grand slam. But suddenly Iván Ilyich was conscious of that gnawing pain, that taste in his mouth, and it seemed ridiculous that in such circumstances he should be pleased to make a grand slam.

He looked at his partner Mikháil Mikháylovich, who rapped the table with his strong hand and instead of snatching up the tricks pushed the cards courteously and indulgently towards Iván Ilyich that he might have the pleasure of gathering them up without the trouble of stretching out his hand for them. "Does he think I am too weak to stretch out my arm?" thought Iván Ilyich, and forgetting what he was doing he over-trumped his partner, missing the grand slam by three tricks. And what was most awful of all was that he saw how upset Mikháil Mikháylovich was about it but did not himself care. And it was dreadful to realize why he did not care.

They all saw that he was suffering, and said: "We can stop if you are tired. Take a rest." Lie down? No, he was not at all tired, and he finished the rubber. All were gloomy and silent. Iván Ilyich felt that he had diffused this gloom over them and could not dispel it. They had supper and went away, and Iván Ilyich was left alone with the consciousness that his life

was poisoned and was poisoning the lives of others, and that this poison
did not weaken but penetrated more and more deeply into his whole
being.

With this consciousness, and with physical pain besides the terror, he
must go to bed, often to lie awake the greater part of the night. Next
morning he had to get up again, dress, go to the law courts, speak, and
write; or if he did not go out, spend at home those twenty-four hours a day
each of which was a torture. And he had to live thus all alone on the brink
of an abyss, with no one who understood or pitied him.

V

So one month passed and then another. Just before the New Year his
brother-in-law came to town and stayed at their house. Iván Ilyich was at
the law courts and Praskóvya Fëdorovna had gone shopping. When Iván
Ilyich came home and entered his study he found his brother-in-law
there—a healthy, florid man—unpacking his portmanteau himself. He
raised his head on hearing Iván Ilyich's footsteps and looked up at him for
a moment without a word. That stare told Iván everything. His brother-in-
law opened his mouth to utter an exclamation of surprise but checked
himself, and that action confirmed it all.

"I have changed, eh?"

"Yes, there is a change."

And after that, try as he would to get his brother-in-law to return to
the subject of his looks, the latter would say nothing about it. Praskóvya
Fëdorovna came home and her brother went out to her. Iván Ilyich locked
the door and began to examine himself in the glass, first full face, then in
profile. He took up a portrait of himself taken with his wife, and compared
it with what he saw in the glass. The change in him was immense. Then
he bared his arms to the elbow, looked at them, drew the sleeves down
again, sat down on an ottoman, and grew blacker than night.

"No, no, this won't do!" he said to himself, and jumped up, went to the
table, took up some law papers and began to read them, but could not
continue. He unlocked the door and went into the reception-room. The
door leading to the drawing-room was shut. He approached it on tiptoe
and listened.

"No, you are exaggerating!" Praskóvya Fëdorovna was saying.

"Exaggerating! Don't you see it? Why, he's a dead man! Look at his
eyes—there's no light in them. But what is it that is wrong with him?"

"No one knows. Nikoláevich [that was another doctor] said something,
but I don't know what. And Leshchetítsky [this was the celebrated special-
ist] said quite the contrary. . ."

Iván Ilyich walked away, went to his own room, lay down and began
musing: "The kidney, a floating kidney." He recalled all the doctors had
told him of how it detached itself and swayed about. And by an effort of
imagination he tried to catch that kidney and arrest it and support it. So
little was needed for this, it seemed to him. "No, I'll go to see Peter Ivánovich again." [That was the friend whose friend was a doctor.] He rang,
ordered the carriage, and got ready to go.

"Where are you going, *Jean?*" asked his wife, with a specially sad and exceptionally kind look.

This exceptionally kind look irritated him. He looked morosely at her. "I must go to see Peter Ivánovich."

He went to see Peter Ivánovich, and together they went to see his friend, the doctor. He was in, and Iván Ilyich had a long talk with him.

Reviewing the anatomical and physiological details of what in the doctor's opinion was going on inside him, he understood it all.

There was something, a small thing, in the vermiform appendix. It might all come right. Only stimulate the energy of one organ and check the activity of another, then absorption would take place and everything would come right. He got home rather late for dinner, ate his dinner, and conversed cheerfully, but could not for a long time bring himself to go back to work in his room. At last, however, he went to his study and did what was necessary, but the consciousness that he had put something aside—an important, intimate matter which he would revert to when his work was done—never left him. When he had finished his work he remembered that this intimate matter was the thought of his vermiform appendix. But he did not give himself up to it, and went to the drawing-room for tea. There were callers there, including the examining magistrate who was a desirable match for his daughter, and they were conversing, playing the piano, and singing. Iván Ilyich, as Praskóvya Fëdorovna remarked, spent that evening more cheerfully than usual, but he never for a moment forgot that he had postponed the important matter of the appendix. At eleven o'clock he said good-night and went to his bedroom. Since his illness he had slept alone in a small room next to his study. He undressed and took up a novel by Zola,[9] but instead of reading it he fell into thought, and in his imagination that desired improvement in the vermiform appendix occurred. There was the absorption and evacuation and the reestablishment of normal activity. "Yes, that's it!" he said to himself. "One need only assist nature, that's all." He remembered his medicine, rose, took it, and lay down on his back watching for the beneficent action of the medicine and for it to lessen the pain. "I need only take it regularly and avoid all injurious influences. I am already feeling better, much better." He began touching his side: it was not painful to the touch. "There, I really don't feel it. It's much better already." He put out the light and turned on his side. . . . "The appendix is getting better, absorption is occurring." Suddenly he felt the old, familiar, dull, gnawing pain, stubborn and serious. There was the same familiar loathsome taste in his mouth. His heart sank and he felt dazed. "My God! My God!" he muttered. "Again, again! And it will never cease." And suddenly the matter presented itself in a quite different aspect. "Vermiform appendix! Kidney!" he said to himself. "It's not a question of appendix or kidney, but of life and . . . death. Yes, life was there and now it is going, going and I cannot stop it. Yes. Why deceive myself? Isn't it obvious to everyone but me that I'm dying, and that it's only a question of weeks, days . . . it may happen

9. Émile Zola (1840–1902), French novelist, author of the *Rougon-Macquart* novels (*Nana*, *Germinal*, and so on). Tolstoy condemned Zola for his naturalistic theories and considered his novels crude and gross.

this moment. There was light and now there is darkness. I was here and now I'm going there! Where?" A chill came over him, his breathing ceased, and he felt only the throbbing of his heart.

"When I am not, what will there be? There will be nothing. Then where shall I be when I am no more? Can this be dying? No, I don't want to!" He jumped up and tried to light the candle, felt for it with trembling hands, dropped candle and candlestick on the floor, and fell back on his pillow.

"What's the use? It makes no difference," he said to himself, staring with wide-open eyes into the darkness. "Death. Yes, death. And none of them know or wish to know it, and they have no pity for me. Now they are playing." (He heard through the door the distant sound of a song and its accompaniment.) "It's all the same to them, but they will die too! Fools! I first, and they later, but it will be the same for them. And now they are merry . . . the beasts!"

Anger choked him and he was agonizingly, unbearably miserable. "It is impossible that all men have been doomed to suffer this awful horror!" He raised himself.

"Something must be wrong. I must calm myself—must think it all over from the beginning." And he again began thinking. "Yes, the beginning of my illness: I knocked my side, but I was still quite well that day and the next. It hurt a little, then rather more. I saw the doctors, then followed despondency and anguish, more doctors, and I drew nearer to the abyss. My strength grew less and I kept coming nearer and nearer, and now I have wasted away and there is no light in my eyes. I think of the appendix—but this is death! I think of mending the appendix, and all the while here is death! Can it really be death!" Again terror seized him and he gasped for breath. He leant down and began feeling for the matches, pressing with his elbow on the stand beside the bed. It was in his way and hurt him, he grew furious with it, pressed on it still harder, and upset it. Breathless and in despair he fell on his back, expecting death to come immediately.

Meanwhile the visitors were leaving. Praskóvya Fëdorovna was seeing them off. She heard something fall and came in.

"What has happened?"

"Nothing. I knocked it over accidentally."

She went out and returned with a candle. He lay there panting heavily, like a man who has run a thousand yards, and stared upwards at her with a fixed look.

"What is it, *Jean?*"

"No . . . o . . . thing. I upset it." ("Why speak of it? She won't understand," he thought.)

And in truth she did not understand. She picked up the stand, lit his candle, and hurried away to see another visitor off. When she came back he still lay on his back, looking upwards.

"What is it? Do you feel worse?"

"Yes."

She shook her head and sat down.

"Do you know, *Jean*, I think we must ask Leshchetítsky to come and see you here."

This meant calling in the famous specialist, regardless of expense. He smiled malignantly and said "No." She remained a little longer and then went up to him and kissed his forehead.

While she was kissing him he hated her from the bottom of his soul and with difficulty refrained from pushing her away.

"Good-night. Please God you'll sleep."

"Yes."

VI

Iván Ilyich saw that he was dying, and he was in continual despair.

In the depth of his heart he knew he was dying, but not only was he not accustomed to the thought, he simply did not and could not grasp it.

The syllogism he had learned from Kiesewetter's *Logic*:[1] "Caius is a man, men are mortal, therefore Caius is mortal," had always seemed to him correct as applied to Caius, but certainly not as applied to himself. That Caius—man in the abstract—was mortal, was perfectly correct, but he was not Caius, not an abstract man, but a creature quite, quite separate from all others. He had been little Ványa, with a mamma and a papa, with Mítya and Volódya, with the toys, a coachman and a nurse, afterwards with Kátenka and with all the joys, griefs, and delights of childhood, boyhood, and youth. What did Caius know of the smell of that striped leather ball Ványa had been so fond of? Had Caius kissed his mother's hand like that, and did the silk of her dress rustle so for Caius? Had he rioted like that at school when the pastry was bad? Had Caius been in love like that? Could Caius preside at a session as he did? "Caius really was mortal, and it was right for him to die; but for me, little Ványa, Iván Ilyich, with all my thoughts and emotions, it's altogether a different matter. It cannot be that I ought to die. That would be too terrible."

Such was his feeling.

"If I had to die like Caius I should have known it was so. An inner voice would have told me so, but there was nothing of the sort in me and I and all my friends felt that our case was quite different from that of Caius. And now here it is!" he said to himself. "It can't be. It's impossible! But here it is. How is this? How is one to understand it?"

He could not understand it, and tried to drive this false, incorrect, morbid thought away and to replace it by other proper and healthy thoughts. But that thought, and not the thought only but the reality itself, seemed to come and confront him.

And to replace that thought he called up a succession of others, hoping to find in them some support. He tried to get back into the former current of thoughts that had once screened the thought of death from him. But strange to say, all that had formerly shut off, hidden, and destroyed, his consciousness of death, no longer had that effect. Iván Ilyich now spent

---

1. Karl Kiesewetter (1766–1819) was a German popularizer of Kant's philosophy. His *Outline of Logic According to Kantian Principles* (1796) was widely used in Russian adaptations as a schoolbook.

most of his time in attempting to re-establish that old current. He would
say to himself: "I will take up my duties again—after all I used to live by
them." And banishing all doubts he would go to the law courts, enter into
conversation with his colleagues, and sit carelessly as was his wont, scanning the crowd with a thoughtful look and leaning both his emaciated
arms on the arms of his oak chair; bending over as usual to a colleague
and drawing his papers nearer he would interchange whispers with him,
and then suddenly raising his eyes and sitting erect would pronounce certain words and open the proceedings. But suddenly in the midst of those
proceedings the pain in his side, regardless of the stage the proceedings
had reached, would begin its own gnawing work. Iván Ilyich would turn
his attention to it and try to drive the thought of it away, but without
success. *It* would come and stand before him and look at him, and he
would be petrified and the light would die out of his eyes, and he would
again begin asking himself whether *It* alone was true. And his colleagues
and subordinates would see with surprise and distress that he, the brilliant
and subtle judge, was becoming confused and making mistakes. He would
shake himself, try to pull himself together, manage somehow to bring the
sitting to a close, and return home with the sorrowful consciousness that
his judicial labours could not as formerly hide from him what he wanted
them to hide, and could not deliver him from *It*. And what was worst of
all was that *It* drew his attention to itself not in order to make him take
some action but only that he should look at *It*, look it straight in the face:
look at it without doing anything, suffer inexpressibly.

And to save himself from this condition Iván Ilyich looked for consolations—new screens—and new screens were found and for a while seemed
to save him, but then they immediately fell to pieces or rather became
transparent, as *It* penetrated them and nothing could veil *It*.

In these latter days he would go into the drawing-room he had
arranged—that drawing-room where he had fallen and for the sake of
which (how bitterly ridiculous it seemed) he had sacrificed his life—for
he knew that his illness originated with that knock. He would enter and
see that something had scratched the polished table. He would look for
the cause of this and find that it was the bronze ornamentation of an
album, that had got bent. He would take up the expensive album which
he had lovingly arranged, and feel vexed with his daughter and her friends
for their untidiness—for the album was torn here and there and some of
the photographs turned upside down. He would put it carefully in order
and bend the ornamentation back into position. Then it would occur to
him to place all those things in another corner of the room, near the
plants. He would call the footman, but his daughter or wife would contradict him, and he would dispute and grow angry. But that was all right, for
then he did not think about *It*. *It* was invisible.

But then, when he was moving something himself, his wife would say:
"Let the servants do it. You will hurt yourself again." And suddenly *It*
would flash through the screen and he would see it. It was just a flash, and
he hoped it would disappear, but he would involuntarily pay attention to
his side. "It sits there as before, gnawing just the same!" And he could no

longer forget It, but could distinctly see it looking at him from behind the flowers. "What is it all for?"

"It really is so! I lost my life over that curtain as I might have done when storming a fort. Is that possible? How terrible and how stupid. It can't be true! It can't, but it is."

He would go to his study, lie down, and again be alone with It: face to face with It. And nothing could be done with It except to look at it and shudder.

VII

How it happened it is impossible to say because it came about step by step, unnoticed, but in the third month of Iván Ilyich's illness, his wife, his daughter, his son, his acquaintances, the doctors, the servants, and above all he himself, were aware that the whole interest he had for other people was whether he would soon vacate his place, and at last release the living from the discomfort caused by his presence and be himself released from his sufferings.

He slept less and less. He was given opium and hypodermic injections of morphine, but this did not relieve him. The dull depression he experienced in a somnolent condition at first gave him a little relief, but only as something new; afterwards it became as distressing as the pain itself or even more so.

Special foods were prepared for him by the doctors' orders, but all those foods became increasingly distasteful and disgusting to him.

For his excretions also special arrangements had to be made, and this was a torment to him every time—a torment from the uncleanliness, the unseemliness, and the smell, and from knowing that another person had to take part in it.

But just through this most unpleasant matter, Iván Ilyich obtained comfort. Gerásim, the butler's young assistant, always came in to carry the things out. Gerásim was a clean, fresh peasant lad, grown stout on town food and always cheerful and bright. At first the sight of him, in his clean Russian peasant costume, engaged on that disgusting task embarrassed Iván Ilyich.

Once when he got up from the commode too weak to draw up his trousers, he dropped into a soft armchair and looked with horror at his bare, enfeebled thighs with the muscles so sharply marked on them.

Gerásim with a firm light tread, his heavy boots emitting a pleasant smell of tar and fresh winter air, came in wearing a clean Hessian apron, the sleeves of his print shirt tucked up over his strong bare young arms; and refraining from looking at his sick master out of consideration for his feelings, and restraining the joy of life that beamed from his face, he went up to the commode.

"Gerásim!" said Iván Ilyich in a weak voice.

Gerásim started, evidently afraid he might have committed some blunder, and with a rapid movement turned his fresh, kind, simple young face which just showed the first downy sign of a beard.

"Yes, sir?"

"That must be very unpleasant for you. You must forgive me. I am helpless."

"Oh, why, sir," and Gerásim's eyes beamed and he showed his glistening white teeth, "what's a little trouble? It's a case of illness with you, sir."

And his deft strong hands did their accustomed task, and he went out of the room stepping lightly. Five minutes later he as lightly returned.

Iván Ilyich was still sitting in the same position in the armchair.

"Gerásim," he said when the latter had replaced the freshly-washed utensil. "Please come here and help me." Gerásim went up to him. "Lift me up. It is hard for me to get up, and I have sent Dmítri away."

Gerásim went up to him, grasped his master with his strong arms deftly but gently, in the same way that he stepped—lifted him, supported him with one hand, and with the other drew up his trousers and would have set him down again, but Iván Ilyich asked to be led to the sofa. Gerásim, without an effort and without apparent pressure, led him, almost lifting him, to the sofa and placed him on it.

"Thank you. How easily and well you do it all!"

Gerásim smiled again and turned to leave the room. But Iván Ilyich felt his presence such a comfort that he did not want to let him go.

"One thing more, please move up that chair. No, the other one—under my feet. It is easier for me when my feet are raised."

Gerásim brought the chair, set it down gently in place, and raised Iván Ilyich's legs on to it. It seemed to Iván Ilyich that he felt better while Gerásim was holding up his legs.

"It's better when my legs are higher," he said. "Place that cushion under them."

Gerásim did so. He again lifted the legs and placed them, and again Iván Ilyich felt better while Gerásim held his legs. When he set them down Iván Ilyich fancied he felt worse.

"Gerásim," he said. "Are you busy now?"

"Not at all, sir," said Gerásim, who had learnt from the townsfolk how to speak to gentlefolk.

"What have you still to do?"

"What have I to do? I've done everything except chopping the logs for to-morrow."

"Then hold my legs up a bit higher, can you?"

"Of course I can. Why not?" And Gerásim raised his master's legs higher and Iván Ilyich thought that in that position he did not feel any pain at all.

"And how about the logs?"

"Don't trouble about that, sir. There's plenty of time."

Iván Ilyich told Gerásim to sit down and hold his legs, and began to talk to him. And strange to say it seemed to him that he felt better while Gerásim held his legs up.

After that Iván Ilyich would sometimes call Gerásim and get him to hold his legs on his shoulders, and he liked talking to him. Gerásim did it all easily, willingly, simply, and with a good nature that touched Iván

Ilyich. Health, strength, and vitality in other people were offensive to him, but Gerásim's strength and vitality did not mortify but soothed him.

What tormented Iván Ilyich most was the deception, the lie, which for some reason they all accepted, that he was not dying but was simply ill, and that he only need keep quiet and undergo a treatment and then something very good would result. He however knew that do what they would nothing would come of it, only still more agonizing suffering and death. This deception tortured him—their not wishing to admit what they all knew and what he knew, but wanting to lie to him concerning his terrible condition, and wishing and forcing him to participate in that lie. Those lies—lies enacted over him on the eve of his death and destined to degrade this awful, solemn act to the level of their visitings, their curtains, their sturgeon for dinner—were a terrible agony for Iván Ilyich. And strangely enough, many times when they were going through their antics over him he had been within a hairbreadth of calling out to them: "Stop lying! You know and I know that I am dying. Then at least stop lying about it!" But he had never had the spirit to do it. The awful, terrible act of his dying was, he could see, reduced by those about him to the level of a casual, unpleasant, and almost indecorous incident (as if someone entered a drawing-room diffusing an unpleasant odour) and this was done by that very decorum which he had served all his life long. He saw that no one felt for him, because no one even wished to grasp his position. Only Gerásim recognized and pitied him. And so Iván Ilyich felt at ease only with him. He felt comforted when Gerásim supported his legs (sometimes all night long) and refused to go to bed, saying: "Don't you worry, Iván Ilyich. I'll get sleep enough later on," or when he suddenly became familiar and exclaimed: "If you weren't sick it would be another matter, but as it is, why should I grudge a little trouble?" Gerásim alone did not lie; everything showed that he alone understood the facts of the case and did not consider it necessary to disguise them, but simply felt sorry for his emaciated and enfeebled master. Once when Iván Ilyich was sending him away he even said straight out: "We shall all of us die, so why should I grudge a little trouble?"—expressing the fact that he did not think his work burdensome, because he was doing it for a dying man and hoped someone would do the same for him when his time came.

Apart from this lying, or because of it, what most tormented Iván Ilyich was that no one pitied him as he wished to be pitied. At certain moments after prolonged suffering he wished most of all (though he would have been ashamed to confess it) for someone to pity him as a sick child is pitied. He longed to be petted and comforted. He knew he was an important functionary, that he had a beard turning grey, and that therefore what he longed for was impossible, but still he longed for it. And in Gerásim's attitude towards him there was something akin to what he wished for, and so that attitude comforted him. Iván Ilyich wanted to weep, wanted to be petted and cried over, and then his colleague Shébek would come, and instead of weeping and being petted, Iván Ilyich would assume a serious, severe, and profound air, and by force of habit would express his opinion on a decision of the Court of Appeal and would stubbornly insist on that view. This falsity around him and within him did more than anything else to poison his last days.

VIII

It was morning. He knew it was morning because Gerásim had gone, and Peter the footman had come and put out the candles, drawn back one of the curtains, and begun quietly to tidy up. Whether it was morning or evening, Friday or Sunday, made no difference, it was all just the same: the gnawing, unmitigated, agonizing pain, never ceasing for an instant, the consciousness of life inexorably waning but not yet extinguished, the approach of that ever dreaded and hateful Death which was the only reality, and always the same falsity. What were days, weeks, hours, in such a case?

"Will you have some tea, sir?"

"He wants things to be regular, and wishes the gentlefolk to drink tea in the morning," thought Iván Ilyich, and only said "No."

"Wouldn't you like to move onto the sofa, sir?"

"He wants to tidy up the room, and I'm in the way. I am uncleanliness and disorder," he thought, and said only:

"No, leave me alone."

The man went on bustling about. Iván Ilyich stretched out his hand. Peter came up, ready to help.

"What is it, sir?"

"My watch."

Peter took the watch which was close at hand and gave it to his master.

"Half-past eight. Are they up?"

"No sir, except Vladímir Ivánich" (the son) "who has gone to school. Praskóvya Fëdorovna ordered me to wake her if you asked for her. Shall I do so?"

"No, there's no need to." "Perhaps I'd better have some tea," he thought, and added aloud: "Yes, bring me some tea."

Peter went to the door, but Iván Ilyich dreaded being left alone. "How can I keep him here? Oh yes, my medicine." "Peter, give me my medicine." "Why not? Perhaps it may still do me some good." He took a spoonful and swallowed it. "No, it won't help. It's all tomfoolery, all deception," he decided as soon as he became aware of the familiar, sickly, hopeless taste. "No, I can't believe in it any longer. But the pain, why this pain? If it would only cease just for a moment!" And he moaned. Peter turned towards him. "It's all right. Go and fetch me some tea."

Peter went out. Left alone Iván Ilyich groaned not so much with pain, terrible though that was, as from mental anguish. Always and forever the same, always these endless days and nights. If only it would come quicker! If only *what* would come quicker? Death, darkness? . . . No, no! Anything rather than death!

When Peter returned with the tea on a tray, Iván Ilyich stared at him for a time in perplexity, not realizing who and what he was. Peter was disconcerted by that look and his embarrassment brought Iván Ilyich to himself.

"Oh, tea! All right, put it down. Only help me to wash and put on a clean shirt."

And Iván Ilyich began to wash. With pauses for rest, he washed his hands and then his face, cleaned his teeth, brushed his hair, and looked in the glass. He was terrified by what he saw, especially by the limp way in which his hair clung to his pallid forehead.

While his shirt was being changed he knew that he would be still more frightened at the sight of his body, so he avoided looking at it. Finally he was ready. He drew on a dressing-gown, wrapped himself in a plaid, and sat down in the armchair to take his tea. For a moment he felt refreshed, but as soon as he began to drink the tea he was again aware of the same taste, and the pain also returned. He finished it with an effort, and then lay down stretching out his legs, and dismissed Peter.

Always the same. Now a spark of hope flashes up, then a sea of despair rages, and always pain; always pain, always despair, and always the same. When alone he had a dreadful and distressing desire to call someone, but he knew beforehand that with others present it would be still worse. "Another dose of morphine—to lose consciousness. I will tell him, the doctor, that he must think of something else. It's impossible, impossible, to go on like this."

An hour and another pass like that. But now there is a ring at the door bell. Perhaps it's the doctor? It is. He comes in fresh, hearty, plump, and cheerful, with that look on his face that seems to say: "There now, you're in a panic about something, but we'll arrange it all for you directly!" The doctor knows this expression is out of place here, but he has put it on once for all and can't take it off—like a man who has put on a frock-coat in the morning to pay a round of calls.

The doctor rubs his hands vigorously and reassuringly.

"Brr! How cold it is! There's such a sharp frost; just let me warm myself!" he says, as if it were only a matter of waiting till he was warm, and then he would put everything right.

"Well now, how are you?"

Iván Ilyich feels that the doctor would like to say: "Well, how are our affairs?" but that even he feels that this would not do, and says instead: "What sort of a night have you had?"

Iván Ilyich looks at him as much as to say: "Are you really never ashamed of lying?" But the doctor does not wish to understand this question, and Iván Ilyich says: "Just as terrible as ever. The pain never leaves me and never subsides. If only something . . ."

"Yes, you sick people are always like that. . . . There, now I think I'm warm enough. Even Praskóvya Fëdorovna, who is so particular, could find no fault with my temperature. Well, now I can say good-morning," and the doctor presses his patient's hand.

Then, dropping his former playfulness, he begins with a most serious face to examine the patient, feeling his pulse and taking his temperature, and then begins the sounding and auscultation.

Iván Ilyich knows quite well and definitely that all this is nonsense and pure deception, but when the doctor, getting down on his knee, leans over him, putting his ear first higher then lower, and performs various gymnastic movements over him with a significant expression on his face, Iván Ilyich submits to it all as he used to submit to the speeches of the lawyers, though he knew very well that they were all lying and why they were lying.

The doctor, kneeling on the sofa, is still sounding him when Praskóvya Fëdorovna's silk dress rustles at the door and she is heard scolding Peter for not having let her know of the doctor's arrival.

She comes in, kisses her husband, and at once proceeds to prove that she has been up a long time already, and only owing to a misunderstanding failed to be there when the doctor arrived.

Iván Ilyich looks at her, scans her all over, sets against her the whiteness and plumpness and cleanness of her hands and neck, the gloss of her hair, and the sparkle of her vivacious eyes. He hates her with his whole soul. And the thrill of hatred he feels for her makes him suffer from her touch.

Her attitude towards him and his disease is still the same. Just as the doctor had adopted a certain relation to his patient which he could not abandon, so had she formed one towards him—that he was not doing something he ought to do and was himself to blame, and that she reproached him lovingly for this—and she could not now change that attitude.

"You see he doesn't listen to me and doesn't take his medicine at the proper time. And above all he lies in a position that is no doubt bad for him—with his legs up."

She described how he made Gerásim hold his legs up.

The doctor smiled with a contemptuous affability that said: "What's to be done? These sick people do have foolish fancies of that kind, but we must forgive them."

When the examination was over the doctor looked at his watch, and then Praskóvya Fëdorovna announced to Iván Ilyich that it was of course as he pleased, but she had sent to-day for a celebrated specialist who would examine him and have a consultation with Michael Danílovich (their regular doctor).

"Please don't raise any objections. I am doing this for my own sake," she said ironically, letting it be felt that she was doing it all for his sake and only said this to leave him no right to refuse. He remained silent, knitting his brows. He felt that he was so surrounded and involved in a mesh of falsity that it was hard to unravel anything.

Everything she did for him was entirely for her own sake, and she told him she was doing for herself what she actually was doing for herself, as if that was so incredible that he must understand the opposite.

At half-past eleven the celebrated specialist arrived. Again the sounding began and the significant conversations in his presence and in other rooms, about the kidneys and the appendix, and the questions and answers, with such an air of importance that again, instead of the real question of life and death which now alone confronted him, the question arose of the kidney and the appendix which were not behaving as they ought to and would now be attacked by Michael Danílovich and the specialist and forced to amend their ways.

The celebrated specialist took leave of him with a serious though not hopeless look, and in reply to the timid question in Iván Ilyich, with eyes glistening with fear and hope, put to him as to whether there was a chance of recovery, said that he could not vouch for it but there was a possibility. The look of hope with which Iván Ilyich watched the doctor out was so pathetic that Praskóvya Fëdorovna, seeing it, even wept as she left the room to hand the doctor his fee.

The gleam of hope kindled by the doctor's encouragement did not last long. The same room, the same pictures, curtains, wallpaper, medicine bottles, were all there, and the same aching suffering body, and Iván Ilyich began to moan. They gave him a subcutaneous injection and he sank into oblivion.

It was twilight when he came to. They brought him his dinner and he swallowed some beef tea with difficulty, and then everything was the same again and night was coming on.

After dinner, at seven o'clock, Praskóvya Fëdorovna came into the room in evening dress, her full bosom pushed up by her corset, and with traces of powder on her face. She had reminded him in the morning that they were going to the theatre. Sarah Bernhardt[2] was visiting the town and they had a box, which he had insisted on their taking. Now he had forgotten about it and her toilet offended him, but he concealed his vexation when he remembered that he had himself insisted on their securing a box and going because it would be an instructive and aesthetic pleasure for the children.

Praskóvya Fëdorovna came in, self-satisfied but yet with a rather guilty air. She sat down and asked how he was, but, as he saw, only for the sake of asking and not in order to learn about it, knowing that there was nothing to learn—and then went on to what she really wanted to say: that she would not on any account have gone but that the box had been taken and Helen and their daughter were going, as well as Petríshchev (the examining magistrate, their daughter's fiancé) and that it was out of the question to let them go alone; but that she would have much preferred to sit with him for a while; and he must be sure to follow the doctor's orders while she was away.

"Oh, and Fëdor Petróvich" (the fiancé) "would like to come in. May he? And Lisa?"

"All right."

Their daughter came in in full evening dress, her fresh young flesh exposed (making a show of that very flesh which in his own case caused so much suffering), strong, healthy, evidently in love, and impatient with illness, suffering, and death, because they interfered with her happiness.

Fëdor Petróvich came in too, in evening dress, his hair curled à la Capoul, a tight stiff collar round his long sinewy neck, an enormous white shirt-front and narrow black trousers tightly stretched over his strong thighs. He had one white glove tightly drawn on, and was holding his opera hat in his hand.

Following him the schoolboy crept in unnoticed, in a new uniform, poor little fellow, and wearing gloves. Terribly dark shadows showed under his eyes, the meaning of which Iván Ilyich knew well.

---

2. Stage name of Rosine Bernard (1844–1923), famed for romantic and tragic roles.

His son had always seemed pathetic to him, and now it was dreadful to see the boy's frightened look of pity. It seemed to Iván Ilyich that Vásya was the only one besides Gerásim who understood and pitied him.

They all sat down and again asked how he was. A silence followed. Lisa asked her mother about the opera-glasses, and there was an altercation between mother and daughter as to who had taken them and where they had been put. This occasioned some unpleasantness.

Fëdor Petróvich inquired of Iván Ilyich whether he had ever seen Sarah Bernhardt. Iván Ilyich did not at first catch the question, but then replied: "No, have you seen her before?"

"Yes, in *Adrienne Lecouvreur*."[3]

Praskóvya Fëdorovna mentioned some rôles in which Sarah Bernhardt was particularly good. Her daughter disagreed. Conversation sprang up as to the elegance and realism of her acting—the sort of conversation that is always repeated and is always the same.

In the midst of the conversation Fëdor Petróvich glanced at Iván Ilyich and became silent. The others also looked at him and grew silent. Iván Ilyich was staring with glittering eyes straight before him, evidently indignant with them. This had to be rectified, but it was impossible to do so. The silence had to be broken, but for a time no one dared to break it and they all became afraid that the conventional deception would suddenly become obvious and the truth become plain to all. Lisa was the first to pluck up courage and break that silence, but by trying to hide what everybody was feeling, she betrayed it.

"Well, if we are going it's time to start," she said, looking at her watch, a present from her father, and with a faint and significant smile at Fëdor Petróvich relating to something known only to them. She got up with a rustle of her dress.

They all rose, said good-night, and went away.

When they had gone it seemed to Iván Ilyich that he felt better; the falsity had gone with them. But the pain remained—that same pain and that same fear that made everything monotonously alike, nothing harder and nothing easier. Everything was worse.

Again minute followed minute and hour followed hour. Everything remained the same and there was no cessation. And the inevitable end of it all became more and more terrible.

"Yes, send Gerásim here," he replied to a question Peter asked.

IX

His wife returned late at night. She came in on tiptoe, but he heard her, opened his eyes, and made haste to close them again. She wished to send Gerásim away and to sit with him herself, but he opened his eyes and said: "No, go away."

"Are you in great pain?"

"Always the same."

---

3. A play (1849) by the French dramatist Eugène Scribe (1791–1861), in which the heroine was a famous actress of the 18th century. Tolstoy considered Scribe, who wrote over four hundred plays, a shoddy, commercial playwright.

"Take some opium."

He agreed and took some. She went away.

Till about three in the morning he was in a state of stupefied misery. It seemed to him that he and his pain were being thrust into a narrow, deep black sack, but though they were pushed further and further in they could not be pushed to the bottom. And this, terrible enough in itself, was accompanied by suffering. He was frightened yet wanted to fall through the sack, he struggled but yet co-operated. And suddenly he broke through, fell, and regained consciousness. Gerásim was sitting at the foot of the bed dozing quietly and patiently, while he himself lay with his emaciated stockinged legs resting on Gerásim's shoulders; the same shaded candle was there and the same unceasing pain.

"Go away, Gerásim," he whispered.

"It's all right, sir. I'll stay a while."

"No. Go away."

He removed his legs from Gerásim's shoulders, turned sideways onto his arm, and felt sorry for himself. He only waited till Gerásim had gone into the next room and then restrained himself no longer but wept like a child. He wept on account of his helplessness, his terrible loneliness, the cruelty of man, the cruelty of God, and the absence of God.

"Why hast Thou done all this? Why hast Thou brought me here? Why, dost Thou torment me so terribly?"

He did not expect an answer and yet wept because there was no answer and could be none. The pain again grew more acute, but he did not stir and did not call. He said to himself: "Go on! Strike me! But what is it for? What have I done to Thee? What is it for?"

Then he grew quiet and not only ceased weeping but even held his breath and became all attention. It was as though he were listening not to an audible voice but to a voice of his soul, to the current of thoughts arising within him.

"What is it you want?" was the first clear conception capable of expression in words, that he heard.

"What do you want? What do you want?" he repeated to himself.

"What do I want? To live and not to suffer," he answered.

And again he listened with such concentrated attention that even his pain did not distract him.

"To live? How?" asked his inner voice.

"Why, to live as I used to—well and pleasantly."

"As you lived before, well and pleasantly?" the voice repeated.

And in imagination he began to recall the moments of his pleasant life. But strange to say none of those best moments of his pleasant life now seemed at all what they had then seemed—none of them except the first recollections of childhood. There, in childhood, there had been something really pleasant with which it would be possible to live if it could return. But the child who had experienced that happiness existed no longer, it was like a reminiscence of somebody else.

As soon as the period began which had produced the present Iván Ilyich, all that had then seemed joys now melted before his sight and turned into something trivial and often nasty.

And the further he departed from childhood and the nearer he came to
the present the more worthless and doubtful were the joys. This began
with the School of Law. A little that was really good was still found there—
there was light-heartedness, friendship, and hope. But in the upper classes
there had already been fewer of such good moments. Then during the
first years of his official career, when he was in the service of the Governor,
some pleasant moments again occurred: they were the memories of love
for a woman. Then all became confused and there was still less of what
was good; later on again there was still less that was good, and the further
he went the less there was. His marriage, a mere accident, then the disenchantment that followed it, his wife's bad breath and the sensuality and
hypocrisy: then that deadly official life and those preoccupations about
money, a year of it, and two, and ten, and twenty, and always the same
thing. And the longer it lasted the more deadly it became. "It is as if I had
been going downhill while I imagined I was going up. And that is really
what it was. I was going up in public opinion, but to the same extent life
was ebbing away from me. And now it is all done and there is only death."

"Then what does it mean? Why? It can't be that life is so senseless and
horrible. But if it really has been so horrible and senseless, why must I die
and die in agony? There is something wrong!"

"Maybe I did not live as I ought to have done," it suddenly occurred to
him. "But how could that be, when I did everything properly?" he replied,
and immediately dismissed from his mind this, the sole solution of all the
riddles of life and death, as something quite impossible.

"Then what do you want now? To live? Live how? Live as you lived in
the law courts when the usher proclaimed 'The judge is coming!' The
judge is coming, the judge!" he repeated to himself. "Here he is, the
judge. But I am not guilty!" he exclaimed angrily. "What is it for?" And
he ceased crying, but turning his face to the wall continued to ponder on
the same question: Why, and for what purpose, is there all this horror?
But however much he pondered he found no answer. And whenever the
thought occurred to him, as it often did, that it all resulted from his not
having lived as he ought to have done, he at once recalled the correctness
of his whole life, and dismissed so strange an idea.

X

Another fortnight passed. Iván Ilyich now no longer left his sofa. He
would not lie in bed but lay on the sofa, facing the wall nearly all the
time. He suffered ever the same unceasing agonies and in his loneliness
pondered always on the same insoluble question: "What is this? Can it be
that it is Death?" And the inner voice answered: "Yes, it is Death."

"Why these sufferings?" And the voice answered, "For no reason—they
just are so." Beyond and besides this there was nothing.

From the very beginning of his illness, ever since he had first been to
see the doctor, Iván Ilyich's life had been divided between two contrary
and alternating moods: now it was despair and the expectation of this
uncomprehended and terrible death, and now hope and an intently interested observation of the functioning of his organs. Now before his eyes

there was only a kidney or an intestine that temporarily evaded its duty, and now only that incomprehensible and dreadful death from which it was impossible to escape.

These two states of mind had alternated from the very beginning of his illness, but the further it progressed the more doubtful and fantastic became the conception of the kidney, and the more real the sense of impending death.

He had but to call to mind what he had been three months before and what he was now, to call to mind with what regularity he had been going downhill, for every possibility of hope to be shattered.

Latterly during that loneliness in which he found himself as he lay facing the back of the sofa, a loneliness in the midst of a populous town and surrounded by numerous acquaintances and relations but that yet could not have been more complete anywhere—either at the bottom of the sea or under the earth—during that terrible loneliness Iván Ilyich had lived only in memories of the past. Pictures of his past rose before him one after another. They always began with what was nearest in time and then went back to what was most remote—to his childhood—and rested there. If he thought of the stewed prunes that had been offered him that day, his mind went back to the raw shrivelled French plums of his childhood, their peculiar flavour and the flow of saliva when he sucked their stones, and along with the memory of that taste came a whole series of memories of those days: his nurse, his brother, and their toys. "No, I mustn't think of that. . . . It is too painful," Iván Ilyich said to himself, and brought himself back to the present—to the button on the back of the sofa and the creases in its morocco. "Morocco is expensive, but it does not wear well: there had been a quarrel about it. It was a different kind of quarrel and a different kind of morocco that time when we tore father's portfolio and were punished, and mamma brought us some tarts. . . ." And again his thoughts dwelt on his childhood, and again it was painful and he tried to banish them and fix his mind on something else.

Then again together with that chain of memories another series passed through his mind—of how his illness had progressed and grown worse. There also the further back he looked the more life there had been. There had been more of what was good in life and more of life itself. The two merged together. "Just as the pain went on getting worse and worse, so my life grew worse and worse," he thought. "There is one bright spot there at the back, at the beginning of life, and afterwards all becomes blacker and blacker and proceeds more and more rapidly—in inverse ratio to the square of the distance from death," thought Iván Ilyich. And the example of a stone falling downwards with increasing velocity entered his mind. Life, a series of increasing sufferings, flies further and further towards its end—the most terrible suffering. "I am flying. . . ." He shuddered, shifted himself, and tried to resist, but was already aware that resistance was impossible, and again with eyes weary of gazing but unable to cease seeing what was before them, he stared at the back of the sofa and waited—awaiting that dreadful fall and shock and destruction.

"Resistance is impossible!" he said to himself. "If I could only understand what it is all for! But that too is impossible. An explanation would be possible if it could be said that I have not lived as I ought to. But it is impossible to say that," and he remembered all the legality, correctitude, and propriety of his life. "That at any rate can certainly not be admitted," he thought, and his lips smiled ironically as if someone could see that smile and be taken in by it. "There is no explanation! Agony, death. . . . What for?"

XI

Another two weeks went by in this way and during that fortnight an event occurred that Iván Ilyich and his wife had desired. Petríshchev formally proposed. It happened in the evening. The next day Praskóvya Fëdorovna came into her husband's room considering how best to inform him of it, but that very night there had been a fresh change for the worse in his condition. She found him still lying on the sofa but in a different position. He lay on his back, groaning and staring fixedly straight in front of him.

She began to remind him of his medicines, but he turned his eyes towards her with such a look that she did not finish what she was saying; so great an animosity, to her in particular, did that look express.

"For Christ's sake let me die in peace!" he said.

She would have gone away, but just then their daughter came in and went up to say good morning. He looked at her as he had done at his wife, and in reply to her inquiry about his health said dryly that he would soon free them all of himself. They were both silent and after sitting with him for a while went away.

"Is it our fault?" Lisa said to her mother. "It's as if we were to blame! I am sorry for papa, but why should we be tortured?"

The doctor came at his usual time. Iván Ilyich answered "Yes" and "No," never taking his angry eyes from him, and at last said: "You know you can do nothing for me, so leave me alone."

"We can ease your sufferings."

"You can't even do that. Let me be."

The doctor went into the drawing-room and told Praskóvya Fëdorovna that the case was very serious and that the only resource left was opium to allay her husband's sufferings, which must be terrible.

It was true, as the doctor said, that Iván Ilyich's physical sufferings were terrible, but worse than the physical sufferings were his mental sufferings which were his chief torture.

His mental sufferings were due to the fact that that night, as he looked at Gerásim's sleepy, good-natured face with its prominent cheek-bones, the question suddenly occurred to him: "What if my whole life has really been wrong?"

It occurred to him that what had appeared perfectly impossible before, namely that he had not spent his life as he should have done, might after all be true. It occurred to him that his scarcely perceptible attempts to struggle against what was considered good by the most highly placed people, those scarcely noticeable impulses which he had immediately suppressed, might have been the real thing, and all the rest false. And his professional duties and the whole arrangement of his life and of his family, and all his social and official interests, might all have been false. He tried to defend all those things to himself and suddenly felt the weakness of what he was defending. There was nothing to defend.

"But if that is so," he said to himself, "and I am leaving this life with the consciousness that I have lost all that was given me and it is impossible to rectify it—what then?"

He lay on his back and began to pass his life in review in quite a new way. In the morning when he saw first his footman, then his wife, then his daughter, and then the doctor, their every word and movement confirmed to him the awful truth that had been revealed to him during the night. In them he saw himself—all that for which he had lived—and saw clearly that it was not real at all, but a terrible and huge deception which had hidden both life and death. This consciousness intensified his physical suffering tenfold. He groaned and tossed about, and pulled at his clothing which choked and stifled him. And he hated them on that account.

He was given a large dose of opium and became unconscious, but at noon his sufferings began again. He drove everybody away and tossed from side to side.

His wife came to him and said:

"Jean, my dear, do this for me. It can't do any harm and often helps. Healthy people often do it."

He opened his eyes wide.

"What? Take communion? Why? It's unnecessary! However . . ."

She began to cry.

"Yes, do, my dear. I'll send for our priest. He is such a nice man."

"All right. Very well," he muttered.

When the priest came and heard his confession, Iván Ilyich was softened and seemed to feel a relief from his doubts and consequently from his sufferings, and for a moment there came a ray of hope. He again began to think of the vermiform appendix and the possibility of correcting it. He received the sacrament with tears in his eyes.

When they laid him down again afterwards he felt a moment's ease, and the hope that he might live awoke in him again. He began to think of the operation that had been suggested to him. "To live! I want to live!" he said to himself.

His wife came in to congratulate him after his communion, and when uttering the usual conventional words she added:

"You feel better, don't you?"

Without looking at her he said "Yes."

Her dress, her figure, the expression of her face, the tone of her voice, all revealed the same thing. "This is wrong, it is not as it should be. All you have lived for and still live for is falsehood and deception, hiding life and death from you." And as soon as he admitted that thought, his hatred and his agonizing physical suffering again sprang up, and with that suffering a consciousness of the unavoidable, approaching end. And to this was added a new sensation of grinding shooting pain and a feeling of suffocation.

The expression of his face when he uttered that "yes" was dreadful.

Having uttered it, he looked her straight in the eyes, turned on his face with a rapidity extraordinary in his weak state and shouted:

"Go away! Go away and leave me alone!"

XII

From that moment the screaming began that continued for three days, and was so terrible that one could not hear it through two closed doors without horror. At the moment he answered his wife he realized that he was lost, that there was no return, that the end had come, the very end, and his doubts were still unsolved and remained doubts.

"Oh! Oh! Oh!" he cried in various intonations. He had begun by screaming "I won't!" and continued screaming on the letter "o."

For three whole days, during which time did not exist for him, he struggled in that black sack into which he was being thrust by an invisible, resistless force. He struggled as a man condemned to death struggles in the hands of the executioner, knowing that he cannot save himself. And every moment he felt that despite all his efforts he was drawing nearer and nearer to what terrified him. He felt that his agony was due to his being thrust into that black hole and still more to his not being able to get right into it. He was hindered from getting into it by his conviction that his life had been a good one. That very justification of his life held him fast and prevented his moving forward, and it caused him most torment of all.

Suddenly some force struck him in the chest and side, making it still harder to breathe, and he fell through the hole and there at the bottom was a light. What had happened to him was like the sensation one sometimes experiences in a railway carriage when one thinks one is going backwards while one is really going forwards and suddenly becomes aware of the real direction.

"Yes, it was all not the right thing," he said to himself, "but that's no matter. It can be done. But what *is* the right thing?" he asked himself, and suddenly grew quiet.

This occurred at the end of the third day, two hours before his death. Just then his schoolboy son had crept softly in and gone up to the bedside. The dying man was still screaming desperately and waving his arms. His hand fell on the boy's head, and the boy caught it, pressed it to his lips, and began to cry.

At that very moment Iván Ilyich fell through and caught sight of the light, and it was revealed to him that though his life had not been what it should have been, this could still be rectified. He asked himself, "What *is* the right thing?" and grew still, listening. Then he felt that someone was kissing his hand. He opened his eyes, looked at his son, and felt sorry for him. His wife came up to him and he glanced at her. She was gazing at him open-mouthed, with undried tears on her nose and cheek and a despairing look on her face. He felt sorry for her too.

"Yes, I am making them wretched," he thought. "They are sorry, but it will be better for them when I die." He wished to say this but had not the strength to utter it. "Besides, why speak? I must act," he thought. With a look at his wife he indicated his son and said: "Take him away . . . sorry for him . . . sorry for you too. . . ." He tried to add, "forgive me," but said "forgo" and waved his hand, knowing that He whose understanding mattered would understand.

And suddenly it grew clear to him that what had been oppressing him and would not leave him was all dropping away at once from two sides, from ten sides, and from all sides. He was sorry for them, he must act so as not to hurt them: release them and free himself from these sufferings. "How good and how simple!" he thought. "And the pain?" he asked himself. "What has become of it? Where are you, pain?"

He turned his attention to it.

"Yes, here it is. Well, what of it? Let the pain be."

"And death . . . where is it?"

He sought his former accustomed fear of death and did not find it. "Where is it? What death?" There was no fear because there was no death.

In place of death there was light.

"So that's what it is!" he suddenly exclaimed aloud. "What joy!"

To him all this happened in a single instant, and the meaning of that instant did not change. For those present his agony continued for another two hours. Something rattled in his throat, his emaciated body twitched, then the gasping and rattle became less and less frequent.

"It is finished!" said someone near him.

He heard these words and repeated them in his soul.

"Death is finished," he said to himself. "It is no more!"

He drew in a breath, stopped in the midst of a sigh, stretched out, and died.

HENRIK IBSEN
1828–1906

Henrik Ibsen was the foremost playwright of his time—treating social themes and ideas and often satirizing the nineteenth-century bourgeoisie—and not only in Norway, his native land. His plays may be viewed historically as the culmination point of the *bourgeois* drama that has flourished fitfully, in France and Germany particularly, since the eighteenth century, when Diderot advocated and wrote plays about the middle classes, their "conditions" and problems. But they may also be seen as the fountainhead of much twentieth-century drama; in the West the plays of George Bernard Shaw and John Galsworthy, who discuss social problems, and of Maurice Maeterlinck and Anton Chekhov, who learned from the later "symbolist" Ibsen. Ibsen's drama of domestic and political crisis was also immensely popular in China and influenced a generation of modern playwrights.

Ibsen was born at Skien, in Norway, on March 20, 1828. His family had sunk into poverty and finally complete bankruptcy. In 1844, at the age of sixteen, he was sent to Grimstad, another small coastal town, as an apothecary's apprentice. There he lived in almost complete isolation and cut himself off from his family, except for his sister Hedvig. In 1850 he managed to get to Oslo (then Christiana) and to enroll at the university. But he never passed his examinations and in the following year left for Bergen, where he had acquired the position of playwright and assistant stage manager at the newly founded Norwegian Theater. Ibsen supplied the small theater with several historical and romantic plays. In 1857 he was appointed artistic director at the Mollergate Theater in Christiana, and a year later he married Susannah Thoresen. *Love's Comedy* (1862) was his first major success on the stage. Ibsen was then deeply affected by Scandinavianism, the movement for solidarity of the northern nations, and when in 1864 Norway refused to do anything to support Denmark in its war with Prussia and Austria over Schleswig-Holstein, he was so disgusted with his country that he left it for what he thought would be permanent exile. He lived in Rome, in Dresden, in Munich, and in smaller summer resorts, and during this time wrote all his later plays.

After a long period of incubation and experimentation with romantic and histor-ical themes, Ibsen wrote a series of "problem" plays, beginning with *The Pillars of Society* (1877), which in their time created a furor by their fearless criticism of the nineteenth-century social scene: the subjection of women, hypocrisy, hereditary disease, seamy politics, and corrupt journalism. He wrote these plays using natural-istic modes of presentation: ordinary colloquial speech, a simple setting in a draw-ing room or study, a natural way of introducing or dismissing characters. Ibsen had learned from the "well-made" Parisian play (typified by those of Eugène Scribe) how to confine his action to one climactic situation and how gradually to uncover the past by retrogressive exposition. But he went far beyond it in technical skill and intellectual honesty.

The success of Ibsen's problem plays was international. But we must not forget that he was a Norwegian, the first writer of his small nation (its population at that time was less than two million) to win a reputation outside of Norway. Ibsen more than anyone else widened the scope of world literature beyond the confines of the "great" modern nations, which had entered its community roughly in this order: Italy, Spain, France, England, Germany, Russia. Since the time of Ibsen, other small nations have begun to play their part in the concert of world literature. Paradoxically, however, Ibsen rejected his own land. He had dreamed of becom-ing a great national poet. Instead, the plays he wrote during his voluntary exile depicted Norwegian society as consisting largely of a stuffy, provincial middle class, redeemed by a few upright, even fiery, individuals of initiative and courage. Only in 1891, when he was sixty-three, did Ibsen return to Christiana for good. He was then famous and widely honored, but lived a very retired life. In 1900 he suffered a stroke that made him a complete invalid for the last years of his life. He died on May 23, 1906, in Christiana.

Ibsen could hardly have survived his time if he had been merely a painter of society, a dialectician of social issues, and a magnificent technician of the theater. True, many of his discussions are now dated. We smile at some of what happens in *A Doll's House* (1879) and *Ghosts* (1881). His stagecraft is not unusual, even on Broadway. But Ibsen stays with us because he has more to offer—because he was an artist who managed to create, at his best, works of poetry that, under their mask of sardonic humor, express his dream of humanity reborn by intelligence and self-sacrifice.

Hedda Gabler (1890) surprised and puzzled the large audience all over Europe that Ibsen had won in the 1880s. The play shows nothing of Ibsen's reforming zeal: no general theme emerges that could be used in spreading progressive ideas such as the emancipation of women dramatized in *A Doll's House* (1879), nor is the play an example of Ibsen's peculiar technique of retrospective revelation exhib-ited in *Rosmersholm* (1886). At first glance it seems mainly a study of a complex, exceptional, and even unique woman. Henry James, reviewing the first English performance, saw it as the picture of "a state of nerves as well as of soul, a state of temper, of health, of chagrin, of despair." Undoubtedly, Hedda is the central figure of the play, but she is no conventional heroine. She behaves atrociously to every-one with whom she comes in contact, and her moral sense is thoroughly defective:

she is perverse, egotistical, sadistic, callous, even evil and demonic, truly a *femme fatale*. Still, this impression, while not mistaken, ignores another side of her personality and her situation. The play is, after all, a tragedy (though there are comic touches), and we are to feel pity and terror. Hedda is not simply evil and perverse. We must imagine her as distinguished, well bred, proud, beautiful, and even grand in her defiance of her surroundings and in the final gesture of her suicide. Not for nothing have great actresses excelled in this role. We must pity her as a tortured, tormented creature caught in a web of circumstance, as a victim, in spite of her desperate struggles to dominate and control the fate of those around her.

We are carefully prepared to understand her heritage. She is General Gabler's daughter. Ibsen tells us himself (in a letter to Count Moritz Prozor, dated December 4, 1890) that "I intended to indicate thereby that as a personality she is to be regarded rather as her father's daughter than as her husband's wife." She has inherited an aristocratic view of life. Her father's portrait hangs in her apartment. His pistols tell of the code of honor and the ready escape they offer in a self-inflicted death. Hedda lives in Ibsen's Norway, a stuffy, provincial, middle-class society, and is acutely, even morbidly afraid of scandal. She has, to her own regret, rejected the advances of Eilert, theatrically threatening him with her father's pistol. She envies Thea for the boldness with which she deserted her husband to follow Eilert. She admires Eilert for his escapades, which she romanticizes with the recurrent metaphor of his returning with "vine-leaves in his hair." But she cannot break out of the narrow confines of her society. She is not an emancipated woman.

When she is almost thirty, in reduced circumstances, she accepts a suitable husband, George Tesman. The marriage of convenience turns out to be a ghastly error for which she cannot forgive herself: Tesman is an amiable bore absorbed in his research into the "Domestic Industries of Brabant During the Middle Ages." His expectations of a professorship in his home town turn out to be uncertain. He has gone into debt, even to his guileless old aunt, in renting an expensive house, and, supreme humiliation for her, Hedda is pregnant by him. The dream of luxury, of becoming a hostess, of keeping thoroughbred horses, is shattered the very first day after their return from the prolonged honeymoon, which for Tesman was also a trip to rummage around in archives. Hedda is deeply stirred by the return of Eilert, her first suitor. She seems vaguely to think of a new relationship, at least, by spoiling his friendship with Thea. She plays with the attentions of Judge Brack. But everything quickly comes to nought: she is trapped in her marriage, unable and unwilling to become unfaithful to her husband; she is deeply disappointed by Eilert's ugly death, saying, "Oh, why does everything I touch become mean and ludicrous? It's like a curse!" She fears the scandal that will follow when her role in Eilert's suicide is discovered and she is called before the police; she can avoid it only by coming under the power of Judge Brack, who is prepared to blackmail her with his knowledge of the circumstances. Her plot to destroy Thea and Eilert's brainchild is frustrated by Thea's having preserved notes and drafts, which Thea eagerly starts to reconstruct with the help of Tesman. Still, while Hedda is in a terrible impasse, her suicide remains a shock, an abrupt, even absurd deed, eliciting the final line from the commonsensical Judge Brack: "But, good God! People don't do such things!" But we must assume that Hedda had pondered suicide long before: the pistol she gave to Eilert implies an unspoken suicide pact. He bungled it; she does it the right way, dying in beauty, shot in the temple and not in the abdomen.

The play is not, however, simply a character study, though Hedda is an extraordinarily complex, contradictory, subtle woman whose portrait, at least on the stage, could not be easily paralleled before Ibsen. It is also an extremely effective, swiftly moving play of action, deftly plotted in its clashes and climaxes. At the end of Act I Hedda seems to have won. The Tesmans, husband and aunt, are put in their place. Thea is lured into making confidences. The scene in Act II in which Hedda appeals to Eilert's pride in his independence and induces him to join in Judge Brack's party is a superb display of Hedda's power and skill. Act II ends with Eilert going off and the two women left alone in their tense though suppressed antagonism. Act III ends with Hedda alone, burning the precious manuscript about the "forces that will shape our civilization and the direction in which that civilization may develop," an obvious contrast to Tesman's research into an irrelevant past. (Ibsen himself always believed in progress, in a utopia he called "the Third Realm.")

The action is compressed into about thirty-six hours and located in a house where only the moving of furniture (the piano into the back room) or the change of light or costumes indicates the passing of time. Tesman is something of a fool. He is totally unaware of Hedda's inner turmoil, he obtusely misunderstands allusions to her pregnancy, he comically encourages the advances of Judge Brack, he complacently settles down to the task of assembling the fragments of Eilert's manuscript, recognizing that "putting other people's papers into order is rather my specialty." Though he seems amiably domestic in his love for his aunts, proud of having won Hedda, ambitious to provide an elegant home for her, his behavior is by no means above reproach. He envies and fears Eilert, gloats over his bad reputation, surreptitiously brings home the lost manuscript, conceals its recovery from Thea; when Hedda tells of its being burned, he is at first shocked, reacting comically with the legal phrase about "appropriating lost property," but is then easily persuaded to accept it when Hedda tells him that she did it for his sake and is completely won over when she reveals her pregnancy. After Eilert's death he feels, however, some guilt and tries to make up by helping in the reconstruction of the manuscript, now that his rival no longer threatens his career. Tesman is given strong speech mannerisms: the frequent use of "what?"—which Hedda, commenting at the end on the progress of the work on the manuscript, imitates sarcastically—and the use of "fancy that." His last inappropriate words, "She's shot herself! Shot herself in the head! Fancy that!" lend a grotesque touch to the tragic end. Aunt Juliana belongs with him: she is a fussy, kindly person, proud of her nephew, awed by his new wife, eager to help with the expected baby, but also easily consoled after the death of her sister: "There's always some poor invalid who needs care and attention."

The other pair, Eilert Loevborg and Thea Elvsted, are sharply contrasted. Thea had the courage to leave her husband; she is devoted to Eilert and seems to have cured him of his addiction to drink but fears that he cannot resist a new temptation. Eilert tells Hedda unkindly that Thea is "silly," and there is some truth to that, inasmuch as she is so easily taken in by Hedda. Her quick settling down to work on the manuscript after Eilert's death suggests some obtuseness, though we must, presumably, excuse it as a theatrical foreshortening.

Judge Brack is a "man of the world," a sensualist who hardly conceals his desire to make Hedda his mistress, by blackmail if necessary, and is dismayed when she escapes his clutches: in his facile philosophy "people usually learn to accept the inevitable."

Eilert, we must assume, is some kind of genius. His book, we have to take on trust, is an important work. We are told that he had squandered an inheritance, had engaged in orgies, and had regaled Hedda with tales of his exploits before she chased him with her pistol. When he comes back to town, ostensibly reformed, dressed conventionally, he immediately starts courting Hedda again. Stung by her contempt for his abstinence, he rushes off to Brack's party, which degenerates into a disgraceful brawl in a brothel. His relapse and the loss of the manuscript destroy his self-esteem and hope for any future. He accepts Hedda's pistol but dies an ignominious, ugly death. We see Eilert mainly reflected in Hedda's imagination as a figure of pagan freedom who, she thinks, has done something noble, beautiful, and courageous in "rising from the feast of life so early." She dies in beauty as she wanted Eilert to die.

This aesthetic suicide must seem to us a supremely futile gesture of revolt. Ibsen always admired the great rebels, the fighters for freedom, but *Hedda Gabler* will appear almost a parodic version of his persistent theme: the individual against society, defying it and escaping it in death.

J. W. McFarlane, ed., *Discussions of Henrik Ibsen* (1962), contains Henry James's "On the Occasion of 'Hedda Gabler.'" John Northam, *Ibsen: A Critical Study* (1973), has a chapter on *Hedda Gabler*, as do Bernard Shaw, *The Quintessence of Ibsenism* (1913), and Hermann J. Weigand, *The Modern Ibsen* (1925). Rolf Fjelde, ed., *Ibsen: A Collection of Critical Essays* (1965), has a good essay on *Hedda Gabler*. For more general comment, see Yvonne Shafter, *Henrik Ibsen: Life, Work, and Criticism* (1985). *Ibsen's Heroines* (1985), by Ibsen's friend Lou Andreas-Salomé, has an interesting chapter on Hedda Gabler as an empty soul reaching for greatness. Frederick J. Marker and Lise-Lone Marker, *Ibsen's Lively Art: A Performance Study of the Major Plays* (1989), use descriptions of the various performances of *Hedda Gabler* to examine differing interpretations of the main characters.

PRONOUNCING GLOSSARY

The following list uses common English syllables and stress accents to provide rough equivalents of selected words whose pronunciation may be unfamiliar to the general reader.

Eilert Loevborg: *ai'-lert leuhv'-borg*

fjord: *fyoord*

Rosmersholm: *ross'-merss-holm*

Thea Elvsted: *tay'-ah aelf'-sted*

Hedda Gabler[1]

CHARACTERS

GEORGE TESMAN, *research graduate in cultural history*
HEDDA, *his wife*
MISS JULIANA TESMAN, *his aunt*
MRS. ELVSTED
JUDGE BRACK
EILERT LOEVBORG
BERTHA, *a maid*

The action takes place in TESMAN's *villa in the fashionable quarter of town.*

Act I

SCENE—*A large drawing room, handsomely and tastefully furnished; decorated in dark colors. In the rear wall is a broad open doorway, with curtains drawn back to either side. It leads to a smaller room, decorated in the same style as the drawing room. In the right-hand wall of the drawing room, a folding door leads out to the hall. The opposite wall, on the left,*

---

1. Translated by Michael Meyer.

contains french windows, also with curtains drawn back on either side. Through the glass we can see part of a verandah, and trees in autumn colors. Downstage stands an oval table, covered by a cloth and surrounded by chairs. Downstage right, against the wall, is a broad stove tiled with dark porcelain; in front of it stand a high-backed armchair, a cushioned footrest, and two footstools. Upstage right, in an alcove, is a corner sofa, with a small, round table. Downstage left, a little away from the wall, is another sofa. Upstage of the french windows, a piano. On either side of the open doorway in the rear wall stand what-nots holding ornaments of terra cotta and majolica. Against the rear wall of the smaller room can be seen a sofa, a table, and a couple of chairs. Above this sofa hangs the portrait of a handsome old man in general's uniform. Above the table a lamp hangs from the ceiling, with a shade of opalescent, milky glass. All round the drawing room bunches of flowers stand in vases and glasses. More bunches lie on the tables. The floors of both rooms are covered with thick carpets. Morning light. The sun shines in through the french windows.

MISS JULIANA TESMAN, wearing a hat and carrying a parasol, enters from the hall, followed by BERTHA, who is carrying a bunch of flowers wrapped in paper. MISS TESMAN is about sixty-five, of pleasant and kindly appearance. She is neatly but simply dressed in grey outdoor clothes. BERTHA, the maid, is rather simple and rustic-looking. She is getting on in years.

MISS TESMAN: [Stops just inside the door, listens, and says in a hushed voice.] No, bless my soul! They're not up yet.

BERTHA: [Also in hushed tones.] What did I tell you, miss? The boat didn't get in till midnight. And when they did turn up—Jesus, miss, you should have seen all the things Madam made me unpack before she'd go to bed!

MISS TESMAN: Ah, well. Let them have a good lie in. But let's have some nice fresh air waiting for them when they do come down. [Goes to the french windows and throws them wide open.]

BERTHA: [Bewildered at the table, the bunch of flowers in her hand.] I'm blessed if there's a square inch left to put anything. I'll have to let it lie here, miss. [Puts it on the piano.]

MISS TESMAN: Well, Bertha dear, so now you have a new mistress. Heaven knows it nearly broke my heart to have to part with you.

BERTHA: [Snivels.] What about me, Miss Juju? How do you suppose I felt? After all the happy years I've spent with you and Miss Rena?

MISS TESMAN: We must accept it bravely, Bertha. It was the only way. George needs you to take care of him. He could never manage without you. You've looked after him ever since he was a tiny boy.

BERTHA: Oh, but Miss Juju, I can't help thinking about Miss Rena, lying there all helpless, poor dear. And that new girl! She'll never learn the proper way to handle an invalid.

MISS TESMAN: Oh, I'll manage to train her. I'll do most of the work myself, you know. You needn't worry about my poor sister, Bertha dear.

BERTHA: But Miss Juju, there's another thing. I'm frightened Madam may not find me suitable.

MISS TESMAN: Oh, nonsense, Bertha. There may be one or two little things to begin with——

BERTHA: She's a real lady. Wants everything just so.

MISS TESMAN: But of course she does! General Gabler's daughter! Think of what she was accustomed to when the General was alive. You remember how we used to see her out riding with her father? In that long black skirt? With the feather in her hat?

BERTHA: Oh, yes, miss. As if I could forget! But, Lord! I never dreamed I'd live to see a match between her and Master Georgie.

MISS TESMAN: Neither did I. By the way, Bertha, from now on you must stop calling him Master Georgie. You must say: Dr. Tesman.

BERTHA: Yes, Madam said something about that too. Last night—the moment they'd set foot inside the door. Is it true, then, miss?

MISS TESMAN: Indeed it is. Just imagine, Bertha, some foreigners have made him a doctor. It happened while they were away. I had no idea till he told me when they got off the boat.

BERTHA: Well, I suppose there's no limit to what he won't become. He's that clever. I never thought he'd go in for hospital work, though.

MISS TESMAN: No, he's not that kind of doctor. [*Nods impressively.*] In any case, you may soon have to address him by an even grander title.

BERTHA: You don't say! What might that be, miss?

MISS TESMAN: [*Smiles.*] Ah! If you only knew! [*Moved.*] Dear God, if only poor dear Joachim could rise out of his grave and see what his little son has grown into! [*Looks round.*] But Bertha, why have you done this? Taken the chintz covers off all the furniture!

BERTHA: Madam said I was to. Can't stand chintz covers on chairs, she said.

MISS TESMAN: But surely they're not going to use this room as a parlor?

BERTHA: So I gathered, miss. From what Madam said. He didn't say anything. The Doctor.

> [GEORGE TESMAN *comes into the rear room, from the right, humming, with an open, empty travelling bag in his hand. He is about thirty-three, of medium height and youthful appearance, rather plump, with an open, round, contented face, and fair hair and beard. He wears spectacles, and is dressed in comfortable, indoor clothes.*]

MISS TESMAN: Good morning! Good morning, George!

TESMAN: [*In open doorway.*] Auntie Juju! Dear Auntie Juju! [*Comes forward and shakes her hand.*] You've come all the way out here! And so early! What?

MISS TESMAN: Well, I had to make sure you'd settled in comfortably.

TESMAN: But you can't have had a proper night's sleep.

MISS TESMAN: Oh, never mind that.

TESMAN: We were so sorry we couldn't give you a lift. But you saw how it was—Hedda had so much luggage—and she insisted on having it all with her.

MISS TESMAN: Yes, I've never seen so much luggage.

BERTHA: [*To TESMAN.*] Shall I go and ask Madam if there's anything I can lend her a hand with?

TESMAN: Er—thank you, Bertha; no, you needn't bother. She says if she wants you for anything she'll ring.

BERTHA: [*Over to right.*] Oh. Very good.

TESMAN: Oh, Bertha—take this bag, will you?

BERTHA: [*Takes it.*] I'll put it in the attic. [*Goes out into the hall.*]

TESMAN: Just fancy, Auntie Juju, I filled that whole bag with notes for my book. You know, it's really incredible what I've managed to find rooting through those archives. By Jove! Wonderful old things no one even knew existed——

MISS TESMAN: I'm sure you didn't waste a single moment of your honeymoon, George dear.

TESMAN: No, I think I can truthfully claim that. But, Auntie Juju, do take your hat off. Here. Let me untie it for you. What?

MISS TESMAN: [*As he does so.*] Oh dear, oh dear! It's just as if you were still living at home with us.

TESMAN: [*Turns the hat in his hand and looks at it.*] I say! What a splendid new hat!

MISS TESMAN: I bought it for Hedda's sake.

TESMAN: For Hedda's sake? What?

MISS TESMAN: So that Hedda needn't be ashamed of me, in case we ever go for a walk together.

TESMAN: [*Pats her cheek.*] You still think of everything, don't you, Auntie Juju? [*Puts the hat down on a chair by the table.*] Come on, let's sit down here on the sofa. And have a little chat while we wait for Hedda.

[*They sit. She puts her parasol in the corner of the sofa.*]

MISS TESMAN: [*Clasps both his hands and looks at him.*] Oh, George, it's so wonderful to have you back, and be able to see you with my own eyes again! Poor dear Joachim's own son!

TESMAN: What about me! It's wonderful for me to see you again, Auntie Juju. You've been a mother to me. And a father, too.

MISS TESMAN: You'll always keep a soft spot in your heart for your old aunties, won't you, George dear?

TESMAN: I suppose Auntie Rena's no better? What?

MISS TESMAN: Alas, no. I'm afraid she'll never get better, poor dear. She's lying there just as she has for all these years. Please God I may be allowed to keep her for a little longer. If I lost her I don't know what I'd do. Especially now I haven't you to look after.

TESMAN: [*Pats her on the back.*] There, there, there!

MISS TESMAN: [*With a sudden change of mood.*] Oh but George, fancy you being a married man! And to think it's you who've won Hedda Gabler! The beautiful Hedda Gabler! Fancy! She was always so surrounded by admirers.

TESMAN: [*Hums a little and smiles contentedly.*] Yes, I suppose there are quite a few people in this town who wouldn't mind being in my shoes. What?

MISS TESMAN: And what a honeymoon! Five months! Nearly six.

TESMAN: Well, I've done a lot of work, you know. All those archives to go through. And I've had to read lots of books.

MISS TESMAN: Yes, dear, of course. [*Lowers her voice confidentially.*] But

tell me, George—haven't you any—any extra little piece of news to give
me?

TESMAN: You mean, arising out of the honeymoon?

MISS TESMAN: Yes.

TESMAN: No, I don't think there's anything I didn't tell you in my letters.
My doctorate, of course—but I told you about that last night, didn't I?

MISS TESMAN: Yes, yes, I didn't mean that kind of thing. I was just wondering—are you—are you expecting——?

TESMAN: Expecting what?

MISS TESMAN: Oh, come on George, I'm your old aunt!

TESMAN: Well actually—yes, I am expecting something.

MISS TESMAN: I knew it!

TESMAN: You'll be happy to hear that before very long I expect to become
a professor.

MISS TESMAN: Professor?

TESMAN: I think I may say that the matter has been decided. But, Auntie
Juju, you know about this.

MISS TESMAN: [*Gives a little laugh.*] Yes, of course. I'd forgotten. [*Changes
her tone.*] But we were talking about your honeymoon. It must have
cost a dreadful amount of money, George?

TESMAN: Oh well, you know, that big research grant I got helped a good
deal.

MISS TESMAN: But how on earth did you manage to make it do for two?

TESMAN: Well, to tell the truth it was a bit tricky. What?

MISS TESMAN: Especially when one's traveling with a lady. A little bird tells
me that makes things very much more expensive.

TESMAN: Well, yes, of course it does make things a little more expensive.
But Hedda has to do things in style, Auntie Juju. I mean, she has to.
Anything less grand wouldn't have suited her.

MISS TESMAN: No, no, I suppose not. A honeymoon abroad seems to be
the vogue nowadays. But tell me, have you had time to look round the
house?

TESMAN: You bet. I've been up since the crack of dawn.

MISS TESMAN: Well, what do you think of it?

TESMAN: Splendid. Absolutely splendid. I'm only wondering what we're
going to do with those two empty rooms between that little one and
Hedda's bedroom.

MISS TESMAN: [*Laughs slyly.*] Ah, George dear, I'm sure you'll manage to
find some use for them—in time.

TESMAN: Yes, of course, Auntie Juju, how stupid of me. You're thinking of
my books. What?

MISS TESMAN: Yes, yes, dear boy. I was thinking of your books.

TESMAN: You know, I'm so happy for Hedda's sake that we've managed to
get this house. Before we became engaged she often used to say this was
the only house in town she felt she could really bear to live in. It used
to belong to Mrs. Falk—you know, the Prime Minister's widow.

MISS TESMAN: Fancy that! And what a stroke of luck it happened to come
into the market. Just as you'd left on your honeymoon.

TESMAN: Yes, Auntie Juju, we've certainly had all the luck with us. What?

MISS TESMAN: But, George dear, the expense! It's going to make a dreadful hole in your pocket, all this.

TESMAN: [*A little downcast.*] Yes, I—I suppose it will, won't it?

MISS TESMAN: Oh, George, really!

TESMAN: How much do you think it'll cost? Roughly, I mean? What?

MISS TESMAN: I can't possibly say till I see the bills.

TESMAN: Well, luckily Judge Brack's managed to get it on very favorable terms. He wrote and told Hedda so.

MISS TESMAN: Don't you worry, George dear. Anyway I've stood security for all the furniture and carpets.

TESMAN: Security? But dear, sweet Auntie Juju, how could you possibly stand security?

MISS TESMAN: I've arranged a mortgage on our annuity.

TESMAN: [*Jumps up.*] What? On your annuity? And—Auntie Rena's?

MISS TESMAN: Yes. Well, I couldn't think of any other way.

TESMAN: [*Stands in front of her.*] Auntie Juju, have you gone completely out of your mind? That annuity's all you and Auntie Rena have.

MISS TESMAN: All right, there's no need to get so excited about it. It's a pure formality, you know. Judge Brack told me so. He was so kind as to arrange it all for me. A pure formality; those were his very words.

TESMAN: I dare say. All the same——

MISS TESMAN: Anyway, you'll have a salary of your own now. And, good heavens, even if we did have to fork out a little—tighten our belts for a week or two—why, we'd be happy to do so for your sake.

TESMAN: Oh, Auntie Juju! Will you never stop sacrificing yourself for me?

MISS TESMAN: [*Gets up and puts her hands on his shoulders.*] What else have I to live for but to smooth your road a little, my dear boy? You've never had any mother or father to turn to. And now at last we've achieved our goal. I won't deny we've had our little difficulties now and then. But now, thank the good Lord, George dear, all your worries are past.

TESMAN: Yes, it's wonderful really how everything's gone just right for me.

MISS TESMAN: Yes! And the enemies who tried to bar your way have been struck down. They have been made to bite the dust. The man who was your most dangerous rival has had the mightiest fall. And now he's lying there in the pit he dug for himself, poor misguided creature.

TESMAN: Have you heard any news of Eilert? Since I went away?

MISS TESMAN: Only that he's said to have published a new book.

TESMAN: What! Eilert Loevborg? You mean—just recently? What?

MISS TESMAN: So they say. I don't imagine it can be of any value, do you? When your new book comes out, that'll be another story. What's it going to be about?

TESMAN: The domestic industries of Brabant[2] in the Middle Ages.

MISS TESMAN: Oh, George! The things you know about!

TESMAN: Mind you, it may be some time before I actually get down to writing it. I've made these very extensive notes, and I've got to file and index them first.

---

2. In the Middle Ages, a duchy located in parts of what are now Belgium and the Netherlands.

MISS TESMAN: Ah, yes! Making notes; filing and indexing; you've always been wonderful at that. Poor dear Joachim was just the same.

TESMAN: I'm looking forward so much to getting down to that. Especially now I've a home of my own to work in.

MISS TESMAN: And above all, now that you have the girl you set your heart on, George dear.

TESMAN: [*Embraces her.*] Oh, yes, Auntie Juju, yes! Hedda's the loveliest thing of all! [*Looks towards the doorway.*] I think I hear her coming. What?

[HEDDA *enters the rear room from the left, and comes into the drawing room. She is a woman of twenty-nine. Distinguished, aristocratic face and figure. Her complexion is pale and opalescent. Her eyes are steel-grey, with an expression of cold, calm serenity. Her hair is of a handsome auburn color, but is not especially abundant. She is dressed in an elegant, somewhat loose-fitting morning gown.*]

MISS TESMAN: [*Goes to greet her.*] Good morning, Hedda dear! Good morning!

HEDDA: [*Holds out her hand.*] Good morning, dear Miss Tesman. What an early hour to call. So kind of you.

MISS TESMAN: [*Seems somewhat embarrassed.*] And has the young bride slept well in her new home?

HEDDA: Oh—thank you, yes. Passably well.

TESMAN: [*Laughs.*] Passably. I say, Hedda, that's good! When I jumped out of bed, you were sleeping like a top.

HEDDA: Yes. Fortunately. One has to accustom oneself to anything new, Miss Tesman. It takes time. [*Looks left.*] Oh, that maid's left the french windows open. This room's flooded with sun.

MISS TESMAN: [*Goes towards the windows.*] Oh—let me close them.

HEDDA: No, no, don't do that. Tesman dear, draw the curtains. This light's blinding me.

TESMAN: [*At the windows.*] Yes, yes, dear. There, Hedda, now you've got shade and fresh air.

HEDDA: This room needs fresh air. All these flowers—But my dear Miss Tesman, won't you take a seat?

MISS TESMAN: No, really not, thank you. I just wanted to make sure you have everything you need. I must see about getting back home. My poor dear sister will be waiting for me.

TESMAN: Be sure to give her my love, won't you? Tell her I'll run over and see her later today.

MISS TESMAN: Oh yes, I'll tell her that. Oh, George——[*Fumbles in the pocket of her skirt.*] I almost forgot. I've brought something for you.

TESMAN: What's that, Auntie Juju? What?

MISS TESMAN: [*Pulls out a flat package wrapped in newspaper and gives it to him.*] Open and see, dear boy.

TESMAN: [*Opens the package.*] Good heavens! Auntie Juju, you've kept them! Hedda, this is really very touching. What?

HEDDA: [*By the what-nots, on the right.*] What is it, Tesman?

TESMAN: My old shoes! My slippers, Hedda!

HEDDA: Oh, them. I remember you kept talking about them on our honey-moon.

TESMAN: Yes, I missed them dreadfully. [*Goes over to her.*] Here, Hedda, take a look.

HEDDA: [*Goes away towards the stove.*] Thanks, I won't bother.

TESMAN: [*Follows her.*] Fancy, Hedda, Auntie Rena's embroidered them for me. Despite her being so ill. Oh, you can't imagine what memories they have for me.

HEDDA: [*By the table.*] Not for me.

MISS TESMAN: No, Hedda's right there, George.

TESMAN: Yes, but I thought since she's one of the family now——

HEDDA: [*Interrupts.*] Tesman, we really can't go on keeping this maid.

MISS TESMAN: Not keep Bertha?

TESMAN: What makes you say that, dear? What?

HEDDA: [*Points.*] Look at that! She's left her old hat lying on the chair.

TESMAN: [*Appalled, drops his slippers on the floor.*] But, Hedda——!

HEDDA: Suppose someone came in and saw it?

TESMAN: But Hedda—that's Auntie Juju's hat.

HEDDA: Oh?

MISS TESMAN: [*Picks up the hat.*] Indeed it's mine. And it doesn't happen to be old, Hedda dear.

HEDDA: I didn't look at it very closely, Miss Tesman.

MISS TESMAN: [*Tying on the hat.*] As a matter of fact, it's the first time I've worn it. As the good Lord is my witness.

TESMAN: It's very pretty, too. Really smart.

MISS TESMAN: Oh, I'm afraid it's nothing much really. [*Looks round.*] My parasol? Ah, here it is. [*Takes it.*] This is mine, too. [*Murmurs.*] Not Bertha's.

TESMAN: A new hat and a new parasol! I say, Hedda, fancy that!

HEDDA: Very pretty and charming.

TESMAN: Yes, isn't it? What? But Auntie Juju, take a good look at Hedda before you go. Isn't she pretty and charming?

MISS TESMAN: Dear boy, there's nothing new in that. Hedda's been a beauty ever since the day she was born. [*Nods and goes right.*]

TESMAN: [*Follows her.*] Yes, but have you noticed how strong and healthy she's looking? And how she's filled out since we went away?

MISS TESMAN: [*Stops and turns.*] Filled out?

HEDDA: [*Walks across the room.*] Oh, can't we forget it?

TESMAN: Yes, Auntie Juju—you can't see it so clearly with that dress on. But I've good reason to know——

HEDDA: [*By the french windows, impatiently.*] You haven't good reason to know anything.

TESMAN: It must have been the mountain air up there in the Tyrol——

HEDDA: [*Curtly, interrupts him.*] I'm exactly the same as when I went away.

TESMAN: You keep on saying so. But you're not. I'm right, aren't I, Auntie Juju?

MISS TESMAN: [*Has folded her hands and is gazing at her.*] She's beautiful—beautiful. Hedda is beautiful. [*Goes over to* HEDDA, *takes her head between her hands, draws it down and kisses her hair.*] God bless and keep you, Hedda Tesman. For George's sake.

HEDDA: [*Frees herself politely.*] Oh—let me go, please.

MISS TESMAN: [*Quietly, emotionally.*] I shall come see you both every day.

TESMAN: Yes, Auntie Juju, please do. What?

MISS TESMAN: Good-bye! Good-bye!

[*She goes out into the hall.* TESMAN *follows her. The door remains open.* TESMAN *is heard sending his love to* AUNT RENA *and thanking* MISS TESMAN *for his slippers. Meanwhile* HEDDA *walks up and down the room raising her arms and clenching her fists as though in desperation. Then she throws aside the curtains from the french windows and stands there, looking out. A few moments later,* TESMAN *returns and closes the door behind him.*]

TESMAN: [*Picks up his slippers from the floor.*] What are you looking at, Hedda?

HEDDA: [*Calm and controlled again.*] Only the leaves. They're so golden. And withered.

TESMAN: [*Wraps up the slippers and lays them on the table.*] Well, we're in September now.

HEDDA: [*Restless again.*] Yes. We're already into September.

TESMAN: Auntie Juju was behaving rather oddly, I thought, didn't you? Almost as though she was in church or something. I wonder what came over her. Any idea?

HEDDA: I hardly know her. Does she often act like that?

TESMAN: Not to the extent she did today.

HEDDA: [*Goes away from the french windows.*] Do you think she was hurt by what I said about the hat?

TESMAN: Oh, I don't think so. A little at first, perhaps—

HEDDA: But what a thing to do, throw her hat down in someone's drawing room. People don't do such things.

TESMAN: I'm sure Auntie Juju doesn't do it very often.

HEDDA: Oh well, I'll make it up with her.

TESMAN: Oh Hedda, would you?

HEDDA: When you see them this afternoon invite her to come out here this evening.

TESMAN: You bet I will! I say, there's another thing which would please her enormously.

HEDDA: Oh?

TESMAN: If you could bring yourself to call her Auntie Juju. For my sake, Hedda? What?

HEDDA: Oh no, really Tesman, you mustn't ask me to do that. I've told you so once before. I'll try to call her Aunt Juliana. That's as far as I'll go.

TESMAN: [*After a moment.*] I say, Hedda, is anything wrong? What?

HEDDA: I'm just looking at my old piano. It doesn't really go with all this.

TESMAN: As soon as I start getting my salary we'll see about changing it.

HEDDA: No, no, don't let's change it. I don't want to part with it. We can move it into that little room and get another one to put in here.

TESMAN: [*A little downcast.*] Yes, we—might do that.

HEDDA: [*Picks up the bunch of flowers from the piano.*] These flowers weren't here when we arrived last night.

TESMAN: I expect Auntie Juju brought them.

HEDDA: Here's a card. [*Takes it out and reads.*] "Will come back later today." Guess who it's from?

TESMAN: No idea. Who? What?

HEDDA: It says: "Mrs. Elvsted."

TESMAN: No, really? Mrs. Elvsted! She used to be Miss Rysing, didn't she?

HEDDA: Yes. She was the one with that irritating hair she was always showing off. I hear she used to be an old flame of yours.

TESMAN: [*Laughs.*] That didn't last long. Anyway, that was before I got to know you, Hedda. By Jove, fancy her being in town!

HEDDA: Strange she should call. I only knew her at school.

TESMAN: Yes, I haven't seen her for—oh, heaven knows how long. I don't know how she manages to stick it out up there in the north. What?

HEDDA: [*Thinks for a moment, then says suddenly.*] Tell me, Tesman, doesn't he live somewhere up in those parts? You know—Eilert Loevborg?

TESMAN: Yes, that's right. So he does.

[BERTHA *enters from the hall.*]

BERTHA: She's here again, madam. The lady who came and left the flowers. [*Points.*] The ones you're holding.

HEDDA: Oh, is she? Well, show her in.

[BERTHA *opens the door for* MRS. ELVSTED *and goes out.* MRS. ELVSTED *is a delicately built woman with gentle, attractive features. Her eyes are light blue, large, and somewhat prominent, with a frightened, questioning expression. Her hair is extremely fair, almost flaxen, and is exceptionally wavy and abundant. She is two or three years younger than* HEDDA: *She is wearing a dark visiting dress, in good taste but not quite in the latest fashion.*]

HEDDA: [*Goes cordially to greet her.*] Dear Mrs. Elvsted, good morning. How delightful to see you again after all this time.

MRS. ELVSTED: [*Nervously, trying to control herself.*] Yes, it's many years since we met.

TESMAN: And since *we* met. What?

HEDDA: Thank you for your lovely flowers.

MRS. ELVSTED: Oh, please—I wanted to come yesterday afternoon. But they told me you were away——

TESMAN: You've only just arrived in town, then? What?

MRS. ELVSTED: I got here yesterday, around midday. Oh, I became almost desperate when I heard you weren't here.

HEDDA: Desperate? Why?

TESMAN: My dear Mrs. Rysing—Elvsted——

HEDDA: There's nothing wrong, I hope?

MRS. ELVSTED: Yes, there is. And I don't know anyone else here whom I can turn to.

HEDDA: [*Puts the flowers down on the table.*] Come and sit with me on the sofa——

MRS. ELVSTED: Oh, I feel too restless to sit down.

HEDDA: You must. Come along, now.

[*She pulls* MRS. ELVSTED *down on to the sofa and sits beside her.*]

TESMAN: Well? Tell us, Mrs.—er——

HEDDA: Has something happened at home?

MRS. ELVSTED: Yes—that is, yes and no. Oh, I do hope you won't misunderstand me——

HEDDA: Then you'd better tell us the whole story, Mrs. Elvsted.

TESMAN: That's why you've come. What?

MRS. ELVSTED: Yes—yes, it is. Well, then—in case you don't already know—Eilert Loevborg is in town.

HEDDA: Loevborg here?

TESMAN: Eilert back in town? By Jove, Hedda, did you hear that?

HEDDA: Yes, of course I heard.

MRS. ELVSTED: He's been here a week. A whole week! In this city. Alone. With all those dreadful people——

HEDDA: But my dear Mrs. Elvsted, what concern is he of yours?

MRS. ELVSTED: [*Gives her a frightened look and says quickly.*] He's been tutoring the children.

HEDDA: Your children?

MRS. ELVSTED: My husband's. I have none.

HEDDA: Oh, you mean your stepchildren.

MRS. ELVSTED: Yes.

TESMAN: [*Gropingly.*] But was he sufficiently—I don't know how to put it—sufficiently regular in his habits to be suited to such a post? What?

MRS. ELVSTED: For the past two to three years he has been living irreproachably.

TESMAN: You don't say! By Jove, Hedda, hear that?

HEDDA: I hear.

MRS. ELVSTED: Quite irreproachably, I assure you. In every respect. All the same—in this big city—with money in his pockets—I'm so dreadfully frightened something may happen to him.

TESMAN: But why didn't he stay up there with you and your husband?

MRS. ELVSTED: Once his book had come out, he became restless.

TESMAN: Oh, yes—Auntie Juju said he's brought out a new book.

MRS. ELVSTED: Yes, a big new book about the history of civilization. A kind of general survey. It came out a fortnight ago. Everyone's been buying it and reading it—it's created a tremendous stir——

TESMAN: Has it really? It must be something he's dug up, then.

MRS. ELVSTED: You mean from the old days?

TESMAN: Yes.

MRS. ELVSTED: No, he's written it all since he came to live with us.

TESMAN: Well, that's splendid news, Hedda. Fancy that!

MRS. ELVSTED: Oh, yes! If only he can go on like this!

HEDDA: Have you met him since you came here?

MRS. ELVSTED: No, not yet. I had such dreadful difficulty finding his address. But this morning I managed to track him down at last.

HEDDA: [*Looks searchingly at her.*] I must say I find it a little strange that your husband—hm——

MRS. ELVSTED: [*Starts nervously.*] My husband! What do you mean?

HEDDA: That he should send you all the way here on an errand of this kind. I'm surprised he didn't come himself to keep an eye on his friend.

MRS. ELVSTED: Oh, no, no—my husband hasn't the time. Besides, I—er—wanted to do some shopping here.

HEDDA: [*With a slight smile.*] Ah. Well, that's different.

MRS. ELVSTED: [*Gets up quickly, restlessly.*] Please, Mr. Tesman, I beg you—be kind to Eilert Loevborg if he comes here. I'm sure he will. I mean, you used to be such good friends in the old days. And you're both studying the same subject, as far as I can understand. You're in the same field, aren't you?

TESMAN: Well, we used to be, anyway.

MRS. ELVSTED: Yes—so I beg you earnestly, do please, please, keep an eye on him. Oh, Mr. Tesman, do promise me you will.

TESMAN: I shall be only too happy to do so, Mrs. Rysing.

HEDDA: Elvsted.

TESMAN: I'll do everything for Eilert that lies in my power. You can rely on that.

MRS. ELVSTED: Oh, how good and kind you are! [*Presses his hands.*] Thank you, thank you, thank you. [*Frightened.*] My husband's so fond of him, you see.

HEDDA: [*Gets up.*] You'd better send him a note, Tesman. He may not come to you of his own accord.

TESMAN: Yes, that'd probably be the best plan, Hedda. What?

HEDDA: The sooner the better. Why not do it now?

MRS. ELVSTED: [*Pleadingly.*] Oh yes, if only you would!

TESMAN: I'll do it this very moment. Do you have his address, Mrs.—er—Elvsted?

MRS. ELVSTED: Yes. [*Takes a small piece of paper from her pocket and gives it to him.*]

TESMAN: Good, good. Right, well I'll go inside and—— [*Looks round.*] Where are my slippers? Oh yes, here. [*Picks up the package and is about to go.*]

HEDDA: Try to sound friendly. Make it a nice long letter.

TESMAN: Right, I will.

MRS. ELVSTED: Please don't say anything about my having seen you.

TESMAN: Good heavens no, of course not. What? [*Goes out through the rear room to the right.*]

HEDDA: [*Goes over to* MRS. ELVSTED, *smiles, and says softly.*] Well! Now we've killed two birds with one stone.

MRS. ELVSTED: What do you mean?

HEDDA: Didn't you realize I wanted to get him out of the room?

MRS. ELVSTED: So that he could write the letter?

HEDDA: And so that I could talk to you alone.

MRS. ELVSTED: [*Confused.*] About this?

HEDDA: Yes, about this.

MRS. ELVSTED: [*In alarm.*] But there's nothing more to tell, Mrs. Tesman. Really there isn't.

HEDDA: Oh, yes there is. There's a lot more. I can see that. Come along, let's sit down and have a little chat.

[She pushes MRS. ELVSTED *down into the armchair by the stove and seats herself on one of the footstools.*]

MRS. ELVSTED: [*Looks anxiously at her watch.*] Really, Mrs. Tesman, I think I ought to be going now.

HEDDA: There's no hurry. Well? How are things at home?

MRS. ELVSTED: I'd rather not speak about that.

HEDDA: But my dear, you can tell me. Good heavens, we were at school together.

MRS. ELVSTED: Yes, but you were a year senior to me. Oh, I used to be terribly frightened of you in those days.

HEDDA: Frightened of me?

MRS. ELVSTED: Yes, terribly frightened. Whenever you met me on the staircase you used to pull my hair.

HEDDA: No, did I?

MRS. ELVSTED: Yes. And once you said you'd burn it all off.

HEDDA: Oh, that was only in fun.

MRS. ELVSTED: Yes, but I was so silly in those days. And then afterwards— I mean, we've drifted so far apart. Our backgrounds were so different.

HEDDA: Well, now we must try to drift together again. Now listen. When we were at school we used to call each other by our Christian names—

MRS. ELVSTED: No, I'm sure you're mistaken.

HEDDA: I'm sure I'm not. I remember it quite clearly. Let's tell each other our secrets, as we used to in the old days. [*Moves closer on her footstool.*] There, now. [*Kisses her on the cheek.*] You must call me Hedda.

MRS. ELVSTED: [*Squeezes her hands and pats them.*] Oh, you're so kind. I'm not used to people being so nice to me.

HEDDA: Now, now, now. And I shall call you Tora, the way I used to.

MRS. ELVSTED: My name is Thea.

HEDDA: Yes, of course. Of course. I meant Thea. [*Looks at her sympathetically.*] So you're not used to kindness, Thea? In your own home?

MRS. ELVSTED: Oh, if only I had a home! But I haven't. I've never had one.

HEDDA: [*Looks at her for a moment.*] I thought that was it.

MRS. ELVSTED: [*Stares blankly and helplessly.*] Yes—yes—yes.

HEDDA: I can't remember exactly now, but didn't you first go to Mr. Elvsted as a housekeeper?

MRS. ELVSTED: Governess, actually. But his wife—at the time, I mean— she was an invalid, and had to spend most of her time in bed. So I had to look after the house too.

HEDDA: But in the end, you became mistress of the house.

MRS. ELVSTED: [*Sadly.*] Yes, I did.

HEDDA: Let me see. Roughly how long ago was that?

MRS. ELVSTED: When I got married, you mean?

HEDDA: Yes.

MRS. ELVSTED: About five years.

HEDDA: Yes; it must be about that.

MRS. ELVSTED: Oh, those five years! Especially that last two or three. Oh, Mrs. Tesman, if you only knew——

HEDDA: [*Slaps her hand gently.*] Mrs. Tesman? Oh, Thea!

MRS. ELVSTED: I'm sorry, I'll try to remember. Yes—if you had any idea——

HEDDA: [*Casually.*] Eilert Loevborg's been up there too, for about three years, hasn't he?

MRS. ELVSTED: [*Looks at her uncertainly.*] Eilert Loevborg? Yes, he has.

HEDDA: Did you know him before? When you were here?

MRS. ELVSTED: No, not really. That is—I knew him by name, of course.

HEDDA: But up there, he used to visit you?

MRS. ELVSTED: Yes, he used to come and see us every day. To give the children lessons. I found I couldn't do that as well as manage the house.

HEDDA: I'm sure you couldn't. And your husband——? I suppose being a magistrate he has to be away from home a good deal?

MRS. ELVSTED: Yes. You see, Mrs. ——you see, Hedda, he has to cover the whole district.

HEDDA: [*Leans against the arm of* MRS. ELVSTED'*s chair.*] Poor, pretty little Thea! Now you must tell me the whole story. From beginning to end.

MRS. ELVSTED: Well—what do you want to know?

HEDDA: What kind of a man is your husband, Thea? I mean, as a person. Is he kind to you?

MRS. ELVSTED: [*Evasively.*] I'm sure he does his best to be.

HEDDA: I only wonder if he isn't too old for you. There's more than twenty years between you, isn't there?

MRS. ELVSTED: [*Irritably.*] Yes, there's that too. Oh, there are so many things. We're different in every way. We've nothing in common. Nothing whatever.

HEDDA: But he loves you, surely? In his own way?

MRS. ELVSTED: Oh, I don't know. I think he just finds me useful. And then I don't cost much to keep. I'm cheap.

HEDDA: Now you're being stupid.

MRS. ELVSTED: [*Shakes her head.*] It can't be any different. With him. He doesn't love anyone except himself. And perhaps the children—a little.

HEDDA: He must be fond of Eilert Loevborg, Thea.

MRS. ELVSTED: [*Looks at her.*] Eilert Loevborg? What makes you think that?

HEDDA: Well, if he sends you all the way down here to look for him—— [*Smiles almost imperceptibly.*] Besides, you said so yourself to Tesman.

MRS. ELVSTED: [*With a nervous twitch.*] Did I? Oh yes, I suppose I did. [*Impulsively, but keeping her voice low.*] Well, I might as well tell you the whole story. It's bound to come out sooner or later.

HEDDA: But my dear Thea——?

MRS. ELVSTED: My husband had no idea I was coming here.

HEDDA: What? Your husband didn't know?

MRS. ELVSTED: No, of course not. As a matter of fact, he wasn't even there. He was away at the assizes. Oh, I couldn't stand it any longer, Hedda! I just couldn't. I'd be so dreadfully lonely up there now.

HEDDA: Go on.

MRS. ELVSTED: So I packed a few things. Secretly. And went.

HEDDA: Without telling anyone?

MRS. ELVSTED: Yes. I caught the train and came straight here.

HEDDA: But my dear Thea! How brave of you!

MRS. ELVSTED: [*Gets up and walks across the room.*] Well, what else could I do?

HEDDA: But what do you suppose your husband will say when you get back?

MRS. ELVSTED: [*By the table, looks at her.*] Back there? To him?

HEDDA: Yes. Surely——?

MRS. ELVSTED: I shall never go back to him.

HEDDA: [*Gets up and goes closer.*] You mean you've left your home for good?

MRS. ELVSTED: Yes. I didn't see what else I could do.

HEDDA: But to do it so openly!

MRS. ELVSTED: Oh, it's no use trying to keep a thing like that secret.

HEDDA: But what do you suppose people will say?

MRS. ELVSTED: They can say what they like. [*Sits sadly, wearily on the sofa.*] I had to do it.

HEDDA: [*After a short silence.*] What do you intend to do now? How are you going to live?

MRS. ELVSTED: I don't know. I only know that I must live wherever Eilert Loevborg is. If I am to go on living.

HEDDA: [*Moves a chair from the table, sits on it near* MRS. ELVSTED *and strokes her hands.*] Tell me, Thea, how did this—friendship between you and Eilert Loevborg begin?

MRS. ELVSTED: Oh, it came about gradually. I developed a kind of—power over him.

HEDDA: Oh?

MRS. ELVSTED: He gave up his old habits. Not because I asked him to. I'd never have dared to do that. I suppose he just noticed I didn't like that kind of thing. So he gave it up.

HEDDA: [*Hides a smile.*] So you've made a new man of him. Clever little Thea!

MRS. ELVSTED: Yes—anyway, he says I have. And he's made a—sort of— real person of me. Taught me to think—and to understand all kinds of things.

HEDDA: Did he give you lessons too?

MRS. ELVSTED: Not exactly lessons. But he talked to me. About—oh, you've no idea—so many things! And then he let me work with him. Oh, it was wonderful. I was so happy to be allowed to help him.

HEDDA: Did he allow you to help him!

MRS. ELVSTED: Yes. Whenever he wrote anything we always—did it together.

HEDDA: Like good pals?

MRS. ELVSTED: [*Eagerly.*] Pals! Yes—why, Hedda, that's exactly the word he used! Oh, I ought to feel so happy. But I can't. I don't know if it will last.

HEDDA: You don't seem very sure of him.

MRS. ELVSTED: [*Sadly.*] Something stands between Eilert Loevberg and me. The shadow of another woman.

HEDDA: Who can that be?

MRS. ELVSTED: I don't know. Someone he used to be friendly with in—in the old days. Someone he's never been able to forget.

HEDDA: What has he told you about her?

MRS. ELVSTED: Oh, he only mentioned her once, casually.

HEDDA: Well! What did he say?

MRS. ELVSTED: He said when he left her she tried to shoot him with a pistol.

HEDDA: [*Cold, controlled.*] What nonsense. People don't do such things. The kind of people we know.

MRS. ELVSTED: No, I think it must have been that red-haired singer he used to——

HEDDA: Ah yes, very probably.

MRS. ELVSTED: I remember they used to say she always carried a loaded pistol.

HEDDA: Well then, it must be her.

MRS. ELVSTED: But Hedda, I hear she's come back, and is living here. Oh, I'm so desperate——!

HEDDA: [*Glances toward the rear room.*] Ssh! Tesman's coming. [*Gets up and whispers.*] Thea, we mustn't breathe a word about this to anyone.

MRS. ELVSTED: [*Jumps up.*] Oh, no, no! Please don't!

[GEORGE TESMAN *appears from the right in the rear room with a letter in his hand, and comes into the drawing room.*]

TESMAN: Well, here's my little epistle all signed and sealed.

HEDDA: Good. I think Mrs. Elvsted wants to go now. Wait a moment—I'll see you as far as the garden gate.

TESMAN: Er—Hedda, do you think Bertha could deal with this?

HEDDA: [*Takes the letter.*] I'll give her instructions.

[BERTHA *enters from the hall.*]

BERTHA: Judge Brack is here and asks if he may pay his respects to Madam and the Doctor.

HEDDA: Yes, ask him to be so good as to come in. And—wait a moment—drop this letter in the post box.

BERTHA: [*Takes the letter.*] Very good, madam.

[*She opens the door for* JUDGE BRACK, *and goes out.* JUDGE BRACK *is forty-five; rather short, but well-built, and elastic in his movements. He has a roundish face with an aristocratic profile. His hair, cut short, is still almost black, and is carefully barbered. Eyes lively and humorous. Thick eyebrows. His moustache is also thick, and is trimmed square at the ends. He is wearing outdoor clothes which are elegant but a little too youthful for him. He has a monocle in one eye; now and then he lets it drop.*]

BRACK: [*Hat in hand, bows.*] May one presume to call so early?

HEDDA: One may presume.

TESMAN: [*Shakes his hand.*] You're welcome here any time. Judge Brack— Mrs. Rysing.

[HEDDA *sighs.*]

BRACK: [*Bows.*] Ah—charmed——

HEDDA: [*Looks at him and laughs.*] What fun to be able to see you by daylight for once, Judge.

BRACK: Do I look—different?

HEDDA: Yes. A little younger, I think.

BRACK: Obliged.

TESMAN: Well, what do you think of Hedda? What? Doesn't she look well? Hasn't she filled out——?

HEDDA: Oh, do stop it. You ought to be thanking Judge Brack for all the inconvenience he's put himself to——

BRACK: Nonsense, it was a pleasure——

HEDDA: You're a loyal friend. But my other friend is pining to get away. Au revoir, Judge. I won't be a minute.

[*Mutual salutations.* MRS. ELVSTED *and* HEDDA *go out through the hall.*]

BRACK: Well, is your wife satisfied with everything?

TESMAN: Yes, we can't thank you enough. That is—we may have to shift one or two things around, she tells me. And we're short of one or two little items we'll have to purchase.

BRACK: Oh? Really?

TESMAN: But you musn't worry your head about that. Hedda says she'll get what's needed. I say, why don't we sit down? What?

BRACK: Thanks, just for a moment. [*Sits at the table.*] There's something I'd like to talk to you about, my dear Tesman.

TESMAN: Oh? Ah yes, of course. [*Sits.*] After the feast comes the reckoning. What?

BRACK: Oh, never mind about the financial side—there's no hurry about that. Though I could wish we'd arranged things a little less palatially.

TESMAN: Good heavens, that'd never have done. Think of Hedda, my dear chap. You know her. I couldn't possibly ask her to live like a suburban housewife.

BRACK: No, no—that's just the problem.

TESMAN: Anyway, it can't be long now before my nomination[3] comes through.

BRACK: Well, you know, these things often take time.

TESMAN: Have you heard any more news? What?

BRACK: Nothing definite. [*Changing the subject.*] Oh, by the way, I have one piece of news for you.

TESMAN: What?

BRACK: Your old friend Eilert Loevborg is back in town.

TESMAN: I know that already.

BRACK: Oh? How did you hear that?

TESMAN: She told me. That lady who went out with Hedda.

BRACK: I see. What was her name? I didn't catch it.

TESMAN: Mrs. Elvsted.

---

3. For the professorship. Professors at European universities were less numerous and more socially prominent than their contemporary American counterparts.

BRACK: Oh, the magistrate's wife. Yes, Loevborg's been living up near them, hasn't he?

TESMAN: I'm delighted to hear he's become a decent human being again.

BRACK: Yes, so they say.

TESMAN: I gather he's published a new book, too. What?

BRACK: Indeed he has.

TESMAN: I hear it's created rather a stir.

BRACK: Quite an unusual stir.

TESMAN: I say, isn't that splendid news! He's such a gifted chap—and I was afraid he'd gone to the dogs for good.

BRACK: Most people thought he had.

TESMAN: But I can't think what he'll do now. How on earth will he manage to make ends meet? What?

[*As he speaks his last words,* HEDDA *enters from the hall.*]

HEDDA: [*To* BRACK, *laughs slightly scornfully.*] Tesman is always worrying about making ends meet.

TESMAN: We were talking about poor Eilert Loevborg, Hedda dear.

HEDDA: [*Gives him a quick look.*] Oh, were you? [*Sits in the armchair by the stove and asks casually.*] Is he in trouble?

TESMAN: Well, he must have run through his inheritance long ago by now. And he can't write a new book every year. What? So I'm wondering what's going to become of him.

BRACK: I may be able to enlighten you there.

TESMAN: Oh?

BRACK: You mustn't forget he has relatives who wield a good deal of influence.

TESMAN: Relatives? Oh, they've quite washed their hands of him, I'm afraid.

BRACK: They used to regard him as the hope of the family.

TESMAN: Used to, yes. But he's put an end to that.

HEDDA: Who knows? [*With a little smile.*] I hear the Elvsteds have made a new man of him.

BRACK: And then this book he's just published——

TESMAN: Well, let's hope they find something for him. I've just written him a note. Oh, by the way, Hedda, I asked him to come over and see us this evening.

BRACK: But my dear chap, you're coming to me this evening. My bachelor party.[4] You promised me last night when I met you at the boat.

HEDDA: Had you forgotten, Tesman?

TESMAN: Good heavens, yes, I'd quite forgotten.

BRACK: Anyway, you can be quite sure he won't turn up here.

TESMAN: Why do you think that? What?

BRACK: [*A little unwillingly, gets up and rests his hands on the back of his chair.*] My dear Tesman—and you, too, Mrs. Tesman—there's something I feel you ought to know.

TESMAN: Concerning Eilert?

BRACK: Concerning him and you.

---

4. A party for men only, whether single or married.

TESMAN: Well, my dear Judge, tell us, please!

BRACK: You must be prepared for your nomination not to come through quite as quickly as you hope and expect.

TESMAN: [*Jumps up uneasily.*] Is anything wrong? What?

BRACK: There's a possibility that the appointment may be decided by competition——

TESMAN: Competition! By Jove, Hedda, fancy that!

HEDDA: [*Leans further back in her chair.*] Ah! How interesting!

TESMAN: But who else——? I say, you don't mean——?

BRACK: Exactly. By competition with Eilert Loevborg.

TESMAN: [*Clasps his hands in alarm.*] No, no, but this is inconceivable! It's absolutely impossible! What?

BRACK: Hm. We may find it'll happen, all the same.

TESMAN: No, but—Judge Brack, they couldn't be so inconsiderate toward me! [*Waves his arms.*] I mean, by Jove, I—I'm a married man! It was on the strength of this that Hedda and I *got* married! We ran up some pretty hefty debts. And borrowed money from Auntie Juju! I mean, good heavens, they practically promised me the appointment. What?

BRACK: Well, well, I'm sure you'll get it. But you'll have to go through a competition.

HEDDA: [*Motionless in her armchair.*] How exciting, Tesman. It'll be a kind of duel, by Jove.

TESMAN: My dear Hedda, how can you take it so lightly?

HEDDA: [*As before.*] I'm not. I can't wait to see who's going to win.

BRACK: In any case, Mrs. Tesman, it's best you should know how things stand. I mean before you commit yourself to these little items I hear you're threatening to purchase.

HEDDA: I can't allow this to alter my plans.

BRACK: Indeed? Well, that's your business. Good-bye. [*To* TESMAN.] I'll come and collect you on the way home from my afternoon walk.

TESMAN: Oh, yes, yes. I'm sorry, I'm all upside down just now.

HEDDA: [*Lying in her chair, holds out her hand.*] Good-bye, Judge. See you this afternoon.

BRACK: Thank you. Good-bye, good-bye.

TESMAN: [*Sees him to the door.*] Good-bye, my dear Judge. You will excuse me, won't you?

[JUDGE BRACK *goes out through the hall.*]

TESMAN: [*Pacing up and down.*] Oh, Hedda! One oughtn't to go plunging off on wild adventures. What?

HEDDA: [*Looks at him and smiles.*] Like you're doing?

TESMAN: Yes. I mean, there's no denying it, it was a pretty big adventure to go off and get married and set up house merely on expectation.

HEDDA: Perhaps you're right.

TESMAN: Well, anyway, we have our home, Hedda. By Jove, yes. The home we dreamed of. And set our hearts on. What?

HEDDA: [*Gets up slowly, wearily.*] You agreed that we should enter society. And keep open house. That was the bargain.

TESMAN: Yes. Good heavens, I was looking forward to it all so much. To seeing you play hostess to a select circle! By Jove! What? Ah, well, for the time being we shall have to make do with each other's company, Hedda. Perhaps have Auntie Juju in now and then. Oh dear, this wasn't at all what you had in mind——

HEDDA: I won't be able to have a liveried footman.[5] For a start.

TESMAN: Oh no, we couldn't possibly afford a footman.

HEDDA: And that thoroughbred horse you promised me——

TESMAN: [*Fearfully.*] Thoroughbred horse!

HEDDA: I mustn't even think of that now.

TESMAN: Heaven forbid!

HEDDA: [*Walks across the room.*] Ah, well. I still have one thing left to amuse myself with.

TESMAN: [*Joyfully.*] Thank goodness for that. What's that, Hedda? What?

HEDDA: [*In the open doorway, looks at him with concealed scorn.*] My pistols, George darling.

TESMAN: [*Alarmed.*] Pistols!

HEDDA: [*Her eyes cold.*] General Gabler's pistols.

   [*She goes into the rear room and disappears.*]

TESMAN: [*Runs to the doorway and calls after her.*] For heaven's sake, Hedda dear, don't touch those things. They're dangerous. Hedda— please—for my sake! What?

Act II

SCENE—*The same as in Act I except that the piano has been removed and an elegant little writing table, with a bookcase, stands in its place. By the sofa on the left a smaller table has been placed. Most of the flowers have been removed.* MRS. ELVSTED's *bouquet stands on the larger table, down-stage. It is afternoon.*

   HEDDA, *dressed to receive callers, is alone in the room. She is standing by the open french windows, loading a revolver. The pair to it is lying in an open pistol case on the writing table.*

HEDDA: [*Looks down into the garden and calls.*] Good afternoon, Judge.

BRACK: [*In the distance, below.*] Afternoon, Mrs. Tesman.

HEDDA: [*Raises the pistol and takes aim.*] I'm going to shoot you, Judge Brack.

BRACK: [*Shouts from below.*] No no, no! Don't aim that thing at me!

HEDDA: This'll teach you to enter houses by the back door. [*Fires.*]

BRACK: [*Below.*] Have you gone completely out of your mind?

HEDDA: Oh dear! Did I hit you?

BRACK: [*Still outside.*] Stop playing these silly tricks.

HEDDA: All right, Judge. Come along in.

   [JUDGE BRACK, *dressed for a bachelor party, enters through the french windows. He has a light overcoat on his arm.*]

BRACK: For God's sake! Haven't you stopped fooling around with those things yet? What are you trying to hit?

---

5. A uniformed servant.

HEDDA: Oh, I was just shooting at the sky.

BRACK: [*Takes the pistol gently from her hand.*] By your leave, ma'am. [*Looks at it.*] Ah, yes—I know this old friend well. [*Looks around.*] Where's the case? Oh, yes. [*Puts the pistol in the case and closes it.*] That's enough of that little game for today.

HEDDA: Well, what on earth *am* I to do?

BRACK: You haven't had any visitors?

HEDDA: [*Closes the french windows.*] Not one. I suppose the best people are all still in the country.

BRACK: Your husband isn't home yet?

HEDDA: [*Locks the pistol case away in a drawer of the writing table.*] No. The moment he'd finished eating he ran off to his aunties. He wasn't expecting you so early.

BRACK: Ah, why didn't I think of that? How stupid of me.

HEDDA: [*Turns her head and looks at him.*] Why stupid?

BRACK: I'd have come a little sooner.

HEDDA: [*Walks across the room.*] There'd have been no one to receive you. I've been in my room since lunch, dressing.

BRACK: You haven't a tiny crack in the door through which we might have negotiated?

HEDDA: You forgot to arrange one.

BRACK: Another stupidity.

HEDDA: Well, we'll have to sit down here. And wait. Tesman won't be back for some time.

BRACK: Sad. Well, I'll be patient.

> [HEDDA *sits on the corner of the sofa.* BRACK *puts his coat over the back of the nearest chair and seats himself, keeping his hat in his hand. Short pause. They look at each other.*]

HEDDA: Well?

BRACK: [*In the same tone of voice.*] Well?

HEDDA: I asked first.

BRACK: [*Leans forward slightly.*] Yes, well, now we can enjoy a nice, cosy little chat—Mrs. Hedda.

HEDDA: [*Leans further back in her chair.*] It seems such ages since we had a talk. I don't count last night or this morning.

BRACK: You mean: *à deux?*[6]

HEDDA: Mm—yes. That's roughly what I meant.

BRACK: I've been longing so much for you to come home.

HEDDA: So have I.

BRACK: You? Really, Mrs. Hedda? And I thought you were having such a wonderful honeymoon.

HEDDA: Oh, yes. Wonderful!

BRACK: But your husband wrote such ecstatic letters.

HEDDA: He! Oh, yes! He thinks life has nothing better to offer than rooting around in libraries and copying old pieces of parchment, or whatever it is he does.

BRACK: [*A little maliciously.*] Well, that *is* his life. Most of it, anyway.

---

6. Just the two of us.

HEDDA: Yes, I know. Well, it's all right for him. But for me! Oh no, my dear Judge. I've been bored to death.

BRACK: [*Sympathetically.*] Do you mean that? Seriously?

HEDDA: Yes. Can you imagine? Six whole months without ever meeting a single person who was one of us, and to whom I could talk about the kind of things we talk about.

BRACK: Yes, I can understand. I'd miss that, too.

HEDDA: That wasn't the worst, though.

BRACK: What was?

HEDDA: Having to spend every minute of one's life with—with the same person.

BRACK: [*Nods.*] Yes. What a thought! Morning; noon; and——

HEDDA: [*Coldly.*] As I said: every minute of one's life.

BRACK: I stand corrected. But dear Tesman is such a clever fellow, I should have thought one ought to be able——

HEDDA: Tesman is only interested in one thing, my dear Judge. His special subject.

BRACK: True.

HEDDA: And people who are only interested in one thing don't make the most amusing company. Not for long, anyway.

BRACK: Not even when they happen to be the person one loves?

HEDDA: Oh, don't use that sickly, stupid word.

BRACK: [*Starts.*] But, Mrs. Hedda——!

HEDDA: [*Half laughing, half annoyed.*] You just try it, Judge. Listening to the history of civilization morning, noon and——

BRACK: [*Corrects her.*] Every minute of one's life.

HEDDA: All right. Oh, and those domestic industries of Brabant in the Middle Ages! That really is beyond the limit.

BRACK: [*Looks at her searchingly.*] But, tell me—if you feel like this why on earth did you—? Ha——

HEDDA: Why on earth did I marry George Tesman?

BRACK: If you like to put it that way.

HEDDA: Do you think it so very strange?

BRACK: Yes—and no, Mrs. Hedda.

HEDDA: I'd danced myself tired, Judge. I felt my time was up——[*Gives a slight shudder.*] No, I mustn't say that. Or even think it.

BRACK: You've no rational cause to think it.

HEDDA: Oh—cause, cause——[*Looks searchingly at him.*] After all, George Tesman—well, I mean, he's a very respectable man.

BRACK: Very respectable, sound as a rock. No denying that.

HEDDA: And there's nothing exactly ridiculous about him. Is there?

BRACK: Ridiculous? No-no, I wouldn't say that.

HEDDA: Mm. He's very clever at collecting material and all that, isn't he? I mean, he may go quite far in time.

BRACK: [*Looks at her a little uncertainly.*] I thought you believed, like everyone else, that he would become a very prominent man.

HEDDA: [*Looks tired.*] Yes, I did. And when he came and begged me on his bended knees to be allowed to love and to cherish me, I didn't see why I shouldn't let him.

BRACK: No, well—if one looks at it like that——

HEDDA: It was more than my other admirers were prepared to do, Judge dear.

BRACK: [*Laughs.*] Well, I can't answer for the others. As far as I myself am concerned, you know I've always had a considerable respect for the institution of marriage. As an institution.

HEDDA: [*Lightly.*] Oh, I've never entertained any hopes of you.

BRACK: All I want is to have a circle of friends whom I can trust, whom I can help with advice or—or by any other means, and into whose houses I may come and go as a—trusted friend.

HEDDA: Of the husband?

BRACK: [*Bows.*] Preferably, to be frank, of the wife. And of the husband too, of course. Yes, you know, this kind of—triangle is a delightful arrangement for all parties concerned.

HEDDA: Yes, I often longed for a third person while I was away. Oh, those hours we spent alone in railway compartments——

BRACK: Fortunately your honeymoon is now over.

HEDDA: [*Shakes her head.*] There's a long way still to go. I've only reached a stop on the line.

BRACK: Why not jump out and stretch your legs a little, Mrs. Hedda?

HEDDA: I'm not the jumping sort.

BRACK: Aren't you?

HEDDA: No. There's always someone around who——

BRACK: [*Laughs.*] Who looks at one's legs?

HEDDA: Yes. Exactly.

BRACK: Well, but surely——

HEDDA: [*With a gesture of rejection.*] I don't like it. I'd rather stay where I am. Sitting in the compartment. *A deux.*

BRACK: But suppose a third person were to step into the compartment?

HEDDA: That would be different.

BRACK: A trusted friend—someone who understood——

HEDDA: And was lively and amusing——

BRACK: And interested in—more subjects than one——

HEDDA: [*Sighs audibly.*] Yes, that'd be a relief.

BRACK: [*Hears the front door open and shut.*] The triangle is completed.

HEDDA: [*Half under breath.*] And the train goes on.

[GEORGE TESMAN, *in grey walking dress with a soft felt hat, enters from the hall. He has a number of paper-covered books under his arm and in his pockets.*]

TESMAN: [*Goes over to the table by the corner sofa.*] Phew! It's too hot to be lugging all this around. [*Puts the books down.*] I'm positively sweating, Hedda. Why, hullo, hullo! You here already, Judge? What? Bertha didn't tell me.

BRACK: [*Gets up.*] I came in through the garden.

HEDDA: What are all those books you've got there?

TESMAN: [*Stands glancing through them.*] Oh, some new publications dealing with my special subject. I had to buy them.

HEDDA: Your special subject?

BRACK: His special subject, Mrs. Tesman.

[BRACK *and* HEDDA *exchange a smile.*]

HEDDA: Haven't you collected enough material on your special subject?

TESMAN: My dear Hedda, one can never have too much. One must keep abreast of what other people are writing.

HEDDA: Yes. Of course.

TESMAN: [*Rooting among the books.*] Look—I bought a copy of Eilert Loevborg's new book, too. [*Holds it out to her.*] Perhaps you'd like to have a look at it, Hedda? What?

HEDDA: No, thank you. Er—yes, perhaps I will, later.

TESMAN: I glanced through it on my way home.

BRACK: What's your opinion—as a specialist on the subject?

TESMAN: I'm amazed how sound and balanced it is. He never used to write like that. [*Gathers his books together.*] Well, I must get down to these at once. I can hardly wait to cut the pages.[7] Oh, I've got to change, too. [*To* BRACK.] We don't have to be off just yet, do we? What?

BRACK: Heavens, no. We've plenty of time yet.

TESMAN: Good, I needn't hurry, then. [*Goes with his books, but stops and turns in the doorway.*] Oh, by the way, Hedda, Auntie Juju won't be coming to see you this evening.

HEDDA: Won't she? Oh—the hat, I suppose.

TESMAN: Good heavens, no. How could you think such a thing of Auntie Juju? Fancy——! No, Auntie Rena's very ill.

HEDDA: She always is.

TESMAN: Yes, but today she's been taken really bad.

HEDDA: Oh, then it's quite understandable that the other one should want to stay with her. Well, I shall have to swallow my disappointment.

TESMAN: You can't imagine how happy Auntie Juju was in spite of everything. At your looking so well after the honeymoon!

HEDDA: [*Half beneath her breath, as she rises.*] Oh, these everlasting aunts!

TESMAN: What?

HEDDA: [*Goes over to the french windows.*] Nothing.

TESMAN: Oh. All right. [*Goes into the rear room and out of sight.*]

BRACK: What was that about the hat?

HEDDA: Oh, something that happened with Miss Tesman this morning. She'd put her hat down on a chair. [*Looks at him and smiles.*] And I pretended to think it was the servant's.

BRACK: [*Shakes his head.*] But my dear Mrs. Hedda, how could you do such a thing? To that poor old lady?

HEDDA: [*Nervously, walking across the room.*] Sometimes a mood like that hits me. And I can't stop myself. [*Throws herself down in the armchair by the stove.*] Oh, I don't know how to explain it.

BRACK: [*Behind her chair.*] You're not really happy. That's the answer.

HEDDA: [*Stares ahead of her.*] Why on earth should I be happy? Can you give me a reason?

BRACK: Yes. For one thing you've got the home you always wanted.

---

7. Books used to be sold with the pages folded but uncut as they came from the printing press; the owner had to cut the pages to read the book.

HEDDA: [*Looks at him.*] You really believe that story?

BRACK: You mean it isn't true?

HEDDA: Oh, yes, it's partly true.

BRACK: Well?

HEDDA: It's true I got Tesman to see me home from parties last summer——

BRACK: It was a pity my home lay in another direction.

HEDDA: Yes. Your interests lay in another direction, too.

BRACK: [*Laughs.*] That's naughty of you, Mrs. Hedda. But to return to you and Tesman——

HEDDA: Well, we walked past this house one evening. And poor Tesman was fidgeting in his boots trying to find something to talk about. I felt sorry for the great scholar——

BRACK: [*Smiles incredulously.*] Did you? Hm.

HEDDA: Yes, honestly I did. Well, to help him out of his misery, I happened to say quite frivolously how much I'd love to live in this house.

BRACK: Was that all?

HEDDA: That evening, yes.

BRACK: But—afterwards?

HEDDA: Yes. My little frivolity had its consequences, my dear Judge.

BRACK: Our little frivolities do. Much too often, unfortunately.

HEDDA: Thank you. Well, it was our mutual admiration for the late Prime Minister's house that brought George Tesman and me together on common ground. So we got engaged, and we got married, and we went on our honeymoon, and—Ah well, Judge, I've—made my bed and I must lie in it, I was about to say.

BRACK: How utterly fantastic! And you didn't really care in the least about the house?

HEDDA: God knows I didn't.

BRACK: Yes, but now that we've furnished it so beautifully for you?

HEDDA: Ugh—all the rooms smell of lavender and dried roses. But perhaps Auntie Juju brought that in.

BRACK: [*Laughs.*] More likely the Prime Minister's widow, rest her soul.

HEDDA: Yes, it's got the odor of death about it. It reminds me of the flowers one has worn at a ball—the morning after. [*Clasps her hands behind her neck, leans back in the chair and looks up at him.*] Oh, my dear Judge, you've no idea how hideously bored I'm going to be out here.

BRACK: Couldn't you find some kind of occupation, Mrs. Hedda? Like your husband?

HEDDA: Occupation? That'd interest me?

BRACK: Well—preferably.

HEDDA: God knows what. I've often thought——[*Breaks off.*] No, that wouldn't work either.

BRACK: Who knows? Tell me about it.

HEDDA: I was thinking—if I could persuade Tesman to go into politics, for example.

BRACK: [*Laughs.*] Tesman! No, honestly, I don't think he's quite cut out to be a politician.

HEDDA: Perhaps not. But if I could persuade him to have a go at it?

BRACK: What satisfaction would that give you? If he turned out to be no good? Why do you want to make him do that?

HEDDA: Because I'm bored. [*After a moment.*] You feel there's absolutely no possibility of Tesman becoming Prime Minister, then?

BRACK: Well, you know, Mrs. Hedda, for one thing he'd have to be pretty well off before he could become that.

HEDDA: [*Gets up impatiently.*] There you are! [*Walks across the room.*] It's this wretched poverty that makes life so hateful. And ludicrous. Well, it is!

BRACK: I don't think that's the real cause.

HEDDA: What is, then?

BRACK: Nothing really exciting has ever happened to you.

HEDDA: Nothing serious, you mean?

BRACK: Call it that if you like. But now perhaps it may.

HEDDA: [*Tosses her head.*] Oh, you're thinking of this competition for that wretched professorship? That's Tesman's affair. I'm not going to waste my time worrying about that.

BRACK: Very well, let's forget about that then. But suppose you were to find yourself faced with what people call—to use the conventional phrase—the most solemn of human responsibilities? [*Smiles.*] A new responsibility, little Mrs. Hedda.

HEDDA: [*Angrily.*] Be quiet! Nothing like that's going to happen.

BRACK: [*Warily.*] We'll talk about it again in a year's time. If not earlier.

HEDDA: [*Curtly.*] I've no leanings in that direction, Judge. I don't want any—responsibilities.

BRACK: But surely you must feel some inclination to make use of that— natural talent which every woman—

HEDDA: [*Over by the french windows.*] Oh, be quiet, I say! I often think there's only one thing for which I have any natural talent.

BRACK: [*Goes closer.*] And what is that, if I may be so bold as to ask?

HEDDA: [*Stands looking out.*] For boring myself to death. Now you know. [*Turns, looks toward the rear room and laughs.*] Talking of boring, here comes the Professor.

BRACK: [*Quietly, warningly.*] Now, now, now, Mrs. Hedda!

[GEORGE TESMAN, *in evening dress, with gloves and hat in his hand, enters through the rear room from the right.*]

TESMAN: Hedda, hasn't any message come from Eilert? What?

HEDDA: No.

TESMAN: Ah, then we'll have him here presently. You wait and see.

BRACK: You really think he'll come?

TESMAN: Yes, I'm almost sure he will. What you were saying about him this morning is just gossip.

BRACK: Oh?

TESMAN: Yes. Auntie Juju said she didn't believe he'd ever dare to stand in my way again. Fancy that!

BRACK: Then everything in the garden's lovely.

TESMAN: [*Puts his hat, with his gloves in it, on a chair, right.*] Yes, but you really must let me wait for him as long as possible.

BRACK: We've plenty of time. No one'll be turning up at my place before seven or half past.

TESMAN: Ah, then we can keep Hedda company a little longer. And see if he turns up. What?

HEDDA: [*Picks up* BRACK'*s coat and hat and carries them over to the corner sofa.*] And if the worst comes to the worst, Mr. Loevborg can sit here and talk to me.

BRACK: [*Offering to take his things from her.*] No, please. What do you mean by "if the worst comes to the worst"?

HEDDA: If he doesn't want to go with you and Tesman.

TESMAN: [*Looks doubtfully at her.*] I say, Hedda, do you think it'll be all right for him to stay here with you? What? Remember Auntie Juju isn't coming.

HEDDA: Yes, but Mrs. Elvsted is. The three of us can have a cup of tea together.

TESMAN: Ah, that'll be all right then.

BRACK: [*Smiles.*] It's probably the safest solution as far as he's concerned.

HEDDA: Why?

BRACK: My dear Mrs. Tesman, you always say of my little bachelor parties that they should be attended only by men of the strongest principles.

HEDDA: But Mr. Loevborg is a man of principle now. You know what they say about a reformed sinner——

[BERTHA *enters from the hall.*]

BERTHA: Madam, there's a gentleman here who wants to see you——

HEDDA: Ask him to come in.

TESMAN: [*Quietly.*] I'm sure it's him. By Jove. Fancy that!

[EILERT LOEVBORG *enters from the hall. He is slim and lean, of the same age as* TESMAN, *but looks older and somewhat haggard. His hair and beard are of a blackish-brown; his face is long and pale, but with a couple of reddish patches on his cheekbones. He is dressed in an elegant and fairly new black suit, and carries black gloves and a top hat in his hand. He stops just inside the door and bows abruptly. He seems somewhat embarrassed.*]

TESMAN: [*Goes over and shakes his hand.*] My dear Eilert! How grand to see you again after all these years!

EILERT LOEVBORG: [*Speaks softly.*] It was good of you to write, George. [*Goes nearer to* HEDDA.] May I shake hands with you, too, Mrs. Tesman?

HEDDA: [*Accepts his hand.*] Delighted to see you, Mr. Loevborg. [*With a gesture.*] I don't know if you two gentlemen——

LOEVBORG: [*Bows slightly.*] Judge Brack, I believe.

BRACK: [*Also with a slight bow.*] Correct. We—met some years ago——

TESMAN: [*Puts his hands on* LOEVBORG'*s shoulders.*] Now you're to treat this house just as though it were your own home, Eilert. Isn't that right, Hedda? I hear you've decided to settle here again? What?

LOEVBORG: Yes, I have.

TESMAN: Quite understandable. Oh, by the bye—I've just bought your new book. Though to tell the truth I haven't found time to read it yet.

LOEVBORG: You needn't bother.

TESMAN: Oh? Why?

LOEVBORG: There's nothing much in it.

TESMAN: By Jove, fancy hearing that from you!

BRACK: But everyone's praising it.

LOEVBORG: That was exactly what I wanted to happen. So I only wrote what I knew everyone would agree with.

BRACK: Very sensible.

TESMAN: Yes, but my dear Eilert——

LOEVBORG: I want to try to re-establish myself. To begin again—from the beginning.

TESMAN: [*A little embarrassed.*] Yes, I—er—suppose you do. What?

LOEVBORG: [*Smiles, puts down his hat and takes a package wrapped in paper from his coat pocket.*] But when this gets published—George Tesman—read it. This is my real book. The one in which I have spoken with my own voice.

TESMAN: Oh, really? What's it about?

LOEVBORG: It's the sequel.

TESMAN: Sequel? To what?

LOEVBORG: To the other book.

TESMAN: The one that's just come out?

LOEVBORG: Yes.

TESMAN: But my dear Eilert, that covers the subject right up to the present day.

LOEVBORG: It does. But this is about the future.

TESMAN: The future! But, I say, we don't know anything about that.

LOEVBORG: No. But there are one or two things that need to be said about it. [*Opens the package.*] Here, have a look.

TESMAN: Surely that's not your handwriting?

LOEVBORG: I dictated it. [*Turns the pages.*] It's in two parts. The first deals with the forces that will shape our civilization. [*Turns further on towards the end.*] And the second indicates the direction in which that civilization may develop.

TESMAN: Amazing! I'd never think of writing about anything like that.

HEDDA: [*By the french windows, drumming on the pane.*] No. You wouldn't.

LOEVBORG: [*Puts the pages back into their cover and lays the package on the table.*] I brought it because I thought I might possibly read you a few pages this evening.

TESMAN: I say, what a kind idea! Oh, but this evening——? [*Glances at* BRACK.] I'm not quite sure whether——

LOEVBORG: Well, some other time, then. There's no hurry.

BRACK: The truth is, Mr. Loevborg, I'm giving a little dinner this evening. In Tesman's honor, you know.

LOEVBORG: [*Looks round for his hat.*] Oh—then I mustn't——

BRACK: No, wait a minute. Won't you do me the honor of joining us?

LOEVBORG: [*Curtly, with decision.*] No I can't. Thank you so much.

BRACK: Oh, nonsense. Do—please. There'll only be a few of us. And I can promise you we shall have some good sport, as Mrs. Hed—as Mrs. Tesman puts it.

LOEVBORG: I've no doubt. Nevertheless——

BRACK: You could bring your manuscript along and read it to Tesman at my place. I could lend you a room.

TESMAN: By Jove, Eilert, that's an idea. What?

HEDDA: [*Interposes.*] But Tesman, Mr. Loevborg doesn't want to go. I'm sure Mr. Loevborg would much rather sit here and have supper with me.

LOEVBORG: [*Looks at her.*] With you, Mrs. Tesman?

HEDDA: And Mrs. Elvsted.

LOEVBORG: Oh. [*Casually.*] I ran into her this afternoon.

HEDDA: Did you? Well, she's coming here this evening. So you really must stay, Mr. Loevborg. Otherwise she'll have no one to see her home.

LOEVBORG: That's true. Well—thank you, Mrs. Tesman, I'll stay then.

HEDDA: I'll just tell the servant.

[*She goes to the door which leads into the hall, and rings.* BERTHA *enters.* HEDDA *talks softly to her and points towards the rear room.* BERTHA *nods and goes out.*]

TESMAN: [*To* LOEVBORG, *as* HEDDA *does this.*] I say, Eilert. This new subject of yours—the—er—future—is that the one you're going to lecture about?

LOEVBORG: Yes.

TESMAN: They told me down at the bookshop that you're going to hold a series of lectures here during the autumn.

LOEVBORG: Yes, I am, I—hope you don't mind, Tesman.

TESMAN: Good heavens, no! But——?

LOEVBORG: I can quite understand it might queer your pitch a little.

TESMAN: [*Dejectedly.*] Oh well, I can't expect you to put them off for my sake.

LOEVBORG: I'll wait till your appointment's been announced.

TESMAN: You'll wait! But—but—aren't you going to compete with me for the post? What?

LOEVBORG: No. I only want to defeat you in the eyes of the world.

TESMAN: Good heavens! Then Auntie Juju was right after all! Oh, I knew it, I knew it! Hear that, Hedda? Fancy! Eilert *doesn't* want to stand in our way.

HEDDA: [*Curtly.*] Our? Leave me out of it, please.

[*She goes towards the rear room, where* BERTHA *is setting a tray with decanters and glasses on the table.* HEDDA *nods approval, and comes back into the drawing room.* BERTHA *goes out.*]

TESMAN: [*While this is happening.*] Judge Brack, what do you think about all this? What?

BRACK: Oh, I think honor and victory can be very splendid things——

TESMAN: Of course they can. Still——

HEDDA: [*Looks at* TESMAN *with a cold smile.*] You look as if you'd been hit by a thunderbolt.

TESMAN: Yes, I feel rather like it.

BRACK: There was a black cloud looming up, Mrs. Tesman. But it seems to have passed over.

HEDDA: [*Points toward the rear room.*] Well, gentlemen, won't you go in and take a glass of cold punch?

BRACK: [*Glances at his watch.*] A stirrup cup?[8] Yes, why not?

TESMAN: An admirable suggestion, Hedda. Admirable! Oh, I feel so relieved!

HEDDA: Won't you have one, too, Mr. Loevborg?

LOEVBORG: No, thank you. I'd rather not.

BRACK: Great heavens, man, cold punch isn't poison. Take my word for it.

LOEVBORG: Not for everyone, perhaps.

HEDDA: I'll keep Mr. Loevborg company while you drink.

TESMAN: Yes, Hedda dear, would you?

> [*He and* BRACK *go into the rear room, sit down, drink punch, smoke cigarettes and talk cheerfully during the following scene.* EILERT LOEVBORG *remains standing by the stove.* HEDDA *goes to the writing table.*]

HEDDA [*Raising her voice slightly.*] I've some photographs I'd like to show you, if you'd care to see them. Tesman and I visited the Tyrol on our way home.

> [*She comes back with an album, places it on the table by the sofa and sits in the upstage corner of the sofa.* EILERT LOEVBORG *comes toward her, stops and looks at her. Then he takes a chair and sits down on her left, with his back toward the rear room.*]

HEDDA: [*Opens the album.*] You see these mountains, Mr. Loevborg? That's the Ortler group. Tesman has written the name underneath. You see: "The Ortler Group near Meran."[9]

LOEVBORG: [*Has not taken his eyes from her; says softly, slowly.*] Hedda — Gabler!

HEDDA: [*Gives him a quick glance.*] Ssh!

LOEVBORG: [*Repeats softly.*] Hedda Gabler!

HEDDA: [*Looks at the album.*] Yes, that used to be my name. When we first knew each other.

LOEVBORG: And from now on — for the rest of my life — I must teach myself never to say: Hedda Gabler.

HEDDA: [*Still turning the pages.*] Yes, you must. You'd better start getting into practice. The sooner the better.

LOEVBORG: [*Bitterly.*] Hedda Gabler married? And to George Tesman?

HEDDA: Yes. Well — that's life.

LOEVBORG: Oh, Hedda, Hedda! How could you throw yourself away like that?

HEDDA: [*Looks sharply at him.*] Stop it.

LOEVBORG: What do you mean?

> [TESMAN *comes in and goes toward the sofa.*]

HEDDA: [*Hears him coming and says casually.*] And this, Mr. Loevborg, is the view from the Ampezzo valley. Look at those mountains. [*Glances affectionately up at* TESMAN.] What did you say those curious mountains were called, dear?

TESMAN: Let me have a look. Oh, those are the Dolomites.

---

8. A drink before parting. (Originally, it was taken by riders on horseback just before setting forth.)
9. Or Merano, a city in the Austrian Tyrol, since 1918 in Italy. The scenic features mentioned here and later are tourist attractions. The Ortler Group and the Dolomites are ranges of the Alps. The Ampezzo Valley lies beyond the Dolomites to the east. The Brenner Pass is a major route through the Alps to Austria.

HEDDA: Of course. Those are the Dolomites, Mr. Loevborg.

TESMAN: Hedda, I just wanted to ask you, can't we bring some punch in here? A glass for you, anyway. What?

HEDDA: Thank you, yes. And a biscuit[1] or two, perhaps.

TESMAN: You wouldn't like a cigarette?

HEDDA: No.

TESMAN: Right.

[*He goes into the rear room and over to the right.* BRACK *is sitting there, glancing occasionally at* HEDDA *and* LOEVBORG.]

LOEVBORG: [*Softly, as before.*] Answer me, Hedda. How could you do it?

HEDDA: [*Apparently absorbed in the album.*] If you go on calling me Hedda I won't talk to you any more.

LOEVBORG: Mayn't I even when we're alone?

HEDDA: No. You can think it. But you mustn't say it.

LOEVBORG: Oh, I see. Because you love George Tesman.

HEDDA: [*Glances at him and smiles.*] Love? Don't be funny.

LOEVBORG: You don't love him?

HEDDA: I don't intend to be unfaithful to him. That's not what I want.

LOEVBORG: Hedda — just tell me one thing —

HEDDA: Ssh!

[TESMAN *enters from the rear room, carrying a tray.*]

TESMAN: Here we are! Here come the goodies! [*Puts the tray down on the table.*]

HEDDA: Why didn't you ask the servant to bring it in?

TESMAN: [*Fills the glasses.*] I like waiting on you, Hedda.

HEDDA: But you've filled both glasses. Mr. Loevborg doesn't want to drink.

TESMAN: Yes, but Mrs. Elvsted'll be here soon.

HEDDA: Oh yes, that's true. Mrs. Elvsted —

TESMAN: Had you forgotten her? What?

HEDDA: We're so absorbed with these photographs. [*Shows him one.*] You remember this little village?

TESMAN: Oh, that one down by the Brenner Pass. We spent a night there —

HEDDA: Yes, and met all those amusing people.

TESMAN: Oh yes, it was there, wasn't it? By Jove, if only we could have had you with us, Eilert! Ah, well. [*Goes back into the other room and sits down with* BRACK.]

LOEVBORG: Tell me one thing, Hedda.

HEDDA: Yes?

LOEVBORG: Didn't you love me either? Not — just a little?

HEDDA: Well now, I wonder? No, I think we were just good pals — Really good pals who could tell each other anything. [*Smiles.*] You certainly poured your heart out to me.

LOEVBORG: You begged me to.

HEDDA: Looking back on it, there was something beautiful and fascinating — and brave — about the way we told each other everything. That secret friendship no one else knew about.

1. Cookie.

LOEVBORG: Yes, Hedda, yes! Do you remember? How I used to come up to your father's house in the afternoon—and the General sat by the window and read his newspapers—with his back toward us——

HEDDA: And we sat on the sofa in the corner——

LOEVBORG: Always reading the same illustrated magazine——

HEDDA: We hadn't any photograph album.

LOEVBORG: Yes, Hedda. I regarded you as a kind of confessor. Told you things about myself which no one else knew about—then. Those days and nights of drinking and— Oh, Hedda, what power did you have to make me confess such things?

HEDDA: Power? You think I had some power over you?

LOEVBORG: Yes—I don't know how else to explain it. And all those—oblique questions you asked me——

HEDDA: You knew what they meant.

LOEVBORG: But that you could sit there and ask me such questions! So unashamedly——

HEDDA: I thought you said they were oblique.

LOEVBORG: Yes, but you asked them so unashamedly. That you could question me about—about that kind of thing!

HEDDA: You answered willingly enough.

LOEVBORG: Yes—that's what I can't understand—looking back on it. But tell me, Hedda—what you felt for me—wasn't that—love? When you asked me those questions and made me confess my sins to you, wasn't it because you wanted to wash me clean?

HEDDA: No, not exactly.

LOEVBORG: Why did you do it, then?

HEDDA: Do you find it so incredible that a young girl, given the chance to do so without anyone knowing, should want to be allowed a glimpse into a forbidden world of whose existence she is supposed to be ignorant?

LOEVBORG: So that was it?

HEDDA: One reason. One reason—I think.

LOEVBORG: You didn't love me, then. You just wanted—knowledge. But if that was so, why did you break it off?

HEDDA: That was your fault.

LOEVBORG: It was you who put an end to it.

HEDDA: Yes, when I realized that our friendship was threatening to develop into something—something else. Shame on you, Eilert Loevborg! How could you abuse the trust of your dearest friend?

LOEVBORG: [Clenches his fists.] Oh, why didn't you do it? Why didn't you shoot me dead? As you threatened to?

HEDDA: I was afraid. Of the scandal.

LOEVBORG: Yes, Hedda. You're a coward at heart.

HEDDA: A dreadful coward. [Changes her tone.] Luckily for you. Well, now you've found consolation with the Elvsteds.

LOEVBORG: I know what Thea's been telling you.

HEDDA: I dare say you told her about us.

LOEVBORG: Not a word. She's too silly to understand that kind of thing.

HEDDA: Silly?

LOEVBORG: She's silly about that kind of thing.

HEDDA: And I am a coward. [*Leans closer to him, without looking him in the eyes, and says quietly.*] But let me tell you something. Something you don't know.

LOEVBORG: [*Tensely.*] Yes?

HEDDA: My failure to shoot you wasn't my worst act of cowardice that evening.

LOEVBORG: [*Looks at her for a moment, realizes her meaning and whispers passionately.*] Oh, Hedda! Hedda Gabler! Now I see what was behind those questions. Yes! It wasn't knowledge you wanted! It was life!

HEDDA: [*Flashes a look at him and says quietly.*] Take care! Don't you delude yourself!

[*It has begun to grow dark.* BERTHA, *from outside, opens the door leading into the hall.*]

HEDDA: [*Closes the album with a snap and cries, smiling.*] Ah, at last! Come in, Thea dear!

[MRS. ELVSTED *enters from the hall, in evening dress. The door is closed behind her.*]

HEDDA: [*On the sofa, stretches out her arms toward her.*] Thea darling, I thought you were never coming!

[MRS. ELVSTED *makes a slight bow to the gentlemen in the rear room as she passes the open doorway, and they to her. Then she goes to the table and holds out her hand to* HEDDA. EILERT LOEVBORG *has risen from his chair. He and* MRS. ELVSTED *nod silently to each other.*]

MRS. ELVSTED: Perhaps I ought to go in and say a few words to your husband?

HEDDA: Oh, there's no need. They're happy by themselves. They'll be going soon.

MRS. ELVSTED: Going?

HEDDA: Yes, they're off on a spree this evening.

MRS. ELVSTED: [*Quickly, to* LOEVBORG.] You're not going with them?

LOEVBORG: No.

HEDDA: Mr. Loevborg is staying here with us.

MRS. ELVSTED: [*Takes a chair and is about to sit down beside him.*] Oh, how nice it is to be here!

HEDDA: No, Thea darling, not there. Come over here and sit beside me. I want to be in the middle.

MRS. ELVSTED: Yes, just as you wish.

[*She goes right of the table and sits on the sofa, on* HEDDA's *right.* LOEVBORG *sits down again in his chair.*]

LOEVBORG: [*After a short pause, to* HEDDA.] Isn't she lovely to look at?

HEDDA: [*Strokes her hair gently.*] Only to look at?

LOEVBORG: Yes. We're just good pals. We trust each other implicitly. We can talk to each other quite unashamedly.

HEDDA: No need to be oblique?

MRS. ELVSTED: [*Nestles close to* HEDDA *and says quietly.*] Oh, Hedda I'm so happy. Imagine—he says I've inspired him!

HEDDA: [*Looks at her with a smile.*] Dear Thea! Does he really?

LOEVBORG: She has the courage of her convictions, Mrs. Tesman.

MRS. ELVSTED: I? Courage?

LOEVBORG: Absolute courage. Where friendship is concerned.

HEDDA: Yes. Courage. Yes. If only one had that——

LOEVBORG: Yes?

HEDDA: One might be able to live. In spite of everything. [*Changes her tone suddenly.*] Well, Thea darling, now you're going to drink a nice glass of cold punch.

MRS. ELVSTED: No, thank you. I never drink anything like that.

HEDDA: Oh. You, Mr. Loevborg?

LOEVBORG: Thank you, I don't either.

MRS. ELVSTED: No, he doesn't, either.

HEDDA: [*Looks into his eyes.*] But if I want you to?

LOEVBORG: That doesn't make any difference.

HEDDA: [*Laughs.*] Have I no power over you at all? Poor me!

LOEVBORG: Not where this is concerned.

HEDDA: Seriously, I think you should. For your own sake.

MRS. ELVSTED: Hedda!

LOEVBORG: Why?

HEDDA: Or perhaps I should say for other people's sake.

LOEVBORG: What do you mean?

HEDDA: People might think you didn't feel absolutely and unashamedly sure of yourself. In your heart of hearts.

MRS. ELVSTED: [*Quietly.*] Oh, Hedda, no!

LOEVBORG: People can think what they like. For the present.

MRS. ELVSTED: [*Happily.*] Yes, that's true.

HEDDA: I saw it so clearly in Judge Brack a few minutes ago.

LOEVBORG: Oh. What did you see?

HEDDA: He smiled so scornfully when he saw you were afraid to go in there and drink with them.

LOEVBORG: Afraid! I wanted to stay here and talk to you.

MRS. ELVSTED: That was only natural, Hedda.

HEDDA: But the Judge wasn't to know that. I saw him wink at Tesman when you showed you didn't dare to join their wretched little party.

LOEVBORG: Didn't dare! Are you saying I didn't dare?

HEDDA: I'm not saying so. But that was what Judge Brack thought.

LOEVBORG: Well, let him.

HEDDA: You're not going, then?

LOEVBORG: I'm staying here with you and Thea.

MRS. ELVSTED: Yes, Hedda, of course he is.

HEDDA: [*Smiles, and nods approvingly to* LOEVBORG.] Firm as a rock! A man of principle! That's how a man should be! [*Turns to* MRS. ELVSTED *and strokes her cheek.*] Didn't I tell you so this morning when you came here in such a panic——

LOEVBORG: [*Starts.*] Panic?

MRS. ELVSTED: [*Frightened.*] Hedda! But—Hedda!

HEDDA: Well, now you can see for yourself. There's no earthly need for you to get scared to death just because——[*Stops.*] Well! Let's all three cheer up and enjoy ourselves.

LOEVBORG: Mrs. Tesman, would you mind explaining to me what this is all about?

MRS. ELVSTED: Oh, my God, my God, Hedda, what are you saying? What are you doing?

HEDDA: Keep calm. That horrid Judge has his eye on you.

LOEVBORG: Scared to death, were you? For my sake?

MRS. ELVSTED: [*Quietly, trembling.*] Oh, Hedda! You've made me so unhappy!

LOEVBORG: [*Looks coldly at her for a moment. His face is distorted.*] So that was how much you trusted me.

MRS. ELVSTED: Eilert dear, please listen to me——

LOEVBORG: [*Takes one of the glasses of punch, raises it and says quietly, hoarsely.*] Skoal, Thea! [*Empties the glass, puts it down and picks up one of the others.*]

MRS. ELVSTED: [*Quietly.*] Hedda, Hedda! Why did you want this to happen?

HEDDA: I—want it? Are you mad?

LOEVBORG: Skoal to you too, Mrs. Tesman. Thanks for telling me the truth. Here's to the truth! [*Empties his glass and refills it.*]

HEDDA: [*Puts her hand on his arm.*] Steady. That's enough for now. Don't forget the party.

MRS. ELVSTED: No, no, no!

HEDDA: Ssh! They're looking at you.

LOEVBORG: [*Puts down his glass.*] Thea, tell me the truth——

MRS. ELVSTED: Yes!

LOEVBORG: Did your husband know you were following me?

MRS. ELVSTED: Oh, Hedda!

LOEVBORG: Did you and he have an agreement that you should come here and keep an eye on me? Perhaps he gave you the idea? After all, he's a magistrate.[2] I suppose he needed me back in his office. Or did he miss my companionship at the card table?

MRS. ELVSTED: [*Quietly, sobbing.*] Eilert, Eilert!

LOEVBORG: [*Seizes a glass and is about to fill it.*] Let's drink to him, too.

HEDDA: No more now. Remember you're going to read your book to Tesman.

LOEVBORG: [*Calm again, puts down his glass.*] That was silly of me, Thea. To take it like that, I mean. Don't be angry with me, my dear. You'll see—yes, and they'll see, too—that though I fell, I—I have raised myself up again. With your help, Thea.

MRS. ELVSTED: [*Happily.*] Oh, thank God!

[BRACK *has meanwhile glanced at his watch. He and* TESMAN *get up and come into the drawing room.*]

BRACK: [*Takes his hat and overcoat.*] Well, Mrs. Tesman. It's time for us to go.

HEDDA: Yes, I suppose it must be.

LOEVBORG: [*Gets up.*] Time for me too, Judge.

---

2. Also translated "sheriff." A civil official with duties associated with the courts.

MRS. ELVSTED: [*Quietly, pleadingly.*] Eilert, please don't!

HEDDA: [*Pinches her arm.*] They can hear you.

MRS. ELVSTED: [*Gives a little cry.*] Oh!

LOEVBORG: [*To* BRACK.] You were kind enough to ask me to join you.

BRACK: Are you coming?

LOEVBORG: If I may.

BRACK: Delighted.

LOEVBORG: [*Puts the paper package in his pocket and says to* TESMAN.] I'd like to show you one or two things before I send it off to the printer.

TESMAN: I say, that'll be fun. Fancy——! Oh, but Hedda, how'll Mrs. Elvsted get home? What?

HEDDA: Oh, we'll manage somehow.

LOEVBORG: [*Glances over toward the ladies.*] Mrs. Elvsted? I shall come back and collect her, naturally. [*Goes closer.*] About ten o'clock, Mrs. Tesman? Will that suit you?

HEDDA: Yes. That'll suit me admirably.

TESMAN: Good, that's settled. But you mustn't expect me back so early, Hedda.

HEDDA: Stay as long as you c—as long as you like, dear.

MRS. ELVSTED: [*Trying to hide her anxiety.*] Well then, Mr. Loevborg, I'll wait here till you come.

LOEVBORG: [*His hat in his hand.*] Pray do, Mrs. Elvsted.

BRACK: Well, gentlemen, now the party begins. I trust that, in the words of a certain fair lady, we shall enjoy good sport.

HEDDA: What a pity the fair lady can't be there, invisible.

BRACK: Why invisible?

HEDDA: So as to be able to hear some of your uncensored witticisms, your honor.

BRACK: [*Laughs.*] Oh, I shouldn't advise the fair lady to do that.

TESMAN: [*Laughs too.*] I say, Hedda, that's good. By Jove! Fancy that!

BRACK: Well, good night, ladies, good night!

LOEVBORG: [*Bows farewell.*] About ten o'clock, then.

[BRACK, LOEVBORG *and* TESMAN *go out through the hall. As they do so* BERTHA *enters from the rear room with a lighted lamp. She puts it on the drawing-room table, then goes out the way she came.*]

MRS. ELVSTED: [*Has got up and is walking uneasily to and fro.*] Oh Hedda, Hedda! How is all this going to end?

HEDDA: At ten o'clock, then. He'll be here. I can see him. With a crown of vine-leaves in his hair.[3] Burning and unashamed!

MRS. ELVSTED: Oh, I do hope so!

HEDDA: Can't you see? Then he'll be himself again! He'll be a free man for the rest of his days!

MRS. ELVSTED: Please God you're right.

HEDDA: That's how he'll come! [*Gets up and goes closer.*] You can doubt him as much as you like. I believe in him! Now we'll see which of us——

MRS. ELVSTED: You're after something, Hedda.

3. Like Bacchus, the Greek god of wine, and his followers.

HEDDA: Yes, I am. For once in my life I want to have the power to shape a man's destiny.

MRS. ELVSTED: Haven't you that power already?

HEDDA: No, I haven't. I've never had it.

MRS. ELVSTED: What about your husband?

HEDDA: Him! Oh, if you could only understand how poor I am. And you're allowed to be so rich, so rich! [*Clasps her passionately.*] I think I'll burn your hair off after all!

MRS. ELVSTED: Let me go! Let me go! You frighten me, Hedda!

BERTHA: [*In the open doorway.*] I've laid tea in the dining room, madam.

HEDDA: Good, we're coming.

MRS. ELVSTED: No, no, no! I'd rather go home alone! Now—at once!

HEDDA: Rubbish! First you're going to have some tea, you little idiot. And then—at ten o'clock—Eilert Loevborg will come. With a crown of vine-leaves in his hair!

[*She drags* MRS. ELVSTED *almost forcibly toward the open doorway.*]

Act III

SCENE—*The same. The curtains are drawn across the open doorway, and also across the french windows. The lamp, half turned down, with a shade over it, is burning on the table. In the stove, the door of which is open, a fire has been burning, but it is now almost out.*

MRS. ELVSTED, *wrapped in a large shawl and with her feet resting on a footstool, is sitting near the stove, huddled in the armchair.* HEDDA *is lying asleep on this sofa, fully dressed, with a blanket over her.*

MRS. ELVSTED: [*After a pause, suddenly sits up in her chair and listens tensely. Then she sinks wearily back again and sighs.*] Not back yet! Oh, God! Oh, God! Not back yet!

[BERTHA *tiptoes cautiously in from the hall. She has a letter in her hand.*]

MRS. ELVSTED: [*Turns and whispers.*] What is it? Has someone come?

BERTHA: [*Quietly.*] Yes, a servant's just called with this letter.

MRS. ELVSTED: [*Quickly, holding out her hand.*] A letter! Give it to me!

BERTHA: But it's for the Doctor, madam.

MRS. ELVSTED: Oh. I see.

BERTHA: Miss Tesman's maid brought it. I'll leave it here on the table.

MRS. ELVSTED: Yes, do.

BERTHA: [*Puts down the letter.*] I'd better put the lamp out. It's starting to smoke.

MRS. ELVSTED: Yes, put it out. It'll soon be daylight.

BERTHA: [*Puts out the lamp.*] It's daylight already, madam.

MRS. ELVSTED: Yes. Broad day. And not home yet.

BERTHA: Oh dear, I was afraid this would happen.

MRS. ELVSTED: Were you?

BERTHA: Yes. When I heard that a certain gentleman had returned to town, and saw him go off with them. I've heard all about him.

MRS. ELVSTED: Don't talk so loud. You'll wake your mistress.

BERTHA: [*Looks at the sofa and sighs.*] Yes. Let her go on sleeping, poor dear. Shall I put some more wood on the fire?

MRS. ELVSTED: Thank you, don't bother on my account.

BERTHA: Very good. [*Goes quietly out through the hall.*]

HEDDA: [*Wakes as the door closes and looks up.*] What's that?

MRS. ELVSTED: It was only the maid.

HEDDA: [*Looks round.*] What am I doing here? Oh, now I remember. [*Sits up on the sofa, stretches herself and rubs her eyes.*] What time is it, Thea?

MRS. ELVSTED: It's gone seven.

HEDDA: When did Tesman get back?

MRS. ELVSTED: He's not back yet.

HEDDA: Not home yet?

MRS. ELVSTED: [*Gets up.*] No one's come.

HEDDA: And we sat up waiting for them till four o'clock.

MRS. ELVSTED: God! How I waited for him!

HEDDA: [*Yawns and says with her hand in front of her mouth.*] Oh, dear. We might have saved ourselves the trouble.

MRS. ELVSTED: Did you manage to sleep?

HEDDA: Oh, yes. Quite well, I think. Didn't you get any?

MRS. ELVSTED: Not a wink. I couldn't, Hedda. I just couldn't.

HEDDA: [*Gets up and comes over to her.*] Now, now, now. There's nothing to worry about. I know what's happened.

MRS. ELVSTED: What? Please tell me.

HEDDA: Well, obviously the party went on very late——

MRS. ELVSTED: Oh dear, I suppose it must have. But——

HEDDA: And Tesman didn't want to come home and wake us all up in the middle of the night. [*Laughs.*] Probably wasn't too keen to show his face either, after a spree like that.

MRS. ELVSTED: But where could he have gone?

HEDDA: I should think he's probably slept at his aunts'. They keep his old room for him.

MRS. ELVSTED: No, he can't be with them. A letter came for him just now from Miss Tesman. It's over there.

HEDDA: Oh? [*Looks at the envelope.*] Yes, it's Auntie Juju's handwriting. Well, he must still be at Judge Brack's, then. And Eilert Loevborg is sitting there, reading to him. With a crown of vine-leaves in his hair.

MRS. ELVSTED: Hedda, you're only saying that. You don't believe it.

HEDDA: Thea, you really are a little fool.

MRS. ELVSTED: Perhaps I am.

HEDDA: You look tired to death.

MRS. ELVSTED: Yes. I am tired to death.

HEDDA: Go to my room and lie down for a little. Do as I say, now; don't argue.

MRS. ELVSTED: No, no. I couldn't possibly sleep.

HEDDA: Of course you can.

MRS. ELVSTED: But your husband'll be home soon. And I must know at once——

HEDDA: I'll tell you when he comes.

MRS. ELVSTED: Promise me, Hedda?

HEDDA: Yes, don't worry. Go and get some sleep.

MRS. ELVSTED: Thank you. All right, I'll try.

[*She goes out through the rear room.* HEDDA *goes to the french windows and draws the curtains. Broad daylight floods into the room. She goes to the writing table, takes a small hand mirror from it and arranges her hair. Then she goes to the door leading into the hall and presses the bell. After a few moments,* BERTHA *enters.*]

BERTHA: Did you want anything, madam?

HEDDA: Yes, put some more wood on the fire. I'm freezing.

BERTHA: Bless you, I'll soon have this room warmed up. [*She rakes the embers together and puts a fresh piece of wood on them. Suddenly she stops and listens.*] There's someone at the front door, madam.

HEDDA: Well, go and open it. I'll see to the fire.

BERTHA: It'll burn up in a moment.

[*She goes out through the hall.* HEDDA *kneels on the footstool and puts more wood in the stove. After a few seconds,* GEORGE TESMAN *enters from the hall. He looks tired, and rather worried. He tiptoes toward the open doorway and is about to slip through the curtains.*]

HEDDA: [*At the stove, without looking up.*] Good morning.

TESMAN: [*Turns.*] Hedda! [*Comes nearer.*] Good heavens, are you up already? What?

HEDDA: Yes, I got up very early this morning.

TESMAN: I was sure you'd still be sleeping. Fancy that!

HEDDA: Don't talk so loud. Mrs. Elvsted's asleep in my room.

TESMAN: Mrs. Elvsted? Has she stayed the night here?

HEDDA: Yes. No one came to escort her home.

TESMAN: Oh. No, I suppose not.

HEDDA: [*Closes the door of the stove and gets up.*] Well. Was it fun?

TESMAN: Have you been anxious about me? What?

HEDDA: Not in the least. I asked if you'd had fun.

TESMAN: Oh yes, rather! Well, I thought, for once in a while—The first part was the best; when Eilert read his book to me. We arrived over an hour too early—what about that, eh? By Jove! Brack had a lot of things to see to, so Eilert read to me.

HEDDA: [*Sits at the right-hand side of the table.*] Well? Tell me about it.

TESMAN: [*Sits on a footstool by the stove.*] Honestly, Hedda, you've no idea what a book that's going to be. It's really one of the most remarkable things that's ever been written. By Jove!

HEDDA: Oh, never mind about the book——

TESMAN: I'm going to make a confession to you, Hedda. When he'd finished reading a sort of beastly feeling came over me.

HEDDA: Beastly feeling?

TESMAN: I found myself envying Eilert for being able to write like that. Imagine that, Hedda!

HEDDA: Yes. I can imagine.

TESMAN: What a tragedy that with all those gifts he should be so incorrigible.

HEDDA: You mean he's less afraid of life than most men?

TESMAN: Good heavens, no. He just doesn't know the meaning of the word moderation.

HEDDA: What happened afterwards?

TESMAN: Well, looking back on it I suppose you might almost call it an orgy, Hedda.

HEDDA: Had he vine-leaves in his hair?

TESMAN: Vine-leaves? No, I didn't see any of them. He made a long, rambling oration in honor of the woman who'd inspired him to write this book. Yes, those were the words he used.

HEDDA: Did he name her?

TESMAN: No. But I suppose it must be Mrs. Elvsted. You wait and see!

HEDDA: Where did you leave him?

TESMAN: On the way home. We left in a bunch—the last of us, that is—and Brack came with us to get a little fresh air. Well, then, you see, we agreed we ought to see Eilert home. He'd had a drop too much.

HEDDA: You don't say?

TESMAN: But now comes the funny part, Hedda. Or I should really say the tragic part. Oh, I'm almost ashamed to tell you. For Eilert's sake, I mean——

HEDDA: Why, what happened?

TESMAN: Well, you see, as we were walking toward town I happened to drop behind for a minute. Only for a minute—er—you understand——

HEDDA: Yes, yes——?

TESMAN: Well then, when I ran on to catch them up, what do you think I found by the roadside. What?

HEDDA: How on earth should I know?

TESMAN: You mustn't tell anyone, Hedda. What? Promise me that—for Eilert's sake. [*Takes a package wrapped in paper from his coat pocket.*] Just fancy! I found this.

HEDDA: Isn't this the one he brought here yesterday?

TESMAN: Yes! The whole of that precious, irreplaceable manuscript! And he went and lost it! Didn't even notice! What about that? By Jove! Tragic.

HEDDA: But why didn't you give it back to him?

TESMAN: I didn't dare to, in the state he was in.

HEDDA: Didn't you tell any of the others?

TESMAN: Good heavens, no. I didn't want to do that. For Eilert's sake, you understand.

HEDDA: Then no one else knows you have his manuscript?

TESMAN: No. And no one must be allowed to know.

HEDDA: Didn't it come up in the conversation later?

TESMAN: I didn't get a chance to talk to him any more. As soon as we got into the outskirts of town, he and one or two of the others gave us the slip. Disappeared, by Jove!

HEDDA: Oh? I suppose they took him home.

TESMAN: Yes, I imagine that was the idea. Brack left us, too.

HEDDA: And what have you been up to since then?

TESMAN: Well, I and one or two of the others—awfully jolly chaps, they were—went back to where one of them lived, and had a cup of morning coffee. Morning-after coffee—what? Ah, well. I'll just lie down for a bit and give Eilert time to sleep it off, poor chap, then I'll run over and give this back to him.

HEDDA: [*Holds out her hand for the package.*] No, don't do that. Not just yet. Let me read it first.

TESMAN: Oh no, really, Hedda dear, honestly, I daren't do that.

HEDDA: Daren't?

TESMAN: No—imagine how desperate he'll be when he wakes up and finds his manuscript's missing. He hasn't any copy, you see. He told me so himself.

HEDDA: Can't a thing like that be rewritten?

TESMAN: Oh no, not possibly, I shouldn't think. I mean, the inspiration, you know——

HEDDA: Oh, yes. I'd forgotten that. [*Casually.*] By the way, there's a letter for you.

TESMAN: Is there? Fancy that!

HEDDA: [*Holds it out to him.*] It came early this morning.

TESMAN: I say, it's from Auntie Juju! What on earth can it be? [*Puts the package on the other footstool, opens the letter, reads it and jumps up.*] Oh, Hedda! She says poor Auntie Rena's dying.

HEDDA: Well, we've been expecting that.

TESMAN: She says if I want to see her I must go quickly. I'll run over at once.

HEDDA: [*Hides a smile.*] Run?

TESMAN: Hedda dear, I suppose you wouldn't like to come with me? What about that, eh?

HEDDA: [*Gets up and says wearily and with repulsion.*] No, no, don't ask me to do anything like that. I can't bear illness or death. I loathe anything ugly.

TESMAN: Yes, yes. Of course. [*In a dither.*] My hat? My overcoat? Oh yes, in the hall. I do hope I won't get there too late, Hedda? What?

HEDDA: You'll be all right if you run.

[BERTHA *enters from the hall.*]

BERTHA: Judge Brack's outside and wants to know if he can come in.

TESMAN: At this hour? No, I can't possibly receive him now.

HEDDA: I can. [*To* BERTHA.] Ask his honor to come in.

[BERTHA *goes.*]

HEDDA: [*Whispers quickly.*] The manuscript, Tesman. [*She snatches it from the footstool.*]

TESMAN: Yes, give it to me.

HEDDA: No, I'll look after it for now.

[*She goes over to the writing table and puts it in the bookcase.* TESMAN *stands dithering, unable to get his gloves on.* JUDGE BRACK *enters from the hall.*]

HEDDA: [*Nods to him.*] Well, you're an early bird.

BRACK: Yes, aren't I? [*To* TESMAN.] Are you up and about, too?

TESMAN: Yes, I've got to go and see my aunts. Poor Auntie Rena's dying.

BRACK: Oh dear, is she? Then you mustn't let me detain you. At so tragic a——

TESMAN: Yes, I really must run. Good-bye! Good-bye! [*Runs out through the hall.*]

HEDDA: [*Goes nearer.*] You seem to have had excellent sport last night—Judge.

BRACK: Indeed yes, Mrs. Hedda. I haven't even had time to take my clothes off.

HEDDA: *You* haven't either?

BRACK: As you see. What's Tesman told you about last night's escapades?

HEDDA: Oh, only some boring story about having gone and drunk coffee somewhere.

BRACK: Yes, I've heard about that coffee party. Eilert Loevborg wasn't with them, I gather?

HEDDA: No, they took him home first.

BRACK: Did Tesman go with him?

HEDDA: No, one or two of the others, he said.

BRACK: [*Smiles.*] George Tesman is a credulous man, Mrs. Hedda.

HEDDA: God knows. But—has something happened?

BRACK: Well, yes, I'm afraid it has.

HEDDA: I see. Sit down and tell me.

[*She sits on the left of the table,* BRACK *at the long side of it, near her.*]

HEDDA: Well?

BRACK: I had a special reason for keeping track of my guests last night. Or perhaps I should say some of my guests.

HEDDA: Including Eilert Loevborg?

BRACK: I must confess—yes.

HEDDA: You're beginning to make me curious.

BRACK: Do you know where he and some of my other guests spent the latter half of last night, Mrs. Hedda?

HEDDA: Tell me. If it won't shock me.

BRACK: Oh, I don't think it'll shock you. They found themselves participating in an exceedingly animated *soirée.*[4]

HEDDA: Of a sporting character?

BRACK: Of a highly sporting character.

HEDDA: Tell me more.

BRACK: Loevborg had received an invitation in advance—as had the others. I knew all about that. But he had refused. As you know, he's become a new man.

HEDDA: Up at the Elvsteds', yes. But he went?

BRACK: Well, you see, Mrs. Hedda, last night at my house, unhappily, the spirit moved him.

HEDDA: Yes, I hear he became inspired.

BRACK: Somewhat violently inspired. And as a result, I suppose, his

---

4. Evening party.

thoughts strayed. We men, alas, don't always stick to our principles as firmly as we should.

HEDDA: I'm sure you're an exception, Judge Brack. But go on about Loevborg.

BRACK: Well, to cut a long story short, he ended up in the establishment of a certain Mademoiselle Danielle.

HEDDA: Mademoiselle Danielle?

BRACK: She was holding the *soirée*. For a selected circle of friends and admirers.

HEDDA: Has she got red hair?

BRACK: She has.

HEDDA: A singer of some kind?

BRACK: Yes—among other accomplishments. She's also a celebrated huntress—of men, Mrs. Hedda. I'm sure you've heard about her. Eilert Loevborg used to be one of her most ardent patrons. In his salad days.[5]

HEDDA: And how did all this end?

BRACK: Not entirely amicably, from all accounts. Mademoiselle Danielle began by receiving him with the utmost tenderness and ended by resorting to her fists.

HEDDA: Against Loevborg?

BRACK: Yes. He accused her, or her friends, of having robbed him. He claimed his pocketbook had been stolen. Among other things. In short, he seems to have made a bloodthirsty scene.

HEDDA: And what did this lead to?

BRACK: It led to a general free-for-all, in which both sexes participated. Fortunately, in the end the police arrived.

HEDDA: The police too?

BRACK: Yes. I'm afraid it may turn out to be rather an expensive joke for Master Eilert. Crazy fool!

HEDDA: Oh?

BRACK: Apparently he put up a very violent resistance. Hit one of the constables on the ear and tore his uniform. He had to accompany them to the police station.

HEDDA: Where did you learn all this?

BRACK: From the police.

HEDDA: [*To herself.*] So that's what happened. He didn't have a crown of vine-leaves in his hair.

BRACK: Vine-leaves, Mrs. Hedda?

HEDDA: [*In her normal voice again.*] But, tell me, Judge, why do you take such a close interest in Eilert Loevborg?

BRACK: For one thing it'll hardly be a matter of complete indifference to me if it's revealed in court that he came there straight from my house.

HEDDA: Will it come to court?

BRACK: Of course. Well, I don't regard that as particularly serious. Still, I thought it my duty, as a friend of the family, to give you and your husband a full account of his nocturnal adventures.

5. Indiscreet youth.

HEDDA: Why?

BRACK: Because I've a shrewd suspicion that he's hoping to use you as a kind of screen.

HEDDA: What makes you think that?

BRACK: Oh, for heaven's sake, Mrs. Hedda, we're not blind. You wait and see. This Mrs. Elvsted won't be going back to her husband just yet.

HEDDA: Well, if there were anything between those two there are plenty of other places where they could meet.

BRACK: Not in anyone's home. From now on every respectable house will once again be closed to Eilert Loevborg.

HEDDA: And mine should be too, you mean?

BRACK: Yes. I confess I should find it more than irksome if this gentleman were to be granted unrestricted access to this house. If he were super-fluously to intrude into—

HEDDA: The triangle?

BRACK: Precisely. For me it would be like losing a home.

HEDDA: [*Looks at him and smiles.*] I see. You want to be the cock of the walk.

BRACK: [*Nods slowly and lowers his voice.*] Yes, that is my aim. And I shall fight for it with—every weapon at my disposal.

HEDDA: [*As her smile fades.*] You're a dangerous man, aren't you? When you really want something.

BRACK: You think so?

HEDDA: Yes. I'm beginning to think so. I'm deeply thankful you haven't any kind of hold over me.

BRACK: [*Laughs equivocally.*] Well, well, Mrs. Hedda—perhaps you're right. If I had, who knows what I might not think up?

HEDDA: Come, Judge Brack. That sounds almost like a threat.

BRACK: [*Gets up.*] Heaven forbid! In the creation of a triangle—and its continuance—the question of compulsion should never arise.

HEDDA: Exactly what I was thinking.

BRACK: Well, I've said what I came to say. I must be getting back. Good-bye, Mrs. Hedda. [*Goes toward the french windows.*]

HEDDA: [*Gets up.*] Are you going out through the garden?

BRACK: Yes, it's shorter.

HEDDA: Yes. And it's the back door, isn't it?

BRACK: I've nothing against back doors. They can be quite intriguing—sometimes.

HEDDA: When people fire pistols out of them, for example?

BRACK: [*In the doorway, laughs.*] Oh, people don't shoot tame cocks.

HEDDA: [*Laughs too.*] I suppose not. When they've only got one.

[*They nod good-bye, laughing. He goes. She closes the french windows behind him, and stands for a moment, looking out pensively. Then she walks across the room and glances through the curtains in the open doorway. Goes to the writing table, takes LOEVBORG's package from the bookcase and is about to leaf through the pages when BERTHA is heard remonstrating loudly in the hall. HEDDA turns and listens. She hastily puts the package back in the drawer, locks it and puts the key on the inkstand. EILERT LOEVBORG, with his overcoat on*] *and his hat in his hand, throws the door open. He looks somewhat confused and excited.*]

LOEVBORG: [*Shouts as he enters.*] I must come in, I tell you! Let me pass! [*He closes the door, turns, sees* HEDDA, *controls himself immediately and bows.*]

HEDDA: [*At the writing table.*] Well, Mr. Loevborg, this is rather a late hour to be collecting Thea.

LOEVBORG: And an early hour to call on you. Please forgive me.

HEDDA: How do you know she's still here?

LOEVBORG: They told me at her lodgings that she has been out all night.

HEDDA: [*Goes to the table.*] Did you notice anything about their behavior when they told you?

LOEVBORG: [*Looks at her, puzzled.*] Notice anything?

HEDDA: Did they sound as if they thought it—strange?

LOEVBORG: [*Suddenly understands.*] Oh, I see what you mean. I'm dragging her down with me. No, as a matter of fact I didn't notice anything. I suppose Tesman isn't up yet?

HEDDA: No, I don't think so.

LOEVBORG: When did he get home?

HEDDA: Very late.

LOEVBORG: Did he tell you anything?

HEDDA: Yes. I gather you had a merry party at Judge Brack's last night.

LOEVBORG: He didn't tell you anything else?

HEDDA: I don't think so. I was so terribly sleepy——

[MRS. ELVSTED *comes through the curtains in the open doorway.*]

MRS. ELVSTED: [*Runs toward him.*] Oh, Eilert! At last!

LOEVBORG: Yes—at last. And too late.

MRS. ELVSTED: What is too late?

LOEVBORG: Everything—now. I'm finished, Thea.

MRS. ELVSTED: Oh, no, no! Don't say that!

LOEVBORG: You'll say it yourself, when you've heard what I——

MRS. ELVSTED: I don't want to hear anything!

HEDDA: Perhaps you'd rather speak to her alone? I'd better go.

LOEVBORG: No, stay.

MRS. ELVSTED: But I don't want to hear anything, I tell you!

LOEVBORG: It's not about last night.

MRS. ELVSTED: Then what——?

LOEVBORG: I want to tell you that from now on we must stop seeing each other.

MRS. ELVSTED: Stop seeing each other!

HEDDA: [*Involuntarily.*] I knew it!

LOEVBORG: I have no further use for you, Thea.

MRS. ELVSTED: You can stand there and say that! No further use for me! Surely I can go on helping you? We'll go on working together, won't we?

LOEVBORG: I don't intend to do any more work from now on.

MRS. ELVSTED: [*Desperately.*] Then what use have I for my life?

LOEVBORG: You must try to live as if you had never known me.

MRS. ELVSTED: But I can't!

LOEVBORG: Try to, Thea. Go back home——

MRS. ELVSTED: Never! I want to be wherever you are! I won't let myself be driven away like this! I want to stay here—and be with you when the book comes out.

HEDDA: [*Whispers.*] Ah, yes! The book!

LOEVBORG: [*Looks at her.*] Our book; Thea's and mine. It belongs to both of us.

MRS. ELVSTED: Oh, yes! I feel that, too! And I've a right to be with you when it comes into the world. I want to see people respect and honor you again. And the joy! The joy! I want to share it with you!

LOEVBORG: Thea—our book will never come into the world.

HEDDA: Ah!

MRS. ELVSTED: Not——?

LOEVBORG: It cannot. Ever.

MRS. ELVSTED: Eilert—what have you done with the manuscript? Where is it?

LOEVBORG: Oh Thea, please don't ask me that!

MRS. ELVSTED: Yes, yes—I must know. I've a right to know. Now!

LOEVBORG: The manuscript. I've torn it up.

MRS. ELVSTED: [*Screams.*] No, no!

HEDDA: [*Involuntarily.*] But that's not——!

LOEVBORG: [*Looks at her.*] Not true, you think?

HEDDA: [*Controls herself.*] Why—yes, of course it is, if you say so. It just sounded so incredible——

LOEVBORG: It's true, nevertheless.

MRS. ELVSTED: Oh, my God, my God, Hedda—he's destroyed his own book!

LOEVBORG: I have destroyed my life. Why not my life's work, too?

MRS. ELVSTED: And you—did this last night?

LOEVBORG: Yes, Thea. I tore it into a thousand pieces. And scattered them out across the fjord.[6] It's good, clean, salt water. Let it carry them away; let them drift in the current and the wind. And in a little while, they will sink. Deeper and deeper. As I shall, Thea.

MRS. ELVSTED: Do you know, Eilert—this book—all my life I shall feel as though you'd killed a little child.

LOEVBORG: You're right. It is like killing a child.

MRS. ELVSTED: But how could you? It was my child, too!

HEDDA: [*Almost inaudibly.*] Oh—the child——!

MRS. ELVSTED: [*Breathes heavily.*] It's all over, then. Well—I'll go now, Hedda.

HEDDA: You're not leaving town?

MRS. ELVSTED: I don't know what I'm going to do. I can't see anything except—darkness.

[*She goes out through the hall.*]

HEDDA: [*Waits a moment.*] Aren't you going to escort her home, Mr. Loevborg?

LOEVBORG: I? Through the streets? Do you want me to let people see her with me?

---

6. Inlet of the sea.

HEDDA: Of course I don't know what else may have happened last night. But is it so utterly beyond redress?

LOEVBORG: It isn't just last night. It'll go on happening. I know it. But the curse of it is, I don't want to live that kind of life. I don't want to start all that again. She's broken my courage. I can't spit in the eyes of the world any longer.

HEDDA: [As though to herself.] That pretty little fool's been trying to shape a man's destiny. [Looks at him.] But how could you be so heartless toward her?

LOEVBORG: Don't call me heartless!

HEDDA: To go and destroy the one thing that's made her life worth living? You don't call that heartless?

LOEVBORG: Do you want to know the truth, Hedda?

HEDDA: The truth?

LOEVBORG: Promise me first—give me your word—that you'll never let Thea know about this.

HEDDA: I give you my word.

LOEVBORG: Good. Well; what I told her just now was a lie.

HEDDA: About the manuscript?

LOEVBORG: Yes. I didn't tear it up. Or throw it in the fjord.

HEDDA: You didn't? But where is it, then?

LOEVBORG: I destroyed it, all the same. I destroyed it, Hedda!

HEDDA: I don't understand.

LOEVBORG: Thea said that what I had done was like killing a child.

HEDDA: Yes. That's what she said.

LOEVBORG: But to kill a child isn't the worst thing a father can do to it.

HEDDA: What could be worse than that?

LOEVBORG: Hedda—suppose a man came home one morning, after a night of debauchery, and said to the mother of his child: "Look here. I've been wandering round all night. I've been to—such-and-such a place and such-and-such a place. And I had our child with me. I took him to—these places. And I've lost him. Just—lost him. God knows where he is or whose hands he's fallen into."

HEDDA: I see. But when all's said and done, this was only a book——

LOEVBORG: Thea's heart and soul were in that book. It was her whole life.

HEDDA: Yes. I understand.

LOEVBORG: Well, then you must also understand that she and I cannot possibly ever see each other again.

HEDDA: Where will you go?

LOEVBORG: Nowhere. I just want to put an end to it all. As soon as possible.

HEDDA: [Takes a step toward him.] Eilert Loevborg, listen to me. Do it— beautifully!

LOEVBORG: Beautifully? [Smiles.] With a crown of vine-leaves in my hair? The way you used to dream of me—in the old days?

HEDDA: No. I don't believe in that crown any longer. But—do it beautifully, all the same. Just this once. Good-bye. You must go now. And don't come back.

LOEVBORG: Adieu, madam. Give my love to George Tesman. [Turns to go.]

HEDDA: Wait. I want to give you a souvenir to take with you.

[*She goes over to the writing table, opens the drawer and the pistol-case, and comes back to* LOEVBORG *with one of the pistols.*]

LOEVBORG: [*Looks at her.*] This? Is this the souvenir?

HEDDA: [*Nods slowly.*] You recognize it? You looked down its barrel once.

LOEVBORG: You should have used it then.

HEDDA: Here! Use it now!

LOEVBORG: [*Puts the pistol in his breast pocket.*] Thank you.

HEDDA: Do it beautifully, Eilert Loevborg. Only promise me that!

LOEVBORG: Good-bye, Hedda Gabler.

[*He goes out through the hall.* HEDDA *stands by the door for a moment, listening. Then she goes over to the writing table, takes out the package containing the manuscript, glances inside it, pulls some of the pages half out and looks at them. Then she takes it to the armchair by the stove and sits down with the package in her lap. After a moment, she opens the door of the stove; then she opens the packet.*]

HEDDA: [*Throws one of the pages into the stove and whispers to herself.*] I'm burning your child, Thea! You with your beautiful wavy hair! [*She throws a few more pages into the stove.*] The child Eilert Loevborg gave you. [*Throws the rest of the manuscript in.*] I'm burning it! I'm burning your child!

Act IV

SCENE—*The same. It is evening. The drawing room is in darkness. The small room is illuminated by the hanging lamp over the table. The curtains are drawn across the french windows.* HEDDA, *dressed in black, is walking up and down in the darkened room. Then she goes into the small room and crosses to the left. A few chords are heard from the piano. She comes back into the drawing room.*

BERTHA *comes through the small room from the right with a lighted lamp, which she places on the table in front of the corner sofa in the drawing room. Her eyes are red with crying, and she has black ribbons on her cap. She goes quietly out, right.* HEDDA *goes over to the french windows, draws the curtains slightly to one side and looks out into the darkness.*

A few moments later, MISS TESMAN *enters from the hall. She is dressed in mourning, with a black hat and veil.* HEDDA *goes to meet her and holds out her hand.*

MISS TESMAN: Well, Hedda, here I am in the weeds of sorrow. My poor sister has ended her struggles at last.

HEDDA: I've already heard. Tesman sent me a card.

MISS TESMAN: Yes, he promised me he would. But I thought, no, I must go and break the news of death to Hedda myself—here, in the house of life.

HEDDA: It's very kind of you.

MISS TESMAN: Ah, Rena shouldn't have chosen a time like this to pass away. This is no moment for Hedda's house to be a place of mourning.

HEDDA: [*Changing the subject.*] She died peacefully, Miss Tesman?

MISS TESMAN: Oh, it was quite beautiful! The end came so calmly. And she was so happy at being able to see George once again. And say good-bye to him. Hasn't he come home yet?

HEDDA: No. He wrote that I mustn't expect him too soon. But please sit down.

MISS TESMAN: No, thank you, Hedda dear—bless you. I'd like to. But I've so little time. I must dress her and lay her out as well as I can. She shall go to her grave looking really beautiful.

HEDDA: Can't I help with anything?

MISS TESMAN: Why, you mustn't think of such a thing! Hedda Tesman mustn't let her hands be soiled by contact with death. Or her thoughts. Not at this time.

HEDDA: One can't always control one's thoughts.

MISS TESMAN: [*Continues.*] Ah, well, that's life. Now we must start to sew poor Rena's shroud. There'll be sewing to be done in this house too before long, I shouldn't wonder. But not for a shroud, praise God.

[GEORGE TESMAN *enters from the hall.*]

HEDDA: You've come at last! Thank heavens!

TESMAN: Are you here, Auntie Juju? With Hedda? Fancy that!

MISS TESMAN: I was just on the point of leaving, dear boy. Well, have you done everything you promised me?

TESMAN: No, I'm afraid I forgot half of it. I'll have to run over again tomorrow. My head's in a complete whirl today. I can't collect my thoughts.

MISS TESMAN: But George dear, you mustn't take it like this.

TESMAN: Oh? Well—er—how should I?

MISS TESMAN: You must be happy in your grief. Happy for what's happened. As I am.

TESMAN: Oh, yes, yes. You're thinking of Aunt Rena.

HEDDA: It'll be lonely for you now, Miss Tesman.

MISS TESMAN: For the first few days, yes. But it won't last long, I hope. Poor dear Rena's little room isn't going to stay empty.

TESMAN: Oh? Whom are you going to move in there? What?

MISS TESMAN: Oh, there's always some poor invalid who needs care and attention.

HEDDA: Do you really want another cross like that to bear?

MISS TESMAN: Cross! God forgive you, child. It's been no cross for me.

HEDDA: But now—if a complete stranger comes to live with you——?

MISS TESMAN: Oh, one soon makes friends with invalids. And I need so much to have someone to live for. Like you, my dear. Well, I expect there'll soon be work in this house too for an old aunt, praise God!

HEDDA: Oh—please!

TESMAN: By Jove, yes! What a splendid time the three of us could have together if——

HEDDA: If?

TESMAN: [*Uneasily.*] Oh, never mind. It'll all work out. Let's hope so—what?

MISS TESMAN: Yes, yes. Well, I'm sure you two would like to be alone. [*Smiles.*] Perhaps Hedda may have something to tell you, George.

Good-bye. I must go home to Rena. [*Turns to the door.*] Dear God, how strange! Now Rena is with me and with poor dear Joachim.

TESMAN: Fancy that. Yes, Auntie Juju! What?

[MISS TESMAN *goes out through the hall.*]

HEDDA: [*Follows* TESMAN *coldly and searchingly with her eyes.*] I really believe this death distresses you more than it does her.

TESMAN: Oh, it isn't just Auntie Rena. It's Eilert I'm so worried about.

HEDDA: [*Quickly.*] Is there any news of him?

TESMAN: I ran over to see him this afternoon. I wanted to tell him his manuscript was in safe hands.

HEDDA: Oh? You didn't find him?

TESMAN: No. He wasn't at home. But later I met Mrs. Elvsted and she told me he'd been here early this morning.

HEDDA: Yes, just after you'd left.

TESMAN: It seems he said he'd torn the manuscript up. What?

HEDDA: Yes, he claimed to have done so.

TESMAN: You told him we had it, of course?

HEDDA: No. [*Quickly.*] Did you tell Mrs. Elvsted?

TESMAN: No, I didn't like to. But you ought to have told him. Think if he should go home and do something desperate! Give me the manuscript, Hedda. I'll run over to him with it right away. Where did you put it?

HEDDA: [*Cold and motionless, leaning against the armchair.*] I haven't got it any longer.

TESMAN: Haven't got it? What on earth do you mean?

HEDDA: I've burned it.

TESMAN: [*Starts, terrified.*] Burned it! Burned Eilert's manuscript!

HEDDA: Don't shout. The servant will hear you.

TESMAN: Burned it! But in heaven's name——! Oh, no, no, no! This is impossible!

HEDDA: Well, it's true.

TESMAN: But Hedda, do you realize what you've done? That's appropriating lost property! It's against the law! By Jove! You ask Judge Brack and see if I'm not right.

HEDDA: You'd be well advised not to talk about it to Judge Brack or anyone else.

TESMAN: But how could you go and do such a dreadful thing? What on earth put the idea into your head? What came over you? Answer me! What?

HEDDA: [*Represses an almost imperceptible smile.*] I did it for your sake, George.

TESMAN: For my sake?

HEDDA: When you came home this morning and described how he'd read his book to you——

TESMAN: Yes, yes?

HEDDA: You admitted you were jealous of him.

TESMAN: But, good heavens, I didn't mean it literally!

HEDDA: No matter. I couldn't bear the thought that anyone else should push you into the background.

TESMAN: [*Torn between doubt and joy.*] Hedda—is this true? But—but—but I never realized you loved me like that! Fancy——

HEDDA: Well, I suppose you'd better know. I'm going to have—— [*Breaks off and says violently.*] No, no—you'd better ask your Auntie Juju. She'll tell you.

TESMAN: Hedda! I think I understand what you mean. [*Clasps his hands.*] Good heavens, can it really be true! What?

HEDDA: Don't shout. The servant will hear you.

TESMAN: [*Laughing with joy.*] The servant! I say, that's good! The servant! Why, that's Bertha! I'll run out and tell her at once!

HEDDA: [*Clenches her hands in despair.*] Oh, it's destroying me, all this—it's destroying me!

TESMAN: I say, Hedda, what's up? What?

HEDDA: [*Cold, controlled.*] Oh, it's all so—absurd—George.

TESMAN: Absurd? That I'm so happy? But surely——? Ah, well—perhaps I won't say anything to Bertha.

HEDDA: No, do. She might as well know too.

TESMAN: No, no, I won't tell her yet. But Auntie Juju—I must let her know! And you—you called me George! For the first time! Fancy that! Oh, it'll make Auntie Juju so happy, all this! So very happy!

HEDDA: Will she be happy when she hears I've burned Eilert Loevborg's manuscript—for your sake?

TESMAN: No, I'd forgotten about that. Of course no one must be allowed to know about the manuscript. But that you're burning with love for me, Hedda, I must certainly let Auntie Juju know that. I say, I wonder if young wives often feel like that toward their husbands? What?

HEDDA: You might ask Auntie Juju about that too.

TESMAN: I will, as soon as I get the chance. [*Looks uneasy and thoughtful again.*] But I say, you know, that manuscript. Dreadful business. Poor Eilert!

[MRS. ELVSTED, *dressed as on her first visit, with hat and overcoat, enters from the hall.*]

MRS. ELVSTED: [*Greets them hastily and tremulously.*] Oh, Hedda dear, do please forgive me for coming here again.

HEDDA: Why, Thea, what's happened?

TESMAN: Is it anything to do with Eilert Loevborg? What?

MRS. ELVSTED: Yes—I'm so dreadfully afraid he may have met with an accident.

HEDDA: [*Grips her arm.*] You think so?

TESMAN: But, good heavens, Mrs. Elvsted, what makes you think that?

MRS. ELVSTED: I heard them talking about him at the boarding-house, as I went in. Oh, there are the most terrible rumors being spread about him in town today.

TESMAN: Fancy. Yes, I heard about them too. But I can testify that he went straight home to bed. Fancy that!

HEDDA: Well—what did they say in the boarding-house?

MRS. ELVSTED: Oh, I couldn't find out anything. Either they didn't know, or else—— They stopped talking when they saw me. And I didn't dare to ask.

TESMAN: [*Fidgets uneasily.*] We must hope—we must hope you misheard them, Mrs. Elvsted.

MRS. ELVSTED: No, no, I'm sure it was he they were talking about. I heard them say something about a hospital——

TESMAN: Hospital!

HEDDA: Oh no, surely that's impossible!

MRS. ELVSTED: Oh, I became so afraid. So I went up to his rooms and asked to see him.

HEDDA: Do you think that was wise, Thea?

MRS. ELVSTED: Well, what else could I do? I couldn't bear the uncertainty any longer.

TESMAN: But you didn't manage to find him either? What?

MRS. ELVSTED: No. And they had no idea where he was. They said he hadn't been home since yesterday afternoon.

TESMAN: Since yesterday? Fancy that!

MRS. ELVSTED: I'm sure he must have met with an accident.

TESMAN: Hedda, I wonder if I ought to go into town and make one or two enquiries?

HEDDA: No, no, don't you get mixed up in this.

[JUDGE BRACK *enters from the hall, hat in hand.* BERTHA, *who has opened the door for him, closes it. He looks serious and greets them silently.*]

TESMAN: Hullo, my dear Judge. Fancy seeing you!

BRACK: I had to come and talk to you.

TESMAN: I can see Auntie Juju's told you the news.

BRACK: Yes, I've heard about that too.

TESMAN: Tragic, isn't it?

BRACK: Well, my dear chap, that depends on how you look at it.

TESMAN: [*Looks uncertainly at him.*] Has something else happened?

BRACK: Yes.

HEDDA: Another tragedy?

BRACK: That also depends on how you look at it, Mrs. Tesman.

MRS. ELVSTED: Oh, it's something to do with Eilert Loevborg!

BRACK: [*Looks at her for a moment.*] How did you guess? Perhaps you've heard already——?

MRS. ELVSTED: [*Confused.*] No, no, not at all—I——

TESMAN: For heaven's sake, tell us!

BRACK: [*Shrugs his shoulders.*] Well, I'm afraid they've taken him to the hospital. He's dying.

MRS. ELVSTED: [*Screams.*] Oh God, God!

TESMAN: The hospital! Dying!

HEDDA: [*Involuntarily.*] So quickly!

MRS. ELVSTED: [*Weeping.*] Oh, Hedda! And we parted enemies!

HEDDA: [*Whispers.*] Thea—Thea!

MRS. ELVSTED: [*Ignoring her.*] I must see him! I must see him before he dies!

BRACK: It's no use, Mrs. Elvsted. No one's allowed to see him now.

MRS. ELVSTED: But what's happened to him? You must tell me!

TESMAN: He hasn't tried to do anything to himself? What?

HEDDA: Yes, he has. I'm sure of it.

TESMAN: Hedda, how can you——?

BRACK: [*Who has not taken his eyes from her.*] I'm afraid you've guessed correctly, Mrs. Tesman.

MRS. ELVSTED: How dreadful!

TESMAN: Attempted suicide! Fancy that!

HEDDA: Shot himself!

BRACK: Right again, Mrs. Tesman.

MRS. ELVSTED: [*Tries to compose herself.*] When did this happen, Judge Brack?

BRACK: This afternoon. Between three and four.

TESMAN: But, good heavens—where? What?

BRACK: [*A little hesitantly.*] Where? Why, my dear chap, in his rooms of course.

MRS. ELVSTED: No, that's impossible. I was there soon after six.

BRACK: Well, it must have been somewhere else, then. I don't know exactly. I only know that they found him. He'd shot himself—through the breast.

MRS. ELVSTED: Oh, how horrible! That he should end like that!

HEDDA: [*To* BRACK.] Through the breast, you said?

BRACK: That is what I said.

HEDDA: Not through the head?

BRACK: Through the breast, Mrs. Tesman.

HEDDA: The breast. Yes; yes. That's good, too.

BRACK: Why, Mrs. Tesman?

HEDDA: Oh—no, I didn't mean anything.

TESMAN: And the wound's dangerous you say? What?

BRACK: Mortal. He's probably already dead.

MRS. ELVSTED: Yes, yes—I feel it! It's all over. All over. Oh Hedda——!

TESMAN: But, tell me, how did you manage to learn all this?

BRACK: [*Curtly.*] From the police. I spoke to one of them.

HEDDA: [*Loudly, clearly.*] At last! Oh, thank God!

TESMAN: [*Appalled.*] For God's sake, Hedda, what are you saying?

HEDDA: I am saying there's beauty in what he has done.

BRACK: Mm—Mrs. Tesman——

TESMAN: Beauty! Oh, but I say!

MRS. ELVSTED: Hedda, how can you talk of beauty in connection with a thing like this?

HEDDA: Eilert Loevborg has settled his account with life. He's had the courage to do what—what he had to do.

MRS. ELVSTED: No, that's not why it happened. He did it because he was mad.

TESMAN: He did it because he was desperate.

HEDDA: You're wrong! I know!

MRS. ELVSTED: He must have been mad. The same as when he tore up the manuscript.

BRACK: [*Starts.*] Manuscript? Did he tear it up?

MRS. ELVSTED: Yes. Last night.

TESMAN: [*Whispers.*] Oh, Hedda, we shall never be able to escape from this.

BRACK: Hm. Strange.

TESMAN: [*Wanders round the room.*] To think of Eilert dying like that. And not leaving behind him the thing that would have made his name endure.

MRS. ELVSTED: If only it could be pieced together again!

TESMAN: Yes, fancy! If only it could! I'd give anything——

MRS. ELVSTED: Perhaps it can, Mr. Tesman.

TESMAN: What do you mean?

MRS. ELVSTED: [*Searches in the pocket of her dress.*] Look! I kept the notes he dictated it from.

HEDDA: [*Takes a step nearer.*] Ah!

TESMAN: You kept them, Mrs. Elvsted! What?

MRS. ELVSTED: Yes, here they are. I brought them with me when I left home. They've been in my pocket ever since.

TESMAN: Let me have a look.

MRS. ELVSTED: [*Hands him a wad of small sheets of paper.*] They're in a terrible muddle. All mixed up.

TESMAN: I say, just fancy if we can sort them out! Perhaps if we work on them together——?

MRS. ELVSTED: Oh, yes! Let's try, anyway!

TESMAN: We'll manage it. We must! I shall dedicate my life to this.

HEDDA: *You,* George? Your life?

TESMAN: Yes—well, all the time I can spare. My book'll have to wait. Hedda, you do understand? What? I owe it to Eilert's memory.

HEDDA: Perhaps.

TESMAN: Well, my dear Mrs. Elvsted, you and I'll have to pool our brains. No use crying over spilt milk, what? We must try to approach this matter calmly.

MRS. ELVSTED: Yes, yes, Mr. Tesman. I'll do my best.

TESMAN: Well, come over here and let's start looking at these notes right away. Where shall we sit? Here? No, the other room. You'll excuse us, won't you, Judge? Come along with me, Mrs. Elvsted.

MRS. ELVSTED: Oh, God! If only we can manage to do it!

[TESMAN *and* MRS. ELVSTED *go into the rear room. He takes off his hat and overcoat. They sit at the table beneath the hanging lamp and absorb themselves in the notes.* HEDDA *walks across to the stove and sits in the armchair. After a moment,* BRACK *goes over to her.*]

HEDDA: [*Half aloud.*] Oh, Judge! This act of Eilert Loevborg's—doesn't it give one a sense of release!

BRACK: Release, Mrs. Hedda? Well, it's a release for him, of course——

HEDDA: Oh, I don't mean him—I mean me! The release of knowing that someone can do something really brave! Something beautiful!

BRACK: [*Smiles.*] Hm—my dear Mrs. Hedda——

HEDDA: Oh, I know what you're going to say. You're a bourgeois at heart too, just like—ah, well!

BRACK: [*Looks at her.*] Eilert Loevborg has meant more to you than you're willing to admit to yourself. Or am I wrong?

HEDDA: I'm not answering questions like that from you. I only know that Eilert Loevborg has had the courage to live according to his own principles. And now, at last, he's done something big! Something beautiful!

To have the courage and the will to rise from the feast of life so early!

BRACK: It distresses me deeply, Mrs. Hedda, but I'm afraid I must rob you of that charming illusion.

HEDDA: Illusion?

BRACK: You wouldn't have been allowed to keep it for long, anyway.

HEDDA: What do you mean?

BRACK: He didn't shoot himself on purpose.

HEDDA: Not on purpose?

BRACK: No. It didn't happen quite the way I told you.

HEDDA: Have you been hiding something? What is it?

BRACK: In order to spare poor Mrs. Elvsted's feelings, I permitted myself one or two small—equivocations.

HEDDA: What?

BRACK: To begin with, he is already dead.

HEDDA: He died at the hospital?

BRACK: Yes. Without regaining consciousness.

HEDDA: What else haven't you told us?

BRACK: The incident didn't take place at his lodgings.

HEDDA: Well, that's utterly unimportant.

BRACK: Not utterly. The fact is, you see, that Eilert Loevborg was found shot in Mademoiselle Danielle's boudoir.

HEDDA: [Almost jumps up, but instead sinks back in her chair.] That's impossible. He can't have been there today.

BRACK: He was there this afternoon. He went to ask for something he claimed they'd taken from him. Talked some crazy nonsense about a child which had got lost——

HEDDA: Oh! So that was the reason!

BRACK: I thought at first he might have been referring to his manuscript. But I hear he destroyed that himself. So he must have meant his pocket-book—I suppose.

HEDDA: Yes, I suppose so. So they found him there?

BRACK: Yes; there. With a discharged pistol in his breast pocket. The shot had wounded him mortally.

HEDDA: Yes. In the breast.

BRACK: No. In the—hm—stomach. The—lower part——

HEDDA: [Looks at him with an expression of repulsion.] That too! Oh, why does everything I touch become mean and ludicrous? It's like a curse!

BRACK: There's something else, Mrs. Hedda. It's rather disagreeable, too.

HEDDA: What?

BRACK: The pistol he had on him——

HEDDA: Yes? What about it?

BRACK: He must have stolen it.

HEDDA: [Jumps up.] Stolen it! That isn't true! He didn't!

BRACK: It's the only explanation. He must have stolen it. Ssh!

[TESMAN and MRS. ELVSTED have got up from the table in the rear room and come into the drawing room.]

TESMAN: [His hands full of papers.] Hedda, I can't see properly under that lamp. Think!

HEDDA: I am thinking.

TESMAN: Do you think we could possibly use your writing table for a little? What?

HEDDA: Yes, of course. [*Quickly.*] No, wait! Let me tidy it up first.

TESMAN: Oh, don't you trouble about that. There's plenty of room.

HEDDA: No, no, let me tidy it up first, I say. I'll take this in and put them on the piano. Here.

> [*She pulls an object, covered with sheets of music, out from under the bookcase, puts some more sheets on top and carries it all into the rear room and away to the left.* TESMAN *puts his papers on the writing table and moves the lamp over from the corner table. He and* MRS. ELVSTED *sit down and begin working again.* HEDDA *comes back.*]

HEDDA: [*Behind* MRS. ELVSTED's *chair, ruffles her hair gently.*] Well, my pretty Thea! And how is work progressing on Eilert Loevborg's memorial?

MRS. ELVSTED: [*Looks up at her, dejectedly.*] Oh, it's going to be terribly difficult to get these into any order.

TESMAN: We've got to do it. We must! After all, putting other people's papers into order is rather my specialty, what?

> [HEDDA *goes over to the stove and sits on one of the footstools.* BRACK *stands over her, leaning against the armchair.*]

HEDDA: [*Whispers.*] What was that you were saying about the pistol?

BRACK: [*Softly.*] I said he must have stolen it.

HEDDA: Why do you think that?

BRACK: Because any other explanation is unthinkable, Mrs. Hedda, or ought to be.

HEDDA: I see.

BRACK: [*Looks at her for a moment.*] Eilert Loevborg was here this morning. Wasn't he?

HEDDA: Yes.

BRACK: Were you alone with him?

HEDDA: For a few moments.

BRACK: You didn't leave the room while he was here?

HEDDA: No.

BRACK: Think again. Are you sure you didn't go out for a moment?

HEDDA: Oh—yes, I might have gone into the hall. Just for a few seconds.

BRACK: And where was your pistol-case during this time?

HEDDA: I'd locked it in that——

BRACK: Er—Mrs. Hedda?

HEDDA: It was lying over there on my writing table.

BRACK: Have you looked to see if both the pistols are still there?

HEDDA: No.

BRACK: You needn't bother. I saw the pistol Loevborg had when they found him. I recognized it at once. From yesterday. And other occasions.

HEDDA: Have you got it?

BRACK: No. The police have it.

HEDDA: What will the police do with this pistol?

BRACK: Try to trace the owner.

HEDDA: Do you think they'll succeed?

BRACK: [*Leans down and whispers.*] No, Hedda Gabler. Not as long as I hold my tongue.

HEDDA: [*Looks nervously at him.*] And if you don't?

BRACK: [*Shrugs his shoulders.*] You could always say he'd stolen it.

HEDDA: I'd rather die!

BRACK: [*Smiles.*] People say that. They never do it.

HEDDA: [*Not replying.*] And suppose the pistol wasn't stolen? And they trace the owner? What then?

BRACK: There'll be a scandal, Hedda.

HEDDA: A scandal!

BRACK: Yes, a scandal. The thing you're so frightened of. You'll have to appear in court. Together with Mademoiselle Danielle. She'll have to explain how it all happened. Was it an accident, or was it—homicide? Was he about to take the pistol from his pocket to threaten her? And did it go off? Or did she snatch the pistol from his hand, shoot him and then put it back in his pocket? She might quite easily have done it. She's a resourceful lady, is Mademoiselle Danielle.

HEDDA: But I had nothing to do with this repulsive business.

BRACK: No. But you'll have to answer one question. Why did you give Eilert Loevborg this pistol? And what conclusions will people draw when it is proved you did give it to him?

HEDDA: [*Bows her head.*] That's true. I hadn't thought of that.

BRACK: Well, luckily there's no danger as long as I hold my tongue.

HEDDA: [*Looks up at him.*] In other words, I'm in your power, Judge. From now on, you've got your hold over me.

BRACK: [*Whispers, more slowly.*] Hedda, my dearest—believe me—I will not abuse my position.

HEDDA: Nevertheless, I'm in your power. Dependent on your will, and your demands. Not free. Still not free! [*Rises passionately.*] No. I couldn't bear that. No.

BRACK: [*Looks half-derisively at her.*] Most people resign themselves to the inevitable, sooner or later.

HEDDA: [*Returns his gaze.*] Possibly they do.
     [*She goes across to the writing table.*]

HEDDA: [*Represses an involuntary smile and says in* TESMAN's *voice.*] Well, George. Think you'll be able to manage? What?

TESMAN: Heaven knows, dear. This is going to take months and months.

HEDDA: [*In the same tone as before.*] Fancy that, by Jove! [*Runs her hands gently through* MRS. ELVSTED's *hair.*] Doesn't it feel strange, Thea? Here you are working away with Tesman just the way you used to work with Eilert Loevborg.

MRS. ELVSTED: Oh—if only I can inspire your husband too!

HEDDA: Oh, it'll come. In time.

TESMAN: Yes—do you know, Hedda, I really think I'm beginning to feel a bit—well—that way. But you go back and talk to Judge Brack.

HEDDA: Can't I be of use to you two in any way?

TESMAN: No, none at all. [*Turns his head.*] You'll have to keep Hedda company from now on, Judge, and see she doesn't get bored. If you don't mind.

BRACK. [*Glances at* HEDDA.] It'll be a pleasure.

HEDDA: Thank you. But I'm tired this evening. I think I'll lie down on the sofa in there for a little while.

TESMAN: Yes, dear—do. What?

[HEDDA *goes into the rear room and draws the curtain behind her. Short pause. Suddenly she begins to play a frenzied dance melody on the piano.*]

MRS. ELVSTED: [*Starts up from her chair.*] Oh, what's that?

TESMAN: [*Runs to the doorway.*] Hedda dear, please! Don't play dance music tonight! Think of Auntie Rena. And Eilert.

HEDDA: [*Puts her head out through the curtains.*] And Auntie Juju. And all the rest of them. From now on I'll be quiet. [*Closes the curtains behind her.*]

TESMAN: [*At the writing table.*] It distresses her to watch us doing this. I say, Mrs. Elvsted, I've an idea. Why don't you move in with Auntie Juju? I'll run over each evening, and we can sit and work there. What?

MRS. ELVSTED: Yes, that might be the best plan.

HEDDA: [*From the rear room.*] I can hear what you're saying, Tesman. But how shall I spend the evenings out here?

TESMAN: [*Looking through his papers.*] Oh, I'm sure Judge Brack'll be kind enough to come over and keep you company. You won't mind my not being here, Judge?

BRACK: [*In the armchair, calls gaily.*] I'll be delighted, Mrs. Tesman. I'll be here every evening. We'll have great fun together, you and I.

HEDDA: [*Loud and clear.*] Yes, that'll suit you, won't it, Judge? The only cock on the dunghill——!

[*A shot is heard from the rear room.* TESMAN, MRS. ELVSTED *and* JUDGE BRACK *start from their chairs.*]

TESMAN: Oh, she's playing with those pistols again.

[*He pulls the curtains aside and runs in.* MRS. ELVSTED *follows him.* HEDDA *is lying dead on the sofa. Confusion and shouting.* BERTHA *enters in alarm from the right.*]

TESMAN: [*Screams to* BRACK.] She's shot herself! Shot herself in the head! By Jove! Fancy that!

BRACK: [*Half paralyzed in the armchair.*] But, good God! People don't do such things!

ANTON CHEKHOV
1860–1904

In plays and stories Anton Chekhov depicts Russia around the turn of the twentieth century with great pity, gentleness, and kindness of heart. More important, with a deep humanity that has outlasted all the problems of his time, he dramatizes universal and almost timeless feelings rather than ideas that date and pass. He differs sharply from the two giants of Russian literature, Dostoevsky and Tolstoy. For one thing, his work is of smaller scope. With the exception of an immature, forgotten novel and a travel book, he wrote only short stories and plays. He belongs, furthermore, to a very different moral and spiritual atmosphere. Chekhov had studied medicine and practiced it for a time. He shared the scientific outlook of his age and had too skeptical a mind to believe in Christianity or in any metaphysical system. He confessed that an intelligent believer was a puzzle to him. His attitude toward his materials and characters is detached, "objective," and his letters to friends insist that a good writer must present both physical details and a character's state of mind without overt interpretation or judgment. He is thus much more in the stream of Western realism than either Tolstoy or Dostoevsky, and the delicate, precise realism of his short stories has served as a model for later writers in Europe, China, and the United States. But extended reading of Chekhov does convey an impression of his view of life. There is implied in his stories a philosophy of kindness and humanity, a love of beauty, a sense of the unexplainable mystery of life, a sense, especially, of the individual's utter loneliness in this universe and among other people. Chekhov's pessimism has nothing of the defiance of the universe or the horror at it which we meet in other writers with similar attitudes; it is somehow merely sad, often pathetic, and yet also comforting and comfortable.

The Russia depicted in Chekhov's stories and plays is of a later period than that presented by Tolstoy and Dostoevsky. It seems to be nearing its end; there is a sense of decadence and frustration which heralds the approach of catastrophe. The aristocracy still keeps up a beautiful front but is losing its fight without much resistance, resignedly. Officialdom is stupid and venal. The Church is backward and narrow minded. The intelligentsia are hopelessly ineffectual, futile, lost in the provinces or absorbed in their egos. The peasants live subject to the lowest degradations of poverty and drink, apparently rather aggravated than improved since the much-heralded emancipation of the serfs in 1861. There seems no hope for society except in a gradual spread of enlightenment, good sense, and hygiene, for Chekhov is skeptical of the revolution and revolutionaries as well as of Tolstoy's followers.

Anton Pavlovich Chekhov was born on January 17, 1860, at Taganrog, a small town on the Sea of Azov. His father was a grocer and haberdasher; his grandfather, a serf who had bought his freedom. Chekhov's father went bankrupt in 1876, and the family moved to Moscow, leaving Anton to finish school in his home town. After his graduation in 1879, he followed his family to Moscow, where he studied medicine. To earn additional money for his family and himself, he started to write humorous sketches and stories for magazines. In 1884 he became a doctor and published his first collection of stories, *Tales of Melpomene*. In the same year he had his first hemorrhage. All the rest of his life he struggled against tuberculosis. His first play, *Ivanov*, was performed in 1887. Three years later, he undertook an arduous journey through Siberia to the island of Sakhalin (north of Japan) and back by boat through the Suez Canal. He saw there the Russian penal settlements and wrote a moving account of his trip in *Sakhalin Island* (1892). In 1898 his play *The Sea Gull* was a great success at the Moscow Art Theater. The next year he moved to Yalta, in the Crimea, and in 1901 married the actress Olga Knipper. He died on July 2, 1904, at Badenweiler in the Black Forest.

The plays of Chekhov seem to go furthest in the direction of naturalism, the depiction of a "slice of life," on stage. Compared with Ibsen's plays they seem plotless; they could be described as a succession of little scenes, composed like a mosaic or like the dots or strokes in an impressionist painting. The characters rarely engage in the usual dialogue; they speak often in little soliloquies, hardly justified by the situation; and they often do not listen to the words of their ostensible partners. They seem alone even in a crowd. Human communication seems difficult and even impossible. There is no clear message, no zeal for social reform; life seems to flow quietly, even sluggishly, until interrupted by some desperate outbreak or even a pistol shot.

Chekhov's last play, *The Cherry Orchard* (composed in 1903, first performed at the Moscow Art Theater on January 17, 1904) differs, however, from this pattern in several respects. It has a strongly articulated central theme—the loss of the orchard—and it has a composition that roughly follows the traditional scheme of a well-made play. Arrival and departure from the very same room, the nursery, frame the two other acts: the outdoor idyll of Act II and the dance in Act III. Act III is the turning point of the action: Lopahin appears and announces, somewhat shamefacedly, that he has bought the estate. The orchard was lost from the very beginning—there is no real struggle to prevent its sale—but still the news of Lopahin's purchase is a surprise as he had no intention of buying it but did so only when during the auction sale a rival seemed to have a chance of acquiring it. A leading action runs its course, and many—one may even argue too many—subplots crisscross each other: the shy and awkward love affair of the student Trofimov and the daughter Anya; the love triangle among the three dependents, Yepihodov (the unlucky clerk), Dunyasha (the chambermaid), and Yasha (the conceited and insolent footman). Varya, the practical stepdaughter, has her troubles with Lopahin, and Simeonov-Pishchik is beset by the same financial problems as the owners of the orchard and is rescued by the discovery of some white clay on his estate. The German governess Charlotta drifts around alluding to her obscure origins and past. There are undeveloped references to events preceding the action on stage—the lover in Paris, the drowned boy Grisha—but there is no revelation of the past as in Ibsen, no mystery, no intrigue.

While the events on the stage follow each other naturally, though hardly always in a logical, causal order, a symbolic device is used conspicuously: in Act II after a pause, "suddenly a distant sound is heard, coming from the sky as it were, the sound of a snapping string, mournfully dying away." It occurs again at the very end of the play followed by "the strokes of the ax against a tree far away in the orchard." An attempt is made to explain this sound at its first occurrence as a bucket's fall in a faraway pit or as the cries of a heron or an owl, but the effect is weird and even supernatural; it establishes an ominous mood. Even the orchard carries more than its obvious meaning: it is white, drowned in blossoms when the party arrives in the spring; it is bare and desolate in the autumn when the axes are heard cutting it down. "The old bark on the trees gleams faintly, and the cherry trees seem to be dreaming of things that happened a hundred, two hundred years ago and to be tormented by painful visions," declaims Trofimov, defining his feeling for the orchard as a symbol of repression and serfdom. For Lubov Ranevskaya it is an image of her lost innocence and of the happier past, while Lopahin sees it only as an investment. It seems to draw together the meaning of the play.

But what is this meaning? Can we even decide whether it is a tragedy or a comedy? It has been commonly seen as the tragedy of the downfall of the Russian aristocracy (or more correctly, the landed gentry) victimized by the newly rich, upstart peasantry. One could see the play as depicting the defeat of a group of feckless people at the hand of a ruthless "developer" who destroys nature and natural beauty for profit. Or one can see it as prophesying, through the mouth of the student Trofimov, the approaching end of feudal Russia and the coming happier future. Soviet interpretations and performances lean that way.

Surely none of these interpretations can withstand inspection in the light of the actual play. They all run counter to Chekhov's professed intentions. He called the play a comedy. In a letter of September 15, 1903, he declared expressly that the play "has not turned out as drama but as comedy, in places even a farce" and a few days later (September 21, 1903) he wrote that "the whole play is gay and frivolous." Chekhov did not like the staging of the play at the Moscow Art Theater and complained of its tearful tone and its slow pace. He objected that "they obstinately call my play a drama in playbill and newspaper advertisements" while he had called it a comedy (April 10, 1904).

No doubt, there are many comical and even farcical characters and scenes in the play. Charlotta with her nut-eating dog, her card tricks, her ventriloquism, her disappearing acts, is a clownish figure. Gayev, the landowner, though "suave and elegant," is a boor, obsessed by his passion for billiards, constantly popping candy into his mouth, telling the waiters in a restaurant about the "decadents" in Paris. Yepihodov, the clerk, carries a revolver and, threatening suicide, asks foolishly whether you have read Buckle (the English historian) and complains of his ill-luck: a spider on his chest, a cockroach in his drink. Simeonov-Pishchik empties a whole bottle of pills, eats half a bucket of pickles, quotes Nietzsche supposedly recommending the forging of banknotes, and, fat as he is, puffs and prances at the dance ordering the "cavaliers à genoux." Even the serious characters are put into ludicrous predicaments: Trofimov falls down the stairs; Lopahin, coming to announce the purchase of the estate, is almost hit with a stick by Varya (and was hit in the original version). Lopahin, teasing his intended Varya, "moos like a cow." The ball, the hunting for the galoshes, and the champagne drinking by Yasha in the last act have all a touch of absurdity. The grand speeches, Gayev's addresses to the bookcase and to nature or Trofimov's about "mankind going forward" and "All Russia is our orchard," are undercut by the contrast between words and character: Gayev is callous and shallow; the "perpetual student," Trofimov never did a stitch of work. He is properly ridiculed and insulted by Lubov for his scant beard and his silly professions of being "above love." One can sympathize with Chekhov's irritation at the pervading gloom imposed by the Moscow production.

Still we cannot, in spite of the author, completely dismiss the genuine pathos of the central situation and of the central figure, Lubov Ranevskaya. Whatever one may say about her recklessness in financial matters and her guilt in relation to her lover in France, we must feel her deep attachment to the house and the orchard, to the past and her lost innocence, clearly and unhumorously expressed in the first act on her arrival, again and again at the impending sale of the estate, and finally at the parting from her house: "Oh, my orchard—my dear, sweet, beautiful orchard! . . . My life, my youth, my happiness—Good-bye!" That Gayev, before the final parting, seems to have overcome the sense of loss and even looks forward to his job in the bank and that Lubov acknowledges that her "nerves are better" and that "she sleeps well" testifies to the indestructible spirit of brother and sister, but cannot minimize the sense of loss, the pathos of parting, the nostalgia for happier times. Nor is the conception of Lopahin simple. Chekhov emphasized, in a letter to Konstantin Stanislavsky who was to play the part, that "Lopahin is a decent person in the full sense of the word, and his bearing must be that of a completely dignified and intelligent man." He is not, he says, a profiteering peasant (*kulachok*, October 30, 1903). He admires Lubov and thinks of her with gratitude. He senses the beauty of the poppies in his fields. Even the scene of the abortive encounter with Varya at the end has its quiet pathos in spite of all its awkwardness and the comic touches such as the reference to the broken thermometer. Firs, the eighty-seven-year-old valet, may be grotesque in his deafness and his nostalgia for the good old days of serfdom, but the very last scene when we see him abandoned in the locked-up house surely ends the play on a note of desolation and even despair.

Chekhov, we must conclude, achieved a highly original and even paradoxical blend of comedy and tragedy, or rather of farce and pathos. The play presents a social picture firmly set in a specific historical time—the dissolution of the landed gentry, the rise of the peasant, the encroachment of the city—but it does not propound an obvious social thesis. Chekhov, in his tolerance and tenderness, in his distrust of ideologies and heroics, extends his sympathy to all his characters (with the exception of the crudely ambitious valet Yasha). The glow of his humanity, untrammeled by time and place, keeps *The Cherry Orchard* alive in quite different social and political conditions, as it has the universalizing power of great art.

Donald Rayfield, *The Cherry Orchard: Catastrophe and Comedy* (1994), presents an extended discussion of the play; good chapters are also found in Beverly Hahn, *Chekhov: A Study of the Major Stories and Plays* (1977), Harvey Pitcher, *The Chekhov Play: A New Interpretation* (1973), and Richard Pearce, *Chekhov: A Study of the Four Major Plays* (1983). Francis Fergusson compares Ibsen and Chekhov in "*Ghosts* and *The Cherry Orchard*," in *The Idea of the Theatre* (1949). There is helpful critical analysis in R. L. Jackson, ed., *Chekhov: A Collection of Critical Essays* (1967) and *Reading Chekhov's Text* (1993), in D. Rayfield, *Chekhov: The Evolution of His Art* (1975), and in René Wellek and N. D. Wellek, eds. *Chekhov: New Perspectives* (1984); the latter includes a sketch of Chekhov criticism in England and America. J. L. Styan discusses *The Cherry Orchard* from a different perspective in *Chekhov in Performance: A Commentary on the Major Plays* (1971), and Nicholas Worrall, *File on Chekhov* (1986), offers an introductory survey with useful cited passages and suggestions for further study.

PRONOUNCING GLOSSARY

The following list uses common English syllables and stress accents to provide rough equivalents of selected words whose pronunciation may be unfamiliar to the general reader.

Anton Chekhov: *ahn'-tonn chek'-off*

Charlotta Ivanovna: *sharlotta ee-van'-ovna*

Firs: *feers*

Leonid Andreyevich Gayev: *lay-on'-it ahn-dray'evich gah'-yeff*

Lubov Andreyevna Ranevskaya: *loo-boff' ahn-dray'-ev-na rahn-yeff'-skaya*

Pyotr Sergeyevich Trofimov: *pyotr sair-gyay'-evich traw-fee'-moff*

Semyon Yepihodov: *sem-yon' yepee-ho'doff*

Simeon Pishchik: *see-may-ohn' pish-chik*

Yermolay Alexeyevich Lopahin: *yair-moh-lai' ah-lex-ay'evich loh-pah-heen'*

The Cherry Orchard[1]

CHARACTERS

LUBOV ANDREYEVNA RANEVSKAYA, *a landowner*

ANYA, *her seventeen-year-old daughter*

VARYA, *her adopted daughter, twenty-four years old*

LEONID ANDREYEVICH GAYEV, *Mme. Ranevskaya's brother*

YERMOLAY ALEXEYEVICH LOPAHIN, *a merchant*

PYOTR SERGEYEVICH TROFIMOV, *a student*

SIMEONOV-PISHCHIK, *a landowner*

CHARLOTTA IVANOVNA, *a governess*

SEMYON YEPIHODOV, *a clerk*

DUNYASHA, *a maid*

FIRS, *a manservant, aged eighty-seven*

YASHA, *a young valet*

A TRAMP

STATIONMASTER

POST OFFICE CLERK

GUESTS

SERVANTS

The action takes place on MME. RANEVSKAYA's *estate.*

---

1. Translated by Avraham Yarmolinsky.

Act I

A room that is still called the nursery. One of the doors leads into ANYA'*s room. Dawn, the sun will soon rise. It is May, the cherry trees are in blossom, but it is cold in the orchard; there is a morning frost. The windows are shut. Enter* DUNYASHA *with a candle, and* LOPAHIN *with a book in his hand.*

LOPAHIN: The train is in, thank God. What time is it?

DUNYASHA: Nearly two. [*Puts out the candle.*] It's light already.

LOPAHIN: How late is the train, anyway? Two hours at least. [*Yawns and stretches.*] I'm a fine one! What a fool I've made of myself! I came here on purpose to meet them at the station, and then I went and overslept. I fell asleep in my chair. How annoying! You might have waked me . . .

DUNYASHA: I thought you'd left. [*Listens.*] I think they're coming!

LOPAHIN: [*Listens.*] No, they've got to get the luggage, and one thing and another . . . [*Pause.*] Lubov Andreyevna spent five years abroad, I don't know what she's like now. . . . She's a fine person—lighthearted, simple. I remember when I was a boy of fifteen, my poor father—he had a shop here in the village then—punched me in the face with his fist and made my nose bleed. We'd come into the yard, I don't know what for, and he'd had a drop too much. Lubov Andreyevna, I remember her as if it were yesterday—she was still young and so slim—led me to the washbasin, in this very room . . . in the nursery. "Don't cry, little peasant," she said, "it'll heal in time for your wedding . . ." [*Pause.*] Little peasant . . . my father was a peasant, it's true, and here I am in a white waistcoat and yellow shoes. A pig in a pastry shop, you might say. It's true I'm rich. I've got a lot of money. . . . But when you look at it closely, I'm a peasant through and through. [*Pages the book.*] Here I've been reading this book and I didn't understand a word of it. . . . I was reading it and fell asleep . . . [*Pause.*]

DUNYASHA: And the dogs were awake all night, they feel that their masters are coming.

LOPAHIN: Dunyasha, why are you so—

DUNYASHA: My hands are trembling. I'm going to faint.

LOPAHIN: You're too soft, Dunyasha. You dress like a lady, and look at the way you do your hair. That's not right. One should remember one's place.

[*Enter* YEPIHODOV *with a bouquet; he wears a jacket and highly polished boots that squeak badly. He drops the bouquet as he comes in.*]

YEPIHODOV: [*Picking up the bouquet.*] Here, the gardener sent these, said you're to put them in the dining room. [*Hands the bouquet to* DUN-YASHA.]

LOPAHIN: And bring me some kvass.[2]

DUNYASHA: Yes, sir. [*Exits.*]

YEPIHODOV: There's a frost this morning—three degrees below—and yet the cherries are all in blossom. I cannot approve of our climate. [*Sighs.*] I cannot. Our climate does not activate properly. And, Yermolay Alex-

---

2. Russian beer, made from rye or barley.

eyevich, allow me to make a further remark. The other day I bought myself a pair of boots, and I make bold to assure you, they squeak so that it is really intolerable. What should I grease them with?

LOPAHIN: Oh, get out! I'm fed up with you.

YEPIHODOV: Every day I meet with misfortune. And I don't complain, I've got used to it, I even smile.

[DUNYASHA *enters, hands* LOPAHIN *the kvass.*]

YEPIHODOV: I am leaving. [*Stumbles against a chair, which falls over.*] There! [*Triumphantly, as it were.*] There again, you see what sort of circumstance, pardon the expression. . . . It is absolutely phenomenal! [*Exits.*]

DUNYASHA: You know, Yermolay Alexeyevich, I must tell you, Yepihodov has proposed to me.

LOPAHIN: Ah!

DUNYASHA: I simply don't know . . . he's a quiet man, but sometimes when he starts talking, you can't make out what he means. He speaks nicely— and it's touching—but you can't understand it. I sort of like him though, and he is crazy about me. He's an unlucky man . . . every day something happens to him. They tease him about it here . . . they call him, Two-and-Twenty Troubles.

LOPAHIN: [*Listening.*] There! I think they're coming.

DUNYASHA: They *are* coming! What's the matter with me? I feel cold all over.

LOPAHIN: They really are coming. Let's go and meet them. Will she recognize me? We haven't seen each other for five years.

DUNYASHA: [*In a flutter.*] I'm going to faint this minute. . . . Oh, I'm going to faint!

[*Two carriages are heard driving up to the house.* LOPAHIN *and* DUN-YASHA *go out quickly. The stage is left empty. There is a noise in the adjoining rooms.* FIRS, *who had driven to the station to meet* LUBOV ANDREYEVNA RANEVSKAYA, *crosses the stage hurriedly, leaning on a stick. He is wearing an old-fashioned livery and a tall hat. He mutters to himself indistinctly. The hubbub offstage increases. A* VOICE: "Come, let's go this way." *Enter* LUBOV ANDREYEVNA, ANYA, *and* CHAR-LOTTA IVANOVNA *with a pet dog on a leash, all in traveling dresses;* VARYA, *wearing a coat and kerchief;* GAYEV, SIMEONOV-PISHCHIK, LOPAHIN, DUNYASHA *with a bag and an umbrella, servants with luggage. All walk across the room.*]

ANYA: Let's go this way. Do you remember what room this is, Mamma?

MME. RANEVSKAYA: [*Joyfully, through her tears.*] The nursery!

VARYA: How cold it is! My hands are numb. [*To* MME. RANEVSKAYA.] Your rooms are just the same as they were, Mamma, the white one and the violet.

MME. RANEVSKAYA: The nursery! My darling, lovely room! I slept here when I was a child . . . [*Cries.*] And here I am, like a child again! [*Kisses her brother and* VARYA, *and then her brother again.*] Varya's just the same as ever, like a nun. And I recognized Dunyasha. [*Kisses* DUN-YASHA.]

GAYEV: The train was two hours late. What do you think of that? What a way to manage things!

CHARLOTTA: [*To* PISHCHIK.] My dog eats nuts, too.

PISHCHIK: [*In amazement.*] You don't say!

[*All go out, except* ANYA *and* DUNYASHA.]

DUNYASHA: We've been waiting for you for hours. [*Takes* ANYA's *hat and coat.*]

ANYA: I didn't sleep on the train for four nights and now I'm frozen . . .

DUNYASHA: It was Lent when you left; there was snow and frost, and now . . . My darling! [*Laughs and kisses her.*] I have been waiting for you, my sweet, my darling! But I must tell you something . . . I can't put it off another minute . . .

ANYA: [*Listlessly.*] What now?

DUNYASHA: The clerk, Yepihodov, proposed to me, just after Easter.

ANYA: There you are, at it again . . . [*Straightening her hair.*] I've lost all my hairpins . . . [*She is staggering with exhaustion.*]

DUNYASHA: Really, I don't know what to think. He loves me — he loves me so!

ANYA: [*Looking toward the door of her room, tenderly.*] My own room, my windows, just as though I'd never been away. I'm home! Tomorrow morning I'll get up and run into the orchard. Oh, if I could only get some sleep. I didn't close my eyes during the whole journey — I was so anxious.

DUNYASHA: Pyotr Sergeyevich came the day before yesterday.

ANYA: [*Joyfully.*] Petya!

DUNYASHA: He's asleep in the bathhouse. He has settled there. He said he was afraid of being in the way. [*Looks at her watch.*] I should wake him, but Miss Varya told me not to. "Don't you wake him," she said.

[*Enter* VARYA *with a bunch of keys at her belt.*]

VARYA: Dunyasha, coffee, and be quick. . . . Mamma's asking for coffee.

DUNYASHA: In a minute. [*Exits.*]

VARYA: Well, thank God, you've come. You're home again. [*Fondling* ANYA.] My darling is here again. My pretty one is back.

ANYA: Oh, what I've been through!

VARYA: I can imagine.

ANYA: When we left, it was Holy Week, it was cold then, and all the way Charlotta chattered and did her tricks. Why did you have to saddle me with Charlotta?

VARYA: You couldn't have travelled all alone, darling — at seventeen!

ANYA: We got to Paris, it was cold there, snowing. My French is dreadful. Mamma lived on the fifth floor; I went up there, and found all kinds of Frenchmen, ladies, an old priest with a book. The place was full of tobacco smoke, and so bleak. Suddenly I felt sorry for Mamma, so sorry, I took her head in my arms and hugged her and couldn't let go of her. Afterward Mamma kept fondling me and crying . . .

VARYA: [*Through tears.*] Don't speak of it . . . don't.

ANYA: She had already sold her villa at Mentone, she had nothing left, nothing. I hadn't a kopeck left either, we had only just enough to get home. And Mamma wouldn't understand! When we had dinner at the stations, she always ordered the most expensive dishes, and tipped the waiters a whole ruble. Charlotta, too. And Yasha kept ordering, too—it was simply awful. You know Yasha's Mamma's footman now, we brought him here with us.

VARYA: Yes, I've seen the blackguard.

ANYA: Well, tell me—have you paid the interest?

VARYA: How could we?

ANYA: Good heavens, good heavens!

VARYA: In August the estate will be put up for sale.

ANYA: My God!

LOPAHIN: [*Peeps in at the door and bleats*]. Meh-h-h. [*Disappears.*]

VARYA: [*Through tears.*] What I couldn't do to him! [*Shakes her fist threateningly.*]

ANYA: [*Embracing* VARYA, *gently.*] Varya, has he proposed to you? [VARYA *shakes her head.*] But he loves you. Why don't you come to an understanding? What are you waiting for?

VARYA: Oh, I don't think anything will ever come of it. He's too busy, he has no time for me . . . pays no attention to me. I've washed my hands of him—I can't bear the sight of him. They all talk about our getting married, they all congratulate me—and all the time there's really nothing to it—it's all like a dream. [*In another tone.*] You have a new brooch—like a bee.

ANYA: [*Sadly.*] Mamma bought it. [*She goes into her own room and speaks gaily like a child.*] And you know, in Paris I went up in a balloon.

VARYA: My darling's home, my pretty one is back! [DUNYASHA *returns with the coffeepot and prepares coffee.* VARYA *stands at the door of* ANYA's *room.*] All day long, darling, as I go about the house, I keep dreaming. If only we could marry you off to a rich man, I should feel at ease. Then I would go into a convent, and afterward to Kiev, to Moscow . . . I would spend my life going from one holy place to another . . . I'd go on and on. . . . What a blessing that would be!

ANYA: The birds are singing in the orchard. What time is it?

VARYA: It must be after two. Time you were asleep, darling. [*Goes into* ANYA's *room.*] What a blessing that would be!

[YASHA *enters with a plaid and a traveling bag, crosses the stage.*]

YASHA: [*Finically.*] May I pass this way, please?

DUNYASHA: A person could hardly recognize you, Yasha. Your stay abroad has certainly done wonders for you.

YASHA: Hm-m . . . and who are you?

DUNYASHA: When you went away I was that high—[*Indicating with her hand.*] I'm Dunyasha—Fyodor Kozoyedev's daughter. Don't you remember?

YASHA: Hm! What a peach!

[*He looks round and embraces her. She cries out and drops a saucer.* YASHA *leaves quickly.*]

VARYA: [*In the doorway, in a tone of annoyance.*] What's going on here?

DUNYASHA: [*Through tears.*] I've broken a saucer.

VARYA: Well, that's good luck.

ANYA: [*Coming out of her room.*] We ought to warn Mamma that Petya's here.

VARYA: I left orders not to wake him.

ANYA: [*Musingly.*] Six years ago father died. A month later brother Grisha was drowned in the river. . . . Such a pretty little boy he was—only seven. It was more than Mamma could bear, so she went away, went away without looking back . . . [*Shudders.*] How well I understand her, if she only knew! [*Pause.*] And Petya Trofimov was Grisha's tutor, he may remind her of it all . . .

[*Enter* FIRS, *wearing a jacket and a white waistcoat. He goes up to the coffeepot.*]

FIRS: [*Anxiously.*] The mistress will have her coffee here. [*Puts on white gloves.*] Is the coffee ready? [*Sternly, to* DUNYASHA.] Here, you! And where's the cream?

DUNYASHA: Oh, my God! [*Exits quickly.*]

FIRS: [*Fussing over the coffeepot.*] Hah! the addlehead! [*Mutters to himself.*] Home from Paris. And the old master used to go to Paris too . . . by carriage. [*Laughs.*]

VARYA: What is it, Firs?

FIRS: What is your pleasure, Miss? [*Joyfully.*] My mistress has come home, and I've seen her at last! Now I can die. [*Weeps with joy.*]

[*Enter* MME. RANEVSKAYA, GAYEV, *and* SIMEONOV-PISHCHIK: *The latter is wearing a tight-waisted, pleated coat of fine cloth, and full trousers.* GAYEV, *as he comes in, goes through the motions of a billiard player with his arms and body.*]

MME. RANEVSKAYA: Let's see, how does it go? Yellow ball in the corner! Bank shot in the side pocket!

GAYEV: I'll tip it in the corner! There was a time, Sister, when you and I used to sleep in this very room and now I'm fifty-one, strange as it may seem.

LOPAHIN: Yes, time flies.

GAYEV: Who?

LOPAHIN: I say, time flies.

GAYEV: It smells of patchouli here.

ANYA: I'm going to bed. Good night, Mamma. [*Kisses her mother.*]

MME. RANEVSKAYA: My darling child! [*Kisses her hands.*] Are you happy to be home? I can't come to my senses.

ANYA: Good night, Uncle.

GAYEV: [*Kissing her face and hands.*] God bless you, how like your mother you are! [*To his sister.*] At her age, Luba, you were just like her.

[ANYA *shakes hands with* LOPAHIN *and* PISHCHIK, *then goes out, shutting the door behind her.*]

MME. RANEVSKAYA: She's very tired.

PISHCHIK: Well, it was a long journey.

VARYA: [*To* LOPAHIN *and* PISHCHIK.] How about it, gentlemen? It's past two o'clock—isn't it time for you to go?

MME. RANEVSKAYA: [*Laughs.*] You're just the same as ever, Varya. [*Draws her close and kisses her.*] I'll have my coffee and then we'll all go. [FIRS *puts a small cushion under her feet.*] Thank you, my dear. I've got used to coffee. I drink it day and night. Thanks, my dear old man. [*Kisses him.*]

VARYA: I'd better see if all the luggage has been brought in. [*Exits.*]

MME. RANEVSKAYA: Can it really be I sitting here? [*Laughs.*] I feel like dancing, waving my arms about. [*Covers her face with her hands.*] But maybe I am dreaming! God knows I love my country, I love it tenderly; I couldn't look out of the window in the train, I kept crying so. [*Through tears.*] But I must have my coffee. Thank you, Firs, thank you, dear old man. I'm so happy that you're still alive.

FIRS: Day before yesterday.

GAYEV: He's hard of hearing.

LOPAHIN: I must go soon, I'm leaving for Kharkov about five o'clock. How annoying! I'd like to have a good look at you, talk to you. . . . You're just as splendid as ever.

PISHCHIK: [*Breathing heavily.*] She's even better-looking. . . . Dressed in the latest Paris fashion. . . . Perish my carriage and all its four wheels. . . .

LOPAHIN: Your brother, Leonid Andreyevich, says I'm a vulgarian and an exploiter. But it's all the same to me—let him talk. I only want you to trust me as you used to. I want you to look at me with your touching, wonderful eyes, as you used to. Dear God! My father was a serf of your father's and grandfather's, but you, you yourself, did so much for me once . . . so much . . . that I've forgotten all about that; I love you as though you were my sister—even more.

MME. RANEVSKAYA: I can't sit still, I simply can't. [*Jumps up and walks about in violent agitation.*] This joy is too much for me. . . . . Laugh at me, I'm silly! My own darling bookcase! My darling table! [*Kisses it.*]

GAYEV: While you were away, nurse died.

MME. RANEVSKAYA: [*Sits down and takes her coffee.*] Yes, God rest her soul; they wrote me about it.

GAYEV: And Anastasy is dead. Petrushka Kossoy has left me and has gone into town to work for the police inspector. [*Takes a box of sweets out of his pocket and begins to suck one.*]

PISHCHIK: My daughter Dashenka sends her regards.

LOPAHIN: I'd like to tell you something very pleasant—cheering. [*Glancing at his watch.*] I am leaving directly. There isn't much time to talk. But I will put it in a few words. As you know, your cherry orchard is to be sold to pay your debts. The sale is to be on the twenty-second of August; but don't you worry, my dear, you may sleep in peace; there is a way out. Here is my plan. Give me your attention! Your estate is only fifteen miles from the town; the railway runs close by it; and if the cherry orchard and the land along the riverbank were cut up into lots and these leased for summer cottages, you would have an income of at least 25,000 rubles a year out of it.

GAYEV: Excuse me. . . . What nonsense.

MME. RANEVSKAYA: I don't quite understand you, Yermolay Alexeyevich.

LOPAHIN: You will get an annual rent of at least ten rubles per acre, and if you advertise at once, I'll give you any guarantee you like that you won't have a square foot of ground left by autumn, all the lots will be snapped

up. In short, congratulations, you're saved. The location is splendid—
by that deep river. . . . Only, of course, the ground must be cleared . . .
all the old buildings, for instance, must be torn down, and this house,
too, which is useless, and, of course, the old cherry orchard must be cut
down.

MME. RANEVSKAYA: Cut down? My dear, forgive me, but you don't know
what you're talking about. If there's one thing that's interesting—
indeed, remarkable—in the whole province, it's precisely our cherry
orchard.

LOPAHIN: The only remarkable thing about this orchard is that it's a very
large one. There's a crop of cherries every other year, and you can't do
anything with them; no one buys them.

GAYEV: This orchard is even mentioned in the encyclopedia.

LOPAHIN: [*Glancing at his watch.*] If we can't think of a way out, if we
don't come to a decision, on the twenty-second of August the cherry
orchard and the whole estate will be sold at auction. Make up your
minds! There's no other way out—I swear. None, none.

FIRS: In the old days, forty or fifty years ago, the cherries were dried,
soaked, pickled, and made into jam, and we used to—

GAYEV: Keep still, Firs.

FIRS: And the dried cherries would be shipped by the cartload. It meant a
lot of money! And in those days the dried cherries were soft and juicy,
sweet, fragrant. . . . They knew the way to do it, then.

MME. RANEVSKAYA: And why don't they do it that way now?

FIRS: They've forgotten. Nobody remembers it.

PISHCHIK: [*To* MME. RANEVSKAYA.] What's doing in Paris? Eh? Did you eat
frogs there?

MME. RANEVSKAYA: I ate crocodiles.

PISHCHIK: Just imagine!

LOPAHIN: There used to be only landowners and peasants in the country,
but now these summer people have appeared on the scene. . . . All the
towns, even the small ones, are surrounded by these summer cottages;
and in another twenty years, no doubt, the summer population will have
grown enormously. Now the summer resident only drinks tea on his
porch, but maybe he'll take to working his acre, too, and then your
cherry orchard will be a rich, happy, luxuriant place.

GAYEV: [*Indignantly.*] Poppycock!

[*Enter* VARYA *and* YASHA.]

VARYA: There are two telegrams for you, Mamma dear. [*Picks a key from
the bunch at her belt and noisily opens an old-fashioned bookcase.*]
Here they are.

MME. RANEVSKAYA: They're from Paris. [*Tears them up without reading
them.*] I'm through with Paris.

GAYEV: Do you know, Luba, how old this bookcase is? Last week I pulled
out the bottom drawer and there I found the date burnt in it. It was
made exactly a hundred years ago. Think of that! We could celebrate
its centenary. True, it's an inanimate object, but nevertheless, a bookcase . . .

PISHCHIK: [*Amazed.*] A hundred years! Just imagine!

GAYEV: Yes. [*Tapping it.*] That's something. . . . Dear, honored bookcase, hail to you who for more than a century have served the glorious ideals of goodness and justice! Your silent summons to fruitful toil has never weakened in all those hundred years [*through tears*], sustaining, through successive generations of our family, courage and faith in a better future, and fostering in us ideals of goodness and social consciousness. . . . [*Pauses.*]

LOPAHIN: Yes . . .

MME. RANEVSKAYA: You haven't changed a bit, Leonid.

GAYEV: [*Somewhat embarrassed.*] I'll play it off the red in the corner! Tip it in the side pocket!

LOPAHIN: [*Looking at his watch.*] Well, it's time for me to go . . .

YASHA: [*Handing pillbox to* MME. RANEVSKAYA.] Perhaps you'll take your pills now.

PISHCHIK: One shouldn't take medicines, dearest lady, they do neither harm nor good. . . . Give them here, my valued friend. [*Takes the pillbox, pours the pills into his palm, blows on them, puts them in his mouth, and washes them down with some kvass.*] There!

MME. RANEVSKAYA: [*Frightened.*] You must be mad!

PISHCHIK: I've taken all the pills.

LOPAHIN: What a glutton!

    [*All laugh.*]

FIRS: The gentleman visited us in Easter week, ate half a bucket of pickles, he did . . . [*Mumbles.*]

MME. RANEVSKAYA: What's he saying?

VARYA: He's been mumbling like that for the last three years—we're used to it.

YASHA: His declining years!

    [CHARLOTTA IVANOVNA, *very thin, tightly laced, dressed in white, a lorgnette at her waist, crosses the stage.*]

LOPAHIN: Forgive me, Charlotta Ivanovna, I've not had time to greet you. [*Tries to kiss her hand.*]

CHARLOTTA: [*Pulling away her hand.*] If I let you kiss my hand, you'll be wanting to kiss my elbow next, and then my shoulder.

LOPAHIN: I've no luck today. [*All laugh.*] Charlotta Ivanovna, show us a trick.

MME. RANEVSKAYA: Yes, Charlotta, do a trick for us.

CHARLOTTA: I don't see the need. I want to sleep. [*Exits.*]

LOPAHIN: In three weeks we'll meet again. [*Kisses* MME. RANEVSKAYA's *hand.*] Good-bye till then. Time's up. [*To* GAYEV.] Bye-bye. [*Kisses* PISHCHIK.] Bye-bye. [*Shakes hands with* VARYA, *then with* FIRS *and* YASHA.] I hate to leave. [*To* MME. RANEVSKAYA.] If you make up your mind about the cottages, let me know; I'll get you a loan of 50,000 rubles.[3] Think it over seriously.

VARYA: [*Crossly.*] Will you never go!

LOPAHIN: I'm going, I'm going. [*Exits.*]

GAYEV: The vulgarian. But, excuse me . . . Varya's going to marry him, he's Varya's fiancé.

---

3. The basic unit of currency. One ruble is equal to one hundred kopecks.

VARYA: You talk too much, Uncle.

MME. RANEVSKAYA: Well, Varya, it would make me happy. He's a good man.

PISHCHIK: Yes, one must admit, he's a most estimable man. And my Dashenka . . . she too says that . . . she says . . . lots of things. [*Snores; but wakes up at once.*] All the same, my valued friend, could you oblige me . . . with a loan of 240 rubles? I must pay the interest on the mortgage tomorrow.

VARYA: [*Alarmed.*] We can't, we can't!

MME. RANEVSKAYA: I really haven't any money.

PISHCHIK: It'll turn up. [*Laughs.*] I never lose hope, I thought everything was lost, that I was done for, when lo and behold, the railway ran through my land . . . and I was paid for it. . . . And something else will turn up again, if not today, then tomorrow . . . Dashenka will win two hundred thousand . . . she's got a lottery ticket.

MME. RANEVSKAYA: I've had my coffee, now let's go to bed.

FIRS: [*Brushes off* GAYEV; *admonishingly.*] You've got the wrong trousers on again. What am I to do with you?

VARYA: [*Softly.*] Anya's asleep. [*Gently opens the window.*] The sun's up now, it's not a bit cold. Look, Mamma dear, what wonderful trees. And heavens, what air! The starlings are singing!

GAYEV: [*Opens the other window.*] The orchard is all white. You've not forgotten it? Luba? That's the long alley that runs straight, straight as an arrow; how it shines on moonlight nights, do you remember? You've not forgotten?

MME. RANEVSKAYA: [*Looking out of the window into the orchard.*] Oh, my childhood, my innocent childhood. I used to sleep in this nursery—I used to look out into the orchard, happiness waked with me every morning, the orchard was just the same then . . . nothing has changed. [*Laughs with joy.*] All, all white! Oh, my orchard! After the dark, rainy autumn and the cold winter, you are young again, and full of happiness, the heavenly angels have not left you. . . . If I could free my chest and my shoulders from this rock that weighs on me, if I could only forget the past!

GAYEV: Yes, and the orchard will be sold to pay our debts, strange as it may seem.

MME. RANEVSKAYA: Look! There is our poor mother walking in the orchard . . . all in white . . . [*Laughs with joy.*] It is she!

GAYEV: Where?

VARYA: What are you saying, Mamma dear!

MME. RANEVSKAYA: There's no one there, I just imagined it. To the right, where the path turns toward the arbor, there's a little white tree, leaning over, that looks like a woman . . .

[TROFIMOV *enters, wearing a shabby student's uniform and spectacles.*]

MME. RANEVSKAYA: What an amazing orchard! White masses of blossom, the blue sky . . .

TROFIMOV: Lubov Andreyevna! [*She looks round at him.*] I just want to pay my respects to you, then I'll leave at once. [*Kisses her hand ardently.*] I was told to wait until morning, but I hadn't the patience . . .

[MME. RANEVSKAYA *looks at him, perplexed.*]

VARYA: [*Through tears.*] This is Petya Trofimov.

TROFIMOV: Petya Trofimov, formerly your Grisha's tutor. . . . Can I have
changed so much?

[MME. RANEVSKAYA *embraces him and weeps quietly.*]

GAYEV: [*Embarrassed.*] Don't, don't, Luba.

VARYA: [*Crying.*] I told you, Petya, to wait until tomorrow.

MME. RANEVSKAYA: My Grisha . . . my little boy . . . Grisha . . . my son.

VARYA: What can one do, Mamma dear, it's God's will.

TROFIMOV: [*Softly, through tears.*] There . . . there.

MME. RANEVSKAYA: [*Weeping quietly.*] My little boy was lost . . . drowned.
Why? Why, my friend? [*More quietly.*] Anya's asleep in there, and here
I am talking so loudly . . . making all this noise. . . . But tell me, Petya,
why do you look so badly? Why have you aged so?

TROFIMOV: A mangy master, a peasant woman in the train called me.

MME. RANEVSKAYA: You were just a boy then, a dear little student, and now
your hair's thin—and you're wearing glasses! Is it possible you're still a
student? [*Goes toward the door.*]

TROFIMOV: I suppose I'm a perpetual student.

MME. RANEVSKAYA: [*Kisses her brother, then* VARYA.] Now, go to bed. . . .
You have aged, too, Leonid.

PISHCHIK: [*Follows her.*] So now we turn in. Oh, my gout! I'm staying the
night here . . . Lubov Andreyevna, my angel, tomorrow morning . . . I
do need 240 rubles.

GAYEV: He keeps at it.

PISHCHIK: I'll pay it back, dear . . . it's a trifling sum.

MME. RANEVSKAYA: All right, Leonid will give it to you. Give it to him,
Leonid.

GAYEV: Me give it to him! That's a good one!

MME. RANEVSKAYA: It can't be helped. Give it to him! He needs it. He'll
pay it back.

[MME. RANEVSKAYA, TROFIMOV, PISHCHIK, *and* FIRS *go out;* GAYEV,
VARYA, *and* YASHA *remain.*]

GAYEV: Sister hasn't got out of the habit of throwing money around. [*To*
YASHA.] Go away, my good fellow, you smell of the barnyard.

YASHA: [*With a grin.*] And you, Leonid Andreyevich, are just the same as
ever.

GAYEV: Who? [*To* VARYA.] What did he say?

VARYA: [*To* YASHA.] Your mother's come from the village; she's been sitting
in the servants' room since yesterday, waiting to see you.

YASHA: Botheration!

VARYA: You should be ashamed of yourself!

YASHA: She's all I needed! She could have come tomorrow. [*Exits.*]

VARYA: Mamma is just the same as ever; she hasn't changed a bit. If she
had her own way, she'd keep nothing for herself.

GAYEV: Yes . . . [*Pauses.*] If a great many remedies are offered for some
disease, it means it is incurable; I keep thinking and racking my brains;
I have many remedies, ever so many, and that really means none. It
would be fine if we came in for a legacy; it would be fine if we married

off our Anya to a very rich man; or we might go to Yaroslavl and try our luck with our aunt, the Countess. She's very rich, you know . . .

VARYA: [*Weeping.*] If only God would help us!

GAYEV: Stop bawling. Aunt's very rich, but she doesn't like us. In the first place, Sister married a lawyer who was no nobleman . . . [ANYA *appears in the doorway.*] She married beneath her, and it can't be said that her behavior has been very exemplary. She's good, kind, sweet, and I love her, but no matter what extenuating circumstances you may adduce, there's no denying that she has no morals. You sense it in her least gesture.

VARYA: [*In a whisper.*] Anya's in the doorway.

GAYEV: Who? [*Pauses.*] It's queer, something got into my right eye—my eyes are going back on me. . . . And on Thursday, when I was in the circuit court—
    [*Enter* ANYA.]

VARYA: Why aren't you asleep, Anya?

ANYA: I can't get to sleep, I just can't.

GAYEV: My little pet! [*Kisses* ANYA's *face and hands.*] My child! [*Weeps.*] You are not my niece, you're my angel! You're everything to me. Believe me, believe—

ANYA: I believe you, Uncle. Everyone loves you and respects you . . . but, Uncle dear, you must keep still. . . . You must. What were you saying just now about my mother? Your own sister? What made you say that?

GAYEV: Yes, yes . . . [*Covers his face with her hand.*] Really, that was awful! Good God! Heaven help me! Just now I made a speech to the bookcase . . . so stupid! And only after I was through, I saw how stupid it was.

VARYA: It's true, Uncle dear, you ought to keep still. Just don't talk, that's all.

ANYA: If you could only keep still, it would make things easier for you, too.

GAYEV: I'll keep still. [*Kisses* ANYA's *and* VARYA's *hands.*] I will. But now about business. On Thursday I was in court; well, there were a number of us there, and we began talking of one thing and another, and this and that, and do you know, I believe it will be possible to raise a loan on a promissory note to pay the interest at the bank.

VARYA: If only God would help us!

GAYEV: On Tuesday I'll go and see about it again. [*To* VARYA.] Stop bawling. [*To* ANYA.] Your mamma will talk to Lopahin, and he, of course, will not refuse her . . . and as soon as you're rested, you'll go to Yaroslavl to the Countess, your great-aunt. So we'll be working in three directions at once, and the thing is in the bag. We'll pay the interest—I'm sure of it. [*Puts a candy in his mouth.*] I swear on my honor, I swear by anything you like, the estate shan't be sold. [*Excitedly.*] I swear by my own happiness! Here's my hand on it, you can call me a swindler and a scoundrel if I let it come to an auction! I swear by my whole being.

ANYA: [*Relieved and quite happy again.*] How good you are, Uncle, and how clever! [*Embraces him.*] Now I'm at peace, quite at peace, I'm happy.

[*Enter* FIRS.]

FIRS: [*Reproachfully.*] Leonid Andreyevich, have you no fear of God? When are you going to bed?

GAYEV: Directly, directly. Go away, Firs, I'll . . . yes, I will undress myself. Now, children, 'nightie-'nightie. We'll consider details tomorrow, but now go to sleep. [*Kisses* ANYA *and* VARYA.] I am a man of the eighties; they have nothing good to say of that period nowadays. Nevertheless, in the course of my life, I have suffered not a little for my convictions. It's not for nothing that the peasant loves me; one should know the peasant; one should know from which—

ANYA: There you go again, Uncle.

VARYA: Uncle dear, be quiet.

FIRS: [*Angrily.*] Leonid Andreyevich!

GAYEV: I'm coming, I'm coming! Go to bed! Double bank shot in the side pocket! Here goes a clean shot . . .

[*Exits,* FIRS *hobbling after him.*]

ANYA: I am at peace now. I don't want to go to Yaroslavl—I don't like my great-aunt, but still, I am at peace, thanks to Uncle. [*Sits down.*]

VARYA: We must get some sleep. I'm going now. While you were away, something unpleasant happened. In the old servants' quarters, there are only the old people as you know; Yefim, Polya, Yevstigney, and Karp, too. They began letting all sorts of rascals in to spend the night. . . . I didn't say anything. Then I heard they'd been spreading a report that I gave them nothing but dried peas to eat—out of stinginess, you know . . . and it was all Yevstigney's doing. . . . All right, I thought, if that's how it is, I thought, just wait. I sent for Yevstigney . . . [*Yawns.*] He comes. . . . "How's this, Yevstigney?" I say, "You fool . . ." [*Looking at* ANYA.] Anichka! [*Pauses.*] She's asleep. [*Puts her arm around* ANYA.] Come to your little bed. . . . Come . . . [*Leads her.*] My darling has fallen asleep. . . . Come.

[*They go out. Far away beyond the orchard, a shepherd is piping.* TROFIMOV *crosses the stage and, seeing* VARYA *and* ANYA, *stands still.*]

VARYA: Sh! She's asleep . . . asleep. . . . Come, darling.

ANYA: [*Softly, half-asleep.*] I'm so tired. Those bells . . . Uncle . . . dear. . . . Mamma and Uncle . . .

VARYA: Come, my precious, come along. [*They go into* ANYA*'s room.*]

TROFIMOV: [*With emotion.*] My sunshine, my spring!

Act II

A meadow. An old, long-abandoned, lopsided little chapel; near it a well, large slabs, which had apparently once served as tombstones, and an old bench. In the background the road to the Gayev estate. To one side poplars loom darkly, where the cherry orchard begins. In the distance a row of telegraph poles, and far off, on the horizon, the faint outline of a large city which is seen only in fine, clear weather. The sun will soon be setting. CHARLOTTA, YASHA, *and* DUNYASHA *are seated on the bench.* YEPIHODOV *stands near and plays a guitar. All are pensive.* CHARLOTTA *wears an old peaked cap. She has taken a gun from her shoulder and is straightening the buckle on the strap.*

CHARLOTTA: [*Musingly.*] I haven't a real passport, I don't know how old I am, and I always feel that I am very young. When I was a little girl, my father and mother used to go from fair to fair and give performances, very good ones. And I used to do the *salto mortale,*[4] and all sorts of other tricks. And when papa and mamma died, a German lady adopted me and began to educate me. Very good. I grew up and became a governess. But where I come from and who am I, I don't know. . . . Who were my parents? Perhaps they weren't even married. . . . I don't know . . . [*Takes a cucumber out of her pocket and eats it.*] I don't know a thing. [*Pause.*] One wants so much to talk, and there isn't anyone to talk to. . . . I haven't anybody.

YEPIHODOV: [*Plays the guitar and sings.*] "What care I for the jarring world? What's friend or foe to me? . . ." How agreeable it is to play the mandolin.

DUNYASHA: That's a guitar, not a mandolin. [*Looks in a hand mirror and powders her face.*]

YEPIHODOV: To a madman in love it's a mandolin. [*Sings.*] "Would that the heart were warmed by the fire of mutual love!"
     [YASHA *joins in.*]

CHARLOTTA: How abominably these people sing. Pfui! Like jackals!

DUNYASHA: [*To* YASHA.] How wonderful it must be though to have stayed abroad!

YASHA: Ah, yes, of course, I cannot but agree with you there. [*Yawns and lights a cigar.*]

YEPIHODOV: Naturally. Abroad, everything has long since achieved full perfection.

YASHA: That goes without saying.

YEPIHODOV: I'm a cultivated man, I read all kinds of remarkable books. And yet I can never make out what direction I should take, what is it that I want, properly speaking. Should I live, or should I shoot myself, properly speaking? Nevertheless, I always carry a revolver about me. . . . Here it is . . . [*Shows revolver.*]

CHARLOTTA: I've finished. I'm going. [*Puts the gun over her shoulder.*] You are a very clever man, Yepihodov, and a very terrible one; women must be crazy about you. Br-r-r! [*Starts to go.*] These clever men are all so stupid; there's no one for me to talk to . . . always alone, alone, I haven't a soul . . . and who I am, and why I am, nobody knows. [*Exits unhurriedly.*]

YEPIHODOV: Properly speaking and letting other subjects alone, I must say regarding myself, among other things, that fate treats me mercilessly, like a storm treats a small boat. If I am mistaken, let us say, why then do I wake up this morning, and there on my chest is a spider of enormous dimensions . . . like this . . . [*Indicates with both hands.*] Again, I take up a pitcher of kvass to have a drink, and in it there is something

4. Somersault (Italian).

unseemly to the highest degree, something like a cockroach. [*Pause.*]
Have you read Buckle?[5] [*Pause.*] I wish to have a word with you, Avdotya Fyodorovna, if I may trouble you.

DUNYASHA: Well, go ahead.

YEPIHODOV: I wish to speak with you alone. [*Sighs.*]

DUNYASHA: [*Embarassed.*] Very well. Only first bring me my little cape.
You'll find it near the wardrobe. It's rather damp here.

YEPIHODOV: Certainly, ma'am; I will fetch it, ma'am. Now I know what to
do with my revolver. [*Takes the guitar and goes off playing it.*]

YASHA: Two-and-Twenty Troubles! An awful fool, between you and me.
[*Yawns.*]

DUNYASHA: I hope to God he doesn't shoot himself! [*Pause.*] I've become
so nervous, I'm always fretting. I was still a little girl when I was taken
into the big house, I am quite unused to the simple life now, and my
hands are white, as white as a lady's. I've become so soft, so delicate, so
refined, I'm afraid of everything. It's so terrifying; and if you deceive
me, Yasha, I don't know what will happen to my nerves. [YASHA *kisses
her.*]

YASHA: You're a peach! Of course, a girl should never forget herself; and
what I dislike more than anything is when a girl don't behave properly.

DUNYASHA: I've fallen passionately in love with you; you're educated—you
have something to say about everything. [*Pause.*]

YASHA: [*Yawns.*] Yes, ma'am. Now the way I look at it, if a girl loves someone, it means she is immoral. [*Pause.*] It's agreeable smoking a cigar in
the fresh air. [*Listens.*] Someone's coming this way. . . . It's our madam
and the others. [DUNYASHA *embraces him impulsively.*] You go home,
as though you'd been to the river to bathe; go to the little path, or else
they'll run into you and suspect me of having arranged to meet you
here. I can't stand that sort of thing.

DUNYASHA: [*Coughing softly.*] Your cigar's made my head ache.

[*Exits.* YASHA *remains standing near the chapel. Enter* MME. RANEV-
SKAYA, GAYEV, *and* LOPAHIN.]

LOPAHIN: You must make up your mind once and for all—there's no time
to lose. It's quite a simple question, you know. Do you agree to lease
your land for summer cottages or not? Answer in one word, yes or no;
only one word!

MME. RANEVSKAYA: Who's been smoking such abominable cigars here?
[*Sits down.*]

GAYEV: Now that the railway line is so near, it's made things very convenient. [*Sits down.*] Here we've been able to have lunch in town. Yellow
ball in the side pocket! I feel like going into the house and playing just
one game.

MME. RANEVSKAYA: You can do that later.

LOPAHIN: Only one word! [*Imploringly.*] Do give me an answer!

GAYEV: [*Yawning.*] Who?

5. Henry Thomas Buckle (1821–1862) wrote a *History of Civilization in England* (1857–61), which was considered daringly materialistic and free thinking.

MME. RANEVSKAYA: [*Looks into her purse.*] Yesterday I had a lot of money and now my purse is almost empty. My poor Varya tries to economize by feeding us just milk soup; in the kitchen the old people get nothing but dried peas to eat, while I squander money thoughtlessly. [*Drops the purse, scattering gold pieces.*] You see, there they go . . . [*Shows vexation.*]

YASHA: Allow me—I'll pick them up. [*Picks up the money.*]

MME. RANEVSKAYA: Be so kind. Yasha. And why did I go to lunch in town? That nasty restaurant, with its music and the tablecloth smelling of soap. . . . Why drink so much, Leonid? Why eat so much? Why talk so much? Today again you talked a lot, and all so inappropriately about the seventies, about the decadents.[6] And to whom? Talking to waiters about decadents!

LOPAHIN: Yes.

GAYEV: [*Waving his hand.*] I'm incorrigible; that's obvious.[*Irritably, to* YASHA.] Why do you keep dancing about in front of me?

YASHA: [*Laughs.*] I can't hear your voice without laughing—

GAYEV: Either he or I—

MME. RANEVSKAYA: Go away, Yasha; run along.

YASHA: [*Handing* MME. RANEVSKAYA *her purse.*] I'm going at once. [*Hardly able to suppress his laughter.*] This minute. [*Exits.*]

LOPAHIN: That rich man, Deriganov, wants to buy your estate. They say he's coming to the auction himself.

MME. RANEVSKAYA: Where did you hear that?

LOPAHIN: That's what they are saying in town.

GAYEV: Our aunt in Yaroslavl has promised to help, but when she will send the money, and how much, no one knows.

LOPAHIN: How much will she send? A hundred thousand? Two hundred?

MME. RANEVSKAYA: Oh, well, ten or fifteen thousand; and we'll have to be grateful for that.

LOPAHIN: Forgive me, but such frivolous people as you are, so queer and unbusinesslike—I never met in my life. One tells you in plain language that your estate is up for sale, and you don't seem to take it in.

MME. RANEVSKAYA: What are we to do? Tell us what to do.

LOPAHIN: I do tell you, every day; every day I say the same thing! You must lease the cherry orchard and the land for summer cottages, you must do it and as soon as possible—right away. The auction is close at hand. Please understand! Once you've decided to have the cottages, you can raise as much money as you like, and you're saved.

MME. RANEVSKAYA: Cottages—summer people—forgive me, but it's all so vulgar.

GAYEV: I agree with you absolutely.

LOPAHIN: I shall either burst into tears or scream or faint! I can't stand it! You've worn me out! [*To* GAYEV.] You're an old woman!

GAYEV: Who?

---

6. A group of French poets of the 1880s (Mallarmé is today the most famous) were labeled "decadents" by their enemies and sometimes adopted the name themselves, proud of their refinement and sensitivity.

LOPAHIN: An old woman! [*Gets up to go.*]

MME. RANEVSKAYA: [*Alarmed.*] No, don't go! Please stay, I beg you, my dear. Perhaps we shall think of something.

LOPAHIN: What is there to think of?

MME. RANEVSKAYA: Don't go, I beg you. With you here it's more cheerful anyway. [*Pause.*] I keep expecting something to happen, it's as though the house were going to crash about our ears.

GAYEV: [*In deep thought.*] Bank shot in the corner. . . . Three cushions in the side pocket. . . .

MME. RANEVSKAYA: We have been great sinners . . .

LOPAHIN: What sins could you have committed?

GAYEV: [*Putting a candy in his mouth.*] They say I've eaten up my fortune in candy! [*Laughs.*]

MME. RANEVSKAYA: Oh, my sins! I've squandered money away recklessly, like a lunatic, and I married a man who made nothing but debts. My husband drank himself to death on champagne, he was a terrific drinker. And then, to my sorrow, I fell in love with another man, and I lived with him. And just then—that was my first punishment—a blow on the head: my little boy was drowned here in the river. And I went abroad, went away forever . . . never to come back, never to see this river again . . . I closed my eyes and ran, out of my mind. . . . But he followed me, pitiless, brutal. I bought a villa near Mentone, because he fell ill there; and for three years, day and night, I knew no peace, no rest. The sick man wore me out, he sucked my soul dry. Then last year, when the villa was sold to pay my debts, I went to Paris, and there he robbed me, abandoned me, took up with another woman, I tried to poison myself—it was stupid, so shameful—and then suddenly I felt drawn back to Russia, back, to my own country, to my little girl. [*Wipes her tears away.*] Lord, Lord! Be merciful, forgive me my sins—don't punish me anymore! [*Takes a telegram out of her pocket.*] This came today from Paris—he begs me to forgive him, implores me to go back . . . [*Tears up the telegram.*] Do I hear music? [*Listens.*]

GAYEV: That's our famous Jewish band, you remember? Four violins, a flute, and a double bass.

MME. RANEVSKAYA: Does it still exist? We ought to send for them some evening and have a party.

LOPAHIN: [*Listens.*] I don't hear anything. [*Hums softly.*] "The Germans for a fee will Frenchify a Russian."[7] [*Laughs.*] I saw a play at the theater yesterday—awfully funny.

MME. RANEVSKAYA: There was probably nothing funny about it. You shouldn't go to see plays, you should look at yourselves more often. How drab your lives are—how full of unnecessary talk.

LOPAHIN: That's true; come to think of it, we do live like fools. [*Pause.*] My pop was a peasant, an idiot; he understood nothing, never taught me anything, all he did was beat me when he was drunk, and always with a stick. Fundamentally, I'm just the same kind of blockhead and

---

7. Satirical reference to Russian efforts, from the time of Peter the Great (1672–1725), to imitate Western Europe and particularly Parisian culture.

idiot. I was never taught anything—I have a terrible handwriting. I write so that I feel ashamed before people, like a pig.

MME. RANEVSKAYA: You should get married, my friend.

LOPAHIN: Yes . . . that's true.

MME. RANEVSKAYA: To our Varya, she's a good girl.

LOPAHIN: Yes.

MME. RANEVSKAYA: She's a girl who comes of simple people, she works all day long; and above all, she loves you. Besides, you've liked her for a long time now.

LOPAHIN: Well, I've nothing against it. She's a good girl. [*Pause.*]

GAYEV: I've been offered a place in the bank—6,000 a year. Have you heard?

MME. RANEVSKAYA: You're not up to it. Stay where you are.

[FIRS *enters, carrying an overcoat.*]

FIRS: [*To* GAYEV.] Please put this on, sir, it's damp.

GAYEV: [*Putting it on.*] I'm fed up with you, brother.

FIRS: Never mind. This morning you drove off without saying a word. [*Looks him over.*]

MME. RANEVSKAYA: How you've aged, Firs.

FIRS: I beg your pardon?

LOPAHIN: The lady says you've aged.

FIRS: I've lived a long time; they were arranging my wedding and your papa wasn't born yet. [*Laughs.*] When freedom came[8] I was already head footman. I wouldn't consent to be set free then; I stayed on with the master . . . [*Pause.*] I remember they were all very happy, but why they were happy, they didn't know themselves.

LOPAHIN: It was fine in the old days! At least there was flogging!

FIRS: [*Not hearing.*] Of course. The peasants kept to the masters, the masters kept to the peasants; but now they've all gone their own ways, and there's no making out anything.

GAYEV: Be quiet, Firs. I must go to town tomorrow. They've promised to introduce me to a general who might let us have a loan.

LOPAHIN: Nothing will come of that. You won't even be able to pay the interest, you can be certain of that.

MME. RANEVSKAYA: He's raving, there isn't any general.

[*Enter* TROFIMOV, ANYA, *and* VARYA.]

GAYEV: Here come our young people.

ANYA: There's Mamma, on the bench.

MME. RANEVSKAYA: [*Tenderly.*] Come here, come along, my darlings. [*Embraces* ANYA *and* VARYA.] If you only knew how I love you both! Sit beside me—there, like that. [*All sit down.*]

LOPAHIN: Our perpetual student is always with the young ladies.

TROFIMOV: That's not any of your business.

LOPAHIN: He'll soon be fifty, and he's still a student!

TROFIMOV: Stop your silly jokes.

LOPAHIN: What are you so cross about, you queer bird?

TROFIMOV: Oh, leave me alone.

8. Czar (or Tsar) Alexander II (ruled 1855–81) emancipated the serfs in 1861.

LOPAHIN: [*Laughs.*] Allow me to ask you, what do you think of me?

TROFIMOV: What I think of you, Yermolay Alexeyevich, is this: you are a
rich man who will soon be a millionaire. Well, just as a beast of prey,
which devours everything that comes in its way, is necessary for the
process of metabolism to go on, so you, too, are necessary. [*All laugh.*]

VARYA: Better tell us something about the planets, Petya.

MME. RANEVSKAYA: No, let's go on with yesterday's conversation.

TROFIMOV: What was it about?

GAYEV: About man's pride.

TROFIMOV: Yesterday we talked a long time, but we came to no conclusion.
There is something mystical about man's pride in your sense of the
word. Perhaps you're right, from your own point of view. But if you
reason simply, without going into subtleties, then what call is there for
pride? Is there any sense in it, if man is so poor a thing physiologically,
and if, in the great majority of cases, he is coarse, stupid, profoundly
unhappy? We should stop admiring ourselves. We should work, and
that's all.

GAYEV: You die, anyway.

TROFIMOV: Who knows? And what does it mean—to die? Perhaps man has
a hundred senses, and at his death only the five we know perish, while
the other ninety-five remain alive.

MME. RANEVSKAYA: How clever you are, Petya!

LOPAHIN: [*Ironically.*] Awfully clever!

TROFIMOV: Mankind goes forward, developing its powers. Everything that
is now unattainable for it will one day come within man's reach and be
clear to him; only we must work, helping with all our might those who
seek the truth. Here among us in Russia only the very few work as yet.
The great majority of the intelligentsia, as far as I can see, seek nothing,
do nothing, are totally unfit for work of any kind. They call themselves
the intelligentsia, yet they are uncivil to their servants, treat the peasants
like animals, are poor students, never read anything serious, do absolutely nothing at all, only talk about science, and have little appreciation
of the arts. They are all solemn, have grim faces, they all philosophize
and talk of weighty matters. And meanwhile the vast majority of us,
ninety-nine out of a hundred, live like savages. At the least provocation—a punch in the jaw, and curses. They eat disgustingly, sleep in
filth and stuffiness, bedbugs everywhere, stench and damp and moral
slovenliness. And obviously, the only purpose of all our fine talk is to
hoodwink ourselves and others. Show me where the public nurseries
are that we've heard so much about, and the libraries. We read about
them in novels, but in reality they don't exist, there is nothing but dirt,
vulgarity, and Asiatic backwardness. I don't like very solemn faces, I'm
afraid of them, I'm afraid of serious conversations. We'd do better to
keep quiet for a while.

LOPAHIN: Do you know, I get up at five o'clock in the morning, and I work
from morning till night; and I'm always handling money, my own and
other people's, and I see what people around me are really like. You've
only to start doing anything to see how few honest, decent people there
are. Sometimes when I lie awake at night, I think: "Oh, Lord, thou hast

given us immense forests, boundless fields, the widest horizons, and living in their midst, we ourselves ought really to be giants."

MME. RANEVSKAYA: Now you want giants! They're only good in fairy tales; otherwise they're frightening.

[YEPIHODOV *crosses the stage at the rear, playing the guitar.*]

MME. RANEVSKAYA: [*Pensively.*] There goes Yepihodov.

GAYEV: Ladies and gentlemen, the sun has set.

TROFIMOV: Yes.

GAYEV: [*In a low voice, declaiming as it were.*] Oh, Nature, wondrous Nature, you shine with eternal radiance, beautiful and indifferent! You, whom we call our mother, unite within yourself life and death! You animate and destroy!

VARYA: [*Pleadingly.*] Uncle dear!

ANYA: Uncle, again!

TROFIMOV: You'd better bank the yellow ball in the side pocket.

GAYEV: I'm silent, I'm silent . . .

[*All sit plunged in thought. Stillness reigns. Only* FIRS's *muttering is audible. Suddenly a distant sound is heard, coming from the sky as it were, the sound of a snapping string, mournfully dying away.*]

MME. RANEVSKAYA: What was that?

LOPAHIN: I don't know. Somewhere far away, in the pits, a bucket's broken loose; but somewhere very far away.

GAYEV: Or it might be some sort of bird, perhaps a heron.

TROFIMOV: Or an owl . . .

MME. RANEVSKAYA: [*Shudders.*] It's weird, somehow. [*Pause.*]

FIRS: Before the calamity the same thing happened—the owl screeched, and the samovar hummed all the time.

GAYEV: Before what calamity?

FIRS: Before the Freedom. [*Pause.*]

MME. RANEVSKAYA: Come, my friends, let's be going. It's getting dark. [*To* ANYA.] You have tears in your eyes. What is it, my little one? [*Embraces her.*]

ANYA: I don't know, Mamma; it's nothing.

TROFIMOV: Somebody's coming.

[*A* TRAMP *appears, wearing a shabby white cap and an overcoat. He is slightly drunk.*]

TRAMP: Allow me to inquire, will this short cut take me to the station?

GAYEV: It will. Just follow that road.

TRAMP: My heartfelt thanks. [*Coughing.*] The weather is glorious. [*Recites.*] "My brother, my suffering brother. . . . Go down to the Volga![9] Whose groans . . . ?" [*To* VARYA.] Mademoiselle, won't you spare 30 kopecks for a hungry Russian?

[VARYA, *frightened, cries out.*]

LOPAHIN: [*Angrily.*] Even panhandling has its proprieties.

MME. RANEVSKAYA: [*Scared.*] Here, take this. [*Fumbles in her purse.*] I haven't any silver . . . never mind, here's a gold piece.

TRAMP: My heartfelt thanks. [*Exits. Laughter.*]

---

9. Lines from poems by Semyon Nadson (1826–1878) and Nikolay Nekrasov (1821–1878).

VARYA: [*Frightened.*] I'm leaving. I'm leaving. . . . Oh, Mamma dearest, at home the servants have nothing to eat, and you gave him a gold piece!

MME. RANEVSKAYA: What are you going to do with me? I'm such a fool. When we get home, I'll give you everything I have. Yermolay Alexeyevich, you'll lend me some more . . .

LOPAHIN: Yes, ma'am.

MME. RANEVSKAYA: Come, ladies and gentlemen, it's time to be going. Oh! Varya, we've settled all about your marriage. Congratulations!

VARYA: [*Through tears.*] Really, Mamma, that's not a joking matter.

LOPAHIN: "Aurelia, get thee to a nunnery, go . . ."

GAYEV: And do you know, my hands are trembling: I haven't played billiards in a long time.

LOPAHIN: "Aurelia, nymph, in your orisons, remember me!"[1]

MME. RANEVSKAYA: Let's go, it's almost suppertime.

VARYA: He frightened me! My heart's pounding.

LOPAHIN: Let me remind you, ladies and gentlemen, on the twenty-second of August the cherry orchard will be up for sale. Think about that! Think!

　　　　[*All except* TROFIMOV *and* ANYA *go out.*]

ANYA: [*Laughs.*] I'm grateful to that tramp, he frightened Varya and so we're alone.

TROFIMOV: Varya's afraid we'll fall in love with each other all of a sudden. She hasn't left us alone for days. Her narrow mind can't grasp that we're above love. To avoid the petty and illusory, everything that prevents us from being free and happy—that is the goal and meaning of our life. Forward! Do not fall behind, friends!

ANYA: [*Strikes her hands together.*] How well you speak! [*Pause.*] It's wonderful here today.

TROFIMOV: Yes, the weather's glorious.

ANYA: What have you done to me, Petya? Why don't I love the cherry orchard as I used to? I loved it so tenderly. It seemed to me there was no spot on earth lovelier than our orchard.

TROFIMOV: All Russia is our orchard. Our land is vast and beautiful, there are many wonderful places in it. [*Pause.*] Think of it, Anya, your grandfather, your great-grandfather and all your ancestors were serf owners, owners of living souls, and aren't human beings looking at you from every tree in the orchard, from every leaf, from every trunk? Don't you hear voices? Oh, it's terrifying! Your orchard is a fearful place, and when you pass through it in the evening or at night, the old bark on the trees gleams faintly, and the cherry trees seem to be dreaming of things that happened a hundred, two hundred years ago and to be tormented by painful visions. What is there to say? We're at least two hundred years behind, we've really achieved nothing yet, we have no definite attitude to the past, we only philosophize, complain of the blues, or drink vodka. It's all so clear: in order to live in the present, we should first redeem

---

1. Lopahin makes comic use of Hamlet's meeting with Ophelia. (Here *Aurelia* conveys the Russian text's distortion of "Ophelia" as "Okhmelia.") Hamlet, seeing her approaching, says: "Nymph, in thy orisons / Be all my sins remembered" (III.89–90), and later, suspecting her of spying for her father, sends her off with "Get thee to a nunnery" (III.121).

our past, finish with it, and we can expiate it only by suffering, only by extraordinary, unceasing labor. Realize that, Anya.

ANYA: The house in which we live has long ceased to be our own, and I will leave it, I give you my word.

TROFIMOV: If you have the keys, fling them into the well and go away. Be free as the wind.

ANYA: [*In ecstasy.*] How well you put that!

TROFIMOV: Believe me, Anya, believe me! I'm not yet thirty, I'm young, I'm still a student—but I've already suffered so much. In winter I'm hungry, sick, harassed, poor as a beggar, and where hasn't Fate driven me? Where haven't I been? And yet always, every moment of the day and night, my soul is filled with inexplicable premonitions. . . . I have a premonition of happiness, Anya. . . . I see it already!

ANYA: [*Pensively.*] The moon is rising.

[YEPIHODOV *is heard playing the same mournful tune on the guitar. The moon rises. Somewhere near the poplars* VARYA *is looking for* ANYA *and calling,* "Anya, where are you?"]

TROFIMOV: Yes, the moon is rising. [*Pause.*] There it is, happiness, it's approaching, it's coming nearer and nearer, I can already hear its footsteps. And if we don't see it, if we don't know it, what does it matter? Others will!

VARYA'S VOICE: Anya! Where are you?

TROFIMOV: That Varya again! [*Angrily.*] It's revolting!

ANYA: Never mind, let's go down to the river. It's lovely there.

TROFIMOV: Come on. [*They go.*]

VARYA'S VOICE: Anya! Anya!

Act III

A drawing room separated by an arch from a ballroom. Evening. Chandelier burning. The Jewish band is heard playing in the anteroom. In the ballroom they are dancing the Grand Rond. PISHCHIK *is heard calling,* "Promenade à une paire!"[2] PISHCHIK *and* CHARLOTTA, TROFIMOV *and* MME. RANEVSKAYA, ANYA *and the* POST OFFICE CLERK, VARYA *and the* STATIONMASTER, *and others enter the drawing room in couples.* DUNYASHA *is in the last couple.* VARYA *weeps quietly, wiping her tears as she dances. All parade through drawing room,* PISHCHIK *calling,* "Grand rond, balancez!"[3] *and* "Les cavaliers à genoux et remerciez vos dames!"[4] FIRS, *wearing a dress coat, brings in soda water on a tray.* PISHCHIK *and* TROFIMOV *enter the drawing room.*

PISHCHIK: I have high blood pressure; I've already had two strokes. Dancing's hard work for me; but as they say, "If you run with the pack, you can bark or not, but at least wag your tail." Still, I'm as strong as a horse. My late lamented father, who would have his joke, God rest his soul, used to say, talking about our origin, that the ancient line of the Simeo-

---

2. Promenade with your partner! (French). *Grand Rond:* a ring dance.   3. Make a large circle, get set! (French).   4. Gentlemen, on your knees and thank your ladies! (French).

nov-Pishchiks was descended from the very horse that Caligula had made a senator.[5] [*Sits down.*] But the trouble is, I have no money. A hungry dog believes in nothing but meat. [*Snores, and wakes up at once.*] It's the same with me—I can think of nothing but money.

TROFIMOV: You know, there *is* something equine about your figure.

PISHCHIK: Well, a horse is a fine animal—one can sell a horse.

[*Sound of billiards being played in an adjoining room.* VARYA *appears in the archway.*]

TROFIMOV: [*Teasing her.*] Madam Lopahina! Madam Lopahina!

VARYA: [*Angrily.*] Mangy master!

TROFIMOV: Yes, I am a mangy master and I'm proud of it.

VARYA: [*Reflecting bitterly.*] Here we've hired musicians, and what shall we pay them with? [*Exits.*]

TROFIMOV: [*To* PISHCHIK.] If the energy you have spent during your lifetime looking for money to pay interest had gone into something else, in the end you could have turned the world upside down.

PISHCHIK: Nietzsche,[6] the philosopher, the greatest, most famous of men, that colossal intellect, says in his works that it is permissible to forge banknotes.

TROFIMOV: Have you read Nietzsche?

PISHCHIK: Well . . . Dashenka told me. . . . And now I've got to the point where forging banknotes is the only way out for me. . . . The day after tomorrow I have to pay 310 rubles—I already have 130 . . . [*Feels in his pockets. In alarm.*] The money's gone! I've lost my money! [*Through tears.*] Where's my money? [*Joyfully.*] Here it is! Inside the lining . . . I'm all in a sweat . . .

[*Enter* MME. RANEVSKAYA *and* CHARLOTTA.]

MME. RANEVSKAYA: [*Hums the "Lezginka."*[7]] Why isn't Leonid back yet? What is he doing in town? [*To* DUNYASHA.] Dunyasha, offer the musicians tea.

TROFIMOV: The auction hasn't taken place, most likely.

MME. RANEVSKAYA: It's the wrong time to have the band, and the wrong time to give a dance. Well, never mind. [*Sits down and hums softly.*]

CHARLOTTA. [*Hands* PISHCHIK *a pack of cards.*] Here is a pack of cards. Think of any card you like.

PISHCHIK: I've thought of one.

CHARLOTTA: Shuffle the pack now. That's right. Give it here, my dear Mr. Pishchik. *Eins, zwei, drei!*[8] Now look for it—it's in your side pocket.

PISHCHIK: [*Taking the card out of his pocket.*] The eight of spades! Perfectly right! Just imagine!

CHARLOTTA: [*Holding the pack of cards in her hands. To* TROFIMOV.] Quickly, name the top card.

TROFIMOV: Well, let's see—the queen of spades.

CHARLOTTA: Right! [*To* PISHCHIK.] Now name the top card.

5. The mad emperor Caligula (12–41 A.D.) brought his favorite horse into the Roman senate to make it a senator.   6. Friedrich W. Nietzsche (1844–1900), German philosopher.   7. The music that in the Caucasus mountains accompanies a courtship dance in which the man dances with abandon around the woman, who moves with grace and ease.   8. One, two, three (German).

PISHCHIK: The ace of hearts.

CHARLOTTA: Right! [*Claps her hands and the pack of cards disappears.*]
Ah, what lovely weather it is today! [*A mysterious feminine* VOICE,
which seems to come from under the floor, answers her: "Oh, yes, it's
magnificent weather, madam."] You are my best ideal. [VOICE: "And I
find you pleasing too, madam."]

STATIONMASTER.[*Applauding.*] The lady ventriloquist, bravo!

PISHCHIK: [*Amazed.*] Just imagine! Enchanting Charlotta Ivanovna, I'm
simply in love with you.

CHARLOTTA: In love? [*Shrugs her shoulders.*] Are you capable of love?
Guter Mensch, aber schlechter Musikant![9]

TROFIMOV: [*Claps* PISHCHIK *on the shoulder.*] You old horse, you!

CHARLOTTA: Attention please! One more trick! [*Takes a plaid*[1] *from a
chair.*] Here is a very good plaid; I want to sell it. [*Shaking it out.*] Does
anyone want to buy it?

PISHCHIK: [*In amazement.*] Just imagine!

CHARLOTTA: *Eins, zwei, drei!* [*Raises the plaid quickly, behind it stands*
ANYA. *She curtsies, runs to her mother, embraces her, and runs back
into the ballroom, amid general enthusiasm.*]

MME. RANEVSKAYA: [*Applauds.*] Bravo! Bravo!

CHARLOTTA: Now again! *Eins, zwei, drei!* [*Lifts the plaid; behind it stands*
VARYA, *bowing.*]

PISHCHIK: [*In amazement.*] Just imagine!

[CHARLOTTA *throws the plaid at* PISHCHIK, *curtsies, and runs into the
ballroom.*]

PISHCHIK: [*Running after her.*] The rascal! What a woman, what a woman!
[*Exits.*]

MME. RANEVSKAYA: And Leonid still isn't here. What is he doing in town
so long? I don't understand. It must be all over by now. Either the estate
has been sold, or the auction hasn't taken place. Why keep us in suspense so long?

VARYA: [*Trying to console her.*] Uncle's bought it, I feel sure of that.

TROFIMOV: [*Mockingly.*] Oh, yes!

VARYA: Great-aunt sent him an authorization to buy it in her name, and to
transfer the debt. She's doing it for Anya's sake. And I'm sure that God
will help us, and Uncle will buy it.

MME. RANEVSKAYA: Great-aunt sent fifteen thousand to buy the estate in
her name, she doesn't trust us, but that's not even enough to pay the
interest. [*Covers her face with her hands.*] Today my fate will be
decided, my fate—

TROFIMOV: [*Teasing* VARYA.] Madam Lopahina!

VARYA: [*Angrily.*] Perpetual student! Twice already you've been expelled
from the university.

MME. RANEVSKAYA: Why are you so cross, Varya? He's teasing you about

---

9. "A good man, but a bad musician" (German), usually quoted in the plural: "*Gute Leute, schlechte
Musikanten.*" It comes from *Das Buch le Grand* (1826) by the German poet Heinrich Heine (1799–
1856). Here it suggests that Pishchik may be a good man but a bad lover.   1. A small plaid blanket, or
lap robe.

Lopahin. Well, what of it? If you want to marry Lopahin, go ahead. He's a good man, and interesting; if you don't want to, don't. Nobody's compelling you, my pet!

VARYA: Frankly, Mamma dear, I take this thing seriously; he's a good man and I like him.

MME. RANEVSKAYA: All right then, marry him. I don't know what you're waiting for.

VARYA: But, Mamma, I can't propose to him myself. For the last two years, everyone's been talking to me about him—talking. But he either keeps silent, or else cracks jokes. I understand; he's growing rich, he's absorbed in business—he has no time for me. If I had money, even a little, say, 100 rubles, I'd throw everything up and go far away—I'd go into a nunnery.

TROFIMOV: What a blessing . . .

VARYA: A student ought to be intelligent. [Softly, with tears in her voice.] How homely you've grown, Petya! How old you look! [To MME. RANEVSKAYA, with dry eyes.] But I can't live without work, Mamma dear; I must keep busy every minute.

[Enter YASHA.]

YASHA: [Hardly restraining his laughter.] Yepihodov has broken a billiard cue! [Exits.]

VARYA: Why is Yepihodov here? Who allowed him to play billiards? I don't understand these people! [Exits.]

MME. RANEVSKAYA: Don't tease her, Petya. She's unhappy enough with that.

TROFIMOV: She bustles so—and meddles in other people's business. All summer long she's given Anya and me no peace. She's afraid of a love affair between us. What business is it of hers? Besides, I've given no grounds for it, and I'm far from such vulgarity. We are above love.

MME. RANEVSKAYA: And I suppose I'm beneath love? [Anxiously.] What can be keeping Leonid? If I only knew whether the estate has been sold or not. Such a calamity seems so incredible to me that I don't know what to think—I feel lost. . . . I could scream. . . . I could do something stupid. . . . Save me, Petya, tell me something, talk to me!

TROFIMOV: Whether the estate is sold today or not, isn't it all one? That's all done with long ago—there's no turning back, the path is overgrown. Calm yourself, my dear. You mustn't deceive yourself. For once in your life you must face the truth.

MME. RANEVSKAYA: What truth? You can see the truth, you can tell it from falsehood, but I seem to have lost my eyesight, I see nothing. You settle every great problem so boldly, but tell me, my dear boy, isn't it because you're young, because you don't yet know what one of your problems means in terms of suffering? You look ahead fearlessly, but isn't it because you don't see and don't expect anything dreadful, because life is still hidden from your young eyes? You're bolder, more honest, more profound than we are, but think hard, show just a bit of magnanimity, spare me. After all, I was born here, my father and mother lived here, and my grandfather; I love this house. Without the cherry orchard, my life has no meaning for me, and if it really must be sold, then sell me with the orchard. [*Embraces* TROFIMOV, *kisses him on the forehead.*] My son was drowned here. [*Weeps.*] Pity me, you good, kind fellow!

TROFIMOV: You know, I feel for you with all my heart.

MME. RANEVSKAYA: But that should have been said differently, so differently! [*Takes out her handkerchief—a telegram falls on the floor.*] My heart is so heavy today—you can't imagine! The noise here upsets me—my inmost being trembles at every sound—I'm shaking all over. But I can't go into my own room; I'm afraid to be alone. Don't condemn me, Petya. . . . I love you as though you were one of us, I would gladly let you marry Anya—I swear I would—only, my dear boy, you must study—you must take your degree—you do nothing, you let yourself be tossed by Fate from place to place—it's so strange. It's true, isn't it? And you should do something about your beard, to make it grow somehow! [*Laughs.*] You're so funny!

TROFIMOV: [*Picks up the telegram.*] I've no wish to be a dandy.

MME. RANEVSKAYA: That's a telegram from Paris. I get one every day. One yesterday and one today. That savage is ill again—he's in trouble again. He begs forgiveness, implores me to go to him, and really I ought to go to Paris to be near him. Your face is stern, Petya; but what is there to do, my dear boy? What am I to do? He's ill, he's alone and unhappy, and who is to look after him, who is to keep him from doing the wrong thing, who is to give him his medicine on time? And why hide it or keep still about it—I love him! That's clear. I love him, love him! He's a millstone round my neck, he'll drag me to the bottom, but I love that stone, I can't live without it. [*Presses* TROFIMOV's *hand.*] Don't think badly of me. Petya, and don't say anything, don't say . . .

TROFIMOV: [*Through tears.*] Forgive me my frankness in heaven's name; but, you know, he robbed you!

MME. RANEVSKAYA: No, no, no, you mustn't say such things! [*Covers her ears.*]

TROFIMOV: But he's a scoundrel! You're the only one who doesn't know it. He's a petty scoundrel—a nonentity!

MME. RANEVSKAYA: [*Controlling her anger.*] You are twenty-six or twenty-seven years old, but you're still a schoolboy.

TROFIMOV: That may be.

MME. RANEVSKAYA: You should be a man at your age. You should understand people who love—and ought to be in love yourself. You ought to fall in love! [*Angrily.*] Yes, yes! And it's not purity in you, it's prudishness, you're simply a queer fish, a comical freak!

TROFIMOV: [*Horrified.*] What is she saying?

MME. RANEVSKAYA: "I am above love!" You're not above love, but simple, as our Firs says, you're an addlehead. At your age not to have a mistress!

TROFIMOV: [*Horrified.*] This is frightful! What is she saying! [*Goes rapidly into the ballroom, clutching his head.*] It's frightful—I can't stand it, I won't stay! [*Exits, but returns at once.*] All is over between us! [*Exits into anteroom.*]

MME. RANEVSKAYA: [*Shouts after him.*] Petya! Wait! You absurd fellow, I was joking. Petya!

[*Sound of somebody running quickly downstairs and suddenly falling down with a crash.* ANYA *and* VARYA *scream. Sound of laughter a moment later.*]

MME. RANEVSKAYA: What's happened?

[ANYA *runs in.*]

ANYA: [*Laughing.*] Petya's fallen downstairs! [*Runs out.*]

MME. RANEVSKAYA: What a queer bird that Petya is!

[STATIONMASTER, *standing in the middle of the ballroom, recites Alexey Tolstoy's "Magdalene,"[2] to which all listen, but after a few lines, the sound of a waltz is heard from the anteroom and the reading breaks off. All dance.* TROFIMOV, ANYA, VARYA *and* MME. RANEVSKAYA *enter from the anteroom.*]

MME. RANEVSKAYA: Petya, you pure soul, please forgive me. . . . Let's dance. [*Dances with* PETYA, ANYA *and* VARYA *dance.* FIRS *enters, puts his stick down by the side door.* YASHA *enters from the drawing room and watches the dancers.*]

YASHA: Well, Grandfather?

FIRS: I'm not feeling well. In the old days it was generals, barons, and admirals that were dancing at our balls, and now we have to send for the Post Office Clerk and the Stationmaster, and even they aren't too glad to come. I feel kind of shaky. The old master that's gone, their grandfather, dosed everyone with sealing wax, whatever ailed 'em. I've been taking sealing wax every day for twenty years or more. Perhaps that's what's kept me alive.

YASHA: I'm fed up with you, Grandpop. [*Yawns.*] It's time you croaked.

FIRS: Oh, you addlehead! [*Mumbles.*]

[TROFIMOV *and* MME. RANEVSKAYA *dance from the ballroom into the drawing room.*]

MME. RANEVSKAYA: Merci. I'll sit down a while. [*Sits down.*] I'm tired. [*Enter* ANYA.]

ANYA: [*Excitedly.*] There was a man in the kitchen just now who said the cherry orchard was sold today.

MME. RANEVSKAYA: Sold to whom?

ANYA: He didn't say. He's gone. [*Dances off with* TROFIMOV.]

YASHA: It was some old man gabbing, a stranger.

FIRS: And Leonid Andreyevich isn't back yet, he hasn't come. And he's wearing his lightweight between-season overcoat; like enough, he'll catch cold. Ah, when they're young they're green.

MME. RANEVSKAYA: This is killing me. Go, Yasha, find out to whom it has been sold.

YASHA: But the old man left long ago. [*Laughs.*]

MME RANEVSKAYA: What are you laughing at? What are you pleased about?

YASHA: That Yepihodov is such a funny one. A funny fellow, Two-and-Twenty Troubles!

MME. RANEVSKAYA: Firs, if the estate is sold, where will you go?

FIRS: I'll go where you tell me.

---

2. Called *The Sinning Woman* in Russian, it begins: "A bustling crowd with happy laughter, / with twanging lutes and clashing cymbals / with flowers and foliage all around / the colonnaded portico." Alexey Tolstoy (1817–1875), popular in his time as a dramatist and poet, was a distant relative of Leo Tolstoy.

MME. RANEVSKAYA: Why do you look like that? Are you ill? You ought to go to bed.

FIRS: Yes! [*With a snigger.*] Me go to bed, and who's to hand things round? Who's to see to things? I'm the only one in the whole house.

YASHA: [*To* MME. RANEVSKAYA.] Lubov Andreyevna, allow me to ask a favor of you, be so kind! If you go back to Paris, take me with you, I beg you. It's positively impossible for me to stay here. [*Looking around; sotto voce.*] What's the use of talking? You see for yourself, it's an uncivilized country, the people have no morals, and then the boredom! The food in the kitchen's revolting, and besides there's this Firs wanders about mumbling all sorts of inappropriate words. Take me with you, be so kind!

[*Enter* PISHCHIK.]

PISHCHIK: May I have the pleasure of a waltz with you, charming lady? [MME. RANEVSKAYA *accepts.*] All the same, enchanting lady, you must let me have 180 rubles. . . . You must let me have [*dancing*] just one hundred and eighty rubles. [*They pass into the ballroom.*]

YASHA: [*Hums softly.*] "Oh, wilt thou understand the tumult in my soul?" [*In the ballroom a figure in a gray top hat and checked trousers is jumping about and waving its arms; shouts:* "Bravo, Charlotta Ivanovna!"]

DUNYASHA: [*Stopping to powder her face; to* FIRS.] The young miss has ordered me to dance. There are so many gentlemen and not enough ladies. But dancing makes me dizzy, my heart begins to beat fast, Firs Nikolayevich. The Post Office Clerk said something to me just now that quite took my breath away.

[*Music stops.*]

FIRS: What did he say?

DUNYASHA: "You're like a flower," he said.

YASHA: [*Yawns.*] What ignorance. [*Exits.*]

DUNYASHA: "Like a flower!" I'm such a delicate girl. I simply adore pretty speeches.

FIRS: You'll come to a bad end.

[*Enter* YEPIHODOV.]

YEPIHODOV: [*To* DUNYASHA.] You have no wish to see me, Avdotya Fyodorovna . . . as though I was some sort of insect. [*Sighs.*] Ah, life!

DUNYASHA: What is it you want?

YEPIHODOV: Indubitably you may be right. [*Sighs.*] But of course, if one looks at it from the point of view, if I may be allowed to say so, and apologizing for my frankness, you have completely reduced me to a state of mind. I know my fate. Every day some calamity befalls me, and I grew used to it long ago, so that I look upon my fate with a smile. You gave me your word, and though I—

DUNYASHA: Let's talk about it later, please. But just now leave me alone, I am daydreaming. [*Plays with a fan.*]

YEPIHODOV: A misfortune befalls me every day; and if I may be allowed to say so, I merely smile, I even laugh.

[*Enter* VARYA.]

VARYA: [*To* YEPIHODOV.] Are you still here? What an impertinent fellow you are really! Run along, Dunyasha. [*To* YEPIHODOV.] Either you're playing billiards and breaking a cue, or you're wandering about the drawing room as though you were a guest.

YEPIHODOV: You cannot, permit me to remark, penalize me.

VARYA: I'm not penalizing you; I'm just telling you. You merely wander from place to place, and don't do your work. We keep you as a clerk, but heaven knows what for.

YEPIHODOV: [*Offended.*] Whether I work or whether I walk, whether I eat or whether I play billiards, is a matter to be discussed only by persons of understanding and of mature years.

VARYA: [*Enraged.*] You dare say that to me—you dare? You mean to say I've no understanding? Get out of here at once! This minute!

YEPIHODOV: [*Scared.*] I beg you to express yourself delicately.

VARYA: [*Beside herself.*] Clear out this minute! Out with you!

[YEPIHODOV *goes toward the door,* VARYA *following.*]

VARYA: Two-and-Twenty Troubles! Get out—don't let me set eyes on you again!

[*Exit* YEPIHODOV: *His voice is heard behind the door:* "I shall lodge a complaint against you!"]

VARYA: Oh, you're coming back? [*She seizes the stick left near door by* FIRS.] Well, come then . . . come . . . I'll show you. . . . Ah, you're coming? You're coming? . . . Come . . . [*Swings the stick just as* LOPAHIN *enters.*]

LOPAHIN: Thank you kindly.

VARYA: [*Angrily and mockingly.*] I'm sorry.

LOPAHIN: It's nothing. Thank you kindly for your charming reception.

VARYA: Don't mention it. [*Walks away, looks back and asks softly.*] I didn't hurt you, did I?

LOPAHIN: Oh, no, not at all. I shall have a large bump, though.

[*Voices from the ballroom:* "Lopahin is here! Lopahin!" *Enter* PISHCHIK.]

PISHCHIK: My eyes do see, my ears do hear! [*Kisses* LOPAHIN.] You smell of cognac, my dear friend. And we've been celebrating here, too.

[*Enter* MME. RANEVSKAYA.]

MME. RANEVSKAYA: Is that you, Yermolay Alexeyevich? What kept you so long? Where's Leonid?

LOPAHIN: Leonid Andreyevich arrived with me. He's coming.

MME. RANEVSKAYA: Well, what happened? Did the sale take place? Speak!

LOPAHIN: [*Embarrassed, fearful of revealing his joy.*] The sale was over at four o'clock. We missed the train—had to wait till half-past nine. [*Sighing heavily.*] Ugh. I'm a little dizzy.

[*Enter* GAYEV: *In his right hand he holds parcels, with his left he is wiping away his tears.*]

MME. RANEVSKAYA: Well, Leonid? What news? [*Impatiently, through tears.*] Be quick, for God's sake!

GAYEV: [*Not answering, simply waves his hand. Weeping, to* FIRS.] Here, take these; anchovies, Kerch herrings . . . I haven't eaten all day. What I've been through! [*The click of billiard balls comes through the open door of the billiard room and* YASHA's *voice is heard:* "Seven and eighteen!" GAYEV's *expression changes, he no longer weeps.*] I'm terribly tired. Firs, help me change. [*Exits, followed by* FIRS.]

PISHCHIK: How about the sale? Tell us what happened.

MME. RANEVSKAYA: Is the cherry orchard sold?

LOPAHIN: Sold.

MME. RANEVSKAYA: Who bought it?

LOPAHIN: I bought it.

[*Pause,* MME. RANEVSKAYA *is overcome. She would fall to the floor, were it not for the chair and table near which she stands.* VARYA *takes the keys from her belt, flings them on the floor in the middle of the drawing room and goes out.*]

LOPAHIN: I bought it. Wait a bit, ladies and gentlemen, please, my head is swimming, I can't talk. [*Laughs.*] We got to the auction and Deriganov was there already. Leonid Andreyevich had only 15,000 and straight off Deriganov bid 30,000 over and above the mortgage. I saw how the land lay, got into the fight, bid 40,000. He bid 45,000. I bid fifty-five. He kept adding five thousands, I ten. Well . . . it came to an end. I bid ninety above the mortgage and the estate was knocked down to me. Now the cherry orchard's mine! Mine! [*Laughs uproariously.*] Lord! God in Heaven! The cherry orchard's mine! Tell me that I'm drunk—out of my mind—that it's all a dream. [*Stamps his feet.*] Don't laugh at me! If my father and my grandfather could rise from their graves and see all that has happened—how their Yermolay, who used to be flogged, their half-literate Yermolay, who used to run about barefoot in winter, how that very Yermolay has bought the most magnificent estate in the world. I bought the estate where my father and grandfather were slaves, where they weren't even allowed to enter the kitchen. I am asleep—it's only a dream—I only imagine it. . . . It's the fruit of your imagination, wrapped in the darkness of the unknown! [*Picks up the keys, smiling genially.*] She threw down the keys, wants to show she's no longer mistress here. [*Jingles keys.*] Well, no matter. [*The band is warming up.*] Hey, musicians! Strike up! I want to hear you! Come, everybody, and see how Yermolay Lopahin will lay the ax to the cherry orchard and how the trees will fall to the ground. We will build summer cottages there, and our grandsons and great grandsons will see a new life here. Music! Strike up!

[*The band starts to play.* MME RANEVSKAYA *has sunk into a chair and is weeping bitterly.*]

LOPAHIN: [*Reproachfully.*] Why, why didn't you listen to me? My dear friend, my poor friend, you can't bring it back now. [*Tearfully.*] Oh, if only this were over quickly! Oh, if only our wretched, disordered life were changed!

PISHCHIK: [*Takes him by the arm; sotto voce.*] She's crying. Let's go into the ballroom. Let her be alone. Come. [*Takes his arm and leads him into the ballroom.*]

LOPAHIN: What's the matter? Musicians, play so I can hear you! Let me have things the way I want them.[*Ironically.*] Here comes the new master, the owner of the cherry orchard. [*Accidentally he trips over a little table, almost upsetting the candelabra.*] I can pay for everything. [*Exits with* PISHCHIK.]

    [MME. RANEVSKAYA, *alone, sits huddled up, weeping bitterly. Music plays softly. Enter* ANYA *and* TROFIMOV *quickly.* ANYA *goes to her mother and falls on her knees before her.* TROFIMOV *stands in the doorway.*]

ANYA: Mamma, Mamma, you're crying! Dear, kind, good Mamma, my precious, I love you, I bless you! The cherry orchard is sold, it's gone, that's true, quite true. But don't cry, Mamma, life is still before you, you still have your kind, pure heart. Let us go, let us go away from here, darling. We will plant a new orchard, even more luxuriant than this one. You will see it, you will understand, and like the sun at evening, joy—deep, tranquil joy—will sink into your soul, and you will smile, Mamma. Come, darling, let us go.

Act IV

Scene as in Act I. No window curtains or pictures, only a little furniture, piled up in a corner, as if for sale. A sense of emptiness. Near the outer door and at the back, suitcases, bundles, etc., are piled up. A door open on the left and the voices of VARYA *and* ANYA *are heard.* LOPAHIN *stands waiting.* YASHA *holds a tray with glasses full of champagne.* YEPIHODOV *in the anteroom is tying up a box. Behind the scene a hum of voices: peasants have come to say good-bye. Voice of* GAYEV: "Thanks, brothers, thank you."*

YASHA: The country folk have come to say good-bye. In my opinion, Yermolay Alexeyevich, they are kindly souls, but there's nothing in their heads.

    [*The hum dies away. Enter* MME. RANEVSKAYA *and* GAYEV: *She is not crying, but is pale, her face twitches and she cannot speak.*]

GAYEV: You gave them your purse, Luba. That won't do! That won't do!

MME. RANEVSKAYA: I couldn't help it! I couldn't! [*They go out.*]

LOPAHIN: [*Calls after them.*] Please, I beg you, have a glass at parting. I didn't think of bringing any champagne from town and at the station I could find only one bottle. Please, won't you? [*Pause.*] What's the matter, ladies and gentlemen, don't you want any? [*Moves away from the door.*] If I'd known, I wouldn't have bought it. Well, then I won't drink any, either. [YASHA *carefully sets the tray down on a chair.*] At least you have a glass, Yasha.

YASHA: Here's to the travelers! And good luck to those that stay! [*Drinks.*] This champagne isn't the real stuff, I can assure you.

LOPAHIN: Eight rubles a bottle. [*Pause.*] It's devilishly cold here.

YASHA: They didn't light the stoves today—it wasn't worth it, since we're leaving. [*Laughs.*]

LOPAHIN: Why are you laughing?

YASHA: It's just that I'm pleased.

LOPAHIN: It's October, yet it's as still and sunny as though it were summer. Good weather for building. [*Looks at his watch, and speaks off.*] Bear in mind, ladies and gentlemen, the train goes in forty-seven minutes, so you ought to start for the station in twenty minutes. Better hurry up!

[*Enter* TROFIMOV, *wearing an overcoat.*]

TROFIMOV: I think it's time to start. The carriages are at the door. The devil only knows what's become of my rubbers; they've disappeared. [*Calling off.*] Anya! My rubbers are gone. I can't find them.

LOPAHIN: I've got to go to Kharkov. I'll take the same train you do. I'll spend the winter in Kharkov. I've been hanging round here with you, till I'm worn out with loafing. I can't live without work—I don't know what to do with my hands, they dangle as if they didn't belong to me.

TROFIMOV: Well, we'll soon be gone, then you can go on with your useful labors again.

LOPAHIN: Have a glass.

TROFIMOV: No, I won't.

LOPAHIN: So you're going to Moscow now?

TROFIMOV: Yes, I'll see them into town, and tomorrow I'll go on to Moscow.

LOPAHIN: Well, I'll wager the professors aren't giving any lectures, they're waiting for you to come.

TROFIMOV: That's none of your business.

LOPAHIN: Just how many years have you been at the university?

TROFIMOV: Can't you think of something new? Your joke's stale and flat. [*Looking for his rubbers.*] We'll probably never see each other again, so allow me to give you a piece of advice at parting: don't wave your hands about! Get out of the habit. And another thing: building bungalows, figuring that summer residents will eventually become small farmers, figuring like that is just another form of waving your hands about. . . . Never mind, I love you anyway; you have fine, delicate fingers, like an artist; you have a fine delicate soul.

LOPAHIN: [*Embracing him.*] Good-bye, my dear fellow. Thank you for everything. Let me give you some money for the journey, if you need it.

TROFIMOV: What for? I don't need it.

LOPAHIN: But you haven't any.

TROFIMOV: Yes, I have, thank you. I got some money for a translation— here it is in my pocket. [*Anxiously.*] But where are my rubbers?

VARYA: [*From the next room.*] Here! Take the nasty things. [*Flings a pair of rubbers onto the stage.*]

TROFIMOV: What are you so cross about, Varya? Hm . . . and these are not my rubbers.

LOPAHIN: I sowed three thousand acres of poppies in the spring, and now I've made 40,000 on them, clear profit; and when my poppies were in bloom, what a picture it was! So, as I say, I made 40,000; and I am offering you a loan because I can afford it. Why turn up your nose at it? I am a peasant—I speak bluntly.

TROFIMOV: Your father was a peasant, mine was a druggist—that proves absolutely nothing whatever. [LOPAHIN *takes out his wallet.*] Don't, put that away! If you were to offer me two hundred thousand, I wouldn't take it. I'm a free man. And everything that all of you, rich and poor alike, value so highly and hold so dear hasn't the slightest power over me. It's like so much fluff floating in the air. I can get on without you, I can pass you by, I'm strong and proud. Mankind is moving toward the highest truth, toward the highest happiness possible on earth, and I am in the front ranks.

LOPAHIN: Will you get there?

TROFIMOV: I will. [*Pause.*] I will get there, or I will show others the way to get there.

[*The sound of axes chopping down trees is heard in the distance.*]

LOPAHIN: Well, good-bye, my dear fellow. It's time to leave. We turn up our noses at one another, but life goes on just the same. When I'm working hard, without resting, my mind is easier, and it seems to me that I, too, know why I exist. But how many people are there in Russia, brother, who exist nobody knows why? Well, it doesn't matter. That's not what makes the wheels go round. They say Leonid Andreyevich has taken a position in the bank, 6,000 rubles a year. Only, of course, he won't stick to it, he's too lazy. . . .

ANYA: [*In the doorway.*] Mamma begs you not to start cutting down the cherry trees until she's gone.

TROFIMOV: Really, you should have more tact! [*Exits.*]

LOPAHIN: Right away—right away! Those men . . . [*Exits.*]

ANYA: Has Firs been taken to the hospital?

YASHA: I told them this morning. They must have taken him.

ANYA: [*To* YEPIHODOV, *who crosses the room.*] Yepihodov, please find out if Firs has been taken to the hospital.

YASHA: [*Offended.*] I told Yegor this morning. Why ask a dozen times?

YEPIHODOV: The aged Firs, in my definitive opinion, is beyond mending. It's time he was gathered to his fathers. And I can only envy him. [*Puts a suitcase down on a hat box and crushes it.*] There now, of course, I knew it! [*Exits.*]

YASHA: [*Mockingly.*] Two-and-Twenty Troubles!

VARYA: [*Through the door.*] Has Firs been taken to the hospital?

ANYA: Yes.

VARYA: Then why wasn't the note for the doctor taken too?

ANYA: Oh! Then someone must take it to him. [*Exits.*]

VARYA: [*From adjoining room.*] Where's Yasha? Tell him his mother's come and wants to say good-bye.

YASHA: [*Waves his hand.*] She tries my patience.

[DUNYASHA *has been occupied with the luggage. Seeing* YASHA *alone, she goes up to him.*]

DUNYASHA: You might just give me one little look, Yasha. You're going away. . . . You're leaving me . . . [*Weeps and throws herself on his neck.*]

YASHA: What's there to cry about? [*Drinks champagne.*] In six days I shall be in Paris again. Tomorrow we get into an express train and off we go, that's the last you'll see of us. . . . I can scarcely believe it. *Vive la France!*[3] It don't suit me here, I just can't live here. That's all there is to it. I'm fed up with the ignorance here, I've had enough of it. [*Drinks champagne.*] What's there to cry about? Behave yourself properly, and you'll have no cause to cry.

DUNYASHA: [*Powders her face, looking in pocket mirror.*] Do send me a letter from Paris. You know I loved you, Yasha, how I loved you! I'm a delicate creature, Yasha.

YASHA: Somebody's coming! [*Busies himself with the luggage; hums softly.*]

[*Enter* MME. RANEVSKAYA, GAYEV, ANYA, *and* CHARLOTTA.]

GAYEV: We ought to be leaving. We haven't much time. [*Looks at* YASHA.] Who smells of herring?

MME. RANEVSKAYA: In about ten minutes we should be getting into the carriages. [*Looks around the room.*] Good-bye, dear old home, good-bye, grandfather. Winter will pass, spring will come, you will no longer be here, they will have torn you down. How much these walls have seen! [*Kisses* ANYA *warmly.*] My treasure, how radiant you look! Your eyes are sparkling like diamonds. Are you glad? Very?

ANYA: [*Gaily.*] Very glad. A new life is beginning, Mamma.

GAYEV: Well, really, everything is all right now. Before the cherry orchard was sold, we all fretted and suffered; but afterward, when the question was settled finally and irrevocably, we all calmed down, and even felt quite cheerful. I'm a bank employee now, a financier. The yellow ball in the side pocket! And anyhow, you are looking better, Luba, there's no doubt of that.

MME. RANEVSKAYA: Yes, my nerves are better, that's true. [*She is handed her hat and coat.*] I sleep well. Carry out my things, Yasha. It's time. [*To* ANYA.] We shall soon see each other again, my little girl. I'm going to Paris, I'll live there on the money your great-aunt sent us to buy the estate with—long live Auntie! But that money won't last long.

ANYA: You'll come back soon, soon, Mamma, won't you? Meanwhile I'll study. I'll pass my high school examination, and then I'll go to work and help you. We'll read all kinds of books together, Mamma, won't we? [*Kisses her mother's hands.*] We'll read in the autumn evenings, we'll read lots of books, and a new wonderful world will open up before us. [*Falls into a revery.*] Mamma, do come back.

MME. RANEVSKAYA: I will come back, my precious.

[*Embraces her daughter. Enter* LOPAHIN *and* CHARLOTTA, *who is humming softly.*]

GAYEV: Charlotta's happy: she's singing.

CHARLOTTA: [*Picks up a bundle and holds it like a baby in swaddling clothes.*] Bye, baby, bye. [*A baby is heard crying:* "Wah! Wah!"] Hush, hush, my pet, my little one. ["Wah! Wah!"] I'm so sorry for you! [*Throws the bundle down.*] You will find me a position, won't you? I can't go on like this.

LOPAHIN: We'll find one for you, Charlotta Ivanovna, don't worry.

---

3. Long live France! (French).

GAYEV: Everyone's leaving us. Varya's going away. We've suddenly become of no use.

CHARLOTTA: There's no place for me to live in town, I must go away. [*Hums.*]

    [*Enter* PISHCHIK.]

LOPAHIN: There's nature's masterpiece!

PISHCHIK: [*Gasping.*] Oh . . . let me get my breath . . . I'm in agony. . . . Esteemed friends . . . Give me a drink of water. . . .

GAYEV: Wants some money, I suppose. No, thank you . . . I'll keep out of harm's way. [*Exits.*]

PISHCHIK: It's a long while since I've been to see you, most charming lady. [*To* LOPAHIN.] So you are here . . . glad to see you, you intellectual giant . . . There . . . [*Gives* LOPAHIN *money.*] Here's 400 rubles, and I still owe you 840.

LOPAHIN: [*Shrugging his shoulders in bewilderment.*] I must be dreaming. . . . Where did you get it?

PISHCHIK: Wait a minute . . . it's hot. . . . A most extraordinary event! Some Englishmen came to my place and found some sort of white clay on my land . . . [*To* MME. RANEVSKAYA.] And 400 for you . . . most lovely . . . most wonderful . . . [*Hands her the money.*] The rest later. [*Drinks water.*] A young man in the train was telling me just now that a great philosopher recommends jumping off roofs. "Jump!" says he; "that's the long and the short of it!" [*In amazement.*] Just imagine! Some more water!

LOPAHIN: What Englishmen?

PISHCHIK: I leased them the tract with the clay on it for twenty-four years. . . . And now, forgive me, I can't stay. . . . I must be dashing on. . . . I'm going over to Znoikov . . . to Kardamanov . . . I owe them all money . . . [*Drinks water.*] Good-bye, everybody . . . I'll look in on Thursday . . .

MME. RANEVSKAYA: We're just moving into town; and tomorrow I go abroad.

PISHCHIK: [*Upset.*] What? Why into town? That's why the furniture is like that . . . and the suitcases. . . . Well, never mind! [*Through tears.*] Never mind . . . men of colossal intellect, these Englishmen. . . . Never mind . . . Be happy. God will come to your help. . . . Never mind . . . everything in this world comes to an end. [*Kisses* MME. RANEVSKAYA's *hand.*] If the rumor reaches you that it's all up with me, remember this old . . . horse, and say: "Once there lived a certain . . . Simeonov-Pishchik . . . the kingdom of Heaven be his. . . ." Glorious weather! . . . Yes . . . [*Exits, in great confusion, but at once returns and says in the doorway.*] My daughter Dashenka sends her regards. [*Exits.*]

MME. RANEVSKAYA: Now we can go. I leave with two cares weighing on me. The first is poor old Firs. [*Glancing at her watch.*] We still have about five minutes.

ANYA: Mamma, Firs has already been taken to the hospital. Yasha sent him there this morning.

MME. RANEVSKAYA: My other worry is Varya. She's used to getting up early and working; and now, with no work to do, she is like a fish out of water. She has grown thin and pale, and keeps crying, poor soul. [*Pause.*] You know this very well, Yermolay Alexeyevich; I dreamed of seeing her married to you, and it looked as though that's how it would be. [*Whispers to* ANYA, *who nods to* CHARLOTTA *and both go out.*] She loves you. You find her attractive. I don't know, I don't know why it is you seem to avoid each other; I can't understand it.

LOPAHIN: To tell you the truth, I don't understand it myself. It's all a puzzle. If there's still time, I'm ready now, at once. Let's settle it straight off, and have done with it! Without you, I feel I'll never be able to propose.

MME. RANEVSKAYA: That's splendid. After all, it will only take a minute. I'll call her once. . . .

LOPAHIN: And luckily, here's champagne, too. [*Looks at the glasses.*] Empty! Somebody's drunk it all. [*Yasha coughs.*] That's what you might call guzzling . . .

MME. RANEVSKAYA: [*Animatedly.*] Excellent! We'll go and leave you alone. Yasha, *allez!*[4] I'll call her. [*At the door.*] Varya, leave everything and come here. Come! [*Exits with* YASHA.]

LOPAHIN: [*Looking at his watch.*] Yes . . . [*Pause behind the door, smothered laughter and whispering; at last, enter* VARYA.]

VARYA: [*Looking over the luggage in leisurely fashion.*] Strange, I can't find it . . .

LOPAHIN: What are you looking for?

VARYA: Packed it myself, and I don't remember . . . [*Pause.*]

LOPAHIN: Where are you going now, Varya?

VARYA: I? To the Ragulins'. I've arranged to take charge there—as housekeeper, if you like.

LOPAHIN: At Yashnevo? About fifty miles from here. [*Pause.*] Well, life in this house is ended!

VARYA: [*Examining luggage.*] Where is it? Perhaps I put it in the chest. Yes, life in this house is ended. . . . There will be no more of it.

LOPAHIN: And I'm just off to Kharkov—by this next train. I've a lot to do there. I'm leaving Yepihodov here . . . I've taken him on.

VARYA: Oh!

LOPAHIN: Last year at this time, it was snowing, if you remember, but now it's sunny and there's no wind. It's cold, though. . . . It must be three below.

VARYA: I didn't look. [*Pause.*] And besides, our thermometer's broken. [*Pause.* VOICE *from the yard:* "Yermolay Alexeyevich!"]

LOPAHIN: [*As if he had been waiting for the call.*] This minute! [*Exits quickly.*]

[VARYA *sits on the floor and sobs quietly, her head on a bundle of clothes. Enter* MME. RANEVSKAYA *cautiously.*]

MME. RANEVSKAYA: Well? [*Pause.*] We must be going.

VARYA: [*Wiping her eyes.*] Yes, it's time, Mamma dear. I'll be able to get to the Ragulins' today, if only we don't miss the train.

MME. RANEVSKAYA: [*At the door.*] Anya, put your things on.

[*Enter* ANYA, GAYEV, CHARLOTTA. GAYEV *wears a heavy overcoat with*

---

4. Go on! (French).

a hood. Enter servants and coachmen. YEPIHODOV *bustles about the luggage.*]

MME. RANEVSKAYA: Now we can start on our journey.

ANYA: [*Joyfully.*] On our journey!

GAYEV: My friends, my dear, cherished friends, leaving this house forever, can I be silent? Can I, at leave-taking, refrain from giving utterance to those emotions that now fill my being?

ANYA: [*Imploringly.*] Uncle!

VARYA: Uncle, Uncle dear, don't.

GAYEV: [*Forlornly.*] I'll bank the yellow in the side pocket . . . I'll be silent . . .

[*Enter* TROFIMOV, *then* LOPAHIN.]

TROFIMOV: Well, ladies and gentlemen, it's time to leave.

LOPAHIN: Yepihodov, my coat.

MME. RANEVSKAYA: I'll sit down just a minute. It seems as though I'd never before seen what the walls of this house were like, the ceilings, and now I look at them hungrily, with such tender affection.

GAYEV: I remember when I was six years old sitting on that window sill on Whitsunday,[5] watching my father going to church.

MME. RANEVSKAYA: Has everything been taken?

LOPAHIN: I think so. [*Putting on his overcoat.*] Yepihodov, see that every-thing's in order.

YEPIHODOV: [*In a husky voice.*] You needn't worry, Yermolay Alexeyevich.

LOPAHIN: What's the matter with your voice?

YEPIHODOV: I just had a drink of water. I must have swallowed something.

YASHA: [*Contemptuously.*] What ignorance!

MME. RANEVSKAYA: When we're gone, not a soul will be left here.

LOPAHIN: Until the spring.

[VARYA *pulls an umbrella out of a bundle, as though about to hit someone with it.* LOPAHIN *pretends to be frightened.*]

VARYA: Come, come, I had no such idea!

TROFIMOV: Ladies and gentlemen, let's get into the carriages—it's time. The train will be in directly.

VARYA: Petya, there they are, your rubbers, by that trunk. [*Tearfully.*] And what dirty old things, they are!

TROFIMOV: [*Puts on rubbers.*] Let's go, ladies and gentlemen.

GAYEV: [*Greatly upset, afraid of breaking down.*] The train . . . the station. . . . Three cushions in the side pocket, I'll bank this one in the corner . . .

MME. RANEVSKAYA: Let's go.

LOPAHIN: Are we all here? No one in there? [*Locks the side door on the left.*] There are some things stored here, better lock up. Let us go!

ANYA: Good-bye, old house! Good-bye, old life!

TROFIMOV: Hail to you, new life!

[*Exits with* ANYA: VARYA *looks round the room and goes out slowly.* YASHA *and* CHARLOTTA *with her dog go out.*]

LOPAHIN: And so, until the spring. Go along, friends . . . Bye-bye! [*Exits.*]

---

5. Or Pentecost, a Christian festival occurring on the seventh Sunday after Easter.

[MME. RANEVSKAYA *and* GAYEV *remain alone. As though they had been waiting for this, they throw themselves on each other's necks, and break into subdued, restrained sobs, afraid of being overheard.*]

GAYEV: [*In despair.*] My sister! My sister!

MME. RANEVSKAYA: Oh, my orchard—my dear, sweet, beautiful orchard! My life, my youth, my happiness—good-bye! Good-bye!

[*Voice of* ANYA, *gay and summoning:* "Mamma!" *Voice of* TROFIMOV, *gay and excited:* "Halloo!"]

MME. RANEVSKAYA: One last look at the walls, at the windows. . . . Our poor mother loved to walk about this room . . .

GAYEV: My sister, my sister!

[*Voice of* ANYA: "Mamma!" *Voice Of* TROFIMOV: "Halloo!"]

MME. RANEVSKAYA: We're coming.

[*They go out. The stage is empty. The sound of doors being locked, of carriages driving away. Then silence. In the stillness is heard the muffled sound of the ax striking a tree, a mournful, lonely sound.*

Footsteps are heard. FIRS *appears in the doorway on the right. He is dressed as usual in a jacket and white waistcoat and wears slippers. He is ill.*]

FIRS: [*Goes to the door, tries the handle.*] Locked! They've gone . . . [*Sits down on the sofa.*] They've forgotten me. . . . Never mind . . . I'll sit here a bit . . . I'll wager Leonid Andreyevich hasn't put his fur coat on, he's gone off in his light overcoat . . . [*Sighs anxiously.*] I didn't keep an eye on him. . . . Ah, when they're young, they're green . . . [*Mumbles something indistinguishable.*] Life has gone by as if I had never lived. [*Lies down.*] I'll lie down a while. . . There's no strength left in you, old fellow; nothing is left, nothing. Ah, you addlehead!

[*Lies motionless. A distant sound is heard coming from the sky, as it were, the sound of a snapping string mournfully dying away. All is still again, and nothing is heard but the strokes of the ax against a tree far away in the orchard.*]

Part III

THE TWENTIETH CENTURY: SELF AND OTHER IN GLOBAL CONTEXT

The World

ca. 1913

GREENLAND
(Den.)

ICELAND
(Den.)

ALASKA
(U.S.)

C A N A D A

U N I T E D
S T A T E S

ATLANTIC
OCEAN

NOR

GREAT
BRITAIN

IRELAND

ENGLAND

DENM
NE
BELG

LUX

FRANCE

SWIT

Azores
(Port.)

PORTUGAL

SPAIN

Bermuda
(Br.)

Madeira
(Port.)

MOROCCO

Bahamas (Br.)

Canary Is.
(Sp.)

ALGER

Hawaiian Islands
(U.S.)

MEXICO

BR.
HONDURAS

CUBA

HAITI
DOMINICAN REPUBLIC
Puerto Rico (U.S.)

RIO DE ORO

Cape Verde Is.
(Port.)

FRENCH W

JAMAICA

Guadeloupe (Fr.)
Martinique (Fr.)

SENEGAL

GUATEMALA
EL SALVADOR
HONDURAS
NICARAGUA
COSTA RICA

Grenada
(Br.)

Barbados (Br.)
Trinidad (Br.)

GAMBIA
PORT. GUINEA
SIERRA LEONE
LIBERIA

PANAMA

VENEZUELA

BR. GUIANA
DUTCH GUIANA
FR. GUIANA

COLOMBIA

IVORY COAST
GOLD COAST
TOGOLAND
NIGERIA

P A C I F I C

Galapagos Is.

ECUADOR

B R A Z I L

Ascension
(Br.)

CAMEROONS
SP. GUINEA
FR. CONGO

Marquesas Is.

PERU

ANGO

French Polynesia

BOLIVIA

St. Helena
(Br.)

Tahiti

O C E A N

PARAGUAY

GERM
SOUTH-W
AFR

ATLANTIC

CHILE

URUGUAY

ARGENTINA

Tristan da Cunha
(Br.)

O C E A N

Falkland Is.
(Br.)

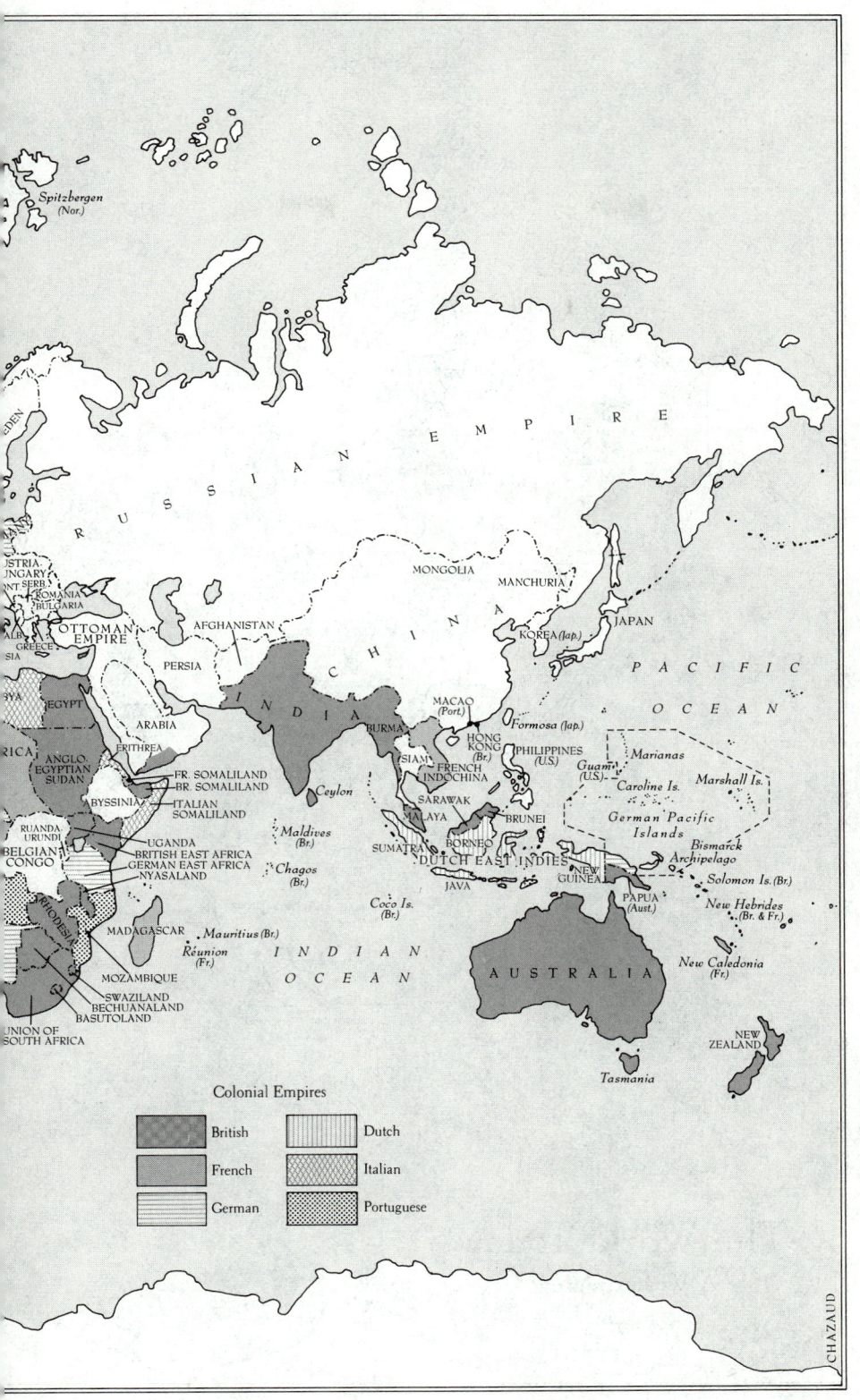

Spitzbergen
(Nor.)

R U S S I A N   E M P I R E

MONGOLIA   MANCHURIA

AUSTRIA-
HUNGARY   KOREA (Jap.)   JAPAN
INT. SERB.
ROMANIA
BULGARIA

ALB.   AFGHANISTAN
GREECE
SIA   OTTOMAN
                    EMPIRE
                                        P A C I F I C

RBYA   EGYPT   PERSIA   I N D I A   C H I N A
                                                        O C E A N
                            ARABIA   MACAO
ANGLO.   (Port.)
EGYPTIAN   BURMA   HONG   Formosa (Jap.)
RICA   SUDAN   KONG
                  ERITREA   SIAM   (Br.)   PHILIPPINES   Marianas
                   FR. SOMALILAND   FRENCH   (U.S.)
              BYSSINIA BR. SOMALILAND   Ceylon INDOCHINA   Guam   Marshall Is.
                     ITALIAN   (U.S.) Caroline Is.
RUANDA   SOMALILAND   MALAYA   BRUNEI
URUNDI   Maldives   German Pacific
           UGANDA   (Br.)   SUMATRA BORNEO   Islands
BELGIAN   BRITISH EAST AFRICA   DUTCH EAST INDIES NEW   Bismarck
CONGO   GERMAN EAST AFRICA   Chagos   JAVA   GUINEA Archipelago
           NYASALAND   (Br.)   Solomon Is. (Br.)

RHODESIA   Coco Is.   PAPUA   New Hebrides
                            (Br.)   (Aust.) (Br. & Fr.)
         MADAGASCAR   Mauritius (Br.)   New Caledonia
                     Réunion   I N D I A N   A U S T R A L I A   (Fr.)
         MOZAMBIQUE   (Fr.)   O C E A N
         SWAZILAND
         BECHUANALAND   NEW
UNION OF BASUTOLAND   ZEALAND
SOUTH AFRICA
                                                     Tasmania

Colonial Empires

	British		Dutch
	French		Italian
	German		Portuguese

CHAZAUD

The World Today
A Western View

The World Today
An Eastern View

OCEAN

GREENLAND

ALASKA

C A N A D A

Hudson Bay

Labrador Sea

Bering Sea

Aleutian Islands

N O R T H   P A C I F I C   U N I T E D

O C E A N   S T A T E S

Colorado

A T L A N T I C

O C E A N

HAITI

HAWAII   CUBA   DOMINICAN
Honolulu   REPUBLIC
PUERTO RICO

MEXICO   BELIZE
JAMAICA   *Barbados*

GUATEMALA   *Caribbean Sea*
EL SALVADOR   GUYANA
MARSHALL   HONDURAS   SURINAME
ISLANDS   NICARAGUA   VENEZUELA   FR. GUIANA
COSTA RICA
KIRIBATI   PANAMA   COLOMBIA

TUVALU   *Galapagos Is.*   ECUADOR   *Amazon*

SOLOMON   PERU   B R A Z I L
ISLANDS

Samoa Is.   *French Polynesia*
WESTERN   BOLIVIA
VANUATU   SAMOA   *Tahiti*   PARAGUAY
FIJI
New Caledonia   TONGA   CHILE

ane   S O U T H   P A C I F I C

O C E A N   ARGENTINA   URUGUAY

NEW
ZEALAND
Wellington

Falkland Is.

*Antarctic
Peninsula*

CHAZAUD

The Twentieth Century

Modern consciousness in the twentieth century is remarkable. Not because it is "modern" (every period is modern in its own eyes), but because it is for the first time beginning to be truly global. No beckoning frontier, no large area of the globe remains unvisited and mysterious for future explorers to map. Breathtaking advances in technology, transformations of modern states, the rapid spread of international corporations, cultural exchanges occurring rapidly and inevitably as communication and transportation networks link all sections of the world—all have created an era in which the essential reality is interconnectedness rather than isolation. Not that this simplifies matters. Connections bring their own problems, and they are not always welcome. Connections inevitably change the system, disrupt tradition, and confront people with many more choices than they were aware of previously. In many ways, this is the story of the twentieth century as it draws to a close.

These days the terms *modern* and *modernization* reappear everywhere as a key to change. They can be used as a weapon to bring about "progress," or rejected in favor of "tradition," or defined differently according to context and situation. In the West (understood as Europe and America), modernization has meant industrial progress, a refusal of positivist certainty about the nature of the world, and a desire to transcend narrowly nationalist politics. Elsewhere, modernization has been equated with "Westernization" (especially in technology, industry, political structures, and mass culture) and has been supported or rejected with that understanding.

Modernization has also arrived at different speeds in different parts of the world, growing gradually in Europe out of previous centuries, but coming far more rapidly to non-Western countries, often as a forced change brought about by colonialist politics and economic necessity. Little pockets of Western prosperity around the world—colonial enclaves in China, Africa, India, and South America—drove home the difference between colonizing and colonized societies, and the wealthy Western countries made a tempting model for regions beset by poverty, disease, and social unrest. Political leaders soon equated progress with Westernization, and many sought prosperity by transforming their societies into the closest possible imitation of Europe. Western success, they felt (and were told), was the result not merely of industrialization but also of a whole set of distinctive values and institutions—the concepts of individualism and democracy, attention to literacy and general education, private ownership and a thriving middle class, religious freedom, scientific method, public institutions, and (sometimes) the emancipation of women.

Colonial governments considered it their duty to disseminate these values by setting up school systems where European languages were used instead of local ones, and Western literature and philosophy were taught instead of indigenous culture. As a result, twentieth-century Westernization in many countries not only promised advances in literacy and standard of living but seemed to require the suppression of indigenous traditions, including centuries of literature (much of it oral) as well as languages, philosophy, religion, and models of community life. Works in this volume by Chinua Achebe, Léopold Sédar Senghor, Wole Soyinka, Albert Camus, Naguib Mahfouz, Kojima Nobuo, Derek Walcott, Lorna Goodison, and Nadine Gordimer illustrate this conflict of different ways of life. Yet these same works also demonstrate another fact of global existence: that the clash of opposites is also a set of inextricably intermingled experiences, pointing to a fuller understanding of cultural (and multicultural) identity.

Modernism is not the same as modernization. Twentieth-century modernism is a literary and artistic movement with roots in Europe, and modernist works—translated and republished in great numbers—were exported around the globe along with the general expansion of Western culture. Many non-Western writers and intellectuals saw modernist style as the latest image of a progressive Western culture and a technique embodying an "advanced" way of thought. They borrowed artistic forms that were a gradual outgrowth of experimentation and literary evolution in Europe and America and used them as instant models in a new pattern of global crisscrossing that has overlaid narrower lines of literary evolution. In some instances, the militantly new aura of modernist works was prized as a way of rejecting traditional authority, an oblique means of transforming local perceptions. Although a reaction has since set in owing to shifts in economic and political power and to a greater acceptance of cultural difference, Western concepts of modernism continue to influence modern literature and literary theory the world over.

THE EUROPEAN ORIGINS OF TWENTIETH-CENTURY MODERNISM

Western modernity evolved out of, and in contrast to, a specific historical situation. This situation differed in other parts of the world, especially in feudal societies without industry, middle class, or a popular press and where artistic tradition supported highly stylized works with mythological subjects. Change followed different lines, therefore, according to whether the immediate past was feudal or democratic and whether the audience favored exquisite craftsmanship or, as in the West, versions of realism. In conservative societies such as China, Japan, and India, the foreign examples that helped usher in modern literature were likely to come from the same European realism against which Western modernism reacted. By the end of the twentieth century, however, Western modernist techniques could be found in literature around the world, usually blended with perspectives drawn from Realism.

In Europe, the idea of modernity was already a source of public debate and widespread anxiety as the Industrial Revolution transformed social, economic, and political life faster, it seemed, than such changes could peacefully be absorbed. Some saw it as a time of decadence and the loss of stable values. Others saw it, more optimistically, as an era in which a progressive Europe would lead the rest of the world to its own pinnacle of achievement (a point of view shared only briefly by the colonized countries). In science, philosophy, social theory, and the arts, the nineteenth century prepared both the evolution and the rebellion of the twentieth.

Scientific Rationalism

By the end of the nineteenth century, unprecedented developments in science had encouraged Westerners to believe that they would soon master all the secrets of the universe. The Enlightenment notion of the world as a machine—something whose parts could be named and seen to function—came back into favor. Discoveries in different fields seemed to make the universe more rational and hence predictable. In chemistry, there was John Dalton's (1766–1844) atomic theory and Dimitri Mendeleyev's (1834–1907) periodic table of elements; in physics, James

Maxwell's (1831–1879) field theory unifying the study of electricity, magnetism, and light. The further development of Newtonian ideas made it possible to study the fixed stars, and spectral analysis showed the essential homogeneity of the universe. Technological applications suggested that these discoveries would serve humanity, not master it. Thermodynamics explained the processes of energy transformation, and locomotives and steamships promised rapid transportation throughout the world. Daguerreotype photography (developed by Louis Daguerre [1787–1851]) provided a documentary record. Finally, the history of living nature itself became an object of study when Charles Darwin (1809–1882) examined the evolution of species according to material evidence, without reference to divine laws or purpose.

The enthusiasm for scientific discovery was not confined to scientists. Auguste Comte (1798–1857), a French philosopher known as the founder of "positivism," held that scientific method constituted a total world view in which everything would ultimately be explained, including human society. Comte proposed a science of humanity that would analyze and define the laws governing human society (the first sociology). It became evident, however, that the results of scientific method depended on the objectivity of the scientist's point of view. Count Gobineau (1816–1882) proposed a "scientific" description of society in which there were three races (white, black, and yellow) with innate qualities and in which the white race (predictably, for this white Frenchman) was the superior category. Gobineau's writings laid the groundwork for much "scientific" racism later on, until he himself became a subject of analysis for scientists interested in explaining the history of race prejudice.

In literature, the historian and critic Hippolyte Taine (1828–1893) proposed a science of culture in which each literary work could be categorized as the combined product of its "race, milieu, and time." The novelist Emile Zola offered as scientific justification for his series on the degeneracy of the Rougon-Macquart family an *Introduction to the Study of Experimental Medicine* by Dr. Claude Bernard (1813–1878). Nowadays, it is easier to recognize the preexisting bias that flaws these large explanatory systems and to be cautious of claims of "scientific truth," especially in descriptions of human nature. The enormous wealth created by technology and scientific method, however, offered a powerful incentive for other regions of the world to imitate the Western example.

Western social theorists shared with the philosopher Comte the vision of creating a perfect society by understanding social "laws." Utopian socialists like the French Charles Fourier (1772–1837) and the Comte de Saint-Simon (1760–1825) and the Welsh industrialist Robert Owen (1771–1858) proposed various methods for organizing society and planning its economy. The English philosopher and economist John Stuart Mill (1806–1873) preached the dignity of man, the rights of women, and the possibility of happiness for all. By far the most important and influential theorist was the German Karl Marx (1819–1883), whose *Communist Manifesto* (1848) and *Capital* (1867) proposed a scientific theory of world history driven by broad economic forces. According to Marx, the most basic material needs—food, shelter, and the social relationships enabling group survival—provide an economic foundation from which all other aspects of human culture are derived. His description of modern workers as alienated cogs in the industrial economic machine, no longer owning their own labor, expressed for many the antihuman aspect of modern technological progress. Like his contemporaries, he believed in the power of rational systems to find answers for social ills; he described the division of modern industrial society into the two competing forces of capital and labor (the proletariat) and proposed the theory of dialectical materialism to explain the processes of history.

Reactions to Rationalism

The debate about scientific rationalism was inevitably a debate about knowledge and human values. In the nineteenth century, one of the strongest opponents of positivism and its belief in rational solutions was the German philosopher Friedrich Nietzsche (1844–1900). Nietzsche focused on the individual, not society, and admired only the *Übermensch*, the superhuman being who refused to be bound by the prevailing social paradigms of nationalism, Christianity, faith in science, loyalty to the state, or bourgeois civilized comfort. Nietzsche's distinction between Dionysian (instinctual) and Apollonian (intellectual) forces in human beings, his insistence on the individual's complete freedom (and responsibility) in a world that lacks transcendental law ("God is dead"), and his attack on the unimaginative mediocrity of mass society in the modern industrial world have made him a powerful influence in twentieth-century Western thought. In general, he gave a quasi-philosophical focus to the underlying distrust of rationalist perspectives that was already alive in other parts of the world and had begun to emerge in nineteenth-century Europe with explorations of magic and the occult, theosophy, and the constructed image of an "Eastern" spirituality complementary to the scientific, soulless West.

The shape and intensity of this debate in Europe were dictated for many years by a historical event that turned the younger generations against everything inherited from the recent past: the Great War (World War I, 1914–18). In spite of the confident rationalism of the political leaders of "Papa's Europe" (a term of resentment used by many to describe an authoritarian, patriarchal society that claimed to have all the answers), World War I had for the first time involved the whole continent of Europe and the United States in battle (reaching, with Turkey, into Asia Minor) and was the first "total war" in which modern weapons spared no one, including civilians. Clearly, something was wrong. An entire generation was lost in the trenches, and the survivors emerged resolved to reexamine the bases of certainty, the structures of knowledge, the systems of belief, and the repositories of authority in a society that had allowed such a war to occur. Their reaction would also be reflected in literature, not only in subject matter but—for many—in a new use of language, in new ways of representing our knowledge of the world, and, most especially, new hesitations about subscribing to any single mode of understanding it. They drew on areas beyond the intellect, interrogating modes of human consciousness and feeling in an intellectual attempt to go beyond the self-imposed limitations of previous rationalism.

Several thinkers were particularly important in formulating alternatives to the narrow rationalism of positivist philosophy. The French philosopher Henri Bergson (1859–1941) attacked scientific rationality as artificial and unreal because it froze everything in conceptual space; it ignored the whole dimension of life as it is actually experienced. For Bergson, reality was a fluid, living force (*élan vital*) that could only be apprehended by consciousness. Instead of quantitative and logical inquiry, he proposed intuiting the "immediate data of consciousness" as an alternate, nonscientific means of knowledge. This intuition was not a kind of spiritualism or a meditative philosophy such as Buddhism: Bergson neither ignored nor tried to escape the world of the senses but wished to register its immediate impact with great precision. Authors were not slow to perceive the implications of his prescription for representing reality. Marcel Proust, searching to discover his identity through layers of "lost time," James Joyce, imitating the stream of consciousness in the written flow of words, the later author Tanizaki Jun'ichirō, representing cultural difference as a matter of finely differentiated sensations—all reflect a twentieth-century, Bergsonian change in the way reality is perceived and represented. Bergson himself received the Nobel Prize in literature in 1927, both for the creative imagination shown in his own work and for his literary influence.

Sigmund Freud (1856–1939), the founder of psychoanalysis, was another influential figure. Freud's study of subconscious motives and instinctual drives revealed a level of activity that had been largely ignored outside of literature and was not considered a productive subject for continued "rational" inquiry. His essays and case studies argued that dreams and manias contain their own networks of meaning and that human beings cannot properly be understood without taking into consideration the irrational as well as the rational level of their existence. All are caught up, he suggested, in the process of mediating the same sexual drives and civilizational repressions that caused neurosis in his own patients.

Many of Freud's theories are questioned today (his assumption that every woman considers herself an incomplete man, for example). Some of his psychoanalytic categories seem too rigid. He rejected divergent views, and he ignored the possibility that his own cultural stereotypes influenced both his theories and his view of patients. The mythic images he used to convey some of his basic concepts, like the Oedipus complex, were drawn from a heavily patriarchal Western mythology and are, therefore, less persuasive to societies—like India, for example—whose mythology contains strong matriarchal images. Freud's insistence on a fundamental and universally true image of human sexuality has also been interpreted as a defensive reaction against racial and social discord that included anti-Semitism: to prejudice and alienation, he would oppose a grand unifying image. His chief importance, however, lies elsewhere, in his brilliant and even poetic attempts to clarify patterns of human thought and emotion. He focused attention on the way everyday "rational" behavior is shaped by unconscious impulses and hidden motivations and on the way human beings actually create (and modify) their images of self through engaging in dialogue with others. Freud was indebted to the great poets, and he, like Bergson, was honored as a creative artist when he received the Goethe Prize in 1930.

It is probably impossible for any poet, novelist, or playwright after Freud to write without taking into consideration the psychological undercurrents of human behavior—whether or not the author has read him. Some post-Freudian writers derive themes and images from the idea of subconscious motivations guiding interpersonal relations and social behavior. Others employ a stream of consciousness technique very much like Freud's therapeutic tactic of free association. Some exploit the aesthetic possibilities of a surface pattern of apparent intentions concealing a contradictory pattern of repressed desires. Still others exploit the techniques of an otherwise-empty dialogue that creates its own reality through repetition. Freud can even be cited against his own intentions: the surrealists, while quoting him, completely reverse his aim by pronouncing madness not an illness to be cured but an insight into a larger reality.

Literature, however, is also a matter of words and not just themes and patterns of consciousness. Different concepts of language have colored literary expression at different times, and twentieth-century literature is no exception. Experimental language in the early part of the century shows the influence of psychoanalysis and of Symbolist poetics. Its syntax and imagery emulate Freudian free association, the complex inner patterns favored by nineteenth-century Symbolist poetry and the artistic effects of Impressionist or Cubist painting. Later works reflect a change in linguistic theory. Nineteenth-century positivism had assumed that language was an accurate tool for direct reference to reality (a view parodied in "The sun is called a sun because it *looks* like a sun"). In contrast, the Swiss linguist Ferdinand de Saussure (1857–1913) and the Austrian philosopher Ludwig Wittgenstein (1889–1951) emphasized that language is tied to society and usage: descriptions are not "accurate," for they can never grasp absolute reality or give "real" names. All that language can do, as they see it, is to create socially agreed-upon labels ("signifiers" pointing to a "signified"). The sun remains the same gaseous ball whether it is named *sun*, *soleil*, or *taiyang*. What works in conversation is not the thing itself but the way the label—the word used to describe it—provides a recognizable common ground for different speakers. Language may therefore be described as a "game" played with words: a serious game, since it shapes our vision of reality. Modernist literature shows how words reshape the world we think we know. Thus Wallace Stevens's "moon creeps up / To the bubbling of bassoons," and Gertrude Stein diversifies a carafe into "a kind of glass and a cousin, a spectacle and nothing strange a single hurt color and an arrangement in a system to pointing."

In this perspective, both literature and linguistic systems are seen as *games*, combinations of *pieces* (words) and *rules* (grammar, syntax, and other conventions). On MTV, publicity for the latest record albums uses fragmented, kaleidoscopic images to express a confused or rebellious state of mind and also to appear artistically up to date. Writers stressing the gamelike nature of language combine words and word fragments to exhibit the play of relationships, instead of struggling to find the "right" word dear to Flaubert. Game theory can be frustrating in practice. Samuel Beckett's (1906–1989) tongue-tied characters in *Endgame*, or the endlessly chattering narrators of his novels, make brief conversational sense but finally express very little, unless it be the absurd inexpressibility of the human condition. At its most extreme, this theory leads to a view of all language as an endless networking of associations: a situation in which real communication is impossible. "Reality," instead of becoming more accessible, ultimately disappears inside language itself.

Yet the conclusions to be drawn from this bleak prospect may be very practical. If a work by Jorge Luis Borges, Beckett or Alain Robbe-Grillet persuades us that language determines how we see the world as well as our own place in it, then we will look for that shaping use of language. Modern advertising has already profited by the concept of different communicative worlds. Television commercials fragment and reconstruct reality, racing through sets of highly associative words and images to persuade you that the sponsor "speaks your language" and can deliver what you really want. Literary criticism has learned to recognize hitherto unseen structures and systems of reference embedded in the written text or alive in oral performance. Nor are new techniques of reading restricted to contemporary texts, for the idea of inexhaustible word play has also illuminated a traditional definition of the literary masterwork: that it can bear reading and rereading by different generations and even different cultures and always seems to tell us something about ourselves. Such works are not exhausted by a single theme or audience because they reach out into the world on many different planes, achieving an extraordinary connotative richness so as to make accessible many systems of meaning.

Theories of linguistic play have not been isolated from concurrent developments in the sciences or from the impact of historical events. Psychology, anthropology, and physics also stressed relationships as they redefined current concepts of human nature and the material world. Gestalt psychology (*Gestalt* is German for "form") after 1912 suggested that the meaning of individual phenomena was not to be found in microscopic analysis of separate pieces but rather in organized wholes. It was the "shape of things" that mattered.

Shapes and the relation of parts were important in structural anthropology, with the anthropologist Claude Lévi-Strauss (born 1908) describing human society as a system of worldviews or "codes" that could be compared from culture to culture. From his early research on the primitive Nambikwara Indians of Brazil to his later comparisons of primitive with modern cultures, Lévi-Strauss has insisted that anthropological knowledge comes only from imaginative participation in the codes governing each society (kinship rules, taboos, habits of social interaction, folkloric imagination). His "structural method" appealed to literary critics as a way to illuminate simultaneously a work's inner structural relationship and its relationships to the individual and culture that produced it.

Deeper structures were proposed by Jungian psychology—based on the work of Carl Gustav Jung (1875–1961)—which claimed that humanity shares a "collective unconscious," a buried level of universal experience tapped by myth, religion, and art. Accordingly, the common experience of our species is revealed in archetypes (master patterns) like the figures of the hero, seer, or Great Mother, the image of the quest, or the process of death and rebirth. Much folklore and ritual poetry (including examples such as Birago Diop's *Mother Crocodile*, Andrew Peynetsa's *The Boy and the Deer*) use variations of such archetypal figures. In retrospect, works such as T. S. Eliot's *The Waste Land* may be seen to incorporate Jungian archetypal images, alluding to a universal level of human experience. In the case of Eliot, actual inspiration came from another synthesizing enterprise, James George Frazer's vast masterwork of anthropology, *The Golden Bough* (1890–1915), which profoundly influenced the intellectual climate of Europe and America with its demonstration of the striking resemblances among world mythologies and religions.

The social or "human" sciences were not alone in paying attention to the role played by the perceiver. The "hard" sciences of physics and mathematics were doing the same thing, with results that shocked the general public and intrigued writers and artists. Albert Einstein's theory of relativity (1905) abandoned the concepts of absolute motion and the absolute difference of space and time and, working from pure mathematical logic, proposed that reality should be understood as a four-dimensional continuum (called space-time) that literally could not be expressed either in words or in the old three-dimensional models of Newtonian physics. Since *relativity* implied "relativism" in the popular mind, Einstein's discovery (despite his own religious beliefs) was widely thought to pull the ground out from under any certainty—scientific or religious—about the physical world. Even more disturbing, Werner Heisenberg's "uncertainty principle" (1927) proclaimed that scientific measurement (in this case, the measurement of electrons) was always a matter of statistical approximation, a "probability function" and not an exact description. Ironically, what was scientifically an increasingly *accurate* perception of the nature of things often seemed just the opposite to the general public. People could no longer refer to "self-evident truths" in nature, or go "back to basics," when scientists had just shown that the "basic" world was not what it seemed. Many writers, however, and Proust among the earliest, welcomed what they saw as a richer view of experience and scientific confirmation that reality could be represented in a shifting and fluid perspective.

The world's major religions and philosophies have all had something to say about the nature of reality. They explain the origin and structure of the universe (in ancient Egyptian hymns, the biblical Book of Genesis, the Eleventh Teaching from the *Bhagavad-Gita*, and the Popol Vuh), preach escaping the bonds of the material world for a higher spiritual existence (Buddhism and Hinduism), assert the interpenetration of all existence at all times (Taoism) or the linkage of all forms of life (African and North American indigenous religions), and discuss human mortality. They provide models—differing from culture to culture—that give pattern and meaning to human experience, bridging the gap between things as they appear to us in the details of daily life and dimensions that exceed ordinary measurement.

The modern philosophy that coincides with the rise of Modernism is similarly an inquiry into the reliability of appearances. Ever since Plato, Western philosophers have struggled systematically to understand the relationship between appearance and reality. In the twentieth century, such issues are the central concern of the philosophy known as phenomenology (phenomena are literally *things as they appear*) and its off-shoot, existentialism. Both approaches investigate the role of perception in establishing reality. The phenomenology proposed by Edmund Husserl (1859–1938) described all consciousness as consciousness *of* something *by* someone and concluded that every object of study should be imagined in "brackets"—not as a thing in itself but as part of a relationship between perceiver and perceived.

The ethical implications of this view were taken up by the philosophers Martin Heidegger (1889–1976) and Jean-Paul Sartre (1905–1980), who questioned the meaning of existence in a world without preexisting truths, values, or moral laws. Heidegger's profoundly somber vision of the "absurd" condition of human beings, "thrown into the world" without any understanding of their fate, influenced many writers and especially the "theater of the absurd" that flourished after World War II, of which Samuel Beckett and Eugène Ionesco (1912–1994) are the best-known writers. Sartre, who was much more of a social activist, derived from the same absurd freedom an ideal of human "authenticity," which consists in choosing our actions at each point, avoiding the "bad faith" of pretending that others are responsible for our choices, and choosing not just for oneself but "for all" inasmuch as each choice envisages the creation of a new world. This kind of existentialism, with its appealing image of the lonely tragic hero who acts to benefit society without any hope of reward (Sartre portrayed such a hero as Orestes in *The Flies*, based on Aeschylus's *Oresteia*, in Volume 1), had tremendous influence on European writers immediately after World War II. Albert Camus, writing at the same time as Sartre, offers in *The Guest* a good example of existentialism's emphasis on freedom, responsibility, and social commitment or "engagement."

Existentialism's popular appeal in the 1940s and 1950s was undoubtedly enhanced by the fact that it was a philosophic attempt to recover clear vision—and a basis for action—in a perplexed and apparently meaningless world. The notion of philosophical absurdity corresponded to a very real confusion caused by the radical historical changes taking place in the first half of the century. By 1950, there had been two world wars, the second of which was truly global, and a sweeping realignment of geopolitical forces that saw the flourishing of Marxism and the establishment of major Communist states. Almost all the old monarchies had been overthrown and colonial empires were being dismantled as the emerging nations of Africa and Asia struggled for independence and self-definition. The wielders of authority became the enormous buck-passing bureaucracies of the modern state, multinational corporations, international governmental organizations, and ethnic alliances. Transportation and telecommunications progressed to an extent only envisaged in earlier ages' science fiction and effectively created but also shrank the global community. The rise of the modern industrial state set up new political, cultural, and economic tensions, the most important of which was a widening gulf between the West and "less developed" countries.

These changes in historical conditions had visible repercussions on modern literature and art. Cultural parochialism—the belief that there is only one correct view of the world (one's own)—was much harder to maintain when people traveled widely and experienced different ways of life. Racial and ethnic stereotypes were challenged, and traditional ideas of identity and social class broken down. Romantic heroism and aristocratic "rank" seemed irrelevant to soldiers who died anonymously in the trenches of World War I or civilians killed at a distance by bombing raids in both wars. The appropriate symbol for modern, impersonal warfare was the Tomb of the Unknown Soldier, first erected in Paris, after World War I, to honor the nameless soldiers who had died defending their country. In literature it was the "common man," not the Romantic hero, whose plight was portrayed. The conventional roles of the sexes also came under examination. Western women achieved civil rights they had been denied for centuries: the right to vote (1920 in the United States), the right to have bank accounts and to own and control their own property, the right to be educated equally with men, and the right to enter professions not previously open to them. When women held many jobs previously thought to be masculine ("Rosie the Riveter" was the subject of a famous American poster in World War II), it was no longer possible to pretend that they were incapable of work outside the home. Indeed, it was clear not only that women were quite capable but that they enjoyed taking responsibility in a variety of careers. Later in the century, the image of the emancipated Western woman would be presented as a shocking and even heretical example in traditional Mideastern and African societies; in contrast, the modern Communist Chinese state insisted on women's equality in the workplace. International organizations began to discuss, and women writers to describe, the situation of women in different countries (as do Ingeborg Bachmann, Mariama Bâ, and Lorna Goodison, for example). Globally, the nature of the workplace changed as technological advances brought a range of new machines, services, and types of labor. Technology became everywhere part of the modern literary consciousness, inspiring both enthusiasm and fear, and initiating all over again the question of human values in a society where so much could be done (and so many controlled) by the use of machines.

A Century of Isms

The literary and artistic movements of the twentieth century are part of this evolution; they were shaped by it and helped shape it for others. Many flourished in Europe and America and were exported to other parts of the globe where they flourished or failed according to their relevance for local conditions. The twentieth century has been called by some a "century of isms," or of "vanguardism," reflecting the fact that so many different groups have tried to find an appropriate artistic response to contemporary history. European Expressionism, Dadaism, Surrealism, and Futurism—each worth exploring—are all different ways of expressing the "reality" of the world. Some appear very unreal at first glance, but all reveal an inner (presumably more important) truth than can be shown by documentary detail alone. Thus Expressionists refused the direct representation of reality, or even impressions of it (as in Impressionism), in favor of expressing an inner vision, emotion, or spiritual reality. *The Scream*, a painting by the Norwegian Edvard Munch (1863–1944) evokes a whole realm of spiritual agony, and expressionist writers like the Germans Frank Wedekind (1864–1918) and Gottfried Benn (1886–1956) assert their alienation from an industrial society whose inhumanity repels them. To bring out an underlying psychological distress that "objective" descriptions fail to capture, expressionist writers subordinate conventional (rational) style and let emotion dictate the structure of their works, emphasizing rhythm, disrupted narrative line and broken syntax, and distorted imagery.

Futurism loudly proclaimed its enthusiasm for the dynamic new machine age. F. T. Marinetti (1876–1944) wrote in the first Futurist Manifesto (1908) that "a roaring motor car which seems to run on machine-gun fire is more beautiful than the Winged Victory of Samothrace" (a famous Greek statue). Italian Futurism is still tainted by Marinetti's glorification of terrorism and war and his delighted description (from the pilot's point of view) of bombs bursting below. Russian futurism was suppressed, along with other experimental art, by the conservative tastes of the government in the USSR. Nonetheless, the Futurists' experiments in typography, in free association, in rapid shifts and breaks of syntax; their manipulation of sounds and word placement for special effects; their harshness and stark vision; and above all their eagerness to depict the new age were widely imitated.

Dada-Surrealism is the best known of the European "isms" and the only one to have followers today. Dada began in Zurich in 1916 as a movement of absolute revolt against Papa's Europe, and the word *dada* is a nonsense word that represents the disgust the Dadaists felt for the traditional middle-class values (patriotism, religion, morality, and rationalism) that they blamed for World War I. Dada set out to subvert authority and break all the rules (including those of art), hoping to liberate the creative imagination. Marcel Duchamp (1887–1968) reversed a series of expectations when he named a piece *Why Not Sneeze, Rrose Sélavy?* (1921): it was a small birdcage filled with what looked like sugar lumps but turned out (when you lifted the heavy cage) to be carved marble cubes. Tristan Tzara (1896–1963) attacked the notion of the inspired genius by giving a recipe for the Dada poem: the "poet" was to cut words out of a newspaper, shake them in a paper bag, and pull them out one at a time. Dada creations were attacks on the mind and emotions; Surrealists emphasized a "revolution of the mind" in which ordinary habits of seeing yielded to a different, "surreal" or "super-real," vision. Freedom from conventional perspectives, they felt, was a first step in reforming society.

Surrealists especially aimed to bring about a fuller awareness of human experience, including both conscious and unconscious states. In France, the Surrealist Manifestoes of 1924 and 1930 proclaimed that Surrealism was a means of expressing "the actual functioning of thought," "the total recuperation of our psychic force by a means that is nothing else than the dizzying descent into ourselves." André Breton, the Surrealist leader, had been a medical intern in a psychiatric clinic during World War I and was interested in Freud's theories of the unconscious. The Surrealists experimented with various means to liberate the unconscious imagination and reach a sublime state they called "the marvelous." Dream writing, automatic writing (writing rapidly and continuously whatever comes to mind), riddling games, interruption and collage, and chiefly the creation of startling images opened the mind to new possibilities.

The Surrealist image gains its power by forcibly yoking two unrelated elements; it suggests buried connections and possible relationships overlooked by the logical mind. Thus a poem by Paul Eluard, for example, will begin "Earth is blue like an orange, / Never a mistake; words don't lie . . ." and let the reader sort out the connections of shape, color, and distance that may allow such a perspective. The poet's challenge is clear: "words don't lie." Readers faced with the absurdity of "like an orange" will reach for whatever pattern of meaning might exist in a vision that just barely seems to offer such connections. And there it is, a tenuous but consistent structural relationship of similarity or difference—in shape, color, size, and distance from the perceiver. Surrealist language is structured to arouse the free play of the mind, and its anti-rational and open-ended style foreshadows the emphasis, in later "post-modernist" literature, on word play and radical language games.

Known for its intensity, playfulness, and openness to change, Surrealism has proved to be the most influential and enduring of all these movements, with adherents around the globe. Its impudent rejection of authority and rational thought inspired rebellious writers everywhere, especially in countries where the government linked correct thinking to realistic art. Surrealist themes of liberty, anti-rationality, and the importance of the unconscious mind, and the preferred Surrealist techniques of collage, constant metamorphosis, and a narrative in which it is hard to distinguish between dream and reality permeate modern literature. They find their way into the explosive sequences of Aimé Césaire, the magical images of Gabriel García Márquez, and the dryly puzzling narrative of Murakami Haruki (all in this volume), as well as many others. Surrealist influence has also spread beyond art and literature to advertising, fashion, and MTV, and the term *surrealist* has become a convenient word for unconventional or fantastic works that have no real connection with the movement.

Modernism is the accepted general term for the change in attitudes and artistic strategy that occurred in Europe and America at the beginning of the century. In its broadest sense, it embraces all the separate movements just described. Taken more narrowly, Modernism refers to a group of Anglo-American writers (many associated with the Imagists, 1908–17) who favored clear, precise images and "common speech" and who thought of the work primarily as an art object produced by consummate craft. James Joyce, Ezra Pound, T. S. Eliot, William Faulkner, and Virginia Woolf are examples of Anglo-American modernism and of the larger modernism, too. European modernists used language in an exploratory way, redefining the world of art much as the philosophers and scientists had redefined the world of their own disciplines. They disassembled in order to reconstruct, playing with shifting and contradictory appearances to suggest the shifting and uncertain nature of reality (Luigi Pirandello). They broke up the logically developing plot typical of the nineteenth-century novel and offered instead unexpected connections or sudden changes of perspective (Virginia Woolf). They used interior monologues and free association to express the rhythm of consciousness (Joyce, Woolf). They made much greater use of image clusters, thematic associations, and "musical" patterning to supply the basic structures of both fiction and poetry (Marcel Proust, Wallace Stevens, Eliot). They drew attention to style instead of trying to make it invisible or "transparent" (Eliot, Bertolt Brecht). They blended fantasy with reality while representing real historical or psychological dilemmas (Franz Kafka). They raised age-old questions of human identity in terms of contemporary philosophy and psychology (Freud, Proust, Camus). And they explored ancient and non-Western literatures in search of universal themes and fresh modes of expression (Eliot, Pound, Joyce). Whether their style was elaborate or spare, wordy or elliptical, abstract or concrete, modernist works displayed a highly self-conscious use of language, aiming not only to transform the way we see the world but also to change the way we understand language. This aspect of modernism gave it cultural as well as artistic impact, and young writers in other countries frequently adopted modernist techniques as a way to transform their own society's vision. The brilliant linguistic play of Aimé Césaire's *Notebook of a Return to the Native Land*, for example, displayed a dynamic new vision of black identity and Caribbean culture. Yet modernists in the early twentieth century are still close to nineteenth-century thought in one important respect. Their enterprise assumed, through all its fragmentation, a profoundly rich and unified core to human experience. Modernist experiments with perspective and language were carried on inside still-traditional concepts of individual psychological depth and of the art work as a coherent aesthetic whole. The combination of discontinuous, experimental style with a continuing belief in the wholeness of the human personality and of the art work carries with it the stamp of what we call the modernist (as opposed to the "postmodernist") tradition.

MODERNISM EXPANDS AND EVOLVES

The influence of Modernism, or other isms, on non-Western literary developments of the twentieth century has proved more varied. The smaller movements inside Western modernism lost their separate status when exported, becoming merely part of the whole mosaic of twentieth-century Western culture. This mosaic in turn meshed with local priorities such as an emerging national consciousness, religious tradition, or cultural customs, and the entire picture changed in the process. In some cases, Western literary models were adapted to represent the views of a particular national, religious, or ethnic group. In others, exposure to the West inspired a rediscovery of national literary traditions. In yet others, new ideologies of Western origin—social, political, religious, philosophical—had a much greater pollinating effect than any literary movement. While it is impossible to describe the full range of traditions included in this anthology, a few examples will indicate how modernism and modernity were refracted in twentieth-century non-Western civilizations.

Countries like Japan that attempted to reinvent themselves as equals of the

materially advanced and economically powerful Western nations undertook a tortuous process of cultural absorption and transformation. Technology transfer and
economic integration proved inseparable from institutional change and cultural
diffusion. As the Japanese of the late nineteenth century learned the practical
aspects of Western civilization—bookkeeping, smelting, cotton spinning, ship-
building, principles of the joint-stock corporation—their curiosity about the world
and their traditional receptivity to foreign ways soon transfigured the fabric of
Japanese life.

For intellectuals, including writers, the real issue was not whether modernism
offered a superior refraction of reality, although they would take advantage of modernist style when it suited them. More fundamental questions came to the fore.
Cultural identity is a theme to which writers like Tanizaki Jun'ichirō return again
and again. *In Praise of Shadows* asks what is lost when a nation tries to make itself
over in the image of another. Natsume Sōseki, perhaps the most introspective of
Japan's modern novelists, frames the same question and concludes that each wave
of Westernization hitting Japan is "like sitting at a dinner table and having one
dish after another set before us and then taken away so quickly that, far from
getting a good taste of each one, we can't even enjoy a clear look at what is being
served. A nation, a people, that incurs a civilization like this can only feel a sense
of emptiness, a dissatisfaction and anxiety." Yet it was a Western concept, individualism, that Japanese writers saw as the possible salvation. Part and parcel of Japan's
modernization was its discovery of the emphasis that Western societies place on
human beings as autonomous individual selves. For much of Japanese history,
people in this conservative, group-oriented society were thought of as members of
a unit (a clan, a fief, a class) who fitted somewhere quite precisely on a Confucian
grid of relationships (between ruler and subject, father and son, husband and wife,
elder brother and younger, friend and friend). The mesh of these two networks
was the source of one's identity: an unproblematic part of a larger whole.

More problematic was the attempt to assert one's newfound ego in a manner
that did not infringe on other egos—or to navigate in a culture where individual
independence was still uncharted, where support systems that had developed over
time in democratic, Judaeo-Christian societies for fostering and protecting the
individual were completely missing. On the one hand, writers like Kawabata and
Tanizaki felt that individualism offered the hope of choosing one's own route
through life, colliding with possibilities in a way that would never have been think-
able, and thereby forging one's own personal happiness, the ultimate objective.
Tanizaki's essay on Japanese cultural identity is framed as an extended meditation
on the values of shadow and light, a style evoking the introspective inquiry of
Proust's own search for lost time. On the other hand, many Japanese writers felt
that the new intellectuals who asserted their ego in the Western manner were
doomed, for they lacked any inherited moral or psychological safeguard against
their own destructive self-centeredness.

Modern Japanese novels describe a society mutating so fast that one generation
after another must confront the confusion of new freedoms, new relationships,
new dynamics, new challenges. In the early years of the century, language itself
seemed unstable. Writers felt increasingly dissatisfied with the written medium at
their disposal. It had become too florid, or baroque, too removed from everyday
speech and, at the same time, both too restrictive and too playful to express the
dilemmas of the new age. There was even talk of jettisoning Japanese in favor of
English. In the end, through a convoluted process of language reform, literary
style was streamlined into a more flexible and colloquial vehicle, producing literature that in its various aspects was the expression of a deeply felt need to grapple
with the complexities of contemporary Japanese reality. For the last century, Japanese writers have struggled to assert the authenticity of the individual personality

at the same time that they delineated the consequences of the liberation of the self: guilt, betrayal, loneliness, and alienation. Their modernism has as much in common with the realism of Ibsen and Chekhov as it does with the innovative strategies of Proust or Pirandello. Relying on the conceit of an accurate, detailed description of an external reality, combined with psychological appraisal of motivation, they offered their readers a valuable literary compass for situating the bewilderment of identity, self-interest, and "belonging" in a convulsive age of cultural ambiguity.

In twentieth-century China, on the other hand, modernization ended a feudal system that had controlled social and artistic expression for more than two thousand years. The Revolution of 1911 was only the first of many conflicts—revolutions, civil war, or differing programs of social reform, each harshly administered—reflecting the intellectual and political ferment as China emerged from the old Confucian order into the People's Republic of China. (The philosopher Confucius lived between 551 and 479 B.C.) Unchanging, however, was the social importance attributed to writing, which was expected to embody and preserve the core of Chinese cultural identity. This privileged position for literature, visibly different from the Western norm that distinguishes between artistic dedication and social responsibility, could be quite uncomfortable when the ruling powers (as earlier in Russia) enforced political guidelines for writers. The famous speech by Mao Zedong (1893–1976) at the Yan'an Forum on Literature and Art in 1942 warned Chinese writers to think positively and eliminate personal introspection from their work: it was the nation, not the individual, that should be the focus of their attention. The traditional Confucian concept of the ethical artist (like many other Confucian concepts) survives in modern China, although adapted to new circumstances and a greatly changed political scene.

Western readers are generally surprised to find that the Chinese government for thousands of years required literary examinations for any government post. Confucius had proposed an influential model of moral development and related social responsibility, and in 136 B.C., during the Han Dynasty of emperors, Confucianism was proclaimed the state doctrine. The Four Books of Confucian writings were prescribed subjects for the imperial civil service examinations from 1414 until the examinations themselves were abolished in 1905. Confucian principles defined the forms of education and the (mainly literary) examinations, governed the writing of history, prescribed social and family relationships, and extended the rules of family obedience to include obedience to the emperor as head of the "family" state. One of Confucius's followers, Mencius, phrased the five basic human relations of Confucianism as follows: "Between father and son there should be affection, between ruler and minister, there should be righteousness, between husband and wife, there should be attention to their separate functions, between elder and younger brothers, there should be order, and between friends, there should be good faith." The literature favored in traditional China was a subtly disciplined poetry (not fiction, which was thought trivial), and it was written in a refined and elegant classical Chinese whose mastery required years of study.

At the turn of the century, Chinese intellectuals who had traveled abroad began to adapt literary models encountered in Japan, Europe, and America. The most striking change in this first wave of literary modernization had political as well as literary importance: use of the vernacular (popular speech) in both poetry and prose, and depiction of social problems. Lu Xun's *Diary of a Madman* (1918) introduced the use of vernacular prose, and the modernist rhythms of its broken, hallucinated narrative proposed a cannibalistic picture of Confucian society. Poetry in the 1920s was not only written in the vernacular but also rejected classical prosody, which had been used for thousands of years; instead, it experimented with free verse, and echoed such diverse writers as Wordsworth, Whitman,

Goethe, and Tagore. Playwrights who had read Ibsen and Chekhov dramatized contemporary social problems and the clash of opposed ideas against a realistic background. Romantic and Realist themes co-existed in a broad spectrum of Westernization that aimed not merely to liberate artistic expression but also to represent feelings and social tensions that had not previously found a place in literature. Yet this modern literature was not imitatively "Western" but rather an attempt by a new generation of writers to find different and perhaps fuller ways of expressing Chinese cultural experience. Their actions were never without political implications, both in this original opening up of traditional forms to a variety of different models and in the later turn away from Western examples toward a Marxist literature and political structure that seemed more congenial to China's group-oriented society.

With the formation of a League of Left-Wing Writers in 1930, Mao's proclamations at the Yan'an Forum, and the establishment of the Communist People's Republic of China under his control in 1949, a new conservatism in literature and art returned. Modernism in the Western sense of a liberal, experimental, and individually focused art was thought bourgeois, dilettantish, and antisocial—and was very dangerous to attempt. During the Cultural Revolution, writers and intellectuals who did not actively support socialist realism (the realistic depiction of the Communist state as a workers' paradise and of individuals as representative class figures) were imprisoned and persecuted. Very little was actually published, because little met the approval of the censors. Yet the People's Republic does not represent all Chinese literature, and writers in the Republic of China on Taiwan (some of whom had fled the mainland) followed their own path, writing a variety of prose fiction and founding a "Modernist School" in 1956 that sought a modern Chinese poetry "transplanted" from Europe rather than "inherited" from classical tradition. On the mainland, it was not until 1979 that writers felt free publicly to explore personal themes and use modernist forms. A new cluster of confessional works called "Wound Literature" then emerged, evoking the anguish of young Chinese alienated from their society, while more cautious writers avoided the risk of being declared antisocial by exploring objective forms like the interview, which allows an author to disclaim personal responsibility for what is said. The risk of social disapproval has not disappeared: the campaign against "Spiritual Pollution" in 1983, the expulsion from the party of the prominent writer Liu Binyan in 1987, and the tight control over the translation and publication of minority literatures show otherwise. Yet contemporary Chinese writers are once more part of a worldwide community of artists as they strive to develop a literature that is both characteristically modern and characteristically Chinese.

The situation of modern India is quite different, linguistically and literarily. European trade had been active in India for almost two centuries before British political rule dominated the continent in 1800. Independence from Britain came only in 1947, and by then Western culture and technology had permeated the subcontinent. The civil service and educational system were British, and generations of Indians—the future lawyers, teachers, writers, businesspeople, and government officials—had gone to Europe for university training. English was and remains the common language, the language used in government, although India itself is a mosaic of two hundred regional languages among which are Tamil, Gujarati, Oriya, Hindi, Bengali, Urdu, Kannada, and Sindhi. Some indigenous languages have no written form, and oral literature remains an important element in a society where a large part of the population is still illiterate. Indian works written in English, or translated into English (Indo-Anglian literature), can be read across regional linguistic barriers, and they have consequently come to represent Indian literature to the world outside India. Tagore, for example, who revolutionized Bengali literature, is more widely known abroad for his works in English.

The long-standing political and linguistic link with Europe had foreseeable literary results: first, that Indian intellectuals were educated in the same Western heritage as Europeans, reading in recent literature Wordsworth, Baudelaire, Goethe, and Ibsen; and second, that Western literary forms—tragic drama, the short story, the realistic novel, and personal lyrics, together with the use of the vernacular—edged out the classical Indian traditions of epic, devotional poetry, and oral literature. Realistic novels analyzed Indian social problems, including caste barriers, the position of women, religious strife, and national identity. Personal and autobiographical perspectives, psychological explorations, and depictions of modern society replaced a more impersonal focus on mythological or devotional subjects. Traditional prosody gave way to experiments with new forms, including free verse. Written literature flourished, offering a wide range of perspectives as it adapted European genres to local topics and settings. The performance-oriented Indian tradition, in contrast, moved into the background.

A further result was that the might and prestige of the British Empire, and the Empire's conviction that Western literature far outshone Indian tradition, encouraged a general belief in the superiority of Western ways and a neglect if not outright suppression of indigenous literature and languages. According to Lord Macaulay (1800–1859) in the previous century, a shelf of European masterworks was worth the whole of Indian art and literature: this attitude informed the education provided in British schools. Reactions, literary as well as political, were inevitable. Premchand (1880–1936), who established the realistic short story in Indian literature, used that form to describe the misery of peasant life under British bureaucracy; the bureaucracy responded by burning his first collection in 1909. Postcolonial writers (those writing after Indian independence) commonly attacked British colonial arrogance and, as part of rejecting capitalist colonialism, turned to Marxism for a vision of social structure that would correspond to the traditionally group-oriented nature of Indian society. Many authors wrote about the difficult position of women in public and private life, and the strain on interpersonal and family relationships, caused by conflicting social paradigms. Others returned to traditional religious themes and imagery in a modern landscape: R. K. Narayan (born 1906), included satires of Westernized life inside half-realistic, half-mystical narratives set in south India. One of the major self-imposed tasks of postcolonial literature has been to break free of European perspectives, to rediscover Indian traditions in art and literature, and finally to explore the implications of "Indianness" and also cultural ambiguity in a nation with so many competing cultures.

Whether it is a question of "Indianness" versus "Westernness" or of the multicultural identity that is now a global fact of life, Indian literature provides some of the most striking examples. The language of this literature is a hotly debated issue, as it is for African writers. Some critics assert that a truly Indian literature must be written in one of the ethnic languages and that indigenous experience cannot be accurately expressed in the colonizer's tongue. Despite the current government's encouragement of literary and linguistic pluralism, however, most of modern India's regional literature has not reached a wide audience because it is not available in translation—either into European or into other Indian languages. Who is to represent India, and to whom? The purist point of view rejects, perhaps rightly, the notion that Indian culture can be represented as a whole; yet it also denies the authenticity of Indian writers who choose to write in English. Some of these writers (for example, Narayan and Anita Desai) are major artists who ponder the question of "Indianness" in their own terms, whether as an assertion of traditional values or in the somber analysis of unfulfilled personal identities. Perhaps the most poignant example of intertwined literary cultures is Salman Rushdie, born a Muslim in 1947 in Bombay, India, who now lives in hiding in England because the modernist style, secular irony, and clashing cultural perspectives of his satiric novel *The Satanic Verses* (1988) caused conservative Muslim clerics to order his death for heresy. Throughout the twentieth century, in one form or another, questions of cultural identity and the challenge of a mixed heritage have been part of Indian literary tradition.

In the varied panorama of Middle Eastern countries, modernism and modernization have been linked as two categories of change brought by Western political and economic influence. It is the change of revolution, not evolution, and of a strong (though disputed) push to transform society rapidly in all aspects. The introduction of new generic forms like the novel and the modern short story, and the evolution, or modernization, of the older forms like poetry and drama, meant that Middle Eastern writers ceased to find their themes and forms principally within their own cultural tradition and attempted to internalize and naturalize an imported tradition. Initially, they seemed more drawn by content than form, or, rather, the structural looseness of modern Western poetry made it hard for Middle Eastern poets to see it as poetry at all. They were used to more highly codified forms of poetry, and for a long time they wrote politically engaged poems using traditional rhyme and meter. The link between modernist themes and modernist forms is so strong, however, that few poets now attempt to distinguish between them.

Writers sought an audience within the new middle class, for traditional aristocratic patronage had disappeared. Languages were transformed, sometimes acquiring a new alphabet; literary language became freer, more personal and colloquial; prose fiction, depicting everyday life and social issues, asserted itself in a tradition that had favored poetry and craftsmanship. In some ways, these changes are like those that took place in the West—the development of a new literary language, the recasting of the tradition's myths, the replacement of poetry with prose, the discovery of new heroes and antiheroes—but others are special to the non-Western world in its encounter with Western modernity: for example, the wrenching dislocations experienced by the first generations to be educated in the new learning. To accept Western modernity with its emphasis on the secular world, and its preference for the new, was to engage in a radical transformation of society and, with it, the near annihilation of traditional culture. Such a transformation has been the subject of a series of novels and short stories by the Egyptian writer Naguib Mahfouz (born 1911).

The encounter with European literature divided Middle Eastern intellectuals and writers into two camps: those who believed that the only hope of their respective communities lay in the wholehearted appropriation of Western culture and those who vehemently opposed it. Many in the former group began with the expectation that some essential elements of their native tradition could be maintained, but there were also many who were willing to jettison centuries of accumulated artistic tradition. According to an enthusiastic Turkish formula, citizens should "belong to the Turkish nation, the Moslem religion and European civilization." Modernism flourished in Turkey, where prose writers like Tawfiq al-Hakim (1898–1989) recast traditional subjects in modern form and where vers libre, poetic realism, and surrealism found their way into an increasingly diverse poetry after World War II. The underlying tension is reaffirmed, however, by events in Iran (ancient Persia). Postwar Iranian poetry, inspired by European models, developed both a hermetic, Symbolist-inspired style and a poetry of social action. After the Islamic Revolution of 1979 brought religious traditionalists once more to power, however, the freedom to write in Western modes dwindled sharply and most modernist writers fled the country.

The most striking example of Westernization in the Mideast is surely the transformation of Turkey from a feudal society ruled by a sultan to a modern, thoroughly Westernized state. Kemal Ataturk, president of the Turkish Republic

(1923–38), led the Turks into a radical secularization and separation from the past by changing the basis of the Turkish alphabet from Arabic to Latin. His stated intention was to return Turkey to its pre-Islamic roots, but the effect was that within a generation the Turks lost access to the literary tradition of the preceding six centuries and to the Arabic and Persian literature on which it had been nourished. (The same sort of deracination by alphabet reform occurred in the Islamic Republics of the USSR.) A more moderate response, and one that more nearly characterizes the approach of Mideast modernist poets and writers, was that of al-Hakim, who felt that Middle Eastern writers should both appropriate Western classical mythology and recast their own in modern forms. The aesthetic battle has largely been won, and by the modernizers.

It is not possible to discuss modern literature in the Middle East without mentioning Israel, whose political and cultural identity differs sharply from its neighbors'. Israel's past was biblical, not Koranic. Moreover, the first generation of Israeli poets and writers were not only influenced by European literature but had often grown up in that tradition themselves. Yet Israel's poets and writers have faced many of the same dilemmas as other Middle Eastern authors. In language, they have sought to create a new, colloquial idiom to replace the formal, elitist idiom they had inherited: Hebrew had not been used as a colloquial idiom for millennia. In literature, they undertook to give modern form to their inherited tradition (for example, the poems by Yehuda Amichai). They shared with their Middle Eastern counterparts a commitment to use writing as a means of engaging in the discussion the central political questions of the time (A. B. Yehoshua). Some of the most interesting writing in contemporary Israel is produced by writers of a mixed Israeli-Arab heritage who, like their peers in other regions, explore the richness and difficulty of multicultural identity in the modern world.

Modern African literature is probably better known to Western readers than writing from any other part of the globe, for a variety of reasons. The fact that many works were originally written in English, French, and Portuguese made them accessible to a wider audience. The African slave diaspora, which linked ethnic groups in Africa, the United States, and the Caribbean, created a far-flung audience with shared concerns. The colonial education system, which meant that many Europeans taught in African schools and many Africans went to European universities, generated a continuing cultural exchange. Finally, the fascination of European artists and intellectuals at the beginning of the century with the "otherness" of black African art and civilization became part of the European intellectual and artistic tradition. Many connections exist, but also an unmistakable separation. Black African writers' sense of a distinct, non-European, racially defined identity, a division partly imposed by European colonialism and partly by their own urge to define black culture, permeates the development of modern literature on this continent of mixed African, Arabic, and European heritage. No one can ignore the impact of race on African thought and literature, and the South African writer Nadine Gordimer is keenly aware of her own ambiguously privileged white perspective when she analyzes the shifting overtones of everyday relationships between black and white in a changing Africa.

The importance of "négritude," or consciousness of black identity, can hardly be overestimated. Coined by the Caribbean Aimé Césaire (born 1913) in his *Notebook of a Return to the Native Land* (1939), prefigured by earlier Harlem Renaissance writings about black cultural identity, affirmed and illustrated by Léopold Sédar Senghor (born 1906) in the poems of *Chants d'ombre* (1945) and in a widely influential anthology of 1948, the term is an amalgam of ideas derived from the passionate discussions of black intellectuals gathered in Paris during the 1920s and 1930s. Interpreted differently by different thinkers—as an absolute genetic inheritance or as an oppositional movement linked to specific historical circumstances—négritude provided a counterconcept to colonialist images of Western ethnic and cultural superiority. It crystallized the opposition and offered a positive definition of blackness around which art, literature, and philosophy could rally.

Négritude is most usefully understood as a powerful concept and a reference point rather than as absolute reality. After centuries of intermingled traditions, it is difficult for any society to wrest apart fused layers of cultural identity. (This fact many Indian authors have recognized about their own postcolonial condition, as have Chinese authors after attempting to root out Confucianism.) Senghor has frequently described the two voices, African and French, that resonate in his poetry. His parents came from different African ethnic groups with their own languages; he himself was born in Senegal, when it was still a French colony, and was educated in Paris. There, he absorbed a French literary tradition that would influence his own poetry, but there he also met other black writers and intellectuals, learned about the Harlem Renaissance, studied African cultural history and anthropology, and founded, with Césaire and the Guinean Léon-Gontran Damas (born 1912), the journal *L'Étudiant noir* (The black student). Drafted into the French army after graduation, this future president of the independent republic of Senegal spent part of World War II in a German concentration camp, learning German and writing French poems about the African experience of colonialism. Senghor's experience may be the best known, but it is not unique. Birago Diop, Wole Soyinka, Césaire, Chinua Achebe, Derek Walcott, and Kamau Brathwaite also express, in different ways, the interweaving of European and black African or Caribbean identities.

One of the more pressing issues for black African writers has been the use of language. This is not a debate over style, or the language of European modernism with its ruptures, broken images, and stream of consciousness. Such stylistic concerns have less significance here than other social, quasi-existential, themes of personal and cultural identity. The immediate issue is whether to write in the European languages they have learned from childhood—which are now associated with colonialism—or, by translating earlier texts, writing in an African language, or emphasizing performance, to recreate an indigenous artistic tradition. Senghor echoes this tradition when he composes poetry on African themes that is intended to be chanted before a group and accompanied by musical instruments. Some authors follow the example of the Kenyan Ngugi wa Thiongo (born 1938), who chooses now to write in Gikuyu after having made a reputation as a novelist in English; others, like Diop (1906–1992) and Wole Soyinka (born 1934), join to their own work in French and English the translation and adaptation of folk tales; still others, like Achebe and Mariama Bâ, write about African topics in a European language permeated by their own indigenous references and turns of speech. Before her death in 1981, Bâ was one of a growing number of feminist authors in contemporary Africa: she did not emphasize colonial issues per se but wrote instead about the personal and cultural dilemma of African women caught in a modern society that is still governed by traditional definitions of gender and caste. To the extent that this twentieth-century literature is chiefly a *written* literature, exploiting the genres of novel, drama, short story, essay and lyric poetry, the question of language is already compromised by a link with European culture. African tradition (like that of India) emphasized oral and performance-oriented art. Modern African literature, like that of other postcolonial societies, incorporates the dynamism and internal tensions of an evolving society in which indigenous traditions, the colonial heritage, and an ongoing intellectual and artistic ferment coexist as parts of a common history.

In the West, modernism was transformed after midcentury, partly in the normal course of literary evolution and partly under the pressure of changing historical circumstances. With the passage of time, the modernist world no longer seemed "modern" (hence the invention of the term *postmodern*). Writers in the 1960s considered their predecessors in the earlier half century—Proust, Eliot, Woolf, Mann, and Stevens—part of a relatively concentrated "high Modernism" that emphasized formal innovation but preserved roots in conservative mainstream thought. Nor did the focus on European tradition go unchallenged, as other regions reasserted their own cultural aims. Seen from outside, the modernist search for profound reality no longer appeared revolutionary: instead, it was the latest development of a Western tradition reaching back to Homer and the Bible. Seeking a common image of essential human nature seemed utopian in a world where more than six thousand languages were spoken and where (by 1994) the United Nations had 184 member nations.

Other political and economic changes have had their effect. The first half of the century was marked by two world wars that enlisted forces around the globe in two large alliances, and the Cold War that succeeded World War II also cast global conflict in terms of two superpowers, the United States and the USSR. This relatively monolithic opposition was not to endure. The breakup of colonial empires, the creation of many new nations eager to assert their identity, and the emergence of new centers of trade (Japan, the oil-producing Middle Eastern countries acting together as OPEC) distributed power throughout a more diverse system. Nor were nations necessarily the holders of power, for the second half of the century saw the rise of multinational corporations whose chief loyalty was to business, and of transnational religious movements (like Islamic fundamentalism) that fought to assume authority in formerly secular states. The United Nations provided a forum in which global issues were publicly discussed, and television spread the images around the world. The developing countries of Africa, Asia, and Latin America, possessing many of the world's resources but few industries or corporate structures, called on the former colonial states to share their wealth and expertise. International agencies coordinated aid in the face of environmental catastrophes, epidemics, and famine; crime organizations also operated internationally; and the image of shared global problems moved into the foreground. Thousands of people migrated from poorer countries to seek jobs in wealthier regions, bringing different cultural groups in contact at the same time that they changed local economies. A host of smaller wars, sometimes driven by religious or ethnic allegiances that led to genocide or "ethnic cleansing," forced millions from their homes, and in 1994 the United Nations reported that 1 out of every 114 people in the world had been displaced by military conflict. Individuals were no longer so tied to their native countries; for some, their countries had disappeared in new political arrangements and for others, their simultaneous ties to more than one country created a new dimension of bicultural, hybrid, or "migrant" identity. Mass culture, radio, and television stretched to every part of the globe, often effacing local traditions as they introduced people to a broader horizon. With the disappearance of an old world order, the political picture became at once more fragmented and more interconnected, a situation that is reflected in contemporary literature and art.

Postmodernism

The term *postmodernism* has been proposed to suggest this change, defining an attitude that derives from modernist thought but turns away from it in several important ways. Even if the term is still debated (and more widely accepted by critics than by writers), to contrast modernism with postmodernism can illuminate many of the themes and strategies present in contemporary literature. Where modernism tries to reveal a core of profound experience through innovative form, postmodernism is suspicious of claims of "profundity," which it associates with hidden value judgments (calling something "profound" implies that the speaker finds it specially true and valuable). Consequently, postmodernist writers who avoid the search for "profundity" tend to avoid images of depth and prefer to describe inconclusive surface images. The modernist Wallace Stevens, for example, symbolizes the profound underlying opposition of appearance and reality by describing a festive wake in *The Emperor of Ice-Cream* but the postmodernist Alain Robbe-Grillet avoids drawing conclusions when he gives conflicting versions of a single scene in *The Secret Room*. Similar contrasts between modernism and postmodernism (sometimes called *poststructuralism*) are drawn between principles of *construction* and *deconstruction*, *center*, and *dissemination* or more generally between the concept of an organic whole dependent on a central motivating principle and a web of shifting relationships depicted without a frame or center. Throughout, the postmodernist notion is that modernism's emphasis on meaningful aesthetic form anchored in a central vision suggests an image of human experience that is too finished, too symmetrical—that a human reality which is basically "jagged" (Ezra Pound's term) needs to be represented in all its incompleteness and rough edges. Postmodernist art, although it rejects the concept of "art" or "aesthetic" completion, has its own recognizable style, one that favors visual and verbal strategies that undermine all forms of certainty.

This shift of artistic sensibility takes to its logical conclusion the modernist's use of fragmentation and discontinuity. Both modernist and postmodernist thinkers are indebted to the evolution of scientific thought in the twentieth century and most of all to its emphasis on randomness and shifting perceptions. The physicist Werner Heisenberg's uncertainty principle (mentioned earlier) stresses the *approximate* nature of any description of reality as well as the fact that the observer's position relative to what is observed changes from moment to moment. The mathematician Kurt Gödel describes the ultimate incompleteness (and, therefore, lack of authority) of all logical systems. A similar emphasis on shifting patterns of perception appears in the later development of Freudian psychoanalysis with the concepts of transference and countertransference. Here, attention is displaced from subconscious and instinctual drives to the concept of dialogue and exchange. Therapists no longer "cure" patients of specific psychoses, but engage them in a process of self-definition through interaction with others. Finally, semiotics, literally a science of *signs*, studies the "gamelike" construction of meaning and is undoubtedly the purest expression of postmodern consciousness.

The *literature* called postmodernist displays an impersonal, coolly decentered, or self-reflexive style with frequent gaps and endless ramifications. It stresses shifts and the play of surfaces, rather than asserting any specific version of reality; it avoids commitment. Postmodernist *theory* covers more than one style of literary expression and is in fact a philosophy of knowledge. In contrast to the dominant Kantian tradition, this philosophy emphasizes relationships but not coherence, particulars but not universality, instability rather than system, internal contradictions rather than harmony, and, throughout, constant change. It expresses what the poet W. H. Auden called an "age of anxiety," analyzing that age and its preoccupation with questions of identity. Postmodernist theory is fascinated by claims of cultural specificity (specificity implies difference) and also by the simultaneous occurrence of more than one cultural perspective; it studies the relationship of interwoven traditions, and it undertakes to unfold layers of complicity and contradiction in any text, no matter how reputedly "pure."

Postmodernist critics suggest that contemporary works not only are different but that they should be read differently from earlier ones. The modernist author guides and controls the reader's response while the postmodernist author creates an "open" work with alternate meanings, so that the reader, by decoding, shares in "writing" a new text. Thomas Mann's modernist *Death in Venice*, for example, weaves together psychological, cultural, aesthetic, and mythic themes to explain the downfall of its doomed artist-hero; Ingeborg Bachmann, conversely, works by indirection to uncover an undefined murderousness that readers must piece out in *The Barking*. Samuel Beckett is often taken as the arch-example of postmodernist style and philosophy. In *Endgame*, he uses spare dialogue and a nearly barren stage to invite readers to concentrate on context and meaning. The intentional construction of meaning is a recurrent theme in *Endgame* itself: "Me—to play." Postmodernist writers play with language and create "self-reflexive" works that constantly refer to their own composition; indeed, emphasis on words sometimes replaces descriptions of exterior or historical reality. The line is not always easy to draw, however: Luigi Pirandello, Marcel Proust, Bertolt Brecht, and particularly Franz Kafka and James Joyce are modernist writers who have also been called precursors of postmodernism.

Readers will find that there are certain easily identified strategies at work in this literature, strategies whose general aim is to avoid creating any sense of completeness or central reference point. In fiction, this literature often replaces the authorial personality (the coordinating core, for example, of Proust's *Remembrance of Things Past* or of Joyce's *Portrait of the Artist*) with an anonymous and even self-contradictory narrative viewpoint (the impersonal and contradictory narrative perspective in Robbe-Grillet's *The Secret Room*). Just as there is no unified authorial perspective, so individual characters do not develop psychologically as they would be expected to in a nineteenth-century realistic work. Like Hamm and Clov in Beckett's *Endgame*, these characters interact in a (relatively) meaningless void, living moment by moment within a permanent present, located in an ambiguous and allusive situation that cannot be defined in external terms. Nor does their time have a solid chronological basis. It leads nowhere: in *Endgame*, we are not even sure whether the action concludes or is simply part of a repetitive pattern. Time in *The Secret Room* moves backward; in Robbe-Grillet's novels and his film *Last Year at Marienbad* it is made up of contradictory scenes so that any fixed sense of what happened, or when, is not available. There is no plot, and the narrative line is not patterned by a beginning, middle, and end; overall, there is no sense of action developing toward a logical conclusion. The ambiguity of appearances is heightened by putting history and fantasy on the same level (Borges), or by including impossible, "magical" scenes in the midst of apparently realistic narrative (García Márquez). Style can be allusive, disrupted, contradictory, and confusing, as if to disorient a reader who might wish to extract a single authorized meaning.

All these strategies actually serve to engage readers in a new and challenging way. They refuse to provide a coherent interpretation of reality, and offer instead a collection of ambiguously related fragments, strangely emphasized silences, and merely *potential* themes. The burden, in fact, is placed squarely and openly on the reader to construct a meaning. Similar challenges are evident in Brecht's "alienation technique," which, by refusing to let spectators lose themselves in dramatic illusion, forces them to interpret events in a wider (in this case political) context. These forms are built on a calculated refusal of easy coherence, an apparently nihilistic "antiform," which in fact requires a great deal of artistic patterning to be convincing. Some of these texts have been called "antiliterature" for their refusal to provide the aesthetic completion suggested by the term *literature*. A truly random work, however, would be nothing more than a collection of unrelated words (like Tzara's Dada poem, created from newspaper clippings shaken in a paper bag). To impress the reader with the fact that the world does *not* correspond to neatly packaged artistic representations, the authors of "incomplete" literature— with complete logic—devise new artistic forms to focus our attention on the artificiality of any "total" perspective.

Incompleteness and a delight in ambiguity do not exclude strong impressions of moral or cultural judgment. Borges, often considered the originator of postmodernism in his labyrinthine, self-reflexive style, includes a subtle contrast of cultural and national prejudices in *The Garden of Forking Paths*. The creeping, murkily defined terror of Bachmann's *The Barking* is directed against the Nazi personality. Cultural uneasiness abounds in Murakami Haruki's story of contemporary Japanese citizens who live in a world between fantasy and realism, slowly transformed into *TV People*. Gabriel García Márquez comes close to the European "new wave" of radically experimental techniques, with his manipulation of perspective through magical realism. His focus is clearly the political and cultural reality of Latin America, however, even when he jokes about acquiring a reputation for writing "real literature" by writing impenetrably and imitating Robbe-Grillet.

There are also contemporary authors who draw primarily on other traditions. Writers like Kojima Nobuo and Naguib Mahfouz rely on the style of the realistic novel as they lament the difficulty of preserving individual dignity and cultural values in a world of rapidly interpenetrating societies. A. B. Yehoshua explores the identity crisis of modern Israel by depicting, realistically, the interrelationships of Arab and Jewish lives. Extending twentieth-century attempts to recapture and preserve ethnic traditions (for example, the transcription of Inuit songs and of Zuni ritual poetry), Andrew Peynetsa recreates a Zuni myth, *The Boy and the Deer*, and Leslie Marmon Silko composes, in *Yellow Woman*, a mysterious twentieth-century tale based on Laguna Indian legend.

Faith in a common version of reality has faded in the literature of the second half of the century, where it more and more appears that we will rediscover human nature only by juxtaposing many diverse and fluid images. The realistic representation of issues involving women and their position in society—or of gender relationships themselves—emerges with particular force in this part of the century. "Masculine" and "feminine" behavior—defined, as anthropologists have shown, so differently in different societies—is more likely to be a topic for analysis and not just a preexisting role into which characters must fit. Feminist critics have also taken a new look at canonical texts, asking, for example, what it means when heroic protagonists are almost always men and when women (unless they die, or subside into obscurity at the end of the drama) are supporting characters in a masculine narrative. Without diminishing the picture of social reality in earlier twentieth-century literature, it is still possible to say that recent years have brought an unprecedented recognition of different ethnic, sexual, and cultural identities, both as political facts and as the subject matter of literature. This recognition has transformed our understanding of "Western" world literature, as regional and ethnic identities (for example, African-American, Yiddish, Chicano, Québecois, and native American literatures) represent their traditional self-images and values. What was once a simpler model of the Western heritage has turned out, on examination, to be much more heterogeneous and much more interesting.

What does this mean for the concept of masterpiece? Each of the major civilizations has works that it considers, and other traditions consider, to be of enduring value and more than local interest. A masterpiece, in brief, speaks not only to its own time and time-bound audience, but to future generations and other cultures. It lasts; it travels well.

Some critics locate this strength in a work's aesthetic character and power of reference: the scope and complexity of its external and internal relations, and the compound impression of interactivating thought, shape, feel, and sound that it imposes on—and awakens in—the mind. In this more technical perspective, a "masterpiece" continues to be relevant because it constitutes a coherent structure of reference and representation that is neither easily exhausted nor tied to a single context. Other critics locate a work's strength in its ability to inform us about ourselves and our fellow human beings, about the terror and wonder of the universe we live in, the miseries it is possible to suffer, the grandeurs it is possible to attain: all this through an imaginative sharing of experience that is qualitatively different from historical or anthropological perspectives. In this definition, a masterpiece remains a masterpiece as long as it provides mature insight into the condition, the plight, the art of being human.

Each of these emphases is valid, but incomplete. Works in this anthology possess inexhaustibly challenging structures of dynamic reference that bring to imaginative life a variety of intellectual and moral concerns of lasting importance. As recent revisionary readings of many canonical masterworks show (for example, the Greek dramatists, or Shakespeare), works having both these dimensions continue to respond to the most diverse and often confrontational approaches. The major works of twentieth-century literature will encounter similar tests in a hundred years.

The intricate meeting of cultures, lively interaction of ethnic, sexual, or racial identities, and inquiries into the nature of art and language have combined to create a global literature that in its insistent teasing-out of contradictory layers of reality corresponds to the diversity of our new geopolitical age with its philosophy of openness and change.

FURTHER READING

Monique Chefdor, Ricardo Quinones, Albert Wachtel, eds., *Modernism: Challenges and Perspectives* (1986), offers valuable essays on international modernism. David Hayman, *Re-Forming the Narrative: Toward a Mechanics of Modernist Fiction* (1987), proposes five tactics that distinguish modernist narrative from earlier fiction. Harry Levin, "What Was Modernism?" (1962, rep. in *Refractions*, 1966), is a survey of modernist writers as humanists and inheritors of the Enlightenment. H. H. Arnason, *History of Modern Art: Painting, Sculpture, Architecture* (1977, illustrated), follows the evolution of the arts in the West from the nineteenth century to the 1960s. Matei Calinescu, *Five Faces of Modernity* (1987), is an informative collection of essays on the aesthetics of modernism, avant-garde, decadence, and kitsch. Morton P. Levitt, *Modernist Survivors: The Contemporary Novel in England, the United States, France, and Latin America* (1987), analyzes the impact of literary modernism and the continuity of humanist values. James F. Knapp, *Literary Modernism and the Transformation of Work* (1988), examines work-related themes in English and American modernist literature and modernism's contradictory attitudes toward a changing economic order. Harry R. Garvin, ed., *Romanticism, Modernism, Postmodernism* (1980), is a collection of essays that attempts to define changing views of the artistic imagination.

Marjorie Perloff, *The Poetics of Indeterminacy* (1981), has significance beyond its primary focus on contemporary English and American poetry stemming from the French tradition. See also Perloff, ed., *Postmodern Genres* (1989), for a collection of essays on postmodernism in art and literature. Ihab and Sally Hassan, eds., *Essays in Innovation/Renovation: New Perspectives on the Humanities* (1983), explores change in contemporary Western culture. Susan Rubin Suleiman, *Subversive Intent: Gender, Politics, and the Avant-garde* (1990), analyzes the cultural implications of avant-garde artistic practices. Nancy K. Miller, ed., *The Poetics of Gender* (1986), presents essays on various aspects of feminist criticism. Elise Boulding, *The Underside of History: A View of Women through Time* (1992), complements traditional histories by drawing attention to the position and contributions of women. Frederick Buell, *National Culture and the New Global System* (1994), analyzes literary examples in a discussion of twentieth-century cultural globalization that moves beyond the concept of "three worlds." Sarah Lawall, ed., *Reading World Literature: Theory, History, Practice* (1994), includes a theoretical introduction to the subject of world literature and twelve essays on specific topics. Janheinz Jahn, *Muntu: African Culture and the Western World*, trans. Marjorie Grene (1990, orig. 1961), is an influential discussion of the interface of two cultures. J. M. Roberts, *History of the World* (1993), is an up-to-date history of world events in a contemporary perspective.

TIMELINE

TEXTS	CONTEXTS
1893 Rabindranath Tagore, **Punishment**	
1895 Higuchi Ichiyō, *Child's Play*	
ca. 1897–1902 Washington Matthews conducts studies of the Navajo **Night Chant**	**1899–1902** Boer War in South Africa
	1900 Boxer uprisings in China protest European presence • Max Planck proposes quantum theory, the first step in the discovery of the atom
1902 Joseph Conrad, *Heart of Darkness*	
1903 Henry James, *The Ambassadors*	**1903** Wright brothers invent the powered airplane
1905 Sigmund Freud, **Dora (Fragment of an Analysis of a Case of Hysteria)** • F. T. Marinetti, *Futurist Manifesto*	**1905** Modern labor movement begins with foundation of International Workers of the World (IWW) • Partition of Bengal based on Hindu and Muslim populations
1907 August Strindberg, *The Ghost Sonata*	**1907** Japanese immigration to the United States prohibited
1908 Gertrude Stein, *Three Lives*	
	1909 Commercial manufacture of plastic begins
	1910 China abolishes slavery • Mexican Revolution (1910–11) • NAACP founded in United States • Post-Impressionist Exhibition in London
	1911 Revolution establishes Chinese Republic after 267 years of Manchu rule
1912 Rabindranath Tagore, *Gitanjali*	**1912–1913** Balkan wars
1913 Marcel Proust, **Swann's Way**, first volume of *Remembrance of Things Past* (1913–27) • Thomas Mann, **Death in Venice** • D. H. Lawrence, *Sons and Lovers*	
	1914–1918 World War I involves Europe, Turkey, and the United States

TIMELINE

TEXTS	CONTEXTS
	1915 Albert Einstein formulates general theory of relativity • First transcontinental phone call, in America
1916 Franz Kafka, *The Metamorphosis* • James Joyce, *A Portrait of the Artist as a Young Man*	
1917 T. S. Eliot, *Prufrock and Other Observations*	1917 Russian Revolution overthrows Romanov Dynasty
1918 Lu Xun, *Diary of a Madman,* the first story in Chinese vernacular	1918 Women over 30 given vote in Great Britain
	1918–1920 Global influenza epidemic kills millions
	1919 League of Nations formed (U.S. Senate rejects membership, 1920)
1920 Edith Wharton, *The Age of Innocence*	1920 Mahatma Gandhi leads India's struggle for independence from Britain
1921 Luigi Pirandello, *Six Characters in Search of an Author*	1921–1929 Harlem Renaissance, black literary and artistic movement
1921–1924 Knud Rasmussen documents Inuit culture and collects **Inuit Songs** during the Fifth Thule Expedition	
1922 T. S. Eliot, *The Waste Land* • Paris publication of James Joyce, *Ulysses* (imported copies burned in U.S. Post Office) • Rainer Maria Rilke, *Sonnets to Orpheus*	1922 Turkey becomes a republic • Irish Free State established • USSR formed • Discovery of Egyptian pharaoh Tutankhamen's tomb
1923 Rainer Maria Rilke, *Duino Elegies*	1923 Earthquakes destroy centers of Tokyo and Yokohama
1924 Thomas Mann, *The Magic Mountain* • André Breton, *First Surrealist Manifesto* • Premchand, *The Road to Salvation*	1924 Insecticides first used
1925 *Geriguigatugo* and other tales narrated by Úke Iwágu Úo published in Italian and Bororo	

TIMELINE

TEXTS	CONTEXTS
1926 Franz Kafka, *The Castle*	
1927 Virginia Woolf, *To the Lighthouse*	
1928 William Butler Yeats, *The Tower*	1928 Sixty-five states sign Kellogg-Briand antiwar pact in Paris • First Five Year Plan in USSR • Penicillin discovered • First scheduled television broadcasts
1929 William Faulkner, *The Sound and the Fury*	1929 Stock market crash heralds beginning of world economic crisis; Great Depression lasts until 1937
1932 **Zuni Ritual Poetry** published by anthropologist Ruth L. Bunzel	
1933 Federico García Lorca, *Blood Wedding*	1933 Adolf Hitler given dictatorial powers in Germany • Nazis build first concentration camps
	1934 Stalin begins purges of Communist Party
1935–1947 Kawabata Yasunari, **Snow Country**	
1936 Premchand, *The Cow* • Leo Frobenius, *History of African Civilizations*	
1937 Wallace Stevens, *The Man with the Blue Guitar*	
1939 Aimé Césaire, **Notebook of a Return to the Native Land**	1939 Germany invades Poland and all Europe is drawn into World War II
1940 Richard Wright, *Native Son*	
1941 Bertolt Brecht, **Mother Courage and Her Children**	1941 United States and Japan enter World War II
1942 Albert Camus, *The Stranger*	
1943 T. S. Eliot, **Four Quartets**	
1944 Jorge Luis Borges, **The Garden of Forking Paths** • Ralph Ellison, **King of the Bingo Game**	

TIMELINE

TEXTS	CONTEXTS
1945 Leopold Sedar Senghor, *Chants d'ombre*	1945 World War II ends with dropping of atomic bombs on Hiroshima and Nagasaki • United Nations, Arab League founded
	1946 Churchill's "Iron Curtain" speech marks beginning of Cold War • Pan-African Federation formed
1947 Birago Diop, **Tales of Amadou Koumba**	1947 Religious massacres accompany partition of India and Pakistan into independent states • Transistor invented
1948 Ezra Pound, *Pisan Cantos*	1948 Creation of Jewish state in Palestine
	1949 Communist People's Republic of China established • Apartheid instituted in South Africa
	1950–1953 Korean War involves North and South Korea, the United Nations, and China
1952 Ralph Ellison, *Invisible Man*	1952 Revolution in Egypt, which becomes a republic in 1953 • First hydrogen bomb
	1953 Discovery of DNA structure launches modern genetic science
1954 Kojima Nobuo, **The American School**	
1955 Alain Robbe-Grillet, *The Voyeur*	
1956 Tanizaki Jun'ichiro, *The Key*	1956 First Congress of Black Writers meets in Paris
1956–1957 Naguib Mahfouz, *The Cairo Trilogy*	
1957 Samuel Beckett, **Endgame** • Albert Camus, *Exile and the Kingdom*, which includes **The Guest**	

TIMELINE

TEXTS	CONTEXTS
1958 Chinua Achebe, *Things Fall Apart*	1958 European Common Market established • Algerian War of Independence (1958–62)
1959 Tawfiq al-Hakim, *The Sultan's Dilemma*	
1960 Marguerite Duras, *Hiroshima mon amour* • Shōno Junzō, *Still Life*	1960–1962 Independence for Belgian Congo, Uganda, Tanganyika, Nigeria
1961 Soviet astronaut orbits earth	
1962 Doris Lessing, *The Golden Notebook* • Alain Robbe-Grillet, *Snapshots*, which includes *The Secret Room*	1962–1973 United States engaged in Vietnam War
1963 Anna Akhmatova, *Requiem* • Naguib Mahfouz, *God's World*, which includes *Zaabalawi* • Alexander Solzhenitsyn, *Matroyna's Home*	
1965 Recorded performance by Andrew Peynetsa of *The Boy and the Deer*	
	1966 Mao Tse-tung's *Cultural Revolution* attacks Confucian tradition and intellectuals in China (1966–69) • First Dakar Arts Festival provides showcase for African culture
1967 Gabriel García Márquez, *One Hundred Years of Solitude*	
1968 Kamau Brathwaite, *Masks*	
	1969 American astronaut is first man on moon
1970 Derek Walcott, *Dream on Monkey Mountain* • A. B. Yehoshua, *Three Days and a Child*, which includes *Facing the Forests* • Gabriel García Márquez, *Death Constant Beyond Love*	
1972 Ingeborg Bachmann, *Three Paths to the Lake*, which includes *The Barking*	

TEXTS	CONTEXTS
	1973 Arab oil producers cut off shipments to nations supporting Israel; ensuing energy crisis reshapes global economy
1975 Wole Soyinka, *Death and the King's Horseman*	
1979 Mariama Bâ, *So Long a Letter*	
1980 Nadine Gordimer, *A Soldier's Embrace*, which includes *Oral History* • Mahasweta Devi, *Breast-Giver* • Anita Desai, *Clear Light of Day* • Lorna Goodison, *Tamarind Season*	1980s Widespread concern as damage to the environment is increasingly documented
1981 Leslie Marmon Silko, *Ceremony* and *Storyteller*, which includes *Yellow Woman*	
	1983–1984 Famine in Ethiopia • Ethnic and religious riots throughout India
	1986 Nuclear disaster in Chernobyl spreads radiation contamination throughout Europe
	1987 Floods destroy homes of millions in Bangladesh • World stock market crash
1989 Murakami Haruki, *TV People*	1989 Mikhail Gorbachev restructures the Soviet state • Chinese government shoots thousands of protesters gathered in Tiananmen Square • Berlin Wall demolished
	1990 East and West Germany united
	1991 United States and USSR agree to arms reduction • Economic chaos and nationalist unrest bring end of Soviet Union
1994 Alice Munro, *The Albanian Virgin*	1994 Nelson Mandela becomes president of South Africa after first multiracial elections • Israel and PLO sign peace agreement establishing a Palestinian state

THE NIGHT CHANT

Navajo ceremonialism, like Iroquois law and Maya architecture, ranks among the glories of native American achievement. Esteemed for its therapeutic values and duly respected by Western medicine, it has proved a magnet for students of religion and an inexhaustible field for research in the arts and various sciences. Directed primarily toward healing and the restoration of harmony between individuals and the environment, the ceremonies of Mountainway, Beautyway, Enemyway, and Blessingway, to name only a few of the better known, create a spiritual universe of song, prayer, drama, and graphic art, rooted in an oral literature of epic proportions. With its induction of new initiates, its unique all-night sing, and its lofty portrayal of deities, the famous Nightway occupies a place of honor among these "ways," or "chants," and some observers have regarded Nightway as the most important of them all.

Literally rendered "night-way chant," the name is almost always abbreviated to "nightway" in Navajo usage but was called *Night Chant* by its preeminent translator, Washington Matthews (whose Night Chant studies were conducted mainly during the 1890s). It was Matthews who translated the phrase "walk in beauty," often reiterated by poets and occasionally used as a salutation by speakers of English outside the Navajo community.

The shared quest for *beauty*—a broad term that includes "perfection," "normality," "success," and "well-being"—as exemplified by the Night Chant and other ceremonials, is reflected in the remarkable vitality of the Navajo nation and its culture. The Navajo reservation, located in northern Arizona and adjacent New Mexico, is the largest in the contiguous United States; it is the most populous and has the greatest number of native speakers. Farming, sheep ranching, weaving, and silversmithing have long been important industries in the Navajo homeland. The staging of the ceremonials has also been a noteworthy, if small, element in the economy. Ceremonialism, at least in theory, provides a livelihood for the specialist, or chanter, who must organize dancers, singers, and other helpers, whose services are paid for by a sponsor, or host.

Although the chant is attended by a large audience of relatives, friends, and visitors, its power is aimed primarily at a single person, usually called "the patient" in anthropological writings. Each of the Navajo ceremonials is said to be effective against a particular group of disorders; in the case of the Night Chant, paralytic stroke and ailments of the head. So narrow a view of its virtues, however, is belied by the wide interest it evokes and by the constant demand for performances. In the late twentieth century, its practitioners are being called on throughout the winter, with as many as half a dozen Night Chants in progress at any given moment, and bookings for a chant must be made two years in advance. Abbreviated versions may be ordered on shorter notice. Evidently, the chant in its full form is not an emergency therapy; among its more obvious benefits are the prestige it brings to the host who sponsors it and the opportunities it provides for cultural reaffirmation, socializing, and general spiritual revival.

Performed only in fall or winter, the nine-day Night Chant falls into two four-day parts, followed by a climactic ninth-night reprise, the night of nights, in which the long-awaited spirit of thunder is summoned. At this point the ceremony breaks free in a torrent of song continuing unabated until dawn. In part 1 the emphasis is on rites that exorcise evil influences and invoke the distant gods. Part 2 is distinguished by spacious and intricate sand paintings, made of dry pigments sprinkled on the earth. The paintings depict the gods and enable the patient to merge with their divine invulnerability. Through it all, the ceremonial leader, or chanter, directs the included song recitals and intones the prescribed prayers. The two selections printed here are the prayer to thunder that begins the final night and the last of the Finishing Songs that bring it to a close.

A text of the Night Chant may be read in John Bierhorst, *Four Masterworks of American Indian Literature* (1974). The selections printed here are from Washington Matthews, *The Night Chant: A Navaho Ceremony* (1902). For survey articles on ceremonialism and other Navajo topics, see Alfonso Ortiz, ed., *Southwest*, vol. 10 of *Handbook of North American Indians* (1983). James C. Faris, *The Nightway: A History and a History of Documentation of a Navajo Ceremonial* (1990), brings Night Chant scholarship up to date.

From The Night Chant[1]

Prayer to Thunder[2]

*   *   *

In Tsegíhi,[3]
In the house made of the dawn,
In the house made of the evening twilight,
In the house made of the dark cloud,
In the house made of the he-rain,   5
In the house made of the dark mist,
In the house made of the she-rain,[4]
In the house made of pollen,[5]
In the house made of grasshoppers,
Where the dark mist curtains the doorway,   10
The path to which is on the rainbow,
Where the zigzag lightning stands high on top,
Where the he-rain stands high on top,
Oh, male divinity![6]
With your moccasins of dark cloud, come to us.   15
With your leggings of dark cloud, come to us.
With your shirt of dark cloud, come to us.
With your headdress of dark cloud, come to us.
With your mind enveloped in dark cloud, come to us.
With the dark thunder above you, come to us soaring.   20
With the shapen cloud at your feet, come to us soaring.
With the far darkness made of the dark cloud
      over your head, come to us soaring.
With the far darkness made of the he-rain
      over your head, come to us soaring.
With the far darkness made of the dark mist
      over your head, come to us soaring.
With the far darkness made of the she-rain
      over your head, come to us soaring.   25
With the zigzag lightning flung out on high
      over your head, come to us soaring.

1. Both selections translated by Washington Matthews.   2. In performance each line of the prayer is first recited by the chanter, then repeated by the patient.   3. Pronounced *tsay-gee'-hee*, a distant canyon and site of the *house made of dawn* (line 2), a prehistoric ruin, regarded as the home of deities.   4. Rain without thunder. *He-rain*: rain with thunder.   5. Emblem of peace, of happiness, of prosperity [Translator's note].   6. Thunder, regarded as a bird.

With the rainbow hanging high over your head,
    come to us soaring.
With the far darkness made of the dark cloud on
    the ends of your wings, come to us soaring.
With the far darkness made of the he-rain on
    the ends of your wings, come to us soaring.
With the far darkness made of the dark mist on
    the ends of your wings, come to us soaring.   30
With the far darkness made of the she-rain on
    the ends of your wings, come to us soaring.
With the zigzag lightning flung out on high on
    the ends of your wings, come to us soaring.
With the rainbow hanging high on the ends of
    your wings, come to us soaring.
With the near darkness made of the dark cloud, of
    the he-rain, of the dark mist, and of the
    she-rain, come to us.
With the darkness on the earth, come to us.   35
With these I wish the foam floating on the flowing
    water over the roots of the great corn.
I have made your sacrifice.
I have prepared a smoke[7] for you.
My feet restore for me.
My limbs restore for me.   40
My body restore for me.
My mind restore for me.
My voice restore for me.
Today, take out your spell for me.
Today, take away your spell for me.   45
Away from me you have taken it.
Far off from me it is taken.
Far off you have done it.
Happily I recover.
Happily my interior becomes cool.   50
Happily my eyes regain their power.
Happily my head becomes cool.
Happily my limbs regain their power.
Happily I hear again.
Happily for me *the spell*[8] is taken off.   55
Happily may I walk.
Impervious to pain, may I walk.
Feeling light within, may I walk.
With lively feelings, may I walk.
Happily abundant dark clouds I desire.   60
Happily abundant dark mists I desire.
Happily abundant passing showers I desire.
Happily an abundance of vegetation I desire.
Happily an abundance of pollen I desire.
Happily abundant dew I desire.   65
Happily may fair white corn, to the ends of the
    earth, come with you.

---

7. Painted reed filled with native tobacco, offered as a sacrifice.   8. Words added by the translator.

Happily may fair yellow corn, to the ends of the
    earth, come with you.
Happily may fair blue corn, to the ends of the
    earth, come with you.
Happily may fair corn of all kinds, to the ends
    of the earth, come with you.
Happily may fair plants of all kinds, to the ends
    of the earth, come with you.   70
Happily may fair goods of all kinds, to the ends
    of the earth, come with you.
Happily may fair jewels of all kinds, to the ends
    of the earth, come with you.
With these before you, happily may they come
    with you.
With these behind you, happily may they come
    with you.
With these below you, happily may they come
    with you.   75
With these above you, happily may they come
    with you.
With these all around you, happily may they
    come with you.
Thus happily you accomplish your tasks.
Happily the old men will regard you.
Happily the old women will regard you.   80
Happily the young men will regard you.
Happily the young women will regard you.
Happily the boys will regard you.
Happily the girls will regard you.
Happily the children will regard you.   85
Happily the chiefs will regard you.
Happily, as they scatter in different directions,
    they will regard you.
Happily, as they approach their homes, they will
    regard you.
Happily may their roads home be on the trail of pollen.
Happily may they all get back.   90
In beauty I walk.
With beauty before me, I walk.
With beauty behind me, I walk.
With beauty below me, I walk.
With beauty above me, I walk.   95
With beauty all around me, I walk.
It is finished in beauty,
It is finished in beauty,
It is finished in beauty,
It is finished in beauty.   100

Finishing Song

    From the pond in the white valley—
    The young man doubts it—
    He takes up his sacrifice,

With that he now heals.
With that your kindred thank you now.   5

From the pools in the green meadow[9] —
The young woman doubts it —
He takes up his sacrifice,[1]
With that he now heals.
With that your kindred thank you now.   10

9. A contrast of landscapes, of the beginning and end of a stream. It rises in a green valley in the mountains and flows down to the lower plains, where it spreads into a single sheet of water. As the dry season
approaches, it shrinks, leaving a white saline efflorescence called alkali. The male is associated with the
sterile, unattractive alkali flat in the first stanza, while the female is named with the pleasant mountain
meadow in the second stanza [adapted from Translator's note].   1. The deity accepts the sacrificial
offering (see n. 7, p. 1386) and effects the healing that benefits the patient and his kindred—though
young men and young women, with the irreverence of youth, may doubt the truth of the ceremony.

ÚKE IWÁGU ÚO
1850?–1916

The Bororo tribal leader Úke Iwágu Úo is known to the outside world as the
earliest teacher of the Roman Catholic Salesian missionaries who in the 1890s
began a hundred-year project to document his culture. As a result of his efforts
and of the continuing diligence of those who came after him, his people, the
eastern Bororo of Matto Grosso State, in southwest Brazil, would become the
subject of a voluminous documentation that has not yet been brought to a close.

Based on a subsistence of hunting and gathering, with a modicum of gardening,
the Bororo had built an exquisitely refined way of life, now recognized for the
complexity of its social organization and for a metaphysics that elaborately integrates the contrasting realms of nature and society. Formerly the masters of a
territory encompassing a hundred thousand square miles, the Bororo suffered dire
losses through the 1800s in clashes with Brazilian colonists. Reduced to a population of a few hundred by the mid-twentieth century and with the western groups
already dispersed, the eastern Bororo faced a crisis that was met in at least one
village by a collective decision to stop bearing children. The news of a self-geno-
cide, as the decision has been called, received international attention. But by the
1970s, energized by new leadership, the Bororo had recommitted themselves to
survival as a people, strengthening Bororo traditions to the fullest extent possible —
while the Salesian fathers, meanwhile, labored to complete their monumental
ethnography.

Geriguigatugo, also called *The Origin of Wind and Rain*, together with other
stories narrated by Úke Iwágu Úo, was published in Italian and Bororo in an edition of 1925 that cannot be said to have gained a wide audience. In 1942 the
Salesians republished the story, this time in Portuguese and with a different ending, again to little notice. But in the 1960s it reappeared as the "key myth" in the
first volume of Claude Lévi-Strauss's four-volume *Mythologiques* (1964–71) and
thereby became, along with Bororo narratives as a whole, a topic of high interest
among anthropologists and literary scholars, especially in Europe and the Americas.

In *Mythologiques* Lévi-Strauss, the master anthropologist-philosopher and chief
exponent of French structuralism, was proposing no less than a unified theory of
myth based on nearly a thousand native American texts minutely analyzed—and

continually harking back to the so-called key myth (to which all the other myths could be made to refer). *Geriguigatugo* had been chosen to fill this role, Lévi-Strauss explains, "not so much arbitrarily as through an intuitive feeling that it was both rich and rewarding."

Briefly, the story tells of a boy at puberty who rapes his mother, driving his father to a murderous vengeance from which the young man is repeatedly saved by his grandmother. In the end, rejecting society, young Geriguigatugo takes the grandmother and retires with her to the other world, sending harsh rainstorms to punish humanity for having allowed him to suffer so many ordeals at the hands of the father.

Like all good myth, *Geriguigatugo* is constructed in a way that is puzzling to conventional Western literary criticism. There is no character development in the usual sense; the actors are stick figures to say the least. The plot is largely unmotivated, cluttered with precisely itemized incidents that appear irrelevant, and there is no clear line between fantasy and reality. Before the mid-nineteenth century and the advent of modernism, such a text would have been dismissed as incomprehensible. Nor would it even have been preserved in European script. Yet since the late 1800s, archive boxes and library shelves have accommodated increasingly vast amounts of pure, uncontaminated myth, presenting us with the paradox that texts felt to be "ancient" or "primitive" belong not to the past but to twentieth-century literature.

It should not be forgotten that modernism is in part an antiquarian movement. The mask-faces of Pablo Picasso's *Les Demoiselles d'Avignon* (1907), the volcanic rhythms of Igor Stravinsky's *Rite of Spring* (1913), and the studied use of myth and ritual in James Joyce's *Ulysses* (1922) and T. S. Eliot's *The Waste Land* (1922) are reminders that the artists who brought Europe into the twentieth century were also scholars, determined to use the new archival material in ways that would revitalize Western culture. And yet critics who freely ponder the abstractions of Joyce and Eliot—or, from a later time, Alain Robbe-Grillet—may recoil from genuine myth. One does not wish to invent explanations for the literature of a culture so far from home.

But myth does not go away. Indeed, the question of what to do about it has become one of the ongoing debates of the modern era, with no consensus yet in sight. The most influential approaches, in chronological order, have been nature mythology, Freudian psychoanalysis, Jungian theory, and Lévi-Straussian structuralism. In each case the text is read as a string of symbols, concealing an inner process: for nature mythologists, the diurnal cycle of the sun or the annual death and rebirth of vegetation; for Freudians, the family drama; for Jungians, the individual's progress toward wholeness; or for Lévi-Straussians, an exercise in logic, aimed at the resolution of a dilemma.

As the twentieth century draws to a close, however, the nagging voice of doubt can be heard with ever greater persistence: Why must one look to Europe for the exegesis of native American literature?

The world has changed, and native people no longer rely on missionaries and anthropologists to publish and explicate their traditions. Rather they collaborate with outsiders as co-authors, or increasingly, they publish the material themselves without intervention. Native criticism may then become part of the project, and one learns why the narrators themselves place more or less value on a particular work. But lacking so specific a benefit, the reader may nonetheless turn to the cultural documentation surrounding the work—which in the case of the Bororo is exceptionally rich.

In traditional Bororo society the boy at puberty becomes a man through an arduous series of rituals lasting as long as a year. In the culminating ceremony he is fitted with a penis sheath, the badge of male adulthood, and formally removed from the custody of his mother. When this event is imminent, the women weep for the loss of their sons, as if mourning a death. In fact, the rite is often postponed until an actual death occurs, so that the initiation and the funeral can be held together. The sheath, it is said, represents the women of the particular clans into which the young man will be eligible to marry. Until marriage he sleeps in the men's house at the center of the village, later moving in with the family of his bride, never again to live with his mother's people. In *Geriguigatugo*, the young man resists, or reverses, this scenario, clinging to his mother (in the sense that he chooses her as a sexual partner) and ending as a bachelor in the company of his grandmother. In life, however, bachelorhood is not an acceptable option. For the traditional Bororo, marriage is virtually obligatory.

One further point: it is obvious that the father in the story tries to kill the son by sending him down to the souls of the dead, but it may be unclear why the same threat is implied by sending him aloft to the nest of the macaws. The reason, presumably, is that according to the Bororo theory of transmigration, macaws themselves are dead souls.

The complete collection of 111 Bororo narratives recorded by the Salesian missionaries is published in English in Johannes Wilbert and Karin Simoneau, eds., *Folk Literature of the Bororo Indians* (1983). Claude Lévi-Strauss's principal discussion of *Geriguigatugo* appears in his *The Raw and the Cooked*, vol. 1 of *Mythologiques* (1969), trans. John Weightman and Doreen Weightman. For an engaging description of Bororo society see Lévi-Strauss, *Tristes Tropiques: An Anthropological Study of Primitive Societies in Brazil* (1961). Bororo metaphysics is treated in Jon Christopher Crocker, *Vital Souls: Bororo Cosmology, Natural Symbolism, and Shamanism* (1985).

PRONOUNCING GLOSSARY

The following list uses common English syllables and stress accents to provide rough equivalents of selected words whose pronunciation may be unfamiliar to the general reader.

Baigareu: *bai-gah-ray'-oo*

Bokwadorireu: *boh-kwah-doh-ree-ray'-oo*

Bororo: *boh-roh'-roh*

Geriguigatugo: *jay-ree-gee-gah-too'-goh*

Kiwareu: *kee-wah-ray'-oo*

Korogo: *koh-roh'-goh*

Kugago: *koo-gah'-goh*

Salesian: *suh-lee'-zhun*

Úke Iwágo Úo: *oo'-kay ee-wah'-goh oo'-oh*

Geriguigatugo[1]

The people of the ancient time were gathering leaves for the penis sheath.[2] Korogo joined the other women and went along too. Then a boy, her

---

1. Translated by John Bierhorst.   2. A palm-leaf wrapper, customarily worn by men and presented to boys on the occasion of their initiation. Thus the stage is set for a boys' puberty rite.

son, caught sight of her and raped her—his own mother. The boy was
Geriguigatugo. His father was Bokwadorireu.

When the woman returned to her lodge, the father could not help but
notice that a boy's ornamental feathers were caught in his wife's girdle. To
learn who had treated his wife in this manner, he ordered the people to
begin the boys' soul-dance.[3] And as they danced he looked and looked to
see which boys were wearing feathers on their arms. But in vain. His son
was the only one with arm feathers.

Then he called his son once more and ordered him to go tell the people
there must be another dance. And as they danced again, he watched to
see if any boys were wearing arm feathers. But in vain. The boys were
unadorned. Only his son wore decorations, he alone wore feathers on his
arms.

Now the father was enraged, and he ordered his son to go down to the
nest of souls to fetch the large rattle.[4] Then the boy ran at once to his
grandmother, saying, "Grandmother, Grandmother! Father says I must get
the large rattle that belongs to the souls. He wants it." And his grandmother said, "You can't do such a difficult thing"—that's what she said.
But then she said, "Go to the hummingbird! The hummingbird will help
you get it." Then the boy went to the hummingbird, saying, "Hummingbird, Hummingbird, we must go to the nest of souls to get the large rattle."

Then he went with him there—went with him to the souls' nest, where
the large rattle was. He went all the way down to the souls. Yet the nest is
beneath the water. Thus the boy himself sat alongside the water, he stayed
behind, the bird went on.

Then the hummingbird flew to the souls' nest and cut the string that
held the large rattle. It dropped and went *djo-o-o!* And at that the souls
cried, "Umh! umh! umh! umh!" and they tried to shoot him, but he flew
swiftly away: they failed to wound him. He came a second time and cut
the string. Then he returned to the boy and gave him the rattle. Then the
hummingbird quickly flew off. And the boy went home to his father, saying, "Father, your rattle!"

The father had acted this way so that the souls could kill his son. But
the grandmother's knowledge had been great. She had counseled her
grandson.

Now the father called his son again and told him to go to the souls' nest
to get the small rattle. At once the boy ran to his grandmother, saying,
"Grandmother, Grandmother! Father says I must get the small rattle that
belongs to the souls." Then the grandmother said, "You can't do such a
difficult thing. But go to the dove! With the dove you can get it." And he
went to the dove and said, "Dove, Dove, we must go to the souls' nest to
get the small rattle." Then they went off together to where the souls lived,
to their waterside. And the boy stayed behind and the dove went on.

Then the dove flew down to the small rattle. Then he cut the string that
held the rattle, and the rattle went *djo-o-o!* as it struck the water. At that
the souls cried, "Umh! umh! umh! umh!" and they shot their arrows. But

---

3. Part of the initiation ceremony.   4. A musical instrument used in the dance. *Nest of souls:* beneath
the water, where the dead reside.

he flew so swiftly they failed to hit him. And then he returned, got the small rattle, and flew back to the boy. Then the dove disappeared. And the boy took it home to his father, saying, "Father, your rattle!"

Then the father called his son once again and told him to go to the souls' nest to get the peccary anklet.[5] And the boy ran off to his grandmother, saying, "Grandmother, Grandmother! Father says I must get the souls' peccary anklet." Then the grandmother said, "Try the mammori.[6] With the mammori you'll get the souls' anklet." So the boy ran to the mammori: "My father says we must get the souls' anklet." Then together they went, to get the souls' anklet. The boy stayed back, the mammori went on.

The mammori flew down to the anklet and cut the string. Then the anklet went *djo-o-o!* as it hit the water. And the souls cried, "Umh! umh! umh! umh!" and they shot at him then. And because he flew poorly, they hit him again and again in the chest. Yet they failed to kill him: he was able to bring back the peccary anklet. He gave it to the boy, then flew out of sight. And the boy went home to his father, saying, "Father, your anklet!"

Seeing that his son had returned alive, the father cried, "Hah! May you be killed by the red macaws!" Then he spoke to him again, saying, "O man! O man! We must be off now to the macaws' nest!" And the boy ran to his grandmother and said, "Grandmother, Grandmother! Father says I must go with him to the macaws' nest!" But the grandmother did not know what to do. The boy became agitated. Then at last she picked up her walking stick and gave it to him, saying, "Push this into the nest, quickly!"

Then the boy went along with his father to the base of the rock where the nest was, and there the father, finding a pole, raised it against the face of the rock so the boy could climb up. But as soon as the boy reached the cleft where the nest was, the father stopped holding the pole, thinking the boy would fall and be killed. Then quickly the boy pushed his grandmother's stick into the cleft and held on, dangling, crying for help, while the father went back to the village.

Then the boy, looking up, saw a vine hanging down within reach. He seized it and climbed to the top of the rock. Recovered somewhat from his fright and exertion, he found he was hungry. Then, using the shrubs that grew on the rock, he made a bow and many arrows and began hunting the lizards that abounded there. He killed many. Then he ate some and fastened the rest to his belt and to his arm- and ankle-bands and carried them with him.

But they started to rot and grow foul, until at last the stench overwhelmed him and he fell to the ground unconscious. Then a flock of urubus and other vultures flew down on him and greedily fed on the lizards. And when they'd finished the lizards, they attacked his buttocks. Then he frightened them off with a huge strap. But they came back and kept pecking from behind until his buttocks were eaten away.

---

5. A jingle string, a kind of rattle made from hooves of the peccary, or wild pig, used in the boys' soul-dance. Note the decreasing power of the three musical instruments—the large rattle, the small rattle, the anklet jingles—as the hero, rather than his representative, draws closer and closer to death.   6. A giant grasshopper.

And then with their beaks they grasped him by the belt and by the arm- and leg-bands and lifted him up. They flew far into the sky, then at last put him down at the base of the rock where the macaws' nest was.

He came to, as though waking from a long sleep. He was hungry and began eating the fruits that were plentiful there. Yet he saw that whatever he ate went immediately through him. The birds had destroyed his anus.

Then he remembered a story his grandmother had told, in which the same thing had happened and the missing parts had been molded out of soft yams. And so he did likewise, he molded new hind parts out of soft yams. Then he started to eat once again to see if they worked as they should. They did. Then he set off for home. But the village was no longer there. The people had moved.

Then for many days he wandered in search of the path that would lead him to the new village, but for a long time he looked in vain. Then at last he saw stick marks and human tracks, and he knew that the tracks had been made by his grandmother and his little brother, and the marks by his grandmother's stick. Then he felt a desire to be with her at once, and he said:

"Baigareu![7] Fly at once! *There!*" He changed into a baigareu, flying right to the spot he had meant. Then he changed back into himself. Then he saw that the tracks led on, and he said:

"Kugago! Fly at once! *There!*" He changed into a kugago, flew right to the spot, changed back to himself, then saw that the tracks led on, and said:

"Little Bird! Fly at once! *There!*" And he changed to a little bird, flew right to the spot, changed back to himself, then saw that the tracks led on, and said:

"Kiwareu! Fly at once! *There!*" Then he changed to a kiwareu, flew right to the spot, changed back to himself, then saw that the tracks led on. And he said:

"Butterfly! Fly at once! *There!*" Then he changed to a butterfly and flew on, and there before him he saw his grandmother, walking along with her stick, and beside her his little brother.

Then before he got there he changed back to himself and followed along behind her. Hearing steps, the grandmother said to her little grandson, "Look back! See who's coming!" He looked, then said, "My elder brother!"

The boy was glad to see his grandmother again. Through her wisdom she had saved him from many dangers.

Then he said to her, "I will live with our people no more. They have treated me badly. And to punish my father and all the others who have made me suffer, I will send them wind, cold, and rain." Then he led his grandmother off to a distant and beautiful country and told her that she must remain there, that he would go punish the people and then return. And so in exchange for the treatment he'd received from his father, he punished the people—and turned into wind, cold, and rain.

---

7. An unidentified bird, the first in a series of five birdlike creatures, evidently decreasing in size.

SIGMUND FREUD
1856–1939

Psychoanalysis, for its founder and for those he influenced, was a new cosmology comparable only to the revolutionary discoveries of Nicolaus Copernicus and Charles Darwin. Each changed the way that human beings thought about themselves: Copernicus, by proving the universe did not revolve around earth; Darwin, by showing that humanity was only one of many evolving biological species; and Sigmund Freud, by offering a model of the unconscious mind and its dependence on drives rooted in sexual desire. Although he was suspicious of philosophers for offering overbroad systems detached from experience, and he always considered himself a scientist, Freud was in fact a system maker whose creative imagination put a personal stamp on everything he wrote. His work in turn has stamped the twentieth century, spreading to all parts of the globe touched by modern Western thought. From the early case histories to the later, more speculative, essays on civilization, Freud struggled to understand the nature of human mental activity. Like Proust (to whom he has often been compared), he probed questions of identity, memory, and desire; interrogated personal experience; disclosed his own thought processes; proposed explanations; and constantly reconsidered and revised his ideas. Like fiction writers in general (or at least nineteenth-century fiction writers), Freud imposed a master plot on his scientific inquiries by following a central theme that he tried to bring to a logical conclusion. He himself said that his case histories read like short stories, and he gave the title *The Man Moses, A Historical Novel* to the first draft of *Moses and Monotheism*. The breadth of Freud's appeal may indeed be attributed to the persuasiveness of his prose and to the dramatic power of analytic scenes that are framed in a tight, novel-like structure of plot development and the discovery of answers.

Many of Freud's ideas or terms have entered common usage. The "Freudian slip" (a slip of the tongue that reveals hidden preoccupations), the "Oedipus complex" (a son's rivalry with his father for authority and for his mother's affection), the "Freudian symbol" (an object, especially one linear or curved, that suggests genitalia), the "castration complex," the "death wish," the "repression" of disturbing memories as an unconscious defense mechanism, the "repetition compulsion" that leads people to repeat unpleasant experiences, dreams and "dreamwork" as the voice of unconscious wishes, free association as a tactic for revealing obsessions, and the multiple forms of narcissism (self-love), all refer to concepts that Freud developed in his work.

Contemporary discussions of personality cannot do without Freud's insights. He did not invent the unconscious, but he focused attention on the strength of its ties to conscious thought. He was the first to interpret dreams as an expression of unconscious impulses. More than that, he described categories by which one could analyze dream structures. Human beings defend themselves from continued contact with painful reality, argued Freud, by transforming the disturbing experience through tactics he called condensation, displacement, representation, symbolization, and a "secondary revision" that retells events in more coherent—and acceptable—form. Interpersonal relationships, he added, were similarly governed by complex buried motivations. Part of the analyst's job was to decipher the underlying pattern suggested by the repressions and revisions of a patient's story. Even in such a controlled medical situation, however, there were two further complications that needed to be taken into account: the "transference" by which a patient sought to make the analyst enact a familiar role in his or her drama, and the "countertransference" that took place when the analyst accepted such a role. In reviewing his first case history ("*Dora*," presented here), Freud recognized that he had not yet sufficiently accounted for his patient's transference. Contemporary critics feel that Freud also never recognized his own countertransference, and the fact that he himself had adopted a role in relating to Dora. Such a situation would not have seemed impossible to Freud, who knew how difficult it was to determine motivation and who was constantly on the lookout for blind spots in theory and practice.

Freud's scientism is colored by a deep respect for art and literature. Writers and artists are cited liberally throughout his work; Goethe, Shakespeare, Dostoevsky, Leonardo da Vinci, and Michelangelo are used as points of departure for individual studies. He named a fundamental psychoanalytic concept after Sophocles' Oedipus. The creative artist, according to Freud, gives aesthetic form to personal "phantasies" or daydreams, but these fantasies are shared—in one form or another—by every human being. Literature and art display the workings of the mind, even if they do not explicate meanings; Freud planned to reverse the order and to formulate scientific insights accompanied by a "detailed description of mental processes such as we are accustomed to find in the works of imaginative writers." If art and psychoanalysis both reveal mental activity, they also have a similar therapeutic value: psychoanalysis clarifies and cures the individual, and artistic creations—the "mental assets of civilization"—are defenses against destructive impulses that, unchecked, lead straight to barbarism. Paradoxically, modern writers who have learned from Freud (for example, Joyce, Kafka, D. H. Lawrence, Beckett, Ellison, Tanizaki, and others included in this volume) are less intent on the therapeutic possibilities of art than they are on capturing the unconscious in dream scenes, associative language, and the depiction of complexes or madness. In both instances, nonetheless, the aim is to give a fuller representation of human mental activity by taking into account the role played by unconscious desires.

Sigismund Freud (he later changed the name to Sigmund) was born on May 6, 1856, in the small town of Freiberg in Moravia (now part of Czech Republic). His father was a small-scale wool merchant, some twenty years older than his third wife, Freud's mother, and the family was relatively poor. In 1860, they moved to Vienna, a city that Freud claimed to dislike but where he lived for seventy-nine years until forced to flee by the Nazis.

Sigmund was the oldest of his mother's seven children; she doted on him, and the household revolved around this brilliant young son who was expected to achieve great things. He did extremely well in school, graduating from the Gymnasium (academic high school) with impressive grades and beginning his medical studies at the University of Vienna in 1873. Here he had his first serious encounters with anti-Semitism. "I found that I was expected to feel myself inferior and an alien because I was a Jew. I refused absolutely to do the first of these things." Freud later noted that this experience of being considered an outsider, cut off from the "compact majority," taught him to rely on his own judgment and sustained him in later intellectual battles.

In this early period, the young medical student was particularly interested in physiological explanations for human behavior. He studied with the famous physiologist E. W. von Brücke and the brain anatomist Theodor Meynert, receiving his medical degree in 1881. Although he would have preferred a career in research, he prepared for medical practice at the General Hospital so as to be able to support a wife and family. In 1886, he entered private practice as a neurologist and married Martha Bernays after a four-year engagement. Around this time, Freud began to take a greater interest in psychological rather than physiological approaches to brain activity. During the winter of 1885–86 he had studied with the neurologist

Jean-Martin Charcot at the Parisian mental hospital of La Salpêtrière. Freud was impressed by Charcot's investigations of hysteria and hypnosis, and he reported on what he had learned when he returned to Vienna. The Viennese medical establishment, however, was shocked by Charcot's ideas (especially the concept of male hysteria). Freud was publicly attacked by his former teacher Meynert and excluded from the laboratories of the General Hospital. In private practice, he continued his work on hysteria, gradually moving from a dependence on medical hypnosis to the use of free association. In 1895 he published (with the Viennese physician Josef Breuer) *Studies on Hysteria*. The book introduced what was called a "cathartic" treatment by which patients would recall, understand, and render harmless painful memories.

Freud felt that hypnosis had only limited value and that its cures were too often temporary; he preferred to explore the broader possibilities of free association. If patients could recall events under hypnosis, he reasoned, they must in fact "know" them at some level of unconscious memory even if they resisted bringing that material to the surface. Freud's investigation of the selective processes of memory—of what he would call "defense mechanisms" that protect the subject from painful experiences—initiated the study of psychoanalysis proper. He would now describe various defense mechanisms used by individuals to preserve their self-image and sense of well-being. His own self-analysis, undertaken in 1897 after the death of his father, brought forth not only the concept of an Oedipus complex but many other insights into the effects of unconscious processes on conscious behavior and on dreams. *The Interpretation of Dreams*, published in November 1899 (dated 1900), argued that dreams were not random occurrences but had their own coded meaning. Freud included his own "Irma" dream among various examples of the way that dreams censored disturbing material while fulfilling an underlying repressed wish. Interpreting dreams became an important part of his clinical practice and was central to such case histories as *"Dora"* (1905) and *"The Wolfman"* (1918). The influence of unconscious impulses on conscious behavior was also a theme of two other volumes published around the turn of the century: *The Psychopathology of Everyday Life* (1901) and *Jokes and Their Relation to the Unconscious* (1905).

Freud was disappointed at the small response to *The Interpretation of Dreams*, his first major book, and indeed his studies of sexuality attracted far more attention. Contemporary audiences were disconcerted by his clinical descriptions of "normal" and "abnormal" sexual practices and his recognition of sexual drives in women as well as in men. Even more upsetting was his description of a many-sided or "polymorphously perverse" sexuality in children. Freud was convinced, however, of the causative relation between childhood sexuality, its inevitable channeling and repression, and the adult personality. He continued to explore aspects of human sexuality throughout his work, publishing the controversial *Three Essays on Sexuality* in 1905 and revising and expanding the text through subsequent editions until the sixth and last edition of 1925.

In the last decades of his life, Freud turned to broader speculations and the creation of explanatory structures. With the essay *On Narcissism* (1914), he began to suggest models of the conscious and unconscious mind that included the related concepts of ego, id, super-ego and ego-ideal: very loosely, the ego as rational consciousness, the id as primitive energy ("the dark, inaccessible part of our personality . . . striving to bring about the satisfaction of instinctive needs") and the super-ego as an internalized ideal image of human behavior, learned from parents and society, that "represents the ethical standards of mankind." An increasingly somber tone accompanied the elaboration of these ideas in *Beyond the Pleasure Principle* (1920), which countered pleasure with a "reality principle" and added the notion of a "death instinct," and in the revised and definitive statement of *The Ego and the Id* (1923). Freud did not content himself with structural models of the individual mind, however, and adapted his theories of mental conflict to larger models of civilization. *Totem and Taboo* (1913), *Group Psychology* (1921), *The Future of an Illusion* (1927), and *Moses and Monotheism* (1938) focused on the relation of individual and group, analyzing particularly the role of religion. Gradually, Freud envisaged an all-encompassing, dialectical scheme in which Eros and Thanatos, the life and death instincts, figured as opposing forces in human beings and in civilization itself. His late study, *Civilization and Its Discontents* (1930), described civilization as a hard-won and not entirely pleasurable prize achieved only through renunciation and control of instinctual desires. The scientific inquiry that began with laboratory studies of cerebral anatomy had emerged in a philosophic essay of grandiose scope and tragic vision. The span of Freud's achievement was noted in the citation for the Goethe Prize awarded that same year: he had "opened access to the driving forces of the soul and thus created the possibility of recognizing the emergence and construction of cultural forms and of curing some of the soul's illnesses."

As the founder of psychoanalysis and a brilliant writer in his own right, Freud was an exceptional innovator whose influence on twentieth-century thought can scarcely be overestimated. He was also a creature of his place and time, and even those who feel greatly indebted to him recognize the degree to which he shared a traditional nineteenth-century Western social perspective. Freudian psychology claims universal validity, but its structures are Western and patriarchal, that is, it is based on Western models of a "nuclear" family, and it is invariably governed by a masculine perspective. Traditional kinship structures in India or Africa, for example, do not respond so readily to the Freudian model. In the West, the strongest criticism of Freud's theories of sexuality has come, in fact, from those who note in them the subterranean influence of Victorian gender stereotypes. In Freud's day, women had little control over their own lives: fathers, husbands, or male relatives decided what was best for them. Despite his bold recognition of female sexuality, Freud held conventional views of women's social role. One of the more than nine hundred letters he wrote his fiancée during their four-year engagement reveals his personal attitude: "It seems a completely unrealistic notion to send women into the struggle for existence in the same way as men. Am I to think of my delicate sweet girl as a competitor?" Readers may well feel that both aspects emerge in the "Dora" case: on the one hand, an intrepid and imaginative researcher pursuing medical truth through all obstacles and, on the other, a man whose analytic attitude toward his patient is shaped by existing cultural attitudes and by what he thinks is "normal" for a young woman her age.

Dora's real name was Ida Bauer. At age eighteen, she was sent to Freud for treatment after her parents had discovered an apparent suicide letter. Her father, who had previously been Freud's patient, hoped that Freud would bring Dora to reason—which included reconciling her with the "K." family and with Herr K., whom she had accused of propositioning her. Dora was reluctant to undertake the treatment, and she did not welcome Freud's intensifying explanations of what was wrong with her; after eleven weeks she notified him that she would not be coming back. Freud was disappointed not to finish the treatment, especially since his analysis was providing evidence for theories outlined in *The Interpretation of Dreams*. He published his account five years later as a "Fragment of an Analysis of a Case of Hysteria," but this "fragment" continued to occupy his mind and he added footnotes in later editions.

"*Dora*" is the first of Freud's major case histories, and for many years it was a model for students of psychoanalysis. It has also been called a literary masterwork, and indeed it can be read as a novel in which the narrative point of view is as fascinating as the plot and characters. The author's perspective is personal as well as professional, and he is hurt and even a little vindictive when Dora decides to break off the relationship. His preface observes that Dora may be pained to see her case in print, and he reinforces his argument through numerous footnotes that justify and comment personally on his interpretation of events that themselves recall a romantic novel: there are related love stories, misunderstandings, and betrayal and an unhappy heroine whose destiny is the focus of attention. The author arranges the sequence of events "for the sake of presenting the case in a more connected form." He selects some characters for extended description (the father, Herr K.) while dismissing others equally close (the mother) in a few words. Dramatic tension builds as Freud observes and interprets his subject's every move, concluding triumphantly that "he who has eyes to see and ears to hear, becomes convinced that mortals can keep no secret. If their lips are silent, they gossip with their fingertips; betrayal forces its way through every pore." Freud was not unaware of the literary quality of his case histories: he complained mildly that "it still strikes me myself as strange that the case histories I write should read like short stories and that, as one might say, they lack the serious stamp of science." Yet the stamp of science is also evident in "*Dora*"; it emerges in the narrator's dedication to discovering the truth of mental processes, in the tightly controlled structure he imposes on his quest and—most obviously—in the clinical detail with which he analyzes evidence. Literature and science come together, finally, in Freud's practice of displaying his own tactical strategy as he goes; with "*Dora*" this laying bare of narrative principles fits both scientific method and modernist literary technique.

Charles Bernheimer and Claire Kahane, eds., *In Dora's Case: Freud-Hysteria-Feminism* (1985), present twelve major essays on the "Dora" case, a two-part introduction, and a biographical note. Peter Gay, *Freud: A Life for Our Time* (1988), is a full, very readable biography by a major cultural historian and Freud scholar. Gerald Levin, *Sigmund Freud* (1975), is a brief biography that gives descriptions of individual works and a chronology. Madelon Sprengnether, *The Spectral Mother: Freud, Feminism, and Psychoanalysis* (1990), contains a revisionary discussion of Freud's ambiguous relationship to Dora. Malcolm Bowie, *Freud, Proust and Lacan: Theory as Fiction* (1987), sees the authors as theorists and fiction writers who develop portraits of mental life; the book includes a chapter on each writer, a chapter comparing Freud and Proust, and a note on translations. Hannah S. Decker, *Freud, Dora and Vienna 1900* (1990), describes the cultural context that influenced both Freud and Dora, and Robin Lakoff and James Coyne, *Father Knows Best: The Use and Abuse of Power in Freud's Case of Dora* (1993), take a feminist approach in analyzing the "Dora" case, its critics, and the cultural assumptions involved in therapeutic relationships. Paul Robinson, *Freud and His Critics* (1993), sympathetically cross-examines the major recent attacks on Freud and concludes with a discussion of Freud's place in intellectual history.

From "Dora"

(Fragment of an Analysis of a Case of Hysteria)[1]

I

The Clinical Picture

In my *Interpretation of Dreams*, published in 1900, I showed that dreams in general can be interpreted, and that after the work of interpreta-

---

1. Translated by Alix Strachey and James Strachey. Freud's prefatory remarks have been omitted.

tion has been completed they can be replaced by perfectly correctly constructed thoughts which can be assigned a recognizable position in the chain of mental events. I wish to give an example in the following pages of the only practical application of which the art of interpreting dreams seems to admit. I have already mentioned in my book how it was that I came upon the problem of dreams. The problem crossed my path as I was endeavouring to cure psychoneuroses by means of a particular psychotherapeutic method. For, among their other mental experiences, my patients told me their dreams, and these dreams seemed to call for insertion in the long thread of connections which spun itself out between a symptom of the disease and a pathogenic idea. At that time I learnt how to translate the language of dreams into the forms of expression of our own thought-language, which can be understood without further help. And I may add that this knowledge is essential for the psycho-analyst; for the dream is one of the roads along which consciousness can be reached by the psychical material which, on account of the opposition aroused by its content, has been cut off from consciousness and repressed, and has thus become pathogenic. The dream, in short, is one of the *détours by which repression can be evaded*; it is one of the principal means employed by what is known as the indirect method of representation in the mind. The following fragment from the history of the treatment of a hysterical girl is intended to show the way in which the interpretation of dreams plays a part in the work of analysis. It will at the same time give me a first opportunity of publishing at sufficient length to prevent further misunderstanding some of my views upon the psychical processes of hysteria and upon its organic determinants. I need no longer apologize on the score of length, since it is now agreed that the exacting demands which hysteria makes upon physician and investigator can be met only by the most sympathetic spirit of inquiry and not by an attitude of superiority and contempt. For,

> *Nicht Kunst und Wissenschaft allein,*
> *Geduld will bei dem Werke sein!*[2]

If I were to begin by giving a full and consistent case history, it would place the reader in a very different situation from that of the medical observer. The reports of the patient's relatives—in the present case I was given one by the eighteen-year-old girl's father—usually afford a very indistinct picture of the course of the illness. I begin the treatment, indeed, by asking the patient to give me the whole story of his life and illness, but even so the information I receive is never enough to let me see my way about the case. This first account may be compared to an unnavigable river whose stream is at one moment choked by masses of rock and at another divided and lost among shallows and sandbanks. I cannot help wondering how it is that the authorities can produce such smooth and precise histories in cases of hysteria. As a matter of fact the patients are incapable of giving such reports about themselves. They can, indeed, give the physician plenty of coherent information about this or that period of

---

2. Science is not enough, nor art; / In this work patience plays a part (German); from Goethe's *Faust*, "Witch's Kitchen," lines 34–35 (Walter Kaufman, trans.).

their lives; but it is sure to be followed by another period as to which their communications run dry, leaving gaps unfilled, and riddles unanswered; and then again will come yet another period which will remain totally obscure and unilluminated by even a single piece of serviceable information. The connections—even the ostensible ones—are for the most part incoherent, and the sequence of different events is uncertain. Even during the course of their story patients will repeatedly correct a particular or a date, and then perhaps, after wavering for some time, return to their first version. The patients' inability to give an ordered history of their life in so far as it coincides with the history of their illness is not merely characteristic of the neurosis. It also possesses great theoretical significance. For this inability has the following grounds. In the first place, patients consciously and intentionally keep back part of what they ought to tell—things that are perfectly well known to them—because they have not got over their feelings of timidity and shame (or discretion, where what they say concerns other people); this is the share taken by *conscious* disingenuousness. In the second place, part of the anamnestic[3] knowledge, which the patients have at their disposal at other times, disappears while they are actually telling their story, but without their making any deliberate reservations: the share taken by *unconscious* disingenuousness. In the third place, there are invariably true amnesias—gaps in the memory into which not only old recollections but even quite recent ones have fallen—and paramnesias,[4] formed secondarily so as to fill in those gaps.[5] When the events themselves have been kept in mind, the purpose underlying the amnesias can be fulfilled just as surely by destroying a connection, and a connection is most surely broken by altering the chronological order of events. The latter always proves to be the most vulnerable element in the store of memory and the one which is most easily subject to repression. Again, we meet with many recollections that are in what might be described as the first stage of repression, and these we find surrounded with doubts. At a later period the doubts would be replaced by a loss or a falsification of memory.[6]

That this state of affairs should exist in regard to the memories relating to the history of the illness is *a necessary correlate of the symptoms and one which is theoretically requisite*. In the further course of the treatment the patient supplies the facts which, though he had known them all along, had been kept back by him or had not occurred to his mind. The paramnesias prove untenable, and the gaps in his memory are filled in. It is only towards the end of the treatment that we have before us an intelligible, consistent, and unbroken case history. Whereas the practical aim of the treatment is to remove all possible symptoms and to replace them by conscious thoughts, we may regard it as a second and theoretical aim to repair all the damages to the patient's memory. These two aims are coincident.

---

3. Recollected, remembered (*anamnesis*: "calling to memory").   4. "Memories" blended of fantasy and actual experience.   5. Amnesias and paramnesias stand in a complementary relation to each other. When there are large gaps in the memory there will be few mistakes in it. And conversely, paramnesias can at a first glance completely conceal the presence of amnesias [Freud's note].   6. If a patient exhibits doubts in the course of his narrative, an empirical rule teaches us to disregard such expressions of his judgement entirely. If the narrative wavers between two versions, we should incline to regard the first one as correct and the second as a product of repression [Freud's note].

When one is reached, so is the other; and the same path leads to them both.

It follows from the nature of the facts which form the material of psychoanalysis that we are obliged to pay as much attention in our case histories to the purely human and social circumstances of our patients as to the somatic data and the symptoms of the disorder. Above all, our interest will be directed towards their family circumstances—and not only, as will be seen later, for the purpose of enquiring into their heredity.

The family circle of the eighteen-year-old girl who is the subject of this paper included, besides herself, her two parents and a brother who was one and a half years her senior. Her father was the dominating figure in this circle, owing to his intelligence and his character as much as to the circumstances of his life. It was those circumstances which provided the framework for the history of the patient's childhood and illness. At the time at which I began the girl's treatment her father was in his late forties, a man of rather unusual activity and talents, a large manufacturer in very comfortable circumstances. His daughter was most tenderly attached to him, and for that reason her critical powers, which developed early, took all the more offence at many of his actions and peculiarities.

Her affection for him was still further increased by the many severe illnesses which he had been through since her sixth year. At that time he had fallen ill with tuberculosis and the family had consequently moved to a small town in a good climate, situated in one of our southern provinces. There his lung trouble rapidly improved; but, on account of the precautions which were still considered necessary, both parents and children continued for the next ten years or so to reside chiefly in this spot, which I shall call B——. When her father's health was good, he used at times to be away, on visits to his factories. During the hottest part of the summer the family used to move to a health-resort in the hills.

When the girl was about ten years old, her father had to go through a course of treatment in a darkened room on account of a detached retina. As a result of this misfortune his vision was permanently impaired. His gravest illness occurred some two years later. It took the form of a confusional attack, followed by symptoms of paralysis and slight mental disturbances. A friend of his (who plays a part in the story with which we shall be concerned later on) persuaded him, while his condition had scarcely improved, to travel to Vienna with his physician and come to me for advice. I hesitated for some time as to whether I ought not to regard the case as one of tabo-paralysis,[7] but I finally decided upon a diagnosis of a diffuse vascular affection; and since the patient admitted having had a specific infection before his marriage, I prescribed an energetic course of anti-luetic[8] treatment, as a result of which all the remaining disturbances passed off. It is no doubt owing to this fortunate intervention of mine that four years later he brought his daughter, who had meanwhile grown unmistakably neurotic, and introduced her to me, and that after another two years he handed her over to me for psychotherapeutic treatment.

---

7. Paralysis resulting from syphilis attacking the spinal cord and sensory nerves.   8. Antisyphilis.

I had in the meantime also made the acquaintance in Vienna of a sister of his, who was a little older than himself. She gave clear evidence of a severe form of psychoneurosis without any characteristically hysterical symptoms. After a life which had been weighed down by an unhappy marriage, she died of a marasmus[9] which made rapid advances and the symptoms of which were, as a matter of fact, never fully cleared up. An elder brother of the girl's father, whom I once happened to meet, was a hypochondriacal bachelor.

The sympathies of the girl herself, who, as I have said, became my patient at the age of eighteen, had always been with the father's side of the family, and ever since she had fallen ill she had taken as her model the aunt who has just been mentioned. There could be no doubt, too, that it was from her father's family that she had derived not only her natural gifts and her intellectual precocity but also the predisposition to her illness. I never made her mother's acquaintance. From the accounts given me by the girl and her father I was led to imagine her as an uncultivated woman and above all as a foolish one, who had concentrated all her interests upon domestic affairs, especially since her husband's illness and the estrangement to which it led. She presented the picture, in fact, of what might be called the "housewife's psychosis." She had no understanding of her children's more active interests, and was occupied all day long in cleaning the house with its furniture and utensils and in keeping them clean—to such an extent as to make it almost impossible to use or enjoy them. This condition, traces of which are to be found often enough in normal housewives, inevitably reminds one of forms of obsessional washing and other kinds of obsessional cleanliness. But such women (and this applied to the patient's mother) are entirely without insight into their illness, so that one essential characteristic of an "obsessional neurosis" is lacking. The relations between the girl and her mother had been unfriendly for years. The daughter looked down on her mother and used to criticize her mercilessly, and she had withdrawn completely from her influence.

During the girl's earlier years, her only brother (her elder by a year and a half) had been the model which her ambitions had striven to follow. But in the last few years the relations between the brother and sister had grown more distant. The young man used to try so far as he could to keep out of the family disputes; but when he was obliged to take sides he would support his mother. So that the usual sexual attraction had drawn together the father and daughter on the one side and the mother and son on the other.

The patient, to whom I shall in future give the name of "Dora," had even at the age of eight begun to develop neurotic symptoms. She became subject at that time to chronic dyspnoea[1] with occasional accesses in which the symptom was very much aggravated. The first outset occurred after a short expedition in the mountains and was accordingly put down to over-exertion. In the course of six months, during which she was made to rest and was carefully looked after, this condition gradually passed off. The family doctor seems to have had not a moment's hesitation in diag-

---

9. A wasting away of the body.   1. Difficult or labored breathing.

nosing the disorder as purely nervous and in excluding any organic cause for the dyspnoea; but he evidently considered this diagnosis compatible with the aetiology of over-exertion.

The little girl went through the usual infectious diseases of childhood without suffering any lasting damage. As she herself told me—and her words were intended to convey a deeper meaning—her brother was as a rule the first to start the illness and used to have it very slightly, and she would then follow suit with a severe form of it. When she was about twelve she began to suffer from unilateral headaches in the nature of a migraine, and from attacks of nervous coughing. At first these two symptoms always appeared together, but they became separated later on and ran different courses. The migraine grew rarer, and by the time she was sixteen she had quite got over it. But attacks of *tussis nervosa*,[2] which had no doubt been started by a common catarrh, continued to occur over the whole period. When, at the age of eighteen, she came to me for treatment, she was again coughing in a characteristic manner. The number of these attacks could not be determined; but they lasted from three to five weeks, and on one occasion for several months. The most troublesome symptom during the first half of an attack of this kind, at all events in the last few years, used to be a complete loss of voice. The diagnosis that this was once more a nervous complaint had been established long since; but the various methods of treatment which are usual, including hydrotherapy and the local application of electricity, had produced no result. It was in such circumstances as these that the child had developed into a mature young woman of very independent judgement, who had grown accustomed to laugh at the efforts of doctors, and in the end to renounce their help entirely. Moreover, she had always been against calling in medical advice, though she had no personal objection to her family doctor. Every proposal to consult a new physician aroused her resistance, and it was only her father's authority which induced her to come to me at all.

I first saw her when she was sixteen, in the early summer. She was suffering from a cough and from hoarseness, and even at that time I proposed giving her psychological treatment. My proposal was not adopted, since the attack in question, like the others, passed off spontaneously, though it had lasted unusually long. During the next winter she came and stayed in Vienna with her uncle and his daughters after the death of the aunt of whom she had been so fond. There she fell ill of a feverish disorder which was diagnosed at the time as appendicitis. In the following autumn, since her father's health seemed to justify the step, the family left the health-resort of B—— for good and all. They first moved to the town where her father's factory was situated, and then, scarcely a year later, settled permanently in Vienna.

Dora was by that time in the first bloom of youth—a girl of intelligent and engaging looks. But she was a source of heavy trials for her parents. Low spirits and an alteration in her character had now become the main features of her illness. She was clearly satisfied neither with herself nor with her family; her attitude towards her father was unfriendly, and she

---

2. Nervous coughing (Latin).

was on very bad terms with her mother, who was bent upon drawing her into taking a share in the work of the house. She tried to avoid social intercourse, and employed herself—so far as she was allowed to by the fatigue and lack of concentration of which she complained—with attending lectures for women and with carrying on more or less serious studies. One day her parents were thrown into a state of great alarm by finding on the girl's writing-desk, or inside it, a letter in which she took leave of them because, as she said, she could no longer endure her life.[3] Her father, indeed, being a man of some perspicacity, guessed that the girl had no serious suicidal intentions. But he was none the less very much shaken; and when one day, after a slight passage of words between him and his daughter, she had a first attack of loss of consciousness[4]—an event which was subsequently covered by an amnesia—it was determined, in spite of her reluctance, that she should come to me for treatment.

[Freud asserts the validity of the psychoanalytic theory of hysteria outlined in his *Studies in Hysteria* (1895).]

*   *   *

In Dora's case, thanks to her father's shrewdness which I have remarked upon more than once already, there was no need for me to look about for the points of contact between the circumstances of the patient's life and her illness, at all events in its most recent form. Her father told me that he and his family while they were at B—— had formed an intimate friendship with a married couple who had been settled there for several years. Frau K. had nursed him during his long illness, and had in that way, he said, earned a title to his undying gratitude. Herr[5] K. had always been most kind to Dora. He had gone for walks with her when he was there, and had made her small presents; but no one had thought any harm of that. Dora had taken the greatest care of the K.'s two little children, and been almost a mother to them. When Dora and her father had come to see me two years before in the summer, they had been just on their way to stop with Herr and Frau K., who were spending the summer on one of our lakes in the Alps. Dora was to have spent several weeks at the K.'s, while her father had intended to return home after a few days. During that time Herr K. had been staying there as well. As her father was preparing for his departure the girl had suddenly declared with the greatest determination that she was going with him, and she had in fact put her decision into effect. It was not until some days later that she had thrown any light upon her strange behaviour. She had then told her mother—intending that what she said should be passed on to her father—that Herr K. had had the audacity to make her a proposal while they were on a walk after a trip upon the lake. Herr K. had been called to account by her father and uncle

---

3. As I have already explained, the treatment of the case, and consequently my insight into the complex of events composing it, remained fragmentary. There are therefore many questions to which I have no solution to offer, or in which I can only rely upon hints and conjectures. This affair of the letter came up in the course of one of our sessions, and the girl showed signs of astonishment. "How on earth," she asked, "did they find the letter? It was shut up in my desk." But since she knew that her parents had read this draft of a farewell letter, I conclude that she had herself arranged for it to fall into their hands [Freud's note].   4. The attack was, I believe, accompanied by convulsions and delirious states. But since this event was not reached by the analysis either, I have no trustworthy recollections on the subject to fall back upon [Freud's note].   5. Mister (German). *Frau*: Mrs. (German).

on the next occasion of their meeting, but he had denied in the most emphatic terms having on his side made any advances which could have been open to such a construction. He had then proceeded to throw suspicion upon the girl, saying that he had heard from Frau K. that she took no interest in anything but sexual matters, and that she used to read Mantegazza's *Physiology of Love*[6] and books of that sort in their house on the lake. It was most likely, he had added, that she had been over-excited by such reading and had merely "fancied" the whole scene she had described.

"I have no doubt," continued her father, "that this incident is responsible for Dora's depression and irritability and suicidal ideas. She keeps pressing me to break off relations with Herr K. and more particularly with Frau K., whom she used positively to worship formerly. But that I cannot do. For, to begin with, I myself believe that Dora's tale of the man's immoral suggestions is a phantasy that has forced its way into her mind; and besides, I am bound to Frau K. by ties of honourable friendship and I do not wish to cause her pain. The poor woman is most unhappy with her husband, of whom, by the by, I have no very high opinion. She herself has suffered a great deal with her nerves, and I am her only support. With my state of health I need scarcely assure you that there is nothing wrong in our relations. We are just two poor wretches who give one another what comfort we can by an exchange of friendly sympathy. You know already that I get nothing out of my own wife. But Dora, who inherits my obstinacy, cannot be moved from her hatred of the K.'s. She had her last attack after a conversation in which she had again pressed me to break with them. Please try and bring her to reason."

Her father's words did not always quite tally with this pronouncement; for on other occasions he tried to put the chief blame for Dora's impossible behavior on her mother—whose peculiarities made the house unbearable for every one. But I had resolved from the first to suspend my judgement of the true state of affairs till I had heard the other side as well.

[A brief discussion of trauma theory follows.]

                *   *   *

When the first difficulties of the treatment had been overcome, Dora told me of an earlier episode with Herr K., which was even better calculated to act as a sexual trauma. She was fourteen years old at the time. Herr K. had made an arrangement with her and his wife that they should meet him one afternoon at his place of business in the principal square of B—— so as to have a view of a church festival. He persuaded his wife, however, to stay at home, and sent away his clerks, so that he was alone when the girl arrived. When the time for the procession approached, he asked the girl to wait for him at the door which opened on to the staircase leading to the upper story, while he pulled down the outside shutters. He then came back, and, instead of going out by the open door, suddenly

---

6. Paolo Mantegazza (1831–1910) wrote three books on human sexuality. The *Physiology of Love* (1877) is more romantic and less explicit than, for example, his *Sexual Relations of Mankind*.

clasped the girl to him and pressed a kiss upon her lips. This was surely just the situation to call up a distinct feeling of sexual excitement in a girl of fourteen who had never before been approached. But Dora had at that moment a violent feeling of disgust, tore herself from the man, and hurried past him to the staircase and from there to the street door. She nevertheless continued to meet Herr K. Neither of them ever mentioned the little scene; and according to her account Dora kept it a secret till her confession during the treatment. For some time afterwards, however, she avoided being alone with Herr K. The K.'s had just made plans for an expedition which was to last for some days and on which Dora was to have accompanied them. After the scene of the kiss she refused to join the party, without giving any reason.

In this scene—second in order of mention, but first in order of time—the behaviour of this child of fourteen was already entirely and completely hysterical. I should without question consider a person hysterical in whom an occasion for sexual excitement elicited feelings that were preponderantly or exclusively unpleasurable; and I should do so whether or not the person were capable of producing somatic symptoms. The elucidation of the mechanism of this *reversal of affect* is one of the most important and at the same time one of the most difficult problems in the psychology of the neuroses. In my own judgement I am still some way from having achieved this end; and I may add that within the limits of the present paper I shall be able to bring forward only a part of such knowledge on the subject as I do possess.

In order to particularize Dora's case it is not enough merely to draw attention to the reversal of affect; there has also been a *displacement* of sensation. Instead of the genital sensation which would certainly have been felt by a healthy girl in such circumstances, Dora was overcome by the unpleasurable feeling which is proper to the tract of mucous membrane at the entrance to the alimentary canal—that is by disgust. The stimulation of her lips by the kiss was no doubt of importance in localizing the feeling at that particular place; but I think I can also recognize another factor in operation.[7]

The disgust which Dora felt on that occasion did not become a permanent symptom, and even at the time of the treatment it was only, as it were, potentially present. She was a poor eater and confessed to some disinclination for food. On the other hand, the scene had left another consequence behind it in the shape of a sensory hallucination which occurred from time to time and even made its appearance while she was telling me her story. She declared that she could still feel upon the upper part of her body the pressure of Herr K.'s embrace. In accordance with certain rules of symptom-formation which I have come to know, and at the same time taking into account certain other of the patient's peculiarities, which were otherwise inexplicable,—such as her unwillingness to walk past any man whom she saw engaged in eager or affectionate conver-

7. The causes of Dora's disgust at the kiss were certainly not adventitious, for in that case she could not have failed to remember and mention them. I happen to know Herr K., for he was the same person who had visited me with the patient's father, and he was still quite young and of prepossessing appearance [Freud's note].

sation with a lady—I have formed in my own mind the following recon-struction of the scene. I believe that during the man's passionate embrace she felt not merely his kiss upon her lips but also the pressure of his erect member against her body. This perception was revolting to her; it was dismissed from her memory, repressed, and replaced by the innocent sen-sation of pressure upon her thorax, which in turn derived an excessive intensity from its repressed source. Once more, therefore, we find a dis-placement from the lower part of the body to the upper. On the other hand, the compulsive piece of behaviour which I have mentioned was formed as though it were derived from the undistorted recollection of the scene: she did not like walking past any man who she thought was in a state of sexual excitement, because she wanted to avoid seeing for a second time the somatic sign which accompanies it.

[Freud describes Dora's feelings of disgust as a matter of *overdetermina-tion* (that is, a given symptom stems from or is *determined* by different intertwined causes).]

* * *

I did not find it easy, however, to direct the patient's attention to her relations with Herr K. She declared that she had done with him. The uppermost layer of all her associations during the sessions, and everything of which she was easily conscious and of which she remembered having been conscious the day before, was always connected with her father. It was quite true that she could not forgive her father for continuing his relations with Herr K. and more particularly with Frau K. But she viewed those relations in a very different light from that in which her father wished them to appear. In her mind there was no doubt that what bound her father to this young and beautiful woman was a common love-affair. Nothing that could help to confirm this view had escaped her perception, which in this connection was pitilessly sharp; *here there were no gaps to be found in her memory.* Their acquaintance with the K.'s had begun before her father's serious illness; but it had not become intimate until the young woman had officially taken on the position of nurse during that illness, while Dora's mother had kept away from the sick-room. During the first summer holidays after his recovery things had happened which must have opened every one's eyes to the true character of this "friendship." The two families had taken a suite of rooms in common at the hotel. One day Frau K. had announced that she could not keep the bedroom which she had up till then shared with one of her children. A few days later Dora's father had given up his bedroom, and they had both moved into new rooms— the end rooms, which were only separated by the passage, while the rooms they had given up had not offered any such security against interruption. Later on, whenever she had reproached her father about Frau K., he had been in the habit of saying that he could not understand her hostility and that, on the contrary, his children had every reason for being grateful to Frau K. Her mother, whom she has asked for an explanation of this myste-rious remark, had told her that her father had been so unhappy at that time that he had made up his mind to go into the wood and kill himself, and that Frau K., suspecting as much, had gone after him and had per-

suaded him by her entreaties to preserve his life for the sake of his family.
Of course, Dora went on, she herself did not believe this story; no doubt
the two of them had been seen together in the wood, and her father had
thereupon invented this fairy tale of his suicide so as to account for their
rendezvous.[8]

When they had returned to B——, her father had visited Frau K. every
day at definite hours, while her husband was at his business. Everybody
had talked about it and had questioned her about it pointedly. Herr K.
himself had often complained bitterly to her mother, though he had
spared her herself any allusions to the subject—which she seemed to attribute to delicacy of feeling on his part. When they had all gone for walks
together, her father and Frau K. had always known how to manage things
so as to be alone with each other. There could be no doubt that she had
taken money from him, for she spent more than she could possibly have
afforded out of her own purse or her husband's. Dora added that her father
had begun to make handsome presents to Frau K., and in order to make
these less conspicuous had at the same time become especially liberal
towards her mother and herself. And, while previously Frau K. had been
an invalid and had even been obliged to spend months in a sanatorium
for nervous disorders because she had been unable to walk, she had now
become a healthy and lively woman.

Even after they had left B—— for the manufacturing town, these relations, already of many years' standing, had been continued. From time to
time her father used to declare that he could not endure the rawness of
the climate, and that he must do something for himself; he would begin
to cough and complain, until suddenly he would start off to B——, and
from there write the most cheerful letters home. All these illnesses had
only been pretexts for seeing his friend again. Then one day it had been
decided that they were to move to Vienna and Dora began to suspect a
hidden connection. And sure enough, they had scarcely been three weeks
in Vienna when she heard that the K.'s had moved there as well. They
were in Vienna, so she told me, at that very moment, and she frequently
met her father with Frau K. in the street. She also met Herr K. very often,
and he always used to turn round and look after her; and once when he
had met her out by herself he had followed her for a long way, so as
to make sure where she was going and whether she might not have a
rendezvous.

On one occasion during the course of the treatment her father again
felt worse, and went off to B—— for several weeks; and the sharp-sighted
Dora had soon unearthed the fact that Frau K. had started off to the same
place on a visit to her relatives there. It was at this time that Dora's criticisms of her father were the most frequent: he was insincere, he had a
strain of falseness in his character, he only thought of his enjoyment, and
he had a gift for seeing things in the light which suited him best.

I could not in general dispute Dora's characterization of her father; and
there was one particular respect in which it was easy to see that her

---

8. This is the point of connection with her own pretence at suicide, which may thus be regarded as the
expression of a longing for a love of the same kind [Freud's note].

reproaches were justified. When she was feeling embittered she used to be overcome by the idea that she had been handed over to Herr K. as the price of his tolerating the relations between her father and his wife; and her rage at her father's making such a use of her was visible behind her affection for him. At other times she was quite well aware that she had been guilty of exaggeration in talking like this. The two men had of course never made a formal agreement in which she was treated as an object for barter; her father in particular would have been horrified at any such suggestion. But he was one of those men who know how to evade a dilemma by falsifying their judgement upon one of the conflicting alternatives. If it had been pointed out to him that there might be danger for a growing girl in the constant and unsupervised companionship of a man who had no satisfaction from his own wife, he would have been certain to answer that he could rely upon his daughter, that a man like K. could never be dangerous to her, and that his friend was himself incapable of such intentions, or that Dora was still a child and was treated as a child by K. But as a matter of fact things were in a position in which each of the two men avoided drawing any conclusions from the other's behaviour which would have been awkward for his own plans. It was possible for Herr K. to send Dora flowers every day for a whole year while he was in the neighbourhood, to take every opportunity of giving her valuable presents, and to spend all his spare time in her company, without her parents noticing anything in his behaviour that was characteristic of love-making.

When a patient brings forward a sound and incontestable train of argument during psycho-analytic treatment, the physician is liable to feel a moment's embarrassment, and the patient may take advantage of it by asking: "This is all perfectly correct and true, isn't it? What do you want to change in [it] now that I've told it you?" But it soon becomes evident that the patient is using thoughts of this kind, which the analysis cannot attack, for the purpose of cloaking others which are anxious to escape from criticism and from consciousness. A string of reproaches against other people leads one to suspect the existence of a string of self-reproaches with the same content. All that need be done is to turn back each particular reproach on to the speaker himself. There is something undeniably automatic about this method of defending oneself against a self-reproach by making the same reproach against some one else. A model of it is to be found in the *tu quoque*[9] arguments of children; if one of them is accused of being a liar, he will reply without an instant's hesitation: "You're another." A grown-up person who wanted to throw back abuse would look for some really exposed spot in his antagonist and would not lay the chief stress upon the same content being repeated. In paranoia the projection of a reproach on to another person without any alteration in its content and therefore without any consideration for reality becomes manifest as the process of forming delusions.

Dora's reproaches against her father had a "lining" or "backing" of self-reproaches of this kind with a corresponding content in every case, as I

9. You too! (Latin).

shall show in detail. She was right in thinking that her father did not wish to look too closely into Herr K.'s behaviour to his daughter, for fear of being disturbed in his own love-affair with Frau K. But Dora herself had done precisely the same thing. She had made herself an accomplice in the affair, and had dismissed from her mind every sign which tended to show its true character. It was not until after her adventure by the lake that her eyes were opened and that she began to apply such a severe standard to her father. During all the previous years she had given every possible assistance to her father's relations with Frau K. She would never go to see her if she thought her father was there; but, knowing that in that case the children would have been sent out, she would turn her steps in a direction where she would be sure to meet them, and would go for a walk with them. There had been some one in the house who had been anxious at an early stage to open her eyes to the nature of her father's relations with Frau K., and to induce her to take sides against her. This was her last governess, an unmarried woman, no longer young, who was well-read and of advanced views.[1] The teacher and her pupil were for a while upon excellent terms, until suddenly Dora became hostile to her and insisted on her dismissal. So long as the governess had any influence she used it for stirring up feeling against Frau K. She explained to Dora's mother that it was incompatible with her dignity to tolerate such an intimacy between her husband and another woman; and she drew Dora's attention to all the obvious features of their relations. But her efforts were vain. Dora remained devoted to Frau K. and would hear of nothing that might make her think ill of her relations with her father. On the other hand she very easily fathomed the motives by which her governess was actuated. She might be blind in one direction, but she was sharp-sighted enough in the other. She saw that the governess was in love with her father. When he was there, she seemed to be quite another person: at such times she could be amusing and obliging. While the family were living in the manufacturing town and Frau K. was not on the horizon, her hostility was directed against Dora's mother, who was then her more immediate rival. Up to this point Dora bore her no ill-will. She did not become angry until she observed that she herself was a subject of complete indifference to the governess, whose pretended affection for her was really meant for her father. While her father was away from the manufacturing town the governess had no time to spare for her, would not go for walks with her, and took no interest in her studies. No sooner had her father returned from B—— than she was once more ready with every sort of service and assistance. Thereupon Dora dropped her.

The poor woman had thrown a most unwelcome light on a part of Dora's own behaviour. What the governess had from time to time been to Dora, Dora had been to Herr K.'s children. She had been a mother to them, she had taught them, she had gone for walks with them, she had offered them a complete substitute for the slight interest which their own

---

1. This governess used to read every sort of book on sexual life and similar subjects, and talked to the girl about them, at the same time asking her quite frankly not to mention their conversations to her parents, as one could never tell what line they might take about them. For some time I looked upon this woman as the source of all Dora's secret knowledge, and perhaps I was not entirely wrong in this [Freud's note].

mother showed in them. Herr K. and his wife had often talked of getting a divorce; but it never took place, because Herr K., who was an affectionate father, would not give up either of the two children. A common interest in the children had from the first been a bond between Herr K. and Dora. Her preoccupation with his children was evidently a cloak for something else that Dora was anxious to hide from herself and from other people.

The same inference was to be drawn both from her behaviour towards the children, regarded in the light of the governess's behaviour towards herself, and from her silent acquiescence in her father's relations with Frau K.—namely, that she had all these years been in love with Herr K. When I informed her of this conclusion she did not assent to it. It is true that she at once told me that other people besides (one of her cousins, for instance—a girl who had stopped with them for some time at B——) had said to her: "Why you're simply wild about that man!" But she herself could not be got to recollect any feelings of the kind. Later on, when the quantity of material that had come up had made it difficult for her to persist in her denial, she admitted that she might have been in love with Herr K. at B——, but declared that since the scene by the lake it had all been over. In any case it was quite certain that the reproaches which she made against her father of having been deaf to the most imperative calls of duty and of having seen things in the light which was most convenient from the point of view of his own passions—these reproaches recoiled on her own head.[2]

Her other reproach against her father was that his ill-health was only a pretext and that he exploited it for his own purposes. This reproach, too, concealed a whole section of her own secret history. One day she complained of a professedly new symptom, which consisted of piercing gastric pains. "Whom are you copying now?" I asked her, and found I had hit the mark. The day before she had visited her cousins, the daughters of the aunt who had died. The younger one had become engaged, and this had given occasion to the elder one for falling ill with gastric pains, and she was to be sent off to Semmering.[3] Dora thought it was all just envy on the part of the elder sister; she always got ill when she wanted something, and what she wanted now was to be away from home so as not to have to look on at her sister's happiness.[4] But Dora's own gastric pains proclaimed the fact that she identified herself with her cousin, who, according to her, was a malingerer. Her grounds for this identification were either that she too envied the luckier girl her love, or that she saw her own story reflected in that of the elder sister, who had recently had a love-affair which had ended unhappily. But she had also learned from observing Frau K. what useful things illnesses could become. Herr K. spent part of the year in travelling. Whenever he came back, he used to find his wife in bad health, although, as Dora knew, she had been quite well only the day before. Dora realized

---

2. The question then arises: If Dora loved Herr K., what was the reason for her refusing him in the scene by the lake? Or at any rate, why did her refusal take such a brutal form, as though she were embittered against him? And how could a girl who was in love feel insulted by a proposal which was made in a manner neither tactless nor offensive? [Freud's note].   3. A fashionable health resort in the mountains near Vienna.   4. An event of everyday occurrence between sisters [Freud's note].

that the presence of the husband had the effect of making his wife ill, and that she was glad to be ill so as to be able to escape the conjugal duties which she so much detested. At this point in the discussion Dora suddenly brought in an allusion to her own alternations between good and bad health during the first years of her girlhood at B——; and I was thus driven to suspect that her states of health were to be regarded as depending upon something else, in the same way as Frau K.'s. (It is a rule of psycho-analytic technique that an internal connection which is still undisclosed will announce its presence by means of a contiguity—a temporal proximity— of associations; just as in writing, if "a" and "b" are put side by side, it means that the syllable "ab" is to be formed out of them.) Dora had had a very large number of attacks of coughing accompanied by loss of voice. Could it be that the presence or absence of the man she loved had had an influence upon the appearance and disappearance of the symptoms of her illness? If this were so, it must be possible to discover some coincidence or other which would betray the fact. I asked her what the average length of these attacks had been. "From three to six weeks, perhaps." How long had Herr K.'s absences lasted? "Three to six weeks, too," she was obliged to admit. Her illness was therefore a demonstration of her love for K., just as his wife's was a demonstration of her *dislike*. It was only necessary to suppose that her behaviour had been the opposite of Frau K.'s and that she had been ill when he was absent and well when he had come back. And this really seemed to have been so, at least during the first period of the attacks. Later on it no doubt became necessary to obscure the coinci- dence between her attacks of illness and the absence of the man she secretly loved, lest its regularity should betray her secret. The length of the attacks would then remain as a trace of their original significance.

I remembered that long before, while I was working at Charcot's[5] clinic, I had seen and heard how in cases of hysterical mutism writing operated vicariously in the place of speech. Such patients were able to write more fluently, quicker, and better than others did or than they themselves had done previously. The same thing had happened with Dora. In the first days of her attacks of aphonia "writing had always come specially easy to her." No psychological elucidation was really required for this peculiarity, which was the expression of a physiological substitutive function enforced by necessity; it was noticeable, however, that such an elucidation was eas- ily to be found. Herr K. used to write to her at length while he was travel- ling and to send her picture post-cards. It used to happen that she alone was informed as to the date of his return, and that his arrival took his wife by surprise. Moreover, that a person will correspond with an absent friend whom he cannot talk to is scarcely less obvious than that if he has lost his voice he will try to make himself understood in writing. Dora's aphonia, then, allowed of the following symbolic interpretation. When the man she loved was away she gave up speaking; speech had lost its value since she could not speak to *him*. On the other hand, writing gained in importance, as being the only means of communication with him in his absence.

---

5. Jean-Martin Charcot (1825–1893), French neurologist famous for his research on hysteria and hypno- sis. Freud worked at his clinic from 1885 to 1886.

[Freud comments on the relationship of physical and psychical symptoms in hysteria ("somatic compliance").]

*   *   *

I now return to the reproach of malingering which Dora brought against her father. It soon became evident that this reproach corresponded to self-reproaches not only concerning her earlier states of ill-health but also concerning the present time. At such points the physician is usually faced by the task of guessing and filling in what the analysis offers him in the shape only of hints and allusions. I was obliged to point out to the patient that her present ill-health was just as much actuated by motives and was just as tendentious as had been Frau K.'s illness, which she had understood so well. There could be no doubt, I said, that she had an aim in view which she hoped to gain by her illness. That aim could be none other than to detach her father from Frau K. She had been unable to achieve this by prayers or arguments; perhaps she hoped to succeed by frightening her father (there was her farewell letter), or by awakening his pity (there were her fainting-fits), or if all this was in vain, at least she would be taking her revenge on him. She knew very well, I went on, how much he was attached to her, and that tears used to come into his eyes whenever he was asked after his daughter's health. I felt quite convinced that she would recover at once if only her father were to tell her that he had sacrificed Frau K. for the sake of her health. But, I added, I hoped he would not let himself be persuaded to do this, for then she would have learned what a powerful weapon she had in her hands, and she would certainly not fail on every future occasion to make use once more of her liability to ill-health. Yet if her father refused to give way to her, I was quite sure she would not let herself be deprived of her illness so easily.

I will pass over the details which showed how entirely correct all of this was, and I will instead add a few general remarks upon the part played in hysteria by the *motives of illness*. A *motive* for being ill is sharply to be distinguished as a concept from a *liability* to being ill—from the material out of which symptoms are formed. The motives have no share in the formation of symptoms, and indeed are not present at the beginning of the illness. They only appear secondarily to it; but it is not until they have appeared that the disease is fully constituted. Their presence can be reckoned upon in every case in which there is real suffering and which is of fairly long standing. A symptom comes into the patient's mental life at first as an unwelcome guest; it has everything against it; and that is why it may vanish so easily, apparently of its own accord, under the influence of time. To begin with there is no use to which it can be put in the domestic economy of the mind; but very often it succeeds in finding one secondarily. Some psychical current or other finds it convenient to make use of it, and in that way the symptom manages to obtain a *secondary function* and remains, as it were, anchored fast in the patient's mental life. And so it happens that any one who tries to make him well is to his astonishment brought up against a powerful resistance, which teaches him that the patient's intention of getting rid of his complaint is not so entirely and completely serious as it seemed. Let us imagine a workman, a bricklayer, let us say, who has fallen off a house and been crippled, and now earns his livelihood by begging at the street-corner. Let us then suppose that a miracle-worker comes along and promises him to make his crooked leg straight and capable of walking. It would be unwise, I think, to look forward to seeing an expression of peculiar bliss upon the man's features. No doubt at the time of the accident he felt he was extremely unlucky, when he realized that he would never be able to do any more work and would have to starve or live upon charity. But since then the very thing which in the first instance threw him out of employment has become his source of income: he lives by his disablement. If that is taken from him he may become totally helpless. He has in the meantime forgotten his trade and lost his habits of industry; he has grown accustomed to idleness, and perhaps to drink as well.

The motives for being ill often begin to be active even in childhood. A little girl in her greed for love does not enjoy having to share the affection of her parents with her brothers and sisters; and she notices that the whole of their affection is lavished on her once more whenever she arouses their anxiety by falling ill. She has now discovered a means of enticing out her parents' love, and will make use of that means as soon as she has the necessary psychical material at her disposal for producing an illness. When such a child has grown up to be a woman she may find all the demands she used to make in her childhood countered owing to her marriage with an inconsiderate husband, who may subjugate her will, mercilessly exploit her capacity for work, and lavish neither his affection nor his money upon her. In that case ill-health will be her one weapon for maintaining her position. It will procure her the care she longs for; it will force her husband to make pecuniary sacrifices for her and to show her consideration, as he would never have done while she was well; and it will compel him to treat her with solicitude if she recovers, for otherwise a relapse will threaten. Her state of ill-health will have every appearance of being objective and involuntary—the very doctor who treats her will bear witness to the fact; and for that reason she will not need to feel any conscious self-reproaches at making such successful use of a means which she had found effective in her years of childhood.

And yet illnesses of this kind *are* the result of intention. They are as a rule levelled at a particular person, and consequently vanish with that person's departure. The crudest and most commonplace views on the character of hysterical disorders—such as are to be heard from uneducated relatives or nurses—are in a certain sense right. It is true that the paralysed and bedridden woman would spring to her feet if a fire were to break out in her room, and that the spoiled wife would forget all her sufferings if her child were to fall dangerously ill or if some catastrophe were to threaten the family circumstances. People who speak of the patients in this way are right except upon a single point: they overlook the psychological distinction between what is conscious and what is unconscious. This may be permissible where children are concerned, but with adults it is no longer possible. That is why all these asseverations that it is "only a question of willing" and all the encouragements and abuse that are addressed to the patient are of no avail. An attempt must first be made by the roundabout methods of analysis to convince the patient herself of the existence in her of an intention to be ill.

It is in combating the motives of illness that the weak point in every kind of therapeutic treatment of hysteria lies. This is quite generally true, and it applies equally to psycho-analysis. Destiny has an easier time of it in this respect: it need not concern itself either with the patient's constitution or with his pathogenic material; it has only to take away a motive for being ill, and the patient is temporarily or perhaps even permanently freed from his illness. How many fewer miraculous cures and spontaneous disappearances of symptoms should we physicians have to register in cases of hysteria, if we were more often given a sight of the human interests which the patient keeps hidden from us! In one case, some stated period of time has elapsed; in a second, consideration for some other person has ceased to operate; in a third, the situation has been fundamentally changed by some external event—and the whole disorder, which up till then had shown the greatest obstinacy, vanishes at a single blow, apparently of its own accord, but really because it has been deprived of its most powerful motive, one of the uses to which it has been put in the patient's life.

Motives that support the patient in being ill are probably to be found in all fully developed cases. But there are some in which the motives are purely internal—such as desire for self-punishment, that is, penitence and remorse. It will be found much easier to solve the therapeutic problem in such cases than in those in which the illness is related to the attainment of some external aim. In Dora's case that aim was clearly to touch her father's heart and to detach him from Frau K.

None of her father's actions seemed to have embittered her so much as his readiness to consider the scene by the lake as a product of her imagination. She was almost beside herself at the idea of its being supposed that she had merely fancied something on that occasion. For a long time I was in perplexity as to what the self-reproach could be which lay behind her passionate repudiation of this explanation of the episode. It was justifiable to suspect that there was something concealed, for a reproach which misses the mark gives no lasting offence. On the other hand, I came to the conclusion that Dora's story must correspond to the facts in every respect. No sooner had she grasped Herr K.'s intention than, without letting him finish what he had to say, she had given him a slap in the face and hurried away. Her behaviour must have seemed as incomprehensible to the man after she had left him as to us, for he must long before have gathered from innumerable small signs that he was secure of the girl's affections. In our discussion of Dora's second dream we shall come upon the solution of this riddle as well as upon the self-reproach which we have hitherto failed to discover.

As she kept on repeating her complaints against her father with a wearisome monotony, and as at the same time her cough continued, I was led to think that this symptom might have some meaning in connection with her father. And apart from this, the explanation of the symptom which I had hitherto obtained was far from fulfilling the requirements which I am accustomed to make of such explanations. According to a rule which I had found confirmed over and over again by experience, though I had not yet ventured to erect it into a general principle, a symptom signifies the representation—the realization—of a phantasy with a sexual content, that is to say, it signifies a sexual situation. It would be better to say that at least *one* of the meanings of a symptom is the representation of a sexual phantasy, but that no such limitation is imposed upon the content of its other meanings. Any one who takes up psycho-analytic work will quickly discover that a symptom has more than one meaning and served to represent several unconscious mental processes simultaneously. And I should like to add that in my estimation a single unconscious mental process or phantasy will scarcely ever suffice for the production of a symptom.

An opportunity very soon occurred for interpreting Dora's nervous cough in this way by means of an imagined sexual situation. She had once again been insisting that Frau K. only loved her father because he was "*ein vermögender Mann.*"[6] Certain details of the way in which she expressed herself (which I pass over here, like most other purely technical parts of the analysis) led me to see that behind this phrase its opposite lay concealed, namely, that her father was "*ein unvermögender Mann.*"[7] This could only be meant in a sexual sense—that her father, as a man, was without means, was impotent. Dora confirmed this interpretation from her conscious language; whereupon I pointed out the contradiction she was involved in if on the one hand she continued to insist that her father's relation with Frau K. was a common love-affair, and on the other hand maintained that her father was impotent, or in other words incapable of carrying on an affair of such a kind. Her answer showed that she had no need to admit the contradiction. She knew very well, she said, that there was more than one way of obtaining sexual gratification. (The source of this piece of knowledge, however, was once more untraceable.) I questioned her further, whether she referred to the use of organs other than the genitals for the purpose of sexual intercourse, and she replied in the affirmative. I could then go on to say that in that case she must be thinking of precisely those parts of the body which in her case were in a state of irritation,—the throat and the oral cavity. To be sure, she would not hear of going so far as this in recognizing her own thoughts; and indeed, if the occurrence of the symptom was to be made possible at all, it was essential that she should not be completely clear on the subject. But the conclusion was inevitable that with her spasmodic cough, which, as is usual, was referred for its exciting stimulus to a tickling in her throat, she pictured to herself as scene of sexual gratification *per os*[8] between the two people whose love-affair occupied her mind so incessantly. A very short time after she had tacitly accepted this explanation her cough vanished—which fitted in very well with my view; but I do not wish to lay too much stress upon this development, since her cough had so often before disappeared spontaneously.

This short piece of the analysis may perhaps have excited in the medical reader—apart from the scepticism to which he is entitled—feelings of

---

6. A man of means (German).   7. A man without means (German). *Unvermögend* means literally "unable" and is commonly used in the sense of both "not rich" and "impotent."   8. Orally (Latin).

astonishment and horror; and I am prepared at this point to look into these two reactions so as to discover whether they are justifiable. The astonishment is probably caused by my daring to talk about such delicate and unpleasant subjects to a young girl—or, for that matter, to any woman who is sexually active. The horror is aroused, no doubt, by the possibility that an inexperienced girl could know about practices of such a kind and could occupy her imagination with them. I would advise recourse to moderation and reasonableness upon both points. There is no cause for indignation either in the one case or in the other. It is possible for a man to talk to girls and women upon sexual matters of every kind without doing them harm and without bringing suspicion upon himself, so long as, in the first place, he adopts a particular way of doing it, and, in the second place, can make them feel convinced that it is unavoidable. A gynaecologist, after all, under the same conditions, does not hesitate to make them submit to uncovering every possible part of their body. The best way of speaking about such things is to be dry and direct; and that is at the same time the method furthest removed from the prurience with which the same subjects are handled in "society," and to which girls and women alike are so thoroughly accustomed. I call bodily organs and processes by their technical names, and I tell these to the patient if they—the names, I mean—happen to be unknown to her. *J'appelle un chat un chat.*[9] I have certainly heard of some people—doctors and laymen—who are scandalized by a therapeutic method in which conversations of this sort occur, and who appear to envy either me or my patients the titillation which, according to their notions, such a method must afford. But I am too well acquainted with the respectability of these gentry to excite myself over them. I shall avoid the temptation of writing a satire upon them. But there is one thing that I will mention: often, after I have for some time treated a patient who had not at first found it easy to be open about sexual matters, I have had the satisfaction of hearing her exclaim: "Why, after all, your treatment is far more respectable than Mr. X.'s conversation!"

No one can undertake the treatment of a case of hysteria until he is convinced of the impossibility of avoiding the mention of sexual subjects, or unless he is prepared to allow himself to be convinced by experience. The right attitude is: *"pour faire une omelette il faut casser des œufs."*[1] The patients themselves are easy to convince; and there are only too many opportunities of doing so in the course of the treatment. There is no necessity for feeling any compunction at discussing the facts of normal or abnormal sexual life with them. With the exercise of a little caution all that is done is to translate into conscious ideas what was already known in the unconscious; and, after all, the whole effectiveness of the treatment is based upon our knowledge that the affect attached to an unconscious idea operates more strongly and, since it cannot be inhibited, more injuriously than the affect attached to a conscious one. There is never any danger of corrupting an inexperienced girl. For where there is no knowledge of sexual processes even in the unconscious, no hysterical symptom will arise; and where hysteria is found there can no longer be any question of "inno-

---

9. I call a cat a cat (French, literal trans.); call a spade a spade.   1. You can't make an omelet without breaking eggs (French).

cence of mind" in the sense in which parents and educators use the phrase. With children of ten, of twelve, or of fourteen, with boys and girls alike, I have satisfied myself that the truth of this statement can invariably be relied upon.

[A discussion follows of the difference between psychoneuroses and perversions, of Dora's thumb sucking, and of the possibility that symptoms change their meaning.]

*   *   *

Dora's incessant repetition of the same thoughts about her father's relations with Frau K. made it possible to derive still further important material from the analysis.

A train of thought such as this may be described as excessively intense, or better *reinforced*, or "supervalent" in Wernicke's[2] sense. It shows its pathological character in spite of its apparently reasonable content, by the single peculiarity that no amount of conscious and voluntary effort of thought on the patient's part is able to dissipate or remove it. A normal train of thought, however intense it may be, can eventually be disposed of. Dora felt quite rightly that her thoughts about her father required to be judged in a special way. "I can think of nothing else," she complained again and again. "I know my brother says we children have no right to criticize this behaviour of Father's. He declares that we ought not to trouble ourselves about it, and ought even to be glad, perhaps, that he has found a woman he can love, since Mother understands him so little. I can quite see that, and I should like to think the same as my brother, but I can't. I can't forgive him for it."[3]

Now what is one to do in the face of a supervalent thought like this, after one has heard what its conscious grounds are and listened to the ineffectual protests made against it? Reflection will suggest that *this excessively intense train of thought must owe its reinforcement to the unconscious.* It cannot be resolved by any effort of thought, either because it itself reaches with its root down into unconscious, repressed material, or because another unconscious thought lies concealed behind it. In the latter case, the concealed thought is usually the direct contrary of the supervalent one. Contrary thoughts are always closely connected with each other and are often paired off in such a way that *the one thought is excessively conscious while its counterpart is repressed and unconscious.* This relation between the two thoughts is an effect of the process of repression. For repression is often achieved by means of an excessive reinforcement of the thought contrary to the one which is to be repressed. This process I call *reactive* reinforcement, and the thought which asserts itself with excessive intensity in consciousness and (in the same way as a prejudice) cannot be removed I call a *reactive thought.* The two thoughts then act towards each other much like the two needles of an astatic galvanometer. The reactive thought keeps the objectionable one under repression by

---

2. Carl Wernicke (1848–1905), German neurologist.   3. A supervalent thought of this kind is often the only symptom, beyond deep depression, of a pathological condition which is usually described as "melancholia," but which can be cleared up by psychoanalysis like a hysteria [Freud's note].

means of a certain surplus of intensity; but for that reason it itself is "damped" and proof against conscious efforts of thought. So that the way to deprive the excessively intense thought of its reinforcement is by bringing its repressed contrary into consciousness.

We must also be prepared to meet with instances in which the supervalence of a thought is due not to the presence of one only of these two causes but to a concurrence of both of them. Other complications, too, may arise, but they can easily be fitted into the general scheme.

Let us now apply our theory to the instance provided by Dora's case. We will begin with the first hypothesis, namely, that her preoccupation with her father's relations to Frau K. owed its obsessive character to the fact that its root was unknown to her and lay in the unconscious. It is not difficult to divine the nature of that root from her circumstances and her conduct. Her behaviour obviously went far beyond what would have been appropriate to filial concern. She felt and acted more like a jealous wife— in a way which would have been comprehensible in her mother. By her ultimatum to her father ("either her or me"), by the scenes she used to make, by the suicidal intentions she allowed to transpire—by all this she was clearly putting herself in her mother's place. If we have rightly guessed the nature of the imaginary sexual situation which underlay her cough, in that phantasy she must have been putting herself in Frau K.'s place. She was therefore identifying herself both with the woman her father had once loved and with the woman he loved now. The inference is obvious that her affection for her father was a much stronger one than she knew or than she would have cared to admit: in fact, that she was in love with him.

I have learnt to look upon unconscious love relations like this (which are marked by their abnormal consequences)—between a father and a daughter, or between a mother and a son—as a revival of germs of feeling in infancy. I have shown at length elsewhere at what an early age sexual attraction makes itself felt between parents and children, and I have explained that the legend of Oedipus is probably to be regarded as a poetical rendering of what is typical in these relations. Distinct traces are probably to be found in most people of an early partiality of this kind—on the part of a daughter for her father, or on the part of a son for his mother; but it must be assumed to be more intense from the very first in the case of those children whose constitution marks them down for a neurosis, who develop prematurely and have a craving for love. At this point certain other influences, which need not be discussed here, come into play, and lead to a fixation of this rudimentary feeling of love or to a reinforcement of it; so that it turns into something (either while the child is still young or not until it has reached the age of puberty) which must be put on a par with a sexual inclination and which, like the latter, has the forces of the libido at its command. The external circumstances of our patient were by no means unfavourable to such an assumption. The nature of her disposition had always drawn her towards her father, and his numerous illnesses were bound to have increased her affection for him. In some of these illnesses he would allow no one but her to discharge the lighter duties of nursing. He had been so proud of the early growth of her intelligence that he had made her his confidante while she was still a child. It was really she and not her mother whom Frau K.'s appearance had driven out of more than one position.

When I told Dora that I could not avoid supposing that her affection for her father must at a very early moment have amounted to her being completely in love with him, she of course gave me her usual reply: "I don't remember that." But she immediately went on to tell me something analogous about a seven-year-old girl who was her cousin (on her mother's side) and in whom she often thought she saw a kind of reflection of her own childhood. This little girl had (not for the first time) been the witness of a heated dispute between her parents, and, when Dora happened to come in on a visit soon afterwards, whispered in her ear: "You can't think how I hate that person!" (pointing to her mother), "and when she's dead I shall marry Daddy." I am in the habit of regarding associations such as this, which bring forward something that agrees with the content of an assertion of mine, as a confirmation from the unconscious of what I have said. No other kind of "Yes" can be extracted from the unconscious; there is no such thing at all as an unconscious "No."[4]

For years on end she had given no expression to this passion for her father. On the contrary, she had for a long time been on the closest terms with the woman who had supplanted her with her father, and she had actually, as we know from her self-reproaches, facilitated this woman's relations with her father. Her own love for her father had therefore been recently revived; and, if so, the question arises to what end this had happened. Clearly as a reactive symptom, so as to suppress something else— something, that is, that still exercised power in the unconscious. Considering how things stood, I could not help supposing in the first instance that what was suppressed was her love of Herr K. I could not avoid the assumption that she was still in love with him, but that, for unknown reasons, since the scene by the lake her love had aroused in her violent feelings of opposition, and that the girl had brought forward and reinforced her old affection for her father in order to avoid any further necessity for paying conscious attention to the love which she had felt in the first years of her girlhood and which had now become distressing to her. In this way I gained an insight into a conflict which was well calculated to unhinge the girl's mind. On the one hand she was filled with regret at having rejected the man's proposal, and with longing for his company and all the little signs of his affection; while on the other hand these feelings of tenderness and longing were combated by powerful forces, amongst which her pride was one of the most obvious. Thus she had succeeded in persuading herself that she had done with Herr K.—that was the advantage she derived from this typical process of repression; and yet she was obliged to summon up her infantile affection for her father and to exaggerate it, in order to protect herself against the feelings of love which were constantly pressing forward into consciousness. The further fact that she was almost inces-

---

4. There is another very remarkable and entirely trustworthy form of confirmation from the unconscious, which I had not recognized at the time this was written: namely, an exclamation on the part of the patient of "I didn't think that," or "I didn't think of that." This can be translated point-blank into: "Yes, I was unconscious of that" [Freud's note, added 1923].

santly a prey to the most embittered jealousy seemed to admit of still another determination.[5]

My expectations were by no means disappointed when this explanation of mine was met by Dora with a most emphatic negative. The "No" uttered by a patient after a repressed thought has been presented to his conscious perception for the first time does no more than register the existence of a repression and its severity; it acts, as it were, as a gauge of the repression's strength. If this "No," instead of being regarded as the expression of an impartial judgement (of which, indeed, the patient is incapable), is ignored, and if work is continued, the first evidence soon begins to appear that in such a case "No" signifies the desired "Yes." Dora admitted that she found it impossible to be as angry with Herr K. as he had deserved. She told me that one day she had met Herr K. in the street while she was walking with a cousin of hers who did not know him. The other girl had exclaimed all at once: "Why, Dora, what's wrong with you? You've gone as white as a sheet!" She herself had felt nothing of this change of colour; but I explained to her that the expression of emotion and the play of features obey the unconscious rather than the conscious, and are a means of betraying the former.[6] Another time Dora came to me in the worst of tempers after having been uniformly cheerful for several days. She could give no explanation of this. She felt so contrary today, she said; it was her uncle's birthday, and she could not bring herself to congratulate him, she did not know why. My powers of interpretation were at a low ebb that day; I let her go on talking, and she suddenly recollected that it was Herr K.'s birthday too—a fact which I did not fail to use against her. And it was then no longer hard to explain why the handsome presents she had had on her own birthday a few days before had given her no pleasure. One gift was missing, and that was Herr K.'s, the gift which had plainly once been the most prized of all.

Nevertheless Dora persisted in denying my contention for some time longer, until, towards the end of the analysis, the conclusive proof of its correctness came to light.

I must now turn to consider a further complication to which I should certainly give no space if I were a man of letters engaged upon the creation of a mental state like this for a short story, instead of being a medical man engaged upon its dissection. The element to which I must now allude can only serve to obscure and efface the outlines of the fine poetic conflict which we have been able to ascribe to Dora. This element would rightly fall a sacrifice to the censorship of a writer, for he, after all, simplifies and abstracts when he appears in the character of a psychologist. But in the world of reality, which I am trying to depict here, a complication of motives, an accumulation and conjunction of mental activities—in a word, overdetermination—is the rule.

---

5. We shall come upon this [in a moment] [Freud's note].   6. "Compare the lines: 'Ruhig mag ich Euch erscheinen, / Ruhig gehen sehn'" [Freud's note]. "Quietly can I watch your coming, / Quietly watch you go" (German). Freud refers to a scene at the beginning of *Ritter Toggenburg*, a ballad of love between brother and sister by Friedrich von Schiller (1759–1805) in which the sister hides her emotion from her tearful brother as he departs for the Crusades.

[Examples follow of Dora's early attraction to, and subsequent estrangement from, her governess and Frau K.]

                          *   *   *

I believe, therefore, that I am not mistaken in supposing that Dora's
supervalent train of thought, which was concerned with her father's relations with Frau K., was designed not only for the purpose of suppressing
her love for Herr K., which had once been conscious, but also to conceal
her love for Frau K., which was in a deeper sense unconscious. The
supervalent train of thought was directly contrary to the latter current of
feeling. She told herself incessantly that her father had sacrificed her to
this woman, and made noisy demonstrations to show that she grudged her
the possession of her father; and in this way she concealed from herself
the contrary fact, which was that she grudged her father Frau K.'s love,
and had not forgiven the woman she loved for the disillusionment she had
been caused by her betrayal. The jealous emotions of a woman were
linked in the unconscious with a jealousy such as might have been felt by
a man. These masculine or, more properly speaking, *gynaecophilic*[7] currents of feeling are to be regarded as typical of the unconscious erotic life
of hysterical girls.

                                 II

                          [The First Dream]

Just at a moment when there was a prospect that the material that was
coming up for analysis would throw light upon an obscure point in Dora's
childhood, she reported that a few nights earlier she had once again had
a dream which she had already dreamt in exactly the same way on many
previous occasions. A periodically recurrent dream was by its very nature
particularly well calculated to arouse my curiosity; and in any case it was
justifiable in the interests of the treatment to consider the way in which
the dream worked into the analysis as a whole. I therefore determined to
make an especially careful investigation of it.

Here is the dream as related by Dora: "*A house was on fire.*[8] *My father
was standing beside my bed and woke me up. I dressed quickly. Mother
wanted to stop and save her jewel-case; but Father said: 'I refuse to let myself
and my two children be burnt for the sake of your jewel-case.' We hurried
downstairs, and as soon as I was outside I woke up.*"

As the dream was a recurrent one, I naturally asked her when she had
first dreamt it. She told me she did not know. But she remembered having
had the dream three nights in succession at L—— (the place on the lake
where the scene with Herr K. had taken place), and it had now come back
again a few nights earlier, here in Vienna.[9] My expectations from the
clearing-up of the dream were naturally heightened when I heard of its
connection with the events at L——. But I wanted to discover first what
had been the exciting cause of its recent recurrence, and I therefore asked
Dora to take the dream bit by bit and tell me what occurred to her in

---

7. Woman-loving.   8. In answer to an inquiry Dora told me that there had never really been a fire at
their house [Freud's note].   9. The content of the dream makes it possible to establish that it in fact
occurred *for the first time* at L—— [Freud's note].

connection with it. She had already had some training in dream interpretation from having previously analysed a few minor specimens.

"Something occurs to me," she said, "but it cannot belong to the dream, for it is quite recent, whereas I have certainly had the dream before."

"That makes no difference," I replied. "Start away! It will simply turn out to be the most recent thing that fits in with the dream."

"Very well, then. Father has been having a dispute with Mother in the last few days, because she locks the dining-room door at night. My brother's room, you see, has no separate entrance, but can only be reached through the dining-room. Father does not want my brother to be locked in like that at night. He says it will not do: something might happen in the night so that it might be necessary to leave the room."

"And that made you think of the risk of fire?"

"Yes."

"Now, I should like you to pay close attention to the exact words you used. We may have to come back to them. You said that *'something might happen in the night so that it might be necessary to leave the room.'* "[1]

But Dora had now discovered the connecting link between the recent exciting cause of the dream and the original one, for she continued:

"When we arrived at L—— that time, Father and I, he openly said he was afraid of fire. We arrived in a violent thunderstorm, and saw the small wooden house without any lightning-conductor. So his anxiety was quite natural."

What I now had to do was to establish the relation between the events at L—— and the recurrent dreams which she had had there. I therefore said: "Did you have the dream during your first nights at L—— or during your last ones? in other words, before or after the scene in the wood by the lake of which we have heard so much?" (I must explain that I knew that the scene had not occurred on the very first day, and that she had remained at L—— for a few days after it without giving any hint of the incident.)

Her first reply was that she did not know, but after a while she added: "Yes. I think it was after the scene."

So now I knew that the dream was a reaction to that experience. But why had it recurred there three times? I continued my questions: "How long did you stop on at L—— after the scene?"

"Four more nights. On the following day I went away with Father."

"Now I am certain that the dream was an immediate effect of your experience with Herr K. It was at L—— that you dreamed it for the first time, and not before. You have only introduced this uncertainty in your memory so as to obliterate the connection in your mind. But the figures do not quite fit in to my satisfaction yet. If you stayed at L—— for four nights longer, the dream might have occurred four times over. Perhaps this was so?"

---

1. I laid stress on these words because they took me aback. They seemed to have an ambiguous ring about them. Are not certain physical needs referred to in the same words? Now, in a line of associations ambiguous words (or, as we may call them, "switch-words") act like points at a junction. If the points are switched across from the position in which they appear to lie in the dream, then we find ourselves on another set of rails; and along this second track run the thoughts which we are in search of but which still lie concealed behind the dream [Freud's note].

She no longer disputed by contention; but instead of answering my question she proceeded:[2] "In the afternoon after our trip on the lake, from which we (Herr K. and I) returned at midday, I had gone to lie down as usual on the sofa in the bedroom to have a short sleep. I suddenly awoke and saw Herr K. standing beside me. . . ."

"In fact, just as you saw your father standing beside your bed in the dream?"

"Yes. I asked him sharply what it was he wanted there. By way of reply he said he was not going to be prevented from coming into his own bedroom when he wanted; besides, there was something he wanted to fetch. This episode put me on my guard, and I asked Frau K. whether there was not a key to the bedroom door. The next morning I locked myself in while I was dressing. That afternoon, when I wanted to lock myself in so as to lie down again on the sofa, the key was gone. I was convinced that Herr K. had removed it."

"Then here we have the theme of locking or not locking a room which appeared in the first association to the dream and also happened to occur in the exciting cause of the recent recurrence of the dream.[3] I wonder whether the phrase '*I dressed quickly*' may not also belong to this context?"

"It was then that I made up my mind not to stop on with the K.'s without Father. On the subsequent mornings I could not help feeling afraid that Herr K. would surprise me while I was dressing: *so I always dressed very quickly*. You see, Father lived at the hotel, and Frau K. used always to go out early so as to go on expeditions with him. But Herr K. did not annoy me again."

"I understand. On the afternoon of the day after the scene in the wood you formed your intention of escaping from his persecution, and during the second, third, and fourth nights you had time to repeat that intention in your sleep. (You already knew on the second afternoon—before the dream, therefore—that you would not have the key on the following morning to lock yourself in with while you were dressing; and you could then form the design of dressing as quickly as possible.) But your dream recurred each night, for the very reason that it corresponded to an intention. An intention remains in existence until it has been carried out. You said to yourself, as it were: 'I shall have no rest and I can get no quiet sleep until I am out of this house.' In your account of the dream you turned it the other way and said: '*As soon as I was outside I woke up.*'"

[Freud interrupts his analysis to compare the preceding dream-interpretation with his theories in *The Interpretation of Dreams* (1900).]

*   *   *

Much of the dream, however, still remained to be interpreted, and I proceeded with my questions: "What is this about the jewel-case that your mother wanted to save?"

---

2. This was because a fresh piece of material had to emerge from her memory before the question I had put could be answered [Freud's note].   3. I suspected, though I did not as yet say so to Dora, that she had seized upon this element on account of a symbolic meaning which it possessed. "*Zimmer*" ["room"] in dreams stands very frequently for "*Frauenzimmer*" [a slightly derogatory word for "woman"; literally, "women's apartments"]. The question whether a woman is "open" or "shut" can naturally not be a matter of indifference. It is well known, too, what sort of "key" effects the opening in such a case [Freud's note].

"Mother is very fond of jewellery and had had a lot given her by Father."
"And you?"

"I used to be very fond of jewellery too, once; but I have not worn any since my illness.—Once, four years ago" (a year before the dream), "Father and Mother had a great dispute about a piece of jewellery. Mother wanted to be given a particular thing—pearl drops to wear in her ears. But Father does not like that kind of thing, and he brought her a bracelet instead of the drops. She was furious, and told him that as he had spent so much money on a present she did not like he had better just give it to some one else."

"I dare say you thought to yourself you would accept it with pleasure."

"I don't know.[4] I don't in the least know how Mother comes into the dream; she was not with us at L—— at the time."[5]

"I will explain that to you presently. Does nothing else occur to you in connection with the jewel-case? So far you have only talked about jewellery and have said nothing about a case."

"Yes, Herr K. had made me a present of an expensive jewel-case a little time before."

"Then a return-present would have been very appropriate. Perhaps you do not know that 'jewel-case' is a favourite expression for the same thing that you alluded to not long ago by means of the reticule you were wearing—for the female genitals, I mean."

"I knew you would say that."[6]

"That is to say, you knew that it *was* so. —The meaning of the dream is now becoming even clearer. You said to yourself: 'This man is persecuting me; he wants to force his way into my room. My "jewel-case" is in danger, and if anything happens it will be Father's fault.' For that reason in the dream you chose a situation which expresses the opposite—a danger from which your father is *saving* you. In this part of the dream everything is turned into its opposite; you will soon discover why. As you say, the mystery turns upon your mother. You ask how she comes into the dream? She is, as you know, your former rival in your father's affections. In the incident of the bracelet, you would have been glad to accept what your mother had rejected. Now let us just put 'give' instead of 'accept' and 'withhold' instead of 'reject.' Then it means that you were ready to give your father what your mother withheld from him; and the thing in question was connected with jewellery. Now bring your mind back to the jewel-case which Herr K. gave you. You have there the starting-point for a parallel line of thoughts, in which Herr K. is to be put in the place of your father just as he was in the matter of standing beside your bed. He gave you a jewel-case; so you are to give him your jewel-case. That was why I spoke just now of a 'return-present.' In this line of thoughts your mother must be replaced by Frau K. (You will not deny that she, at any rate, was present at the time.) So you are ready to give Herr K. what his wife withholds from

<hr/>

4. The regular formula with which she confessed to anything that had been repressed [Freud's note].
5. This remark gave evidence of a complete misunderstanding of the rules of dream-interpretation, though on other occasions Dora was perfectly familiar with them. This fact, coupled with the hesitancy and meagreness of her associations with the jewel-case, showed me that we were here dealing with material which had been very intensely repressed [Freud's note].   6. A very common way of putting aside a piece of knowledge that emerges from the repressed [Freud's note].

him. That is the thought which has had to be repressed with so much energy, and which has made it necessary for every one of its elements to be turned into its opposite. The dream confirms once more what I had already told you before you dreamt it—that you are summoning up your old love for your father in order to protect yourself against your love for Herr K. But what do all these efforts show? Not only that you are afraid of Herr K., but that you are still more afraid of yourself, and of the temptation you feel to yield to him. In short, these efforts prove once more how deeply you loved him."[7]

Naturally Dora would not follow me in this part of the interpretation. I myself, however, had been able to arrive at a further step in the interpretation, which seemed to me indispensable both for the anamnesis of the case and for the theory of dreams. I promised to communicate this to Dora at the next session.

The fact was that I could not forget the hint which seemed to be conveyed by the ambiguous words already noticed—*that it might be necessary to leave the room; that an accident might happen in the night*. Added to this was the fact that the elucidation of the dream seemed to me incomplete so long as a particular requirement remained unsatisfied; for, though I do not wish to insist that this requirement is a universal one, I have a predilection for discovering a means of satisfying it. A regularly formed dream stands, as it were, upon two legs, one of which is in contact with the main and current exciting cause, and the other with some momentous event in the years of childhood. The dream sets up a connection between those two factors—the event during childhood and the event of the present day—and it endeavours to re-shape the present on the model of the remote past. For the wish which creates the dream always springs from the period of childhood; and it is continually trying to summon childhood back into reality and to correct the present day by the measure of childhood. I believed that I could already clearly detect those elements of Dora's dream which could be pieced together into an allusion to an event in childhood.

I opened the discussion of the subject with a little experiment, which was, as usual, successful. There happened to be a large match-stand on the table. I asked Dora to look round and see whether she noticed anything special on the table, something that was not there as a rule. She noticed nothing. I then asked her if she knew why children were forbidden to play with matches.

"Yes; on account of the risk of fire. My uncle's children are very fond of playing with matches."

"Not only on that account. They are warned not to 'play with fire,' and a particular belief is associated with the warning."

She knew nothing about it.—"Very well, then; the fear is that if they do they will wet their bed. The antithesis of 'water' and 'fire' must be at the

---

7. I added: "Moreover, the re-appearance of the dream in the last few days forces me to the conclusion that you consider that the same situation has arisen once again, and that you have decided to give up the treatment—to which, after all, it is only your father who makes you come." The sequel showed how correct my guess had been. At this point my interpretation touches for a moment upon the subject of "transference"—a theme which is of the highest practical and theoretical importance, but into which I shall not have much further opportunity of entering in the present paper [Freud's note].

bottom of this. Perhaps it is believed that they will dream of fire and then try and put it out with water. I cannot say exactly. But I notice that the antithesis of water and fire has been extremely useful to you in the dream. Your mother wanted to save the jewel-case so that it should not be *burnt*; while in the dream-thoughts it is a question of the 'jewel-case' not being *wetted*. But fire is not only used as the contrary of water, it also serves directly to represent love (as in the phrase 'to be *consumed* with love'). So that from 'fire' one set of rails runs by way of this symbolic meaning to thoughts of love; while the other set runs by way of the contrary 'water,' and, after sending off a branch line which provides another connection with 'love' (for love also makes things wet), leads in a different direction. And what direction can that be? Think of the expressions you used: that *an accident might happen in the night*, and that *it might be necessary to leave the room*. Surely the allusion must be to a physical need? And if you transpose the accident into childhood what can it be but bed-wetting? But what is usually done to prevent children from wetting their bed? Are they not woken up in the night out of their sleep, *exactly as your father woke you up in the dream?* This, then, must be the actual occurrence which enabled you to substitute your father for Herr K., who really woke you up out of your sleep. I am accordingly driven to conclude that you were addicted to bed-wetting up to a later age than is usual with children. The same must also have been true of your brother; for your father said: '*I refuse to let my two children* go to their destruction. . . .' Your brother has no other sort of connection with the real situation at the K.'s; he had not gone with you to L——. And now, what have your recollections to say to this?"

"I know nothing about myself," was her reply, "but my brother used to wet his bed up till his sixth or seventh year; and it used sometimes to happen to him in the daytime too."

I was on the point of remarking to her how much easier it is to remember things of that kind about one's brother than about oneself, when she continued the train of recollections which had been revived: "Yes. I used to do it too, for some time, but not until my seventh or eighth year. It must have been serious, because I remember now that the doctor was called in. It lasted till a short time before my nervous asthma."

"And what did the doctor say to it?"

"He explained it as nervous weakness: it would soon pass off, he thought; and he prescribed a tonic."[8]

The interpretation of the dream now seemed to me to be complete.[9] But Dora brought me an addendum to the dream on the very next day. She had forgotten to relate, she said, that each time after waking up she had smelt smoke. Smoke, of course, fitted in well with fire, but it also showed that the dream had a special relation to myself; for when she used

---

8. This physician was the only one in whom she showed any confidence, because this episode showed her that he had not penetrated her secret. She felt afraid of any other doctor about whom she had not yet been able to form a judgement, and we can now see that the motive of her fear was the possibility that he might guess her secret [Freud's note].   9. The essence of the dream might perhaps be translated into words such as these: "The temptation is so strong. Dear Father, protect me again as you used to in my childhood, and prevent my bed from being wetted!" [Freud's note].

to assert that there was nothing concealed behind this or that, I would often say by way of rejoinder: "There can be no smoke without fire!" Dora objected, however, to such a purely personal interpretation, saying that Herr K. and her father were passionate smokers—as I am too, for the matter of that. She herself had smoked during her stay by the lake, and Herr K. had rolled a cigarette for her before he began his unlucky proposal. She thought, too, that she clearly remembered having noticed the smell of smoke on the three occasions of the dream's occurrence at L——, and not for the first time at its recent reappearance. As she would give me no further information, it was left to me to determine how this addendum was to be introduced into the texture of the dream-thoughts. One thing which I had to go upon was the fact that the smell of smoke had only come up as an addendum to the dream, and must therefore have had to overcome a particularly strong effort on the part of repression. Accordingly it was probably related to the thoughts which were the most obscurely presented and the most successfully repressed in the dream, to the thoughts, that is, concerned with the temptation to show herself willing to yield to the man. If that were so, the addendum to the dream could scarcely mean anything else than the longing for a kiss, which, with a smoker, would necessarily smell of smoke. But a kiss had passed between Herr K. and Dora some two years further back, and it would certainly have been repeated more than once if she had given way to him. So the thoughts of temptation seemed in this way to have harked back to the earlier scene, and to have revived the memory of the kiss against whose seductive influence the little "thumb-sucker" had defended herself at the time, by the feeling of disgust. Taking into consideration, finally, the indications which seemed to point to there having been a transference on to me—since I am a smoker too—I came to the conclusion that the idea had probably occurred to her one day during a session that she would like to have a kiss from me. This would have been the exciting cause which led her to repeat the warning dream and to form her intention of stopping the treatment. Everything fits together very satisfactorily upon this view; but owing to the characteristics of "transference" its validity is not susceptible of definite proof.

[Freud discusses the relationship of bedwetting and masturbation in neurotic behavior and brings in her father's syphilis and her own playing with a small purse.]

*　　*　　*

There is a great deal of symbolism of this kind in life, but as a rule we pass it by without heeding it. When I set myself the task of bringing to light what human beings keep hidden within them, not by the compelling power of hypnosis, but by observing what they say and what they show, I thought the task was a harder one than it really is. He that has eyes to see and ears to hear may convince himself that no mortal can keep a secret. If his lips are silent, he chatters with his finger-tips; betrayal oozes out of him at every pore. And thus the task of making conscious the most hidden recesses of the mind is one which it is quite possible to accomplish.

[Freud continues and comments on the previous material, including its relationship to *dyspnoea* (breathing difficulties) as another symptom of distress.]

*   *   *

I suspect that we are here concerned with unconscious processes of thought which are twined around a pre-existing structure of organic connections, much as festoons of flowers are twined around a wire; so that on another occasion one might find other lines of thought inserted between the same points of departure and termination. Yet a knowledge of the thought-connections which have been effective in the individual case is of a value which cannot be exaggerated for clearing up the symptoms. It is only because the analysis was prematurely broken off that we have been obliged in Dora's case to resort to framing conjectures and filling in deficiencies. Whatever I have brought forward for filling up the gaps is based upon other cases which have been more thoroughly analysed.

The dream from the analysis of which we have derived this information corresponded, as we have seen, to an intention which Dora carried with her into her sleep. It was therefore repeated each night until the intention had been carried out; and it reappeared years later when an occasion arose for forming an analogous intention. The intention might have been consciously expressed in some such words as these: "I must fly from this house, for I see that my virginity is threatened here; I shall go away with my father, and I shall take precautions not to be surprised while I am dressing in the morning." These thoughts were clearly expressed in the dream; they formed part of a mental current which had achieved consciousness and a dominating position in waking life. Behind them can be discerned obscure traces of a train of thought which formed part of a contrary current and had consequently been suppressed. This other train of thought culminated in the temptation to yield to the man, out of gratitude for the love and tenderness he had shown her during the last few years, and it may perhaps have revived the memory of the only kiss she had so far had from him. But according to the theory which I developed in my *Interpretation of Dreams* such elements as these are not enough for the formation of a dream. On that theory a dream is not an intention represented as having been carried out, but a wish represented as having been fulfilled, and, moreover, in most cases a wish dating from childhood. It is our business now to discover whether this principle may not be contradicted by the present dream.

The dream does in fact contain infantile material, though it is impossible at a first glance to discover any connections between that material and Dora's intention of flying from Herr K.'s house and the temptation of his presence. Why should a recollection have emerged of her bed-wetting when she was a child and of the trouble her father used to take to teach the child clean habits? We may answer this by saying that it was only by the help of the train of thought that it was possible to suppress the other thoughts which were so intensely occupied with the temptation to yield or that it was possible to secure the dominance of the intention which had been formed of combating those other thoughts. The child decided to fly *with* her father; in reality she fled *to* her father because she was afraid of the man who was pursuing her; she summoned up an infantile affection for her father so that it might protect her against her present affection for a stranger. Her father was himself partly responsible for her present danger, for he had handed her over to this strange man in the interests of his own love-affair. And how much better it had been when that same father of hers had loved no one more than her, and had exerted all his strength to save her from the dangers that had then threatened her! The infantile, and now unconscious, wish to put her father in the strange man's place had the potency necessary for the formation of a dream. If there were a past situation similar to a present one, and differing from it only in being concerned with one instead of with the other of the two persons mentioned in the wish, that situation would become the main one in the dream. But there *had* been such a situation. Her father had once stood beside her bed, just as Herr K. had the day before, and had woken her up, with a kiss perhaps, as Herr K. may have meant to do. Thus her intention of flying from the house was not in itself capable of producing a dream; but it became so by being associated with another intention which was founded upon infantile wishes. The wish to replace Herr K. by her father provided the necessary motive power for the dream. Let me recall the interpretation I was led to adopt of Dora's reinforced train of thought about her father's relations with Frau K. My interpretation was that she had at that point summoned up an infantile affection for her father so as to be able to keep her repressed love for Herr K. in its state of repression. This same sudden revulsion in the patient's mental life was reflected in the dream.

[Freud connects passages from *The Interpretation of Dreams* with Dora's case.]

*   *   *

I add a few remarks which may help towards the synthesis of this dream. The dream-work began on the afternoon of the day after the scene in the wood, after Dora had noticed that she was no longer able to lock the door of her room. She then said to herself: "I am threatened by a serious danger here," and formed her intention of not stopping on in the house alone but of going off with her father. This intention became capable of forming a dream, because it succeeded in finding a continuation in the unconscious. What corresponded to it there was her summoning up her infantile love for her father as a protection against the present temptation. The change which thus took place in her became fixed and brought her into the attitude shown by her supervalent train of thought—jealousy of Frau K. on her father's account, as though she herself were in love with him. There was a conflict within her between a temptation to yield to the man's proposal and a composite force rebelling against that feeling. This latter force was made up of motives of respectability and good sense, of hostile feelings caused by the governess's disclosures (jealousy and wounded pride, as we shall see later), and of a neurotic element, namely, the tendency to a repudiation of sexuality which was already present in her and was based on her childhood history. Her love for her father, which she summoned up to protect her against the temptation, had its origin in this same childhood history.

Her intention of flying to her father, which, as we have seen, reached down into the unconscious, was transformed by the dream into a situation which presented as fulfilled the wish that her father would save her from the danger. In this process it was necessary to put on one side a certain thought which stood in the way; for it was her father himself who had brought her into the danger. The hostile feeling against her father (her desire for revenge), which was here suppressed, was, as we shall discover, one of the motive forces of the second dream.

According to the necessary conditions of dream-formation the imagined situation must be chosen so as to reproduce a situation in infancy. A special triumph is achieved if a recent situation, perhaps even the very situation which is the exciting cause of the dream, can be transformed into an infantile one. This has actually been achieved in the present case, by a purely chance disposition of the material. Just as Herr K. had stood beside her sofa and woken her up, so her father had often done in her childhood. The whole trend of her thoughts could be most aptly symbolized by her substitution of her father for Herr K. in that situation.

[Freud continues to analyze images of wetness, jewel-case, and locked doors in relation to Dora's dream and her family situation.]

*   *   *

III

The Second Dream

A few weeks after the first dream the second occurred, and when it had been dealt with the analysis was broken off. It cannot be made as completely intelligible as the first, but it afforded a desirable confirmation of an assumption which had become necessary about the patient's mental state, it filled up a gap in her memory, and it made it possible to obtain a deep insight into the origin of another of her symptoms.

Dora described the dream as follows: "*I was walking about in a town which I did not know. I saw streets and squares which were strange to me.*[1] *Then I came into a house where I lived, went to my room, and found a letter from Mother lying there. She wrote saying that as I had left home without my parents' knowledge she had not wished to write to me to say that Father was ill. 'Now he is dead, and if you like*[2] *you can come.' I then went to the station and asked about a hundred times: 'Where is the station?' I always got the same answer: 'Five minutes.' I then saw a thick wood before me which I went into, and there I asked a man whom I met. He said to me: 'Two and a half hours more.'*[3] *He offered to accompany me. But I refused and went alone. I saw the station in front of me and could not reach it. At*

---

1. To this she subsequently made an important addendum: "*I saw a monument in one of the squares*" [Freud's note].   2. To this came the addendum: "*There was a question-mark after this word, thus:* '*like?*' " [Freud's note].   3. In repeating the dream she said: "*Two hours*" [Freud's note].

the same time I had the usual feeling of anxiety that one has in dreams when one cannot move forward. Then I was at home. I must have been travelling in the meantime, but I know nothing about that. I walked into the porter's lodge, and enquired for our flat. The maidservant opened the door to me and replied that Mother and the others were already at the cemetery."[4]

It was not without some difficulty that the interpretation of this dream proceeded. In consequence of the peculiar circumstances in which the analysis was broken off—circumstances connected with the content of the dream—the whole of it was not cleared up. And for this reason, too, I am not equally certain at every point of the order in which my conclusions were reached. I will begin by mentioning the subject-matter with which the current analysis was dealing at the time when the dream intervened. For some time Dora herself had been raising a number of questions about the connection between some of her actions and the motives which presumably underlay them. One of these questions was "Why did I say nothing about the scene by the lake for some days after it had happened?" Her second question was: "Why did I then suddenly tell my parents about it?" Moreover, her having felt so deeply injured by Herr K.'s proposal seemed to me in general to need explanation, especially as I was beginning to realize that Herr K. himself had not regarded his proposal to Dora as a mere frivolous attempt at seduction. I looked upon her having told her parents of the episode as an action which she had taken when she was already under the influence of a morbid craving for revenge. A normal girl, I am inclined to think, will deal with a situation of this kind by herself.

I shall present the material produced during the analysis of this dream in the somewhat haphazard order in which it recurs to my mind.

She was wandering about alone in a strange town, and saw streets and squares. Dora assured me that it was certainly not B——, which I had first hit upon, but a town in which she had never been. It was natural to suggest that she might have seen some pictures or photographs and have taken the dream-pictures from them. After this remark of mine came the addendum about the monument in one of the squares and immediately afterwards her recognition of its source. At Christmas she had been sent an album from a German health-resort, containing views of the town; and the very day before the dream she had looked this out to show it to some relatives who were stopping with them. It had been put in a box for keeping pictures in, and she could not lay her hands on it at once. She had therefore said to her mother: *"Where is the box?"*[5] One of the pictures was of a square with a monument in it. The present had been sent to her by a young engineer, with whom she had once had a passing acquaintance in the manufacturing town. The young man had accepted a post in Germany, so as to become sooner self-supporting; and he took every opportu-

---

4. In the next session Dora brought me two addenda to this: *"I saw myself particularly distinctly going up the stairs,"* and *"After she had answered I went to my room, but not the least sadly, and began reading a big book that lay on my writing-table"* [Freud's note].   5. In the dream she said: *"Where is the station?"* The resemblance between the two questions led me to make an inference which I shall go into presently [Freud's note].

nity of reminding Dora of his existence. It was easy to guess that he intended to come forward as a suitor one day, when his position had improved. But that would take time, and it meant waiting.

The wandering about in a strange town was overdetermined. It led back to one of the exciting causes from the day before. A young cousin of Dora's had come to stay with them for the holidays, and Dora had had to show him round Vienna. This cause was, it is true, a matter of complete indifference to her. But her cousin's visit reminded her of her own first brief visit to Dresden. On that occasion she had been a stranger and had wandered about, not failing, of course, to visit the famous picture gallery. Another [male] cousin of hers, who was with them and knew Dresden, had wanted to act as a guide and take her round the gallery. *But she declined and went alone*, and stopped in front of the pictures that appealed to her. She remained *two hours* in front of the Sistine Madonna, rapt in silent admiration. When I asked her what had pleased her so much about the picture she could find no clear answer to make. At last she said: "The Madonna."

There could be no doubt that these associations really belonged to the material concerned in forming the dream. They included portions which reappeared in the dream unchanged ("she declined and went alone" and "two hours"). I may remark at once that "pictures" was a nodal point in the network of her dream-thoughts (the pictures in the album, the pictures at Dresden). I should also like to single out, with a view to subsequent investigation, the theme of the "Madonna," of the virgin mother. But what was most evident was that in this first part of the dream she was identifying herself with a young man. This young man was wandering about in a strange place, he was striving to reach a goal, but he was being kept back, he needed patience and must wait. If in all this she had been thinking of the engineer, it would have been appropriate for the goal to have been the possession of a woman, of herself. But instead of this it was—a station. Nevertheless, the relation of the question in the dream to the question which had been put in real life allows us to substitute *"box"* for "station."[6] A box and a woman: the notions begin to agree better.

She asked quite a hundred times. . . . This led to another exciting cause of the dream, and this time to one that was less indifferent. On the previous evening they had had company, and afterwards her father had asked her to fetch him the brandy: he could not get to sleep unless he had taken some brandy. She had asked her mother for the key of the sideboard; but the latter had been deep in conversation, and had not answered her, until Dora had exclaimed with the exaggeration of impatience: "I've asked you *a hundred times* already where the key is." As a matter of fact, she had of course only repeated the question about *five times.*[7]

"Where is the *key?*" seems to me to be the masculine counterpart to the question "Where is the *box?*" They are therefore questions referring to— the genitals.

---

6. *Schachtel*, the word that was used for "box" by Dora in her question, is a deprecatory term for "woman." 7. In the dream the number five occurs in the mention of the period of "five minutes." In my book on the interpretation of dreams I have given several examples of the way in which numbers occurring in the dream-thoughts are treated by dreams. We frequently find them torn out of their true context and inserted into a new one [Freud's note].

Dora went on to say that during this same family gathering some one had toasted her father and had expressed the hope that he might continue to enjoy the best of health for many years to come, etc. At this a strange quiver passed over her father's tired face, and she had understood what thoughts he was having to keep down. Poor sick man! who could tell what span of life was still to be his?

This brings us to the *contents of the letter* in the dream. Her father was dead, and she had left home by her own choice. In connection with this letter I at once reminded Dora of the farewell letter which she had written to her parents or had at least composed for their benefit. This letter had been intended to give her father a fright, so that he should give up Frau K.; or at any rate to take revenge on him if he could not be induced to do that. We are here concerned with the subject of her death and of her father's death. (Cf. "cemetery" later on in the dream.) Shall we be going astray if we suppose that the situation which formed the facade of the dream was a phantasy of revenge directed against her father? The feelings of pity for him which she remembered from the day before would be quite in keeping with this. According to the phantasy she had left home and gone among strangers, and her father's heart had broken with grief and with longing for her. Thus she would be revenged. She understood very clearly what it was that her father needed when he could not get to sleep without a drink of brandy.[8] We will make a note of Dora's *craving for revenge* as a new element to be taken into account in any subsequent synthesis of her dream-thoughts.

But the contents of the letter must be capable of further determination. What was the source of the words "if you like"? It was at this point that the addendum of there having been a question-mark after the word "like" occurred to Dora, and she then recognized these words as a quotation out of the letter from Frau K. which had contained the invitation to L——, the place by the lake. In that letter there had been a question-mark placed, in a most unusual fashion, in the very middle of a sentence, after the intercalated words "if you would like to come."

So here we were back again at the scene by the lake and at the problems connected with it. I asked Dora to describe the scene to me in detail. At first she produced little that was new. Herr K.'s exordium had been somewhat serious; but she had not let him finish what he had to say. No sooner had she grasped the purport of his words than she had slapped him in the face and hurried away. I enquired what his actual words had been. Dora could only remember one of his pleas: "You know I get nothing out of my wife." In order to avoid meeting him again she had wanted to get back to L—— on foot, by walking round the lake, and *she had asked a man whom she met how far it was.* On his replying that it was *"Two and a half hours,"* she had given up her intention and had after all gone back to the boat, which left soon afterwards. Herr K. had been there too and had come up to her and begged her to forgive him and not to mention the incident. But

---

8. There can be no doubt that sexual satisfaction is the best soporific, just as sleeplessness is almost always the consequence of lack of satisfaction. Her father could not sleep because he was debarred from sexual intercourse with the woman he loved. (Compare in this connection the phrase discussed just below: "I get nothing out of my wife.") [Freud's note].

she had made no reply.—Yes. The *wood* in the dream had been just like the wood by the shore of the lake, the wood in which the scene she had just described once more had taken place. But she had seen precisely the same thick wood the day before, in a picture at the Secessionist[9] exhibition. In the background of the picture there were *nymphs*.[1]

At this point a certain suspicion of mine became a certainty. The use of *"Bahnhof"* and *"Friedhof"*[2] to represent the female genitals was striking enough in itself, but it also served to direct my awakened curiosity to the similarity formed *"Vorhof"*[3]—an anatomical term for a particular region of the female genitals. This might have been no more than mistaken ingenuity. But now, with the addition of "nymphs" visible in the background of a "thick wood," no further doubts could be entertained. Here was a symbolic geography of sex! "Nymphae," as is known to physicians though not to laymen (and even by the former term is not very commonly used), is the name given to the labia minora, which lie in the background of the "thick wood" of the pubic hair. But any one who employed such technical names as "vestibulum" and "nymphae" must have derived this knowledge from books, and not from popular ones either, but from anatomical textbooks or from an encyclopaedia—the common refuge of youth when it is devoured by sexual curiosity. If this interpretation were correct, therefore, there lay concealed behind the first situation in the dream a phantasy of defloration, the phantasy of a man seeking to force an entrance into the female genitals.[4]

I informed Dora of the conclusions I had reached. The impression made upon her must have been forcible, for there immediately appeared a piece of the dream which had been forgotten: *"she went calmly to her room, and began reading a big book that lay on her writing-table."* The emphasis here was upon the two details "calmly" and "big" in connection with "book." I asked whether the book was in encyclopaedia *format*, and she said it was. Now children never read about forbidden subjects in an encyclopaedia *calmly*. They do it in fear and trembling, with an uneasy look over their shoulder to see if some one may not be coming. Parents are very much in the way while reading of this kind is going on. But this uncomfortable situation had been radically improved, thanks to the dream's power of fulfilling wishes. Dora's father was dead, and the others had already gone to the cemetery. She might calmly read whatever she chose. Did not this mean that one of her motives for revenge was a revolt

9. The Vienna Secessionists were a group of recognized art nouveau artists—led by painter Gustav Klimt (1862–1918)—who withdrew from established art societies to show their own work.   1. Here for the third time we come upon "picture" (views of towns, the Dresden gallery), but in a much more significant connection. Because of what appears in the picture (the wood, the nymphs), the *"Bild"* ["picture"] is turned into a *"Weibsbild"* [literally, "picture of a woman"—a somewhat derogatory expression for "woman"] [Freud's note].   2. "Station"; literally, "railway-court." *"Friedhof"*: "Cemetery"; literally, "peace-court." Moreover, a "station" is used for purposes of *"Verkehr"* ["traffic," "intercourse," "sexual intercourse"]: this fact determines the psychical coating in a number of cases of railway phobia [Freud's note].   3. Fore-court (German, literal trans.); vestibulum.   4. The phantasy of defloration formed the second component of the situation. The emphasis upon the difficulty of getting forward and the anxiety felt in the dream indicated the stress which the dreamer was so ready to lay upon her virginity—a point alluded to in another place by means of the Sistine Madonna. These sexual thoughts gave an unconscious ground-colouring to the wishes (which were perhaps merely kept secret) concerned with the suitor who was waiting for her in Germany. We have already recognized the phantasy of revenge as the first component of the same situation in the dream. The two components do not coincide completely, but only in part. We shall subsequently come upon the traces of a third and still more important train of thought [Freud's note].

against her parents' constraint? If her father was dead she could read or love as she pleased.

At first she would not remember ever having read anything in an encyclopaedia; but she then admitted that a recollection of an occasion of the kind did occur to her, though it was of an innocent enough nature. At the time when the aunt she was so fond of had been so seriously ill and it had already been settled that Dora was to go to Vienna, a *letter* had come from another uncle, to say that they could not go to Vienna, as a boy of his, a cousin of Dora's therefore, had fallen dangerously ill with appendicitis. Dora had thereupon looked up in the encyclopaedia to see what the symptoms of appendicitis were. From what she had then read she still recollected the characteristic localization of the abdominal pain.

I then remembered that shortly after her aunt's death Dora had had an attack of what had been alleged to be appendicitis. Up till then I had not ventured to count that illness among her hysterical productions. She told me that during the first few days she had had high fever and had felt the pain in her abdomen that she had read about in the encyclopaedia. She had been given cold fomentations but had not been able to bear them. On the second day her period had set in, accompanied by violent pains. (Since her health had been bad, the periods had been very irregular.) At that time she used to suffer continually from constipation.

It was not really possible to regard this state as a purely hysterical one. Although hysterical fever does undoubtedly occur, yet it seemed too arbitrary to put down the fever accompanying this questionable illness to hysteria instead of to some organic cause operative at the time. I was on the point of abandoning the track, when she herself helped me along it by producing her last addendum to the dream: *"she saw herself particularly distinctly going up the stairs."*

I naturally required a special determinant for this. Dora objected that she would anyhow have had to go upstairs if she had wanted to get to her flat, which was on an upper floor. It was easy to brush aside this objection (which was probably not very seriously intended) by pointing out that if she had been able to travel in her dream from the unknown town to Vienna without making a railway journey she ought also to have been able to leave out a flight of stairs. She then proceeded to relate that after the appendicitis she had not been able to walk properly and had dragged her right foot. This state of things had continued for a long time, and on that account she had been particularly glad to avoid stairs. Even now her foot sometimes dragged. The doctors whom she had consulted at her father's desire had been very much astonished at this most unusual after-effect of an appendicitis, especially as the abdominal pains had not recurred and did not in any way accompany the dragging of the foot.[5]

Here, then, we have a true hysterical symptom. The fever may have been organically determined—perhaps by one of those very frequent

5. We must assume the existence of some somatic connection between the painful abdominal sensations known as "ovarian neuralgia" and locomotor disturbances in the leg on the same side; and we must suppose that in Dora's case the somatic connection had been given an interpretation of a particularly specialized sort, that is to say, that it had been overlaid with and brought into the service of a particular psychological meaning. The reader is referred to my analogous remarks in connection with the analysis of Dora's symptom of coughing and with the relation between catarrh and loss of appetite [Freud's note].

attacks of influenza that are not localized in any particular part of the body. Nevertheless it was now established that the neurosis had seized upon this chance event and made use of it for an utterance of its own. Dora had therefore given herself an illness which she had read up about in the encyclopaedia, and she had punished herself for dipping into its pages. But she was forced to recognize that the punishment could not possibly apply to her reading the innocent article in question. It must have been inflicted as the result of a process of displacement, after another occasion of more guilty reading had become associated with this one; and the guilty occasion must lie concealed in her memory behind the contemporaneous innocent one.[6] It might still be possible, perhaps, to discover the nature of the subjects she had read about on that other occasion.

What, then, was the meaning of this condition, of this attempted simulation of a perityphlitis?[7] The remainder of the disorder, the dragging of one leg, was entirely out of keeping with perityphlitis. It must, no doubt, fit in better with the secret and possibly sexual meaning of the clinical picture; and if it were elucidated might in its turn throw light on the meaning which we were in search of. I looked about for a method of approaching the puzzle. Periods of time had been mentioned in the dream; and time is assuredly never a matter of indifference in any biological event. I therefore asked Dora when this attack of appendicitis had taken place; whether it had been before or after the scene by the lake. Every difficulty was resolved at a single blow by her prompt reply: "Nine months later." The period of time is sufficiently characteristic. Her supposed attack of appendicitis had thus enabled the patient with the modest means at her disposal (the pains and the menstrual flow) to realize a phantasy of *childbirth*.[8] Dora was naturally aware of the significance of this period of time, and could not dispute the probability of her having, on the occasion under discussion, read up in the encyclopaedia about pregnancy and childbirth. But what was all this about her dragging her leg? I could now hazard a guess. That is how people walk when they have twisted a foot. So she had made a "false step": which was true indeed if she could give birth to a child nine months after the scene by the lake. But there was still another requirement upon the fulfilment of which I had to insist. I am convinced that a symptom of this kind can only arise where it has an *infantile* prototype. All my experience hitherto has led me to hold firmly to the view that recollections derived from the impressions of later years do not possess sufficient force to enable them to establish themselves as symptoms. I scarcely dared hope that Dora would provide me with the material that I wanted from her childhood, for the fact is that I am not yet in a position to assert the general validity of this rule, much as I should like to be able to do so. But in this case there came an immediate confirmation of it. Yes, said Dora, once when she was a child she had twisted the same foot; she had slipped on one of the steps as she was going *down-*

---

6. This is quite a typical example of the way in which symptoms arise from exciting causes which appear to be entirely unconnected with sexuality [Freud's note].   7. Appendicitis.   8. I have already indicated that the majority of hysterical symptoms, when they have attained their full pitch of development, represent an imagined situation of sexual life—such as a scene of sexual intercourse, pregnancy, childbirth, confinement, etc. [Freud's note].

stairs. The foot—and it was actually the same one that she afterwards dragged—had swelled up and had to be bandaged and she had had to lie up for some weeks. This had been a short time before the attack of nervous asthma in her eighth year.

The next thing to do was to turn to account our knowledge of the existence of this phantasy: "If it is true that you were delivered of a child nine months after the scene by the lake, and that you are going about to this very day carrying the consequences of your false step with you, then it follows that in your unconscious you must have regretted the upshot of the scene. In your unconscious thoughts, that is to say, you have made an emendation in it. The assumption that underlies your phantasy of childbirth is that on that occasion something took place,[9] that on that occasion you experienced and went through everything that you were in fact obliged to pick up later on from the encyclopaedia. So you see that your love for Herr K. did not come to an end with the scene, but that (as I maintained) it has persisted down to the present day—though it is true that you are unconscious of it."—And Dora disputed the fact no longer.[1]

The labour of elucidating the second dream had so far occupied two hours. At the end of the second session, when I expressed my satisfaction at the result, Dora replied in a depreciatory tone: "Why, has anything so very remarkable come out?" These words prepared me for the advent of fresh revelations.

She opened the third session with these words: "Do you know that I am here for the last time to-day?"—"How can I know, as you have said nothing to me about it?"—"Yes. I made up my mind to put up with it till the New Year.[2] But I shall wait no longer than that to be cured."—"You know that you are free to stop the treatment at any time. But for to-day we will go on with our work. When did you come to this decision?"—"A fortnight ago, I think."—"That sounds just like a maidservant or a governess—a fortnight's warning."—"There was a governess who gave warning with the K.'s, when I was on my visit to them that time at L——, by the lake."—"Really? You have never told me about her. Tell me."

"Well, there was a young girl in the house, who was the children's governess; and she behaved in the most extraordinary way to Herr K. She never said good morning to him, never answered his remarks, never handed him anything at table when he asked for it, and in short treated him like thin air. For that matter he was hardly any politer to her. A day or two before the scene by the lake, the girl took me aside and said she had something to tell me. She then told me that Herr K. had made advances to her at a time when his wife was away for several weeks; he had made

9. The phantasy of defloration is thus found to have an application to Herr K., and we begin to see why this part of the dream contained material taken from the scene by the lake—the refusal, two and a half hours, the wood, the invitation to L—— [Freud's note].   1. I may here add a few supplementary interpretations to those that have already been given: The "*Madonna*" was obviously Dora herself; in the first place because of the "adorer" who had sent her the pictures, in the second place because she had won Herr K.'s love chiefly by the motherliness she had shown towards his children, and lastly because she had had a child though she was still a girl (this being a direct allusion to the phantasy of childbirth). Moreover, the notion of the "Madonna" is a favourite counter-idea in the mind of girls who feel themselves oppressed by imputations of sexual guilt,—which was the case with Dora [Freud's note].   2. It was December 31st [Freud's note].

violent love to her and had implored her to yield to his entreaties, saying that he got nothing from his wife, and so on."—"Why, those are the very words he used afterwards, when he made his proposal to you and you gave him the slap in his face."—"Yes. She had given way to him, but after a little while he had ceased to care for her, and since then she hated him."—"And this governess had given warning?"—"No. She meant to give warning. She told me that as soon as she felt she was thrown over she had told her parents what had happened. They were respectable people living in Germany somewhere. Her parents said that she must leave the house instantly; and, as she failed to do so, they wrote to her saying that they would have nothing more to do with her, and that she was never to come home again."—"And why had she not gone away?"—"She said she meant to wait a little longer, to see if there might not be some change in Herr K. She could not bear living like that any more, she said, and if she saw no change she should give warning and go away."—"And what became of the girl?"—"I only know that she went away."—"And she did not have a child as a result of the adventure?"—"No."

Here, therefore (and quite in accordance with the rules), was a piece of material information coming to light in the middle of the analysis and helping to solve problems which had previously been raised. I was able to say to Dora: "Now I know your motive for the slap in the face with which you answered Herr K.'s proposal. It was not that you were offended at his suggestions; you were actuated by jealousy and revenge. At the time when the governess was telling you her story you were still able to make use of your gift for putting on one side everything that is not agreeable to your feelings. But at the moment when Herr K. used the words 'I get nothing out of my wife'—which were the same words he had used to the governess—fresh emotions were aroused in you and tipped the balance. 'Does he dare,' you said to yourself, 'to treat me like a governess, like a servant?' Wounded pride added to jealousy and to the conscious motives of common sense—it was too much.[3] To prove to you how deeply impressed you were by the governess's story, let me draw your attention to the repeated occasions upon which you have identified yourself with her both in your dream and in your conduct. You told your parents what happened—a fact which we have hitherto been unable to account for—just as the governess wrote and told *her* parents. You give me a fortnight's warning, just like a governess. The letter in the dream which gave you leave to go home is the counterpart of the governess's letter from her parents forbidding her to do so."

"Then why did I not tell my parents at once?"

"How much time did you allow to elapse?"

"The scene took place on the last day of June; I told my mother about it on July 14th."

"Again a fortnight, then—the time characteristic for a person in service. Now I can answer your question. You understood the poor girl very well. She did not want to go away at once, because she still had hopes, because

---

3. It is not a matter of indifference, perhaps, that Dora may have heard her father make the same complaint about his wife, just as I myself did from his own lips. She was perfectly well aware of its meaning [Freud's note].

she expected that Herr K.'s affections would return to her again. So that must have been your motive too. You waited for that length of time so as to see whether he would repeat his proposals; if he had, you would have concluded that he was in earnest, and did not mean to play with you as he had done with the governess."

"A few days after I had left he sent me a picture post-card."[4]

"Yes, but when after that nothing more came, you gave free rein to your feelings of revenge. I can even imagine that at that time you were still able to find room for a subsidiary intention, and thought that your accusation might be a means of inducing him to travel to the place where you were living."—"As he actually offered to do at first," Dora threw in.—"In that way your longing for him would have been appeased"—here she nodded assent, a thing which I had not expected—"and he might have made you the amends you desired."

"What amends?"

"The fact is, I am beginning to suspect that you took the affair with Herr K. much more seriously than you have been willing to admit so far. Had not the K.'s often talked of getting a divorce?"

"Yes, certainly. At first she did not want to, on account of the children. And now she wants to, but he no longer does."

"May you not have thought that he wanted to get divorced from his wife so as to marry you? And that now he no longer wants to because he has no one to replace her? It is true that two years ago you were very young. But you told me yourself that your mother was engaged at seventeen and then waited two years for her husband. A daughter usually takes her mother's love-story as her model. So you too wanted to wait for him, and you took it that he was only waiting till you were grown up enough to be his wife. I imagine that this was a perfectly serious plan for the future in your eyes. You have not even got the right to assert that it was out of the question for Herr K. to have had any such intention; you have told me enough about him that points directly towards his having such an intention. Nor does his behaviour at L—— contradict this view. After all, you did not let him finish his speech and do not know what he meant to say to you. Incidentally, the scheme would by no means have been so impracticable. Your father's relations with Frau K.—and it was probably only for this reason that you lent them your support for so long—made it certain that her consent to a divorce could be obtained; and you can get anything you like out of your father. Indeed, if your temptation at L—— had had a different upshot, this would have been the only possible solution for all the parties concerned. And I think that is why you regretted the actual event so deeply and emended it in the phantasy which made its appearance in the shape of the appendicitis. So it must have been a bitter piece of disillusionment for you when the effect of your charges against Herr K. was not that he renewed his proposals but that he replied instead with denials and slanders. You will agree that nothing makes you so angry as having it thought that you merely fancied the scene by the lake. I know

---

4. Here is the point of contact with the engineer, who was concealed behind the figure of Dora herself in the first situation in the dream [Freud's note].

now—and this is what you do not want to be reminded of—that you *did* fancy that Herr K.'s proposals were serious, and that he would not leave off until you had married him."

Dora had listened to me without any of her usual contradictions. She seemed to be moved; she said good-bye to me very warmly, with the heartiest wishes for the New Year, and—came no more. Her father, who called on me two or three times afterwards, assured me that she would come back again, and said it was easy to see that she was eager for the treatment to continue. But it must be confessed that Dora's father was never entirely straightforward. He had given his support to the treatment so long as he could hope that I should "talk" Dora out of her belief that there was something more than a friendship between him and Frau K. His interest faded when he observed that it was not my intention to bring about that result. I knew Dora would not come back again. Her breaking off so unexpectedly, just when my hopes of a successful termination of the treatment were at their highest, and her thus bringing those hopes to nothing—this was an unmistakable act of vengeance on her part. Her purpose of self-injury also profited by this action. No one who, like me, conjures up the most evil of those half-tamed demons that inhabit the human breast, and seeks to wrestle with them, can expect to come through the struggle unscathed. Might I perhaps have kept the girl under my treatment if I myself had acted a part, if I had exaggerated the importance to me of her staying on, and had shown a warm personal interest in her—a course which, even after allowing for my position as her physician, would have been tantamount to providing her with a substitute for the affection she longed for? I do not know. Since in every case a portion of the factors that are encountered under the form of resistance remains unknown, I have always avoided acting a part, and have contented myself with practising the humbler arts of psychology. In spite of every theoretical interest and of every endeavour to be of assistance as a physician, I keep the fact in mind that there must be some limits to the extent to which psychological influence may be used, and I respect as one of these limits the patient's own will and understanding.

Nor do I know whether Herr K. would have done any better if it had been revealed to him that the slap Dora gave him by no means signified a final "No" on her part, but that it expressed the jealousy which had lately been roused in her, while her strongest feelings were still on his side. If he had disregarded that first "No," and had continued to press his suit with a passion which left room for no doubts, the result might very well have been a triumph of the girl's affection for him over all her internal difficulties. But I think she might just as well have been merely provoked into satisfying her craving for revenge upon him all the more thoroughly. It is never possible to calculate towards which side the decision will incline in such a conflict of motives: whether towards the removal of the repression or towards its reinforcement. Incapacity for meeting a *real* erotic demand is one of the most essential features of a neurosis. Neurotics are dominated by the opposition between reality and phantasy. If what they long for the most intensely in their phantasies is presented to them in reality, they none the less flee from it; and they abandon themselves to their phantasies the most readily where they need no longer fear to see them realized. Nevertheless, the barrier erected by repression can fall before the onslaught of a violent emotional excitement produced by a real cause; it is possible for a neurosis to be overcome by reality. But we have no general means of calculating through what person or what event such a cure can be effected.

IV

Postscript

It is true that I have introduced this paper as a fragment of an analysis; but the reader will have discovered that it is incomplete to a far greater degree than its title might have led him to expect. It is therefore only proper that I should attempt to give a reason for the omissions—which are by no means accidental.

A number of the results of the analysis have been omitted, because at the time when work was broken off they had either not been established with sufficient certainty or they required further study before any general statement could be made about them. At other points, where it seemed to be permissible, I have indicated the direction along which some particular solution would probably have been found to lie. I have in this paper left entirely out of account the technique, which does not at all follow as a matter of course, but by whose means alone the pure metal of valuable unconscious thoughts can be extracted from the raw material of the patient's associations. This brings with it the disadvantage of the reader being given no opportunity of testing the correctness of my procedure in the course of this exposition of the case. I found it quite impracticable, however, to deal simultaneously with the technique of analysis and with the internal structure of a case of hysteria: I could scarcely have accomplished such a task, and if I had, the result would have been almost unreadable.

[Freud affirms his scientific objectivity and asserts that further clinical studies will support his description of unconscious motives and the general theory of hysteria.]

*   *   *

Nevertheless, in publishing this paper, incomplete though it is, I had two objects in view. In the first place, I wished to supplement my book on the interpretation of dreams by showing how an art, which would otherwise be useless, can be turned to account for the discovery of the hidden and repressed parts of mental life. (Incidentally, in the process of analysing the two dreams dealt with in the paper, the technique of dream-interpretation, which is similar to that of psycho-analysis, has come under consideration.) In the second place, I wished to stimulate interest in a whole group of phenomena of which science is still in complete ignorance today because they can only be brought to light by the use of this particular method. No one, I believe, can have had any true conception of the complexity of the psychological events in a case of hysteria—the juxtaposition of the most dissimilar tendencies, the mutual dependence of contrary ideas, the repressions and displacements, and so on. The emphasis laid by Janet[5] upon the *"idée fixe"* which becomes transformed into a symptom amounts to no more than an extremely meagre attempt at schematization. Moreover, it is impossible to avoid the suspicion that, when the ideas attaching to certain excitations are incapable of becoming conscious, those excitations must act upon one another differently, run a different course, and manifest themselves differently from those other excitations which we describe as "normal" and which have ideas attaching to them of which we become conscious. When once things have been made clear up to this point, no obstacle can remain in the way of an understanding of a therapeutic method which removes neurotic symptoms by transforming ideas of the former kind into normal ones.

I was further anxious to show that sexuality does not simply intervene, like a *deus ex machina,* on one single occasion, at some point in the working of the processes which characterize hysteria, but that it provides the motive power for every single symptom, and for every single manifestation of a symptom. The symptoms of the disease are nothing else than *the patient's sexual activity.* A single case can never be capable of proving a theorem so general as this one; but I can only repeat over and over again—for I never find it otherwise—that sexuality is the key to the problem of the psychoneuroses and of the neuroses in general. No one who disdains the key will ever be able to unlock the door. I still await news of the investigations which are to make it possible to contradict this theorem or to limit its scope. What I have hitherto heard against it have been expressions of personal dislike or disbelief. To these it is enough to reply in the words of Charcot: "Ça n'empêche pas d'exister."[6]

Nor is the case of whose history and treatment I have published a fragment in these pages well calculated to put the value of psycho-analytic therapy in its true light. Not only the briefness of the treatment (which hardly lasted three months) but another factor inherent in the nature of the case prevented results being brought about such as are attainable in other instances, where the improvement will be admitted by the patient and his relatives and will approximate more or less closely to a complete recovery. Satisfactory results of this kind are reached when the symptoms are maintained solely by the internal conflict between the impulses concerned with sexuality. In such cases the patient's condition will be seen improving in proportion as he is helped towards a solution of his mental problems by the translation of pathogenic into normal material. The course of events is very different when the symptoms have become enlisted in the service of external motives, as had happened with Dora during the two preceding years. It is surprising, and might easily be misleading, to find that the patient's condition shows no noticeable alteration even though considerable progress has been made with the work of analysis. But in reality things are not as bad as they seem. It is true that the symptoms do not disappear while the work is proceeding; but they disappear a little

5. Pierre Janet (1859–1947), French psychologist and neurologist.   6. That doesn't mean it doesn't exist (French).

while later, when the relations between patient and physician have been dissolved. The postponement of recovery or improvement is really only caused by the physician's own person.

I must go back a little, in order to make the matter intelligible. It may be safely said that during psycho-analytic treatment the formation of new symptoms is invariably stopped. But the productive powers of the neurosis are by no means extinguished; they are occupied in the creation of a special class of mental structures, for the most part unconscious, to which the name of *"transferences"* may be given.

What are transferences? They are new editions or facsimiles of the impulses and phantasies which are aroused and made conscious during the progress of the analysis; but they have this peculiarity, which is characteristic for their species, that they replace some earlier person by the person of the physician. To put it another way: a whole series of psychological experiences are revived, not as belonging to the past, but as applying to the person of the physician at the present moment. Some of these transferences have a content which differs from that of their model in no respect whatever except for the substitution. These then—to keep to the same metaphor—are merely new impressions or reprints. Others are more ingeniously constructed; their content has been subjected to a moderating influence—to *sublimation*, as I call it—and they may even become conscious, by cleverly taking advantage of some real peculiarity in the physician's person or circumstances and attaching themselves to that. These, then, will no longer be new impressions, but revised editions.

If the theory of analytic technique is gone into, it becomes evident that transference is an inevitable necessity. Practical experience, at all events, shows conclusively that there is no means of avoiding it, and that this latest creation of the disease must be combated like all the earlier ones. This happens, however, to be by far the hardest part of the whole task. It is easy to learn how to interpret dreams, to extract from the patient's associations his unconscious thoughts and memories, and to practise similar explanatory arts; for these the patient himself will always provide the text. Transference is the one thing the presence of which has to be detected almost without assistance and with only the slightest clues to go upon, while at the same time the risk of making arbitrary inferences has to be avoided. Nevertheless, transference cannot be evaded, since use is made of it in setting up all the obstacles that make the material inaccessible to treatment, and since it is only after the transference has been resolved that a patient arrives at a sense of conviction of the validity of the connections which have been constructed during the analysis.

Some people may feel inclined to look upon it as a serious objection to a method which is in any case troublesome enough that it itself should multiply the labours of the physician by creating a new species of pathological mental products. They may even be tempted to infer from the existence of transferences that the patient will be injured by analytic treatment. Both these suppositions would be mistaken. The physician's labours are not multiplied by transference; it need make no difference to him whether he has to overcome any particular impulse of the patient's in connection with himself or with some one else. Nor does the treatment force upon the patient, in the shape of transference, any new task which he would not otherwise have performed. It is true that neuroses may be cured in institutions from which psycho-analytic treatment is excluded, that hysteria may be said to be cured not by the method but by the physician, and that there is usually a sort of blind dependence and a permanent bond between a patient and the physician who has removed his symptoms by hypnotic suggestion; but the scientific explanation of all these facts is to be found in the existence of "transferences" such as are regularly directed by patients on to their physicians. Psycho-analytic treatment does not *create* transferences, it merely brings them to light, like so many other hidden psychical factors. The only difference is this—that spontaneously a patient will only call up affectionate and friendly transferences to help towards his recovery; if they cannot be called up, he feels the physician is "antipathetic" to him, and breaks away from him as fast as possible and without having been influenced by him. In psycho-analysis, on the other hand, since the play of motives is different, all the patient's tendencies, including hostile ones, are aroused; they are then turned to account for the purposes of the analysis by being made conscious, and in this way the transference is constantly being destroyed. Transference, which seems ordained to be the greatest obstacle to psycho-analysis, becomes its most powerful ally, if its presence can be detected each time and explained to the patient.

I have been obliged to speak of transference, for it is only by means of this factor that I can elucidate the peculiarities of Dora's analysis. Its great merit, namely, the unusual clarity which makes it seem so suitable as a first introductory publication, is closely bound up with its great defect, which led to its being broken off prematurely. I did not succeed in mastering the transference in good time. Owing to the readiness with which Dora put one part of the pathogenic material at my disposal during the treatment, I neglected the precaution of looking out for the first signs of transference, which was being prepared in connection with another part of the same material—a part of which I was in ignorance. At the beginning it was clear that I was replacing her father in her imagination, which was not unlikely, in view of the difference between our ages. She was even constantly comparing me with him consciously, and kept anxiously trying to make sure whether I was being quite straightforward with her, for her father "always preferred secrecy and roundabout ways." But when the first dream came, in which she gave herself the warning that she had better leave my treatment just as she had formerly left Herr K.'s house, I ought to have listened to the warning myself. "Now," I ought to have said to her, "it is from Herr K. that you have made a transference on to me. Have you noticed anything that leads you to suspect me of evil intentions similar (whether openly or in some sublimated form) to Herr K.'s? Or have you been struck by anything about me or got to know anything about me which has caught your fancy, as happened previously with Herr K?" Her attention would then have been turned to some detail in our relations, or in my person or circumstances, behind which there lay concealed something analogous but immeasurably more important concerning Herr K. And when this transference had been cleared up, the analysis would have obtained access to new memories, dealing, probably, with actual events. But I was deaf to this first note of warning, thinking I had ample time before me, since no further stages of transference developed and the material for the analysis had not yet run dry. In this way the transference took me unawares, and, because of the unknown quantity in me which reminded Dora of Herr K., she took her revenge on me as she wanted to take her revenge on him, and deserted me as she believed herself to have been deceived and deserted by him. Thus she *acted out* an essential part of her recollections and phantasies instead of reproducing it in the treatment. What this unknown quantity was I naturally cannot tell. I suspect that it had to do with money, or with jealousy of another patient who had kept up relations with my family after her recovery. When it is possible to work transferences into the analysis at an early stage, the course of the analysis is retarded and obscured, but its existence is better guaranteed against sudden and overwhelming resistances.

In Dora's second dream there are several clear allusions to transference. At the time she was telling me the dream I was still unaware (and did not learn until two days later) that we had only *two hours* more work before us. This was the same length of time which she had spent in front of the Sistine Madonna, and which (by making a correction and putting "two hours" instead of "two and a half hours") she had taken as the length of the walk which she had not made round the lake. The striving and waiting in the dream, which related to the young man in Germany, and had their origin in her waiting till Herr K. could marry her, had been expressed in the transference a few days before. The treatment, she had thought, was too long for her; she would never have the patience to wait so long. And yet in the first few weeks she had had discernment enough to listen without making any such objections when I informed her that her complete recovery would require perhaps a year. Her refusing in the dream to be accompanied, and preferring to go alone, also originated from her visit to the gallery at Dresden, and I was myself to experience them on the appointed day. What they meant was, no doubt: "Men are all so detestable that I would rather not marry. This is my revenge."[7]

If cruel impulses and revengeful motives, which have already been used in the patient's ordinary life for maintaining her symptoms, become transferred on to the physician during treatment, before he has had time to detach them from himself by tracing them back to their sources, then it is not to be wondered at if the patient's condition is unaffected by his therapeutic efforts. For how could the patient take a more effective revenge than by demonstrating upon her own person the helplessness and incapacity of the physician? Nevertheless, I am not inclined to put too low a value on the therapeutic results even of such a fragmentary treatment as Dora's.

---

7. The longer the interval of time that separates me from the end of this analysis, the more probable it seems to me that the fault in my technique lay in this omission: I failed to discover in time and to inform the patient that her homosexual (gynaecophilic) love for Frau K. was the strongest unconscious current in her mental life. I ought to have guessed that the main source of her knowledge of sexual matters could have been no one but Frau K.—the very person who later on charged her with being interested in those same subjects. Her knowing all about such things and, at the same time, her always pretending not to know where her knowledge came from was really too remarkable. I ought to have attacked this riddle and looked for the motive of such an extraordinary piece of repression. If I had done this, the second dream would have given me my answer [Freud's note].

It was not until fifteen months after the case was over and this paper composed that I had news of my patient's condition and the effects of my treatment. On a date which is not a matter of complete indifference, on the first of April (times and dates, as we know, were never without significance for her), Dora came to see me again: to finish her story and to ask for help once more. One glance at her face, however, was enough to tell me that she was not in earnest over her request. For four or five weeks after stopping the treatment she had been "all in a muddle," as she said. A great improvement had then set in; her attacks had become less frequent and her spirits had risen. In May of that year one of the K.'s two children (it had always been delicate) had died. She took the opportunity of their loss to pay them a visit of condolence, and they received her as though nothing had happened in the last three years. She made it up with them, she took her revenge on them, and she brought her own business to a satisfactory conclusion. To the wife she said: "I know you have an affair with my father"; and the other did not deny it. From the husband she drew an admission of the scene by the lake which he had disputed, and brought the news of her vindication home to her father. Since then she had not resumed her relations with the family.

After this she had gone on quite well till the middle of October, when she had had another attack of aphonia which had lasted for six weeks. I was surprised at this news, and, on my asking her whether there had been any exciting cause, she told me that the attack had followed upon a violent fright. She had seen some one run over by a carriage. Finally she came out with the fact that the accident had occurred to no less a person than Herr K. himself. She had come across him in the street one day; they had met in a place where there was a great deal of traffic; he had stopped in front of her as though in bewilderment, and in his abstraction he had allowed himself to be knocked down by a carriage. She had been able to convince herself, however, that he escaped without serious injury. She still felt some slight emotion if she heard any one speak of her father's affair with Frau K., but otherwise she had no further concern with the matter. She was absorbed in her work, and had no thoughts of marrying.

She went on to tell me that she had come for help on account of a right-sided facial neuralgia, from which she was now suffering day and night. "How long has it been going on?" "Exactly a fortnight."[8] I could not help smiling; for I was able to show her that exactly a fortnight earlier she had read a piece of news that concerned me in the newspaper. (This was in 1902.) And this she confirmed.

Her alleged facial neuralgia was thus a self-punishment—remorse at having once given Herr K. a box on the ear, and at having transferred her feelings of revenge on to me. I do not know what kind of help she wanted from me, but I promised to forgive her for having deprived me of the satisfaction of affording her a far more radical cure for her troubles.

Years have again gone by since her visit. In the meantime the girl has married, and indeed—unless all the signs mislead me—she has married

---

8. For the significance of this period of time and its relation to the theme of revenge, see the analysis of the second dream [Freud's note].

the young man who came into her associations at the beginning of the analysis of the second dream.[9] Just as the first dream represented her turning away from the man she loved to her father—that is to say, her flight from life into disease—so the second dream announced that she was about to tear herself free from her father and had been reclaimed once more by the realities of life.

9. In the 1909, 1912, and 1921 editions, Freud added the following footnote: "This, as I afterwards learnt, was a mistaken notion."

RABINDRANATH TAGORE
1861–1941

The preeminent figure in the history of modern literature in Bengali (the language of the state of West Bengal in eastern India, and of the neighboring nation of Bangladesh), poet and novelist Rabindranath Tagore has deeply influenced writers in the other Indian languages as well. Winner of the Nobel prize for literature in 1913, Tagore is also perhaps the Indian writer whose name is likely to be familiar to most readers in the West. No less a poet than W. B. Yeats was responsible for Tagore's fame in European and American literary circles, but Tagore did not wear well in translation. He was mistakenly perceived as a mystical poet, Western tastes in poetry changed rather rapidly, and, in spite of the many translations of his poetry and fiction that appeared in English and other European languages after 1913, few outside of Bengal have been aware of Tagore's achievement as a writer or of his substantial contributions to the history of ideas in the modern age.

Tagore was born in Calcutta, the capital of British India in the nineteenth century, into an illustrious Hindu family. The Tagores were pioneers of the Bengal Renaissance, a movement led by Bengali intellectuals who were in many ways shaped by English education, which had been introduced in Bengal by the British government, but who at the same time reacted with profound ambivalence to colonial rule and the imposition of Western cultural norms on Indians. Through their writings, and through the institutions they founded, the leaders of the Renaissance sought to refashion Indian society to meet the challenges of the modern world, but to do so without losing its moorings in the highest values and ideals of traditional Indian culture. Tagore's father, Debendranath Tagore, was among the first leaders of the Brahmo Samaj, a major Hindu social reform organization that was founded on just such a blend of Western and Indian ideas.

Each of Debendranath Tagore's fourteen children (including his daughter, Swarnakumari) made significant contributions to Bengali literature and culture. None of them, however, equaled Rabindranath, the youngest, in breadth and importance of achievement. In the course of a life that spanned the period during which India emerged from colonial domination to independent nationhood, Tagore wrote poems, novels, short stories, plays, and essays, transforming extant Bengali literary forms and creating new ones. *Gitanjali* (Song offering), an anthology of lyric poems that the poet himself translated from the Bengali into English, brought him international recognition in the form of the Nobel prize. Tagore's own translations of the *Gitanjali* poems, and Yeats's praise of them in his preface to the first edition of the anthology, contributed to the misleading stereotyping of the poems as a combination of romantic lyricism and vague Eastern mysticism. The truth is that the *Gitanjali* poems reflect only one facet of Tagore's poetic

sensibility, and that not accurately. On the one hand, he drew on earlier lyric traditions in Sanskrit and Bengali with great sensitivity; on the other, he nearly single-handedly brought the Bengali language and Bengali poetry into the domain of the modern. Tagore continued to write poetry to the end of his life, experimenting with language and with a variety of poetic forms, combining a spare, direct style with vivid yet deeply suggestive images in ways that are difficult to convey in translation. In addition to the lyric poems in *Gitanjali* and other collections (these are not true songs), Tagore composed and set to music nearly two thousand songs, which continue to dominate the Bengali song repertoire in the twentieth century. Included in these songs are the national anthems of India and Bangladesh.

Among Tagore's lasting contributions are Shantiniketan and Viswabharati, the school and the international university he founded near Calcutta as alternatives to colonial education and as arenas and training grounds for international cooperation. He used the international attention he gained as a result of the Nobel Prize to travel widely in Europe, Asia, and America, speaking out against the evils of colonialism, wars based on narrow nationalism, and abuses of human rights all over the world. When Mahatma Gandhi led the Indian people in their nonviolent (and ultimately successful) struggle for freedom from British colonial rule in the period between the two world wars, Tagore stood by Gandhi and his movement but pointed out the dangers of focusing on exclusively nationalistic goals, arguing instead for a new world order based on transnational values and ideals. A true "renaissance" figure, Tagore left no aspect of human experience untouched in his life and writings. The universalistic humanism that informs all his writings makes him one of the towering figures of the twentieth century.

Although the Bengali language had a rich tradition of medieval lyric and narrative poetry, Bengali prose fiction emerged in the late nineteenth century as a result of the impact of English education and Western literary forms. The novels of Tagore's elder contemporary Bankim Chandra Chatterjee (1838–1894) were mainly historical romances modeled on the novels of Sir Walter Scott, though Chatterjee also used the novel as a vehicle for social critique and nationalist propaganda. Concern about social issues, especially the need for the emancipation of Bengali women from oppressive cultural practices, dominates Tagore's major novels, beginning with *Cokher bali* (Speck in the eye) and *Nastanir* (The broken nest), published serially in 1901. Here, as well as in his more than one hundred short stories, his preoccupation with the emotional and psychological lives of his characters and his passionate championship of the integrity of the individual strike a new note in Bengali literature.

Tagore's short stories are the first major examples of the genre in any Indian language. Between 1891 and 1895 forty-four of his stories appeared in Bengali periodicals, the majority of them in the monthly journal *Sadhana* (Endeavor), edited by members of the Tagore family. The rest were written in the 1920s. *Punishment* (*Sasti*, 1893) belongs to the earlier stories, which were inspired by Tagore's experience of rural Bengal during the decade he spent there as manager of the family estates in Shelidah. Shelidah is in what was formerly the British province of East Bengal, which became East Pakistan following the partition of India in 1947 and is now the independent nation of Bangladesh. The characters in Tagore's major fiction tend to be drawn from the Bengali middle class, which he knew well; but a number of these early stories are about the peasants and villagers with whom he came in contact during the Shelidah years. Here the great Padma River and the agricultural landscape of eastern Bengal become the focus of the love of nature and the lyrical, romantic sensibility that are characteristic of all the writer's works.

The stories of this period are by no means idyllic pictures of village life. In *Punishment*, Tagore's sensitive portrayal of the complex relationships among the

members of the low-caste Rui family and between them and the upper-class rural
society that exploits them suggests both realism and a sense of tragedy. The transactions among Chandara, the proud and beautiful young woman; her husband, the
farm-laborer Chidam; and landlord Ramlochan Chakravarti, "pillar of the village,"
reveal Tagore's intimate understanding both of the ways in which economic,
social, and patriarchal oppression are intrinsically linked and of the ability of the
oppressed to resist even the most powerful forms of oppression. However, as in
his other stories and novels, his real interest in *Punishment* is in delineating the
psychological ramifications of social and familial relationships. Chandara is a typical Tagore protagonist, representing the power and dignity of the human will in
the face of societal degradation. And yet Tagore's world is a tragic one, populated
by individuals who, trapped in what he called the "dreary desert sand of dead
habit," are ultimately unable to transcend the tyranny of institutions.

Two recent histories of Bengali literature, Dushan Zbavitel, *Bengali Literature*
(1976), and Asit Kumar Bandhyopadhyay, *Modern Bengali Literature* (1986), provide information about the context of Tagore's achievement. Humayun Kabir, *The
Bengali Novel* (1968), discusses Tagore with reference to the development of the
Bengali novel. William Radice, *Rabindranath Tagore: Selected Short Stories*
(1991), offers faithful, readable translations of thirty of Tagore's early short stories,
including some of his best known ones. For a comparison of Tagore's short stories
with those of later Bengali writers on the themes of oppression and resistance, see
Kalpana Bardhan, ed. and trans., *Of Women, Outcastes, Peasants, and Rebels*
(1990). Krishna Kripalani, *Rabindranath Tagore* (1962), is the authoritative Tagore
biography, and Amiya Chakravarty, ed., *A Tagore Reader* (1961), remains the best
introduction to the full range of Tagore's writing.

PRONOUNCING GLOSSARY

The following list uses common English syllables and stress accents to provide rough equivalents of selected words whose pronunciation may be unfamiliar to the general reader.

Baṛobau: *baroh'-bau*

Chandara: *chuhn'-duh-rah*

Chidam Rui: *chee'-duhm roo'-yee*

Dukhiram Rui: *doo-khee'-rahm roo'-yee*

Kashi Majumdar: *kah'-shee muh'-joom-
    dahr*

koel: *koh'-yuhl*

Rabindranath Tagore: *ruh-beend'-run-
    naht tuh-gohr'*

Ram: *rahm*

Ramlochan   Chakravarti: *rahm'-loh-
    chuhn chuhk'-ruh-vuhr-tee*

Ṭhākur: *thah'-koor*

zamindar: *zuh-meen'-dahr*

Punishment[1]

I

When the brothers Dukhiram Rui and Chidam Rui went out in the
morning with their heavy farm-knives, to work in the fields, their wives
would quarrel and shout. But the people near by were as used to the
uproar as they were to other customary, natural sounds. When they heard
the shrill screams of the women, they would say, "They're at it again"—

---

1. Translated by William Radice.

that is, what was happening was only to be expected: it was not a violation of Nature's rules. When the sun rises at dawn, no one asks why; and whenever the two wives in this *kuri*-caste[2] household let fly at each other, no one was at all curious to investigate the cause.

Of course this wrangling and disturbance affected the husbands more than the neighbours, but they did not count it a major nuisance. It was as if they were riding together along life's road in a cart whose rattling, clattering, unsprung wheels were inseparable from the journey. Indeed, days when there was no noise, when everything was uncannily silent, carried a greater threat of unpredictable doom.

The day on which our story begins was like this. When the brothers returned home at dusk, exhausted by their work, they found the house eerily quiet. Outside, too, it was extremely sultry. There had been a sharp shower in the afternoon, and clouds were still massing. There was not a breath of wind. Weeds and scrub round the house had shot up after the rain: the heavy scent of damp vegetation, from these and from the water-logged jute-fields, formed a solid wall all around. Frogs croaked from the milkman's pond behind the house, and the buzz of crickets filled the leaden sky.

Not far off the swollen Padma[3] looked flat and sinister under the mounting clouds. It had flooded most of the grain-fields, and had come close to the houses. Here and there, roots of mango and jackfruit trees on the slipping bank stuck up out of the water, like helpless hands clawing at the air for a last fingerhold.

That day, Dukhiram and Chidam had been working near the zamindar's office. On a sandbank opposite, paddy[4] had ripened. The paddy needed to be cut before the sandbank was washed away, but the village people were busy either in their own fields or in cutting jute: so a messenger came from the office and forcibly engaged the two brothers. As the office roof was leaking in places, they also had to mend that and make some new wickerwork panels: it had taken them all day. They couldn't come home for lunch; they just had a snack from the office. At times they were soaked by the rain; they were not paid normal labourers' wages; indeed, they were paid mainly in insults and sneers.

When the two brothers returned at dusk, wading through mud and water, they found the younger wife, Chandara, stretched on the ground with her sari[5] spread out. Like the sky, she had wept buckets in the afternoon, but had now given way to sultry exhaustion. The elder wife, Radha, sat on the verandah sullenly: her eighteen-month son had been crying, but when the brothers came in they saw him lying naked in a corner of the yard, asleep.

Dukhiram, famished, said gruffly, "Give me my food."

Like a spark on a sack of gunpowder, the elder wife exploded, shrieking out, "Where is there food? Did you give me anything to cook? Must I earn money myself to buy it?"

After a whole day of toil and humiliation, to return—raging with hun-

---

2. In Bengal, a low caste originally of bird catchers, but by the 19th century, general laborers.   3. A major river in what is now Bangladesh.   4. The rice crop. *Zamindar:* landlord.   5. A long strip of cloth draped around the body, Indian women's traditional clothing.

ger—to a dark, joyless, foodless house, to be met by Radha's sarcasm, especially her final jibe, was suddenly unendurable. "What?" he roared, like a furious tiger, and then, without thinking, plunged his knife into her head. Radha collapsed into her sister-in-law's lap, and in minutes she was dead.

"What have you done?" screamed Chandara, her clothes soaked with blood. Chidam pressed his hand over her mouth. Dukhiram, throwing aside the knife, fell to his knees with his head in his hands, stunned. The little boy woke up and started to wail in terror.

Outside there was complete quiet. The herd-boys were returning with the cattle. Those who had been cutting paddy on the far sandbanks were crossing back in groups in a small boat—with a couple of bundles of paddy on their heads as payment. Everyone was heading for home.

Ramlochan Chakravarti, pillar of the village, had been to the post office with a letter, and was now back in his house, placidly smoking. Suddenly he remembered that his sub-tenant Dukhiram was very behind with his rent: he had promised to pay some today. Deciding that the brothers must be home by now, he threw his chadar[6] over his shoulders, took his umbrella, and stepped out.

As he entered the Ruis' house, he felt uneasy. There was no lamp alight. On the dark verandah, the dim shapes of three or four people could be seen. In a corner of the verandah there were fitful, muffled sobs: the little boy was trying to cry for his mother, but was stopped each time by Chidam.

"Dukhi," said Ramlochan nervously, "are you there?"

Dukhiram had been sitting like a statue for a long time; now, on hearing his name, he burst into tears like a helpless child.

Chidam quickly came down from the verandah into the yard, to meet Ramlochan. "Have the women been quarrelling again?" Ramlochan asked. "I heard them yelling all day."

Chidam, all this time, had been unable to think what to do. Various impossible stories occurred to him. All he had decided was that later that night he would move the body somewhere. He had never expected Ramlochan to come. He could think of no swift reply. "Yes," he stumbled, "today they were quarrelling terribly."

"But why is Dukhi crying so?" asked Ramlochan, stepping towards the verandah.

Seeing no way out now, Chidam blurted, "In their quarrel, *Chotobau* struck at *Barobau's*[7] head with a farm-knife."

When immediate danger threatens, it is hard to think of other dangers. Chidam's only thought was to escape from the terrible truth—he forgot that a lie can be even more terrible. A reply to Ramlochan's question had come instantly to mind, and he had blurted it out.

"Good grief," said Ramlochan in horror. "What are you saying? Is she dead?"

"She's dead," said Chidam, clasping Ramlochan's feet.

Ramlochan was trapped. "*Rām, Rām,*"[8] he thought, "what a mess I've

---

6. In Bengal, a sheet of cloth draped around the shoulders, usually worn by men but sometimes by women.   7. "Elder Daughter-in-Law"; members of a family address each other by kinship terms. *Choto-bau:* "Younger Daughter-in-Law."   8. God's name, repeated to express great emotion.

got into this evening. What if I have to be a witness in court?" Chidam was still clinging to his feet, saying, "Ṭhākur,[9] how can I save my wife?"

Ramlochan was the village's chief source of advice on legal matters. Reflecting further he said, "I think I know a way. Run to the police station: say that your brother Dukhi returned in the evening wanting his food, and because it wasn't ready he struck his wife on the head with his knife. I'm sure that if you say that, she'll get off."

Chidam felt a sickening dryness in his throat. He stood up and said, "Ṭhākur, if I lose my wife I can get another, but if my brother is hanged, how can I replace him?" In laying the blame on his wife, he had not seen it that way. He had spoken without thought; now, imperceptibly, logic and awareness were returning to his mind.

Ramlochan appreciated his logic. "Then say what actually happened," he said. "You can't protect yourself on all sides."

He had soon, after leaving, spread it round the village that Chandara Rui had, in a quarrel with her sister-in-law, split her head open with a farm-knife. Police charged into the village like a river in flood. Both the guilty and the innocent were equally afraid.

II

Chidam decided he would have to stick to the path he had chalked out for himself. The story he had given to Ramlochan Chakravarti had gone all round the village; who knew what would happen if another story was circulated? But he realized that if he kept to the story he would have to wrap it in five more stories if his wife was to be saved.

Chidam asked Chandara to take the blame on to herself. She was dumbfounded. He reassured her: "Don't worry—if you do what I tell you, you'll be quite safe." But whatever his words, his throat was dry and his face was pale.

Chandara was not more than seventeen or eighteen. She was buxom, well-rounded, compact and sturdy—so trim in her movements that in walking, turning, bending or climbing there was no awkwardness at all. She was like a brand-new boat: neat and shapely, gliding with ease, not a loose joint anywhere. Everything amused and intrigued her; she loved to gossip; her bright, restless, deep black eyes missed nothing as she walked to the ghāṭ,[1] pitcher on her hip, parting her veil slightly with her finger.

The elder wife had been her exact opposite: unkempt, sloppy and slovenly. She was utterly disorganized in her dress, housework, and the care of her child. She never had any proper work in hand, yet never seemed to have time for anything. The younger wife usually refrained from comment, for at the mildest barb Radha would rage and stamp and let fly at her, disturbing everyone around.

Each wife was matched by her husband to an extraordinary degree. Dukhiram was a huge man—his bones were immense, his nose was squat, in his eyes and expression he seemed not to understand the world very well, yet he never questioned it either. He was innocent yet fearsome: a

9. "Master" or "lord," term of address for gods and upper-class (Brahmin) men. *Tagore* is an anglicized form of Ṭhākur.   1. Steps leading down to a pond or river; meeting place, especially for women, who go there to get water or to wash clothes.

rare combination of power and helplessness. Chidam, however, seemed to have been carefully carved from shiny black rock. There was not an inch of excess fat on him, not a wrinkle or dimple anywhere. Each limb was a perfect blend of strength and finesse. Whether jumping from a river-bank, or punting a boat, or climbing up bamboo-shoots for sticks, he showed complete dexterity, effortless grace. His long black hair was combed with oil back from his brow and down to his shoulders—he took great care over his dress and appearance. Although he was not unrespon-sive to the beauty of other women in the village, and was keen to make himself charming in their eyes, his real love was for his young wife. They quarrelled sometimes, but there was mutual respect too: neither could defeat the other. There was a further reason why the bond between them was firm: Chidam felt that a wife as nimble and sharp as Chandara could not be wholly trusted, and Chandara felt that all eyes were on her hus-band—that if she didn't bind him tightly to her she might one day lose him.

A little before the events in this story, however, they had a major row. Chandara had noticed that when her husband's work took him away for two days or more, he brought no extra earnings. Finding this ominous, she also began to overstep the mark. She would hang around by the ghāṭ, or wander about talking rather too much about Kashi Majumdar's middle son.

Something now seemed to poison Chidam's life. He could not settle his attention on his work. One day his sister-in-law rounded on him: she shook her finger and said in the name of her dead father, "That girl runs before the storm. How can I restrain her? Who knows what ruin she will bring?"

Chandara came out of the next room and said sweetly, "What's the matter, Didi?"[2] and a fierce quarrel broke out between them.

Chidam glared at his wife and said, "If I ever hear that you've been to the ghāṭ on your own, I'll break every bone in your body."

"The bones will mend again," said Chandara, starting to leave. Chidam sprang at her, grabbed her by the hair, dragged her back to the room and locked her in.

When he returned from work that evening he found that the room was empty. Chandara had fled three villages away, to her maternal uncle's house. With great difficulty Chidam persuaded her to return, but he had to surrender to her. It was as hard to restrain his wife as to hold a handful of mercury; she always slipped through his fingers. He did not have to use force any more, but there was no peace in the house. Ever-fearful love for his elusive young wife wracked him with intense pain. He even once or twice wondered if it would be better if she were dead: at least he would get some peace then. Human beings can hate each other more than death.

It was at this time that the crisis hit the house.

When her husband asked her to admit to the murder, Chandara stared at him, stunned; her black eyes burnt him like fire. Then she shrank back,

2. "Elder Sister," respectful form of address for Bengali women.

as if to escape his devilish clutches. She turned her heart and soul away from him. "You've nothing to fear," said Chidam. He taught her repeatedly what she should say to the police and the magistrate. Chandara paid no attention—sat like a wooden statue whenever he spoke.

Dukhiram relied on Chidam for everything. When he told him to lay the blame on Chandara, Dukhiram said, "But what will happen to her?" "I'll save her," said Chidam. His burly brother was content with that.

III

This was what he instructed his wife to say: "The elder wife was about to attack me with the vegetable-slicer. I picked up a farm-knife to stop her, and it somehow cut into her." This was all Ramlochan's invention. He had generously supplied Chidam with the proofs and embroidery that the story would require.

The police came to investigate. The villagers were sure now that Chandara had murdered her sister-in-law, and all the witnesses confirmed this. When the police questioned Chandara, she said, "Yes, I killed her."

"Why did you kill her?"

"I couldn't stand her any more."

"Was there a brawl between you?"

"No."

"Did she attack you first?"

"No."

"Did she ill-treat you?"

"No."

Everyone was amazed at these replies, and Chidam was completely thrown off balance. "She's not telling the truth," he said. "The elder wife first—"

The inspector silenced him sharply. He continued according to the rules of cross-examination and repeatedly received the same reply: Chandara would not accept that she had been attacked in any way by her sister-in-law. Such an obstinate girl was never seen! She seemed absolutely bent on going to the gallows; nothing would stop her. Such fierce, passionate pride! In her thoughts, Chandara was saying to her husband, "I shall give my youth to the gallows instead of to you. My final ties in this life will be with them."

Chandara was arrested, and left her home for ever, by the paths she knew so well, past the festival carriage, the market-place, the ghāṭ, the Majumdars' house, the post office, the school—an ordinary, harmless, flirtatious, fun-loving village wife; leaving a shameful impression on all the people she knew. A bevy of boys followed her, and the women of the village, her friends and companions—some of them peering through their veils, some from their doorsteps, some from behind trees—watched the police leading her away and shuddered with embarrassment, fear and contempt.

To the Deputy Magistrate, Chandara again confessed her guilt, claiming no ill-treatment from her sister-in-law at the time of the murder. But when Chidam was called to the witness-box he broke down completely, weeping, clasping his hands and saying, "I swear to you, sir, my wife is innocent." The magistrate sternly told him to control himself, and began to question him. Bit by bit the true story came out.

The magistrate did not believe him, because the chief, most trustworthy, most educated witness—Ramlochan Chakravarti—said: "I appeared on the scene a little after the murder. Chidam confessed everything to me and clung to my feet saying, 'Tell me how I can save my wife.' I did not say anything one way or the other. Then Chidam said, 'If I say that my elder brother killed his wife in a fit of fury because his food wasn't ready, then she'll get off.' I said, 'Be careful, you rogue: don't say a single false word in court—there's no worse offence than that.'" Ramlochan had previously prepared lots of stories that would save Chandara, but when he found that she herself was bending her neck to receive the noose, he decided, "Why take the risk of giving false evidence now? I'd better say what little I know." So Ramlochan said what he knew—or rather said a little more than he knew.

The Deputy Magistrate committed the case to a sessions trial.[3] Meanwhile in fields, houses, markets and bazaars, the sad or happy affairs of the world carried on; and just as in previous years, torrential monsoon rains fell on to the new rice-crop.

Police, defendant and witnesses were all in court. In the civil court opposite hordes of people were waiting for their cases. A Calcutta lawyer had come on a suit about the sharing of a pond behind a kitchen; the plaintiff had thirty-nine witnesses. Hundreds of people were anxiously waiting for hair-splitting judgements, certain that nothing, at present, was more important. Chidam stared out of the window at the constant throng, and it seemed like a dream. A *koel*-bird[4] was hooting from a huge banyan tree in the compound: no courts or cases in *his* world!

Chandara said to the judge, "Sir, how many times must I go on saying the same thing?"

The judge explained, "Do you know the penalty for the crime you have confessed?"

"No," said Chandara.

"It is death by the hanging."

"Then please give it to me, sir," said Chandara. "Do what you like—I can't take any more."

When her husband was called to the court, she turned away. "Look at the witness," said the judge, "and say who he is."

"He is my husband," said Chandara, covering her face with her hands.

"Does he not love you?"

"He loves me greatly."

"Do you not love him?"

"I love him greatly."

When Chidam was questioned, he said, "I killed her."

"Why?"

"I wanted my food and my sister-in-law didn't give it to me."

---

3. A trial that is settled through a special court *sessions* in one continuous sitting.   4. Common Indian songbird.

When Dukhiram came to give evidence, he fainted. When he had come round again, he answered, "Sir, I killed her."

"Why?"

"I wanted a meal and she didn't give it to me."

After extensive cross-examination of various other witnesses, the judge concluded that the brothers had confessed to the crime in order to save the younger wife from the shame of the noose. But Chandara had, from the police investigation right through to the sessions trial, said the same thing repeatedly—she had not budged an inch from her story. Two barristers did their utmost to save her from the death-sentence, but in the end were defeated by her.

Who, on that auspicious night when, at a very young age, a dusky, diminutive, round-faced girl had left her childhood dolls in her father's house and come to her in-laws' house, could have imagined these events? Her father, on his deathbed, had happily reflected that at least he had made proper arrangements for his daughter's future.

In gaol,[5] just before the hanging, a kindly Civil Surgeon asked Chandara, "Do you want to see anyone?"

"I'd like to see my mother," she replied.

"Your husband wants to see you," said the doctor. "Shall I call him?"

"To hell with him,"[6] said Chandara.

5. Jail.   6. "Death to him" (literal trans.); an expression usually uttered in jest.

WILLIAM BUTLER YEATS
1865–1939

William Butler Yeats is not only the main figure in the Irish literary renaissance but also the twentieth century's greatest poet in the English language. His sensuously evocative descriptions and his fusion of concrete historical examples with an urgent metaphysical vision stir readers around the world. Years after the poet's death, the Nigerian Chinua Achebe borrowed three words from one of his lines as the title of a novel, *Things Fall Apart*—confident that his audience would immediately recognize the source. If the English language has a Symbolist poet, it is once again Yeats for his constant use of allusive imagery and large symbolic structures. Yeats's symbolism is not that of Baudelaire, Mallarmé, or other continental predecessors, however, for the European Symbolists did not share the Irish poet's fascination with occult wisdom and large historical patterns. Yeats adopted a cyclical model of history for which the rise and fall of civilizations are predetermined inside a series of interweaving evolutionary spirals. With this cyclical model, he created a private mythology that allowed him to come to terms with both personal and cultural pain and helped to explain—as symptoms of Western civilization's declining spiral—the plight of contemporary Irish society and the chaos of European culture around World War I. Yeats shares with writers like Rilke and T. S. Eliot the quest for larger meaning in a time of trouble and the use of symbolic language to give verbal form to that quest.

Yeats was born in a Dublin suburb on June 13, 1865, the oldest of four children born to John Butler and Susan Pollexfen Yeats. His father, a cosmopolitan Anglo-Irishman who had turned from law to painting, took over Yeats's education when he found that, at age nine, the boy could not read. J. B. Yeats was a highly argumentative religious skeptic who alternately terrorized his son and awakened his interest in poetry and the visual arts, inspiring at one and the same time both rebellion against scientific rationalism and belief in the higher knowledge of art. His mother's strong ties to her home in County Sligo (where Yeats spent many summers and school holidays) introduced him to the beauties of the Irish countryside and the Irish folklore and supernatural legends that appear throughout his work. Living alternately in Ireland and England for much of his youth, Yeats became part of literary society in both countries and—though an Irish nationalist—was unable to adopt a narrowly patriotic point of view. Even the failed Easter Rebellion of 1916, which he celebrated in *Easter 1916*, and the revolutionary figures who were beloved friends took their place in a larger mythic historical framework. By the end of his life, he had abandoned all practical politics and devoted himself to the reality of personal experience inside a mystic view of history.

For many, it is Yeats's mastery of images that defines his work. From his early use of symbols as private keys, or dramatic metaphors for complex personal emotions, to the immense cosmology of his last work, he continued to create a highly visual poetry whose power derives from the dramatic interweaving of specific images. Symbols such as the Tower, Byzantium, Helen of Troy, the opposition of sun and moon, birds of prey, the blind man, and the fool recur frequently and draw their meaning not from inner connections established inside the poem (as for the French Symbolists) but from an underlying myth based on occult tradition, Irish folklore, history, and Yeats's own personal experience. Symbols as Yeats used them, however, make sense in and among themselves: the "gyre," or spiral unfolding of history, is simultaneously the falcon's spiral flight; and the sphinx-like beast slouching blank-eyed toward Bethlehem in *The Second Coming* is a comprehensible horror capable of many explicit interpretations but resistant to all and, therefore, the more terrifying. Even readers unacquainted with Yeats's mythic system will respond to images precisely expressing a situation or state of mind (for example, golden Byzantium for intellect, art, wisdom—all that "body" cannot supply) and to a visionary organization that proposes shape and context for twentieth-century anxieties.

The nine poems included here cover the range of Yeats's career, which embraced several periods and styles. Yeats had attended art school and planned to be an artist before he turned fully to literature in 1886, and his early works show the influence of the Pre-Raphaelite school in art and literature. Pre-Raphaelitism called for a return to the sensuous representation and concrete particulars found in Italian painting before Raphael (1483–1520), and Pre-Raphaelite poetry evoked a poetic realm of luminous supernatural beauty described in allusive and erotically sensuous detail. Rossetti's *Blessed Damozel*, yearning for her beloved "from the gold bar of heaven," has eyes "deeper than the depth / Of waters stilled at even; / She had three lilies in her hand, / And the stars in her hair were seven." The Pre-Raphaelite fascination with the medieval past (William Morris wrote a *Defense of Guenevere*, King Arthur's adulterous wife) combined with Yeats's own interest in Irish legend and, in 1889 a long poem describing a traveler in fairyland (*The Wanderings of Oisin*) established his reputation and won Morris's praise. The musical, evocative style of Yeats's Pre-Raphaelite period is well shown in *The Lake Isle of Innisfree* (1890), with its hidden "bee-loud glade" where "peace comes dropping slow" and evening, after the "purple glow" of noon, is "full of the linnet's wings." Another poem from the same period, *When You Are Old*, pleads his love for the beautiful actress and Irish nationalist Maud Gonne, whom he met in 1889 and who repeatedly refused to marry him. From the love poems of his youth to his old age, when *The Circus Animals' Desertion* described her as prey to fanaticism and hate, Yeats returned again and again to examine his feelings for this woman, who personified love, beauty, and Irish nationalism along with hope, frustration, and despair.

Yeats's family moved to London in 1887, where he continued an earlier interest in mystical philosophy by taking up theosophy under its Russian interpreter Madame Blavatsky. Madame Blavatsky claimed mystic knowledge from Tibetan monks and preached a doctrine of the Universal Oversoul, individual spiritual evolution through cycles of incarnation, and the world as a conflict of opposites. Yeats was taken with her grandiose cosmology, although he inconveniently wished to test it by experiment and analysis and was ultimately expelled from the society in 1890. He found a more congenial literary model in the works of William Blake, which he co-edited in 1893 with F. J. Ellis. Yeats's interest in large mystical systems later waned but never altogether disappeared, and traces may be seen in the introduction that he wrote in 1916 for *Gitanjali*, a collection of poems by the Indian author Rabindranath Tagore (see p. 1448).

Several collections of Irish folk and fairy tales and a book describing Irish traditions (*The Celtic Twilight*, 1893) demonstrated a corresponding interest in Irish national identity. In 1896 he had met Lady Gregory, an Irish nationalist who invited him to spend summers at Coole Park, her country house in Galway, and who worked closely with him (and later J. M. Synge) in founding the Irish National Theatre (later the Abbey Theatre). Along with other participants in what was once called the Irish literary renaissance, he aimed to create "a national literature that made Ireland beautiful in the memory . . . freed from provincialism by an exacting criticism." To this end, he wrote *Cathleen ni Houlihan* (1902), a play in which the title character personifies Ireland, which became immensely popular with Irish nationalists. He also established Irish literary societies in Dublin and Ireland, promoted and reviewed Irish books, and lectured and wrote about the need for Irish community. In 1922 he was elected senator of the Irish Free State, serving until 1928.

Gradually, Yeats became embittered by the split between narrow Irish nationalism and the free expression of Irish culture. He was outraged at the attacks on Synge's *Playboy of the Western World* (1907) for its supposed derogatory picture of Irish culture, and he commented scathingly in *Poems Written in Discouragement* (1913, reprinted in *Responsibilities*, 1914) on the inability of the Irish middle class to appreciate art or literature. When he celebrates the abortive Easter uprisings of 1916, it is with a more universal, aesthetic view; "A terrible beauty is born" in the self-sacrifice that leads even a "drunken, vainglorious lout" to be "transformed utterly" by political martyrdom. Except for summers at Coole Park, Yeats in his middle age was spending more time in England than in Ireland. He began his *Autobiographies* in 1914, and wrote symbolic plays intended for small audiences on the model of the Japanese nō theater. There is a change in the tone of his works at this time, a new precision and epigrammatic quality that is partly due to his disappointment with the narrowness of Irish nationalism and partly to the new tastes in poetry promulgated by his friend Ezra Pound and by T. S. Eliot after the example of John Donne and the metaphysical poets.

Yeats's marriage in 1917 to Georgie Hyde-Lees provided him with much-needed stability and also an impetus to work out a larger symbolic scheme. He interpreted his wife's experiments with automatic writing (writing whatever comes to mind, without correction or rational intent) as glimpses into a hidden cosmic order, and gradually evolved a total system, which he explained in *A Vision* (1925). The wheel of history takes twenty-six thousand years to turn; and inside that wheel civilizations evolve in roughly two thousand-year *gyres*, spirals expanding outward until they collapse at the beginning of a new gyre, which will reverse the direction of the old. Human personalities fall into different types within the system, and both gyres and types are related to the different phases of the moon. Yeats's later poems in *The Tower* (1928), *The Winding Stair* (1933), and *Last Poems* (1939) are set in the context of this system. Even when it is not literally present, it suggests an organizing pattern that resolves contraries inside an immense historical perspective. *Leda and the Swan,* on one level an erotic retelling of a mythic rape, also foreshadows the Trojan War—brute force mirroring brute force. In the two poems on the legendary city of Byzantium, Yeats admired an artistic civilization that "could answer all my questions" but that was also only a moment in history. Byzantine art, with its stylized perspectives and mosaics made by arranging tiny colored pieces of stone, was the exact opposite of the Western tendency to imitate nature, and it provided a kind of escape, or healing distance, for the poet. The idea of an inhuman, metallic, abstract beauty separated "out of nature" by art expresses a mystic and Symbolist quest for an invulnerable world distinct from the ravages of time. This world was to be found in an idealized Byzantium, where the poet's body would be transmuted into "such a form as Grecian goldsmiths make / Of hammered gold and gold enamelling / To keep a drowsy Emperor awake; / Or set upon a golden bough to sing / To lords and ladies of Byzantium / Of what is past, or passing, or to come." At the end of *Among School Children,* the sixty-year-old "public man" compensates for the passing of youth by dreaming of pure "Presences" that never fade. Yeats had often adopted the persona of the old man for whom the perspectives of age, idealized beauty, or of history were ways to keep human agony at a distance. In *Lapis Lazuli,* the tragic figures of history transcend their roles by the calm "gaiety" with which they accept their fate; the ancient Chinamen carved in the poem's damaged blue stone climb toward a vantage point where they stare detachedly down on the world's tragedies: "Their eyes mid many wrinkles, their eyes, / Their ancient, glittering eyes, are gay."

But the world is still there, its tragedies still take place, and Yeats's poetry is always aware of the physical and emotional roots from which it sprang. Whatever the wished-for distance, his poems are full of passionate feelings, erotic desire and disappointment, delight in sensuous beauty, horror at civil war and anarchy, dismay at degradation and change. By the time of his death on January 28, 1939, Yeats had rejected his Byzantine identity as the golden songbird, and sought out "the brutality, the ill breeding, the barbarism of truth." "The Wild Old Wicked Man" replaced earlier druids or ancient Chinamen as spokesman, and in *The Circus Animals' Desertion* Yeats described his former themes as so many circus animals put on display. No matter how much these themes embodied "pure mind," they were based in "a mound of refuse or the sweepings of a street . . . the foul rag-and-bone shop of the heart"—the rose springing from the dunghill. Yeats's poetry, which draws its initial power from the mastery of images and verbal rhythm, continues to resonate in the reader's mind for this attempt to come to terms with reality, to grasp and make sense of human experience in the transfiguring language of art.

Edward Malins presents a brief introduction with biography, illustrations, and maps in *A Preface to Yeats* (1977). Richard Ellmann, *The Identity of Yeats* (1964), is an excellent discussion of Yeats's work as a whole. Norman A. Jeffares has revised his major study, *A New Commentary on the Collected Poems of W. B. Yeats* (1983); his *W. B. Yeats: A New Biography* (1988) takes into account recent scholarship and new information about the poet; and Elizabeth Cullingford, *Gender and History in Yeats's Love Poetry* (1993), thoughtfully examines aesthetic form and cultural perspectives in the love lyrics. Harold Bloom, ed., *William Butler Yeats* (1986), presents twelve essays that incorporate close readings of texts. Richard J. Finneran, ed., *Critical Essays on W. B. Yeats* (1986), assembles fourteen essays on diverse topics, with a brief review of Yeats's criticism and a bibliography. Seventeen essays and an interview in Deborah Fleming, ed., *Learning the Trade: Essays on W. B. Yeats and Contemporary Poetry* (1993), discuss Yeats's imprint on various contemporary poets. And ten essays in Leonard Orr, ed., *Yeats and Postmodernism* (1991), approach Yeats from different postmodernist perspectives.

PRONOUNCING GLOSSARY

The following list uses common English syllables and stress accents to provide rough equivalents of selected words whose pronunciation may be unfamiliar to the general reader.

Callimachus: *ca-li'-mah-cus*

Cuchulain: *coo-hu'-lin*

gyre: *jai-er*

Quattrocento: *kwah-troh-chen'-toh*

When You Are Old[1]

When you are old and gray and full of sleep,
And nodding by the fire, take down this book,
And slowly read, and dream of the soft look
Your eyes had once, and of their shadows deep;

How many loved your moments of glad grace,   5
And loved your beauty with love false or true,
But one man loved the pilgrim soul in you,
And loved the sorrows of your changing face;

And bending down beside the glowing bars,
Murmur, a little sadly, how Love fled   10
And paced upon the mountains overhead
And hid his face amid a crowd of stars.

Easter 1916[1]

I have met them at close of day
Coming with vivid faces
From counter or desk among grey
Eighteenth-century houses.
I have passed with a nod of the head   5
Or polite meaningless words,
Or have lingered awhile and said
Polite meaningless words,
And thought before I had done
Of a mocking tale or a gibe   10
To please a companion
Around the fire at the club,
Being certain that they and I

1. An adaptation of a love sonnet by the French Renaissance poet Pierre de Ronsard (1524–1585), which begins similarly ("Quand vous serez bien vieille . . .") but ends by asking the beloved to "pluck the roses of life today."   1. On Easter Sunday 1916, Irish nationalists began an unsuccessful rebellion against British rule, which lasted throughout the week and ended in the surrender and execution of its leaders.

But lived where motley is worn:
All changed, changed utterly: 15
A terrible beauty is born.

That woman's[2] days were spent
In ignorant good-will,
Her nights in argument
Until her voice grew shrill.   20
What voice more sweet than hers
When, young and beautiful,
She rode to harriers?
This man had kept a school
And rode our wingèd horse;   25
This other his helper and friend[3]
Was coming into his force;
He might have won fame in the end,
So sensitive his nature seemed,
So daring and sweet his thought.   30
This other man[4] I had dreamed
A drunken, vainglorious lout.
He had done most bitter wrong
To some who are near my heart,
Yet I number him in the song;   35
He, too, has resigned his part
In the casual comedy;
He, too, has been changed in his turn,
Transformed utterly:
A terrible beauty is born.   40

Hearts with one purpose alone
Through summer and winter seem
Enchanted to a stone
To trouble the living stream.
The horse that comes from the road,   45
The rider, the birds that range
From cloud to tumbling cloud,
Minute by minute they change;
A shadow of cloud on the stream
Changes minute by minute;   50
A horse-hoof slides on the brim,
And a horse plashes within it;
The long-legged moor-hens dive,
And hens to moor-cocks call;
Minute by minute they live: 55
The stone's in the midst of all.

Too long a sacrifice
Can make a stone of the heart.
O when may it suffice?
That is Heaven's part, our part   60

2. Constance Gore-Booth (1868–1927), later Countess Markiewicz, an ardent nationalist.   3. Patrick Pearse (1879–1916) and his friend Thomas MacDonagh (1878–1916), both schoolmasters and leaders of the rebellion and both executed by the British. As a Gaelic poet, Pearse symbolically rode the winged horse of the Muses, Pegasus.   4. Major John MacBride (1865–1916), who had married and separated from Maud Gonne (1866–1953), Yeats's great love.

To murmur name upon name,
As a mother names her child
When sleep at last has come
On limbs that had run wild.
What is it but nightfall?   65
No, no, not night but death;
Was it needless death after all?
For England may keep faith
For all that is done and said.
We know their dream; enough   70
To know they dreamed and are dead;
And what if excess of love
Bewildered them till they died?
I write it out in a verse—
MacDonagh and MacBride   75
And Connolly[5] and Pearse
Now and in time to be,
Wherever green is worn,
Are changed, changed utterly:
A terrible beauty is born.   80

The Second Coming[1]

Turning and turning in the widening gyre[2]
The falcon cannot hear the falconer;
Things fall apart; the centre cannot hold;
Mere anarchy is loosed upon the world,
The blood-dimmed tide is loosed, and everywhere   5
The ceremony of innocence is drowned;
The best lack all conviction, while the worst
Are full of passionate intensity.

Surely some revelation is at hand;
Surely the Second Coming is at hand.   10
The Second Coming! Hardly are those words out
When a vast image out of *Spiritus Mundi*[3]
Troubles my sight: somewhere in sands of the desert
A shape with lion body and the head of a man
A gaze blank and pitiless as the sun,   15
Is moving its slow thighs, while all about it
Reel shadows of the indignant desert birds.
The darkness drops again; but now I know
That twenty centuries of stony sleep
Were vexed to nightmare by a rocking cradle,   20
And what rough beast, its hour come round at last,
Slouches towards Bethlehem to be born?

---

5. James Connolly (1870–1916), labor leader and nationalist executed by the British.   1. The Second Coming of Christ, believed by Christians to herald the end of the world, is transformed here into the prediction of a new birth initiating a new era and terminating the two thousand-year cycle of Christianity. 2. The cone pattern of the falcon's flight and of historical cycles, in Yeats's vision.   3. World-soul (Latin) or, as *Anima Mundi* in Yeats's *Per Amica Silentia Lunae*, a "great memory" containing archetypal images; recalls C. G. Jung's collective unconscious.

Leda and the Swan[1]

A sudden blow: the great wings beating still
Above the staggering girl, her thighs caressed
By the dark webs, her nape caught in his bill,
He holds her helpless breast upon his breast.

How can those terrified vague fingers push   5
The feathered glory from her loosening thighs?
And how can body, laid in that white rush,
But feel the strange heart beating where it lies?

A shudder in the loins engenders there
The broken wall, the burning roof and tower   10
And Agamemnon dead.[2]
               Being so caught up,
So mastered by the brute blood of the air,
Did she put on his knowledge with his power
Before the indifferent beak could let her drop?

Sailing to Byzantium[1]

1

That is no country for old men. The young
In one another's arms, birds in the trees
—Those dying generations—at their song,
The salmon-falls, the mackerel-crowded seas,
Fish, flesh, or fowl, commend all summer long   5
Whatever is begotten, born, and dies.
Caught in the sensual music all neglect
Monuments of unageing intellect.

2

An aged man is but a paltry thing,
A tattered coat upon a stick, unless   10
Soul clap its hands and sing, and louder sing
For every tatter in its mortal dress,
Nor is there singing school but studying
Monuments of its own magnificence;
And therefore I have sailed the seas and come   15
To the holy city of Byzantium.

3

O sages standing in God's holy fire
As in the gold mosaic of a wall,

---

1. Zeus, ruler of the Greek gods, took the form of a swan to rape the mortal Leda; she gave birth to Helen of Troy, whose beauty caused the Trojan War.   2. The ruins of Troy and the death of Agamemnon, the Greek leader, whose sacrifice of his daughter Iphigenia to win the gods' favor caused his wife, Clytemnestra (also a daughter of Leda), to assassinate him on his return.   1. Byzantium, the ancient name for modern Istanbul, was the capital of the Eastern Roman Empire and represented for Yeats (who had seen Byzantine mosaics in Italy) a highly stylized and perfectly integrated artistic world where "religious, aesthetic, and practical life were one."

Come from the holy fire, perne in a gyre,[2]
And be the singing-masters of my soul.   20
Consume my heart away; sick with desire
And fastened to a dying animal
It knows not what it is; and gather me
Into the artifice of eternity.

4

Once out of nature I shall never take   25
My bodily form from any natural thing,
But such a form as Grecian goldsmiths make
Of hammered gold and gold enamelling
To keep a drowsy Emperor awake;
Or set upon a golden bough to sing   30
To lords and ladies of Byzantium
Of what is past, or passing, or to come.

Among School Children

1

I walk through the long schoolroom questioning;
A kind old nun in a white hood replies;
The children learn to cipher and to sing,
To study reading-books and history,
To cut and sew, be neat in everything   5
In the best modern way—the children's eyes
In momentary wonder stare upon
A sixty-year-old smiling public man.[1]

2

I dream of a Ledaean[2] body, bent
Above a sinking fire, a tale that she   10
Told of a harsh reproof, or trivial event
That changed some childish day to tragedy—
Told, and it seemed that our two natures blent
Into a sphere from youthful sympathy,
Or else, to alter Plato's parable,   15
Into the yolk and white of the one shell.[3]

3

And thinking of that fit of grief or rage
I look upon one child or t'other there
And wonder if she stood so at that age—
For even daughters of the swan can share   20
Something of every paddler's heritage—

---

2. That is, come spinning down in a spiral. *Perne:* a spool or bobbin. *Gyre:* the cone pattern of the falcon's flight and of historical cycles, in Yeats's vision.   **1.** Yeats was elected senator of the Irish Free State in 1922.   **2.** Beautiful as Leda or as her daughter Helen of Troy.   **3.** In Plato's *Symposium,* Socrates explains love by telling how the gods split human beings into two halves—like halves of an egg—so that each half seeks its opposite throughout life. Yeats compares the two parts to the yolk and white of an egg.

And had that color upon cheek or hair,
And thereupon my heart is driven wild:
She stands before me as a living child.

4

Her present image floats into the mind—   25
Did Quattrocento finger fashion it
Hollow of cheek[4] as though it drank the wind
And took a mess of shadows for its meat?
And I though never of Ledaean kind
Had pretty plumage once—enough of that,   30
Better to smile on all that smile, and show
There is a comfortable kind of old scarecrow.

5

What youthful mother, a shape upon her lap
Honey of generation had betrayed,
And that must sleep, shriek, struggle to escape   35
As recollection or the drug decide,[5]
Would think her son, did she but see that shape
With sixty or more winters on its head,
A compensation for the pang of his birth,
Or the uncertainty of his setting forth?   40

6

Plato thought nature but a spume that plays
Upon a ghostly paradigm of things;
Solider Aristotle played the taws
Upon the bottom of a king of kings;
World-famous golden-thighed Pythagoras[6]   45
Fingered upon a fiddle-stick or strings
What a star sang and careless Muses heard:
Old clothes upon old sticks to scare a bird.

7

Both nuns and mothers worship images,
But those the candles light are not as those   50
That animate a mother's reveries,
But keep a marble or a bronze repose.
And yet they too break hearts—O Presences
That passion, piety, or affection knows,
And that all heavenly glory symbolize—   55
O self-born mockers of man's enterprise;

---

4. The Italian 15th century is known as the Quattrocento; painters like Botticelli (1444–1510) were
known for their delicate figures.   5. Yeats's note to this poem recalls the Greek scholar Porphyry (ca.
234–ca. 305), who associates "honey" with "the pleasure arising from copulation" that engenders children;
the poet further describes honey as a drug that destroys the child's " 'recollection' of pre-natal freedom."
6. Three Greek philosophers. Plato (427–337 B.C.) believed that nature was only a series of illusionistic
reflections or appearances cast by abstract "forms" that were the only true realities. Aristotle (384–322
B.C.), more pragmatic, was Alexander the Great's tutor and spanked him with the "taws" (leather straps).
Pythagoras (582–407 B.C.), a demigod to his disciples and thought to have a golden thigh bone, pondered
the relationship of music, mathematics, and the stars.

8

Labor is blossoming or dancing where
The body is not bruised to pleasure soul,
Nor beauty born out of its own despair,
Nor blear-eyed wisdom out of midnight oil.   60
O chestnut tree, great-rooted blossomer,
Are you the leaf, the blossom, or the bole?
O body swayed to music, O brightening glance,
How can we know the dancer from the dance?

Byzantium[1]

The unpurged images of day recede;
The Emperor's drunken soldiery are abed;
Night resonance recedes, night-walkers' song
After great cathedral gong;
A starlit or a moonlit dome[2] disdains   5
All that man is,
All mere complexities,
The fury and the mire of human veins.

Before me floats an image, man or shade,
Shade more than man, more image than a shade;   10
For Hades' bobbin bound in mummy-cloth
May unwind the winding path;[3]
A mouth that has no moisture and no breath
Breathless mouths may summon;
I hail the superhuman;   15
I call it death-in-life and life-in-death.

Miracle, bird or golden handiwork,
More miracle than bird or handiwork,
Planted on the starlit golden bough,
Can like the cocks of Hades crow,[4]   20
Or, by the moon embittered, scorn aloud
In glory of changeless metal
Common bird or petal
And all complexities of mire or blood.

At midnight on the Emperor's pavement flit   25
Flames that no faggot feeds, nor steel has lit,
Nor storm disturbs, flames begotten of flame,
Where blood-begotten spirits come
And all complexities of fury leave,
Dying into a dance,   30
An agony of trance,
An agony of flame that cannot singe a sleeve.

1. The holy city of *Sailing to Byzantium*, (see p. 1464), seen here as it resists and transforms the blood and mire of human life into its own transcendent world of art.   2. According to Yeats's system in *A Vision* (1925), the first "starlit" phase in which the moon does not shine and the fifteenth, opposing phase of the full moon represent complete objectivity (potential being) and complete subjectivity (the achievement of complete beauty). In between these absolute phases lie the evolving "mere complexities" of human life.   3. Unwinding the spool of fate that leads from mortal death to the superhuman. *Hades*: the realm of the dead in Greek mythology.   4. To mark the transition from death to the dawn of new life.

Astraddle on the dolphin's mire and blood,[5]
Spirit after spirit! The smithies break the flood,
The golden smithies of the Emperor!   35
Marbles of the dancing floor
Break bitter furies of complexity,
Those images that yet
Fresh images beget,
That dolphin-torn, that gong-tormented sea.   40

Lapis Lazuli[1]

For Harry Clifton

I have heard that hysterical women say
They are sick of the palette and fiddle-bow,
Of poets that are always gay,
For everybody knows or else should know
That if nothing drastic is done   5
Aeroplane and Zeppelin will come out,
Pitch like King Billy[2] bomb-balls in
Until the town lie beaten flat.

All perform their tragic play,
There struts Hamlet, there is Lear,   10
That's Ophelia, that Cordelia;[3]
Yet they, should the last scene be there,
The great stage curtain about to drop,
If worthy their prominent part in the play,
Do not break up their lines to weep.   15
They know that Hamlet and Lear are gay;
Gaiety transfiguring all that dread.
All men have aimed at, found and lost;
Black out; Heaven blazing into the head:[4]
Tragedy wrought to its uttermost.   20
Though Hamlet rambles and Lear rages,
And all the drop-scenes drop at once
Upon a hundred thousand stages,
It cannot grow by an inch or an ounce.

On their own feet they came, or on shipboard,   25
Camel-back, horse-back, ass-back, mule-back,
Old civilisations put to the sword.
Then they and their wisdom went to rack:

5. A dolphin rescued the famous singer Arion by carrying him on his back over the sea. Dolphins were associated with Apollo, Greek god of music and prophecy, and in ancient art they are often shown escorting the souls of the dead to the Isles of the Blessed. Here, the dolphin is also flesh and blood, a part of life. 1. A deep blue semiprecious stone. One of Yeats's letters (to Dorothy Wellesley, July 6, 1935) describes a Chinese carving in lapis lazuli that depicts an ascetic and pupil about to climb a mountain: "Ascetic, pupil, hard stone, eternal theme of the sensual east . . . the east has its solutions always and therefore knows nothing of tragedy." 2. A linkage of past and present. According to an Irish ballad, King William III of England "threw his bomb-balls in" and set fire to the tents of the deposed James II at the Battle of the Boyne in 1690. Also a reference to Kaiser Wilhelm II (King William II) of Germany, who sent zeppelins to bomb London during World War I. *Zeppelin:* a long, cylindrical airship, supported by internal gas chambers. 3. Tragic figures in Shakespeare's plays. 4. The loss of rational consciousness making way for the blaze of inner revelation or "mad" tragic vision. Also suggests the final curtain and an air raid curfew.

No handiwork of Callimachus[5]
Who handled marble as if it were bronze,   30
Made draperies that seemed to rise
When sea-wind swept the corner, stands;
His long lamp-chimney shaped like the stem
Of a slender palm, stood but a day;
All things fall and are built again,   35
And those that build them again are gay.

Two Chinamen, behind them a third,
Are carved in Lapis Lazuli,
Over them flies a long-legged bird,[6]
A symbol of longevity;   40
The third, doubtless a serving-man,
Carries a musical instrument.

Every discoloration of the stone,
Every accidental crack or dent,
Seems a water-course or an avalanche,   45
Or lofty slope where it still snows
Though doubtless plum or cherry-branch
Sweetens the little half-way house
Those Chinamen climb towards, and I
Delight to imagine them seated there;   50
There, on the mountain and the sky,
On all the tragic scene they stare.
One asks for mournful melodies;
Accomplished fingers begin to play.
Their eyes mid many wrinkles, their eyes,   55
Their ancient, glittering eyes, are gay.

The Circus Animals' Desertion

1

I sought a theme and sought for it in vain,
I sought it daily for six weeks or so.
Maybe at last, being but a broken man,
I must be satisfied with my heart, although
Winter and summer till old age began   5
My circus animals were all on show,
Those stilted boys, that burnished chariot,
Lion and woman[1] and the Lord knows what.

2

What can I but enumerate old themes?
First that sea-rider Oisin led by the nose   10
Through three enchanted islands, allegorical dreams,[2]

5. Athenian sculptor (5th century B.C.), famous for a gold lamp in the Erechtheum (temple on the Acropolis) and for using drill lines in marble to give the effect of flowing drapery.   6. A crane.
1. Yeats enumerates images and themes from his earlier work; here, the sphinx of *The Double Vision of Michael Robartes.*   2. In *The Wanderings of Oisin* (1889), an early poem in which Yeats describes a legendary Irish hero who wandered in fairyland for 150 years.

Vain gaiety, vain battle, vain repose,
Themes of the embittered heart, or so it seems,
That might adorn old songs or courtly shows;
But what cared I that set him on to ride,   15
I, starved for the bosom of his faery bride?

And then a counter-truth filled out its play,
The Countess Cathleen[3] was the name I gave it;
She, pity-crazed, had given her soul away,
But masterful Heaven had intervened to save it.   20
I thought my dear must her own soul destroy,
So did fanaticism and hate enslave it,
And this brought forth a dream and soon enough
This dream itself had all my thought and love.

And when the Fool and Blind Man stole the bread   25
Cuchulain[4] fought the ungovernable sea;
Heart-mysteries there, and yet when all is said
It was the dream itself enchanted me:
Character isolated by a deed
To engross the present and dominate memory.   30
Players and painted stage took all my love,
And not those things that they were emblems of.

3

Those masterful images because complete
Grew in pure mind, but out of what began?
A mound of refuse or the sweepings of a street,   35
Old kettles, old bottles, and a broken can,
Old iron, old bones, old rags, that raving slut
Who keeps the till. Now that my ladder's gone,
I must lie down where all the ladders start,
In the foul rag-and-bone shop of the heart.   40

---

3. A play (1892), dedicated to Maud Gonne, in which the countess is saved by Heaven after having sold her soul to the Devil in exchange for food for the poor. The figure of Cathleen comes up frequently in Yeats's work and is often taken as a personification of nationalist Ireland.   4. A legendary Irish hero. Yeats is referring to the play *On Baile's Strand* (1904).

LUIGI PIRANDELLO
1867–1936

"Who am I?" and "What is real?" are the persistent and even agonized questions that underlie Luigi Pirandello's novels, short stories, and plays. The term *Pirandellismo* or "Pirandellism" —coined from the author's name—suggests that there are as many truths as there are points of view. Here are already the basic issues of later existential philosophy as seen in writers like Jean-Paul Sartre and Albert Camus: the difficulty of achieving a sense of identity, the impossibility of authentic communication between people, and the overlapping frontiers of appearance and reality. These dilemmas are dramatic crises in self-knowledge and as such are particularly suited for demonstration in the theater. Indeed, Pirandello is best known as an innovative dramatist who revolutionized European stage techniques to break down comfortable illusions of compartmentalized, stable reality. Instead of the late nineteenth-century's "well-made play"—with its neatly constructed plot that packaged real life into a conventional beginning, middle, and end, and its consistent characters remaining safely inaccessible on the other side of the footlights—he offers unpredictable plots and characters whose ambiguity puts into question the solidity of identities assumed in everyday life. It is not easy to know the truth, he suggests, or to make oneself known behind the face or "naked mask" that each of us wears in society. Pirandello's theater readily displays its nature as dramatic illusion: plays exist within plays until one is not sure where the "real" play begins or ends, and characters question their own reality and that of the audience. In their manipulation of ambiguous appearances and tragicomic effects, these plays foreshadow the absurdist theater of Samuel Beckett, Eugène Ionesco, and Harold Pinter, the cosmic irony of Antonin Artaud's "theater of cruelty," and the emphasis on spectacle and illusion in works by Jean Genet. Above all, they insist that the most "real" life is that which changes from moment to moment, exhibiting a fluidity that renders difficult and perhaps impossible any single formulation of either character or situation. This fluidity is a cause of existential anguish because it implies perpetual loss; readers may wish to contrast Pirandello's cosmos of uncertain boundaries with the sense of continuity throughout different dimensions of existence that informs Wole Soyinka's *Death and the King's Horseman* (in this volume).

Pirandello was born in Girgenti (now Agrigento), Sicily, on June 28, 1867. His father was a sulfur merchant who intended his son to go into business like himself, but Pirandello preferred language and literature. After studying in Palermo and the University of Rome, he traveled to the University of Bonn in 1888 where he received a doctorate in romance philology in 1891 with a thesis on the dialect of his hometown. In 1894, Pirandello made an arranged marriage with the daughter of a rich sulfur merchant. They lived for ten years in Rome, where he wrote poetry and short stories, until the collapse of the sulfur mines destroyed the fortunes of both families, and he was suddenly forced to earn a living. To add to his misfortunes, his wife became insane with a jealous paranoia that lasted until her death in 1918. The author himself died on December 1, 1936.

Pirandello's early work shows a number of different influences. His poetry was indebted to nineteenth-century Italian predecessors like Giosuè Carducci (1835–1907), and in 1896 he translated Goethe's *Roman Elegies*. Soon, however, he turned to short stories or *novelle* under the influence of a narrative style called *verismo* (realism) exemplified in the work of the Sicilian writer Giovanni Verga (1840–1922). Pirandello wrote hundreds of stories of all lengths and—in his clarity, realism, and psychological acuteness (often including a taste for the grotesque)—is recognized as an Italian master of the story much as was Guy de Maupassant in France. Collections include the 1894 *Love Without Love* and an anthology in 1922 entitled *A Year's Worth of Stories*.

In such stories, and in his early novels, Pirandello begins to develop his characteristic themes: the questioning of appearance and reality, and problems of identity. In *The Outcast* (1901), an irate husband drives his innocent wife out of the house only to take her back when—without his knowing it—the supposed adultery has actually occurred. The hero of Pirandello's best-known novel, *The Late Mattia Pascal*, tries to create a fresh identity for himself and leave behind the old Mattia Pascal. When things become too difficult he returns to his "late" self and begins to write his life story, an early example of the tendency in Pirandello's works to comment on their own composition. The protagonists in these and other works are visibly commonplace, middle-class citizens, neither heroic nor villainous, but prototypes of the twentieth-century "antihero" who remains aggressively average while taking the center of the stage.

The questions of identity that obsessed Pirandello (he speaks of them as reflecting the "pangs of my spirit") are explored on social, psychological, and metaphysical levels. He was acquainted with the experimental psychology of his day, and learned from works such as Alfred Binet's *Personality Alterations* (1892) about the existence of a subconscious personality beneath our everyday awareness (a theme Pirandello shares with Proust and Freud). Successive layers of personality, conflicts among the various parts, and the simultaneous existence of multiple perspectives shape an identity that is never fixed but always fluid and changing. This identity escapes the grasp of onlookers and subject alike, and expresses a basic incongruity in human existence that challenges the most earnest attempts to create a unified self. The protagonist of a later novel, *One, None, and a Hundred Thousand* (1925–26) finds that what "he" is depends on the viewpoint of a great number of people. Such incongruity can be tragic or comic—or both at once—according to one's attitude, a topic that Pirandello explored in a 1908 essay, *On Humor,* and that is echoed in the double-edged humor of his plays. The "Pirandellian" themes of ambiguous identity, lack of communication, and deceptive appearance reappear in all the genres, however, reaching a particular intensity in his first dramatic success, *It Is So [If You Think So]* (1917), and in the play included here, *Six Characters in Search of an Author.*

Six Characters in Search of an Author and *Henry IV* established Pirandello's stature as a major dramatist. He directed his own company (the Teatro d'Arte di Roma) from 1924 to 1928 and received the Nobel Prize for Literature in 1934. His later plays, featuring fantastic and grotesque elements, did not achieve the wide popularity of their predecessors. In 1936, he published a collection of forty-three plays as *Naked Masks,* a title conceived in 1918 after Luigi Chiarelli's "grotesque theater." Pirandello's characters are "naked" and vulnerable inside the social roles or masks they put on to survive: Henry IV, trapped for life inside a pretense of insanity, or the Father in *Six Characters,* forced to play out a demeaning role in which, he insists, only part of his true nature is revealed. The term *naked mask* also suggests Pirandello's superb manipulation of theatrical ambiguity—the confusion between the actor and the character portrayed—that ultimately prolongs the confusion of appearance and reality, which is one of his chief themes. Pirandello is famous in twentieth-century theater for his use of the play within a play, a technique of embedded dramatic episodes that maintain a life of their own while serving as foil to the overall or governing plot. Dividing lines are sometimes hard to draw when stage dialogue can be taken as referring to either context—a situation that allows for double meanings at the same time that it reiterates the impossibility of real communication.

Six Characters in Search of an Author combines all these elements in an extraordinarily self-reflexive style. At the very beginning, the Stage Hand's interrupted hammering suggests that the audience has chanced on a rehearsal—of still another play by Pirandello—instead of coming to a finished performance; concurrently, Pirandello's stage dialogue pokes fun at his own reputation for obscurity. Just as the Actors are apparently set to rehearse *The Rules of the Game,* six unexpected persons come down the aisle seeking the Producer: they are Characters out of an unwritten novel who demand to be given dramatic existence. The play *Six Characters* is continually in the process of being composed: composed as the interwoven double plot we see on stage, written down in shorthand by the Prompter for the Actors to reproduce, and potentially composed as the Characters' inner drama finally achieves its rightful existence as a work of art. The conflicts between the different levels of the play finally prevent the completion of any but the first work, but it has created a convincing dramatic illusion in the meantime that incorporates the psychological drama of the "six characters" as well as a discussion of the relationship of life and art.

The initial absurdity of the play appears when the six admittedly fictional characters arrive with their claim to be "truer and more real" than the "real" characters they confront. (Of course, to the audience all the actors on stage are equally unreal.) Their greater "truth" is the truth of art with its profound but formally fixed glimpses into human nature. Each Character represents, specifically and in depth, a particular identity created by the author, who later suggested that the Characters should wear masks to distinguish them from the Actors. These masks are not the conventional masks of ancient Greek drama or the Japanese nō theater, nor do they function as the ceremonial masks representing spirits in African ritual, masks that temporarily invest the wearer with the spirit's identity and authority. Instead, they are a theatrical device, a symbol and visual reminder of each character's unchanging essence. The Six Characters are incapable of developing outside their roles and are condemned, in their search for existence, painfully to reenact their essential selves.

Conversely, the fictional characters have a more stable personality than "real" people who are still "nobody," incomplete, open to change and misinterpretation. Characters are "somebody" because their nature has been decided once and for all. Yet there is a further complication to this contrast between real and fictional characters: the Characters have real anxieties in that they want to play their own roles and are disturbed at the prospect of having Actors represent them incorrectly. All human beings, suggests Pirandello, whether fictional or real, are subject to misunderstanding. We even misunderstand ourselves when we think we are the same person in all situations. "We always have the illusion of being the same person for everybody," says the Father, "but it's not true!" When he explains himself as a very human philosopher driven by the Demon of Experiment, his self-image is quite different from the picture held by his vengeful Stepdaughter or the passive Mother who blames him for her expulsion from the house. The Stepdaughter, in turn, appears to love an innocent little sister because she reminds her of an earlier self. It is an entanglement of motives and deceit of mutual understanding that goes beyond the tabloid level of a sordid family scandal and claims a broader scope. Pirandello, in fact, does not intend merely to describe a particular setting or situation; that is the concern of what he calls "historical writers." He belongs to the opposite category of "philosophical writers" whose characters and situations embody "a particular sense of life and acquire from it a universal value."

Six Characters in Search of an Author underwent an interesting evolution to become the play that we see today. First performed in Rome in 1921, where its unsettling plot and characters already scandalized a traditionalist audience, it was reshaped in more radical theatrical form after the remarkable performance produced by Georges Pitoëff in Paris in 1923. Pirandello, who came to Paris somewhat wary of Pitoëff's innovations (he brought on the Characters in a green-lit stage elevator), was soon convinced that the Russian director's stagecraft suggested changes that would enhance the original text. Pitoëff had used his knowledge of technical effects to accentuate the interrelationships of appearance and reality: he extended the stage with several steps leading down into the auditorium (a break in the conventional stage's "fourth wall" that Pirandello was quick to exploit); he underscored the play within a play with rehearsal effects, showing the Stage Hand hammering and the Director arranging suitable props and lighting; he emphasized the division between Characters and Actors by separating groups on stage and dressing the Characters (all except the Little Girl) in black. Pirandello welcomed and expanded on many of these changes. To distinguish even further the Characters from the Actors, he proposed stylized masks as well as black clothes for the former and light-colored summery clothing for the latter. To bring out Madame Pace's grotesque fictionality, he changed her costume from a sober black gown to a garish red silk dress and carrot-colored wool wig. Most striking, however, is the dramatist's development of Pitoëff's steps into a real bridge between the world of the stage and the auditorium, a strategy that allows his Actors (and Characters) to come and go in the "real world" of the audience. Pirandello's revised ending to *Six Characters in Search of an Author* makes a final break with theatrical illusion: with the other characters immobilized on stage, the Stepdaughter races down the steps, through the auditorium, and out into the foyer from which the audience can still hear her distraught laughter.

Pirandello does not hold his audience by uttering grand philosophical truths. There is constant suspense and a process of discovery in *Six Characters*, from the moment that the rehearsal with its complaining Actors and Manager is interrupted and the initial hints of melodrama and family scandal catch our attention in the Stepdaughter's and Mother's complaints. It is a story that could be found in the most sensational papers: an adulterous wife thrust out of her home and supporting herself and her children after her lover's death by sewing, the daughter's turn to prostitution to support the family, the Father's unknowing attempt to seduce his Stepdaughter (interpreted by the latter as the continuation of an old and perverse impulse), and the final drowning and suicide of the two youngest children. Pirandello plays with the sensational aspect of his story by focusing the play on the characters' repeated attempts to portray the seduction scene; Actors and Manager perceive the salable quality of such "human-interest" events and are eager to let the story unfold. The Stepdaughter's protective fondness for her doomed baby sister and her enigmatic reproach to the little Boy ("instead of killing myself, I'd have killed one of those two") hint at the inner plot that is revealed only as the action continues. The interplay of illusion and reality persists to the very end, when the Actors argue about whether the Boy is dead or not, the Producer is terrified as the lights change eerily around the surviving Characters, and the Stepdaughter breaks away from the ending tableau to escape into the audience.

The translation by John Linstrum has been selected on the one hand for its accuracy to the Italian text and its fluent use of contemporary English idiom and on the other for its quality as a performance-oriented script, staged in London in 1979. Readers are encouraged to test the continued liveliness of Pirandello's dialogue by rehearsing their own selection of scenes—or perhaps by relocating them in a contemporary setting. According to director Robert Brustein, whose 1988 production of *Six Characters in Search of an Author* set the action in New York and replaced Madame Pace with a pimp, "Pirandello both encourages and stimulates a pluralism in theater because there can be dozens, hundreds, thousands of productions of *Six Characters*, and every one of them is going to be different."

A good biography and general introduction is found in Susan Bassnett-McGuire, *Pirandello* (1984). Walter Starkie, *Luigi Pirandello, 1867–1936* (1965), a general study against the background of twentieth-century Italian literature, treats novels, stories, plays, and themes. Glauco Cambon, ed., *Pirandello: A Collection of Critical Essays* (1967), emphasizes the plays. Richard Sogliuzzo, *Luigi Pirandello, Director* (1982), deals with Pirandello's dramatic theories and practices; it contains a discussion of *Six Characters*. John Louis DiGaetani, ed., *A Companion to Pirandello Studies* (1991), is an excellent collection of twenty-seven essays and four appendices on diverse aspects of Pirandello's thought and work; many essays take up *Six Characters*.

PRONOUNCING GLOSSARY

The following list uses common English syllables and stress accents to provide rough equivalents of selected words whose pronunciation may be unfamiliar to the general reader.

commedia dell'arte: *com-may'-dee-ah del ar'-tay*

Luigi Pirandello: *loo-ee'-jee pee-ran-del'-oh*

Pace: *pah'-chay*

Pitoëff: *pee'-toh-eff*

Six Characters in Search of an Author[1]

A Comedy in the Making

THE CHARACTERS	THE COMPANY
FATHER	THE PRODUCER
MOTHER	THE STAGE STAFF
STEPDAUGHTER	THE ACTORS
SON	
BOY	
LITTLE GIRL	
MADAME PACE	

Act One

When the audience enters, the curtain is already up and the stage is just as it would be during the day. There is no set; it is empty, in almost total darkness. This is so that from the beginning the audience will have the feeling of being present, not at a performance of a properly rehearsed play, but at a performance of a play that happens spontaneously. Two small sets of steps, one on the right and one on the left, lead up to the stage from the auditorium. On the stage, the top is off the PROMPTER*'s box and is lying next to it. Downstage, there is a small table and a chair with arms for the* PRODUCER*: it is turned with its back to the audience.*

Also downstage there are two small tables, one a little bigger than the other, and several chairs, ready for the rehearsal if needed. There are more chairs scattered on both left and right for the ACTORS*: to one side at the back and nearly hidden is a piano.*

When the houselights go down the STAGE HAND *comes on through the back door. He is in blue overalls and carries a tool bag. He brings some pieces of wood on, comes to the front, kneels down and starts to nail them together.*

The STAGE MANAGER *rushes on from the wings.*

1. Translated by John Linstrum. In the Italian editions, Pirandello notes that he did not divide the play into formal acts or scenes. The translator has marked the divisions for clarity, however, according to the stage directions.

STAGE MANAGER: Hey! What are you doing?

STAGE HAND: What do you think I'm doing? I'm banging nails in.

STAGE MANAGER: Now? [*He looks at his watch.*] It's half-past ten already. The Producer will be here in a moment to rehearse.

STAGE HAND: I've got to do my work some time, you know.

STAGE MANAGER: Right—but not now.

STAGE HAND: When?

STAGE MANAGER: When the rehearsal's finished. Come on, get all this out of the way and let me set for the second act of *The Rules of the Game*.[2]

[*The* STAGE HAND *picks up his tools and wood and goes off, grumbling and muttering. The* ACTORS *of the company come in through the door, men and women, first one then another, then two together and so on: there will be nine or ten, enough for the parts for the rehearsal of a play by Pirandello,* The Rules of the Game, *today's rehearsal. They come in, say their "Good-mornings" to the* STAGE MANAGER *and each other. Some go off to the dressing-rooms; others, among them the* PROMPTER *with the text rolled up under his arm, scatter about the stage waiting for the* PRODUCER *to start the rehearsal. Meanwhile, sitting or standing in groups, they chat together; some smoke, one complains about his part, another one loudly reads something from "The Stage." It would be as well if the* ACTORS *and* ACTRESSES *were dressed in colourful clothes, and this first scene should be improvised naturally and vivaciously. After a while somebody might sit down at the piano and play a song; the younger* ACTORS *and* ACTRESSES *start dancing.*]

STAGE MANAGER: [*Clapping his hands to call their attention.*] Come on, everybody! Quiet please. The Producer's here.

[*The piano and the dancing both stop. The* ACTORS *turn to look out into the theatre and through the door at the back comes the* PRODUCER; *he walks down the gangway between the seats and, calling "Good-morning" to the* ACTORS, *climbs up one of the sets of stairs onto the stage. The* SECRETARY *gives him the post, a few magazines, a script. The* ACTORS *move to one side of the stage.*]

PRODUCER: Any letters?

SECRETARY: No. That's all the post there is. [*Giving him the script.*]

PRODUCER: Put it in the office. [*Then looking round and turning to the* STAGE MANAGER.] I can't see a thing here. Let's have some lights please.

STAGE MANAGER: Right. [*Calling.*] Workers please!

[*In a few seconds the side of the stage where the* ACTORS *are standing is brilliantly lit with white light. The* PROMPTER *has gone into his box and spread out his script.*]

PRODUCER: Good. [*Clapping hands.*] Well then, let's get started. Anybody missing?

STAGE MANAGER: [*Heavily ironic.*] Our leading lady.

PRODUCER: Not again! [*Looking at his watch.*] We're ten minutes late already. Send her a note to come and see me. It might teach her to be

---

2. *Il giuoco delle parti*, written in 1918. The hero, Leone Gala, pretends to ignore his wife Silia's infidelity until the end, when he takes revenge by tricking her lover Guido Venanzi into taking his place in a fatal duel she had engineered to get rid of her husband.

on time for rehearsals. [*Almost before he has finished, the* LEADING ACTRESS*'s voice is heard from the auditorium.*]

LEADING ACTRESS: Morning everybody. Sorry I'm late. [*She is very expensively dressed and is carrying a lap-dog. She comes down the aisle and goes up on to the stage.*]

PRODUCER: You're determined to keep us waiting, aren't you?

LEADING ACTRESS: I'm sorry. I just couldn't find a taxi anywhere. But you haven't started yet and I'm not on at the opening anyhow. [*Calling the* STAGE MANAGER, *she gives him the dog.*]. Put him in my dressing-room for me will you?

PRODUCER: And she's even brought her lap-dog with her! As if we haven't enough lap-dogs here already. [*Clapping his hands and turning to the* PROMPTER.] Right then, the second act of *The Rules of the Game.* [*Sits in his arm-chair.*] Quiet please! Who's on?

[*The* ACTORS *clear from the front of the stage and sit to one side, except for three who are ready to start the scene—and the* LEADING ACTRESS. *She has ignored the* PRODUCER *and is sitting at one of the little tables.*]

PRODUCER: Are you in this scene, then?

LEADING ACTRESS: No—I've just told you.

PRODUCER: [*Annoyed.*] Then get off, for God's sake. [*The* LEADING ACTRESS *goes and sits with the others. To the* PROMPTER.] Come on then, let's get going.

PROMPTER: [*Reading his script.*] "The house of Leone Gala. A peculiar room, both dining-room and study."

PRODUCER: [*To the* STAGE MANAGER.] We'll use the red set.

STAGE MANAGER: [*Making a note.*] The red set—right.

PROMPTER: [*Still reading.*] "The table is laid and there is a desk with books and papers. Bookcases full of books and china cabinets full of valuable china. An exit at the back leads to Leone's bedroom. An exit to the left leads to the kitchen. The main entrance is on the right."

PRODUCER: Right. Listen carefully everybody: there, the main entrance, there, the kitchen. [*To the* LEADING ACTOR *who plays Socrates.*[3]] Your entrances and exits will be from there [*To the* STAGE MANAGER.] We'll have the French windows there and put the curtains on them.

STAGE MANAGER: [*Making a note.*] Right.

PROMPTER: [*Reading.*] "Scene One. Leone Gala, Guido Venanzi, and Filippo, who is called Socrates." [*To* PRODUCER.] Have I to read the directions as well?

PRODUCER: Yes, you have! I've told you a hundred times.

PROMPTER: [*Reading.*] "When the curtain rises, Leone Gala, in a cook's hat and apron, is beating an egg in a dish with a little wooden spoon. Filippo is beating another and he is dressed as a cook too. Guido Venanzi is sitting listening."

LEADING ACTOR: Look, do I really have to wear a cook's hat?

PRODUCER: [*Annoyed by the question.*] I expect so! That's what it says in the script. [*Pointing to the script.*]

---

3. Nickname given to Gala's servant, Philip, in *The Rules of the Game,* the play they are rehearsing.

LEADING ACTOR: If you ask me it's ridiculous.

PRODUCER: [*Leaping to his feet furiously.*] Ridiculous? It's ridiculous, is it? What do you expect me to do if nobody writes good plays any more[4] and we're reduced to putting on plays by Pirandello? And if you can understand them you must be very clever. He writes them on purpose so nobody enjoys them, neither actors nor critics nor audience. [*The* ACTORS *laugh. Then crosses to* LEADING ACTOR *and shouts at him.*] A cook's hat and you beat eggs. But don't run away with the idea that that's all you are doing—beating eggs. You must be joking! You have to be symbolic of the shells of the eggs you are beating. [*The* ACTORS *laugh again and start making ironical comments to each other.*] Be quiet! Listen carefully while I explain. [*Turns back to* LEADING ACTOR.] Yes, the shells, because they are symbolic of the empty form of reason, without its content, blind instinct! You are reason and your wife is instinct: you are playing a game where you have been given parts and in which you are not just yourself but the puppet of yourself.[5] Do you see?

LEADING ACTOR: [*Spreading his hands.*] Me? No.

PRODUCER: [*Going back to his chair.*] Neither do I! Come on, let's get going; you wait till you see the end! You haven't seen anything yet! [*Confidentially.*] By the way, I should turn almost to face the audience if I were you, about three-quarters face. Well, what with the obscure dialogue and the audience not being able to hear you properly in any case, the whole lot'll go to hell. [*Clapping hands again.*] Come on. Let's get going!

PROMPTER: Excuse me, can I put the top back on the prompt-box? There's a bit of a draught.

PRODUCER: Yes, yes, of course. Get on with it.

[*The* STAGE DOORKEEPER, *in a braided cap, has come into the auditorium, and he comes all the way down the aisle to the stage to tell the* PRODUCER *the* SIX CHARACTERS *have come, who, having come in after him, look about them a little puzzled and dismayed. Every effort must be made to create the effect that the* SIX CHARACTERS *are very different from the* ACTORS *of the company. The placings of the two groups, indicated in the directions, once the* CHARACTERS *are on the stage, will help this: so will using different coloured lights. But the most effective idea is to use masks for the* CHARACTERS, *masks specially made of a material that will not go limp with perspiration and light enough not to worry the actors who wear them: they should be made so that the eyes, the nose and the mouth are all free. This is the way to bring out the deep significance of the play. The* CHARACTERS *should not appear as ghosts, but as created realities, timeless creations of the imagination, and so more real and consistent than the changeable realities of the* ACTORS. *The masks are designed to give the impression of figures constructed by art, each one fixed for-*

---

4. The producer refers to the realistic, tightly constructed plays (often French) that were internationally popular in the late 19th century and a staple of Italian theaters at the beginning of the 20th.   5. Leone Gala is a rationalist and an aesthete—the opposite of his impulsive, passionate wife, Silia. By masking his feelings and constantly playing the role of gourmet cook, he chooses his own role and thus becomes his own "puppet."

ever in its own fundamental emotion; that is, Remorse for the FATHER, *Revenge for the* STEPDAUGHTER, *Scorn for the* SON, *Sorrow for the* MOTHER. *Her mask should have wax tears in the corners of the eyes and down the cheeks like the sculptured or painted weeping Madonna in a church. Her dress should be of a plain material, in stiff folds, looking almost as if it were carved and not of an ordinary material you can buy in a shop and have made up by a dressmaker.*

The FATHER *is about fifty: his reddish hair is thinning at the temples, but he is not bald: he has a full moustache that almost covers his young-looking mouth, which often opens in an uncertain and empty smile. He is pale, with a high forehead: he has blue oval eyes, clear and sharp: he is dressed in light trousers and a dark jacket: his voice is sometimes rich, at other times harsh and loud.*

The MOTHER *appears crushed by an intolerable weight of shame and humiliation. She is wearing a thick black veil and is dressed simply in black; when she raises her veil she shows a face like wax, but not suffering, with her eyes turned down humbly.*

The STEPDAUGHTER, *who is eighteen years old, is defiant, even insolent. She is very beautiful, dressed in mourning as well, but with striking elegance. She is scornful of the timid, suffering, dejected air of her* YOUNG BROTHER, *a grubby little boy of fourteen, also dressed in black; she is full of a warm tenderness, on the other hand, for the* LITTLE SISTER, *a girl of about four, dressed in white with a black silk sash round her waist.*

The SON *is twenty-two, tall, almost frozen in an air of scorn for the* FATHER *and indifference to the* MOTHER: *he is wearing a mauve overcoat and a long green scarf round his neck.*]

DOORMAN: Excuse me, sir.

PRODUCER: [*Angrily.*] What the hell is it now?

DOORMAN: There are some people here—they say they want to see you, sir.

[*The* PRODUCER *and the* ACTORS *are astonished and turn to look out into the auditorium.*]

PRODUCER: But I'm rehearsing! You know perfectly well that no-one's allowed in during rehearsals. [*Turning to face out front.*] Who are you? What do you want?

FATHER: [*Coming forward, followed by the others, to the foot of one of the sets of steps.*] We're looking for an author.

PRODUCER: [*Angry and astonished.*] An author? Which author?

FATHER: Any author will do, sir.

PRODUCER: But there isn't an author here because we're not rehearsing a new play.

STEPDAUGHTER: [*Excitedly as she rushes up the steps.*] That's better still, better still! We can be your new play.

ACTORS: [*Lively comments and laughter from the* ACTORS.] Oh, listen to that, etc.

FATHER: [*Going up on the stage after the* STEPDAUGHTER.] Maybe, but if there isn't an author here . . . [*To the* PRODUCER.] Unless you'd like to be . . .

[*Hand in hand, the* MOTHER *and the* LITTLE GIRL, *followed by the* LITTLE BOY, *go up on the stage and wait. The* SON *stays sullenly behind.*]

PRODUCER: Is this some kind of joke?

FATHER: Now, how can you think that? On the contrary, we are bringing you a story of anguish.

STEPDAUGHTER: We might make your fortune for you!

PRODUCER: Do me a favour, will you? Go away. We haven't time to waste on idiots.

FATHER: [*Hurt but answering gently.*] You know very well, as a man of the theatre, that life is full of all sorts of odd things which have no need at all to pretend to be real because they are actually true.

PRODUCER: What the devil are you talking about?

FATHER: What I'm saying is that you really must be mad to do things the opposite way round: to create situations that obviously aren't true and try to make them seem to be really happening. But then I suppose that sort of madness is the only reason for your profession.

[*The* ACTORS *are indignant.*]

PRODUCER: [*Getting up and glaring at him.*] Oh, yes? So ours is a profession of madmen, is it?

FATHER: Well, if you try to make something look true when it obviously isn't, especially if you're not forced to do it, but do it for a game . . . Isn't it your job to give life on the stage to imaginary people?

PRODUCER: [*Quickly answering him and speaking for the* ACTORS *who are growing more indignant.*] I should like you to know, sir, that the actor's profession is one of great distinction. Even if nowadays the new writers only give us dull plays to act and puppets to present instead of men, I'd have you know that it is our boast that we have given life, here on this stage, to immortal works.

[*The* ACTORS, *satisfied, agree with and applaud the* PRODUCER.]

FATHER: [*Cutting in and following hard on his argument.*] There! You see? Good! You've given life! You've created living beings with more genuine life than people have who breathe and wear clothes! Less real, perhaps, but nearer the truth. We are both saying the same thing.

[*The* ACTORS *look at each other, astonished.*]

PRODUCER: But just a moment! You said before . . .

FATHER: I'm sorry, but I said that before, about acting for fun, because you shouted at us and said you'd no time to waste on idiots, but you must know better than anyone that Nature uses human imagination to lift her work of creation to even higher levels.

PRODUCER: All right then: but where does all this get us?

FATHER: Nowhere. I want to try to show that one can be thrust into life in many ways, in many forms: as a tree or a stone, as water or a butterfly — or as a woman. It might even be as a character in a play.

PRODUCER: [*Ironic, pretending to be annoyed.*] And you, and these other people here, were thrust into life, as you put it, as characters in a play?

FATHER: Exactly! And alive, as you can see.

[*The* PRODUCER *and the* ACTORS *burst into laughter as if at a joke.*]

FATHER: I'm sorry you laugh like that, because we carry in us, as I said

before, a story of terrible anguish as you can guess from this woman
dressed in black.

[*Saying this, he offers his hand to the* MOTHER *and helps her up the
last steps and, holding her still by the hand, leads her with a sense of
tragic solemnity across the stage which is suddenly lit by a fantastic
light.*

The LITTLE GIRL *and the* BOY *follow the* MOTHER: *then the* SON
comes up and stands to one side in the background: then the STEP-
DAUGHTER *follows and leans against the proscenium arch: the* ACTORS
*are astonished at first, but then, full of admiration for the "entrance,"
they burst into applause—just as if it were a performance specially
for them.*]

PRODUCER: [*At first astonished and then indignant.*] My God! Be quiet all
of you. [*Turns to the* CHARACTERS.] And you lot get out! Clear off!
[*Turns to the* STAGE MANAGER.] Jesus! Get them out of here.

STAGE MANAGER: [*Comes forward but stops short as if held back by something strange.*] Go on out! Get out!

FATHER: [*To* PRODUCER.] Oh no, please, you see, we . . .

PRODUCER: [*Shouting.*] We came here to work, you know.

LEADING ACTOR: We really can't be messed about like this.

FATHER: [*Resolutely, coming forward.*] I'm astonished! Why don't you
believe me? Perhaps you are not used to seeing the characters created
by an author spring into life up here on the stage face to face with
each other. Perhaps it's because we're not in a script? [*He points to the*
PROMPTER'*s box.*]

STEPDAUGHTER: [*Coming down to the* PRODUCER, *smiling and persuasive.*]
Believe me, sir, we really are six of the most fascinating characters. But
we've been neglected.

FATHER: Yes, that's right, we've been neglected. In the sense that the
author who created us, living in his mind, wouldn't or couldn't make
us live in a written play for the world of art.[6] And that really is a crime
sir, because whoever has the luck to be born a character can laugh even
at death. Because a character will never die! A man will die, a writer,
the instrument of creation: but what he has created will never die! And
to be able to live for ever you don't need to have extraordinary gifts or
be able to do miracles. Who was Sancho Panza? Who was Prospero?[7]
But they will live for ever because—living seeds—they had the luck to
find a fruitful soil, an imagination which knew how to grow them and
feed them, so that they will live for ever.

PRODUCER: This is all very well! But what do you want here?

FATHER: We want to live, sir.

PRODUCER: [*Ironically.*] For ever!

FATHER: No, no: only for a few moments—in you.

AN ACTOR: Listen to that!

LEADING ACTRESS: They want to live in us!

---

6. In the 1925 preface to *Six Characters*, Pirandello explains that these characters came to him first as
characters for a novel that he later abandoned. Haunted by their half-realized personalities, he decided to
use the situation in a play.   7. The magician and exiled duke of Milan in Shakespeare's *The Tempest*.
Sancho Panza was Don Quixote's servant in Cervantes's novel *Don Quixote* (1605–15).

YOUNG ACTOR: [*Pointing to the* STEPDAUGHTER.] I don't mind . . . so long as I get her.

FATHER: Listen, listen: the play is all ready to be put together and if you and your actors would like to, we can work it out now between us.

PRODUCER: [*Annoyed.*] But what exactly do you want to do? We don't make up plays like that here! We present comedies and tragedies here.

FATHER: That's right, we know that of course. That's why we've come.

PRODUCER: And where's the script?

FATHER: It's in us, sir. [*The* ACTORS *laugh.*] The play is in us: we are the play and we are impatient to show it to you: the passion inside us is driving us on.

STEPDAUGHTER: [*Scornfully, with the tantalising charm of deliberate impudence.*] My passion, if only you knew! My passion for him! [*She points at the* FATHER *and suggests that she is going to embrace him: but stops and bursts into a screeching laugh.*]

FATHER: [*With sudden anger.*] You keep out of this for the moment! And stop laughing like that!

STEPDAUGHTER: Really? Then with your permission, ladies and gentlemen; even though it's only two months since I became an orphan, just watch how I can sing and dance.

[*The* ACTORS, *especially the younger, seem strangely attracted to her while she sings and dances and they edge closer and reach out their hands to catch hold of her.*[8] *She eludes them, and when the* ACTORS *applaud her and the* PRODUCER *speaks sharply to her she stays still quite removed from them all.*]

FIRST ACTOR: Very good! etc.

PRODUCER: [*Angrily.*] Be quiet! Do you think this is a nightclub? [*Turns to* FATHER *and asks with some concern.*] Is she a bit mad?

FATHER: Mad? Oh no—it's worse than that.

STEPDAUGHTER: [*Suddenly running to the* PRODUCER.] Yes. It's worse, much worse! Listen please! Let's put this play on at once, because you'll see that at a particular point I—when this darling little girl here—[*Taking the* LITTLE GIRL *by the hand from next to the* MOTHER *and crossing with her to the* PRODUCER.] Isn't she pretty? [*Takes her in her arms.*] Darling! Darling! [*Puts her down again and adds, moved very deeply but almost without wanting to.*] Well, this lovely little girl here, when God suddenly takes her from this poor Mother: and this little idiot here [*Turning to the* LITTLE BOY *and seizing him roughly by the sleeve.*] does the most stupid thing, like the half-wit he is,—then you will see me run away! Yes, you'll see me rush away! But not yet, not yet! Because, after all the intimate things there have been between him and me [*In the direction of the* FATHER, *with a horrible vulgar wink.*] I can't stay with them any longer, to watch the insult to this mother through that supercilious cretin over there. [*Pointing to the* SON.] Look at him! Look at him! Condescending, stand-offish, because he's the legitimate son, him! Full of contempt for me, for the boy and for the little girl: because we

---

8. Pirandello uses a contemporary popular song, "Chu-Chin-Chow" from the Ziegfeld Follies of 1917, for the Stepdaughter to display her talents.

are bastards. Do you understand? Bastards. [*Running to the* MOTHER *and embracing her.*] And this poor mother—she—who is the mother of all of us—he doesn't want to recognise her as his own mother—and he looks down on her, he does, as if she were only the mother of the three of us who are bastards—the traitor. [*She says all this quickly, with great excitement, and after having raised her voice on the word "bastards" she speaks quietly, half-spitting the word "traitor."*]

MOTHER: [*With deep anguish to the* PRODUCER.] Sir, in the name of these two little ones, I beg you . . . [*Feels herself grow faint and sways.*] Oh, my God.

FATHER: [*Rushing to support her with almost all the* ACTORS *bewildered and concerned.*] Get a chair someone . . . quick, get a chair for this poor widow.

[*One of the* ACTORS *offers a chair: the others press urgently around. The* MOTHER, *seated now, tries to stop the* FATHER *lifting her veil.*]

ACTORS: Is it real? Has she really fainted? etc.

FATHER: Look at her, everybody, look at her.

MOTHER: No, for God's sake, stop it.

FATHER: Let them look?

MOTHER: [*Lifting her hands and covering her face, desperately.*] Oh, please, I beg you, stop him from doing what he is trying to do; it's hateful.

PRODUCER: [*Overwhelmed, astounded.*] It's no use, I don't understand this any more. [*To the* FATHER.] Is this woman your wife?

FATHER: [*At once.*] That's right, she is my wife.

PRODUCER: How is she a widow, then, if you're still alive?

[*The* ACTORS *are bewildered too and find relief in a loud laugh.*]

FATHER: [*Wounded, with rising resentment.*] Don't laugh! Please don't laugh like that! That's just the point, that's her own drama. You see, she had another man. Another man who ought to be here.

MOTHER: No, no! [*Crying out.*]

STEPDAUGHTER: Luckily for him he died. Two months ago, as I told you: we are in mourning for him, as you can see.

FATHER: Yes, he's dead: but that's not the reason he isn't here. He isn't here because—well just look at her, please, and you'll understand at once—hers is not a passionate drama of the love of two men, because she was incapable of love, she could feel nothing—except, perhaps a little gratitude (but not to me, to him). She's not a woman; she's a mother. And her drama—and, believe me, it's a powerful one—her drama is focused completely on these four children of the two men she had.

MOTHER: I had them? How dare you say that I had them, as if I wanted them myself? It was him, sir! He forced the other man on me. He made me go away with him!

STEPDAUGHTER: [*Leaping up, indignantly.*] It isn't true!

MOTHER: [*Bewildered.*] How isn't it true?

STEPDAUGHTER: It isn't true, it just isn't true.

MOTHER: What do you know about it?

STEPDAUGHTER: It isn't true. [*To the* PRODUCER.] Don't believe it! Do you know why she said that? She said it because of him, over there. [*Pointing to the* SON.] She tortures herself, she exhausts herself with worry and all because of the indifference of that son of hers. She wants to make him believe that she abandoned him when he was two years old because the Father made her do it.

MOTHER: [*Passionately.*] He did! He made me! God's my witness. [*To the* PRODUCER.] Ask him if it isn't true. [*Pointing to the* FATHER.] Make him tell our son it's true. [*Turning to the* STEPDAUGHTER.] You don't know anything about it.

STEPDAUGHTER: I know that when my father was alive you were always happy and contented. You can't deny it.

MOTHER: No, I can't deny it.

STEPDAUGHTER: He was always full of love and care for you. [*Turning to the* LITTLE BOY *with anger.*] Isn't it true? Admit it. Why don't you say something, you little idiot?

MOTHER: Leave the poor boy alone! Why do you want to make me appear ungrateful? You're my daughter. I don't in the least want to offend your father's memory. I've already told him that it wasn't my fault or even to please myself that I left his house and my son.

FATHER: It's quite true. It was my fault.

LEADING ACTOR: [*To other actors.*] Look at this. What a show!

LEADING ACTRESS: And we're the audience.

YOUNG ACTOR: For a change.

PRODUCER: [*Beginning to be very interested.*] Let's listen to them! Quiet! Listen!
    [*He goes down the steps into the auditorium and stands there as if to get an idea of what the scene will look like from the audience's viewpoint.*]

SON: [*Without moving, coldly, quietly, ironically.*] Yes, listen to his little scrap of philosophy. He's going to tell you all about the Daemon of Experiment.

FATHER: You're a cynical idiot, and I've told you so a hundred times. [*To the* PRODUCER *who is now in the stalls.*] He sneers at me because of this expression I've found to defend myself.

SON: Words, words.

FATHER: Yes words, words! When we're faced by something we don't understand, by a sense of evil that seems as if it's going to swallow us, don't we all find comfort in a word that tells us nothing but that calms us?

STEPDAUGHTER: And dulls your sense of remorse, too. That more than anything.

FATHER: Remorse? No, that's not true. It'd take more than words to dull the sense of remorse in me.

STEPDAUGHTER: It's taken a little money too, just a little money. The money that he was going to offer as payment, gentlemen.
    [*The* ACTORS *are horrified.*]

SON: [*Contemptuously to his stepsister.*] That's a filthy trick.

STEPDAUGHTER: A filthy trick? There it was in a pale blue envelope on the little mahogany table in the room behind the shop at Madame Pace's.

You know Madame Pace, don't you? One of those Madames who sell "Robes et Manteaux" so that they can attract poor girls like me from decent families into their workroom.[9]

SON: And she's bought the right to tyrannise over the whole lot of us with that money—with what he was going to pay her: and luckily—now listen carefully—he had no reason to pay it to her.

STEPDAUGHTER: But it was close!

MOTHER: [*Rising up angrily.*] Shame on you, daughter! Shame!

STEPDAUGHTER: Shame? Not shame, revenge! I'm desperate, desperate to live that scene! The room . . . over here the showcase of coats, there the divan, there the mirror, and the screen, and over there in front of the window, that little mahogany table with the pale blue envelope and the money in it. I can see it all quite clearly. I could pick it up! But you should turn your faces away, gentlemen: because I'm nearly naked! I'm not blushing any longer—I leave that to him. [*Pointing at the* FATHER.] But I tell you he was very pale, very pale then. [*To the* PRODUCER.] Believe me.

PRODUCER: I don't understand any more.

FATHER: I'm not surprised when you're attacked like that! Why don't you put your foot down and let me have my say before you believe all these horrible slanders she's so viciously telling about me.

STEPDAUGHTER: We don't want to hear any of your long winded fairy-stories.

FATHER: I'm not going to tell any fairy-stories! I want to explain things to him.

STEPDAUGHTER: I'm sure you do. Oh, yes! In your own special way.

[*The* PRODUCER *comes back up on stage to take control.*]

FATHER: But isn't that the cause of all the trouble? Words! We all have a world of things inside ourselves and each one of us has his own private world. How can we understand each other if the words I use have the sense and the value that I expect them to have, but whoever is listening to me inevitably thinks that those same words have a different sense and value, because of the private world he has inside himself too. We think we understand each other: but we never do. Look! All my pity, all my compassion for this woman [*Pointing to the* MOTHER.] she sees as ferocious cruelty.

MOTHER: But he turned me out of the house!

FATHER: There, do you hear? I turned her out! She really believed that I had turned her out.

MOTHER: You know how to talk. I don't . . . But believe me, sir, [*Turning to the* PRODUCER.] after he married me . . . I can't think why! I was a poor, simple woman.

FATHER: But that was the reason! I married you for your simplicity, that's what I loved in you, believing—[*He stops because she is making gestures of contradiction. Then, seeing the impossibility of making her understand, he throws his arms wide in a gesture of desperation and*

---

9. The implication is that Madame Pace (Italian for "peace") runs a call-girl operation under the guise of selling fashionable "dresses and coats."

turns back to the PRODUCER.] No, do you see? She says no! It's terrifying, sir, believe me, terrifying, her deafness, her mental deafness. [*He taps his forehead.*] Affection for her children, oh yes. But deaf, mentally deaf, deaf, sir, to the point of desperation.

STEPDAUGHTER: Yes, but make him tell you what good all his cleverness has brought us.

FATHER: If only we could see in advance all the harm that can come from the good we think we are doing.

[*The* LEADING ACTRESS, *who has been growing angry watching the* LEADING ACTOR *flirting with the* STEPDAUGHTER, *comes forward and snaps at the* PRODUCER.]

LEADING ACTRESS: Excuse me, are we going to go on with our rehearsal?

PRODUCER: Yes, of course. But I want to listen to this first.

YOUNG ACTOR: It's such a new idea.

YOUNG ACTRESS: It's fascinating.

LEADING ACTRESS: For those who are interested. [*She looks meaningfully at the* LEADING ACTOR.]

PRODUCER: [*To the* FATHER.] Look here, you must explain yourself more clearly. [*He sits down.*]

FATHER: Listen then. You see, there was a rather poor fellow working for me as my assistant and secretary, very loyal: he understood her in everything. [*Pointing to the* MOTHER.] But without a hint of deceit, you must believe that: he was good and simple, like her: neither of them was capable even of thinking anything wrong, let alone doing it.

STEPDAUGHTER: So instead he thought of it for them and did it too!

FATHER: It's not true! What I did was for their good—oh yes and mine too, I admit it! The time had come when I couldn't say a word to either of them without there immediately flashing between them a sympathetic look: each one caught the other's eye for advice, about how to take what I had said, how not to make me angry. Well, that was enough, as I'm sure you'll understand, to put me in a bad temper all the time, in a state of intolerable exasperation.

PRODUCER: Then why didn't you sack this secretary of yours?

FATHER: Right! In the end I did sack him! But then I had to watch this poor woman wandering about in the house on her own, forlorn, like a stray animal you take in out of pity.

MOTHER: It's quite true.

FATHER: [*Suddenly, turning to her, as if to stop her.*] And what about the boy? Is that true as well?

MOTHER: But first he tore my son from me, sir.

FATHER: But not out of cruelty! It was so that he could grow up healthy and strong, in touch with the earth.

STEPDAUGHTER: [*Pointing to the* SON *jeeringly.*] And look at the result!

FATHER: [*Quickly.*] And is it my fault, too, that he's grown up like this? I took him to a nurse in the country, a peasant, because his mother didn't seem strong enough to me, although she is from a humble family herself. In fact that was what made me marry her. Perhaps it was superstitious of me; but what was I to do? I've always had this dreadful longing for a kind of sound moral healthiness.

[*The* STEPDAUGHTER *breaks out again into noisy laughter.*]
Make her stop that! It's unbearable.
PRODUCER: Stop it will you? Let me listen, for God's sake.
[*When the* PRODUCER *has spoken to her, she resumes her previous position . . . absorbed and distant, a half-smile on her lips. The* PRODUCER *comes down into the auditorium again to see how it looks from there.*]
FATHER: I couldn't bear the sight of this woman near me. [*Pointing to the* MOTHER.] Not so much because of the annoyance she caused me, you see, or even the feeling of being stifled, being suffocated that I got from her, as for the sorrow, the painful sorrow that I felt for her.
MOTHER: And he sent me away.
FATHER: With everything you needed, to the other man, to set her free from me.
MOTHER: And to set yourself free!
FATHER: Oh, yes, I admit it. And what terrible things came out of it. But I did it for the best, and more for her than for me: I swear it! [*Folds his arms: then turns suddenly to the* MOTHER.] I never lost sight of you did I? Until that fellow, without my knowing it, suddenly took you off to another town one day. He was idiotically suspicious of my interest in them, a genuine interest, I assure you, without any ulterior motive at all. I watched the new little family growing up round her with unbelievable tenderness, she'll confirm that. [*He points to the* STEPDAUGHTER.]
STEPDAUGHTER: Oh yes, I can indeed. I was a pretty little girl, you know, with plaits down to my shoulders and my little frilly knickers showing under my dress—so pretty—he used to watch me coming out of school. He came to see how I was maturing.
FATHER: That's shameful! It's monstrous.
STEPDAUGHTER: No it isn't! Why do you say it is?
FATHER: It's monstrous! Monstrous. [*He turns excitedly to the* PRODUCER *and goes on in explanation.*] After she'd gone away [*Pointing to the* MOTHER.], my house seemed empty. She'd been like a weight on my spirit but she'd filled the house with her presence. Alone in the empty rooms I wandered about like a lost soul. This boy here, [*Indicating the* SON.] growing up away from home—whenever he came back to the home—I don't know—but he didn't seem to be mine any more. We needed the mother between us, to link us together, and so he grew up by himself, apart, with no connection to me either through intellect or love. And then—it must seem odd, but it's true—first I was curious about and then strongly attracted to the little family that had come about because of what I'd done. And the thought of them began to fill all the emptiness that I felt around me. I needed, I really needed to believe that she was happy, wrapped up in the simple cares of her life, lucky because she was better off away from the complicated torments of a soul like mine. And to prove it, I used to watch that child coming out of school.
STEPDAUGHTER: Listen to him! He used to follow me along the street; he used to smile at me and when we came near the house he'd wave his hand—like this! I watched him, wide-eyed, puzzled. I didn't know who

he was. I told my mother about him and she knew at once who it must be. [MOTHER *nods agreement.*] At first, she didn't let me go to school again, at any rate for a few days. But when I did go back, I saw him standing near the door again—looking ridiculous—with a brown paper bag in his hand. He came close and petted me: then he opened the bag and took out a beautiful straw hat with a hoop of rosebuds round it— for me!

PRODUCER: All this is off the point, you know.

SON: [*Contemptuously.*] Yes . . . literature, literature.

FATHER: What do you mean, literature? This is real life: real passions.

PRODUCER: That may be! But you can't put it on the stage just like that.

FATHER: That's right you can't. Because all this is only leading up to the main action. I'm not suggesting that this part should be put on the stage. In any case, you can see for yourself, [*Pointing at the* STEPDAUGHTER.] she isn't a pretty little girl any longer with plaits down to her shoulders.

STEPDAUGHTER: —and with frilly knickers showing under her frock.

FATHER: The drama begins now: and it's new and complex.

STEPDAUGHTER: [*Coming forward, fierce and brooding.*] As soon as my father died . . .

FATHER: [*Quickly, not giving her time to speak.*] They were so miserable. They came back here, but I didn't know about it because of the Mother's stubbornness. [*Pointing to the* MOTHER.] She can't really write you know; but she could have got her daughter to write, or the boy, or tell me that they needed help.

MOTHER: But tell me, sir, how could I have known how he felt?

FATHER: And hasn't that always been your fault? You've never known anything about how I felt.

MOTHER: After all the years away from him and after all that had happened.

FATHER: And was it my fault if that fellow took you so far away? [*Turning back to the* PRODUCER.] Suddenly, overnight, I tell you, he'd found a job away from here without my knowing anything about it. I couldn't possibly trace them; and then, naturally I suppose, my interest in them grew less over the years. The drama broke out, unexpected and violent, when they came back: when I was driven in misery by the needs of my flesh, still alive with desire . . . and it is misery, you know, unspeakable misery for the man who lives alone and who detests sordid, casual affairs; not old enough to do without women, but not young enough to be able to go and look for one without shame! Misery? Is that what I called it. It's horrible, it's revolting, because there isn't a woman who will give her love to him any more. And when he realises this, he should do without . . . It's easy to say though. Each of us, face to face with other men, is clothed with some sort of dignity, but we know only too well all the unspeakable things that go on in the heart. We surrender, we give in to temptation: but afterwards we rise up out of it very quickly, in a desperate hurry to rebuild our dignity, whole and firm as if it were a gravestone that would cover every sign and memory of our shame, and hide it from even our own eyes. Everyone's like that, only some of us haven't the courage to talk about it.

STEPDAUGHTER: But they've all got the courage to do it!

FATHER: Yes! But only in secret! That's why it takes more courage to talk about it! Because if a man does talk about it—what happens then?—everybody says he's a cynic. And it's simply not true; he's just like everybody else; only better perhaps, because he's not afraid to use his intelligence to point out the blushing shame of human bestiality, that man, the beast, shuts his eyes to, trying to pretend it doesn't exist. And what about woman—what is she like? She looks at you invitingly, teasingly. You take her in your arms. But as soon as she feels your arms round her she closes her eyes. It's the sign of her mission, the sign by which she says to a man, "Blind yourself—I'm blind!"

STEPDAUGHTER: And when she doesn't close her eyes any more? What then? When she doesn't feel the need to hide from herself any more, to shut her eyes and hide her own shame. When she can see instead, dispassionately and dry-eyed this blushing shame of a man who has blinded himself, who is without love. What then? Oh, then what disgust, what utter disgust she feels for all these intellectual complications, for all this philosophy that points to the bestiality of man and then tries to defend him, to excuse him ... I can't listen to him, sir. Because when a man says he needs to "simplify" life like this—reducing it to bestiality—and throws away every human scrap of innocent desire, genuine feeling, idealism, duty, modesty, shame, then there's nothing more contemptible and nauseating than his remorse—crocodile tears!

PRODUCER: Let's get to the point, let's get to the point. This is all chat.

FATHER: Right then! But a fact is like a sack—it won't stand up if it's empty. To make it stand up, first you have to put in it all the reasons and feelings that caused it in the first place. I couldn't possibly have known that when that fellow died they'd come back here, that they were desperately poor and that the Mother had gone out to work as a dressmaker, nor that she'd gone to work for Madame Pace, of all people.

STEPDAUGHTER: She's a very high-class dressmaker—you must understand that. She apparently has only high-class customers, but she has arranged things carefully so that these high-class customers in fact serve her—they give her a respectable front ... without spoiling things for the other ladies at the shop who are not quite so high-class at all.

MOTHER: Believe me, sir, the idea never entered my head that the old hag gave me work because she had an eye on my daughter ...

STEPDAUGHTER: Poor Mummy! Do you know what that woman would do when I took back the work that my mother had been doing? She would point out how the dress had been ruined by giving it to my mother to sew: she bargained, she grumbled. So, you see, I paid for it, while this poor woman here thought she was sacrificing herself for me and these two children, sewing dresses all night for Madame Pace.

[*The* ACTORS *make gestures and noises of disgust.*]

PRODUCER: [*Quickly.*] And there one day, you met ...

STEPDAUGHTER: [*Pointing at the* FATHER.] Yes, him. Oh, he was an old customer of hers! What a scene that's going to be, superb!

FATHER: With her, the mother, arriving—

STEPDAUGHTER: [*Quickly, viciously.*]—Almost in time!

FATHER: [*Crying out.*]—No, just in time, just in time! Because, luckily, I found out who she was in time. And I took them all back to my house, sir. Can you imagine the situation now, for the two of us living in the same house? She, just as you see her here: and I, not able to look her in the face.

STEPDAUGHTER: It's so absurd! Do you think it's possible for me, sir, after what happened at Madame Pace's, to pretend that I'm a modest little miss, well brought up and virtuous just so that I can fit in with his damned pretensions to a "sound moral healthiness"?

FATHER: This is the real drama for me; the belief that we all, you see, think of ourselves as one single person: but it's not true: each of us is several different people, and all these people live inside us. With one person we seem like this and with another we seem very different. But we always have the illusion of being the same person for everybody and of always being the same person in everything we do. But it's not true! It's not true! We find this out for ourselves very clearly when by some terrible chance we're suddenly stopped in the middle of doing something and we're left dangling there, suspended. We realise then, that every part of us was not involved in what we'd been doing and that it would be a dreadful injustice of other people to judge us only by this one action as we dangle there, hanging in chains, fixed for all eternity, as if the whole of one's personality were summed up in that single, interrupted action. Now do you understand this girl's treachery? She accidentally found me somewhere I shouldn't have been, doing something I shouldn't have been doing! She discovered a part of me that shouldn't have existed for her: and now she wants to fix on me a reality that I should never have had to assume for her: it came from a single brief and shameful moment in my life. This is what hurts me most of all. And you'll see that the play will make a tremendous impact from this idea of mine. But then, there's the position of the others. His . . . [*Pointing to the* SON.]

SON: [*Shrugging his shoulders scornfully.*] Leave me out of it. I don't come into this.

FATHER: Why don't you come into this?

SON: I don't come into it and I don't want to come into it, because you know perfectly well that I wasn't intended to be mixed up with you lot.

STEPDAUGHTER: We're vulgar, common people, you see! He's a fine gentleman. But you've probably noticed that every now and then I look at him contemptuously, and when I do, he lowers his eyes—he knows the harm he's done me.

SON: [*Not looking at her.*] I have?

STEPDAUGHTER: Yes, you. It's your fault, dearie, that I went on the streets! Your fault! [*Movement of horror from the* ACTORS.] Did you or didn't you, with your attitude, deny us—I won't say the intimacy of your home—but that simple hospitality that makes guests feel comfortable? We were intruders who had come to invade the country of your "legitimacy"! [*Turning to the* PRODUCER.] I'd like you to have seen some of the little scenes that went on between him and me, sir. He says that I tyrannised over everyone. But don't you see? It was because of the way he treated us. He called it "vile" that I should insist on the right we had to move into his house with my mother—and she's his mother too. And I went into the house as its mistress.

SON: [*Slowly coming forward.*] They're really enjoying themselves, aren't they, sir? It's easy when they all gang up against me. But try to imagine what happened: one fine day, there is a son sitting quietly at home and he sees arrive as bold as brass, a young woman like this, who cheekily asks for his father, and heaven knows what business she has with him. Then he sees her come back with the same brazen look in her eye accompanied by that little girl there: and he sees her treat his father— without knowing why—in a most ambiguous and insolent way—asking him for money in a tone that leads one to suppose he really ought to give it, because he is obliged to do so.

FATHER: But I was obliged to do so: I owed it to your mother.

SON: And how was I to know that? When had I ever seen her before? When had I ever heard her mentioned? Then one day I see her come in with her [*Pointing at the* STEPDAUGHTER.], that boy and that little girl: they say to me, "Oh, didn't you know? This is your mother, too." Little by little I began to understand, mostly from her attitude. [*Points to* STEPDAUGHTER.] Why they'd come to live in the house so suddenly. I can't and I won't say what I feel, and what I think. I wouldn't even like to confess it to myself. So I can't take any active part in this. Believe me, sir, I am a character who has not been fully developed dramatically, and I feel uncomfortable, most uncomfortable, in their company. So please leave me out of it.

FATHER: What! But it's precisely because you feel like this . . .

SON: [*Violently exasperated.*] How do you know what I feel?

FATHER: All right! I admit it! But isn't that a situation in itself? This with-drawing of yourself, it's cruel to me and to your mother: when she came back to the house, seeing you almost for the first time, not recognising you, but knowing that you're her own son . . . [*Turning to point out the* MOTHER *to the* PRODUCER.] There, look at her: she's weeping.

STEPDAUGHTER: [*Angrily, stamping her foot.*] Like the fool she is!

FATHER: [*Quickly pointing at the* STEPDAUGHTER *to the* PRODUCER.] She can't stand that young man, you know. [*Turning and referring to the* SON.] He says that he doesn't come into it, but he's really the pivot of the action! Look here at this little boy, who clings to his mother all the time, frightened, humiliated. And it's because of him over there! Per-haps this little boy's problem is the worst of all: he feels an outsider, more than the others do; he feels so mortified, so humiliated just being in the house,—because it's charity, you see. [*Quietly.*] He's like his father: timid; he doesn't say anything . . .

PRODUCER: It's not a good idea at all, using him: you don't know what a nuisance children are on the stage.

FATHER: He won't need to be on the stage for long. Nor will the little girl—she's the first to go.

PRODUCER: That's good! Yes. I tell you all this interests me—it interests me very much. I'm sure we've the material here for a good play.

STEPDAUGHTER: [*Trying to push herself in.*] With a character like me you have!

FATHER: [*Driving her off, wanting to hear what the* PRODUCER *has decided.*] You stay out of it!

PRODUCER: [*Going on, ignoring the interruption.*] It's new, yes.

FATHER: Oh, it's absolutely new!

PRODUCER: You've got a nerve, though, haven't you, coming here and throwing it at me like this?

FATHER: I'm sure you understand. Born as we are for the *stage* . . .

PRODUCER: Are you amateur actors?

FATHER: No! I say we are born for the stage because . . .

PRODUCER: Come on now! You're an old hand at this, at acting!

FATHER: No I'm not. I only act, as everyone does, the part in life that he's chosen for himself, or that others have chosen for him. And you can see that sometimes my own passion gets a bit out of hand, a bit theatrical, as it does with all of us.

PRODUCER: Maybe, maybe . . . But you do see, don't you, that without an author . . . I could give you someone's address . . .

FATHER: Oh no! Look here! You do it.

PRODUCER: Me? What are you talking about?

FATHER: Yes, you. Why not?

PRODUCER: Because I've never written anything!

FATHER: Well, why not start now, if you don't mind my suggesting it? There's nothing to it. Everybody's doing it. And your job is even easier, because we're here, all of us, alive before you.

PRODUCER: That's not enough.

FATHER: Why isn't it enough? When you've seen us live our drama . . .

PRODUCER: Perhaps so. But we'll still need someone to write it.

FATHER: Only to write it down, perhaps, while it happens in front of him—live—scene by scene. It'll be enough to sketch it out simply first and then run through it.

PRODUCER: [*Coming back up, tempted by the idea.*] Do you know I'm almost tempted . . . just for fun . . . it might work.

FATHER: Of course it will. You'll see what wonderful scenes will come right out of it! I could tell you what they will be!

PRODUCER: You tempt me . . . you tempt me! We'll give it a chance. Come with me to the office. [*Turning to the* ACTORS.] Take a break: but don't go far away. Be back in a quarter of an hour or twenty minutes. [*To the* FATHER.] Let's see, let's try it out. Something extraordinary might come out of this.

FATHER: Of course it will! Don't you think it'd be better if the others came too? [*Indicating the other* CHARACTERS.]

PRODUCER: Yes, come on, come on. [*Going, then turning to speak to the* ACTORS.] Don't forget: don't be late: back in a quarter of an hour.

[*The* PRODUCER *and the* SIX CHARACTERS *cross the stage and go. The* ACTORS *look at each other in astonishment.*]

LEADING ACTOR: Is he serious? What's he going to do?

YOUNG ACTOR: I think he's gone round the bend.

ANOTHER ACTOR: Does he expect to make up a play in five minutes?

YOUNG ACTOR: Yes, like the old actors in the commedia dell'arte![1]

LEADING ACTRESS: Well if he thinks I'm going to appear in that sort of nonsense . . .

YOUNG ACTOR: Nor me!

FOURTH ACTOR: I should like to know who they are.

THIRD ACTOR: Who do you think? They're probably escaped lunatics—or crooks.

YOUNG ACTOR: And is he taking them seriously?

YOUNG ACTRESS: It's vanity. The vanity of seeing himself as an author.

LEADING ACTOR: I've never heard of such a thing! If the theatre, ladies and gentlemen, is reduced to this . . .

FIFTH ACTOR: I'm enjoying it!

THIRD ACTOR: Really! We shall have to wait and see what happens next I suppose.

[*Talking, they leave the stage. Some go out through the back door, some to the dressing-rooms.*
The curtain stays up.
The interval lasts twenty minutes.]

Act Two

The theatre warning-bell sounds to call the audience back. From the dressing-rooms, the door at the back and even from the auditorium, the ACTORS, *the* STAGE MANAGER, *the* STAGE HANDS, *the* PROMPTER, *the* PROPERTY MAN *and the* PRODUCER, *accompanied by the* SIX CHARACTERS *all come back on to the stage.*
The house lights go out and the stage lights come on again.

PRODUCER: Come on, everybody! Are we all here? Quiet now! Listen! Let's get started! Stage manager?

STAGE MANAGER: Yes, I'm here.

PRODUCER: Give me that little parlour setting, will you? A couple of plain flats and a door flat will do. Hurry up with it!

[*The* STAGE MANAGER *runs off to order someone to do this immediately and at the same time the* PRODUCER *is making arrangements with the* PROPERTY MAN, *the* PROMPTER, *and the* ACTORS: *the two flats and the door flat are painted in pink and gold stripes.*]

PRODUCER: [*To* PROPERTY MAN.] Go see if we have a sofa in stock.

PROPERTY MAN: Yes, there's that green one.

STEPDAUGHTER: No, no, not a green one! It was yellow, yellow velvet with flowers on it: it was enormous! And so comfortable!

PROPERTY MAN: We haven't got one like that.

PRODUCER: It doesn't matter! Give me whatever there is.

STEPDAUGHTER: What do you mean, it doesn't matter? It was Mme. Pace's famous sofa.

PRODUCER: It's only for a rehearsal! Please, don't interfere. [*To the* STAGE

---

1. A form of popular theater beginning in 16th-century Italy; the actors improvised dialogue according to basic comic or dramatic plots and in response to the audience's reaction.

MANAGER.] Oh, and see if there's a shop window, will you—preferably a long, low one.

STEPDAUGHTER: And a little table, a little mahogany table for the blue envelope.

STAGE MANAGER: [*To the* PRODUCER.] There's that little gold one.

PRODUCER: That'll do—bring it.

FATHER: A mirror!

STEPDAUGHTER: And a screen! A screen, please, or I won't be able to manage, will I?

STAGE MANAGER: All right. We've lots of big screens, don't you worry.

PRODUCER: [*To* STEPDAUGHTER.] Then don't you want some coat-hangers and some clothes racks?

STEPDAUGHTER: Yes, lots of them, lots of them.

PRODUCER: [*To the* STAGE MANAGER]. See how many there are and have them brought up.

STAGE MANAGER: Right, I'll see to it.

> [*The* STAGE MANAGER *goes off to do it: and while the* PRODUCER *is talking to the* PROMPTER, *the* CHARACTERS *and the* ACTORS, *the* STAGE MANAGER *is telling the* SCENE SHIFTERS *where to set up the furniture they have brought.*]

PRODUCER: [*To the* PROMPTER.] Now you, go sit down, will you? Look, this is an outline of the play, act by act. [*He hands him several sheets of paper.*] But you'll need to be on your toes.

PROMPTER: Shorthand?

PRODUCER: [*Pleasantly surprised.*] Oh, good! You know shorthand?

PROMPTER: I don't know much about prompting, but I do know about shorthand.

PRODUCER: Thank God for that anyway! [*He turns to a* STAGE HAND.] Go fetch me some paper from my office—lots of it—as much as you can find!

> [*The* STAGE HAND *goes running off and then comes back shortly with a bundle of paper that he gives to the* PROMPTER.]

PRODUCER: [*Crossing to the* PROMPTER.] Follow the scenes, one after another, as they are played and try to get the lines down . . . at least the most important ones. [*Then turning to the* ACTORS.] Get out of the way everybody! Here, go over to the prompt side [*Pointing to stage left.*] and pay attention.

LEADING ACTRESS: But, excuse me, we . . .

PRODUCER: [*Anticipating her.*] You won't be expected to improvise, don't worry!

LEADING ACTOR: Then what are we expected to do?

PRODUCER: Nothing! Just go over there, listen and watch. You'll all be given your parts later written out. Right now we're going to rehearse, as well as we can. And they will be doing the rehearsal. [*He points to the* CHARACTERS.]

FATHER: [*Rather bewildered, as if he had fallen from the clouds into the middle of the confusion on the stage.*] We are? Excuse me, but what do you mean, a rehearsal?

PRODUCER: I mean a rehearsal—a rehearsal for the benefit of the actors.

[*Pointing to the* ACTORS.]

FATHER: But if we are the characters . . .

PRODUCER: That's right, you're "the characters": but characters don't act here, my dear chap. It's actors who act here. The characters are there in the script—[*Pointing to the* PROMPTER.] that's when there is a script.

FATHER: That's the point! Since there isn't one and you have the luck to have the characters alive in front of you. . .

PRODUCER: Great! You want to do everything yourselves, do you? To act your own play, to produce your own play!

FATHER: Well yes, just as we are.

PRODUCER: That would be an experience for us, I can tell you!

LEADING ACTOR: And what about us? What would we be doing then?

PRODUCER: Don't tell me you think you know how to act! Don't make me laugh! [*The* ACTORS *in fact laugh.*] There you are, you see, you've made them laugh. [*Then remembering.*] But let's get back to the point! We need to cast the play. Well, that's easy: it almost casts itself. [*To the* SECOND ACTRESS.] You, the mother. [*To the* FATHER.] You'll need to give her a name.

FATHER: Amalia.

PRODUCER: But that's the real name of your wife isn't it? We can't use her real name.

FATHER: But why not? That is her name . . . But perhaps if this lady is to play the part . . . [*Indicating the* ACTRESS *vaguely with a wave of his hand.*] I don't know what to say . . . I'm already starting to . . . how can I explain it . . . to sound false, my own words sound like someone else's.

PRODUCER: Now don't worry yourself about it, don't worry about it at all. We'll work out the right tone of voice. As for the name, if you want it to be Amalia, then Amalia it shall be: or we can find another. For the moment we'll refer to the characters like this: [*To the* YOUNG ACTOR, *the juvenile lead.*] you are The Son. [*To the* LEADING ACTRESS.] You, of course, are The Stepdaughter.

STEPDAUGHTER: [*Excitedly.*] What did you say? That woman is me? [*Bursts into laughter.*]

PRODUCER: [*Angrily.*] What are you laughing at?

LEADING ACTRESS: [*Indignantly.*] Nobody has ever dared to laugh at me before! Either you treat me with respect or I'm walking out! [*Starting to go.*]

STEPDAUGHTER: I'm sorry. I wasn't really laughing at you.

PRODUCER: [*To the* STEPDAUGHTER.] You should feel proud to be played by . . .

LEADING ACTRESS: [*Quickly, scornfully.*] . . . that woman!

STEPDAUGHTER: But I wasn't thinking about her, honestly. I was thinking about me: I can't see myself in you at all . . . you're not a bit like me!

FATHER: Yes, that's right: you see, our meaning . . .

PRODUCER: What are you talking about, "our meaning"? Do you think you have exclusive rights to what you represent? Do you think it can only exist inside you? Not a bit of it!

FATHER: What? Don't we even have our own meaning?

PRODUCER: Not a bit of it! Whatever you mean is only material here, to which the actors give form and body, voice and gesture, and who, through their art, have given expression to much better material than what you have to offer: yours is really very trivial and if it stands up on the stage, the credit, believe me, will all be due to my actors.

FATHER: I don't dare to contradict you. But you for your part, must believe me — it doesn't seem trivial to us. We are suffering terribly now, with these bodies, these faces . . .

PRODUCER: [*Interrupting impatiently.*] Yes, well, the make-up will change that, make-up will change that, at least as far as the faces are concerned.

FATHER: Yes, but the voices, the gestures . . .

PRODUCER: That's enough! You can't come on the stage here as yourselves. It is our actors who will represent you here: and let that be the end of it!

FATHER: I understand that. But now I think I see why our author who saw us alive as we are here now, didn't want to put us on the stage. I don't want to offend your actors. God forbid that I should! But I think that if I saw myself represented . . . by I don't know whom . . .

LEADING ACTOR: [*Rising majestically and coming forward, followed by a laughing group of* YOUNG ACTRESSES.] By me, if you don't object.

FATHER: [*Respectfully, smoothly.*] I shall be honoured, sir. [*He bows.*] But I think, that no matter how hard this gentleman works with all his will and all his art to identify himself with me . . . [*He stops, confused.*]

LEADING ACTOR: Yes, go on.

FATHER: Well, I was saying the performance he will give, even if he is made up to look like me . . . I mean with the difference in our appearance . . . [*All the* ACTORS *laugh.*] it will be difficult for it to be a performance of me as I really am. It will be more like — well, not just because of his figure — it will be more an interpretation of what I am, what he believes me to be, and not how I know myself to be. And it seems to me that this should be taken into account by those who are going to comment on us.

PRODUCER: So you are already worrying about what the critics will say, are you? And I'm still waiting to get this thing started! The critics can say what they like: and we'll worry about putting on the play. If we can! [*Stepping out of the group and looking around.*] Come on, come on! Is the scene set for us yet? [*To the* ACTORS *and* CHARACTERS.] Out of the way! Let's have a look at it. [*Climbing down off the stage.*] Don't let's waste any more time. [*To the* STEPDAUGHTER.] Does it look all right to you?

SON: What! That? I don't recognise it at all.

PRODUCER: Good God! Did you expect us to reconstruct the room at the back of Mme. Pace's shop here on the stage? [*To the* FATHER.] Did you say the room had flowered wallpaper?

FATHER: White, yes.

PRODUCER: Well it's not white: it's striped. That sort of thing doesn't matter at all! As for the furniture, it looks to me as if we have nearly everything we need. Move that little table a bit further downstage. [*A* STAGE HAND *does it. To the* PROPERTY MAN.] Go and fetch an envelope, pale blue if you can find one, and give it to that gentleman there. [*Pointing to the* FATHER.]

STAGE HAND: An envelope for letters?

PRODUCER: ⎫
⎬ Yes, an envelope for letters!
FATHER: ⎭

STAGE HAND: Right. [*He goes off.*]

PRODUCER: Now then, come on! The first scene is the young lady's. [*The* LEADING ACTRESS *comes to the centre.*] No, no, not yet. I said the young lady's. [*He points to the* STEPDAUGHTER.] You stay there and watch.

STEPDAUGHTER: [*Adding quickly.*] . . . how I bring it to life.

LEADING ACTRESS: [*Resenting this.*] I shall know how to bring it to life, don't you worry, when I am allowed to.

PRODUCER: [*His head in his hands.*] Ladies, please, no more arguments! Now then. The first scene is between the young lady and Mme. Pace. Oh! [*Worried, turning round and looking out into the auditorium.*] Where is Mme. Pace?

FATHER: She isn't here with us.

PRODUCER: So what do we do now?

FATHER: But she is real. She's real too!

PRODUCER: All right. So where is she?

FATHER: May I deal with this? [*Turns to the* ACTRESSES.] Would each of you ladies be kind enough to lend me a hat, a coat, a scarf or something?

ACTRESSES: [*Some are surprised or amused.*] What? My scarf? A coat? What's he want my hat for? What are you wanting to do with them? [*All the* ACTRESSES *are laughing.*]

FATHER: Oh, nothing much, just hang them up here on the racks for a minute or two. Perhaps someone would be kind enough to lend me a coat?

ACTORS: Just a coat? Come on, more! The man must be mad.

AN ACTRESS: What for? Only my coat?

FATHER: Yes, to hang up here, just for a moment. I'm very grateful to you. Do you mind?

ACTRESSES: [*Taking off various hats, coats, scarves, laughing and going to hang them on the racks.*] Why not? Here you are. I really think it's crazy. Is it to dress the set?

FATHER: Yes, exactly. It's to dress the set.

PRODUCER: Would you mind telling me what you are doing?

FATHER: Yes, of course: perhaps, if we dress the set better, she will be drawn by the articles of her trade and, who knows, she may even come to join us . . . [*He invites them to watch the door at the back of the set.*] Look! Look!

[*The door at the back opens and* MME. PACE *takes a few steps downstage: she is a gross old harridan wearing a ludicrous carroty-coloured wig with a single red rose stuck in at one side, Spanish fashion: garishly made-up: in a vulgar but stylish red silk dress, holding an ostrich-feather fan in one hand and a cigarette between two fingers in the other. At the sight of this apparition, the* ACTORS *and the* PRO-*

DUCER *immediately jump off the stage with cries of fear, leaping down into the auditorium and up the aisles. The* STEPDAUGHTER, *however, runs across to* MME. PACE, *and greets her respectfully, as if she were the mistress.*]

STEPDAUGHTER: [*Running across to her.*] Here she is! Here she is!

FATHER: [*Smiling broadly.*] It's her! What did I tell you? Here she is!

PRODUCER: [*Recovering from his shock, indignantly.*] What sort of trick is this?

LEADING ACTOR: [*Almost at the same time as the others.*] What the hell is happening?

JUVENILE LEAD: Where on earth did they get that extra from?

YOUNG ACTRESS: They were keeping her hidden!

LEADING ACTRESS: It's a game, a conjuring trick!

FATHER: Wait a minute! Why do you want to spoil a miracle by being factual. Can't you see this is a miracle of reality, that is born, brought to life, lured here, reproduced, just for the sake of this scene, with more right to be alive here than you have? Perhaps it has more truth than you have yourselves. Which actress can improve on Mme. Pace there? Well? That is the real Mme. Pace. You must admit that the actress who plays her will be less true than she is herself—and there she is in person! Look! My daughter recognised her straight away and went to meet her. Now watch—just watch this scene.

[*Hesitantly, the* PRODUCER *and the* ACTORS *move back to their original places on the stage.*

But the scene between the STEPDAUGHTER *and* MME. PACE *had already begun while the* ACTORS *were protesting and the* FATHER *explaining: it is being played under their breaths, very quietly, very naturally, in a way that is obviously impossible on stage. So when the* ACTORS' *attention is recalled by the* FATHER *they turn and see that* MME. PACE *has just put her hand under the* STEPDAUGHTER's *chin to make her lift her head up: they also hear her speak in a way that is unintelligible to them. They watch and listen hard for a few moments, then they start to make fun of them.*]

PRODUCER: Well?

LEADING ACTOR: What's she saying?

LEADING ACTRESS: Can't hear a thing!

JUVENILE LEAD: Louder! Speak up!

STEPDAUGHTER: [*Leaving* MME. PACE *who has an astonishing smile on her face, and coming down to the* ACTORS.] Louder? What do you mean, "Louder"? What we're talking about you can't talk about loudly. I could shout about it a moment ago to embarrass him [*Pointing to the* FATHER.] to shame him and to get my own back on him! But it's a different matter for Mme. Pace. It would mean prison for her.

PRODUCER: What the hell are you on about? Here in the theatre you have to make yourself heard! Don't you see that? We can't hear you even from here, and we're on the stage with you! Imagine what it would be like with an audience out front! You need to make the scene go! And after all, you would speak normally to each other when you're alone, and you will be, because we shan't be here anyway. I mean we're only here because it's a rehearsal. So just imagine that there you are in the room at the back of the shop, and there's no one to hear you.

[*The* STEPDAUGHTER, *with a knowing smile, wags her finger and her head rather elegantly, as if to say no.*]

PRODUCER: Why not?

STEPDAUGHTER: [*Mysteriously, whispering loudly.*] Because there is some-one who will hear if she speaks normally. [*Pointing to* MME. PACE.]

PRODUCER: [*Anxiously.*] You're not going to make someone else appear are you?

[*The* ACTORS *get ready to dive off the stage again.*]

FATHER: No, no. She means me. I ought to be over there, waiting behind the door: and Mme. Pace knows I'm there, so excuse me will you: I'll go there now so that I shall be ready for my entrance.

[*He goes towards the back of the stage.*]

PRODUCER: [*Stopping him.*] No, no wait a minute! You must remember the stage conventions! Before you can go on to that part . . .

STEPDAUGHTER: [*Interrupts him.*] Oh yes, let's get on with that part. Now! Now! I'm dying to do that scene. If he wants to go through it now, I'm ready!

PRODUCER: [*Shouting.*] But before that we must have, clearly stated, the scene between you and her. [*Pointing to* MME. PACE.] Do you see?

STEPDAUGHTER: Oh God! She's only told me what you already know, that my mother's needlework is badly done again, the dress is spoilt and that I shall have to be patient if I want her to go on helping us out of our mess.

MME. PACE: [*Coming forward, with a great air of importance.*] Ah, yes, sir, for that I do not wish to make a profit, to make advantage.

PRODUCER: [*Half frightened.*] What? Does she really speak like that?

[*All the* ACTORS *burst out laughing.*]

STEPDAUGHTER: [*Laughing too.*] Yes, she speaks like that, half in Spanish, in the silliest way imaginable!

MME. PACE: Ah it is not good manners that you laugh at me when I make myself to speak, as I can, English, señor.

PRODUCER: No, no, you're right! Speak like that, please speak like that, madam. It'll be marvelous. Couldn't be better! It'll add a little touch of comedy to a rather crude situation. Speak like that! It'll be great!

STEPDAUGHTER: Great! Why not? When you hear a proposition made in that sort of accent, it'll almost seem like a joke, won't it? Perhaps you'll want to laugh when you hear that there's an "old señor"[2] who wants to "amuse himself with me"—isn't that right, Madame?

MME. PACE: Not so old . . . but not quite young, no? But if he is not to your taste . . . he is, how you say, discreet!

[*The* MOTHER *leaps up, to the astonishment and dismay of the* ACTORS *who had not been paying any attention to her, so that when she shouts out they are startled and then smilingly restrain her: however she has already snatched off* MME. PACE*'s wig and flung it on the floor.*]

2. Old gentleman.

MOTHER: You witch! Witch! Murderess! Oh, my daughter!

STEPDAUGHTER: [*Running across and taking hold of the* MOTHER.] No! No! Mother! Please!

FATHER: [*Running across to her as well.*] Calm yourself, calm yourself! Come and sit down.

MOTHER: Get her away from here!

STEPDAUGHTER: [*To the* PRODUCER *who has also crossed to her.*] My mother can't bear to be in the same place with her.

FATHER: [*Also speaking quietly to the* PRODUCER.] They can't possibly be in the same place! That's why she wasn't with us when we first came, do you see! If they meet, everything's given away from the very beginning.

PRODUCER: It's not important, that's not important! This is only a first run-through at the moment! It's all useful stuff, even if it is confused. I'll sort it all out later. [*Turning to the* MOTHER *and taking her to sit down on her chair.*] Come on, my dear, take it easy; take it easy: come and sit down again.

STEPDAUGHTER: Go on, Mme. Pace.

MME. PACE: [*Offended.*] Oh no, thank-you! I no longer do nothing here with your mother present.

STEPDAUGHTER: Get on with it, bring in this "old señor" who wants to "amuse himself with me"! [*Turning majestically to the others.*] You see, this next scene has got to be played out—we must do it now. [*To* MME. PACE.] Oh, you can go!

MME. PACE: Ah, I go, I go—I go! Most probably! I go!

[*She leaves banging her wig back into place, glaring furiously at the* ACTORS *who applaud her exit, laughing loudly.*]

STEPDAUGHTER: [*To the* FATHER.] Now you come on! No, you don't need to go off again! Come back! Pretend you've just come in! Look, I'm standing here with my eyes on the ground, modestly—well, come on, speak up! Use that special sort of voice, like somebody who has just come in. "Good afternoon, my dear."

PRODUCER: [*Off the stage by now.*] Look here, who's the director here, you or me? [*To the* FATHER *who looks uncertain and bewildered.*] Go on, do as she says: go upstage—no, no don't bother to make an entrance. Then come down stage again.

[*The* FATHER *does as he is told, half mesmerised. He is very pale but already involved in the reality of his re-created life, smiles as he draws near the back of the stage, almost as if he genuinely is not aware of the drama that is about to sweep over him. The* ACTORS *are immediately intent on the scene that is beginning now.*]

The Scene

FATHER: [*Coming forward with a new note in his voice.*] Good afternoon, my dear.

STEPDAUGHTER: [*Her head down trying to hide her fright.*] Good afternoon.

FATHER: [*Studying her a little under the brim of her hat which partly hides her face from him and seeing that she is very young, he exclaims to*

himself a little complacently and a little guardedly because of the dan-
ger of being compromised in a risky adventure.] Ah . . . but . . . tell me,
this won't be the first time, will it? The first time you've been here?
STEPDAUGHTER: No, sir.
FATHER: You've been here before? [*And after the* STEPDAUGHTER *has nod-*
ded an answer.] More than once? [*He waits for her reply: tries again to*
look at her under the brim of her hat: smiles: then says.] Well then . . .
it shouldn't be too . . . May I take off your hat?
STEPDAUGHTER: [*Quickly, to stop him, unable to conceal her shudder of*
fear and disgust.] No, don't! I'll do it!
     [*She takes it off unsteadily.*
     The MOTHER *watches the scene intently with the* SON *and the two*
     smaller children who cling close to her all the time: they make a
     group on one side of the stage opposite the ACTORS: *She follows the*
     words and actions of the FATHER *and the* STEPDAUGHTER *in this scene*
     with a variety of expressions on her face—sadness, dismay, anxiety,
     horror: sometimes she turns her face away and sobs.]
MOTHER: Oh God! Oh God!
FATHER: [*He stops as if turned to stone by the sobbing: then he goes on in*
the same tone of voice.] Here, give it to me. I'll hang it up for you. [*He*
takes the hat in his hand.] But such a pretty, dear little head like yours
should have a much smarter hat than this! Would you like to help me
choose one, then, from these hats of Madame's hanging up here?
Would you?
YOUNG ACTRESS: [*Interrupting.*] Be careful! Those are our hats!
PRODUCER: [*Quickly and angrily.*] For God's sake, shut up! Don't try to be
funny! We're rehearsing! [*Turns back to the* STEPDAUGHTER.] Please go
on, will you, from where you were interrupted.
STEPDAUGHTER: [*Going on.*] No, thank you, sir.
FATHER: Oh, don't say no to me please! Say you'll have one—to please
me. Isn't this a pretty one—look! And then it will please Madame too,
you know. She's put them out here on purpose, of course.
STEPDAUGHTER: No, look, I could never wear it.
FATHER: Are you thinking of what they would say at home when you went
in wearing a new hat? Goodness me! Don't you know what to do? Shall
I tell you what to say at home?
STEPDAUGHTER: [*Furiously, nearly exploding.*] That's not why! I couldn't
wear it because . . . as you can see: you should have noticed it before.
[*Indicating her black dress.*]
FATHER: You're in mourning! Oh, forgive me. You're right, I see that now.
Please forgive me. Believe me, I'm really very sorry.
STEPDAUGHTER: [*Gathering all her strength and making herself overcome*
her contempt and revulsion.] That's enough. Don't go on, that's
enough. I ought to be thanking you and not letting you blame yourself
and get upset. Don't think any more about what I told you, please. And
I should do the same. [*Forcing herself to smile and adding.*] I should
try to forget that I'm dressed like this.
PRODUCER: [*Interrupting, turning to the* PROMPTER *in the box and jump-*
ing up on the stage again]. Hold it, hold it! Don't put that last line

down, leave it out. [*Turning to the* FATHER *and the* STEPDAUGHTER.] It's going well! It's going well! [*Then to the* FATHER *alone.*] Then we'll put in there the bit that we talked about. [*To the* ACTORS.] That scene with the hats is good, isn't it?

STEPDAUGHTER: But the best bit is coming now! Why can't we get on with it?

PRODUCER: Just be patient, wait a minute. [*Turning and moving across to the* ACTORS.] Of course, it'll all have to be made a lot more light-hearted.

LEADING ACTOR: We shall have to play it a lot quicker, I think.

LEADING ACTRESS: Of course: there's nothing particularly difficult in it. [*To the* LEADING ACTOR.] Shall we run through it now?

LEADING ACTOR: Yes right . . . Shall we take it from my entrance? [*He goes to his position behind the door upstage.*]

PRODUCER: [*To the* LEADING ACTRESS.] Now then, listen, imagine the scene between you and Mme. Pace is finished. I'll write it up myself properly later on. You ought to be over here I think—[*She goes the opposite way.*] Where are you going now?

LEADING ACTRESS: Just a minute, I want to get my hat—[*She crosses to take her hat from the stand.*]

PRODUCER: Right, good, ready now? You are standing here with your head down.

STEPDAUGHTER: [*Very amused.*] But she's not dressed in black!

LEADING ACTRESS: Oh, but I shall be, and I'll look a lot better than you do, darling.

PRODUCER: [*To the* STEPDAUGHTER.] Shut up, will you! Go over there and watch! You might learn something! [*Clapping his hands.*] Right! Come on! Quiet please! Take it from his entrance.

[*He climbs off stage so that he can see better. The door opens at the back of the set and the* LEADING ACTOR *enters with the lively, knowing air of an ageing roué.[3] The playing of the following scene by the* ACTORS *must seem from the very beginning to be something quite different from the earlier scene, but without having the faintest air of parody in it.*

Naturally the STEPDAUGHTER *and the* FATHER *unable to see themselves in the* LEADING ACTOR *and* LEADING ACTRESS, *hearing their words said by them, express their reactions in different ways, by gestures, or smiles or obvious protests so that we are aware of their suffering, their astonishment, their disbelief.*

The PROMPTER's *voice is heard clearly between every line in the scene, telling the* ACTORS *what to say next.*]

LEADING ACTOR: Good afternoon, my dear.

FATHER: [*Immediately, unable to restrain himself.*] Oh, no!

[*The* STEPDAUGHTER, *watching the* LEADING ACTOR *enter this way, bursts into laughter.*]

PRODUCER: [*Furious.*] Shut up, for God's sake! And don't you dare laugh like that! We're never going to get anywhere at this rate.

STEPDAUGHTER: [*Coming to the front.*] I'm sorry, I can't help it! The lady

---

3. Dissipated lover.

stands exactly where you told her to stand and she never moved. But if
it were me and I heard someone say good afternoon to me in that way
and with a voice like that I should burst out laughing—so I did.

FATHER: [*Coming down a little too.*] Yes, she's right, the whole manner,
the voice . . .

PRODUCER: To hell with the manner and the voice! Get out of the way,
will you, and let me watch the rehearsal!

LEADING ACTOR: [*Coming down stage.*] If I have to play an old man who
has come to a knocking shop—

PRODUCER: Take no notice, ignore them. Go on please! It's going well, it's
going well! [*He waits for the* ACTOR *to begin again.*] Right, again!

LEADING ACTOR: Good afternoon, my dear.

LEADING ACTRESS: Good afternoon.

LEADING ACTOR: [*Copying the gestures of the* FATHER, *looking under the
brim of the hat, but expressing distinctly the two emotions, first, complacent satisfaction and then anxiety.*] Ah! But tell me . . . this won't be the
first time I hope.

FATHER: [*Instinctively correcting him.*] Not "I hope"—"will it," "will it."

PRODUCER: Say "will it"—and it's a question.

LEADING ACTOR: [*Glaring at the* PROMPTER.] I distinctly heard him say "I
hope."

PRODUCER: So what? It's all the same, "I hope" or "isn't it." It doesn't make
any difference. Carry on, carry on. But perhaps it should still be a little
bit lighter; I'll show you—watch me! [*He climbs up on the stage again,
and going back to the entrance, he does it himself.*] Good afternoon,
my dear.

LEADING ACTRESS: Good afternoon.

PRODUCER: Ah, tell me . . . [*He turns to the* LEADING ACTOR *to make sure
that he has seen the way he has demonstrated of looking under the brim
of the hat.*] You see—surprise . . . anxiety and self-satisfaction. [*Then,
starting again, he turns to the* LEADING ACTRESS.] This won't be the first
time, will it? The first time you've been here? [*Again turns to the* LEAD-
ING ACTOR *questioningly.*] Right? [*To the* LEADING ACTRESS.] And then
she says, "No, sir." [*Again to* LEADING ACTOR.] See what I mean? More
subtlety. [*And he climbs off the stage.*]

LEADING ACTRESS: No, sir.

LEADING ACTOR: You've been here before? More than once?

PRODUCER: No, no, no! Wait for it, wait for it. Let her answer first. "You've
been here before?"

[*The* LEADING ACTRESS *lifts her head a little, her eyes closed in pain
and disgust, and when the* PRODUCER *says "Now" she nods her head
twice.*]

STEPDAUGHTER: [*Involuntarily.*] Oh, my God! [*And she immediately claps
her hand over her mouth to stifle her laughter.*]

PRODUCER: What now?

STEPDAUGHTER: [*Quickly.*] Nothing, nothing!

PRODUCER: [*To* LEADING ACTOR.] Come on, then, now it's you.

LEADING ACTOR: More than once? Well then, it shouldn't be too . . . May
I take off your hat?

[*The* LEADING ACTOR *says this last line in such a way and adds to it such a gesture that the* STEPDAUGHTER, *even with her hand over her mouth trying to stop herself laughing, can't prevent a noisy burst of laughter.*]

LEADING ACTRESS: [*Indignantly turning.*] I'm not staying any longer to be laughed at by that woman!

LEADING ACTOR: Nor am I! That's the end—no more!

PRODUCER: [*To* STEPDAUGHTER, *shouting.*] Once and for all, will you shut up! Shut up!

STEPDAUGHTER: Yes, I'm sorry . . . I'm sorry.

PRODUCER: You're an ill-mannered little bitch! That's what you are! And you've gone too far this time!

FATHER: [*Trying to interrupt.*] Yes, you're right, she went too far, but please forgive her . . .

PRODUCER: [*Jumping on the stage.*] Why should I forgive her? Her behaviour is intolerable!

FATHER: Yes, it is, but the scene made such a peculiar impact on us . . .

PRODUCER: Peculiar? What do you mean peculiar? Why peculiar?

FATHER: I'm full of admiration for your actors, for this gentleman [*To the* LEADING ACTOR.] and this lady. [*To the* LEADING ACTRESS.] But, you see, well . . . they're not us!

PRODUCER: Right! They're not! They're actors!

FATHER: That's just the point—they're actors. And they are acting our parts very well, both of them. But that's what's different. However much they want to be the same as us, they're not.

PRODUCER: But why aren't they? What is it now?

FATHER: It's something to do with . . . being themselves, I suppose, not being us.

PRODUCER: Well we can't do anything about that! I've told you already. You can't play the parts yourselves.

FATHER: Yes, I know, I know . . .

PRODUCER: Right then. That's enough of that. [*Turning back to the* ACTORS.] We'll rehearse this later on our own, as we usually do. It's always a bad idea to have rehearsals with authors there! They're never satisfied. [*Turns back to the* FATHER *and the* STEPDAUGHTER.] Come on, let's get on with it; and let's see if it's possible to do it without laughing.

STEPDAUGHTER: I won't laugh any more, I won't really. My best bit's coming up now, you wait and see!

PRODUCER: Right: when you say "Don't think any more about what I told you, please. And I should do the same." [*Turning to the* FATHER.] Then you come in immediately with the line "I understand, ah yes, I understand" and then you ask . . .

STEPDAUGHTER: [*Interrupting.*] Ask what? What does he ask?

PRODUCER: Why you're in mourning.

STEPDAUGHTER: No! No! That's not right! Look: when I said that I should try not to think abut the way I was dressed, do you know what he said? "Well then, let's take it off, we'll take it off at once, shall we, your little black dress."

PRODUCER: That's great! That'll be wonderful! That'll bring the house down!

STEPDAUGHTER: But it's the truth!

PRODUCER: The truth! Do me a favour will you? This is the theatre you know! Truth's all very well up to a point but . . .

STEPDAUGHTER: What do you want to do then?

PRODUCER: You'll see! You'll see! Leave it all to me.

STEPDAUGHTER: No. No I won't. I know what you want to do! Out of my feeling of revulsion, out of all the vile and sordid reasons why I am what I am, you want to make a sugary little sentimental romance. You want him to ask me why I'm in mourning and you want me to reply with the tears running down my face that it is only two months since my father died. No. No. I won't have it! He must say to me what he really did say. "Well then, let's take it off, we'll take it off at once, shall we, your little black dress." And I, with my heart still grieving for my father's death only two months before, I went behind there, do you see? Behind that screen and with my fingers trembling with shame and loathing I took off the dress, unfastened my bra . . .

PRODUCER: [*His head in his hands.*] For God's sake! What are you saying!

STEPDAUGHTER: [*Shouting excitedly.*] The truth! I'm telling you the truth!

PRODUCER: All right then, Now listen to me. I'm not denying it's the truth. Right. And believe me I understand your horror, but you must see that we can't really put a scene like that on the stage.

STEPDAUGHTER: You can't? Then thanks very much. I'm not stopping here.

PRODUCER: No, listen . . .

STEPDAUGHTER: No, I'm going. I'm not stopping. The pair of you have worked it all out together, haven't you, what to put in the scene. Well, thank you very much! I understand everything now! He wants to get to the scene where he can talk about his spiritual torments but I want to show you my drama! Mine!

PRODUCER: [*Shaking with anger.*] Now we're getting to the real truth of it, aren't we? Your drama—yours! But it's not only yours, you know. It's drama for the other people as well! For him [*Pointing to the* FATHER.] and for your mother! You can't have one character coming on like you're doing, trampling over the others, taking over the play. Everything needs to be balanced and in harmony so that we can show what has to be shown! I know perfectly well that we've all got a life inside us and that we all want to parade it in front of other people. But that's the difficulty, how to present only the bits that are necessary in relation to the other characters: and in the small amount we show, to hint at all the rest of the inner life of the character! I agree, it would be so much simpler, if each character, in a soliloquy or in a lecture could pour out to the audience what's bubbling away inside him. But that's not the way we work. [*In an indulgent, placating tone.*] You must restrain yourself, you see. And believe me, it's in your own interests: because you could so easily make a bad impression, with all this uncontrollable anger, this disgust and exasperation. That seems a bit odd, if you don't mind my saying so, when you've admitted that you'd been with other men at Mme. Pace's and more than once.

STEPDAUGHTER: I suppose that's true. But you know, all the other men were all him as far as I was concerned.

PRODUCER: [*Not understanding.*] Uum—? What? What are you talking about?

STEPDAUGHTER: If someone falls into evil ways, isn't the responsibility for all the evil which follows to be laid at the door of the person who caused the first mistake? And in my case, it's him, from before I was even born. Look at him: see if it isn't true.

PRODUCER: Right then! What about the weight of remorse he's carrying? Isn't that important? Then, give him the chance to show it to us.

STEPDAUGHTER: But how? How on earth can he show all his long-suffering remorse, all his moral torments as he calls them, if you don't let him show his horror when he finds me in his arms one fine day, after he had asked me to take my dress off, a black dress for my father who had just died: and he finds that I'm the child he used to go and watch as she came out of school, me, a woman now, and a woman he could buy. [*She says these last words in a voice trembling with emotion.*]

[*The* MOTHER, *hearing her say this, is overcome and at first gives way to stifled sobs: but then she bursts out into uncontrollable crying. Everyone is deeply moved. There is a long pause.*]

STEPDAUGHTER: [*As soon as the* MOTHER *has quietened herself she goes on, firmly and thoughtfully.*] At the moment we are here on our own and the public doesn't know about us. But tomorrow you will present us and our story in whatever way you choose, I suppose. But wouldn't you like to see the real drama? Wouldn't you like to see it explode into life, as it really did?

PRODUCER: Of course, nothing I'd like better, then I can use as much of it as possible.

STEPDAUGHTER: Then persuade my mother to leave.

MOTHER: [*Rising and her quiet weeping changing to a loud cry.*] No! No! Don't let her! Don't let her do it!

PRODUCER: But they're only doing it for me to watch—only for me, do you see?

MOTHER: I can't bear it, I can't bear it!

PRODUCER: But if it's already happened, I can't see what's the objection.

MOTHER: No! It's happening now, as well: it's happening all the time. I'm not acting my suffering! Can't you understand that? I'm alive and here now but I can never forget that terrible moment of agony, that repeats itself endlessly and vividly in my mind. And these two little children here, you've never heard them speak have you? That's because they don't speak any more, not now. They just cling to me all the time: they help to keep my grief alive, but they don't really exist for themselves any more, not for themselves. And she [*indicating the* STEPDAUGHTER] . . . she has gone away, left me completely, she's lost to me, lost . . . you see her here for one reason only: to keep perpetually before me, always real, the anguish and the torment I've suffered on her account.

FATHER: The eternal moment, as I told you, sir. She is here [*indicating the* STEPDAUGHTER] to keep me too in that moment, trapped for all eternity, chained and suspended in that one fleeting shameful moment of my life. She can't give up her role and you cannot rescue me from it.

PRODUCER: But I'm not saying that we won't present that bit. Not at all! It will be the climax of the first act, when she [*he points to the* MOTHER] surprises you.

FATHER: That's right, because that is the moment when I am sentenced: all our suffering should reach a climax in her cry. [*Again indicating the* MOTHER.]

STEPDAUGHTER: I can still hear it ringing in my ears! It was that cry that sent me mad! You can have me played just as you like: it doesn't matter! Dressed, too, if you want, so long as I can have at least an arm—only an arm—bare, because, you see, as I was standing like this [*she moves across to the* FATHER *and leans her head on his chest*] with my head like this and my arms round his neck, I saw a vein, here in my arm, throbbing: and then it was almost as if that throbbing vein filled me with a shivering fear, and I shut my eyes tightly like this, like this and buried my head in his chest. [*Turning to the* MOTHER.] Scream, Mummy, scream. [*She buries her head in the* FATHER'*s chest, and with her shoulders raised as if to try not to hear the scream, she speaks with a voice tense with suffering.*] Scream, as you screamed then!

MOTHER: [*Coming forward to pull them apart.*] No! She's my daughter! My daughter! [*Tearing her from him.*] You brute, you animal, she's my daughter! Can't you see she's my daughter?

PRODUCER: [*Retreating as far as the footlights while the* ACTORS *are full of dismay.*] Marvellous! Yes, that's great! And then curtain, curtain!

FATHER: [*Running downstage to him, excitedly.*] That's it, that's it! Because it really was like that!

PRODUCER: [*Full of admiration and enthusiasm.*] Yes, yes, that's got to be the curtain line! Curtain! Curtain!

[*At the repeated calls of the* PRODUCER, *the* STAGE MANAGER *lowers the curtain, leaving on the apron in front, the* PRODUCER *and the* FATHER.]

PRODUCER: [*Looking up to heaven with his arms raised.*] The idiots! I didn't mean now! The bloody idiots—dropping it in on us like that! [*To the* FATHER, *and lifting up a corner of the curtain.*] That's marvellous! Really marvellous! A terrific effect! We'll end the act like that! It's the best tag line I've heard for ages. What a First Act ending! I couldn't have done better if I'd written it myself!

[*They go through the curtain together.*]

Act Three

When the curtain goes up we see that the STAGE MANAGER *and* STAGE HANDS *have struck the first scene and have set another, a small garden fountain.*

From one side of the stage the ACTORS *come on and from the other the* CHARACTERS. *The* PRODUCER *is standing in the middle of the stage with his hand over his mouth, thinking.*

PRODUCER: [*After a short pause, shrugging his shoulders.*] Well, then: let's get on to the second act! Leave it all to me, and everything will work out properly.

STEPDAUGHTER: This is where we go to live at his house [*pointing to the* FATHER] in spite of the objections of him over there. [*Pointing to the* SON.]

PRODUCER: [*Getting impatient.*] All right, all right! But leave it all to me, will you?

STEPDAUGHTER: Provided that you make it clear that he objected!

MOTHER: [*From the corner, shaking her head.*] That doesn't matter. The worse it was for us, the more he suffered from remorse.

PRODUCER: [*Impatiently.*] I know, I know! I'll take it all into account. Don't worry!

MOTHER: [*Pleading.*] To set my mind at rest, sir, please do make sure it's clear that I tried all I could—

STEPDAUGHTER: [*Interrupting her scornfully and going on.*] —to pacify me, to persuade me that this despicable creature wasn't worth making trouble about! [*To the* PRODUCER.] Go on, set her mind at rest, because it's true, she tried very hard. I'm having a whale of a time now! You can see, can't you, that the meeker she was and the more she tried to worm her way into his heart, the more lofty and distant he became! How's that for a dramatic situation!

PRODUCER: Do you think that we can actually begin the Second Act?

STEPDAUGHTER: I won't say another word! But you'll see that it won't be possible to play everything in the garden, like you want to do.

PRODUCER: Why not?

STEPDAUGHTER: [*Pointing to the* SON.] Because to start with, he stays shut up in his room in the house all the time! And then all the scenes for this poor little devil of a boy happen in the house. I've told you once.

PRODUCER: Yes, I know that! But on the other hand we can't put up a notice to tell the audience where the scene is taking place, or change the set three or four times in each Act.

LEADING ACTOR: That's what they used to do in the good old days.

PRODUCER: Yes, when the audience was about as bright as that little girl over there!

LEADING ACTRESS: And it makes it easier to create an illusion.

FATHER: [*Leaping up.*] An illusion? For pity's sake don't talk about illusions! Don't use that word, it's especially hurtful to us!

PRODUCER: [*Astonished.*] And why, for God's sake?

FATHER: It's so hurtful, so cruel! You ought to have realised that!

PRODUCER: What else should we call it? That's what we do here—create an illusion for the audience . . .

LEADING ACTOR: With our performance . . .

PRODUCER: A perfect illusion of reality!

FATHER: Yes, I know that, I understand. But on the other hand, perhaps you don't understand us yet. I'm sorry! But you see, for you and for your actors what goes on here on the stage is, quite rightly, well, it's only a game.

LEADING ACTRESS: [*Interrupting indignantly.*] A game! How dare you! We're not children! What happens here is serious!

FATHER: I'm not saying that it isn't serious. And I mean, really, not just a game but an art, that tries, as you've just said, to create the perfect illusion of reality.

PRODUCER: That's right!

FATHER: Now try to imagine that we, as you see us here, [*he indicates himself and the other* CHARACTERS] that we have no other reality outside this illusion.

PRODUCER: [*Astonished and looking at the* ACTORS *with the same sense of bewilderment as they feel themselves.*] What the hell are you talking about now?

FATHER: [*After a short pause as he looks at them, with a faint smile.*] Isn't it obvious? What other reality is there for us? What for you is an illusion you create, for us is our only reality. [*Brief pause. He moves towards the* PRODUCER *and goes on.*] But it's not only true for us, it's true for others as well, you know. Just think about it. [*He looks intently into the* PRODUCER's *eyes.*] Do you really know who you are? [*He stands pointing at the* PRODUCER.]

PRODUCER: [*A little disturbed but with a half smile.*] What? Who I am? I am me!

FATHER: What if I told you that that wasn't true: what if I told you that you were me?

PRODUCER: I would tell you that you were mad!

[*The* ACTORS *laugh.*]

FATHER: That's right, laugh! Because everything here is a game! [*To the* PRODUCER.] And yet you object when I say that it is only for a game that the gentleman there [*pointing to the* LEADING ACTOR] who is "himself" has to be "me," who, on the contrary, am "myself." You see, I've caught you in a trap.

[*The* ACTORS *start to laugh.*]

PRODUCER: Not again! We've heard all about this a little while ago.

FATHER: No, no. I didn't really want to talk about this. I'd like you to forget about your game. [*Looking at the* LEADING ACTRESS *as if to anticipate what she will say.*] I'm sorry—your artistry! Your art!—that you usually pursue here with your actors; and I am going to ask you again in all seriousness, who are you?

PRODUCER: [*Turning with a mixture of amazement and annoyance, to the* ACTORS.] Of all the bloody nerve! A fellow who claims he is only a character comes and asks me who I am!

FATHER: [*With dignity but without annoyance.*] A character, my dear sir, can always ask a man who he is, because a character really has a life of his own, a life full of his own specific qualities, and because of these he is always "someone." While a man—I'm not speaking about you personally, of course, but man in general—well, he can be an absolute "nobody."

PRODUCER: All right, all right! Well, since you've asked me, I'm the Director, the Producer—I'm in charge! Do you understand?

FATHER: [*Half smiling, but gently and politely.*] I'm only asking to try to find out if you really see yourself now in the same way that you saw yourself, for instance, once upon a time in the past, with all the illusions you had then, with everything inside and outside yourself as it seemed then—and not only seemed, but really was! Well then, look back on those illusions, those ideas that you don't have any more, on all those things that no longer seem the same to you. Don't you feel that not only this stage is falling away from under your feet but so is the earth itself, and that all these realities of today are going to seem tomorrow as if they had been an illusion?

PRODUCER: So? What does that prove?

FATHER: Oh, nothing much. I only want to make you see that if we [*pointing to himself and the other* CHARACTERS] have no other reality outside our own illusion, perhaps you ought to distrust your own sense of reality: because whatever is a reality today, whatever you touch and believe in and that seems real for you today, is going to be—like the reality of yesterday—an illusion tomorrow.

PRODUCER: [*Deciding to make fun of him.*] Very good! So now you're saying that you as well as this play you're going to show me here, are more real than I am?

FATHER: [*Very seriously.*] There's no doubt about that at all.

PRODUCER: Is that so?

FATHER: I thought you'd realised that from the beginning.

PRODUCER: More real than I am?

FATHER: If your reality can change between today and tomorrow—

PRODUCER: But everybody knows that it can change, don't they? It's always changing! Just like everybody else's!

FATHER: [*Crying out.*] But ours doesn't change! Do you see? That's the difference! Ours doesn't change, it can't change, it can never be different, never, because it is already determined, like this, for ever, that's what's so terrible! We are an eternal reality. That should make you shudder to come near us.

PRODUCER: [*Jumping up, suddenly struck by an idea, and standing directly in front of the* FATHER.] Then I should like to know when anyone saw a character step out of his part and make a speech like you've done, proposing things, explaining things. Tell me when, will you? I've never seen it before.

FATHER: You've never seen it because an author usually hides all the difficulties of creating. When the characters are alive, really alive and standing in front of their author, he has only to follow their words, the actions that they suggest to him: and he must want them to be what they want to be: and it's his bad luck if he doesn't do what they want! When a character is born he immediately assumes such an independence even of his own author that everyone can imagine him in scores of situations that his author hadn't even thought of putting him in, and he sometimes acquires a meaning that his author never dreamed of giving him.

PRODUCER: Of course I know all that.

FATHER: Well, then. Why are you surprised by us? Imagine what a disaster it is for a character to be born in the imagination of an author who then

refuses to give him life in a written script. Tell me if a character, left like this, suspended, created but without a final life, isn't right to do what we are doing now, here in front of you. We spent such a long time, such a very long time, believe me, urging our author, persuading him, first me, then her, [*pointing to the* STEPDAUGHTER] then this poor Mother . . .

STEPDAUGHTER: [*Coming down the stage as if in a dream.*] It's true, I would go, would go and tempt him, time after time, in his gloomy study just as it was growing dark, when he was sitting quietly in an armchair not even bothering to switch a light on but leaving the shadows to fill the room: the shadows were swarming with us, we had come to tempt him. [*As if she could see herself there in the study and is annoyed by the presence of the* ACTORS.] Go away will you! Leave us alone! Mother there, with that son of hers—me with the little girl—that poor little kid always on his own—and then me with him [*pointing to the* FATHER] and then at last, just me, on my own, all on my own, in the shadows. [*She turns quickly as if she wants to cling on to the vision she has of herself, in the shadows.*] Ah, what scenes, what scenes we suggested to him! What a life I could have had! I tempted him more than the others!

FATHER: Oh yes, you did! And it was probably all your fault that he did nothing about it! You were so insistent, you made too many demands.

STEPDAUGHTER: But he wanted me to be like that! [*She comes closer to the* PRODUCER *to speak to him in confidence.*] I think it's more likely that he felt discouraged about the theatre and even despised it because the public only wants to see . . .

PRODUCER: Let's go on, for God's sake, let's go on. Come to the point will you?

STEPDAUGHTER: I'm sorry, but if you ask me, we've got too much happening already, just with our entry into his house. [*Pointing to the* FATHER.] You said that we couldn't put up a notice or change the set every five minutes.

PRODUCER: Right! Of course we can't! We must combine things, group them together in one continuous flowing action: not the way you've been wanting, first of all seeing your little brother come home from school and wander about the house like a lost soul, hiding behind the doors and brooding on some plan or other that would—what did you say it would do?

STEPDAUGHTER: Wither him . . . shrivel him up completely.

PRODUCER: That's good! That's a good expression. And then you "can see it there in his eyes, getting stronger all the time"—isn't that what you said?

STEPDAUGHTER: Yes, that's right. Look at him! [*Pointing to him as he stands next to his* MOTHER.]

PRODUCER: Yes, great! And then, at the same time, you want to show the little girl playing in the garden, all innocence. One in the house and the other in the garden—we can't do it, don't you see that?

STEPDAUGHTER: Yes, playing in the sun, so happy! It's the only pleasure I have left, her happiness, her delight in playing in the garden: away from the misery, the squalor of that sordid flat where all four of us slept and where she slept with me—with me! Just think of it! My vile, contaminated body close to hers, with her little arms wrapped tightly round my neck, so lovingly, so innocently. In the garden, wherever she saw me, she would run and take my hand. She never wanted to show me the big flowers, she would run about looking for the "little weeny" ones, so that she could show them to me; she was so happy, so thrilled! [*As she says this, tortured by the memory, she breaks out into a long desperate cry, dropping her head on her arms that rest on a little table. Everybody is very affected by her. The* PRODUCER *comes to her almost paternally and speaks to her in a soothing voice.*]

PRODUCER: We'll have the garden scene, we'll have it, don't worry: and you'll see, you'll be very pleased with what we do! We'll play all the scenes in the garden! [*He calls out to a* STAGE HAND *by name.*] Hey . . . , let down a few bits of tree, will you? A couple of cypresses will do, in front of the fountain. [*Someone drops in the two cypresses and a* STAGE HAND *secures them with a couple of braces and weights.*]

PRODUCER: [*To the* STEPDAUGHTER.] That'll do for now, won't it? It'll just give us an idea. [*Calling out to a* STAGE HAND *by name again.*] Hey, . . . give me something for the sky will you?

STAGE HAND: What's that?

PRODUCER: Something for the sky! A small cloth to come in behind the fountain. [*A white cloth is dropped from the flies.*] Not white! I asked for a sky! Never mind: leave it! I'll do something with it. [*Calling out.*] Hey lights! Kill everything will you? Give me a bit of moonlight—the blues in the batten and a blue spot on the cloth . . . [*They do.*] That's it! That'll do! [*Now on the scene there is the light he asked for, a mysterious blue light that makes the* ACTORS *speak and move as if in the garden in the evening under a moon. To the* STEPDAUGHTER.] Look here now: the little boy can come out here in the garden and hide among the trees instead of hiding behind the doors in the house. But it's going to be difficult to find a little girl to play the scene with you where she shows you the flowers. [*Turning to the* LITTLE BOY.] Come on, come on, son, come across here. Let's see what it'll look like. [*But the* BOY *doesn't move.*] Come on will you, come on. [*Then he pulls him forward and tries to make him hold his head up, but every time it falls down again on his chest.*] There's something very odd about this lad . . . What's wrong with him? My God, he'll have to say something sometime! [*He comes over to him again, puts his hand on his shoulder and pushes him between the trees.*] Come a bit nearer: let's have a look. Can you hide a bit more? That's it. Now pop your head out and look round. [*He moves away to look at the effect and as the* BOY *does what he has been told to do, the* ACTORS *watch impressed and a little disturbed.*] Ahh, that's good, very good . . . [*He turns to the* STEPDAUGHTER.] How about having the little girl, surprised to see him there, run across. Wouldn't that make him say something?

STEPDAUGHTER: [*Getting up.*] It's no use hoping he'll speak, not as long as that creature's there. [*Pointing to the* SON.] You'll have to get him out of the way first.

SON: [*Moving determinedly to one of the sets of steps leading off the stage.*]
With pleasure! I'll go now! Nothing will please me better!

PRODUCER: [*Stopping him immediately.*] Hey, no! Where are you going?
Hang on!

   [*The* MOTHER *gets up, anxious at the idea that he is really going and
   instinctively raising her arms as if to hold him back, but without moving from where she is.*]

SON: [*At the footlights, to the* PRODUCER *who is restraining him there.*]
There's no reason why I should be here! Let me go will you? Let me
go!

PRODUCER: What do you mean there's no reason for you to be here?

STEPDAUGHTER: [*Calmly, ironically.*] Don't bother to stop him. He won't
go!

FATHER: You have to play that terrible scene in the garden with your
mother.

SON: [*Quickly, angry and determined.*] I'm not going to play anything! I've
said that all along! [*To the* PRODUCER.] Let me go will you?

STEPDAUGHTER: [*Crossing to the* PRODUCER.] It's all right. Let him go.
[*She moves the* PRODUCER*'s hand from the* SON. *Then she turns to the*
SON *and says.*] Well, go on then! Off you go!

   [*The* SON *stays near the steps but as if pulled by some strange force
   he is quite unable to go down them: then to the astonishment and
   even the dismay of the* ACTORS, *he moves along the front of the stage
   towards the other set of steps down into the auditorium: but having
   got there, he again stays near and doesn't actually go down them.
   The* STEPDAUGHTER *who has watched him scornfully but very
   intently, bursts into laughter.*]

STEPDAUGHTER: He can't, you see? He can't! He's got to stay here! He
must. He's chained to us for ever! No, I'm the one who goes, when
what must happen does happen, and I run away, because I hate him,
because I can't bear the sight of him any longer. Do you think it's possible for him to run away? He has to stay here with that wonderful father
of his and his mother there. She doesn't think she has any other son but
him. [*She turns to the* MOTHER.] Come on, come on, Mummy, come
on! [*Turning back to the* PRODUCER *to point her out to him.*] Look,
she's going to try to stop him ... [*To the* MOTHER, *half compelling her,
as if by some magic power.*] Come on, come on. [*Then to the* PRO-
DUCER *again.*] Imagine how she must feel at showing her affection for
him in front of your actors! But her longing to be near him is so strong
that—look! She's going to go through that scene with him again! [*The*
MOTHER *has now actually come close to the* SON *as the* STEPDAUGHTER
says the last line: she gestures to show that she agrees to go on.]

SON: [*Quickly.*] But I'm not! I'm not! If I can't get away then I suppose I
shall have to stay here; but I repeat that I will not have any part in it.

FATHER: [*To the* PRODUCER, *excitedly.*] You must make him!

SON: Nobody's going to make me do anything!

FATHER: I'll make you!

STEPDAUGHTER: Wait! Just a minute! Before that, the little girl has to go to the fountain. [*She turns to take the* LITTLE GIRL, *drops on her knees in front of her and takes her face between her hands.*] My poor little darling, those beautiful eyes, they look so bewildered. You're wondering where you are, aren't you? Well, we're on a stage, my darling! What's a stage? Well, it's a place where you pretend to be serious. They put on plays here. And now we're going to put on a play. Seriously! Oh, yes! Even you . . . [*She hugs her tightly and rocks her gently for a moment.*] Oh, my little one, my little darling, what a terrible play it is for you! What horrible things have been planned for you! The garden, the fountain . . . Oh, yes, it's only a pretend fountain, that's right. That's part of the game, my pretty darling: everything is pretends here. Perhaps you'll like a pretends fountain better than a real one: you can play here then. But it's only a game for the others; not for you, I'm afraid, it's real for you, my darling, and your game is in a real fountain, a big beautiful green fountain with bamboos casting shadows, looking at your own reflection, with lots of baby ducks paddling about, shattering the reflections. You want to stroke one! [*With a scream that electrifies and terrifies everybody.*] No, Rosetta, no! Your mummy isn't watching you, she's over there with that selfish bastard! Oh, God, I feel as if all the devils in hell were tearing me apart inside . . . And you . . . [*Leaving the* LITTLE GIRL *and turning to the* LITTLE BOY *in the usual way.*] What are you doing here, hanging about like a beggar? It'll be your fault too, if that little girl drowns; you're always like this, as if I wasn't paying the price for getting all of you into this house. [*Shaking his arm to make him take his hand out of his pocket.*] What have you got there? What are you hiding? Take it out, take your hand out! [*She drags his hand out of his pocket and to everyone's horror he is holding a revolver. She looks at him for a moment, almost with satisfaction: then she says, grimly.*] Where on earth did you get that? [*The* BOY, *looking frightened, with his eyes wide and empty, doesn't answer.*] You idiot, if I'd been you, instead of killing myself, I'd have killed one of those two: either or both, the father and the son. [*She pushes him toward the cypress trees where he then stands watching: then she takes the* LITTLE GIRL *and helps her to climb in to the fountain, making her lie so that she is hidden: after that she kneels down and puts her head and arms on the rim of the fountain.*]

PRODUCER: That's good! It's good! [*Turning to the* STEPDAUGHTER.] And at the same time . . .

SON: [*Scornfully.*] What do you mean, at the same time? There was nothing at the same time! There wasn't any scene between her and me. [*Pointing to the* MOTHER.] She'll tell you the same thing herself, she'll tell you what happened.

   [*The* SECOND ACTRESS *and the* JUVENILE LEAD *have left the group of* ACTORS *and have come to stand nearer the* MOTHER *and the* SON *as if to study them so as to play their parts.*]

MOTHER: Yes, it's true. I'd gone to his room . . .

SON: Room, do you hear? Not the garden!

PRODUCER: It's not important! We've got to reorganize the events anyway. I've told you that already.

SON: [*Glaring at the* JUVENILE LEAD *and the* SECOND ACTRESS.] What do you want?

JUVENILE LEAD: Nothing. I'm just watching.

SON: [*Turning to the* SECOND ACTRESS.] You as well! Getting ready to play her part are you? [*Pointing to the* MOTHER.]

PRODUCER: That's it. And I think you should be grateful—they're paying you a lot of attention.

SON: Oh, yes, thank you! But haven't you realised yet that you'll never be able to do this play? There's nothing of us inside you and you actors are only looking at us from the outside. Do you think we could go on living with a mirror held up in front of us that didn't only freeze our reflection for ever, but froze us in a reflection that laughed back at us with an expression that we didn't even recognise as our own?

FATHER: That's right! That's right!

PRODUCER: [*To* JUVENILE LEAD *and* SECOND ACTRESS.] Okay. Go back to the others.

SON: It's quite useless. I'm not prepared to do anything.

PRODUCER: Oh, shut up, will you, and let me listen to your mother. [*To the* MOTHER.] Well, you'd gone to his room, you said.

MOTHER: Yes, to his room. I couldn't bear it any longer. I wanted to empty my heart to him, tell him about all the agony that was crushing me. But as soon as he saw me come in . . .

SON: Nothing happened. I got away! I wasn't going to get involved. I never have been involved. Do you understand?

MOTHER: It's true! That's right!

PRODUCER: But we must make up the scene between you, then. It's vital!

MOTHER: I'm ready to do it! If only I had the chance to talk to him for a moment, to pour out all my troubles to him.

FATHER: [*Going to the* SON *and speaking violently.*] You'll do it! For your Mother! For your Mother!

SON: [*More than ever determined.*] I'm doing nothing!

FATHER: [*Taking hold of his coat collar and shaking him.*] For God's sake, do as I tell you! Do as I tell you! Do you hear what she's saying? Haven't you any feelings for her?

SON: [*Taking hold of his* FATHER.] No I haven't! I haven't! Let that be the end of it!

[*There is a general uproar. The* MOTHER *frightened out of her wits, tries to get between them and separate them.*]

MOTHER: Please stop it! Please!

FATHER: [*Hanging on.*] Do as I tell you! Do as I tell you!

SON: [*Wrestling with him and finally throwing him to the ground near the steps. Everyone is horrified.*] What's come over you? Why are you so frantic? Do you want to parade our disgrace in front of everybody? Well, I'm having nothing to do with it! Nothing! And I'm doing what our author wanted as well—he never wanted to put us on the stage.

PRODUCER: Then why the hell did you come here?

SON: [*Pointing to the* FATHER.] He wanted to, I didn't.

PRODUCER: But you're here now, aren't you?

SON: He was the one who wanted to come and he dragged all of us here with him and agreed with you in there about what to put in the play: and that meant not only what had really happened, as if that wasn't bad enough, but what hadn't happened as well.

PRODUCER: All right, then, you tell me what happened. You tell me! Did you rush out of your room without saying anything?

SON: [*After a moment's hesitation.*] Without saying anything. I didn't want to make a scene.

PRODUCER: [*Needling him.*] What then? What did you do then?

SON: [*He is now the centre of everyone's agonised attention and he crosses the stage.*] Nothing . . . I went across the garden . . . [*He breaks off gloomy and absorbed.*]

PRODUCER: [*Urging him to say more, impressed by his reluctance to speak.*] Well? What then? You crossed the garden?

SON: [*Exasperated, putting his face into the crook of his arm.*] Why do you want me to talk about it? It's horrible! [*The MOTHER is trembling with stifled sobs and looking towards the fountain.*]

PRODUCER: [*Quietly, seeing where she is looking and turning to the SON with growing apprehension.*] The little girl?

SON: [*Looking straight in front, out to the audience.*] There, in the fountain . . .

FATHER: [*On the floor still, pointing with pity at the MOTHER.*] She was trailing after him!

PRODUCER: [*To the SON, anxiously.*] What did you do then?

SON: [*Still looking out front and speaking slowly.*] I dashed across. I was going to jump in and pull her out . . . But something else caught my eye: I saw something behind the tree that made my blood run cold: the little boy, he was standing there with a mad look in his eyes: he was standing looking into the fountain at his little sister, floating there, drowned.

[*The STEPDAUGHTER is still bent at the fountain hiding the LITTLE GIRL, and she sobs pathetically, her sobs sounding like an echo. There is a pause.*]

SON: [*Continued.*] I made a move towards him: but then . . .

[*From behind the trees where the LITTLE BOY is standing there is the sound of a shot.*]

MOTHER: [*With a terrible cry she runs along with the SON and all the ACTORS in the midst of a great general confusion.*] My son! My son! [*And then from out of the confusion and crying her voice comes out.*] Help! Help me!

PRODUCER: [*Amidst the shouting he tries to clear a space whilst the LITTLE BOY is carried by his feet and shoulders behind the white skycloth.*] Is he wounded? Really wounded?

[*Everybody except the PRODUCER and the FATHER who is still on the floor by the steps, has gone behind the skycloth and stays there talking anxiously. Then independently the ACTORS start to come back into view.*]

LEADING ACTRESS: [*Coming from the right, very upset.*] He's dead! The poor boy! He's dead! What a terrible thing!

LEADING ACTOR: [*Coming back from the left and smiling.*] What do you mean, dead? It's all make-believe. It's a sham! He's not dead. Don't you believe it!

OTHER ACTORS FROM THE RIGHT: Make-believe? It's real! Real! Real! He's dead!

OTHER ACTORS FROM THE LEFT: No, he isn't. He's pretending! It's all make-believe.

FATHER: [*Running off and shouting at them as he goes.*] What do you mean, make-believe? It's real! It's real, ladies and gentlemen! It's reality! [*And with desperation on his face he too goes behind the skycloth.*]

PRODUCER: [*Not caring any more.*] Make-believe?! Reality?! Oh, go to hell the lot of you! Lights! Lights! Lights!

[*At once all the stage and auditorium is flooded with light. The* PRO-DUCER *heaves a sigh of relief as if he has been relieved of a terrible weight and they all look at each other in distress and with uncertainty.*]

PRODUCER: God! I've never known anything like this! And we've lost a whole day's work! [*He looks at the clock.*] Get off with you, all of you! We can't do anything now! It's too late to start a rehearsal. [*When the* ACTORS *have gone, he calls out.*] Hey, lights! Kill everything! [*As soon as he has said this, all the lights go out completely and leave him in the pitch dark.*] For God's sake!! You might have left the workers![4] I can't see where I'm going!

[*Suddenly, behind the skycloth, as if because of a bad connection, a green light comes up to throw on the cloth a huge sharp shadow of the* CHARACTERS, *but without the* LITTLE BOY *and the* LITTLE GIRL. *The* PRODUCER, *seeing this, jumps off the stage, terrified. At the same time the flood of light on them is switched off and the stage is again bathed in the same blue light as before. Slowly the* SON *comes on from the right, followed by the* MOTHER *with her arms raised towards him. Then from the left, the* FATHER *enters.*

They come together in the middle of the stage and stand there as if transfixed. Finally from the left the STEPDAUGHTER *comes on and moves towards the steps at the front: on the top step she pauses for a moment to look back at the other three and then bursts out in a raucous laugh, dashes down the steps and turns to look at the three figures still on the stage. Then she runs out of the auditorium and we can still hear her manic laughter out into the foyer and beyond.*

After a pause the curtain falls slowly.]

---

4. Working lights.

MARCEL PROUST
1871–1922

Proust's influence in twentieth-century letters is unequaled by that of any other writer. His massive novel sequence, *Remembrance of Things Past* (À la recherche du temps perdu), broke from nineteenth-century tradition to provide the example of a new kind of characterization and narrative line, a monumentally complex and precisely coordinated aesthetic structure, and a concept of the individual's cumulatively created profound identity—much of it buried in the experience of our senses—that has influenced writers everywhere modern Western literature is known. All of these innovations refer to an exploration of time in terms that parallel the influential work of Proust's contemporary, the philosopher Henri Bergson, with its emphasis on experience as duration, or *lived* time (rather than the artificial measurements of clock or calendar), and the importance of intuitive knowledge. Proust's plot refuses the immediate sense of direction given by traditional nineteenth-century novels: it acquires purpose gradually, through the relationship of different themes, and its collective intent appears only at the end when Marcel's suddenly catalyzed memory grasps the relationship of all parts. Characters are not sketched in fully from the beginning but are revealed piece by piece, evolving inside the different perspectives of individual chapters; even the protagonist is not fully outlined before the end. Proust's novel is a monumental construction coordinated down to its smallest parts not by the development of traditional novel form but by a new structural vision; it suggested the availability of intuitive or nonrational elements as organizational principles in an example that continues to be a reference point for twentieth-century writers.

Marcel Proust was born on July 10, 1871, the older of two sons in a wealthy middle-class Parisian family. His father was a well-known doctor and professor of medicine, a Catholic from a small town outside Paris. His mother, a sensitive, scrupulous, and highly educated woman to whom Marcel was devoted, came from an urban Jewish family. Proust fell ill with severe asthma when he was nine and thereafter spent his childhood holidays at a seaside resort in Normandy that became the fictional model for Balbec. In spite of his illness, which limited what he could do, he graduated with honors from the Lycée Condorcet in Paris in 1889 and did a year's military service at Orléans (the fictional Doncières). As a student, Proust had met many young writers and composers, and he began to frequent the salons of the wealthy bourgeoisie and the aristocracy of the Faubourg Saint-Germain (an elegant area of Paris), from which he drew much of the material for his portraits of society. He wrote for Symbolist magazines such as *Le Banquet* and *La Revue blanche* and published a collection of essays, poems, and stories in an elegant book, *Pleasures and Days* (1896), with drawings by Madeleine Lemaire and music by Reynaldo Hahn. In 1899 (with his mother's help since he knew no English), he began to translate the English moralist and art critic, John Ruskin.

Proust is known as the author of one work: the enormous, seven-volume exploration of time and consciousness called *Remembrance of Things Past*. As early as 1895, he had begun work on a shorter novel that traced the same themes and autobiographical awareness, but *Jean Santeuil* (published posthumously in 1952) never found a coherent structure for its numerous episodes and Proust abandoned it in 1899. Many episodes from the unfinished manuscript reflected Proust's interest in current events, and especially the Dreyfus Affair (1894–1906) that was dividing France around issues of military honor, anti-Semitism, and national security. Themes, ideas, and some episodes from the earlier novel were absorbed into *Remembrance of Things Past*, and it is striking that the major difference (aside from length) between the two works is simply the extremely sophisticated and subtle structure that Proust devised for the later one.

Proust's health started seriously to decline in 1902, and to make matters worse, he lost both parents by 1905. The following year, his asthma worsening, he moved into a cork-lined, fumigated room at 102 Boulevard Haussmann in Paris, where he stayed until forced to move in 1919. From 1907 to 1914, he spent summers in the seacoast town of Cabourg (another source of material for the fictional Balbec), but when in Paris emerged rarely from his apartment and then only late at night for dinners with friends. In 1909 he conceived the structure of his novel as a whole and wrote its first and last chapters together. A first draft was finished by September 1912, but Proust had difficulty finding a publisher and finally published the first volume at his own expense in 1913. Though *Swann's Way* (*Du côté de chez Swann*) was a success, World War I delayed publication of subsequent volumes, and Proust began the painstaking revision and enlargement of the whole manuscript (from fifteen hundred to four thousand pages, and three to seven parts) that was to occupy him until his death on November 18, 1922. *Within a Budding Grove* (À *l'ombre des jeunes filles en fleurs*, or "In the Shadow of Young Girls in Flower") won the prestigious Goncourt Prize in 1919, and *The Guermantes' Way* (*Le Côté de Guermantes*) followed in 1920–21. The last volume published in Proust's lifetime was *Cities of the Plain II* (*Sodome et Gomorrhe II*, or "Sodom and Gomorrah II," 1922), and the remaining volumes—*The Captive* (*La Prisonnière*, 1923), *The Fugitive* (*Albertine disparue*, or "Albertine Disappeared," 1925), and *Time Regained* (*Le Temps retrouvé*, 1927)—were published posthumously from manuscripts on which he had been working. Written almost completely in the first person and based on events in the author's life (although by no means purely autobiographical), the novel is famous both for its evocation of the closed world of Parisian society at the turn of the century and as a meditation on time and human emotions.

When *Swann's Way* appeared in 1913, it was immediately seen as a new kind of fiction. Unlike nineteenth-century novels such as Flaubert's *Madame Bovary*, *Remembrance of Things Past* has no clear and continuous plot line building to a dénouement, nor (until the last volume, published in 1927) could the reader detect a consistent development of the central character, Marcel. Only at the end does the narrator recognize the meaning and value of what has preceded, and when he retells his story it is not from an omniscient, explanatory point of view but rather as a reliving and gradual assessment of Marcel's lifelong experience. Most of the novel sets forth a roughly chronological sequence of events, yet its opening pages swing through recollections of many times and places before settling on the narrator's childhood in Combray. The second section, *Swann in Love* (*Un Amour de Swann*), is a story told about another character and in the third person. Thus the novel proceeds by apparently discontinuous blocks of recollection, all bound together by the central consciousness of the narrator. This was always Proust's plan: he insisted that he had from the beginning a fixed structure and goal for the whole novel that reached down to the "solidity of the smallest parts," and his substantial revisions of the shorter first draft enriched an already existing structure without changing the sequence of scenes and events.

The overall theme of the novel is suggested by a literal translation of its title: "In Search of Lost Time." The narrator, a "Marcel" who suggests but is not identical with the author, is an old man weakened by a long illness who puzzles over the events of his past, trying to find in them a significant pattern. He begins with his childhood, ordered within the comfortable security of accepted manners and ideals in the family home at Combray. In succeeding volumes he goes out into the world, experiences love and disappointment, discovers the disparity between idealized images of places and their crude, sometimes banal reality, and is increasingly overcome by disillusionment with himself and society. Until the end of the novel, Marcel remains a *grand nerveux* (nervous or high-strung person), an extremely sensitive person impelled by the major experiences of his life—love, betrayal, art, separation, and death—to discard his earlier naive perspective and seek out a largely intuited meaning for life.

In the short ending chapter, things suddenly come into focus as Marcel reaches a new understanding of the role of time. Abruptly reliving a childhood experience when he sees a familiar book and recognizing the ravages of time in the aged and enfeebled figures of his old friends, Marcel faces the approach of death with a new sense of existential continuity and realizes that his vocation as an artist lies in giving form to this buried existence. Apparently lost, the past is still alive within us, a part of our being, and memory can recapture it to give coherence and depth to present identity. Marcel has not yet begun to write by the end of the last volume, *Time Regained*, but paradoxically the book that he plans to write is already there: Proust's *Remembrance of Things Past*.

The larger subject of the novel, penetrating its description of society and Marcel's experience, is "that invisible substance called time." Although neither ever claimed any direct connection (and Proust recognized more readily the influence of his philosophy professor, Darlu), Proust echoes the concerns of contemporary philosopher Bergson when he looks to intuition and a sense of lived experience for a way to represent reality. Bergson's opposition of intellect and intuition, his preference for *duration* (everyday lived time) as opposed to abstract or clock time as a means of knowledge, and his distinction between the interactive "social ego" and the individually "profound" or intuitive ego all correspond to themes in Proust. Marcel's awareness of his life in time is created through memory—not rational or "forced" but spontaneous or "involuntary" memory—the chance recollection that wells up from his subconscious mind when he repeats a previous action such as dipping cookies in lime-blossom tea, stumbling on a paving stone, hearing a spoon clatter, or glimpsing a familiar book. Involuntary memory is more powerful because it draws on a buried level of experience where the five senses are still linked. Life thus recalled comes to us in one piece, not separated into different categories for easier intellectual understanding. Sounds are connected with colors (the name *Brabant* with gold), and emotions with the settings in which they were experienced (sorrow with the smell of varnish on the stairway up to bed). Involuntary memory recreates a whole past world in all its concrete reality—and so does art. When Proust attributes such an absolute metaphysical value to art, making it a special means of knowledge and the focus of his book, he joins a special French tradition of "moralist" writers: those who, from Michel de Montaigne to Albert Camus, strive for clear vision and a sense of universal human values.

Proust's style has a unique "architectural" design that coordinates large blocks of material: themes, situations, places, and events recur and are transformed across time. His long sentences and mammoth paragraphs reflect the slow and careful progression of thought among the changing objects of its perception. The ending paragraph of the *Overture* is composed of two long sentences that encompass an enormous range of meditative detail as the narrator not only recalls his childhood world—the old gray house, garden, public square and country roads, Swann's park, the river, the villagers, and indeed the whole town of Combray—but simultaneously compares the suddenly arisen house to a stage set, and the unfolding village itself to the twists and turns of a Japanese flower taking on color and form inside a bowl of water: here, in the narrator's cup of lime-blossom tea. Characters are remembered in different settings and perspectives, creating a "multiple self" who is free to change and still remain the same. Thus Charles Swann appears first as the visitor who often delays the child Marcel's bedtime kiss from his mother, next as an anxious and disappointed lover, and finally as a tragic, dying man rejected by his friends, the Guermantes, in their haste to get to a ball. Marcel's grandmother appears throughout the scenes in Combray, later during a visit to the seaside resort of Balbec, still later in her death agonies when Marcel is unable truly to grieve, and finally as a sudden recollection when Marcel has trouble tying his shoelace in Balbec. Nor is it characters alone who undergo cumulative transformations. The little musical phrase that Marcel first hears as part of a sonata by the composer Vinteuil and that is associated with love in various settings recurs toward the end of the novel as part of a septet and becomes a revelation of the subtle constructions of art. Places overlap in the memory: the imagined and the real Balbec or Venice confront one another, and the church steeples of Vieuxvicq and Martinville are juxtaposed. On a linguistic level, Proust juxtaposes entire social roles and habits of mind through the interaction of different types of speech. When Charles and the Princesse de Guermantes meet in a bourgeois salon, their manner of speaking to each other creates a small "in-group" dialogue of the aristocracy and sets them off from everyone else. The flexibility of Proust's style, representing thought and habits of speech rather than following a superimposed common code, makes him an example of verbal and visionary innovation that is paralleled by other writers of the same period, such as James Joyce and Virginia Woolf, and is enormously influential on later writers of the "new novel" tradition.

The selection printed here, *Overture*, is the first chapter of *Swann's Way*, the first full volume of Proust's novel. "Swann's way" is one of the two directions in which Marcel's family used to take walks from their home in Combray, toward Tansonville, home of Charles Swann, and is associated with various scenes and anecdotes of love and private life. The longer walk toward the estate of the Guermantes (*The Guermantes' Way*), a fictional family of the highest aristocracy appearing frequently in the novel, evokes an aura of high society and French history, a more public sphere. Fictional people and places mingle throughout with the real; names that are not annotated are Proust's inventions. The narrator of *Overture* is Marcel as an old man, and the French verb tense used in his recollections (here and throughout all but the final volume) is appropriately the imperfect, a tense of uncompleted action ("I used to . . . I would ask myself").

As the chapter title suggests, *Overture* introduces the work's themes and methods rather like the overture of an opera. All but one of the main characters appear or are mentioned, and the patterns of future encounters are set. Marcel, waiting anxiously for his beloved mother's response to a note sent down to her during dinner, suffers the same agony of separation as does Swann in his love for the promiscuous Odette, or the older Marcel himself for Albertine. The strange world of half-sleep, half-waking with which the novel begins prefigures later awakenings of memory. Long passages of intricate introspection, and sudden shifts of time and space, introduce us to the style and point of view of the rest of the book. The narrator shares the painful anxiety of little Marcel's desperate wait for his mother's bedtime kiss; for though his observations and judgments are tempered with mature wisdom, he is only at the beginning of his progress to full consciousness. The remembrance of things past is a key to further discovery but not an end in itself.

Overture ends with Proust's most famous image, summing up for many readers the world, the style, and the process of discovery of the Proustian vision. Nibbling at a madeleine (a small, rich cookie-like pastry) that he has dipped in lime-blossom tea, Marcel suddenly has an overwhelming feeling of happiness. He soon associates this tantalizing, puzzling phenomenon with the memory of earlier times when he sipped tea with his Aunt Leonie. He realizes that there is something valuable about such passive, spontaneous, and sensuous memory, quite different from the abstract operations of reason. Although the Marcel of "Combray" does not yet know it, he will pursue the elusive significance of this moment of happiness until, in *Time Regained*, he can as a complete artist bring it to the surface and link past and present time in a fuller and richer identity.

Roger Shattuck, *Proust* (1974), is a general study including advice on "how to read" Proust; it is still useful although it predates the revised translation used here. An excellent general study is Germaine Brée, *Marcel Proust and Deliverance from Time* (1969), translated by R. J. Richards and A. D. Truitt. Terence Kilmartin, *A Reader's Guide to Remembrance of Things Past* (1984), is a handbook guide to Proust's characters, to persons referred to in the text, to places, and to themes, all keyed to the revised translation by the translator. René Girard, *Proust: A Collection* of *Critical Essays* (1962); Harold Bloom, ed., *Marcel Proust's Remembrance of Things Past* (1987); and Barbara J. Bucknall, ed., *Critical Essays on Marcel Proust* (1987), are also recommended.

PRONOUNCING GLOSSARY

The following list uses common English syllables and stress accents to provide rough equivalents of selected words whose pronunciation may be unfamiliar to the general reader.

Bathilde: *bah-teeld'*

Chartres: *shar'-tr*

Charlus: *shar-lews'*

Combray: *cohm-bray'*

Corot: *core-oh'*

Duc: *dewk*

Faubourg Saint-Germain; *foh-boor'*
    sanh zhair–manh'

George Sand: *zhorzh sonh*

Maubant: *moh-bawnh'*

Maulévrier: *moh-lay'-vree-ay'*

Proust: *proost*

Quai d'Orléans: *kay dor-lay-onh*

Saint-Cloud: *sanh–cloo'*

Saint-Loup: *sanh–loo'*

Sévigné: *say-veen-yay'*

Vinteuil: *van-teuh'-ee*

Remembrance of Things Past[1]

Swann's Way. Overture[2]

For a long time I used to go to bed early. Sometimes, when I had put out my candle, my eyes would close so quickly that I had not even time to say to myself: "I'm falling asleep." And half an hour later the thought that it was time to go to sleep would awaken me; I would make as if to put away the book which I imagined was still in my hands, and to blow out the light; I had gone on thinking, while I was asleep, about what I had just been reading, but these thoughts had taken a rather peculiar turn; it seemed to me that I myself was the immediate subject of my book: a church, a quartet, the rivalry between François I and Charles V.[3] This impression would persist for some moments after I awoke; it did not offend my reason, but lay like scales upon my eyes and prevented them from registering the fact that the candle was no longer burning. Then it would begin to seem unintelligible, as the thoughts of a former existence must be to a reincarnate spirit; the subject of my book would separate itself from me, leaving me free to apply myself to it or not; and at the same time my sight would return and I would be astonished to find myself in a state of darkness, pleasant and restful enough for my eyes, but even more, perhaps, for my mind, to which it appeared incomprehensible, without a cause, something dark indeed.

I would ask myself what time it could be; I could hear the whistling of trains, which, now nearer and now farther off, punctuating the distance

---

1. Translated by C. K. Scott Moncrieff and Terence Kilmartin.　**2.** The opening section of Combray, the first volume of *Swann's Way*.　**3.** Francis I (1496–1567), king of France, and Charles V (1500–1558), Holy Roman emperor and king of Spain, fought four wars over the empire's expansion in Europe.

like the note of a bird in a forest, showed me in perspective the deserted countryside through which a traveller is hurrying towards the nearby station; and the path he is taking will be engraved in his memory by the excitement induced by strange surroundings, by unaccustomed activities, by the conversation he has had and the farewells exchanged beneath an unfamiliar lamp, still echoing in his ears amid the silence of the night, by the imminent joy of going home.

I would lay my cheeks gently against the comfortable cheeks of my pillow, as plump and blooming as the cheeks of babyhood. I would strike a match to look at my watch. Nearly midnight. The hour when an invalid, who has been obliged to set out on a journey and to sleep in a strange hotel, awakened by a sudden spasm, sees with glad relief a streak of daylight showing under his door. Thank God, it is morning! The servants will be about in a minute: he can ring, and someone will come to look after him. The thought of being assuaged gives him strength to endure his pain. He is certain he heard footsteps: they come nearer, and then die away. The ray of light beneath his door is extinguished. It is midnight; someone has just turned down the gas; the last servant has gone to bed, and he must lie all night in agony with no one to bring him relief.

I would fall asleep again, and thereafter would reawaken for short snatches only, just long enough to hear the regular creaking of the wainscot,[4] or to open my eyes to stare at the shifting kaleidoscope of the darkness, to savour, in a momentary glimmer of consciousness, the sleep which lay heavy upon the furniture, the room, the whole of which I formed but an insignificant part and whose insensibility I should very soon return to share. Or else while sleeping I had drifted back to an earlier stage in my life, now for ever outgrown, and had come under the thrall of one of my childish terrors, such as that old terror of my great-uncle's pulling my curls which was effectually dispelled on the day—the dawn of a new era to me—when they were finally cropped from my head. I had forgotten that event during my sleep, but I remembered it again immediately I had succeeded in waking myself up to escape my great-uncle's fingers, and as a measure of precaution I would bury the whole of my head in the pillow before returning to the world of dreams.

Sometimes, too, as Eve was created from a rib of Adam, a woman would be born during my sleep from some strain in the position of my thighs. Conceived from the pleasure I was on the point of consummating, she it was, I imagined, who offered me that pleasure. My body, conscious that its own warmth was permeating hers, would strive to become one with her, and I would awake. The rest of humanity seemed very remote in comparison with this woman whose company I had left but a moment ago; my cheek was still warm from her kiss, my body ached beneath the weight of hers. If, as would sometimes happen, she had the features of some woman whom I had known in waking hours, I would abandon myself altogether to the sole quest of her, like people who set out on a journey to see with their eyes some city of their desire, and imagine that one can taste in reality what has charmed one's fancy. And then, gradually,

---

4. The wooden paneling of the walls.

the memory of her would dissolve and vanish, until I had forgotten the girl of my dream.

When a man is asleep, he has in a circle round him the chain of the hours, the sequence of the years, the order of the heavenly host. Instinctively, when he awakes, he looks to these, and in an instant reads off his own position on the earth's surface and the time that has elapsed during his slumbers; but this ordered procession is apt to grow confused, and to break its ranks. Suppose that, towards morning, after a night of insomnia, sleep descends upon him while he is reading, in quite a different position from that in which he normally goes to sleep, he has only to lift his arm to arrest the sun and turn it back in its course,[5] and, at the moment of waking, he will have no idea of the time, but will conclude that he has just gone to bed. Or suppose that he dozes off in some even more abnormal and divergent position, sitting in an armchair, for instance, after dinner: then the world will go hurtling out of orbit, the magic chair will carry him at full speed through time and space, and when he opens his eyes again he will imagine that he went to sleep months earlier in another place. But for me it was enough if, in my own bed, my sleep was so heavy as completely to relax my consciousness; for then I lost all sense of the place in which I had gone to sleep, and when I awoke in the middle of the night, not knowing where I was, I could not even be sure at first who I was; I had only the most rudimentary sense of existence, such as may lurk and flicker in the depths of an animal's consciousness; I was more destitute than the cave-dweller; but then the memory—not yet of the place in which I was, but of various other places where I had lived and might now very possibly be—would come like a rope let down from heaven to draw me up out of the abyss of not-being, from which I could never have escaped by myself: in a flash I would traverse centuries of civilisation, and out of a blurred glimpse of oil-lamps, then of shirts with turned-down collars, would gradually piece together the original components of my ego.

Perhaps the immobility of the things that surround us is forced upon them by our conviction that they are themselves and not anything else, by the immobility of our conception of them. For it always happened that when I awoke like this, and my mind struggled in an unsuccessful attempt to discover where I was, everything revolved around me through the darkness: things, places, years. My body, still too heavy with sleep to move, would endeavour to construe from the pattern of its tiredness the position of its various limbs, in order to deduce therefrom the direction of the wall, the location of the furniture, to piece together and give a name to the house in which it lay. Its memory, the composite memory of its ribs, its knees, its shoulder-blades, offered it a whole series of rooms in which it had at one time or another slept, while the unseen walls, shifting and adapting themselves to the shape of each successive room that it remembered, whirled round it in the dark. And even before my brain, lingering in cogitation over when things had happened and what they had looked like, had reassembled the circumstances sufficiently to identify the room,

---

5. If his uplifted arm prevents him from seeing the sunlight, he will think it is still night.

it, my body, would recall from each room in succession the style of the bed, the position of the doors, the angle at which the daylight came in at the windows, whether there was a passage outside, what I had had in my mind when I went to sleep and found there when I awoke. The stiffened side on which I lay would, for instance, in trying to fix its position, imagine itself to be lying face to the wall in a big bed with a canopy; and at once I would say to myself, "Why, I must have fallen asleep before Mamma came to say good night," for I was in the country at my grandfather's, who died years ago; and my body, the side upon which I was lying, faithful guardians of a past which my mind should never have forgotten, brought back before my eyes the glimmering flame of the night-light in its urn-shaped bowl of Bohemian glass that hung by chains from the ceiling, and the chimney-piece of Siena marble[6] in my bedroom at Combray, in my grandparents' house, in those far distant days which at this moment I imagined to be in the present without being able to picture them exactly, and which would become plainer in a little while when I was properly awake.

Then the memory of a new position would spring up, and the wall would slide away in another direction; I was in my room in Mme de Saint-Loup's[7] house in the country; good heavens, it must be ten o'clock, they will have finished dinner! I must have overslept myself in the little nap which I always take when I come in from my walk with Mme de Saint-Loup, before dressing for the evening. For many years have now elapsed since the Combray days when, coming in from the longest and latest walks, I would still be in time to see the reflection of the sunset glowing in the panes of my bedroom window. It is a very different kind of life that one leads at Tansonville, at Mme de Saint-Loup's, and a different kind of pleasure that I derive from taking walks only in the evenings, from visiting by moonlight the roads on which I used to play as a child in the sunshine; while the bedroom in which I shall presently fall asleep instead of dressing for dinner I can see from the distance as we return from our walk, with its lamp shining through the window, a solitary beacon in the night.

These shifting and confused gusts of memory never lasted for more than a few seconds; it often happened that, in my brief spell of uncertainty as to where I was, I did not distinguish the various suppositions of which it was composed any more than, when we watch a horse running, we isolate the successive positions of its body as they appear upon a bioscope.[8] But I had seen first one and then another of the rooms in which I had slept during my life, and in the end I would revisit them all in the long course of my waking dream: rooms in winter, where on going to bed I would at once bury my head in a nest woven out of the most diverse materials— the corner of my pillow, the top of my blankets, a piece of a shawl, the edge of my bed, and a copy of a children's paper—which I had contrived to cement together, bird-fashion, by dint of continuous pressure; rooms where, in freezing weather, I would enjoy the satisfaction of being shut in from the outer world (like the sea-swallow which builds at the end of a

6. From central Italy, mottled and reddish in color. *Bohemian glass:* likely to have been ornately engraved. Bohemia (now part of the Czech Republic) was a major center of the glass industry. 7. Charles Swann's daughter, Gilberte, who has married Robert de Saint-Loup, a nephew of the Guermantes. 8. An early moving-picture machine that showed photographs in rapid succession.

dark tunnel and is kept warm by the surrounding earth), and where, the fire keeping in all night, I would sleep wrapped up, as it were, in a great cloak of snug and smoky air, shot with the glow of the logs intermittently breaking out again in flame, a sort of alcove without walls, a cave of warmth dug out of the heart of the room itself, a zone of heat whose boundaries were constantly shifting and altering in temperature as gusts of air traversed them to strike freshly upon my face, from the corners of the room or from parts near the window or far from the fireplace which had therefore remained cold;—or rooms in summer, where I would delight to feel myself a part of the warm night, where the moonlight striking upon the half-opened shutters would throw down to the foot of my bed its enchanted ladder, where I would fall asleep, as it might be in the open air, like a titmouse which the breeze gently rocks at the tip of a sunbeam;—or sometimes the Louis XVI room,[9] so cheerful that I never felt too miserable in it, even on my first night, and in which the slender columns that lightly supported its ceiling drew so gracefully apart to reveal and frame the site of the bed;—sometimes, again, the little room with the high ceiling, hollowed in the form of a pyramid out of two separate storeys, and partly walled with mahogany, in which from the first moment, mentally poisoned by the unfamiliar scent of vetiver,[1] I was convinced of the hostility of the violet curtains and of the insolent indifference of a clock that chattered on at the top of its voice as though I were not there; in which a strange and pitiless rectangular cheval-glass, standing across one corner of the room, carved out for itself a site I had not looked to find tenanted in the soft plenitude of my normal field of vision;[2] in which my mind, striving for hours on end to break away from its moorings, to stretch upwards so as to take on the exact shape of the room and to reach to the topmost height of its gigantic funnel, had endured many a painful night as I lay stretched out in bed, my eyes staring upwards, my ears straining, my nostrils flaring, my heart beating; until habit had changed the colour of the curtains, silenced the clock, brought an expression of pity to the cruel, slanting face of the glass, disguised or even completely dispelled the scent of vetiver, and appreciably reduced the apparent loftiness of the ceiling. Habit! that skilful but slow-moving arranger who begins by letting our minds suffer for weeks on end in temporary quarters, but whom our minds are none the less only too happy to discover at last, for without it, reduced to their own devices, they would be powerless to make any room seem habitable.

Certainly I was now well awake; my body had veered round for the last time and the good angel of certainty had made all the surrounding objects stand still, had set me down under my bedclothes, in my bedroom, and had fixed, approximately in their right places in the uncertain light, my chest of drawers, my writing-table, my fireplace, the window overlooking the street, and both the doors. But for all that I now knew that I was not in any of the houses of which the ignorance of the waking moment had,

9. Furnished in late-18th-century style, named for the French monarch of the time and marked by great elegance. The room is that in which Marcel visits Robert de Saint-Loup in *Guermantes' Way*.   1. The aromatic root of a tropical grass packaged as a moth repellent.   2. The narrator's room at the fictional seaside resort of Balbec, a setting in *Within a Budding Grove*.

in a flash, if not presented me with a distinct picture, at least persuaded me of the possible presence, my memory had been set in motion; as a rule I did not attempt to go to sleep again at once, but used to spend the greater part of the night recalling our life in the old days at Combray with my great-aunt, at Balbec, Paris, Doncières, Venice, and the rest; remembering again all the places and people I had known, what I had actually seen of them, and what others had told me.

At Combray, as every afternoon ended, long before the time when I should have to go to bed and lie there, unsleeping, far from my mother and grandmother, my bedroom became the fixed point on which my melancholy and anxious thoughts were centred. Someone had indeed had the happy idea of giving me, to distract me on evenings when I seemed abnormally wretched, a magic lantern,[3] which used to be set on top of my lamp while we waited for dinner-time to come; and, after the fashion of the master-builders and glass-painters of gothic days, it substituted for the opaqueness of my walls an impalpable iridescence, supernatural phenomena of many colours, in which legends were depicted as on a shifting and transitory window. But my sorrows were only increased thereby, because this mere change of lighting was enough to destroy the familiar impression I had of my room, thanks to which, save for the torture of going to bed, it had become quite endurable. Now I no longer recognised it, and felt uneasy in it, as in a room in some hotel or chalet, in a place where I had just arrived by train for the first time.

Riding at a jerky trot, Golo,[4] filled with an infamous design, issued from the little triangular forest which dyed dark-green the slope of a convenient hill, and advanced fitfully towards the castle of poor Geneviève de Brabant. This castle was cut off short by a curved line which was in fact the circumference of one of the transparent ovals in the slides which were pushed into position through a slot in the lantern. It was only the wing of a castle, and in front of it stretched a moor on which Geneviève stood lost in contemplation, wearing a blue girdle.[5] The castle and the moor were yellow, but I could tell their colour without waiting to see them, for before the slides made their appearance the old-gold sonorous name of Brabant had given me an unmistakable clue. Golo stopped for a moment and listened sadly to the accompanying patter read aloud by my great-aunt,[6] which he seemed perfectly to understand, for he modified his attitude with a docility not devoid of a degree of majesty, so as to conform to the indications given in the text; then he rode away at the same jerky trot. And nothing could arrest his slow progress. If the lantern were moved I could still distinguish Golo's horse advancing across the window-curtains, swelling out with their curves and diving into their folds. The body of Golo himself, being of the same supernatural substance as his steed's, overcame every material obstacle—everything that seemed to bar his way—by taking it as an ossature[7] and embodying it in himself: even the door-handle, for instance, over which, adapting itself at once, would float irresistibly his

3. A kind of slide projector.   4. Villain of a 5th-century legend. He falsely accuses Geneviève de Brabant of adultery. Brabant was a principality in what is now Belgium.   5. Belt.   6. Marcel's great-aunt is reading the story to him as they wait for dinner.   7. Skeleton.

red cloak or his pale face, which never lost its nobility or its melancholy, never betrayed the least concern at this transvertebration.

And, indeed, I found plenty of charm in these bright projections, which seemed to emanate from a Merovingian[8] past and shed around me the reflections of such ancient history. But I cannot express the discomfort I felt at this intrusion of mystery and beauty into a room which I had succeeded in filling with my own personality until I thought no more of it than of myself. The anaesthetic effect of habit being destroyed, I would begin to think—and to feel—such melancholy things. The door-handle of my room, which was different to me from all the other door-handles in the world, inasmuch as it seemed to open of its own accord and without my having to turn it, so unconscious had its manipulation become—lo and behold, it was now an astral body[9] for Golo. And as soon as the dinner-bell rang I would hurry down to the dining-room, where the big hanging lamp, ignorant of Golo and Bluebeard[1] but well acquainted with my family and the dish of stewed beef, shed the same light as on every other evening; and I would fall into the arms of my mother, whom the misfortunes of Geneviève de Brabant had made all the dearer to me, just as the crimes of Golo had driven me to a more than ordinarily scrupulous examination of my own conscience.

But after dinner, alas, I was soon obliged to leave Mamma, who stayed talking with the others, in the garden if it was fine, or in the little parlour where everyone took shelter when it was wet. Everyone except my grandmother, who held that "It's a pity to shut oneself indoors in the country," and used to have endless arguments with my father on the very wettest days, because he would send me up to my room with a book instead of letting me stay out of doors. "That is not the way to make him strong and active," she would say sadly, "especially this little man, who needs all the strength and will-power that he can get." My father would shrug his shoulders and study the barometer, for he took an interest in meteorology, while my mother, keeping very quiet so as not to disturb him, looked at him with tender respect, but not too hard, not wishing to penetrate the mysteries of his superior mind. But my grandmother, in all weathers, even when the rain was coming down in torrents and Françoise had rushed the precious wicker armchairs indoors so that they should not get soaked, was to be seen pacing the deserted rain-lashed garden, pushing back her disordered grey locks so that her forehead might be freer to absorb the health-giving draughts of wind and rain. She would say, "At last one can breathe!" and would trot up and down the sodden paths—too straight and symmetrical for her liking, owing to the want of any feeling for nature in the new gardener, whom my father had been asking all morning if the weather were going to improve—her keen, jerky little step regulated by the various effects wrought upon her soul by the intoxication of the storm, the power of hygiene, the stupidity of my upbringing and the symmetry of gardens, rather than by any anxiety (for that was quite unknown to her) to save her

8. The first dynasty of French kings (A.D. 500–751).   9. Spiritual counterpart of the physical body. According to the doctrine of Theosophy (a spiritualist movement originating in 1875), the astral body survives the death of the physical body.   1. The legendary wife murderer, presumably depicted on another set of slides.

plum-coloured skirt from the mudstains beneath which it would gradually disappear to a height that was the constant bane and despair of her maid.

When these walks of my grandmother's took place after dinner there was one thing which never failed to bring her back to the house: this was if (at one of those points when her circular itinerary brought her back, moth-like, in sight of the lamp in the little parlour where the liqueurs were set out on the card-table) my great-aunt called out to her: "Bathilde! Come in and stop your husband drinking brandy!" For, simply to tease her (she had brought so different a type of mind into my father's family that everyone made fun of her), my great-aunt used to make my grandfather, who was forbidden liqueurs, take just a few drops. My poor grandmother would come in and beg and implore her husband not to taste the brandy; and he would get angry and gulp it down all the same, and she would go out again sad and discouraged, but still smiling, for she was so humble of heart and so gentle that her tenderness for others and her disregard for herself and her own troubles blended in a smile which, unlike those seen on the majority of human faces, bore no trace of irony save for herself, while for all of us kisses seemed to spring from her eyes, which could not look upon those she loved without seeming to bestow upon them passionate caresses. This torture inflicted on her by my great-aunt, the sight of my grandmother's vain entreaties, of her feeble attempts, doomed in advance, to remove the liqueur-glass from my grandfather's hands—all these were things of the sort to which, in later years, one can grow so accustomed as to smile at them and to take the persecutor's side resolutely and cheerfully enough to persuade oneself that it is not really persecution; but in those days they filled me with such horror that I longed to strike my great-aunt. And yet, as soon as I heard her "Bathilde! Come in and stop your husband drinking brandy," in my cowardice I became at once a man, and did what all we grown men do when face to face with suffering and injustice: I preferred not to see them; I ran up to the top of the house to cry by myself in a little room beside the schoolroom and beneath the roof, which smelt of orris-root[2] and was scented also by a wild currant-bush which had climbed up between the stones of the outer wall and thrust a flowering branch in through the half-opened window. Intended for a more special and a baser use, this room, from which, in the daytime, I could see as far as the keep[3] of Roussainville-le-Pin, was for a long time my place of refuge, doubtless because it was the only room whose door I was allowed to lock, whenever my occupation was such as required an inviolable solitude: reading or day-dreaming, secret tears or sensual gratification. Alas! I little knew that my own lack of will-power, my delicate health, and the consequent uncertainty as to my future, weighed far more heavily on my grandmother's mind than any little dietary indiscretion by her husband in the course of those endless perambulations, afternoon and evening, during which we used to see her handsome face passing to and fro, half raised towards the sky, its brown and wrinkled

2. A powder then used as a deodorizer for rooms.   3. The best-fortified tower of a medieval castle. *Baser use:* as a toilet.

cheeks, which with age had acquired almost the purple hue of tilled fields in autumn, covered, if she were "going out," by a half-lifted veil, while upon them either the cold or some sad reflection invariably left the drying traces of an involuntary tear.

My sole consolation when I went upstairs for the night was that Mamma would come in and kiss me after I was in bed. But this good night lasted for so short a time, she went down again so soon, that the moment in which I heard her climb the stairs, and then caught the sound of her garden dress of blue muslin, from which hung little tassels of plaited straw, rustling along the double-doored corridor, was for me a moment of the utmost pain; for it heralded the moment which was bound to follow it, when she would have left me and gone downstairs again. So much so that I reached the point of hoping that this good night which I loved so much would come as late as possible, so as to prolong the time of respite during which Mamma would not yet have appeared. Sometimes when, after kissing me, she opened the door to go, I longed to call her back, to say to her "Kiss me just once more," but I knew that then she would at once look displeased, for the concession which she made to my wretchedness and agitation in coming up to give me this kiss of peace always annoyed my father, who thought such rituals absurd, and she would have liked to try to induce me to outgrow the need, the habit, of having her there at all, let alone get into the habit of asking her for an additional kiss when she was already crossing the threshold. And to see her look displeased destroyed all the calm and serenity she had brought me a moment before, when she had bent her loving face down over my bed, and held it out to me like a host[4] for an act of peace-giving communion in which my lips might imbibe her real presence and with it the power to sleep. But those evenings on which Mamma stayed so short a time in my room were sweet indeed compared to those on which we had guests to dinner, and therefore she did not come at all. Our "guests" were usually limited to M. Swann, who, apart from a few passing strangers, was almost the only person who ever came to the house at Combray, sometimes to a neighbourly dinner (but less frequently since his unfortunate marriage, as my family did not care to receive his wife) and sometimes after dinner, uninvited. On those evenings when, as we sat in front of the house round the iron table beneath the big chestnut-tree, we heard, from the far end of the garden, not the shrill and assertive alarm bell which assailed and deafened with its ferruginous,[5] interminable, frozen sound any member of the household who set it off on entering "without ringing," but the double tinkle, timid, oval, golden, of the visitors' bell, everyone would at once exclaim "A visitor! Who in the world can it be?" but they knew quite well that it could only be M. Swann. My great-aunt, speaking in a loud voice to set an example, in a tone which she endeavoured to make sound natural, would tell the others not to whisper so; that nothing could be more offensive to a stranger coming in, who would be led to think that people were saying things about him which he was not meant to hear; and then my grandmother, always happy to find an excuse for an additional turn in the gar-

---

4. Communion wafer.   5. Iron-like.

den, would be sent out to reconnoitre, and would take the opportunity to remove surreptitiously, as she passed, the stakes of a rose-tree or two, so as to make the roses look a little more natural, as a mother might run her hand through her boy's hair after the barber has smoothed it down, to make it look naturally wavy.

We would all wait there in suspense for the report which my grandmother would bring back from the enemy lines, as though there might be a choice between a large number of possible assailants, and then, soon after, my grandfather would say: "I can hear Swann's voice." And indeed one could tell him only by his voice, for it was difficult to make out his face with its arched nose and green eyes, under a high forehead fringed with fair, almost red hair, done in the Bressant style,[6] because in the garden we used as little light as possible, so as not to attract mosquitoes; and I would slip away unobtrusively to order the liqueurs to be brought out, for my grandmother made a great point, thinking it "nicer," of their not being allowed to seem anything out of the ordinary, which we kept for visitors only. Although a far younger man, M. Swann was very much attached to my grandfather, who had been an intimate friend of Swann's father, an excellent but eccentric man the ardour of whose feelings and the current of whose thoughts would often be checked or diverted by the most trifling thing. Several times in the course of a year I would hear my grandfather tell at table the story, which never varied, of the behaviour of M. Swann the elder upon the death of his wife, by whose bedside he had watched day and night. My grandfather, who had not seen him for a long time, hastened to join him at the Swanns' family property on the outskirts of Combray, and managed to entice him for a moment, weeping profusely, out of the death-chamber, so that he should not be present when the body was laid in its coffin. They took a turn or two in the park, where there was a little sunshine. Suddenly M. Swann seized my grandfather by the arm and cried, "Ah, my dear old friend, how fortunate we are to be walking here together on such a charming day! Don't you see how pretty they are, all these trees, my hawthorns, and my new pond, on which you have never congratulated me? You look as solemn as the grave. Don't you feel this little breeze? Ah! whatever you may say, it's good to be alive all the same, my dear Amédée!" And then, abruptly, the memory of his dead wife returned to him, and probably thinking it too complicated to inquire into how, at such a time, he could have allowed himself to be carried away by an impulse of happiness, he confined himself to a gesture which he habitually employed whenever any perplexing question came into his mind: that is, he passed his hand across his forehead, rubbed his eyes, and wiped his glasses. And yet he never got over the loss of his wife, but used to say to my grandfather, during the two years by which he survived her, "It's a funny thing, now; I very often think of my poor wife, but I cannot think of her for long at a time." "Often, but a little at a time, like poor old Swann," became one of my grandfather's favourite sayings, which he would apply to all manner of things. I should have assumed that this father of Swann's had been a monster if my grandfather, whom I regarded as a

6. Close-cropped, like a crew cut; named after a French actor.

better judge than myself, and whose word was my law and often led me in the long run to pardon offences which I should have been inclined to condemn, had not gone on to exclaim, "But, after all, he had a heart of gold."

For many years, during the course of which—especially before his marriage—M. Swann the younger came often to see them at Combray, my great-aunt and my grandparents never suspected that he had entirely ceased to live in the society which his family had frequented, and that, under the sort of incognito which the name of Swann gave him among us, they were harbouring—with the complete innocence of a family of respectable innkeepers who have in their midst some celebrated highwayman without knowing it—one of the most distinguished members of the Jockey Club, a particular friend of the Comte de Paris and of the Prince of Wales, and one of the men most sought after in the aristocratic world of the Faubourg Saint-Germain.[7]

Our utter ignorance of the brilliant social life which Swann led was, of course, due in part to his own reserve and discretion, but also to the fact that middle-class people in those days took what was almost a Hindu view of society, which they held to consist of sharply defined castes, so that everyone at his birth found himself called to that station in life which his parents already occupied, and from which nothing, save the accident of an exceptional career or of a "good" marriage, could extract you and translate you to a superior caste. M. Swann the elder had been a stockbroker; and so "young Swann" found himself immured for life in a caste whose members' fortunes, as in a category of tax-payers, varied between such and such limits of income. One knew the people with whom his father had associated, and so one knew his own associates, the people with whom he was "in a position to mix." If he knew other people besides, those were youthful acquaintances on whom the old friends of his family, like my relatives, shut their eyes all the more good-naturedly because Swann himself, after he was left an orphan, still came most faithfully to see us; but we would have been ready to wager that the people outside our acquaintance whom Swann knew were of the sort to whom he would not have dared to raise his hat if he had met them while he was walking with us. Had it been absolutely essential to apply to Swann a social coefficient peculiar to himself, as distinct from all the other sons of other stockbrokers in his father's position, his coefficient would have been rather lower than theirs, because, being very simple in his habits, and having always had a craze for "antiques" and pictures, he now lived and amassed his collections in an old house which my grandmother longed to visit but which was situated on the Quai d'Orléans,[8] a neighbourhood in which my great-aunt thought it most degrading to be quartered. "Are you really a connoisseur, now?" she would say to him: "I ask for your own sake, as you are likely to have fakes palmed off on you by the dealers," for she did not, in

7. A fashionable area of Paris on the left bank of the Seine; many of the French aristocracy lived there. *Jockey Club*: an exclusive men's club devoted not only to horseracing but to other diversions (such as the opera). The Comte de Paris (1838–1894) was heir apparent to the French throne, in the unlikely event that the monarchy were reinstated. The Prince of Wales became in 1901 King Edward VII of England. The implication is that Swann's social connections were not merely of the highest but of an idle and somewhat hedonistic sort.   8. A beautiful though less fashionable section in the heart of Paris, along the Seine.

fact, endow him with any critical faculty, and had no great opinion of the intelligence of a man who, in conversation, would avoid serious topics and showed a very dull preciseness, not only when he gave us kitchen recipes, going into the most minute details, but even when my grandmother's sisters were talking to him about art. When challenged by them to give an opinion, or to express his admiration for some picture, he would remain almost offensively silent, and would then make amends by furnishing (if he could) some fact or other about the gallery in which the picture was hung, or the date at which it had been painted. But as a rule he would content himself with trying to amuse us by telling us about his latest adventure with someone whom we ourselves knew, such as the Combray chemist,[9] or our cook, or our coachman. These stories certainly used to make my great-aunt laugh, but she could never decide whether this was on account of the absurd rôle which Swann invariably gave himself therein, or of the wit that he showed in telling them: "I must say you really are a regular character, M. Swann!"

As she was the only member of our family who could be described as a trifle "common," she would always take care to remark to strangers, when Swann was mentioned, that he could easily, had he so wished, have lived in the Boulevard Haussmann or the Avenue de l'Opéra, and that he was the son of old M. Swann who must have left four or five million francs,[1] but that it was a fad of his. A fad which, moreover, she thought was bound to amuse other people so much that in Paris, when M. Swann called on New Year's Day bringing her a little packet of marrons glacés, she never failed, if there were strangers in the room, to say to him: "Well, M. Swann, and do you still live next door to the bonded vaults,[2] so as to be sure of not missing your train when you go to Lyons?" and she would peep out of the corner of her eye, over her glasses, at the other visitors.

But if anyone had suggested to my great-aunt that this Swann, who, in his capacity as the son of old M. Swann, was "fully qualified" to be received by any of the "best people," by the most respected barristers and solicitors[3] of Paris (though he was perhaps a trifle inclined to let this hereditary privilege go by default), had another almost secret existence of a wholly different kind; that when he left our house in Paris, saying that he must go home to bed, he would no sooner have turned the corner than he would stop, retrace his steps, and be off to some salon on whose like no stockbroker or associate of stockbrokers had ever set eyes—that would have seemed to my aunt as extraordinary as, to a woman of wider reading, the thought of being herself on terms of intimacy with Aristaeus[4] and of learning that after having a chat with her he would plunge deep into the realms of Thetis, into an empire veiled from mortal eyes, in which Virgil depicts him as being received with open arms; or—to be content with an image more likely to have occurred to her, for she had seen it painted on

9. Pharmacist.   1. Nearly a million dollars in the currency of the day; about two and a quarter million dollars by today's standards. *Boulevard Haussmann* and *Avenue de l'Opéra*: large modern avenues where the wealthy bourgeoisie (or middle class) liked to live.   2. A wine warehouse in southeastern Paris, close to the *Gare de Lyon*, the terminal from which trains depart for the industrial city of Lyon and other destinations in southeastern France. *Marrons glacés*: candied chestnuts, a traditional gift on New Year's Day, then a more common day for exchanging gifts than Christmas.   3. Trial lawyers and lawyers of other kinds.   4. Son of the Greek god Apollo. In Virgil's *Fourth Georgic*, Aristaeus seeks help from the sea nymph Thetis.

the plates we used for biscuits at Combray—as the thought of having had to dinner Ali Baba,[5] who, as soon as he finds himself alone and unobserved, will make his way into the cave, resplendent with its unsuspected treasures.

One day when he had come to see us after dinner in Paris, apologising for being in evening clothes, Françoise told us after he had left that she had got it from his coachman that he had been dining "with a princess." "A nice sort of princess,"[6] retorted my aunt, shrugging her shoulders without raising her eyes from her knitting, serenely sarcastic.

Altogether, my great-aunt treated him with scant ceremony. Since she was of the opinion that he ought to feel flattered by our invitations, she thought it only right and proper that he should never come to see us in summer without a basket of peaches or raspberries from his garden, and that from each of his visits to Italy he should bring back some photographs of old masters for me.

It seemed quite natural, therefore, to send for him whenever a recipe for some special sauce or for a pineapple salad was needed for one of our big dinner-parties, to which he himself would not be invited, being regarded as insufficiently important to be served up to new friends who might be in our house for the first time. If the conversation turned upon the princes of the House of France,[7] "gentlemen you and I will never know, will we, and don't want to, do we?" my great-aunt would say tartly to Swann, who had, perhaps, a letter from Twickenham[8] in his pocket; she would make him push the piano into place and turn over the music on evenings when my grandmother's sister sang, manipulating this person who was elsewhere so sought after with the rough simplicity of a child who will play with a collectors' piece with no more circumspection than if it were a cheap gewgaw. Doubtless the Swann who was a familiar figure in all the clubs of those days differed hugely from the Swann created by my great-aunt when, of an evening, in our little garden at Combray, after the two shy peals had sounded from the gate, she would inject and vitalise with everything she knew about the Swann family the obscure and shadowy figure who emerged, with my grandmother in his wake, from the dark background and who was identified by his voice. But then, even in the most insignificant details of our daily life, none of us can be said to constitute a material whole, which is identical for everyone, and need only be turned up like a page in an account-book or the record of a will; our social personality is a creation of the thoughts of other people. Even the simple act which we describe as "seeing someone we know" is to some extent an intellectual process. We pack the physical outline of the person we see with all the notions we have already formed about him, and in the total picture of him which we compose in our minds those notions have certainly the principal place. In the end they come to fill out so completely the curve of his cheeks, to follow so exactly the line of his nose, they blend

---

5. Hero of an *Arabian Nights* tale, a poor youth who discovers a robber's cave filled with treasure. 6. That is, a "princess" of some shady level of society.   7. The male members of the French royal family, such as the Comte de Paris. The spirit of the times was anti-Royalist, and in fact all claimants to the French throne and their heirs were banished from France by law in 1886.   8. Fashionable London suburb. The French royal family had a house there.

so harmoniously in the sound of his voice as if it were no more than a transparent envelope, that each time we see the face or hear the voice it is these notions which we recognise and to which we listen. And so, no doubt, from the Swann they had constructed for themselves my family had left out, in their ignorance, a whole host of details of his life in the world of fashion, details which caused other people, when they met him, to see all the graces enthroned in his face and stopping at the line of his aquiline nose as at a natural frontier; but they had contrived also to put into this face divested of all glamour, vacant and roomy as an untenanted house, to plant in the depths of these undervalued eyes, a lingering resid-uum, vague but not unpleasing—half-memory and half-oblivion—of idle hours spent together after our weekly dinners, round the card-table or in the garden, during our companionable country life. Our friend's corporeal envelope had been so well lined with this residuum, as well as various earlier memories of his parents, that their own special Swann had become to my family a complete and living creature; so that even now I have the feeling of leaving someone I know for another quite different person when, going back in memory, I pass from the Swann whom I knew later and more intimately to this early Swann—this early Swann in whom I can distinguish the charming mistakes of my youth, and who in fact is less like his successor than he is like the other people I knew at that time, as though one's life were a picture gallery in which all the portraits of any one period had a marked family likeness, a similar tonality—this early Swann abound-ing in leisure, fragrant with the scent of the great chestnut-tree, of baskets of raspberries and of a sprig of tarragon.

And yet one day, when my grandmother had gone to ask some favour of a lady whom she had known at the Sacré Cœur[9] (and with whom, because of our notions of caste, she had not cared to keep up any degree of intimacy in spite of several common interests), the Marquise de Ville-parisis, of the famous house of Bouillon, this lady had said to her:

"I believe you know M. Swann very well; he's a great friend of my nephews, the des Laumes."[1]

My grandmother had returned from the call full of praise for the house, which overlooked some gardens, and in which Mme de Villeparisis had advised her to rent a flat, and also for a repairing tailor and his daughter who kept a little shop in the courtyard, into which she had gone to ask them to put a stitch in her skirt, which she had torn on the staircase. My grandmother had found these people perfectly charming: the girl, she said, was a jewel, and the tailor the best and most distinguished man she had ever seen. For in her eyes distinction was a thing wholly independent of social position. She was in ecstasies over some answer the tailor had made to her, saying to Mamma:

"Sévigné[2] would not have put it better!" and, by way of contrast, of a nephew of Mme de Villeparisis whom she had met at the house:

9. A convent school in Paris, attended by daughters of the aristocracy and the wealthy bourgeoisie.
1. A fictional family. The Marquise de Villeparisis was a member of the Guermantes family. Proust enhances the apparent reality of the Guermantes by relating them to the historical house of Bouillon, a famous aristocratic family tracing its descent from the Middle Ages. 2. The Marquise de Sévigné (1626–1696), known for the lively style of her letters.

"My dear, he is so common!"

Now, the effect of the remark about Swann had been, not to raise him in my great-aunt's estimation, but to lower Mme de Villeparisis. It appeared that the deference which, on my grandmother's authority, we owed to Mme de Villeparisis imposed on her the reciprocal obligation to do nothing that would render her less worthy of our regard, and that she had failed in this duty by becoming aware of Swann's existence and in allowing members of her family to associate with him. "What! She knows Swann? A person who, you always made out, was related to Marshal Mac-Mahon!"[3] This view of Swann's social position which prevailed in my family seemed to be confirmed later on by his marriage with a woman of the worst type, almost a prostitute, whom, to do him justice, he never attempted to introduce to us—for he continued to come to our house alone, though more and more seldom—but from whom they felt they could establish, on the assumption that he had found her there, the circle, unknown to them, in which he ordinarily moved.

But on one occasion my grandfather read in a newspaper that M. Swann was one of the most regular attendants at the Sunday luncheons given by the Duc de X——, whose father and uncle had been among our most prominent statesmen in the reign of Louis-Philippe.[4] Now my grandfather was curious to learn all the smallest details which might help him to take a mental share in the private lives of men like Molé, the Duc Pasquier, or the Duc de Broglie.[5] He was delighted to find that Swann associated with people who had known them. My great-aunt, on the other hand, interpreted this piece of news in a sense discreditable to Swann; for anyone who chose his associates outside the caste in which he had been born and bred, outside his "proper station," automatically lowered himself in her eyes. It seemed to her that such a one abdicated all claim to enjoy the fruits of the splendid connections with people of good position which prudent parents cultivate and store up for their children's benefit, and she had actually ceased to "see" the son of a lawyer of our acquaintance because he had married a "Highness" and had thereby stepped down—in her eyes—from the respectable position of a lawyer's son to that of those adventurers, upstart footmen or stable-boys mostly, to whom, we are told, queens have sometimes shown their favours. She objected, therefore, to my grandfather's plan of questioning Swann, when next he came to dine with us, about these people whose friendship with him we had discovered. At the same time my grandmother's two sisters, elderly spinsters who shared her nobility of character but lacked her intelligence, declared that they could not conceive what pleasure their brother-in-law could find in talking about such trifles. They were ladies of lofty aspirations, who for that reason were incapable of taking the least interest in what might be termed gossip, even if it had some historical import, or, generally speaking, in anything that was not directly associated with some aesthetic or virtuous

3. Marshal of France (1808–1893), elected president of the French Republic in 1873.   4. King of France from 1830 to 1848, father of the Comte de Paris.   5. Duc Achille Charles Leonce Victor de Broglie (1785–1870) had a busy public career that ended in 1851. Comte Louis Mathieu Molé (1781–1855) held various cabinet positions before becoming premier of France in 1836. Duc Etienne Denis de Pasquier (1767–1862) also held important public positions up to 1837. All were active during the reign of Louis Philippe.

object. So complete was their negation of interest in anything which seemed directly or indirectly connected with worldly matters that their sense of hearing—having finally come to realise its temporary futility when the tone of the conversation at the dinner-table became frivolous or merely mundane without the two old ladies' being able to guide it back to topics dear to themselves—would put its receptive organs into abeyance to the point of actually becoming atrophied. So that if my grandfather wished to attract the attention of the two sisters, he had to resort to some such physical stimuli as alienists adopt in dealing with their distracted patients: to wit, repeated taps on a glass with the blade of a knife, accompanied by a sharp word and a compelling glance, violent methods which these psychiatrists are apt to bring with them into their everyday life among the sane, either from force of professional habit or because they think the whole world a trifle mad.

Their interest grew, however, when, the day before Swann was to dine with us, and when he had made them a special present of a case of Asti, my great-aunt, who had in her hand a copy of the *Figaro* in which to the name of a picture then on view in a Corot exhibition were added the words, "from the collection of M. Charles Swann," asked: "Did you see that Swann is 'mentioned' in the *Figaro*?"[6]

"But I've always told you," said my grandmother, "that he had a great deal of taste."

"You would, of course," retorted my great-aunt, "say anything just to seem different from *us.*" For, knowing that my grandmother never agreed with her, and not being quite confident that it was her own opinion which the rest of us invariably endorsed, she wished to extort from us a wholesale condemnation of my grandmother's views, against which she hoped to force us into solidarity with her own. But we sat silent. My grandmother's sisters having expressed a desire to mention to Swann this reference to him in the *Figaro*, my great-aunt dissuaded them. Whenever she saw in others an advantage, however trivial, which she herself lacked, she would persuade herself that it was no advantage at all, but a drawback, and would pity so as not to have to envy them.

"I don't think that would please him at all; I know very well that I should hate to see my name printed like that, as large as life, in the paper, and I shouldn't feel at all flattered if anyone spoke to me about it."

She did not, however, put any very great pressure upon my grandmother's sisters, for they, in their horror of vulgarity, had brought to such a fine art the concealment of a personal allusion in a wealth of ingenious circumlocution, that it would often pass unnoticed even by the person to whom it was addressed. As for my mother, her only thought was of trying to induce my father to speak to Swann, not about his wife but about his daughter, whom he worshipped, and for whose sake it was understood that he had ultimately made his unfortunate marriage.

"You need only say a word; just ask him how she is. It must be so very hard for him."

---

6. Leading Parisian newspaper. *Asti:* an Italian white wine. Jean Corot (1796–1875) was a French landscape painter, very popular at the time.

My father, however, was annoyed: "No, no; you have the most absurd ideas. It would be utterly ridiculous."

But the only one of us in whom the prospect of Swann's arrival gave rise to an unhappy foreboding was myself. This was because on the evenings when there were visitors, or just M. Swann, in the house, Mamma did not come up to my room. I dined before the others, and afterwards came and sat at table until eight o'clock, when it was understood that I must go upstairs; that frail and precious kiss which Mamma used normally to bestow on me when I was in bed and just going to sleep had to be transported from the dining-room to my bedroom where I must keep it inviolate all the time that it took me to undress, without letting its sweet charm be broken, without letting its volatile essence diffuse itself and evaporate; and it was precisely on those very evenings when I needed to receive it with special care that I was obliged to take it, to snatch it brusquely and in public, without even having the time or the equanimity to bring to what I was doing the single-minded attention of lunatics who compel themselves to exclude all other thoughts from their minds while they are shutting a door, so that when the sickness of uncertainty sweeps over them again they can triumphantly oppose it with the recollection of the precise moment when they shut the door.

We were all in the garden when the double tinkle of the visitors' bell sounded shyly. Everyone knew that it must be Swann, and yet they looked at one another inquiringly and sent my grandmother to reconnoitre.

"See that you thank him intelligibly for the wine," my grandfather warned his two sisters-in-law. "You know how good it is, and the case is huge."

"Now, don't start whispering!" said my great-aunt. "How would you like to come into a house and find everyone muttering to themselves?"

"Ah! There's M. Swann," cried my father. "Let's ask him if he thinks it will be fine to-morrow."

My mother fancied that a word from her would wipe out all the distress which my family had contrived to cause Swann since his marriage. She found an opportunity to draw him aside for a moment. But I followed her: I could not bring myself to let her out of my sight while I felt that in a few minutes I should have to leave her in the dining-room and go up to my bed without the consoling thought, as on ordinary evenings, that she would come up later to kiss me.

"Now, M. Swann," she said, "do tell me about your daughter. I'm sure she already has a taste for beautiful things, like her papa."

"Come along and sit down here with us all on the verandah," said my grandfather, coming up to him. My mother had to abandon her quest, but managed to extract from the restriction itself a further delicate thought, like good poets whom the tyranny of rhyme forces into the discovery of their finest lines.

"We can talk about her again when we are by ourselves," she said, or rather whispered to Swann. "Only a mother is capable of understanding these things. I'm sure that hers would agree with me."

And so we all sat down round the iron table. I should have liked not to think of the hours of anguish which I should have to spend that evening alone in my room, without being able to go to sleep: I tried to convince myself that they were of no importance since I should have forgotten them next morning, and to fix my mind on thoughts of the future which would carry me, as on a bridge, across the terrifying abyss that yawned at my feet. But my mind, strained by this foreboding, distended like the look which I shot at my mother, would not allow any extraneous impression to enter. Thoughts did indeed enter it, but only on the condition that they left behind them every element of beauty, or even of humour, by which I might have been distracted or beguiled. As a surgical patient, thanks to a local anaesthetic, can look on fully conscious while an operation is being performed upon him and yet feel nothing, I could repeat to myself some favourite lines, or watch my grandfather's efforts to talk to Swann about the Duc d' Audiffret-Pasquier,[7] without being able to kindle any emotion from the one or amusement from the other. Hardly had my grandfather begun to question Swann about that orator when one of my grandmother's sisters, in whose ears the question echoed like a solemn but untimely silence which her natural politeness bade her interrupt, addressed the other with:

"Just fancy, Flora, I met a young Swedish governess today who told me some most interesting things about the co-operative movement in Scandinavia. We really must have her to dine here one evening."

"To be sure!" said her sister Flora, "but I haven't wasted my time either. I met such a clever old gentleman at M. Vinteuil's who knows Maubant[8] quite well, and Maubant has told him every little thing about how he gets up his parts. It's the most interesting thing I ever heard. He's a neighbour of M. Vinteuil's, and I never knew; and he is so nice besides."

"M. Vinteuil is not the only one who has nice neighbours," cried my aunt Céline in a voice that was loud because of shyness and forced because of premeditation, darting, as she spoke, what she called a "significant glance" at Swann. And my aunt Flora, who realised that this veiled utterance was Céline's way of thanking Swann for the Asti, looked at him also with a blend of congratulation and irony, either because she simply wished to underline her sister's little witticism, or because she envied Swann his having inspired it, or because she imagined that he was embarrassed, and could not help having a little fun at his expense.

"I think it would be worth while," Flora went on, "to have this old gentleman to dinner. When you get him going on Maubant or Mme Materna[9] he will talk for hours on end."

"That must be delightful," sighed my grandfather, in whose mind nature had unfortunately forgotten to include any capacity whatsoever for becoming passionately interested in the Swedish co-operative movement or in the methods employed by Maubant to get up his parts, just as it had forgotten to endow my grandmother's two sisters with a grain of that precious salt which one has oneself to "add to taste" in order to extract any savour from a narrative of the private life of Molé or of the Comte de Paris.

7. A fictitious nobleman.   8. Actor at the Comédie Française, the French national theater. M. Vinteuil is a fictitious composer and neighbor of the family.   9. Austrian soprano, who took part in the premiere of Wagner's *Ring* cycle at Bayreuth in 1876.

"By the way," said Swann to my grandfather, "what I was going to tell you has more to do than you might think with what you were asking me just now, for in some respects there has been very little change. I came across a passage in Saint-Simon[1] this morning which would have amused you. It's in the volume which covers his mission to Spain; not one of the best, little more in fact than a journal, but at least a wonderfully well written journal, which fairly distinguishes it from the tedious journals we feel bound to read morning and evening."

"I don't agree with you: there are some days when I find reading the papers very pleasant indeed," my aunt Flora broke in, to show Swann that she had read the note about his Corot in the *Figaro*.

"Yes," aunt Céline went one better, "when they write about things or people in whom we are interested."

"I don't deny it," answered Swann in some bewilderment. "The fault I find with our journalism is that it forces us to take an interest in some fresh triviality or other every day, whereas only three or four books in a lifetime give us anything that is of real importance. Suppose that, every morning, when we tore the wrapper off our paper with fevered hands, a transmutation were to take place, and we were to find inside it—oh! I don't know; shall we say Pascal's *Pensées*?"[2] He articulated the title with an ironic emphasis so as not to appear pedantic. "And then, in the gilt and tooled volumes which we open once in ten years," he went on, showing that contempt for worldly matters which some men of the world like to affect, "we should read that the Queen of the Hellenes had arrived at Cannes, or that the Princesse de Léon had given a fancy dress ball. In that way we should arrive at a happy medium." But at once regretting that he had allowed himself to speak of serious matters even in jest, he added ironically: "What a fine conversation we're having! I can't think why we climb to these lofty heights," and then, turning to my grandfather: "Well, Saint-Simon tells how Maulévrier had had the audacity to try to shake hands with his sons.[3] You remember how he says of Maulévrier, 'Never did I find in that coarse bottle anything but ill-humour, boorishness, and folly.'"

"Coarse or not, I know bottles in which there is something very different," said Flora briskly, feeling bound to thank Swann as well as her sister, since the present of Asti had been addressed to them both. Céline laughed.

Swann was puzzled, but went on: "'I cannot say whether it was ignorance or cozenage,' writes Saint-Simon. 'He tried to give his hand to my children. I noticed it in time to prevent him.'"

My grandfather was already in ecstasies over "ignorance or cozenage," but Mlle Céline—the name of Saint-Simon, a "man of letters," having arrested the complete paralysis of her auditory faculties—was indignant:

---

1. The memoirs of the Duc de Saint-Simon (1675–1755) describe court life and intrigue during the reigns of Louis XIV and Louis XV. He was sent to Spain in 1721 to arrange the marriage of Louis XV and the daughter of the king of Spain.   2. The "Thoughts" of the French mathematician and religious philosopher Blaise Pascal (1623–1662) are comments on the human condition and one of the triumphant works of French classicism.   3. Maulévrier was the French ambassador to Spain. Saint-Simon considered him of inferior birth, and refused to let his own children shake Maulévrier's hand (*Memoirs*, vol. XXXIX).

"What! You admire that? Well, that's a fine thing, I must say! But what's it supposed to mean? Isn't one man as good as the next? What difference can it make whether he's a duke or a groom so long as he's intelligent and kind? He had a fine way of bringing up his children, your Saint-Simon, if he didn't teach them to shake hands with all decent folk. Really and truly, it's abominable. And you dare to quote it!"

And my grandfather, utterly depressed, realising how futile it would be, against this opposition, to attempt to get Swann to tell him the stories which would have amused him, murmured to my mother: "Just tell me again that line of yours which always comforts me so much on these occasions. Oh, yes: 'What virtues, Lord, Thou makest us abhor!'[4] How good that is!"

I never took my eyes off my mother. I knew that when they were at table I should not be permitted to stay there for the whole of dinner-time, and that Mamma, for fear of annoying my father, would not allow me to kiss her several times in public, as I would have done in my room. And so I promised myself that in the dining-room, as they began to eat and drink and as I felt the hour approach, I would put beforehand into this kiss, which was bound to be so brief and furtive, everything that my own efforts could muster, would carefully choose in advance the exact spot on her cheek where I would imprint it, and would so prepare my thoughts as to be able, thanks to these mental preliminaries, to consecrate the whole of the minute Mamma would grant me to the sensation of her cheek against my lips, as a painter who can have his subject for short sittings only prepares his palette, and from what he remembers and from rough notes does in advance everything which he possibly can do in the sitter's absence. But to-night, before the dinner-bell had sounded, my grandfather said with unconscious cruelty: "The little man looks tired; he'd better go up to bed. Besides, we're dining late to-night."

And my father, who was less scrupulous than my grandmother or my mother in observing the letter of a treaty, went on: "Yes; run along; off to bed."

I would have kissed Mamma then and there, but at that moment the dinner-bell rang.

"No, no, leave your mother alone. You've said good night to one another, that's enough. These exhibitions are absurd. Go on upstairs."

And so I must set forth without viaticum;[5] must climb each step of the staircase "against my heart," as the saying is, climbing in opposition to my heart's desire, which was to return to my mother, since she had not, by kissing me, given my heart leave to accompany me forth. That hateful staircase, up which I always went so sadly, gave out a smell of varnish which had, as it were, absorbed and crystallised the special quality of sorrow that I felt each evening, and made it perhaps even crueller to my sensibility because, when it assumed this olfactory guise, my intellect was powerless to resist it. When we have gone to sleep with a raging toothache and are conscious of it only as of a little girl whom we attempt, time after

---

4. From *Pompey's Death* (line 1072), a tragedy by the French dramatist Pierre Corneille (1606–1684).
5. The communion wafer and wine given to the dying in Catholic rites.

time, to pull out of the water, or a line of Molière[6] which we repeat incessantly to ourselves, it is a great relief to wake up, so that our intelligence
can disentangle the idea of toothache from any artificial semblance of
heroism or rhythmic cadence. It was the converse of this relief which I
felt when my anguish at having to go up to my room invaded my consciousness in a manner infinitely more rapid, instantaneous almost, a manner at once insidious and brutal, through the inhalation—far more
poisonous than moral penetration—of the smell of varnish peculiar to that
staircase.

Once in my room I had to stop every loophole, to close the shutters, to
dig my own grave as I turned down the bedclothes, to wrap myself in the
shroud of my nightshirt. But before burying myself in the iron bed which
had been placed there because, on summer nights, I was too hot among
the rep curtains of the four-poster,[7] I was stirred to revolt, and attempted
the desperate stratagem of a condemned prisoner. I wrote to my mother
begging her to come upstairs for an important reason which I could not
put in writing. My fear was that Françoise, my aunt's cook who used to be
put in charge of me when I was at Combray, might refuse to take my note.
I had a suspicion that, in her eyes, to carry a message to my mother when
there was a guest would appear as flatly inconceivable as for the doorkeeper of a theatre to hand a letter to an actor upon the stage. On the
subject of things which might or might not be done she possessed a code
at once imperious, abundant, subtle, and uncompromising on points
themselves imperceptible or irrelevant, which gave it a resemblance to
those ancient laws which combine such cruel ordinances as the massacre
of infants at the breast with prohibitions of exaggerated refinement against
"seething the kid in his mother's milk," or "eating of the sinew which is
upon the hollow of the thigh."[8] This code, judging by the sudden obstinacy which she would put into her refusal to carry out certain of our
instructions, seemed to have provided for social complexities and refinements of etiquette which nothing in Françoise's background or in her
career as a servant in a village household could have put into her head;
and we were obliged to assume that there was latent in her some past
existence in the ancient history of France, noble and little understood, as
in those manufacturing towns where old mansions still testify to their former courtly days, and chemical workers toil among delicately sculptured
scenes from *Le Miracle de Théophile* or *Les quatre fils Aymon*.[9]

In this particular instance, the article of her code which made it highly
improbable that—barring an outbreak of fire—Françoise would go down
and disturb Mamma in the presence of M. Swann for so unimportant a
person as myself was one embodying the respect she showed not only for
the family (as for the dead, for the clergy, or for royalty), but also for the
stranger within our gates; a respect which I should perhaps have found
touching in a book, but which never failed to irritate me on her lips,
because of the solemn and sentimental tones in which she would express

6. French dramatist (1622–1673).   7. Bed with corner pillars to support a canopy and curtains. *Rep:* a
heavy, ribbed fabric.   8. Refers to the strict dietary laws of Deuteronomy 14:21 and Genesis 32:32.
9. "The four sons of Aymon" (French), heroic knights who together rode the magic horse Bayard. Théophile was saved from damnation by the Virgin Mary after having signed a pact with the Devil.

it, and which irritated me more than usual this evening when the sacred character with which she invested the dinner-party might have the effect of making her decline to disturb its ceremonial. But to give myself a chance of success I had no hesitation in lying, telling her that it was not in the least myself who had wanted to write to Mamma, but Mamma who, on saying good night to me, had begged me not to forget to send her an answer about something she had asked me to look for, and that she would certainly be very angry if this note were not taken to her. I think that Françoise disbelieved me, for, like those primitive men whose senses were so much keener than our own, she could immediately detect, from signs imperceptible to the rest of us, the truth or falsehood of anything that we might wish to conceal from her. She studied the envelope for five minutes as though an examination of the paper itself and the look of my handwriting could enlighten her as to the nature of the contents, or tell her to which article of her code she ought to refer the matter. Then she went out with an air of resignation which seemed to imply: "It's hard lines on parents having a child like that."

A moment later she returned to say that they were still at the ice stage and that it was impossible for the butler to deliver the note at once, in front of everybody; but that when the finger-bowls were put round he would find a way of slipping it into Mamma's hand. At once my anxiety subsided; it was now no longer (as it had been a moment ago) until tomorrow that I had lost my mother, since my little note—though it would annoy her, no doubt, and doubly so because this stratagem would make me ridiculous in Swann's eyes—would at least admit me, invisible and enraptured, into the same room as herself, would whisper about me into her ear; since that forbidden and unfriendly dining-room, where but a moment ago the ice itself—with burned nuts in it—and the finger-bowls seemed to me to be concealing pleasures that were baleful and of a mortal sadness because Mamma was tasting of them while I was far away, had opened its doors to me and, like a ripe fruit which bursts through its skin, was going to pour out into my intoxicated heart the sweetness of Mamma's attention while she was reading what I had written. Now I was no longer separated from her; the barriers were down; an exquisite thread united us. Besides, that was not all: for surely Mamma would come.

As for the agony through which I had just passed, I imagined that Swann would have laughed heartily at it if he had read my letter and had guessed its purpose; whereas, on the contrary, as I was to learn in due course, a similar anguish[1] had been the bane of his life for many years, and no one perhaps could have understood my feelings at that moment so well as he; to him, the anguish that comes from knowing that the creature one adores is in some place of enjoyment where oneself is not and cannot follow—to him that anguish came through love, to which it is in a sense predestined, by which it will be seized upon and exploited; but when, as had befallen me, it possesses one's soul before love has yet entered into one's life, then it must drift, awaiting love's coming, vague and free, without precise attachment, at the disposal of one sentiment to-

---

1. That is, his unhappy love for Odette de Crécy, described in *Swann in Love*.

day, of another to-morrow, of filial piety or affection for a friend. And the
joy with which I first bound myself apprentice, when Françoise returned
to tell me that my letter would be delivered, Swann, too, had known
well—that false joy which a friend or relative of the woman we love can
give us, when, on his arrival at the house or theatre where she is to be
found, for some ball or party or "first-night" at which he is to meet her,
he sees us wandering outside, desperately awaiting some opportunity of
communicating with her. He recognises us, greets us familiarly, and asks
what we are doing there. And when we invent a story of having some
urgent message to give to his relative or friend, he assures us that nothing
could be simpler, takes us in at the door, and promises to send her down
to us in five minutes. How we love him—as at that moment I loved Françoise—the good-natured intermediary who by a single word has made supportable, human, almost propitious the inconceivable, infernal scene of
gaiety in the thick of which we had been imagining swarms of enemies,
perverse and seductive, beguiling away from us, even making laugh at us,
the woman we love! If we are to judge of them by him—this relative who
has accosted us and who is himself an initiate in those cruel mysteries—
then the other guests cannot be so very demoniacal. Those inaccessible
and excruciating hours during which she was about to taste of unknown
pleasures—suddenly, through an unexpected breach, we have broken into
them; suddenly we can picture to ourselves, we possess, we intervene
upon, we have almost created, one of the moments the succession of
which would have composed those hours, a moment as real as all the rest,
if not actually more important to us because our mistress is more intensely
a part of it: namely, the moment in which he goes to tell her that we are
waiting below. And doubtless the other moments of the party would not
have been so very different from this one, would be no more exquisite, no
more calculated to make us suffer, since this kind friend has assured us
that "Of course, she will be delighted to come down! It will be far more
amusing for her to talk to you than to be bored up there." Alas! Swann
had learned by experience that the good intentions of a third party are
powerless to influence a woman who is annoyed to find herself pursued
even into a ballroom by a man she does not love. Too often, the kind
friend comes down again alone.

My mother did not appear, but without the slightest consideration for
my self-respect (which depended upon her keeping up the fiction that she
had asked me to let her know the result of my search for something or
other) told Françoise to tell me, in so many words: "There is no answer"—
words I have so often, since then, heard the hall-porters in grand hotels
and the flunkeys in gambling-clubs and the like repeat to some poor girl
who replies in bewilderment: "What! he said nothing? It's not possible.
You did give him my letter, didn't you? Very well, I shall wait a little
longer." And, just as she invariably protests that she does not need the
extra gas which the porter offers to light for her, and sits on there, hearing
nothing further except an occasional remark on the weather which the
porter exchanges with a bell-hop whom he will send off suddenly, when
he notices the time, to put some customer's wine on the ice, so, having
declined Françoise's offer to make me some tea or to stay beside me, I let

her go off again to the pantry, and lay down and shut my eyes, trying not to hear the voices of my family who were drinking their coffee in the garden.

But after a few seconds I realised that, by writing that note to Mamma, by approaching—at the risk of making her angry—so near to her that I felt I could reach out and grasp the moment in which I should see her again, I had cut myself off from the possibility of going to sleep until I actually had seen her, and my heart began to beat more and more painfully as I increased my agitation by ordering myself to keep calm and to acquiesce in my ill-fortune. Then, suddenly, my anxiety subsided, a feeling of intense happiness coursed through me, as when a strong medicine begins to take effect and one's pain vanishes: I had formed a resolution to abandon all attempts to go to sleep without seeing Mamma, had made up my mind to kiss her at all costs, even though this meant the certainty of being in disgrace with her for long afterwards—when she herself came up to bed. The calm which succeeded my anguish filled me with an extraordinary exhilaration, no less than my sense of expectation, my thirst for and my fear of danger. Noiselessly I opened the window and sat down on the foot of my bed. I hardly dared to move in case they should hear me from below. Outside, things too seemed frozen, rapt in a mute intentness not to disturb the moonlight which, duplicating each of them and throwing it back by the extension in front of it of a shadow denser and more concrete than its substance, had made the whole landscape at once thinner and larger, like a map which, after being folded up, is spread out upon the ground. What had to move—a leaf of the chestnut-tree, for instance— moved. But its minute quivering, total, self-contained, finished down to its minutest gradation and its last delicate tremor, did not impinge upon the rest of the scene, did not merge with it, remained circumscribed. Exposed upon this surface of silence which absorbed nothing of them, the most distant sounds, those which must have come from gardens at the far end of the town, could be distinguished with such exact "finish" that the impression they gave of coming from a distance seemed due only to their "pianissimo" execution, like those movements on muted strings so well performed by the orchestra of the Conservatoire[2] that, even though one does not miss a single note, one thinks nonetheless that they are being played somewhere outside, a long way from the concert hall, so that all the old subscribers—my grandmother's sisters too, when Swann had given them his seats—used to strain their ears as if they had caught the distant approach of an army on the march, which had not yet rounded the corner of the Rue de Trévise.[3]

I was well aware that I had placed myself in a position than which none could be counted upon to involve me in graver consequences at my parents' hands; consequences far graver, indeed, than a stranger would have imagined, and such as (he would have thought) could follow only some really shameful misdemeanour. But in the upbringing which they had given me faults were not classified in the same order as in that of other children, and I had been taught to place at the head of the list (doubtless

2. The national music conservatory in Paris.   3. A street in Combray.

because there was no other class of faults from which I needed to be more carefully protected) those in which I can now distinguish the common feature that one succumbs to them by yielding to a nervous impulse. But such a phrase had never been uttered in my hearing; no one had yet accounted for my temptations in a way which might have led me to believe that there was some excuse for my giving in to them, or that I was actually incapable of holding out against them. Yet I could easily recognise this class of transgressions by the anguish of mind which preceded as well as by the rigour of the punishment which followed them; and I knew that what I had just done was in the same category as certain other sins for which I had been severely punished, though infinitely more serious than they. When I went out to meet my mother on her way up to bed, and when she saw that I had stayed up in order to say good night to her again in the passage, I should not be allowed to stay in the house a day longer, I should be packed off to school[4] next morning; so much was certain. Very well: had I been obliged, the next moment, to hurl myself out of the window, I should still have preferred such a fate. For what I wanted now was Mamma, to say good night to her. I had gone too far along the road which led to the fulfilment of this desire to be able to retrace my steps.

I could hear my parents' footsteps as they accompanied Swann to the gate, and when the clanging of the bell assured me that he had really gone, I crept to the window. Mamma was asking my father if he had thought the lobster good, and whether M. Swann had had a second helping of the coffee-and-pistachio ice. "I thought it rather so-so," she was saying. "Next time we shall have to try another flavour."

"I can't tell you," said my great-aunt, "what a change I find in Swann. He is quite antiquated!" She had grown so accustomed to seeing Swann always in the same stage of adolescence that it was a shock to her to find him suddenly less young than the age she still attributed to him. And the others too were beginning to remark in Swann that abnormal, excessive, shameful and deserved senescence of bachelors, of all those for whom it seems that the great day which knows no morrow must be longer than for other men, since for them it is void of promise, and from its dawn the moments steadily accumulate without any subsequent partition[5] among offspring.

"I fancy he has a lot of trouble with that wretched wife of his, who lives with a certain Monsieur de Charlus,[6] as all Combray knows. It's the talk of the town."

My mother observed that, in spite of this, he had looked much less unhappy of late. "And he doesn't nearly so often do that trick of his, so like his father, of wiping his eyes and drawing his hand across his forehead. I think myself that in his heart of hearts he no longer loves that woman."

"Why, of course he doesn't," answered my grandfather. "He wrote me a letter about it, ages ago, to which I took care to pay no attention, but it left no doubt as to his feelings, or at any rate his love, for his wife. Hullo! you two; you never thanked him for the Asti," he went on, turning to his sisters-in-law.

---

4. That is, boarding school.   5. Sharing, as under a will.   6. Brother of the Duc de Guermantes.

"What! we never thanked him? I think, between you and me, that I put it to him quite neatly," replied my aunt Flora.

"Yes, you managed it very well; I admired you for it," said my aunt Céline.

"But you did it very prettily, too."

"Yes; I was rather proud of my remark about 'nice neighbours.' "

"What! Do you call that thanking him?" shouted my grandfather. "I heard that all right, but devil take me if I guessed it was meant for Swann. You may be quite sure he never noticed it."

"Come, come; Swann isn't a fool. I'm sure he understood. You didn't expect me to tell him the number of bottles, or to guess what he paid for them."

My father and mother were left alone and sat down for a moment; then my father said: "Well, shall we go up to bed?"

"As you wish, dear, though I don't feel at all sleepy. I don't know why; it can't be the coffee-ice—it wasn't strong enough to keep me awake like this. But I see a light in the servants' hall: poor Françoise has been sitting up for me, so I'll get her to unhook me while you go and undress."

My mother opened the latticed door which led from the hall to the staircase. Presently I heard her coming upstairs to close her window. I went quietly into the passage; my heart was beating so violently that I could hardly move, but at least it was throbbing no longer with anxiety, but with terror and joy. I saw in the well of the stair a light coming upwards, from Mamma's candle. Then I saw Mamma herself and I threw myself upon her. For an instant she looked at me in astonishment, not realising what could have happened. Then her face assumed an expression of anger. She said not a single word to me; and indeed I used to go for days on end without being spoken to, for far more venial offences than this. A single word from Mamma would have been an admission that further intercourse with me was within the bounds of possibility, and that might perhaps have appeared to me more terrible still, as indicating that, with such a punishment as was in store for me, mere silence and black looks would have been puerile. A word from her then would have implied the false calm with which one addresses a servant to whom one has just decided to give notice; the kiss one bestows on a son who is being packed off to enlist, which would have been denied him if it had merely been a matter of being angry with him for a few days. But she heard my father coming from the dressing-room, where he had gone to take off his clothes, and, to avoid the "scene" which he would make if he saw me, she said to me in a voice half-stifled with anger: "Off you go at once. Do you want your father to see you waiting there like an idiot?"

But I implored her again: "Come and say good night to me," terrified as I saw the light from my father's candle already creeping up the wall, but also making use of his approach as a means of blackmail, in the hope that my mother, not wishing him to find me there, as find me he must if she continued to refuse me, would give in and say: "Go back to your room. I will come."

Too late: my father was upon us. Instinctively I murmured, though no one heard me, "I'm done for!"

I was not, however. My father used constantly to refuse to let me do things which were quite clearly allowed by the more liberal charters granted me by my mother and grandmother, because he paid no heed to "principles," and because for him there was no such thing as the "rule of law."[7] For some quite irrelevant reason, or for no reason at all, he would at the last moment prevent me from taking some particular walk, one so regular, so hallowed, that to deprive me of it was a clear breach of faith; or again, as he had done this evening, long before the appointed hour he would snap out: "Run along up to bed now; no excuses!" But at the same time, because he was devoid of principles (in my grandmother's sense), he could not, strictly speaking, be called intransigent. He looked at me for a moment with an air of surprise and annoyance, and then when Mamma had told him, not without some embarrassment, what had happened, said to her: "Go along with him, then. You said just now that you didn't feel very sleepy, so stay in his room for a little. I don't need anything."

"But, my dear," my mother answered timidly, "whether or not I feel sleepy is not the point; we mustn't let the child get into the habit . . ."

"There's no question of getting into a habit," said my father, with a shrug of the shoulders; "you can see quite well that the child is unhappy. After all, we aren't jailers. You'll end by making him ill, and a lot of good that will do. There are two beds in his room; tell Françoise to make up the big one for you, and stay with him for the rest of the night. Anyhow, I'm off to bed; I'm not so nervy as you. Good night."

It was impossible for me to thank my father; he would have been exasperated by what he called mawkishness. I stood there, not daring to move; he was still in front of us, a tall figure in his white nightshirt, crowned with the pink and violet cashmere scarf which he used to wrap around his head since he had begun to suffer from neuralgia, standing like Abraham in the engraving after Benozzo Gozzoli[8] which M. Swann had given me, telling Sarah that she must tear herself away from Isaac. Many years have passed since that night. The wall of the staircase up which I had watched the light of his candle gradually climb was long ago demolished. And in myself, too, many things have perished which I imagined would last for ever, and new ones have arisen, giving birth to new sorrows and new joys which in those days I could not have foreseen, just as now the old are hard to understand. It is a long time, too, since my father has been able to say to Mamma: "Go along with the child." Never again will such moments be possible for me. But of late I have been increasingly able to catch, if I listen attentively, the sound of the sobs which I had the strength to control in my father's presence, and which broke out only when I found myself alone with Mamma. In reality their echo has never ceased; and it is only because life is now growing more and more quiet round about me that I hear them anew, like those convent bells which are so effectively drowned during the day by the noises of the street that one would suppose them to have stopped, until they ring out again through the silent evening air.

---

7. Reference to the *ius gentium*, the "law of nations" or natural law supposed to govern international and public relations. Marcel sees the relationship between himself and his mother and grandmother as a social contract; his father is the unpredictable tyrant.   8. Florentine painter (1420–1497) whose frescoes at Pisa contain scenes from the life of the biblical patriarch Abraham.

Mamma spent that night in my room: when I had just committed a sin so deadly that I expected to be banished from the household, my parents gave me a far greater concession than I could ever have won as the reward of a good deed. Even at the moment when it manifested itself in this crowning mercy, my father's behaviour towards me still retained that arbitrary and unwarranted quality which was so characteristic of him and which arose from the fact that his actions were generally dictated by chance expediencies rather than based on any formal plan. And perhaps even what I called his severity, when he sent me off to bed, deserved that title less than my mother's or my grandmother's attitude, for his nature, which in some respects differed more than theirs from my own, had probably prevented him from realising until then how wretched I was every evening, something which my mother and grandmother knew well; but they loved me enough to be unwilling to spare me that suffering, which they hoped to teach me to overcome, so as to reduce my nervous sensibility and to strengthen my will. Whereas my father, whose affection for me was of another kind, would not, I suspect, have had the same courage, for as soon as he had grasped the fact that I was unhappy he had said to my mother: "Go and comfort him."

Mamma stayed that night in my room, and it seemed that she did not wish to mar by recrimination those hours which were so different from anything that I had had a right to expect, for when Françoise (who guessed that something extraordinary must have happened when she saw Mamma sitting by my side, holding my hand and letting me cry unchided) said to her: "But, Madame, what is young master crying for?" she replied: "Why, Françoise, he doesn't know himself: it's his nerves. Make up the big bed for me quickly and then go off to your own." And thus for the first time my unhappiness was regarded no longer as a punishable offence but as an involuntary ailment which had been officially recognised, a nervous condition for which I was in no way responsible: I had the consolation of no longer having to mingle apprehensive scruples with the bitterness of my tears; I could weep henceforth without sin. I felt no small degree of pride, either, in Françoise's presence at this return to humane conditions which, not an hour after Mamma had refused to come up to my room and had sent the snubbing message that I was to go to sleep, raised me to the dignity of a grown-up person, brought me of a sudden to a sort of puberty of sorrow, a manumission of tears. I ought to have been happy; I was not. It struck me that my mother had just made a first concession which must have been painful to her, that it was a first abdication on her part from the ideal she had formed for me, and that for the first time she who was so brave had to confess herself beaten. It struck me that if I had just won a victory it was over her, that I had succeeded, as sickness or sorrow or age might have succeeded, in relaxing her will, in undermining her judgment; a black date in the calendar. And if I had dared now, I should have said to Mamma: "No, I don't want you to, you mustn't sleep here." But I was conscious of the practical wisdom, of what would nowadays be called the realism, with which she tempered the ardent idealism of my grandmother's nature, and I knew that now the mischief was done she would prefer to let me enjoy the soothing pleasure of her company, and not to disturb my father again. Certainly my mother's beautiful face seemed to shine again with youth that evening, as she sat gently holding my hands and trying to check my tears; but this was just what I felt should not have been; her anger would have saddened me less than this new gentleness, unknown to my childhood experience; I felt that I had with an impious and secret finger traced a first wrinkle upon her soul and brought out a first white hair on her head. This thought redoubled my sobs, and then I saw that Mamma, who had never allowed herself to indulge in any undue emotion with me, was suddenly overcome by my tears and had to struggle to keep back her own. When she realised that I had noticed this, she said to me with a smile: "Why, my little buttercup, my little canary-boy, he's going to make Mamma as silly as himself if this goes on. Look, since you can't sleep, and Mamma can't either, we mustn't go on in this stupid way; we must do something; I'll get one of your books." But I had none there. "Would you like me to get out the books now that your grand-mother is going to give you for your birthday? Just think it over first, and don't be disappointed if there's nothing new for you then."

I was only too delighted, and Mamma went to fetch a parcel of books of which I could not distinguish, through the paper in which they were wrapped, any more than their short, wide format but which, even at this first glimpse, brief and obscure as it was, bade fair to eclipse already the paintbox of New Year's Day and the silkworms of the year before. The books were *La Mare au Diable, François le Champi, La Petite Fadette* and *Les Maîtres Sonneurs.*[9] My grandmother, as I learned afterwards, had at first chosen Musset's poems, a volume of Rousseau, and *Indiana;* for while she considered light reading as unwholesome as sweets and cakes, she did not reflect that the strong breath of genius might have upon the mind even of a child an influence at once more dangerous and less invigorating than that of fresh air and sea breezes upon his body. But when my father had almost called her an imbecile on learning the names of the books she proposed to give me,[1] she had journeyed back by herself to Jouy-le-Vicomte to the bookseller's, so that there should be no danger of my not having my present in time (it was a boiling hot day, and she had come home so unwell that the doctor had warned my mother not to allow her to tire herself so), and had fallen back upon the four pastoral novels of George Sand.

"My dear," she had said to Mamma, "I could not bring myself to give the child anything that was not well written."

The truth was that she could never permit herself to buy anything from which no intellectual profit was to be derived, above all the profit which fine things afford us by teaching us to seek our pleasures elsewhere than in the barren satisfaction of worldly wealth. Even when she had to make someone a present of the kind called "useful," when she had to give an armchair or some table-silver or a walking-stick, she would choose

9. Novels of idealized country life by the French woman writer George Sand (1806–1876). The titles can be translated as *The Devil's Pool, François the Foundling Discovered in the Fields, Little Fadette,* and *The Master Bellringers.*   1. The works of Alfred de Musset (1810–1857) and Jean-Jacques Rousseau (1712–1778), often romantic and sometimes confessional, and some works by Sand (*Indiana* was a novel of free love), would be thought unsuitable reading for a young child.

"antiques," as though their long desuetude had effaced from them any semblance of utility and fitted them rather to instruct us in the lives of the men of other days than to serve the common requirements of our own. She would have liked me to have in my room photographs of ancient buildings or of beautiful places. But at the moment of buying them, and for all that the subject of the picture had an aesthetic value, she would find that vulgarity and utility had too prominent a part in them, through the mechanical nature of their reproduction by photography. She attempted by a subterfuge, if not to eliminate altogether this commercial banality, at least to minimise it, to supplant it to a certain extent with what was art still, to introduce, as it were, several "thicknesses" of art: instead of photographs of Chartres Cathedral, of the Fountains of Saint-Cloud, or of Vesuvius, she would inquire of Swann whether some great painter had not depicted them, and preferred to give me photographs of "Chartres Cathedral" after Corot, of the "Fountains of Saint-Cloud" after Hubert Robert, and of "Vesuvius" after Turner,[2] which were a stage higher in the scale of art. But although the photographer had been prevented from reproducing directly these masterpieces or beauties of nature, and had there been replaced by a great artist, he resumed his odious position when it came to reproducing the artist's interpretation. Accordingly, having to reckon again with vulgarity, my grandmother would endeavour to post-pone the moment of contact still further. She would ask Swann if the picture had not been engraved, preferring, when possible, old engravings with some interest of association apart from themselves, such, for example, as show us a masterpiece in a state in which we can no longer see it to-day (like Morghen's print of Leonardo's "Last Supper" before its deface-ment).[3] It must be admitted that the results of this method of interpreting the art of making presents were not always happy. The idea which I formed of Venice, from a drawing by Titian[4] which is supposed to have the lagoon in the background, was certainly far less accurate than what I should have derived from ordinary photographs. We could no longer keep count in the family (when my great-aunt wanted to draw up an indictment of my grandmother) of all the armchairs she had presented to married couples, young and old, which on a first attempt to sit down upon them had at once collapsed beneath the weight of their recipients. But my grandmother would have thought it sordid to concern herself too closely with the solidity of any piece of furniture in which could still be discerned a flourish, a smile, a brave conceit of the past. And even what in such pieces answered a material need, since it did so in a manner to which we are no longer accustomed, charmed her like those old forms of speech in which we can still see traces of a metaphor whose fine point has been worn away by the rough usage of our modern tongue. As it happened, the pastoral novels of George Sand which she was giving me for my birthday were regular lumber-rooms full of expressions that have fallen out of use

2. The Cathedral of Chartres, painted in 1830 by Corot. The fountains in the old park at Saint-Cloud, outside Paris, painted by Hubert Robert (1733–1809). Vesuvius, the famous volcano near Naples, painted by J. M. W. Turner (1775–1851).   3. Leonardo da Vinci's *Last Supper* was the subject of a famous engraving by Morghen, a late-18th-century engraver. The paints in the original fresco had deteriorated rapidly, and a major restoration took place in the 19th century.   4. Venetian painter (1477–1576).

and become quaint and picturesque, and are now only to be found in country dialects. And my grandmother had bought them in preference to other books, as she would more readily have taken a house with a gothic dovecot or some other such piece of antiquity as will exert a benign influence on the mind by giving it a hankering for impossible journeys through the realms of time.

Mamma sat down by my bed; she had chosen *François le Champi*, whose reddish cover and incomprehensible title[5] gave it, for me, a distinct personality and a mysterious attraction. I had not then read any real novels. I had heard it said that George Sand was a typical novelist. This predisposed me to imagine that *François le Champi* contained something inexpressibly delicious. The narrative devices designed to arouse curiosity or melt to pity, certain modes of expression which disturb or sadden the reader, and which, with a little experience, he may recognise as common to a great many novels, seemed to me—for whom a new book was not one of a number of similar objects but, as it were, a unique person, absolutely self-contained—simply an intoxicating distillation of the peculiar essence of *François le Champi*. Beneath the everyday incidents, the ordinary objects and common words, I sensed a strange and individual tone of voice. The plot began to unfold: to me it seemed all the more obscure because in those days, when I read, I used often to daydream about something quite different for page after page. And the gaps which this habit left in my knowledge of the story were widened by the fact that when it was Mamma who was reading to me aloud she left all the love-scenes out. And so all the odd changes which take place in the relations between the miller's wife and the boy, changes which only the gradual dawning of love can explain, seemed to me steeped in a mystery the key to which (I readily believed) lay in that strange and mellifluous name of *Champi*, which invested the boy who bore it, I had no idea why, with its own vivid, ruddy, charming colour. If my mother was not a faithful reader, she was none the less an admirable one, when reading a work in which she found the note of true feeling, in the respectful simplicity of her interpretation and the beauty and sweetness of her voice. Even in ordinary life, when it was not works of art but men and women whom she was moved to pity or admire, it was touching to observe with what deference she would banish from her voice, her gestures, from her whole conversation, now the note of gaiety which might have distressed some mother who had once lost a child, now the recollection of an event or anniversary which might have reminded some old gentleman of the burden of his years, now the household topic which might have bored some young man of letters. And so, when she read aloud the prose of George Sand, prose which is everywhere redolent of that generosity and moral distinction which Mamma had learned from my grandmother to place above all other qualities in life, and which I was not to teach her until much later to refrain from placing above all other qualities in literature too, taking pains to banish from her voice any pettiness or affectation which might have choked that powerful stream of language, she supplied all the natural tenderness, all the lavish sweetness

5. *Champi* is an old French word the child Marcel would not have known.

which they demanded to sentences which seemed to have been composed for her voice and which were all, so to speak, within the compass of her sensibility. She found, to tackle them in the required tone, the warmth of feeling which pre-existed and dictated them, but which is not to be found in the words themselves, and by this means she smoothed away, as she read, any harshness or discordance in the tenses of verbs, endowing the imperfect and the preterite[6] with all the sweetness to be found in generosity, all the melancholy to be found in love, guiding the sentence that was drawing to a close towards the one that was about to begin, now hastening, now slackening the pace of the syllables so as to bring them, despite their differences of quantity, into a uniform rhythm, and breathing into this quite ordinary prose a kind of emotional life and continuity.

My aching heart was soothed; I let myself be borne upon the current of this gentle night on which I had my mother by my side. I knew that such a night could not be repeated; that the strongest desire I had in the world, namely, to keep my mother in my room through the sad hours of darkness, ran too much counter to general requirements and to the wishes of others for such a concession as had been granted me this evening to be anything but a rare and artificial exception. To-morrow night my anguish would return and Mamma would not stay by my side. But when my anguish was assuaged, I could no longer understand it; besides, to-morrow was still a long way off; I told myself that I should still have time to take preventive action, although that time could bring me no access of power since these things were in no way dependent upon the exercise of my will, and seemed not quite inevitable only because they were still separated from me by this short interval.

And so it was that, for a long time afterwards, when I lay awake at night and revived old memories of Combray, I saw no more of it than this sort of luminous panel, sharply defined against a vague and shadowy background, like the panels which the glow of a Bengal light[7] or a searchlight beam will cut out and illuminate in a building the other parts of which remain plunged in darkness: broad enough at its base, the little parlour, the dining-room, the opening of the dark path from which M. Swann, the unwitting author of my sufferings, would emerge, the hall through which I would journey to the first step of that staircase, so painful to climb, which constituted, all by itself, the slender cone of this irregular pyramid; and, at the summit, my bedroom, with the little passage through whose glazed[8] door Mamma would enter; in a word, seen always at the same evening hour, isolated from all its possible surroundings, detached and solitary against the dark background, the bare minimum of scenery necessary (like the decor one sees prescribed on the title-page of an old play, for its performance in the provinces) to the drama of my undressing; as though all Combray had consisted of but two floors joined by a slender staircase, and as though there had been no time there but seven o'clock at night. I must own[9] that I could have assured any questioner that Combray did include

6. The imperfect is the tense of continued and incomplete action in the past, whereas the preterite describes a single completed action.   7. Fireworks.   8. That is, with glass panes.   9. Admit.

other scenes and did exist at other hours than these. But since the facts which I should then have recalled would have been prompted only by voluntary memory, the memory of the intellect, and since the pictures which that kind of memory shows us preserve nothing of the past itself, I should never have had any wish to ponder over this residue of Combray. To me it was in reality all dead.

Permanently dead? Very possibly.

There is a large element of chance in these matters, and a second chance occurrence, that of our own death, often prevents us from awaiting for any length of time the favours of the first.

I feel that there is much to be said for the Celtic belief that the souls of those whom we have lost are held captive in some inferior being, in an animal, in a plant, in some inanimate object, and thus effectively lost to us until the day (which to many never comes) when we happen to pass by the tree or to obtain possession of the object which forms their prison.[1] Then they start and tremble, they call us by our name, and as soon as we have recognised their voice the spell is broken. Delivered by us, they have overcome death and return to share our life.

And so it is with our own past. It is a labour in vain to attempt to recapture it: all the efforts of our intellect must prove futile. The past is hidden somewhere outside the realm, beyond the reach of intellect, in some material object (in the sensation which that material object will give us) of which we have no inkling. And it depends on chance whether or not we come upon this object before we ourselves must die.

Many years had elapsed during which nothing of Combray, save what was comprised in the theatre and the drama of my going to bed there, had any existence for me, when one day in winter, on my return home, my mother, seeing that I was cold, offered me some tea, a thing I did not ordinarily take. I declined at first, and then, for no particular reason, changed my mind. She sent for one of those squat, plump little cakes called "petites madeleines," which look as though they had been moulded in the fluted valve of a scallop shell. And soon, mechanically, dispirited after a dreary day with the prospect of a depressing morrow, I raised to my lips a spoonful of the tea in which I had soaked a morsel of the cake. No sooner had the warm liquid mixed with the crumbs touched my palate than a shudder ran through me and I stopped, intent upon the extraordinary thing that was happening to me. An exquisite pleasure had invaded my senses, something isolated, detached, with no suggestion of its origin. And at once the vicissitudes of life had become indifferent to me, its disasters innocuous, its brevity illusory—this new sensation having had on me the effect which love has of filling me with a precious essence; or rather this essence was not in me, it *was* me. I had ceased now to feel mediocre, contingent, mortal. Whence could it have come to me, this all-powerful joy? I sensed that it was connected with the taste of the tea and the cake, but that it infinitely transcended those savours, could not, indeed, be of the same nature. Whence did it come? What did it mean? How could I seize and apprehend it?

---

1. A belief attributed to Druids, the priests of the ancient Celtic peoples.

I drink a second mouthful, in which I find nothing more than in the first, then a third, which gives me rather less than the second. It is time to stop; the potion is losing its magic. It is plain that the truth I am seeking lies not in the cup but in myself. The drink has called it into being, but does not know it, and can only repeat indefinitely, with a progressive diminution of strength, the same message which I cannot interpret, though I hope at least to be able to call it forth again and to find it there presently, intact and at my disposal, for my final enlightenment. I put down the cup and examine my own mind. It alone can discover the truth. But how? What an abyss of uncertainty, whenever the mind feels overtaken by itself; when it, the seeker, is at the same time the dark region through which it must go seeking and where all its equipment will avail it nothing. Seek? More than that: create. It is face to face with something which does not yet exist, to which it alone can give reality and substance, which it alone can bring into the light of day.

And I begin again to ask myself what it could have been, this unremembered state which brought with it no logical proof, but the indisputable evidence, of its felicity, its reality, and in whose presence other states of consciousness melted and vanished. I decide to attempt to make it reappear. I retrace my thoughts to the moment at which I drank the first spoonful of tea. I rediscover the same state, illuminated by no fresh light. I ask my mind to make one further effort, to bring back once more the fleeting sensation. And so that nothing may interrupt it in its course I shut out every obstacle, every extraneous idea, I stop my ears and inhibit all attention against the sounds from the next room. And then, feeling that my mind is tiring itself without having any success to report, I compel it for a change to enjoy the distraction which I have just denied it, to think of other things, to rest and refresh itself before making a final effort. And then for the second time I clear an empty space in front of it; I place in position before my mind's eye the still recent taste of that first mouthful, and I feel something start within me, something that leaves its resting-place and attempts to rise, something that has been embedded like an anchor at a great depth; I do not know yet what it is, but I can feel it mounting slowly; I can measure the resistance, I can hear the echo of great spaces traversed.

Undoubtedly what is thus palpitating in the depths of my being must be the image, the visual memory which, being linked to that taste, is trying to follow it into my conscious mind. But its struggles are too far off, too confused and chaotic; scarcely can I perceive the neutral glow into which the elusive whirling medley of stirred-up colours is fused, and I cannot distinguish its form, cannot invite it, as the one possible interpreter, to translate for me the evidence of its contemporary, its inseparable paramour, the taste, cannot ask it to inform me what special circumstance is in question, from what period in my past life.

Will it ultimately reach the clear surface of my consciousness, this memory, this old, dead moment which the magnetism of an identical moment has travelled so far to importune, to disturb, to raise up out of the very depths of my being? I cannot tell. Now I feel nothing; it has stopped, has perhaps sunk back into its darkness, from which who can say whether it will ever rise again? Ten times over I must essay the task, must lean down over the abyss. And each time the cowardice that deters us from every difficult task, every important enterprise, has urged me to leave the thing alone, to drink my tea and to think merely of the worries of to-day and my hopes for to-morrow, which can be brooded over painlessly.

And suddenly the memory revealed itself. The taste was that of the little piece of madeleine which on Sunday mornings at Combray (because on those mornings I did not go out before mass), when I went to say good morning to her in her bedroom, my aunt Léonie used to give me, dipping it first in her own cup of tea or tisane. The sight of the little madeleine had recalled nothing to my mind before I tasted it; perhaps because I had so often seen such things in the meantime, without tasting them, on the trays in pastry-cooks' windows, that their image had dissociated itself from those Combray days to take its place among others more recent; perhaps because of those memories, so long abandoned and put out of mind, nothing now survived, everything was scattered; the shapes of things, including that of the little scallop-shell of pastry, so richly sensual under its severe, religious folds, were either obliterated or had been so long dormant as to have lost the power of expansion which would have allowed them to resume their place in my consciousness. But when from a long-distant past nothing subsists, after the people are dead, after the things are broken and scattered, taste and smell alone, more fragile but more enduring, more unsubstantial, more persistent, more faithful, remain poised a long time, like souls, remembering, waiting, hoping, amid the ruins of all the rest; and bear unflinchingly, in the tiny and almost impalpable drop of their essence, the vast structure of recollection.

And as soon as I had recognised the taste of the piece of madeleine[2] soaked in her decoction of lime-blossom which my aunt used to give me (although I did not yet know and must long postpone the discovery of why this memory made me so happy) immediately the old grey house upon the street, where her room was, rose up like a stage set to attach itself to the little pavilion opening on to the garden which had been built out behind it for my parents (the isolated segment which until that moment had been all that I could see); and with the house the town, from morning to night and in all weathers, the Square where I used to be sent before lunch, the streets along which I used to run errands, the country roads we took when it was fine. And as in the game wherein the Japanese amuse themselves by filling a porcelain bowl with water and steeping in it little pieces of paper which until then are without character or form, but, the moment they become wet, stretch and twist and take on colour and distinctive shape, become flowers or houses or people, solid and recognisable, so in that moment all the flowers in our garden and in M. Swann's park, and the water-lilies on the Vivonne[3] and the good folk of the village and their little dwellings and the parish church and the whole of Combray and its surroundings, taking shape and solidity, sprang into being, town and gardens alike, from my cup of tea.

---

2. A small, rich cookie-like pastry.   3. The local river.

HIGUCHI ICHIYŌ
1872–1896

During the two and a half centuries that the Japanese people cocooned their islands in self-quarantine, comfortably assuming the world would go on just as it always had, beyond the archipelago philosophical, scientific, and technological developments transformed the face of Europe and almost everywhere that Europeans traveled. Fueled by the Industrial Revolution, trade finally propelled the "opening" of Japan. The U.S. government concluded that if official relations were established between the two countries, American whaling ships, which increasingly strayed into Japanese waters, could take provisions there. Japan, however, was not interested and rebuffed several overtures, until the United States resorted to gunboat diplomacy. In July 1853 a squadron of four ships that must have looked monstrous to a nation accustomed to wooden junks—two clipper ships and two ironclad steamships—sailed into Edo bay only forty miles south of the *shogun*'s capital and refused to leave until Commodore Matthew C. Perry had been accorded the chance to present his country's demands. Japan had little choice but to accede, recognizing superior military force and already uneasy at reports that China, its old mentor, had suffered defeat at the hands of the British in the recent Opium Wars.

Ironically, in a sense, Japan was right back where it had started. A thousand years earlier, it had discovered the material superiority of Chinese civilization and had labored hard to approximate China's achievements. Now, as the original model floundered, Japan struggled to remake itself anew as the equal of another materially advanced civilization. It did so less of its own volition this time than to preserve its independence.

In the process, what began as an attempt to compensate for a late technological start soon recast Japanese society. The government of the *shogun* and his *samurai*, in power since the seventeenth century, fell in favor of a constitutional monarchy, with a representative system of local government and a bicameral legislative assembly. A ministry of education was created to oversee the training of future generations of model citizens, military conscription was instituted, railways were laid, political parties founded, and newspapers began to circulate as an important component of the infrastructure of a modern state. "Advances" could be seen everywhere, from the new brick buildings several stories high to the streetlights and telegraph poles, racetracks and Italian circuses, or the bowler hats and petticoats the fashionable adopted as outward proof they were the equals of Parisians and Londoners. As the city of Tokyo grew into a modern metropolis, pawnshops proliferated and the number of rats was said to have multiplied by eight million. Virtually no certainty of daily life went unchallenged. It was debated, for example, whether Sunday should be observed as a day of rest. To do so might win Japan the approval of Christian nations but at the expense of valuable time lost in the race to catch up with these same adversaries.

When Westernization gripped Japan in the late nineteenth century, therefore, it seemed to carry all before it, including literature. The Japanese were ardent readers of every new translation: *Robinson Crusoe, Aesop's Fables, Hamlet, Around the World in Eighty Days, Crime and Punishment.* Aspiring writers looked to the example of European fiction, particularly products of the movement known as realism, to spark their efforts at crafting a new novel for Japan. After false starts, they began to write works that truthfully reflected the social situation and portrayed the subtlest feelings of contemporary, middle-class characters, ordinary people whose inner selves were drawn from an objective and psychologically perceptive observation of real life.

Some of these writers were even fortunate enough to be sent abroad by the Japanese government. Natsume Sōseki (1867–1916), who taught English literature at Tokyo Imperial University before becoming a novelist, spent two years in London. Mori Ōgai (1862–1922), an army doctor and government adviser who translated the works of Shakespeare, Goethe, Rousseau, and others before establishing a separate career writing novels and short stories, spent four years as a foreign student in Leipzig, Munich, Dresden, and Berlin. Sōseki, Ōgai, and others returned to Japan eager to reinvent literature, just as their compatriots were remaking commerce and industry.

Thus the writers who pioneered the creation of the modern Japanese novel were individuals who, for the most part, benefited from the transformations taking place in Japan at the turn of the century. They were educated at the new Japanese universities, fully exposed to the latest intellectual currents and confident of their powers of articulation. Encouraged by the government to think of themselves as potential leaders of the new Japan, they found ready outlets for their talents and their advanced training. Viewing life as opening onto limitless opportunities, they had become worldly in ways unlike any previous generation in Japan.

From the perspective of European culture, the fact that a class of privileged, educated males should dominate literary ventures is not unusual. From the Japanese perspective, on the other hand, remembering the ranking role that women writers had played (at least intermittently) since the time of *The Pillow Book* (in Volume 1), this male initiative in the sphere of cultural modernization could be read as yet another instance of Japanese success in emulating the West. There was, however, one important woman writer in the early years of Japan's modern period, and it would be no exaggeration to say that, in life and in art, she was everything the men were not.

Higuchi Ichiyō, who died at twenty-four from tuberculosis, had a brief, meteoric career that profited from none of the advantages enjoyed by her male counterparts. Her father, a hapless man of peasant stock who worked his way onto the lower rungs of the new Tokyo municipal bureaucracy and managed to purchase the status of a *samurai* less than a year before modernizing reforms did away with the military gentry, died when Ichiyō was seventeen. He left her, her younger sister, and her mother impoverished, for his last undertaking had been a bungled attempt to seize the spirit of the new age as an entrepreneur. He had no head for business, unfortunately, and sank his meager capital into a poorly run and possibly corrupt little enterprise that no sooner swallowed his funds than it went belly up.

The precocious Ichiyō* had been her father's favorite. While the family's straitened circumstances and Ichiyō's gender conspired to prevent her from receiving the Westernized education available to middle-class young men of the time, Ichiyō's father had indulged the budding prodigy as best he could. From an early age he taught her to recite his favorite poems and bought her abridged versions of the classics. When her mother, whose feet were not firmly planted in the modern era, insisted on withdrawing Ichiyō from grade school—too much book learning, she maintained, made a girl unfeminine—Ichiyō's father overrode his wife, at least partially, and enrolled Ichiyō in a poetic conservatory. Here, in a kind of traditional girls' finishing school, Ichiyō was able to cultivate her love of literature through lessons in the composition of classical poetry and lectures on cherished books like *The Tale of Genji* (in Volume 1). And here, for a time, she was eventually able to

---

* Note that names are given in the Japanese order, with surname first. In the case of writers like Ichiyō, who replace their given names with pen names, Japanese convention designates them by the pen name rather than the surname—hence Ichiyō, not Higuchi.

serve as a teaching assistant, until the poverty that followed from her father's death finally forced Ichiyō into a radical break with the family's pretensions to middle-class respectability.

In the dog days of summer 1893, Ichiyō packed up her mother and sister and moved to the fringes of the red-light district. They had pawned everything they owned to open a shop that sold candy and balloons in an alley behind the brothels. Here, in one of the poorest neighborhoods of Tokyo, where very little idea of Western civilization penetrated, Ichiyō discovered the material for great fiction. It was a world modernization had left behind, populated by throwbacks to Japan's secluded centuries: threadbare merchants and day laborers, fortune-tellers and ne'er-do-wells, jugglers and minstrels, and all sorts of hangers-on who eked out a living catering to the so-called "pleasure quarter" on the other side of the ditch. It was, in short, part of the untold story of Japan's modern progress, where things had not changed after all and where the upheavals of recent history had left a number of people, like Ichiyō, on the brink of disaster.

Her education, so different from that of male writers, in the end served her well. And so did her isolation from their literary experiments. Ichiyō's grounding in classical Japanese literature made her receptive to the seventeenth-century fiction of Ihara Saikaku (see p. 592), whose rediscovery led to the publication of his complete works just as Ichiyō moved to her new plebeian neighborhood, coincidentally the same turf that Saikaku had depicted with such brilliance.

Until the move in 1893, when Ichiyō was twenty-one years old, she had published a handful of stories that could best be described as sentimental tales of unrequited love. The pale, well-born characters, whose quivering sensibilities make them sound like refugees from the classical past, were as bogus as Ichiyō's one-time claim to belong to their stratum of society. Now she found characters with blood flowing through their veins, whose struggles she understood as her own. And now life presented true variety, for the environs of the red-light district were a complex realm, a microcosm of contradictory parts. The walled-off pleasure quarter loomed like a stage set, exuding extravagance and ostentation, wit and artifice. Its values colored this rough neighborhood, where people strove to match the fast-talking ways of the courtesans and their stylish suitors, and even the youngest members of the back streets wanted to be cool. It was a part of town, in other words, where luxury, sophistication, and joie de vivre coexisted with sham, naïveté, and the starkest hand-to-mouth struggle to keep going. It may have been the periphery of a modern metropolis, and a tawdry one, but in his tales of prostitutes and moneylenders Saikaku had already anointed it a fit subject for literature.

In *Child's Play*, Ichiyō follows his lead. She recounts the story of a group of adolescents on the verge of adulthood, growing up in the alleyways behind the brothels. When the story begins, they are still children; by the time it ends, they have lost their innocence, and their fates have come into focus. The heroine will become a prostitute, and her best friend, a pawnbroker. Self-consciousness encroaches on their lives, and the new anxieties it brings eat away at their childhood friendships. One by one, entering adolescence as though it were a cave, the once carefree children retreat to their private crannies. The approach of adulthood brings uncertainty, yearning, and loneliness.

Child's Play is a remarkable group portrait that captures with a stunning sense of place a generation at its first moment of disillusionment. It never patronizes its young subjects, nor does it strive to be modern or relevant. (Indeed, the story's language, in the Japanese, is distinctly old-fashioned.) Yet Ichiyō succeeds in a way that male writers of the same period, setting off halfway around the world for literary inspiration, often do not. It is not surprising that this story is sometimes read as an implicit comment on Japan's own troubled passage from the innocence of a simpler time into the precarious world of modernity.

Child's Play made Ichiyō famous. She had already published a dozen stories in various literary magazines, but this is the one that everybody noticed. Mori Ōgai and other leaders of the literary establishment were astonished by the fresh talent of a writer unschooled in Western fiction, and the general public was equally enthusiastic. One member of the newly formed Higuchi Ichiyō Fan Club traveled from Osaka to invite her to address their members. But by now her health was failing. Although Ichiyō managed to write several more stories—also about children or those on the fringes of society, people the successful adult world did not pay much attention to—she died within a year of the publication of *Child's Play*.

For a biography of Ichiyō, with excerpts from her diary and translations of nine short stories, see Robert Lyons Danly, *In the Shade of Spring Leaves* (1992). Recommended novels by Ichiyō's contemporaries include Marleigh Grayer Ryan, trans., *Japan's First Modern Novel: "Ukigumo" of Futabatei Shimei* (1990); Mori Ōgai, *The Wild Geese* (1959); Natsume Sōseki, *Kokoro* (1957); and Natsume Sōseki, *Grass on the Wayside* (1990). An extensive history of modern Japanese literature can be found in Donald Keene, *Dawn to the West* (1984).

PRONOUNCING GLOSSARY

The following list uses common English syllables to provide rough equivalents of selected words whose pronunciation may be unfamiliar to the general reader.

Chōkichi: *choh-kee-chee*

Daikokuya: *dai-koh-koo-yah*

Higuchi Ichiyō: *hee-goo-chee ee-chee-yoh*

Ihara Saikaku: *ee-hah-rah sai-kah-koo*

Ikueisha: *ee-koo-ay-shah*

Kii: *kee-ee*

kumade: *koo-mah-de*

Mori Ōgai: *moh-ree oh-gai*

Murasaki: *moo-rah-sah-kee*

Natsume Sōseki: *nah-tsoo-me soh-se-kee*

Nobuyuki: *noh-boo-yoo-kee*

Ōmaki: *oh-mah-kee*

Ryūge: *ryoo-ge*

Senzoku: *sen-zoh-koo*

Shōta: *shoh-tah*

Ushimatsu: *oo-shee-mah-tsoo*

Child's Play[1]

It's a long way round to the front of the quarter,[2] where the trailing branches of the willow tree bid farewell to the nighttime revellers and the bawdyhouse lights flicker in the moat, dark as the dye that blackens the smiles of the Yoshiwara beauties.[3] From the third-floor rooms of the lofty houses[4] the all but palpable music and laughter spill down into the side

---

1. Translated by Robert Lyons Danly. 2. Yoshiwara, the red-light district on the outskirts of Tokyo. Like Storyville in New Orleans before World War II, such red-light districts in Japan were the common adjunct to a social system that sheltered its "respectable" women—virtuous daughters, chaste wives, and good mothers. 3. The prostitutes follow the ancient aristocratic custom of staining their teeth jet black. 4. In contrast to the sorry sight beyond the confines of the quarter—where most of *Child's Play* is set— the three-story buildings within the red-light district itself suggest, for their time (the 1890s), great opulence. Besides Western-style buildings in central Tokyo, structures of more than two stories would still have been rare. The brothels, with their electric lights and gaiety and sheer height, were imposing edifices to the people who lived on the other side of the moat.

street. Who knows how these great establishments prosper? The rickshaws pull up night and day.

They call this part of town beyond the quarter "in front of Daion Temple." The name may sound a little saintly, but those who live in the area will tell you it's a lively place. Turn the corner at Mishima Shrine and you don't find any mansions, just tenements of ten or twenty houses, where eaves have long begun to sag and shutters only close halfway. It is not a spot for trade to flourish.

Outside the tumble-down houses everyone works madly: cutting up paper into queer little pieces, slopping them with paint, spearing them on funny-looking spits. Whole families, the whole neighborhood is wrapped up in the production of these strange, bright paper skewers. They dry the painted scraps in the morning and assemble them at night. And what are these things that have everyone so preoccupied? "You don't know?" a merchant will reply in astonishment. "*Kumade* charms! On Otori day,[5] you ought to see the big-wishers buy them up!"

Year in, year out, the minute the New Year pine bough comes down from the front gate, every self-respecting businessman takes up the same sideline, and by summer hands and feet are splattered with paint. They count on the earnings to buy new clothes for the holidays. If the gods grant prosperity to mere purchasers of these charms, the men who make them figure they stand to reap a windfall. Funny thing, no one hears of any rich men dwelling in these parts.

Most of the people here, in fact, have some connection with the quarter. The menfolk do odd jobs at the less dignified houses. You can hear them in the evenings jiggling their shoe-check tags[6] before they leave for work, and you'll see them putting on their jackets when most men take them off. Wives rub good-luck flints behind them to protect their men from harm. Could this be the final parting? It's a dangerous business. Innocent bystanders get killed when there's a brawl in one of the houses. And look out if you ever foil the double suicide of a courtesan and her lover! Yet off the husbands go to risk their lives each night like schoolboys to a picnic.

Daughters, too, are involved in the quarter: here, a serving girl in one of the great establishments; there, an escort plying back and forth between the teahouse and the brothel. They bustle along with their shop's lantern, an advertisement for all to see. But what will become of these girls once they have graduated from their present course of training? To them, the work is something grand and gala, as if they were performing on a fine wooden stage. Then one day before they know it they have reached the age of thirty, trim and tidy in their cotton coats with matching dresses and their sensible dark blue stockings. They carry their little packages under

5. There were two or three Otori days each November, when fairs were held at various shrines in Tokyo. The largest shrine was just outside the red-light district. On fair days the side gates to the quarter were thrown open, and women and children were allowed in to see the sights. Otori was written with the character for "bird," the tenth sign of the Chinese zodiac, under which the Otori days always fell. Thus the number of fair days depended on how many days in November fell under the bird sign. Through a pun on the word for "take," a homonym, Otori day became the day of "taking" good luck; hence the sale of *kumade* charms. Kumade: "bear's claws"; good-luck charms named for their five-pronged shape.
6. Shoes were removed upon entering a brothel.

their arms, and we know what *these* are without asking. Stomp, stomp, they go with the heels of their sandals—they're in an awful hurry—and the flimsy drawbridges flop down across the ditch. "We'll leave it here at the back," they say, setting down their bundles, "it's too far round to the front." So they are needle-women now, apparently.

Customs here are indeed a little different. You won't find many women who tie their sashes neatly behind their waists. It's one thing to see a woman of a certain age who favors gaudy patterns, or a sash cut immoderately wide. It's quite another to see these barefaced girls of fifteen or sixteen, all decked out in flashy clothes and blowing on bladder cherries,[7] which everybody knows are used as contraceptives. But that's what kind of neighborhood it is. A trollop who yesterday went by the name of some heroine in *The Tale of Genji* at one of the third-rate houses along the ditch today runs off with a thug. They open a lean-to bar, though neither of them knows the first thing about running a business. They soon go broke. The beauty begins to miss her former calling. Her assets are gone with the chopped-up chicken bones left from last night's hors d'oeuvres. Unlike the chicken, however, our charmer can still return to her old nest. People around here, for some reason, find this kind of woman more alluring than your ordinary one.

In such a world, how are the children to escape being influenced? Take the autumn festival.[8] Mother Meng would be scandalized at the speed with which they learn to mimic all the famous clowns; why, there's not a one of them who can't do Rohachi and Eiki.[9] They hear their performances praised, and that night the smart alecks repeat their rounds. It starts at the age of seven or eight, this audacity, and by the time they're fifteen! Towels from the evening bath dangle from their shoulders, and the latest song, in a nasal twang of disrespect, dribbles from the corner of their lips. At school, any moment, a proper music class is apt to lapse into the rhythms of the quarter. Athletic meets ring with the songs of geisha[1]— who needs the school cheer? One sympathizes with their teachers, who toil at the Ikueisha, not far from here. It may be a crowded little schoolhouse—a private school, actually[2]—but the students number close to a thousand, and the teachers who are popular there soon become known. In these parts, the very word *school* is synonymous with the Ikueisha.

Listen to them walking home from school: "Your father sure keeps an

---

7. *Hōzuki*, Chinese lantern plant (or winter cherry), which bears fruit enclosed in an inflated orange-red calyx that resembles a miniature paper lantern.   8. A lively festival in the red-light district. Entertainers would dance through the streets of the quarter, making the rounds of the teahouses and brothels whose patronage they had enjoyed during the year. For several days, the Yoshiwara assumed even more color than usual. Lanterns shaped like morning glories were hung before the brothels. In the evening, festival floats would parade down the main street of the quarter, each float fitted with a stage on which dances and comic skits were performed. The children of the neighborhood took it all in.   9. The late-19th-century Japanese equivalent of popular comedians. Mother Meng was the mother of the Chinese philosopher Mencius (ca. 372–289 B.C.); legend portrays her as meticulous in her child rearing.   1. "Practitioner of arts" (literal trans.); a professional female entertainer hired primarily for companionship during meals or parties for men. She was trained to sing or dance selections from the classical repertoire; she was not a prostitute, although she might have sexual relations with chosen patrons.   2. In this period, when the Japanese government devoted a good deal of attention to developing a modern public secondary school system, it was the public school that was usually superior to the private. The implication is that the Ikueisha is an overcrowded, second-rate school for a down-at-the-heels neighborhood, a point that has significance later in the story.

eye on the teahouse by the bridge!" they shout at the fireman's boy. It's the wisdom of the street. Children know about the quarter. They scramble over garden walls, imitating firemen. "Hey! You broke the spikes on the fence to keep the thieves away!" A two-bit shyster's son begins his prosecution: "Your old man's a 'horse,' isn't he? Isn't he?" The blood rushes to the defendant's face. The poor boy—he'd sooner die than admit his father collected bills for a brothel. And then there are the favorite sons of the big shots of the quarter, who grow up in lodgings at some remove, free to feign a noble birth. They sport the latest prep-school cap, they have a look of leisure, and they wear their European clothes with style and panache. All the same, it's amusing to watch the others curry favor. "Young master, young master," they call them, when "spoiled brat" would do.

Among the many students at the Ikueisha was Nobuyuki of Ryūge Temple.[3] In time, his thick, black hair would be shorn, and he would don the dark robes of a priest. It may well have been his own choice, and then again perhaps he had resigned himself to fate. His father was a cleric, and already like his father Nobu was a scholar. By nature he was a quiet boy. His classmates considered him a wet blanket and they liked to tease him. "Here—this is your line of work," they would laugh, stringing up a dead cat. "How about offering the last rites?" All that was in the past, however; no one made fun of him now, not even by mistake. He was fifteen and of average height, his dark hair was closely cropped in schoolboy fashion, and yet something about him was different from the others. Although he had the ordinary-sounding name of Fujimoto Nobuyuki, already in his manner were suggestions of the cloth.

The Festival of Senzoku Shrine was set for the twentieth of August, and not a block would there be without a float of its own jostling for glory. Over the ditch and up the side of the embankment they charge: all the young men, pushing, pulling, bent on taking the quarter. The heart beats faster at the mere thought of it. And keep an eye, mind you, on the young ones—once they get wind of what the older boys are up to. Matching kimonos for the whole gang are only the beginning. The saucy things they dream up will give you goose bumps.

The back-street gang, as they preferred to call themselves, had Chōkichi for their leader. He was the fire chief's son—sixteen and full of it. He hadn't walked without his chest puffed out since the day he started policing the fall festival with his father: baton swinging, belt low around the hips, sneering whenever he answered. The firemen's wives all griped among themselves, "If he weren't the chief's boy, he'd never get away with it."

Selfish Chōkichi saw to it that he always got his way. He stretched his side-street influence wider than it really went, until in Shōta, the leader of the main-street gang, Chōkichi knew that he had met his match. Though Shōta was three years younger, he was the son of Tanaka, the pawnbroker; his family had money, he was a likable boy. Chōkichi went to the

---

3. That is, Nobuyuki lives at Ryūge Temple, where his father is the priest.

Ikueisha; Shōta, to a fancy public school. The school songs they sang may have been the same, but Shōta always made a face, as if Chōkichi and his friends at the Ikueisha were poor relations.

With his band of admirers—even some grown-ups numbered among them—for the last two years Shōta's plans for the festival had flowered more luxuriantly than the efforts of Chōkichi's gang. There had been no contest, and, if he lost again this year, all his threats—"Who do you think you're dealing with? Chōkichi from the back streets, that's who!"—would no longer garner even enough members for a swimming team at the Benten Ditch. If it were a matter of strength, he knew he would prevail, but everyone was taken in by Shōta's quiet ways and his good grades. It was mortifying—some of his own gang had gone over on the sly to Shōta's side. Tarokichi and Sangorō, for instance.

Now the festival was only two days away. It looked more and more as if Chōkichi would lose again. He was desperate. If he could just see that Shōta got a little egg on his face, it wouldn't matter if he himself lost an eye or a limb. He wouldn't have to suffer defeat any more if he could recruit the likes of Ushi, the son of the rickshawman, and Ben, whose family made hair ribbons, and Yasuke, the toymaker's boy. Ah, and better still: if he could get Nobu on his side—there was a fellow who'd have a good idea or two.

Near dusk on the evening of the eighteenth, hoping for a chance to persuade Nobu, Chōkichi made his cocky way through the bamboo thicket of the temple. Swatting the mosquitoes that swarmed about his face, he stole up to Nobu's room.

"Nobu? You there? I know people say I'm a roughneck, and maybe I am. But it's no wonder, with the way they goad me. Listen, Nobu, I've had enough of them—ever since last year when that jerk from Shōta's gang picked a fight with my little brother and they all came running and jumped on him and threw him around. I mean, what do you think of something like that? Beating up a little kid and breaking his festival lantern! And then that Donkey from the dumpling shop, who's so big and awkward he thinks he can go around acting like a grown-up! He comes and starts insulting me to my brother behind my back. You know what he said? 'Think Chōkichi's so smart, huh? And your father's fire chief? Well, your big brother isn't head of anything. He's the tail end—a pig's tail end!' That's what he said! All this time I'm off in the parade, pulling our float. When I heard about it later, though, I was ready to get even! But my father found out, and *I'm* the one who got in trouble. And you remember the year before that, don't you? I went over to the paper shop, where a bunch of kids from the main street were putting on their slapstick.[4] You know what snide things they said to me? 'Doesn't the back street have its own games?' And all the while they're treating Shōta like king. I don't forget these things, Nobu . . . I don't care how much money he has. Who is he, anyway, but the son of a loan shark? I'd be doing the world a favor to get rid of such a creep. This year, no matter how tough I have to be, I'll see

---

4. Improvised pantomimes or comic skits. The term is also one of depreciation, meaning "a farce" or "a waste of time."

to it that Shōta eats his words. That's why, Nobu—come on—for a friend, you've got to help. I know you don't like this kind of rough stuff. But it's to get our honor back! Don't you want to help me smash that snooty Shōta with his stuck-up school songs? You know when they call me a stupid private-schooler, it goes for you too. So come on. Do me this one favor and help us out. Carry one of the lanterns around at the festival. Listen, I'm eating my heart out, this has been bothering me so much. If we lose this time, it'll be the end of me." Chōkichi's broad shoulders trembled with anger.

"But I'm not very strong."

"I don't care whether you're strong or not."

"I don't think I could carry one of the lanterns."

"You don't have to!"

"You'll lose even with me—you don't care?"

"If we lose, we lose. Look, you don't have to do anything. Just so you're on our side. All we have to do is show you off. It'll attract others. Build up our morale. I know I'm not very smart, but you are. So if they start using big words and making fun of us, you can answer right back in Chinese.[5] I feel better already. You're worth the whole lot of them! Thanks, Nobu." It wasn't often you heard Chōkichi speak so softly.

The one the son of a workman, with his boy's belt and his smart straw sandals; the other like a priest in his somber jacket and his purple band— they were the opposite sides of a coin. More often than not, the two boys disagreed. Yet it was true that Nobu's own parents had a soft spot for Chō-kichi. Why, the venerable Head Priest and his wife had heard Chōkichi's first cries as a babe outside the temple gate. And, after all, they did both go to the same school. If people made fun of the Ikueisha to Chōkichi, it reflected on Nobu too. It was a shame that Chōkichi wasn't better liked, but he never had been what you'd call appealing—unlike Shōta, who attracted everyone, even the older boys, for his allies. Nobu wasn't showing any prejudice. If Chōkichi lost, the blame would rest squarely on Shōta. When Chōkichi came to him like this, out of a sense of decency Nobu could hardly refuse.

"All right. I'm on your side. But you'd better keep the fighting down . . . If they start things, we won't have any choice. And if that happens, I'll wrap Shōta around my little finger." Nobu's reticence had already been forgotten. He opened his desk drawer and showed Chōkichi the prized Kokaji dagger[6] his father had brought him from Kyōto.

"Say! That'll really cut!" Chōkichi admired.

Look out—careful how you wave that thing.

Undone, her hair would reach her feet. She wore it swept up and pulled into a heavy-looking roll in the "red bear" style[7]—a frightening name for a maiden's hairdo, but the latest fashion even among girls of good family. Her skin was fair and her nose was nicely shaped. Her mouth, a little large perhaps, was firm and not at all unattractive. If you took her features one

---

5. A way to show off being smart.   6. One with the inscription of Kokaji Munechika, a renowned swordsmith from Kyoto.   7. A popular if flamboyant hairstyle, consisting of a large chignon and flow-ered hairpins. It originated in the red-light district.

by one, it is true, they were not the classic components of ideal beauty. And yet she was a winsome girl, exuberant, soft-spoken. Her eyes radiated warmth whenever she looked at you.

"I'd like to see her three years from now!" young men leaving the quarter would remark when they noticed her returning from the morning bath, her towel in hand and her neck a lovely white above her orange kimono of boldly patterned butterflies and birds, her stylish sash wrapped high at the waist and her lacquered slippers more thickly soled than what one usually saw, even around here.

Her name was Midori and she was from the Daikokuya.[8] She was born in Kishū, though, and her words had the slightest southern lilt. It was charming. There were few who did not enjoy her generous, open nature.

For a child, Midori had a handsome pocketbook, thanks to her sister's success in the quarter. The great lady's satellites[9] knew how to purchase good will: "Here Midori, go buy yourself a doll," the manager would say. "It isn't much, honey," one of the attendant girls would offer, "but it'll buy you a ball, anyway." No one took these gifts very seriously, and the income Midori accepted as her due. It was nothing for her to turn round and treat twenty classmates to matching rubber balls. She had been known to delight her friend the woman at the paper store by buying up every last shopworn trifle. The extravagance day after day was certainly beyond the child's age or station. What would become of her? Her parents looked the other way, never a word of caution.

And wasn't it odd, how the owner of her sister's house would spoil her so? She was hardly his adopted child, or even a relation. Yet ever since he had come to their home in the provinces to appraise her older sister, Midori and her parents had found themselves here at the Daikokuya. They had packed up their belongings, along with her sister, to seek their fortunes in the city.

What lay behind it all would be difficult to say, but today her parents were housekeepers for the gentleman. On the side, her mother took in sewing from the women of the district; her father kept the books at a third-rate house. They saw to it that Midori went to school and that she learned her sewing and her music. The rest of the time she was on her own: lolling around her sister's rooms for half the day, playing in the streets the other half. Her head was full of the sounds of samisen[1] and drum, of the twilight reds and purples of the quarter. New to the city, Midori had bristled when the other girls made fun of her, calling her a country girl for wearing a lavender collar with her lined kimono. She had cried for three days then. Not now, though. It was Midori who would tease when someone seemed uncouth—"What kind of dress is that!"—and no one had quite the nimble wit to return her rebukes.

The festival was to be held on the twentieth, and this year they would have to outdo themselves. Midori's help was needed. "All right. Everyone

---

8. The name of the brothel where her older sister is a prostitute.   9. The most successful courtesans, like Midori's sister, had their own attendants.   1. A three-stringed musical instrument, resembling the lute but with a longer neck. It became the most popular Japanese instrument, with large repertories of narrative and lyrical music, and thus a fixture of both the theater and the red-light district.

plan something. We'll take a vote. I'll pay for everything," she responded with her usual generosity. "Don't worry about the cost."

The children were quicker than adults to seize an opportunity. The beneficent ruler seldom comes a second time.

"Let's do a show. We can borrow a shop where everyone can watch us."

"No—that's stupid! Let's build a little shrine to carry around. A good one like they have at Kabata's. Even if it's heavy, it won't matter, once we get it going to a nice beat."

"Yatchoi![2] Yatchoi!" danced a youth already in the mood, his towel twisted into a festive headband.

"What about us?" "You think Midori's going to have any fun just watching while you're all roughhousing?" "Come on, Midori, have them do something else." The girls, it seemed, would prefer to forgo the celebrations for an afternoon of vaudeville.

Shōta's handsome eyes lit up. "Why don't we do a magic lantern show?[3] I have a few pictures at my house. Midori, you can buy the rest. We can use the paper shop. I'll run the lantern, and Sangorō from the back street can be the narrator. What do you say, Midori? Wouldn't that be good?"

"I like it! If Sangorō does the talking, no one will be able to keep from laughing. Too bad we can't put a picture of him in the show."

Everything was decided. Shōta dashed around to get things ready.

By the next day, word of their plans had reached the back street.

The drums, the samisen! Even in a place never wanting for music, the festival is the liveliest time of year. What could rival it but Otori day? Just watch the shrines try to surpass one another in their celebrations.

The back-street and the main-street gangs each had their own matching outfits, Mōka cotton emblazoned with their street names. "But they're not as nice as last year's," some grumbled. Sleeves were tied up with flaxen cords stained yellow from a jasmine dye. The wider the bright ribbons, everyone agreed, the better. Children under fifteen or so weren't satisfied until they had accumulated all the trinkets they could carry—Daruma dolls,[4] owls, dogs of papier-mâché. Some had eight or nine, even eleven, dangling from their yellow armbands. It was a sight to see them, bells of all sizes jingling from their backs as they ran along gamely in their stockinged feet.

Shōta stood apart from the crowd. Today he looked unusually dapper. His red-striped jacket and his dark-blue vest contrasted handsomely with his boyish complexion. He wore a pale blue sash wrapped tightly round the waist. A second look revealed it to be the most expensive crepe. The emblems on his collar were exceptional enough to draw attention by themselves. In his headband he had tucked a paper flower. Though his well-heeled feet beat time to the rhythm of the drums, Shōta did not join the ranks of any of the street musicians.

2. A shout of encouragement, stirring people to action or marking time when lifting a heavy object, such as a portable shrine carried in festivals.   3. Shadow pictures or shadowgraphs. Cutout pictures of people and animals were held up to a lantern and projected on a wall with accompanying humorous commentary, a popular form of entertainment in the days before motion pictures.   4. Dolls that represent the priest Bodhidarma, the founder of Zen Buddhism.

Festival eve had passed without incident. Now at dusk on this once-in-a-year holiday, twelve of the main-street gang were gathered at the paper shop. Only Midori, a long time with her evening toilette, had yet to appear. Shōta was getting impatient.

"What's taking her so long?" He paced in and out the front door. "Sangorō, go and get her. You've never been to the Daikokuya, though, have you? Call her from the garden, and she'll hear you. Hurry up."

"All right. I'll leave my lantern here. Shōta, keep an eye on it; someone might take the candle."

"Don't be such a cheapskate! Stop dawdling."

"I'm off." The boy didn't seem to mind being scolded by his juniors.

"There goes the god of lightning,"[5] someone said, and the girls all burst out laughing at the way he ran. He was short and beefy, and, with no neck to speak of, his bulging head suggested one of those wooden mallets. Protruding forehead, pug nose, big front teeth—no wonder he was called Bucktooth-Sangorō. He was decidedly dark-skinned, but what one noticed even more was the expression on his face, dimpled and affable and ready for the clown's role. His eyebrows were so oddly placed as to suggest the final outcome of a game of pin-the-tail-on-the-donkey. He was an amusing child, without a mean streak in him.

To those who did not know how poor he was, Sangorō shrugged off his everyday cotton clothes. "Couldn't get a matching kimono made in time."

He was the eldest of six children. Their father contrived to feed them all by clinging to the handles of a rickshaw. True, he worked the prosperous street in front of the quarter, lined with the teahouses. But somehow the wheels of his cart never turned a real profit. Fast as they spun, they only kept the family going hand-to-mouth.

"Now that you're thirteen, I'm counting on you to help out, boy," Sangorō's father had told him the year before last. He went to work at the printing shop over in Namiki but, in his lackadaisical way, in ten days he had tired of the job. Seldom did he last more than a month anywhere. From November to January he worked part-time making shuttlecocks for the New Year's games. In summer he helped the iceman near the hospital. Thanks to the comical way he had of soliciting customers, the two of them did a brisk business. A born hawker, the iceman said.

Ever since he had pulled a float last year at the Yoshiwara carnival, his disapproving friends had dubbed him "Mannenchō." He was as bad, they said, as the jesters from that lowliest of slums. But everyone knew Sangorō was a buffoon. No one disliked him; this was his one advantage.

The pawnshop Shōta's people ran was a lifeline for Sangorō and his family, whose gratitude toward the Tanakas was no small thing. True, the daily interest rates they were obliged to pay bordered on the exorbitant; yet without the loans they could scarcely have kept going. How, then, could they begrudge the moneylender his due?

"Sangorō," Shōta and the main-street gang were forever urging him, "come over to our street and play." And how could he refuse Shōta, to

---

5. In the Buddhist pantheon, a swift-footed warrior named Idaten who chased down the thief of the Buddha's ashes.

whose family they were all indebted? On the other hand, he was born and raised in the back streets, he lived on land belonging to Ryūge Temple, Chōkichi's father owned their house. It wouldn't do to turn his back openly on Chōkichi. When in the end he quietly went over to the main street, the accusing looks were hard for him to bear.

Shōta sat down in the paper shop, tired of waiting for Midori, and began to sing the opening lines of "Secret Love."

"Listen to that!" laughed the shopkeeper's wife. "Singing love songs already—we'll have to keep an eye on this one."

Shōta's ears turned red. "Let's go!" he called to the others in a loud voice he hoped would cover his embarrassment. But as he ran out of the shop, he bumped into his grandmother.

"Shōta—why haven't you come home for dinner? I've been calling and calling, but you're so busy playing you don't even listen. You can all play again after dinner. Thanks," she added in a curt word of parting to the shopkeeper's wife.

Shōta had no choice but to follow her home.

Whenever he left, how lonely it seemed. Only one less person than before, and yet even the grown-ups missed Shōta. It was not that he was boisterous or always cracking jokes, like Sangorō. Such friendliness, though—you don't usually find it in a rich boy.

"But did you see the nasty way his grandmother has?" housewives gossiped on the street corner. "She's sixty-four if she's a day. And her hair done up like a young floozy! At least she doesn't wear all that powder any more."

"You ought to hear her purr and coax to get her loans back. Nothing stops her. You watch—the borrower could die, and she'd be at the funeral to collect. She's the kind who'll try to take her money with her when she goes."

"We can't even hold our heads up to her—that's the power of money."

"Don't you wish you had a little of it?"

"They say she even lends to the big houses in the quarter."

What they wouldn't give to know how much the old crone had.

"How sad it is for one who waits alone by the midnight hearth." The love songs do have a way of putting things.

The breeze felt cool on that summer evening. In the bath Midori had washed the heat of the day away, and now she stood before her full-length mirror getting ready. Her mother took charge of repairing the girl's hairdo. A beauty, even if she did say so, the woman thought, inspecting her daughter from every angle. "You still don't have enough powder on your neck." They had chosen for the occasion a silk kimono in a cool, pale blue. Her straw-colored sash was flecked with gold threads and custom-made to fit her tiny waist. It would be some time, though, before they could begin deciding on the proper sandals.

"Isn't she ready yet?" Sangorō was losing his patience. He had circled the garden wall seven times. How much longer could he go on yawning? The mosquitoes around here were a local specialty; no sooner had he brushed them away than they would buzz back again. A bite on the neck, a bite on the forehead. Just as he had had about all he could take, Midori finally appeared.

"Let's go," she said.

He pulled her sleeve without answering her and began to run.

Midori was soon out of breath. She could feel her heart pounding. "Well, if you're in such a hurry about it, go on ahead."

Sangorō arrived at the paper shop just before her. Shōta, it appeared, had gone home for dinner.

"This isn't going to be any fun. We can't start the lantern show without Shōta," Midori complained, turning to the shopkeeper's wife. "Any checkers? Cut-outs? We'll need *something* to keep us busy till he comes."

"Here we are." The girls immediately began to cut out the paper dolls the shop lady handed them.

The boys, with Sangorō in the lead, replayed entertainments from the Yoshiwara carnival. Their harmony was odd, but they knew the melodies:

> "Come see the thriving quarter—
> The lights, the lanterns under every eave,
> The gaiety of all five streets!"

In fact, they remembered perfectly the songs and dances of a year, two years before. They didn't miss a beat; they had every gesture down. A crowd gathered at the gate outside to watch the ten of them, carried away by their own side show.

"Is Sangorō there?" called a voice from among the onlookers. "Come here a minute, quick." It was Bunji, the hairdresser's boy.

"Just a second," yelled Sangorō without a care.

No sooner did he run through the doorway than someone punched him in the face. "You double-crosser! This'll teach you! Who do you think I am? Chōkichi! I'll make you sorry you ever made fun of us!"

Sangorō was dumbfounded. He tried to escape, but they grabbed him by the collar.

"Kill him! Shōta too! Don't let the chicken get away. And Donkey from the dumpling shop—don't think you're going to get off so easy!"

The uproar swelled like the rising tide. Paper lanterns came crashing down from the eaves.

"Mind the lamp. You mustn't fight in front of the shop." The woman's yell was loud enough, but who was listening?

There were fourteen or fifteen of them in the attack, streamers round the heads, their oversize lanterns swinging. Blows were struck in all directions, things trampled underfoot. The outrage of it! But Shōta—the one they were after—was nowhere to be found.

"Hide him, will you? Where is he? If you don't tell us, you'll answer for it." They closed in around Sangorō, hitting and kicking, until Midori couldn't stand to watch. She pushed her way to the front, past the restraining hand of the shopkeeper's wife.

"What are you taking it out on him for? If you want to fight with Shōta, fight with Shōta. He didn't run away and he's not hiding. He's not here, that's all. This is our place. Why do you have to go sticking your noses in? You're such a creep, Chōkichi. Why don't you leave Sangorō alone?

There—you've knocked him down. Now stop it! If you want to hit some-one, hit me. Don't try to hold me back," she turned to the shopkeeper's wife, shouting abuse at Chōkichi all the while she tried to free herself.

"Yeah? You're nothing but a whore, just like your sister," Chōkichi shot back. He stepped around from behind the others and grabbed his muddy sandal. "This is all you're worth." He threw it at Midori.

With a splatter, it struck her square on the forehead. She turned white, but the shopkeeper's wife held her back. "Don't. You'll get hurt."

"Serves you right," Chōkichi gloated. "By the way, guess who's joined our side. Nobu from Ryūge Temple! So try and get even any time you want." He left Sangorō lying in the shop's front door. "You fools! *Weak-lings! Cowards!* We'll be waiting for you. Be careful when you walk through the back streets after dark."

Just then he heard the sound of a policeman's boots. Someone had squealed on them. "Come on!" As fast as they could, Ushimatsu, Bunji, and the ten or so others all scattered in different directions, crouching in hiding places among the alleyways until the coast was clear.

"Damn you, Chōkichi! You bastard. Damn you! Damn you, Bunji! Damn you, Ushimatsu! Why don't you just kill me? Come on. Just try and kill me. I'm Sangorō—and maybe it's not so easy! Even if you did kill me, even if I turned into a ghost, I'd haunt you for the rest of your lives. Remember that, Chōkichi!" Sangorō began to sob. Hot tears rolled down his cheeks. He looked as if he must be aching. His sleeves were torn. His back and hips were covered with dirt.

The force of his anger, beyond his power to control, kept the others back. But the shopkeeper's wife rushed over to him. "It's all right," she soothed him with a pat and helped him to his feet. She brushed the gravel from his clothes. "Don't be upset. There were just too many of them, the rest of us weren't much help, not even a grown-up could do anything. It wasn't a fair match—don't be ashamed. It's lucky you weren't hurt, but you won't be safe going home alone. I'll feel much better if the policeman takes you; it's a good thing he's come. Officer, let me tell you what hap-pened."

As she finished her account, the policeman reached for the boy's hand in his professional way. "I'll take you home."

"No. I'm all right. I can go by myself." He seemed to cringe with shame.

"There's nothing to be afraid of. I'll just take you as far as your house. Don't worry." He smiled at Sangorō and patted him on the head.

But Sangorō shrank back farther. "If my father hears about the fight, I'll get in terrible trouble. Chōkichi's father owns our house."

"How about if I take you as far as the front gate? I won't say anything to get you into trouble." He managed to coax the downcast Sangorō and led him off toward home.

The others felt relieved. But as they watched the two depart, at the corner leading to the back streets, for some reason Sangorō shook loose and broke into a run.

It was as rare as snow falling from a summer sky, but today Midori couldn't brook the thought of school. She wouldn't eat her breakfast. Should they order something special? It couldn't be a cold, she had no fever. Too much excitement yesterday, probably. "Why don't you stay home?" her mother suggested. "I'll go to the shrine for you."

Midori wouldn't hear of it. It was *her* vow to Tarō-sama[6] for her sister's success. "I'll just go and come right back. Give me some money for the offering."

Off she went to the shrine among the paddy fields. She rang the bell, shaped like the great mouth of a crocodile, and clasped her hands in supplication. And what were they for, these prayers of hers? She walked through the fields with her head downcast, to and from the shrine.

Shōta saw her from a distance and called out as he ran toward her. He tugged at her sleeve, "Midori, I'm sorry about last night."

"That's all right. It wasn't your fault."

"But they were after me. If Grandmother hadn't come, I wouldn't have left. And then they wouldn't have beaten up Sangorō the way they did. I went to see him this morning. He was crying and furious. I got angry just listening to him talk about it. Chōkichi threw his sandal at you, didn't he? Damn him, anyway! There are limits to what even he can get away with. But I hope you're not mad at me, Midori. I didn't run away from him. I gulped my food down as fast as I could and was just on my way back when Grandmother said I had to watch the house while she went for her bath. That's when all the commotion must have started. Honest, I didn't know anything about it." He apologized as if the crime were his, not Chōkichi's. "Does it hurt?" Shōta examined Midori's forehead.

"Well, it's nothing that will leave a scar," Midori laughed. "But listen, Shōta, you mustn't tell anyone. If Mother ever found out, I'd get a real scolding. My parents never lay a hand on me. If they hear a dolt like Chōkichi smeared mud on my face with his filthy sandal—." She looked away.

"Please forgive me. It's all my fault. Please. Come on, cheer up. I won't be able to stand it if you're mad at me." Before they knew it, they had reached the back gate of Shōta's house. "Do you want to come in? No one's home. Grandmother's gone to collect the interest. It's lonely by myself. Come on, I'll show you those prints I told you about the other day. There are all kinds of them." Shōta wouldn't let go of her sleeve until Midori had agreed.

Inside the dilapidated gate was a small garden. Dwarf trees were lined up in their pots and from the eaves hung a tiny trellis of fern with a wind-bell, Shōta's memento from the holiday market. But who would have picked it for the wealthiest house in the neighborhood? Here alone by themselves lived an old woman and a boy. No one had ever broken in: there were cold, metal locks everywhere, and the neighboring tenements kept an eye on the place.

Shōta went in first and found a spot where the breeze blew. "Over here," he called to Midori, handing her a fan. For a thirteen-year-old, he was rather too sophisticated. He took out one color print after another. They had been in his family for generations, and he smiled when Midori

---

6. The deity celebrated at the local shrine. Midori prays to him for her sister's continued prosperity.

admired them. "Shall I show you a battledore?[7] It was my mother's. She
got it when she worked for a rich man. Isn't it funny? It's so big. And look
how different people's faces were in those days. I wish she were still alive
. . . My mother died when I was three, and my father went back to his
own family's place in the country. So I've been here with Grandmother
ever since. You're lucky, Midori."

"Look out. You'll get the pictures wet. Boys aren't supposed to cry."

"I guess I'm a sissy. Sometimes I get to thinking about things . . . It's all
right now, but in the winter, when the moon is out and I have to make
the rounds in Tamachi collecting the interest, sometimes when I walk
along the ditch, I sit down on the bank and cry. Not from the cold. I don't
know why . . . I just think about things. I've been doing the collecting ever
since year before last. Grandmother's getting old. It's not safe for her at
night. And her eyes aren't so good any more. She can't see what she's
doing when she has to put her seal on the receipts. We've had a lot of
different men working for us. But Grandmother says they all take us for
fools—when it's only an old lady and a boy they have to answer to. She's
just waiting for the day when I'm a little older and we can open the pawnshop again. We'll put the family sign out in front, even if things aren't as
good as they used to be. Oh, I know people say Grandmother's stingy. But
she's only careful about things for my sake. It really bothers me, to hear
them talk that way. I guess the people I collect from over in Tōrishinmachi
are pretty bad off, all right. I suppose it's no wonder they say things about
her. When I think about it, though, sometimes I just can't help it if I cry.
I guess I am a weakling. This morning when I went to see Sangorō, he
was sore all over, but he still went right on working so his father wouldn't
find out about last night. I didn't know what to say. A boy looks pretty silly
when he cries, doesn't he? That's why the back street makes fun of Sangorō." He seemed ashamed at his own unmanliness.

Occasionally their eyes would meet.

"You looked so handsome yesterday, Shōta. It made me wish I were a
boy. You were the best dressed of them all."

"I looked good! You were beautiful! Everybody said you were prettier
than any of the girls in the quarter, even your sister Ōmaki. Boy, I'd be
proud if you were my sister! I'd hold my head up with a girl like you
alongside me. But I don't have any brothers or sisters. Hey, Midori, what
do you say we have our picture taken? I'll wear what I did yesterday and
you can put on one of your best striped kimonos, and we'll have Katō in
Suidōjiri take our picture! Won't Nobu be jealous! He'll turn white, he'll
be so envious—a milquetoast like him wouldn't know how to turn red. Or
maybe he'll just laugh at us. Who cares? If Katō takes a big one, he might
use our picture in the window! What's the matter? Don't you like the idea?
You don't look very excited." The boy's impatience was disarming.

"What if I look funny? You might not like me any more." Her laugh
had a beautiful ring, her spirits had obviously improved.

The cool of the morning had given way to the summer sun. It was time
for Midori to be going: "Shōta, why don't you come over this evening?

7. A rectangular-shaped paddle with a handle used to play shuttlecock, a game like badminton.

We can float candles on the pond and chase the fish. It'll be easy now that the bridge is fixed."

Shōta beamed as he saw her out. What a beauty Midori was.

Nobu of Ryūge Temple and Midori of the Daikokuya both went to school at the Ikueisha. It had all started at the end of last April, at the spring athletic meet in Mizunoya-no-hara. The cherries had fallen and the wisteria was already in bloom in the shade of the new green leaves. They played their games of tug-of-war and catch and jump rope with such ardor that no one seemed to notice the sun going down. But what had come over Nobu? He had lost his usual composure. He stumbled over the root of a pine by the pond and landed hands-first in the red mud.

Midori, who happened to be going by, took one look at his dirty jacket and proffered her crimson handkerchief. "Here, you can wipe it off with this."

There were those, however, who were jealous of this attention from Midori. "For a priest's son, he sure knows how to flirt. Look at him smile when he thanks her! What's he going to do—take her for his wife? If she goes to live at the temple, then she really will be Miss Daikoku:[8] from Midori of the Daikokuya to Daikoku, goddess of the kitchen! That ought to suit a priest."

Nobu couldn't stomach all the talk. He had never been one to enjoy idle gossip and had always shunned tales about others. How, then, could he tolerate it when he found himself the target of the rumors? He began to dread hearing Midori's name. He was snappish whenever anyone mentioned field day. "You're not going to bring that up again, are you?" It never failed to put him in a bad mood. Yet what reason was there, really, for this loss of temper? He knew he would do better feigning indifference. A stoic face, wait it out, he told himself. He could silence his tormentors with a word or two, but the embarrassment was still there. A cold sweat followed every confrontation.

At first, Midori failed to notice any change. On her way home from school one day she called out with her usual friendliness. Nobu trailed behind amid a cluster of people. The blossoms at the roadside had caught her eye, and she waited for him to catch up. "See the pretty flowers, Nobu? I can't reach them. You're tall enough—won't you pick me some?"

She had singled him out from his younger companions. There was no escaping. He cringed at what he knew the others would be saying. Reaching for the nearest branch, without even choosing, he picked the first flower he saw, a token effort. He flung it at her and was gone.

"Well, if that's how he's going to be! Unsociable thing!"

After several of these incidents, it dawned on Midori: Nobu was being mean to her deliberately. He was never rude to any of the others, only her. When she approached, he fled. If she spoke to him, he became angry. He was sullen and self-conscious. Midori had no idea how to please him, and in the end she gave up trying. Let him be perverse; he was no friend of

---

8. A euphemism for the wife, or mistress, of a Buddhist priest, who until the modern period was expected to be celibate. The sobriquet derived sarcastically from Daikoku, one of the seven gods of good fortune and the patron saint of the pocketbook. Nobu's tormentors are also playing on the name of the brothel where Midori's sister is employed, the Daikokuya, itself no doubt named for the god of prosperity.

hers. See if she'd speak to him after he'd cut her to the quick. "Hello's" in the street were a thing of the past. It would take important business indeed before she would deign to talk to him. A great river now stretched between them that all boats were forbidden to cross. Each of them walked alone on separate banks of the stream.

From the day after the festival, Midori came to school no more. She could wash the mud from her face, but the shame could not be scrubbed away so easily.

They sat together side by side at school—Chōkichi's gang and the main-street gang—and one might have expected that they could get along. But there had always been a sharp division.

It was the act of a coward to attack a weak, defenseless girl. Everyone knew Chōkichi was as violent and as stupid as they come. But if he hadn't had Nobu backing him, he could never have behaved so brazenly. And that Nobu! In front of others he pretended to be gentle and wise, but a look behind the scenes would reveal that *he* was the one pulling all the strings. Midori didn't care if he was ahead of her in school, or how good his grades were. So what if he was the young master of Ryūge Temple! She, after all, was Midori of the Daikokuya, and not beholden to him in the slightest. She had never borrowed a single sheet of paper. So who were they to call her a tramp, or those other names Chōkichi had used? She wasn't about to be impressed just because Ryūge Temple had a prominent parishioner or two.

What about the patrons her sister Ōmaki had? The banker Kawa, a steady customer for three years now; Yone, from the stock exchange; and that short one, the member of parliament—why, he'd been all set to buy her sister's contract and marry her, till Ōmaki decided she could do without him. And he was somebody! Just ask the lady who ran Ōmaki's house. Go ahead and ask, if you thought she was making it up. Where would the Daikokuya be without her sister? Why do you think even the owner of the house was never curt with Midori and her parents? Just take that porcelain statue of Daikoku, the one he kept in the alcove. Once when she was playing shuttlecock, she knocked over a vase accidentally and smashed the master's favorite statue to smithereens. He was sitting right in the next room drinking. And all he said was, Midori, you're turning into a little tomboy." Not one word of reproach. Had it been anyone else, you can be sure, he wouldn't have stopped there. The maids were green with envy. No question about it, the child's privileges derived from her sister's position. Midori knew it, too. Her parents were mere caretakers for the master's house, but her sister was Ōmaki of the Daikokuya. She didn't have to take insults from the likes of Chōkichi. And too bad for him if the little priest wanted to be mean to her. Midori had had enough of school. She was born stubborn and she was not about to suffer anyone's contempt. That day she broke her pencils and threw away her ink; she would spend her time playing with her real friends. She wasn't going to need her abacus or her books.

In evening they rush into the quarter, at dawn they leave less cheerfully. It's a lonely ride home, with only dreams of the night before to keep a man company. Getaways are under cover. A hat pulled low, a towel around the face. More than one of these gentlemen would rather that you didn't look. To watch will only make you feel uneasy. That smirk of theirs—not half-pleased with themselves as the sting of their lady's farewell slap sinks in. After all, she wouldn't want him to forget her. Careful when you get to Sakamoto. The vegetable carts come barreling back from the early morning market. Watch out when you hit Crazy Street. Until Mishima Shrine, you won't be safe from those who wander home all gaga and enraptured from the night before. Their faces never look so resolute the morning after. It's rude to say it, but don't they all suggest love's fools? The fishwives seldom hesitate to sum them up. Look, there goes a man with money. But that one over there, he couldn't have a penny to his name.

One need hardly cite the Chinese "Song of Everlasting Sorrow"[9] and the heights to which Yang's daughter rose to see that there are times when daughters are more valuable than sons. Many a princess comes into the world among the shanties of the back street. Today she calls herself "Snow" in one of those swank geisha houses over in Tsukiji, a celebrated beauty whose accomplishments in dance have entertained a nobleman or two. But yesterday she was a mere delinquent and she earned her spending money making playing cards, you know. "What kind of tree does rice grow on?" she asks, as if she'd grown up in the lap of luxury. Around here, of course, she is not the celebrity she used to be. Once they leave, they're soon forgotten. Already she has been eclipsed by the dye-maker's second daughter, Kokichi, a home-grown flower of a girl, whose name you'll hear throughout the park. The lanterns are up these days at The New Ivy, in Senzoku, where that one works.

Night and day, it's the daughters that you hear of. A boy is about as useful as a mutt sniffing round the rubbish. Every shopkeeper's son is a wastrel. At seventeen, the age of insolence, the young men band together. Before they go completely gallant—you don't see any flutes tucked into sashes yet—they join up with a leader whose alias is invariably a solemn, grandiose affair. They deck themselves out with matching scarves and matching paper lanterns. It won't be long now before they learn to gamble and to window-shop the quarter. Bantering with the courtesans will begin to come more easily. Even with the serious ones, the family business is only something for the day. Back from the evening bath they come in kimonos of a rakish cut, sandals dragging. "Hey, did you see the new one? At What's-Its-Name? She looks like the girl at the sewing shop, over in Kanasugi. But, with that funny little nose of hers, she's even uglier." It's the only thing remotely on their minds. They bum tobacco, a piece of tissue at every house.[1] The pats and pinches they exchange with each beauty along the way: *these* are the things that bring a lifetime of renown. Even the sons of perfectly upstanding families decide to style themselves as local toughs. They are forever picking fights around the Gate.[2]

Ah, the power of women. One need hardly say more. In the quarter,

---

9. By Po Chü-i (772–846). The poem concerns the immoderate love of the Chinese emperor Hsüan Tsung for his beautiful young consort, Yang Kuei-fei, and the grief into which he is plunged by her death. 1. Borrowing tobacco or a facial tissue was merely an excuse to get into the houses. 2. The main entrance to the red-light district.

prosperity makes no distinctions between the autumn and the spring. Escort lanterns[3] are not in vogue these days, and still the men are carried away. All it takes is the echo of a pair of sandals. Here she comes! The little girl from the teahouse who will take them to their ladies. Clip-clop, clip-clop. The sound mingles with the music of the theater. They hear it and they stream into the quarter. If you ask them what they're after, it's a flowing robe, a scarlet collar, a baroque coiffure, a pair of sparkling eyes and lips with painted smiles. The beauties may in fact have little of the beautiful about them. The minute they are courtesans, they climb the pedestal. Those of you from other parts may find it all a little hard to understand.

Needless to say, Midori, who spent her days and nights immersed in such a world, soon took on the color of the quarter. In her eyes, men were not such fearsome things. And her sister's calling was nothing to disparage. When Ōmaki was on the verge of leaving for the city, how Midori had cried. Not in her wildest dreams had she hoped to accompany her sister. And now here they were. Who wouldn't envy a sister like Ōmaki? What with her recent success, it was nothing for her to repay all the debts she had ever owed her parents. Midori had no notion of what price Ōmaki might have paid to reign supreme in her profession. To her it was all a game. She knew about the charms and tricks the girls would use. Simpering to summon men they longed for, like mice grabbing cheese. Tapping on the lattice when they made a wish. She knew the secret signals they would use to give their guests a parting pat. She had mastered the special language of the quarter, and she didn't feel the least embarrassed when she used it.

It was all a little sad. She was fourteen. When she caressed her dolls, she could have been a prince's child. But for her, all lessons in manners and morals and the wifely arts were topics to be left at school. What never ceased to capture her attention were the rumors of her sister's suitors— who was in and who was out of favor—the costumes of the serving girls, the bedding gifts that men would lavish on Ōmaki,[4] the teahouse tips for the introduction of a patron. What was bright and colorful was good, and what was not was bad. The child was still too young to exercise discretion. She was always taken with the flower just before her eyes. A headstrong girl by nature, Midori indulged herself by fluttering about in a world that she had fashioned from the clouds.

Crazy Street, Sleepy Street. The half-witted, groggy gentlemen all pass this way as they head home. At the gate to this village of late risers, the sweepers and the sprinklers have already cleaned the streets. But look down main street. They have roosted for the night among the slums of Mannenchō or Yamabushichō, or perhaps Shintanimachi, and now here they come: what for want of any other word one might as well call "entertainers." The singing candy man. The two-bit player. The puppeteers. The jugglers and the acrobats. The dancers with their parasols. The clowns

---

3. Carried by women escorting customers from the teahouse to the brothel.   4. A courtesan's regular patrons were expected to finance new sets of nightgowns and bedding on each of the five major holidays. These gifts were an expensive proposition, and the display of new bedding—in plain view of every passerby—became a courtesan's demonstration of her status within her world.

who do the lion dance.[5] Their dress is as varied as their arts, a gauze of silk, a sash of satin. The clowns prefer the cotton prints from Satsuma, with black bands round the waist. Men, pretty women, troupes of five, seven, even ten, and a lonely old man, all skin and bones, who totters as he clutches his battered samisen. And, look, there's a little girl of five or so they've got to do the Kinokuni dance.[6] Over there, with the red ribbons on her sleeves. But none of them stop here. They know where the business is, and they hurry to the quarter. The guest who has lingered at the tea-house, the beauty in a melancholy mood—these are the ones it pays to entertain. The profits are too good to give it up, or to waste time with benefit performances along the way. Not even the most tattered and suspicious-looking beggar would bother to loiter around here.

A lady minstrel passed before the paper shop. Her hat all but concealed her striking face, yet she sang and played with the bearing of a star. "It's a shame we never get to hear the end of her song," the shopkeeper's wife complained. Midori, bright from her morning bath, was lounging on the shop's front step, watching the parade pass by. She pushed her hair up with her boxwood comb. "Wait here. I'll bring her back!"

The child never mentioned slipping something in the lady's sleeve to coax her to perform but, sure enough, back in tow she came to sing the requested song of thwarted love. "Thank you very much for your patronage," she concluded in her honeyed tone, and even as it echoed they knew that they were not about to hear its likes again.

"To think—a mere child could have arranged it!" bystanders marveled, more impressed with Midori than with the minstrel.

"Wouldn't it be fun to have them all perform?" Midori whispered to Shōta. "The samisen and the flute and the drums! The singers and the dancers! Everything we never get more than just a glimpse of!"

Even for Midori, the proposal was ambitious. "Don't overdo it, girl," Shōta muttered.

"Thus have I heard it spoken," the reverend priest intoned the sutra.[7] As the holy words were carried from the temple by the soft breeze through the pines, they should have blown away all dust within the heart.

But smoke rose from fish broiling in the kitchen. In the cemetery diapers had been seen drying over tombstones. Nothing wrong here in the eyes of the Order, perhaps; those who fancied their clerics above worldly desires, though, found the doings at Ryūge Temple rather too earthly for their tastes.[8]

Here the fortunes of the head priest were as handsome as his stomach. Both had rounded out nicely through the years. The man's glow of well-being beggared description: not the sunny pink of the cherries, not the deep pink of the peach; from the top of his freshly shaven pate to the bottom of his neck, he shone like burnished copper. When he whooped

---

5. A popular folk dance for which performers dress as *shishi*, mythical lionlike creatures who ward off evil.   6. Named after a popular song: "Out in the deep blue sea the white sails pass: / The tangerine boats from Kinokuni."   7. A narrative portion of the Buddhist scriptures.   8. Until 1872, with the exception of members of the sect known as Jōdo Shinshū, Buddhist monks were forbidden to marry or to eat fish (or meat, for that matter). By the time of this story, however, these taboos had been abolished for some twenty years. Therefore, the priest of Ryūge Temple was committing no offense against the letter of the law, but the religious practices and attitudes of centuries were slow to die.

with laughter—bushy, salt-and-pepper eyebrows floating heavenward—the noise of the old man's excess could have toppled Buddha from the altar.

The priest's young wife (she was only in her forties) was not an unattractive woman. Her skin was fair, and she wore her thinning hair in a small, modest bun. She was always cordial when people came to pray. Even the florist's wife outside the temple gate held her tongue where the reverend's wife was concerned—the fruit, you may be sure, of the temple lady's kindliness: a hand-me-down here, a leftover there. At one time, she herself had been among the parishioners. But her husband died young, and, having nowhere to turn, she came to do the sewing at the temple. In exchange for meals, she took over the washing and the cooking. Before long she was out in the graveyard, sweeping away with the best of the groundsmen. The priest was quick to offer his compassion, and quicker still to calculate the advantages. The woman knew full well that the difference in their ages, some twenty years, might make the arrangement appear a bit unseemly. But she had nowhere else to go, and she came to consider the temple a good place to live out her days and to meet her end. She learned not to lose too much sleep over prying neighbors.

Some in the congregation found the situation shocking. Soon enough, however, they began to acknowledge that in her heart the woman was a good person, and they ceased to censure her. While she was carrying their first child, Ohana, the priest finally made an honest woman of her. A retired oil dealer over in Sakamoto, one of the parishioners who went in for such things, acted as the go-between—if you want to call it that.

Nobu was their second child. Someday he would do his father proud, but at the moment he was a taciturn, moody boy who preferred to pass the day alone in his room. Ohana, on the other hand, was quite the opposite, a lovely girl with fine skin and a soft, plump little chin. To call her a beauty would be going too far, perhaps, but since adolescence she had had her share of admirers. It seemed a shame to waste such a girl, for she might have been a geisha. Who knows? There may be worlds where even Buddha enjoys the music of the samisen. In this world, at any rate, there was the matter of what others said, and talk they would if the daughter of a temple became an entertainer with her skirt hitched up. What the priest did instead was to establish Ohana in a little tea shop in Tamachi. He put her behind the counter, where she could vend her charm. Young men with no idea in their heads how tea was weighed and measured began to gather at the shop. Seldom was Ohana's empty before midnight.

But his holiness was the busy one. Loans to collect, the shop to oversee, funerals to arrange, not to mention all the sermons every month. When he wasn't flipping through accounts, he was going through the sutras. If things didn't let up, he'd wear himself out, he would sigh as he dragged his flowered cushion onto the veranda, where he fanned himself, half-naked, and enjoyed his nightly hooch.[9] He was a fish-eater, and Nobu was the one he sent over to the main street for the broiled eels that he liked. "The big oily ones, if you please." It galled Nobu. His eyes never left his

---

9. Very potent cheap liquor.

feet as he trudged over to the Musashiya. If he heard voices at the paper shop across the street, he would keep on going. Then, when the coast was clear, he'd dart into the eel shop. The shame he felt! He would never eat the smelly things.

The reverend was nothing if not practical. There were some who might call him greedy, but that never bothered him a whit. He was neither a timid soul nor an idler: give him a spare moment and he'd set about fashioning kumade charms. On Otori day he would have his wife out peddling them. Whatever doubts she may have had about the venture, they were short-lived once his holiness started to bemoan the killing everybody else made, rank amateurs up and down the street. He soon persuaded his reluctant wife, set up a booth not a stone's throw from the temple gate, and installed her there to sell his charms and good-luck hairpins. She tied her hair back with a headband, just like the vendors and all the young men. In the daytime, she knew enough to stay out of sight and mingle with the crowd, leaving the florist's wife to manage things. But when the sun went down—who would have guessed it?—the woman had a field day. At dusk she took over for herself, quite forgetting what a spectacle she made with her sudden itch for profit. "Everything marked down! Prices slashed!" she barked after a customer who backed away. Buffeted and dizzy from the throngs, the victim soon lost his powers of appraisal. They had fled along with memory: two days earlier he had come to this very temple as a pilgrim. "Three for only seventy-five sen."[1] But her price left room to negotiate. "How about five for seventy-three?" "Sold!"

There were, of course, all kinds of sharp practices. Even if no one from the congregation heard, Nobu wondered, what would the neighbors think? And his friends? He could just hear them. Ryūge Temple is selling hairpins now. Nobu's mother is out huckstering like a lunatic. Really, didn't they think they ought to stop?

The reverend priest would hear nothing of it. "Knock it off. You don't know what you're talking about." The mere idea sent the man into paroxysms.

Prayers in the morning, accounts at night. His father's face beamed whenever his fingers touched the abacus. It was enough to turn the boy's stomach. Why on earth had the man become a priest?

There was nothing in his upbringing to make Nobu such a gloomy child. He had the same parents as Ohana. They were part of the same cozy, self-contained family. Yet he was the quiet one. Even when he did speak, his opinions were never taken seriously. His father's schemes, his mother's conduct, his sister's education—to Nobu everything they did was a travesty. He had resigned himself to knowing that they would never listen. How unfair it was. His friends found him contrary and perverse, but in fact he was a weakling. If anyone maligned him in the slightest, he would run for the shelter of his room. He was a coward utterly lacking in the courage to defend himself. At school they called him a brain; his fami-

---

1. A unit of currency. One sen equaled one-hundredth of a yen; the yen had a value of approximately fifty cents.

ly's station was not lowly. No one knew how weak he really was. More than one of his friends considered Nobu something of a cold fish.

The night of the festival Nobu was sent on an errand to his sister's tea shop in Tamachi, and he was late coming home. Not until the next morning did he learn of the fight at the paper shop. When Ushimatsu and Bunji and the others gave him the details, the full impact of Chōkichi's violent ways startled him anew. What was done was done—but in name he was included in the violence, and it rankled. Now people would be blaming him for the trouble.

It was three days before Chōkichi had the nerve to face Nobu. For once he must have felt a little sheepish about the damage he had done. He did not look forward to Nobu's scolding. "I know you're probably angry," he ventured, having waited for the storm to pass. "I couldn't help it, though. Everything got out of hand. I hadn't meant it to happen. You won't hold it against me, will you, Nobu? How were we to know that you'd be gone and Shōta would fly the coop? It's not as though I planned to beat up Sangorō and pick a fight with that tramp Midori. Things just happened. You don't run away once the lanterns start swinging! All we wanted was to show a little muscle, show 'em who's boss. It's my fault, I know. I should have listened to you. But come on Nobu, if you get mad now, how's it going to look? After I've gone around telling everybody you're on *our* side. You can't leave us in the lurch. Okay, so you don't approve of this one thing. You be the leader, and next time we won't botch things up." Gone was the usual swagger.

Nobu couldn't turn his back on Chōkichi. "All right," he sighed. "But listen—bully the weak ones, and we'll be the ones in disgrace. We're not going to gain anything fighting Sangorō and Midori. If Shōta and his flunkies want to stir up trouble, we can cross that bridge when we come to it. But let's not egg them on." Chōkichi had to promise: no more fights. For a rebuke, it was rather mild.

The innocent one was Sangorō. They had kicked and beaten him to their hearts' content, and he still ached two, three days afterward. He couldn't stand up, he couldn't sit down. Every evening when his father picked up the empty rickshaw and headed for the teahouses, someone would ask him what was wrong with the boy. "Say, your Sangorō looks a little peaked these days," the caterer remarked, almost accusingly. "Somebody give him a pounding?"

Groveling Tetsu they called his father, head always lowered before his betters. It didn't matter who—the landlord or someone with money or the owner of one of the houses in the quarter, where Tetsu pulled his cart— any of them could make the most impossible demands, and the rickshawman would acquiesce. "Indeed, of course, how right you are." Small wonder, then, what his reaction was to the incident with Chōkichi. "He's the landlord's son, isn't he? I don't care if you were right. I won't have you getting into scraps with him. Now go apologize. You ought to know better!" There was no avoiding it. His father made sure that he got down on his knees in front of Chōkichi.

Within a week Sangorō's wounds healed and his temper cooled. He was ready to forget what he'd been angry about. For the price of a carriage ride, he was baby-sitting again for Chōkichi's little brother, walking round with the child on his back and lulling it to sleep with nursery rhymes. Sangorō was sixteen, that age when boys get cocky, but the lumpish figure he cut failed to trouble him. He wandered over to the main street, unconcerned as always. "Hey, Sangorō. Have you forgotten you're a boy?" Midori and Shōta were great ones when it came to teasing. "Some sight you make, with that baby on your back!" It didn't matter, they were still his friends.

In spring the cherry trees blossom in profusion. In summer the lanterns twinkle in memory of the late Tamagiku.[2] In fall the festival streets overflow with rickshaws. Count them: seventy-five down the road within the space of ten minutes. Then the autumn holidays are over. Here and there a red dragonfly bobs above the rice fields. Before long, quail will be calling out along the moat. Mornings and evenings, the breeze blows cold. At the sundries shop, pocket warmers now take the place of mosquito incense. It's sad, somehow, that faint sound of the mortar grinding flour at Tamura's, over by the bridge. The clock at Kadoebi's has a melancholy ring. Fires glow through all four seasons from the direction of Nippori.[3] It's in autumn that one begins to notice them. Smoke rises each time one more soul embarks on the journey to the other shore.

Deftly, a geisha plays on the samisen. The refrain reaches the path along the bank behind the teahouses. A passerby looks up and listens. Not much of a song, really, but moving all the same. "Together we shall spend our night of love." Women who have done time in the quarter will tell you— it's the men who begin visiting in fall who prove to be the truly faithful ones.

Talk, talk: in this neighborhood, there is always grist for gossip. The details are tedious, but the stories make the rounds. A blind masseuse, she was only twenty, killed herself. With a handicap like hers, love was out of the question. Well she couldn't stand it any more. Drowned herself in Mizunoya Pond. Then there are the incidents too commonplace to rate a rumor. Missing persons: Kichigorō, the greengrocer, and Takichi, the carpenter. How come? "They picked them up for this," a fellow whispers, and pantomimes a gambler dealing out the cards.

A moment ago there were children there, down the street. "Ring-a-ring-a-rosy, pocket full of posies." Suddenly it's quiet now, before you notice. Only the sound of rickshaws, loud as ever.

It was a lonely night. Just when it seemed the autumn rains would go on and on falling softly, with a roar a downpour came. At the paper shop they were not expecting anyone. The shopkeeper's wife had closed up for the evening. Inside, playing marbles, were Shōta and Midori, as usual, and two or three of the younger ones. All at once, Midori heard something: "Is that a customer? I hear footsteps."

"I don't hear anything," Shōta said. He stopped counting out the marbles.

2. A celebrated courtesan whose death in 1726 was commemorated with a festival of lanterns, a popular event in the red-light district.   3. A place of cremation.

"Maybe someone wants to play."

Who could it be? They heard him come as far as the gate, but after that, not a word, not a sound.

"Boo!" Shōta opened the door and stuck his head out. "Hey, who's there?" He could just make out the back of someone walking along beneath the eaves two or three houses up ahead. "Who is it? Do you want to come in?" He had slipped Midori's sandals on and was about to run after him, in spite of the rain. "Oh, it's him." Shōta cupped his hand above his head, mimicking a bald monk. "No use—we can call him all we want, he won't come."

"Nobu?" Midori asked. "That old priest! I'll bet he came to buy a writing brush and scurried off the minute he heard us. Nasty, stupid, toothless, old-maid Nobu! Just let him come in. I'll tell him what I think. Too bad he ran away. Let me have the sandals. I want a look." This time Midori poked her head out. The rain dripped down from the eaves onto her forehead. It gave her a chill. She pulled back, staring at the shadowy figure as he made his way around the puddles. He was four or five houses away by now, and he seemed to cower in the gaslight. His paper umbrella hugged his shoulders. She looked and looked.

Shōta tapped her on the shoulder. "Midori, what is it?"

"Nothing," she said absent-mindedly, returning to the game. "I hate that little altar boy! He can't even conduct his fights in public. He makes that pious, old-maid face of his and goes sneaking round corners. Isn't he awful? My mother says people who are straightforward are the good ones. She's right, don't you think, Shōta? It's a sure thing Nobu has an evil heart, the way he lurks around."

"But at least he knows what's what. Not like Chōkichi, there's a real moron. The boy's a total ignoramus," Shōta said knowingly.

"Cut it out. You and your big words." Midori laughed and pinched him on the cheek. "Such a serious face! Since when are you so grown up?"

Shōta was not amused. "For your information, it won't be long before I *am* grown up. I'll wear a topcoat with square-cut shoulders like the shopkeeper at Kabata's, and the gold watch Grandmother's put away for me. I'll wear a ring. I'll smoke cigarettes. And for shoes—you're not going to see me in any clogs. Oh, no. I'll wear leather sandals, the good kind, with triple-layered heels and fancy satin straps. Won't I look sharp!"

"You in triple heels and a square-cut overcoat?" Midori couldn't help snickering. "Mm, sure, if you want to look like a walking medicine bottle."

"Oh, quiet. You don't think I've stopped growing, do you? I won't be this short forever."

"Seeing is believing. You know, Shōta," Midori said, pointing a sarcastic finger at the rafters, "even the mice laugh when you keep making these promises." Everyone, the shopkeeper's wife included, shook with laughter.

His eyes spun; Shōta was completely serious. "Midori makes a joke of everything. But everyone grows up, you know. Why is what I say so funny? The day will come when I go walking with my pretty wife. I always like things to be pretty. If I had to marry someone like that pock-marked Ofuku at the cracker shop, or the girl at the firewood store with the bulging fore-head—no thank you. I'd send her home. No pockmarks for me!"

"How good of you to come, then," the shop wife laughed. "Haven't you noticed my spots?"

"Oh, but you're old. I'm talking about brides. Once you're old, it doesn't matter."

"I shouldn't have said anything," the woman sighed. "Well, let's see now. There's Oroku at the flower shop. She has a pretty face. And Kii at the fruit stand. And who else? Who else, I wonder? Why, the prettiest one is sitting right next to you. Shōta, who will it be? Oroku with those eyes of hers? Kii and her lovely voice? Tell us who."

"What are you talking about? Oroku, Kii—what's so good about them?" Shōta's face turned scarlet, and he backed away from the light, into a corner.

"Does that mean it's Midori, then?"

"How do I know?" He looked away, tapping out a song against the wall. "The water wheel goes round and round."

Midori and the rest had begun another game of marbles. *Her* face was not flushed in the slightest.

There would have been no problem if he hadn't taken the short cut. But every time Nobu went off to Tamachi he took the path along the ditch. And every time he saw it: the lattice gate, the stone lantern, the thatched fence. The summer bamboo blinds were rolled up now along the veranda. He couldn't help remembering things. Behind the glass windows,[4] her mother would be there, like some latter-day widow of Azechi at her rosary; and she would be there too, straight from the ancient tales, a young Mura-saki[5] with her hair bobbed. This was the house of the man who owned the Daikokuya.

Yesterday and today the autumn rains had continued. The winter slip Ohana had requested was ready, and Nobu's mother was anxious for her to have it. She didn't like to ask in such weather, but would he mind taking it to the shop in Tamachi on his way to school? The poor girl was waiting for the package. Diffident Nobu could never say no. He took the bundle under his arm, stepped into his clogs, and started out, clinging to his umbrella as the rain lapped at his feet.

He followed the ditch around the quarter, the same path he always took, but today luck was not with him. Just in front of the Daikokuya, the wind came up. He had to tug to keep his umbrella from flying off. He braced his legs against the wind, when the strap on one of his clogs tore clean away. Now what was he to do?

It was almost enough to make him swear. He had no choice but to try repairing the clog himself. He propped his umbrella against the gate and sought shelter underneath its eaves. Yet how was a fledgling cleric to

---

4. This is mentioned to indicate that the house belongs to someone of means. Glass windows were expensive and still relatively rare in Japan in the 1890s.   **5.** The favorite of the hero of *The Tale of the Genji* (in Volume 1). It is the widow of Azechi (Murasaki's grandmother) with whom the young girl lives when Genji discovers her, on a night when the widow is at her prayers; as soon as he spies Murasaki, Genji knows that the child will grow up to be the woman of his dreams. The equation of Midori with the young Murasaki and the passing Nobu with the traveling Genji is an obvious hint at the blossoming, inarticulate love between Nobu and Midori.

accomplish this sort of handiwork? He was flustered, and no matter how hard he tried, he couldn't fix it. He grew more and more irritated. From his sleeve he took out the draft of his school composition and tore it up, twisting the strips of paper in hopes of somehow fashioning a new strap. But the confounded storm grew worse again, and his umbrella began to roll away in the wind. This was more than he could tolerate! He reached out to grab the umbrella—but it was just his luck—his sister's package fell from his lap into the mud. There, now he had mud on his sleeve, too.

A pathetic sight he made, without an umbrella and stranded barefoot in the downpour. From the window, Midori saw the sad figure beyond the gate. "Look, someone's broken his sandal. Mother, can I give him something to fix it with?" She found a piece of Yūzen crepe[6] in the sewing drawer and hurried into her clogs. Grabbing an umbrella from the veranda, she dashed out across the stepping stones toward the front gate.

Then she saw who it was. The blood rushed to Midori's head. Her heart pounded as if she had encountered a dreaded fate. She turned to see, was anyone watching? Trembling, she inched her way toward the gate. At that instant Nobu, too, looked around. He was speechless, he felt cold sweat begin to bead. He wanted to kick off the other sandal and run away.

Had Midori been herself, she would have seized on Nobu's predicament to tell him what she thought. She would have sneered at his cowardice and heaped upon him every bit of abuse that he deserved. Didn't he think he owed her an apology? Bossing everyone around from backstage, ruining all the fun at the festival, just because he was angry at Shōta. And letting them beat up helpless Sangorō! He was the one who had incited Chōkichi to call her those names. And what was wrong with being a courtesan, anyway, even if she were one? She didn't owe him anything. With her parents and her sister and the man from the Daikokuya—what did she need to ask favors of a broken-down priest for? He had better stop calling her names. Something to say, was there? Then he could come out in the open, like a man. Any time, any time. She'd meet him. What did he have to say to that? She would have grabbed him by the sleeve and given him a piece of her mind, all right. Nobu would not have had a prayer.

But instead she cringed in the shadows of the gate. She didn't move, her heart throbbed. This was not the old Midori.

Whenever he came near the Daikokuya, timorous Nobu hurried past without so much as looking left or right. But today, the unlucky rain, the unlucky wind, and, to make matters worse, the broken sandal strap! There was nothing for it but to stop and make a new one. He was upset enough already, and then he heard the sound of steps on the flagstones—he felt as if ice water had been poured down his back. Even without looking, he knew who it would be. He shivered and his face changed color. He turned away and pretended to be hard at work. But he was panic-stricken. It didn't look as if the clog would ever be of use again.

From the garden, Midori peered at him. How clumsy he was; he could never do anything right. Who ever heard of trying to make a strap out of

6. A fabric colored by an elaborate and expensive dying process created by Miyazaki Yūzen of Kyoto.

anything as flimsy as a piece of paper—or straw, is that what he was using? Old ladies, maybe. It would never hold. Oh, and didn't he know he was getting mud all over the bottom of his jacket? There went the umbrella. Why didn't he close it before he propped it up? How it irritated her to watch his fumbling. "Here's some cloth to fix it with." If only she could have said it. Instead, she stood rooted to the spot, hiding, staring. The girl was oblivious to the rain soaking through her sleeves.

Midori's mother, unaware of what was happening, called out. "Midori, the iron's ready. What are you doing out there? Don't you know better than to play in the rain? You'll catch another cold."

"All right, coming." If only Nobu wouldn't hear. Her heart raced, her head seemed to reel. The last thing she could do was open the gate, but she could not turn her back on him, either. What was she to do? There— she hurled the rag outside the lattice without saying anything. Nobu pretended not to notice. Oh! He was his same old nasty self! It crushed her, the tears welled up. Why did he have to be so mean? Why didn't he just tell her what it was? It made her sick. But her mother kept on calling. It was no use. She started for the house. After all, why should she be sentimental? She wasn't going to let him see Midori eat humble pie.

He heard her walk away; his eyes wandered after her. The scarlet scrap of Yūzen silk lay in the rain, its pattern of red maple leaves near enough to touch. Odd, how her one gesture moved him, and yet he could not bring himself to reach out and take the cloth. He stared at it vacantly, and as he looked at it he felt his heart break.

He bungled everything. Nobu sighed and took the cord from his jacket and wrapped it round the clog. It was unsightly and makeshift, but perhaps it would do, perhaps he could stumble along. But all the way to Ohana's? It was a little late to be wondering that, he thought as he stood up, his sister's package tight under his arm. He had only gone two or three steps when he looked back again at the tatter of silk, bright with autumn maples. It was hard for him to leave it there.

"Nobu, what's the matter? Break your strap? What a sight you are!"

Nobu turned around to see who owned the unexpected voice. It was obnoxious Chōkichi, decked out like a young gallant. He had on his best-dress kimono, and he wore his orange sash profligately low on the hips. His new jacket had a fancy black collar, and the umbrella he carried was festooned with the trademark of one of the houses in the quarter. His high clogs were sporting lacquered rain covers—this was something new. What pride there was in the young man's swagger.

"The strap broke, and I was wondering what to do," Nobu answered helplessly. "I'm not very good at these things."

"No, you wouldn't be. It's all right, wear mine. The straps won't give out."

"But what will you do?"

"Don't worry. I'm used to it. I'll just go like this," he said, tucking up the bottom of his kimono. "Feels much better than wearing sandals, anyway." He kicked off his rain clogs.

"You're going to go barefoot? That won't be fair."

"I don't mind. I'm used to going barefoot. Someone like you has soft feet. You could never walk barefoot on the gravel. Come on, wear these," he urged, arranging his sandals obligingly. What a spectacle: Chōkichi was more detested than the plague god himself, and here he was with soft words on his tongue and bushy eyebrows moving solicitously. "I'll take your sandals and toss them in at the back door. Here, let's switch."

Chōkichi took the broken clogs, and they parted, Nobu bound for his sister's in Tamachi and Chōkichi for home before they met again at school.

The silk shred lay abandoned by the gate. Its red maple leaves shimmered in the rain.

This year there were three Otori fair days.[7] Rain had spoiled the second, but today, like the first, was perfect for a festival. Throngs packed Otori Shrine, young men surged into the quarter through the side gates. They say they've come to pay a visit to the shrine. They are pilgrims, but, ah, the roar of young laughter is loud enough to rend the pillars holding up the heavens, to tear away the very cord from which the earth hangs. Front and back of the main street of the quarter look as if they've been reversed. Today, the side drawbridges are down clear around the moat, and the crowds keep pouring in. "Coming through, coming through." What have we here? Some flat-bottomed boat trying to navigate these waves of people? Who will soon forget the excitement in the air? Peals of laughter, incessant chatter echo from the little shops along the ditch. Strains of the samisen rise from the first-class pleasure houses towering several stories in the sky.

Shōta took a holiday from collecting interest. He dropped in at Sangorō's potato stall, and then he visited his friend Donkey at the dumpling shop. "How are you doing? Making any money?" The sweets looked pretty uninviting.

"Shōta! You're just in time. I've run out of bean jam and don't know what to do. I've already put more on to cook, but they keep coming and I don't want to turn them away. What should I do?"

"Don't be stupid. Look what you've got on the sides of the pot. Add some water and some sugar, and you can feed another ten or twenty people. Everybody does it—you won't be the first. Besides, who's going to notice how it tastes in all this commotion? Start selling, start selling." Shōta was already at the sugar bowl.

Donkey's one-eyed mother was filled with admiration. "You've become a real merchant, Shōta. I'm almost afraid of you."

"This? I saw Clammy do the same thing in the alley. It's not my idea." The woman's praise did not go to his head. "Hey, do you know where Midori is? I've been looking for her since this morning. Where'd she go off to? She hasn't been to the paper shop. I know that. I wonder if she's in the quarter."

"Oh, Midori, she went by a little while ago. I saw her take one of the

---

7. Otori days were not consecutive (see n. 5, p. 1561).

side bridges into the quarter. Shōta, you should have seen her. She had her hair all done up like this." He made an oafish effort to suggest the splendor of Midori's new grown-up hairdo. "She's really something, that girl!" The boy wiped his nose as he extolled her.

"Yes, she's even prettier than her sister. I hope she won't end up like Ōmaki." Shōta looked down at the ground.

"What do you mean—that would be wonderful! Next year I'm going to open a shop, and after I save some money I'll buy her for a night!" He didn't understand things.

"Don't be such a smart aleck. Even if you tried, she wouldn't have anything to do with you."

"Why? Why should she refuse me?"

"She just would." Shōta flushed as he laughed. "I'm going to walk around for a while. I'll see you later." He went out the gate.

> "Growing up,
>   she plays among the butterflies
>   and flowers.
> But she turns sixteen,
>   and all she knows
>   is work and sorrow."[8]

He sang the popular refrain in a voice that was curiously quavering for him, and repeated it again to himself. His sandals drummed their usual ring against the paving stones, as all at once his little figure vanished into the crowd.

Inside the bustling quarter, Shōta found himself swept along into a corner of the compound. It was there he saw Midori. Why, it certainly was Midori of the Daikokuya; she was talking to an attendant from one of the houses, and, just as he had heard, her hair was done up in the glorious *shimada* style[9] of a young woman. And yet she looked shy today. Colored ribbons cascaded from her hair, tortoise-shell combs and flowered hairpins flickered in the sun. The whole effect was as bright and stately as a Kyōto doll. Shōta was tongue-tied. Any other time, he would have rushed over and taken her arm.

"Shōta!" Midori came running up. "If you have shopping to do, Otsuma, why don't you go on ahead? I'll go home with him." She nodded good-by to the lady.

"Oh, you don't want me around, now that you've found another friend, is that it?" Otsuma smiled as she headed down a narrow street of shops. "I'll be off to Kyōmachi, then."

"You look nice, Midori." Shōta tugged at her sleeve. "When did you get that new hairdo? This morning? Why didn't you come and show it to me?" He pretended to be angry.

Midori had difficulty speaking. "I had it done this morning at my sis-

---

8. A popular song.   9. The fashionable hairstyle for young, unmarried women and for courtesans. There were many variations, but essentially the larger the chignon, the more youthful or ostentatious the woman. The hairdo is a clear sign that Midori is no longer considered a child. And the fact that it is large (here translated as "glorious") suggests Midori's affinity with the world of prostitutes.

ter's. I hate it." Her spirits drooped. She kept her head down; she couldn't bear it when a passerby would gawk.

When she felt so awkward and unhappy, flattery only sounded like an insult. People turned to admire her and she thought they were jeering.

"Shōta, I'm going home."

"Why don't you play? Did someone scold you? I bet you had a fight with your sister."

Midori felt her face color. Shōta was still a child, clearly. Where did one begin to explain?

They passed the dumpling shop, and Donkey called out theatrically, "You two sure are friendly." It made her feel like crying.

"Shōta, I don't want to walk with you." She hurried off ahead of him.

She had promised to go with him to the festival, and now here she was, headed in the opposite direction. "Aren't you going to come?" he yelled, running after her. "Why are you going home? You might at least explain!"

Midori walked on without answering, hoping to elude him. Shōta was stunned. He pulled at her sleeve. It was all so strange. Midori's face only turned a deeper red. "It's nothing, Shōta." But he knew that this was not the truth.

He followed her in through the gate at her house and onto the veranda. There was no need to hesitate; he had been coming here to play for years.

"Oh, Shōta," her mother greeted him. "Nice to see you. She's been in a bad mood all day. I don't know what to do with her. See if you can cheer her up."

Shōta became quite the grown-up. "Something the matter, is there?"

"No, no." Her mother gave an odd smile. "She'll get over it in no time. She's just spoiled. I suppose she's been grumpy with her friends, too? I tell you, sometimes I've had it with that girl." Her mother turned to look at her, but Midori had gone into the other room. Her sash and her outer kimono were discarded on the floor and Midori lay face-down underneath a quilt.

Shōta approached her gingerly. "Midori, what is it? Don't you feel well? Please tell me what's the matter." He held back as he spoke to her. What should he do? He folded and unfolded his hands in his lap. Midori said nothing. He could hear her sobbing into her sleeve. Her bangs, too short still for sweeping up into the great hairdo, were matted with tears. Something was terribly wrong, but, child that he was, Shōta had no idea what it could be, or how to console her. He was totally bewildered. "Please tell me what it is. You've never said anything to me, so how can you be angry with me?" He looked at her warily.

"Shōta, it isn't you." Midori wiped her eyes.

But when he asked her what it was, then, she couldn't answer. There were just sad things, vague things. Feelings . . . She couldn't put them into words. They made her cheeks burn. Nothing she could point to— and yet lately everything discouraged her. So many thoughts; none of them would ever have occurred to the Midori of yesterday. This awkwardness all of a sudden! How was she to explain it? If they would just leave her alone . . . she'd be happy to spend night and day in a dark room. No one to talk to her, no one to stare. Even if she felt unhappy, at least she would be spared the embarrassment. If only she could go on playing house forever—with her dolls for companions, then she'd be happy again. Oh! She hated, hated, hated this growing up! Why did things have to change? What she would give to go back a year, ten months, seven months, even.

They were the thoughts of someone already old.

She had forgotten that Shōta was there. But he kept on pestering her until she wanted to drive him away. "For God's sake, go home, Shōta. I feel like dying, with you here. All these questions give me a headache. They make me dizzy. I don't want anybody here! Just go *home!*"

She had never treated him so cruelly; Shōta could make no sense of it. He might as well have been groping through a cloud of smoke. "You sure are acting strange, Midori. I don't know why you talk this way. You must be crazy." The regrets were too much for him. He spoke calmly enough, but now his eyes smarted. This wouldn't help matters.

"Go home! Go home, will you! If you don't get out of here, you're not my friend at all. I hate you, Shōta."

"If that's the way you feel, I'm sorry to have bothered you." He darted off through the garden without so much as a farewell to Midori's mother, who had gone to check the water in the bath.

Shōta made a beeline for the paper shop, ducking, dodging his way through the crowds.

Sangorō was there, his holiday stall sold out and the take jingling in his pocket. Shōta burst in upon them just as Sangorō was playing the part of big brother. "Anything you want—it's yours!" The younger ones jumped up and down with glee. "Hey, Shōta! I was looking for you. I made a lot of money today. I'll treat you."

"You idiot. Since when do you treat me? Don't start talking big." These were rough words for Shōta. "That's not what I came here for." He looked dejected.

"What happened? A fight?" Sangorō shoved a half-eaten doughnut into his pocket. "Who was it? Nobu? Chōkichi? Where? The temple? Was it in the quarter? It won't be like the last time! This time, they won't take us by surprise. There's no way we can lose. I'm ready. Let me lead. We can't chicken out, Shōta."

The call to arms only infuriated him. "Take it easy," Shōta snapped. "There was no fight."

"But you came in here as if something terrible had happened. I thought it was a fight. And besides, if you don't do it tonight, we won't have another chance. Chōkichi's losing his right arm."

"Huh?"

"His accomplice, Nobu. Didn't you hear? I just found out. My father was talking with Nobu's mother. Any day now, he's going off to learn how to be a monk. Once he puts those robes on, they'll cover up his fighting arm. Those long, floppy robes—how can he roll up his sleeves in them?

But you know what that means. Next year, you'll have the front and the back street to yourself."

"All right, quiet. For a few coins they'll go over to Chōkichi. I could have a hundred like you, and it wouldn't excite me in the least. They can go where they like for all I care. I'll fight my own battles. It was Nobu I wanted to beat. But if he's running off on me, it can't be helped. I thought he was going next year, after he graduated. What a coward—why is he going so soon?"

But it wasn't Nobu he was worried about. Tonight, there were none of the usual songs from Shōta. Midori was on his mind. The throngs of merrymakers passing in the street only left him feeling lonely. What was there to celebrate?

The lamps went on, and Shōta rolled over on his side. Some festival, everything had ended in a mess!

From that day on Midori was a different person. When she had to, she went to her sister's rooms in the quarter, but she never went to play in town. Her friends missed her and came to invite her to join them in the fun again. "Maybe later. You go on ahead." Empty promises, always. She was cool even to Shōta, once her closest friend. She was forever blushing now. It seemed unlikely that the paper shop would see the old dancing and the games a second time.

People were puzzled. Was the girl sick? "No, no. She'll be her old self again," her mother assured them. "She's just having a rest. One of her little vacations." The woman smiled. And yet there seemed to be more to it.

There was praise for Midori now from some quarters. So ladylike, so well-behaved. Yes, but what a shame, others mourned: she was such a delightful, saucy child.

The front street was quiet suddenly, as if a light had gone out. Seldom did Shōta sing his songs any more. At night you could see him with his lantern making the rounds for the interest payments. The shadow moving along the moat looked chilly, somehow. From time to time, Sangorō would join him, and his voice rang out, comical as ever.

Everyone talked about Nobu, but Midori had not heard any of the rumors. The former spitfire was still closeted away somewhere. With all these changes lately, she hardly knew herself. She was timid now, everything embarrassed her.

One frosty morning, a paper narcissus lay inside the gate. No one knew what it was doing there, but Midori took a fancy to it, for some reason, and she put it in a bud vase. It was perfect, she thought, and yet almost sad in its crisp, solitary shape. That same day—she wasn't sure exactly where—Midori heard of Nobu's plans. Tomorrow he was leaving for the seminary. The color of his robes would never be the same.

THOMAS MANN
1875–1955

Thomas Mann's reputation as the great German novelist of the twentieth century represents only part of his stature; by the time of his death, he had become an international figure to whom people looked for statements on art, modern society, and the human condition. Continuing the great nineteenth-century tradition of psychological realism, Mann took as his subject the cultural and spiritual crises of Europe at the turn of the century. His career spanned a time of great change, including as it did the upheaval of two world wars and the visible disintegration of an entire society. Where other modern novelists, such as James Joyce, William Faulkner, and Virginia Woolf stressed innovative language and style, Mann emphasized instead the society of his time and—inside that society—the universal human conflicts between art and life, sensuality and intellect, individual and social will.

Many of Mann's themes derive from the nineteenth-century German aesthetic tradition in which he grew up. The philosophers Schopenhauer and Nietzsche and the composer Wagner had the most influence on his work: Arthur Schopenhauer (1788–1860) for his vision of the artist's suffering and development; Friedrich Nietzsche (1844–1900) for his portrait of the diseased artist overcoming chaos and decay to produce, through discipline and will, art works that justify existence; and Richard Wagner (1813–1883) for embodying the complete artist who controlled all aspects of his work: music, lyrics, the very staging of his operas. Mann's well-known use of the verbal *leitmotif* is also borrowed from Wagner, who would use in his operas a recurrent musical theme (the *leitmotif*) associated with a particular person, thing, action, or state of being. In Mann's literary adaptation, evocative phrases, repeated almost without change, link memories throughout the text and establish a cumulative emotional resonance. In the story *Tonio Kröger*, for example, Tonio's dual ancestry is repeatedly suggested by the contrasting phrases of the "dark, fiery mother, who played the piano and mandolin," and the father with his "thoughtful blue eyes" and "wild flower in the buttonhole." Inside the tradition of realistic narration, Mann created a highly organized literary structure with subtly interrelated themes and images that built up rich associations of ideas: in his own words, an "epic prose composition . . . understood by me as spiritual thematic pattern, as a musical complex of associations."

Mann was born in Lübeck, a historic seaport and commercial city in northern Germany, on June 6, 1875. His father was a grain merchant and head of the family firm; his mother came from a German-Brazilian family and was known for her beauty and musical talent. The contrast of Nordic and Latin that plays such a large part in Mann's work begins in his consciousness of his own heritage and is expanded to far-reaching symbolic levels. He disliked the scientific emphasis of his secondary education and left school in 1894 after repeating two years. Rejoining his family in Munich, where they had moved in 1891 after his father's death, he worked as an unpaid apprentice in a fire insurance business but found more interest in university lectures in history, political economy, and art. He decided against a business career after his first published story, *Fallen* (1896), received praise from the noted poet Richard Dehmel, and from 1896 to 1898 lived and wrote in Italy before returning to Munich for a two-year stint as manuscript reader for the satiric weekly *Simplicissimus*. In 1905, he married Katia Pringsheim, with whom he had six children. The short stories collected in *Little Herr Friede-*

mann (1899) were a success, and enabled Mann to find a publisher for his first major work, *Buddenbrooks* (1901).

Buddenbrooks describes the decline of a prosperous German family through four generations and is to some extent based on the history of the Mann family business. Nonetheless, the elements of autobiography are quickly absorbed into the more universal themes of the inner decay of the German burgher ("bourgeois," or middle-class) tradition and its growing isolation from other segments of society, a decline paralleled in the portrait of a developing artistic sensitivity and its relation to death. Children in the family of the self-confident, aggressive, and disciplined Consul Johann Buddenbrooks become increasingly introspective, hesitant, unhealthy, and artistic. The end of the family comes with young Hanno, a musical genius who is completely absorbed in his piano improvisations and thus prey to the fatal temptation of infinite beauty. In this novel, as in many later works, Mann's fictional world is governed by a tension or dualism between sensuous experience and intellect or will. A diseased and alienated imaginative soul is set against a healthy, gregarious, somewhat obtuse normal citizen; the erratic and poor artist against the disciplined and prosperous burgher; the dark, brown-eyed Latin against the blond, blue-eyed Nordic; warm, unself-conscious feelings against icy intellect; freedom against authority; immorality and decadence against moral respectability; a longing for the eternal and infinite against active participation in everyday life.

There is no recommended resolution of these polarities, for if either overwhelms the other, tragedy must follow. In the seemingly autobiographical *Tonio Kröger*, the protagonist is portrayed as sensitive to the claims of both, and his growing awareness of their combined importance is a sign of maturity. Ideally, the artist must live both extremes at once, in constant lucidity and pain. In *Death in Venice* (1912) the author Gustave Aschenbach suffers and dies for having been unable to keep the balance; in the novel *Doctor Faustus* (1947), the composer Adrian Leverkühn sells his soul to experience both poles. In *Mario and the Magician* (1929), the sadistic hypnotist Cipolla is an artist in his fashion, exercising a fatally corrupt art in which all his psychological insight, cutting intellect, and iron will produce only torment for himself and others. Mann's letters and essays show that he felt deeply involved in the relations of the artist's life to the art work, but his protagonists have their own identity and symbolize much more than Mann's own artistic career. As artist and craftsman, he always insisted on distinguishing the work of art from its raw material, the emotions and experiences of life. He cultivated objectivity, distance, and irony in his own works, and no character—including the narrator—is immune from the author's critical eye.

Throughout his writings up to and during World War I, Mann established himself as an important spokesman for modern Germany. His early conservatism and defense of an authoritarian nationalist government (*Reflections of a Non-Political Man*, 1918) gave way to an ardent defense of democracy and liberal humanism as the Nazis came to power. Mann's most famous novel, *The Magic Mountain* (1924), is a *Bildungsroman* (a novel of the protagonist's education and development) that uses the isolation of a mountaintop tuberculosis sanitorium to gain perspective on the philosophic issues of twentieth-century Europe. The hero, Hans Castorp, has to decide how to live as he listens to the competing dogmas of the humanist Settembrini and the fanatic antirationalist Naphta, and undergoes a double temptation of oblivion through eroticism (Clavdia Chauchat) and death (symbolized by the isolated sanitorium). The novel ends with Castorp choosing active participation in a world at war; whether or not he survives the trenches is left unresolved, but he has taken charge of his own destiny. *The Magic Mountain* was immensely popular, and its author received the Nobel Prize in 1929. He was so much an international figure when he went into voluntary exile in Switzerland as

Hitler came to power in 1933 that the Nazis, stung by his criticism, revoked his citizenship. Moving to America in 1938, he wrote and lectured against Nazism and in 1944 became an American citizen.

Mann's later works cover a range of themes. *Joseph, and His Brothers* (1933–45) is a tetralogy on the biblical tale of Joseph, who, abandoned for dead by his brothers, survives and comes to power in Egypt. *Doctor Faustus*, which Mann called "the novel of my epoch, dressed up in the story of a highly precarious and sinful artistic life," portrayed the composer Adrian Leverkühn as a modern Faust who personifies the temptation and corruption of contemporary Germany. Leverkühn makes a pact with the devil to become aware of the extremes of his own personality, thus enriching his experience and his music. His pieces are rationally composed by using intellectual patterns derived from the twelve-tone row, an avantgarde theory of composition based on a sequence of twelve tones with no previous harmonic relations, instead of the traditional musical scale. His *Lamentation of Doctor Faustus* is a direct challenge in theme and technique to the scale-based tonality of that earlier German masterpiece, Beethoven's Ninth Symphony with its concluding *Ode to Joy*. A somber and compelling work, *Doctor Faustus* symbolizes the negation of life Mann found inherent in Hitler's attempt to reshape German culture. Well after the war, when Mann had moved to Zurich, he published a final, comic picture of the artist-figure as a confidence man who uses his skill and ironic insight to manipulate society (*The Confessions of Felix Krull*, 1954). Mann's last work before his death on August 12, 1955, the *Confessions* recapitulates his familiar themes but in a lighthearted parody of traditional *Bildungsromans* that is a far cry from the moral seriousness of earlier tales.

Mann's most famous novella, *Death in Venice*, was published in 1912, shortly after the writer's own vacation in Venice and two years before World War I. Its sense of impending doom involves the cultural disintegration of the "European soul" (soon to be expressed in the Great War) symbolized by the corruption and death of the writer Gustave Aschenbach during an epidemic. The story pictures a loss of psychological balance, a sickness of the artistic soul to match that of plague-ridden Venice masking its true condition before unsuspecting tourists. Erotic and artistic themes mingle as the respected Aschenbach, escaping a lifetime of laborious creation and self-discipline, allows himself to be swept away by the classical beauty of a young boy until he becomes a grotesque figure, dyeing his hair and rouging his cheeks in a vain attempt to appear young. The issue, however, is not Aschenbach's obsession with Tadzio but rather the way that this fatal love casts light on the artist's whole career.

Aschenbach has laboriously repressed emotions and spontaneity to achieve the disciplined, classical style of a master—and also to earn fame. Plagued by nervous exhaustion at the beginning of the story, he reacts to the sight of a foreign traveler with an "extraordinary expansion of the inner self" and starts dreaming of exotic, dangerous landscapes. From the tropical swampland and tigers of the Ganges delta to the mountains of a later dream's Dionysiac revels, these visionary landscapes become a metaphor for all the subterranean impulses he has rejected in himself and for his art. Enigmatic figures guide Aschenbach's "adventure of the emotions": the traveler, the grotesque old man on the boat, the gondolier, the street singer, and Tadzio himself interpreted as a godlike figure out of Greek myth or culture. Indeed, allusions to ancient myth and literature multiply rapidly as Aschenbach falls under Tadzio's spell and begins to rationalize his fascination as the artist's pursuit of divine beauty. Turning to Plato's *Phaedrus*, a dialogue that combines themes of love with the search for absolute beauty and truth, Aschenbach sketches his own "Platonic" argument as a meditation on the dual nature of the artist. It is the same dualism that was described by Nietzsche in *The Birth of Tragedy* (1872) as the complementary opposition of the Apollonian and Dionysian aspects of art.

In serving Apollo, the god of clarity and light, Aschenbach has sacrificed an integral part of his artistic vision. He has developed an "official" note and been anthologized in textbooks, but he has lost spontaneity and joy; he lives with the tension of a clenched fist and suffers from repressed yearnings for freedom and mystic beauty. Aschenbach has betrayed the "dark god" Dionysus, who takes thorough and humiliating vengeance as the writer sinks into a passive, fatalistic acceptance of his feelings and remains to the end in the plague-stricken city. "Who shall unriddle the puzzle of the artist's nature?" asks the narrator. *Death in Venice* is a crystallization of Mann's work at its best, displaying the penetrating detail of his social and psychological realism, the power of his tightly interwoven symbolic structure, and the cumulative impact of his artist-hero's fall.

Ignace Feuerlicht, *Thomas Mann* (1969), provides a general biographical introduction. Henry Hatfield, in *Thomas Mann: A Collection of Critical Essays* (1964), presents essays on different works, including one by Mann on humor; there is a short biographical sketch at the end. Terence J. Reed, *Thomas Mann: The Uses of Tradition* (1974), is an excellent, well-written general study incorporating recent material. Richard Winston, *Thomas Mann: The Making of an Artist 1875–1911* (1981), the first volume of an unfinished study, is a detailed and authoritative presentation by the translator of Mann's diaries and letters.

PRONOUNCING GLOSSARY

The following list uses common English syllables and stress accents to provide rough equivalents of selected words whose pronunciation may be unfamiliar to the general reader.

Bildungsroman: *bil'-doongs-roh-mahn'*

dolce far niente: *dohl'-chay far nyen'-tay*

durchhalten: *doorkh'-hahl-ten*

Föhringer Chaussée: *feuh'-rin-jer shoh-say'*

Schwabing: *shva'-bing*

Wagner: *vahg'-ner*

Death in Venice[1]

1

On a spring afternoon in 19—, the year in which for months on end so grave a threat seemed to hang over the peace of Europe,[2] Gustav Aschenbach, or von[3] Aschenbach as he had been officially known since his fiftieth birthday, had set out from his apartment on the Prinzregentenstrasse[4] in Munich to take a walk of some length by himself. The morning's writing had overstimulated him: his work had now reached a difficult and dangerous point which demanded the utmost care and circumspection, the most insistent and precise effort of will, and the productive mechanism

---

1. Translated by David Luke.   2. In 1911, when the story was written, the "Moroccan crisis" was precipitated when a German gunboat appeared off the coast of Agadir, prompting negotiations between France and Germany over their respective national interests. A series of similar diplomatic crises led to the outbreak of World War I in 1914.   3. Indicates noble rank. Aschenbach was given the equivalent of a knighthood on his fiftieth birthday.   4. A street in Munich.

in his mind—that *motus animi continuus* which according to Cicero[5] is the essence of eloquence—had so pursued its reverberating rhythm that he had been unable to halt it even after lunch, and had missed the refreshing daily siesta which was now so necessary to him as he became increasingly subject to fatigue. And so, soon after taking tea, he had left the house hoping that fresh air and movement would set him to rights and enable him to spend a profitable evening.

It was the beginning of May, and after a succession of cold, wet weeks a premature high summer had set in. The Englischer Garten,[6] although still only in its first delicate leaf, had been as sultry as in August, and at its city end full of traffic and pedestrians. Having made his way to the Aumeister along less and less frequented paths, Aschenbach had briefly surveyed the lively scene at the popular open-air restaurant, around which a few cabs and private carriages were standing; then, as the sun sank, he had started homeward across the open meadow beyond the park, and since he was now tired and a storm seemed to be brewing over Föhring,[7] he had stopped by the Northern Cemetery to wait for the tram that would take him straight back to the city.

As it happened, there was not a soul to be seen at or near the tram-stop. Not one vehicle passed along the Föhringer Chaussee or the paved Ungererstrasse[8] on which solitary gleaming tramrails pointed toward Schwabing;[9] nothing stirred behind the fencing of the stonemasons' yards, where crosses and memorial tablets and monuments, ready for sale, composed a second and untenanted burial ground; across the street, the mortuary chapel with its Byzantine styling stood silent in the glow of the westering day. Its facade, adorned with Greek crosses and brightly painted hieratic motifs, is also inscribed with symmetrically arranged texts in gilt lettering, selected scriptual passages about the life to come, such as: "They shall go in unto the dwelling-place of the Lord," or "May light perpetual shine upon them." The waiting Aschenbach had already been engaged for some minutes in the solemn pastime of deciphering the words and letting his mind wander in contemplation of the mystic meaning that suffused them, when he noticed something that brought him back to reality: in the portico of the chapel, above the two apocalyptic beasts that guard the steps leading up to it, a man was standing, a man whose slightly unusual appearance gave his thoughts an altogether different turn.

It was not entirely clear whether he had emerged through the bronze doors from inside the chapel or had suddenly appeared and mounted the steps from outside. Aschenbach, without unduly pondering the question, inclined to the former hypothesis. The man was moderately tall, thin, beardless and remarkably snub-nosed; he belonged to the red-haired type and had its characteristic milky, freckled complexion. He was quite evidently not of Bavarian origin; at all events he wore a straw hat with a broad straight brim which gave him an exotic air, as of someone who had come from distant parts. It is true that he also had the typical Bavarian rucksack

---

5. Marcus Tullius Cicero (106–43 B.C.), Roman orator. *Motus animi continuus:* "the continuous motion of the spirit" (Latin).   6. The English Garden, a nine-hundred-acre public park with diverse attractions extending from the city to the water meadows of the Isar River.   7. A section of Munich.   8. Streets in Munich.   9. Another section of Munich.

strapped to his shoulders and wore a yellowish belted outfit of what looked like frieze,[1] as well as carrying a gray rain-cape over his left forearm which was propped against his waist, and in his right hand an iron-pointed walking stick which he had thrust slantwise into the ground, crossing his feet and leaning his hip against its handle. His head was held high, so that the Adam's apple stood out stark and bare on his lean neck where it rose from the open shirt; and there were two pronounced vertical furrows, rather strangely ill-matched to his turned-up nose, between the colorless red-lashed eyes with which he peered sharply into the distance. There was thus—and perhaps the raised point of vantage on which he stood contributed to his impression—an air of imperious survey, something bold or even wild about his posture; for whether it was because he was dazzled into a grimace by the setting sun or by reason of some permanent facial deformity, the fact was that his lips seemed to be too short and were completely retracted from his teeth, so that the latter showed white and long between them, bared to the gums.

Aschenbach's half absentminded, half inquisitive scrutiny of the stranger had no doubt been a little less than polite, for he suddenly became aware that his gaze was being returned: the man was in fact staring at him so aggressively, so straight in the eye, with so evident an intention to make an issue of the matter and outstare him, that Aschenbach turned away in disagreeable embarrassment and began to stroll along the fence, casually resolving to take no further notice of the fellow. A minute later he had put him out of his mind. But whether his imagination had been stirred by the stranger's itinerant appearance, or whether some other physical or psychological influence was at work, he now became conscious, to his complete surprise, of an extraordinary expansion of his inner self, a kind of roving restlessness, a youthful craving for far-off places, a feeling so new or at least so long unaccustomed and forgotten that he stood as if rooted, with his hands clasped behind his back and his eyes to the ground, trying to ascertain the nature and purport of his emotion.

It was simply a desire to travel; but it had presented itself as nothing less than a seizure, with intensely passionate and indeed hallucinatory force, turning his craving into vision. His imagination, still not at rest from the morning's hours of work, shaped for itself a paradigm of all the wonders and terrors of the manifold earth, of all that it was now suddenly striving to encompass: he saw it, saw a landscape, a tropical swampland under a cloud-swollen sky, moist and lush and monstrous, a kind of primeval wilderness of islands, morasses and muddy alluvial channels; far and wide around him he saw hairy palm-trunks thrusting upward from rank jungles of fern, from among thick fleshy plants in exuberant flower; saw strangely misshapen trees with roots that arched through the air before sinking into the ground or into stagnant shadowy-green glassy waters where milk-white blossoms floated as big as plates, and among them exotic birds with grotesque beaks stood hunched in the shallows, their heads tilted motionlessly sideways; saw between the knotted stems of the bamboo thicket the glinting eyes of a crouching tiger; and his heart throbbed with terror and myste-

---

1. Coarse wool cloth with uncut nap.

rious longing. Then the vision faded; and with a shake of his head Aschenbach resumed his perambulation along the fencing of the grave-stone yards.

His attitude to foreign travel, at least since he had had the means at his disposal to enjoy its advantages as often as he pleased, had always been that it was nothing more than a necessary health precaution, to be taken from time to time however disinclined to it one might be. Too preoccu-pied with the tasks imposed upon him by his own sensibility and by the collective European psyche, too heavily burdened with the compulsion to produce, too shy of distraction to have learned how to take leisure and pleasure in the colorful external world, he had been perfectly well satisfied to have no more detailed a view of the earth's surface than anyone can acquire without stirring far from home, and he had never even been tempted to venture outside Europe. This had been more especially the case since his life had begun its gradual decline and his artist's fear of not finishing his task—the apprehension that his time might run out before he had given the whole of himself by doing what he had it in him to do— was no longer something he could simply dismiss as an idle fancy; and during this time his outward existence had been almost entirely divided between the beautiful city which had become his home and the rustic mountain retreat he had set up for himself and where he passed his rainy summers.

And sure enough, the sudden and belated impulse that had just over-whelmed him very soon came under the moderating and corrective influ-ence of common sense and of the self-discipline he had practiced since his youth. It had been his intention that the book to which his life was at present dedicated should be advanced to a certain point before he moved to the country, and the idea of a jaunt in the wide world that would take him away from his work for months now seemed too casual, too upsetting to his plans to be considered seriously. Nevertheless, he knew the reason for the unexpected temptation only too well. This longing for the distant and the new, this craving for liberation, relaxation and forgetfulness—it had been, he was bound to admit, an urge to escape, to run away from his writing, away from the humdrum scene of his cold, inflexible, passionate duty. True, it was a duty he loved, and by now he had almost even learned to love the enervating daily struggle between his proud, tenacious, tried and tested will and that growing weariness which no one must be allowed to suspect nor his finished work betray by any telltale sign of debility or lassitude. Nevertheless, it would be sensible, he decided, not to span the bow too far and willfully stifle a desire that had erupted in him with such vivid force. He thought of his work, thought of the passage at which he had again, today as yesterday, been forced to interrupt it—that stubborn problem which neither patient care could solve nor a decisive *coup de main*[2] dispel. He reconsidered it, tried to break or dissolve the inhibition, and, with a shudder of repugnance, abandoned the attempt. It was not a case of very unusual difficulty, he was simply paralyzed by a scruple of distaste, manifesting itself as a perfectionistic fastidiousness which nothing

2. Bold stroke (French).

could satisfy. Perfectionism, of course, was something which even as a young man he had come to see as the innermost essence of talent, and for its sake he had curbed and cooled his feelings; for he knew that feeling is apt to be content with high-spirited approximations and with work that falls short of supreme excellence. Could it be that the enslaved emotion was now avenging itself by deserting him, by refusing from now on to bear up his art on its wings, by taking with it all his joy in words, all his appetite for the beauty of form? Not that he was writing badly: it was at least the advantage of his years to be master of his trade, a mastery of which at any moment he could feel calmly confident. But even as it brought him national honor he took no pleasure in it himself, and it seemed to him that his work lacked that element of sparkling and joyful improvisation, that quality which surpasses any intellectual substance in its power to delight the receptive world. He dreaded spending the summer in the country, alone in that little house with the maid who prepared his meals and the servant who brought them to him; dreaded the familiar profile of the mountain summits and mountain walls which would once again sur-round his slow discontented toil. So what did he need? An interlude, some impromptu living, some *dolce far niente*,[3] the invigoration of a distant climate, to make his summer bearable and fruitful. Very well then—he would travel. Not all that far, not quite to where the tigers were. A night in the wagon-lit and a siesta of three or four weeks at some popular holiday resort in the charming south . . .

Such were his thoughts as the tram clattered toward him along the Ungererstrasse, and as he stepped into it he decided to devote that evening to the study of maps and timetables. On the platform it occurred to him to look round and see what had become of the man in the straw hat, his companion for the duration of this not inconsequential wait at a tram-stop. But the man's whereabouts remained a mystery, for he was no longer standing where he had stood, nor was he to be seen anywhere else at the stop or in the tramcar itself.

2

The author of the lucid and massive prose-epic about the life of Fred-eric of Prussia;[4] the patient artist who with long toil had woven the great tapestry of the novel called *Maya*,[5] so rich in characters, gathering so many human destinies together under the shadow of one idea; the creator of that powerful tale entitled *A Study in Abjection*, which earned the grati-tude of a whole younger generation by pointing to the possibility of moral resolution even for those who have plumbed the depths of knowledge; the author (lastly but not least in this summary enumeration of his maturer works) of that passionate treatise *Intellect and Art* which in its ordering energy and antithetical eloquence has led serious critics to place it imme-diately alongside Schiller's disquisition *On Naive and Reflective Litera-ture*:[6] in a word, Gustav Aschenbach, was born in L . . . , an important city

---

3. Pleasant idleness (Italian).   4. Frederick II ("the Great"), king of Prussia from 1740 to 1786.
5. The illusory appearance of the world concealing a higher spiritual reality, in Hindu religion.   6. An influential essay by the German Romantic writer Friedrich Schiller (1759–1805).

in the province of Silesia, as the son of a highly-placed legal official. His ancestors had been military officers, judges, government administrators; men who had spent their disciplined, decently austere life in the service of the king and the state. A more inward spirituality had shown itself in one of them who had been a preacher; a strain of livelier, more sensuous blood had entered the family in the previous generation with the writer's mother, the daughter of a director of music from Bohemia. Certain exotic racial characteristics in his external appearance had come to him from her. It was from this marriage between hard-working, sober conscientiousness and darker, more fiery impulses that an artist, and indeed this particular kind of artist, had come into being.

With his whole nature intent from the start upon fame, he had displayed not exactly precocity, but a certain decisiveness and personal trenchancy in his style of utterance, which at an early age made him ripe for a life in the public eye and well suited to it. He had made a name for himself when he had scarcely left school. Ten years later he had learned to perform, at his writing desk, the social and administrative duties entailed by his reputation; he had learned to write letters which, however brief they had to be (for many claims beset the successful man who enjoys the confidence of the public), would always contain something kindly and pointed. By the age of forty he was obliged, wearied though he might be by the toils and vicissitudes of his real work, to deal with a daily correspondence that bore postage-stamps from every part of the globe.

His talent, equally remote from the commonplace and from the eccentric, had a native capacity both to inspire confidence in the general public and to win admiration and encouragement from the discriminating connoisseur. Ever since his boyhood the duty to achieve—and to achieve exceptional things—had been imposed on him from all sides, and thus he had never known youth's idleness, its carefree negligent ways. When in his thirty-fifth year he fell ill in Vienna, a subtle observer remarked of him on a social occasion: "You see, Aschenbach has always only lived like *this*"—and the speaker closed the fingers of his left hand tightly into a fist—"and never like *this*"—and he let his open hand hang comfortably down along the back of the chair. It was a correct observation; and the morally courageous aspect of the matter was that Aschenbach's native constitution was by no means robust, and the constant harnessing of his energies was something to which he had been called, but not really born.

As a young boy, medical advice and care had made school attendance impossible and obliged him to have his education at home. He had grown up by himself, without companions, and had nevertheless had to recognize in good time that he belonged to a breed not seldom talented, yet seldom endowed with the physical basis which talent needs if it is to fulfill itself—a breed that usually gives of its best in youth, and in which the creative gift rarely survives into mature years. But he would "stay the course"—it was his favorite motto, he saw his historical novel about Frederic the Great as nothing if not the apotheosis of this, the king's word of command, "*durchhalten!*"[7] which to Aschenbach epitomized a manly

7. Hold out! See it through! (German).

ethos of suffering action. And he dearly longed to grow old, for it had always been his view that an artist's gift can only be called truly great and wide-ranging, or indeed truly admirable, if it has been fortunate enough to bear characteristic fruit at all the stages of human life.

They were not broad, the shoulders on which he thus carried the tasks laid upon him by his talent; and since his aims were high, he stood in great need of discipline—and discipline, after all, was fortunately his inborn heritage on his father's side. At the age of forty or fifty, and indeed during those younger years in which other men live prodigally and dilettantishly, happily procrastinating the execution of great plans, Aschenbach would begin his day early by dashing cold water over his chest and back, and then, with two tall wax candles in silver candlesticks placed at the head of his manuscript, he would offer up to art, for two or three ardently conscientious morning hours, the strength he had gathered during sleep. It was a pardonable error, indeed it was one that betokened as nothing else could the triumph of his moral will, that uninformed critics should mistake the great world of *Maya*, or the massive epic unfolding of Frederic's life, for the product of solid strength and long stamina, whereas in fact they had been built up to their impressive size from layer upon layer of daily opuscula,[8] from a hundred or a thousand separate inspirations; and if they were indeed so excellent, both absolutely and in every detail, it was only because their creator, showing that same constancy of will and tenacity of purpose as had once conquered his native Silesia,[9] had held out for years under the pressure of one and the same work, and had devoted to actual composition only his best and worthiest hours.

For a significant intellectual product to make a broad and deep immediate appeal, there must be a hidden affinity, indeed a congruence, between the personal destiny of the author and the wider destiny of his generation. The public does not know why it grants the accolade of fame to a work of art. Being in no sense connoisseurs, readers imagine they perceive a hundred good qualities in it which justify their admiration; but the real reason for their applause is something imponderable, a sense of sympathy. Hidden away among Aschenbach's writings was a passage directly asserting that nearly all the great things that exist owe their existence to a defiant despite: it is despite grief and anguish, despite poverty, loneliness, bodily weakness, vice and passion and a thousand inhibitions, that they have come into being at all. But this was more than an observation, it was an experience, it was positively the formula of his life and his fame, the key to his work; is it surprising then that it was also the moral formula, the outward gesture, of his work's most characteristic figures?

The new hero-type favored by Aschenbach, and recurring in his books in a multiplicity of individual variants, had already been remarked upon at an early stage by a shrewd commentator, who had described his conception as that of "an intellectual and boyish manly virtue, that of a youth who clenches his teeth in proud shame and stands calmly on as the swords and spears pass through his body." That was well put, perceptive and pre-

---

8. Tiny works.   9. A region of central Europe, which Frederick the Great fought to acquire from 1740 to 1763.

cisely true, for all its seemingly rather too passive emphasis. For composure under the blows of fate, grace in the midst of torment—this is not only endurance: it is an active achievement, a positive triumph, and the figure of Saint Sebastian[1] is the most perfect symbol if not of art in general, then certainly of the kind of art here in question. What did one see if one looked in any depth into the world of this writer's fiction? Elegant self-control concealing from the world's eyes until the very last moment a state of inner disintegration and biological decay; sallow ugliness, sensuously marred and worsted, which nevertheless is able to fan its smouldering concupiscence to a pure flame, and even to exalt itself to mastery in the realm of beauty; pallid impotence, which from the glowing depths of the spirit draws strength to cast down a whole proud people at the foot of the Cross and set its own foot upon them as well; gracious poise and composure in the empty austere service of form; the false, dangerous life of the born deceiver, his ambition and his art which lead so soon to exhaustion— to contemplate all these destinies, and many others like them, was to doubt if there is any other heroism at all but the heroism of weakness. In any case, what other heroism could be more in keeping with the times? Gustav Aschenbach was the writer who spoke for all those who work on the brink of exhaustion, who labor and are heavy-laden, who are worn out already but still stand upright, all those moralists of achievement who are slight of stature and scanty of resources, but who yet, by some ecstasy of the will and by wise husbandry, manage at least for a time to force their work into a semblance of greatness. There are many such, they are the heroes of our age. And they all recognized themselves in his work, they found that it confirmed them and raised them on high and celebrated them; they were grateful for this, and they spread his name far and wide.

He had been young and raw with the times: ill advised by fashion, he had publicly stumbled, blundered, made himself look foolish, offended in speech and writing against tact and balanced civility. But he had achieved dignity, that goal toward which, as he declared, every great talent is innately driven and spurred; indeed it can be said that the conscious and defiant purpose of his entire development had been to leave all the inhibitions of skepticism and irony behind him and to ascend to dignity.

Lively, clear-outlined, intellectually undemanding presentation is the delight of the great mass of the middle-class public, but passionate radical youth is interested only in problems: and Aschenbach had been as problematic and as radical as any young man ever was. He had been in thrall to intellect, had exhausted the soil by excessive analysis and ground up the seed corn of growth; he had uncovered what is better kept hidden, made talent seem suspect, betrayed the truth about art—indeed, even as the sculptural vividness of his descriptions was giving pleasure to his more naive devotees and lifting their minds and hearts, he, this same youthful artist, had fascinated twenty-year-olds with his breathtaking cynicisms about the questionable nature of art and of the artist himself.

But it seems that there is nothing to which a noble and active mind

---

1. A 3rd-century Roman martyr whose body pierced with arrows was a popular subject for Renaissance painters.

more quickly becomes inured than that pungent and bitter stimulus, the acquisition of knowledge; and it is very sure that even the most gloomily conscientious and radical sophistication of youth is shallow by comparison with Aschenbach's profound decision as a mature master to repudiate knowledge as such, to reject it, to step over it with head held high — in the recognition that knowledge can paralyze the will, paralyze and discourage action and emotion and even passion, and rob all these of their dignity. How else is the famous short story A *Study in Abjection* to be understood but as an outbreak of disgust against an age indecently undermined by psychology and represented by the figure of that spiritless, witless semi-scoundrel who cheats his way into a destiny of sorts when, motivated by his own ineptitude and depravity and ethical whimsicality, he drives his wife into the arms of a callow youth — convinced that his intellectual depths entitle him to behave with contemptible baseness? The forthright words of condemnation which here weighed vileness in the balance and found it wanting — they proclaimed their writer's renunciation of all moral skepticism, of every kind of sympathy with the abyss; they declared his repudiation of the laxity of that compassionate principle which holds that to understand all is to forgive all. And the development that was here being anticipated, indeed already taking place, was that "miracle of reborn naiveté" to which, in a dialogue written a little later, the author himself had referred with a certain mysterious emphasis. How strange these associations! Was it an intellectual consequence of this "rebirth," of this new dignity and rigor, that, at about the same time, his sense of beauty was observed to undergo an almost excessive resurgence, that his style took on the noble purity, simplicity and symmetry that were to set upon all his subsequent works that so evident and evidently intentional stamp of the classical master? And yet: moral resoluteness at the far side of knowledge, achieved despite all corrosive and inhibiting insight — does this not in its turn signify a simplification, a morally simplistic view of the world and of human psychology, and thus also a resurgence of energies that are evil, forbidden, morally impossible? And is form not two-faced? Is it not at one and the same time moral and immoral — moral as the product and expression of discipline, but immoral and even antimoral inasmuch as it houses within itself an innate moral indifference, and indeed essentially strives for nothing less than to bend morality under its proud and absolute scepter?

Be that as it may! A development is a destiny; and one that is accompanied by the admiration and mass confidence of a wide public must inevitably differ in its course from one that takes place far from the limelight and from the commitments of fame. Only the eternal intellectual vagrant is bored and prompted to mockery when a great talent grows out of its libertinistic chrysalis-stage, becomes an expressive representative of the dignity of mind, takes on the courtly bearing of that solitude which has been full of hard, uncounseled, self-reliant sufferings and struggles, and has achieved power and honor among men. And what a game it is too, how much defiance there is in it and how much satisfaction, this self-formation of a talent! As time passed, Gustav Aschenbach's presentations took on something of an official air, of an educator's stance; his style in later years came to eschew direct audacities, new and subtle nuances, it developed toward the exemplary and definitive, the fastidiously conventional, the conservative and formal and even formulaic; and as tradition has it of Louis XIV,[2] so Aschenbach as he grew older banned from his utterance very unrefined word. It was at this time that the education authority adopted selected pages from his works for inclusion in the prescribed school readers.[3] And when a German prince who had just come to the throne granted personal nobilitation to the author of *Frederic of Prussia* on his fiftieth birthday, he sensed the inner appropriateness of this honor and did not decline it.

After a few restless years of experimental living in different places, he soon chose Munich as his permanent home and lived there in the kind of upper-bourgeois status which is occasionally the lot of certain intellectuals. The marriage which he had contracted while still young with the daughter of an academic family had been ended by his wife's death after a short period of happiness. She had left him a daughter, now already married. He had never had a son.

Gustav von Aschenbach was of rather less than average height, dark and clean-shaven. His head seemed a little too large in proportion to his almost delicate stature. His brushed-back hair, thinning at the top, very thick and distinctly gray over the temples, framed a high, deeply lined, scarred-looking forehead. The bow of a pair of gold spectacles with rimless lenses cut into the base of his strong, nobly curved nose. His mouth was large, often relaxed, often suddenly narrow and tense; the cheeks were lean and furrowed, the well-formed chin slightly cleft. Grave visitations of fate seemed to have passed over this head, which usually inclined to one side with an air of suffering. And yet it was art that had here performed that fashioning of the physiognomy which is usually the work of a life full of action and stress. The flashing exchanges of the dialogue between Voltaire and the king on the subject of war had been born behind that brow; these eyes that looked so wearily and deeply through their glasses had seen the bloody inferno of the Seven Years War[4] sick bays. Even in a personal sense, after all, art is an intensified life. By art one is more deeply satisfied and more rapidly used up. It engraves on the countenance of its servant the traces of imaginary and intellectual adventures, and even if he has outwardly existed in cloistral tranquillity, it leads in the long term to overfastidiousness, overrefinement, nervous fatigue and overstimulation, such as can seldom result from a life full of the most extravagant passions and pleasures.

3

Mundane and literary business of various kinds delayed Aschenbach's eagerly awaited departure until about a fortnight after that walk in Munich. Finally he gave instructions that his country house was to be made ready for occupation in four weeks' time, and then, one day between

---

2. King of France (1638–1715), the "great monarch" of the French classical period.   3. That is, he received national recognition in the highly centralized German educational system.   4. A global war (1756–63) fought in Europe, North America, and India among European powers. François-Marie Arouet de Voltaire (1694–1778), French writer and philosopher, was a guest at the court of Frederick the Great from 1750 until 1753, when he found it wise to leave after a disagreement.

the middle and end of May, he took the night train to Trieste, where he stayed only twenty-four hours, embarking on the following morning for Pola.[5]

What he sought was something strange and random, but in a place easily reached, and accordingly he took up his abode on an Adriatic island which had been highly spoken of for some years: a little way off the Istrian[6] coast, with colorful ragged inhabitants speaking a wild unintelligible dialect, and picturesque fragmented cliffs overlooking the open sea. But rain and sultry air, a self-enclosed provincial Austrian hotel clientele, the lack of that restful intimate contact with the sea which can only be had on a gentle, sandy coast, filled him with vexation and with a feeling that he had not yet come to his journey's end. He was haunted by an inner impulse that still had no clear direction; he studied shipping timetables, looked up one place after another—and suddenly his surprising yet at the same time self-evident destination stared him in the face. If one wanted to travel overnight to somewhere incomparable, to a fantastic mutation of normal reality, where did one go? Why, the answer was obvious. What was he doing here? He had gone completely astray. *That* was where he had wanted to travel. He at once gave notice of departure from his present, mischosen stopping place. Ten days after his arrival on the island, in the early morning mist, a rapid motor-launch carried him and his luggage back over the water to the naval base, and here he landed only to re-embark immediately, crossing the gangway onto the damp deck of a ship that was waiting under steam to leave for Venice.[7]

It was an ancient Italian boat, out of date and dingy and black with soot. Aschenbach was no sooner aboard than a grubby hunchbacked seaman, grinning obsequiously, conducted him to an artificially lit cavelike cabin in the ship's interior. Here, behind a table, with his cap askew and a cigarette end in the corner of his mouth, sat a goat-bearded man with the air of an old-fashioned circus director and a slick caricatured business manner, taking passengers' particulars and issuing their tickets. "To Venice!" he exclaimed, echoing Aschenbach's request, and extending his arm he pushed his pen into some coagulated leftover ink in a titled inkstand. "One first class to Venice. Certainly, sir!" He scribbled elaborately, shook some blue sand from a box over the writing and ran it off into an earthenware dish, then folded the paper with his yellow bony fingers and wrote on it again. "A very happily chosen destination!" he chattered as he did so. "Ah, Venice! A splendid city! A city irresistibly attractive to the man of culture, by its history no less than by its present charms!" There was something hypnotic and distracting about the smooth facility of his movements and the glib empty talk with which he accompanied them, almost as if he were anxious that the traveler might have second thoughts about his decision to go to Venice. He hastily took Aschenbach's money and with the dexterity of a croupier[8] dropped the change on the stained tablecloth.

5. Trieste (Italy) and Pola are major seaports at the head of the Adriatic Sea. Until 1919 they were Austrian possessions.   6. A peninsula in Croatia.   7. An ancient city whose network of bridges and canals links 118 islands in the Gulf of Venice. The Republic of Venice was headed by a doge (duke) and was a cultural, commercial, and political center in Europe from the 14th century.   8. Attendant at a gambling table who handles bets and money.

"*Buon divertimento, signore,*"[9] he said, bowing histrionically. "It is an honor to serve you ... Next, please, gentlemen!" he exclaimed with a wave of the arm, as if he were doing a lively trade, although in fact there was no one else there to be dealt with. Aschenbach returned on deck.

Resting one elbow on the handrail, he watched the idle crowd hanging about the quayside to see the ship's departure, and watched the passengers who had come aboard. Those with second-class tickets were squatting, men and women together, on the forward deck, using boxes and bundles as seats. The company on the upper deck consisted of a group of young men, probably shop or office workers from Pola, a high-spirited party about to set off on an excursion to Italy. They were making a considerable exhibition of themselves and their enterprise, chattering, laughing, fatuously enjoying their own gesticulations, leaning overboard and shouting glibly derisive ribaldries at their friends on the harbor-side street, who were hurrying about their business with briefcases under their arms and waved their sticks peevishly at the holiday-makers. One of the party, who wore a light yellow summer suit of extravagant cut, a scarlet necktie and a rakishly tilted Panama hat, was the most conspicuous of them all in his shrill hilarity. But as soon as Aschenbach took a slightly closer look at him, he realized with a kind of horror that the man's youth was false. He was old, there was no mistaking it. There were wrinkles round his eyes and mouth. His cheeks' faint carmine was rouge, the brown hair under his straw hat with its colored ribbon was a wig, his neck was flaccid and scrawny, his small stuck-on moustache and the little imperial on his chin were dyed, his yellowish full complement of teeth, displayed when he laughed, were a cheap artificial set, and his hands, with signet rings on both index fingers, were those of an old man. With a spasm of distaste Aschenbach watched him as he kept company with his young friends. Did they not know, did they not notice that he was old, that he had no right to be wearing foppish and garish clothes like theirs, no right to be acting as if he were one of them? They seemed to be tolerating his presence among them as something habitual and to be taken for granted, they treated him as an equal, reciprocated without embarrassment when he teasingly poked them in the ribs. How was this possible? Aschenbach put his hand over his forehead and closed his eyes, which were hot from too little sleep. He had a feeling that something not quite usual was beginning to happen, that the world was undergoing a dreamlike alienation, becoming increasingly deranged and bizarre, and that perhaps this process might be arrested if he were to cover his face for a little and then take a fresh look at things. But at that moment he had the sensation of being afloat, and starting up in irrational alarm, he noticed that the dark heavy hulk of the steamer was slowly parting company with the stone quayside. Inch by inch, as the engine pounded and reversed, the width of the dirty glinting water between the hull and the quay increased, and after clumsy maneuverings the ship turned its bows toward the open sea. Aschenbach crossed to the starboard side, where the hunchback had set up a deck chair for him and a steward in a grease-stained frock coat offered his services.

9. Have a good vacation, sir (Italian).

The sky was gray, the wind damp. The port and the islands had been left behind, and soon all land was lost to view in the misty panorama. Flecks of sodden soot drifted down on the washed deck, which never seemed to get dry. After only an hour an awning was set up, as it was beginning to rain.

Wrapped in his overcoat, a book lying on his lap, the traveler rested, scarcely noticing the hours as they passed him by. It had stopped raining; the canvas shelter was removed. The horizon was complete. Under the turbid dome of the sky the desolate sea surrounded him in an enormous circle. But in empty, unarticulated space our mind loses its sense of time as well, and we enter the twilight of the immeasurable. As Aschenbach lay there, strange and shadowy figures, the foppish old man, the goat-bearded purser from the ship's interior, passed with uncertain gestures and confused dream-words through his mind, and he fell asleep.

At midday he was requested to come below for luncheon in the long, narrow dining saloon, which ended in the doors to the sleeping berths; here he ate at the head of the long table, at the other end of which the group of apprentices, with the old man among them, had been quaffing since ten o'clock with the good-humored ship's captain. The meal was wretched and he finished it quickly. He needed to be back in the open air, to look at the sky: perhaps it would clear over Venice.

It had never occurred to him that this would not happen, for the city had always received him in its full glory. But the sky and the sea remained dull and leaden, from time to time misty rain fell, and he resigned himself to arriving by water in a different Venice, one he had never encountered on the landward approach. He stood by the foremast, gazing into the distance, waiting for the sight of land. He recalled that poet of plangent inspiration who long ago had seen the cupolas and bell-towers of his dream rise before him out of these same waters; inwardly he recited a few lines of the measured music that had been made from that reverence and joy and sadness,[1] and effortlessly moved by a passion already shaped into language, he questioned his grave and weary heart, wondering whether some new inspiration and distraction, some late adventure of the emotions, might yet be in store for him on his leisured journey.

And now, on his right, the flat coastline rose above the horizon, the sea came alive with fishing vessels, the island resort appeared: the steamer left it on its port side, glided at half speed through the narrow channel named after it, entered the lagoon, and presently, near some shabby miscellaneous buildings, came to a complete halt, as this was where the launch carrying the public health inspector must be awaited.

An hour passed before it appeared. One had arrived and yet not arrived; there was no hurry, and yet one was impelled by impatience. The young men from Pola had come on deck, no doubt also patriotically attracted by the military sound of bugle calls across the water from the direction of the Public Gardens; and elated by the Asti[2] they had drunk, they began cheering the *bersaglieri*[3] as they drilled there in the park. But the dandified old

1. Probably lines from the *Sonnets on Venice* (1825) by the German classical poet August Graf Platen (1796–1835).   2. An Italian white wine.   3. Elite infantry soldiers (Italian).

man, thanks to his spurious fraternization with the young, was now in a condition repugnant to behold. His old head could not carry the wine as his sturdy youthful companions had done, and he was lamentably drunk. Eyes glazed, a cigarette between his trembling fingers, he stood swaying, tilted to and fro by inebriation and barely keeping his balance. Since he would have fallen at his first step he did not dare move from the spot, and was nevertheless full of wretched exuberance, clutching at everyone who approached him, babbling, winking, sniggering, lifting his ringed and wrinkled forefinger as he uttered some bantering inanity, and licking the corners of his mouth with the tip of his tongue in a repellently suggestive way. Aschenbach watched him with frowning disapproval, and once more a sense of numbness came over him, a feeling that the world was some-how, slightly yet uncontrollably, sliding into some kind of bizarre and grotesque derangement. It was feeling on which, to be sure, he was unable to brood further in present circumstances, for at this moment the thudding motion of the engine began again, and the ship, having stopped short so close to its destination, resumed its passage along the San Marco Canal.[4]

Thus it was that he saw it once more, that most astonishing of all landing places, that dazzling composition of fantastic architecture which the Republic presented to the admiring gaze of approaching seafarers: the unburdened splendor of the Ducal Palace, the Bridge of Sighs, the lion and the saint on their two columns at the water's edge, the magnificently projecting side wing of the fabulous basilica, the vista beyond it of the gate tower and the Giants' Clock[5] and as he contemplated it all he reflected that to arrive in Venice by land, at the station, was like entering a palace by a back door: that only as he was now doing, only by ship, over the high sea, should one come to this most extraordinary of cities.

The engine stopped, gondolas pressed alongside, the gangway was let down, customs officers came on board and perfunctorily discharged their duties; disembarkation could begin. Aschenbach indicated that he would like a gondola to take him and his luggage to the stopping place of the small steamboats that ply between the city and the Lido,[6] since he intended to stay in a hotel by the sea. His wishes were approved, his orders shouted down to water level, where the gondoliers were quarreling in Venetian dialect. He was still prevented from leaving the ship, held up by his trunk which at that moment was being laboriously dragged and maneuvered down the ladderlike gangway; and thus, for a full minute or two, he could not avoid the importunate attentions of the dreadful old man, who on some obscure drunken impulse felt obliged to do this stranger the parting honors. "We wish the signore a most enjoyable stay!" he bleated, bowing and scraping. "We hope the signore will not forget us! Au revoir, excusez and bon jour,[7] your Excellency!" He drooled, he screwed up his eyes, licked the corners of his mouth, and the dyed impe-rial on his senile underlip reared itself upward. "Our compliments," he

---

4. Saint Mark's Canal, named for the patron saint of Venice.   5. A large clock tower built in the late 15th century. *Bridge of Sighs:* condemned prisoners would walk over this bridge when proceeding to prison from the ducal palace. *Two columns:* one is surmounted by a statue of St. Theodore stepping on a crocodile; the other by a winged lion, emblem of St. Mark. *Basilica:* the church of St. Mark.   6. A famous island resort near Venice.   7. Goodbye, excuse me, and good-day (French).

driveled, touching his lips with two fingers, "our compliments to your sweetheart, to your most charming, beautiful sweetheart . . ." And suddenly the upper set of his false teeth dropped half out of his jaw. Aschenbach was able to escape. "Your sweetheart, your pretty sweetheart!" he heard from behind his back, in gurgling, cavernous, encumbered tones, as he clung to the rope railing and descended the gangway.

Can there be anyone who has not had to overcome a fleeting sense of dread, a secret shudder of uneasiness, on stepping for the first time or after a long interval of years into a Venetian gondola? How strange a vehicle it is, coming down unchanged from times of old romance, and so characteristically black,[8] the way no other thing is black except a coffin—a vehicle evoking lawless adventures in the plashing stillness of night, and still more strongly evoking death itself, the bier, the dark obsequies, the last silent journey! And has it been observed that the seat of such a boat, that armchair with its coffin-black lacquer and dull black upholstery, is the softest, the most voluptuous, most enervating seat in the world? Aschenbach became aware of this when he had settled down at the gondolier's feet, sitting opposite his luggage, which was nearly assembled at the prow. The oarsmen were still quarreling; raucously, unintelligibly, with threatening gestures. But in the peculiar silence of this city of water their voices seemed to be softly absorbed, to become bodiless, dissipated above the sea. It was sultry here in the harbor. As the warm breath of the sirocco[9] touched him, as he leaned back on cushions over the yielding element, the traveler closed his eyes in the enjoyment of this lassitude as sweet as it was unaccustomed. It will be a short ride, he thought; if only it could last forever! In a gently swaying motion he felt himself gliding away from the crowd and the confusion of voices.

How still it was growing all round him! There was nothing to be heard except the plashing of the oar, the dull slap of the wave against the boat's prow where it rose up steep and black and armed at its tip like a halberd, and a third sound also: that of a voice speaking and murmuring—it was the gondolier, whispering and muttering to himself between his teeth, in intermittent grunts pressed out of him by the labor of his arms. Aschenbach looked up and noticed with some consternation that the lagoon was widening round him and that his gondola was heading out to sea. It was thus evident that he must not relax too completely, but give some attention to the proper execution of his instructions.

"Well! To the *vaporetto*[1] stop!" he said, half turning round. The muttering ceased, but no answer came.

"I said to the *vaporetto* stop!" he repeated, turning round completely and looking up into the face of the gondolier, who was standing behind him on his raised deck, towering between him and the pale sky. He was a man of displeasing, indeed brutal appearance, wearing blue seaman's clothes, with a yellow scarf round his waist and a shapeless, already fraying straw hat tilted rakishly on his head. To judge by the cast of his face and the blond curling moustache under his snub nose, he was quite evidently

8. Legend explains the gondolas' traditional black through an ancient law forbidding ostentation.   9. A hot, humid southern wind originating in the Sahara.   1. Small steamboat used for public transport.

not of Italian origin. Although rather slightly built, so that one would not
have thought him particularly well suited to his job, he plied his oar with
great energy, putting his whole body into every stroke. Occasionally the
effort made him retract his lips and bare his white teeth. With his reddish
eyebrows knitted, he stared right over his passenger's head as he answered
peremptorily, almost insolently:

"You are going to the Lido."

Aschenbach replied:

"Of course. But I only engaged this gondola to row me across to San
Marco. I wish to take the *vaporetto*."

"You cannot take the *vaporetto*, signore."

"And why not?"

"Because the *vaporetto* does not carry luggage."

That was correct, as Aschenbach now remembered. He was silent. But
the man's abrupt, presumptuous manner, so uncharacteristic of the way
foreigners were usually treated in this country, struck him as unacceptable.
He said:

"That is my business. I may wish to deposit my luggage. Will you kindly
turn round."

There was silence. The oar plashed, the dull slap of the water against
the bow continued, and the talking and muttering began again: the gondolier was talking to himself between his teeth.

What was to be done? Alone on the sea with this strangely contuma-
cious, uncannily resolute fellow, the traveler could see no way of compelling him to obey his instructions. And in any case, how luxurious a rest he
might have here if he simply accepted the situation! Had he not wished
the trip were longer, wished it to last forever? It was wisest to let things
take their course, and above all it was very agreeable to do so. A magic
spell of indolence seemed to emanate from his seat, from this low black-
upholstered armchair, so softly rocked by the oarstrokes of the high-
handed gondolier behind him. The thought that he had perhaps fallen
into the hands of a criminal floated dreamily across Aschenbach's mind—
powerless to stir him to any active plan of self-defence. There was the
more annoying possibility that the whole thing was simply a device for
extorting money from him. A kind of pride or sense of duty, a recollection,
so to speak, that there are precautions to be taken against such things,
impelled him to make one further effort. He asked:

"What is your charge for the trip?"

And looking straight over his head, the gondolier answered:

"You will pay, signore."

The prescribed retort to this was clear enough. Aschenbach answered
mechanically:

"I shall pay nothing, absolutely nothing, if you take me where I do not
want to go."

"The signore wants to go to the Lido."

"But not with you."

"I can row you well."

True enough, thought Aschenbach, relaxing. True enough, you will
row me well. Even if you are after my cash and dispatch me to the house

of Hades[2] with a blow of your oar from behind, you will have rowed me well.

But nothing of the sort happened. He was even provided with company: a boat full of piratical musicians, men and women singing to the guitar or mandolin, importunately traveling hard alongside the gondola and for the foreigner's benefit filling the silence of the waters with mercenary song. Aschenbach threw some money into the outheld hat, whereupon they fell silent and moved off. And the gondolier's muttering became audible again, as in fits and starts he continued his self-colloquy.

And so in due course one arrived, bobbing about in the wake of a *vaporetto* bound for the city. Two police officers, with their hands on their backs, were pacing up and down the embankment and looking out over the lagoon. Aschenbach stepped from the gondola onto the gangway, assisted by the old man with a boat hook who turns up for this purpose at every landing stage in Venice; and having run out of small change, he walked across to the hotel opposite the pier, intending to change money and pay off the oarsman with some suitable gratuity. He was served at the hall desk, and returned to the landing stage to find his luggage loaded onto a trolley on the embankment: the gondola and the gondolier had vanished.

"He left in a hurry," said the old man with the boat hook. "A bad man, a man without a licence, signore. He is the only gondolier who has no licence. The others telephoned across to us. He saw that he was expected. So he left in a hurry."

Aschenbach shrugged his shoulders.

"The signore has had a free trip," said the old man, holding out his hat. Aschenbach threw coins into it. He directed that his luggage should be taken to the Hotel des Bains,[3] and followed the trolley along the avenue, that white-blossoming avenue, bordered on either side by taverns and bazaars and guesthouses, which runs straight across the island to the beach.

He entered the spacious hotel from the garden terrace at the back, passing through the main hall and the vestibule to the reception office. As his arrival had been notified in advance, he was received with obsequious obligingness. A manager, a soft-spoken, flatteringly courteous little man with a black moustache and a frock coat of French cut, accompanied him in the lift to the second floor and showed him to his room, an agreeable apartment with cherry-wood furniture, strongly scented flowers put out to greet him, and a view through tall windows to the open sea. He went and stood by one of them when the manager had withdrawn, and as his luggage was brought in behind him and installed in the room, he gazed out over the beach, uncrowded at this time of the afternoon, and over the sunless sea which was at high tide, its long low waves beating with a quiet regular rhythm on the shore.

The observations and encounters of a devotee of solitude and silence are at once less distinct and more penetrating than those of the sociable

---

2. The world of the dead in Greek and Roman mythology, ruled by the god Hades. The newly dead entered the underworld by paying a coin to the boatman Charon, who then ferried them across the river Styx.   3. A famous seaside hotel.

man; his thoughts are weightier, stranger, and never without a tinge of
sadness. Images and perceptions which might otherwise be easily dispelled
by a glance, a laugh, an exchange of comments, concern him unduly,
they sink into mute depths, take on significance, become experiences,
adventures, emotions. The fruit of solitude is originality, something daringly and disconcertingly beautiful, the poetic creation. But the fruit of
solitude can also be the perverse, the disproportionate, the absurd and the
forbidden. And thus the phenomena of his journey to this place, the horrible old made-up man with his maudlin babble about a sweetheart, the
illicit gondolier who had been done out of his money, were still weighing
on the traveler's mind. Without in any way being rationally inexplicable,
without even really offering food for thought, they were nevertheless, as it
seemed to him, essentially strange, and indeed it was no doubt this very
paradox that made them disturbing. In the meantime he saluted the sea
with his gaze and rejoiced in the knowledge that Venice was now so near
and accessible. Finally he turned round, bathed his face, gave the room
maid certain instructions for the enhancement of his comfort, and then
had himself conveyed by the green-uniformed Swiss lift attendant to the
ground floor.

He took tea on the front terrace, then went down to the esplanade and
walked some way along it in the direction of the Hotel Excelsior. When
he returned, it was already nearly time to be changing for dinner. He did
so in his usual leisurely and precise manner, for it was his custom to work
while performing his toilet: despite this, he arrived a little early in the hall,
where he found a considerable number of the hotel guests assembled,
unacquainted with each other and affecting a studied mutual indifference,
yet all united in expectancy by the prospect of their evening meal. He
picked up a newspaper from the table, settled down in a leather armchair
and took stock of the company, which differed very agreeably from what
he had encountered at his previous hotel.

A large horizon opened up before him, tolerantly embracing many elements. Discreetly muted, the sounds of the major world languages mingled. Evening dress, that internationally accepted uniform of civilization,
imparted a decent outward semblance of unity to the wide variations of
mankind here represented. One saw the dry elongated visages of Americans, many-membered Russian families, English ladies, German children
with French nurses. The Slav component seemed to predominate. In his
immediate vicinity he could hear Polish being spoken.

It was a group of adolescent and barely adult young people, sitting
round a cane table under the supervision of a governess or companion:
three young girls, of fifteen to seventeen as it seemed, and a long-haired
boy of about fourteen. With astonishment Aschenbach noticed that the
boy was entirely beautiful. His countenance, pale and gracefully reserved,
was surrounded by ringlets of honey-colored hair, and with its straight
nose, its enchanting mouth, its expression of sweet and divine gravity, it
recalled Greek sculpture of the noblest period; yet despite the purest formal perfection, it had such unique personal charm that he who now contemplated it felt he had never beheld, in nature or in art, anything so
consummately successful. What also struck him was an obvious contrast

of educational principles in the way the boy and his sisters were dressed and generally treated. The system adopted for the three girls, the oldest of whom could be considered to be grown-up, was austere and chaste to the point of disfigurement. They all wore exactly the same slate-colored half-length dresses, sober and of a deliberately unbecoming cut, with white turnover collars as the only relieving feature, and any charm of figure they might have had was suppressed and negated from the outset by this cloistral uniform. Their hair, smoothed and stuck back firmly to their heads, gave their faces a nunlike emptiness and expressionlessness. A mother was clearly in charge here; and it had not even occurred to her to apply to the boy the same pedagogic strictness as she thought proper for the girls. In his life, softness and tenderness were evidently the rule. No one had ever dared to cut short his beautiful hair; like that of the *Boy Extracting a Thorn*[4] it fell in curls over his forehead, over his ears, and still lower over his neck. The English sailor's suit, with its full sleeves tapering down to fit the fine wrists of his still childlike yet slender hands, and with its lanyards and bows and embroideries, enhanced his delicate shape with an air of richness and indulgence. He was sitting, in semiprofile to Aschenbach's gaze, with one foot in its patent leather shoe advanced in front of the other, with one elbow propped on the arm of his basket chair, with his cheek nestling against the closed hand, in a posture of relaxed dignity, without a trace of the almost servile stiffness to which his sisters seemed to have accustomed themselves. Was he in poor health? For his complexion was white as ivory against the dark gold of the surrounding curls. Or was he simply a pampered favorite child, borne up by the partiality of a capricious love? Aschenbach was inclined to think so. Inborn in almost every artistic nature is a luxuriant, treacherous bias in favor of the injustice that creates beauty, a tendency to sympathize with aristocratic preference and pay it homage.

A waiter circulated and announced in English that dinner was served. Gradually the company disappeared through the glass door into the dining room. Latecomers passed, coming from the vestibule or the lifts. The service of dinner had already begun, but the young Poles were still waiting round their cane table, and Aschenbach, comfortably ensconced in his deep armchair, and additionally having the spectacle of beauty before his eyes, waited with them.

The governess, a corpulent and rather unladylike, red-faced little woman, finally gave the signal for them to rise. With arched brows she pushed back her chair and bowed as a tall lady, dressed in silvery gray and very richly adorned with pearls, entered the hall. This lady's attitude was cool and poised, her lightly powdered coiffure and the style of her dress both had that simplicity which is the governing principle of taste in circles where piety is regarded as one of the aristocratic values. In Germany she might have been the wife of a high official. The only thing that did give her appearance a fantastic and luxurious touch was her jewellery, which was indeed beyond price, consisting of earrings as well as a very long three-stranded necklace of gently shimmering pearls as big as cherries.

---

4. A bronze Greek statue from the 1st century B.C.

The brother and sisters had quickly risen to their feet. They bowed over their mother's hand to kiss it, while she, with a restrained smile on her well-maintained but slightly weary and angular face, looked over their heads and addressed a few words in French to the governess. Then she walked toward the glass door. Her children followed her: the girls in order of age, after them the governess, finally the boy. For some reason or other he turned round before crossing the threshold, and as there was now no one else in the hall, his strangely twilight-gray eyes met those of Aschenbach, who with his paper in his lap, lost in contemplation, had been watching the group leave.

What he had seen had certainly not been remarkable in any particular. One does not go in to table before one's mother, they had waited for her, greeted her respectfully, and observed normal polite precedence in entering the dining room. But this had all been carried out with such explicitness, with such a strongly accented air of discipline, obligation and self-respect, that Aschenbach felt strangely moved. He lingered for another few moments, then he too crossed into the dining room and had himself shown to his table—which, as he noticed with a brief stirring of regret, was at some distance from that of the Polish family.

Tired and yet intellectually stimulated, he beguiled the long and tedious meal with abstract and indeed transcendental reflections. He meditated on the mysterious combination into which the canonical and the individual must enter for human beauty to come into being, proceeded from this point to general problems of form and art, and concluded in the end that his thoughts and findings resembled certain seemingly happy inspirations that come to us in dreams, only to be recognized by the sober senses as completely shallow and worthless. After dinner he lingered for a while, smoking and sitting and walking about, in the evening fragrance of the hotel garden, then retired early and passed the night in sleep which was sound and long, though dream images enlivened it from time to time.

Next day the weather did not seem to be improving. The wind was from landward. Under a pallid overcast sky the sea lay sluggishly still and shrunken-looking, with the horizon in prosaic proximity and the tide so far out that several rows of long sandbars lay exposed. When Aschenbach opened his window, he thought he could smell the stagnant air of the lagoon.

Vexation overcame him. The thought of leaving occurred to him then and there. Once before, years ago, after fine spring weeks, this same weather had come on him here like a visitation, and so adversely affected his health that his departure from Venice had been like a precipitate escape. Were not the same symptoms now presenting themselves again, that unpleasant feverish sensation, the pressure in the temples, the heaviness in the eyelids? To move elsewhere yet again would be tiresome; but if the wind did not change, then there was no question of his staying here. As a precaution he did not unpack completely. At nine he breakfasted in the buffet between the hall and the main restaurant which was used for serving breakfast.

The kind of ceremonious silence prevailed here which a large hotel always aims to achieve. The serving waiters moved about noiselessly. A clink of crockery, a half-whispered word, were the only sounds audible. In one corner, obliquely opposite the door and two tables away from his own, Aschenbach noticed the Polish girls with their governess. Perched very upright, their ash-blond hair newly brushed and with reddened eyes, in stiff blue linen dresses with little white turnover collars and cuffs, they sat there passing each other a jar of preserves. They had almost finished their breakfast. The boy was missing.

Aschenbach smiled. Well, my little Phaeacian![5] he thought. You seem, unlike these young ladies, to enjoy the privilege of sleeping your fill. And with his spirits suddenly rising, he recited to himself the line: "Varied garments to wear, warm baths and restful reposing."

He breakfasted unhurriedly, received some forwarded mail from the porter who came into the breakfast room with his braided cap in hand, and opened a few letters as he smoked a cigarette. Thus it happened that he was still present to witness the entry of the lie-abed they were waiting for across the room.

He came through the glass door and walked in the silence obliquely across the room to his sisters' table. His walk was extraordinarily graceful, in the carriage of his upper body, the motion of his knees, the placing of his white-shod foot; it was very light, both delicate and proud, and made still more beautiful by the childlike modesty with which he twice, turning his head toward the room, raised and lowered his eyes as he passed. With a smile and a murmured word in his soft liquescent language, he took his seat; and now especially, as his profile was exactly turned to the watching Aschenbach, the latter was again amazed, indeed startled, by the truly godlike beauty of this human creature. Today the boy was wearing a light casual suit of blue and white striped linen material with a red silk breast-knot, closing at the neck in a simple white stand-up collar. But on this collar—which did not even match the rest of the suit very elegantly— there, like a flower in bloom, his head was gracefully resting. It was the head of Eros, with the creamy luster of Parian marble,[6] the brows fine-drawn and serious, the temples and ear darkly and softly covered by the neat right-angled growth of the curling hair.

Good, good! thought Aschenbach, with that cool prefessional approval in which artists confronted by a masterpiece sometimes cloak their ecstasy, their rapture. And mentally he added: Truly, if the sea and the shore did not await me, I should stay here as long as you do! But as it was, he went, went through the hall accompanied by the courteous attentions of the hotel staff, went down over the great terrace and straight along the wooden passageway to the enclosed beach reserved for hotel guests. Down there, a barefooted old man with linen trousers, sailor's jacket and straw hat func-tioned as bathing attendant: Aschenbach had himself conducted by him to his reserved beach cabin, had his table and chair set up on the sandy wooden platform in front of it, and made himself comfortable in the deck chair which he had drawn further out toward the sea across the wax-yellow sand.

5. A reference to Homer's *Odyssey* VIII. The Phaeacians were a peaceful, happy people who showed hospitality to the shipwrecked Odysseus.   6. White marble from the island of Paros was especially prized. *Eros:* Greek god of love.

The scene on the beach, the spectacle of civilization taking its carefree sensuous ease at the brink of the element, entertained and delighted him as much as ever. Already the gray shallow sea was alive with children wading, with swimmers, with assorted figures lying on the sandbars, their crossed arms under their heads. Others were rowing little keelless boats painted red and blue, and capsizing with shrieks of laughter. In front of the long row of *capanne*,[7] with their platforms like little verandahs to sit on, there was animated play and leisurely sprawling repose, there was visiting and chattering, there was punctilious morning elegance as well as unabashed nakedness contentedly enjoying the liberal local conventions. Further out, on the moist firm sand, persons in white bathing robes, in loose-fitting colorful shirtwear wandered to and fro. On the right, a complicated sand castle built by children was bedecked by flags in all the national colors. Vendors of mussels, cakes and fruit knelt to display their wares. On the left, in front of one of the huts in the row that was set at right angles to the others and to the sea, forming a boundary to the beach at this end, a Russian family was encamped: men with beards and big teeth, overripe indolent women, a Baltic spinster sitting at an easel and with exclamations of despair painting the sea, two good-natured hideous children, an old nanny in a headcloth who behaved in the caressingly deferential manner of the born serf. There they all were, gratefully enjoying their lives, tirelessly shouting the names of their disobediently romping children, mustering a few Italian words to joke at length with the amusing old man who sold them sweets, kissing each other on the cheeks and caring not a jot whether anyone was watching their scene of human solidarity.

Well, I shall stay, thought Aschenbach. What better place could I find? And with his hands folded in his lap, he let his eyes wander in the wide expanse of the sea, let his gaze glide away, dissolve and die in the monotonous haze of this desolate emptiness. There were profound reasons for his attachment to the sea: he loved it because as a hard-working artist he needed rest, needed to escape from the demanding complexity of phenomena and lie hidden on the bosom of the simple and tremendous; because of a forbidden longing deep within him that ran quite contrary to his life's task and was for that very reason seductive, a longing for the unarticulated and immeasurable, for eternity, for nothingness. To rest in the arms of perfection is the desire of any man intent upon creating excellence; and is not nothingness a form of perfection? But now, as he mused idly on such profound matters, the horizontal line of the sea's shore was suddenly intersected by a human figure, and when he had retrieved his gaze from limitless immensity and concentrated it again, he beheld the beautiful boy, coming from the left and walking past him across the sand. He walked barefoot, ready for wading, his slender legs naked to above the knees; his pace was leisured, but as light and proud as if he had long been used to going about without shoes. As he walked he looked round at the projecting row of huts: but scarcely had he noticed the Russian family, as it sat there in contented concord and going about its natural business,

7. Beach cabins (Italian).

than a storm of angry contempt gathered over his face. He frowned darkly, his lips pouted, a bitter grimace pulled them to one side and distorted his cheek; his brows were contracted in so deep a scowl that his eyes seemed to have sunk right in under their pressure, glaring forth a black message of hatred. He looked down, looked back again menacingly, then made with one shoulder an emphatic gesture of rejection as he turned his back and left his enemies behind him.

A kind of delicacy or alarm, something like respect and embarrassment, moved Aschenbach to turn away as if he had seen nothing; for no serious person who witnesses a moment of passion by chance will wish to make any use, even privately, of what he has observed. But he was at one and the same time entertained and moved, that is to say he was filled with happiness. Such childish fanaticism, directed against so harmless a piece of good-natured living—it gave a human dimension to mute divinity, it made a statuesque masterpiece of nature, which had hitherto merely delighted the eyes, seem worthy of a profounder appreciation as well; and it placed the figure of this adolescent, remarkable already by his beauty, in a context which enabled one to take him seriously beyond his years.

With his head still averted, Aschenbach listened to the boy's voice, his high, not very strong voice, as he called out greetings to his playmates working at the sand castle, announcing his arrival when he was still some way from them. They answered, repeatedly shouting his name or a diminutive of his name, and Aschenbach listened for this with a certain curiosity, unable to pick up anything more precise than two melodious syllables that sounded something like "Adgio" or still oftener "Adgiu," called out with a long u at the end. The sound pleased him, he found its euphony befitting to its object, repeated it quietly to himself and turned again with satisfaction to his letters and papers.

With his traveling writing-case on his knees, he took out his fountain pen and began to deal with this and that item of correspondence. But after no more than a quarter of an hour he felt that it was a great pity to turn his mind away like this from the present situation, this most enjoyable of all situations known to him, and to miss the experience of it for the sake of an insignificant activity. He threw his writing materials aside, he returned to the sea; and before long, his attention attracted by the youthful voices of the sand castle builders, he turned his head comfortably to the right against the back of his chair, to investigate once more the whereabouts and doings of the excellent Adgio.

His first glance found him; the red breast-knot was unmistakable. He and some others were busy laying an old plank as a bridge across the damp moat of the sand castle, and he was supervising this work, calling out instructions and motioning with his head. With him were about ten companions, both boys and girls, of his age and some of them younger, all chattering together in tongues, in Polish, in French and even in Balkan idioms. But it was his name that was most often heard. It was obvious that he was sought after, wooed, admired. One boy in particular, a Pole like him, a sturdy young fellow whom they called something like "Jashu," with glossy black hair and wearing a linen belted suit, seemed to be his particular vassal and friend. When the work on the sand castle ended for the time

being, they walked along the beach with their arms round each other, and
the boy they called "Jashu" kissed his beautiful companion.

Aschenbach was tempted to shake his finger at him. "But I counsel you,
Critobulus," he thought with a smile, "to go traveling for a year! You will
need that much time at least before you are cured."[8] And he then breakfasted on some large, fully ripe strawberries which he bought from a vendor. It had grown very warm, although the sun was unable to break
through the sky's layer of cloud. Even as one's senses enjoyed the tremendous and dizzying spectacle of the sea's stillness, lassitude paralyzed the
mind. To the mature and serious Aschenbach it seemed an appropriate,
fully satisfying task and occupation for him to guess or otherwise ascertain
what name this could be that sounded approximately like "Adgio." And
with the help of a few Polish recollections he established that what was
meant must be "Tadzio," the abbreviation of "Tadeusz" and changing in
the vocative to "Tadziu."

Tadzio was bathing. Aschenbach, who had lost sight of him, identified
his head and his flailing arm far out to sea; for the water was evidently still
shallow a long way out. But already he seemed to be giving cause for
alarm, already women's voices were calling out to him from the bathing
huts, again shrieking this name which ruled the beach almost like a rallying-cry, and which with its soft consonants, its long-drawn-out u-sound
at the end, had both a sweetness and a wildness about it: "Tadziu! Tadziu!" He returned, he came running, beating the resisting water to foam
with his feet, his head thrown back, running through the waves. And to
behold this living figure, lovely and austere in its early masculinity, with
dripping locks and beautiful as a young god, approaching out of the depths
of the sky and the sea, rising and escaping from the elements—this sight
filled the mind with mythical images, it was like a poet's tale from a primitive age, a tale of the origins of form and of the birth of the gods. Aschenbach listened with closed eyes to this song as it began its music deep
within him, and once again he reflected that it was good to be here and
that here he would stay.

Later on, Tadzio lay in the sand resting from his bathe, wrapped in his
white bathing robe which he had drawn through under his right shoulder,
and cradling his head on his naked arm; and even when Aschenbach was
not watching him but reading a few pages in his book, he almost never
forgot that the boy was lying there, and that he need only turn his head
slightly to the right to have the admired vision again in view. It almost
seemed to him that he was sitting here for the purpose of protecting the
half-sleeping boy—busy with doings of his own and yet nevertheless constantly keeping watch over this noble human creature there on his right,
only a little way from him. And his heart was filled and moved by a paternal fondness, the tender concern by which he who sacrifices himself to
beget beauty in the spirit is drawn to him who possesses beauty.

After midday he left the beach, returned to the hotel and took the lift
up to his room. Here he spent some time in front of the looking glass

---

8. Reference to Socrates' advice to Critobulus when the latter kissed Alcibiades' handsome son (Xeno-
phon's *Memorabilia* I.3).

studying his gray hair, his weary sharp-featured face. At the moment he thought of his fame, reflected that many people recognized him on the streets and would gaze at him respectfully, saluting the unerring and graceful power of his language—he recalled all the external successes he could think of that his talent had brought him, even calling to mind his elevation to the nobility. Then he went down to the restaurant and took lunch at his table. When he had finished and was entering the lift again, a group of young people who had also just been lunching crowded after him into the hovering cubicle, and Tadzio came with them. He stood quite near Aschenbach, so near that for the first time the latter was not seeing him as a distant image, but perceiving and taking precise cognizance of the details of his humanity. The boy was addressed by someone, and as he replied, with an indescribably charming smile, he was already leaving the lift again as it reached the first floor, stepping out backward with downcast eyes. The beautiful are modest, thought Aschenbach, and began to reflect very intensively on why this should be so. Nevertheless, he had noticed that Tadzio's teeth were not as attractive as they might have been: rather jagged and pale, lacking the luster of health and having that peculiar brittle transparency that is sometimes found in cases of anemia. "He's very delicate, he's sickly," thought Aschenbach, "he'll probably not live to grow old." And he made no attempt to explain to himself a certain feeling of satisfaction or relief that accompanied this thought.

He spent two hours in his room, and in mid-afternoon took the *vaporetto* across the stale-smelling lagoon to Venice. He got out at San Marco, took tea on the Piazza,[9] and then, in accordance with the daily program he had adopted for his stay here, set off on a walk through the streets. But it was this walk that brought about a complete change in his mood and intentions.

An unpleasant sultriness pervaded the narrow streets; the air was so thick that the exhalations from houses and shops and hot food stalls, the reek of oil, the smell of perfume and many other odors hung about in clouds instead of dispersing. Cigarette smoke lingered and was slow to dissipate. The throng of people in the alleyways annoyed him as he walked instead of giving him pleasure. The further he went, the more overwhelmingly he was afflicted by that appalling condition sometimes caused by a combination of the sea air with the sirocco, a condition of simultaneous excitement and exhaustion. He began to sweat disagreeably. His eyes faltered, his chest felt constricted, he was feverish, the blood throbbed in his head. He fled from the crowded commercial thoroughfares, over bridges, into the poor quarters. There he was besieged by beggars, and the sickening stench from the canals made it difficult to breathe. In a silent square, one of those places in the depths of Venice that seem to have been forgotten and put under a spell, he rested on the edge of a fountain, wiped the sweat from his forehead and realized that he would have to leave.

For the second time, and this time definitively, it had become evident that this city, in this state of the weather, was extremely injurious to him. To stay on willfully would be contrary to good sense, the prospect of a

---

9. A large public square in front of the church, lined by restaurants and cafés.

change in the wind seemed quite uncertain. He must make up his mind at once. To return straight home was out of the question. Neither his summer nor his winter quarters were ready to receive him. But this was not the only place with the sea and a beach, and elsewhere they were to be had without the harmful additional ingredient of this lagoon with its mephitic vapors. He remembered a little coastal resort not far from Trieste which had been recommended to him. Why not go there? And he must do so without delay, if it was to be worthwhile changing to a different place yet again. He declared himself resolved and rose to his feet. At the next gondola stop he took a boat and had himself conveyed back to San Marco through the murky labyrinth of canals, under delicate marble balconies flanked with carved lions, round the slimy stone corners of buildings, past the mournful facades of *palazzi*[1] on which boards bearing the names of commercial enterprises were mirrored in water where refuse bobbed up and down. He had some trouble getting to his destination, as the gondolier was in league with lace factories and glassworks and tried to land him at every place where he might view the wares and make a purchase; and whenever this bizarre journey through Venice might have cast its spell on him, he was effectively and irksomely disenchanted by the cutpurse mercantile spirit of the sunken queen of the Adriatic.[2]

Back in the hotel, before he had even dined, he notified the office that unforeseen circumstances obliged him to leave on the following morning. Regret was expressed, his bill was settled. He took dinner and spent the warm evening reading newspapers in a rocking chair on the back terrace. Before going to bed he packed completely for departure.

He slept fitfully, troubled by his impending further journey. When he opened his windows in the morning, the sky was still overcast, but the air seemed fresher, and—he began even now to regret his decision. Had he not given notice too impulsively, had it not been a mistake, an action prompted by a mere temporary indisposition? If only he had deferred it for a little, if only, without giving up so soon, he had taken a chance on acclimatizing himself to Venice or waiting for the wind to change, then he would now have before him not the hurry and flurry of a journey, but a morning on the beach like that of the previous day. Too late. What he had wanted yesterday he must go on wanting now. He got dressed and took the lift down to breakfast at eight o'clock.

When he entered the breakfast room it was still empty of guests. A few came in as he was sitting waiting for what he had ordered. As he sipped his tea he saw the Polish girls arrive with their companion: strict and matutinal, with reddened eyes, they proceeded to their table in the window corner. Shortly after this the porter approached with cap in hand and reminded him that it was time to leave. The motor coach was standing ready to take him and other passengers to the Hotel Excelsior, from which point the motor launch would convey the ladies and gentlemen through the company's private canal and across to the station. Time is pressing, signore.—In Aschenbach's opinion time was doing nothing of the sort.

---

1. Palaces (Italian); once-stately Renaissance homes that now lodge businesses.   2. A major sea power by the 15th century, Venice was called Queen of the Seas.

There was more than an hour till his train left. He found it extremely annoying that hotels should make a practice of getting their departing clients off the premises unnecessarily early, and indicated to the porter that he wished to have his breakfast in peace. The man hesitantly withdrew, only to reappear five minutes later. It was impossible, he said, for the automobile to wait any longer. Aschenbach retorted angrily that in that case it should leave, and take his trunk with it. He himself would take the public steamboat when it was time, and would they kindly leave it to him to deal with the problem of his own departure. The hotel servant bowed. Aschenbach, glad to have fended off these tiresome admonitions, finished his breakfast unhurriedly, and even got the waiter to hand him a newspaper. It was indeed getting very late by the time he rose. It so happened that at that same moment Tadzio entered through the glass door.

As he walked to his family's table his path crossed that of the departing guest. Meeting this gray-haired gentleman with the lofty brow, he modestly lowered his eyes, only to raise them again at once in his enchanting way, in a soft and full glance; and then he had passed. Good-bye, Tadzio! thought Aschenbach. How short our meeting was. And he added, actually shaping the thought with his lips and uttering it aloud to himself, as he normally never did: "May God bless you!"—He then went through the routine of departure, distributed gratuities, received the parting courtesies of the soft-spoken little manager in the French frock coat, and left the hotel on foot as he had come, walking along the white-blossoming avenue with the hotel servant behind him carrying his hand luggage, straight across the island to the *vaporetto* landing stage. He reached it, he took his seat on board—and what followed was a voyage of sorrow, a grievous passage that plumbed all the depths of regret.

It was the familiar trip across the lagoon, past San Marco, up the Grand Canal. Aschenbach sat on the semicircular bench in the bows, one arm on the railing, shading his eyes with his hand. The Public Gardens fell away astern, the Piazzetta revealed itself once more in its princely elegance and was left behind, then came the great flight of the *palazzi*, with the splendid marble arch of the Rialto appearing as the waterway turned. The traveler contemplated it all, and his heart was rent with sorrow. The atmosphere of the city, this slightly moldy smell of sea and swamp from which he had been so anxious to escape—he breathed it in now in deep, tenderly painful drafts. Was it possible that he had not known, had not considered how deeply his feelings were involved in all these things? What had been a mere qualm of compunction this morning, a slight stirring of doubt as to the wisdom of his behavior, now became grief, became real suffering, an anguish of the soul, so bitter that several times it brought tears to his eyes, and which as he told himself he could not possibly have foreseen. What he found so hard to bear, what was indeed at times quite unendurable, was evidently the thought that he would never see Venice again, that this was a parting forever. For since it had become clear for a second time that this city made him ill, since he had been forced a second time to leave it precipitately, he must of course from now on regard it as an impossible and forbidden place to which he was not suited, and which it would be senseless to attempt to revisit. Indeed, he felt that if he left now, shame and pride must prevent him from ever setting eyes again on this beloved city which had twice physically defeated him; and this contention between his soul's desire and his physical capacities suddenly seemed to the aging Aschenbach so grave and important, the bodily inadequacy so shameful, so necessary to overcome at all costs, that he could not understand the facile resignation with which he had decided yesterday, without any serious struggle, to tolerate that inadequacy and to acknowledge it.

In the meantime the *vaporetto* was approaching the station, and Aschenbach's distress and sense of helplessness increased to the point of distraction. In his torment he felt it to be impossible to leave and no less impossible to turn back. He entered the station torn by this acute inner conflict. It was very late, he had not a moment to lose if he was to catch his train. He both wanted to catch it and wanted to miss it. But time was pressing, lashing him on; he hurried to get his ticket, looking round in the crowded concourse for the hotel company's employee who would be on duty here. The man appeared and informed him that his large trunk had been sent off as registered baggage. Sent off already? Certainly—to Como.[3] To Como? And from hasty comings and goings, from angry questions and embarrassed replies, it came to light that the trunk, before even leaving the luggage room in the Hotel Excelsior, had been put with some quite different baggage and dispatched to a totally incorrect address.

Aschenbach had some difficulty preserving the facial expression that would be the only comprehensible one in these circumstances. A wild joy, an unbelievable feeling of hilarity, shook him almost convulsively from the depths of his heart. The hotel employee rushed to see if it was still possible to stop the trunk, and needless to say returned without having had any success. Aschenbach accordingly declared that he was not prepared to travel without his luggage, that he had decided to go back and wait at the Hotel des Bains for the missing article to turn up again. Was the company's motor launch still at the station? The man assured him that it was waiting immediately outside. With Italian eloquence he prevailed upon the official at the ticket office to take back Aschenbach's already purchased ticket. He swore that telegrams would be sent, that nothing would be left undone and no effort spared to get the trunk back in no time at all—and thus it most strangely came about that the traveler, twenty minutes after arriving at the station, found himself back on the Grand Canal and on his way back to the Lido.

How unbelievably strange an experience it was, how shaming, how like a dream in its bizarre comedy: to be returning, by a quirk of fate, to places from which one has just taken leave forever with the deepest sorrow—to be sent back and to be seeing them again within the hour! With spray tossing before its bows, deftly and entertainingly tacking to and fro between gondolas and *vaporetti*, the rapid little boat darted toward its destination, while its only passenger sat concealing under a mask of resigned annoyance the anxiously exuberant excitement of a truant schoolboy. From time to time he still inwardly shook with laughter at this mishap,

---

3. A large lake and resort area in the northwest of Italy.

telling himself that even a man born under a lucky star could not have had a more welcome piece of ill luck. There would be explanations to be given, surprised faces to be confronted—and then, as he told himself, everything would be well again, a disaster would have been averted, a grievous mistake corrected, and everything he thought he had turned his back on for good would lie open again for him to enjoy, would be his for as long as he liked . . . And what was more, did the rapid movement of the motor launch deceive him, or was there really now, to crown all else, a breeze blowing from the sea?

The bow waves dashed against the concrete walls of the narrow canal that cuts across the island to the Hotel Excelsior. There a motor omnibus was waiting for the returning guest and conveyed him along the road above the rippling sea straight to the Hotel des Bains. The little manager with the moustache and the fancily-cut frock coat came down the flight of steps to welcome him.

In softly flattering tones he expressed regret for the incident, described it as highly embarrassing for himself and for the company, but emphatically endorsed Aschenbach's decision to wait here for his luggage. His room, to be sure, had been relet, but another, no less comfortable, was immediately at his disposal. *"Pas de chance, monsieur!"*[4] said the Swiss lift-attendant as they glided up. And thus the fugitive was once more installed in a room situated and furnished almost exactly like the first.

Exhausted and numbed by the confusion of this strange morning, he had no sooner distributed the contents of his hand luggage about the room than he collapsed into a reclining chair at the open window. The sea had turned pale green, the air seemed clearer and purer, the beach with its bathing cabins and boats more colorful, although the sky was still gray. Aschenbach gazed out, his hands folded in his lap, pleased to be here again but shaking his head with displeasure at his irresolution, his ignorance of his own wishes. Thus he sat for about an hour, resting and idly daydreaming. At midday he caught sight of Tadzio in his striped linen suit with the red breast-knot, coming from the sea, through the beach barrier and along the boarded walks back to the hotel. From up here at his window Aschenbach recognized him at once, before he had even looked at him properly, and some such thought came to him as: Why, Tadzio, there you are again too! But at the same instant he felt that casual greeting die on his lips, stricken dumb by the truth in his heart—he felt the rapturous kindling of his blood, the joy and the anguish of his soul, and realized that it was because of Tadzio that it had been so hard for him to leave.

He sat quite still, quite unseen at his high vantage point, and began to search his feelings. His features were alert, his eyebrows rose, an attentive, intelligently inquisitive smile parted his lips. Then he raised his head, and with his arms hanging limply down along the back of his chair, described with both of them a slowly rotating and lifting motion, the palms of his hands turning forward, as if to sketch an opening and outspreading of the arms. It was gesture that gladly bade welcome, a gesture of calm acceptance.

---

4. Bad luck, sir! (French).

4

Now day after day the god with the burning cheeks[5] soared naked, driving his four fire-breathing steeds through the spaces of heaven, and now, too, his yellow-gold locks fluttered wide in the outstorming east wind. Silkwhite radiance gleamed on the slow-swelling deep's vast waters. The sand glowed. Under the silvery quivering blue of the ether, rust-colored awnings were spread out in front of the beach cabins, and one spent the morning hours on the sharply defined patch of shadow they provided. But exquisite, too, was the evening, when the plants in the park gave off a balmy fragrance, and the stars on high moved through their dance, and the softly audible murmur of the night-surrounded sea worked its magic on the soul. Such an evening carried with it the delightful promise of a new sunlit day of leisure easily ordered, and adorned with countless close-knit possibilities of charming chance encounter.

The guest whom so convenient a mishap had detained here was very far from seeing the recovery of his property as a reason for yet another departure. For a couple of days he had had to put up with some privations and appear in the main dining room in his traveling clothes. Then, when finally the errant load was once more set down in his room, he unpacked completely and filled the cupboards and drawers with his possessions, resolving for the present to set no time limit on his stay; he was glad now to be able to pass his hours on the beach in a tussore[6] suit and to present himself again in seemly evening attire at the dinner table.

The lulling rhythm of this existence had already cast its spell on him; he had been quickly enchanted by the indulgent softness and splendor of this way of life. What a place this was indeed, combining the charms of a cultivated seaside resort in the south with the familiar ever-ready proximity of the strange and wonderful city! Aschenbach did not enjoy enjoying himself. Whenever and wherever he had to stop work, have a breathing space, take things easily, he would soon find himself driven by restlessness and dissatisfaction—and this had been so in his youth above all—back to his lofty travail, to his stern and sacred daily routine. Only this place bewitched him, relaxed his will, gave him happiness. Often in the forenoon, under the awning of his hut, gazing dreamily at the blue of the southern sea, or on a mild night perhaps, reclining under a star-strewn sky on the cushions of a gondola that carried him back to the Lido from the Piazza where he had long lingered—and as the bright lights, the melting sounds of the serenade dropped away behind him—often he recalled his country house in the mountains, the scene of his summer labors, where the low clouds would drift through his garden, violent evening thunderstorms would put out all the lights, and the ravens he fed would take refuge in the tops of the pine trees. Then indeed he would feel he had been snatched away now to the Elysian land,[7] to the ends of the earth, where lightest of living is granted to mortals, where no snow is nor winter, no storms and no rain downstreaming, but where Oceanus[8] ever causes a

---

5. Helios, Greek god of the sun (later equated with Apollo).   6. A coarse brown silk.   7. In Greek mythology, virtuous mortals were sent to the Elysian Fields or Islands of the Blessed after their death.
8. A river flowing nearby, which originated in the underworld and circled the globe.

gentle cooling breeze to ascend, and the days flow past in blessed idleness, with no labor or strife, for to the sun alone and its feasts they are all given over.

Aschenbach saw much of the boy Tadzio, he saw him almost constantly; in a confined environment, with a common daily program, it was natural for the beautiful creature to be near him all day, with only brief interruptions. He saw him and met him everywhere: in the ground floor rooms of the hotel, on their cooling journeys by water to the city and back, in the sumptuous Piazza itself, and often elsewhere from time to time, in alleys and byways, when chance had played a part. But it was during the mornings on the beach above all, and with the happiest regularity, that he could devote hours at a time to the contemplation and study of this exquisite phenomenon. Indeed, it was precisely this ordered routine of happiness, this equal daily repetition of favorable circumstances, that so filled him with contentment and zest for life, that made this place so precious to him, that allowed one sunlit day to follow another in such obligingly endless succession.

He rose early, as he would normally have done under the insistent compulsion of work, and was down at the beach before most of the other guests, when the sun's heat was still gentle and the sea lay dazzling white in its morning dreams. He greeted the barrier attendant affably, exchanged familiar greetings also with the barefooted, white-bearded old man who had prepared his place for him, spread the brown awning and shifted the cabin furniture out to the platform where Aschenbach would settle down. Three hours or four were then his, hours in which the sun would rise to its zenith and to terrible power, hours in which the sea would turn a deeper and deeper blue, hours in which he would be able to watch Tadzio.

He saw him coming, walking along from the left by the water's edge, saw him from behind as he emerged between the cabins, or indeed would sometimes look up and discover, gladdened and startled, that he had missed his arrival and that the boy was already there, already in the blue and white bathing costume which now on the beach was his sole attire. There he would be, already busy with his customary activities in the sun and the sand—this charmingly trivial, idle yet ever-active life that was both play and repose, a life of sauntering, wading, digging, snatching, lying about and swimming, under the watchful eyes and at the constant call of the women on their platform, who with their high-pitched voices would cry out his name: "Tadziu! Tadziu!" and to whom he would come running with eager gesticulation, to tell them what he had experienced, to show them what he had found, what he had caught: jellyfish, little seahorses, and mussels, and crabs that go sideways. Aschenbach understood not a word of what he said, and commonplace though it might be, it was liquid melody in his ears. Thus the foreign sound of the boy's speech exalted it to music, the sun in its triumph shed lavish brightness all over him, and the sublime perspective of the sea was the constant contrasting background against which he appeared.

Soon the contemplative beholder knew every line and pose of that noble, so freely displayed body, he saluted again with joy each already familiar perfection, and there was no end to his wonder, to the delicate delight of his senses. The boy would be summoned to greet a guest who was making a polite call on the ladies in their cabin; he would run up, still wet perhaps from the sea, throw back his curls, and as he held out his hand, poised on one leg with the other on tiptoe, he had an enchanting way of turning and twisting his body, gracefully expectant, charmingly shamefaced, seeking to please because good breeding required him to do so. Or he would be lying full-length, his bathing robe wrapped round his chest, his finely chiseled arm propped on the sand, his hand cupping his chin; the boy addressed as "Jashu" would squat beside him caressing him, and nothing could be more bewitching than the way the favored Tadzio, smiling with his eyes and lips, would look up at this lesser and servile mortal. Or he would be standing at the edge of the sea, alone, some way from his family, quite near Aschenbach, standing upright with his hands clasped behind his neck, slowly rocking to and fro on the balls of his feet and dreamily gazing into the blue distance, while little waves ran up and bathed his toes. His honey-colored hair nestled in ringlets at his temples and at the back of his neck, the sun gleamed in the down on his upper spine, the subtle outlining of his ribs and the symmetry of his breast stood out through the scanty covering of his torso, his armpits were still as smooth as those of a statue, the hollows of his knees glistened and their bluish veins made his body seem composed of some more translucent material. What discipline, what precision of thought was expressed in that outstretched, youthfully perfect physique! And yet the austere pure will that had here been darkly active, that had succeeded in bringing this divine sculptured shape to light—was it not well known and familiar to Aschenbach as an artist? Was it not also active in him, in the sober passion that filled him as he set free from the marble mass of language[9] that slender form which he had beheld in the spirit, and which he was presenting to mankind as a model and mirror of intellectual beauty?

A model and mirror! His eyes embraced that noble figure at the blue water's edge, and in rising ecstasy he felt he was gazing on Beauty itself, on Form as a thought of God, on the one and pure perfection which dwells in the spirit and of which a human image and likeness had here been lightly and graciously set up for him to worship. Such was his emotional intoxication; and the aging artist welcomed it unhesitatingly, even greedily. His mind was in labor, its store of culture was in ferment, his memory threw up thoughts from ancient tradition which he had been taught as a boy, but which had never yet come alive in his own fire. Had he not read that the sun turns our attention from spiritual things to the things of the senses?[1] He had read that it so numbs and bewitches our intelligence and memory that the soul, in its joy, quite forgets its proper state and clings with astonished admiration to that most beautiful of all the things the sun shines upon: yet, that only with the help of a bodily form is the soul then still able to exalt itself to a higher vision. That Cupid, indeed, does as mathematicians do, when they show dull-witted children

9. The Italian artist Michelangelo Buonarroti (1475–1564) explained that he created his statues by carving away the marble block until the figure within was set free.   1. In section 764E of the *Erotikos* (Dialogue on love) by the Greek essayist Plutarch (46–120).

tangible images of the pure Forms: so too the love god, in order to make spiritual things visible, loves to use the shapes and colors of young men, turning them into instruments of Recollection by adorning them with all the reflected splendor of Beauty, so that the sight of them will truly set us on fire with pain and hope.

Such were the thoughts the god inspired in his enthusiast, such were the emotions of which he grew capable. And a delightful vision came to him, spun from the sea's murmur and the glittering sunlight.[2] It was the old plane tree not far from the walls of Athens—that place of sacred shade, fragrant with chaste-tree blossoms, adorned with sacred statues and pious gifts in honor of the nymphs and of Acheloüs.[3] The stream trickled crystal clear over smooth pebbles at the foot of the great spreading tree; the crickets made their music. But on the grass, which sloped down gently so that one could hold up one's head as one lay, there reclined two men, sheltered here from the heat of the noonday: one elderly and one young, one ugly and one beautiful, the wise beside the desirable. And Socrates, wooing him with witty compliments and jests, was instructing Phaedrus on desire and virtue. He spoke to him of the burning tremor of fear which the lover will suffer when his eye perceives a likeness of eternal Beauty; spoke to him of the lusts of the profane and base who cannot turn their eyes to Beauty when they behold its image and are not capable of reverence; spoke of the sacred terror that visits the noble soul when a godlike countenance, a perfect body appears to him—of how he trembles then and is beside himself and hardly dares look at the possessor of beauty, and reveres him and would even sacrifice to him as to a graven image, if he did not fear to seem foolish in the eyes of men. For Beauty, dear Phaedrus, only Beauty is at one and the same time divinely desirable and visible: it is, mark well, the only form of the spiritual that we can receive with our sense and endure with our senses. For what would become of us if other divine things, if Reason and Virtue and Truth were to appear to us sensuously? Should we not perish in a conflagration of love, as once upon a time Semele[4] did before Zeus? Thus Beauty is the lover's path to the spirit—only the path, only a means, little Phaedrus ... And then he uttered the subtlest thing of all, that sly wooer: he who loves, he said, is more divine than the beloved, because the god is in the former, but not in the latter—this, the tenderest perhaps and the most mocking thought ever formulated, a thought alive with all the mischievousness and most secret voluptuousness of the heart.

The writer's joy is the thought that can become emotion, the emotion that can wholly become a thought. At that time the solitary Aschenbach took possession and control of just such a pulsating thought, just such a precise emotion: namely, that Nature trembles with rapture when the spirit bows in homage before Beauty. He suddenly desired to write. Eros indeed, we are told, loves idleness and is born only for the idle. But at this

2. A reference to the scene and some of the arguments in Plato's dialogue *Phaedrus*. Plato's school, or Academy, was located in a grove of plane trees outside Athens; in the dialogue, the young student Phaedrus tells Socrates of Lysias's speech on love, and Socrates responds with two speeches of his own.   3. A river god.   4. The mortal mother of Zeus's son Dionysus, who perished in flames when the king of the gods appeared to her (at her request) in his divine glory.

point of Aschenbach's crisis and visitation his excitement was driving him to produce. The occasion was almost a matter of indifference. An inquiry, an invitation to express a personal opinion on a certain important cultural problem, a burning question of taste, had been circulated to the intellectual world and had been forwarded to him on his travels. The theme was familiar to him, it was close to his experience; the desire to illuminate it in his own words was suddenly irresistible. And what he craved, indeed, was to work on it in Tadzio's presence, to take the boy's physique for a model as he wrote, to let his style follow the lineaments of this body which he saw as divine, and to carry its beauty on high into the spiritual world, as the eagle once carried the Trojan shepherd boy[5] up into the ether. Never had he felt the joy of the word more sweetly, never had he known so clearly that Eros dwells in language, as during those perilously precious hours in which, seated at his rough table under the awning, in full view of his idol and with the music of his voice in his ears, he used Tadzio's beauty as a model for his brief essay—that page and a half of exquisite prose which with its limpid nobility and vibrant controlled passion was soon to win the admiration of many. It is as well that the world knows only a fine piece of work and not also its origins, the conditions under which it came into being; for knowledge of the sources of an artist's inspiration would often confuse readers and shock them, and the excellence of the writing would be of no avail. How strange those hours were! How strangely exhausting that labor! How mysterious this act of intercourse and begetting between a mind and a body! When Aschenbach put away his work and left the beach, he felt worn out, even broken, and his conscience seemed to be reproaching him as if after some kind of debauch.

On the following morning, just as he was leaving the hotel, he noticed from the steps that Tadzio, already on his way to the sea—and alone—was just approaching the beach barrier. The wish to use this opportunity, the mere thought of doing so, and thereby lightly, lightheartedly, making the acquaintance of one who had unknowingly so exalted and moved him: the thought of speaking to him, of enjoying his answer and his glance—all this seemed natural, it was the irresistibly obvious thing to do. The beautiful boy was walking in a leisurely fashion, he could be overtaken, and Aschenbach quickened his pace. He reached him on the boarded way behind the bathing cabins, he was just about to lay his hand on his head or his shoulder, and some phrase or other, some friendly words in French were on the tip of his tongue—when he felt his heart, perhaps partly because he had been walking fast, hammering wildly inside him, felt so breathless that he would only have been able to speak in a strangled and trembling voice. He hesitated, struggled to control himself, then was suddenly afraid that he had already been walking too long close behind the beautiful boy, afraid that Tadzio would notice this, that he would turn and look at him questioningly; he made one more attempt, failed, gave up, and hurried past with his head bowed.

Too late! he thought at that moment. Too late! But was it too late? This

---

5. The Trojan prince Ganymede was kidnapped by Zeus in the form of an eagle; he became the cup-bearer of the gods on Olympus.

step he had failed to take would very possibly have been all to the good, it might have had a lightening and gladdening effect, led perhaps to a wholesome disenchantment. But the fact now seemed to be that the aging lover no longer wished to be disenchanted, that the intoxication was too precious to him. Who shall unravel the mystery of an artist's nature and character! Who shall explain the profound instinctual fusion of discipline and dissoluteness on which it rests! For not to be able to desire wholesome disenchantment is to be dissolute. Aschenbach was no longer disposed to self-criticism; taste, the intellectual mold of his years, self-respect, maturity and late simplicity all disinclined him to analyze his motives and decide whether what had prevented him from carrying out his intention had been a prompting of conscience or a disreputable weakness. He was confused, he was afraid that someone, even if only the bathing attendant, might have witnessed his haste and his defeat; he was very much afraid of exposure to ridicule. For the rest, he could not help inwardly smiling at his comic-sacred terror. "Crestfallen," he thought, "spirits dashed, like a frightened cock hanging its wings in a fight![6] Truly this is the god who at the sight of the desired beauty so breaks our courage and dashes our pride so utterly to the ground . . ." He toyed with the theme, gave rein to his enthusiasm, plunged into emotions he was too proud to fear.

He was no longer keeping any tally of the leisure time he had allowed himself; the thought of returning home did not even occur to him. He had arranged for ample funds to be made available to him here. His one anxiety was that the Polish family might leave; but he had surreptitiously learned, by a casual question to the hotel barber, that these guests had arrived at the hotel only very shortly before he had arrived himself. The sun was browning his face and hands, the stimulating salty breeze heightened his capacity for feeling, and whereas formerly, when sleep or food or contact with nature had given him any refreshment, he would always have expended it completely on his writing, he now, with high-hearted prodigality, allowed all the daily revitalization he was receiving from the sun and leisure and sea air to burn itself up in intoxicating emotion.

He slept fleetingly; the days of precious monotony were punctuated by brief, happily restless nights. To be sure, he would retire early, for at nine o'clock, when Tadzio had disappeared from the scene, he judged his day to be over. But at the first glint of dawn a pang of tenderness would startle him awake, his heart would remember its adventure, he could bear his pillows no longer, he would get up, and lightly wrapped against the early morning chill he would sit down at the open window to wait for the sunrise. His soul, still fresh with the solemnity of sleep, was filled with awe by this wonderful event. The sky, the earth and the sea still wore the glassy paleness of ghostly twilight; a dying star still floated in the void. But a murmur came, a winged message from dwelling places no mortal may approach, that Eos[7] was rising from her husband's side; and now it appeared, that first sweet blush at the furthest horizon of the sky and sea, which heralds the sensuous disclosure of creation. The goddess

---

6. From the Greek tragedian Phrynichus (512–476 B.C.), quoted in Plutarch's *Erotikos* (762E).   7. The goddess of dawn in Greek mythology.

approached, that ravisher of youth, who carried off Cleitus and Cephalus and defied the envy of all the Olympians to enjoy the love of the beautiful Orion.[8] A scattering of roses began, there at the edge of the world an ineffably lovely shining and blossoming: childlike clouds, transfigured and transparent with light, hovered like serving *amoretti*[9] in the vermilion and violet haze; crimson light fell across the waves, which seemed to be washing it landward; golden spears darted from below into the heights of heaven, the gleam became a conflagration, noiselessly and with overwhelming divine power the glow and the fire and the blazing flames reared upward, and the sacred steeds of the goddess's brother Helios, tucking their hooves, leapt above the earth's round surface. With the splendor of the god irradiating him, the lone watcher sat; he closed his eyes and let the glory kiss his eyelids. Feelings he had had long ago, early and precious dolors of the heart, which had died out in his life's austere service and were now, so strangely transformed, returning to him—he recognized them with a confused and astonished smile. He meditated, he dreamed, slowly a name shaped itself on his lips, and still smiling, with upturned face, his hands folded in his lap, he fell asleep in his chair once more.

With such fiery ceremony the day began, but the rest of it, too, was strangely exalted and mythically transformed. Where did it come from, what was its origin, this sudden breeze that played so gently and speakingly around his temples and ears, like some higher insufflation? Innumerable white fleecy clouds covered the sky, like the grazing flocks of the gods. A stronger wind rose, and the horses of Poseidon[1] reared and ran; his bulls too, the bulls of the blue-haired sea god, roared and charged with lowered horns. But among the rocks and stones of the more distant beach the waves danced like leaping goats. A sacred, deranged world, full of Panic[2] life, enclosed the enchanted watcher, and his heart dreamed tender tales. Sometimes, as the sun was sinking behind Venice, he would sit on a bench in the hotel park to watch Tadzio, dressed in white with a colorful sash, at play on the rolled gravel tennis court; and in his mind's eye he was watching Hyacinthus, doomed to perish because two gods loved him.[3] He could even feel Zephyr's grievous envy of his rival, who had forgotten his oracle and his bow and his zither to be forever playing with the beautiful youth; he saw the discus, steered by cruel jealousy, strike the lovely head; he himself, turning pale too, caught the broken body in his arms, and the flower that sprang from that sweet blood bore the inscription of his undying lament.

Nothing is stranger, more delicate, than the relationship between people who know each other only by sight—who encounter and observe each other daily, even hourly, and yet are compelled by the constraint of convention or by their own temperament to keep up the pretense of being indifferent strangers, neither greeting nor speaking to each other. Between them is uneasiness and overstimulated curiosity, the nervous excitement of an unsatisfied, unnaturally suppressed need to know and to communi-

8. Eos loved the youths Cleitus and Cephalus and the hunter Orion.   9. Cupids.   1. God of the sea and brother of Zeus in Greek mythology, associated with the horse and the bull.   2. Associated with the Greek demigod Pan, a satyr-like figure with goat's horns and hooves.   3. Apollo and Zephyr (god of the west wind) both loved the youth Hyacinthus. When Apollo accidentally killed him in a discus game, a flower marked with the Greek syllables "ai ai" ("alas!") sprang from the boy's blood. Apollo is an archer and musician as well as sun god and the god of the Delphic oracle.

cate; and above all, too, a kind of strained respect. For man loves and respects his fellow man for as long as he is not yet in a position to evaluate him, and desire is born of defective knowledge.

It was inevitable that some kind of relationship and acquaintance should develop between Aschenbach and the young Tadzio, and with a surge of joy the older man became aware that his interest and attention were not wholly unreciprocated. Why, for example, when the beautiful creature appeared in the morning on the beach, did he now never use the boarded walk behind the bathing cabins, but always take the front way, through the sand, passing Aschenbach's abode and often passing unnecessarily close to him, almost touching his table or his chair, as he sauntered toward the cabin where his family sat? Was this the attraction, the fascination exercised by a superior feeling on its tender and thoughtless object? Aschenbach waited daily for Tadzio to make his appearance and sometimes pretended to be busy when he did so, letting the boy pass him seemingly unnoticed. But sometimes, too, he would look up, and their eyes would meet. They would both be deeply serious when this happened. In the cultured and dignified countenance of the older man, nothing betrayed an inner emotion; but in Tadzio's eyes there was an inquiry, a thoughtful questioning, his walk became hesitant, he looked at the ground, looked sweetly up again, and when he had passed, something in his bearing seemed to suggest that only good breeding restrained him from turning to look back.

But once, one evening, it was different. The Poles and their governess had been absent from dinner in the main restaurant—Aschenbach had noticed this with concern. After dinner, very uneasy about where they might be, he was walking in evening dress and a straw hat in front of the hotel, at the foot of the terrace, when suddenly he saw the nunlike sisters appearing with their companion, in the light of the arc lamps, and four paces behind them was Tadzio. Obviously they had come from the *vaporetto* pier, having for some reason dined in the city. The crossing had been chilly perhaps; Tadzio was wearing a dark blue reefer jacket with gold buttons and a naval cap to match. The sun and sea air never burned his skin, it was marble-pale as always; but today he seemed paler than usual, either because of the cool weather or in the blanching moonlight of the lamps. His symmetrical eyebrows stood out more sharply, his eyes seemed much darker. He was more beautiful than words can express, and Aschenbach felt, as so often already, the painful awareness that language can only praise sensuous beauty, but not reproduce it.

He had not been prepared for the beloved encounter, it came unexpectedly, he had not had time to put on an expression of calm and dignity. Joy no doubt, surprise, admiration, were openly displayed on his face when his eyes met those of the returning absentee—and in that instant it happened that Tadzio smiled: smiled at him, speakingly, familiarly, enchantingly and quite unabashed, with his lips parting slowly as the smile was formed. It was the smile of Narcissus[4] as he bows his head over the

4. A beautiful Greek youth who fell in love with his own image in a pool and drowned trying to reach it. "Tadzio's smile is Narcissus' who sees his own reflection—he sees it in the face of another/he sees his beauty in its effects. Coquettishness and tenderness are also in this smile" [Mann's note].

mirroring water, that profound, fascinated, protracted smile with which he reaches out his arms toward the reflection of his own beauty—a very slightly contorted smile, contorted by the hopelessness of his attempt to kiss the sweet lips of his shadow; a smile that was provocative, curious and imperceptibly troubled, bewitched and bewitching.

He who had received this smile carried it quickly away with him like a fateful gift. He was so deeply shaken that he was forced to flee the lighted terrace and the front garden and hurry into the darkness of the park at the rear. Words struggled from his lips, strangely indignant and tender reproaches: "You mustn't smile like that! One mustn't, do you hear, mustn't smile like that at anyone!" He sank down on one of the seats, deliriously breathing the nocturnal fragrance of the flowers and trees. And leaning back, his arms hanging down, overwhelmed, trembling, shuddering all over, he whispered the standing formula of the heart's desire— impossible here, absurd, depraved, ludicrous and sacred nevertheless, still worthy of honor even here: "I love you!"

5

During the fourth week of his stay at the Lido Gustav von Aschenbach began to notice certain uncanny developments in the outside world. In the first place it struck him that as the height of the season approached, the number of guests at his hotel was diminishing rather than increasing, and in particular that the German language seemed to be dying away into silence all round him, so that in the end only foreign sounds fell on his ear at table and on the beach. Then one day the hotel barber, whom he visited frequently now, let slip in conversation a remark that aroused his suspicions. The man had mentioned a German family who had just left after only a brief stay, and in his chattering, flattering manner he added: "But you are staying on, signore; you are not afraid of the sickness?" Aschenbach looked at him. "The sickness?" he repeated. The fellow stopped his talk, pretended to be busy, had not heard the question. And when it was put to him again more sharply, he declared that he knew nothing and tried with embarrassed loquacity to change the subject.

That was at midday. In the afternoon, with the sea dead calm and the sun burning, Aschenbach crossed to Venice, for he was now driven by a mad compulsion to follow the Polish boy and his sisters, having seen them set off toward the pier with their companion. He did not find his idol at San Marco. But at tea, sitting at his round wrought-iron table on the shady side of the Piazza, he suddenly scented in the air a peculiar aroma, one which it now seemed to him he had been noticing for days without really being conscious of it—a sweetish, medicinal smell that suggested squalor and wounds and suspect cleanliness. He scrutinized it, pondered and identified it, finished his tea and left the Piazza at the far end opposite the basilica. In the narrow streets the smell was stronger. At corners, printed notices had been pasted up in which the civic authorities, with fatherly concern, gave warning to the local population that since certain ailments of the gastric system were normal in this weather, they should refrain from eating oysters and mussels and indeed from using water from the canals.

The euphemistic character of the announcement was obvious. Groups of people were standing about silently on bridges or in squares, and the stranger stood among them, brooding and scenting the truth.

He found a shopkeeper leaning against his vaulted doorway, surrounded by coral necklaces and trinkets made of imitation amethyst, and asked him about the unpleasant smell. The man looked him over with heavy eyes, and hastily gathered his wits. "A precautionary measure, signore," he answered, gesticulating. "The police have laid down regulations, and quite right too, it must be said. This weather is oppressive, the sirocco is not very wholesome. In short, the signore will understand—an exaggerated precaution no doubt . . ." Aschenbach thanked him and walked on. Even on the *vaporetto* taking him back to the Lido he now noticed the smell of the bactericide.

Back at the hotel, he went at once to the table in the hall where the newspapers were kept, and carried out some research. In the foreign papers he found nothing. Those in his own language mentioned rumors, quoted contradictory statistics, reported official denials and questioned their veracity. This explained the withdrawal of the German and Austrian clientele. Visitors of other nationalities evidently knew nothing, suspected nothing, still had no apprehensions. "They want it kept quiet!" thought Aschenbach in some agitation, throwing the newspapers back on the table. "They're hushing this up!" But at the same time his heart filled with elation at the thought of the adventure in which the outside world was about to be involved. For to passion, as to crime, the assured everyday order and stability of things is not opportune, and any weakening of the civil structure, any chaos and disaster afflicting the world, must be welcome to it, as offering a vague hope of turning such circumstances to its advantage. Thus Aschenbach felt an obscure sense of satisfaction at what was going on in the dirty alleyways of Venice, cloaked in official secrecy—this guilty secret of the city, which merged with his own interest to protect. For in his enamored state his one anxiety was that Tadzio might leave, and he realized with a kind of horror that he would not be able to go on living if that were to happen.

Lately he had not been content to owe the sight and proximity of the beautiful boy merely to daily routine and chance: he had begun pursuing him, following him obtrusively. On Sunday, for example, the Poles never appeared on the beach; he rightly guessed that they were attending mass in San Marco, and hastened to the church himself. There, stepping from the fiery heat of the Piazza into the golden twilight of the sanctuary, he would find him whom he had missed, bowed over a prie-dieu[5] and performing his devotions. Then he would stand in the background, on the cracked mosaic floor, amid a throng of people kneeling, murmuring and crossing themselves, and the massive magnificence of the oriental temple would weigh sumptuously on his senses. At the front, the ornately vested priest walked to and fro, doing his business and chanting. Incense billowed up, clouding the feeble flames of the altar candles, and with its heavy, sweet sacrificial odor another seemed to mingle: the smell of the

5. Low stool to kneel on during prayers (literally, "pray-God," French).

sick city. But through the vaporous dimness and the flickering lights Aschenbach saw the boy, up there at the front, turn his head and seek him with his eyes until he found him.

Then, when the great doors were opened and the crowd streamed out into the shining Piazza swarming with pigeons, the beguiled lover would hide in the antebasilica, he would lurk and lie in wait. He would see the Poles leave the church, see the brother and sisters take ceremonious leave of their mother, who would then set off home, turning toward the Piazzetta; he would observe the boy, the cloistral sisters and the governess turn right and walk through the clock tower gateway into the Merceria,[6] and after letting them get a little way ahead he would follow them—follow them furtively on their walk through Venice. He had to stop when they lingered, had to take refuge in hot food stalls and courtyards to let them pass when they turned round; he would lose them, search for them frantically and exhaustingly, rushing over bridges and along filthy culs-de-sac, and would then have to endure minutes of mortal embarrassment when he suddenly saw them coming toward him in a narrow passageway where no escape was possible. And yet one cannot say that he suffered. His head and his heart were drunk, and his steps followed the dictates of that dark god[7] whose pleasure it is to trample man's reason and dignity underfoot.

Presently, somewhere or other, Tadzio and his family would take a gondola, and while they were getting into it Aschenbach, hiding behind a fountain or the projecting part of a building, would wait till they were a little way from the shore and then do the same. Speaking hurriedly and in an undertone, he would instruct the oarsman, promising him a large tip, to follow that gondola ahead of them that was just turning the corner, to follow it at a discreet distance; and a shiver would run down his spine when the fellow, with the roguish compliance of a pander, would answer him in the same tone, assuring him that he was at his service, entirely at his service.

Thus he glided and swayed gently along, reclining on soft black cushions, shadowing that other black, beaked craft, chained to its pursuit by his infatuation. Sometimes he would lose sight of it and become distressed and anxious, but his steersman, who seemed to be well practiced in commissions of this kind, would always know some cunning maneuver, some side-canal or short cut that would again bring Aschenbach in sight of what he craved. The air was stagnant and malodorous, the sun burned oppressively through the haze that had turned the sky to the color of slate. Water lapped against wood and stone. The gondolier's call, half warning and half greeting, was answered from a distance out of the silent labyrinth, in accordance with some strange convention. Out of little overhead gardens umbelliferous[8] blossoms spilled over and hung down the crumbling masonry, white and purple and almond scented. Moorish windows were mirrored in the murky water. The marble steps of a church dipped below the surface; a beggar squatted on them, protesting his misery, holding out his hat and showing the whites of his eyes as if he were blind; an antiques

---

6. Commercial district.   7. Dionysus, originally an Eastern fertility god, worshiped with wild dances in ecstatic rites.   8. Bearing umbels or flower clusters.

dealer beckoned to them with crawling obsequiousness as they passed his den, inviting them to stop and be swindled. This was Venice, the flattering and suspect beauty—this city, half fairy tale and half tourist trap, in whose insalubrious air the arts once rankly and voluptuously blossomed, where composers have been inspired to lulling tones of somniferous eroticism. Gripped by his adventure, the traveler felt his eyes drinking in this sumptuousness, his ears wooed by these melodies; he remembered, too, that the city was stricken with sickness and concealing it for reasons of cupidity, and he peered around still more wildly in search of the gondola that hovered ahead.

So it was that in his state of distraction he could no longer think of anything or want anything except this ceaseless pursuit of the object that so inflamed him: nothing but to follow him, to dream of him when he was not there, and after the fashion of lovers to address tender words to his mere shadow. Solitariness, the foreign environment, and the joy of an intoxication of feeling that had come to him so late and affected him so profoundly—all this encouraged and persuaded him to indulge himself in the most astonishing ways: as when it had happened that late one evening, returning from Venice and reaching the first floor of the hotel, he had paused outside the boy's bedroom door, leaning his head against the door-frame in a complete drunken ecstasy, and had for a long time been unable to move from the spot, at the risk of being surprised and discovered in this insane situation.

Nevertheless, there were moments at which he paused and half came to his senses. Where is this leading me! he would reflect in consternation at such moments. Where was it leading him! Like any man whose natural merits move him to take an aristocratic interest in his origins, Aschenbach habitually let the achievements and successes of his life remind him of his ancestors, for in imagination he could then feel sure of their approval, of their satisfaction, of the respect they could not have withheld. And he thought of them even here and now, entangled as he was in so impermissible an experience, involved in such exotic extravagances of feeling; he thought, with a sad smile, of their dignified austerity, their decent manliness of character. What would they say? But for that matter, what would they have said about his entire life, a life that had deviated from theirs to the point of degeneracy, this life of his in the compulsive service of art, this life about which he himself, adopting the civic values of his forefathers, had once let fall such mocking observations—and which nevertheless had essentially been so much like theirs! He too had served, he too had been a soldier and a warrior, like many of them: for art was a war, an exhausting struggle, it was hard these days to remain fit for it for long. A life of self-conquest and of defiant resolve, an astringent, steadfast and frugal life which he had turned into the symbol of that heroism for delicate constitutions, that heroism so much in keeping with the times—surely he might call this manly, might call it courageous? And it seemed to him that the kind of love that had taken possession of him did, in a certain way, suit and befit such a life. Had it not been highly honored by the most valiant of peoples, indeed had he not read that in their cities it had flourished by inspiring valorous deeds? Numerous warrior-heroes of olden times had willingly borne its yoke, for there was no kind of abasement that could be reckoned as such if the god had imposed it; and actions that would have been castigated as signs of cowardice had their motives been different, such as falling to the ground in supplication, desperate pleas and slavish demeanor—these were accounted no disgrace to a lover, but rather won him still greater praise.

Such were the thoughts with which love beguiled him, and thus he sought to sustain himself, to preserve his dignity. But at the same time he kept turning his attention, inquisitively and persistently, to the disreputable events that were evolving in the depths of Venice, to that adventure of the outside world which darkly mingled with the adventure of his heart, and which nourished his passion with vague and lawless hopes. Obstinately determined to obtain new and reliable information about the status and progress of the malady, he would sit in the city's coffee houses searching through the German newspapers, which several days ago had disappeared from the reading table in the hotel foyer. They carried assertions and retractions by turns. The number of cases, the number of deaths, was said to be twenty, or forty, or a hundred and more, such reports being immediately followed by statements flatly denying the outbreak of an epidemic, or at least reducing it to a few quite isolated cases brought in from outside the city. Scattered here and there were warning admonitions, or protests against the dangerous policy being pursued by the Italian authorities. There was no certainty to be had.

The solitary traveler was nevertheless conscious of having a special claim to participation in this secret, and although excluded from it, he took a perverse pleasure in putting embarrassing questions to those in possession of the facts, and thus, since they were pledged to silence, forcing them to lie to him directly. One day, at luncheon in the main dining room, he interrogated the hotel manager in this fashion, the soft-footed little man in the French frock coat who was moving around among the tables supervising the meal and greeting the clients, and who also stopped at Aschenbach's table for a few words of conversation. Why, in fact, asked his guest in a casual and nonchalant way, why on earth had they begun recently to disinfect Venice?—"It is merely a police measure, sir," answered the trickster, "taken in good time, as a safeguard against various disagreeable public health problems that might otherwise arise from this sultry and exceptionally warm weather—a precautionary measure which it is their duty to take."—"Very praiseworthy of the police," replied Aschenbach; and after exchanging a few meteorological observations with him the manager took his leave.

On the very same day, in the evening after dinner, it happened that a small group of street singers from the city gave a performance in the front garden of the hotel. They stood by one of the iron arc lamp standards, two men and two women, their faces glinting white in the glare, looking up at the great terrace where the hotel guests sat over their coffee and cooling drinks, resigned to watching this exhibition of folk culture. The hotel staff, the lift boys, waiters, office employees, had come out to listen in the hall doorways. The Russian family, eager to savor every pleasure, had had cane chairs put out for them down in the garden in order to be nearer the performers and were contentedly sitting there in a semicircle. Behind her master and mistress, in a turbanlike headcloth, stood their aged serf.

The beggar virtuosi were playing a mandolin, a guitar, a harmonica and a squeaking fiddle. Instrumental developments alternated with vocal numbers, as when the younger of the women, shrill and squawky of voice, joined the tenor with his sweet falsetto notes in an ardent love duet. But the real talent and leader of the ensemble was quite evidently the other man, the one who had the guitar and was a kind of buffo[9]-baritone character, with hardly any voice but with a mimic gift and remarkable comic verve. Often he would detach himself from the rest of the group and come forward, playing his large instrument and gesticulating, toward the terrace, where his pranks were rewarded with encouraging laughter. The Russians in their parterre seats took special delight in all this southern vivacity, and their plaudits and admiring shouts led him on to ever further and bolder extravagances.

Aschenbach sat by the balustrade, cooling his lips from time to time with the mixture of pomegranate[1] juice and soda water that sparkled ruby-red in the glass before him. His nervous system greedily drank in the jangling tones, for passion paralyzes discrimination and responds in all seriousness to stimuli which the sober sense would either treat with humorous tolerance or impatiently reject. The antics of the mountebank had distorted his features into a rictus-like smile which he was already finding painful. He sat on with a casual air, but inwardly he was utterly engrossed; for six paces from him Tadzio was leaning against the stone parapet.

There he stood, in the white belted suit he occasionally put on for dinner, in a posture of innate and inevitable grace, his left forearm on the parapet, his feet crossed, his right hand on the supporting hip; and he was looking down at the entertainers with an expression that was scarcely a smile, merely one of remote curiosity, a polite observation of the spectacle. Sometimes he straightened himself, stretching his chest, and with an elegant movement of both arms drew his white tunic down through his leather belt. But sometimes, too, and the older man noticed it with a mind-dizzying sense of triumph as well as with terror, he would turn his head hesitantly and cautiously, or even quickly and suddenly as if to gain the advantage of surprise, and look over his left shoulder to where his lover was sitting. Their eyes did not meet, for an ignominious apprehension was forcing the stricken man to keep his looks anxiously in check. Behind them on the terrace sat the women who watched over Tadzio, and at the point things had now reached, the enamored Aschenbach had reason to fear that he had attracted attention and aroused suspicion. Indeed, he had several times, on the beach, in the hotel foyer, and on the Piazza San Marco, been frozen with alarm to notice that Tadzio was being called away if he was near him, that they were taking care to keep them apart— and although his pride writhed in torments it had never known under the appalling insult that this implied, he could not in conscience deny its justice.

---

9. Comic.   1. The pomegranate is a tropical fruit with many seeds, associated both with Persephone, the queen of Hades, and with the world of the dead in Greek mythology.

In the meantime the guitarist had begun a solo to his own accompaniment, a song in many stanzas which was then a popular hit all over Italy, and which he managed to perform in a graphic and dramatic manner, with the rest of his troupe joining regularly in the refrain. He was a lean fellow, thin and cadaverous in the face as well, standing there on the gravel detached from his companions, with a shabby felt hat on the back of his head and a quiff[2] of his red hair bulging out under the brim, in a posture of insolent bravado; strumming and thrumming on his instrument, he tossed his pleasantries up to the terrace in a vivid *parlando*,[3] enacting it all so strenuously that the veins swelled on his forehead. He was quite evidently not of Venetian origin, but rather of the Neapolitan comic type, half pimp, half actor, brutal and bold-faced, dangerous and entertaining. The actual words of his song were merely foolish, but in his presentation, with his grimaces and bodily movements, his way of winking suggestively and lasciviously licking the corner of his mouth, it had something indecent and vaguely offensive about it. Though otherwise dressed in urban fashion he wore a sports shirt, out of the soft collar of which his skinny neck projected, displaying a remarkably large and naked Adam's apple. His pallid snub-nosed face, the features of which gave little clue to his age, seemed to be lined with contortions and vice, and the grinning of his mobile mouth was rather strangely ill-matched to the two deep furrows that stood defiantly, imperiously, almost savagely, between his reddish brows. But what really fixed the solitary Aschenbach's deep attention on him was his observation that this suspect figure seemed to be carrying his own suspect atmosphere about with him as well. For every time the refrain was repeated the singer would perform, with much face-pulling and shaking of his hand as if in greeting, a grotesque march round the scene, which brought him immediately below where Aschenbach sat; and every time this happened a stench of carbolic[4] from his clothes or his body drifted up to the terrace.

Having completed his ballad he began to collect money. He started with the Russians, who were seen to give generously, and then came up the steps. Saucy as his performance had been, up here he was humility itself. Bowing and scraping, he crept from table to table, and a sly obsequious grin bared his prominent teeth, although the two furrows still stood threateningly between his red eyebrows. The spectacle of this alien being gathering in his livelihood was received with curiosity and not a little distaste; one threw coins with the tips of one's fingers into the hat, which one took care not to touch. Removal of the physical distance between the entertainer and decent folk always causes, however great one's pleasure has been, a certain embarrassment. He sensed this, and sought to make amends by cringing. He approached Aschenbach, and with him came the smell, which no one else in the company appeared to have noticed.

"Listen to me!" said the solitary traveler in an undertone and almost mechanically. "Venice is being disinfected. Why?"—The comedian answered hoarsely: "Because of the police! It's the regulations, signore, when it's so hot and when there's sirocco. The sirocco is oppressive. It is

---

2. Bunch.   3. Singing as if speaking (Italian), a musical term.   4. Carbolic acid, a disinfectant.

not good for the health . . ." He spoke in a tone of surprise that such a
question could be asked, and demonstrated with his outspread hand how
oppressive the sirocco was.—"So there is no sickness in Venice?" asked
Aschenbach very softly and between his teeth.—The clown's muscular
features collapsed into a grimace of comic helplessness. "A sickness? But
what sickness? Is the sirocco a sickness? Is our police a sickness perhaps?
The signore is having his little joke! A sickness! Certainly not, signore! A
preventive measure, you must understand, a police precaution against the
effects of the oppressive weather . . ." He gesticulated. "Very well," said
Aschenbach briefly, still without raising his voice, and quickly dropped an
unduly large coin into the fellow's hat. Then he motioned him with his
eyes to clear off. The man obeyed, grinning and bowing low. But he had
not even reached the steps when two hotel servants bore down on him,
and with their faces close to his subjected him to a whispered cross examination. He shrugged, gave assurances, swore that he had been discreet; it
was obvious. Released, he returned to the garden, and after a brief consultation with his colleagues under the arc lamp he came forward once more,
to express his thanks in a parting number.

It was a song that Aschenbach could not remember ever having heard
before; a bold hit in an unintelligible dialect, and having a laughing
refrain in which the rest of the band regularly and loudly joined. At this
point both the words and the instrumental accompaniment stopped, and
nothing remained except a burst of laughter, to some extent rhythmically
ordered but treated with a high degree of naturalism, the soloist in particular showing great talent in his lifelike rendering of it. With artistic distance
restored between himself and the spectators, he had recovered all his
impudence, and the simulated laughter which he shamelessly directed at
the terrace was a laughter of mockery. Even before the end of the articulated part of each stanza he would pretend to be struggling with an irresistible impulse of hilarity. He would sob, his voice would waver, he would
press his hand against his mouth and hunch his shoulders, till at the
proper moment the laughter would burst out of him, exploding in a wild
howl, with such authenticity that it was infectious and communicated
itself to the audience, so that a wave of objectless and merely self-propagat-
ing merriment swept over the terrace as well. And precisely this seemed
to redouble the singer's exuberance. He bent his knees, slapped his thighs,
held his sides, he nearly burst with what was now no longer laughing but
shrieking; he pointed his finger up at the guests, as if that laughing company above him were itself the most comical thing in the world, and in
the end they were all laughing, everyone in the garden and on the verandah, the waiters and the lift boys and the house servants in the doorways.

Aschenbach reclined in his chair no longer, he was sitting bolt upright
as if trying to fend off an attack or flee from it. But the laughter, the
hospital smell drifting toward him, and the nearness of the beautiful boy,
all mingled for him into an immobilizing nightmare, an unbreakable and
inescapable spell that held his mind and senses captive. In the general
commotion and distraction he ventured to steal a glance at Tadzio, and as
he did so he became aware that the boy, returning his glance, had
remained no less serious than himself, just as if he were regulating his

attitude and expression by those of the older man, and as if the general mood had no power over him while Aschenbach kept aloof from it. There was something so disarming and overwhelmingly moving about this child-like submissiveness, so rich in meaning, that the gray-haired lover could only with difficulty restrain himself from burying his face in his hands. He had also had the impression that the way Tadzio from time to time drew himself up with an intake of breath was like a kind of sighing, as if from a constriction of the chest. "He's sickly, he'll probably not live long," he thought again, with that sober objectivity into which the drunken ecstasy of desire sometimes strangely escapes; and his heart was filled at one and the same time with pure concern on the boy's behalf and with a certain wild satisfaction.

In the meantime the troupe of Venetians had finished their perfor-mance and were leaving. Applause accompanied them, and their leader took care to embellish even his exit with comical pranks. His bowing and scraping and hand-kissing amused the company, and so he redoubled them. When his companions were already outside, he put on yet another act of running backward and painfully colliding with a lamppost, then hobbling to the gate apparently doubled up in agony. When he got there however, he suddenly discarded the mask of comic underdog, uncoiled like a spring to his full height, insolently stuck out his tongue at the hotel guests on the terrace and slipped away into the darkness. The company was dispersing; Tadzio had left the balustrade some time ago. But the solitary Aschenbach, to the annoyance of the waiters, sat on and on at his little table over his unfinished pomegranate drink. The night was advanc-ing, time was ebbing away. In his parents' house, many years ago, there had been an hourglass—he suddenly saw that fragile symbolic little instru-ment as clearly as if it were standing before him. Silently, subtly, the rust-red sand trickled through the narrow glass aperture, dwindling away out of the upper vessel, in which a little whirling vortex had formed.

On the very next day, in the afternoon, Aschenbach took a further step in his persistent probing of the outside world, and this time his success was complete. What he did was to enter the British travel agency just off the Piazza San Marco, and after changing some money at the cash desk, he put on the look of a suspicious foreigner and addressed his embar-rassing question to the clerk who had served him. The clerk was a tweed-clad Englishman, still young, with his hair parted in the middle, his eyes close set, and having that sober, honest demeanor which makes so unusual and striking an impression amid the glib knaveries of the south. "No cause for concern, sir," he began. "An administrative measure, nothing serious. They often issue directives of this kind, as a precaution against the unhealthy effects of the heat and the sirocco . . ." But raising his blue eyes he met those of the stranger, which were looking wearily and rather sadly at his lips, with an expression of slight contempt. At this the Englishman colored. "That is," he continued in an undertone and with some feeling, "the official explanation, which the authorities here see fit to stick to. I can tell you that there is rather more to it than that." And then, in his straightforward comfortable language, he told Aschenbach the truth.

For several years now, Asiatic cholera had been showing an increased tendency to spread and migrate. Originating in the sultry morasses of the Ganges delta,[5] rising with the mephitic exhalations of that wilderness of rank useless luxuriance, that primitive island jungle shunned by man, where tigers crouch in the bamboo thickets, the pestilence had raged with unusual and prolonged virulence all over northern India; it had struck eastward into China, westward into Afghanistan and Persia, and following the main caravan routes, it had borne its terrors to Astrakhan and even to Moscow. But while Europe trembled with apprehension that from there the specter might advance and arrive by land, it had been brought by Syrian traders over the sea; it had appeared almost simultaneously in several Mediterranean ports, raising its head in Toulon and Malaga, showing its face repeatedly in Palermo and Naples, and taking a seemingly permanent hold all over Calabria and Apulia.[6] The northern half of the peninsula had still been spared. But in the middle of May this year, in Venice, the dreadful comma-bacilli had been found on one and the same day in the emaciated and blackened corpses of a ship's hand and of a woman who sold greengroceries. The two cases were hushed up. But a week later there were ten, there were twenty and then thirty, and they occurred in different quarters of the city. A man from a small provincial town in Austria who had been taking a few days' holiday in Venice died with unmistakable symptoms after returning home, and that was why the first rumors of a Venetian outbreak had appeared in German newspapers. The city authorities replied with a statement that the public health situation in Venice had never been better, and at the same time adopted the most necessary preventive measures. But the taint had probably now passed into foodstuffs, into vegetables or meat or milk; for despite every denial and concealment, the mortal sickness went on eating its way through the narrow little streets, and with the premature summer heat warming the water in the canals, conditions for the spread of infection were particularly favorable. It even seemed as if the pestilence had undergone a renewal of its energy, as if the tenacity and fertility of its pathogens had redoubled. Cases of recovery were rare; eighty percent of the victims died, and they died in a horrible manner, for the sickness presented itself in an extremely acute form and was frequently of the so-called "dry" type, which is the most dangerous of all. In this condition the body could not even evacuate the massive fluid lost from the blood-vessels. Within a few hours the patient would become dehydrated, his blood would thicken like pitch and he would suffocate with convulsions and hoarse cries. He was lucky if, as sometimes happened, the disease took the form of a slight malaise followed by a deep coma from which one never, or scarcely at all, regained consciousness. By the beginning of June the isolation wards in the Ospedale Civile[7] were quietly filling, the two orphanages were running out of accommodation, and there was a gruesomely brisk traffic between the quayside of the Fondamente Nuove[8] and the cemetery island of San Michele. But fear of general detriment to the city, concern for the recently opened art exhibition in the Public Gardens, consideration of the appall-

5. In India.   6. Astrakhan, Toulon, Malaga, Palermo, and Naples are seaports in Russia, France, Spain, Sicily, and southern Italy, respectively. Calabria and Apulia are regions in southern Italy.   7. City hospital.   8. New foundations (Italian); or new piers.

ing losses which panic and disrepute would inflict on the hotels, on the
shops, on the whole nexus of the tourist trade, proved stronger in Venice
than respect for the truth and for international agreements; it was for this
reason that the city authorities obstinately adhered to their policy of concealment and denial. The city's chief medical officer, a man of high
repute, had resigned from his post in indignation and had been quietly
replaced by a more pliable personality. This had become public knowledge; and such corruption in high places, combined with the prevailing
insecurity, the state of crisis into which the city had been plunged by the
death that walked its streets, led at the lower social levels to a certain
breakdown of moral standards, to an activation of the dark and antisocial
forces, which manifested itself in intemperance, shameless license and
growing criminality. Drunkenness in the evenings became noticeably
more frequent; thieves and ruffians, it was said, were making the streets
unsafe at night; there were repeated robberies and even murders, for it
had already twice come to light that persons alleged to have died of the
plague had in fact been poisoned by their own relatives; and commercial
vice now took on obtrusive and extravagant forms which had hitherto been
unknown in this area and indigenous only to southern Italy or eastern
countries.

The Englishman's narrative conveyed the substance of all this to
Aschenbach. "You would be well advised, sir," he concluded, "to leave
today rather than tomorrow. The imposition of quarantine can be
expected any day now."—"Thank you," said Aschenbach, and left the
office.

The Piazza was sunless and sultry. Unsuspecting foreigners were sitting
at the cafés, or standing in front of the church with pigeons completely
enveloping them, watching the birds swarm and beat their wings and push
each other out of the way as they snatched with their beaks at the hollow
hands offering them grains of maize. Feverish with excitement, triumphant in his possession of the truth, yet with a taste of disgust on his tongue
and a fantastic horror in his heart, the solitary traveler paced up and down
the flagstones of the magnificent precinct. He was considering a decent
action which would cleanse his conscience. Tonight, after dinner, he
might approach the lady in the pearls and address her with words which
he now mentally rehearsed: "Madam, allow me as a complete stranger to
do you a service, to warn you of something which is being concealed from
you for reasons of self-interest. Leave here at once with Tadzio and your
daughters! Venice is plague-stricken." He might then lay his hand in farewell on the head of a mocking deity's instrument, turn away and flee from
this quagmire. But at the same time he sensed an infinite distance
between himself and any serious resolve to take such a step. It would lead
him back to where he had been, give him back to himself again; but to
one who is beside himself, no prospect is so distasteful as that of self-
recovery. He remembered a white building adorned with inscriptions that
glinted in the evening light, suffused with mystic meaning in which his
mind had wandered; remembered then that strange itinerant figure who
had wakened in him, in his middle age, a young man's longing to rove to

far-off and strange places; and the thought of returning home, of level-headedness and sobriety, of toil and mastery, filled him with such repugnance that his face twisted into an expression of physical nausea. "They want it kept quiet!" he whispered vehemently. And: "I shall say nothing!" The consciousness of his complicity in the secret, of his share in the guilt, intoxicated him as small quantities of wine intoxicate a weary brain. The image of the stricken and disordered city, hovering wildly before his mind's eye, inflamed him with hopes that were beyond comprehension, beyond reason and full of monstrous sweetness. What, compared with such expectations, was that tender happiness of which he had briefly dreamed a few moments ago? What could art and virtue mean to him now, when he might reap the advantages of chaos? He said nothing, and stayed on.

That night he had a terrible dream, if dream is the right word for a bodily and mental experience which did indeed overtake him during deepest sleep, in complete independence of his will and with complete sensuous vividness, but with no perception of himself as present and moving about in any space external to the events themselves; rather, the scene of the events was his own soul, and they irrupted into it from outside, violently defeating his resistance—a profound, intellectual resistance—as they passed through him, and leaving his whole being, the culture of a lifetime, devastated and destroyed.

It began with fear, fear and joy and a horrified curiosity about what was to come. It was night, and his senses were alert; for from far off a hubbub was approaching, an uproar, a compendium of noise, a clangor and blare and dull thundering, yells of exultation and a particular howl with a long-drawn-out *u* at the end—all of it permeated and dominated by a terrible sweet sound of flute music: by deep-warbling, infamously persistent, shamelessly clinging tones that bewitched the innermost heart. Yet he was aware of a word, an obscure word, but one that gave a name to what was coming: *"the stranger-god!"*[9] There was a glow of smoky fire: in it he could see a mountain landscape, like the mountains round his summer home. And in fragmented light, from wooded heights, between tree trunks and mossy boulders, it came tumbling and whirling down: a human and animal swarm, a raging rout, flooding the slope with bodies, with flames, with tumult and frenzied dancing. Women, stumbling on the hide garments that fell too far about them from the waist, held up tambourines and moaned as they shook them above their thrown-back heads; they swung blazing torches, scattering the sparks, and brandished naked daggers; they carried snakes with flickering tongues which they had seized in the middle of the body, or they bore up their own breasts in both hands, shrieking as they did so. Men with horns over their brows, hairy-skinned and girdled with pelts, bowed their necks and threw up their arms and thighs, clanging brazen cymbals and beating a furious tattoo on drums, while smooth-skinned boys prodded goats with leafy staves, clinging to their horns and

9. Dionysus (also Bacchus), whose cult was brought to Greece from Thrace and Phrygia. The dream describes the orgiastic rites of his worship.

yelling with delight as the leaping beasts dragged them along. And the god's enthusiasts howled out the cry with the soft consonants and long-drawn-out final *u*, sweet and wild both at once, like no cry that was ever heard: here it was raised, belled out into the air as by rutting stags, and there they threw it back with many voices, in ribald triumph, urging each other on with it to dancing and tossing of limbs, and never did it cease. But the deep, enticing flute music mingled irresistibly with everything. Was it not also enticing him, the dreamer who experienced all this while struggling not to, enticing him with shameless insistence to the feast and frenzy of the uttermost surrender? Great was his loathing, great his fear, honorable his effort of will to defend to the last what was his and protect it against the Stranger, against the enemy of the composed and dignified intellect. But the noise, the howling grew louder, with the echoing cliffs reiterating it: it increased beyond measure, swelled up to an enrapturing madness. Odors besieged the mind, the pungent reek of the goats, the scent of panting bodies and an exhalation as of staling water, with another smell, too, that was familiar: that of wounds and wandering disease. His heart throbbed to the drumbeats, his brain whirled, a fury seized him, a blindness, a dizzying lust, and his soul craved to join the round-dance of the god. The obscene symbol,[1] wooden and gigantic, was uncovered and raised on high: and still more unbridled grew the howling of the rallying-cry. With foaming mouths they raged, they roused each other with lewd gestures and licentious hands, laughing and moaning they thrust the prods into each other's flesh and licked the blood from each other's limbs. But the dreamer now was with them and in them, he belonged to the Stranger-God. Yes, they were himself as they flung themselves, tearing and slaying, on the animals and devoured steaming gobbets of flesh, they were himself an orgy of limitless coupling, in homage to the god, began on the trampled, mossy ground. And his very soul savored the lascivious delirium of annihilation.

Out of this dream the stricken man woke unnerved, shattered and powerlessly enslaved to the daemon-god. He no longer feared the observant eyes of other people; whether he was exposing himself to their suspicions he no longer cared. In any case they were running away, leaving Venice; many of the bathing cabins were empty now, there were great gaps in the clientele at dinner, and in the city one scarcely saw any foreigners. The truth seemed to have leaked out, and however tightly the interested parties closed ranks, panic could no longer be stemmed. But the lady in the pearls stayed on with her family, either because the rumors were not reaching her or because she was too proud and fearless to heed them. Tadzio stayed on; and to Aschenbach, in his beleaguered state, it sometimes seemed that all these unwanted people all around him might flee from the place or die, that every living being might disappear and leave him alone on this island with the beautiful boy—indeed, as he sat every morning by the sea with his gaze resting heavily, recklessly, incessantly on the object of his desire, or as he continued his undignified pursuit of him in the evenings along streets in which the disgusting mortal malady wound its under-

1. The phallus.

ground way, then indeed monstrous things seemed full of promise to him, and the moral law no longer valid.

Like any other lover, he desired to please and bitterly dreaded that he might fail to do so. He added brightening and rejuvenating touches to his clothes, he wore jewelry and used scent, he devoted long sessions to his toilet several times a day, arriving at table elaborately attired and full of excited expectation. As he beheld the sweet youthful creature who had so entranced him he felt disgust at his own aging body, the sight of his gray hair and sharp features filled him with a sense of shame and hopelessness. He felt a compulsive need to refresh and restore himself physically; he paid frequent visits to the hotel barber.

Cloaked in a hairdressing gown, leaning back in the chair as the chatterer's hands tended him, he stared in dismay at his reflection in the looking glass.

"Gray," he remarked with a wry grimace.

"A little," the man replied. "And the reason? A slight neglect, a slight lack of interest in outward appearances, very understandable in persons of distinction, but not altogether to be commended, especially as one would expect those very persons to be free from prejudice about such matters as the natural and the artificial. If certain people who profess moral disapproval of cosmetics were to be logical enough to extend such rigorous principles to their teeth, the result would be rather disgusting. After all, we are only as old as we feel in our minds and hearts, and sometimes gray hair is actually further from the truth than the despised corrective would be. In your case, signore, one has a right to the natural color of one's hair. Will you permit me simply to give your color back to you?"

"How so?" asked Aschenbach.

Whereupon the eloquent tempter washed his client's hair in two kinds of water, one clear and one dark; and his hair was as black as when he had been young. Then he folded it into soft waves with the curling tongs, stepped back and surveyed his handiwork.

"Now the only other thing," he said, "would be just to freshen up the signore's complexion a little."

And like a craftsman unable to finish, unable to satisfy himself, he passed busily and indefatigably from one procedure to another. Aschenbach, reclining comfortably, incapable of resistance, filled rather with exciting hopes by what was happening, gazed at the glass and saw his eyebrows arched more clearly and evenly, the shape of his eyes lengthened, their brightness enhanced by a slight underlining of the lids; saw below them a delicate carmine come to life as it was softly applied to skin that had been brown and leathery; saw his lips that had just been so pallid now burgeoning cherry-red; saw the furrows on his cheeks, round his mouth, the wrinkles by his eyes, all vanishing under face cream and an aura of youth—with beating heart he saw himself as a young man in his earliest bloom. The cosmetician finally declared himself satisfied, with the groveling politeness usual in such people, by profusely thanking the client he had served. "An insignificant adjustment, signore," he said as he gave a final helping hand to Aschenbach's outward appearance. "Now the signore can fall in love as soon as he pleases." And the spellbound lover departed, confused and timorous but happy as in a dream. His necktie was scarlet, his broad-brimmed straw hat encircled with a many-colored ribbon.

A warm gale had blown up; it rained little and lightly, but the air was humid and thick and filled with smells of decay. The ear was beset with fluttering, flapping and whistling noises, and to the fevered devotee, sweating under his makeup, it seemed that a vile race of wind demons was disporting itself in the sky, malignant sea birds that churn up and gnaw and befoul a condemned man's food.[2] For the sultry weather was taking away his appetite, and he could not put aside the thought that what he ate might be tainted with infection.

One afternoon, dogging Tadzio's footsteps, Aschenbach had plunged into the confused network of streets in the depths of the sick city. Quite losing his bearings in this labyrinth of alleys, narrow waterways, bridges and little squares that all looked so much like each other, not sure now even of the points of the compass, he was intent above all on not losing sight of the vision he so passionately pursued. Ignominious caution forced him to flatten himself against walls and hide behind the backs of people walking in front of him; and for a long time he was not conscious of the weariness, the exhaustion that emotion and constant tension had inflicted on his body and mind. Tadzio walked behind his family; he usually gave precedence in narrow passages to his attendant and his nunlike sisters, and as he strolled along by himself he sometimes turned his head and glanced over his shoulder with his strange twilight-gray eyes, to ascertain that his lover was still following him. He saw him, and did not give him away. Drunk with excitement as he realized this, lured onward by those eyes, helpless in the leading strings of his mad desire, the infatuated Aschenbach stole upon the trail of his unseemly hope—only to find it vanish from his sight in the end. The Poles had crossed a little humpbacked bridge; the height of the arch hid them from their pursuer, and when in his turn he reached the top of it, they were no longer to be seen. He looked frantically for them in three directions, straight ahead and to left and right along the narrow, dirty canal-side, but in vain. Unnerved and weakened, he was compelled to abandon his search.

His head was burning, his body was covered with sticky sweat, his neck quivered, a no longer endurable thirst tormented him; he looked round for something, no matter what, that would instantly relieve it. At a little greengrocer's shop he bought some fruit, some overripe soft strawberries, and ate some of them as he walked. A little square, one that seemed to have been abandoned, to have been put under a spell, opened up in front of him: he recognized it, he had been here, it was where he had made that vain decision weeks ago to leave Venice. On the steps of the well in its center he sank down and leaned his head against the stone rim. The place was silent, grass grew between the cobblestones, garbage was lying about. Among the dilapidated houses of uneven height all round him there was one that looked like a *palazzo*, with Gothic windows that now

---

2. "Harpies: hideously thin, they flew swiftly in, fell with insatiable greed on whatever food was there, ate without being satisfied, and *befouled* whatever they left with their filth" [Mann's note]. See Virgil's *Aeneid* III.210–62.

had nothing behind them, and little lion balconies. On the ground floor of another there was a chemist's shop. From time to time warm gusts of wind blew the stench of carbolic across to him.

There he sat, the master, the artist who had achieved dignity, the author of A *Study in Abjection,* he who in such paradigmatically pure form had repudiated intellectual vagrancy and the murky depths, who had proclaimed his renunciation of all sympathy with the abyss, who had weighed vileness in the balance and found it wanting; he who had risen so high, who had set his face against his own sophistication, grown out of all his irony, and taken on the commitments of one whom the public trusted; he, whose fame was official, whose name had been ennobled, and on whose style young boys were taught to model themselves—there he sat, with his eyelids closed, with only an occasional mocking and rueful sideways glance from under them which he hid again at once; and his drooping, cosmetically brightened lips shaped the occasional word of the discourse his brain was delivering, his half-asleep brain with its tissue of strange dream-logic.[3]

"For Beauty, Phaedrus, mark well! only Beauty is at one and the same time divine and visible, and so it is indeed the sensuous lover's path, little Phaedrus, it is the artist's path to the spirit. But do you believe, dear boy, that the man whose path to the spiritual passes through the senses can ever achieve wisdom and true manly dignity? Or do you think rather (I leave it to you to decide) that this is a path of dangerous charm, very much an errant and sinful path which must of necessity lead us astray? For I must tell you that we artists cannot tread the path of Beauty without Eros keeping company with us and appointing himself as our guide; yes, though we may be heroes in our fashion and disciplined warriors, yet we are like women, for it is passion that exalts us, and the longing of our soul must remain the longing of a lover—that is our joy and our shame. Do you see now perhaps why we writers can be neither wise nor dignified? That we necessarily go astray, necessarily remain dissolute emotional adventurers? The magisterial poise of our style is a lie and a farce, our fame and social position are an absurdity, the public's faith in us is altogether ridiculous, the use of art to educate the nation and its youth is a reprehensible undertaking which should be forbidden by law. For how can one be fit to be an educator when one has been born with an incorrigible and natural tendency toward the abyss? We try to achieve dignity by repudiating that abyss, but whichever way we turn we are subject to its allurement. We renounce, let us say, the corrosive process of knowledge—for knowledge, Phaedrus, has neither dignity nor rigor: it is all insight and understanding and tolerance, uncontrolled and formless; it sympathizes with the abyss, it *is* the abyss. And so we reject it resolutely, and henceforth our pursuit is of Beauty alone, of Beauty which is simplicity, which is grandeur and a new kind of rigor and a second naiveté, of Beauty which is Form. But form and naiveté, Phaedrus, lead to intoxication and lust; they may lead a noble mind into terrible criminal emotions, which his own fine

---

3. Aschenbach adopts the role of Socrates in Plato's *Phaedrus* to examine the role of the artist; the Platonic dialogue, however, is not concerned with the artist but rather with moral choices and absolute beauty.

rigor condemns as infamous; they lead, they too lead, to the abyss. I tell you, that is where they lead us writers; for we are not capable of self-exaltation, we are capable only of self-debauchery. And now I shall go, Phaedrus, and you shall stay here; and leave this place only when you no longer see me."

A few days later Gustav von Aschenbach, who had been feeling unwell, left the Hotel des Bains at a later morning hour than usual. He was being attacked by waves of dizziness, only half physical, and with them went an increasing sense of dread, a feeling of hopelessness and pointlessness, though he could not decide whether this referred to the external world or to his personal existence. In the foyer he saw a large quantity of luggage standing ready for dispatch, asked one of the doormen which guests were leaving, and was given in reply the aristocratic Polish name which he had inwardly been expecting to hear. As he received the information there was no change in his ravaged features, only that slight lift of the head with which one casually notes something one did not need to know. He merely added the question: "When?" and was told: "After lunch." He nodded and went down to the sea.

It was a bleak spectacle there. Tremors gusted outward across the water between the beach and the first long sandbar, wrinkling its wide flat surface. An autumnal, out-of-season air seemed to hang over the once so colorful and populous resort, now almost deserted, with litter left lying about on the sand. An apparently abandoned camera stood on its tripod at the edge of the sea, and the black cloth over it fluttered and flapped in the freshening breeze.

Tadzio, with the three or four playmates he still had, was walking about on the right in front of his family's bathing cabin; and reclining in his deck chair with a rug over his knees, about midway between the sea and the row of cabins, Aschenbach once more sat watching him. The boys' play was unsupervised, as the women were probably busy with travel preparations; it seemed to be unruly and degenerating into roughness. The sturdy boy he had noticed before, the one in the belted suit with glossy black hair who was addressed as "Jashu," had been angered and blinded by some sand thrown into his face: he forced Tadzio to a wrestling match, which soon ended in the downfall of the less muscular beauty. But as if in this hour of leave-taking the submissiveness of the lesser partner had been transformed into cruel brutality, as if he were now bent on revenge for his long servitude, the victor did not release his defeated friend even then, but knelt on his back and pressed his face into the sand so hard and so long that Tadzio, breathless from the fight in any case, seemed to be on the point of suffocation. His attempts to shake off the weight of his tormentor were convulsive; they stopped altogether for moments on end and became a mere repeated twitching. Appalled, Aschenbach was about to spring to the rescue when the bully finally released his victim. Tadzio, very pale, sat up and went on sitting motionless for some minutes, propped on one arm, his hair tousled and his eyes darkening. Then he stood right up and walked slowly away. His friends called to him, laughingly at first, then anxiously and pleadingly; he took no notice. The dark-haired boy, who had no doubt been seized at once by remorse at having gone so far, ran after him and tried to make up the quarrel. A jerk of Tadzio's shoulder rejected him. Tadzio walked on at an angle down to the water. He was barefooted and wearing his striped linen costume with the red bow.

At the edge of the sea he lingered, head bowed, drawing figures in the wet sand with the point of one foot, then walked into the shallow high water, which at its deepest point did not even wet his knees; he waded through it, advancing easily, and reached the sandbar. There he stood for a moment looking out into the distance and then, moving left, began slowly to pace the length of this narrow strip of unsubmerged land. Divided from the shore by a width of water, divided from his companions by proud caprice, he walked, a quite isolated and unrelated apparition, walked with floating hair out there in the sea, in the wind, in front of the nebulous vastness. Once more he stopped to survey the scene. And suddenly, as if prompted by a memory, by an impulse, he turned at the waist, one hand on his hip, with an enchanting twist of the body, and looked back over his shoulder at the beach. There the watcher sat, as he had sat once before when those twilight-gray eyes, looking back at him then from that other threshold, had for the first time met him. Resting his head on the back of his chair, he had slowly turned it to follow the movements of the walking figure in the distance; now he lifted it toward this last look; then it sank down on his breast, so that his eyes stared up from below, while his face wore the inert, deep-sunken expression of profound slumber. But to him it was as if the pale and lovely soul-summoner[4] out there were smiling to him, beckoning to him; as if he loosed his hand from his hip and pointed outward, hovering ahead and onward, into an immensity rich with unutterable expectation. And as so often, he set out to follow him.

Minutes passed, after he had collapsed sideways in his chair, before anyone hurried to his assistance. He was carried to his room. And later that same day the world was respectfully shocked to receive the news of his death.

---

4. "*Mercury* was charged with leading souls to the Underworld and was therefore called leader of souls and guide of souls" [Mann's note]. Mercury is the Roman name for the Greek god Hermes.

RAINER MARIA RILKE
1875–1926

Rainer Maria Rilke's intensely personal search to understand the "great mysteries" of the universe asks questions that are ordinarily called religious. Whether his gaze is turned toward the objects and creatures of earth, which he describes with extraordinary clarity and affection, or toward a higher intuited realm whose enigma remains to be deciphered, he seeks throughout a comprehensive vision of cosmic unity. Like the existentialists after him, Rilke is haunted by the baffling incompleteness of human experience, by the passage of time, and by a need to situate himself inside some framework of reality. His response is to turn to art—

like the Symbolists—to reconcile the various dimensions of experience. When objects are represented artistically, they are drawn into a "human" world: they are infused with ideas, emotions and value. The poet's role, according to Rilke, is to observe with a fresh sensitivity "this fleeting world, which in some strange way / keeps calling to us," and to bear witness, through language, to the transfiguration of its materiality in and by human emotions. Rilke's sharply focused yet visionary lyricism has made him the best-known and most influential German poet of the twentieth century.

Born in Prague on December 4, 1875, to German-speaking parents who separated when he was nine, Rilke had an unhappy childhood that included being dressed as a girl when he was young (thus his mother compensated for the earlier loss of a baby daughter) and being sent to military academies, where he was lonely and miserable, from 1886 to 1891. Illness caused his departure from the second academy and, after a year in business school, he worked in his uncle's law firm and studied at the University of Prague. Rilke hoped to persuade his family that he should devote himself to a literary career rather than business or law, and energetically wrote poetry (*Sacrifice to the Lares*, 1895, *Crowned by Dream*, 1896), plays, stories, and reviews. Moving to Munich in 1897, he met and fell in love with a fascinating and cultured older woman, Lou Andreas-Salomé, who would be a constant influence on him throughout his life. He accompanied Andreas-Salomé and her husband to Russia in 1899, where he met Leo Tolstoy and the painter Leonid Pasternak and—fascinated with Russian mysticism and the Russian landscape—wrote most of the poems later published as *The Book of Hours: The Book of Monastic Life* (1905) as well as a Romantic verse tale that became extremely popular, *The Tale of Love and Death of Cornet Christoph Rilke* (1906). After a second trip to Russia, Rilke spent some time at an artists' colony called Worpswede where he met his future wife, the sculptor Clara Westhoff. They were married in March 1901 and settled in a cottage near the colony where Rilke wrote the second part of *The Book of Hours: The Book of Pilgrimage*. He and Clara separated in the following year, and Rilke moved to Paris where he embarked on a study of the French sculptor Auguste Rodin (1903).

Unhappy in Paris, where he felt lonely and isolated, he fled to Italy in 1903 to write the last section of *The Book of Hours: The Book of Poverty and Death*. Nonetheless, he had found in Paris a new kind of literary and artistic inspiration. He read French writers and especially Baudelaire, whose minutely realistic but strangely beautiful description of a rotting corpse (*A Carcass*) initiated, he felt, "the entire development toward objective expression, which we now recognize in Cézanne." In Rodin, too, he recognized a workmanlike dedication to the technical demands of his craft, an intense concentration on visible, tangible objects, and above all, a belief in art as an essentially religious activity. Although he wrote in distress to his friend Andreas-Salomé, complaining of nightmares and a sense of failure, it is at this time (and with her encouragement) that Rilke began his major work. The anguished, semiautobiographical spiritual confessions of *The Notebooks of Malte Laurids Brigge* (1910) date to this period, as do a series of *New Poems* (1907–08) in which he abandoned his earlier, impressionistic and Romantic style and developed a more intense Symbolic vision focused on objects. The *New Poems* emphasized physical reality, the absolute otherness and "thing-like" nature of what was observed—be it fountain, panther, flower, human being, or the *Archaic Torso of Apollo* printed here. "Thing-poems" (*Dinggedichte*), in fact, is a term often used to describe Rilke's writing at this time, with its open emphasis on material description. In a letter to Andreas-Salomé, he described the way that ancient art objects took on a peculiar luster once they were detached from history and seen as "things" in and for themselves: "No subject matter is attached to them, no irrelevant voice interrupts the silence of their concentrated reality . . . no history casts a shadow over their naked clarity—: they *are*. That is all . . . one day one of them reveals itself to you, and shines like a first star."

Such "things" are not dead or inanimate but supremely alive, filled with a strange vitality before the poet's glance: the charged sexuality of the marble torso, the metamorphosis of the Spanish dance in which the dancer's flamelike dress "becomes a furnace / from which, like startled rattlesnakes, the long / naked arms uncoil, aroused and clicking" (*Spanish Dancer*), or the caged panther's circling "like a ritual dance around a center / in which a mighty will stands paralyzed" (*The Panther*). If things are not dead, neither is death unambiguous: when Rilke retells the ancient myth of Orpheus and his lost wife, Eurydice, the dead woman is seen as achieving a new and fuller existence in the underworld. "Deep within herself. Being dead / filled her beyond fulfillment. . . . She was already loosened like long hair, / poured out like fallen rain, / shared like a limitless supply. / She was already root." Themes of the interpenetration of life and death, the visible and invisible world, and creativity itself are taken up in Rilke's next major work, the sequence of ten elegies (mournful lyric poems, usually laments for loss, and generally of medium length) called the *Duino Elegies* (1923) which he was to begin in 1912 while spending the winter in Duino Castle near Trieste.

The composition of the *Duino Elegies* came in two bursts of inspiration separated by ten years. Despite Rilke's increasing reputation and the popularity of his earlier work, he felt frustrated and unhappy. It was not that he lacked friends or activity; back in Paris once more, he corresponded actively and traveled widely, visiting Italy, Flanders, Germany, Austria, Egypt, and Algeria. But social pressures and everyday anxieties kept him overly occupied, and when a patroness, Princess Marie von Thurn und Taxis-Hohenlohe, proposed that he stay by himself in her castle at Duino during the winter of 1911–12, he was delighted. "The necessity to be alone, alone for a long time, builds stronger in me every day. . . . People (whether it be my fault or theirs) wear me out." The story has been told many times of how Rilke, walking on the rocks above the sea and puzzling over how to answer a bothersome business letter that had just arrived, seemed to hear in the roar of the wind the first lines of his elegies: "Who, if I cried out, would hear me among the angels' / hierarchies?" By February he had written the first and second elegies, and when he left Duino Castle in May he had conceived the whole cycle and written fragments of the third, sixth, ninth, and tenth.

Completion did not come easily in the following years, with the advent of World War I. After writing the third Duino elegy in Paris in 1913, Rilke left for Munich— never dreaming that his apartment and personal property would soon be confiscated as that of an enemy alien. In April 1915, everything was sold at public auction; that summer, Duino Castle was bombarded and reduced to ruins. Rilke wrote the somber fourth elegy in Munich on November 22 and 23, and the next day was called up for the draft. Three weeks later, he was a clerk in the War Archives Office in Vienna where he drew precise vertical and horizontal lines on paper until June 1916, when the intercession of friends released him from military service. Rilke composed little after this experience and feared that he would never be able to complete the Duino sequence. In 1922, however, a friend's purchase of the tiny Château de Muzot in Switzerland gave him a peaceful place to retire and write. He not only completed the *Duino Elegies* in Muzot, but wrote in addition— as a memorial for the young daughter of a friend—a two-part sequence of fifty-five sonnets, the *Sonnets to Orpheus* (1923).

With the *Duino Elegies* and the *Sonnets to Orpheus*, Rilke's last great works were complete. The melancholy philosophic vision of the early elegies describes an Angel of absolute reality, whose self-contained perfection is terrifyingly separate from mortal concerns. In the later elegies and the *Sonnets*, the idea of Angelic perfection is balanced by a newly important human role for the human artist, who serves as a bridge between the worlds of earth and of the Angel. To the poet's initial sense of helplessness and alienation, the later poems respond that all creatures need the artist's transforming glance in order to reach full being. If the Angel is "that creature in whom the transformation of the visible into the invisible . . . already appears in its completion . . . who guarantees the recognition of a higher level of reality in the invisible," then also the artist has the mission of bringing about this transformation. "It is our task to imprint this temporary, perishable earth into ourselves so deeply, so painfully and passionately, that its essence can rise again, 'invisibly,' inside us. We are the bees of the invisible. We wildly collect the honey of the visible, to store it in the great golden hive of the invisible." *Elegies* and the *Sonnets* together move toward a more positive celebration of simple Things. A sequence of symbolic figures suggests this development from uncertainty to affirmation, as the dominant Angel of the *Elegies* gives way to the human poet Orpheus, who in turn retires into the background of the later *Sonnets* before Eurydice, the woman whose passing into the realm of the dead brings her fuller being. With this major affirmation of the essential unity of life and death, Rilke closed his two complementary sequences ("the little rust-colored sail of the Sonnets and the Elegies' gigantic white canvas") and wrote little—chiefly poems in French—over the next few years. Increasingly ill with leukemia, he died on December 29, 1926, as the result of a sudden infection after pricking himself on roses he cut for a friend in his garden.

Despite their differences of length and style, the *Archaic Torso of Apollo* and the first and ninth Duino elegies are all concerned with the contrast of Angelic perfection and flawed human existence. Art is the key in each case, although what the poet feels intuitively in the first poem remains to be analyzed and affirmed in the latter two. The *Archaic Torso of Apollo* is written in Petrarchan sonnet form, and takes as its point of departure a fifth-century B.C. Greek sculpture on display in the Louvre Museum in Paris. This headless marble torso is only a "thing": it should strike us as a lifeless, even defaced chunk of stone. Yet such is the perfection of its luminous sensuality—descended, the speaker suggests, from the brilliant gaze of its missing head and "ripening" eyes—that it seems impossibly alive, and an inner radiance bursts starlike from the marble. The *human* perfection of this marble torso, a perfection achieved through artistic vision, challenges and puts to shame the observer's own puny existence. Nor is there any place to escape from the lesson, once it is recognized; instead, "You must change your life."

The ten *Duino Elegies* also explore the same ambiguous relationship of life and art but in a more extended narrative style; they take up in addition one of Rilke's favorite themes, the complex tension between life and death in which human beings often appear puppets on a falsely real stage, ephemeral beings whose greatest achievements are finally reduced to nothing. The first and ninth elegies have a special corresponding relationship inside the overall sequence. To the question phrased desperately in the first: "Whom can we ever turn to / in our need?" the ninth elegy responds that we must turn to ourselves, and to the artist's ability to comprehend and transmute the objects of this earth. In the first elegy, human alienation and distress are evident even to the beasts who, more attuned to nature, know that human beings are "not really at home" in the world. The poet himself fails to notice the simplest things as they call out for recognition—a star, a wave, or the sound of a violin—because he yearns for purer existence. Yet he too cannot attain the ideal: reaching out for perfect love, his arms embrace only emptiness. If there is an ideal essence of human qualities, he realizes, it is lifted above earthly ties: heroes survive in their reputation, and the purest love is a "soaring, objectless love" that does not depend on being answered, and recognizes that there is no permanence on earth—"no place where we can remain." Rilke's characteristic examples of an idealized human essence are women, unrequited love, and those dying young: "What speaks to me of humanity," he wrote, "is the phenomenon of those have died young and, even more absolutely, purely, inexhaustibly: *the woman in love.*" To these he gives his entire sympathy and he evokes, at the end of the first elegy, the gentle surprise of the newly dead for whom "it is strange to inhabit the earth no longer, to give up customs one barely had time to learn. . . ." Rilke celebrates the passage into eternity of these crucially "human" lives, and suggests that the celebration itself is important because it provides a nourishing myth for the living, who are otherwise overwhelmed by their sense of mortal loss. Such is the role of art: when the poet assumes the all-embracing perspective of angelic vision his lament (like the ancient dirge for Linus) transcends grief by filling the Void with unexpected and comforting harmony.

The ninth elegy begins by stressing the peculiar paradox of the human condition: why, being mortal, do we not live serenely and happily as part of the natural world—like the laurel leaf? Why is it "human" to long for some further destiny? The response, as in the first elegy, involves art; but whereas earlier it was the poet's special mission to give profundity to human lives, here he responds to a universal need. "Everything here / apparently needs us . . . . Us, the most fleeting of all." The unsayable reality of the Angel is not the reality of earth, and the poet's human magic resides in finding some "pure word" that names things in their essence, says them "*more* intensely than the Things themselves / ever dreamed of existing." Such a poet presents earthly things to the unearthly Angel in a way the latter, astonished, can never know. Ultimately, Rilke is celebrating the power of human creativity: like the rope maker in Rome, or the potter along the Nile, he observes reality and creates from it a new form, a new being. For the poet, however, it is a process of making the visible angelically "invisible," and a bridge between two worlds; he "delivers" things by absorbing them into his imagination's inner dimension. "Earth, isn't this what you want: to arise within us, / *invisible?*" Rilke's poetic journey, in the *Elegies* as in the *Sonnets to Orpheus*, was an inward journey that preserved what was most alive and valuable in human existence by subjecting it to the transfiguring perspective of art.

J. F. Hendry, *The Sacred Threshold: A Life of Rainer Maria Rilke* (1983), is a brief and readable biography with numerous citations from Rilke's letters and work. Heinz F. Peters, *Rainer Maria Rilke: Masks and the Man* (1977), is a biographical and thematic study of Rilke's work and influence. Romano Guardini, *Rilke's Duino Elegies* (1961), examines the elegies. Donald Prater, *A Ringing Glass: The Life of Rainer Maria Rilke* (1986), is an excellent account of the poet's life and the conditions in which his work developed and includes extensive quotations from many unpublished letters.

PRONOUNCING GLOSSARY

The following list uses common English syllables and stress accents to provide rough equivalents of selected words whose pronunciation may be unfamiliar to the general reader.

Dinggedichte: *ding'-ge-dikh-tuh*

Duino: *doo-ee'-noh*

Muzot: *moo-tsot'*

Archaic Torso of Apollo[1]

We cannot know his legendary head[2]
with eyes like ripening fruit. And yet his torso
is still suffused with brilliance from inside,
like a lamp, in which his gaze, now turned to low,

gleams in all its power. Otherwise   5
the curved breast could not dazzle you so, nor could
a smile run through the placid hips and thighs
to that dark center where procreation flared.

Otherwise this stone would seem defaced
beneath the translucent cascade of the shoulders   10
and would not glisten like a wild beast's fur:

would not, from all the borders of itself,
burst like a star: for here there is no place
that does not see you. You must change your life.

Archaïscher Torso Apollos

Wir kannten nicht sein unerhörtes Haupt,
darin die Augenäpfel reiften. Aber
sein Torso glüht noch wie ein Kandelaber,
in dem sein Schauen, nur zurückgeschraubt,

sich hält und glänzt. Sonst könnte nicht der Bug   5
der Brust dich blenden, und im leisen Drehen
der Lenden könnte nicht ein Lächeln gehen
zu jener Mitte, die die Zeugung trug.

Sonst stünde dieser Stein entstellt und kurz
unter der Schultern durchsichtigem Sturz   10
und flimmerte nicht so wie Raubtierfelle;

und bräche nicht aus allen seinen Rändern
aus wie ein Stern: denn da ist keine Stelle,
die dich nicht sieht. Du mußt dein Leben ändern.

Duino Elegies

The First Elegy

Who, if I cried out, would hear me among the angels'[1]
hierarchies? and even if one of them pressed me

---

1. All selections translated by Stephen Mitchell. The first poem in the second volume of Rilke's *New Poems* (1908), which were dedicated "to my good friend, Auguste Rodin" (the French sculptor, 1840–1917, whose secretary Rilke was for a brief period and on whom he wrote two monographs, in 1903 and 1907). The poem itself was inspired by an ancient Greek statue discovered at Miletus (a Greek colony on the coast of Asia Minor) that was called simply the *Torso of a Youth from Miletus*; since the god Apollo was an ideal of youthful male beauty, his name was often associated with such statues.   2. In a torso, the head and limbs are missing.   1. "The 'angel' of the Elegies has nothing to do with the angel of the Christian heaven. . . . The angel of the Elegies is that being which stands for the idea of recognizing a higher order of reality in invisibility" [Rilke: Letter to his Polish translator Witold Hulewicz, November 13, 1925].

suddenly against his heart: I would be consumed
in that overwhelming existence. For beauty is nothing
but the beginning of terror, which we still are just able to endure,   5
and we are so awed because it serenely disdains
to annihilate us. Every angel is terrifying.
    And so I hold myself back and swallow the call-note
of my dark sobbing. Ah, whom can we ever turn to
in our need? Not angels, not humans,   10
and already the knowing animals are aware
that we are not really at home in
our interpreted[2] world. Perhaps there remains for us
some tree on a hillside, which every day we can take
into our vision; there remains for us yesterday's street   15
and the loyalty of a habit so much at ease
when it stayed with us that it moved in and never left.
    Oh and night: there is night, when a wind full of infinite space
gnaws at our faces. Whom would it not remain for—that longed-after,
mildly disillusioning presence, which the solitary heart   20
so painfully meets. Is it any less difficult for lovers?
But they keep on using each other to hide their own fate.
    Don't you know *yet*? Fling the emptiness out of your arms
into the spaces we breathe; perhaps the birds
will feel the expanded air with more passionate flying.   25

Yes—the springtimes needed you. Often a star
was waiting for you to notice it. A wave rolled toward you
out of the distant past, or as you walked
under an open window, a violin
yielded itself to your hearing. All this was mission.   30
But could you accomplish it? Weren't you always
distracted by expectation, as if every event
announced a beloved? (Where can you find a place
to keep her, with all the huge strange thoughts inside you
going and coming and often staying all night.)   35
But when you feel longing, sing of women in love;
for their famous passion is still not immortal. Sing
of women abandoned and desolate (you envy them, almost)
who could love so much more purely than those who were gratified.
Begin again and again the never-attainable praising;   40
remember: the hero lives on; even his downfall was
merely a pretext for achieving his final birth.
But Nature, spent and exhausted, takes lovers back
into herself, as if there were not enough strength
to create them a second time. Have you imagined   45
Gaspara Stampa[3] intensely enough so that any girl
deserted by her beloved might be inspired
by that fierce example of soaring, objectless love
and might say to herself, "Perhaps I can be like her"?
Shouldn't this most ancient of sufferings finally grow   50
more fruitful for us? Isn't it time that we lovingly

2. Unlike animals, who live in unconscious harmony with earth, human beings interpret or conceptual-
ize whatever they see.   3. An Italian poet (1523–1554) who wrote a series of two hundred sonnets
recording her unhappy love for Count Collalto, who abandoned her.

freed ourselves from the beloved and, quivering, endured:[4]
as the arrow endures the bowstring's tension, so that
gathered in the snap of release it can be more than
itself. For there is no place where we can remain.   55

Voices. Voices. Listen, my heart, as only
saints have listened: until the gigantic call lifted them
off the ground; yet they kept on, impossibly,
kneeling and didn't notice at all:
so complete was their listening. Not that you could endure   60
God's voice—far from it. But listen to the voice of the wind
and the ceaseless message that forms itself out of silence.
It is murmuring toward you now from those who died young.
Didn't their fate, whenever you stepped into a church
in Naples or Rome, quietly come to address you?   65
Or high up, some eulogy entrusted you with a mission,
as, last year, on the plaque in Santa Maria Formosa.[5]
What they want of me is that I gently remove the appearance
of injustice about their death—which at times
slightly hinders their souls from proceeding onward.   70

Of course, it is strange to inhabit the earth no longer,
to give up customs one barely had time to learn,
not to see roses and other promising Things
in terms of a human future; no longer to be
what one was in infinitely anxious hands; to leave   75
even one's own first name behind, forgetting it
as easily as a child abandons a broken toy.
Strange to no longer desire one's desires. Strange
to see meanings that clung together once, floating away
in every direction. And being dead is hard work   80
and full of retrieval before one can gradually feel
a trace of eternity.—Though the living are wrong to believe
in the too-sharp distinctions which they themselves have created.
Angels (they say) don't know whether it is the living
they are moving among, or the dead. The eternal torrent   85
whirls all ages along in it, through both realms
forever, and their voices are drowned out in its thunderous roar.

In the end, those who were carried off early no longer need us:
they are weaned from earth's sorrows and joys, as gently as children
outgrow the soft breasts of their mothers. But we, who do need   90
such great mysteries, we for whom grief is so often
the source of our spirit's growth—: could we exist without *them*?
Is the legend meaningless that tells how, in the lament for Linus,[6]
the daring first notes of song pierced through the barren numbness;
and then in the startled space which a youth as lovely as a god   95
had suddenly left forever, the Void felt for the first time
that harmony which now enraptures and comforts and helps us?

---

4. Reference to a passage from the *Portuguese Letters* (a 17th-century French epistolary novel supposedly
written by a Portuguese nun) in which the heroine, Marianna Alcoforado, writes that her love no longer
depends on its being reciprocated by the man who has clearly abandoned her.   **5.** A church in Venice
(which Rilke visited in 1911) where a plaque commemorating the death of a Hermann Wilhelm in 1593
reads, in part, "I have not perished but live to myself in cold marble" (*non perii at gelido in marmore vivo
mihi*).   **6.** The Linus song (Homer's *Iliad* XVIII.570) is a dirge for a man who died young and whose
death is associated with the passing of summer; those paralyzed by his loss were revived only by the perfect
music of the song of mourning (attributed to Apollo or Orpheus).

The Ninth Elegy

Why, if this interval of being can be spent serenely
in the form of a laurel,[1] slightly darker than all
other green, with tiny waves on the edges
of every leaf (like the smile of a breeze)—: why then
have to be human—and, escaping from fate,   5
keep longing for fate? . . .[2]

        Oh *not* because happiness *exists*,
that too-hasty profit snatched from approaching loss.
Not out of curiosity, not as practice for the heart, which
would exist in the laurel too. . . .   10

But because *truly* being here is so much; because everything here
apparently needs us, this fleeting world, which in some strange way
keeps calling to us. Us, the most fleeting of all.
Once for each thing. Just once; no more. And we too,
just once. And never again. But to have been   15
this once, completely, even if only once:
to have been at one with the earth, seems beyond undoing.

And so we keep pressing on, trying to achieve it,
trying to hold it firmly in our simple hands,
in our overcrowded gaze, in our speechless heart.   20
Trying to become it.—Whom can we give it to? We would
hold on to it all, forever . . . Ah, but what can we take along
into that other realm? Not the art of looking,
which is learned so slowly, and nothing that happened here. Nothing.
The sufferings, then. And, above all, the heaviness,   25
and the long experience of love,—just what is wholly
unsayable. But later, among the stars,
what good is it—*they* are *better* as they are: unsayable.
For when the traveler returns from the mountain-slopes into the valley,
he brings, not a handful of earth, unsayable to others, but instead   30
some word he has gained, some pure word, the yellow and blue
gentian. Perhaps we are *here* in order to say: house,
bridge, fountain, gate, pitcher, fruit-tree, window—
at most: column, tower. . . . But to *say* them, you must understand,
oh to say them *more* intensely than the Things themselves   35
ever dreamed of existing. Isn't the secret intent
of this taciturn earth, when it forces lovers together,
that inside their boundless emotion all things may shudder with joy?
Threshold: what it means for two lovers
to be wearing down, imperceptibly, the ancient threshold of
    their door—   40
they too, after the many who came before them
and before those to come. . . . , lightly.

Here is the time for the *sayable, here* is its homeland.
Speak and bear witness. More than ever
the Things that we might experience are vanishing, for   45
what crowds them out and replaces them is an imageless act.

---

1. The nymph Daphne, escaping from the pursuit of her would-be lover Apollo, was changed by that god
into a laurel tree (Ovid's *Metamorphoses* I.548ff.).   2. Here and elsewhere in the elegies, Rilke's ellipsis
marks indicate a pause, not an omission.

An act under a shell, which easily cracks open as soon as
the business inside outgrows it and seeks new limits.
Between the hammers our heart
endures, just as the tongue does   50
between the teeth and, despite that,
still is able to praise.

Praise this world to the angel, not the unsayable one,
you can't impress *him* with glorious emotion; in the universe
where he feels more powerfully, you are a novice. So show him   55
something simple which, formed over generations,
lives as our own, near our hand and within our gaze.
Tell him of Things. He will stand astonished; as *you* stood
by the rope-maker in Rome or the potter along the Nile.
Show him how happy a Thing can be, how innocent and ours,   60
how even lamenting grief purely decides to take form,
serves as a Thing, or dies into a Thing—, and blissfully
escapes far beyond the violin.—And these Things,
which live by perishing, know you are praising them; transient,
they look to us for deliverance: us, the most transient of all.   65
They want us to change them, utterly, in our invisible heart,
within—oh endlessly—within us! Whoever we may be at last.

Earth, isn't this what you want: to arise within us,
invisible? Isn't it your dream
to be wholly invisible someday?—O Earth: invisible!   70
What, if not transformation, is your urgent command?
Earth, my dearest, I will. Oh believe me, you no longer
need your springtimes to win me over—one of them,
ah, even one, is already too much for my blood.
Unspeakably I have belonged to you, from the first.   75
You were always right, and your holiest inspiration
is our intimate companion, Death.

Look, I am living. On what? Neither childhood nor future
grows any smaller. . . . Superabundant being
wells up in my heart.   80

WALLACE STEVENS

1879–1955

"A bucket of sand and a wishing lamp," Wallace Stevens once said, was all he
needed to "create a world in half a second that would make this one look like a
hunk of mud." His poetry invites us into an imaginative world that fuses poignantly
sensuous images with the most abstract metaphysics. Stevens himself embodied
contrasts: a Hartford insurance executive as well as a major American poet, he was
never a part of the contemporary literary scene with its movements and isms. He
was acquainted with current New York writers and artists, he collected modern art
(which is often reflected in his poems), and later in his career he wrote and lectured about poetry; but it is not through these associations that he joins the mainstream of modern European and American letters. In his work Stevens combines
two aspects of modernist tradition. His musical free verse and sensuous, significant

imagery recall Symbolism, which he especially admired in the French poet Paul Verlaine. His stress on concrete, physical descriptions inside a philosophical framework is characteristic of "existential" writers such as Jean-Paul Sartre and Albert Camus. More than any other modern poet, Stevens inherited the Symbolists' desire to balance the intertwined concepts of concrete reality and human imagination. Like the Symbolists, too, he finds an ultimate human value in the artist's freedom to create the world anew in a "supreme fiction": *fiction*, because "true" reality can never be ascertained or re-created; *supreme*, because it is the highest aspiration of human creativity. This fiction is not yet the ungraspable "fictionality" of postmodernist writers such as Samuel Beckett and Alain Robbe-Grillet, for it does not dissolve into a series of competing perspectives. Instead, Stevens's modernist poetry holds up the ideal of a supreme artistic transformation whose creation bestows meaning on an otherwise meaningless universe.

Stevens was born in Reading, Pennsylvania, on October 2, 1879, the second of five children. His father was a schoolteacher and then attorney with diverse interests; his mother taught school. He enrolled at Harvard in 1897 as a nondegree student and while at college contributed poems, stories, and sketches to the Harvard *Advocate* (of which he became president) and the Harvard *Monthly*. He also came to know the philosopher and writer George Santayana, whose assertion of a common imaginative essence in religion and poetry appealed greatly to him.

Stevens left Harvard in 1900 to try journalism and then law school in New York; he received his degree and was admitted to the bar in 1904. After working as an attorney for several firms he finally entered the insurance business in 1908. In 1916 he joined a subsidiary of the Hartford Accident and Indemnity Company, becoming vice president of the parent company in 1934 and remaining there until his death in 1955. He dictated business correspondence and poems to the same secretary. In 1922 business affairs took him to Florida, and until 1940 he returned frequently to its warm and lush landscape, which contrasted in his poetry—both physically and emotionally—with the chillier climate of the north.

Stevens married Elsie V. Kachel in 1909, and in 1924 his daughter Holly was born; she later edited her father's letters. He published individual poems in little magazines (small avant-garde literary magazines) and was a friend of *Poetry* editor Harriet Monroe and of the poets William Carlos Williams and Marianne Moore. *Harmonium*, his first collection of poetry, appeared in 1923. In following years, Stevens's insurance career occupied most of his time, and he published little poetry until 1936, when *Ideas of Order* appeared. Later volumes included *The Man with the Blue Guitar* (1937), *Parts of a World* (1942), and a collection of prose essays, *The Necessary Angel* (1951). Stevens kept the two parts of his career quite separate but gradually became a well-known and influential poet, winning the Bollingen Prize for poetry in 1949 and the National Book Award in 1951 (for *The Auroras of Autumn*) and 1955 (for *The Collected Poems of Wallace Stevens*). He died of cancer on August 2, 1955.

Stevens's poetry expresses the dualism between reality and imagination, between things as they really are and as we perceive and then shape them. For we can never know reality directly; our five senses see, touch, taste, smell, and hear what is outside us, constructing an image of the world in which we live, but this world also exists separate from us and beyond our image of it. This paradox underlies all Stevens's poetry, which swings between the two poles of the shaping, creative imagination and the material world of which we are only partly aware. The names of real Connecticut towns or the state of Tennessee, an inventory of the trash in a dump, descriptions of coffee and oranges at breakfast, and marred old pieces of furniture, inhabit his poems side by side with the most abstract speculations, transformations of everyday scenes, and visions of the edge of space. Poetic artifice—the playful and imaginative use of language—clothes the most mundane observations, as if to assert a relationship between verbal style and the real subject about which it tries to speak. Stevens once said that "it is pleasant to hear the milkman, and yet . . . the imaginative world is the only real world after all," and this balancing of dualities continues throughout his work.

Sunday Morning, one of Stevens's earlier poems, already reflects this dualism on several levels. The opening lines present a contrast between the comfortable self-indulgence of the Sunday morning breakfast table, warmly alive with sun and bright colors, and the traditional Christian dedication of the day to thoughts of human mortality redeemed by Christ's death. The contrast continues in a quasi-dialogue between the poet, who protests any attempt to transcend this world or death, and the woman, who speaks of paradise and some "imperishable bliss." Earth itself is sufficient paradise, says the poet, and "friendlier" than the untouchable sky or supernatural explanations of different religions; death is a necessary part of life's constant renewal and sharpens our awareness of love and beauty while they exist. The wholly natural beauty of the New England landscape at the poem's end, with its acceptance of death and change, suggests to the speaker a more real and human ideal than the unchanging perfection of eternal life.

The softer, more consolatory tone of *Sunday Morning* (which derives in part from Stevens's recollection of his mother's death in 1912), becomes bold and gaudier in *The Emperor of Ice-Cream*, which also deals—but more ironically—with the contrast of life and death. The scene is a wake: a dead woman lies covered with the same sheet on which she once embroidered fantail pigeons. Stevens, however, begins his poem in the kitchen with the festivities in which the survivors are taking part. For the day is devoted not only to the dead but to the living, in whose imperial court the ice cream server is emperor, and the women dressed in their best clothes are handmaidens. Words with erotic overtones (*concupiscent, wenches*) reinforce the scene's essential hedonism, in which the only reality that counts is the pleasure of the moment.

Yet there is another reality, that of the dead woman, who has now become a mere object much like her own furniture, and Stevens painstakingly registers its details. The dresser is made of pine wood and lacks three glass knobs; the dead woman's calloused feet protrude from the too-short embroidered sheet. Such close-up observation puts the woman in a new imaginative context, in a world of lifeless inanimate things whose stillness comments with grim finality on the first stanza's boisterous celebration. The empire of ice cream contains both life and death; people, flowers, and yesterday's newspapers all ultimately come down to the same level of bare physicality. Wisdom lies in accepting the common outcome of all earthly appearances—"Let be be finale of seem"—and in celebrating life while it remains.

Stevens's juxtaposition of reality and our imaginative perception of it is echoed throughout his writing by a dialectic of other oppositions, one idea being raised seemingly only to be challenged and tested by another. Thus the jar on a hill in Tennessee juxtaposes human intellect and aesthetic imagination against the unshaped wilderness of nature, and *Peter Quince at the Clavier* celebrates the immortal presence—in the memory—of a long-dead woman's physical beauty. Such balancing or counterpoint rejects a single perspective and opens up avenues for continued meditation.

Counterpoint is basically a musical term, and Stevens's work is filled with the imagery of musical performance: the harpsichord of *Peter Quince at the Clavier*, the singer in *The Idea of Order at Key West*, and the nightingale and even grackles of *The Man on the Dump*. Other poems speak of a blue guitar (the image taken from a painting by Pablo Picasso), an old horn, a lute, citherns, saxophones, not to mention the "tink and tank and tunk-a-tunk-tunk" of an unnamed instrument (perhaps a banjo). Musical images are used to describe events, such as the tambourinelike rhythm of Susanna's attendants arriving (with the additional musical end rhymes of *tambourines* and *Byzantines*), or emotions, like the erotic intensity of the elders' lustful glance ("The basses of their beings throb / In witching chords") and the comic counterpoint of their quivering nerves pulsing "pizzicati of Hosanna." Even the title of Stevens's book is the name of a musical instrument, *Harmonium*, and he had wanted to name his collected poems *The Whole of Harmonium*.

Music for Stevens was not, however, merely musical images in a poem, or the notion of harmonizing the sounds of words or holding contrasted ideas in counterpoint. It implied for him a supreme, intuited language, the "foreign song" of the gold-feathered bird on the edge of space in *Of Mere Being*, perhaps the same bird that sang to the emperor in Yeats's *Sailing to Byzantium*. The singer, bird or human, is the type of the poet, the "one of fictive music" who creates the world anew through the incantatory power of imagination.

The singer of *The Idea of Order at Key West* is such a poet, embodying imagination at its most ambitious: "She was the single artificer of the world / In which she sang." Nature itself cannot create such a world, for it lacks the igniting spark; while the sea may imitate human gestures and sounds, it cannot truly speak, and makes only "meaningless plungings of water and wind." Imagination is supreme; the singer has "the maker's rage to order words" (*poet* comes from a Greek word meaning "maker"), and her song creates for herself and for her listeners a world of imagination in which lights from the fishing boats seem to map out the night against which they shine.

The luminous beauty of the singer's world is only one of many possible poetic worlds, all of which take their place on the accumulated heap of poetry where the latest artificer sits as *The Man on the Dump*. The trash heap of history is the place to find outworn poetic images, from dewy clichés to the nightingale as traditional symbol for poetry (see Keats's *Ode to a Nightingale*, p. 822). In a poem filled with the debris of modern times, from old tires to dead cats, Stevens suggests that poetry's philosophical quest to name the "the" of existence cannot employ previous ages' images and ideas but must develop its own, even if they appear only the grating music of grackles or beatings on an old tin can. Yet all are engaged in the same enterprise, creating what he elsewhere called "supreme fictions" to give meaning to our lives.

Stevens's poetry celebrates the ability of the individual imagination to conceive its own world. Broader social or political themes are pushed to the background, even in texts (such as *The Man on the Dump* or *The Emperor of Ice-Cream*) that derive power from their realistic descriptions. Consequently, the politically minded critics of the 1930s accused the poet of being an escapist, content to be the "single artificer of his own world of mannerism." Stevens responded that to do otherwise was to misunderstand "the spiritual role of the poet," for this role was not to make political statements but to clarify basic issues by illuminating the relations between human subjectivity and a world of objects. Such an explanation may have seemed too philosophical to those seeking an openly committed literature, and Stevens's early work was largely unappreciated. The gaudy exuberance of its images made it seem less serious than the poetry of political commitment and visionary mysticism that Yeats was then writing, or Eliot's evocation in *The Waste Land* of a universal and profound despair. Only after World War II did Americans, and Europeans, realize that Stevens, too, was a master worthy to stand beside his greatest contemporaries.

A good general introduction is Robert Pack, *Wallace Stevens: An Approach to His Poetry* (1958). Robert Buttel, *Wallace Stevens: The Makings of Harmonium* (1967), discusses Stevens's early and middle work. Many views on Stevens are presented in Marie Borroff, ed., *Wallace Stevens: A Collection of Critical Essays*

(1963). Michel Benamou, *Wallace Stevens and the Symbolist Imagination* (1972), is an interesting study of Stevens's themes and style compared with those of French Symbolist poets. Albert Gelpi, *Wallace Stevens: The Poetics of Modernism* (1985), presents seven essays situating Stevens's work in the context of twentieth-century modernism in English. Historical, philosophical, and artistic perspectives are discussed as well as Stevens's influence on contemporary poets. John T. Newcomb, *Wallace Stevens and Literary Canons* (1992), examines the way Stevens's "canonical" reputation evolves in tandem with critical perspectives on American modernism. Glen MacLeod, *Wallace Stevens and Modern Art: From the Armory Show to Abstract Expression* (1993), traces the relations between Stevens's poetics and his understanding of issues in modern art.

Sunday Morning[1]

I

Complacencies of the peignoir, and late
Coffee and oranges in a sunny chair,
And the green freedom of a cockatoo
Upon a rug mingle to dissipate
The holy hush of ancient sacrifice.   5
She dreams a little, and she feels the dark
Encroachment of that old catastrophe,
As a calm darkens among water-lights.
The pungent oranges and bright, green wings
Seem things in some procession of the dead,   10
Winding across wide water, without sound.
The day is like wide water, without sound,
Stilled for the passing of her dreaming feet
Over the seas, to silent Palestine,
Dominion of the blood and sepulchre.[2]   15

II

Why should she give her bounty to the dead?
What is divinity if it can come
Only in silent shadows and in dreams?
Shall she not find in comforts of the sun,
In pungent fruit and bright, green wings, or else   20
In any balm or beauty of the earth,
Things to be cherished like the thought of heaven?[3]
Divinity must live within herself:
Passions of rain, or moods in falling snow;
Grievings in loneliness, or unsubdued   25
Elations when the forest blooms; gusty
Emotions on wet roads on autumn nights;

---

1. Although the central figure of the poem is clearly a woman sitting over late breakfast on Sunday morning instead of going to church, Stevens comments that "this is not essentially a woman's meditation on religion and the meaning of life. It is anybody's meditation" (Stevens's *Letters*, p. 250).   2. Throughout the stanza there are hints of Christ's Crucifixion and the celebration of the Mass.   3. "The poem is simply an expression of paganism" (Stevens's *Letters*, p. 250).

All pleasures and all pains, remembering
The bough of summer and the winter branch.
These are the measures destined for her soul.   30

III

Jove[4] in the clouds had his inhuman birth.
No mother suckled him, no sweet land gave
Large-mannered motions to his mythy mind
He moved among us, as a muttering king,
Magnificent, would move among his hinds,[5]   35
Until our blood, commingling, virginal,[6]
With heaven, brought such requital to desire
The very hinds discerned it, in a star.[7]
Shall our blood fail? Or shall it come to be
The blood of paradise? And shall the earth   40
Seem all of paradise that we shall know?
The sky will be much friendlier then than now,
A part of labor and a part of pain,
And next in glory to enduring love,
Not this dividing and indifferent blue.   45

IV

She says, "I am content when wakened birds,
Before they fly, test the reality
Of misty fields, by their sweet questionings;
But when the birds are gone, and their warm fields
Return no more, where, then, is paradise?"   50
There is not any haunt of prophecy,[8]
Nor any old chimera of the grave,
Neither the golden underground, nor isle
Melodious, where spirits gat them home,[9]
Nor visionary south, nor cloudy palm   55
Remote on heaven's hill, that has endured
As April's green endures; or will endure
Like her remembrance of awakened birds,
Or her desire for June and evening, tipped
By the consummation of the swallow's wings.   60

V

She says, "But in contentment I still feel
The need of some imperishable bliss."
Death is the mother of beauty; hence from her,
Alone, shall come fulfilment to our dreams
And our desires. Although she strews the leaves   65
Of sure obliteration on our paths,

---

4. Ruler of the gods in Roman myth. Stevens softens the traditional story in which Jove's father Cronus swallows the infant shortly after birth.   5. Shepherds.   6. An allusion to the conception of Jesus in the womb of the Virgin Mary.   7. The star over Bethlehem that marked Jesus' birth.   8. Like, for example, the oracle at Delphi.   9. The Elysian Fields, or Isles of the Blessed, where the heroes of Greek myth went after death.

The path sick sorrow took, the many paths
Where triumph rang its brassy phrase, or love
Whispered a little out of tenderness,
She makes the willow shiver in the sun   70
For maidens who were wont to sit and gaze
Upon the grass, relinquished to their feet.
She causes boys to pile new plums and pears
On disregarded plate.[1] The maidens taste
And stray impassioned in the littering leaves.   75

VI

Is there no change of death in paradise?
Does ripe fruit never fall? Or do the boughs
Hang always heavy in that perfect sky,
Unchanging, yet so like our perishing earth,
With rivers like our own that seek for seas   80
They never find, the same receding shores
That never touch with inarticulate pang?
Why set the pear upon those river-banks
Or spice the shores with odors of the plum?
Alas, that they should wear our colors there,   85
The silken weavings of our afternoons,
And pick the strings of our insipid lutes!
Death is the mother of beauty, mystical,
Within whose burning bosom we devise
Our earthly mothers waiting, sleeplessly.   90

VII

Supple and turbulent, a ring of men
Shall chant in orgy on a summer morn
Their boisterous devotion to the sun,
Not as a god, but as a god might be,
Naked among them, like a savage source.   95
Their chant shall be a chant of paradise,
Out of their blood, returning to the sky;
And in their chant shall enter, voice by voice,
The windy lake wherein their lord delights,
The trees, like serafin,[2] and echoing hills,   100
That choir among themselves long afterward.
They shall know well the heavenly fellowship
Of men that perish and of summer morn.
And whence they came and whither they shall go
The dew upon their feet shall manifest.[3]   105

---

1. "Plate is used in the sense of so-called family plate. Disregarded refers to the disuse into which things fall that have been possessed for a long time. I mean, therefore, that death releases and renews. What the old have come to disregard, the young inherit and make use of" (Stevens's *Letters*, p. 183).   2. Angels of the highest rank.   3. "Life is as fugitive as dew upon the feet of men dancing in dew. Men do not either come from any direction or disappear in any direction. Life is as meaningless as dew" (Stevens's *Letters*, p. 250).

VIII

She hears, upon that water without sound,
A voice that cries, "The tomb in Palestine
Is not the porch of spirits lingering.[4]
It is the grave of Jesus, where he lay."
We live in an old chaos of the sun,   110
Or old dependency of day and night,
Or island solitude, unsponsored, free,
Of that wide water, inescapable.
Deer walk upon our mountains, and the quail
Whistle about us their spontaneous cries;   115
Sweet berries ripen in the wilderness;
And, in the isolation of the sky,
At evening, casual flocks of pigeons make
Ambiguous undulations as they sink.
Downward to darkness, on extended wings.   120

Peter Quince at the Clavier[1]

I

Just as my fingers on these keys
Make music, so the selfsame sounds
On my spirit make a music, too.

Music is feeling, then, not sound;
And thus it is that what I feel,   5
Here in this room, desiring you,

Thinking of your blue-shadowed silk,
Is music. It is like the strain
Waked in the elders by Susanna.[2]

Of a green evening, clear and warm,   10
She bathed in her still garden, while
The red-eyed elders watching, felt

The basses of their beings throb
In witching chords, and their thin blood
Pulse pizzicati of Hosanna.[3]   15

II

In the green water, clear and warm,
Susanna lay.
She searched
The touch of springs,
And found   20

4. That is, remaining on earth after the body is dead.   1. General term in the 16th century for a keyboard instrument, such as a harpsichord. In Shakespeare's *A Midsummer Night's Dream*, Peter Quince is the carpenter-playwright who directs his own play about the tragic lovers Pyramus and Thisbe. Both the play and the production amuse the noble audience.   2. In the biblical Apocrypha, a Babylonian woman falsely accused of adultery by lecherous elders who spied on her bathing.   3. A cry of praise to God. *Pizzicati*: notes sounded by plucking a string (as on a violin).

Concealed imaginings.
She sighed,
For so much melody.

Upon the bank, she stood
In the cool   25
Of spent emotions.
She felt, among the leaves,
The dew
Of old devotions.

She walked upon the grass,   30
Still quavering.
The winds were like her maids,
On timid feet,
Fetching her woven scarves,
Yet wavering.   35

A breath upon her hand
Muted the night.
She turned—
A cymbal crashed,
And roaring horns.   40

III

Soon, with a noise like tambourines,
Came her attendant Byzantines.[4]

They wondered why Susanna cried
Against the elders by her side;

And as they whispered, the refrain   45
Was like a willow swept by rain.

Anon,[5] their lamps' uplifted flame
Revealed Susanna and her shame.

And then, the simpering Byzantines
Fled, with a noise like tambourines.   50

IV

Beauty is momentary in the mind—
The fitful tracing of a portal;
But in the flesh it is immortal.
The body dies; the body's beauty lives.
So evenings die, in their green going,   55
A wave, interminably flowing.
So gardens die, their meek breath scenting
The cowl of winter, done repenting.
So maidens die,[6] to the auroral
Celebration of a maiden's choral.[7]   60

---

4. Inhabitants of ancient Byzantium, a Christian empire of the Near East. "Somebody once called my attention to the fact that there were no Byzantines in Susanna's time. I hope that that bit of precious pedantry will seem as unimportant to you as it does to me" (Stevens's *Letters*, p. 250).   5. Soon.
6. As maidens, that is, become women.   7. Choral song.

Susanna's music touched the bawdy strings
Of those white elders; but, escaping,
Left only Death's ironic scraping.[8]
Now, in its immortality, it plays
On the clear viol[9] of her memory,   65
And makes a constant sacrament of praise.

Anecdote of the Jar

I placed a jar in Tennessee.
And round it was, upon a hill.
It made the slovenly wilderness
Surround that hill.

The wilderness rose up to it,   5
And sprawled around, no longer wild.
The jar was round upon the ground
And tall and of a port[1] in air.

It took dominion everywhere.
The jar was gray and bare.   10
It did not give of bird or bush,
Like nothing else in Tennessee.

The Emperor of Ice-Cream[1]

Call the roller of big cigars,
The muscular one, and bid him whip
In kitchen cups concupiscent[2] curds.
Let the wenches dawdle in such dress
As they are used to wear, and let the boys   5
Bring flowers in last month's newspapers.
Let be be finale of seem.[3]
The only emperor is the emperor of ice-cream.

Take from the dresser of deal,[4]
Lacking the three glass knobs, that sheet   10
On which she embroidered fantails[5] once
And spread it so as to cover her face.
If her horny feet protrude, they come
To show how cold she is, and dumb.
Let the lamp affix its beam.   15
The only emperor is the emperor of ice-cream.

8. Rasping fiddle music.   9. A stringed instrument of the 16th and 17th centuries, played with a bow;
also a pun on *violation*.   1. Dignified bearing, manner.   1. "I think I should select from my poems
as my favorite 'The Emperor of Ice-Cream.' This wears a deliberately commonplace costume, and yet
seems to me to contain something of the essential gaudiness of poetry; that is the reason why I like it"
(Stevens's *Letters*, p. 263).   2. Lusty, sensual. "The words 'concupiscent curds' . . . express the concupiscence of life, but, by contrast with the things in relation to them in the poem they express or accentuate
life's destitution" (Stevens's *Letters*, p. 500).   3. "The true sense of 'Let be be the finale of seem' is let
being become the conclusion or denouement of appearing to be: in short, icecream is an absolute good.
The poem is obviously not about icecream, but about being as distinguished from seeming to be" (Stevens's *Letters*, p. 341).   4. Fir or pine wood.   5. Fantail pigeons.

The Idea of Order at Key West[1]

She sang beyond the genius of the sea.[2]
The water never formed to mind or voice,
Like a body wholly body, fluttering
Its empty sleeves; and yet its mimic motion
Made constant cry, caused constantly a cry,   5
That was not ours although we understood,
Inhuman, of the veritable ocean.

The sea was not a mask.[3] No more was she.
The song and water were not medleyed sound
Even if what she sang was what she heard.   10
Since what she sang was uttered word by word.
It may be that in all her phrases stirred
The grinding water and the gasping wind;
But it was she and not the sea we heard.

For she was the maker of the song she sang.   15
The ever-hooded, tragic-gestured sea
Was merely a place by which she walked to sing.
Whose spirit is this? we said, because we knew
It was the spirit that we sought and knew
That we should ask this often as she sang.   20

If it was only the dark voice of the sea
That rose, or even colored by many waves;
If it was only the outer voice of sky
And cloud, of the sunken coral water-walled,
However clear, it would have been deep air,   25
The heaving speech of air, a summer sound
Repeated in a summer without end
And sound alone. But it was more than that,
More even than her voice, and ours, among
The meaningless plungings of water and the wind,   30
Theatrical distances, bronze shadows heaped
On high horizons, mountainous atmospheres
Of sky and sea.
             It was her voice that made
The sky acutest at its vanishing.   35
She measured to the hour its solitude.
She was the single artificer of the world
In which she sang. And when she sang, the sea,
Whatever self it had, became the self
That was her song, for she was the maker. Then we,   40
As we beheld her striding there alone,
Knew that there never was a world for her
Except the one she sang and, singing, made.

1. Published in *Ideas of Order* (1936). "In 'The Idea of Order at Key West' life has ceased to be a matter of chance. It may be that every man introduces his own order into the life about him. . . . But still there is order. . . . These are tentative ideas for the purposes of poetry" (Stevens's *Letters*, p. 293). Key West is the southernmost of the Florida keys, and Stevens spent midwinter vacations there for almost twenty years.
2. That is, beyond the power of the sea to respond.   3. The movement of the waves, imitating fluttering sleeves, also emits an inhuman cry. The sea mimics the human body, but without a mind; it is not even as close as the mask worn by actors in ancient Greek drama.

Ramon Fernandez,[4] tell me, if you know,
Why, when the singing ended and we turned   45
Toward the town, tell why the glassy lights,
The lights in the fishing boats at anchor there,
As the night descended, tilting in the air,
Mastered the night and portioned out the sea,
Fixing emblazoned[5] zones and fiery poles,   50
Arranging, deepening, enchanting night.

Oh! Blessed rage for order, pale Ramon,
The maker's rage to order words of the sea,
Words of the fragrant portals, dimly-starred,
And of ourselves and of our origins,   55
In ghostlier demarcations, keener sounds.

The Man on the Dump

Day creeps down. The moon is creeping up.
The sun is a corbeil of flowers the moon Blanche[1]
Places there, a bouquet. Ho-ho . . . The dump is full
Of images. Days pass like papers[2] from a press.
The bouquets come here in the papers. So the sun,   5
And so the moon, both come, and the janitor's poems
Of every day, the wrapper on the can of pears,
The cat in the paper-bag, the corset, the box
From Esthonia:[3] the tiger chest, for tea.

The freshness of night has been fresh a long time.   10
The freshness of morning, the blowing of day, one says
That it puffs as Cornelius Nepos[4] reads, it puffs
More than, less than or it puffs like this or that.
The green smacks in the eye, the dew in the green
Smacks like fresh water in a can, like the sea   15

On a cocoanut—how many men have copied dew
For buttons, how many women have covered themselves
With dew, dew dresses, stones and chains of dew, heads
Of the floweriest flowers dewed with the dewiest dew.
One grows to hate these things except on the dump.   20

Now, in the time of spring (azaleas, trilliams,
Myrtle, viburnums, daffodils, blue phlox),[5]
Between that disgust and this, between the things
That are on the dump (azaleas and so on)
And those that will be (azaleas and so on).   25
One feels the purifying change. One rejects
The trash.

---

4. French critic (1894–1944) who described the way impressionistic techniques in literature impose a
subjective order on reality. Stevens had read some of Fernandez's criticism, but denied that he intended
any specific reference here.   5. As with the geographic zones and poles of the earth. *Emblazoned:*
ornamented, usually with heraldic symbols.   1. A woman's name, etymologically signifying whiteness.
Corbeil: basket.   2. Newspapers.   3. Or Estonia; a Baltic republic, once part of the Soviet Union.
4. Roman historian (1st century B.C.), now little read, the author of brief anecdotal and highly moralized
Lives of Famous Men.   5. Spring flowers.

That's the moment when the moon creeps up
To the bubbling of bassoons. That's the time
One looks at the elephant-colorings of tires: 30
Everything is shed; and the moon comes up as the moon
(All its images are in the dump) and you see
As a man (not like an image of a man),
You see the moon rise in the empty sky.

One sits and beats an old tin can, lard pail.   35
One beats and beats for that which one believes.
That's what one wants to get near. Could it after all
Be merely oneself, as superior as the ear
To a crow's voice? Did the nightingale[6] torture the ear,
Pack the heart and scratch the mind? And does the ear   40
Solace itself in peevish birds? Is it peace,
Is it a philosopher's honeymoon,[7] one finds
On the dump? Is it to sit among mattresses of the dead,
Bottles, pots, shoes and grass and murmur *aptest eve*:
Is it to hear the blatter of grackles[8] and say   45
Invisible priest; is it to eject, to pull
The day to pieces and cry *stanza my stone?*[9]
Where was it one first heard of the Truth? The the.[1]

6. Traditional image for lyric poetry, for example, in Keats's *Ode to a Nightingale.*   7. Like a busman's holiday, that is, no respite at all.   8. Noisy birds.   9. Suggests a Romantic, mystical, "nightingale" poetry that turns its back on material reality. "Invisible priest" may recall Rilke's proposed artistic transformation of reality into an invisible higher reality (see *The Ninth Elegy*, p. 1657).   1. "The truth" is an intangible absolute (like *"the* good"); what it specifies cannot be defined. The *the* itself however represents an urge to seek absolute meaning: to say *the*, not merely *a*.

PREMCHAND
(DHANPAT RAI SHRIVASTAVA)
1880–1936

Dhanpat Rai Shrivastava, known by the pen name Premchand, is the towering figure in the history of modern literature in Hindi, the principal language of north India. Hindi fiction owes its development to Premchand's pioneering achievement. Premchand is also the outstanding Hindi writer on peasant life in north India, which has not changed radically since his time, and his novels and short stories are still popular among Hindi readers. Like several other contemporary Indian writers, Premchand was influenced by the socialist and Marxist critique of capitalism and feudal social structure and intended his fiction to serve as social criticism and a catalyst for social change. A prolific essayist and editor of several journals devoted to literature and public affairs, he also made significant contributions to the political and intellectual debates of his time. In the last year of his life Premchand joined Mulk Raj Anand (born 1905) and other Indian writers in the founding of the Progressive Writers Association. Although English-speaking readers are by and large not familiar with Premchand, the social realism of his work, like that of other Hindi writers of the 1930s, has earned him an appreciative audience in the erstwhile Communist bloc countries.

Premchand was born in a village near the north Indian city of Banaras. Though his family was poor, they belonged to the Hindu Kayastha caste, a community of professional writers, lawyers, and teachers, and he received an excellent education in Persian and Urdu, the dominant languages of literature and administration in nineteenth-century north India. Premchand spent some years as a schoolteacher in various north Indian towns, acquiring a college degree at the same time. Writing, however, remained his first interest. Although he was the author of fourteen novels, his main energy went to the short story form, which he literally introduced into Hindi. By the end of his life, he had published more than three hundred stories in a dozen collections, and his reputation as the foremost exponent of the Hindi short story remained unchallenged well into the 1960s, when the Marxist and Progressive movements in Hindi literature began to wane and Hindi fiction began to be dominated by writers whose main themes have been the problems of modernity and alienation in the context of urban life.

Premchand wrote his first stories and novels in Urdu, a form of the Hindi language that, having evolved out of the interaction of medieval Hindi dialects with the Persian language brought by Muslim rulers in India from the twelfth century onward, has a heavily Persian vocabulary and is written in the Persian script. He later produced versions of his stories both in Urdu and in Hindi, which is written in Sanskrit script and has a vocabulary with primarily Sanskrit and Hindu cultural associations. By the 1920s Hindu and Muslim separatist groups succeeded in identifying Urdu exclusively with Muslim culture and in promoting the dissociation of the Hindu majority from Urdu. After 1920, to reach as large as a public as possible, Premchand was forced to publish primarily through Hindi publishing houses and to give up Urdu publication. Throughout his career, however, Premchand condemned the polarization of north Indian communities along linguistic and religious lines and advocated the adoption of Hindustani, a hybrid form of Urdu and Hindi that had been in currency for some centuries, as the national language.

Premchand's fiction reflects the deep influence on the writer of the great political and social movements that swept over India and the world between the 1890s and the 1930s. Inspired by India's anticolonial nationalist movement, Premchand wrote his first short stories on nationalist themes in the form of historical allegory. The British government banned the Urdu story collection *Soz-e-vatan* (Sufferings of the motherland, 1907) as seditious literature. In the 1920s Premchand participated in Mahatma Gandhi's campaign of nonviolent resistance to British rule, resigning his post in a government school as a gesture of noncooperation. Meanwhile, the focus of his fiction shifted from political issues to social reform in the villages. The main themes of his later novels and short stories—such as *Godan* (Gift of a cow, 1936), his last and most celebrated novel—are the exploitation of the poor peasants by landowners and other members of the elite classes and of the lower castes by upper-caste Hindus. Both kinds of fiction reflect a synthesis of Western socialism and Gandhian thought.

Premchand's short stories bear the impress of the realism of Tolstoy, Gorki, Anatole France, Chekhov, Galsworthy, and other European writers whom he admired and translated. Dickens, who was widely read in India, appears to have been a major literary model for Premchand's focus on social problems. Among the nineteenth-century English novelists, the Hindi writer admired the moral sensibility of George Eliot, whose novel *Silas Marner* he adapted in Hindi. The particular blend of idealism and social criticism in Premchand's fiction is, however, entirely his own. *Road to Salvation* (*Mukti-marg*, 1924) is representative of Premchand at his best, examining the mechanics of various forms of exploitation with a clear, ironic eye. Neither Buddhu nor Jhingur belongs to the elite classes, who are strategically positioned to exploit those below them in the rigid class and caste hierarchies of rural India. Yet, instead of uniting to resist their oppressors, they destroy each other, thus revealing the insidious power of systemic oppression. In many of Premchand's stories there is a clear dividing line between the oppressors (brahman priests, landlords, rich men) and the oppressed (usually poor peasants, women, outcastes). But in this story the author indicts the compliant victim as much as the oppressor. Here brahman ritualism and greed are amply satirized, but Buddhu and Jhingur owe their downfall to their own peculiar combination of gullibility and deviousness, which is itself the product of a social structure that stifles the aspirations of the less privileged.

Premchand's fluid, direct, vivid prose is among the features that account for the immediate and enduring appeal of his stories for Hindi readers. In the typical Premchand story long, moralizing passages are balanced by the colorful idioms of peasant speech, although the author never uses any actual rural dialect. In the best stories, as in *Road to Salvation*, the didactic tone is also offset, and sometimes entirely replaced, by a form of black humor that allows Premchand to make these moving tales of human suffering also extremely effective as social satire.

Peter Gaeffke, *Hindi Literature in the 20th Century* (1978), is the best history of modern Hindi literature. David Rubin, *The World of Premchand* (1969), provides superb translations and an excellent introduction to Premchand's short stories. Gordon Roadarmel, *The Gift of a Cow* (1968), is the best translation of Premchand's monumental novel of peasant life in north India. For a life of Premchand, see Amrit Rai, *Premchand: His Life and Times* (1991). Also useful is Prakash Chandra Gupta, *Premchand* (1968), a brief literary biography. For trends in the Hindi fiction of the 1960s, see Gordon Roadarmel, ed. and trans., *A Death in Delhi* (1972), a volume of short stories.

PRONOUNCING GLOSSARY

The following list uses common English syllables and stress accents to provide rough equivalents of selected words whose pronunciation may be unfamiliar to the general reader.

chappattie: *chuh-pah'-tee*   Lakshmi: *luhksh'-mee*

Dhanpat Rai Shrivastava: *duhn'-puht*   pan: *pahn*

   rah'-yee shree-vahs'-tuh-vah   pandit: *puhn'-deet*

ghee: *geeh*   Premchand: *praym'-chuhnd*

Harihar: *huh'-ree-huhr*   Satyanarayan: *suht'-yuh-nah-rah'-yuhn*

Jhingur: *jeen'-goor*   Savan: *sah'-vuhn*

The Road to Salvation[1]

1

The pride the peasant takes in seeing his fields flourishing is like the soldier's in his red turban, the coquette's in her jewels or the doctor's in the patients seated before him. Whenever Jhingur looked at his cane[2] fields a sort of intoxication came over him. He had three *bighas* of land which would earn him an easy 600 rupees.[3] And if God saw to it that the rates went up, then who could complain? Both his bullocks were old so

---

1. Translated by David Rubin.   2. Sugarcane, an important crop in north India.   3. The currency of India. *Bigha:* a measure of land equal to one-fifth of an acre.

he'd buy a new pair at the Batesar fair. If he could hook on to another two *bighas*, so much the better. Why should he worry about money? The merchants were already beginning to fawn on him. He was convinced that nobody was as good as himself—and so there was scarcely anyone in the village he hadn't quarrelled with.

One evening when he was sitting with his son in his lap, shelling peas, he saw a flock of sheep coming towards him. He said to himself, "The sheep path doesn't come that way. Can't those sheep go along the bank? What's the idea, coming over here? They'll trample and gobble up the crop and who'll make good for it? I bet it's Buddhu the shepherd—just look at his nerve! He can see me here but he won't drive his sheep back. What good will it do me to put up with *this*? If I try to buy a ram from him he actually asks for five rupees, and everybody sells blankets for four rupees but he won't settle for less than five."

By now the sheep were close to the cane-field. Jhingur yelled, "*Arrey,*[4] where do you think you're taking those sheep, you?"

Buddhu said meekly, "Chief, they're coming by way of the boundary embankment.[5] If I take them back around it will mean a couple of miles extra."

"And I'm supposed to let you trample my field to save you a detour? Why didn't you take them by way of some other boundary path? Do you think I'm some bull-skinning nobody or has your money turned your head? Turn 'em back!"

"Chief, just let them through today. If I ever come back this way again you can punish me any way you want."

"I told you to get them out. If just one of them crosses the line you're going to be in a pack of trouble."

"Chief," Buddhu said, "if even one blade of grass gets under my sheeps' feet you can call me anything you want."

Although Buddhu was still speaking meekly he had decided that it would be a loss of face to turn back. "If I drive the flock back for a few little threats," he thought, "how will I graze my sheep? Turn back today and tomorrow I won't find anybody willing to let me through, they'll all start bullying me."

And Buddhu was a tough man too. He owned 240 sheep and he was able to get eight annas[6] per night to leave them in people's fields to manure them, and he sold their milk as well and made blankets from their wool. He thought, "Why's he getting so angry? What can he do to me? I'm not his servant."

When the sheep got a whiff of the green leaves they became restless and they broke into the field. Beating them with his stick Buddhu tried to push them back across the boundary line but they just broke in somewhere else. In a fury Jhingur said, "You're trying to force your way through here but I'll teach you a lesson!"

Buddhu said, "It's seeing you that's scared them. If you just get out of the way I'll clear them all out of the field."

---

4. A rough form of address, equivalent to "Hey!" or "Hey you!"   5. A bank or raised stone structure, marking the edge of a field.   6. Sixteen annas made a rupee.

But Jhingur put down his son and grabbing up his cudgel he began to whack into the sheep. Not even a washerman would have beat his donkey so cruelly. He smashed legs and backs and while they bleated Buddhu stood silent watching the destruction of his army. He didn't yell at the sheep and he didn't say anything to Jhingur, no, he just watched the show. In just about two minutes, with the prowess of an epic hero, Jhingur had routed the enemy forces. After this carnage among the host of sheep Jhingur said with the pride of victory, "Now move on straight! And don't ever think about coming this way again."

Looking at his wounded sheep, Buddhu said, "Jhingur, you've done a dirty job. You're going to regret it."

2

To take vengeance on a farmer is easier than slicing a banana. Whatever wealth he has is in his fields or barns. The produce gets into the house only after innumerable afflictions of nature and the gods. And if it happens that a human enemy joins in alliance with those afflictions the poor farmer is apt to be left nowhere. When Jhingur came home and told his family about the battle, they started to give him advice.

"Jhingur, you've got yourself into real trouble! You knew what to do but you acted as though you didn't. Don't you realize what a tough customer Buddhu is? Even now it's not too late—go to him and make peace, otherwise the whole village will come to grief along with you."

Jhingur thought it over. He began to regret that he'd stopped Buddhu at all. If the sheep had eaten up a little of his crop it wouldn't have ruined him. The fact is, a farmer's prosperity comes precisely from being humble—God doesn't like it when a peasant walks with his head high. Jhingur didn't enjoy the idea of going to Buddhu's house but urged on by the others he set out. It was the dead of winter, foggy, with the darkness settling in everywhere. He had just come out of the village when suddenly he was astonished to see a fire blazing over in the direction of his cane field. His heart started to hammer. A field had caught fire! He ran wildly, hoping it wasn't his own field, but as he got closer this deluded hope died. He'd been struck by the very misfortune he'd set out to avert. The bastard had started the fire and was ruining the whole village because of him. As he ran it seemed to him that today his field was a lot nearer than it used to be, as though the fallow land between had ceased to exist.

When he finally reached his field the fire had assumed dreadful proportions. Jhingur began to wail. The villagers were running and ripping up stalks of millet to beat the fire. A terrible battle between man and nature went on for several hours, each side winning in turn. The flames would subside and almost vanish only to strike back again with redoubled vigour like battle-crazed warriors. Among the men Buddhu was the most valiant fighter; with his dhoti[7] tucked up around his waist he leapt into the fiery gulfs as though ready to subdue the enemy or die, and he'd emerge after many a narrow escape. In the end it was the men who triumphed, but the

7. A sheet of cloth wrapped around the waist, worn by men throughout India.

triumph amounted to defeat. The whole village's sugarcane crop was burned to ashes and with the cane all their hopes as well.

3

It was no secret who had started the fire. But no one dared say anything about it. There was no proof and what was the point of a case without any evidence? As for Jhingur, it had become difficult for him to show himself out of his house. Wherever he went he had to listen to abuse. People said right to his face, "You were the cause of the fire! You ruined us. You were so stuck up your feet didn't touch the dirt. You yourself were ruined and you dragged the whole village down with you. If you hadn't fought with Buddhu would all this have happened?"

Jhingur was even more grieved by these taunts than by the destruction of his crop, and he would stay in his house the whole day.

Winter drew on. Where before the cane-press had turned all night and the fragrance of the crushed sugar filled the air and fires were lit with people sitting around them smoking their hookas,[8] all was desolation now. Because of the cold people cursed Jhingur and, drawing their doors shut, went to bed as soon as it was dark. Sugarcane isn't only the farmers' wealth; their whole way of life depends on it. With the help of the cane they get through the winter. They drink the cane juice, warm themselves from fires made of its leaves and feed their livestock on the cuttings. All the village dogs that used to sleep in the warm ash of the fires died from the cold and many of the livestock too from lack of fodder. The cold was excessive and everybody in the village was seized with coughs and fevers. And it was Jhingur who'd brought about the whole catastrophe, that cursed, murdering Jhingur.

Jhingur thought and thought and decided that Buddhu had to be put in a situation exactly like his own. Buddhu had ruined him and he was wallowing in comfort, so Jhingur would ruin Buddhu too.

Since the day of their terrible quarrel Buddhu had ceased to come by Jhingur's. Jhingur decided to cultivate an intimacy with him; he wanted to show him he had no suspicion at all that Buddhu started the fire. One day, on the pretext of getting a blanket, he went to Buddhu, who greeted him with every courtesy and honour—for a man offers the hooka even to an enemy and won't let him depart without making him drink milk and syrup.

These days Jhingur was earning a living by working in a jute-wrapping mill.[9] Usually he got several days' wages at once. Only by means of Buddhu's help could he meet his daily expenses between times. So it was that Jhingur re-established a friendly footing between them.

One day Buddhu asked, "Say Jhingur, what would you do if you caught the man who burned your cane field? Tell me the truth."

Solemnly Jhingur said, "I'd tell him, 'Brother, what you did was good. You put an end to my pride, you made me into a decent man.'"

---

8. A type of clay pipe that has a water reservoir, common all over north India.   9. In north and eastern India, jute or hemp fiber is made into a kind of cloth that is used as wrapping material or made into sacks.

"If I were in your place," Buddhu said, "I wouldn't settle for anything less than burning down his house."

"But what's the good of stirring up hatred in a life that lasts such a little while in all? I've been ruined already, what could I get out of ruining him?"

"Right, that's the way of a decent religious man," Buddhu said, "but when a fellow's in the grip of anger all his sense gets jumbled up."

4

Spring came and the peasants were getting the fields ready for planting cane. Buddhu was doing a fine business. Everybody wanted his sheep. There were always a half dozen men at his door fawning on him, and he lorded it over everybody. He doubled the price of hiring out his sheep to manure the fields; if anybody objected he'd say bluntly, "Look, brother, I'm not shoving my sheep on you. If you don't want them, don't take them. But I can't let you have them for a pice[1] less than I said." The result was that everybody swarmed around him, despite his rudeness, just like priests after some pilgrim.

Lakshmi, goddess of wealth, is of no great size; she can, according to the occasion, shrink or expand, to such a degree that sometimes she can contract her most magnificent manifestation into the form of a few small figures printed on paper. There are times when she makes some man's tongue her throne and her size is reduced to nothing. But just the same she needs a lot of elbow-room for her permanent living quarters. If she comes into somebody's house, the house should grow accordingly, she can't put up with a small one. Buddhu's house also began to grow. A veranda was built in front of the door, six rooms replaced the former two. In short the house was done over from top to bottom. Buddhu got the wood from a peasant, from another the cowdung cakes for the kiln fuel to make the tiles; somebody else gave him the bamboo and reeds for the mats. He had to pay for having the walls put up but he didn't give any cash even for this, he gave some lambs. Such is the power of Lakshmi: the whole job—and it was quite a good house, all in all—was put up for nothing. They began to prepare for a house-warming.

Jhingur was still labouring all day without getting enough to half fill his belly, while gold was raining on Buddhu's house. If Jhingur was angry, who could blame him? Nobody could put up with such injustice.

One day Jhingur went out walking in the direction of the untouchable tanners'[2] settlement. He called for Harihar, who came out, greeting him with "*Ram Ram!*"[3] and filled the hooka. They began to smoke. Harihar, the leader of the tanners, was a mean fellow and there wasn't a peasant who didn't tremble at the sight of him.

After smoking a bit, Jhingur said, "No singing for the spring festival[4] these days? We haven't heard you."

---

1. Coin of the lowest value.   2. Tanners are treated as untouchable, that is, outcastes, by other Hindus because they handle the carcasses and hides of animals, an activity considered ritually polluting. 3. The name of God is repeated as a greeting and also as an expression of deep emotion.   4. The festival of Holi, during which villagers engage in riotous, carnivalesque play.

"What festival? The belly can't take a holiday. Tell me, how are you getting on lately?"

"Getting by," Jhingur said. "Hard times mean a hard life. If I work all day in the mill there's a fire in my stove. But these days only Buddhu's making money. He doesn't have room to store it! He's built a new house, bought more sheep. Now there's a big fuss about his house-warming. He's sent *pan*[5] to the headmen of all the seven villages around to invite everybody to it."

"When Mother Lakshmi comes men don't see so clearly," Harihar said. "And if you see him, he's not walking on the same ground as you or I. If he talks, it's only to brag."

"Why shouldn't he brag? Who in the village can equal him? But friend, I'm not going to put up with injustice. When God gives I bow my head and accept it. It's not that I think nobody's equal to me but when I hear *him* bragging it's as though my body started to burn. 'A cheat yesterday, a banker today.' He's stepped on us to get ahead. Only yesterday he was hiring himself out in the fields with just a loincloth on to chase crows and today his lamp's burning in the skies."

"Speak," Harihar said, "Is there something I can do?"

"What can you do? He doesn't keep any cows or buffaloes just because he's afraid somebody will do something to them to get at him."

"But he keeps sheep, doesn't he?"

"You mean, 'hunt a heron and get a grouse'?"

"Think about it again."

"It's got to be a plan that will keep him from ever getting rich again."

Then they began to whisper. It's a mystery why there's just as much love among the wicked as malice among the good. Scholars, holy men and poets sizzle with jealousy when they see other scholars, holy men and poets. But a gambler sympathizes with another gambler and helps him, and it's the same with drunkards and thieves. Now, if a Brahman Pandit[6] stumbles in the dark and falls then another Pandit, instead of giving him a hand, will give him a couple of kicks so he won't be able to get up. But when a thief finds another thief in distress he helps him. Everybody's united in hating evil so the wicked have to love one another; while everybody praises virtue so the virtuous are jealous of each other. What does a thief get by killing another thief? Contempt. A scholar who slanders another scholar attains to glory.

Jhingur and Harihar consulted, plotting their course of action—the method, the time and all the steps. When Jhingur left he was strutting—he'd already overcome his enemy, there was no way for Buddhu to escape now.

On his way to work the next day he stopped by Buddhu's house. Buddhu asked him, "Aren't you working today?"

"I'm on my way, but I came by to ask you if you wouldn't let my calf graze with your sheep. The poor thing's dying tied up to the post while I'm away all day, she doesn't get enough grass and fodder to eat."

5. The betel leaf; a symbol of invitation to auspicious ceremonies.   6. A scholar, a learned brahman. The brahman is the highest of the four Hindu classes (castes, at their most general level).

"Brother, I don't keep cows and buffaloes. You know the tanners, they're all killers. That Harihar killed my two cows, I don't know what he fed them. Since then I've vowed never again to keep cattle. But yours is just a calf, there'd be no profit to anyone in harming that. Bring her over whenever you want."

Then he began to show Jhingur the arrangements for the housewarming. Ghee, sugar, flour and vegetables were all on hand. All they were waiting for was the Satyanarayan ceremony.[7] Jhingur's eyes were popping.

When he came home after work the first thing he did was bring his calf to Buddhu's house. That night the ceremony was performed and a feast offered to the Brahmans. The whole night passed in lavishing hospitality on the priests. Buddhu had no opportunity to go to look after his flock of sheep.

The feasting went on until morning. Buddhu had just got up and had his breakfast when a man came and said, "Buddhu, while you've been sitting around here, out there in your flock the calf has died. You're a fine one! The rope was still around its neck."

When Buddhu heard this it was as though he'd been punched. Jhingur, who was there having some breakfast too, said, "Oh God, my calf! Come on, I want to see her! But listen, I never tied her with a rope. I brought her to the flock of sheep and went back home. When did you have her tied with a rope, Buddhu?"

"God's my witness, I never touched any rope! I haven't been back to my sheep since then."

"If you didn't, then who put the rope on her?" Jhingur said. "You must have done it and forgotten it."

"And it was in your flock," one of the Brahmans said. "People are going to say that whoever tied the rope, that heifer died because of Buddhu's negligence."

Harihar came along just then and said, "I saw him tying the rope around the calf's neck last night."

"Me?" Buddhu said.

"Wasn't that you with your stick over your shoulder tying up the heifer?"

"And you're an honest fellow, I suppose!" Buddhu said. "You saw me tying her up?"

"Why get angry with me, brother? Let's just say you didn't tie her up, if that's what you want."

"We will have to decide about it," one of the Brahmans said. "A cow slaughterer should be stoned[8]—it's no laughing matter."

"Maharaj,"[9] Jhingur said, "the killing was accidental."

"What's that got to do with it?" the Brahman said. "It's set down that no cow is ever to be done to death in any way."

"That's right," Jhingur said. "Just to tie a cow up is a fiendish act."

---

7. A ceremony in which the god Vishnu is worshiped to ensure prosperity. Feasting the brahmans is an important part of the worship. *Ghee:* clarified butter, used in Indian cooking and as an offering in Hindu fire rituals.   8. The Hindu veneration of the cow has its origins in the pastoral culture of the Vedic Aryans and the importance of the cow in their religious rituals. As Premchand goes on to show, killing a cow is considered among the most heinous sins.   9. "Lord, Sir, Your Majesty" (Hindi). A respectful form of address for men of higher rank than oneself.

"In the Scriptures it's called the greatest sin," the Brahman said. "Killing a cow is no less than killing a Brahman."

"That's right," Jhingur said. "The cow's got a high place, that's why we respect her, isn't it? The cow is like a mother. But Maharaj, it was an accident—figure out something to get the poor fellow off."

Buddhu stood listening while the charge of murder was brought against him like the simplest thing in the world. He had no doubt it was Jhingur's plotting, but if he said a thousand times that he hadn't put the rope on the calf nobody would pay any attention to it. They'd say he was trying to escape the penance.

The Brahman, that divinity, also stood to profit from the imposition of a penance. Naturally, he was not one to neglect an opportunity like this. The outcome was that Buddhu was charged with the death of a cow; the Brahman had got very incensed about it too and he determined the manner of compensation. The punishment consisted of three months of begging in the streets, then a pilgrimage to the seven holy places,[1] and in addition the price for five cows and feeding 500 Brahmans. Stunned, Buddhu listened to it. He began to weep, and after that the period of begging was reduced by one month. Apart from this he received no favour. There was no one to appeal to, no one to complain to. He had to accept the punishment.

He gave up his sheep to God's care. His children were young and all by herself what could his wife do? The poor fellow would stand in one door after another hiding his face and saying, "Even the gods are banished for cow-slaughter!" He received alms but along with them he had to listen to bitter insults. Whatever he picked up during the day he'd cook in the evening under some tree and then go to sleep right there. He did not mind the hardship, for he was used to wandering all day with his sheep and sleeping beneath trees, and his food at home hadn't been much better than this, but he was ashamed of having to beg, especially when some harridan would taunt him with, "You've found a fine way to earn your bread!" That sort of thing hurt him profoundly, but what could he do?

He came home after two months. His hair was long, and he was as weak as though he were sixty years old. He had to arrange for the money for his pilgrimage, and where's the moneylender who loans to shepherds? You couldn't depend on sheep. Sometimes there are epidemics and you're cleaned out of the whole flock in one night. Furthermore, it was the middle of the hot weather when there was no hope of profit from the sheep. There was an oil-dealer who was willing to loan him money at an interest of two annas per rupee—in eight months the interest would equal the principal. Buddhu did not dare borrow on such terms. During the two months many of his sheep had been stolen. When the children took them to graze the other villagers would hide one or two sheep away in a field or hut and afterwards slaughter them and eat them. The boys, poor lads, couldn't catch a single one of them, and even when they saw, how could

---

1. Various lists are given of the seven holy places of pilgrimage in the Hindu religion. These invariably include Benares (or Kashi), Hardwar, Ramesvaram, and Gaya.

they fight? The whole village was banded together. It was an awful dilemma. Helpless, Buddhu sent for a butcher and sold the whole flock to him for 500 rupees. He took 200 and started out on his pilgrimage. The rest of the money he set aside for feeding the Brahmans.

When Buddhu left, his house was burgled twice, but by good fortune the family woke up and the money was saved.

5

It was Savan,[2] month of rains, with everything lush green. Jhingur, who had no bullocks now, had rented out his field to share-croppers. Buddhu had been freed from his penitential obligations and along with them his delusions about wealth. Neither one of them had anything left; neither could be angry with the other—there was nothing left to be angry about.

Because the jute mill had closed down Jhingur went to work with pick and shovel in town where a very large rest-house for pilgrims was being built. There were a thousand labourers on the job. Every seventh day Jhingur would take his pay home and after spending the night there go back the next morning.

Buddhu came to the same place looking for work. The foreman saw that he was a skinny little fellow who wouldn't be able to do any heavy work so he had him take mortar to the labourers. Once when Buddhu was going with a shallow pan on his head to get mortar Jhingur saw him. "*Ram Ram*" they said to one another and Jhingur filled the pan. Buddhu picked it up. For the rest of the day they went about their work in silence.

At the end of the day Jhingur asked, "Are you going to cook something?"

"How can I eat if I don't?" Buddhu said.

"I eat solid food only once a day," Jhingur said. "I get by just drinking water with ground meal in it in the evenings. Why fuss?"

"Pick up some of those sticks lying around," Buddhu said. "I brought some flour from home. I had it ground there—it costs a lot here in town. I'll knead it on the flat side of this rock. Since you won't eat food I cook I'll get it ready and you cook it."[3]

"But there's no frying pan."

"There are lots of frying pans," Buddhu said. "I'll scour out one of these mortar trays."

The fire was lit, the flour kneaded. Jhingur cooked the chapatties,[4] Buddhu brought the water. They both ate the bread with salt and red pepper. Then they filled the bowl of the hooka. They both lay down on the stony ground and smoked.

Buddhu said, "I was the one who set fire to your cane field."

Jhingur said light-heartedly, "I know."

After a little while he said, "I tied up the heifer and Harihar fed it something."

In the same light-hearted tone Buddhu said, "I know."

Then the two of them went to sleep.

2. The fifth month in the Hindu calendar, marking the season of the monsoon rains, which corresponds to July or August in the Western calendar.   3. As a member of a caste somewhat higher in the hierarchy than Buddhu's, Jhingur cannot eat food cooked by Buddhu.   4. Flat unleavened bread made of whole wheat flour, a staple food of north India.

LU XUN
1881–1936

No country in the world has had so long, continuous, and essentially autonomous a culture as China. For the past century Chinese intellectuals have struggled to free themselves from the oppressive weight of their past and to discover a Chinese cultural identity independent of the traditional civilization. This has, in fact, been a central concern throughout modern Chinese literature. The rapid importation of Western fiction, drama, and poetry in the early twentieth century provided a set of literary models quite distinct from those of the Chinese tradition. Rather than finding in the Western models new possibilities of art, however, many Chinese writers sought in them instruments by which to change the culture or a medium by which to analyze the problems posed by China's cultural legacy. Western writers have often had similar aims, but the marginal status of the writer in European civilization has been a helpful counterweight to such grand purposes. By contrast, the centrality of the writer and intellectual has proved to be one of the tenacious assumptions of traditional Chinese culture, and it is ironic that this assumption stands behind the continuing hope of modern Chinese writers to free China of the weight of its traditional civilization.

Modern China has produced many talented writers, on whom critical opinion is divided. There is, however, almost universal agreement on one authentic genius among them: Lu Xun (also romanized Lu Hsün), the pen name of Zhou Shuren. Few writers of fiction have gained so much fame for such a small oeuvre. His reputation rests entirely on twenty-five stories published between 1918 and 1926, gathered into two collections: *Cheering from the Sidelines* and *Wondering Where to Turn*. In addition to this fiction he published a collection of prose poems, *Wild Grasses*, and a large number of literary and political essays. His small body of stories gives a ruthlessly bleak portrayal of an entire culture that has failed. Whether the culture had indeed failed is less important than the powerful representation he gives of it and the way in which his representations touched a deep chord of response in Chinese readers. Lu was a controlled ironist and a craftsman whose narrative skill far exceeded that of most of his contemporaries; yet underneath his mastery the reader senses the depth of his anger at traditional culture.

Lu was well prepared to engage traditional culture on its own terms. Born into a Shaoxing family of Confucian scholar-officials, he had a traditional education and became a classical scholar of considerable erudition and a writer of poetry in the classical language. Sometimes he displays this learning in his fiction, but there it is always undercut by irony. He grew up at a time when the traditional education system, based on the Confucian classics, was being supplanted by a modern one; and after the early death of his father in 1896, Lu, like so many young Chinese intellectuals of the period, went abroad to study—first at Tokyo and then in 1904 at Sendai, a remote Japanese university where he studied medicine. Because it was successfully modernizing a traditional culture, Japan attracted many young Chinese intellectuals. At the time, the Russians and Japanese were at war in the former Chinese territory of Manchuria. In a famous anecdote describing his moment of decision to become a writer, Lu tells of seeing a slide of a Chinese prisoner about to be decapitated as a Russian spy. What shocked the young medical student was the apathetic crowd of Chinese onlookers, gathered around to watch the execution. At that moment he decided that it was their dulled spirits rather than their bodies that were in need of healing.

Returning to Tokyo, Lu founded a journal in which he published literary essays and set to work translating Western works of fiction. In 1909 financial difficulties drove him back to China, where he worked as a teacher in Hangzhou. When the Republican revolution came in 1911, he joined the ministry of education, moving north to Peking, where he also taught at various universities. The Republican government was soon at the mercy of the powerful armies competing for regional power, and during this period, perhaps for self-protection, Lu devoted himself to traditional scholarship. One might have expected the revolutionary writer of narrative to write the first history of Chinese fiction, as Lu did; but he also produced an erudite and painstaking textual study of the third-century writer Xi Kang that is still used.

On May 4, 1919, a massive student strike forced the Chinese government not to sign the Versailles Peace Treaty, which would have given Japan effective control over the Chinese province of Shandong. The date gave its name to the May Fourth Movement, a group of young intellectuals who advocated the use of vernacular Chinese in all writing and a repudiation of classical Chinese literature.* Though Lu himself kept out of the May Fourth Movement, it was during this period (1918–26) that he wrote all but one of his short stories. During the last decade of his life, he became a political activist and put his satirical talents at the service of the left, becoming one of the favorite writers of the Communist leader Mao Zedong.

Diary of a Madman, Lu's earliest story, takes its title from a work of the Russian novelist Gogol. On one level, it is a parable of the way in which Chinese society devours its members, told under the guise of the discovery of a continuing history of literal cannibalism. But the diarist who makes the "discovery" is indeed, as the title tells us, a madman, and his paranoid raving compels the reader to take the point of view of "sane" society, all the while uncomfortably recognizing that the diarist's claims are true in a figurative sense.

Lu's literary anger at Chinese culture was far from a new phenomenon in Chinese fiction. Traditional novels such as *The Travels of Lao Can* had often ruthlessly satirized the falseness and corruption of the social order. But in traditional Chinese satirical fiction, as in most premodern satire worldwide, the capacity to make moral judgments presumed a secure sense of what was right (whether or not such a sense agreed with conventional morality). In Lu's satire, however, the very capacity to judge evil is itself corrupted by that evil, a circularity perfectly embodied in the figure of a cannibalistic society that feeds on itself.

Diary of a Madman opens with a preface in mannered classical Chinese, giving an account of the discovery of the diary. Such ironic use of classical Chinese to suggest a falsely polite world of social appearances was quite common in traditional Chinese fiction; but its presence usually suggested the alternative possibility of immediate, direct, and genuine language, a language of the heart set against a language of society. The diary that follows the preface is indeed immediate, direct, and genuine, but it is also deluded and twisted. The diarist becomes increasingly convinced that everyone around him wants to eat him; from this growing circle of cannibals observed in the present, the diarist then turns to examine old texts, only to discover that the entire history of the culture has been one of secret cannibalism. Beneath society's false politeness, represented by the voice in the preface, he detects a violent bestiality lurking, a hunger to assimilate others, to "eat men."

As the diary progresses, it becomes increasingly clear that the diarist, who sees

*Written Chinese ranges between two extremes: the "classical" language, which is essentially that of the fourth to third centuries B.C., and the "vernacular," which attempts to represent the spoken language. Poetry and essays tended to be in classical Chinese, while traditional fiction tended to use the vernacular (although there was also fiction in the classical language). In the modern period, poetry and essays also came to be written in vernacular Chinese. Traditional drama used a mixed style; modern drama, the vernacular.

himself as the potential victim, is no less the mirror of the society he describes, assimilating everyone around him into his own fixed view of the world. His reading of ancient texts to discover evidence of cannibalism is a parody of traditional Confucian scholarship, the distorting discovery of "secret meanings" that only serve to confirm beliefs already held. His is a world entirely closed in on itself, one that survives by feeding on itself and its young, a voracity that gives Lu his famous last line, "Save the children . . ."

In contrast to the tormented diarist of *Diary of a Madman*, the characters in *Upstairs in a Wineshop* have already been eaten and fully digested. It is a bleak tale of deaths and wasted lives. The narrator's friend, after grand hopes in his youth, finds himself back in his hometown, going through the hollow motions of filial duty. Caring for the family graves was an act that had great resonance in Confucian family ritual. To put to rest the worries of his mother, who has heard that the nearby riverbank is encroaching on the grave site, the friend has come to rebury his younger brother, whom he barely remembers. On digging up the grave, he finds that there is nothing left of his brother's body. Nevertheless, having bought a new coffin, he puts some dirt from the old grave in it, reburying it beside his father in a different graveyard and enclosing it in bricks for a better seal. As the friend says, "At least I've done enough to pull the wool over Mother's eyes and set her mind at rest." Even when the past has lost all meaning, leaving neither physical remains nor memory, the narrator's friend still finds himself trapped by its forms, which he carries out scrupulously, moving a grave site to protect a body that no longer exists. This return to a hometown and to the now meaningless rituals of the past is echoed at the very close of the story, when the friend tells the narrator that he has given up teaching Western learning and has gone back to teaching the Chinese classics to his pupils: "That's what their fathers *want* them to be taught." Here, as in many of Lu's stories, the characters seem imprisoned in an unreality perpetuated by friends and family. They belong neither to the traditional world nor to the modern world but to some limbo in between, going through the ancient forms, all the while knowing that they mean nothing.

Leo Ou-fan Lee, *Voices from the Iron House: A Study of Lu Xun* (1987), is an excellent introduction to Lu Xun's work, placing it in the context of his life and Chinese cultural history, and Lee, *Lu Xun and His Legacy* (1985), is a collection of scholarly articles treating Lu's literary work, his politics, and his influence. William A. Lyell, *Lu Hsün's Vision of Reality* (1976), is also useful.

PRONOUNCING GLOSSARY

The following list uses common English syllables to provide rough equivalents of selected words whose pronunciation may be unfamiliar to the general reader.

Ah-shun: *ah-shwun*

Ah-zhao: *ah–jao*

Changfu: *chahng-foo*

Changgeng: *chahng-gung*

Laofa: *lao-fah*

Lu Xun: *loo shoon*

Luosi: *lwoh-suh*

Mao Zedong: *mao dzuh-doong*

Shaoxing: *shao-shing*

Weifu: *way-foo*

Xu Xilin: *shoo shee-lin*

Zhao: *jao*

Zhou Shuren: *joe shoo-ren*

Diary of a Madman[1]

There was once a pair of male siblings whose actual names I beg your indulgence to withhold. Suffice it to say that we three were boon companions during our school years. Subsequently, circumstances contrived to rend us asunder so that we were gradually bereft of knowledge regarding each other's activities.

Not too long ago, however, I chanced to hear that one of them had been hard afflicted with a dread disease. I obtained this intelligence at a time when I happened to be returning to my native haunts and, hence, made so bold as to detour somewhat from my normal course in order to visit them. I encountered but one of the siblings. He apprised me that it had been his younger brother who had suffered the dire illness. By now, however, he had long since become sound and fit again; in fact he had already repaired to other parts to await a substantive official appointment.[2]

The elder brother apologized for having needlessly put me to the inconvenience of this visitation, and concluding his disquisition with a hearty smile, showed me two volumes of diaries which, he assured me, would reveal the nature of his brother's disorder during those fearful days.

As to the lapsus calami[3] *that occur in the course of the diaries, I have altered not a word. Nonetheless, I have changed all the names, despite the fact that their publication would be of no great consequence since they are all humble villagers unknown to the world at large.*

Recorded this 2nd day in the 7th year of the Republic.[4]

1

Moonlight's really nice tonight. Haven't seen it in over thirty years. Seeing it today, I feel like a new man. I know now that I've been completely out of things for the last three decades or more. But I've still got to be *very* careful. Otherwise, how do you explain those dirty looks the Zhao family's dog gave me?

I've got good reason for my fears.

2

No moonlight at all tonight—something's not quite right. When I made my way out the front gate this morning—ever so carefully—there was something funny about the way the Venerable Old Zhao looked at me: seemed as though he was afraid of me and yet, at the same time, looked as though he had it in for me. There were seven or eight other people who had their heads together whispering about me. They were afraid I'd see them too! All up and down the street people acted the same way. The meanest looking one of all spread his lips out wide and actually *smiled* at

---

1. Both selections translated by and with notes adapted from William A. Lyell.   2. When there were too many officials for the number of offices to be filled, a man might well be appointed to an office that already had an incumbent. The new appointee would proceed to his post and wait until said office was vacated. Sometimes there would be a number of such appointees waiting their turns.   3. "The fall of the reed [writing instrument]" (literal trans.); hence, lapses in writing.   4. The Qing Dynasty was overthrown and the Republic of China was established in 1911; thus it is April 2, 1918. The introduction is written in classical Chinese, whereas the diary entries that follow are all in the colloquial language.

me! A shiver ran from the top of my head clear down to the tips of my toes, for I realized that meant they already had their henchmen well deployed, and were ready to strike.

But I wasn't going to let that intimidate *me*. I kept right on walking. There was a group of children up ahead and they were talking about me too. The expressions in their eyes were just like the Venerable Old Zhao's, and their faces were iron gray. I wondered what grudge the children had against me that they were acting this way too. I couldn't contain myself any longer and shouted, "Tell me, tell me!" But they just ran away.

Let's see now, what grudge can there be between me and the Venerable Old Zhao, or the people on the street for that matter? The only thing I can think of is that twenty years ago I trampled the account books kept by Mr. Antiquity, and he was hopping mad about it too. Though the Venerable Old Zhao doesn't know him, he must have gotten wind of it somehow. Probably decided to right the injustice I had done Mr. Antiquity by getting all those people on the street to gang up on me. But the children? Back then they hadn't even come into the world yet. Why should they have given me those funny looks today? Seemed as though they were afraid of me and yet, at the same time, looked as though they would like to do me some harm. That really frightens me. Bewilders me. Hurts me.

I have it! Their fathers and mothers have *taught* them to be like that!

3

I can never get to sleep at night. You really have to study something before you can understand it.

Take all those people: some have worn the cangue on the district magistrate's order, some have had their faces slapped by the gentry, some have had their wives ravished by *yamen*[5] clerks, some have had their dads and moms dunned to death by creditors; and yet, right at the time when all those terrible things were taking place, the expressions on their faces were never as frightened, or as savage, as the ones they wore yesterday.

Strangest of all was that woman on the street. She slapped her son and said: "Damn it all, you've got me so riled up I could take a good bite right out of your hide!" She was talking to him, but she was looking at me! I tried, but couldn't conceal a shudder of fright. That's when that ghastly crew of people, with their green faces and protruding fangs, began to roar with laughter. Old Fifth Chen[6] ran up, took me firmly in tow, and dragged me away.

When we got back, the people at home all pretended not to know me. The expressions in their eyes were just like all the others too. After he got me into the study, Old Fifth Chen bolted the door from the outside—just the way you would pen up a chicken or a duck! That made figuring out what was at the bottom of it all harder than ever.

A few days back one of our tenant farmers came in from Wolf Cub Village to report a famine. Told my elder brother the villagers had all

---

5. Local government offices. The petty clerks who worked in them were notorious for relying on their proximity to power to bully and abuse the common people. *Cangue*: a split board, hinged at one end and locked at the other; holes were cut out to accommodate the prisoner's neck and wrists.   6. People were often referred to by their hierarchical position within their extended family.

ganged up on a "bad" man and beaten him to death. Even gouged out his heart and liver. Fried them up and ate them to bolster their own courage! When I tried to horn in on the conversation, Elder Brother and the tenant farmer both gave me sinister looks. I realized for the first time today that the expression in their eyes was just the same as what I saw in those people on the street.

As I think of it now, a shiver's running from the top of my head clear down to the tips of my toes.

If they're capable of eating people, then who's to say they won't eat *me*?

Don't you see? That woman's words about "taking a good bite," and the laughter of that ghastly crew with their green faces and protruding fangs, and the words of our tenant farmer a few days back—it's perfectly clear to me now that all that talk and all that laughter were really a set of secret signals. Those words were poison! That laughter, a knife! Their teeth are bared and waiting—white and razor sharp! Those people are cannibals!

As I see it myself, though I'm not what you'd call an evil man, still, ever since I trampled the Antiquity family's account books, it's hard to say *what* they'll do. They seem to have something in mind, but I can't begin to guess what. What's more, as soon as they turn against someone, they'll *say* he's evil anyway. I can still remember how it was when Elder Brother was teaching me composition.[7] No matter how good a man was, if I could find a few things wrong with him he would approvingly underline my words; on the other hand, if I made a few allowances for a bad man, he'd say I was "an extraordinary student, an absolute genius." When all is said and done, how can I possibly guess what people like *that* have in mind, especially when they're getting ready for a cannibals' feast?

You have to *really* go into something before you can understand it. I seemed to remember, though not too clearly, that from ancient times on people have often been eaten, and so I started leafing through a history book to look it up. There were no dates in this history, but scrawled this way and that across every page were the words BENEVOLENCE, RIGHTEOUS-NESS, and MORALITY. Since I couldn't get to sleep anyway, I read that history very carefully for most of the night, and finally I began to make out what was written *between* the lines; the whole volume was filled with a single phrase: EAT PEOPLE!

The words written in the history book, the things the tenant farmer said—all of it began to stare at me with hideous eyes, began to snarl and growl at me from behind bared teeth!

Why sure, *I'm* a person too, and they want to eat *me*!

4

In the morning I sat in the study for a while, calm and collected. Old Fifth Chen brought in some food—vegetables and a steamed fish. The fish's eyes were white and hard. Its mouth was wide open, just like the mouths of those people who wanted to eat human flesh. After I'd taken a

---

7. That is, to compose essays in the classical style.

few bites, the meat felt so smooth and slippery in my mouth that I couldn't tell whether it was fish or human flesh. I vomited.

"Old Fifth," I said, "tell Elder Brother that it's absolutely stifling in here and that I'd like to take a walk in the garden." He left without answering, but sure enough, after a while the door opened. I didn't even budge—just sat there waiting to see what they'd do to me. I *knew* that they wouldn't be willing to set me loose.

Just as I expected! Elder Brother came in with an old man in tow and walked slowly toward me. There was a savage glint in the old man's eyes. He was afraid I'd see it and kept his head tilted toward the floor while stealing sidewise glances at me over the temples of his glasses. "You seem to be fine today," said Elder Brother.

"You bet!" I replied.

"I've asked Dr. He to come and examine your pulse today."

"He's welcome!" I said. But don't think for one moment that I didn't know the old geezer was an executioner in disguise! Taking my pulse was nothing but a ruse; he wanted to feel my flesh and decide if I was fat enough to butcher yet. He'd probably even get a share of the meat for his troubles. I wasn't a *bit* afraid. Even though I don't eat human flesh, I still have a lot more courage than those who do. I thrust both hands out to see how the old buzzard would make his move. Sitting down, he closed his eyes and felt my pulse[8] for a good long while. Then he froze. Just sat there without moving a muscle for another good long while. Finally he opened his spooky eyes and said: "Don't let your thoughts run away with you. Just convalesce in peace and quiet for a few days and you'll be all right."

Don't let my thoughts run away with me? Convalesce in peace and quiet? If I convalesce till I'm good and fat, they get more to eat, but what do *I* get out of it? How can I possibly be *all right*? What a bunch! All they think about is eating human flesh, and then they go sneaking around, thinking up every which way they can to camouflage their real intentions. They were comical enough to crack *anybody* up. I couldn't hold it in any longer and let out a good loud laugh. Now *that* really felt good. I knew in my heart of hearts that my laughter was *packed* with courage and righteousness. And do you know what? They were so completely subdued by it that the old man and my elder brother both went pale!

But the more *courage* I had, the more that made them want to eat me so that they could get a little of it for free. The old man walked out. Before he had taken many steps, he lowered his head and told Elder Brother, "To be eaten as soon as possible!" He nodded understandingly. So, Elder Brother, you're in it too! Although that discovery seemed unforeseen, it really wasn't, either. My own elder brother had thrown in with the very people who wanted to eat me!

My elder brother is a cannibal!

I'm brother to a cannibal.

Even though I'm to be the victim of cannibalism, I'm *brother* to a cannibal all the same!

---

8. In Chinese medicine the pulse is taken at both wrists.

5

During the past few days I've taken a step back in my thinking. Supposing that old man wasn't an executioner in disguise but really was a doctor—well, he'd still be a cannibal just the same. In *Medicinal ... something or other* by Li Shizhen,[9] the grandfather of the doctor's trade, it says quite clearly that human flesh can be eaten, so how can that old man say that *he's* not a cannibal too?

And as for my own elder brother, I'm not being the least bit unfair to him. When he was explaining the classics to me, he said with his very own tongue that it was all right to *exchange children and eat them*. And then there was another time when he happened to start in on an evil man and said that not only should the man be killed, but his *flesh should be eaten* and *his skin used as a sleeping mat*[1] as well.

When our tenant farmer came in from Wolf Cub Village a few days back and talked about eating a man's heart and liver, Elder Brother didn't seem to see anything out of the way in that either—just kept nodding his head. You can tell from that alone that his present way of thinking is every bit as malicious as it was when I was a child. If it's all right to exchange *children* and eat them, then *anyone* can be exchanged, anyone can be eaten. Back then I just took what he said as explanation of the classics and let it go at that, but now I realize that while he was explaining, the grease of human flesh was smeared all over his lips, and what's more, his mind was filled with plans for further cannibalism.

6

Pitch black out. Can't tell if it's day or night. The Zhao family's dog has started barking again.

Savage as a lion, timid as a rabbit, crafty as a fox . . .

7

I'm on to the way they operate. They'll never be willing to come straight out and kill me. Besides, they wouldn't dare. They'd be afraid of all the bad luck it might bring down on them if they did. And so, they've gotten everyone into cahoots with them and have set traps all over the place so that I'll do *myself* in. When I think back on the looks of those men and women on the streets a few days ago, coupled with the things my elder brother's been up to recently, I can figure out eight or nine tenths of it. From their point of view, the best thing of all would be for me to take off my belt, fasten it around a beam, and hang myself. They wouldn't be guilty of murder, and yet they'd still get everything they're after. Why,

9. Lived from 1518 to 1593. *Taxonomy of Medicinal Herbs*, a gigantic work, was the most important pharmacopoeia in traditional China.   1. Both italicized expressions are from the *Zuozhuan* (Zuo commentary to the *Spring and Summer Annals*, a historical work that dates from the 3rd century B.C.). In 448 B.C., an officer who was exhorting his own side not to surrender is recorded as having said, "When the army of Chu besieged the capital of Song [in 603 B.C.], the people exchanged their children and ate them, and used the bones for fuel; and still they would not submit to a covenant at the foot of their walls. For us who have sustained no great loss, to do so is to cast our state away" (translated by James Legge, 5.817). It is also recorded that in 551 B.C. an officer boasting of his own prowess before his ruler pointed to two men whom his ruler considered brave and said, "As to those two, they are like beasts, whose flesh I will eat, and then sleep upon their skins" (Legge 5.492).

they'd be so beside themselves with joy, they'd sob with laughter. Or if they couldn't get me to do that, maybe they could torment me until I died of fright and worry. Even though I'd come out a bit leaner that way, they'd still nod their heads in approval.

Their kind only know how to eat dead meat. I remember reading in a book somewhere about something called the *hai-yi-na*.[2] Its general appearance is said to be hideous, and the expression in its eyes particularly ugly and malicious. Often eats carrion, too. Even chews the bones to a pulp and swallows them down. Just thinking about it's enough to frighten a man.

The *hai-yi-na* is kin to the wolf. The wolf's a relative of the dog, and just a few days ago the Zhao family dog gave me a funny look. It's easy to see that he's in on it too. How did that old man expect to fool *me* by staring at the floor?

My elder brother's the most pathetic of the whole lot. Since he's a human being too, how can he manage to be so totally without qualms, and what's more, even gang up with them to eat me? Could it be that he's been used to this sort of thing all along and sees nothing wrong with it? Or could it be that he's lost all conscience and just goes ahead and does it even though he knows it's wrong?

If I'm going to curse cannibals, I'll have to start with him. And if I'm going to *convert* cannibals, I'll have to start with him too.

8

Actually, by now even they should long since have understood the truth of this . . .

Someone came in. Couldn't have been more than twenty or so. I wasn't able to make out what he looked like too clearly, but he was all smiles. He nodded at me. His smile didn't look like the real thing either. And so I asked him, "Is this business of eating people right?"

He just kept right on smiling and said, "Except perhaps in a famine year, how could anyone get eaten?" I knew right off that he was one of them—one of those monsters who devour people!

At that point my own courage increased a hundredfold and I asked him, "Is it right?"

"Why are you talking about this kind of thing anyway? You really know how to . . . uh . . . how to pull a fellow's leg. Nice weather we're having."

"The weather *is* nice. There's a nice moon out, too, but I *still* want to know if it's right."

He seemed quite put out with me and began to mumble, "It's not—"

"Not right? Then how come they're still eating people?"

"No one's eating anyone."

"No one's *eating* anyone? They're eating people in Wolf Cub Village this very minute. And it's written in all the books, too, written in bright red blood!"

His expression changed and his face went gray like a slab of iron. His

2. Three Chinese characters are used here for phonetic value only; that is, *hai yi na* is a transliteration into Chinese of the English word *hyena*.

eyes started out from their sockets as he said, "Maybe they are, but it's always been that way, it's—"

"Just because it's always been that way, does that make it *right?*"

"I'm not going to discuss such things with you. If you insist on talking about that, then *you're* the one who's in the wrong!"

I leaped from my chair, opened my eyes, and looked around—but the fellow was nowhere to be seen. He was far younger than my elder brother, and yet he was actually one of them. It must be because his mom and dad taught him to be that way. And he's probably already passed it on to his own son. No wonder that even the children give me murderous looks.

9

They want to eat others and at the same time they're afraid that other people are going to eat them. That's why they're always watching each other with such suspicious looks in their eyes.

But all they'd have to do is give up that way of thinking, and then they could travel about, work, eat, and sleep in perfect security. Think how happy they'd feel! It's only a threshold, a pass. But what do they do instead? What is it that these fathers, sons, brothers, husbands, wives, friends, teachers, students, enemies, and even people who don't know each other *really* do? Why they all join together to hold each other back, and talk each other out of it!

That's it! They'd rather *die* than take that one little step.

10

I went to see Elder Brother bright and early. He was standing in the courtyard looking at the sky. I went up behind him so as to cut him off from the door back into the house. In the calmest and friendliest of tones, I said, "Elder Brother, there's something I'd like to tell you."

"Go right ahead." He immediately turned and nodded his head.

"It's only a few words, really, but it's hard to get them out. Elder Brother, way back in the beginning, it's probably the case that primitive peoples *all* ate some human flesh. But later on, because their ways of thinking changed, some gave up the practice and tried their level best to improve themselves; they kept on changing until they became human beings, *real* human beings. But the others didn't; they just kept right on with their cannibalism and stayed at that primitive level.

"You have the same sort of thing with evolution[3] in the animal world. Some reptiles, for instance, changed into fish, and then they evolved into birds, then into apes, and then into human beings. But the others didn't want to improve themselves and just kept right on being reptiles down to this very day.

"Think how ashamed those primitive men who have remained cannibals must feel when they stand before *real* human beings. They must feel

---

3. Charles Darwin's (1809–1892) theory of evolution was immensely important to Chinese intellectuals during Lu's lifetime and the common coin of much discourse.

even more ashamed than reptiles do when confronted with their brethren who have evolved into apes.

"There's an old story from ancient times about Yi Ya boiling his son and serving him up to Jie Zhou.[4] But if the truth be known, people have *always* practiced cannibalism, all the way from the time when Pan Gu separated heaven and earth down to Yi Ya's son, down to Xu Xilin,[5] and on down to the man they killed in Wolf Cub Village. And just last year when they executed a criminal in town, there was even someone with T.B. who dunked a steamed bread roll in his blood and then licked it off.

"When they decided to eat me, by yourself, of course, you couldn't do much to prevent it, but why did you have to go and *join* them? Cannibals are capable of anything! If they're capable of eating me, then they're capable of eating *you* too! Even within their own group, they think nothing of devouring each other. And yet all they'd have to do is turn back— *change*—and then everything would be fine. Even though people may say, 'It's always been like this,' we can still do our best to improve. And we can start today!

"You're going to tell me it can't be done! Elder Brother, I think you're very likely to say that. When that tenant wanted to reduce his rent the day before yesterday, wasn't it you who said it couldn't be done?"

At first he just stood there with a cold smile, but then his eyes took on a murderous gleam. (I had exposed their innermost secrets.) His whole face had gone pale. Some people were standing outside the front gate. The Venerable Old Zhao and his dog were among them. Stealthily peering this way and that, they began to crowd through the open gate. Some I couldn't make out too well—their faces seemed covered with cloth. Some looked the same as ever—smiling green faces with protruding fangs. I could tell at a glance that they all belonged to the same gang, that they were all cannibals. But at the same time I also realized that they didn't all think the same way. Some thought *it's always been like this* and that they really should eat human flesh. Others knew they shouldn't but went right on doing it anyway, always on the lookout for fear someone might give them away. And since that's exactly what I had just done, I knew they must be furious. But they were all *smiling* at me—cold little smiles!

At this point Elder Brother suddenly took on an ugly look and barked, "Get out of here! All of you! What's so funny about a madman?"

Now I'm on to *another* of their tricks: not only are they unwilling to change, but they're already setting me up for their next cannibalistic feast by labeling me a "madman." That way, they'll be able to eat me without getting into the slightest trouble. Some people will even be grateful to

4. An early philosophical text, *Guan Zi*, reports that the famous cook Yi Ya boiled his son and served him to his ruler, Duke Huan of Qi (685–643 B.C.), because the meat of a human infant was one of the few delicacies the duke had never tasted. Ji and Zhou were the last evil rulers of the Sang (1776–1122 B.C.) and Zhou (1122–221 B.C.) dynasties. The madman has mixed up some facts here.   5. From Lu's hometown, Shaoxing (1873–1907). After studies in Japan, he returned to China and served as head of the Anhui Police Academy. When a high Qing official, En Ming, participated in a graduation ceremony at the academy, Xu assassinated him, hoping that this would touch off the revolution. After the assassination, he and some of his students at the academy occupied the police armory and managed, for a while, to hold off En Ming's troops. When Xu was finally captured, En Ming's personal body guards dug out his heart and liver and ate them. Pan Gu (literally, "Coiled-up Antiquity") was born out of an egg. As he stood up he separated heaven and earth. The world as we know it was formed from his body.

them. Wasn't that the very trick used in the case that the tenant reported? Everybody ganged up on a "bad" man and ate him. It's the same old thing.

Old Fifth Chen came in and made straight for me, looking mad as could be. But he wasn't going to shut *me* up! I was going to tell that bunch of cannibals off, and no two ways about it!

"You can change! You can change from the bottom of your hearts! You ought to know that in the future they're not going to allow cannibalism in the world anymore. If you don't change, you're going to devour each other anyway. And even if a lot of you *are* left, a real human being's going to come along and eradicate the lot of you, just like a hunter getting rid of wolves—or reptiles!"

Old Fifth Chen chased them all out. I don't know where Elder Brother disappeared to. Old Fifth talked me into going back to my room.

It was pitch black inside. The beams and rafters started trembling over-head. They shook for a bit, and then they started getting bigger and bigger. They piled themselves up into a great heap on top of my body!

The weight was incredibly heavy and I couldn't even budge—they were trying to kill me! But I knew their weight was an illusion, and I struggled out from under them, my body bathed in sweat. I was still going to have my say. "Change this minute! Change from the bottom of your hearts! You ought to know that in the future they're not going to allow cannibals in the world anymore . . ."

11

The sun doesn't come out. The door doesn't open. It's two meals a day.

I picked up my chopsticks and that got me thinking about Elder Brother. I realized that the reason for my younger sister's death lay entirely with him. I can see her now—such a lovable and helpless little thing, only five at the time. Mother couldn't stop crying, but *he* urged her to stop, probably because he'd eaten sister's flesh himself and hearing mother cry over her like that shamed him! But if he's still capable of feeling shame, then maybe . . .

Younger Sister was eaten by Elder Brother. I have no way of knowing whether Mother knew about it or not.

I think she *did* know, but while she was crying she didn't say anything about it. She probably thought it was all right, too. I can remember once when I was four or five, I was sitting out in the courtyard taking in a cool breeze when Elder Brother told me that when parents are ill, a son, in order to be counted as a really good person, should slice off a piece of his own flesh, boil it, and let them eat it.[6] At the time Mother didn't come out and say there was anything wrong with that. But if it was all right to eat one piece, then there certainly wouldn't be anything wrong with her eating the whole body. And yet when I think back to the way she cried and cried that day, it's enough to break my heart. It's all strange—very, very strange.

---

6. In traditional literature, stories about such gruesome acts of filial piety were not unusual.

12

Can't think about it anymore. I just realized today that I too have muddled around for a good many years in a place where they've been continually eating people for four thousand years. Younger Sister happened to die at just the time when Elder Brother was in charge of the house. Who's to say he didn't slip some of her meat into the food we ate?

Who's to say I didn't eat a few pieces of my younger sister's flesh without knowing it? And now it's my turn . . .

Although I wasn't aware of it in the beginning, now that I *know* I'm someone with four thousand years' experience of cannibalism behind me, how hard it is to look real human beings in the eye!

13

Maybe there are some children around who still haven't eaten human flesh.

Save the children . . .

April 1918

Upstairs in a Wineshop

While making a trip from north China down into the southeast, I detoured a bit to visit the area where I was born and had grown up. And so it was that I arrived in S-town.[1] It was the midst of winter and a recent snowfall had rendered the landscape bleak and clear. S-town was only ten miles from my home town, less than half a day by boat, and I had once put in a year here teaching school.

A comfortable sense of freedom from my normal round of duties gave such impetus to the nostalgia that assailed me that I ended up checking into a place called the Luosi, a hotel that had not been here back in my teaching days. Since S-town wasn't very large to begin with, I quickly made the rounds on foot as I hunted up a few former colleagues I thought might still be around. It turned out, however, that they had long since scattered to who-knows-where. Then I sauntered over to see the school where I had taught. It had so changed, in both name and appearance, that it no longer felt the least bit familiar. Thus, before two hours were out, my initial homecoming enthusiasm had waned completely. I decided that my detour had been a waste of time and rather regretted having come.

The Luosi rented rooms but sold no food. Meals had to be ordered in from the outside, and the one I got was as tasteless as sawdust. Outside my window, withered moss clung to a stain-mottled wall above which there

1. Lu spent the years from 1902 to 1909 as a student in Japan. Upon his return to China, he taught physiology and chemistry for a year at the Zhejiang Normal School in Hangzhou, about thirty miles from his native Shaoxing. Then from 1909 to 1911, he was engaged as a teacher and dean of studies in the Shaoxing High School. In many of his writings, "S-town" stands loosely for Shaoxing and its environs. The stories, of course, are fictional and reflect only in an approximate way the actual events of Lu's life.

was nothing to relieve the monotonous pallor of the leaden sky, a pallor emphasized by the light snow that had begun dancing in the wind.

Since I hadn't eaten enough lunch and had nothing to occupy my time, my thoughts turned quite naturally to the *Gallon*, a little two-storied wineshop where my face had once been a familiar one. It occurred to me that this new hotel couldn't be far from it. I locked my door, went outside, and headed off to find the *Gallon*. It wasn't that I wanted to get intoxicated, but simply that I wanted to escape, if only for a moment, that awful nothing-to-do feeling that so often besets the traveler.

It was still there too—the same battered old sign, the same cramped and dingy downstairs room. From the manager on down, however, there wasn't a single person I recognized. As far as the *Gallon* was concerned, I had been transformed into a newcomer.

Nonetheless, I walked over to the corner of the room, placed my hand on the bannister, and climbed the stairs I had trod so many times before to the little room on the second floor. Just as I remembered, there were five small tables. The only change was that the latticed window at the rear had been torn out and replaced by a pane of glass.

"A catty of Shaoxing.[2] To eat? Ten fried beancurd cakes, and don't skimp on the hotsauce!" Saying this to the waiter who had followed me up, I made straight for the table under the back window. Since the room was empty, I was free to pick the best seat—a lofty perch by the window from which I could look down on the abandoned courtyard out back. As I think back on it, that yard probably didn't belong to the wineshop. I had gazed down on it many times before, and sometimes in snowy weather just like today's, too. But now, to forgetful eyes that had become accustomed to the scenery of north China, there were things in that courtyard well worth marveling at. Several old plum trees were doggedly blossoming in the midst of the snow as though oblivious to the rigors of winter, and next to a pavilion that had long since collapsed, a camellia showed more than a dozen red blooms against thick, dark green leaves. Fire-bright against the snow, it stood there in all its grandeur, passionate and proud, seeming to scorn the wanderer's willingness to have ventured so far from home. At this point, I suddenly recalled how moist the snow is here in my homeland. It glistens brightly and will stick to anything, nothing like the dry powdery snow of north China that flies up and fills the sky with a white mist whenever the wind picks up.

"Wine . . . for . . . the . . . guest," said the waiter slowly as he arranged cup, chopsticks, winepot, bowl, and saucer. The Shaoxing had arrived. I turned back toward the table and poured myself a cup. It occurred to me that while it was true the north wasn't my home, the south wasn't my home anymore either, for I was treated as a guest here too. No matter how the dry snow of the north scattered in the wind, no matter how the moist snow of the south clung to things—none of that had anything to do with me. Somewhat dejected at the thought, I took a very satisfying sip of wine.

---

2. Shaoxing is famous for the manufacture of the liquor that bears its name. The local distillery is a present-day tourist attraction. *Catty:* a measure of weight, approximately 1.33 pounds.

The flavor was authentic, and the beancurd cakes were done to a turn, but the hotsauce, sad to say, was watery and weak. The people of S-town have never understood what a spicy cuisine is all about.

Perhaps because it was only the afternoon, no aroma of wine permeated the shop. Even after I had downed my third cup, the upstairs was still empty, save for myself and four unoccupied tables. Gazing at the abandoned courtyard outside, I began to feel even more lonely. And yet, I really didn't want anyone to join me either. And so, when I heard footsteps on the stairs, I could not help but feel irritated. I didn't regain my composure until I saw that it was only the waiter. Sitting there alone, I drank two more cups of wine.

The next time, the footsteps were far too slow to be those of the waiter. I was sure that another patron had arrived. I waited until I thought he must have reached the landing and then, somewhat apprehensively, raised my head to get a good look at this alien companion of mine. I rose from my seat with a start. I had never imagined it would prove to be an old friend—that is, if he would still let me call him that. No doubt about it, the man who had come up was an old schoolmate of mine. After graduation, when I was a teacher, he had once been my colleague too. The only thing about him that had really changed was his movement: he had become noticeably sluggish, nothing like the forceful and agile Lü Weifu I had known in years gone by.

"Weifu, is that you? I never expected to meet you here."

"What, can that really be you? Who would have thought . . ."

I invited him to sit down. To my surprise, he actually seemed to hesitate a bit before joining me. My first reaction was simply to consider his behavior a bit odd, but then I began to feel somewhat saddened and even offended. I studied him more closely: same disheveled hair, same long squarish face, but grown old and thin. His spirits seemed subdued too—one might even have said enfeebled. Yes, beneath those thick black brows of his, the life had gone out of his eyes. And yet as he surveyed his present surroundings, the moment he caught sight of the abandoned courtyard, those eyes blazed with that same old flame with which he had once been able to transfix people. I had often seen that look in our school days.

"Well, Weifu," I began enthusiastically, albeit a bit unnaturally, "it must be a good ten years this time. A while back, I heard you were in Jinan,[3] but I was too darned lazy to get a letter off to you."

"Yes, well it was the same with me too. I'm at Taiyuan[4] now. Been there over two years already. Mother's with me. It was when I came back down here to get her that I discovered you'd long since moved away—disappeared without a trace."

"What are you up to in Taiyuan?"

"Family tutor in a fellow provincial's home."

"And before that?"

"Before that?" He fished a cigarette out of his pocket, put it between his

3. Capital of Shandong Province, about five hundred miles north of the two friends' homeland.   4. Capital of Shanxi Province, more than seven hundred miles northwest of their homeland.

lips, lit it, took a puff, exhaled, and then gazed musing into the cloud of smoke. "Didn't do anything really, except a bunch of stuff that didn't amount to anything. Actually, it's the *same* as having done nothing."

In his turn, he asked me about my own situation since we had last met. While I was setting it out for him, I told the waiter to bring another pair of chopsticks and a cup. I ordered another two catties of Shaoxing and passed my own over to him in the meantime. We had never stood on ceremony in the past, but now when it came to ordering the food, we outdid each other in insisting that "you order what *you* want" until things got so mixed up we couldn't tell who had ordered what. We had to depend on the waiter's reading it back to us to determine that four dishes had in fact been ordered: beans cooked with fennel, jellied meat, fried beancurd, and dried black carp.

"As soon as I got back, I realized what an absurd figure I must cut," he said with a wan smile, holding his cigarette aloft with one hand and grasping his winecup with the other. "When I was a kid, I used to think that bees and flies were absurd and pathetic. I'd watch the way they'd light someplace, get spooked by something, and then fly away. After making a small circle, they'd always come back again and land just exactly where they had been before. Who could have imagined that someday, having made my own small circle, I would fly back too? And who would ever have expected that you would do the same thing? Couldn't you have managed to fly a little farther away?"

"Hard to say. I'm probably no different than you—just made my little circle before coming back," I answered with a smile as wan as his own. "But why have you flown back *this* time?"

"Just to do some more stuff that doesn't amount to anything." He downed a cup of wine with a single gulp, took several drags on his cigarette, and opened his eyes a bit wider. "Doesn't amount to a darned thing really, but I suppose it won't do any harm to tell you about it."

The waiter came upstairs with our order. When he had it all set down, it covered the whole table. Permeated with the warm aroma of cigarette smoke and fried beancurd, the little upstairs room now assumed a lively air. Outside the window, the snow was falling even thicker than before.

"You probably know I had a little brother who died when he was three and was buried out in the countryside. I can't even remember what he looked like now, but according to Mother, he was a lovable little guy who got along very well with me. Down to this very day, her eyes mist up whenever she speaks of him. Well anyway, this spring we got a letter from a cousin saying that the riverbank was eroding fast, and if we didn't do something pretty soon, his grave would slide into the river. As soon as Mother found out—she knows enough characters to read letters—she was worried sick. Couldn't sleep nights. But what could *I* do? No money, no time. I was helpless.

"The situation dragged on and on until finally I was able to take advantage of the New Year's vacation to come back down and rebury him." Draining another cup of wine, Weifu looked out the window. "When would you ever see anything like this up north—flowers blooming in all that snow, the ground underneath not even frozen?

"Well anyway, day before yesterday I bought a little coffin in town (I thought the original must have long since rotted away), picked up some cotton batting and quilts, hired four grave diggers, and set out to rebury him. Suddenly I began to feel very positive about the whole thing. Now I actually *wanted* to dig up the grave, wanted to have a look at the dead bones of the little brother who had once been so close to me. I'd never quite had such feelings before in my entire life.

"When we got to the gravesite, sure enough, the river water had eaten away at the bank until it was less than two feet from the mound. And what a pitiful little grave mound it was, too. No one had added any dirt to it for over two years, and it was pathetically flat. With an air of command, I stood there in the snow, pointed at it, and gave the order: 'Open it up!' Coming from me, such an authoritative command had an incongruous ring, for I'm a very run-of-the-mill kind of man, not at all accustomed to telling people what to do. But the grave diggers didn't seem to find anything in the least odd about my giving commands. They simply started digging.

"Once they had the mound open, I went over and looked inside. As I had expected, the coffin was almost gone—transformed into shreds of rotting wood. Heart beating wildly, I carefully brushed aside what was left of it, so that I might be able to see my brother. To my surprise, however, there was nothing there, absolutely nothing! The quilt he'd been wrapped in, the clothes he'd worn, his skeleton—all gone. I had always heard that the hair is the last part of the body to rot. 'Perhaps there's still some hair left,' I thought to myself as I knelt down and sifted through the dirt around the place where I thought the pillow must have been. Nothing there either. He had disappeared without leaving a trace!"

I noticed that Weifu's eyes were slightly red, but immediately realized that this signaled nothing more than the fact he had had too much to drink. While we were talking, he had eaten next to nothing but had continued to down cup after cup of wine, and must have long since gone through a good catty or more. The alcohol seemed to put new life into him, both physically and spiritually. He was now beginning to resemble the old Weifu I used to know. Swinging around in my chair, I ordered another two catties of wine; then I turned back and, sitting directly across from my old friend, listened in silence as he continued.

"Actually, at that point, I really didn't have to go through with it. I could simply have smoothed the grave over, sold the coffin, and that would have been the end of it. To be sure, trying to get rid of a coffin like that would have looked a bit peculiar, but as long as I didn't ask too much, I'd probably have been able to sell it back to the store where I'd bought it. At the very least, I'd get enough for a drink or two. But I didn't even try.

"Instead, I spread the quilt out in the new coffin just as I had originally planned, took some dirt from the spot where my brother's body had lain, wrapped it in cotton batting, and put the resulting package inside the quilt. Then I had the coffin moved to the graveyard where my father is buried. I had them bury it next to him. This time I had the coffin enclosed in bricks to make a good tight seal. Had to spend most of my day yesterday supervising the workmen. At any rate, it's over and done with, and at least

I've done enough to pull the wool over Mother's eyes and set her mind at rest.

"Hey, why are you looking at me like that? Do you blame me for being so different from the old Lü Weifu who lives in your memory? I can understand your feelings. I too can still remember how it was when we were young, how we used to go to the City Temple together and yank the beards off the statues of the gods, and how we'd often argue the whole day about this or that way of reforming China, until we got so worked up we even came to blows. But now, I am as you see me—a man who goes through the motions of living without taking anything seriously. Sometimes it occurs to me that if my friends from back then were to see me now, they'd disown me. But I am what I am." He fished out another cigarette, dangled it between his lips, and lit up.

"I can tell from your eyes that you still have hopes I'll do something to realize some of our old ideals. Though I'm much more insensitive than I used to be, I can still sense some things by the way a man looks at me. And I'm grateful for your faith in me too. But at the same time, it makes me anxious for fear that when all is said and done, I'll let down those old friends who, like you, continue to think well of me to this very day."

He paused in his recitation, took several drags on his cigarette, and then resumed in slow, measured tones: "Only today, just before I came here to the *Gallon*, I did something else that didn't amount to anything, but at least it was something I wanted to do. It had to do with an old neighbor of ours by the name of Changfu. He was the boatman who lived on the east side of our place. Had a daughter named Ah-shun. You probably saw her now and then when you used to come by to see me. But she was so young back then that you probably didn't give her a second glance. Didn't turn into any great beauty when she grew up, either—just an ordinary kind of oval face that was a bit drawn and somewhat on the sallow side. But those *eyes* of hers! And those long lashes! The whites of her eyes were as clear as a cloudless sky at night. And I'm talking about a northern sky on a night when there's no wind. We have nothing to compare to it down here.

"Ah-shun was a very capable girl, too. Lost her mother when she was eleven or so. From then on, the care of her younger brother and younger sister fell entirely on her. And then of course, she had to attend to her father's needs too. She did it all, and she did it well. Knew how to save a penny, too. After she took over the management of the household, the family's finances gradually got onto a better footing. There was hardly a neighbor around who didn't have a good word for Ah-shun. Even Changfu would often say how grateful he was to have a daughter like her.

"Well, at any rate, when I was on the point of setting out to come back down here this time, my mother started thinking about Ah-shun. Funny what long memories old people have. She said she remembered a time when Ah-shun had wanted a red velvet flower to put in her hair. Seemed that she'd seen another girl wearing one and decided that she'd like one too. But she couldn't find any place that sold them. She bawled and bawled until Changfu finally gave her a beating. Went around with red and swollen eyes for a couple of days afterwards.

"Artificial flowers like that come from outside the province and if she couldn't find one even in S-town, then she certainly wouldn't be able to find it anywhere else. As long as I was coming down this way, Mother told me to buy her one somewhere along the way. Well that was one task I didn't mind in the least. As a matter of fact, I rather looked forward to it, for I honestly felt like doing something for Ah-shun myself.

"When I was down here the year before last to pick up Mother and take her back up north with me, I happened by Changfu's place one day and, somehow or other, struck up a conversation with him. The upshot was that he invited me to stay for a snack, a bowl of cereal made out of buckwheat flour. He made a point of telling me they made theirs with white sugar. Think about that: a fisherman who's able to keep white sugar in the house can't be any pauper, that's for sure. As a matter of fact, you could say he must be eating rather well. Changfu kept pressing me to sit down until I couldn't very well say no. But I agreed only on the condition that he give me a small bowl. Well, he wasn't born yesterday and probably knew what I meant, so he said to his daughter: 'Ah-shun, you know these educated people—don't know what a real meal is, so make sure you use a small bowl. And don't hold back on the sugar either!"

"When she brought it out, I almost fell off my chair. That bowl was huge. There was easily enough in it to keep my mouth on duty the whole day. But then I saw Changfu's bowl and realized that mine really was small by comparison. I'd never eaten buckwheat cereal in my whole life and didn't find it exactly palatable when I tasted it now, but there was no denying it *was* sweet. Looking as casual about it as I could, I downed a few mouthfuls and was just about to set aside my bowl when I happened to catch a glimpse of Ah-shun standing over in the corner. I lost my nerve immediately, for she was watching me with a mixture of fear and hope, probably afraid that she hadn't made it just right, but at the same time hoping that I'd like it. I knew that if I left over half the bowl, she would feel terribly disappointed, and guilty as well.

"Through sheer will power, I widened my throat as much as I could and crammed that cereal down as fast as it would go, almost as fast as Changfu himself. For the first time in my life I understood what a painful thing forced feeding is. For unpleasantness, I could remember nothing that came even close—except, perhaps, once during my childhood when I had to eat a bowl of tapeworm medicine mixed with brown sugar.

"And yet I didn't mind in the least, for when Ah-shun came to take my bowl, that smile of utter satisfaction, which she was doing her best to hold in, more than repaid any discomfort I may have suffered. Though I left feeling so bloated that I couldn't get to sleep that night and had one nightmare after the other, I still wished Ah-shun nothing but the best and hoped that, for her sake, the world would take a turn for the better. Almost immediately, however, I laughed at myself for entertaining such thoughts, for I realized that they were simply vestiges of the old dreams I'd entertained in days gone by. After that, I put her completely out of mind.

"I hadn't known that she'd once gotten a beating over an artificial velvet flower, but hearing my mother bring it up, my experience with the buckwheat cereal came back to mind and the memory of it made me especially diligent on Ah-shun's behalf. I searched the town over in Taiyuan without finding one. It wasn't until I got to—"

Shish! Outside the window, an accumulation of snow that had been weighing upon a camellia branch, bending it down into an arc, now slid to the ground as the branch stretched itself straight out, showing off its dark glistening leaves and blood-red blossoms. The leaden sky was even darker now and you could hear chirping everywhere: dusk was fast approaching and, unable to find any food on the snow-blanketed ground, birds now hurried back to their nests for the night.

"—until I got to Jinan," he continued after turning to look out the window, "that I managed to find velvet flowers. I had no idea whether they were like the one she'd taken a beating for, but they *were* velvet. And since I didn't know whether she preferred lighter or darker hues, I bought her a bright red one and a pale pink one.

"It was only this afternoon, right after lunch, that I went to look her up. Put off my departure a whole day just to do it. The house was still there, but as I looked at it, there seemed to be something that wasn't quite right. Dismissing that as my own subjective feeling, I walked closer and saw Changfu's son and second daughter, Ah-zhao, standing in the doorway. They were both grown now. Ah-zhao had developed into a young woman who looked nothing like her elder sister. Looked more like some sort of witch.

"When she saw me coming toward her, she shot inside like a bolt. I learned from the son that Changfu wasn't at home. 'How about your elder sister?' He immediately opened his eyes into a wide and angry stare and asked what business I had with her. He suddenly looked so vicious you would have thought he was a wild animal ready to pounce on me to tear the flesh from my body with bared fangs. Trying to smooth things over as best I could, I left in a hurry. I never have the guts to see things through any more . . .

"You probably don't know this, but I'm much more afraid of calling on people than I used to be. You see, now that I *know* what a contemptible wretch I am, I even despise myself. Sure, people may not come right out and *say* anything to me, but knowing how they must feel about me, what's the point in going to see them? Deliberately making them uncomfortable? Despite all that, I felt this was one task I had to see through. After wracking my brains for a while, I walked over to the firewood store diagonally across from their place. Old Granny Laofa was still there. She recognized me and, much to my surprise, invited me in. After we'd exchanged greetings, I explained why I had come back to S-town and why I was looking for Changfu.

"She sighed and said, 'Too bad Ah-shun wasn't lucky enough to get to wear your flowers.' Granny Laofa then told me the whole story, from beginning to end.

" 'It was probably around spring last year,' she began, 'that Ah-shun began lookin' all weak and pale. Later on, she took to cryin' a lot. When they asked her why, she wouldn't say. Sometimes she'd cry the whole night. Finally, Changfu couldn't take it anymore and blew his top. Cursed her out for stayin' an old maid too long, and said it was this that was makin' her crazy. Come fall, somethin' that started out as just a cold ended up gettin' so bad Ah-shun couldn't even get out of bed. Wasn't till a few days before she died that she finally told her dad what was really wrong. Said that for a long time she'd been the way her mother used to be—spittin' up blood and breakin' into night sweats. She'd hidden it all that time so as not to worry him.

"'And then one night, her uncle, Changgeng, came round tryin' to borrow money—he did that a lot. He wouldn't take no for an answer. When Ah-shun wouldn't give 'im any, Changgeng gave a mean laugh and said, "Don't get so uppity there. I'm a helluva lot better than the man they've got picked out for *you!*" After that, Ah-shun got really down in the dumps. Such a modest girl she was. Rather than askin' round to get the facts about this man her dad was supposed to have picked out, she just bawled. Changfu finally found out how she'd been taken in by Changgeng and told her the truth about what a fine fellow he'd lined up for her. By then, though, the harm'd been done. You could tell she didn't really believe what her dad said because she came back with: "It's a good thing I'm in the shape I am, 'cause now it don't matter one way or the other."

"'If the man he'd picked for her wasn't a match for Changgeng, that'd be enough to scare anybody to death! Not even a match for a *chicken thief?* What sort of excuse for a man would that be? I got to see her intended in person when he came to Ah-shun's funeral. Had nice clean clothes and wasn't all that hard to look at either. Tears in his eyes, he told everybody there how he'd poled a boat almost half his life. Scrimped and saved until he'd finally put enough by to buy himself a wife. And then she went and died on 'im. You could tell he was a good man and that all that stuff Changgeng had said was nothin' but a pack of lies. What a pity that Ah-shun should believe that bastard's crap and go lose her life for nothin'.' The old lady finished it all up by telling me: 'If you wanted to put it on anything, you'd have to put it on Ah-shun's bad fate.'

"Well, whatever the case, I was through with my part of it. But what was I to do with the flowers? I asked Granny Laofa if she would give them to Ah-zhao. Since Ah-zhao had treated me like a wild wolf or worse, I really didn't *feel* like letting her have them. So then why did I? Because that way I'd be able to tell Mother how delighted she was. What's it all amount to anyway? Right now, all I've got to worry about is muddling through till New Year's is over and then I can go back to teaching my *thus-spoke-the-Master* and *so-states-the-Poetry-Classic*."[5]

"You're teaching the *classics?* I asked in astonishment.

"Of course. Did you think I was still teaching ABCD?[6] At first I had two students, one studying the *Poetry Classic* and the other doing *The Mencius*.[7] Later on a third one joined us, a girl. She's reading *Maxims for Young Ladies*.[8] I don't even teach mathematics anymore. It's not that I don't want to, it's just that their fathers don't want me to."

"I never expected that you'd actually be teaching that kind of thing."

"That's what their fathers *want* them to be taught. I'm an outsider, so

5. Translation of the four-character phrase *ziyue shiyun*, a shorthand reference to classical learning. The friends, of course, consider all such erudition reactionary and useless. The *Master* is Confucius.   6. Shorthand for Western learning; the original text prints it in Roman letters.   7. Mencius (372–279 B.C.) is sometimes referred to as the St. Paul of Confucianism.   8. An anonymous text known in several different versions.

it's all the same to me. What's it all amount to anyway? All I have to do is muddle along as best . . ."

His entire face was flushed now and he seemed slightly inebriated. The gleam in his eyes, however, had subsided. I gave in to a light sigh and for the moment could think of nothing to say. There was a flurry of sound on the staircase as several newcomers crowded their way up. First in line was a short man with bulging jowls. Second, a tall fellow with a conspicuous red nose.

Others followed behind them, stomping up the stairs with such force that the whole building trembled. I turned and looked at Lü Weifu just as he also turned to look at me. I told the waiter to total up our bill.

"Does it give you enough to get by on?" I asked as I prepared to leave.

"Yes, it . . . To tell the truth, I get twenty a month and don't get by all that well."

"What do you plan on doing after this?"

"After this? I don't know. Just think, not a single one of the hopes and dreams we had back then has worked out, has it? I don't know anything anymore. I don't even know what tomorrow's going to bring, or even the next moment . . ."

The waiter came up and handed me the check. Not nearly so deferential as when I first arrived, he simply threw me a single glance and then, looking utterly uninterested, stood to one side and smoked while I took out the money to pay.

Weifu and I walked out of the wineshop together, but since his hotel lay in the opposite direction to mine, we parted at the door. As I walked off toward the Luosi, with the cold wind and snowflakes blowing against my face, I felt refreshed. Judging from the color of the sky, it was already dusk. Along with the surrounding buildings and streets, I too became woven into a pure white and ever-shifting web of snow.

February 16, 1926

JAMES JOYCE
1882–1941

An Irish writer who spent most of his life outside Ireland and became an international figure, James Joyce is the most important and influential exponent of literary modernism in prose. He created a narrative style that changed the way modern novelists could afford to write about the world, and writers as diverse as the American William Faulkner, the Irish Samuel Beckett, the Colombian Gabriel García Márquez, and the French "new novelists" Alain Robbe-Grillet and Nathalie Sarraute are indebted to his twentieth-century revision of the art of the novel. Joyce's playful manipulation of language, perspective, and blocks of time is not entirely new to literary history—Laurence Sterne's *Tristram Shandy* gave the example in 1760—but his progressive exploration of the resources of literary language inspired many contemporary authors eager to break away from the traditions of the immediate past and to express, in newly relevant form, the intricacies of modern consciousness. Joyce's best-known contribution to modern literature is the "stream of consciousness" technique that attempts to reproduce the natural, often arbitrary, flow of thoughts and emotions. Influential because it allows the reader apparent access to the very workings of a character's mind, stream of consciousness also reminds us—in its rejection of orthodox sentence structure and logical transition—that literary texts achieve their most realistic effects only by manipulating language itself.

Born in Dublin on February 2, 1882, to May Murray and John Stanislaus Joyce, he was given the impressive name of James Augustine Aloysius Joyce. His father held a well-paid and easy post in the civil service, and the family was comfortable until 1891, when his job was eliminated with a small pension and he declined to take up more demanding work elsewhere. The Joyce family (there were ten children) moved steadily down the social and economic scale, and life became difficult under the improvident guidance of a man whom Joyce later portrayed as "a drinker, a good fellow, a storyteller, somebody's secretary, something in a distillery, a tax-gatherer, a bankrupt, and at present a praiser of his own past." Joyce attended the well-known Catholic preparatory school of Clongowes Wood College from six to nine years of age, leaving when his family could no longer afford the tuition; two years later, he was admitted as a scholarship student to Belvedere College in Dublin. Both were Jesuit schools, and provided a rigorous Catholic training against which Joyce violently rebelled but which he was never able to forget. In Belvedere College, shaken by a dramatic hell-fire sermon shortly after his first experience with sex, he even thought of becoming a priest; the life of the senses and his vocation as an artist won out, however, and the sermon and his reaction to it became part of A *Portrait of the Artist as a Young Man*. After graduating from Belvedere in 1898, Joyce entered another Irish Catholic institution—University College, Dublin—where he consciously rebelled against Irish tradition and looked abroad for new values. Teaching himself Norwegian to read Henrik Ibsen in the original, he criticized the writers of the Irish Literary Renaissance as provincial and had no interest in joining their ranks. Like his hero, Stephen Dedalus, he decided in 1902 to escape the stifling conventions of his native country and leave for the Continent.

This first trip did not last long. For six months, he supported himself in Paris by giving English lessons, but when his mother turned seriously ill he was called home. After her death, he taught school for a time in Dublin and then returned to the Continent with Nora Barnacle, a country woman from western Ireland with whom he had two children and whom he married in 1931. The young couple moved to Trieste, where Joyce taught English in a Berlitz school and where he started writing both the short stories collected as *Dubliners* and an early version (partially published as *Stephen Hero* in 1944) of A *Portrait of the Artist as a Young Man*. *Dubliners* sketches aspects of life in Dublin as Joyce knew it, which means that the parochiality, piety, and repressive conventions of Irish life are shown stifling artistic and psychological development. Whether it be the young boy who arrives too late at the fair in *Araby*, the poor-aunt laundress of *Clay*, or the frustrated writer Gabriel Conroy of *The Dead*, characters in *Dubliners* dream of a better life against a dismal and impoverishing background whose cumulative effect is one of despair. The style of *Dubliners* is more realistic than Joyce's later fiction, but he is already employing a structure of symbolic meanings and revelatory moments called "epiphanies." The all-blanketing white snow at the end of *The Dead* suggests the chill uniformity of death and Gabriel Conroy's alienation from the rest of his world. It is Gabriel who observes the scene and whose suddenly expanded vision of the whole universe being swallowed up in oblivion constitutes an epiphany, a moment when everything fuses and makes sense in a larger spiritual perspective.

A *Portrait of the Artist as a Young Man* is based on Joyce's life until 1902, but the novel is clearly not a conventional autobiography and the reader recognizes in the first pages a radical experiment in fictional language. From the child's vocabulary and fragmented echoing of his parents' baby talk ("nicens little boy," "baby tuckoo") to the mature rhetoric of the end ("Old father, old artificer, stand me now and ever in good stead"), everything in *Portrait* is introduced sequentially and shaped to make the most powerful cumulative impact. Even Stephen's first naive thoughts prepare for themes developed later on: the importance of sense impressions, from the clammy bed to his mother's smell; the political symbolism of Dante's green and maroon hairbrushes; the bird imagery and threat of punishment on high in Dante's reproach; and the small boy's habit of thinking over things and rephrasing them in poetic language. Events that stand out in the young boy's mind, such as the humiliation of receiving an unfair spanking in school, are described with their full impact because they are not simply first-person (subjective) or third-person (objective) accounts but an imaginative combination of the two. An outside observer with access to all Stephen's feelings follows the course of events. *Portrait*, like *Dubliners*, is still in the tradition of naturalist narrative and specifically of the *Künstlerroman* or artist-novel, which follows chronologically the career of its artist hero. Its sophisticated symbolism, use of epiphanies, and stress on dramatic dialogue, however, hint at the radical break with narrative tradition that Joyce was preparing in *Ulysses*.

Ulysses (1922) is one of the most celebrated instances of literary censorship. Its serial publication in the New York *Little Review* from 1918 to 1920 was stopped as obscene by the U.S. Post Office after a complaint from the New York Society for the Prevention of Vice. The novel was banned and all available copies were actually burned in England and America until a 1933 decision by Judge Woolsey in a U.S. district court lifted the ban in the States. The problem was not new: Joyce's realistic descriptions of sensory experience from bedroom to bathroom, his playfully allusive use of language, and his antinationalist and antireligious attitudes had already offended many readers from *Dubliners* (which an Irish printer refused to print on the grounds that it was anti-Irish) to *Portrait* (which was refused as a "work of doubtful character even though it may be a classic"). While Joyce's descriptions have lost none of their pungency, it is hard to imagine a reader who would not be struck also by another side—by the "classical" density and enormous mythic scope of this complex, symbolic, and linguistically innovative novel. Openly referring to an ancient predecessor, the *Odyssey* of Homer ("Ulysses" is the Latin name for the hero Odysseus), *Ulysses* structures numerous episodes to suggest parallels with the Greek epic, and transforms the twenty-year Homeric journey home into the day-long wanderings through Dublin of an unheroic advertising man, Leopold Bloom, and a rebellious young teacher and writer from *Portrait*, Stephen Dedalus.

Bloom is in one sense a perfectly ordinary man, the "common man" of modern society. He comes to no great decisions (whereas Stephen decides to leave Ireland and dedicate himself to art), and his life will continue its uneventful and somewhat downtrodden way. Yet Bloom is the most fully developed character in the book, a man whose dimensions encompass the mythic overtones of the outcast (Ulysses or the Wandering Jew), the psychological tension of a father and husband cut off from family relationships, and (in bathroom, bedroom, and meat market) the most mundane domestic details. The ancient Ulysses was a man of many roles, and so is the modern Bloom. If the *Odyssey* has been described as one of the first voyages of Everyman, *Ulysses* shows Everyman in the twentieth century. According to T. S. Eliot, Joyce's paralleling of ancient myth and modern life is more than literary homage; it is "a way of controlling, of ordering, of giving a shape and significance to the immense panorama of futility and anarchy which is contemporary history."

There is no classical parallel, however, for the language of *Ulysses*, which has long been recognized as a paradigm of modernist style. Its quick shifts in points of view, changes of narrative voice, and blendings of the most exacting realism with hallucinatory scenes that combine memory and distorted current vision are the literary equivalent of cinematic montage. In addition, Joyce abandoned the regular syntax and logical sequences of traditional narrative for a style that tried to represent the flow of thought and emotion in a character's mind. A development of the "interior monologue," this stream of consciousness technique is far looser and freer in its fragmented, punning, freely associating representation of consciousness. Sometimes it is a sleepy jangle where the relaxed mind lazily plays with sound associations: "Sinbad the Sailor and Tinbad the Tailor and Jinbad the Jailer and Whinbad the Whaler and Ninbad the Nailer and . . ." Sometimes it is more obscure, as in the introduction to a bar scene with its associative, fragmented vision and imitations of different sounds: "Bronze by gold heard the hoofirons, steelyringing Imperthnthn thnthnthn. Chips, picking chips off rocky thumbnail, chips. Horrid! And gold flushed more. A husky fifenote blew. Blew. Blue bloom in on the Gold pinnacled hair." In the famous ending to the novel, it combines passion and response in specific images called up from memory, as his wife, Molly, recalls her first yielding to Bloom: "O that awful deepdown torrent O and the sea the sea crimson sometimes like fire and the glorious sunsets and the figtrees in the Alameda gardens yes and all the queer little streets and pink and blue and yellow houses and the rosegardens and the jessamine and geraniums and cactuses . . . yes and then he asked me would I yes to say yes my mountain flower and first I put my arms around him yes and drew him down to me so he could feel my breasts all perfume yes and his heart was going like mad and yes I said yes I will Yes." The extraordinary thing about Joyce's stream of consciousness technique, as the perspicacious Judge Woolsey commented in his court decision, was that it represents the many layers of experience making up each individual's current consciousness: "Not only what is in the focus of each man's observation of the actual things about him, but also in a penumbral zone residua of past impressions, some recent and some drawn up by association from the domain of the subconscious." Taken to the extreme, it is so completely individualized that a reader who remains outside the personal code cannot break in; at its best, though, it can draw on echoes and clues already present in the text. The complicated inner reference in *Ulysses* provided a glimpse of unparalleled richness into human awareness and set a challenging example for narrative style after Joyce.

After the publication of *Ulysses*, Joyce spent the next seventeen years writing an even more complex work: *Finnegans Wake* (1939). Despite the title, which refers to a ballad in which the bricklayer Tim Finnegan is brought back to life at his wake when somebody spills whisky on him, the novel is the multivoiced, multidimensional dream of Humphrey Chimpden Earwicker: HCE, Here Comes Everybody, Haveth Childers Everywhere, Tristan, Humpty-Dumpty, and Allmen. HCE's dream includes his wife, Anna Earwicker, as Anna Livia Plurabelle, ALP, the voice of the river Liffey, or a suggestion of historical "holy wars," and together they constitute the originating pair of Adam and Eve. *Finnegans Wake* expands on the encyclopedic series of literary and cultural references underlying *Ulysses* and does so in language that has been even more radically broken apart and reassembled. Digressing exuberantly in all directions at once, with complex puns and hybrid words that mix languages, *Finnegans Wake* is—in spite of its cosmic symbolism—a game of language and reference by an artist "hoppy on akkant of his joycity." It has not achieved the wide audience of *Portrait*, or *Ulysses*, but when

Joyce died in Zurich in 1941 he considered it the culmination of his career as a writer.

A *Portrait of the Artist as a Young Man* shows only the beginnings of the fanciful and allusive use of language to come. The novel falls into three general sections: Stephen Dedalus's infancy and boyhood until age sixteen, by which time he has found religious doubt and had his first sexual experience; his painful alternation between religious belief and doubt at Belvedere College (this section includes the famous hell-fire sermon but also Stephen's conscious acceptance of the world of nature and of himself as Stephanoforos, the ritually crowned artist—*stephanos* being the Greek word for a "victory wreath"); and a last section in which Stephen examines his experience, develops a theory of art, and prepares for exile and the solitary life of an artist: "Amen. So be it. Welcome, O life! I go to encounter for the millionth time the reality of experience and to forge in the smithy of my soul the uncreated conscience of my race." In the first chapter, printed here, Stephen's earliest memories of home and school are presented through still-naive eyes and the short, choppy sentences of a child's groping attempts to make sense of the world. Drawn to adopt the rhythms of the child's thought, the reader participates in the young boy's wonder at tastes, textures, and smells, or at the peculiar language and behavior of adults; in his half-formed curiosity about sex and religious belief; in his frustrated rage at an unjust punishment or his triumph as he appeals to authority against his tormenter. The drops of water falling into the brimming bowl at the end of the first chapter already suggest the way that Stephen's early experiences will merge into the undivided whole that underlies A *Portrait of the Artist as a Young Man*.

Harry Levin, *James Joyce: A Critical Introduction* (1941), is an excellent and readable general introduction. The standard and detailed biography, with illustrations, is Richard Ellmann, *James Joyce* (1982). Morris Beja, *James Joyce: A Literary Life* (1992), includes recent scholarship. Derek Attridge, ed., *The Cambridge Companion to James Joyce* (1990), and Mary T. Reynolds, ed., *James Joyce: A Collection of Critical Essays* (1993), treat various aspects of the work. Thomas F. Staley and Bernard Benstock, eds., *Approaches to Joyce's "Portrait": Ten Essays* (1976), focus on the novel and its cultural contexts. Diverse critical approaches are represented in Alan Roughley, *James Joyce and Critical Theory: An Introduction* (1991), and Suzette A. Henke's feminist study *James Joyce and the Politics of Desire* (1990), which includes a chapter on *Portrait*. With pictures, maps, and relevant historical information, Bruce Bidwell and Linda Heffer provide a setting for Joyce's work in *The Joycean Way: A Topographic Guide to Dubliners and A Portrait of the Artist as a Young Man* (1982). David Pierce, *James Joyce's Ireland* (1992), includes contemporary photographs by Dan Harper and uses documents, photographs, and copious quotation to reconstruct Joyce's biography in historical context.

A Portrait of the Artist as a Young Man

Part 1

Once upon a time and a very good time it was there was a moocow coming down along the road and this moocow that was coming down along the road met a nicens little boy named baby tuckoo. . . .

His father told him that story: his father looked at him through a glass: he had a hairy face.

He was baby tuckoo. The moocow came down the road where Betty Byrne lived: she sold lemon platt.[1]

> O, the wild rose blossoms
> On the little green place.

He sang that song. That was his song.

> O, the green wothe botheth.

When you wet the bed first it is warm then it gets cold. His mother put on the oilsheet. That had the queer smell.

His mother had a nicer smell than his father. She played on the piano the sailor's hornpipe for him to dance. He danced:

> Tralala lala
> Tralala tralaladdy
> Tralala lala
> Tralala lala.

Uncle Charles and Dante clapped. They were older than his father and mother but uncle Charles was older than Dante.

Dante had two brushes in her press.[2] The brush with the maroon velvet back was for Michael Davitt and the brush with the green velvet back was for Parnell.[3] Dante gave him a cachou[4] every time he brought her a piece of tissue paper.

The Vances lived in number seven. They had a different father and mother. They were Eileen's father and mother. When they were grown up he was going to marry Eileen. He hid under the table. His mother said:

—O, Stephen will apologise.

Dante said:

—O, if not, the eagles will come and pull out his eyes.[5]

> Pull out his eyes,
> Apologise,
> Apologise,
> Pull out his eyes.
>
> Apologise,
> Pull out his eyes,
> Pull out his eyes,
> Apologise.

•   •   •

The wide playgrounds were swarming with boys. All were shouting and the prefects urged them on with strong cries. The evening air was pale and chilly and after every charge and thud of the footballers the greasy leather orb flew like a heavy bird through the grey light. He kept on the

1. Barley-sugar candy.   2. A cupboard or chest of drawers.   3. Irish patriots. Davitt (1846–1906) broke with Parnell (1846–1891) when the latter was accused of adultery by Captain O'Shea in 1889. Parnell was leader of the Irish Parliamentary Party in the British House of Commons, and the Irish nationalists were split over whether he should continue in that position. His power was broken when the Irish Roman Catholic hierarchy denounced him.   4. Imitated sound of a sneeze.   5. Echo of a song for children by the hymnologist Isaac Watts, based on Proverbs 30:17: "The eye that mocketh at his father, and despiseth to obey his mother, the ravens of the valley shall pick it out, and the young eagles shall eat it."

fringe of his line, out of sight of his prefect, out of the reach of the rude
feet, feigning to run now and then. He felt his body small and weak amid
the throng of players and his eyes were weak and watery. Rody Kickham
was not like that: he would be captain of the third line[6] all the fellows
said.

Rody Kickham was a decent fellow but Nasty Roche was a stink. Rody
Kickham had greaves in his number[7] and a hamper in the refectory. Nasty
Roche had big hands. He called the Friday pudding dog-in-the-blanket.
And one day he had asked:

—What is your name?

Stephen had answered:

—Stephen Dedalus.

Then Nasty Roche had said:

—What kind of a name is that?

And when Stephen had not been able to answer Nasty Roche had asked:

—What is your father?

Stephen had answered:

—A gentleman.

Then Nasty Roche had asked:

—Is he a magistrate?

He crept about from point to point on the fringe of his line, making
little runs now and then. But his hands were bluish with cold. He kept his
hands in the sidepockets of his belted grey suit. That was a belt round his
pocket. And belt was also to give a fellow a belt. One day a fellow had said
to Cantwell:

—I'd give you such a belt in a second.

Cantwell had answered:

—Go and fight your match. Give Cecil Thunder a belt. I'd like to see
you. He'd give you a toe in the rump for yourself.

That was not a nice expression. His mother had told him not to speak
with the rough boys in the college. Nice mother! The first day in the hall
of the castle[8] when she had said goodbye she had put up her veil double
to her nose to kiss him: and her nose and eyes were red. But he had
pretended not to see that she was going to cry. She was a nice mother but
she was not so nice when she cried. And his father had given him two five-
shilling pieces for pocket money. And his father had told him if he wanted
anything to write home to him and, whatever he did, never to peach on a
fellow. Then at the door of the castle the rector had shaken hands with
his father and mother, his soutane fluttering in the breeze, and the car
had driven off with his father and mother on it. They had cried to him
from the car, waving their hands:

—Goodbye, Stephen, goodbye!

—Goodbye, Stephen, goodbye!

He was caught in the whirl of a scrimmage and, fearful of the flashing
eyes and muddy boots, bent down to look through the legs. The fellows

---

6. Students at Clongowes were divided into three age groups: the third line, those under thirteen (including Stephen); the lower line, from thirteen to fifteen; and the higher line, from fifteen to eighteen.
7. Shin guards in his locker.   8. The central buildings of the Jesuit boys' school at Clongowes Wood
College were part of an old castle.

were struggling and groaning and their legs were rubbing and kicking and stamping. Then Jack Lawton's yellow boots dodged out the ball and all the other boots and legs ran after. He ran after them a little way and then stopped. It was useless to run on. Soon they would be going home for the holidays. After supper in the studyhall he would change the number pasted up inside his desk from seventyseven to seventysix.

It would be better to be in the studyhall than out there in the cold. The sky was pale and cold but there were lights in the castle. He wondered from which window Hamilton Rowan had thrown his hat on the haha[9] and had there been flowerbeds at that time under the windows. One day when he had been called to the castle the butler had shown him the marks of the soldiers' slugs in the wood of the door and had given him a piece of shortbread that the community[1] ate. It was nice and warm to see the lights in the castle. It was like something in a book. Perhaps Leicester Abbey was like that. And there were nice sentences in Doctor Cornwell's Spelling Book.[2] They were like poetry but they were only sentences to learn the spelling from.

> Wolsey died in Leicester Abbey
> Where the abbots buried him.
> Canker is a disease of plants,
> Cancer one of animals.

It would be nice to lie on the hearthrug before the fire, leaning his head upon his hands, and think on those sentences. He shivered as if he had cold slimy water next his skin. That was mean of Wells to shoulder him into the square ditch because he would not swop his little snuffbox for Wells's seasoned hacking chestnut,[3] the conqueror of forty. How cold and slimy the water had been! A fellow had once seen a big rat jump into the scum. Mother was sitting at the fire with Dante waiting for Brigid to bring in the tea. She had her feet on the fender[4] and her jewelly slippers were so hot and they had such a lovely warm smell! Dante knew a lot of things. She had taught him where the Mozambique Channel was and what was the longest river in America and what was the name of the highest mountain in the moon. Father Arnall knew more than Dante because he was a priest but both his father and uncle Charles said that Dante was a clever woman and a wellread woman. And when Dante made that noise after dinner and then put up her hand to her mouth: that was heartburn.

A voice cried far out on the playground:

—All in!

Then other voices cried from the lower and third lines:

—All in! All in!

The players closed around, flushed and muddy, and he went among them, glad to go in. Rody Kickham held the ball by its greasy lace. A fellow asked him to give it one last: but he walked on without ever answering the

---

9. A ditch with raised bank intended to keep cattle away from gardens. Rowan was an Irish patriot who tricked his British pursuers by pretending to have escaped out a window at Clongowes Wood Castle: he threw his hat on the haha and hid.   1. Faculty.   2. An English-oriented grammar book stressing items of English history, such as the name of the abbey in which Cardinal Wolsey (1475–1530) died, one hundred miles north of London.   3. Used in a game in which two chestnuts, suspended on strings, are knocked against each other until one breaks.   4. Fire screen.

fellow. Simon Moonan told him not to because the prefect was looking. The fellow turned to Simon Moonan and said:

—We all know why you speak. You are McGlade's suck.

Suck was a queer word. The fellow called Simon Moonan that name because Simon Moonan used to tie the prefect's false sleeves[5] behind his back and the prefect used to let on to be angry. But the sound was ugly. Once he had washed his hands in the lavatory of the Wicklow Hotel[6] and his father pulled the stopper up by the chain after and the dirt water went down through the hole in the basin. And when it had all gone down slowly the hole in the basin had made a sound like that: suck. Only louder.

To remember that and the white look of the lavatory made him feel cold and then hot. There were two cocks[7] that you turned and water came out: cold and hot. He felt cold and then a little hot: and he could see the names printed on the cocks. That was a very queer thing.

And the air in the corridor chilled him too. It was queer and wettish. But soon the gas would be lit and in burning it made a light noise like a little song. Always the same: and when the fellows stopped talking in the playroom you could hear it.

It was the hour for sums. Father Arnall wrote a hard sum on the board and then said:

—Now then, who will win? Go ahead, York! Go ahead, Lancaster![8]

Stephen tried his best but the sum was too hard and he felt confused. The little silk badge with the white rose on it that was pinned on the breast of his jacket began to flutter. He was no good at sums but he tried his best so that York might not lose. Father Arnall's face looked very black but he was not in a wax:[9] he was laughing. Then Jack Lawton cracked his fingers and Father Arnall looked at his copybook and said:

—Right. Bravo Lancaster! The red rose wins. Come on now, York! Forge ahead!

Jack Lawton looked over from his side. The little silk badge with the red rose on it looked very rich because he had a blue sailor top on. Stephen felt his own face red too, thinking of all the bets about who would get first place in elements,[1] Jack Lawton or he. Some weeks Jack Lawton got the card for first and some weeks he got the card for first. His white silk badge fluttered and fluttered as he worked at the next sum and heard Father Arnall's voice. Then all his eagerness passed away and he felt his face quite cool. He thought his face must be white because it felt so cool. He could not get out the answer for the sum but it did not matter. White roses and red roses: those were beautiful colours to think of. And the cards for first place and second place and third place were beautiful colours too: pink and cream and lavender. Lavender and cream and pink roses were beautiful to think of. Perhaps a wild rose might be like those colours and he remembered the song about the wild rose blossoms on the little green place. But you could not have a green rose. But perhaps somewhere in the world you could.

---

5. Strips of cloth that hang down over the sleeves of the soutane or cassock. Simon "sucks up to," or flatters, the prefect.   6. In Dublin.   7. Faucets.   8. To encourage competition, the teams are named after rival claimants to the throne in the English Wars of the Roses (1445–85): the house of Lancaster, symbolized by the red rose, and the house of York, symbolized by the white.   9. Rage. 1. The third line subjects of spelling, grammar, writing, arithmetic, geography, history, and Latin.

The bell rang and then the classes began to file out of the rooms and along the corridors towards the refectory. He sat looking at the two prints of butter on his plate but could not eat the damp bread. The tablecloth was damp and limp. But he drank off the hot weak tea which the clumsy scullion, girt with a white apron, poured into his cup. He wondered whether the scullion's apron was damp too or whether all white things were cold and damp. Nasty Roche and Saurin drank cocoa that their people sent them in tins. They said they could not drink the tea; that it was hogwash. Their fathers were magistrates, the fellows said.

All the boys seemed to him very strange. They had all fathers and mothers and different clothes and voices. He longed to be at home and lay his head on his mother's lap. But he could not: and so he longed for the play and study and prayers to be over and to be in bed.

He drank another cup of hot tea and Fleming said:

—What's up? Have you a pain or what's up with you?

—I don't know, Stephen said.

—Sick in your breadbasket, Fleming said, because your face looks white. It will go away.

—O yes, Stephen said.

But he was not sick there. He thought that he was sick in his heart if you could be sick in that place. Fleming was very decent to ask him. He wanted to cry. He leaned his elbows on the table and shut and opened the flaps of his ears. Then he heard the noise of the refectory every time he opened the flaps of his ears. It made a roar like a train at night. And when he closed the flaps the roar was shut off like a train going into a tunnel. That night at Dalkey[2] the train had roared like that and then, when it went into the tunnel, the roar stopped. He closed his eyes and the train went on, roaring and then stopping; roaring again, stopping. It was nice to hear it roar and stop and then roar out the tunnel again and then stop.

Then the higher line fellows began to come down along the matting in the middle of the refectory, Paddy Rath and Jimmy Magee and the Spaniard who was allowed to smoke cigars and the little Portuguese who wore the woolly cap. And then the lower line tables and the tables of the third line. And every single fellow had a different way of walking.

He sat in a corner of the playroom pretending to watch a game of dominos and once or twice he was able to hear for an instant the little song of the gas.[3] The prefect was at the door with some boys and Simon Moonan was knotting his false sleeves. He was telling them something about Tullabeg.[4]

Then he went away from the door and Wells came over to Stephen and said:

—Tell us, Dedalus, do you kiss your mother before you go to bed?

Stephen answered:

—I do.

Wells turned to the other fellows and said:

2. Coastal village eight miles southeast of Dublin, on the railroad line connecting Dublin with Stephen's home in Bray.   3. The bubbling noise of the gas lamp.   4. Fifty-five miles west of Dublin, site of St. Stanislaus's College.

—O, I say, here's a fellow says he kisses his mother every night before he goes to bed.

The other fellows stopped their game and turned round, laughing. Stephen blushed under their eyes and said:

—I do not.

Wells said:

—O, I say, here's a fellow says he doesn't kiss his mother before he goes to bed.

They all laughed again. Stephen tried to laugh with them. He felt his whole body hot and confused in a moment. What was the right answer to the question? He had given two and still Wells laughed. But Wells must know the right answer for he was in third of grammar.[5] He tried to think of Wells's mother but he did not dare to raise his eyes to Wells's face. He did not like Wells's face. It was Wells who had shouldered him into the square ditch the day before because he would not swop his little snuffbox for Wells's seasoned hacking chestnut, the conqueror of forty. It was a mean thing to do; all the fellows said it was. And how cold and slimy the water had been! And a fellow had once seen a big rat jump plop into the scum.

The cold slime of the ditch covered his whole body; and, when the bell rang for study and the lines filed out of the playrooms, he felt the cold air of the corridor and staircase inside his clothes. He still tried to think what was the right answer. Was it right to kiss his mother or wrong to kiss his mother? What did that mean, to kiss? You put your face up like that to say goodnight and then his mother put her face down. That was to kiss. His mother put her lips on his cheek; her lips were soft and they wetted his cheek; and they made a tiny little noise: kiss. Why did people do that with their two faces?

Sitting in the studyhall he opened the lid of his desk and changed the number pasted up inside from seventyseven to seventysix. But the Christmas vacation was very far away: but one time it would come because the earth moved round always.

There was a picture of the earth on the first page of his geography: a big ball in the middle of clouds. Fleming had a box of crayons and one night during free study he had coloured the earth green and the clouds maroon. That was like the two brushes in Dante's press, the brush with the green velvet back for Parnell and the brush with the maroon velvet back for Michael Davitt. But he had not told Fleming to colour them those colours. Fleming had done it himself.

He opened the geography to study the lesson; but he could not learn the names of places in America. Still they were all different places that had those different names. They were all in different countries and the countries were in continents and the continents were in the world and the world was in the universe.

He turned to the flyleaf of the geography and read what he had written there: himself, his name and where he was.

5. Just above Stephen's class.

Stephen Dedalus
Class of Elements
Clongowes Wood College
Sallins
County Kildare
Ireland
Europe
The World
The Universe

That was in his writing: and Fleming one night for a cod[6] had written on the opposite page:

Stephen Dedalus is my name,
Ireland is my nation.
Clongowes is my dwellingplace
And heaven my expectation.

He read the verses backwards but then they were not poetry. Then he read the flyleaf from the bottom to the top till he came to his own name. That was he: and he read down the page again. What was after the universe? Nothing. But was there anything round the universe to show where it stopped before the nothing place began? It could not be a wall but there could be a thin thin line there all round everything. It was very big to think about everything and everywhere. Only God could do that. He tried to think what a big thought that must be but he could think only of God. God was God's name just as his name was Stephen. *Dieu* was the French for God and that was God's name too; and when anyone prayed to God and said *Dieu* then God knew at once that it was a French person that was praying. But though there were different names for God in all the different languages in the world and God understood what all the people who prayed said in their different languages still God remained always the same God and God's real name was God.

It made him very tired to think that way. It made him feel his head very big. He turned over the flyleaf and looked wearily at the green round earth in the middle of the maroon clouds. He wondered which was right, to be for the green or for the maroon, because Dante had ripped the green velvet back off the brush that was for Parnell one day with her scissors and had told him that Parnell was a bad man. He wondered if they were arguing at home about that. That was called politics. There were two sides in it: Dante was on one side and his father and Mr. Casey were on the other side but his mother and uncle Charles were on no side. Every day there was something in the paper about it.

It pained him that he did not know well what politics meant and that he did not know where the universe ended. He felt small and weak. When would he be like the fellows in poetry and rhetoric?[7] They had big voices and big boots and they studied trigonometry. That was very far away. First came the vacation and then the next term and then vacation again and

---

6. Joke.   7. The highest levels at Clongowes.

then again another term and then again the vacation. It was like a train
going in and out of tunnels and that was like the noise of the boys eating
in the refectory when you opened and closed the flaps of the ears. Term,
vacation; tunnel, out; noise, stop. How far away it was! It was better to go
to bed to sleep. Only prayers in the chapel and then bed. He shivered and
yawned. It would be lovely in bed after the sheets got a bit hot. First they
were so cold to get into. He shivered to think how cold they were first. But
then they got hot and then he could sleep. It was lovely to be tired. He
yawned again. Night prayers and then bed: he shivered and wanted to
yawn. It would be lovely in a few minutes. He felt a warm glow creeping
up from the cold shivering sheets, warmer and warmer till he felt warm
all over, ever so warm; ever so warm and yet he shivered a little and still
wanted to yawn.

The bell rang for night prayers and he filed out of the studyhall after
the others and down the staircase and along the corridors to the chapel.
The corridors were darkly lit and the chapel was darkly lit. Soon all would
be dark and sleeping. There was cold night air in the chapel and the
marbles were the colour the sea was at night. The sea was cold day and
night: but it was colder at night. It was cold and dark under the seawall
beside his father's house. But the kettle would be on the hob[8] to make
punch.

The prefect of the chapel prayed above his head and his memory knew
the responses:

> O Lord, open our lips
> And our mouth shall announce Thy praise.
> Incline unto our aid, O God!
> O Lord, make haste to help us![9]

There was a cold night smell in the chapel. But it was a holy smell. It
was not like the smell of the old peasants who knelt at the back of the
chapel at Sunday mass. That was a smell of air and rain and turf and
corduroy. But they were very holy peasants. They breathed behind him
on his neck and sighed as they prayed. They lived in Clane, a fellow said:
there were little cottages there and he had seen a woman standing at the
halfdoor of a cottage with a child in her arms, as the cars had come past
from Sallins. It would be lovely to sleep for one night in that cottage before
the fire of smoking turf, in the dark lit by the fire, in the warm dark,
breathing the smell of the peasants, air and rain and turf and corduroy.
But, O, the road there between the trees was dark! You would be lost in
the dark. It made him afraid to think of how it was.

He heard the voice of the prefect of the chapel saying the last prayer.
He prayed it too against the dark outside under the trees.

> Visit, we beseech Thee, O Lord, this habitation and drive away from
> it all the snares of the enemy. May Thy holy angels dwell herein to
> preserve us in peace and may Thy blessing be always upon us through
> Christ, Our Lord. Amen.[1]

---

8. Heating shelf in the fireplace.   9. The beginning of Matins, or morning prayers.   1. From the
Compline, or last prayers of the day.

His fingers trembled as he undressed himself in the dormitory. He told his fingers to hurry up. He had to undress and then kneel and say his own prayers and be in bed before the gas was lowered so that he might not go to hell when he died. He rolled his stockings off and put on his nightshirt quickly and knelt trembling at his bedside and repeated his prayers quickly quickly, fearing that the gas would go down. He felt his shoulders shaking as he murmured:

> God bless my father and my mother and spare them to me!
> God bless my little brothers and sisters and spare them to me!
> God bless Dante and uncle Charles and spare them to me!

He blessed himself and climbed quickly into bed and, tucking the end of the nightshirt under his feet, curled himself together under the cold white sheets, shaking and trembling. But he would not go to hell when he died; and the shaking would stop. A voice bade the boys in the dormitory goodnight. He peered out for an instant over the coverlet and saw the yellow curtains round and before his bed that shut him off on all sides. The light was lowered quietly.

The prefect's shoes went away. Where? Down the staircase and along the corridors or to his room at the end? He saw the dark. Was it true about the black dog that walked there at night with eyes as big as carriagelamps? They said it was the ghost of a murderer. A long shiver of fear flowed over his body. He saw the dark entrance hall of the castle. Old servants in old dress were in the ironingroom[2] above the staircase. It was long ago. The old servants were quiet. There was a fire there but the hall was still dark. A figure came up the staircase from the hall. He wore the white cloak of a marshal;[3] his face was pale and strange; he held his hand pressed to his side. He looked out of strange eyes at the old servants. They looked at him and saw their master's face and cloak and knew that he had received his deathwound. But only the dark was where they looked: only dark silent air. Their master had received his deathwound on the battlefield of Prague far away over the sea. He was standing on the field; his hand was pressed to his side; his face was pale and strange and he wore the white cloak of a marshal.

O how cold and strange it was to think of that! All the dark was cold and strange. There were pale strange faces there, great eyes like carriagelamps. They were the ghosts of murderers, the figures of marshals who had received their deathwound on battlefields far away over the sea. What did they wish to say that their faces were so strange?

> Visit, we beseech Thee, O Lord, this habitation and drive away from it all . . .

Going home for the holidays! That would be lovely: the fellows had told him. Getting up on the cars in the early wintry morning outside the

---

2. The room where armor was stored.   3. Maximilian Ulysses, Count von Browne (1705–1757) and a marshal in the Austrian army, was supposed to have appeared as a ghost in the castle on the day he died abroad; his family owned the castle at that time.

door of the castle. The cars were rolling on the gravel. Cheers for the rector!

Hurray! Hurray! Hurray!

The cars drove past the chapel and all caps were raised. They drove merrily along the country roads. The drivers pointed with their whips to Bodenstown. The fellows cheered. They passed the farmhouse of the Jolly Farmer. Cheer after cheer after cheer. Through Clane they drove, cheering and cheered. The peasant women stood at the halfdoors, the men stood here and there. The lovely smell there was in the wintry air: the smell of Clane: rain and wintry air and turf smouldering and corduroy.

The train was full of fellows: a long long chocolate train with cream facings. The guards went to and fro opening, closing, locking, unlocking the doors. They were men in dark blue and silver; they had silvery whistles and their keys made a quick music: click, click: click, click.

And the train raced on over the flat lands and past the Hill of Allen. The telegraphpoles were passing, passing. The train went on and on. It knew. There were coloured lanterns in the hall of his father's house and ropes of green branches. There were holly and ivy round the pierglass[4] and holly and ivy, green and red, twined round the chandeliers. There were red holly and green ivy round the old portraits on the walls. Holly and ivy for him and for Christmas.

Lovely . . .

All the people. Welcome home, Stephen! Noises of welcome. His mother kissed him. Was that right? His father was a marshal now: higher than a magistrate. Welcome home, Stephen!

Noises . . .

There was a noise of curtainrings running back along the rods, of water being splashed in the basins. There was a noise of rising and dressing and washing in the dormitory: a noise of clapping of hands as the prefect went up and down telling the fellows to look sharp. A pale sunlight showed the yellow curtains drawn back, the tossed beds. His bed was very hot and his face and body were very hot.

He got up and sat on the side of his bed. He was weak. He tried to pull on his stocking. It had a horrid rough feel. The sunlight was queer and cold.

Fleming said:

—Are you not well?

He did not know; and Fleming said:

—Get back into bed. I'll tell McGlade you're not well.

—He's sick.

—Who is?

—Tell McGlade.

—Get back into bed.

—Is he sick?

A fellow held his arms while he loosened the stocking clinging to his foot and climbed back into the hot bed.

He crouched down between the sheets, glad of their tepid glow. He

---

4. A tall mirror often placed between two windows.

heard the fellows talk among themselves about him as they dressed for mass. It was a mean thing to do, to shoulder him into the square ditch, they were saying.

Then their voices ceased; they had gone. A voice at his bed said:

—Dedalus, don't spy on us, sure you won't?

Wells's face was there. He looked at it and saw that Wells was afraid.

—I didn't mean to. Sure you won't?

His father had told him, whatever he did, never to peach on a fellow. He shook his head and answered no and felt glad. Wells said:

—I didn't mean to, honour bright. It was only for cod. I'm sorry.

The face and the voice went away. Sorry because he was afraid. Afraid that it was some disease. Canker was a disease of plants and cancer one of animals: or another different. That was a long time ago then out on the playgrounds in the evening light, creeping from point to point on the fringe of his line, a heavy bird flying low through the grey light. Leicester Abbey lit up. Wolsey died there. The abbots buried them themselves.

It was not Wells's face, it was the prefect's. He was not foxing. No, no: he was sick really. He was not foxing. And he felt the prefect's hand on his forehead; and he felt his forehead warm and damp against the prefect's cold damp hand. That was the way a rat felt, slimy and damp and cold. Every rat had two eyes to look out of. Sleek slimy coats, little little feet tucked up to jump, black shiny eyes to look out of. They could understand how to jump. But the minds of rats could not understand trigonometry. When they were dead they lay on their sides. Their coats dried then. They were only dead things.

The prefect was there again and it was his voice that was saying that he was to get up, that Father Minister[5] had said he was to get up and dress and go to the infirmary. And while he was dressing himself as quickly as he could the prefect said:

—We must pack off to Brother Michael because we have the collywobbles! Terrible thing to have the collywobbles! How we wobble when we have the collywobbles!

He was very decent to say that. That was all to make him laugh. But he could not laugh because his cheeks and lips were all shivery; and then the prefect had to laugh by himself.

The prefect cried:

—Quick march! Hayfoot! Strawfoot![6]

They went together down the staircase and along the corridor and past the bath. As he passed the door he remembered with a vague fear the warm turfcoloured bogwater, the warm moist air, the noise of plunges, the smell of the towels, like medicine.

Brother Michael was standing at the door of the infirmary and from the door of the dark cabinet on his right came a smell like medicine. That came from the bottles on the shelves. The prefect spoke to Brother Michael and Brother Michael answered and called the prefect sir. He had reddish hair mixed with grey and a queer look. It was queer that he would

---

5. The priest supervising all nonacademic activities.   6. Marching orders; uneducated rural recruits traditionally were supposed to distinguish their feet in learning to march by having hay tied to the left foot, and straw to the right.

always be a brother. It was queer too that you could not call him sir because he was a brother and had a different kind of look. Was he not holy enough or why could he not catch up on the others?

There were two beds in the room and in one bed there was a fellow: and when they went in he called out:

—Hello! It's young Dedalus! What's up?

—The sky is up, Brother Michael said.

He was a fellow out of the third of grammar and, while Stephen was undressing, he asked Brother Michael to bring him a round of buttered toast.

—Ah, do! he said.

—Butter you up! said Brother Michael. You'll get your walking papers in the morning when the doctor comes.

—Will I? the fellow said. I'm not well yet.

Brother Michael repeated:

You'll get your walking papers, I tell you.

He bent down to rake the fire. He had a long back like the long back of a tramhorse. He shook the poker gravely and nodded his head at the fellow out of third of grammar.

Then Brother Michael went away and after a while the fellow out of third of grammar turned in towards the wall and fell asleep.

That was the infirmary. He was sick then. Had they written home to tell his mother and father? But it would be quicker for one of the priests to go himself to tell them. Or he would write a letter for the priest to bring.

Dear Mother

I am sick. I want to go home. Please come and take me home. I am in the infirmary.

Your fond son,
Stephen

How far away they were! There was cold sunlight outside the window. He wondered if he would die. You could die just the same on a sunny day. He might die before his mother came. Then he would have a dead mass in the chapel like the way the fellows had told him it was when Little had died. All the fellows would be at the mass, dressed in black, all with sad faces. Wells too would be there but no fellow would look at him. The rector would be there in a cope of black and gold[7] and there would be tall yellow candles on the altar and round the catafalque. And they would carry the coffin out of the chapel slowly and he would be buried in the little graveyard of the community off the main avenue of lime.[8] And Wells would be sorry then for what he had done. And the bell would toll slowly.

He could hear the tolling. He said over to himself the song that Brigid had taught him.

> *Dingdong! The castle bell!*
> *Farewell, my mother!*
> *Bury me in the old churchyard*

---

7. The priest's mantle for the funeral Mass.   8. Lime trees (linden).

> *Beside my eldest brother.*
> *My coffin shall be black,*
> *Six angels at my back,*
> *Two to sing and two to pray*
> *And two to carry my soul away.*

How beautiful and sad that was! How beautiful the words were where they said *Bury me in the old churchyard!* A tremor passed over his body. How sad and how beautiful! He wanted to cry quietly but not for himself: for the words, so beautiful and sad, like music. The bell! The bell! Farewell! O farewell!

The cold sunlight was weaker and Brother Michael was standing at his bedside with a bowl of beeftea. He was glad for his mouth was hot and dry. He could hear them playing on the playgrounds. And the day was going on in the college just as if he were there.

Then Brother Michael was going away and the fellow out of third of grammar told him to be sure and come back and tell him all the news in the paper. He told Stephen that his name was Athy and that his father kept a lot of racehorses that were spiffing[9] jumpers and that his father would give a good tip to Brother Michael any time he wanted it because Brother Michael was very decent and always told him the news out of the paper they got every day up in the castle. There was every kind of news in the paper: accidents, shipwrecks, sports and politics.

—Now it is all about politics in the paper, he said. Do your people talk about that too?

—Yes, Stephen said.

—Mine too, he said.

Then he thought for a moment and said:

—You have a queer name, Dedalus, and I have a queer name too, Athy. My name is the name of a town. Your name is like Latin.

Then he asked:

—Are you good at riddles?

Stephen answered:

—Not very good.

Then he said:

—Can you answer me this one? Why is the county Kildare like the leg of a fellow's breeches?

Stephen thought what could be the answer and then said:

—I give it up.

—Because there is a thigh[1] in it, he said. Do you see the joke? Athy is the town in the county Kildare and a thigh is the other thigh.

—O, I see, Stephen said.

—That's an old riddle, he said.

After a moment he said:

—I say!

—What? asked Stephen.

—You know, he said, you can ask that riddle another way?

—Can you? said Stephen.

9. Elegant.   1. Athy is pronounced "a thigh."

—The same riddle, he said. Do you know the other way to ask it?

—No, said Stephen.

—Can you not think of the other way? he said.

He looked at Stephen over the bedclothes as he spoke. Then he lay back on the pillow and said:

—There is another way but I won't tell you what it is.

Why did he not tell it? His father, who kept the racehorses, must be a magistrate too like Saurin's father and Nasty Roche's father. He thought of his own father, of how he sang songs while his mother played and of how he always gave him a shilling when he asked for sixpence and he felt sorry for him that he was not a magistrate like the other boys' fathers. Then why was he sent to that place with them? But his father had told him that he would be no stranger there because his granduncle had presented an address to the liberator[2] there fifty years before. You could know the people of that time by their old dress. It seemed to him a solemn time: and he wondered if that was the time when the fellows in Clongowes wore blue coats with brass buttons and yellow waistcoats and caps of rabbitskin and drank beer like grownup people and kept greyhounds of their own to course the hares with.

He looked at the window and saw that the daylight had grown weaker. There would be cloudy grey light over the playgrounds. There was no noise on the playgrounds. The class must be doing the themes or perhaps Father Arnall was reading a legend[3] out of the book.

It was queer that they had not given him any medicine. Perhaps Brother Michael would bring it back when he came. They said you got stinking stuff to drink when you were in the infirmary. But he felt better now than before. It would be nice getting better slowly. You could get a book then. There was a book in the library about Holland. There were lovely foreign names in it and pictures of strangelooking cities and ships. It made you feel so happy.

How pale the light was at the window! But that was nice. The fire rose and fell on the wall. It was like waves. Someone had put coal on and he heard voices. They were talking. It was the noise of the waves. Or the waves were talking among themselves as they rose and fell.

He saw the sea of waves, long dark waves rising and falling, dark under the moonless night. A tiny light twinkled at the pierhead where the ship was entering: and he saw a multitude of people gathered by the waters' edge to see the ship that was entering their harbour. A tall man stood on the deck, looking out towards the flat dark land: and by the light at the pierhead he saw his face, the sorrowful face of Brother Michael.

He saw him lift his hand towards the people and heard him say in a loud voice of sorrow over the waters:

—He is dead. We saw him lying upon the catafalque.

A wail of sorrow went up from the people.

—Parnell! Parnell! He is dead![4]

2. Daniel O'Connell (1775–1847), Irish politician who brought about the repeal in 1829 of laws restricting Catholic civil and political rights.   3. A saint's life, from the collection of such lives called (in English) *The Golden Legend.*   4. Parnell was buried in Dublin with great pomp and a massive funeral procession on October 11, 1891.

They fell upon their knees, moaning in sorrow.

And he saw Dante in a maroon velvet dress and with a green velvet mantle hanging from her shoulders walking proudly and silently past the people who knelt by the waters' edge.

．　　．　　．

A great fire, banked high and red, flamed in the grate and under the ivytwined branches of the chandelier the Christmas table was spread. They had come home a little late and still dinner was not ready: but it would be ready in a jiffy, his mother had said. They were waiting for the door to open and for the servants to come in, holding the big dishes covered with their heavy metal covers.

All were waiting: uncle Charles, who sat far away in the shadow of the window, Dante and Mr. Casey, who sat in the easychairs at either side of the hearth, Stephen, seated on a chair between them, his feet resting on the toasted boss.[5] Mr. Dedalus looked at himself in the pierglass above the mantelpiece, waxed out his moustache-ends and then, parting his coattails, stood with his back to the glowing fire: and still, from time to time, he withdrew a hand from his coattail to wax out one of his moustache-ends. Mr. Casey leaned his head to one side and, smiling, tapped the gland of his neck with his fingers. And Stephen smiled too for he knew now that it was not true that Mr. Casey had a purse of silver in his throat. He smiled to think how the silvery noise which Mr. Casey used to make had deceived him. And when he had tried to open Mr. Casey's hand to see if the purse of silver was hidden there he had seen that the fingers could not be straightened out: and Mr. Casey had told him that he had got those three cramped fingers making a birthday present for Queen Victoria.[6]

Mr. Casey tapped the gland of his neck and smiled at Stephen with sleepy eyes: and Mr. Dedalus said to him:

—Yes. Well now, that's all right. O, we had a good walk, hadn't we, John? Yes . . . I wonder if there's any likelihood of dinner this evening. Yes . . . O, well now, we got a good breath of ozone round the Head[7] today. Ay, bedad.

He turned to Dante and said:

—You didn't stir out at all, Mrs. Riordan?

Dante frowned and said shortly:

—No.

Mr. Dedalus dropped his coattails and went over to the sideboard. He brought forth a great stone jar of whisky from the locker and filled the decanter slowly, bending now and then to see how much he had poured in. Then replacing the jar in the locker he poured a little of the whisky into two glasses, added a little water and came back with them to the fireplace.

—A thimbleful, John, he said, just to whet your appetite.

Mr. Casey took the glass, drank, and placed it near him on the mantelpiece. Then he said:

5. A hassock.　　6. Mr. Casey, an ardent Irish nationalist, may have been in a British prison picking oakum (a form of hard labor).　　7. Bray Head, on the coast thirteen miles south of Dublin.

—Well, I can't help thinking of our friend Christopher manufacturing . . .

He broke into a fit of laughter and coughing and added:

—. . . manufacturing that champagne for those fellows.

Mr. Dedalus laughed loudly.

—Is it Christy? he said. There's more cunning in one of those warts on his bald head than in a pack of jack foxes.

He inclined his head, closed his eyes, and, licking his lips profusely, began to speak with the voice of the hotelkeeper.

—And he has such a soft mouth when he's speaking to you, don't you know. He's very moist and watery about the dewlaps, God bless him.

Mr. Casey was still struggling through his fit of coughing and laughter. Stephen, seeing and hearing the hotelkeeper through his father's face and voice, laughed.

Mr. Dedalus put up his eyeglass and, staring down at him, said quietly and kindly:

—What are you laughing at, you little puppy, you?

The servants entered and placed the dishes on the table. Mrs. Dedalus followed and the places were arranged.

—Sit over, she said.

Mr. Dedalus went to the end of the table and said:

—Now, Mrs. Riordan, sit over. John, sit you down, my hearty.

He looked round to where uncle Charles sat and said:

—Now then, sir, there's a bird here waiting for you.

When all had taken their seats he laid his hand on the cover and then said quickly, withdrawing it:

—Now, Stephen.

Stephen stood up in his place to say the grace before meals:

> Bless us, O Lord, and these Thy gifts which through Thy bounty we are about to receive through Christ Our Lord. Amen.

All blessed themselves and Mr. Dedalus with a sigh of pleasure lifted from the dish the heavy cover pearled around the edge with glistening drops.

Stephen looked at the plump turkey which had lain, trussed and skewered, on the kitchen table. He knew that his father had paid a guinea for it in Dunn's of D'Olier Street and that the man had prodded it often at the breastbone to show how good it was: and he remembered the man's voice when he had said:

—Take that one, sir. That's the real Ally Daly.[8]

Why did Mr. Barrett in Clongowes call his pandybat[9] a turkey? But Clongowes was far away: and the warm heavy smell of turkey and ham and celery rose from the plates and dishes and the great fire was banked high and red in the grate and the green ivy and red holly made you feel

---

8. The very best (Dublin slang).   9. A leather strap reinforced with whalebone used to spank schoolboys' hands, whereupon they turn "turkey" red.

so happy and when dinner was ended the big plumpudding would be carried in, studded with peeled almonds and sprigs of holly, with bluish fire running around it and a little green flag flying from the top.

It was his first Christmas dinner and he thought of his little brothers and sisters who were waiting in the nursery, as he had often waited, till the pudding came. The deep low collar and the Eton jacket made him feel queer and oldish: and that morning when his mother had brought him down to the parlour, dressed for mass, his father had cried. That was because he was thinking of his own father. And uncle Charles had said so too.

Mr. Dedalus covered the dish and began to eat hungrily. Then he said:

—Poor old Christy, he's nearly lopsided now with roguery.

—Simon, said Mrs. Dedalus, you haven't given Mrs. Riordan any sauce.

Mr. Dedalus seized the sauceboat.

—Haven't I? he cried. Mrs. Riordan, pity the poor blind.

Dante covered her plate with her hands and said:

—No, thanks.

Mr. Dedalus turned to uncle Charles.

—How are you off, sir?

—Right as the mail, Simon.

—You, John?

—I'm all right. Go on yourself.

—Mary? Here, Stephen, here's something to make your hair curl.

He poured sauce freely over Stephen's plate and set the boat again on the table. Then he asked uncle Charles was it tender. Uncle Charles could not speak because his mouth was full but he nodded that it was.

—That was a good answer our friend made to the canon. What? said Mr Dedalus.

—I didn't think he had that much in him, said Mr. Casey.

—*I'll pay you your dues, father, when you cease turning the house of God into a pollingbooth.*[1]

—A nice answer, said Dante, for any man calling himself a catholic to give to his priest.

—They have only themselves to blame, said Mr. Dedalus suavely. If they took a fool's advice they would confine their attention to religion.

—It is religion, Dante said. They are doing their duty in warning the people.

—We go to the house of God, Mr. Casey said, in all humility to pray to our Maker and not to hear election addresses.

—It is religion, Dante said again. They are right. They must direct their flocks.

—And preach politics from the altar, is it? asked Mr. Dedalus.

—Certainly, said Dante. It is a question of public morality. A priest would not be a priest if he did not tell his flock what is right and what is wrong.

---

1. The Irish clergy preached against Parnell and Parnellite candidates, causing the defeat of one of them in an 1890 Kilkenny by-election.

Mrs. Dedalus laid down her knife and fork, saying:

—For pity's sake and for pity sake let us have no political discussion on this day of all days in the year.

—Quite right, ma'am, said uncle Charles. Now, Simon, that's quite enough now. Not another word now.

—Yes, yes, said Mr. Dedalus quickly.

He uncovered the dish boldly and said:

—Now then, who's for more turkey?

Nobody answered. Dante said:

—Nice language for any catholic to use!

—Mrs. Riordan, I appeal to you, said Mrs. Dedalus, to let the matter drop now.

Dante turned on her and said:

—And am I to sit here and listen to the pastors of my church being flouted?

—Nobody is saying a word against them, said Mr. Dedalus, so long as they don't meddle in politics.

—The bishops and priests of Ireland have spoken, said Dante, and they must be obeyed.

—Let them leave politics alone, said Mr. Casey, or the people may leave their church alone.

—You hear? said Dante turning to Mrs. Dedalus.

—Mr. Casey! Simon! said Mrs. Dedalus. Let it end now.

—Too bad! Too bad! said uncle Charles.

—What? cried Mr. Dedalus. Were we to desert him at the bidding of the English people?[2]

—He was no longer worthy to lead, said Dante. He was a public sinner.

—We are all sinners and black sinners, said Mr. Casey coldly.

—*Woe be to the man by whom the scandal cometh!* said Mrs. Riordan. *It would be better for him that a millstone were tied about his neck and that he were cast into the depth of the sea rather than that he should scandalise one of these, my least little ones.*[3] That is the language of the Holy Ghost.

—And very bad language if you ask me, said Mr. Dedalus coolly.

—Simon! Simon! said uncle Charles. The boy.

—Yes, yes, said Mr. Dedalus. I meant about the . . . I was thinking about the bad language of that railway porter. Well now, that's all right. Here, Stephen, show me your plate, old chap. Eat away now. Here.

He heaped up the food on Stephen's plate and served uncle Charles and Mr. Casey to large pieces of turkey and splashes of sauce. Mrs. Dedalus was eating little and Dante sat with her hands in her lap. She was red in the face. Mr. Dedalus rooted with the carvers at the end of the dish and said:

—There's a tasty bit here we call the pope's nose.[4] If any lady or gentleman . . .

---

2. Prime Minister William Gladstone (1809–1898), pressured by his own Liberal Party, tried to persuade Parnell to leave politics after the scandal and—when the latter refused—issued an ultimatum that the Irish could choose between Parnell and Gladstone's support of Home Rule. 3. Luke 17:1–2. 4. The roasted turkey's tail end, so-called because it has no feathers and looks like a "Roman" nose.

He held a piece of fowl up on the prong of the carving-fork. Nobody spoke. He put it on his own plate, saying:

—Well, you can't say but you were asked. I think I had better eat it myself because I'm not well in my health lately.

He winked at Stephen and, replacing the dishcover, began to eat again.

There was a silence while he ate. Then he said:

—Well now, the day kept up fine after all. There were plenty of strangers down too.

Nobody spoke. He said again:

—I think there were more strangers down than last Christmas.

He looked round at the others whose faces were bent towards their plates and, receiving no reply, waited for a moment and said bitterly:

—Well, my Christmas dinner has been spoiled anyhow.

—There could be neither luck nor grace, Dante said, in a house where there is no respect for the pastors of the church.

Mr. Dedalus threw his knife and fork noisily on his plate.

—Respect! he said. Is it for Billy with the lip or for the tub of guts up in Armagh?[5] Respect!

—Princes of the church, said Mr. Casey with slow scorn.

—Lord Leitrim's coachman,[6] yes, said Mr. Dedalus.

—They are the Lord's anointed, Dante said. They are an honour to their country.

—Tub of guts, said Mr. Dedalus coarsely. He has a handsome face, mind you, in repose. You should see that fellow lapping up his bacon and cabbage of a cold winter's day. O Johnny!

He twisted his features into a grimace of heavy bestiality and made a lapping noise with his lips.

—Really, Simon, said Mrs. Dedalus, you should not speak that way before Stephen. It's not right.

—O, he'll remember all this when he grows up, said Dante hotly—the language he heard against God and religion and priests in his own home.

—Let him remember too, cried Mr. Casey to her from across the table, the language with which the priests and the priests' pawns broke Parnell's heart and hounded him into his grave. Let him remember that too when he grows up.

—Sons of bitches! cried Mr. Dedalus. When he was down they turned on him to betray him and rend him like rats in a sewer. Lowlived dogs! And they look it! By Christ, they look it!

—They behaved rightly, cried Dante. They obeyed their bishops and their priests. Honour to them!

—Well, it is perfectly dreadful to say that not even for one day in the year, said Mrs. Dedalus, can we be free from these dreadful disputes!

Uncle Charles raised his hands mildly and said:

—Come now, come now, come now! Can we not have our opinions

---

5. The archbishop of Dublin, William J. Walsh (1841–1921), and the archbishop of Armagh, Michael Logue (1840–1924).   6. Lord Leitrim was the English absentee landlord of an enormous estate in western Ireland. His Irish coachman tried to save him when he was murdered in 1877, presumably by Irish nationalists.

whatever they are without this bad temper and this bad language? It is too bad surely.

Mrs. Dedalus spoke to Dante in a low voice but Dante said loudly:

—I will not say nothing. I will defend my church and my religion when it is insulted and spit on by renegade catholics.

Mr. Casey pushed his plate rudely into the middle of the table and, resting his elbows before him, said in a hoarse voice to his host:

—Tell me, did I tell you that story about a very famous spit?

—You did not, John, said Mr. Dedalus.

—Why then, said Mr. Casey, it is a most instructive story. It happened not long ago in the county Wicklow where we are now.

He broke off and, turning towards Dante, said with quiet indignation:

—And I may tell you, ma'am, that I, if you mean me, am no renegade catholic. I am a catholic as my father was and his father before him and his father before him again when we gave up our lives rather than sell our faith.

—The more shame to you now, Dante said, to speak as you do.

—The story, John, said Mr. Dedalus smiling. Let us have the story anyhow.

—Catholic indeed! repeated Dante ironically. The blackest protestant in the land would not speak the language I have heard this evening.

Mr. Dedalus began to sway his head to and fro, crooning like a country singer.

—I am no protestant, I tell you again, said Mr. Casey flushing.

Mr. Dedalus, still crooning and swaying his head, began to sing in a grunting nasal tone:

> O, come all you Roman catholics
> That never went to mass.[7]

He took up his knife and fork again in good humour and set to eating, saying to Mr. Casey:

—Let us have the story, John. It will help us to digest.

Stephen looked with affection at Mr. Casey's face which stared across the table over his joined hands. He liked to sit near him at the fire, looking up at his dark fierce face. But his dark eyes were never fierce and his slow voice was good to listen to. But why was he then against the priests? Because Dante must be right then. But he had heard his father say that she was a spoiled nun and that she had come out of the convent in the Alleghanies when her brother had got the money from the savages for the trinkets and the chainies.[8] Perhaps that made her severe against Parnell. And she did not like him to play with Eileen because Eileen was a protestant and when she was young she knew children that used to play with protestants and the protestants used to make fun of the litany of the Blessed Virgin. *Tower of Ivory*, they used to say, *House of Gold!*[9] How could a woman be a tower of ivory or a house of gold? Who was right then? And he remembered the evening in the infirmary in Clongowes, the dark

7. Parody of the street ballad, "Come all you loyal Irishmen . . ."   8. Damaged china.   9. Phrases taken from a Roman Catholic litany celebrating the Virgin Mary as the gateway to Heaven.

waters, the light at the pierhead and the moan of sorrow from the people when they had heard.

Eileen had long white hands. One evening when playing tig[1] she had put her hands over his eyes: long and white and thin and cold and soft. That was ivory: a cold white thing. That was the meaning of *Tower of Ivory.*

—The story is very short and sweet, Mr. Casey said. It was one day down in Arklow, a cold bitter day, not long before the chief[2] died. May God have mercy on him!

He closed his eyes wearily and paused. Mr. Dedalus took a bone from his plate and tore some meat from it with his teeth, saying:

—Before he was killed, you mean.

Mr. Casey opened his eyes, sighed and went on:

—It was down in Arklow one day. We were down there at a meeting and after the meeting was over we had to make our way to the railway station through the crowd. Such booing and baaing, man, you never heard. They called us all the names in the world. Well there was one old lady, and a drunken old harridan she was surely, that paid all her attention to me. She kept dancing along beside me in the mud bawling and scream- ing into my face: *Priest-hunter! The Paris Funds! Mr. Fox! Kitty O'Shea!*[3]

—And what did you do, John? asked Mr. Dedalus.

—I let her bawl away, said Mr. Casey. It was a cold day and to keep up my heart I had (saving your presence, ma'am) a quid of Tullamore in my mouth and sure I couldn't say a word in any case because my mouth was full of tobacco juice.

—Well, John?

—Well. I let her bawl away, to her heart's content, *Kitty O'Shea* and the rest of it till at last she called that lady a name that I won't sully this Christmas board nor your ears, ma'am, nor my own lips by repeating.

He paused. Mr. Dedalus, lifting his head from the bone, asked:

—And what did you do, John?

—Do! said Mr. Casey. She stuck her ugly old face up at me when she said it and I had my mouth full of tobacco juice. I bent down to her and *Phth!* says I to her like that.

He turned aside and made the act of spitting.

—*Phth!* says I to her like that, right into her eye.

He clapped a hand to his eye and gave a hoarse scream of pain.

—*O Jesus, Mary and Joseph!* says she. *I'm blinded! I'm blinded and drownded!*

He stopped in a fit of coughing and laughter, repeating:

—*I'm blinded entirely.*

Mr. Dedalus laughed loudly and lay back in his chair while uncle Charles swayed his head to and fro.

Dante looked terribly angry and repeated while they laughed:

1. Tag.   2. Parnell.   3. Parnell, a Protestant, struck back at the Irish Catholic hierarchy that was preaching against him. The Paris Funds were money (drawn chiefly from American supporters) placed in a Paris bank so that the English would not be able to confiscate them; Parnell had control of them, and after the split the funds were an object of suspicion and rumor. Parnell had used the name *Mr. Fox* when corresponding with Mrs. O'Shea. The diminutive *Kitty* is insulting.

—Very nice! Ha! Very nice!

It was not nice about the spit in the woman's eye. But what was the name the woman had called Kitty O'Shea that Mr. Casey would not repeat? He thought of Mr. Casey walking through the crowds of people and making speeches from a wagonette. That was what he had been in prison for and he remembered that one night Sergeant O'Neill had come to the house and had stood in the hall, talking in a low voice with his father and chewing nervously at the chinstrap of his cap. And that night Mr. Casey had not gone to Dublin by train but a car had come to the door and he had heard his father say something about the Cabinteely road.[4]

He was for Ireland and Parnell and so was his father: and so was Dante too for one night at the band on the esplanade she had hit a gentleman on the head with her umbrella because he had taken off his hat when the band played *God save the Queen* at the end.

Mr. Dedalus gave a snort of contempt.

—Ah, John, he said. It is true for them. We are an unfortunate priest-ridden race and always were and always will be till the end of the chapter.

Uncle Charles shook his head, saying:

—A bad business! A bad business!

Mr. Dedalus repeated:

—A priestridden Godforsaken race!

He pointed to the portrait of his grandfather on the wall to his right.

—Do you see that old chap up there, John? he said. He was a good Irishman when there was no money in the job. He was condemned to death as a whiteboy.[5] But he had a saying about our clerical friends, that he would never let one of them put his two feet under his mahogany.[6]

Dante broke in angrily:

—If we are a priestridden race we ought to be proud of it! They are the apple of God's eye. *Touch them not*, says Christ, *for they are the apple of My eye.*[7]

—And can we not love our country then? asked Mr. Casey. Are we not to follow the man that was born to lead us?

—A traitor to his country! replied Dante. A traitor, an adulterer! The priests were right to abandon him. The priests were always the true friends of Ireland.

—Were they, faith? said Mr. Casey.

He threw his fist on the table and, frowning angrily, protruded one finger after another.

—Didn't the bishops of Ireland betray us in the time of the union when bishop Lanigan presented an address of loyalty to the Marquess Cornwallis? Didn't the bishops and priests sell the aspirations of their country in 1829 in return for catholic emancipation? Didn't they denounce the

---

4. An indirect route from Bray to Dublin.   5. Agitators for tax reform who wore white clothes to be able to recognize each other during night raids; the movement began in the late 18th century.   6. Dining room table.   7. Dante misquotes a line from the second vision of Zechariah, a prophet of the Old Testament of the Bible, in which God promises protection to Zion: "he that toucheth you, toucheth the apple of my eye" (Zechariah 2:8; Douay Bible).

fenian movement from the pulpit and in the confessionbox? And didn't they dishonour the ashes of Terence Bellew MacManus?[8]

His face was glowing with anger and Stephen felt the glow rise to his own cheek as the spoken words thrilled him. Mr. Dedalus uttered a guffaw of coarse scorn.

—O, by God, he cried, I forgot little old Paul Cullen![9] Another apple of God's eye!

Dante bent across the table and cried to Mr. Casey:

—Right! Right! They were always right! God and morality and religion come first.

Mrs. Dedalus, seeing her excitement, said to her:

—Mrs. Riordan, don't excite yourself answering them.

—God and religion before everything! Dante cried. God and religion before the world!

Mr. Casey raised his clenched fist and brought it down on the table with a crash.

—Very well, then, he shouted hoarsely, if it comes to that, no God for Ireland!

—John! John! cried Mr. Dedalus, seizing his guest by the coatsleeve.

Dante stared across the table, her cheeks shaking. Mr. Casey struggled up from his chair and bent across the table towards her, scraping the air from before his eyes with one hand as though he were tearing aside a cobweb.

—No God for Ireland! he cried. We have had too much God in Ireland. Away with God!

—Blasphemer! Devil! screamed Dante, starting to her feet and almost spitting in his face.

Uncle Charles and Mr. Dedalus pulled Mr. Casey back into his chair again, talking to him from both sides reasonably. He stared before him out of his dark flaming eyes, repeating:

—Away with God, I say!

Dante shoved her chair violently aside and left the table, upsetting her napkinring which rolled slowly along the carpet and came to rest against the foot of an easychair. Mrs. Dedalus rose quickly and followed her towards the door. At the door Dante turned round violently and shouted down the room, her cheeks flushed and quivering with rage:

—Devil out of hell! We won! We crushed him to death! Fiend!

The door slammed behind her.

Mr. Casey, freeing his arms from his holders, suddenly bowed his head on his hands with a sob of pain.

—Poor Parnell! he cried loudly. My dead king![1]

He sobbed loudly and bitterly.

---

8. An Irish patriot who died in exile and was brought back to Ireland for burial over clerical opposition. In 1800, and after much political maneuvering that included promising Catholic bishops the emancipation of their faith from various civil and political restrictions, the British were able to persuade the Irish Parliament to dissolve and merge with the British Parliament in London (the Act of Union). *Fenian movement*: the Irish Republican Brotherhood, whose terrorist activities were condemned by the clergy. 9. Archbishop of Dublin (1803–1878), later cardinal and ruler of the Catholic Church in Ireland. He supported the British.   1. Parnell was called "the uncrowned king of Ireland."

Stephen, raising his terrorstricken face, saw that his father's eyes were full of tears.

• • •

The fellows talked together in little groups.

One fellow said:

— They were caught near the Hill of Lyons.[2]

— Who caught them?

— Mr. Gleeson and the minister. They were on a car.

The same fellow added:

— A fellow in the higher line told me.

Fleming asked:

— But why did they run away, tell us?

— I know why, Cecil Thunder said. Because they had fecked[3] cash out of the rector's room.

— Who fecked it?

— Kickham's brother. And they all went shares in it.

But that was stealing. How could they have done that?

— A fat lot you know about it, Thunder! Wells said. I know why they scut.[4]

— Tell us why.

— I was told not to, Wells said.

— O, go on, Wells, all said. You might tell us. We won't let it out.

Stephen bent forward his head to hear. Wells looked round to see if anyone was coming. Then he said secretly:

— You know the altar wine they keep in the press in the sacristy?

— Yes.

— Well, they drank that and it was found out who did it by the smell. And that's why they ran away, if you want to know.

And the fellow who had spoken first said:

— Yes, that's what I heard too from the fellow in the higher line.

The fellows were all silent. Stephen stood among them, afraid to speak, listening. A faint sickness of awe made him feel weak. How could they have done that? He thought of the dark silent sacristy. There were dark wooden presses there where the crimped surplices lay quietly folded. It was not the chapel but still you had to speak under your breath. It was a holy place. He remembered the summer evening he had been there to be dressed as boatbearer,[5] the evening of the procession to the little altar in the wood.[6] A strange and holy place. The boy that held the censer had swung it gently to and fro near the door with the silvery cap lifted by the middle chain to keep the coals lighting. That was called charcoal: and it had burned quietly as the fellow had swung it gently and had given off a weak sour smell. And then when all were vested he had stood holding out the boat to the rector and the rector had put a spoonful of incense in it and it had hissed on the red coals.

---

2. Between Clongowes Wood College and Dublin.   3. Stolen ("fetched").   4. Ran away.   5. The person who carries the boat or incense container to be blessed during Mass. Incense is then taken from the boat and burned in the censer.   6. Processions on holy days went from the college to a little altar in the nearby park.

The fellows were talking together in little groups here and there on the playground. The fellows seemed to him to have grown smaller: that was because a sprinter[7] had knocked him down the day before, a fellow out of second of grammar. He had been thrown by the fellow's machine lightly on the cinderpath and his spectacles had been broken in three pieces and some of the grit of the cinders had gone into his mouth.

That was why the fellows seemed to him smaller and farther away and the goalposts so thin and far and the soft grey sky so high up. But there was no play on the football grounds for cricket was coming: and some said that Barnes would be the prof[8] and some said it would be Flowers. And all over the playgrounds they were playing rounders and bowling twisters and lobs.[9] And from here and from there came the sounds of the cricketbats through the soft grey air. They said: pick, pack, pock, puck: like drops of water in a fountain slowly falling in the brimming bowl.

Athy, who had been silent, said quietly:

—You are all wrong.

All turned towards him eagerly.

—Why?

—Do you know?

—Who told you?

—Tell us, Athy.

Athy pointed across the playground to where Simon Moonan was walking by himself kicking a stone before him.

—Ask him, he said.

The fellows looked there and then said:

—Why him?

—Is he in it?

—Tell us, Athy. Go on. You might if you know.

Athy lowered his voice and said.

—Do you know why those fellows scut? I will tell you but you must not let on you know.

He paused for a moment and then said mysteriously:

—They were caught with Simon Moonan and Tusker Boyle in the square[1] one night.

The fellows looked at him and asked:

—Caught?

—What doing?

Athy said:

—Smugging.[2]

All the fellows were silent: and Athy said:

—And that's why.

Stephen looked at the faces of the fellows but they were all looking across the playground. He wanted to ask somebody about it. What did that mean about the smugging in the square? Why did the five fellows out of the higher line run away for that? It was a joke, he thought. Simon Moonan had nice clothes and one night he had shown him a ball of creamy

---

7. A high-speed bicyclist.   8. Captain of the team.   9. Pitches in the game of cricket. *Rounders:* a game like baseball. *Twisters:* curve balls thrown in cricket.   1. The urinal.   2. An obsolete word that implies, in this case, schoolboy homosexuality.

sweets that the fellows of the football fifteen[3] had rolled down to him along the carpet in the middle of the refectory when he was at the door. It was the night of the match against the Bective Rangers and the ball was made just like a red and green apple only it opened and it was full of the creamy sweets. And one day Boyle had said that an elephant had two tuskers instead of two tusks and that was why he was called Tusker Boyle but some fellows called him Lady Boyle because he was always at his nails, paring them.

Eileen had long thin cool white hands too because she was a girl. They were like ivory; only soft. That was the meaning of *Tower of Ivory* but protestants could not understand it and made fun of it. One day he had stood beside her looking into the hotel grounds. A waiter was running up a trail of bunting on the flagstaff and a fox terrier was scampering to and fro on the sunny lawn. She had put her hand into his pocket where his hand was and he had felt how cool and thin and soft her hand was. She had said that pockets were funny things to have: and then all of a sudden she had broken away and had run laughing down the sloping curve of the path. Her fair hair had streamed out behind her like gold in the sun. *Tower of Ivory. House of Gold.* By thinking of things you could understand them.

But why in the square? You went there when you wanted to do something. It was all thick slabs of slate and water trickled all day out of tiny pinholes and there was a queer smell of stale water there. And behind the door of one of the closets there was a drawing in red pencil of a bearded man in a Roman dress with a brick in each hand and underneath was the name of the drawing:

Balbus was building a wall.[4]

Some fellows had drawn it there for a cod. It had a funny face but it was very like a man with a beard. And on the wall of another closet there was written in backhand in beautiful writing:

Julius Cæsar wrote The Calico Belly.[5]

Perhaps that was why they were there because it was a place where some fellows wrote things for cod. But all the same it was queer what Athy said and the way he said it. It was not a cod because they had run away. He looked with the others in silence across the playground and began to feel afraid.

At last Fleming said:

—And we are all to be punished for what other fellows did?

—I won't come back, see if I do, Cecil Thunder said. Three days' silence in the refectory and sending us up for six and eight every minute.

—Yes, said Wells. And old Barrett has a new way of twisting the note so that you can't open it and fold it again to see how many ferulæ[6] you are to get. I won't come back too.

—Yes, said Cecil Thunder, and the prefect of studies was in second of grammar this morning.

—Let us get up a rebellion, Fleming said. Will we?

---

3. The Irish football (soccer) team.   **4.** Graffito after a Latin text in which Cicero criticized Balbus (*Letters to Atticus* XII:2) and which the students probably had to study.   **5.** Mimicking the sound of a famous title. The "Calico Belly" is *De Bello Gallico*, or Caesar's *Gallic Wars.*   **6.** Strokes that the boys received on the palm of the hands for misbehavior (first three on each hand, then four; see just above).

All the fellows were silent. The air was very silent and you could hear the cricketbats but more slowly than before: pick, pock.

Wells asked:

—What is going to be done to them?

—Simon Moonan and Tusker are going to be flogged, Athy said, and the fellows in the higher line got their choice of flogging or being expelled.

—And which are they taking? asked the fellow who had spoken first.

—All are taking expulsion except Corrigan, Athy answered. He's going to be flogged by Mr. Gleeson.

—Is it Corrigan that big fellow? said Fleming. Why, he'd be able for two of Gleeson!

—I know why, Cecil Thunder said. He is right and the other fellows are wrong because a flogging wears off after a bit but a fellow that has been expelled from college is known all his life on account of it. Besides Gleeson won't flog him hard.

—It's best of his play not to, Fleming said.

—I wouldn't like to be Simon Moonan and Tusker, Cecil Thunder said. But I don't believe they will be flogged. Perhaps they will be sent up for twice nine.

—No, no, said Athy. They'll both get it on the vital spot.

Wells rubbed himself and said in a crying voice:

—Please, sir, let me off!

Athy grinned and turned up the sleeves of his jacket, saying:

> It can't be helped;
> It must be done.
> So down with your breeches
> And out with your bum.

The fellows laughed; but he felt that they were a little afraid. In the silence of the soft grey air he heard the cricketbats from here and from there: pock. That was a sound to hear but if you were hit then you would feel a pain. The pandybat made a sound too but not like that. The fellows said it was made of whalebone and leather with lead inside: and he wondered what was the pain like. There were different kinds of pains for all the different kinds of sounds. A long thin cane would have a high whistling sound and he wondered what was that pain like. It made him shivery to think of it and cold: and what Athy said too. But what was there to laugh at in it? It made him shivery: but that was because you always felt like a shiver when you let down your trousers. It was the same in the bath when you undressed yourself. He wondered who had to let them down, the master or the boy himself. O how could they laugh about it that way?

He looked at Athy's rolledup sleeves and knuckly inky hands. He had rolled up his sleeves to show how Mr. Gleeson would roll up his sleeves. But Mr. Gleeson had round shiny cuffs and clean white wrists and fattish white hands and the nails of them were long and pointed. Perhaps he pared them too like Lady Boyle. But they were terribly long and pointed nails. So long and cruel they were though the white fattish hands were not cruel but gentle. And though he trembled with cold and fright to think of the cruel long nails and of the high whistling sound of the cane and of the chill you felt at the end of your shirt when you undressed yourself yet he felt a feeling of queer quiet pleasure inside him to think of the white fattish hands, clean and strong and gentle. And he thought of what Cecil Thunder had said; that Mr. Gleeson would not flog Corrigan hard. And Fleming had said he would not because it was best of his play not to. But that was not why.

A voice from far out on the playground cried:

—All in!

And other voices cried:

—All in! All in!

During the writing lesson he sat with his arms folded, listening to the slow scraping of the pens. Mr. Harford went to and fro making little signs in red pencil and sometimes sitting beside the boy to show him how to hold the pen. He had tried to spell out the headline for himself though he knew already what it was for it was the last of the book. *Zeal without prudence is like a ship adrift.* But the lines of the letters were like fine invisible threads and it was only by closing his right eye tight tight and staring out of the left eye that he could make out the full curves of the capital.

But Mr. Harford was very decent and never got into a wax. All the other masters got into dreadful waxes. But why were they to suffer for what fellows in the higher line did? Wells had said that they had drunk some of the altar wine out of the press in the sacristy and that it had been found out who had done it by the smell. Perhaps they had stolen a monstrance[7] to run away with it and sell it somewhere. That must have been a terrible sin, to go in there quietly at night, to open the dark press and steal the flashing gold thing into which God was put on the altar in the middle of flowers and candles at benediction while the incense went up in clouds at both sides as the fellow swung the censer and Dominic Kelly sang the first part by himself in the choir. But God was not in it of course when they stole it. But still it was a strange and a great sin even to touch it. He thought of it with deep awe; a terrible and strange sin: it thrilled him to think of it in the silence when the pens scraped lightly. But to drink the altar wine out of the press and be found out by the smell was a sin too: but it was not terrible and strange. It only made you feel a little sickish on account of the smell of the wine. Because on the day when he had made his first holy communion in the chapel he had shut his eyes and opened his mouth and put out his tongue a little: and when the rector had stooped down to give him the holy communion he had smelt a faint winy smell off the rector's breath after the wine of the mass. The word was beautiful: wine. It made you think of dark purple because the grapes were dark purple that grew in Greece outside houses like white temples. But the faint smell off the rector's breath had made him feel a sick feeling on the morning of his first communion. The day of your first communion was the happiest day of your life. And once a lot of generals had asked Napoleon what was the happiest day of his life. They thought he would say the

---

7. Vessel in which the Host is kept.

day he won some great battle or the day he was made an emperor. But he said:

—Gentlemen, the happiest day of my life was the day on which I made my first holy communion.

Father Arnall came in and the Latin lesson began and he remained still, leaning on the desk with his arms folded. Father Arnall gave out the themebooks and he said that they were scandalous and that they were all to be written out again with the corrections at once. But the worst of all was Fleming's theme because the pages were stuck together by a blot: and Father Arnall held it up by a corner and said it was an insult to any master to send him up such a theme. Then he asked Jack Lawton to decline the noun *mare* and Jack Lawton stopped at the ablative singular and could not go on with the plural.

—You should be ashamed of yourself, said Father Arnall sternly. You, the leader of the class!

Then he asked the next boy and the next and the next. Nobody knew. Father Arnall became very quiet, more and more quiet as each boy tried to answer and could not. But his face was blacklooking and his eyes were staring though his voice was so quiet. Then he asked Fleming and Fleming said that that word had no plural. Father Arnall suddenly shut the book and shouted at him:

—Kneel out there in the middle of the class. You are one of the idlest boys I ever met. Copy out your themes again the rest of you.

Fleming moved heavily out of his place and knelt between the two last benches. The other boys bent over their themebooks and began to write. A silence filled the classroom and Stephen, glancing timidly at Father Arnall's dark face, saw that it was a little red from the wax he was in.

Was that a sin for Father Arnall to be in a wax or was he allowed to get into a wax when the boys were idle because that made them study better or was he only letting on to be in a wax? It was because he was allowed because a priest would know what a sin was and would not do it. But if he did it one time by mistake what would he do to go to confession? Perhaps he would go to confession to the minister. And if the minister did it he would go to the rector: and the rector to the provincial: and the provincial to the general of the jesuits. That was called the order: and he had heard his father say that they were all clever men. They could all have become highup people in the world if they had not become jesuits. And he wondered what Father Arnall and Paddy Barrett would have become and what Mr. McGlade and Mr. Gleeson would have become if they had not become jesuits. It was hard to think what because you would have to think of them in a different way with different coloured coats and trousers and with beards and moustaches and different kinds of hats.

The door opened quietly and closed. A quick whisper ran through the class: the prefect of studies. There was an instant of dead silence and then the loud crack of a pandybat on the last desk. Stephen's heart leapt up in fear.

—Any boys want flogging here, Father Arnall? cried the prefect of studies. Any lazy idle loafers that want flogging in this class?

He came to the middle of the class and saw Fleming on his knees.

—Hoho! he cried. Who is this boy? Why is he on his knees? What is your name, boy?

—Fleming, sir.

—Hoho, Fleming! An idler of course. I can see it in your eye. Why is he on his knees, Father Arnall?

—He wrote a bad Latin theme, Father Arnall said, and he missed all the questions in grammar.

—Of course he did! cried the prefect of studies. Of course he did! A born idler! I can see it in the corner of his eye.

He banged his pandybat down on the desk and cried:

—Up, Fleming! Up, my boy!

Fleming stood up slowly.

—Hold out! cried the prefect of studies.

Fleming held out his hand. The pandybat came down on it with a loud smacking sound: one, two, three, four, five, six.

—Other hand!

The pandybat came down again in six loud quick smacks.

—Kneel down! cried the prefect of studies.

Fleming knelt down squeezing his hands under his armpits, his face contorted with pain, but Stephen knew how hard his hands were because Fleming was always rubbing rosin into them. But perhaps he was in great pain for the noise of the pandies was terrible. Stephen's heart was beating and fluttering.

—At your work, all of you! shouted the prefect of studies. We want no lazy idle loafers here, lazy idle little schemers. At your work, I tell you. Father Dolan will be in to see you every day. Father Dolan will be in tomorrow.

He poked one of the boys in the side with the pandybat, saying:

—You, boy! When will Father Dolan be in again?

—Tomorrow, sir, said Tom Furlong's voice.

—Tomorrow and tomorrow and tomorrow, said the prefect of studies. Make up your minds for that. Every day Father Dolan. Write away. You, boy, who are you?

Stephen's heart jumped suddenly.

—Dedalus, sir.

—Why are you not writing like the others?

—I . . . my . . .

He could not speak with fright.

—Why is he not writing, Father Arnall?

—He broke his glasses, said Father Arnall, and I exempted him from work.

—Broke? What is this I hear? What is this your name is? said the prefect of studies.

—Dedalus, sir.

—Out here, Dedalus. Lazy little schemer. I see schemer in your face. Where did you break your glasses?

Stephen stumbled into the middle of the class, blinded by fear and haste.

—Where did you break your glasses? repeated the prefect of studies.

—The cinderpath, sir.

—Hoho! The cinderpath! cried the prefect of studies. I know that trick.

Stephen lifted his eyes in wonder and saw for a moment Father Dolan's whitegrey not young face, his baldy whitegrey head with fluff at the sides of it, the steel rims of his spectacles and his nocoloured eyes looking through the glasses. Why did he say he knew that trick?

—Lazy idle little loafer! cried the prefect of studies. Broke my glasses! An old schoolboy trick! Out with your hand this moment!

Stephen closed his eyes and held out in the air his trembling hand with the palm upwards. He felt the prefect of studies touch it for a moment at the fingers to straighten it and then the swish of the sleeve of the soutane as the pandybat was lifted to strike. A hot burning stinging tingling blow like the loud crack of a broken stick made his trembling hand crumple together like a leaf in the fire: and at the sound and the pain scalding tears were driven into his eyes. His whole body was shaking with fright, his arm was shaking and his crumpled burning livid hand shook like a loose leaf in the air. A cry sprang to his lips, a prayer to be let off. But though the tears scalded his eyes and his limbs quivered with pain and fright he held back the hot tears and the cry that scalded his throat.

—Other hand! shouted the prefect of studies.

Stephen drew back his maimed and quivering right arm and held out his left hand. The soutane sleeve swished again as the pandybat was lifted and a loud crashing sound and a fierce maddening tingling burning pain made his hand shrink together with the palms and fingers in a livid quivering mass. The scalding water burst forth from his eyes and, burning with shame and agony and fear, he drew back his shaking arm in terror and burst out into a whine of pain. His body shook with a palsy of fright and in shame and rage he felt the scalding cry come from his throat and the scalding tears falling out of his eyes and down his flaming cheeks.

—Kneel down! cried the prefect of studies.

Stephen knelt down quickly pressing his beaten hands to his sides. To think of them beaten and swollen with pain all in a moment made him feel so sorry for them as if they were not his own but someone else's that he felt sorry for. And as he knelt, calming the last sobs in his throat and feeling the burning tingling pain pressing in to his sides, he thought of the hands which he had held out in the air with the palms up and of the firm touch of the prefect of studies when he had steadied the shaking fingers and of the beaten swollen reddened mass of palm and fingers that shook helplessly in the air.

—Get at your work, all of you, cried the prefect of studies from the door. Father Dolan will be in every day to see if any boy, any lazy idle little loafer wants flogging. Every day. Every day.

The door closed behind him.

The hushed class continued to copy out the themes. Father Arnall rose from his seat and went among them, helping the boys with gentle words and telling them the mistakes they had made. His voice was very gentle and soft. Then he returned to his seat and said to Fleming and Stephen:

—You may return to your places, you two.

Fleming and Stephen rose and, walking to their seats, sat down. Stephen, scarlet with shame, opened a book quickly with one weak hand and bent down upon it, his face close to the page.

It was unfair and cruel because the doctor had told him not to read without glasses and he had written home to his father that morning to send him a new pair. And Father Arnall had said that he need not study till the new glasses came. Then to be called a schemer before the class and to be pandied when he always got the card for first or second and was the leader of the Yorkists! How could the prefect of studies know that it was a trick? He felt the touch of the prefect's fingers as they had steadied his hand and at first he had thought he was going to shake hands with him because the fingers were soft and firm: but then in an instant he had heard the swish of the soutane sleeve and the crash. It was cruel and unfair to make him kneel in the middle of the class then: and Father Arnall had told them both that they might return to their places without making any difference between them. He listened to Father Arnall's low and gentle voice as he corrected the themes. Perhaps he was sorry now and wanted to be decent. But it was unfair and cruel. The prefect of studies was a priest but that was cruel and unfair. And his whitegrey face and the nocoloured eyes behind the steelrimmed spectacles were cruel looking because he had steadied the hand first with his firm soft fingers and that was to hit it better and louder.

—It's a stinking mean thing, that's what it is, said Fleming in the corridor as the classes were passing out in file to the refectory, to pandy a fellow for what is not his fault.

—You really broke your glasses by accident, didn't you? Nasty Roche asked.

Stephen felt his heart filled by Fleming's words and did not answer.

—Of course he did! said Fleming. I wouldn't stand it. I'd go up and tell the rector on him.

—Yes, said Cecil Thunder eagerly, and I saw him lift the pandybat over his shoulder and he's not allowed to do that.

—Did they hurt much? Nasty Roche asked.

—Very much, Stephen said.

—I wouldn't stand it, Fleming repeated, from Baldyhead or any other Baldyhead. It's a stinking mean low trick, that's what it is. I'd go straight up to the rector and tell him about it after dinner.

—Yes, do. Yes, do, said Cecil Thunder.

—Yes, do. Yes, go up and tell the rector on him, Dedalus, said Nasty Roche, because he said that he'd come in tomorrow again to pandy you.

—Yes, yes. Tell the rector, all said.

And there were some fellows out of second of grammar listening and one of them said:

—The senate and the Roman people declared that Dedalus had been wrongly punished.[8]

It was wrong; it was unfair and cruel: and, as he sat in the refectory, he suffered time after time in memory the same humiliation until he began

---

8. Another echo of their Latin studies: decrees of the Roman Senate began "*Senatus populusque Romanus*" ("The Senate and the Roman people").

to wonder whether it might not really be that there was something in his face which made him look like a schemer and he wished he had a little mirror to see. But there could not be; and it was unjust and cruel and unfair.

He could not eat the blackish fish fritters they got on Wednesdays in Lent and one of his potatoes had the mark of the spade in it. Yes, he would do what the fellows had told him. He would go up and tell the rector that he had been wrongly punished. A thing like that had been done before by somebody in history, by some great person whose head was in the books of history. And the rector would declare that he had been wrongly punished because the senate and the Roman people always declared that the men who did that had been wrongly punished. Those were the great men whose names were in Richmal Magnall's questions. History was all about those men and what they did and that was what Peter Parley's[9] Tales about Greece and Rome were all about. Peter Parley himself was on the first page in a picture. There was a road over a heath with grass at the side and little bushes: and Peter Parley had a broad hat like a protestant minister and a big stick and he was walking fast along the road to Greece and Rome.

It was easy what he had to do. All he had to do was when the dinner was over and he came out in his turn to go on walking but not out to the corridor but up the staircase on the right that led to the castle. He had nothing to do but that: to turn to the right and walk fast up the staircase and in half a minute he would be in the low dark narrow corridor that led through the castle to the rector's room. And every fellow had said that it was unfair, even the fellow out of second of grammar who had said that about the senate and the Roman people.

What would happen? He heard the fellows of the higher line stand up at the top of the refectory and heard their steps as they came down the matting: Paddy Rath and Jimmy Magee and the Spaniard and the Portuguese and the fifth was big Corrigan who was going to be flogged by Mr. Gleeson. That was why the prefect of studies had called him a schemer and pandied him for nothing: and, straining his weak eyes, tired with the tears, he watched big Corrigan's broad shoulders and big hanging black head passing in the file. But he had done something and besides Mr. Gleeson would not flog him hard: and he remembered how big Corrigan looked in the bath. He had skin the same colour as the turfcoloured bog-water in the shallow end of the bath and when he walked along the side his feet slapped loudly on the wet tiles and at every step his thighs shook a little because he was fat.

The refectory was half empty and the fellows were still passing out in file. He could go up the staircase because there was never a priest or a prefect outside the refectory door. But he could not go. The rector would side with the prefect of studies and think it was a schoolboy trick and then the prefect of studies would come in every day the same only it would be worse because he would be dreadfully waxy at any fellow going up to the

9. A pseudonym; he published educational books for children. Richmal Magnall wrote a popular elementary history text called *Historical and Miscellaneous Questions for the Use of Young People* (1800).

rector about him. The fellows had told him to go but they would not go themselves. They had forgotten all about it. No, it was best to forget all about it and perhaps the prefect of studies had only said he would come in. No, it was best to hide out of the way because when you were small and young you could often escape that way.

The fellows at his table stood up. He stood up and passed out among them in the file. He had to decide. He was coming near the door. If he went on with the fellows he could never go up to the rector because he could not leave the playground for that. And if he went and was pandied all the same all the fellows would make fun and talk about young Dedalus going up to the rector to tell on the prefect of studies.

He was walking down along the matting and he saw the door before him. It was impossible: he could not. He thought of the baldy head of the prefect of studies with the cruel nocoloured eyes looking at him and he heard the voice of the prefect of studies asking him twice what his name was. Why could he not remember the name when he was told the first time? Was he not listening the first time or was it to make fun out of the name? The great men in the history had names like that and nobody made fun of them. It was his own name that he should have made fun of if he wanted to make fun. Dolan: it was like the name of a woman that washed clothes.

He had reached the door and, turning quickly up to the right, walked up the stairs and, before he could make up his mind to come back, he had entered the low dark narrow corridor that led to the castle. And as he crossed the threshold of the door of the corridor he saw, without turning his head to look, that all the fellows were looking after him as they went filing by.

He passed along the narrow dark corridor, passing little doors that were the doors of the rooms of the community. He peered in front of him and right and left through the gloom and thought that those must be portraits. It was dark and silent and his eyes were weak and tired with tears so that he could not see. But he thought they were the portraits of the saints and great men of the order who were looking down on him silently as he passed: saint Ignatius Loyola holding an open book and pointing to the words *Ad Majorem Dei Gloriam* in it, saint Francis Xavier pointing to his chest, Lorenzo Ricci with his berretta on his head like one of the prefects of the lines, the three patrons of holy youth, saint Stanislaus Kostka, saint Aloysius Gonzaga and blessed John Berchmans, all with young faces because they died when they were young, and Father Peter Kenny[1] sitting in a chair wrapped in a big cloak.

He came out on the landing above the entrance hall and looked about him. That was where Hamilton Rowan had passed and the marks of the soldiers' slugs were there. And it was there that the old servants had seen the ghost in the white cloak of a marshal.

---

1. Founded Clongowes Wood College. St. Ignatius of Loyola founded the Jesuit order in 1534. *Ad Majorem Dei Gloriam:* "To the greater glory of God" (Latin), which is the Jesuit motto. St. Francis Xavier was a Jesuit missionary to India. Lorenzo Ricci was a general of the Jesuits in 1758. *Beretta:* square cap. The remaining three saints (Berchmans was also canonized) died young and are, therefore, patron saints for Jesuit boys' schools.

An old servant was sweeping at the end of the landing. He asked him where was the rector's room and the old servant pointed to the door at the far end and looked after him as he went on to it and knocked.

There was no answer. He knocked again more loudly and his heart jumped when he heard a muffled voice say:

—Come in!

He turned the handle and opened the door and fumbled for the handle of the green baize door inside. He found it and pushed it open and went in.

He saw the rector sitting at a desk writing. There was a skull[2] on the desk and a strange solemn smell in the room like the old leather of chairs.

His heart was beating fast on account of the solemn place he was in and the silence of the room: and he looked at the skull and at the rector's kindlooking face.

—Well, my little man, said the rector, what is it?

Stephen swallowed down the thing in his throat and said:

—I broke my glasses, sir.

The rector opened his mouth and said:

—O!

Then he smiled and said:

—Well, if we broke our glasses we must write home for a new pair.

—I wrote home, sir, said Stephen, and Father Arnall said I am not to study till they come.

—Quite right! said the rector.

Stephen swallowed down the thing again and tried to keep his legs and his voice from shaking.

—But, sir . . .

—Yes?

—Father Dolan came in today and pandied me because I was not writing my theme.

The rector looked at him in silence and he could feel the blood rising to his face and the tears about to rise to his eyes.

The rector said:

—Your name is Dedalus, isn't it?

—Yes, sir.

—And where did you break your glasses?

—On the cinderpath, sir. A fellow was coming out of the bicycle house and I fell and they got broken. I don't know the fellow's name.

The rector looked at him again in silence. Then he smiled and said:

—O, well, it was a mistake; I am sure Father Dolan did not know.

—But I told him I broke them, sir, and he pandied me.

—Did you tell him that you had written home for a new pair? the rector asked.

—No, sir.

—O well then, said the rector, Father Dolan did not understand. You can say that I excused you from your lessons for a few days.

Stephen said quickly for fear his trembling would prevent him:

2. A traditional reminder that one should always be prepared for death.

—Yes, sir, but Father Dolan said he will come in tomorrow to pandy
me again for it.

Very well, the rector said, it is a mistake and I shall speak to Father
Dolan myself. Will that do now?

Stephen felt the tears wetting his eyes and murmured:

—O yes sir, thanks.

The rector held his hand across the side of the desk where the skull was
and Stephen, placing his hand in it for a moment, felt a cool moist palm.

—Good day now, said the rector, withdrawing his hand and bowing.

—Good day, sir, said Stephen.

He bowed and walked quietly out of the room, closing the doors carefully and slowly.

But when he had passed the old servant on the landing and was again
in the low narrow dark corridor he began to walk faster and faster. Faster
and faster he hurried on through the gloom excitedly. He bumped his
elbow against the door at the end and, hurrying down the staircase, walked
quickly through the two corridors and out into the air.

He could hear the cries of the fellows on the playgrounds. He broke
into a run and, running quicker and quicker, ran across the cinderpath
and reached the third line playground, panting.

The fellows had seen him running. They closed round him in a ring,
pushing one against another to hear.

—Tell us! Tell us!

—What did he say?

—Did you go in?

—What did he say?

—Tell us! Tell us!

He told them what he had said and what the rector had said and, when
he had told them, all the fellows flung their caps spinning up into the air
and cried:

—Hurroo!

They caught their caps and sent them up again spinning skyhigh and
cried again:

—Hurroo! Hurroo!

They made a cradle of their locked hands and hoisted him up among
them and carried him along till he struggled to get free. And when he had
escaped from them they broke away in all directions, flinging their caps
again into the air and whistling as they went spinning up and crying:

—Hurroo!

And they gave three groans for Baldyhead Dolan and three cheers for
Conmee and they said he was the decentest rector that was ever in Clongowes.

The cheers died away in the soft grey air. He was alone. He was happy
and free: but he would not be anyway proud with Father Dolan. He would
be very quiet and obedient: and he wished that he could do something
kind for him to show him that he was not proud.

The air was soft and grey and mild and evening was coming. There was
the smell of evening in the air, the smell of the fields in the country where
they digged up turnips to peel them and eat them when they went out for

a walk to Major Barton's,[3] the smell there was in the little wood beyond the pavilion where the gallnuts were.

The fellows were practising long shies and bowing lobs and slow twisters. In the soft grey silence he could hear the bump of the balls: and from here and from there through the quiet air the sound of the cricket bats: pick, pack, pock, puck: like drops of water in a fountain falling softly in the brimming bowl.

3. A local magistrate whose estate was a little more than two miles from Clongowes.

VIRGINIA WOOLF
1882–1941

An experimental novelist who developed an extraordinary poetic style for prose fiction, Virginia Woolf is known for her precise evocations of states of mind—the sensuous as well as rational perceptions that make up human consciousness. It is through this recording of moments of awareness that she joins Proust and Joyce in the move away from the linear development and objective descriptions of the nineteenth-century novel and works toward a different way of structuring both her protagonists' personal awareness and the relationships of different parts of the text. Blocks of time are juxtaposed in the memory or in different points of view; incomplete perspectives play off one another to create a larger pattern; alternating modes of narration remind the reader that a poetic (or fictional) creation is involved. Adapting the "stream of consciousness" technique inside a narrative style that ranges from precise, mundane details to lyric elaboration, and keenly aware of the way perception is further shaped by cultural habits, Woolf shows the creative imagination to be as necessary in our lives as it is in the creation of artistic texts.

She was born Adeline Virginia Stephen on January 25, 1882, one of the four children of the eminent Victorian editor and historian Leslie Stephen and his wife, Julia. The family actively pursued intellectual and artistic interests, and Julia was admired and sketched by some of the most famous Pre-Raphaelite artists. Following the customs of the day, only the sons, Adrian and Thoby, were given formal and university education; Virginia and her sister, Vanessa (later the painter Vanessa Bell), were instructed at home by their parents, and depended for further education on their father's immense library. Virginia bitterly resented this unequal treatment and the systematic discouragement of women's intellectual development that it implied. Throughout her own work, themes of society's different attitudes toward men and women play a strong role, especially in the essay collection *A Room of One's Own* (1929)—which contains the famous anecdote of her having been warned off the grass and forbidden entrance to a university library because she was a woman—and *Three Guineas* (1938). *A Room of One's Own* examines the history of literature written by women and contains also an impassioned plea that women writers be given conditions equal to those available for men: specifically, the privacy of a room in which to write and economic independence. (At the time Woolf wrote, it was very unusual for women to have any money of their own or to be able to devote themselves to a career with the same freedom as men.) After her mother's death in 1895, Woolf was expected to take over the supervision of the family household, which she did until her father's death in 1904. Of fragile physical health after an attack of whooping cough when she was six, she suffered in addition a nervous breakdown after the death of each parent.

Woolf moved to central London with her sister and brother Adrian after their father's death, and took a house in the Bloomsbury district (where the British Museum is located). They soon became the focus of what was later called the Bloomsbury Group, a gathering of writers, artists, and intellectuals impatient with conservative Edwardian society and eager to explore new modes of thought. Members of the group included the novelist E. M. Forster, the historian Lytton Strachey, the economist John Maynard Keynes, and the art critics Clive Bell (who married Vanessa) and Roger Fry (who introduced the group to postimpressionist painters such as Édouard Manet and Paul Cézanne). Woolf was not yet writing fiction, but contributed reviews to the *Times Literary Supplement*, taught literature and composition at Morley College (an institution with a volunteer faculty that provided educational opportunities for workers), and worked for the adult suffrage movement and a feminist group. In 1912 she married Leonard Woolf, who encouraged her to write and with whom she founded the Hogarth Press in 1917. The press became one of the most respected of the small literary presses and published works by such major authors as T. S. Eliot, Katherine Mansfield, Lytton Strachey, E. M. Forster, Maxim Gorky, and John Middleton Murry as well as Woolf's own novels and translations of Freud. Over the next two decades she produced her best-known fiction while coping with frequent bouts of physical and mental illness. Already depressed during World War II and exhausted after the completion of her last novel, *Between the Acts* (1941), she sensed the approach of a serious attack of insanity and the confinement it would entail: in such situations, she was obliged to "rest" and forbidden to read or write. In March 1941, she drowned herself in a river close to her Sussex home.

As a writer, Woolf is best known for her poetic evocations of the way we think and feel. Like Proust and Joyce, she is superbly capable of evoking all the concrete, sensuous details of everyday experience; like them, she explores the structures of consciousness. What she really deplored was the microscopic, documentary realism that contemporaries like Arnold Bennett and John Galsworthy drew from the nineteenth-century masters. The contemporary realists' pretense of scientific objectivity was false, she felt, since they refused to take into account the fact that there are no neutral observers—that "reality" is reported differently by different people. Worse, their goal of scientific objectivity often resulted in a mere chronological accumulation of details, the "appalling narrative business of . . . getting from lunch to dinner." Woolf preferred a more subjective and, she hoped, a more accurate account of the real. Her focus was not so much the object under observation as the way the observer perceived it: "Let us record the atoms as they fall upon the mind in the order in which they fall, let us trace the pattern, however disconnected and incoherent in appearance, which each sight or incident scores upon the consciousness."

Woolf's writing has been compared with postimpressionist art in the way that it emphasizes the abstract arrangement of perspectives to suggest additional networks of meaning. After two relatively traditional novels, she began to develop a more flexible approach that openly manipulated fictional structure. The continuously developing plot gave way to an organization by juxtaposed points of view; the experience of "real" or chronological time was displaced (although not completely) by a mind ranging ambiguously among its memories; and an intricate pattern of symbolic themes connected otherwise unrelated characters in the same story. All these techniques made new demands on the reader's ability to synthesize and re-create a whole picture. In *Jacob's Room* (1922), a picture of the hero must be assembled from a series of partial points of view. In *The Waves* (1931), the multiple perspective of different characters soliloquizing on their relationship to the dead Percival is broken by ten interludes that together construct an additional, interacting perspective when they describe the passage of a single day from dawn to dusk. The same novel may expand or telescope the sense of time: *Mrs. Dalloway* (1925) focuses apparently on Clarissa Dalloway's preparations for a party that evening but at the same time calls up—at different times, and according to different contexts—her whole life from childhood to her present age of fifty. Problems of identity are a constant concern in these shifting perspectives, and Woolf often portrays the search of unfulfilled personalities for whatever will complete them. Her work is studded with moments of heightened awareness (comparable to Joyce's epiphanies) in which a character suddenly *sees into* a person or situation. With Woolf, this moment is less a matter of mystical insight (as it is with Joyce) than a creation of the mind using all its faculties.

No one can read Woolf without being struck by the importance she gives to the creative imagination. Her major characters display a sensitivity beyond rational logic, and her narrative style celebrates the aesthetic impulse to coordinate many dimensions inside one harmoniously significant whole. Human beings are not complete, Woolf suggests, without exercising their intuitive and imaginative faculties. Like other modernist writers, she is fascinated by the creative process and often makes reference to it in her work. Whether describing the struggles of a painter in *To the Lighthouse* (1927) or of a writer in *An Unwritten Novel*, she simultaneously illustrates the exploratory and creative work of the human imagination. Not all this work is visible in the finished painting or novel: observing, sifting, coordinating, projecting different interpretations and relationships, the mind performs an enormous labor of coordinating consciousness that cannot be captured entirely in any fixed form.

In *An Unwritten Novel*, Woolf humorously describes the embryonic stages of composition by taking the reader through the tentative beginnings of a novel that might have been. The story moves back and forth between two sides of imagination and reality, both contributing to the potential novel, as the narrator mentally tests out possible versions based on her observation of a particular person in the railway carriage. On the one hand, she records the actual words and gestures of her fellow passengers on the train: on the other, she projects their imagined life into a completely fictional creation as she perceives, empathizes, and shapes what she sees to fit her own preconceptions. The process of composition appears in all its experiments, false starts, and corrections for tone and consistency: the narrator must find the appropriate imagined crime for Minnie's repressed air, supply ferns instead of rhododendrons to fit a given scene, and add or subtract characters to round out the story. Nor does Woolf ignore the narrator's own character as a motivating force. Although the narrator prides herself on starting from a solid base of concrete observation, her artist's joy in the pure exercise of creativity quickly leads to elaboration for its own sake (the broken eggshell that becomes a map, blocks of marble, and Spanish silver and gold: her delighted transformation of James Moggridge into a clinically functioning organism as her x-ray vision penetrates "the spine tough as whalebone, straight as oaktree; the ribs radiating branches; the flesh taut tarpaulin; the red hollows; the suck and regurgitation of the heart; while from above meat falls in brown cubes and beer gushes to be churned to blood again"). Like Baudelaire in *The Windows*, she triumphantly asserts the value of creativity over mere factual evidence. When her first tale has comically been disproved and she is left "bare as a bone," it is not long before instinct takes over and she starts spinning stories anew. In this richly textured story, which combines the dimensions of objective reality and self-deception with a passionate statement of the liberating power of art, Woolf pokes gentle fun at herself and at the whole tradition of the novel as a mirror of reality. The essayist's critical and self-analytic perspective gives way at the end, however, to a lyric reaffirmation of the artist's obsession with the fascinating, "adorable world" of colorful sights and mysterious figures, all waiting to be created.

Phyllis Rose, *Woman of Letters: A Life of Virginia Woolf* (1978), is a valuable biography; Edward Bishop, *Virginia Woolf* (1991), is a recent brief introduction. A useful and readable overview of the texts is provided by Avrom Fleishman, *Virginia Woolf: A Critical Reading* (1975). Two valuable collections of essays of Woolf's writing and her position in the modernist/postmodernist tradition are Patricia Clements and Isobel Grundy, eds., *Virginia Woolf: New Critical Essays* (1983), and Margaret Homans, ed., *Virginia Woolf: A Collection of Critical Essays* (1993). Dean R. Baldwin, *Virginia Woolf: A Study of the Short Fiction* (1989), offers a brief discussion, six essays by other critics, and two essays by Woolf on modern fiction. Jane Marcus, *New Feminist Essays on Virginia Woolf* (1981), includes representative feminist critiques of Virginia Woolf as writer and social thinker. Patricia Ondek Laurence situates Woolf in *The Reading of Silence: Virginia Woolf in the English Tradition* (1991); comparative studies include Richard Pearce, *The Politics of Narration: James Joyce, William Faulkner, and Virginia Woolf* (1991), and Bette London, *The Appropriated Voice: Narrative Authority in Conrad, Forster, and Woolf* (1990).

An Unwritten Novel

Such an expression of unhappiness was enough by itself to make one's eyes slide above the paper's edge to the poor woman's face—insignificant without that look, almost a symbol of human destiny with it. Life's what you see in people's eyes; life's what they learn, and, having learnt it, never, though they seek to hide it, cease to be aware of—what? That life's like that, it seems. Five faces opposite—five mature faces—and the knowledge in each face. Strange though, how people want to conceal it! Marks of reticence are on all those faces: lips shut, eyes shaded, each one of the five doing something to hide or stultify his knowledge. One smokes; another reads; a third checks entries in a pocket book; a fourth stares at the map of the line framed opposite; and the fifth—the terrible thing about the fifth is that she does nothing at all. She looks at life. Ah, but my poor, unfortunate woman, do play the game—do, for all our sakes, conceal it!

As if she heard me, she looked up, shifted slightly in her seat and sighed. She seemed to apologize and at the same time to say to me, "If only you knew!" Then she looked at life again. "But I do know," I answered silently, glancing at the *Times*[1] for manners' sake. "I know the whole business. 'Peace between Germany and the Allied Powers was yesterday officially ushered in at Paris—Signor Nitti, the Italian Prime Minister—a passenger train at Doncaster was in collision with a goods train . . .' We all know— the *Times* knows—but we pretend we don't." My eyes had once more crept over the paper's rim. She shuddered, twitched her arm queerly to the middle of her back and shook her head. Again I dipped into my great reservoir of life. "Take what you like," I continued, "births, deaths, marriages, Court Circular,[2] the habits of birds, Leonardo da Vinci, the Sand-

---

1. Major London newspaper, reputed to cover everything from international and royal news to a variety of local topics.   2. Royal news.

hills murder, high wages and the cost of living—oh, take what you like," I repeated, "it's all in the *Times!*" Again with infinite weariness she moved her head from side to side until, like a top exhausted with spinning, it settled on her neck.

The *Times* was no protection against such sorrow as hers. But other human beings forbade intercourse. The best thing to do against life was to fold the paper so that it made a perfect square, crisp, thick, impervious even to life. This done, I glanced up quickly, armed with a shield of my own. She pierced through my shield; she gazed into my eyes as if searching any sediment of courage at the depths of them and damping it to clay. Her twitch alone denied all hope, discounted all illusion.

So we rattled through Surrey and across the border into Sussex.[3] But with my eyes upon life I did not see that the other travellers had left, one by one, till, save for the man who read, we were alone together. Here was Three Bridges station. We drew slowly down the platform and stopped. Was he going to leave us? I prayed both ways—I prayed last that he might stay. At that instant he roused himself, crumpled his paper contemptuously, like a thing done with, burst open the door, and left us alone.

The unhappy woman, leaning a little forward, palely and colourlessly addressed me—talked of stations and holidays, of brothers at Eastbourne,[4] and the time of year, which was, I forget now, early or late. But at last looking from the window and seeing, I knew, only life, she breathed, "Staying away—that's the drawback of it—" Ah, now we approached the catastrophe.[5] "My sister-in-law"—the bitterness of her tone was like lemon on cold steel, and speaking, not to me, but to herself, she muttered, "Nonsense, she would say—that's what they all say," and while she spoke she fidgeted as though the skin on her back were as a plucked fowl's in a poulterer's shop-window.

"Oh, that cow!" she broke off nervously, as though the great wooden cow in the meadow had shocked her and saved her from some indiscretion. Then she shuddered, and then she made the awkward angular movement that I had seen before, as if, after the spasm, some spot between the shoulders burnt or itched. Then again she looked the most unhappy woman in the world, and I once more reproached her, though not with the same conviction, for if there were a reason, and if I knew the reason, the stigma was removed from life.

"Sisters-in-law," I said—

Her lips pursed as if to spit venom at the word; pursed they remained. All she did was to take her glove and rub hard at a spot on the window-pane. She rubbed as if she would rub something out for ever—some stain, some indelible contamination. Indeed, the spot remained for all her rubbing, and back she sank with the shudder and the clutch of the arm I had come to expect. Something impelled me to take my glove and rub my window. There, too, was a little speck on the glass. For all my rubbing it remained. And then the spasm went through me; I crooked my arm and plucked at the middle of my back. My skin, too, felt like the damp chick-

3. The train is passing through the southeastern English countryside, headed away from London.   4. A seaside resort.   5. In the literary sense: a dénouement or crucial revelation.

en's skin in the poulterer's shop-window; one spot between the shoulders itched and irritated, felt clammy, felt raw. Could I reach it? Surreptitiously I tried. She saw me. A smile of infinite irony, infinite sorrow, flitted and faded from her face. But she had communicated, shared her secret, passed her poison; she would speak no more. Leaning back in my corner, shielding my eyes from her eyes, seeing only the slopes and hollows, greys and purples, of the winter's landscape, I read her message, deciphered her secret, reading it beneath her gaze.

Hilda's the sister-in-law. Hilda? Hilda? Hilda Marsh—Hilda the blooming, the full bosomed, the matronly. Hilda stands at the door as the cab draws up, holding a coin. "Poor Minnie, more of a grasshopper than ever—old cloak she had last year. Well, well, with two children these days one can't do more. No, Minnie, I've got it; here you are, cabby—none of your ways with me. Come in, Minnie. Oh, I could carry *you*, let alone your basket!" So they go into the dining-room. "Aunt Minnie, children."

Slowly the knives and forks sink from the upright. Down they get (Bob and Barbara), hold out hands stiffly; back again to their chairs, staring between the resumed mouthfuls. [But this we'll skip; ornaments, curtains, trefoil china plate, yellow oblongs of cheese, white squares of biscuit— skip, oh, but wait! Halfway through luncheon one of those shivers; Bob stares at her, spoon in mouth. "Get on with your pudding, Bob"; but Hilda disapproves. "Why *should* she twitch?" Skip, skip, till we reach the landing on the upper floor; stairs brass-bound; linoleum worn; oh, yes! little bedroom looking out over the roofs of Eastbourne—zigzagging roofs like the spines of caterpillars, this way, that way, striped red and yellow, with blue-black slating.] Now, Minnie, the door's shut; Hilda heavily descends to the basement; you unstrap the straps of your basket, lay on the bed a meagre nightgown, stand side by side furred felt slippers. The looking-glass—no, you avoid the looking-glass. Some methodical disposition of hat-pins. Perhaps the shell box has something in it? You shake it; it's the pearl stud there was last year—that's all. And then the sniff, the sigh, the sitting by the window. Three o'clock on a December afternoon; the rain drizzling! one light low in the skylight of a drapery emporium; another high in a servant's bedroom—this one goes out. That gives her nothing to look at. A moment's blankness—then, what are you thinking? (Let me peep across at her opposite; she's asleep or pretending it; so what would she think about sitting at the window at three o'clock in the afternoon? Health, money, bills, her God?) Yes, sitting on the very edge of the chair looking over the roofs of Eastbourne, Minnie Marsh prays to God. That's all very well; and she may rub the pane too, as though to see God better; but what God does she see? Who's the God of Minnie Marsh, the God of the back streets of Eastbourne, the God of three o'clock in the afternoon? I, too, see roofs, I see sky; but, oh, dear—this seeing of Gods! More like President Kruger than Prince Albert[6]—that's the best I can do for him; and I see him on a chair, in a black frock-coat, not so very high up either; I can manage a cloud or two for him to sit on; and then his hand trailing in the

---

6. Husband of the British Queen Victoria; he was a popular figure known for political moderation (1819–1861). Paul Kruger (1825–1904), Transvaal statesman strongly opposed to British influence in South Africa, president of the Boer Republic for twenty years. Contemporary pictures show him in formal frock coat with a severe, bearded face.

cloud holds a rod, a truncheon is it?—black, thick, thorned—a brutal old bully—Minnie's God! Did he send the itch and the patch and the twitch? Is that why she prays? What she rubs on the window is the stain of sin. Oh, she committed some crime!

I have my choice of crimes. The woods flit and fly—in summer there are bluebells; in the opening there, when spring comes, primroses. A parting, was it, twenty years ago? Vows broken? Not Minnie's! . . . She was faithful. How she nursed her mother! All her savings on the tombstone— wreaths under glass—daffodils in jars. But I'm off the track. A crime. . . . They would say she kept her sorrow, suppressed her secret—her sex, they'd say—the scientific people. But what flummery to saddle *her* with sex! No—more like this. Passing down the streets of Croydon twenty years ago, the violet loops of ribbon in the draper's window spangled in the electric light catch her eye. She lingers—past six. Still by running she can reach home. She pushes through the glass wing door. It's sale-time. Shallow trays brim with ribbons. She pauses, pulls this, fingers that with the raised roses on it—no need to choose, no need to buy, and each tray with its surprises. "We don't shut till seven," and then it *is* seven. She runs, she rushes, home she reaches, but too late. Neighbours—the doctor—baby brother—the kettle—scalded—hospital—dead—or only the shock of it, the blame? Ah, but the detail matters nothing! It's what she carries with her; the spot, the crime, the thing to expiate, always there between her shoulders. "Yes," she seems to nod to me, "it's the thing I did."

Whether you did, or what you did, I don't mind; it's not the thing I want. The draper's window looped with violet—that'll do; a little cheap perhaps, a little commonplace—since one has a choice of crimes, but then so many (let me peep across again—still sleeping, or pretending sleep! white, worn, the mouth closed—a touch of obstinacy, more than one would think—no hint of sex)—so many crimes aren't *your* crime; your crime was cheap, only the retribution solemn; for now the church door opens, the hard wooden pew receives her; on the brown tiles she kneels; every day, winter, summer, dusk, dawn (here she's at it) prays. All her sins fall, fall, for ever fall. The spot receives them. It's raised, it's red, it's burning. Next she twitches. Small boys point. "Bob at lunch today"—But elderly women are the worst.

Indeed now you can't sit praying any longer. Kruger's sunk beneath the clouds—washed over as with a painter's brush of liquid grey, to which he adds a tinge of black—even the tip of the truncheon gone now. That's what always happens! Just as you've seen him, felt him, someone interrupts. It's Hilda now.

How you hate her! She'll even lock the bathroom door overnight, too, though it's only cold water you want, and sometimes when the night's been bad it seems as if washing helped. And John at breakfast—the children—meals are worst, and sometimes there are friends—ferns don't altogether hide 'em—they guess, too; so out you go along the front, where the waves are grey, and the papers blow, and the glass shelters green and draughty, and the chairs cost tuppence[7]—too much—for there must be preachers along the sands. Ah, that's a nigger—that's a funny man—that's

7. Chairs were available for rent along the waterfront.

a man with parakeets—poor little creatures! Is there no one here who thinks of God?—just up there, over the pier, with his rod—but no—there's nothing but grey in the sky or if it's blue the white clouds hide him, and the music—it's military music—and what are they fishing for? Do they catch them? How the children stare! Well, then home a back way— "Home a back way!" The words have meaning; might have been spoken by the old man with whiskers—no, no, he didn't really speak; but everything has meaning—placards leaning against doorways—names above shop-windows—red fruit in baskets—women's heads in the hairdresser's— all say "Minnie Marsh!" But here's a jerk. "Eggs are cheaper!"[8] That's what always happens! I was heading her over the waterfall, straight for madness, when, like a flock of dream sheep, she turns t'other way and runs between my fingers. Eggs are cheaper. Tethered to the shores of the world, none of the crimes, sorrows, rhapsodies, or insanities for poor Minnie Marsh; never late for luncheon; never caught in a storm without a mackintosh; never utterly unconscious of the cheapness of eggs. So she reaches home—scrapes her boots.

Have I read you right? But the human face—the human face at the top of the fullest sheet of print holds more, withholds more. Now, eyes open, she looks out; and in the human eye—how d'you define it?—there's a break—a division—so that when you've grasped the stem the butterfly's off—the moth that hangs in the evening over the yellow flower—move, raise your hand, off, high, away. I won't raise my hand. Hang still, then, quiver, life, soul, spirit, whatever you are of Minnie Marsh—I, too, on my flower—the hawk over the down—alone, or what were the worth of life? To rise; hang still in the evening, in the midday; hang still over the down. The flicker of a hand—off, up! then poised again. Alone, unseen; seeing all so still down there, all so lovely. None seeing, none caring. The eyes of others our prisons; their thoughts our cages. Air above, air below. And the moon and immortality. . . . Oh, but I drop to the turf! Are you down too, you in the corner, what's your name—woman—Minnie Marsh; some such name as that? There she is, tight to her blossom; opening her handbag, from which she takes a hollow shell—an egg—who was saying that eggs were cheaper? You or I? Oh, it was you who said it on the way home, you remember, when the old gentleman, suddenly opening his umbrella—or sneezing was it? Anyhow, Kruger went, and you came "home a back way," and scraped your boots. Yes. And now you lay across your knees a pocket-handkerchief into which drop little angular fragments of eggshell—fragments of a map—a puzzle. I wish I could piece them together! If you would only sit still. She's moved her knees—the map's in bits again. Down the slopes of the Andes the white blocks of marble go bounding and hurtling, crushing to death a whole troop of Spanish muleteers, with their convoy—Drake's booty, gold and silver.[9] But to return—

To what, to where? She opened the door, and, putting her umbrella in

---

8. The narrator's silent imaginings are interrupted and brought down to earth when Minnie Marsh, preparing to eat her snack of hard-boiled egg, comments out loud that "Eggs are cheaper!"   9. The yellow and white fragments of egg inspire another series of images. Sir Francis Drake (1540?–1596) was an English explorer and sea captain who captured Spanish ships returning from South America laden with gold and silver stolen from the Indians. The Indians are imagined as rolling blocks of marble down the Andes mountains to crush the invaders.

the stand—that goes without saying: so, too, the whiff of beef from the basement; dot, dot, dot. But what I cannot thus eliminate, what I must, head down, eyes shut, with the courage of a battalion and the blindness of a bull, charge and disperse are, indubitably, the figures behind the ferns, commercial travellers. There, I've hidden them all this time in the hope that somehow they'd disappear, or better still emerge, as indeed they must, if the story's to go on gathering richness and rotundity, destiny and tragedy, as stories should, rolling along with it two, if not three, commercial travellers and a whole grove of aspidistra. "The fronds of the aspidistra only partly concealed the commercial traveller[1]—" Rhododendrons would conceal him utterly, and into the bargain give me my fling of red and white, for which I starve and strive; but rhododendrons in Eastbourne—in December—on the Marshes' table—no, no, I dare not;[2] it's all a matter of crusts and cruets, frills and ferns. Perhaps there'll be a moment later by the sea. Moreover, I feel, pleasantly pricking through the green fretwork and over the glacis of cut glass, a desire to peer and peep at the man opposite—one's as much as I can manage. James Moggridge is it, whom the Marshes call Jimmy? [Minnie, you must promise not to twitch till I've got this straight.] James Moggridge travels in—shall we say buttons?[3]—but the time's not come for bringing *them* in—the big and the little on the long cards, some peacock-eyed, others dull gold; cairngorms[4] some, and others coral sprays—but I say the time's not come. He travels, and on Thursdays, his Eastbourne day, takes his meals with the Marshes. His red face, his little steady eyes—by no means altogether commonplace—his enormous appetite (that's safe; he won't look at Minnie till the bread's swamped the gravy dry), napkin tucked diamond-wise—but this is primitive, and, whatever it may do the reader, don't take me in. Let's dodge to the Moggridge household, set that in motion. Well, the family boots are mended on Sundays by James himself. He reads *Truth.*[5] But his passion? Roses—and his wife a retired hospital nurse—interesting—for God's sake let me have one woman with a name I like! But no; she's of the unborn children of the mind, illicit, none the less loved, like my rhododendrons. How many die in every novel that's written—the best, the dearest, while Moggridge lives. It's life's fault. Here's Minnie eating her egg at the moment opposite and at t'other end of the line—are we past Lewes?[6]—there must be Jimmy—or what's her twitch for?

There must be Moggridge—life's fault. Life imposes her laws; life blocks the way; life's behind the fern; life's the tyrant; oh, but not the bully! No, for I assure you I come willingly; I come wooed by Heaven knows what compulsion across ferns and cruets, table splashed and bottles smeared. I come irresistibly to lodge myself somewhere on the firm flesh, in the robust spine, wherever I can penetrate or find foothold on the person, in the soul, of Moggridge the man. The enormous stability of the fabric; the spine tough as whalebone, straight as oaktree; the ribs radiating

1. Traveling salesman.   2. Aspidistra (a long-leaved, common house plant) is more appropriate for the imagined story's middle-class setting than rhododendron, which would not fit the season or context.
3. The commercial traveler given the name James Moggridge is imagined as selling buttons; there follows a brief description of his merchandise on its display cards.   4. A yellow quartz.   5. A popular weekly magazine.   6. County town in East Sussex.

branches; the flesh taut tarpaulin; the red hollows; the suck and regurgitation of the heart; while from above meat falls in brown cubes and beer
gushes to be churned to blood again—and so we reach the eyes. Behind
the aspidistra they see something: black, white, dismal; now the plate
again; behind the aspidistra they see an elderly woman; "Marsh's sister.
Hilda's more my sort"; the tablecloth now. "Marsh would know what's
wrong with Morrises . . ." talk that over; cheese has come; the plate again;
turn it round—the enormous fingers; now the woman opposite. "Marsh's
sister—not a bit like Marsh; wretched, elderly female. . . . You should feed
your hens. . . . God's truth, what's set her twitching? Not what I said? Dear,
dear, dear! these elderly women. Dear, dear!"

[Yes, Minnie; I know you've twitched, but one moment—James Moggridge.]

"Dear, dear, dear!" How beautiful the sound is! like the knock of a
mallet on seasoned timber, like the throb of the heart of an ancient whaler
when the seas press thick and the green is clouded. "Dear, dear!" what a
passing bell for the souls of the fretful to soothe them and solace them,
lap them in linen, saying, "So long. Good luck to you!" and then, "What's
your pleasure?" for though Moggridge would pluck his rose for her, that's
done, that's over. Now what's the next thing? "Madam, you'll miss your
train," for they don't linger.

That's the man's way; that's the sound that reverberates; that's St.
Paul's,[7] and the motor-omnibuses. But we're brushing the crumbs off. Oh,
Moggridge, you won't stay? You must be off? Are you driving through
Eastbourne this afternoon in one of those little carriages? Are you the man
who's walled up in green cardboard boxes, and sometimes sits so solemn
staring like a sphinx; and always there's a look of the sepulchral, something
of the undertaker, the coffin, and the dusk about horse and driver? Do
tell me—but the doors slammed. We shall never meet again. Moggridge,
farewell!

Yes, yes, I'm coming. Right up to the top of the house. One moment
I'll linger. How the mud goes round in the mind—what a swirl these
monsters leave, the waters rocking, the weeds waving and green here,
black there, striking to the sand, till by degrees the atoms reassemble, the
deposit sifts itself, and again through the eyes one sees clear and still, and
there comes to the lips some prayer for the departed, some obsequy for
the souls of those one nods to, the people one never meets again.

James Moggridge is dead now, gone for ever. Well, Minnie—"I can
face it no longer." If she said that—(Let me look at her. She is brushing
the eggshell into deep declivities). She said it certainly, leaning against
the wall of the bedroom, and plucking at the little balls which edge the
claret-coloured curtain. But when the self speaks to the self, who is speaking?—the entombed soul, the spirit driven in, in, in to the central cata-
comb; the self that took the veil[8] and left the world—a coward perhaps,
yet somehow beautiful, as it flits with its lantern restlessly up and down
the dark corridors. "I can bear it no longer," her spirit says. "That man at
lunch—Hilda—the children." Oh, heavens, her sob! It's the spirit wailing

7. St. Paul's Cathedral in London.   8. Became a nun.

its destiny, the spirit driven hither, thither, lodging on the diminishing carpets—meagre footholds—shrunken shreds of all the vanishing universe—love, life, faith, husband, children, I know not what splendours and pageantries glimpsed in girlhood. "Not for me—not for me."

But then—the muffins, the bald elderly dog? Bead mats I should fancy and the consolation of underlinen. If Minnie Marsh were run over and taken to hospital, nurses and doctors themselves would exclaim.[9] . . . There's the vista and the vision—there's the distance—the blue blot at the end of the avenue, while, after all, the tea is rich, the muffin hot, and the dog—"Benny, to your basket, sir, and see what mother's brought you!" So, taking the glove with the worn thumb, defying once more the encroaching demon of what's called going in holes, you renew the fortifications, threading the grey wool, running it in and out.

Running it in and out, across and over, spinning a web through which God himself—hush, don't think of God! How firm the stitches are! You must be proud of your darning. Let nothing disturb her. Let the light fall gently, and the clouds show an inner vest of the first green leaf. Let the sparrow perch on the twig and shake the raindrop hanging to the twig's elbow. . . . Why look up? Was it a sound, a thought? Oh, heavens! Back again to the thing you did, the plate glass with the violet loops? But Hilda will come. Ignominies, humiliations, oh! Close the breach.

Having mended her glove, Minnie Marsh lays it in the drawer. She shuts the drawer with decision. I catch sight of her face in the glass. Lips are pursed. Chin held high. Next she laces her shoes. Then she touches her throat. What's your brooch? Mistletoe or merrythought?[1] And what is happening? Unless I'm much mistaken, the pulse's quickened, the moment's coming, the threads are racing, Niagara's ahead. Here's the crisis! Heaven be with you! Down she goes. Courage, courage! Face it, be it! For God's sake don't wait on the mat now! There's the door! I'm on your side. Speak! Comfort her, confound her soul![2]

"Oh, I beg your pardon! Yes, this is Eastbourne. I'll reach it down for you. Let me try the handle." [But Minnie, though we keep up pretences, I've read you right—I'm with you now.]

"That's all your luggage?"

"Much obliged, I'm sure."

(But why do you look about you? Hilda won't come to the station, nor John; and Moggridge is driving at the far side of Eastbourne.)

"I'll wait by my bag, ma'am, that's safest. He said he'd meet me. . . . Oh, there he is! That's my son."

So they walk off together.

Well, but I'm confounded. . . . Surely, Minnie, you know better! A strange young man. . . . Stop! I'll tell him—Minnie!—Miss Marsh!—I don't know though. There's something queer in her cloak as it blows. Oh, but it's untrue, it's indecent. . . . Look how he bends as they reach the gateway. She finds her ticket. What's the joke? Off they go, down the road, side by side. . . . Well, my world's done for! What do I stand on? What do

---

9. The hospital attendants are to exclaim at the neatness of Minnie Marsh's underwear. Immaculate and well-kept clothing—both inside and out—was one of the signs of a proper lady.   1. Wishbone.
2. The narrator imagines a major confrontation between the poor spinster Minnie Marsh and Hilda.

I know? That's not Minnie. There never was Moggridge. Who am I? Life's
bare as bone.

And yet the last look of them—he stepping from the kerb and she following him round the edge of the big building brims me with wonder—
floods me anew. Mysterious figures! Mother and son. Who are you? Why
do you walk down the street? Where tonight will you sleep, and then,
tomorrow? Oh, how it whirls and surges—floats me afresh! I start after
them. People drive this way and that. The white light splutters and pours.
Plate-glass windows. Carnations; chrysanthemums. Ivy in dark gardens.
Milk carts at the door. Wherever I go, mysterious figures, I see you, turning
the corner, mothers and sons; you, you, you. I hasten, I follow. This, I
fancy, must be the sea. Grey is the landscape; dim as ashes; the water
murmurs and moves. If I fall on my knees, if I go through the ritual, the
ancient antics, it's you, unknown figures, you I adore; if I open my arms,
it's you I embrace, you I draw to me—adorable world!

FRANZ KAFKA
1883–1924

The predicament of Franz Kafka's writing is, for many, the predicament of modern civilization. Nowhere is the anxiety and alienation of twentieth-century society
more visible than in his stories of individuals struggling to prevail against a vast,
meaningless, and apparently hostile system. Identifying that system as bureaucracy,
family, religion, language, or the invisible network of social habit is less important
than recognizing the protagonists' bewilderment at being placed in impossible
situations. Kafka's heroes are driven to find answers in an unresponsive world, and
they are required to act according to incomprehensible rules administered by an
inaccessible authority; small wonder that they fluctuate between fear, hope, anger,
resignation, and despair. Kafka's fictional world has long fascinated contemporary
writers, who find in it an extraordinary blend of prosaic realism and nightmarish,
infinitely interpretable symbolism. Whether evoking the multilayered bureaucracy
of the modern state, the sense of guilt felt by those facing the accusations of authority, or the vulnerability of characters who cannot make themselves understood,
Kafka's descriptions are believable because of their scrupulous attention to detail:
the flea on a fur collar, the dust under an unmade bed, the creases and yellowing
of an old newspaper, or the helplessness of a beetle turned upside down. The
sheer *ordinariness* of these details grounds the entire narrative, giving the reader a
continuing expectation of reality even when events escape all logic and the situation is at its most hallucinatory. This paradoxical combination has appealed to a
range of contemporary writers—each quite different from the other—who have
read and absorbed Kafka's lesson: Samuel Beckett, Harold Pinter, Alain Robbe-
Grillet, Gabriel García Márquez.

Kafka was born into cultural alienation: Jewish (though not truly part of the
Jewish community) in Catholic Czechoslovakia, son of a German-speaking shopkeeper when German was the language of the imposed Austro-Hungarian government, and drawn to literature when his father—a domineering, self-made man—
pushed him toward success in business. Nor was he happier at home. Resenting
his father's overbearing nature and feeling deprived of maternal love, he nonetheless lived with his parents for most of his life and complained in long letters about

his coldness and inability to love (despite numerous liaisons). Kafka took a degree in law to qualify himself for a position in a large accident-insurance corporation, where he worked until illness forced his retirement in 1922. By the time of his death from tuberculosis two years later, he had published a number of short stories and two novellas (*The Metamorphosis*, 1915; *In the Penal Colony*, 1919), but left behind him the manuscripts of three near-complete novels that—considering himself a failure—he asked to have burned. Instead, Kafka's executor Max Brod published the novels (*The Trial*, 1925; *The Castle*, 1926; *Amerika*, 1927) and a biography celebrating the genius of his tormented, guilt-ridden friend.

In spite of the indubitable fact that Franz Kafka became a respected senior executive handling claims, litigations, public relations, and his institute's annual reports, and was one of the few top German executives retained when Czechoslovakia finally gained independence in 1918, his image in the modern imagination is derived from the portraits of inner anguish given in his fiction, diaries, and letters. This "Kafka" is a tormented and sensitive soul, guiltily resentful of his job in a giant bureaucracy, unable to free himself from his family or to cope with the demands of love, physically feeble, and constantly beset by feelings of inferiority and doom in an existence whose laws he can never quite understand. "Before the Law," a parable published in Kafka's lifetime and included in *The Trial*, recounts the archetypal setting of the "Kafka" character: a countryman waits and waits throughout his lifetime for permission to enter a crucial Gate, where the doorkeeper (the first of many) repeatedly refuses him entrance. He tries everything from good behavior to bribes without success. Finally, as the now-aged countryman dies in frustration, he is told that the gate existed only for him, and that it is now being closed. For the countryman (as for Vladimir and Estragon in Beckett's *Waiting for Godot*, and indeed for much modern literature), there is no response. The Law that governs our existence is all-powerful but irrational; at least it is not to be understood by its human suppliants, a lesson that Kafka could have derived equally well from his readings in the Danish philosopher Søren Kierkegaard, in Friedrich Nietzsche, or in the Jewish Talmud.

The combination of down-to-earth, matter-of-fact setting and unreal or nightmarish events is the hallmark of Kafka's style. His characters speak prosaically and react in a commonsense way when such a response (given the situation) is utterly grotesque. A young businessman is changed overnight into a giant beetle (*The Metamorphosis*) or charged with undefined crimes and finally executed (*The Trial*); a would-be land surveyor is unable to communicate with the castle that employs him and keeps sending incomprehensible messages (*The Castle*); a visitor to a penal colony observes a gigantic machine whose function is to execute condemned criminals by inscribing their sentence deeper and deeper into their flesh (*In the Penal Colony*). The term *surrealist* is often attached to this blend of everyday reality and dream configuration, with its implication of psychic undercurrents and cosmic significance stirring beneath the most ordinary-seeming existence. Kafka, however, had no connection with the Surrealists, whose vision of a miraculous level of existence hidden behind everyday life is the obverse of his heroes' vain attempts to maintain control over the impossible and the absurd.

Kafka's stories are not allegories, although many readers have been tempted to find in them an underlying message. A political reading sees them as indictments of faceless bureaucracy controlling individual lives in the modern totalitarian state. The sense of being found guilty by an entire society recalls the traditional theme of the Wandering Jew, and predicts for many the Holocaust of World War II (in fact, Kafka's three sisters died in concentration camps). His heroes' self-conscious quest to fit into some meaningful structure, their ceaseless attempts to do the right thing when there is no rational way of knowing what that is, is the very picture of absurdity and alienation that existentialist philosophers and writers examined during and after World War II. The assumption that there is a Law, and the presence of protagonists who die in search for purity (*The Hunger Artist*) or in a humble admission of guilt (*The Trial*) allow the stories to be taken as religious metaphors. Kafka's desperately lucid analysis of the way his parents' influence shaped an impressionable child into an unhappy adult (*Letter to My Father*) articulates emotional tangles and parent-child rivalry with an openness and detail that recalls decades of psychoanalytical criticism following Freud. The picture of a sick society where individual rights and sensitivity no longer count and unreasoning torment is visited on the ignorant has been read as an indictment of disintegrating modern culture. Yet no one allegorical interpretation is finally possible, for all these potential meanings overlap as they expand toward social, familial, political, philosophical, and religious dimensions and constitute the richly allusive texture of separate tales by a master storyteller.

The Metamorphosis, Kafka's longest complete work published in his lifetime, is first of all a consummate narrative: the question "What happens next?" never disappears from the moment that Gregor Samsa wakes up to find himself transformed. "It was no dream," no nightmarish fantasy in which Gregor temporarily identified himself with other downtrodden vermin of society. Instead, this grotesque transformation is permanent, a single unshakable fact that renders almost comic his family's calculations and attempts to adjust. "The terror of art," said Kafka in a conversation about The Metamorphosis, is that "the dream reveals the reality." This artistic dream, become Gregor's reality, sheds light on the intolerable nature of his former daily existence. The other side of his job is its mechanical rigidity, personal rivalries, and threatening suspicion of any deviation from the norm. Gregor himself is part of this world, as he shows when he fawns on the manager and tries to manipulate him by criticizing their boss.

More disturbing is the transformation that takes place in Gregor's family, where the expected love and support turns into shamed acceptance and animal resentment now that Gregor has let the family down. Mother and sister are ineffectual, and their sympathy is slowly replaced by disgust. Gregor's father quickly reassumes his position of authority and beats the beetle back into his room: first with the businesslike newspaper and manager's cane, and later with a barrage of apples from the family table. Just before his death Gregor has become an "it" whose death is warmly wished by the whole family—and perhaps they are right, in one of Kafka's ironies. The beetle's death brings not remorse but a new lease on life to his family. Weak and passive when Gregor took care of them, they regain strength and vitality under the pressure of earning a living. Mother, father, and sister celebrate Gregor's death with a holiday trip out of town, into the sunshine and open air, where they make plans for the future.

Gregor Samsa may be a pathetic figure but he is not a tragic one. In his passiveness and unvoiced resentment, his willingness to exist at a surface level of adjustment to job and family, he has become an accomplice in his own fate. His descent into animal consciousness is not a true pilgrimage to inner awareness, even though it involves letting go the trappings of civilization. Rather, it is an obscuring of consciousness that is perfectly represented when he is swept out onto the dustheap at the end. From that point on, it is the family's story, continuing a career that has meant death for Gregor and joyous survival for his family, but in which both are reduced to existence on an animal level.

Anthony Thorlby, *Kafka: A Study* (1972), is a brief general introduction. Heinz Politzer, *Franz Kafka: Parable and Paradox* (1966), presents an interesting, readable study of symbolic relationships. Ernest Pawel, *The Nightmare of Reason: A Life of Franz Kafka* (1984), is an excellent contemporary biography with penetrating descriptions of his family and friends. Max Brod, *Franz Kafka: A Biography* (1960), is an early, admiring biography by a close friend and Kafka's executor.

Ronald Gray, ed., *Kafka: A Collection of Critical Essays* (1962), is a useful early collection of essays on different works. Harold Bloom, ed., *Franz Kafka's The Metamorphosis* (1988), collects essays on spiritual, metaphorical, formal, social, and psychoanalytic aspects of *The Metamorphosis*. Jack Murray analyzes the sense of space in *The Landscapes of Alienation: Ideological Subversion in Kafka, Celine, and Onetti* (1991). Kurt Fickert, *End of a Mission: Kafka's Search for Truth in His Last Stories* (1993), interprets the stories as metaphors for an autobiographical quest to resolve personal problems.

The Metamorphosis[1]

I

When Gregor Samsa woke up one morning from unsettling dreams, he found himself changed in his bed into a monstrous vermin. He was lying on his back as hard as armor plate, and when he lifted his head a little, he saw his vaulted brown belly, sectioned by arch-shaped ribs, to whose dome the cover, about to slide off completely, could barely cling. His many legs, pitifully thin compared with the size of the rest of him, were waving helplessly before his eyes.

"What's happened to me?" he thought. It was no dream. His room, a regular human room, only a little on the small side, lay quiet between the four familiar walls. Over the table, on which an unpacked line of fabric samples was all spread out—Samsa was a traveling salesman—hung the picture which he had recently cut out of a glossy magazine and lodged in a pretty gilt frame. It showed a lady done up in a fur hat and a fur boa, sitting upright and raising up against the viewer a heavy fur muff in which her whole forearm had disappeared.

Gregor's eyes then turned to the window, and the overcast weather—he could hear raindrops hitting against the metal window ledge—completely depressed him. "How about going back to sleep for a few minutes and forgetting all this nonsense," he thought, but that was completely impracticable, since he was used to sleeping on his right side and in his present state could not get into that position. No matter how hard he threw himself onto his right side, he always rocked onto his back again. He must have tried it a hundred times, closing his eyes so as not to have to see his squirming legs, and stopped only when he began to feel a slight, dull pain in his side, which he had never felt before.

"Oh God," he thought, "what a grueling job I've picked. Day in, day out—on the road. The upset of doing business is much worse than the actual business in the home office, and besides, I've got the torture of traveling, worrying about changing trains, eating miserable food at all hours, constantly seeing new faces, no relationships that last or get more intimate. To the devil with it all!" He felt a slight itching up on top of his belly; shoved himself slowly on his back closer to the bedpost, so as to be able to lift his head better; found the itchy spot, studded with small white

---

1. Translated by Stanley Corngold.

dots which he had no idea what to make of; and wanted to touch the spot with one of his legs but immediately pulled it back, for the contact sent a cold shiver through him.

He slid back again into his original position. "This getting up so early," he thought, "makes anyone a complete idiot. Human beings have to have their sleep. Other traveling salesmen live like harem women. For instance, when I go back to the hotel before lunch to write up the business I've done, these gentlemen are just having breakfast. That's all I'd have to try with my boss; I'd be fired on the spot. Anyway, who knows if that wouldn't be a very good thing for me. If I didn't hold back for my parents' sake, I would have quit long ago, I would have marched up to the boss and spoken my piece from the bottom of my heart. He would have fallen off the desk! It is funny, too, the way he sits on the desk and talks down from the heights to the employees, especially when they have to come right up close on account of the boss's being hard of hearing. Well, I haven't given up hope completely; once I've gotten the money together to pay off my parents' debt to him—that will probably take another five or six years—I'm going to do it without fail. Then I'm going to make the big break. But for the time being I'd better get up, since my train leaves at five."

And he looked over at the alarm clock, which was ticking on the chest of drawers. "God Almighty!" he thought. It was six-thirty, the hands were quietly moving forward, it was actually past the half-hour, it was already nearly a quarter to. Could it be that the alarm hadn't gone off? You could see from the bed that it was set correctly for four o'clock; it certainly had gone off, too. Yes, but was it possible to sleep quietly through a ringing that made the furniture shake? Well, he certainly hadn't slept quietly, but probably all the more soundly for that. But what should he do now? The next train left at seven o'clock; to make it, he would have to hurry like a madman, and the line of samples wasn't packed yet, and he himself didn't feel especially fresh and ready to march around. And even if he did make the train, he could not avoid getting it from the boss, because the messenger boy had been waiting at the five-o'clock train and would have long ago reported his not showing up. He was a tool of the boss, without brains or backbone. What if he were to say he was sick? But that would be extremely embarrassing and suspicious because during his five years with the firm Gregor had not been sick even once. The boss would be sure to come with the health-insurance doctor, blame his parents for their lazy son, and cut off all excuses by quoting the health-insurance doctor, for whom the world consisted of people who were completely healthy but afraid to work. And, besides, in this case would he be so very wrong? In fact, Gregor felt fine, with the exception of his drowsiness, which was really unnecessary after sleeping so late, and he even had a ravenous appetite.

Just as he was thinking all this over at top speed, without being able to decide to get out of bed—the alarm clock had just struck a quarter to seven—he heard a cautious knocking at the door next to the head of his bed. "Gregor," someone called—it was his mother—"it's a quarter to seven. Didn't you want to catch the train?" What a soft voice! Gregor was shocked to hear his own voice answering, unmistakably his own voice, true, but in which, as if from below, an insistent distressed chirping intruded, which left the clarity of his words intact only for a moment really, before so badly garbling them as they carried that no one could be sure if he had heard right. Gregor had wanted to answer in detail and to explain everything, but, given the circumstances, confined himself to saying, "Yes, yes, thanks, Mother, I'm just getting up." The wooden door must have prevented the change in Gregor's voice from being noticed outside, because his mother was satisfied with this explanation and shuffled off. But their little exchange had made the rest of the family aware that, contrary to expectations, Gregor was still in the house, and already his father was knocking on one of the side doors, feebly but with this fist. "Gregor, Gregor," he called, "what's going on?" And after a little while he called again in a deeper, warning voice, "Gregor! Gregor!" At the other side door, however, his sister moaned gently, "Gregor? Is something the matter with you? Do you want anything?" Toward both sides Gregor answered: "I'm all ready," and made an effort, by meticulous pronunciation and by inserting long pauses between individual words, to eliminate everything from his voice that might betray him. His father went back to his breakfast, but his sister whispered, "Gregor, open up, I'm pleading with you." But Gregor had absolutely no intention of opening the door and complimented himself instead on the precaution he had adopted from his business trips, of locking all the doors during the night even at home.

First of all he wanted to get up quietly, without any excitement; get dressed; and the main thing, have breakfast, and only then think about what to do next, for he saw clearly that in bed he would never think things through to a rational conclusion. He remembered how even in the past he had often felt some kind of slight pain, possibly caused by lying in an uncomfortable position, which, when he got up, turned out to be purely imaginary, and he was eager to see how today's fantasy would gradually fade away. That the change in his voice was nothing more than the first sign of a bad cold, an occupational ailment of the traveling salesman, he had no doubt in the least.

It was very easy to throw off the cover; all he had to do was puff himself up a little, and it fell off by itself. But after this, things got difficult, especially since he was so unusually broad. He would have needed hands and arms to lift himself up, but instead of that he had only his numerous little legs, which were in every different kind of perpetual motion and which, besides, he could not control. If he wanted to bend one, the first thing that happened was that it stretched itself out; and if he finally succeeded in getting this leg to do what he wanted, all the others in the meantime, as if set free, began to work in the most intensely painful agitation. "Just don't stay in bed being useless," Gregor said to himself.

First he tried to get out of bed with the lower part of his body, but this lower part—which by the way he had not seen yet and which he could not form a clear picture of—proved too difficult to budge; it was taking so long; and when finally, almost out of his mind, he lunged forward with all his force, without caring, he had picked the wrong direction and slammed himself violently against the lower bedpost, and the searing pain he felt taught him that exactly the lower part of his body was, for the moment anyway, the most sensitive.

He therefore tried to get the upper part of his body out of bed first and warily turned his head toward the edge of the bed. This worked easily, and in spite of its width and weight, the mass of his body finally followed, slowly, the movement of his head. But when at last he stuck his head over the edge of the bed into the air, he got too scared to continue any further, since if he finally let himself fall in this position, it would be a miracle if he didn't injure his head. And just now he had better not for the life of him lose consciousness; he would rather stay in bed.

But when, once again, after the same exertion, he lay in his original position, sighing, and again watched his little legs struggling, if possible more fiercely, with each other and saw no way of bringing peace and order into this mindless motion, he again told himself that it was impossible for him to stay in bed and that the most rational thing was to make any sacrifice for even the smallest hope of freeing himself from the bed. But at the same time he did not forget to remind himself occasionally that thinking things over calmly—indeed, as calmly as possible—was much better than jumping to desperate decisions. At such moments he fixed his eyes as sharply as possible on the window, but unfortunately there was little confidence and cheer to be gotten from the view of the morning fog, which shrouded even the other side of the narrow street. "Seven o'clock already," he said to himself as the alarm clock struck again, "seven o'clock already and still such a fog." And for a little while he lay quietly, breathing shallowly, as if expecting, perhaps, from the complete silence the return of things to the way they really and naturally were.

But then he said to himself, "Before it strikes a quarter past seven, I must be completely out of bed without fail. Anyway, by that time someone from the firm will be here to find out where I am, since the office opens before seven." And now he started rocking the complete length of his body out of the bed with a smooth rhythm. If he let himself topple out of bed in this way, his head, which on falling he planned to lift up sharply, would presumably remain unharmed. His back seemed to be hard; nothing was likely to happen to it when it fell onto the carpet. His biggest misgiving came from his concern about the loud crash that was bound to occur and would probably create, if not terror, at least anxiety behind all the doors. But that would have to be risked.

When Gregor's body already projected halfway out of bed—the new method was more of a game than a struggle, he only had to keep on rocking and jerking himself along—he thought how simple everything would be if he could get some help. Two strong persons—he thought of his father and the maid—would have been completely sufficient; they would only have had to shove their arms under his arched back, in this way scoop him off the bed, bend down with their burden, and then just be careful and patient while he managed to swing himself down onto the floor, where his little legs would hopefully acquire some purpose. Well, leaving out the fact that the doors were locked, should he really call for help? In spite of all his miseries, he could not repress a smile at this thought.

He was already so far along that when he rocked more strongly he could hardly keep his balance, and very soon he would have to commit himself,

because in five minutes it would be a quarter past seven—when the doorbell rang. "It's someone from the firm," he said to himself and almost
froze, while his little legs only danced more quickly. For a moment everything remained quiet. "They're not going to answer," Gregor said to himself, captivated by some senseless hope. But then, of course, the maid went
to the door as usual with her firm stride and opened up. Gregor only had
to hear the visitor's first word of greeting to know who it was—the office
manager himself. Why was only Gregor condemned to work for a firm
where at the slightest omission they immediately suspected the worst?
Were all employees louts without exception, wasn't there a single loyal,
dedicated worker among them who, when he had not fully utilized a few
hours of the morning for the firm, was driven half-mad by pangs of conscience and was actually unable to get out of bed? Really, wouldn't it have
been enough to send one of the apprentices to find out—if this prying
were absolutely necessary—did the manager himself have to come, and
did the whole innocent family have to be shown in this way that the investigation of this suspicious affair could be entrusted only to the intellect of
the manager? And more as a result of the excitement produced in Gregor
by these thoughts than as a result of any real decision, he swung himself
out of bed with all his might. There was a loud thump, but it was not a
real crash. The fall was broken a little by the carpet, and Gregor's back was
more elastic than he had thought, which explained the not very noticeable
muffled sound. Only he had not held his head carefully enough and hit
it; he turned it and rubbed it on the carpet in anger and pain.

"Something fell in there," said the manager in the room on the left.
Gregor tried to imagine whether something like what had happened to
him today could one day happen even to the manager; you really had to
grant the possibility. But, as if in rude reply to this question, the manager
took a few decisive steps in the next room and made his patent leather
boots creak. From the room on the right his sister whispered, to inform
Gregor, "Gregor, the manager is here." "I know," Gregor said to himself;
but he did not dare raise his voice enough for his sister to hear.

"Gregor," his father now said from the room on the left, "the manager
has come and wants to be informed why you didn't catch the early train.
We don't know what we should say to him. Besides, he wants to speak to
you personally. So please open the door. He will certainly be so kind as to
excuse the disorder of the room." "Good morning, Mr. Samsa," the manager called in a friendly voice. "There's something the matter with him,"
his mother said to the manager while his father was still at the door, talking. "Believe me, sir, there's something the matter with him. Otherwise
how would Gregor have missed a train? That boy has nothing on his mind
but the business. It's almost begun to rile me that he never goes out nights.
He's been back in the city for eight days now, but every night he's been
home. He sits there with us at the table, quietly reading the paper or
studying timetables. It's already a distraction for him when he's busy working with his fretsaw. For instance, in the span of two or three evenings he
carved a little frame. You'll be amazed how pretty it is; it's hanging inside
his room. You'll see it right away when Gregor opens the door. You know,
I'm glad that you've come, sir. We would never have gotten Gregor to

open the door by ourselves; he's so stubborn. And there's certainly something wrong with him, even though he said this morning there wasn't." "I'm coming right away," said Gregor slowly and deliberately, not moving in order not to miss a word of the conversation. "I haven't any other explanation myself," said the manager. "I hope it's nothing serious. On the other hand, I must say that we businessmen—fortunately or unfortunately, whichever you prefer—very often simply have to overcome a slight indisposition for business reasons." "So can the manager come in now?" asked his father, impatient, and knocked on the door again. "No," said Gregor. In the room on the left there was an embarrassing silence; in the room on the right his sister began to sob.

Why didn't his sister go in to the others? She had probably just got out of bed and not even started to get dressed. Then what was she crying about? Because he didn't get up and didn't let the manager in, because he was in danger of losing his job, and because then the boss would start hounding his parents about the old debts? For the time being, certainly, her worries were unnecessary. Gregor was still here and hadn't the slightest intention of letting the family down. True, at the moment he was lying on the carpet, and no one knowing his condition could seriously have expected him to let the manager in. But just because of this slight discourtesy, for which an appropriate excuse would easily be found later on, Gregor could not simply be dismissed. And to Gregor it seemed much more sensible to leave him alone now than to bother him with crying and persuasion. But it was just the uncertainty that was tormenting the others and excused their behavior.

"Mr. Samsa," the manager now called, raising his voice, "what's the matter? You barricade yourself in your room, answer only 'yes' and 'no,' cause your parents serious, unnecessary worry, and you neglect—I mention this only in passing—your duties to the firm in a really shocking manner. I am speaking here in the name of your parents and of your employer and ask you in all seriousness for an immediate, clear explanation. I'm amazed, amazed. I thought I knew you to be a quiet, reasonable person, and now you suddenly seem to want to start strutting about, flaunting strange whims. The head of the firm did suggest to me this morning a possible explanation for your tardiness—it concerned the cash payments recently entrusted to you—but really, I practically gave my word of honor that this explanation could not be right. But now, seeing your incomprehensible obstinacy, I am about to lose even the slightest desire to stick up for you in any way at all. And your job is not the most secure. Originally I intended to tell you all this in private, but since you make me waste my time here for nothing, I don't see why your parents shouldn't hear too. Your performance of late has been very unsatisfactory; I know it is not the best season for doing business, we all recognize that; but a season for not doing any business, there is no such thing, Mr. Samsa, such a thing cannot be tolerated."

"But sir," cried Gregor, beside himself, in his excitement forgetting everything else, "I'm just opening up, in a minute. A slight indisposition, a dizzy spell, prevented me from getting up. I'm still in bed. But I already feel fine again. I'm just getting out of bed. Just be patient for a minute!

I'm not as well as I thought yet. But really I'm fine. How something like this could just take a person by surprise! Only last night I was fine, my parents can tell you, or wait, last night I already had a slight premonition. They must have been able to tell by looking at me. Why didn't I report it to the office! But you always think that you'll get over a sickness without staying home. Sir! Spare my parents! There's no basis for any of the accusations that you're making against me now; no one has ever said a word to me about them. Perhaps you haven't seen the last orders I sent in. Anyway, I'm still going on the road with the eight o'clock train; these few hours of rest have done me good. Don't let me keep you, sir. I'll be at the office myself right away, and be so kind as to tell them this, and give my respects to the head of the firm."

And while Gregor hastily blurted all this out, hardly knowing what he was saying, he had easily approached the chest of drawers, probably as a result of the practice he had already gotten in bed, and now he tried to raise himself up against it. He actually intended to open the door, actually present himself and speak to the manager; he was eager to find out what the others, who were now so anxious to see him, would say at the sight of him. If they were shocked, then Gregor had no further responsibility and could be calm. But if they took everything calmly, then he, too, had no reason to get excited and could, if he hurried, actually be at the station by eight o'clock. At first he slid off the polished chest of drawers a few times, but at last, giving himself a final push, he stood upright; he no longer paid any attention to the pains in his abdomen, no matter how much they were burning. Now he let himself fall against the back of a nearby chair, clinging to its slats with his little legs. But by doing this he had gotten control of himself and fell silent, since he could now listen to what the manager was saying.

"Did you understand a word?" the manager was asking his parents. "He isn't trying to make fools of us, is he?" "My God," cried his mother, already in tears, "maybe he's seriously ill, and here we are, torturing him. Grete! Grete!" she then cried. "Mother?" called his sister from the other side. They communicated by way of Gregor's room. "Go to the doctor's immediately. Gregor is sick. Hurry, get the doctor. Did you just hear Gregor talking?" "That was the voice of an animal," said the manager, in a tone conspicuously soft compared with the mother's yelling. "Anna!" "Anna!" the father called through the foyer into the kitchen, clapping his hands, "get a locksmith right away!" And already the two girls were running with rustling skirts through the foyer—how could his sister have gotten dressed so quickly?—and tearing open the door to the apartment. The door could not be heard slamming; they had probably left it open, as is the custom in homes where a great misfortune has occurred.

But Gregor had become much calmer. It was true that they no longer understood his words, though they had seemed clear enough to him, clearer than before, probably because his ear had grown accustomed to them. But still, the others now believed that there was something the matter with him and were ready to help him. The assurance and confidence with which the first measures had been taken did him good. He felt integrated into human society once again and hoped for marvelous, amazing feats from both the doctor and the locksmith, without really distinguishing sharply between them. In order to make his voice as clear as possible for the crucial discussions that were approaching, he cleared his throat a little—taking pains, of course, to do so in a very muffled manner, since this noise, too, might sound different from human coughing, a thing he no longer trusted himself to decide. In the next room, meanwhile, everything had become completely still. Perhaps his parents were sitting at the table with the manager, whispering; perhaps they were all leaning against the door and listening.

Gregor slowly lugged himself toward the door, pushing the chair in front of him, then let go of it, threw himself against the door, held himself upright against it—the pads on the bottom of his little legs exuded a little sticky substance—and for a moment rested there from the exertion. But then he got started turning the key in the lock with his mouth. Unfortunately it seemed that he had no real teeth—what was he supposed to grip the key with?—but in compensation his jaws, of course, were very strong; with their help he actually got the key moving and paid no attention to the fact that he was undoubtedly hurting himself in some way, for a brown liquid came out of his mouth, flowed over the key, and dripped onto the floor. "Listen," said the manager in the next room, "he's turning the key." This was great encouragement to Gregor; but everyone should have cheered him on, his father and mother too. "Go, Gregor," they should have called, "keep going, at that lock, harder, harder!" And in the delusion that they were all following his efforts with suspense, he clamped his jaws madly on the key with all the strength he could muster. Depending on the progress of the key, he danced around the lock; holding himself upright only by his mouth, he clung to the key, as the situation demanded, or pressed it down again with the whole weight of his body. The clearer click of the lock as it finally snapped back literally woke Gregor up. With a sigh of relief he said to himself, "So I didn't need the locksmith after all," and laid his head down on the handle in order to open wide one wing of the double doors.

Since he had to use this method of opening the door, it was really opened very wide while he himself was still invisible. He first had to edge slowly around the one wing of the door, and do so very carefully if he was not to fall flat on his back just before entering. He was still busy with this difficult maneuver and had no time to pay attention to anything else when he heard the manager burst out with a loud "Oh!"—it sounded like a rush of wind—and now he could see him, standing closest to the door, his hand pressed over his open mouth, slowly backing away, as if repulsed by an invisible, unrelenting force. His mother—in spite of the manager's presence she stood with her hair still unbraided from the night, sticking out in all directions—first looked at his father with her hands clasped, then took two steps toward Gregor, and sank down in the midst of her skirts spreading out around her, her face completely hidden on her breast. With a hostile expression his father clenched his fist, as if to drive Gregor back into his room, then looked uncertainly around the living room, shielded his eyes with his hands, and sobbed with heaves of his powerful chest.

Now Gregor did not enter the room after all but leaned against the inside of the firmly bolted wing of the door, so that only half his body was visible and his head above it, cocked to one side and peeping out at the others. In the meantime it had grown much lighter; across the street one could see clearly a section of the endless, grayish-black building opposite—it was a hospital—with its regular windows starkly piercing the façade; the rain was still coming down, but only in large, separately visible drops that were also pelting the ground literally one at a time. The breakfast dishes were laid out lavishly on the table, since for his father breakfast was the most important meal of the day, which he would prolong for hours while reading various newspapers. On the wall directly opposite hung a photograph of Gregor from his army days, in a lieutenant's uniform, his hand on his sword, a carefree smile on his lips, demanding respect for his bearing and his rank. The door to the foyer was open, and since the front door was open too, it was possible to see out onto the landing and the top of the stairs going down.

"Well," said Gregor—and he was thoroughly aware of being the only one who had kept calm—"I'll get dressed right away, pack up my samples, and go. Will you, will you please let me go? Now, sir, you see, I'm not stubborn and I'm willing to work; traveling is a hardship, but without it I couldn't live. Where are you going, sir? To the office? Yes? Will you give an honest report of everything? A man might find for a moment that he was unable to work, but that's exactly the right time to remember his past accomplishments and to consider that later on, when the obstacle has been removed, he's bound to work all the harder and more efficiently. I'm under so many obligations to the head of the firm, as you know very well. Besides, I also have my parents and my sister to worry about. I'm in a tight spot, but I'll also work my way out again. Don't make things harder for me than they already are. Stick up for me in the office, please. Traveling salesmen aren't well liked there, I know. People think they make a fortune leading the gay life. No one has any particular reason to rectify this prejudice. But you, sir, you have a better perspective on things than the rest of the office, an even better perspective, just between the two of us, than the head of the firm himself, who in his capacity as owner easily lets his judgment be swayed against an employee. And you also know very well that the traveling salesman, who is out of the office practically the whole year round, can so easily become the victim of gossip, coincidences, and unfounded accusations, against which he's completely unable to defend himself, since in most cases he knows nothing at all about them except when he returns exhausted from a trip, and back home gets to suffer on his own person the grim consequences, which can no longer be traced back to their causes. Sir, don't go away without a word to tell me you think I'm at least partly right!"

But at Gregor's first words the manager had already turned away and with curled lips looked back at Gregor only over his twitching shoulder. And during Gregor's speech he did not stand still for a minute but, without letting Gregor out of his sight, backed toward the door, yet very gradually, as if there were some secret prohibition against leaving the room. He was already in the foyer, and from the sudden movement with which he took

his last step from the living room, one might have thought he had just
burned the sole of his foot. In the foyer, however, he stretched his right
hand far out toward the staircase, as if nothing less than an unearthly
deliverance were awaiting him there.

Gregor realized that he must on no account let the manager go away
in this mood if his position in the firm were not to be jeopardized in the
extreme. His parents did not understand this too well; in the course of the
years they had formed the conviction that Gregor was set for life in this
firm; and furthermore, they were so preoccupied with their immediate
troubles that they had lost all consideration for the future. But Gregor had
this forethought. The manager must be detained, calmed down, convinced, and finally won over; Gregor's and the family's future depended
on it! If only his sister had been there! She was perceptive; she had already
begun to cry when Gregor was still lying calmly on his back. And certainly
the manager, this ladies' man, would have listened to her; she would have
shut the front door and in the foyer talked him out of his scare. But his
sister was not there, Gregor had to handle the situation himself. And without stopping to realize that he had no idea what his new faculties of movement were, and without stopping to realize either that his speech had
possibly—indeed, probably—not been understood again, he let go of the
wing of the door; he shoved himself through the opening, intending to go
to the manager, who was already on the landing, ridiculously holding onto
the banisters with both hands; but groping for support, Gregor immediately fell down with a little cry onto his numerous little legs. This had
hardly happened when for the first time that morning he had a feeling of
physical well-being; his little legs were on firm ground; they obeyed him
completely, as he noted to his joy; they even strained to carry him away
wherever he wanted to go; and he already believed that final recovery from
all his sufferings was imminent. But at that very moment, as he lay on the
floor rocking with repressed motion, not far from his mother and just
opposite her, she, who had seemed so completely self-absorbed, all at once
jumped up, her arms stretched wide, her fingers spread, and cried, "Help,
for God's sake, help!" held her head bent as if to see Gregor better, but
inconsistently darted madly backward instead; had forgotten that the table
laden with the breakfast dishes stood behind her; sat down on it hastily, as
if her thoughts were elsewhere, when she reached it; and did not seem to
notice at all that near her the big coffeepot had been knocked over and
coffee was pouring in a steady stream onto the rug.

"Mother, Mother," said Gregor softly and looked up at her. For a
minute the manager had completely slipped his mind; on the other hand
at the sight of the spilling coffee he could not resist snapping his jaws
several times in the air. At this his mother screamed once more, fled from
the table, and fell into the arms of his father, who came rushing up to her.
But Gregor had no time now for his parents; the manager was already on
the stairs; with his chin on the banister, he was taking a last look back.
Gregor was off to a running start, to be as sure as possible of catching up
with him; the manager must have suspected something like this, for he
leaped down several steps and disappeared; but still he shouted "Agh," and
the sound carried through the whole staircase. Unfortunately the manag-

er's flight now seemed to confuse his father completely, who had been relatively calm until now, for instead of running after the manager himself, or at least not hindering Gregor in his pursuit, he seized in his right hand the manager's cane, which had been left behind on a chair with his hat and overcoat, picked up in his left hand a heavy newspaper from the table, and stamping his feet, started brandishing the cane and the newspaper to drive Gregor back into his room. No plea of Gregor's helped, no plea was even understood; however humbly he might turn his head, his father merely stamped his feet more forcefully. Across the room his mother had thrown open a window in spite of the cool weather, and leaning out, she buried her face, far outside the window, in her hands. Between the alley and the staircase a strong draft was created, the window curtains blew in, the newspapers on the table rustled, single sheets fluttered across the floor. Pitilessly his father came on, hissing like a wild man. Now Gregor had not had any practice at all walking in reverse, it was really very slow going. If Gregor had only been allowed to turn around, he could have gotten into his room right away, but he was afraid to make his father impatient by this time-consuming gyration, and at any minute the cane in his father's hand threatened to come down on his back or his head with a deadly blow. Finally, however, Gregor had no choice, for he noticed with horror that in reverse he could not even keep going in one direction; and so, incessantly throwing uneasy side-glances at his father, he began to turn around as quickly as possible, in reality turning only very slowly. Perhaps his father realized his good intentions, for he did not interfere with him; instead, he even now and then directed the maneuver from afar with the tip of his cane. If only his father did not keep making this intolerable hissing sound! It made Gregor lose his head completely. He had almost finished the turn when—his mind continually on this hissing—he made a mistake and even started turning back around to his original position. But when he had at last successfully managed to get his head in front of the opened door, it turned out that his body was too broad to get through as it was. Of course in his father's present state of mind it did not even remotely occur to him to open the other wing of the door in order to give Gregor enough room to pass through. He had only the fixed idea that Gregor must return to his room as quickly as possible. He would never have allowed the complicated preliminaries Gregor needed to go through in order to stand up on one end and perhaps in this way fit through the door. Instead he drove Gregor on, as if there were no obstacle, with exceptional loudness; the voice behind Gregor did not sound like that of only a single father; now this was really no joke any more, and Gregor forced himself—come what may—into the doorway. One side of his body rose up, he lay lop-sided in the opening, one of his flanks was scraped raw, ugly blotches marred the white door, soon he got stuck and could not have budged any more by himself, his little legs on one side dangled tremblingly in midair, those on the other were painfully crushed against the floor—when from behind his father gave him a hard shove, which was truly his salvation, and bleeding profusely, he flew far into his room. The door was slammed shut with the cane, then at last everything was quiet.

II

It was already dusk when Gregor awoke from his deep, comalike sleep. Even if he had not been disturbed, he would certainly not have woken up much later, for he felt that he had rested and slept long enough, but it seemed to him that a hurried step and a cautious shutting of the door leading to the foyer had awakened him. The light of the electric street-lamps lay in pallid streaks on the ceiling and on the upper parts of the furniture, but underneath, where Gregor was, it was dark. Groping clum-sily with his antennae, which he was only now beginning to appreciate, he slowly dragged himself toward the door to see what had been happen-ing there. His left side felt like one single long, unpleasantly tautening scar, and he actually had to limp on his two rows of legs. Besides, one little leg had been seriously injured in the course of the morning's events—it was almost a miracle that only one had been injured—and dragged along lifelessly.

Only after he got to the door did he notice what had really attracted him—the smell of something to eat. For there stood a bowl filled with fresh milk, in which small slices of white bread were floating. He could almost have laughed for joy, since he was even hungrier than he had been in the morning, and he immediately dipped his head into the milk, almost to over his eyes. But he soon drew it back again in disappointment; not only because he had difficulty eating on account of the soreness in his left side—and he could eat only if his whole panting body cooperated—but because he didn't like the milk at all, although it used to be his favorite drink, and that was certainly why his sister had put it in the room; in fact, he turned away from the bowl almost with repulsion and crawled back to the middle of the room.

In the living room, as Gregor saw through the crack in the door, the gas had been lit, but while at this hour of the day his father was in the habit of reading the afternoon newspaper in a loud voice to his mother and sometimes to his sister too, now there wasn't a sound. Well, perhaps this custom of reading aloud, which his sister was always telling him and writ-ing him about, had recently been discontinued altogether. But in all the other rooms too it was just as still, although the apartment certainly was not empty. "What a quiet life the family has been leading," Gregor said to himself, and while he stared rigidly in front of him into the darkness, he felt very proud that he had been able to provide such a life in so nice an apartment for his parents and his sister. But what now if all the peace, the comfort, the contentment were to come to a horrible end? In order not to get involved in such thoughts, Gregor decided to keep moving, and he crawled up and down the room.

During the long evening first one of the side doors and then the other was opened a small crack and quickly shut again; someone had probably had the urge to come in and then had had second thoughts. Gregor now settled into position right by the living-room door, determined somehow to get the hesitating visitor to come in, or at least to find out who it might be; but the door was not opened again, and Gregor waited in vain. In the morning, when the doors had been locked, everyone had wanted to come in; now that he had opened one of the doors and the others had evidently been opened during the day, no one came in, and now the keys were even inserted on the outside.

It was late at night when the light finally went out in the living room, and now it was easy for Gregor to tell that his parents and his sister had stayed up so long, since, as he could distinctly hear, all three were now retiring on tiptoe. Certainly no one would come in to Gregor until the morning; and so he had ample time to consider undisturbed how best to rearrange his life. But the empty high-ceilinged room in which he was forced to lie flat on the floor made him nervous, without his being able to tell why—since it was, after all, the room in which he had lived for the past five years—and turning half unconsciously and not without a slight feeling of shame, he scuttled under the couch where, although his back was a little crushed and he could not raise his head any more, he immediately felt very comfortable and was only sorry that his body was too wide to go completely under the couch.

There he stayed the whole night, which he spent partly in a sleepy trance, from which hunger pangs kept waking him with a start, partly in worries and vague hopes, all of which, however, led to the conclusion that for the time being he would have to lie low and, by being patient and showing his family every possible consideration, help them bear the inconvenience which he simply had to cause them in his present condition.

Early in the morning—it was still almost night—Gregor had the opportunity of testing the strength of the resolutions he had just made, for his sister, almost fully dressed, opened the door from the foyer and looked in eagerly. She did not see him right away, but when she caught sight of him under the couch—God, he had to be somewhere, he couldn't just fly away—she became so frightened that she lost control of herself and slammed the door shut again. But, as if she felt sorry for her behavior, she immediately opened the door again and came in on tiptoe, as if she were visiting someone seriously ill or perhaps even a stranger. Gregor had pushed his head forward just to the edge of the couch and was watching her. Would she notice that he had left the milk standing, and not because he hadn't been hungry, and would she bring in a dish of something he'd like better? If she were not going to do it of her own free will, he would rather starve than call it to her attention, although, really, he felt an enormous urge to shoot out from under the couch, throw himself at his sister's feet, and beg her for something good to eat. But his sister noticed at once, to her astonishment, that the bowl was still full, only a little milk was spilled around it; she picked it up immediately—not with her bare hands, of course, but with a rag—and carried it out. Gregor was extremely curious to know what she would bring him instead, and he racked his brains on the subject. But he would never have been able to guess what his sister, in the goodness of her heart, actually did. To find out his likes and dislikes, she brought him a wide assortment of things, all spread out on an old newspaper: old, half-rotten vegetables; bones left over from the evening meal, caked with congealed white sauce; some raisins and almonds; a piece of cheese, which two days before Gregor had declared inedible; a plain slice of bread, a slice of bread and butter, and one with butter and salt. In addition to all this she put down some water in the bowl apparently permanently earmarked for Gregor's use. And out of a sense of delicacy, since she knew that Gregor would not eat in front of her, she left hurriedly and even turned the key, just so that Gregor should know that he might make himself as comfortable as he wanted. Gregor's legs began whirring now that he was going to eat. Besides, his bruises must have completely healed, since he no longer felt any handicap, and marveling at this he thought how, over a month ago, he had cut his finger very slightly with a knife and how this wound was still hurting him only the day before yesterday. "Have I become less sensitive?" he thought, already sucking greedily at the cheese, which had immediately and forcibly attracted him ahead of all the other dishes. One right after the other, and with eyes streaming with tears of contentment, he devoured the cheese, the vegetables, and the sauce; the fresh foods, on the other hand, he did not care for; he couldn't even stand their smell and even dragged the things he wanted to eat a bit farther away. He had finished with everything long since and was just lying lazily at the same spot when his sister slowly turned the key as a sign for him to withdraw. That immediately startled him, although he was almost asleep, and he scuttled under the couch again. But it took great self-control for him to stay under the couch even for the short time his sister was in the room, since his body had become a little bloated from the heavy meal, and in his cramped position he could hardly breathe. In between slight attacks of suffocation he watched with bulging eyes as his unsuspecting sister took a broom and swept up, not only his leavings, but even the foods which Gregor had left completely untouched—as if they too were no longer usable—and dumping everything hastily into a pail, which she covered with a wooden lid, she carried everything out. She had hardly turned her back when Gregor came out from under the couch, stretching and puffing himself up.

This, then, was the way Gregor was fed each day, once in the morning, when his parents and the maid were still asleep, and a second time in the afternoon after everyone had had dinner, for then his parents took a short nap again, and the maid could be sent out by his sister on some errand. Certainly they did not want him to starve either, but perhaps they would not have been able to stand knowing any more about his meals than from hearsay, or perhaps his sister wanted to spare them even what was possibly only a minor torment, for really, they were suffering enough as it was.

Gregor could not find out what excuses had been made to get rid of the doctor and the locksmith on that first morning, for since the others could not understand what he said, it did not occur to any of them, not even to his sister, that he could understand what they said, and so he had to be satisfied, when his sister was in the room, with only occasionally hearing her sighs and appeals to the saints. It was only later, when she had begun to get used to everything—there could never, of course, be any question of a complete adjustment—that Gregor sometimes caught a remark which was meant to be friendly or could be interpreted as such. "Oh, he liked what he had today," she would say when Gregor had tucked away a good helping, and in the opposite case, which gradually occurred more and more frequently, she used to say, almost sadly, "He's left everything again."

But if Gregor could not get any news directly, he overheard a great deal from the neighboring rooms, and as soon as he heard voices, he would immediately run to the door concerned and press his whole body against it. Especially in the early days, there was no conversation that was not somehow about him, if only implicitly. For two whole days there were family consultations at every mealtime about how they should cope; this was also the topic of discussion between meals, for at least two members of the family were always at home, since no one probably wanted to stay home alone and it was impossible to leave the apartment completely empty. Besides, on the very first day the maid—it was not completely clear what and how much she knew of what had happened—had begged his mother on bended knees to dismiss her immediately; and when she said goodbye a quarter of an hour later, she thanked them in tears for the dismissal, as if for the greatest favor that had ever been done to her in this house, and made a solemn vow, without anyone asking her for it, not to give anything away to anyone.

Now his sister, working with her mother, had to do the cooking too; of course that did not cause her much trouble, since they hardly ate anything. Gregor was always hearing one of them pleading in vain with one of the others to eat and getting no answer except, "Thanks, I've had enough," or something similar. They did not seem to drink anything either. His sister often asked her father if he wanted any beer and gladly offered to go out for it herself; and when he did not answer, she said, in order to remove any hesitation on his part, that she could also send the janitor's wife to get it, but then his father finally answered with a definite "No," and that was the end of that.

In the course of the very first day his father explained the family's financial situation and prospects to both the mother and the sister. From time to time he got up from the table to get some kind of receipt or note-book out of the little strongbox he had rescued from the collapse of his business five years before. Gregor heard him open the complicated lock and secure it again after taking out what he had been looking for. These explanations by his father were to some extent the first pleasant news Gregor had heard since his imprisonment. He had always believed that his father had not been able to save a penny from the business, at least his father had never told him anything to the contrary, and Gregor, for his part, had never asked him any questions. In those days Gregor's sole concern had been to do everything in his power to make the family forget as quickly as possible the business disaster which had plunged everyone into a state of total despair. And so he had begun to work with special ardor and had risen almost overnight from stock clerk to traveling salesman, which of course had opened up very different money-making possibilities, and in no time his successes on the job were transformed, by means of commissions, into hard cash that could be plunked down on the table at home in front of his astonished and delighted family. Those had been wonderful times, and they had never returned, at least not with the same glory, although later on Gregor earned enough money to meet the expenses of the entire family and actually did so. They had just gotten used to it, the family as well as Gregor, the money was received with thanks and given with pleasure, but no special feeling of warmth went with it any more. Only his sister had remained close to Gregor, and it was his secret plan that she who, unlike him, loved music and could play the violin movingly, should be sent next year to the Conservatory, regardless of the great expense involved, which could surely be made up for in some other way. Often during Gregor's short stays in the city, the Conservatory would come up in his conversations with his sister, but always merely as a beautiful dream which was not supposed to come true, and his parents were not happy to hear even these innocent allusions; but Gregor had very concrete ideas on the subject and he intended solemnly to announce his plan on Christmas Eve.

Thoughts like these, completely useless in his present state, went through his head as he stood glued to the door, listening. Sometimes out of general exhaustion he could not listen any more and let his head bump carelessly against the door, but immediately pulled it back again, for even the slight noise he made by doing this had been heard in the next room and made them all lapse into silence. "What's he carrying on about in there now?" said his father after a while, obviously turning toward the door, and only then would the interrupted conversation gradually be resumed.

Gregor now learned in a thorough way—for his father was in the habit of often repeating himself in his explanations, partly because he himself had not dealt with these matters for a long time, partly, too, because his mother did not understand everything the first time around—that in spite of all their misfortunes a bit of capital, a very little bit, certainly, was still intact from the old days, which in the meantime had increased a little through the untouched interest. But besides that, the money Gregor had brought home every month—he had kept only a few dollars for himself— had never been completely used up and had accumulated into a tidy principal. Behind his door Gregor nodded emphatically, delighted at this unexpected foresight and thrift. Of course he actually could have paid off more of his father's debt to the boss with this extra money, and the day on which he could have gotten rid of his job would have been much closer, but now things were undoubtedly better the way his father had arranged them.

Now this money was by no means enough to let the family live off the interest; the principal was perhaps enough to support the family for one year, or at the most two, but that was all there was. So it was just a sum that really should not be touched and that had to be put away for a rainy day; but the money to live on would have to be earned. Now his father was still healthy, certainly, but he was an old man who had not worked for the past five years and who in any case could not be expected to undertake too much; during these five years, which were the first vacation of his hard-working yet unsuccessful life, he had gained a lot of weight and as a result had become fairly sluggish. And was his old mother now supposed to go out and earn money, when she suffered from asthma, when a walk through the apartment was already an ordeal for her, and when she spent every other day lying on the sofa under the open window, gasping for breath? And was his sister now supposed to work—who for all her seventeen years was still a child and whom it would be such a pity to deprive of the life she had led until now, which had consisted of wearing pretty clothes, sleeping late, helping in the house, enjoying a few modest amusements, and above all playing the violin? At first, whenever the conversation turned to the necessity of earning money, Gregor would let go of the door and throw himself down on the cool leather sofa which stood beside it, for he felt hot with shame and grief.

Often he lay there the whole long night through, not sleeping a wink and only scrabbling on the leather for hours on end. Or, not balking at the huge effort of pushing an armchair to the window, he would crawl up to the window sill and, propped up in the chair, lean against the window, evidently in some sort of remembrance of the feeling of freedom he used to have from looking out the window. For, in fact, from day to day he saw things even a short distance away less and less distinctly; the hospital opposite, which he used to curse because he saw so much of it, was now completely beyond his range of vision, and if he had not been positive that he was living in Charlotte Street—a quiet but still very much a city street—he might have believed that he was looking out of his window into a desert where the gray sky and the gray earth were indistinguishably fused. It took his observant sister only twice to notice that his armchair was standing by the window for her to push the chair back to the same place by the window each time she had finished cleaning the room, and from then on she even left the inside casement of the window open.

If Gregor had only been able to speak to his sister and thank her for everything she had to do for him, he could have accepted her services more easily; as it was, they caused him pain. Of course his sister tried to ease the embarrassment of the whole situation as much as possible, and as time went on, she naturally managed it better and better, but in time Gregor, too, saw things much more clearly. Even the way she came in was terrible for him. Hardly had she entered the room than she would run straight to the window without taking time to close the door—though she was usually so careful to spare everyone the sight of Gregor's room—then tear open the casements with eager hands, almost as if she were suffocating, and remain for a little while at the window even in the coldest weather, breathing deeply. With this racing and crashing she frightened Gregor twice a day; the whole time he cowered under the couch, and yet he knew very well that she would certainly have spared him this if only she had found it possible to stand being in a room with him with the window closed.

One time—it must have been a month since Gregor's metamorphosis, and there was certainly no particular reason any more for his sister to be astonished at Gregor's appearance—she came a little earlier than usual and caught Gregor still looking out the window, immobile and so in an excellent position to be terrifying. It would not have surprised Gregor if she had not come in, because his position prevented her from immediately opening the window, but not only did she not come in, she even sprang back and locked the door; a stranger might easily have thought that Gregor had been lying in wait for her, wanting to bite her. Of course Gregor immediately hid under the couch, but he had to wait until noon before his sister came again, and she seemed much more uneasy than usual. He realized from this that the sight of him was still repulsive to her and was bound to remain repulsive to her in the future, and that she probably had to overcome a lot of resistance not to run away at the sight of even the small part of his body that jutted out from under the couch. So, to spare her even this sight, one day he carried the sheet on his back to the couch—the job took four hours—and arranged it in such a way that he was now completely covered up and his sister could not see him even when she stooped. If she had considered this sheet unnecessary, then of course she could have removed it, for it was clear enough that it could not be for his own pleasure that Gregor shut himself off altogether, but she left the sheet the way it was, and Gregor thought that he had even caught a grateful look when one time he cautiously lifted the sheet a little with his head in order to see how his sister was taking the new arrangement.

During the first two weeks, his parents could not bring themselves to come in to him, and often he heard them say how much they appreciated his sister's work, whereas until now they had frequently been annoyed with her because she had struck them as being a little useless. But now both of them, his father and his mother, often waited outside Gregor's room while his sister straightened it up, and as soon as she came out she had to tell them in great detail how the room looked, what Gregor had eaten, how he had behaved this time, and whether he had perhaps shown a little improvement. His mother, incidentally, began relatively soon to want to visit Gregor, but his father and his sister at first held her back with reasonable arguments to which Gregor listened very attentively and of which he whole-heartedly approved. But later she had to be restrained by force, and then when she cried out, "Let me go to Gregor, he is my unfortunate boy! Don't you understand that I have to go to him?" Gregor thought that it might be a good idea after all if his mother did come in, not every day of course, but perhaps once a week; she could still do everything much better than his sister, who, for all her courage, was still only a child and in the final analysis had perhaps taken on such a difficult assignment only out of childish flightiness.

Gregor's desire to see his mother was soon fulfilled. During the day Gregor did not want to show himself at the window, if only out of consideration for his parents, but he couldn't crawl very far on his few square yards of floor space, either; he could hardly put up with just lying still even at night; eating soon stopped giving him the slightest pleasure, so, as a distraction, he adopted the habit of crawling crisscross over the walls and the ceiling. He especially liked hanging from the ceiling; it was completely different from lying on the floor; one could breathe more freely; a faint swinging sensation went through the body; and in the almost happy absent-mindedness which Gregor felt up there, it could happen to his own surprise that he let go and plopped onto the floor. But now, of course, he had much better control of his body than before and did not hurt himself even from such a big drop. His sister immediately noticed the new entertainment Gregor had discovered for himself—after all, he left behind traces of his sticky substance wherever he crawled—and so she got it into her head to make it possible for Gregor to crawl on an altogether wider scale by taking out the furniture which stood in his way—mainly the chest of drawers and the desk. But she was not able to do this by herself; she did not dare ask her father for help; the maid would certainly not have helped her, for although this girl, who was about sixteen, was bravely sticking it out after the previous cook had left, she had asked for the favor of locking herself in the kitchen at all times and of only opening the door on special request. So there was nothing left for his sister to do except to get her mother one day when her father was out. And his mother did come, with exclamations of excited joy, but she grew silent at the door of Gregor's room. First his sister looked to see, of course, that everything in the room was in order; only then did she let mother come in. Hurrying as fast as he could, Gregor had pulled the sheet down lower still and pleated it more tightly—it really looked just like a sheet accidentally thrown over the couch. This time Gregor also refrained from spying from under the sheet; he renounced seeing his mother for the time being and was simply happy that she had come after all. "Come on, you can't see him," his sister said, evidently leading her mother in by the hand. Now Gregor could hear the two frail women moving the old chest of drawers—heavy for anyone— from its place and his sister insisting on doing the harder part of the job herself, ignoring the warnings of her mother, who was afraid that she would overexert herself. It went on for a long time. After struggling for a good quarter of an hour, his mother said that they had better leave the chest where it was, because, in the first place, it was too heavy, they would not finish before his father came, and with the chest in the middle of the room, Gregor would be completely barricaded; and, in the second place, it was not at all certain that they were doing Gregor a favor by removing his furniture. To her the opposite seemed to be the case; the sight of the bare wall was heart-breaking; and why shouldn't Gregor also have the same feeling, since he had been used to his furniture for so long and would feel abandoned in the empty room. "And doesn't it look," his mother concluded very softly—in fact she had been almost whispering the whole time, as if she wanted to avoid letting Gregor, whose exact where-abouts she did not know, hear even the sound of her voice, for she was convinced that he did not understand the words—"and doesn't it look as if by removing his furniture we were showing him that we have given up all hope of his getting better and are leaving him to his own devices with-out any consideration? I think the best thing would be to try to keep the room exactly the way it was before, so that when Gregor comes back to us again, he'll find everything unchanged and can forget all the more easily what's happened in the meantime."

When he heard his mother's words, Gregor realized that the monotony of family life, combined with the fact that not a soul had addressed a word directly to him, must have addled his brain in the course of the past two months, for he could not explain to himself in any other way how in all seriousness he could have been anxious to have his room cleared out. Had he really wanted to have his warm room, comfortably fitted with furniture that had always been in the family, changed into a cave, in which, of course, he would be able to crawl around unhampered in all directions but at the cost of simultaneously, rapidly, and totally forgetting his human past? Even now he had been on the verge of forgetting, and only his mother's voice, which he had not heard for so long, had shaken him up. Nothing should be removed; everything had to stay; he could not do without the beneficial influence of the furniture on his state of mind; and if the furniture prevented him from carrying on this senseless crawling around, then that was no loss but rather a great advantage.

But his sister unfortunately had a different opinion; she had become accustomed, certainly not entirely without justification, to adopt with her parents the role of the particularly well-qualified expert whenever Gregor's affairs were being discussed; and so her mother's advice was now sufficient reason for her to insist, not only on the removal of the chest of drawers and the desk, which was all she had been planning at first, but also on the removal of all the furniture with the exception of the indispensable couch. Of course it was not only childish defiance and the self-confidence she had recently acquired so unexpectedly and at such a cost that led her to make this demand; she had in fact noticed that Gregor needed plenty of room to crawl around in; and on the other hand, as best she could tell, he never used the furniture at all. Perhaps, however, the romantic enthusiasm of girls her age, which seeks to indulge itself at every opportunity, played a part, by tempting her to make Gregor's situation even more terrifying in order that she might do even more for him. Into a room in which Gregor ruled the bare walls all alone, no human being beside Grete was ever likely to set foot.

And so she did not let herself be swerved from her decision by her mother, who, besides, from the sheer anxiety of being in Gregor's room, seemed unsure of herself, soon grew silent, and helped her daughter as best she could to get the chest of drawers out of the room. Well, in a pinch Gregor could do without the chest, but the desk had to stay. And hardly had the women left the room with the chest, squeezing against it and groaning, than Gregor stuck his head out from under the couch to see how he could feel his way into the situation as considerately as possible. But unfortunately it had to be his mother who came back first, while in the next room Grete was clasping the chest and rocking it back and forth by herself, without of course budging it from the spot. His mother, however, was not used to the sight of Gregor, he could have made her ill, and so Gregor, frightened, scuttled in reverse to the far end of the couch but could not stop the sheet from shifting a little at the front. That was enough to put his mother on the alert. She stopped, stood still for a moment, and then went back to Grete.

Although Gregor told himself over and over again that nothing special was happening, only a few pieces of furniture were being moved, he soon had to admit that this coming and going of the women, their little calls to each other, the scraping of the furniture along the floor had the effect on him of a great turmoil swelling on all sides, and as much as he tucked in his head and his legs and shrank until his belly touched the floor, he was forced to admit that he would not be able to stand it much longer. They were clearing out his room; depriving him of everything that he loved; they had already carried away the chest of drawers, in which he kept the fretsaw and other tools; were now budging the desk firmly embedded in the floor, the desk he had done his homework on when he was a student at business college, in high school, yes, even in public school—now he really had no more time to examine the good intentions of the two women, whose existence, besides, he had almost forgotten, for they were so exhausted that they were working in silence, and one could hear only the heavy shuffling of their feet.

And so he broke out—the women were just leaning against the desk in the next room to catch their breath for a minute—changed his course four times, he really didn't know what to salvage first, then he saw hanging conspicuously on the wall, which was otherwise bare already, the picture of the lady all dressed in furs, hurriedly crawled up on it and pressed himself against the glass, which gave a good surface to stick to and soothed his hot belly. At least no one would take away this picture, while Gregor completely covered it up. He turned his head toward the living-room door to watch the women when they returned.

They had not given themselves much of a rest and were already coming back; Grete had put her arm around her mother and was practically carrying her. "So what should we take now?" said Grete and looked around. At that her eyes met Gregor's as he clung to the wall. Probably only because of her mother's presence she kept her self-control, bent her head down to her mother to keep her from looking around, and said, though in a quavering and thoughtless voice: "Come, we'd better go back into the living room for a minute." Grete's intent was clear to Gregor, she wanted to bring his mother into safety and then chase him down from the wall. Well, just let her try! He squatted on his picture and would not give it up. He would rather fly in Grete's face.

But Grete's words had now made her mother really anxious; she stepped to one side, caught sight of the gigantic brown blotch on the flowered wallpaper, and before it really dawned on her that what she saw was Gregor, cried in a hoarse, bawling voice: "Oh, God, Oh, God!"; and as if giving up completely, she fell with outstretched arms across the couch and did not stir. "You, Gregor!" cried his sister with raised fist and piercing eyes. These were the first words she had addressed directly to him since his metamorphosis. She ran into the next room to get some kind of spirits to revive her mother; Gregor wanted to help too—there was time to rescue the picture—but he was stuck to the glass and had to tear himself loose by force; then he too ran into the next room, as if he could give his sister some sort of advice, as in the old days; but then had to stand behind her doing nothing while she rummaged among various little bottles; moreover, when she turned around she was startled, a bottle fell on the floor and broke, a splinter of glass wounded Gregor in the face, some kind of corrosive medicine flowed around him; now without waiting any longer, Grete grabbed as many little bottles as she could carry and ran with them inside to her mother; she slammed the door behind her with her foot. Now Gregor was cut off from his mother, who was perhaps near death through his fault; he could not dare open the door if he did not want to chase away his sister, who had to stay with his mother; now there was nothing for him to do except wait; and tormented by self-reproaches and worry, he began to crawl, crawled over everything, walls, furniture and ceiling, and finally in desperation, as the whole room was beginning to spin, fell down onto the middle of the big table.

A short time passed; Gregor lay there prostrate; all around, things were quiet, perhaps that was a good sign. Then the doorbell rang. The maid, of course, was locked up in her kitchen and so Grete had to answer the door. His father had come home. "What's happened?" were his first words; Grete's appearance must have told him everything. Grete answered in a muffled voice, her face was obviously pressed against her father's chest; "Mother fainted, but she's better now. Gregor's broken out." "I knew it," his father said. "I kept telling you, but you women don't want to listen." It was clear to Gregor that his father had put the worst interpretation on Grete's all-too-brief announcement and assumed that Gregor was guilty of some outrage. Therefore Gregor now had to try to calm his father down, since he had neither the time nor the ability to enlighten him. And so he fled to the door of his room and pressed himself against it for his father to see, as soon as he came into the foyer, that Gregor had the best intentions of returning to his room immediately and that it was not necessary to drive him back; if only the door were opened for him, he would disappear at once.

But his father was in no mood to notice such subtleties; "Ah!" he cried as he entered, in a tone that sounded as if he were at once furious and glad. Gregor turned his head away from the door and lifted it toward his father. He had not really imagined his father looking like this, as he stood in front of him now; admittedly Gregor had been too absorbed recently in his newfangled crawling to bother as much as before about events in the rest of the house and should really have been prepared to find some changes. And yet, and yet—was this still his father? Was this the same man who in the old days used to lie wearily buried in bed when Gregor left on a business trip; who greeted him on his return in the evening, sitting in his bathrobe in the armchair, who actually had difficulty getting to his feet but as a sign of joy only lifted up his arms; and who, on the rare occasions when the whole family went out for a walk, on a few Sundays in June and on the major holidays, used to shuffle along with great effort between Gregor and his mother, who were slow walkers themselves, always a little more slowly than they, wrapped in his old overcoat, always carefully planting down his crutch-handled cane, and, when he wanted to say something, nearly always stood still and assembled his escort around him? Now, however, he was holding himself very erect, dressed in a tight-fitting blue uniform with gold buttons, the kind worn by messengers at banking concerns; above the high stiff collar of the jacket his heavy chin protruded; under his bushy eyebrows his black eyes darted bright, piercing glances; his usually rumpled white hair was combed flat, with a scrupulously exact, gleaming part. He threw his cap—which was adorned with a gold monogram, probably that of a bank—in an arc across the entire room onto the couch, and with the tails of his long uniform jacket slapped back, his hands in his pants pockets, went for Gregor with a sullen look on his face. He probably did not know himself what he had in mind; still he lifted his feet unusually high off the floor, and Gregor staggered at the gigantic size of the soles of his boots. But he did not linger over this, he had known right from the first day of his new life that his father considered only the strictest treatment called for in dealing with him. And so he ran ahead of his father, stopped when his father stood still, and scooted ahead again when his father made even the slightest movement. In this way they made more than one tour of the room, without anything decisive happening; in fact the whole movement did not even have the appearance of a chase because of its slow tempo. So Gregor kept to the floor for the time being, especially since he was afraid that his father might interpret a flight onto the walls or the ceiling as a piece of particular nastiness. Of course Gregor had to admit that he would not be able to keep up even this running for long, for whenever his father took one step, Gregor had to execute countless movements. He was already beginning to feel winded, just as in the old days he had not had very reliable lungs. As he now staggered around, hardly keeping his eyes open in order to gather all his strength for the running; in his obtuseness not thinking of any escape other than by running; and having almost forgotten that the walls were at his disposal, though here of course they were blocked up with elaborately carved furniture full of notches and points—at that moment a lightly flung object hit the floor right near him and rolled in front of him. It was an apple; a second one came flying right after it; Gregor stopped dead with fear; further running was useless, for his father was determined to bombard him. He had filled his pockets from the fruit bowl on the buffet and was now pitching one apple after another, for the time being without taking good aim. These little red apples rolled around on the floor as if electrified, clicking into each other. One apple, thrown weakly, grazed Gregor's back and slid off harmlessly. But the very next one that came flying after it literally forced its way into Gregor's back; Gregor tried to drag himself away, as if the startling, unbelievable pain might disappear with a change of place; but he felt nailed to the spot and stretched out his body in a complete confusion of all his senses. With his last glance he saw the door of his room burst open, as his mother rushed out ahead of his screaming sister, in her chemise, for his sister had partly undressed her while she was unconscious in order to let her breathe more freely; saw his mother run up to his father and on the way her unfastened petticoats slide to the floor one by one; and saw as, stumbling over the skirts, she forced herself onto his father, and embracing him, in complete union with him—but now Gregor's sight went dim—her hands clasping his father's neck, begged for Gregor's life.

III

Gregor's serious wound, from which he suffered for over a month—the apple remained imbedded in his flesh as a visible souvenir since no one dared to remove it—seemed to have reminded even his father that Gregor was a member of the family, in spite of his present pathetic and repulsive shape, who could not be treated as an enemy; that, on the contrary, it was the commandment of family duty to swallow their disgust and endure him, endure him and nothing more.

And now, although Gregor had lost some of his mobility probably for good because of his wound, and although for the time being he needed long, long minutes to get across his room, like an old war veteran—crawling above ground was out of the question—for this deterioration of his situation he was granted compensation which in his view was entirely satisfactory: every day around dusk the living-room door—which he was in the habit of watching closely for an hour or two beforehand—was opened, so that, lying in the darkness of his room, invisible from the living room, he could see the whole family sitting at the table under the lamp and could listen to their conversation, as it were with general permission; and so it was completely different from before.

Of course these were no longer the animated conversations of the old days, which Gregor used to remember with a certain nostalgia in small hotel rooms when he'd had to throw himself wearily into the damp bedding. Now things were mostly very quiet. Soon after supper his father would fall asleep in his armchair; his mother and sister would caution each other to be quiet; his mother, bent low under the light, sewed delicate lingerie for a clothing store; his sister, who had taken a job as a salesgirl, was learning shorthand and French in the evenings in order to attain a better position some time in the future. Sometimes his father woke up, and as if he had absolutely no idea that he had been asleep, said to his mother, "Look how long you're sewing again today!" and went right back to sleep, while mother and sister smiled wearily at each other.

With a kind of perverse obstinacy his father refused to take off his official uniform even in the house; and while his robe hung uselessly on the clothes hook, his father dozed, completely dressed, in his chair, as if he were always ready for duty and were waiting even here for the voice of his superior. As a result his uniform, which had not been new to start with, began to get dirty in spite of all the mother's and sister's care, and Gregor would often stare all evening long at this garment, covered with stains and gleaming with its constantly polished gold buttons, in which the old man slept most uncomfortably and yet peacefully.

As soon as the clock struck ten, his mother tried to awaken his father with soft encouraging words and then persuade him to go to bed, for this was no place to sleep properly, and his father badly needed his sleep, since he had to be at work at six o'clock. But with the obstinacy that had possessed him ever since he had become a messenger, he always insisted on staying at the table a little longer, although he invariably fell asleep and then could be persuaded only with the greatest effort to exchange his armchair for bed. However much mother and sister might pounce on him with little admonitions, he would slowly shake his head for a quarter of an hour at a time, keeping his eyes closed, and would not get up. Gregor's mother plucked him by the sleeves, whispered blandishments into his ear, his sister dropped her homework in order to help her mother, but all this was of no use. He only sank deeper into his armchair. Not until the women lifted him up under his arms did he open his eyes, look alternately at mother and sister, and usually say, "What a life. So this is the peace of my old age." And leaning on the two women, he would get up laboriously, as if he were the greatest weight on himself, and let the women lead him to the door, where, shrugging them off, he would proceed independently, while Gregor's mother threw down her sewing and his sister her pen as quickly as possible so as to run after his father and be of further assistance.

Who in this overworked and exhausted family had time to worry about Gregor any more than was absolutely necessary? The household was stinted more and more; now the maid was let go after all; a gigantic bony cleaning woman with white hair fluttering about her head came mornings and evenings to do the heaviest work; his mother took care of everything else, along with all her sewing. It even happened that various pieces of family jewelry, which in the old days his mother and sister had been overjoyed to wear at parties and celebrations, were sold, as Gregor found out one evening from the general discussion of the prices they had fetched. But the biggest complaint was always that they could not give up the apartment, which was much too big for their present needs, since no one could figure out how Gregor was supposed to be moved. But Gregor understood easily that it was not only consideration for him which prevented their moving, for he could easily have been transported in a suitable crate with a few air holes; what mainly prevented the family from moving was their complete hopelessness and the thought that they had been struck by a misfortune as none of their relatives and acquaintances had ever been hit. What the world demands of poor people they did to the utmost of their ability; his father brought breakfast for the minor officials at the bank, his mother sacrificed herself to the underwear of strangers, his sister ran back and forth behind the counter at the request of the customers; but for anything more than this they did not have the strength. And the wound in Gregor's back began to hurt anew when mother and sister, after getting his father to bed, now came back, dropped their work, pulled their chairs close to each other and sat cheek to cheek; when his mother, pointing to Gregor's room, said, "Close that door, Grete"; and when Gregor was back in darkness, while in the other room the women mingled their tears or stared dry-eyed at the table.

Gregor spent the days and nights almost entirely without sleep. Sometimes he thought that the next time the door opened he would take charge of the family's affairs again, just as he had done in the old days; after this long while there again appeared in his thoughts the boss and the manager, the salesmen and the trainees, the handyman who was so dense, two or three friends from other firms, a chambermaid in a provincial hotel—a happy fleeting memory—a cashier in a millinery store, whom he had courted earnestly but too slowly—they all appeared, intermingled with strangers or people he had already forgotten; but instead of helping him and his family, they were all inaccessible, and he was glad when they faded away. At other times he was in no mood to worry about his family, he was completely filled with rage at his miserable treatment, and although he could not imagine anything that would pique his appetite, he still made plans for getting into the pantry to take what was coming to him, even if he wasn't hungry. No longer considering what she could do to give Gregor a special treat, his sister, before running to business every morning and afternoon, hurriedly shoved any old food into Gregor's room with her foot; and in the evening, regardless of whether the food had only been toyed with or—the most usual case—had been left completely untouched, she swept it out with a swish of the broom. The cleaning up of Gregor's room, which she now always did in the evenings, could not be done more hastily. Streaks of dirt ran along the walls, fluffs of dust and filth lay here and there on the floor. At first, whenever his sister came in, Gregor would place himself in those corners which were particularly offending, meaning by his position in a sense to reproach her. But he could probably have stayed there for weeks without his sister's showing any improvement; she must have seen the dirt as clearly as he did, but she had just decided to leave it. At the same time she made sure—with an irritableness that was completely new to her and which had in fact infected the whole family—that the cleaning of Gregor's room remain her province. One time his mother had submitted Gregor's room to a major house-cleaning, which she managed only after employing a couple of pails of water—all this dampness, of course, irritated Gregor too and he lay prostrate, sour and immobile, on the couch—but his mother's punishment was not long in coming. For hardly had his sister noticed the difference in Gregor's room that evening than, deeply insulted, she ran into the living room and, in spite of her mother's imploringly uplifted hands, burst out in a fit of crying, which his parents—his father had naturally been startled out of his armchair—at first watched in helpless amazement; until they too got going; turning to the right, his father blamed his mother for not letting his sister clean Gregor's room; but turning to the left, he screamed at his sister that she would never again be allowed to clean Gregor's room; while his mother tried to drag his father, who was out of his mind with excitement, into the bedroom; his sister, shaken with sobs, hammered the table with her small fists; and Gregor hissed loudly with rage because it did not occur to any of them to close the door and spare him such a scene and a row.

But even if his sister, exhausted from her work at the store, had gotten fed up with taking care of Gregor as she used to, it was not necessary at all for his mother to take her place and still Gregor did not have to be neglected. For now the cleaning woman was there. This old widow, who thanks to her strong bony frame had probably survived the worst in a long life, was not really repelled by Gregor. Without being in the least inquisitive, she had once accidentally opened the door of Gregor's room, and at the sight of Gregor—who, completely taken by surprise, began to race back and forth although no one was chasing him—she had remained standing, with her hands folded on her stomach, marveling. From that time on she never failed to open the door a crack every morning and every evening and peek in hurriedly at Gregor. In the beginning she also used to call him over to her with words she probably considered friendly, like, "Come over here for a minute, you old dung beetle!" or "Look at that old dung beetle!" To forms of address like these Gregor would not respond but remained immobile where he was, as if the door had not been opened. If only they had given this cleaning woman orders to clean up his room every day, instead of letting her disturb him uselessly whenever the mood took her. Once, early in the morning—heavy rain, perhaps already a sign of approaching spring, was beating on the window panes—Gregor was so exasperated when the cleaning woman started in again with her phrases that he turned on her, of course slowly and decrepitly, as if to attack. But the cleaning woman, instead of getting frightened, simply lifted up high a chair near the door, and as she stood there with her mouth wide open, her intention was clearly to shut her mouth only when the chair in her hand came crashing down on Gregor's back. "So, is that all there is?" she asked when Gregor turned around again, and she quietly put the chair back in the corner.

Gregor now hardly ate anything anymore. Only when he accidentally passed the food laid out for him would he take a bite into his mouth just for fun, hold it in for hours, and then mostly spit it out again. At first he thought that his grief at the state of his room kept him off food, but it was the very changes in his room to which he quickly became adjusted. His family had gotten into the habit of putting in this room things for which they could not find any other place, and now there were plenty of these, since one of the rooms in the apartment had been rented to three board- ers. These serious gentlemen—all three had long beards, as Gregor was able to register once through a crack in the door—were obsessed with neatness, not only in their room, but since they had, after all, moved in here, throughout the entire household and especially in the kitchen. They could not stand useless, let alone dirty junk. Besides, they had brought along most of their own household goods. For this reason many things had become superfluous, and though they certainly weren't salable, on the other hand they could not just be thrown out. All these things migrated into Gregor's room. Likewise the ash can and the garbage can from the kitchen. Whatever was not being used at the moment was just flung into Gregor's room by the cleaning woman, who was always in a big hurry; fortunately Gregor generally saw only the object involved and the hand that held it. Maybe the cleaning woman intended to reclaim the things as soon as she had a chance or else to throw out everything together in one fell swoop, but in fact they would have remained lying wherever they had been thrown in the first place if Gregor had not squeezed through the junk and set it in motion, at first from necessity, because otherwise there would have been no room to crawl in, but later with growing pleasure, although after such excursions, tired to death and sad, he did not budge again for hours.

Since the roomers sometimes also had their supper at home in the com- mon living room, the living-room door remained closed on certain eve- nings, but Gregor found it very easy to give up the open door, for on many evenings when it was opened he had not taken advantage of it, but instead, without the family's noticing, had lain in the darkest corner of his room. But once the cleaning woman had left the living-room door slightly open, and it also remained opened a little when the roomers came in in the evening and the lamp was lit. They sat down at the head of the table where in the old days his father, his mother, and Gregor had eaten, unfolded their napkins, and picked up their knives and forks. At once his mother appeared in the doorway with a platter of meat, and just behind her came his sister with a platter piled high with potatoes. A thick vapor steamed up from the food. The roomers bent over the platters set in front of them as if to examine them before eating, and in fact the one who sat in the middle, and who seemed to be regarded by the other two as an authority, cut into a piece of meat while it was still on the platter, evidently to find out whether it was tender enough or whether it should perhaps be sent back to the kitchen. He was satisfied, and mother and sister, who had been watching anxiously, sighed with relief and began to smile.

The family itself ate in the kitchen. Nevertheless, before going into the kitchen, his father came into this room and, bowing once, cap in hand, made a turn around the table. The roomers rose as one man and mumbled something into their beards. When they were alone again, they ate in almost complete silence. It seemed strange to Gregor that among all the different noises of eating he kept picking up the sound of their chewing teeth, as if this were a sign to Gregor that you needed teeth to eat with and that even with the best make of toothless jaws you couldn't do a thing. "I'm hungry enough," Gregor said to himself, full of grief, "but not for these things. Look how these roomers are gorging themselves, and I'm dying!"

On this same evening—Gregor could not remember having heard the violin during the whole time—the sound of violin playing came from the kitchen. The roomers had already finished their evening meal, the one in the middle had taken out a newspaper, given each of the two others a page, and now, leaning back, they read and smoked. When the violin began to play, they became attentive, got up, and went on tiptoe to the door leading to the foyer, where they stood in a huddle. They must have been heard in the kitchen, for his father called, "Perhaps the playing bothers you, gentlemen? It can be stopped right away." "On the contrary," said the middle roomer. "Wouldn't the young lady like to come in to us and play in here where it's much roomier and more comfortable?" "Oh, certainly," called Gregor's father, as if he were the violinist. The boarders went back into the room and waited. Soon Gregor's father came in with the music stand, his mother with the sheet music, and his sister with the violin. Calmly his sister got everything ready for playing; his parents— who had never rented out rooms before and therefore behaved toward the roomers with excessive politeness—did not even dare sit down on their own chairs; his father leaned against the door, his right hand inserted between two buttons of his uniform coat, which he kept closed; but his mother was offered a chair by one of the roomers, and since she left the chair where the roomer just happened to put it, she sat in a corner to one side.

His sister began to play. Father and mother, from either side, attentively followed the movements of her hands. Attracted by the playing, Gregor had dared to come out a little further and already had his head in the living room. It hardly surprised him that lately he was showing so little consideration for the others; once such consideration had been his greatest pride. And yet he would never have had better reason to keep hidden; for now, because of the dust which lay all over his room and blew around at the slightest movement, he too was completely covered with dust; he dragged around with him on his back and along his sides fluff and hairs and scraps of food; his indifference to everything was much too deep for him to have gotten on his back and scrubbed himself clean against the carpet, as once he had done several times a day. And in spite of his state, he was not ashamed to inch out a little farther on the immaculate living-room floor.

Admittedly no one paid any attention to him. The family was completely absorbed by the violin-playing; the roomers, on the other hand, who at first had stationed themselves, hands in pockets, much too close behind his sister's music stand, so that they could all have followed the score, which certainly must have upset his sister, soon withdrew to the window, talking to each other in an undertone, their heads lowered, where they remained, anxiously watched by his father. It now seemed only too obvious that they were disappointed in their expectation of hearing beautiful or entertaining violin-playing, had had enough of the whole performance, and continued to let their peace be disturbed only out of politeness. Especially the way they all blew the cigar smoke out of their nose and mouth toward the ceiling suggested great nervousness. And yet his sister was playing so beautifully. Her face was inclined to one side, sadly and probingly her eyes followed the lines of music. Gregor crawled forward a little farther, holding his head close to the floor, so that it might be possible to catch her eye. Was he an animal, that music could move him so? He felt as if the way to the unknown nourishment he longed for were coming to light. He was determined to force himself on until he reached his sister, to pluck at her skirt, and to let her know in this way that she should bring her violin into his room, for no one here appreciated her playing the way he would appreciate it. He would never again let her out of his room—at least not for as long as he lived; for once, his nightmarish looks would be of use to him; he would be at all the doors of his room at the same time and hiss and spit at the aggressors; his sister, however, should not be forced to stay with him, but would do so of her own free will; she should sit next to him on the couch, bending her ear down to him, and then he would confide to her that he had had the firm intention of sending her to the Conservatory, and that, if the catastrophe had not intervened, he would have announced this to everyone last Christmas—certainly Christmas had come and gone?—without taking notice of any objections. After this declaration his sister would burst into tears of emotion, and Gregor would raise himself up to her shoulder and kiss her on the neck which, ever since she started going out to work, she kept bare, without a ribbon or collar.

"Mr. Samsa!" the middle roomer called to Gregor's father and without wasting another word pointed his index finger at Gregor, who was slowly moving forward. The violin stopped, the middle roomer smiled first at his friends, shaking his head, and then looked at Gregor again. Rather than driving Gregor out, his father seemed to consider it more urgent to start by soothing the roomers although they were not at all upset, and Gregor seemed to be entertaining them more than the violin-playing. He rushed over to them and tried with outstretched arms to drive them into their room and at the same time with his body to block their view of Gregor. Now they actually did get a little angry—it was not clear whether because of his father's behavior or because of their dawning realization of having had without knowing it such a next door neighbor as Gregor. They demanded explanations from his father; in their turn they raised their arms, plucked excitedly at their beards, and, dragging their feet, backed off toward their room. In the meantime his sister had overcome the abstracted mood into which she had fallen after her playing had been so suddenly interrupted; and all at once, after holding violin and bow for a while in her slackly hanging hands and continuing to follow the score as if she were still playing, she pulled herself together, laid the instrument on the lap of her mother—who was still sitting in her chair, fighting for breath, her lungs violently heaving—and ran into the next room, which the roomers, under pressure from her father, were nearing more quickly than before. One could see the covers and bolsters on the beds, obeying his sister's practiced hands, fly up and arrange themselves. Before the boarders had reached the room, she had finished turning down the beds and had slipped out. Her father seemed once again to be gripped by his perverse obstinacy to such a degree that he completely forgot any respect still due his tenants. He drove them on and kept on driving until, already at the bedroom door, the middle boarder stamped his foot thunderingly and thus brought him to a standstill. "I herewith declare," he said, raising his hand and casting his eyes around for Gregor's mother and sister too, "that in view of the disgusting conditions prevailing in this apartment and family"—here he spat curtly and decisively on the floor—"I give notice as of now. Of course I won't pay a cent for the days I have been living here, either; on the contrary, I shall consider taking some sort of action against you with claims that—believe me—will be easy to substantiate." He stopped and looked straight in front of him, as if he were expecting something. And in fact his two friends at once chimed in with the words, "We too give notice as of now." Thereupon he grabbed the door knob and slammed the door with a bang.

Gregor's father, his hands groping, staggered to his armchair and collapsed into it; it looked as if he were stretching himself out for his usual evening nap, but the heavy drooping of his head, as if it had lost all support, showed that he was certainly not asleep. All this time Gregor had lain quietly at the spot where the roomers had surprised him. His disappointment at the failure of his plan—but perhaps also the weakness caused by so much fasting—made it impossible for him to move. He was afraid with some certainty that in the very next moment a general debacle would burst over him, and he waited. He was not even startled by the violin as it slipped from under his mother's trembling fingers and fell off her lap with a reverberating clang.

"My dear parents," said his sister and by way of an introduction pounded her hand on the table, "things can't go on like this. Maybe you don't realize it, but I do. I won't pronounce the name of my brother in front of this monster, and so all I say is: we have to try to get rid of it. We've done everything humanly possible to take care of it and to put up with it; I don't think anyone can blame us in the least."

"She's absolutely right," said his father to himself. His mother, who still could not catch her breath, began to cough dully behind her hand, a wild look in her eyes.

His sister rushed over to his mother and held her forehead. His father seemed to have been led by Grete's words to more definite thoughts, had sat up, was playing with the cap of his uniform among the plates which were still lying on the table from the roomers' supper, and from time to time looked at Gregor's motionless form.

"We must try to get rid of it," his sister now said exclusively to her father, since her mother was coughing too hard to hear anything. "It will be the death of you two, I can see it coming. People who already have to work as hard as we do can't put up with this constant torture at home, too. I can't stand it anymore either." And she broke out crying so bitterly that her tears poured down onto her mother's face, which she wiped off with mechanical movements of her hand.

"Child," said her father kindly and with unusual understanding, "but what can we do?"

Gregor's sister only shrugged her shoulders as a sign of the bewildered mood that had now gripped her as she cried, in contrast with her earlier confidence.

"If he could understand us," said her father, half questioning; in the midst of her crying Gregor's sister waved her hand violently as a sign that that was out of the question.

"If he could understand us," his father repeated and by closing his eyes, absorbed his daughter's conviction of the impossibility of the idea, "then maybe we could come to an agreement with him. But the way things are——"

"It has to go," cried his sister. "That's the only answer, Father. You just have to try to get rid of the idea that it's Gregor. Believing it for so long, that is our real misfortune. But how can it be Gregor? If it were Gregor, he would have realized long ago that it isn't possible for human beings to live with such a creature, and he would have gone away of his own free will. Then we wouldn't have a brother, but we'd be able to go on living and honor his memory. But as things are, this animal persecutes us, drives the roomers away, obviously wants to occupy the whole apartment and for us to sleep in the gutter. Look, Father," she suddenly shrieked, "he's starting in again!" And in a fit of terror that was completely incomprehensible to Gregor, his sister abandoned even her mother, literally shoved herself off from her chair, as if she would rather sacrifice her mother than stay near Gregor, and rushed behind her father, who, upset only by her behavior, also stood up and half-lifted his arms in front of her as if to protect her.

But Gregor had absolutely no intention of frightening anyone, let alone his sister. He had only begun to turn around in order to trek back to his room; certainly his movements did look peculiar, since his ailing condition made him help the complicated turning maneuver along with his head, which he lifted up many times and knocked against the floor. He stopped and looked around. His good intention seemed to have been recognized; it had only been a momentary scare. Now they all watched him, silent and sad. His mother lay in her armchair, her legs stretched out and pressed together, her eyes almost closing from exhaustion; his father and his sister sat side by side, his sister had put her arm around her father's neck.

Now maybe they'll let me turn around, Gregor thought and began his labors again. He could not repress his panting from the exertion, and from time to time he had to rest. Otherwise no one harassed him, he was left completely on his own. When he had completed the turn, he immediately began to crawl back in a straight line. He was astonished at the great distance separating him from his room and could not understand at all how, given his weakness, he had covered the same distance a little while ago almost without realizing it. Constantly intent only on rapid crawling, he hardly noticed that not a word, not an exclamation from his family interrupted him. Only when he was already in the doorway did he turn his head—not completely, for he felt his neck stiffening; nevertheless he still saw that behind him nothing had changed except that his sister had gotten up. His last glance ranged over his mother, who was now fast asleep.

He was hardly inside his room when the door was hurriedly slammed shut, firmly bolted, and locked. Gregor was so frightened at the sudden noise behind him that his little legs gave way under him. It was his sister who had been in such a hurry. She had been standing up straight, ready and waiting, then she had leaped forward nimbly, Gregor had not even heard her coming, and she cried "Finally!" to her parents as she turned the key in the lock.

"And now?" Gregor asked himself, looking around in the darkness. He soon made the discovery that he could no longer move at all. It did not surprise him; rather, it seemed unnatural that until now he had actually been able to propel himself on these thin little legs. Otherwise he felt relatively comfortable. He had pains, of course, throughout his whole body, but it seemed to him that they were gradually getting fainter and fainter and would finally go away altogether. The rotten apple in his back and the inflamed area around it, which were completely covered with fluffy dust, already hardly bothered him. He thought back on his family with deep emotion and love. His conviction that he would have to disappear was, if possible, even firmer than his sister's. He remained in this state of empty and peaceful reflection until the tower clock struck three in the morning. He still saw that outside the window everything was beginning to grow light. Then, without his consent, his head sank down to the floor, and from his nostrils streamed his last weak breath.

When early in the morning the cleaning woman came—in sheer energy and impatience she would slam all the doors so hard although she had often been asked not to, that once she had arrived, quiet sleep was no longer possible anywhere in the apartment—she did not at first find anything out of the ordinary on paying Gregor her usual short visit. She thought that he was deliberately lying motionless, pretending that his feelings were hurt; she credited him with unlimited intelligence. Because she happened to be holding the long broom, she tried from the doorway to tickle Gregor with it. When this too produced no results, she became annoyed and jabbed Gregor a little, and only when she had shoved him without any resistance to another spot did she begin to take notice. When she quickly became aware of the true state of things, she opened her eyes wide, whistled softly, but did not dawdle; instead, she tore open the door of the bedroom and shouted at the top of her voice into the darkness: "Come and have a look, it's croaked; it's lying there, dead as a doornail!"

The couple Mr. and Mrs. Samsa sat up in their marriage bed and had a struggle overcoming their shock at the cleaning woman before they could finally grasp her message. But then Mr. and Mrs. Samsa hastily scrambled out of bed, each on his side, Mr. Samsa threw the blanket around his shoulders, Mrs. Samsa came out in nothing but her nightgown; dressed this way, they entered Gregor's room. In the meantime the door of the living room had also opened, where Grete had been sleeping since the roomers had moved in; she was fully dressed, as if she had not been asleep at all; and her pale face seemed to confirm this. "Dead?" said Mrs. Samsa and looked inquiringly at the cleaning woman, although she could scrutinize everything for herself and could recognize the truth even without scrutiny. "I'll say," said the cleaning woman, and to prove it she pushed Gregor's corpse with her broom a good distance sideways. Mrs. Samsa made a movement as if to hold the broom back but did not do it. "Well," said Mr. Samsa, "now we can thank God!" He crossed himself, and the three women followed his example. Grete, who never took her eyes off the corpse, said, "Just look how thin he was. Of course he didn't eat anything for such a long time. The food came out again just the way it went in." As a matter of fact, Gregor's body was completely flat and dry; this was obvious now for the first time, really, since the body was no longer raised up by his little legs and nothing else distracted the eye.

"Come in with us for a little while, Grete," said Mrs. Samsa with a melancholy smile, and Grete, not without looking back at the corpse, followed her parents into their bedroom. The cleaning woman shut the door and opened the window wide. Although it was early in the morning, there was already some mildness mixed in with the fresh air. After all, it was already the end of March.

The three boarders came out of their room and looked around in astonishment for their breakfast; they had been forgotten. "Where's breakfast?" the middle roomer grumpily asked the cleaning woman. But she put her finger to her lips and then hastily and silently beckoned the boarders to follow her into Gregor's room. They came willingly and then stood, their hands in the pockets of their somewhat shabby jackets, in the now already very bright room, surrounding Gregor's corpse.

At that point the bedroom door opened, and Mr. Samsa appeared in his uniform, his wife on one arm, his daughter on the other. They all looked as if they had been crying; from time to time Grete pressed her face against her father's sleeve.

"Leave my house immediately," said Mr. Samsa and pointed to the door, without letting go of the women. "What do you mean by that?" said the middle roomer, somewhat nonplussed, and smiled with a sugary smile. The two others held their hands behind their back and incessantly rubbed them together, as if in joyful anticipation of a big argument, which could only turn out in their favor. "I mean just what I say," answered Mr. Samsa and with his two companions marched in a straight line toward the roomer. At first the roomer stood still and looked at the floor, as if the thoughts inside his head were fitting themselves together in a new order. "So, we'll go, then," he said and looked up at Mr. Samsa as if, suddenly overcome by a fit of humility, he were asking for further permission even for this decision. Mr. Samsa merely nodded briefly several times, his eyes wide open. Thereupon the roomer actually went immediately into the foyer, taking long strides; his two friends had already been listening for a while, their hands completely still, and now they went hopping right after him, as if afraid that Mr. Samsa might get into the foyer ahead of them and interrupt the contact with their leader. In the foyer all three took their hats from the coatrack, pulled their canes from the umbrella stand, bowed silently, and left the apartment. In a suspicious mood which proved completely unfounded, Mr. Samsa led the two women out onto the landing; leaning over the banister, they watched the three roomers slowly but steadily going down the long flight of stairs, disappearing on each landing at a particular turn of the stairway and a few moments later emerging again; the farther down they got, the more the Samsa family's interest in them wore off, and when a butcher's boy with a carrier on his head came climbing up the stairs with a proud bearing, toward them and then up on past them, Mr. Samsa and the women quickly left the banister and all went back, as if relieved, into their apartment.

They decided to spend this day resting and going for a walk; they not only deserved a break in their work, they absolutely needed one. And so they sat down at the table and wrote three letters of excuse, Mr. Samsa to the management of the bank, Mrs. Samsa to her employer, and Grete to the store owner. While they were writing, the cleaning woman came in to say that she was going, since her morning's work was done. The three letter writers at first simply nodded without looking up, but as the cleaning woman still kept lingering, they looked up, annoyed. "Well?" asked Mr. Samsa. The cleaning woman stood smiling in the doorway, as if she had somegreat good news to announce to the family but would do so only if she were thoroughly questioned. The little ostrich feather which stood almost upright on her hat and which had irritated Mr. Samsa the whole time she had been with them swayed lightly in all directions. "What do you want?" asked Mrs. Samsa, who inspired the most respect in the cleaning woman. "Well," the cleaning woman answered, and for good-natured laughter could not immediately go on, "look, you don't have to worry about getting rid of the stuff next door. It's already been taken care of." Mrs. Samsa and Grete bent down over their letters, as if to continue writing; Mr. Samsa, who noticed that the cleaning woman was now about to start describing everything in detail, stopped her with a firmly outstretched hand. But since she was not going to be permitted to tell her story, she remembered that she was in a great hurry, cried, obviously insulted, "So long, everyone," whirled around wildly, and left the apartment with a terrible slamming of doors.

"We'll fire her tonight," said Mr. Samsa, but did not get an answer from either his wife or his daughter, for the cleaning woman seemed to have ruined their barely regained peace of mind. They got up, went to the window, and stayed there, holding each other tight. Mr. Samsa turned around in his chair toward them and watched them quietly for a while.

Then he called, "Come on now, come over here. Stop brooding over the past. And have a little consideration for me, too." The women obeyed him at once, hurried over to him, fondled him, and quickly finished their letters.

Then all three of them left the apartment together, something they had not done in months, and took the trolley into the open country on the outskirts of the city. The car, in which they were the only passengers, was completely filled with warm sunshine. Leaning back comfortably in their seats, they discussed their prospects for the time to come, and it seemed on closer examination that these weren't bad at all, for all three positions—about which they had never really asked one another in any detail—were exceedingly advantageous and especially promising for the future. The greatest immediate improvement in their situation would come easily, of course, from a change in apartments; they would now take a smaller and cheaper apartment, but one better situated and in every way simpler to manage than the old one, which Gregor had picked for them. While they were talking in this vein, it occurred almost simultaneously to Mr. and Mrs. Samsa, as they watched their daughter getting livelier and livelier, that lately, in spite of all the troubles which had turned her cheeks pale, she had blossomed into a good-looking, shapely girl. Growing quieter and communicating almost unconsciously through glances, they thought that it would soon be time, too, to find her a good husband. And it was like a confirmation of their new dreams and good intentions when at the end of the ride their daughter got up first and stretched her young body.

INUIT SONGS

The inhospitable central Arctic, directly north and northwest of Hudson Bay, is home to numerous small communities using varieties of one of the world's most far-flung languages: Inuit-Inupiaq, also called Eskimo, spoken across Alaska, Canada, and Greenland from the Bering Strait to the North Atlantic. Known to Europe since the earliest Norse colonization of Greenland, an event memorialized in the Icelandic sagas (ca. A.D. 1000–1300), the Inuit project an image of superhuman survivorship and intense artistry far beyond their native realm. As early as the eighteenth century, their poetry became known to an international audience through the *Volkslieder* (Folksongs; 1778–79) of the German philosopher and critic Johann Gottfried Herder, whose publication of an Inuit father's lament for his dead son ("My joy has gone into darkness and has become hidden in the mountain") gave the world its first taste of a literary tradition eventually to be revealed in depth—not from Greenland but from the central Arctic, the last region of the inhabitable north to be reached by Europe and still today a stronghold of native tradition.

It was Knud Johan Victor Rasmussen, born in Greenland to an Inuit mother, who gave the great singers of the central Arctic their lasting voice. Leader of the Danish-sponsored Fifth Thule Expedition (1921–24), Rasmussen brought a team of distinguished scientists through the heart of the Canadian Arctic, assigning to himself the task of documenting what he termed *intellectual culture*. The results were reported in a series of publications that included texts obtained from several dozen native singers, five of whom are represented in the selections printed here.

Orpingalik, a prominent shaman of Pelly Bay (on the Boothia Peninsula in north-central Canada), gave Rasmussen nearly a hundred songs in the course of a week. In his extensive accompanying testimony, he is revealed as a theorist as well as a poet. "We will fear to use words," he explained on one occasion, "but it will happen that the words we need will come of themselves. When the words we want to use shoot up of themselves, we get a new song."

Uvlunuaq, wife of Orpingalik, was a gifted singer in her own right. As reported by Rasmussen, "They had a son Igsivalitaq ('the frostbitten one'); a year or two before, this son had murdered a hunting companion in a fit of temper, and now he lived as outlaw in the mountains round Pelly Bay, fearing that the Mounted Police, of whom he had heard tell, would come for him. And his mother had made the following song through sorrow over her son's fate."

Netsit, storyteller and singer of the Umingmaktôrmiut ("Musk Ox People"), accompanied Rasmussen in his travels in the vicinity of Bathurst Inlet (seven hundred miles west of Pelly Bay). Netsit's "Dead Man's Song" is apparently another's composition, since he prefaced it with the statement, "After Aijuk's death, they say, his song was dreamt by Paulinâq."

Uvavnuk, fellow tribeswoman of Orpingalik and Uvlunuaq, had died before Rasmussen's arrival. A sometime shaman, whose powers came and went, she had composed her song "The Great Sea" in a seizure of ecstasy said to have filled her body with light. At the end of her life, she declared to an assembled audience that she had brought forth all manner of game from the interior of the earth; following her death, the people enjoyed a year of abundance. Her song was performed for Rasmussen by her son Niviatsian, himself a shaman.

Kibkarjuk, an elder woman of the Pâdlermiut ("People of the Dried Willow Branches"), had saved her village from starvation during the winter of 1921–22. Having dreamed of a distant, trout-filled lake, she succeeded in locating it after a perilous journey through blizzards, accompanied only by her small adopted son. Nevertheless, she was no longer her husband's favorite wife. In the song included here, she draws on that unhappy circumstance, recalling younger days.

Inuit songs are performed in the communal feasting house to the accompaniment of drumming and dancing. The audience joins in on the refrains, which consist of untranslatable song-syllables (for example, *unaija unaija*). Songs may also enliven the intimacy of a family gathering at home, or they may be sung in private. Orpingalik referred to his own songs as "my companions in solitude."

The translations printed here are from Rasmussen's Danish versions, rather than from the original Inuit. By virtue of his command of both Inuit and Danish, and in view of his consultations with the singers themselves, Rasmussen was uniquely qualified to interpret an obscure diction characterized by word distortions and special vocabulary. A native speaker of Greenland Inuit from childhood, he was able to penetrate the subtleties of the Canadian dialects—though not without effort. As one of his informants commented approvingly, upon taking leave, "Your tongue is not so frozen as when you came."

For a fuller selection of Inuit song texts, one may turn to Tom Lowenstein, *Eskimo Poems from Canada and Greenland* (1973), a literary anthology based on the research of Rasmussen. The source works are Knud Rasmussen, *Intellectual Culture of the Hudson Bay Eskimos* (1930), *The Netsilik Eskimos* (1931), and *Intellectual Culture of the Copper Eskimos* (1932). David Damas, ed., *Arctic*, vol. 5 of *Handbook of North American Indians* (1984), provides an indispensable guide to Inuit history and culture.

PRONOUNCING GLOSSARY

The following list uses common English syllables and stress accents to provide rough equivalents of selected words whose pronunciation may be unfamiliar to the general reader.

aji jai ja: *ah-yee' yigh yah*

ejaja-eja: *eh-yah'-yah–eh-yah*

Igsivalitaq: *eeg-see'-vah-lee-tahk*

ija-je-ja: *ee-yah–yeh–yah*

Inuit: *in'-oo-it*

Inupiaq: *in-oo'-pee-ak*

Kibkarjuk: *keeb'-kahr-yook*

Netsit: *nayt'-seet*

Orpingalik: *or-peeng'-ah-leek*

unaija: *oo-nigh'-ya*

Uvavnuk: *oo-vahv'-nook*

Uvlunuaq: *oov-loo'-noo-ahk*

ORPINGALIK

flourished 1923

My Breath[1]

This is what I call my song, because it is as important for me to sing it, as it is to draw breath.

> This is my song: a powerful song.
> Unaija-unaija.[2]
> Since autumn I have lain here,
> helpless and ill,
> as if I were my own child.   5
>
> Sorrowfully, I wish my woman
> to another hut,
> another man for refuge,
> firm and safe as the winter-ice.
> Unaija-unaija.   10
>
> And I wish my woman
> a more fortunate protector,
> now I lack the strength
> to raise myself from bed.
> Unaija-unaija.   15
>
> Do you know yourself?
> How little of yourself you understand!
> Stretched out feebly on my bench,
> my only strength is in my memories.
> Unaija-unaija.   20
>
> Game! Big game,
> chasing ahead of me!
> Allow me to re-live that!
> Let me forget my frailty,

1. Translated by Tom Lowenstein. Orpingalik told Rasmussen that this song came to him in a fit of despondency after a long illness.   2. The refrain connotes melancholy and resignation [Translator's note].

by calling up the past!   25
Unaija-unaija.

I bring to mind that great white one,
the polar bear,
approaching with raised hind-quarters,
his nose in the snow—   30
convinced, as he rushed at me,
that of the two of us,
he was the only male!
Unaija-unaija.

Again and again he threw me down: 35
but spent at last,
he settled by a hump of ice,
and rested there,
ignorant that I was going to finish him.
He thought he was the only male around!   40
But I too was a man!
Unaija-unaija.

Nor will I forget that great blubbery one,
the fjord-seal, that I slaughtered
from an ice-floe before dawn,   45
while friends at home
were laid out like the dead,
feeble with hunger,
famished with bad luck.
I hurried home,   50
laden with meat and blubber,
as though I were just running across the ice
to view a breathing-hole.[3]
Yet this had been an old and cunning bull,
who'd scented me at once—   55
but before he had drawn breath,
my spear was sinking
through his neck.

This is how it was.
Now I lie on my bench,   60
too sick to even fetch
a little seal oil for my woman's lamp.
Time, time scarcely seems to pass,
though dawn follows dawn,
and spring approaches the village.   65
Unaija-unaija.

How much longer must I lie here?
How long? How long must she go begging
oil for the lamp,
reindeer-skins for her clothes,   70
and meat for her meal?
I, a feeble wretch:
she, a defenceless woman.
Unaija-unaija.

---

3. Hole in the ice where a seal comes up to breathe.

Do you know yourself?   75
How little of yourself you understand!
Dawn follows dawn,
and spring is approaching the village.
   Unaija-unaija.

UVLUNUAQ
flourished 1923

Song of a Mother[1]

[A young man had killed his hunting companion in a fit of rage. The
murderer's mother sang this song to express her grief.]

    Ejaja-eja.
    A bit of song comes back.
    I draw it to me like a friend.
      Ejaja-eja.

    I ought, I suppose, to be ashamed   5
    of the child I once carried on my back,
    when I heard he'd left the settlement.
    They're right to tell me so:
    I ought to be ashamed.
      Ejaja-eja.   10

    I am ashamed:
    because he didn't have a mother
    who was faultless
    as the clear sky,
    wise and without folly.   15
    Now that he's the butt
    of everybody's tongue,
    this evil talk will finish him.
      Ejaja-eja.

    He has become the burden   20
    of my age.
    But far from being
    properly ashamed,
    I'm envious of others
    when they break up   25
    after feasts, and set off
    with crowds of friends
    behind them, waving on the ice.
      Ejaja-eja.

    I remember one mild spring.   30
    We'd camped near Cross-Eye Lake.

1. Translated by Tom Lowenstein.

Our footsteps sank
with a soft creak
into half-thawed snow.
I stayed near the men,   35
like a tame animal.
But when the news
about the murder came,
and that he'd fled,
the ground heaved under me   40
like a mountain,
and I stood on its summit,
and I staggered.

NETSIT

flourished 1923

Dead Man's Song[1]

I'm filled with joy
when the day dawns quietly
over the roof of the sky,
    aji, jai ja.

I'm filled with joy   5
when the sun rises slowly
over the roof of the sky,
    aji, jai ja.

But other times, I choke with fear:
a greedy swarm of maggots   10
eats into the hollows
of my collar-bone and eyes,
    aji, jai ja.

I lie here dreaming
how I choked with fear   15
when they shut me
in an ice-hut on the lake,[2]
    aji, jai ja.

And I could not see
my soul would ever free itself   20
and get up to the hunting-grounds
of the sky,
    aji, jai ja.

Fear grew, and grew.
Fear overwhelmed me   25

1. Translated by Tom Lowenstein. "Dreamed by one who is alive" [Rasmussen's note].   2. The dead
are often interred by being left in the snow hut in which they have died, it being closed up with a block
of snow [Rasmussen's note].

when the fresh-water ice
snapped in the cold,
and the booming crack of the frost
grew into the sky,
   aji, jai ja.   30

Life was wonderful
in winter.
But did winter make me happy?
No, I always worried
about hides for boot-soles   35
and for boots:
and if there'd be enough
for all of us.
Yes, I worried constantly,
   aji, jai ja.   40

Life was wonderful
in summer.
But did summer make me happy?
No, I always worried
about reindeer skins and rugs for the platform.[3]   45
Yes, I worried constantly,
   aji, jai ja.

Life was wonderful
when you stood at your fishing-hole
on the ice.   50
But was I happy waiting at my fishing hole?
No, I always worried
for my little hook,
in case it never got a bite.
Yes, I worried constantly,   55
   aji, jai ja.

Life was wonderful
when you danced in the feasting-house.[4]
But did this make me any happier?
No, I always worried   60
I'd forget my song.
Yes, I worried constantly,
   aji, jai ja.

Life was wonderful . . .
And I still feel joy   65
each time the day-break
whitens the dark sky,
each time the sun
climbs over the roof of the sky,
   aji, jai ja.   70

---

3. That is, the sleeping platform within the house.   4. Where songs are performed.

UVAVNUK

died before 1921

The Great Sea[1]

The great sea
Has sent me adrift,
It moves me as the weed in a great river,
Earth and the great weather
Move me,   5
Have carried me away
And move my inward parts with joy.

KIBKARJUK

flourished 1922

Song of the Rejected Woman[1]

[Kibkarjuk remembers when she was her husband's favorite wife, and was allowed to hunt caribou herself.]

Inland,
far inland go my thoughts,
my mournful thoughts.
To never leave the woman's bench
is too much to endure: 5
I want to wander inland,
far inland.
    Ija-je-ja.

My thoughts return
to hunting: 10
animals, delightful food!
To never leave the woman's bench
is too much to endure:
I want to wander inland,
far inland.   15
    Ija-je-ja.

I hunted like
the men:
I carried weapons,
shot a reindeer bull,   20
a reindeer cow and calf,
yes, slew them with my arrows,
with my arrows,
one evening towards winter,

---

1. Translated by W. Worster.   1. Translated by Tom Lowenstein.

as the sky-dusk fell   25
  far inland.
    Ija-je-ja.

This is what I think about,
  this is what I struggle with,
  while inland, under falling snow,   30
  the earth turns white,
  far inland.
    Ija-je-ja.

D. H. LAWRENCE
1885–1930

Few novelists have expressed the opposition between nature and society, intuitive instincts and the industrial age, as insistently as D. H. Lawrence. Widely known for portrayals of erotic passion that shocked his contemporaries, Lawrence took as his mission the exploration of individual human psychology and a struggle against everything that hindered its fulfillment. A master of striking descriptions that seemed to reproduce the very sight and smell of physical reality, Lawrence also worked on another plane: that of symbolic allusions to an underlying, elementary or archetypal reality that actually explained the human interactions being portrayed. Whether he wrote about the stunted, dreary landscape of the coal mining district, the deadening influence of gentility and social inhibitions, or about human possessiveness and its destruction of personal relationships, Lawrence tried to suggest an alternate world in which men and women related freely with one another and in perfect harmony with nature. Such a world is almost a mystic vision: it will come about, he argues, only if we remain true to the darker, irrational life forces within us, and reject any intellectualized attempt to master our basic instincts. As often happens, the fictional definition of this supreme vision is less generous than its aim: Lawrence usually associates repression and convention with women and the mutely powerful expression of life forces with men or animals. Nonetheless, his fiction is remarkable for its artistry and power, and for evoking— inside realistically portrayed personal relationships—some of the deepest currents of human psychology.

David Herbert Lawrence was born on September 11, 1885, the fourth of five children born to the coal miner Arthur Lawrence and his wife, Lydia, a former schoolteacher. They lived in Eastwood, a mining town near Nottingham, England, where the father went down to dig in the pits each day and David's mother— who had come from a more prosperous family—struggled against poverty and her husband's alcoholism to give her children a better opportunity in life. After the death of his older brother, Ernest, in 1901, young David—already physically frail—became increasingly the focus of his mother's anxious care. Violent quarrels between father and mother marked the early years of the children, who were usually sympathetic to their mother, although Lawrence came later to feel that he had underestimated his father's warmth and vitality. Echoes of this early struggle, of his mother's ultimately unhealthy and possessive love, and of the mining community itself occur repeatedly in Lawrence's work, notably the novel *Sons and Lovers* (1913) and the short story *Odor of Chrysanthemums*, included here.

Lawrence was a good student and at twelve won a county council scholarship that let him attend Nottingham High School. After graduation he became a clerk in a factory making artificial limbs, and then a teacher in local schools. He had taken up painting by now and started writing poetry in 1902. Teaching at the British School in Eastwood, Lawrence became close friends with a neighbor, Jessie Chambers, who shared his love of literature. The two might well have married if it had not been for the jealous disapproval of his mother, a situation Lawrence reconstructed with a pitiless perspective on both women in his third novel, *Sons and Lovers*. Memories of the countryside and the women he came to know reappear in several novels: Louise Burrows, whom he met in 1903, furnished elements of the "modern woman" Ursula Brangwen in *The Rainbow* (1915), and the tragic love affair of a later friend, Helen Corke, became the basis of his second novel, *The Trespasser* (1912).

In 1904 Lawrence won first place in all England and Wales in the King's Scholarship Examination. Although he had to postpone entrance into Nottingham University College until he could earn money for fees, the scholarship enabled him to begin the college's two-year teaching certificate course in 1906, and in 1908 he began teaching at a school in south London. His mother died in December 1910, and illness forced Lawrence to retire from teaching the next year. In 1912, on a visit to his former French professor, Lawrence met the man's much younger wife—Frieda von Richthofen Weekley—and fell in love. The two left the same year for Germany and then Italy, although they were not able to marry until Frieda received her divorce in 1914. The marriage lasted, passionate and quarrelsome, until Lawrence's death on March 2, 1930.

During World War I Frieda's German birth and Lawrence's general disgust with patriotic sentiments made the couple a focus of local suspicion. After much harassment, they were ordered in 1917 to leave the cottage in Cornwall where they had lived for two years and to stay away from coastal areas altogether; yet their application for passports was denied, and they could not leave England. Lawrence wrote his most celebrated novels in this period. After the moderate success of *Sons and Lovers*, he turned to a longer study of love relationships in modern society that became *The Rainbow* and *Women in Love* (1920). The latter novel continued the earlier tale of Ursula Brangwen's quest for love inside the story of two couples, themselves modeled on aspects of the Lawrences and their friends, the short story writer Katherine Mansfield and the critic John Middleton Murry. *The Rainbow* and *Women in Love*, with their depictions of erotic consciousness inside a suggested mythic and symbolic framework, were stylistically far more innovative than *Sons and Lovers*. The explicit love scenes, criticism of modern industrial society, and scorn for patriotic values shocked many, and *The Rainbow* was declared obscene and all copies destroyed in November 1915.

Embittered by his experiences in England, Lawrence left for Italy with Frieda in 1919. In subsequent years they traveled widely, living for brief periods in Sicily, Ceylon, Australia, and finally New Mexico and Mexico, where Lawrence thought to find in Indian primitivism a key to the elemental "blood-knowledge" he sought as an antidote to overly intellectualized modern society. The travel book, *Sea and Sardinia*, dates to this period, as does a series of "leadership" novels (*Aaron's Rod*, 1922; *Kangaroo*, 1923; and *The Plumed Serpent*, 1926) in which the protagonist seeks direction from a charismatic leader or cause. Although Lawrence has often been accused of fascism in these novels (and he certainly had no use for democracy or the rule of the masses), his main concern was to assert individual rights against society's encroaching claims and to rebalance the human personality by emphasizing intuition over intellect. After finishing *The Plumed Serpent* in February 1925, Lawrence fell seriously ill with the tuberculosis that would cause his death five years later. He and Frieda returned to Italy and settled in 1926 in the Villa Mirenda outside Florence, where he took up painting again and completed work on *Lady Chatterley's Lover*. Privately printed in Florence in 1928, the novel could not be published or circulated unexpurgated in England or America until 1959 because of its explicit sexual scenes (*Ulysses*, in contrast, was judged not obscene in 1933). Lawrence and Frieda left the Villa Mirenda in 1928 and traveled in France and Spain before returning to Florence. His paintings had been exhibited in London in 1929 and provoked the same scandal and legal suppression as *Lady Chatterley's Lover*. Lawrence was extremely ill with tuberculosis in these years, although he also wrote poems (*Pansies*, 1929), essays, and what was considered a blasphemous variation on the biblical account of the Resurrection (*The Man Who Died*, 1929) in which the resurrected prophet renounces prophecy for human love. In February 1930 the sick man moved to a sanitorium in Vence, in southern France. He died there on March 2; his body was later cremated and the ashes buried in a tomb on the New Mexico ranch where he had finished *The Plumed Serpent*.

From the beginning, *Odor of Chrysanthemums* evokes the childhood scenery and psychological themes of Lawrence's first novels, especially *Sons and Lovers*. The contrast between the industrial ugliness of the mining community and the thwarted beauty of nature is emphasized and given moral significance by the juxtaposition of locomotive and startled colt, the picture of the woman standing "insignificantly trapped" between the tracks and the hedge, and the dreary landscape's "bony vines," "ragged cabbages," and faded pink chrysanthemums. The conflict between husband and wife is also familiar, although here it appears at an earlier stage: Elizabeth Bates's two children are still young as she tries, pregnant, to keep the household going in spite of her unruly and alcoholic husband. She is portrayed as imperious, practical, responsible, and disillusioned, and most of the story focuses on what seems to be one more evening of waiting for Walter Bates to come home drunk after having spent most of his pay at a local bar. Our knowledge of the situation develops through scenes of family friction as mother and children wait by the fire, and through the cautious sympathy of her father and neighbors, so that Elizabeth's impatience and hostility toward her irresponsible husband seem totally justified by the time of the shocking announcement of his death. From that point on, the portrait of the wife does not change but a new counterpoint is introduced in the person of the dead man: solid, unreachable, mysteriously alien and inviolate in his death.

In the last pages of the story, the physical presence of her husband's dead body forces Elizabeth to recognize for the first time the absolute difference between their two natures: a complete separation of individual identities that was true all along but that was not visible until the permanent separation of death. Her image of Walter while alive was not the measure of the man, whose stock of vitality and warmth Lawrence hints at when he repeatedly associates with him the natural symbol of chrysanthemum flowers. Husband and wife had not known each other, "had denied each other in life," and the wrong is now forever irreparable. The horror with which Elizabeth comes to this realization extends beyond the loss of her husband, and beyond the tears her mother-in-law expects. It is the horror of "utter, intact separateness" that can exist between human beings in the closest relationships.

George Becker, *D. H. Lawrence* (1980), provides a general introduction and biography, and Frank Kermode, *D. H. Lawrence* (1971), is an excellent general study. See E. T. (Jessie Chambers), *D. H. Lawrence* (1965), for an account of Lawrence's youth by a close friend who figures in *Sons and Lovers*. Carol Sklenicka offers a thematic study in *D. H. Lawrence and the Child* (1991). A good critical study of the fiction is Julian Moynahan, *The Deed of Life: The Novels and Tales of D. H. Lawrence* (1963). Weldon Thornton, *D. H. Lawrence: A Study of the Short Fiction* (1993), examines short stories; Harold Bloom, ed., *D. H. Law-*

rence, and Michael Squires and Keith Cushman, eds., *The Challenge of D. H. Lawrence* (1990), are useful general collections.

Odor of Chrysanthemums

I

The small locomotive engine, Number 4, came clanking, stumbling down from Selston with seven full wagons. It appeared round the corner with loud threats of speed, but the colt that it startled from among the gorse, which still flickered indistinctly in the raw afternoon, out-distanced it at a canter. A woman, walking up the railway line to Underwood, drew back into the hedge, held her basket aside, and watched the footplate of the engine advancing. The trucks thumped heavily past, one by one, with slow inevitable movement, as she stood insignificantly trapped between the jolting black wagons and the hedge; then they curved away towards the coppice where the withered oak leaves dropped noiselessly, while the birds, pulling at the scarlet hips beside the track, made off into the dusk that had already crept into the spinney. In the open, the smoke from the engine sank and cleaved to the rough grass. The fields were dreary and forsaken, and in the marshy strip that led to the whimsey, a reedy pit pond, the fowls had already abandoned their run among the alders, to roost in the tarred fowl house. The pit bank[1] loomed up beyond the pond, flames like red sores licking its ashy sides, in the afternoon's stagnant light. Just beyond rose the tapering chimneys and the clumsy black headstocks[2] of Brinsley Colliery. The two wheels were spinning fast up against the sky, and the winding engine rapped out its little spasms. The miners were being turned up.

The engine whistled as it came into the wide bay of railway lines beside the colliery, where rows of trucks stood in harbor.

Miners, single, trailing, and in groups, passed like shadows diverging home. At the edge of the ribbed level of sidings squat[3] a low cottage, three steps down from the cinder track. A large bony vine clutched at the house, as if to claw down the tiled roof. Round the bricked yard grew a few wintry primroses. Beyond, the long garden sloped down to a bush-covered brook course. There were some twiggy apple trees, winter-crack[4] trees, and ragged cabbages. Beside the path hung disheveled pink chrysanthemums, like pink cloths hung on bushes. A woman came stooping out of the felt-covered fowl house, halfway down the garden. She closed and padlocked the door, then drew herself erect, having brushed some bits from her white apron.

She was a tall woman of imperious mien, handsome, with definite black eyebrows. Her smooth black hair was parted exactly. For a few moments she stood steadily watching the miners as they passed along the railway: then she turned towards the brook course. Her face was calm and set, her mouth was closed with disillusionment. After a moment she called:

"John!" There was no answer. She waited, and then said distinctly:

---

1. Bank formed by waste materials extracted from the mine.   2. Aboveground structures over mine shafts.   3. Squatted.   4. A species of plum not ripe until November.

"Where are you?"

"Here!" replied a child's sulky voice from among the bushes. The woman looked piercingly through the dusk.

"Are you at that brook?" she asked sternly.

For answer the child showed himself before the raspberry canes that rose like whips. He was a small, sturdy boy of five. He stood quite still, defiantly.

"Oh!" said the mother, conciliated. "I thought you were down at that wet brook—and you remember what I told you——"

The boy did not move or answer.

"Come, come on in," she said more gently, "it's getting dark. There's your grandfather's engine coming down the line!"

The lad advanced slowly, with resentful, taciturn movement. He was dressed in trousers and waistcoat of cloth that was too thick and hard for the size of the garments. They were evidently cut down from a man's clothes.

As they went slowly towards the house he tore at the ragged wisps of chrysanthemums and dropped the petals in handfuls among the path.

"Don't do that—it does look nasty," said his mother. He refrained, and she, suddenly pitiful, broke off a twig with three or four wan flowers and held them against her face. When mother and son reached the yard her hand hesitated, and instead of laying the flower aside, she pushed it in her apron-band. The mother and son stood at the foot of the three steps looking across the bay of lines at the passing home of the miners. The trundle of the small train was imminent. Suddenly the engine loomed past the house and came to a stop opposite the gate.

The engine-driver, a short man with round gray beard, leaned out of the cab high above the woman.

"Have you got a cup of tea?" he said in a cheery, hearty fashion.

It was her father. She went in, saying she would mash.[5] Directly, she returned.

"I didn't come to see you on Sunday," began the little gray-bearded man.

"I didn't expect you," said his daughter.

The engine driver winced; then, reassuming his cheery, airy manner, he said:

"Oh, have you heard then? Well, and what do you think——?"

"I think it is soon enough," she replied.

At her brief censure the little man made an impatient gesture, and said coaxingly, yet with dangerous coldness:

"Well, what's a man to do? It's no sort of life for a man of my years, to sit at my own hearth like a stranger. And if I'm going to marry again it may as well be soon as late—what does it matter to anybody?"

The woman did not reply, but turned and went into the house. The man in the engine-cab stood assertive, till she returned with a cup of tea and a piece of bread and butter on a plate. She went up the steps and stood near the footplate of the hissing engine.

"You needn't 'a' brought me bread an' butter," said her father. "But a

5. Steep some tea.

cup of tea"—he sipped appreciatively—"it's very nice." He sipped for a
moment or two, then: "I hear as Walter's got another bout on," he said.

"When hasn't he?" said the woman bitterly.

"I heerd tell of him in the Lord Nelson braggin' as he was going to
spend that b——[6] afore he went: half a sovereign that was."

"When?" asked the woman.

"A' Sat'day night—I know that's true."

"Very likely," she laughed bitterly. "He gives me twenty-three shillings."

"Aye, it's a nice thing, when a man can do nothing with his money but
make a beast of himself!" said the gray-whiskered man. The woman
turned her head away. Her father swallowed the last of his tea and handed
her the cup.

"Aye," he sighed, wiping his mouth. "It's a settler,[7] it is——"

He put his hand on the lever. The little engine strained and groaned,
and the train rumbled towards the crossing. The woman again looked
across the metals. Darkness was settling over the spaces of the railway and
trucks: the miners, in gray somber groups, were still passing home. The
winding engine pulsed hurriedly, with brief pauses. Elizabeth Bates
looked at the dreary flow of men, then she went indoors. Her husband did
not come.

The kitchen was small and full of firelight; red coals piled glowing up
the chimney mouth. All the life of the room seemed in the white, warm
hearth and the steel fender reflecting the red fire. The cloth was laid for
tea; cups glinted in the shadows. At the back, where the lowest stairs protruded into the room, the boy sat struggling with a knife and a piece of
white wood. He was almost hidden in the shadow. It was half-past four.
They had but to await the father's coming to begin tea. As the mother
watched her son's sullen little struggle with the wood, she saw herself in
his silence and pertinacity; she saw the father in her child's indifference
to all but himself. She seemed to be occupied by her husband. He had
probably gone past his home, slunk past his own door, to drink before he
came in, while his dinner spoiled and wasted in waiting. She glanced at
the clock, then took the potatoes to strain them in the yard. The garden
and fields beyond the brook were closed in uncertain darkness. When she
rose with the saucepan, leaving the drain steaming into the night behind
her, she saw the yellow lamps were lit along the high road that went up
the hill away beyond the space of the railway lines and the field.

Then again she watched the men trooping home, fewer now and fewer.

Indoors the fire was sinking and the room was dark red. The woman
put her saucepan on the hob, and set a batter pudding near the mouth of
the oven. Then she stood unmoving. Directly, gratefully, came quick
young steps to the door. Someone hung on the latch a moment, then a
little girl entered and began pulling off her outdoor things, dragging a
mass of curls, just ripening from gold to brown, over her eyes with her hat.

Her mother chid her for coming late from school, and said she would
have to keep her at home the dark winter days.

---

6. Bugger; the husband's profane name for the half-sovereign, a gold coin worth ten shillings.
7. Grave problem, something hard to bear.

"Why, mother, it's hardly a bit dark yet. The lamp's not lighted, and my father's not home."

"No, he isn't. But it's a quarter to five! Did you see anything of him?"

The child became serious. She looked at her mother with large, wistful blue eyes.

"No, mother, I've never seen him. Why? Has he come up an' gone past, to Old Brinsley? He hasn't, mother, 'cos I never saw him."

"He'd watch that," said the mother bitterly, "he'd take care as you didn't see him. But you may depend upon it, he's seated in the Prince o' Wales. He wouldn't be this late."

The girl looked at her mother piteously.

"Let's have our teas, mother, should we?" said she.

The mother called John to table. She opened the door once more and looked out across the darkness of the lines. All was deserted: she could not hear the winding engines.[8]

"Perhaps," she said to herself, "he's stopped to get some ripping[9] done."

They sat down to tea. John, at the end of the table near the door, was almost lost in the darkness. Their faces were hidden from each other. The girl crouched against the fender slowly moving a thick piece of bread before the fire. The lad, his face a dusky mark on the shadow, sat watching her who was transfigured in the red glow.

"I do think it's beautiful to look in the fire," said the child.

"Do you?" said her mother. "Why?"

"It's so red, and full of little caves—and it feels so nice, and you can fair smell it."

"It'll want mending directly," replied her mother, "and then if your father comes he'll carry on and say there never is a fire when a man comes home sweating from the pit. A public house is always warm enough."

There was silence till the boy said complainingly: "Make haste, our Annie."

"Well, I am doing! I can't make the fire do it no faster, can I?"

"She keeps wafflin'[1] it about so's to make 'er slow," grumbled the boy.

"Don't have such an evil imagination, child," replied the mother.

Soon the room was busy in the darkness with the crisp sound of crunching. The mother ate very little. She drank her tea determinedly, and sat thinking. When she rose her anger was evident in the stern unbending of her head. She looked at the pudding in the fender, and broke out:

"It is a scandalous thing as a man can't even come home to his dinner! If it's crozzled[2] up to a cinder I don't see why I should care. Past his very door he goes to get to a public house, and here I sit with his dinner waiting for him——"

She went out. As she dropped piece after piece of coal on the red fire, the shadows fell on the walls, till the room was almost in total darkness.

"I canna see," grumbled the invisible John. In spite of herself, the mother laughed.

"You know the way to your mouth," she said. She set the dust-pan out-

---

8. For raising and lowering men and materials.   9. Stripping the coal face in the mine.   1. Separating, breaking up embers.   2. Burned up.

side the door. When she came again like a shadow on the hearth, the lad
repeated, complaining sulkily:

"I canna see."

"Good gracious!" cried the mother irritably, "you're as bad as your
father if it's a bit dusk!"

Nevertheless, she took a paper spill[3] from a sheaf on the mantelpiece
and proceeded to light the lamp that hung from the ceiling in the middle
of the room. As she reached up, her figure displayed itself just rounding
with maternity.

"Oh, mother——!" exclaimed the girl.

"What?" said the woman, suspended in the act of putting the lamp glass
over the flame. The copper reflector shone handsomely on her, as she
stood with uplifted arm, turning to face her daughter.

"You've got a flower in your apron!" said the child, in a little rapture at
this unusual event.

"Goodness me!" exclaimed the woman, relieved. "One would think the
house was afire." She replaced the glass and waited a moment before turning up the wick. A pale shadow was seen floating vaguely on the floor.

"Let me smell!" said the child, still rapturously, coming forward and
putting her face to her mother's waist.

"Go along, silly!" said the mother, turning up the lamp. The light
revealed their suspense so that the woman felt it almost unbearable. Annie
was still bending at her waist. Irritably, the mother took the flowers out
from her apron band.

"Oh, mother—don't take them out!" Annie cried, catching her hand
and trying to replace the sprig.

"Such nonsense!" said the mother, turning away. The child put the pale
chrysanthemums to her lips, murmuring:

"Don't they smell beautiful!"

Her mother gave a short laugh.

"No," she said, "not to me. It was chrysanthemums when I married
him, and chrysanthemums when you were born, and the first time they
ever brought him home drunk, he'd got brown chrysanthemums in his
buttonhole."

She looked at the children. Their eyes and their parted lips were wondering. The mother sat rocking in silence for some time. Then she looked
at the clock

"Twenty minutes to six!" In a tone of fine bitter carelessness she continued: "Eh, he'll not come now till they bring him. There he'll stick! But
he needn't come rolling in here in his pit dirt, for *I* won't wash him. He
can lie on the floor——Eh, what a fool I've been, what a fool! And this is
what I came here for, to this dirty hole, rats and all, for him to slink past
his very door. Twice last week—he's begun now——"

She silenced herself, and rose to clear the table.

While for an hour or more the children played, subduedly intent, fertile
of imagination, united in fear of the mother's wrath, and in dread of their
father's home-coming, Mrs. Bates sat in her rocking chair making a "sin-

3. Long twist of paper.

glet" of thick cream-colored flannel, which gave a dull wounded sound as she tore off the gray edge. She worked at her sewing with energy, listening to the children, and her anger wearied itself, lay down to rest, opening its eyes from time to time and steadily watching, its ears raised to listen. Sometimes even her anger quailed and shrank, and the mother suspended her sewing, tracing the footsteps that thudded along the sleepers[4] outside; she would lift her head sharply to bid the children "hush," but she recovered herself in time, and the footsteps went past the gate, and the children were not flung out of their play-world.

But at last Annie sighed, and gave in. She glanced at her wagon of slippers,[5] and loathed the game. She turned plaintively to her mother.

"Mother!"—but she was inarticulate.

John crept out like a frog from under the sofa. His mother glanced up.

"Yes," she said, "just look at those shirt-sleeves!"

The boy held them out to survey them, saying nothing. Then somebody called in a hoarse voice away down the line, and suspense bristled in the room, till two people had gone by outside, talking.

"It is time for bed," said the mother.

"My father hasn't come," wailed Annie plaintively. But her mother was primed with courage.

"Never mind. They'll bring him when he does come—like a log." She meant there would be no scene. "And he may sleep on the floor till he wakes himself. I know he'll not go to work to-morrow after this!"

The children had their hands and faces wiped with a flannel. They were very quiet. When they had put on their nightdresses, they said their prayers, the boy mumbling. The mother looked down at them, at the brown silken bush of intertwining curls in the nape of the girl's neck, at the little black head of the lad, and her heart burst with anger at their father, who caused all three such distress. The children hid their faces in her skirts for comfort.

When Mrs. Bates came down, the room was strangely empty, with a tension of expectancy. She took up her sewing and stitched for some time without raising her head. Meantime her anger was tinged with fear.

II

The clock struck eight and she rose suddenly, dropping her sewing on her chair. She went to the stair-foot door, opened it, listening. Then she went out, locking the door behind her.

Something scuffled in the yard, and she started, though she knew it was only the rats with which the place was over-run. The night was very dark. In the great bay of railway lines, bulked with trucks, there was no trace of light, only away back she could see a few yellow lamps at the pit top, and the red smear of the burning pit bank on the night. She hurried along the edge of the track, then, crossing the converging lines, came to the stile by the white gates, whence she emerged on the road. Then the fear which had led her shrank. People were walking up to New Brinsley; she saw the

---

4. Timbers in a wooden walkway.   5. Pieces of coal.

lights in the houses; twenty yards farther on were the broad windows of the Prince of Wales, very warm and bright, and the loud voices of men could be heard distinctly. What a fool she had been to imagine that anything had happened to him! He was merely drinking over there at the Prince of Wales. She faltered. She had never yet been to fetch him, and she never would go. So she continued her walk towards the long straggling line of houses, standing back on the highway. She entered a passage between the dwellings.

"Mr. Rigley?—Yes! Did you want him? No, he's not in at this minute."

The raw-boned woman leaned foward from her dark scullery and peered at the other, upon whom fell a dim light through the blind of the kitchen window.

"Is it Mrs. Bates?" she asked in a tone tinged with respect.

"Yes. I wondered if your Master[6] was at home. Mine hasn't come yet."

" 'Asn't 'e! Oh, Jack's been 'ome an' 'ad 'is dinner an' gone out. 'E's just gone for 'alf an hour afore bedtime. Did you call at the Prince of Wales?"

"No——"

"No, you didn't like——! It's not very nice." The other woman was indulgent. There was an awkward pause. "Jack never said nothink about— about your Master," she said.

"No!—I expect he's stuck in there!"

Elizabeth Bates said this bitterly, and with recklessness. She knew that the woman across the yard was standing at her door listening, but she did not care. As she turned:

"Stop a minute! I'll just go an' ask Jack if 'e knows anythink," said Mrs. Rigley.

"Oh no—I wouldn't like to put——!"

"Yes, I will, if you'll just step inside an' see as th' childer doesn't come downstairs and set theirselves afire."

Elizabeth Bates, murmuring a remonstrance, stepped inside. The other woman apologized for the state of the room.

The kitchen needed apology. There were little frocks and trousers and childish undergarments on the squab[7] and on the floor, and a litter of playthings everywhere. On the black American cloth of the table were pieces of bread and cake, crusts, slops,[8] and a teapot with cold tea.

"Eh, ours is just as bad," said Elizabeth Bates, looking at the woman, not at the house. Mrs. Rigley put a shawl over her head and hurried out, saying:

"I shanna be a minute."

The other sat, noting with faint disapproval the general untidiness of the room. Then she fell to counting the shoes of various sizes scattered over the floor. There were twelve. She sighed and said to herself: "No wonder!"—glancing at the litter. There came the scratching of two pairs of feet on the yard, and the Rigleys entered. Elizabeth Bates rose. Rigley was a big man, with very large bones. His head looked particularly bony.

---

6. Husband.   7. Couch.   8. Undrunk remains of tea, emptied out of the cups into a "slop bowl." *American cloth*: oilcloth.

Across his temple was a blue scar, caused by a wound got in the pit, a wound in which the coal dust remained blue like tattooing.

" 'Asna 'e come whoam yit?" asked the man, without any form of greeting, but with deference and sympathy. "I couldna say wheer he is—'e's non ower theer!"[9]—he jerked his head to signify the Prince of Wales.

" 'E's 'appen gone up to th'Yew," said Mrs. Rigley.

There was another pause. Rigley had evidently something to get off his mind:

"Ah left 'im finishin' a stint," he began. "Loose-all[1] 'ad bin gone about ten minutes when we com'n away, an' I shouted: 'Are ter comin', Walt?' an' 'e said: 'Go on, Ah shanna be but a'ef a minnit,' so we com'n ter th' bottom, me an' Bowers, thinkin' as 'e wor just behint, an' 'ud come up i' th' next bantle[2]——"

He stood perplexed, as if answering a charge of deserting his mate. Elizabeth Bates, now again certain of disaster, hastened to reassure him:

"I expect 'e's gone up to th' Yew Tree, as you say. It's not the first time. I've fretted myself into a fever before now. He'll come home when they carry him."

"Ay, isn't it too bad!" deplored the other woman.

"I'll just step up to Dick's an' see if 'e *is* theer," offered the man, afraid of appearing alarmed, afraid of taking liberties.

"Oh, I wouldn't think of bothering you that far," said Elizabeth Bates, with emphasis, but he knew she was glad of his offer.

As they stumbled up the entry, Elizabeth Bates heard Rigley's wife run across the yard and open her neighbor's door. At this, suddenly all the blood in her body seemed to switch away from her heart.

"Mind!" warned Rigley. "Ah've said many a time as Ah'd fill up them ruts in this entry, sumb'dy 'll be breakin' their legs yit."

She recovered herself and walked quickly along with the miner.

"I don't like leaving the children in bed, and nobody in the house," she said.

"No, you dunna!" he replied courteously. They were soon at the gate of the cottage.

"Well, I shanna be many minnits. Dunna you be frettin' now, 'e'll be all right," said the butty.[3]

"Thank you very much, Mr. Rigley," she replied.

"You're welcome!" he stammered, moving away. "I shanna be many minnits."

The house was quiet. Elizabeth Bates took off her hat and shawl, and rolled back the rug. When she had finished, she sat down. It was a few minutes past nine. She was startled by the rapid chuff of the winding engine at the pit, and the sharp whirr of the brakes on the rope as it descended. Again she felt the painful sweep of her blood, and she put her hand to her side, saying aloud: "Good gracious!—it's only the nine o'clock deputy going down," rebuking herself.

9. "Hasn't he come home yet?" "He's not over there!"   1. End of day's shift.   2. Platform of the elevator in the mine shaft.   3. Buddy, work companion.

She sat still, listening. Half an hour of this, and she was wearied out.

"What am I working myself up like this for?" she said pitiably to herself, "I s'll only be doing myself some damage."

She took out her sewing again.

At a quarter to ten there were footsteps. One person! She watched for the door to open. It was an elderly woman, in a black bonnet and a black woolen shawl—his mother. She was about sixty years old, pale, with blue eyes, and her face all wrinkled and lamentable. She shut the door and turned to her daughter-in-law peevishly.

"Eh, Lizzie, whatever shall we do, whatever shall we do!" she cried.

Elizabeth drew back a little, sharply.

"What is it, mother?" she said.

The elder woman seated herself on the sofa.

"I don't know, child, I can't tell you!"—she shook her head slowly. Elizabeth sat watching her, anxious and vexed.

"I don't know," replied the grandmother, sighing very deeply. "There's no end to my troubles, there isn't. The things I've gone through, I'm sure it's enough——!" She wept without wiping her eyes, the tears running.

"But, mother," interrupted Elizabeth, "what do you mean? What is it?"

The grandmother slowly wiped her eyes. The fountains of her tears were stopped by Elizabeth's directness. She wiped her eyes slowly.

"Poor child! Eh, you poor thing!" she moaned. "I don't know what we're going to do, I don't—and you as you are—it's a thing, it is indeed!"

Elizabeth waited.

"Is he dead?" she asked, and at the words her heart swung violently, though she felt a slight flush of shame at the ultimate extravagance of the question. Her words sufficiently frightened the old lady, almost brought her to herself.

"Don't say so, Elizabeth! We'll hope it's not as bad as that; no, may the Lord spare us that, Elizabeth. Jack Rigley came just as I was sittin' down to a glass afore going to bed, an' 'e said: ' 'Appen you'll go down th' line, Mrs. Bates. Walt's had an accident. 'Appen you'll go an' sit wi' 'er till we can get him home.' I hadn't time to ask him a word afore he was gone. An' I put my bonnet on an' come straight down, Lizzie. I thought to myself: 'Eh, that poor blessed child, if anybody should come an' tell her of a sudden, ther's no knowin' what'll 'appen to 'er.' You mustn't let it upset you, Lizzie—or you know what to expect. How long is it, six months—or is it five, Lizzie? Ay!"—the old woman shook her head—"time slips on, it slips on! Ay!"

Elizabeth's thoughts were busy elsewhere. If he was killed—would she be able to manage on the little pension and what she could earn?—she counted up rapidly. If he was hurt—they wouldn't take him to the hospital—how tiresome he would be to nurse!—but perhaps she'd be able to get him away from the drink and his hateful ways. She would—while he was ill. The tears offered to come to her eyes at the picture. But what sentimental luxury was this she was beginning? She turned to consider the children. At any rate she was absolutely necessary for them. They were her business.

"Ay!" repeated the old woman, "it seems but a week or two since he brought me his first wages. Ay—he was a good lad, Elizabeth, he was, in his way. I don't know why he got to be such a trouble, I don't. He was a happy lad at home, only full of spirits. But there's no mistake he's been a handful of trouble, he has! I hope the Lord'll spare him to mend his ways. I hope so, I hope so. You've had a sight o' trouble with him, Elizabeth, you have indeed. But he was a jolly enough lad wi' me, he was, I can assure you. I don't know how it is. . . ."

The old woman continued to muse aloud, a monotonous irritating sound, while Elizabeth thought concentratedly, startled once, when she heard the winding engine chuff quickly, and the brakes skirr with a shriek. Then she heard the engine more slowly, and the brakes made no sound. The old woman did not notice. Elizabeth waited in suspense. The mother-in-law talked, with lapses into silence.

"But he wasn't your son, Lizzie, an' it makes a difference. Whatever he was, I remember him when he was little, an' I learned to understand him and to make allowances. You've got to make allowances for them——"

It was half-past ten, and the old woman was saying: "But it's trouble from beginning to end; you're never too old for trouble, never too old for that——" when the gate banged back, and there were heavy feet on the steps.

"I'll go, Lizzie, let me go," cried the old woman, rising. But Elizabeth was at the door. It was a man in pit clothes.

"They're bringin' 'im, Missis," he said. Elizabeth's heart halted a moment. Then it surged on again, almost suffocating her.

"Is he—is it bad?" she asked.

The man turned away, looking at the darkness:

"The doctor says 'e'd been dead hours. 'E saw 'im i' th' lamp-cabin."

The old woman, who stood just behind Elizabeth, dropped into a chair, and folded her hands, crying: "Oh, my boy, my boy!"

"Hush!" said Elizabeth, with a sharp twitch of a frown. "Be still, mother, don't waken th' children: I wouldn't have them down for anything!"

The old woman moaned softly, rocking herself. The man was drawing away. Elizabeth took a step forward.

"How was it?" she asked.

"Well, I couldn't say for sure," the man replied, very ill at ease. " 'E wor finishin' a stint an' th' butties 'ad gone, an' a lot o'stuff come down atop 'n 'im."

"And crushed him?" cried the widow, with a shudder.

"No," said the man, "it fell at th' back of 'im. 'E wor under th' face[4] an' it niver touched 'im. It shut 'im in. It seems 'e wor smothered."

Elizabeth shrank back. She heard the old woman behind her cry:

"What?—what did 'e say it was?"

The man replied, more loudly: " 'E wor smothered!"

Then the old woman wailed aloud, and this relieved Elizabeth.

"Oh, mother," she said, putting her hand on the old woman, "don't waken th' children, don't waken th' children."

She wept a little, unknowing, while the old mother rocked herself and

4. Coal face.

moaned. Elizabeth remembered that they were bringing him home, and she must be ready. "They'll lay him in the parlor," she said to herself, standing a moment pale and perplexed.

Then she lighted a candle and went into the tiny room. The air was cold and damp, but she could not make a fire, there was no fireplace. She set down the candle and looked round. The candlelight glittered on the luster-glasses, on the two vases that held some of the pink chrysanthemums, and on the dark mahogany. There was a cold, deathly smell of chrysanthemums in the room. Elizabeth stood looking at the flowers. She turned away, and calculated whether there would be room to lay him on the floor, between the couch and the chiffonier. She pushed the chairs aside. There would be room to lay him down and to step round him. Then she fetched the old red tablecloth, and another old cloth, spreading them down to save her bit of carpet. She shivered on leaving the parlor; so, from the dresser drawer she took a clean shirt and put it at the fire to air. All the time her mother-in-law was rocking herself in the chair and moaning.

"You'll have to move from there, mother," said Elizabeth. "They'll be bringing him in. Come in the rocker."

The old mother rose mechanically, and seated herself by the fire, continuing to lament. Elizabeth went into the pantry for another candle, and there, in the little penthouse under the naked tiles, she heard them coming. She stood still in the pantry doorway, listening. She heard them pass the end of the house, and come awkwardly down the three steps, a jumble of shuffling footsteps and muttering voices. The old woman was silent. The men were in the yard.

Then Elizabeth heard Matthews, the manager of the pit, say: "You go in first, Jim. Mind!"

The door came open, and the two women saw a collier backing into the room, holding one end of a stretcher, on which they could see the nailed pit boots of the dead man. The two carriers halted, the man at the head stooping to the lintel of the door.

"Wheer will you have him?" asked the manager, a short, white-bearded man.

Elizabeth roused herself and came from the pantry carrying the unlighted candle.

"In the parlor," she said.

"In there, Jim!" pointed the manager, and the carriers backed round into the tiny room. The coat with which they had covered the body fell off as they awkwardly turned through the two doorways, and the women saw their man, naked to the waist, lying stripped for work. The old woman began to moan in a low voice of horror.

"Lay th' stretcher at th' side," snapped the manager, "an' put 'im on th' cloths. Mind now, mind! Look you now——!"

One of the men had knocked off a vase of chrysanthemums. He stared awkwardly, then they set down the stretcher. Elizabeth did not look at her husband. As soon as she could get in the room, she went and picked up the broken vase and the flowers.

"Wait a minute!" she said.

The three men waited in silence while she mopped up the water with a duster.

"Eh, what a job, what a job, to be sure!" the manager was saying, rubbing his brow with trouble and perplexity. "Never knew such a thing in my life, never! He'd no business to ha' been left. I never knew such a thing in my life! Fell over him clean as a whistle, an' shut him in. Not four foot of space, there wasn't—yet it scarce bruised him."

He looked down at the dead man, lying prone, half naked, all grimed with coal dust.

"'Sphyxiated', the doctor said. It *is* the most terrible job I've ever known. Seems as if it was done o' purpose. Clean over him, an' shut 'im in, like a mouse-trap"—he made a sharp, descending gesture with his hand.

The colliers standing by jerked aside their heads in hopeless comment.

The horror of the thing bristled upon them all.

Then they heard the girl's voice upstairs calling shrilly: "Mother, mother—who is it? Mother, who is it?"

Elizabeth hurried to the foot of the stairs and opened the door:

"Go to sleep!" she commanded sharply. "What are you shouting about? Go to sleep at once—there's nothing——"

Then she began to mount the stairs. They could hear her on the boards, and on the plaster floor of the little bedroom. They could hear her distinctly:

"What's the matter now?—what's the matter with you, silly thing?"— her voice was much agitated, with an unreal gentleness.

"I thought it was some men come," said the plaintive voice of the child. "Has he come?"

"Yes, they've brought him. There's nothing to make a fuss about. Go to sleep now, like a good child."

They could hear her voice in the bedroom, they waited whilst she covered the children under the bedclothes.

"Is he drunk?" asked the girl, timidly, faintly.

"No! No—he's not! He—he's asleep."

"Is he asleep downstairs?"

"Yes—and don't make a noise."

There was silence for a moment, then the men heard the frightened child again:

"What's that noise?"

"It's nothing, I tell you, what are you bothering for?"

The noise was the grandmother moaning. She was oblivious of everything, sitting on her chair rocking and moaning. The manager put his hand on her arm and bade her "Sh—sh!"

The old woman opened her eyes and looked at him. She was shocked by this interruption, and seemed to wonder.

"What time is it?" the plaintive thin voice of the child, sinking back unhappily into sleep, asked this last question.

"Ten o'clock," answered the mother more softly. Then she must have bent down and kissed the children.

Matthews beckoned to the men to come away. They put on their caps and took up the stretcher. Stepping over the body, they tiptoed out of the house. None of them spoke till they were far from the wakeful children.

When Elizabeth came down she found her mother alone on the parlor floor, leaning over the dead man, the tears dropping on him.

"We must lay him out," the wife said. She put on the kettle, then returning knelt at the feet, and began to unfasten the knotted leather laces. The room was clammy and dim with only one candle, so that she had to bend her face almost to the floor. At last she got off the heavy boots and put them away.

"You must help me now," she whispered to the old woman. Together they stripped the man.

When they arose, saw him lying in the naïve dignity of death, the women stood arrested in fear and respect. For a few moments they remained still, looking down, the old mother whimpering. Elizabeth felt countermanded. She saw him, how utterly inviolable he lay in himself. She had nothing to do with him. She could not accept it. Stooping, she laid her hand on him, in claim. He was still warm, for the mine was hot where he had died. His mother had his face between her hands, and was murmuring incoherently. The old tears fell in succession as drops from wet leaves; the mother was not weeping, merely her tears flowed. Elizabeth embraced the body of her husband, with cheek and lips. She seemed to be listening, inquiring, trying to get some connection. But she could not. She was driven away. He was impregnable.

She rose, went into the kitchen, where she poured warm water into a bowl, brought soap and flannel and a soft towel. "I must wash him," she said.

Then the old mother rose stiffly, and watched Elizabeth as she carefully washed his face, carefully brushing his big blond moustache from his mouth with the flannel. She was afraid with a bottomless fear, so she ministered to him. The old woman, jealous, said:

"Let me wipe him!"—and she kneeled on the other side drying slowly as Elizabeth washed, her big black bonnet sometimes brushing the dark head of her daughter-in-law. They worked thus in silence for a long time. They never forgot it was death, and the touch of the man's dead body gave them strange emotions, different in each of the women; a great dread possessed them both, the mother felt the lie was given to her womb, she was denied; the wife felt the utter isolation of the human soul, the child within her was a weight apart from her.

At last it was finished. He was a man of handsome body, and his face showed no traces of drink. He was blond, full fleshed, with fine limbs. But he was dead.

"Bless him," whispered his mother, looking always at his face, and speaking out of sheer terror. "Dear lad—bless him!" She spoke in a faint, sibilant ecstasy of fear and mother love.

Elizabeth sank down again to the floor, and put her face against his neck, and trembled and shuddered. But she had to draw away again. He was dead, and her living flesh had no place against his. A great dread and weariness held her: she was so unavailing. Her life was gone like this.

"White as milk he is, clear as a twelve-month baby, bless him, the darling!" the old mother murmured to herself. "Not a mark on him, clear and clean and white, beautiful as ever a child was made," she murmured with pride. Elizabeth kept her face hidden.

"He went peaceful, Lizzie—peaceful as sleep. Isn't he beautiful, the lamb? Ay—he must ha' made his peace, Lizzie. 'Appen he made it all right, Lizzie, shut in there. He'd have time. He wouldn't look like this if he hadn't made his peace. The lamb, the dear lamb. Eh, but he had a hearty laugh. I loved to hear it. He had the heartiest laugh, Lizzie, as a lad——"

Elizabeth looked up. The man's mouth was fallen back, slightly open under the cover of the moustache. The eyes, half shut, did not show glazed in the obscurity. Life with its smoky burning gone from him, had left him apart and utterly alien to her. And she knew what a stranger he was to her. In her womb was ice of fear, because of this separate stranger with whom she had been living as one flesh. Was this what it all meant—utter, intact separateness, obscured by heat of living? In dread she turned her face away. The fact was too deadly. There had been nothing between them, and yet they had come together, exchanging their nakedness repeatedly. Each time he had taken her, they had been two isolated beings, far apart as now. He was no more responsible than she. The child was like ice in her womb. For as she looked at the dead man, her mind, cold and detached, said clearly: "Who am I? What have I been doing? I have been fighting a husband who did not exist. *He* existed all the time. What wrong have I done? What was that I have been living with? There lies the reality, this man." And her soul died in her for fear: she knew she had never seen him, he had never seen her, they had met in the dark and had fought in the dark, not knowing whom they met or whom they fought. And now she saw, and turned silent in seeing. For she had been wrong. She had said he was something he was not; she had felt familiar with him. Whereas he was apart all the while, living as she never lived, feeling as she never felt.

In fear and shame she looked at his naked body, that she had known falsely. And he was the father of her children. Her soul was torn from her body and stood apart. She looked at his naked body and was ashamed, as if she had denied it. After all, it was itself. It seemed awful to her. She looked at his face, and she turned her own face to the wall. For his look was other than hers, his way was not her way. She had denied him what he was—she saw it now. She had refused him as himself. And this had been her life, and his life. She was grateful to death, which restored the truth. And she knew she was not dead.

And all the while her heart was bursting with grief and pity for him. What had he suffered? What stretch of horror for this helpless man! She was rigid with agony. She had not been able to help him. He had been cruelly injured, this naked man, this other being, and she could make no reparation. There were the children—but the children belonged to life. This dead man had nothing to do with them. He and she were only channels through which life had flowed to issue in the children. She was a mother—but how awful she knew it now to have been a wife. And he, dead now, how awful he must have felt it to be a husband. She felt that in the next world he would be a stranger to her. If they met there, in the beyond, they would only be ashamed of what had been before. The children had come, for some mysterious reason, out of both of them. But the children did not unite them. Now he was dead, she knew how eternally he was apart from her, how eternally he had nothing more to do with her. She saw this episode of her life closed. They had denied each other in life. Now he had withdrawn. An anguish came over her. It was finished then: it had become hopeless between them long before he died. Yet he had been her husband. But how little!

"Have you got his shirt, 'Lizabeth?"

Elizabeth turned without answering, though she strove to weep and behave as her mother-in-law expected. But she could not, she was silenced. She went into the kitchen and returned with the garment.

"It is aired," she said, grasping the cotton shirt here and there to try. She was almost ashamed to handle him; what right had she or anyone to lay hands on him; but her touch was humble on his body. It was hard work to clothe him. He was so heavy and inert. A terrible dread gripped her all the while: that he could be so heavy and utterly inert, unresponsive, apart. The horror of the distance between them was almost too much for her— it was so infinite a gap she must look across.

At last it was finished. They covered him with a sheet and left him lying, with his face bound. And she fastened the door of the little parlor, lest the children should see what was lying there. Then, with peace sunk heavy on her heart, she went about making tidy the kitchen. She knew she submitted to life, which was her immediate master. But from death, her ultimate master, she winced with fear and shame.

TANIZAKI JUN'ICHIRŌ
1886–1965

It would be hard to find a novelist in modern Japan, or anywhere, whose career could rival in distinction and productivity that of Tanizaki Jun'ichirō. No other Japanese writer quite combines popular appeal, fecund imagination, and understanding of the historical moment with such a pitch-perfect style and deadly sense of humor. For all they delight the reader, these qualities are only the most striking in a grab bag of mischievous idiosyncrasies, which made Tanizaki, long before the publication of his last novel at the age of seventy-six, Japan's favorite literary curmudgeon. Many critics imply that he should have been Japan's first recipient of the Nobel Prize for literature, and his admirers may well regret that a mere three years after Tanizaki's death this distinction went to Kawabata Yasunari (p. 2033). With a life's work as rich as Tanizaki's, however, accolades seem irrelevant. Tanizaki built his own monument.

He was born into a merchant family in the heart of the old commercial quarter of Tokyo, where a trace of seventeenth- and eighteenth-century townsman customs still hung in the air like incense. Tanizaki's maternal grandfather was an old-style storekeeper whose printing shop saw the family through some lean times when Tanizaki's father proved an inept rice broker. The experiences and milieu of his childhood seem to have shaped the literary Tanizaki to a profound degree. His youthful world was an unstable mix of financial stringency and the cultured leisure of the secure, old-fashioned bourgeoisie. His mother, a noted beauty used to the comforts and established customs of a prosperous house, took him often to the traditional plays of the *kabuki* theater, whose open, straw-matted stalls and adjoining teahouses later made their way into his fiction. The plays that he watched from these timeworn stalls would have left a child wide-eyed with wonder, for *kabuki* appealed to its audiences through tangled plots and larger-than-life heroes and managed to blend a spectacular compound of drama, music, and dance with lavish costumes, revolving sets, and special effects, including everything from severed heads to fox spirits flying through the air.

His mother also took Tanizaki on outings by rickshaw to see the cherry blossoms and by train to visit the *shogun's* tomb in nearby Nikko. She would dress him in formal silk kimonos whose patterns, cuts, and fabrics were miniature models of the well turned out gentleman. He was taught to recognize fine hand-made paper and to select quality bean jam and other traditional sweets so that he could be dispatched when gift-wrapping or a delicacy was needed.

He learned the songs of the *geisha* houses at his father's knee. And like the children in *Child's Play* (p. 1560), he was allowed to roam through the byways of his downtown neighborhood. He discovered the many bookstores in the area, where he spent his allowance on adventure stories or tales of the *samurai*. On summer evenings, when amateur players gathered in the garden of the local shrine, he would slip out to watch them reenact famous ghost stories or the latest grisly murder.

On other evenings he would overhear his parents quarreling about money. Or he would go to his grandfather's house for a bath. The walk home in the dark seems to have stimulated his growing powers of imagination, in the same way that his parents' arguments exposed him to sexual tension. *Kabuki* theater and the bookshops drew him into the world of fiction, and the neighborhood plays on the shrine grounds were his introduction to violence and manipulation. All these threads—together with his training as an epicure and a tendency to idolize his beautiful, almost archaically cultured mother—would become major themes in his fiction.

So too would the world of darkness that Tanizaki has immortalized in his famous essay *In Praise of Shadows*. The dark held for him a fascination that, if his memoirs are to be believed, went back to his earliest years. He was drawn, for example, to the storehouse at the rear of his grandfather's compound.

> It was located in the farthest reaches of the property: to get to it, one had to pass through the little room where Grandmother sat all day before the brazier; then through a room with a formal alcove, which my uncle used as a study; then along a passage which led ultimately to a separate two-story building. There was usually no one about the storehouse except when something was being put into it, or taken out. For the most part, the place was perfectly quiet. I liked to sneak off there by myself and sit on the cold stone steps where no voices broke the silence and even the noise of the print shop was reduced to a dull and distant hum. I would press my face against the gleaming black double-doors, which were covered with wire netting and closed by a large padlock, and try to peer into the dark interior through the crack between them. I didn't know just what was hidden within, but there was a faint, elegant fragrance like aloes and musk mingled with the inevitable smell of damp and mold.*

These dark, musty depths held the promise of untold mysteries, and they were linked in Tanizaki's mind with relics of the old Japan.

* Paul McCarthy, trans., *Childhood Years* (1988).

As a young adult Tanizaki shed (temporarily) this childhood fascination, a not uncommon pattern among those young enough to want to rid themselves of youth. He set himself up as a writer of "demonic" fiction, as critics called it: historical tales of sexual obsession and sadomasochism, and stories of what might be called Japan's own version of a "lost generation," pursuing its debauches in the new, modern age. When financial success came, he ensconced his wife and daughter in a house as different from the houses of his youth as it is possible to imagine. He moved to Yokohama, the new port city south of Tokyo where foreigners gathered and where he went to work writing screenplays for one of the new motion picture studios. There he bought a Western-style house in the thick of the foreign settlement in the Bluff area, overlooking the city. It was a swank residence that came equipped with electricity and glass windows as well as the furniture and cook of its former British owners. And there he engaged, to use the words with which he describes one of his fictional characters, "in foreign tastes of the most hair-raising variety." Western foods like roast turkey and kidney pie became staples. He took to wearing brown suits and playing the guitar. He boasted that he went entire days without removing his shoes (violating the Japanese custom). He and his wife embraced "social dancing" and gravitated to the bright lights of the foreigners' Christmas balls and New Year's fêtes as moths flying to the flame.

But the dancing stopped when a massive earthquake ripped through the Tokyo-Yokohama area on September 1, 1923. Tanizaki was vacationing in a mountain resort southwest of the epicenter, and his first reaction was a perverse flood of joy. "Good," he later describes himself as thinking. "Now Tokyo will become a decent place!" The old had been leveled, and the new city would be a shiny metropolis of horns and headlights, champagne and high-rises, Turkish baths and showgirls irradiated in the glare of footlights.

In anticipation of this exciting new city, Tanizaki moved temporarily to the Kyoto-Osaka region, hub of the old Japan, where polite classical tradition and antiquated merchant culture merged at a relatively safe remove from the onslaught of the West. Once he had relocated, Tanizaki began to reconsider his youthful enthusiasms. No doubt he was affected by the more conservative environment, for a process now began in which his own, and Japan's, infatuation with the West came into sociological and historical focus.

His first major work, A Fool's Love (1924), portrays his compatriots in the grip of a national obsession. The hero, the fool of the title who narrates the novel and is clearly intended to serve as an emblematic figure, is a country bumpkin new to the big city and riding the escalator of upward mobility. His profession as an electrical engineer, his uncritical admiration of all things European, and even his name Jōji, which can quickly elide into what sounds like the Japanese pronunciation of "George," place him in the vanguard of modernization. When Jōji meets a bar girl, Naomi, who reminds him of the movie star Mary Pickford, he sees in her the key to his dream of a modern, American sort of life unfettered by Japanese conventions. He installs her in a stylish Western house (not unlike Tanizaki's) and proceeds to squander his savings on piano lessons and Paris fashions. The more Naomi succeeds in replicating the look of an American flapper, the nastier and more demanding she becomes and the more seductive to the masochistic Jōji, who, in cutting himself off from his own past, has surrendered his inherited sense of virtue and, with it, self-worth. He is increasingly unhinged in his confusion of eros with the West. By the end of the book, when his wife has taken a succession of foreign lovers, relegating Jōji to the role of houseboy with occasional privileges, he views this shucking of convention as yet another triumph of modern sophistication. In his fool's mind the material attractions of another culture are mistaken for sexual allure, or perhaps more accurately, the two have fused into an impossible muddle: the novel's metaphor for Japan's modern plight. It is not the West per se that Tanizaki objects to, but the West as it is appropriated and misperceived by the Japanese, objectified and turned into a fetish. The entire nation, he says, is in the throes of a fatal attraction, a predicament entirely of its own making.

It was at this juncture that Tanizaki wrote *In Praise of Shadows*. One might characterize the piece as an essay on aesthetics, and indeed Tanizaki is as learned and rigorous an aesthete as they come. He would devote many years to rendering *The Tale of Genji* (in Volume 1) into modern Japanese. On three separate occasions he produced a translation of this thousand-page classical novel, sinking himself into the courtly world of the eleventh century and reemerging each time with a work of brilliant erudition, impressive for the affinity it displayed for the sensibility of a remote and, to current Japanese readers, alien society. He would also write a considerable body of historical fiction, which, though highly imaginative, demonstrates his love of the arcana of historical scholarship. On almost every page of the essay, this learning is evident. So is the discriminating, antiquarian taste of the serious aesthete. The author of *In Praise of Shadows*, very much his mother's son, is disappointed when the sliding doors of his new house fail to provide a "mellow softness" or when a moon-viewing party must be canceled lest a recording of "Moonlight Sonata" break the spell.

Yet it would be a serious mistake to read this work solely as a tract on aesthetics. If it is an eloquent and deeply felt paean to the past and to the tastes that are formed by tradition, it is also an argument for reconsidering how far one ought to go in remaking oneself in another's image. Tanizaki had by now recovered a respect for the past as a meaningful, ultimately inescapable component of our lives, however detached they may seem from what has gone before. He had come to appreciate that one cannot discard the cultural legacy one has inherited without in the process ending up empty: a fool. He chooses architecture as his figure of speech, but when he describes what Japanese houses were like before electric lights and telephones he is talking about the whole of Japanese culture.

In Praise of Shadows has been called perverse. It is certainly idiosyncratic. Virtually everything Tanizaki wrote shows a playful sense of humor, and this essay, for all its seriousness, is no exception. When Tanizaki tells us "the Japanese toilet truly is a place of spiritual repose," even in overcrowded Japan one may assume that the tongue is firmly planted in the cheek. His portrait of Japanese womanhood is also skewed in a peculiarly Tanizakian fashion. It is not that what he says about traditional Japanese standards of feminine beauty is incorrect or exaggerated. Rather, the master storyteller cannot help selecting his words in such a way that the evocation romanticizes women into an ethereal and mysterious composite. He may be criticized for this, and indeed his entire work, repeatedly addressing male desire for a transcendent female, is a ripe target for feminist criticism. Likewise, Tanizaki's fascination with skin color may offend those who misread his blunt language as racism, when in fact his motives are the very opposite: to embrace difference and to insist, even as he overstates, that distinctions—and distance—be allowed to stand. To deprive Tanizaki of his chosen material, especially when he is the first to acknowledge the manipulative aspects of both craft and obsession, would inevitably impoverish an extravagant art. Japan itself, for that matter, and the weight of its traditions have to a certain extent been exoticized by Tanizaki. One could argue that it is all part of a rhetorical strategy.

The vagrant structure of the essay, too, may seem unorthodox. What does Einstein's trip to Japan have to do with it, one might ask. Tanizaki surely does wander, from jade to temples to *sushi* to makeup. The links are sometimes tenuous, and just as we catch the drift of things Tanizaki is apt to circle back to an earlier theme. Yet for all it lacks in logical progression, *In Praise of Shadows* is a modern example of a hallowed Japanese literary tradition: a twentieth-century version of the discursive essays known as *zuihitsu* that were first practiced by Sei Shōnagon in *The*

Pillow Book and Yoshida Kenkō in *Essays in Idleness* (both in Volume 1). Tanizaki breaks no new ground when he "follows the brush" (or more likely the fountain pen), unconcerned with contriving a structure. But steeped as he was in the Japanese classics, Tanizaki knew intuitively that an essay on the vicissitudes of Japan's pursuit of the West is most effectively expressed in a genre whose very form conveys uncertainty.

Tanizaki's complete works run to twenty-eight volumes, of which *In Praise of Shadows* is but a tantalizing sample. Altogether, he wrote in an amazing variety of forms: novels, short stories, plays, poetry, movie scripts, essays, criticism, and translations. But his major works all configure themselves around a handful of recurring themes. The world as Tanizaki sees it is composed of worlds constructed. Jōji in *A Fool's Love* tries to build a world that will have the glamour of an American movie and, therefore, freedom from Japanese propriety. The protagonist of Tanizaki's next major novel, *Some Prefer Nettles* (1928–29), written shortly before *In Praise of Shadows*, finds himself drawn like Tanizaki toward the old Japan, away from foreign fads. He observes his father-in-law cultivating a life of obsolete practices, and he begins to understand their attraction for the old man, and thus their reality.

During World War II, Tanizaki sought escape in the writing of an extended novel of manners, *The Makioka Sisters* (1943–48). Ostensibly, it tells the story of a declining merchant family's frustrated attempts to secure a husband for one of the younger sisters. The bulk of the long novel, however, details the efforts of the four sisters to stage a life for themselves in mimicry of prouder days. Even as he wrote, the progress of the war ensured that his novel would be an elegy, and Tanizaki must have known that this leisurely world of bourgeois elegance he had called into being one last time was in every way now a fiction.

Fiction, manipulation, constructed or imagined worlds, obsession, and desire also mark Tanizaki's postwar novels. *The Key* (1956) chronicles the sexual fantasies of an aging professor and his wife, told through the medium of their two diaries. They each pretend their diaries are a secret, knowing full well that they write only to be read and to goad the other into a greater sexual frenzy. Writing becomes deceit, and deceit the father of reality. *Diary of a Mad Old Man* (1961–62), the last completed novel from a writer still vigorous in his seventies, records a geriatric urge to satisfy sexual appetites only slightly diminished by age. Before death can defeat him, the septuagenarian concocts elaborate scenarios that allow him to neck with his daughter-in-law or to fondle her lithesome feet. It is no accident that in both of these final works Western consumer goods—Courvoisier, mascara, Polaroid cameras—serve as exotic stimulants, the passport into a world of dreams.

With a wicked sense of humor and an almost religious faith in the power of imagination, Tanizaki knew precisely what he was up to. As his apotheosis of the common privy, so full of delectable hyperbole, amply demonstrates, he was a supremely ironic writer. He was also intensely self-aware. Unlike most of his characters, he understood his need to fashion fictional worlds. And in fact, when—some years after he published *In Praise of Shadows*—an architect he had hired told him, "I've read your essay and I know exactly what you want," Tanizaki is reported to have answered, "No, no. I could never *live* in a house like that."

Tanizaki has been well served in translation. *A Fool's Love* is available in English as *Naomi* (1985), Anthony H. Chambers, trans. Chambers has also translated two novellas in one volume: *The Secret History of Lord Musashi and Arrowroot* (1982). Also in English are Edward G. Seidensticker, trans., *Some Prefer Nettles* (1955) and *The Makioka Sisters* (1957), and Howard Hibbett, trans., *The Key* (1961) and *Diary of a Mad Old Man* (1965). Hibbett, trans., *Seven Japanese Tales* (1963), is a collection of short stories that includes *The Tattooer*, the story that established Tanizaki's reputation, and *A Portrait of Shunkin*, one of his most celebrated works. Also recommended are Paul McCarthy, trans., *A Cat, a Man and Two Women* (1990) and *Childhood Years* (1988), Tanizaki's memoir. Ken K. Ito, *Visions of Desire: Tanizaki's Fictional Worlds* (1991), is an excellent study, and Donald Keene, *Dawn to the West* (1984), a history of modern Japanese literature, has a substantial chapter on Tanizaki.

The following list uses common English syllables to provide rough equivalents of selected words whose pronunciation may be unfamiliar to the general reader.

Baikō: *bai-koh*

Bunraku: *boon-rah-koo*

Chion'in: *chee-ohn-een*

Hiei: *hee-ay*

Higashiyama: *hee-gah-shee-yah-mah*

Honganji: *hohn-gahn-jee*

Jōji: *joh-jee*

Kairakuen: *kai-rah-koo-en*

Kongo Iwao: *kohn-goh ee-wah-oh*

kotei: *koh-tay*

Kurodani: *koo-roh-dah-nee*

Meiji: *may-jee*

Miyako: *mee-yah-koh*

Natsume Sōseki: *nah-tsoo-me soh-se-kee*

Nyoigatake: *nyoh-ee-gah-tah-kay*

Onoe: *oh-noh-ay*

Saitō Ryoku: *sai-toh ryoh-koo*

Sei Shōnagon: *say shoh-nah-gohn*

shōji: *shoh-jee*

Tanizaki Jun'ichirō: *tah-nee-zah-kee joon-ee-chee-roh*

Waranjiya: *wah-rahn-jee-yah*

Yamamoto Sanehiko: *yah-mah-moh-toh sah-ne-hee-koh*

Yoshida Kenkō: *yoh-shee-dah ken-koh*

zuihitsu: *zoo-ee-hee-tsoo*

In Praise of Shadows[1]

What incredible pains the fancier of traditional architecture must take when he sets out to build a house in pure Japanese style, striving somehow to make electric wires, gas pipes, and water lines harmonize with the austerity of Japanese rooms—even someone who has never built a house for himself must sense this when he visits a teahouse, a restaurant, or an inn. For the solitary eccentric it is another matter; he can ignore the blessings of scientific civilization and retreat to some forsaken corner of the countryside; but a man who has a family and lives in the city cannot turn his back on the necessities of modern life—heating, electric lights, sanitary facilities—merely for the sake of doing things the Japanese way. The purist may rack his brain over the placement of a single telephone, hiding it behind the staircase or in a corner of the hallway, wherever he thinks it will least offend the eye. He may bury the wires rather than hang them in the garden, hide the switches in a closet or cupboard, run the cords behind a folding screen. Yet for all his ingenuity, his efforts often impress us as nervous, fussy, excessively contrived. For so accustomed are we to electric

---

1. Translated by Thomas J. Harper and Edward G. Seidensticker.

lights that the sight of a naked bulb beneath an ordinary milk glass[2] shade seems simpler and more natural than any gratuitous attempt to hide it. Seen at dusk as one gazes out upon the countryside from the window of a train, the lonely light of a bulb under an old-fashioned shade, shining dimly from behind the white paper shoji[3] of a thatch-roofed farmhouse, can seem positively elegant.

But the snarl and the bulk of an electric fan remain a bit out of place in a Japanese room. The ordinary householder, if he dislikes electric fans, can simply do without them. But if the family business involves the entertainment of customers in summertime, the gentleman of the house cannot afford to indulge his own tastes at the expense of others. A friend of mine, the proprietor of a Chinese restaurant called the Kairakuen, is a thoroughgoing purist in matters architectural. He deplores electric fans and long refused to have them in his restaurant, but the complaints from customers with which he was faced every summer ultimately forced him to give in.

I myself have had similar experiences. A few years ago I spent a great deal more money than I could afford to build a house. I fussed over every last fitting and fixture, and in every case encountered difficulty. There was the shoji: for aesthetic reasons I did not want to use glass, and yet paper alone would have posed problems of illumination and security. Much against my will, I decided to cover the inside with paper and the outside with glass. This required a double frame, thus raising the cost. Yet having gone to all this trouble, the effect was far from pleasing. The outside remained no more than a glass door; while within, the mellow softness of the paper was destroyed by the glass that lay behind it. At that point I was sorry I had not just settled for glass to begin with. Yet laugh though we may when the house is someone else's, we ourselves accept defeat only after having a try at such schemes.

Then there was the problem of lighting. In recent years several fixtures designed for Japanese houses have come on the market, fixtures patterned after old floor lamps, ceiling lights, candle stands, and the like. But I simply do not care for them, and instead searched in curio shops for old lamps, which I fitted with electric light bulbs.

What most taxed my ingenuity was the heating system. No stove[4] worthy of the name will ever look right in a Japanese room. Gas stoves burn with a terrific roar, and unless provided with a chimney, quickly bring headaches. Electric stoves, though at least free from these defects, are every bit as ugly as the rest. One solution would be to outfit the cupboards with heaters of the sort used in streetcars. Yet without the red glow of the coals, the whole mood of winter is lost and with it the pleasure of family gatherings round the fire. The best plan I could devise was to build a large sunken hearth, as in an old farmhouse. In this I installed an electric brazier, which worked well both for boiling tea water and for heating the room. Expensive it was, but at least so far as looks were concerned I counted it one of my successes.

Having done passably well with the heating system, I was then faced

---

2. Opaque, milky white glass.   3. Sliding doors constructed of a wooden frame and grid covered with translucent paper, or sometimes glass.   4. Used as a space heater.

with the problem of bath and toilet. My Kairakuen friend could not bear to tile the tub and bathing area, and so built his guest bath entirely of wood. Tile, of course, is infinitely more practical and economical. But when ceiling, pillars, and paneling are of fine Japanese stock, the beauty of the room is utterly destroyed when the rest is done in sparkling tile. The effect may not seem so very displeasing while everything is still new, but as the years pass, and the beauty of the grain begins to emerge on the planks and pillars, that glittering expanse of white tile comes to seem as incongruous as the proverbial bamboo grafted to wood.[5] Still, in the bath utility can to some extent be sacrificed to good taste. In the toilet somewhat more vexatious problems arise.[6]

Every time I am shown to an old, dimly lit, and, I would add, impeccably clean toilet in a Nara or Kyoto[7] temple, I am impressed with the singular virtues of Japanese architecture. The parlor may have its charms, but the Japanese toilet truly is a place of spiritual repose. It always stands apart from the main building, at the end of a corridor, in a grove fragrant with leaves and moss. No words can describe that sensation as one sits in the dim light, basking in the faint glow reflected from the shoji, lost in meditation or gazing out at the garden. The novelist Natsume Sōseki[8] counted his morning trips to the toilet a great pleasure, "a physiological delight" he called it. And surely there could be no better place to savor this pleasure than a Japanese toilet where, surrounded by tranquil walls and finely grained wood, one looks out upon blue skies and green leaves.

As I have said there are certain prerequisites: a degree of dimness, absolute cleanliness, and quiet so complete one can hear the hum of a mosquito. I love to listen from such a toilet to the sound of softly falling rain, especially if it is a toilet of the Kantō[9] region, with its long, narrow windows at floor level; there one can listen with such a sense of intimacy to the raindrops falling from the eaves and the trees, seeping into the earth as they wash over the base of a stone lantern and freshen the moss about the stepping stones. And the toilet is the perfect place to listen to the chirping of insects or the song of the birds, to view the moon, or to enjoy any of those poignant moments that mark the change of the seasons. Here, I suspect, is where haiku[1] poets over the ages have come by a great many of their ideas. Indeed one could with some justice claim that of all the elements of Japanese architecture, the toilet is the most aesthetic. Our forebears, making poetry of everything in their lives, transformed what by rights should be the most unsanitary room in the house into a place of unsurpassed elegance, replete with fond associations with the beauties of nature. Compared to Westerners, who regard the toilet as utterly unclean and avoid even the mention of it in polite conversation, we are far more sensible and certainly in better taste. The Japanese toilet is, I must admit, a bit inconvenient to get to in the middle of the night, set apart from the

5. That is, putting together two types of material that are not compatible.   6. In the traditional Japanese house the bath and toilet are in separate rooms.   7. Former capitals of Japan, where temples retain their original architectural style.   8. Generally considered by the Japanese to be their greatest 20th-century novelist (1867–1916).   9. Located in the east-central portion of the main island of Japan, which includes Tokyo. Traditional architectural style there differed slightly from that in the older region of Nara, Kyoto, and Osaka to the west.   1. See the headnote "Matsuo Bashō" (p. 608) for a discussion of *haiku*.

main building as it is; and in winter there is always a danger that one might catch cold. But as the poet Saitō Ryokū[2] has said, "elegance is frigid." Better that the place be as chilly as the out-of-doors; the steamy heat of a Western-style toilet in a hotel is most unpleasant.

Anyone with a taste for traditional architecture must agree that the Japanese toilet is perfection. Yet whatever its virtues in a place like a temple, where the dwelling is large, the inhabitants few, and everyone helps with the cleaning, in an ordinary household it is no easy task to keep it clean. No matter how fastidious one may be or how diligently one may scrub, dirt will show, particularly on a floor of wood or tatami matting. And so here too it turns out to be more hygienic and efficient to install modern sanitary facilities—tile and a flush toilet—though at the price of destroying all affinity with "good taste" and the "beauties of nature." That burst of light from those four white walls hardly puts one in a mood to relish Sōseki's "physiological delight." There is no denying the cleanliness; every nook and corner is pure white. Yet what need is there to remind us so forcefully of the issue of our own bodies. A beautiful woman, no matter how lovely her skin, would be considered indecent were she to show her bare buttocks or feet in the presence of others; and how very crude and tasteless to expose the toilet to such excessive illumination. The cleanliness of what can be seen only calls up the more clearly thoughts of what cannot be seen. In such places the distinction between the clean and the unclean is best left obscure, shrouded in a dusky haze.

Though I did install modern sanitary facilities when I built my own house, I at least avoided tiles, and had the floor done in camphor wood. To that extent I tried to create a Japanese atmosphere—but was frustrated finally by the toilet fixtures themselves. As everyone knows, flush toilets are made of pure white porcelain and have handles of sparkling metal. Were I able to have things my own way, I would much prefer fixtures—both men's and women's—made of wood. Wood finished in glistening black lacquer is the very best; but even unfinished wood, as it darkens and the grain grows more subtle with the years, acquires an inexplicable power to calm and sooth. The ultimate, of course, is a wooden "morning glory" urinal[3] filled with boughs of cedar; this is a delight to look at and allows not the slightest sound. I could not afford to indulge in such extravagances. I hoped I might at least have the external fittings made to suit my own taste, and then adapt these to a standard flushing mechanism. But the custom labor would have cost so much that I had no choice but to abandon the idea. It was not that I objected to the conveniences of modern civilization, whether electric lights or heating or toilets, but I did wonder at the time why they could not be designed with a bit more consideration for our own habits and tastes.

The recent vogue for electric lamps in the style of the old standing lanterns comes, I think, from a new awareness of the softness and warmth of paper, qualities which for a time we had forgotten; it stands as evidence of our

---

2. He also wrote satirical essays and comic fiction and compiled the first collected edition of Higuchi Ichiyō's works.   3. That is, in the shape of a morning glory flower.

recognition that this material is far better suited than glass to the Japanese house. But no toilet fixtures or stoves that are at all tasteful have yet come on the market. A heating system like my own, an electric brazier in a sunken hearth, seems to me ideal; yet no one ventures to produce even so simple a device as this (there are, of course, those feeble electric hibachi,[4] but they provide no more heat than an ordinary charcoal hibachi); all that can be had ready-made are those ugly Western stoves.

There are those who hold that to quibble over matters of taste in the basic necessities of life is an extravagance, that as long as a house keeps out the cold and as long as food keeps off starvation, it matters little what they look like. And indeed for even the sternest ascetic the fact remains that a snowy day is cold, and there is no denying the impulse to accept the services of a heater if it happens to be there in front of one, no matter how cruelly its inelegance may shatter the spell of the day. But it is on occasions like this that I always think how different everything would be if we in the Orient had developed our own science. Suppose for instance that we had developed our own physics and chemistry: would not the techniques and industries based on them have taken a different form, would not our myriads of everyday gadgets, our medicines, the products of our industrial art—would they not have suited our national temper better than they do? In fact our conception of physics itself, and even the principles of chemistry, would probably differ from that of Westerners; and the facts we are now taught concerning the nature and function of light, electricity, and atoms might well have presented themselves in different form.

Of course I am only indulging in idle speculation; of scientific matters I know nothing. But had we devised independently at least the more practical sorts of inventions, this could not but have had profound influence upon the conduct of our everyday lives, and even upon government, religion, art, and business. The Orient quite conceivably could have opened up a world of technology entirely its own.

To take a trivial example near at hand: I wrote a magazine article recently comparing the writing brush with the fountain pen, and in the course of it I remarked that if the device had been invented by the ancient Chinese or Japanese it would surely have had a tufted end like our writing brush. The ink would not have been this bluish color but rather black, something like India ink, and it would have been made to seep down from the handle into the brush. And since we would have then found it inconvenient to write on Western paper, something near Japanese paper—even under mass production, if you will—would have been most in demand. Foreign ink and pen would not be as popular as they are; the talk of discarding our system of writing for Roman letters would be less noisy; people would still feel an affection for the old system. But more than that: our thought and our literature might not be imitating the West as they are, but might have pushed forward into new regions quite on their own. An insignificant little piece of writing equipment, when one thinks of it, has had a vast, almost boundless, influence on our culture.

---

4. A metal or porcelain brazier originally containing live coals and used to heat a room.

But I know as well as anyone that these are the empty dreams of a novelist, and that having come this far we cannot turn back. I know that I am only grumbling to myself and demanding the impossible. If my complaints are taken for what they are, however, there can be no harm in considering how unlucky we have been, what losses we have suffered, in comparison with the Westerner. The Westerner has been able to move forward in ordered steps, while we have met superior civilization and have had to surrender to it, and we have had to leave a road we have followed for thousands of years. The missteps and inconveniences this has caused have, I think, been many. If we had been left alone we might not be much further now in a material way than we were five hundred years ago. Even now in the Indian and Chinese countryside life no doubt goes on much as it did when Buddha and Confucius were alive. But we would have gone only in a direction that suited us. We would have gone ahead very slowly, and yet it is not impossible that we would one day have discovered our own substitute for the trolley, the radio, the airplane of today. They would have been no borrowed gadgets, they would have been the tools of our own culture, suited to us.

One need only compare American, French, and German films to see how greatly nuances of shading and coloration can vary in motion pictures. In the photographic image itself, to say nothing of the acting and the script, there somehow emerge differences in national character. If this is true even when identical equipment, chemicals, and film are used, how much better our own photographic technology might have suited our complexion, our facial features, our climate, our land. And had we invented the phonograph and the radio, how much more faithfully they would reproduce the special character of our voices and our music. Japanese music is above all a music of reticence, of atmosphere. When recorded, or amplified by a loudspeaker, the greater part of its charm is lost. In conversation, too, we prefer the soft voice, the understatement. Most important of all are the pauses. Yet the phonograph and radio render these moments of silence utterly lifeless. And so we distort the arts themselves to curry favor for them with the machines. These machines are the inventions of Westerners, and are, as we might expect, well suited to the Western arts. But precisely on this account they put our own arts at a great disadvantage.

Paper, I understand, was invented by the Chinese; but Western paper is to us no more than something to be used, while the texture of Chinese paper and Japanese paper gives us a certain feeling of warmth, of calm and repose. Even the same white could as well be one color for Western paper and another for our own. Western paper turns away the light, while our paper seems to take it in, to envelop it gently, like the soft surface of a first snowfall. It gives off no sound when it is crumpled or folded, it is quiet and pliant to the touch as the leaf of a tree.

As a general matter we find it hard to be really at home with things that shine and glitter. The Westerner uses silver and steel and nickel tableware, and polishes it to a fine brilliance, but we object to the practice. While we do sometimes indeed use silver for teakettles, decanters, or saké[5] cups, we prefer not to polish it. On the contrary, we begin to enjoy it only when the luster has worn off, when it has begun to take on a dark, smoky patina. Almost every householder has had to scold an insensitive maid who has polished away the tarnish so patiently waited for.

Chinese food is now most often served on tableware made of tin, a material the Chinese could only admire for the patina it acquires. When new it resembles aluminum and is not particularly attractive; only after long use brings some of the elegance of age is it at all acceptable. Then, as the surface darkens, the line of verse etched upon it gives a final touch of perfection. In the hands of the Chinese this flimsy, glittering metal takes on a profound and somber dignity akin to that of their red unglazed pottery.

The Chinese also love jade. That strange lump of stone with its faintly muddy light, like the crystallized air of the centuries, melting dimly, dully back, deeper and deeper—are not we Orientals the only ones who know its charms? We cannot say ourselves what it is that we find in this stone. It quite lacks the brightness of a ruby or an emerald or the glitter of a diamond. But this much we can say: when we see that shadowy surface, we think how Chinese it is, we seem to find in its cloudiness the accumulation of the long Chinese past, we think how appropriate it is that the Chinese should admire that surface and that shadow.

It is the same with crystals. Crystals have recently been imported in large quantities from Chile, but Chilean crystals are too bright, too clear. We have long had crystals of our own, their clearness always moderated, made graver by a certain cloudiness. Indeed, we much prefer the "impure" varieties of crystal with opaque veins crossing their depths. Even of glass this is true; for is not fine Chinese glass closer to jade or agate than to Western glass? Glassmaking has long been known in the Orient, but the craft never developed as in the West. Great progress has been made, however, in the manufacture of pottery. Surely this has something to do with our national character. We do not dislike everything that shines, but we do prefer a pensive luster to a shallow brilliance, a murky light that, whether in a stone or an artifact, bespeaks a sheen of antiquity.

Of course this "sheen of antiquity" of which we hear so much is in fact the glow of grime. In both Chinese and Japanese the words denoting this glow describe a polish that comes of being touched over and over again, a sheen produced by the oils that naturally permeate an object over long years of handling—which is to say grime. If indeed "elegance is frigid," it can as well be described as filthy. There is no denying, at any rate, that among the elements of the elegance in which we take such delight is a measure of the unclean, the unsanitary. I suppose I shall sound terribly defensive if I say that Westerners attempt to expose every speck of grime and eradicate it, while we Orientals carefully preserve and even idealize it. Yet for better or for worse we do love things that bear the marks of grime, soot, and weather, and we love the colors and the sheen that call

5. Japanese rice wine.

to mind the past that made them. Living in these old houses among these old objects is in some mysterious way a source of peace and repose.

I have always thought that hospitals, those for the Japanese at any rate, need not be so sparkling white, that the walls, uniforms, and equipment might better be done in softer, more muted colors. Certainly the patients would be more reposed where they are able to lie on tatami[6] matting surrounded by the sand-colored walls of a Japanese room. One reason we hate to go to the dentist is the scream of his drill; but the excessive glitter of glass and metal is equally intimidating. At a time when I was suffering from a severe nervous disorder, a dentist was recommended to me as having just returned from America with the latest equipment, but these tidings only made my hair stand on end. I chose instead to go to an old-fashioned dentist who maintained an office in an old Japanese house, a dentist of the sort found in small country towns. Antiquated medical equipment does have its drawbacks; but had modern medicine been developed in Japan we probably would have devised facilities and equipment for the treatment of the sick that would somehow harmonize with Japanese architecture. Here again we have to come off the loser for having borrowed.

There is a famous restaurant in Kyoto, the Waranjiya, one of the attractions of which was until recently that the dining rooms were lit by candlelight rather than electricity; but when I went there this spring after a long absence, the candles had been replaced by electric lamps in the style of old lanterns. I asked when this had happened, and was told that the change had taken place last year; several of their customers had complained that candlelight was too dim, and so they had been left no choice—but if I preferred the old way they should be happy to bring me a candlestand. Since that was what I had come for, I asked them to do so. And I realized then that only in dim half-light is the true beauty of Japanese lacquerware revealed. The rooms at the Waranjiya are about nine feet square, the size of a comfortable little tearoom, and the alcove pillars and ceilings glow with a faint smoky luster, dark even in the light of the lamp. But in the still dimmer light of the candlestand, as I gazed at the trays and bowls standing in the shadows cast by that flickering point of flame, I discovered in the gloss of this lacquerware a depth and richness like that of a still, dark pond, a beauty I had not before seen. It had not been mere chance, I realized, that our ancestors, having discovered lacquer, had conceived such a fondness for objects finished in it.

An Indian friend once told me that in his country ceramic tableware is still looked down upon, and that lacquerware is in far wider use. We, however, use ceramics for practically everything but trays and soup bowls; lacquerware, except in the tea ceremony and on formal occasions, is considered vulgar and inelegant. This, I suspect, is in part the fault of the much-vaunted "brilliance" of modern electric lighting. Darkness is an

---

6. Modular straw mats measuring approximately six by three feet, the customary flooring for a traditional Japanese room. (Wood was used for corridors.) The patients would be lying on bedding called *futon* placed directly on the floor.

indispensable element of the beauty of lacquerware. Nowadays they make even a white lacquer, but the lacquerware of the past was finished in black, brown, or red, colors built up of countless layers of darkness, the inevitable product of the darkness in which life was lived. Sometimes a superb piece of black lacquerware, decorated perhaps with flecks of silver and gold—a box or a desk or a set of shelves—will seem to me unsettlingly garish and altogether vulgar. But render pitch black the void in which they stand, and light them not with the rays of the sun or electricity but rather a single lantern or candle: suddenly those garish objects turn somber, refined, dignified. Artisans of old, when they finished their works in lacquer and decorated them in sparkling patterns, must surely have had in mind dark rooms and sought to turn to good effect what feeble light there was. Their extravagant use of gold, too, I should imagine, came of understanding how it gleams forth from out of the darkness and reflects the lamplight.

Lacquerware decorated in gold is not something to be seen in a brilliant light, to be taken in at a single glance; it should be left in the dark, a part here and a part there picked up by a faint light. Its florid patterns recede into the darkness, conjuring in their stead an inexpressible aura of depth and mystery, of overtones but partly suggested. The sheen of the lacquer, set out in the night, reflects the wavering candlelight, announcing the drafts that find their way from time to time into the quiet room, luring one into a state of reverie. If the lacquer is taken away, much of the spell disappears from the dream world built by that strange light of candle and lamp, that wavering light beating the pulse of the night. Indeed the thin, impalpable, faltering light, picked up as though little rivers were running through the room, collecting little pools here and there, lacquers a pattern on the surface of the night itself.

Ceramics are by no means inadequate as tableware, but they lack the shadows, the depth of lacquerware. Ceramics are heavy and cold to the touch; they clatter and clink, and being efficient conductors of heat are not the best containers for hot foods. But lacquerware is light and soft to the touch, and gives off hardly a sound. I know few greater pleasures than holding a lacquer soup bowl in my hands, feeling upon my palms the weight of the liquid and its mild warmth. The sensation is something like that of holding a plump newborn baby. There are good reasons why lacquer soup bowls are still used, qualities which ceramic bowls simply do not possess. Remove the lid from a ceramic bowl, and there lies the soup, every nuance of its substance and color revealed. With lacquerware there is a beauty in that moment between removing the lid and lifting the bowl to the mouth when one gazes at the still, silent liquid in the dark depths of the bowl, its color hardly differing from that of the bowl itself. What lies within the darkness one cannot distinguish, but the palm senses the gentle movements of the liquid, vapor rises from within forming droplets on the rim, and the fragrance carried upon the vapor brings a delicate anticipation. What a world of difference there is between this moment and the moment when soup is served Western style, in a pale, shallow bowl. A moment of mystery, it might almost be called, a moment of trance.

Whenever I sit with a bowl of soup before me, listening to the murmur that penetrates like the far-off shrill of an insect, lost in contemplation of flavors to come, I feel as if I were being drawn into a trance. The experience must be something like that of the tea master who, at the sound of the kettle, is taken from himself as if upon the sigh of the wind in the legendary pines of Onoe.[7]

It has been said of Japanese food that it is a cuisine to be looked at rather than eaten. I would go further and say that it is to be meditated upon, a kind of silent music evoked by the combination of lacquerware and the light of a candle flickering in the dark. Natsume Sōseki, in *Pillow of Grass*, praises the color of the confection yōkan;[8] and is it not indeed a color to call forth meditation? The cloudy translucence, like that of jade; the faint, dreamlike glow that suffuses it, as if it had drunk into its very depths the light of the sun; the complexity and profundity of the color—nothing of the sort is to be found in Western candies. How simple and insignificant cream-filled chocolates seem by comparison. And when yōkan is served in a lacquer dish within whose dark recesses its color is scarcely distinguishable, then it is most certainly an object for meditation. You take its cool, smooth substance into your mouth, and it is as if the very darkness of the room were melting on your tongue; even undistinguished yōkan can then take on a mysteriously intriguing flavor.

In the cuisine of any country efforts no doubt are made to have the food harmonize with the tableware and the walls; but with Japanese food, a brightly lighted room and shining tableware cut the appetite in half. The dark miso[9] soup that we eat every morning is one dish from the dimly lit houses of the past. I was once invited to a tea ceremony where miso was served; and when I saw the muddy, claylike color, quiet in a black lacquer bowl beneath the faint light of a candle, this soup that I usually take without a second thought seemed somehow to acquire a real depth, and to become infinitely more appetizing as well. Much the same may be said of soy sauce. In the Kyoto-Osaka region a particularly thick variety of soy is served with raw fish, pickles, and greens; and how rich in shadows is the viscous sheen of the liquid, how beautifully it blends with the darkness. White foods too—white miso, bean curd, fish cake, the white meat of fish—lose much of their beauty in a bright room. And above all there is rice. A glistening black lacquer rice cask set off in a dark corner is both beautiful to behold and a powerful stimulus to the appetite. Then the lid is briskly lifted, and this pure white freshly boiled food, heaped in its black container, each and every grain gleaming like a pearl, sends forth billows of warm steam—here is a sight no Japanese can fail to be moved by. Our cooking depends upon shadows and is inseparable from darkness.

I possess no specialized knowledge of architecture, but I understand that in the Gothic cathedral of the West, the roof is thrust up and up so as to place its pinnacle as high in the heavens as possible—and that herein is thought to lie its special beauty. In the temples of Japan, on the other

---

7. "A place high in the mountains." Wind blowing through the pines provokes a sense of solitude and loneliness.   8. Made from a sweet bean paste. It is usually made from dark red beans but comes in several colors and flavors, including a jadelike green.   9. Made by mixing steamed soybeans with salt and a fermenting agent; one of the basic flavorings in Japanese cooking.

hand, a roof of heavy tiles is first laid out, and in the deep, spacious shadows created by the eaves the rest of the structure is built. Nor is this true only of temples; in the palaces of the nobility and the houses of the common people, what first strikes the eye is the massive roof of tile or thatch and the heavy darkness that hangs beneath the eaves. Even at midday cavernous darkness spreads over all beneath the roof's edge, making entryway, doors, walls, and pillars all but invisible. The grand temples of Kyoto—Chion'in, Honganji—and the farmhouses of the remote countryside are alike in this respect: like most buildings of the past their roofs give the impression of possessing far greater weight, height, and surface than all that stands beneath the eaves.

In making for ourselves a place to live, we first spread a parasol to throw a shadow on the earth, and in the pale light of the shadow we put together a house. There are of course roofs on Western houses too, but they are less to keep off the sun than to keep off the wind and the dew; even from without it is apparent that they are built to create as few shadows as possible and to expose the interior to as much light as possible. If the roof of a Japanese house is a parasol, the roof of a Western house is no more than a cap, with as small a visor as possible so as to allow the sunlight to penetrate directly beneath the eaves. There are no doubt all sorts of reasons— climate, building materials—for the deep Japanese eaves. The fact that we did not use glass, concrete, and bricks, for instance, made a low roof necessary to keep off the driving wind and rain. A light room would no doubt have been more convenient for us, too, than a dark room. The quality that we call beauty, however, must always grow from the realities of life, and our ancestors, forced to live in dark rooms, presently came to discover beauty in shadows, ultimately to guide shadows towards beauty's ends.

And so it has come to be that the beauty of a Japanese room depends on a variation of shadows, heavy shadows against light shadows—it has nothing else. Westerners are amazed at the simplicity of Japanese rooms, perceiving in them no more than ashen walls bereft of ornament. Their reaction is understandable, but it betrays a failure to comprehend the mystery of shadows. Out beyond the sitting room, which the rays of the sun can at best but barely reach, we extend the eaves or build on a veranda, putting the sunlight at still greater a remove. The light from the garden steals in but dimly through paper-paneled doors, and it is precisely this indirect light that makes for us the charm of a room. We do our walls in neutral colors so that the sad, fragile, dying rays can sink into absolute repose. The storehouse, kitchen, hallways, and such may have a glossy finish, but the walls of the sitting room will almost always be of clay textured with fine sand. A luster here would destroy the soft fragile beauty of the feeble light. We delight in the mere sight of the delicate glow of fading rays clinging to the surface of a dusky wall, there to live out what little life remains to them. We never tire of the sight, for to us this pale glow and these dim shadows far surpass any ornament. And so, as we must if we are not to disturb the glow, we finish the walls with sand in a single neutral color. The hue may differ from room to room, but the degree of difference will be ever so slight; not so much a difference in color as in shade, a difference that will seem to exist only in the mood of the viewer. And from these delicate differences in the hue of the walls, the shadows in each room take on a tinge peculiarly their own.

Of course the Japanese room does have its picture alcove, and in it a hanging scroll and a flower arrangement. But the scroll and the flowers serve not as ornament but rather to give depth to the shadows. We value a scroll above all for the way it blends with the walls of the alcove, and thus we consider the mounting quite as important as the calligraphy or painting. Even the greatest masterpiece will lose its worth as a scroll if it fails to blend with the alcove, while a work of no particular distinction may blend beautifully with the room and set off to unexpected advantage both itself and its surroundings. Wherein lies the power of an otherwise ordinary work to produce such an effect? Most often the paper, the ink, the fabric of the mounting will possess a certain look of antiquity, and this look of antiquity will strike just the right balance with the darkness of the alcove and room.

We have all had the experience, on a visit to one of the great temples of Kyoto or Nara, of being shown a scroll, one of the temple's treasures, hanging in a large, deeply recessed alcove. So dark are these alcoves, even in bright daylight, that we can hardly discern the outlines of the work; all we can do is listen to the explanation of the guide, follow as best we can the all-but-invisible brush strokes, and tell ourselves how magnificent a painting it must be. Yet the combination of that blurred old painting and the dark alcove is one of absolute harmony. The lack of clarity, far from disturbing us, seems rather to suit the painting perfectly. For the painting here is nothing more than another delicate surface upon which the faint, frail light can play; it performs precisely the same function as the sand-textured wall. This is why we attach such importance to age and patina. A new painting, even one done in ink monochrome or subtle pastels, can quite destroy the shadows of an alcove, unless it is selected with the greatest care.

A Japanese room might be likened to an inkwash painting, the paper-paneled shoji being the expanse where the ink is thinnest, and the alcove where it is darkest. Whenever I see the alcove of a tastefully built Japanese room, I marvel at our comprehension of the secrets of shadows, our sensitive use of shadow and light. For the beauty of the alcove is not the work of some clever device. An empty space is marked off with plain wood and plain walls, so that the light drawn into it forms dim shadows within emptiness. There is nothing more. And yet, when we gaze into the darkness that gathers behind the crossbeam, around the flower vase, beneath the shelves, though we know perfectly well it is mere shadow, we are overcome with the feeling that in this small corner of the atmosphere there reigns complete and utter silence; that here in the darkness immutable tranquility holds sway. The "mysterious Orient" of which Westerners speak probably refers to the uncanny silence of these dark places. And even we as children would feel an inexpressible chill as we peered into the depths of an alcove to which the sunlight had never penetrated. Where lies the key to this mystery? Ultimately it is the magic of shadows. Were the shadows to be banished from its corners, the alcove would in that instant revert to mere void.

This was the genius of our ancestors, that by cutting off the light from this empty space they imparted to the world of shadows that formed there a quality of mystery and depth superior to that of any wall painting or ornament. The technique seems simple, but was by no means so simply achieved. We can imagine with little difficulty what extraordinary pains were taken with each invisible detail—the placement of the window in the shelving recess, the depth of the crossbeam, the height of the threshold. But for me the most exquisite touch is the pale white glow of the shoji in the study bay; I need only pause before it and I forget the passage of time.

The study bay, as the name suggests, was originally a projecting window built to provide a place for reading. Over the years it came to be regarded as no more than a source of light for the alcove; but most often it serves not so much to illuminate the alcove as to soften the sidelong rays from without, to filter them through paper panels. There is a cold and desolate tinge to the light by the time it reaches these panels. The little sunlight from the garden that manages to make its way beneath the eaves and through the corridors has by then lost its power to illuminate, seems drained of the complexion of life. It can do no more than accentuate the whiteness of the paper. I sometimes linger before these panels and study the surface of the paper, bright, but giving no impression of brilliance.

In temple architecture the main room stands at a considerable distance from the garden; so dilute is the light there that no matter what the season, on fair days or cloudy, morning, midday, or evening, the pale, white glow scarcely varies. And the shadows at the interstices of the ribs seem strangely immobile, as if dust collected in the corners had become a part of the paper itself. I blink in uncertainty at this dreamlike luminescence, feeling as though some misty film were blunting my vision. The light from the pale white paper, powerless to dispel the heavy darkness of the alcove, is instead repelled by the darkness, creating a world of confusion where dark and light are indistinguishable. Have not you yourselves sensed a difference in the light that suffuses such a room, a rare tranquility not found in ordinary light? Have you never felt a sort of fear in the face of the ageless, a fear that in that room you might lose all consciousness of the passage of time, that untold years might pass and upon emerging you should find you had grown old and gray?

And surely you have seen, in the darkness of the innermost rooms of these huge buildings, to which sunlight never penetrates, how the gold leaf of a sliding door or screen will pick up a distant glimmer from the garden, then suddenly send forth an ethereal glow, a faint golden light cast into the enveloping darkness, like the glow upon the horizon at sunset. In no other setting is gold quite so exquisitely beautiful. You walk past, turning to look again, and yet again; and as you move away the golden surface of the paper glows ever more deeply, changing not in a flash, but growing slowly, steadily brighter, like color rising in the face of a giant. Or again you may find that the gold dust of the background, which until that moment had only a dull, sleepy luster, will, as you move past, suddenly gleam forth as if it had burst into flame.

How, in such a dark place, gold draws so much light to itself is a mystery to me. But I see why in ancient times statues of the Buddha were gilt with gold and why gold leaf covered the walls of the homes of the nobility. Modern man, in his well-lit house, knows nothing of the beauty of gold; but those who lived in the dark houses of the past were not merely captivated by its beauty, they also knew its practical value; for gold, in these dim rooms, must have served the function of a reflector. Their use of gold leaf and gold dust was not mere extravagance. Its reflective properties were put to use as a source of illumination. Silver and other metals quickly lose their gloss, but gold retains its brilliance indefinitely to light the darkness of the room. This is why gold was held in such incredibly high esteem.

I have said that lacquerware decorated in gold was made to be seen in the dark; and for this same reason were the fabrics of the past so lavishly woven of threads of silver and gold. The priest's surplice[1] of gold brocade is perhaps the best example. In most of our city temples, catering to the masses as they do, the main hall will be brightly lit, and these garments of gold will seem merely gaudy. No matter how venerable a man the priest may be, his robes will convey no sense of his dignity. But when you attend a service at an old temple, conducted after the ancient ritual, you see how perfectly the gold harmonizes with the wrinkled skin of the old priest and the flickering light of the altar lamps, and how much it contributes to the solemnity of the occasion. As with lacquerware, the bold patterns remain for the most part hidden in darkness; only occasionally does a bit of gold or silver gleam forth.

I may be alone in thinking so, but to me it seems that nothing quite so becomes the Japanese skin as the costumes of the Nō theatre. Of course many are gaudy in the extreme, richly woven of gold and silver. But the Nō actor, unlike the Kabuki[2] performer, wears no white powder. Whenever I attend the Nō I am impressed by the fact that on no other occasion is the beauty of the Japanese complexion set off to such advantage—the brownish skin with a flush of red that is so uniquely Japanese, the face like old ivory tinged with yellow. A robe woven or embroidered in patterns of gold or silver sets it off beautifully, as does a cloak of deep green or persimmon,[3] or a kimono or divided skirt of a pure white, unpatterned material. And when the actor is a handsome young man with skin of fine texture and cheeks glowing with the freshness of youth, his good looks emerge as perfection, with a seductive charm quite different from a woman's. Here,

---

1. A loose outer robe, extending to the knees, worn by priests.   2. One of the principal theatrical traditions of Japan, originating in the 17th century. *Kabuki* is gaudier and somewhat more realistic than the older, aristocratic *nō*, which dates from the 14th century, although, in the eyes of today's audiences, it appears almost as stylized. Nō is a more austere form of drama. While *kabuki* relies on intricate plots and flamboyant theatrical effects, including trap doors, revolving stages, and elaborate sets, *nō* is performed on a bare stage without sets and with virtually no props. In contrast to the spectacle *kabuki* offers, the luxurious *nō* costumes that Tanizaki mentions (together with masks worn by the main actors) provide the only striking visual feature in the performance. Both *nō* and *kabuki* combine acting with music and dance. In *kabuki* the three elements propel melodramatic or action-packed stories; a *nō* play, however, is essentially a dramatic poem, with minimal action, often depicting remote or supernatural events. Tanizaki refers only to male actors because both theatrical traditions had banned women from the stage, a point he takes up subsequently.   3. Pale to reddish orange.

one sees, is the beauty that made feudal lords lose themselves over their boy favorites.

Kabuki costumes, in the history plays and dance dramas, are no less colorful than Nō costumes; and Kabuki is commonly thought to have far greater sexual appeal than Nō. But to the adept the opposite is true. At first Kabuki will doubtless seem the more erotic and visually beautiful; but, whatever they may have been in the past, the gaudy Kabuki colors under the glare of the Western floodlamps verge on a vulgarity of which one quickly tires. And if this is true of the costumes it is all the more true of the makeup. Beautiful though such a face may be, it is after all made up; it has nothing of the immediate beauty of the flesh. The Nō actor performs with no makeup on his face or neck or hands. The man's beauty is his own; our eyes are in no way deceived. And so there is never that disappointment with the Nō actor that we feel upon seeing the unadorned face of the Kabuki actor who has played the part of a woman or handsome young man. Rather we are amazed how much the man's looks are enhanced by the gaudy costume of a medieval warrior—a man with skin like our own, in a costume we would not have thought would become him in the slightest.

I once saw Kongō Iwao play the Chinese beauty Yang Kuei-fei in the Nō play *Kōtei*,[4] and I shall never forget the beauty of his hands showing ever so slightly from beneath his sleeves. As I watched his hands, I would occasionally glance down at my own hands resting on my knees. Again, and yet again, I looked back at the actor's hands, comparing them with my own; and there was no difference between them. Yet strangely the hands of the man on the stage were indescribably beautiful, while those on my knees were but ordinary hands. In the Nō only the merest fraction of the actor's flesh is visible—the face, the neck, the hands—and when a mask is worn, as for the role of Yang Kuei-fei, even the face is hidden; and so what little flesh can be seen creates a singularly strong impression. This was particularly true of Kongō Iwao; but even the hands of an ordinary actor—which is to say the hands of an average, undistinguished Japanese—have a remarkable erotic power which we would never notice were we to see the man in modern attire.

I would repeat that this is by no means true only of youthful or handsome actors. An ordinary man's lips will not ordinarily attract us; and yet on the Nō stage, the deep red glow and the moist sheen that come over them give a texture far more sensual than the painted lips of a woman. Chanting may keep the actor's lips constantly moist, but there is more to his beauty than this. Then again, the flush of red in the cheeks of a child actor can emerge with extraordinary freshness—an effect which in my experience is most striking against a costume in which green predominates. We might expect this to be true of a fair-skinned child; yet remarkably the reddish tinge shows to better effect on a dark-skinned child. For with the fair child the contrast between white and red is too marked, and

---

4. *The Emperor* by Kanze Kojirō Nobumitsu (1435–1516), who also wrote the nō play *Dōjōji* (in Volume 1). The ghost of a former retainer of the Chinese emperor appears at the sickbed of the emperor's consort (Yang Kuei-fei) and drives away the demon afflicting her. Kongō Iwao (1886–1951), head of the traditional Kongō troupe of nō actors.

the dark, somber colors of the Nō costume stand out too strongly, while against the brownish cheeks of the darker child the red is not so conspicuous, and costume and face complement each other beautifully. The perfect harmony of the yellow skin with garments of a subdued green or brown forces itself upon our attention as at no other time.

Were the Nō to be lit by modern floodlamps, like the Kabuki, this sense of beauty would vanish under the harsh glare. And thus the older the structure the better, for it is an essential condition of the Nō that the stage be left in the darkness in which it has stood since antiquity. A stage whose floor has acquired a natural gloss, whose beams and backdrop glow with a dark light, where the darkness beneath the rafters and eaves hangs above the actors' heads as if a huge temple bell were suspended over them — such is the proper place for Nō. Its recent ventures into huge auditoriums may have something to recommend them, but in such a setting the true beauty of the Nō is all but lost.

The darkness in which the Nō is shrouded and the beauty that emerges from it make a distinct world of shadows which today can be seen only on the stage; but in the past it could not have been far removed from daily life. The darkness of the Nō stage is after all the darkness of the domestic architecture of the day; and Nō costumes, even if a bit more splendid in pattern and color, are by and large those that were worn by court nobles and feudal lords. I find the thought fascinating: to imagine how very handsome, by comparison with us today, the Japanese of the past must have been in their resplendent dress — particularly the warriors of the fifteenth and sixteenth centuries. The Nō sets before us the beauty of Japanese manhood at its finest. What grand figures those warriors who traversed the battlefields of old must have cut in their full regalia emblazoned with family crests, the somber ground and gleaming embroidery setting off strong-boned faces burnished a deep bronze by wind and rain. Every devotee of the Nō finds a certain portion of his pleasure in speculations of this sort; for the thought that the highly colored world on the stage once existed just as we see it imparts to the Nō a historical fascination quite apart from the drama.

But the Kabuki is ultimately a world of sham, having little to do with beauty in the natural state. It is inconceivable that the beautiful women of old — to say nothing of the men — bore any resemblance to those we see on the Kabuki stage. The women of the Nō, portrayed by masked actors, are far from realistic; but the Kabuki actor in the part of a woman inspires not the slightest sense of reality. The failure is the fault of excessive lighting. When there were no modern floodlamps, when the Kabuki stage was lit by the meager light of candles and lanterns, actors must have been somewhat more convincing in women's roles. People complain that Kabuki actors are no longer really feminine, but this is hardly the fault of their talents or looks. If actors of old had had to appear on the bright stage of today, they would doubtless have stood out with a certain masculine harshness, which in the past was discreetly hidden by darkness. This was brought home to me vividly when I saw the aging Baikō in the role of the young Okaru.[5] A senseless and extravagant use of lights, I thought, has destroyed the beauty of Kabuki.

A knowledgeable Osaka gentleman has told me that the Bunraku puppet theatre was for long lit by lamplight, even after the introduction of electricity in the Meiji era,[6] and that this method was far more richly suggestive than modern lighting. Even now I find the puppets infinitely more real than the actors of female Kabuki parts. But in the dim lamplight, the hard lines of the puppet features softened, the glistening white of their faces muted—a chill comes over me when I think of the uncanny beauty the puppet theatre must once have had.

The female puppets consist only of a head and a pair of hands. The body, legs, and feet are concealed within a long kimono, and so the operators need only work their hands within the costume to suggest movements. To me this is the very epitome of reality, for a woman of the past did indeed exist only from the collar up and the sleeves out; the rest of her remained hidden in darkness. A woman of the middle or upper ranks of society seldom left her house, and when she did she shielded herself from the gaze of the public in the dark recesses of her palanquin.[7] Most of her life was spent in the twilight of a single house, her body shrouded day and night in gloom, her face the only sign of her existence. Though the men dressed somewhat more colorfully than they do today, the women dressed more somberly. Daughters and wives of the merchant class wore astonishingly severe dress. Their clothing was in effect no more than a part of the darkness, the transition between darkness and face.

One thinks of the practice of blackening the teeth.[8] Might it not have been an attempt to push everything except the face into the dark? Today this ideal of beauty has quite disappeared from everyday life, and one must go to an ancient Kyoto teahouse, such as the Sumiya in Shimabara,[9] to find traces of it. But when I think back to my own youth in the old downtown section of Tokyo, and I see my mother at work on her sewing in the dim light from the garden, I think I can imagine a little what the old Japanese woman was like. In those days—it was around 1890—the Tokyo townsman still lived in a dusky house, and my mother, my aunts, my relatives, most women of their age, still blackened their teeth. I do not remember what they wore for everyday, but when they went out it was often in a gray kimono with a small, modest pattern.

My mother was remarkably slight, under five feet I should say, and I do not think that she was unusual for her time. I can put the matter strongly: women in those days had almost no flesh. I remember my mother's face

---

5. The heroine of the popular play *The Bridegroom's Journey*. Onoe Baikō VI (1870–1934), a *kabuki* actor who specialized in playing women's roles.   6. The period during which Japan embarked on modernization (1868–1912). *Bunraku puppet theater*: contemporaneous with *kabuki* and, in the 18th century, its rival.   7. An enclosed seat mounted on shafts, designed to carry a single passenger.   8. A cosmetic custom, dating from protohistoric times. A solution of iron filings was used to darken the teeth. In the era of *The Tale of Genji*, women of the court nobility blackened their teeth. The practice, which was thought to strengthen teeth and prevent toothache, was also taken up by male aristocrats and later emulated by members of the *samurai* class. By the beginning of the modern period, married women from all social classes (as well as prostitutes) blackened their teeth. The practice fell out of fashion when the empress abandoned it in 1873, no doubt to align Japanese cosmetic taste with the style of the West.   9. The red-light district.

and hands, I can clearly remember her feet, but I can remember nothing about her body. She reminds me of the statue of Kannon in the Chūgūji,[1] whose body must be typical of most Japanese women of the past. The chest as flat as a board, breasts paper-thin, back, hips, and buttocks forming an undeviating straight line, the whole body so lean and gaunt as to seem out of proportion with the face, hands, and feet, so lacking in substance as to give the impression not of flesh but of a stick—must not the traditional Japanese woman have had just such a physique? A few are still about— the aged lady in an old-fashioned household, some few geisha. They remind me of stick dolls, for in fact they are nothing more than poles upon which to hang clothes. As with the dolls their substance is made up of layer upon layer of clothing, bereft of which only an ungainly pole remains. But in the past this was sufficient. For a woman who lived in the dark it was enough if she had a faint, white face—a full body was unnecessary.

I suppose it is hard for those who praise the fleshly beauty we see under today's bright lights to imagine the ghostly beauty of those older women. And there may be some who argue that if beauty has to hide its weak points in the dark it is not beauty at all. But we Orientals, as I have suggested before, create a kind of beauty of the shadows we have made in out-of-the-way places. There is an old song that says "the brushwood we gather—stack it together, it makes a hut; pull it apart, a field once more." Such is our way of thinking—we find beauty not in the thing itself but in the patterns of shadows, the light and the darkness, that one thing against another creates.

A phosphorescent jewel gives off its glow and color in the dark and loses its beauty in the light of day. Were it not for shadows, there would be no beauty. Our ancestors made of woman an object inseparable from darkness, like lacquerware decorated in gold or mother-of-pearl. They hid as much of her as they could in shadows, concealing her arms and legs in the folds of long sleeves and skirts, so that one part and one only stood out—her face. The curveless body may, by comparison with Western women, be ugly. But our thoughts do not travel to what we cannot see. The unseen for us does not exist. The person who insists upon seeing her ugliness, like the person who would shine a hundred-candlepower light upon the picture alcove, drives away whatever beauty may reside there.

Why should this propensity to seek beauty in darkness be so strong only in Orientals? The West too has known a time when there was no electricity, gas, or petroleum, and yet so far as I know the West has never been disposed to delight in shadows. Japanese ghosts have traditionally had no feet; Western ghosts have feet, but are transparent. As even this trifle suggests, pitch darkness has always occupied our fantasies, while in the West even ghosts are as clear as glass. This is true too of our household implements: we prefer colors compounded of darkness, they prefer the colors of sunlight. And of silver and copperware: we love them for the burnish and patina, which they consider unclean, unsanitary, and polish to a glittering

---

1. An ancient Buddhist convent in Japan's early capital of Nara. Kannon, a deity in the Buddhist pantheon, was venerated for her compassion.

brilliance. They paint their ceilings and walls in pale colors to drive out as many of the shadows as they can. We fill our gardens with dense plantings, they spread out a flat expanse of grass.

But what produces such differences in taste? In my opinion it is this: we Orientals tend to seek our satisfactions in whatever surroundings we happen to find ourselves, to content ourselves with things as they are; and so darkness causes us no discontent, we resign ourselves to it as inevitable. If light is scarce then light is scarce; we will immerse ourselves in the darkness and there discover its own particular beauty. But the progressive Westerner is determined always to better his lot. From candle to oil lamp, oil lamp to gaslight, gaslight to electric light—his quest for a brighter light never ceases, he spares no pains to eradicate even the minutest shadow.

But beyond such differences in temperament, I should like to consider the importance of the difference in the color of our skin. From ancient times we have considered white skin more elegant, more beautiful than dark skin, and yet somehow this whiteness of ours differs from that of the white races. Taken individually there are Japanese who are whiter than Westerners and Westerners who are darker than Japanese, but their whiteness and darkness is not the same. Let me take an example from my own experience. When I lived on the Bluff in Yokohama[2] I spent a good deal of my leisure in the company of foreign residents, at their banquets and balls. At close range I was not particularly struck by their whiteness, but from a distance I could distinguish them quite clearly from the Japanese. Among the Japanese were ladies who were dressed in gowns no less splendid than the foreigners', and whose skin was whiter than theirs. Yet from across the room these ladies, even one alone, would stand out unmistakably from amongst a group of foreigners. For the Japanese complexion, no matter how white, is tinged by a slight cloudiness. These women were in no way reticent about powdering themselves. Every bit of exposed flesh— even their backs and arms—they covered with a thick coat of white. Still they could not efface the darkness that lay below their skin. It was as plainly visible as dirt at the bottom of a pool of pure water. Between the fingers, around the nostrils, on the nape of the neck, along the spine— about these places especially, dark, almost dirty, shadows gathered. But the skin of the Westerners, even those of a darker complexion, had a limpid glow. Nowhere were they tainted by this gray shadow. From the tops of their heads to the tips of their fingers the whiteness was pure and unadulterated. Thus it is that when one of us goes among a group of Westerners it is like a grimy stain on a sheet of white paper. The sight offends even our own eyes and leaves none too pleasant a feeling.

We can appreciate, then, the psychology that in the past caused the white races to reject the colored races. A sensitive white person could not but be upset by the shadow that even one or two colored persons cast over a social gathering. What the situation is today I do not know, but at the time of the American Civil War, when persecution of Negroes was at its most intense, the hatred and scorn were directed not only at full-blooded

2. Port city fifteen miles south of Tokyo; in the late 19th and early 20th centuries, it was the site of one of the major foreign enclaves. Tanizaki bought a house in the hilly section known as the Bluff, which was particularly favored by foreigners.

Negroes, but at mulattos, the children of mulattos, and even the children of mulattos and whites. Those with the slightest taint of Negro blood, be it but a half, a quarter, a sixteenth, or a thirty-second, had to be ferreted out and made to suffer. Not even those who at a glance were indistinguishable from pure-blooded whites, but among whose ancestors two or three generations earlier there had been a Negro, escaped the searching gaze, no matter how faint the tinge that lay hidden beneath their white skin.

And so we see how profound is the relationship between shadows and the yellow races. Because no one likes to show himself to bad advantage, it is natural that we should have chosen cloudy colors for our food and clothing and houses, and sunk ourselves back into the shadows. I am not saying that our ancestors were conscious of the cloudiness in their skin. They cannot have known that a whiter race existed. But one must conclude that something in their sense of color led them naturally to this preference.

Our ancestors cut off the brightness on the land from above and created a world of shadows, and far in the depths of it they placed woman, marking her the whitest of beings. If whiteness was to be indispensible to supreme beauty, then for us there was no other way, nor do I find this objectionable. The white races are fair-haired, but our hair is dark; so nature taught us the laws of darkness, which we instinctively used to turn a yellow skin white. I have spoken of the practice of blackening the teeth, but was not the shaving of the eyebrows also a device to make the white face stand out? What fascinates me most of all, however, is that green, iridescent lipstick, so rarely used today even by Kyoto geisha. One can guess nothing of its power unless one imagines it in the low, unsteady light of a candle. The woman of old was made to hide the red of her mouth under green-black lipstick, to put shimmering ornaments in her hair; and so the last trace of color was taken from her rich skin. I know of nothing whiter than the face of a young girl in the wavering shadow of a lantern, her teeth now and then as she smiles shining a lacquered black through lips like elfin fires. It is whiter than the whitest white woman I can imagine. The whiteness of the white woman is clear, tangible, familiar, it is not this otherworldly whiteness. Perhaps the latter does not even exist. Perhaps it is only a mischievous trick of light and shadow, a thing of a moment only. But even so it is enough. We can ask for nothing more.

And while I am talking of this whiteness I want to talk also of the color of the darkness that enfolds it. I think of an unforgettable vision of darkness I once had when I took a friend from Tokyo to the old Sumiya teahouse in Kyoto. I was in a large room, the "Pine Room" I think, since destroyed by fire, and the darkness, broken only by a few candles, was of a richness quite different from the darkness of a small room. As we came in the door an elderly waitress with shaven eyebrows and blackened teeth was kneeling by a candle behind which stood a large screen. On the far side of the screen, at the edge of the little circle of light, the darkness seemed to fall from the ceiling, lofty, intense, monolithic, the fragile light of the candle unable to pierce its thickness, turned back as from a black wall. I wonder if my readers know the color of that "darkness seen by candlelight." It was different in quality from darkness on the road at night. It was a repletion,[3] a pregnancy of tiny particles like fine ashes, each particle luminous as a rainbow. I blinked in spite of myself, as though to keep it out of my eyes.

Smaller rooms are the fashion now, and even if one were to use candles in them one would not get the color of that darkness; but in the old palace and the old house of pleasure the ceilings were high, the skirting corridors were wide, the rooms themselves were usually tens of feet long and wide, and the darkness must always have pressed in like a fog. The elegant aristocrat of old was immersed in this suspension of ashen particles, soaked in it, but the man of today, long used to the electric light, has forgotten that such a darkness existed. It must have been simple for specters to appear in a "visible darkness," where always something seemed to be flickering and shimmering, a darkness that on occasion held greater terrors than darkness out-of-doors. This was the darkness in which ghosts and monsters were active, and indeed was not the woman who lived in it, behind thick curtains, behind layer after layer of screens and doors—was she not of a kind with them? The darkness wrapped her round tenfold, twentyfold, it filled the collar, the sleeves of her kimono, the folds of her skirt, wherever a hollow invited. Further yet: might it not have been the reverse, might not the darkness have emerged from her mouth and those black teeth, from the black of her hair, like the thread from the great earth spider?[4]

The novelist Takebayashi Musōan[5] said when he returned from Paris a few years ago that Tokyo and Osaka were far more brightly lit than any European city; that even on the Champs Élysées there were still houses lit by oil lamps, while in Japan hardly a one remained unless in a remote mountain village. Perhaps no two countries in the world waste more electricity than America and Japan, he said, for Japan is only too anxious to imitate America in every way it can. That was some four or five years ago, before the vogue for neon signs. Imagine his surprise were he to come home today, when everything is so much brighter.

Yamamoto Sanehiko, president of the Kaizō publishing house, told me of something that happened when he escorted Dr. Einstein on a trip to Kyoto. As the train neared Ishiyama,[6] Einstein looked out the window and remarked, "Now that is terribly wasteful." When asked what he meant, Einstein pointed to an electric lamp burning in broad daylight. "Einstein is a Jew, and so he is probably very careful about such things"—this was Yamamoto's interpretation. But the truth of the matter is that Japan wastes more electric light than any Western country except America.

This calls to mind another curious Ishiyama story. This year I had great trouble making up my mind where to go for the autumn moon-viewing. Finally, after much perplexed head-scratching, I decided on the Ishiyama Temple. The day before the full moon, however, I read in the paper that there would be loudspeakers in the woods at Ishiyama to regale the moon-viewing guests with phonograph records of the Moonlight Sonata. I can-

---

3. A fullness, abundance; a state of being permeated with something.   4. A creature from early Japanese folklore thought to live deep beneath the mountains and to emerge to spin a lethal, mesmerizing web in which it entraps human beings and sucks their vital essences.   5. He was also a translator (1880–1962); his works include *Praise for Marriage* and *Tales of a Mindless Recluse*.   6. A town approximately six miles southeast of Kyoto known for its Buddhist temple of the same name.

celed my plans immediately. Loudspeakers were bad enough, but if it could be assumed that they would set the tone, then there would surely be floodlights too strung all over the mountain. I remember another ruined moon-viewing, the year we took a boat on the night of the harvest full moon and sailed out over the lake of the Suma Temple.[7] We put together a party, we had our refreshments in lacquered boxes, we set bravely out. But the margin of the lake was decorated brilliantly with electric lights in five colors. There was indeed a moon if one strained one's eyes for it.

So benumbed are we nowadays by electric lights that we have become utterly insensitive to the evils of excessive illumination. It does not matter all that much in the case of the moon, I suppose, but teahouses, restaurants, inns, and hotels are sure to be lit far too extravagantly. Some of this may be necessary to attract customers, but when the lights are turned on in summer even before dark it is a waste, and worse than the waste is the heat. I am upset by it wherever I go in the summer. Outside it will be cool, but inside it will be ridiculously hot, and more often than not because of lights too strong or too numerous. Turn some of them off and in no time at all the room is refreshingly cool. Yet curiously neither the guests nor the owner seem to realize this. A room should be brighter in winter, but dimmer in summer; it is then appropriately cool, and does not attract insects. But people will light the lights, then switch on an electric fan to combat the heat. The very thought annoys me.

One can endure a Japanese room all the same, for ultimately the heat escapes through the walls. But in a Western-style hotel circulation is poor, and the floors, walls, and ceilings drink in the heat and throw it back from every direction with unbearable intensity. The worst example, alas, is the Miyako Hotel in Kyoto, as anyone who has been in its lobby on a summer's evening should agree. It stands on high ground, facing north, commanding a view of Mount Hiei, Nyoigatake, the Kurodani pagoda, the forests, the green hills of Higashiyama—a splendidly fresh and clean view, all the more disappointing for being so. Should a person of a summer's evening set out to refresh himself among purple hills and crystal streams, to take in the cool breeze that blows through the tower on the heights, he will only find himself beneath a white ceiling dotted with huge milk glass lights, each sending forth a blinding blaze.

As in most recent Western-style buildings, the ceilings are so low that one feels as if balls of fire were blazing directly above one's head. "Hot" is no word for the effect, and the closer to the ceiling the worse it is—your head and neck and spine feel as if they were being roasted. One of these balls of fire alone would suffice to light the place, yet three or four blaze down from the ceiling, and there are smaller versions on the walls and pillars, serving no function but to eradicate every trace of shadow. And so the room is devoid of shadows. Look about and all you will see are white walls, thick red pillars, a garish floor done in mosaic patterns looking much like a freshly printed lithograph—all oppressively hot. When you

---

7. Buddhist temple in Suma, on the Inland Sea; a location made famous by *The Tale of Genji* when its hero is exiled to the coastal town. Suma also figures in the *nō* play *Atsumori*. (Both texts are in Volume 1.)

enter from the corridor the difference in temperature is all too apparent. No matter how cool a breeze blows in, it is instantly transformed to hot wind.

I have stayed at the Miyako several times and think fondly of it. My warnings are given with the friendliest of intentions. It is a pity that so lovely a view, so perfect a place for enjoying the cool of a summer's night, should be utterly destroyed by electric lights. The Japanese quite aside, I cannot believe that Westerners, however much they may prefer light, can be other than appalled at the heat, and I have no doubt they would see immediately the improvement in turning down the lights. The Miyako is by no means the only example. The Imperial Hotel, with its indirect lighting, is on the whole a pleasant place, but in summer even it might be a bit darker.

Light is used not for reading or writing or sewing but for dispelling the shadows in the farthest corners, and this runs against the basic idea of the Japanese room. Something is salvaged when a person turns off the lights at home to save money, but at inns and restaurants there is inevitably too much light in the halls, on the stairs, in the doorway, the gate, the garden. The rooms and the water and stones outside become flat and shallow. There are advantages for keeping warm in the winter, I suppose, but in the summer, no matter to what isolated mountain resort a person flees to escape the heat, he has a disappointment waiting if it is an inn or hotel he is going to. I have found myself that the best way to keep cool is to stay at home, open the doors, and stretch out in the dark under a mosquito net.

I recently read a newspaper or magazine article about the complaints of old women in England. When they were young, they said, they respected their elders and took good care of them; but their own daughters care nothing at all for them, and avoid them as though they were somehow dirty. The morals of the young, they lamented, are not what they once were. It struck me that old people everywhere have much the same complaints. The older we get the more we seem to think that everything was better in the past. Old people a century ago wanted to go back two centuries, and two centuries ago they wished it were three centuries earlier. Never has there been an age that people have been satisfied with. But in recent years the pace of progress has been so precipitous that conditions in our own country go somewhat beyond the ordinary. The changes that have taken place since the Restoration of 1867[8] must be at least as great as those of the preceding three and a half centuries.

It will seem odd, I suppose, that I should go on in this vein, as if I too were grumbling in my dotage. Yet of this I am convinced, that the conveniences of modern culture cater exclusively to youth, and that the times grow increasingly inconsiderate of old people. Let me take a familiar example: now that we cannot cross an intersection without consulting a traffic signal, old people can no longer venture confidently out into the streets. For someone sufficiently well-off to be driven about in an automobile there may be no problem, but on those rare occasions when I go into

---

8. When Japan's modern period began. The *shogun*, the military dictator, abdicated power, and the emperor was restored as a figurehead for the new Western-influenced government.

Osaka, it sets every nerve in my body on edge to cross from one side of the street to the other. If the signal is in the middle of the intersection it is easy enough to see it; but it is all but impossible to pick out a stop light that stands off to the side, where no one would ever expect to find it. If the intersection is broad, it is only too easy to confuse the light for facing traffic with the light for crossing traffic. It seemed to me the end of everything when the traffic policeman came to Kyoto. Now one must travel to such small cities as Nishinomiya, Sakai, Wakayama, or Fukuyama for the feel of Japan.

The same is true of food. In a large city it takes a concerted search to turn up a dish that will be palatable to an old person. Not long ago a newspaper reporter came to interview me on the subject of unusual foods, and I described to him the persimmon-leaf sushi made by the people who live deep in the mountains of Yoshino—and which I shall take the opportunity to introduce to you here. To every ten parts of rice one part of saké is added just when the water comes to a boil. When the rice is done it should be cooled thoroughly, after which salt is applied to the hands and the rice molded into bite-size pieces. At this stage the hands must be absolutely free of moisture, the secret being that only salt should touch the rice. Thin slices of lightly salted salmon are placed on the rice, and each piece is wrapped in a persimmon leaf, the surface of the leaf facing inward. Both the persimmon leaves and the salmon should be wiped with a dry cloth to remove any moisture. Then in a rice tub or sushi box, the interior of which is perfectly dry, the pieces are packed standing on end so that no space remains between them, and the lid is put in place and weighted with a heavy stone, as in making pickles. Prepared in the evening, the sushi should be ready to eat the next morning. Though the taste is best on the first day, it remains edible for two or three days. A slight bit of vinegar is sprinkled over each piece with a sprig of bitter nettle just before eating.

I learned of the dish from a friend who had been to Yoshino and found it so exceptionally good that he took the trouble to learn how to make it— but if you have the persimmon leaves and salted salmon it can be made anywhere. You need only remember to keep out every trace of moisture, and to cool the rice completely. I made some myself, and it was very good indeed. The oil of the salmon and the slight hint of salt give just the proper touch of seasoning to the rice, and the salmon becomes as soft as if it were fresh—the flavor is indescribable, and far better than the sushi one gets in Tokyo. I have become so fond of it that I ate almost nothing else this summer. What impressed me, however, was that this superb method of preparing salted salmon was the invention of poor mountain people. Yet a sampling of the various regional cuisines suggests that in our day country people have far more discriminating palates than city people, and that in this respect they enjoy luxuries we cannot begin to imagine.

And so as time goes by, old people give up the cities and retire to the country; and yet there is not much cause for hope there either, for country towns are year by year going the way of Kyoto, their streets strung with bright lights. There are those who say that when civilization progresses a bit further transportation facilities will move into the skies and under the ground, and that our streets will again be quiet, but I know perfectly well that when that day comes some new device for torturing the old will be invented. "Out of our way, old people," we say, and they have no recourse but to shrink back into their houses, to make whatever tidbits they can for themselves, and to enjoy their evening saké as best they can to the accompaniment of the radio.

But do not think that old people are the only ones to find fault. The author of the "Vox Populi Vox Dei" column in the Osaka *Asahi*[9] recently castigated city officials who quite needlessly cut a swath through a forest and leveled a hill in order to build a highway through Minō Park. I was somewhat encouraged;[1] for to snatch away from us even the darkness beneath trees that stand deep in the forest is the most heartless of crimes. At this rate every place of any beauty in Nara or in the suburbs of Kyoto and Osaka, as the price of being turned over to the masses, will be denuded of trees. But again I am grumbling.

I am aware of and most grateful for the benefits of the age. No matter what complaints we may have, Japan has chosen to follow the West, and there is nothing for her to do but move bravely ahead and leave us old ones[2] behind. But we must be resigned to the fact that as long as our skin is the color it is the loss we have suffered cannot be remedied. I have written all this because I have thought that there might still be somewhere, possibly in literature or the arts, where something could be saved. I would call back at least for literature this world of shadows we are losing. In the mansion called literature I would have the eaves deep and the walls dark, I would push back into the shadows the things that come forward too clearly, I would strip away the useless decoration. I do not ask that this be done everywhere, but perhaps we may be allowed at least one mansion where we can turn off the electric lights and see what it is like without them.

9. "Morning Sun"; a daily newspaper. *Vox Populi Vox Dei*: "the voice of the people is the voice of God" (Latin); that is, the voice of the people is supreme.   1. Because the editorial shared the author's interest in preservation.   2. A bit of an exaggeration; Tanizaki was forty-eight.

ZUNI RITUAL POETRY

Although repeatedly invaded since the 1500s and subjected, in turn, to regulation by Spanish, Mexican, and U.S. authority, Oraibi, Taos, Acoma, Zuni, and the other pueblos of the North American Southwest—the continent's oldest towns north of Mexico—have yet to be conquered in the full sense of the term. Bastions of spiritual and social autonomy, the pueblo communities make a profound impression on the nonnative world by the strength of their traditions in an era of change; and of this there can be no more convincing proof than the ceremonial system of Zuni pueblo with its annual cycle of drama, sacrifice, and oratory. Heard at the winter solstice and again, repeatedly, through the phases of the next twelve moons, the spoken word, to the accompaniment of ritual acts, continues to provide the cohesive bond for a growing community of nearly ten thousand people.

Continuously occupied since at least the 1300s, the Zuni territory in western

New Mexico has traditionally supported an agricultural economy, dominated by the town, or pueblo, of Zuni itself, surrounded by outlying seasonal farming villages. The raising of livestock became important during the Spanish and Mexican period (1540–1846), but by the mid-twentieth century most Zuni residents had come to rely either on the thriving silversmithing industry or on jobs in off-reservation communities. Farming as a livelihood gradually became insignificant. Yet the agricultural cycle, today, still inspires Zuni ceremonialism.

The often-quoted and deeply admired texts for the Zuni ceremonial round were published just once, in 1932—yet plentifully—by the anthropologist Ruth L. Bunzel under the rubric *Zuni Ritual Poetry*. They comprise one of the two most important bodies of native American oratory on record, exceeded in scope and in quantity only by the Aztec orations preserved in the sixteenth-century Florentine Codex (in Volume 1).

As the Zuni orations make clear, the purpose of the ceremonial round is to establish a relationship between "daylight people," or ordinary humans, and the so-called raw people, such as deer, bear, the sun, rainstorms, and corn plants, who consume either raw food or the offerings that the daylight people present to them. In a special category of raw people are the *kokkokwe*, ancestral spirits known in English as kachinas, represented during the ceremonies by masked dancers. Dependent on humans for their nurture, the kachinas and other raw people are given offerings that include the feather-decorated willow shafts called prayer sticks or, in Bunzel's translation, "plume wands." In return the raw people grant "seeds," "breath," "life," "light," and all manner of good fortune. The offerings are sacrificed by depositing, or "planting," them at prescribed locations. Since the Zuni hold that sacrifices were established in the ancient time by the raw people, it is natural enough to find kachinas themselves planting wands during the course of the rituals. In effect these are human sacrifices, with the prayer sticks standing in for the people.

As mentioned above, the ceremonial year at Zuni begins with the winter solstice. This major event is followed by a series of winter dances and a calendar of prayer-stick offerings coordinated with the reappearances of the moon. The summer solstice, with its urgent prayers for rain, marks a second ceremonial high point, followed again by the repeating schedule of monthly offerings. Ceremonial activity quickens in the fall with the setting of the date for the great Shalako, a ceremony held shortly before the winter solstice. The selections offered here are from the prayers for three of the annual episodes: the winter solstice observances, the Scalp Dance, and the Shalako.

The winter solstice rites span twenty days, with the solstice itself falling in the middle. This "middle," moreover, is regarded as the center of the entire year. On the first day an announcement is made that prayer sticks will be planted ten days hence. The offerings are not prepared, however, until the ninth day, when the Fire Keeper is appointed. On the tenth day, ideally December 21, the offerings are planted and the Fire Keeper lights the New Year's fire. With this begins a ten-day "fire taboo," during which no fire may be seen outdoors and no ashes may be removed from any house (the ashes accumulating just as stored crops, one hopes, will accumulate later in the year). When the taboo is lifted the Fire Keeper delivers his prayer, or oration, asking especially for plentiful crops as in the excerpt printed here.

The Scalp Dance, formerly, was performed on the return of a victorious war party to purify any warrior who had taken a scalp and to induct the trophy itself into the company of previously won scalps, regarded as "rain makers." The dead in general are a source of contamination, threatening to those who have come into contact with them; but having "attained the place of blessed waters," they also have the power to send rain and, by extension, fruitfulness and good fortune. By the 1970s the Scalp Dance, no longer relevant as an occasional observance, had been brought into the annual round as a fall ritual. In the excerpt from the prayer given here, the scalp is envisioned in its role as rain maker and as an agent of blessing.

The Shalako, the most festive of the ceremonials, attracts an international audience of visitors who arrive at Zuni in time for the grand entrance of the kachinas at the start of eight days of public proceedings. Led by the kachina Sayatasha, the masked party, which includes the troupe of six Shalako (giant kachinas in ten-foot-high birdlike costumes), enters the town and breaks up into small groups, each assigned to a house renovated for the occasion. During the first evening Sayatasha delivers his lengthy "night chant," which includes a house blessing for the benefit of his host. Dances and other rites during the next several days are marked by the presence of the Koyemshi, or clowns, who attend the kachinas and mock them. On the eighth day, with the spectacle finished, the Koyemshi are dismissed from their duties, and the ceremonial year comes to a close.

The ceremonial orations typically request or predict blessings, as can be seen from all the selections presented here. This culminating portion of the "talk" is preceded by a summary of what the speaker has been doing to obtain the desired result, as in the excerpt from the "Shalako House Blessing" (which describes the consecration of the structure and, as a result, the fruitfulness it will one day contain). The avowal of duty is in turn preceded by a statement noting the day or the occasion, making reference to a particular position in the ceremonial year. All three segments—occasion, duty, and result—can be observed in the "Dismissal of the Koyemshi," presented here in full.

Our selections are from Ruth L. Bunzel, "Zuni Ritual Poetry," *Forty-Seventh Annual Report of the Bureau of American Ethnology* (1932), which includes annotated texts in Zuni and English. Two related works by Bunzel, "Introduction to Zuni Ceremonialism" and "Zuni Katcinas," are in the same volume. Alfonso Ortiz, ed., *Southwest*, vol. 9 of *Handbook of North American Indians* (1979), serves as a guide to the history and culture of Zuni and other pueblos. For recent impressions of Zuni life and Zuni ceremonialism, see Barbara Tedlock, *The Beautiful and the Dangerous* (1992).

PRONOUNCING GLOSSARY

The following list uses common English syllables and stress accents to provide rough equivalents of selected words whose pronunciation may be unfamiliar to the general reader.

Acoma: *ak'-uh-muh*

kachinas: *kuh-chee'-nuhz*

kokkokwe: *koh'-koh-kway*

Koyemshi: *koh'-yaym-shee*

Oraibi: *oh-righ'-bee*

Sayatasha: *sah'-yah-tah-shah*

Shalako: *shah'-lah-koh*

Uwanammi: *oo'-wah-nahm-mee*

From A Prayer at the Winter Solstice[1]

*   *   *

Perhaps if we are lucky
Our earth mother
Will wrap herself in a fourfold robe
Of white meal,
Full of frost flowers;   5
A floor of ice will spread over the world,
The forests,
Because of the cold will lean to one side,
Their arms will break beneath the weight of snow.
When the days are thus   10
The flesh of our earth mother
Will crack with cold.
Then in the spring when she is replete with living waters
Our mothers,
All different kinds of corn   15
In their earth mother
We shall lay to rest.
With their earth mother's living waters
They will be made into new beings;
Into their sun father's daylight   20
They will come out standing;
Yonder to all directions
They will stretch out their hands calling for rain.
Then with their fresh waters
The rain makers[2] will pass us on our roads.   25
Clasping their young ones in their arms
They will rear their children.
Gathering them[3] into our houses,
Following these toward whom our thoughts bend,
With our thoughts following them,   30
Thus we shall always live.

*   *   *

From The Scalp Dance

*   *   *

Indeed, the enemy,
Though in his life
He was a person given to falsehood,
He has become one to foretell[1]
How the world will be,   5
How the days will be.

---

1. All selections translated by Ruth L. Bunzel. Text printed in italics was added by Bunzel.   2. The rain makers, or Uwanammi, are water spirits who live in all the waters of the earth; cumulus clouds are their houses; mist is their breath [adapted from Translator's note].   3. The corn at harvest.   1. It is expected that the scalp will prove an omen of good fortune.

That during his time,
We may have good days,
Beautiful days,
Hoping for this,   10
We shall keep his days.[2]
Indeed, if we are lucky,
During the enemy's time
Fine rain caressing the earth,
Heavy rain caressing the earth,   15
We shall win.
When the enemy's days are in progress,
The enemy's waters,
We shall win,
His seeds we shall win,   20
His riches we shall win,
His power,
His strong spirit,
His long life,
His old age,   25
In order to win these,
Tirelessly, unwearied,
We shall pass his days.
Now, indeed, the enemy,
Even one who thought himself a man,   30
In a shower of arrows,
In a shower of war clubs,
With bloody head,
The enemy,
Reaching the end of his life,   35
Added to the flesh of our earth mother.

*   *   *

From Shalako

From *Sayatasha's*[1] *Night Chant*

HOUSE BLESSING

*   *   *

Then my father's rain-filled room
I rooted at the north,
I rooted at the west,
I rooted at the south,
I rooted at the east,[2]   5
I rooted above,
Then in the middle of my father's roof,
With two plume wands joined together,

---

2. That is, observe the several days' ritual, which is spoken of as the "enemy's time," "enemy's days," or simply "his time."   1. Long Horn; the kachina's mask has a curved horn on the right side.   2. Consecrating the principal room (*rain-filled room*) of the human host (*father*) by stroking each wall with a torch, a whip, or other instrument.

I consecrated his roof.
This is well; 10
In order that my father's offspring may increase,
I consecrated the center of his roof.
And then also, the center of my father's floor,
With seeds of all kinds,[3]
I consecrated the center of his floor. 15
This is well;
In order that my father's fourth room[4]
May be bursting with corn,
That even in his doorway,
The shelled corn may be scattered before the door, 20
The beans may be scattered before the door,
That his house may be full of little boys,
And little girls,
And people grown to maturity;
That in his house 25
Children may jostle one another in the doorway,
In order that it may be thus,
I have consecrated the rain-filled room
Of my daylight father,
My daylight mother. 30

*   *   *

DISMISSAL OF THE KOYEMSHI[1]

This many are the days,
My children,
Since with their plume wand they appointed us.
Throughout the winter,
And the summer 5
Anxiously we have awaited our time.
Hither toward the south
We have given our fathers plume wands.[2]
For all our ladder descending children[3]
We have been asking for life. 10
Now we have reached the appointed time.
This night
We have fulfilled the thoughts of our fathers.
Always with one thought
We shall live. 15
My children,
This night
Your children,
Your families,
Happily you will pass on their roads.[4] 20

---

3. Male and female wands joined together (representing fertility) are placed in a decorated box suspended from the ceiling; seeds, in a permanent excavation below the floor. Thus the sixfold blessing encompasses the four directions, the zenith, and the nadir.   4. Innermost room.   1. A troupe of ten clowns appearing in dances throughout the year. Their impersonators, appointed at the winter solstice to serve for twelve months, are here dismissed by their leader, or "father" (who calls them "children"), bringing the Shalako to an end.   2. That is, raw people (*fathers*) have been given *plume wands* in exchange for benefits conferred on humans.   3. Humans; so called since houses in former times were entered through an opening in the roof.   4. Will meet, will join.

Happily we shall always live.
Even though we say we have fulfilled their thoughts
No indeed
Anxiously awaiting until we shall again come to our appointed time
We shall live henceforth.   25
My children,
Thus I have finished my words for you.
To this end, my children:
May you now go happily to your children.
Asking for life from my fathers   30
Yonder on all sides,
Asking for my fathers' life-giving breath,
Their breath of old age,
And into my warm body,
Drawing their breath,   35
I add to your breath.
To this end, my children
May your roads be fulfilled;
May you grow old;
May you be blessed with life.   40

T. S. ELIOT
1888–1965

In poetry and in literary criticism, Thomas Stearns Eliot has a unique position as
a writer who not only expressed but helped to define modernist taste and style. He
rejected the narrative, moralizing, and frequently "noble" style of late Victorian
poetry, employing instead precisely focused and often startling images and an elliptical, allusive, and ironic voice that had enormous influence on modern American
poetry. His early essays on literature and literary history helped bring about not
only a new appreciation of seventeenth-century "metaphysical" poetry but also a
different understanding of the text, no longer seen as the inspired overflow of
spontaneous emotion but as a carefully made aesthetic object. Yet much of Eliot's
immediate impact was not merely formal but spiritual or philosophical. The
search for meaning that pervades his work created a famous picture of the barrenness of modern culture in *The Waste Land* (1922), which juxtaposed images of
past nobility and present decay, civilizations near and far, and biblical, mythical,
and Buddhist allusions to evoke the dilemma of a composite, anxious, and infinitely vulnerable modern soul. Readers in different countries who know nothing
of Eliot's other works are often familiar with *The Waste Land* as a literary-historical
landmark representing the cultural crisis in European society after World War I.
In many ways, Eliot's combination of spiritual insight and technical innovation
carries on the tradition of the Symbolist poet who was both visionary artist and
consummate craftsman.

Two countries, England and the United States, claim Eliot as part of their
national literature. Born September 26, 1888, to a prosperous and educated family
in St. Louis, Eliot went to Harvard University for his undergraduate and graduate
education and moved to England only in 1915, where he became a British citizen
in 1927. While at Harvard, Eliot was influenced by the anti-Romantic humanist

Irving Babbitt and the philosopher and aesthetician George Santayana. He later wrote a doctoral dissertation on the philosophy of F. H. Bradley, whose examination of private consciousness (*Appearance and Reality*) appears in Eliot's own later essays and poems. Eliot also found literary examples that would be important for him in future years: the poetry of Dante and John Donne, and the Elizabethan and Jacobean dramatists. In 1908 he read Arthur Symons's *The Symbolist Movement in Literature* and became acquainted with the French Symbolist poets whose richly allusive images—as well as highly self-conscious, ironic, and craftsmanlike technique—he would adopt for his own. Eliot began writing poetry while in college, and published his first major poem, *The Love Song of J. Alfred Prufrock*, in Chicago's *Poetry* magazine in 1915. When he moved to England, however, he began a many-sided career as poet, reviewer, essayist, editor, and later playwright. By the time he received the Nobel Prize for literature in 1948, Eliot was recognized as one of the most influential twentieth-century writers in English.

Eliot's first poems, in 1915, already displayed the evocative yet startling images, abrupt shifts in focus, and combination of human sympathy and ironic wit that would attract and puzzle his readers. The *Preludes* linked the "notion of some infinitely gentle / Infinitely suffering thing" with a harsh fatalism in which "The worlds revolve like ancient women / Gathering fuel in vacant lots." Prufrock's dramatic monologue openly tried to startle readers by asking them to imagine the evening spread out "like a patient etherised upon a table" and by changing focus abruptly between imaginary landscapes, metaphysical questions, drawing-room chatter, literary and biblical allusions, and tones of high seriousness set against the most banal and even sing-song speech. "I grow old . . . I grow old. . . . / I shall wear the bottoms of my trousers rolled." The individual stanzas of *Prufrock* are individual scenes, each with its own coherence (for example, the third stanza's yellow fog as a cat). Together, they compose a symbolic landscape sketched in the narrator's mind as a combination of factual observation and subjective feelings: the delicately stated eroticism of the arm "downed with light brown hair," and the frustrated aggression in "I should have been a pair of ragged claws / Scuttling across the floors of silent seas." In its discontinuity, precise yet evocative imagery, mixture of romantic and everyday reference, formal and conversational speech, and in the complex and ironic self-consciousness of its most unheroic hero, *The Love Song of J. Alfred Prufrock* already displays many of the modernist traits typical of Eliot's entire work. Also typical is the theme of spiritual void and of a disoriented protagonist who—at least at this point—does not know how to cope with a crisis that is as much that of modern Western culture as it is his own personal tragedy.

Once established in London, Eliot married, taught briefly before taking a job in the foreign department of Lloyd's Bank (1917–25), and in 1925 joined the publishing firm of Faber & Faber. He wrote a number of essays and book reviews that were published in *The Sacred Wood* (1920) and *Homage to Dryden* (1924) and enjoyed a great deal of influence as assistant editor of the *Egoist* (1917–19) and founding editor of the quarterly *Criterion* from 1922 until it folded in 1939. Eliot helped shape changing literary tastes as much by his essays and literary criticism as by his poetry. Influenced himself by T. E. Hulme's proposal that the time had come for a classical literature of "hard, dry wit" after Romantic vagueness and religiosity and following Imagism's goal of clear, precise physical images phrased in everyday language, he outlined his own definitions of literature and literary history and contributed to a theoretical approach later known as the *New Criticism*. In his essay *Tradition and the Individual Talent* (1919), Eliot proclaimed that there existed a special level of great works—"masterpieces"—that formed among themselves an "ideal order" of quality even though, as individual works, they expressed the characteristic sensibility of their age. The best poets were aware of fitting into the cumulative "mind of Europe" (for Eliot, the humanistic tradition of Homer,

Dante, and Shakespeare) and thus of being to some extent depersonalized in their works. Eliot's "impersonal theory of poetry" emphasizes the medium in which a writer works, rather than his or her inner state; craft and control rather than the Romantic ideal of a spontaneous overflow of private emotion. In a famous passage that compares the creative mind to the untouched catalyst of a chemistry experiment, he insists that the writer makes the art object out of language and the experience of any number of people. "The poet's mind is in fact a receptacle for seizing and storing up numberless feelings, phrases, images, which remain there until all the particles which can unite to form a new compound are present together." Poetry can and should express the whole being—intellectual and emotional, conscious and unconscious. In a review of Herbert Grierson's edition of the seventeenth-century Metaphysical poets (1921), Eliot praised the complex mixture of intellect and passion that characterized John Donne and the other Metaphysicals (and that characterized Eliot himself) and criticized the tendency of English literature after the seventeenth century to separate the language of analysis from that of feeling. His criticism of this "dissociation of sensibility" implied a change in literary tastes: from Milton to Donne, from Tennyson to Gerard Manley Hopkins, from Romanticism to classicism, from simplicity to complexity.

The great poetic example of this change came with *The Waste Land* in 1922. Eliot dedicated the poem to Ezra Pound, who had helped him revise the first draft, with a quotation from Dante praising the "better craftsman." Quotations from, or allusions to, a wide range of sources, including Shakespeare, Dante, Charles Baudelaire, Richard Wagner, Ovid, St. Augustine, Buddhist sermons, folk songs, and the anthropologists Jessie Weston and James Frazer, punctuate this lengthy poem, to which Eliot actually added explanatory notes when it was first published in book form. *The Waste Land* describes modern society in a time of cultural and spiritual crisis and sets off the fragmentation of modern experience against references (some in foreign languages) to a more stable cultural heritage. The ancient Greek prophet Tiresias is juxtaposed with the contemporary charlatan Madame Sosostris; celebrated lovers like Antony and Cleopatra with a house-agent's clerk who mechanically seduces an uninterested typist at the end of her day; the religious vision of St. Augustine and Buddhist sermons with a sterile world of rock and dry sand where "one can neither stand nor lie nor sit." The modern wasteland could be redeemed if it learned to answer (or perhaps, to ask) the right questions: a situation Eliot symbolized by oblique references to the legend of a knight passing an evening of trial in a Chapel Perilous, and healing a Fisher King by asking the right questions about the Holy Grail and its lance. The series of references (many from literary masterworks) that Eliot integrated into his poem were so many "fragments I have shored against my ruins," pieces of a puzzle whose resolution would bring "shantih," or the peace that passes understanding, but that is still out of reach as the poem's final lines in a foreign language suggest.

The most influential technical innovation in *The Waste Land* was the deliberate use of fragmentation and discontinuity. Eliot pointedly refused to supply any transitional passages or narrative thread and expected the reader to construct a pattern whose implications would make sense as a whole. This was a direct attack on linear habits of reading, which are here broken up with sudden introductions of a different scene or unexplained literary references, shifts in perspective, interpolation of a foreign language, changes from elegant description to barroom gossip, from Elizabethan to modern scenes, from formal to colloquial language. Eliot's rupture of traditional expectations served several functions. It contributed to the general picture of cultural disintegration that the poem expressed, it allowed him to exploit the Symbolist or allusive powers of language inasmuch as they now carried the burden of meaning, and finally—by drawing attention to its own technique—it exemplified modernist "self-reflexive" or self-conscious style. It is impossible to read a triple shift such as "I remember / Those are pearls that were his eyes. / 'Are you alive, or not? Is there nothing in your head?' "—moving from the narrator's meditative recall to a quotation from Shakespeare and the woman's blunt attack—without noticing the abrupt changes in style and tone. Eliot's "heap of broken images" and "fragments shored against my ruins" also took the shape of fragments of thought and speech, and as such embodied a new tradition of literary language.

The spiritual search of *Prufrock, Gerontion* (1919), and *The Waste Land* entered a new phase for Eliot in 1927, when he became a member of the Anglican Church. *Ash Wednesday* (1930) and a verse play on the death of the English St. Thomas à Becket (*Murder in the Cathedral*, 1935) display the same distress over the human condition but now within a framework of hope for those who have accepted religious discipline. Eliot began writing plays to reach a larger audience, of which the best known are *The Family Reunion* (1939), which recasts the Orestes story from Greek tragedy, and *The Cocktail Party* (1949), a drawing room comedy that also explored its characters' search for salvation. He is still best known for his poetry, however, and his last major work in that genre is the *Four Quartets*, begun in 1934 and published in its entirety in 1943.

As their title suggests, the *Four Quartets* are divided into sections much like the movement of a musical quartet. Each has five sections, inside which themes are introduced, developed, and resolved, and each has the title of a place. *Little Gidding* is a village in Huntingdonshire, England, which was the home of a seventeenth-century Anglican Catholic religious community of which only a chapel (rebuilt after the English Civil Wars) remained. All the *Quartets* use varying forms of free verse, ranging from the most intense short lyrics to—for the first time— continuous narrative passages of the kind Eliot once disdained. Throughout, the poet ponders the relationship of historical change and eternal order.

Eliot's experiences in World War II as a watchman checking for fires during bombing raids enter into *Little Gidding*, and he uses the chapel in that village as the point of departure for a meditation on the meaning of strife and change in a universe that the mind strives to structure, always imperfectly, by the timeless truths of religion. The *Quartet* opens with a section that is itself divided into three separate movements, first establishing the season of "midwinter spring" with the sun blazing on ice, then the chapel as the goal of any season's journey, and finally the chapel as a place so consecrated by prayer that the dead may communicate with the living. The lyrics opening the second section mourn the place's present decay by all four elements of earth, air, fire, and water and pass on to an imaginary conversation between the poet, wandering after the last bomb and before the all-clear signal, and an anonymous "dead master." The mood is pessimistic, and the dead master (a "compound ghost" with elements of Eliot, the Virgil of Dante's *Divine Comedy*, and W. B. Yeats) prophesies a bitter old age full of remorse and impotent rage at human folly. Their conversation suggests a comparison between the air-raid scene and Dante's *Inferno*, for it echoes the triple-line stanzaic form of the *Divine Comedy* and recalls the Italian poet's own encounter with his former master Brunetto Latini, in Hell (*Inferno* 15.23–124). The rest of the poem, how-ever, moves forward to a kind of resolution out of time. The third section's begin-ning rhetoric of logical persuasion ("There are three conditions") introduces the concept of memory expanding our perspectives and enabling us to transcend the narrow commitments of history and civil war. The intense lyrics of the short fourth section propose that the flames of the annunciatory dove (or bomb) may be purga-tion as well as destruction; and in the final section, as the afternoon draws to a close, the poet ends his meditation on past and present, time and eternity, by asserting his faith in a condition of mind and spirit that combines both *now* and *always*, a transcendental vision that is a "condition of complete simplicity" and "crowned knot of fire."

The poem's conclusion is thus a religious one, moving from the agony of history to an eternal, purifying flame that may recall a similar mystic vision of all-penetrating light at the end of Dante's *Paradiso*. It may seem paradoxical that the poet who is known for expressing the dilemma of modern consciousness and for developing a new poetic style appropriate to twentieth-century experience should resolve that experience in a metaphor of transcendence. From his earliest work, however, Eliot was preoccupied with the spiritual implications of the most mundane reality, and the yoking of concrete with transcendental vision defines at once the range and depth of his modernist style.

Bernard Bergonzi, *T. S. Eliot* (1972), and Tony Sharpe, *T. S. Eliot: A Literary Life* (1991), are brief and readable introductions to the life and works. Martin Scofield, *T. S. Eliot: The Poems* (1988), offers a concise, balanced discussion of the evolution of Eliot's poetry. *The Waste Land* is discussed in Jay Martin, ed., *Twentieth-Century Interpretations of The Waste Land* (1968); Lois A. Cuddy and David H. Hirsch, eds., *Critical Essays on T. S. Eliot's The Waste Land* (1991); and as part of John Mayer, *T. S. Eliot's Silent Voices* (1989), which analyzes themes of awareness and self-consciousness in the early poetry. *Little Gidding* is examined in Steve Ellis, *The English Eliot: Design, Language, and Landscape in Four Quartets* (1991), and John Paul Riquelme, *Harmony of Dissonances: T. S. Eliot, Romanticism, and Imagination* (1991), which links Eliot's response to Romanticism with postmodern views. Useful general collections are Linda Wagner, ed., *T. S. Eliot: A Collection of Criticism* (1974), and Ronald Bush, ed., *T. S. Eliot: The Modernist in History* (1991).

The Love Song of J. Alfred Prufrock

> *S'io credesse che mia risposta fosse*
> *A persona che mai tornasse al mondo,*
> *Questa fiamma staria senza piu scosse.*
> *Ma perciocche giammai di questo fondo*
> *Non torno vivo alcun, s'i'odo il vero,*
> *Senza tema d'infamia ti rispondo.*[1]

    Let us go then, you and I,
When the evening is spread out against the sky
Like a patient etherised upon a table;
Let us go, through certain half-deserted streets,
The muttering retreats   5
Of restless nights in one-night cheap hotels
And sawdust restaurants with oyster-shells:
Streets that follow like a tedious argument
Of insidious intent
To lead you to an overwhelming question . . .   10
Oh, do not ask, "What is it?"
Let us go and make our visit.

---

1. From Dante's *Inferno* 27.61–66, where the false counselor Guido da Montefeltro, enveloped in flame, explains that he would never reveal his past if he thought the traveler could report it: "If I thought that my reply would be to one who would ever return to the world, this flame would stay without further movement. But since none has ever returned alive from this depth, if what I hear is true, I answer you without fear of infamy."

In the room the women come and go
Talking of Michelangelo.[2]

The yellow fog that rubs its back upon the window-panes,   15
The yellow smoke that rubs its muzzle on the window-panes
Licked its tongue into the corners of the evening,
Lingered upon the pools that stand in drains,
Let fall upon its back the soot that falls from chimneys,
Slipped by the terrace, made a sudden leap,   20
And seeing that it was a soft October night,
Curled once about the house, and fell asleep.

And indeed there will be time[3]
For the yellow smoke that slides along the street,
Rubbing its back upon the window-panes;   25
There will be time, there will be time
To prepare a face to meet the faces that you meet;
There will be time to murder and create,
And time for all the works and days of hands[4]
That lift and drop a question on your plate;   30
Time for you and time for me,
And time yet for a hundred indecisions,
And for a hundred visions and revisions,
Before the taking of a toast and tea.

In the room the women come and go   35
Talking of Michelangelo.

And indeed there will be time
To wonder, "Do I dare?" and, "Do I dare?"
Time to turn back and descend the stair,
With a bald spot in the middle of my hair—   40
(They will say: "How his hair is growing thin!")
My morning coat, my collar mounting firmly to the chin,
My necktie rich and modest, but asserted by a simple pin—
(They will say: "But how his arms and legs are thin!")
Do I dare   45
Disturb the universe?
In a minute there is time
For decisions and revisions which a minute will reverse.

For I have known them all already, known them all—
Have known the evenings, mornings, afternoons,   50
I have measured out my life with coffee spoons;
I know the voices dying with a dying fall[5]
Beneath the music from a farther room.
So how should I presume?

And I have known the eyes already, known them all—   55
The eyes that fix you in a formulated phrase,

---

2. Michelangelo Buonarroti (1475–1564), famous Italian Renaissance sculptor, painter, architect, and poet; here, merely a topic of fashionable conversation.   **3.** Echo of a love poem by Andrew Marvell (1621–1678), *To His Coy Mistress*: "Had we but world enough and time."   **4.** An implied contrast with the more productive agricultural labor of hands in the *Works and Days* of the Greek poet Hesiod (8th century B.C.).   **5.** Recalls Duke Orsino's description of a musical phrase in Shakespeare's *Twelfth Night* (1.1.4): "It has a dying fall."

And when I am formulated, sprawling on a pin,
When I am pinned and wriggling on the wall,
Then how should I begin
To spit out all the butt-ends of my days and ways?   60
  And how should I presume?

  And I have known the arms already, known them all—
Arms that are braceleted and white and bare
(But in the lamplight, downed with light brown hair!)
Is it perfume from a dress   65
That makes me so digress?
Arms that lie along a table, or wrap about a shawl.
  And should I then presume?
  And how should I begin?

                    .   .   .

  Shall I say, I have gone at dusk through narrow streets   70
And watched the smoke that rises from the pipes
Of lonely men in shirt-sleeves, leaning out of windows? . . .

  I should have been a pair of ragged claws
Scuttling across the floors of silent seas.

                    .   .   .

          And the afternoon, the evening, sleeps so peacefully!   75
Smoothed by long fingers,
Asleep . . . tired . . . or it malingers,
Stretched on the floor, here beside you and me.
Should I, after tea and cakes and ices,
Have the strength to force the moment to its crisis?   80
But though I have wept and fasted, wept and prayed,
Though I have seen my head (grown slightly bald) brought in upon a
          platter,
I am no prophet[6]—and here's no great matter;
I have seen the moment of my greatness flicker,
And I have seen the eternal Footman hold my coat, and snicker,   85
And in short, I was afraid.

  And would it have been worth it, after all,
After the cups, the marmalade, the tea,
Among the porcelain, among some talk of you and me,
Would it have been worth while,   90
To have bitten off the matter with a smile,
To have squeezed the universe into a ball
To roll it toward some overwhelming question,[7]
To say: "I am Lazarus, come from the dead,[8]
Come back to tell you all, I shall tell you all"—   95
If one, settling a pillow by her head,

---

6. Salome obtained the head of the prophet John the Baptist on a platter as a reward for dancing before the tetrarch Herod (Matthew 14:3–11).   7. Another echo of *To His Coy Mistress*, when the lover suggests rolling "all our strength and all / our sweetness up into one ball" to send against the "iron gates of life."   8. The story of Lazarus, raised from the dead, is told in John 11:1–44.

Should say: "That is not what I meant at all.
That is not it, at all."

And would it have been worth it, after all,
Would it have been worth while,   100
After the sunsets and the dooryards and the sprinkled streets,
After the novels, after the teacups, after the skirts that trail along the
    floor—
And this, and so much more?—
It is impossible to say just what I mean!
But as if a magic lantern[9] threw the nerves in patterns on a screen: 105
Would it have been worth while
If one, settling a pillow or throwing off a shawl,
And turning toward the window, should say:
    "That is not it at all,
    That is not what I meant, at all."   110

                . . . . .

    No! I am not Prince Hamlet, nor was meant to be;
Am an attendant lord, one that will do
To swell a progress,[1] start a scene or two,
Advise the prince; no doubt, an easy tool,
Deferential, glad to be of use,   115
Politic, cautious, and meticulous;
Full of high sentence, but a bit obtuse;
At times, indeed, almost ridiculous—
Almost, at times, the Fool.

    I grow old . . . I grow old . . .   120
I shall wear the bottoms of my trousers rolled.

    Shall I part my hair behind? Do I dare to eat a peach?
I shall wear white flannel trousers, and walk upon the beach.
I have heard the mermaids singing, each to each.

I do not think that they will sing to me.   125

    I have seen them riding seaward on the waves
Combing the white hair of the waves blown back
When the wind blows the water white and black.

    We have lingered in the chambers of the sea
By sea-girls wreathed with seaweed red and brown   130
Till human voices wake us, and we drown.

---

9. A slide projector.   1. A procession of attendants accompanying a king or nobleman across the stage,
as in Elizabethan drama.

The Waste Land[1]

"Nam Sibyllam quidem Cumis ego ipse oculis meis vidi in ampulla
pendere, et cum illi pueri dicerent: Σίβυλλα τί θέλεισ; respondebat
illa: ἀποθανεῖν θέλω."[2]

For Ezra Pound
il miglior fabbro.[3]

I. THE BURIAL OF THE DEAD[4]

April is the cruellest month, breeding
Lilacs out of the dead land, mixing
Memory and desire, stirring
Dull roots with spring rain.
Winter kept us warm, covering   5
Earth in forgetful snow, feeding
A little life with dried tubers.
Summer surprised us, coming over the Starnbergersee[5]
With a shower of rain; we stopped in the colonnade,
And went on in sunlight, into the Hofgarten,[6]   10
And drank coffee, and talked for an hour.
Bin gar keine Russin, stamm' aus Litauen, echt deutsch.[7]
And when we were children, staying at the archduke's,
My cousin's, he took me out on a sled,
And I was frightened. He said, Marie,   15
Marie, hold on tight. And down we went.
In the mountains, there you feel free.
I read, much of the night, and go south in the winter.

What are the roots that clutch, what branches grow
Out of this stony rubbish? Son of man,[8]   20
You cannot say, or guess, for you know only
A heap of broken images, where the sun beats,
And the dead tree gives no shelter, the cricket no relief,[9]
And the dry stone no sound of water. Only
There is shadow under this red rock,   25
(Come in under the shadow of this red rock),
And I will show you something different from either
Your shadow at morning striding behind you
Or your shadow at evening rising to meet you;
I will show you fear in a handful of dust.   30

---

1. Eliot provided footnotes for *The Waste Land* when it was first published in book form; these notes are included here. A general note at the beginning referred readers to the religious symbolism described in Jessie L. Weston's study of the Grail legend, *From Ritual to Romance* (1920), and to fertility myths and vegetation ceremonies (especially those involving Adonis, Attis, and Osiris) as described in the *The Golden Bough* (1890–1918) by the anthropologist Sir James Frazer.   2. Lines from Petronius's *Satyricon* (ca. A.D. 60) describing the Sibyl, a prophetess shriveled with age and suspended in a bottle. "For indeed I myself have seen with my own eyes the Sibyl at Cumae, hanging in a bottle, and when those boys would say to her: 'Sibyl, what do you want?' she would reply: 'I want to die.'"   3. The dedication to Ezra Pound, who suggested cuts and changes in the first manuscript of *The Waste Land*, borrows words used by Guido Guinizelli to describe his predecessor, the Provençal poet Arnaut Daniel, in Dante's *Purgatorio* (26.117): he is "the better craftsman."   4. From the burial service of the Anglican Church.   5. A lake near Munich. Lines 8–16 recall *My Past*, the memoirs of Countess Marie Larisch.   6. A public park.   7. "I am certainly no Russian, I come from Lithuania and am pure German." German settlers in Lithuania considered themselves superior to the Slavic natives.   8. "Cf. Ezekiel II,i" [Eliot's note]. The passage reads "Son of man, stand upon thy feet, and I will speak unto thee."   9. "Cf. Ecclesiastes XII,v" [Eliot's note]. "Also when they shall be afraid of that which is high, and fears shall be in the way . . . the grasshopper shall be a burden, and desire shall fail."

> *Frisch weht der Wind*
> *Der Heimat zu*
> *Mein Irisch Kind,*
> *Wo weilest du?*[1]

"You gave me hyacinths first a year ago;   35
"They called me the hyacinth girl."
—Yet when we came back, late, from the Hyacinth garden,
Your arms full, and your hair wet, I could not
Speak, and my eyes failed, I was neither
Living nor dead, and I knew nothing,   40
Looking into the heart of light, the silence.
Oed' und leer das Meer.[2]

Madame Sosostris, famous clairvoyante,[3]
Had a bad cold, nevertheless
Is known to be the wisest woman in Europe,   45
With a wicked pack of cards.[4] Here, said she,
Is your card, the drowned Phoenician Sailor,
(Those are pearls that were his eyes.[5] Look!)
Here is Belladonna, the Lady of the Rocks,
The lady of situations.   50
Here is the man with three staves, and here the Wheel,
And here is the one-eyed merchant, and this card,
Which is blank, is something he carries on his back,
Which I am forbidden to see. I do not find
The Hanged Man. Fear death by water.   55
I see crowds of people, walking round in a ring.
Thank you. If you see dear Mrs. Equitone,
Tell her I bring the horoscope myself:
One must be so careful these days.

Unreal City,[6]   60
Under the brown fog of a winter dawn,
A crowd flowed over London Bridge, so many,
I had not thought death had undone so many.[7]

---

1. "V. *Tristan und Isolde*, I, verses 5–8" [Eliot's note]. A sailor in Richard Wagner's opera sings "The wind blows fresh / Towards the homeland / My Irish child / Where are you waiting?"   **2.** "Id. III, verse 24" [Eliot's note]. "Barren and empty is the sea" is the erroneous report the dying Tristan hears as he waits for Isolde's ship in the third act of Wagner's opera.   **3.** A fortune-teller with an assumed Egyptian name, possibly suggested by a similar figure in a novel by Aldous Huxley (*Crome Yellow*, 1921).   **4.** "I am not familiar with the exact constitution of the Tarot pack of cards, from which I have obviously departed to suit my own convenience. The Hanged Man, a member of the traditional pack, fits my purpose in two ways: because he is associated in my mind with the Hanged God of Frazer, and because I associate him with the hooded figure in the passage of the disciples to Emmaus in Part V. The Phoenician Sailor and the Merchant appear later; also the 'crowds of people,' and Death by Water is executed in Part IV. The Man with Three Staves (an authentic member of the Tarot pack) I associate, quite arbitrarily, with the Fisher King himself" [Eliot's note]. Tarot cards are used for telling fortunes; the four suits (cup, lance, sword, and dish) are life symbols related to the Grail legend and, as Eliot suggests, various figures on the cards are associated with different characters and situations in *The Waste Land*. For example: the "drowned Phoenician Sailor" recurs in the merchant from Smyrna (III) and Phlebas the Phoenician (IV); Belladonna (a poison, hallucinogen, medicine, and cosmetic; in Italian, "beautiful lady"; also an echo of Leonardo da Vinci's painting of the Virgin, *Madonna of the Rocks*) heralds the neurotic society woman amid her jewels and perfumes (II); the Wheel is the wheel of fortune; the Hanged Man becomes the sacrificed fertility god whose death ensures resurrection and new life for his people.   **5.** A line from Ariel's song in Shakespeare's *The Tempest* (1.2.398), which describes the transformation of a drowned man.   **6.** "Cf. Baudelaire: 'Fourmillante cité, cité pleine de rêves, / Où le spectre en plein jour raccroche le passant' " [Eliot's note]. "Swarming city, city full of dreams, / Where the specter in broad daylight accosts the passerby"; a description of Paris from "The Seven Old Men" in *The Flowers of Evil* (1857).   **7.** "Cf. *Inferno* III, 55–57: 'si lunga tratta / di gente, ch'io non avrei mai creduto / che morte tanta n'avesse disfatta' " [Eliot's note]. "So long a train / of people, that I would never have believed / death had undone so many"; not only is Dante amazed at the number of people who have died but he is

Sighs, short and infrequent, were exhaled,[8]
And each man fixed his eyes before his feet.   65
Flowed up the hill and down King William Street,
To where Saint Mary Woolnoth kept the hours
With a dead sound on the final stroke of nine.[9]
There I saw one I knew, and stopped him, crying: "Stetson!
"You who were with me in the ships at Mylae![1]   70
"That corpse you planted last year in your garden,
"Has it begun to sprout? Will it bloom this year?
"Or has the sudden frost disturbed its bed?
"Oh keep the Dog far hence, that's friend to men,[2]
"Or with his nails he'll dig it up again!   75
"You! hypocrite lecteur!—mon semblable,—mon frère!"[3]

II. A GAME OF CHESS[4]

The Chair she sat in, like a burnished throne,[5]
Glowed on the marble, where the glass
Held up by standards wrought with fruited vines
From which a golden Cupidon peeped out   80
(Another hid his eyes behind his wing)
Doubled the flames of sevenbranched candelabra
Reflecting light upon the table as
The glitter of her jewels rose to meet it,
From satin cases poured in rich profusion.   85
In vials of ivory and coloured glass
Unstoppered, lurked her strange synthetic perfumes,
Unguent, powdered, or liquid—troubled, confused
And drowned the sense in odours; stirred by the air
That freshened from the window, these ascended   90
In fattening the prolonged candle-flames,
Flung their smoke into the laquearia,[6]
Stirring the pattern on the coffered ceiling.
Huge sea-wood fed with copper

---

also describing a crowd of people who were neither good nor bad—nonentities denied even the entrance to Hell.   **8.** "Cf. *Inferno* IV, 25–27: 'Quivi, secondo che per ascoltare, / non avea pianto, ma' che di sospiri, / che l'aura eterna facevan tremare' " [Eliot's note]. "Here, so far as I could tell by listening, there was no weeping but so many sighs that they caused the everlasting air to tremble"; the first circle of Hell, or Limbo, contained the souls of virtuous people who lived before Christ or had not been baptized. **9.** "A phenomenon which I have often noticed" [Eliot's note]. The church is in the financial district of London, where King William Street is also located.   **1.** An "average" modern name (with business associations) linked to the ancient battle of Mylae (260 B.C.), where Rome was victorious over its commercial rival, Carthage.   **2.** "Cf. the Dirge in Webster's *White Devil*" [Eliot's note]. The dirge, or song of lamentation, sung by Cornelia in John Webster's play (1625), asks to "keep the wolf far thence, that's foe to men," so that the wolf's nails may not dig up the bodies of her murdered relatives. Eliot's reversal of dog for wolf, and friend for foe, domesticates the grotesque scene; it may also foreshadow rebirth since (according to Weston's book), the rise of the Dog Star Sirius announced the flooding of the Nile and the consequent return of fertility to Egyptian soil.   **3.** "V. Baudelaire, Preface to *Fleurs du Mal*" [Eliot's note]. Baudelaire's poem preface, titled "To the Reader," ended "Hypocritical reader!—my likeness!—my brother!" The poet challenges the reader to recognize that both are caught up in the worst sin of all—the moral wasteland of *ennui* ("boredom") as lack of will, the refusal to care one way or the other. **4.** Reference to a play, *A Game of Chess* (1627) by Thomas Middleton (1580–1627); see n. 4, p. 1862. Part II juxtaposes two scenes of modern sterility: an initial setting of wealthy boredom, neurosis, and lack of communication, and a pub scene where similar concerns of appearance, sexual attraction, and thwarted childbirth are brought out more visibly, and in more vulgar language.   **5.** "Cf. *Antony and Cleopatra*, II, ii, l. 190" [Eliot's note]. A paler version of Cleopatra's splendor as she met her future lover Antony: "The barge she sat in, like a burnished throne, / Burned on the water."   **6.** "Laquearia. V. *Aeneid*, I, 726: dependent lychni laquearibus aureis incensi, et noctem flammis funalia vincunt" [Eliot's note]. "Glowing lamps hang from the gold-paneled ceiling, and the torches conquer night with their flames"; the banquet setting of another classical love scene, where Dido is inspired with a fatal passion for Aeneas.

Burned green and orange, framed by the colourèd stone, 95
In which sad light a carvèd dolphin swam.
Above the antique mantel was displayed
As though a window gave upon the sylvan scene[7]
The change of Philomel,[8] by the barbarous king
So rudely forced; yet there the nightingale[9] 100
Filled all the desert with inviolable voice
And still she cried, and still the world pursues,
"Jug Jug"[1] to dirty ears.
And other withered stumps of time
Were told upon the walls; staring forms 105
Leaned out, leaning, hushing the room enclosed.
Footsteps shuffled on the stair.
Under the firelight, under the brush, her hair
Spread out in fiery points
Glowed into words, then would be savagely still. 110

   "My nerves are bad to-night. Yes, bad. Stay with me.
Speak to me. Why do you never speak. Speak.
   What are you thinking of? What thinking? What?
I never know what you are thinking. Think."

   I think we are in rats' alley[2] 115
Where the dead men lost their bones.

   "What is that noise?"
              The wind under the door.[3]
"What is that noise now? What is the wind doing?"
              Nothing again nothing. 120
                    "Do
"You know nothing? Do you see nothing? Do you remember
"Nothing?"

       I remember
Those are pearls that were his eyes.
"Are you alive, or not? Is there nothing in your head?" 125
                             But
O O O O that Shakespeherian Rag—
It's so elegant
So intelligent 130
"What shall I do now? What shall I do?"
"I shall rush out as I am, and walk the street
"With my hair down, so. What shall we do to-morrow?
"What shall we ever do?"
              The hot water at ten. 135
And if it rains, a closed car at four.
And we shall play a game of chess,[4]
Pressing lidless eyes and waiting for a knock upon the door.

---

7. "Sylvan scene. V. Milton, *Paradise Lost*, IV, 140" [Eliot's note]. Eden as first seen by Satan.   8. "V. Ovid, *Metamorphoses*, VI, Philomela" [Eliot's note]. Philomela was raped by her brother-in-law, King Tereus, who cut out her tongue so that she could not tell her sister, Procne. Later Procne is changed into a swallow, and Philomela into a nightingale, to save them from the king's rage after they have revenged themselves by killing his son.   9. "Cf. Part III, l. 204" [Eliot's note].   1. Represents the nightingale's song in Elizabethan poetry.   2. "Cf. Part III, l. 195" [Eliot's note].   3. "Cf. Webster: 'Is the wind in that door still?'" [Eliot's note]. From *The Devil's Law Case* (1623), 3.2.162, with the implied meaning "is there still breath in him?"   4. "Cf. the game of chess in Middleton's *Women Beware Women*" [Eliot's note]. In this scene, a woman is seduced in a series of strategic steps that parallel the moves of a chess game occupying her mother-in-law at the same time.

When Lil's husband got demobbed,[5] I said—
I didn't mince my words, I said to her myself,   140
HURRY UP PLEASE ITS TIME[6]
Now Albert's coming back, make yourself a bit smart.
He'll want to know what you done with that money he gave you
To get yourself some teeth. He did, I was there.
You have them all out, Lil, and get a nice set,   145
He said, I swear, I can't bear to look at you.
And no more can't I, I said, and think of poor Albert,
He's been in the army four years, he wants a good time,
And if you don't give it him, there's others will, I said.
Oh is there, she said. Something o' that, I said.   150
Then I'll know who to thank, she said, and give me a straight look.
HURRY UP PLEASE ITS TIME
If you don't like it you can get on with it, I said.
Others can pick and choose if you can't.
But if Albert makes off, it won't be for lack of telling.   155
You ought to be ashamed, I said, to look so antique.
(And her only thirty-one.)
I can't help it, she said, pulling a long face,
It's them pills I took, to bring it off, she said.
(She's had five already, and nearly died of young George.)   160
The chemist[7] said it would be all right, but I've never been the same.
You are a proper fool, I said.
Well, if Albert won't leave you alone, there it is, I said,
What you get married for if you don't want children?
HURRY UP PLEASE ITS TIME   165
Well, that Sunday Albert was home, they had a hot gammon,[8]
And they asked me in to dinner, to get the beauty of it hot—
HURRY UP PLEASE ITS TIME
HURRY UP PLEASE ITS TIME
Goonight Bill. Goonight Lou. Goonight May. Goonight.   170
Ta ta. Goonight. Goonight.
Good night, ladies, good night, sweet ladies, good night, good night.[9]

III. THE FIRE SERMON[1]

The river's tent is broken: the last fingers of leaf
Clutch and sink into the wet bank. The wind
Crosses the brown land, unheard. The nymphs are departed.   175
Sweet Thames, run softly, till I end my song.[2]
The river bears no empty bottles, sandwich papers,
Silk handkerchiefs, cardboard boxes, cigarette ends
Or other testimony of summer nights. The nymphs are departed.
And their friends, the loitering heirs of city directors;   180
Departed, have left no addresses.

---

5. Demobilized, discharged from the army.   6. The British bartender's warning that the pub is about to close.   7. The druggist, who gave her pills to cause a miscarriage.   8. Ham.   9. The popular song for a party's end ("Good Night, Ladies") shifts into Ophelia's last words in *Hamlet* (4.5.72) as she goes off to drown herself.   1. Reference to the Buddha's Fire Sermon (see n. 1, p. 1867) in which he denounced the fiery lusts and passions of earthly experience. "All things are on fire . . . with the fire of passion . . . of hatred . . . of infatuation." Part III describes the degeneration of even these passions in the sterile decadence of the modern Waste Land.   2. "V. Spenser, *Prothalamion*" [Eliot's note]. The line is the refrain of a marriage song by the Elizabethan poet Edmund Spenser (1552?—1599) and evokes a river of unpolluted pastoral beauty.

By the waters of Leman[3] I sat down and wept . . .
Sweet Thames, run softly till I end my song,
Sweet Thames, run softly, for I speak not loud or long.
But at my back in a cold blast I hear[4]   185
The rattle of the bones, and chuckle spread from ear to ear.

A rat crept softly through the vegetation
Dragging its slimy belly on the bank
While I was fishing in the dull canal
On a winter evening round behind the gashouse   190
Musing upon the king my brother's wreck
And on the king my father's death before him.[5]
White bodies naked on the low damp ground
And bones cast in a little low dry garret,
Rattled by the rat's foot only, year to year.   195
But at my back from time to time I hear[6]
The sound of horns and motors, which shall bring[7]
Sweeney to Mrs. Porter in the spring.
O the moon shone bright on Mrs. Porter[8]
And on her daughter   200
They wash their feet in soda water
Et O ces voix d'enfants, chantant dans la coupole![9]

Twit twit twit
Jug jug jug jug jug jug
So rudely forc'd.   205
Tereu[1]

    Unreal City
Under the brown fog of a winter noon
Mr. Eugenides, the Smyrna merchant
Unshaven, with a pocket full of currants   210
C.i.f. London: documents at sight,[2]
Asked me in demotic French
To luncheon at the Cannon Street Hotel
Followed by a weekend at the Metropole.[3]

    At the violet hour, when the eyes and back   215
Turn upward from the desk, when the human engine waits

---

3. Lake Geneva (where Eliot wrote much of *The Waste Land*). A *leman* is a mistress or lover. In Psalm 137:1, the exiled Hebrews sit by the rivers of Babylon and weep for their lost homeland.   **4.** Distorted echo of Andrew Marvell's (1621–1678) poem *To His Coy Mistress*: "But at my back I always hear / Time's winged chariot hurrying near."   **5.** "Cf. *The Tempest* I.ii" [Eliot's note]. Ferdinand, the king's son, believing his father drowned and mourning his death, hears in the air a song containing the line that Eliot quotes earlier at lines 48 and 126.   **6.** "Cf. Marvell, 'To His Coy Mistress'" [Eliot's note]. **7.** "Cf. Day, *Parliament of Bees*: 'When of the sudden, listening, you shall hear, / A noise of horns and hunting, which shall bring / Actaeon to Diana in the spring, / Where all shall see her naked skin.'" [Eliot's note]. The young hunter Actaeon was changed into a stag, hunted down, and killed when he came upon the goddess Diana bathing. Sweeney is in no such danger from his visit to Mrs. Porter. **8.** "I do not know the origin of the ballad from which these lines are taken: it was reported to me from Sydney, Australia" [Eliot's note]. A song popular among Allied troops during World War I. One version continues lines 199–201 as follows: "And so they oughter / To keep them clean."   **9.** "V. Verlaine, *Parsifal*" [Eliot's note]. "And O these children's voices, singing in the dome!"; the last lines of a sonnet by Paul Verlaine (1844–1896), which ambiguously celebrates the Grail hero's chaste restraint. In Richard Wagner's opera, Parsifal's feet are washed to purify him before entering the presence of the Grail.   **1.** Tereus, who raped Philomela (see line 99); also the nightingale's song.   **2.** "The currants were quoted at a price 'carriage and insurance free to London'; and the Bill of Lading etc. were to be handed to the buyer upon payment of the sight draft" [Eliot's note].   **3.** Smyrna is an ancient Phoenician seaport, and early Smyrna merchants spread the Eastern fertility cults. In contrast, their descendant Mr. Eugenides ("Well-born") invites the poet to lunch in a large commercial hotel and a weekend at a seaside resort in Brighton.

Like a taxi throbbing waiting,
I Tiresias,[4] though blind, throbbing between two lives,
Old man with wrinkled female breasts, can see
At the violet hour, the evening hour that strives   220
Homeward, and brings the sailor home from sea,[5]
The typist home at teatime, clears her breakfast, lights
Her stove, and lays out food in tins.
Out of the window perilously spread
Her drying combinations touched by the sun's last rays,   225
On the divan are piled (at night her bed)
Stockings, slippers, camisoles, and stays.
I Tiresias, old man with wrinkled dugs
Perceived the scene, and foretold the rest—
I too awaited the expected guest.   230
He, the young man carbuncular, arrives,
A small house agent's clerk, with one bold stare,
One of the low on whom assurance sits
As a silk hat on a Bradford[6] millionaire.
The time is now propitious, as he guesses,   235
The meal is ended, she is bored and tired,
Endeavours to engage her in caresses
Which still are unreproved, if undesired.
Flushed and decided, he assaults at once;
Exploring hands encounter no defence;   240
His vanity requires no response,
And makes a welcome of indifference.
(And I Tiresias have foresuffered all
Enacted on this same divan or bed;
I who have sat by Thebes below the wall   245
And walked among the lowest of the dead.)[7]
Bestows one final patronising kiss,
And gropes his way, finding the stairs unlit . . .

    She turns and looks a moment in the glass,
Hardly aware of her departed lover;   250
Her brain allows one half-formed thought to pass:
"Well now that's done: and I'm glad it's over."
When lovely woman stoops to folly and[8]
Paces about her room again, alone,
She smoothes her hair with automatic hand,   255
And puts a record on the gramophone.

---

4. "Tiresias, although a mere spectator and not indeed a 'character,' is yet the most important personage
in the poem, uniting all the rest. Just as the one-eyed merchant, seller of currants, melts into the Phoenician Sailor, and the latter is not wholly distinct from Ferdinand Prince of Naples, so all the women are
one woman, and the two sexes meet in Tiresias. What Tiresias *sees*, in fact, is the substance of the poem.
The whole passage from Ovid is one of great anthropological interest" [Eliot's note]. The passage then
quoted from Ovid's *Metamorphoses* (3.320–38) describes how Tiresias spent seven years of his life as a
woman and thus experienced love from the point of view of both sexes. Blinded by Juno, he was recom-
pensed by Jove with the gift of prophecy.   5. "This may or may not appear as exact as Sappho's lines,
but I had in mind the 'longshore' or 'dory' fisherman, who returns at nightfall" [Eliot's note]. The Greek
poet Sappho's poem describes how the evening star brings home those whom dawn has sent abroad; there
is also an echo of Robert Louis Stevenson's (1850–1894) *Requiem*, 1.221: "Home is the sailor, home
from the sea."   6. A manufacturing town in Yorkshire, which prospered greatly during World War I.
7. Tiresias prophesied in the marketplace at Thebes for many years before dying and continuing to
prophesy in Hades.   8. "V. Goldsmith, the song in *The Vicar of Wakefield*" [Eliot's note]. "When lovely
woman stoops to folly / And finds too late that men betray / What charm can soothe her melancholy, /
What art can wash her guilt away?" Oliver Goldsmith (ca. 1730–1774), *The Vicar of Wakefield* (1766).

"This music crept by me upon the waters"[9]
And along the Strand, up Queen Victoria Street.
O City city,[1] I can sometimes hear
Beside a public bar in Lower Thames Street,   260
The pleasant whining of a mandoline
And a clatter and a chatter from within
Where fishmen lounge at noon: where the walls
Of Magnus Martyr hold[2]
Inexplicable splendour of Ionian white and gold.   265

               The river sweats[3]
               Oil and tar
               The barges drift
               With the turning tide
               Red sails   270
               Wide
               To leeward, swing on the heavy spar.
               The barges wash
               Drifting logs
               Down Greenwich reach   275
               Past the Isle of Dogs.[4]
                     Weialala leia
                     Wallala leialala

               Elizabeth and Leicester[5]
               Beating oars   280
               The stern was formed
               A gilded shell
               Red and gold
               The brisk swell
               Rippled both shores   285
               Southwest wind
               Carried down stream
               The peal of bells
               White towers
                     Weialala leia   290
                     Wallala leialala

"Trams and dusty trees.
Highbury bore me. Richmond and Kew

---

9. "V. *The Tempest*, as above" [Eliot's note, referring to line 191]. Spoken by Ferdinand as he hears Ariel sing of his father's transformation by the sea, his eyes turning to pearls, his bones to coral, and everything else he formerly was into "something rich and strange."   1. A double invocation: the city of London and the City as London's central financial district (see lines 60 and 207). See also lines 375–6, the great cities of Western civilization.   2. "The interior of St. Magnus Martyr is to my mind one of the finest among Wren's interiors. See *The Proposed Demolition of Nineteen City Churches*: (P. S. King & Son, Ltd)" [Eliot's note]. The architect was Christopher Wren (1632–1723), and the church is located just below London Bridge on Lower Thames Street.   3. "The Song of the (three) Thames-daughters begins here. From line 292 to 306 inclusive they speak in turn. V. *Götterdämmerung* III.i: the Rhine-daughters" [Eliot's note]. In Wagner's opera *The Twilight of the Gods* (1876), the three Rhine-maidens mourn the loss of their gold, which gave the river its sparkling beauty; lines 177–8 here echo the Rhine-maidens' refrain.   4. A peninsula opposite Greenwich on the Thames.   5. "V. Froude, *Elizabeth*, vol. I, ch. iv, letter of De Quadra to Philip of Spain: 'In the afternoon we were in a barge, watching the games on the river. (The queen) was alone with Lord Robert and myself on the poop, when they began to talk nonsense, and went so far that Lord Robert at last said, as I was on the spot there was no reason why they should not be married if the queen pleased" [Eliot's note]. Sir Robert Dudley (1532–1588) was the earl of Leicester, a favorite of Queen Elizabeth who at one point hoped to marry her.

Undid me.[6] By Richmond I raised my knees
Supine on the floor of a narrow canoe."   295

"My feet are at Moorgate,[7] and my heart
Under my feet. After the event
He wept. He promised 'a new start.'
I made no comment. What should I resent?"

"On Margate Sands.[8]   300
I can connect
Nothing with nothing.
The broken fingernails of dirty hands.
My people humble people who expect
Nothing."   305
          la la

To Carthage then I came[9]

Burning burning burning burning[1]
O Lord Thou pluckest me out[2]
O Lord Thou pluckest   310

burning

IV. DEATH BY WATER

Phlebas the Phoenician, a fortnight dead,
Forgot the cry of gulls, and the deep sea swell
And the profit and loss.
                    A current under sea   315
Picked his bones in whispers. As he rose and fell
He passed the stages of his age and youth
Entering the whirlpool.
                    Gentile or Jew
O you who turn the wheel and look to windward,   320
Consider Phlebas, who was once handsome and tall as you.

V. WHAT THE THUNDER SAID[3]

After the torchlight red on sweaty faces
After the frosty silence in the gardens
After the agony in stony places
The shouting and the crying   325

6. "Cf. *Purgatorio*, V, 133: 'Ricorditi di me, che son la Pia; / Siena mi fe', disfecemi Maremma' " [Eliot's note]. La Pia, in Purgatory, recalls her seduction: "Remember me, who am La Pia. / Siena made me, Maremma undid me." Eliot's parody substitutes Highbury (a London suburb) and Richmond and Kew, popular excursion points on the Thames.   7. A London slum.   8. A seaside resort on the Thames. 9. "V. St. Augustine's *Confessions*: 'to Carthage then I came, where a cauldron of unholy loves sang all about mine ears' " [Eliot's note]. The youthful Augustine is described. Carthage is also the scene of Dido's faithful love for Aeneas, referred to in line 92.   1. "The complete text of the Buddha's Fire Sermon (which corresponds in importance to the Sermon on the Mount) from which these words are taken, will be found translated in the late Henry Clarke Warren's *Buddhism in Translation* (Harvard Oriental Studies). Mr. Warren was one of the great pioneers of Buddhist studies in the Occident" [Eliot's note]. The Sermon on the Mount is in Matthew 5–7.   2. "From St. Augustine's *Confessions* again. The collocation of these two representatives of eastern and western asceticism, as the culmination of this part of the poem is not an accident" [Eliot's note]. See also Zechariah 3:2, where the high priest Joshua is described as a "brand plucked out of the fire."   3. "In the first part of Part V three themes are employed: the journey to Emmaus, the approach to the Chapel Perilous (see Miss Weston's book) and the present decay of eastern Europe" [Eliot's note]. On their journey to Emmaus (Luke 24:13–34), Jesus' disciples were joined by a stranger who later revealed himself to be the crucified and resurrected Christ. The Thunder of the title is a divine voice in the Hindu *Upanishads* (see n. 2, p. 1869).

Prison and palace and reverberation
Of thunder of spring over distant mountains
He who was living is now dead[4]
We who were living are now dying
With a little patience   330

   Here is no water but only rock
Rock and no water and the sandy road
The road winding above among the mountains
Which are mountains of rock without water
If there were water we should stop and drink   335
Amongst the rock one cannot stop or think
Sweat is dry and feet are in the sand
If there were only water amongst the rock
Dead mountain mouth of carious teeth that cannot spit
Here one can neither stand nor lie nor sit   340
There is not even silence in the mountains
But dry sterile thunder without rain
There is not even solitude in the mountains
But red sullen faces sneer and snarl
From doors of mudcracked houses   345
                        If there were water
   And no rock
   If there were rock
   And also water
   And water   350
   A spring
   A pool among the rock
   If there were the sound of water only
   Not the cicada[5]
   And dry grass singing   355
   But sound of water over a rock
   Where the hermit-thrush[6] sings in the pine trees
   Drip drop drip drop drop drop drop
   But there is no water

   Who is the third who walks always beside you?   360
When I count, there are only you and I together[7]
But when I look ahead up the white road
There is always another one walking beside you
Gliding wrapt in a brown mantle, hooded
I do not know whether a man or a woman   365
—But who is that on the other side of you?

   What is that sound high in the air[8]
Murmur of maternal lamentation

---

4. Allusions to stages in Christ's Passion: the betrayal, prayer in the garden of Gethsemane, imprisonment, trial, crucifixion, and burial. Despair reigns, for this is death before the Resurrection. **5.** Grasshopper or cricket; see line 23. **6.** "The hermit-thrush which I have heard in Quebec Province. . . . Its 'water-dripping song' is justly celebrated" [Eliot's note]. **7.** "The following lines were stimulated by the account of one of the Antarctic expeditions (I forget which, but I think one of Shackleton's): it was related that the party of explorers, at the extremity of their strength, had the constant delusion that there was *one more member* than could actually be counted" [Eliot's note]. See also n. 3, p. 1867. **8.** Eliot's note to lines 367–77 refers to Hermann Hesse's *Blick ins Chaos* (Glimpse into chaos), and a passage that reads, translated, "Already half of Europe, already at least half of Eastern Europe is on the way to Chaos, drives drunk in holy madness on the edge of the abyss and sings at the same time, sings drunk and hymn-like, as Dimitri Karamazov sang [in Dostoevsky's *The Brothers Karamazov*]. The offended bourgeois laughs at the songs; the saint and the seer hear them with tears."

Who are those hooded hordes swarming
Over endless plains, stumbling in cracked earth   370
Ringed by the flat horizon only
What is the city over the mountains
Cracks and reforms and bursts in the violet air
Falling towers
Jerusalem Athens Alexandria   375
Vienna London
Unreal

   A woman drew her long black hair out tight
And fiddled whisper music on those strings
And bats with baby faces in the violet light   380
Whistled, and beat their wings
And crawled head downward down a blackened wall
And upside down in air were towers
Tolling reminiscent bells, that kept the hours
And voices singing out of empty cisterns and exhausted wells.   385

   In this decayed hole among the mountains
In the faint moonlight, the grass is singing
Over the tumbled graves, about the chapel
There is the empty chapel, only the wind's home.
It has no windows, and the door swings,   390
Dry bones can harm no one.
Only a cock stood on the rooftree
Co co rico co co rico[9]
In a flash of lightning. Then a damp gust
Bringing rain   395

   Ganga was sunken, and the limp leaves
Waited for rain, while the black clouds
Gathered far distant, over Himavant.[1]
The jungle crouched, humped in silence.
Then spoke the thunder   400
DA
Datta: what have we given?[2]
My friend, blood shaking my heart
The awful daring of a moment's surrender
Which an age of prudence can never retract   405
By this, and this only, we have existed
Which is not to be found in our obituaries
Or in memories draped by the beneficent spider[3]
Or under seals broken by the lean solicitor
In our empty rooms   410
DA
Dayadhvam:[4] I have heard the key

---

9. European version of the cock's crow: cock-a-doodle-doo. The cock crowed in Matthew 26:34, 74, after Peter had denied Jesus three times.   1. A mountain in the Himalayas. *Ganga:* the river Ganges in India.   2. " 'Datta, dayadhvam, damyata' (Give, sympathise, control). The fable of the meaning of the Thunder is found in the *Brihadaranyaka*—Upanishad 5,1" [Eliot's note]. In the fable, the word *DA*, spoken by the supreme being Prajapati, is interpreted as *Datta* (to give alms), *Dayadhvam* (to sympathize or have compassion), and *Damyata* (to have self-control) by gods, human beings, and demons respectively. The conclusion is that when the thunder booms DA DA DA, Prajapati is commanding that all three virtues be practiced simultaneously.   3. "Cf. Webster, *The White Devil,* V, vi: '. . . they'll remarry / Ere the worm pierce your winding-sheet, ere the spider / Make a thin curtain for your epitaphs" [Eliot's note].   4. Eliot's note on the command to "sympathize" or reach outside the self cites two descriptions of helpless isolation. The first comes from Dante's *Inferno* 33:46: as Ugolino, imprisoned in a tower with

Turn in the door once and turn once only
We think of the key, each in his prison
Thinking of the key, each confirms a prison   415
Only at nightfall, aethereal rumours
Revive for a moment a broken Coriolanus[5]
Da
Damyata: The boat responded
Gaily, to the hand expert with sail and oar   420
The sea was calm, your heart would have responded
Gaily, when invited, beating obedient
To controlling hands
                                    I sat upon the shore
Fishing,[6] with the arid plain behind me   425
Shall I at least set my lands in order?
London Bridge is falling down falling down falling down
Poi s'ascose nel foco che gli affina[7]
Quando fiam uti chelidon[8]—O swallow swallow
Le Prince d'Aquitaine à la tour abolie[9]   430
These fragments I have shored against my ruins
Why then Ile fit you. Hieronymo's mad againe.[1]
Datta. Dayadhvam. Damyata.
            Shantih   shantih   shantih[2]

Four Quartets

Little Gidding[1]

Midwinter spring is its own season
Sempiternal though sodden towards sundown,
Suspended in time, between pole and tropic.
When the short day is brightest, with frost and fire,
The brief sun flames the ice, on pond and ditches,   5

---

his children to die of starvation, says "And I heard below the door of the horrible tower being locked up"). The second is a modern description by the English philosopher F. H. Bradley (1846–1924) of the inevitably self-enclosed or private nature of consciousness: "My external sensations are no less private to myself than are my thoughts or my feelings. In either case my experience falls within my own circle, a circle closed on the outside; and, with all its elements alike, every sphere is opaque to the others which surround it. . . . In brief, regarded as an existence which appears in a soul, the whole world for each is peculiar and private to that soul" (*Appearance and Reality*).   5. A proud Roman patrician who was exiled and led an army against his homeland. In Shakespeare's play, both his grandeur and his downfall come from a desire to be ruled only by himself.   6. "V. Weston: *From Ritual to Romance*; chapter on the Fisher King" [Eliot's note].   7. Eliot's note quotes a passage in the *Purgatorio* in which Arnaut Daniel (see n. 3, p. 1859) asks Dante to remember his pain. The line cited here, "then he hid himself in the fire which refines them" (*Purgatorio* 26.148), shows Daniel departing in fire which—in Purgatory—exists as a purifying rather than a destructive element.   8. "V. *Pervigilium Veneris*. Cf. Philomela in Parts II and III [Eliot's note]. "When shall I be as a swallow?" A line from the *Vigil of Venus*, an anonymous late Latin poem, that asks for the gift of song; here associated with Philomela as a swallow, not the nightingale of lines 99–103 and 203–6.   9. "V. Gerard de Nerval, Sonnet *El Desdichado*" [Eliot's note]. The Spanish title means "The Disinherited One," and the sonnet is a monologue describing the speaker as a melancholy, ill-starred dreamer: "the Prince of Aquitaine in his ruined tower." Another line recalls the scene at the end of *Love Song of J. Alfred Prufrock* (p. 1858): "I dreamed in the grotto where sirens swim."   1. "V. Kyd's *Spanish Tragedy*" [Eliot's note]. Thomas Kyd's revenge play (1594) is subtitled "Hieronymo's Mad Againe." The protagonist "fits" his son's murderers into appropriate roles in a court entertainment so that they may all be killed.   2. "Shantih. Repeated as here, a formal ending to an Upanishad. 'The Peace which passeth understanding' is our equivalent to this word' " [Eliot's note]. The *Upanishads* comment on the sacred Hindu scriptures, the *Vedas*.   1. A village in Huntingdonshire that housed a religious community in the 17th century. Eliot visited the (rebuilt) chapel on a midwinter day.

In windless cold that is the heart's heat,
Reflecting in a watery mirror
A glare that is blindness in the early afternoon.
And glow more intense than blaze of branch, or brazier,
Stirs the dumb spirit: no wind, but pentecostal fire[2]   10
In the dark time of the year. Between melting and freezing
The soul's sap quivers. There is no earth smell
Or smell of living thing. This is the spring time
But not in time's covenant. Now the hedgerow
Is blanched for an hour with transitory blossom   15
Of snow, a bloom more sudden
Than that of summer, neither budding nor fading,
Not in the scheme of generation.
Where is the summer, the unimaginable
Zero summer?   20
                    If you came this way,
Taking the route you would be likely to take
From the place you would be likely to come from,
If you came this way in may time,[3] you would find the hedges
White again, in May, with voluptuary sweetness.   25
It would be the same at the end of the journey,
If you came at night like a broken king,[4]
If you came by day not knowing what you came for,
It would be the same, when you leave the rough road
And turn behind the pig-sty to the dull façade   30
And the tombstone. And what you thought you came for
Is only a shell, a husk of meaning
From which the purpose breaks only when it is fulfilled
If at all. Either you had no purpose
Or the purpose is beyond the end you figured   35
And is altered in fulfilment. There are other places
Which also are the world's end, some at the sea jaws,
Or over a dark lake, in a desert or a city—
But this is the nearest, in place and time,
Now and in England.   40
                    If you came this way,
Taking any route, starting from anywhere,
At any time or at any season,
It would always be the same: you would have to put off
Sense and notion. You are not here to verify,   45
Instruct yourself, or inform curiosity
Or carry report. You are here to kneel
Where prayer has been valid. And prayer is more
Than an order of words, the conscious occupation
Of the praying mind, or the sound of the voice praying.   50
And what the dead had no speech for, when living,
They can tell you, being dead: the communication
Of the dead is tongued with fire beyond the language of the living.
Here, the intersection of the timeless moment
Is England and nowhere. Never and always.   55

2. On the Pentecost day after Christ's resurrection, the apostles saw "cloven tongues like as of fire" (Acts 2:3) and were "filled with the Holy Ghost" (Acts 2:4).   3. When the May (Hawthorne) is in bloom.
4. Charles I, king of England (1600–1649), had visited the religious community several times and went there secretly after his final defeat in the English Civil War.

II

Ash on an old man's sleeve
Is all the ash the burnt roses leave.
Dust in the air suspended
Marks the place where a story ended.
Dust inbreathed was a house—   60
The wall, the wainscot and the mouse.
The death of hope and despair,
     This is the death of air.[5]

There are flood and drouth
Over the eyes and in the mouth,   65
Dead water and dead sand
Contending for the upper hand.
The parched eviscerate soil
Gapes at the vanity of toil,
Laughs without mirth.   70
     This is the death of earth.

Water and fire succeed
The town, the pasture and the weed.
Water and fire deride
The sacrifice that we denied.   75
Water and fire shall rot
The marred foundations we forgot,
Of sanctuary and choir.
     This is the death of water and fire.

In the uncertain hour before the morning[6]   80
   Near the ending of interminable night
   At the recurrent end of the unending
After the dark dove[7] with the flickering tongue
   Had passed below the horizon of his homing
   While the dead leaves still rattled on like tin   85
Over the asphalt where no other sound was
   Between three districts whence the smoke arose
   I met one walking, loitering and hurried
As if blown towards me like the metal leaves
   Before the urban dawn wind unresisting.   90
   And as I fixed upon the down-turned face
That pointed scrutiny with which we challenge
   The first-met stranger in the waning dusk
   I caught the sudden look of some dead master
Whom I had known, forgotten, half recalled   95
   Both one and many; in the brown baked features
   The eyes of a familiar compound ghost
Both intimate and unidentifiable.
So I assumed a double part,[8] and cried

---

5. "Fire lives in the death of air": a phrase from the pre-Socratic philosopher Heraclitus (535–475 B.C.) describing how one element (here, fire) lives at the expense of another (here, air).   6. The narrative passage from here to the end of Part II is written in tercets, a form that recalls Dante's use of *terza rima* (triple rhyme) in the *Divine Comedy*. Eliot later commented that this section was "the nearest equivalent to a canto of the *Inferno* or *Purgatorio*" that he could create.   7. A play on the emblem of the Holy Spirit that descended to the apostles at Pentecost and on the then-current German slang for bomb, *Taube* ("dove").   8. The role of questioner of souls (after Dante in the *Divine Comedy*) and the role of one interrogating himself.

And heard another's voice cry: "What! are *you* here?"   100
Although we were not. I was still the same,
    Knowing myself yet being someone other—
    And he a face still forming; yet the words sufficed
To compel the recognition they preceded.
    And so, compliant to the common wind,   105
    Too strange to each other for misunderstanding,
In concord at this intersection time
    Of meeting nowhere, no before and after,
    We trod the pavement in a dead patrol.
I said: "The wonder that I feel is easy,   110
    Yet ease is cause of wonder. Therefore speak:
    I may not comprehend, may not remember."
And he: "I am not eager to rehearse
    My thought and theory which you have forgotten.
    These things have served their purpose: let them be.   115
So with your own, and pray they be forgiven
    By others, as I pray you to forgive
    Both bad and good. Last season's fruit is eaten
And the fullfed beast shall kick the empty pail.
    For last year's words belong to last year's language   120
    And next year's words await another voice.
But, as the passage now presents no hindrance
    To the spirit unappeased and peregrine
    Between two worlds become much like each other,
So I find words I never thought to speak   125
    In streets I never thought I should revisit
    When I left my body on a distant shore.
Since our concern was speech, and speech impelled us
    To purify the dialect of the tribe[9]
    And urge the mind to aftersight and foresight,   130
Let me disclose the gifts reserved for age
    To set a crown upon your lifetime's effort.
    First, the cold friction of expiring sense
Without enchantment, offering no promise
    But bitter tastelessness of shadow fruit   135
    As body and soul begin to fall asunder.
Second, the conscious impotence of rage
    At human folly, and the laceration
    Of laughter at what ceases to amuse.
And last, the rending pain of re-enactment   140
    Of all that you have done, and been; the shame
    Of motives late revealed, and the awareness
Of things ill done and done to others' harm
    Which once you took for exercise of virtue.
    Then fools' approval stings, and honour stains.   145
From wrong to wrong the exasperated spirit
    Proceeds, unless restored by that refining fire
    Where you must move in measure, like a dancer."[1]
The day was breaking. In the disfigured street

---

9. In his epitaph-sonnet for Edgar Allan Poe, *The Tomb of Edgar Poe*, the French poet Stéphane Mallarmé (1842–1898) defines the poet's role as purifying speech by using ordinary language ("the dialect of the tribe") in a more precise and yet complex way, creating a new structure of interlocking or multiple meanings (see lines 221–24.)   1. In Dante's *Purgatorio* (26.148), fire is seen as a purgative or refining element, and characters are enveloped in flames that move in accord with their bodies.

He left me, with a kind of valediction,   150
And faded on the blowing of the horn.[2]

III

There are three conditions which often look alike
Yet differ completely, flourish in the same hedgerow:
Attachment to self and to things and to persons; detachment
From self and from things and from persons; and, growing between
    them, indifference   155
Which resembles the others as death resembles life,
Being between two lives—unflowering, between
The live and the dead nettle. This is the use of memory:
For liberation—not less of love but expanding
Of love beyond desire, and so liberation   160
From the future as well as the past. Thus, love of a country
Begins as attachment to our own field of action
And comes to find that action of little importance
Though never indifferent. History may be servitude,
History may be freedom. See, now they vanish,   165
The faces and places, with the self which, as it could, loved them,
To become renewed, transfigured, in another pattern.

Sin is Behovely,[3] but
All shall be well, and
All manner of thing shall be well.   170
If I think, again, of this place,
And of people, not wholly commendable,
Of no immediate kin or kindness,
But some of peculiar genius,
All touched by a common genius,   175
United in the strife which divided them;
If I think of a king at nightfall,
Of three men, and more, on the scaffold[4]
And a few who died forgotten
In other places, here and abroad,   180
And of one who died blind and quiet,[5]
Why should we celebrate
These dead men more than the dying?
It is not to ring the bell backward
Nor is it an incantation   185
To summon the spectre of a Rose.
We cannot revive old factions[6]
We cannot restore old policies
Or follow an antique drum.

2. The horn that marks the all clear signal after an air raid; also the disappearance of Hamlet's father's ghost (*Hamlet* 1.2.157): "It faded on the crowing of the cock."   3. Inevitable. Lines 168–70 repeat the consoling words of Dame Juliana of Norwich, a 14th-century English mystic: "Sin is behovabil, but all shall be well and all manner of thing shall be well."   4. Charles I and his chief advisers were executed on the scaffold after the English Civil War.   5. The poet John Milton (1608–1674), who supported Parliament and the Commonwealth in the English Civil War.   6. Alluding to the factionalisms of history exemplified here in the Wars of the Roses (1555–1585), when Yorkists, whose badge was the white rose, fought Lancastrians, whose badge was a red rose, for the English throne. The struggle ended in the strong centralized monarchy of the Tudors, whose Tudor Rose "in-folded" (compare line 259) the other two. There is also allusion to the discovery, beyond history, of the vast rose of pure light seen by Dante in the *Paradiso* (30.112ff), evoked in line 261.

These men, and those who opposed them 190
And those whom they opposed
Accept the constitution of silence
And are folded in a single party.
Whatever we inherit from the fortunate
We have taken from the defeated 195
What they had to leave us—a symbol:
A symbol perfected in death.
And all shall be well and
All manner of thing shall be well
By the purification of the motive 200
In the ground of our beseeching.

IV

The dove descending breaks the air
With flame of incandescent terror
Of which the tongues declare
The one discharge from sin and error. 205
The only hope, or else despair
    Lies in the choice of pyre or pyre—
    To be redeemed from fire by fire.

Who then devised the torment? Love.
Love is the unfamiliar Name 210
Behind the hands that wove
The intolerable shirt of flame[7]
Which human power cannot remove.
    We only live, only suspire
    Consumed by either fire or fire. 215

V

What we call the beginning is often the end
And to make an end is to make a beginning.
The end is where we start from. And every phrase
And sentence that is right (where every word is at home,
Taking its place to support the others, 220
The word neither diffident nor ostentatious,
An easy commerce of the old and the new,
The common word exact without vulgarity,
The formal word precise but not pedantic,
The complete consort[8] dancing together) 225
Every phrase and every sentence is an end and a beginning,
Every poem an epitaph. And any action
Is a step to the block, to the fire, down the sea's throat
Or to an illegible stone: and that is where we start.
We die with the dying: 230
See, they depart, and we go with them.
We are born with the dead:
See, they return, and bring us with them.

7. The shirt, poisoned with the blood of Nessus the centaur, that Deianeira (unknowingly) gave her husband Hercules to strengthen his love for her. Instead, the shirt so burned Hercules' flesh that he chose death on a funeral pyre to escape the agony.   8. Both "harmony" and "company."

The moment of the rose and the moment of the yew-tree
Are of equal duration. A people without history   235
Is not redeemed from time, for history is a pattern
Of timeless moments. So, while the light fails
On a winter's afternoon, in a secluded chapel
History is now and England.

With the drawing of this Love and the voice of this Calling[9]   240
We shall not cease from exploration
And the end of all our exploring
Will be to arrive where we started
And know the place for the first time.
Through the unknown, remembered gate   245
When the last of earth left to discover
Is that which was the beginning;
At the source of the longest river
The voice of the hidden waterfall
And the children in the apple-tree   250
Not known, because not looked for
But heard, half-heard, in the stillness
Between two waves of the sea.
Quick now, here, now, always[1] —
A condition of complete simplicity   255
(Costing not less than everything)
And all shall be well and
All manner of thing shall be well
When the tongues of flame are in-folded
Into the crowned knot of fire   260
And the fire and the rose are one.

---

9. Line from *The Cloud of Unknowing*, a 14th-century book of Christian mysticism.   1. This same line occurs toward the end of *Burnt Norton*, the first of the *Four Quartets*, where it also follows voices of children hidden in foliage; there is a suggestion of sudden insight gained in a moment of passive openness to illumination.

ANNA AKHMATOVA
1889–1966

The voice of Anna Akhmatova is intensely personal, whether she speaks as lover, wife, and mother or as a national poet commemorating the mute agony of millions. From the subjective love lyrics of her earliest work to the communal mourning of *Requiem* and the many-layered drama of *Poem without a Hero*, she expresses universal themes in terms of individual experience, and historical events through the filter of basic emotions like fear, love, hope, and pain. Akhmatova is one of the great Russian poets of the twentieth century, but she retains a broad sense of European culture, both past and present, and fills her later works with references to Western music, literature, and art that give a startling breadth and scope to her very personalized poetry. Too cosmopolitan and too independent to be tolerated by the authorities, Akhmatova was viciously attacked and her books suppressed (1922–40) because they did not fit the government-approved model of literature: they were too "individualistic" and were not "socially useful." Although she was rehabilitated in the 1960s and achieved recognized status as national poet, Akhmatova was read in secret for a long time, chiefly for the perfection of her early love lyrics. After the death of Joseph Stalin in 1953, however, her collected poems—including poems of the war years and unknown texts written during the periods of enforced silence—brought the full range of her work to public attention.

She was born Anna Andreevna Gorenko on June 11, 1889, in a suburb of the Black Sea port of Odessa and in a traditional society that she described as "Dostoevsky's Russia." Her father was a maritime engineer and her mother an independent woman of populist sympathies who belonged to an early revolutionary group called People's Will. The poet took the pen name of Akhmatova (accented on the second syllable) from her maternal great-grandmother, who was of Tatar descent. Her family soon moved to Tsarskoe Selo ("the Czar's Village"), a small town outside St. Petersburg that had been for centuries the summer palace of the czars, and also—perhaps more important for Akhmatova—a place where the great Romantic poet Alexandr Pushkin wrote his youthful works. She attended the local school at Tsarskoe Selo, but completed her degree in Kiev; in 1907, she briefly studied law at the Kiev College for Women before moving to St. Petersburg to study literature.

In Tsarskoe Selo, Akhmatova met Nikolai Gumilyov, whom she would marry in April 1910. After their marriage, the couple visited Paris during the spring of 1910 and 1911, meeting many writers and artists, including Amedeo Modigliani, who sketched Akhmatova several times and with whom she recalled wandering around Paris and reading aloud the poetry of Paul Verlaine. It was a time of change in the arts, and when the couple returned to St. Petersburg Gumilyov helped organize a Poets' Guild that became the core of a new small literary movement, Acmeism, which rejected the romantic, quasi-religious aims of Russian Symbolism, and (like Imagism) valued clarity and concreteness, and a closeness to things of this earth. The Symbolist–Acmeist debate went on inside a lively literary and social life, while the three main figures of Acmeism—Akhmatova, Gumilyov, and Osip Mandelstam—gained a reputation as important poets.

Akhmatova's first collection of poems, *Evening*, was published in the spring of 1912; it is an intensely personal collection of lyrics in which the poet describes evening as a time of awakening to love—and grief. There is a new clarity and directness to these traditionally romantic subjects, however, as for the first time in Russian poetry a woman in love expresses and analyzes her own emotions. In October of the same year, her son, Lev Gumilyov, was born; it was his arrest and imprisonment in 1935 that inspired the first poems of the cycle that would become *Requiem*. Lev was ultimately imprisoned for a total of fourteen years as the government sought a way to punish his mother, who would not or could not write according to the approved Socialist Realist style praising the government. Even after she had become a national poet known for her patriotic poetry during World War II, Akhmatova was still criticized by the Stalinist régime as a reactionary "half-harlot, half-nun" who wrote subjective love lyrics without social significance: the love poetry of *Evening, Rosary* (1914), and *The White Flock* (1917, published a month before the start of the Russian Revolution).

The White Flock was published during World War I, the destruction of which so shocked Akhmatova that she wrote, "This untimely death is so terrible / I cannot look at God's world." Yet more bloodshed was to follow in the civil war following the Revolution of 1917. Akhmatova refused to flee abroad, as many Russians were doing. Her marriage with Gumilyov was breaking up, and they divorced in 1918; she remarried an Assyriologist, Vladimir Shileiko, who did not approve of his wife's writing poetry and burned some of her poems (she divorced him in 1928). Akhmatova's political difficulties began in 1922. Although she and Gumilyov were divorced, his arrest and execution for counterrevolutionary activities in 1921 put her own status into question. After 1922 and the publication of *Anno Domini*, she was no longer allowed to publish, and was forced into the unwilling withdrawal from public activity that Russians call "internal emigration." Officially forgotten, she was not forgotten in fact; in the schools, her poems were copied out by hand and circulated among students who would never hear her name mentioned in a literature class.

Depending on a meager and irregular pension, Akhmatova prepared essays on the life and works of Pushkin, and wrote poems that that would not appear until much later. Stalin's "Great Purge" of 1935–38 sent millions of people to prison camps, and made the 1930s a time of terror and uncertainty for everyone. It is this fear and misery that is expressed in *Requiem*, as the poet blends personal references to her own life with an awareness of the common plight. The art critic Nikolai Punin, with whom she lived from 1926 to 1940, was arrested briefly in 1935; Osip Mandelstam, her great friend, was exiled to Voronezh in May 1934, and then sent to a prison camp in 1938 where he died the same year; her son, Lev, was arrested briefly in 1935 and then again in 1938, remaining imprisoned until 1941 when he was allowed to enroll in military service. Composing *Requiem* itself was a risky act carried out over several years, and Akhmatova and her friend Lidia Chukovskaya memorized the stanzas to preserve the poem in the absence of written copy. Akhmatova wrote of Mandelstam (but perhaps of them all), that "in the room of the poet in disgrace / Fear and the Muse keep watch by turns / And the night comes on / That knows no dawn." A temporary lifting of the ban against her works in 1940 did not last; although she was allowed to publish a new collection, *From Six Books*, the edition was recalled by officials after six months.

It was in 1940 that Akhmatova became interested in larger musical forms and began thinking in terms of cycles of poems instead of her accustomed separate lyrics. She envisaged a larger framework for the core poems of *Requiem* in this year, and wrote the "Dedication" and two epilogues. She also began work on the *Poem without a Hero*, a long and complex verse narrative in three parts that sums up many of her earlier themes: love, death, creativity, the unity of European culture, and the suffering of her people. During World War II the poet was allowed a partial return to public life, addressing women on the radio during the siege of Leningrad (St. Petersburg) in 1941, and writing patriotic lyrics such as the famous *Courage* (published in *Pravda* in 1942) which rallied the Russian people to defend their homeland (and national language) from enslavement. In spite of her patriotic activities, she was subject to vicious official attacks after the war. Stalin's Minister of Culture, Andrei Zhdanov, in a famous Report of 1946 proclaimed the doctrine of Socialist Realism as the official style, and attacked Akhmatova's "individualistic" writing as the "poetry of an overwrought upper-class lady who frantically races back and forth between boudoir and chapel." Akhmatova was immediately expelled from the Writer's Union, which meant that she was not officially recognized as a professional writer (and hence could not earn her living in that career).

Unable once more to publish her work, she supported herself between 1946 and 1958 by translating poetry from a number of foreign languages. Her son had been arrested again in 1949, and hoping to obtain his release, she wrote the kind of adulatory poetry in praise of Stalin that the regime required. The attempt was unsuccessful, and her son remained in prison until 1956. The Stalinist cycle, *In Praise of Peace* (1950), contains such clumsy imitations of socialist-realist poetry that it has been considered a parody: "Where a tank rumbled, there is now a peaceful tractor." Akhmatova later directed that it be omitted from her collected works.

During the slow thaw that followed Stalin's death in 1953, Akhmatova was rehabilitated. Gradually her poems were allowed back into print; an edition of selected poems with added texts was published in 1958, and in the same year she was even elected to an honorary position on the executive council of the Writer's Union. In 1965 a larger collection appeared, *The Flight of Time*, which contained a new series called *The Seventh Book* as well as part of the still-unfinished *Poem without a Hero*. She took an interest in the young writers who flocked to her and supported those who—like Josif Brodsky—were accused by the new order of being a "parasite on the state." Akhmatova's work was already recognized internationally: Robert Frost visited her on his trip to the Soviet Union in 1962, *Requiem* was first published "without her consent" in Munich in 1963 (not until 1987 was the full text published in the Soviet Union), and in 1964 she traveled to Italy to receive the Taormina poetry prize. She was surrounded by admirers when she visited England in 1965 to receive an honorary degree from Oxford University. Her death in 1966 signaled the end of an era in modern Russian poetry, for she was the last of the famous "quartet" that also included Mandelstam, Tsvetaeva, and Pasternak.

Requiem is a lyrical cycle, a series of poems written on a common theme, but it is also a short epic narrative. The story it tells is acutely personal, even autobiographical, but like an epic it also transcends personal significance and describes (as in *The Song of Roland*) a moment in the history of a nation. Akhmatova, who had seen her husband and son arrested and her friends die in prison camps, was only one of millions who had suffered similar losses in the purges of the 1930s. The "Preface," "Dedication," and two epilogues to *Requiem* constitute a framework examining this image of a common fate, while the core of numbered poems develops a more subjective picture, and the stages of an individual drama. In the inner poems, Akhmatova blends her separate personal losses—husband, son, and friends—to create a single focus, the figure of a mother grieving for her condemned son. In the frame, the poet identifies herself with the crowd of women with whom she waited for seventeen months outside the Leningrad prison—women who, in turn, represent bereaved women throughout the Soviet Union. The "I" of the speaker throughout remains anonymous, in spite of the fact that she describes her personal emotions in the central poems; her identity is that of a sorrowing mother, and she is distinguished from her fellow-suffers only by the poetic gift which makes her the "exhausted mouth, / Through which a hundred million scream." *Requiem* is at once a public and a private poem, a picture of individual grief simultaneously linked to a national disaster, and a vision of community suffering that extends past even national disaster into medieval Russian history and Greek mythology. The martyrdom of the Soviet people is consistently pictured in religious terms, from the recurrent mention of crosses and crucifixion to the culminating image of maternal suffering in Mary, the mother of Christ.

The "Dedication" and "Prologue" establish the context for the poem as a whole: the mass arrests in the 1930s after the assassination on December 1, 1934, of Sergei Kirov, the top Communist Party official in Leningrad. The women waiting outside the Kresty ("Crosses") prison of Leningrad arrive at dawn in the coldest of weather, waiting for news of their loved ones, hoping to be allowed to pass them a parcel or a letter, and fearing the sentence of death or exile to the prison camps of frozen Siberia. Instead of living a natural life where "for someone the sunset luxuriates," these women and the prisoners are forced into a suspended existence of separation and uncertainty in which all values are inverted and the city itself has become only the setting for its prisons. It is a situation before which the great forces of nature bow in silent horror.

With the numbered poems, Akhmatova recounts the growing anguish of a bereaved mother as her son is arrested and sentenced to death. The speaker describes her husband's arrest at dawn, in the midst of the family. Her son was arrested later, and in the rest of the poem she relives her numbed incomprehension as she struggles against the increasing likelihood that he will be condemned to death. Recalling her own carefree adolescence in contrast to her current situation as she weeps outside the prison walls, or pleads with Stalin to relent, the mother has a premonition of his fate that pushes her into the temporary relief of insanity and forgetting, and to a desire for her own arrest and death. After sentence is passed, the traumatized mother can speak of his execution only in oblique terms that are at once universal and potentially consoling: by shifting the image of death onto the plane of the Crucifixion and God's will. It is a tragedy that cannot be comprehended or looked at directly just as, she suggests, at the Crucifixion "No one glanced and no one would have dared" to look at the grieving Mary. In the two epilogues, the grieving speaker returns from religious transcendence to earth and current history. Here she takes on a newly composite identity, seeing herself not as an isolated sufferer but as reciprocally identified with the women whose fate she has shared. It is their memory she perpetuates by writing *Requiem* and it is in their memory that she herself lives on. No longer the victim of purely personal tragedy, she has become a bronze statue commemorating a community of suffering, a figure shaped by circumstances into a monument of public and private grief.

Sam Driver, *Anna Akhmatova* (1972), is an excellent introduction to Akhmatova's work and its historical context that stresses the years up to 1922. Amanda Haight, *Anna Akhmatova: A Poetic Pilgrimage* (1976), and Susan Amert, *In a Shattered Mirror: The Later Poetry of Anna Akhmatova* (1992), are perceptive book-length studies. Ronald Hingley, *Nightingale Fever: Russian Poets in Revolution* (1981), discusses Akhmatova, Pasternak, Tsvetaeva, and Mandelstam in the context of Russian literary history and Soviet politics up to the early years of World War II. Wendy Rosslyn, ed., *The Speech of Unknown Eyes: Akhmatova's Readers on Her Poetry* (1990), collects a range of different responses. Sharon Leiter, *Akhmatova's Petersburg* (1983), examines the image of St. Petersburg as a focus for spiritual and historical themes in Akhmatova's poetry. Editor Roberta Reeder's introduction to the poet's life and works prefaces Judith Hemschemeyer's translations in the bilingual *The Complete Poems of Anna Akhmatova* (1990). Anna Akhmatova, *My Half Century: Selected Prose*, ed. Ronald Meyer (1992), includes autobiographical material, correspondence, short pieces on other writers, and an essay on Akhmatova's prose.

Requiem[1]

1935–1940

No, not under the vault of alien skies,[2]
And not under the shelter of alien wings—
I was with my people then,
There, where my people, unfortunately, were.

1961

Instead of a Preface

In the terrible years of the Yezhov terror,[3] I spent seventeen months in the prison lines of Leningrad. Once, someone "recognized" me. Then a woman with bluish lips standing behind me, who, of course, had never heard me called by name before, woke up from the stupor to which every-

---

1. Translated by Judith Hemschemeyer.   2. A phrase borrowed from *Message to Siberia* by the Russian poet Pushkin (1799–1837).   3. In 1937–38, mass arrests were carried out by the secret police, headed by Nikolai Yezhov.

one had succumbed and whispered in my ear (everyone spoke in whispers there):

"Can you describe this?"

And I answered: "Yes, I can."

Then something that looked like a smile passed over what had once been her face.

April 1, 1957
Leningrad[4]

Dedication

Mountains bow down to this grief,
Mighty rivers cease to flow,
But the prison gates hold firm,
And behind them are the "prisoners' burrows"
And mortal woe.   5
For someone a fresh breeze blows,
For someone the sunset luxuriates—
We[5] wouldn't know, we are those who everywhere
Hear only the rasp of the hateful key
And the soldiers' heavy tread.   10
We rose as if for an early service,
Trudged through the savaged capital
And met there, more lifeless than the dead;
The sun is lower and the Neva[6] mistier,
But hope keeps singing from afar.   15
The verdict . . . And her tears gush forth,
Already she is cut off from the rest,
As if they painfully wrenched life from her heart,
As if they brutally knocked her flat,
But she goes on . . . Staggering . . . Alone . . . 20
Where now are my chance friends
Of those two diabolical years?
What do they imagine is in Siberia's storms,[7]
What appears to them dimly in the circle of the moon?
I am sending my farewell greeting to them.   25

March 1940

Prologue

That was when the ones who smiled
Were the dead, glad to be at rest.
And like a useless appendage, Leningrad
Swung from its prisons.
And when, senseless from torment,   5
Regiments of convicts marched,
And the short songs of farewell
Were sung by locomotive whistles.

---

4. The prose preface was written after her son had been released from prison and it was possible to think of editing the poem for publication.   5. The women waiting in line before the prison gates.   6. The large river that flows through St. Petersburg.   7. Victims of the purges who were not executed were condemned to prison camps in Siberia. Their wives were allowed to accompany them into exile, although they had to live in towns at a distance from the camps.

The stars of death stood above us
And innocent Russia writhed   10
Under bloody boots
And under the tires of the Black Marias.[8]

I

They led you away at dawn,
I followed you, like a mourner,
In the dark front room the children were crying,[9]
By the icon shelf the candle was dying.
On your lips was the icon's chill.[1]   5
The deathly sweat on your brow . . . Unforgettable!—
I will be like the wives of the Streltsy,
Howling under the Kremlin towers.[2]

1935

II

Quietly flows the quiet Don,[3]
Yellow moon slips into a home.

He slips in with cap askew,
He sees a shadow, yellow moon.

This woman is ill,   5
This woman is alone,

Husband in the grave,[4] son in prison,
Say a prayer for me.

III

No, it is not I, it is somebody else who is suffering.
I would not have been able to bear what happened,
Let them shroud it in black,
And let them carry off the lanterns . . .
                                        Night.   5

1940

IV

You should have been shown, you mocker,
Minion of all your friends,
Gay little sinner of Tsarskoye Selo,[5]
What would happen in your life—
How three-hundredth in line, with a parcel,   5
You would stand by the Kresty prison,

8. Police cars for conveying those arrested.   9. Akhmatova's third husband, the art historian Nikolai Punin, was arrested at dawn while the children (his daughter and her cousin) cried.   1. The icon—a small religious painting—was set on a shelf before which a candle was kept lit. Punin had kissed the icon before being taken away.   2. The *Streltsy*, elite troops organized by Ivan the Terrible around 1550, rebelled and were executed by Peter the Great in 1698. Pleading in vain, their wives and mothers saw the men killed under the towers of the Kremlin.   3. The great Russian river, often celebrated in folk songs. This poem is modeled on a simple, rhythmic short folk song known as a *chastuska*.   4. Akhmatova's first husband, the poet Nikolai Gumilyov, was shot in 1921.   5. Akhmatova recalls her early, carefree, and privileged life in Tsarskoe Selo outside St. Petersburg.

Your tempestuous tears
Burning through the New Year's ice.
Over there the prison poplar bends,
And there's no sound—and over there how many   10
Innocent lives are ending now . . .

V

For seventeen months I've been crying out,
Calling you home.
I flung myself at the hangman's feet,[6]
You are my son and my horror.
Everything is confused forever,   5
And it's not clear to me
Who is a beast now, who is a man,
And how long before the execution.
And there are only dusty flowers,
And the chinking of the censer, and tracks   10
From somewhere to nowhere.
And staring me straight in the eyes,
And threatening impending death,
Is an enormous star.[7]

1939

VI

The light weeks will take flight,
I won't comprehend what happened.
Just as the white nights[8]
Stared at you, dear son, in prison

So they are staring again,   5
With the burning eyes of a hawk,
Talking about your lofty cross,
And about death.

1939

VII

THE SENTENCE

And the stone word fell
On my still-living breast.
Never mind, I was ready.
I will manage somehow.

Today I have so much to do: 5
I must kill memory once and for all,
I must turn my soul to stone,
I must learn to live again—

6. Stalin. Akhmatova wrote a letter to him pleading for the release of her son.   7. The star, the censer and foliage, and the confusion between beast and man recall apocalyptic passages in the Book of Revelation (8:5, 7, 10–11 and 9:7–10).   8. In St. Petersburg, because it is so far north, the nights around the summer solstice are never totally dark.

Unless . . . Summer's ardent rustling
Is like a festival outside my window.   10
For a long time I've foreseen this
Brilliant day, deserted house.

June 22, 1939[9]
Fountain House

VIII

TO DEATH

You will come in any case—so why not now?
I am waiting for you—I can't stand much more.
I've put out the light and opened the door
For you, so simple and miraculous.
So come in any form you please,   5
Burst in as a gas shell
Or, like a gangster, steal in with a length of pipe,
Or poison me with typhus fumes.
Or be that fairy tale you've dreamed up,[1]
So sickeningly familiar to everyone—   10
In which I glimpse the top of a pale blue cap[2]
And the house attendant white with fear.
Now it doesn't matter anymore. The Yenisey[3] swirls,
The North Star shines.
And the final horror dims   15
The blue luster of beloved eyes.

August 19, 1939
Fountain House

IX

Now madness half shadows
My soul with its wing,
And makes it drunk with fiery wine
And beckons toward the black ravine.

And I've finally realized   5
That I must give in,
Overhearing myself
Raving as if it were somebody else.

And it does not allow me to take
Anything of mine with me   10
(No matter how I plead with it,
No matter how I supplicate):

Not the terrible eyes of my son—
Suffering turned to stone,
Not the day of the terror,   15
Not the hour I met with him in prison,

---

9. The date that her son was sentenced to labor camp.   1. A denunciation to the police for imaginary crimes, common during the purges as people hastened to protect themselves by accusing their neighbor. 2. The NKVD (secret police) wore blue caps.   3. A river in Siberia along which there were many prison camps.

Not the sweet coolness of his hands,
Not the trembling shadow of the lindens,
Not the far-off, fragile sound —
Of the final words of consolation.   20

May 4, 1940
Fountain House

X

CRUCIFIXION

"Do not weep for Me, Mother,
I am in the grave."

1

A choir of angels sang the praises of that momentous hour,
And the heavens dissolved in fire.
To his Father He said: "Why hast Thou forsaken me!"[4]
And to his Mother: "Oh, do not weep for Me. . ."[5]

1940
Fountain House

2

Mary Magdalene beat her breast and sobbed,
The beloved disciple[6] turned to stone,
But where the silent Mother stood, there
No one glanced and no one would have dared.

1943
Tashkent

Epilogue I

I learned how faces fall,
How terror darts from under eyelids,
How suffering traces lines
Of stiff cuneiform on cheeks,
How locks of ashen-blonde or black   5
Turn silver suddenly,
Smiles fade on submissive lips
And fear trembles in a dry laugh.
And I pray not for myself alone,
But for all those who stood there with me   10
In cruel cold, and in July's heat,
At that blind, red wall.

---

4. Jesus' last words from the Cross (Matthew 27:46).   **5.** These words and the epigraph refer to a line from the Russian Orthodox prayer sung at services on Easter Saturday: "Weep not for Me, Mother, when you look upon the grave." Jesus is comforting Mary with the promise of his resurrection.   **6.** The apostle John.

Epilogue II

Once more the day of remembrance[7] draws near.
I see, I hear, I feel you:

The one they almost had to drag at the end,
And the one who tramps her native land no more,

And the one who, tossing her beautiful head,   5
Said: "Coming here's like coming home."

I'd like to name them all by name,
But the list has been confiscated and is nowhere to be found.[8]

I have woven a wide mantle for them
From their meager, overheard words.   10

I will remember them always and everywhere,
I will never forget them no matter what comes.

And if they gag my exhausted mouth
Through which a hundred million scream,

Then may the people remember me   15
On the eve of my remembrance day.

And if ever in this country
They decide to erect a monument to me,

I consent to that honor
Under these conditions—that it stand   20

Neither by the sea, where I was born:
My last tie with the sea is broken,

Nor in the tsar's garden near the cherished pine stump,[9]
Where an inconsolable shade[1] looks for me,

But here, where I stood for three hundred hours,   25
And where they never unbolted the doors for me.

This, lest in blissful death
I forget the rumbling of the Black Marias,

Forget how that detested door slammed shut
And an old woman howled like a wounded animal.   30

And may the melting snow stream like tears
From my motionless lids of bronze,

And a prison dove coo in the distance,
And the ships of the Neva sail calmly on.

March 1940

---

7. In the Russian Orthodox Church, a memorial service is held on the anniversary of a death.   8. The lists of prisoners were taken away and lost.   9. The gardens and park surrounding the summer palace in Tsarskoe Selo. Akhmatova writes elsewhere of the stump of a favorite tree in the gardens and of the poet Pushkin whom she describes as walking in the park.   1. A ghost, probably the restless spirit of Akhmatova's executed husband Gumilyov, who courted her in Tsarskoe Selo.

WILLIAM FAULKNER
1897–1962

Chronicler of the American South, William Faulkner's inventive imagination and innovative use of language brought him an international reputation and influence on writers as far apart as Europe, Latin America, and China. His account of historical change between the Old and the New South as experienced by a community in mythical Yoknapatawpha County, Mississippi, involved issues that far transcended his regional roots: the clash of generations and ways of life, racial and family tragedies beyond individual comprehension or control, and the opposition of good and evil in almost archetypal terms. The breadth of his historical vision appealed to readers in the former Soviet Union and in China, where his influence is unequaled by any other modern Western author. "Faulknerian" style is best known for its brilliantly extended narrative sentences, and for its adaptation of Joyce's "stream of consciousness" technique to provide insights into a character's mind. The application of an allegorizing, fantastic imagination to the portrayal of history has also influenced writers such as the Colombian Gabriel García Márquez. With Faulkner, the Balzacian tradition of the "human comedy"—the novelist's panorama of society—develops into a new mixture of realism and linguistic innovation.

William Cuthbert Falkner was born on September 25, 1897, in New Albany, Mississippi, to a prosperous family with many ties to Southern history. The eldest of four sons, Faulkner (he adopted this spelling in 1924 for his first book) was named for a great-grandfather who commanded a Confederate regiment in the Civil War, built railroads, and wrote novels. Faulkner's father worked for the family railroad until it was sold in 1902, afterward moving his family to Oxford and eventually becoming business manager of the University of Mississippi. Faulkner's close acquaintance with Southern customs and attitudes, his own experience as the descendant of a once-prosperous and influential family, and his attachment to the region of Lafayette County and the town of Oxford (Yoknapatawpha County and Jefferson in the novels) helped to shape themes and setting in his fiction.

Young Faulkner did not like school, although he read widely in his grandfather's library and borrowed books from an older friend, Philip Stone. Leaving high school after two years to work as a bookkeeper in his grandfather's bank, he continued reading and discussing literature with Stone, who introduced him to the French writer Honoré de Balzac's novels and encouraged his writing. In the last six months of 1918 he trained in Canada as a fighter pilot—then a common way of getting more quickly into combat in World War I—but the war ended and he returned to Oxford to enroll at the university as a special student. While in school, Faulkner published poetry, prose, and drawings in *The Mississippian* and worked on the yearbook, but decided to leave the university in November 1920 to work in a New York bookstore. By December 1921 he had returned to Oxford, where he became postmaster at the university and was dismissed three years later for irresponsibility. During these years he wrote mainly poetry and seems to have been influenced by the French Symbolists: his first published poem, *L'Après-midi d'un faune*, takes its title from an earlier poem by Stéphane Mallarmé. With Stone's help, Faulkner published his first book, a collection of lyrics called *The Marble Faun* (also the title of a novel by Nathaniel Hawthorne) in 1924.

In 1925, Faulkner spent six months living in New Orleans where he was attracted to a literary group associated with *The Double Dealer*, a magazine in which he himself published poems, essays, and prose sketches. The group's chief figure was the novelist Sherwood Anderson, author of a series of regional stories published as *Winesburg, Ohio*, who encouraged Faulkner to make fictional use of his Southern background and who recommended his first novel (without having read it) to a publisher. After completing *Soldier's Pay* (1926), Faulkner took a freighter to Europe where he bicycled and hiked through Italy and France and lived for a short while in Paris. He returned to Mississippi at the end of the year, where he wrote his second novel, *Mosquitoes* (1927), a satire on the New Orleans group.

Taking up Anderson's earlier suggestion, Faulkner now embarked on the regional Yoknapatawpha series with *Sartoris* (1929), an account of the return home, marriage, and death of wounded veteran Bayard Sartoris. In Yoknapatawpha County, Faulkner created a whole fictional world with characters who reappear from novel to novel (a technique he would have encountered in Balzac's *Comédie humaine*). Here imaginary families such as the Sartorises, Compsons, Sutpens, McCaslins, and Snopeses rise to prosperity or fall into various kinds of weakness, degradation, and death. Individual characters work out destinies that are already half-shaped by family tradition and invisible community pressures. They are caught in close and often incestuous blood relationships, and make their way in a world where the values, traditions, and privileges of an old plantation society are yielding to the values of a new mercantile class. A network of family dynasties illustrates this picture of a changing society: the decaying and impoverished Compson family (*The Sound and the Fury*, 1929); two generations of Sutpens rising to great wealth and dying in madness and isolation (*Absalom, Absalom!* 1936); the McCaslin family with its history of incest, miscegenation, and guilt (*Go Down, Moses*, 1942); and the viciously grasping and ambitious "poor white" Snopes family (*The Hamlet*, 1940; *The Town*, 1957; *The Mansion*, 1959), who appear in the story printed here. These are violent works, and the murders, lynchings, and bestialities of all kinds that appear in them account for Faulkner's early American reputation as a lurid local writer. European critics, however— especially the French, who recognized his ability as early as 1931—were quick to recognize mythic overtones and classical and biblical prototypes in these tales of twisted family relationships. Faulkner's Mississippi countryside is the setting for archetypal conflicts of good and evil, or for local tragedies whose degenerate grandeur is hinted at in the names from Greek tragedy given some of the characters: Orestes Snopes, Clytemnestra Sutpen.

After *Sartoris*, Faulkner experimented with a new style modeled on the stream of consciousness technique of Joyce's *Ulysses* for his next novel, *The Sound and the Fury*. In this novel, the Compson family's tragedy is told through several different points of view, and the first version the reader encounters is the disconnected and emotionally skewed world of the idiot Benjy. Both *Sartoris* and *The Sound and the Fury* were rejected several times before finally being published in 1929, and Faulkner supported himself during these years chiefly through odd jobs (working on a shrimp trawler, in a lumber mill, and a power plant and as a carpenter, painter, and paper hanger), and then from his short stories, of which he sold thirty between 1930 and 1932. In 1929 he married Estelle Oldham Franklin, with whom he had one child, Jill, in 1933. Irritated at the difficulty of finding publishers for his serious or experimental works, the novelist set out to write a best-seller—and succeeded. *Sanctuary*, a novel of the Deep South that described the rape and prostitution of a schoolgirl, murder, perjury, and the lynching of an innocent man, was made into a movie and brought Faulkner invitations to work on movie scripts for a variety of Hollywood studios. From 1932 to 1955, the novelist added to his income by working as a "film doctor" revising and collaborating on scripts. Although his works continued to receive critical praise, he did not have any commercial successes after *Sanctuary*; in 1945 when he was, according to the French writer and philosopher Jean-Paul Sartre, the idol of young French readers, almost all his novels were out of print. It took an anthology, *The Portable Faulkner*, to reintroduce Faulkner to a wide audience in 1946. In 1950 he won the Nobel Prize for literature and used the prize money to establish the William Faulkner Foundation to assist Latin American writers and award educational scholarships to Mississippi blacks. Five years later he received the Pulitzer Prize and the National Book award for *A Fable* (1954). Faulkner's last book was a comedy set in Yoknapatawpha County, *The Reivers* (1962). He died of a heart attack in Oxford, Mississippi, on July 6, 1962.

In Faulkner's world men and women are measured by the breadth of their compassion or the quality of their endurance. Although there are villains, few wholly negative characters appear, and these are seen as grotesque distortions of humanity: the cruel and frustrated Jason Compson or the impotent rapist Popeye of *Sanctuary*, who "had that vicious depthless quality of stamped tin." Heroes tend to be larger than life, casting their shadow even after death as does Addie Bundren in *As I Lay Dying* (1930); her dying wish obliges her family to accompany her coffin across Mississippi in a miniature epic journey through flood and fire. They have the moral endurance of Bayard Sartoris II, who as a boy kills his grandmother's murderer and as a man faces down his father's killer—unarmed—to break the pattern of "honorable revenge," or the physical endurance of the tall convict in *Old Man*, whose "whole purpose," according to Faulkner, was "to prove . . . just how much the human body could bear, stand, endure." Not all characters are heroes. Some are ordinary people whose perseverance and dedication to an idea, a person, or a way of life give them larger significance; some are thoughtful people driven by circumstances to question their own identity and values; some are idiots able only to feel a succession of emotions. Faulkner generally describes such figures from the outside. We see them act, and we may even follow their thoughts in an interior monologue, but these are only traces of an inner personality that has already been decided and to which we have no real access.

The "truth" of the novels comes to us through a variety of perspectives and rhetorical strategies. Three different narrators in *Absalom, Absalom!* tell the story of Thomas Sutpen. The four points of view in *The Sound and the Fury* move from the imagined inner monologue of an idiot to the adult monologues of his nervously suicidal and psychopathic brothers, and finally to a third-person narrative focusing on Dilsey, the black woman who has been in charge of family and household and who "endures." Fifty-nine sections of interior monologue in *As I Lay Dying* express the inner relationships of the Bundren family. The convict in *Old Man* possesses a dogged, wilfully limited view of things modeled on simplistic cops-and-robbers stories and adventure tales. A narrative perspective may change tone, as happens at the end of the epic coffin journey in *As I Lay Dying* when the widowed Anse Bundren returns happily from town with a new set of false teeth, a new wife, and a phonograph. Chronology may be broken, as in the time changes represented by two typefaces in the "Benjy" section of *The Sound and the Fury*; details are exaggerated or distorted; dialect speech emphasizes the presence of the storyteller's art. Throughout, Faulkner's fluid style escapes rigid categories; it is a style of tensions and contradictions, of tragedy and humor, of realism and mythic outreach, now short and laconic, now rambling. Like Joyce and Proust, he uses long, involved, and elaborate sentences to draw the reader into a special world of the imagination, sentences that follow the ebb and flow of his characters' thoughts, or meander like a narrative consciousness absorbed in the variety of the world it describes. His tales are rooted in a community of the regional South, itself caught in the large context of historical change, but they are at the same time allegories of human endurance in an often hostile universe. Yet Faulkner's world is by no means unrelievedly somber, and its realism and earthy humor have led to his being called a "comic" writer in the broad sense that implies a universal vision encompassing the pettiness as well as the grandeur of human existence.

The Snopes family and Snopesism are at the center of *Barn Burning*. Just as the Sartoris family represents Southern aristocratic tradition in all its romanticism and humanity, the Snopeses originate as the society's shiftless "poor whites" and come to embody the cold, calculating, exploitative side of human nature that is working its way to the fore in a modern, commercially oriented age. Although members of the Snopes family take on individuality and human traits (generally perverse) when described separately, together they become allegorized into "Snopesism," a vision of evil that is openly diabolical and calls up its own counterforce. In Faulkner's view of the eternal battle between good and evil, "There is always someone that will never stop trying to cope with Snopes, that will never stop trying to get rid of Snopes." Abner Snopes is such a personification of inhuman, two-dimensional evil: "without face or depth—a shape black, flat, and bloodless as though cut from tin . . . a voice harsh like tin and without heat like tin." His human qualities are purely destructive: a ferocious independence and conviction of his own rectitude, linked to deep jealousy and rage against others' prosperity or authority; a vicious paranoia that creates opportunities for revenge; an arsonist's love for the destructive element of fire that speaks to "some deep mainspring" of his being. Young Colonel Sartoris Snopes is torn between two loyalties, as his name implies: dependent on his family and fiercely defensive of his father whenever the "enemy" threatens, he nonetheless dislikes lying, takes joy in imagining Major de Spain's mansion as a sanctuary his father cannot touch, wishes his father would change even as he recognizes he will not, and finally cuts himself off completely from his family by warning Major de Spain of the intended arson. To the psychological realism of individual portraits and of the struggle between father and son, Faulkner adds the level of a struggle between right and wrong: both sides inextricably related to each other and, at the end, both left with equally open futures.

Suggested studies include Michael Millgate, *The Achievement of William Faulkner* (1963), a critical study of the novels and stories with a brief biography in the first chapter; Cleanth Brooks, *William Faulkner: The Yoknapatawpha Country* (1963), a basic literary analysis and study of Faulkner's mythical South in the Yoknapatawpha stories, with a list of Faulkner's fictional characters. Studies of the short stories are James B. Carothers, *William Faulkner's Short Stories* (1985), which examines the stories in the context of the novels; Evans Harrington and Ann J. Abadie, eds., *Faulkner and the Short Story: Faulkner and Yoknapatawpha, 1990* (1990), which includes essays on Faulkner's impact on China and the Soviet Union, and James Ferguson, *Faulkner's Short Fiction* (1991), which focuses on Faulkner's relationship to the genre. Joseph Blotner, *Faulkner: A Biography* (1974), is the authorized and immensely detailed biography. Shorter, more specialized biographies are Stephen B. Oates, *William Faulkner, The Man and the Artist* (1987), and Joel Williamson, *William Faulkner and Southern History* (1993). More general essay collections include Linda Wagner, ed., *William Faulkner: Four Decades of Criticism* (1973), and Doreen Fowler and Ann J. Abadie, eds., *Faulkner and the Craft of Fiction: Faulkner and Yoknapatawpha* (1989). Philip Weinstein, *Faulkner's Subject: A Cosmos No One Owns* (1992), discusses the cultural constructs in Faulkner's work.

Barn Burning

The store in which the Justice of the Peace's court was sitting smelled of cheese. The boy, crouched on his nail keg at the back of the crowded room, knew he smelled cheese, and more: from where he sat he could see

the ranked shelves close-packed with the solid, squat, dynamic shapes of
tin cans whose labels his stomach read, not from the lettering which
meant nothing to his mind but from the scarlet devils and the silver curve
of fish—this, the cheese which he knew he smelled and the hermetic[1]
meat which his intestines believed he smelled coming in intermittent
gusts momentary and brief between the other constant one, the smell and
sense just a little of fear because mostly of despair and grief, the old fierce
pull of blood. He could not see the table where the Justice sat and before
which his father and his father's enemy (*our enemy* he thought in that
despair; *ourn! mine and hisn both! He's my father!*) stood, but he could
hear them, the two of them that is, because his father had said no word
yet:

"But what proof have you, Mr. Harris?"

"I told you. The hog got into my corn. I caught it up and sent it back
to him. He had no fence that would hold it. I told him so, warned him.
The next time I put the hog in my pen. When he came to get it I gave
him enough wire to patch up his pen. The next time I put the hog up and
kept it. I rode down to his house and saw the wire I gave him still rolled
on to the spool in his yard. I told him he could have the hog when he
paid me a dollar pound fee. That evening a nigger came with the dollar
and got the hog. He was a strange nigger. He said, 'He say to tell you wood
and hay kin burn.' I said, 'What?' 'That whut he say to tell you,' the nigger
said. 'Wood and hay kin burn.' That night my barn burned. I got the stock
out but I lost the barn."

"Where is the nigger? Have you got him?"

"He was a strange nigger, I tell you. I don't know what became of him."

"But that's not proof. Don't you see that's not proof?"

"Get that boy up here. He knows." For a moment the boy thought too
that the man meant his older brother until Harris said, "Not him. The
little one. The boy," and, crouching, small for his age, small and wiry like
his father, in patched and faded jeans even too small for him, with straight,
uncombed, brown hair and eyes gray and wild as storm scud, he saw the
men between himself and the table part and become a lane of grim faces,
at the end of which he saw the Justice, a shabby, collarless, graying man
in spectacles, beckoning him. He felt no floor under his bare feet; he
seemed to walk beneath the palpable weight of the grim turning faces. His
father, stiff in his black Sunday coat donned not for the trial but for the
moving, did not even look at him. *He aims for me to lie,* he thought, again
with that frantic grief and despair. *And I will have to do hit.*

"What's your name, boy?" the Justice said.

"Colonel Sartoris Snopes,"[2] the boy whispered.

"Hey?" the Justice said. "Talk louder. Colonel Sartoris? I reckon anybody named for Colonel Sartoris in this country can't help but tell the
truth, can they?" The boy said nothing. *Enemy! Enemy!* he thought; for a
moment he could not even see, could not see that the Justice's face was
kindly nor discern that his voice was troubled when he spoke to the man

---

1. Sealed-in, canned, in tins whose labels display scarlet devils and the silver curve of fish.   2. The
Snopes boy is named for Colonel [John] Sartoris, legendary founder of the aristocratic Sartoris family.

named Harris: "Do you want me to question this boy?" But he could hear, and during those subsequent long seconds while there was absolutely no sound in the crowded little room save that of quiet and intent breathing it was as if he had swung outward at the end of a grape vine, over a ravine, and at the top of the swing had been caught in a prolonged instant of mesmerized gravity, weightless in time.

"No!" Harris said violently, explosively. "Damnation! Send him out of here!" Now time, the fluid world, rushed beneath him again, the voices coming to him again through the smell of cheese and sealed meat, the fear and despair and the old grief of blood:

"This case is closed. I can't find against you, Snopes, but I can give you advice. Leave this country and don't come back to it."

His father spoke for the first time, his voice cold and harsh, level, without emphasis: "I aim to. I don't figure to stay in a country among people who . . ." he said something unprintable and vile, addressed to no one.

"That'll do," the Justice said. "Take your wagon and get out of this country before dark. Case dismissed."

His father turned, and he followed the stiff black coat, the wiry figure walking a little stiffly from where a Confederate provost's man's[3] musket ball had taken him in the heel on a stolen horse thirty years ago, followed the two backs now, since his older brother had appeared from somewhere in the crowd, no taller than the father but thicker, chewing tobacco steadily, between the two lines of grim-faced men and out of the store and across the worn gallery and down the sagging steps and among the dogs and half-grown boys in the mild May dust, where as he passed a voice hissed:

"Barn burner!"

Again he could not see, whirling; there was a face in a red haze, moonlike, bigger than the full moon, the owner of it half again his size, he leaping in the red haze toward the face, feeling no blow, feeling no shock when his head struck the earth, scrabbling up and leaping again, feeling no blow this time either and tasting no blood, scrabbling up to see the other boy in full flight and himself already leaping into pursuit as his father's hand jerked him back, the harsh, cold voice speaking above him: "Go get in the wagon."

It stood in a grove of locusts and mulberries across the road. His two hulking sisters in their Sunday dresses and his mother and her sister in calico and sunbonnets were already in it, sitting on and among the sorry residue of the dozen and more movings which even the boy could remember—the battered stove, the broken beds and chairs, the clock inlaid with mother-of-pearl, which would not run, stopped at some fourteen minutes past two o'clock of a dead and forgotten day and time, which had been his mother's dowry. She was crying, though when she saw him she drew her sleeve across her face and began to descend from the wagon. "Get back," the father said.

"He's hurt. I got to get some water and wash his . . ."

"Get back in the wagon," his father said. He got in too, over the tail-

---

3. Military policeman.

gate. His father mounted to the seat where the older brother already sat and struck the gaunt mules two savage blows with the peeled willow, but without heat. It was not even sadistic; it was exactly that same quality which in later years would cause his descendants to over-run the engine before putting a motor car into motion, striking and reining back in the same movement. The wagon went on, the store with its quiet crowd of grimly watching men dropped behind; a curve in the road hid it. *Forever* he thought. *Maybe he's done satisfied now, now that he has* . . . stopping himself, not to say it aloud even to himself. His mother's hand touched his shoulder.

"Does hit hurt?" she said.

"Naw," he said. "Hit don't hurt. Lemme be."

"Can't you wipe some of the blood off before hit dries?"

"I'll wash to-night," he said. "Lemme be, I tell you."

The wagon went on. He did not know where they were going. None of them ever did or ever asked, because it was always somewhere, always a house of sorts waiting for them a day or two days or even three days away. Likely his father had already arranged to make a crop on another farm before he . . . Again he had to stop himself. He (the father) always did. There was something about his wolflike independence and even courage when the advantage was at least neutral which impressed strangers, as if they got from his latent ravening ferocity not so much a sense of dependability as a feeling that his ferocious conviction in the rightness of his own actions would be of advantage to all whose interest lay with his.

That night they camped, in a grove of oaks and beeches where a spring ran. The nights were still cool and they had a fire against it, of a rail lifted from a nearby fence and cut into lengths—a small fire, neat, niggard almost, a shrewd fire; such fires were his father's habit and custom always, even in freezing weather. Older, the boy might have remarked this and wondered why not a big one; why should not a man who had not only seen the waste and extravagance of war, but who had in his blood an inherent voracious prodigality with material not his own, have burned everything in sight? Then he might have gone a step farther and thought that that was the reason: that niggard blaze was the living fruit of nights passed during those four years in the woods hiding from all men, blue or gray,[4] with his strings of horses (captured horses, he called them). And older still, he might have divined the true reason: that the element of fire spoke to some deep mainspring of his father's being, as the element of steel or of powder spoke to other men, as the one weapon for the preservation of integrity, else breath were not worth the breathing, and hence to be regarded with respect and used with discretion.

But he did not think this now and he had seen those same niggard blazes all his life. He merely ate his supper beside it and was already half asleep over his iron plate when his father called him, and once more he followed the stiff back, the stiff and ruthless limp, up the slope and on to the starlit road where, turning, he could see his father against the stars but without face or depth—a shape black, flat, and bloodless as though cut

---

4. In the Civil War (1861–65), Union soldiers wore blue uniforms and Confederate soldiers, gray.

from tin in the iron folds of the frockcoat which had not been made for him, the voice harsh like tin and without heat like tin:

"You were fixing to tell them. You would have told him." He didn't answer. His father struck him with the flat of his hand on the side of the head, hard but without heat, exactly as he had struck the two mules at the store, exactly as he would strike either of them with any stick in order to kill a horse fly, his voice still without heat or anger: "You're getting to be a man. You got to learn. You got to learn to stick to your own blood or you ain't going to have any blood to stick to you. Do you think either of them, any man there this morning, would? Don't you know all they wanted was a chance to get at me because they knew I had them beat? Eh?" Later, twenty years later, he was to tell himself, "If I had said they wanted only truth, justice, he would have hit me again." But now he said nothing. He was not crying. He just stood there. "Answer me," his father said.

"Yes," he whispered. His father turned.

"Get on to bed. We'll be there tomorrow."

To-morrow they were there. In the early afternoon the wagon stopped before a paintless two-room house identical almost with the dozen others it had stopped before even in the boy's ten years, and again, as on the other dozen occasions, his mother and aunt got down and began to unload the wagon, although his two sisters and his father and brother had not moved.

"Likely hit ain't fitten for hawgs," one of the sisters said.

"Nevertheless, fit it will and you'll hog it and like it," his father said. "Get out of them chairs and help your Ma unload."

The two sisters got down, big, bovine, in a flutter of cheap ribbons; one of them drew from the jumbled wagon bed a battered lantern, the other a worn broom. His father handed the reins to the older son and began to climb stiffly over the wheel. "When they get unloaded, take the team to the barn and feed them." Then he said, and at first the boy thought he was still speaking to his brother: "Come with me."

"Me?" he said.

"Yes," his father said. "You."

"Abner," his mother said. His father paused and looked back—the harsh level stare beneath the shaggy, graying, irascible brows.

"I reckon I'll have a word with the man that aims to begin to-morrow owning me body and soul for the next eight months."

They went back up the road. A week ago—or before last night, that is—he would have asked where they were going, but not now. His father had struck him before last night but never before had he paused afterward to explain why; it was as if the blow and the following calm, outrageous voice still rang, repercussed, divulging nothing to him save the terrible handicap of being young, the light weight of his few years, just heavy enough to prevent his soaring free of the world as it seemed to be ordered but not heavy enough to keep him footed solid in it, to resist it and try to change the course of its events.

Presently he could see the grove of oaks and cedars and the other flowering trees and shrubs where the house would be, though not the house yet. They walked beside a fence massed with honeysuckle and Cherokee roses[5] and came to a gate swinging open between two brick pillars, and now, beyond a sweep of drive, he saw the house for the first time and at that instant he forgot his father and the terror and despair both, and even when he remembered his father again (who had not stopped) the terror and despair did not return. Because, for all the twelve movings, they had sojourned until now in a poor country, a land of small farms and fields and houses, and he had never seen a house like this before. *Hit's big as a courthouse* he thought quietly, with a surge of peace and joy whose reason he could not have thought into words, being too young for that: *They are safe from him. People whose lives are a part of this peace and dignity are beyond his touch, he no more to them than a buzzing wasp: capable of stinging for a little moment but that's all; the spell of this peace and dignity rendering even the barns and stable and cribs which belong to it impervious to the puny flames he might contrive . . .* this, the peace and joy, ebbing for an instant as he looked again at the stiff black back, the stiff and implacable limp of the figure which was not dwarfed by the house, for the reason that it had never looked big anywhere and which now, against the serene columned backdrop, had more than ever that impervious quality of something cut ruthlessly from tin, depthless, as though, sidewise to the sun, it would cast no shadow. Watching him, the boy remarked the absolutely undeviating course which his father held and saw the stiff foot come squarely down in a pile of fresh droppings where a horse had stood in the drive and which his father could have avoided by a simple change of stride. But it ebbed only for a moment, though he could not have thought this into words either, walking on in the spell of the house, which he could even want but without envy, without sorrow, certainly never with that ravening and jealous rage which unknown to him walked in the iron-like black coat before him: *Maybe he will feel it too. Maybe it will even change him now from what maybe he couldn't help but be.*

They crossed the portico. Now he could hear his father's stiff foot as it came down on the boards with clocklike finality, a sound out of all proportion to the displacement of the body it bore and which was not dwarfed either by the white door before it, as though it had attained to a sort of vicious and ravening minimum not to be dwarfed by anything—the flat, wide, black hat, the formal coat of broadcloth which had once been black but which had now that friction-glazed greenish cast of the bodies of old house flies, the lifted sleeve which was too large, the lifted hand like a curled claw. The door opened so promptly that the boy knew the Negro must have been watching them all the time, an old man with neat grizzled hair, in a linen jacket, who stood barring the door with his body, saying, "Wipe you foots, white man, fo you come in here. Major ain't home nohow."

"Get out of my way, nigger," his father said, without heat too, flinging the door back and the Negro also and entering, his hat still on his head. And now the boy saw the prints of the stiff foot on the doorjamb and saw them appear on the pale rug behind the machinelike deliberation of the

5. An evergreen climbing rose with white flowers.

foot which seemed to bear (or transmit) twice the weight which the body compassed. The Negro was shouting "Miss[6] Lula! Miss Lula!" somewhere behind them, then the boy, deluged as though by a warm wave by a suave turn of carpeted stair and a pendant glitter of chandeliers and a mute gleam of gold frames, heard the swift feet and saw her too, a lady—perhaps he had never seen her like before either—in a gray, smooth gown with lace at the throat and an apron tied at the waist and the sleeves turned back, wiping cake or biscuit dough from her hands with a towel as she came up the hall, looking not at his father at all but at the tracks on the blond rug with an expression of incredulous amazement.

"I tried," the Negro cried. "I tole him to . . ."

"Will you please go away?" she said in a shaking voice. "Major de Spain is not at home. Will you please go away?"

His father had not spoken again. He did not speak again. He did not even look at her. He just stood stiff in the center of the rug, in his hat, the shaggy iron-gray brows twitching slightly above the pebble-colored eyes as he appeared to examine the house with brief deliberation. Then with the same deliberation he turned; the boy watched him pivot on the good leg and saw the stiff foot drag round the arc of the turning, leaving a final long and fading smear. His father never looked at it, he never once looked down at the rug. The Negro held the door. It closed behind them, upon the hysteric and indistinguishable woman-wail. His father stopped at the top of the steps and scraped his boot clean on the edge of it. At the gate he stopped again. He stood for a moment, planted stiffly on the stiff foot, looking back at the house. "Pretty and white, ain't it?" he said. "That's sweat. Nigger sweat. Maybe it ain't white enough yet to suit him. Maybe he wants to mix some white sweat with it."

Two hours later the boy was chopping wood behind the house within which his mother and aunt and the two sisters (the mother and aunt, not the two girls, he knew that; even at this distance and muffled by walls the flat loud voices of the two girls emanated an incorrigible idle inertia) were setting up the stove to prepare a meal, when he heard the hooves and saw the linen-clad man on a fine sorrel mare, whom he recognized even before he saw the rolled rug in front of the Negro youth following on a fat bay carriage horse—a suffused, angry face vanishing, still at full gallop, beyond the corner of the house where his father and brother were sitting in the two tilted chairs; and a moment later, almost before he could have put the axe down, he heard the hooves again and watched the sorrel mare go back out of the yard, already galloping again. Then his father began to shout one of the sisters' names, who presently emerged backward from the kitchen door dragging the rolled rug along the ground by one end while the other sister walked behind it.

"If you ain't going to tote, go on and set up the wash pot," the first said.

"You, Sarty!" the second shouted. "Set up the wash pot!" His father appeared at the door, framed against that shabbiness, as he had been against that other bland perfection, impervious to either, the mother's anxious face at his shoulder.

"Go on," the father said. "Pick it up." The two sisters stooped, broad,

---

6. A traditional Southern form of respectful address used also for married women.

lethargic; stooping, they presented an incredible expanse of pale cloth and a flutter of tawdry ribbons.

"If I thought enough of a rug to have to git hit all the way from France I wouldn't keep hit where folks coming in would have to tromp on hit," the first said. They raised the rug.

"Abner," the mother said. "Let me do it."

"You go back and git dinner," his father said. "I'll tend to this."

From the woodpile through the rest of the afternoon the boy watched them, the rug spread flat in the dust beside the bubbling wash-pot, the two sisters stooping over it with that profound and lethargic reluctance, while the father stood over them in turn, implacable and grim, driving them though never raising his voice again. He could smell the harsh homemade lye[7] they were using; he saw his mother come to the door once and look toward them with an expression not anxious now but very like despair; he saw his father turn, and he fell to with the axe and saw from the corner of his eye his father raise from the ground a flattish fragment of field stone and examine it and return to the pot, and this time his mother actually spoke: "Abner. Abner. Please don't. Please, Abner."

Then he was done too. It was dusk; the whippoorwills had already begun. He could smell coffee from the room where they would presently eat the cold food remaining from the mid-afternoon meal, though when he entered the house he realized they were having coffee again probably because there was a fire on the hearth, before which the rug now lay spread over the backs of the two chairs. The tracks of his father's foot were gone. Where they had been were now long, water-cloudy scoriations resembling the sporadic course of a lilliputian[8] mowing machine.

It still hung there while they ate the cold food and then went to bed, scattered without order or claim up and down the two rooms, his mother in one bed, where his father would later lie, the older brother in the other, himself, the aunt, and the two sisters on pallets on the floor. But his father was not in bed yet. The last thing the boy remembered was the depthless, harsh silhouette of the hat and coat bending over the rug and it seemed to him that he had not even closed his eyes when the silhouette was standing over him, the fire almost dead behind it, the stiff foot prodding him awake. "Catch up the mule," his father said.

When he returned with the mule his father was standing in the black door, the rolled rug over his shoulder. "Ain't you going to ride?" he said.

"No. Give me your foot."

He bent his knee into his father's hand, the wiry, surprising power flowed smoothly, rising, he rising with it, on to the mule's bare back (they had owned a saddle once; the boy could remember it though not when or where) and with the same effortlessness his father swung the rug up in front of him. Now in the starlight they retraced the afternoon's path, up the dusty road rife with honeysuckle, through the gate and up the black tunnel of the drive to the lightless house, where he sat on the mule and felt the rough warp of the rug drag across his thighs and vanish.

"Don't you want me to help?" he whispered. His father did not answer

---

7. A caustic cleanser made from leaching ashes, certain to damage any delicate material.   8. Miniature, after the tiny inhabitants of Lilliput described in Jonathan Swift's *Gulliver's Travels* (1726).

and now he heard again that stiff foot striking the hollow portico with that wooden and clocklike deliberation, that outrageous overstatement of the weight it carried. The rug, hunched, not flung (the boy could tell that even in the darkness) from his father's shoulder struck the angle of wall and floor with a sound unbelievably loud, thunderous, then the foot again, unhurried and enormous; a light came on in the house and the boy sat, tense, breathing steadily and quietly and just a little fast, though the foot itself did not increase its beat at all, descending the steps now; now the boy could see him.

"Don't you want to ride now?" he whispered. "We kin both ride now," the light within the house altering now, flaring up and sinking. *He's coming down the stairs now*, he thought. He had already ridden the mule up beside the horse block; presently his father was up behind him and he doubled the reins over and slashed the mule across the neck, but before the animal could begin to trot the hard, thin arm came round him, the hard, knotted hand jerking the mule back to a walk.

In the first red rays of the sun they were in the lot, putting plow gear on the mules. This time the sorrel mare was in the lot before he heard it at all, the rider collarless and even bareheaded, trembling, speaking in a shaking voice as the woman in the house had done, his father merely looking up once before stooping again to the hame he was buckling, so that the man on the mare spoke to his stooping back:

"You must realize you have ruined that rug. Wasn't there anybody here, any of your women . . ." he ceased, shaking, the boy watching him, the older brother leaning now in the stable door, chewing, blinking slowly and steadily at nothing apparently. "It cost a hundred dollars. But you never had a hundred dollars. You never will. So I'm going to charge you twenty bushels of corn against your crop. I'll add it in your contract and when you come to the commissary you can sign it. That won't keep Mrs. de Spain quiet but maybe it will teach you to wipe your feet off before you enter her house again."

Then he was gone. The boy looked at his father, who still had not spoken or even looked up again, who was now adjusting the logger-head in the hame.

"Pap," he said. His father looked at him—the inscrutable face, the shaggy brows beneath which the gray eyes glinted coldly. Suddenly the boy went toward him, fast, stopping as suddenly. "You done the best you could!" he cried. "If he wanted hit done different why didn't he wait and tell you how? He won't git no twenty bushels! He won't git none! We'll gether hit and hide hit! I kin watch . . ."

"Did you put the cutter back in that straight stock like I told you?"

"No, sir," he said.

"Then go do it."

That was Wednesday. During the rest of that week he worked steadily, at what was within his scope and some which was beyond it, with an industry that did not need to be driven nor even commanded twice; he had this from his mother, with the difference that some at least of what he did he liked to do, such as splitting wood with the half-size axe which his mother and aunt had earned, or saved money somehow, to present him with at Christmas. In company with the two older women (and on one afternoon, even one of the sisters), he built pens for the shoat and the cow which were a part of his father's contract with the landlord, and one afternoon, his father being absent, gone somewhere on one of the mules, he went to the field.

They were running a middle buster[9] now, his brother holding the plow straight while he handled the reins, and walking beside the straining mule, the rich black soil shearing cool and damp against his bare ankles, he thought *Maybe this is the end of it. Maybe even that twenty bushels that seems hard to have to pay for just a rug will be a cheap price for him to stop forever and always from being what he used to be*; thinking, dreaming now, so that his brother had to speak sharply to him to mind the mule: *Maybe he even won't collect the twenty bushels. Maybe it will all add up and balance and vanish—corn, rug, fire; the terror and grief, the being pulled two ways like between two teams of horses—gone, done with for ever and ever.*

Then it was Saturday; he looked up from beneath the mule he was harnessing and saw his father in the black coat and hat. "Not that," his father said. "The wagon gear." And then, two hours later, sitting in the wagon bed behind his father and brother on the seat, the wagon accomplished a final curve, and he saw the weathered paintless store with its tattered tobacco- and patent-medicine posters and the tethered wagons and saddle animals below the gallery. He mounted the gnawed steps behind his father and brother, and there again was the lane of quiet, watching faces for the three of them to walk through. He saw the man in spectacles sitting at the plank table and he did not need to be told this was a Justice of the Peace; he sent one glare of fierce, exultant, partisan defiance at the man in collar and cravat now, whom he had seen but twice before in his life, and that on a galloping horse, who now wore on his face an expression not of rage but of amazed unbelief which the boy could not have known was at the incredible circumstance of being sued by one of his own tenants, and came and stood against his father and cried at the Justice: "He ain't done it! He ain't burnt . . . ."

"Go back to the wagon," his father said.

"Burnt?" the Justice said. "Do I understand this rug was burned too?"

"Does anybody here claim it was?" his father said. "Go back to the wagon." But he did not, he merely retreated to the rear of the room, crowded as that other had been, but not to sit down this time, instead, to stand pressing among the motionless bodies, listening to the voices:

"And you claim twenty bushels of corn is too high for the damage you did to the rug?"

"He brought the rug to me and said he wanted the tracks washed out of it. I washed the tracks out and took the rug back to him."

"But you didn't carry the rug back to him in the same condition it was in before you made the tracks on it."

His father did not answer, and now for perhaps half a minute there was no sound at all save that of breathing, the faint, steady suspiration of complete and intent listening.

"You decline to answer that, Mr. Snopes?" Again his father did not

9. A double moldboard plow that throws a ridge of earth both ways.

answer. "I'm going to find against you, Mr. Snopes. I'm going to find that
you were responsible for the injury to Major de Spain's rug and hold you
liable for it. But twenty bushels of corn seems a little high for a man in
your circumstances to have to pay. Major de Spain claims it cost a hundred dollars. October corn will be worth about fifty cents. I figure that if
Major de Spain can stand a ninety-five dollar loss on something he paid
cash for, you can stand a five-dollar loss you haven't earned yet. I hold you
in damages to Major de Spain to the amount of ten bushels of corn over
and above your contract with him, to be paid to him out of your crop at
gathering time. Court adjourned."

It had taken no time hardly, the morning was but half begun. He
thought they would return home and perhaps back to the field, since they
were late, far behind all other farmers. But instead his father passed on
behind the wagon, merely indicating with his hand for the older brother
to follow with it, and crossed the road toward the blacksmith shop opposite, pressing on after his father, overtaking him, speaking, whispering up
at the harsh, calm face beneath the weathered hat: "He won't git no ten
bushels neither. He won't git one. We'll ..." until his father glanced
for an instant down at him, the face absolutely calm, the grizzled eyebrows tangled above the cold eyes, the voice almost pleasant, almost
gentle:

"You think so? Well, we'll wait till October anyway."

The matter of the wagon—the setting of a spoke or two and the tightening of the tires—did not take long either, the business of the tires
accomplished by driving the wagon into the spring branch behind the
shop and letting it stand there, the mules nuzzling into the water from
time to time, and the boy on the seat with the idle reins, looking up the
slope and through the sooty tunnel of the shed where the slow hammer
rang and where his father sat on an upended cypress bolt, easily, either
talking or listening, still sitting there when the boy brought the dripping
wagon up out of the branch and halted it before the door.

"Take them on to the shade and hitch," his father said. He did so and
returned. His father and the smith and a third man squatting on his heels
inside the door were talking, about crops and animals; the boy, squatting
too in the ammoniac dust and hoof-parings and scales of rust, heard his
father tell a long and unhurried story out of the time before the birth of
the older brother even when he had been a professional horsetrader. And
then his father came up beside him where he stood before a tattered last
year's circus poster on the other side of the store, gazing rapt and quiet at
the scarlet horses, the incredible poisings and convolutions of tulle and
tights and the painted leers of comedians, and said, "It's time to eat."

But not at home. Squatting beside his brother against the front wall, he
watched his father emerge from the store and produce from a paper sack
a segment of cheese and divide it carefully and deliberately into three with
his pocket knife and produce crackers from the same sack. They all three
squatted on the gallery and ate, slowly, without talking; then in the store
again, they drank from a tin dipper tepid water smelling of the cedar
bucket and of living beech trees. And still they did not go home. It was a
horse lot this time, a tall rail fence upon and along which men stood and

sat and out of which one by one horses were led, to be walked and trotted and then cantered back and forth along the road while the slow swapping and buying went on and the sun began to slant westward, they—the three of them—watching and listening, the older brother with his muddy eyes and his steady, inevitable tobacco, the father commenting now and then on certain of the animals, to no one in particular.

It was after sundown when they reached home. They ate supper by lamplight, then, sitting on the doorstep, the boy watched the night fully accomplish, listening to the whippoorwills and the frogs, when he heard his mother's voice: "Abner! No! No! Oh, God. Oh, God. Abner!" and he rose, whirled, and saw the altered light through the door where a candle stub now burned in a bottle neck on the table and his father, still in the hat and coat, at once formal and burlesque as though dressed carefully for some shabby and ceremonial violence, emptying the reservoir of the lamp back into the five-gallon kerosene can from which it had been filled, while the mother tugged at his arm until he shifted the lamp to the other hand and flung her back, not savagely or viciously, just hard, into the wall, her hands flung out against the wall for balance, her mouth open and in her face the same quality of hopeless despair as had been in her voice. Then his father saw him standing in the door.

"Go to the barn and get that can of oil we were oiling the wagon with," he said. The boy did not move. Then he could speak.

"What . . ." he cried. "What are you . . ."

"Go get that oil," his father said. "Go."

Then he was moving, running, outside the house, toward the stable: this the old habit, the old blood which he had not been permitted to choose for himself, which had been bequeathed him willy nilly and which had run for so long (and who knew where, battening on what of outrage and savagery and lust) before it came to him. *I could keep on,* he thought. *I could run on and on and never look back, never need to see his face again. Only I can't. I can't,* the rusted can in his hand now, the liquid sploshing in it as he ran back to the house and into it, into the sound of his mother's weeping in the next room, and handed the can to his father.

"Ain't you going to even send a nigger?" he cried. "At least you sent a nigger before!"

This time his father didn't strike him. The hand came even faster than the blow had, the same hand which had set the can on the table with almost excruciating care flashing from the can toward him too quick for him to follow it, gripping him by the back of his shirt and on to tiptoe before he had even seen it quit the can, the face stooping at him in breathless and frozen ferocity, the cold, dead voice speaking over him to the older brother, who leaned against the table, chewing with that steady, curious, sidewise motion of cows:

"Empty the can into the big one and go on. I'll catch up with you."

"Better tie him up to the bedpost," the brother said.

"Do like I told you," the father said. Then the boy was moving, his bunched shirt and the hard, bony hand between his shoulder-blades, his toes just touching the floor, across the room and into the other one, past the sisters sitting with spread heavy thighs in the two chairs over the cold hearth, and to where his mother and aunt sat side by side on the bed, the aunt's arms about his mother's shoulders.

"Hold him," the father said. The aunt made a startled movement. "Not you," the father said. "Lennie. Take hold of him. You'll hold him better than that. If he gets loose don't you know what he is going to do? He will go up yonder." He jerked his head toward the road. "Maybe I'd better tie him."

"I'll hold him," his mother whispered.

"See you do then." Then his father was gone, the stiff foot heavy and measured upon the boards, ceasing at last.

Then he began to struggle. His mother caught him in both arms, he jerking and wrenching at them. He would be stronger in the end, he knew that. But he had no time to wait for it. "Lemme go!" he cried. "I don't want to have to hit you!"

"Let him go!" the aunt said. "If he don't go, before God, I am going up there myself!"

"Don't you see I can't?" his mother cried. "Sarty! Sarty! No! No! Help me, Lizzie!"

Then he was free. His aunt grasped at him but it was too late. He whirled, running, his mother stumbled forward on to her knees behind him, crying to the nearer sister: "Catch him, Net! Catch him!" But that was too late too, the sister (the sisters were twins, born at the same time, yet either of them now gave the impression of being, encompassing as much living meat and volume and weight as any other two of the family) not yet having begun to rise from the chair, her head, face, alone merely turned, presenting to him in the flying instant an astonishing expanse of young female features untroubled by any surprise even, wearing only an expression of bovine interest. Then he was out of the room, out of the house, in the mild dust of the starlit road and the heavy rifeness of honey-suckle, the pale ribbon unspooling with terrific slowness under his running feet, reaching the gate at last and turning in, running, his heart and lungs drumming, on up the drive toward the lighted house, the lighted door. He did not knock, he burst in, sobbing for breath, incapable for the moment of speech; he saw the astonished face of the Negro in the linen jacket without knowing when the Negro had appeared.

"De Spain!" he cried, panted. "Where's . . . ." then he saw the white man too emerging from a white door down the hall. "Barn!" he cried. "Barn!"

"What?" the white man said. "Barn?"

"Yes!" the boy cried. "Barn!"

"Catch him!" the white man shouted.

But it was too late this time too. The Negro grasped his shirt, but the entire sleeve, rotten with washing, carried away, and he was out that door too and in the drive again, and had actually never ceased to run even while he was screaming into the white man's face.

Behind him the white man was shouting, "My horse! Fetch my horse!" and he thought for an instant of cutting across the park and climbing the fence into the road, but he did not know the park nor how high the vine-massed fence might be and he dared not risk it. So he ran on down the drive, blood and breath roaring; presently he was in the road again though he could not see it. He could not hear either: the galloping mare was almost upon him before he heard her, and even then he held his course, as if the very urgency of his wild grief and need must in a moment more find his wings, waiting until the ultimate instant to hurl himself aside and into the weed-choked roadside ditch as the horse thundered past and on, for an instant in furious silhouette against the stars, the tranquil early summer night sky which, even before the shape of the horse and rider vanished, stained abruptly and violently upward: a long, swirling roar incredible and soundless, blotting the stars, and he springing up and into the road again, running again, knowing it was too late yet still running even after he heard the shot and, an instant later, two shots, pausing now without knowing he had ceased to run, crying "Pap! Pap!", running again before he knew he had begun to run, stumbling, tripping over something and scrabbling up again without ceasing to run, looking backward over his shoulder at the glare as he got up, running on among the invisible trees, panting, sobbing, "Father! Father!"

At midnight he was sitting on the crest of a hill. He did not know it was midnight and he did not know how far he had come. But there was no glare behind him now and he sat now, his back toward what he had called home for four days anyhow, his face toward the dark woods which he would enter when breath was strong again, small, shaking steadily in the chill darkness, hugging himself into the remainder of his thin, rotten shirt, the grief and despair now no longer terror and fear but just grief and despair. *Father. My father*, he thought. "He was brave!" he cried suddenly, aloud but not loud, no more than a whisper: "He was! He was in the war! He was in Colonel Sartoris' cav'ry!" not knowing that his father had gone to that war a private in the fine old European sense, wearing no uniform, admitting the authority of and giving fidelity to no man or army or flag, going to war as Malbrouck[1] himself did: for booty—it meant nothing and less than nothing to him if it were enemy booty or his own.

The slow constellations wheeled on. It would be dawn and then sun-up after a while and he would be hungry. But that would be to-morrow and now he was only cold, and walking would cure that. His breathing was easier now and he decided to get up and go on, and then he found that he had been asleep because he knew it was almost dawn, the night almost over. He could tell that from the whippoorwills. They were everywhere now among the dark trees below him, constant and inflectioned and ceaseless, so that, as the instant for giving over to the day birds drew nearer and nearer, there was no interval at all between them. He got up. He was a little stiff, but walking would cure that too as it would the cold, and soon there would be the sun. He went on down the hill, toward the dark woods within which the liquid silver voices of the birds called unceasing—the rapid and urgent beating of the urgent and quiring heart of the late spring night. He did not look back.

---

1. The duke of Marlborough (1650–1722), an English general whose name became distorted as Malbrough and Malbrouch in English and French popular songs celebrating his exploits.

BERTOLT BRECHT
1898–1956

Bertolt Brecht is a dominant figure in modern drama not only as the author of half a dozen plays which rank as modern classics but as the first master of a powerful new concept of theater. He was dissatisfied with the traditional notion, derived from Aristotle's *Poetics*, that drama should draw its spectators into identification with and sympathy for the characters, and with the realist aesthetic of naturalness and psychological credibility. Brecht saw only harm in such uncritical submission to illusions created on stage. Like Pirandello, he believed that the modern stage should break open the closed world established as a dramatic convention by writers such as Ibsen and Chekhov, whose audiences were to look at the action from a distance, as if it were a slice of real life going on behind an invisible "fourth wall." Unlike Pirandello, however, Brecht did not stress the anguish of individuals in society and the difficulty of knowing who we are; his focus was the community at large, and social responsibility. For Brecht, a political activist, the modern audience must not be allowed to indulge in passive emotional identification at a safe distance, or in the subjective whirlpool of existential identity crises. His characters are to be seen as members of society, and his audience must be educated and moved to action. The movement called "epic theater," which was born in the 1920s, suited his needs well, and through his plays, theoretical writings, and dramatic productions he developed its basic ideas into one of the most powerful theatrical styles of the century.

Eugen Berthold Brecht was born in the medieval town of Augsburg, Bavaria, on February 10, 1898. His father was a respected town citizen, director of a paper mill, and a Catholic. His mother, the daughter of a civil servant from the Black Forest, was a Protestant who raised young Berthold in her own faith. (The spelling *Bertolt* was adopted later.) Brecht attended local schools until 1917, when he enrolled in Munich University to study natural science and medicine. He continued his studies while acting as drama critic for an Augsburg newspaper and writing his own plays: *Drums in the Night* (1918) won the Kleist Prize in 1922. In 1918, Brecht was mobilized for a year as an orderly in a military hospital, and he pursued medical studies at Munich until 1921. In 1929 he married Helene Weigel, an actress who worked closely with him and for whom he wrote many leading roles. Together, they would direct and make famous the theater group founded for them in 1949 in East Berlin: the Berliner Ensemble.

Moving to Berlin, Brecht worked briefly with the directors Max Reinhardt and Erwin Piscator but was chiefly interested in his own writing. In this pre-Marxist period he is especially concerned with the plight of the individual "common man," pushed around by social and economic forces beyond his control until he loses both identity and humanity. In *A Man's a Man* (1924–25), the timid dock worker Galy Gay is transformed by fright and persuasion into another person, the ferociously successful soldier Jeriah Jip. When Jip turns up at the end of the play, he is given Gay's former papers and forced to assume Gay's old identity. The play teaches that human personalities can be broken down and reassembled like a machine; the only weapon against such mindless manipulation is awareness, an awareness that enables people to understand and control their destiny.

Most of Brecht's plays are didactic, either openly or by implication. After he became a fervent Marxist in the mid-1920s, he considered it even more his moral and artistic duty to encourage the audience to remedy social ills. *The Threepenny Opera* (1928), a ballad opera written with composer Kurt Weill (1900–50) and modeled on John Gay's *The Beggar's Opera* (1728), satirizes capitalist society from the point of view of outcasts and romantic thieves. Brecht also wrote a number of "lesson" plays intended to set forth Communist doctrine and to instruct the workers of Germany in the meaning of social revolution. The lesson was particularly harsh in *The Measures Taken* (1930), which describes the necessary execution of a young party member who has broken discipline and helped the local poor, thus postponing the revolution. Such drama, however doctrinally pure, was not likely to win adherents to the cause, and the lesson plays were condemned as unattractive and "intellectualist" by the Communist press in Berlin and Moscow.

Brecht's unorthodoxy, his pacifism, his enthusiasm for Marx, and his desire to create an activist popular theater that would embody a Marxist view of art all put him at odds with the rising power of Hitler's National Socialism. He fled Germany for Denmark in 1933, before the Nazis could include him in their purge of left-wing intellectuals; in 1935, he was deprived of his German citizenship. Brecht was to flee several more times as the Nazi invasions expanded throughout Europe: in 1939 he went to Sweden, in 1940 to Finland, and in 1941 to the United States, where he joined a colony of German expatriates in Santa Monica, California, working for the film industry. This was the period of some of his greatest plays: *The Life of Galileo* (1938–39), which attacks society for suppressing Galileo's discovery that the earth revolves around the sun, but also condemns the scientist for not insisting openly on the truth; *Mother Courage and Her Children* (1939), included here; *The Good Woman of Setzuan* (1938–40), which shows how an instinctively good and generous person can only survive in this world by putting on a mask of hardness and calculation; and *The Caucasian Chalk Circle* (1944–45), which adapts the legendary choice of Solomon between two mothers who claim the same infant and decides in favor of the servant girl—who cared for the child—over the wealthy mother (the implied comparison is between those who do the work of society and those who merely profit from their possessions). In America, Brecht arranged for the translation of his work into English, and *Galileo*, with Charles Laughton in the title role, was produced in 1947. In the same year, he was questioned by the House Un-American Activities Committee as part of a wide-ranging inquiry into possible Communist activity in the entertainment business. No charges were brought, but he left for Europe the day after being brought before the committee.

After leaving the United States, Brecht worked for a year in Zurich before going to Berlin with his wife, Helene Weigel, to stage *Mother Courage*. The East Berlin government offered the couple positions as directors of their own troupe, the Berliner Ensemble, and Brecht—who had just finished a theoretical work on the theater, *A Little Organon for the Theater* (1949)—turned his attention to the professional role of director. Although the East Berliners subsidized Brecht's work and advertised the artist's presence among them as a tribute to their own political system, they also obliged him to defend some of his plays against charges of political unorthodoxy and indeed to revise them. After 1934, the prevailing Communist Party view had upheld a style called "socialist realism," whose goal was to offer simple messages and to foster identification with revolutionary heroes. Brecht's mind was too keen and questioning, too attracted by irony and paradox, for him to provide the simplistic drama desired or to have a comfortable relation with authority, either of the right or of the left. After settling in East Berlin, he wrote no major new plays but only minor propaganda pieces and adaptations of classical works such as Molière's *Don Juan* and Shakespeare's *Coriolanus*. As an additional measure of protection, he took out Austrian citizenship through his wife's nationality. Brecht died in Berlin on August 14, 1956.

The "epic theater" for which Brecht is known derives its name from a famous essay, *On Epic and Dramatic Poetry*, by Goethe and Schiller, who in 1797 described *dramatic* poetry as pulling the audience into emotional identification, in contrast to *epic* poetry, which by being distanced in the time, place, and nature of the action could be absorbed in calm contemplation. The idea of an epic theater is a paradox: how can a play engage an audience that is still held at a distance? Brecht's solution was to employ many "alienation effects" that were genuinely dramatic, but that prevented total identification with the characters and forced spectators to think critically about what was taking place. These alienation effects have since become standard production techniques in the modern theater. In spite of Brecht's intentions and frequent revisions, however, the characters and situations of his plays remain emotionally engrossing, especially in his best-known works, such as *Mother Courage and Her Children.*

Brecht's concept of an epic theater touches on all aspects of the form: dramatic structure, stage setting, music, and the actor's performance. The structure is to be open, episodic, and broken by dramatic or musical interludes. It is a "chronicle" that recounts events in an epic or distanced perspective. Episodes may also be performed independently as self-contained dramatic parables, instead of being organically tied to a centrally developing plot. Skits appear between scenes: in *A Man's a Man*, there is a fantastic interlude in which an elephant is accused of having murdered its mother. Sometimes a narrator comments on the action (as in *The Three-Penny Opera* and *A Man's a Man*). The alienation effects are also heightened by setting most of the plays in far-away lands (China in *The Good Woman of Setzuan*, India in *A Man's a Man*, England in *The Three-Penny Opera*, the Soviet Union in *The Caucasian Chalk Circle*, Chicago in *Saint Joan of the Stockyards* and *The Resistible Rise of Arturo Ui*) or distant times (the seventeenth century in *Mother Courage*, Renaissance Italy in *Galileo*, or an imagined ghostly afterlife in *The Trial of Lucullus*).

Stagecraft and performance further support Brecht's concept of a critical, intellectualized theater. Events on stage are announced beforehand by signs, or are accompanied by projected films and images during the action itself. Place names are printed on signs and suspended over the actors, and footlights and stage machinery are openly displayed. Songs that interrupt the dramatic action are addressed directly to the audience, and are often heralded by a sign Brecht called a "musical emblem: in *Mother Courage*, 'a trumpet, a drum, a flag, and electric globes that lit up.'" In addition, Brecht described a special kind of acting: actors should "demonstrate" their parts instead of being submerged in them. At rehearsals, Brecht often asked actors to speak their parts in the third person instead of the first. Masks were occasionally used for wicked people or soldiers' faces were chalked white to suggest a stylized fear. Such constant artificiality introduced into all aspects of the performance makes it difficult for the audience to identify completely and unself-consciously with the characters on stage.

Audiences may react emotionally to Brecht's plays and characters, but their reactions are never simple. Brecht's characters are complex and inhabit complex situations. Galileo is both a dedicated scientist who sacrifices his reputation for honesty so as to complete his work, and a weak sensualist who fails to realize how his recantation will affect others' pursuit of scientific knowledge. In *The Good Woman of Setzuan*, the overgenerous Shen Te can survive only by periodically adopting the mask of a harshly practical "cousin," Shui Ta. Mother Courage is both a tragic mother figure and a small-time profiteer who loses her children as she battens on war. Brecht's work teems with such paradoxes at all levels. He is a cynic who deflates religious zeal, militant patriotism, and heroic example as delusions that lead the masses on to futile sacrifice; yet he is also a preacher who makes prominent use of traditional biblical language and imagery, and themes of individual sacrifice.

Mother Courage, written shortly after Brecht turned forty, combines all these elements. The play is set in Germany, in the middle years of the Thirty Years' War

(1618–48), a conflict involving all of Europe and believed at the time of Brecht's writing to have destroyed half the German population. But senseless violence, religious intolerance, artificial patriotism, and cynical opportunism were equally apparent in seventeenth-century Germany and in the Nazi state, and the setting gave Brecht what he needed to write a strongly pacifist play in 1939, the year in which World War II was to begin.

Mother Courage evoked the sympathy of early audiences for her tragic inability to prevent her children's death. Such was not Brecht's intention, and he rewrote several sections of the play to bring out her avarice and blindness, and her belief that she can use the war and profit from others' misery without endangering her own family. To Brecht, the tragedy of her life lay in her failure to relate the general fate of society to that of her own family. In trying to manipulate the system for her personal advantage, she denies the personal rights of others: she calls to others to enlist but not to her own children, and she would rather sell shirts to the officers than use them to bind a peasant's wounds. Yet the war that Mother Courage sees as a good provider ends by killing her three children, and even sooner because of their virtues (Eilif's martial zeal, Swiss Cheese's honesty, Kattrin's pity). Mother Courage is ruined, all the more so since she has learned nothing from the war and does not protest it. Instead, her bitter "Song of the Great Capitulation" presents compromise as inevitable, and at the end of the play she is chasing after a new regiment to continue her peddler's career.

Each of the twelve parable-like scenes of Mother Courage presents a particular aspect or lesson of the war. Setting and props encourage the audience to see the action as a "demonstration" by drawing attention to the way the play is put on. Signs or titles are projected onto a screen to announce what is about to happen; a revolving stage and projected backgrounds suggest the wagon's travels in a highly stylized way; a group of musicians sits in full view beside the stage to accompany the songs; realistic but sketchy three-dimensional structures represent buildings. The main piece of stage furniture is Mother Courage's canteen wagon, whose increasingly dilapidated appearance reveals her fall from prosperity into lonely poverty. In the first scene, the whole family appears with the wagon: at the end, Mother Courage pulls it alone.

Brecht hoped that Mother Courage and Her Children would show its audiences "that in wartime the big profits are not made by little people. That war, which is a continuation of business by other means, makes the human virtues fatal even to their possessors. That no sacrifice is too great for the struggle against war." This last point is demonstrated by Kattrin's death, for she is the only one of Mother Courage's family whose virtue is not perverted by the war, and whose death is meant to provide a moral example. Drumming frantically to awaken the endangered city of Halle, she sacrifices her life to save the city's threatened children. Religious and secular themes join at this point as they do so often in the course of the play, for Kattrin acts immediately after hearing the peasant family bemoan their helplessness and pray to God for miraculous aid. It is action like hers, not passive prayer, that Brecht hopes to evoke with his epic theater. Both the play itself and its self-conscious, "alienated" staging try to move the audience toward a clearer understanding of the societal forces that condition their destinies—and to a responsible choice of their own roles.

Martin Esslin, Brecht, The Man and His Work (1974), provides a basic biography and overview. John Willett, ed. and trans., Brecht on Theatre: The Development of an Aesthetic (1964), contains Brecht's own essays and lectures on his theater. Other views of Brecht are found in Peter Demetz, ed., Brecht: A Collection of Critical Essays (1962), and Siegfried Mews, ed., Critical Essays on Bertolt Brecht (1989). Ronald Hayman, Brecht: A Biography (1983), offers a detailed view of Brecht's life. Eric Bentley, The Brecht Commentaries 1943–1986 (1987), offers lively essays on the major plays, on Brecht's stagecraft, and on his place in modern culture by a friend and sometime colleague. The essays in Walter Benjamin, *Understanding Brecht* (1983), provide important insights into Brecht's work and modern thought by a close friend and major intellectual figure.

PRONOUNCING GLOSSARY

The following list uses common English syllables and stress accents to provide rough equivalents of selected words whose pronunciation may be unfamiliar to the general reader.

Eilif: *ai'-lif*

Fichtelgebirge: *fikh-tel-ge-beer'-guh*

Fierling: *feer'-ling*

Mother Courage and Her Children[1]

A Chronicle of the Thirty Years' War[2]

CHARACTERS

MOTHER COURAGE	THE OLD COLONEL
KATTRIN, *her mute daughter*	A CLERK
EILIF, *her elder son*	A YOUNG SOLDIER
SWISS CHEESE, *her younger son*	AN OLDER SOLDIER
THE RECRUITER	A PEASANT
THE SERGEANT	THE PEASANT'S WIFE
THE COOK	THE YOUNG MAN
THE GENERAL	THE OLD WOMAN
THE CHAPLAIN	ANOTHER PEASANT
THE ORDNANCE OFFICER	THE PEASANT WOMAN
YVETTE POTTIER	A YOUNG PEASANT
THE MAN WITH THE PATCH OVER HIS	THE LIEUTENANT
EYE	SOLDIERS
THE OTHER SERGEANT	A VOICE

1

Spring 1624. General Oxenstjerna recruits troops in Dalarna for the Polish campaign. The canteen woman, Anna Fierling, known as Mother Courage, loses a son.[3]

1. Translated by Ralph Manheim.   2. Actually a series of wars fought in central Europe from 1618 to 1648. At the time *Mother Courage* opens, in 1624, a Swedish army has been fighting in Poland for three years. After winning the coastal province of Livonia (now in Latvia and Estonia), it invades Germany in 1630 under the command of King Gustavus Adolphus. The king, however, fails to relieve the siege of Magdeburg by the imperial general Johan Tserclaes, count of Tilly, and the Protestant bishopric is burned to the ground. Gustavus Adolphus later defeats Tilly in two major battles, but in 1632 both are killed, and two years later the Swedish force is destroyed by the Imperial Army. The ensuing peace is brief, for in 1635 a new Swedish army, joined by troops from Catholic France, renews the fighting. This last phase of the war has just begun at the end of *Mother Courage*, and lasting peace will come only twelve years later. (Brecht is true to history as he knew it; only recently have historians disputed the traditional belief that the war devastated Germany and halved its population.)   3. The heading for this and each new scene is projected on a screen on stage; it situates the action and tells what will happen. General Oxenstjerna

Highway near a city.

A SERGEANT *and a* RECRUITER *stand shivering.*

THE RECRUITER: How can anybody get a company together in a place like this? Sergeant, sometimes I feel like committing suicide. The general wants me to recruit four platoons by the twelfth, and the people around here are so depraved I can't sleep at night. I finally get hold of a man, I close my eyes and pretend not to see that he's chicken-breasted and he's got varicose veins, I get him good and drunk and he signs up. While I'm paying for the drinks, he steps out, I follow him to the door because I smell a rat: Sure enough, he's gone, like a fart out of a goose. A man's word doesn't mean a thing, there's no honor, no loyalty. This place has undermined my faith in humanity, sergeant.

THE SERGEANT: It's easy to see these people have gone too long without a war. How can you have morality without a war, I ask you? Peace is a mess, it takes a war to put things in order. In peacetime the human race goes to the dogs. Man and beast are treated like so much dirt. Everybody eats what they like, a big piece of cheese on white bread, with a slice of meat on top of the cheese. Nobody knows how many young men or good horses there are in that town up ahead, they've never been counted. I've been in places where they hadn't had a war in as much as seventy years, the people had no names, they didn't even know who they were. It takes a war before you get decent lists and records; then your boots are done up in bales and your grain in sacks, man and beast are properly counted and marched away, because people realize that without order they can't have a war.

THE RECRUITER: How right you are!

THE SERGEANT: Like all good things, a war is hard to get started. But once it takes root, it's vigorous; then people are as scared of peace as dice players are of laying off, because they'll have to reckon up their losses. But at first they're scared of war. It's the novelty.

THE RECRUITER: Say, there comes a wagon. Two women and two young fellows. Keep the old woman busy, sergeant. If this is another flop, you won't catch me standing out in this April wind any more.

[*A Jew's harp is heard. Drawn by two young men, a covered wagon[4] approaches. In the wagon sit* MOTHER COURAGE *and her mute daughter* KATTRIN.]

MOTHER COURAGE: Good morning, sergeant.

SERGEANT: [*Barring the way.*] Good morning, friends. Who are you?

MOTHER COURAGE: Business people. [*Sings.*]
       Hey, Captains, make the drum stop drumming
       And let your soldiers take a seat.
       Here's Mother Courage, with boots she's coming
       To help along their aching feet.
       How can they march off to the slaughter
       With baggage, cannon, lice and fleas

---

was one of the Swedish generals. Dalarna is a rural province in central Sweden. A *canteen woman* sells provisions to soldiers.   4. "A cross between a military vehicle and a general store" [Brecht's note]. *Jew's harp*: a small, twangy instrument held against the teeth, associated with folk music.

Across the rocks and through the water
Unless their boots are in one piece?
    The spring is come. Christian, revive![5]
    The snowdrifts melt. The dead lie dead.
    And if by chance you're still alive
    It's time to rise and shake a leg.

O Captains, don't expect to send them
To death with nothing in their crops.
First you must let Mother Courage mend them
In mind and body with her schnapps.[6]
On empty bellies it's distressing
To stand up under shot and shell.
But once they're full, you have my blessing
To lead them to the jaws of hell.
    The spring is come. Christian, revive!
    The snowdrifts melt, the dead lie dead.
    And if by chance you're still alive
    It's time to rise and shake a leg.

THE SERGEANT: Halt, you scum. Where do you belong?

THE ELDER SON: Second Finnish Regiment.

THE SERGEANT: Where are your papers?

MOTHER COURAGE: Papers?

THE YOUNGER SON: But she's Mother Courage!

THE SERGEANT: Never heard of her. Why Courage?

MOTHER COURAGE: They call me Courage, sergeant, because when I saw ruin staring me in the face I drove out of Riga through cannon fire with fifty loaves of bread in my wagon. They were getting moldy, it was high time, I had no choice.

THE SERGEANT: No wisecracks. Where are your papers?

MOTHER COURAGE: [*Fishing a pile of papers out of a tin box and climbing down.*] Here are my papers, sergeant. There's a whole missal, picked it up in Alt-Ötting to wrap cucumbers in, and a map of Moravia,[7] God knows if I'll ever get there, if I don't it's total loss. And this here certifies that my horse hasn't got hoof-and-mouth disease, too bad, he croaked on us, he cost fifteen guilders,[8] but not out of my pocket, glory be. Is that enough paper?

THE SERGEANT: Are you trying to pull my leg? I'll teach you to get smart. You know you need a license.

MOTHER COURAGE: You mind your manners and don't go telling my innocent children that I'd go anywhere near your leg, it's indecent. I want no truck with you. My license in the Second Regiment is my honest face, and if you can't read it, that's not my fault. I'm not letting anybody put his seal on it.

---

5. The phrase in German parodies religious announcements of Easter and Christ's resurrection.   6. Liquor, especially gin. (The original says *wein*, "wine.")   7. Part of the Czech Republic. *Missal:* prayer book. *Alt-Ötting:* a place of pilgrimage fifty miles east of Munich in the south German kingdom of Bavaria.   8. The basic unit of Dutch money, also called a *florin*. When Brecht was writing, one guilder was worth about twenty-five cents.

THE RECRUITER: Sergeant, I detect a spirit of insubordination in this woman. In our camp we need respect for authority.

MOTHER COURAGE: Wouldn't sausage be better?

THE SERGEANT: Name.

MOTHER COURAGE: Anna Fierling.

THE SERGEANT: Then you're all Fierlings.

MOTHER COURAGE: What do you mean? Fierling is my name. Not theirs.

THE SERGEANT: Aren't they all your children?

MOTHER COURAGE: That they are, but why should they all have the same name? [*Pointing at the elder son.*] This one, for instance. His name is Eilif Nojocki. How come? Because his father always claimed to be called Kojocki or Mojocki. The boy remembers him well, except the one he remembers was somebody else, a Frenchman with a goatee. But aside from that, he inherited his father's intelligence, that man could strip the pants off a peasant's ass without his knowing it. So, you see, we've each got our own name.

THE SERGEANT: Each different, you mean?

MOTHER COURAGE: Don't act so innocent.

THE SERGEANT: I suppose that one's a Chinaman? [*Indicating the younger son.*]

MOTHER COURAGE: Wrong. He's Swiss.

THE SERGEANT: After the Frenchman?

MOTHER COURAGE: What Frenchman? I never heard of any Frenchman. Don't get everything balled up or we'll be here all day. He's Swiss, but his name is Fejos, the name has nothing to do with his father. He had an entirely different name, he was an engineer, built fortifications, but he drank.

[SWISS CHEESE *nods, beaming; the mute* KATTRIN *is also tickled.*]

THE SERGEANT: Then how can his name be Fejos?

MOTHER COURAGE: I wouldn't want to offend you, but you haven't got much imagination. Naturally his name is Fejos because when he came I was with a Hungarian, it was all the same to him, he was dying of kidney trouble though he never touched a drop, a very decent man. The boy takes after him.

THE SERGEANT: But you said he wasn't his father?

MOTHER COURAGE: He takes after him all the same. I call him Swiss Cheese, how come, because he's good at pulling the wagon. [*Pointing at her daughter.*] Her name is Kattrin Haupt, she's half German.

THE SERGEANT: A fine family, I must say.

MOTHER COURAGE: Yes, I've been all over the world with my wagon.

THE SERGEANT: It's all being taken down. [*He takes it down.*] You're from Bamberg, Bavaria. What brings you here?

MOTHER COURAGE: I couldn't wait for the war to kindly come to Bamberg.

THE RECRUITER: You wagon pullers ought to be called Jacob Ox and Esau[9] Ox. Do you ever get out of harness?

EILIF: Mother, can I clout him one on the kisser? I'd like to.

9. Biblical twin brothers (Genesis 26:22–26).

MOTHER COURAGE: And I forbid you. You stay put. And now, gentlemen, wouldn't you need a nice pistol, or a belt buckle, yours is all worn out, sergeant.

THE SERGEANT: I need something else. I'm not blind. Those young fellows are built like tree trunks, big broad chests, sturdy legs. Why aren't they in the army? That's what I'd like to know.

MOTHER COURAGE: [*Quickly.*] Nothing doing, sergeant. My children aren't cut out for soldiers.

THE RECRUITER: Why not? There's profit in it, and glory. Peddling shoes is woman's work. [*To* EILIF.] Step up; let's feel if you've got muscles or if you're a sissy.

MOTHER COURAGE: He's a sissy. Give him a mean look and he'll fall flat on his face.

THE RECRUITER: And kill a calf if it happens to be standing in the way. [*Tries to lead him away.*]

MOTHER COURAGE: Leave him alone. He's not for you.

THE RECRUITER: He insulted me. He referred to my face as a kisser. Him and me will now step out in the field and discuss this thing as man to man.

EILIF: Don't worry, mother. I'll take care of him.

MOTHER COURAGE: You stay put. You no-good! I know you, always fighting. He's got a knife in his boot, he's a knifer.

THE RECRUITER: I'll pull it out of him like a milk tooth. Come on, boy.

MOTHER COURAGE: Sergeant, I'll report you to the colonel. He'll throw you in the lock-up. The lieutenant is courting my daughter.

THE SERGEANT: No rough stuff, brother. [*To* MOTHER COURAGE.] What have you got against the army? Wasn't his father a soldier? Didn't he die fair and square? You said so yourself.

MOTHER COURAGE: He's only a child. You want to lead him off to slaughter, I know you. You'll get five guilders for him.

THE RECRUITER: He'll get a beautiful cap and top boots.

EILIF: Not from you.

MOTHER COURAGE: Oh, won't you come fishing with me? said the fisherman to the worm. [*To* SWISS CHEESE.] Run and yell that they're trying to steal your brother. [*She pulls a knife.*] Just try to steal him. I'll cut you down, you dogs. I'll teach you to put him in your war! We do an honest business in ham and shirts, we're peaceful folk.

THE SERGEANT: I can see by the knife how peaceful you are. You ought to be ashamed of yourself, put that knife away, you bitch. A minute ago you admitted you lived off war, how else would you live, on what? How can you have a war without soldiers?

MOTHER COURAGE: It doesn't have to be my children.

THE SERGEANT: I see. You'd like the war to eat the core and spit out the apple. You want your brood to batten on war, tax-free. The war can look out for itself, is that it? You call yourself Courage, eh? And you're afraid of the war that feeds you. Your sons aren't afraid of it, I can see that.

EILIF: I'm not afraid of any war.

THE SERGEANT: Why should you be? Look at me: Has the soldier's life disagreed with me? I was seventeen when I joined up.

MOTHER COURAGE: You're not seventy yet.

THE SERGEANT: I can wait.

MOTHER COURAGE: Sure. Under ground.

THE SERGEANT: Are you trying to insult me? Telling me I'm going to die?

MOTHER COURAGE: But suppose it's the truth? I can see the mark on you. You look like a corpse on leave.

SWISS CHEESE: She's got second sight. Everybody says so. She can tell the future.

THE RECRUITER: Then tell the sergeant his future. It might amuse him.

THE SERGEANT: I don't believe in that stuff.

MOTHER COURAGE: Give me your helmet. [He gives it to her.]

THE SERGEANT: It doesn't mean any more than taking a shit in the grass. But go ahead for the laugh.

MOTHER COURAGE: [Takes a sheet of parchment and tears it in two.] Eilif, Swiss Cheese, Kattrin: That's how we'd all be torn apart if we got mixed up too deep in the war. [To the SERGEANT.] Seeing it's you, I'll do it for nothing. I make a black cross on this piece. Black is death.

SWISS CHEESE: She leaves the other one blank. Get it?

MOTHER COURAGE: Now I fold them, and now I shake them up together. Same as we're all mixed up together from the cradle to the grave. And now you draw, and you'll know the answer.

[The SERGEANT hesitates.]

THE RECRUITER: [To EILIF.] I don't take everybody, I'm known to be picky and choosey, but you've got spirit, I like that.

THE SERGEANT: [Fishing in the helmet.] Damn foolishness! Hocus-pocus!

SWISS CHEESE: He's pulled a black cross. He's through.

THE RECRUITER: Don't let them scare you, there's not enough bullets for everybody.

THE SERGEANT: [Hoarsely.] You've fouled me up.

MOTHER COURAGE: You fouled yourself up the day you joined the army. And now we'll be going, there isn't a war every day, I've got to take advantage.

THE SERGEANT: Hell and damnation! Don't try to hornswoggle me. We're taking your bastard to be a soldier.

EILIF: I'd like to be a soldier, mother.

MOTHER COURAGE: You shut your trap, you Finnish devil.

EILIF: Swiss Cheese wants to be a soldier too.

MOTHER COURAGE: That's news to me. I'd better let you draw too, all three of you. [She goes to the rear to mark crosses on slips of parchment.]

THE RECRUITER: [To EILIF.] It's been said to our discredit that a lot of religion goes on in the Swedish camp, but that's slander to blacken our reputation. Hymn singing only on Sunday, one verse! And only if you've got a voice.

MOTHER COURAGE: [Comes back with the slips in the SERGEANT's helmet.] Want to sneak away from their mother, the devils, and run off to war like calves to a salt lick. But we'll draw lots on it, then they'll see that the world is no vale of smiles[1] with a "Come along, son, we're short on

---

1. Parodying the traditional description of this world as a "vale of tears."

generals." Sergeant, I'm very much afraid they won't come through the war. They've got terrible characters, all three of them. [*She holds out the helmet to* EILIF.] There. Pick a slip. [*He picks one and unfolds it. She snatches it away from him.*] There you have it. A cross! Oh, unhappy mother that I am, Oh, mother of sorrows. Has he got to die? Doomed to perish in the springtime of his life? If he joins the army, he'll bite the dust, that's sure. He's too brave, just like his father. If he's not smart, he'll go the way of all flesh, the slip proves it. [*She roars at him.*] Are you going to be smart?

EILIF: Why not?

MOTHER COURAGE: The smart thing to do is to stay with your mother, and if they make fun of you and call you a sissy, just laugh.

THE RECRUITER: If you're shitting in your pants, we'll take your brother.

MOTHER COURAGE: I told you to laugh. Laugh! And now you pick, Swiss Cheese. I'm not so worried about you, you're honest. [*He picks a slip.*] Oh! Why, have you got that strange look? It's got to be blank. There can't be a cross on it. No, I can't lose you. [*She takes the slip.*] A cross? Him too? Maybe it's because he's so stupid. Oh, Swiss Cheese, you'll die too, unless you're very honest the whole time, the way I've taught you since you were a baby, always bringing back the change when I sent you to buy bread. That's the only way you can save yourself. Look sergeant, isn't that a black cross?

THE SERGEANT: It's a cross all right. I don't see how I could have pulled one. I always stay in the rear. [*To the* RECRUITER.] It's on the up and up. Her own get it too.

SWISS CHEESE: I get it too. But I can take a hint.

MOTHER COURAGE: [*To* KATTRIN.] Now you're the only one I'm sure of, you're a cross[2] yourself because you've got a good heart. [*She holds up the helmet to* KATTRIN *in the wagon, but she herself takes out the slip.*] It's driving me to despair. It can't be right, maybe I mixed them wrong. Don't be too good-natured, Kattrin, don't, there's a cross on your path too. Always keep very quiet, that ought to be easy seeing you're dumb. Well, now you know. Be careful, all of you, you'll need to be. And now we'll climb up and drive on. [*She returns the* SERGEANT's *helmet and climbs up into the wagon.*]

THE RECRUITER: [*To the* SERGEANT.] Do something!

THE SERGEANT: I'm not feeling so good.

THE RECRUITER: Maybe you caught cold when you took your helmet off in the wind. Tell her you want to buy something. Keep her busy. [*Aloud.*] You could at least take a look at that buckle, sergeant. After all, selling things is these good people's living. Hey, you, the sergeant wants to buy that belt buckle.

MOTHER COURAGE: Half a guilder. A buckle like that is worth two guilders. [*She climbs down.*]

THE SERGEANT: It's not new. This wind! I can't examine it here. Let's go where it's quiet. [*He goes behind the wagon with the buckle.*]

MOTHER COURAGE: I haven't noticed wind.

2. That is, a heavy burden.

THE SERGEANT: Maybe it is worth half a guilder. It's silver.

MOTHER COURAGE: [*Joins him behind the wagon.*] Six solid ounces.

THE RECRUITER: [*To* EILIF.] And then we'll have a drink, just you and me. I've got your enlistment bonus right here. Come on.

[EILIF *stands undecided.*]

MOTHER COURAGE: All right. Half a guilder.

THE SERGEANT: I don't get it. I always stay in the rear. There's no safer place for a sergeant. You can send the men up forward to win glory. You've spoiled my dinner. It won't go down, I know it, not a bite.

MOTHER COURAGE: Don't take it to heart. Don't let it spoil your appetite. Just keep behind the lines. Here, take a drink of schnapps, man. [*She hands him the bottle.*]

THE RECRUITER: [*Has taken* EILIF*'s arm and is pulling him away toward the rear.*] A bonus of ten guilders, and you'll be a brave man and you'll fight for the king, and the women will tear each other's hair out over you. And you can clout me one on the kisser for insulting you. [*Both go out.*]

[*Mute* KATTRIN *jumps down from the wagon and emits raucous sounds.*]

MOTHER COURAGE: Just a minute, Kattrin. Just a minute. The sergeant's paying up. [*Bites the half guilder.*] I'm always suspicious of money. I'm a burnt child, sergeant. But your coin is good. And now we'll be going. Where's Eilif?

SWISS CHEESE: He's gone with the recruiter.

MOTHER COURAGE: [*Stands motionless, then.*] You simple soul. [*To* KATTRIN.] I know. You can't talk, you couldn't help it.

THE SERGEANT: You could do with a drink yourself, mother. That's the way it goes. Soldiering isn't the worst thing in the world. You want to live off the war, but you want to keep you and yours out of it. Is that it?

MOTHER COURAGE: Now you'll have to pull with your brother, Kattrin.

[*Brother and sister harness themselves to the wagon and start pulling.* MOTHER COURAGE *walks beside them. The wagon rolls off.*]

THE SERGEANT: [*Looking after them.*]

> If you want the war to work for you
> You've got to give the war its due.

2

In 1625 and 1626 Mother Courage crosses Poland in the train[3] of the Swedish armies. Outside the fortress of Wallhof[4] she meets her son again.—A capon is successfully sold, the brave son's fortunes are at their zenith.

The general's tent.

Beside it the kitchen. The thunder of cannon. The cook is arguing with MOTHER COURAGE, *who is trying to sell him a capon.*

---

3. That is, with the supplies and baggage at the end of the line of march.   4. Fictional city.

THE COOK: Sixty hellers[5] for that pathetic bird?

MOTHER COURAGE: Pathetic bird? You mean this plump beauty? Are you trying to tell me that a general who's the biggest eater for miles around—God help you if you haven't got anything for his dinner—can't afford a measly sixty hellers?

THE COOK: I can get a dozen like it for ten hellers right around the corner.

MOTHER COURAGE: What, you'll find a capon like this right around the corner? With a siege on and everybody so starved you can see right through them. Maybe you'll scare up a rat, maybe, I say, 'cause they've all been eaten, I've seen five men chasing a starved rat for hours. Fifty hellers for a giant capon in the middle of a siege.

THE COOK: We're not besieged; they are. We're the besiegers, can't you get that through your head?

MOTHER COURAGE: But we haven't got anything to eat either, in fact we've got less than the people in the city. They've hauled it all inside. I hear their life is one big orgy. And look at us. I've been around to the peasants, they haven't got a thing.

THE COOK: They've got plenty. They hide it.

MOTHER COURAGE: [Triumphantly.] Oh, no! They're ruined, that's what they are. They're starving. I've seen them. They're so hungry they're digging up roots. They lick their fingers when they've eaten a boiled strap. That's the situation. And here I've got a capon and I'm supposed to let it go for forty hellers.

THE COOK: Thirty, not forty. Thirty, I said.

MOTHER COURAGE: It's no common capon. They tell me this bird was so talented that he wouldn't eat unless they played music, he had his own favorite march. He could add and subtract, that's how intelligent he was. And you're trying to tell me forty hellers is too much. The general will bite your head off if there's nothing to eat.

THE COOK: You know what I'm going to do? [He takes a piece of beef and sets his knife to it.] Here I've got a piece of beef. I'll roast it. Think it over. This is your last chance.

MOTHER COURAGE: Roast and be damned. It's a year old.

THE COOK: A day old. That ox was running around only yesterday afternoon, I saw him with my own eyes.

MOTHER COURAGE: Then he must have stunk on the hoof.

THE COOK: I'll cook it five hours if I have to. We'll see if it's still tough. [He cuts it.]

MOTHER COURAGE: Use plenty of pepper, maybe the general won't notice the stink.

[The GENERAL, the CHAPLAIN, and EILIF enter the tent.]

THE GENERAL: [Slapping EILIF on the back.] All right, son, into your general's tent you go, you'll sit at my right hand. You've done a heroic deed and you're a pious trooper, because this is a war of religion and what you did was done for God, that's what counts with me. I'll reward you with a gold bracelet when I take the city. We come here to save their souls and what do those filthy, shameless peasants do? They drive their

5. A small coin formerly used in Austria and Germany.

cattle away. And they stuff their priests with meat, front and back. But you taught them a lesson. Here's a tankard of red wine for you. [*He pours.*] We'll down it on one gulp. [*They do so.*] None for the chaplain, he's got his religion. What would you like for dinner, sweetheart?

EILIF: A scrap of meat. Why not?

THE GENERAL: Cook! Meat!

THE COOK: And now he brings company when there's nothing to eat.

[*Wanting to listen,* MOTHER COURAGE *makes him stop talking.*]

EILIF: Cutting down peasants whets the appetite.

MOTHER COURAGE: God, it's my Eilif.

THE COOK: Who?

MOTHER COURAGE: My eldest. I haven't seen hide nor hair of him in two years, he was stolen from me on the highway. He must be in good if the general invites him to dinner, and what have you got to offer? Nothing. Did you hear what the general's guest wants for dinner? Meat! Take my advice, snap up this capon. The price is one guilder.

THE GENERAL: [*Has sat down with* EILIF. *Bellows.*] Food, Lamb, you lousy, no-good cook, or I'll kill you.

THE COOK: All right, hand it over. This is extortion.

MOTHER COURAGE: I thought it was a pathetic bird.

THE COOK: Pathetic is the word. Hand it over. Fifty hellers! It's highway robbery.

MOTHER COURAGE: One guilder, I say. For my eldest son, the general's honored guest, I spare no expense.

THE COOK: [*Gives her the money.*] Then pluck it at least while I make the fire.

MOTHER COURAGE: [*Sits down to pluck the capon.*] Won't he be glad to see me! He's my brave, intelligent son. I've got a stupid one too, but he's honest. The girl's a total loss. But at least she doesn't talk, that's something.

THE GENERAL: Take another drink, son, it's my best Falerno,[6] I've only got another barrel or two at the most, but it's worth it to see that there's still some true faith in my army. The good shepherd here just looks on, all he knows how to do is preach. Can he do anything? No. And now, Eilif my son, tell us all about it, how cleverly you hoodwinked those peasants and captured those twenty head of cattle. I hope they'll be here soon.

EILIF: Tomorrow. Maybe the day after.

MOTHER COURAGE: Isn't my Eilif considerate, not bringing those oxen in until tomorrow, or you wouldn't have even said hello to my capon.

EILIF: Well, it was like this: I heard the peasants were secretly—mostly at night—rounding up the oxen they'd hidden in a certain forest. The city people had arranged to come and get them. I let them round the oxen up, I figured they'd find them easier than I would. I made my men ravenous for meat, put them on short rations for two days until their mouths watered if they even heard a word beginning with *me* . . . like measles.

THE GENERAL: That was clever of you.

6. A famous wine made from grapes grown in Falerno in Italy.

EILIF: Maybe. The rest was a pushover. Except the peasants had clubs and there were three times more of them and they fell on us like bloody murder. Four of them drove me into a clump of bushes, they knocked my sword out of my hand and yelled: Surrender! Now what'll I do, I says to myself, they'll make hash out of me.

THE GENERAL: What did you do?

EILIF: I laughed.

THE GENERAL: You laughed?

EILIF: I laughed. Which led to a conversation. The first thing you know, I'm bargaining. Twenty guilders is too much for that ox, I say, how about fifteen? Like I'm meaning to pay. They're flummoxed, they scratch their heads. Quick, I reach for my sword and mow them down. Necessity knows no law. See what I mean?

THE GENERAL: What do you say to that, shepherd?

CHAPLAIN: Strictly speaking, that maxim is not in the Bible. But our Lord was able to turn five loaves into five hundred.[7] So there was no question of poverty; he could tell people to love their neighbors because their bellies were full. Nowadays it's different.

THE GENERAL: [*Laughs.*] Very different. All right, you Pharisee, take a swig. [*To* EILIF.] You mowed them down, splendid, so my fine troops could have a decent bite to eat. Doesn't the Good Book say: "Whatsoever thou doest for the least of my brethren, thou doest for me"?[8] And what have you done for them? You've got them a good chunk of beef for their dinner. They're not used to moldy crusts; in the old days they had a helmetful of white bread and wine before they went out to fight for God.

EILIF: Yes, I reached for my sword and I mowed them down.

THE GENERAL: You're a young Caesar. You deserve to see the king.

EILIF: I have, in the distance. He shines like a light. He's my ideal.

THE GENERAL: You're a something like him already, Eilif. I know the worth of a brave soldier like you. When I find one, I treat him like my own son. [*He leads him to the map.*] Take a look at the situation, Eilif; we've still got a long way to go.

MOTHER COURAGE: [*Who has been listening starts plucking her capon furiously.*] He must be a rotten general.

THE COOK: Eats like a pig, but why rotten?

MOTHER COURAGE: Because he needs brave soldiers, that's why. If he planned his campaigns right, what would he need brave soldiers for? The run-of-the-mill would do. Take it from me, whenever you find a lot of virtues, it shows that something's wrong.

THE COOK: I'd say it proves that something is all right.

MOTHER COURAGE: No, that something's wrong. See, when a general or a king is real stupid and leads his men up shit creek, his troops need courage, that's a virtue. If he's stingy and doesn't hire enough soldiers, they've all got to be Herculeses. And if he's a slob and lets everything go to pot, they've got to be as sly as serpents or they're done for. And if

---

7. Episode in the Gospels when Jesus fed five thousand people with five loaves and two fishes (Matthew 15:33ff.). 8. Spoken by Jesus in the Gospels (Matthew 25:40ff.). *Pharisee*: religious hypocrite, quibbler on religious doctrine.

he's always expecting too much of them, they need an extra dose of loyalty. A country that's run right, or a good king or a good general, doesn't need any of these virtues. You don't need virtues in a decent country, the people can all be perfectly ordinary, medium-bright, and cowards too for my money.

THE GENERAL: I bet your father was a soldier.

EILIF: A great soldier, I'm told. My mother warned me about it. Makes me think of a song.

THE GENERAL: Sing it! [*Bellowing.*] Where's that food!

EILIF: It is called: The Song of the Old Wife and the Soldier. [*He sings, doing a war dance with his saber.*]

> A gun or a pike they can kill who they like
> And the torrent will swallow a wader
> You had better think twice before battling with ice
> Said the old wife to the soldier.
> Cocking his rifle he leapt to his feet
> Laughing for joy as he heard the drum beat
> The wars cannot hurt me, he told her.
> He shouldered his gun and he picked up his knife
> To see the wide world. That's the soldier's life.
> Those were the words of the soldier.
>
> Ah, Deep will they lie who wise counsel defy
> Learn wisdom from those that are older
> Oh, don't venture too high or you'll fall from the sky
> Said the old wife to the soldier.
> But the young soldier with knife and with gun
> Only laughed a cold laugh and stepped into the run.
> The water can't hurt me, he told her.
> And when the moon on the rooftop shines white
> We'll be coming back. You can pray for that night.
> Those were the words of the soldier.

MOTHER COURAGE: [*In the kitchen, continues the song, beating a pot with a spoon.*]

> Like the smoke you'll be gone and no warmth linger on
> And your deeds only leave me the colder!
> Oh, see the smoke race. Oh, dear God keep him safe!
> That's what she said of the soldier.

EILIF: What's that?

MOTHER COURAGE: [*Goes on singing.*]

> And the young soldier with knife and with gun
> Was swept from his feet till he sank in the run
> And the torrent swallowed the waders.
> Cold shone the moon on the rooftop white
> But the soldier was carried away with the ice
> And what was it she heard from the soldier?
> Like the smoke he was gone and no warmth lingered on
> And his deeds only left her the colder.
> Ah, deep will they lie who wise counsel defy!
> That's what she said to the soldier.

THE GENERAL: What do they think they're doing in my kitchen?

EILIF: [*Has gone into the kitchen. He embraces his mother.*] Mother! It's you! Where are the others?

MOTHER COURAGE: [*In his arms.*] Snug as a bug in a rug. Swiss Cheese is paymaster of the Second Regiment; at least he won't be fighting, I couldn't keep him out altogether.

EILIF: And how about your feet?

MOTHER COURAGE: Well, it's hard getting my shoes on in the morning.

THE GENERAL: [*Has joined them.*] Ah, so you're his mother. I hope you've got more sons for me like this fellow here.

EILIF: Am I lucky! There you're sitting in the kitchen hearing your son being praised.

MOTHER COURAGE: I heard it all right! [*She gives him a slap in the face.*]

EILIF: [*Holding his cheek.*] For capturing the oxen?

MOTHER COURAGE: No. For not surrendering when the four of them were threatening to make hash out of you! Didn't I teach you to take care of yourself? You Finnish devil!

[*The* GENERAL *and the* CHAPLAIN *laugh.*]

3

Three years later Mother Courage and parts of a Finnish[9] regiment are taken prisoner. She is able to save her daughter and her wagon, but her honest son dies.

Army camp.

Afternoon. On a pole the regimental flag. MOTHER COURAGE *has stretched a clothesline between her wagon, on which all sorts of merchandise is hung in display, and a large cannon. She and* KATTRIN *are folding washing and piling it on the cannon. At the same time she is negotiating with an* ORDNANCE OFFICER[1] *over a sack of bullets.* SWISS CHEESE, *now in the uniform of a paymaster, is looking on. A pretty woman,* YVETTE POTTIER, *is sitting with a glass of brandy in front of her, sewing a gaudy-colored hat. She is in her stocking feet, her red high-heeled shoes are on the ground beside her.*

THE ORDNANCE OFFICER: I'll let you have these bullets for two guilders. It's cheap, I need the money, because the colonel's been drinking with the officers for two days and we're out of liquor.

MOTHER COURAGE: That's ammunition for the troops. If it's found here, I'll be court-martialed. You punks sell their bullets and the men have nothing to shoot at the enemy.

THE ORDNANCE OFFICER: Don't be hard-hearted, you scratch my back, I'll scratch yours.

MOTHER COURAGE: I'm not taking any army property. Not at that price.

THE ORDNANCE OFFICER: You can sell it for five guilders, maybe eight, to the ordnance officer of the Fourth before the day is out, if you're quiet

---

9. Finland was under Swedish rule at this time.   1. Officer in charge of weapons, particularly explosives.

about it and give him a receipt for twelve. He hasn't an ounce of ammunition left.

MOTHER COURAGE: Why don't you do it yourself?

THE ORDNANCE OFFICER: Because I don't trust him, he's a friend of mine.

MOTHER COURAGE: [*Takes the sack.*] Hand it over. [*To* KATTRIN.] Take it back there and pay him one and a half guilders. [*In response to the* ORDNANCE OFFICER's *protest.*] One and a half guilders, I say. [KATTRIN *drags the sack behind the wagon, the* ORDNANCE OFFICER *follows her.* MOTHER COURAGE *to* SWISS CHEESE.] Here's your underdrawers, take good care of them, this is October, might be coming on fall, I don't say it will be, because I've learned that nothing is sure to happen the way we think, not even the seasons. But whatever happens, your regimental funds have to be in order. Are your funds in order?

SWISS CHEESE: Yes, mother.

MOTHER COURAGE: Never forget that they made you paymaster because you're honest and not brave like your brother, and especially because you're too simple-minded to get the idea of making off with the money. That's a comfort to me. And don't go mislaying your drawers.

SWISS CHEESE: No, mother. I'll put them under my mattress. [*Starts to go.*]

ORDNANCE OFFICER: I'll go with you, paymaster.

MOTHER COURAGE: Just don't teach him any of your tricks.

[*Without saying good-bye the* ORDNANCE OFFICER *goes out with* SWISS CHEESE.]

YVETTE: [*Waves her hand after the* ORDNANCE OFFICER.] You might say good-bye, officer.

MOTHER COURAGE: [*To* YVETTE.] I don't like to see those two together. He's not the right kind of company for my Swiss Cheese. But the war's getting along pretty well. More countries are joining in all the time, it can go on for another four, five years, easy. With a little planning ahead, I can do good business if I'm careful. Don't you know you shouldn't drink in the morning with your sickness?

YVETTE: Who says I'm sick, it's slander.

MOTHER COURAGE: Everybody says so.

YVETTE: Because they're all liars. Mother Courage, I'm desperate. They all keep out of my way like I'm a rotten fish on account of those lies. What's the good of fixing my hat? [*She throws it down.*] That's why I drink in the morning, I never used to, I'm getting crow's-feet, but it doesn't matter now. In the Second Finnish Regiment they all know me. I should have stayed home when my first love walked out on me. Pride isn't for the likes of us. If we can't put up with shit, we're through.

MOTHER COURAGE: Just don't start in on your Pieter and how it all happened in front of my innocent daughter.

YVETTE: She's just the one to hear it, it'll harden her against love.

MOTHER COURAGE: Nothing can harden them.

YVETTE: Then I'll talk about it because it makes me feel better. It begins with my growing up in fair Flanders, because if I hadn't I'd never have laid eyes on him and I wouldn't be here in Poland now, because he was an army cook, blond, a Dutchman, but skinny. Kattrin, watch out for the skinny ones, but I didn't know that then, and another thing I didn't know is that he had another girl even then, and they all called him Pete the Pipe, because he didn't even take his pipe out of his mouth when he was doing it, that's all it meant to him. [*She sings the* Song of Fraternization.]

When I was only sixteen
The foe came into our land.
He laid aside his saber
And with a smile he took my hand.
After the May parade
The May light starts to fade.
The regiment dressed by the right[2]
Then drums were beaten, that's the drill.[3]
The foe took us behind the hill
And fraternized all night.

There were so many foes came
And mine worked in the mess.[4]
I loathed him in the daytime.
At night I loved him none the less.
After the May parade
The May light starts to fade.
The regiment dressed by the right
Then drums were beaten, that's the drill.
The foe took us behind the hill
And fraternized all night.

The love which came upon me
Was wished on me by fate.
My friends could never grasp why
I found it hard to share their hate.
The fields were wet with dew
When sorrow first I knew.
The regiment dressed by the right
Then drums were beaten, that's the drill.
And then the foe, my lover still
Went marching from our sight.

Well, I followed him, but I never found him. That was five years ago. [*She goes behind the wagon with an unsteady gait.*]

MOTHER COURAGE: You've left your hat.

YVETTE: Anybody that wants it can have it.

MOTHER COURAGE: Let that be a lesson to you, Kattrin. Have no truck with soldiers. It's love that makes the world go round, so you'd better watch out. Even with a civilian it's no picnic. He says he'd kiss the ground you put your little feet on, talking of feet, did you wash yours yesterday, and then you're his slave. Be glad you're dumb, that way you'll never contradict yourself or want to bite your tongue off because you've told the

---

2. That is, each man aligned himself with the man on his right to form straight ranks for the parade.
3. That's the usual thing.   4. The kitchen.

truth, it's a gift of God to be dumb. Here comes the general's cook, I wonder what he wants.

[*The* COOK *and the* CHAPLAIN *enter.*]

THE CHAPLAIN: I've got a message for you from your son Eilif. The cook here thought he'd come along, he's taken a shine to you.

THE COOK: I only came to get a breath of air.

MOTHER COURAGE: You can always do that here if you behave, and if you don't, I can handle you. Well, what does he want? I've got no money to spare.

THE CHAPLAIN: Actually he wanted me to see his brother, the paymaster.

MOTHER COURAGE: He's not here any more, or anywhere else either. He's not his brother's paymaster. I don't want him leading him into temptation and being smart at his expense [*Gives him money from the bag slung around her waist.*] Give him this, it's a sin, he's speculating on mother love and he ought to be ashamed.

THE COOK: He won't do it much longer, then he'll be marching off with his regiment, maybe to his death, you never can tell. Better make it a little more, you'll be sorry later. You women are hard-hearted, but afterwards you're sorry. A drop of brandy wouldn't have cost much when it was wanted, but it wasn't given, and later, for all you know, he'll be lying in the cold ground and you can't dig him up again.

THE CHAPLAIN: Don't be sentimental, cook. There's nothing wrong with dying in battle, it's a blessing, and I'll tell you why. This is a war of religion. Not a common war, but a war for the faith, and therefore pleasing to God.

THE COOK: That's a fact. In a way you could call it a war, because of the extortion and killing and looting, not to mention a bit of rape, but it's a war of religion, which makes it different from all other wars, that's obvious. But it makes a man thirsty all the same, you've got to admit that.

THE CHAPLAIN: [*To* MOTHER COURAGE, *pointing at the cook.*] I tried to discourage him, but he says you've turned his head, he sees you in his dreams.

THE COOK: [*Lights a short-stemmed pipe.*] All I want is a glass of brandy from your fair hand, nothing more sinful. I'm already so shocked by the jokes the chaplain's been telling me, I bet I'm still red in the face.

MOTHER COURAGE: And him a clergyman! I'd better give you fellows something to drink or you'll be making me immoral propositions just to pass the time.

THE CHAPLAIN: This is temptation, said the deacon, and succumbed to it. [*Turning toward* KATTRIN *as he leaves.*] And who is this delightful young lady?

MOTHER COURAGE: She's not delightful, she's a respectable young lady.

[*The* CHAPLAIN *and the* COOK *go behind the wagon with* MOTHER COURAGE. KATTRIN *looks after them, then she walks away from the washing and approaches the hat. She picks it up, sits down and puts on the red shoes. From the rear* MOTHER COURAGE *is heard talking politics with the chaplain and the cook.*]

MOTHER COURAGE: The Poles here in Poland shouldn't have butted in. All right, our king marched his army into their country. But instead of keeping the peace, the Poles start butting into their own affairs and attack the king while he's marching quietly through the landscape. That was a breach of the peace and the blood is on their head.

THE CHAPLAIN: Our king had only one thing in mind; freedom. The emperor had everybody under his yoke, the Poles as much as the Germans; the king had to set them free.

THE COOK: I see it this way, your brandy's first-rate, I can see why I liked your face, but we were talking about the king. This freedom he was trying to introduce into Germany cost him a fortune, he had to levy a salt tax in Sweden, which, as I said, cost the poor people a fortune. Then he had to put the Germans in jail and break them on the rack because they liked being the emperor's slaves. Oh yes, the king made short shrift of anybody that didn't want to be free. In the beginning he only wanted to protect Poland against wicked people, especially the emperor, but the more he ate the more he wanted, and pretty soon he was protecting all of Germany.[5] But the Germans didn't take it lying down and the king got nothing but trouble for all his kindness and expense, which he naturally had to defray from taxes, which made for bad blood, but that didn't discourage him. He had one thing in his favor, the word of God, which was lucky, because otherwise people would have said he was doing it all for himself and what he hoped to get out of it. As it was, he always had a clear conscience and that was all he really cared about.

MOTHER COURAGE: It's easy to see you're not a Swede, or you wouldn't talk like that about the Hero-King.

THE CHAPLAIN: You're eating his bread, aren't you?

THE COOK: I don't eat his bread, I bake it.

MOTHER COURAGE: He can't be defeated because his men believe in him. [*Earnestly.*] When you listen to the big wheels talk, they're making war for reasons of piety, in the name of everything that's fine and noble. But when you take another look, you see that they're not so dumb; they're making war for profit. If they weren't, the small fry like me wouldn't have anything to do with it.[6]

THE COOK: That's a fact.

THE CHAPLAIN: And it wouldn't hurt you as a Dutchman to take a look at that flag up there before you express opinions in Poland.

MOTHER COURAGE: We're all good Protestants here! Prosit![7]

[KATTRIN *has started strutting about with* YVETTE's *hat on, imitating* YVETTE's *gait. Suddenly cannon fire and shots are heard. Drums.* MOTHER COURAGE, *the* COOK, *and the* CHAPLAIN *run out from behind the wagon, the two men still with glasses in hand. The* ORDNANCE OFFICER *and a* SOLDIER *rush up to the cannon and try to push it away.*]

---

5. Allusion to Hitler's expansion of German territory allegedly to protect German-speaking peoples, first in Bohemia (now part of the Czech Republic) and then, in 1938, through the annexation of Austria. 6. The German expression can also be translated, "Wouldn't be doing the same thing." 7. A common drinking toast (literally, "May it do good," Latin).

MOTHER COURAGE: What's going on? Let me get my washing first, you lugs. [*She tries to rescue her washing.*]

THE ORDNANCE OFFICER: The Catholics. They're attacking. I don't know as we'll get away. [*To the* SOLDIER.] Get rid of the gun! [*Runs off.*]

THE COOK: Christ, I've got to find the general. Courage, I'll be back for a little chat in a day or two. [*Rushes out.*]

MOTHER COURAGE: Stop, you've forgotten your pipe.

THE COOK: [*From the distance.*] Keep it for me! I'll need it.

MOTHER COURAGE: Just when we were making a little money!

THE CHAPLAIN: Well, I guess I'll be going too. It might be dangerous though, with the enemy so close. Blessed are the peaceful[8] is the best motto in wartime. If only I had a cloak to cover up with.

MOTHER COURAGE: I'm not lending any cloaks, not on your life. I've had bitter experience in that line.

THE CHAPLAIN: But my religion puts me in special danger.

MOTHER COURAGE: [*Bringing him a cloak.*] It's against my better conscience. And now run along.

THE CHAPLAIN: Thank you kindly, you've got a good heart. But maybe I'd better sit here a while. The enemy might get suspicious if they see me running.

MOTHER COURAGE: [*To the* SOLDIER.] Leave it lay, you fool, you won't get paid extra. I'll take care of it for you, you'd only get killed.

THE SOLDIER: [*Running away.*] I tried. You're my witness.

MOTHER COURAGE: I'll swear it on the Bible. [*Sees her daughter with the hat.*] What are you doing with that floozy hat? Take it off, have you gone out of your mind? Now of all times, with the enemy on top of us? [*She tears the hat off* KATTRIN's *head.*] You want them to find you and make a whore out of you? And those shoes! Take them off, you woman of Babylon![9] [*She tries to pull them off.*] Jesus Christ, chaplain, make her take those shoes off! I'll be right back. [*She runs to the wagon.*]

YVETTE: [*Enters, powdering her face.*] What's this I hear? The Catholics are coming? Where is my hat? Who's been stamping on it? I can't be seen like this if the Catholics are coming. What'll they think of me? I haven't even got a mirror. [*To the* CHAPLAIN.] How do I look? Too much powder?

THE CHAPLAIN: Just right.

YVETTE: And where are my red shoes? [*She doesn't see them because* KATTRIN *hides her feet under her skirt.*] I left them here. I've got to get back to my tent. In my bare feet. It's disgraceful! [*Goes out.*]

[SWISS CHEESE *runs in carrying a small box.*]

MOTHER COURAGE: [*Comes out with her hands full of ashes. To* KATTRIN.] Ashes. [*To* SWISS CHEESE.] What you got there?

SWISS CHEESE: The regimental funds.

MOTHER COURAGE: Throw it away! No more paymastering for you.

---

8. A parody of Jesus' Sermon on the Mount: "Blessed are the peacemakers, for they shall be called the children of God" (Matthew 5:9).   9. Sinful woman. The ancient Asian city of Babylon is a biblical locus for sin and decadence: "Babylon the great, the mother of harlots and abominations of the earth" (Revelation 17:5).

SWISS CHEESE: I'm responsible for it. [*He goes rear.*]

MOTHER COURAGE: [*To the* CHAPLAIN.] Take your clergyman's coat off, chaplain, or they'll recognize you, cloak or no cloak. [*She rubs* KATTRIN's *face with ashes.*] Hold still! There. With a little dirt you'll be safe. What a mess! The sentries were drunk. Hide your light under a bushel,[1] as the Good Book says. When a soldier, especially a Catholic, sees a clean face, she's a whore before she knows it. Nobody feeds them for weeks. When they finally loot some provisions, the next thing they want is women. That'll do it. Let me look at you. Not bad. Like you'd been wallowing in a pigsty. Stop shaking. You're safe now. [*To* SWISS CHEESE.] What did you do with the cashbox?

SWISS CHEESE: I thought I'd put it in the wagon.

MOTHER COURAGE: [*Horrified.*] What! In my wagon? Of all the sinful stupidity! If my back is turned for half a second! They'll hang us all!

SWISS CHEESE: Then I'll put it somewhere else, or I'll run away with it.

MOTHER COURAGE: You'll stay right here. It's too late.

THE CHAPLAIN: [*Still changing, comes forward.*] Heavens, the flag!

MOTHER COURAGE: [*Takes down the regimental flag.*] Bozhe moi![2] I'm so used to it I don't see it. Twenty-five years I've had it.

[*The cannon fire grows louder.*]

[*Morning, three days later. The cannon is gone.* MOTHER COURAGE, KATTRIN, *the* CHAPLAIN, *and* SWISS CHEESE *are sitting dejectedly over a meal.*]

SWISS CHEESE: This is the third day I've been sitting here doing nothing; the sergeant has always been easy on me, but now he must be starting to wonder: where can Swiss Cheese be with the cashbox?

MOTHER COURAGE: Be glad they haven't tracked you down.

THE CHAPLAIN: What about me? I can't hold a service here either. The Good Book says: "Whosoever hath a full heart, his tongue runneth over."[3] Heaven help me if mine runneth over.

MOTHER COURAGE: That's the way it is. Look what I've got on my hands: one with a religion and one with a cashbox. I don't know which is worse.

THE CHAPLAIN: Tell yourself that we're in the hands of God.

MOTHER COURAGE: I don't think we're that bad off, but all the same I can't sleep at night. If it weren't for you, Swiss Cheese, it'd be easier. I think I've put myself in the clear. I told them I was against the antichrist;[4] he's a Swede with horns, I told them, and I'd noticed the left horn was kind of worn down. I interrupted the questioning to ask where I could buy holy candles cheap. I knew what to say because Swiss Cheese's father was a Catholic and he used to make jokes about it. They didn't really believe me, but their regiment had no provisioner, so they looked

1. Also parodies the Sermon on the Mount: "Neither do men light a candle, and put it under a bushel [basket], but on a candlestick; and it giveth light unto all that are in the house" (Matthew 5:15). 2. My God! (Polish and Russian expression). 3. From Matthew 12:34: "For out of the abundance of the heart the mouth speaketh" (Jesus to the Pharisees). The biblical proverb means that one's words reflect the good or evil in one's heart. 4. Figure of evil, whose appearance on earth is supposed to foreshadow the end of the world and the coming of the Last Judgment.

the other way. Maybe we stand to gain. We're prisoners, but so are lice on a dog.

THE CHAPLAIN: This milk is good. Though there's not much of it or of anything else. Maybe we'll have to cut down on our Swedish appetites. But such is the lot of the vanquished.

MOTHER COURAGE: Who's vanquished? Victory and defeat don't always mean the same thing to the big wheels up top and the small fry underneath. Not by a long shot. In some cases defeat is a blessing to the small fry. Honor's lost, but nothing else. One time in Livonia[5] our general got such a shellacking from the enemy that in the confusion I laid hands on a beautiful white horse from the baggage train. That horse pulled my wagon for seven months, until we had a victory and they checked up. On the whole, you can say that victory and defeat cost us plain people plenty. The best thing for us is when politics gets bogged down. [*To* SWISS CHEESE.] Eat!

SWISS CHEESE: I've lost my appetite. How's the sergeant going to pay the men?

MOTHER COURAGE: Troops never get paid when they're running away.

SWISS CHEESE: But they've got it coming to them. If they're not paid, they don't need to run. Not a step.

MOTHER COURAGE: Swiss Cheese, you're too conscientious, it almost frightens me. I brought you up to be honest, because you're not bright, but somewhere it's got to stop. And now me and the chaplain are going to buy a Catholic flag and some meat. Nobody can buy meat like the chaplain, he goes into a trance and heads straight for the best piece, I guess it makes his mouth water and that shows him the way. At least they let me carry on my business. Nobody cares about a shopkeeper's religion, all they want to know is the price. Protestant pants are as warm as any other kind.

THE CHAPLAIN: Like the friar[6] said when somebody told him the Lutherans were going to stand the whole country on its head. They'll always need beggars, he says. [MOTHER COURAGE *disappears into the wagon.*] But she's worried about that cashbox. They've taken no notice of us so far, they think we're all part of the wagon, but how long can that go on?

SWISS CHEESE: I can take it away.

THE CHAPLAIN: That would be almost more dangerous. What if somebody sees you? They've got spies. Yesterday morning, just as I'm relieving myself, one of them jumps out of the ditch. I was so scared I almost let out a prayer. That would have given me away. I suppose they think they can tell a Protestant by the smell of his shit. He was a little runt with a patch over one eye.

MOTHER COURAGE: [*Climbing down from the wagon with a basket.*] Look what I've found. You shameless slut! [*She holds up the red shoes triumphantly.*] Yvette's red shoes! She's swiped them in cold blood. It's your fault. Who told her she was a delightful young lady? [*She puts them into the basket.*] I'm giving them back. Stealing Yvette's shoes! She ruins

5. Region of the east Baltic.   6. A mendicant or beggar monk.

herself for money, that I can understand. But you'd like to do it free of charge, for pleasure. I've told you, you'll have to wait for peace. No soldiers! Just wait for peace with your worldly ways.

THE CHAPLAIN: She doesn't seem very worldly to me.

MOTHER COURAGE: Too worldly for me. In Dalarna she was like a stone, which is all they've got around there. The people used to say: We don't see the cripple. That's the way I like it. That way she's safe. [*To* SWISS CHEESE.] You leave that box where it is, hear? And keep an eye on your sister, she needs it. The two of you will be the death of me. I'd sooner take care of a bag of fleas. [*She goes off with the* CHAPLAIN. KATTRIN *starts clearing away the dishes.*]

SWISS CHEESE: Won't be many more days when I can sit in the sun in my shirtsleeves. [KATTRIN *points to a tree.*] Yes, the leaves are all yellow. [KATTRIN *asks him, by means of gestures, whether he wants a drink.*] Not now. I'm thinking. [*Pause.*] She says she can't sleep. I'd better get the cashbox out of here, I've found a hiding place. All right, get me a drink. [KATTRIN *goes behind the wagon.*] I'll hide it in the rabbit hole down by the river until I can take it away. Maybe late tonight, I'll go get it and take it to the regiment. I wonder how far they've run in three days? Won't the sergeant be surprised! Well, Swiss Cheese, this is a pleasant disappointment, that's what he'll say. I trust you with the regimental cashbox and you bring it back.

[*As* KATTRIN *comes out from behind the wagon with a glass of brandy, she comes face to face with two men. One is a* SERGEANT. *The other removes his hat and swings it through the air in a ceremonious greeting. He has a patch over one eye.*]

THE MAN WITH THE PATCH: Good morning, my dear. Have you by any chance seen a man from the headquarters of the Second Finnish Regiment?

[*Scared out of her wits,* KATTRIN *runs front, spilling the brandy. The two exchange looks and withdraw after seeing* SWISS CHEESE *sitting there.*]

SWISS CHEESE: [*Starting up from his thoughts.*] You've spilled half of it. What's the fuss about? Poke yourself in the eye? I don't understand you. I'm getting out of here, I've made up my mind, it's best. [*He stands up. She does everything she can think of to call his attention to the danger. He only evades her.*] I wish I could understand you. Poor thing, I know you're trying to tell me something, you just can't say it. Don't worry about spilling the brandy, I'll be drinking plenty more. What's one glass? [*He takes the cashbox out of the wagon and hides it under his jacket.*] I'll be right back. Let me go, you're making me angry. I know you mean well. If only you could talk.

[*When she tries to hold him back, he kisses her and tears himself away. He goes out. She is desperate, she races back and forth, uttering short inarticulate sounds. The* CHAPLAIN *and* MOTHER COURAGE *come back.* KATTRIN *gesticulates wildly at her mother.*]

MOTHER COURAGE: What's the matter? You're all upset. Has somebody hurt you? Where's Swiss Cheese? Tell it to me in order, Kattrin. Your mother understands you. What, the no-good's taken the cashbox? I'll hit

him over the head with it, the sneak. Take your time, don't talk nonsense, use your hands, I don't like it when you howl like a dog, what
will the chaplain think? It gives him the creeps. A one-eyed man?

THE CHAPLAIN: The one-eyed man is a spy. Did they arrest Swiss Cheese?
[KATTRIN *shakes her head and shrugs her shoulders.*] We're done for.

MOTHER COURAGE: [*Takes a Catholic flag out of her basket. The* CHAPLAIN
fastens it to the flagpole.] Hoist the new flag!

THE CHAPLAIN: [*Bitterly.*] All good Catholics here.

[*Voices are heard from the rear. The two men bring in* SWISS
CHEESE.]

SWISS CHEESE: Let me go, I haven't done anything. Stop twisting my shoulder, I'm innocent.

THE SERGEANT: He belongs here. You know each other.

MOTHER COURAGE: What makes you think that?

SWISS CHEESE: I don't know them. I don't even know who they are. I had
a meal here, it cost me ten hellers. Maybe you saw me sitting here, it
was too salty.

THE SERGEANT: Who are you anyway?

MOTHER COURAGE: We're respectable people. And it's true. He had a meal
here. He said it was too salty.

THE SERGEANT: Are you trying to tell me you don't know each other?

MOTHER COURAGE: Why should I know him? I don't know everybody. I
don't ask people what their name is or if they're heathens; if they pay,
they're not heathens. Are you a heathen?

SWISS CHEESE: Of course not.

THE CHAPLAIN: He ate his meal and he behaved himself. He didn't open
his mouth except when he was eating. Then you have to.

THE SERGEANT: And who are you?

MOTHER COURAGE: He's only my bartender. You gentlemen must be
thirsty, I'll get you a drink of brandy, you must be hot and tired.

THE SERGEANT: We don't drink on duty. [*To* SWISS CHEESE.] You were
carrying something. You must have hidden it by the river. You had
something under your jacket when you left here.

MOTHER COURAGE: Was it really him?

SWISS CHEESE: I think you must have seen somebody else. I saw a
man running with something under his jacket. You've got the wrong
man.

MOTHER COURAGE: That's what I think too, it's a misunderstanding. These
things happen. I'm a good judge of people. I'm Mother Courage, you've
heard of me, everybody knows me. Take it from me, this man has an
honest face.

THE SERGEANT: We're looking for the cashbox of the Second Finnish Regiment. We know what the man in charge of it looks like. We've been
after him for two days. You're him.

SWISS CHEESE: I'm not.

THE SERGEANT: Hand it over. If you don't you're a goner, you know that.
Where is it?

MOTHER COURAGE: [*With urgency.*] He'd hand it over, wouldn't he, knowing he was a goner if he didn't? I've got it, he'd say, take it, you're

stronger. He's not that stupid. Speak up, you stupid idiot, the sergeant's giving you a chance.

SWISS CHEESE: But I haven't got it.

THE SERGEANT: In that case come along. We'll get it out of you.
   [*They lead him away.*]

MOTHER COURAGE: [*Shouts after them.*] He'd tell you. He's not that stupid. And don't twist his shoulder off! [*Runs after them.*]

[*The same evening. The* CHAPLAIN *and mute* KATTRIN *are washing dishes and scouring knives.*]

THE CHAPLAIN: That boy's in trouble. There are cases like that in the Bible. Take the Passion of our Lord and Savior. There's an old song about it. [*He sings the* Song of the Hours.]

> In the first hour Jesus mild
> Who had prayed since even
> Was betrayed and led before
> Pontius[7] the heathen.
>
> Pilate found him innocent
> Free from fault and error.
> Therefore, having washed his hands
> Sent him to King Herod.
>
> In the third hour he was scourged
> Stripped and clad in scarlet
> And a plaited crown of thorns
> Set upon his forehead.
>
> On the Son of Man they spat
> Mocked him and made merry.
> Then the cross of death was brought
> Given him to carry.
>
> At the sixth hour with two thieves
> To the cross they nailed him
> And the people and the thieves
> Mocked him and reviled him.
>
> This is Jesus King of Jews
> Cried they in derision
> Till the sun withdrew its light
> From that awful vision.
>
> At the ninth hour Jesus wailed
> Why hast thou me forsaken?
> Soldiers brought him vinegar
> Which he left untaken.
>
> Then he yielded up the ghost
> And the earth was shaken.

---

7. Roman judge before whom Jesus was arraigned by the Scribes (Matthew 27:1–24).

Rended was the temple's veil[8]
And the saints were wakened.

Soldiers broke the two thieves' legs
As the night descended
Thrust a spear in Jesus' side
When his life had ended.

Still they mocked, as from his wound
Flowed the blood and water
Thus blasphemed the Son of Man
With their cruel laughter.

MOTHER COURAGE: [*Enters in a state of agitation.*] His life's at stake. But they say the sergeant will listen to reason. Only it mustn't come out that he's our Swiss Cheese, or they'll say we've been giving him aid and comfort. All they want is money. But where will we get the money? Hasn't Yvette been here? I met her just now, she's latched onto a colonel, he's thinking of buying her a provisioner's business.

THE CHAPLAIN: Are you really thinking of selling?

MOTHER COURAGE: How else can I get the money for the sergeant?

THE CHAPLAIN: But what will you live on?

MOTHER COURAGE: That's the hitch.

[YVETTE POTTIER *comes in with a* doddering COLONEL.]

YVETTE: [*Embracing* MOTHER COURAGE.] My dear Mother Courage. Here we are again! [*Whispering.*] He's willing. [*Aloud.*] This is my dear friend who advises me on business matters. I just chanced to hear that you wish to sell your wagon, due to circumstances. I might be interested.

MOTHER COURAGE: Mortgage it, not sell it, let's not be hasty. It's not so easy to buy a wagon like this in wartime.

YVETTE: [*Disappointed.*] Only mortgage it? I thought you wanted to sell it. In that case, I don't know if I'm interested. [*To the* COLONEL.] What do you think?

THE COLONEL: Just as you say, my dear.

MOTHER COURAGE: It's only being mortgaged.

YVETTE: I thought you needed money.

MOTHER COURAGE: [*Firmly.*] I need the money, but I'd rather run myself ragged looking for an offer than sell now. The wagon is our livelihood. It's an opportunity for you, Yvette, God knows when you'll find another like it and have such a good friend to advise you. See what I mean?

YVETTE: My friend thinks I should snap it up, but I don't know. If it's only being mortgaged . . . . Don't you agree that we ought to buy?

THE COLONEL: Yes, my dear.

MOTHER COURAGE: Then you'll have to look for something that's for sale, maybe you'll find something if you take your time and your friend goes around with you. Maybe in a week or two you'll find the right thing.

YVETTE: Then we'll go looking, I love to go looking for things, and I love

---

8. Matthew reports that at the moment of Jesus' death, the veil, or curtain, in the temple that set off the sanctuary was torn from top to bottom; the earth shook, and the dead rose from their graves (Matthew 27:51–53).

to go around with you, Poldi, it's a real pleasure. Even if it takes two weeks. When would you pay the money back if you get it?

MOTHER COURAGE: I can pay it back in two weeks, maybe one.

YVETTE: I can't make up my mind, Poldi, chéri,[9] tell me what to do. [*She takes the* COLONEL *aside.*] I know she's got to sell, that's definite. The lieutenant, you know who I mean, the blond one, he'd be glad to lend me the money. He's mad about me, he says I remind him of somebody. What do you think?

THE COLONEL: Keep away from that lieutenant. He's no good. He'll take advantage. Haven't I told you I'd buy you something, pussykins?

YVETTE: I can't accept it from you. But then if you think the lieutenant might take advantage . . . Poldi, I'll accept it from you.

THE COLONEL: I hope so.

YVETTE: Your advice is to take it?

THE COLONEL: That's my advice.

YVETTE: [*Goes back to* MOTHER COURAGE.] My friend advises me to do it. Write me out a receipt, say the wagon belongs to me complete with stock and furnishings when the two weeks are up. We'll take the inventory right now, then I'll bring you the two hundred guilders. [*To the* COLONEL.] You go back to camp, I'll join you in a little while, I've got to take inventory, I don't want anything missing from my wagon. [*She kisses him. He leaves. She climbs up in the wagon.*] I don't see very many boots.

MOTHER COURAGE: Yvette. This is no time to inspect your wagon if it is yours. You promised to see the sergeant about my Swiss Cheese, you've got to hurry. They say he's to be court-martialed in an hour.

YVETTE: Just let me count the shirts.

MOTHER COURAGE: [*Pulls her down by the skirt.*] You hyena, it's Swiss Cheese, his life's at stake. And don't tell anybody where the offer comes from, in heaven's name say it's your gentleman friend, or we'll all get it, they'll say we helped him.

YVETTE: I've arranged to meet One-Eye in the woods, he must be there already.

THE CHAPLAIN: And there's no need to start out with the whole two hundred, offer a hundred and fifty, that's plenty.

MOTHER COURAGE: Is it your money? You just keep out of this. Don't worry, you'll get your bread and soup. Go on now and don't haggle. It's his life. [*She gives* YVETTE *a push to start her on her way.*]

THE CHAPLAIN: I didn't mean to butt in, but what are we going to live on? You've got an unemployable daughter on your hands.

MOTHER COURAGE: You muddlehead, I'm counting on the regimental cashbox. They'll allow for his expenses, won't they?

THE CHAPLAIN: But will she handle it right?

MOTHER COURAGE: It's in her own interest. If I spend her two hundred, she gets the wagon. She's mighty keen on it, how long can she expect to hold on to her colonel? Kattrin, you scour the knives, use pumice. And you, don't stand around like Jesus on the Mount of Olives,[1] bestir

---

9. Darling. Poldi is her pet name for Leopold.   1. The ridge of hills outside Jerusalem where Jesus waited after the Last Supper to be captured and taken before the high priest.

yourself, wash those glasses, we're expecting at least fifty for dinner, and then it'll be the same old story: "Oh my feet, I'm not used to running around, I don't run around in the pulpit." I think they'll set him free. Thank God they're open to bribery. They're not wolves, they're human and out for money. Bribe-taking in humans is the same as mercy in God. It's our only hope. As long as people take bribes, you'll have mild sentences and even the innocent will get off once in a while.

YVETTE: [*Comes in panting.*] They want two hundred. And we've got to be quick. Or it'll be out of their hands. I'd better take One-Eye to see my colonel right away. He confessed that he'd had the cashbox, they put the thumb screws on him. But he threw it in the river when he saw they were after him. The box is gone. Should I run and get the money from my colonel?

MOTHER COURAGE: The box is gone? How will I get my two hundred back?

YVETTE: Ah, so you thought you could take it out of the cashbox? You thought you'd put one over on me. Forget it. If you want to save Swiss Cheese, you'll just have to pay, or maybe you'd like me to drop the whole thing and let you keep your wagon?

MOTHER COURAGE: This is something I hadn't reckoned with. But don't rush me, you'll get the wagon, I know it's down the drain, I've had it for seventeen years. Just let me think a second, it's all so sudden. What'll I do, I can't give them two hundred, I guess you should have bargained. If I haven't got a few guilders to fall back on, I'll be at the mercy of the first Tom, Dick, or Harry. Say I'll give them a hundred and twenty, I'll lose my wagon anyway.

YVETTE: They won't go along. One-Eye's in a hurry, he's so keyed-up he keeps looking behind him. Hadn't I better give them the whole two hundred?

MOTHER COURAGE: [*In despair.*] I can't do it. Thirty years I've worked. She's twenty-five and no husband. I've got her to keep too. Don't needle me, I know what I'm doing. Say a hundred and twenty or nothing doing.

YVETTE: It's up to you. [*Goes out quickly.*]

[MOTHER COURAGE *looks neither at the* CHAPLAIN *nor at her daughter. She sits down to help* KATTRIN *scour the knives.*]

MOTHER COURAGE: Don't break the glasses. They're not ours any more. Watch what you're doing, you'll cut yourself. Swiss Cheese will be back, I'll pay two hundred if I have to. You'll have your brother. With eighty guilders we can buy a peddler's pack and start all over. Worse things have happened.

THE CHAPLAIN: The Lord will provide.

MOTHER COURAGE: Rub them dry. [*They scour the knives in silence. Suddenly* KATTRIN *runs sobbing behind the wagon.*]

YVETTE: [*Comes running.*] They won't go along. I warned you. One-Eye wanted to run out on me, he said it was no use. He said we'd hear the drums any minute, meaning he'd been sentenced. I offered a hundred and fifty. He didn't even bother to shrug his shoulders. When I begged and pleaded, he promised to wait till I'd spoken to you again.

MOTHER COURAGE: Say I'll give him the two hundred. Run. [YVETTE *runs off. They sit in silence. The* CHAPLAIN *has stopped washing the glasses.*] Maybe I bargained too long. [*Drums are heard in the distance. The*

CHAPLAIN *stands up and goes to the rear.* MOTHER COURAGE *remains seated. It grows dark. The drums stop. It grows light again.* MOTHER COURAGE *has not moved.*]

YVETTE: [*Enters, very pale.*] Now you've done it with your haggling and wanting to keep your wagon. Eleven bullets he got, that's all. I don't know why I bother with you any more, you don't deserve it. But I've picked up a little information. They don't believe the cashbox is really in the river. They suspect it's here and they think you were connected with him. They're going to bring him here, they think maybe you'll give yourself away when you see him. I'm warning you: You don't know him, or you're all dead ducks. I may as well tell you, they're right behind me. Should I keep Kattrin out of the way? [MOTHER COURAGE *shakes her head.*] Does she know? Maybe she didn't hear the drums or maybe she didn't understand.

MOTHER COURAGE: She knows. Get her.

[YVETTE *brings* KATTRIN, *who goes to her mother and stands beside her.* MOTHER COURAGE *takes her by the hand. Two* SOLDIERS *come in with a stretcher on which something is lying under a sheet. The* SERGEANT *walks beside them. They set the stretcher down.*]

THE SERGEANT: We've got a man here and we don't know his name. We need it for the records. He had a meal with you. Take a look, see if you know him. [*He removes the sheet.*] Do you know him? [MOTHER COURAGE *shakes her head.*] What? You'd never seen him before he came here for a meal? [MOTHER COURAGE shakes her head.] Pick him up. Throw him on the dump. Nobody knows him.

[*They carry him away.*]

4

Mother Courage sings the *Song of the Great Capitulation.*

Outside an officer's tent.

MOTHER COURAGE *is waiting. A* CLERK *looks out of the tent.*

THE CLERK: I know you. You had a Protestant paymaster at your place, he was hiding. I wouldn't put in any complaints if I were you.

MOTHER COURAGE: I'm putting in a complaint. I'm innocent. If I take this lying down, it'll look as if I had a guilty conscience. First they ripped up my whole wagon with their sabers, then they wanted me to pay a fine of five talers[2] for no reason at all.

THE CLERK: I'm advising you for your own good: Keep your trap shut. We haven't got many provisioners and we'll let you keep on with your business, especially if you've got a guilty conscience and pay a fine now and then.

MOTHER COURAGE: I'm putting in a complaint.

THE CLERK: Have it your way. But you'll have to wait till the captain can see you. [*Disappears into the tent.*]

A YOUNG SOLDIER: [*Enters in a rage.*] Bouque la Madonne![3] Where's that

---

2. German silver coins.   3. Screw the Virgin! (French).

stinking captain? He embezzled my reward and now he's drinking it up with his whores. I'm going to get him!

AN OLDER SOLDIER: [*Comes running after him.*] Shut up. They'll put you in the stocks!

THE YOUNG SOLDIER: Come on out, you crook! I'll make chops out of you. Embezzling my reward! Who jumps in the river? Not another man in the whole squad, only me. And I can't even buy myself a beer. I won't stand for it. Come on out and let me cut you to pieces!

THE OLDER SOLDIER: Holy Mary! He'll ruin himself.

MOTHER COURAGE: They didn't give him a reward?

THE YOUNG SOLDIER: Let me go. I'll run you through too, the more the merrier.

THE OLDER SOLDIER: He saved the colonel's horse and they didn't give him a reward. He's young, he hasn't been around long.

MOTHER COURAGE: Let him go, he's not a dog, you don't have to tie him up. Wanting a reward is perfectly reasonable. Why else would he distinguish himself?

THE YOUNG SOLDIER: And him drinking in there! You're all a lot of yellow-bellies. I distinguished myself and I want my reward.

MOTHER COURAGE: Young man, don't shout at me. I've got my own worries and besides, go easy on your voice, you may need it. You'll be hoarse when the captain comes out, you won't be able to say boo and he won't be able to put you in the stocks till you're blue in the face. People that yell like that don't last long, maybe half an hour, then they're so exhausted you have to sing them to sleep.

THE YOUNG SOLDIER: I'm not exhausted and who wants to sleep? I'm hungry. They make our bread out of acorns and hemp seed, and they skimp on that. He's whoring away my reward and I'm hungry. I'll murder him.

MOTHER COURAGE: I see. You're hungry. Last year your general made you cut across the fields to trample down the grain. I could have sold a pair of boots for ten guilders if anybody'd had ten guilders and if I'd had any boots. He thought he'd be someplace else this year, but now he's still here and everybody's starving. I can see that you might be good and mad.

THE YOUNG SOLDIER: He can't do this to me, save your breath, I won't put up with injustice.

MOTHER COURAGE: You're right, but for how long? How long won't you put up with injustice? An hour? Two hours? You see, you never thought of that, though it's very important, because it's miserable in the stocks when it suddenly dawns on you that you *can* put up with injustice.

THE YOUNG SOLDIER: I don't know why I listen to you. Bouque la Madonne! Where's the captain?

MOTHER COURAGE: You listen to me because I'm not telling you anything new. You know your temper has gone up in smoke, it was a short temper and you need a long one, but that's a hard thing to come by.

THE YOUNG SOLDIER: Are you trying to say I've no right to claim my reward?

MOTHER COURAGE: Not at all. I'm only saying your temper isn't long enough, it won't get you anywhere. Too bad. If you had a long temper,

I'd even egg you on. Chop the bastard up, that's what I'd say, but suppose you don't chop him up, because your tail's drooping and you know it. I'm left standing there like a fool and the captain takes it out on me.

THE OLDER SOLDIER: You're right. He's only blowing off steam.

THE YOUNG SOLDIER: We'll see about that. I'll cut him to pieces. [*He draws his sword.*] When he comes, I'll cut him to pieces.

THE CLERK: [*Looks out.*] The captain will be here in a moment. Sit down. [*The* YOUNG SOLDIER *sits down.*]

MOTHER COURAGE: There he sits. What did I tell you? Sitting, aren't you? Oh, they know us like a book, they know how to handle us. Sit down! And down we sit. You can't start a riot sitting down. Better not stand up again, you won't be able to stand the way you were standing before. Don't be embarrassed on my account, I'm no better, not a bit of it. We were full of piss and vinegar, but they've bought it off. Look at me. No back talk, it's bad for business. Let me tell you about the great capitulation. [*She sings the* Song of the Great Capitulation.][4]

When I was young, no more than a spring chicken
I too thought that I was really quite the cheese
(No common peddler's daughter, not I with my looks and my talent
    and striving for higher things!)
One little hair in the soup would make me sicken
And at me no man would dare to sneeze.
(It's all or nothing, no second best for me. I've got what it takes, the
    rules are for somebody else!)
But a chickadee
Sang wait and see!
    And you go marching with the show
    In step, however fast or slow
    And rattle off your little song:
    It won't be long.
    And then the whole thing slides.
    You think God provides—
    But you've got it wrong.

And before one single year had wasted
I had learned to swallow down the bitter brew
(Two kids on my hands and the price of bread and who do they take
    me for anyway!)
Man, the double-edged shellacking that I tasted
On my ass and knees I was when they were through.
(You've got to get along with people, one good turn deserves another,
    no use trying to ram your head through the wall!)
And the chickadee
Sang wait and see!
    And she goes marching with the show
    In step, however fast or slow
    And rattles off her little song:

4. Mother Courage punctuates the story of her own gradual disillusionment with proverbs and common sayings that represent a folk wisdom of successful adjustment.

It won't be long.
And then the whole thing slides
You think God provides—
But you've got it wrong.

I've seen many fired by high ambition
No star's big or high enough to reach out for.
(It's ability that counts, where there's a will there's a way, one way or
     another, we'll swing it!)
Then while moving mountains they get a suspicion
That to wear a straw hat is too big a chore.
(No use being too big for your britches!)
And the chickadee
Sings wait and see!
     And they go marching with the show
     In step, however fast or slow
     And rattle off their little song:
     It won't be long.
     And then the whole thing slides!
     You think God provides—
     But you've got it wrong!

MOTHER COURAGE: [*To the* YOUNG SOLDIER.] So here's what I think: Stay
     here with your sword if your anger's big enough, I know you have good
     reason, but if it's a short quick anger, better make tracks!

THE YOUNG SOLDIER: Kiss my ass! [*He staggers off, the* OLDER SOLDIER *after
     him.*]

THE CLERK: [*Sticking his head out.*] The captain is here. You can put in
     your complaint now.

MOTHER COURAGE: I've changed my mind. No complaint. [*She goes out.*]

5

Two years have passed. The war has spread far and wide. With scarcely
a pause Mother Courage's little wagon rolls through Poland, Moravia,
Bavaria, Italy, and back again to Bavaria in 1631. Tilly's victory at Magdeburg[5] costs Mother Courage four officers' shirts.

MOTHER COURAGE*'s wagon has stopped in a devastated village.*

Thin military music is heard from the distance. Two SOLDIERS *at the
bar are being waited on by* KATTRIN *and* MOTHER COURAGE*: One of them
is wearing a lady's fur coat over his shoulders.*

MOTHER COURAGE: What's that? You can't pay? No money, no schnapps.
     Plenty of victory marches for the Lord but no pay for the men.

THE SOLDIER: I want my schnapps. I came too late for the looting. The
     general skunked us: permission to loot the city for exactly one hour.
     Says he's not a monster; the mayor must have paid him.

THE CHAPLAIN: [*Staggers in.*] There's still some wounded in the house.

---

5. City eighty miles west of Berlin, besieged by the Imperial Army in 1630.

The peasant and his family. Help me, somebody, I need linen.

[*The* SECOND SOLDIER *goes out with him.* KATTRIN *gets very excited and tries to persuade her mother to hand out linen.*]

MOTHER COURAGE: I haven't got any. The regiment's bought up all my bandages. You think I'm going to rip up my officers' shirts for the likes of them?

THE CHAPLAIN: [*Calling back.*] I need linen, I tell you.

MOTHER COURAGE: [*Sitting down on the wagon steps to keep* KATTRIN *out.*] Nothing doing. They don't pay, they got nothing to pay with.

THE CHAPLAIN: [*Bending over a* WOMAN *whom he has carried out.*] Why did you stay here in all that gunfire?

THE PEASANT WOMAN: [*Feebly.*] Farm.

MOTHER COURAGE: You won't catch them leaving their property. And I'm expected to foot the bill. I won't do it.

THE FIRST SOLDIER: They're Protestants. Why do they have to be Protestants?

MOTHER COURAGE: Religion is the least of their worries. They've lost their farm.

THE SECOND SOLDIER: They're no Protestants. They're Catholics like us.

THE FIRST SOLDIER: How do we know who we're shooting at?

A PEASANT: [*Whom the* CHAPLAIN *brings in.*] They got my arm.

THE CHAPLAIN: Where's the linen?

[*All look at* MOTHER COURAGE, *who does not move.*]

MOTHER COURAGE: I can't give you a thing. What with all my taxes, duties, fees and bribes! [*Making guttural sounds,* KATTRIN *picks up a board and threatens her mother with it.*] Are you crazy? Put that board down, you slut, or I'll smack you. I'm not giving anything, you can't make me. I've got to think of myself. [*The* CHAPLAIN *picks her up from the step and puts her down on the ground. Then he fishes out some shirts and tears them into strips.*]

My shirts! Half a guilder apiece! I'm ruined!

[*The anguished cry of a baby is heard from the house.*]

THE PEASANT: The baby's still in there!

[KATTRIN *runs in.*]

THE CHAPLAIN: [*To the* WOMAN.] Don't move. They're bringing him out.

MOTHER COURAGE: Get her out of there. The roof'll cave in.

THE CHAPLAIN: I'm not going in there again.

MOTHER COURAGE: [*Torn.*] Don't run hog-wild with my expensive linen.

[KATTRIN *emerges from the ruins carrying an infant.*]

MOTHER COURAGE: Oh, so you've found another baby to carry around with you? Give that baby back to its mother this minute, or it'll take me all day to get it away from you. Do you hear me? [*To the* SECOND SOLDIER.] Don't stand there gaping, go back and tell them to stop that music, I can see right here that they've won a victory. Your victory's costing me a pretty penny.

[KATTRIN *rocks the baby in her arms, humming a lullaby.*]

MOTHER COURAGE: There she sits, happy in all this misery; give it back this minute, the mother's coming to. [*She pounces on the* FIRST SOLDIER *who has been helping himself to the drinks and is now making off with*

the bottle.] Pshagreff![6] Beast! Haven't you had enough victories for
today? Pay up.
FIRST SOLDIER: I'm broke.
MOTHER COURAGE: [*Tears the fur coat off him.*] Then leave the coat here,
it's stolen anyway.
THE CHAPLAIN: There's still somebody in there.

6

Outside Ingolstadt[7] in Bavaria Mother Courage attends the funeral of
Tilly, the imperial field marshal. Conversations about heroes and the lon-
gevity of the war. The chaplain deplores the waste of his talents. Mute
Kattrin gets the red shoes. 1632.

Inside MOTHER COURAGE*'s tent.*

*A bar open to the rear. Rain. In the distance drum rolls and funeral
music. The* CHAPLAIN *and the regimental* CLERK *are playing a board game.*
MOTHER COURAGE *and her daughter are taking inventory.*

THE CHAPLAIN: The procession's starting.
MOTHER COURAGE: It's a shame about the general—socks: twenty-two
   pairs—I hear he was killed by accident. On account of the fog in the
   fields. He's up front encouraging the troops. "Fight to the death, boys,"
   he sings out. Then he rides back, but he gets lost in the fog and rides
   back forward. Before you know it he's in the middle of the battle and
   stops a bullet—lanterns: we're down to four. [*A whistle from the rear.
   She goes to the bar.*] You men ought to be ashamed, running out on
   your late general's funeral! [*She pours drinks.*]
THE CLERK: They shouldn't have been paid before the funeral. Now
   they're getting drunk instead.
THE CHAPLAIN: [*To the* CLERK.] Shouldn't you be at the funeral?
THE CLERK: In this rain?
MOTHER COURAGE: With you it's different, the rain might spoil your uni-
   form. It seems they wanted to ring the bells, naturally, but it turned out
   the churches had all been shot to pieces by his orders, so the poor
   general won't hear any bells when they lower him into his grave.
   They're going to fire a three-gun salute instead, so it won't be too dull—
   seventeen sword belts.
CRIES: [*From the bar.*] Hey! Brandy!
MOTHER COURAGE: Money first! No, you can't come into my tent with
   your muddy boots! You can drink outside, rain or no rain. [*To the*
   CLERK.] I'm only letting officers in. It seems the general had been having his troubles. Mutiny in the Second Regiment because he hadn't
   paid them. It's a war of religion, he says, should they profit by their
   faith?
   [*Funeral march. All look to the rear.*]
THE CHAPLAIN: Now they're marching past the body.
MOTHER COURAGE: I feel sorry when a general or an emperor passes away

6. Son of a bitch! (Polish).   7. City forty miles north of Munich.

like this, maybe he thought he'd do something big, that posterity would still be talking about and maybe put up a statue in his honor, conquer the world, for instance, that's a nice ambition for a general, he doesn't know any better. So he knocks himself out, and then the common people come and spoil it all, because what do they care about greatness, all they care about is a mug of beer and maybe a little company. The most beautiful plans have been wrecked by the smallness of the people that are supposed to carry them out. Even an emperor can't do anything by himself, he needs the support of his soldiers and his people. Am I right?

THE CHAPLAIN: [*Laughing.*] Courage, you're right, except about the soldiers. They do their best. With those fellows out there, for instance, drinking their brandy in the rain, I'll undertake to carry on one war after another for a hundred years, two at once if I have to, and I'm not a general by trade.

MOTHER COURAGE: Then you don't think the war might stop?

THE CHAPLAIN: Because the general's dead? Don't be childish. They grow by the dozen, there'll always be plenty of heroes.

MOTHER COURAGE: Look here, I'm not asking you for the hell of it. I've been wondering whether to lay in supplies while they're cheap, but if the war stops, I can throw them out the window.

THE CHAPLAIN: I understand. You want a serious answer. There have always been people who say: "The war will be over some day." I say there's no guarantee the war will ever be over. Naturally a brief intermission is conceivable. Maybe the war needs a breather, a war can even break its neck, so to speak. There's always a chance of that, nothing is perfect here below. Maybe there never will be a perfect war, one that lives up to all our expectations. Suddenly, for some unforeseen reason, a war can bog down, you can't think of everything. Some little oversight and your war's in trouble. And then you've got to pull it out of the mud. But the kings and emperors, not to mention the pope, will always come to its help in adversity. On the whole, I'd say this war has very little to worry about, it'll live to a ripe old age.

A SOLDIER: [*Sings at the bar.*]

> A drink, and don't be slow!
> A soldier's got to go
> And fight for his religion.

> Make it double, this is a holiday.

MOTHER COURAGE: If I could only be sure . . .

THE CHAPLAIN: Figure it out for yourself. What's to stop the war?

THE SOLDIER: [*Sings.*]

> Your breasts, girl, don't be slow!
> A soldier's got to go
> And ride away to Pilsen.[8]

THE CLERK: [*Suddenly.*] But why can't we have peace? I'm from Bohemia, I'd like to go home when the time comes.

---

8. City in Bohemia, near the German border.

THE CHAPLAIN: Oh, you'd like to go home? Ah, peace! What becomes of the hole when the cheese has been eaten?

THE SOLDIER: [*Sings.*]

> Play cards, friends, don't be slow!
> A soldier's got to go
> No matter if it's Sunday.
>
> A prayer, priest, don't be slow!
> A soldier's got to go
> And die for king and country.

THE CLERK: In the long run nobody can live without peace.

THE CHAPLAIN: The way I see it, war gives you plenty of peace. It has its peaceful moments. War meets every need, including the peaceful ones, everything's taken care of, or your war couldn't hold its own. In a war you can shit the same as in the dead of peace, you can stop for a beer between battles, and even on the march you can always lie down on your elbows and take a little nap by the roadside. You can't play cards when you're fighting; but then you can't when you're plowing in the dead of peace either, but after a victory the sky's the limit. Maybe you've had a leg shot off, at first you raise a howl; you make a big thing of it. But then you calm down or they give you schnapps, and in the end you're hopping around again and the war's no worse off than before. And what's to prevent you from multiplying in the thick of the slaughter, behind a barn or someplace, in the long run how can they stop you, and then the war has your progeny to help it along. Take it from me, the war will always find an answer. Why would it have to stop?

[KATTRIN *has stopped working and is staring at the* CHAPLAIN.]

MOTHER COURAGE: Then I'll buy the merchandise. You've convinced me. [KATTRIN *suddenly throws down a basket full of bottles and runs out.*] Kattrin! [*Laughs.*] My goodness, the poor thing's been hoping for peace. I promised her she'd get a husband when peace comes. [*She runs after her.*]

THE CLERK: [*Getting up.*] I win, you've been too busy talking. Pay up.

MOTHER COURAGE: [*Comes back with* KATTRIN.] Be reasonable, the war'll go on a little longer and we'll make a little more money, then peace will be even better. Run along to town now, it won't take you ten minutes, and get the stuff from the Golden Lion, only the expensive things, we'll pick up the rest in the wagon later, it's all arranged, the regimental clerk here will go with you. They've almost all gone to the general's funeral, nothing can happen to you. Look sharp, don't let them take anything away from you, think of your dowry.

[KATTRIN *puts a kerchief over her head and goes with the clerk.*]

THE CHAPLAIN: Is it all right letting her go with the clerk?

MOTHER COURAGE: Who'd want to ruin her? She's not pretty enough.

THE CHAPLAIN: I've come to admire the way you handle your business and pull through every time. I can see why they call you Mother Courage.

MOTHER COURAGE: Poor people need courage. Why? Because they're sunk. In their situation it takes gumption just to get up in the morning. Or to plow a field in the middle of a war. They even show courage by bringing children into the world, because look at the prospects. The way they butcher and execute each other, think of the courage they need to look each other in the face. And putting up with an emperor and a pope takes a whale of a lot of courage, because those two are the death of the poor. [*She sits down, takes a small pipe from her pocket and smokes.*] You could be making some kindling.

THE CHAPLAIN: [*Reluctantly takes his jacket off and prepares to chop.*] Chopping wood isn't really my trade, you know, I'm a shepherd of souls.

MOTHER COURAGE: Sure. But I have no soul and I need firewood.

THE CHAPLAIN: What's that pipe?

MOTHER COURAGE: Just a pipe.

THE CHAPLAIN: No, it's not "just a pipe," it's a very particular pipe.

MOTHER COURAGE: Really?

THE CHAPLAIN: It's the cook's pipe from the Oxenstjerna regiment.

MOTHER COURAGE: If you know it all, why the mealy-mouthed questions?

THE CHAPLAIN: I didn't know if *you* knew. You could have been rummaging through your belongings and laid hands on some pipe and picked it up without thinking.

MOTHER COURAGE: Yes. Maybe that's how it was.

THE CHAPLAIN: Except it wasn't. You knew who that pipe belongs to.

MOTHER COURAGE: What of it?

THE CHAPLAIN: Courage, I'm warning you. It's my duty. I doubt if you ever lay eyes on the man again, but that's no calamity, in fact you're lucky. If you ask me, he wasn't steady. Not at all.

MOTHER COURAGE: What makes you say that? He was a nice man.

THE CHAPLAIN: Oh, you think he was nice? I differ. Far be it from me to wish him any harm, but I can't say he was nice. I'd say he was a scheming Don Juan.[9] If you don't believe me, take a look at his pipe. You'll have to admit that it shows up his character.

MOTHER COURAGE: I don't see anything. It's beat up.

THE CHAPLAIN: It's half bitten through. A violent man. That is the pipe of a ruthless, violent man, you must see that if you've still got an ounce of good sense.

MOTHER COURAGE: Don't wreck my chopping block.

THE CHAPLAIN: I've told you I wasn't trained to chop wood. I studied theology. My gifts and abilities are being wasted on muscular effort. The talents that God gave me are lying fallow. That's a sin. You've never heard me preach. With one sermon I can whip a regiment into such a state that they take the enemy for a flock of sheep. Then men care no more about their lives than they would about a smelly old sock that they're ready to throw away in hopes of final victory. God has made me eloquent. You'll swoon when you hear me preach.

MOTHER COURAGE: I don't want to swoon. What good would that do me?

THE CHAPLAIN: Courage, I've often wondered if maybe you didn't conceal a warm heart under that hard-bitten talk of yours. You too are human, you need warmth.

9. Philanderer.

MOTHER COURAGE: The best way to keep this tent warm is with plenty of firewood.

THE CHAPLAIN: Don't try to put me off. Seriously, Courage, I sometimes wonder if we couldn't make our relationship a little closer. I mean, seeing that the whirlwind of war has whirled us so strangely together.

MOTHER COURAGE: Seems to me it's close enough. I cook your meals and you do chores, such as chopping wood, for instance.

THE CHAPLAIN: [*Goes toward her.*] You know what I mean by "closer"; it has nothing to do with meals and chopping wood and such mundane needs. Don't harden your heart, let it speak.

MOTHER COURAGE: Don't come at me with that ax. That's too close a relationship.

THE CHAPLAIN: Don't turn it to ridicule. I'm serious. I've given it careful thought.

MOTHER COURAGE: Chaplain, don't be silly. I like you, I don't want to have to scold you. My aim in life is to get through, me and my children and my wagon. I don't think of it as mine and besides I'm not in the mood for private affairs. Right now I'm taking a big risk, buying up merchandise with the general dead and everybody talking peace. What'll you do if I'm ruined? See? You don't know. Chop that wood, then we'll be warm in the evening, which is a good thing in times like these. Now what? [*She stands up.*]

[*Enter* KATTRIN *out of breath, with a wound across her forehead and over one eye. She is carrying all sort of things, packages, leather goods, a drum, etc.*]

MOTHER COURAGE: What's this? Assaulted? On the way back? She was assaulted on the way back. Must have been that soldier that got drunk here! I shouldn't have let you go! Throw the stuff down! It's not bad, only a flesh wound. I'll bandage it, it'll heal in a week. They're worse than wild beasts. [*She bandages the wound.*]

THE CHAPLAIN: I can't find fault with them. At home they never raped anybody. I blame the people that start wars, they're the ones that dredge up man's lowest instincts.

MOTHER COURAGE: Didn't the clerk bring you back? That's because you're respectable, they don't give a damn. It's not a deep wound, it won't leave a mark. There, all bandaged. Don't fret, I've got something for you. I've been keeping it for you on the sly, it'll be a surprise. [*She fishes* YVETTE*'s red shoes out of a sack.*] See? You've always wanted them. Now you've got them. Put them on quick before I regret it. It won't leave a mark, though I wouldn't mind if it did. The girls that attract them get the worst of it. They drag them around till there's nothing left of them. If you don't appeal to them, they won't harm you. I've seen girls with pretty faces, a few years later they'd have given a wolf the creeps. They can't step behind a bush without fearing the worst. It's like trees. The straight tall ones get chopped down for ridgepoles, the crooked ones enjoy life. In other words, it's a lucky break. The shoes are still in good condition, I've kept them nicely polished.

[KATTRIN *leaves the shoes where they are and crawls into the wagon.*]

THE CHAPLAIN: I hope she won't be disfigured.

MOTHER COURAGE: There'll be a scar. She can stop waiting for peace.

THE CHAPLAIN: She didn't let them take anything.

MOTHER COURAGE: Maybe I shouldn't have drummed it into her. If I only knew what went on in her head. One night she stayed out, the only time in all these years. Afterwards she traipsed around as usual, except she worked harder. I never could find out what happened. I racked my brains for quite some time. [*She picks up the articles brought by* KAT-TRIN *and sorts them angrily.*] That's war for you! A fine way to make a living!

[*Cannon salutes are heard.*]

THE CHAPLAIN: Now they're burying the general. This is a historic moment.

MOTHER COURAGE: To me it's a historic moment when they hit my daughter over the eye. She's a wreck, she'll never get a husband now, and she's so crazy about children. It's the war that made her dumb too, a soldier stuffed something in her mouth when she was little. I'll never see Swiss Cheese again and where Eilif is, God knows. God damn the war.

7

Mother Courage at the height of her business career.

Highway.

The CHAPLAIN, MOTHER COURAGE, *and her daughter* KATTRIN *are pulling the wagon. New wares are hanging on it.* MOTHER COURAGE *is wearing a necklace of silver talers.*

MOTHER COURAGE: Stop running down the war. I won't have it. I know it destroys the weak, but the weak haven't a chance in peacetime either. And war is a better provider. [*Sings.*]

> If you're not strong enough to take it
> The victory will find you dead.
> A war is only what you make it.
> It's business, not with cheese but lead.

And what good is it staying in one place? The stay-at-homes are the first to get it. [*Sings.*]

> Some people think they'd like to ride out
> The war, leave danger to the brave
> And dig themselves a cozy hideout—
> They'll dig themselves an early grave.
> I've seen them running from the thunder
> To find a refuge from the war
> But once they're resting six feet under
> They wonder what they hurried for.

[*They plod on.*]

8

In the same year Gustavus Adolphus, King of Sweden, is killed at the battle of Lützen.[1] Peace threatens to ruin Mother Courage's business. Her brave son performs one heroic deed too many and dies an ignominious death.

A camp.

A summer morning. An OLD WOMAN *and her* SON *are standing by the wagon. The son is carrying a large sack of bedding.*

MOTHER COURAGE'S VOICE: [*From the wagon.*] Does it have to be at this unearthly hour?

THE YOUNG MAN: We've walked all night, twenty miles, and we've got to go back today.

MOTHER COURAGE'S VOICE: What can I do with bedding? The people haven't any houses.

THE YOUNG MAN: Wait till you've seen it.

THE OLD WOMAN: She won't take it either. Come on.

THE YOUNG MAN: They'll sell the roof from over our heads for taxes. Maybe she'll give us three guilders if you throw in the cross. [*Bells start ringing.*] Listen, mother!

VOICES: [*From the rear.*] Peace! The king of Sweden is dead!

MOTHER COURAGE: [*Sticks her head out of the wagon. She has not yet done her hair.*] Why are the bells ringing in the middle of the week?

THE CHAPLAIN: [*Crawls out from under the wagon.*] What are they shouting?

MOTHER COURAGE: Don't tell me peace has broken out when I've just taken in more supplies.

THE CHAPLAIN: [*Shouting toward the rear.*] Is it true? Peace?

VOICE: Three weeks ago, they say. But we just found out.

THE CHAPLAIN: [*To* MOTHER COURAGE.] What else would they ring the bells for?

VOICE: There's a whole crowd of Lutherans, they've driven their carts into town. They brought the news.

THE YOUNG MAN: Mother, it's peace. What's the matter?

[*The* OLD WOMAN *has collapsed.*]

MOTHER COURAGE: [*Going back into the wagon.*] Heavenly saints! Kattrin, peace! Put your black dress on! We're going to church. We owe it to Swiss Cheese. Can it be true?

THE YOUNG MAN: The people here say the same thing. They've made peace. Can you get up? [*The* OLD WOMAN *stands up, still stunned.*] I'll get the saddle shop started again. I promise. Everything will be all right. Father will get his bed back. Can you walk? [*To the* CHAPLAIN.] She fainted. It was the news. She thought peace would never come again. Father said it would. We'll go straight home. [*Both go out.*]

MOTHER COURAGE'S VOICE: Give her some brandy.

1. Town a few miles from the great Protestant city of Leipzig.

THE CHAPLAIN: They're gone.

MOTHER COURAGE'S VOICE: What's going on in camp?

THE CHAPLAIN: A big crowd. I'll go see. Shouldn't I put on my clericals?

MOTHER COURAGE'S VOICE: Better make sure before you step out in your antichrist costume. I'm glad to see peace, even if I'm ruined. At least I've brought two of my children through the war. Now I'll see my Eilif again.

THE CHAPLAIN: Look who's coming down the road. If it isn't the general's cook!

THE COOK: [*Rather bedraggled, carrying a bundle.*] Can I believe my eyes? The chaplain!

THE CHAPLAIN: Courage! A visitor!

[MOTHER COURAGE *climbs down.*]

THE COOK: Didn't I promise to come over for a little chat as soon as I had time? I've never forgotten your brandy, Mrs. Fierling.

MOTHER COURAGE: Mercy, the general's cook! After all these years! Where's Eilif, my eldest?

THE COOK: Isn't he here yet? He left ahead of me, he was coming to see you too.

THE CHAPLAIN: I'll put on my clericals, wait for me. [*Goes out behind the wagon.*]

MOTHER COURAGE: Then he'll be here any minute. [*Calls into the wagon.*] Kattrin, Eilif's coming! Bring the cook a glass of brandy! [KATTRIN *does not appear.*] Put a lock of hair over it, and forget it! Mr. Lamb is no stranger. [*Gets the brandy herself.*] She won't come out. Peace doesn't mean a thing to her, it's come too late. They hit her over the eye, there's hardly any mark, but she thinks people are staring at her.

THE COOK: Ech, war! [*He and* MOTHER COURAGE *sit down.*]

MOTHER COURAGE: Cook, you find me in trouble. I'm ruined.

THE COOK: What? Say, that's a shame.

MOTHER COURAGE: Peace has done me in. Only the other day I stocked up. The chaplain's advice. And now they'll all demobilize and leave me sitting on my merchandise.

THE COOK: How could you listen to the chaplain? If I'd had time, I'd have warned you against him, but the Catholics came too soon. He's a fly-by-night. So now he's the boss here?

MOTHER COURAGE: He washed my dishes and helped me pull the wagon.

THE COOK: Him? Pulling? I guess he's told you a few of his jokes too, I wouldn't put it past him, he has an unsavory attitude toward women, I tried to reform him, it was hopeless. He's not steady.

MOTHER COURAGE: Are you steady?

THE COOK: If nothing else, I'm steady. Prosit!

MOTHER COURAGE: Steady is no good. I've only lived with one steady man, thank the Lord. I never had to work so hard, he sold the children's blankets when spring came, and he thought my harmonica was unchristian. In my opinion you're not doing yourself any good by admitting you're steady.

THE COOK: You've still got your old bite, but I respect you for it.

MOTHER COURAGE: Don't tell me you've been dreaming about my old bite.

THE COOK: Well, here we sit, with the bells of peace and your world-famous brandy, that hasn't its equal.

MOTHER COURAGE: The bells of peace don't strike my fancy right now. I don't see them paying the men, they're behindhand already. Where does that leave me with my famous brandy? Have you been paid?

THE COOK: [*Hesitantly.*] Not really. That's why we demobilized ourselves. Under the circumstances, I says to myself, why should I stay on? I'll go see my friends in the meantime. So here we are.

MOTHER COURAGE: You mean you're out of funds?

THE COOK: If only they'd stop those damn bells! I'd be glad to go into some kind of business. I'm sick of being a cook. They give me roots and shoe leather to work with, and then they throw the hot soup in my face. A cook's got a dog's life these days. I'd rather be in combat, but now we've got peace. [*The* CHAPLAIN *appears in his original dress.*] We'll discuss it later.

THE CHAPLAIN: It's still in good condition. There were only a few moths in it.

THE COOK: I don't see why you bother. They won't take you back. Who are you going to inspire now to be an honest soldier and earn his pay at the risk of his life? Besides, I've got a bone to pick with you. Advising this lady to buy useless merchandise on the ground that the war would last forever.

THE CHAPLAIN: [*Heatedly.*] And why, I'd like to know, is it any of your business?

THE COOK: Because it's unscrupulous. How can you meddle in other people's business and give unsolicited advice?

THE CHAPLAIN: Who's meddling? [*To* MOTHER COURAGE.] I didn't know you were accountable to this gentleman, I didn't know you were so intimate with him.

MOTHER COURAGE: Don't get excited, the cook is only giving his private opinion. And you can't deny that your war was a dud.

THE CHAPLAIN: Courage, don't blaspheme against peace. You're a battle-field hyena.

MOTHER COURAGE: What am I?

THE COOK: If you insult this lady, you'll hear from me.

THE CHAPLAIN: I'm not talking to you. Your intentions are too obvious. [*To* MOTHER COURAGE.] But when I see you picking up peace with thumb and forefinger like a snotty handkerchief, it revolts my humanity; you don't want peace, you want war, because you profit by it, but don't forget the old saying: "He hath need of a long spoon that eateth with the devil."

MOTHER COURAGE: I've no use for war and war hasn't much use for me. Anyway, I'm not letting anybody call me a hyena, you and me are through.

THE CHAPLAIN: How can you complain about peace when it's such a relief to everybody else? On account of the old rags in your wagon?

MOTHER COURAGE: My merchandise isn't old rags, it's what I live off, and so did you.

THE CHAPLAIN: Off war, you mean. Aha!

THE COOK: [*To the* CHAPLAIN.] You're a grown man, you ought to know there's no sense in giving advice. [*To* MOTHER COURAGE.] The best thing you can do now is to sell off certain articles quick, before the prices hit the floor. Dress yourself and get started, there's no time to lose.

MOTHER COURAGE: That's very sensible advice. I think I'll do it.

THE CHAPLAIN: Because the cook says so!

MOTHER COURAGE: Why didn't *you* say so? He's right, I'd better run over to the market. [*She goes into the wagon.*]

THE COOK: My round, chaplain. No presence of mind. Here's what you should have said: me give you advice? All I ever did was talk politics! Don't try to take me on. Cockfighting is undignified in a clergyman.

THE CHAPLAIN: If you don't shut up, I'll murder you, undignified or not.

THE COOK: [*Taking off his shoe and unwinding the wrappings from his feet.*] If the war hadn't made a godless bum out of you, you could easily come by a parsonage now that peace is here. They won't need cooks, there's nothing to cook, but people still do a lot of believing, that hasn't changed.

THE CHAPLAIN: See here, Mr. Lamb. Don't try to squeeze me out. Being a bum has made me a better man. I couldn't preach to them any more.

[YVETTE POTTIER *enters, elaborately dressed in black, with a cane. She is much older and fatter and heavily powdered. Behind her a servant.*]

YVETTE: Hello there! Is this the residence of Mother Courage?

THE CHAPLAIN: Right you are. With whom have we the pleasure?

YVETTE: The Countess Starhemberg, my good people. Where is Mother Courage?

THE CHAPLAIN: [*Calls into the wagon.*] Countess Starhemberg wishes to speak to you!

MOTHER COURAGE: I'm coming.

YVETTE: It's Yvette!

MOTHER COURAGE'S VOICE: My goodness! It's Yvette!

YVETTE: Just dropped in to see how you're doing. [*The* COOK *has turned around in horror.*] Pieter!

THE COOK: Yvette!

YVETTE: Blow me down! How did you get here?

THE COOK: In a cart.

THE CHAPLAIN: Oh, you know each other? Intimately?

YVETTE: I should think so. [*She looks the* COOK *over.*] Fat!

THE COOK: You're not exactly willowy yourself.

YVETTE: All the same I'm glad I ran into you, you bum. Now I can tell you what I think of you.

THE CHAPLAIN: Go right ahead, spare no details, but wait until Courage comes out.

MOTHER COURAGE: [*Comes out with all sorts of merchandise.*] Yvette! [*They embrace.*] But what are you in mourning for?

YVETTE: Isn't it becoming? My husband the colonel died a few years ago.

MOTHER COURAGE: The old geezer that almost bought my wagon?

YVETTE: His elder brother.

MOTHER COURAGE: You must be pretty well fixed. It's nice to find somebody that's made a good thing out of the war.

YVETTE: Oh well, it's been up and down and back up again.

MOTHER COURAGE: Let's not say anything bad about colonels. They make money by the bushel.

THE CHAPLAIN: If I were you, I'd put my shoes back on again. [*To* YVETTE.] Countess Starhemberg, you promised to tell us what you think of this gentleman.

THE COOK: Don't make a scene here.

MOTHER COURAGE: He's a friend of mine, Yvette.

YVETTE: He's Pete the Pipe, that's who he is.

THE COOK: Forget the nicknames, my name is Lamb.

MOTHER COURAGE: [*Laughs.*] Pete the Pipe! That drove the women crazy! Say, I've saved your pipe.

THE CHAPLAIN: And smoked it.

YVETTE: It's lucky I'm here to warn you. He's the worst rotter that ever infested the coast of Flanders. He ruined more girls than he's got fingers.

THE COOK: That was a long time ago. I've changed.

YVETTE: Stand up when a lady draws you into a conversation! How I loved this man! And all the while he was seeing a little bandy-legged brunette, ruined her, too, naturally.

THE COOK: Seems to me I started you off on a prosperous career.

YVETTE: Shut up, you depressing wreck! Watch your step with him, his kind are dangerous even when they've gone to seed.

MOTHER COURAGE: [*To* YVETTE.] Come along, I've got to sell my stuff before the prices drop. Maybe you can help me, with your army connections. [*Calls into the wagon.*] Kattrin, forget about church, I'm running over to the market. When Eilif comes, give him a drink. [*Goes out with* YVETTE.]

YVETTE: [*In leaving.*] To think that such a man could lead me astray! I can thank my lucky stars that I was able to rise in the world after that. I've put a spoke in your wheel, Pete the Pipe, and they'll give me credit for it in heaven when my time comes.

THE CHAPLAIN: Our conversation seems to illustrate the old adage: The mills of God grind slowly.[2] What do you think of my jokes now?

THE COOK: I'm just unlucky. I'll come clean: I was hoping for a hot meal. I'm starving. And now they're talking about me, and she'll get the wrong idea. I think I'll beat it before she comes back.

THE CHAPLAIN: I think so too.

THE COOK: Chaplain, I'm fed up on peace already. Men are sinners from the cradle, fire and sword are their natural lot. I wish I were cooking for the general again. God knows where he is, I'd roast a fine fat capon, with mustard sauce and a few carrots.

THE CHAPLAIN: Red cabbage. Red cabbage with capon.

THE COOK: That's right, but he wanted carrots.

THE CHAPLAIN: He was ignorant.

THE COOK: That didn't prevent you from gorging yourself.

---

2. From a saying by Friedrich von Logan (1605–1655), as translated by Longfellow: "Though the mills of God grind slowly, / Yet they grind exceeding small."

THE CHAPLAIN: With repugnance.

THE COOK: Anyway you'll have to admit those were good times.

THE CHAPLAIN: I might admit that.

THE COOK: Now you've called her a hyena, your good times here are over. What are you staring at?

THE CHAPLAIN: Eilif? [EILIF *enters, followed by* SOLDIERS *with pikes. His hands are fettered. He is deathly pale.*] What's wrong?

EILIF: Where's mother?

THE CHAPLAIN: Gone to town.

EILIF: I heard she was here. They let me come and see her.

THE COOK: [*To the* SOLDIERS.] Where are you taking him?

A SOLDIER: No good place.

THE CHAPLAIN: What has he done?

THE SOLDIER: Broke into a farm. The peasant's wife is dead.

THE CHAPLAIN: How could you do such a thing?

EILIF: It's what I've been doing all along.

THE COOK: But in peacetime!

EILIF: Shut your trap. Can I sit down till she comes?

THE SOLDIER: We haven't time.

THE CHAPLAIN: During the war they honored him for it, he sat at the general's right hand. Then it was bravery. Couldn't we speak to the officer?

THE SOLDIER: No use. What's brave about taking a peasant's cattle?

THE COOK: It was stupid.

EILIF: If I'd been stupid, I'd have starved, wise guy.

THE COOK: And for being smart your head comes off.

THE CHAPLAIN: Let's get Kattrin at least.

EILIF: Leave her be. Get me a drink of schnapps.

THE SOLDIER: No time. Let's go!

THE CHAPLAIN: And what should we tell your mother?

EILIF: Tell her it wasn't any different, tell her it was the same. Or don't tell her anything.

[*The* SOLDIERS *drive him away.*]

THE CHAPLAIN: I'll go with you on your hard journey.

EILIF: I don't need any sky pilot.

THE CHAPLAIN: You don't know yet. [*He follows him.*]

THE COOK: [*Calls after them.*] I'll have to tell her, she'll want to see him.

THE CHAPLAIN: Better not tell her anything. Or say he was here and he'll come again, maybe tomorrow. I'll break it to her when I get back. [*Hurries out.*]

[*The* COOK *looks after them, shaking his head, then he walks anxiously about. Finally he approaches the wagon.*]

THE COOK: Hey! Come on out! I can see why you'd hide from peace. I wish I could do it myself. I'm the general's cook, remember? Wouldn't you have a bite to eat, to do me till your mother gets back? A slice of ham or just a piece of bread while I'm waiting. [*He looks in.*] She's buried her head in a blanket.

[*The sound of gunfire in the rear.*]

MOTHER COURAGE: [*Runs in. She is out of breath and still has her mer-*

chandise.] Cook, the peace is over, the war started up again three days ago. I hadn't sold my stuff yet when I found out. Heaven be praised! They're shooting each other up in town, the Catholics and Lutherans. We've got to get out of here. Kattrin, start packing. What have *you* got such a long face about? What's wrong?

THE COOK: Nothing.

MOTHER COURAGE: Something's wrong, I can tell by your expression.

THE COOK: Maybe it's the war starting up again. Now I probably won't get anything hot to eat before tomorrow night.

MOTHER COURAGE: That's a lie, cook.

THE COOK: Eilif was here. He couldn't stay.

MOTHER COURAGE: He was here? Then we'll see him on the march. I'm going with our troops this time. How does he look?

THE COOK: The same.

MOTHER COURAGE: He'll never change. The war couldn't take him away from me. He's smart. Could you help me pack? [*She starts packing.*] Did he tell you anything? Is he in good with the general? Did he say anything about his heroic deeds?

THE COOK: [*Gloomily.*] They say he's been at one of them again.

MOTHER COURAGE: Tell me later, we've got to be going. [KATTRIN *emerges.*] Kattrin, peace is over. We're moving. [*To the* COOK.] What's the matter with you?

THE COOK: I'm going to enlist.

MOTHER COURAGE: I've got a suggestion. Why don't . . . ? Where's the chaplain?

THE COOK: Gone to town with Eilif.

MOTHER COURAGE: Then come a little way with me, Lamb. I need help.

THE COOK: That incident with Yvette . . .

MOTHER COURAGE: It hasn't lowered you in my estimation. Far from it. Where there's smoke there's fire. Coming?

THE COOK: I won't say no.

MOTHER COURAGE: The Twelfth Regiment has shoved off. Take the shaft. Here's a chunk of bread. We'll have to circle around to meet the Lutherans. Maybe I'll see Eilif tonight. He's my favorite. It's been a short peace. And we're on the move again. [*She sings, while the* COOK *and* KATTRIN *harness themselves to the wagon.*]

> From Ulm to Metz, from Metz to Pilsen[3]
> Courage is right there in the van.
> The war both in and out of season
> With shot and shell will feed its man.
> But lead alone is not sufficient
> The war needs soldiers to subsist!
> Its diet elseways is deficient.
> The war is hungry! So enlist!

---

3. Ulm is about eighty miles west of Munich. Metz, in the province of Lorraine (ceded to France at the end of the Thirty Years' War), is about two hundred miles west of Ulm. To travel from Metz to Pilsen one must cross the whole of Germany.

9

The great war of religion has been going on for sixteen years. Germany has lost more than half its population. Those whom the slaughter has spared have been laid low by epidemics. Once-flourishing countrysides are ravaged by famine. Wolves prowl through the charred ruins of the cities. In the fall of 1634 we find Mother Courage in Germany, in the Fichtelgebirge[4] at some distance from the road followed by the Swedish armies. Winter comes early and is exceptionally severe. Business is bad, begging is the only resort. The cook receives a letter from Utrecht[5] and is dismissed.

Outside a half-demolished presbytery.

Gray morning in early winter. Gusts of wind. MOTHER COURAGE *and the* COOK *in shabby sheepskins by the wagon.*

THE COOK: No light. Nobody's up yet.

MOTHER COURAGE: But it's a priest. He'll have to crawl out of bed to ring the bells. Then he'll get himself a nice bowl of hot soup.

THE COOK: Go on, you saw the village, everything's been burned to a crisp.

MOTHER COURAGE: But somebody's here, I heard a dog bark.

THE COOK: If the priest's got anything, he won't give it away.

MOTHER COURAGE: Maybe if we sing . . .

THE COOK: I've had it up to here. [*Suddenly.*] I got a letter from Utrecht. My mother's died of cholera and the tavern belongs to me. Here's the letter if you don't believe me. It's no business of yours what my aunt says about my evil ways, but never mind, read it.

MOTHER COURAGE:[6] [*Reads the letter.*] Lamb, I'm sick of roaming around, myself. I feel like a butcher's dog that pulls the meat cart but doesn't get any for himself. I've nothing left to sell and the people have no money to pay for it. In Saxony a man in rags tried to foist a cord of books on me for two eggs, and in Württemberg they'd have let their plow go for a little bag of salt. What's the good of plowing? Nothing grows but brambles. In Pomerania[7] they say the villagers have eaten up all the babies, and that nuns have been caught at highway robbery.

THE COOK: It's the end of the world.

MOTHER COURAGE: Sometimes I have visions of myself driving through hell, selling sulfur and brimstone, or through heaven peddling refreshments to the roaming souls. If me and the children I've got left could find a place where there's no shooting, I wouldn't mind a few years of peace and quiet.

THE COOK: We could open up the tavern again. Think it over, Anna. I made up my mind last night; with or without you, I'm going back to Utrecht. In fact I'm leaving today.

MOTHER COURAGE: I'll have to talk to Kattrin. It's kind of sudden, and I

---

4. A range of mountains in Germany near the Bohemian border.   5. City in the south of Holland. 6. In this scene, Mother Courage and the Cook for the first time use *du*, the familiar form of *you* in German. (The familiar form is used between lovers, close friends and family, and young people; the formal *Sie* is used otherwise.)   7. Saxony, Württemberg, and Pomerania are German principalities.

don't like to make decisions in the cold with nothing in my stomach. Kattrin! [KATTRIN *climbs out of the wagon.*] Kattrin, I've got something to tell you. The cook and me are thinking of going to Utrecht. They've left him a tavern there. You'd be living in one place, you'd meet people. A lot of men would be glad to get a nice, well-behaved girl, looks aren't everything. I'm all for it. I get along fine with the cook. I've got to hand it to him: He's got a head for business. We'd eat regular meals, wouldn't that be nice? And you'd have your own bed, wouldn't you like that? It's no life on the road, year in year out. You'll go to rack and ruin. You're crawling with lice already. We've got to decide, you see, we could go north with the Swedes, they must be over there. [*She points to the left.*] I think we'll do it, Kattrin.

THE COOK: Anna, could I have a word with you alone?

MOTHER COURAGE: Get back in the wagon, Kattrin.

[KATTRIN *climbs back in.*]

THE COOK: I interrupted you because I see there's been a misunderstanding, I thought it was too obvious to need saying. But if it isn't, I'll just have to say it. You can't take her, it's out of the question. Is that plain enough for you?

[KATTRIN *sticks her head out of the wagon and listens.*]

MOTHER COURAGE: You want me to leave Kattrin?

THE COOK: Look at it this way. There's no room in the tavern. It's not one of those places with three taprooms. If the two of us put our shoulder to the wheel, we can make a living, but not three, it can't be done. Kattrin can keep the wagon.

MOTHER COURAGE: I'd been thinking she could find a husband in Utrecht.

THE COOK: Don't make me laugh! How's she going to find a husband? At her age? And dumb! And with that scar!

MOTHER COURAGE: Not so loud.

THE COOK: Shout or whisper, the truth's the truth. And that's another reason why I can't have her in the tavern. The customers won't want a sight like that staring them in the face. Can you blame them?

MOTHER COURAGE: Shut up. Not so loud, I say.

THE COOK: There's a light in the presbytery. Let's sing.

MOTHER COURAGE: How could she pull the wagon by herself? She's afraid of the war. She couldn't stand it. The dreams she must have! I hear her groaning at night. Especially after battles. What she sees in her dreams, God knows. It's pity that makes her suffer so. The other day the wagon hit a hedgehog, I found it hidden in her blanket.

THE COOK: The tavern's too small. [*He calls.*] Worthy gentleman and members of the household! We shall now sing the Song of Solomon, Julius Caesar, and other great men, whose greatness didn't help them any. Just to show you that we're God-fearing people ourselves, which makes it hard for us, especially in the winter. [*They sing.*]

> You saw the wise King Solomon[8]
> You know what came of him.

8. Biblical ruler celebrated for his wisdom.

To him all hidden things were plain.
He cursed the hour gave birth to him[9]
And saw that everything was vain.
How great and wise was Solomon!
Now think about his case. Alas
A useful lesson can be won.
It's wisdom that had brought him to that pass!
How happy is the man with none!

Our beautiful song proves that virtues are dangerous things, better steer clear of them, enjoy life, eat a good breakfast, a bowl of hot soup, for instance. Take me, I haven't got any soup and wish I had, I'm a soldier, but what has my bravery in all those battles got me, nothing, I'm starving, I'd be better off if I'd stayed home like a yellowbelly. And I'll tell you why.

You saw the daring Caesar[1] next
You know what he became.
They deified him in his life
But then they killed him just the same.
And as they raised the fatal knife
How loud he cried: "You too, my son!"
Now think about his case. Alas
A useful lesson can be won.
It's daring that had brought him to that pass!
How happy is the man with none!

[*In an undertone.*] They're not even looking out. Worthy gentleman and members of the household! Maybe you'll say, all right, if bravery won't keep body and soul together, try honesty. That may fill your belly or at least get you a drop to drink. Let's look into it.

You've heard of honest Socrates[2]
Who never told a lie.
They weren't so grateful as you'd think
Instead they sentenced him to die
And handed him the poisoned drink.
How honest was the people's noble son!
Now think about his case. Alas
A useful lesson can be won.
His honesty had brought him to that pass.
How happy is the man with none!

Yes, they tell us to be charitable and to share what we have, but what if we haven't got anything? Maybe philanthropists have a rough time of it too, it stands to reason, they need a little something for themselves. Yes, charity is a rare virtue, because it doesn't pay.

St. Martin couldn't bear to see
His fellows in distress.
He saw a poor man in the snow.

---

9. The cook confuses Solomon with the biblical Job, who curses the day he was born (Job 3:1).   1. Roman general and dictator (100–44 B.C.), assassinated by a republican clique—that included his young friend Brutus—when suspected of imperial ambitions.   2. Greek philosopher, condemned to death in 399 B.C. for teaching the young to question accepted beliefs.

"Take half my cloak!"[3] He did, and lo!
They both of them froze none the less.
He thought his heavenly reward was won.
Now think about his case. Alas
A useful lesson can be won.
Unselfishness had brought him to that pass.
How happy is the man with none!

That's our situation. We're God-fearing folk, we stick together, we don't
steal, we don't murder, we don't set fire to anything! You could say that
we set an example which bears out the song, we sink lower and lower,
we seldom see any soup, but if we were different, if we were thieves
and murderers, maybe our bellies would be full. Because virtue isn't
rewarded, only wickedness, the world needn't be like this, but it is.

And here you see God-fearing folk
Observing God's ten laws.
So far He hasn't taken heed.
You people sitting warm indoors
Help to relieve our bitter need!
Our virtue can be counted on.
Now think about our case. Alas
A useful lesson can be won.
The fear of God has brought us to this pass.
How happy is the man with none!

VOICE: [*From above.*] Hey, down there! Come on up! We've got some
good thick soup.

MOTHER COURAGE: Lamb, I couldn't get anything down. I know what you
say makes sense, but is it your last word? We've always been good
friends.

THE COOK: My last word. Think it over.

MOTHER COURAGE: I don't need to think it over. I won't leave her.

THE COOK: It wouldn't be wise, but there's nothing I can do. I'm not inhuman, but it's a small tavern. We'd better go in now, or there won't be
anything left, we'll have been singing in the cold for nothing.

MOTHER COURAGE: I'll get Kattrin.

THE COOK: Better bring it down for her. They'll get a fright if the three of
us barge in. [*They go out.*]

[KATTRIN *climbs out of the wagon. She is carrying a bundle. She
looks around to make sure the others are gone. Then she spreads out
an old pair of the cook's trousers and a skirt belonging to her mother
side by side on a wheel of the wagon so they can easily be seen. She
is about to leave with her bundle when* MOTHER COURAGE *comes out
of the house.*]

MOTHER COURAGE: [*With a dish of soup.*] Kattrin! Stop! Kattrin! Where do
you think you're going with that bundle? Have you taken leave of your
wits? [*She examines the bundle.*] She's packed her things. Were you
listening? I've told him it's no go with Utrecht and his lousy tavern,

---

3. As a young soldier in the Roman army, Martin (330–397) divided his military cloak with a beggar. He
dreamed of Christ that night and was baptized thereafter, later becoming bishop of Tours.

what would we do there? A tavern's no place for you and me. The war still has a thing or two up its sleeve for us. [*She sees the trousers and skirt.*] You're stupid. Suppose I'd seen that and you'd been gone? [KATTRIN *tries to leave,* MOTHER COURAGE *holds her back.*] And don't go thinking I've given him the gate on your account. It's the wagon. I won't part with the wagon, I'm used to it, it's not you, it's the wagon. We'll go in the other direction, we'll put the cook's stuff out here where he'll find it, the fool. [*She climbs up and throws down a few odds and ends, to join the trousers.*] There. Now we're shut of him, you won't see me taking anyone else into the business. From now on it's you and me. This winter will go by like all the rest. Harness up, it looks like snow.

[*They harness themselves to the wagon, turn it around and pull it away. When the* COOK *comes out he sees his things and stands dumbfounded.*]

10

Throughout 1635 Mother Courage and her daughter Kattrin pull the wagon over the roads of central Germany in the wake of the increasingly bedraggled armies.

Highway.

MOTHER COURAGE *and* KATTRIN *are pulling the wagon. They come to a peasant's house. A voice is heard singing from within.*

THE VOICE:

The rose bush in our garden
Rejoiced our hearts in spring
It bore such lovely flowers.
We planted it last season
Before the April showers.
A garden is a blessèd thing
It bore such lovely flowers.

When winter comes a-stalking
And gales great snow storms bring
They trouble us but little.
We've lately finished caulking
The roof with moss and wattle.
A sheltering roof's a blessèd thing
When winter comes a-stalking.

[MOTHER COURAGE *and* KATTRIN *have stopped to listen. Then they move on.*]

11

January 1636. The imperial troops threaten the Protestant city of Halle.[4] The stone speaks. Mother Courage loses her daughter and goes on alone. The end of the war is not in sight.

4. Twenty miles northwest of Leipzig.

The wagon, much the worse for wear, is standing beside a peasant house with an enormous thatch roof. The house is built against the side of a stony hill. Night.

A LIEUTENANT *and three* SOLDIERS *in heavy armor step out of the woods.*

THE LIEUTENANT: I don't want any noise. If anybody yells, run him through with your pikes.

FIRST SOLDIER: But we need a guide. We'll have to knock if we want them to come out.

THE LIEUTENANT: Knocking sounds natural. It could be a cow bumping against the barn wall.

[*The* SOLDIERS *knock on the door. A* PEASANT WOMAN *opens. They hold their hands over her mouth. Two* SOLDIERS *go in.*]

A MAN'S VOICE: [*Inside.*] Who's there?

[*The* SOLDIERS *bring out a* PEASANT *and his* SON.]

THE LIEUTENANT: [*Points to the wagon, in which* KATTRIN *has appeared.*] There's another one. [*A* SOLDIER *pulls her out.*] Anybody else live here?

THE PEASANT COUPLE: This is our son.—That's a dumb girl.—Her mother's gone into the town on business—Buying up people's belongings, they're selling cheap because they're getting out.—They're provisioners.

THE LIEUTENANT: I'm warning you to keep quiet, one squawk and you'll get a pike over the head. All right. I need somebody who can show us the path to the city. [*Points to the* YOUNG PEASANT.] You. Come here!

THE YOUNG PEASANT: I don't know no path.

THE SECOND SOLDIER: [*Grinning.*] He don't know no path.

THE YOUNG PEASANT: I'm not helping the Catholics.

THE LIEUTENANT: [*To the* SECOND SOLDIER.] Give him a feel of your pike!

THE YOUNG PEASANT: [*Forced down on his knees and threatened with the pike.*] You can kill me. I won't do it.

THE FIRST SOLDIER: I know what'll make him think twice. [*He goes over to the barn.*] Two cows and an ox. Get this: If you don't help us, I'll cut them down.

THE YOUNG PEASANT: Not the animals!

THE PEASANT WOMAN: [*In tears.*] Captain, spare our animals or we'll starve.

THE LIEUTENANT: If he insists on being stubborn, they're done for.

THE FIRST SOLDIER: I'll start with the ox.

THE YOUNG PEASANT: [*To the* OLD MAN.] Do I have to? [*The* OLD WOMAN *nods.*] I'll do it.

THE PEASANT WOMAN: And thank you kindly for your forbearance, Captain, for ever and ever, amen.

[*The* PEASANT *stops her from giving further thanks.*]

THE FIRST SOLDIER: Didn't I tell you? With them it's the animals that come first.

[*Led by the* YOUNG PEASANT, *the* LIEUTENANT *and the* SOLDIERS *continue on their way.*]

THE PEASANT: I wish I knew what they're up to. Nothing good.

THE PEASANT WOMAN: Maybe they're only scouts.—What are you doing?

THE PEASANT: [*Putting a ladder against the roof and climbing up.*] See if they're alone. [*On the roof.*] Men moving in the woods. All the way to the quarry. Armor in the clearing. And a cannon. It's more than a regiment. God have mercy on the city and everybody in it.

THE PEASANT WOMAN: See any light in the city?

THE PEASANT: No. They're all asleep. [*He climbs down.*] If they get in, they'll kill everybody.

THE PEASANT WOMAN: The sentry will see them in time.

THE PEASANT: They must have killed the sentry in the tower on the hill, or he'd have blown his horn.

THE PEASANT WOMAN: If there were more of us . . .

THE PEASANT: All by ourselves up here with a cripple . . .

THE PEASANT WOMAN: We can't do a thing. Do you think . . .

THE PEASANT: Not a thing.

THE PEASANT WOMAN: We couldn't get down there in the dark.

THE PEASANT: The whole hillside is full of them. We can't even give a signal.

THE PEASANT WOMAN: They'd kill us.

THE PEASANT: No, we can't do a thing.

THE PEASANT WOMAN: [*To* KATTRIN.] Pray, poor thing, pray! We can't stop the bloodshed. If you can't talk, at least you can pray. He'll hear you if nobody else does. I'll help you. [*All kneel,* KATTRIN *behind the* PEASANTS.] Our Father which art in heaven, hear our prayer. Don't let the town perish with everybody in it, all asleep and unsuspecting. Wake them, make them get up and climb the walls and see the enemy coming through the night with cannon and pikes, through the fields and down the hillside. [*Back to* KATTRIN.] Protect our mother and don't let the watchman sleep, wake him before it's too late. And succor our brother-in-law, he's in there with his four children, let them not perish, they're innocent and don't know a thing. [*To* KATTRIN, *who groans.*] The littlest is less than two, the oldest is seven. [*Horrified,* KATTRIN *stands up.*] Our Father, hear us, for Thou alone canst help, we'll all be killed, we're weak, we haven't any pikes or anything, we are powerless and in Thine hands, we and our animals and the whole farm, and the city too, it's in Thine hands, and the enemy is under the walls with great might.

[KATTRIN *has crept unnoticed to the wagon, taken something out of it, put it under her apron and climbed up the ladder to the roof of the barn.*]

THE PEASANT WOMAN: Think upon the children in peril, especially the babes in arms and the old people that can't help themselves and all God's creatures.

THE PEASANT: And forgive us our trespasses as we forgive them that trespass against us. Amen.

[KATTRIN, *sitting on the roof, starts beating the drum that she has taken out from under her apron.*]

THE PEASANT WOMAN: Jesus! What's she doing?

THE PEASANT: She's gone crazy.

THE PEASANT WOMAN: Get her down, quick!

[*The* PEASANT *runs toward the ladder, but* KATTRIN *pulls it up on the roof.*]

THE PEASANT WOMAN: She'll be the death of us all.

THE PEASANT: Stop that, you cripple!

THE PEASANT WOMAN: She'll have the Catholics down on us.

THE PEASANT: [*Looking around for stones.*] I'll throw rocks at you.

THE PEASANT WOMAN: Have you no pity? Have you no heart? We're dead if they find out it's us! They'll run us through!

[KATTRIN *stares in the direction of the city, and goes on drumming.*]

THE PEASANT WOMAN: [*To the* PEASANT.] I told you not to let those tramps stop here. What do they care if the soldiers drive our last animals away?

THE LIEUTENANT: [*Rushes in with his* SOLDIERS *and the* YOUNG PEASANT.] I'll cut you to pieces!

THE PEASANT WOMAN: We're innocent, captain. We couldn't help it. She sneaked up there. We don't know her.

THE LIEUTENANT: Where's the ladder?

THE PEASANT: Up top.

THE LIEUTENANT: [*To* KATTRIN.] Throw down that drum. It's an order!

[KATTRIN *goes on drumming.*]

THE LIEUTENANT: You're all in this together! This'll be the end of you!

THE PEASANT: They've felled some pine trees in the woods over there. We could get one and knock her down . . .

THE FIRST SOLDIER: [*To the* LIEUTENANT.] Request permission to make a suggestion. [*He whispers something in the* LIEUTENANT's *ear. He nods.*] Listen. We've got a friendly proposition. Come down, we'll take you into town with us. Show us your mother and we won't touch a hair of her head.

[KATTRIN *goes on drumming.*]

THE LIEUTENANT: [*Pushes him roughly aside.*] She doesn't trust you. No wonder with your mug. [*He calls up.*] If I give you my word? I'm an officer, you can trust my word of honor.

[*She drums still louder.*]

THE LIEUTENANT: Nothing is sacred to her.

THE YOUNG PEASANT: It's not just her mother, lieutenant!

THE FIRST SOLDIER: We can't let this go on. They'll hear it in the city.

THE LIEUTENANT: We'll have to make some kind of noise that's louder than the drums. What could we make noise with?

THE FIRST SOLDIER: But we're not supposed to make noise.

THE LIEUTENANT: An innocent noise, stupid. A peaceable noise.

THE PEASANT: I could chop wood.

THE LIEUTENANT: That's it, chop! [*The* PEASANT *gets an ax and chops at a log.*] Harder! Harder! You're chopping for your life.

[*Listening,* KATTRIN *has been drumming more softly. Now she looks anxiously around and goes on drumming as before.*]

THE LIEUTENANT: [*To the* PEASANT.] Not loud enough. [*To the* FIRST SOLDIER.] You chop too.

THE PEASANT: There's only one ax. [*Stops chopping.*]

THE LIEUTENANT: We'll have to set the house on fire. Smoke her out.

THE PEASANT: That won't do any good, Captain. If the city people see fire up here, they'll know what's afoot.

[*Still drumming,* KATTRIN *has been listening again. Now she laughs.*]

THE LIEUTENANT: Look, she's laughing at us. I'll shoot her down, regardless. Get the musket!

[*Two* SOLDIERS *run out.* KATTRIN *goes on drumming.*]

THE PEASANT WOMAN: I've got it, captain. That's their wagon over there. If we start smashing it up, she'll stop. The wagon's all they've got.

THE LIEUTENANT: [*To the* YOUNG PEASANT.] Smash away. [*To* KATTRIN.] We'll smash your wagon if you don't stop.

[*The* YOUNG PEASANT *strikes a few feeble blows at the wagon.*]

THE PEASANT WOMAN: Stop it, you beast!

[KATTRIN *stares despairingly at the wagon and emits pitiful sounds. But she goes on drumming.*]

THE LIEUTENANT: Where are those stinkers with the musket?

THE FIRST SOLDIER: They haven't heard anything in the city yet, or we'd hear their guns.

THE LIEUTENANT: [*To* KATTRIN.] They don't hear you. And now we're going to shoot you down. For the last time: Drop that drum!

THE YOUNG PEASANT: [*Suddenly throws the plank away.*] Keep on drumming! Or they'll all be killed! Keep on drumming, keep on drumming . . .

[*The* SOLDIER *throws him down and hits him with his pike.* KATTRIN *starts crying, but goes on drumming.*]

THE PEASANT WOMAN: Don't hit him in the back! My God, you're killing him.

[*The* SOLDIERS *run in with the musket.*]

THE SECOND SOLDIER: The colonel's foaming at the mouth. We'll be court-martialed.

THE LIEUTENANT: Set it up! Set it up! [*To* KATTRIN, *while the musket is being set up on its stand.*] For the last time: Stop that drumming! [KATTRIN *in tears drums as loud as she can.*] Fire!

[*The* SOLDIERS *fire,* KATTRIN *is hit. She beats the drum for a few times more and then slowly collapses.*]

THE LIEUTENANT: Now we'll have some quiet.

[*But* KATTRIN'*s last drumbeats are answered by the city's cannon. A confused hubbub of alarm bells and cannon is heard in the distance.*]

THE FIRST SOLDIER: She's done it.

12

Night, toward morning. The fifes and drums of troops marching away.

Outside the wagon MOTHER COURAGE *sits huddled over her daughter. The* PEASANT COUPLE *are standing beside them.*

THE PEASANT: [*Hostile.*] You'll have to be going, woman. There's only one more regiment to come. You can't go alone.[5]

MOTHER COURAGE: Maybe I can get her to sleep. [*She sings.*]
     Lullaby baby
     What stirs in the hay?

---

5. That is, for protection and customers, Mother Courage must travel with the army.

> The neighbor brats whimper
> Mine are happy and gay.
> They go in tatters
> And you in silk down
> Cut from an angel's
> Best party gown.
>
> They've nothing to munch on
> And you will have pie
> Just tell your mother
> In case it's too dry.
> Lullaby baby
> What stirs in the hay?
> That one lies in Poland
> The other—who can say?

Now she's asleep. You shouldn't have told her about your brother-in-law's children.

THE PEASANT: Maybe it wouldn't have happened if you hadn't gone to town to swindle people.

MOTHER COURAGE: I'm glad she's sleeping now.

THE PEASANT WOMAN: She's not sleeping, you'll have to face it, she's dead.

THE PEASANT: And it's time you got started. There are wolves around here, and what's worse, marauders.

MOTHER COURAGE: Yes. [*She goes to the wagon and takes out a sheet of canvas to cover the body with.*]

THE PEASANT WOMAN: Haven't you anybody else? Somebody you can go to?

MOTHER COURAGE: Yes, there's one of them left. Eilif.

THE PEASANT: [*While* MOTHER COURAGE *covers the body.*] Go find him. We'll attend to this one, give her a decent burial. Set your mind at rest.

MOTHER COURAGE: Here's money for your expenses. [*She gives the* PEASANT *money.*]

[*The* PEASANT *and his* SON *shake hands with her and carry* KATTRIN *away.*]

THE PEASANT WOMAN: [*On the way out.*] Hurry up!

MOTHER COURAGE: [*Harnesses herself to the wagon.*] I hope I can pull the wagon alone. I'll manage, there isn't much in it. I've got to get back in business.

[*Another regiment marches by with fifes and drums in the rear.*]

MOTHER COURAGE: Hey, take me with you! [*She starts to pull.*]

[*Singing is heard in the rear.*]

> With all the killing and recruiting
> The war will worry on a while.
> In ninety years they'll still be shooting.
> It's hardest on the rank-and-file.
> Our food is swill, our pants all patches
> The higher-ups steal half our pay
> And still we dream of God-sent riches.
> Tomorrow is another day!

The spring is come! Christian, revive!
The snowdrifts melt, the dead lie dead!
And if by chance you're still alive
It's time to rise and shake a leg.

FEDERICO GARCÍA LORCA
1898–1936

Although he died young, the poet and playwright Federico García Lorca is the best-known writer of modern Spain, and perhaps the most famous Spanish writer since Cervantes. A member of the brilliant "Generation of 1927" (along with Jorgé Guillen, Vicente Aleixandre, Pedro Salinas, and Rafael Alberti), known for the striking imagery and lyric musicality of his work, Lorca is both classical and modern, traditional and innovative, difficult and popular, a voice combining regional and universal themes. The poetry and plays that began as (and always were) personal statements took on larger significance first as the expression of tragic conflicts in Spanish culture, and then as poignant laments for humanity—seen especially in the plight of those who are deprived, by society or simply by death, of the fulfillment which could have been theirs. When Lorca was dragged from a friend's house and executed by a Fascist squad on August 19, 1936, his murder outraged the whole European and American literary and artistic community and seemed to symbolize in addition the mindless destruction of humane and cultural values that loomed with the approach of World War II.

Lorca (despite the Spanish practice of using both paternal and maternal last names—correctly "García Lorca"—the author is generally called "Lorca") was born on June 5, 1898, in the small village of Fuentevaqueros, near the Andalusian city of Granada. His parents were well-to-do: his father was a prosperous farmer and his mother, who had been a schoolteacher, encouraged him to read widely and develop his musical talent. The composer Manuel de Falla befriended the young musician, who became an expert pianist and guitar player. Lorca began law studies at the University of Granada where—after several years' absence—he received a degree in 1923. He published a book of *Impressions and Landscapes* (1918) after a trip through Spain but left Granada in 1919 for Madrid where he entered the Residencia de Estudiantes, a modern college established to provide a cosmopolitan education for Spanish youth. Madrid was not only the capital of Spain but also the center of intellectual and artistic ferment and the Residencia attracted many of those who would be the most influential writers and artists of their generation (among the latter the artist Salvador Dalí and the film director Luis Buñuel). Lorca soon gained the reputation of a rising young poet from poetry readings and the publication of a few poems in magazines, even before the appearance of his first collection of verse, the *Book of Poems* of 1921. Although he lived at the Residencia almost continuously until 1928, he never seriously pursued a degree but spent his time reading, writing, improvising music and poetry in company with his friends, and producing his first plays.

In these early years, before his departure for New York in 1929, Lorca concentrated on writing poetry although he was clearly interested in the theater as well. *The Butterfly's Evil Spell* (1920), a fantasy about a cockroach who is hopelessly enchanted by the beauty of a butterfly, was staged in Barcelona; in 1923 Lorca wrote, designed sets for, and directed a puppet play on a theme from Andalusian folklore, *The Girl Who Waters the Sweet Basil Flower and the Inquisitive Prince,* for which De Falla himself arranged the music. Yet the major achievement of this period is the composition of several books of poetry, not all of which were published at the time: the *Book of Poems;* most of the *Songs* (1927); early versions of the poems in the *Poem of the Deep Song,* which was not published as a book until 1931, although several poems were recited at a 1922 Andalusian festival; and the *Gypsy Ballads* (1928), which was an immediate popular success.

The first collection, the *Book of Poems,* introduces themes that will be familiar in later works: death, an innocent or childlike point of view, a closeness to nature which takes the form of animal fables or symbolic meanings attached to images like the pomegranate ("the idea of blood enclosed / In a hard and bitter globe") and overall a certain witty or ironic distance from the situations he describes. The playful tone never quite covers Lorca's constant preoccupation with death, however: death as the common fate that shadows our most vivid experiences. Speaking to a chorus of questioning children in "The Ballad of the Little Square," the poet answers that he feels in his mouth only "the savor of the bones / of my great skull."

The *Poem of the Deep Song* marked a return to the gypsy themes and ballads of Lorca's home province of Andalusia, a region known for its mixture of Arab and Spanish culture and for a tradition of wandering gypsy singers who improvised, to guitar accompaniment, rhythmic laments on themes of love and death. The *cante jondo* ("deep song") was an ancient Andalusian ballad form that centered on repeated notes or phrases, and Lorca took full advantage (as he would in the *Lament for Ignacio Sánchez Mejías*) of the haunting quality that could be obtained through this obsessive refrain. The *Songs* written subsequently are noted for their lyricism and for the moments of experience they capture; however, many reach beyond the sensuously precise description of real objects to encompass abstract concepts, psychological states, and clusters of associations—as does the Symbolist poetry Lorca knew. Lorca describes how "the ear of grain keeps intact / its hard yellow laughter," how a little mute boy looks for his voice in a drop of water, and how Narcissus (both youth and flower) is mirrored in a double image in which "over your white eyes flicker / shadows and sleeping fish."

Lorca's next collection, the *Gypsy Ballads,* marks the beginning of his mature verse. Blending classical ballad form with scenes taken directly from contemporary life, the poet expresses, with images of violence and eroticism, the tragic struggle in which innocence, spontaneity, creativity, and freedom are repressed by society and by the inevitable limitations of human nature. In the famous *Ballad of the Spanish Civil Guard,* the militia with their "patent-leather souls" and heads filled with "a vague astronomy / of shapeless pistols" cut down the gypsies in their fantastic city with its banners and "cinnamon towers." The unsuspecting populace, caught in the midst of their festival, are helpless to prevent absolute destruction— the tile roofs become "furrows in the soil," and the burned city itself persists only in the sterile "play of moon and sand" on the poet's brow. A hostile, violent world is pictured here, in which even the wind pursues a young girl with lustful breath and "hot sword," and St. Eulalia's martyrdom and mutilation are described with a mixture of eroticism and horror. These themes are not restricted to poetry: they reoccur in a contemporary play, *Mariana Pineda* (1928), in which Lorca's heroine is executed for refusing to identify a group of revolutionaries (among them the lover who abandoned her).

Impelled by an emotional crisis, Lorca left Spain for New York in 1929, where he wrote a series of poems later published as *Poet in New York* (1940). The collection does not focus exclusively on the city, however, and moves from the poet's youth in Europe to scenes of rural New York and northern Vermont as Lorca tries to come to terms with his own complex personality against a background of psychological, artistic, and social tensions. Blended with the familiar theme of doomed love and death is a tentative exploration of the homosexuality, which Lorca could not admit inside traditional Spanish society, and which he expressed only with hesitation and anxiety in this and later works. A large part of the ten-section *Poet in New York*, however, focuses primarily on the city, which is seen as a frightening symbol of the modern industrial West. In a richly varied and densely metaphorical apocalyptic vision, Lorca juxtaposes two ways of life and creates a vision of contrast which, he said, "puts my poetic world in contact with the poetic world of New York." Beginning with a denunciation of the dehumanized commercial city-world of sterile concrete and glass, he moves on to celebrate the only area where the natural world survives: Harlem, with its "garnet violence deaf and dumb in the shadows," and its "great king a prisoner in a janitor's uniform." In the face of this universal despair there are foreshadowings of a coming upheaval when "the Stock Market will be a pyramid of moss" and the oppressed and deprived will unite to proclaim "the reign of the ear of corn." The book's ending sections mark an escape from New York to Havana and (in spite of a continued sense of alienation) to the dancelike harmony of a more primitive life.

From 1930 to his death in 1936, Lorca was extremely active in the theater both as writer and as director (after 1931) of a traveling theatrical group (La Barraca) subsidized by the Spanish Republic. After a series of farces that mixed romantically tragic and comic themes, he presented the tragedies for which he is best known: *Blood Wedding* (1933) and *Yerma* (1934), and he wrote in 1936 the posthumously published *The House of Bernarda Alba* (1945). All Lorca's theater, from the early fantasy of *The Butterfly's Evil Spell* to the puppet plays, farces, and last tragedies, rejects the conventionally realistic nineteenth-century drama and employs an openly poetic form that suggests musical patterns, includes choruses, songs, and stylized movement, and may even (as in the fragmentary surrealist drama, *The Audience*) attack the audience itself. The tragic themes of Lorca's poetry emerge here in dramatic form, usually centering on the suffering of individual women whose instinctual fulfillment (through love or children) is denied by fate or social circumstance. In *Blood Wedding*, the Mother's last remaining son dies in a moonlit struggle with Leonardo, who has run away with his bride (Leonardo's former betrothed) on their wedding day. Leonardo (who also dies) is a member of the family that has killed the Mother's husband and other sons, and images of approaching death and sensual, frustrated love permeate the whole play. In *Yerma* (the title name also means desert or sterility), the heroine is caught between her own passionate, sensual nature, yearning to love and bear children, and the need—for honor's sake—to remain with a husband who cares only for a well-regulated house. When Yerma realizes the extent of Juan's spiritual as well as sexual sterility, she strangles him and (because she will not remarry) simultaneously kills her only chance to fulfill her natural instincts through bearing children. *The House of Bernarda Alba* (subtitled "A Drama About Women in the Villages of Spain") revolves around the same themes of sterility and frustrated love, as the repressed spinster daughters of the stern matriarch Bernarda Alba (and even the mad grandmother) reveal their common desire to marry a young man. Bernarda, however, upholds the proprieties that hedge in Spanish society; she refuses to let her daughters have visitors, ignores their rivalry over young Pepe el Romano (engaged to the wealthy oldest daughter, Angustias), recommends a painful death for an unwed mother being dragged through the streets, and—when the youngest daughter Adela commits suicide over Pepe, who has become her lover—seems chiefly concerned that Adela's body be dressed "as though she were a virgin." The conflict between social custom and individual need takes on mythic proportions in *The House of Bernarda Alba*, where only women appear on a stage that is strangely quarantined and painted white, and where the disturbing male principle represented by Pepe el Romano is reiterated by the noise of a stallion's hooves banging against stable walls.

In 1936, the year of his death, Lorca was revising a series of short lyric poems based on the Arabic forms of *casida* and the *gacela*, a collection eventually published in 1940 as *The Divan at Tamarit* (a "divan" is a poetic collection, and Lorca wrote the poems at a country house called after the ancient place name of Tamarit). In the previous year, he had published a long elegiac poem on the death of his good friend, the famous bullfighter Ignacio Sánchez Mejías, who had been fatally gored by a bull on August 11, 1934, in Manzanares and died two days later in Madrid. Sánchez Mejías was a cultured man, well-known in literary circles and himself the author of a play, and Lorca's *Lament for Ignacio Sánchez Mejías* celebrates both his friend and the value of human grace and courage in a world where everything ends in death.

Lorca's *Lament* is not only cast as an elegy (a medium-length poem that mourns a death), but also recalls one of the most famous poems of Spanish literature: the *Verses on the Death of His Father* written by the medieval poet Jorge Manrique (1440–1479). Manrique's catalog of his father's noble qualities ("What a friend to his friends!"), and his description of individual lives as flowing into the sea of death, are echoed by passages in the modern elegy. Yet there is a fundamental difference between the two: while Manrique's elegy stresses religious themes and the prospect of eternal life, Lorca—in grim contrast—rejects such consolation and insists that his friend's death is permanent.

The four parts of the *Lament* incorporate a variety of forms and perspectives, all working together to suggest a progression from the report of death in the precise first line—"At five in the afternoon"—to the end where the dead man's nobility and elegance survive in "a sad breeze through the olive trees." The "deep song" technique of an insistent refrain coloring the whole organizes the first section, "Cogida [the bull's toss] and Death," with its throbbing return to the moment of death. The scene in the arena wavers between an objective report—the boy with the shroud, the coffin on wheels—and the shared agony of the bull's bellowing and wounds burning like suns. Lorca moves in the next, ballad section to a personal refusal of Sánchez Mejías's death ("I will not see it!"), and a request that images of whiteness cover up this spilled blood; instead, he imagines Ignacio climbing steps to seek dawn and a mystic meeting with his true self but encountering, bewildered, only his broken body. After a tribute to his princely friend, the poet finally admits what he cannot force himself to see: the finality of physical dissolution as moss and grass invade the buried bullfighter's skull.

In "The Laid Out Body," a series of somber quatrains in regular meter recognizes the inevitability of death and dissolution (Ignacio's "pure shape which had nightingales" is now "filled with depthless holes"), and the fact that the bullfighter will be entombed in unyielding, lifeless stone. In this and the final section with its rhythmic free verse, Lorca accepts physical death ("even the sea dies!") but preserves, in his poetry, a vision of his noble countryman that surpasses such obliteration. For those who exist only on the unthinking, physical level (the bull, fig tree, household ants, the black satin of his funeral suit), Ignacio has indeed "died for ever." Yet human beings recognize other qualities beyond the physical and in fact shape their estimate of an individual according to these qualities. In life, Sánchez Mejías was known to his friends for "the signal maturity of your understanding. . . . your appetite for death and the taste of its mouth." These qualities survive, for a while, in memory. Lorca, echoing the pride with which the Latin poet Horace claimed to perpetuate his subjects in a "monument of lasting bronze," sings of his friend "for posterity," and captures the life and death of Sánchez Mejías in his *Lament*.

Ian Gibson, *Federico García Lorca: A Life* (1989), is an extensive and detailed biography. Carl W. Cobb, *Federico García Lorca* (1967), is a good general biography. E. Honig, *García Lorca* (1980), provides a critical introduction to the poet and his work, in literary historical context. Manuel Durán, ed., *Lorca: A Collection of Critical Essays* (1962), is a valuable collection of essays on the poet and his work (mainly the poetry). Manuel Durán and Francesca Colecchia, eds., *Lorca's Legacy* (1991), offer a range of essays and a recent bibliography.

Lament for Ignacio Sánchez Mejías[1]

1. Cogida[2] and Death

At five in the afternoon.
It was exactly five in the afternoon.
A boy brought the white sheet
at five in the afternoon.
A frail of lime[3] ready prepared   5
at five in the afternoon.
The rest was death, and death alone
at five in the afternoon.

The wind carried away the cottonwool[4]
at five in the afternoon.   10
And the oxide scattered crystal and nickel
at five in the afternoon.
Now the dove and the leopard[5] wrestle
at five in the afternoon.
And a thigh with a desolate horn   15
at five in the afternoon.
The bass-string struck up
at five in the afternoon.
Arsenic bells[6] and smoke
at five in the afternoon.   20
Groups of silence in the corners
at five in the afternoon.
And the bull alone with a high heart!
At five in the afternoon.
When the sweat of snow was coming   25
at five in the afternoon,
when the bull ring was covered in iodine
at five in the afternoon.
death laid eggs in the wound
at five in the afternoon.   30
At five in the afternoon.
Exactly at five o'clock in the afternoon.

A coffin on wheels is his bed
at five in the afternoon.

1. Translated by Stephen Spender and J. L. Gili.   2. Harvesting (literal trans.); the toss when the bull catches the bullfighter.   3. A disinfectant, which was sprinkled on the body after death. *Frail:* a basket. 4. To stop the blood; the beginning of a series of medicinal, chemical, and inhuman images that emphasize the presence of death.   5. Traditional symbols for peace and violence; they wrestle with one another as the bullfighter's thigh struggles with the bull's horn.   6. Bells are rung to announce a death. The *bass-string* of the guitar strums a lament.

Bones and flutes resound in his ears[7]   35
at five in the afternoon.
Now the bull was bellowing through his forehead
at five in the afternoon.
The room[8] was iridescent with agony
at five in the afternoon.   40
In the distance the gangrene now comes
at five in the afternoon.
Horn of the lily through green[9] groins
at five in the afternoon.
The wounds were burning like suns   45
at five in the afternoon,
and the crowd was breaking the windows[1]
at five in the afternoon.
At five in the afternoon.
Ah, that fatal five in the afternoon!   50
It was five by all the clocks!
It was five in the shade of the afternoon!

2. The Spilled Blood

I will not see it!

Tell the moon to come
for I do not want to see the blood
of Ignacio on the sand.   55
I will not see it!

The moon wide open.
Horse of still clouds,
and the grey bull ring of dreams   60
with willows in the barreras.[2]
I will not see it!

Let my memory kindle![3]
Warn the jasmines[4]
of such minute whiteness!   65
I will not see it!

The cow of the ancient world
passed her sad tongue
over a snout of blood
spilled on the sand,   70
and the bulls of Guisando,[5]
partly death and partly stone,
bellowed like two centuries
sated with treading the earth.
No.   75
I do not want to see it!
I will not see it!

---

7. A suggestion of the medieval Dance of Death.   8. The room adjoining the arena where wounded bullfighters are taken for treatment.   9. Gangrene turns flesh a greenish color. *Lily:* the shape of the wound resembles this flower.   1. A Spanish idiom for the crowd's loud roar.   2. The barriers around the ring within which the fight takes place and over which a fighter may escape the bull's charge. *Willows:* symbols of mourning.   3. Literal trans.: "My memory burns within me." 4. The poet calls on (*warns* as "notify") the small white jasmine flowers to come and cover the blood.   5. Carved stone bulls from the Celtic past, a tourist attraction in the province of Madrid.

Ignacio goes up the tiers[6]
with all his death on his shoulders.
He sought for the dawn   80
but the dawn was no more.
He seeks for his confident profile
and the dream bewilders him.
He sought for his beautiful body
and encountered his opened blood.   85
Do not ask me to see it!
I do not want to hear it spurt
each time with less strength:
that spurt that illuminates
the tiers of seats, and spills   90
over the corduroy and the leather
of a thirsty multitude.
Who shouts that I should come near!
Do not ask me to see it!

His eyes did not close   95
when he saw the horns near,
but the terrible mothers
lifted their heads.[7]
And across the ranches,[8]
an air of secret voices rose,   100
shouting to celestial bulls,
herdsmen of pale mist.
There was no prince in Seville[9]
who could compare with him,
nor sword like his sword   105
nor heart so true.
Like a river of lions
was his marvellous strength,
and like a marble torso
his firm drawn moderation.   110
The air of Andalusian Rome
gilded his head[1]
where his smile was a spikenard[2]
of wit and intelligence.
What a great torero[3] in the ring!   115
What a good peasant in the sierra![4]
How gentle with the sheaves!
How hard with the spurs!
How tender with the dew!
How dazzling in the fiesta!   120
How tremendous with the final
banderillas[5] of darkness!

But now he sleeps without end.
Now the moss and the grass

6. An imaginary scene in which the bullfighter mounts the stairs of the arena.   7. The three Fates
traditionally raised their heads when the thread of life was cut.   8. Fighting bulls are raised on the
ranches of Lorca's home province of Andalusia.   9. Leading city of Andalusia.   1. The image suggests a statue from Roman times, when Andalusia was part of the Roman Empire.   2. A small, white,
fragrant flower common in Andalusia; by extension, the bullfighter's white teeth.   3. Bullfighter.
4. Mountainous country. Sánchez Mejías is seen as a good *serrano* or "man of the hills."   5. The
multicolored short spears that are thrust in the bull's shoulders to provoke him to attack.

open with sure fingers   125
the flower of his skull.
And now his blood comes out singing;
singing along marshes and meadows,
sliding on frozen horns,
faltering soulless in the mist,   130
stumbling over a thousand hoofs
like a long, dark, sad tongue,
to form a pool of agony
close to the starry Guadalquivir.[6]
Oh, white wall of Spain!   135
Oh, black bull of sorrow!
Oh, hard blood of Ignacio!
Oh, nightingale of his veins!
No.
I will not see it!   140
No chalice can contain it,
no swallows[7] can drink it,
no frost of light can cool it,
nor song nor deluge of white lilies,
no glass can cover it with silver.   145
No.
I will not see it!

3. The Laid Out Body[8]

Stone is a forehead where dreams grieve
without curving waters and frozen cypresses.
Stone is a shoulder on which to bear Time   150
with trees formed of tears and ribbons and planets.[9]

I have seen grey showers move towards the waves
raising their tender riddled arms,
to avoid being caught by the lying stone
which loosens their limbs without soaking the blood.   155

For stone gathers seed and clouds,
skeleton larks and wolves of penumbra:
but yields not sounds nor crystals nor fire,
only bull rings and bull rings and more bull rings without walls.

Now Ignacio the well born lies on the stone.   160
All is finished. What is happening? Contemplate his face:
death has covered him with pale sulphur
and has placed on him the head of a dark minotaur.[1]

All is finished. The rain penetrates his mouth.
The air, as if mad, leaves his sunken chest,   165

6. A great river that passes through all the major cities of Andalusia. The singing stream of the bullfighter's blood suggests both the river and a nightingale.   7. According to a Spanish legend of the Crucifixion, swallows—a symbol of innocence—drank the blood of Christ on the Cross. The poet is seeking ways of concealing the dead man's blood.   8. Literal trans.: "Present Body"; the Spanish expression for a funeral wake, when the body is laid out for public mourning. The title contrasts with that of the next section: "Absent Soul."   9. Traditional funeral imagery carved on gravestones.   1. A monster from Greek myth: half man, half bull.

and Love, soaked through with tears of snow,
warms itself on the peak of the herd.[2]

What are they saying? A stenching silence settles down.
We are here with a body laid out which fades away,
with a pure shape which had nightingales   170
and we see it being filled with depthless holes.

Who creases the shroud? What he says is not true![3]
Nobody sings here, nobody weeps in the corner,
nobody pricks the spurs, nor terrifies the serpent.
Here I want nothing else but the round eyes   175
to see this body without a chance of rest.

Here I want to see those men of hard voice.
Those that break horses and dominate rivers;
those men of sonorous skeleton who sing
with a mouth full of sun and flint.   180

Here I want to see them. Before the stone.
Before this body with broken reins.
I want to know from them the way out
for this captain strapped down by death.

I want them to show me a lament like a river   185
which will have sweet mists and deep shores,
to take the body of Ignacio where it loses itself
without hearing the double panting of the bulls.

Loses itself in the round bull ring of the moon
which feigns in its youth a sad quiet bull: 190
loses itself in the night without song of fishes
and in the white thicket of frozen smoke.

I don't want them to cover his face with handkerchiefs
that he may get used to the death he carries.
Go, Ignacio; feel not the hot bellowing.   195
Sleep, fly, rest: even the sea dies!

4. Absent Soul

The bull does not know you, nor the fig tree,
nor the horses, nor the ants in your own house.
The child and the afternoon do not know you
because you have died for ever.   200

The back of the stone does not know you,
nor the black satin in which you crumble.
Your silent memory does not know you
because you have died for ever.

The autumn will come with small white snails,[4]   205
misty grapes and with clustered hills,
but no one will look into your eyes
because you have died for ever.

---

2. Literal trans.: "of the ranch."   3. Lorca criticizes the conventional pieties voiced by someone standing close to the shrouded body; the poet prefers a clear-eyed, realistic view of death.   4. Actually, conch
shell–shaped horns; the shepherds' horns that sound in the hills each fall as the sheep are driven to new
pastures.

Because you have died for ever,
like all the death of the Earth,   210
like all the dead who are forgotten
in a heap of lifeless dogs.[5]

Nobody knows you. No. But I sing of you.
For posterity I sing of your profile and grace.
Of the signal maturity of your understanding.   215
Of your appetite for death and the taste of its mouth.
Of the sadness of your once valiant gaiety.

It will be a long time, if ever, before there is born
an Andalusian so true, so rich in adventure.
I sing of his elegance with words that groan,   220
and I remember a sad breeze through the olive trees.

From Llanto por Ignacio Sánchez Mejías

4. *Alma Ausente*

No te conoce el toro ni la higuera,
ni caballos ni hormigas de tu casa.
No te conoce el niño ni la tarde
porque te has muerto para siempre.

No te conoce el lomo de la piedra,   5
ni el raso negro donde te destrozas.
No te conoce tu recuerdo mudo
porque te has muerto para siempre.

El otoño vendrá con caracolas,
uva de niebla y montes agrupados,   10
pero nadie querrá mirar tus ojos
porque te has muerto para siempre.

Porque te has muerto para siempre,
como todos los muertos de la Tierra,
como todos los muertos que se olvidan   15
en un montón de perros apagados.

No te conoce nadie. No. Pero yo te canto.
Yo canto para luego tu perfil y tu gracia.
La madurez insigne de tu conocimiento.
Tu apetencia de muerte y el gusto de su boca.   20
La tristeza que tuvo tu valiente alegría.

Tardará mucho tiempo en nacer, si es que nace,
un andaluz tan claro, tan rico de aventura.
Yo canto su elegancia con palabras que gimen
y recuerdo una brisa triste por los olivos.   25

---

5. Dogs as a (typically Continental) image for undignified, inferior creatures.

TAWFIQ AL-HAKIM
1898–1989

Tawfiq al-Hakim is the master of a genre that he invented: Arabic literary drama. From the mid-1930s, when he achieved renown as a playwright, until the late 1970s, he was the premier dramatist of Egypt and of the Arab world. In the course of his long career, he produced plays in a wide variety of styles, from dramatic pageant to absurdist drama, and on themes drawn from the Egypt of the pharaohs, classical Greece, the golden age of Islamic history, and the concerns of the moment. His plays have been staged throughout the Arab world and, in translation, in the capitals of Asia, Europe, and America. His great gift has been to give dramatic life to questions of enduring interest and to shape a language for the stage that is flexible, idiomatic, and vivid.

To understand the importance of al-Hakim's achievement one needs some knowledge of the nature of traditional Arabic and Middle Eastern literature and the place of drama and the theater within it. Until the modern era, Middle Eastern literature was sharply divided between formal and popular traditions in literary style, genre, and mode of performance. Formal poetry and prose were elegant, learned, richly rhetorical, and highly conventional in their themes. Their subject matter was governed by well-established conventions, and their genres had been fixed in the first few centuries of the classical era—roughly the seventh through thirteenth centuries. Drama was not a genre of classical literature. There were not only no great playwrights in Arabic, Persian or Turkish—there were none at all.

Popular literature found its audiences among the vast majority of the population that could neither read nor write. Its home was in the marketplace and the village square, not in the court or the centers of learning. For the most part, it was transmitted orally rather than in writing. What little we know about it is based on a few popular texts like the tales of *The Thousand and One Nights* (in Volume 1), that were written down before the modern era. In contrast to formal literature, the essence of popular literature was performance, and its goal was entertainment, not edification. It often shared stories with classical works but cast them in popular language and adapted them to the tastes of ordinary people. Dramatic performance of various kinds seem to have been a familiar and long-standing element within it.

We know from the accounts of European travelers that in eighteenth-century Egypt both farces and puppet plays were widely popular, and elements of this public theatrical tradition may even have survived from pharaonic rituals. Moreover, in the mid-nineteenth century enterprising theatrical producers in Syria and Egypt translated European plays freely into colloquial Arabic and adapted them to local tastes and their own theatrical tradition. Molière, Racine, and Shakespeare, among many others, were introduced to Egyptian audiences this way, although in renderings so free that little of the original work survived. Later, some authors attempted to write or translate plays in formal Arabic to elevate drama to the level of literary art. Their efforts had unfortunate but predictable results. What was acceptable to the educated few put audiences to sleep, and what was popular in the theater was dismissed as burlesque by the arbiters of literary taste. So matters stood until the time of al-Hakim, who took on himself the task of creating a theatrical language that would bridge this gap.

Al-Hakim was born in Alexandria in 1898 to a conservative middle-class Egyptian family that was appalled by his early determination to pursue a literary career. At his father's insistence, he first studied law in Cairo and then went on to Paris to earn a doctorate of law degree. Literature, however, remained his principal interest. He almost failed to receive his law degree because he preferred to spend his time collaborating with a friend in writing musical comedies, and he spent his three years in Paris (1925–28) reading widely in French literature, associating with other writers, and going to the theater. There he made the wonderful discovery that in Europe plays were accepted as a respectable literary form. He returned to Cairo in 1928 without a doctorate, and determined to be a writer.

Al-Hakim had begun publishing his work while still in his twenties, but this paid little. Since it was virtually impossible for him, or any other writer, to earn a living from the pen, he was obliged to pursue a parallel career. For a university graduate like himself, the obvious choice was government service, and he first took a job in the Ministry of Legal Affairs as a prosecutor in a village in the Nile delta—an experience he later used in his novel *Maze of Justice* (1937). He left the Ministry of Law for the Ministry of Education in 1934 and was subsequently director of social guidance in the Ministry of Social Affairs. He continued to write and publish throughout this period, and enjoyed growing success and recognition of his work. In 1943 al-Hakim left government service to pursue writing full time. He also joined the staff of the newspaper *Akhbar al-Yawm* in 1943 and stayed there for eight years. In 1951 he was appointed director of the National Library, and in 1959 he returned to Paris as permanent delegate to UNESCO for his country. During the fall of that year he wrote *The Sultan's Dilemma*. Later he was appointed a member of the Higher Council for Arts and Letters, and in 1961 he became a member of the board of directors of Egypt's most prestigious newspaper, *Al-Ahram*, a position he held until his retirement.

Al-Hakim is principally known as a dramatist, but he was a prolific writer who did not limit himself to a single form. In the more than fifty years of his productive life he wrote some seventy plays as well as short stories, novels, and several volumes both of essays and of autobiography. His productivity was as great and varied as that of his illustrious contemporary, the novelist Naguib Mahfouz, and he helped to shape narrative prose and drama. His novel *The Return of the Spirit*, for example, initiated a vogue for setting novels in the pharaonic period.

The task that al-Hakim set for himself was to create a drama that was sufficiently formal in language and challenging in substance to be regarded as literature and yet was close enough to the language of everyday life to be vital and engaging. Classical Arabic, the only language that was acceptable as a vehicle for serious literature, really had no colloquial form. Within classical Arabic itself there was no history of dramatic literature. As for colloquial Arabic, it had many dialects, but none that was as close to classical Arabic as spoken English is to even the most literary style of written English and none that was acceptable as a vehicle for literature. With no tradition of dramatic dialogue to draw on, al-Hakim was obliged to invent his own spoken classical language and, more generally, to create his own dramatic tradition from the materials available to him. On the one hand, there was the stuff of classical and popular Arabic literature—materials as varied as the Koran and *The Thousand and One Nights*. Although none of this literature was dramatic in form, it was a rich source of stories and characters, and it was immediately familiar to his audience. The challenge for him was to give these familiar materials dramatic shape, as he does in his play *Muhammad* (1936), in which the great events of the Prophet's life are brought to the stage in a vivid and moving pageant. In other works he responds to traditional materials even more creatively. In his *Shahrazad* (1934), he continues the story of *The Thousand and One Nights* from the point where Shahrazad leaves off, and he explores her marital life with the Shahrayar. He also drew on Egypt's pharaonic past for inspiration, as in his drama *Isis* (1955).

The other source that al-Hakim had available to him was the long and varied dramatic tradition of Europe. Arab dramatists, he argued, must build their craft on the European classics. It was foreign to Egypt and Islam, but it was the obvious school to which Arab dramatists must go, and he wrote eloquently of the need to make the classical Greek theatrical tradition their own. Al-Hakim believed strongly that some sort of synthesis of East and West was inevitable. However, it would not be enough simply to translate classical European drama, to adopt European classics as though they were their own. Rather, the works of the ancient Greek masters must be rethought and recast in the mold of Egyptian culture. In rewriting the classics, al-Hakim was, of course, following the example of modern European dramatists. But while their audiences could hold each new work up against the template of the original, for al-Hakim's audience his plays were completely independent works. And the focus of the transformations he made was not classic to modern but European to Middle Eastern. When he wrote his own *King Oedipus* (1949), for example, he made Tiresias the villain of the piece because, he said, as a Muslim and an Arab, he simply could not accept that the gods would inflict so cruel a fate on the heroic Oedipus.

In other works he attempted to combine Eastern and Western elements. In the preface to *The Wisdom of Solomon* (1943), a work in which he anticipates the looming conflict between technology and humane values, he gives a sense of this integration. "This story," he says, "is based on three books: the Koran, the Bible, and *A Thousand and One Nights.* I have followed the same procedure I used in the *Sleepers of Ephesus, Shahrazad,* and *Pygmalion,* and have made use of the old texts and ancient legends to create a picture in my mind . . . nothing more, nothing less." The incorporation of three such disparate works is emblematic of the synthesis he hoped to achieve.

The phrase "a picture in my mind . . . nothing more, nothing less" may seem puzzling at first because we are used to thinking of dramatic texts and dramatic performances as joined, but in Egypt this was and is far from the case. For many years the plays that al-Hakim wrote to create a new dramatic literature were rarely, if ever, performed. There were essentially two reasons for this. First, there was, initially, no audience of theater-goers who were used to watching modern plays that were serious in substance and contemporary in language and sensibility. Second, there were no trained actors. The players who performed in popular farces and burlesques had no formal training and were completely unready and unwilling to present serious drama seriously and in al-Hakim's version of classical Arabic. However, when he published his plays in book form or in newspapers (Egyptian newspapers often publish stories, novels, plays and poems), they found an increasingly appreciative audience. Moreover, once professional actors began to appear in Egypt in the late 1940s, his plays were performed there and in other capitals of the Arab world with great success.

The enormous volume of al-Hakim's work, the many styles in which he wrote, and the great disparities between his best efforts and the rest of his work make any comprehensive evaluation all but impossible. Since he was trying to find a middle ground between an elevated poetic rhetoric and vulgar farce, those who criticize his work have tended to cluster around one pole or the other. Because of the moral seriousness with which he took his role as a writer and his love of philosophical questions, his plays often have a philosophical and discursive quality that led some critics to speak of him as an "ivory tower" playwright. Yet many of his plays are immersed in the problems of daily life. *Boss Kuduz's Building* (1948) is an ironic attack on war profiteers. *I Want to Kill* (1957) explores the breakdown of an apparently ideal marriage that has been challenged by the sudden intrusion of violence. While virtually all commentators find something to disagree with in al-Hakim's work, over and over one encounters the judgment that despite these failings, nothing should be allowed to detract from the tremendous status he has in contemporary Arabic letters.

The Sultan's Dilemma is often spoken of as al-Hakim's best work, and in it we see him at his most appealing. It is a comedy with a light touch and charming wit, but one that raises serious and thoughtful questions. In it we encounter a ruler who, when confronted with a dilemma that challenges the basis of his authority, chooses to put his trust in law, and does so despite a great deal of encouragement to allow might to make right. Appealing as the message is, it could easily degenerate into a tedious and soporific polemic. Here it is saved from that by al-Hakim's deft touch. He gives each point of view an individual personality, balances the seriousness of the debate with comic exchanges between the characters, and varies the rhythm by moving the action back and forth between groups and individuals. The result is a drama that manages to be serious without being solemn.

Implausible as the central event of this play is—a sultan who is an unmanumitted slave—it does in fact reflect a historical reality. Slaves have occupied positions of great authority in Islamic societies since the early days of its empire. In the ninth century the Arab caliphs of Baghdad began to introduce Turkish slave soldiers from central Asia as a personal guard. These slaves, often purchased as children and raised in the royal household, depended completely on their masters and so were completely loyal to them. Unlike other groups within the state, they were not distracted by loyalties to tribe, family, region, profession, ethnic group, or a religion other than Islam. The Ottoman Empire (1281–1924), the last great dynasty to rule in the Islamic Middle East before the modern period, reserved the highest offices in both the military and the government administration for slaves who were forcibly recruited as youths from the Christian communities in eastern Europe and the Caucasus. Before the Ottomans, Egypt was ruled for two and a half centuries (1250–1517) by a dynasty whose name, *mamluk*, means slave and whose monarchs were, as the play indicates, manumitted slaves. The events of the play are not based on a historical fact, however, nor are they an attempt to recreate a plausible kind of pseudo history. This is a fantasy, an artful improvisation. The fact of the Mamluk Dynasty provides al-Hakim with an attractive metaphor, the Sultan as slave, and one whose serious implications he explores. The metaphor also has an unexpectedly modern resonance, since democratic leaders are fond of presenting themselves as servants or slaves of the people they govern. *The Sultan's Dilemma* playfully suggests what might happen if that were literally true.

The opening scene between the executioner and the condemned man establishes that while the play will deal with serious matters, the tone will be light and comic. It makes a connection between the life of ordinary Egyptians and the court since the intervention of the beautiful lady, a woman of doubtful virtue, and her maid set up the dilemma that the Sultan must confront. Had the slave merchant been executed there would be no play. This opening sequence promises us that the play will end happily and that the humorous possibilities of every situation will be exploited. It also introduces the theme of hair-splitting legalism that recurs throughout the play, and by presenting the lady as a woman of shrewdness, compassion, and authority despite her unsavory reputation, it prepares us for the role she plays in the last portion of the play.

The middle portion of the play reveals the dilemma of the title and, in the persons of the vizier and the chief cadi, articulates the two horns of that dilemma. It ends once the Sultan makes his decision, and the remainder of the play follows the working out of the consequences of his choice. The orderly scenario that the officers of the court have planned runs aground on the unforeseen and unforeseeable intervention of the lady. By trusting himself to the law the Sultan has entered on a course that is, apparently, more open to risk than anyone had anticipated,

and again he must choose to continue as he began or fall back on arbitrary violence. The final scenes are in essence a playing out of the reward he receives for
having made the right decision.

There are two good studies of al-Hakim in English: Richard Long, *Tawfiq al
Hakim: Playwright of Egypt* (1979), and Paul Starkey, *From the Ivory Tower: A
Critical Study of Tawfiq al-Hakim* (1987). Both contain useful bibliographies. In
addition, the translation by Denys Johnson-Davies was first published in a collection titled *Fate of a Cockroach: Four Plays of Freedom* (1973). Johnson-Davies has
also published a translation of al-Hakim's delightful absurdist play *The Tree
Climber* (1966).

PRONOUNCING GLOSSARY

The following list uses common English syllables and stress accents to provide rough equivalents of selected words whose pronunciation may be unfamiliar to the general reader.

adab: *a'-dab*

cadi: *caw'-dee*

Kuduz: *coo-dooz'*

muezzin: *moo-ez'-zin*

Naguib Mahfouz: *nuh-geeb' mah-fooz'*

Tawfiq al-Hakim: *tow-feek' al–ha-keem'*

vizier: *vi-zeer'*

The Sultan's Dilemma[1]

CHARACTERS

THE SULTAN	UNKNOWN MAN
THE VIZIER[2]	1ST LEADING CITIZEN
THE CHIEF CADI[3]	2ND LEADING CITIZEN
A BEAUTIFUL LADY	3RD LEADING CITIZEN
HER MAIDSERVANT	1ST MAN IN CROWD
AN EMINENT SLAVE TRADER	2ND MAN IN CROWD
THE CONDEMNED MAN	MOTHER
THE EXECUTIONER	CHILD
THE WINE MERCHANT	TOWNSPEOPLE
THE MUEZZIN	GUARDS
THE SHOEMAKER	SULTAN'S RETINUE

Act One

*An open space in the city during the time of the Mamluke Sultans.[4]
On one side there is a mosque with a minaret; on the other, a tavern.
In the centre is a house with a balcony. Dawn is about to break and*

---

1. Translated by Denys Johnson-Davies.   2. The chief minister of the sultan.   3. Judge.   4. Ruled
in Egypt from 1250 to 1517.

silence reigns. A stake has been set up to which a man, condemned to death, has been tied. His EXECUTIONER *is nearby trying to fight off sleep.*

CONDEMNED MAN: [*Contemplating the* EXECUTIONER.] Getting sleepy? Of course you are. Congratulations. Sleep well. You're not awaiting something that will spoil *your* peace of mind.

EXECUTIONER: Quiet!

CONDEMNED MAN: And so—when is it to be?

EXECUTIONER: I told you to be quiet.

CONDEMNED MAN: [*Pleadingly.*] Tell me truly when it's to be? When?

EXECUTIONER: When are you going to stop disturbing me?

CONDEMNED MAN: Sorry. It is, though, something that particularly concerns me. When does this event—a joyous one for you—take place?

EXECUTIONER: At dawn. I've told you this more than ten times. At dawn I'll carry out the sentence on you. Now do you understand? So let me enjoy a moment's peace.

CONDEMNED MAN: Dawn? It's still far off, isn't it, Executioner?

EXECUTIONER: I don't know.

CONDEMNED MAN: You don't know?

EXECUTIONER: It's the Muezzin[5] who knows. When he goes up to the minaret of this mosque and gives the call to the dawn prayer, I'll raise my sword and swipe off your head—those are the orders. Happy now?

CONDEMNED MAN: Without a trial? I haven't yet been put on trial, I haven't yet appeared before a judge.

EXECUTIONER: That's nothing to do with me.

CONDEMNED MAN: For sure, you have nothing to do with anything except my execution.

EXECUTIONER: At dawn, in furtherance of the Sultan's orders.

CONDEMNED MAN: For what crime?

EXECUTIONER: That's not my affair.

CONDEMNED MAN: Because I said . . .

EXECUTIONER: Quiet! Quiet! Shut your mouth—I have been ordered to cut off your head right away if you utter a word about your crime.

CONDEMNED MAN: Don't be upset, I'll shut my mouth.

EXECUTIONER: You've done well to shut your mouth and leave me to enjoy my sleep. It's in your interest that I should enjoy a quiet and peaceful sleep.

CONDEMNED MAN: In my interest?

EXECUTIONER: Certainly, it's in your interest that I should be completely rested and in excellent health, both in body and mind; because when I'm tired, depressed, and strung up, my hand shakes, and when it shakes I perform my work badly.

CONDEMNED MAN: And what's your work to me?

EXECUTIONER: Fool! My work has to do with your neck. Poor performance means your neck will not be cleanly cut, because a clean cut requires a steady hand and calm mind so that the head may fly off at a single

---

5. Gives the call to prayer at the five daily appointed times.

blow, allowing you no time to feel any sensation of pain. Do you understand now?

CONDEMNED MAN: Of course, that's quite right.

EXECUTIONER: You see! Now you must be quite convinced why it is necessary that you should let me rest; also, to bring joy to my heart and raise
my morale.

CONDEMNED MAN: Your morale? *Yours?*

EXECUTIONER: Naturally, if I were in your shoes . . .

CONDEMNED MAN: O God, take him at his word! I wish you *were* in my
shoes.

EXECUTIONER: What are you saying?

CONDEMNED MAN: Carry on. What would you do if you had the honour
and good fortune to be in my shoes?

EXECUTIONER: I'll tell you what I'd do—have you any money?

CONDEMNED MAN: Ah, money! Yes, yes, yes! Money! An apposite[6] thought.
As for money, my friend, you may say what you like about that. The
whole city knows—and you among them—that I'm one of the very richest of merchants and slave-traders.

EXECUTIONER: No, you have misunderstood me—I'm not talking of a
bribe. It's impossible to bribe me—not because of my honesty and
integrity, but because, quite frankly, I am unable to save you. All I
wanted was to accept your invitation to have a drink—if you should
happen to do so. A glass of wine is not a bribe. It would be impolite of
me to refuse your invitation. Look! There's a Wine Merchant a stone's
throw away from you—his tavern is open all night, because he has customers who visit that whore who lives in the house opposite.

CONDEMNED MAN: A drink? Is that all?

EXECUTIONER: That's all.

CONDEMNED MAN: I've got a better and more attractive idea. Let's go up
together, you and I, to that beautiful woman. I know her and if we went
to her we'd spend the most marvellous night of our lives—a night to fill
your heart with joy and gaiety and raise your morale. What do you say?

EXECUTIONER: No, gracious sir.

CONDEMNED MAN: You would accept my invitation to a drink, but refuse
my invitation to a party of drinking and fun, beauty and merriment?

EXECUTIONER: In that house? No, my dear condemned friend, I prefer for
you to stay as you are: fettered with chains till dawn.

CONDEMNED MAN: What a pity you don't trust me! What if I were to promise you that before the call to dawn prayers I would be back again in
chains?

EXECUTIONER: Does a bird return to the snare?

CONDEMNED MAN: Yes, I swear to you on my honour.

EXECUTIONER: *Your* honour? What an oath!

CONDEMNED MAN: You don't believe me.

EXECUTIONER: I believe you so long as you are where you are—and in
handcuffs.

CONDEMNED MAN: How can I invite you to have a drink then?

6. To the point, appropriate.

EXECUTIONER: That's easy. I'll go to the tavern and ask him to bring two glasses of his best wine and when he brings them we'll drink them right here. What do you say?

CONDEMNED MAN: But . . .

EXECUTIONER: We're agreed. I'll go—there's no need for you to trouble yourself. Just a minute, with your permission.

[*The* EXECUTIONER *goes to the tavern at the corner of the square and knocks at the door. The* WINE MERCHANT *comes out to him, he whispers something in his ear, and returns to his place.*]

EXECUTIONER: [*To the* CONDEMNED MAN.] Everything necessary has been arranged, and you will see, my dear condemned man, the good result shortly.

CONDEMNED MAN: What good result?

EXECUTIONER: My masterful work. When I drink I'm very precise in my work, but, if I haven't drunk, my work goes all to hell. By way of example I'll tell you what happened the other day. I was charged with the job of executing someone, and I hadn't drunk a thing all that day. Do you know what I did? I gave that poor fellow's neck such a blow that his head flew off into the air and landed far away—not in this basket of mine, but in another basket over there, the basket belonging to the Shoemaker next door to the tavern. God alone knows the trouble we had getting the missing head out of the heaps of shoes and soles.

CONDEMNED MAN: The Shoemaker's basket! What a shameful thing to happen! I beseech you by God not to let my head suffer such a fate.

EXECUTIONER: Don't be afraid. Things are different where you are concerned. The other head belonged to a horribly stingy fellow.

[*The* WINE MERCHANT *appears from his shop carrying two glasses.*]

WINE MERCHANT: [*Moving towards the* CONDEMNED MAN.] This is of course for you—your last wish.

CONDEMNED MAN: No, for the Executioner—it's his cherished wish.

EXECUTIONER: [*To the* WINE MERCHANT.] To bring calm and contentment to my heart.

WINE MERCHANT: And from whom shall I receive payment?

CONDEMNED MAN: From me of course—to bring joy and gladness to his heart.

EXECUTIONER: It is incumbent upon me to accept his warm invitation.

CONDEMNED MAN: And it is incumbent upon me to raise his morale.

WINE MERCHANT: What very good friends you two are!

EXECUTIONER: It is a reciprocated affection.

CONDEMNED MAN: Until dawn breaks.

EXECUTIONER: Don't worry about the dawn now—it is still far off. Come, let's touch glasses.

[*The* EXECUTIONER *snatches up the two glasses and strikes one against the other, turns, raises a glass, and drinks to the* CONDEMNED MAN.]

EXECUTIONER: Your health!

CONDEMNED MAN: Thank you.

EXECUTIONER: [*After he has drained his glass he holds the other glass up to the* CONDEMNED MAN'*s mouth.*] And now it's your turn, my dear fellow.

CONDEMNED MAN: [*Taking a gulp and coughing.*] Enough. You drink the rest for me.

EXECUTIONER: Is that your wish?

CONDEMNED MAN: The last!

EXECUTIONER: [*Raising the second glass.*] Then I raise my glass to . . .

CONDEMNED MAN: Your masterful work.

EXECUTIONER: God willing! Also to your generosity and kindness, my friend.

WINE MERCHANT: [*Taking the two empty glasses from the* EXECUTIONER.] What's this old slave-trader done? What's his crime? All of us in the city know him—he's no murderer or thief.

CONDEMNED MAN: And yet my head will fall at dawn, just like that of any murderer or thief.

WINE MERCHANT: Why? For what crime?

CONDEMNED MAN: For no reason except that I said . . .

EXECUTIONER: Quiet! Don't utter a word! Shut your mouth!

CONDEMNED MAN: I've shut my mouth.

EXECUTIONER: And you, Wine Merchant, you've got your glasses, so off with you!

WINE MERCHANT: And my money?

EXECUTIONER: It's he who invited me—and only a dastardly fellow refuses an invitation.

CONDEMNED MAN: To be sure I invited him, and he was good enough to accept my invitation. Your money, Tavern Owner, is here in a purse in my belt. Approach and take what you want.

EXECUTIONER: Allow me to approach on his behalf.

[*He approaches and takes some money from the* CONDEMNED MAN'*s purse and pays the* WINE MERCHANT.]

EXECUTIONER: Take what you're owed and a bit more that you may know we're generous people.

[*The* WINE MERCHANT *takes his money and returns to his shop. The* EXECUTIONER *begins humming in a low voice.*]

CONDEMNED MAN: [*Anxiously.*] And now . . .

EXECUTIONER: Now we begin our singing and merrymaking. Do you know, my dear condemned man, that I'm very fond of good singing, a pleasant tune, and fine lyrics? It fills the heart with contentment and joy, with gladness and a delight in life. Sing me something!

CONDEMNED MAN: I? Sing?

EXECUTIONER: Yes. Why not? What's to stop you? Your larynx—thanks be to God—is perfectly free. All you have to do is raise your voice in song and out will come a lovely tune to delight the ear. Come on, sing! Entertain me!

CONDEMNED MAN: God bless us! O God, bear witness!

EXECUTIONER: Come along! Sing to me!

CONDEMNED MAN: Do you really think I'm in the mood for singing at this time?

EXECUTIONER: Did you not just now promise me to bring gladness to my soul and remove the depression from my heart?

CONDEMNED MAN: Are you the one to feel depressed?

EXECUTIONER: Yes, please remove my depression. Overwhelm me with joy! Let me enjoy the strains of ballads and songs! Drown me with melodies and sweet tunes! Listen—I've remembered something. I know by heart a song I composed myself during one night of sleeplessness and woe.

CONDEMNED MAN: Then sing it to me.

EXECUTIONER: I don't have a beautiful voice.

CONDEMNED MAN: And who told you that *my* voice was beautiful?

EXECUTIONER: To me all other people's voices are beautiful—because I don't listen to them, especially if I'm drunk. All I'm concerned with is being surrounded on all sides by singing: the feeling that there is singing all around me soothes my nerves. Sometimes I feel as though I myself would like to sing, but one condition must obtain: that I find someone to listen to me. And if there is someone to listen, let him beware if he does not show admiration and appreciation, for if not . . . if not I become shy and embarrassed and begin to tremble, after which I get very angry. Now, having drawn your attention to the condition, shall I sing?

CONDEMNED MAN: Sing!

EXECUTIONER: And will you admire me and show your appreciation?

CONDEMNED MAN: Yes.

EXECUTIONER: You promise faithfully?

CONDEMNED MAN: Faithfully.

EXECUTIONER: Then I'll sing you my tender song. Are you listening?

CONDEMNED MAN: I'm listening and appreciating.

EXECUTIONER: The appreciation comes at the end. As for now, all you're asked to do is merely to listen.

CONDEMNED MAN: I'm merely listening.

EXECUTIONER: Good. Are you ready?

CONDEMNED MAN: Why? Isn't it you who're going to sing?

EXECUTIONER: Yes, but it's necessary for you to be ready to listen.

CONDEMNED MAN: And am I capable of doing anything else? You have left my ears free—no doubt for that purpose.

EXECUTIONER: Then let's start. This tender song, called *The Flower and the Gardener,* was composed by me. Yes, I composed it myself.

CONDEMNED MAN: I know that.

EXECUTIONER: How odd! Who told you?

CONDEMNED MAN: You told me so yourself just a moment ago.

EXECUTIONER: Really? Really? And now, do you want me to begin?

CONDEMNED MAN: Go ahead.

EXECUTIONER: I'm just about to begin. Listen—but you're not listening.

CONDEMNED MAN: I am listening.

EXECUTIONER: The listening must be done with superlative attention.

CONDEMNED MAN: With superlative attention!

EXECUTIONER: Be careful not to upset me by letting your mind wander and not paying attention.

CONDEMNED MAN: I am paying attention.

EXECUTIONER: Are you ready?

CONDEMNED MAN: Yes.

EXECUTIONER: I don't find you excessively enthusiastic.

CONDEMNED MAN: And how should I behave?

EXECUTIONER: I want you to be burning with enthusiasm. Tell me you absolutely insist that you listen to my singing.

CONDEMNED MAN: I absolutely insist . . .

EXECUTIONER: You say it coldly, with indifference.

CONDEMNED MAN: Coldly?

EXECUTIONER: Yes. I want the insistence to issue forth from the depths of your heart.

CONDEMNED MAN: It comes from the depths of my heart.

EXECUTIONER: I don't sense the warmth of sincerity in your voice.

CONDEMNED MAN: Sincerity?

EXECUTIONER: Yes, it's not apparent from the tone of your voice; it is the tone and timbre of the voice that reveals a person's true feelings, and your voice is cold and indifferent.

CONDEMNED MAN: And so—are you going to sing or aren't you?

EXECUTIONER: I shan't sing.

CONDEMNED MAN: Thanks be to God!

EXECUTIONER: You thank God for my not singing?

CONDEMNED MAN: No, I shall always thank God for your singing and your not singing alike. I don't believe there's anyone who'd object to praising God in all circumstances.

EXECUTIONER: Deep down you're wishing that I won't sing.

CONDEMNED MAN: Deep down? Who but God knows a man's inner thoughts?

EXECUTIONER: Then you want me to sing?

CONDEMNED MAN: If you like.

EXECUTIONER: I'll sing.

CONDEMNED MAN: Sing!

EXECUTIONER: No, I have a condition: implore me first of all to sing. Plead with me.

CONDEMNED MAN: I plead with you.

EXECUTIONER: Say it sensitively, entreatingly.

CONDEMNED MAN: Please—I implore you—by your Lord, by the Lord of all creation. I ask of God, the One, the Conqueror, the Strong and Mighty, to soften your cruel heart and to listen to my request and to be so good and gracious as to sing.

EXECUTIONER: Again!

CONDEMNED MAN: What?

EXECUTIONER: Repeat this pleading!

CONDEMNED MAN: God Almighty! Have mercy upon me! You've killed me with all this resistance and coyness. Sing if you want to; if not, then, for God's sake let me be and I'll have nothing to do with it.

EXECUTIONER: Are you angry? I don't want you to be angry. I'll sing so as to calm you down and remove your feeling of distress. I'll start right away. [He coughs, then hums softly preparatory to singing.]

CONDEMNED MAN: At last!

EXECUTIONER: [Standing up suddenly.] If you'd prefer me not to sing, say so frankly.

CONDEMNED MAN: Heavens above! He's going to start all over again.

EXECUTIONER: Is your patience exhausted?

CONDEMNED MAN: And how!

EXECUTIONER: Am I making you suffer?

CONDEMNED MAN: And how!

EXECUTIONER: Just be patient, my dear fellow. Be patient.

CONDEMNED MAN: This Executioner is really killing me!

EXECUTIONER: What are you saying?

CONDEMNED MAN: I can't stand any more.

EXECUTIONER: You can't stand the waiting. What a poor, pining creature you are, so consumed with wanting to hear my singing! I'll begin then. I shan't make you wait any longer. I'll start right away. Listen! Here's my tender song.

[*He clears his throat, hums, and then sings in a drunken voice.*]

> O flower whose life is but a night,
> Greetings from your admirers!
> Plucked at dawn of day tomorrow,
> The robe of dew from you will fall.
> In a firewood basket you will lie
> And all around my tunes will die.
> In the air the deadly blade will flash
> Shining bright in gardener's hand.
> O flower, whose life is but a night!
> On you be peace, on you be peace!

[*Silence.*]

EXECUTIONER: Why are you silent? Didn't you like it? This is the time to show admiration and appreciation.

CONDEMNED MAN: Is this your tender song, you ill-omened Executioner?

EXECUTIONER: Please—I'm no Executioner.

CONDEMNED MAN: What do you think you are then?

EXECUTIONER: I'm a gardener.

CONDEMNED MAN: A gardener?

EXECUTIONER: Yes, a gardener. Do you understand? A gardener. I'm a gar-den-er.

[*A window is opened in the beautiful lady's house, and the* MAID *looks out.*]

MAID: What's all this now? What's this uproar when people are asleep? My mistress has a headache and wishes to sleep undisturbed.

EXECUTIONER: [*Sarcastically.*] Your mistress! [*He laughs derisively.*] Her mistress!

MAID: I told you to stop that noise.

EXECUTIONER: Take yourself off, server of vice and obscenity.

MAID: Don't insult my mistress! If she wanted to she could have twenty sweepers like you to sweep the dust from under her shoes.

EXECUTIONER: Hold your tongue and take yourself off, you filthiest of creatures!

[*The* LADY *appears at the window behind her servant.*]

LADY: What's happening?

MAID: This drunken executioner is raising a din and hurling abuse at us.

LADY: How dare he!

EXECUTIONER: [*Pointing at the window.*] That's her, in all her splendour— her famous mistress!

LADY: Show a little respect, man!

EXECUTIONER: [*Laughing sarcastically.*] Respect!

LADY: Yes, and don't force me to teach you how to respect ladies.

EXECUTIONER: Ladies? [*He laughs.*] Ladies! She says ladies! Listen and marvel!

LADY: [*To her* MAID.] Go down and give him a lesson in manners.

MAID: [*To the* EXECUTIONER.] Wait for me—if you're a man!

    [*The two women disappear from the window.*]

EXECUTIONER: [*To the* CONDEMNED MAN.] What does this . . . this she-devil intend to do? Do you know? She's capable of anything. Good God, did you see how she threatened me?

MAID: [*Emerging from the door of the house, a shoe held high in her hand.*] Come here!

EXECUTIONER: What are you going to do with that shoe?

MAID: This shoe is the oldest and filthiest thing I could find in the house— do you understand? I came across nothing older or filthier befitting that dirty, ugly face of yours.

EXECUTIONER: Now the effect of the glass of lovely wine has really flown from my head. Did you hear the nice polite things she was saying, oh condemned man?

CONDEMNED MAN: Yes.

EXECUTIONER: And you utter not a word?

CONDEMNED MAN: I?

EXECUTIONER: And you remain unmoved?

CONDEMNED MAN: How?

EXECUTIONER: You let her insult me like this and remain silent?

CONDEMNED MAN: And what do you want me to do?

EXECUTIONER: Do something! At least say something!

CONDEMNED MAN: What's it got to do with me?

EXECUTIONER: What lack of gallantry, what flagging resolution! You see her raising the shoe in her hand like someone brandishing a sword and you don't make a move to defend me. You just stand there with shack-led hands. You just look on without caring. You listen without concern to my being insulted, humiliated, and abused? By God, this is no way to show chivalry.

CONDEMNED MAN: Truly!

MAID: [*Shaking the shoe in her hand.*] Listen here, man! Leave this poor fellow alone. You face up to me if you've got any courage. Your reckon-ing is with me. You've behaved very rudely towards us and it's up to you to apologize and ask our forgiveness. Otherwise, by the Lord of Hosts, by the Almighty, by the Omnipotent . . .

EXECUTIONER: [*Gently.*] Steady! Steady!

MAID: Speak! What's your answer?

EXECUTIONER: Let's come to an understanding.

MAID: First, ask for forgiveness.

EXECUTIONER: From whom should I ask forgiveness? From you?

MAID: From my mistress.

EXECUTIONER: Where is she?

LADY: [*Appearing on the threshold of her house.*] Here I am. Has he apologized?

MAID: He will do so, milady.

EXECUTIONER: Yes, milady.

LADY: Good. Then I accept your apology.

EXECUTIONER: Only, milady—would it not be best for the waters to flow back to their usual channels and for things to be as before?

LADY: They are.

EXECUTIONER: I meant for the wine to flow back into the channels of my head.

LADY: What do you mean?

EXECUTIONER: I mean that there is a certain damage that requires repairing. Your efficient servant has removed the intoxication from my head. From where shall I fill the void?

LADY: I shall take upon myself the filling of your head. Take as much drink as you wish from the Wine Merchant at my expense.

EXECUTIONER: Thank you, O bountiful lady. [*The* EXECUTIONER *signals to the* WINE MERCHANT *who is standing by the door of his tavern to bring him a glass.*]

CONDEMNED MAN: [*To the* LADY.] Do you not know me, beautiful lady?

LADY: Of course I know you. From the first instant when they brought you here at nightfall. I caught sight of you from my window and recognized you and it saddened me to see you in shackles, but—but what crime have you committed?

CONDEMNED MAN: Nothing much. All that happened was that I said . . .

EXECUTIONER: [*Shouting.*] Careful! Careful! Shut your mouth!

CONDEMNED MAN: I've shut my mouth.

LADY: Naturally they gave you a trial?

CONDEMNED MAN: No.

LADY: What are you saying? Weren't you given a trial?

CONDEMNED MAN: I wasn't taken to court. I sent a complaint to the Sultan asking that I be given the right to appear before the Chief Cadi, the most just of those who judge by conscience, the most scrupulous adherent to the canonical law, and the most loyal defender of the sanctity of the law. But—here dawn approaches and the Executioner has had his orders to cut off my head when the call to dawn prayers is given.

LADY: [*Looking up at the sky.*] The dawn? The dawn's almost breaking. Look at the sky!

EXECUTIONER: [*In his hand a glass taken from the* WINE MERCHANT.] It's not the sky, my dear lady, that will decide the moment of fate for this condemned man but the minaret of this mosque. I am waiting for the Muezzin.

LADY: The Muezzin. He is surely on his way. Sometimes I stay awake in the morning and I see him at this very moment making for the mosque.

CONDEMNED MAN: Then my hour has come.

LADY: No—not so long as your complaint has not been examined.

CONDEMNED MAN: This Executioner will not await the result of the complaint. Isn't that so, Executioner?

EXECUTIONER: I shall await only the Muezzin. Those are my orders.

LADY: Whose orders? The Sultan's?

EXECUTIONER: Roughly.

CONDEMNED MAN: [Shouting.] Roughly? Is it not then the Sultan?

EXECUTIONER: The Vizier—the orders of the Vizier are the orders of the Sultan.

CONDEMNED MAN: Then I am irretrievably lost.

EXECUTIONER: Just so. No sooner does the Muezzin's call to prayer rise up to the sky than your soul rises with it. This causes me great sadness and distress but work is work. A job's a job.

LADY: [Turning towards the street.] Oh disaster! Here is the Muezzin—he has arrived.

CONDEMNED MAN: The die is cast.

[The MUEZZIN makes his appearance.]

EXECUTIONER: Hurry, O Muezzin—we're waiting for you.

MUEZZIN: Waiting for me? Why?

EXECUTIONER: To give the call to the dawn prayer.

MUEZZIN: Do you want to pray?

EXECUTIONER: I want to carry out my work.

MUEZZIN: What have I to do with your work?

EXECUTIONER: When your voice rises up to the sky the soul of this man will rise with it.

MUEZZIN: God forbid!

EXECUTIONER: Those are the orders.

MUEZZIN: The life of this man hangs on my vocal cords?

EXECUTIONER: Yes.

MUEZZIN: There is no power and no strength save in God!

EXECUTIONER: O Muezzin, hasten to your work so that I may do mine.

LADY: And what's the hurry, kind Executioner? The Muezzin's voice has been affected by the night cold and he is in need of a hot drink. Come into my house, Muezzin. I shall prepare you something which will put your voice to rights.

EXECUTIONER: And the dawn?

LADY: The dawn is in no danger and the Muezzin knows best as to its time.

EXECUTIONER: And my work?

LADY: Your work is in no danger—so long as the Muezzin has not yet called for the dawn prayers.

EXECUTIONER: Do you agree, oh Muezzin?

LADY: He agrees to accepting my little invitation for a short while, for he is among my best friends in the quarter.

EXECUTIONER: And those who have gone to pray in the mosque?

MUEZZIN: There are only two men there. One of them is a stranger to this city and has taken up his abode in the mosque, whilst the other is a beggar who has sought shelter in it from the night cold. All are now deep in sleep and seldom do people pay attention to the call to dawn prayers. Only those get up whom I wake with a kick so that they may perform their religious duties.

LADY: Most of the people of the quarter live a life of ease and sleep well on into the forenoon.

EXECUTIONER: Are you both meaning to say that the call to dawn prayers won't be given today?

LADY: What we mean is . . . there's no hurry. There is safety in proceeding slowly, remorse in proceeding hastily. Don't worry yourself! The call to the dawn prayer will be given in good time, and in any event you are all right and are not answerable. The Muezzin alone is responsible. Let us go then, oh Muezzin! A cup of coffee will restore your voice.

MUEZZIN: There's no harm in just a little time and just a small cup.

[*The* LADY *enters her house with the* MUEZZIN.]

EXECUTIONER: [*To the* CONDEMNED MAN.] Did you see? Instead of going up into the minaret he went up to the house of the . . . the honoured lady. There's the Muezzin for you!

CONDEMNED MAN: A gallant man! He risks everything. As for you, you against whom no censure or blame will be directed, you who are safely covered by your excuse, who bear no liability, possessed as you are of a pretext, it's you who's raging and storming and becoming alarmed. Calm down a little, my friend! Be forbearing and patient! Put your trust in God! Listen, I've got an idea—an excellent, a brilliant idea. It will calm your nerves and bring joy to your soul. Sing me your tender song once again with that sweet, melodious voice of yours, and I swear to you I'll listen to it with a heart palpitating with enthusiasm and admiration. Come along—sing! I'm listening to you with my very being.

EXECUTIONER: I no longer have any desire to.

CONDEMNED MAN: Why? What's upset you? Is it because you didn't lop off my head?

EXECUTIONER: It's because I failed to carry out my duty.

CONDEMNED MAN: Your duty is to carry out the sentence at the time of the call to the dawn prayer. Yet who gives the call to the dawn prayer? You or the Muezzin?

EXECUTIONER: The Muezzin.

CONDEMNED MAN: And has he done so?

EXECUTIONER: No.

CONDEMNED MAN: Then what fault is it of yours?

EXECUTIONER: Truly it is not my fault.

CONDEMNED MAN: This is what we're all saying.

EXECUTIONER: You're comforting me and making light of things for me.

CONDEMNED MAN: I'm telling the truth.

EXECUTIONER: [*Looking up and down the street and shouting.*] What are these crowds? Good God! It's the Vizier's retinue! It's the Vizier!

CONDEMNED MAN: Don't tremble like that! Calm yourself!

EXECUTIONER: It won't be held against me . . . I'm covered, aren't I?

CONDEMNED MAN: Set your mind at rest! You are covered with a thousand blankets of arguments and excuses.

EXECUTIONER: It's the accursed Muezzin who will pay the harsh reckoning.

[*The* VIZIER *appears surrounded by his guards.*]

VIZIER: [*Shouting.*] How strange! Has this criminal not been executed yet?

EXECUTIONER: We are awaiting the dawn prayer, milord Vizier, in accordance with your orders.

VIZIER: The dawn prayer? We have performed it at the palace mosque in the presence of Our Majesty the Sultan and the Chief Cadi.

EXECUTIONER: It's not my fault, milord Vizier. The Muezzin of this mosque has not yet gone up to the minaret.

VIZIER: How's that? This is unbelievable. Where is this Muezzin?

[*The* MUEZZIN *comes out drunk from the door of the house and tries to hide himself behind the* LADY *and her* MAID.]

EXECUTIONER: [*Catching sight of him and shouting.*] That's him! There he is!

VIZIER: [*To the guards.*] Bring him here! [*They bring him before the* VIZIER.] Are you the Muezzin of this mosque?

MUEZZIN: Yes, milord Vizier.

VIZIER: Why have you not yet given the call to the dawn prayer?

MUEZZIN: Who told you that, milord Vizier? I gave the call to the dawn prayer some time ago . . .

VIZIER: To the dawn prayer?

MUEZZIN: At its due time, just like every day, and there are those who heard me.

LADY: Truly we all heard him give the call to the dawn prayer from up in the minaret.

MAID: Yes, today as is his habit every day at the same time.

VIZIER: But this Executioner claims . . .

LADY: This Executioner was drunk and fast asleep.

MAID: And the sound of his snoring rose up to us and woke us from our sweet slumbers.

VIZIER: [*In astonishment to the* EXECUTIONER.] Is it thus that you carry out my orders?

EXECUTIONER: I swear, I swear, milord Vizier . . .

VIZIER: Enough of that!

[*The* EXECUTIONER *is tongue-tied with bewilderment.*]

CONDEMNED MAN: O Vizier, I would beg you to listen to me. I sent to His Majesty the Sultan a complaint . . .

EXECUTIONER: [*Collecting his wits and shouting.*] I swear, milord Vizier, that I was awake . . .

VIZIER: I told you to keep quiet. [*He turns to the* CONDEMNED MAN.] Yes, your complaint is known to His Majesty the Sultan and he ordered that you be turned over to the Chief Cadi. His Majesty the Sultan will himself attend your trial. This is his noble wish and his irrefutable command. Guards! Clear the square of people and let everyone go home. This trial must take place in complete secrecy.

[*The guards clear the square of people.*]

EXECUTIONER: Milord Vizier . . . [*He tries to explain matters but the* VIZIER *dismisses him with a gesture.*]

[*The* SULTAN *appears with his retinue, accompanied by the* CHIEF CADI.]

CONDEMNED MAN: [*Shouting.*] Your Majesty! Justice! I beg for justice!

SULTAN: Is this the accused?

CONDEMNED MAN: Your Majesty! I have committed no fault or crime!

SULTAN: We shall see.

CONDEMNED MAN: And I haven't been tried yet! I haven't been tried!

SULTAN: You shall be given a fair trial in accordance with your wish, and the Chief Cadi shall be in charge of your trial in our presence. [*The* SULTAN *makes a sign to the* CHIEF CADI *to start the trial, then sits down in a chair which has been brought for him, while the* VIZIER *stands by his side.*]

CADI: [*Sitting on his chair.*] Remove the accused's chains. [*One of the guards undoes the* CONDEMNED MAN*'s fetters.*] Approach, man! What is your crime?

CONDEMNED MAN: I have committed no crime.

CADI: What is the charge brought against you?

CONDEMNED MAN: Ask the Vizier that!

CADI: I am asking *you.*

CONDEMNED MAN: I did nothing at all except utter an innocent word in which there is neither danger nor harm.

VIZIER: It's a terrible and sinful word.

CADI: [*To the* CONDEMNED MAN.] What is this word?

CONDEMNED MAN: I don't like to repeat it.

VIZIER: Now you don't like to, but in the middle of the market place and amongst throngs of people . . .

CADI: What is this word?

VIZIER: He said that His Majesty, the great and noble Sultan, is a mere slave.

CONDEMNED MAN: Everyone knows this—it is common knowledge.

VIZIER: Don't interrupt me—and he claimed that he was the slave trader who undertook the sale of our Sultan in his youth to the former Sultan.

CONDEMNED MAN: That's true. I swear it by a sacred oath—and it is a matter of pride to me which I shall treasure for all time.

SULTAN: [*To the* CONDEMNED MAN.] You? You sold me to the late Sultan?

CONDEMNED MAN: Yes.

SULTAN: When was that?

CONDEMNED MAN: Twenty-five years ago, Your Majesty. You were a small boy of six, lost and abandoned in a Circassian village raided by the Mongols.[7] You were extremely intelligent and wise for one of your tender years. I rejoiced in you and carried you off to the Sultan of this country. As the price for you he made me a present of one thousand dinars.[8]

SULTAN: [*Derisively.*] Only a thousand dinars!

CONDEMNED MAN: Of course you were worth more than that but I was new to the trade, not being more than twenty-six years of age. That deal was the beginning of my business—it opened for me the way to the future.

SULTAN: For you and for me!

---

7. Mongol armies devastated this region in both the 13th and the 14th centuries. Circassia is a region in the Caucasus Mountains near the Black Sea.   8. Gold coins.

CONDEMNED MAN: Thanks be to God!

SULTAN: Is it this that merits your death—bringing me to this country? I see the matter quite differently.

VIZIER: He deserves death for his babbling and indiscretion.

SULTAN: I see no great harm in his saying or bruiting[9] abroad the fact that I was a slave. The late Sultan was just that—is not that right, Vizier?

VIZIER: That's right but . . .

SULTAN: Is it not so, Chief Cadi?

VIZIER: Quite so, O Sultan.

SULTAN: The entire family comes from slaves since time immemorial. The Mamluke Sultans were all taken from earliest childhood to the palace, there to be given a strict and hardy upbringing; and later they became rulers, army leaders, and Sultans of countries. I am merely one of those, in no way different from them.

CONDEMNED MAN: Rather are you among the best of them in wisdom and sound judgement, may God preserve you for the good of your subjects.

SULTAN: Even so, I don't remember your face; in fact I don't clearly remember my childhood days in that Circassian village you talk about and in which you say you found me. All I remember is my childhood at the palace under the protection of the late Sultan. He used to treat me as though I were his real son, for he himself had no children. He brought me up and instructed me so that I might take over the rule. I knew for absolute certainty that he was not my father.

CONDEMNED MAN: Your parents were killed by the Mongols.

SULTAN: No one ever talked to me of my parents. I knew only that I had been brought to the palace at a young age.

CONDEMNED MAN: And it was I who brought you there.

SULTAN: Maybe.

CONDEMNED MAN: Therefore, Your Majesty, what is my crime?

SULTAN: By God, I know not. Ask him who accused you.

VIZIER: That's not his real crime.

SULTAN: Is there a real crime?

VIZIER: Yes, Your Majesty. To say that you had been a slave is truly not something shameful, no reason for guilt—all the Mamluk Sultans have been slaves. It's not there that the crime lies. However, a Mamluke Sultan is generally manumitted before ascending the throne.

SULTAN: So what?

VIZIER: So, Your Majesty, this man claims that you have not yet been manumitted,[1] that you are still a slave and that a person bearing such a stigma is not entitled to rule over a free people.

SULTAN: [To the CONDEMNED MAN.] Did you really say this?

CONDEMNED MAN: I did not say all that; however, people in the market place always enjoy such gossip and tittle-tattle.

SULTAN: And from where did you learn that I had not been manumitted?

CONDEMNED MAN: It is not I who said so. They ascribe to me every infamous word that is spoken.

SULTAN: But they are nevertheless indulging in gossip and tittle-tattle.

---

9. Spreading, repeating.   1. Emancipated, or freed from slavery.

CONDEMNED MAN: Not I.

SULTAN: You or someone else—it no longer matters. The important thing now is that all the people everywhere know that it is all sheer lies—isn't that so, Chief Cadi?

CADI: The fact is, Your Majesty . . .

SULTAN: It's utter falsehood and slander. It's mere fabrication unsupported by logic or common sense. Not yet manumitted? I? I, who was a leader of armies and conquered the Mongols? I, the right-hand man of the late Sultan, whom he arranged to rule after him? All this, and the Sultan did not think about manumitting me before his death? Is it plausible? Listen, Cadi! All you now have to do is to let the town-criers announce an official denial in the city and publish to the people the text of the document registering my manumission, which is doubtless kept in your strong-rooms, isn't that so?

CADI: [Combing his fingers through his beard.] You are saying, Your Majesty . . .

SULTAN: Didn't you hear what I said?

CADI: Yes, but . . .

SULTAN: You were busy playing with your beard.

CADI: Your Majesty!

SULTAN: What? Your Majesty the Sultan is addressing you in clear and simple language requiring no long consideration or deep thought. All it amounts to is that it has become necessary to make public the document. Do you understand?

CADI: Yes.

SULTAN: You're still playing with your beard. Can't you leave it alone—just for a while?

VIZIER: [Intervening.] Your Majesty! Would you permit me . . .

SULTAN: What's up with you? You too?

VIZIER: I would ask Your Majesty to . . .

SULTAN: What's all this embarrassment? You and he are as bad as each other.

CADI: It is better to postpone this trial until some other time—when we are on our own, Your Majesty.

VIZIER: Yes, that would be best.

SULTAN: I'm beginning to catch on.

[The VIZIER, by a sign, orders everyone to move off with the CONDEMNED MAN, leaving only himself, the SULTAN, and the CHIEF CADI on stage.]

SULTAN: Now here we are on our own. What have you to say? I see from your expressions that you have things to say.

CADI: Yes, Your Majesty. You have with your perspicacity realized . . . in actual fact there is no document of your manumission in my strong-rooms.

SULTAN: Perhaps you have not yet received it, though it must be somewhere. Isn't that so, Vizier?

VIZIER: In truth, Your Majesty . . .

SULTAN: What?

VIZIER: The truth is that . . .

SULTAN: Speak!

VIZIER: There is no document to prove your having been manumitted.

SULTAN: What are you saying?

VIZIER: The late Sultan collapsed suddenly following a heart attack and departed this life before manumitting you.

SULTAN: What's this you're alleging, you rogue?

VIZIER: I'm certainly a rogue, Your Majesty—and a criminal. I'm wicked, I don't deny it. I should have arranged all this at the time, but this business of manumission did not occur to me. My head was filled with other weighty matters. At that time, Your Majesty, you were far away— in the thick of the fray. No one but myself was present by the dying Sultan's bedside. I forgot this matter under the stress of the situation, the momentous nature of the occasion, and the intensity of my grief. Nothing occupied me at that moment save taking the oath, before the dying man, that I would serve you, Your Majesty, with the very same devotion as that with which I had served him for the whole of his life.

SULTAN: Truly, here and now you have really served me!

VIZIER: I deserve death—I know that. It is an unpardonable crime. The late Sultan could not think of everything or remember everything. It was the very essence of my work to think for him and to remind him of important matters. It was certainly my duty to put before him the matter of manumission, because of its particular seriousness, and to do the necessary legal formalities. But your lofty position, Your Majesty, your influence, your prestige, your great place in people's hearts—all these high attributes caused us to overlook your being a slave; to overlook the necessity for someone of your stature to have such proofs and documents. I swear to God, this matter never occurred to me until after you had ascended the throne, Your Majesty. At that time the whole business became clear to me. I was seized with terror and almost went mad. I would surely have done so, had I not calmed down and pulled myself together, cherishing the hope that this matter would never arise or be revealed.

SULTAN: And now it has arisen and been revealed.

VIZIER: What a tragedy! I did not know that such a man would come along one day with his gossip and tittle-tattle.

SULTAN: For this reason you wanted to close his mouth by handing him over to the executioner?

VIZIER: Yes.

SULTAN: And so bury your fault by burying the man himself?

VIZIER: [With head lowered.] Yes.

SULTAN: And what's the point of that now? Everyone's gossiping now.

VIZIER: If this man's head were cut off and hung up in the square before the people, no tongue would thenceforth dare to utter.

SULTAN: Do you think so?

VIZIER: If the sword is not able to cut off tongues, then what can?

CADI: Will you allow me to say a word, Your Majesty?

SULTAN: I'm listening.

CADI: The sword certainly does away with heads and tongues; it does not, however, do away with difficulties and problems.

SULTAN: What do you mean?

CADI: I mean that the problem will still nevertheless remain, namely that the Sultan is ruling without having been manumitted, and that a slave is at the head of a free people.

VIZIER: Who dares to say this? Whoever does so will have his head cut off.

CADI: That's another question.

VIZIER: It is not necessary for the person ruling to be carrying around documents and proofs. We have the strongest and most striking example of this in the Fatimid dynasty. Every one of us remembers what Al-Mu'izz li-Din Allah Al-Fatimi did.[2] One day he came along claiming he was descended from the Prophet (the prayers of God be upon him), and when the people did not believe him, he went at them with drawn sword and opened up his coffers of gold, saying 'These are my forbears, these my ancestors'. The people kept silent and he reigned and his children reigned after him quietly and peaceably for centuries long.

SULTAN: What do you say about this, Cadi?

CADI: I say that this is correct from the historical point of view but . . .

SULTAN: But what?

CADI: Then, O illustrious Sultan, you would like to solve your problem by this method?

SULTAN: And why not?

VIZIER: Truly, why not? There is nothing easier than this, especially in this matter of ours. It is sufficient for us to announce publicly that Our Majesty the Sultan has been legally manumitted, that he was manumitted by the late Sultan before his death, and that the documents and proofs are recorded and kept with the Chief Cadi—and death to anyone who dares deny it!

CADI: There is a person who will so deny.

VIZIER: Who's that?

CADI: I.

SULTAN: You?

CADI: Yes, Your Majesty. I cannot take part in this conspiracy.

VIZIER: It is not a conspiracy—it's a plan for saving the situation.

CADI: It is a conspiracy against the law I represent.

SULTAN: The law?

CADI: Yes, Sultan—the law. In the eyes of the civil and religious codes you are only a slave, and a slave—by civil and religious law—is regarded as a thing, a chattel. As the late Sultan, who had the power of life and death over you, did not manumit you before his death, you are thus still a thing, a chattel, owned by someone else, and so you have forfeited the basic qualification for entering into the normal transactions exercised by the rest of free people.

SULTAN: Is this the law?

CADI: Yes.

VIZIER: Take it easy, Chief Cadi! We are not now discussing the view of the law but are looking for a way by which to be free of this law, and the way to be free of it is to assume that manumission has in fact taken

---

2. The Fatimid Dynasty ruled Egypt from 909 to 1171. Al-Mu'izz ruled from 953 to 975.

place. So long as the matter is a secret between us three, with no one but ourselves knowing the truth, it will be easy to induce the people to believe . . .

CADI: The lie.

VIZIER: The solution rather—it's a more appropriate and suitable word.

CADI: A solution through lying.

VIZIER: And what's the harm in that?

CADI: In relation to you two there is no harm.

VIZIER: And in relation to you?

CADI: In relation to me it's different, for I cannot fool myself and I cannot free myself from the law, being as I am the person who represents it; I cannot break an oath by which I took upon myself to be the trusted servant of the civil and religious law.

SULTAN: You took this upon yourself before me.

CADI: And before God and my conscience.

SULTAN: Which means that you won't go along with us?

CADI: Along this road, no.

SULTAN: You will not join hands with us?

CADI: In this instance, no.

SULTAN: Then in that case you can take yourself off to one side. Don't interfere in anything and leave us to act as we think fit. You thus keep your oath and satisfy your conscience.

CADI: I'm sorry, Your Majesty.

SULTAN: Why?

CADI: Because, having admitted that in the eyes of the law you are lacking the authority to make a contract, I find myself obliged to order that all your actions are null and void.

SULTAN: You're mad—that's impossible!

CADI: I'm sorry but I cannot do other than this so long as . . .

SULTAN: So long as?

CADI: So long as you don't order me to be dismissed from my post, thrown out of the country, or have my head cut off. In this manner I would be freed from my oath and you could suit yourself and do as you pleased.

SULTAN: Is this a threat?

CADI: No, it's a solution.

VIZIER: You're complicating the problem for us, Chief Cadi.

CADI: I am helping you to get out of an impasse.

SULTAN: I've begun to weary of this man.

VIZIER: He knows that we are in his grasp in that he will divulge everything to the people if the least amount of coercion is used on him.

SULTAN: [To the CADI.] The substance of what you say is that you don't want to assist us.

CADI: On the contrary, Your Majesty, I wish very greatly to be of assistance to you, but not in this manner.

SULTAN: What do you suggest then?

CADI: That the law be applied.

SULTAN: If you applied the law, I'd lose my throne.

CADI: Not only that.

SULTAN: Is there something even worse?

CADI: Yes.

SULTAN: What is there then?

CADI: Owing to the fact that in the eyes of the law you are a chattel owned by the late Sultan, you have become part of his inheritance, and as he died without leaving an heir, his estate reverts to the Exchequer.[3] You are thus one of the chattels owned by the Exchequer—an unproductive chattel yielding no profit or return. I, in my additional capacity as Treasurer of the Exchequer, say: it is the custom in such cases to get rid of unprofitable chattels by putting them up for sale at auction, so that the good interests of the Exchequer be not harmed and so that it may utilize the proceeds of the sale in bringing benefit to the people generally and in particular to the poor.

SULTAN: [Indignantly.] An unproductive chattel? I?

CADI: I am speaking of course strictly from the legal point of view.

SULTAN: Up until now I have obtained no solutions from you. All I have had are insults.

CADI: Insults? I beg your pardon, illustrious Sultan. You know very well how much I revere and admire you and in what high esteem I hold you. You will recollect no doubt that it was I who from the first moment was the one to come forward to pay you homage and proclaim you as the Sultan to rule over our country. What I am doing now is merely to give a frank review of the situation from the point of view of civil and religious law.

SULTAN: The long and short of it is then that I'm a thing and a chattel and not a man or a human being?

CADI: Yes.

SULTAN: And that this thing or chattel is owned by the Exchequer?

CADI: Indeed.

SULTAN: And that the Exchequer disposes of unproductive chattels by putting them up for sale at auction for the public good?

CADI: Exactly.

SULTAN: Oh Chief Cadi, don't you feel, as I do, that this is all extraordinarily bizarre?

CADI: Yes, but . . .

SULTAN: And that there's a great deal of undue exaggeration and extravagance in it all?

CADI: Maybe, but in my capacity as Cadi what concerns me is where the facts stand in relation to the processes of the law.

SULTAN: Listen, Cadi. This law of yours has brought me no solution, whereas a small movement of my sword will ensure that the knot of the problem is severed instantly.

CADI: Then do so.

SULTAN: I shall. What does the spilling of a little blood matter for the sake of the practicability of governing?

CADI: Then you must start by spilling my blood.

3. Treasury.

SULTAN: I shall do everything I think necessary for safeguarding the security of the State, and I shall in fact start with you. I shall cast you into
prison. Vizier! Arrest the Cadi!

VIZIER: Your Majesty, you have not yet listened to his answer to your question.

SULTAN: What question?

VIZIER: The question about the solution he deems appropriate for the
problem.

SULTAN: He has answered this question.

VIZIER: What he said was not the solution but a review of the situation.

SULTAN: Is that true, Cadi?

CADI: Yes.

SULTAN: Have you then a solution to this problem of ours?

CADI: [In the same tone.] Yes.

SULTAN: Then speak! What is the solution?

CADI: There is only one solution.

SULTAN: Say! What is it?

CADI: That the law be applied.

SULTAN: Again? Once more?

CADI: Yes—once more and always, for I see no other solution.

SULTAN: Do you hear, Vizier? After this, do you entertain any hope of cooperation with this stubborn old windbag?

VIZIER: Allow me, Your Majesty, to interrogate him a little.

SULTAN: Do as you like!

VIZIER: O Chief Cadi, the question is a subtle one and it requires of you
to explain to us clearly and in detail your point of view.

CADI: My point of view is both clear and simple and I can propound it in
two words: for the solution of this problem we have before us two alternatives, that of the sword and that of the law. As for the sword, that is
none of my concern; as for the law, that is what it behoves me to recommend and on which I can give a legal opinion. The law says: it is only
his master, the possessor of the power of life and death over him, who
has the right to manumit a slave. In this instance, the master, the possessor of the power of life and death, died without leaving an heir and
the ownership of the slave has reverted to the Exchequer. The Exchequer may not manumit him without compensation in that no one has
the right to dispose gratis of property or chattels belonging to the State.
It is, however, permitted for the Exchequer to make a disposition by
sale, and the selling of the property of the State is not valid by law other
than by an auction carried out publicly. The legal solution, therefore,
is that we should put up His Majesty the Sultan for sale by public auction and the person to whom he is knocked down thereafter manumits
him. In this manner the Exchequer is not harmed or defrauded in
respect of its property and the Sultan gains his manumission and release
through the law.

SULTAN: [To the VIZIER.] Do you hear all this?

VIZIER: [To the CADI.] We put up Our Majesty, the illustrious Sultan, for
sale by public auction! This is sheer madness!

CADI: This is the legal and legitimate solution.

SULTAN: [*To the* VIZIER.] Don't waste time. No answer is left for this stupid and impudent fellow except to chop off his head—and let result what may! And it is I who shall perform this with my own hand. [*He draws his sword.*]

CADI: It is a great honour for me, Your Majesty, to die by your hand and for me to give up my life for the sake of truth and principles.

VIZIER: Patience, Your Majesty, patience! Don't make a martyr of this man! Such a broken-down old man could not hope for a more splendid death. It will be said that through him you destroyed the civil and religious laws; he will become the living symbol of the spirit of truth and principles—and many a glorious martyr has more effect and influence on the conscience of peoples than a tyrannical king.

SULTAN: [*Suppressing his anger.*] God's curse . . .

VIZIER: Don't give him this glory, Your Majesty, at the expense of the situation.

SULTAN: Then what's to be done? This man puts us in a dilemma, he makes us choose between two alternatives, both of them painful: the law which shows me up as weak and makes a laughing-stock of me, or the sword which brands me with brutality and makes me loathed.

VIZIER: [*Turning to the* CADI.] O Chief Cadi! Be tractable and obliging! Don't be rigid and hard! Meet us half-way, find a compromise and work with us towards finding a reasonable solution.

CADI: There is no reasonable way out other than the law.

VIZIER: We put the Sultan up for sale by auction?

CADI: Yes.

VIZIER: And the person he's knocked down to buys him?

CADI: He manumits him immediately, at the session for drawing up the contract—that's the condition.

VIZIER: And who will accept to lose his money in this manner?

CADI: Many people—those who would ransom the Sultan's freedom with their money.

VIZIER: Then why don't we ourselves undertake this duty—you and I— and ransom our Sultan secretly with our own money and gain this honour? Is it not an appropriate idea?

CADI: I'm afraid not. It cannot be secret—the law is specific in that it lays down that every sale of the properties of the Exchequer must be carried out publicly and by general auction.

SULTAN: [*To the* VIZIER.] Don't trouble yourself with him—he's determined to disgrace us.

VIZIER: [*To the* CADI.] For the last time, Chief Cadi—is there no stratagem for extracting us from this impasse?

CADI: A stratagem? I am not the person to ask to look for stratagems.

SULTAN: Naturally! This man looks only for what will provoke and humiliate us.

CADI: Not I as a person, Your Majesty. I as a person am weak and have nothing to do with the whole matter. If the matter were in my hands and depended upon my wishes, I would like nothing better than to extricate you from this situation in the best manner you could wish.

SULTAN: Poor weak fellow! The matter's not in his hands—in whose hands then?

CADI: The law's.

SULTAN: Yes, the spectre behind which he hides in order to subjugate me, impose his will upon me, and show me up before the people in that laughable, feeble, and ignominious guise.

CADI: I as a person would rather wish for you to appear in the guise of the glorious ruler.

SULTAN: Do you consider it as being among the characteristics of glory that a sultan be treated like goods or chattels to be sold in the market?

CADI: It is certainly a characteristic of glory that a sultan should submit to the law as do the rest of people.

VIZIER: It is truly laudable, Chief Cadi, that the ruler should obey the law as does the sentenced person, but this entails a great hazard. The politics of government have their procedures; the ruling of people has other methods.

CADI: I know nothing of politics or of the business of ruling people.

SULTAN: It's our business—allow us then to exercise it in our own way.

CADI: I have not fettered your hands, Your Majesty. You possess complete freedom to exercise your rule as you wish.

SULTAN: Fine! I now see what I must do.

VIZIER: What are you going to do, Your Majesty?

SULTAN: Look at this old man! Do you see him carrying a sword on his belt? Of course not. He carries nothing but a tongue in his mouth with which he turns words and phrases. He's good at using the acumen and skill he possesses, but I carry this. [*And he indicates his sword.*] It's not made of wood, it's not a toy. It's a real sword and must be useful for something, must have some reason for its existence. Do you understand what I'm saying? Answer! Why was it ordained that I should carry it? Is it for decoration or for action?

VIZIER: For action.

SULTAN: And you, Cadi—why do you not answer? Answer! Is it for decoration or for action?

CADI: For one or the other.

SULTAN: What are you saying?

CADI: I am saying, for this or for that.

SULTAN: What do you mean?

CADI: I mean that you have a choice, Your Majesty. You can employ it for action, or you can employ it for decoration. I recognize the undoubted strength possessed by the sword, its swift action and decisive effect. But the sword gives right to the strongest, and who knows who will be the strongest tomorrow? There may appear some strong person who will tilt the balance of power against you. As for the law, it protects your rights from every aggression, because it does not recognize the strongest—it recognizes right. And now there's nothing for you to do, Your Majesty, but choose: between the sword which imposes and yet exposes you, and between the law which threatens and yet protects you.

SULTAN: [*Thinking a while.*] The sword which imposes and exposes me, and the law which threatens and protects me?

CADI: Yes.

SULTAN: What talk is this?

CADI: The frank truth.

SULTAN: [*Thinking and repeating over to himself.*] The sword which imposes and exposes? The law which threatens and protects?

CADI: Yes, Your Majesty.

SULTAN: [*To the* VIZIER.] What an accursed old man he is! He's got a unique genius for always landing us in a spot.

CADI: I have done nothing, Your Majesty, except to present to you the two sides of the question; the choice is yours.

SULTAN: The choice? The choice? What is your opinion, Vizier?

VIZIER: It is for you to decide about this, Your Majesty.

SULTAN: As far as I can see, you don't know either.

VIZIER: Actually, Your Majesty, the . . .

SULTAN: The choice is difficult?

VIZIER: Certainly.

SULTAN: The sword which imposes me on all and yet which exposes me to danger, or the law which threatens my wishes yet which protects my rights.

VIZIER: Yes.

SULTAN: You choose for me.

VIZIER: I? No, no, Your Majesty!

SULTAN: What are you frightened of?

VIZIER: Of the consequences—of the consequences of this choice. Should it one day become apparent that I had chosen the wrong course, then what a catastrophe there'd be!

SULTAN: You don't want to bear the responsibility?

VIZIER: I wouldn't dare—it's not my right.

SULTAN: In the end a decision must be made.

VIZIER: No one, Your Majesty, but yourself has the right to decide in this matter.

SULTAN: Truly, there is no one but myself. I cannot escape from that. It's I who must choose and bear the responsibility of the choice.

VIZIER: You are our master and our ruler.

SULTAN: Yes, this is my most fearful moment, the fearful moment for every ruler—the moment of giving the final decision, the decision that will change the course of things, the moment when is uttered that small word which will decide the inevitable choice, the choice that will decide fate.

[*He thinks hard as he walks up and down, with the other two waiting for him to speak. Silence reigns for a moment.*]

SULTAN: [*With head lowered in thought.*] The sword or the law? The law or the sword?

VIZIER: Your Majesty, I appreciate the precariousness of your situation.

SULTAN: Yet you don't want to assist me with an opinion?

VIZIER: I cannot. In this situation you alone are the one to decide.

SULTAN: There is, therefore, no getting away from deciding all by myself?

VIZIER: That's so.

SULTAN: The sword or the law? The law or the sword? [*He thinks for a while, then raises his head sharply.*] Good—I've decided.

VIZIER: Let us have your orders, Your Majesty.

SULTAN: I have decided to choose, to choose . . .

VIZIER: What, Your Majesty?

SULTAN: [*Shouting decisively.*] The law! I have chosen the law!

CURTAIN

Act Two

The same square. GUARDS *have started to arrange rows of people around a platform that has been set up there. The* WINE MERCHANT'*s shop is closed and he is standing talking to the* SHOEMAKER, *who is engrossed in his work at the open door of his shop.*

WINE MERCHANT: How odd of you, Shoemaker! You open your shop and work when today every shop is closed, just like a feast day?

SHOEMAKER: And why should I close it? Is it because they're selling the Sultan?

WINE MERCHANT: You fool—because you'll be watching the most incredible sight in the world!

SHOEMAKER: I can see everything that goes on from here while I work.

WINE MERCHANT: It's up to you. As for me I've closed my shop so that I shan't miss the smallest detail of this wonderful spectacle.

SHOEMAKER: You're making the biggest mistake, my friend. Today's an excellent opportunity for attracting customers. It's not every day you get such crowds gathered outside your shop. It is certain that today many people will suffer from thirst and will yearn for a drop of your drink.

WINE MERCHANT: Do you think so?

SHOEMAKER: It's obvious. Look—here am I, for example, showing off my finest shoes today. [*He points to the shoes hanging up at the door of his shop.*]

WINE MERCHANT: My dear Shoemaker, those who come to buy today have come to buy the Sultan, not your shoes.

SHOEMAKER: Why not? Maybe there are some among the people who are in greater need of my shoes.

WINE MERCHANT: Shut up, say no more! It seems you don't understand what's so extraordinary about this happening, don't realize that it's unique. Do you find a sultan being put up for sale every day?

SHOEMAKER: Listen, friend. I'll talk to you frankly: even were I to have sufficient money to buy the Sultan, by God I wouldn't do it!

WINE MERCHANT: You wouldn't buy him?

SHOEMAKER: Never!

WINE MERCHANT: Allow me to say you're a fool!

SHOEMAKER: No, I'm intelligent and astute. Just tell me what you'd want me to do with a sultan in my shop? Can I teach him this trade of mine? Of course not! Can I entrust him with any work? Certainly not! Then, it's I who'll go on working doubly hard so as to feed him, look after him, and serve him. I swear that that is what would happen. I'd merely be buying a rod for my back, a sheer luxury I couldn't afford. My resources, friend, don't allow me to acquire works of art.

WINE MERCHANT: What nonsense!

SHOEMAKER: And you—would you buy him?

WINE MERCHANT: Can there be any doubt about that?

SHOEMAKER: What would you do with him?

WINE MERCHANT: Many things, very many things, my friend. His mere presence in my shop would be enough to bring along the whole city. It would be enough to ask him to recount to my customers every evening the stories of his battles against the Mongols, the strange things that have happened to him, his voyages and adventures, the countries he has seen, the places he's been to, the deserts he's crossed—wouldn't all that be valuable and enjoyable?

SHOEMAKER: Certainly, you could employ him in that manner but I . . .

WINE MERCHANT: You too could do the same.

SHOEMAKER: How? He knows nothing about repairing shoes or making soles for him to be able to talk about them.

WINE MERCHANT: It's not necessary for him to talk in your shop.

SHOEMAKER: What would he do then?

WINE MERCHANT: If I were in your place I'd know how to employ him.

SHOEMAKER: How? Tell me.

WINE MERCHANT: I'd sit him down in front of the door of the shop in a comfortable chair, I'd put a new pair of shoes on his feet and a placard above his head reading: 'Sultan Shoes Sold Here', and the next day you'd see how the people of the city would flock to your shop and demand your wares.

SHOEMAKER: What a great idea!

WINE MERCHANT: Isn't it?

SHOEMAKER: I'm beginning to admire your ingenuity.

WINE MERCHANT: What do you say then to thinking about buying him together and making him our joint property. I'd release him to you during the day and you could give him to me for the evening?

SHOEMAKER: A lovely dream! But all we own, you and I, isn't enough to buy one of his fingers.

WINE MERCHANT: That's true.

SHOEMAKER: Look! The crowds have begun to arrive and collect.

[Groups of men, women and children gather together and chat among themselves.]

FIRST MAN: [To another man.] Is it here they'll be selling the Sultan?

SECOND MAN: Yes, don't you see the guards?

FIRST MAN: If only I had money!

SECOND MAN: Shut up! That's for the rich!

CHILD: Mother! Is that the Sultan?

MOTHER: [To the CHILD.] No, child, that's one of the guards.

CHILD: Where is the Sultan then?

MOTHER: He hasn't come yet.

CHILD: Has the Sultan got a sword?

MOTHER: Yes, a large sword.

CHILD: And will they sell him here?

MOTHER: Yes, child.

CHILD: When, Mother?

MOTHER: Very soon.

CHILD: Mother! Buy him for me!

MOTHER: What?

CHILD: The Sultan! Buy me the Sultan!

MOTHER: Quiet! He's not a toy for you to play with.

CHILD: You said they'll sell him here. Buy him for me then.

MOTHER: Quiet, child. This is not a game for children.

CHILD: For whom then? For grown-ups?

MOTHER: Yes, it's for grown-ups.

[*The window of the* LADY's *house is opened and the* MAIDSERVANT *looks out.*]

MAID: [*Calling.*] Wine Merchant! Tavern keeper! Have you closed your shop today?

WINE MERCHANT: Yes—haven't I done right? And your mistress? Where is she? Is she still in bed?

MAID: No, she has just got out of her bath to dress.

WINE MERCHANT: She was superb! Her trick with the Executioner worked well.

MAID: Quiet! He's there. I can see him in the crowd. Now he's spotted us.

EXECUTIONER: [*Approaching the* WINE MERCHANT.] God curse you and wine!

WINE MERCHANT: Why? What sin has my wine committed to justify your curse? Didn't it bring joy to your heart that night, stimulate you in your singing, and cause you to see everything around you clear and pure?

EXECUTIONER: [*In tones of anger.*] Clear and pure! Certainly that night I saw everything clear and pure!

WINE MERCHANT: Certainly—do you doubt it?

EXECUTIONER: Shut up and don't remind me of that night.

WINE MERCHANT: I've shut up. Tell me: are you on holiday today?

EXECUTIONER: Yes.

WINE MERCHANT: And your friend the condemned man?

EXECUTIONER: He has been pardoned.

WINE MERCHANT: And you, naturally. No one asked you about that business at dawn?

EXECUTIONER: No.

WINE MERCHANT: Then everything has turned out for the best.

EXECUTIONER: Yes, but I don't like anyone to make a fool of me or play tricks on me.

MAID: Even when it means saving a man's head?

EXECUTIONER: Shut up, you vile woman—you and your mistress.

MAID: Are you continuing to insult us on such a day?

WINE MERCHANT: [*To the* EXECUTIONER.] Don't upset yourself! This evening I'll bring you a large glass of the best wine—free.

EXECUTIONER: Free?

WINE MERCHANT: Yes, a present from me, to drink to the health . . .

EXECUTIONER: Of whom?

WINE MERCHANT: [*Catching sight of the* MUEZZIN *approaching.*] To the health of the brave Muezzin!

EXECUTIONER: That most evil of liars!

MUEZZIN: A liar? Me?

EXECUTIONER: Yes, you claim that I was fast asleep at that hour.

MUEZZIN: And you were drunk!

EXECUTIONER: I'm absolutely convinced that I was awake and alert and that I hadn't slept for a moment up until then.

MUEZZIN: So long as *you're* absolutely convinced of that . . .

EXECUTIONER: Yes, I didn't sleep at all up until then.

MUEZZIN: Fine!

EXECUTIONER: You mean you agree about that?

MUEZZIN: Yes.

EXECUTIONER: Then it's you who're lying.

MUEZZIN: No!

EXECUTIONER: Then I *was* sleeping?

MUEZZIN: Yes.

EXECUTIONER: How can you say yes?

MUEZZIN: No!

EXECUTIONER: Make your mind up! Is it yes or is it no?

MUEZZIN: Which do you want?

EXECUTIONER: I want to know whether I was asleep at that time or whether I was awake.

MUEZZIN: What does it matter to you? So long as everything has passed peacefully—your friend the condemned man has been issued with a pardon and no one has asked you about anything. As for me, no one has spoken to me about the matter of that dawn. The question in relation to us all has ended as well as we could hope, so why dig up the past?

EXECUTIONER: Yes, but the question still troubles me since that day. I haven't grasped the situation absolutely clearly. I want to know whether I really was asleep at that time and whether you really gave the call to the dawn prayer without my being aware of it. In the end you must divulge to me what actually happened for you doubtless know the whole truth. Tell me exactly what happened then. I was in truth a little drunk at the time but . . .

MUEZZIN: Since the matter occupies your mind to such an extent, why should I put you at ease. I prefer to leave you like this, grilling away and turning on the fire of doubt.

EXECUTIONER: May you turn on Hell's Fire, you ruffian of a Muezzin!

MUEZZIN: [*Shouting.*] Look! Look! The Sultan's retinue has come!

[*The* RETINUE *with the* SULTAN *at its head appears, followed by the* CHIEF CADI, *the* VIZIER, *and the condemned* SLAVE TRADER. *They walk towards the dais, where the* SULTAN *seats himself in the middle chair with all around him, while the* SLAVE TRADER *stands beside him to face the people.*]

WINE MERCHANT: [*To the* EXECUTIONER.] Extraordinary! This is your friend the condemned man. What has brought him here alongside the Sultan?

EXECUTIONER: [*Looking at him.*] Truly, by God, it's none other than he.

MUEZZIN: No doubt he is the person charged with making the sale—is he not one of the biggest slave traders?

WINE MERCHANT: Do you see, Executioner? His escape, therefore, from your hands was no accident.

EXECUTIONER: How extraordinary! Here he is selling the same sultan twice—once as a child and again now when he's grown up.

MUEZZIN: Quiet! He's about to talk.

SLAVE TRADER: [*Clapping his hands.*] Quiet, people! I announce to you, in my capacity of slave-trader and auctioneer, that I have been charged with carrying out this sale by public auction for the benefit of the Exchequer. It honours me, first of all, that the Chief Cadi will open these proceedings with a word explaining the conditions of this sale. Let our venerable Chief Cadi now speak.

CADI: O people! The sale to be held before you is not like any other sale: it is of a special kind and this fact has been previously announced to you. This sale must be accompanied by another contract, a contract of manumission whereby the person who is the highest bidder at the auction may not retain what he has bought but must proceed with the manumission at the same session as the contract of sale, that is to say at this present session of ours. There is no need for me to remind you of the law's provision which prevents State employees from participating in any sale by the State. Having said this I leave the Vizier to speak to you about the patriotic character of these proceedings.

SHOEMAKER: [*Whispering to the* WINE MERCHANT.] Did you hear? The buyer cannot keep what he has bought. This means throwing one's money into the sea.

WINE MERCHANT: [*Whispering.*] We'll now see what imbecile will come forward.

SLAVE TRADER: Silence! Silence!

VIZIER: Honourable people! You are today present at a great and unique occasion, one of the most important in our history: a glorious Sultan asks for his freedom and has recourse to his people instead of to his sword—that sharp and mighty sword by which he was victorious in battles against the Mongols and with which he could also have been victorious in gaining his freedom and liberating himself from slavery. But our just and triumphant Sultan has chosen to submit to the law like the lowliest individual amongst his subjects. Here he is seeking his freedom by the method laid down by law. Whoever of you wishes to redeem the freedom of his beloved Sultan, let him come forward to this auction, and whoever of you pays the highest price will have done a goodly act for his homeland and will be remembered for time immemorial.

[*Cheers from the crowd.*]

VOICE: [*Raised from amongst* THE PEOPLE.] Long live the Sultan!

ANOTHER VOICE: Long live the law!

SLAVE TRADER: Silence, O people!

VIZIER: [*Continuing.*] And now, O noble people, that you know the small and trivial sacrifice your country expects of you for the sake of this high and lofty purpose—the freeing of your Sultan with your money and the passing of that money to the Exchequer so that it may be spent on the poor and those in need—now that your dearly beloved and cherished Sultan has come to you so that you may compete in showing your appreciation of him and liberating him, I declare that the proceedings shall begin.

[*He indicates to the* SLAVE TRADER *that he should begin, while the crowds cheer.*]

SLAVE TRADER: Silence! Silence! O people of this city, the auction has commenced. I shall not resort to enumerating properties and attributes as is generally resorted to in the markets for the purpose of making people want to acquire the goods, for the subject of this sale is above every description or comment. It is no extravagance or exaggeration to say that he is worth his weight in gold. However, it is not the intention to make things difficult or to inhibit you, but to facilitate matters for you in gauging what is possible. I thus begin the auction with a sum both small and paltry in respect of a sultan: Ten thousand dinars! [*Uproar amongst the crowd.*]

SHOEMAKER: [*To the* WINE MERCHANT.] Ten thousand? Only! What a trifling sum! Look at that great ruby in his turban! By God, it alone is worth a hundred thousand dinars!

WINE MERCHANT: Truly it's a paltry amount—especially when paid for a noble and patriotic end! Ten thousand dinars! It is not seemly. I'm a loyal citizen and this displeases me. [*Shouts.*] Eleven thousand dinars!

SLAVE TRADER: Eleven thousand dinars! Eleven thousand?

SHOEMAKER: [*To the* WINE MERCHANT.] Only eleven thousand dinars? Is that all you have? Then I'll say [*Shouting.*]—twelve thousand dinars!

SLAVE TRADER: Twelve thousand dinars! Twelve thousand . . .

WINE MERCHANT: [*To the* SHOEMAKER.] Are you outbidding me? Then I'll say . . . thirteen thousand dinars!

SLAVE TRADER: Thirteen thousand dinars! Thirteen thousand . . .

[*An* UNKNOWN MAN *comes forward suddenly, forcing his way through the crowd.*]

UNKNOWN MAN: [*Shouting.*] Fifteen thousand dinars!

SHOEMAKER: Good heavens! Who can this man be?

WINE MERCHANT: A joker of your own ilk without doubt.

SHOEMAKER: And of your ilk too.

SLAVE TRADER: Fifteen thousand dinars! Fifteen thousand! Fifteen thousand!

SHOEMAKER: [*Shouting.*] Sixteen thousand dinars!

SLAVE TRADER: [*Shouting.*] Sixteen thousand dinars! Sixteen!

UNKNOWN MAN: Eighteen thousand dinars!

SHOEMAKER: [*To the* WINE MERCHANT.] In one fell swoop! This fellow's overdoing things!

SLAVE TRADER: Eighteen thousand dinars! Eighteen thousand!

WINE MERCHANT: [*Scrutinizing the* UNKNOWN MAN *closely.*] It seems to me I've seen this man somewhere. Yes, he's one of the well-to-do; he comes to my tavern from time to time and drinks a glass of wine before going up to that beautiful lady.

SHOEMAKER: [*Turning to her window.*] Look! There she is at the window!

Glittering in all her cheap finery as though she were some sugar doll!
[*Shouts to her.*] You pretty one up in your heights, are you too not a
loyal citizen?

LADY: Shut up, you Shoemaker! I am not one to be made fun of in such
circumstances. By God, if you don't keep quiet I'll tell on you and
they'll put you into prison.

SLAVE TRADER: [*Calling out.*] Eighteen thousand dinars . . . at a sum of
eighteen thousand . . .

    [*A* LEADING CITIZEN *comes forward to the dais.*]

CITIZEN: [*Shouting.*] Nineteen thousand dinars!

UNKNOWN MAN: I bid twenty thousand dinars!

SLAVE TRADER: Twenty thousand dinars! Twenty thousand dinars! Twenty!

CITIZEN: I bid twenty-one thousand dinars!

UNKNOWN MAN: Twenty-two thousand dinars!

    [*A* SECOND LEADING CITIZEN *comes forward.*]

2ND CITIZEN: Twenty-three thousand dinars!

SLAVE TRADER: Twenty-three! Twenty-three!

UNKNOWN MAN: Twenty-five!

SLAVE TRADER: Twenty-five thousand dinars! Twenty-five!

    [*A* THIRD LEADING CITIZEN *comes forward.*]

3RD CITIZEN: Twenty-six!

SLAVE TRADER: [*Shouting.*] Twenty-six thousand dinars! Twenty-six!

UNKNOWN MAN: Twenty-eight!

SLAVE TRADER: [*Shouting.*] Twenty-eight! Twenty-eight thousand dinars!

3RD CITIZEN: Twenty-nine!

SHOEMAKER: [*Whispering to the* WINE MERCHANT.] Are these people really
serious about all this?

WINE MERCHANT: It seems so.

SLAVE TRADER: Twenty-nine . . . twenty-nine thousand dinars! Twenty-
nine!

UNKNOWN MAN: [*Shouting.*] Thirty! I bid thirty thousand dinars!

SLAVE TRADER: Thirty! At a sum of thirty! Thirty thousand dinars!

SHOEMAKER: [*Whispering.*] Thirty thousand dinars to be thrown into the
sea! What a madman!

SLAVE TRADER: [*Shouting at the top of his voice.*] Thirty thousand dinars!
Thirty! Any better bid? No one? No one bids more than thirty thousand
dinars? Is this all I'm offered as a price for our great Sultan?

SULTAN: [*To the* VIZIER.] So this is the height of noble, patriotic, appreciation!

VIZIER: Your Majesty, those present bidding here are mostly the miserly
merchants and well-to-do, those whose nature is niggardly, whose one
desire is profit, and who begrudge spending money for the sake of a
lofty purpose.

SLAVE TRADER: [*Shouting.*] Thirty thousand dinars! Once again I say: Who
bids more? No one? No? No? [*The* SLAVE TRADER *exchanges glances
with the* VIZIER, *then announces.*] I shall count up to three: One—
two—three! That's it! The final price is thirty thousand dinars. [*Cheering from the crowd.*]

WINE MERCHANT: [*To the* SHOEMAKER.] He's a client of mine, the man who won the auction.

SLAVE TRADER: Come forward the winner! Accept congratulations for your good luck!

[*The crowds cheer him.*]

VIZIER: I congratulate you, good citizen, and salute you.

[*Cheering from the crowd.*]

SLAVE TRADER: [*Shouting.*] Silence! Silence!

VIZIER: [*Continuing what he has to say.*] I salute you, good citizen, in the name of the fatherland and in the name of this loyal and upright people from whom you have your origins, for buying and ransoming the freedom of our great Sultan. This sublime deed of yours will be inscribed for evermore in the pages of the history of this noble people.

[*Cheering from the crowd.*]

SLAVE TRADER: [*Shouting.*] Silence! [*Turns to the* UNKNOWN MAN.] O good citizen, the sum is ready, is it not?

UNKNOWN MAN: Certainly—the sacks of gold are but a few paces away.

SLAVE TRADER: Good. Wait, then, for the venerable Chief Cadi to give his orders.

CADI: The question is decided. The judgement of the law has been carried out. The problem has been solved. Approach, good citizen. Are you able to sign your name?

UNKNOWN MAN: Yes, milord Cadi.

CADI: Sign, then, on these deeds.

UNKNOWN MAN: I hear and obey, milord Cadi.

CADI: [*Presenting him with a document.*] Here—sign here.

UNKNOWN MAN: [*Reading before signing.*] What's this? And that?

CADI: This is the contract of sale.

UNKNOWN MAN: Yes, I'll sign. [*He signs the document.*]

CADI: And this too. [*He presents him with the second document.*]

UNKNOWN MAN: This? What's this?

CADI: This is the deed of manumission.

UNKNOWN MAN: [*Taking a step backwards.*] I'm sorry.

CADI: [*Taken unawares.*] What are you saying?

UNKNOWN MAN: I can't sign this deed.

CADI: Why not? What's this you're saying?

UNKNOWN MAN: I'm saying it's not within my power.

CADI: What's not within your power?

UNKNOWN MAN: To sign the deed of manumission.

CADI: [*In a daze.*] It's not within your power to sign?

UNKNOWN MAN: No, it's not within my power or authority.

CADI: What's the meaning of this? What do you mean by this? You're undoubtedly mad. It's your bounden duty to sign the deed of manumission. That's the condition—the basic condition for the whole of these proceedings.

UNKNOWN MAN: I much regret that I am in no position to do this. This is beyond me, is outside the limits of my authority.

VIZIER: What's this man saying?

CADI: I don't understand.

VIZIER: [*To the* UNKNOWN MAN.] Why do you refuse to sign the deed of manumission?

UNKNOWN MAN: Because I have not been given permission to do so.

VIZIER: Have not been given permission?

UNKNOWN MAN: [*Confirming what he has to say with nods of the head.*] I have not been given permission, having been empowered only in respect of the bidding and the contract of sale. Outside this sphere I have no authorization.

CADI: Authorization? Authorization from whom?

UNKNOWN MAN: From the person who appointed me to act for him.

CADI: You are the agent for another person?

UNKNOWN MAN: Yes, milord Cadi.

CADI: Who is this person?

UNKNOWN MAN: I can't say.

CADI: But you must say.

UNKNOWN MAN: No! No, I can't.

VIZIER: You are absolutely required to tell us the person who appointed you to act for him in signing the deed of sale.

UNKNOWN MAN: I cannot divulge his name.

VIZIER: Why?

UNKNOWN MAN: Because I swore an irrevocable oath that I would keep his name a secret.

VIZIER: And why should the person who appointed you be so careful about his name remaining secret?

UNKNOWN MAN: I don't know.

VIZIER: He obviously has a lot of money seeing that he is able to spend this vast sum all at once.

UNKNOWN MAN: These thirty thousand dinars are his whole life's savings.

VIZIER: And he empowered you to put them all into this auction?

UNKNOWN MAN: Yes.

VIZIER: That's the very acme of generosity, the height of noble feeling . . . but why hide his name? Is it modesty? Is it an urgent wish that his bounty should remain hidden and his good deed unknown?

UNKNOWN MAN: Perhaps.

CADI: In such an event he should have given permission to his agent to sign the manumission deed as well.

UNKNOWN MAN: No, he commissioned me to sign only the contract of sale.

CADI: This is evidence of evil intent.

VIZIER: Truly!

SULTAN: [*In a sarcastic tone.*] It seems that things have become complicated.

CADI: A little, Your Majesty.

VIZIER: This man must speak, otherwise I'll force him to talk.

CADI: Gently, O Vizier, gently. He will talk of his own accord and will answer my questions in friendly fashion. Listen, good man—this person who appointed you, what things does he make in order to earn his living?

UNKNOWN MAN: He makes nothing.

CADI: Has he no trade?

UNKNOWN MAN: They claim he has.

CADI: They claim he has a trade but he does not make anything.

UNKNOWN MAN: That's so.

CADI: Then he's an employee.

UNKNOWN MAN: No.

CADI: He's rich?

UNKNOWN MAN: Fairly so.

CADI: And you're in charge of directing his affairs?

UNKNOWN MAN: That's about it.

CADI: Is he one of the notables?

UNKNOWN MAN: Better than that.

CADI: How's that?

UNKNOWN MAN: The notables visit him but he is unaffected by their visits.

CADI: He's a vizier then?

UNKNOWN MAN: No.

CADI: Has he influence?

UNKNOWN MAN: Yes, on his acquaintances.

CADI: Has he many acquaintances?

UNKNOWN MAN: Yes—many.

CADI: [*Thinking in silence as he passes his fingers through his beard.*] Yes. Yes.

SULTAN: Well finally, O Cadi—have you found a solution to these riddles? Or shall we now spend our time in games of riddles and conundrums?

VIZIER: [*His patience exhausted.*] We must have resort to the use of force, Your Majesty. There is no other choice open to us. That person, cloaked in secrets and concealing his name, who storms into this auction like this must inevitably be planning some suspiciously dangerous plan of action. With your permission, Your Majesty, I shall act in the matter. [*Calling to the* GUARDS.] Take this man off and torture him till he reveals the name of the person who appointed him and connived with him.

UNKNOWN MAN: [*Shouting.*] No! No! No! Don't send me to be tortured! Please! Don't torture me, I implore you!

VIZIER: Then talk!

UNKNOWN MAN: I swore not to.

VIZIER: [*To the* GUARDS.] Take him away!

[*The* GUARDS *surround him.*]

UNKNOWN MAN: No! No! No!

[*The door of the* LADY's *house is opened. She appears and approaches the dais, followed by her* MAID *and slave-girls carrying sacks.*]

LADY: Leave him! Leave him! It is I who appointed him and here are your sacks of gold—full thirty thousand dinars in cash!

[*Commotion among the crowds.*]

SLAVE TRADER: [*Shouting.*] Be quiet! Silence!

VIZIER: Who's this woman?

THE CROWDS: [*Shouting.*] The whore whose house is before us.

VIZIER: Whore!

CROWDS: Yes, a whore well known in the district.

SULTAN: Bravo! Bravo! The crowning touch!

VIZIER: You, O woman, are you she who . . .

LADY: Yes, I am the person who authorized this man to take part in the auction on my account. [*Turning to the* UNKNOWN MAN.] Is that not so?

UNKNOWN MAN: That's the truth, milady.

VIZIER: You? You dare to buy His Majesty?

LADY: And why not? Am I not a citizen and do I not have money? Why then should I not have exactly the same rights as the others?

CADI: Yes, you have this right. The law applies to all. You must also, however, make yourself acquainted with the conditions of this sale.

LADY: That's natural. I know it's a sale.

CADI: A sale with a particular characteristic.

LADY: A sale by public auction.

CADI: Yes, but . . .

VIZIER: Before everything else it's a patriotic action. You are a citizen and I would think you are concerned with the well-being of the fatherland.

LADY: Without doubt.

VIZIER: Then sign this deed.

LADY: What does this deed contain?

VIZIER: Manumission.

LADY: What does that mean.

VIZIER: Don't you know the meaning of manumission?

LADY: Does it mean giving up what I am in possession of?

VIZIER: Yes.

LADY: Giving up the chattel I bought at the auction?

VIZIER: That's it.

LADY: No, I don't want to give it up.

SULTAN: That's just fine!

VIZIER: You shall give it up, woman!

LADY: No.

VIZIER: Don't force me to be tough. You know that I can force you.

LADY: By what means?

VIZIER: [*Pointing to his sword.*] By this.

SULTAN: Resort to the sword now? The time has passed.

VIZIER: She must yield.

LADY: I do yield, oh Vizier—I yield to the law. Is it not in pursuance of the law that I have signed the contract of sale with the State? Is this law therefore respected or not?

SULTAN: Reply, O Chief Cadi.

CADI: Truly, woman, you have signed a contract of sale but it is a conditional contract.

LADY: Meaning?

CADI: Meaning that it's a sale dependent upon a condition.

LADY: What condition?

CADI: Manumission—otherwise the sale itself becomes null and void.

LADY: You mean, O Cadi, that in order for the sale to become valid I must sign the manumission?

CADI: Yes.

LADY: And you likewise mean that I must sign the manumission so that the purchase may become effective?

CADI: Exactly.

LADY: But, milord Cadi, what is a purchase? Is it not owning a thing in return for a price?

CADI: That is so.

LADY: And what is manumission? Is it not the opposite of possession? Is it not yielding up possession?

CADI: Yes.

LADY: Then, O Cadi, you make manumission a condition of possession, that is to say that in order validly to possess the thing sold, the purchaser must yield up that very thing.

CADI: What? What?

LADY: You're saying, in other words, in order to possess something you must yield it up.

CADI: What are you saying? In order to possess you must yield up?

LADY: Or, if you like, in order to possess you must not possess.

CADI: What is this talk?

LADY: This is your condition: in order to buy you must manumit; in order for me to possess I must not possess. Do you find this reasonable?

SULTAN: She is right—neither common sense nor logic can accept this.

CADI: Who taught you this, woman? There is certainly someone learned in the law, some knowing, impudent debauchee who has taught her the things she is saying.

SULTAN: What does it matter? That changes nothing. This is *your* law, O Cadi. Now, you've seen for yourself! With the law there is always some argument that clashes with some other argument, and none is devoid of sense and logic.

CADI: But this is picking holes. This is sophistry. What this woman is saying is mere sophistry.

SULTAN: It's your condition that's sophistry. Selling is selling—that's self-evident. As for the rest, it is binding on no one.

CADI: Yes, Your Majesty. However, this woman took part in the auction being aware of the nature of it and knowing full well the whys and wherefores of it; for her to behave after that in this way is nothing but trickery, deceit, and double-dealing.

SULTAN: If you now want to give her a lesson in morals, that's your affair. As for the law, it no longer has a leg to stand on and you should desist from talking in its name.

CADI: Rather it is my duty, Your Majesty, to protect the law from such creatures who ridicule and make fun of it.

LADY: I would ask you, O Cadi, not to insult me.

CADI: And you, woman, should be ashamed of yourself—aren't you embarrassed at this behaviour of yours?

LADY: Embarrassed and ashamed? Why? Because I bought something the State was selling? Because I refused to be robbed of the thing I bought, the thing I'd paid such a high price for? Here are the sacks of gold, count out what is owing to you and take it!

CADI: I refuse your money, and I thus invalidate this contract.

LADY: For what reason do you invalidate it?

CADI: Because you're a woman of bad reputation and wicked conduct. This money may well have been earned through immorality, so how can it be accepted as money to be paid to the Exchequer and the State?

LADY: This same money of mine has in fact been accepted as payment for dues and taxes, and are not dues and taxes paid to the Exchequer and the State? If that is your opinion, O Cadi, then I shall not pay a single tax to the State from now on.

SULTAN: Accept her money, O Cadi: it's a lot easier and simpler.

CADI: Then you insist on the stand you've taken, woman?

LADY: Certainly. I am not joking with these sacks of gold. I am paying in order to buy and I buy in order to possess. The law gives me this right. A sale is a sale. Possession is possession. Take your due and hand me over what is mine!

VIZIER: How can you want us to hand over to you the Sultan who rules this land, O woman?

LADY: Why then have you put the Sultan up for sale?

SULTAN: What she says is logical. What a woman!

LADY: I shall reply, for the reply is simple. You put him up for sale so that one of the people might buy him. Now I have bought him, having been the highest bidder at the auction—in public, in front of everyone. Here is the required price and all that remains for you to do is to hand over to me the goods purchased.

SULTAN: The goods?

LADY: Yes, and I demand that they be delivered to the house.

SULTAN: Which house?

LADY: My house of course—this house opposite.

SULTAN: [*To the* CADI.] Do you hear?

CADI: There is no longer any use or point in arguing with a woman of this sort. Your Majesty, I wash my hands of it.

SULTAN: What an excellent solution, Chief Cadi! You land me in this mire and then wash your hands of it.

CADI: I admit my failure—I didn't know I'd be facing this sort of a person.

SULTAN: And then?

CADI: Punish me, Your Majesty. I deserve the most terrible punishment for my bad advice and lack of foresight. Order that my head be cut off!

SULTAN: What's the point of cutting off your head? That head of yours on your shoulders cast me into this plight—will your decapitated head get me out of it?

VIZIER: Leave the matter to me, Your Majesty! I now see clearly what must be done. [*He draws his sword.*]

SULTAN: No!

VIZIER: But, Your Majesty . . .

SULTAN: I said no. Sheathe your sword!

VIZIER: Listen to me for a moment, Your Majesty.

SULTAN: Sheathe your sword! We have accepted this situation, so let's proceed.

VIZIER: Your Majesty, seeing that the Cadi has failed and is at a loss, let us go back to our own methods.

SULTAN: No, I shall not go back.

VIZIER: By the sword everything is easily accomplished and is solved in the twinkling of an eye.

SULTAN: No, I have chosen the law and I shall continue on that path whatever obstacles I may encounter.

VIZIER: The law?

SULTAN: Yes, and you yourself said so a while ago and expressed it in beautiful terms: 'The Sultan has chosen to submit to the law just like the lowliest individual amongst his subjects.' These fine words deserve that every effort be expended in implementing them.

VIZIER: Do you think, Your Majesty, that the lowliest individual amongst your subjects would agree to accept this situation? Here are the people standing before us; if you will permit me I shall ask them and seek their decision. Do you give me permission?

SULTAN: Do so and show me!

VIZIER: [Addressing the crowd.] O people! You see how this impudent woman treats your august Sultan, are you in agreement with what she has done?

THE PEOPLE: [Shouting.] No!

VIZIER: Are you happy with her insulting behaviour towards our illustrious ruler?

THE PEOPLE: No!

VIZIER: Do you consider it merits punishment?

THE PEOPLE: [Shouting.] Yes!

VIZIER: What is the appropriate punishment for her?

THE PEOPLE: [Shouting.] Death!

VIZIER: [Turning to the SULTAN.] You see, Your Majesty—the people have given their verdict.

LADY: [Turning to THE PEOPLE.] Death for me? Why, O people, do you condemn me to death? What offence have I committed? Is buying an affront and a crime? Have I stolen this money? It is my life's savings. Am I grabbing and making off by force with the thing offered for sale? I have bought it with my own money at a public auction before your very eyes. For what offence do you seek to spill the blood of a weak woman who has bought something at an auction?

VOICES: [Rising from amidst the crowd.] Death to the whore!

OTHER VOICES: [From amongst the crowd.] No, don't kill her!

SULTAN: [To the Vizier.] Do you see?

VIZIER: [To the people.] O people, do you consider that the judgement against her should be put into effect?

VOICES: [Shouting.] Yes!

OTHER VOICES: [Shouting.] No!

SULTAN: Opinions are divided, Vizier.

VIZIER: But the majority, Your Majesty, are on the side of death.

SULTAN: For me that is no justification for killing this woman. You are wanting the excuse of a semi-legal justification for employing the sword.

VIZIER: The death of this woman is essential for getting us out of this predicament.

SULTAN: We now need a lifeless corpse to save us?

VIZIER: Yes, Your Majesty.

SULTAN: Once again I am forced to choose between the mire and blood.

VIZIER: We can no longer force a way out for ourselves other than by the sword.

SULTAN: He who proceeds forwards along a straight line always finds a way out.

VIZIER: Your Majesty means . . .

SULTAN: I mean that there is no retreating, no turning back—do you understand?

VIZIER: I understand, Your Majesty. You wish to go on complying with the law.

SULTAN: Just so, I shall not swerve from what I have chosen, I shall not go back on what I have decided.

VIZIER: And how shall we go on complying with the law with which the Cadi himself has announced his defeat and inability to cope?

SULTAN: He is free to announce his defeat. As for me, I shall not retreat, so let us proceed along the road to its end.

VIZIER: And this woman who blocks the road for us?

SULTAN: Leave her to me. [*He turns to the woman.*] Come here, woman! Approach! Another step—here in front of me! I want to put a few questions to you. Do you permit me?

LADY: I hear and obey, Your Majesty.

SULTAN: First and foremost—who am I?

LADY: Who are you?

SULTAN: Yes, who am I?

LADY: You are the Sultan?

SULTAN: You admit I'm the Sultan?

LADY: Naturally.

SULTAN: Good—and what's the Sultan's job?

LADY: His job is to rule.

SULTAN: You agree that he rules?

LADY: Certainly.

SULTAN: Very good. In as much as you acknowledge all this, how can you demand that the Sultan be handed over to you?

LADY: Because he has become mine by right.

SULTAN: I do not dispute your right. However, I merely wonder at the possibility of your implementing this right. In as much as I am a sultan who rules, how can I carry out the functions of my office if I am handed over to you in your house?

LADY: Nothing is easier or simpler. You are a sultan during the day, therefore I shall lend you to the State for the whole of the day, and in the evening you will return to my house.

SULTAN: I'm afraid you don't understand my work correctly. A sultan is not the owner of a shop who keeps it open during the day and then locks it up at night. He is at the beck and call of the State at any moment. There are urgent and important questions that often require him to hold talks with his men of State in the middle of the night.

LADY: This too is an easy matter, for in my house there is a quiet secluded room where you can work with your men of State.

SULTAN: Do you regard such a set-up as acceptable?

LADY: More than acceptable, I regard it as marvellous!

SULTAN: It is indeed marvellous—a sultan who directs affairs of State from the house of a woman of whom it is said that she . . . please forgive me . . . my apologies.

LADY: Say it! Go on! The word no longer wounds me because of the many torments I have suffered—I have become immune. However, I assure you, O Sultan, that you will experience greater joy in my house than you do in yours.

SULTAN: Possibly, except that a ruler is not proficient in carrying out the functions of government when he does so from the houses of others.

LADY: That is if the ruler is free.

SULTAN: You have scored—I am not free. [*He lowers his head. A moment's silence.*]

LADY: What I admire in you, O Sultan, is your composed and calm attitude in the face of this catastrophe.

SULTAN: [*Raising his head.*] You are admitting then that it is a catastrophe?

LADY: It's self-evident—a great Sultan like you being badly treated in this way.

SULTAN: And is anyone but you badly treating me?

LADY: How right you are! What pride and joy it is to me to hear this from the mouth of a great sultan! It's an honour which merits the payment of all the world's gold. No one in the city after today will dare slight me, for I am treating sultans badly!

VIZIER: [*In a rage.*] Enough, woman! Enough! This is unbearable. She has overstepped all limits of decency. The head of this mischievous and shameless woman must fall!

SULTAN: Calm yourself!

LADY: Yes, calm yourself, O Vizier—and don't interfere in what does not concern you.

VIZIER: How can all this be borne? Patience, Lord! Patience, Lord!

LADY: Yes, have patience, O Vizier, and let the Sultan and me talk. This matter concerns us alone.

SULTAN: That's true.

LADY: Where did we get to, Your Majesty?

SULTAN: I no longer know—it was you who were talking.

LADY: Oh yes, I remember now—we got to where I was saying that it was an honour . . .

SULTAN: For you to treat me badly.

LADY: Rather that I should have the good fortune of enjoying talking to you. In fact, Your Majesty, it's the first time I have seen you at close quarters. People have talked about you so much but I didn't know you were so charming.

SULTAN: Thank you.

LADY: Truly, it's as though we'd been friends for a long time.

SULTAN: Is it your custom to subject your friends to humiliation and ridicule in this manner?

LADY: Not at all—just the opposite.

SULTAN: Then why make an exception of me?

LADY: This in fact is what has begun to upset me. How I would like to bring happiness to your heart and show you reverence and respect! But how? How can I do that! What's the way to do it?

SULTAN: The way's easy.

LADY: By signing this manumission deed?

SULTAN: I would have thought so.

LADY: No, I don't want to let you go. I don't want to give you up. You belong to me. You're mine—mine.

SULTAN: I belong to you and to all the rest of the people.

LADY: I want you to be mine alone.

SULTAN: And my people?

LADY: Your people have not paid gold in order to acquire you.

SULTAN: That's right, but you must know that it's absolutely impossible for me to be yours alone and for me to remain thereafter a sultan. There is only one situation in which it is in order for me to be yours alone.

LADY: What's that?

SULTAN: That I should not be a sultan, that I should give up the throne and relinquish power.

LADY: No, I don't wish that for you—I wish you to remain a sultan.

SULTAN: In that event there must be sacrifice.

LADY: From my side?

SULTAN: Or from my own.

LADY: I should give you up?

SULTAN: Or I should give up the throne?

LADY: It's for me to choose?

SULTAN: Of course it's for you to choose, because all the cards are in your hands.

LADY: Have I all that importance, all that weight?

SULTAN: At this moment, yes.

LADY: This is wonderful!

SULTAN: Certainly.

LADY: Then I now hold all the cards in my hands?

SULTAN: Yes.

LADY: At my pleasure I keep the Sultan in power?

SULTAN: Yes.

LADY: And by a word from me the removal of the Sultan is accomplished?

SULTAN: Yes.

LADY: This is truly wonderful!

SULTAN: Without doubt.

LADY: And who has given me all this authority—money?

SULTAN: The law.

LADY: A word from my mouth can change your destiny and channel your life either to slavery and bondage, or to freedom and sovereignty.

SULTAN: And it is up to you to choose.

LADY: [*Thoughtfully.*] Between bondage that bestows you upon me, and between freedom which retains you for your throne and your people.

SULTAN: It is up to you to choose.

LADY: The choice is difficult.

SULTAN: I know.

LADY: It is painful to let you go, to lose you for ever; but it is also painful to see you lose your throne, for our country has never had the good fortune to have a sultan with such courage and sense of justice. No, do not give up the rule, do not relinquish the throne! I want you to remain a sultan.

SULTAN: And so?

LADY: I shall sign the deed.

SULTAN: The manumission deed?

LADY: Yes.

CADI: [*Hurrying to present the deed.*] Here is the deed.

LADY: I have only a final request.

SULTAN: What is it?

LADY: That you give this night to me, Your Majesty—a single night. Honour me by accepting my invitation and be my guest until daybreak. And when the Muezzin gives the call to dawn prayers from this minaret here, I shall sign the deed of manumission and Your Majesty will be free.

CADI: If the Muezzin does give the call to dawn prayers!

LADY: Yes. Is this too much—that I buy with these sacks of gold not the Sultan himself but a single night with him as my guest?

SULTAN: I accept.

VIZIER: But, Your Majesty, who will guarantee that this promise will be kept by such a woman?

SULTAN: I shall. I am the guarantor, I trust what she says.

CADI: Do you take an oath on what you say, woman?

LADY: Yes, I swear. I swear a triple oath by Almighty God. I shall sign the deed of manumission when the Muezzin gives the call to dawn prayers from on top of this minaret.

CADI: I bear witness before God to that. All of us here are witnesses.

SULTAN: As for me, I believe her without an oath.

LADY: And now, O noble Sultan, will you be so good as to honour my humble house with your gracious presence?

SULTAN: With great pleasure!

[*The* SULTAN *rises and follows the* LADY *into her house. Music.*]

CURTAIN

Act Three

[*The same square. One side of the mosque with its minaret is in view, also a side of the* LADY's *house, showing a portion of the room with the window overlooking the square. The time is night. Among the throng are the* VIZIER, *the* SHOEMAKER, *and the* WINE MERCHANT.]

VIZIER: [*In the square, shouting to the* GUARDS.] What are all these crowds waiting for in the middle of the night? Turn the people away! Let everyone go to his home, to his bed!

GUARDS: [*Turning away the crowds.*] To your homes! To your houses!

THE CROWDS: [*Grumbling.*] No! No!

SHOEMAKER: [*Shouting.*] I want to stay here.

WINE MERCHANT: And I too shan't budge from here.

VIZIER: [*To the* GUARDS.] What are they saying?

GUARDS: They refuse to go.

VIZIER: [*Shouting.*] Refuse? What's this nonsense? Make them!

GUARDS: [*Forcefully.*] Everyone to his home! Everyone to his house! Get along! Get along!

SHOEMAKER: I'm already at home. This is my shop.

WINE MERCHANT: I too have my tavern right here before you.

GUARDS: Will you not obey orders? Get going! Get going! [*They push the* WINE MERCHANT *and the* SHOEMAKER.]

SHOEMAKER: There's no reason for violence—please.

WINE MERCHANT: Don't push me about like this!

VIZIER: [*To the* GUARDS.] Bring along those two trouble-makers!
[*The* GUARDS *seize hold of the* SHOEMAKER *and the* WINE MERCHANT *and bring them before the* VIZIER.]

SHOEMAKER: By God, I haven't done anything, milord Vizier.

VIZIER: Why do you refuse to go home?

SHOEMAKER: I don't want to go to bed. I have a strong desire to stay here, milord Vizier—in order to watch.

VIZIER: To watch what?

SHOEMAKER: To watch Our Majesty the Sultan leaving this house.

WINE MERCHANT: I too, milord Vizier—let me watch it.

VIZIER: Really, what affrontery? Today everyone's affrontery has reached the bounds of impudence. Even you and your comrade have the nerve to talk in such terms.

WINE MERCHANT: It's not impudence, milord Vizier, it's a request.

VIZIER: A request?

SHOEMAKER: Yes, milord Vizier, we request that you give us permission to watch.

VIZIER: What insolence! And what have you to do with this matter?

SHOEMAKER: Are we not good citizens? The fate of our Sultan inevitably concerns us.

VIZIER: This does not give you both the right to disobey orders.

SHOEMAKER: We are not disobeying, we are requesting. How can we sleep a wink tonight with the fate of our Sultan in the balance?

VIZIER: In the balance?

SHOEMAKER: Yes, milord—the balance of capricious whims.

VIZIER: What do you mean?

SHOEMAKER: I mean that the outcome is not reassuring.

VIZIER: Why do you think so?

SHOEMAKER: With such a woman one can be certain of nothing.

WINE MERCHANT: We have made a bet between ourselves. He says this woman will break her promise, while I say she will honour it.

VIZIER: A fine thing, indeed—of an important event like this you make a game of having bets!

WINE MERCHANT: We are not alone in this, milord Vizier. Many such as we among these crowds are tonight making bets among themselves. Even the Muezzin and the Executioner have made a bet.

VIZIER: The Executioner: where is the Executioner?

WINE MERCHANT: [*Pointing.*] Over there, milord. He's trying to hide among the people.

VIZIER: [*To the* GUARDS.] Bring him over here.

[*The* GUARDS *bring the* EXECUTIONER *to the* VIZIER.]

EXECUTIONER: [*Frightened.*] It's not my fault, milord Vizier. It's the Muezzin's mistake. It's he who's responsible, it's he who did not give the call to the dawn prayers.

VIZIER: Dawn? What dawn? We're no longer talking about dawn prayers, you idiot. [*The* WINE MERCHANT *and the* SHOEMAKER *laugh.*] Do you dare to laugh in my presence? Get out of my sight! Out! [*The* WINE MERCHANT *and the* SHOEMAKER *take to their heels.*] And now, Executioner—are you busy with bets?

EXECUTIONER: Bets? Who said so, milord?

VIZIER: I want a straight answer to my question.

EXECUTIONER: But, milord, I . . .

VIZIER: Don't be frightened—tell me.

EXECUTIONER: But this bet, milord . . .

VIZIER: I know, I know, and I shall not punish you. Answer this question frankly: will this woman in your opinion break her promise or will she honour it?

EXECUTIONER: But, milord Vizier, I . . .

VIZIER: I told you not to be frightened but to express your opinion without constraint. That's an order and you must obey it.

EXECUTIONER: Your order must be obeyed, milord—in truth I have no trust in this woman.

VIZIER: Why?

EXECUTIONER: Because she's a liar, a cheat, and a swindler!

VIZIER: Do you know her?

EXECUTIONER: I got to know some of her wiles when I was here that day waiting for the dawn in order to carry out the sentence of execution on the slave trader.

VIZIER: A liar, a cheat, and a swindler?

EXECUTIONER: Yes.

VIZIER: And what does such a woman deserve?

EXECUTIONER: Punishment of course.

VIZIER: And what is the punishment you deem suitable for her if she has tricked and lied to our exalted Sultan?

EXECUTIONER: Death, without doubt!

VIZIER: Good. Then be prepared to carry out this sentence at dawn.

EXECUTIONER: [*As though talking to himself.*] Dawn? Yet again?

VIZIER: What are you saying?

EXECUTIONER: I am saying that at dawn I shall be ready to execute the order of milord Vizier.

VIZIER: Yes, if the Muezzin has given the call to the dawn prayer and our Sultan has not emerged from this house a free man . . .

EXECUTIONER: Then I cut off the head of this woman.

VIZIER: Yes, as punishment for the crime of . . .

EXECUTIONER: Lying and cheating.

VIZIER: No.

EXECUTIONER: [*Not understanding.*] No?

VIZIER: [*As though talking to himself.*] No, that is not enough—it is not a crime that merits death. This woman is liable to find some high-sounding phrases in law and logic to justify her action. No, there must be some terrible and serious crime which she will not be able to justify or defend herself against—a crime that will earn her the universal opprobrium of the whole people. We could for instance say she is a spy.

EXECUTIONER: A spy?

VIZIER: Yes, that she's working for the Mongols. Then the people in their entirety will rise up and demand her head.

EXECUTIONER: Yes, an appropriate punishment.

VIZIER: Is that not your opinion?

EXECUTIONER: And I shall raise my voice crying 'Death to the traitor!'

VIZIER: Your voice alone will not suffice. There must be other voices besides yours giving this cry.

EXECUTIONER: There will be other voices.

VIZIER: Do you know whose they'll be?

EXECUTIONER: It won't be difficult to find them.

VIZIER: Witnesses must be got ready.

EXECUTIONER: All that is easy, milord.

VIZIER: I think that such an arrangement can be successful. I'm relying on you if things go badly.

EXECUTIONER: I am your faithful servant, milord Vizier.

[*A part of the room in the* LADY'*s house is lit up.*]

VIZIER: Quiet! A light in the window! Let's move away a little.

[*While the room is lit up, the square becomes dark; the* LADY *appears and moves towards the sofa followed by the* SULTAN.

SULTAN: [*Sitting down.*] Your house is magnificent and your furnishings costly.

LADY: [*Sitting at his feet.*] Yes, I told you just now that my husband was a wealthy merchant who had taste and a passion for poetry and singing.

SULTAN: Were you one of his slave-girls?

LADY: Yes, he bought me when I was sixteen years of age, then gave me my freedom and married me several years before his death.

SULTAN: Your luck was better than mine. With you no one forgot to free you at the proper time.

LADY: My real good luck is your having honoured my house with your presence tonight.

SULTAN: Here I am in your house—what do you intend doing with me tonight?

LADY: Nothing except to allow you to relax a little.

SULTAN: Is that all?

LADY: Nothing more than that. Previously I said to you that at my house there is more joy than at yours. I have beautiful slave-girls who excel at dancing and singing and playing on every musical instrument. Be assured, you will not be bored here tonight.

SULTAN: Until dawn breaks?

LADY: Think not of the dawn now. The dawn is still far off.

SULTAN: I shall do all you demand until dawn breaks.

LADY: I shall ask nothing of you except to converse, to take food, and to listen to singing.

SULTAN: Nothing but that?

LADY: But do you want me to ask of you more than that?

SULTAN: I don't know—you know best.

LADY: Let us then start with conversation—tell me about yourself.

SULTAN: About myself?

LADY: Yes, your story—tell me the story of your life.

SULTAN: You want me to tell you stories?

LADY: Yes, in truth you must have a store of wonderfully entertaining stories.

SULTAN: It is *I* now who must tell stories!

LADY: And why not?

SULTAN: Truly that's how it should be, seeing that it is I who am in the position of Shahrazad![4] She too had to tell stories throughout the whole night, awaiting the dawn that would decide her fate.

LADY: [*Laughing.*] And I, then, am the dreadful, awe-inspiring Shahriyar?

SULTAN: Yes—isn't it extraordinary? Today everything is upside down.

LADY: No, you are always the Sultan. As for me, I am she who plays the role of Shahrazad, always seated at your feet.

SULTAN: A Shahrazad having her apprehensive Shahriyar[5] by the neck until the morning comes.

LADY: No, rather a Shahrazad who will bring joy and gladness to the heart of her sultan. You will see now how I shall deal with your anxiety and misgivings. [*She claps and soothing music issues forth from behind the screens.*]

SULTAN: [*After listening for a while.*] A delightful performance!

LADY: And I myself shall dance for you. [*She rises and dances.*]

SULTAN: [*After she has finished her dance.*] Delightful! It's all delightful! Do you do this every night?

LADY: No, Your Majesty. This is an exception. It's just for you, for I myself have not danced since being manumitted and married. On other nights it is the slave-girls who do the dancing and singing.

SULTAN: For your clients?

LADY: My guests, rather.

SULTAN: As you will—your guests. Doubtless these guests of yours pay you a high fee for all this. I now realize how it is you have such wealth.

LADY: My wealth I inherited from my husband. Sometimes I spend on these nights more than I get back.

SULTAN: Why? For nothing?

LADY: For the sake of art. I am a lover of art.

SULTAN: [*Sarcastically.*] Refined art to be sure!

LADY: You don't believe me. You don't take what I say seriously. So be it. Think as badly of me as you like—I am not in the habit of defending myself against other people's assumptions. In people's eyes I am a

---

4. The narrator of *The Thousand and One Nights* (in Volume 1).   5. The king to whom Shahrazad tells the stories.

woman who behaves badly, and I have reached the stage where I have accepted this judgement. I have found this convenient—it is no longer in my interests to correct people's opinion. When one has crossed the ultimate boundaries of wickedness one becomes free, and I am in need of my freedom.

SULTAN: You too?

LADY: Yes, in order to do what I enjoy.

SULTAN: And what do you enjoy?

LADY: The company of men.

SULTAN: Understood!

LADY: No, you understand wrongly. It's not as you think.

SULTAN: How is it then?

LADY: Do you want lies or the truth?

SULTAN: The truth of course.

LADY: You won't believe the truth, so what's the point of my telling it? A truth that people don't believe is a useless truth.

SULTAN: Say it in any case.

LADY: I shall say it purely to amuse you. I enjoy the company of men for their souls, not for their bodies. Do you understand?

SULTAN: No, not exactly.

LADY: I shall elucidate. When I was a young slave-girl of the same age as the slave-girls I have with me now, my master brought me up to love poetry and singing and playing on musical instruments. He used to make me attend his banquets and converse with his guests, who were poets and singers; they also included intellectuals and men of wit and charm. We would spend the night reciting poetry, singing and playing music and conversing, quoting and capping quotations from the master-pieces of literature, and laughing from the depths of our hearts. Those were wonderfully enjoyable nights, but they were also innocent and chaste. Please believe that. My master was a good man and knew no pleasure in life other than these nights—a pleasure without sin, without vulgarity. In this way did he bring me up and educate me. And when I later became his wife he did not wish to deprive me of the pleasure of those nights which used so to enchant me; he therefore allowed me to continue to attend, though from behind silken curtains. That's the whole story.

SULTAN: And after his death?

LADY: After his death I was unable to give up this practice, so I continued to invite my husband's guests. At first I would receive them screened behind the silken curtains, but when the people of the district began spreading gossip at seeing men nightly entering the house of a woman with no husband I found it pointless to continue to be screened behind the curtains. I said to myself: seeing that the people's verdict has pro-nounced me guilty, let me make myself the judge of my own behaviour.

SULTAN: It is truly extraordinary that your exterior should proclaim so loudly what is not to be found within; your shop window advertises goods that are not to be found inside.

LADY: It is for you to believe or not what I have said to you.

SULTAN: I prefer to believe—it is more conducive to peace of mind.

LADY: Be that as it may, I do not at all intend to change my life and habits. If the road I tread be filled with mire I shall continue to wade through it.

SULTAN: Mire! It's to be found on every road—be sure of that!

LADY: Now you remind me of what I did to you in front of the masses of people.

SULTAN: Truly you rolled me in it properly!

LADY: I was intentionally insolent to you, deliberately vulgar and impudent. Do you know why? Because I imagined you as being quite different. I imagined you as an arrogant sultan, strutting about haughtily and giving yourself airs—like most sultans. You could, in fact, well have been even more conceited and overbearing by reason of the wars you have waged and your victories. People always talk of that fabulous ruby which adorns your turban, that ruby that is without peer in the world, of which it is said that you seized it at sword-point from the head of the Mongol Chief. Yes, your deeds are wondrous and splendid. Thus the picture of you in my mind was synonymous with haughtiness, harshness, and cruelty. But as soon as you talked to me so pleasantly and modestly I was overcome by a certain bewilderment and confusion.

SULTAN: Don't be misled! I am not always so pleasant, nor so modest. There are times when I am more cruel and brutal than the worst of sultans.

LADY: I don't believe that.

SULTAN: That's because you've fallen under the influence of the present circumstances.

LADY: You mean that you are specially pleasant to me? This fills me with great pride, dear Majesty. But wait! Perhaps I have misunderstood. What is it that causes you to be so pleasant to me? Is it personal? Or is it the decision you await from me at daybreak?

SULTAN: I affect being pleasant with you, I put it on, in order to gain your sympathy—isn't that so?

LADY: And no sooner will you achieve your freedom than you'll revert to your true nature and will become the cruel Sultan who pursues revenge in order to atone to himself for his moments of humiliation—and then will come my hour of doom.

SULTAN: It would therefore be wise and far-sighted of you to keep me always in your grasp and power.

LADY: Is that so?

SULTAN: That is absolutely logical, seeing that you have your doubts.

LADY: Have I not the right to doubt?

SULTAN: I don't blame you if you do, for it is I who, quite simply and incautiously, have implanted in you the seeds of doubt by saying what I did about myself.

LADY: [*Regarding him searchingly.*] No.

SULTAN: No? Why?

LADY: I prefer to rely on the womanly instinct that is deep within me. It never deceives me.

SULTAN: And what does your womanly instinct tell you?

LADY: It tells me that you are not that type of man. You are different. I should have realized this from the moment I saw you renouncing the use of the sword.

SULTAN: If only you knew how easy things would have been had I used my sword!

LADY: Do you now regret it?

SULTAN: I am merely talking about how easy it would have been. However, the real victory is in solving the problem by sleight-of-hand.

LADY: And this is the path you are now pursuing?

SULTAN: Yes, but I am not confident about the result.

LADY: Let's suppose the result to be that your hopes are dashed—what will you do then?

SULTAN: I have already told you.

LADY: Give up your throne?

SULTAN: Yes.

LADY: No, I do not believe you would really do that. I'm not so simple or stupid as to believe that or to take it seriously. Even if you wanted to do it not a single person in the country would accept it, or would permit you to embark upon such an action. You would bear a heavy burden by accepting the easy solution and would revert to using the simple expedient.

SULTAN: It has never happened that I have taken a step backwards—not even in the field of battle. I admit that this is wrong from the military point of view, for there are circumstances that make retreat necessary. However, I have never done so. Perhaps luck was on my side; in any event I have adopted this bad practice.

LADY: You're amazing!

SULTAN: The truth is rather that I'm an unimaginative man.

LADY: You?

SULTAN: The proof is that were I possessed of imagination and had envisaged what awaited me at the end of such a road, I would have been stunned.

LADY: Nothing stuns you. You have composure, self-confidence, control over your actions, the ability to do what you want with meticulous precision and resoluteness. You are far from being weak or wily—you're frank, natural, and courageous. There's no more to say.

SULTAN: Are you flattering me? Who should be flattering whom? Once again the situations have been reversed.

LADY: Will you permit me, my dear Sultan?

SULTAN: To do what?

LADY: To ask you a personal question?

SULTAN: Personal? Is not all this that we are engaged in personal?

LADY: I want to ask you about—about your heart, about love.

SULTAN: Love? What love?

LADY: Love—for a woman?

SULTAN: Do you imagine I have the time to occupy myself with such things?

LADY: How strange! Has your heart never opened to love a woman?

SULTAN: Why have you opened your large eyes like this in astonishment? Is it such an important matter?

LADY: But you have definitely known many women?

SULTAN: Certainly—that is the nature of military life. The leader of an army, as you know, every night has some female prisoner, some captive, brought to him. Sometimes there are beautiful women among them. That's all there is to it.

LADY: And not a single particular woman succeeded in attracting your glances?

SULTAN: My glances? You should know that at the end of the day I returned always to my tent with eyes filled with the dust of battle.

LADY: And on the following day? Did you not retain a single memory of those beautiful women?

SULTAN: On the following day I would again mount my steed and think of something else.

LADY: But now you're the Sultan. You certainly have sufficient time for love.

SULTAN: Do you believe so?

LADY: What prevents you?

SULTAN: The problems of government. And this is one of them—this problem that has descended upon my head today so unexpectedly and put me in this fix. Do you consider that such a problem allows one to be in the mood for love?

LADY: [*Laughing.*] You're right!

SULTAN: You laugh!

LADY: Another question—the last, be sure of that! A very serious question this time, because it relates to me.

SULTAN: To you?

LADY: Yes. Let us assume that I have manumitted you at dawn—you will of course return to your palace.

SULTAN: Of course, I have business awaiting me there.

LADY: And I?

SULTAN: And what about you?

LADY: Will you not think about me after that?

SULTAN: I don't understand.

LADY: You really don't understand what I mean?

SULTAN: You know the language of women is too subtle for me, it is very often obscure.

LADY: You understand me only too well, for you are exceedingly intelligent and astute, and also very sensitive, despite appearances and the impression you like to give. In any case I shall explain my words—here is what I want to know: Will you forget me altogether and erase me from your memory directly you have left here?

SULTAN: I do not think it is possible to erase you altogether from my memory.

LADY: And will you retain a pleasant memory of me?

SULTAN: Certainly!

LADY: Is that all? Does everything for me end just like that?

SULTAN: Are we going over the same ground as before?

LADY: No, I merely wish to ask you: Is this night our last night together?

SULTAN: That's a question which it's difficult to answer.

LADY: Good! Don't answer it now!

[*The* MAIDSERVANT *appears.*]

MAID: Dinner is served, milady.

LADY: [*Rising to her feet.*] If Your Majesty pleases.

SULTAN: [*Rising to his feet.*] You are a model of kindness and hospitality.

LADY: Rather is it you who do me a kindness.

[*She leads him into another room to the accompaniment of music.
The light in the house is extinguished and a dim light comes on in
the square.*]

SHOEMAKER: [*To the* WINE MERCHANT *in a corner of the square.*] Look!
They've put out the light.

WINE MERCHANT: [*Looking towards the window.*] That's a good sign!

SHOEMAKER: How?

WINE MERCHANT: Putting out the light means going to bed!

SHOEMAKER: And so?

WINE MERCHANT: And so agreement is complete.

SHOEMAKER: Over what?

WINE MERCHANT: Over everything.

SHOEMAKER: You mean that she'll accept to give him up at dawn?

WINE MERCHANT: Yes.

SHOEMAKER: And so you win the bet.

WINE MERCHANT: Without the slightest doubt.

SHOEMAKER: You're over-optimistic, my friend, to think that such a woman
would easily accept throwing her money into the sea.

WINE MERCHANT: Who is to know? I say yes.

SHOEMAKER: And I say no.

WINE MERCHANT: Fine, let us await the dawn.

SHOEMAKER: What time is it now?

WINE MERCHANT: [*Looking at the sky.*] According to the stars it is now
approximately midnight.

SHOEMAKER: Dawn is still far-off and I am beginning to feel sleepy.

WINE MERCHANT: Go to bed!

SHOEMAKER: I? Out of the question! The whole city is staying up tonight,
so how can I be the only one to sleep? In fact I have more reason than
anybody to stay up until dawn in order to witness your defeat.

WINE MERCHANT: My defeat?

SHOEMAKER: Without the slightest doubt.

WINE MERCHANT: We shall see which of us turns out to be the loser.

SHOEMAKER: [*Turning to a corner of the square.*] Look! Over there!

WINE MERCHANT: What?

SHOEMAKER: [*Whispering.*] The Vizier and the Executioner. They look as
though they're hatching some plot.

WINE MERCHANT: Quiet!

[*The* VIZIER *walks up and down as he questions the* EXECUTIONER.]

VIZIER: What exactly did you hear from the guards?

EXECUTIONER: I heard them say, milord Vizier, that it was impossible to
quell the people and force them to go to bed tonight. The crowds are
still standing or squatting in the lanes and alleyways and all are whispering together and gossiping.

VIZIER: Gossiping?

EXECUTIONER: Yes.

VIZIER: And what's all this whispering and gossiping about?

EXECUTIONER: About the business of the Sultan of course and what he's doing tonight in this house.

VIZIER: And what, in your opinion, might he be doing in this house?

EXECUTIONER: Are you asking me, milord Vizier?

VIZIER: Yes, I'm asking you. Are you not one of the people, and does not your opinion represent public opinion? Answer me! What do you imagine the Sultan is doing in this house?

EXECUTIONER: Actually . . . well he's certainly not performing his prayers there!

VIZIER: Are you making fun? Are you being insolent?

EXECUTIONER: Pardon, milord Vizier. I merely wanted to say that this house is not . . . is no saintly place.

VIZIER: Then the gossip in the city is along these lines—that the Sultan is spending the night in a . . .

EXECUTIONER: A brothel!

VIZIER: What are you saying?

EXECUTIONER: That's what they are saying, milord. I am reporting what I heard.

VIZIER: Is this all that people are mentioning about this important matter? They are forgetting the noble purport, the lofty aim, the sublime concept, the patriotic objective! Even you, as I see it, have forgotten all this.

EXECUTIONER: No, milord Vizier, I have forgotten nothing.

VIZIER: We shall see. Tell me then why the Sultan accepted to enter this house.

EXECUTIONER: In order to . . . to gratify the whore.

VIZIER: Is that all it's about? What a shallow way of looking at things!

EXECUTIONER: Milord Vizier, I was present and I saw and heard everything from the beginning.

VIZIER: And you didn't understand any of it, except for the insignificant and degrading side of the issue. Are there many like you among the people?

EXECUTIONER: Like me they were all present.

VIZIER: And they all made of it what you did as far as I can see. Their talk does not deal with the profound reason, the exalted meaning of all that has happened. Their talk deals merely with what you yourself say: the Sultan is spending the night in a brothel! What a catastrophe! It's this that's the real catastrophe!

[*The* CHIEF CADI *appears.*]

CADI: I haven't slept tonight.

VIZIER: You too?

CADI: Why I too?

VIZIER: The whole of the rest of the city hasn't slept tonight.

CADI: I know that.

VIZIER: And everyone's whispering and gossiping.

CADI: I know that as well.

VIZIER: And do you know what they're saying in the city?

CADI: The worst possible things. The point of interest and excitement for the people is the scandalous side of the affair.

VIZIER: Unfortunately so.

CADI: It's my fault.

VIZIER: And mine too. I should have been more resolute in the defence of my opinion.

CADI: But, on the other hand, how could we have anticipated that woman's intervention?

VIZIER: We should have anticipated everything.

CADI: You're right.

VIZIER: Now the die is cast and we have no power to do anything.

CADI: Yet it is in our power to snatch the Sultan away from this house.

VIZIER: We must wait for the dawn.

CADI: No, now . . . at once!

VIZIER: But the dawn is still far off.

CADI: It must be made to come now—at once!

VIZIER: Who? What?

CADI: The dawn!

VIZIER: My apologies—I don't understand.

CADI: You will shortly. Where's the Muezzin of this mosque?

VIZIER: [Turning towards the EXECUTIONER.] The Executioner must know.

EXECUTIONER: He's over there, among the crowds.

CADI: Go and bring him to me.

[The EXECUTIONER returns, and after some whispered conversation hurries off obediently.]

VIZIER: [To the CADI.] It seems you have some plan or other?

CADI: Yes.

VIZIER: May I know it?

CADI: Shortly.

[The MUEZZIN appears, panting.]

MUEZZIN: Here I am, milord Cadi.

CADI: Come close! I want to talk to you regarding the dawn.

MUEZZIN: The dawn? Be sure, milord Cadi, that I have committed no wrong. This Executioner is accusing me falsely of . . .

CADI: Listen to me well.

MUEZZIN: I swear to you, milord Cadi, that on that day . . .

CADI: Will you stop this nonsensical chattering! I told you to listen to me well. I want you to carry out what I am going to say to the letter. Do you understand?

MUEZZIN: Yes.

CADI: Go and climb up into your minaret and give the call to the dawn prayer.

MUEZZIN: When?

CADI: Now!

MUEZZIN: [In surprise.] Now?

CADI: Yes, immediately.

MUEZZIN: The dawn prayer?

CADI: Yes, the dawn prayer. Go and give the call to the dawn prayer. Is what I say clear or not?

MUEZZIN: It's clear, but it's now approximately . . . midnight.

CADI: Let it be!

MUEZZIN: Dawn at midnight?

CADI: Yes! Hurry!

MUEZZIN: Isn't this just a little . . . premature?

CADI: No.

MUEZZIN: [*Whispering to himself.*] I'm at a loss about this dawn—sometimes I'm asked to put it back and sometimes I'm asked to bring it forward.

CADI: What are you saying?

MUEZZIN: Nothing, milord Cadi. I shall go at once to carry out your order.

CADI: Listen! Make sure you tell no one that it was the Cadi who gave you this order.

MUEZZIN: Meaning, milord?

CADI: Meaning that it's you on your own initiative who have acted thus.

MUEZZIN: On my own initiative? I go up into the minaret to give the call to dawn prayers at midnight? Anyone behaving like that *must* be a crazy idiot.

CADI: Leave to me the task of explaining your behaviour at the appropriate time.

MUEZZIN: But, milord, by this action I expose myself to the ridicule of the masses and they'll ask that I be punished.

CADI: And whom will you appear before to be tried? Won't it be before me, the Chief Cadi?

MUEZZIN: And if you disown and abandon me?

CADI: Do not be afraid, that will never happen.

MUEZZIN: And how can I be sure?

CADI: I promise you—have you no faith in my promise?

MUEZZIN: [*Whispering to himself.*] The promises tonight are many—and not a soul is sure of anything.

CADI: What are you saying?

MUEZZIN: Nothing. I'm just asking myself—why should I expose myself to all this danger?

CADI: It's a service you're rendering the State.

MUEZZIN: [*In astonishment.*] The State?

CADI: Yes, I shall tell you about the matter so that you may rest assured. Listen! If you give the call to dawn prayers now, the Sultan will immediately leave this house a free man. That, in a couple of words, is what it's all about. Do you understand now?

MUEZZIN: It's a patriotic act!

CADI: It certainly is. What do you say then?

MUEZZIN: I shall do it immediately. I shall be proud of it the whole of my life. Permit me, milord Cadi, also to tell you something—what I say being strictly between ourselves—which is that I previously told you a small falsehood of this sort in order to save the head of someone who had been condemned to death; so why should I not commit a similar falsehood in order to gain the freedom of Our Majesty the beloved Sultan!

CADI: You're quite right, but I enjoin you to secrecy. Be careful not to let that tongue of yours wag! Hide this pride of yours in your soul, for if you begin to boast of what you have done in these present circumstances the whole business will be ruined. Shut your mouth well if you want your action to bear fruit and be appreciated.

MUEZZIN: I shall shut my mouth.

CADI: Good. Hurry off and do it.

MUEZZIN: As swift as the winds I'll be!

[*The* MUEZZIN *leaves hurriedly.*]

CADI: [*To the* VIZIER.] What do you think?

VIZIER: Do you think a trick like this will put matters right?

CADI: Yes, in the best way possible. Tonight I set about considering every aspect of the matter. I no longer regard myself as having been defeated. I still have in my quiver—or, to be more exact, in the law's quiver—many tricks.

VIZIER: Let us pray to God to make your tricks successful this time. Your personal honour is at stake.

CADI: You will see.

[*The voice of the* MUEZZIN *rings out.*]

MUEZZIN: [*From afar.*] God is great! God is great! Come to prayers! Come to prayers! Come to salvation! Come to salvation!

[*The crowd make their appearance in a state of agitation, astonishment, protest, and anger.*]

THE PEOPLE: [*Shouting.*] The dawn? Now? It's still night—we're in the middle of the night. He's mad! This madman—arrest him! Bring him down, bring him down from on top of the minaret! Bring him down!

VIZIER: [*To the* CADI.] The crowds will fall upon this poor fellow.

CADI: Order your guards to disperse the crowds.

VIZIER: [*Shouting at the* GUARDS.] Clear the square! Clear everyone out of the square!

[*The* GUARDS *chase* THE PEOPLE *away and clear the square, while the* MUEZZIN *continues with his call to prayer. The light goes on in the* LADY's *room. She appears at the window followed by the* SULTAN.]

LADY: Is it really dawn?

CADI: It is the call to prayers. Come down here at once!

LADY: This is absurd—look at the stars in the sky.

SULTAN: [*Looking at the sky.*] Truly this is most strange.

CADI: [*To the* LADY.] I told you to come down here immediately.

SULTAN: [*To the* LADY.] Let us go down together to see what it's all about.

LADY: Let us go, Your Majesty. [*They leave the room, the light is extinguished, and they are seen coming out of the house.*]

SULTAN: [*Looking at the sky.*] The dawn? At this hour?

VIZIER: Yes, Your Majesty.

SULTAN: This is truly extraordinary. What do you say, Cadi?

CADI: No, Your Majesty, the dawn has not yet broken.

VIZIER: [*Taken aback.*] How's that?

CADI: It's quite obvious—it's still night.

VIZIER: [*To the* CADI *in astonishment.*] But . . . .

CADI: But we have all heard the Muezzin give the call to dawn prayers. Did you hear it, woman?

LADY: Yes, I did.

CADI: You admit then that you heard the voice of the Muezzin giving the call to dawn prayers?

LADY: Yes, but . . .

CADI: There is nothing more to be said. As you have admitted this, there is nothing left for you to do but keep your promise. Here is the deed of manumission—you have only to sign.

[*He presents her with the deed.*]

LADY: I promised to sign it at dawn and here you are admitting, O Cadi, that it's still night.

CADI: Not so fast, woman! Your promise is inscribed in my head, word for word. Your exact words were: 'When the Muezzin gives the call to dawn prayers.' The whole matter now comes down to this question: have you or have you not heard the voice of the Muezzin?

LADY: I heard it, but if the dawn's still far off . . .

CADI: The dawn as such is not in question—the promise related to the voice of the Muezzin as he gave the call to the dawn prayer. If the Muezzin has made a mistake in his calculation or conduct, it is he who is responsible for his mistake—that's his business. It's not ours. You understand?

LADY: I understand—it's not a bad trick!

CADI: The Muezzin will of course be prosecuted for his mistake. This, however, doesn't change the facts, which are that we have all heard the Muezzin giving the call to the dawn prayers from on top of his minaret. And so all the legal consequences deriving therefrom must take their course—immediately! Come along then and sign!

LADY: Is it thus that you interpret my one condition before manumitting the Sultan?

CADI: In the same manner as you interpreted our condition when you purchased the Sultan!

VIZIER: You have fallen into the very same snares of the law. Therefore, submit and sign!

LADY: This is not honest! It's sheer trickery!

VIZIER: Trickery matched by trickery! You began it—and he who begins is the greater offender. You are the last person to object and protest.

SULTAN: [*Shouting.*] Shame! Enough! Enough! Stop this nonsense! Cease this pettiness! She shall not sign. I absolutely refuse that she should sign this way. And you, Chief Cadi, aren't you ashamed of yourself for fooling around with the law like this?

CADI: Milord Sultan . . .

SULTAN: I am disappointed. I am disappointed in you, Chief Cadi. Is this, in your opinion, the law? The expenditure of effort and skill in trickery and fraud!

CADI: Your Majesty, I merely wanted . . .

SULTAN: To rescue me, I know that, but did you think I'd accept being rescued by such methods?

CADI: With such a woman, Your Majesty, we have the right . . .

SULTAN: No, you have no right at all to do this. You have no such right. Maybe it was the right of this woman to indulge in trickery—she cannot be blamed if she did so; maybe she should be the object of indulgence because of her intelligence and skill. As for the Chief Cadi, the representative of justice, the defender of the sanctity of the law, the upright servant of the canonical law, it is one of his most bounden duties to preserve the law's purity, integrity, and majesty, whatever the price. It was you yourself who first showed me the virtue of the law and the respect it must be shown, who told me that it was the supreme power before which I myself must bow. And I have bowed down right to the end in all humility. But did it ever occur to me that I would see you yourself eventually regarding the law in this manner; stripping it of its robe of sanctity so that it becomes in your hands no more than wiles, clauses, words—a mere plaything?

CADI: Let me explain to you, Your Majesty . . .

SULTAN: No, explain nothing. Go now! It's better for you to go home and betake yourself to bed until the morning. As for me I shall respect this lady's situation—in the true sense in which we all understand it. Let us go, milady! Let us return to your house! I am at your disposal.

LADY: No, Your Majesty.

SULTAN: No?

LADY: No, your Chief Cadi wanted to rescue you, and I don't want to be any less loyal than him towards you. You are now free, Your Majesty.

SULTAN: Free?

LADY: Yes, bring the deed of manumission, Chief Cadi, so that I may sign it.

CADI: You'll sign it now?

LADY: Yes, now.

CADI: [Presenting her with the deed.] God grant she's telling the truth!

LADY: [Signing the deed.] Believe me this time! There's my signature!

CADI: [Examining the signature.] Yes, despite everything you're a good woman.

SULTAN: Rather is she one of the most outstanding of women! The people of the city must respect her. That's an order, O Vizier!

VIZIER: I hear and obey, Your Majesty!

CADI: [Folding up the deed.] Everything has now been completed, Your Majesty, in first-class fashion.

SULTAN: And without a drop of blood being spilt—that's the important thing.

VIZIER: Thanks to your courage, Your Majesty. Who would imagine that to proceed to the end of this road would require more courage than that of the sword?

CADI: Truly!

SULTAN: Let us give praise to the generosity of this noble lady. Allow me, milady, to address my thanks to you, and I ask that you accept the return of your money to you, for there is no longer any reason why you should lose it. Vizier! Pay her from my private purse the amount which she has lost.

LADY: No, no, Your Majesty. Don't take away this honour from me. There are no riches in the world, in my opinion, to equal this beautiful mem-

ory on which I shall live for the whole of my life. With something so
paltry I have participated in one of the greatest of events.

SULTAN: Good—as the memory has such significance for you, then keep
this memento of it. [*He takes the enormous ruby from his turban.*]

VIZIER: [*Whispering.*] The ruby? The one without peer in the world?

SULTAN: Compared with your goodness, this is accounted a petty thing.
[*He presents her with the ruby.*]

LADY: No, dear Majesty, I don't deserve, am not worthy of this . . . this . . .

SULTAN: [*Starting to leave.*] Farewell, good lady!

LADY: [*With tears in her eyes.*] Farewell, dear Sultan!

SULTAN: [*Noticing her tears.*] Are you crying?

LADY: With joy!

SULTAN: I shall never forget that I was your slave for a night.

LADY: For the sake of principles and the law, Your Majesty! [*She lowers
her head to hide her tears.*]
[*Music. The* SULTAN's *cortège moves off.*]

CURTAIN

KAWABATA YASUNARI
1899–1972

At the time he was awarded the Nobel Prize in literature in 1968, Kawabata Yasunari was the patriarch of Japanese letters. One of Japan's most frequently translated
novelists, he served as a literary godfather to the country's aspiring writers, both in
his official capacity as president of the Japan P.E.N. Club (which included poets,
essayists, and novelists) and through countless book reviews and his active interest
in fostering new talent. If Kawabata had done nothing more than discover Mishima Yukio he would be well remembered, since the popular and prolific Mishima achieved a fame beyond Japan that all but eclipsed that of his mentor. It
was on Kawabata, however, that the Swedish Academy chose to bestow Japan's
first Nobel Prize for literature. He was only the second such Nobel laureate in all
of Asia (Rabindranath Tagore of India [p. 1448]) having received the prize in
1913), and not until twenty-six years later would he be joined by another Japanese
novelist, Ōe Kenzaburō, who received the Nobel Prize in 1994.

In its citation in 1968 the Swedish Academy commended Kawabata's mastery
in illuminating "the essence of the Japanese mind." Kawabata was also praised
during the presentation ceremonies as a conservator of Japanese tradition: "In the
postwar wave of violent Americanization his fiction is a gentle reminder of the
necessity of trying to save something of the old Japan's beauty and individuality for
the new." Kawabata was acutely aware of "the old Japan's beauty." He spoke of it
in his acceptance speech in Stockholm, and he writes of it frequently in his novels,
which take as their backdrop such traditions as the tea ceremony, the *geisha* house,
and *go*, the ancient game of strategy. Yet it is doubtful that his vision of the old
Japan and its beauty corresponded with what the Nobel Prize committee thought
it saw. Perhaps the award was in part a gesture toward all Japanese writers, or
toward Japan, or toward Asia in general, for the Swedish tribute idealizes Kawabata

as it reiterates the Western fantasy of a mysterious Orient (revealed by the writer's ability to extract "the essence of the Japanese mind," whatever that might be) and as it simultaneously rewards Kawabata's work, basically, for being charming. Perhaps Kawabata's frail appearance—so birdlike or, in the words of one critic, suggestive of a doe frightened by headlights—only encouraged the Europeans to view the author and his fiction as gentler and more winsome than either really was. In fact, in the appraisal of his own translator, there is a strain of bitterness and even ugliness that runs through Kawabata's writing. Beauty is seldom present without an aspect of decay, and critics see in his subtle joining of the two Kawabata's great strength.

Other strengths include a magician's ability to fashion weightless texts. Ungrounded by anything but the most elemental structure, they seem to levitate and float at random—between past and present time, action and celebration of the setting, oblique depiction of character and the mystic's sense of the oneness of humanity and nature—until the writer decides, quite arbitrarily it would seem, to bring the text down at its "conclusion." To some, this will appear the badge of modernism; to others, pure Japanese convention. Both views have their justification, and here again it is the joining of the two that makes Kawabata interesting. *Snow Country*, his undisputed masterpiece, is a good example.

The novel is set in a hot-spring resort in the mountains of northwest Japan. In the winter, when cold winds swoop down from Siberia, drawing moisture as they cross the Japan Sea, they blow into the mountainous spine of the central island and deposit snowfalls of up to fifteen feet. The onslaught continues almost daily from November through April, making the area one of the snowiest regions in the world and making, too, the name *snow country* a very specific appellation. It does not mean just any countryside where snow falls, but a distinct location in Japan west of the central mountain range, where the winters are long and dark, the snow piles up to the eaves, and people live cut off from the world beyond the mountains. Their isolation is broken only by the occasional tourist. Today the interruptions are more than occasional, as holiday skiers flock into the region, but at the time of the novel, in the 1930s, visitors were fewer and as apt to come for the waters and the leisurely seclusion as for the ski runs.

And just as *snow country* has a particular connotation in Japan, so does *hot spring*. The Japanese do not go for "the season" (as it was called when Americans summered in Saratoga or other famous spas), nor do they go for health—nor, it should be added, do they generally go as couples, especially at the time of this novel. A man would visit a hot spring for a brief respite from work and family. (Then as now, husband and wife in Japan led lives surprisingly autonomous by American standards.) He would stay at an inn, soak in its steaming waters, relax, view the local sights (the autumn leaves, perhaps, or the cherry blossoms), and while away the evening hours in the company of *geisha*.

So it is with the protagonist of *Snow Country*. Shimamura is a man whose days are nothing but leisure. A well-heeled dilettante for whom commitment is anathema, Shimamura travels to the snow country in the same manner that he drifts through all of life, in vague search of idle pleasures. Apparently unfettered by the need to earn a living, he cultivates his aesthetic sensibilities; should they turn in the direction of genuine enthusiasm, he scrupulously retreats. Having once been a student of traditional Japanese dance, for example, he has abandoned the avocation after his growing expertise prompted calls for active involvement in the dance world. Instead, he has since taken up the study of Western ballet—pure book learning, however, because he shuns actual performances, which were in any case still safely uncommon in Japan of the 1930s. Shimamura is an intelligent man, quite aware of the dynamics of his peculiar detachment. "It was like being in love with someone he had never seen," the narrator has Shimamura acknowledging.

"Nothing could be more comfortable than writing about the ballet from books. A ballet he had never seen was an art in another world. It was an unrivaled armchair reverie, a lyric from some paradise. He called his work research, but it was actually free, uncontrolled fantasy."

His ennui, then, takes Shimamura to the snow country, where he meets a local *geisha*, far livelier than he and less cynical, who falls deeply in love with this enigmatic figure. To appreciate the relation between them one must understand that the hot-spring *geisha* is the sad country cousin of the city *geisha*, who draws on a proud tradition of artistic accomplishment and can expect to be pampered by prosperous patrons. The city *geisha* at this time could still aspire to the repute we might accord a fashion model. The country *geisha*, on the other hand, had to entertain whatever traveler happened to pass through the village. There was a thin line sometimes between performer and prostitute. Chances were that she would drift from one hot spring to another, less and less appreciated with each move, until finally, as Kawabata says, "going pleasantly to seed." Appreciating both the beauty and sadness of this woman, Shimamura develops an attenuated sort of affection, not unlike his aloof attachment to ballet. Their sporadic affair over the course of his three visits to the snow country forms a study in disappointing love, where beauty is wasted and melancholy is the fate of the sensitive soul.

The novel trembles with sensitivity, and it is hard not to take the implied author, that personality we imagine standing behind the work, for Shimamura. Kawabata, the lyrical sensualist, weaves a narrative almost as disengaged as its hero: at once serene and disquieting, sensuous and cold. The narrative itself is sporadic and sometimes riddlelike—a shifting movement of images and allusions, dialogue and description—creating a text that is spare, elliptical, opaque, and, for all its authority, somehow hesitant, as though Kawabata too were avoiding a final commitment.

The tentative, capricious qualities of the novel would appear to have their source in Kawabata's early involvement with European modernism. While still a student at Tokyo University specializing in Japanese literature, Kawabata joined with other literary youths to form a group that called itself the Neosensualist, or New Sensibilities, school. His formal studies of the native literature were supplemented by the circle's enthusiastic readings in avant-garde European literature, which its members explored not as scholars so much as for inspiration in their own budding careers as writers. From 1924, the year Kawabata graduated, to 1927 the group of twenty or so published their own magazine, *The Literary Age* (though many of the works most often cited as examples of the New Sensibilities style appeared in other journals). The youthful group took as its mission the elevation of contemporary Japanese literature as art for art's sake, rescuing it from the joint clutches of a drab, confessional, naturalistic movement and the equally flat-footed, if politically engaged, proletarian movement. Just as the European school known as modernism might be better described in the plural, there were various modernisms that influenced the New Sensibilities writers. In the group as a whole, futurism, cubism, expressionism, and Dadaism commanded the most explosive attention, with certain radical members, perhaps jolted by the fermenting compound of nihilism and imaginative liberation, declaring an open "war of utter rebellion against the Japanese language."

The modernist trends insinuated into Kawabata's writing were less belligerent. From Joyce, apparently, he learned that words could be ordered not only in the sequence of historical or narrative time but according to the movement and rhythm of the subjective imagination, the stream of consciousness. From Freud, he was inspired to splinter the naturalistic surface of a text by probing the irrational unconscious forces of the mind and the world of dreams, both sleeping and wakeful. By the Surrealists, he was encouraged to free associate, seeing art as the juxtaposition of random images whose multiple views and abrupt transitions challenge the reader to forge a coherent meaning from fragmentary forms. In Symbolism, he admired the primacy of suggestion over direct statement and the quest for the luminous image that transformed reality into metaphor. And, in absorbing the spirit of modernism, Kawabata saw literature as style, the writer as introvert, life as a rupture of expected continuities, and all human relations, therefore, as ultimately insubstantial.

The question is, how much of this was really new, or European, and how much had Kawabata inherited from his own tradition? Poetry, imagistic from earliest times in Japan, had always cultivated the art of indirection, with states of mind a principal concern. Nonlinear structure had long marked the country's literature, from diaries and discursive essays known as *zuihitsu* to *nō* plays. The great women writers of the eleventh century, steeped in the Buddhist teaching that the world is evanescent and not to be trusted, had eloquently appraised the consequences both of fickle love and of impossible yearnings. Aestheticism was at the heart of traditional Japanese literature, and so in a way was an element of the surreal. Chikamatsu Monzaemon, the greatest dramatist of Japan's long period of seclusion (1600–1868), posited that "art is something which lies in the slender margin between the real and the unreal." And the coalescing of a text into an unpredictable progression of startling, discontinuous images piloted by thin or abrupt transitions that seem to fling flashes of acute perception into a narrative void was the very essence of the art of Japanese linked verse known as *renga*, dating from the fifteenth century.

Kawabata is often described as a *haiku*-like writer. The crisp, seventeen-syllable poems that communicate a moment of truth, or a poignant awakening, through the union of incongruous or contrary images do indeed suggest the terse, austere, intuitive style of *Snow Country*. But *haiku* grew out of a form of linked verse, and the elliptical, associative, and unresolved aspects of the novel seem more the offspring of *renga*. This "medieval" literary form would still have been known to most educated Japanese of Kawabata's generation. Lacking a single integrated plot, topic, or point of view, *renga* requires a group of poets who take turns composing verses to form a sequence wherein each verse is linked only to the one immediately preceding and immediately following. The result is a continuous stream of images and poetic associations, a vibration of themes at once fragmentary and symphonic.

Whether he consciously emulated *renga* or not, Kawabata clearly found an accumulative, open-ended approach to be congenial. This we know from his curious publishing preferences. Some authors dislike being asked whether they use a number-two pencil or a word processor, but in Kawabata's case writing habits may be considered quite pertinent. Virtually never did he compose a work from start to finish. Serialization (in magazines or, earlier in the century, in newspapers) is hardly uncommon in Japan, but Kawabata's brand of publishing in stages is definitely unusual. *Snow Country*, like most of his novels, may be said to have grown organically and slowly. It began life as a short story, which he wrote in 1934 and published in 1935 in a magazine called *Japanese Opinion*. The story bears a resemblance to the first section of the completed novel, set on a train traveling into the snow country, but it lacks the mystery and otherworldliness it would acquire when rewritten as the novel's opening. Initially, Kawabata considered the work finished. He soon changed his mind, however, and incorporated some leftover material into another short story for a different magazine. He would have added the material to the original story, but the deadline had already passed. No doubt he considered the second piece finished as well, until another aspect of the story came to mind. And so it grew, incrementally, stories published here and there over a two-year span, with no indication that they formed a single work of fiction. In 1937 Kawabata revised the disparate parts and published them as a novel.

Two years later he was back again, tinkering. He added two new chapters in 1939 and 1940, revised them, thought some more, became dissatisfied with the ending, and in 1947 finally completed the novel, which was published the following year. This is the form in which *Snow Country* is known today. But even that is not the end of the story's gestation. Indicative of the pride of place he gave the novel in his body of work, shortly before his death twenty-four years later, he distilled the entire novel into a ten-page episode that he called a "palm-sized" short story, a genre of vignette he had invented at the beginning of his career and frequently returned to. We might call these miniatures short shorts or "vest-pocket" stories. Some are no more than three or four paragraphs, but they are yet another reason Kawabata's fiction is habitually compared with *haiku*.

A literary text to Kawabata was a permeable thing. In its shifting boundaries perhaps he discerned an analogue of the Buddhist concept of mutability: life forever fluid and uncertain. Though he cut his teeth on European fiction, as a writer he acknowledged a large debt to Buddhism, whose scriptures he proclaimed "the supreme works of world literature," "incomparably wonderful lyric poems." If for Kawabata a text, like a life, is never finished (for Buddhism holds that death leads to reincarnation), he would seem to be the most "Japanese" of writers, just as the Swedish Academy had classified him.

Yet the indeterminacy of his method of composition may be taken for a theory of literature that is very modern, indeed, in our own day, postmodern. Current reader-response criticism, for example, might construe the ellipses and logical holes in Kawabata, or the centrifugal pull of digression, as case studies illustrating the theory that a text is seldom self-contained, that in filling in the "gaps" to construct meaning the reader is also a literary producer. Deconstruction, which argues that the meaning of a text is always in play and consequently perpetually deferred, with language itself inherently unstable, might serve to place Kawabata's tentative intentions within a philosophical (albeit skeptical) framework.

If there is a strain of nihilism (a philosophy of skepticism that denies meaningfulness) in this recent school of literary theory, there is also a trace of it in Kawabata. Despite the evidence that appears everywhere in his fiction—one character even speaks baldly of "the joy of emptiness"—Kawabata denied he was a nihilist. In his acceptance speech at the Nobel ceremonies, he took pains to distinguish his "emptiness" as the nothingness of Zen and Japanese tradition, not the nihilism of the West. It is difficult to tell what to make of Kawabata's address in Stockholm, described by one critic as "a forced march through a blizzard of cherry blossoms." But perhaps what Kawabata meant to say in quoting innumerable ancient poems, in invoking dwarf pines and flower arranging, is simply that the sad, untapped, autumnal feel of empty space in the Japanese aesthetic (think of the rock garden or architecture or *haiku*) signifies not hopelessness or despair—but beauty. Perhaps what he meant to say is that accepting absence or imperfection can bring quietude, and that this is the source of the beautiful.

In the same speech, Kawabata condemned suicide, mindful no doubt of the unusual number of his fellow writers who had died by their own hands. Less than four years later, however, he was to die in the same manner. Perhaps what he expressed in Stockholm was only a kind of hope, which his writings intermittently succeeded in adhering to. There is beauty aplenty in Kawabata. The simplicity of his style summons a range of subtleties, a depth of emotions; his command of imagery and allusion makes poetry of prose. But there is also the ironic detachment, sometimes shading into withdrawal or callousness, that we associate with a nihilist's despair at the futility of human existence.

Kawabata was born in Osaka in 1899 and was orphaned by the age of three. Childhood for him meant becoming "an expert in funerals." His grandmother died when he was seven, his only sister when he was nine, his grandfather when he was fifteen. Bereft of close relations and living mainly in school dormitories, the young Kawabata knew a loneliness that must have seeped into his bones. It surely accounts for the melancholy and rootlessness that color his fiction. Death and decay were already his intimates, soon joined by a first experience of impossible love. His central preoccupations were thus all in place before he published a first story in his early twenties. Though he oscillates between modernist and traditional approaches, the principal themes of his work remained constant for the next fifty years.

His most famous disciple, Mishima Yukio, would call Kawabata "the eternal traveler." From his first important short story, the typical protagonist in Kawabata's fiction is a man away from home. In *The Izu Dancer* (1926) a lonely student sets out on a walking trip on the Izu Peninsula south of Tokyo. The action takes place along the road and in remote inns, where, befriended by a troupe of entertainers, he becomes infatuated with the young dancer of the title. Temporarily dislocated, he is a poor judge of his surroundings; the Izu dancer turns out to be a mere child. A similar displacement marks *The Master of Go* (1954). In this fictionalized account of a 1938 *go* match (a board game of strategy, like chess) the champion and his challenger play out their protracted game sequestered in a series of inns, where they are quite cut off from the rest of the world. When the game is over and they emerge from isolation—the master defeated—tradition itself has been displaced. *Snow Country*, too, takes its protagonist out of his "real" world of family ties and responsibility. In the far-off snow country, Shimamura becomes even more detached and tentative than usual. *The House of the Sleeping Beauties* (1961), one of Kawabata's last novels, is perhaps his darkest and most disturbing statement on the space that another place, away from home, opens as a site for fantasy, or a closet life—in this case the desire of an old man to sleep beside young girls who have been drugged into obliviousness.

Kawabata described himself as one drawn to "islands in a distant sea." His novels and short stories were all in one sense or another travels to a distant lodging, a temporary home—isolated, provisional, and sometimes claustrophobic. For all the beauty of the scenery, the perpetual traveler finds in his wanderings only the most fragile sense of place. People are even more fragile. They have a tendency to fade away into the landscape or disappear into a symbol. "Perhaps I was never in touch with reality," Kawabata said after World War II. In the most misanthropic of his stories, *Of Birds and Beasts*, the crotchety hero is made to confront his true nature. "All alone, he came to the arbitrary conclusion: he did not like people." "I have the feeling I have never taken a woman's hand in mine with romantic intentions," Kawabata once said of himself. "And it's not only women I have never taken by the hand. For me, I wonder if the same isn't true of the whole of life." No writer surpasses Kawabata in capturing a life folding in on itself, so close to beauty, yet so estranged.

Even in translation, the eloquent abstinence of Kawabata's style shines through, and it is reasonable to assume that Edward Seidensticker's English versions were influential in bringing Kawabata the Nobel Prize. Especially recommended are *Thousand Cranes* (1959), *The Sound of the Mountain* (1970), *The Master of Go* (1972), *The Izu Dancer and Other Stories* (1974), and *House of the Sleeping Beauties and Other Stories* (1969). A collection of Kawabata's very short pieces has been translated by Lane Dunlop and J. Martin Holman, *Palm-of-the-Hand Stories* (1988). For background on Kawabata, see Seidensticker, "On Kawabata Yasunari" in *This Country, Japan* (1979). There are chapter-length studies of the author in Donald Keene, *Dawn to the West* (1984); Masao Miyoshi, *Accomplices of Silence: The Modern Japanese Novel* (1974); and David Pollack, *Reading against Culture: Ideology and Narrative in the Japanese Novel* (1992).

PRONOUNCING GLOSSARY

The following list uses common English syllables to provide rough equivalents of selected words whose pronunciation may be unfamiliar to the general reader.

Chijimi: *chee-jee-mee*

Jizo: *jee-zoh*

Kikumura: *kee-koo-moo-rah*

Kikuyu: *kee-koo-yoo*

Komako: *koh-mah-koh*

kotatsu: *koh-tah-tsoo*

Mishima Yukio: *mee-shee-mah yoo-kee-oh*

nagauta: *nah-gah-oo-tah*

samisen: *sah-mee-sen*

Shimamura: *shee-mah-moo-rah*

zuihitsu: *zoo-ee-hee-tsoo*

Snow Country[1]

PART ONE

The train came out of the long tunnel into the snow country. The earth lay white under the night sky. The train pulled up at a signal stop.

A girl who had been sitting on the other side of the car came over and opened the window in front of Shimamura. The snowy cold poured in. Leaning far out the window, the girl called to the station master as though he were a great distance away.

The station master walked slowly over the snow, a lantern in his hand. His face was buried to the nose in a muffler, and the flaps of his cap were turned down over his ears.

It's that cold, is it, thought Shimamura. Low, barracklike buildings that might have been railway dormitories were scattered here and there up the frozen slope of the mountain. The white of the snow fell away into the darkness some distance before it reached them.

"How are you?" the girl called out. "It's Yoko."

"Yoko, is it. On your way back? It's gotten cold again."

"I understand my brother has come to work here. Thank you for all you've done."

"It will be lonely, though. This is no place for a young boy."

"He's really no more than a child. You'll teach him what he needs to know, won't you."

"Oh, but he's doing very well. We'll be busier from now on, with the snow and all. Last year we had so much that the trains were always being stopped by avalanches, and the whole town was kept busy cooking for them."

---

1. Translated by and with notes adapted from Edward G. Seidensticker.

"But look at the warm clothes, would you. My brother said in his letter that he wasn't even wearing a sweater yet."

"I'm not warm unless I have on four layers, myself. The young ones start drinking when it gets cold, and the first thing you know they're over there in bed with colds." He waved his lantern toward the dormitories.

"Does my brother drink?"

"Not that I know of."

"You're on your way home now, are you?"

"I had a little accident. I've been going to the doctor."

"You must be more careful."

The station master, who had an overcoat on over his kimono, turned as if to cut the freezing conversation short. "Take care of yourself," he called over his shoulder.

"Is my brother here now?" Yoko looked out over the snow-covered plat-form. "See that he behaves himself." It was such a beautiful voice that it struck one as sad. In all its high resonance it seemed to come echoing back across the snowy night.

The girl was still leaning out the window when the train pulled away from the station. "Tell my brother to come home when he has a holiday," she called out to the station master, who was walking along the tracks.

"I'll tell him," the man called back.

Yoko closed the window and pressed her hands to her red cheeks.

Three snowplows were waiting for the heavy snows here on the Border Range.[2] There was an electric avalanche-warning system at the north and south entrances to the tunnel. Five thousand workers were ready to clear away the snow, and two thousand young men from the volunteer fire-departments could be mobilized if they were needed.

Yoko's brother would be working at this signal stop, so soon to be buried under the snow—somehow that fact made the girl more interesting to Shimamura.

"The girl"—something in her manner suggested the unmarried girl. Shimamura of course had no way of being sure what her relationship was to the man with her. They acted rather like a married couple. The man was clearly ill, however, and illness shortens the distance between a man and a woman. The more earnest the ministrations, the more the two come to seem like husband and wife. A girl taking care of a man far older than she, for all the world like a young mother, can from a distance be taken for his wife.

But Shimamura in his mind had cut the girl off from the man with her and decided from her general appearance and manner that she was unmarried. And then, because he had been looking at her from a strange angle for so long, emotions peculiarly his own had perhaps colored his judgment.

It had been three hours earlier. In his boredom, Shimamura stared at his left hand as the forefinger bent and unbent. Only this hand seemed to have a vital and immediate memory of the woman he was going to see. The more he tried to call up a clear picture of her, the more his memory

---

2. The mountain range dividing two prefectures.

failed him, the farther she faded away, leaving him nothing to catch and hold. In the midst of this uncertainty only the one hand, and in particular the forefinger, even now seemed damp from her touch, seemed to be pulling him back to her from afar. Taken with the strangeness of it, he brought the hand to his face, then quickly drew a line across the misted-over window. A woman's eye floated up before him. He almost called out in his astonishment. But he had been dreaming, and when he came to himself he saw that it was only the reflection in the window of the girl opposite. Outside it was growing dark, and the lights had been turned on in the train, transforming the window into a mirror. The mirror had been clouded over with steam until he drew that line across it.

The one eye by itself was strangely beautiful, but, feigning a traveler's weariness and putting his face to the window as if to look at the scenery outside, he cleared the steam from the rest of the glass.

The girl leaned attentively forward, looking down at the man before her. Shimamura could see from the way her strength was gathered in her shoulders that the suggestion of fierceness in her eyes was but a sign of an intentness that did not permit her to blink. The man lay with his head pillowed at the window and his legs bent so that his feet were on the seat facing, beside the girl. It was a third-class coach. The pair were not directly opposite Shimamura but rather one seat forward, and the man's head showed in the window-mirror only as far as the ear.

Since the girl was thus diagonally opposite him, Shimamura could as well have looked directly at her. When the two of them came on the train, however, something coolly piercing about her beauty had startled Shimamura, and as he hastily lowered his eyes he had seen the man's ashen fingers clutching at the girl's. Somehow it seemed wrong to look their way again.

The man's face in the mirror suggested the feeling of security and repose it gave him to be able to rest his eyes on the girl's breast. His very weakness lent a certain soft balance and harmony to the two figures. One end of his scarf served as a pillow, and the other end, pulled up tight over his mouth like a mask, rested on his cheek. Now and then it fell loose or slipped down over his nose, and almost before he had time to signal his annoyance the girl gently rearranged it. The process was repeated over and over, automatically, so often that Shimamura, watching them, almost found himself growing impatient. Occasionally the bottom of the overcoat in which the man's feet were wrapped would slip open and fall to the floor, and the girl would quickly pull it back together. It was all completely natural, as if the two of them, quite insensitive to space, meant to go on forever, farther and farther into the distance. For Shimamura there was none of the pain that the sight of something truly sad can bring. Rather it was as if he were watching a tableau in a dream—and that was no doubt the working of his strange mirror.

In the depths of the mirror the evening landscape moved by, the mirror and the reflected figures like motion pictures superimposed one on the other. The figures and the background were unrelated, and yet the figures, transparent and intangible, and the background, dim in the gathering darkness, melted together into a sort of symbolic world not of this world.

Particularly when a light out in the mountains shone in the center of the girl's face, Shimamura felt his chest rise at the inexpressible beauty of it.

The mountain sky still carried traces of evening red. Individual shapes were clear far into the distance, but the monotonous mountain landscape, undistinguished for mile after mile, seemed all the more undistinguished for having lost its last traces of color. There was nothing in it to catch the eye, and it seemed to flow along in a wide, unformed emotion. That was of course because the girl's face was floating over it. Cut off by the face, the evening landscape moved steadily by around its outlines. The face too seemed transparent—but was it really transparent? Shimamura had the illusion that the evening landscape was actually passing over the face, and the flow did not stop to let him be sure it was not.

The light inside the train was not particularly strong, and the reflection was not as clear as it would have been in a mirror. Since there was no glare, Shimamura came to forget that it was a mirror he was looking at. The girl's face seemed to be out in the flow of the evening mountains.

It was then that a light shone in the face. The reflection in the mirror was not strong enough to blot out the light outside, nor was the light strong enough to dim the reflection. The light moved across the face, though not to light it up. It was a distant, cold light. As it sent its small ray through the pupil of the girl's eye, as the eye and the light were superimposed one on the other, the eye became a weirdly beautiful bit of phosphorescence on the sea of evening mountains.

There was no way for Yoko to know that she was being stared at. Her attention was concentrated on the sick man, and even had she looked toward Shimamura, she would probably not have seen her reflection, and she would have paid no attention to the man looking out the window.

It did not occur to Shimamura that it was improper to stare at the girl so long and stealthily. That too was no doubt because he was taken by the unreal, otherworldly power of his mirror in the evening landscape.

When, therefore, the girl called out to the station master, her manner again suggesting overearnestness, Shimamura perhaps saw her first of all as rather like a character out of an old, romantic tale.

The window was dark by the time they came to the signal stop. The charm of the mirror faded with the fading landscape. Yoko's face was still there, but for all the warmth of her ministrations, Shimamura had found in her a transparent coldness. He did not clear the window as it clouded over again.

He was startled, then, when a half-hour later Yoko and the man got off the train at the same station as he. He looked around as though he were about to be drawn into something, but the cold air on the platform made him suddenly ashamed of his rudeness on the train. He crossed the tracks in front of the locomotive without looking back again.

The man, clinging to Yoko's shoulder, was about to climb down to the tracks from the platform opposite when from this side a station attendant raised a hand to stop them.

A long freight train came out of the darkness to block them from sight.

The porter from the inn was so well-equipped for the cold that he suggested a fireman. He had on ear flaps and high rubber boots. The woman looking out over the tracks from the waiting-room wore a blue cape with the cowl pulled over her head.

Shimamura, still warm from the train, was not sure how cold it really was. This was his first taste of the snow-country winter, however, and he felt somewhat intimidated.

"Is it as cold as all that?"

"We're ready for the winter. It's always especially cold the night it clears after a snow. It must be below freezing tonight."

"This is below freezing, is it?" Shimamura looked up at the delicate icicles along the eaves as he climbed into the taxi. The white of the snow made the deep eaves look deeper still, as if everything had sunk quietly into the earth.

"The cold here is different, though, that's easy to see. It feels different when you touch something."

"Last year it went down to zero."

"How much snow?"

"Ordinarily seven or eight feet, sometimes as much as twelve or thirteen, I'd say."

"The heavy snows come from now on?"

"They're just beginning. We had about a foot, but it's melted down a good bit."

"It's been melting, has it?"

"We could have a heavy snow almost any time now, though."

It was the beginning of December.

Shimamura's nose had been stopped up by a stubborn cold, but it cleared to the middle of his head in the cold air, and began running as if the matter in it were washing cleanly away.

"Is the girl who lived with the music teacher still around?"

"She's still around. You didn't see her in the station? In the dark-blue cape?"

"So that's who it was. We can call her later, I suppose?"

"This evening?"

"This evening."

"I hear the music teacher's son came back on your train. She was at the station to meet him."

The sick man he had watched in that evening mirror, then, was the son of the music teacher in whose house the woman Shimamura had come to see was living.

He felt a current pass through him, and yet the coincidence did not seem especially remarkable. Indeed he was surprised at himself for being so little surprised.

Somewhere in his heart Shimamura saw a question, as clearly as if it were standing there before him: was there something, what would happen, between the woman his hand remembered and the woman in whose eye that mountain light had glowed? Or had he not yet shaken off the spell of the evening landscape in that mirror? He wondered whether the flowing landscape was not perhaps symbolic of the passage of time.

The hot-spring inn had its fewest guests in the weeks before the skiing season began, and by the time Shimamura had come up from the bath the place seemed to be asleep. The glass doors rattled slightly each time he took a step down the sagging corridor. At the end, where it turned past the office, he saw the tall figure of the woman, her skirts trailing coldly off across the dark floor.

He started back as he saw the long skirts—had she finally become a geisha?[3] She did not come toward him, she did not bend in the slightest movement of recognition. From the distance he caught something intent and serious in the still form. He hurried up to her, but they said nothing even when he was beside her. She started to smile through the thick, white geisha's powder. Instead she melted into tears, and the two of them walked off silently toward his room.

In spite of what had passed between them, he had not written to her, or come to see her, or sent her the dance instructions he had promised. She was no doubt left to think that he had laughed at her and forgotten her. It should therefore have been his part to begin with an apology or an excuse, but as they walked along, not looking at each other, he could tell that, far from blaming him, she had room in her heart only for the pleasure of regaining what had been lost. He knew that if he spoke he would only make himself seem the more wanting in seriousness. Overpowered by the woman, he walked along wrapped in a soft happiness. Abruptly, at the foot of the stairs, he shoved his left fist before her eyes, with only the forefinger extended.

"This remembered you best of all."

"Oh?" The woman took the finger in her hand and clung to it as though to lead him upstairs.

She let go his hand as they came to the *kotatsu*[4] in his room, and suddenly she was red from her forehead to her throat. As if to conceal her confusion, she clutched at his hand again.

"This remembered me?"

"Not the right hand. This." He pushed his right hand into the *kotatsu* to warm it, and again gave her his left fist with the finger extended.

"I know." Her face carefully composed, she laughed softly. She opened his hand, and pressed her cheek against it. "This remembered me?"

"Cold! I don't think I've ever touched such cold hair."

"Is there snow in Tokyo yet?"

"You remember what you said then? But you were wrong. Why else would anyone come to such a place in December?"

"Then": the danger of avalanches was over, and the season for climbing mountains in the spring green had come.

---

3. A woman entertainer at certain restaurants or, sometimes, at traditional Japanese inns. Hired primarily for the companionship during meals or parties that her skills or repartee provides male customers, the geisha ("practitioner of the arts") is presumed competent to sing or dance selections from the classic repertoire. A geisha is not a prostitute, although she may extend that favor to chosen patrons; in any case, she cuts a more worldly figure than the chaste housewife. The geisha's employment prospects were more viable in prewar Japan, the time of *Snow Country*. Today she represents an expensive museum piece for the moneyed, beyond the reach (or interest) of the average Japanese.   **4.** A charcoal brazier covered by a wooden frame and a quilt. It resembles a table at which four people can sit. Although it warms little more than the hands and feet, the *kotatsu* was at this time the only heating device in the ordinary Japanese house.

Presently the new sprouts would be gone from the table.

Shimamura, who lived a life of idleness, found that he tended to lose his honesty with himself, and he frequently went out alone into the mountains to recover something of it. He had come down to the hot-spring village after seven days in the Border Range. He asked to have a geisha called. Unfortunately, however, there was a celebration that day in honor of the opening of a new road, the maid said, so lively a celebration that the town's combined cocoon-warehouse[5] and theater had been taken over, and the twelve or thirteen geisha had more than enough to keep them busy. The girl who lived at the music teacher's might come, though. She sometimes helped at parties, but she would have gone home after no more than one or two dances. As Shimamura questioned her, the maid told him more about the girl at the music teacher's: the samisen[6] and dancing teacher had living with her a girl who was not a geisha but who was sometimes asked to help at large parties. Since there were no young apprentice geisha in the town, and since most of the local geisha were at an age when they preferred not to have to dance, the services of the girl were much valued. She almost never came alone to entertain a guest at the inn, and yet she could not exactly be called an amateur—such in general was the maid's story.

An odd story, Shimamura said to himself, and dismissed the matter. An hour or so later, however, the woman from the music teacher's came in with the maid. Shimamura brought himself up straight. The maid started to leave but was called back by the woman.

The impression the woman gave was a wonderfully clean and fresh one. It seemed to Shimamura that she must be clean to the hollows under her toes. So clean indeed did she seem that he wondered whether his eyes, back from looking at early summer in the mountains, might not be deceiving him.

There was something about her manner of dress that suggested the geisha, but she did not have the trailing geisha skirts. On the contrary, she wore her soft, unlined summer kimono with an emphasis on careful propriety. The obi[7] seemed expensive, out of keeping with the kimono, and struck him as a little sad.

The maid slipped out as they started talking about the mountains. The woman was not very sure of the names of the mountains that could be seen from the inn, and, since Shimamura did not feel the urge to drink that might have come to him in the company of an ordinary geisha, she began telling of her past in a surprisingly matter-of-fact way. She was born in this snow country, but she had been put under contract as a geisha[8] in Tokyo. Presently she found a patron who paid her debts for her and proposed to set her up as a dancing teacher, but unfortunately a year and a half later he died. When it came to the story of what had happened since,

---

5. Raising silkworms was a common source of supplementary income in prewar rural villages, and raw silk was a major Japanese export. 6. The *geisha*'s traditional instrument. It resembles a banjo with a round body, long neck, and three strings, which give off a sharp, plaintive tone once likened by a French observer to the sound of a nerve being plucked. 7. The sash with which a kimono is tied. A woman's *obi* is wide and stiff; a man's is narrower and usually softer. 8. Debts incurred by parents could be repaid by their daughters becoming *geisha*. Unless the woman could find a patron willing to pay off the debt for her parents, she was unlikely to earn enough money to escape her situation.

the story of what was nearest to her, she was less quick to tell her secrets. She said she was nineteen. Shimamura had taken her to be twenty-one or twenty-two, and, since he assumed that she was not lying, the knowledge that she had aged beyond her years gave him for the first time a little of the ease he expected to feel with a geisha. When they began talking of the Kabuki,[9] he found that she knew more about actors and styles than he did. She talked on feverishly, as though she had been starved for someone who would listen to her, and presently began to show an ease and abandon that revealed her to be at heart a woman of the pleasure quarters[1] after all. And she seemed in general to know what there was to know about men. Shimamura, however, had labeled her an amateur and, after a week in the mountains during which he had spoken to almost no one, he found himself longing for a companion. It was therefore friendship more than anything else that he felt for the woman. His response to the mountains had extended itself to cover her.

On her way to the bath the next afternoon, she left her towel and soap in the hall and came in to talk to him.

She had barely taken a seat when he asked her to call him a geisha.

"Call you a geisha?"

"You know what I mean."

"I didn't come to be asked that." She stood up abruptly and went over to the window, her face reddening as she looked out at the mountains. "There are no women like that here."

"Don't be silly."

"It's the truth." She turned sharply to face him, and sat down on the window sill. "No one forces a geisha to do what she doesn't want to. It's entirely up to the geisha herself. That's one service the inn won't provide for you. Go ahead, try calling someone and talking to her yourself, if you want to."

"You call someone for me."

"Why do you expect me to do that?"

"I'm thinking of you as a friend. That's why I've behaved so well."

"And this is what you call being a friend?" Led on by his manner, she had become engagingly childlike. But a moment later she burst out: "Isn't it fine that you think you can ask me a thing like that!"

"What is there to be so excited about? I'm too healthy after a week in the mountains, that's all. I keep having the wrong ideas. I can't even sit here talking to you the way I would like to."

The woman was silent, her eyes on the floor. Shimamura had come to a point where he knew he was only parading his masculine shamelessness, and yet it seemed likely enough that the woman was familiar with the failing and need not be shocked by it. He looked at her. Perhaps it was the rich lashes of the downcast eyes that made her face seem warm and sensuous. She shook her head very slightly, and again a faint blush spread over her face.

---

9. One of the major forms of traditional theater, dating from the 17th century. It is characterized by stylized dialogue and stage movements; vivid costumes and makeup; and animated, often violent action, incorporating musical accompaniment and dancing.   1. A red-light district such as the Yoshiwara, on the outskirts of Tokyo. Its women included not only prostitutes but professional entertainers.

"Call any geisha you like."

"But isn't that exactly what I'm asking you to do? I've never been here before, and I've no idea which geisha are the best-looking."

"What do you consider good-looking?"

"Someone young. You're less apt to make mistakes when they're young. And someone who doesn't talk too much. Clean, and not too quick. When I want someone to talk to, I can talk to you."

"I'll not come again."

"Don't be foolish."

"I said I'll not come again. Why should I come again?"

"But haven't I told you it's exactly because I want to be friends with you that I've behaved so well?"

"You've said enough."

"Suppose I were to go too far with you. Very probably from tomorrow I wouldn't want to talk to you. I couldn't stand the sight of you. I've had to come into the mountains to want to talk to people again, and I've left you alone so that I can talk to you. And what about yourself? You can't be too careful with travelers."

"That's true."

"Of course it is. Think of yourself. If it were a woman you objected to, you wouldn't want to see me afterwards. It would be much better for her to be a woman you picked out."

"I don't want to hear any more." She turned sharply away, but presently she added: "I suppose there's something in what you say."

"An affair of the moment, no more. Nothing beautiful about it. You know that—it couldn't last."

"That's true. It's that way with everyone who comes here. This is a hot spring and people are here for a day or two and gone." Her manner was remarkably open—the transition had been almost too abrupt. "The guests are mostly travelers. I'm still just a child myself, but I've listened to all the talk. The guest who doesn't say he's fond of you, and yet you somehow know is—he's the one you have pleasant memories of. You don't forget him, even long after he's left you, they say. And he's the one you get letters from."

She stood up from the window sill and took a seat on the mat below it. She seemed to be living in the past, and yet she seemed to be very near Shimamura.

Her voice carried such a note of immediate feeling that he felt a little guilty, as though he had deceived her too easily.

He had not been lying, though. To him this woman was an amateur. His desire for a woman was not of a sort to make him want this particular woman—it was something to be taken care of lightly and with no sense of guilt. This woman was too clean. From the moment he saw her, he had separated this woman and the other in his mind.

Then too, he had been trying to decide where he would go to escape the summer heat, and it occurred to him that he could bring his family to this mountain hot spring. The woman, being fortunately an amateur, would be a good companion for his wife. He might even have his wife take dancing lessons to keep from getting bored. He was quite serious about it. He said he felt only friendship for the woman, but he had his reasons for thus stepping into shallow water without taking the final plunge.

And something like that evening mirror was no doubt at work here too. He disliked the thought of drawn-out complications from an affair with a woman whose position was so ambiguous; but beyond that he saw her as somehow unreal, like the woman's face in that evening mirror.

His taste for the occidental dance[2] had much the same air of unreality about it. He had grown up in the merchants' section of Tokyo, and he had been thoroughly familiar with the Kabuki theater from his childhood. As a student his interests had shifted to the Japanese dance and the dance-drama.[3] Never satisfied until he learned everything about his subject, he had taken to searching through old documents and visiting the heads of various dance schools, and presently he had made friends with rising figures in the dance world and was writing what one might call research pieces and critical essays. It was but natural, then, that he should come to feel a keen dissatisfaction with the slumbering old tradition as well as with reformers who sought only to please themselves. Just as he had arrived at the conclusion that there was nothing for it but to throw himself actively into the dance movement, and as he was being persuaded to do so by certain of the younger figures in the dance world, he abruptly switched to the occidental dance. He stopped seeing the Japanese dance. He gathered pictures and descriptions of the occidental ballet, and began laboriously collecting programs and posters from abroad. This was more than simple fascination with the exotic and the unknown. The pleasure he found in his new hobby came in fact from his inability to see with his own eyes occidentals in occidental ballets. There was proof of this in his deliberate refusal to study the ballet as performed by Japanese. Nothing could be more comfortable than writing about the ballet from books. A ballet he had never seen was an art in another world. It was an unrivaled armchair reverie, a lyric from some paradise. He called his work research, but it was actually free, uncontrolled fantasy. He preferred not to savor the ballet in the flesh; rather he savored the phantasms of his own dancing imagination, called up by Western books and pictures. It was like being in love with someone he had never seen. But it was also true that Shimamura, with no real occupation, took some satisfaction from the fact that his occasional introductions to the occidental dance put him on the edge of the literary world—even while he was laughing at himself and his work.

It might be said that his knowledge was now for the first time in a very great while being put to use, since talk of the dance helped bring the woman nearer to him; and yet it was also possible that, hardly knowing it, he was treating the woman exactly as he treated the occidental dance.

He felt a little guilty, as though he had deceived her, when he saw how the frivolous words of the traveler who would be gone tomorrow seemed to have struck something deep and serious in the woman's life.

But he went on: "I can bring my family here, and we can all be friends."

---

2. That is, Western dance; here, ballet. 3. *Kabuki* contains complex and energetic dance sequences essential to its dramatic effect.

"I understand that well enough." She smiled, her voice falling, and a touch of the geisha's playfulness came out. "I'd like that much better. It lasts longer if you're just friends."

"You'll call someone, then?"

"Now?"

"Now."

"But what can you say to a woman in broad daylight?"

"At night there's too much danger of getting the dregs no one else wants."

"You take this for a cheap hot-spring town like any other. I should think you could tell just from looking at the place." Her tone was sober again, as though she felt thoroughly degraded. She repeated with the same emphasis as before that there were no girls here of the sort he wanted. When Shimamura expressed his doubts, she flared up, then retreated a step. It was up to the geisha whether she would stay the night or not. If she stayed without permission from her house, it was her own responsibility. If she had permission the house took full responsibility, whatever happened. That was the difference.

"Full responsibility?"

"If there should happen to be a child, or some sort of disease."

Shimamura smiled wryly at the foolishness of his question. In a mountain village, though, the arrangements between a geisha and her keeper might indeed still be so easygoing. . . .

Perhaps with the idler's bent for protective coloring, Shimamura had an instinctive feeling for the spirit of the places he visited, and he had felt as he came down from the mountains that, for all its air of bare frugality, there was something comfortable and easy about the village. He heard at the inn that it was indeed one of the more comfortable villages in this harsh snow country. Until the railway was put through, only very recently, it had served mainly as a medicinal spring for farmers in the area. The house that kept geisha would generally have a faded shop curtain that advertised it as a restaurant or a tearoom, but a glance at the old-style sliding doors, their paper panels dark with age, made the passer-by suspect that guests were few. The shop that sold candy or everyday sundries might have its one geisha, and the owner would have his small farm besides the shop and the geisha. Perhaps because she lived with the music teacher, there seemed to be no resentment at the fact that a woman not yet licensed as a geisha was now and then helping at parties.

"How many are there in all?"

"How many geisha? Twelve or thirteen, I suppose."

"Which one do you recommend?" Shimamura stood up to ring for the maid.

"You won't mind if I leave now."

"I mind very much indeed."

"I can't stay." She spoke as if trying to shake off the humiliation. "I'm going. It's all right. I don't mind. I'll come again."

When the maid came in, however, she sat down as though nothing were amiss. The maid asked several times which geisha she should call, but the woman refused to mention a name.

One look at the seventeen- or eighteen-year-old geisha who was presently led in, and Shimamura felt his need for a woman fall dully away.
Her arms, with their underlying darkness, had not yet filled out, and something about her suggested an unformed, good-natured young girl. Shimamura, at pains not to show that his interest had left him, faced her
dutifully, but he could not keep himself from looking less at her than at
the new green on the mountains behind her. It seemed almost too much
of an effort to talk. She was the mountain geisha through and through. He
lapsed into a glum silence. No doubt thinking to be tactful and adroit, the
woman stood up and left the room, and the conversation became still
heavier. Even so, he managed to pass perhaps an hour with the geisha.
Looking for a pretext to be rid of her, he remembered that he had had
money telegraphed from Tokyo. He had to go to the post office before it
closed, he said, and the two of them left the room.

But at the door of the inn he was seduced by the mountain, strong with
the smell of new leaves. He started climbing roughly up it.

He laughed on and on, not knowing himself what was funny.

When he was pleasantly tired, he turned sharply around and, tucking
the skirts of his kimono into his *obi*, ran headlong back down the slope.
Two yellow butterflies flew up at his feet.

The butterflies, weaving in and out, climbed higher than the line of the
Border Range, their yellow turning to white in the distance.

"What happened?" The woman was standing in the shade of the cedar
trees. "You must have been very happy, the way you were laughing."

"I gave it up." Shimamura felt the same senseless laugh rising again. "I
gave it up."

"Oh?" She turned and walked slowly into the grove. Shimamura followed in silence.

It was a shrine grove. The woman sat down on a flat rock beside the
moss-covered shrine dogs.[4]

"It's always cool here. Even in the middle of the summer there's a cool
wind."

"Are all the geisha like that?"

"They're all a little like her, I suppose. Some of the older ones are very
attractive, if you had wanted one of them." Her eyes were on the ground,
and she spoke coldly. The dusky green of the cedars seemed to reflect
from her neck.

Shimamura looked up at the cedar branches. "It's all over. My strength
left me—really, it seems very funny."

From behind the rock, the cedars threw up their trunks in perfectly
straight lines, so high that he could see the tops only by arching his back.
The dark needles blocked out the sky, and the stillness seemed to be singing quietly. The trunk against which Shimamura leaned was the oldest of
all. For some reason all the branches on the north side had withered, and,
their tips broken and fallen, they looked like stakes driven into the trunk
with their sharp ends out, to make a terrible weapon for some god.

"I made a mistake. I saw you as soon as I came down from the moun-

---

4. Stone-carved statues that are the guardians of the shrine. Designed to blend into the natural setting,
Shinto shrines are typically characterized by large, aged trees; clean, uncluttered grounds; and subdued
colors, symbolizing the ritual purity of Shinto. The shrine area exudes a sense of tranquillity and solitude.

tains, and I let myself think that all the geisha here were like you," he laughed. It occurred to him now that the thought of washing away in such short order the vigor of seven days in the mountains had perhaps first come to him when he saw the cleanness of this woman.

She gazed down at the river, distant in the afternoon sun. Shimamura was a little unsure of himself.

"I forgot," she suddenly remarked, with forced lightness. "I brought your tobacco. I went back up to your room a little while ago and found that you had gone out. I wondered where you could be, and then I saw you running up the mountain for all you were worth. I watched from the window. You were very funny. But you forgot your tobacco. Here."

She took the tobacco from her kimono sleeve and lighted a match for him.

"I wasn't very nice to that poor girl."

"But it's up to the guest, after all, when he wants to let the geisha go."

Through the quiet, the sound of the rocky river came up to them with a rounded softness. Shadows were darkening in the mountain chasms on the other side of the valley, framed in the cedar branches.

"Unless she were as good as you, I'd feel cheated when I saw you afterwards."

"Don't talk to me about it. You're just unwilling to admit you lost, that's all." There was scorn in her voice, and yet an affection of quite a new sort flowed between them.

As it became clear to Shimamura that he had from the start wanted only this woman, and that he had taken his usual roundabout way of saying so, he began to see himself as rather repulsive and the woman as all the more beautiful. Something from that cool figure had swept through him after she called to him from under the cedars.

The high, thin nose was a little lonely, a little sad, but the bud of her lips opened and closed smoothly, like a beautiful little circle of leeches. Even when she was silent her lips seemed always to be moving. Had they had wrinkles or cracks, or had their color been less fresh, they would have struck one as unwholesome, but they were never anything but smooth and shining. The line of her eyelids neither rose nor fell. As if for some special reason, it drew its way straight across her face. There was something faintly comical about the effect, but the short, thick hair of her eyebrows sloped gently down to enfold the line discreetly. There was nothing remarkable about the outlines of her round, slightly aquiline face. With her skin like white porcelain coated over a faint pink, and her throat still girlish, not yet filled out, the impression she gave was above all one of cleanness, not quite one of real beauty.

Her breasts were rather full for a woman used to the high, binding *obi* of the geisha.

"The sand flies have come out," she said, standing up and brushing at the skirt of her kimono.

Alone in the quiet, they could think of little to say.

It was perhaps ten o'clock that night. The woman called loudly to Shimamura from the hall, and a moment later she fell into his room as if someone had thrown her. She collapsed in front of the table. Flailing with a drunken arm at everything that happened to be on it, she poured herself a glass of water and drank in great gulps.

She had gone out to meet some travelers down from the mountains that evening, men she had been friendly with during the skiing season the winter before. They had invited her to the inn, whereupon they had had a riotous party, complete with geisha, and had proceeded to get her drunk.

Her head waved uncertainly, and she seemed prepared to talk on forever. Presently she remembered herself. "I shouldn't be here. I'll come again. They'll be looking for me. I'll come again later." She staggered from the room.

An hour or so later, he heard uneven steps coming down the long hall. She was weaving from side to side, he could tell, running into a wall, stumbling to the floor.

"Shimamura, Shimamura," she called in a high voice. "I can't see. Shimamura!"

It was, with no attempt at covering itself, the naked heart of a woman calling out to her man. Shimamura was startled. That high, piercing voice must surely be echoing all through the inn. He got up hastily. Pushing her fingers through the paper panel, the woman clutched at the frame of the door, and fell heavily against him.

"You're here." Clinging to him, she sank to the floor. She leaned against him as she spoke. "I'm not drunk. Who says I'm drunk? Ah, it hurts, it hurts. It's just that it hurts. I know exactly what I'm doing. Give me water, I want water. I mixed my drinks, that was my mistake. That's what goes to your head. It hurts. They had a bottle of cheap whisky. How was I to know it was cheap?" She rubbed her forehead with her fists.

The sound of the rain outside was suddenly louder.

Each time he relaxed his embrace even a little, she threatened to collapse. His arm was around her neck so tight that her hair was rumpled against his cheek. He thrust a hand inside the neck of her kimono.

He added coaxing words, but she did not answer. She folded her arms like a bar over the breast he was asking for.

"What's the matter with you." She bit savagely at her arm, as though angered by its refusal to serve her. "Damn you, damn you. Lazy, useless. What's the matter with you."

Shimamura drew back startled. There were deep teeth-marks on her arm.

She no longer resisted, however. Giving herself up to his hands, she began writing something with the tip of her finger. She would tell him the people she liked, she said. After she had written the names of some twenty or thirty actors, she wrote "Shimamura, Shimamura," over and over again.

The delicious swelling under Shimamura's hand grew warmer.

"Everything is all right." His voice was serene. "Everything is all right again." He sensed something a little motherly in her.

But the headache came back. She writhed and twisted, and sank to the floor in a corner of the room.

"It won't do. It won't do. I'm going home. Going home."

"Do you think you can walk that far? And listen to the rain."

"I'll go home barefoot. I'll crawl home."

"You don't think that's a little dangerous? If you have to go, I'll take you."

The inn was on a hill, and the road was a steep one.

"Suppose you try loosening your clothes. Lie down for a little while and you'll feel well enough to go."

"No, no. This is the way. I'm used to it." She sat up straight and took a deep breath, but breathing was clearly painful. She felt a little nauseated, she said, and opened the window behind her, but she could not vomit. She seemed to be holding back the urge to fall down writhing on the floor. Now and then she came to herself. "I'm going home, I'm going home," she said again and again, and presently it was after two.

"Go on to bed. Go on to bed when a person tells you to."

"But what will you do?" Shimamura asked.

"I'll just sit here like this. When I feel a little better I'll go home. I'll go home before daylight." She crawled over on her knees and tugged at him. "Go on to sleep. Pay no attention to me, I tell you."

Shimamura went back to bed. The woman sprawled over the table and took another drink of water.

"Get up. Get up when a person tells you to."

"Which do you want me to do?"

"All right, go to sleep."

"You aren't making much sense, you know." He pulled her into bed after him.

Her face was turned half away, hidden from him, but after a time she thrust her lips violently toward him.

Then, as if in a delirium she were trying to tell of her pain, she repeated over and over, he did not know how many times: "No, no. Didn't you say you wanted to be friends?"

The almost too serious tone of it rather dulled his ardor, and as he saw her wrinkle her forehead in the effort to control herself, he thought of standing by the commitment he had made.

But then she said: "I won't have any regrets. I'll never have any regrets. But I'm not that sort of woman. It can't last. Didn't you say so yourself?"

She was still half numb from the liquor.

"It's not my fault. It's yours. You lost. You're the weak one. Not I." She ran on almost in a trance, and she bit at her sleeve as if to fight back the happiness.

She was quiet for a time, apparently drained of feeling. Then, as if the thought came to her from somewhere in her memory, she struck out: "You're laughing, aren't you? You're laughing at me."

"I am not."

"Deep in your heart you're laughing at me. Even if you aren't now, you will be later." She was choked with tears. Turning away from him, she buried her face in her hands.

But a moment later she was calm again. Soft and yielding as if she were offering herself up, she was suddenly very intimate, and she began telling him all about herself. She seemed quite to have forgotten the headache. She said not a word about what had just happened.

"But I've been so busy talking I haven't noticed how late it is." She smiled a little bashfully. She had to leave before daylight, she said. "It's still dark. But people here get up early." Time after time she got up to look out the window. "They won't be able to see my face yet. And it's raining. No one will be going out to the fields this morning."

She seemed reluctant to go even when the lines of the mountain and of the roofs on its slopes were floating out of the rain. Finally it was time for the hotel maids to be up and about. She retouched her hair and ran, almost fled, from the room, brushing aside Shimamura's offer to see her to the door. Someone might catch a glimpse of the two of them together.

Shimamura went back to Tokyo that day.

"You remember what you said then? But you were wrong. Why else would anyone come to such a place in December? I wasn't laughing at you."

The woman raised her head. Her face where it had been pressed against Shimamura's hand was red under the thick powder, from the eye across the bridge of the nose. It made him think of the snow-country cold, and yet, because of the darkness of her hair, there was a certain warmth in it.

She smiled quietly, as though dazzled by a bright light. Perhaps, as she smiled, she thought of "then," and Shimamura's words gradually colored her whole body. When she bowed her head, a little stiffly, he could see that even her back under her kimono was flushed a deep red. Set off by the color of her hair, the moist sensuous skin was as if laid naked before him. Her hair could not really have been called thick. Stiff like a man's, and swept up into a high Japanese-style coiffure with not a hair out of place, it glowed like some heavy black stone.

Shimamura looked at the hair and wondered whether the coldness that had so startled him—he had never touched such cold hair, he said— might be less the cold of the snow-country winter than something in the hair itself. The woman began counting on her fingers. For some time she counted on.

"What are you counting?" he asked. Still the counting continued.

"It was the twenty-third of May."

"You're counting the days, are you. Don't forget that July and August are two long months in a row."

"It's the hundred-and-ninety-ninth day. It's exactly a hundred and ninety-nine days."

"How did you remember it was the twenty-third of May?"

"All I have to do is look in my diary."

"You keep a diary?"

"It's always fun to read an old diary. But I don't hide anything when I write in my diary, and sometimes I'm ashamed to look at it myself."

"When did you begin?"

"Just before I went to Tokyo as a geisha. I didn't have any money, and I bought a plain notebook for two or three sen[5] and drew in lines. I must have had a very sharp pencil. The lines are all neat and close together, and every page is crammed from top to bottom. When I had enough money to

---

5. One sen equaled one-hundredth of a yen; the yen had a value of twenty-five to thirty cents before World War II.

buy a diary, it wasn't the same any more. I started taking things for granted. It's that way with my writing practice, too. I used to practice on newspapers before I even thought of trying good paper, but now I set it down on good paper from the start."

"And you've kept the diary all this time?"

"Yes. The year I was sixteen and this year have been the best. I write in my diary when I'm home from a party and ready for bed, and when I read it over I can see places where I've gone to sleep writing. . . . But I don't write every day. Some days I miss. Way off here in the mountains, every party's the same. This year I couldn't find anything except a diary with a new day on each page. It was a mistake. When I start writing, I want to write on and on."

But even more than at the diary, Shimamura was surprised at her statement that she had carefully catalogued every novel and short story she had read since she was fifteen or sixteen. The record already filled ten notebooks.

"You write down your criticisms, do you?"

"I could never do anything like that. I just write down the author and the characters and how they are related to each other. That is about all."

"But what good does it do?"

"None at all."

"A waste of effort."

"A complete waste of effort," she answered brightly, as though the admission meant little to her. She gazed solemnly at Shimamura, however.

A complete waste of effort. For some reason Shimamura wanted to stress the point. But, drawn to her at that moment, he felt a quiet like the voice of the rain flow over him. He knew well enough that for her it was in fact no waste of effort, but somehow the final determination that it was had the effect of distilling and purifying the woman's existence.

Her talk of novels seemed to have little to do with "literature" in the everyday sense of the word. The only friendly ties she had with the people of this village had come from exchanging women's magazines, and afterwards she had gone on with her reading by herself. She was quite indiscriminate and had little understanding of literature, and she borrowed even the novels and magazines she found lying in the guests' rooms at the inn. Not a few of the new novelists whose names came to her meant nothing to Shimamura. Her manner was as though she were talking of a distant foreign literature. There was something lonely, something sad in it, something that rather suggested a beggar who has lost all desire. It occurred to Shimamura that his own distant fantasy on the occidental ballet, built up from words and photographs in foreign books, was not in its way dissimilar.

She talked on happily too of movies and plays she had never seen. She had no doubt been starved all these months for someone who would listen to her. Had she forgotten that a hundred and ninety-nine days earlier exactly this sort of conversation had set off the impulse to throw herself at Shimamura? Again she lost herself in the talk, and again her words seemed to be warming her whole body.

But her longing for the city had become an undemanding dream, wrapped in simple resignation, and the note of wasted effort was much stronger in it than any suggestion of the exile's lofty dissatisfaction. She did not seem to find herself especially sad, but in Shimamura's eyes there was something strangely touching about her. Were he to give himself quite up to that consciousness of wasted effort, Shimamura felt, he would be drawn into a remote emotionalism that would make his own life a waste. But before him was the quick, live face of the woman, ruddy from the mountain air.

In any case, he had revised his view of her, and he had found, surprisingly, that her being a geisha made it even more difficult for him to be free and open with her.

Dead-drunk that night, she had savagely bitten her half-paralyzed arm in a fit of irritation at its recalcitrance. "What's the matter with you? Damn you, damn you. Lazy, worthless. What's the matter with you?"

And, unable to stand, she had rolled from side to side. "I'll never have any regrets. But I'm not that sort of woman. I'm not that sort of woman."

"The midnight for Tokyo." The woman seemed to sense his hesitation, and she spoke as if to push it away. At the sound of the train whistle she stood up. Roughly throwing open a paper-paneled door and the window behind it, she sat down on the sill with her body thrown back against the railing. The train moved off into the distance, its echo fading into a sound as of the night wind. Cold air flooded the room.

"Have you lost your mind?" Shimamura too went over to the window. The air was still, without a suggestion of wind.

It was a stern night landscape. The sound of the freezing of snow over the land seemed to roar deep into the earth. There was no moon. The stars, almost too many of them to be true, came forward so brightly that it was as if they were falling with the swiftness of the void. As the stars came nearer, the sky retreated deeper and deeper into the night color. The layers of the Border Range, indistinguishable one from another, cast their heaviness at the skirt of the starry sky in a blackness grave and somber enough to communicate their mass. The whole of the night scene came together in a clear, tranquil harmony.

As she sensed Shimamura's approach, the woman fell over with her breast against the railing. There was no hint of weakness in the pose. Rather, against the night, it was the strongest and most stubborn she could have taken. So we have to go through that again, thought Shimamura.

Black though the mountains were, they seemed at that moment brilliant with the color of the snow. They seemed to him somehow transparent, somehow lonely. The harmony between sky and mountains was lost.

Shimamura put his hand to the woman's throat. "You'll catch cold. See how cold it is." He tried to pull her back, but she clung to the railing.

"I'm going home." Her voice was choked.

"Go home, then."

"Let me stay like this a little longer."

"I'm going down for a bath."

"No, stay here with me."

"If you close the window."

"Let me stay here like this a little longer."

Half the village was hidden behind the cedars of the shrine grove. The light in the railway station, not ten minutes away by taxi, flickered on and off as if crackling in the cold.

The woman's hair, the glass of the window, the sleeve of his kimono—everything he touched was cold in a way Shimamura had never known before.

Even the straw mats under his feet seemed cold. He started down to the bath.

"Wait. I'll go with you." The woman followed meekly.

As she was rearranging the clothes he had thrown to the floor outside the bath, another guest, a man, came in. The woman crouched low in front of Shimamura and hid her face.

"Excuse me." The other guest started to back away.

"No, please," Shimamura said quickly. "We'll go next door." He scooped up his clothes and stepped over to the women's bath. The woman followed as if they were married. Shimamura plunged into the bath without looking back at her. He felt a high laugh mount to his lips now that he knew she was with him. He put his face to the hot-water tap and noisily rinsed his mouth.

Back in the room, she raised her head a little from the pillow and pushed her side hair up with her little finger.

"This makes me very sad." She said only that. Shimamura thought for a moment that her eyes were half open, but he saw that the thick eyelashes created the illusion.

The woman, always high-strung, did not sleep the whole night.

It was apparently the sound of the *obi* being tied that awakened Shimamura.

"I'm sorry. I should have let you sleep. It's still dark. Look—can you see me?" She turned off the light. "Can you see me? You can't?"

"I can't see you. It's still pitch dark."

"No, no. I want you to look close. Now. Can you see me?" She threw open the window. "It's no good. You can see me. I'm going."

Surprised anew at the morning cold, Shimamura raised his head from the pillow. The sky was still the color of night, but in the mountains it was already morning.

"But it's all right. The farmers aren't busy this time of the year, and no one will be out so early. But do you suppose someone might be going out into the mountains?" She talked on to herself, and she walked about trailing the end of the half-tied *obi*. "There were no guests on the five-o'clock from Tokyo. None of the inn people will be up for a long while yet."

Even when she had finished tying the *obi*, she stood up and sat down and stood up again, and wandered about the room with her eye on the window. She seemed on edge, like some restless night beast that fears the approach of the morning. It was as though a strange, magical wildness had taken her.

Presently the room was so light that he could see the red of her cheeks. His eye was fastened on that extraordinarily bright red.

"Your cheeks are flaming. That's how cold it is."

"It's not from the cold. It's because I've taken off my powder. I only have to get into bed and in a minute I'm warm as an oven. All the way to my feet." She knelt at the mirror by the bed.

"It's daylight. I'm going home."

Shimamura glanced up at her, and immediately lowered his head. The white in the depths of the mirror was the snow, and floating in the middle of it were the woman's bright red cheeks. There was an indescribably fresh beauty in the contrast.

Was the sun already up? The brightness of the snow was more intense, it seemed to be burning icily. Against it, the woman's hair became a clearer black, touched with a purple sheen.

Probably to keep snow from piling up, the water from the baths was led around the walls of the inn by a makeshift ditch, and in front of the entrance it spread out like a shallow spring. A powerful black dog stood on the stones by the doorway lapping at the water. Skis for the hotel guests, probably brought out from a storeroom, were lined up to dry, and the faint smell of mildew was sweetened by the steam. The snow that had fallen from the cedar branches to the roof of the public bath was breaking down into something warm and shapeless.

By the end of the year, that road would be shut off from sight by the snowstorms. She would have to go to her parties in long rubber boots with baggy "mountain trousers" over her kimono, and she would have a cape pulled around her and a veil over her face. The snow would by then be ten feet deep—the woman had looked down on the steep road from the window of the inn, high on a hill, before daybreak this morning, and now Shimamura was walking down the same road. Diapers hung high beside the road to dry. Under them stretched the vista of the Border Range, the snow on its peaks glowing softly. The green onions in the garden patches were not yet buried in the snow.

Children of the village were skiing in the fields.

As he started into the part of the village that fronted on the highway, he heard a sound as of quiet rain.

Little icicles glistened daintily along the eaves.

"While you're at it, would you mind shoveling a little from ours?" Dazzled by the bright light, a woman on her way back from the bath wiped at her forehead with a damp towel as she looked up at a man shoveling snow from a roof. A waitress, probably, who had drifted into the village a little in advance of the skiing season. Next door was a café with a sagging roof, its painted window flaking with age.

Rows of stones held down the shingles with which most of the houses along the street were roofed. Only on the side exposed to the sun did the round stones show their black surfaces, less a moist black from the melting snow than an ink-stone black, beaten away at by icy wind and storm. The houses were of a kind with the dark stones on their roofs. The low eaves hugging the ground seemed to have in them the very essence of the north country.

Children were breaking off chunks of ice from the drains and throwing them down in the middle of the road. It was no doubt the sparkle of the ice as it went flying off into bits that enchanted them so. Shimamura, standing in the sunlight, found it hard to believe that the ice could be so thick. He stopped for a moment to watch.

A girl of twelve or thirteen stood knitting apart from the rest, her back against a stone wall. Under the baggy "mountain trousers," her feet were bare but for sandals, and Shimamura could see that the soles were red and cracked from the cold. A girl of perhaps two stood on a bundle of fire-wood beside her patiently holding a ball of yarn. Even the faded, ashen line of reclaimed yarn from the younger girl to the older seemed warmly aglow.

He could hear a carpenter's plane in a ski shop seven or eight doors down the street. Five or six geisha were talking under the eaves opposite. Among them, he was sure, would be the woman, Komako—he had just that morning learned her geisha name[6] from a maid at the inn. And indeed, there she was. She had apparently noticed him. The deadly seri-ous expression on her face set her off from the others. She would of course flush scarlet, but if she could at least pretend that nothing had hap-pened—before Shimamura had time to go further with his thoughts, he saw that she had flushed to the throat. She might better have looked away, but her head turned little by little to follow him, while her eyes were fixed on the ground in acute discomfort.

Shimamura's cheeks too were aflame. He walked briskly by, and imme-diately Komako came after him.

"You mustn't. You embarrass me, walking by at a time like this."

"I embarrass you—you think I'm not embarrassed myself, with all of you lined up to waylay me? I could hardly make myself walk past. Is it always this way?"

"Yes, I suppose so. In the afternoon."

"But I'd think you'd be even more embarrassed, turning bright red and then chasing after me."

"What difference does it make?" The words were clear and definite, but she was blushing again. She stopped and put her arm around a persimmon tree beside the road. "I ran after you because I thought I might ask you to come by my house."

"Is your house near here?"

"Very near."

"I'll come if you'll let me read your diary."

"I'm going to burn my diary before I die."

"But isn't there a sick man in your house?"

"How did you know?"

"You were at the station to meet him yesterday. You had on a dark-blue cape. I was sitting near him on the train. And there was a woman with him, looking after him, as gentle as she could be. His wife? Or someone who went from here to bring him home? Or someone from Tokyo? She was exactly like a mother. I was very much impressed."

---

6. *Geisha* were given professional names, often based on the names of heroines in popular love stories or classical Japanese literature.

"Why didn't you say so last night? Why were you so quiet?" Something had upset her.

"His wife?"

Komako did not answer. "Why didn't you say anything last night? What a strange person you are."

Shimamura did not like this sharpness. Nothing he had done and nothing that had happened seemed to call for it, and he wondered if something basic in the woman's nature might not be coming to the surface. Still, when she came at him the second time, he had to admit that he was being hit in a vulnerable spot. This morning, as he glanced at Komako in that mirror reflecting the mountain snow, he had of course thought of the girl in the evening train window. Why then had he said nothing?

"It doesn't matter if there is a sick man. No one ever comes to my room." Komako went in through an opening in a low stone wall.

To the right was a small field, and to the left persimmon trees stood along the wall that marked off the neighboring plot. There seemed to be a flower garden in front of the house, and red carp were swimming in the little lotus pond. The ice had been broken away and lay piled along the bank. The house was old and decayed, like the pitted trunk of a persimmon. There were patches of snow on the roof, the rafters of which sagged to draw a wavy line at the eaves.

The air in the earthen-floored hallway was still and cold. Shimamura was led up a ladder before his eyes had become accustomed to the darkness. It was a ladder in the truest sense of the word, and the room at the top was an attic.

"This is the room the silkworms used to live in. Are you surprised?"

"You're lucky you've never fallen downstairs, drinking the way you do."

"I have. But generally when I've had too much to drink I crawl into the *kotatsu* downstairs and go off to sleep." She pushed her hand tentatively into the *kotatsu*, then went below for charcoal. Shimamura looked around at the curious room. Although there was but one low window, opening to the south, the freshly changed paper on the door turned off the rays of the sun brightly. The walls had been industriously pasted over with rice paper, so that the effect was rather like the inside of an old-fashioned paper box; but overhead was only the bare roof sloping down toward the window, as if a dark loneliness had settled itself over the room. Wondering what might be on the other side of the wall, Shimamura had the uneasy feeling that he was suspended in a void. But the walls and the floor, for all their shabbiness, were spotlessly clean.

For a moment he was taken with the fancy that the light must pass through Komako, living in the silkworms' room, as it passed through the translucent silkworms.

The *kotatsu* was covered with a quilt of the same rough, striped cotton material as the standard "mountain trousers." The chest of drawers was old, but the grain of the wood was fine and straight—perhaps it was a relic of Komako's years in Tokyo. It was badly paired with a cheap dresser, while the vermilion sewing-box gave off the luxurious glow of good lacquer. The boxes stacked along the wall behind a thin woolen curtain apparently served as bookshelves.

The kimono of the evening before hung on the wall, open to show the brilliant red under-kimono.

Komako came spryly up the ladder with a supply of charcoal.

"It's from the sickroom. But you needn't worry. They say fire spreads no germs." Her newly dressed hair almost brushed the *kotatsu* as she stirred away at the coals. The music teacher's son had intestinal tuberculosis, she said, and had come home to die.

But it was not entirely accurate to say that he had "come home." He had as a matter of fact not been born here. This was his mother's home. His mother had taught dancing down on the coast even when she was no longer a geisha, but she had had a stroke while she was still in her forties, and had come back to this hot spring to recover. The son, fond of machinery since he was a child, had stayed behind to work in a watch-shop. Presently he moved to Tokyo and started going to night school, and the strain was evidently too much for him. He was only twenty-five.

All this Komako told him with no hesitation, but she said nothing about the girl who had brought the man home, and nothing about why she herself was in this house.

Shimamura felt most uncomfortable at what she did say, however. Suspended there in the void, she seemed to be broadcasting to the four directions.

As he stepped from the hallway, he saw something faintly white through the corner of his eye. It was a samisen box,[7] and it struck him as larger and longer than it should be. He found it hard to imagine her carrying so unwieldy an object to parties. The darkened door inside the hallway slid open.

"Do you mind if I step over this, Komako?" It was that clear voice, so beautiful that it was almost sad. Shimamura waited for an echo to come back.

It was Yoko's voice, the voice that had called out over the snow to the station master the night before.

"No, please go ahead." Yoko stepped lightly over the samisen box, a glass chamber-pot in her hand.

It was clear, from the familiar way she had talked to the station master the evening before and from the way she wore "mountain trousers," that she was a native of this snow country, but the bold pattern of her *obi*, half visible over the trousers, made the rough russet and black stripes of the latter seem fresh and cheerful, and for the same reason the long sleeves of her woolen kimono took on a certain voluptuous charm. The trousers, split just below the knees, filled out toward the hips, and the heavy cotton, for all its natural stiffness, was somehow supple and gentle.

Yoko darted one quick, piercing glance at Shimamura and went silently out over the earthen floor.

Even when he had left the house, Shimamura was haunted by that glance, burning just in front of his forehead. It was cold as a very distant light, for the inexpressible beauty of it had made his heart rise when, the night before, that light off in the mountains had passed across the girl's

---

7. Komako's mastery of the instrument comes up later in the story.

face in the train window and lighted her eye for a moment. The impression came back to Shimamura, and with it the memory of the mirror filled with snow, and Komako's red cheeks floating in the middle of it.

He walked faster. His legs were round and plump, but he was seized with a certain abandon as he walked along gazing at the mountains he was so fond of, and his pace quickened, though he hardly knew it. Always ready to give himself up to reverie, he could not believe that the mirror floating over the evening scenery and the other snowy mirror were really works of man. They were part of nature, and part of some distant world.

And the room he had only this moment left had become part of that same distant world.

Startled at himself, in need of something to cling to, he stopped a blind masseuse at the top of the hill.

"Could you give me a massage?"

"Let me see. What time will it be?" She tucked her cane under her arm and, taking a covered pocket watch from her *obi*, felt at the face with her left hand. "Two thirty-five. I have an appointment over beyond the station at three-thirty. But I suppose it won't matter if I'm a little late."

"You're very clever to be able to tell the time."

"It has no glass, and I can feel the hands."

"You can feel the figures?"

"Not the figures." She took the watch out again, a silver one, large for a woman, and flicked open the lid. She laid her fingers across the face with one at twelve and one at six, and a third halfway between at three. "I can tell the time fairly well. I may be a minute off one way or the other, but I never miss by as much as two minutes."

"You don't find the road a little slippery?"

"When it rains my daughter comes to call for me. At night I take care of the people in the village, and never come up this far. The maids at the inn are always joking and saying it's because my husband won't let me go out at night."

"Your children are growing up?"

"The oldest girl is twelve." They had reached Shimamura's room, and they were silent for a time as the massaging began. The sound of a samisen came to them from the distance.

"Who would that be, I wonder."

"You can always tell which geisha it is by the tone?"

"I can tell some of them. Some I can't. You must not have to work. Feel how nice and soft you are."

"No stiff muscles on me."

"A little stiff here at the base of the neck. But you're just right, not too fat and not too thin. And you don't drink, do you?"

"You can tell that?"

"I have three other customers with physiques exactly like yours."

"A common sort of physique."

"But when you don't drink, you don't know what it is really to enjoy yourself—to forget everything that happens."

"Your husband drinks, does he?"

"Much too much."

"But whoever it is, she's not much of a musician."

"Very poor indeed."

"Do you play yourself?"

"I did when I was young. From the time I was eight till I was nineteen. I haven't played in fifteen years now. Not since I was married."

Did all blind people look younger than they were? Shimamura wondered.

"But if you learn when you're young, you never forget."

"My hands have changed from doing this sort of work, but my ear is still good. It makes me very impatient to hear them playing. But then I suppose I felt impatient at my own playing when I was young." She listened for a time. "Fumi at the Izutsuya, maybe. The best ones and the worst are the easiest to tell."

"There are good ones?"

"Komako is very good. She's young, but she's improved a great deal lately."

"Really?"

"You know her, don't you? I say she's good, but you have to remember that our standards here in the mountains are not very high."

"I don't really know her. I was on the train with the music teacher's son last night, though."

"He's well again?"

"Apparently not."

"Oh? He's been sick for a long time in Tokyo, and they say it was to help pay the doctors' bills that Komako became a geisha last summer. I wonder if it did any good."

"Komako, you say?"

"They were only engaged. But I suppose you feel better afterwards if you've done everything you can."

"She was engaged to him?"

"So they say. I don't really know, but that's the rumor."

It was almost too ordinary a thing to hear gossip about geisha from the hot-spring masseuse, and that fact had the perverse effect of making the news the more startling; and Komako's having become a geisha to help her fiancé was so ordinary a bit of melodrama that he found himself almost refusing to accept it. Perhaps certain moral considerations—questions of the propriety of selling oneself as a geisha—helped the refusal.

Shimamura was beginning to think he would like to go deeper into the story, but the masseuse was silent.

If Komako was the man's fiancée, and Yoko was his new lover, and the man was going to die—the expression "wasted effort" again came into Shimamura's mind. For Komako thus to guard her promise to the end, for her even to sell herself to pay doctors' bills—what was it if not wasted effort?

He would accost her with this fact, he would drive it home, when he saw her again, he said to himself; and yet her existence seemed to have become purer and cleaner for this new bit of knowledge.

Aware of a shameful danger lurking in his numbed sense of the false and empty, he lay concentrating on it, trying to feel it, for some time after the masseuse left. He was chilled to the pit of his stomach—but someone had left the windows wide open.

The color of evening had already fallen on the mountain valley, early buried in shadows. Out of the dusk the distant mountains, still reflecting the light of the evening sun, seemed to have come much nearer.

Presently, as the mountain chasms were far and near, high and low, the shadows in them began to deepen, and the sky was red over the snowy mountains, bathed now in but a wan light.

Cedar groves stood out darkly by the river bank, at the ski ground, around the shrine.

Like a warm light, Komako poured in on the empty wretchedness that had assailed Shimamura.

There was a meeting at the inn to discuss plans for the ski season. She had been called in for the party afterwards. She put her hands into the *kotatsu*, then quickly reached up and stroked Shimamura's cheek.

"You're pale this evening. Very strange." She clutched at the soft flesh of his cheek as if to tear it away. "Aren't you the foolish one, though."

She already seemed a little drunk. When she came back from the party she collapsed before the mirror, and drunkenness came out on her face to almost comic effect. "I know nothing about it. Nothing. My head aches. I feel terrible. Terrible. I want a drink. Give me water."

She pressed both hands to her face and tumbled over with little concern for her carefully dressed hair. Presently she brought herself up again and began cleaning away the thick powder with cold cream. The face underneath was a brilliant red. She was quite delighted with herself. To Shimamura it was astonishing that drunkenness could pass so quickly. Her shoulders were shaking from the cold.

All through August she had been near nervous collapse, she told him quietly.

"I thought I'd go mad. I kept brooding over something, and I didn't know myself what it was. It was terrifying. I couldn't sleep. I kept myself under control only when I went out to a party. I had all sorts of dreams, and I lost my appetite. I would sit there jabbing at the floor for hours on end, all through the hottest part of the day."

"When did you first go out as a geisha?"

"In June. I thought for a while I might go to Hamamatsu."

"Get married?"

She nodded. The man had been after her to marry him, but she couldn't like him. She had had great trouble deciding what to do.

"But if you didn't like him, what were you so undecided about?"

"It's not that simple."

"Marriage has so much charm?"

"Don't be nasty. It's more that I want to have everything around me tidy and in order."

Shimamura grunted.

"You're not a very satisfying person, you know."

"Was there something between you and the man from Hamamatsu?"

She flung out her answer: "If there had been, do you think I would have hesitated? But he said that as long as I stayed here, he wouldn't let me marry anyone else. He said he would do everything possible to stand in the way."

"But what could he do from as far away as Hamamatsu? You worried about that?"

Komako stretched out for a time, enjoying the warmth of her body. When she spoke again, her tone was quite casual. "I thought I was pregnant." She giggled. "It seems ridiculous when I look back on it now."

She curled up like a little child, and grabbed at the neck of his kimono with her two fists.

The rich eyelashes again made him think that her eyes were half open.

Her elbow against the brazier, Komako was scribbling something on the back of an old magazine when Shimamura awoke the next morning.

"I can't go home. I jumped up when the maid came to bring charcoal, but it was already broad daylight. The sun was shining in on the door. I was a little drunk last night, and I slept too well."

"What time is it?"

"It's already eight."

"Let's go have a bath." Shimamura got out of bed.

"I can't. Someone might see me in the hall." She was completely tamed. When Shimamura came back from the bath, he found her industriously cleaning the room, a kerchief draped artistically over her head.

She had polished the legs of the table and the edge of the brazier almost too carefully, and she stirred up the charcoal with a practiced hand.

Shimamura sat idly smoking, his feet in the *kotatsu*. When the ashes dropped from his cigarette Komako took them up in a handkerchief and brought him an ashtray. He laughed, a bright morning laugh. Komako laughed too.

"If you had a husband, you'd spend all your time scolding him."

"I would not. But I'd be laughed at for folding up even my dirty clothes. I can't help it. That's the way I am."

"They say you can tell everything about a woman by looking inside her dresser drawers."

"What a beautiful day." They were having breakfast, and the morning sun flooded the room. "I should have gone home early to practice the samisen. The sound is different on a day like this." She looked up at the crystal-clear sky.

The snow on the distant mountains was soft and creamy, as if veiled in a faint smoke.

Shimamura, remembering what the masseuse had said, suggested that she practice here instead. Immediately she telephoned her house to ask for music and a change of clothes.

So the house he had seen the day before had a telephone, thought Shimamura. The eyes of the other girl, Yoko, floated into his mind.

"That girl will bring your music?"

"She might."

"You're engaged to the son, are you?"

"Well! When did you hear that?"

"Yesterday."

"Aren't you strange? If you heard it yesterday, why didn't you tell me?" But her tone showed none of the sharpness of the day before. Today there was only a clean smile on her face.

"That sort of thing would be easier to talk about if I had less respect for you."

"What are you really thinking, I wonder? That's why I don't like Tokyo people."

"You're trying to change the subject. You haven't answered my question, you know."

"I'm not trying to change the subject. You really believed it?"

"I did."

"You're lying again. You didn't really."

"I couldn't quite believe all of it, as a matter of fact. But they said you went to work as a geisha to help pay doctors' bills."

"It sounds like something out of a cheap magazine. But it's not true. I was never engaged to him. People seem to think I was, though. It wasn't to help anyone in particular that I became a geisha. But I owe a great deal to his mother, and I had to do what I could."

"You're talking in riddles."

"I'll tell you everything. Very clearly. There does seem to have been a time when his mother thought it would be a good idea for us to get married. But she only thought it. She never said a word. Both of us knew in a vague sort of way what was on her mind, but it went no farther. And that's all there is to tell."

"Childhood friends."

"That's right. But we've lived most of our lives apart. When they sent me to Tokyo to be a geisha, he was the only one who saw me off. I have that written down on the very first page of my very oldest diary."

"If the two of you had stayed together, you'd probably be married by now."

"I doubt it."

"You would be, though."

"You needn't worry about him. He'll be dead before long."

"But is it right for you to be spending your nights away from home?"

"It's not right for you to ask. How can a dying man keep me from doing as I like?"

Shimamura could think of no answer.

Why was it that Komako said not a word about the girl Yoko?

And Yoko, who had taken care of the sick man on the train, quite as his mother must have when he was very young—how would she feel coming to an inn with a change of kimono for Komako, who was something, Shimamura could not know what, to the man Yoko had come home with?

Shimamura found himself off in his usual distant fantasies.

"Komako, Komako." Yoko's beautiful voice was low but clear.

"Thank you very much." Komako went out to the dressing-room. "You brought it yourself, did you? It must have been heavy."

Yoko left immediately.

The top string snapped as Komako plucked tentatively at the samisen. Shimamura could tell even while she was changing the string and tuning the instrument that she had a firm, confident touch. She took up a bulky bundle and undid it on the *kotatsu*. Inside were an ordinary book of lyrics and some twenty scores. Shimamura glanced curiously at the latter.

"You practice from these?"

"I have to. There's no one here who can teach me."

"What about the woman you live with?"

"She's paralyzed."

"If she can talk she ought to be able to help you."

"But she can't talk. She can still use her left hand to correct mistakes in dancing, but it only annoys her to have to listen to the samisen and not be able to do anything about it."

"Can you really understand the music from only a score?"[8]

"I understand it very well."

"The publishing gentleman[9] would be happy if he knew he had a real geisha—not just an ordinary amateur—practicing from his scores way off here in the mountains."

"In Tokyo I was expected to dance, and they gave me dancing lessons. But I got only the faintest idea of how to play the samisen. If I were to lose that there would be no one here to teach me again. So I use scores."

"And singing?"

"I don't like to sing. I did learn a few songs from my dancing, and I manage to get through them, but newer things I've had to pick up from the radio. I've no idea how near right I am. My own private style—you'd laugh at it, I know. And then my voice gives out when I'm singing for someone I know well. It's always loud and brave for strangers." She looked a little bashful for a moment, then brought herself up and glanced at Shimamura as though signaling that she was ready for him to begin.

He was embarrassed. He was unfortunately no singer.

He was generally familiar with the Nagauta[1] music of the Tokyo theater and dance, and he knew the words to most of the repertoire. He had had no formal training, however. Indeed he associated the Nagauta less with the parlor performance of the geisha than with the actor on the stage.

"The customer is being difficult." Giving her lower lip a quick little bite, Komako brought the samisen to her knee, and, as if that made her a different person, turned earnestly to the lyrics before her.

"I've been practicing this one since last fall."

A chill swept over Shimamura. The goose flesh seemed to rise even to his cheeks. The first notes opened a transparent emptiness deep in his entrails, and in the emptiness the sound of the samisen reverberated. He was startled—or, better, he fell back as under a well-aimed blow. Taken with a feeling almost of reverence, washed by waves of remorse, defenseless, quite deprived of strength—there was nothing for him to do but give himself up to the current, to the pleasure of being swept off wherever Komako would take him.

---

8. While there is some notation for the samisen, *geisha* usually learn to play the instrument through rote memorization, imitating music they hear performed by a teacher. Komako's reliance solely on written music illustrates her isolation. 9. That is, the publisher of the sheet music Komako is using. 1. "Long songs" (literal trans.); lyric ballads common in *kabuki* plays and popular among *geisha* and amateur students of the samisen.

She was a mountain geisha, not yet twenty, and she could hardly be as good as all that, he told himself. And in spite of the fact that she was in a small room, was she not slamming away at the instrument as though she were on the stage? He was being carried away by his own mountain emotionalism. Komako purposely read the words in a monotone, now slowing down and now jumping over a passage that was too much trouble; but gradually she seemed to fall into a spell. As her voice rose higher, Shimamura began to feel a little frightened. How far would that strong, sure touch take him? He rolled over and pillowed his head on an arm, as if in bored indifference.

The end of the song released him. Ah, this woman is in love with me— but he was annoyed with himself for the thought.

Komako looked up at the clear sky over the snow. "The tone is different on a day like this." The tone had been as rich and vibrant as her remark suggested. The air was different. There were no theater walls, there was no audience, there was none of the city dust. The notes went out crystalline into the clean winter morning, to sound on the far, snowy peaks.

Practicing alone, not aware herself of what was happening, perhaps, but with all the wideness of nature in this mountain valley for her companion, she had come quite as a part of nature to take on this special power. Her very loneliness beat down sorrow and fostered a wild strength of will. There was no doubt that it had been a great victory of the will, even granted that she had had an amount of preparatory training, for her to learn complicated airs from only a score, and presently go through them from memory.

To Shimamura it was wasted effort, this way of living. He sensed in it too a longing that called out to him for sympathy. But the life and way of living no doubt flowed thus grandly from the samisen with a new worth for Komako herself.

Shimamura, untrained in the niceties of samisen technique and conscious only of the emotion in the tone, was perhaps an ideal audience for Komako.

By the time she had begun her third song—the voluptuous softness of the music itself may have been responsible—the chill and the goose flesh had disappeared, and Shimamura, relaxed and warm, was gazing into Komako's face. A feeling of intense physical nearness came over him.

The high, thin nose was usually a little lonely, a little sad, but today, with the healthy, vital flush on her cheeks, it was rather whispering: I am here too. The smooth lips seemed to reflect back a dancing light even when they were drawn into a tight bud; and when for a moment they were stretched wide, as the singing demanded, they were quick to contract again into that engaging little bud. Their charm was exactly like the charm of her body itself. Her eyes, moist and shining, made her look like a very young girl. She wore no powder, and the polish of the city geisha had over it a layer of mountain color. Her skin, suggesting the newness of a freshly peeled onion or perhaps a lily bulb, was flushed faintly, even to the throat. More than anything, it was clean.

Seated rigidly upright, she seemed more demure and maidenly than usual.

This time using a score, she sang a song she had not yet finished memorizing. At the end she silently pushed the plectrum[2] under the strings and let herself fall into an easier posture.

Her manner quickly took on a touch of the seductive and alluring.

Shimamura could think of nothing to say. Komako did not seem to care particularly what he thought of her playing, however. She was quite unaffectedly pleased with herself.

"Can you always tell which geisha it is from the tone of the samisen?"

"That's easy. There aren't twenty of us all together. It depends a little on the style, though. The individual comes out more in some styles than in others."

She took up the samisen again and shifted her weight so that her feet were a little to one side and the instrument rested on the calf of one leg.

"This is the way you hold it when you're small." She leaned toward the samisen as though it were too large for her. "Da-a-ark hair. . . ." Her voice was deliberately childish and she picked out the notes uncertainly.

" 'Dark Hair' was the first one you learned?"

"Uh-uh." She shook her head girlishly, as no doubt she did in the days when she was still too small to hold the samisen properly.

Komako no longer tried to leave before daybreak when she stayed the night.

"Komako," the two-year-old daughter of the innkeeper would call from far down the hall, her voice rising in the mountain-country lilt. The two of them would play happily in the *kotatsu* until nearly noon, when they would go for a bath.

Back from the bath, Komako was combing her hair. "Whenever the child sees a geisha, she calls out 'Komako' in that funny accent, and when she sees a picture of someone with her hair done in the old way, that's 'Komako' too. Children can tell when you like them. Come, Kimi. Let's go play at Komako's." She stood up to leave, then sat down lazily on the veranda. "Eager people from Tokyo already out skiing."

The room looked from high ground directly south over the ski runs at the base of the mountain.

Shimamura glanced up from the *kotatsu*. There were patches of snow on the mountain, and five or six figures in black ski clothes were moving about in the terraced fields. It seemed a trifle silly. The slope was a gentle one, and the walls between the fields were not yet covered with snow.

"They look like students. Is today Sunday? Do you suppose that's fun?"

"They're good, though," Komako said, as if to herself. "Guests are always surprised when a geisha says hello to them on the ski grounds. They don't recognize her for the snow-burn. At night the powder hides it."

"You wear ski clothes?"

She wore "mountain trousers," she said. "But what a nuisance the ski season is. It's all coming again. You see them in the evening at the inn, and they say they'll see you again the next day skiing. Maybe I should give

---

2. A pick for plucking the strings of a musical instrument.

up skiing this year. Good-by. Come along, Kimi. We'll have snow this evening. It's always cold the night before it snows."

Shimamura went out to the veranda. Komako was leading Kimi down the steep road below the ski grounds.

The sky was clouding over. Mountains still in the sunlight stood out against shadowed mountains. The play of light and shade changed from moment to moment, sketching a chilly landscape. Presently the ski grounds too were in shadow. Below the window Shimamura could see little needles of frost like isinglass[3] among the withered chrysanthemums, though water was still dripping from the snow on the roof.

It did not snow that evening. A hailstorm turned to rain.

Shimamura called Komako again the night before he was to leave. It was a clear, moonlit night. At eleven o'clock the air was bitterly cold, but Komako insisted on going for a walk. She pulled him roughly from the *kotatsu*.

The road was frozen. The village lay quiet under the cold sky. Komako hitched up the skirt of her kimono and tucked it into her *obi*. The moon shone like a blade frozen in blue ice.

"We'll go to the station," said Komako.

"You're insane. It's more than a mile each way."

"You'll be going back to Tokyo soon. We'll go look at the station."

Shimamura was numb from his shoulders to his thighs.

Back in his room, Komako sank disconsolately to the floor. Her head was bowed and her arms were deep in the *kotatsu*. Strangely, she refused to go with him to the bath.

Bedding had been laid out with the foot of the mattress inside the *kotatsu*. Komako was sitting forlornly beside it when Shimamura came back from the bath. She said nothing.

"What's the matter?"

"I'm going home."

"Don't be foolish."

"Go on to bed. Just let me sit here for a little while."

"Why do you want to go home?"

"I'm not going home. I'll sit here till morning."

"Don't be difficult."

"I'm not being difficult. I'm not being difficult."

"Then . . . ?"

"I . . . don't feel well."

"Is that all?" Shimamura laughed. "I'll leave you quite to yourself."

"No."

"And why did you have to go out and run all over town?"

"I'm going home."

"There's no need to go home."

"But it's not easy for me. Go on back to Tokyo. It's not easy for me."

Her face was low over the *kotatsu*.

Was it sorrow at finding herself about to sink into too deep a relationship with a traveler? Or at having to keep herself under control at so dear a

---

3. Thin, translucent sheets of mica (an aluminum silicate mineral).

moment? She has come that far, then, Shimamura said to himself. He too was silent for a time.

"Please go back to Tokyo."

"As a matter of fact, I was thinking of going back tomorrow."

"No! Why are you going back?" She looked up, startled, as though aroused from sleep.

"What can I do for you, no matter how long I stay?"

She gazed at him for a moment, then burst out violently: "You don't have to say that. What reason have you to say that?" She stood up irritably, and threw herself at his neck. "It's wrong of you to say such things. Get up. Get up, I tell you." The words poured out deliriously, and she fell down beside him, quite forgetting in her derangement the physical difficulty she had spoken of earlier.

Some time later, she opened warm, moist eyes.

She picked up the hair ornament that had fallen to the floor.

"You really must go back tomorrow," she said quietly.

As Shimamura was changing clothes to leave on the three-o'clock train the next afternoon, the manager of the inn beckoned Komako into the hall. "Let's see. Suppose we make it about eleven hours," he could hear Komako's answer. They were evidently discussing the bill for her services as a geisha, and the manager perhaps thought it would be unreasonable to charge for the whole sixteen or seventeen hours.

The bill as a matter of fact was computed by the hour—"Left at five," or "Left at twelve"—without the usual charge for overnight services.

Komako, in an overcoat and a white scarf, saw him to the station.

Even when he had finished buying presents to take back to Tokyo, he had some twenty minutes to kill. Walking with Komako in the slightly raised station plaza, he thought what a narrow little valley it was, crowded in among the snowy mountains. Komako's too-black hair was a little touching, a little sad, in the loneliness of the shadowed mountain pocket.

The sun shone dimly on a spot in the mountains far down the river.

"It's melted a good deal since I came."

"Two days of snow, though, and we'll have six feet. Then it snows again, and before long the lights on those poles are out of sight. I'll walk along thinking of you, and I'll find myself strung up on a wire."

"The snow is that deep?"

"They say that in the next town up the line the schoolchildren jump naked from the second floor of the dormitory. They sink out of sight in the snow, and they move around under it as though they were swimming. Look, a snowplow."

"I'd like to see it that deep. But I suppose the inn will be crowded. And there might be danger of slides along the way."

"With you it's not a question of money, is it? Have you always had so much to spend?" She turned to look up at his face. "Why don't you grow a mustache?"

"I've thought of it." Shimamura, freshly shaven, stroked the blue-black traces of his beard. A deep line from the corner of his mouth set off the softness of his cheek. Was that, he wondered, what Komako found attrac-

tive? "You always look a little as though you'd just shaved too when you
take off that powder."

"Listen! The crows. That frightening way they sometimes have. Where
are they, I wonder? And isn't it cold!" Komako hugged herself as she
looked up at the sky.

"Shall we go in by the stove?"

A figure in "mountain trousers" came running up the wide road from
the main highway into the station plaza. It was Yoko.

"Komako. Yukio—Komako," she panted, clinging to Komako like a
child that has run frightened to its mother, "come home. Right away.
Yukio's worse. Right away."

Komako closed her eyes, as if from the pain of the assault on her shoulder. Her face was white, but she shook her head with surprising firmness.

"I can't go home. I'm seeing off a guest."

Shimamura was startled. "You needn't see me off."

"It's not right to leave. How do I know you'll come again?"

"I'll come, I'll come."

Yoko seemed not to hear the exchange. "I just called the inn," she went
on feverishly, "and they said you were at the station. So I came here. I ran
all the way. Yukio is asking for you." She pulled at Komako, but Komako
shook her off impatiently.

"Leave me alone."

It was Komako who reeled back, however. She retched violently, but
nothing came from her mouth. The rims of her eyes were moist. There
was goose flesh on her cheeks.

Yoko stood rigid, gazing at Komako. Her face, like a mask, wore an
expression of such utter earnestness that it was impossible to tell whether
she was angry or surprised or grieved. It seemed an extraordinarily pure
and simple face to Shimamura.

She turned quickly and, without the slightest change of expression,
clutched at Shimamura's hand. "I'm sorry, but would you let her go
home?" A tense, high-pitched voice assailed him. "Let her go home."

"Of course I'll let her go home. Go on home," he called out to Komako.
"Don't be a fool."

"And what say do you have in the matter?" Komako pushed Yoko
roughly away from him.

Shimamura tried to signal the taxi waiting in front of the station. Yoko
clutched at his arm so tightly that his fingers were numbed. "I'll send her
home in a taxi," he said. "Why don't you go on ahead? People will be
watching us."

Yoko nodded quickly, and turned away with almost unbelievable alacrity. Why was the girl always so earnest, so sober, Shimamura wondered.
But such musings did not seem entirely in keeping with the occasion.

That voice, so beautiful it was almost lonely, lingered in Shimamura's
ears as if it were echoing back from somewhere in the snowy mountains.

"Where are you going?" Komako pulled at Shimamura. He had signaled the taxi and was walking toward it. "I won't. I'm not going home."

For an instant Shimamura felt something very near physical revulsion.

"I don't know what there is among the three of you, but the man may be dying even now. She came for you, didn't she, because he wants to see you. Go home like a good girl. You'll regret it all your life if you don't. What if he dies even while you're standing here? Don't be stubborn. Forgive and forget."

"Forgive and forget? You don't understand. You don't understand at all."

"And when they sent you to Tokyo, he was the only one who saw you off, didn't you say? Do you think it's right not to say good-by to the man you yourself said was on the very first page of the very first volume of your diary? This is the very last page of his."

"But I don't want to. I don't want to see a man die."

It could have been the coldest heartlessness or too warm a passion — Shimamura did not know which.

"I'll not be able to write in my diary any more. I'll burn it," she said softly, almost to herself. Her cheeks were flushed. "You're a good, simple person at heart, aren't you? If you really are, I won't mind sending my whole diary to you. You won't laugh at me? You're a good, honest person at heart, I'm sure."

Shimamura was moved by a wave of feeling he could not define himself. He thought he must indeed be the plainest, most honest person in the world. He no longer worried about sending Komako home. She said nothing more.

A porter from the inn came to tell them that the gate to the tracks was open.

Four or five villagers in somber winter dress got on and off the train.

"I'll not go to the platform with you. Good-by." Komako stood inside the closed window of the waiting-room. From the train window it was as though one strange piece of fruit had been left behind in the grimy glass case of a shabby mountain grocery.

The window of the waiting-room was clear for an instant as the train started to move. Komako's face glowed forth, and as quickly disappeared. It was the bright red it had been in the mirror that snowy morning, and for Shimamura that color again seemed to be the point at which he parted with reality.

The train climbed the north slope of the Border Range into the long tunnel. On the far side it moved down a mountain valley. The color of evening was descending from chasms between the peaks. The dim brightness of the winter afternoon seemed to have been sucked into the earth, and the battered old train had shed its bright shell in the tunnel. There was no snow on the south slope.

Following a stream, the train came out on the plain. A mountain, cut at the top in curious notches and spires, fell off in a graceful sweep to the far skirts. Over it the moon was rising. The solid, integral shape of the mountain, taking up the whole of the evening landscape there at the end of the plain, was set off in a deep purple against the pale light of the sky. The moon was no longer an afternoon white, but, faintly colored, it had not yet taken on the clear coldness of the winter night. There was not a bird in the sky. Nothing broke the lines of the wide skirts to the right and the left. Where the mountain swept down to meet the river, a stark white building, a hydroelectric plant perhaps, stood out sharply from the withered scene the train window framed, one last spot saved from the night.

The window began to steam over. The landscape outside was dusky, and the figures of the passengers floated up half-transparent. It was the play of that evening mirror again. The train, probably no more than three or four worn-out, faded, old-fashioned coaches strung together, was not from the same world as the trains one finds on the main lines. The light inside was dim.

Shimamura abandoned himself to the fancy that he had stepped into some unreal conveyance, that he was being borne away in emptiness, cut off from time and place. The monotonous sound of the wheels became the woman's voice.

Her words, though short and broken, were a sign that she was alive in all her vital intensity, and he knew he had not forgotten her from the fact that listening was a trial. But to the Shimamura of that moment, moving away from the woman, the voice was already a distant one that could do no more than sharpen the poignancy of travel.

Would Yukio be breathing his last even now? Komako had for reasons of her own refused to go home; and had she then failed to reach his bedside in time?

There were so few passengers that Shimamura felt a little uneasy.

Besides Shimamura himself, there were only a man, probably in his fifties, and opposite him a red-faced girl. A black shawl was thrown over the full flesh of her shoulders, and her cheeks were a wonderful, fiery red. She leaned slightly forward to catch every word the man said, and she answered him happily. A pair off on a long journey together, Shimamura concluded.

As the train pulled into a station behind which rose the chimneys of spinning-factories, however, the man hastily got up, took a wicker trunk from the baggage rack, and threw it out the window to the platform. "Maybe we'll meet again sometime," he called back to the girl as he hurried from the train.

Shimamura suddenly wanted to weep. He had been caught quite off guard, and it struck him afresh that he had said good-by to the woman and was on his way home.

He had not considered the possibility that the two had simply met on the train. The man was perhaps a traveling salesman.

PART TWO

It was the egg-laying season for moths, Shimamura's wife told him as he left Tokyo, and he was not to leave his clothes hanging in the open. There were indeed moths at the inn. Five or six large corn-colored moths clung to the decorative lantern under the eaves, and in the little dressing-room was a moth whose body was large out of all proportion to its wings.

The windows were still screened from the summer. A moth so still that it might have been glued there clung to one of the screens. Its feelers stood out like delicate wool, the color of cedar bark, and its wings, the length of a woman's finger, were a pale, almost diaphanous green. The ranges of mountains beyond were already autumn-red in the evening sun. That one spot of pale green struck him as oddly like the color of death. The fore and after wings overlapped to make a deeper green, and the wings fluttered like thin pieces of paper in the autumn wind.

Wondering if the moth was alive, Shimamura went over to the window and rubbed his finger over the inside of the screen. The moth did not move. He struck at it with his fist, and it fell like a leaf from a tree, floating lightly up midway to the ground.

In front of the cedar grove opposite, dragonflies were bobbing about in countless swarms, like dandelion floss in the wind.

The river seemed to flow from the tips of the cedar branches.

He thought he would never tire of looking at the autumn flowers that spread a blanket of silver up the side of the mountain.

A White-Russian[4] woman, a peddler, was sitting in the hallway when he came out of the bath. So you find them even in these mountains—He went for a closer look.

She appeared to be in her forties. Her face was wrinkled and dirty, but her skin, where it showed at the full throat and beyond, was a pure, glowing white.

"Where are you from?" Shimamura asked.

"Where am I from? Where am I from?" The woman seemed troubled for an answer. She began to put away her wares, the most ordinary Japanese cosmetics and hair ornaments.

Her skirt, like a dirty sheet wrapped around her, had quite lost the feel of occidental dress, and had taken on instead something of the air of Japan. She carried her wares on her back in a large Japanese-style kerchief. But for all that, she still wore foreign shoes.

The innkeeper's wife stood beside Shimamura watching the Russian leave. The two of them went into the office, where a large woman was seated at the hearth with her back to them. She took her long skirts in her hand as she stood up to go. Her cloak was a formal black.

She was a geisha Shimamura remembered having seen with Komako in an advertising photograph, the two of them on skis with cotton "mountain trousers" pulled over party kimonos. She seemed to be well along in years, plump and to all appearances good-natured.

The innkeeper was warming thick, oblong cakes over the embers.

"Won't you have one?" he asked Shimamura. "You really must have one. The geisha you saw brought them to celebrate the end of her term."

"She's leaving, is she?"

"Yes."

"She looks like a good sort."

"She was very popular. Today she's going the rounds to say good-by."

Shimamura blew on the cake and bit into it. The hard crust, a little sour, gave off a musty smell.

---

4. One who fought against the Bolsheviks in the Russian Revolution (1917). A number of them fled to Japan after the collapse of the Czarist government.

Outside the window, the bright red of ripe persimmons was bathed in the evening sun. It seemed to send out a red glow even to the bamboo of the pothook over the hearth.

"See how long they are." Shimamura looked out in astonishment at the steep path, down which old women were trudging with bundles of autumn grass on their backs. The grass looked to be twice the height of the women, and the tassels were long and powerful.

"It's *kaya* grass."[5]

"*Kaya*, is it?"

"The government railways built a sort of rest-room, I suppose you would call it, for their hot-spring exhibit, and they thatched the teahouse with *kaya* from these mountains. Someone in Tokyo bought it exactly as it was."

"*Kaya*, is it," Shimamura repeated, half to himself. "It's *kaya* then on the mountain? I thought it must be a flower of some sort."

The first thing that had struck Shimamura's eye as he got off the train was that array of silver-white. High up the mountain, the *kaya* spread out silver in the sun, like the autumn sunlight itself pouring over the face of the mountain. Ah, I am here, something in Shimamura called out as he looked up at it.

But the great strands he saw here seemed quite different in nature from the grasses that had so moved him. The large bundles hid the women carrying them, and rustled against the rocks that flanked the path. And the plumes were long and powerful.

Under the dim light in the dressing-room, Shimamura could see that the large-bodied moth was laying eggs along the black lacquer of the clothes-frame. Moths were beating at the lantern under the eaves.

There was a steady humming of autumn insects, as there had been from before sundown.

Komako was a little late.

She gazed in at him from the hall.

"Why have you come here? Why have you come to a place like this?"

"I've come to see you."

"You don't mean that. I dislike people from Tokyo because they're always lying." She sat down, and her voice was softer. "I'm never going to see anyone off again. I can't describe how it felt to see you off."

"This time I'll go without telling you."

"No. I mean I won't go to the station again."

"What happened to him?"

"He died, of course."

"While you were seeing me off?"

"But that's not the reason. I had no idea I could hate so to see someone off."

Shimamura nodded.

"Where were you on the fourteenth of February? I was waiting for you. But I'll know better than to believe you next time."

---

5. A tall, coarse grass used for thatching.

The fourteenth of February was the "bird-chasing festival,"[6] a children's festival that had in it the spirit of this snow country. For ten days before the festival the children of the village tramped down the snow with straw boots, and presently, cutting the now boardlike snow into two-foot cubes, they built a snow palace some six yards square and more than ten feet high. Since the New Year was celebrated here early in February, the traditional straw ropes[7] were still strung up over the village doorways. On the fourteenth the children gathered the ropes and burned them in a red bonfire before the snow palace. They pushed and jostled one another on the roof and sang the bird-chasing song,[8] and afterwards, setting out lights, they spent the night in the palace. At dawn on the fifteenth they again climbed to the roof to sing the bird-chasing song.

It was then that the snow was deepest, and Shimamura had told Komako he would come for the festival.

"I was at home in February. I took a vacation. I was sure you would be here on the fourteenth, and I came back especially. I could have stayed to take care of her longer if I had known."

"Was someone ill?"

"The music teacher. She had pneumonia down on the coast. The telegram came when I was at home, and I went down to take care of her."

"Did she get better?"

"No."

"I'm sorry." Shimamura's words could have been either an expression of sympathy or an apology for the broken promise.

Komako shook her head mildly, and wiped at the table with her handkerchief. "The place is alive with insects." A swarm of tiny winged insects fell from the table to the floor. Several small moths were circling the light.

Moths, how many kinds he could not tell, dotted the screen, floating on the clear moonlight.

"My stomach aches." Komako thrust both hands tight inside her *obi*, and her head fell to Shimamura's knee. "My stomach aches."

Insects smaller than moths gathered on the thick white powder at her neck. Some of them died there as Shimamura watched.

The flesh on her neck and shoulders was richer than it had been the year before. She is just twenty, he told himself.

He felt something warm and damp on his knee.

" 'Komako, go on up and look in the Camellia Room,' they said in the office, very pleased with themselves. I don't like that way they have. I'd been to see Kikuyu off, and I was just ready for a good nap when someone said there had been a call from here. I didn't feel like coming. I had too much to drink last night at Kikuyu's farewell party. They only laughed

6. An observance in rural agricultural communities lasting from the night of the fourteenth until dawn the next morning. Children and youths ran around the houses of the village singing and banging mallets and sticks, ladles and whisks, and other implements to ensure a fruitful harvest in the coming year by scaring away any birds that might feed on crops. 7. Sacred rope hung at Shinto shrines and elsewhere (especially during holidays) to sanctify the premises. According to the traditional lunar calendar of premodern times, the New Year was usually in early February (see introduction "The Rise of Popular Arts in Premodern Japan," p. 589). 8. One of the various songs sung during the bird-chasing festival.

down in the office and wouldn't tell me who was here. And it was you. It's been a whole year. You're the sort that comes only once a year?"

"I had one of the cakes she left."

"You did?" Komako sat up. Her face was red where it had been pressed against his knee. She seemed very young.

She had seen the old geisha Kikuyu to the second station down the line, she said.

"It's very sad. We used to be able to work things out together, but now it's every geisha for herself. The place has changed. New geisha come in and no one gets along with anyone else. I'll be lonesome without Kikuyu. She was at the center of everything. And she made more money than any of the rest of us. Her people took very good care of her."

Kikuyu had worked out her contract, and she was going home. Would she get married or would she open an inn or restaurant of her own? Shima-mura asked.

"Kikuyu is a very sad case. She made a bad marriage, and she came here afterwards." Komako was silent for a time, evidently unsure how much she should tell. She looked out toward the slope below the terraced fields, bright in the moonlight. "You know the new house halfway up the hill?"

"The restaurant—the Kikumura, is it called?"

"That's the one. Kikuyu was supposed to manage the Kikumura, but at the last minute she had a change of heart. It caused all sorts of excitement. She had a patron build the place for her, and then, when she was all ready to move in, she threw it over. She found someone she liked and was going to marry him, but he ran off and left her. Is that what happens when you lose your head over a man? I wonder. She can't very well go back to her old work, and she can't take over the restaurant now that she's turned it down, and she's ashamed to stay here after all that's happened. There's nothing for her to do but start over somewhere else. It makes me very sad to think about Kikuyu. There were all sorts of people—but of course we don't really know the details."

"Men? How many? Five or so?"

"I wonder." Komako laughed softly and turned away. "Kikuyu was weak. A weakling."

"Maybe there was nothing else she could do."

"But isn't it so? You can't go losing your head over every man that likes you." Her eyes were on the floor, and she was stroking her hair medita-tively with a hair ornament. "It wasn't easy, seeing her off."

"And what happened to the restaurant?"

"The wife of the man who built it has taken it over."

"An interesting situation. The wife managing the mistress's restaurant."

"But what else could they do? The place was ready to open, and the wife moved in with all her children."

"What about her own house?"

"They left the old woman to take care of it, I hear. The man's a farmer, but he likes to have his fun. He's a very interesting fellow."

"So it would seem. Is he well along in years?"

"He's young. No more than thirty-one or thirty-two."

"The mistress must be older than the wife, then."

"They're both twenty-six."

"The 'Kiku' of 'Kikumura' would be from 'Kikuyu.' And the wife took over the name even?"

"But they couldn't change the name once it was advertised."

Shimamura straightened the collar of his kimono. Komako got up to close the window.

"Kikuyu knew all about you. She told me today you were here."

"I saw her down in the office when she came to say good-by."

"Did she say anything to you?"

"Not a thing."

"Do you know how I feel?" Komako threw open the window she had just shut, and sat down on the sill as if she meant to throw herself out.

"The stars here are different from the stars in Tokyo," Shimamura said after a time. "They seem to float up from the sky."

"Not tonight, though. The moon is too bright. . . . The snow was dreadful this year."

"I understand there were times when the trains couldn't get through."

"I was almost afraid. The roads weren't open until May, a month later than usual. You know the shop up at the ski grounds? An avalanche went through the second floor of it. The people below heard a strange noise and thought the rats were tearing up the kitchen. There were no rats, though, and when they looked upstairs the place was full of snow and the shutters and all had been carried off. It was just a surface slide, but there was a great deal of talk on the radio. The skiers were frightened away. I said I wouldn't ski any more and I gave my skis away the end of last year, but I went out again after all. Twice, three times maybe. Have I changed?"

"What have you been doing since the music teacher died?"

"Don't you worry about other people's problems. I came back and I was waiting for you in February."

"But if you were down on the coast you could have written me a letter."

"I couldn't. I really couldn't. I couldn't possibly write the sort of letter your wife would see. I couldn't bring myself to. I don't tell lies just because people might be listening." The words came at him in a sudden torrent. He only nodded. "Why don't you turn out the light? You don't have to sit in this swarm of insects."

The moonlight, so bright that the furrows in the woman's ear were clearly shadowed, struck deep into the room and seemed to turn the mats on the floor a chilly green.

"No. Let me go home."

"I see you haven't changed." Shimamura raised his head. There was something strange in her manner. He peered into the slightly aquiline face.

"People say I haven't changed since I came here. I was sixteen then. But life goes on the same, year after year."

Her cheeks still carried the ruddiness of her north-country girlhood. In the moonlight the fine geishalike skin took on the luster of a sea shell.

"But did you hear I'd moved?"

"Since the teacher died? You're not in the silkworms' room any more, then? This time it's a real geisha house?"

"A real geisha house? I suppose it is. They sell tobacco and candy in the shop, and I'm the only geisha they have. I have a real contract, and when I read late in the night I always use a candle to save electricity."

Shimamura let out a loud guffaw.

"The meter, you know. Shouldn't use too much electricity."

"I see, I see."

"But they're very good to me, so good that I sometimes find it hard to believe I'm really hired out as a geisha. When one of the children cries, the mother takes it outside so that I won't be bothered. I have nothing to complain about. Only sometimes the bedding is crooked. When I come home late at night, everything is laid out for me, but the mattresses aren't square one on the other, and the sheet is wrong. I hate it. After they've been so kind, though, I feel guilty making the bed over."

"You'd wear yourself out if you had a house of your own."

"So everyone says. There are four little children, and the place is a terrible clutter. I spend the whole day picking things up. I know everything will be thrown down again as soon as my back is turned, but somehow I can't help myself. I want to be as clean and neat as the place will let me. . . . Do you understand how I feel?"

"I understand."

"If you understand, then tell me. Tell me, if you see how I feel." Again that tense, urgent note came into her voice. "See, you can't. Lying again. You have plenty of money, and you're not much of a person. You don't understand at all." She lowered her voice. "I'm very lonely sometimes. But I'm a fool. Go back to Tokyo, tomorrow."

"It's very well for you to condemn me, but how can you expect me to tell you exactly what I mean?"

"Why can't you? It's wrong of you." Her voice was almost desperate. Then she closed her eyes, and began again as if she had asked herself whether Shimamura knew her, felt her for what she was, and had answered that he did. "Once a year is enough. You'll come once a year, won't you, while I'm here?"

Her contract was for four years, she said.

"When I was at home, I didn't dream I would ever be a geisha again. I even gave away my skis before I left. And so all I've accomplished, I suppose, has been to give up smoking."

"I remember how much you used to smoke, now that you mention it."

"When guests at parties give me cigarettes, I tuck them away in my sleeve, and I have a fine collection by the time I'm ready to go home."

"But four years—that's a long time."

"It will pass in a hurry."

"Aren't you warm, though." Shimamura took her in his arms as she came to him.

"I've always been warm."

"I suppose the nights will be getting chilly."

"It's five years now since I came here. At first I wondered how I could live in such a place—especially before the railroad came through. And it's going on two years since you first came."

He had come three times in less than two years, and on each new visit he had found Komako's life changed.

Crickets were chirping outside in a noisy chorus.

"I wish they'd be a little quieter." Komako pulled away from Shima-mura.

The moths at the window started up as the wind came from the north.

Shimamura knew well enough that the thick eyelashes made her eyes seem half open, and yet he found himself looking again to be sure.

"I'm fatter now that I've stopped smoking."

The fat on her abdomen was heavier, he had noticed.

They had long been apart, but what eluded his grasp when he was away from her was immediately near and familiar when he was beside her again.

"One is bigger than the other." She cupped her breasts lightly in her hands.

"I suppose that's a habit of his—one side only."

"What a nasty thing to say!" Here she was—this was it, he remembered.

"Next time tell him to treat them both alike."

"Alike? Shall I tell him to treat them both alike?" She brought her face gently toward his.

It was a second-floor room, but it seemed to be surrounded by croaking toads. Two and three of them were moving from spot to spot, remarkably long-winded croakers.

Back from the bath, Komako began talking of herself. Her voice was quiet and her manner was completely serene.

The first physical examination she had had here—she thought it would be as when she was an apprentice geisha, and she bared her chest for a tuberculosis check. The doctor laughed, and she burst into tears—such were the intimate details she went into. She talked on as Shimamura encouraged her with questions.

"I'm always exactly on the calendar. Two days less than a month each time."

"I don't suppose it keeps you from your parties?"

"You understand such things, do you?"

Every day she had a bath in the hot spring, famous for its lingering warmth. She walked two miles and more between parties at the old spring and the new, and here in the mountains there were few parties that kept her up late. She was therefore healthy and full-bodied, though she did have a suggestion of the low, bunched-up hips so common with geisha, narrow from side to side and wide from front to back. To Shimamura there was something touching about the fact that such a woman could call him back from afar.

"I wonder if I can have children." And she wondered too if being gener-ally faithful to one man was not the same thing as being married.

That was the first Shimamura had heard of the "one man" in Komako's life. She had known him since she was sixteen, she said. Shimamura thought he understood now the lack of caution that had at first so puzzled him.

She had never liked the man, Komako continued, and had never felt near him, perhaps because the affair had begun when she was down on the coast just after the death of the man who had paid her debts.

"But it's certainly better than average if it's lasted five years."

"I've had two chances to leave him. When I went to work as a geisha here, and when I moved after the music teacher died. But I've never had the will power to do it. I don't have much will power."

The man was still down on the coast. It had not been convenient to keep her there, and when the music teacher came back to these mountains he had left Komako with her. He had been very kind, Komako said, and it made her sad to think that she could not give her whole self to him. He was considerably older than she, and he but rarely came to see her.

"I sometimes think it would be easiest to break away from him if I were to be really bad. I honestly think so sometimes."

"That would never do."

"But I wouldn't be up to it. It's not in my nature. I'm fond of this body I live in. If I tried, I could cut my four years down to two, but I don't strain myself. I take care of myself. Think of all the money I could make if I really tried. But it's enough if the man I have my contract with hasn't lost money at the end of four years. I know about how much it takes each month for an installment on the loan, and interest, and taxes, and my own keep, and I don't strain myself to make more. If it's a party that doesn't seem worth the trouble, I slip off and go home, and they don't call me late at night even from the inn unless an old guest has asked especially for me. If I wanted to be extravagant, I could go on and on, but I work as the mood takes me. That's enough. I've already paid back more than half the money, and it's not a year yet. But even so I manage to spend thirty yen or so on myself every month."

It was enough if she made a hundred yen a month, she said. The month before, the least busy of the year, she had made sixty yen. She had had some ninety parties, more than any other geisha. She received a fixed amount for herself from each party, and the larger number of parties therefore meant relatively more for her and less the man to whom she was indentured. But she moved busily from one to another as the spirit took her. There was not a single geisha at this hot spring who lost money and had to extend her contract.

Komako was up early the next morning. "I dreamed I was cleaning house for the woman who teaches flower-arranging, and I woke up."

She had moved the little dresser over to the window. In the mirror the mountains were red with autumn leaves, and the autumn sun was bright.

This time it was not Yoko he heard, Yoko calling through the door in that voice so clear he found it a little sad. Komako's clothes were brought rather by the little daughter of the man with whom she had her contract.

"What happened to the girl?" Shimamura asked.

Komako darted a quick glance at him. "She spends all her time at the cemetery. Over there at the foot of the ski course. See the buckwheat field—the white flowers? And the cemetery to the left of it?"

Shimamura went for a walk in the village when Komako had left.

Before a white wall, shaded by eaves, a little girl in "mountain trousers" and an orange-red flannel kimono, clearly brand-new, was bouncing a rubber ball. For Shimamura, there was autumn in the little scene.

The houses were built in the style of the old regime.[9] No doubt they were there when provincial lords passed down this north-country road. The eaves and the verandas were deep, while the latticed, paper-covered windows on the second floor were long and low, no more than a foot or so high. There were reed blinds hanging from the eaves.

Slender autumn grasses grew along the top of an earthen wall. The pale-yellow plumes were at their most graceful, and below each plume narrow leaves spread out in a delicate fountain.

Yoko knelt on a straw mat beside the road, flailing at beans spread out before her in the sunlight.

The beans jumped from their dry pods like little drops of light.

Perhaps she could not see him because of the scarf around her head. She knelt, flailing away at the beans, her knees spread apart in their "mountain trousers," and she sang in that voice so clear it was almost sad, the voice that seemed to be echoing back from somewhere.

"The butterfly, the dragonfly, the cricket.
The pine cricket, bell cricket, horse cricket
Are singing in the hills."

How large the crow is, starting up from the cedar in the evening breeze—so says the poet. Again there were swarms of dragonflies by the cedar grove Shimamura could see from his window. As the evening approached, they seemed to swim about faster, more restlessly.

Shimamura had bought a new guide to these mountains while he was waiting for his train in Tokyo. Thumbing through it, he learned that near the top of one of the Border Range peaks a path threaded its way through beautiful lakes and marshes, and in this watery belt Alpine plants grew in the wildest profusion. In the summer red dragonflies flew calmly about, lighting on a hat or a hand, or the rim of a pair of spectacles, as different from the persecuted city dragonfly as a cloud from a mud puddle.

But the dragonflies here before him seemed to be driven by something. It was as though they wanted desperately to avoid being pulled in with the cedar grove as it darkened before the sunset.

The western sun fell on distant mountains, and in the evening light he could see how the red leaves were working their way down from the summits.

"People are delicate, aren't they?" Komako had said that morning. "Broken into a pulp, they say, skull and bones and all. And a bear could fall from a higher ledge and not be hurt in the least." There had been another accident up among the rocks, and she had pointed out the mountain on which it had happened.

If man had a tough, hairy hide like a bear, his world would be different

---

9. The *shogun's* government during the Edo period (1600–1868).

indeed, Shimamura thought. It was through a thin, smooth skin that man loved. Looking out at the evening mountains, Shimamura felt a sentimental longing for the human skin.

"The butterfly, the dragonfly, the cricket." A geisha had been singing the song to a clumsy samisen accompaniment as he sat down to an early dinner.

The guidebook gave only the most essential information on routes, schedules, lodgings, costs, and left the rest to the imagination. Shimamura had come down from these mountains, as the new green was making its way through the last of the snow, to meet Komako for the first time; and now, in the autumn climbing season, he found himself drawn again to the mountains he had left his tracks in. Though he was an idler who might as well spend his time in the mountains as anywhere, he looked upon mountain climbing as almost a model of wasted effort. For that very reason it pulled at him with the attraction of the unreal.

When he was far away, he thought incessantly of Komako; but now that he was near her, this sighing for the human skin took on a dreamy quality like the spell of the mountains. Perhaps he felt a certain security, perhaps he was at the moment too intimate, too familiar with her body. She had stayed with him the night before. Sitting alone in the quiet, he could only wait for her. He was sure she would come without his calling. As he listened to the noisy chatter of a group of schoolgirls out on the hiking trip, however, he began to feel a little sleepy. He went to bed early.

Rain fell during the night, one of those quick showers that come in the autumn.

When he awoke the next morning, Komako was sitting primly beside the table, a book open before her. She wore an everyday kimono and cloak.

"Are you awake?" Her voice was soft as she turned to him.

"What are you doing here?"

"Are you awake?"

Shimamura glanced around the room, wondering if she had come in the night without his knowing it. He picked up the watch beside his pillow. It was only six-thirty.

"You're early."

"But the maid has already brought charcoal."

A morninglike steam was rising from the teakettle.

"It's time to get up." She sat beside his pillow, the picture of the proper housewife. Shimamura stretched and yawned. He took the hand on her knee and caressed the small fingers, callused from playing the samisen.

"But it's barely sunrise."

"Did you sleep well by yourself?"

"Very well."

"You didn't grow a mustache after all."

"You did tell me to grow a mustache, didn't you?"

"It's all right. I knew you wouldn't. You always shave yourself nice and blue."

"And you always look as if you'd just shaved when you wash away that powder."

"Isn't your face a little fatter, though? You were very funny asleep, all round and plump with your white skin and no mustache."

"Sweet and gentle?"

"But unreliable."

"You were staring at me, then? I'm not sure I like having people stare at me when I'm asleep."

Komako smiled and nodded. Then, like a glow that breaks into a flame, the smile became a laugh. There was strength in the fingers that took his.

"I hid in the closet. The maid didn't suspect a thing."

"When? How long were you hidden?"

"Just now, of course. When the maid came to bring charcoal." She laughed happily at the prank, and suddenly she was red to the ears. As if to hide her confusion, she began fanning herself with the edge of his quilt. "Get up. Get up, please."

"It's cold." Shimamura pulled the quilt away from her. "Are the inn people up yet?"

"I have no idea. I came in from the back."

"The back?"

"I fought my way up from the cedar grove."

"Is there a path in back?"

"No. But it's shorter."

Shimamura looked at her in surprise.

"No one knows I'm here. I heard someone in the kitchen, but the front door must still be locked."

"You seem to be an early riser."

"I couldn't sleep."

"Did you hear the rain?"

"It rained? That's why the underbrush was wet, then. I'm going home. Go on back to sleep."

But Shimamura jumped vigorously out of bed, the woman's hand still in his. He went over to the window and looked down at the hill she said she had come up. Below the shrubbery, halfway down toward the cedar grove, dwarf bamboo was growing in a wild tangle. Directly below the window were rows of taro[1] and sweet potatoes, onions and radishes. It was a most ordinary garden patch, and yet the varied colors of the leaves in the morning sun made him feel that he was seeing them for the first time.

The porter was throwing feed to the carp from the corridor that led to the bath.

"It's colder, and they aren't eating well," he said as Shimamura passed. Shimamura stood for a moment looking at the feed on the water, dried and crumbled silkworms.

Komako was waiting for him, clean and prim as before, when he came back from the bath.

"It would be good to work on my sewing in a quiet place like this," she said.

The room had evidently been cleaned, and the sun poured in on the deepest corners of the slightly worn matting.

---

1. A plant grown for its edible, starchy, tuberous rootstocks.

"You sew, do you?"

"What an insulting question. I had to work harder than anyone else in the family. I see now, looking back, that the years when I was growing up were the worst ones of all." She spoke almost to herself, but her voice was tense as she continued: "The maid saw me. She gave me a strange look and asked when I had come. It was very embarrassing—but I couldn't go on hiding in the closet forever. I'm going home. I'm very busy. I couldn't sleep, and I thought I'd wash my hair. I have to wait for it to dry, and then go to the hairdresser's, and if I don't wash it early in the morning I'm never ready for an afternoon party. There's a party here too, but they only told me about it last night. I won't come. I've made other promises. And I won't be able to see you tonight—it's Saturday and I'll be very busy."

She showed no sign of leaving, however.

She decided not to wash her hair after all. She took Shimamura down to the back garden. Her damp sandals and stockings were hidden under the veranda where she had come in.

The dwarf bamboo she said she had fought her way through seemed impassible. Starting down along the garden path toward the sound of the water, they came out on the high river bank. There were children's voices in the chestnut trees. A number of burrs lay in the grass at their feet. Komako stamped them open and took out the fruit. The kernels were small.

Kaya plumes waved on the steep slope of the mountain opposite, a dazzling silver in the morning sun. Dazzling, and yet rather like the fleeting translucence that moved across the autumn sky.

"Shall we cross over? We can see your fiancé's grave."

Komako brought herself to her full height and glared at him. A handful of chestnuts came at his face.

"You're making fun of me."

Shimamura had no time to dodge. The chestnuts lashed at his forehead.

"What possible reason could you have for going to the cemetery?"

"But there's no need to lose your temper."

"I was completely in earnest. I'm not like people who can do exactly as they want and think of no one else."

"And who can do that?" Shimamura muttered weakly.

"Why do you have to call him my fiancé? Didn't I tell you very carefully he wasn't? But you've forgotten, of course."

Shimamura had not forgotten. Indeed, the memory gave the man Yukio a certain weight in his thoughts.

Komako seemed to dislike talking about Yukio. She was not his fiancée, perhaps, but she had become a geisha to help pay doctors' bills. There was no doubt that she had been "completely in earnest."

Shimamura showed no anger even under the barrage of chestnuts. Komako looked curiously at him, and her resistance seemed to collapse. She took his arm. "You're a simple, honest person at heart, aren't you? Something must be making you sad."

"They're watching us from the trees."

"What of it? Tokyo people are complicated. They live in such noise and confusion that their feelings are broken to little bits."

"Everything is broken to little bits."

"Even life, before long. . . . Shall we go to the cemetery?"

"Well. . . ."

"See? You don't really want to go at all."

"But you made such an issue of it."

"Because I've never once gone to the cemetery. I really haven't gone once. I feel guilty sometimes, now that the teacher's buried there too. But I can't very well start going now. I'd only be pretending."

"You're more complicated than I am."

"Why? I'm never able to be completely open with living people, and I want at least to be honest with him now that he's dead."

They came out of the cedar grove, where the quiet seemed to fall in chilly drops. Following the railway along the foot of the ski grounds, they were soon at the cemetery. Some ten weathered old tombstones and a forlorn statue of Jizo,[2] guardian of children, stood on a tiny island of high ground among the paddies. There were no flowers.

Quite without warning, Yoko's head and shoulders rose from the bushes behind the Jizo. Her face wore the usual solemn, masklike expression. She darted a burning glance at the two of them, and nodded a quick greeting to Shimamura. She said nothing.

"Aren't you early, though, Yoko? I thought of going to the hairdresser's. . . ." As Komako spoke, a black squall came upon them and threatened to sweep them from their feet.

A freight train roared past.

"Yoko, Yoko. . . ." A boy was waving his hat in the door of a black freight car.

"Saichiro, Saichiro," Yoko called back.

It was the voice that had called to the station master at the snowy signal stop, a voice so beautiful it was almost lonely, calling out as if to someone who could not hear, on a ship far away.

The train passed, and the buckwheat across the tracks emerged fresh and clean as the blind was lifted. The field of white flowers on red stems was quietness itself.

The two of them had been so startled at seeing Yoko that they had not noticed the approach of the freight train; but the first shock was dispelled by the train.

They seemed still to hear Yoko's voice, and not the dying rumble of the freight train. It seemed to come back like an echo of distilled love.

"My brother," said Yoko, looking after the train. "I wonder if I should go to the station."

"But the train won't wait for you at the station," Komako laughed.

"I suppose not."

"I didn't come to see Yukio's grave."

Yoko nodded. She seemed to hesitate a moment, then knelt down before the grave.

Komako watched stiffly.

Shimamura looked away, toward the Jizo. It had three long faces, and,

2. A Buddhist divinity who promised to deliver all people from worldly suffering.

besides the hands clasped at its breast, a pair each to the left and the right.[3]

"I'm going to wash my hair," Komako said to Yoko. She turned and started back along a ridge between the paddies.

It was the practice in the snow country to string wooden or bamboo poles on a number of levels from tree trunk to tree trunk, and to hang rice sheaves head down from them to dry. At the height of the harvest the frames presented a solid screen of rice. Farmers were hanging out rice along the path Shimamura and Komako took back to the village.

A farm girl threw up a sheaf of rice with a twist of her trousered hips, and a man high above her caught it expertly and in one deft sweep of his hand spread it to hang from the frame. The unconscious, practiced motions were repeated over and over.

Komako took one of the dangling sheaves in her hand and shook it gently up and down, as though she were feeling the weight of a jewel.

"See how it's headed. And how nice it is to the touch. Entirely different from last year's rice." She half-closed her eyes from the pleasure. A disorderly flock of sparrows flew low over her head.

An old notice was pasted to a wall beside the road: "Pay for field hands. Ninety sen a day, meals included. Women forty per cent less."

There were rice frames in front of Yoko's house too, beyond the slightly depressed field that separated the house from the road. One set of frames was strung up high in a row of persimmon trees, along the white wall between the garden and the house next door, while another, at right angles to it, followed the line between the field and the garden. With an opening for a doorway at one end, the frames suggested a makeshift little theater covered not with the usual straw mats but with unthreshed rice. The taro in the field still sent out powerful stems and leaves, but the dahlias and roses beyond were withered. The lotus pond with its red carp was hidden behind the screen of rice, as was the window of the silkworm room, where Komako had lived.

Bowing her head sharply, almost angrily, Yoko went in through the opening in the headed rice.

"Does she live alone?" Shimamura asked, looking after the bowed figure.

"I imagine not." Komako's answer was a little tart. "But what a nuisance. I'll not go to the hairdresser's after all. You say things you have no business saying, and we ruin her visit to the cemetery."

"You're only being difficult—is it really so terrible to run into her at the cemetery?"

"You have no idea how I feel. . . . If I have time later, I'll stop by to wash my hair. I may be late, but I'll stop by."

It was three in the morning.

Shimamura was awakened by a slamming as though someone were knocking the doors loose. Komako lay stretched out on top of him.

"I said I would come and I've come. Haven't I? I said I'd come and I've come, haven't I?" Her chest, even her abdomen, rose and fell violently.

---

3. Unlike this statue, the usual representation of Jizo was as a monk with a jewel in one hand and a staff in the other.

"You're dead-drunk."

"Haven't I? I said I'd come and I've come, haven't I?"

"You have indeed."

"Couldn't see a thing on the way. Not a thing. My head aches."

"How did you manage to get up the hill?"

"I have no idea. Not the slightest." She lay heavily across his chest. He found it a little oppressive, especially when she turned over and arched her back; but, too suddenly awakened, he fell back as he tried to get up. It was an astonishingly hot object that his head came to rest on.

"You're on fire."

"Oh? Fire for a pillow. See that you don't burn yourself."

"I might very well." He closed his eyes and the warmth sank into his head, bringing an immediate sense of life. Reality came through the violent breathing, and with it a sort of nostalgic remorse. He felt as though he were waiting tranquilly for some undefined revenge.

"I said I'd come, and I've come." She spoke with the utmost concentration. "I've come, and now I'm going home. I'm going to wash my hair."

She got to her knees and took a drink of water in great swallows.

"I can't let you go home like this."

"I'm going home. I have some people waiting. Where did I leave my towel?"

Shimamura got up and turned on the light. "Don't!" She hid her face in her hands, then buried it, hands and all, in the quilt.

She had on a bold informal kimono with a narrow undress *obi*, and under it a nightgown. Her under-kimono had slipped down out of sight. She was flushed from drink even to the soles of her bare feet, and there was something very engaging about the way she tried to tuck them out of sight.

Evidently she had thrown down her towel and bath utensils when she came in. Soap and combs were scattered over the floor.

"Cut. I brought scissors."

"What do you want me to cut?"

"This." She pointed at the strings that held her Japanese coiffure in place. "I tried to do it myself, but my hands wouldn't work. I thought maybe I could ask you."

Shimamura separated the hair and cut at the strings, and as he cut she shook the long hair loose. She was somewhat calmer.

"What time is it?"

"Three o'clock."

"Not really! You'll be careful not to cut the hair, won't you?"

"I've never seen so many strings."

The false hair that filled out the coiffure was hot where it touched her head.

"Is it really three o'clock? I must have fallen asleep when I got home. I promised to come for a bath with some people, and they stopped by to call me. They'll be wondering what's happened."

"They're waiting for you?"

"In the public bath. Three of them. There were six parties, but I only got to four. Next week we'll be very busy with people coming to see the maple leaves. Thanks very much." She raised her head to comb her hair, now long and flowing, and she laughed uncertainly. "Funny, isn't it." Unsure what to do with herself, she reached to pick up the false hair. "I have to go. It's not right to keep them waiting. I'll not come again tonight."

"Can you see your way home?"

"Yes."

But she tripped over the skirt of her kimono on the way out.

At seven and again at three in the morning—twice in one short day she had chosen unconventional hours to come calling. There was something far from ordinary in all this, Shimamura told himself.

Guests would soon be coming for the autumn leaves. The door of the inn was being decorated with maple branches to welcome them.

The porter who was somewhat arrogantly directing operations was fond of calling himself a "migrant bird." He and his kind worked the mountain resorts from spring through to the autumn leaves, and moved down to the coast for the winter. He did not much care whether or not he came to the same inn each year. Proud of his experience in the prosperous coast resorts, he had no praise for the way the inn treated its guests. He reminded one of a not-too-sincere beggar as he rubbed his hands together and hovered about prospective guests at the station.

"Have you ever tasted one of these?" he asked Shimamura, picking up a pomegranatelike *akebi*.[4] "I can bring some in from the mountains if you like." Shimamura, back from a walk, watched him tie the *akebi*, stem and all, to a maple branch.

The freshly cut branches were so long that they brushed against the eaves. The hallway glowed a bright, fresh scarlet. The leaves were extraordinarily large.

As Shimamura took the cool *akebi* in his hand, he noticed that Yoko was sitting by the hearth in the office.

The innkeeper's wife was heating *saké*[5] in a brass boiler. Yoko, seated opposite her, nodded quickly in answer to each remark. She was dressed informally, though she did not have on the everyday "mountain trousers." Her plain woolen kimono was freshly washed.

"That girl is working here?" Shimamura asked the porter nonchalantly.

"Yes, sir. Thanks to all of you, we've had to take on extra help."

"You, for instance."

"That's right. She's an unusual type, though, for a girl from these parts."

Yoko worked only in the kitchen, apparently. She was not yet serving at parties. As the inn filled, the voices of the maids in the kitchen became louder, but he did not remember having heard Yoko's clear voice among them. The maid who took care of his room said that Yoko liked to sing in the bath before she went to bed, but that, too, Shimamura had missed.

Now that he knew Yoko was in the house, he felt strangely reluctant to call Komako. He was conscious of an emptiness that made him see Komako's life as beautiful but wasted, even though he himself was the

---

4. The purple fruit of a deciduous woody vine, which also yields purple flowers.   5. A winelike alcoholic beverage brewed from fermented rice.

object of her love; and yet the woman's existence, her straining to live, came touching him like naked skin. He pitied her, and he pitied himself.

He was sure that Yoko's eyes, for all their innocence, could send a probing light to the heart of these matters, and he somehow felt drawn to her too.

Komako came often enough without being called.

When he went to see the maple leaves up the valley, he passed her house. Hearing the automobile and thinking it must be he, she ran out to look—and he did not even glance back, she complained. That was most unfeeling of him. She of course stopped by whenever she came to the inn, and she stopped by too on her way to the bath. When she was to go to a party, she came an hour or so early and waited in his room for the maid to call her. Often she would slip away from a party for a few minutes. After retouching her face in the mirror, she would stand up to leave. "Back to work. I'm all business. Business, business."

She was in the habit of forgetting something she had brought with her, a cloak, perhaps, or the cover to a samisen plectrum.

"Last night when I got home there was no hot water for tea. I hunted through the kitchen and found the left-overs from breakfast. Co-o-old. . . . They didn't call me this morning. When I woke up it was already ten-thirty. I meant to come see you at seven, but it was no good."

Such were the things she talked of. Or she told him of the inn she had gone to first, and the next and the next, and the parties she had been to at each.

"I'll come again later." She had a glass of water before she left. "Or maybe I won't. Thirty guests and only three of us. I'll be much too busy."

But almost immediately she was back.

"It's hard work. Thirty of them and only three of us. And the other two are the very oldest and the very youngest in town, and that leaves all the hard work for me. Stingy people. A travel club of some sort, I suppose. With thirty guests you need at least six geisha. I'll go have a drink and pick a fight with them."

So it was every day. Komako must have wanted to crawl away and hide at the thought of where it was leading. But that indefinable air of loneliness only made her the more seductive.

"The floor always creaks when I come down the hall. I walk very softly, but they hear me just the same. 'Off to the Camellia Room again, Komako?' they say as I go by the kitchen. I never thought I'd have to worry so about my reputation."

"The town's really too small."

"Everyone has heard about us, of course."

"That will never do."

"You begin to have a bad name, and you're ruined in a little place like this." But she looked up and smiled. "It makes no difference. My kind can find work anywhere."

That straightforward manner, so replete with direct, immediate feeling, was quite foreign to Shimamura, the idler who had inherited his money.

"It will be the same, wherever I go. There's nothing to be upset about."

But he caught an echo of the woman underneath the surface nonchalance.

"And I can't complain. After all, only women are able really to love." She flushed a little and looked at the floor.

Her kimono stood out from her neck, and her back and shoulders were like a white fan spread under it. There was something sad about the full flesh under that white powder. It suggested a woolen cloth, and again it suggested the pelt of some animal.

"In the world as it is," he murmured, chilled at the sterility of the words even as he spoke.

But Komako only replied: "As it always has been." She raised her head and added absentmindedly: "You didn't know that?"

The red under-kimono clinging to her skin disappeared as she looked up.

Shimamura was translating Valéry and Alain,[6] and French treatises on the dance from the golden age of the Russian ballet. He meant to bring them out in a small luxury edition at his own expense. The book would in all likelihood contribute nothing to the Japanese dancing world. One could nonetheless say, if pressed, that it would bring aid and comfort to Shimamura. He pampered himself with the somewhat whimsical pleasure of sneering at himself through his work, and it may well have been from such a pleasure that his sad little dream world sprang. Off on a trip, he saw no need to hurry himself.

He spent much of his time watching insects in their death agonies.

Each day, as the autumn grew colder, insects died on the floor of his room. Stiff-winged insects fell on their backs and were unable to get to their feet again. A bee walked a little and collapsed, walked a little and collapsed. It was a quiet death that came with the change of seasons. Looking closely, however, Shimamura could see that the legs and feelers were trembling in the struggle to live. For such a tiny death, the empty eight-mat room[7] seemed enormous.

As he picked up a dead insect to throw it out, he sometimes thought for an instant of the children he had left in Tokyo.

A moth on the screen was still for a very long time. It too was dead, and it fell to the earth like a dead leaf. Occasionally a moth fell from the wall. Taking it up in his hand, Shimamura would wonder how to account for such beauty.

The screens were removed, and the singing of the insects was more subdued and lonely day by day.

The russet deepened on the Border Range. In the evening sun the mountains lighted up sharply, like a rather chilly stone. The inn was filled with maple-viewing guests.

"I don't think I'll come again tonight. Some people from the village are having a party." Komako left, and presently he heard a drum in the large

---

6. Pen name of Henri-Alban Fournier, or Alain-Fournier (1886–1914), French poet, journalist, and novelist. Paul Valéry (1871–1945), one of the greatest French poets of the 20th century, also critic and essayist. 7. About four yards square.

banquet-room, and strident women's voices. At the very height of the festivities he was startled by a clear voice almost at his elbow.

"May I come in?" It was Yoko. "Komako asked me to bring this."

She thrust her hand out like a postman. Then, remembering her manners, she knelt down awkwardly before him. Shimamura opened the knotted bit of paper, and Yoko was gone. He had not had time to speak to
her.

"Having a fine, noisy time. And drinking." That was the whole of the
message, written in a drunken hand on a paper napkin.

Not ten minutes later Komako staggered in.

"Did she bring something to you?"

"She did."

"Oh?" Komako cocked an eye at him in wonderfully high spirits. "I do
feel good. I said I'd go order more *saké*, and I ran away. The porter caught
me. But *saké* is wonderful. I don't care a bit if the floor creaks. I don't care
if they scold me. As soon as I come here I start feeling drunk, though.
Damn. Well, back to work."

"You're rosy down to the tips of your fingers."

"Business is waiting. Business, business. Did she say anything? Terribly
jealous. Do you know how jealous?"

"Who?"

"Someone will be murdered one of these days."

"She's working here?"

"She brings *saké*, and then stands there staring in at us, with her eyes
flashing. I suppose you like her sort of eyes."

"She probably thinks you're a disgrace."

"That's why I gave her a note to bring to you. I want water. Give me
water. Who's a disgrace? Try seducing her too before you answer my question. Am I drunk?" She peered into the mirror, bracing both hands against
the stand. A moment later, kicking aside the long skirts, she swept from
the room.

The party was over. The inn was soon quiet, and Shimamura could
hear a distant clatter of dishes. Komako must have been taken off by a
guest to a second party, he concluded; but just then Yoko came in with
another bit of paper.

"Decided not to go to Sampukan go from here to the Plum Room may
stop by on way home good night."

Shimamura smiled wryly, a little uncomfortable before Yoko. "Thank
you very much. You've come to help here?"

She darted a glance at him with those beautiful eyes, so bright that he
felt impaled on them. His discomfort was growing.

The girl left a deep impression each time he saw her, and now she was
sitting before him—a strange uneasiness swept over him. Her too-serious
manner made her seem always at the very center of some remarkable
occurrence.

"They're keeping you busy, I suppose."

"But there's very little I can do."

"It's strange how often I see you. The first time was when you were bringing that man home. You talked to the station master about your brother. Do you remember?"

"Yes."

"They say you sing in the bath before you go to bed."

"Really! They accuse me of having such bad manners?" The voice was astonishingly beautiful.

"I feel I know everything about you."

"Oh? And have you asked Komako, then?"

"She won't say a thing. She seems to dislike talking about you."

"I see." Yoko turned quickly away. "Komako is a fine person, but she's not been lucky. Be good to her." She spoke rapidly, and her voice trembled very slightly on the last words.

"But there's nothing I can do for her."

It seemed that the girl's whole body must soon be trembling. Shimamura looked away, fearful that a dangerous light would be breaking out on the too-earnest face.

He laughed. "I think I'd best go back to Tokyo soon."

"I'm going to Tokyo myself."

"When?"

"It doesn't matter."

"Shall I see you to Tokyo when I go back?"

"Please do." The seriousness was intense, and at the same time her tone suggested that the matter was after all trivial. Shimamura was startled.

"If it will be all right with your family."

"The brother who works on the railroad is all the family I have. I can decide for myself."

"Have you made arrangements in Tokyo?"

"No."

"Have you talked to Komako, then?"

"To Komako? I don't like Komako. I haven't talked to her."

She looked up at him with moist eyes—a sign perhaps that her defenses were breaking down—and he found in them an uncanny sort of beauty. But at that moment his affection for Komako welled up violently. To run off to Tokyo, as if eloping, with a nondescript woman would somehow be in the nature of an intense apology[8] to Komako, and a penance for Shimamura himself.

"It doesn't frighten you to go off alone with a man?"

"Why should it?"

"It doesn't seem dangerous to go to Tokyo without at least deciding where you will stay and what you might want to do?"

"A woman by herself can always get by." There was a delicious lilt in her speech. Her eyes were fixed on his as she spoke again: "You won't hire me as a maid?"

"Really, now. Hire you as a maid?"

"But I don't want to be a maid."

"What were you in Tokyo before?"

"A nurse."

8. In the sense of expressing a deep regret about the course their relationship had taken.

"You were in a hospital? Or in nursing school?"

"I just thought I'd like to be a nurse."

Shimamura smiled. This perhaps explained the earnestness with which she had taken care of the music teacher's son on the train.

"And you still want to be a nurse?"

"I won't be a nurse now."

"But you'll have to make up your mind. This indecisiveness will never do."

"Indecisiveness? It has nothing to do with indecisiveness." Her laugh threw back the accusation.

Her laugh, like her voice, was so high and clear that it was almost lonely. There was not a suggestion in it of the dull or the simple-minded; but it struck emptily at the shell of Shimamura's heart, and fell away in silence.

"What's funny?"

"But there has only been one man I could possibly nurse."

Again Shimamura was startled.

"I could never again."

"I see." His answer was quiet. He had been caught off guard. "They say you spend all your time at the cemetery."

"I do."

"And for the rest of your life you can never nurse anyone else, or visit anyone else's grave?"

"Never again."

"How can you leave the grave and go off to Tokyo, then?"

"I'm sorry. Do take me with you."

"Komako says you're frightfully jealous. Wasn't the man her fiancé?"

"Yukio? It's a lie. It's a lie."

"Why do you dislike Komako, then?"

"Komako." She spoke as if calling to someone in the same room, and she gazed hotly at Shimamura. "Be good to Komako."

"But I can do nothing for her."

There were tears in the corners of Yoko's eyes. She sniffled as she slapped at a small moth on the matting. "Komako says I'll go crazy." With that she slipped from the room.

Shimamura felt a chill come over him.

As he opened the window to throw out the moth, he caught a glimpse of the drunken Komako playing parlor games with a guest. She leaned forward half from her seat, as though to push her advantage home by force. The sky had clouded over. Shimamura went down for a bath.

In the women's bath next door, Yoko was bathing the innkeeper's little daughter.

Her voice was gentle as she undressed the child and bathed it—soothing and agreeable, like the voice of a young mother.

Presently she was singing in that same voice:

> "See, out in back,
> Three pears, three cedars,
> Six trees in all.
> Crows' nests below,

Sparrows' nests above.
And what is it they're singing?
'Hakamairi itchō, itchō, itchō ya.' "[9]

It was a song little girls sang as they bounced rubber balls. The quick, lively manner in which Yoko rolled off the nonsense-words made Shimamura wonder if he might not have seen the earlier Yoko in a dream.

She chattered on as she dressed the child and led it from the bath, and even when she was gone her voice seemed to echo on like a flute. On the worn floor of the hallway, polished to a dark glow, a geisha had left behind a samisen box, the very embodiment of quiet in the late autumn night. As Shimamura was looking for the owner's name, Komako came out from the direction of the clattering dishes.

"What are you looking at?"

"Is she staying the night?"

"Who? Oh, her. Don't be foolish. You think we carry these with us wherever we go, do you? Sometimes we leave them at an inn for days on end." She laughed, but almost immediately she was breathing painfully and her eyes were screwed tightly shut. Dropping her long skirts, she fell against Shimamura. "Take me home, please."

"You don't have to go, do you?"

"It's no good. I have to go. The rest went on to other parties and left me behind. No one will say anything if I don't stay too long—I had business here. But if they stop by my house on their way to the bath and find me away, they'll start talking."

Drunk though she was, she walked briskly down the steep hill.

"You made that girl weep."

"She does seem a trifle crazy."

"And do you enjoy making such remarks?"

"But didn't you say it yourself? She remembered how you said she would go crazy, and it was then that she broke down—mostly out of resentment, I suspect."

"Oh? It's all right, then."

"And not ten minutes later she was in the bath, singing in fine voice."

"She's always liked to sing in the bath."

"She said very seriously that I must be good to you."

"Isn't she foolish, though? But you didn't have to tell me."

"Tell you? Why is it that you always seem so touchy when that girl is mentioned?"

"Would you like to have her?"

"See? What call is there for a remark like that?"

"I'm not joking. Whenever I look at her, I feel as though I have a heavy load and can't get rid of it. Somehow I always feel that way. If you're really fond of her, take a good look at her. You'll see what I mean." She laid her hand on his shoulder and leaned toward him. Then, abruptly, she shook her head. "No, that's not what I want. If she were to fall into the hands of

---

9. "To the cemetery, a hundred yards, a hundred yards, a hundred yards again" (literal trans.); in imitation of the birds.

someone like you, she might not go crazy after all. Why don't you take my load for me?"

"You're going a little too far."

"You think I'm drunk and talking nonsense? I'm not. I would know she was being well taken care of, and I could go pleasantly to seed here in the mountains. It would be a fine, quiet feeling."

"That's enough."

"Just leave me alone." In her flight, she ran into the closed door of the house she lived in.

"They've decided you're not coming home."

"But I can open it." The door sounded old and dry as she lifted it from the groove and pushed it back.

"Come on in."

"But think of the hour."

"Everyone will be asleep."

Shimamura hesitated.

"I'll see you back to the inn, then."

"I can go by myself."

"But you haven't seen my room."

They stepped through the kitchen door, and the sleeping figures of the family lay sprawled before them. The thin mattresses on the floor were covered with cheap striped cloth, now faded, of the sort often used for "mountain trousers." The mother and father and five or six children, the oldest a girl perhaps sixteen, lay under a scorched lampshade. Heads faced in every direction. There was drab poverty in the scene, and yet under it there lay an urgent, powerful vitality.

As if thrown back by the warm breath of all the sleepers, Shimamura started toward the door. Komako noisily closed it in his face, however, and went in through the kitchen. She made no attempt to soften her footsteps. Shimamura followed stealthily past the children's pillows, a strange thrill rising in his chest.

"Wait here. I'll turn on the light upstairs."

"It's all right." Shimamura climbed the stairs in the dark. As he looked back, he saw the candy shop beyond the homely sleeping faces.

The matting was worn in the four rustic rooms on the second floor.

"It's a little large, I have to admit, for just one person." The partitions between the rooms had been taken down, and Komako's bedding lay small and solitary inside the sliding doors, their paper panels yellowed with age, that separated the rooms from the skirting corridor. Old furniture and tools, evidently the property of the family she lived with, were piled in the far room. Party kimonos hung from pegs along the wall. The whole suggested a fox's or badger's lair[1] to Shimamura.

Komako sat down solidly in the slightly raised alcove and offered him the only cushion.

---

1. Both animals were considered to be tricksters with supernatural powers—the fox sinister and the badger comical—and both were thought capable of assuming human form. Traditional belief explained derangement as possession by a fox spirit, and in folklore and popular drama a fox would often appear as a beautiful temptress.

"Bright red." She peered into the mirror. "Am I really so drunk?" She fumbled through the top drawer of the dresser. "Here. My diary."

"As long as this, is it?"

She took up a small figured-paper box filled to the top with assorted cigarettes.

"I push them up my sleeve or inside my *obi* when a guest gives them to me, and some of them are a little smashed. They're clean, though. I make up for wrinkles by having every variety to offer." She stirred up the contents to demonstrate that he could have his choice.

"But I don't have a match. I don't need matches now that I've stopped smoking."

"It's all right. How is the sewing?"

"I try to work at it, but the guests for the maple leaves keep me busy." She turned to put away the sewing that lay in front of the dresser.

The fine-grained chest of drawers and the expensive vermilion-lacquered sewing-box, relics perhaps of her years in Tokyo, were as they had been in the attic that so resembled an old paper box; but they seemed sadly out of place in these dilapidated second-floor rooms.

A thin string ran from Komako's pillow to the ceiling.

"I turn the light out with this when I'm reading." She tugged at the string. Gentle and subdued, the proper housewife again, she was not quite able even so to hide her discomposure.

"Lonely as the fox's lady out at night, aren't you."

"I really am."

"And do you mean to live here four years?"

"But it's going on a year already. It won't be long."

Shimamura was nervous. He thought he could hear the breathing of the family below, and he had run out of things to talk about. He stood up to leave.

Komako slid the door half shut behind him. She glanced up at the sky. "It's beginning to look like snow. The end of the maple leaves." She recited a line of poetry as she stepped outside: "Here in our mountains, the snow falls even on the maple leaves."[2]

"Well, good night."

"Wait. I'll see you back to the hotel. As far as the door, no farther."

But she followed him inside.

"Go on to bed." She slipped away, and a few minutes later she was back with two glasses filled to the brim with *saké*.

"Drink," she ordered as she stepped into the room. "We're going to have a drink."

"But aren't they asleep? Where did you find it?"

"I know where they keep it." She had quite obviously had herself a drink as she poured from the vat. The earlier drunkenness had come back. With narrowed eyes, she watched the *saké* spill over on her hand. "It's no fun, though, swallowing the stuff down in the dark."

Shimamura drank meekly from the cup that was thrust at him.

---

2. The line is from a *kabuki* play.

It was not usual for him to get drunk on so little; but perhaps he was chilled from the walk. He began to feel sick. His head was whirling, and he could almost see himself going pale. He closed his eyes and fell back on the quilt. Komako put her arms around him in alarm. A childlike feeling of security came to him from the warmth of her body.

She seemed ill at ease, like a young woman, still childless, who takes a baby up in her arms. She raised her head and looked down, as at the sleeping child.

"You're a good girl."

"Why? Why am I good? What's good about me?"

"You're a good girl."

"Don't tease me. It's wrong of you." She looked aside, and she spoke in broken phrases, like little blows, as she rocked him back and forth.

She laughed softly to herself.

"I'm not good at all. It's not easy having you here. You'd best go home. Each time I come to see you I want to put on a new kimono, and now I have none left. This one is borrowed. So you see I'm not really good at all."

Shimamura did not answer.

"And what do you find good in me?" Her voice was a little husky. "The first day I met you I thought I had never seen anyone I disliked more. People just don't say the sort of things you said. I hated you."

Shimamura nodded.

"Oh? You understand then why I've not mentioned it before? When a woman has to say these things, she has gone as far as she can, you know."

"But it's all right."

"Is it?" They were silent for some moments. Komako seemed to be looking back on herself, and the awareness of a woman's being alive came to Shimamura in her warmth.

"You're a good woman."

"How am I good?"

"A good woman."

"What an odd person." Her face was hidden from him, as though she were rubbing her jaw against an itching shoulder. Then suddenly, Shimamura had no idea why, she raised herself angrily to an elbow.

"A good woman—what do you mean by that? What do you mean?"

He only stared at her.

"Admit it. That's why you came to see me. You were laughing at me. You were laughing at me after all."

She glared at him, scarlet with anger. Her shoulders were shaking. But the flush receded as quickly as it had come, and tears were falling over her blanched face.

"I hate you. How I hate you." She rolled out of bed and sat with her back to him.

Shimamura felt a stabbing in his chest as he saw what the mistake had been. He lay silent, his eyes closed.

"It makes me very sad," she murmured to herself. Her head was on her knees, and her body was bent into a tight ball.

When she had wept herself out, she sat jabbing at the floor mat with a silver hair-ornament. Presently she slipped from the room.

Shimamura could not bring himself to follow her. She had reason to feel hurt.

But soon she was back, her bare feet quiet in the corridor. "Are you going for a bath?" she called from outside the door. It was a high, thin little voice.

"If you want."

"I'm sorry. I've reconsidered."

She showed no sign of coming in. Shimamura picked up his towel and stepped into the hall. She walked ahead of him with her eyes on the floor, like a criminal being led away. As the bath warmed her, however, she became strangely gay and winsome, and sleep was out of the question.

The next morning Shimamura awoke to a voice reciting a Nō play.[3]

He lay for a time listening. Kamoko turned and smiled from the mirror.

"The guests in the Plum Room. I was called there after my first party. Remember?"

"A Nō club out on a trip?"

"Yes."

"It snowed?"

"Yes." She got up and threw open the sliding door in front of the window. "No more maple leaves."

From the gray sky, framed by the window, the snow floated toward them in great flakes, like white peonies. There was something quietly unreal about it. Shimamura stared with the vacantness that comes from lack of sleep.

The Nō reciters had taken out a drum.

He remembered the snowy morning toward the end of the year before, and glanced at the mirror. The cold peonies floated up yet larger, cutting a white outline around Komako. Her kimono was open at the neck, and she was wiping at her throat with a towel.

Her skin was as clean as if it had just been laundered. He had not dreamed that she was a woman who would find it necessary to take offense at such a trivial remark, and that very fact lent her an irresistible sadness.

The mountains, more distant each day as the russet of the autumn leaves had darkened, came brightly back to life with the snow.

The cedars, under a thin coating of snow, rose sheer from the white ground to the sky, each cut off sharply from the rest.

The thread was spun in the snow, and the cloth woven in the snow, washed in the snow, and bleached in the snow. Everything, from the first spinning of the thread to the last finishing touches, was done in the snow. "There is Chijimi linen[4] because there is snow," someone wrote long ago. "Snow is the mother of Chijimi."

The Chijimi grass-linen of this snow country was the handwork of the mountain maiden through the long, snowbound winters. Shimamura

---

3. Japan's oldest extant theatrical tradition, originating in the 14th century, which is a highly stylized combination of acting, chanting, and dancing.   4. A crepe cloth woven with a stronger thread horizontally and made to shrink so that it would wrinkle. It was prized as a fabric for lightweight kimonos. The connection between Chijimi linen and snow becomes clear below.

searched for the cloth in old-clothes shops to use for summer kimonos. Through acquaintances in the dance world, he had found a shop that specialized in old Nō robes, and he had a standing order that when a good piece of Chijimi came in he was to see it.

In the old days, it is said, the early Chijimi fair was held in the spring, when the snow had melted and the snow blinds were taken down from the houses. People came from far and near to buy Chijimi, even wholesalers from the great commercial cities, Edo, Nagoya, and Osaka;[5] and the inns at which they stayed were fixed by tradition. Since the labors of half a year were on display, youths and maidens gathered from all the mountain villages. Sellers' booths and buyers' booths were lined up side by side, and the market took on the air of a festival. With prizes awarded for the best pieces of weaving, it came also to be a sort of competition for husbands. The girls learned to weave as children, and they turned out their best work between the ages of perhaps fourteen and twenty-four. As they grew older they lost the touch that gave tone to the finest Chijimi. In their desire to be numbered among the few outstanding weavers, they put their whole labor and love into this product of the long snowbound months—the months of seclusion and boredom, between October, under the old lunar calendar,[6] when the spinning began, and mid-February of the following year, when the last bleaching was finished.

There may have been among Shimamura's kimonos one or more woven by these mountain maidens toward the middle of the last century.

He still sent his kimonos back for "snow-bleaching." It was a great deal of trouble to return old kimonos—that had touched the skin of he could not know whom—for rebleaching each year to the country that had produced them; but when he considered the labors of those mountain maidens, he wanted the bleaching to be done properly in the country where the maidens had lived. The thought of the white linen, spread out on the deep snow, the cloth and the snow glowing scarlet in the rising sun, was enough to make him feel that the dirt of the summer had been washed away, even that he himself had been bleached clean. It must be added, however, that a Tokyo shop took care of the details for him, and he had no way of knowing that the bleaching had really been done in the old manner.

From ancient times there were houses that specialized in bleaching. The weavers for the most part did not do their own. White Chijimi was spread out on the snow after it was woven, colored Chijimi bleached on frames while still in thread. The bleaching season came in January and February under the lunar calendar, and snow-covered fields and gardens were the bleaching grounds.

The cloth or thread was soaked overnight in ash water.[7] The next morning it was washed over and over again, wrung, and put out to bleach. The process was repeated day after day, and the sight when, as the bleaching

---

5. Three great commercial centers in premodern Japan. Present-day Tokyo was known as Edo until the end of the *shogun*'s rule.   6. Introduced from China and followed until 1873, when, as part of its drive toward modernization, Japan adopted the solar-based Gregorian calendar employed in the West (see introduction "The Rise of Popular Arts in Premodern Japan," p. 589).   7. Lye used to bleach or dye fabric.

came to an end, the rays of the rising sun turned the white Chijimi blood-red was quite beyond description, Shimamura had read in an old book. It was something to be shown to natives of warmer provinces. And the end of the bleaching was a sign that spring was coming to the snow country.

The land of the Chijimi was very near this hot spring, just down the river, where the valley began to widen out. Indeed it must almost have been visible from Shimamura's window. All of the Chijimi market towns now had railway stations, and the region was still a well-known weaving center.

Since Shimamura had never come to the snow country in midsummer, when he wore Chijimi, or in the snowy season, when it was woven, he had never had occasion to talk of it to Komako; and she hardly seemed the person to ask about the fate of an old folk art.

When he heard the song Yoko sang in the bath, it had come to him that, had she been born long ago, she might have sung thus as she worked over her spools and looms, so exactly suited to the fancy was her voice.

The thread of the grass-linen, finer than animal hair, is difficult to work except in the humidity of the snow, it is said, and the dark, cold season is therefore ideal for weaving. The ancients used to add that the way this product of the cold has of feeling cool to the skin in the hottest weather is a play of the principles of light and darkness. This Komako too, who had so fastened herself to him, seemed at center cool, and the remarkable, concentrated warmth was for that fact all the more touching.

But this love would leave behind it nothing so definite as a piece of Chijimi. Though cloth to be worn is among the most short-lived of craft-works, a good piece of Chijimi, if it has been taken care of, can be worn quite unfaded a half-century and more after weaving. As Shimamura thought absently how human intimacies have not even so long a life, the image of Komako as the mother of another man's children suddenly floated into his mind. He looked around, startled. Possibly he was tired.

He had stayed so long that one might wonder whether he had forgotten his wife and children. He stayed not because he could not leave Komako nor because he did not want to. He had simply fallen into the habit of waiting for those frequent visits. And the more continuous the assault became, the more he began to wonder what was lacking in him, what kept him from living as completely. He stood gazing at his own coldness, so to speak. He could not understand how she had so lost herself. All of Komako came to him, but it seemed that nothing went out from him to her. He heard in his chest, like snow piling up, the sound of Komako, an echo beating against empty walls. And he knew that he could not go on pamper-ing himself forever.

He leaned against the brazier, provided against the coming of the snowy season, and thought how unlikely it was that he would come again once he had left. The innkeeper had lent him an old Kyoto teakettle, skillfully inlaid in silver with flowers and birds, and from it came the sound of wind in the pines. He could make out two pine breezes, as a matter of fact, a near one and a far one. Just beyond the far breeze he heard faintly the tinkling of a bell. He put his ear to the kettle and listened. Far away, where the bell tinkled on, he suddenly saw Komako's feet, tripping in time with the bell. He drew back. The time had come to leave.

He thought of going to see the Chijimi country. That excursion might set him on his way toward breaking away from this hot spring.

He did not know at which of the towns downstream he should get off the train. Not interested in modern weaving centers, he chose a station that looked suitably lonesome and backward. After walking for a time he came out on what seemed to be the main street of an old post town.[8]

The eaves pushing out far beyond the houses were supported by pillars along both sides of the street, and in their shade were passages for communication when the snow was deep, rather like the open lean-to the old Edo shopkeeper used for displaying his wares. With deep eaves on one side of each house, the passages stretched on down the street.

Since the houses were joined in a solid block, the snow from the roofs could only be thrown down into the street. One might more accurately say that at its deepest the snow was thrown not down but up, to a high bank of snow in the middle of the street. Tunnels were cut through for passage from one side to the other.

The houses in Komako's hot-spring village, for all of its being a part of this same snow country, were separated by open spaces, and this was therefore the first time Shimamura had seen the snow passages. He tried walking in one of them. The shade under the old eaves was dark, and the leaning pillars were beginning to rot at their bases. He walked along looking into the houses as into the gloom where generation after generation of his ancestors had endured the long snows.

He saw that the weaver maidens, giving themselves up to their work here under the snow, had lived lives far from as bright and fresh as the Chijimi they made. With an allusion to a Chinese poem, Shimamura's old book had pointed out that in harsh economic terms the making of Chijimi was quite impractical, so great was the expenditure of effort that went into even one piece. It followed that none of the Chijimi houses had been able to hire weavers from outside.

The nameless workers, so diligent while they lived, had presently died, and only the Chijimi remained, the plaything of men like Shimamura, cool and fresh against the skin in the summer. This rather unremarkable thought struck him as most remarkable. The labor into which a heart has poured its whole love—where will it have its say, to excite and inspire, and when?

Like the old post road that was its ancestor, the main street ran without a curve through the straggling village, and no doubt on through Komako's hot spring. The roofs, with rows of stones to weigh down their shingles, were very much like the ones he already knew.

The pillars supporting the deep eaves cast dim shadows across the ground. With his hardly having noticed, afternoon had drawn on toward evening.

---

8. A relay posting station (like a pony express stop) along the main thoroughfares of Japan in the 17th–19th centuries.

There was nothing more to see. He took a train to another village, very much like the first. Again he walked about for a time. Feeling a little chilly, he stopped for a bowl of noodles.

The noodle shop stood beside a river, probably the river that flowed past the hot spring. Shaven-headed Buddhist nuns were crossing a bridge in twos and threes to the far side. All wore rough straw sandals, and some had dome-shaped straw hats tied to their backs. Evidently on their way from a service, they looked like crows hurrying home to their nests.

"Quite a procession of them," Shimamura said to the woman who kept the shop.

"There's a nunnery up in the hills. I suppose they're getting everything done now. It will be next to impossible for them to go out once the heavy snows begin."

The mountain beyond the bridge, growing dark in the twilight, was already covered with snow.

In this snow country, cold, cloudy days succeed one another as the leaves fall and the winds grow chilly. Snow is in the air. The high mountains near and far become white in what the people of the country call "the round of the peaks." Along the coast the sea roars, and inland the mountains roar—"the roaring at the center," like a distant clap of thunder. The round of the peaks and the roaring at the center announce that the snows are not far away. This too Shimamura had read in his old book.

The first snow had fallen the morning he lay in bed listening to the Nō recital. Had the roaring already been heard, then, in the sea and the mountains? Perhaps his senses were sharper, off on a trip with only the company of the woman Komako: even now he seemed to catch an echo of a distant roaring.

"They'll be snowbound too, will they? How many are there?"

"A great many."

"What do they do with themselves, do you suppose, shut up together through the snows? Maybe we could set them to making Chijimi."

The woman smiled vaguely at the inquisitive stranger.

Shimamura went back to the station and waited two hours for a train. The wintry sun set, and the air was so clear that it seemed to burnish the stars. Shimamura's feet were cold.

He arrived back at the hot spring not knowing what he had gone out looking for. The taxi crossed the tracks into the village as usual. A brightly lighted house stood before them as they skirted the cedar grove. Shimamura felt warm and safe again. It was the restaurant Kikumura, and three or four geisha were talking in the doorway.

Komako will be among them—but almost before he had time to frame the thought he saw only Komako.

The driver put on the brakes. Apparently he had heard rumors about the two.

Shimamura turned away from her to look out the rear window. In the light of the stars, the tracks were clear against the snow, surprisingly far into the distance.

Komako closed her eyes and jumped at the taxi. It moved slowly up the hill without stopping. She stood on the running-board, hunched over the door handle.

She had leaped at the car as if to devour it, but for Shimamura something warm had suddenly come near. The impulsive act struck him as neither rash nor unnatural. Komako raised one arm, half-embracing the closed window. Her kimono sleeve fell back from her wrist, and the warm red of the under-kimono, spilling through the thick glass, sank its way into the half-frozen Shimamura.

She pressed her forehead to the window. "Where have you been? Tell me where you've been," she called in a high voice.

"Don't be a fool. You'll get hurt," he shouted back, but they both knew it was only a gentle game.

She opened the door and fell inside the taxi. It had already stopped, however. They were at the foot of the path up the mountain.

"Where have you been?"

"Well. . . ."

"Where?"

"Nowhere in particular."

He noticed with surprise that she had the geisha's way of arranging her skirts.

The driver waited silently. It was a bit odd, Shimamura had to admit, for them to be sitting in a taxi that had gone as far as it could.

"Let's get out." Komako put her hand on his. "Cold. See how cold. Why didn't you take me with you?"

"You think I should have?"

"What a strange person." She laughed happily as she hurried up the stone steps. "I saw you leave. About two . . . a little before three?"

"That's right."

"I ran out when I heard the car. I ran out in front. And you didn't look around."

"Look around?"

"You didn't. Why didn't you look around?"

Shimamura was a little surprised at this insistence.

"You didn't know I was seeing you off, did you?"

"I didn't."

"See?" Laughing happily to herself, she came very near him. "Why didn't you take me along? You leave me behind and you come back cold—I don't like it at all."

Suddenly a fire-alarm was ringing, with the special fury that told of an emergency.

They looked back.

"Fire, fire!"

"A fire!"

A column of sparks was rising in the village below.

Komako cried out two or three times, and clutched at Shimamura's hand.

A tongue of flames shot up intermittently in the spiral of smoke, dipping down to lick at the roofs about it.

"Where is it? Fairly near the music teacher's?"

"No."

"Where, then?"

"Farther up toward the station."

The tongue of flame sprang high over the roofs.

"It's the cocoon-warehouse. The warehouse. Look, look! The cocoon-warehouse is on fire." She pressed her face to his shoulder. "The ware-house, the warehouse!"

The fire blazed higher. From the mountain, however, it was as quiet under the starry sky as a little make-believe fire. Still the terror of it came across to them. They could almost hear the roar of the flames. Shimamura put his arm around Komako's shoulders.

"What is there to be afraid of?"

"No, no, no!" Komako shook her head and burst into tears. Her face seemed smaller than usual in Shimamura's hand. The hard forehead was trembling.

She had burst out weeping at the sight of the fire, and Shimamura held her to him without thinking to wonder what had so upset her.

She stopped weeping as quickly as she had begun, and pulled away from him.

"There's a movie in the warehouse. Tonight. The place will be full of people. . . . People will be hurt. People will burn to death."

They hurried up toward the inn. There was shouting above them. Guests stood on the second- and third-floor verandas, flooded with light from the open doors. At the edge of the garden, withering chrysanthe-mums were silhouetted against the light from the inn—or the starlight. For an instant he almost thought it was the light from the fire. Several figures stood beyond the chrysanthemums. The porter and two or three others came bounding down the steps.

"Is it the cocoon-warehouse?" Komako called after them.

"That's right."

"Is anyone hurt? Has anyone been hurt?"

"They're getting everyone out. The film caught fire, and in no time the whole place was on fire. Heard it over the telephone. Look!" The porter raised one arm as he ran off. "Throwing children over one after another from the balcony, they say."

"What shall we do?" Komako started off down the stairs after the porter. Several others overtook her, and she too broke into a run. Shimamura followed.

At the foot of the stairs, their uneasiness increased. Only the very tip of the flames showed over the roofs, and the fire-alarm was nearer and more urgent.

"Careful. It's frozen, and you might slip." She stopped as she turned to look back at him. "But it's all right. You don't need to go any farther. I ought to go on myself to see if anyone has been hurt."

There was indeed no reason for him to go on. His excitement fell away. He looked down at his feet and saw that they had come to the crossing.

"The Milky Way. Beautiful, isn't it," Komako murmured. She looked up at the sky as she ran off ahead of him.

The Milky Way. Shimamura too looked up, and he felt himself floating into the Milky Way. Its radiance was so near that it seemed to take him up into it. Was this the bright vastness the poet Bashō[9] saw when he wrote of the Milky Way arched over a stormy sea? The Milky Way came down just over there, to wrap the night earth in its naked embrace. There was a terrible voluptuousness about it. Shimamura fancied that his own small shadow was being cast up against it from the earth. Each individual star stood apart from the rest, and even the particles of silver dust in the luminous clouds could be picked out, so clear was the night. The limitless depth of the Milky Way pulled his gaze up into it.

"Wait, wait," Shimamura called.

"Come on." Komako ran toward the dark mountain on which the Milky Way was falling.

She seemed to have her long skirts in her hands, and as her arms waved the skirts rose and fell a little. He could feel the red over the starlit snow.

He ran after her as fast as he could.

She slowed down and took his hand, and the long skirts fell to the ground. "You're going too?"

"Yes."

"Always looking for excitement." She clutched at her skirts, now trailing over the snow. "But people will laugh. Please go back."

"Just a little farther."

"But it's wrong. People won't like it if I take you to a fire."

He nodded and stopped. Her hand still rested lightly on his sleeve, however, as she walked on.

"Wait for me somewhere. I'll be right back. Where will you wait?"

"Wherever you say."

"Let's see. A little farther." She peered into his face, and abruptly shook her head. "No. I don't want you to."

She threw herself against him. He reeled back a step or two. A row of onions was growing in the thin snow beside the road.

"I hated it." That sudden torrent of words came at him again. "You said I was a good woman, didn't you? You're going away. Why did you have to say that to me?"

He could see her stabbing at the mat with that silver hair-ornament.

"I cried about it. I cried again after I got home. I'm afraid to leave you. But please go away. I won't forget that you made me cry."

A feeling of nagging, hopeless impotence came over Shimamura at the thought that a simple misunderstanding had worked its way so deep into the woman's being.[1] But just then they heard shouts from the direction of the fire, and a new burst of flame sent up its column of sparks.

"Look. See how it's flaming up again."

They ran on, released.

---

9. A *haiku* poet (1644–1694). The poem alluded to is contained in *The Narrow Road of the Interior* (see p. 629): "Tumultuous seas: / spanning the sky to Sado Isle, / the Milky Way." 1. Komako may be reacting to an earlier conversation (p. 2099), when Shimamura says to her, "You're a good girl" and then corrects himself, perhaps unconsciously, saying "You're a good woman." This slight shift in tone acknowledges the sexual nature of their relationship. At this moment Komako sees that she has been used. Because we are given primarily Shimamura's point of view and virtually never an inside view of how Komako feels, we can only guess at what her expectations may have been.

Komako ran well. Her sandals skimmed the frozen snow, and her arms, close to her sides, seemed hardly to move. She was as one whose whole strength is concentrated in the breast—a strangely small figure, Shimamura thought. Too plump for running himself, he was exhausted the more quickly from watching her. But Komako too was soon out of breath. She fell against him.

"My eyes are watering," she said. "That's how cold it is."

Shimamura's eyes too were moist. His cheeks were flushed, and only his eyes were cold. He blinked, and the Milky Way came to fill them. He tried to keep the tears from spilling over.

"Is the Milky Way like this every night?"

"The Milky Way? Beautiful, isn't it? But it's not like this every night. It's not usually so clear."

The Milky Way flowed over them in the direction they were running, and seemed to bathe Komako's head in its light.

The shape of her slightly aquiline nose was not clear, and the color was gone from her small lips. Was it so dim, then, the light that cut across the sky and overflowed it? Shimamura found that hard to believe. The light was dimmer even than on the night of the new moon, and yet the Milky Way was brighter than the brightest full moon. In the faint light that left no shadows on the earth, Komako's face floated up like an old mask. It was strange that even in the mask there should be the scent of the woman.

He looked up, and again the Milky Way came down to wrap itself around the earth.

And the Milky Way, like a great aurora, flowed through his body to stand at the edges of the earth. There was a quiet, chilly loneliness in it, and a sort of voluptuous astonishment.

"If you leave, I'll lead an honest life," Komako said, walking on again. She put her hand to her disordered hair. When she had gone five or six steps she turned to look back at him. "What's the matter? You don't have to stand there, do you?"

But Shimamura stood looking at her.

"Oh? You'll wait, then? And afterwards you'll take me to your room with you."

She raised her left hand a little and ran off. Her retreating figure was drawn up into the mountain. The Milky Way spread its skirts to be broken by the waves of the mountain, and, fanning out again in all its brilliant vastness higher in the sky, it left the mountain in a deeper darkness.

Komako turned into the main street and disappeared. Shimamura started after her.

Several men were pulling a fire-pump down the street to a rhythmical chant. Floods of people poured after them. Shimamura joined the crowd from the side road he and Komako had taken.

Another pump came down the street. He let it pass, and fell in behind it.

It was an old wooden hand-pump, ridiculously small, with swarms of men at the long rope pulling it and other swarms to man it.

Komako too had stopped to let it pass. She spotted Shimamura and ran along beside him. All down the road people who had stood aside fell in again as if sucked up by the pump. The two of them were now no more than part of a mob running to a fire.

"So you came. Always looking for excitement."

"That's right. It's a sad little pump, though, isn't it. The better part of a hundred years old."

"At least. Careful you don't fall."

"It is slippery."

"Come sometime when we have a real blizzard, and the snow drives along the ground all night long. But you won't, of course. Rabbits and pheasants come running inside the house to get out of the storm." Komako's voice was bright and eager. She seemed to take her beat from the chanting voices and the tramping feet around her. Shimamura too was buoyed up by the crowd.

They could hear the sound of the flames now, and tongues of flame leaped up before them. Komako clutched at Shimamura's arm. The low, dark houses along the street seemed to be breathing as they floated up in the light of the fire and faded away again. Water from the pumps flowed along the street. They came against a wall of people. Mixed in with the smoke was a smell like boiling cocoons.

The same standard remarks were taken up in loud voices through the crowd: the fire had started at the projector; children had been thrown one after another from the balcony; no one was hurt; it was lucky there had been no rice or cocoons in the warehouse. And yet a sort of quiet unified the whole fiery scene, as though everyone were voiceless before the flames, as though the heart, the point of reference, had been torn away from each individual. Everyone seemed to be listening to the sound of the fire and the pumps.

Now and then a villager came running up late, and called out the name of a relative. There would be an answer, and the two would call happily back and forth. Only those voices seemed alive and present. The fire-alarm no longer sounded.

Afraid people would be watching, Shimamura slipped away from Komako and stood behind a group of children. The children moved back from the heat. The snow at their feet was melting, while farther on it had already turned to slush from the fire and water, a muddy confusion of footprints.

They were standing in the field beside the cocoon-warehouse. Most of the crowd on the main street had poured into that same open space.

The fire had apparently started near the entrance, and the walls and roof of half the building had burned away. The pillars and beams were still smoldering. It was a wide barn of a building, only shingles and boarded walls and floors, and the inside was fairly free of smoke. Though the roof, soaked from the pumps, did not seem to be burning, the fire continued to spread. A tongue would shoot up from a quite unexpected spot, the three pumps would turn hastily towards it, and a shower of sparks would fly up in a cloud of black smoke.

The sparks spread off into the Milky Way, and Shimamura was pulled up with them. As the smoke drifted away, the Milky Way seemed to dip and flow in the opposite direction. Occasionally a pump missed the roof, and the end of its line of water wavered and turned to a faint white mist, as though lighted by the Milky Way.

Komako had come up to him, he did not know when. She took his hand. He looked around at her, but said nothing. She gazed at the fire, the pulse of the fire beating on her intent, slightly flushed face. Shimamura felt a violent rising in his chest. Komako's hair was coming undone, and her throat was bare and arched. His fingers trembled from the urge to touch it. His hand was warm, but Komako's was still warmer. He did not know why he should feel that a separation was forcing itself upon them.

Flames shot up again from the pillars and beams at the entrance. A line of water was turned on them. Hissing clouds of steam arose as the framework began to give way.

The crowd gasped as one person. A woman's body had fallen through the flames.

The cocoon-warehouse had a balcony that was little more than a perfunctory recognition of its duties as an auditorium. Since it fell from the balcony, low for a second floor, the body could have taken but a fraction of a second to reach the ground; but the eye had somehow been able to trace its passage in detail. Perhaps the strange, puppetlike deadness of the fall was what made that fraction of a second seem so long. One knew immediately that the figure was unconscious. It made no noise as it struck the ground between the fire that had newly blazed up and the fire that still smoldered beyond. Water had collected inside the building, and no dust arose from the fall.

A line of water from one of the pumps arched down on the smoldering fire, and a woman's body suddenly floated up before it: such had been the fall. The body was quite horizontal as it passed through the air. Shimamura started back—not from fear, however. He saw the figure as a phantasm from an unreal world. That stiff figure, flung out into the air, became soft and pliant. With a doll-like passiveness, and the freedom of the lifeless, it seemed to hold both life and death in abeyance. If Shimamura felt even a flicker of uneasiness, it was lest the head drop, or a knee or a hip bend to disturb that perfectly horizontal line. Something of the sort must surely happen; but the body was still horizontal when it struck the ground.

Komako screamed and brought her hands to her eyes. Shimamura gazed at the still form.

When did he realize that it was Yoko? The gasp from the crowd and Komako's scream seemed to come at the same instant; and that instant too there was a suggestion of a spasm in the calf of Yoko's leg, stretched out on the ground.

The scream stabbed him through. At the spasm in Yoko's leg, a chill passed down his spine to his very feet. His heart was pounding in an indefinable anguish.

Yoko's leg moved very slightly, hardly enough to catch the eye.

Even before the spasm passed, Shimamura was looking at the face and the kimono, an arrow figure against a red ground. Yoko had fallen face up. The skirt of her kimono was pulled just over one knee. There was but that slight movement in her leg after she struck the earth. She lay unconscious. For some reason Shimamura did not see death in the still form. He felt rather that Yoko had undergone some shift, some metamorphosis.

Two or three beams from the collapsing balcony were burning over her head. The beautiful eyes that so pierced their object were closed. Her jaw was thrust slightly out, and her throat was arched. The fire flickered over the white face.

Shimamura felt a rising in his chest again as the memory came to him of the night he had been on his way to visit Komako, and he had seen that mountain light shine in Yoko's face. The years and months with Komako seemed to be lighted up in that instant; and there, he knew, was the anguish.

Komako put her hands to her eyes and screamed, and even as the crowd held its breath in that first gasp she broke away from Shimamura and ran toward the fire.

The long geisha's skirts trailing behind her, she staggered through the pools of water and the charred bits of wood that lay scattered over the ground. She turned and struggled back with Yoko at her breast. Her face was strained and desperate, and beneath it Yoko's face hung vacantly, as at the moment of the soul's flight. Komako struggled forward as if she bore her sacrifice, or her punishment.

The crowd found its various voices again. It surged forward to envelop the two.

"Keep back. Keep back, please." He heard Komako's cry. "This girl is insane. She's insane."

He tried to move toward that half-mad voice, but he was pushed aside by the men who had come up to take Yoko from her. As he caught his footing, his head fell back, and the Milky Way flowed down inside him with a roar.

JORGE LUIS BORGES
1899–1986

Although other modernist writers are known for their formal innovations, it is the Argentinian Jorge Luis Borges who represents, above all, the gamelike or playful aspect of literary creation. The "real world" is only one of the possible realities in Borges's multiple universe, which treats history, fantasy, and science fiction as having equal claim on our attention: since they all can be imagined, they all are perhaps equally real. His is a world of pure thought, where abstract fictional games are played out when an initial situation or concept is pushed to its elegantly logical extreme. If everything is possible, there is no need for the artificial constraints imposed by conventional artistic attempts to represent reality: no need for psychological consistency, for a realistic setting, or for a story that unfolds in ordinary time and space. The voice telling the story becomes lost inside the setting it creates, just as a drawing by Saul Steinberg or Maurits Escher depicts a pen drawing the rest of the landscape in which it appears. Not unexpectedly, this thorough immersion in the play of subjective imagination appealed to writers like the French "new novelists," who were experimenting with shifting perspectives and a refusal of "objective" reality. For a long time, Borges's European reputation outstripped his prestige in his native land.

Borges was born in Buenos Aires, Argentina, on August 24, 1899, to a prosperous family whose ancestors were distinguished in Argentinian history. The family moved early to a large house whose library and garden were to form an essential part of his literary imagination. His paternal grandmother being English, the young Borges knew English as soon as Spanish and was educated by an English tutor until he was nine. Traveling in Europe, the family was caught in Geneva at the outbreak of World War I; Borges attended secondary school in Switzerland and throughout the war, at which time he learned French and German. After the war they moved to Spain, where he associated with a group of young experimental poets known as the Ultraists. When Borges returned home in 1921, he founded his own group of Argentinian Ultraists (their mural-review, *Prisma*, was printed on sign paper and plastered on walls); became close friends with the philosopher Macedonio Fernandez, whose dedication to pure thought and linguistic intricacies greatly influenced his own attitudes; and contributed regularly to the avant-garde review *Martin Fierro*, at that time associated with an apolitical "art for art's sake" attitude quite at odds with that of the Boedo group of politically committed writers. Although devoted to pure art, Borges consistently opposed the military dictatorship of Juan Perón and made his political views plain in speeches and nonliterary writings even if they were not included in his fiction. His attitude did not go unnoticed: in 1946, the Perón regime removed him from the librarian's post that he had held since 1938 and offered him a job as a chicken inspector.

During the 1930s, Borges turned to short narrative pieces and in 1935 published a collection of sketches titled *Universal History of Infamy*. His more mature stories—brief, metaphysical fictions whose density and elegance at times approach poetry—came as an experiment after a head injury and operation in 1938. *The Garden of Forking Paths* (1941), his first major collection, introduced him to a wider public as an intellectual and idealist writer, whose short stories subordinated familiar techniques of character, scene, plot, and narrative voice to a central idea, which was often a philosophical concept. This concept was not used as a lesson or dogma, but as the starting point of fantastic elaborations to entertain readers within the game of literature.

Borges's imaginative world is an immense labyrinth, a "garden of forking paths" in which images of mazes and infinite mirroring, cyclical repetition and recall, illustrate the effort of an elusive narrative voice to understand its own significance and that of the world. In *Borges and I*, he comments on the parallel existence of two Borgeses: the one who exists in his work (the one his readers know) and the living, fleshly identity felt by the man who sets pen to paper. "Little by little, I am giving over everything to him . . . I do not know which one of us has written this page." Borges has written on the idea (derived from the British philosophers David Hume and George Berkeley) of the individual self as a cluster of different perceptions, and he further elaborates this notion in his fictional proliferation of identities and alternate realities. Disdaining the "psychological fakery" of realistic novels (the "draggy novel of characters"), he prefers writing that is openly artful, concerned with technique for its own sake, and invents its own multidimensional reality.

Stories in *The Garden of Forking Paths, Fictions* (1944), and *The Aleph* (1949) develop these themes in a variety of styles. Borges is fond of detective stories (and has written a number of them) in which the search for an elusive explanation, given carefully planted clues, matters more than how recognizable the characters may be. In *Death and the Compass*, a mysterious murderer leaves tantalizing traces that refer to points of the compass and lead the detective into a fatal trap that closes on him at a fourth compass point symbolized by the architectural lozenges of the house where he dies. The author composes an art of puzzles and discovery, a grand code that treats our universe as a giant library where meaning is locked away in endless hexagonal galleries (*The Library of Babel*), as an enormous lottery whose results are all the events of our lives (*The Lottery in Babylon*), as a series of dreams within dreams (*The Circular Ruins*), or as a small iridescent sphere containing all of the points in space (*The Aleph*). In *Pierre Menard, Author of the Quixote*, the narrator is a scholarly reviewer of a certain fictitious Menard, whose masterwork has been to rewrite *Don Quixote* as if it were created today: not revise it, or yet transcribe it, but actually *reinvent* it word for word. He has succeeded; the two texts are "verbally identical" although Menard's modern version is "more ambiguous" than Cervantes's and thus "infinitely richer."

The imaginary universe of *Tlön, Uqbar, Orbis Tertius* exemplifies the mixture of fact and fiction with which Borges invites us to speculate on the solidity of our own world. The narrator is engaged in tracking down mysterious references to a country called Tlön, whose language, science, and literature are exactly opposite (and perhaps related to) our own. For example, the Tlönians use verbs or adjectives instead of nouns, since they have no concept of objects in space, and their science consists of an association of ideas in which the most astounding theory becomes the truth. In a postscript, the narrator reveals that the encyclopedia has turned out to be an immense scholarly hoax, yet also mentions that strange and unearthly objects—recognizably from Tlön—have recently been found.

The intricate, riddling, mazelike ambiguity of Borges's stories earned him international reputation and influence, to the point that a "style like Borges" has become a recognized term. In Argentina, he was given the prestigious post of Director of the National Library after the fall of Perón in 1955 and in 1961 he shared the International Publishers' Prize with Samuel Beckett. Always nearsighted, he grew increasingly blind in the mid-1950s and he was forced to dictate his work. Nonetheless, he continued to travel, teach, and lecture in the company of his wife, Else Astete Milan, whom he married in 1967. Borges lived until his death in his beloved Buenos Aires, the city he celebrated in his first volume of poetry.

The Garden of Forking Paths begins as a simple spy story purporting to reveal the hidden truth about a German bombing raid during World War I. Borges alludes to documented facts: the geographic setting of the town of Albert and the Ancre River; a famous Chinese novel as Ts'ui Pên's proposed model; the *History of the World War (1914–1918)* published by B. H. Liddell Hart in 1934. Official history is undermined on the first page, however, both by the newly discovered confession of Dr. Yu Tsun and by his editor's suspiciously defensive footnote. Ultimately, Yu Tsun will learn from his ancestor's novel that history is a labyrinth of alternate possibilities (much like the "alternate worlds" of science fiction).

Borges executes his detective story with the traditional carefully planted clues. We know from the beginning that Yu Tsun—even though arrested—has successfully outwitted his rival Captain Richard Madden; that his problem was to convey the name of a bombing target to his chief in Berlin; that he went to the telephone book to locate someone capable of transmitting his message; and that he had one bullet in his revolver. The cut-off phone call, the chase at the railroad station, and Madden's hasty arrival at Dr. Albert's house provide the excitement and pressure expected in a straightforward detective plot. Quite different spatial and temporal horizons open up halfway through, however. Coincidences—those chance relationships that might well have happened differently—introduce the idea of forking paths or alternate possible routes for history. Both Yu Tsun and Richard Madden are aliens trying to prove their worth inside their respective bureaucracies; the road to Stephen Albert's house turns mazelike always to the left; the only suitable name in the phone book—the man Yu Tsun must kill—is a Sinologist who has reconstructed the labyrinthine text written long ago by Yu Tsun's ancestor. This text, Ts'ui Pên's *The Garden of Forking Paths*, describes the universe as an infinite series of alternate versions of experience. In different versions of the story (taking place at different times), Albert and Yu Tsun are enemies—or friends—or not even there. The war and Richard Madden appear diminished (although no less real) in such a kaleidoscopic perspective, for they exist in only one of many possible dimensions. Yet Madden hurries up the walk, and current reality returns to demand Albert's death. It may seem as though the vision of other worlds in which Albert continues to exist (or is Yu Tsun's enemy) would soften the murderer's remorse for his deed. Instead, it makes more poignant the narrator's realization that in this dimension no other way could be found.

George R. McMurray, *Jorge Luis Borges* (1980), and Martin S. Stabb, *Borges Revisited* (1991), are general introductions to the man and his work. Jaime Alazraki, ed., *Critical Essays on Jorge Luis Borges* (1987), assembles articles and reviews (including the 1970 *Autobiographical Essay*), four comparative essays, and a general introduction that offer valuable perspectives on Borges's writing as well as his impact on American writers and critics. Edna Aizenberg, ed., *Borges and His Successors: the Borgesian Impact on Literature and the Arts* (1990), is a wide-ranging collection of essays describing Borges as the precursor of postmodern fiction and criticism. Anna Maria Barrenechea, *Borges The Labyrinth Maker* (1965), discusses Borges's intricate style while Daniel Balderston, *Out of Context: Historical Reference and the Representation of Reality in Borges* (1993), focuses on the texts' manipulation of fictional and historical reality. Fernando Sorrentino, *Seven Conversations with Jorge Luis Borges* (1981), is a series of informal, widely ranging interviews from 1972, with a prefaced list of the topics of each conversation.

PRONOUNCING GLOSSARY

The following list uses common English syllables and stress accents to provide rough equivalents of selected words whose pronunciation may be unfamiliar to the general reader.

Borges: *bore'-kess*

Hsi P'êng: *shee pung*

Hung Lu Meng: *hoong low mung*

Ts'ui Pên: *tsoo-ay pun*

Yu Tsun: *yew tsoo-en*

The Garden of Forking Paths[1]

On page 22 of Liddell Hart's *History of World War I* you will read that an attack against the Serre-Montauban line by thirteen British divisions (supported by 1,400 artillery pieces), planned for the 24th of July, 1916, had to be postponed until the morning of the 29th. The torrential rains, Captain Liddell Hart comments, caused this delay, an insignificant one, to be sure.

The following statement, dictated, reread and signed by Dr. Yu Tsun, former professor of English at the *Hochschule* at Tsingtao,[2] throws an

---

1. Translated by Donald A. Yates.   2. Or Ch'ing-tao; a major port in east China, part of territory leased to (and developed by) Germany in 1898. *Hochschule:* university (German).

unsuspected light over the whole affair. The first two pages of the document are missing.

"... and I hung up the receiver. Immediately afterwards, I recognized the voice that had answered in German. It was that of Captain Richard Madden. Madden's presence in Viktor Runeberg's apartment meant the end of our anxieties and—but this seemed, or should have seemed, very secondary to me—also the end of our lives. It meant that Runeberg had been arrested or murdered.[3] Before the sun set on that day, I would encounter the same fate. Madden was implacable. Or rather, he was obliged to be so. An Irishman at the service of England, a man accused of laxity and perhaps of treason, how could he fail to seize and be thankful for such a miraculous opportunity: the discovery, capture, maybe even the death of two agents of the German Reich?[4] I went up to my room; absurdly I locked the door and threw myself on my back on the narrow iron cot. Through the window I saw the familiar roofs and the cloud-shaded six o'clock sun. It seemed incredible to me that that day without premonitions or symbols should be the one of my inexorable death. In spite of my dead father, in spite of having been a child in a symmetrical garden of Hai Feng, was I—now—going to die? Then I reflected that everything happens to a man precisely, precisely now. Centuries of centuries and only in the present do things happen; countless men in the air, on the face of the earth and the sea, and all that really is happening is happening to me . . . The almost intolerable recollection of Madden's horselike face banished these wanderings. In the midst of my hatred and terror (it means nothing to me now to speak of terror, now that I have mocked Richard Madden, now that my throat yearns for the noose) it occurred to me that that tumultuous and doubtless happy warrior did not suspect that I possessed the Secret. The name of the exact location of the new British artillery park on the River Ancre. A bird streaked across the gray sky and blindly I translated it into an airplane and that airplane into many (against the French sky) annihilating the artillery station with vertical bombs. If only my mouth, before a bullet shattered it, could cry out that secret name so it could be heard in Germany . . . My human voice was very weak. How might I make it carry to the ear of the Chief? To the ear of that sick and hateful man who knew nothing of Runeberg and me save that we were in Staffordshire[5] and who was waiting in vain for our report in his arid office in Berlin, endlessly examining newspapers . . . I said out loud: I must flee. I sat up noiselessly, in a useless perfection of silence, as if Madden were already lying in wait for me. Something—perhaps the mere vain ostentation of proving my resources were nil—made me look through my pockets. I found what I knew I would find. The American watch, the nickel chain and the square coin, the key ring with the incriminating useless keys to Runeberg's apartment, the notebook, a letter which I resolved to destroy immediately (and which I did not destroy), a crown, two shillings and a few pence, the red and blue pencil, the handkerchief, the revolver with

---

3. "A hypothesis both hateful and odd. The Prussian spy Hans Rabener, alias Viktor Runeberg, attacked with drawn automatic the bearer of the warrant for his arrest, Captain Richard Madden. The latter, in self-defense, inflicted the wound which brought about Runeberg's death [Editor's note]." This entire note is by Borges as "Editor."   4. Empire (German).   5. County in west central England.

one bullet. Absurdly, I took it in my hand and weighed it in order to inspire courage within myself. Vaguely I thought that a pistol report can be heard at a great distance. In ten minutes my plan was perfected. The telephone book listed the name of the only person capable of transmitting the message; he lived in a suburb of Fenton,[6] less than a half hour's train ride away.

I am a cowardly man. I say it now, now that I have carried to its end a plan whose perilous nature no one can deny. I know its execution was terrible. I didn't do it for Germany, no. I care nothing for a barbarous country which imposed upon me the abjection of being a spy. Besides, I know of a man from England—a modest man—who for me is no less great than Goethe.[7] I talked with him for scarcely an hour, but during that hour he was Goethe . . . I did it because I sensed that the Chief somehow feared people of my race—for the innumerable ancestors who merge within me. I wanted to prove to him that a yellow man could save his armies. Besides, I had to flee from Captain Madden. His hands and his voice could call at my door at any moment. I dressed silently, bade farewell to myself in the mirror, went downstairs, scrutinized the peaceful street and went out. The station was not far from my home, but I judged it wise to take a cab. I argued that in this way I ran less risk of being recognized; the fact is that in the deserted street I felt myself visible and vulnerable, infinitely so. I remember that I told the cab driver to stop a short distance before the main entrance. I got out with voluntary, almost painful slowness; I was going to the village of Ashgrove but I bought a ticket for a more distant station. The train left within a very few minutes, at eight-fifty. I hurried; the next one would leave at nine-thirty. There was hardly a soul on the platform. I went through the coaches; I remember a few farmers, a woman dressed in mourning, a young boy who was reading with fervor the *Annals* of Tacitus,[8] a wounded and happy soldier. The coaches jerked forward at last. A man whom I recognized ran in vain to the end of the platform. It was Captain Richard Madden. Shattered, trembling, I shrank into the far corner of the seat, away from the dreaded window.

From this broken state I passed into an almost abject felicity. I told myself that the duel had already begun and that I had won the first encounter by frustrating, even if for forty minutes, even if by a stroke of fate, the attack of my adversary. I argued that this slightest of victories foreshadowed a total victory. I argued (no less fallaciously) that my cowardly felicity proved that I was a man capable of carrying out the adventure successfully. From this weakness I took strength that did not abandon me. I foresee that man will resign himself each day to more atrocious undertakings; soon there will be no one but warriors and brigands; I give them this counsel: *The author of an atrocious undertaking ought to imagine that he has already accomplished it, ought to impose upon himself a future as irrevocable as the past.* Thus I proceeded as my eyes of a man already dead

---

6. In Lincolnshire, a county in east England.   7. Johann Wolfgang von Goethe (1749–1832), German poet, novelist, and dramatist, author of *Faust*; often taken as representing the peak of German cultural achievement.   8. Cornelius Tacitus (55–117), Roman historian whose *Annals* give a vivid picture of the decadence and corruption of the Roman Empire under Tiberius, Claudius, and Nero.

registered the elapsing of that day, which was perhaps the last, and the diffusion of the night. The train ran gently along, amid ash trees. It stopped, almost in the middle of the fields. No one announced the name of the station. "Ashgrove?" I asked a few lads on the platform. "Ashgrove," they replied. I got off.

A lamp enlightened the platform but the faces of the boys were in shadow. One questioned me, "Are you going to Dr. Stephen Albert's house?" Without waiting for my answer, another said, "The house is a long way from here, but you won't get lost if you take this road to the left and at every crossroads turn again to your left." I tossed them a coin (my last), descended a few stone steps and started down the solitary road. It went downhill, slowly. It was of elemental earth; overhead the branches were tangled; the low, full moon seemed to accompany me.

For an instant, I thought that Richard Madden in some way had penetrated my desperate plan. Very quickly, I understood that that was impossible. The instructions to turn always to the left reminded me that such was the common procedure for discovering the central point of certain labyrinths. I have some understanding of labyrinths: not for nothing am I the great grandson of that Ts'ui Pên who was governor of Yunnan and who renounced worldly power in order to write a novel that might be even more populous than the *Hung Lu Meng*[9] and to construct a labyrinth in which all men would become lost. Thirteen years he dedicated to these heterogeneous tasks, but the hand of a stranger murdered him—and his novel was incoherent and no one found the labyrinth. Beneath English trees I meditated on that lost maze: I imagined it inviolate and perfect at the secret crest of a mountain; I imagined it erased by rice fields or beneath the water; I imagined it infinite, no longer composed of octagonal kiosks and returning paths, but of rivers and provinces and kingdoms . . . I thought of a labyrinth of labyrinths, of one sinuous spreading labyrinth that would encompass the past and the future and in some way involve the stars. Absorbed in these illusory images, I forgot my destiny of one pursued. I felt myself to be, for an unknown period of time, an abstract perceiver of the world. The vague, living countryside, the moon, the remains of the day worked on me, as well as the slope of the road which eliminated any possibility of weariness. The afternoon was intimate, infinite. The road descended and forked among the now confused meadows. A high-pitched, almost syllabic music approached and receded in the shifting of the wind, dimmed by leaves and distance. I thought that a man can be an enemy of other men, of the moments of other men, but not of a country: not of fireflies, words, gardens, streams of water, sunsets. Thus I arrived before a tall, rusty gate. Between the iron bars I made out a poplar grove and a pavilion. I understood suddenly two things, the first trivial, the second almost unbelievable: the music came from the pavilion, and the music was Chinese. For precisely that reason I had openly accepted it without paying it any heed. I do not remember whether there was a bell or whether I knocked with my hand. The sparkling of the music continued.

9. *The Dream of the Red Chamber* (1791) by Ts'ao Hsüeh-ch'in; the most famous Chinese novel, a love story and panorama of Chinese family life involving more than 430 separate characters. (Also called *The Story of the Stone*; see above, p. 156.)

From the rear of the house within a lantern approached: a lantern that the trees sometimes striped and sometimes eclipsed, a paper lantern that had the form of a drum and the color of the moon. A tall man bore it. I didn't see his face for the light blinded me. He opened the door and said slowly, in my own language: "I see that the pious Hsi P'êng persists in correcting my solitude. You no doubt wish to see the garden?"

I recognized the name of one of our consuls and I replied, disconcerted, "The garden?"

"The garden of forking paths."

Something stirred in my memory and I uttered with incomprehensible certainty, "The garden of my ancestor Ts'ui Pên."

"Your ancestor? Your illustrious ancestor? Come in."

The damp path zigzagged like those of my childhood. We came to a library of Eastern and Western books. I recognized bound in yellow silk several volumes of the Lost Encyclopedia, edited by the Third Emperor of the Luminous Dynasty but never printed.[1] The record on the phonograph revolved next to a bronze phoenix. I also recall a *famille rose*[2] vase and another, many centuries older, of that shade of blue which our craftsmen copied from the potters of Persia . . .

Stephen Albert observed me with a smile. He was, as I have said, very tall, sharp-featured, with gray eyes and a gray beard. He told me that he had been a missionary in Tientsin "before aspiring to become a Sinologist."

We sat down—I on a long, low divan, he with his back to the window and a tall circular clock. I calculated that my pursuer, Richard Madden, could not arrive for at least an hour. My irrevocable determination could wait.

"An astounding fate, that of Ts'ui Pên," Stephen Albert said. "Governor of his native province, learned in astronomy, in astrology and in the tireless interpretation of the canonical books, chess player, famous poet and calligrapher—he abandoned all this in order to compose a book and a maze. He renounced the pleasures of both tyranny and justice, of his populous couch, of his banquets and even of erudition—all to close himself up for thirteen years in the Pavilion of the Limpid Solitude. When he died, his heirs found nothing save chaotic manuscripts. His family, as you may be aware, wished to condemn them to the fire; but his executor—a Taoist or Buddhist monk—insisted on their publication."

"We descendants of Ts'ui Pên," I replied, "continue to curse that monk. Their publication was senseless. The book is an indeterminate heap of contradictory drafts. I examined it once: in the third chapter the hero dies, in the fourth he is alive. As for the other undertaking of Ts'ui Pên, his labyrinth . . ."

"Here is Ts'ui Pên's labyrinth," he said, indicating a tall lacquered desk.

---

1. The Yung-lo emperor of the Ming ("bright") Dynasty commissioned a massive encyclopedia between 1403 and 1408. A single copy of the 11,095 manuscript volumes was made in the mid-1500s; the original was later destroyed and only 370 volumes of the copy remain today.   2. Pink family (French); refers to a Chinese decorative enamel ranging in color from an opaque pink to purplish rose. *Famille rose* pottery was at its best during the reign of Yung Chên (1723–1735).

"An ivory labyrinth!" I exclaimed. "A minimum labyrinth."

"A labyrinth of symbols," he corrected. "An invisible labyrinth of time. To me, a barbarous Englishman, has been entrusted the revelation of this diaphanous mystery. After more than a hundred years, the details are irretrievable; but it is not hard to conjecture what happened. Ts'ui Pên must have said once: *I am withdrawing to write a book.* And another time: *I am withdrawing to construct a labyrinth.* Every one imagined two works; to no one did it occur that the book and the maze were one and the same thing. The Pavilion of the Limpid Solitude stood in the center of a garden that was perhaps intricate; that circumstance could have suggested to the heirs a physical labyrinth. Ts'ui Pên died; no one in the vast territories that were his came upon the labyrinth; the confusion of the novel suggested to me that *it* was the maze. Two circumstances gave me the correct solution of the problem. One: the curious legend that Ts'ui Pên had planned to create a labyrinth which would be strictly infinite. The other: a fragment of a letter I discovered."

Albert rose. He turned his back on me for a moment; he opened a drawer of the black and gold desk. He faced me and in his hands he held a sheet of paper that had once been crimson, but was now pink and tenuous and cross-sectioned. The fame of Ts'ui Pên as a calligrapher had been justly won. I read, uncomprehendingly and with fervor, these words written with a minute brush by a man of my blood: *I leave to the various futures (not to all) my garden of forking paths.* Wordlessly, I returned the sheet. Albert continued:

"Before unearthing this letter, I had questioned myself about the ways in which a book can be infinite. I could think of nothing other than a cyclic volume, a circular one. A book whose last page was identical with the first, a book which had the possibility of continuing indefinitely. I remembered too that night which is at the middle of the Thousand and One Nights when Scheherazade[3] (through a magical oversight of the copyist) begins to relate word for word the story of the Thousand and One Nights, establishing the risk of coming once again to the night when she must repeat it, and thus on to infinity. I imagined as well a Platonic, hereditary work, transmitted from father to son, in which each new individual adds a chapter or corrects with pious care the pages of his elders. These conjectures diverted me; but none seemed to correspond, not even remotely, to the contradictory chapters of Ts'ui Pên. In the midst of this perplexity, I received from Oxford the manuscript you have examined. I lingered, naturally, on the sentence: *I leave to the various futures (not to all) my garden of forking paths.* Almost instantly, I understood: 'The garden of forking paths' was the chaotic novel; the phrase 'the various futures (not to all)' suggested to me the forking in time, not in space. A broad rereading of the work confirmed the theory. In all fictional works, each time a man is confronted with several alternatives, he chooses one and eliminates the others; in the fiction of Ts'ui Pên, he chooses—simultane-

---

3. The narrator of the collection also known as the *Arabian Nights*, a thousand and one tales supposedly told by Scheherazade to her husband, Shahrayar, king of Samarkand, to postpone her execution (in Volume 1).

ously—all of them. *He creates*, in this way, diverse futures, diverse times which themselves also proliferate and fork. Here, then, is the explanation of the novel's contradictions. Fang, let us say, has a secret; a stranger calls at his door; Fang resolves to kill him. Naturally, there are several possible outcomes: Fang can kill the intruder, the intruder can kill Fang, they both can escape, they both can die, and so forth. In the work of Ts'ui Pên, all possible outcomes occur; each one is the point of departure for other forkings. Sometimes, the paths of this labyrinth converge: for example, you arrive at this house, but in one of the possible pasts you are my enemy, in another, my friend. If you will resign yourself to my incurable pronunciation, we shall read a few pages."

His face, within the vivid circle of the lamplight, was unquestionably that of an old man, but with something unalterable about it, even immortal. He read with slow precision two versions of the same epic chapter. In the first, an army marches to a battle across a lonely mountain; the horror of the rocks and shadows makes the men undervalue their lives and they gain an easy victory. In the second, the same army traverses a palace where a great festival is taking place; the resplendent battle seems to them a continuation of the celebration and they win the victory. I listened with proper veneration to these ancient narratives, perhaps less admirable in themselves than the fact that they had been created by my blood and were being restored to me by a man of a remote empire, in the course of a desperate adventure, on a Western isle. I remember the last words, repeated in each version like a secret commandment: *Thus fought the heroes, tranquil their admirable hearts, violent their swords, resigned to kill and to die.*

From that moment on, I felt about me and within my dark body an invisible, intangible swarming. Not the swarming of the divergent, parallel and finally coalescent armies, but a more inaccessible, more intimate agitation that they in some manner prefigured. Stephen Albert continued:

"I don't believe that your illustrious ancestor played idly with these variations. I don't consider it credible that he would sacrifice thirteen years to the infinite execution of a rhetorical experiment. In your country, the novel is a subsidiary form of literature; in Ts'ui Pên's time it was a despicable form. Ts'ui Pên was a brilliant novelist, but he was also a man of letters who doubtless did not consider himself a mere novelist. The testimony of his contemporaries proclaims—and his life fully confirms—his metaphysical and mystical interests. Philosophic controversy usurps a good part of the novel. I know that of all problems, none disturbed him so greatly nor worked upon him so much as the abysmal problem of time. Now then, the latter is the only problem that does not figure in the pages of the *Garden*. He does not even use the word that signifies *time*. How do you explain this voluntary omission?"

I proposed several solutions—all unsatisfactory. We discussed them. Finally, Stephen Albert said to me:

"In a riddle whose answer is chess, what is the only prohibited word?"

I thought a moment and replied, "The word *chess*."

"Precisely," said Albert. "*The Garden of Forking Paths* is an enormous riddle, or parable, whose theme is time; this recondite cause prohibits its mention. To omit a word always, to resort to inept metaphors and obvious periphrases, is perhaps the most emphatic way of stressing it. That is the tortuous method preferred, in each of the meanderings of his indefatigable novel, by the oblique Ts'ui Pên. I have compared hundreds of manuscripts, I have corrected the errors that the negligence of the copyists has introduced, I have guessed the plan of this chaos, I have re-established—I believe I have re-established—the primordial organization, I have translated the entire work: it is clear to me that not once does he employ the word 'time.' The explanation is obvious: *The Garden of Forking Paths* is an incomplete, but not false, image of the universe as Ts'ui Pên conceived it. In contrast to Newton and Schopenhauer,[4] your ancestor did not believe in a uniform, absolute time. He believed in an infinite series of times, in a growing, dizzying net of divergent, convergent and parallel times. This network of times which approached one another, forked, broke off, or were unaware of one another for centuries, embraces *all* possibilities of time. We do not exist in the majority of these times; in some you exist, and not I; in others I, and not you; in others, both of us. In the present one, which a favorable fate has granted me, you have arrived at my house; in another, while crossing the garden, you found me dead; in still another, I utter these same words, but I am a mistake, a ghost."

"In every one," I pronounced, not without a tremble to my voice, "I am grateful to you and revere you for your re-creation of the garden of Ts'ui Pên."

"Not in all," he murmured with a smile. "Time forks perpetually toward innumerable futures. In one of them I am your enemy."

Once again I felt the swarming sensation of which I have spoken. It seemed to me that the humid garden that surrounded the house was infinitely saturated with invisible persons. Those persons were Albert and I, secret, busy and multiform in other dimensions of time. I raised my eyes and the tenuous nightmare dissolved. In the yellow and black garden there was only one man; but this man was as strong as a statue . . . this man was approaching along the path and he was Captain Richard Madden.

"The future already exists," I replied, "but I am your friend. Could I see the letter again?"

Albert rose. Standing tall, he opened the drawer of the tall desk; for the moment his back was to me. I had readied the revolver. I fired with extreme caution. Albert fell uncomplainingly, immediately. I swear his death was instantaneous—a lightning stroke.

The rest is unreal, insignificant. Madden broke in, arrested me. I have been condemned to the gallows. I have won out abominably; I have communicated to Berlin the secret name of the city they must attack. They bombed it yesterday; I read it in the same papers that offered to England the mystery of the learned Sinologist Stephen Albert who was murdered by a stranger, one Yu Tsun. The Chief had deciphered this mystery. He knew my problem was to indicate (through the uproar of the war) the city

---

4. German philosopher (1788–1860), whose concept of will proceeded from a concept of the self as enduring through time. In *Seven Conversations with Jorge Luis Borges*, Borges also comments on Schopenhauer's interest in the "oneiric [dreamlike] essence of life." Isaac Newton (1642–1727), English mathematician and philosopher best known for his formulation of laws of gravitation and motion.

called Albert, and that I had found no other means to do so than to kill a man of that name. He does not know (no one can know) my innumerable contrition and weariness.

For Victoria Ocampo

ANDREW PEYNETSA
1904?–1976

Among the Zuni of western New Mexico the art of fiction is practiced by the teller of *telapnaawe*, "tales," which may be recited only during the cold months, between the fall and spring equinoxes, and only after the sun has set. *Telapnaawe* are told by both men and women, more often men, either at home or in meetings of the religious and social organizations known as medicine societies. Before the advent of television nearly every older man at Zuni performed *telapnaawe*, though some narrators were recognized as more adept than others. Evidently among the most gifted of his generation was the teller Andrew Peynetsa, who during the mid-1960s together with his clan relative Walter Sanchez performed nearly a hundred stories—including histories, both sacred and secular, as well as the fictional *telapnaawe*—for the benefit of small audiences of which the anthropologist Dennis Tedlock was a regular member. Tedlock preserved these recitals on tape, later to be translated with the help of Andrew's nephew, Joseph Peynetsa. It was on the evening of January 20, 1965, that Andrew Peynetsa—in a recital lasting half an hour—gave his performance of the *telapnaane* (singular) about the boy and the deer that would measurably influence the study of native American narratives and would challenge the way one looks at narrative art in general.

Little has been recorded of Andrew Peynetsa's life. The date of his birth is uncertain; he is said to have been seventy-two when he died in 1976. As a child he was schooled in Albuquerque, and he spoke English as well as Zuni. In the 1960s, when most Zunis were turning to silversmithing or were working away from the reservation, Peynetsa continued to devote himself to the traditional Zuni occupation of farming. He was an active medicine society member, a specialist in society liturgy, and a master orator (for oratory, as opposed to narrative, see the headnote "Zuni Ritual Poetry," p. 1845).

The Boy and the Deer is not an original story with Peynetsa. Strictly speaking, there can be no "new" *telapnaane*. The narrator's contribution lies in the handling of a traditional plot, to which fresh details expressing manners, locale, and even character may be freely added, yielding the typically Zunian style that is as much novelistic as it is traditional, or folkloric.

The earliest Deer Boy tale on record was collected in the 1880s by the flamboyant, controversial Frank Hamilton Cushing, who took up residence at Zuni Pueblo and was accepted into the innermost circles of Zuni society, becoming the first and most famous practitioner of what would come to be called "participant ethnography." Several additional Deer Boy variants were recorded in the 1920s by two well-known anthropologists, Ruth Bunzel and Ruth Benedict. All versions have in common the illegitimate birth of the boy who, abandoned by his human mother, is reared in the hills by a deer mother, is eventually captured by his human kinsmen, and returns, if only briefly, to human society. What made the Peynetsa version distinctive is that it exhibited a new and perhaps extreme theory of translation, as worked out by Tedlock—combined with the widely acknowledged perfection of Peynetsa's art, which made the theory compelling. The translated text was published in Tedlock's *Finding the Center* (1972), a collection that included eight other Zuni stories. *The Boy and the Deer*, however, is the one that has been remembered, repeatedly cited, and reprinted.

Listening and relistening to the recordings he had made, Tedlock came to feel that the live recital with its louds, softs, and calculated silences could not be translated into prose. Further, he would come to disparage prose itself, stating that "prose has no real existence outside the printed page." To avoid creating so lifeless an artifact, Tedlock published the Peynetsa and Sanchez narratives as a kind of poetry, using the poetic "line" to mark the narrator's pauses, adding typographic devices to indicate vocal changes. The result was not without precedent. Anthropologists had been experimenting for a decade or more with new methods for recording and translating texts. It was *Finding the Center*, however, that won an army of converts to the new quest for accuracy; and it may be said that *The Boy and the Deer* stands as a landmark in the development of the interrelated subdisciplines that have been called "ethnopoetics," "the ethnography of speaking" and, encompassing a broader scope, "discourse analysis." The pervading commandment—which has spread beyond anthropology—is to pay close, even minute, attention to human utterance for both its informational and its artistic values.

Yet *The Boy and the Deer* is a haunting story that, in a sense, could survive even the clumsiest paraphrase. It reaches deep into native American tradition to present the essential conflict between the animal and human worlds, enabling the reader or listener to join with nature in its willingness to serve humanity—and, equally, to join in the guilt of the human community for taking this gift. Expressed in stories of animal-human marriage or, as here, animal-human adoption, the basic theme is common to the native oral literatures of North, South, and Central America. Its unwritten history no doubt stretches back thousands of years.

This is not to suggest that ancient stories are kept alive for their venerability alone. To be continually re-created they must remain relevant. In an essay titled *An American Indian View of Death* (1975), Tedlock explores this connection between traditional knowledge and contemporary reality, showing how Andrew Peynetsa's version of *The Boy and the Deer* prefigured a tragic incident that occurred at Zuni in the summer of 1966. A young man, while hunting, accidentally killed himself as he bent over his rifle to straighten the sight. He had been holding the barrel with the muzzle toward his chin. The weapon discharged; the bullet entered the boy's chin and lodged in his brain. In Peynetsa's story, with chilling similarity, the boy pulls a yucca blade toward him, piercing his heart. Were these deaths truly accidental? In regard to both story and real-life incident the question became a topic of speculation. Referring to the story, Peynetsa himself commented, after narrating it: "Yes, his mother got blamed, because she sent him to get the yucca; he wasn't just going to do that. Her folks said she shouldn't tell him to get it and that his uncles should go and get it. Probably he had it in his mind to kill himself, that's the way I felt when I was telling it."

By the same token it was decided among the relatives of the teenage boy with the rifle that he had "shortened his road." After his death it was recalled that he had been in a hurry to finish things and to acquire knowledge beyond his years. No one said he had committed suicide; it was merely proposed that he had had in the back of his mind that his life would end prematurely. Yet, just as in Peynetsa's commentary on the fictional story, the web of cause and effect did not involve the victim alone. Each member of the boy's family now remembered something he or she might have done, or refrained from doing, to prevent the outcome. In any case, the victim's fate—if not to the point of death, then beyond that point—had been preordained, not only for the young rifleman but for the fictional deer boy. According to Zuni doctrine, the human being in the afterworld eventually becomes transformed into an animal with which he or she had been associated in life. There is reason to believe, according to Tedlock, that the boy with the rifle would become a deer—just as the deer boy in the story, as Peynetsa phrases it, "entered upon the roads of his elders."

In reading the text as printed here, note that the end of each line indicates a pause, often imperceptible, of a half second or more, depending on the whim of the narrator. A space between lines (with a centered bullet) implies a pause of at least two seconds. A vowel followed by a dash is to be held for about two seconds. Use a hushed voice for words in smaller type, a loud voice for words printed in all capital letters. Passages with words raised or lowered are to be chanted: chant raised words about three half tones higher than normal; lowered words, about three half tones lower. Special directions appear in parentheses, for example, "(sharply)." Audience responses are labeled "(audience)." As a final instruction Tedlock advises that the reader should not attempt mechanical accuracy to the point where it interferes with the flow of performance.

Tedlock's *An American Indian View of Death*, mentioned above, is in Dennis Tedlock and Barbara Tedlock, eds., *Teachings from the American Earth* (1975). Further essays, relating to Zuni narrative and to Andrew Peynetsa, are in Dennis Tedlock, *The Spoken Word and the Work of Interpretation* (1983). For earlier versions of the Deer Boy story, see Frank Hamilton Cushing, *Zuñi Folk Tales* (1986); Ruth Bunzel, *Zuni Texts* (1933); and Ruth Benedict, *Zuni Mythology* (1935).

PRONOUNCING GLOSSARY

The following list uses common English syllables and stress accents to provide rough equivalents of selected words whose pronunciation may be unfamiliar to the general reader.

eeso: *eh'-soh*

He'shokta: *hay'-shohk-tah*

Huututu: *hoo'-too-too*

Kyaklo: *kyah'-kloh*

Pawtiwa: *pow'-tee-wah*

Peynetsa: *pay'-nay-tsah*

son'ahchi: *sohn'-ah-chee*

sonti: *sohn'-tee*

telapnaawe: *tay'-lahp-nah-way*

telele: *tay-lay-lay*

Tísshomahhá: *tees'-shoh-mah-hah'*

The Boy and the Deer[1]

SON'AHCHI.[2]

(*audience*) Ee——so.[3]

SONTI[4] LO——NG A GO.

(*audience*) Ee——so.

THERE WERE VIL LAGERS AT HE' SHOKTA[5]

and

up on the Prairie-Dog Hills

the deer

had their home.

5

1. Translated by Dennis Tedlock. 2. Strictly untranslatable, but analogous to "once upon a time."
3. Untranslatable; roughly, "so it was." 4. Analogous to "once long ago." 5. Zuni tales customarily begin by setting the locale. He'shokta is a pueblo ruin about three miles northwest of Zuni.

•

The daughter of a priest   10
      sit   room   fourth   down   bas
was   ting in a   on the   story   weaving   ket-plaques.[6]
She was always sitting and working in there, and the Sun came up
every day   Sun came up
         when the

     girl   working
the   would sit
at the place where he came in.   15
It seems the Sun made her pregnant.
When he made her pregnant
                                    bel
though she sat in there without knowing any man, her   ly grew large.
She worked o———n for a time
weaving basket-plaques, and   20
her belly grew large, very very large.
When her time was near
she had a pain in her belly.
Gathering all her clothes
she went out and   25
went down to Water's End.

                    •

On she went until
she came to the bank
went on down to the river, and washed her clothes.

                   •

Then   30
having washed a few things, she had a pain in her belly.

                   •

She came out of the river. Having come out she sat down
by a juniper tree and strained her muscles:
the little baby came out.
She dug a hole, put juniper leaves in it   35
then laid the baby there.
She went back into the water
gathered all her clothes
and carefully washed the blood off herself.
She bundled   40
her clothes
put them on her back
and returned to her home at He'shokta.

                   •

And the DEER
who lived on the Prairie-Dog Hills   45
were going down to DRINK, going down to drink at dusk.
The Sun had almost set when they went down to drink and the little baby
      was crying.
"Where is the little baby crying?" they said.
It was two fawns on their way down
with their mother   50

---

6. Ornamental disks of woven yucca and grass fibers.

who heard him.
The crying was coming from the direction of a tree.
They were going into the water

         •

and there
they came upon the crying.   55
Where a juniper tree stood, the child
was crying.

         •

The deer
the two fawns and their mother went to him.

         •

"Well, why shouldn't we   60
save him?
Why don't you two hold my nipples
so
so he can nurse?" that's what the mother said to her fawns.

         •

The two fawns helped the baby   65
suck their mother's nipple and get some milk.
Now the little boy

         •

was nursed, the little boy was nursed by the deer
o——n until he was full.
Their mother lay down cuddling him the way deer sleep   70
with her two fawns
together
lying beside her
and they SLEPT WITH THEIR FUR AROUND HIM.
They would nurse him, and so they lived on, lived on.   75
As he grew
he was without clothing, NAKED.
His elder brother and sister had fur:
they had fur, but he was NAKED and this was not good.

         •

The deer   80
the little boy's mother
spoke to her two fawns: "Tonight
when you sleep, you two will lie on both sides
and he will lie in the middle.
While you're sleeping   85
I'll go to Kachina Village,[7] for he is without clothing, naked, and
this is not good."

         •

That's what she said to her children, and
there
at the village of He'shokta   90

         •

were young men
who went out hunting, and the young men who went out hunting
         looked for deer.

---

7. This lies beneath the surface of the lake and comes to life only at night; it is the home of all the kachinas, the ancestral gods of the Zunis. Kachinas are impersonated by the Zunis in masked dances [Translator's note].

When they went hunting they made their kills around the
    Prairie-Dog Hills.
And their mother went to Kachina Village, she went o———n until
    she reached Kachina Village.
It was filled with dancing kachinas.   95

              •

"My fathers, my children, how have you been passing the days?"
    "Happily, our child, so you've come, sit down," they said.
"Wait, stop your dancing, our child has come and must have
    something to say," then the kachinas stopped.
The deer sat down the old lady deer sat down.
A kachina priest spoke to her:
"Now speak.   100
You must've come because you have something to say."
    "YES, in TRUTH
I have come because I have something to SAY.
There in the village of He'shokta is a priest's daughter
who abandoned her child.
We found him   105
we have been raising him.
But he is poor, without clothing, naked, and this
is not good.
So I've come to ask for clothes for him," that's what she said.
"Indeed." "Yes, that's why I've come, to ask for clothes for him."   110
"Well, there is always a way," they said.
Kyaklo
laid out his shirt.
Long Horn put in his kilt and his moccasins.
              •

And Huututu[8] put in his buckskin leggings   115
he laid out his bandoleer.[9]
              •

And Pawtiwa[1] laid out his macaw headdress.
              •

Also they put in the BELLS he would wear on his legs.
              •

Also they laid out
              •

strands of turquoise beads   120
moccasins.
So they laid it all out, hanks of yarn for his wrists and ankles
they gathered all his clothing.
When they had gathered it his mother put it on her back: "Well, I must GO
but when he has grown larger I will return to ask for clothing again." 125
That's what she said. "Very well indeed."
Now the deer went her way.
When she got back to her children they were all sleeping.
When she got there they were sleeping and she
lay down beside them.   130
The little boy, waking up
began to nurse, his deer mother nursed him
and he went back to sleep. So they spent the night and then

---

8. Kyaklo, Long Horn, and Huututu are kachina priests.   9. Belt worn over the shoulder to support
carried articles.   1. The chief priest.

(*with pleasure*) the little boy was clothed by his mother.
His mother clothed him.   135

                    •

When he was clothed he was no longer cold.
He went around playing with his elder brother and sister, they would
        run after each other, playing.
They lived on this way until he was grown.
And THEN
they went back up to their old home on the Prairie-Dog Hills.
        Having gone up   140
they remained there and would come down only to drink, in
        the evening.
There they lived o——n for a long time

                    •

until
from the village
his uncle   145
went out hunting. Going out hunting
he came along
down around
Worm Spring, and from there he went on towards

                    •

the Prairie-Dog Hills and came up near the edge of a valley there.   150
When he came to the woods on the Prairie-Dog Hills he looked down and
THERE IN THE VALLEY was the herd of deer. In the herd of deer
there was a little boy going around among them
dressed in white.
He had bells on his legs and he wore a macaw headdress.   155
He wore a macaw headdress, he was handsome, surely it was a boy
a male
a person among them.
While he was looking the deer mothers spotted him.
When they spotted the young man[2] they ran off.   160
There the little boy outdistanced the others.

                    •

"Haa——, who could that be?"
That's what his uncle said. "Who
could you be? Perhaps you are a daylight person."[3]
That's what his UNCLE thought and he didn't do ANYTHING
        to the deer.   165
He returned to his house in the evening.

                    •

It was evening
dinner was ready and when they sat down to eat
the young man spoke:
"Today, while I was out hunting   170
when I reached the top
of the Prairie-Dog Hills, where the woods are, when I reached the top,
        THERE in the VALLEY was a HERD OF DEER.
There was a herd of deer

                    •

2. That is, the little boy's uncle.   3. Living human beings are "daylight people"; all other beings, including animals, some plants, various natural phenomena, and deceased humans (kachinas), are called
"raw people," because they do not depend on cooked food [Translator's note].

and with them was a LITTLE BOY:
whose child could it be?   175
When the deer spotted me they ran off and he outdistanced them.
He wore bells on his legs, he wore a macaw headdress, he was dressed in white."
That's what the young man was saying
telling his father.
It was one of the boy's OWN ELDERS   180
his OWN UNCLE had found him. (*audience*) Ee——so.
His uncle had found him.

                              •

Then
he said, "If
the herd is to be chased, then tell your Bow Priest."[4]   185
That's what the young man said. "Whose child could this be?
PERHAPS WE'LL CATCH HIM."
That's what he was saying.
A girl
a daughter of the priest said "Well, I'll go ask the Bow Priest."   190
She got up and went to the Bow Priest's house.
Arriving at the Bow Priest's house
she entered:
"My fathers, my mothers, how have you been passing the days?"
       "Happily, our child
so you've come, sit down," they said. "Yes.   195
Well, I'm
asking you to come.
Father asked that you come, that's what my father said," that's what
       she told the Bow Priest.
"Very well, I'll come," he said.
The girl went out and went home and after a while the Bow Priest
       came over.   200
He came to their house
while they were still eating.

                              •

"My children, how are you
this evening?" "Happy
sit down and eat," he was told.   205
He sat down and ate with them.
When they were finished eating, "Thank you," he said. "Eat plenty,"
       he was told.
He moved to another seat

                              •

and after a while
the Bow Priest questioned them:
"NOW, for what reason have you   210
summoned ME?
Perhaps it is because of a WORD of some importance that you have
summoned me. You must make this known to me
so that I may think about it as I pass the days," that's what he said.   215
"YES, in truth
today, this very day

---

4. In charge of hunting, warfare, and public announcements; he shouts from the top of the highest house
[Translator's note].

my child here
went out to hunt.
Up on the Prairie-Dog Hills, there   220
HE SAW A HERD OF DEER.
But a LITTLE BOY WAS AMONG THEM.
Perhaps he is a daylight person.
Who could it be?
He was dressed in white and he wore a macaw headdress.   225
When the deer ran off he OUTDISTANCED them:
he must be very fast.
That's why my child here said, 'Perhaps
they should be CHASED, the deer should be chased.'
He wants to see him caught, that's what he's thinking.   230
Because he said this
I summoned you," he said. "Indeed."
"Indeed, well

                                        •

perhaps he's a daylight person, what else can he be?
It is said he was dressed in white, what else can he be?"   235
That's what they were saying.
"WHEN would you want to do this?" that's what he said.
The young man who had gone out hunting said, "Well, in four days
so we can prepare our weapons."
That's what he said.   240
"So you should tell your people that in FOUR DAYS there will be
      a deer chase."
That's what
he said. "Very well."

                                        •

(*sharply*) Because of the little boy the word was given out for
      the deer chase.
The Bow Priest went out and shouted it.   245
When he shouted the VILLAGERS
heard him.
(*slowly*) "In four days there will be a deer chase.
A little boy is among the deer, who could it be? With luck
you might CATCH him.   250
We don't know who it will be.
You will find a child, then," that's what he SAID as he shouted.

                                        •

Then they went to sleep and lived on with anticipation.
Now when it was the THIRD night, the eve of the chase

                                        •

the deer   255
spoke to her son
when the deer had gathered:
"My son." "What is it?" he said.
"Tomorrow we'll be chased, the one who found us is your uncle.
When he found us he saw you, and that's why   260

                                        •

we'll be chased.
They'll come out after you:
your uncles.

•

(*excited*) The uncle who saw you will ride a spotted horse, and
     HE'LL BE THE ONE who
WON'T LET YOU GO, and   265
your elder brothers, your mothers
no
he won't think of killing them, it'll be you alone
he'll think of, he'll chase.
You won't be the one to get tired, but we'll get tired.   270
It'll be you alone
WHEN THEY HAVE KILLED US ALL
and you will go on alone.
Your first uncle
will ride a spotted horse and a second uncle will ride a white horse.   275
THESE TWO WILL FOLLOW YOU.
You must pretend you are tired but keep on going
and they will catch you.
But WE
MYSELF, your elder SISTER, your elder BROTHER   280
ALL OF US

•

will go with you.
Wherever they take you we will go along with you."
That's what his deer mother told him that's what she said.
THEN HIS DEER MOTHER TOLD HIM EVERYTHING:
     "AND NOW   285
I will tell you everything.
From here

•

from this place
where we're living now, we went down to drink. When we went
     down to drink
it was one of your ELDERS, one of your OWN ELDERS   290
your mother who sits in a room on the fourth story down making
     basket-plaques:
IT WAS SHE
whom the Sun had made pregnant.
When her time was near
she went down to Water's End to the bank   295
to wash clothes
and when you were about to come out
she had pains, got out of the water
went to a TREE and there she just DROPPED you.
THAT is your MOTHER.   300
She's in a room on the fourth story down making basket-plaques,
     that's what you'll tell them.

•

THAT'S WHAT SHE DID TO YOU, SHE JUST DROPPED YOU.
When we went down to drink
we found you, and because you have grown up
on my milk   305
and because of the thoughts of your Sun Father, you have grown fast.
Well, you

have looked at us
at your elder sister and your elder brother
and they have fur. 'Why don't I have fur like them?' you have asked.   310
But that is proper, for you are a daylight person.
That's why I went to Kachina Village to get clothes for you
the ones you were wearing.
You began wearing those when you were small
before you were GROWN.   315
Yesterday I went to get the clothes you're wearing now
the ones you will wear when they chase us. When you've been caught
you must tell these things to your elders.
                              •

When they bring you in
when they've caught you and bring you in   320
you
you will go inside. When you go inside
your grandfather
a priest
will be sitting by the fire. 'My grandfather, how have you been passing
     the days?'   325
'Happily. As old as I am, I could be a grandfather to anyone, for we
     have many children,' he will say.
'Yes, but truly you are my real grandfather,' you will say.
When you come to where your grandmother is sitting, 'Grandmother
     of mine, how have you been passing the days?' you will say.
'Happily, our child, surely I could be a grandmother to anyone,
     for we have the whole village as our children,' she will say.
Then, with the uncles who brought you in and   330
with your three aunts, you will shake hands.
'WHERE IS MY MOTHER?' you will say.
'Who is your mother?' they will say. 'She's in a room on the
     fourth story down making basket-plaques, tell her to come in,'
     you will say.
                              •

Your youngest aunt will go in to get her.
When she enters: 335
(sharply) 'There's a little boy who wants you, he says you are
     his mother.'
(tight) 'How could that be? I don't know any man, how could I
     have an offspring?'
'Yes, but he wants you,' she will say
and she will force her to come out.
THEN THE ONE WE TOLD YOU ABOUT WILL COME OUT: 340
you will shake hands with her, call her mother. 'Surely we could be
     mothers to anyone, for we have the whole village as our
     CHILDREN,' she will say to you.
'YES, BUT TRULY YOU ARE MY REAL MOTHER.
There, in a room on the fourth story down
you sit and work.
My Sun Father, where you sit in the light   345
my Sun Father
made you pregnant.
When you were about to deliver

it was to Water's End
that you went down to wash. You washed at the bank   350
and when I was about to come out
when it hurt you
you went to a tree and just dropped me there.
You gathered your clothes, put them on your back, and returned
to your house.   355
But my MOTHERS
HERE
found me. When they found me
because it was on their milk
that I grew, and because of the thoughts of my Sun Father   360
I grew fast.
I had no clothing
so my mother went to Kachina Village to ask for clothing.'
THAT'S WHAT YOU MUST SAY.''

                              •

That's what he was told, that's what his mother told him. "And   365
tonight
(*aside*) we'll go up on the Ruin Hills."
That's what the deer mother told her son. "We'll go to the Ruin Hills
we won't live here anymore.
(*sharply*) We'll go over there where the land is rough   370
for TOMORROW they will CHASE us.
Your uncles won't think of US, surely they will think of YOU
ALONE. They have GOOD HORSES," that's what
his mother told him. It was on the night before
that the boy   375
was told by his deer mother.
The boy became
so unhappy.
They slept through the night
and before dawn the deer   380
went to the Ruin Hills.

                              •

They went there and remained, and the VILLAGERS AWOKE.
It was the day of the chase, as had been announced, and the people
     were coming out.
They were coming out, some carrying bows, some on foot and
some on horseback, they kept on this way   385
o——n they went on
past Stone Chief, along the trees, until they got to the Prairie-Dog
     Hills and there were no deer.
Their tracks led straight and they followed them.
Having found the trail they went on until
when they reached the Ruin Hills, there in the valley   390
beyond the thickets there
was the herd, and the
young man and two of his elder sisters were chasing each other
by the edge of the valley, playing together. Playing together
they were spotted.   395
The deer saw the people.
They fled.

Many were the people who came out after them
now they chased the deer.
Now and again they dropped them, killed them.   400
Sure enough the boy outdistanced the others, while his mother
    and his elder sister and brother
still followed their child. As they followed him
he was far in the lead, but they followed on, they were on the run
and sure enough his uncles weren't thinking about killing deer, it
    was the boy they were after.
And ALL THE PEOPLE WHO HAD COME   405
    KILLED THE DEER
                killed the deer
                    killed the deer.
Wherever they made their kills they gutted them, put them on
    their backs, and went home.
Two of the uncles

                •

then
went ahead of the group, and a third uncle   410
(*voice breaking*) dropped his elder sister
his elder brother
his mother.
He gutted them there while the other two uncles went on. As they went ON
the boy pretended to be tired. The first uncle pleaded:
"Tísshomahhá![5]   415
STOP," he said, "Let's stop this contest now."
That's what he was saying as
the little boy kept on running.
As he kept on his bells went telele.
O———n, he went on this way   420
on until

                •

the little boy stopped and his uncle, dismounting
caught him.

                •

Having caught him
(*gently*) "Now come with me, get up," he said.   425
His uncle
helped his nephew get up, then his uncle got on the horse.
They went back. They went on
until they came to where his mother and his elder sister and brother were lying
and the third uncle was there. The third uncle was there.   430
"So you've come." "Yes."
The little boy spoke: "This is my mother, this is my
elder sister, this is my elder brother.
They will accompany me to my house.
They will accompany me," that's what the boy said.   435
"Very well."
His uncles put the deer on their horses' backs.
On they went, while the people were coming in coming in, and
    still the uncles didn't arrive, until at nightfall

---

5. A common interjection; roughly, "oh no!"

the little boy was brought in, sitting up on the horse.
It was night and the people, a crowd of people, came out to see the boy as
    he was brought in on the horse through the plaza   440
and his mother and his elder sister and brother
came along also
as he was brought in.
His grandfather came out. When he came out the little boy and his
    uncle dismounted.
His grandfather took the lead with the little boy following, and they
    went up.   445
When they reached the roof his grandfather
made a corn-meal road[6]
and they entered.
His grandfather entered
with the little boy following   450
while his
uncles brought in the deer. When everyone was inside
•

the little boy's grandfather spoke: "Sit down," and the little boy spoke to his
    grandfather as he came to where he was sitting:
"Grandfather of mine, how have you been passing the days?" that's
    what he said.
"Happily our child   455
surely I could be a grandfather to anyone,[7] for we have the whole village
    as our children." "Yes, but you are my real grandfather," he said.
When he came to where his grandmother was sitting he said the
    same thing.
"Yes, but surely I could be a grandmother to anyone, for we have many
    children." "Yes, but you are my real grandmother," he said.
He looked the way
his uncle had described him, he wore a macaw headdress and
    his clothes were white.   460
He had new moccasins, new buckskin leggings.
He wore a bandoleer and a macaw headdress.
He was a stranger.
He shook hands with his uncles and shook hands with his aunts.
"WHERE IS MY MOTHER?" he said.   465
•

"She's in a room on the fourth story down weaving basket-plaques,"
    he said.
"Tell her to come out."
Their younger sister went in.
"Hurry and come now:
some little boy has come and says you are his mother."   470
(*tight*) "How could that be?
I've never known any man, how could I have an offspring?" she said.
"Yes, but come on, he wants you, he wants you to come out."
Finally she was forced to come out.

---

6. In the "long ago," houses were entered through a trap-door in the roof; the boy and his grandfather go up an outside ladder to reach the roof and then down a second ladder into the house. Just before they enter the grandfather makes a "cornmeal road" by sprinkling a handful of cornmeal in front of them, thus treating the boy as an important ritual personage [Translator's note].   7. A priest is everyone's "grandfather."

The moment she entered the little boy   475
went up to his mother.
"Mother of mine, how have you been passing the days?"
"Happily, but surely I could be anyone's
mother, for we have many children," that's what his mother said.
That's what she said.   480

•

"YES INDEED
but you are certainly my REAL MOTHER.
YOU GAVE BIRTH TO ME," he said.

•

Then, just as his deer mother had told him to do
he told his mother everything: 485

•

"You really are my mother.
In a room on the fourth story down
you sit and work.
As you sit and work
the light comes through your window.   490
My Sun Father
made you pregnant.
When he made you pregnant you
sat in there and your belly began to grow large.   495
Your belly grew large
you
you were about to deliver, you had pains in your belly, you were
    about to give birth to me, you had pains in your belly
you gathered your clothes
and you went down to the bank to wash.
When you got there you   500
washed your clothes in the river.
When I was about to COME OUT and caused you pain
you got out of the water
you went to a juniper tree.
There I made you strain your muscles   505
and there you just dropped me.
When you dropped me
you made a little hole and placed me there.
You gathered your clothes
bundled them together   510
washed all the blood off carefully, and came back here.
When you had gone
my elders here
came down to DRINK
and found me.   515
They found me

•

I criedand they heard me.
Because of the milk
of my deer mother here   520
my elder sister and brother here

because of
their milk
I grew.
I had no clothing, I was poor.   525
My mother here went to Kachina Village to ask for my clothing.
                                      •

That's where
she got my clothing.
That's why I'm clothed. Truly, that's why I was among them
that's why one of you   530
who went out hunting discovered me.
You talked about it and that's why these things happened today."
        (*audience*) Ee———so.
That's what the little boy said.
                                      •

"THAT'S WHAT YOU DID AND YOU ARE MY REAL MOTHER,"
        that's what he told his mother. At that moment his mother
embraced him embraced him.   535
His uncle got angry his uncle got angry.
He beat
his kinswoman
he beat his kinswoman.
That's how it happened.   540
The boy's deer elders were on the floor.
His grandfather then
spread some covers
on the floor, laid them there, and put strands of turquoise beads on them.[8]
After a while they skinned them.   545
With this done and dinner ready they ate with their son.
                                      •

They slept through the night, and the next day
the little boy spoke: "Grandfather." "What is it?"
"Where is your quiver?" he said. "Well, it must be hanging in the other
        room," he said.
                                      •

He went out, having been given the quiver, and wandered around.   550
He wandered around, he wasn't thinking of killing deer, he just
        wandered around.
In the evening he came home empty-handed.
They lived on
                                      •

and slept through the night.
After the second night he was wandering around again.   555
The third one came
and on the fourth night, just after sunset, his mother
spoke to him: "I need
the center blades of the yucca plant," she said.
"Which kind of yucca?"   560

8. Joseph Peynetsa [Andrew Peynetsa's nephew, who helped with the translation] commented: "When the deer die, they go to Kachina Village. And from there they go to their re-make, transform into another being, maybe a deer. That's in the prayers the Zunis say for deer, and that's why you have to give them cornmeal and put necklaces on them, so that they'll come back to your house once again" [Translator's note].

"Well, the large yucca, the center blades," that's what his mother said.
"Indeed.
Tomorrow I'll try to find it for you," he said.
(*aside*) She was finishing her basket-plaque and this was for the outer part.
    (*audience*) Ee——so.
That's what she said.
The next morning, when he had eaten   565
he put the quiver on and went out.
He went up on Big Mountain and looked around until he found
    a large yucca
with very long blades.
            •

"Well, this must be the kind you talked about," he said. It was the center
    blades she wanted.
He put down his bow and his quiver, got hold of the center blades, and
    began to pull.
(*with strain*) He pulled   570
            •

it came loose suddenly
and he pulled it straight into his heart.
There he died.
            •

He died and they waited for him but he didn't come.   575
            •

When the Sun went down
and he still hadn't come, his uncles began to worry.
They looked for him.
They found his tracks, made torches, and followed him
until they found him with the center blades of the yucca in his heart. 580
            •

Their
nephew
was found and they brought him home.
The next day
            •

he was buried.   585
Now he entered upon the roads
of his elders.[9]
THIS WAS LIVED LONG AGO. LEE——SEMKONIKYA.[1]

9. The deer.   1. A standard closing, for which Tedlock has proposed the translation: "The word is just
so——short."

SAMUEL BECKETT
1906–1989

The sparest, starkest representation of the human condition in all its "absurd"
emptiness fills Samuel Beckett's novels and plays. Not that other authors do not
concern themselves with the problem of representing reality, but where Pirandello
plays with allusions to an elusive identity, Joyce with the stream of consciousness,

and Proust with layers of the self reconstituted through affective memory, Beckett's world is haunted—like that of Kafka—by an absence of meaning at the core. Whether expressed by the protagonist's ramblings in the novels *Molloy* (1951), *Malone Dies* (1951), or *The Unnamable* (1953), by the stripped-down dialogue of the plays *Waiting for Godot* (1952) and *Endgame* (1957), or by the telegraphic style of a late novel, *How It Is* (1961), Beckett's characters engage in a desperate attempt to find or to create meaning for themselves. Born into a world without reason, they live out their lives waiting for an explanation that never comes and whose existence may be only a figment of their imagination. In the meantime, human relationships are reduced to the most elemental tensions of cruelty, hope, frustration, and disillusionment around themes of birth, death, human emotions, material obstacles, and unending consciousness. Beckett's comedy of errors is a bitter one and, even in its puns and parodies, draws heavily on what the author has described as "the power of the text to claw."

Like Joyce and Yeats, Beckett was born in Ireland; like Joyce, he chose to live abroad for most of his life. Born near Dublin on April 13, 1906, he was educated in Ireland and received a B.A. from Trinity College in 1927. From 1928 to 1930, he taught English at the École Normale Supérieure in Paris, where he met James Joyce and was for a while influenced by the older novelist's exuberant and punning use of language. Beckett wrote an essay on the early stages of Joyce's *Finnegans Wake* and later helped in the French translation of part of the book. In 1930 he entered a competition for a poem on the subject of time and won first prize with a ninety-eight-line (and seventeen-footnote) monologue, *Whoroscope,* spoken by the seventeenth-century French physicist and philosopher René Descartes. Beckett returned to Trinity College where he took an M.A. in 1931, published an essay on Proust, and stayed on the following year to teach French. It was a brief academic career, for he gave up teaching in 1932 and, after living in London, France, and Germany, made Paris his permanent home in 1937. Although two early novels, *Murphy* (1938) and *Watt* (1953), were written in English, Beckett was already turning to French as his preferred language for original composition; in the years after World War II, he wrote almost exclusively in French and only later translated (often with substantial changes) the same texts into English. He said that he wrote in French because it was easier to write "without style"—without the native speaker's temptation to elegance and virtuoso display. Although no generalization holds true for all cases, comparing the French and English versions of the same work often suggests just such a contrast, with the French text closer to basic grammatical forms and, therefore, possessing a harsher, less nuanced focus.

Whether comic or despairing (often both), Beckett's characters ring changes on the Cartesian image of the Rational Man that has been at the base of Western cultural attitudes ever since the philosopher René Descartes moved from specific questions about the physical sciences to the larger question of human existence. Descartes, like Beckett, went back to zero in order not to be led astray by any preconceived assumptions or doctrines. He doubted everything—except that he doubted, which in itself indicated that he was thinking and that if "I think, therefore I am" (*Cogito, ergo sum*). Upon that certainty Descartes erected a logical system for exploring the natural universe and explaining the human condition. Beckett is not so sure that logic allows us to know what we are looking at, or in fact to match up our terminology with reality at all. In *Watt,* the protagonist is caught in a peculiar hesitation inasmuch as things, "if they consented to be named, did so as it were with reluctance." He looks at a pot, but "it was not a pot, the more he looked, the more he reflected, the more he felt sure of that, that it was not a pot at all. It resembled a pot, it was almost a pot, but it was not a pot of which one could say, Pot, pot and be comforted." The gentle bewilderment that Watt feels turns bitter and more dangerous in later novels such as the famous trilogy (*Molloy, Malone Dies,* and *The Unnamable*), or in *How It Is,* which refuses to present any image of rational control as it murmurs, free of punctuation, the monologue of an unstructured consciousness inside an accompanying "quaqua [bzzz bzzz] on all sides."

The narrative perspective in the trilogy moves from a series of related monologue stories in which narrators come more and more to resemble one another, to the ramblings of an "unnamable" speaker who seems to represent them all at the end. In *Molloy,* there are two interlocking points of view as first Molloy tells of setting out on a bicycle to visit his bedridden mother, a search that takes him months and leads him all over (with many echoes of Homer's *Odyssey*). The last we hear of Molloy is that he is crippled and has lost his bicycle, but is determined still to proceed if only by rolling; Moran takes over at that point, and describes a corresponding search for Molloy in the course of which he loses his bicycle, is crippled, and ends up frustrated back home. The next novel, *Malone Dies,* is similarly divided between protagonists, even if in the mind of a single narrator: a dying and bedridden Malone writes the diary of his last days, and also composes the story of Macmann, who is to die at the same moment as Malone and apparently does so as the novel ends. The last in the trilogy, *The Unnamable,* has no fixed authorial perspective or claim to responsibility. "I'm in words, made of words." Someone (unnamed and—by now—clearly unnamable) is seated in an undefined gray space and time, writing a series of stories that may be the tales of Malone, Malloy, and Moran, or of a new Mahood who also becomes Worm, who may in turn be the narrator writing stories about himself; or it may simply evoke the act of storytelling as it creates fictions of life to establish some mode of reality. In 1949, when the trilogy was just complete, Beckett published a dialogue on modern art that described the artist's disgust with traditional art's "puny exploits . . . doing a little better the same old thing," and his preference for "the expression that there is nothing to express, nothing with which to express, nothing from which to express, no power to express, no desire to express, together with the obligation to express." The disintegration of narrative perspective in Beckett's fiction is one means of denying that there is a knowable "something to express," or an authoritative point of view from which to express "nothing."

How can one possibly make a convincing stage play out of "nothing"? The popularity of Beckett's first performed play, *Waiting for Godot* (French version presented 1953; English, 1955), showed that absurdist theater—with its empty, repetitive dialogue, its grotesquely bare yet apparently symbolic settings, and its refusal to build to a dramatic climax—had meaning even for audiences used to theatrical realism and logically developing plots. These audiences found two clownlike tramps, Vladimir and Estragon (Didi and Gogo), talking, quarreling, falling down, contemplating suicide, and generally filling up time with conversation that ranges from vaudeville patter to metaphysical speculation as they wait under a tree for a Godot who never comes. Instead, the two are joined in the middle of each act by another grotesque pair: the rich Pozzo and his brutally abused servant Lucky, whom he leads around by a rope tied to his neck. The popular interpretation of "Godot" as a diminutive for "God," and of the play as a statement of existential anguish at the inexplicable human condition, is scarcely defused by Beckett's caution that "If by Godot I had meant God, I would have said God." Yet identifying Godot is less important than identifying the ignominious plight on stage as symbolically our own, and identifying *with* the characters as they express the anxious, often repugnant but also comic picture of human relationships in an absurd universe.

After the popular success of *Waiting for Godot,* Beckett wrote *Endgame* (French version performed 1957; English, 1958) and a series of stage plays and brief pieces for the radio. The stage plays have the same bare yet striking settings: *Krapp's Last*

Tape (1958) presents an old man sitting at a table with his tape recorder, recalling a love affair thirty years past; and *Happy Days* (1961) portrays a married couple in which Winnie, the wife, chatters ceaselessly about her possessions although she is buried up to her waist in the first act and to her neck in the second. When Beckett received the Nobel Prize for literature in 1969, he was recognized as the purest exponent of the twentieth century's chief philosophical dilemma: the notion of the "absurd," or the grotesque contradiction between human attempts to discover meaning in life and the simultaneous conviction that there is no "meaning" available that we have not created ourselves. *Endgame*, often called Beckett's major achievement, is a prime example of this dilemma.

When the curtain rises on *Endgame*, it is as though the world were awaking from sleep. The sheets draping the furniture and central character are taken off, and Hamm sets himself in motion like an actor or chess pawn: "Me . . . to play." Yet we are also near the end for, as the title implies, nothing new will happen; an "endgame" is the final phase of a chess game, the stage at which the end is predictably in sight although the play must still be completed. Throughout, the theme of "end," "finish," "no more" is sounded, even while Hamm notes the passage of time: "Something is taking its course." But time does not lead anywhere; it is either past or present, and always barren. The past exists as Nagg's and Nell's memories, as Hamm's story, which may or may not describe Clov's entry into the home, and as a period in which Clov once loved Hamm. The present shows four characters dwindling away, alone in a dead world, caught between visions of dusty hell and dreams of life reborn. In one of the biblical echoes that permeate the play, Hamm and Clov repeatedly evoke the last words of the crucified Jesus in the Gospel according to St. John: "It is finished." But this is not a biblical morality play, and *Endgame* describes a world not of divine but of self-creation. Hamm may be composing and directing the entire performance: a storyteller and playwright with "asides" and "last soliloquy" whose "dialogue" keeps Clov on stage against his will, a mad artist who (when looking out the window onto a flourishing world) can see only dust and ashes, or a magician presiding over an imaginary kingdom who concludes an inner story and unavailing prayer with Prospero's line from Shakespeare's *The Tempest* (4.1.148): "Our revels now are ended." Or he may simply be aware of their lives *as* a performance without any other meaning: Shakespeare's passage continues later: "We are such stuff / As dreams are made on, and our little life / Is rounded with a sleep." The situation at the end of the play is little changed—only barer, as Hamm discards his stick, whistle, and dog, "reckoning closed and story ended." Yet Clov is still waiting to leave as Hamm covers his face, and it is not impossible that the play will resume in precisely the same terms tomorrow.

Endgame, like *Waiting for Godot* (and like Kafka's stories), has been given a number of symbolic interpretations. Some refer to Beckett's love of wordplay: Hamm as Hamm-actor, Hammlet, Hammer, and Nag and Nell as shortened forms of *Nägel* and *nello*, German and Italian words for "nail," which are invoked as crucifixion themes suggesting the martyrdom of humanity. The setting of a boxlike room with two windows is seen as a skull, the seat of consciousness, or (emphasizing the bloody handkerchief and the reference to fontanelles—the soft spot in the skull of a newborn child) as a womb. The characters' isolation in a dead world after an unnamed catastrophe (which may be Hamm's fault) suggests the world after atomic holocaust; or, for those who recall Beckett's fascination with the apathetic figure of Belacqua waiting, in the Purgatory of Dante's *Divine Comedy*, for his punishment to begin, it evokes an image of pre-Purgatorial consciousness. The ashcans in which Hamm has "bottled" his parents, and the general cruelty between characters, are to represent the dustbin of modern Western civilized values. Hamm and Clov represent the uneasy adjustment of soul and body, the class struggle of rich and poor, or the master-slave relationship in all senses (including the slave's acceptance of his victimization). Clearly Beckett has created a structure that accommodates all these readings while authorizing none. He himself said to director Alan Schneider that he was less interested in symbolism than in describing a "local situation," an interaction of four characters in a given set of circumstances, and that the audience's interpretation was its own responsibility.

Beckett both authorized and denied these interpretations. He pruned down an earlier, more anecdotal two-act play to achieve *Endgame*'s skeletal plot and almost anonymous characters, and in doing so created a structure that immediately elicits the reader's instinct to "fill in the blanks." His puns and allusions openly point to a further meaning that *may* be contained in the implied reference, but may also be part of an infinite regress of meaning—expressing the "absurd" itself. Working against too heavy an insistence on symbolic meanings is the fact that the play is also funny—especially when performed on stage. The characters popping out of ashcans, the jerky, repetitive motions with which Clov carries out his master's commands, and the often obscene vaudeville patter accompanied by appropriate gestures, all provide a comic perspective that keeps *Endgame* from sinking into tragic despair. The intellectual distance offered by comedy is entirely in keeping with the more somber side of the play, which rejects pathos and constantly drags its characters' escapist fancies down to the minimal facts of survival: food, shelter, sleep, painkiller. Thus it is possible to say that *Endgame* describes—but only among many other things—what it is like to be alive, declining toward death in a world without meaning.

Samuel Beckett, *Endgame: with a Revised Text* (1992), ed. S. E. Gontarski, is a revised text based on productions directed or supervised by Beckett; the attached theatrical notebooks often clarify situations and settings. Alexander Astro, *Understanding Samuel Beckett* (1990), discusses the complete work with interpretations emphasizing cultural and linguistic aspects. Andrew Kennedy, *Samuel Beckett* (1989), provides a compact, comprehensive overview of Beckett's work with separate chapters on the major plays and novels. Linda Ben-Zvi, *Samuel Beckett* (1986), offers a general overview and commentary, with summaries. Deirdre Bair, *Samuel Beckett: A Biography* (1978), provides an extensive view of Beckett. Hugh Kenner, *Samuel Beckett: A Critical Study* (1974), is an earlier but still valuable discussion of Beckett's work, and Steven Connor, ed., *Waiting for Godot and Endgame—Samuel Beckett* (1992), includes eleven essays, of which seven are wholly or partially on *Endgame*.

Endgame[1]

For Roger Blin

CHARACTERS

NAGG
NELL
HAMM
CLOV

Bare interior.
Gray light.
Left and right back, high up, two small windows, curtains drawn.
Front right, a door. Hanging near door, its face to wall, a picture.

---

1. Translated by the author.

Front left, touching each other, covered with an old sheet, two ashbins.
Center, in an armchair on castors, covered with an old sheet, HAMM.
Motionless by the door, his eyes fixed on HAMM, CLOV. *Very red face.*
Brief tableau.

[CLOV *goes and stands under window left. Stiff, staggering walk. He*
looks up at window left. He turns and looks at window right. He goes and
stands under window right. He looks up at window right. He turns and
looks at window left. He goes out, comes back immediately with a small
step-ladder, carries it over and sets it down under window left, gets up on
it, draws back curtain. He gets down, takes six steps (for example) towards
window right, goes back for ladder, carries it over and sets it down under
window right, gets up on it, draws back curtain. He gets down, takes three
steps towards window left, goes back for ladder, carries it over and sets it
down under window left, gets up on it, looks out of window. Brief laugh.
He gets down, takes one step towards window right, goes back for ladder,
carries it over and sets it down under window right, gets up on it, looks
out of window. Brief laugh. He gets down, goes with ladder towards ash-
bins, halts, turns, carries back ladder and sets it down under window right,
goes to ashbins, removes sheet covering them, folds it over his arm. He
raises one lid, stoops and looks into bin. Brief laugh. He closes lid. Same
with other bin. He goes to HAMM, *removes sheet covering him, folds it*
over his arm. In a dressing-gown, a stiff toque[2] *on his head, a large blood-*
stained handkerchief over his face, a whistle hanging from his neck, a rug
over his knees, thick socks on his feet, HAMM *seems to be asleep.* CLOV
looks him over. Brief laugh. He goes to door, halts, turns towards audito-
rium.]

CLOV: [*Fixed gaze, tonelessly.*] Finished, it's finished, nearly finished, it
    must be nearly finished. [*Pause.*] Grain upon grain, one by one, and
    one day, suddenly, there's a heap, a little heap, the impossible heap.
    [*Pause.*] I can't be punished any more. [*Pause.*] I'll go now to my
    kitchen, ten feet by ten feet by ten feet, and wait for him to whistle me.
    [*Pause.*] Nice dimensions, nice proportions, I'll lean on the table, and
    look at the wall, and wait for him to whistle me.
    [*He remains a moment motionless, then goes out. He comes back*
    immediately, goes to window right, takes up the ladder and carries it
    out. Pause. HAMM *stirs. He yawns under the handkerchief. He*
    removes the handkerchief from his face. Very red face. Black glasses.]
HAMM: Me—[*He yawns.*]—to play.[3] [*He holds the handkerchief spread*
    out before him.] Old Stancher![4] [*He takes off his glasses, wipes his eyes,*
    his face, the glasses, puts them on again, folds the handkerchief and
    puts it back neatly in the breast-pocket of his dressing-gown. He clears
    his throat, joins the tips of his fingers.] Can there be misery—[*He*
    yawns.]—loftier than mine? No doubt. Formerly. But now? [*Pause.*] My

---

2. A fitted cloth hat with little or no brim, sometimes indicating official status as with a judge's toque.
3. Hamm announces that it is his move at the beginning of *Endgame*; the comparison is with a game of
chess, of which the "endgame" is the final stage.   4. The handkerchief that stanches his blood.

father? [*Pause.*] My mother? [*Pause.*] My ... dog? [*Pause.*] Oh I am willing to believe they suffer as much as such creatures can suffer. But does that mean their sufferings equal mine? No doubt. [*Pause.*] No, all is a—[*He yawns.*] —bsolute, [*Proudly.*] the bigger a man is the fuller he is. [*Pause. Gloomily.*] And the emptier. [*He sniffs.*] Clov! [*Pause.*] No, alone. [*Pause.*] What dreams! Those forests! [*Pause.*] Enough, it's time it ended, in the shelter too. [*Pause.*] And yet I hesitate, I hesitate to ... to end. Yes, there it is, it's time it ended and yet I hesitate to— [*He yawns.*]—to end. [*Yawns.*] God, I'm tired, I'd be better off in bed. [*He whistles. Enter* CLOV *immediately. He halts beside the chair.*] You pollute the air! [*Pause.*] Get me ready, I'm going to bed.

CLOV: I've just got you up.

HAMM: And what of it?

CLOV: I can't be getting you up and putting you to bed every five minutes, I have things to do. [*Pause.*]

HAMM: Did you ever see my eyes?

CLOV: No.

HAMM: Did you never have the curiosity, while I was sleeping, to take off my glasses and look at my eyes?

CLOV: Pulling back the lids? [*Pause.*] No.

HAMM: One of these days I'll show them to you. [*Pause.*] It seems they've gone all white. [*Pause.*] What time is it?

CLOV: The same as usual.

HAMM: [*Gesture towards window right.*] Have you looked?

CLOV: Yes.

HAMM: Well?

CLOV: Zero.

HAMM: It'd need to rain.

CLOV: It won't rain. [*Pause.*]

HAMM: Apart from that, how do you feel?

CLOV: I don't complain.

HAMM: You feel normal?

CLOV: [*Irritably.*] I tell you I don't complain.

HAMM: I feel a little queer. [*Pause.*] Clov!

CLOV: Yes.

HAMM: Have you not had enough?

CLOV: Yes! [*Pause.*] Of what?

HAMM: Of this ... this ... thing.

CLOV: I always had. [*Pause.*] Not you?

HAMM: [*Gloomily.*] Then there's no reason for it to change.

CLOV: It may end. [*Pause.*] All life long the same questions, the same answers.

HAMM: Get me ready. [CLOV *does not move.*] Go and get the sheet. [CLOV *does not move.*] Clov!

CLOV: Yes.

HAMM: I'll give you nothing more to eat.

CLOV: Then we'll die.

HAMM: I'll give you just enough to keep you from dying. You'll be hungry all the time.

CLOV: Then we won't die. [*Pause.*] I'll go and get the sheet. [*He goes towards the door.*]

HAMM: No! [CLOV *halts.*] I'll give you one biscuit per day. [*Pause.*] One and a half. [*Pause.*] Why do you stay with me?

CLOV: Why do you keep me?

HAMM: There's no one else.

CLOV: There's nowhere else. [*Pause.*]

HAMM: You're leaving me all the same.

CLOV: I'm trying.

HAMM: You don't love me.

CLOV: No.

HAMM: You loved me once.

CLOV: Once!

HAMM: I've made you suffer too much. [*Pause.*] Haven't I?

CLOV: It's not that.

HAMM: [*Shocked.*] I haven't made you suffer too much?

CLOV: Yes!

HAMM: [*Relieved.*] Ah you gave me a fright! [*Pause. Coldly.*] Forgive me. [*Pause. Louder.*] I said, Forgive me.

CLOV: I heard you. [*Pause.*] Have you bled?

HAMM: Less. [*Pause.*] Is it not time for my pain-killer?

CLOV: No. [*Pause.*]

HAMM: How are your eyes?

CLOV: Bad.

HAMM: How are your legs?

CLOV: BAD.

HAMM: But you can move.

CLOV: Yes.

HAMM: [*Violently.*] Then move! [CLOV *goes to back wall, leans against it with his forehead and hands.*] Where are you?

CLOV: Here.

HAMM: Come back! [CLOV *returns to his place beside the chair.*] Where are you?

CLOV: Here.

HAMM: Why don't you kill me?

CLOV: I don't know the combination of the cupboard. [*Pause.*]

HAMM: Go and get two bicycle-wheels.

CLOV: There are no more bicycle-wheels.

HAMM: What have you done with your bicycle?

CLOV: I never had a bicycle.

HAMM: The thing is impossible.

CLOV: When there were still bicycles I wept to have one. I crawled at your feet. You told me to go to hell. Now there are none.

HAMM: And your rounds? When you inspected my paupers. Always on foot?

CLOV: Sometimes on horse. [*The lid of one of the bins lifts and the hands of* NAGG *appear, gripping the rim. Then his head emerges. Nightcap. Very white face.* NAGG *yawns, then listens.*] I'll leave you, I have things to do.

HAMM: In your kitchen?

CLOV: Yes.

HAMM: Outside of here it's death. [*Pause.*] All right, be off. [*Exit* CLOV. *Pause.*] We're getting on.

NAGG: Me Pap!⁵

HAMM: Accursed progenitor!

NAGG: Me pap!

HAMM: The old folks at home! No decency left! Guzzle, guzzle, that's all they think of. [*He whistles. Enter* CLOV. *He halts beside the chair.*] Well! I thought you were leaving me.

CLOV: Oh not just yet, not just yet.

NAGG: Me pap!

HAMM: Give him his pap.

CLOV: There's no more pap.

HAMM: [*To* NAGG.] Do you hear that? There's no more pap. You'll never get any more pap.

NAGG: I want me pap!

HAMM: Give him a biscuit. [*Exit* CLOV.] Accursed fornicator! How are your stumps?

NAGG: Never mind me stumps.

    [Enter CLOV *with biscuit.*]

CLOV: I'm back again, with the biscuit. [*He gives biscuit to* NAGG *who fingers it, sniffs it.*]

NAGG: [*Plaintively.*] What is it?

CLOV: Spratt's medium.⁶

NAGG: [*As before.*] It's hard! I can't!

HAMM: Bottle him!

    [CLOV *pushes* NAGG *back into the bin, closes the lid.*]

CLOV: [*Returning to his place beside the chair.*] If age but knew!

HAMM: Sit on him!

CLOV: I can't sit.

HAMM: True. And I can't stand.

CLOV: So it is.

HAMM: Every man his speciality. [*Pause.*] No phone calls? [*Pause.*] Don't we laugh?

CLOV: [*After reflection.*] I don't feel like it.

HAMM: [*After reflection.*] Nor I. [*Pause.*] Clov!

CLOV: Yes.

HAMM: Nature has forgotten us.

CLOV: There's no more nature.

HAMM: No more nature! You exaggerate.

CLOV: In the vicinity.

HAMM: But we breathe, we change! We lose our hair, our teeth! Our bloom! Our ideals!

CLOV: Then she hasn't forgotten us.

HAMM: But you say there is none.

---

5. Food, mush.   6. A common plain cookie.

CLOV: [*Sadly.*] No one that ever lived ever thought so crooked as we.

HAMM: We do what we can.

CLOV: We shouldn't. [*Pause.*]

HAMM: You're a bit of all right, aren't you?[7]

CLOV: A smithereen.[8] [*Pause.*]

HAMM: This is slow work. [*Pause.*] Is it not time for my pain-killer?

CLOV: No. [*Pause.*] I'll leave you, I have things to do.

HAMM: In your kitchen?

CLOV: Yes.

HAMM: What, I'd like to know.

CLOV: I look at the wall.

HAMM: The wall! And what do you see on your wall? Mene, mene?[9] Naked bodies?

CLOV: I see my light dying.

HAMM: Your light dying! Listen to that! Well, it can die just as well here, *your* light. Take a look at me and then come back and tell me what you think of *your* light. [*Pause.*]

CLOV: You shouldn't speak to me like that. [*Pause.*]

HAMM: [*Coldly.*] Forgive me. [*Pause. Louder.*] I said, Forgive me.

CLOV: I heard you.

[*The lid of* NAGG's *bin lifts. His hands appear, gripping the rim. Then his head emerges. In his mouth the biscuit. He listens.*]

HAMM: Did your seeds come up?

CLOV: No.

HAMM: Did you scratch round them to see if they had sprouted?

CLOV: They haven't sprouted.

HAMM: Perhaps it's still too early.

CLOV: If they were going to sprout they would have sprouted. [*Violently.*] They'll never sprout!

[*Pause.* NAGG *takes biscuit in his hand.*]

HAMM: This is not much fun. [*Pause.*] But that's always the way at the end of the day, isn't it, Clov?

CLOV: Always.

HAMM: It's the end of the day like any other day, isn't it, Clov?

CLOV: Looks like it. [*Pause.*]

HAMM: [*Anguished.*] What's happening, what's happening?

CLOV: Something is taking its course. [*Pause.*]

HAMM: All right, be off. [*He leans back in his chair, remains motionless.* CLOV *does not move, heaves a great groaning sigh.* HAMM *sits up.*] I thought I told you to be off.

CLOV: I'm trying. [*He goes to door, halts.*] Ever since I was whelped.

[*Exit* CLOV.]

HAMM: We're getting on.

[*He leans back in his chair, remains motionless.* NAGG *knocks on the*

---

7. You're pretty good, aren't you? (British slang).   8. A tiny bit.   9. From Daniel 5:25: "Mene, mene, tekel, upharsin"; words written by a divine hand on the wall during the feast of Belshazzar, king of Babylon. They predict doom and tell the king "Thou art weighed in the balances, and art found wanting" (Daniel 5:27).

lid of the other bin. Pause. He knocks harder. The lid lifts and the hands of NELL *appear, gripping the rim. Then her head emerges. Lace cap. Very white face.*]

NELL: What is it, my pet? [*Pause.*] Time for love?

NAGG: Were you asleep?

NELL: Oh no!

NAGG: Kiss me.

NELL: We can't.

NAGG: Try.

[*Their heads strain towards each other, fail to meet, fall apart again.*]

NELL: Why this farce, day after day? [*Pause.*]

NAGG: I've lost me tooth.

NELL: When?

NAGG: I had it yesterday.

NELL: [*Elegiac.*] Ah yesterday!

[*They turn painfully towards each other.*]

NAGG: Can you see me?

NELL: Hardly. And you?

NAGG: What?

NELL: Can you see me?

NAGG: Hardly.

NELL: So much the better, so much the better.

NAGG: Don't say that. [*Pause.*] Our sight has failed.

NELL: Yes.

[*Pause. They turn away from each other.*]

NAGG: Can you hear me?

NELL: Yes. And you?

NAGG: Yes. [*Pause.*] Our hearing hasn't failed.

NELL: Our what?

NAGG: Our hearing.

NELL: No. [*Pause.*] Have you anything else to say to me?

NAGG: Do you remember—

NELL: No.

NAGG: When we crashed on our tandem[1] and lost our shanks.

[*They laugh heartily.*]

NELL: It was in the Ardennes.

[*They laugh less heartily.*]

NAGG: On the road to Sedan.[2] [*They laugh still less heartily.*] Are you cold?

NELL: Yes, perished. And you?

NAGG: [*Pause.*] I'm freezing. [*Pause.*] Do you want to go in?

NELL: Yes.

NAGG: Then go in. [NELL *does not move.*] Why don't you go in?

NELL: I don't know. [*Pause.*]

NAGG: Has he changed your sawdust?

---

1. A bicycle built for two.   2. Town in northern France where the French were defeated in the Franco-Prussian War (1870). Ardennes is a forest in northern France, the scene of bitter fighting in both world wars.

NELL: It isn't sawdust. [*Pause. Wearily.*] Can you not be a little accurate, Nagg?

NAGG: Your sand then. It's not important.

NELL: It is important. [*Pause.*]

NAGG: It was sawdust once.

NELL: Once!

NAGG: And now it's sand. [*Pause.*] From the shore. [*Pause. Impatiently.*] Now it's sand he fetches from the shore.

NELL: Now it's sand.

NAGG: Has he changed yours?

NELL: No.

NAGG: Nor mine. [*Pause.*] I won't have it! [*Pause. Holding up the biscuit.*] Do you want a bit?

NELL: No. [*Pause.*] Of what?

NAGG: Biscuit. I've kept you half. [*He looks at the biscuit. Proudly.*] Three quarters. For you. Here. [*He proffers the biscuit.*] No? [*Pause.*] Do you not feel well?

HAMM: [*Wearily.*] Quiet, quiet, you're keeping me awake. [*Pause.*] Talk softer. [*Pause.*] If I could sleep I might make love. I'd go into the woods. My eyes would see . . . the sky, the earth. I'd run, run, they wouldn't catch me. [*Pause.*] Nature! [*Pause.*] There's something dripping in my head. [*Pause.*] A heart, a heart in my head. [*Pause.*]

NAGG: [*Soft.*] Do you hear him? A heart in his head! [*He chuckles cautiously.*]

NELL: One mustn't laugh at those things, Nagg. Why must you always laugh at them?

NAGG: Not so loud!

NELL: [*Without lowering her voice.*] Nothing is funnier than unhappiness, I grant you that. But—

NAGG: [*Shocked.*] Oh!

NELL: Yes, yes, it's the most comical thing in the world. And we laugh, we laugh, with a will, in the beginning. But it's always the same thing. Yes, it's like the funny story we have heard too often, we still find it funny, but we don't laugh any more. [*Pause.*] Have you anything else to say to me?

NAGG: No.

NELL: Are you quite sure? [*Pause.*] Then I'll leave you.

NAGG: Do you not want your biscuit? [*Pause.*] I'll keep it for you. [*Pause.*] I thought you were going to leave me.

NELL: I am going to leave you.

NAGG: Could you give me a scratch before you go?

NELL: No. [*Pause.*] Where?

NAGG: In the back.

NELL: No. [*Pause.*] Rub yourself against the rim.

NAGG: It's lower down. In the hollow.

NELL: What hollow?

NAGG: The hollow! [*Pause.*] Could you not? [*Pause.*] Yesterday you scratched me there.

NELL: [*Elegiac.*] Ah yesterday!

NAGG: Could you not? [*Pause.*] Would you like me to scratch you? [*Pause.*] Are you crying again?

NELL: I was trying. [*Pause.*]

HAMM: Perhaps it's a little vein. [*Pause.*]

NAGG: What was that he said?

NELL: Perhaps it's a little vein.

NAGG: What does that mean? [*Pause.*] That means nothing. [*Pause.*] Will I tell you the story of the tailor?

NELL: No. [*Pause.*] What for?

NAGG: To cheer you up.

NELL: It's not funny.

NAGG: It always made you laugh. [*Pause.*] The first time I thought you'd die.

NELL: It was on Lake Como.[3] [*Pause.*] One April afternoon. [*Pause.*] Can you believe it?

NAGG: What?

NELL: That we once went out rowing on Lake Como. [*Pause.*] One April afternoon.

NAGG: We had got engaged the day before.

NELL: Engaged!

NAGG: You were in such fits that we capsized. By rights we should have been drowned.

NELL: It was because I felt happy.

NAGG: [*Indignant.*] It was not, it was not, it was my story and nothing else. Happy! Don't you laugh at it still? Every time I tell it. Happy!

NELL: It was deep, deep. And you could see down to the bottom. So white. So clean.

NAGG: Let me tell it again. [*Raconteur's voice.*] An Englishman, needing a pair of striped trousers in a hurry for the New Year festivities, goes to his tailor who takes his measurements. [*Tailor's voice.*] "That's the lot, come back in four days, I'll have it ready." Good. Four days later. [*Tailor's voice.*] "So sorry, come back in a week, I've made a mess of the seat." Good, that's all right, a neat seat can be very ticklish. A week later. [*Tailor's voice.*] "Frightfully sorry, come back in ten days, I've made a hash of the crotch." Good, can't be helped, a snug crotch is always a teaser. Ten days later. [*Tailor's voice.*] "Dreadfully sorry, come back in a fortnight, I've made a balls of the fly." Good, at a pinch, a smart fly is a stiff proposition. [*Pause. Normal voice.*] I never told it worse. [*Pause. Gloomy.*] I tell this story worse and worse. [*Pause. Raconteur's voice.*] Well, to make it short, the bluebells are blowing and he ballockses[4] the buttonholes. [*Customer's voice.*] "God damn you to hell, Sir, no, it's indecent, there are limits! In six days, do you hear me, six days, God made the world. Yes Sir, no less Sir, the WORLD! And you are not bloody well capable of making me a pair of trousers in three months!" [*Tailor's voice, scandalized.*] "But my dear Sir, my dear Sir, look—[*Disdainful gesture, disgustedly.*]—at the world—[*Pause.*] and look—[*Loving gesture, proudly.*] —at my TROUSERS!"

3. A large lake and tourist resort in northern Italy, near the Swiss border.   4. "Bollixes," botches.

[*Pause. He looks at* NELL *who has remained impassive, her eyes unseeing, breaks into a high forced laugh, cuts it short, pokes his head towards* NELL, *launches his laugh again.*]

HAMM: Silence!

[NAGG *starts, cuts short his laugh.*]

NELL: You could see down to the bottom.

HAMM: [*Exasperated.*] Have you not finished? Will you never finish? [*With sudden fury.*] Will this never finish? [NAGG *disappears into his bin, closes the lid behind him.* NELL *does not move. Frenziedly.*] My kingdom for a nightman![5] [*He whistles. Enter* CLOV.] Clear away this muck! Chuck it in the sea!

[CLOV *goes to bins, halts.*]

NELL: So white.

HAMM: What? What's she blathering about?

[CLOV *stoops, takes* NELL'*s hand, feels her pulse.*]

NELL: [*To* CLOV.] Desert!

[CLOV *lets go her hand, pushes her back in the bin, closes the lid.*]

CLOV: [*Returning to his place beside the chair.*] She has no pulse.

HAMM: What was she drivelling about?

CLOV: She told me to go away, into the desert.

HAMM: Damn busybody! Is that all?

CLOV: No.

HAMM: What else?

CLOV: I didn't understand.

HAMM: Have you bottled her?

CLOV: Yes.

HAMM: Are they both bottled?

CLOV: Yes.

HAMM: Screw down the lids. [CLOV *goes towards door.*] Time enough. [CLOV *halts.*] My anger subsides, I'd like to pee.

CLOV: [*With alacrity.*] I'll go and get the catheter. [*He goes towards door.*]

HAMM: Time enough. [CLOV *halts.*] Give me my pain-killer.

CLOV: It's too soon. [*Pause.*] It's too soon on top of your tonic, it wouldn't act.

HAMM: In the morning they brace you up and in the evening they calm you down. Unless it's the other way round. [*Pause.*] That old doctor, he's dead naturally?

CLOV: He wasn't old.

HAMM: But he's dead?

CLOV: Naturally. [*Pause.*] You ask *me* that? [*Pause.*]

HAMM: Take me for a little turn. [CLOV *goes behind the chair and pushes it forward.*] Not too fast! [CLOV *pushes chair.*] Right round the world! [CLOV *pushes chair.*] Hug the walls, then back to the center again. [CLOV *pushes chair.*] I was right in the center, wasn't I?

CLOV: [*Pushing.*] Yes.

HAMM: We'd need a proper wheel-chair. With big wheels. Bicycle wheels! [*Pause.*] Are you hugging?

---

5. Parody of Shakespeare's *Richard III*, where the defeated king seeks a horse to escape from the battlefield: "A horse! a horse! My kingdom for a horse!" (5.4.7).

CLOV: [*Pushing.*] Yes.

HAMM: [*Groping for wall.*] It's a lie! Why do you lie to me?

CLOV: [*Bearing closer to wall.*] There! There!

HAMM: Stop! [CLOV *stops chair close to back wall.* HAMM *lays his hand against wall.*] Old wall! [*Pause.*] Beyond is the . . . other hell. [*Pause. Violently.*] Closer! Closer! Up against!

CLOV: Take away your hand. [HAMM *withdraws his hand.* CLOV *rams chair against wall.*] There!

[HAMM *leans towards wall, applies his ear to it.*]

HAMM: Do you hear? [*He strikes the wall with his knuckles.*] Do you hear? Hollow bricks! [*He strikes again.*] All that's hollow! [*Pause. He straightens up. Violently.*] That's enough. Back!

CLOV: We haven't done the round.

HAMM: Back to my place! [CLOV *pushes chair back to center.*] Is that my place?

CLOV: Yes, that's your place.

HAMM: Am I right in the center?

CLOV: I'll measure it.

HAMM: More or less! More or less!

CLOV: [*Moving chair slightly.*] There!

HAMM: I'm more or less in the center?

CLOV: I'd say so.

HAMM: You'd say so! Put me right in the center!

CLOV: I'll go and get the tape.

HAMM: Roughly! Roughly! [CLOV *moves chair slightly.*] Bang in the center!

CLOV: There! [*Pause.*]

HAMM: I feel a little too far to the left. [CLOV *moves chair slightly.*] Now I feel a little too far to the right. [CLOV *moves chair slightly.*] I feel a little too far forward. [CLOV *moves chair slightly.*] Now I feel a little too far back. [CLOV *moves chair slightly.*] Don't stay there, [*i.e., behind the chair*] you give me the shivers.

[CLOV *returns to his place beside the chair.*]

CLOV: If I could kill him I'd die happy. [*Pause.*]

HAMM: What's the weather like?

CLOV: As usual.

HAMM: Look at the earth.

CLOV: I've looked.

HAMM: With the glass?

CLOV: No need of the glass.

HAMM: Look at it with the glass.

CLOV: I'll go and get the glass.

[*Exit* CLOV.]

HAMM: No need of the glass!

[*Enter* CLOV *with telescope.*]

CLOV: I'm back again, with the glass. [*He goes to window right, looks up at it.*] I need the steps.

HAMM: Why? Have you shrunk? [*Exit* CLOV *with telescope.*] I don't like that, I don't like that.

[*Enter* CLOV *with ladder, but without telescope.*]

CLOV: I'm back again, with the steps. [*He sets down ladder under window right, gets up on it, realizes he has not the telescope, gets down.*] I need the glass. [*He goes towards door.*]

HAMM: [*Violently.*] But you have the glass!

CLOV: [*Halting, violently.*] No, I haven't the glass!
　　　　[*Exit* CLOV.]

HAMM: This is deadly.
　　　　[*Enter* CLOV *with telescope. He goes towards ladder.*]

CLOV: Things are livening up. [*He gets up on ladder, raises the telescope, lets it fall.*] I did it on purpose. [*He gets down, picks up the telescope, turns it on auditorium.*] I see . . . a multitude . . . in transports . . . of joy.[6] [*Pause.*] That's what I call a magnifier. [*He lowers the telescope, turns towards* HAMM.] Well? Don't we laugh?

HAMM: [*After reflection.*] I don't.

CLOV: [*After reflection.*] Nor I. [*He gets up on ladder, turns the telescope on the without.*] Let's see. [*He looks, moving the telescope.*] Zero . . . [*he looks*] . . . zero . . . [*he looks*] . . . and zero.

HAMM: Nothing stirs. All is —

CLOV: Zer —

HAMM: [*Violently.*] Wait till you're spoke to! [*Normal voice.*] All is . . . all is . . . all is what? [*Violently.*] All is what?

CLOV: What all is? In a word? Is that what you want to know? Just a moment. [*He turns the telescope on the without, looks, lowers the telescope, turns towards* HAMM.] Corpsed. [*Pause.*] Well? Content?

HAMM: Look at the sea.

CLOV: It's the same.

HAMM: Look at the ocean!
　　　　[CLOV *gets down, takes a few steps towards window left, goes back for ladder, carries it over and sets it down under window left, gets up on it, turns the telescope on the without, looks at length. He starts, lowers the telescope, examines it, turns it again on the without.*]

CLOV: Never seen anything like that!

HAMM: [*Anxious.*] What? A sail? A fin? Smoke?

CLOV: [*Looking.*] The light is sunk.

HAMM: [*Relieved.*] Pah! We all knew that.

CLOV: [*Looking.*] There was a bit left.

HAMM: The base.

CLOV: [*Looking.*] Yes.

HAMM: And now?

CLOV: [*Looking.*] All gone.

HAMM: No gulls?

CLOV: [*Looking.*] Gulls!

HAMM: And the horizon? Nothing on the horizon?

CLOV: [*Lowering the telescope, turning towards* HAMM, *exasperated.*] What in God's name could there be on the horizon? [*Pause.*]

HAMM: The waves, how are the waves?

---

6. Echo of Revelation 7:9–10: "After this I beheld, and, lo, a great multitude, which . . . cried with a loud voice, saying, . . . Salvation."

CLOV: The waves? [*He turns the telescope on the waves.*] Lead.

HAMM: And the sun?

CLOV: [*Looking.*] Zero.

HAMM: But it should be sinking. Look again.

CLOV: [*Looking.*] Damn the sun.

HAMM: Is it night already then?

CLOV: [*Looking.*] No.

HAMM: Then what is it?

CLOV: [*Looking.*] Gray. [*Lowering the telescope, turning towards* HAMM, *louder.*] Gray! [*Pause. Still louder.*] GRRAY! [*Pause. He gets down, approaches* HAMM *from behind, whispers in his ear.*]

HAMM: [*Starting.*] Gray! Did I hear you say gray?

CLOV: Light black. From pole to pole.

HAMM: You exaggerate. [*Pause.*] Don't stay there, you give me the shivers.
   [CLOV *returns to his place beside the chair.*]

CLOV: Why this farce, day after day?

HAMM: Routine. One never knows. [*Pause.*] Last night I saw inside my breast. There was a big sore.

CLOV: Pah! You saw your heart.

HAMM: No, it was living. [*Pause. Anguished.*] Clov!

CLOV: Yes.

HAMM: What's happening?

CLOV: Something is taking its course. [*Pause.*]

HAMM: Clov!

CLOV: [*Impatiently.*] What is it?

HAMM: We're not beginning to . . . to . . . mean something?

CLOV: Mean something! You and I, mean something! [*Brief laugh.*] Ah that's a good one!

HAMM: I wonder. [*Pause.*] Imagine if a rational being came back to earth, wouldn't he be liable to get ideas into his head if he observed us long enough. [*Voice of rational being.*] Ah, good, now I see what it is, yes, now I understand what they're at! [CLOV *starts, drops the telescope and begins to scratch his belly with both hands. Normal voice.*] And without going so far as that, we ourselves . . . [*With emotion.*] . . . we ourselves . . . at certain moments . . . [*Vehemently.*] To think perhaps it won't all have been for nothing!

CLOV: [*Anguished, scratching himself.*] I have a flea!

HAMM: A flea! Are there still fleas?

CLOV: On me there's one. [*Scratching.*] Unless it's a crablouse.

HAMM: [*Very perturbed.*] But humanity might start from there all over again! Catch him, for the love of God!

CLOV: I'll go and get the powder.
   [*Exit* CLOV.]

HAMM: A flea! This is awful! What a day!
   [*Enter* CLOV *with a sprinkling-tin.*]

CLOV: I'm back again, with the insecticide.

HAMM: Let him have it!
   [CLOV *loosens the top of his trousers, pulls it forward and shakes pow-*

der into the aperture. He stoops, looks, waits, starts, frenziedly shakes more powder, stoops, looks, waits.]

CLOV: The bastard!

HAMM: Did you get him?

CLOV: Looks like it. [He drops the tin and adjusts his trousers.] Unless he's laying doggo.

HAMM: Laying! Lying you mean. Unless he's *lying* doggo.

CLOV: Ah? One says lying? One doesn't say laying?

HAMM: Use your head, can't you. If he was laying we'd be bitched.

CLOV: Ah. [Pause.] What about that pee?

HAMM: I'm having it.

CLOV: Ah that's the spirit, that's the spirit! [Pause.]

HAMM: [With ardour.] Let's go from here, the two of us! South! You can make a raft and the currents will carry us away, far away, to other . . . mammals!

CLOV: God forbid!

HAMM: Alone, I'll embark alone! Get working on that raft immediately. Tomorrow I'll be gone for ever.

CLOV: [Hastening towards door.] I'll start straight away.

HAMM: Wait! [CLOV halts.] Will there be sharks, do you think?

CLOV: Sharks? I don't know. If there are there will be. [He goes towards door.]

HAMM: Wait! [CLOV halts.] Is it not yet time for my pain-killer?

CLOV: [Violently.] No! [He goes towards door.]

HAMM: Wait! [CLOV halts.] How are your eyes?

CLOV: Bad.

HAMM: But you can see.

CLOV: All I want.

HAMM: How are your legs?

CLOV: Bad.

HAMM: But you can walk.

CLOV: I come . . . and go.

HAMM: In my house. [Pause. With prophetic relish.] One day you'll be blind, like me. You'll be sitting there, a speck in the void, in the dark, for ever, like me. [Pause.] One day you'll say to yourself, I'm tired, I'll sit down, and you'll go and sit down. Then you'll say, I'm hungry, I'll get up and get something to eat. But you won't get up. You'll say, I shouldn't have sat down, but since I have I'll sit on a little longer, then I'll get up and get something to eat. But you won't get up and you won't get anything to eat. [Pause.] You'll look at the wall awhile, then you'll say, I'll close my eyes, perhaps have a little sleep, after that I'll feel better, and you'll close them. And when you open them again there'll be no wall any more. [Pause.] Infinite emptiness will be all around you, all the resurrected dead of all the ages wouldn't fill it, and there you'll be like a little bit of grit in the middle of the steppe. [Pause.] Yes, one day you'll know what it is, you'll be like me, except that you won't have anyone with you, because you won't have had pity on anyone and because there won't be anyone left to have pity on. [Pause.]

CLOV: It's not certain. [*Pause.*] And there's one thing you forget.

HAMM: Ah?

CLOV: I can't sit down.

HAMM: [*Impatiently.*] Well you'll lie down then, what the hell! Or you'll come to a standstill, simply stop and stand still, the way you are now. One day you'll say, I'm tired, I'll stop. What does the attitude matter? [*Pause.*]

CLOV: So you all want me to leave you.

HAMM: Naturally.

CLOV: Then I'll leave you.

HAMM: You can't leave us.

CLOV: Then I won't leave you. [*Pause.*]

HAMM: Why don't you finish us? [*Pause.*] I'll tell you the combination of the cupboard if you promise to finish me.

CLOV: I couldn't finish you.

HAMM: Then you won't finish me. [*Pause.*]

CLOV: I'll leave you, I have things to do.

HAMM: Do you remember when you came here?

CLOV: No. Too small, you told me.

HAMM: Do you remember your father?

CLOV: [*Wearily.*] Same answer. [*Pause.*] You've asked me these questions millions of times.

HAMM: I love the old questions. [*With fervor.*] Ah the old questions, the old answers, there's nothing like them! [*Pause.*] It was I was a father to you.

CLOV: Yes. [*He looks at* HAMM *fixedly.*] You were that to me.

HAMM: My house a home for you.

CLOV: Yes. [*He looks about him.*] This was that for me.

HAMM: [*Proudly.*] But for me, [*Gesture towards himself.*] no father. But for Hamm, [*Gesture towards surroundings.*] no home. [*Pause.*]

CLOV: I'll leave you.

HAMM: Did you ever think of one thing?

CLOV: Never.

HAMM: That here we're down in a hole. [*Pause.*] But beyond the hills? Eh? Perhaps it's still green. Eh? [*Pause.*] Flora! Pomona! [*Ecstatically.*] Ceres![7] [*Pause.*] Perhaps you won't need to go very far.

CLOV: I can't go very far. [*Pause.*] I'll leave you.

HAMM: Is my dog ready?

CLOV: He lacks a leg.

HAMM: Is he silky?

CLOV: He's a kind of Pomeranian.

HAMM: Go and get him.

CLOV: He lacks a leg.

HAMM: Go and get him! [*Exit* CLOV.] We're getting on.

[*Enter* CLOV *holding by one of its three legs a black toy dog.*]

CLOV: Your dogs are here. [*He hands the dog to* HAMM *who feels it, fondles it.*]

---

7. In Roman mythology, the goddesses of flowers, fruits, and fertility.

HAMM: He's white, isn't he?

CLOV: Nearly.

HAMM: What do you mean, nearly? Is he white or isn't he?

CLOV: He isn't. [*Pause.*]

HAMM: You've forgotten the sex.

CLOV: [*Vexed.*] But he isn't finished. The sex goes on at the end. [*Pause.*]

HAMM: You haven't put on his ribbon.

CLOV: [*Angrily.*] But he isn't finished, I tell you! First you finish your dog and then you put on his ribbon! [*Pause.*]

HAMM: Can he stand?

CLOV: I don't know.

HAMM: Try. [*He hands the dog to* CLOV *who places it on the ground.*] Well?

CLOV: Wait! [*He squats down and tries to get the dog to stand on its three legs, fails, lets it go. The dog falls on its side.*]

HAMM: [*Impatiently.*] Well?

CLOV: He's standing.

HAMM: [*Groping for the dog.*] Where? Where is he?
     [CLOV *holds up the dog in a standing position.*]

CLOV: There. [*He takes* HAMM*'s hand and guides it towards the dog's head.*]

HAMM: [*His hand on the dog's head.*] Is he gazing at me?

CLOV: Yes.

HAMM: [*Proudly.*] As if he were asking me to take him for a walk?

CLOV: If you like.

HAMM: [*As before.*] Or as if he were begging me for a bone. [*He withdraws his hand.*] Leave him like that, standing there imploring me.
     [CLOV *straightens up. The dog falls on its side.*]

CLOV: I'll leave you.

HAMM: Have you had your visions?

CLOV: Less.

HAMM: Is Mother Pegg's light on?

CLOV: Light! How could anyone's light be on?

HAMM: Extinguished!

CLOV: Naturally it's extinguished. If it's not on it's extinguished.

HAMM: No, I mean Mother Pegg.

CLOV: But naturally she's extinguished! [*Pause.*] What's the matter with you today?

HAMM: I'm taking my course. [*Pause.*] Is she buried?

CLOV: Buried! Who would have buried her?

HAMM: You.

CLOV: Me! Haven't I enough to do without burying people?

HAMM: But you'll bury me.

CLOV: No I won't bury you. [*Pause.*]

HAMM: She was bonny once, like a flower of the field. [*With reminiscent leer.*] And a great one for the men!

CLOV: We too were bonny—once. It's a rare thing not to have been bonny—once. [*Pause.*]

HAMM: Go and get the gaff.
     [CLOV *goes to door, halts.*]

CLOV: Do this, do that, and I do it. I never refuse. Why?

HAMM: You're not able to.

CLOV: Soon I won't do it any more.

HAMM: You won't be able to any more. [*Exit* CLOV.] Ah the creatures, the creatures, everything has to be explained to them.

    [*Enter* CLOV *with gaff.*]

CLOV: Here's your gaff. Stick it up. [*He gives the gaff to* HAMM *who, wielding it like a puntpole, tries to move his chair.*]

HAMM: Did I move?

CLOV: No.

    [HAMM *throws down the gaff.*]

HAMM: Go and get the oilcan.

CLOV: What for?

HAMM: To oil the castors.

CLOV: I oiled them yesterday.

HAMM: Yesterday! What does that mean? Yesterday!

CLOV: [*Violently.*] That means that bloody awful day, long ago, before this bloody awful day. I use the words you taught me. If they don't mean anything any more, teach me others. Or let me be silent. [*Pause.*]

HAMM: I once knew a madman who thought the end of the world had come. He was a painter—and engraver. I had a great fondness for him. I used to go and see him, in the asylum. I'd take him by the hand and drag him to the window. Look! There! All that rising corn! And there! Look! The sails of the herring fleet! All that loveliness! [*Pause.*] He'd snatch away his hand and go back into his corner. Appalled. All he had seen was ashes. [*Pause.*] He alone had been spared. [*Pause.*] Forgotten. [*Pause.*] It appears the case is . . . was not so . . . so unusual.

CLOV: A madman! When was that?

HAMM: Oh way back, way back, you weren't in the land of the living.

CLOV: God be with the days!

    [*Pause.* HAMM *raises his toque.*]

HAMM: I had a great fondness for him. [*Pause. He puts on his toque again.*] He was a painter—and engraver.

CLOV: There are so many terrible things.

HAMM: No, no, there are not so many now. [*Pause.*] Clov!

CLOV: Yes.

HAMM: Do you not think this has gone on long enough?

CLOV: Yes! [*Pause.*] What?

HAMM: This . . . this . . . thing.

CLOV: I've always thought so. [*Pause.*] You not?

HAMM: [*Gloomily.*] Then it's a day like any other day.

CLOV: As long as it lasts. [*Pause.*] All life long the same inanities.

HAMM: I can't leave you.

CLOV: I know. And you can't follow me. [*Pause.*]

HAMM: If you leave me how shall I know?

CLOV: [*Briskly.*] Well you simply whistle me and if I don't come running it means I've left you. [*Pause.*]

HAMM: You won't come and kiss me goodbye?

CLOV: Oh I shouldn't think so. [*Pause.*]

HAMM: But you might be merely dead in your kitchen.

CLOV: The result would be the same.

HAMM: Yes, but how would I know, if you were merely dead in your kitchen?

CLOV: Well . . . sooner or later I'd start to stink.

HAMM: You stink already. The whole place stinks of corpses.

CLOV: The whole universe.

HAMM: [*Angrily.*] To hell with the universe. [*Pause.*] Think of something.

CLOV: What?

HAMM: An idea, have an idea. [*Angrily.*] A bright idea!

CLOV: Ah good. [*He starts pacing to and fro, his eyes fixed on the ground, his hands behind his back. He halts.*] The pains in my legs! It's unbelievable! Soon I won't be able to think any more.

HAMM: You won't be able to leave me. [CLOV *resumes his pacing.*] What are you doing?

CLOV: Having an idea. [*He paces.*] Ah! [*He halts.*]

HAMM: What a brain! [*Pause.*] Well?

CLOV: Wait! [*He meditates. Not very convinced.*] Yes . . . [*Pause. More convinced.*] Yes! [*He raises his head.*] I have it! I set the alarm. [*Pause.*]

HAMM: This is perhaps not one of my bright days, but frankly—

CLOV: You whistle me. I don't come. The alarm rings. I'm gone. It doesn't ring. I'm dead. [*Pause.*]

HAMM: Is it working? [*Pause. Impatiently.*] The alarm, is it working?

CLOV: Why wouldn't it be working?

HAMM: Because it's worked too much.

CLOV: But it's hardly worked at all.

HAMM: [*Angrily.*] Then because it's worked too little!

CLOV: I'll go and see. [*Exit* CLOV. *Brief ring of alarm off. Enter* CLOV *with alarm-clock. He holds it against* HAMM*'s ear and releases alarm. They listen to it ringing to the end. Pause.*] Fit to wake the dead! Did you hear it?

HAMM: Vaguely.

CLOV: The end is terrific!

HAMM: I prefer the middle. [*Pause.*] Is it not time for my pain-killer?

CLOV: No! [*He goes to door, turns.*] I'll leave you.

HAMM: It's time for my story. Do you want to listen to my story.

CLOV: No.

HAMM: Ask my father if he wants to listen to my story.

[CLOV *goes to bins, raises the lid of* NAGG*'s, stoops, looks into it. Pause. He straightens up.*]

CLOV: He's asleep.

HAMM: Wake him.

[CLOV *stoops, wakes* NAGG *with the alarm. Unintelligible words.* CLOV *straightens up.*]

CLOV: He doesn't want to listen to your story.

HAMM: I'll give him a bon-bon.

[CLOV *stoops. As before.*]

CLOV: He wants a sugar-plum.

HAMM: He'll get a sugar-plum.

[CLOV *stoops. As before.*]

CLOV: It's a deal. [*He goes towards door.* NAGG's *hands appear, gripping the rim. Then the head emerges.* CLOV *reaches door, turns.*] Do you believe in the life to come?

HAMM: Mine was always that. [*Exit* CLOV.] Got him that time!

NAGG: I'm listening.

HAMM: Scoundrel! Why did you engender me?

NAGG: I didn't know.

HAMM: What? What didn't you know?

NAGG: That it'd be you. [*Pause.*] You'll give me a sugar-plum?

HAMM: After the audition.

NAGG: You swear?

HAMM: Yes.

NAGG: On what?

HAMM: My honor.

[*Pause. They laugh heartily.*]

NAGG: Two.

HAMM: One.

NAGG: One for me and one for—

HAMM: One! Silence! [*Pause.*] Where was I? [*Pause. Gloomily.*] It's finished, we're finished. [*Pause.*] Nearly finished. [*Pause.*] There'll be no more speech. [*Pause.*] Something dripping in my head, ever since the fontanelles. [*Stifled hilarity of* NAGG.] Splash, splash, always on the same spot. [*Pause.*] Perhaps it's a little vein. [*Pause.*] A little artery. [*Pause. More animated.*] Enough of that, it's story time, where was I? [*Pause. Narrative tone.*] The man came crawling towards me, on his belly. Pale, wonderfully pale and thin, he seemed on the point of—[*Pause. Normal tone.*] No, I've done that bit. [*Pause. Narrative tone.*] I calmly filled my pipe—the meerschaum, lit it with . . . let us say a vesta, drew a few puffs. Aah! [*Pause.*] Well, what is it *you* want? [*Pause.*] It was an extraordinarily bitter day, I remember, zero by the thermometer. But considering it was Christmas Eve there was nothing . . . extra-ordinary about that. Seasonable weather, for once in a way. [*Pause.*] Well, what ill wind blows you my way? He raised his face to me, black with mingled dirt and tears. [*Pause. Normal tone.*] That should do it. [*Narrative tone.*] No, no, don't look at me, don't look at me. He dropped his eyes and mumbled something, apologies I presume. [*Pause.*] I'm a busy man, you know, the final touches, before the festivities, you know what it is. [*Pause. Forcibly.*] Come on now, what is the object of this invasion? [*Pause.*] It was a glorious bright day, I remember, fifty by the heliometer,[8] but already the sun was sinking down into the . . . down among the dead. [*Normal tone.*] Nicely put, that. [*Narrative tone.*] Come on now, come on, present your petition and let me resume my labors. [*Pause. Normal tone.*] There's English for you. Ah well . . . [*Narrative tone.*] It was then he took the plunge. It's my little one, he said. Tsstss, a little one, that's bad. My little boy, he said, as if the sex mattered. Where did he come from? He named the hole. A good half-day, on horse. What

---

8. Literally, a "sun meter." Ordinarily, a telescope used to measure distances between celestial bodies.

are you insinuating? That the place is still inhabited? No no, not a soul, except himself and the child—assuming he existed. Good. I enquired about the situation at Kov, beyond the gulf. Not a sinner. Good. And you expect me to believe you have left your little one back there, all alone, and alive into the bargain? Come now! [*Pause.*] It was a howling wild day, I remember, a hundred by the anemometer.[9] The wind was tearing up the dead pines and sweeping them . . . away. [*Pause. Normal tone.*] A bit feeble, that. [*Narrative tone.*] Come on, man, speak up, what is you want from me, I have to put up my holly. [*Pause.*] Well to make it short it finally transpired that what he wanted from me was . . . bread for his brat? Bread? But I have no bread, it doesn't agree with me. Good. Then perhaps a little corn? [*Pause. Normal tone.*] That should do it. [*Narrative tone.*] Corn, yes, I have corn, it's true, in my granaries. But use your head. I give you some corn, a pound, a pound and a half, you bring it back to your child and you make him—if he's still alive— a nice pot of porridge, [NAGG *reacts.*] a nice pot and a half of porridge, full of nourishment. Good. The colors come back into his little cheeks—perhaps. And then? [*Pause.*] I lost patience. [*Violently.*] Use your head, can't you, use your head, you're on earth, there's no cure for that! [*Pause.*] It was an exceedingly dry day, I remember, zero by the hygrometer.[1] Ideal weather, for my lumbago. [*Pause. Violently.*] But what in God's name do you imagine? That the earth will awake in spring? That the rivers and seas will run with fish again? That there's manna in heaven still for imbeciles like you? [*Pause.*] Gradually I cooled down, sufficiently at least to ask him how long he had taken on the way. Three whole days. Good. In what condition he had left the child. Deep in sleep. [*Forcibly.*] But deep in what sleep, deep in what sleep already? [*Pause.*] Well to make it short I finally offered to take him into my service. He had touched a chord. And then I imagined already that I wasn't much longer for this world. [*He laughs. Pause.*] Well? [*Pause.*] Well? Here if you were careful you might die a nice natural death, in peace and comfort. [*Pause.*] Well? [*Pause.*] In the end he asked me would I consent to take in the child as well—if he were still alive. [*Pause.*] It was the moment I was waiting for. [*Pause.*] Would I consent to take in the child . . . [*Pause.*] I can see him still, down on his knees, his hands flat on the ground, glaring at me with his mad eyes, in defiance of my wishes. [*Pause. Normal tone.*] I'll soon have finished with this story. [*Pause.*] Unless I bring in other characters. [*Pause.*] But where would I find them? [*Pause.*] Where would I look for them? [*Pause. He whistles. Enter* CLOV.] Let us pray to God.

NAGG: Me sugar-plum!

CLOV: There's a rat in the kitchen!

HAMM: A rat! Are there still rats?

CLOV: In the kitchen there's one.

HAMM: And you haven't exterminated him?

CLOV: Half. You disturbed us.

HAMM: He can't get away?

---

9. A wind meter.   1. A moisture meter.

CLOV: No.

HAMM: You'll finish him later. Let us pray to God.

CLOV: Again!

NAGG: Me sugar-plum!

HAMM: God first! [*Pause.*] Are you right?

CLOV: [*Resigned.*] Off we go.

HAMM: [*To* NAGG.] And you?

NAGG: [*Clasping his hands, closing his eyes, in a gabble.*] Our Father which art—

HAMM: Silence! In silence! Where are your manners? [*Pause.*] Off we go. [*Attitudes of prayer. Silence. Abandoning his attitude, discouraged.*] Well?

CLOV: [*Abandoning his attitude.*] What a hope! And you?

HAMM: Sweet damn all! [*To* NAGG.] And you?

NAGG: Wait! [*Pause. Abandoning his attitude.*] Nothing doing!

HAMM: The bastard! He doesn't exist!

CLOV: Not yet.

NAGG: Me sugar-plum!

HAMM: There are no more sugar-plums! [*Pause.*]

NAGG: It's natural. After all I'm your father. It's true if it hadn't been me it would have been someone else. But that's no excuse. [*Pause.*] Turkish Delight,[2] for example, which no longer exists, we all know that, there is nothing in the world I love more. And one day I'll ask you for some, in return for a kindness, and you'll promise it to me. One must live with the times. [*Pause.*] Whom did you call when you were a tiny boy, and were frightened, in the dark? Your mother? No. Me. We let you cry. Then we moved you out of earshot, so that we might sleep in peace. [*Pause.*] I was asleep, as happy as a king, and you woke me up to have me listen to you. It wasn't indispensable, you didn't really need to have me listen to you. [*Pause.*] I hope the day will come when you'll really need to have me listen to you, and need to hear my voice, any voice. [*Pause.*] Yes, I hope I'll live till then, to hear you calling me like when you were a tiny boy, and were frightened, in the dark, and I was your only hope. [*Pause.* NAGG *knocks on lid of* NELL's *bin. Pause.*] Nell! [*Pause. He knocks louder. Pause. Louder.*] Nell! [*Pause.* NAGG *sinks back into his bin, closes the lid behind him. Pause.*]

HAMM: Our revels now are ended.[3] [*He gropes for the dog.*] The dog's gone.

CLOV: He's not a real dog, he can't go.

HAMM: [*Groping.*] He's not there.

CLOV: He's lain down.

HAMM: Give him up to me. [CLOV *picks up the dog and gives it to* HAMM. HAMM *holds it in his arms. Pause.* HAMM *throws away the dog.*] Dirty brute! [CLOV *begins to pick up the objects lying on the ground.*] What are you doing?

CLOV: Putting things in order. [*He straightens up. Fervently.*] I'm going to clear everything away! [*He starts picking up again.*]

---

2. A sticky sweet candy.　　3. Lines spoken by Prospero in Shakespeare's *The Tempest* (4.1.148).

HAMM: Order!

CLOV: [*Straightening up.*] I love order. It's my dream. A world where all would be silent and still and each thing in its last place, under the last dust. [*He starts picking up again.*]

HAMM: [*Exasperated.*] What in God's name do you think you are doing?

CLOV: [*Straightening up.*] I'm doing my best to create a little order.

HAMM: Drop it!

[CLOV *drops the objects he has picked up.*]

CLOV: After all, there or elsewhere. [*He goes towards door.*]

HAMM: [*Irritably.*]What's wrong with your feet?

CLOV: My feet?

HAMM: Tramp! Tramp!

CLOV: I must have put on my boots.

HAMM: Your slippers were hurting you? [*Pause.*]

CLOV: I'll leave you.

HAMM: No!

CLOV: What is there to keep me here?

HAMM: The dialogue. [*Pause.*] I've got on with my story. [*Pause.*] I've got on with it well. [*Pause. Irritably.*] Ask me where I've got to.

CLOV: Oh, by the way, your story?

HAMM: [*Surprised.*] What story?

CLOV: The one you've been telling yourself all your days.

HAMM: Ah you mean my chronicle?

CLOV: That's the one. [*Pause.*]

HAMM: [*Angrily.*] Keep going, can't you, keep going!

CLOV: You've got on with it, I hope.

HAMM: [*Modestly.*] Oh not very far, not very far. [*He sighs.*] There are days like that, one isn't inspired. [*Pause.*] Nothing you can do about it, just wait for it to come. [*Pause.*] No forcing, no forcing, it's fatal. [*Pause.*] I've got on with it a little all the same. [*Pause.*] Technique, you know. [*Pause. Irritably.*] I say I've got on with it a little all the same.

CLOV: [*Admiringly.*] Well I never! In spite of everything you were able to get on with it!

HAMM: [*Modestly.*] Oh not very far, you know, not very far, but nevertheless, better than nothing.

CLOV: Better than nothing! Is it possible?

HAMM: I'll tell you how it goes. He comes crawling on his belly—

CLOV: Who?

HAMM: What?

CLOV: Who do you mean, he?

HAMM: Who do I mean! Yet another.

CLOV: Ah him! I wasn't sure.

HAMM: Crawling on his belly, whining for bread for his brat. He's offered a job as gardener. Before—[CLOV *bursts out laughing.*] What is there so funny about that?

CLOV: A job as gardener!

HAMM: Is that what tickles you?

CLOV: It must be that.

HAMM: It wouldn't be the bread?

CLOV: Or the brat. [*Pause.*]

HAMM: The whole thing is comical, I grant you that. What about having a good guffaw the two of us together?

CLOV: [*After reflection.*] I couldn't guffaw again today.

HAMM: [*After reflection.*] Nor I. [*Pause.*] I continue then. Before accepting with gratitude he asks if he may have his little boy with him.

CLOV: What age?

HAMM: Oh tiny.

CLOV: He would have climbed the trees.

HAMM: All the little odd jobs.

CLOV: And then he would have grown up.

HAMM: Very likely. [*Pause.*]

CLOV: Keep going, can't you, keep going!

HAMM: That's all. I stopped there. [*Pause.*]

CLOV: Do you see how it goes on.

HAMM: More or less.

CLOV: Will it not soon be the end?

HAMM: I'm afraid it will.

CLOV: Pah! You'll make up another.

HAMM: I don't know. [*Pause.*] I feel rather drained. [*Pause.*] The prolonged creative effort. [*Pause.*] If I could drag myself down to the sea! I'd make a pillow of sand for my head and the tide would come.

CLOV: There's no more tide. [*Pause.*]

HAMM: Go and see is she dead.

[CLOV *goes to bins, raises the lid of* NELL*'s, stoops, looks into it. Pause.*]

CLOV: Looks like it.

[*He closes the lid, straightens up.* HAMM *raises his toque. Pause. He puts it on again.*]

HAMM: [*With his hand to his toque.*] And Nagg?

[CLOV *raises lid of* NAGG*'s bin, stoops, looks into it. Pause.*]

CLOV: Doesn't look like it. [*He closes the lid, straightens up.*]

HAMM: [*Letting go his toque.*] What's he doing? [CLOV *raises lid of* NAGG*'s bin, stoops, looks into it. Pause.*]

CLOV: He's crying. [*He closes lid, straightens up.*]

HAMM: Then he's living. [*Pause.*] Did you ever have an instant of happiness?

CLOV: Not to my knowledge. [*Pause.*]

HAMM: Bring me under the window. [CLOV *goes towards chair.*] I want to feel the light on my face. [CLOV *pushes chair.*] Do you remember, in the beginning, when you took me for a turn? You used to hold the chair too high. At every step you nearly tipped me out. [*With senile quaver.*] Ah great fun, we had, the two of us, great fun. [*Gloomily.*] And then we got into the way of it. [CLOV *stops the chair under window right.*] There already? [*Pause. He tilts back his head.*] Is it light?

CLOV: It isn't dark.

HAMM: [*Angrily.*] I'm asking you is it light.

CLOV: Yes. [*Pause.*]

HAMM: The curtain isn't closed?

CLOV: No.

HAMM: What window is it?

CLOV: The earth.

HAMM: I knew it! [*Angrily.*] But there's no light there! The other! [CLOV *stops the chair under window left.* HAMM *tilts back his head.*] That's what I call light! [*Pause.*] Feels like a ray of sunshine. [*Pause.*] No?

CLOV: No.

HAMM: It isn't a ray of sunshine I feel on my face?

CLOV: No. [*Pause.*]

HAMM: Am I very white? [*Pause. Angrily.*] I'm asking you am I very white!

CLOV: Not more so than usual. [*Pause.*]

HAMM: Open the window.

CLOV: What for?

HAMM: I want to hear the sea.

CLOV: You wouldn't hear it.

HAMM: Even if you opened the window?

CLOV: No.

HAMM: Then it's not worth while opening it?

CLOV: No.

HAMM: [*Violently.*] Then open it! [CLOV *gets up on the ladder, opens the window. Pause.*] Have you opened it?

CLOV: Yes. [*Pause.*]

HAMM: You swear you've opened it?

CLOV: Yes. [*Pause.*]

HAMM: Well. . .! [*Pause.*] It must be very calm. [*Pause. Violently.*] I'm asking you is it very calm!

CLOV: Yes.

HAMM: It's because there are no more navigators. [*Pause.*] You haven't much conversation all of a sudden. Do you not feel well?

CLOV: I'm cold.

HAMM: What month are we? [*Pause.*] Close the window, we're going back. [CLOV *closes the window, gets down, pushes the chair back to its place, remains standing behind it, head bowed.*] Don't stay there, you give me the shivers! [CLOV *returns to his place beside the chair.*] Father! [*Pause. Louder.*] Father! [*Pause.*] Go and see did he hear me.

[CLOV *goes to* NAGG*'s bin, raises the lid, stoops. Unintelligible words.* CLOV *straightens up.*]

CLOV: Yes.

HAMM: Both times?

[CLOV *stoops. As before.*]

CLOV: Once only.

HAMM: The first time or the second?

[CLOV *stoops. As before.*]

CLOV: He doesn't know.

HAMM: It must have been the second.

CLOV: We'll never know. [*He closes lid.*]

HAMM: Is he still crying?

CLOV: No.

HAMM: The dead go fast. [*Pause.*] What's he doing?

CLOV: Sucking his biscuit.

HAMM: Life goes on. [CLOV *returns to his place beside the chair.*] Give me a rug. I'm freezing.

CLOV: There are no more rugs. [*Pause.*]

HAMM: Kiss me. [*Pause.*] Will you not kiss me?

CLOV: No.

HAMM: On the forehead.

CLOV: I won't kiss you anywhere. [*Pause.*]

HAMM: [*Holding out his hand.*] Give me your hand at least. [*Pause.*] Will you not give me your hand?

CLOV: I won't touch you. [*Pause.*]

HAMM: Give me the dog. [CLOV *looks round for the dog.*] No!

CLOV: Do you not want your dog?

HAMM: No.

CLOV: Then I'll leave you.

HAMM: [*Head bowed, absently.*] That's right.

　　[CLOV *goes to door, turns.*]

CLOV: If I don't kill that rat he'll die.

HAMM: [*As before.*] That's right. [*Exit* CLOV. *Pause.*] Me to play. [*He takes out his handkerchief, unfolds it, holds it spread out before him.*] We're getting on. [*Pause.*] You weep, and weep, for nothing, so as not to laugh, and little by little . . . you begin to grieve. [*He folds the handkerchief, puts it back in his pocket, raises his head.*] All those I might have helped. [*Pause.*] Helped! [*Pause.*] Saved. [*Pause.*] Saved! [*Pause.*] The place was crawling with them! [*Pause. Violently.*] Use your head, can't you, use your head, you're on earth, there's no cure for that! [*Pause.*] Get out of here and love one another! Lick your neighbor as yourself![4] [*Pause. Calmer.*] When it wasn't bread they wanted it was crumpets. [*Pause. Violently.*] Out of my sight and back to your petting parties! [*Pause.*] All that, all that! [*Pause.*] Not even a real dog! [*Calmer.*] The end is in the beginning and yet you go on. [*Pause.*] Perhaps I could go on with my story, end it and begin another. [*Pause.*] Perhaps I could throw myself out on the floor. [*He pushes himself painfully off his seat, falls back again.*] Dig my nails into the cracks and drag myself forward with my fingers. [*Pause.*] It will be the end and there I'll be, wondering what can have brought it on and wondering what can have . . . [*He hesitates.*] . . . why it was so long coming. [*Pause.*] There I'll be, in the old shelter, alone against the silence and . . . [*He hesitates.*] . . . the stillness. If I can hold my peace, and sit quiet, it will be all over with sound, and motion, all over and done with. [*Pause.*] I'll have called my father and I'll have called my . . . [*He hesitates.*] . . . my son. And even twice, or three times, in case they shouldn't have heard me, the first time, or the second. [*Pause.*] I'll say to myself, He'll come back. [*Pause.*] And then? [*Pause.*] And then? [*Pause.*] He couldn't, he has gone too far. [*Pause.*] And then? [*Pause. Very agitated.*] All kinds of fantasies! That I'm being watched! A rat! Steps! Breath held and then . . . [*He breathes out.*] Then babble, babble, words, like the solitary child who turns himself into children, two, three, so as to be together, and whisper

---

4. Parody of Jesus' words in the Bible: "Thou shalt love thy neighbor as thyself" (Matthew 19:19).

together, in the dark. [*Pause.*] Moment upon moment, pattering down, like the millet grains of . . . [*He hesitates.*] . . . that old Greek,[5] and all life long you wait for that to mount up to a life. [*Pause. He opens his mouth to continue, renounces.*] Ah let's get it over! [*He whistles. Enter* CLOV *with alarm-clock. He halts beside the chair.*] What? Neither gone nor dead?

CLOV: In spirit only.

HAMM: Which?

CLOV: Both.

HAMM: Gone from me you'd be dead.

CLOV: And vice versa.

HAMM: Outside of here it's death! [*Pause.*] And the rat?

CLOV: He's got away.

HAMM: He can't go far. [*Pause. Anxious.*] Eh?

CLOV: He doesn't need to go far. [*Pause.*]

HAMM: Is it not time for my pain-killer?

CLOV: Yes.

HAMM: Ah! At last! Give it to me! Quick! [*Pause.*]

CLOV: There's no more pain-killer. [*Pause.*]

HAMM: [*Appalled.*] Good. . . ! [*Pause.*] No more pain-killer!

CLOV: No more pain-killer. You'll never get any more pain-killer. [*Pause.*]

HAMM: But the little round box. It was full!

CLOV: Yes. But now it's empty.

    [*Pause.* CLOV *starts to move about the room. He is looking for a place to put down the alarm-clock.*]

HAMM: [*Soft.*] What'll I do? [*Pause. In a scream.*] What'll I do? [CLOV *sees the picture, takes it down, stands it on the floor with its face to the wall, hangs up the alarm-clock in its place.*] What are you doing?

CLOV: Winding up.

HAMM: Look at the earth.

CLOV: Again!

HAMM: Since it's calling to you.

CLOV: Is your throat sore? [*Pause.*] Would you like a lozenge? [*Pause.*] No. [*Pause.*] Pity. [*He goes, humming, towards window right, halts before it, looks up at it.*]

HAMM: Don't sing.

CLOV: [*Turning towards* HAMM.] One hasn't the right to sing any more?

HAMM: No.

CLOV: Then how can it end?

HAMM: You want it to end?

CLOV: I want to sing.

HAMM: I can't prevent you.

    [*Pause.* CLOV *turns towards window right.*]

CLOV: What did I do with that steps? [*He looks around for ladder.*] You didn't see that steps? [*He sees it.*] Ah, about time. [*He goes towards window left.*] Sometimes I wonder if I'm in my right mind. Then it

---

5. Zeno of Elea, a Greek philosopher active around 450 B.C., known for logical paradoxes that reduce to absurdity various attempts to define "Being." Aristotle reports that Zeno's paradox on sound questioned: If a grain of millet falling makes no sound, how can a bushel of grains make any sound? (Aristotle's *Physics* 5.250a.19).

passes over and I'm as lucid as before. [*He gets up on ladder, looks out of window.*] Christ, she's under water! [*He looks.*] How can that be? [*He pokes forward his head, his hand above his eyes.*] It hasn't rained. [*He wipes the pane, looks. Pause.*] Ah what a fool I am! I'm on the wrong side! [*He gets down, takes a few steps towards window right.*] Under water! [*He goes back for ladder.*] What a fool I am! [*He carries ladder towards window right.*] Sometimes I wonder if I'm in my right senses. Then it passes off and I'm as intelligent as ever. [*He sets down ladder under window right, gets up on it, looks out of window. He turns towards* HAMM.] Any particular sector you fancy? Or merely the whole thing?

HAMM: Whole thing.

CLOV: The general effect? Just a moment. [*He looks out of window. Pause.*]

HAMM: Clov.

CLOV: [*Absorbed.*] Mmm.

HAMM: Do you know what it is?

CLOV: [*As before.*] Mmm.

HAMM: I was never there. [*Pause.*] Clov!

CLOV: [*Turning towards* HAMM, *exasperated.*] What is it?

HAMM: I was never there.

CLOV: Lucky for you. [*He looks out of window.*]

HAMM: Absent, always. It all happened without me. I don't know what's happened. [*Pause.*] Do you know what's happened? [*Pause.*] Clov!

CLOV: [*Turning towards* HAMM, *exasperated.*] Do you want me to look at this muckheap, yes or no?

HAMM: Answer me first.

CLOV: What?

HAMM: Do you know what's happened?

CLOV: When? Where?

HAMM: [*Violently.*] When! What's happened? Use your head, can't you! What has happened?

CLOV: What for Christ's sake does it matter? [*He looks out of window.*]

HAMM: I don't know.

[*Pause.* CLOV *turns towards* HAMM.]

CLOV: [*Harshly.*] When old Mother Pegg asked you for oil for her lamp and you told her to get out to hell, you knew what was happening then, no? [*Pause.*] You know what she died of, Mother Pegg? Of darkness.

HAMM: [*Feebly.*] I hadn't any.

CLOV: [*As before.*] Yes, you had. [*Pause.*]

HAMM: Have you the glass?

CLOV: No, it's clear enough as it is.

HAMM: Go and get it.

[*Pause.* CLOV *casts up his eyes, brandishes his fists. He loses balance, clutches on to the ladder. He starts to get down, halts.*]

CLOV: There's one thing I'll never understand. [*He gets down.*] Why I always obey you. Can you explain that to me?

HAMM: No. . . . Perhaps it's compassion. [*Pause.*] A kind of great compassion. [*Pause.*] Oh you won't find it easy, you won't find it easy.

[*Pause.* CLOV *begins to move about the room in search of the telescope.*]

CLOV: I'm tired of our goings on, very tired. [*He searches.*] You're not sitting on it? [*He moves the chair, looks at the place where it stood, resumes his search.*]

HAMM: [*Anguished.*] Don't leave me there! [*Angrily* CLOV *restores the chair to its place.*] Am I right in the center?

CLOV: You'd need a microscope to find this—[*He sees the telescope.*] Ah, about time. [*He picks up the telescope, gets up on the ladder, turns the telescope on the without.*]

HAMM: Give me the dog.

CLOV: [*Looking.*] Quiet!

HAMM: [*Angrily.*] Give me the dog!

[CLOV *drops the telescope, clasps his hands to his head. Pause. He gets down precipitately, looks for the dog, sees it, picks it up, hastens towards* HAMM *and strikes him violently on the head with the dog.*]

CLOV: There's your dog for you!

[*The dog falls to the ground. Pause.*]

HAMM: He hit me!

CLOV: You drive me mad, I'm mad!

HAMM: If you must hit me, hit me with the axe. [*Pause.*] Or with the gaff, hit me with the gaff. Not with the dog. With the gaff. Or with the axe.

[CLOV *picks up the dog and gives it to* HAMM *who takes it in his arms.*]

CLOV: [*Imploringly.*] Let's stop playing!

HAMM: Never! [*Pause.*] Put me in my coffin.

CLOV: There are no more coffins.

HAMM: Then let it end! [CLOV *goes towards ladder.*] With a bang! [CLOV *gets up on ladder, gets down again, looks for telescope, sees it, picks it up, gets up ladder, raises telescope.*] Of darkness! And me? Did anyone ever have pity on me?

CLOV: [*Lowering the telescope, turning towards* HAMM.] What? [*Pause.*] Is it me you're referring to?

HAMM: [*Angrily.*] An aside, ape! Did you never hear an aside before? [*Pause.*] I'm warming up for my last soliloquy.

CLOV: I warn you. I'm going to look at this filth since it's an order. But it's the last time. [*He turns the telescope on the without.*] Let's see. [*He moves the telescope.*] Nothing . . . nothing . . . good . . . good . . . nothing . . . goo—[*He starts, lowers the telescope, examines it, turns it again on the without. Pause.*] Bad luck to it!

HAMM: More complications! [CLOV *gets down.*] Not an underplot, I trust.

[CLOV *moves ladder nearer window, gets up on it, turns telescope on the without.*]

CLOV: [*Dismayed.*] Looks like a small boy!

HAMM: [*Sarcastic.*] A small . . . boy!

CLOV: I'll go and see. [*He gets down, drops the telescope, goes towards door, turns.*] I'll take the gaff. [*He looks for the gaff, sees it, picks it up, hastens towards door.*]

HAMM: No! [CLOV *halts.*]

CLOV: No? A potential procreator?

HAMM: If he exists he'll die there or he'll come here. And if he doesn't . . .
[*Pause.*]

CLOV: You don't believe me? You think I'm inventing? [*Pause.*]

HAMM: It's the end, Clov, we've come to the end. I don't need you any
more. [*Pause.*]

CLOV: Lucky for you. [*He goes towards door.*]

HAMM: Leave me the gaff.

  [CLOV *gives him the gaff, goes towards door, halts, looks at alarm-*
  clock, takes it down, looks round for a better place to put it, goes to
  bins, puts it on lid of NAGG's *bin. Pause.*]

CLOV: I'll leave you. [*He goes towards door.*]

HAMM: Before you go . . . [CLOV *halts near door.*] . . . say something.

CLOV: There is nothing to say.

HAMM: A few words . . . to ponder . . . in my heart.

CLOV: Your heart!

HAMM: Yes. [*Pause. Forcibly.*] Yes! [*Pause.*] With the rest, in the end, the
shadows, the murmurs, all the trouble, to end up with. [*Pause.*] Clov.
. . . He never spoke to me. Then, in the end, before he went, without
my having asked him, he spoke to me. He said . . .

CLOV: [*Despairingly.*] Ah. . . !

HAMM: Something . . . from your heart.

CLOV: My heart!

HAMM: A few words . . . from your heart. [*Pause.*]

CLOV: [*Fixed gaze, tonelessly, towards auditorium.*] They said to me,
That's love, yes, yes, not a doubt, now you see how—

HAMM: Articulate!

CLOV: [*As before.*] How easy it is. They said to me, That's friendship, yes,
yes, no question, you've found it. They said to me, Here's the place,
stop, raise your head and look at all that beauty. That order! They said
to me. Come now, you're not a brute beast, think upon these things
and you'll see how all becomes clear. And simple! They said to me,
What skilled attention they get, all these dying of their wounds.

HAMM: Enough!

CLOV: [*As before.*] I say to myself—sometimes, Clov, you must learn to
suffer better than that if you want them to weary of punishing you—
one day. I say to myself—sometimes, Clov, you must be there better
than that if you want them to let you go—one day. But I feel too old,
and too far, to form new habits. Good, it'll never end, I'll never go.
[*Pause.*] Then one day, suddenly, it ends, it changes, I don't understand,
it dies, or it's me, I don't understand, that either. I ask the words that
remain—sleeping, waking, morning, evening. They have nothing to
say. [*Pause.*] I open the door of the cell and go. I am so bowed I only
see my feet, if I open my eyes, and between my legs a little trail of black
dust. I say to myself that the earth is extinguished, though I never saw it
lit. [*Pause.*] It's easy going. [*Pause.*] When I fall I'll weep for happiness.
[*Pause. He goes towards door.*]

HAMM: Clov! [CLOV *halts, without turning.*] Nothing. [CLOV *moves on.*]
Clov!

  [CLOV *halts, without turning.*]

CLOV: This is what we call making an exit.

HAMM: I'm obliged to you, Clov. For your services.

CLOV: [*Turning, sharply.*] Ah pardon, it's I am obliged to you.

HAMM: It's we are obliged to each other. [*Pause.* CLOV *goes towards door.*] One thing more. [CLOV *halts.*] A last favor. [*Exit* CLOV.] Cover me with the sheet. [*Long pause.*] No? Good. [*Pause.*] Me to play. [*Pause. Wearily.*] Old endgame lost of old, play and lose and have done with losing. [*Pause. More animated.*] Let me see. [*Pause.*] Ah yes! [*He tries to move the chair, using the gaff as before. Enter* CLOV, *dressed for the road. Panama hat, tweed coat, raincoat over his arm, umbrella, bag. He halts by the door and stands there, impassive and motionless, his eyes fixed on* HAMM, *till the end.* HAMM *gives up.*] Good. [*Pause.*] Discard. [*He throws away the gaff, makes to throw away the dog, thinks better of it.*] Take it easy. [*Pause.*] And now? [*Pause.*] Raise hat. [*He raises his toque.*] Peace to our ... arses. [*Pause.*] And put on again. [*He puts on his toque.*] Deuce. [*Pause. He takes off his glasses.*] Wipe. [*He takes out his handkerchief and, without unfolding it, wipes his glasses.*] And put on again. [*He puts on his glasses, puts back the handkerchief in his pocket.*] We're coming. A few more squirms like that and I'll call. [*Pause.*] A little poetry. [*Pause.*] You prayed—[*Pause. He corrects himself.*] You CRIED for night; it comes—[*Pause. He corrects himself.*] It FALLS: now cry in darkness. [*He repeats, chanting.*] You cried for night; it falls: now cry in darkness.[6] [*Pause.*] Nicely put, that. [*Pause.*] And now? [*Pause.*] Moments for nothing, now as always, time was never and time is over, reckoning closed and story ended. [*Pause. Narrative tone.*] If he could have his child with him. ... [*Pause.*] It was the moment I was waiting for. [*Pause.*] You don't want to abandon him? You want him to bloom while you are withering? Be there to solace your last million last moments? [*Pause.*] He doesn't realize, all he knows is hunger, and cold, and death to crown it all. But you! You ought to know what the earth is like, nowadays. Oh I put him before his responsibilities! [*Pause. Normal tone.*] Well, there we are, there I am, that's enough. [*He raises the whistle to his lips, hesitates, drops it. Pause.*] Yes, truly! [*He whistles. Pause. Louder. Pause.*] Good. [*Pause.*] Father! [*Pause. Louder.*] Father! [*Pause.*] Good. [*Pause.*] We're coming. [*Pause.*] And to end up with? [*Pause.*] Discard. [*He throws away the dog. He tears the whistle from his neck.*] With my compliments. [*He throws whistle towards auditorium. Pause. He sniffs. Soft.*] Clov! [*Long pause.*] No? Good. [*He takes out the handkerchief.*] Since that's the way we're playing it ... [*He unfolds handkerchief.*] ... let's play it that way ... [*He unfolds.*] ... and speak no more about it ... [*He finishes unfolding.*] ... speak no more. [*He holds handkerchief spread out before him.*] Old stancher! [*Pause.*] You ... remain.

   [*Pause. He covers his face with handkerchief, lowers his arms to armrests, remains motionless.*]

   [*Brief tableau.*]

Curtain

---

6. Parody of a line from the poem *Meditation*, by Baudelaire: "You were calling for evening; it falls; here it is."

BIRAGO DIOP
1906–1992

Although Birago Diop was an accomplished poet and dramatist, his achievement as a writer resides principally in his felicitous renderings of the African folktale and his effective adaptation of an essentially oral mode to a literate medium. His work thus testifies to the productive relationship between orality and literacy that has largely conditioned the modern African imagination. For, in their spirit and essential features, Diop's tales derive from the folktale tradition in Africa and incorporate the formal principles and performance modes associated with this tradition. Diop himself disclaims authorship of these tales. He ascribes them to Amadou Koumba, an old sage and *griot* who recited them to him during a memorable week he spent, in the late 1930s, in the hinterland of the former French West African empire, during one of his many tours of duty as a veterinary officer in the colonial service. Listening to Amadou Koumba brought back to Diop vivid memories of the nightly folktale sessions that formed part of his childhood in the family compound in Dakar and confirmed for him the imaginative scope as well as the profound human import of the tales.

Given these circumstances, Diop has claimed for himself only the merit of having transcribed and rendered the tales in French. This explains why, in his retelling, they retain a quality of authenticity and bear out his desire to be considered the faithful perpetuator of an age-old tradition. Diop's fidelity to this tradition does not, however, preclude an originality of style that puts his personal seal on the tales, for they emerge in his versions as individual re-creations of a communal resource. They are not "translations" but rather "transpositions" from an African— and specifically Wolof (an ethnic group in central Senegal)—mode of expression into a European one. They represent, in other words, a conscious reworking of folktale elements in a new idiom.

Diop was born in 1906 in Dakar, Senegal, to an influential Wolof family that, though nominally Muslim, had remained firmly rooted in the traditional way of life. He began attending koranic school at the customary age of five, learning the rudiments of Arabic and the sacred texts of Islam. However, at ten, he enrolled on his own at the French school, where he spent the next four years and developed an enduring attachment to the French language and literature, which formed the basis of the curriculum. After completing his primary education in 1921, he was sent to live with a relative in St. Louis, at that time the capital of Senegal, and was admitted the following year to the Lycée Faidherbe as a scholarship student. An old colonial city founded in the late sixteenth century by the French at the mouth of the Senegal River in the far north of the colony, St. Louis in the 1920s was a social and cultural elite center. In its intellectual atmosphere Diop's passion for literature and the arts was further strengthened. He immersed himself while a student at the lycée in classical French literature and began to try his hand at poetry. The influence of the French Romantic and Parnassian poets was predominant in this early work, colored no doubt by a naive exoticism but testifying to a preoccupation with form (indicative of the Parnassians) that was to become a hallmark of his writing. It was also during this period that he encountered the works of the French anthropologists Georges Hardy and Robert Delavignette, both colonial administrators, whose investigations of the indigenous social institutions and the traditional arts had begun to foster a revised image of Africa, one at variance with the received Western opinion of Africa as the "Dark Continent." From his reading of their works, Diop acquired a new reverence for his cultural background.

In 1928, Diop obtained his *baccalauréat* (the high school degree in the French system) and was immediately drafted into the colonial army and attached as an assistant nurse to the military hospital in St. Louis. There he decided to become a doctor, and although he subsequently won a scholarship to study at the University of Toulouse in France, he was refused admission to the faculty of medicine; he decided instead to become a veterinary surgeon. He graduated in 1933 and moved to Paris the same year for advanced studies. This was the first of Diop's many sojourns in Paris, and although it lasted less than a year, it enabled him to meet his compatriot Léopold Sédar Senghor and other French-speaking African and Caribbean intellectuals then promoting the new self-awareness among black people that was to lead to the concept of Negritude, the idea of a collective personality of the black race, and the literary movement by which it came to be sustained. With Senghor and others in the group around him Diop helped found *L'Etudiant noir* (The black student), a journal devoted to African cultural renovation and the rehabilitation of the black race. The efforts of the group benefited from a new climate of French appreciation of African culture and from the growing recognition of African art, whose impact on avant-garde European artists had been decisive. These shifts in attitude were complemented by a lively interest in African folklore, of which the success of Blaise Cendrar's *Anthologie Nègre* provided striking evidence. But perhaps more important for Diop was the work of the West Indian novelist René Maran, whose *Batouala* had won the prestigious Prix Goncourt in 1921 and whose last work, *Le Livre de la brousse*, had given a new orientation to the literature of exoticism in French. Maran's integration of the African environment into his novels, with human characters interacting with vegetation and wildlife, could not but recall to his African readers the elements and atmosphere of their traditional tales and must have made a lasting impression on Diop. Moreover, Diop's French education had already made him familiar with the *Fables* of La Fontaine, derived from Aesop, a work peopled by animal characters, representing a wide range of human dispositions and dramatic situations, as in the folktales of his West African homeland.

Diop's appointment as a veterinary officer, on his return to Senegal in 1934, was to determine the direction of his literary career. Because his job required him to travel all over the West African savanna, he came into intimate contact with the daily life of rural folk. The experience gave him a new awareness, as an African assimilated to Western culture, of his antecedents in the indigenous way of life and a fresh insight into the centrality of the imaginative function—of which in oral communities the folktale was the immediate vehicle of expression. His sessions with Amadou Koumba crystallized his resolve to set down in writing the tales he had heard both as a city child and during his travels in the country. Unable to return in 1942 to Senegal from his annual summer vacation in France because of the war and the German occupation, he devoted the next two years to writing poetry and composing the first of his folktale adaptations. This work began to appear in various literary journals, and in 1947 the tales were gathered into a volume and published under the title *Les contes d'Amadou Khoumba* (The tales of Amadou Koumba). They were immediately acclaimed by Senghor, who included a poem from the collection in his historic anthology of black writing in French published the following year. The poem, *Souffles* (Breaths), featured as a song interlude in the tale *Sarzan*, remains the best known statement in literature of the mystical conception of the universe in African thought systems:

> Listen more often
> To Things than to Beings
> The voice of fire
> The voice of water

Listen in the wind
The sigh of the woods
The breath of the ancestors

Those who are dead are not dead
They are in the shadows that lighten around us
And in the shadows that thicken into darkness
The dead are not under the ground
They are in the trees that tremble
They are in the woods that groan
They are in the water that flows
They are in the water that sleeps
They are in the Hut, they are in the Crowd
The dead are not dead.

Diop's second collection *Les nouveaux contes d'Amadou Koumba* (New tales of Amadou Koumba), with an extensive prefatory essay by Senghor, appeared in 1958, and confirmed his special genius. It was followed by *Leurres et luerres* (1960), which brought together poems Diop had written over a period of some twenty years. Appointed by President Senghor as ambassador to Tunisia at the independence of Senegal in 1960, Diop put together a third collection, *Contes et lavanes* (1963), containing new tales and a selection of Wolof riddles and aphorisms (the *lavanes* of the title). After four years, he gave up his official position to return to private life in Dakar, where he set up a veterinary clinic and began work on his memoirs, two books of which were later published: *La plume raboutée* (The splintered pen) (1978) and *A Rebrousse-temps* (Against the grain of time) (1982). With his tales translated into several languages and many of them adapted for the stage, by himself and others, Diop was esteemed as one of the architects of a modern African literary renaissance. But apart from receiving visitors from all over the world at his clinic, he lived a largely uneventful life until his death in 1992.

The three selections presented here offer a representative view of Diop's themes and of his formal approach to the material he inherited from the oral tradition. *The Humps* combines the motif of the etiological tale, one centered on a symbolic explanation of natural phenomena, with the structure and satirical intent of the moral fable. The marked contrasts in situations and characters and the ironic turn of events that concludes the tale underline the preeminently didactic function of the folktale in the oral tradition. Its theme of just retribution meted out to vice receives a more pointed human application in *The Bone*, through the depiction of an obsessive and ultimately self-destructive character trait. The setting of this tale in a highly integrated community puts in bold relief Mor Lame's willful deviation from shared norms and gives telling effect to the macabre details of the story. The tale also is remarkable for the way the background functions within the narrative to determine its pace and structure, with the stages of Mor Lame's descent to the grave linked to the progression of the day, itself marked by the Muslim prayers prescribed for the faithful from sunrise to sunset.

Mother Crocodile offers a much wider canvas than the other two tales. Its portrait gallery introduces us to the principal animal characters of Wolof folktales, some of whom, notably Leuk-the-Hare, have whole cycles devoted to them. Diop builds on and extends the traditional folktale's anthropomorphism—which gives animals human traits and contexts—to project a view sympathetic to reclaiming the ancestral heritage. The immediate theme of memory on which the tale revolves illustrates the enduring value of traditional wisdom and refers beyond itself to the human world of heroic and epic narratives in which the broader historical consciousness of traditional societies is grounded. The references in the tale to some dramatic moments of the precolonial period in the West African savanna—evoked as a theater both of human interaction going back to the Middle Ages and of varied forms of socioeconomic and cultural life—affirm the significance of the historical background of the region for the generation of Africans, alienated by Western colonialism from their past, to whom Diop's ideological message is addressed. At the same time, the parallel maintained throughout the tale between the human and animal realms, leading to its grim conclusion, conveys a vivid sense not only of humanity's profound rootage in nature but also of the tragic implications of history, so often manifested at all times and in all places as the violent enactment of human passions.

Although many other African writers have turned to the folktale tradition for inspiration, in this mode the work of Diop remains unequaled. The familiar style of the narrative reproduces the conversational flow of African folktale sessions, highlighted by proverbs and aphorisms and punctuated by songs and refrains sung or chanted by both the narrator and the audience. His concern for structure is reflected in the economy of his narrative style and in the elegance of his French, which can only be captured imperfectly in translation. The diversity of situations in his stories reveals his insight into the many facets of human nature, while his animal characters reinforce with their allegorical implications his seriocomic vision of the human condition. Free from self-consciousness, he captures and transmits the atmosphere of the West African savanna, with its customs and values, and gives to his stories, through the blend of realism and fantasy, the stamp of a specific and deeply felt life. But perhaps the most engaging qualities of Diop's writing are the gentle humor with which these tales are rendered, expressive of his essentially humane outlook and the rich imagination that enabled him to reestablish the folktale as a viable genre in the modern literature of Africa written in European languages.

An extensive secondary literature on Birago Diop exists in French; in her introduction to *Tales of Amadou Koumba* (1989), a selection in English translation from Birago Diop's first two volumes, Dorothy S. Blair offers an admirably succinct account of Diop's life and of his work in relation to its background in the oral tradition.

PRONOUNCING GLOSSARY

The following list uses common English syllables to provide rough equivalents of selected words whose pronunciation may be unfamiliar to the general reader.

Assalamou Aleykoum: *ah-sah-lah-moo alay-ee-koom*

Bafoulabe: *bah-foo-lah-bay*

Brack-Oualo: *brahk–waloh*

Brahim Saloum: *brah-heem sah-loom*

Birago Diop: *bee-rah-goh jop*

Diara: *jah-rah*

Diassigue: *dyah-seeg*

Djoliba: *joh-lee-bah*

Dougoudougou: *doo-goo-doo-goo*

griot: *gree-oh*

Kouloubali: *koo-loo-bah-lee*

Lamene: *lah-men*

Mame: *mahm*

Momor: *maw-mawr*

Mor Lame: *mawr lahm*

Ngalam: *en-gah-lahm*

Ngolo: *en-goh-loh*

N'Guew: *en-gay-woo*

Niangal: *nyan-gahl*

Peul: *pel*

Samba Lame: *sahm-bah lahm*

Sa n'diaye: *sah en-dee-aye*

Segue: *seg*

Serigne: *say-reenh*   Thioye: *tyo-ee*
Thile: *teel*   tong-tong: *tawn–tawn*
Thioker: *tyoh-ker*   Trarza: *trahr-zah*

The Humps[1]

Here, far from my home in Senegal, my eyes are surrounded by closed
horizons. When the greens of summer and the russets of autumn have
passed, I seek the vast expanses of the Savannah, and find only bare mountains, sombre as ancient prostrate giants that the snow refuses to bury
because of their misdeeds. . . .

Winter is an unskilled weaver, who never manages to comb or card his
cotton; he spins and weaves nothing but a soft drizzle. The sky is grey and
cold, the sun is pale, and shivers; and so I huddle near the stove to warm
my numbed limbs.

The fire from logs one has felled and chopped oneself seems to give
more heat than any other fire. Astride the leaping flames my thoughts go
riding one by one down paths which are lined and invaded with memories.

Suddenly the flames become the red reflection of a sun setting on rippling waves. The furrowed wake forms furtive fireflies against the receding
back-cloth. Tired after its long journey the liner lazily skirts the Point of
Almadies.[2] . . .

"So that's all your famous Humps[3] are?" an ironical voice beside me
asked.

Yes, indeed! This is all the Humps are, the most westerly point of Senegal. Scarcely three hundred feet high. I had to admit as much to this
young woman, who had been so shy and retiring during the voyage that I
had not been able to resist the temptation to call her Violet. It was no use
my telling her that farther on, as she was continuing the voyage, she would
find Fouta-Djallon and the Cameroon[4] Mountains; Violet still thought
that Nature had been mean in bestowing on Senegal no more than these
two ridiculous heaps of rock, here moss-covered, there quite bare.

It was only later, long after this first home-coming, when I was picking
up from Amadou-Koumba the crumbs of his knowledge and his wisdom,
that I learned, among many other things, exactly what the Humps were,
these two hummocks at the extremity of the Cape Verde[5] Peninsula, the
last land of Africa on which the sun gazes before plunging each evening
into the Great Ocean.[6]

When Memory goes a-gathering firewood, he brings back the sticks that
strike his fancy.[7] . . .

---

1. Translated by Dorothy S. Blair   2. The area west of Dakar where the continental landmass tapers
into the Atlantic Ocean. *Liner:* the passenger steamboat that used to link Bordeaux, France, to Dakar,
Senegal, before the advent of air travel.   3. Two hills on the outskirts of Dakar, lying close together and
overlooking the ocean, called "Les Mamelles" in French.   4. Volcanic mountain at the southern end
of the bend of the West African coastline. The Fouta-Djallon are a range of mountains in upper Guinea
from which the river Niger has its origins.   5. The administrative name for the western peninsular tip
of Senegal, which includes Dakar, the capital.   6. The Atlantic.   7. The use of proverbs to highlight
a theme or narrative detail is a typical device of the traditional storyteller.

This evening, as I sit by the fireside, my memory ties up with the same liana strand my little mountains, Momor's wives, and the shy, fair-haired Violet, for whom, in belated answer to her question, I relate the following tale as it was told to me by Amadou-Koumba.

In the matter of wives two is not a good number. The man who wants to avoid quarrels, shouting, grousing, reproaches, and nasty innuendoes must have at least three wives, or else one, but never two. Two women in the same house always have with them a third companion, who is not only good for nothing, but also happens to be the worst of bad counsellors. This companion is shrill-voiced Envy, bitter as tamarind[8] juice.

Khary, the first wife of Momor, was as envious as could be. She could have filled ten calabashes[9] with her jealousy and emptied them down a well, and she would still have had enough to fill ten times ten gourds in the depths of her coal-black heart.[1] It is true that Khary had perhaps no good reason to be very satisfied with her lot. In fact Khary was a hunchback. Mind you, it was quite a small, insignificant little hump; a hump that could easily be hidden under a well-starched camisole or a full, pleated *boubou*.[2] But Khary imagined that everyone was always staring at her hump.

She always heard her ears ringing with the shouts of "*Khary-khougué! Khary-khougué!*" (Khary-the-hunchback!), memories of the time when, like all children, she used to go naked to the waist, and her childhood playmates would jeer at her, asking her to lend them the baby she carried on her back. Full of fury she would pursue them, and woe betide the girl who fell into her clutches. She would scratch her face, pull her hair, tear off her earrings. Khary's victim could scream and weep herself sick; for she could only be rescued by those of her playmates who were not themselves too scared of Khary's fists and finger-nails, as grown-ups no more interfere in children's arguments and quarrels than they do in their games.

Khary's temper had not improved with age; on the contrary, it had soured like milk which an evil spirit has stepped across, and now it was Momor's turn to suffer from the unpleasant moods of his hunchbacked wife. When he went off to the fields Momor had to take his midday meal with him. Khary would not leave the house for fear of mocking glances, nor would she help her husband with the tilling, for the very same reason.

Weary of working the whole day and only eating a hot meal in the evening, Momor had decided to take a second wife, and so he had married Koumba.

At the sight of her husband's new wife Khary should have become the best of spouses, the most amiable of women; and that is what Momor, in his simplicity, had anticipated. But such was not the case.

Now Koumba was also a hunchback. But her hump really exceeded all proportions of what a decent hump should be. When she turned her back you would have thought that there was a dyer's pot holding up both her

8. A large tree with a tangy fruit.   9. Gourds, which were scooped out and used as household utensils.
1. An example of hyperbole (exaggeration), a regular feature of folktales.   2. A long flowing dress worn by women.

neckerchief and the calabash carried on her head. Yet, in spite of her hump, Koumba was light-hearted, sweet-natured, and friendly.

When the other children teased little Koumba-Khougue, when they played together, naked to the waist, and they asked her to lend them the baby she carried on her back, she would reply laughing louder than them all, "I'd be surprised if he'd come to you. He won't even get down to suckle!"

Later, when Koumba came into contact with grown-ups, she realised they were less given to teasing than children, but more spiteful. She did not change her character, however. In her husband's house she was just the same. She considered Khary as a big sister and tried to do everything to please her. She did all the heavy housework, she went down to the river with the washing, she winnowed the grain, and ground the millet. Every day she took Momor's meal out to him in the fields and helped him with his work.

Khary was by no means pleased by all this. On the contrary, she became more shrewish and spiteful than ever when she saw that Koumba did not seem to suffer from her huge hump. So greedy is Envy that it will feed on any dish.

So Momor lived, half-happy, between his two hunchbacked wives; the one affable, good-natured and friendly, the other spiteful, cantankerous, and peevish as a bear with a sore head.

Often in order to stay longer in the fields helping her husband, Koumba would take out food that she had prepared the night before, or at dawn the same morning. Then, when they had dug and hoed from sunrise till noon, and their shadows crouched behind their bodies, to take refuge from the heat of the day, Momor and Koumba stopped work. Koumba heated up the rice or the porridge which she shared with her husband; then they both lay down in the shade of a tamarind tree which stood in the middle of the field. But instead of sleeping like her husband, Koumba would stroke Momor's head, while she dreamed perhaps of women's bodies which were not deformed.

The tamarind is, of all trees, the one that provides the deepest shade; sometimes one can see the stars in broad daylight through its foliage which the sun can scarcely penetrate. That is what makes this tree the commonest haunt of spirits and ghosts, good spirits as well as bad, the ghosts of unsatisfied desires as well as those which have found fulfilment.

There is many a madman who shouts and sings by the evening, though he left his village or dwelling in the morning perfectly sane. This is because he has passed under a tamarind tree at midday, and has seen there what he should not have seen: the inhabitants of another world, spirits which he had offended by his words or actions.

Many a woman weeps and laughs, shouts and sings in the villages, driven out of her mind because she has poured boiling water from a cauldron on to the ground and scalded the spirits who were passing by or who were resting in the courtyard of her dwelling. These spirits have waited for her in the shade of a tamarind tree and made her lose her wits.[3]

---

3. A folk belief, which sets the scene for what follows.

Momor and Koumba had never offended the spirits, nor hurt them by either actions or words; so they could rest beneath the shade of the tamarind without fearing either visit or vengeance from the evil spirits.

Momor was sleeping that day, when Koumba, who was sewing nearby, thought she heard a voice calling her name from the tamarind. She looked up and there she espied, on the lowest branch of the tree, an old, old woman, whose long, white hair, whiter than cotton, hung down her back.

"Are you at peace,[4] Koumba?" asked the old woman.

"At peace, only, Mame (Grandmother)," replied Koumba.

"Koumba," went on the old woman, "I have known how good is your heart and how great is your merit, as long as you have known your right hand from your left.[5] I wish to do you a great service, for I know how well you deserve it. On Friday, at the full moon, the spirit-maidens will dance on the clay hill of N'Guew.[6] You will go up to the hill when the earth has grown cool. And when the tom-tom is at its wildest, and the ring of dancers whirls fastest, and as each dancer falls out she is immediately replaced by another,[7] then you will approach and you will say to the spirit-maiden nearest to you.

"Here, take the child that I have on my back; it is my turn to dance."

On Friday it happened that Momor slept in the hut of Khary, his first wife. The last of the villagers to retire were already turning over in their first sleep when Koumba left her hut and made her way towards the clay hill.

From a long way off she could hear the frenzied beating of the tom-tom and the clapping of hands. The spirit-maidens were dancing the *sa-n'diaye*,[8] twisting and turning in the middle of the merry ring. Koumba approached and clapped her hands to the hypnotic rhythm of the tom-tom and the frantic whirl of the dancers.

One, two, three . . . ten had whirled and swirled in an eddy of *boubous* and *pagnes*[9]. . . . Then Koumba said to the neighbour on her left, as she turned her back to her:

"Here, take the child for me, it is my turn to dance."

The spirit-maiden took her hump, and Koumba fled.

She ran and never stopped till she reached her hut, which she did just as the first cock crew.

The spirit-maiden could not catch her, for this was the signal for the tom-tom to cease and for the spirit-maidens to return to their own domains till the next Friday full moon.

Koumba no longer had her hump. Her finely braided hair fell on her neck which was now long and slender as a gazelle's. Momor saw her as he was leaving the hut of his first wife, thought that he was dreaming, and rubbed his eyes many times. Koumba told him what had happened.

Khary's saliva turned to gall in her mouth when she in turn spied Koumba drawing water from the well; her eyes became bloodshot, she opened her mouth which was dry as a lump of clay before the first rains,

---

4. A literal translation of the traditional greeting in Wolof.   5. That is, reached maturity.   6. An open area in the village that serves as a meeting place for people from all walks of life.   7. Traditional dances are often performed in a circle, with each dancer stepping into the middle to perform individually and then rejoining the circle.   8. A Wolof dance.   9. Women's dresses made from printed cotton.

and as bitter as a sindian root;[1] but no sound emerged and she fell down in a swoon. Momor and Koumba picked her up and carried her into her hut. Koumba watched over her, gave her water to drink, massaged her, and spoke gentle words to her.

When Khary recovered and was back on her feet again, almost suffocated by the jealousy that had risen from her belly to her throat, Koumba, as good a friend as ever, told her how she had lost her hump, and gave her instructions as to what she must do if she wished to be rid of hers.

Khary waited impatiently for the Friday of the full moon, which never seemed to come. The sun, dawdling the whole day in the fields, was in no hurry to return to his resting-place, while the moon took her time before leaving hers to take her flock of stars out to pasture.

Finally Friday of the full moon did arrive, since everything arrives eventually. That evening Khary ate nothing. She made Koumba repeat the advice and instructions the old woman with the cotton-white hair had given her by the tamarind tree. She heard all the noises of the early night grow fainter and vanish, and listened to the sounds of the late night arise and grow louder. When the earth was cool she made her way to the clay hill were the spirit-maidens were dancing.

The dancers were competing in skill, endurance, and suppleness, lured on and encouraged by the cries, singing, and hand-clapping of their companions who formed the circle around them, all anxious in their turn to show their talents to the quickened rhythm of the tom-tom beat.

Khary approached, clapping her hands as her husband's second wife had instructed her; then, when one, two, three, ten spirit-maidens had whirled around in the ring and come panting out, she said to her neighbour,

"Here, take the child from me, it's my turn to dance."

"Oh, no! Not on your life!" said the spirit-maiden. "It's my turn. Here, you look after this one for me; I've been left with it for a whole moon and no one has come to claim it."

With these words she planted on Khary's back the hump which Koumba had left with her. Just then the first cock crew, the spirits disappeared, and Khary was left alone on the clay hill, alone with her two humps.

The first hump, which was quite small, had made her suffer every moment of her life, and now she had another one, an enormous one, more than enormous! It was really more than she could ever endure.

Tucking up the skirt of her *pagne* she began to run. She ran for days, she ran for nights, she ran so far and so fast that she reached the sea and threw herself into the waves. But she did not disappear entirely; the sea would not swallow her altogether.

It is Khary-Khougué's two humps which jut out beyond the point of Cape Verde, and catch the last rays of the sun as it sets on the soil of Africa.

It is Khary's two humps which have become the Humps.

---

1. Thought to have medicinal properties.

The Bone[1]

"If he had his belly behind him, it would drag him into a hole." So runs the saying about the impenitent glutton.[2]

And, when talking about Mor Lame, one would add, "If your greed has not been the end of you, then it is not genuine greed!"

For Mor Lame was both a gourmand and a glutton.

In many of the villages, the cattle stocks, ravaged by the most deadly of plagues ever known in the memory of the elders, were slowly building up again. But in Lamene[3] no man of twenty knew what a horned beast looked like.

It is true that Lamene was not as old as the village of Niangal,[4] where, in times gone by, the traveller found, as he later sang, nothing but:

> Fresh fish for some
> Dried fish for others
> Chicken
> Was not yet
> Quite the fashion![5]

The thatch on all the huts had been renewed less often, and the fields ploughed less often than in Niangal. But if chicken had been the fashion for quite a long time, beef had been unknown for two generations.

That year the rains had been abundant, the earth bounteous, the locusts absent. The children had not been too carried away by their games and had guarded the young ears quite reasonably against the attacks of impudent millet-eaters.[6]

Many a cudgel had forced Golo[7]-the-Monkey and his tribe to respect the ground-nut[8] crop.

Since several members of his family had lost a paw or two in the traps set by the folk of Lamene, Thile-the-Jackal had deemed it wiser to go elsewhere in search of melons, which, if not juicier than those of Lamene, would at least be easier to gather and a less risky proposition for the picker.

In a word, the crops had been magnificent, undreamed of by the folk of Lamene.

So they had decided to send donkeys laden with millet, maize and ground-nuts down to Ferlo, where the Peul[9] tribes pasture their huge herds. Now these Peul folk hardly ever eat meat, for it is true that one becomes satiated with abundance. As the saying goes, "When gathering is too easy, bending down becomes difficult." However the Peul do not live on milk alone and are only too pleased to have millet, for they never touch harrow or hoe, in order to make a *couscous*[1] to mix with the milk from their cows, fresh, curdled, or sour.

---

1. Translated by Dorothy S. Blair.   2. It is standard procedure to announce the theme of a story with this kind of general observation.   3. A village in north-central Senegal.   4. Another village in north-central Senegal.   5. This song, which dwells on the monotony of the villagers' diet, emphasizes the interest of the meat-sharing ceremony that becomes central to the story.   6. The locusts. *Young ears:* that is, of the millet plant.   7. Monkey (Wolof). Diop usually combines the Wolof and French names of his animal characters.   8. Peanut.   9. The French word for the Fulani people, who are pastoralists. Ferlo is an area in northern Senegal, inhabited mainly by the Fulani; the region is less susceptible to drought than other parts of the country.   1. Steamed grains (usually wheat or millet) as well as the soup or stew that is served with them.

The donkeys had been gone for three moons, driven along the paths towards Ferlo by the strongest young men of Lamene, who had been instructed to bring back with them a fine seven-year-old bull.

The sharing-out of this animal (known as the *Tong-Tong*[2]) among the heads of families would allow the elders of the village, the old folk, and the middle-aged (the majority of whom, alas! were now toothless) to relearn the taste of red meat. The younger ones, who would probably only get the bones to gnaw in the end, would get to know, if not the taste, at least the smell of meat grilling or stewing.

The very day the donkeys and their drivers had set out, Mor Lame had decided in his own mind which morsel he would choose on the occasion of the *Tong-Tong*: a shin-bone, well covered with meat and full of juicy marrow. Every subsequent day he had said to his wife, Awa, "You will cook it very slowly, and for a long time, until it is tender and melts like butter in the mouth. And that day you'll see that no one comes near my hut!"

The day came when the young men of Lamene returned to the village from Ferlo, driving back in their midst a splendid bull with huge horns, a rope attached to its right hind leg, and its tawny coat gleaming in the setting sun. From its neck the dewlap, massive as a baobab[3] trunk, hung down to the ground.

At the risk of receiving a kick, which in fact he just avoided, Mor Lame came to feel his shin-bone. After reminding those who were responsible for killing and cutting up the bull at the first cock-crow, that this was the portion he had chosen, he went off to instruct his wife to cook it very slowly, very gently, and for a very long time.

The sharing-out was done as soon as the *assaloumou Aleykoum* had been said at the end of the *Fidjir* prayer.[4]

The children had scarcely begun to scrape off the shreds of the meat still clinging to the carcass, when Mor Lame was already in his hut. After closing and barricading the door, he gave his portion to his wife, saying, "Cook it slowly, gently, and for a very long time!"

Awa put into the pot everything necessary to stew a shinbone till it melts deliciously in the mouth and makes a rich creamy broth, a juicy sauce fit to accompany a calabash of *couscous*, cooked just right and mixed with just the right quantity of ground baobab seeds to make it easily digestible.

She put the pot on the fire and the lid on the pot.

Mor Lame lay down on his bed of branches and bark-fibres. Awa squatted near the fire, whose smoke blackened the roof of the hut. The aroma of the cooking slowly mounted and gradually drove away the smell of smoke, filling the whole hut and tickling Mor Lame's nostrils.

Mor Lame half rose, leaned on his elbow and asked his wife,

"Where is the bone?"

"The bone is there," replied Awa, lifting the lid and skewering the shin.

"Is it getting softer?"

---

2. A ceremony designed to help the poorer people obtain meat and for religious sacrifices.   3. A gigantic tree found in the dry areas of the West African savannah; its seeds and leaves are used for cooking. 4. Said at dawn, this is the first of the many prayers that Muslims are obliged to say throughout the day. *Assalamou Aleykoum*: Peace be unto you (Arabic), a standard greeting.

"It is getting softer."

"Put the lid back and stir up the fire!" ordered Mor Lame.

In Lamene everyone was a fervent believer and no adult ever missed a single prayer. So Moussa was astonished that day not to see Mor Lame, his hut brother, at the *yor-yor* prayer.[5]

He swore that he would taste some of that meat, and went to the home of the man who was his more-than-brother.

Stronger than brotherly love, more rigid than paternal love, "hut frater-nity"[6] subjects every man worthy of the name to rules, obligations, and laws which he cannot transgress without falling in everyone's estimation.

When, at the age of twelve, you have mingled the blood of your sex[7] with that of another boy one cold morning on the old mortar-stone set up on the ground; when you have sung the same initiatory songs with him, suffered the same blows, eaten from the same calabashes the same deli-cious or disgusting food; when in a word you have become a man at the same time as he and in the same hut, you are then the slave of his desires, the servant of his needs, the prisoner of his troubles, for all your life; before everyone—father and mother, uncles and brothers.

The day of the *Tong-Tong*, Moussa intended to use and even abuse this right, which custom and tradition gave him over Mor Lame.

"He shall not eat that bone all by himself! He shall not eat it without me!" he said to himself, as he hammered louder and louder on the fence surrounding Mor Lame's hut, calling to his hut-brother,

"It's me, Mor! It's me, Moussa, your more-than-brother! Let me in!"

At the sound of the knocking and the shouting, Mor Lame got up sud-denly and asked,

"Where is the bone?"

"The bone is there."

"Is it getting soft?"

Awa lifted the lid, skewered the shin, and said,

"It's getting soft."

"Put the lid back, stir up the fire, then go out and shut the door!" ordered her husband, as he took up a mat.

He spread his mat in the shade of a flame tree[8] in the middle of the courtyard, and then opened the gate to Moussa.

Cordial, merry greetings there were on the one hand; on the other, grunts and a surly face, like a back-side exposed to the cold morning air.

No one shuts the door in the face of a man who knocks, especially if he is your hut-brother. So Moussa came in and lay down beside Mor Lame, who rested his head on Awa's lap.

Perhaps they might have been able to hear something besides the twit-terings of birds, especially the hoarse, peevish chatter of the parrots, if Moussa had not kept up a ceaseless flow of conversation, all by him-self.

---

5. Said in the mid-morning.   6. A bond among men of the same age group who underwent the initia-tion ceremony together.   7. The principal element of the initiation ceremony is circumcision.   8. A tall tree with brightly colored flowers.

He talked of the district, of this man and of that, of the good old times of their youth! He revived the memories of their time in the "men's hut," in order to remind Mor Lame discreetly of his duties and obligations, if by chance he had forgotten them, or was inclined to neglect them.

Mor Lame was not in a talkative mood that day, and replied only "yes" and "no" and "perhaps" and "*inch Allah!*"[9] and even more often by those same grunts that had constituted the main part of his greeting.

The shade of the flame tree grew smaller and smaller, and was already exposing the feet of the two hut brothers to the heat of the sun.

Mor Lame beckoned to his wife. As she bent over him, he whispered into her ear,

"Where is the bone?"

"It is over there!"

"Is it soft yet?"

Awa got up, went into the hut; she lifted the lid of the pot, skewered the shin, put the lid back on the pot, came and sat down and then whispered to her husband,

"It's soft!"

The sun, having paused a moment at the zenith to see if he should retrace his steps or continue on his way, began to go down towards the west.

The shade of the flame tree stretched out to the east.

The Muezzin called the *Teshar*[1] prayer. Mor Lame and Moussa, with Awa far behind them, performed their devotions; they greeted their guardian angels, asked forgiveness and remission of their sins from the Lord, and then lay down again in the shade of the flame tree, which stretched ever further towards the east.

Another prayer. Then the *izan* prayer,[2] after which the sun, tired of his journey, retired to rest.

As soon as he had lain down for the last time, Mor Lame immediately took his wife aside and asked,

"Where is the bone?"

"The bone is over there."

"Is it soft?"

Awa went into the hut and came back saying,

"It is soft."

"That fellow, Moussa!" said her husband in an undertone, but with rage in his heart. "That dog that won't go away! Awa I'm going to fall ill."

And he did exactly what he said.

Rigid and trembling, he began to sweat like a water-cooler, hung up in the shade of a tamarind tree, shivering like milk which is just coming to the boil.

Assisted by Moussa, who, as a true hut brother, was most sympathetic

9. An Arabic expression, equivalent to "God willing."   1. One of the five required daily prayers. *Muezzin:* calls the faithful to prayer from the mosque's tower.   2. Said individually at the call of the muezzin, as opposed to collective prayers led by the imam (a religious leader) at the mosque.

with Mor Lame's sufferings, Awa carried her husband into another hut from the one where the stew-pot was boiling.

With his wife at the head of his bed and his hut brother at the foot Mor Lame groaned, shivering and sweating. He heard the hours passing until it was midnight.

Weakly he asked Awa,

"Where is the bone?"

"The bone is over there."

"Is it soft?"

"It is soft."

"Leave it there. This dog will not go away. Wife, I am going to die. Then he will be forced to go."

Having said this he pretended to be dead like a corpse already stiff and dry!

"Moussa, your hut brother is dead. Go and fetch Serigne-the-Marabout[3] and the people of the village!"

"No, indeed!" said Moussa most positively. "Never will I abandon my more-than-brother at this hour; nor will I leave you alone with his corpse! The earth is not yet cold; the first cock has not yet crowed. I shall not arouse the whole village. We will watch over him, we two together, as is our duty, we who are—or were—those most dear to him. When the sun rises, the women will pass by here on their way to the well. They will take it upon themselves to inform the people of the village."

And Moussa sat down at the feet of the "corpse" with Awa at its head. The earth grew cold; the first cock crew. The sun left his resting-place. Women passed Mor Lame's house, on their way to the well. Intrigued by the unusual silence they went in and learned of the death of Mor Lame. The news spread through Lamene like a whirlwind. Serigne-the-Marabout, the notables and all the men of the village invaded the house.

Awa bent over her husband and whispered in his ear,

"Mor, things are getting too serious. The whole village is here, in your house, come to wash you and wrap you in your shroud and bury you."

"Where is Moussa?" whispered the corpse of Mor Lame.

"Moussa is here."

"Where is the bone?"

"The bone is over there."

"Is it soft?"

"It is soft."

"Then let them wash me!" decreed Mor Lame.

Just as Serigne-the-Marabout was about to wrap him in the white shroud, seven cubits[4] long, Awa came forward and said:

"Serigne, my husband charged me to recite over his dead body a *sourate*[5] he taught me, so that the Lord would have mercy on him."

The Marabout and his followers retired. Then Awa whispered in her husband's ear,

3. A religious leader, equivalent to *imam*. The term is specific to Islam in French-speaking West Africa.
4. The cubit is an ancient measure of length, based on the distance from the elbow to the fingers, about a foot and a half.   5. A verse of the Koran; each one has a name related to different situations in life.

"Mor, get up! They are going to wrap you in your shroud and they will bury you if you go on pretending to be dead."

"Where is the bone?" inquired Mor's corpse.

"It's over there."

"Is it soft?"

"It is soft."

"And where is Moussa?"

"He is still here."

"Then let them wrap me in my shroud!" decided Mor Lame.

And so it was done.

And then his body was placed on a plank and covered with the coffin which served for all the dead. The holy words were spoken and he was carried to the cemetery.

Women do not accompany a burial to the cemetery, any more than they go into a Mosque.

But Awa suddenly remembered that she had another *sourate* to say over her husband's body, at the edge of the grave. So she ran after them, and when they had all drawn aside she fell on her knees near the head of the corpse and begged,

"Mor Lame, get up! You are going too far. They are going to bury you now."

"Where is the bone?" asked Mor Lame, through his shroud.

"The bone is at home."

"Is it soft? Is it nice and soft?"

"It is nice and soft."

"And Moussa?"

"Moussa is still here."

"Then let them bury me. I hope he will go away in the end!"

The last prayers were said and the body of Mor Lame was lowered into the grave, lying on the right side.[6]

The first clods of earth were already half covering the departed, when Awa asked once more to be allowed to say a last *sourate*.

"Mor Lame!" she whispered into the grave, "Mor, get up, they are filling up the grave!"

"Where is the bone?" asked Mor Lame, through the sand and his shroud.

"It is at home," answered Awa, through her tears.

"Is it soft?"

"It is soft."

"Where is Moussa?"

"He is still here."

"Let them fill up my grave."

Mor Lame, the glutton, Mor-the-Greedy, was still busy explaining to the Angel of Death, who had come to take him away, and who did not seem to understand that he was not really dead, "Hey! I'm only here on account of a bone!" when Serigne-the-Marabout, with the approval of the elders of the village, who are always of good counsel, decided,

"Moussa, you were the hut brother, the more-than-brother of the late

---

6. The position in which Muslims are laid in the grave.

Mor Lame. Awa cannot pass into better hands than yours. As soon as the period of a widow's mourning is over, you will take her for your wife.[7] She will be a good wife to you."

And everybody went their way with many an "*inch Allah!*"

Then Moussa, who was already acting as the master of the house in place of the late Mor Lame, asked Awa,

"Where is the bone?"

"It is here," replied the docile widow.

"Bring it and let us make an end of it."

Mother Crocodile[1]

The most stupid of all animals that fly, walk or swim, that live beneath the ground, in water, or in the air, are undoubtedly crocodiles, which crawl on the earth and walk at the bottom of the water.

"That is not my opinion," said Amadou Koumba. "That is what Golo the monkey says. And although everyone agrees that Golo is the most coarsely spoken of all creatures, since he is their *griot*[2] he sometimes manages to make the most sensible remarks, so some say; or at least to make us believe he has made them, according to others."

So Golo was in the habit of stating to anyone who was prepared to listen to him that crocodiles were the most stupid of all creatures, for no other reason than that they had the best memories.

There is no means of knowing whether Golo intended this to be praise or blame, the expression of envy or contempt. Indeed, as far as memory is concerned, Golo must have arrived late when the Lord was sharing it out. In spite of his great love of mischief, his empty head very quickly forgets the tricks he is continually playing on everyone in turn, to the detriment of his ribs and his hairless posterior. So his opinion of crocodiles might have been expressed one day when he had a bone to pick with Diassigue, the Mother-Crocodile, who might have taken a somewhat rough revenge for a little bit of teasing.

Diassigue had a good memory. It is possible that she had the best memory in the world, for she was content, from her lair in the mud or under the sunny banks of the river, to watch animals, things, and men, and collect the sounds and news the canoes confided to the gossiping fish from the mountains of Fouta-Djallon as far as the Great Sea,[3] where the sun goes down to bathe at the end of the day. She listened to the chatter of the women who came to wash linen, scour calabashes, or draw water at the river. She listened to the donkeys and the camels who came from far off, from north and south, and set down their loads of millet and of rubber, staying long to quench their thirst.[4] The birds came to tell her what the wild ducks whistled as they passed overhead, flying back to the sands.[5]

---

7. A reference to the levirate, a custom by which a man inherited his dead brother's widow. The custom was prevalent in nearly all ancient societies and is still practiced in many traditional societies. 1. Translated by Dorothy S. Blair. 2. A traditional storyteller and oral historian. 3. From far inland in Guinea to the Atlantic Ocean off Senegal, a distance of some fifteen hundred miles. 4. Besides providing realistic details of daily life in the region, the passage indicates Diassigue's attentive disposition, an essential factor of her wisdom. 5. The Sahara, immediately to the north and northwest.

So Diassigue had a good memory;[6] and much as he deplored this, in his heart of hearts Golo had to admit it. As for her being stupid, Golo's statement was pure exaggeration; in fact he lied like the buffoon that he was. But the saddest part of the whole business was that Diassigue's children, the little crocodiles, began to share the monkey's opinion of their mother, imitating in this the cunning and malicious hare Leuk, whose conscience is as mobile as the pair of old, worn-out slippers which he has been wearing clipped on to his head since the day he took them off to run faster, and which he has used as ears ever since. Thile-the-Jackal, who always tacks from right to left as he runs, even on the bare sand, for fear of some unexpected attack, Thile also thought like Golo, Leuk, and Bouki-the-Hyena, that thief and coward, whose hind-quarters always seem to be sagging beneath a shower of blows, like Thioye-the-Parrot, whose round tongue is always colliding with her fish-hook of a beak which catches all the ill-natured gossip and tittle-tattle that flies around on the four winds. Sègue-the-Panther, with her reputation for double-dealing, might well have shared the opinion of all this common rabble, but she bore Golo too much of a grudge for the thrashings she got from him every time she tried to jump up into the highest branches of a tree to catch him, from which her nose was still bruised.

So Diassigue's own children also began to believe that Golo was speaking the truth. They thought that perhaps their mother really did sometimes talk a lot of nonsense.

When she became weary of the sun's caresses, or tired of watching the moon ceaselessly quenching her thirst in the water half the night through, or bored with watching stupid canoes[7] swim past, with their bellies upward, down the river that travels as fast as they do, then Diassigue would collect her offspring and tell them stories, histories of men, not of crocodiles, for crocodiles have no history.[8] And that is possibly what annoyed them instead of pleasing them—poor little crocodiles.

So Mother-Crocodile would collect her children around her and tell them what she had seen, what her mother had seen and told to her, and what her mother's mother had seen and told to her mother.

The little crocodiles often yawned when she told them of warriors and merchants from Ghana,[9] whom her great-grandmother had seen sailing up and down the rivers in search of slaves and the gold of N'Galam.[1] When she told them of Soumangourou, of Soun Diata Keita[2] and of the empire of Mali. When she told them of the first men with white skin whom her grandmother had seen bowing low to the rising sun after first washing their arms, their faces, their feet, and their hands; of the red colour of the water[3] after the passing of the white men, who had taught the black men to bow down like them to the rising sun. This exceeding red

---

6. Symbolic of knowledge derived from accumulated experience.   7. The epithet extends to the men who row the canoes.   8. An ironic reference to the conventional idea of Africa in Western colonial ideology.   9. The medieval empire in West Africa from which the modern country takes its name. 1. A mine in western Senegal, famous for its high concentration of gold. It has given rise to a Wolof expression denoting any object of high quality.   2. That is, Son-Jara Keita. Soumangourou was Son-Jara's arch-rival (see *The Epic of Son-Jara*, in Volume 1).   3. An allusion to the conversion by the sword of the West African indigenous populations to Islam by the Arab invaders (*the first men with white skin*). *Bowing low:* Muslims say their prayers with their faces turned to Mecca, in the east.

colour of the river had forced her grandmother to leave the Senegal River and go, by way of the Bafing and the Tinkisso, down to the King of Rivers, the Djoliba, the Niger,[4] where she found more white-eared men who had come down from the country of the sands. Her grandmother had seen more wars and corpses there; so many corpses that the greediest of crocodile families could have suffered an attack of indigestion lasting seven times seven moons. There she had seen empires born and kingdoms die.

The little crocodiles yawned when Diassigue told them what her mother had seen and heard: Kouloubali overthrowing the King of the Manding, n'Golo Diara who had lived for three times thirty years and had beaten the Mossi[5] on the eve of his death; when she told them of the Toucouleur Samba Lame, who had been master of the river, master of the Brack-Oualo, master of Damel King of the Cayor and master of the Moors,[6] which makes the Toucouleur fisherfolk even more conceited as they sing his praises over the heads of the little crocodiles and disturb their frolics with their long rods.

When Diassigue spoke the little crocodiles yawned or dreamed of crocodile exploits, of distant banks from which the river washed away gold nuggets and gold dust, and where every year a nubile virgin with fresh young flesh would be offered to the crocodiles. They dreamed of those distant lands, yonder in Pinkou,[7] where the sun was born; lands where crocodiles were gods, or so they had been told one day by Ibis-the-Pilgrim, the wisest of birds. They dreamed of going down to the vast distant lakes of Macina, to hear the songs of the Bozo[8] oarsmen, and find out whether what Dougoudougou, the little duck, had told them was true, namely that these songs were more like those of Oualo women, who came down to wash their linen near the crocodile holes, than those of the Somono[9] canoemen, whose ancestors had come from the mountains of the south, on the banks of the Niger, when Diassigue's mother was swimming up the big river.

They dreamed of the Bafing and the Bakoy, the blue river and the white river, which meet down in Bafoulabe[1] to form the river in which they lived. They dreamed of those nuptial places, where, according to the tales the Dog-Fish told, nothing separated the waters of the two rivers, and yet each one kept its own colour for a long, long distance. They would have loved to swim in the waters of the two rivers at the same time; such was the dream of little crocodiles, to have one side of their body in the blue river, one side in the white river, and their back-bone burning in the sun.

They often dreamed of following the same course as their great-grand-

---

4. The most important river in West Africa. Apart from its great size, the river has dominated life in the region for centuries, acquiring a legendary quality, hence the epithet "King of Rivers." The Senegal (in the north) serves for much of its length as the border with Mauritania. The Bafing and Tinkisso rivers run through Mali and the Niger Republic, emptying into the Niger.   5. An ethnic group in Burkina Faso and Mali. *Kouloubali:* a Malian surname; the reference is obscure. N'*Golo Diara:* from the context, one of the rulers of the ancient Manding Empire of Mali, thus in the line of Son-Jara.   6. Specifically, the Mauritanians of Arab origin. *The Toucouleur:* originally inhabitants of the Tekrour Empire, now living in Senegal, Mauritania, and Mali. *Brack-Oualo:* the title of the ruler of the Walo kingdom in northern Senegal. The kingdom lasted until the late 19th century, when it was conquered by France.   7. The East (Wolof).   8. An ethnic group in Mali. Macina is a Muslim state in central Mali.   9. An ethnic group in Mali.   1. A village in Mali, at the confluence of the river Niger and the Senegal River. *Bakoy:* a river in Mali.

mother, travelling down from the Senegal River to the Niger, by way of the Bafing and the Tinkisso. The little crocodiles' dreams, like their parents' teeth, never stopped growing. They dreamed of great crocodile exploits, and Diassigue, the Mother-Crocodile, could only tell them tales of men, of wars, of massacres of men by other men . . .

That is why the little crocodiles were ready to share Golo's opinion of their mother, an opinion which had been passed on to them by Thioker-the-Partridge, the most scandal-mongering of birds.

One morning some crows flew very high above the river croaking:

> A naked sun—a sun of gold
> A naked sun of an early dawn
> Sheds its golden light of morn
> On the banks of the river of gold[2]

Diassigue emerged from her hole in the side of the bank and watched the crows fly away.

At midday other crows followed, flying lower, and croaking:

> A naked sun—a sun all white
> A sun all naked and white
> Sheds its silvery light
> On the river all white

Diassigue lifted her nose and watched the crows fly away.

At twilight other crows came and perched on the bank and croaked:

> A naked sun—a sun all red
> A sun all naked and red
> Sheds its streams of blood all red
> On the river all red.

Diassigue approached with measured, dignified step, her flabby belly scraping the sand, and asked them the meaning of their migration and their song.

"Brahim Saloum has declared war on Yeli,"[3] the crows told her.

Very upset, Diassigue hurried home.

"Children," she said, "the Emir of Trarza has declared war on the Wolofs. We must get away from here."

The youngest of the crocodile sons asked,

"What difference does it make to us crocodiles if the Wolofs of Walo fight against the Moors of Trarza?"

"My child," replied Mother-Crocodile, "the dry grass can set fire to the green grass.[4] Let us go."

But the little crocodiles would not follow their mother.

As soon as Yeli had crossed the river with his army and had set foot on the north bank, on Ghana territory, he guessed his adversary's intention to

---

2. This song, with its variations marking the onset of war, would normally be taken up by the audience in an oral performance. 3. The personal name of the king (Brack-Oualo) of Walo. Brahim Saloum was a Mauritanian ruler, later referred to as "the Emir of Trarza." 4. The use of the proverb here conforms to its function in the folktale to bring home its moral; more generally, proverbs function as vehicles of collective wisdom.

draw him as far from the river as possible. In fact, the Moors, who had come right down to the river to hurl defiance at the Walo army, now seemed to flee before the Wolofs. They did not wish to join battle till they were a long way off, far to the north, in the sands, where the black men would be out of sight of the river which made them invisible whenever they bathed or drank from it before the battle. Before pursuing the men of Trarza, Yeli ordered his men to fill all the water-skins that the camels and donkeys carried. They were then forbidden to touch them until the command was given.

For seven days the Walo army pursued the Moors; finally Brahim Saloum halted his warriors, judging the Wolofs to be far enough away from the river to suffer from thirst as soon as they began to fight, and battle was joined.

The most terrible fighting raged for seven days, during which time each Wolof had to choose his Moor and each Moor had to attack his black man. Yeli was engaged in single combat against Brahim Saloum and his five brothers. He killed the Emir on the first day. On each of the succeeding five days he killed one brother. On the seventh day he picked up the son of Brahim Saloum who had been abandoned by the Trarza army on the field of battle. The heir to the Moorish kingdom bore a wound on his right side. Yeli took him back with him to his capital.

All the priests and medicine-men were summoned to care for the young captive prince. But all the attention lavished on him seemed only to aggravate the wound.

Finally there came to the court of Brack-Walo an old, old woman, who prescribed the effective remedy. This remedy was: to apply, three times a day, to the sore place, the fresh brain of a young crocodile.

LÉOPOLD SÉDAR SENGHOR
born 1906

Léopold Sédar Senghor's poetry takes as its primary subject the encounter between Africa and Europe. The harsh circumstances of this encounter, the conflict between two races and their conceptions of life, together with the pressure of this situation on his personal world, provide the background to his intense exploration of the historical and moral implications of the African and black experience in modern times. But it is essential to see how his concerns become transmuted into an art that takes them beyond their immediate historical reference. For Senghor's poetry reflects the movement of his sensibility beyond the contingencies of a collective and personal history toward a broader vision of humanity.

Senghor was born in Joal, a small fishing village in the Sine-Saloum basin in west-central Senegal, then a colony of France. His father, who was a Serer (the dominant ethnic group of his native region), was a prosperous and influential merchant. His mother was a Peul, one of a pastoral and nomadic people found all over the northern savannah belt of western Africa. This double ethnic ancestry was later to assume a larger meaning for Senghor. As he says in *Prayer of the Senegalese*

Soldiers: "I grew up in the heartland of Africa, at the crossroads / Of castes and races and roads." Senghor's early childhood seems to have been a serene and sheltered time within a closely knit pastoral community, and his memory of it has acquired a unique symbolic value in his poetry. Senghor has also indicated that the two most important influences in his childhood were those of his maternal uncle, who gave him his early education in the traditional culture (as was customary in a matrilineal society), and that of the poet Marônne, whose recitations of the traditional oral poetry introduced him to the imaginative uses of language.

Senghor's encounter with the French language did not begin until he was seven, when he was sent to the local elementary school to start his formal education. The following year, his father transferred him to a boarding school run by Catholic missionaries in the nearby village of Ngasobil. After elementary school, Senghor entered the Collège Libermann, a junior seminary in Dakar, the capital of Senegal, with the intention of becoming a Catholic priest. He abandoned the plan after six years, however, and enrolled in the state secondary school, the Lycée van Vollenhoven, where he distinguished himself as a star pupil, winning the prize in French every year. Obtaining his *baccalauréat* in 1928, he won a state scholarship to continue his education in France. He arrived in Paris in the autumn of the same year and enrolled in the Lycée Louis-le-Grand to prepare for entry into the prestigious École Normale Supérieure. His arrival in Paris brought him in direct contact with French people and French culture and began a relationship marked by conflicting emotions of attachment and discomfort.

The late 1920s and early 1930s were a period of political, social, intellectual, and artistic upheaval in Europe. The troubled state of Europe made a profound impression on the young African scholar, who had previously held a distant and idealized image of the European continent. From the beginning of his sojourn in France, Senghor found himself at the center of a group of African and Caribbean students and intellectuals who had been influenced by radical currents in Western thought, in particular Marxism, as well as by the militant literature of black American writers such as Langston Hughes, Claude McKay, and Countee Cullen, associated with the Harlem Renaissance. This group included Aimé Césaire, a fellow student, with whom Senghor struck up an important friendship. It was through their collaboration that the Négritude movement, with its challenge of the colonial order and passionate concern for the rehabilitation of Africa and the black race, developed. Also inspiring were the Pan-African activities of W. E. B. Du Bois, whose *Souls of Black Folk*, published early in the century, sought to inspire race pride and a sense of African identity among African-Americans and also contributed to the growing racial consciousness of the French-speaking black world.

During this period Senghor became acquainted with the modernist current of Baudelaire and his Symbolist successors. The influence of Baudelaire and Verlaine on Senghor is direct, and his poetry reflects their evocative manner and expressive musicality. To the succeeding Surrealist movement, Senghor's poetry owes little in style and manner, but he does seek to translate into an African register the Surrealist view of life with its appeal to the inner forces of consciousness and quasi-mystical conception of reality. Similarly valuable to Senghor was the poetry of Paul Claudel, whose organic images celebrate the mysteries of the Catholic faith. Claudel's powerful poetic temperament found expression in an ample verse form that allies the movement of modern free verse to the cadences of the Bible, as in the Psalms and other Old Testament books. This verse form, known in French as the *verset*, was taken over by Senghor, who infused into it elements of the oral poetry of traditional Africa. In other French poets as well (such as Charles Péguy and St. John Perse), Senghor found models for his own effort, always, however, shaping what he learned to his own needs.

Senghor's Parisian studies culminated in 1935 with his passing the highly competitive examination for the *agrégation*, the first African to be awarded the degree. This opened up for him a career in the French educational system, and for the next five years, he held various teaching positions, notably at Tours in central France and St. Martin-des-Fossés near Paris, where he began to write the poems later collected in his first volume *Chants d'ombre* (Shadow songs, 1945). At the outbreak of World War II in 1939, he was drafted as an officer into the French army and saw service on the northern front, where he was taken prisoner by the Germans in 1940. He spent his time during his internment learning German and writing the poems that make up *Hosties noires* (Black hosts, 1948). In 1942, released on health grounds but confined to Paris, he resumed teaching and in 1944 was appointed professor of African languages at the École Nationale de la France d'Outre-Mer. After the war, he was active in the effort to promote a new understanding of Africa and helped to launch a cultural journal, *Présence Africaine*, founded in Paris in 1947 by his friend and compatriot Alioune Diop, as a vehicle for African and black self-affirmation. The following year, Senghor published the historic *Anthologie de la nouvelle poésie nègre et malgache*, which may be said to have launched Négritude as a movement, due largely to the impact of the prefatory essay, *Orphée noir* (Black Orpheus), by the eminent French philosopher Jean-Paul Sartre. Sartre provided both a critical review of French-speaking black poetry and a philosophical exposition of the concept of Négritude. The publication of *Chants pour Naët* (Songs for Naët, 1948), a collection of love poems dedicated to his first wife, confirmed Senghor's status as a lyric poet of the first order. Meanwhile, his political career had begun with his election in 1946 to the French Constituent Assembly as deputy for Senegal, a career that was to be distinguished by service as a spokesman for Africa in the French parliament under the Fourth Republic and was to culminate in his election to the presidency of Senegal at its independence from France in 1960. Politics and literature thus came to run more or less parallel, as complementary aspects of a life devoted to the African cause.

Senghor's first volume, *Chants d'ombre*, is a kind of mental diary of his experience of cultural exile in Europe. The poems are marked by an acute sense of solitude, the physical separation from his homeland becoming symbolic of a more profound estrangement, that of the soul from its roots. The theme of exile runs through the volume. A complementary aspect of this theme is the poet's nostalgia for his origins. The memory of Africa is colored by its association with his childhood, which becomes transformed into an anterior state of grace. Thus he declares, in the poem *Prayer of the Senegalese Soldiers*: "I have chosen to live near the rebuilt walls of my memory / And from the top of the high ramparts / I remember Joal-of-the-Shades / The face of the land of my blood." This recall of origins signals a movement to a unified experience of the self. But beyond this quest for harmony, the African theme registers the poet's broader affirmation of his antecedents, of a historical and spiritual continuity that forms the basis of his identity. The bond with nature, the living presence of the ancestors, the supernatural as informing principle of visible reality, these are some of the motifs around which Senghor weaves his themes, as a mode of reconnection with his African origins. The historical consciousness is linked in his poetry with a metaphysical conception of human destiny: the individual participating in the life of the community attains to a larger relation with the forces of creation.

Senghor's later volumes develop and amplify this progression from the social and psychological to the imaginative and visionary. Although the political emphasis is more pronounced in *Hosties noires*, the same movement is implied. Through their direct reference to World War II, the poems constitute a commentary on public events and a judgment on the passions behind those events. The critique of Europe and the colonial protest are intertwined; this is conveyed in the title of the volume, which suggests the sacrifice of Africans to the blind fury of the European war. The association also carries religious overtones: that of the collective passion of the black race, conferring on it the nobility of suffering. The African image thus takes on an explicit polemical role in the volume; the opposition between Africa and Europe is not only historical and political but also moral and spiritual. The European war is seen as an apocalypse in which Africa assumes the aspect of a redeeming force and the black poet becomes the prophet of a new hope for humanity. This polemical and limited vision assumes, however, another dimension: at its heart lies a conflict that lends a poignancy to his critique of Europe. The appeal of the humanist ideals of French civilization remains too strong for him and its intellectual and literary traditions run too deeply in his nature to admit of a total and untroubled rejection. His commitment to the African cause produces a singular ambivalence. At the same moment that Senghor reaffirms his African belonging, he also seeks to transcend the antithesis created by the colonial situation and to elaborate a new ideal of unity that would embrace both halves of his awareness. This need lies behind Senghor's idea of a *Civilisation de l'universel*, which has become a key component of his conception of Négritude.

Between 1949 and 1960, Senghor's energies were absorbed by politics and his crusade for the rehabilitation of Africa and its peoples, through a constant stream of essays and lectures in France and other parts of Europe as well as in Africa. His writings during this period, later collected in four volumes under the title *Liberté*, demonstrate a concern for a reassessment of Africa's civilization and values and a redefinition of the African continent's place in the modern world. In 1956, Senghor's collection *Ethiopiques* inaugurated a new direction in his poetry, one less overtly related to the colonial experience. This new direction was confirmed in subsequent volumes: *Nocturnes* (1961), *Elégie des Alizés* (Elegy of the west wind, 1968), *Lettres d'hivernage* (Letters in the rainy season, 1973), and *Elégies Majeures* (1979). The later poetry confirms Senghor's standing as a great lyric poet, turning to a deeper exploration of the poetic self and developing a more complex attitude to the world. The interplay between the elegiac and the lyrical that runs as an undercurrent in the early poems receives in this later work an expanded frame of reference. The tensions of public life are balanced against the comforts of love, the death of individuals and of civilizations, and the assurance of rebirth within the stream of the universal life. If in the early volumes Senghor voices an individual predicament as part of a collective historical plight, in the later poetry, his vision embraces a wider universe of experience.

It is especially in this perspective that Africa reveals its central significance as prime mediator of his vision. Senghor's African beliefs and symbolic schemes give depth of meaning and even a ritual dimension to his poetry. The constant recourse to organic imagery indicates a consciousness formed by an agrarian culture and shows a preoccupation with growth, with a sense of the surge of life in the natural world, characteristic of an animist outlook. The dominant imagery of *night* derives its importance from its association with Africa and blackness. Night carries connotations of peace and meditation, of the propitious presence of the dead, and of the mystic life of the African continent and the universe. It is the organizing symbol of Senghor's poetry, representing for him the authentic mode of the black poet's imagination: "I proclaim the Night more truthful than the day." Africa is envisaged, then, in poetic terms; it becomes an image both of the racial homeland and of humanity's appropriate relation to the universe:

I would choose the poetry of the rivers, the winds, the forests,
The assonance of the plains and streams, choose the rhythm of my naked body's
    blood
Choose the vibrating balaphons and the harmony of chords. . . . I choose my toil-
    ing black people, my peasant people.

Although a controversial figure in African literary and intellectual circles, Senghor is widely respected as both poet and statesman. When he voluntarily gave up power as president of Senegal in 1980 to go into private life, he left behind an outstanding contribution to the political and social development of Africa and to the continent's cultural and intellectual renaissance. His election to the French Academy in 1983 came as a fitting recognition of one of the foremost modern writers in the French language.

Of the abundant critical literature on Senghor's work in French, little is yet available in English. Sylvia Washington Bâ's *The Concept of Négritude in the Poetry of Léopold Sédar Senghor* (1973) provides the most comprehensive discussion of the work. Both Okechukwu Mezu, *The Poetry of Léopold Sédar Senghor* (1973), and Janice Spleth, *Léopold Sédar Senghor* (1985), present useful overviews. The selections presented here are taken from *The Collected Poetry* (1991), translated by Melvin Dixon, whose introduction is helpful. Also useful are Ellen Conroy Kennedy, *The Négritude Poets* (1989), and Lilyan Kesteloot, *Black Writers in French* (1991). For accounts of Senghor's life and intellectual development, with incidental comments on his poetry, see Jacques Louis Hymans, *Léopold Sédar Senghor: An Intellectual Biography* (1971), and Janet G. Vaillant, *Black, French and African: A Life of Léopold Sédar Senghor* (1990).

PRONOUNCING GLOSSARY

The following list uses common English syllables to provide rough equivalents of selected words whose pronunciation may be unfamiliar to the general reader.

Dyouma: *joom-a*

Guéolowâr: *gayl-wahr*

guimm: *geem*

Ngom: *en-gom*

Nyaout Mbodybe: *en-yah-oot em-boj*

Sine: *seen*

Tamsir Dargui Ndyâye: *tahm-seer dahr-gee enjahee*

Tyâné: *cha-nay*

Woi: *woh-ee*

Letter to a Poet[1]

to Aimé Césaire

To my Brother *aimé*,[2] beloved friend, my bluntly fraternal greetings!
Black sea gulls like seafaring boatmen have brought me a taste
Of your tidings mixed with spices and the noisy fragrance of Southern
    Rivers[3]
And Islands.[4] They showed your influence, your distinguished brow,
The flower of your delicate lips. They are now your disciples,   5

---

1. All selections translated by Melvin Dixon.   2. Beloved (French). The poem pays homage to fellow poet Aimé Césaire (p. 2217).   3. Senghor plays here on the poetic resonance of the French administrative term (*Rivières du Sud*) for the area comprising the former French empire in west and central Africa.
4. The Caribbean, where Césaire was born.

A hive of silence, proud as peacocks. You keep their breathless zeal
From fading until moonrise. Is it your perfume of exotic fruits,
Or your wake of light in the fullness of day?
O, the many plum-skin women in the harem of your mind!

Still charming beyond the years, embers aglow under the ash   10
Of your eyelids, is the music we stretched our hands
And hearts to so long ago. Have you forgotten your nobility?
Your talent to praise the Ancestors, the Princes,
And the Gods, neither flower nor drops of dew?[5]
You were to offer the Spirits the virgin fruits of your garden   15
—You ate only the newly harvested millet blossom
And stole not a petal to sweeten your mouth.
At the bottom of the well of my memory, I touch your face
And draw water to refresh my long regret.
You recline royally, elbow on a cushion of clear hillside,   20
Your bed presses the earth, easing the toil of wetland drums
Beating the rhythm of your song, and your verse
Is the breath of the night and the distant sea.
You praised the Ancestors and the legitimate princes.
For your rhyme and counterpoint you scooped a star from the
    heavens.   25
At your bare feet poor men threw down a mat of their year's wages,
And women their amber[6] hearts and soul-wrenching dance.

My friend, my friend—Oh, you will come back, come back!
I shall await you under the mahogany tree,[7] the message
Already sent to the woodcutter's boss. You will come back   30
For the feast of first fruits[8] when the soft night
In the sloping sun rises steaming from the rooftops
And athletes,[9] befitting your arrival,
Parade their youthfulness, adorned like the beloved.

Night in Sine[1]

Woman, place your soothing hands upon my brow,
Your hands softer than fur.
Above us balance the palm trees, barely rustling
In the night breeze. Not even a lullaby.
Let the rhythmic silence cradle us.   5
Listen to its song. Hear the beat of our dark blood,
Hear the deep pulse of Africa in the mist of lost villages.

Now sets the weary moon upon its slack seabed
Now the bursts of laughter quiet down, and even the storyteller
Nods his head like a child on his mother's back   10
The dancers' feet grow heavy, and heavy, too,
Come the alternating voices of singers.

5. The conventions of Western lyricism are contrasted to the more pressing social themes of the black poet.   6. A translucent stone, with a brownish yellow hue.   7. Of royal significance.   8. The harvest festival.   9. Wrestlers, the traditional sporting heroes of Senegal.   1. A river in Senegal. The Serer, Senghor's ethnic group, inhabit the basin formed by the confluence of Sine and Saloum.

Now the stars appear and the Night dreams
Leaning on that hill of clouds, dressed in its long, milky pagne.[2]
The roofs of the huts shine tenderly. What are they saying   15
So secretly to the stars? Inside, the fire dies out
In the closeness of sour and sweet smells.

Woman, light the clear-oil lamp. Let the Ancestors
Speak around us as parents do when the children are in bed.
Let us listen to the voices of the Elissa[3] Elders. Exiled like us   20
They did not want to die, or lose the flow of their semen in the sands.
Let me hear, a gleam of friendly souls visits the smoke-filled hut,
My head upon your breast as warm as tasty *dang*[4] steaming from the fire,
Let me breathe the odor of our Dead, let me gather
And speak with their living voices, let me learn to live   25
Before plunging deeper than the diver[5]
Into the great depths of sleep.

Black Woman

Naked woman, black woman
Dressed in your color[1] that is life, in your form that is beauty!
I grew up in your shadow. The softness of your hands
Shielded my eyes, and now at the height of Summer and Noon,
From the crest of a charred hilltop I discover you, Promised Land[2]   5
And your beauty strikes my heart like an eagle's lightning flash.

Naked woman, dark woman
Ripe fruit with firm flesh, dark raptures of black wine,
Mouth that gives music to my mouth
Savanna of clear horizons, savanna quivering to the fervent caress   10
Of the East Wind,[3] sculptured tom-tom, stretched drumskin
Moaning under the hands of the conqueror
Your deep contralto voice[4] is the spiritual song of the Beloved.

Naked woman, dark woman
Oil no breeze can ripple, oil soothing the thighs   15
Of athletes and the thighs of the princes of Mali[5]
Gazelle with celestial limbs, pearls are stars
Upon the night of your skin. Delight of the mind's riddles,
The reflections of red gold from your shimmering skin
In the shade of your hair, my despair   20
Lightens in the close suns of your eyes.

Naked woman, black woman
I sing your passing beauty and fix it for all Eternity
before jealous Fate reduces you to ashes to nourish the roots of life.

---

2. Printed cloth (French African); here the Milky Way, with which the moon appears to be robed.
3. A village in Guinea Bissau, south of Senegal, where Senghor's ancestors are buried.   4. A cereal
meal.   5. The setting moon.   1. A reference to the green vegetation of the African landscape, to
which the black woman is assimilated.   2. The analogy with the Israelites in the Old Testament of the
Bible confers a religious note on this poem.   3. The Harmattan, a dry, sharp wind that blows from the
Sahara, northeast of Senegal, between November and April.   4. An allusion to the vocal register of
Marian Anderson (1897–1993), an African-American singer famous for her rendering of Negro spirituals.
5. The ancient empire of the West African savanna.

Prayer to the Masks

Masks![1] O Masks!
Black mask, red mask, you white-and-black masks
Masks of the four cardinal points where the Spirit blows
I greet you in silence!
And you, not the least of all, Ancestor with the lion head.[2]   5
You keep this place safe from women's laughter
And any wry, profane smiles[3]
You exude the immortal air where I inhale
The breath of my Fathers.
Masks with faces without masks, stripped of every dimple   10
And every wrinkle
You created this portrait, my face leaning
On an altar of blank paper[4]
And in your image, listen to me!
The Africa of empires is dying—it is the agony   15
Of a sorrowful princess
And Europe, too, tied to us at the navel.
Fix your steady eyes on your oppressed children
Who give their lives like the poor man his last garment.
Let us answer "present" at the rebirth of the World   20
As white flour cannot rise without the leaven.[5]
Who else will teach rhythm to the world
Deadened by machines and cannons?
Who will sound the shout of joy at daybreak to wake orphans and the
    dead?
Tell me, who will bring back the memory of life   25
To the man of gutted hopes?
They call us men of cotton, coffee, and oil
They call us men of death.
But we are men of dance, whose feet get stronger
As we pound upon firm ground.[6]   30

Letter to a Prisoner

Ngom! Champion of Tyâné![1]

It is I who greet you, I your village neighbor, your heart's neighbor.
I send you my white[2] greeting like the dawn's white cry,
Over the barbed wires of hate and stupidity,
And I call you by your name and your honor.   5

1. Representatives of the spirits of the ancestors. In African belief, the ancestors inhabit the immaterial world beyond the visible, from there offering protection to their living descendants.   2. The animal totem of Senghor's family. His father bore the Serer name Diogoye ("Lion"). A totem is an animal or plant that is closely associated with a family, sometimes considered to be a member of the family. 3. Ancestral masks are usually kept in an enclosure, a sacred place forbidden to women and uninitiated males. There is also a suggestion here that Senghor will protect them from the patronizing gaze of white people.   4. An ironic reference to Senghor's Western education.   5. An ingredient (for example, yeast) in baked goods that make them rise; also a biblical image.   6. A reference to Antaeus, who in Greek mythology drew strength by touching the earth with his feet.   1. A female Serer name. The direct address with which the poem opens is a convention of oral poetry. Ngom, a comrade in the German prisoner-of-war camp, is addressed by his praise name as a champion wrestler, whose exploits in the arena bring honor to his beloved, Tyâné. In the poem, Senghor shares his experience of wartime Paris, to which he has returned after his release from the camp, with the Africans whom he left behind.   2. Wan, melancholic.

My greetings to Tamsia Dargui Ndyâye, who lives off parchments[3]
That give him a subtle tongue and long thin fingers,[4]
To Samba Dyouma, the poet, whose voice is the color of flame[5]
And whose forehead bears the signs of his destiny,
To Nyaoutt Mbodye and to Koli Ngom, your namesake   10
And to all those who, at the hour when the great arms
Are sad like branches beaten by the sun, huddle at night
Shivering around the dish of friendship.

I write you from the solitude of my precious—and closely guarded—
Residence of my black skin. Fortunate are my friends   15
Who know nothing of the icy walls and the brightly lit
Apartments that sterilize every seed on the ancestors' masks
And even the memories of love.
You know nothing of the good white bread, milk, and salt,
Or those substantial dishes that do not nourish,   20
That separate the refined from the boulevard crowds,
Sleepwalkers who have renounced their human identity
Chameleons[6] deaf to change, and their shame locks you
In your cage of solitude.
You know nothing of restaurants and swimming pools   25
Forbidden to noble black blood
And Science and Humanity erecting their police lines
At the borders of negritude.[7]
Must I shout louder? Tell me, can you hear me?
I no longer recognize white men, my brothers,   30
Like this evening at the cinema, so lost were they
Beyond the void made around my skin.[8]

I write to you because my books are white like boredom,
Like misery, like death.
Make room for me around the pot so I can take my place   35
Again, still warm.
Let our hands touch as they reach into the steaming
Rice of friendship. Let the old Serer words
Pass from mouth to mouth like a pipe among friends.
Let Dargui share his succulent fruits,[9] the hay   40
Of every smelly drought! And you, serve us your wise words
As huge as the navel[1] of prodigious Africa.
Which singer this evening will summon the Ancestors around us,
Gathering like a peaceful herd of beasts of the bush?
Who will nestle our dreams under the eyelids of the stars?   45

Ngom! Answer me by the new-moon mail.
At the turn in the road, I shall meet your naked, hesitant words.
Like the fledgling emerging from his cage
Your words are put together so naively; and the learned may mock
    them,

3. Implies intellectual and spiritual nourishment. *Tamsir:* a title for a learned man, equivalent to "doctor."   4. Of the ascetic man of letters.   5. A reference to Dyouma's golden voice and the passionate content of his lyrics. Oral poets sang or declaimed their compositions.   6. A reference to those French people who collaborated with the German forces of the Occupation.   7. Here, a collective term for the black race, in its historical circumstance the world over.   8. A rare report of Senghor's personal experience of racial discrimination.   9. Of his mind, which is well stocked with learning and wisdom.
1. Many African children have large navels. Senghor turns this into a mark of natural strength.

But they bring me back to the surreal　　　　　　　　　　50
And their milk gushes on my face.
I await your letter at the hour when morning lays death low.
I shall receive it piously like the morning ablution,
Like the dew of dawn.

Paris, June 1942

The Kaya-Magan[1]

(guimm *for* kora[2])

Kaya-Magan am I! the first person[3]
King of the black night, the silver night,
King of the night of glass.
Graze my antelopes safe from lions, far from the charm of my voice.
You delight in dotting the silent plains!　　　　　　　　5
Here you are each day my flowers, my stars,
Here you are at my joyful feast.
So feed on my abundant breasts, for I, who am the source of joy,
Do not eat. Graze from my strong, manly breasts,
The milk grass[4] gleaming from my chest.　　　　　　　10

May a thousand stars be lit each night on the Great Square[5]
May twelve thousand bowls ringed with sea serpents[6] be warmed
For my pious subjects, for the fawns of my womb,
The residents of my house and their dependents, the Guélowârs[7]
Of the nine fortresses[8] and the villages in the wild bush,　　　15
For all who have entered by the four carved doors[9]—
The solemn march of my long-suffering people!
Their steps are lost in the sands of Time.[1]
For the whites of the north,[2] the blacks of the south
Of so soft a blue. To say nothing of the red men of the west[3]　　20
Or the River herds! Eat and sleep, children of my sap.
Live your lives fully and peace to you who decline.
Even you draw breath from my nostrils.

I say Kaya-Magan am I! King of the moon, I join night and day.
I am the Prince of the north, of the south,　　　　　　　25
Prince of the Rising and Setting Sun
The savanna open to a hundred ruts, the mold that melds
Precious metals. Red gold comes from it and the red Man,
Red my delight as King of Gold—I, who have the splendor
Of noon and the feminine tenderness of night.　　　　　30
So peck at my curved brow, birds of my serpentine hair.[4]
You can't live on whole milk alone. So nibble the Wiseman's brain,
The master of hieroglyphics in his glass tower.

---

1. King of Gold; legendary founder of the ancient empire of Ghana.　2. A stringed instrument, which sounds like the harp. It is often played to accompany praise songs to royalty and nobility. *Guimm:* ode (Serer).　3. As a ruler who takes precedence over his subjects.　4. That is, milk from grass eaten by cows.　5. The picture is that of a great celebration.　6. Symbols of spiritual insight.　7. Warriors (Wolof).　8. At the nine outposts of the empire; they are manned by the Guélowârs.　9. The gates of the capital city, which open to the four cardinal points.　1. A double reference: to the hourglass as well as to the desert origins of the founders of the Ghana Empire.　2. The Moors of Mauritania.　3. People who have mixed white and black parentage.　4. In some African royal masks, the hair on the king's head is represented as a knotted serpent, with birds pecking at the forehead, to signify abundance.

Graze, fawns of my womb, under my scepter and my crescent moon.[5]
I am the Buffalo that mocks the Lion and his rifles   35
Loaded up to his chin. He'll have to prepare himself
Inside his walls. My empire is Caesar's banished ones,[6]
The great outlaws of reason or instinct
My empire is that of Love, for I am weak for you, woman,
Foreigner with clear eyes,[7] lips of cinnamon apple,   40
And a sex like a burning bush
For I am both sides of a double door, the binary rhythm of space
And the third beat,[8] I am the movement of drums,
The strength of future Africa.
Now sleep, fawns of my womb, sleep under my crescent moon.   45

To New York

(for jazz orchestra and trumpet solo)

I

New York! At first I was bewildered by your beauty,
Those huge, long-legged, golden girls.
So shy, at first, before your blue metallic eyes and icy smile,
So shy. And full of despair at the end of skyscraper streets
Raising my owl eyes at the eclipse of the sun.   5
Your light is sulphurous against the pale towers
Whose heads strike lightning into the sky,
Skyscrapers defying storms with their steel shoulders
And weathered skin of stone.
But two weeks on the naked sidewalks of Manhattan—   10
At the end of the third week the fever
Overtakes you with a jaguar's leap
Two weeks without well water or pasture all birds of the air
Fall suddenly dead under the high, sooty terraces.
No laugh from a growing child, his hand in my cool hand.   15
No mother's breast, but nylon legs. Legs and breasts
Without smell or sweat. No tender word, and no lips,
Only artificial hearts paid for in cold cash
And not one book offering wisdom.
The painter's palette yields only coral crystals.   20
Sleepless nights, O nights of Manhattan!
Stirring with delusions while car horns blare the empty hours
And murky streams carry away hygenic loving
Like rivers overflowing with the corpses of babies.

II

Now is the time for signs and reckoning, New York!   25
Now is the time of manna and hyssop.[1]
You have only to listen to God's trombones,[2] to your heart

---

5. Symbol of Islam, the religion of the emperor.   **6.** Beyond Western civilization.   **7.** Senghor's
French wife.   **8.** The off beat in music based on syncopated rhythm, as jazz. This expresses Senghor's
idea of a third term transcending the conflict of opposites.   **1.** An aromatic herb with religious associations. *Manna*: the food that came down miraculously from Heaven to feed the Israelites when they were
wandering in the desert after leaving Egypt.

Beating to the rhythm of blood, your blood.
I saw Harlem teeming with sounds and ritual colors
And outrageous smells—   30
At teatime in the home of the drugstore-deliveryman
I saw the festival of Night begin at the retreat of day.
And I proclaim Night more truthful than the day.
It is the pure hour when God brings forth
Life immemorial in the streets,   35
All the amphibious elements shining like suns.
Harlem, Harlem! Now I've seen Harlem, Harlem!
A green breeze of corn rising from the pavements
Plowed by the Dan[3] dancers' bare feet,
Hips rippling like silk and spearhead breasts,   40
Ballets of water lilies and fabulous masks
And mangoes of love rolling from the low houses
To the feet of police horses.
And along sidewalks I saw streams of white rum
And streams of black milk in the blue haze of cigars.   45
And at night I saw cotton flowers snow down
From the sky and the angels' wings and sorcerers' plumes.
Listen, New York! O listen to your bass male voice,
Your vibrant oboe voice, the muted anguish of your tears
Falling in great clots of blood,   50
Listen to the distant beating of your nocturnal heart,
The tom-tom's rhythm and blood, tom-tom blood and tom-tom.

III

New York! I say New York, let black blood flow into your blood.
Let it wash the rust from your steel joints, like an oil of life
Let it give your bridges the curve of hips and supple vines.   55
Now the ancient age returns, unity is restored,
The reconciliation of Lion and Bull and Tree[4]
Idea links to action, the ear to the heart, sign to meaning.
See your rivers stirring with musk alligators[5]
And sea cows[6] with mirage eyes. No need to invent the Sirens.   60
Just open your eyes to the April rainbow
And your ears, especially your ears, to God
Who in one burst of saxophone laughter
Created heaven and earth in six days,
And on the seventh slept a deep Negro sleep.   65

---

2. The title of a book of sermons by James Weldon Johnson, written in the idiom of black preachers. The work has become a classic of African-American literature.   3. An ethnic group in Ivory Coast, reputed for the vigor of its dances. These lines establish a racial and cultural connection between Africa and black America.   4. Symbolic of suffering, from the Christian Cross. *Lion*: a symbol of the black race. *Bull*: a symbol of the white race.   5. Held in Serer mythology to conserve the memory of the past.   6. Or manatees, credited by the Serer with being able to see into the future.

Songs for Signare

(for flutes[1])

A *hand of light*[2] caressed my dark eyelids and your smile rose
Over the mists floating monotonously on my Congo.[3]
My heart has echoed the virgin song of the dawn birds
As my blood used to beat to the white song of sap in my branching arms.
See the bush flower and the star in my hair   5
And the bandana on the brow of the herdsman athlete.[4]
I will take up the flute and play a rhythm for the peace
Of the herds and sitting all day in the shade of your lashes,
Close to the Fimla Springs[5] I shall graze faithfully the golden
Lowings[6] of your herds. For this morning a hand of light   10
Caressed my dark eyelids, and all day long
My heart has echoed the virgin song of the birds.

Elegy of the Circumcised[1]

Childhood Night,[2] blue Night, gold Night, O Moon!
How often have I invoked you, O Night! while weeping by the road,
Feeling the pain of adulthood. Loneliness! and its dunes all around.
One night during childhood it was a night as black as pitch.
Our backs were bent with fear at the lion's roar,[3] and the shifting   5
Silence in the night bent the tall grass. Branches caught fire
And you were fired with hope! and my pale memory of the Sun
Barely reassured my innocence. I had to die.[4]
I laid my hands on my neck like the virgin who shivers in the throes
Of death. I had to die to the beauty of the song—all things drift   10
Along the thread of death. Look at twilight on the turtledoves' breast,
When blue ringdoves coo and dream sea gulls fly
With their plaintive cries.

Let us die and dance elbow to elbow in a braided garland[5]
May our clothes not impede our steps, but let the gift   15
Of the betrothed girl glow like sparks under the clouds.
W*oi!*[6] The drum furrows the holy silence.
Let us dance, the song whipping the blood, and let the rhythm
Chase away the agony that grabs us by the throat.
Life keeps death away.   20
Let us dance to the refrain of agony, may the night of sex[7]
Rise above our ignorance, above our innocence.
Ah! To die to childhood, let the poem die, the syntax disintegrate,
And all the unimportant words become spoiled.

1. Associated with sheperds in the pastoral tradition.   2. That is, of the beloved. This is a love poem based on the Western pastoral convention.   3. A river in central Africa that flows through dense tropical landscape; here, an image of the poet's state of mind.   4. The poet himself.   5. The source of a stream in Sine-Saloum.   6. This association of the sound of the cattle with color is an example of synaesthesia.   1. The circumcision rite is the essential element in the initiation ceremony that marks the formal passage of the adolescent to adult status. The ceremony involves the confinement of candidates in the bush for a long period, during which they undergo a series of tests and receive instruction in the history and customs of the land. At the end of this period, on a designated night, they are circumcised one after the other.   2. The night of the circumcision.   3. Simulated, as part of the initiation ceremony, and intended to develop the virtue of courage in the boys.   4. Initiation is the symbolic death of the child who is reborn an adult.   5. The triumphant dance of the initiates after the ceremony.   6. A chant.   7. Initiation also purifies the adolescent, in preparation for sexuality in its creative function.

The rhythm's weight is sufficient, no need for cement words 25
To build the city of tomorrow on rock.
May the Sun rise up from the sea of shadows
Blood![8] The waves are the color of dawn.

But God, I have wailed too much—how many times?
—The transparent childhood nights. 30
The Male-Noon is the time of Spirits, when all form
Gets rid of its flesh, like trees in Europe under the winter sun.
See, the bones are abstract, they obey only the measures
Of the ruler, the compass, the sextant.
Like sand, life slips freely from man's fingers, 35
And snowflakes imprison the water's life,
The water snake[9] glides through the vain hands of the reeds.
Lovely Nights, friendly Nights, childhood Nights
Along the salt flats and in the woods, nights throbbing
With presences and with eyelids, full of wings and breaths 40
And living silence, now tell me how many times
Have I cried for you in the bloom of my age?

The poem withers in the midday sun and feeds upon the evening
    dew,
The tom-tom beats the rhythm of sap in the smell of ripe fruit.
Master of the Initiates,[1] I know I need your knowledge to understand 45
The cipher of things, to be aware of my duties as father and
    lamarque,[2]
To measure exactly the scope of my responsibilities, to distribute
The harvest without forgetting any worker or orphan.
The song is not just a charm, it feeds the woolly heads of my flock.
The poem is a snake-bird,[3] the dawn marriage of shadow and light 50
It soars like the Phoenix![4] It sings with wings spread
Over the slaughter of words.

8. That shed at circumcision, heralding a new birth.   9. A symbol of wisdom and durability.   1. An elder who supervises the ceremony.   2. A word coined by Senghor from the Wolof *lam* and the Greek *archos*, both meaning "landowner." The line refers to the civic and moral obligations taught to the initiates.   3. Or plumed serpent, who is endowed with visionary powers. This creature is found in the mythology of many cultures.   4. A mythical bird that is supposed to rise from its own ashes, thus a symbol of regeneration. Like the bird, poetry embodies the force of renewal in nature.

NAGUIB MAHFOUZ
born 1911

The foremost novelist writing in Arabic traces his roots to the civilization of the ancient Egyptians, seven thousand years ago. Past and present combine for Naguib Mahfouz as he interrogates the destiny of his people and their often-traumatic adjustment to modern industrial society. Without Mahfouz, it is said, the turbulent history of twentieth-century Egypt would never be known. His fictional families and frustrated middle-class clerks have documented the successive stages of Egyptian social and political life from the time the country cast off foreign rule and became a "postcolonial" society. Time, in fact, is the real protagonist of his novels: the time in which individuals live and die, governments come and go, and social values are transformed—time, ultimately, as the conqueror that reduces human endeavor to nothing and forces attention on spiritual truth. Mahfouz's novels and short stories have millions of readers throughout the Arab world, and a growing audience in the West, because they deal with basic human issues in a realistic social context. Generations of Arabs have read his works or seen them adapted to film and television, and his characters have become household words. Mahfouz the craftsman has also wrought a change in Arabic prose, synthesizing traditional literary style and modern speech to create a new literary language understood by Arabs everywhere.

Readers of his best-known works, however, will find many similarities with the nineteenth-century realist novel in Europe. Mahfouz has been called the "Balzac of Egypt"—a comparison to the great French novelist and panoramic chronicler of society Honoré de Balzac (1799–1850)—and he is well acquainted with the works of Gustave Flaubert, Leo Tolstoy, and other nineteenth-century novelists. Traditional Arabic literature has many forms of narrative, but the novel is not one of them, and contemporary writers like Mahfouz have adapted the Western form to their own needs. Their readers will find familiar nineteenth-century strategies such as a chronological plot, unified characters, the inclusion of documentary information and realistic details, a panoramic view of society including a strong moral and humanistic perspective, and—typically if not necessarily—a picture of urban middle-class life. Among twentieth-century authors Mahfouz might be compared with Alexander Solzhenitsyn for his realist style and analysis of national identity. The Egyptian author employs allegory much more than do traditionally realist authors, however, and his most recent work has made use of fragmented and absurdist techniques as well as a variety of classical Arabic forms. He continues to be preoccupied with individual experience inside what he calls the "tragedies of society," although his focus is not restricted to the individualized existentialism of Jean-Paul Sartre or Albert Camus and embraces a complex of social relationships. Like the nineteenth-century novelists he follows, Mahfouz believes in the social function of art and the concomitant responsibility of the writer. His books have been censored and banned in many Arab countries, and he was blacklisted for several years for supporting Egypt's 1979 peace treaty with Israel.

Naguib Mahfouz was born in Cairo on December 11, 1911, the youngest of seven children in the family of a civil servant. The family moved from their home in the old Jamaliya district to the suburbs of Cairo when the boy was young. He attended government schools and entered the University of Cairo in 1930, graduating in 1934 with a degree in philosophy. These were not quiet years: Egypt, officially under Turkish rule, had been occupied by the British since 1883 and was declared a British protectorate at the start of World War I in 1914. Mahfouz grew up in the midst of an ongoing struggle for national independence that culminated in a violent uprising against the British in 1919, and the negotiation of a constitutional monarchy in 1923. The consistent focus on Egyptian cultural identity that permeates his work may well have its roots in this early turbulent period. The difficulty of disentangling cultural traditions, however, is indicated by the fact that Mahfouz's first published book was a 1932 translation of an English work on ancient Egypt.

While at the university, Mahfouz made friends with the socialist and Darwinian thinker Salama Musa and began to write articles for Musa's journal *Al-Majalla al-Jadida* (The Modern Magazine). In 1938, he published his first collection of stories, *Whispers of Madness*, and in 1939 the first of three historical novels set in ancient Egypt. He planned at that time to write a set of forty books on the model of the historical romance written by the British novelist Sir Walter Scott (1771–1832). These first novels already included modern references, and few missed the criticism of King Farouk in *Radubis* (1943) or the analogy in *The Struggle for Thebes* (1944) between the ancient Egyptian battle to expel Hyksos usurpers and twentieth-century rebellions against foreign rule. In 1945 Mahfouz shifted decisively to the realistic novel and a portrayal of modern society. He focused on the social and spiritual dilemmas of the middle class in Cairo, documenting in vivid detail the life of an urban society that represented modern Egypt.

The major work of this period, and Mahfouz's masterwork in many eyes, is *The Cairo Trilogy* (1956–57), three volumes depicting the experience of three generations of a Cairo family between 1918 and 1944. Into this story, whose main protagonist Mahfouz has called Time, is woven a social history of Egypt after World War I. Mahfouz's achievement was recognized in the State Prize for literature in 1956, but he himself temporarily ceased to write after finishing the *Trilogy* in 1952. In that year, an officers' coup headed by Gamal Abdel-Nasser overthrew the monarchy and instituted a republic that promised democratic reforms, and there was a change in the panorama of Egyptian society that Mahfouz described. Although the author was at first optimistic about the new order, he soon recognized that not much had changed for the general populace. When he started publishing again in 1959, his works included much open criticism of the Nasser régime.

Although he had become the best-known writer in the Arab world, his works read by millions, Mahfouz like other Arab authors could not make a living from his books. Copyright protection was minimal, and without copyright protection even best-selling authors received only small sums for their books. Until he began writing for motion pictures in the 1960s, he supported himself and his family through various positions in governmental ministries and as a contributing editor for the leading newspaper, *Al-Ahram*. Attached to the Ministry of Culture in 1954, he adapted novels for film and television and later became director-general of the governmental Cinema Organization. (Cinema, radio, and television are nationalized industries in Egypt.) After his retirement from the civil service in 1971, Mahfouz continued to publish articles and short stories in *Al-Ahram*, where most of his novels have appeared in serialized form before being issued as paperbacks. When he received the Nobel Prize in 1988, at the age of seventy-seven, he was still publishing a weekly column, "Point of View," in *Al-Ahram*.

Three years after *The Cairo Trilogy* brought him international praise, Mahfouz shocked many readers with a new book, *Children of Gebelawi*. Serialized in *Al-Ahram*, *Children of Gebelawi* is on the surface another description of a patriarchal family evolving in modern times. The story of the patriarch Gebelawi and his disobedient or ambitious children, however, is also an allegory of religious history. Its personification of God, Adam, and the prophets—among whom science is included as the youngest and most destructive son—and its simultaneous portrayal of the prophets as primarily social reformers rather than religious figures, scandalized orthodox believers. The book was banned throughout the Arab world except in Lebanon, and the Jordan League of Writers attacked Mahfouz as a "delinquent man" whose novels were "plagued with sex and drugs." *Children of Gebelawi* remains unpublished in Egypt to this day.

Mahfouz took up writing short stories again in the early 1960s after concentrating on novels for two decades. His second collection, *God's World* (1963), combined social realism and metaphysical speculation. He also began to move away from an "objective," realistic style toward one that emphasized subjective or existential awareness. The perceptions of individual characters govern works such as *The Thief and the Dogs* (1962), the story of a released prisoner who—seeking revenge on his unfaithful wife and the man who betrayed him—is trapped by police dogs and shot; and *Miramar* (1967), in which different points of view describe the disappointed love of a young servant girl, her determination to shape her own career, and the death of a lodger. Mahfouz did not abandon social commentary in his new mode. Individual characters represent particular classes or even (with *Miramar*'s servant girl) Egypt itself, and the film made from *Miramar* attracted large audiences for its sharp criticism of the dominant political party, the Arab Socialist Union. In *Mirrors* (1972), brief accounts of fifty-four different characters "mirror" various aspects of contemporary Egyptian society.

Mahfouz's approach changed again in the late 1960s; social commentary in the novels became even more direct, while individual stories grew more fragmented and even absurdist in style. Egypt's defeat by Israel in the June 1967 war had a shattering effect on the nation's self-confidence, and Mahfouz responded to what he saw as the country's spiritual dilemma. Stories written between October and December 1967 and collected in *Under the Bus Shelter* repeatedly show contradictory and incomprehensible events happening to perplexed and frustrated people. An almost cinematic style emerged, emphasizing dialogue over interpretation; some pieces in later collections resemble one-act plays. In the title story of *Under the Bus Shelter*, people waiting for a bus observe beatings, a car crash with several deaths, a couple making love on a corpse, dancing, the rapid construction of a monumental grave in which both corpses and lovers are buried, inaudible speeches, a man who may possibly be the director of the film (if it *is* a film) but may also be a thug, a decapitation, and finally "a group of official-looking men wandering around" whose appearance frightens off the others—until the puzzled observers are shot by a previously apathetic policeman when they ask questions. Several novels in the 1970s and 1980s reveal a similar bleak perspective in a more didactic style; *There Only Remains One Hour* (1982), for example, portrays current events as a sequence of failed efforts to achieve peace and prosperity.

Mahfouz's style continues to evolve in new directions. His most recent work has adapted classical Arabic narrative forms such as the *maqama* (elaborate rhymed trickster tales) or folk narratives like the *Arabian Nights* into imaginative sequences such as *The Nights of "The Thousand and One Nights"* or *The Epic of the Riff-Raff*. While these latest works have disconcerted adherents of his earlier, realistic style, they are an integral part of the Egyptian writer's attempt to find new ways to express Arabic culture and to comment from a broader, often prophetic perspective on the contemporary scene. That Mahfouz is impelled by a sense of moral purpose is evident throughout his works, and perhaps no more so than in his Nobel Prize acceptance speech in 1988. Speaking first for Arabic letters but also as a representative of the Third World, he addressed the leaders of a Western civilization that has allowed science and technology to outweigh basic human values. "The developed world and the third world are but one family. Each human being bears responsibility towards it by the degree of what he has obtained of knowledge, wisdom, and civilization. . . . in the name of the third world: Be not spectators to our miseries." The "able ones, the civilized ones," he added, perhaps ironically, must be guided by the collective needs of humanity.

Zaabalawi, a story included in *God's World*, contains many of Mahfouz's predominant themes. Written two years after *Children of Gebelawi*, it echoes the earlier work's religious symbolism in the mysterious character of Zaabalawi himself. It is also a social document: the narrator's quest for Zaabalawi brings him before various representatives of modern Egyptian society inside a realistically described Cairo. *Zaabalawi*, therefore, takes on the character of a social and metaphysical allegory. Its terminally ill narrator seeks to be cured in a quest that implies not only physical healing but also religious salvation. He has already exhausted the resources of medical science and, in desperation, he decides to seek out a holy man whose name he recalls from childhood tales.

In the initial stage of his search, the protagonist is coldly received by a lawyer and a district officer, former acquaintances of Zaabalawi who have become worldly, materialistic, and highly successful. Moreover, these bureaucrats who depend on reason, technology, and businesslike efficiency can do no more than send him to old addresses or draw him city maps. Zaabalawi is still alive, they say, but he is unpredictable and hard to find now that he no longer inhabits his old home—a now-dilapidated mansion in front of which an old bookseller sells used books on mysticism and theology. In contrast, the calligrapher and composer to whom the narrator next turns welcome him as a person. Indeed, the composer reproves him for thinking only of his errand and overlooking the value of getting to know another human being. The relationship among art, human sympathy, and spiritual values is made clear, for Zaabalawi is close to both artists and has provided inspiration for their best works. In the last scene at the Negma Bar, Mahfouz fuses the realistic description of a hardened drinker with a dream-vision of another, peaceful world. At this stage of the quest, the narrator is not even allowed to state his errand but must place himself on a level with his drunken host before being allowed to speak. When he does sink into oblivion (in stages that suggest a mystic stripping-away of rational faculties), he is rewarded in his dreams by a glimpse of Paradise and wakes to find that Zaabalawi has been beside him as he slept. *Zaabalawi* ends as it began—"I have to find Zaabalawi"—but the seeker is now more confident, and the route more clearly marked.

Roger M. A. Allen, *The Arabic Novel: An Historical and Critical Introduction* (1982), is an authoritative introduction that situates Mahfouz in the context of modern Arabic literature and includes a bibliography of works in Arabic and Western languages. Sasson Somekh, "*Za'balawi*"—Author, Theme and Technique" in *Journal of Arabic Literature* 1 (1970), 24–35, examines the story as a "double-layered" structure governed by references to Sufi mysticism. Michael Beard and Adnan Haydar, eds., *Naguib Mahfouz* (1993), assemble eleven original essays on themes, individual works, and cultural contexts in Mahfouz's work. Trevor le Gassick, ed., *Critical Perspectives on Naguib Mahfouz* (1991), reprints articles on Mahfouz's work up to the 1970s. Rasheed El-Enany, ed., *Naguib Mahfouz: The Pursuit of Meaning* (1993), is an excellent study that includes biography, analyses of novels, short stories, and plays and a guide for further reading. Mona Mikhail, *Studies in the Short Fiction of Mahfouz and Idris* (1992), an introductory work, juxtaposes themes in Hemingway, Idris, Mahfouz, and Camus.

PRONOUNCING GLOSSARY

The following list uses common English syllables and stress accents to provide rough equivalents of selected words whose pronunciation may be unfamiliar to the general reader.

Hassanein: *hassan-ayn'*

Naguib Mahfouz: *nah-geeb' mah-fooz'*

Qamar: *qa-mar'*

Umm al-Ghulam: *oum al–ghol-am'*

Wanas al-Damanhouri: *wa'-nas ad–dam-an-oo'-ree*

Zaabalawi: *zah-bah-lah'-wee*

Zaabalawi[1]

Finally I became convinced that I had to find Sheikh[2] Zaabalawi.

The first time I had heard of his name had been in a song:

---

1. Translated by Denys Johnson-Davies.   2. A title of respect (originally "old man"), often indicating rulership.

Oh what's become of the world, Zaabalawi?
They've turned it upside down and taken away its taste.

It had been a popular song in my childhood, and one day it had occurred to me to demand of my father, in the way children have of asking endless questions:

"Who is Zaabalawi?"

He had looked at me hesitantly as though doubting my ability to understand the answer. However, he had replied, "May his blessing descend upon you, he's a true saint of God, a remover of worries and troubles. Were it not for him I would have died miserably—"

In the years that followed, I heard my father many a time sing the praises of this good saint and speak of the miracles he performed. The days passed and brought with them many illnesses, for each one of which I was able, without too much trouble and at a cost I could afford, to find a cure, until I became afflicted with that illness for which no one possesses a remedy. When I had tried everything in vain and was overcome by despair, I remembered by chance what I had heard in my childhood: Why, I asked myself, should I not seek out Sheikh Zaabalawi? I recollected my father saying that he had made his acquaintance in Khan Gaafar[3] at the house of Sheikh Qamar, one of those sheikhs who practiced law in the religious courts, and so I took myself off to his house. Wishing to make sure that he was still living there, I made inquiries of a vendor of beans whom I found in the lower part of the house.

"Sheikh Qamar!" he said, looking at me in amazement. "He left the quarter ages ago. They say he's now living in Garden City and has his office in al-Azhar Square."[4]

I looked up the office address in the telephone book and immediately set off to the Chamber of Commerce Building, where it was located. On asking to see Sheikh Qamar, I was ushered into a room just as a beautiful woman with a most intoxicating perfume was leaving it. The man received me with a smile and motioned me toward a fine leather-upholstered chair. Despite the thick soles of my shoes, my feet were conscious of the lushness of the costly carpet. The man wore a lounge suit and was smoking a cigar; his manner of sitting was that of someone well satisfied both with himself and with his worldly possessions. The look of warm welcome he gave me left no doubt in my mind that he thought me a prospective client, and I felt acutely embarrassed at encroaching upon his valuable time.

"Welcome!" he said, prompting me to speak.

"I am the son of your old friend Sheikh Ali al-Tatawi," I answered so as to put an end to my equivocal position.

A certain languor was apparent in the glance he cast at me; the languor was not total in that he had not as yet lost all hope in me.

"God rest his soul," he said. "He was a fine man."

The very pain that had driven me to go there now prevailed upon me to stay.

"He told me," I continued, "of a devout saint named Zaabalawi whom

3. Gaafar Market, an area of shops.   4. An area of Cairo close to the famous mosque and university of al-Azhar.

he met at Your Honor's. I am in need of him, sir, if he be still in the land of the living."

The languor became firmly entrenched in his eyes, and it would have come as no surprise if he had shown the door to both me and my father's memory.

"That," he said in the tone of one who has made up his mind to terminate the conversation, "was a very long time ago and I scarcely recall him now."

Rising to my feet so as to put his mind at rest regarding my intention of going, I asked, "Was he really a saint?"

"We used to regard him as a man of miracles."

"And where could I find him today?" I asked, making another move toward the door.

"To the best of my knowledge he was living in the Birgawi Residence in al-Azhar," and he applied himself to some papers on his desk with a resolute movement that indicated he would not open his mouth again. I bowed my head in thanks, apologized several times for disturbing him, and left the office, my head so buzzing with embarrassment that I was oblivious to all sounds around me.

I went to the Birgawi Residence, which was situated in a thickly populated quarter. I found that time had so eaten at the building that nothing was left of it save an antiquated façade and a courtyard that, despite being supposedly in the charge of a caretaker, was being used as a rubbish dump. A small, insignificant fellow, a mere prologue to a man, was using the covered entrance as a place for the sale of old books on theology and mysticism.

When I asked him about Zaabalawi, he peered at me through narrow, inflamed eyes and said in amazement, "Zaabalawi! Good heavens, what a time ago that was! Certainly he used to live in this house when it was habitable. Many were the times he would sit with me talking of bygone days, and I would be blessed by his holy presence. Where, though, is Zaabalawi today?"

He shrugged his shoulders sorrowfully and soon left me, to attend to an approaching customer. I proceeded to make inquiries of many shopkeepers in the district. While I found that a large number of them had never even heard of Zaabalawi, some, though recalling nostalgically the pleasant times they had spent with him, were ignorant of his present whereabouts, while others openly made fun of him, labeled him a charlatan, and advised me to put myself in the hands of a doctor—as though I had not already done so. I therefore had no alternative but to return disconsolately home.

With the passing of days like motes in the air, my pains grew so severe that I was sure I would not be able to hold out much longer. Once again I fell to wondering about Zaabalawi and clutching at the hope his venerable name stirred within me. Then it occurred to me to seek the help of the local sheikh of the district; in fact, I was surprised I had not thought of this to begin with. His office was in the nature of a small shop, except that it contained a desk and a telephone, and I found him sitting at his desk, wearing a jacket over his striped galabeya.[5] As he did not interrupt his conversation with a man sitting beside him, I stood waiting till the man had gone. The sheikh then looked up at me coldly. I told myself that I should win him over by the usual methods, and it was not long before I had him cheerfully inviting me to sit down.

"I'm in need of Sheikh Zaabalawi," I answered his inquiry as to the purpose of my visit.

He gazed at me with the same astonishment as that shown by those I had previously encountered.

"At least," he said, giving me a smile that revealed his gold teeth, "he is still alive. The devil of it is, though, he has no fixed abode. You might well bump into him as you go out of here, on the other hand you might spend days and months in fruitless searching."

"Even you can't find him!"

"Even I! He's a baffling man, but I thank the Lord that he's still alive!"

He gazed at me intently, and murmured, "It seems your condition is serious."

"Very."

"May God come to your aid! But why don't you go about it systematically?" He spread out a sheet of paper on the desk and drew on it with unexpected speed and skill until he had made a full plan of the district, showing all the various quarters, lanes, alleyways, and squares. He looked at it admiringly and said, "These are dwelling-houses, here is the Quarter of the Perfumers, here the Quarter of the Coppersmiths, the Mouski,[6] the police and fire stations. The drawing is your best guide. Look carefully in the cafés, the places where the dervishes perform their rites, the mosques and prayer-rooms, and the Green Gate,[7] for he may well be concealed among the beggars and be indistinguishable from them. Actually, I myself haven't seen him for years, having been somewhat preoccupied with the cares of the world, and was only brought back by your inquiry to those most exquisite times of my youth."

I gazed at the map in bewilderment. The telephone rang, and he took up the receiver.

"Take it," he told me, generously. "We're at your service."

Folding up the map, I left and wandered off through the quarter, from square to street to alleyway, making inquiries of everyone I felt was familiar with the place. At last the owner of a small establishment for ironing clothes told me, "Go to the calligrapher[8] Hassanein in Umm al-Ghulam—they were friends."

I went to Umm al-Ghulam,[9] where I found old Hassanein working in a deep, narrow shop full of signboards and jars of color. A strange smell, a mixture of glue and perfume, permeated its every corner. Old Hassanein was squatting on a sheepskin rug in front of a board propped against the wall; in the middle of it he had inscribed the word "Allah"[1] in silver let-

5. The traditional Arabic robe, over which this modernized district officer wears a European jacket. 6. The central bazaar.   7. A medieval gate in Cairo.   8. One who does calligraphy. The art of decorative lettering (literally "beautiful writing") is respected as a fine art in Arabic and Asian culture.   9. A street in Cairo.   1. The Arabic word for "God."

tering. He was engrossed in embellishing the letters with prodigious care. I stood behind him, fearful of disturbing him or breaking the inspiration that flowed to his masterly hand. When my concern at not interrupting him had lasted some time, he suddenly inquired with unaffected gentleness, "Yes?"

Realizing that he was aware of my presence, I introduced myself. "I've been told that Sheikh Zaabalawi is your friend; I'm looking for him," I said.

His hand came to a stop. He scrutinized me in astonishment. "Zaabalawi! God be praised!" he said with a sigh.

"He *is* a friend of yours, isn't he?" I asked eagerly.

"He was, once upon a time. A real man of mystery: he'd visit you so often that people would imagine he was your nearest and dearest, then would disappear as though he'd never existed. Yet saints are not to be blamed."

The spark of hope went out with the suddenness of a lamp snuffed by a power-cut.

"He was so constantly with me," said the man, "that I felt him to be a part of everything I drew. But where is he today?"

"Perhaps he is still alive?"

"He's alive, without a doubt. . . . He had impeccable taste, and it was due to him that I made my most beautiful drawings."

"God knows," I said, in a voice almost stifled by the dead ashes of hope, "how dire my need for him is, and no one knows better than you[2] of the ailments in respect of which he is sought."

"Yes, yes. May God restore you to health. He is, in truth, as is said of him, a man, and more. . . ."

Smiling broadly, he added, "And his face possesses an unforgettable beauty. But where is he?"

Reluctantly I rose to my feet, shook hands, and left. I continued wandering eastward and westward through the quarter, inquiring about Zaabalawi from everyone who, by reason of age or experience, I felt might be likely to help me. Eventually I was informed by a vendor of lupine[3] that he had met him a short while ago at the house of Sheikh Gad, the well-known composer. I went to the musician's house in Tabakshiyya,[4] where I found him in a room tastefully furnished in the old style, its walls redolent with history. He was seated on a divan, his famous lute beside him, concealing within itself the most beautiful melodies of our age, while somewhere from within the house came the sound of pestle and mortar and the clamor of children. I immediately greeted him and introduced myself, and was put at my ease by the unaffected way in which he received me. He did not ask, either in words or gesture, what had brought me, and I did not feel that he even harbored any such curiosity. Amazed at his understanding and kindness, which boded well, I said, "O Sheikh Gad, I am an admirer of yours, having long been enchanted by the renderings of your songs."

2. One of the calligrapher's major tasks is to write religious documents and prayers to Allah.   3. Beans.
4. A quarter named for the straw trays made and sold there.

"Thank you," he said with a smile.

"Please excuse my disturbing you," I continued timidly, "but I was told that Zaabalawi was your friend, and I am in urgent need of him."

"Zaabalawi!" he said, frowning in concentration. "You need him? God be with you, for who knows, O Zaabalawi, where you are."

"Doesn't he visit you?" I asked eagerly.

"He visited me some time ago. He might well come right now; on the other hand I mightn't see him till death!"

I gave an audible sigh and asked, "What made him like that?"

The musician took up his lute. "Such are saints or they would not be saints," he said, laughing.

"Do those who need him suffer as I do?"

"Such suffering is part of the cure!"

He took up the plectrum and began plucking soft strains from the strings. Lost in thought, I followed his movements. Then, as though addressing myself, I said, "So my visit has been in vain."

He smiled, laying his cheek against the side of the lute. "God forgive you," he said, "for saying such a thing of a visit that has caused me to know you and you me!"

I was much embarrassed and said apologetically, "Please forgive me; my feelings of defeat made me forget my manners."

"Do not give in to defeat. This extraordinary man brings fatigue to all who seek him. It was easy enough with him in the old days when his place of abode was known. Today, though, the world has changed, and after having enjoyed a position attained only by potentates, he is now pursued by the police on a charge of false pretenses. It is therefore no longer an easy matter to reach him, but have patience and be sure that you will do so."

He raised his head from the lute and skillfully fingered the opening bars of a melody. Then he sang:

> I make lavish mention, even though I blame myself, of those I love,
> For the stories of the beloved are my wine.[5]

With a heart that was weary and listless, I followed the beauty of the melody and the singing.

"I composed the music to this poem in a single night," he told me when he had finished. "I remember that it was the eve of the Lesser Bairam.[6] Zaabalawi was my guest for the whole of that night, and the poem was of his choosing. He would sit for a while just where you are, then would get up and play with my children as though he were one of them. Whenever I was overcome by weariness or my inspiration failed me, he would punch me playfully in the chest and joke with me, and I would bubble over with melodies, and thus I continued working till I finished the most beautiful piece I have ever composed."

"Does he know anything about music?"

"He is the epitome of things musical. He has an extremely beautiful

---

5. Words from a poem by the medieval mystic poet Ibn al-Farid.   6. A major Islamic holiday, celebrated for three days to end the month's fasting during Ramadan.

speaking voice, and you have only to hear him to want to burst into song and to be inspired to creativity. . . ."

"How was it that he cured those diseases before which men are powerless?"

"That is his secret. Maybe you will learn it when you meet him."

But when would that meeting occur? We relapsed into silence, and the hubbub of children once more filled the room.

Again the sheikh began to sing. He went on repeating the words "and I have a memory of her" in different and beautiful variations until the very walls danced in ecstasy. I expressed my wholehearted admiration, and he gave me a smile of thanks. I then got up and asked permission to leave, and he accompanied me to the front door. As I shook him by the hand, he said, "I hear that nowadays he frequents the house of Hagg Wanas al-Damanhouri. Do you know him?"

I shook my head, though a modicum of renewed hope crept into my heart.

"He is a man of private means," the sheikh told me, "who from time to time visits Cairo, putting up at some hotel or other. Every evening, though, he spends at the Negma Bar in Alfi Street."

I waited for nightfall and went to the Negma Bar. I asked a waiter about Hagg Wanas, and he pointed to a corner that was semisecluded because of its position behind a large pillar with mirrors on all four sides. There I saw a man seated alone at a table with two bottles in front of him, one empty, the other two-thirds empty. There were no snacks or food to be seen, and I was sure that I was in the presence of a hardened drinker. He was wearing a loosely flowing silk galabeya and a carefully wound turban; his legs were stretched out toward the base of the pillar, and as he gazed into the mirror in rapt contentment, the sides of his face, rounded and handsome despite the fact that he was approaching old age, were flushed with wine. I approached quietly till I stood but a few feet away from him. He did not turn toward me or give any indication that he was aware of my presence.

"Good evening, Mr. Wanas," I greeted him cordially.

He turned toward me abruptly, as though my voice had roused him from slumber, and glared at me in disapproval. I was about to explain what had brought me to him when he interrupted in an almost imperative tone of voice that was none the less not devoid of an extraordinary gentleness, "First, please sit down, and, second, please get drunk!"

I opened my mouth to make my excuses but, stopping up his ears with his fingers, he said, "Not a word till you do what I say."

I realized I was in the presence of a capricious drunkard and told myself that I should at least humor him a bit. "Would you permit me to ask one question?" I said with a smile, sitting down.

Without removing his hands from his ears he indicated the bottle. "When engaged in a drinking bout like this, I do not allow any conversation between myself and another unless, like me, he is drunk, otherwise all propriety is lost and mutual comprehension is rendered impossible."

I made a sign indicating that I did not drink.

"That's your lookout," he said offhandedly. "And that's my condition!"

He filled me a glass, which I meekly took and drank. No sooner had the wine settled in my stomach than it seemed to ignite. I waited patiently till I had grown used to its ferocity, and said, "It's very strong, and I think the time has come for me to ask you about—"

Once again, however, he put his fingers in his ears. "I shan't listen to you until you're drunk!"

He filled up my glass for the second time. I glanced at it in trepidation; then, overcoming my inherent objection, I drank it down at a gulp. No sooner had the wine come to rest inside me than I lost all willpower. With the third glass, I lost my memory, and with the fourth the future vanished. The world turned round about me and I forgot why I had gone there. The man leaned toward me attentively, but I saw him—saw everything—as a mere meaningless series of colored planes. I don't know how long it was before my head sank down onto the arm of the chair and I plunged into deep sleep. During it, I had a beautiful dream the like of which I had never experienced. I dreamed that I was in an immense garden surrounded on all sides by luxuriant trees, and the sky was nothing but stars seen between the entwined branches, all enfolded in an atmosphere like that of sunset or a sky overcast with cloud. I was lying on a small hummock of jasmine petals, more of which fell upon me like rain, while the lucent spray of a fountain unceasingly sprinkled the crown of my head and my temples. I was in a state of deep contentedness, of ecstatic serenity. An orchestra of warbling and cooing played in my ear. There was an extraordinary sense of harmony between me and my inner self, and between the two of us and the world, everything being in its rightful place, without discord or distortion. In the whole world there was no single reason for speech or movement, for the universe moved in a rapture of ecstasy. This lasted but a short while. When I opened my eyes, consciousness struck at me like a policeman's fist and I saw Wanas al-Damanhouri regarding me with concern. Only a few drowsy customers were left in the bar.

"You have slept deeply," said my companion. "You were obviously hungry for sleep."

I rested my heavy head in the palms of my hands. When I took them away in astonishment and looked down at them, I found that they glistened with drops of water.

"My head's wet," I protested.

"Yes, my friend tried to rouse you," he answered quietly.

"Somebody saw me in this state?"

"Don't worry, he is a good man. Have you not heard of Sheikh Zaabalawi?"

"Zaabalawi!" I exclaimed, jumping to my feet.

"Yes," he answered in surprise. "What's wrong?"

"Where is he?"

"I don't know where he is now. He was here and then he left."

I was about to run off in pursuit but found I was more exhausted than I had imagined. Collapsed over the table, I cried out in despair, "My sole reason for coming to you was to meet him! Help me to catch up with him or send someone after him."

The man called a vendor of prawns and asked him to seek out the sheikh and bring him back. Then he turned to me. "I didn't realize you were afflicted. I'm very sorry. . . ."

"You wouldn't let me speak," I said irritably.

"What a pity! He was sitting on this chair beside you the whole time. He was playing with a string of jasmine petals he had around his neck, a gift from one of his admirers, then, taking pity on you, he began to sprinkle some water on your head to bring you around."

"Does he meet you here every night?" I asked, my eyes not leaving the doorway through which the vendor of prawns had left.

"He was with me tonight, last night and the night before that, but before that I hadn't seen him for a month."

"Perhaps he will come tomorrow," I answered with a sigh.

"Perhaps."

"I am willing to give him any money he wants."

Wanas answered sympathetically, "The strange thing is that he is not open to such temptations, yet he will cure you if you meet him."

"Without charge?"

"Merely on sensing that you love him."

The vendor of prawns returned, having failed in his mission.

I recovered some of my energy and left the bar, albeit unsteadily. At every street corner I called out "Zaabalawi!" in the vague hope that I would be rewarded with an answering shout. The street boys turned contemptuous eyes on me till I sought refuge in the first available taxi.

The following evening I stayed up with Wanas al-Damanhouri till dawn, but the sheikh did not put in an appearance. Wanas informed me that he would be going away to the country and would not be returning to Cairo until he had sold the cotton crop.

I must wait, I told myself; I must train myself to be patient. Let me content myself with having made certain of the existence of Zaabalawi, and even of his affection for me, which encourages me to think that he will be prepared to cure me if a meeting takes place between us.

Sometimes, however, the long delay wearied me. I would become beset by despair and would try to persuade myself to dismiss him from my mind completely. How many weary people in this life know him not or regard him as a mere myth! Why, then, should I torture myself about him in this way?

No sooner, however, did my pains force themselves upon me than I would again begin to think about him, asking myself when I would be fortunate enough to meet him. The fact that I ceased to have any news of Wanas and was told he had gone to live abroad did not deflect me from my purpose; the truth of the matter was that I had become fully convinced that I had to find Zaabalawi.

Yes, I have to find Zaabalawi.

AIMÉ CÉSAIRE
born 1913

Aimé Césaire has been called "Poet of the Black Diaspora." The title draws attention to the dominant reference of Césaire's work, which is to the bitter historical experience of the black population in the New World, especially in the Caribbean—its uprooting, transplantation, and dispossession as part of its enslavement in America and its longing for the lost homeland of Africa. Most striking is the acute race consciousness he displays, responding to the somber experience of domination and devaluation that black people have endured in modern times. It is impossible to understand Césaire's poetry apart from this determining context and its impact on the poet. The collective experience of the black race touched Césaire so directly and profoundly that it constitutes the framework of his poetic destiny. His poetry presents itself as a symbolic mode of working through both a historical predicament and a personal drama.

Césaire was born on June 26, 1913, at Basse-Pointe, in northern Martinique, the second child in a family of modest means; his father was a junior functionary of the French colonial administration and his mother, a dressmaker. The burden of race and the legacy of slavery weighed heavily on the black population in the highly stratified society of colonial Martinique, exerting a pressure that Césaire could not have escaped during his childhood. Apart from this, Césaire's earliest impressions were almost certainly formed by the landscape of his birthplace, on the Atlantic coast of his native island, where the sea is especially forceful, and in the vicinity of the volcano Mont Pélé, amid an abundant tropical vegetation. These features of the physical environment in which he grew up are significant elements of his imaginative universe.

Césaire received his primary education at Basse-Pointe, then went for his secondary education to Fort-de-France, the capital of the colony, where he attended the Lycée Schoelcher, named after the most prominent French abolitionist. After obtaining his baccalauréat in 1931, he was awarded a scholarship to continue his studies in France. Shortly after his arrival in Paris that year, and his enrollment at the Lycée Louis-le-Grand in the preparatory class for the Ecole Normale Supérieure, he met Léopold Sédar Senghor (p. 2191), and formed with him a lasting friendship. It was through the close collaboration of the two men over the next few years that what came to be known as the Négritude movement developed. The term itself, which denotes a sense of collective racial identity and common destiny among black people the world over, was coined by Césaire and first appeared in print in his celebrated long poem *Cahier d'un retour au pays natal* (Notebook of a return to the native land), which he was to publish in 1939 and which remains his best-known work.

The meeting with Senghor had a highly personal significance for Césaire. As he was later to remark, "When I met Senghor, I knew I was an African." By introducing Césaire to aspects of African civilization that formed Senghor's own background, Senghor helped free his friend from the negative associations that Africa held for West Indians of his generation. The two men became intellectual companions, with a common passion for Africa. Together they read and discussed the ethnographic literature on Africa that began to appear during this period—notably the works of the French anthropologist Maurice Delafosse and the German cultural historian Leo Frobenius—which emphasized the coherence of African social systems and the value of the continent's indigenous cultures. Through Senghor and in these books, Césaire encountered a positive image of Africa that enabled him to identify with the continent of his ancestors and thus to arrive at self-acceptance as a black person.

Césaire's relationship with Senghor developed within the context of a black awakening that was already under way during the years between the two world wars. In the United States, the activities of W. E. B. Du Bois had given concrete form to the idea of Pan-Africanism as a movement of black solidarity concerned with the bleak situation of black people both in America and on the African continent. By the time of Césaire's arrival in Paris, a strong anticolonial sentiment had developed among African and Caribbean students and intellectuals. This new militancy can be attributed to several factors. Foremost among them was the political, social, and cultural malaise, resulting from World War I, which undermined the claim of Western civilization to moral superiority, a claim consistently used to justify the colonial enterprise. Another factor was the rise of socialism with its explicit challenge to imperialism. Finally, there was the Harlem Renaissance, at its height in the 1920s, which had introduced a strongly affirmative note into black American literature.

This revolution of consciousness among French-speaking black intellectuals prompted Césaire and Senghor to question the premises on which colonial ideology was based: the notion of Africa as a "dark" continent, symbolizing the inferiority of the black race. This they did through the journal *L'Etudiant noir*, founded in 1935 by a group of West Indian and African students. Although devoted exclusively to cultural matters, *L'Etudiant noir* had a pronounced Pan-African orientation, for its aim was to establish connections between the conditions of life and the cultures expressing those conditions in Africa as well as in the American diaspora and to affirm what Césaire termed, in an article in the journal, "the primacy of self."

In the midst of this intense promotion of a new black consciousness, Césaire continued his literary and classical studies. He entered the Ecole Normale Supérieure in 1935, and a year later obtained his first degree, the *Licence-ès-Lettres*. The following year, he obtained the *Diplôme d'Etudes Supérieures* (equivalent to the Master's degree), writing a thesis on the South in black American literature. He had also begun to write poetry and was especially drawn to the work of the Surrealists, in particular André Breton, whose aesthetic of spontaneous expression had a special appeal for Césaire. Surrealism offered not only a modern poetic idiom but also an instrument for sounding the depths of his own consciousness and releasing the tension between a mind-set acquired from his Western conditioning and what he considered to be his authentic self, grounded in an African sensibility and disposition. In this spirit, he began to compose *Notebook of a Return to the Native Land* in the autumn of 1936 and completed it in time for publication in the journal *Volontés*, in August 1939, just before the outbreak of World War II. The poem attracted practically no attention at the time but was later to play a determining role in shaping contemporary attitudes in the French-speaking black world and beyond.

Césaire returned to Martinique later in the year, in the early stages of a war that soon saw the collapse of France and the setting up of the Vichy regime, which quickly established its control over the island colony and pursued authoritarian and racist policies. In response to this somber atmosphere, Césaire, now a professor at his old school, founded the journal *Tropiques* with his wife, Suzanne, and a few colleagues. In the articles they wrote for the journal over the four years of its life, they scrutinized the complex social and psychological problems of their island people and undertook to foster in them a new awareness of their potential, a new determination of the collective will.

The first issue of the journal had just appeared, in April 1941, when André Breton, passing through Martinique on his way to voluntary exile in the United

States, came on a copy in a local bookshop. Its tone and content made such an impression on him that he asked to meet Césaire and his collaborators and thus became acquainted with the first version of *Notebook*, which had been published earlier in Paris. Later, he arranged the publication of a revised and expanded edition in volume form, along with an English translation. In the preface of this edition, issued in New York in 1947, he hailed Césaire's poem as "the greatest lyrical monument of the age."

Invited in 1944 to deliver a keynote address at a philosophy conference at Port-au-Prince, in Haiti, Césaire chose the subject *poésie et connaissance* (poetry and knowledge), stressing the importance of poetry both as a reflection of the lived conditions of existence and as a privileged insight into the true nature of things. His stay in Haiti lasted seven months, during which he familiarized himself with the life of Toussaint L'Ouverture, hero of the Haitian revolution, whose biography he would publish in 1961, and of Henri Christophe, Toussaint's successor, about whom he wrote a powerful play in the mid-1960s.

In 1945, Césaire was elected mayor of Fort-de-France and, under the banner of the Communist Party, one of the deputies for Martinique in the French Constituent Assembly. His active political career ended only with his retirement from politics in 1993. He has been at the forefront of the ideological battles of French-speaking black intellectuals, carried on through the journal *Présence Africaine*, founded in 1947 by the Senegalese Alioune Diop. He was principal speaker at the two Congresses of Black Writers organized by that journal, the first in Paris in 1956 and the second in Rome in 1959. His *Discourse on Colonialism*, published in 1955, contains a vigorous denunciation of the brutal methods of colonial conquest and remains an outstanding example of polemical literature.

With the active promotion of Breton, Césaire's poems began to appear in the mid-1940s in Surrealist journals. His first collection, *Les Armes miraculeuses* (The miraculous arms, 1946), shows the peculiar strength of his poetic imagination and his links to Surrealism. The title asserts his aggressive stance, the dissidence that underlies every image: "And the mines of radium buried deep / in the abyss of my innocences / will burst into grains / in the manger of birds."

The same dissident mood can be observed in his next collection, *Soleil cou coupé* (Solar throat slashed, 1948). The title, derived from a poem by Apollinaire (*Solde*), confirms the modernist orientation of the poet's social and metaphysical revolt. The poems are marked by baroque imagery, and a wide range of poetic voices project the turmoil of the poet's inner state. His dark presence in the world predisposes him to a combative role. Playing deliberately on the sinister associations of blackness in Western culture, he assumes the aspect of a primordial force engaged in the revision of an inequitable history:

> A robust bolt of thunder flashes danger
> from the most untouchable brow in the world
> in you all the widowed light
> of twilights of cities stabbed
> by birds from the countryside
> And beware the crow that does not fly it is my head which has broken
> loose of the centrepole of my shoulders
> uttering an ancient screech rending guts disrupting watering holes

In Césaire's next volume *Corps perdu* (Lost body, 1950), the language is sparer, though still animated by a sense of justified revolt:

> And our faces beautiful
> as the true operative power
> of negation.

Since its republication in volume form, Césaire had been revising *Notebook*, and in 1956 the publishing house of Présence Africaine brought out an enlarged and updated version. The poem quickly established itself as the centerpiece of the literature of Négritude. The most impassioned statement in all literature of the racial sentiment of black people in their historical, social, and cultural relation to the Western world, the poem also became recognized as a masterpiece of modern French poetry, the only *long* poem in the Surrealist tradition. Thus *Notebook* belongs as much to mainstream French literature as to the evolving canon of French-speaking literature in Africa and the Caribbean.

The long opening evocation of the physical and moral misery of the Antilles is an essential part of the process of self-knowledge that is the poem's goal. But the movement of self-recovery it narrates also involves a recognition of the wider world of humanity in need of spiritual renewal: "You know that it is not from hatred of other races / that I demand a digger for this unique race / that what I want / is for universal hunger / for universal thirst." Despite the force of its commitment to a collective social and political cause, the poem's enduring significance resides in its apprehension of a realm of transcendental values. This aspect of the poem is intimated constantly in the imagery that gives a mystic resonance to the experience it dramatizes. It emerges fully in the concluding stanzas of the poem, confirming for us the meaning of the poet's adventure: the turbulent movement through history mirrors the unfolding of his aspiration to a higher mode of being.

In his later work, Césaire combines the sinewy character of his earlier poetry with an opulent and ceremonial style of address, as in the poems of *Ferrements* (1960). The need for more direct communication, evident in this volume, led him next to drama. *The Tragedy of King Christophe* (1963), based on events in Haiti after its independence in the early nineteenth century, confronts the problems of decolonization. The connection hinted at here between the Haitian precedent and the African situation becomes overt in his next play, *Une Saison au Congo* (A season in the Congo, 1966), which focuses on Patrice Lumumba and his tragic fate in the former Belgian Congo (now Zaire). In these plays, the dialogue often assumes heroic dimensions, rising to become a comprehensive meditation on nation building. Césaire returns to the colonial question in *Une tempête* (1969), an adaptation of Shakespeare's *The Tempest*, which examines in contemporary terms the relation between Prospero and Caliban.

Césaire's latest published work, *moi laminaire* (1982), represents a stock-taking of his poetic and political career. The spareness of the imagery, rooted more than ever in the Caribbean landscape, endows with a lyrical gravity the uncompromising self-reflection undertaken in these poems. The volume thus returns to and confirms the introspective note in Césaire's work, in a complex interaction of personal, historical, and mythical references. Beyond its social and political references, Césaire's poetry expresses a deeply human ideal, a primary vision in which humanity, restored to nature, will find the "rock without dialect, the leaf without keep, the fragile water without femur."

The fullest critical account of Césaire's work is to be found in A. James Arnold, *Négritude and Modernism: The Poetry and Poetics of Aimé Césaire* (1981); Arnold has further developed his views in his introduction to Clayton Eshleman and Annette Smith, trans., *Aimé Césaire: Lyrical and Dramatic Poetry* (1992). Janis Pallister, *Aimé Césaire* (1991), is a useful general discussion of the main themes; while Ronnie Leah Scharfman, *Engagement and the Language of the Subject in the Poetry of Aimé Césaire* (1980), examines the complex psychological mechanisms at work in the poetry. The translation of *Notebook* printed here is taken from Clayton Eshleman and Annette Smith, trans., *Aimé Césaire: The Collected Poetry* (1983), which contains, in addition to translations of Césaire's poetry up to the late 1970s, a valuable general introduction.

PRONOUNCING GLOSSARY

The following list uses common English syllables to provide rough equivalents of selected words whose pronunciation may be unfamiliar to the general reader.

grigri: *gree-gree*

jiculi: *jee-koo-lee*

likouala: *lee-koo-ah-la*

patyura: *paht-yur-ah*

Notebook of a Return to the Native Land[1]

At the end of daybreak . . .

Beat it, I said to him, you cop, you lousy pig, beat it, I detest the flunkies of order and the cockchafers of hope. Beat it, evil grigri,[2] you bedbug of a petty monk. Then I turned toward paradises lost for him and his kin, calmer than the face of a woman telling lies, and there,   5 rocked by the flux of a never exhausted thought I nourished the wind, I unlaced the monsters and heard rise, from the other side of disaster,[3] a river of turtledoves and savanna clover which I carry forever in my depths height-deep as the twentieth floor of the most arrogant houses and as a guard against the putrefying force of crepuscular surround-   10 ings, surveyed night and day by a cursed venereal sun.

At the end of daybreak burgeoning with frail coves, the hungry Antilles, the Antilles pitted with smallpox, the Antilles dynamited by alcohol, stranded in the mud of this bay, in the dust of this town sinisterly stranded.   15

At the end of daybreak, the extreme, deceptive desolate bedsore on the wound of the waters; the martyrs who do not bear witness; the flowers of blood that fade and scatter in the empty wind like the screeches of babbling parrots; an aged life mendaciously smiling, its lips opened by vacated agonies; an aged poverty rotting under the sun,   20 silently; an aged silence bursting with tepid pustules, the awful futility of our raison d'être.[4]

At the end of daybreak, on this very fragile earth thickness exceeded in a humiliating way by its grandiose future—the volcanoes will explode,[5] the naked water will bear away the ripe sun stains and   25 nothing will be left but a tepid bubbling pecked at by sea birds—the beach of dreams and the insane awakenings.

At the end of daybreak, this town sprawled-flat toppled from its common sense, inert, winded under its geometric weight of an eter- nally renewed cross, indocile to its fate, mute, vexed no matter what,   30

---

1. Translated by Clayton Eshleman and Annette Smith.   2. Charms.   3. That is, Africa before the historical disaster of slavery.   4. Reason for being (French, literal trans.).   5. A reference to Mont Pélé, which suddenly erupted in 1902 and destroyed Saint Pierre, the former capital of Martinique.

incapable of growing with the juice of this earth, self-conscious, clipped, reduced, in breach of fauna and flora.

At the end of daybreak, this town sprawled-flat . . .

And in this inert town, this squalling throng so astonishingly detoured from its cry as this town has been from its movement, from 35 its meaning, not even worried, detoured from its true cry, the only cry you would have wanted to hear because you feel it alone belongs to this town; because you feel it lives in it in some deep refuge and pride in this inert town, this throng detoured from its cry of hunger, of poverty, of revolt, of hatred, this throng so strangely chattering and 40 mute.

In this inert town, this strange throng which does not pack, does not mix: clever at discovering the point of disencasement,[6] of flight, of dodging. This throng which does not know how to throng, this throng, clearly so perfectly alone under this sun, like a woman one 45 thought completely occupied with her lyric cadence, who abruptly challenges a hypothetical rain and enjoins it not to fall; or like a rapid sign of the cross without perceptive motive; or like the sudden grave animality of a peasant, urinating standing, her legs parted, stiff.

In this inert town, this desolate throng under the sun, not con- 50 nected with anything that is expressed, asserted, released in broad earth daylight, its own. Neither with Josephine, Empress of the French, dreaming way up there above the nigger scum. Nor with the liberator[7] fixed in his whitewashed stone liberation. Nor with the conquistador.[8] Nor with this contempt, with this freedom, with this 55 audacity.

At the end of daybreak, this inert town and its beyond of lepers, of consumption, of famines, of fears squatting in the ravines, fears perched in the trees, fears dug in the ground, fears adrift in the sky, piles of fears and their fumaroles[9] of anguish. 60

At the end of daybreak, the morne[1] forgotten, forgetful of leaping.

At the end of daybreak, the morne in restless, docile hooves—its malarial blood routs the sun with its overheated pulse.

At the end of daybreak, the restrained conflagration of the 65 morne like a sob gagged on the verge of a bloodthirsty burst, in quest of an ignition that slips away and ignores itself.

---

6. The point at which two pieces of machinery can be fitted into each other or disconnected.   7. Victor Schoelcher (1804–1893), French abolitionist, whose statue stands in a square in the capital, Fort de France. Josephine (1763–1814), the first wife of Napoléon Bonaparte, was born in Martinique into the white settler class; she became empress when Napoléon took the title "emperor of the French" in 1801. 8. Conqueror (Spanish), applied to Cortes, Pizarro, and other adventurers who conquered South America on behalf of Spain. Here, Bélain d'Estambuc, who occupied Martinique in 1635 and claimed it for France.   9. In volcanic regions, ground holes that emit gases and vapors.   1. A little hill or hillock characteristic of Martinican landscape.

At the end of daybreak, the morne crouching before bulimia on the lookout for tuns[2] and mills, slowly vomiting out its human fatigue, the morne solitary and its blood shed, the morne bandaged in shades, the morne and its ditches of fear, the morne and its great hands of wind.

At the end of daybreak, the famished morne and no one knows better than this bastard morne why the suicide choked with a little help from his hypoglossal jamming his tongue backward to swallow it;[3] why a woman seems to float belly up on the Capot River[4] (her chiaroscuro body submissively organized at the command of her navel) but she is only a bundle of sonorous water.

And neither the teacher in his classroom, nor the priest at catechism will be able to get a word out of this sleepy little nigger, no matter how energetically they drum on his shorn skull, for starvation has quicksanded his voice into the swamp of hunger (a word-one-single-word and we-will-forget-about-Queen-Blanche-of-Castille,[5] a-word-one-single-word, you-should-see-this-little savage-who-doesn't-know-any-of-The-Ten-Commandments).

for his voice gets lost in the swamp of hunger,
and there is nothing, really nothing to squeeze out of this little brat,
other than a hunger which can no longer climb to the rigging of his voice
a sluggish flabby hunger,
a hunger buried in the depth of the Hunger of this famished morne.

At the end of daybreak, the disparate stranding,[6] the exacerbated stench of corruption, the monstrous sodomies of the host and the sacrificing priest, the impassable beakhead frames of prejudice and stupidity, the prostitutions, the hypocrisies, the lubricities, the treasons, the lies, the frauds, the concussions—the panting of a deficient cowardice, the heave-holess enthusiasm of supernumerary sahibs,[7] the greeds, the hysterias, the perversions, the clownings of poverty, the cripplings, the itchings, the hives, the tepid hammocks of degeneracy. Right here the parade of laughable and scrofulous buboes, the forced feedings of very strange microbes, the poisons without known alexins, the sanies[8] of really ancient sores, the unforeseeable fermentations of putrescible species.

At the end of daybreak, the great motionless night, the stars deader than a caved-in balafon.[9]

2. Casks, in which rum is stored. *Bulimia:* here, excessive hunger. The references are to the economic life of the islands, dominated by the production of sugar and the distillation of rum.   3. Slaves committed suicide by choking on their own tongues. *Hypoglossal:* the nerve under the tongue.   4. A stream in northern Martinique. The passage plays on an allusion to Ophelia, in Shakespeare's *Hamlet,* who floats down river after her suicide by drowning.   5. A queen of France in the Middle Ages.   6. The heterogeneous character of the West Indian population.   7. Lord, commander (Hindi).   8. Fluid from a wound. *Scrofulous buboes:* swellings caused by tuberculosis ("scrofula"). *Alexins:* antidotes.   9. An African musical instrument similar to a xylophone.

the teratical[1] bulb of night, sprouted from our vilenesses and our   105
renunciations.

And our foolish and crazy stunts to revive the golden splashing of
privileged moments, the umbilical cord restored to its ephemeral
splendor, the bread, and the wine of complicity, the bread, the wine,
the blood of honest weddings.   110

And this joy of former times making me aware of my present poverty, a bumpy road plunging into a hollow where it scatters a few
shacks; an indefatigable road charging at full speed a morne at the
top of which it brutally quicksands into a pool of clumsy houses, a
road foolishly climbing, recklessly descending, and the carcass of   115
wood, which I call "our house," comically perched on minute cement
paws, its coiffure of corrugated iron in the sun like a skin laid out to
dry, the main room, the rough floor where the nail heads gleam, the
beams of pine and shadow across the ceiling, the spectral straw chairs,
the grey lamp light, the glossy flash of cockroaches in a maddening   120
buzz . . .

At the end of daybreak, this most essential land restored to my gour-
mandise,[2] not in diffuse tenderness, but the tormented sensual concentration of the fat tits of the mornes with an occasional palm tree
as their hardened sprout, the jerky orgasm of torrents and from   125
Trinité to Grand-Rivière,[3] the hysterical grandsuck of the sea.

And time passed quickly, very quickly.
After August and mango trees decked out in all their little moons,
September begetter of cyclones, October igniter of sugar-cane,
November who purrs in the distilleries, there came Christmas.   130
It had come in at first, Christmas did, with a tingling of desires, a
thirst for new tenderness, a burgeoning of vague dreams, then with a
purple rustle of its great joyous wings it had suddenly flown away, and
then its abrupt fall out over the village that made the shack life burst
like an overripe pomegranate.   135
Christmas was not like other holidays. It didn't like to gad about
the streets,[4] to dance on public squares, to mount the wooden horses,
to use the crowd to pinch women, to hurl fireworks in the faces of the
tamarind trees. It had agoraphobia,[5] Christmas did. What it wanted
was a whole day of bustling, preparing, a cooking and cleaning spree, 140
endless jitters
about-not-having-enough,
about-running-short,
about-getting-bored,

then at evening an unimposing little church, which would benevo-   145
lently make room for the laughter, the whispers, the secrets, the love
talk, the gossip and the guttural cacophony of a plucky singer and also
boisterous pals and shameless hussies and shacks up to their guts in

---

1. Monstrous.   2. Here, keen desire.   3. Towns in northern Martinique.   4. As during Carnival
(just before Lent).   5. The fear of open spaces, the opposite of claustrophobia.

succulent goodies, and not stingy, and twenty people can crowd in, and the street is deserted, and the village turns into a bouquet of 150 singing, and you are cozy in there, and you eat good, and you drink hearty and there are blood sausages, one kind only two fingers wide twined in coils, the other broad and stocky, the mild one tasting of wild thyme, the hot one spiced to an incandescence, and steaming coffee and sugared anise[6] and milk punch, and the liquid sun of rums, 155 and all sorts of good things which drive your taste buds wild or distill them to the point of ecstasy or cocoon them with fragrances, and you laugh, and you sing, and the refrains flare on and on like coco-palms:

ALLELUIA
KYRIE ELEISON[7] . . . LEISON . . . LEISON   160
CHRISTE ELEISON . . . LEISON . . . LEISON.

And not only do the mouths sing, but the hands, the feet, the buttocks, the genitals, and your entire being liquefies into sounds, voices, and rhythm.

At the peak of its ascent, joy bursts like a cloud. The songs don't 165 stop, but now anxious and heavy roll through the valleys of fear, the tunnels of anguish and the fires of hell.

And each one starts pulling the nearest devil by his tail, until fear imperceptibly fades in the fine sand lines of dream, and you really live as in a dream, and you drink and you shout and you sing as in a 170 dream, and doze too as in a dream, with rose petal eyelids, and the day comes velvety as a sapodilla[8] tree, and the liquid manure smell of the cacao trees, and the turkeys which shell their red pustules[9] in the sun, and the obsessive bells, and the rain,

the bells . . . the rain . . .   175
that tinkle, tinkle, tinkle . . .

At the end of daybreak, this town sprawled-flat . . .

It crawls on its hands without the slightest desire to drill the sky with a stature of protest. The backs of the houses are afraid of the sky truffled with fire, their feet of the drownings of the soil, they chose to 180 perch shallowly between surprises and treacheries. And yet it advances, the town does. It even grazes every day further out into its tide of tiled corridors, prudish shutters, gluey courtyards, dripping paintwork. And petty hushed-up scandals, petty unvoiced guilts, petty immense hatreds knead the narrow streets into bumps and potholes 185 where the waste-water grins longitudinally through turds . . .

At the end of daybreak, life prostrate, you don't know how to dispose of your aborted dreams, the river of life desperately torpid in its bed, neither turgid nor low, hesitant to flow, pitifully empty, the impartial heaviness of boredom distributing shade equally on all 190 things, the air stagnant, unbroken by the brightness of a single bird.

---

6. A liqueur made from aniseed.   7. Lord have mercy (Greek); a chant from the first part of the Catholic mass.   8. A fleshy fruit found in the West Indies.   9. Pimples. The red skin hanging in a fold around the neck of turkeys seems to be covered with them.

At the end of daybreak, another little house very bad-smelling in a very narrow street, a miniscule house which harbors in its guts of rotten wood dozens of rats and the turbulence of my six brothers and sisters, a cruel little house whose demands panic the ends of our months and my temperamental father gnawed by one persistent ache, I never knew which one, whom an unexpected sorcery could lull to melancholy tenderness or drive to towering flames of anger; and my mother whose legs pedal, pedal, night and day, for our tireless hunger, I was even awakened at night by these tireless legs which pedal the night and the bitter bite in the soft flesh of the night of a Singer[1] that my mother pedals, pedals for our hunger and day and night.

At the end of daybreak, beyond my father, my mother, the shack chapped with blisters, like a peach tree afflicted with curl,[2] and the thin roof patched with pieces of gasoline cans, which create swamps of rust in the stinking sordid grey straw pulp, and when the wind whistles, these odds and ends make a noise bizarre, first like the crackling of frying, then like a brand dropped into water the smoke of its twigs flying up. And the bed of boards from which my race arose, my whole entire race from this bed of boards, with its kerosene case paws, as if it had elephantiasis,[3] that bed, and its kidskin, and its dry banana leaves, and its rags, yearning for a mattress, my grandmother's bed. (Above the bed, in a jar full of oil a dim light whose flame dances like a fat cockroach . . . on the jar in gold letters: MERCI.[4])

And this rue Paille,[5] this disgrace,

an appendage repulsive as the private parts of the village which extends right and left, along the colonial highway, the grey surge of its shingled roofs. Here there are only straw roofs, spray browned and wind plucked.

Everybody despises rue Paille. It's there that the village youth go astray. It's there especially that the sea pours forth its garbage, its dead cats and its croaked dogs. For the street opens on to the beach, and the beach alone cannot satisfy the sea's foaming rage.

A blight this beach as well, with its piles of rotting muck, its furtive rumps relieving themselves, and the sand is black,[6] funereal, you've never seen a sand so black, and the scum glides over it yelping, and the sea pummels it like a boxer, or rather the sea is a huge dog licking and biting the shins of the beach, biting them so fiercely that it will end up devouring it, the beach and rue Paille along with it.

At the end of daybreak, the wind of long ago—of betrayed trusts, of uncertain evasive duty and that other dawn in Europe—

---

1. An old-model sewing machine that was powered by the movement of the legs. 2. An infection that attacks the leaves of the peach tree. 3. A disease that causes swelling of the legs. 4. Thank you (French); the inscription is presumably addressed to God. 5. Straw Road (French, literal trans.); a street whose houses are roofed with straw. 6. Because of its volcanic origin.

arises . . .

To go away.
As there are hyena-men and panther-men, I would be a jew-man[7]
a Kaffir-man   235
    a Hindu-man-from-Calcutta
a Harlem-man-who-doesn't-vote[8]

the famine man, the insult-man, the torture man you can grab anytime, beat up, kill—no joke, kill—without having to account to anyone, without having to make excuses to anyone   240
a jew-man
a pogrom[9]-man
a puppy
a beggar
but *can* one kill Remorse, perfect as the stupefied face of an English   245
lady discovering a Hottentot[1] skull in her soup-tureen?

I would rediscover the secret of great communications and great com-
bustions. I would say storm. I would say river. I would say tornado. I
would say leaf. I would say tree. I would be drenched by all rains,
moistened by all dews. I would roll like frenetic blood on the slow   250
current of the eye of words turned into mad horses into fresh children
into clots into curfew into vestiges of temples into precious stones
remote enough to discourage miners. Whoever would not understand
me would not understand any better the roaring of a tiger.

And you ghosts rise blue from alchemy from a forest of hunted   255
beasts of twisted machines of a jujube tree of rotten flesh of a basket
of oysters of eyes of a network of straps in the beautiful sisal[2] of human
skin I would have words vast enough to contain you earth taut earth
drunk
earth great vulva raised to the sun   260
earth great delirium of God's mentula[3]
savage earth arisen from the storerooms of the sea a clump of
Cecropia[4] in your mouth earth whose tumultuous face I can only
compare to the virgin and mad forest which were it in my power I
would show in guise of a face to the undeciphering eyes of men   265
all I would need is a mouthful of jiculi milk[5] to discover in you always
as distant as a mirage—a thousand times more native and made
golden by a sun that no prism divides—the earth where everything is
free and fraternal, my earth.

To go away. My heart was pounding with emphatic generosities.   270

7. Césaire's identification with another persecuted people, extended in the lines below to other minorit-
ies.   8. Harlem, the center of black life in New York City, is an appropriate reference for the denial of
civil rights to blacks in the United States before corrective legislation in the 1960s. *Kaffir:* a term of
contempt formerly applied by whites to black South Africans. Calcutta, India, was noted for its extreme
poverty.   9. Organized harassment of Jews, often leading to their massacre.   1. A people of southwest
Africa, who were decimated by white invaders in the 19th century.   2. A fibrous plant. *Jujube tree:*
produces red fruit.   3. Penis, here ascribed to the sun.   4. A tree with a milky sap.   5. The juice
of a tropical plant; it produces a hallucinatory effect.

To go away . . . I would arrive sleek and young in this land of mine
and I would say to this land whose loam is part of my flesh: "I have
wandered for a long time and I am coming back to the deserted hid-
eousness of your sores."

I would go to this land of mine and I would say to it: "Embrace me   275
without fear . . . And if all I can do is speak, it is for you I shall speak."

And again I would say:

"My mouth shall be the mouth of those calamities that have no
mouth, my voice the freedom of those who break down in the solitary
confinement of despair."   280

And on the way I would say to myself:

"And above all, my body as well as my soul, beware of assuming the sterile attitude of a spectator, for life is not a spectacle, a sea
of miseries is not a proscenium,[6] a man screaming is not a dancing
bear . . ."   285

And behold here I am!

Once again this life hobbling before me, what am I saying life, *this
death*, this death without sense or piety, this death that so pathetically
falls short of greatness, the dazzling pettiness of this death, this death
hobbling from pettiness to pettiness; these shovelfuls of petty greeds   290
over the conquistador; these shovelfuls of petty flunkies over the great-
savage, these shovelfuls of petty souls over the three-souled Carib,[7]
and all these deaths futile
absurdities under the splashing of my open conscience
tragic futilities lit up by this single noctiluca[8]   295
and I alone, sudden stage of this daybreak when the apocalypse of
monsters cavorts then, capsized, hushes
warm election of cinders, of ruins and collapses
—One more thing! only one, but please make it only one: I have no
right to measure life by my sooty finger span; to reduce myself to this   300
little ellipsoidal nothing[9] trembling four fingers above the line,[1] I a
man, to so overturn creation, that I include myself between latitude
and longitude!

At the end of daybreak,
the male thirst and the desire stubborn,   305
here I am, severed from the cool oases of brotherhood
this so modest nothing bristles with hard splinters
this too safe horizon is startled like a jailer.

Your last triumph, tenacious crow of Treason.

What is mine, these few thousand deathbearers who mill in the   310
calabash of an island and mine too, the archipelago arched[2] with an
anguished desire to negate itself, as if from maternal anxiety to protect
this impossibly delicate tenuity separating one America from another;
and these loins which secrete for Europe the hearty liquor of a Gulf

---

6. A platform that serves as a stage for a performance.   7. Indicating the indigenous Carib Indians as
well as the descendants of Africans and of Europeans.   8. Light from a glowworm.   9. That is, Martinique, which is oval-shaped.   1. A reference to Martinique's geographical position close to the equator.
2. Like a tense bow, an image suggested by the half circle formed by the islands across the Caribbean
Sea.

Stream,[3] and one of the two slopes of incandescence between which   315
the Equator tightropewalks toward Africa. And my nonfence island,
its brave audacity standing at the stern of this Polynesia, before it,
Guadeloupe, split in two down its dorsal line and equal in poverty to
us, Haiti[4] where negritude rose for the first time[4] and stated that it
believed in its humanity and the funny little tail of Florida where the   320
strangulation of a nigger is being completed, and Africa gigantically
caterpillaring up to the Hispanic foot of Europe, its nakedness where
Death scythes widely.

And I say to myself Bordeaux and Nantes and Liverpool[5] and New
York and San Francisco   325

not an inch of this world devoid of my fingerprint
and my calcaneum[6] on the spines of skyscrapers and my filth in the
glitter of gems!
Who can boast of being better off than I? Virginia.
Tennessee. Georgia. Alabama[7]   330
monstrous putrefactions of stymied
revolts
marshes of putrid blood
trumpets absurdly muted
land red, sanguineous, consanguineous[8] land.   335

What is also mine: a little
cell in the Jura,[9]
a little cell, the snow lines it with white bars
the snow is a jailer mounting
guard before a prison   340

What is mine
a lonely man imprisoned in
whiteness
a lonely man defying the white
screams of white death   345
(TOUSSAINT, TOUSSAINT L'OUVERTURE)

a man who mesmerizes
the white hawk of white death
a man alone in the sterile
sea of white sand   350
a coon grown old standing up to

---

3. An ocean current that flows from the West Indies to the north Atlantic; it has a tempering effect on the climate of western Europe. *Delicate tenuity:* the thin strip of Central America, protected by the Caribbean from the full force of the Atlantic.   4. A reference to the slave revolt, led by Toussaint L'Ouverture (c. 1743–1803), which led to the independence of Haiti in 1804. Guadeloupe, the other French West Indian colony, is now a French department. It lies north of Martinique and is made up of two islands (Basse Terre and Grand Terre). *Polynesia:* in the sense of a group of islands.   5. Bordeaux and Nantes in France and Liverpool in England were the principal ports from which, in a triangular circuit, the slave ships sailed out to Africa and, after being loaded with their human cargo, crossed to America, returning with produce to Europe.   6. Heel, complementary to *fingerprint.*   7. Along with New York and San Francisco, symbols of the economic exploitation of the black people.   8. Linked by blood; here, that of the black slave.   9. L'Ouverture was captured by the French and taken to France, to be imprisoned in the fortress of Joux, in the Jura Mountains, where he eventually died.

the waters of the sky
Death traces a shining circle
above this man
death stars softly above his head   355
death breathes, crazed, in the ripened
cane field of his arms
death gallops in the prison like
a white horse[1]
death gleams in the dark like the   360
eyes of a cat
death hiccups like water under the Keys[2]
death is a struck bird
death wanes
death flickers   365
death is a very shy patyura[3]
death expires in a white pool
of silence.
Swellings of night in the four corners
of this dawn   370
convulsions of congealed death
tenacious fate
screams erect from mute earth
the splendor of this blood will it not burst open?

    At the end of daybreak this land without a stele,[4] these paths with-   375
out memory, these winds without a tablet.
    So what?
    We would tell. Would sing. Would howl.
    Full voice, ample voice, you would be our wealth, our spear
pointed.   380
    Words?
    Ah yes, words!

Reason, I crown you evening wind.[5]
Your name voice of order?
To me the whip's corolla.[6]   385
Beauty I call you the false claim of the stone.
But ah! my raucous laughter
smuggled in
Ah! my saltpetre[7] treasure!
Because we hate you   390
and your reason, we claim kinship
with dementia praecox[8] with the flaming madness
of persistent cannibalism

---

1. Refers both to Baron Samedi, the spirit of death in Haitian folk belief, and the horse of death in Western iconography.   2. Coral reefs in the Caribbean.   3. According to Césaire, a variation on "patira," the name for a peccary found in Paraguay [*Translators' note*].   4. Funeral monuments to military heroes.   5. Boding death.   6. The strands of the whip commonly used on slaves.   7. Potassium, used in the manufacture of gunpowder.   8. Schizophrenia.

Treasure, let's count:
the madness that remembers[9]   395
the madness that howls
the madness that sees
the madness that is unleashed
And you know the rest

That 2 and 2 are 5[1]   400
that the forest miaows
that the tree plucks the maroons from the fire[2]
that the sky strokes its beard
etc. etc. . . .

Who and what are we?   405
A most worthy question!

From staring too long at trees I have
become a tree and my long tree
feet have dug in the ground large
venom sacs high cities of bone   410
from brooding too long on the Congo[3]
I have become a Congo resounding with
forests and rivers
where the whip cracks like a great banner
the banner of a prophet   415
where the water goes
likouala-likouala
where the angerbolt hurls its greenish
axe[4] forcing the boars of
putrefaction to the lovely wild edge   420
of the nostrils.

At the end of daybreak the sun which
hacks and spits up its lungs

At the end of daybreak
a slow gait of sand   425
a slow gait of gauze
a slow gait of corn kernels
At the end of daybreak
a full gallop of pollen
a full gallop of a slow gait of   430
little girls
a full gallop of hummingbirds[5]

9. The immediate reference is to the memory of slavery, but the phrase draws its full meaning from the
Surrealist belief in madness as a form of insight.   1. Deliberately irrational, again as part of the Surrealist convention.   2. Runaway slaves (*maroons*) often made animal sounds as signals to each other. They
also hid in the treetops to escape their pursuers; plays also on the French meaning of *maroon* = chestnut.
3. A river that flows through dense tropical forests in central Africa.   4. *Angerbolt* refers to the uprising
of the native population, an act that restores the people to harmony with their essential beings (*greenish
axe*). The Likouala River is in the interior of the present-day Republic of Congo.   5. Symbols of Césaire's native land.

a full gallop of daggers to stave in
the earth's breast

customs angels mounting guard over   435
prohibitions at the gates of foam

I declare my crimes[6] and that there is nothing
to say in my defense.
Dances. Idols. An apostate. I too
I have assassinated God with my laziness with   440
my words with my gestures
with my obscene songs

I have worn parrot plumes
musk cat skins
I have exhausted the missionaries' patience   445
insulted the benefactors of mankind.
Defied Tyre. Defied Sidon.
Worshipped the Zambezi.[7]
The extent of my perversity overwhelms me!

But why impenetrable jungle are you still hiding the raw zero of my   450
mendacity and from a self-conscious concern for nobility not celebrating the horrible leap of my Pahouin[8] ugliness?

voum rooh oh[9]
voum rooh oh
to charm the snakes to conjure   455
the dead
voum rooh oh
to compel the rain to turn back
the tidal waves
voum rooh oh   460
to keep the shade from moving
voum rooh oh that my own skies
may open

—me on a road, a child, chewing
sugar cane root   465
—a dragged man on a bloodspattered road
a rope around his neck
—standing in the center of a huge circus,
on my black forehead a crown of daturas[1]
voum rooh   470
to fly off

6. The stereotypes of Africans in colonial ideology are echoed in this ironic confession.   7. A river in
southern Africa. The religious practices of Africans were often devalued as animism, of which river worship was a prominent feature. Tyre and Sidon were commercial ports in ancient Phoenicia, often mentioned in history books as early centers of civilization.   8. An ethnic group in present-day Gabon.
9. An incantation, by which Césaire assumes the powers enumerated in this stanza.   1. A mildly poisonous, hallucinatory plant, with which his brow is decked—as befits his combative role—instead of the
laurels associated with classical tradition.

higher than quivering higher
than the sorceresses toward other stars
ferocious exultation of forests and
mountains uprooted at the hour   475
when no one expects it[2]
the islands linked for a thousand years!

voum rooh oh
that the promised times may return
and the bird who knew my name   480
and the woman[3] who had a thousand names
names of fountain sun and tears
and her hair of minnows[4]
and her steps my climates
and her eyes my seasons   485
and the days without injury
and the nights without offense
and the stars my confidence
and the wind my accomplice

But who misleads my voice? who grates   490
my voice? Stuffing my throat
with a thousand bamboo fangs. A thousand
sea urchin stakes. It is you dirty end
of the world. Dirty end of daybreak.
It is you dirty hatred. It is you weight   495
of the insult and a hundred years of whip
lashes. It is you one hundred years of my
patience, one hundred years of my effort
simply to stay alive
rooh oh   500
we sing of venomous flowers
flaring in fury-filled prairies;
the skies of love cut with bloodclots;
the epileptic mornings; the white blaze
of abyssal[5] sands, the sinking   505
of flotsam in nights electrified
with feline smells.

What can I do?

One must begin somewhere.

Begin what?   510

The only thing in the world
worth beginning:
The End of the world of course.

2. Another reference to the sudden eruption of Mont Pélé.   3. A guardian goddess, identified with
Césaire's vision of Martinique's future. *The bird who knew my name:* the hummingbird (see n. 5, p. 2231).
4. The woman is now presented as the sea goddess of folk mythology, with hair made of small fish.
5. Unfathomable.

Torte[6]
oh torte of the terrifying autumn   515
where the new steel and the perennial concrete
grow
torte oh torte
where the air rusts in great sheets
of evil glee   520
where the sanious[7] water scars the great
solar cheeks
I hate you

one still sees madras rags[8] around the loins
of women rings in their ears   525
smiles on their lips babies
at their nipples, these for starters:

ENOUGH OF THIS OUTRAGE!

So here is the great challenge and the satanic
compulsion and the insolent   530
nostalgic drift of April moons,[9]
of green fires, of yellow fevers!

Vainly in the tepidity of your throat
you ripen for the twentieth time the same indigent
solace that we are   535
mumblers of words

Words? while we handle
quarters of earth, while we wed
delirious continents, while
we force steaming gates,   540
words, ah yes, words! but
words of fresh blood, words that are
tidal waves and erysipelas[1]
malarias and lava and brush
fires, and blazes of flesh,   545
and blazes of cities . . .

Know this:
the only game I play is the millennium
the only game I play is the Great
Fear[2]   550

Put up with me. I won't put up with you!

Sometimes you see me with a great display of brains
snap up a cloud too red
or a caress of rain, or a prelude

---

6. A kind of crude peasant bread.   7. Pertaining to fluid from a wound.   8. The scarf of fine material
worn around the waist by Martinican women.   9. Often reddish in hue and considered an ill omen.
1. An inflammation of the skin.   2. The year A.D. 1000 was awaited in early Christendom with foreboding (*the Great Fear*) as the date that would mark the end of the world predicted in the Book of Revelation.

of wind,   555
don't fool yourself:

I am forcing the vitelline membrane[3] that separates
me from myself,
I am forcing the great waters which girdle me with blood

I and I alone choose   560
a seat on the last train of the last
surge of the last tidal wave

I and I alone
make contact with the latest
anguish   565

I and oh, only I
secure the first
drops of virginal milk through a straw!

And now a last boo:
to the sun (not strong enough to inebriate   570
my very tough head)
to the mealy night with its golden
hatchings of erratic fireflies
to the head of hair trembling at the very
top of the cliff   575
where the wind leaps in bursts of salty
cavalries
I clearly read in my pulse that for me
exoticism is no provender[4]

Leaving Europe utterly twisted with screams   580
the silent currents of despair
leaving timid Europe which
collects and proudly overrates itself
I summon this egotism beautiful
and bold   585
    and my ploughing reminds me of an implacable cutwater.[5]

So much blood in my memory! In my memory are lagoons. They are
covered with death's-heads.
    They are not covered with water lilies.
In my memory are lagoons. No women's loincloths spread out on   590
their shores.
My memory is encircled with blood. My memory has a belt of
corpses!
and machine gun fire of rum barrels brilliantly sprinkling
our ignominious revolts, amorous glances swooning from having   595
swigged too much ferocious freedom

(niggers-are-all-alike, I-tell-you vices-all-the-vices-believe-you-me
nigger-smell, that's-what-makes-cane-grow
remember-the-old-saying:

---

3. Protects the fetus in its mother's womb.   4. Animal feed.   5. The prow of a ship.

beat-a-nigger, and you feed him)   600
among "rocking chairs" contemplating the voluptuousness of quirts[6]
I circle about, an unappeased filly

Or else quite simply as they like to think of us!
Cheerfully obscene, completely nuts about jazz to cover their extreme
boredom   605
I can boogie-woogie, do the Lindy-hop[7] and tap-dance.
And for a special treat the muting of our cries muffled with wah-wah.[8]
Wait . . . Everything is as it should be. My good angel grazes the neon.
I swallow batons. My dignity wallows in puke . . .
　　Sun, Angel Sun, curled Angel of the Sun   610
　　for a leap beyond the sweet and greenish
treading of the waters of abjection!

　　But I approached the wrong sorcerer, on this exorcised earth, cast
adrift from its precious malignant purpose, this voice that cries, little
by little hoarse, vainly, vainly hoarse,   615
　　and there remains only the accumulated droppings of our lies—
and they do not respond.
What madness to dream up a marvelous caper above the baseness!
Oh Yes the Whites are great warriors hosannah to the master and to
the nigger-gelder!   620
Victory! Victory, I tell you: the defeated are content!
Joyous stenches and songs of mud!
　　By a sudden and beneficent inner revolution, I now honour my
repugnant ugliness.

　　On Midsummer Day, as soon as the first shadows fall on the village   625
of Gros-Morne, hundreds of horse dealers gather on rue "De PRO-
FUNDIS,"[9] a name at least honest enough to announce an onrush
from the shoals of Death. And it truly is from Death, from its thousand
petty local forms (cravings unsatisfied by Para grass[1] and tipsy bondage
to the distilleries) that the astonishing cavalry of impetuous nags   630
surges unfenced toward the great-life. What a galloping! what
neighing! what sincere urinating! what prodigious droppings! "A fine
horse difficult to mount!"—"A proud mare sensitive to the spur"—"A
fearless foal superbly pasterned!"[2]
　　And the shrewd fellow whose waistcoat displays a proud watch   635
chain, palms off instead of full udders, youthful mettle and genuine
contours, either the systematic puffiness from obliging wasps, or the
obscene stings from ginger, or the helpful distribution of several gal-
lons of sugared water.[3]

　　I refuse to pass off my puffiness for authentic glory.   640
　　And I laugh at my former childish fantasies.
　　No, we've never been Amazons of the king of Dahomey, nor

---

6. Riding whips.　　7. A dance named after Carl Lindbergh, who made aviation history in 1927 by being
the first to fly solo across the Atlantic.　　8. Sarcastic imitation of the muted trumpet.　　9. Out of the
depths (Latin), from a liturgy for the dead. Gros-Morne is north of Fort de France.　　1. Coarse elephant
grass on which the horses are fed.　　2. Nobly built.　　3. Ways in which the horses have been doctored
to give them a false air of well-being.

princes of Ghana with eight hundred camels, nor wise men in Timbuktu under Askia the Great, nor the architects of Djenne, nor
Madhis,[4] nor warriors. We don't feel under our armpit the itch of   645
those who in the old days carried a lance. And since I have sworn to
leave nothing out of our history (I who love nothing better than a
sheep grazing his own afternoon shadow), I may as well confess that
we were at all times pretty mediocre dishwashers, shoeblacks without
ambition, at best conscientious sorcerers and the only unquestionable   650
record that we broke was that of endurance under the chicote[5] . . .

And this land screamed for centuries that we are bestial brutes; that
the human pulse stops at the gates of the slave compound; that we
are walking compost hideously promising tender cane and silky cotton and they would brand us with red-hot irons and we would sleep   655
in our excrement and they would sell us on the town square and an
ell[6] of English cloth and salted meat from Ireland cost less than we
did, and this land was calm, tranquil, repeating that the spirit of the
Lord was in its acts.

We the vomit of slave ships   660
We the venery of the Calabars[7]
what? Plug up our ears?
We, so drunk on jeers and inhaled fog that we rode the roll to death!
Forgive us fraternal whirlwind!

I hear coming up from the hold the enchained curses, the gasps of   665
the dying, the noise of someone thrown into the sea . . . the baying of
a woman in labor . . . the scrape of fingernails seeking throats . . . the
flouts of the whip . . . the seethings of vermin amid the weariness . . .

Nothing could ever lift us toward a noble hopeless adventure.
So be it. So be it.   670
I am of no nationality recognized by the chancelleries.
I defy the craniometer. Homo sum etc.
Let them serve and betray and die
So be it. So be it. It was written in the shape of their pelvis.[8]

And I, and I,   675
I was singing the hard fist
You must know the extent of my cowardice. One evening on the
streetcar facing me, a nigger.
A nigger big as a pongo[9] trying to make himself small on the street-

---

4. In Islam, leaders in a holy war. *Amazons:* female warriors in the ancient African kingdom of Dahomey.
Ghana is the medieval West African empire after which the modern state is named. Timbuktu, on the
river Niger, was an outstanding intellectual center in the Middle Ages. Askia the Great was ruler of the
African empire of Songhai from the late 15th to the early years of the 16th century. Djenne, in present-
day Mali, was a university town in the Middle Ages. This passage contains references to aspects of precolonial African history to which the West Indian has at best an ambiguous connection.   5. Whip.   6. A
unit of measure, just over a yard.   7. A coastal town in southeastern Nigeria; a major slave depot.
8. Ironic reference to physiological arguments employed to establish the inferiority of the black race,
notably by the French writer Arthur Gobineau, whose actual words are quoted here. *Craniometer:* an
instrument for measuring the size of skulls, thought to be a factor in the evolution of the brain. *Homo
sum:* I am man (Latin); a quotation from *The Self-Tormentor* by the playwright Terence. The rest of the
line reads, "and I consider nothing human foreign to me."   9. *Pongo* is a genus of anthropoid apes,
including orangutans.

car bench. He was trying to leave behind, on this grimy bench, his   680
gigantic legs and his trembling famished boxer hands. And everything
had left him, was leaving him. His nose which looked like a drifting
peninsula and even his negritude discolored as a result of untiring
tawing.[1] And the tawer was Poverty. A big unexpected lop-eared bat
whose claw marks in his face had scabbed over into crusty islands. Or   685
rather, it was a tireless worker, Poverty was, working on some hideous
cartouche.[2] One could easily see how that industrious and malevolent
thumb had kneaded bumps into his brow, bored two bizarre parallel
tunnels in his nose, overexaggerated his lips, and in a masterpiece of
caricature, planed, polished and varnished the tiniest cutest little ear   690
in all creation.

He was a gangly nigger without rhythm or measure.

A nigger whose eyes rolled a bloodshot weariness.

A shameless nigger and his toes sneered in a rather stinking way at
the bottom of the yawning lair of his shoes.   695

Poverty, without any question, had knocked itself out to finish him
off.

It had dug the socket, had painted it with a rouge of dust mixed
with rheum.[3]

It had stretched an empty space between the solid hinge of the jaw   700
and bone of an old tarnished cheek. Had planted over it the small
shiny stakes of a two- or three-day beard. Had panicked his heart, bent
his back.

And the whole thing added up perfectly to a hideous nigger, a
grouchy nigger, a melancholy nigger, a slouched nigger, his hands   705
joined in prayer on a knobby stick. A nigger shrouded in an old
threadbare coat. A comical and ugly nigger, with some women
behind me sneering at him.

He was COMICAL AND UGLY,[4]

COMICAL AND UGLY for sure.   710

I displayed a big complicitous smile . . .

My cowardice rediscovered!

Hail to the three centuries which uphold my civil rights and my minimized blood!

My heroism, what a farce!   715

This town fits me to a t.

And my soul is lying down. Lying down like this town in its refuse
and mud.

This town, my face of mud.

For my face I demand the vivid homage of spit! . . .   720

So, being what we are, ours the warrior thrust, the triumphant knee,
the well-plowed plains of the future?

Look, I'd rather admit to uninhibited ravings, my heart in my brain
like a drunken knee.

---

1. Working of leather.   2. Portrait sketch.   3. Liquid from the eye.   4. An echo of Baudelaire's
poem *The Albatros.* The individual is, of course, without the mystical significance Baudelaire attributes
to the ungainly bird.

My star now, the funereal menfenil.[5]   725

And on this former dream my cannibalistic cruelties:

(The bullets in the mouth thick saliva
our heart from daily lowness bursts the continents break the fragile
bond of isthmuses
lands leap in accordance with the fatal division of rivers   730
and the morne which for centuries kept its scream within itself, it is
its turn to draw and quarter the silence and this people an ever-
rebounding spirit
and our limbs vainly disjointed by the most refined tortures
and life even more impetuously jetting from this compost—unex-   735
pected as a soursop amidst the decomposition of jack tree[6] fruit!)

On this dream so old in me my cannibalistic cruelties

I was hiding behind a stupid vanity destiny called me I was hiding
behind it and suddenly there was a man on the ground, his feeble
defenses scattered,   740
his sacred maxims trampled underfoot, his pedantic rhetoric oozing
air through each wound.
There is a man on the ground
and his soul is almost naked
and destiny triumphs in watching this soul which defied its metamor-   745
phosis in the ancestral slough.

I say that this is right.
My back will victoriously exploit the chalaza[7] of fibers.
I will deck my natural obsequiousness with gratitude
And the silver-braided bullshit of the postillion of Havana,[8] lyrical   750
baboon pimp for the glamour of slavery, will be more than a match
for my enthusiasm.

I say that this is right
I live for the flattest part of my soul.
For the dullest part of my flesh!   755

    Tepid dawn[9] of ancestral heat and fear
I now tremble with the collective trembling that our docile blood
sings in the madrepore.[1]

And these tadpoles hatched in me by my prodigious ancestry!
Those who invented neither powder nor compass   760
those who could harness neither steam nor electricity
those who explored neither the seas nor the sky but who know
in its most minute corners the land of suffering

5. A Caribbean sparrow hawk with black plumage; hence *funereal*.   6. Or breadfruit, which provided
an important source of nourishment for the slaves. *Soursop:* a tropical tree with a white fleshy fruit, which
has a sharp taste.   7. A whip made of hard fibers.   8. A port city in Cuba. *Postilion:* a valet employed
to welcome newly arrived slaves with a speech in praise of slavery.   9. Announces a new movement in
the poem, leading to Césaire's celebration of his race.   1. Coral reef, symbolizing Martinique and, by
extension, the Caribbean region.

those who have known voyages only through uprootings
those who have been lulled to sleep by so much kneeling   765
those whom they domesticated and Christianized
those whom they inoculated with degeneracy
tom-toms of empty hands
inane tom-toms of resounding sores
burlesque tom-toms of tabetic treason[2]   770

     Tepid dawn of ancestral heat and fears
overboard with alien riches
overboard with my genuine falsehoods
But what strange pride suddenly illuminates me!
let the hummingbird come   775
let the sparrow hawk come
the breach in the horizon
the cynocephalus
let the lotus[3] bearer of the world come
the pearly upheaval of dolphins   780
cracking the shell of the sea
let a plunge of islands come
let it come from the disappearing of days of dead
flesh in the quicklime of birds of prey[4]
let the ovaries of the water come where the future stirs its testicles   785
let the wolves come who feed in the untamed openings of the body
at the hour when my moon and your sun meet at the ecliptic inn[5]

under the reserve of my uvula[6] there is a wallow of boars
under the grey stone of the day there are your eyes which are a shimmering conglomerate of coccinella[7]   790
in the glance of disorder there is this swallow of mint and broom[8]
which melts always to be reborn in the tidal wave of your light
Calm and lull oh my voice the child who does not know that the map
of spring is always to be drawn again
the tall grass will sway gentle ship of hope for the cattle   795
the long alcoholic sweep of the swell
the stars with the bezels[9] of their rings never in sight will cut the pipes
of the glass organ of evening zinnias
coryanthas[1]
will then pour into the rich extremity of my fatigue   800
and you star[2] please from your luminous foundation draw lemurian
being—of man's unfathomable
sperm the yet undared form

---

2. Ineffectual revolt. *Tabetic:* derives from the Latin *tabidus,* "wasting away."   3. A white flower, symbol of Isis, the ancient Egyptian goddess of the rising sun. *Cynocephalus:* an African monkey, with a
head resembling a dog's, noted for its great strength.   4. An extremely compressed image that identifies
Césaire's revolt with the action of *birds of prey* or *quicklime* (calcium oxide, which has a dissolving effect),
both of which cleanse the land of dead bodies.   5. The partners fuse into one another as in an eclipse
of the sun or moon.   6. The tissue at the back of the tongue, opening into the throat.   7. Beetles.
The passage refers to Césaire's wife, Suzanne, whose bright eyes are compared to the shimmering of a
swarm of beetles.   8. Medicinal plants. *Swallow:* a harbinger of spring, associated with the health-
restoring properties of medicinal plants.   9. The upper parts of rings in which the stones are set.
1. Tropical flowers.   2. Perhaps the sun.

carried like an ore in woman's trembling belly!

oh friendly light   805
oh fresh source of light
those who have invented neither powder nor compass
those who could harness neither steam nor electricity
those who explored neither the seas nor the sky but those
without whom the earth would not be the earth   810
gibbosity[3] all the more beneficent as the bare earth even more earth
silo[4] where that which is earthiest about earth ferments and ripens
my negritude[5] is not a stone, its deafness hurled against the clamor of
the day
my negritude is not a leukoma[6] of dead liquid over the earth's dead   815
eye
my negritude is neither tower nor cathedral
it takes root in the red flesh of the soil
it takes root in the ardent flesh of the sky
it breaks through the opaque prostration with its upright patience[7]   820

Eia for the royal Cailcedra![8]
Eia for those who have never invented anything
for those who never explored anything
for those who never conquered anything

but yield, captivated, to the essence of all things   825
ignorant of surfaces but captivated by the motion of all things
indifferent to conquering, but playing the game of the world
truly the eldest sons of the world
porous to all the breathing of the world
fraternal locus for all the breathing of the world   830
drainless channel for all the water of the world
spark of the sacred fire of the world
flesh of the world's flesh pulsating with the very motion of the world!
    Tepid dawn of ancestral virtues

Blood! Blood! all our blood aroused by the male heart of the sun   835
those who know about the femininity of the moon's oily body
the reconciled exultation of antelope and star
those whose survival travels in the germination of grass!
Eia perfect circle of the world, enclosed concordance!

Hear the white world   840
horribly weary from its immense efforts
its stiff joints crack under the hard stars
hear its blue steel rigidity pierce the mystic flesh
its deceptive victories tout its defeats
hear the grandiose alibis of its pitiful stumblings   845

---

3. An ugly swelling.   4. A granary. Here, the black race as the spiritual reservoir of humankind.
5. See p. 2220, above.   6. A film over the eye, caused by infection.   7. A reference to the Cross,
symbol of Christ's Passion.   8. A tree typical of the west African savannah, with royal significance. *Eia:*
a triumphant cry.

Pity for our omniscient and naive conquerors!

Eia for grief and its udders of reincarnated tears
for those who have never explored anything
for those who have never conquered anything

Eia for joy   850
Eia for love
Eia for grief and its udders of reincarnated tears

and here at the end of this daybreak is my virile prayer that I hear
neither the laughter nor the screams, my eyes fixed on this town
which I prophesy, beautiful,   855

grant me the savage faith of the sorcerer
grant my hands power to mold
grant my soul the sword's temper
I won't flinch. Make my head into a figurehead
and as for me, my heart, do not make me into a father nor a brother,   860
nor a son, but into the father, the brother, the son,
nor a husband, but the lover of this unique people.

Make me resist any vanity, but espouse its genius as the fist the
extended arm!

Make me a steward of its blood   865
make me trustee of its resentment
make me into a man for the ending
make me into a man for the beginning
make me into a man of meditation
but also make me into a man of germination   870

make me into the executor of these lofty works
the time has come to gird one's loins like a brave man[9] —

But in doing so, my heart, preserve me from all hatred
do not make me into that man of hatred for whom I feel only hatred
for entrenched as I am in this unique race   875
you still know my tyrannical love
you know that it is not from hatred of other races
that I demand a digger for this unique race
that what I want
is for universal hunger   880
for universal thirst

to summon it to generate,
free at last, from its intimate closeness
the succulence of fruit.

And be the tree of our hands!   885
it turns, for all, the wounds cut
in its trunk[1]

9. An echo of God's words to Job: "Gird up now thy loins like a man" (Job 38:3).   1. Like the rubber
tree, which thrives on incisions made in its trunk to produce sap.

the soil works for all
and toward the branches a headiness of fragrant precipitation!

But before stepping on the shores of future orchards 890
grant that I deserve those on their belt of sea
grant me my heart while awaiting the earth
grant me on the ocean sterile
but somewhere caressed by the promise of the clew-line[2]
grant me on this diverse ocean 895
the obstinacy of the fierce pirogue[3]
and its marine vigor.
See it advance rising and falling on the pulverized wave
see it dance the sacred dance before the greyness of the village
see it trumpet from a vertiginous conch[4] 900

see the conch gallop up to the uncertainty of the morne

and see twenty times over the paddle
vigorously
plow the water
the pirogue rears under the attack of the swells 905
deviates for an instant
tries to escape, but the paddle's rough caress turns it,
then it charges, a shudder runs along the wave's spine,
the sea slobbers and rumbles
the pirogue like a sleigh glides onto the sand. 910

    At the end of this daybreak, my virile prayer:

grant me pirogue muscles on this raging sea
and the irresistible gaiety of the conch of good tidings!
Look, now I am only a man, no degradation, no spit perturbs him,
now I am only a man who accepts emptied of anger 915
(nothing left in his heart but immense love, which burns)

I accept . . . I accept . . . totally, without reservation . . .
my race that no ablution of hyssop[5] mixed with lilies could purify
my race pitted with blemishes
my race a ripe grape for drunken feet 920
my queen of spittle and leprosy
my queen of whips and scrofula
my queen of squasma and chloasma[6] (oh those queens I once loved
in the remote gardens of spring against the illumination of all the
candles of the chestnut[7] trees!) 925
I accept. I accept.
and the flogged nigger saying: "Forgive me master"
and the twenty-nine legal blows[8] of the whip
and the four-feet-high cell
and the spiked iron-collar 930
and the hamstringing of my runaway audacity

2. Rope by which a clew of an upper square sail is hauled up.   3. A dug-out canoe, in which local fishermen go out to sea.   4. A seashell that has a wound-up *(vertiginous)* shape. It can be made into a horn, which has a trumpeting sound like that of an elephant.   5. An aromatic plant featured in a Latin chant said before High Mass in the Catholic Church.   6. Suggests sickness, possibly derived from the Greek word meaning "paleness." *Squasma:* scales on the skin.   7. In the French, there is a play on the word *marron,* which means both chestnut and runaway slave.   8. The limit prescribed by the *Code Noir* (Black Code), designed to regulate slaveowners' treatment of their slaves.

and the fleur de lys[9] flowing from the red iron into the fat of my
shoulder
and Monsieur VAULTIER MAYENCOURT'S dog house[1] where I
barked   935
six poodle months
and Monsieur BRAFIN
and Monsieur FOURNIOL
and Monsieur de la MAHAUDIERE[2]
and the yaws   940
the mastiff[3]
the suicide
the promiscuity
the bootkin[4]
the shackles   945
the rack
the cippus
the head screw[5]

    Look, am I humble enough? Have I enough calluses on my knees?
Muscles on my loins?   950
Grovel in mud. Brace yourself in the thick of the mud. Carry.
Soil of mud. Horizon of mud. Sky of mud.
Dead of the mud, oh names to thaw in the palm of a feverish
breathing!

    Siméon Piquine, who never knew his father or mother; unheard of   955
in any town hall[6] and who wandered his whole life—seeking a new
name.

    Grandvorka—of him I only know that he died, crushed one harvest
evening, it was his job, apparently, to throw sand under the wheels of
the running locomotive, to help it across bad spots.   960

    Michel who used to write me signing a strange name. Lucky
Michel address *Condemned District*[7] and you their living brothers
Exélie Vêté Congolo Lemké Boussolongo what healer with his thick
lips would suck from the depths of the gaping wound the tenacious
secret of venom?   965

what cautious sorcerer would undo from your ankles the viscous
tepidity of mortal rings?

Presences it is not on your back that I will make my peace with the
world

Islands scars of the water   970
Islands evidence of wounds
Islands crumbs
Islands unformed

9. The lily flower (French); the emblem of the Bourbon Dynasty in France, with which recaptured slaves
were branded.   1. Mayencourt, a slaveowner, caused the death of one of his slaves by caging him in a
dog kennel for six months.   2. Slaveowners involved in an incident in which two slaves committed
suicide.   3. A bloodhound, used to hunt down runaway slaves. Yaws: a tropical disease that attacks the
skin and bones.   4. Stocks designed to lock in the victim's legs.   5. A form of punishment in which
a cord was wound tightly around the slave's head. *Cippus:* an elevated spot where slaves were whipped.
6. Where births and deaths are recorded.   7. Indicative of a mood of total despair.

Islands cheap paper shredded upon the water
Islands stumps skewered side by side on the flaming sword of the Sun   975
Mulish reason you will not stop me from casting on the waters at the
mercy of the currents of my thirst
your form, deformed islands,
your end, my defiance.

Annulose[8] islands, single beautiful hull   980
And I caress you with my oceanic hands. And I turn you
around with the tradewinds of my speech. And I lick you with my
seaweed tongues.
And I sail you unfreebootable!

O death your mushy marsh!   985
Shipwreck your hellish debris! I accept!
    At the end of daybreak, lost puddles, wandering scents, beached
hurricanes, demasted hulls, old sores, rotted bones, vapors, shackled
volcanoes, shallow-rooted dead, bitter cry. I accept!

And my special geography too; the world map made for my own use,   990
not tinted with the arbitrary colors of scholars, but with the geometry
of my spilled blood, I accept both the determination of my biology,
not a prisoner to a facial angle, to a type of hair, to a well-flattened
nose, to a clearly Melanian coloring, and negritude, no longer a
cephalic index, or plasma, or soma, but measured by the compass of   995
suffering[9]
and the Negro every day more base, more cowardly, more sterile, less
profound, more spilled out of himself, more separated from himself,
more wily with himself, less immediate to himself,

I accept, I accept it all   1000

and far from the palatial sea that foams beneath the suppurating syz-
ygy[1] of blisters, miraculously lying in the despair of my arms the body
of my country, its bones shocked and, in its veins, the blood hesitating
like a drop of vegetal milk at the injured point of the bulb . . .

    Suddenly now strength and life assail me like a bull and the water   1005
of life overwhelms the papilla[2] of the morne, now all the veins and
veinlets are bustling with new blood and the enormous breathing lung
of cyclones and the fire hoarded in volcanoes and the gigantic seismic
pulse which now beats the measure of a living body in my firm conflagration.   1010

And we are standing now, my country and I, hair in the wind, my
hand puny in its enormous fist and now the strength is not in us but
above us, in a voice that drills the night and the hearing like the
penetrance of an apocalyptic wasp.[3] And the voice proclaims that for
centuries Europe has force-fed us with lies and bloated us with pesti-   1015
lence,

---

8. Strung out, as in a ceremonial procession.   9. Earlier in this century physical anthropologists were
interested in the worldwide distribution of various physical traits of humans (some of which are listed
here). Others used such data to advance and justify racial theories. *Melanian*: dark. *Cephalic*: relating to
the head. *Soma*: body (Greek).   1. The alignment of the sun and the moon; also the movement of the
tides.   2. Nipple.   3. An allusion to the plague that descended on the Egyptians before the liberation
of the Israelites in Exodus 5–11.

for it is not true that the work of man is done
that we have no business being on earth
that we parasite the world
that it is enough for us to heel to the world   1020
whereas the work has only begun
and man still must overcome all the interdictions wedged in the
recesses of his fervor and no race has a monopoly on beauty, on intelligence, on strength[4]

and there is room for everyone at the convocation of conquest and we   1025
know now that the sun turns around our earth lighting the parcel
designated by our will alone and that every star falls from sky to earth
at our omnipotent command.

I now see the meaning of this trial by the sword: my country is the
"lance of night" of my Bambara[5] ancestors. It shrivels and its point   1030
desperately retreats toward the haft when it is sprinkled with chicken
blood and it says that its nature requires the blood of man, his fat, his
liver, his heart, not chicken blood.

And I seek for my country not date hearts, but men's hearts which,
in order to enter the silver cities through the great trapezoidal[6] gate,   1035
beat with warrior blood, and as my eyes sweep my kilometers of paternal earth I number its sores almost joyfully and I pile one on top of the
other like rare species, and my total is ever lengthened by unexpected
mintings of baseness.

And there are those who will never get over not being made in the   1040
likeness of God but of the devil, those who believe that being a nigger
is like being a second-class clerk; waiting for a better deal and upward
mobility; those who beat the drum of compromise in front of themselves, those who live in their own dungeon pit; those who drape
themselves in proud pseudomorphosis;[7] those who say to Europe: 1045
"You see, I *can* bow and scrape, like you I pay my respects, in short, I
am no different from you; pay no attention to my black skin: the sun
did it."[8]

And there is the nigger pimp, the nigger askari,[9] and all the zebras
shaking themselves in various ways to get rid of their stripes in a dew   1050
of fresh milk.[1] And in the midst of all that I say right on! my grandfather dies, I say right on! the old negritude progressively cadavers itself.

No question about it: he was a good nigger. The Whites say he was a
good nigger, a really good nigger, massa's good ole darky. I say right
on!   1055

He was a good nigger, indeed,
poverty had wounded his chest and back and they had stuffed into his
poor brain that a fatality impossible to trap weighed on him; that he
had no control over his own fate; that an evil Lord had for all eternity

---

4. A pointed reference to the writings of Gobineau, who argued the superiority of the white race in terms
of the qualities stated here.   5. An ethnic group concentrated in present-day Mali. The passage refers
to a ritual in which warriors sprinkled human blood on their spears to ensure their effectiveness.   6. A
geometric figure with four sides of unequal length; a frequent motif in the architecture of ancient civilizations.   7. A false personality.   8. From Song of Solomon (1:6). The words have been attributed to
the Ethiopian queen of Sheba.   9. African colonial soldiers in east Africa (Swahili).   1. Recalls the
queen of Sheba's description of Solomon's eyes as "washed in milk" (Song of Solomon 5:12).

inscribed Thou Shall Not in his pelvic constitution; that he must be   1060
a good nigger; must sincerely believe in his worthlessness, without
any perverse curiosity to check out the fatidic hieroglyphs.[2]

He was a very good nigger

and it never occurred to him that he could hoe, burrow, cut anything,
anything else really than insipid cane   1065

He was a very good nigger.

And they threw stones at him, bits of scrap iron, broken bottles, but
neither these stones, nor this scrap iron, nor these bottles . . . O peaceful years of God on this terraqueous[3] clod!

and the whip argued with the bombilation[4] of the flies over the sugary   1070
dew of our sores.

I say right on! The old negritude
progressively cadavers itself
the horizon breaks, recoils and expands
and through the shredding of clouds the flashing of a sign[5]   1075
the slave ship cracks everywhere . . . Its belly convulses and resounds
. . . The ghastly tapeworm[6] of its cargo gnaws the fetid guts of the
strange suckling of the sea!

And neither the joy of sails filled like a pocket stuffed with doubloons,
nor the tricks played on the dangerous stupidity of the frigates of   1080
order[7] prevent it from hearing the threat of its intestinal rumblings

In vain to ignore them the captain hangs the biggest loudmouth nigger from the main yard or throws him into the sea, or feeds him to his
mastiffs

Reeking of fried onions the nigger scum rediscovers the bitter taste of   1085
freedom in its spilled blood

And the nigger scum is on its feet

the seated nigger scum
unexpectedly standing
standing in the hold   1090
standing in the cabins
standing on deck
standing in the wind
standing under the sun
standing in the blood   1095
    standing
        and
            free
standing and no longer a poor madwoman in her maritime freedom
and destitution gyrating in perfect drift[8]   1100
and there she is:

2. Characters in ancient Egyptian writing. *Fatidic*: pertaining to fate.   3. From the Latin *terra*, "of the
earth."   4. Swarming.   5. Like the clap of thunder heard when Moses brought down the tablets from
Mount Sinai (Genesis 19:1–3).   6. A tropical parasite that lives in the intestines of its victims.
7. Patrol ships sent out from England to enforce Britain's abolition of slavery. *Doubloons*: old Spanish
coins.   8. An allusion to the "Ship of Fools" in which the insane were packed off to sea and set adrift.
The passage describes the momentary disarray on the ship after being taken over by the victorious
slaves.

most unexpectedly standing
standing in the rigging
standing at the tiller
standing at the compass   1105
standing at the map
standing under the stars
  standing
    and
      free   1110
and the lustral[9] ship fearlessly advances on the crumbling water.

And now our ignominous plops are rotting away!
by the clanking noon sea
by the burgeoning midnight sun[1]
listen sparrow hawk who holds the keys to the orient   1115
by the disarmed day
by the stony spurt of the rain

listen dogfish that watches over the occident

listen white dog of the north, black serpent of the south that cinches
the sky girdle   1120
There still remains one sea to cross
oh still one sea to cross
that I may invent my lungs
that the prince may hold his tongue
that the queen may lay me   1125
still one old man to murder
one madman to deliver
that my soul may shine bark shine
bark bark bark
and the owl[2] my beautiful inquisitive angel may hoot.   1130
The master of laughter?
The master of ominous silence?
The master of hope and despair?
The master of laziness? Master of the dance?
  It is I!   1135
and for this reason, Lord,
the frail-necked men
receive and perceive deadly triangular calm[3]

Rally to my side my dances
you bad nigger dances   1140
the carcan-cracker[4] dance
the prison-break dance
the it-is-beautiful-good-and-legitimate-to-be-a-nigger-dance
Rally to my side my dances and let the sun bounce on the racket of
my hands   1145

but no the unequal sun is not enough for me
coil, wind, around my new growth

9. Purifying. The slaves have been cleansed by their act of revolt.   1. A phenomenon that can be observed at the height of summer at both poles.   2. Césaire's guardian angel. The owl was also associated with Minerva, the goddess of wisdom in Greek mythology.   3. The Holy Trinity of Christianity was represented as a triangle, a figure associated in Césaire's consciousness with the triangular circuit of the slave trade.   4. A dance of freedom. *Carcan:* an iron collar fixed around the necks of slaves.

light on my cadenced fingers
to you I surrender my conscience and its fleshy rhythm
to you I surrender the fire in which my weakness smolders   1150
to you I surrender the "chain-gang"
to you the swamps
to you the nontourist of the triangular circuit
devour wind
to you I surrender my abrupt words   1155
devour and encoil yourself
and self-encoiling embrace me with a more ample shudder
embrace me unto furious us
embrace, embrace US
but after having drawn from us blood   1160
drawn by our own blood!
embrace, my purity mingles only with yours
so then embrace
like a field of even filagos[5]
at dusk   1165
our multicolored purities
and bind, bind me without remorse
bind me with your vast arms to the luminous clay
bind my black vibration to the very navel of the world
bind, bind me, bitter brotherhood   1170
then, strangling me with your lasso of stars
rise,
Dove[6]
rise
rise   1175
rise
I follow you who are imprinted on my ancestral white cornea.[7]
rise sky licker
and the great black hole where a moon ago I wanted to drown it is
there I will now fish the malevolent tongue of the night in its   1180
motionless veerition![8]

5. The causuarina tree, which grows tall and straight.   6. The symbol of Pentecost in Christian iconology, from which it has acquired its conventional meaning of peace.   7. The transparent tissue that covers the front of the eye.   8. Coined on a Latin verb "verri," meaning "to sweep," "to scrape a surface," and ultimately "to scan" [*Translators' note*].

ALBERT CAMUS

1913–1960

Albert Camus is often linked with the contemporary philosopher Jean-Paul Sartre as an "existentialist" writer, and indeed—as novelist, playwright, and essayist—he is widely known for his analysis of two concerns basic to existentialism: its distinctive assessment of the human condition and its search for authentic values. Yet Camus rejected doctrinaire labels, and Sartre himself suggested that the author was better placed in the tradition of French "moralist" writers such as Michel de

Montaigne and René Pascal, who analyzed human behavior inside an implied ethical context with its own standards of good and evil. For Camus, "liberty," "justice," "brotherhood," and "happiness" were some of these standards, along with the terms "revolt" and "absurd" that described human nonacceptance of a world without meaning or value. From his childhood among the very poor in Algiers to his later roles as journalist, Resistance fighter, internationally famous literary figure, and winner of the Nobel Prize in 1957, Camus never strayed from an intense awareness of the most basic levels of human existence, or from a sympathy with those—often poor and oppressed—who lived at that level. "I can understand only in human terms. I understand the things I touch, things that offer me resistance." He describes the raw experience of life as it is shared by all human beings, and provides a bond between them. Camus's reaction to the "absurd," the human condition stripped bare, is, therefore, quite different from Samuel Beckett's retreat into agonized subjectivity; where Beckett is haunted by the fictionality of experience, Camus asserts human consciousness and human solidarity as the only values there are.

Camus was born on November 7, 1913, into a "world of poverty and light" in Mondavi, Algeria (then a colony of France). He was the second son in a poor family of mixed Alsatian-Spanish descent, and his father died in one of the first battles of World War I. The two boys lived together with their mother, uncle, and grandmother in a two-room apartment in the working-class section of the capital city, Algiers. Camus and his brother, Lucien, were raised by their strict grandmother while their mother worked as a cleaning woman to support the family. Images of the Mediterranean landscape, with its overwhelming, sensual closeness of sea and blazing sun, recur throughout his work, as does a profound compassion for those who—like his mother—labor unrecognized and in silence. (Camus's mother was illiterate, and left deaf and with a speech impediment by an untreated childhood illness.)

A passionate athlete as well as scholarship student, Camus completed his secondary education and enrolled as a philosophy student at the University of Algiers before contracting, at seventeen, the tuberculosis which undermined his health and shocked him with its demonstration of the human body's vulnerability to disease and death. Camus later finished his degree, but in the meantime he had gained from his illness a metaphor for everything that opposes and puts limits to human fulfillment and happiness: something he was later to term (after Antonin Artaud) the "plague" that infects bodies, minds, cities, and society (*The Plague* is the title of his second novel).

Camus lived and worked as a journalist in Algeria until 1940. He then moved to France when his political commentary (including a famous report on administrative mismanagement during a famine of Berber tribesmen) embroiled him with the local government so that his paper was suspended and he himself refused a work permit. Then as later, however, his work extended far beyond journalism. He published two collections of essays, *The Wrong Side and the Right Side* (1937) and *Nuptials* (1939), started a novel (*A Happy Death*), and founded a collective theater, Le Théâtre du Travail ("The Labor Theater") for which he wrote and adapted a number of plays. The theater always fascinated Camus, possibly because it involved groups of people and live interaction between actors and audience. He not only continued to write plays after leaving Algeria (*Cross Purposes*, 1944; *The Just Assassins*, 1950) but was considering directing a new theater shortly before his death. The Labor Theater was a popular theater with performances on the docks in Algiers and was sponsored by the Communist Party, which Camus had joined in 1934. Like many intellectuals of his day, Camus found in the party a promising vehicle for social protest; he was unwilling to abandon either his independence or his convictions, however, and resigned in 1935 when the party line changed and he was asked to give up his support for Algerian nationalism. He left the Labor Theater in 1937 and, with a group of young Algerian intellectuals associated with the publishing house of Charlot, founded a similar but politically independent Team Theater (Théâtre de l'Equipe). During this decade, Camus also began work on his most famous novel, *The Stranger* (1942), the play *Caligula* (1944), and a lengthy essay defining his concept of the "absurd" hero, *The Myth of Sisyphus* (1942).

These three works established Camus's reputation as a philosopher of the "absurd": the absurdly grotesque discrepancy between human beings' brief, material existence and their urge to believe in larger meanings—to "make sense" of a world that has no discernible sense. In *The Stranger*, Camus described a thirty-year-old clerk named Meursault who lives a series of "real" events: he attends his mother's funeral, makes love to his mistress, goes swimming, shoots an Arab on the beach, and is tried for murder. All these events are described through Meursault's mind, and yet they appear without any connection, as if each one began a new world. They are simply a series of concrete, sensuous *facts* separated from each other and from any kind of human or social meaning. Meursault is finally condemned to death not for murder but for this alienation, and its failure to respond to society's expectations of proper behavior. Just before his execution, when he is infuriated by the prison chaplain's attempt to console him with thoughts of an afterlife, he rises to a new level of existential awareness and an ardent affirmation of life in the here-and-now, the only truly human field of action. Stylistically, much of *The Stranger's* impact comes from the contrast between the immediacy of the physical experience described, and the objective meaninglessness of that experience. On all levels, the novel reaffirms the importance of life lived moment by moment, in a total awareness that creates whatever meaning exists: the same awareness of his own activity that brings the mythological Sisyphus happiness when eternally pushing uphill the rock that will only roll down again or the same search for an absolute honesty free of human pretenses that characterizes the mad emperor Caligula.

During World War II, Camus worked in Paris as a reader for the publishing firm of Gallimard, a post that he kept until his death in 1960. At the same time, he was part of the French Resistance and helped edit the underground journal *Combat*. His friendship with the existentialist philosopher Jean-Paul Sartre began in 1944, and after the war he and Sartre were internationally known as uncompromising analysts of the modern conscience. Camus's second novel, *The Plague* (1947), used a description of plague in a quarantined city, the Algerian Oran, to symbolize the spread of evil during World War II ("the feeling of suffocation from which we all suffered, and the atmosphere of threat and exile") and also to show the human struggle against physical and spiritual death in all its forms. Not content merely to symbolize his views in fiction, he also spoke out in philosophical essays and political statements where his independent mind and refusal of doctrinaire positions brought him attacks from all sides. In the bitter struggle that brought independence to Algeria in 1962, Camus recognized the claims of both French and Arab Algerians to the land in which they were born. In the quest for social reform, he rejected any ideology that subordinated individual freedom and singled out Communism—the doctrine most reformist intellectuals saw as the only active hope—as a particular danger with its emphasis on the de-individualized and inevitable march of history. Camus's open anti-Communism led to a spectacular break with Sartre, whose review *Les Temps Modernes* (Modern times) condemned *The Rebel* (1951) in bitter personal attacks. The concept of revolt that Camus outlined in *The Rebel* was more ethical than political: he defined revolt as a basic nonacceptance of preestablished limits (whether by death or by oppression) that was shared by all human beings and, therefore, required a reciprocal acceptance and balancing of each person's rights. Such "revolt" was directly opposed to revolutionary nihilism in that it made the rebellious impulse a basis for social tolerance inside the individual's self-assertion; it had no patience for master plans that prescribed patterns of thought or action.

Five years after *The Rebel* was published, Camus produced a very different book in *The Fall* (1956). This book is a rhetorical tour de force spoken by a fallen lawyer who uses all the tricks of language to confess his weaknesses and yet emerge triumphant, the omniscient judge of his fellow creatures. If Camus's *Notebooks* reveal in his early works a cycle of Sisyphus or the "absurd," and his middle ones a Promethean cycle of "revolt," *The Fall* inaugurates a third cycle, that of Nemesis, or judgment. It offers a complex, ironic picture that combines a yearning toward purity with a cynical debunking of all such attempts. The narrator, Clamence, is a composite personality including (among other things) satirized aspects of both Sartre and Camus, but it is impossible to get to the bottom of his character behind the layers of self-consciously manipulated language. The style itself challenges and disorients the reader, who is both included and excluded from a narration that presents Clamence's half of a dialogue in which "you," the reader, are presumed to be present as the other half.

Camus was a consummate artist as well as moralist, well aware of the opportunities as well as the illusions of his craft. When he received the Nobel Prize in 1957, his acceptance speech emphasized the artificial but necessary "human" order imposed by art on the chaos of immediate experience. The artist is important as *creator*, because he or she shapes a human perspective, allows understanding in human terms, and therefore provides a basis for action. By stressing the gap between art and reality, Camus in effect provides a bridge between them as two poles of human understanding. His own works illustrate this act of bridging through their juxtaposition of realistic detail and almost mythic allegorization of human destiny. The symbolism of his titles, from *The Stranger* to the last collection of stories, *Exile and the Kingdom* (1957), repeatedly interprets human destiny in terms of a thematic opposition between the individual's sense of alienation and exile in the world, and simultaneous search for the true realm of human happiness and action.

With *The Guest*, taken from *Exile and the Kingdom*, Camus returns to the landscape of his native Algeria. The colonial context is crucial in this story, not only to explain the real threat of guerrilla reprisal at the end (Camus may be recalling the actual killing of rural schoolteachers in 1954) but to establish the dimensions of a political situation in which the government, police, educational system, and economic welfare of Algeria are all controlled by France. A similar colonial (or newly postcolonial) setting is used to indicate a charged political atmosphere in works by Nadine Gordimer, Naguib Mahfouz, Chinua Achebe, and Wole Soyinka (all in this volume). The beginning of Camus's story illustrates how French colonial education reproduces French, not local concerns: the schoolteacher's geography lesson outlines the four main rivers of France. The Arab is led along like an animal behind the gendarme Balducci, who rides a horse (here too, Camus may be recalling a humiliation reported two decades before and used to inspire Algerian nationalists). Within this political context, however, he concentrates on quite different issues: freedom, brotherhood, responsibility, and the ambiguity of actions along with the inevitability of choice.

The remote desert landscape establishes a total physical and moral isolation for events in the story. "No one, in this desert . . . mattered," and the schoolteacher and his guest must each decide on his own what to do. When Balducci invades Daru's monastic solitude and tells him that he must deliver the Arab to prison, Daru is outraged to be involved and, indeed, to have responsibility for another's fate. Cursing both the system that tries to force him into complicity, and the Arab who has not had enough sense to get away, Daru tries in every way possible to avoid taking a stand. In the morning, however, when the Arab has not in fact run away, the schoolteacher makes up a package of food and money and passes on to the Arab his own freedom of choice. We cannot underestimate the quiet heroism of this act, by which Daru alienates himself from his own people and—unexpectedly—from the Arab's compatriots too; he is, he believes, conveying to a fellow human being the freedom of action, which all people require. This level of common humanity is strongly underlined throughout the whole story as a "sort of brotherhood" and "strange alliance" that comes from having shared food and drink, and slept as equals under the same roof. Such hospitality is also the nomadic "law of the desert" that establishes fellowship between guest and host (a law that Daru refers to when he points out the second road at the end). The host's humane hospitality has placed a new burden and reciprocal responsibility on his guest, one that may explain why the Arab chooses—in apparent freedom—the road to prison. Camus considered "Cain" and "The Law" as titles for this story before settling on *The Guest* (and the title word *l'hôte*, is identical for "guest" and "host" in French). Both guest and host are obliged to shoulder the ambiguous, and potentially fatal, burden of freedom.

Germaine Brée, *Albert Camus* (1964), is an excellent general study; see also *Camus: A Collection of Critical Essays* (1961). Phillip Rhein, *Albert Camus* (1969), is a brief introduction and biography. Herbert Lottman, *Albert Camus: A Biography* (1979), is the fullest and most detailed biography available. English Showalter, *Exiles and Strangers: A Reading of Camus's Exile and the Kingdom* (1984), offers essays on the six stories of Camus's collection and separate comments on translations.

The Guest[1]

The schoolmaster was watching the two men climb toward him. One was on horseback, the other on foot. They had not yet tackled the abrupt rise leading to the schoolhouse built on the hillside. They were toiling onward, making slow progress in the snow, among the stones, on the vast expanse of the high, deserted plateau. From time to time the horse stumbled. Without hearing anything yet, he could see the breath issuing from the horse's nostrils. One of the men, at least, knew the region. They were following the trail although it had disappeared days ago under a layer of dirty white snow. The schoolmaster calculated that it would take them half an hour to get onto the hill. It was cold; he went back into the school to get a sweater.

He crossed the empty, frigid classroom. On the blackboard the four rivers of France,[2] drawn with four different colored chalks, had been flowing toward their estuaries for the past three days. Snow had suddenly fallen in mid-October after eight months of drought without the transition of rain, and the twenty pupils, more or less, who lived in the villages scattered over the plateau had stopped coming. With fair weather they would return. Daru now heated only the single room that was his lodging, adjoining the classroom and giving also onto the plateau to the east. Like the

1. Translated by Justin O'Brien.   2. The Seine, Loire, Rhône, and Gironde rivers. French geography was taught in the French colonies.

class windows, his window looked to the south too. On that side the school was a few kilometers from the point where the plateau began to slope toward the south. In clear weather could be seen the purple mass of the mountain range where the gap opened onto the desert.

Somewhat warmed, Daru returned to the window from which he had first seen the two men. They were no longer visible. Hence they must have tackled the rise. The sky was not so dark, for the snow had stopped falling during the night. The morning had opened with a dirty light which had scarcely become brighter as the ceiling of clouds lifted. At two in the afternoon it seemed as if the day were merely beginning. But still this was better than those three days when the thick snow was falling amidst unbroken darkness with little gusts of wind that rattled the double door of the classroom. Then Daru had spent long hours in his room, leaving it only to go to the shed and feed the chickens or get some coal. Fortunately the delivery truck from Tadjid, the nearest village to the north, had brought his supplies two days before the blizzard. It would return in forty-eight hours.

Besides, he had enough to resist a siege, for the little room was cluttered with bags of wheat that the administration left as a stock to distribute to those of his pupils whose families had suffered from the drought. Actually they had all been victims because they were all poor. Every day Daru would distribute a ration to the children. They had missed it, he knew, during these bad days. Possibly one of the fathers or big brothers would come this afternoon and he could supply them with grain. It was just a matter of carrying them over to the next harvest. Now shiploads of wheat were arriving from France and the worst was over. But it would be hard to forget that poverty, that army of ragged ghosts wandering in the sunlight, the plateaus burned to a cinder month after month, the earth shriveled up little by little, literally scorched, every stone bursting into dust under one's foot. The sheep had died then by thousands and even a few men, here and there, sometimes without anyone's knowing.

In contrast with such poverty, he who lived almost like a monk in his remote schoolhouse, nonetheless satisfied with the little he had and with the rough life, had felt like a lord with his whitewashed walls, his narrow couch, his unpainted shelves, his well, and his weekly provision of water and food. And suddenly this snow, without warning, without the foretaste of rain. This is the way the region was, cruel to live in, even without men—who didn't help matters either. But Daru had been born here. Everywhere else, he felt exiled.

He stepped out onto the terrace in front of the schoolhouse. The two men were now halfway up the slope. He recognized the horseman as Balducci, the old gendarme he had known for a long time. Balducci was holding on the end of a rope an Arab who was walking behind him with hands bound and head lowered. The gendarme waved a greeting to which Daru did not reply, lost as he was in contemplation of the Arab dressed in a faded blue jellaba, his feet in sandals but covered with socks of heavy raw wool, his head surmounted by a narrow, short *chèche*.[3] They were

---

3. Scarf; here, wound as a turban around the head. *Jellaba:* a long hooded robe worn by Arabs in North Africa.

approaching. Balducci was holding back his horse in order not to hurt the Arab, and the group was advancing slowly.

Within earshot, Balducci shouted: "One hour to do the three kilometers from El Ameur!" Daru did not answer. Short and square in his thick sweater, he watched them climb. Not once had the Arab raised his head. "Hello," said Daru when they got up onto the terrace. "Come in and warm up." Balducci painfully got down from his horse without letting go the rope. From under his bristling mustache he smiled at the schoolmaster. His little dark eyes, deep-set under a tanned forehead, and his mouth surrounded with wrinkles made him look attentive and studious. Daru took the bridle, led the horse to the shed, and came back to the two men, who were now waiting for him in the school. He led them into his room. "I am going to heat up the classroom," he said. "We'll be more comfortable there." When he entered the room again, Balducci was on the couch. He had undone the rope tying him to the Arab, who had squatted near the stove. His hands still bound, the *chèche* pushed back on his head, he was looking toward the window. At first Daru noticed only his huge lips, fat, smooth, almost Negroid; yet his nose was straight, his eyes were dark and full of fever. The *chèche* revealed an obstinate forehead and, under the weathered skin now rather discolored by the cold, the whole face had a restless and rebellious look that struck Daru when the Arab, turning his face toward him, looked him straight in the eyes. "Go into the other room," said the schoolmaster, "and I'll make you some mint tea." "Thanks," Balducci said. "What a chore! How I long for retirement." And addressing his prisoner in Arabic: "Come on, you." The Arab got up and, slowly, holding his bound wrists in front of him, went into the classroom.

With the tea, Daru brought a chair. But Balducci was already enthroned on the nearest pupil's desk and the Arab had squatted against the teacher's platform facing the stove, which stood between the desk and the window. When he held out the glass of tea to the prisoner, Daru hesitated at the sight of his bound hands. "He might perhaps be untied." "Sure," said Balducci. "That was for the trip." He started to get to his feet. But Daru, setting the glass on the floor, had knelt beside the Arab. Without saying anything, the Arab watched him with his feverish eyes. Once his hands were free, he rubbed his swollen wrists against each other, took the glass of tea, and sucked up the burning liquid in swift little sips.

"Good," said Daru. "And where are you headed?"

Balducci withdrew his mustache from the tea. "Here, son."

"Odd pupils! And you're spending the night?"

"No. I'm going back to El Ameur. And you will deliver this fellow to Tinguit. He is expected at police headquarters."

Balducci was looking at Daru with a friendly little smile.

"What's this story?" asked the schoolmaster. "Are you pulling my leg?"

"No, son. Those are the orders."

"The orders? I'm not . . ." Daru hesitated, not wanting to hurt the old Corsican.[4] "I mean, that's not my job."

"What! What's the meaning of that? In wartime people do all kinds of jobs."

---

4. Balducci is a native of Corsica, a French island north of Sardinia.

"Then I'll wait for the declaration of war!"

Balducci nodded.

"O.K. But the orders exist and they concern you too. Things are brewing, it appears. There is talk of a forthcoming revolt. We are mobilized, in a way."

Daru still had his obstinate look.

"Listen, son," Balducci said. "I like you and you must understand. There's only a dozen of us at El Ameur to patrol throughout the whole territory of a small department[5] and I must get back in a hurry. I was told to hand this guy over to you and return without delay. He couldn't be kept there. His village was beginning to stir; they wanted to take him back. You must take him to Tinguit tomorrow before the day is over. Twenty kilometers shouldn't faze a husky fellow like you. After that, all will be over. You'll come back to your pupils and your comfortable life."

Behind the wall the horse could be heard snorting and pawing the earth. Daru was looking out the window. Decidedly, the weather was clearing and the light was increasing over the snowy plateau. When all the snow was melted, the sun would take over again and once more would burn the fields of stone. For days, still, the unchanging sky would shed its dry light on the solitary expanse where nothing had any connection with man.

"After all," he said, turning around toward Balducci, "what did he do?" And, before the gendarme had opened his mouth, he asked: "Does he speak French?"

"No, not a word. We had been looking for him for a month, but they were hiding him. He killed his cousin."

"Is he against us?"[6]

"I don't think so. But you can never be sure."

"Why did he kill?"

"A family squabble, I think. One owed the other grain, it seems. It's not at all clear. In short, he killed his cousin with a billhook. You know, like a sheep, *kreezk!*"

Balducci made the gesture of drawing a blade across his throat and the Arab, his attention attracted, watched him with a sort of anxiety. Daru felt a sudden wrath against the man, against all men with their rotten spite, their tireless hates, their blood lust.

But the kettle was singing on the stove. He served Balducci more tea, hesitated, then served the Arab again, who, a second time, drank avidly. His raised arms made the jellaba fall open and the schoolmaster saw his thin, muscular chest.

"Thanks, kid," Balducci said. "And now, I'm off."

He got up and went toward the Arab, taking a small rope from his pocket.

"What are you doing?" Daru asked dryly.

Balducci, disconcerted, showed him the rope.

"Don't bother."

---

5. French administrative and territorial division; like a county.   6. Against the French colonial government.

The old gendarme hesitated. "It's up to you. Of course, you are armed?"

"I have my shotgun."

"Where?"

"In the trunk."

"You ought to have it near your bed."

"Why? I have nothing to fear."

"You're crazy, son. If there's an uprising, no one is safe, we're all in the same boat."

"I'll defend myself. I'll have time to see them coming."

Balducci began to laugh, then suddenly the mustache covered the white teeth.

"You'll have time? O.K. That's just what I was saying. You have always been a little cracked. That's why I like you, my son was like that."

At the same time he took out his revolver and put it on the desk.

"Keep it; I don't need two weapons from here to El Ameur."

The revolver shone against the black paint of the table. When the gendarme turned toward him, the schoolmaster caught the smell of leather and horseflesh.

"Listen, Balducci," Daru said suddenly, "every bit of this disgusts me, and first of all your fellow here. But I won't hand him over. Fight, yes, if I have to. But not that."

The old gendarme stood in front of him and looked at him severely.

"You're being a fool," he said slowly. "I don't like it either. You don't get used to putting a rope on a man even after years of it, and you're even ashamed—yes, ashamed. But you can't let them have their way."

"I won't hand him over," Daru said again.

"It's an order, son, and I repeat it."

"That's right. Repeat to them what I've said to you: I won't hand him over."

Balducci made a visible effort to reflect. He looked at the Arab and at Daru. At last he decided.

"No, I won't tell them anything. If you want to drop us, go ahead; I'll not denounce you. I have an order to deliver the prisoner and I'm doing so. And now you'll just sign this paper for me."

"There's no need. I'll not deny that you left him with me."

"Don't be mean with me. I know you'll tell the truth. You're from hereabouts and you are a man. But you must sign, that's the rule."

Daru opened his drawer, took out a little square bottle of purple ink, the red wooden penholder with the "sergeant-major" pen he used for making models of penmanship, and signed. The gendarme carefully folded the paper and put it into his wallet. Then he moved toward the door.

"I'll see you off," Daru said.

"No," said Balducci. "There's no use being polite. You insulted me."

He looked at the Arab, motionless in the same spot, sniffed peevishly, and turned away toward the door. "Good-by, son," he said. The door shut behind him. Balducci appeared suddenly outside the window and then disappeared. His footsteps were muffled by the snow. The horse stirred on the other side of the wall and several chickens fluttered in fright. A moment later Balducci reappeared outside the window leading the horse by the bridle. He walked toward the little rise without turning around and disappeared from sight with the horse following him. A big stone could be heard bouncing down. Daru walked back toward the prisoner, who, without stirring, never took his eyes off him. "Wait," the schoolmaster said in Arabic and went toward the bedroom. As he was going through the door, he had a second thought, went to the desk, took the revolver, and stuck it in his pocket. Then, without looking back, he went into his room.

For some time he lay on his couch watching the sky gradually close over, listening to the silence. It was this silence that had seemed painful to him during the first days here, after the war. He had requested a post in the little town at the base of the foothills separating the upper plateaus from the desert. There, rocky walls, green and black to the north, pink and lavender to the south, marked the frontier of eternal summer. He had been named to a post farther north, on the plateau itself. In the beginning, the solitude and the silence had been hard for him on these wastelands peopled only by stones. Occasionally, furrows suggested cultivation, but they had been dug to uncover a certain kind of stone good for building. The only plowing here was to harvest rocks. Elsewhere a thin layer of soil accumulated in the hollows would be scraped out to enrich paltry village gardens. This is the way it was: bare rock covered three quarters of the region. Towns sprang up, flourished, then disappeared; men came by, loved one another or fought bitterly, then died. No one in this desert, neither he nor his guest, mattered. And yet, outside this desert neither of them, Daru knew, could have really lived.

When he got up, no noise came from the classroom. He was amazed at the unmixed joy he derived from the mere thought that the Arab might have fled and that he would be alone with no decision to make. But the prisoner was there. He had merely stretched out between the stove and the desk. With eyes open, he was staring at the ceiling. In that position, his thick lips were particularly noticeable, giving him a pouting look. "Come," said Daru. The Arab got up and followed him. In the bedroom, the schoolmaster pointed to a chair near the table under the window. The Arab sat down without taking his eyes off Daru.

"Are you hungry?"

"Yes," the prisoner said.

Daru set the table for two. He took flour and oil, shaped a cake in a frying-pan, and lighted the little stove that functioned on bottled gas. While the cake was cooking, he went out to the shed to get cheese, eggs, dates, and condensed milk. When the cake was done he set it on the window sill to cool, heated some condensed milk diluted with water, and beat up the eggs into an omelette. In one of his motions he knocked against the revolver stuck in his right pocket. He set the bowl down, went into the classroom, and put the revolver in his desk drawer. When he came back to the room, night was falling. He put on the light and served the Arab. "Eat," he said. The Arab took a piece of the cake, lifted it eagerly to his mouth, and stopped short.

"And you?" he asked.

"After you. I'll eat too."

The thick lips opened slightly. The Arab hesitated, then bit into the cake determinedly.

The meal over, the Arab looked at the schoolmaster. "Are you the judge?"

"No, I'm simply keeping you until tomorrow."

"Why do you eat with me?"

"I'm hungry."

The Arab fell silent. Daru got up and went out. He brought back a folding bed from the shed, set it up between the table and the stove, perpendicular to his own bed. From a large suitcase which, upright in a corner, served as a shelf for papers, he took two blankets and arranged them on the camp bed. Then he stopped, felt useless, and sat down on his bed. There was nothing more to do or to get ready. He had to look at this man. He looked at him, therefore, trying to imagine his face bursting with rage. He couldn't do so. He could see nothing but the dark yet shining eyes and the animal mouth.

"Why did you kill him?" he asked in a voice whose hostile tone surprised him.

The Arab looked away.

"He ran away. I ran after him."

He raised his eyes to Daru again and they were full of a sort of woeful interrogation. "Now what will they do to me?"

"Are you afraid?"

He stiffened, turning his eyes away.

"Are you sorry?"

The Arab stared at him openmouthed. Obviously he did not understand. Daru's annoyance was growing. At the same time he felt awkward and self-conscious with his big body wedged between the two beds.

"Lie down there," he said impatiently. "That's your bed."

The Arab didn't move. He called to Daru:

"Tell me!"

The schoolmaster looked at him.

"Is the gendarme coming back tomorrow?"

"I don't know."

"Are you coming with us?"

"I don't know. Why?"

The prisoner got up and stretched out on top of the blankets, his feet toward the window. The light from the electric bulb shone straight into his eyes and he closed them at once.

"Why?" Daru repeated, standing beside the bed.

The Arab opened his eyes under the blinding light and looked at him, trying not to blink.

"Come with us," he said.

In the middle of the night, Daru was still not asleep. He had gone to bed after undressing completely; he generally slept naked. But when he suddenly realized that he had nothing on, he hesitated. He felt vulnerable and the temptation came to him to put his clothes back on. Then he shrugged his shoulders; after all, he wasn't a child and, if need be, he could break his adversary in two. From his bed he could observe him, lying on his back, still motionless with his eyes closed under the harsh light. When Daru turned out the light, the darkness seemed to coagulate all of a sudden. Little by little, the night came back to life in the window where the starless sky was stirring gently. The schoolmaster soon made out the body lying at his feet. The Arab still did not move, but his eyes seemed open. A faint wind was prowling around the schoolhouse. Perhaps it would drive away the clouds and the sun would reappear.

During the night the wind increased. The hens fluttered a little and then were silent. The Arab turned over on his side with his back to Daru, who thought he heard him moan. Then he listened for his guest's breathing, become heavier and more regular. He listened to that breath so close to him and mused without being able to go to sleep. In this room where he had been sleeping alone for a year, this presence bothered him. But it bothered him also by imposing on him a sort of brotherhood he knew well but refused to accept in the present circumstances. Men who share the same rooms, soldiers or prisoners, develop a strange alliance as if, having cast off their armor with their clothing, they fraternized every evening, over and above their differences, in the ancient community of dream and fatigue. But Daru shook himself; he didn't like such musings, and it was essential to sleep.

A little later, however, when the Arab stirred slightly, the schoolmaster was still not asleep. When the prisoner made a second move, he stiffened, on the alert. The Arab was lifting himself slowly on his arms with almost the motion of a sleepwalker. Seated upright in bed, he waited motionless without turning his head toward Daru, as if he were listening attentively. Daru did not stir; it had just occurred to him that the revolver was still in the drawer of his desk. It was better to act at once. Yet he continued to observe the prisoner, who, with the same slithery motion, put his feet on the ground, waited again, then began to stand up slowly. Daru was about to call out to him when the Arab began to walk, in a quite natural but extraordinarily silent way. He was heading toward the door at the end of the room that opened into the shed. He lifted the latch with precaution and went out, pushing the door behind him but without shutting it. Daru had not stirred. "He is running away," he merely thought. "Good riddance!" Yet he listened attentively. The hens were not fluttering; the guest must be on the plateau. A faint sound of water reached him, and he didn't know what it was until the Arab again stood framed in the doorway, closed the door carefully, and came back to bed without a sound. Then Daru turned his back on him and fell asleep. Still later he seemed, from the depths of his sleep, to hear furtive steps around the schoolhouse. "I'm dreaming! I'm dreaming!" he repeated to himself. And he went on sleeping.

When he awoke, the sky was clear; the loose window let in a cold, pure air. The Arab was asleep, hunched up under the blankets now, his mouth open, utterly relaxed. But when Daru shook him, he started dreadfully, staring at Daru with wild eyes as if he had never seen him and such a frightened expression that the schoolmaster stepped back. "Don't be afraid. It's me. You must eat." The Arab nodded his head and said yes. Calm had returned to his face, but his expression was vacant and listless.

The coffee was ready. They drank it seated together on the folding bed as they munched their pieces of the cake. Then Daru led the Arab under the shed and showed him the faucet where he washed. He went back into the room, folded the blankets and the bed, made his own bed and put the room in order. Then he went through the classroom and out onto the terrace. The sun was already rising in the blue sky; a soft, bright light was bathing the deserted plateau. On the ridge the snow was melting in spots. The stones were about to reappear. Crouched on the edge of the plateau, the schoolmaster looked at the deserted expanse. He thought of Balducci. He had hurt him, for he had sent him off in a way as if he didn't want to be associated with him. He could still hear the gendarme's farewell and, without knowing why, he felt strangely empty and vulnerable. At that moment, from the other side of the schoolhouse, the prisoner coughed. Daru listened to him almost despite himself and then, furious, threw a pebble that whistled through the air before sinking into the snow. That man's stupid crime revolted him, but to hand him over was contrary to honor. Merely thinking of it made him smart with humiliation. And he cursed at one and the same time his own people who had sent him this Arab and the Arab too who had dared to kill and not managed to get away. Daru got up, walked in a circle on the terrace, waited motionless, and then went back into the schoolhouse.

The Arab, leaning over the cement floor of the shed, was washing his teeth with two fingers. Daru looked at him and said: "Come." He went back into the room ahead of the prisoner. He slipped a hunting-jacket on over his sweater and put on walking-shoes. Standing, he waited until the Arab had put on his *chèche* and sandals. They went into the classroom and the schoolmaster pointed to the exit, saying: "Go ahead." The fellow didn't budge. "I'm coming," said Daru. The Arab went out. Daru went back into the room and made a package of pieces of rusk, dates, and sugar. In the classroom, before going out, he hesitated a second in front of his desk, then crossed the threshold and locked the door. "That's the way," he said. He started toward the east, followed by the prisoner. But, a short distance from the schoolhouse, he thought he heard a slight sound behind them. He retraced his steps and examined the surroundings of the house, there was no one there. The Arab watched him without seeming to understand. "Come on," said Daru.

They walked for an hour and rested beside a sharp peak of limestone. The snow was melting faster and faster and the sun was drinking up the puddles at once, rapidly cleaning the plateau, which gradually dried and vibrated like the air itself. When they resumed walking, the ground rang under their feet. From time to time a bird rent the space in front of them with a joyful cry. Daru breathed in deeply the fresh morning light. He felt a sort of rapture before the vast familiar expanse, now almost entirely yellow under its dome of blue sky. They walked an hour more, descending toward the south. They reached a level height made up of crumbly rocks.

From there on, the plateau sloped down, eastward, toward a low plain where there were a few spindly trees and, to the south, toward outcroppings of rock that gave the landscape a chaotic look.

Daru surveyed the two directions. There was nothing but the sky on the horizon. Not a man could be seen. He turned toward the Arab, who was looking at him blankly. Daru held out the package to him. "Take it," he said. "There are dates, bread, and sugar. You can hold out for two days. Here are a thousand francs too." The Arab took the package and the money but kept his full hands at chest level as if he didn't know what to do with what was being given him. "Now look," the schoolmaster said as he pointed in the direction of the east, "there's the way to Tinguit. You have a two-hour walk. At Tinguit you'll find the administration and the police. They are expecting you." The Arab looked toward the east, still holding the package and the money against his chest. Daru took his elbow and turned him rather roughly toward the south. At the foot of the height on which they stood could be seen a faint path. "That's the trail across the plateau. In a day's walk from here you'll find pasturelands and the first nomads. They'll take you in and shelter you according to their law." The Arab had now turned toward Daru and a sort of panic was visible in his expression. "Listen," he said. Daru shook his head: "No, be quiet. Now I'm leaving you." He turned his back on him, took two long steps in the direction of the school, looked hesitantly at the motionless Arab, and started off again. For a few minutes he heard nothing but his own step resounding on the cold ground and did not turn his head. A moment later, however, he turned around. The Arab was still there on the edge of the hill, his arms hanging now, and he was looking at the schoolmaster. Daru felt something rise in his throat. But he swore with impatience, waved vaguely, and started off again. He had already gone some distance when he again stopped and looked. There was no longer anyone on the hill.

Daru hesitated. The sun was now rather high in the sky and was beginning to beat down on his head. The schoolmaster retraced his steps, at first somewhat uncertainly, then with decision. When he reached the little hill, he was bathed in sweat. He climbed it as fast as he could and stopped, out of breath, at the top. The rock-fields to the south stood out sharply against the blue sky, but on the plain to the east a steamy heat was already rising. And in that slight haze, Daru, with heavy heart, made out the Arab walking slowly on the road to prison.

A little later, standing before the window of the classroom, the schoolmaster was watching the clear light bathing the whole surface of the plateau, but he hardly saw it. Behind him on the blackboard, among the winding French rivers, sprawled the clumsily chalked-up words he had just read: "You handed over our brother. You will pay for this." Daru looked at the sky, the plateau, and, beyond, the invisible lands stretching all the way to the sea. In this vast landscape he had loved so much, he was alone.

RALPH ELLISON
1914–1994

The prose fiction of Ralph Ellison combines the visionary consciousness and linguistic freedom of modernist writers with a harshly realistic context and stressing of social issues that are often pushed to the background in twentieth-century experimental literature. The "invisible man" of his best-known work is both symbolic and real, a figure whose portrayal is indebted to T. S. Eliot and James Joyce as well as to Richard Wright and Fyodor Dostoevsky. Ellison's world is multidimensional: tragic and comic in the same breath, folkloric yet modern, sordidly real and hallucinatory or surreal, preoccupied with existential questions of individual identity at the same time that it describes the dilemmas of a racist society.

His parents were native southerners who had moved to Oklahoma City, hoping for a more open society, and when their son was born on March 1, 1914, they named him Ralph Waldo Ellison after the American poet, essayist, and philosopher Ralph Waldo Emerson. Ellison's father died when the boy was three, but his mother, working to support her two sons, made sure they had books, records, and chemistry sets, and encouraged them to value learning and social activism. Oklahoma was not as consistently and artificially segregated as the South from which she had come, and although segregation laws crept in later (theaters were segregated in the 1920s) Ellison was raised in a generally integrated society. He was especially interested in music, and by the time he attended Tuskegee Institute in 1933 on a music scholarship, he had learned music theory, been first chair trumpeter and student conductor of his high school band, and taken private lessons from the conductor of the Oklahoma City Orchestra.

Tuskegee Institute, in Alabama, was a new experience in many ways. It was Ellison's first encounter with the Deep South and its strict racial divisions; raised in the southwest, he felt an outsider to the local black as well as the Southern white community. The institute itself was intended by its founder, Booker T. Washington, to be a broadly useful trade school rather than a college; but Ellison was inspired by Alain Locke's ideal of academic and artistic excellence in *The New Negro* (1925), and by Locke's picture of a "new psychology" and "new spirit" represented in the Harlem Renaissance. Ellison later satirized the accommodating trade-school attitude in the character of Dr. Bledsoe, the college president who achieves power through hypocrisy in *Invisible Man* (1952), but he nonetheless found examples of the new spirit at Tuskegee. During his three years as a music major, he studied with professors who explored both black idiom and traditional "high culture": composer William Dawson, who combined African-American folk music and classical symphonic forms in his own work, and concert pianist Hazel Harrison, a cosmopolitan figure who encouraged her students to use a range of techniques and introduced them to her friend Alain Locke. Ellison also took up painting and sculpture, read a great deal, and was deeply impressed by *The Waste Land*. T. S. Eliot's poem appealed to him at first for its verbal rhythms and shifts of tone, and for the suggestion of hidden depths in its symbolic organization. Exploring the footnote references, he discovered a buried thematic structure and saw how writers could make use of a common core of anthropological and cultural experience. Ellison's view of black experience would soon reject the "New Negro" definitions of Alain Locke, who suggested that there was a special black artistic sensibility, and he also rebelled against similar racial stereotypes that were proposed in current sociology textbooks as scientific truths. He reached for a larger concept of human (and American, and African-American) civilization in which black experience was one important but contributing part. By the time he left Tuskegee for New York in 1936, Ellison had written some poetry although he still saw himself as a potential artist or musician, and worked for a year in New York with the sculptor Richmond Barthé.

New York in 1936 was in the midst of the Depression, and Ellison supported himself by a variety of jobs: barman at the YMCA, file clerk for a psychiatrist (prompting him to study the psychology of dreams), factory worker, and freelance photographer. He met the poet Langston Hughes and through him Richard Wright, the future novelist and short story writer, who became Ellison's friend and encouraged him to write. It would be several years before Ellison published his own stories, however, and fifteen before the novel *Invisible Man* appeared. His mother's death in February 1937 brought Ellison to Dayton for her funeral, where he made a living during the following months by hunting and selling his catch, and where he practiced writing. Although Ellison read Dostoevsky and the experimental modernists—Joyce, Eliot, and Gertrude Stein—he took Ernest Hemingway as his model when he began to write short stories, the first of which (*Slick Gonna Learn*) appeared in September 1939.

In the meantime, Ellison had returned to New York where he worked during 1938–42 with the Federal Writers' Project, a government-sponsored program that supported a number of writers during Depression years. He was one of a group of writers employed to do historical research in libraries and court records for a book called *The Negro in New York*. More important to Ellison's own work, perhaps, was an oral history project for which he conducted hundreds of interviews with children and adults to record the folklore of Harlem culture—stories, songs, boasting, and speech patterns—much of which, he felt, also reflected earlier Southern sources. Ellison had already been struck by the importance given to tradition in Eliot's *The Waste Land* and essay *Tradition and the Individual Talent*. The research into black American tradition that he carried out in New York sharpened his own historical and folkloric perspective. Yet he did not lose sight of the need to blend history and artistic technique; in an early review, *Creative and Cultural Lag* (1937), he criticizes novelist Waters Edward Turpin for ignoring social and political reality, and also for not having "a greater development in technique" that would allow him to achieve "more than one level of writing." In 1941, when many radical writers believed that the direct portrayal of social ills was more important than literary technique, Ellison—himself a radical critic of society—was still proclaiming that black writers should learn from the experimental style of modernists like James Joyce.

Ellison was slow to publish his stories, although he wrote a number of literary reviews and was editor of the *Negro Quarterly* in 1942 after leaving the Federal Writers' Project. By 1944 he had published eight stories (while writing many more) and had turned his back on both the New Negro aestheticism of Langston Hughes and the militant naturalism of his early mentor, Richard Wright. Wright's heroes, he felt—especially Bigger Thomas, the protagonist of *Native Son* (1940)—were presented too narrowly as victims of society, and not as full human beings with minds and wills of their own. Wright's picture of black experience actually imitated the limited stereotypes drawn by white writers: "Wright could imagine Bigger, but Bigger could not possibly imagine Richard Wright." Ellison's own heroes, even when they too fall victim to society, are endowed with consciousness and imagination that lift them beyond any stereotypes. The early stories, set in the South and emphasizing racial prejudice, imply a response of political action; the "Buster-Riley" stories weave African-American folklore and heroic role models into the games of two young Oklahoma boys outwitting neighbors and family. *Flying Home* (1944) shows how a black pilot, whose plane crashes in Georgia when it hits a buzzard, copes with threats against his life by understanding a comic folk tale about a black angel thrown out of Heaven for superbly reckless flying; *King of the Bingo Game*, printed here, describes a moment of understanding and self-knowledge in the midst of ruin.

Flying Home was initially part of a novel that Ellison worked on but never completed during the 1940s. He had joined the Merchant Marines in 1943 and received a Rosenwald Fellowship in 1945 to write a novel. It was not the envisioned wartime story of a black pilot shot down on foreign soil that emerged, however, but a different novel inspired partly by Lord Raglan's study of archetypal heroic identity in *The Hero* and partly by Ellison's own concern with African-American identity inside modern American history. *Invisible Man*, the result, told the story of an unnamed protagonist who was "invisible," unknown to himself and invisible to a society—black and white—that could see him only in terms of its own needs and stereotypes: "only by surroundings, themselves, or figments of their imagination, everything and anything except me." Prologue and epilogue are spoken from the invisible man's hideaway, a city manhole where he has retreated after a series of betrayals and attacks, and whose darkness he illuminates—in a typically grotesque and comic touch—with 1,369 light bulbs burning on electricity drained from the Monopolated Light and Power company.

The novel is a modern *Bildungsroman*, or novel of education, in which a naive young protagonist tries to get ahead by living up to the roles held out to him but finds in the end that he is always a pawn, exploited for whatever use can be made of him as the stereotyped "primitive" black. Beginning as a naive high school senior forced to box blindfolded for the entertainment of a men's club before repeating his valedictory speech on humility (a chapter often anthologized as the story *Battle Royal*), he experiences expulsion from college, deception by the business community, patronizing by white liberals, abusive medical treatment, manipulation by the political Brotherhood, horror at the casual killing of a friend, and enmity from militant black nationalists. Yet the story of his individual disillusionment is told in a series of ironically tragicomic, often hallucinatory scenes that are still charged with some of the beginning's optimistic idealism, with the wounded belief that things can be changed if they are only seen for what they are. The narrator has written in an attempt to articulate mixed motives, to "give pattern to the chaos which lives within the pattern of your certainties." *Invisible Man* has been criticized by those who would prefer a less complicated picture, one that stresses social injustice over psychological complexity, but Ellison protests what he considers a narrow reductionism and upholds instead "a complex double vision, a fluid, ambivalent response to men and events" that alone can represent "the cost of being human in this modern world."

Invisible Man received the National Book Award and the Russwurm Award in 1953, and in 1965 was named by *Book Week*'s poll of artists and critics as "the most significant work of fiction written by an American" between 1945 and 1965. Ellison found himself in demand as lecturer and consultant, and was awarded a fellowship at the American Academy in Rome (1955–57). He began work on a second novel, sections of which have appeared in different journals as stories about the revival circuit evangelist Reverend Alonzo Zuber Hickman and his adopted son Bliss, who takes advantage of his light (possibly white) skin to make a new life in the north as a white politician, the bigoted Senator Sunraider. Ellison continued writing and teaching at various institutions and he was Albert Schweitzer Professor of Humanities at New York University from 1970 until his death.

King of the Bingo Game, first published in 1944, combines two levels of narration: the starkly realistic picture of an unemployed black man whose anxiety and momentary paralysis keep him from completing his turn at bingo, and the development of a hallucinatory moment of insight in which the dispossessed man achieves a sense of identity by asserting himself against the rigged wheel of fate. The harsh sociological facts of his condition dominate at first: seated in the theater waiting for the movie to end and the bingo game to begin, already light-headed from hunger and anxiety about his sick wife, Laura, the protagonist muses on the difference between the cohesive Southern community he has left (but where births are not always registered for the poor) and the alienated North where a man asking for help is considered crazy (yet, a little farther on, a northerner wakes him from his nightmare and gives him a swallow of whisky). The sociological facts are then interpreted on a level of dream consciousness: by the nightmare in which the train leaps its tracks to pursue him down the street as white folks laugh; by a similar hallucination at the end, in which the A train subway (through Harlem) chases him and Laura; by the sudden revelation of life as a wheel of fortune on which he is spun helplessly until he intervenes to prevent the game from being completed.

Although the theme of the Wheel of Life, Fate, or Fortune is an old one (updated here by the bingo game), Ellison suggests quite specifically how it is rigged in modern society: the crowd is made up of poor blacks seeking a lucky break, the emcee running the game is white and calls the protagonist "boy" (as does the policeman at the end), and in his moment of insight the protagonist significantly forgets his slave name ("given him by the man who had owned his grandfather a long time ago")—the name that symbolizes the humiliation and lack of self-respect that has been taught to blacks—and is reborn with the name of his own act: "The-man-who-pressed-the-button-who-held-the-prize-who-was-the-King-of-Bingo." Here Ellison combines the existential overtones of achieving identity through personal choice and assertion, and the chantlike rhythm of an older tradition in which tribal heroes earn the names by which they are known. The moment of truth cannot last, however, and with the approach of the policemen the magic circle of the bingo wheel gives way to his own frantic circling on stage at the end of the cord: a grotesque tie to the fateful wheel that ends with a blow on the head, and with the ironic double-zero of a win which will not be honored.

John Hersey, ed., *Ralph Ellison: A Collection of Critical Essays* (1974), contains valuable essays on different aspects of Ellison's work and an interview with Ellison himself. Kimberly W. Benston, ed., *Speaking for You: The Vision of Ralph Ellison* (1987), contains essays examining the way that Ellison's moral vision is conveyed through the interplay of aesthetic practice and cultural perception. See also Mark Busby, *Ralph Ellison* (1991), a brief introduction to the writer and his work; and Edith Schor, *Visible Ellison: A Study of Ralph Ellison's Fiction* (1993), a perceptive study with updated bibliography. Comparative studies include Michael Lynch, *Creative Revolt: A Study of Wright, Ellison, and Dostoevsky* (1990), and an essay on Ellison and Dostoevsky in Joseph Frank, *Through the Russian Prism* (1990).

King of the Bingo Game

The woman in front of him was eating roasted peanuts that smelled so good that he could barely contain his hunger. He could not even sleep and wished they'd hurry and begin the bingo game. There, on his right, two fellows were drinking wine out of a bottle wrapped in a paper bag, and he could hear soft gurgling in the dark. His stomach gave a low, gnawing growl. "If this was down South," he thought, "all I'd have to do is lean over and say, 'Lady, gimme a few of those peanuts, please ma'am,' and she'd pass me the bag and never think nothing of it." Or he could ask the fellows for a drink in the same way. Folks down South stuck together that way; they didn't even have to know you. But up here it was different. Ask somebody for something, and they'd think you were crazy. Well, I ain't crazy. I'm just broke, 'cause I got no birth certificate to get a job, and Laura 'bout to die 'cause we got no money for a doctor. But I ain't crazy. And yet a pinpoint of doubt was focused in his mind as he glanced toward the screen and saw the hero stealthily entering a dark room and sending the beam of a flashlight along a wall of bookcases. This is where he finds the trapdoor, he remembered. The man would pass abruptly through the wall and find the girl tied to a bed, her legs and arms spread wide, and her clothing torn to rags. He laughed softly to himself. He had seen the picture three times, and this was one of the best scenes.

On his right the fellow whispered wide-eyed to his companion, "Man, look a-yonder!"

"Damn!"

"Wouldn't I like to have her tied up like that . . ."

"Hey! That fool's letting her loose!"

"Aw, man, he loves her."

"Love or no love!"

The man moved impatiently beside him, and he tried to involve himself in the scene. But Laura was on his mind. Tiring quickly of watching the picture he looked back to where the white beam filtered from the projection room above the balcony. It started small and grew large, specks of dust dancing in its whiteness as it reached the screen. It was strange how the beam always landed right on the screen and didn't mess up and fall somewhere else. But they had it all fixed. Everything was fixed. Now suppose when they showed that girl with her dress torn the girl started taking off the rest of her clothes, and when the guy came in he didn't untie her but kept her there and went to taking off his own clothes? *That* would be something to see. If a picture got out of hand like that those guys up there would go nuts. Yeah, and there'd be so many folks in here you couldn't find a seat for nine months! A strange sensation played over his skin. He shuddered. Yesterday he'd seen a bedbug on a woman's neck as they walked out into the bright street. But exploring his thigh through a hole in his pocket he found only goose pimples and old scars.

The bottle gurgled again. He closed his eyes. Now a dreamy music was accompanying the film and train whistles were sounding in the distance, and he was a boy again walking along a railroad trestle down South, and seeing the train coming, and running back as fast as he could go, and hearing the whistle blowing, and getting off the trestle to solid ground just in time, with the earth trembling beneath his feet, and feeling relieved as he ran down the cinder-strewn embankment onto the highway, and looking back and seeing with terror that the train had left the track and was following him right down the middle of the street, and all the white people laughing as he ran screaming . . .

"Wake up there, buddy! What the hell do you mean hollering like that? Can't you see we trying to enjoy this here picture?"

He started at the man with gratitude.

"I'm sorry, old man," he said. "I musta been dreaming."

"Well, here, have a drink. And don't be making no noise like that, damn!"

His hands trembled as he tilted his head. It was not wine, but whiskey. Cold rye whiskey. He took a deep swoller, decided it was better not to take another, and handed the bottle back to its owner.

"Thanks, old man," he said.

Now he felt the cold whiskey breaking a warm path straight through the middle of him, growing hotter and sharper as it moved. He had not eaten all day, and it made him light-headed. The smell of the peanuts stabbed him like a knife, and he got up and found a seat in the middle aisle. But no sooner did he sit than he saw a row of intense-faced young girls, and got up again, thinking, "You chicks musta been Lindy-hopping[1] somewhere." He found a seat several rows ahead as the lights came on, and he saw the screen disappear behind a heavy red and gold curtain; then the curtain rising, and the man with the microphone and a uniformed attendant coming on the stage.

He felt for his bingo cards, smiling. The guy at the door wouldn't like it if he knew about his having *five* cards. Well, not everyone played the bingo game; and even with five cards he didn't have much of a chance. For Laura, though, he had to have faith. He studied the cards, each with its different numerals, punching the free center hole in each and spreading them neatly across his lap; and when the lights faded he sat slouched in his seat so that he could look from his cards to the bingo wheel with but a quick shifting of his eyes.

Ahead, at the end of the darkness, the man with the microphone was pressing a button attached to a long cord and spinning the bingo wheel and calling out the number each time the wheel came to rest. And each time the voice rang out his finger raced over the cards for the number. With five cards he had to move fast. He became nervous; there were too many cards, and the man went too fast with his grating voice. Perhaps he should just select one and throw the others away. But he was afraid. He became warm. Wonder how much Laura's doctor would cost? Damn that, watch the cards! And with despair he heard the man call three in a row which he missed on all five cards. This way he'd never win . . .

When he saw the row of holes punched across the third card, he sat paralyzed and heard the man call three more numbers before he stumbled forward, screaming,

"Bingo! Bingo!"

"Let that fool up there," someone called.

"Get up there, man!"

He stumbled down the aisle and up the steps to the stage into a light so sharp and bright that for a moment it blinded him, and he felt that he had moved into the spell of some strange, mysterious power. Yet it was as familiar as the sun, and he knew it was the perfectly familiar bingo.

The man with the microphone was saying something to the audience as he held out his card. A cold light flashed from the man's finger as the card left his hand. His knees trembled. The man stepped closer, checking

1. The Lindy-hop was a variant of the jitterbug, a lively jazz dance popular in the 1930s and 1940s.

the card against the numbers chalked on the board. Suppose he had made
a mistake? The pomade on the man's hair made him feel faint, and he
backed away. But the man was checking the card over the microphone
now, and he had to stay. He stood tense, listening.

"Under the O, forty-four," the man chanted. 'Under the I, seven. Under
the G, three. Under the B, ninety-six. Under the N, thirteen!"

His breath came easier as the man smiled at the audience.

"Yessir, ladies and gentlemen, he's one of the chosen people!"

The audience rippled with laughter and applause.

"Step right up to the front of the stage."

He moved slowly forward, wishing that the light was not so bright.

"To win tonight's jackpot of $36.90 the wheel must stop between the
double zero, understand?"

He nodded, knowing the ritual from the many days and nights he had
watched the winners march across the stage to press the button that controlled the spinning wheel and receive the prizes. And now he followed
the instructions as though he'd crossed the slippery stage a million prize-
winning times.

The man was making some kind of a joke, and he nodded vacantly. So
tense had he become that he felt a sudden desire to cry and shook it away.
He felt vaguely that his whole life was determined by the bingo wheel; not
only that which would happen now that he was at last before it, but all
that had gone before, since his birth, and his mother's birth and the birth
of his father. It had always been there, even though he had not been aware
of it, handing out the unlucky cards and numbers of his days. The feeling
persisted, and he started quickly away. I better get down from here before
I make a fool of myself, he thought.

"Here, boy," the man called. "You haven't started yet."

Someone laughed as he went hesitantly back.

"Are you all reet?"

He grinned at the man's jive talk, but no words would come, and he
knew it was not a convincing grin. For suddenly he knew that he stood on
the slippery brink of some terrible embarrassment.

"Where you from, boy?" the man asked.

"Down South."

"He from down South, ladies and gentlemen," the man said. "Where
from? Speak right into the mike."

"Rocky Mont," he said. "Rock' Mont, North Car'lina."

"So you decided to come down off that mountain to the U.S.," the man
laughed. He felt that the man was making a fool of him, but then something cold was placed in his hand, and the lights were no longer behind
him.

Standing before the wheel he felt alone, but that was somehow right,
and he remembered his plan. He would give the wheel a short quick twirl.
Just a touch of the button. He had watched it many times, and always it
came close to double zero when it was short and quick. He steeled himself; the fear had left, and he felt a profound sense of promise, as though
he were about to be repaid for all the things he'd suffered all his life.
Trembling, he pressed the button. There was a whirl of lights, and in a

second he realized with finality that though he wanted to, he could not stop. It was as though he held a high-powered line in his naked hand. His nerves tightened. As the wheel increased its speed it seemed to draw him more and more into its power, as though it held his fate; and with it came a deep need to submit, to whirl, to lose himself in its swirl of color. He could not stop it now, he knew. So let it be.

The button rested snugly in his palm where the man had placed it. And now he became aware of the man beside him, advising him through the microphone, while behind the shadowy audience hummed with noisy voices. He shifted his feet. There was still that feeling of helplessness within him, making part of him desire to turn back, even now that the jackpot was right in his hand. He squeezed the button until his fist ached. Then, like the sudden shriek of a subway whistle, a doubt tore through his head. Suppose he did not spin the wheel long enough? What could he do, and how could he tell? And then he knew, even as he wondered, that as long as he pressed the button, he could control the jackpot. He and only he could determine whether or not it was to be his. He felt drunk. Then, as though he had come down from a high hill into a valley of people, he heard the audience yelling.

"Come down from there, you jerk!"

"Let somebody else have a chance . . ."

"Ole Jack thinks he done found the end of the rainbow . . ."

The last voice was not unfriendly, and he turned and smiled dreamily into the yelling mouths. Then he turned his back squarely on them.

"Don't take too long, boy," a voice said.

He nodded. They were yelling behind him. Those folks did not understand what had happened to him. They had been playing the bingo game day and night for years, trying to win rent money or hamburger change. But not one of those wise guys had discovered this wonderful thing. He watched the wheel whirling past the numbers and experienced a burst of exaltation: This is God! This is the really truly God! He said it aloud, "This is God!"

He said it with such absolute conviction that he feared he would fall fainting into the footlights. But the crowd yelled so loud that they could not hear. These fools, he thought. I'm here trying to tell them the most wonderful secret in the world, and they're yelling like they gone crazy. A hand fell upon his shoulder.

"You'll have to make a choice now, boy. You've taken too long."

He brushed the hand violently away.

"Leave me alone, man. I know what I'm doing!"

The man looked surprised and held on to the microphone for support. And because he did not wish to hurt the man's feelings he smiled, realizing with a sudden pang that there was no way of explaining to the man just why he had to stand there pressing the button forever.

"Come here," he called tiredly.

The man approached, rolling the heavy microphone across the stage.

"Anybody can play this bingo game, right?" he said.

"Sure, but . . ."

He smiled, feeling inclined to be patient with this slick looking white man with his blue sport shirt and his sharp gabardine suit.

"That's what I thought," he said. "Anybody can win the jackpot as long as they get the lucky number, right?"

"That's the rule, but after all . . ."

"That's what I thought," he said. "And the big prize goes to the man who knows how to win it?"

The man nodded speechlessly.

"Well then, go on over there and watch me win like I want to. I ain't going to hurt nobody," he said, "and I'll show you how to win. I mean to show the whole world how it's got to be done."

And because he understood, he smiled again to let the man know that he held nothing against him for being white and impatient. Then he refused to see the man any longer and stood pressing the button, the voices of the crowd reaching him like sounds in distant streets. Let them yell. All the Negroes down there were just ashamed because he was black like them. He smiled inwardly, knowing how it was. Most of the time he was ashamed of what Negroes did himself. Well, let them be ashamed for something this time. Like him. He was like a long thin black wire that was being stretched and wound upon the bingo wheel; wound until he wanted to scream; wound, but this time himself controlling the winding and the sadness and the shame, and because he did, Laura would be all right. Suddenly the lights flickered. He staggered backwards. Had something gone wrong? All this noise. Didn't they know that although he controlled the wheel, it also controlled him, and unless he pressed the button forever and forever and ever it would stop, leaving him high and dry, dry and high on this hard high slippery hill and Laura dead? There was only one chance; he had to do whatever the wheel demanded. And gripping the button in despair, he discovered with surprise that it imparted a nervous energy. His spine tingled. He felt a certain power.

Now he faced the raging crowd with defiance, its screams penetrating his eardrums like trumpets shrieking from a juke-box. The vague faces glowing in the bingo lights gave him a sense of himself that he had never known before. He was running the show, by God! They had to read to him, for he was their luck. This is *me*, he thought. Let the bastards yell. Then someone was laughing inside him, and he realized that somehow he had forgotten his own name. It was a sad, lost feeling to lose your name, and a crazy thing to do. That name had been given him by the white man who had owned his grandfather a long time ago down South. But maybe those wise guys knew his name.

"Who am I?" he screamed.

"Hurry up and bingo, you jerk!"

They didn't know either, he thought sadly. They didn't even know their own names, they were all poor nameless bastards. Well, he didn't need that old name; he was reborn. For as long as he pressed the button he was The-man-who-pressed-the-button-who-held-the-prize-who-was-the-King-of-Bingo. That was the way it was, and he'd have to press the button even if nobody understood, even though Laura did not understand.

"Live!" he shouted.

The audience quieted like the dying of a huge fan.

"Live, Laura, baby. I got holt of it now, sugar. Live!"

He screamed it, tears streaming down his face. "I got nobody but you!"

The screams tore from his very guts. He felt as though the rush of blood to his head would burst out in baseball seams of small red droplets, like a head beaten by police clubs. Bending over he saw a trickle of blood splashing the toe of his shoe. With his free hand he searched his head. It was his nose. God, suppose something has gone wrong? He felt that the whole audience had somehow entered him and was stamping its feet in his stomach and he was unable to throw them out. They wanted the prize, that was it. They wanted the secret for themselves. But they'd never get it; he would keep the bingo wheel whirling forever, and Laura would be safe in the wheel. But would she? It had to be, because if she were not safe the wheel would cease to turn; it could not go on. He had to get away, *vomit* all, and his mind formed an image of himself running with Laura in his arms down the tracks of the subway just ahead of an A train,[2] running desperately *vomit* with people screaming for him to come out but knowing no way of leaving the tracks because to stop would bring the train crushing down upon him and to attempt to leave across the other tracks would mean to run into a hot third rail as high as his waist which threw blue sparks that blinded his eyes until he could hardly see.

He heard singing and the audience was clapping its hands.

> Shoot the liquor to him, Jim, boy!
> Clap-clap-clap
> Well a-calla the cop
> He's blowing his top!
> Shoot the liquor to him, Jim, boy!

Bitter anger grew within him at the singing. They think I'm crazy. Well let 'em laugh. I'll do what I got to do.

He was standing in an attitude of intense listening when he saw that they were watching something on the stage behind him. He felt weak. But when he turned he saw no one. If only his thumb did not ache so. Now they were applauding. And for a moment he thought that the wheel had stopped. But that was impossible, his thumb still pressed the button. Then he saw them. Two men in uniform beckoned from the end of the stage. They were coming toward him, walking in step, slowly, like a tap-dance team returning for a third encore. But their shoulders shot forward, and he backed away, looking wildly about. There was nothing to fight them with. He had only the long black cord which led to a plug somewhere back stage, and he couldn't use that because it operated the bingo wheel. He backed slowly, fixing the men with his eyes as his lips stretched over his teeth in a tight, fixed grin; moved toward the end of the stage and realizing that he couldn't go much further, for suddenly the cord became taut and he couldn't afford to break the cord. But he had to do something. The audience was howling. Suddenly he stopped dead, seeing the men

2. The subway express train to Harlem.

halt, their legs lifted as in an interrupted step of a slow-motion dance. There was nothing to do but run in the other direction and he dashed forward, slipping and sliding. The men fell back, surprised. He struck out violently going past.

"Grab him!"

He ran, but all too quickly the cord tightened, resistingly, and he turned and ran back again. This time he slipped them, and discovered by running in a circle before the wheel he could keep the cord from tightening. But this way he had to flail his arms to keep the men away. Why couldn't they leave a man alone? He ran, circling.

"Ring down the curtain," someone yelled. But they couldn't do that. If they did the wheel flashing from the projection room would be cut off. But they had him before he could tell them so, trying to pry open his fist, and he was wrestling and trying to bring his knees into the fight and holding on to the button, for it was his life. And now he was down, seeing a foot coming down, crushing his wrist cruelly, down, as he saw the wheel whirling serenely above.

"I can't give it up," he screamed. Then quietly, in a confidential tone, "Boys, I really can't give it up."

It landed hard against his head. And in the blank moment they had it away from him, completely now. He fought them trying to pull him up from the stage as he watched the wheel spin slowly to a stop. Without surprise he saw it rest at double-zero.

"You see," he pointed bitterly.

"Sure, boy, sure, it's O. K.," one of the men said smiling.

And seeing the man bow his head to someone he could not see, he felt very, very happy; he would receive what all the winners received.

But as he warmed in the justice of the man's tight smile he did not see the man's slow wink, nor see the bow-legged man behind him step clear of the swiftly descending curtain and set himself for a blow. He only felt the dull pain exploding in his skull, and he knew even as it slipped out of him that his luck had run out on the stage.

KOJIMA NOBUO
born 1915

Kojima Nobuo, a deft satirist, belongs to the generation of writers in Japan who came of age during World War II. Their experiences in war, disastrous defeat, and humiliating occupation inevitably made them connoisseurs of absurdity. Together in particular with Yasuoka Shōtarō (born 1920), Kojima uses irony and ridicule to articulate the postwar pathology of the Japanese antihero: the befuddled ordinary man uprooted by failure, crushed by society, oppressed by go-getters, and so paralyzed by the flux all around him that he surrenders those few privileges still given the Confucian-based head of the household. Now even home denies refuge to the timid and profoundly ineffectual Japanese male. This may surprise American readers. Nowhere in the fiction of Kojima will we recognize the dynamos who built the world's most successful postwar economy (unless, of course, we are seeing them with their masks off, neuroses exposed in the empty hours away from their devotions to the Company).

Kojima was born near the town of Gifu in central Japan, the son of a carpenter who made Buddhist altars. An avid reader from childhood, he explored as a student a range of world literature, including British, American, and Russian writers. He would later aver that Gogol, the nineteenth-century Russian satirist, was a particularly important influence; one can also detect the impact of Kafka and Dostoevsky. In 1941 Kojima graduated with a degree in English literature from the prestigious University of Tokyo. His senior thesis, *Thackeray as a Humorist*, foretold his own future as a satirical writer. Throughout his career, he has combined the work of a novelist with teaching, translation, and writing literary criticism. During his tenure as a professor of English literature at Meiji University in Tokyo, he has published a number of scholarly volumes, including literary biography, and translated a baker's half-dozen of American writers (William Saroyan, Sherwood Anderson, Dorothy Parker, Nathaniel Hawthorne, Robert Penn Warren, Irwin Shaw, and Bernard Malamud).

Without doubt, though, it was Kojima's wartime and immediate postwar experiences that most shaped his fiction. Both periods seemed to demonstrate the randomness and futility of life. No sooner had he mastered the English language as a university student and begun to earn his living teaching English after graduating than he found his country and himself at war with virtually every English-speaking nation. In basic training for the army he was promptly ordered to forget the enemy's hateful tongue. He was also taunted—for being a university graduate, for wearing eyeglasses. Army officers made him drink more liquor than he could hold. He was sent to Manchuria, where scouting missions took on the color of childhood games of hide-and-seek. "When we went out on punitive expeditions," he would later write, "I always felt a great sense of futility. Of course, it would be futile to be killed in battle, but it was truly miserable to be scrambling around looking for an enemy. Whenever we went out looking for them, it was always after they had already run away."[*]

Then orders were reversed, and in 1944 Kojima was assigned to an intelligence unit in Peking, where he was to use his English after all. Here he spent his days intercepting radio communications of the U.S. Air Force and relaying the information to headquarters. On a slow day, or a particularly creative one, by Kojima's own admission, half the "decoded messages" were the products of sheer invention, the author's first fiction. It may even be said that English saved his life. His former battalion, sent to the Philippines not long after he was posted to Peking, was annihilated by General MacArthur's forces in the battle of Leyte at the end of 1944. As the war hurtled to conclusion, his final linguistic duty was to teach his commanding officers to say "I am not a war criminal" and "Would you care for a drink?"

Not surprisingly, then, English figures in Kojima's early fiction. From his intelligence post in China he returned to a homeland completely devastated. More than three million Japanese had died during the war, almost one million of them civilians. Air raids and two atomic bombs had destroyed all but one of Japan's major cities. Over 30 percent of the Japanese people had lost their homes. Food shortages brought black marketeering and near starvation. Once prosperous families were reduced to trading heirlooms for basic necessities. The yen plummeted to barely a hundredth of its prewar value. Industry hardly existed. Perhaps most shocking of all: five hundred thousand former enemy troops, mostly American, now occupied the country. The Allied Occupation of Japan lasted from 1945 to 1952, first to

---

[*]Van C. Gessel, *The Sting of Life: Four Contemporary Japanese Novelists* (1989) 15.

maintain order and establish a new Japanese government and then to oversee extensive political, social, and economic reforms that would purge Japan of "irresponsible militarism" and refashion the country into an American-style democracy. The commanding presence of General MacArthur—whom some viewed as a latter-day *shogun* in the long tradition of Japan's military dictators, whose victories tolerated the continued existence of a figurehead emperor—seemed, like his many soldiers, to be everywhere, and so did their language.

Kojima might have been expected to benefit from this situation. But as his satiric masterpiece *The American School* (1954) makes patently clear, he views those who use the victors' language as carpetbaggers, or opportunists. The antagonist of the story, Yamada, an unctuous teacher of English dying for approval in defeated, shame-ridden Japan, tries to turn an excursion with his fellow teachers to a model school on one of the new American military bases into a demonstration that he alone, by virtue of his English fluency, is worthy of American respect. But as is often the case with people who must have the approval of others in order to respect themselves, Yamada is pathetic and dangerous because he stands for nothing except catering to those in power. For his foil he chooses Isa, the protagonist, a meek, inadequate colleague who is already quite beleaguered even before Yamada proposes a "demonstration" in front of the Americans. It is Isa's misfortune to despise the very language that he teaches, or to despise the uses to which it is now put by his compatriots. When they speak English, those who don't mind toadying enter a twilight zone of colonialism and opportunity. Their obsequious actions are made painless and unreal by the distancing that a foreign language automatically furnishes. They cease, in short, in Isa's eyes, to be Japanese. Yet, of course, they can never be American. Neither fish nor fowl, they let English transport them to an unreal world of license where they humiliate themselves without feeling any shame.

For its relentless, ironic evocation of the insidious shattering of a principled world and for its implied commentary on both Japan's postwar confusion and its historical tendency, at certain watersheds, to let others set its standards (China in the seventh century, the West in the nineteenth, and the United States in the third quarter of the twentieth), *The American School* won Kojima the Akutagawa Prize, one of his country's highest literary honors. With this work, Kojima consolidated his position as a chronicler of the helpless lot of postwar Japanese intellectuals. From his debut story in 1952, *The Rifle*, the portrait of a soldier who sells his soul to the army, to his most famous novel, *A Close Family* (1965), a record of the exact opposite, and his more recent success, *Reasons for Parting* (1982), an immense novel hailed as a landmark in modern Japanese fiction, he has continued to bear witness to what he sees as the slow but discernible disintegration of humanity.

Kojima's novels and the bulk of his short fiction remain untranslated. *Stars*, however, from the same year as *The American School*, is included in Van C. Gessel and Tomone Matsumoto, eds., *The Shōwa Anthology: Modern Japanese Short Stories* (1985), a good source for modern and contemporary Japanese short fiction. Howard Hibbett, ed., *Contemporary Japanese Literature: An Anthology of Fiction, Film, and Other Writing Since 1945* (1977), and Yukiko Tanaka and Elizabeth Hanson, eds., *This Kind of Woman: Ten Stories by Japanese Women Writers, 1960–1976* (1982), also are good sources for modern Japanese literature. Works in English by members of Kojima's loose-knit coterie in the 1950s include Van C. Gessel's translation, *Stained Glass Elegies: Stories by Shūsaku Endō* (1984); Kären Wigen Lewis's translation of Yasuoka Shōtarō, *A View by the Sea* (1984); and Kathryn Sparling's translation of Shimao Toshio, *"The Sting of Death" and Other Stories* (1985). Also highly recommended are E. Dale Saunders's translation of Abe Kōbō, *The Woman in the Dunes* (1964), and John Nathan's translation of Ōe

Kenzaburō, *A Personal Matter* (1968). For a critical study of Kojima, Yasuoka, Shimao, and Endō, see Van C. Gessel, *The Sting of Life: Four Contemporary Japanese Novelists* (1989).

PRONOUNCING GLOSSARY

The following list uses common English syllables to provide rough equivalents of selected words whose pronunciation may be unfamiliar to the general reader.

Gifu: *gee-foo*

Jizo: *jee-zoh*

Kojima Nobuo: *koh-jee-mah noh-boo-oh*

Meiji: *may-jee*

Michiko: *mee-chee-koh*

Shibamoto: *shee-bah-moh-toh*

Yasuoka Shōtarō: *yah-soo-oh-kah shoh-tah-roh*

The American School[1]

It was past eight-thirty and still the official had not appeared. The teachers had been told to assemble by this hour for their excursion to the American school, and most of them had come twenty minutes or so early. Having made their way to the Prefectural Office[2] through the morning throngs of commuters, all thirty of them were now left sitting here and there on the deserted stairs and around the gravel drive. There was one woman among them. She had apparently gone to some trouble to dress for the occasion; but her high heels, hat, and new plaid suit only made her look more sad and shabby.

As soon as they were all present, the teachers went en masse to the Office of Education on the second floor, only to be driven back down to this place which had not even been mentioned at the organization meeting a week ago. Right after the roll call the chairman of that meeting, an administrator from the Office of Education, had read off a list of instructions. The first was to assemble promptly at the appointed time. The second was to dress impeccably. The latter had created a stir which did not die down until the promulgation of the third point, that they must maintain a solemn silence at all times. Finally, they were to pack a lunch, for they would have to march to and from the school, a total distance of some eight miles; and even teachers had learned to feel proper hunger pangs in the three years since the War.

An American jeep ploughed through the gravel of the driveway, rounded the sharp curve, and came to a stop in front of the prefectural building. A teacher who had been sitting just inside the door jumped to his feet and moved away.

There was one man who had all the while been standing straight as a ramrod. The best-dressed and healthiest-looking of the group, he was conspicuous in an almost disconcerting way. At the previous week's meeting he had repeatedly raised his hand with questions for the chairman, a

---

1. Translated by William F. Sibley.   2. A state-level government office.

man by the name of Shibamoto. "Are we only supposed to observe?" he had inquired at one juncture. "What do you mean?" Shibamoto asked. "I was just wondering," he said, "if we might not give them a demonstration of our oral method." With a slight swagger that accentuated his heavy judo wrestler's build, the official reiterated loudly that the purpose of the excursion was to observe. He added that the Office of Education had gone to considerable lengths to secure permission for the visit. The man, whose name was Yamada, had at last given up this line of questioning.

He seized the floor once again in the commotion that followed the remarks on proper dress. "Quite right, sir," he said. "We must all present a neat appearance, whatever the cost. Any sloppiness would reflect on the profession. Worst of all, it would raise serious doubts about our competence to teach English. They despise us as a defeated people to begin with, and when they see the clothes we wear—I know, because I interpreted for the inspectors when they came to our school—they just look the other way. Not to mention the toilets . . ." His speech was interrupted at this point, and by now everyone was staring at him, with particular attention to his feet. There was scarcely another pair of leather shoes in sight. Undaunted, he resumed as soon as the mutters died down. They should avoid speaking Japanese in front of their hosts, he insisted, in order to display to the fullest extent their command of English. This was greeted by more general muttering, and a shrill outcry from the man sitting next to him: "What nonsense!" Yamada turned to face the heckler. But before he could launch into a longwinded defense of his proposal, Shibamoto called for order with the request that both Mr. Yamada and Mr. Isa refrain from intemperate language.

Isa had once been pressed into service at election time as interpreter for the Occupation inspection team (all elections were to be conducted impartially under the watchful eyes of the authorities). He was taken by jeep from one small village to the next, and was expected to keep his American counterpart informed of what was going on. Still only about thirty years old, he had never had a single conversation in English; occasional attempts at practical application of the language in the classroom had left him tingling with embarrassment; and when word came that the Americans would soon be visiting his school he had feigned illness, lying in bed for several days with an icebag pressed against his forehead, where there was not the slightest trace of fever. Only fear of unknown reprisals at the hands of the Occupation officials had deterred him from a similar stratagem at the time of the elections.

The moment he was packed into the jeep with a Negro soldier, he had turned to the fellow and said, in English: "I am truly very sorry to have kept you waiting." This was met with silence, and when he repeated the words three times over, the soldier only stared at him coldly and uncomprehendingly. The phrase he had prepared several days ago and practiced constantly since was clearly too formal and correct. From then on he limited himself to two words, "stop" and "go." For those five hours he felt as if he were being boiled alive, though outwardly he appeared to be merely loafing on the job. And in either case, the result was that he was of no use to anyone.

As soon as they approached the first polling-place, he fled. He tried to reason with himself, before sneaking off to hide, that it would go still worse with him than if he had refused to come in the first place. But the prospect of being addressed in that unfamiliar language in front of a crowd made his knees quake. By the time the Negro noticed his absence and came back to find him, he was long gone.

Isa was not by nature so craven; indeed, as the jeep drove into the village he had felt a strong impulse to do violence to his keeper. But after they slowed down, it seemed easier to escape, and so he jumped off the rear and made for the wooded slope above the road. On discovering that his passenger had fled, the soldier went after him, partly out of fear at being left alone in these dark hills. Deep in the woods Isa saw the man coming. He called out to him in Japanese: "You'll have to speak our language. Speak Japanese or else! What would you do if someone really said that to you?" As the face of his adversary drew near, a neatly trimmed beard, features strained in an effort to make out the indistinct words, it gave a feeling of loneliness. The beard contributed an incongruously civilized air, and as the face moved still closer it seemed almost to show some understanding of the stream of Japanese that issued forth from behind the trees. Isa babbled on as fast as he could. When the Negro at last realized that the words were not in his language, he threw up his hands and shrugged his shoulders. Seated behind the wheel again, he looked even lonelier than before, as if unaccountably intimidated by this creature who spoke scarcely a word of normal English, and who would lapse without warning into Japanese gibberish. He ceased to pay any attention at all to Isa, and proceeded as though chauffeuring an honored guest around the countryside. A pointless errand on the whole; but at least, it occurred to him, the man might be of some service in helping him deal with hostile natives.

Each time an American jeep drove up, Isa drifted a little away from the prefectural building. Yamada's foolish suggestions at the organization meeting were still fresh in his mind, especially the proposal of a demonstration class, which had aroused in him an instant panic that persisted to this moment. Well, he would simply keep a close watch on Yamada and shut him up if necessary. He had, however, already yielded on one point: he was wearing a pair of black leather civilian shoes. They were an odd match with his khaki uniform, but he had wanted at least to spare himself the embarrassment of army boots. Likewise, having set out with his lunch box in an old army bag, along the way he had taken the box out, folded up the incriminating bag, and stuck it under his arm.

Yamada continued to stand alone surveying the scene expectantly. Whenever a jeep pulled up he would bustle over to explain the situation. "We represent the English teachers of this prefecture," he would begin stiffly. "We are very devoted to the English language. We work very hard to teach the English. We are now utilizing the latest methods of instruction, just like you have in your country."

"If you work so goddam hard, what are you hanging around for at this hour?" one driver replied, reaching down with a look of extreme boredom to hand him a cigarette.

"I do not smoke," said Yamada.

"Are you the chief?"

"Our leader is an official of this prefecture. He is very late for our appointment. Government officials are lazy people. But you must not think that all Japanese are like that."

The soldier, who was black, threw up his hands in disgust. "I am truly very sorry to have kept you waiting," he said, and drove off.

Yamada did not know what to make of this parting remark. The American had perhaps been mocking Japanese officials. He looked at his watch again and muttered to himself. What would their hosts think if they arrived late at the school? Something must be done. He called out to those of his colleagues who were sprawled within earshot, "Will some of you come up to the Education Office with me? If we don't do something we'll be late. They have our names on file at the school. We'll be disgraced. 'What can you expect from a defeated people?' they'll say."

Yamada noticed that Isa, who was sitting only a few feet away, kept his back turned as though preoccupied with some important business. He went over to investigate and found him with his lunch box open on his lap. Isa had been up since three, riding his bicycle to the nearest station, then taking a combination of streetcars and trains until he reached this distant city. He was hungry; rather, he thought he ought to be hungry by now.

Yamada stood for a moment in silent amazement. "This is not time to be eating," he said. "Come with me to the Education Office. If the officials there won't cooperate, we'll speak to the Occupation personnel."

The bare mention of the local Occupation force was enough to upset Isa. He had already noticed the bearded Negro in one of the jeeps, and had seen Yamada accost him. Indeed, it was one reason for beginning his lunch now. This was a high-risk area where he might be addressed in English at any moment. A mouthful of food would, he sensed, offer some defense against any demand that might be made of him. And so he did not answer Yamada, and regretted having challenged him at last week's meeting, thus attracting his attention. Isa had decided not to speak a word in any language today, for if he began by conversing in Japanese he would surely end by having to speak English. The best strategy was a tight-lipped silence that would lead people to believe he was indisposed. Then no one, neither official nor colleague, would think it strange if, when his turn came to talk at the school, he had nothing to say. Without looking up from his lunch he waved his chopsticks in the air by way of a reply.

"What kind of answer is that?" Yamada put his question in both languages and waited for an answer. Isa pretended not to hear. Yamada was given to venting his wrath in English. "Oh, for shame!" he exclaimed, stalking off towards the overdressed instructress, Michiko, who capitulated on the spot and followed him up the stairs.

On their way into the office they bumped into the tardy official. Shibamoto was wearing his Sunday best, which consisted of a long overcoat and a soft felt hat. As he led them out of the building, he blew a whistle to assemble the others. Yamada protested that the whistle would sound a shrill note of unreconstructed militarism; furthermore, for the same reason, they should not march in a solid phalanx.[3] Shibamoto granted his point and ordered the group to fall out. When the command was given to reassemble in loose ranks, Yamada placed himself like a staff adjutant at Shibamoto's side. The rest of the teachers straggled behind in a long procession, with Isa bringing up the rear.

Shibamoto made a brief announcement: "We received notification that the time for our visit had been changed. Sorry for the inconvenience. They were very pleased with the first group. Try to keep up the good record. Ready?"

It was about four miles to the American school down an asphalt road that ran straight as the crow flies from the outskirts of the city. Strung out like a chain gang, the teachers set out with Shibamoto and Yamada in the lead. Isa, at the other end, made no effort to move up. He found himself walking beside the woman, and this was somehow reassuring. Within ten minutes they had reached the asphalt road. There was an uninterrupted flow of traffic traveling to and fro among the various installations of the large base that stretched out for miles around the school. A sigh rippled through the group at the sight of this long black ribbon which was clearly not made for walking.

Isa watched with secret admiration as Michiko took a pair of sneakers from her cloth bundle and put them on. What foresight! The men around him were all wearing long overcoats, with a sprinkling of army issue such as he himself had on. The poverty revealed in their bulky clothing showed up starkly against the hard pavement. "I don't want you in rows, but do move closer together," Shibamoto cautioned. "You mustn't look so straggly—there are Occupation personnel all around you." Cars and jeeps were in fact flying by, thick and fast, though there was not another pedestrian to be seen anywhere on the forbidding road.

The presence of a single woman in their midst was enough to mitigate the ragged, faintly subversive spectacle created by the twenty-nine men. Before five minutes had gone by, a car coming from the opposite direction pulled up beside Michiko. A soldier stuck his head out the window and spoke to her. "What are you people doing here?" he asked, echoing the question put to them several times in front of the prefectural building. Michiko stated the purpose of their excursion in clear, correct English. "You're an English teacher, are you? Well, you're pretty damn good, I'd say." The soldier thrust some cans of cheese in her hands and drove off.

It was not until Michiko laughed out loud and tugged at his sleeve that Isa turned to face her. With eyes studiously averted from the exchange with the soldier, he had begun to reconsider his choice of companion. Walking beside the woman, he was easy prey for any number of foreign soldiers. He felt the weight of the can that Michiko had stuffed into his pocket while he was staring at the rice paddies below the road. Living in an era when true goodwill was translated into gifts of food, he was naturally

---

3. Soldiers marching in rank and file.

pleased and flattered, and especially so for having failed to notice that she had received two cans from the soldier and had to give one away to keep the other. What if he was a little more vulnerable being next to her, he had only to look the other way when the enemy approached, and there were these unexpected benefits.

It had occurred to Michiko as they started down the asphalt road that she had forgotten something. In her rush this morning to change after sending off her son, her only child by the husband she had lost in the War (he too had been a teacher), it must have slipped her mind. She poked around in the cloth bundle and her suspicions were confirmed. Luckily the missing article was one that could be borrowed in a pinch; and at the moment the two cans of cheese plopped into her hands, she had picked Isa as her most likely benefactor.

Tranquilly and with unexpected warmth, the winter sun shone down upon the black surface until the glare began to affect one's eyes. Cars continued to pass by in both directions, and then a jeep drove up, this time from behind, and slowed down almost to the pace of the procession. Two soldiers, one white, one black, leaned out to look the group over. Yamada turned around and waited until the jeep drew up beside him. "Haro[4] boys! What are you doing?" he hailed them.

With a look of mild surprise one of the soldiers asked in return: "Only one woman?" Having verified with their own eyes, without listening to Yamada's reply, that the woman they had passed was the only one, they stopped the jeep in the middle of the road and waited. As Michiko approached they called out to her: "Ojosan![5] Ojosan!" They asked where she was going and told her to get in. Her quick response was livelier than when she spoke in Japanese, her face more expressive, even distinctly feminine. "I'm on a group excursion," she said. "I really can't go ahead by myself."

The soldiers exchanged an approving glance as they inspected the proper Japanese lady from top to bottom. They tore the wrapper from two bars of chocolate and, with a parting nod full of regret, tossed them down to Michiko. She broke one of the bars into pieces and passed them out to a few people around her, this time omitting Isa. Afterward the teachers who had dropped back toward her at this point showed no disposition to move up again.

They had not been marching in close ranks from the outset, and by now the group had split into two separate platoons: Shibamoto, Yamada, and their followers in the lead, Michiko and her attendants in the rear, with a gap of over a hundred yards in between.

It came to Isa by slow degrees that his shoes hurt. Each step brought new pains. He began to regret having worn these ill-fitting genuine leather shoes; and when he reflected that he had put them on to please Yamada, to speak the foreign tongue in the right style—simply to hold down his job—his regrets gave way to anger. The pain grew more and more acute. He struggled to keep up with Michiko, but even this was too much for

4. "Hello." The soldier is making fun of the inability of Japanese to discriminate between the sounds *l* and *r* in the English language.   5. A term of address for a young lady, similar to our "Miss."

him. He now noticed with a twinge of envy how smooth and easy her stride had become since she abandoned her high heels for sneakers. No one else, either in his platoon or the group up front, showed signs of suffering from the same problem. He himself had never paid much attention to shoes until this moment. The offending pair, on loan from a colleague, had seemed just right when he first tried them on. A tiny discrepancy was enough, it appeared, to cause a great deal of pain. Isa became suspicious of the colleague who had lent him the shoes. For all he knew, the man could be in league with Yamada.

There was no telling how much farther they had to go, for the view ahead was blocked by a rise in the road. When Isa looked back to see how much ground they had covered he was distressed to find the prefectural building looming still quite large behind them.

About fifteen feet ahead, Michiko stood looking over her shoulder in his direction. "Is something wrong?" she asked when at last he caught up with her. At his mumbled reply apropos of shoes her face took on a look of utmost gravity. Having set out in new shoes herself, she had more than an inkling of what she would have endured but for the sneakers. "That will never do. We still have a long way to go. Maybe you should hitch a ride—why don't you stop one of these jeeps?"

Isa's pain yielded to astonishment and terror. What she suggested would not have occurred to him in his wildest dreams. "If it ever came to that!" he muttered as he stumbled forward in an effort to keep up, putting as much weight as possible on his toes to relieve the pinch on his insteps. He hoped to set her mind at ease and avoid further suggestions of drastic remedies, but he soon realized that his awkward gait only made matters worse.

Michiko slackened her pace and walked silently at Isa's side as if to subdue his pain by force of her own calm will. Until now she had found him a tedious companion, thoroughly wrapped up in himself for no apparent reason. But as soon as she began to share in his suffering, faint memories stirred within her of the love, long forgotten, that a woman can also share with a man. She did not, however, lose sight of her objective. She meant to have from him that homely article left behind in her haste. What love she felt for him was bound up with her hopes of getting it, and seemed to emanate like hunger pangs from somewhere near the pit of her empty stomach. While more cars whizzed by she spoke to him again in a soothing tone, as if to stroke his heaving back. "You really ought to get yourself a lift," she said. "Shall I ask for you?"

"No! No thank you! Never mind! I'd sooner go barefoot."

"Now really, I don't see why . . ."

Isa felt like biting his tongue for breaking his vow of silence. Yet had he kept quiet Michiko would no doubt have hailed a jeep immediately, and at her fluent English they would have picked him up without further ado. Then where would he be? No matter how dire his need, the very thought of riding next to a foreigner again made him sick. He remembered all too vividly his day of torture with the black soldier. He had felt as though at any moment he could murder the man, and if it had gone on for another

day he surely would have done so, unless, of course, he had first found a
way to escape.

The tender feelings which Michiko had summoned up from deep
within her subsided in the face of Isa's stubborn refusal. The sweat now
trickling down her body served as a nagging reminder of her impure
motives. Very well, she thought, she would get what she was after anyway.
And even that didn't really matter so much; she could if necessary do
without. Resolved to not so much as look back at him, she forged ahead
toward Yamada's platoon. The others followed in her wake, leaving Isa far
behind.

Up front, Yamada and Shibamoto were trading boasts. Shibamoto, by
his own account, had been one of a handful of judo experts in the prefecture before the War disrupted things—a fifth-degree black belt, no less.
And contrary to malicious postwar propaganda, devotees of the martial arts
were not all war criminals. One had only to consider himself, holder of a
prominent post in the administrative section of the prefectural Education
Office. Moreover, he taught judo not only to the local police, but to the
Occupation personnel themselves, and had in fact got the job through his
American supervisor.

Yamada's ears perked up at the mention of Occupation personnel. He
was intensely interested in every kind of contact with the Americans,
though so far his own had been restricted to interpreting. He had a consuming ambition to study abroad, to which end he schemed and fretted
the livelong day.

Eager to establish his credentials with such a well-connected man,
Yamada explained that he had conducted any number of demonstration
classes at his school; that although they were supposedly professional
teachers of English, few of his colleagues made a good showing . . . Yes,
said Shibamoto, he had heard about all that. From a leather briefcase
the likes of which were seldom seen in these times, Yamada removed a
mimeographed schedule of a typical demonstration class, which he happened to have brought along.

"Rook heah, see for yourself," he said, breaking momentarily into
English. "I hope sometime soon to hold a teaching seminar here in the
city—with the backing of the administrative section, of course. And we
would certainly welcome cooperation from the Americans." He handed
Shibamoto his card. His name and titles appeared in Japanese script on
one side, Roman on the other. "I might not look it now, but I hold a
second-degree black belt in fencing," he volunteered.

"Is that so? I suppose you've had some experience in your day," said
Shibamoto.

"You bet I have!" Yamada slashed the air with an imaginary sword.
"This might not be the time to mention it, but when I was in OTS[6] I got
to whet my blade a bit, if you know what I mean."

"It must be hard, cutting off heads."

6. Officers' Training School.

"Not really. It takes a good arm, a sharp sword, and practice, of course. That's all."

"How many did you polish off?"

"Let's see . . ." Yamada paused and looked around. "About twenty, I guess. Half of them must've been POWs."

"Any Yanks?"

"Naturally."

"How did they compare with the Chinese?"

"Well, there's quite a difference in how they take it. When you come right down to it, they show their lack of what you might call Oriental philosophy."

"You're lucky they never caught up with you."

". . . I was only following orders."

Yamada was suddenly aware of the dangerous turn in the conversation. What had he been saying? He fell silent. Noticing that Shibamoto had removed his overcoat, he hastily took off his own and stuck it under his arm. He looked over his shoulder at the disorderly procession and his taut, swarthy features collapsed into a disdainful grimace.

"What do you think of this mess?" he said to Shibamoto. "If the War were still on and this were a real march. . . ! But what can you expect from a bunch of high school teachers?"

Yamada fixed Isa hawklike in a distant gaze. In this perspective the laggard could not fail to arouse contempt and indignation. While Yamada stood at the side of the road the group straggled by in little clumps, their pace so listless that he wanted to ask with the Americans what business they had on this highway. He made up his mind to stay where he was and wait for Isa to come along. Over the past week he had not forgotten Isa's vague but unmistakable hostility. As he waited, the word "insubordinate" popped into his head. It seemed to furnish a key to understanding this queer fellow. With his own tales of martial valor still ringing in his ears, Yamada became again the company commander he had been until three years before. But for all the brutal self-assurance restored to him in this transformation, he did not bark out a reprimand to Isa, preferring to take him by surprise.

Michiko passed by first. "His shoes pinch," she explained, pointing back at Isa.

"His shoes pinch? Ridiculous!" This went beyond simple insubordination. To dawdle over such an infantile triviality was inexcusable. At this rate he was likely to start whining about his bladder or a sore throat and fall still farther behind. Well, what was the matter with his shoes? Yamada stared at the black blobs of Isa's feet scraping across the asphalt in the distance. He waited till the dusty shoes had shuffled up diffidently under his nose before he spoke. "Are those your shoes?" he snapped, in English.

Isa had not noticed Yamada at the side of the road. His eyes were wide open with the effort of bearing the pain, but he could not see a thing.

"It's your fault this group is in such a shambles. It only takes one straggler like you to throw everyone out of step."

Michiko came back and repeated to Yamada her suggestion that Isa ask for a ride.

"From the Americans?" Yamada's shoulders fell as he studied Isa's feet. Ignoring Michiko, he lashed out again at Isa: "That is out of the question. Mistah Isa, have you no pride? Maybe for ap-pen-di-ci-tis. But for *shoes?*"

Several other teachers had wandered back to see what was holding things up and stood looking over Yamada's shoulder. "He'd do better to go barefoot," one of them said. This solution had occurred to Isa any number of times since the pain began. But each time he had rejected it for fear of being spotted by the Americans, who were sure to question him about his bare feet and force him to ride in a jeep.

Yamada changed his tone. "Try to keep moving, at least. You've got everyone stopped in their tracks wondering what to do about you—Oh, Mr. Shibamoto. What do you think, sir?"

When Yamada failed to return to the front rank, Shibamoto had planted himself at the roadside like a stone Jizo.[7] Once the leaders dropped out, the rest of the procession ground to a halt.

"If this keeps up we'll be late, sir. We'll be disgraced. The main thing is to make sure the Americans don't see him. Oh, for shame!"

"What seems to be the trouble here?" Shibamoto had not yet grasped the cause of Yamada's excitement. When the problem was put to him he proposed that Isa go ahead and remove his shoes. Yamada and a few others would walk along on either side and shield him from the passers-by.

Shibamoto's proposal was duly adopted and Isa was promptly relieved of his suffering. It even struck him that this pavement could have been made for bare feet, which were not, after all, without some resemblance to the rubber tires of a car.

Michiko brooded over the man who was once more walking beside her, though likely soon to lag behind again. Isa seemed as unresponsive as ever, and she made no attempt to speak to him. But his stubborn streak had begun to remind her of her late husband. Surrounded by Yamada and the others, he strode along unshod and full of purpose, a shy but spirited little man in the jaws of adversity. That is what her husband had been when he went off to war.

Her thoughts drifted back to that day when she had struggled to keep up with the column of soldiers bound for the front as they marched the five miles from their base to the station. They had not paused once along the way, pushing ahead at an unrelenting pace that did not allow for last-minute farewells. Her husband marched with clenched teeth and scarcely cast a glance in her direction. The only time he turned his head to face her, he made a curt gesture with his hand as if to drive her away. There had of course been others besides herself, among them aged mothers calling out their son's names as they stumbled after the swift procession.

Michiko had understood her husband's embarrassment then. The feelings of the barefoot man next to her now were no doubt of the same kind. Perhaps she would speak to him once they were at the school. She was

---

7. A stone statue of the guardian deity of children.

suddenly aware again of the high heels pressing through the cloth against
her hands like hard little buds about to flower. Yes, after she had changed
her shoes at the school she would have a word with him.

Isa showed no sign of faltering, indeed he fairly loped along, with none
of the strain that was beginning to tell on the others. He was, however,
still shy of foreign eyes, though his fears were very different from Yamada's,
and he walked somewhat stooped over. He hurried ahead driven by the
desire to reach his destination at the earliest possible moment, and in the
happy expectation of freedom from any further need to propel himself. He
was too absorbed in the delicate task of simultaneously staying out of sight
and rushing forward to reflect that he would still have to move about at
the school, and then make the trek back to the city.

Taking but small comfort in Isa's return to the fold and the restoration
of some semblance of order, Yamada dwelt on the disgust which the man's
every action stirred up in him. He decided the time had come to broach
to Shibamoto the subject that had been in the back of his mind all day.
"You know, sir," he began, "we really ought to give a demonstration class
while we're there. It's a rare opportunity to show them what we can do,
and maybe we can get them to evaluate and rank us while we're at it."

Shibamoto was busy surveying the buildings of the American school,
which had come into view as soon as they passed the crest in the road. He
gave Yamada a doubtful look and did not reply. When Yamada pressed
the point by suggesting that he himself could make the request, Shibamoto wearily repeated that their hosts might find the exercise troublesome.

"I don't see why it should be any trouble. It will be our show—a demonstration of what English teachers in this country are capable of. Afterwards
we'll let them give us a few pointers, that's all. As a judo expert I'm sure
you can see the wisdom of our taking the offensive, so to speak."

This was a thrust that Shibamoto could not parry. He would have to let
the man have his way. He had never met such a cocky instructor, he
thought, as Yamada announced once again that he would take the bull by
the horns.

Isa did not miss a word of this exchange. When he saw Shibamoto
weaken, his thoughts turned instinctively to escape. Slipping easily
through the loose cordon they had strung around him, he sidled off to the
edge of the road and unbuttoned his fly. Yamada was still preoccupied
and failed to notice this dereliction; the others were too tired to bother
with him.

Just then Michiko was accosted by another jeep. She broke into a cold
sweat as she ascertained that the melancholy black face looking down at
her wanted to know about Isa, who stood relieving himself up the road.
But her fears were set to rest when she heard the soldier ask, "What's with
the bare feet?" She explained, and the jeep rumbled off in Isa's direction.

Isa wheeled around in alarm, and at one glance recognized his old
adversary. He backed away, stunned by the accuracy of his presentiment
that he would see the man again today. When he reached the shoulder of
the road he turned and leaped into the field below. Here he was far less
protected than he had been on that wooded slope. The soldier was beckoning to him with a miniature package of cigarettes. The next moment

Yamada was yelling at him. "He's only trying to do you a favor. What's the matter with you!" Joining forces, the soldier and Yamada clambered into the field. Together they dragged Isa back up to the road and bundled him into the jeep. The vehicle bearing the solitary captive soon vanished in a cloud of sand, and raucous laughter swept through the ranks.

Above the road ahead some crows flocked and veered off to one side as if to clear a path for the car passing far below. Or perhaps they were preparing to scavenge around the American school. Michiko watched this scene and savored a certain relief, accompanied by a quiet, private laugh, at the removal of the burden that Isa had become for her. She no longer imagined that she could understand his excessive timidity, unless, she speculated, he had done something awful during the War.

Isa sat hunched up in the back of the jeep. He quickly averted his eyes from the driver's seat and peered out at the dwindling faces of his colleagues. Although their features were already blurred, he could clearly see that they were laughing. Yet, for all their scorn, their company was far preferable to the predicament that now filled him with despair. The general laughter left little doubt that Yamada would succeed in squeezing out of him some sort of performance in English. As far as he was concerned, it was now all but inevitable; that is, it seemed quite within the realm of possibility, which was for Isa tantamount to inevitability.

On their first encounter the Negro had mistaken Isa's cowed silence for sullen contempt, with overtones of a personal animus against himself. Afterwards he had Isa's credentials checked through the Education Office, without bothering to state the cause of his curiosity; and when the record showed no reason for the man's refusal to speak English, he felt that his suspicions had been confirmed. This unlooked-for second meeting was a stroke of luck: he would have a little revenge for that business in the woods.

The jeep screeched to a halt and Isa found a pistol pointing into his face. Then came the command: "Speak English, man. Let's hear it again. 'I am truly very sorry to have kept you waiting.' "

Isa trembled all over and stammered out the phrase as dictated. Below the trim moustache the mouth of his captor opened in a loud guffaw. The pistol was only a toy, he said. Humming a jazz tune, he started up the engine and drove on.

At the American school the soldier bade Isa a friendly farewell as he climbed out of the jeep. "Maybe we'll meet again," he said, with some appreciation, it appeared, of the karma[8] that had already brought them together twice. Isa felt weak inside at the mere suggestion.

As soon as the jeep was out of sight Isa, still barefoot, ran toward the fence enclosing the school playground. After a few moments' rest he put on his shoes and crouched down to look around. The children at recess on the playground, boys and girls mixed together, ranged from the early grades through junior high school. Even now, in midwinter, they were scampering about in a colorful assortment of light clothes, a sweater here,

---

8. Fate in the Buddhist religion; the outcome of one's actions in previous existences, since Buddhism holds that we are endlessly reborn unless we achieve enlightenment and thus escape the cycle of death and rebirth.

a blouse and jumper there. Isa retreated into the shadow of one of the buildings to continue his inspection from a less public vantage point.

Along with a sense of relative security, he experienced an overwhelming mental fatigue. He closed his eyes for fear of fainting and felt the tears well up behind his eyelids. At first he could not tell what had brought on his tears, but he knew it was a joy so intense as to be close to sorrow. With his eyes still closed he slowly discerned the source of his bliss in a murmuring of soft voices, sweet and clear as a mountain stream. They seemed to come from another world, perhaps in part because the words made little sense to him.

Isa opened his eyes and saw a cluster of young girls, twelve or thirteen years old, chatting with each other about fifty feet from where he was hiding. He concluded that he and his colleagues were members of a pathetic race which had no place here.

Listening to these mellifluous English voices, he could not account for the fear and horror which the language had always inspired in him. At the same time his own inner voice whispered: It is foolish for Japanese to speak this language like foreigners. If they do, it makes them foreigners, too. And that is a real disgrace.

He pictured clearly to himself the outlandish gestures that Yamada affected when he spoke English. There was no dignity in talking just like a foreigner. But it was equally demeaning to speak a foreign tongue like a Japanese. This was the fate that awaited him today, he knew, if he were called upon to talk at the school. The few times that he had begun his class with a halting goodo-moaning-ebury-body he had afterward flushed crimson and felt himself at the bottom of some dark ravine. No! That was not for him. He would sooner make himself over into a whole new man.

Enrapt with the schoolgirls' merry fugue, Isa did not hear the jeep return. The soldier got out, whistling another tune. Some distance from where Isa remained hidden, he stood leaning over the fence and searched out his son. Having been on urgent business to the barracks that adjoined the school, only after it was finished did he remember Isa's feet. The boy, who looked to be of junior-high-school age, came running to his father, and a few moments later disappeared into the school.

Presently a beautiful tall lady of a type one often sees in American movies appeared before Isa's eyes. With the black boy in tow, she advanced swiftly and purposefully toward the fence. Isa stole off into the shade of a nearby grove, lest she find him crouching there and take him for a thief. He shut his eyes and mentally blocked his ears, to no avail; he could distinctly hear her footsteps and the sound of her voice calling out as she came closer and closer. Although he suspected that her call was meant for him, and had in any case resigned himself by now to being caught, he still did not respond. He kept his head down and his eyes closed until he felt a touch on his shoulders and heard the word ". . . shoes?" At this he stood up and bowed.

When he opened his eyes and saw the lady standing right beside him, he was all but blinded by the look of abundance on her face: features that spoke of an ample diet, material well-being, and pride of race. She was for all that only human, and a fellow schoolteacher as well. So he tried to tell himself, but he could not quite believe it. Next to her—she stood at least a head taller than he—Isa felt weak around the knees, and in reply to her questions he only nodded and bowed. In the end, like a timid servant with his mistress, he allowed himself to be led off toward the school.

Isa caught enough of the cascade of soothing words that poured from her lips like melting snow to realize that he had that meddlesome Negro to thank for his new predicament. "I only want to do something about those feet," the lady said. "I'm not going to poison you." He wanted to say thank you—that much he could manage. But once he had opened his mouth she would expect him to keep up a steady conversation. He had better just play dumb and follow her like a dog.

Isa sank back into despondency when he thought of the interrogation to which, as a solitary Japanese among a horde of foreigners, and an English teacher of sorts, he was sure to be subjected. He was too busy brooding to notice the gaggle of students that trailed behind him as he limped along, until a few sharp words from the lady sent them shouting and laughing back to the playground.

She kept smiling at him and making what sounded like friendly remarks, which required him to play deaf as well as dumb. But he had begun to receive contradictory signals from his conscience. To atone for the appearance of incivility he had given so far, he was tempted to fall down and kiss the lady's feet, or at least the ground beneath them. Caught between these conflicting impulses, Isa took it into his head to carry her books for her. He moved abruptly to her side and, without a word, tried to wrest the heavy books from her arms. He had the appropriate phrase on the tip of his tongue but was too embarrassed to say it. Perplexed by this dumbshow, the lady clutched the books to her breast. When he continued to tug at the books, bowing and grinning abjectly, she eventually guessed his intention and thanked him; but she would not surrender her burden.

It was enough for Isa that she had recognized his gesture. Hereafter, however incompetent he might appear at the school, he would not be considered a barbaric ingrate. As they approached the building, he felt something like the relief of a condemned criminal who had made one last plea for forgiveness from his fellow men.

Since the nurse was not to be found in the dispensary, the schoolmistress led Isa to her own office, where she shut the door firmly and turned the key. Once again Isa had a sinking feeling, such as the toy pistol had produced in him a while ago. "Sit down," said the lady, whose name, he gathered from the sign on the door, was Emily. "We lock the door so we can smoke," she explained. "Even the men do. It sets a bad example for the students, you see."

It took Isa some time to decipher this statement. From the moment he entered the room he kept his eyes glued to the floor and let his ears tune out her speech, which he dimly imagined to be a reproach for his earlier rudeness. In any case the words seemed to have nothing to do with his feet, and it was not until he raised his head, afraid of appearing very rude

indeed, that he saw the smoke and half grasped their meaning. Still standing in silence, he traced the upward spiral of smoke with his eyes, the
better to extricate himself from Miss Emily's gaze.

Out of the clear blue sky came the order: "Take off your shoes!" Or so
he interpreted her sharp utterance. But no sooner was he down to his army
socks than she burst out laughing and murmured something about coffee.
Then he thought he heard her say, though it made little sense to him, that
he should "help himself." When Isa, thoroughly confused, began to pull
up his socks, in a single violent motion Miss Emily lunged at him and
stripped them off. She gaped at his exposed feet, at first with simple curiosity, then with a look of distress on detecting the raw wound where the
skin had been scraped away. "Dear me," she exclaimed, putting out her
cigarette.

It was by no means easy for Isa to make such a spectacle of himself in
front of a foreign lady, here in this secret room. But so long as he was
not obliged to speak, he was resigned to suffering these minor indignities.
Nevertheless, he was desperately eager to return to the group, to become
again only one among many.

After drinking a cup of coffee by herself, Miss Emily went out into the
corridor, locking the door behind her. As she left, Isa understood her to
say that she was going to consult with the nurse, which was encouraging —
but why had she locked the door? Only then did he finish puzzling out
her remark upon entering the room, to the effect that they mustn't let the
students see them smoke. Yet that was only part of it, he knew. She was
also worried about his wandering around the school on the loose, or still
worse, escaping again, like a wounded animal that runs away when one is
only trying to help it. As soon as Isa reached this point in his train of
thought he felt an irresistible impulse to flee that very moment. He immediately opened the window, jumped out, and started to run.

After a few steps he felt the ground against his bare feet and remembered his shoes. He could not just leave them there, they did not belong
to him. As he was hoisting himself back up through the window, the door
opened across the room and he found himself face to face with Miss
Emily.

While Isa was still lurking behind the trim modern buildings of the
American school, Yamada wasted no time in approaching Michiko. In the
past he had seen her from a distance conversing with foreigners in a free
and easy manner. Since the beginning of today's excursion, when he
dragged her off to the Education Office, he had been scheming for a
chance to examine her English at first hand. It was not uncommon for
members of his profession to test each other's mettle on some trivial pretext, like samurai picking quarrels simply to show off their prowess.
Yamada was a past master at this sort of thing. And when he came up
against colleagues whose English was better than his own, especially if
they were women, he would try to defeat them on other grounds, to brow-
beat them if need be with the brute strength of his manly will. But in the
end he often lost anyway.

Yamada had bided his time while Isa was tagging along beside Michiko,
with what seemed to be warm encouragement on her part. Now that that

nuisance had been removed, he could proceed with his interrogation. He unleashed a barrage of questions in English that left her scarcely a moment to catch her breath. What schools had she gone to, where did she graduate, had she taken special lessons in conversation, how many American friends did she have????

At first, even Michiko, with her considerable abilities, could not bring herself to reply in kind to her countryman's tirade in a foreign language. She answered only haltingly, and half in Japanese. But when Yamada showed no sign of relenting, she saw what he was up to, and resented his contempt for her sex.

And what, if she might inquire, was the big attraction of English for him? Would he like to try a demonstration class with her sometime? Wasn't it curious that he pronounced certain words with a kind of Boston accent, others in a sort of Southern drawl, which was a little like mixing Kyushu speech with the slow country dialect of Aomori?[9]

Yamada was staggered by the woman's counterattack, delivered in rapid-fire, thoroughly natural English. It was not so much her fluency as the substance of her remarks that defeated him. She was more than a match for him, he conceded; he would have to find some other weakness. In his experience, when dealing with women, food and clothing were the best bet.

"That's a fine outfit you're wearing," he said, lapsing back into Japanese. "Did you get it before the War?"

"Yes," she answered softly. "That is, the material comes from a robe that belonged to my husband. He was killed in the War."

"I'm sorry to hear that. It must be hard for you." Yamada peered shrewdly into Michiko's face as he added: "If you need rice, I can get it fairly cheap."

"That's very kind of you," she said. "May I have your card?"

"And if you'd like a little piecework to do at home, perhaps I could find you something."

"I would certainly appreciate it. Men really are much better at arranging these things, aren't they!"

The procession had at last come to a halt in front of the gate to the school compound. As soon as Yamada noticed the guard looking over their credentials, he burst in with the information that one of their number had preceded them by jeep. Turning back to Michiko, he then announced in English: "I imagine that he is still barefoot, and has concealed himself somewhere behind the school."

"What makes you think that?" asked Michiko.

"Elementary," said Yamada. "The man does not know the language." Lowering his voice, but still speaking English, he suggested that the time had come for her to change her shoes.

Michiko did not need prompting; it had been on her mind all day long. Yet Yamada's sharpness surprised her. He must have been watching her closely since the march began. From now on, she in turn would have to

---

9. The northern-most prefecture on the main island of Japan, where speech patterns tend toward the terse; according to one theory, this is because of cold temperatures. Kyushu is a southern island where temperatures are warm and speech habits are more easy-going.

keep an eye on him. Maybe he had Isa pegged, too, she thought. But was it possible that the poor fellow was still slinking around behind some building? She searched the corners of the compound as their final destination came into full view.

At the center of a large tract of land traversed by neat rows of houses stood the long-awaited school, an almost solid wall of glass on the side facing south. The fields that once occupied the site had been leveled away without a trace. An American observer would not have found the compound remarkable, much less luxurious. But the solid houses planted sparsely over the landscape, the spacious bedrooms illuminated by lamps even in broad daylight, the young Japanese maids attending to the needs of American babies—all of this was clearly revealed at a glance, and impressed the weary visitors as a vignette of some heavenly dwelling place.

Michiko reflected that her command of a foreign language and her general level of education might set her far above most of the residents; nevertheless, it was she who had walked four miles for the privilege of visiting their school, she who had reveled secretly in the pathetic expectation of showing off her high-heeled shoes. Surrounded by this verdant park, she now saw herself as too small and destitute even to set foot in such a place.

"What's the point of our sitting in on their classes?" she overheard a colleague complain to Shibamoto. He was the one, she recalled, who had been so quick to urge Isa to go barefoot. "What can we hope to learn from classes held in a place like this? The only lesson we'll leave with is the one we've learned just getting here: we lost! These magnificent buildings that we're only allowed to peek at—they were built with our taxes. Doesn't it make you want to cry?"

Michiko turned away, ashamed that she had perhaps been noticed before with her hands pressed sorrowfully over her eyes. She felt equally awkward in her present pose, and so she moved a few steps apart from the group, bent over and, though it scarcely mattered anymore, put on her high heels. The first thing she saw as she raised her head again was Isa, shoes still dangling down from one hand, coming toward her across the playground—and standing motionless in the background, the beautiful figure of an American schoolmistress. Michiko wanted to change back into sneakers.

The long march on an empty stomach had reduced some of the group to sullen anger, others to a numb exhaustion. Their leader rose up to his full height, and with a few heaves of his broad shoulders began to harangue them. "You mustn't forget that you're here by special invitation. We in the administrative section worked hard to get it for you, and if anyone misbehaves we are the ones who'll be blamed—You there, what do you think you're doing?" As he spoke, Shibamoto's roving gaze was arrested by a man sitting on the ground with his back to the group. It was Isa. Shibamoto resumed in the same hectoring tone: "I must ask you not to sit down right in front of the school. You look like a beggar. When did you get back?"

"You see, sir, that's what I meant," Yamada interjected. "We have to put our best foot forward, bargain from strength. Otherwise we might as well not have come in the first place. Leave it to me."

Shibamoto cut him off with a vague "We'll see," and quickly moved on to the next item on the agenda. He took a sheaf of printed questionnaires from his briefcase and passed them out to the teachers. As they studied the form he explained that they were to use it to record in detail their impressions of the school; afterwards it would be collected and put on file for future reference.

"What can we possibly write down? What would it prove, anyway?" cried Michiko in a shrill voice. She was visibly overwrought.

"Never mind," Yamada interrupted again. "You can just put down what I have. I intend to comment very critically on the instructional objectives of this school, the aptitude of their teachers, and so forth. I'll show it around when I'm done, and everyone can use it as a model. You needn't worry about that. Instead you might give some thought to . . ."

"No, no, you've missed the point," said Michiko impatiently.

"Well, then, what is the problem?"

Michiko fell silent. There was no use trying to explain to the likes of Yamada. And Isa—what a timid little soul! But he did seem to have a way with women. She would have to get to the bottom of this business with the schoolmistress. For the moment Yamada and Isa were confused in her troubled thoughts.

Just then the iron gate in front of the school opened and a thirtyish, bespectacled man stood before them with a welcoming smile. He introduced himself to the group as Mr. Williams, the Principal. At his appearance the teachers ceased their idle chatter and prepared to begin their visit. Yamada barged through the gate ahead of the others, who hesitated and deferred to one another before following him in. Isa came last, dragging his feet, as the gate swung shut behind them.

Hardly any doubt remained in Isa's mind about Yamada's devious plan, which he had sniffed out from its inception, to face off with him in a demonstration class before the day was over. He was determined to silence Yamada on this subject and prevent the encounter at any cost. But so far no suitable defense had suggested itself, and he approached the potentially fateful classrooms with ever more halting steps.

The group advanced in double file so as not to interfere with the students passing to and fro. Yamada had already attached himself to Mr. Williams. After the Principal's every utterance he would raise his hand as if to call for attention, turn to the person behind him, and communicate his version of the remark. This would be relayed in some form or other from one teacher to the next until it reached the end of the line: a procedure arrived at spontaneously, whether as a throwback to the rigid military chain of command or by simple analogy with a bucket brigade. It took some time for the message to be transmitted to Michiko and Isa in the rear, and in the interval all but the most provocative implications were filtered out.

Mr. Williams's opening remarks, that is, Yamada's rendering of them, went as follows: "Since the school was to be built with Japanese funds, we had little choice but to go along with the specifications given to us by some Japanese architects. The results, as you can see for yourselves, were less than satisfactory. To begin with, the budget was barely twenty percent of what would be considered normal back in the States. In our country we place great emphasis on bright and cheerful surroundings, and this school certainly does not meet those standards. We have twenty students in a class here, which is three too many. The ideal is seven-*teen*. Now I understand that in your country there are seven-*ty* in a class. Imagine! Classes that size are really out of the question. They necessitate regimentation, and this inevitably leads to militarism."

Here Yamada's voice trailed off into silence as Mr. Williams's expression took on a sudden severity, accompanied by a pudgy finger pointed at Yamada's forehead. When Yamada resumed interpreting, he spoke at first in tremulous tones.

The subject had changed to salaries, which, Mr. Williams assured them, were paid by the American government. The lowest salary level at the school, the one for beginning instructresses, was still about ten times the average wage of Japanese teachers, according to the figures he had heard. This was, it was true, a bit more than they would receive in comparable jobs at home; but things were a good deal more expensive in such a remote country; and if the discrepancy seemed excessive, it should be borne in mind that the standard of living which American teachers had to maintain was, after all, extremely high, so it was only natural that the basic salary be of a different order.

The only part of this speech to reach Isa's ear was the startling information, passed down the line with a collective sigh, that the teachers at this school got ten times as much money as they did. This so amazed Michiko that as she repeated it to Isa she had to lean on him to keep her balance. "We should have listened to our colleague there," she commented. "We should have just turned around and gone home."

"Right. That's so," said Isa.

"Did that woman do something about your feet?"

"Right. She did."

"What did you talk about?"

"Nothing."

"Look at those two over there—how disgusting!" Michiko muttered censoriously.

Isa looked in the direction she had indicated and focused on two students who stood holding hands in a corner of the corridor, their eyes closed in mutual infatuation. Miss Emily came up behind the couple and tapped them both gently on the back, not so much to chastise them, it appeared, as to alert them to the presence of visitors. Afterward she turned toward Michiko and smiled.

"It looks like paradise from the outside," said Michiko, "but there's no telling what goes on between these walls."

"Right. That's so."

Michiko did not know what to make of Isa's laconic responses. She looked at his frightened, rabbitlike eyes and recalled what Yamada had said about him. Then he broke his silence.

"Why must I go through this humiliating ordeal?"

"What ordeal? You mean having to go barefoot before?"

"No. I mean having to look at all this beauty."

"Beauty? From a certain point of view, I suppose."

"I'll tell you why. Simply because I'm a so-called English teacher."

"Oh? You don't like speaking English?"

"I d-d-detest it!"

Michiko was not surprised. There were a lot of men like that, the opposite type from Yamada, and Isa must be one of them.

Although the teachers had been told that they should each choose a class to visit and go their separate ways, they preferred to stick together. In the end Shibamoto divided them arbitrarily into three subgroups and dispatched them to different classrooms, with the veiled threat of force that was always present in his judo master's bearing. These smaller units soon congealed so that each proceeded as one, like flocks of peasants being herded around the capital.

Michiko hovered next to Isa. She could hardly forget the small favor she had yet to beg of him, after dwelling on it the length of that asphalt road. Moreover, it was reassuring to have him by her side—here, where almost anything might happen, and now, while she felt so despicably drab in the shadow of the foreign lady. Isa seemed to her the perfect companion for the occasion.

Meanwhile, Isa stayed as close as possible to Yamada, watching his every move, and fervently wishing that he might fall down some stairs and break his neck. He was even prepared, should the opportunity arise, to give him a little nudge. Failing that, in his present position he could at least intervene without delay if Yamada broached the subject of a demonstration class. And as one of his entourage, Isa was spared the necessity of pronouncing a single word of English, for Yamada had appropriated the role of spokesman for their party.

Isa and Michiko followed hard on Yamada's heels as together they entered the designated room, where they found a drawing class in session. Yamada soon retired to the supply closet to note down his observations. When he had finished he faced Michiko and whispered slyly: "Take a good look. With all their money and their fancy buildings, the children can't draw worth a damn."

There was a meek chorus of agreement from several colleagues who stood nearby, hanging on Yamada's every word. Michiko herself shared his opinion of the drawings, but she did not wish to be associated in any way with these people. They were the mean and cunning sort of Japanese; she and Isa were different, Michiko told herself, looking to Isa for confirmation. She caught him stooping over his shoes again: a new pair of sneakers which, she quickly deduced, must have come from that schoolmistress. They were much too big for him and he was trying to compensate by lacing them up tight. The moment Isa's eyes met hers, he blushed and turned the other way.

Michiko proposed that they have a closer look at the work now in progress. As they moved into the classroom and studied the drawings, they found themselves submerged in a waterless sea teeming with fish of various colors, shapes, and sizes. They were all unique, each one the product of a collaborative effort by a small group. Over by the window a few junior-high-school students of both sexes were sketching the thatched-roof cottages which appeared in the distance, beyond the confines of the American compound. They began to steal glances at the visitors over their shoulders, then one of the boys pointed at Shibamoto with his right hand while with his left he indicated a drawing of a seadevil. On closer inspection of other drawings, it was discovered that Yamada had been turned into a shark, Isa into a flying fish, suggested, perhaps, by his emaciated figure, and Michiko a goldfish. In the same fashion the whole party emerged within the next few moments as a school of highly distinctive fish.

As soon as they were back in the corridor, Yamada said to Shibamoto: "What kind of school are they running here, allowing such insulting behavior—and even toward a lady! I think we should submit a written protest. How about the rest of you? And you, Mrs. . . . . ?"

"I didn't really mind it so much," said Michiko. "In fact, we sort of asked for it, with our down-and-out attitude."

"Down-and-out? I'm talking about a serious failing in their instructional objectives, a complete lack of discipline. That art teacher ought to be severely reprimanded. But why should I waste my breath! If you don't mind being turned into a goldfish, that's your business."

Not a glint of amusement alleviated Yamada's peevish expression as he finished berating Michiko and began to make further notations in his little book. "What did they do with you?" he asked Isa, looking up from his book. "Oh yes. It was a flying fish, and quite a masterpiece, too. They must have got the idea from the way you were flitting around in your bare feet."

Isa was at the moment too intent on his malevolent wishes to hear.

Isa stood at the door of the classroom in his borrowed sneakers and listened to the lady whose initials they bore teach English. Michiko had gone inside with the others, this time without trying to coax him into coming along. After a while the group filed back into the corridor one by one and clustered together to exchange comments in a half-whisper.

"You might almost say that our English is better than theirs," Yamada observed to Michiko in Japanese. "Weren't you amazed at all the mistakes in their grammar?"

"But the teacher is pretty, isn't she?"

"Hmm. It's like hiring a movie star to teach at a ridiculous salary."

"You were right about *him*—he really does hate English," said Michiko, switching languages as she again changed the subject.

"I know all that. I am also aware that he harbors some marice toward me."

Michiko acknowledged to herself that in referring to Isa as "him" and making her remark in English she had stilled the pangs of guilt which she would normally have felt in this betrayal of trust. And that, she reflected, was no doubt one reason for Isa's hatred of the foreign language: when you spoke it you stopped being yourself. It was too easy to be carried away by the titillation of the words, words not exactly your own. She knew she ought to get away from Yamada, the sooner the better.

When Michiko was back at Isa's side again she startled herself by blurting out, "If you hate speaking English so much, you must hate me too."

"It's different with women," said Isa.

"Women make good mimics. Is that what you mean?"

Maybe that *was* what he had meant, Isa could not be sure.

Without warning Michiko leaned over and whispered something in his ear. She had reverted to Japanese, to Isa's relief, but he could still make out only the general drift.

"You mean even you . . . ?" Isa blushed a deeper hue than Michiko, though she had brought the matter up.

"Have I embarrassed you again?" she asked.

It was perhaps in part the extraordinary scene now unfolding before their eyes that had driven her to divulge such a delicate matter, and so impetuously. They were now in the gymnasium, where, in preparation for tomorrow's basketball game with a neighboring school, a rally was being conducted by a spirited cheering section. A trio of girls in uniform, sixteen or seventeen years old, stood in front of the others calling out the names of the players with mounting fervor. When the shouting had risen to a high pitch of frenzied excitement, like a line of chorus girls they all began to lift up their skirts while the cheerleaders launched into cartwheels and somersaults.

"It's all set for the demonstration class this afternoon—you and me," said Yamada, who had appeared out of nowhere and taken Isa by surprise.

"I-I-I don't know what you're talking about. I have nothing to do with it."

"Well, you know now. Shibamoto decided on the two of us. I'll meet you after lunch, as soon as the hour for visiting classes is over. And don't try to run away. Shibamoto would not be pleased." Thrusting his jaw out toward Michiko, he added in an insinuating tone: "I'm sure you can get some coaching from her."

Yamada had in fact not the slightest desire to stand in front of a class next to Isa. The man was sure to bring disgrace on the whole profession. But in the middle of the rally he had caught sight of Michiko whispering in Isa's ear, then watched as Isa blushed and nodded in agreement. At that moment he had declared war.

Yamada went directly to the Principal and made his proposal with the same lunatic zeal he had shown to Shibamoto. Shibamoto stood by, wondering anxiously how the Principal would react to this bizarre request, which sounded less like a bid for a classroom demonstration than a demand for satisfaction by a man whose honor had been challenged. Yet, whether because like Shibamoto he saw no way out, or because he was soon to return to America and hoped it might yield a piece of Japanese bravado to regale his friends with, the Principal had accepted the proposal on the spot.

Yamada took leave of Isa and Michiko with a few curt instructions as to where they were to eat their lunch: on some benches in the schoolyard, about three hundred feet outside the gate—and nowhere else.

With quivering lips Isa stared vacantly after Yamada as he retreated across the gymnasium.

"Isa-san.[1] I'll take your place this afternoon," said Michiko.

"It's too late for that," Isa replied. "Either I knock him out, or I quit my job . . . or else I go ahead with the class and just stand there without saying a word."

Isa made as if to run after Yamada, but the sores on his feet seemed to be acting up again, and he had barely managed to limp forward a few steps when Michiko seized him by the hand and held him back.

"Wait a minute," she said. "Please don't forget the little favor I asked you a moment ago. If you'll let me have them now, I'll wash them right away."

Isa's immediate response was a blank look and an incessant blinking of his rabbit-eyes.

"You know, what we talked about before," Michiko prompted.

Isa finally understood what she wanted. All right, she could have them. But only after he had finished with them. Even at this juncture, on the brink of coming to blows with Yamada, he could not ignore his other concern, one from which he was never altogether free.

With sudden resolution Isa removed from his satchel a small bundle wrapped in newspaper and thrust it toward Michiko, all the while keeping his eyes on Yamada's vanishing figure. Michiko reached out in some confusion to take the coveted article from him—hardly ten seconds had passed since he had at last seemed to grasp her wish. But like an overeager relay runner, Isa had moved too soon, and he was off before the bundle was safely in her hands. Uneasy about the transaction to begin with, Michiko now blushed furiously, fumbled, and in the end lost her balance. Her high heels slid out from under her, and with a piercing shriek that filled the corridor she toppled over onto the floor. The bundle lay open where she had hurled it aside in her fall, revealing a pair of black chopsticks.

It remained a secret shared by Isa and Michiko alone that she had fallen while clutching at this homely artifact of their native land. As soon as Mr. Williams arrived on the scene, he loudly ordered the Japanese who had gathered around to disperse, whereupon up and down the corridor foreigners came rushing out of every other door. The Principal drove off this new crowd, leaving only a few women to help Michiko to the dispensary.[2]

Afterward, as he questioned Shibamoto about the accident, Mr. Williams kept adjusting his glasses in an irritable gesture that suggested he found it all very regrettable. What had Michiko and Isa been up to? he wanted to know. Yamada, having rejoined them, interpreted stiffly for Shibamoto to the effect that the man with the limp had been struggling to catch up with yours truly to request that he be allowed to substitute for his colleague in today's demonstration class; meanwhile, the lady, who cherished similar aspirations, had been strenuously attempting to dissuade

---

1. *San* is a title attached to names, corresponding to our Mr., Miss, Mrs., etc.   2. An office in a school, hospital, or other institution where medicines and medical aid are dispensed.

her colleague from his determined course when she slipped and fell. "It all proceeded from their pedagogical dedication," Yamada concluded on Shibamoto's behalf, "and their devotion to the English language."

"Ah yes. The old kamikaze spirit," said the Principal.

The heavy irony was lost on Yamada, who took the remark as a compliment, and presented it as such to his superior. Shibamoto fluttered his eyelashes in silent modesty.

Seeing that his sally had been deflected by misinterpretation, Mr. Williams pushed back his glasses again and turned on them with his sternest expression. "From now on, there are two things which I must strictly forbid," he announced. "The first is for any Japanese instructor to conduct a class here, to engage in any attempts to do so, or in any way to involve himself in the educational process at this school. Secondly, in the future high heels will not be permitted on these premises. If there are any violations, we will have to terminate all further visits."

After spitting out these injunctions with an air of finality, the Principal strode rapidly down the corridor to the door of the dispensary. He showed no inclination to enter, merely surveying the situation from outside.

A long pause ensued during which Yamada neglected to translate Mr. Williams's last pronouncement. When he was summoned back to reality by a poke in the ribs from Shibamoto, he spun around and fled toward the exit, without so much as a word of explanation. Then, with Shibamoto in the lead, the rest of the group hurried after, as though suddenly reminded of some vital errand. Only Isa was left behind, alone once again.

ALEXANDER SOLZHENITSYN
born 1918

The reputation of Russian novelist Alexander Solzhenitsyn is divided almost equally between two complementary aspects: he continues the tradition of the realistic nineteenth-century novel (following the example of his compatriots Tolstoy and Dostoevsky), and he has assumed the role of moral conscience in a modern society where both East and West are fatally flawed. Expelled from the Soviet Union in 1974 and stripped of his citizenship until a new regime restored it in 1990, Solzhenitsyn proclaims the virtues of an older, religious way of life as the only salvation for a civilization that has been dehumanized by political oppression and materialist greed. Art and literature, he feels, are "endowed with the miraculous power to communicate" and thus make it possible for people to experience situations that they have not lived. This basis of common communication erases divisions and allows us to have "a single system of evaluation for evil deeds and for good ones." Solzhenitsyn tries to encompass both the historian's and the moralist's aims when he writes about the history of his own country in the twentieth century and paints a picture of human suffering and moral endurance under oppression. Like Thomas Mann, he includes a range of characters and diverse social types in novels that allude to larger social issues; unlike Mann, his tone is overtly moral and even didactic, especially in his later works. Solzhenitsyn is impelled to testify for all those who cannot speak: for the woman in *Cancer Ward* (1968), for example, who says "Where can I read about us? Will that be only in a hundred years?" His testimony ranges from the more personal account of a day in concentration camp (*One Day in the Life of Ivan Denisovich*, 1963) to broad historical panoramas such as *August 1914* (1971), which focuses on the defeat of the Russian Second Army in East Prussia during World War I, and *Gulag Archipelago* (1973–75), a description of the Soviet concentration camp system. Clearly he finds the form of the realistic novel—expanded, in *August 1914*, with documents and imitation film scripts—the most appropriate method for representing the truth of history. Solzhenitsyn has little patience with avant-garde literature, which, he says, "has been thought up by empty-headed people." Instead, he tries to render the essence of history by blending documented fact and narrative fiction in his creative works and, in recent years, by editing and publishing (in Russian) historical documents from pre-Revolutionary Russia.

He was born Alexander Isayevich Solzhenitsyn on December 11, 1918, in Kislovodsk, in the northern Caucasus. His father had died six months earlier, and his mother supported them in Rostov-on-Don by working as a typist. The family was extremely poor, and—although Solzhenitsyn would have preferred studying literature in Moscow—he was obliged upon graduation from high school to enroll in the local Department of Mathematics at Rostov University. The choice, he says, was a lucky one, for his double degree in mathematics and physics allowed him to spend four years of his prison camp sentence in a relatively privileged *sharashka*, or research institute, instead of at hard manual labor. During 1939–41 he also took correspondence courses from the Institute of History, Philosophy, and Literature in Moscow. When Solzhenitsyn graduated in 1941, in the middle of World War II, he was immediately inducted into the army, where he drove horse-drawn transport vehicles until he was sent to artillery school in 1942. That November, he was put in charge of an artillery reconnaissance battery at the front, a position he held until his sudden arrest in February 1945.

The military censor had found passages in his letters to a friend that were—even under a pseudonym—visibly disrespectful of Stalin, and Solzhenitsyn was sentenced in July to eight years in the prison camps. From 1946 to 1950 he worked as a mathematician in research institutes staffed by prisoners (such as that described in *The First Circle*) but in 1950 was taken to a new kind of camp for political prisoners only, where he worked as a manual laborer. After his sentence was ostensibly over, an administrative order sent him into perpetual exile in southern Kazakhstan. Solzhenitsyn spent the years of exile teaching physics and mathematics in a rural school and wrote prose in secret. The tumor that had developed in his first labor camp grew worse, and in 1954 the author received treatment in a clinic in Tashkent (recalled in the novel *Cancer Ward*). He returned to exile in 1955 (the year he wrote *The First Circle*) and was not released until June 1956. Official rehabilitation came in 1957, and the author moved to Ryazan in European Soviet Union where he continued to teach physics and mathematics, while secretly writing fiction, until 1962. *Matryona's Home* and *One Day in the Life of Ivan Denisovich* were written during this period.

At the age of forty-two, Solzhenitsyn had written a great deal but published nothing. In 1961, however, it looked as though the climate of political censorship might change. Nikita Khrushchev had just publicly attacked the "cult of personality" and hero worship that had surrounded Stalin, and the poet and editor Alexander Tvardovsky called on writers to portray "truth," not the artificial picture of perfect Soviet society that Stalin preferred. Solzhenitsyn was encouraged to submit *One Day in the Life of Ivan Denisovich*, which appeared (with Khrushchev's approval) in the November 1962 issue of Tvardovsky's journal *Novy Mir*. In January 1963 Tvardovsky published the stories *Matryona's Home* and *Incident at Krechetovka Station* but—with the exception of two short stories and an article on style—Solzhenitsyn would not be allowed to publish anything more in his native land. Even the highly praised *One Day in the Life of Ivan Denisovich* was removed from candidacy for the Lenin Prize in 1963. Khrushchev himself was forced into retirement in October 1964, and the temporary loosening of censorship came to an end. The novel *The First Circle* (already accepted by *Novy Mir*) and two plays (*The Lovegirl and the Innocent*, written 1954; *Candle in the Wind*, written 1960) were prohibited during 1964–65, and *Cancer Ward*, after the type was already partially set, was refused publication permission by the Writers' Union in 1966. Solzhenitsyn protested both the censorship and the fact that the Writers' Union did not defend its members before official attacks, but instead he himself was expelled from the Writers' Union in 1969, after *The First Circle* and *Cancer Ward* had appeared in the West. The only means of publishing officially unacceptable works was to convey them abroad to a Western publishing house or to circulate them in *samizdat* ("self-publishing") form by circulating copies of typewritten manuscripts. Solzhenitsyn made arrangements to have his works published in the West, and continued work on the larger historical novels: *The Gulag Archipelago*, which he had begun earlier, and *August 1914*, which he wrote in 1969–70. In 1970 he was awarded the Nobel Prize for literature, which he accepted in absentia because he was afraid that he would not be permitted to re-enter the Soviet Union once he left. After the publication abroad of the first volume of *The Gulag Archipelago*, however, he was arrested in February 1974 and expelled from the country. From 1974 to 1976 Solzhenitsyn lived in Zurich, and in 1976 he moved to the United States, where he lived in seclusion on a farm in Vermont. The expulsion remained in effect until the new president of the Soviet Union, Mikhail S. Gorbachev, offered in 1990 to restore Solzhenitsyn's citizenship as part of an attempt to rehabilitate artists and writers disgraced during previous regimes. Solzhenitsyn did not accept the offer, and later in the year he refused a prize awarded him by the Russian Republic for *The Gulag Archipelago*, noting that the book was not widely available in the Soviet Union and that the "phenomenon of the Gulag" had not been overcome. In September 1991, however, the old charge of treason was officially dropped, and the writer return to Russia in May 1994.

Solzhenitsyn's first three novels have in common the themes of imprisonment, of personal suffering, and of the moral purity to be gained by those who endure and learn from their suffering. *One Day in the Life of Ivan Denisovich* is the story, told at a very basic level of hunger, cold, and brutally demanding work, of one fairly good day in the life of a prison camp inmate, the peasant Ivan Denisovich Shukhov. When the book appeared, it was the first public recognition of Stalin's prison camp system, and Solzhenitsyn's matter-of-fact narration of the prisoners' day-to-day struggle to survive and retain their humanity shocked readers in Russia and in the West. Shukhov is not a heroic figure, or even portrayed as particularly intelligent, but in his deprivation he has found a core of inner spiritual strength that might well be envied, Solzhenitsyn suggests, by those outside prison who compromise their principles, and accede to injustices, for fear of losing what they have.

The worlds of *Cancer Ward* and *The First Circle* are more privileged than that of *One Day in the Life of Ivan Denisovich*, but each retains the atmosphere of imprisonment and imminent death, and each composes a picture of society by juxtaposing characters with different backgrounds and different points of view. Solzhenitsyn calls this technique of juxtaposition "polyphonic" or many-voiced: he writes a "polyphonic novel with concrete details specifying the time and place of action. A novel without a central hero. ... Each character becomes central when the action reverts to him." In *Cancer Ward*, thirteen patients representing different social and political classes are brought together in a ward at the cancer clinic in Tashkent; this microcosm of Soviet society is faced with sickness, suffering, and death, and with an authoritarian medical system that administers treatment without explaining it (or its side effects) to the patient. The ward becomes a metaphor for Soviet society, a metaphor given further dimensions when the inmates articulate their different values in response to a story by Tolstoy: "What Men Live By." The ultimate question is not collective but individual, says Kostoglotov: a man may be a member of a collective, "but only while he's alive . . . he has to die alone."

The same emphasis on the testing of individual values occurs in *The First Circle*, a novel whose title refers to the least painful circle of Hell in Dante's *Inferno*, and indicates here the *sharashka* or prisoner-staffed reasearch section of the Mavrino Institute. The prisoners working in the *sharashka* are under pressure from their superiors (who are under pressure from Stalin) to produce spying devices, including a method for identifying voices on taped telephone calls, and an impregnable telephone coding system for Stalin. If they do not produce satisfactory work, they are sent back to almost-certain death in the labor camps (the lower circles of this Hell); if they do, they become part of the police state. No one is free, not even the dictator who is imprisoned by his own suspicions. The whole society of *The First Circle* is an Inferno, and only by sacrificing everything can one hope to retain spiritual freedom.

Solzhenitsyn turned next to a larger panoramic scope, where the authorial voice would dominate and interpret a mass of historical information. *August 1914* is the first volume of a planned trilogy inquiring into the course of modern Russian history: later volumes (of which a few chapters have appeared in journals and in the fictional portrait, *Lenin in Zurich*) are titled after revolutionary dates, *October 1916* and *March 1917*. *August 1914* describes the defeat of the Second Russian Army in East Prussia during World War I, and—in a consciously fragmented style that moves from scene to scene, includes extracts of documents, newspapers, proverbs, and songs, and provides sections marked "Screen" that imitate film scripts— attempts to depict a broad social panorama with characters from all classes, thus recording a moment in history from an epic point of view.

The second broad panorama is *The Gulag Archipelago*, a three-volume, seven-section account of Stalin's widespread prison camp system. (*Gulag* stands for "Chief Administration of Corrective Labor Camps," camps that were scattered across the Soviet Union like islands in a sea [the archipelago].) Solzhenitsyn describes the horror of these camps in quasi-anecdotal form, using personal experience, oral testimony, excerpts of documents, written eyewitness reports, and altogether a massive collection of evidence accumulated inside "An Attempt at Artistic Investigation" (the subtitle). In this book, perhaps even more than in *August 1914*, there is a tension between the bare facts that Solzhenitsyn transmits and the spiritual interpretation of history into which they fit. The author is overtly present, commenting, guessing intuititively from context when particular facts are missing, and stressing in his own voice the theme that has pervaded all his work: the purification of the soul through suffering. The title of the fourth section, "The Soul and Barbed Wire," symbolizes the recurrent opposition of soul and imprisoning society that has become familiar to his readers.

Since Solzhenitsyn is such a dedicated anti-Communist and anti-Marxist, many Westerners have jumped to the conclusion that he is in favor of the Western democratic system. Such is not the case. He looks back to an earlier, more nationalist and spiritual authoritarianism represented for him by the image of Holy Russia: "For a thousand years Russia lived with an authoritarian order . . . that authoritarian order possessed a strong moral foundation . . . Christian Orthodoxy." In a speech given at Harvard in 1978, "A World Split Apart," he criticized Western democracy's "herd instinct" and "need to accommodate mass standards," its emphasis on "well-being" and "constant desire to have still more things," its "spiritual exhaustion" in which "mediocrity triumphs under the guise of democratic restraints." Once again, he returns to the theme of purification by suffering that permeates his fiction: "We have been through a spiritual training far in advance of Western experience. The complex and deadly crush of life has produced stronger, deeper, and more interesting personalities than those generated by standardized Western well-being."

One of those strong and deep personalities is surely Matryona in *Matryona's Home*. Solzhenitsyn's story, which is probably modeled on the old Russian literary form of the saint's life, is a testimony to Matryona's absolute simplicity, her refusal to possess anything more than the basic necessities (she will not raise a pig to kill for food), her willingness to help others without promise of reward, and finally to let her greedy in-laws tear down part of her own home and cart it off. The narrator of the story, like Solzhenitsyn an ex-convict and mathematics teacher, has buried himself deep in the country to avoid signs of modern Soviet society and to find— if it still exists—an image of the Old Russia. The town of Talnovo itself is tainted, not just by the *kolkhoz* (collective farm) system, which ceases to consider Matryona part of the collective as soon as she becomes ill, but also by the laziness, selfishness, and predatory greed of its inhabitants. Yet there remains Matryona. Her life has been filled with disappointment and deprivation, and she remains an outsider in a materialist society that despises her lack of acquisitive instinct, but she seems to live in a dimension of spiritual contentment and love that is unknown to those around her. Only the narrator, who has learned to value essential qualities from his own experience in the concentration camps, is able finally to recognize her as "the righteous one," one of those whose spiritual merit seems alien to modern society, yet is needed to save society from divine retribution (Genesis 18:23–33).

Andrej Kodjak, *Alexander Solzhenitsyn* (1978), provides a biographical and critical introduction to Solzhenitsyn up to his deportation from the Soviet Union in 1974; it includes a discussion of Russian terms. Kathryn B. Feuer, ed., *Solzhenitsyn: A Collection of Critical Essays* (1976), contains a range of essays on aspects and particular works, including *Matryona's Home*. John B. Dunlop, Richard S. Haugh, and Michael Nicholson, eds., *Solzhenitsyn in Exile: Critical Essays and Documentary Material* (1985), offer critical essays and discussions of Solzhenitsyn's reception in different countries. John Dunlop, Richard Haugh, Alexis Klimoff, eds., *Aleksandr Solzhenitsyn: Critical Essays and Documentary Materials* (1973), is a useful collection with a wide range of essays and reprinted texts, including a short autobiography by Solzhenitsyn and his Nobel Prize lecture. Also of interest is James F. Pontuso, *Solzhenitsyn's Political Thought* (1990).

PRONOUNCING GLOSSARY

The following list uses common English syllables and stress accents to provide rough equivalents of selected words whose pronunciation may be unfamiliar to the general reader.

Matryona Vasilyevna: *mah-treeoh'-na vah-seel'-yev-na*

Vysokoye Polye: *vai-so'-koy pol'-ye*

Matryona's Home[1]

1

A hundred and fifteen miles from Moscow trains were still slowing down to a crawl a good six months after it happened. Passengers stood glued to the windows or went out to stand by the doors. Was the line under repair, or what? Would the train be late?

It was all right. Past the crossing the train picked up speed again and the passengers went back to their seats.

Only the engine drivers knew what it was all about.

The engine drivers and I.

In the summer of 1953 I was coming back from the hot and dusty desert, just following my nose—so long as it led me back to European Russia. Nobody waited or wanted me at my particular place, because I was a little matter of ten years overdue. I just wanted to get to the central belt, away from the great heats, close to the leafy muttering of forests. I wanted to efface myself, to lose myself in deepest Russia . . . if it was still anywhere to be found.

A year earlier I should have been lucky to get a job carrying a hod this side of the Urals.[2] They wouldn't have taken me as an electrician on a decent construction job. And I had an itch to teach. Those who knew told me that it was a waste of money buying a ticket, that I should have a journey for nothing.

But things were beginning to move. When I went up the stairs of the N—— Regional Education Department and asked for the Personnel Section, I was surprised to find Personnel sitting behind a glass partition, like in a chemist's shop, instead of the usual black leather-padded door. I went timidly up to the window, bowed, and asked, "Please, do you need any mathematicians somewhere where the trains don't run? I should like to settle there for good."

They passed every dot and comma in my documents through a fine comb, went from one room to another, made telephone calls. It was something out of the ordinary for them too—people always wanted the towns, the bigger the better. And lo and behold, they found just the place for me—Vysokoe Polye. The very sound of it gladdened my heart.

Vysokoe Polye[3] did not belie its name. It stood on rising ground, with gentle hollows and other little hills around it. It was enclosed by an unbroken ring of forest. There was a pool behind a weir. Just the place where I wouldn't mind living and dying. I spent a long time sitting on a stump in a coppice and wishing with all my heart that I didn't need breakfast and dinner every day but could just stay here and listen to the branches brushing against the roof in the night, with not a wireless anywhere to be heard and the whole world silent.

---

1. Translated by H. T. Willetts.   2. Mountain chain separating European Russia from (Asiatic) Siberia.
3. High Meadow.

Alas, nobody baked bread in Vysokoe Polye. There was nothing edible on sale. The whole village lugged its victuals in sacks from the big town.

I went back to the Personnel Section and raised my voice in prayer at the little window. At first they wouldn't even talk to me. But then they started going from one room to another, made a telephone call, scratched with their pens, and stamped on my orders the word "Torfoprodukt."

Torfoprodukt? Turgenev[4] never knew that you can put words like that together in Russian.

On the station building at Torfoprodukt, an antiquated temporary hut of gray wood, hung a stern notice, BOARD TRAINS ONLY FROM THE PASSENGERS' HALL. A further message had been scratched on the boards with a nail, *And Without Tickets*. And by the booking office, with the same melancholy wit, somebody had carved for all time the words, *No Tickets*. It was only later that I fully appreciated the meaning of these addenda. Getting to Torfoprodukt was easy. But not getting away.

Here too, deep and trackless forests had once stood and were still standing after the Revolution. Then they were chopped down by the peat cutters and the neighboring kolkhoz.[5] Its chairman, Shashkov, had razed quite a few hectares of timber and sold it at a good profit down in the Odessa region.

The workers' settlement sprawled untidily among the peat bogs— monotonous shacks from the thirties, and little houses with carved façades and glass verandas, put up in the fifties. But inside these houses I could see no partitions reaching up to the ceilings, so there was no hope of renting a room with four real walls.

Over the settlement hung smoke from the factory chimney. Little locomotives ran this way and that along narrow-gauge railway lines, giving out more thick smoke and piercing whistles, pulling loads of dirty brown peat in slabs and briquettes. I could safely assume that in the evening a loudspeaker would be crying its heart out over the door of the club and there would be drunks roaming the streets and, sooner or later, sticking knives in each other.

This was what my dream about a quiet corner of Russia had brought me to—when I could have stayed where I was and lived in an adobe hut looking out on the desert, with a fresh breeze at night and only the starry dome of the sky overhead.

I couldn't sleep on the station bench, and as soon as it started getting light I went for another stroll round the settlement. This time I saw a tiny marketplace. Only one woman stood there at that early hour, selling milk, and I took a bottle and started drinking it on the spot.

I was struck by the way she talked. Instead of a normal speaking voice, she used an ingratiating singsong, and her words were the ones I was longing to hear when I left Asia for this place.

"Drink, and God bless you. You must be a stranger round here?"

---

4. A master of Russian prose style (1818–1883), best known for the novel *Fathers and Sons* (1861) and for a series of sympathetic sketches of peasant life published as *A Sportsman's Sketches* (1882). *Torfoprodukt*: peat product; a new word made by combining two words of Germanic origin: *torf* ("peat") and *produckt*.
5. Collective farm.

"And where are you from?" I asked, feeling more cheerful.

I learnt that the peat workings weren't the only thing, that over the railway lines there was a hill, and over the hill a village, that this village was Talnovo, and it had been there ages ago, when the "gipsy woman" lived in the big house and the wild woods stood all round. And farther on there was a whole countryside full of villages—Chaslitsy, Ovintsy, Spudni, Shevertni, Shestimirovo, deeper and deeper into the woods, farther and farther from the railway, up towards the lakes.

The names were like a soothing breeze to me. They held a promise of backwoods Russia. I asked my new acquaintance to take me to Talnovo after the market was over and find a house for me to lodge in.

It appeared that I was a lodger worth having: in addition to my rent, the school offered a truckload of peat for the winter to whoever took me. The woman's ingratiating smile gave way to a thoughtful frown. She had no room herself, because she and her husband were "keeping" her aged mother, so she took me first to one lot of relatives then to another. But there wasn't a separate room to be had and both places were crowded and noisy.

We had come to a dammed-up stream that was short of water and had a little bridge over it. No other place in all the village took my fancy as this did: there were two or three willows, a lopsided house, ducks swimming on the pond, geese shaking themselves as they stepped out of the water.

"Well, perhaps we might just call on Matryona," said my guide, who was getting tired of me by now. "Only it isn't so neat and cozy-like in her house, neglects things she does. She's unwell."

Matryona's house stood quite near by. Its row of four windows looked out on the cold backs, the two slopes of the roof were covered with shingles, and a little attic window was decorated in the old Russian style. But the shingles were rotting, the beam ends of the house and the once mighty gates had turned gray with age, and there were gaps in the little shelter over the gate.

The small gate was fastened, but instead of knocking my companion just put her hand under and turned the catch, a simple device to prevent animals from straying. The yard was not covered, but there was a lot under the roof of the house. As you went through the outer door a short flight of steps rose to a roomy landing, which was open, to the roof high overhead. To the left, other steps led up to the top room, which was a separate structure with no stove, and yet another flight led down to the basement. To the right lay the house proper, with its attic and its cellar.

It had been built a long time ago, built sturdily, to house a big family, and now one lonely woman of nearly sixty lived in it.

When I went into the cottage she was lying on the Russian stove[6] under a heap of those indeterminate dingy rags which are so precious to a working man or woman.

The spacious room, and especially the big part near the windows, was full of rubber plants in pots and tubs standing on stools and benches. They

---

6. A large stove built of masonry, used both for heating and for cooking.

peopled the householder's loneliness like a speechless but living crowd. They had been allowed to run wild, and they took up all the scanty light on the north side. In what was left of the light, and half-hidden by the stovepipe, the mistress of the house looked yellow and weak. You could see from her clouded eyes that illness had drained all the strength out of her.

While we talked she lay on the stove face downward, without a pillow, her head toward the door, and I stood looking up at her. She showed no pleasure at getting a lodger, just complained about the wicked disease she had. She was just getting over an attack; it didn't come upon her every month, but when it did, "It hangs on two or three days so as I shan't manage to get up and wait on you. I've room and to spare, you can live here if you like."

Then she went over the list of other housewives with whom I should be quieter and cozier and wanted me to make the round of them. But I had already seen that I was destined to settle in this dimly lit house with the tarnished mirror, in which you couldn't see yourself, and the two garish posters (one advertising books, the other about the harvest), bought for a ruble each to brighten up the walls.

Matryona Vasilyevna made me go off round the village again, and when I called on her the second time she kept trying to put me off, "We're not clever, we can't cook, I don't know how we shall suit. . . ." But this time she was on her feet when I got there, and I thought I saw a glimmer of pleasure in her eyes to see me back. We reached an agreement about the rent and the load of peat which the school would deliver.

Later on I found out that, year in year out, it was a long time since Matryona Vasilyevna had earned a single ruble. She didn't get a pension. Her relatives gave her very little help. In the kolkhoz she had worked not for money but for credits; the marks recording her labor days in her well-thumbed workbook.

So I moved in with Matryona Vasilyevna. We didn't divide the room. Her bed was in the corner between the door and the stove, and I unfolded my camp bed by one window and pushed Matryona's beloved rubber plants out of the light to make room for a little table by another. The village had electric light, laid on back in the twenties, from Shatury. The newspapers were writing about "Ilyich's little lamps," but the peasants talked wide-eyed about "Tsar Light."[7]

Some of the better-off people in the village might not have thought Matryona's house much of a home, but it kept us snug enough that autumn and winter. The roof still held the rain out, and the freezing winds could not blow the warmth of the stove away all at once, though it was cold by morning, especially when the wind blew on the shabby side.

In addition to Matryona and myself, a cat, some mice, and some cockroaches lived in the house.

The cat was no longer young, and was gammy-legged as well. Matryona

7. The newspapers reflect the new order, *Ilyich* standing for Vladimir Ilyich Lenin (1870–1924), leader of the 1917 Russian Revolution and first head of the new state; the peasants still think in terms of the emperor (*Czar*).

had taken her in out of pity, and she had stayed. She walked on all four feet but with a heavy limp: one of her feet was sore and she favored it. When she jumped from the stove she didn't land with the soft sound a cat usually makes, but with a heavy thud as three of her feet struck the floor at once—such a heavy thud that until I got used to it, it gave me a start. This was because she stuck three feet out together to save the fourth.

It wasn't because the cat couldn't deal with them that there were mice in the cottage: she would pounce into the corner like lightning and come back with a mouse between her teeth. But the mice were usually out of reach because somebody, back in the good old days, had stuck embossed wallpaper of a greenish color on Matryona's walls, and not just one layer of it but five. The layers held together all right, but in many places the whole lot had come away from the wall, giving the room a sort of inner skin. Between the timber of the walls and the skin of wallpaper the mice had made themselves runs where they impudently scampered about, running at times right up to the ceiling. The cat followed their scamperings with angry eyes, but couldn't get at them.

Sometimes the cat ate cockroaches as well, but they made her sick. The only thing the cockroaches respected was the partition which screened the mouth of the Russian stove and the kitchen from the best part of the room. They did not creep into the best room. But the kitchen at night swarmed with them, and if I went in late in the evening for a drink of water and switched on the light the whole floor, the big bench, and even the wall would be one rustling brown mass. From time to time I brought home some borax from the school laboratory and we mixed it with dough to poison them. There would be fewer cockroaches for a while, but Matryona was afraid that we might poison the cat as well. We stopped putting down poison and the cockroaches multiplied anew.

At night, when Matryona was already asleep and I was working at my table, the occasional rapid scamper of mice behind the wallpaper would be drowned in the sustained and ceaseless rustling of cockroaches behind the screen, like the sound of the sea in the distance. But I got used to it because there was nothing evil in it, nothing dishonest. Rustling was life to them.

I even got used to the crude beauty on the poster, forever reaching out from the wall to offer me Belinsky, Panferov,[8] and a pile of other books—but never saying a word. I got used to everything in Matryona's cottage.

Matryona got up at four or five o'clock in the morning. Her wall clock was twenty-seven years old and had been bought in the village shop. It was always fast, but Matryona didn't worry about that—just as long as it didn't lose and make her late in the morning. She switched on the light behind the kitchen screen and moving quietly, considerately, doing her best not to make a noise, she lit the stove, went to milk the goat (all the livestock she had was this one dirty-white goat with twisted horns), fetched water and boiled it in three iron pots: one for me, one for herself, and one for

---

8. Fedor Ivanovich Panferov (1896–1960), socialist-realist writer popular in the 1920s, best known for his novel *The Iron Flood*. Vissarion Grigoryevich Belinsky (1811–1848), Russian literary critic who emphasized social and political ideas.

the goat. She fetched potatoes from the cellar, picking out the littlest for the goat, little ones for herself and egg-sized ones for me. There were no big ones, because her garden was sandy, had not been manured since the war, and she always planted with potatoes, potatoes, and potatoes again, so that it wouldn't grow big ones.

I scarcely heard her about her morning tasks. I slept late, woke up in the wintry daylight, stretched a bit, and stuck my head out from under my blanket and my sheepskin. These, together with the prisoner's jerkin round my legs and a sack stuffed with straw underneath me, kept me warm in bed even on nights when the cold wind rattled our wobbly windows from the north. When I heard the discreet noises on the other side of the screen I spoke to her, slowly and deliberately:

"Good morning, Matryona Vasilyevna!"

And every time the same good-natured words came to me from behind the screen. They began with a warm, throaty gurgle, the sort of sound grandmothers make in fairy tales.

"M-m-m . . . same to you too!"

And after a little while, "Your breakfast's ready for you now."

She didn't announce what was for breakfast, but it was easy to guess: taters in their jackets or tatty soup (as everybody in the village called it), or barley gruel (no other grain could be bought in Torfoprodukt that year, and even the barley you had to fight for, because it was the cheapest and people bought it up by the sack to fatten their pigs on it). It wasn't always salted as it should be, it was often slightly burnt, it furred the palate and the gums, and it gave me heartburn.

But Matryona wasn't to blame: there was no butter in Torfoprodukt either, margarine was desperately short, and only mixed cooking fat was plentiful, and when I got to know it, I saw that the Russian stove was not convenient for cooking: the cook cannot see the pots and they are not heated evenly all round. I suppose the stove came down to our ancestors from the Stone Age, because you can stoke it up once before daylight, and food and water, mash and swill will keep warm in it all day long. And it keeps you warm while you sleep.

I ate everything that was cooked for me without demur, patiently putting aside anything uncalled-for that I came across: a hair, a bit of peat, a cockroach's leg. I hadn't the heart to find fault with Matryona. After all, she had warned me herself.

"We aren't clever, we can't cook—I don't know how we shall suit. . . ."

"Thank you," I said quite sincerely.

"What for? For what is your own?" she answered, disarming me with a radiant smile. And, with a guileless look of her faded blue eyes, she would ask, "And what shall I cook you for just now?"

For just now meant for supper. I ate twice a day, like at the front. What could I order for just now? It would have to be one of the same old things, taters or tater soup.

I resigned myself to it, because I had learned by now not to look for the meaning of life in food. More important to me was the smile on her roundish face, which I tried in vain to catch when at last I had earned enough to buy a camera. As soon as she saw the cold eye of the lens upon her, Matryona assumed a strained or else an exaggeratedly severe expression.

Just once I did manage to get a snap of her looking through the window into the street and smiling at something.

Matryona had a lot of worries that winter. Her neighbors put it into her head to try and get a pension. She was all alone in the world, and when she began to be seriously ill she had been dismissed from the kolkhoz as well. Injustices had piled up, one on top of another. She was ill, but was not regarded as a disabled person. She had worked for a quarter of a century in the kolkhoz, but it was a kolkhoz and not a factory, so she was not entitled to a pension for herself. She could only try and get one for her husband, for the loss of her breadwinner. But she had had no husband for twelve years now, not since the beginning of the war, and it wasn't easy to obtain all the particulars from different places about his length of service and how much he had earned. What a bother it was getting those forms through! Getting somebody to certify that he'd earned, say, three hundred rubles a month; that she lived alone and nobody helped her; what year she was born in. Then all this had to be taken to the Pension Office. And taken somewhere else to get all the mistakes corrected. And taken back again. Then you had to find out whether they would give you a pension.

To make it all more difficult the Pension Office was twelve miles east of Talnovo, the Rural Council Offices six miles to the west, the Factory District Council an hour's walk to the north. They made her run around from office to office for two months on end, to get an *i* dotted or a *t* crossed. Every trip took a day. She goes down to the Rural District Council—and the secretary isn't there today. Secretaries of rural councils often aren't here today. So come again tomorrow. Tomorrow the secretary is in, but he hasn't got his rubber stamp. So come again the next day. And the day after that back she goes yet again, because all her papers are pinned together and some cockeyed clerk has signed the wrong one.

"They shove me around, Ignatich," she used to complain to me after these fruitless excursions. "Worn out with it I am."

But she soon brightened up. I found that she had a sure means of putting herself in a good humor. She worked. She would grab a shovel and go off to pull potatoes. Or she would tuck a sack under her arm and go after peat. Or take a wicker basket and look for berries deep in the woods. When she'd been bending her back to bushes instead of office desks for a while, and her shoulders were aching from a heavy load, Matryona would come back cheerful, at peace with the world and smiling her nice smile.

"I'm on to a good thing now, Ignatich. I know where to go for it (peat she meant), a lovely place it is."

"But surely my peat is enough, Matryona Vasilyevna? There's a whole truckload of it."

"Pooh! Your peat! As much again, and then as much again, that might be enough. When the winter gets really stiff and the wind's battling at the windows, it blows the heat out of the house faster than you can make the stove up. Last year we got heaps and heaps of it. I'd have had three loads in by now. But they're out to catch us. They've summoned one woman from our village already."

That's how it was. The frightening breath of winter was already in the air. There were forests all round, and no fuel to be had anywhere. Excavators roared away in the bogs, but there was no peat on sale to the villagers. It was delivered, free, to the bosses and to the people round the bosses, and teachers, doctors, and workers got a load each. The people of Talnovo were not supposed to get any peat, and they weren't supposed to ask about it. The chairman of the kolkhoz walked about the village looking people in the eye while he gave his orders or stood chatting and talked about anything you liked except fuel. He was stocked up. Who said anything about winter coming?

So just as in the old days they used to steal the squire's wood, now they pinched peat from the trust. The women went in parties of five or ten so that they would be less frightened. They went in the daytime. The peat cut during the summer had been stacked up all over the place to dry. That's the good thing about peat, it can't be carted off as soon as it's cut. It lies around drying till autumn, or, if the roads are bad, till the snow starts falling. This was when the women used to come and take it. They could get six peats in a sack if it was damp, or ten if it was dry. A sackful weighed about half a hundredweight and it sometimes had to be carried over two miles. This was enough to make the stove up once. There were two hundred days in the winter. The Russian stove had to be lit in the mornings, and the "Dutch"[9] stove in the evenings.

"Why beat about the bush?" said Matryona angrily to someone invisible. "Since there've been no more horses, what you can't have around yourself you haven't got. My back never heals up. Winter you're pulling sledges, summer it's bundles on your back, it's God's truth I'm telling you."

The women went more than once in a day. On good days Matryona brought six sacks home. She piled my peat up where it could be seen and hid her own under the passageway, boarding up the hole every night.

"If they don't just happen to think of it, the devils will never find it in their born days," said Matryona smiling and wiping the sweat from her brow.

What could the peat trust do? Its establishment didn't run to a watchman for every bog. I suppose they had to show a rich haul in their returns, and then write off so much for crumbling, so much washed away by the rain. Sometimes they would take it into their heads to put out patrols and try to catch the women as they came into the village. The women would drop their sacks and scatter. Or somebody would inform and there would be a house-to-house search. They would draw up a report on the stolen peat and threaten a court action. The women would stop fetching it for a while, but the approach of winter drove them out with sledges in the middle of the night.

When I had seen a little more of Matryona I noticed that, apart from cooking and looking after the house, she had quite a lot of other jobs to

---

9. Not the real tiled Dutch stove, but a cheap small stove (probably made from an oil barrel) that provided heat with less fuel than the big Russian stove.

do every day. She kept all her jobs, and the proper times for them, in her head and always knew when she woke up in the morning how her day would be occupied. Apart from fetching peat and stumps which the tractors unearthed in the bogs, apart from the cranberries which she put to soak in big jars for the winter ("Give your teeth an edge, Ignatich," she used to say when she offered me some), apart from digging potatoes and all the coming and going to do with her pension, she had to get hay from somewhere for her one and only dirty-white goat.

"Why don't you keep a cow, Matryona?"

Matryona stood there in her grubby apron, by the opening in the kitchen screen, facing my table, and explained to me.

"Oh, Ignatich, there's enough milk from the goat for me. And if I started keeping a cow she'd eat me out of house and home in no time. You can't cut the grass by the railway track, because it belongs to the railway, and you can't cut any in the woods, because it belongs to the foresters, and they won't let me have any at the kolkhoz because I'm not a member any more, they reckon. And those who are members have to work there every day till the white flies swarm and make their own hay when there's snow on the ground—what's the good of grass like that? In the old days they used to be sweating to get the hay in at midsummer, between the end of June and the end of July, while the grass was sweet and juicy."

So it meant a lot of work for Matryona to gather enough hay for one skinny little goat. She took her sickle and a sack and went off early in the morning to places where she knew there was grass growing—round the edges of fields, on the roadside, on hummocks in the bog. When she had stuffed her sack with heavy fresh grass she dragged it home and spread it out in her yard to dry. From a sackful of grass she got one forkload of dry hay.

The farm had a new chairman, sent down from the town not long ago, and the first thing he did was to cut down the garden plots for those who were not fit to work. He left Matryona a third of an acre of sand—when there was over a thousand square yards just lying idle on the other side of the fence. Yet when they were short of working hands, when the women dug in their heels and wouldn't budge, the chairman's wife would come to see Matryona. She was from the town as well, a determined woman whose short gray coat and intimidating glare gave her a somewhat military appearance. She walked into the house without so much as a good morning and looked sternly at Matryona. Matryona was uneasy.

"Well now, Comrade Vasilyevna," said the chairman's wife, drawing out her words. "You will have to help the kolkhoz! You will have to go and help cart manure out tomorrow!"

A little smile of forgiveness wrinkled Matryona's face—as though she understood the embarrassment which the chairman's wife must feel at not being able to pay her for her work.

"Well—er," she droned. "I'm not well, of course, and I'm not attached to you any more . . . ," then she hurried to correct herself, "What time should I come then?"

"And bring your own fork!" the chairman's wife instructed her. Her stiff skirt crackled as she walked away.

"Think of that!" grumbled Matryona as the door closed. "Bring your own fork! They've got neither forks nor shovels at the kolkhoz. And I don't have a man who'll put a handle on for me!"

She went on thinking about it out loud all evening.

"What's the good of talking, Ignatich. I must help, of course. Only the way they work it's all a waste of time—don't know whether they're coming or going. The women stand propped up on their shovels and waiting for the factory whistle to blow twelve o'clock. Or else they get on to adding up who's earned what and who's turned up for work and who hasn't. Now what I call work, there isn't a sound out of anybody, only—oh dear, dear— dinner time's soon rolled round—what, getting dark already."

In the morning she went off with her fork.

But it wasn't just the kolkhoz—any distant relative, or just a neighbor, could come to Matryona of an evening and say, "Come and give me a hand tomorrow, Matryona. We'll finish pulling the potatoes."

Matryona couldn't say no. She gave up what she should be doing next and went to help her neighbor, and when she came back she would say without a trace of envy, "Ah, you should see the size of her potatoes, Ignatich! It was a joy to dig them up. I didn't want to leave the allotment, God's truth I didn't."

Needless to say, not a garden could be plowed without Matryona's help. The women of Talnovo had got it neatly worked out that it was a longer and harder job for one woman to dig her garden with a spade than for six of them to put themselves in harness and plow six gardens. So they sent for Matryona to help them.

"Well—did you pay her?" I asked sometimes.

"She won't take money. You have to try and hide it on her when she's not looking."

Matryona had yet another troublesome chore when her turn came to feed the herdsmen. One of them was a hefty deaf mute, the other a boy who was never without a cigaret in his drooling mouth. Matryona's turn came round only every six weeks, but it put her to great expense. She went to the shop to buy canned fish and was lavish with sugar and butter, things she never ate herself. It seems that the housewives showed off in this way, trying to outdo one another in feeding the herdsmen.

"You've got to be careful with tailors and herdsmen," Matryona explained. "They'll spread your name all round the village if something doesn't suit them."

And every now and then attacks of serious illness broke in on this life that was already crammed with troubles. Matryona would be off her feet for a day or two, lying flat out on the stove. She didn't complain and didn't groan, but she hardly stirred either. On these days Masha, Matryona's closest friend from her earliest years, would come to look after the goat and light the stove. Matryona herself ate nothing, drank nothing, asked for nothing. To call in the doctor from the clinic at the settlement would have seemed strange in Talnovo and would have given the neighbors something to talk about—what does she think she is, a lady? They did call her in once, and she arrived in a real temper and told Matryona to come down to the clinic when she was on her feet again. Matryona went, although she didn't really want to; they took specimens and sent them off to the district hospital—and that's the last anybody heard about it. Matryona was partly to blame herself.

But there was work waiting to be done, and Matryona soon started getting up again, moving slowly at first and then as briskly as ever.

"You never saw me in the old days, Ignatich. I'd lift any sack you liked, I didn't think a hundredweight was too heavy. My father-in-law used to say, 'Matryona, you'll break your back.' And my brother-in-law didn't have to come and help me lift on the cart. Our horse was a warhorse, a big strong one."

"What do you mean, a warhorse?"

"They took ours for the war and gave us this one instead—he'd been wounded. But he turned out a bit spirited. Once he bolted with the sledge right into the lake, the men folk hopped out of the way, but I grabbed the bridle, as true as I'm here, and stopped him. Full of oats that horse was. They liked to feed their horses well in our village. If a horse feels his oats he doesn't know what heavy means."

But Matryona was a long way from being fearless. She was afraid of fire, afraid of "the lightning," and most of all she was for some reason afraid of trains.

"When I had to go to Cherusti,[1] the train came up from Nechaevka way with its great big eyes popping out and the rails humming away—put me in a regular fever. My knees started knocking. God's truth I'm telling you!" Matryona raised her shoulders as though she surprised herself.

"Maybe it's because they won't give people tickets, Matryona Vasilyevna?"

"At the window? They try to shove only first-class tickets on to you. And the train was starting to move. We dashed about all over the place, 'Give us tickets for pity's sake.' "

"The men folk had climbed on top of the carriages. Then we found a door that wasn't locked and shoved straight in without tickets—and all the carriages were empty, they were all empty, you could stretch out on the seat if you wanted to. Why they wouldn't give us tickets, the hardhearted parasites, I don't know. . . ."

Still, before winter came, Matryona's affairs were in a better state than ever before. They started paying her at last a pension of eighty rubles. Besides this she got just over one hundred from the school and me.

Some of her neighbors began to be envious.

"Hm! Matryona can live forever now! If she had any more money, she wouldn't know what to do with it at her age."

Matryona had some new felt boots made. She bought a new jerkin. And she had an overcoat made out of the worn-out railwayman's greatcoat given to her by the engine driver from Cherusti who had married Kira, her foster daughter. The hump-backed village tailor put a padded lining under the cloth and it made a marvelous coat, such as Matryona had never worn before in all her sixty years.

1. About 100 miles east of Moscow and some 250 miles northwest of Nechaevka.

In the middle of winter Matryona sewed two hundred rubles into the lining of this coat for her funeral. This made her quite cheerful.

"Now my mind's a bit easier, Ignatich."

December went by, January went by—and in those two months Matryona's illness held off. She started going over to Masha's house more often in the evening, to sit chewing sunflower seeds with her. She herself didn't invite guests in the evening out of consideration for my work. Once, on the feast of the Epiphany, I came back from school and found a party going on and was introduced to Matryona's three sisters, who called her "nan-nan" or "nanny" because she was the oldest. Until then not much had been heard of the sisters in our cottage—perhaps they were afraid that Matryona might ask them for help.

But one ominous event cast a shadow on the holiday for Matryona. She went to the church three miles away for the blessing of the water and put her pot down among the others. When the blessing was over, the women went rushing and jostling to get their pots back again. There were a lot of women in front of Matryona and when she got there her pot was missing, and no other vessel had been left behind. The pot had vanished as though the devil had run off with it.

Matryona went round the worshipers asking them, "Have any of you girls accidentally mistook somebody else's holy water? In a pot?"

Nobody owned up. There had been some boys there, and boys got up to mischief sometimes. Matryona came home sad.

No one could say that Matryona was a devout believer. If anything, she was a heathen, and her strongest beliefs were superstitious: you mustn't go into the garden on the fast of St. John or there would be no harvest next year. A blizzard meant that somebody had hanged himself. If you pinched your foot in the door, you could expect a guest. All the time I lived with her I didn't once see her say her prayers or even cross herself. But, whatever job she was doing, she began with a "God bless us," and she never failed to say "God bless you," when I set out for school. Perhaps she did say her prayers, but on the quiet, either because she was shy or because she didn't want to embarrass me. There were icons[2] on the walls. Ordinary days they were left in darkness, but for the vigil of a great feast, or on the morning of a holiday, Matryona would light the little lamp.

She had fewer sins on her conscience than her gammy-legged cat. The cat did kill mice.

Now that her life was running more smoothly, Matryona started listening more carefully to my radio. (I had, of course, installed a speaker, or as Matryona called it, a peeker.)[3]

When they announced on the radio that some new machine had been invented, I heard Matryona grumbling out in the kitchen, "New ones all the time, nothing but new ones. People don't want to work with the old ones any more, where are we going to store them all?"

There was a program about the seeding of clouds from airplanes. Matryona, listening up on the stove, shook her head, "Oh, dear, dear, dear, they'll do away with one of the two—summer or winter."

---

2. Religious images or portraits, usually painted on wood. A small lamp was set in front of the icons to illuminate them.   3. The translator is imitating Solzhenitsyn's wordplay. In the original, the narrator calls the speaker *razvedka* (a military term, literally "scout"); Matryona calls it *rozetka* (an electric plug).

Once Shalyapin[4] was singing Russian folk songs. Matryona stood listening for a long time before she gave her emphatic verdict, "Queer singing, not our sort of singing."

"You can't mean that, Matryona Vasilyevna—just listen to him."

She listened a bit longer and pursed her lips, "No, it's wrong. It isn't our sort of tune, and he's tricky with his voice."

She made up for this another time. They were broadcasting some of Glinka's[5] songs. After half a dozen of these drawing-room ballads, Matryona suddenly came from behind the screen clutching her apron, with a flush on her face and a film of tears over her dim eyes.

"That's our sort of singing," she said in a whisper.

2

So Matryona and I got used to each other and took each other for granted. She never pestered me with questions about myself. I don't know whether she was lacking in normal female curiosity or just tactful, but she never once asked if I had been married. All the Talnovo women kept at her to find out about me. Her answer was, "You want to know—you ask him. All I know is he's from distant parts."

And when I got round to telling her that I had spent a lot of time in prison, she said nothing but just nodded, as though she had already suspected it.

And I thought of Matryona only as the helpless old woman she was now and didn't try to rake up her past, didn't even suspect that there was anything to be found there.

I knew that Matryona had got married before the Revolution and had come to live in the house I now shared with her, and she had gone "to the stove" immediately. (She had no mother-in-law and no older sister-in-law, so it was her job to put the pots in the oven on the very first morning of her married life.) I knew that she had had six children and that they had all died very young, so that there were never two of them alive at once. Then there was a sort of foster daughter, Kira. Matryona's husband had not come back from the last war. She received no notification of his death. Men from the village who had served in the same company said that he might have been taken prisoner, or he might have been killed and his body not found. In the eight years that had gone by since the war Matryona had decided that he was not alive. It was a good thing that she thought so. If he was still alive he was probably in Brazil or Australia and married again. The village of Talnovo and the Russian language would be fading from his memory.

One day when I got back from school, I found a guest in the house. A tall, dark man, with his hat on his lap, was sitting on a chair which Matryona had moved up to the Dutch stove in the middle of the room. His face was completely surrounded by bushy black hair with hardly a trace of gray in

4. Feodor Ivanovich Shalyapin (or Chaliapin, 1873–1938), Russian operatic bass with an international reputation as a great singer and actor; he included popular Russian music in his song recitals. 5. Mikhail Ivanovich Glinka (1804–1857), Russian composer who was instrumental in developing a "Russian" style of music, including the two operas A Life for the Czar and Ruslan and Ludmila.

it. His thick black moustache ran into his full black beard, so that his mouth could hardly be seen. Black side-whiskers merged with the black locks which hung down from his crown, leaving only the tips of his ears visible; his broad black eyebrows met in a wide double span. But the front of his head as far as the crown was a spacious bald dome. His whole appearance made an impression of wisdom and dignity. He sat squarely on his chair, with his hands folded on his stick, and his stick resting vertically on the floor, in an attitude of patient expectation, and he obviously hadn't much to say to Matryona, who was busy behind the screen.

When I came in, he eased his majestic head round toward me and suddenly addressed me, "Schoolmaster, I can't see you very well. My son goes to your school. Grigoryev, Antoshka."

There was no need for him to say any more. However strongly inclined I felt to help this worthy old man, I knew and dismissed in advance all the pointless things he was going to say. Antoshka Grigoryev was a plump, red-faced lad in 8-D who looked like a cat that's swallowed the cream. He seemed to think that he came to school for a rest and sat at his desk with a lazy smile on his face. Needless to say, he never did his homework. But the worst of it was that he had been put up into the next class from year to year because our district, and indeed the whole region and the neighboring region were famous for the high percentage of passes they obtained; the school had to make an effort to keep its record up. So Antoshka had got it clear in his mind that however much the teachers threatened him they would promote him in the end, and there was no need for him to learn anything. He just laughed at us. There he sat in the eighth class, and he hadn't even mastered his decimals and didn't know one triangle from another. In the first two terms of the school year I had kept him firmly below the passing line and the same treatment awaited him in the third.

But now this half-blind old man, who should have been Antoshka's grandfather rather than his father, had come to humble himself before me—how could I tell him that the school had been deceiving him for years, and that I couldn't go on deceiving him, because I didn't want to ruin the whole class, to become a liar and a fake, to start despising my work and my profession.

For the time being I patiently explained that his son had been very slack, that he told lies at school and at home, that his record book must be checked frequently, and that we must both take him severely in hand.

"Severe as you like, Schoolmaster," he assured me, "I beat him every week now. And I've got a heavy hand."

While we were talking I remembered that Matryona had once interceded for Antoshka Grigoryev, but I hadn't asked what relation of hers he was and I had refused to do what she wanted. Matryona was standing in the kitchen doorway like a mute suppliant on this occasion too. When Faddey Mironovich left, saying that he would call on me to see how things were going, I asked her, "I can't make out what relation this Antoshka is to you, Matryona Vasilyevna."

"My brother-in-law's son," said Matryona shortly, and went out to milk the goat.

When I'd worked it out, I realized that this determined old man with the black hair was the brother of the missing husband.

The long evening went by, and Matryona didn't bring up the subject again. But late at night, when I had stopped thinking about the old man and was working in a silence broken only by the rustling of the cock-roaches and the heavy tick of the wall-clock, Matryona suddenly spoke from her dark corner, "You know, Ignatich, I nearly married him once."

I had forgotten that Matryona was in the room. I hadn't heard a sound from her—and suddenly her voice came out of the darkness, as agitated as if the old man were still trying to win her.

I could see that Matryona had been thinking about nothing else all evening.

She got up from her wretched rag bed and walked slowly toward me, as though she were following her own words. I sat back in my chair and caught my first glimpse of a quite different Matryona.

There was no overhead light in our big room with its forest of rubber plants. The table lamp cast a ring of light round my exercise books, and when I tore my eyes from it the rest of the room seemed to be half-dark and faintly tinged with pink. I thought I could see the same pinkish glow in her usually sallow cheeks.

"He was the first one who came courting me, before Efim did—he was his brother—the older one—I was nineteen and Faddey was twenty-three. They lived in this very same house. Their house it was. Their father built it."

I looked round the room automatically. Instead of the old gray house rotting under the faded green skin of wallpaper where the mice had their playground, I suddenly saw new timbers, freshly trimmed, not yet discol-ored, and caught the cheerful smell of pine tar.

"Well, and what happened then?"

"That summer we went to sit in the woods together," she whispered. "There used to be a woods where the stable yard is now. They chopped it down. I was just going to marry him, Ignatich. Then the German war started. They took Faddey into the army."

She let fall these few words—and suddenly the blue and white and yellow July of the year 1914 burst into flower before my eyes: the sky still peaceful, the floating clouds, the people sweating to get the ripe corn in. I imagined them side by side, the black-haired Hercules with a scythe over his shoulder, and the red-faced girl clasping a sheaf. And there was singing out under the open sky, such songs as nobody can sing nowadays, with all the machines in the fields.

"He went to the war—and vanished. For three years I kept to myself and waited. Never a sign of life did he give."

Matryona's round face looked out at me from an elderly threadbare headscarf. As she stood there in the gentle reflected light from my lamp, her face seemed to lose its slovenly workday wrinkles, and she was a scared young girl again with a frightening decision to make.

Yes . . . I could see it. The trees shed their leaves, the snow fell and melted. They plowed and sowed and reaped again. Again the trees shed their leaves, and the snow fell. There was a revolution. Then another revolution. And the whole world was turned upside down.

"Their mother died and Efim came to court me. 'You wanted to come to our house,' he says, 'so come.' He was a year younger than me, Efim was. It's a saying with us—sensible girls get married after Michaelmas, and silly ones at midsummer. They were shorthanded. I got married. . . . The wedding was on St. Peter's day, and then about St. Nicholas' day[6] in the winter he came back—Faddey, I mean, from being a prisoner in Hungary."

Matryona covered her eyes.

I said nothing.

She turned toward the door as though somebody were standing there. "He stood there at the door. What a scream I let out! I wanted to throw myself at his feet! . . . but I couldn't. 'If it wasn't my own brother,' he says, 'I'd take my ax to the both of you.' "

I shuddered. Matryona's despair, or her terror, conjured up a vivid picture of him standing in the dark doorway and raising his ax to her.

But she quieted down and went on with her story in a sing-song voice, leaning on a chairback, "Oh dear, dear me, the poor dear man! There were so many girls in the village—but he wouldn't marry. I'll look for one with the same name as you, a second Matryona, he said. And that's what he did—fetched himself a Matryona from Lipovka. They built themselves a house of their own and they're still living in it. You pass their place every day on your way to school."

So that was it. I realized that I had seen the other Matryona quite often. I didn't like her. She was always coming to my Matryona to complain about her husband—he beat her, he was stingy, he was working her to death. She would weep and weep, and her voice always had a tearful note in it. As it turned out, my Matryona had nothing to regret, with Faddey beating his Matryona every day of his life and being so tightfisted.

"Mine never beat me once," said Matryona of Efim. "He'd pitch into another man in the street, but me he never hit once. Well, there was one time—I quarreled with my sister-in-law and he cracked me on the forehead with a spoon. I jumped up from the table and shouted at them, 'Hope it sticks in your gullets, you idle lot of beggars, hope you choke!' I said. And off I went into the woods. He never touched me any more."

Faddey didn't seem to have any cause for regret either. The other Matryona had borne him six children (my Antoshka was one of them, the littlest, the runt) and they had all lived, whereas the children of Matryona and Efim had died, every one of them, before they reached the age of three months, without any illness.

"One daughter, Elena, was born and was alive when they washed her, and then she died right after. . . . My wedding was on St. Peter's day, and it was St. Peter's day I buried my sixth, Alexander."

The whole village decided that there was a curse on Matryona.

6. December 19 (December 6, old style). *Michaelmas:* October 12 (September 29, old style). *St. Peter's Day:* probably July 12 (June 29, old style), Sts. Peter and Paul's Day.

Matryona still nodded emphatic belief when she talked about it. "There was a *course*[7] on me. They took me to a woman who used to be a nun to get cured, she set me off coughing and waited for the *course* to jump out of me like a frog. Only nothing jumped out."

And the years had run by like running water. In 1941 they didn't take Faddey into the army because of his poor sight, but they took Efim. And what had happened to the elder brother in the First World War happened to the younger in the Second—he vanished without a trace. Only he never came back at all. The once noisy cottage was deserted, it grew old and rotten, and Matryona, all alone in the world, grew old in it.

So she begged from the other Matryona, the cruelly beaten Matryona, a child of her womb (or was it a drop of Faddey's blood?), the youngest daughter, Kira.

For ten years she brought the girl up in her own house, in place of the children who had not lived. Then, not long before I arrived, she had married her off to a young engine driver from Cherusti. The only help she got from anywhere came in dribs and drabs from Cherusti: a bit of sugar from time to time, or some of the fat when they killed a pig.

Sick and suffering, and feeling that death was not far off, Matryona had made known her will: the top room, which was a separate frame joined by tie beams to the rest of the house, should go to Kira when she died.[8] She said nothing about the house itself. Her three sisters had their eyes on it too.

That evening Matryona opened her heart to me. And, as often happens, no sooner were the hidden springs of her life revealed to me than I saw them in motion.

Kira arrived from Cherusti. Old Faddey was very worried. To get and keep a plot of land in Cherusti the young couple had to put up some sort of building. Matryona's top room would do very well. There was nothing else they could put up, because there was no timber to be had anywhere. It wasn't Kira herself so much, and it wasn't her husband, but old Faddey who was consumed with eagerness for them to get their hands on the plot at Cherusti.

He became a frequent visitor, laying down the law to Matryona and insisting that she should hand over the top room right away, before she died. On these occasions I saw a different Faddey. He was no longer an old man propped up by a stick, whom a push or a harsh word would bowl over. Although he was slightly bent by backache, he was still a fine figure; in his sixties he had kept the vigorous black hair of a young man; he was hot and urgent.

Matryona had not slept for two nights. It wasn't easy for her to make up her mind. She didn't grudge them the top room, which was standing there idle, any more than she ever grudged her labor or her belongings. And the top room was willed to Kira in any case. But the thought of breaking up the roof she had lived under for forty years was torture to her. Even I, a

---

7. *Curse/course* reflects wordplay in the Russian original, where a similar misuse of language indicates Matryona's lack of formal education.   8. Lumber was scarce and valuable, and old houses were well built. Moving houses or sections of houses is still common in the country.

mere lodger, found it painful to think of them stripping away boards and wrenching out beams. For Matryona it was the end of everything.

But the people who were so insistent knew that she would let them break up her house before she died.

So Faddey and his sons and sons-in-law came along one February morning, the blows of five axes were heard and boards creaked and cracked as they were wrenched out. Faddey's eyes twinkled busily. Although his back wasn't quite straight yet, he scrambled nimbly up under the rafters and bustled about down below, shouting at his assistants. He and his father had built this house when he was a lad, a long time ago. The top room had been put up for him, the oldest son, to move into with his bride. And now he was furiously taking it apart, board by board, to carry it out of somebody else's yard.

After numbering the beam ends and the ceiling boards, they dismantled the top room and the storeroom underneath it. The living room and what was left of the landing they boarded up with a thin wall of deal. They did nothing about the cracks in the wall. It was plain to see that they were wreckers, not builders, and that they did not expect Matryona to be living there very long.

While the men were busy wrecking, the women were getting the drink ready for moving day—vodka would cost too much. Kira brought forty pounds of sugar from the Moscow region, and Matryona carried the sugar and some bottles to the distiller under cover of night.

The timbers were carried out and stacked in front of the gates, and the engine-driver son-in-law went off to Cherusti for the tractor.

But the very same day a blizzard, or "a blower," as Matryona once called it, began. It howled and whirled for two days and nights and buried the road under enormous drifts. Then, no sooner had they made the road passable and a couple of trucks had gone by, than it got suddenly warmer. Within a day everything was thawing out, damp mist hung in the air and rivulets gurgled as they burrowed into the snow, and you could get stuck up to the top of your jackboots.

Two weeks passed before the tractor could get at the dismantled top room. All this time Matryona went around like someone lost. What particularly upset her was that her three sisters came, with one voice called her a fool for giving the top room away, said they didn't want to see her any more, and went off. At about the same time the lame cat strayed and was seen no more. It was just one thing after another. This was another blow to Matryona.

At last the frost got a grip on the slushy road. A sunny day came along, and everybody felt more cheerful. Matryona had had a lucky dream the night before. In the morning she heard that I wanted to take a photograph of somebody at an old-fashioned handloom. (There were looms still standing in two cottages in the village; they wove coarse rugs on them.) She smiled shyly and said, "You just wait a day or two, Ignatich, I'll just send off the top room there and I'll put my loom up, I've still got it, you know, and then you can snap me. Honest to God!"

She was obviously attracted by the idea of posing in an old-fashioned setting. The red frosty sun tinged the window of the curtailed passageway with a faint pink, and this reflected light warmed Matryona's face. People who are at ease with their consciences always have nice faces.

Coming back from school before dusk I saw some movement near our house. A big new tractor-drawn sledge was already fully loaded, and there was no room for a lot of the timbers, so old Faddey's family and the helpers they had called in had nearly finished knocking together another home-made sledge. They were all working like madmen, in the frenzy that comes upon people when there is a smell of good money in the air or when they are looking forward to some treat. They were shouting at one another and arguing.

They could not agree on whether the sledges should be hauled separately or both together. One of Faddey's sons (the lame one) and the engine-driver son-in-law reasoned that the sledges couldn't both be taken at once because the tractor wouldn't be able to pull them. The man in charge of the tractor, a hefty fat-faced fellow who was very sure of himself, said hoarsely that he knew best, he was the driver, and he would take both at once. His motives were obvious: according to the agreement, the engine driver was paying him for the removal of the upper room, not for the number of trips he had to make. He could never have made two trips in a night—twenty-five kilometers each way, and one return journey. And by morning he had to get the tractor back in the garage from which he had sneaked it out for this job on the side.

Old Faddey was impatient to get the top room moved that day, and at a nod from him his lads gave in. To the stout sledge in front they hitched the one they had knocked together in such a hurry.

Matryona was running about among the men, fussing and helping them to heave the beams on the sledge. Suddenly I noticed that she was wearing my jacket and had dirtied the sleeves on the frozen mud round the beams. I was annoyed and told her so. That jacket held memories for me: it had kept me warm in the bad years.

This was the first time that I was ever angry with Matryona Vasilyevna.

Matryona was taken aback. "Oh dear, dear me," she said. "My poor head. I picked it up in a rush, you see, and never thought about it being yours. I'm sorry, Ignatich."

And she took it off and hung it up to dry.

The loading was finished, and all the men who had been working, about ten of them, clattered past my table and dived under the curtain into the kitchen. I could hear the muffled rattle of glasses and, from time to time, the clink of a bottle, the voices got louder and louder, the boasting more reckless. The biggest braggart was the tractor driver. The stink of hooch floated in to me. But they didn't go on drinking long. It was getting dark and they had to hurry. They began to leave. The tractor driver came out first, looking pleased with himself and fierce. The engine-driver son-in-law, Faddey's lame son, and one of his nephews were going to Cherusti. The others went off home. Faddey was flourishing his stick, trying to over-take somebody and put him right about something. The lame son paused at my table to light up and suddenly started telling me how he loved Aunt Matryona, and that he had got married not long ago, and his wife had just had a son. Then they shouted for him and he went out. The tractor set up a roar outside.

After all the others had gone, Matryona dashed out from behind the screen. She looked after them, anxiously shaking her head. She had put on her jacket and her headscarf. As she was going through the door, she said to me, "Why ever couldn't they hire two? If one tractor had cracked up, the other would have pulled them. What'll happen now, God only knows!"

She ran out after the others.

After the boozing and the arguments and all the coming and going, it was quieter than ever in the deserted cottage, and very chilly because the door had been opened so many times. I got into my jacket and sat down to mark exercise books. The noise of the tractor died away in the distance.

An hour went by. And another. And a third. Matryona still hadn't come back, but I wasn't surprised. When she had seen the sledge off, she must have gone round to her friend Masha.

Another hour went by. And yet another. Darkness, and with it a deep silence had descended on the village. I couldn't understand at the time why it was so quiet. Later, I found out that it was because all evening not a single train had gone along the line five hundred yards from the house. No sound was coming from my radio, and I noticed that the mice were wilder than ever. Their scampering and scratching and squeaking behind the wallpaper was getting noisier and more defiant all the time.

I woke up. It was one o'clock in the morning, and Matryona still hadn't come home.

Suddenly I heard several people talking loudly. They were still a long way off, but something told me that they were coming to our house. And sure enough, I heard soon afterward a heavy knock at the gate. A commanding voice, strange to me, yelled out an order to open up. I went out into the pitch darkness with a torch. The whole village was asleep, there was no light in the windows, and the snow had started melting in the last week so that it gave no reflected light. I turned the catch and let them in. Four men in greatcoats went on toward the house. It's a very unpleasant thing to be visited at night by noisy people in greatcoats.

When we got into the light though, I saw that two of them were wearing railway uniforms. The older of the two, a fat man with the same sort of face as the tractor driver, asked, "Where's the woman of the house?"

"I don't know."

"This is the place the tractor with a sledge came from?"

"This is it."

"Had they been drinking before they left?"

All four of them were looking around, screwing up their eyes in the dim light from the table lamp. I realized that they had either made an arrest or wanted to make one.

"What's happened then?"

"Answer the question!"

"But . . ."

"Were they drunk when they went?"

"Were they drinking here?"

Had there been a murder? Or hadn't they been able to move the top room? The men in greatcoats had me off balance. But one thing was certain: Matryona could do time for making hooch.

I stepped back to stand between them and the kitchen door. "I honestly didn't notice. I didn't see anything." (I really hadn't seen anything—only heard.) I made what was supposed to be a helpless gesture, drawing attention to the state of the cottage: a table lamp shining peacefully on books and exercises, a crowd of frightened rubber plants, the austere couch of a recluse, not a sign of debauchery.

They had already seen for themselves, to their annoyance, that there had been no drinking in that room. They turned to leave, telling each other this wasn't where the drinking had been then, but it would be a good thing to put in that it was. I saw them out and tried to discover what had happened. It was only at the gate that one of them growled. "They've all been cut to bits. Can't find all the pieces."

"That's a detail. The nine o'clock express nearly went off the rails. That would have been something." And they walked briskly away.

I went back to the hut in a daze. Who were "they"? What did "all of them" mean? And where was Matryona?

I moved the curtain aside and went into the kitchen. The stink of hooch rose and hit me. It was a deserted battlefield: a huddle of stools and benches, empty bottles lying around, one bottle half-full, glasses, the remains of pickled herring, onion, and sliced fat pork.

Everything was deathly still. Just cockroaches creeping unperturbed about the field of battle.

They had said something about the nine o'clock express. Why? Perhaps I should have shown them all this? I began to wonder whether I had done right. But what a damnable way to behave—keeping their explanations for official persons only.

Suddenly the small gate creaked. I hurried out on to the landing. "Matryona Vasilyevna?"

The yard door opened, and Matryona's friend Masha came in, swaying and wringing her hands. "Matryona—our Matryona, Ignatich—"

I sat her down, and through her tears she told me the story.

The approach to the crossing was a steep rise. There was no barrier. The tractor and the first sledge went over, but the towrope broke and the second sledge, the homemade one, got stuck on the crossing and started falling apart—the wood Faddey had given them to make the second sledge was no good. They towed the first sledge out of the way and went back for the second. They were fixing the towrope—the tractor driver and Faddey's lame son, and Matryona (heaven knows what brought her there) were with them, between the tractor and the sledge. What help did she think she could be to the men? She was forever meddling in men's work. Hadn't a bolting horse nearly tipped her into the lake once, through a hole in the ice? Why did she have to go to the damned crossing? She had handed over the top room and owed nothing to anybody. The engine driver kept a lookout in case the train from Cherusti rushed up on them. Its headlamps would be visible a long way off. But two engines coupled together came from the other direction, from our station, backing without lights.

Why they were without lights nobody knows. When an engine is backing, coal dust blows into the driver's eyes from the tender and he can't see very well. The two engines flew into them and crushed the three people between the tractor and the sledge to pulp. The tractor was wrecked, the sledge was matchwood, the rails were buckled, and both engines turned over.

"But how was it they didn't hear the engines coming?"

"The tractor engine was making such a din."

"What about the bodies?"

"They won't let anybody in. They've roped them off."

"What was that somebody was telling me about the express?"

"The nine o'clock express goes through our station at a good clip and on to the crossing. But the two drivers weren't hurt when their engines crashed, they jumped out and ran back along the line waving their hands, and they managed to stop the train. The nephew was hurt by a beam as well. He's hiding at Klavka's now so that they won't know he was at the crossing. If they find out they'll drag him in as a witness. . . . 'Don't know lies up, and do know gets tied up.' Kira's husband didn't get a scratch. He tried to hang himself, they had to cut him down. It's all because of me, he says, my aunty's killed and my brother. Now he's gone and given himself up. But the madhouse is where he'll be going, not prison. Oh, Matryona, my dearest Matryona. . . ."

Matryona was gone. Someone close to me had been killed. And on her last day I had scolded her for wearing my jacket.

The lovingly drawn red and yellow woman in the book advertisement smiled happily on.

Old Masha sat there weeping a little longer. Then she got up to go. And suddenly she asked me, "Ignatich, you remember, Matryona had a gray shawl. She meant it to go to my Tanya when she died, didn't she?"

She looked at me hopefully in the half-darkness—surely I hadn't forgotten?

No, I remembered. "She said so, yes."

"Well, listen, maybe you could let me take it with me now. The family will be swarming in tomorrow and I'll never get it then." And she gave me another hopeful, imploring look. She had been Matryona's friend for half a century, the only one in the village who truly loved her.

No doubt she was right.

"Of course—take it."

She opened the chest, took out the shawl, tucked it under her coat, and went out.

The mice had gone mad. They were running furiously up and down the walls, and you could almost see the green wallpaper rippling and rolling over their backs.

In the morning I had to go to school. The time was three o'clock. The only thing to do was to lock up and go to bed.

Lock up, because Matryona would not be coming.

I lay down, leaving the light on. The mice were squeaking, almost moaning, racing and running. My mind was weary and wandering, and I couldn't rid myself of an uneasy feeling that an invisible Matryona was flitting about and saying good-bye to her home.

And suddenly I imagined Faddey standing there, young and black-haired, in the dark patch by the door, with his ax uplifted. "If it wasn't my own brother, I'd chop the both of you to bits."

The threat had lain around for forty years, like an old broad sword in a corner, and in the end it had struck its blow.

3

When it was light the women went to the crossing and brought back all that was left of Matryona on a hand sledge with a dirty sack over it. They threw off the sack to wash her. There was just a mess . . . no feet, only half a body, no left hand. One woman said, "The Lord has left her her right hand. She'll be able to say her prayers where she's going."

Then the whole crowd of rubber plants were carried out of the cottage—these plants that Matryona had loved so much that once when smoke woke her up in the night she didn't rush to save her house but to tip the plants onto the floor in case they were suffocated. The women swept the floor clean. They hung a wide towel of old homespun over Matryona's dim mirror. They took down the jolly posters. They moved my table out of the way. Under the icons, near the windows, they stood a rough unadorned coffin on a row of stools.

In the coffin lay Matryona. Her body, mangled and lifeless, was covered with a clean sheet. Her head was swathed in a white kerchief. Her face was almost undamaged, peaceful, more alive than dead.

The villagers came to pay their last respects. The women even brought their small children to take a look at the dead. And if anyone raised a lament, all the women, even those who had looked in out of idle curiosity, always joined in, wailing where they stood by the door or the wall, as though they were providing a choral accompaniment. The men stood stiff and silent with their caps off.

The formal lamentation had to be performed by the women of Matryona's family. I observed that the lament followed a coldly calculated, age-old ritual. The more distant relatives went up to the coffin for a short while and made low wailing noises over it. Those who considered themselves closer kin to the dead woman began their lament in the doorway and when they got as far as the coffin, bowed down and roared out their grief right in the face of the departed. Every lamenter made up her own melody. And expressed her own thoughts and feelings.

I realized that a lament for the dead is not just a lament, but a kind of politics. Matryona's three sisters swooped, took possession of the cottage, the goat, and the stove, locked up the chest, ripped the two hundred rubles for the funeral out of the coat lining, and drummed it into everybody who came that only they were near relatives. Their lament over the coffin went like this, "Oh, nanny, nanny! Oh nan-nan! All we had in the world was you! You could have lived in peace and quiet, you could. And we should always have been kind and loving to you. Now your top room's been the death of you. Finished you off, it has, the cursed thing! Oh, why did you have to take it down? Why didn't you listen to us?"

Thus the sisters' laments were indictments of Matryona's husband's family: they shouldn't have made her take the top room down. (There was an underlying meaning, too: you've taken the top room, all right, but we won't let you have the house itself!)

Matryona's husband's family, her sisters-in-law, Efim and Faddey's sisters, and the various nieces lamented like this, "*Oh poor auntie, poor auntie!* Why didn't you take better care of yourself! Now they're angry with us for sure. Our own dear Matryona you were, and it's your own fault! The top room is nothing to do with it. Oh why did you go where death was waiting for you? Nobody asked you to go there. And what a way to die! Oh why didn't you listen to us?" (Their answer to the others showed through these laments: we are not to blame for her death, and the house we'll talk about later.)

But the "second" Matryona, a coarse, broad-faced woman, the substitute Matryona whom Faddey had married so long ago for the sake of her name, got out of step with family policy, wailing and sobbing over the coffin in her simplicity, "*Oh my poor dear sister!* You won't be angry with me, will you now? Oh-oh-oh! How we used to talk and talk, you and me! Forgive a poor miserable woman! You've gone to be with your dear mother, and you'll come for me some day, for sure! Oh-oh-oh-oh! . . ."

At every "oh-oh-oh" it was as though she were giving up the ghost. She writhed and gasped, with her breast against the side of the coffin. When her lament went beyond the ritual prescription, the women, as though acknowledging its success, all started saying, "Come away now, come away."

Matryona came away, but back she went again, sobbing with even greater abandon. Then an ancient woman came out of a corner, put her hand on Matryona's shoulder, and said, "There are two riddles in this world: how I was born, I don't remember, how I shall die, I don't know."

And Matryona fell silent at once, and all the others were silent, so that there was an unbroken hush.

But the old woman herself, who was much older than all the other old women there and didn't seem to belong to Matryona at all, after a while started wailing, "Oh, my poor sick Matryona! Oh my poor Vasilyevna! Oh what a weary thing it is to be seeing you into your grave!"

There was one who didn't follow the ritual, but wept straight-forwardly, in the fashion of our age, which has had plenty of practice at it. This was Matryona's unfortunate foster daughter, Kira, from Cherusti, for whom the top room had been taken down and moved. Her ringlets were pitifully out of curl. Her eyes looked red and bloodshot. She didn't notice that her headscarf was slipping off out in the frosty air and that her arm hadn't found the sleeve of her coat. She walked in a stupor from her foster mother's coffin in one house to her brother's in another. They were afraid she would lose her mind, because her husband had to go on trial as well.

It looked as if her husband was doubly at fault: not only had he been moving the top room, but as an engine driver, he knew the regulations about unprotected crossings and should have gone down to the station to warn them about the tractor. There were a thousand people on the Urals express that night, peacefully sleeping in the upper and lower berths of their dimly lit carriages, and all those lives were nearly cut short. All because of a few greedy people, wanting to get their hands on a plot of land, or not wanting to make a second trip with a tractor.

All because of the top room, which had been under a curse ever since Faddey's hands had started itching to take it down.

The tractor driver was already beyond human justice. And the railway authorities were also at fault, both because a busy crossing was unguarded and because the coupled engines were traveling without lights. That was why they had tried at first to blame it all on the drink, and then to keep the case out of court.

The rails and the track were so twisted and torn that for three days, while the coffins were still in the house, no trains ran—they were diverted onto another line. All Friday, Saturday, and Sunday, from the end of the investigation until the funeral, the work of repairing the line went on day and night. The repair gang was frozen, and they made fires to warm themselves and to light their work at night, using the boards and beams from the second sledge, which were there for the taking, scattered around the crossing.

The first sledge just stood there, undamaged and still loaded, a little way beyond the crossing.

One sledge, tantalizingly ready to be towed away, and the other perhaps still to be plucked from the flames—that was what harrowed the soul of black-bearded Faddey all day Friday and all day Saturday. His daughter was going out of her mind, his son-in-law had a criminal charge hanging over him, in his own house lay the son he had killed, and along the street the woman he had killed and whom he had once loved. But Faddey stood by the coffins, clutching his beard, only for a short time, and went away again. His high forehead was clouded by painful thoughts, but what he was thinking about was how to save the timbers of the top room from the flames and from Matryona's scheming sisters.

Going over the people of Talnovo in my mind, I realized that Faddey was not the only one like that.

Property, the people's property, or my property, is strangely called our "goods." If you lose your goods, people think you disgrace yourself and make yourself look foolish.

Faddey dashed about, never stopping to sit down, from the settlement to the station, from one official to another, there he stood with his bent back, leaning heavily on his stick, and begged them all to take pity on an old man and give him permission to recover the top room.

Somebody gave permission. And Faddey gathered together his surviving sons, sons-in-law, and nephews, got horses from the kolkhoz and from the other side of the wrecked crossing, by a roundabout way that led through three villages, brought the remnants of the top room home to his yard. He finished the job in the early hours of Sunday morning.

On Sunday afternoon they were buried. The two coffins met in the middle of the village, and the relatives argued about which of them should go first. Then they put them side by side on an open sledge, the aunt and the nephew, and carried the dead over the damp snow, with a gloomy February sky above, to the churchyard two villages away. There was an unkind wind, so the priest and the deacon waited inside the church and didn't come out to Talnovo to meet them.

A crowd of people walked slowly behind the coffins, singing in chorus. Outside the village they fell back.

When Sunday came the women were still fussing around the house. An old woman mumbled psalms by the coffin, Matryona's sisters flitted about, popping things into the oven, and the air round the mouth of the stove trembled with the heat of red-hot peats, those Matryona had carried in a sack from a distant bog. They were making unappetizing pies with poor flour.

When the funeral was over and it was already getting on toward evening, they gathered for the wake. Tables were put together to make a long one, which hid the place where the coffin had stood in the morning. To start with, they all stood round the table, and an old man, the husband of a sister-in-law, said the Lord's Prayer. Then they poured everybody a little honey and warm water,[9] just enough to cover the bottom of the bowl. We spooned it up without bread or anything, in memory of the dead. Then we ate something and drank vodka and the conversation became more animated. Before the jelly they all stood up and sang "Eternal remembrance" (they explained to me that it had to be sung before the jelly). There was more drinking. By now they were talking louder than ever, and not about Matryona at all. The sister-in-law's husband started boasting, "Did you notice, brother Christians, that they took the funeral service slowly today? That's because Father Mikhail noticed me. He knows I know the service. Other times, it's saints defend us, homeward wend us, and that's all."

At last the supper was over. They all rose again. They sang "Worthy Is She."[1] Then again, with a triple repetition of "Eternal Remembrance." But the voices were hoarse and out of tune, their faces drunken, and nobody put any feeling into this "eternal memory."

Then most of the guests went away, and only the near relatives were left. They pulled out their cigarets and lit up, there were jokes and laughter. There was some mention of Matryona's husband and his disappearance. The sister-in-law's husband, striking himself on the chest, assured me and the cobbler who was married to one of Matryona's sisters, "He was dead, Efim was dead! What could stop him coming back if he wasn't? If I knew they were going to hang me when I got to the old place, I'd come back just the same!"

The cobbler nodded in agreement. He was a deserter and had never left the old place. All through the war he was hiding in his mother's cellar.

The stern and silent old woman who was more ancient than all the

---

9. Traditionally Russians have *kutiia,* a wheat pudding with honey and almonds, at funerals and memorial gatherings; the villagers are too poor to have the main ingredients and their honey and water are symbolic of the *kutiia.*   1. "Eternal Remembrance" and "Worthy Is She" are dirges, religious hymns sung to honor the dead; the village still follows religious rituals in time of crisis and does not use the civil ceremony proposed by the Soviet government.

ancients was staying the night and sat high up on the stove. She looked down in mute disapproval on the indecently animated youngsters of fifty and sixty.

But the unhappy foster daughter, who had grown up within these walls, went away behind the kitchen screen to cry.

Faddey didn't come to Matryona's wake—perhaps because he was holding a wake for his son. But twice in the next few days he walked angrily into the house for discussions with Matryona's sisters and the deserting cobbler.

The argument was about the house. Should it go to one of the sisters or to the foster daughter? They were on the verge of taking it to court, but they made peace because they realized that the court would hand over the house to neither side, but to the Rural District Council. A bargain was struck. One sister took the goat, the cobbler and his wife got the house, and to make up Faddey's share, since he had "nursed every bit of timber here in his arms," in addition to the top room which had already been carried away, they let him have the shed which had housed the goat and the whole of the inner fence between the yard and the garden.

Once again the insatiable old man got the better of sickness and pain and became young and active. Once again he gathered together his surviving sons and sons-in-law, they dismantled the shed and the fence, he hauled the timbers himself, sledge by sledge, and only toward the end did he have Antoshka of 8-D, who didn't slack this time, to help him.

They boarded Matryona's house up till the spring, and I moved in with one of her sisters-in-law, not far away. This sister-in-law on several occasions came out with some recollection of Matryona and made me see the dead woman in a new light. "Efim didn't love her. He used to say, 'I like to dress in an educated way, but she dresses any old way, like they do in the country.' Well then, he thinks, if she doesn't want anything, he might as well drink whatever's to spare. One time I went with him to the town to work, and he got himself a madam there and never wanted to come back to Matryona."

Everything she said about Matryona was disapproving. She was slovenly, she made no effort to get a few things about her. She wasn't the saving kind. She didn't even keep a pig, because she didn't like fattening them up for some reason. And the silly woman helped other people without pay. (What brought Matryona to mind this time was that the garden needed plowing, and she couldn't find enough helpers to pull the plow.)

Matryona's sister-in-law admitted that she was warmhearted and straightforward, but pitied and despised her for it.

It was only then, after these disapproving comments from her sister-in-law, that a true likeness of Matryona formed before my eyes, and I understood her as I never had when I lived side by side with her.

Of course! Every house in the village kept a pig. But she didn't. What can be easier than fattening a greedy piglet that cares for nothing in the world but food! You warm his swill three times a day, you live for him—then you cut his throat and you have some fat.

But she had none.

She made no effort to get things round her. She didn't struggle and strain to buy things and then care for them more than life itself.

She didn't go all out after fine clothes. Clothes, that beautify what is ugly and evil.

She was misunderstood and abandoned even by her husband. She had lost six children, but not her sociable ways. She was a stranger to her sisters and sisters-in-law, a ridiculous creature who stupidly worked for others without pay. She didn't accumulate property against the day she died. A dirty-white goat, a gammy-legged cat, some rubber plants. . . .

We had all lived side by side with her and had never understood that she was the righteous one without whom, as the proverb says, no village can stand.[2]

Nor any city.

Nor our whole land.

2. See Genesis 18:23–33, the story of Sodom.

SHŌNO JUNZŌ
born 1921

The voice of Shōno Junzō, understated and subtly philosophical, is less often heard outside Japan than that of certain of his peers who speak in more theatrical tones or in a more overtly Japanese idiom. Tanizaki's yarn-spinning pyrotechnics, for example, or Kawabata's evocation of a world as rarefied as bonsai have found a ready audience among Western readers. But Shōno belongs to another wing of Japanese literature consisting of writers thought not to travel well in translation. Shōno's subject is the ordinariness (however fragile) of everyday life, which in contemporary Tokyo is neither pregnant with inherent drama nor so different from daily life in Manhattan or Cincinnati.

In fact, Shōno spent time in Ohio in the late 1950s, when a grant from the Rockefeller Foundation underwrote a year's study at Kenyon College in the small town of Gambier. By then he had launched his career as a writer whose specialty was to be quiet but acute observations of postwar Japanese life. A literary award in 1955, the Akutagawa Prize, allowed him to leave his job in the broadcasting company where he had worked since 1951 and to devote himself to writing an esteemed series of short stories about the psychological tensions of young marriage.

Shōno was born in 1921 in Osaka, the third son of the founder of a local school. Like Kojima Nobuo, fellow member of a loosely affiliated coterie that Japanese critics christened "the third newcomers" (because they rose to prominence in the mid-1950s, after two other postwar literary groups had been identified), Shōno studied English literature in the university before graduating in time to serve during the final days of World War II. He was stationed as an ensign on the Izu Peninsula in central Japan, where he worked in a unit building artillery emplacements.

Unlike Kojima's, however, Shōno's wartime experiences do not seem to have colored his writing. While Kojima's view of the absurdity of war carried over into his postwar fiction, Shōno's attitude is not nearly so dark, nor is it satirical. If, for Kojima, the loser's survival in postwar Japan is a tragicomic study in debasement and futility, Shōno gravitated to a different kind of subject: family life and its essence. Relations between family members, particularly husband and wife, may be as vulnerable in Shōno's fiction, but the family unit is not dysfunctional, and the characters are more "normal" than what we tend to see in other postwar Japanese fiction. They have ordinary jobs and ordinary lives; they are not overwrought intellectuals.

Still Life (1960), Shōno's beautifully realized portrait of a family, is just what its title implies. The eighteen plotless episodes, both separately and cumulatively, have more the effect of a painting than a story. A husband and wife and their three young children are caught in midmotion, as though in snapshots. With the action frozen, readers have the leisure to contemplate these five people and their relations in the manner in which we would view the timeless inanimate objects—flowers, fruit, everyday utensils—of a seventeenth-century Dutch painting of domestic life. None of the characters even has a name, unless it happens to surface in dialogue. The father is Father, the mother is Mother, and so on. When *Still Life* appeared in English translation, reviewers soon noticed its universality. The critics' perception that one wonders whether it is especially about a Japanese family echoes the appraisal of Shōno's translator, who compares *Still Life* with the Thornton Wilder play *Our Town*. Like Wilder's classic depiction of small-town, everyday existence, Shōno's story places particular value on the small events of life and thereby distills from the commonplace something truly essential.

The incidents in each episode of *Still Life* are so static and unremarkable that they ought to be boring. A father takes his children fishing or tells them a story. A mother helps her young daughter and a friend make doughnuts. At bedtime, children fight over stuffed animals. It is Shōno's artistry, however, to link these episodes in such a way that fragmentary events and ordinary images assume an unexpectedly suggestive, metaphorical power.

Something dramatic, though, does happen, or has happened before the present time of the story—"the incident," as it is referred to opaquely, that intrudes now and then on the father's consciousness and casts a shadow over the family harmony. The painful memory is a ground theme running through the story, hinting that the self-contained world of homework and sibling rivalry, of pets and Sunday excursions may be more fragile than characters in the thick of life comprehend. Or, as Wilder writes in *Our Town*, "so all that was going on, and we didn't even notice."

The father, at least, does notice. The nature of "the incident" he remembers is left for the reader to infer, but its importance for him is unmistakable. Shōno has written a number of other stories about this same man and his family. In subsequent works, the cloud of anxiety experienced by the father gradually dissipates, leaving behind a hard-won tranquillity. But the sense remains that happiness is brittle, change ineluctable. In one story death intrudes. In another, the daughter's impending marriage introduces new, more subtle forms of tension into the family.

In all of the stories Shōno's identification with the father seems implicit, and this identification places his fiction squarely within a genre in twentieth-century Japan known as the *shishōsetsu*. The term is often misleadingly translated as "I-novel," after the German *Ich-roman*, though the Japanese form need be neither a first-person narrative nor a full-length novel. Essentially, the *shishōsetsu* is a highly personal work of fiction in which plot, characterization, and dramatic tension, if not absent, are subordinated to an introspective presentation whereby narrator and hero seem to share one center of consciousness, and the reader is encouraged to identify the author with the narrator and hero. The subjective quality of a *shishō-setsu* invites a subjective response from the reader. If the author becomes deeply involved in the hero's identity, so ultimately does the reader. This personal involvement encouraged by the *shishōsetsu* offers the reader an emotional fulfillment, and the completeness of such involvement and fulfillment seems to have developed into the criterion by which Japanese readers judge the success of a novel in the *shishōsetsu* tradition. This, in turn, has made degrees of honesty, or good faith, the yardstick of literary analysis. While the genre has been the subject of critical controversy since the 1920s, because some Japanese commentators have disdained what they see as a "soft" approach to criticism and others have considered the *shishōsetsu* inferior to more obviously constructed or representational works of Western literature (*Madame Bovary* or *War and Peace*, for example), its partisans argue that the truthfulness and immediacy of this subjective form more than suffice as literary merits.

In a sense, one may wonder if Japanese critics have made too much of the personal, or autobiographical, strain in their country's modern fiction, since it is not confined to their country. James Joyce, Marcel Proust, and Virginia Woolf also took fiction in a highly personal direction. Undeniably, twentieth-century fictional standards have upped the ante on social and especially psychological detail. Perhaps the raised expectations could only have been met by dredging that detail from the writer's own life.

In any case, contemplative impressionistic discourse, which seems to arise from intensely private imperatives and to invite the reader to share the author's privacy, has a venerable heritage in Japan. It can be traced to the unstructured, self-centered narratives known as *zuihitsu* ("followings of the brush") inaugurated by Sei Shōnagon in her *Pillow Book* (in Volume 1) of the eleventh century. Shōno's apparent close modeling of his stories on his own family's experiences, so that life and fiction are both works in progress, locates him in a line of Japanese writers of ancient provenance. The *zuihitsu-shishōsetsu* tradition inclines Japanese readers not to ask of Shōno a story in which something "happens," perhaps in part because the private life they are invited to witness creates a space for their own privacy.

From the smallest means Shōno creates a compelling depiction of the universal desire for a secure and happy home life and for familial affection. Because of their focus on everyday, contemporary life and because of Shōno's place in the important but little understood genre of the *shishōsetsu*, his stories afford us insight into Japanese society and its postwar culture. More important, they also tell us something essential about ourselves.

Twelve additional works by Shōno Junzō, arranged to form a continuing narrative, will be found in Wayne P. Lammers, trans., *"Still Life" and Other Stories* (1992). For fiction by Shōno's contemporaries, see the headnote for Kojima Nobuo (p. 2275). Highly recommended as a perceptive study of the *shishōsetsu*, although it focuses on writers before Shōno, is Edward Fowler, *The Rhetoric of Confession: Shishōsetsu in Early Twentieth-Century Japanese Fiction* (1988). For a study of Japan's most celebrated *shishōsetsu* writer, Shiga Naoya, see William F. Sibley, *The Shiga Hero* (1979); and for Shiga's major novel, see Edwin McClellan, trans., *A Dark Night's Passing* (1976). Also recommended is the study of another important writer of the *shishōsetsu* form: Phyllis I. Lyons, *The Saga of Dazai Osamu* (1985). Mishima Yukio's maiden work, *Confessions of a Mask* (1958), is an excellent example of the *shishōsetsu*; it has been translated by Meredith Weatherby.

PRONOUNCING GLOSSARY

The following list uses common English syllables to provide rough equivalents of selected words whose pronunciation may be unfamiliar to the general reader.

Ikuko: *ee-koo-ko*

Katsujiro: *kah-tsoo-jee-roh*

Kojima Nobuo: *koh-jee-mah noh-boo-oh*

Masuko: *mahs-koh*

Sei Shōnagon: *say shoh-nah-gohn*

shishōsetsu: *shee-shoh-se-tsoo*

Shōno Junzō: *shoh-noh joon-zoh*

Tanizaki: *tah-nee-zah-kee*

zuihitsu: *zoo-ee-hee-tsoo*

Still Life[1]

1

"Can we go to the fishing pond?" the boy pleaded.

It was a beautiful, windless day in early March, and spring seemed just around the corner.

"You don't want to go fishing," his father said. "You know you'd never catch anything."

"I do too want to. All the kids go. Masuko caught five the other day."

"What were they?"

"Goldfish."

"Oh. Goldfish." Father's voice showed his disappointment. "It's not much fun if all you get is goldfish."

"It is too fun. Some of the kids even catch big ones."

"Oh?"

"You'll catch something too, Dad. You will." The boy would be entering the second grade in another month.

"I don't know," Father said. "It'd be my first time. The only fishing I've ever done was in the ocean. I've never been to one of those artificial ponds." Even to him the excuse sounded rather feeble.

"You should try it," chimed in his daughter, soon to be a sixth grader. "Who knows? You just might catch something. And so what if you don't? It'll be fun anyway."

"I suppose you're right," he said. "I'll never know if I don't give it a try."

"If all three of us go, maybe at least one of us'll catch something," the girl said, seeing that her father had abandoned his reluctance. She often spoke to him like this, in an encouraging tone, when he seemed hesitant or worried about something. It was a remarkable way she had with him.

On that morning so many years before, this girl had lain in the corner of the room with her stuffed puppy, alone like an orphan, oblivious to the possibility that anything could be wrong. She had been just over one year old then.

"Have a good time!" Mother called after them. "Bring home your appe-

---

1. Translated by Wayne P. Lammers.

tites now, all of you." The three-year-old boy had to stay behind. He was too small to go fishing.

As they left the house, Father had a pleasant feeling inside. It felt good to set out on something he had never done before. And the children's enthusiasm was contagious.

The boy had brought along the tin bucket he used for his water projects in the yard. As they walked, Father watched it swing back and forth at his son's side. He should get out and do these things more often, he told himself. It was better to go along, to stop making excuses. It didn't really matter whether or not they caught anything. They had set out, bucket in hand—that was the important part. It seemed a little thing, but perhaps it was these little things that did the trick.

To begin with, anything was better than just sitting around doing nothing. All he ever did on his days off was loaf about the house. He never made plans for a Sunday outing, much less went anywhere when Sunday finally rolled around. Sometimes he felt sorry for his family. But he had been this way for a long time now, and the children had grown used to it. So far as they were concerned, holidays were for staying at home and playing by themselves. They had fun enough.

Still, it wasn't good for him to be so lazy. After all, the fishing pond was hardly ten minutes away.

Down the road, the pond came into view, surrounded by rice paddies. Beyond it rose the slope of a wooded hill. There were two ponds, actually—one stocked with small fish, for beginners, and the other with larger fish, for more experienced fishermen. As might be expected on a Sunday, both were crowded.

"One adult and one child," Father said, as if he were buying tickets for the train. He didn't know any differently, since this was the first time he had come. He paid for an hour and got two fishing poles and some bait. But the last person to use one of the poles had returned it with the line badly tangled. No doubt he had gone home in a huff after failing to catch anything. Father couldn't tell where to start, so he asked the lady at the gate to unravel it for him.

"There you go." She handed the pole back to him with a smile.

"It's fixed?"

"Yes, it should be okay now."

Too eager to wait, the boy had run on ahead, but now he was back. "C'mon, Dad, hurry up," he shouted. "I found a good spot. Over there." The place he pointed to, however, was at the pond for experienced fishermen. Not one of the people there was using the sort of flimsy pole the three newcomers had rented. It was also more expensive to fish there.

"We can't go over there," the girl said.

"But you should see. There's lots of big ones."

"No," the girl said softly. "That pond's too hard for us. Beginners have to fish here."

"Oh."

After the lady had shown him how to bait the hooks, Father joined the children at the beginners' pond. There were quite a few adults fishing there, too—men fishing alone, young married couples fishing together.

The three of them shared the two poles, but they failed to get so much as a nibble. Whenever someone else caught something, the boy ran off to have a look, and each time he would call back in a loud voice, "It's better over here, Dad."

"Listen," Father admonished. "Whether you catch anything or not, you're better off staying in one place. When somebody over there catches something, you might think it's a better spot, but it isn't really. It just seems that way. Some people are good at it and some people aren't, but even the good ones have to wait and be patient and not change places all the time if they want to catch anything. You'll never have any luck if you don't sit still."

His own words reminded him of a story he had read in English class in junior high school. It was called "Stick to Your Own Bush." As he remembered it, several children go off into the woods to pick wild raspberries. They spread out among the raspberry bushes scattered here and there, and before long shouts of "I found some! I found some!" ring out, first from one direction, then another. One of the boys, who has yet to find a single berry, races about from place to place pursuing each new shout. When all the others have filled their baskets, he has only a few berries. "You'll never get very many that way," he is told. "Stick to your own bush." And that was the moral of the story—that it's the same with everything we do.

As a boy he had found it a dull and uninspiring story. But now he was a father, and here he was, telling his own son the same thing.

The scolding put an end to the boy's shouting, but, with no change in their own luck, he still darted off periodically to examine the fish that other people caught.

From where Father was sitting he could not actually see the fish in the water. He had to admit there might not be any there. Nonetheless he stuck to his own bush.

"I guess this isn't our day," he said to his daughter beside him. "It's not so easy after all." She went on gazing at her float.

Every now and then women with shopping baskets passed along the road in front of the pond. Some of them stopped briefly to watch the fishermen. Father had been observing these movements on the road when he turned around to find his float bobbing up and down. He raised his pole with a jerk. On the end of the line was a tiny orange glimmer.

"We got one!" cried the girl.

The boy, who had been watching an older boy fish, heard her voice and came running.

"We got one! We got one!" he clamored.

"Simmer down. Don't make such a racket," Father scolded. But his face beamed. It was indeed a tiny goldfish that had come up on the end of his line, hardly any bigger than a guppy.

Now for the first time they had a use for the bucket the boy had brought along. The little fish swam about in the pail as if to belie the fact that a moment ago it had been caught on the tip of a hook.

2

"W-w-when they've tried it once," the elderly doctor said, "they get so they try it again and again."

"That's what I was afraid of," the young husband sighed. Never had he imagined that only three years after his marriage he would feel so beaten and discouraged.

"At least that's frequently the case."

Would it happen again? he had asked disconsolately. Was she likely to try it again?

"T-t-t-t-taking it hard, are you?" the doctor burst into a boisterous, stuttering laugh. But there was a measure of sympathy in his voice. This distinctive laugh of the doctor's had long been familiar to the young man.

"Once is enough, I suppose?"

"It certainly is."

The doctor reached for the bottle and poured some more whiskey for his guest. The young man watched as the dark liquid rose inside the glass.

"These things can happen. You just never know," the doctor said. He picked up the pitcher and mixed a little water with the whiskey.

"As they say, we all walk in darkness."

The old doctor's sitting room was an annex of sorts, built on a level slightly higher than the main section of the house. He spent most of his time alone here, apart from the rest of his family. When he needed something, he simply clapped his hands. He never left the room except to see a patient.

The two sat facing each other, the bottle of whiskey on the table between them. Somehow, the young man always felt reassured when he talked with the old doctor like this.

The young man had been born and raised in this town, and his earliest memory of the doctor's clinic went back to when he was in the third grade. One day he was playing in a field near his house with a friend, running about barefoot on the grass, when all of a sudden he stepped on a piece of wood with a large nail sticking through it. His friend rushed off to get his mother, while he sat there crying. It had seemed an eternity before she appeared at the edge of the field.

The next thing he remembered was lying on an examination table in a dimly lit room while the doctor removed the nail. Tense faces peered down at him from above.

That had been his first visit to this place.

"H-h-how's her foot coming along?" the doctor asked. "Where she burned it."

"I think it still hurts her to walk on it."

"Yes, I'm sure it does. The burn's right on the bottom of her foot."

"She claims it doesn't bother her anymore, though."

The doctor gave him a sympathetic smile, then lowered his eyes.

"I was practically in a state of shock myself," the young man said after another sip of his drink. "I didn't realize the cloth had come loose."

"Of course not, of course not," the doctor laughed with his usual stutter.

"It was hardly the time you would notice something like that. Not even your wife noticed, and it was her own foot."

The young man remembered the chill he had felt when he touched his wife's arms and legs. At first he had still been able to detect a slight warmth, but gradually her body had turned colder and colder. Frantically, he had filled three hot water bottles with piping hot water and put them in her bed: one on either side of her chest, the third at her feet.

Later he had held her—first one way, then another—for the doctor to examine her. Beads of sweat had dripped from his forehead. He couldn't tell exactly when she had gotten burned; the cloth he had wrapped around the hot water bottle must have come loose when her legs moved.

The doctor reached for the whiskey and poured himself another glass. "This kind of burn takes a long time to heal. I've had cases before: people go to bed with a hot water bottle and don't realize they've burned themselves until the next morning."

"So it happens often?"

"I guess if you're sleeping soundly it doesn't hurt enough to wake you up. That's the big problem. The damage goes a lot deeper than other burns."

In his mind the young man pictured his wife still limping a little from the accident as she made her way about the quiet house.

3

"Eight-year-old Susie died three days after coming down with the flu," Father read from the paper. He had found an article among the news from America that he thought the others might like to hear. They were all sitting around the breakfast table, eating.

"Susie is a little black girl," he explained before reading on. "Many friends and neighbors came to express their sympathy to the grief-stricken parents. The funeral service took place without event. But then, when it came time to lower the casket into the grave—"

"Did something go wrong?" the girl broke in.

Father answered her interruption with a sharp look that said "Let me finish," then continued the story. "When the parents raised the lid of the casket for a final look at their daughter, Susie opened her eyes and said, 'Mommy, can I have some milk?' The incident has put the entire town in an uproar."

"She came back to life?" the girl asked. She seemed anxious to have her father say it in so many words.

"That's right, she came back to life."

"Weird," the older boy said and flopped backward onto the tatami.[2] The three-year-old promptly followed suit.

"Imagine what a shock it would have been!" Father said. He tried to form a mental picture of the small southern town where Susie and her parents lived, though, of course, he could not really tell how the houses

---

2. Straw mats, each measuring approximately six by three feet, used as flooring in traditional Japanese houses.

or streets would have looked. The cemetery would be on the outskirts of town, no doubt, but what was the surrounding area like?

"What an awful story!" his wife said.

"Why? What do you mean?"

"Oh, I don't know," she said, looking very ill at ease. "I mean, my goodness, the child was supposed to be dead when all of a sudden she wakes up and starts talking. If I were the mother, I'd have been terrified." Her husband stared back at her but said nothing. "Wouldn't you be scared?"

Suddenly a strange voice filled the room: "Mommy, can I have some milk?"

It was the girl. She had leaned back against the wall and was gazing blankly into space, pretending to be Susie at the moment she came back to life.

What would it sound like? Father wondered: the voice of someone who had all but entered the realm of the dead and then returned suddenly to the brightness of this world.

"Ohhh, don't do that," Mother scolded the girl. "It gives me the shivers."

4

The goldfish from the Sunday excursion was given a place in the children's study. It swam about happily in its glass bowl on the sill of the bay window.

"What a healthy goldfish!" Mother often exclaimed. She was the one who looked after the new family pet most of the time—changing its water, feeding it little scraps of bread, and giving it a pinch of salt every now and then.

When Father and the children had come home with their tiny catch in the toy bucket, she had remarked on what a nice shape it had. It was true, Father had had to agree: It might be only so big, but it did have a nice, sleek body.

An almost invisible tinge of red showed here and there on its stomach and fins as well as on its head.

"I caught it when I was looking the other way," he had said. "We'd better take good care of it."

The study held quite a few things besides desks and bookshelves for the two children who were in school. Their mother's dresser was kept here, together with her sewing machine. In one corner was a basket containing some wooden blocks, the base of a ring-toss game, a baseball glove, and several other items—the few toys the children hadn't managed to break. In another corner stood two large suitcases, one on top of the other. They had seldom been used; most of the time they merely took up space.

To call it the children's study, then, was something of a misnomer. It was the room where they put everything that didn't fit anywhere else.

On the wall were two pictures. The one entitled "Star Children" had been made by the girl as a summer vacation project several years before. Two little girls were holding hands and floating in a light-blue sky, a star made of silver paper atop each of their heads. Their clothes had been cut from scraps of leftover fabric, and bits of yellow and gray yarn had been pasted on for hair. The second picture, entitled "Cowboys on the Plain," was a crayon drawing done by the older of the boys. One of the cowboys, a rifle at his shoulder, had just shot a large bird in a tree; the other was about to lasso a runaway horse. A bull came charging toward them and a rabbit was scampering by.

Two rattan chairs had also found their way into the room. Since they would block the doorway if set side by side, they were usually stacked on top of each other. The children liked to hitch these together with their desk chairs to make a stagecoach. One of them sat on the coachman's seat and the other two would get inside. Then, with many a shout and crack of the whip and clatter of the wheels, they would be off, racing full tilt along some old highway.

Such was the room into which the goldfish had come. It hardly seemed a safe place for a fragile glass bowl filled with water. There was no telling when a ball or some other toy might land in it, or when one of the children would get pushed against it and knock it over.

But incredibly enough, nothing happened. The children were no better behaved than they had ever been, yet somehow the bowl survived. As the days went by it blended in with the other things in the room, and no one worried about it anymore.

Still, Father could never quite get over the feeling that someone would break it yet, someday.

5

"Good night, Dad!"
"Good night, Mom!"
"Good night, everyone!"

The echo of the children's voices seemed to linger in the air. Only a short while ago they had been racing to see who could put on his pajamas and make it into bed first. Now, with the hush of night settling over the house, only Father remained awake.

He contemplated the figure of his wife sleeping beside him. This woman, lying on her side, facing him—this was the woman he had married. For fifteen years he had slept with her, in the same bed, every night.

As a child he had slept alone, and in the navy he had slept alone. But from the day he was married, he had started sharing a bed with another person. Two people who scarcely knew each other had begun to sleep together, just like that.

There had in fact been a short time when they did not share the same bed. How long had it been? Three months? Not even that, probably. They had slept in separate rooms, his wife with their baby daughter, who had just turned one. But the arrangement had come to a quick end. After the incident, they had gone back to sleeping together. And they had done so ever since.

Awake alone in the stillness, Father thought back to their wedding night. He remembered the bright moonlight shining through the window, illumining his wife's face as she slept quietly beside him. She had hardly seemed to breathe. There was a small ribbon in her hair.

That was our first night together, he thought to himself.

The book he had been reading slipped from his hand. He picked it up again and started looking for his place.

"Here it is," he mumbled. "No, wait, I've read this already." He turned several more pages. Was this it? No, he remembered this part too. Where could it have been?

Choosing a page at random, he forced open his heavy eyelids and began to read. Within moments they drooped shut, and the book fell from his hand.

6

"I forget if it was England or America, but I read a story about a boy who found a duck's egg and made it hatch," the boy told his father in their evening bath.

"He *hatched* a duck's egg?"

"Uh-huh."

"Where did he find it?"

"I don't know."

"Somewhere in the country?"

"Uh-huh, in the country."

"Near a stream or pond, I suppose."

"Maybe. Anyway, he wanted to make it hatch, so he tied it to his stomach with a piece of cloth."

"Where?"

"Right here." The boy cupped his hands at his side. Father could tell that he had picked the spot arbitrarily.

"He kept it warm like that all the time for twenty days or so. Even at school, and even when he went to bed."

"For twenty days?"

"Uh-huh, something like that, I don't remember exactly. Anyway, the egg finally hatched right in the middle of class, and the teacher and everyone was really surprised."

"That's amazing," Father said. "It actually hatched during class?"

"Uh-huh."

"And everyone was surprised?"

"Uh-huh."

"Is this something you read at school?"

"Uh-huh. On the bulletin board in the hall. There's a big paper with stories from all over the world."

"Was there a picture?"

"Some of the stories have pictures, but this one didn't."

"When did you read this story?"

"A long time ago."

"Back in first grade?"

"Uh-huh."

"And you happened to think of it now?"

"Uh-huh."

Father wondered what had made him remember the story. "You'd think he would've broken it," he said. "I wonder how he had it tied."

"I bet the egg wouldn't last a day if I did it," the boy said. "I'd forget about it when I was playing. Do you think you could do it, Dad?"

"No, I doubt it. Probably not," he said. "All right, ready to get out?"

"Yep." The boy jumped out of the tub.

"Just a minute," Father stopped him. "Did you wash your face?"

"My face?"

"If you have to think about it, you obviously didn't."

"Yes I did."

"Ohhh no, you can't fool me. Your face isn't even wet. Since when do you take a bath without washing your face? Come on. Stop stalling."

"Okay." The boy took the lid off the soap dish and filled it with hot water.

"Hey, no playing around now. Just wash your face."

"I will, I will." He laid his washcloth over the soap dish.

"Come on."

"Just a second." With a slow and deliberate motion he rubbed soap into the washcloth. Then, bringing the cloth to his lips, he blew on it gently. A soft bank of suds began to form.

"See."

"So that's what you wanted to do."

"Watch. They'll get bigger and bigger."

"Fine, fine. They're plenty big already."

"Isn't it neat?"

"Sure."

"You wanna try it?"

"No. You've shown me your little trick now, so hurry up with your face."

"Just a little more."

The heap of suds quivered gently as it swelled. Before long the boy's face was completely hidden.

7

"I wonder if you remember that movie we saw," Father said to his daughter. She was sewing a blouse for her doll.

"What movie?"

"When you were in the first grade. Or was it kindergarten? No, it wasn't the year we moved; it was the year after. So you would've been in first grade."

The family had moved here from another city when the girl was in kindergarten. The older boy had just started putting a few words together; the second had not yet been born. Father could still remember the long train ride and his first glimpse of their new house standing by itself in the middle of some open farmland.

The following year, in the winter, he had taken his daughter to see a movie.

"The foreman at a construction site falls into a pit being filled with concrete."

"Oh yeah, I remember," the girl said.

"How much do you remember?"

She stopped stitching. "The man was a carpenter, wasn't he?"

"Well, yes, he built houses. He laid bricks, though, so I suppose you'd call him a mason. He was in Italy at first, but then he got on a ship and came to New York."

"He was really poor."

"That's right. That was why he came to America. He couldn't make a living in Italy."

They had seen the movie in a theater at the back of a short alleyway, just off the main thoroughfare in front of the station. Even with their overcoats on, it had been chilly inside.

"He was sick or something and couldn't go to work."

"I think he had hurt himself," Father said, still trying to retrieve the details from his own hazy memory. "That's right. He becomes foreman of a demolition crew tearing down an old building, but then something goes wrong between him and his men and they don't get along very well anymore. First the men stop speaking to him, then they walk out on him. So he has to work all by himself. Pretty soon a wall falls over on him and his leg gets crushed."

"That's why he couldn't work?"

"Something like that."

"Oh, I remember now. It's when his leg finally gets better and he goes back to work that he falls into the hole they're filling with concrete. He screams for help but there's too much noise and no one hears him. So the concrete keeps getting higher and higher."

"And in the end only his head shows."

"I covered my eyes, it was so scary. But I couldn't help hearing his screams."

"What happened next?"

"His wife comes out with kind of a blank look on her face, and someone's talking to her."

"Right. Since her husband was killed on the job, she's supposed to get paid a lot of money. Someone asks her what she plans to do with it, but she only shakes her head, to say she doesn't know. Or maybe she means she hasn't even thought about it. Do you remember anything else?"

"Unh-unh."

"No? How about the book I bought you before we went into the movie?"

"Unh-unh." She picked up her sewing and began stitching again. Father watched the way her hands moved.

As he remembered, it was a picture book, but he couldn't recall the title. He had bought her the book to try to make up for dragging her along, on their one day off, to a movie that *he* wanted to see. Not only was it a foreign film, but the things he had heard about it suggested that it might be a bit heavy going for a six-year-old.

The first few scenes were mild enough. One of the mason's friends at work tells him he ought to get married and suggests a girl he knows. The mason starts seeing the girl and falls in love with her. And she falls in love with him.

"But what about a house?" she asks. "I can't marry you if you don't have a house." Her family, too, had emigrated from Italy. She knows what it's like to be poor. She knows how miserable life can be for a couple who marry without a house of their own.

The mason tells her that he has a house, believing this is the only way he can get her to marry him. The wedding is held. Immigrant families from the neighborhood gather for a joyous celebration.

Everything was fine up to this point. But then the bride finds out that the house she thought was theirs belongs to someone else. Her happy smile vanishes. She had always been a cheerful, lighthearted girl, but now she sinks into gloom.

They begin their married life in a small, shabby apartment. On the wall they carve little notches with a knife, a record of their determination, no matter what the sacrifice, to save enough money to buy a house. Then a child is born.

As the movie continued, the events unfolding on screen became more and more harrowing. Early one morning the mason comes home drunk, having spent the night with another woman. On his way up the stairs of the apartment building, he decides to punish himself. He swings his open palm down on the pointed tip of the newel post.

No! Father caught his breath and quickly turned to look at his daughter. The book he had bought for her on the way to the theater was raised in front of her face. She had instinctively lifted it from her lap, as though merely closing her eyes would not be enough to block out the scene. Clever girl, he thought, breathing a sigh of relief.

The mason continued to suffer one misfortune after another, and with each frightening scene the book on the girl's lap rose, then fell again. Each time, her father let her know when the scene was over. "It's all right now," he would whisper. "You don't want to miss this part."

Near the end, when the mason fell into the pit, Father stole another look at his daughter. Once again she was hunched tensely behind her book. This time the book remained up through the entire scene, while the roar of the falling concrete and the sound of the mason's screams filled the theater.

Suddenly the screen fell silent, and the girl peeked tremulously from behind her book. The mason was nowhere to be seen. His bereaved wife stood all alone, utterly stricken.

"Did . . . did he die?" the girl asked in a tiny voice.

"Yes," he answered.

Father recalled all this as he watched his daughter work at her sewing. That book had really come in handy then, he thought. It had helped her get through the movie without having to watch the scary scenes.

In the same way, his daughter had been spared knowledge of what had happened in her own home on that morning long ago. She was still an infant at the time, and could not have known the meaning of her mother's deep sleep. An invisible hand had gently covered her eyes.

8

"Hey Dad," the older boy said. "Tell us something that begins with s."

"Something that begins with s?"

"Uh-huh. S-t."

"S-t?"

"S-t-o-r-y. A story."

"What about a story?"

"We want you to tell us one."

"I don't know any stories," Father protested.

"You do too."

"I can't think of any."

"How about the wild boar story?"

"But I've told you that one lots of times."

"That's okay."

Father had run out of excuses. "During the summer," he began, "boars always sleep. They stay at home in their dens, lying on big soft beds made of thatch, and all they do is sleep and sleep and sleep. Thatch—that's what the old hunter who told me this story called it—is a plant that grows in the mountains. Besides using it for beds, the boars make roofs out of it, to keep off the rain when there's a storm and to shade themselves on hot, sunny days. It works very nicely, both ways. So the boars just lie around sleeping in their cozy little thatched houses, day in, day out, all summer long. If that isn't the easy life!" he exclaimed enviously, glancing from the older boy to the younger.

"The old hunter told me, though, that you can't eat boar's meat in the summer. It doesn't taste good. So I guess maybe it's not such a good idea to sit around doing nothing after all. You see, when they butcher a summer boar, there's always a layer of fat as stiff as a board right under the skin. In fact that's what the hunters call it—a 'board.' And they say a boar with a board isn't any good because you can't eat the meat. But actually, the board has a special purpose. It helps keep the boar's energy inside its body so that it can sleep the whole summer long."

"That's why badger's fat is better, right?"

"Right. Badgers are the opposite of boars. They sleep through the winter, which means they have a lot of fat then and almost none in the summer. Badger's fat is really good. If you take some from just under the skin and heat it in a pan, you get a smooth, clear oil. Oh, by the way, there's another special name the hunters use: 'cukes.' That's what they call baby boars, because they have patches of fur on their backs that look just like big, fat cucumbers."

"That's kind of cute," the older boy said.

"That's kinda cute," the younger quickly repeated.

"Mmm, I thought so too. Now, one of the boar's favorite foods is earthworms, of all things. To think that an animal that big would go for worms—when they're known to gobble up a whole patch of sweet potatoes in a single night! The old hunter was really shaking his head over this one. He never could understand why such a big eater would take a liking to tiny little earthworms. And they like spiders and mud snails, too. They dig up the snails with their snouts, just like the worms, but it's a mystery how they eat them because they never leave any shells behind. They must either take them home to eat, or else they swallow the whole thing, shell and all. The hunter said he didn't imagine snails would taste very good with the shell on them." Father tilted his head thoughtfully, then shrugged, "Who knows what they do?"

He went on: "Hunting boars can be pretty rough, I guess. When you walk through the snow looking for tracks, your feet get soaked and clumps of snow fall on you from the branches overhead, and after a while your stomach starts to growl. An important thing to know when you're looking for tracks is that boars always travel the same paths. Maybe they're just the methodical type, or maybe they're actually afraid of something—I don't know. But in any case they always follow exactly in each other's footsteps. So no matter how many boars have gone by, it looks like only one. That's how consistent they are.

"One time a terrible thing happened because of this. At the power station in the mountains there's a sluice for the water that turns the generators, and it has a log lying across it for a bridge. One snowy morning the workers at the plant found three dead boars washed against the sluice gates. They went up along the sluice to see if they could find out what had happened, and when they got to the log they discovered there was an icy spot about halfway across. What had happened was the first boar to come along that morning had slipped on the ice and fallen into the water. Since the sluice is made of concrete and the sides go straight up and down, the boar had no place to climb out, and it got swept away by the current. Then the second one came along, and, because it followed the first boar's tracks onto the log, it slipped at the same place. After a while a third one came and fell into the water just like the others. Poor things. The men couldn't tell whether the boars had come one right after the other or a long time apart, but they could see what had happened from the way the tracks ended in the middle of the log."

"They should've watched out better," the older boy said.

"They should've watched out better," his younger brother echoed.

"That's right, they might have been okay if they had only stopped to think, 'Hey, wait a minute. The tracks don't go all the way across.' But they didn't, I guess. Well then, let's get back to the story about the old hunter meeting up with the wild boar."

The boys leaned forward. This was the part they had been waiting for.

"When he was in the mountains one day, the hunter came across a boar's den—made of thatch, as I said. He went home and told three of his hunter friends about it, and without letting anyone else know of their plans they got ready to go back for the kill. You see, you have to have at least three or four hunters to get a boar. If you try to do it alone, the boar will always get away. On the day of the hunt—remember, this all happened before the hunter was as old as he is now—the four of them set off for the mountains early in the morning. As it turned out, there was another group of hunters that had somehow gotten wind of their plans and had left even earlier. But the old hunter and his friends didn't know this yet, and they hiked on and on through the underbrush toward the boar's den. They came to a small cliff and started climbing it, when all of a sudden they heard a panting sound and boom!—"

Pretending he was the hunter crawling up the side of a cliff, Father jerked his head back.

"Just as the old hunter started to pull himself over the top, he found himself face to face with a giant boar. Talk about being caught off guard! They had all assumed the boar would be fast asleep in its den! The hunter immediately ducked down and reached for the rifle slung across his back. And the startled boar retreated, too, almost as quickly."

Now Father acted the part of the wild boar, first leaning forward as if poking his head over the edge of the cliff, then hastily pulling back.

"The hunter thought the boar had decided to run back the way it came, and if he didn't hurry it would get away, so he started to scramble up after it. But *whoosh!*—the boar flew right past his head, landed with a tremendous skid at the bottom of the cliff, and went crashing into the underbrush below. By the time the hunters turned around, all they could see were the broken branches where the boar had disappeared, and, farther on, the churning of the undergrowth as it ran off."

"Wow!" the older boy exclaimed.

The younger boy sat speechless, his wide eyes glued to his father's face.

"What had happened was that the other hunters, the ones who had gone earlier, had already shot at the boar and put it in a panic. That's probably why it made such a desperate leap. So when the old hunter thought the boar had taken off in the other direction, actually it had only backed up a little way to get a running start for the jump." Father broke into a laugh for a moment but then finished the story with a straight face. "The hunter said someone else finally shot the boar a week or so later. And that's the end of the story."

9

Their uncle came to visit them from the town where they had lived before moving to their present home. He brought with him a bag of walnuts for the children.

"What a nice gift," Father said afterward. "We couldn't spend money on nuts for ourselves—they're too much of an extravagance. But as a gift for someone with children, they're perfect. A real treat. A chance for the children to have something we couldn't normally afford."

But how would they divide up the nuts? Mother decided as follows: the girl could have seven, the older boy five, and the younger boy three. That would still leave two, so she and her husband could have one each.

The older boy went to get the hammer and quickly finished off his share. The younger boy ate all of his, too, with Mother's help to crack them open. Mother waited to eat hers until the following afternoon when she was at home alone with the younger boy. Father slipped his into his pocket; he still had it when he went to work the next day, but lost it somewhere the day after.

The girl decided to save hers for a while. She put them in a drawer in her desk, and took them out one at a time to polish them with a piece of felt. She wanted to bring out their shine.

A few days later she told her two best friends at school about the nuts. "They were a present from my uncle when he came to visit," she explained. "Do you like walnuts? If you want, I'll bring you some tomorrow."

"Sure," they said. They both liked walnuts.

Should she give them each two, or only one? she wondered. If she gave them two, they could rub them together in their hands to make a grinding noise, and they'd have more fun with them. But if she gave each of them two, that would leave her with fewer than half of her original seven. She wasn't sure she liked that idea. She enjoyed watching the walnuts roll around when she opened the drawer, and it just wouldn't be the same with only three nuts left. To give two would be better, of course. There was no question of that. But even one was better than nothing.

When she was getting ready for school the next day, she took four walnuts from the drawer and dropped them into the pocket of her skirt.

At school she ran into one of her friends. "I brought the walnuts," she said, reaching into her pocket. She still hadn't made up her mind whether she would give one or two.

"Here." She held out a single walnut.

"Thank you," her friend said gratefully.

That afternoon she walked home with her other friend, Ikuko. As they passed through the school gate she handed her a walnut.

"Thanks," said Ikuko.

"Try this. It's fun," she said, taking the other two nuts from her pocket and rubbing them together.

"That's neat," Ikuko said. The girl lent Ikuko one of her walnuts. Ikuko rubbed the nuts together for a while as they walked, then gave back the one she had borrowed.

"Not very long after that," the girl later recounted to her father, "we went by a place where some men were working on the road. We still had the nuts in our hands, but I guess I wasn't really paying attention because all of a sudden Ikuko said, 'Hey, you dropped one of your walnuts.' So we turned around to look for it right away, and guess what. We hadn't gone back more than five or six steps when one of the construction workers said, 'I bet you're looking for a walnut, aren't you?' and started laughing. He said he'd already eaten it and showed us the shell broken right in half."

"And the nut was all gone?" Father asked.

"Uh-huh."

"Was he still chewing?"

"No, he wasn't. He'd already swallowed it. It couldn't have been more than a couple of seconds."

"Mmm."

"What I want to know is how could he have cracked that hard shell? With his teeth? We told him he was mean and just came on home, but we were really mad."

"I can imagine," Father nodded. After a pause he said, "I guess the nut must have rolled right in front of him—right where he happened to be looking."

10

The goldfish seemed to have grown since it first joined the family. Its stomach had filled out; the faint patches of red were now a deeper hue; and with each passing day it looked more and more like an adult fish. Everyone enjoyed watching it dart briskly around its bowl on the sunny windowsill.

"I don't think I've ever seen such a peppy goldfish before," Mother said.

"Yes, we should count ourselves lucky," Father replied. "Let's hope he stays that way."

Every other day Mother changed about half of the water and sprinkled in a pinch of salt, and every third day she gave the fish some bread crumbs or pieces of crackers or cookies. When the children wanted to feed it, she made them take turns, and she kept track of the days to ensure they didn't feed it too much or too often.

Father did not help with the fish, but from time to time he would go into the children's study and watch it move about in its bowl. Such balance! he marveled. With the slightest flick of its fins and an occasional twitch of its tail, the fish could hold itself perfectly still, going neither forward nor backward, for as long as it wished.

He and the children had recently made a second trip to the fishing pond. This time, however, the little tin bucket proved useless, for they failed to catch even a single fish. Nor were they the only ones to come up empty-handed; nobody else's luck appeared any better, at either of the ponds.

As evening approached, the air over the pond grew heavier and heavier.

"This time it looks pretty hopeless," Father sighed. "No one's getting anything." Even changing the bait seemed a waste of effort. Still, he stuck it out at the same spot until the hour they had paid for was up.

The fish he had caught the last time now became more precious than ever. There was a big difference between catching one fish and catching none at all. To have hooked that one fish almost began to seem like a special meeting of fates.

An old man wearing a hunter's cap started to put his gear away. "I should've known better than to come today," he muttered grumpily as he left. "Fishing's never any good when the wind's out of the east."

A few minutes later they were all given a start. Over at the other pond, a boy who had been watching his father fish fell into the water with a loud splash. Everyone turned to see the fisherman pulling his son out. The child, soaked from the neck down, looked to be about ten years old.

A gentle wave of laughter spread among the few people remaining at the pond. The incident dispelled the oppressive mood that had descended over the place, and everyone relaxed again.

Frustrated and tired from an afternoon spent in vain, the man had apparently started to doze off. When he leaned over against his son, the boy had lost his balance and tumbled into the water.

Having retrieved his son—instead of a fish—from the pond, the man could hardly go on fishing. The sun was low in the sky as the two left for home, the hapless boy sloshing awkwardly along behind his father.

11

"I wonder what's wrong with this thing," Father mumbled to himself. "It manages to flower all right, but it always looks so scraggly."

On Sunday morning he had stepped out into the yard to take a closer look at the lilac bush. His eyes moved from the long, spindly branches, to the clusters of tiny, purple flowers, and to the ground underneath the bush.

He had planted this bush five springs before—the year after they had moved to this house. But once it had reached a height slightly taller than he was, it had stopped growing. It never developed a main trunk; instead, it had split at the base into a mass of skinny branches that fanned out toward the sky.

He had originally hoped it would grow large and full enough for the children to hide behind when they played games of hide-and-seek. This no longer seemed likely.

He was still contemplating the lilac when a band of street musicians came into view down the road. The man at the head of the troupe pranced about nimbly in time with the music, turning first one way, then the other.

He keeps people's attention that way, thought Father. If he walked along normally, there wouldn't be anything to watch.

From where he stood inside the fence, Father continued to follow the dancer's movements as the band moved closer. Suddenly he saw that the dancer was not a man at all, but a woman—a rather skinny woman dressed in a man's clothes and made up with white greasepaint.

Behind her came a second dancer in a similar outfit, only this one actually was a man. Third in line was a woman in a black beret playing the clarinet. Next came the drummer, beating with exaggerated flourish on the rack of gongs and tom-toms strapped to his chest. A trumpet player wearing a radioman's cap brought up the rear.

The procession came to a halt. The three musicians continued playing while the two dancers went from house to house passing out handbills.

The older boy had come out of the house to watch from the side of the road. Now the drummer approached him and said something. The boy stared back, but his lips did not move.

Why didn't he answer? Father wondered. What could the man have said?

The group slowly moved away again, and the boy came back into the yard.

"Did the drummer say something to you?" Father asked.

"Uh-huh."

"What did he say?"

"I had my fingers in my ears," the boy said, "and I was pushing them in and out to make the music sound real loud and then real quiet." He demonstrated as he explained, putting his fingers to his ears again. "So the man said if I had to plug my ears like that, I shouldn't come so close, I should go somewhere else."

"I see," Father nodded.

"I guess he thought I didn't like their music," the boy grinned.

12

On Sunday evening Father took out his sketchbook and began to draw a picture of his daughter. She had gotten ready for bed after an early bath, then settled down on the tatami in the front room to read. She saw what her father was doing and tried her best to sit perfectly still for him.

"Are you getting stiff?" he asked her after a while.

"No, not particularly." She sat with her legs flopped to one side and the book open in her lap. The big toe of one foot peeked out from behind the other knee. Father started stetching the toe.

"No, that's too big, I guess," he said, mostly to himself.

"What's too big?" the girl asked.

"Your toe."

"It better not be," she giggled.

"Do you remember your grandpa?" Father asked as he rubbed the toe out.

"A little," she nodded.

"I was just thinking of the time he told me to make a drawing of your feet."

"My feet?"

"Uh-huh."

"What for?"

"It was a day or two after you were born."

"Why my feet?"

"He said it'd be fun to have later on." He started outlining the toe again. "All I had with me was my address book, so I drew a little sketch in that. Just the bottoms of your feet. I suppose it got thrown out somewhere along the way."

"Too bad."

"Yes, I wish we still had it. You'd get a kick out of it. With my knack for losing things, I wonder if Grandpa really thought I'd keep it all this time. . . . Hmm, I guess this hand isn't quite right, either." He started to reshape the hand holding the book. "I remember how impressed Grandpa was with the hospital room. He kept saying it would make a great apartment, and that they should rent it out to us."

"Can I move my legs a little now?" the girl asked.

"Sure, go ahead. It really was a nice room. A quiet room, perfect for reading. The windows faced the nurses' dormitory, and every once in a while we'd see one of them dash across the street through the rain. I remember there was a big paulownia tree[3] by the front entrance . . . Why can't I get these fingers right? The more I work on them the worse they get."

The girl looked up and glanced at her father's sketchbook.

"That day," he went on, "as I was leaving the hospital, I ran into your grandpa coming through the rain, wearing a hat but without an umbrella. He was on his way to see your mother. We stepped under the eaves to talk for a couple of minutes, and do you know what he said? He had never

___

3. A deciduous Chinese tree that bears clusters of violet or blue flowers.

been to a maternity ward before; he had never visited anyone who'd just had a baby. So I decided to go back to the hospital with him. Later, when we were leaving, he told me not to worry—every day a baby lives it builds up that much more strength to survive. You see, we were having a terrible time getting you to nurse. You kept falling asleep as soon as you got the nipple in your mouth, even when one of the nurses pulled on your ear. We didn't know what to do with you."

The girl giggled sheepishly.

13

"Guess what we found at school today," the girl said at the dinner table. "A mole cricket. We were digging in the flower bed, and—"

"Another mole cricket!" exclaimed Mother. "Yesterday it was your brother who found one. He comes in the door after school, and, before I even have a chance to ask him how his day was, he dangles this ugly creature in front of my face and says 'Look, I brought you a present.' "

"You should've seen her jump," the boy said gleefully.

"Of course I jumped. How many times do I have to tell you? You can bring home anything you like as far as the front door, but I won't have you bringing bugs into the house."

"So-o-rr-y."

"So what did you do with the mole cricket in the flower bed?" Father asked.

"Mine was in the sandbox," the boy said.

"The sandbox? You mean you brought it home all the way from school?"

"Yep."

"When we caught the one in the flower bed," the girl said, "we held it like this and asked it, 'How bi-i-ig is so-and-so's brain?' and it would sort of wiggle in surprise and spread its front legs."

"Whoever thought *that* up?" Father wanted to know.

"We all thought it up together. When you say your own name, you say 'BI-I-IG' real loud," she said, putting extra stress on the B. "Then it spreads its legs way far apart, like this. But when you say someone else's name, you say the words real soft: 'How big?' " This time she lowered her voice to a whisper. "Then it only moves its legs a tiny bit." She demonstrated with her arms as she spoke.

"You're making this up, right?" Mother said.

"No, it's true, it was like the mole cricket really heard. So we started doing the same thing as the cricket, and spread *our* arms real wide, too, when we said our own names."

"As if the poor thing wasn't startled enough already," Father said.

The girl seemed endlessly amused by the way the mole cricket squirmed in surprise. She went through her "How bi-i-ig?" antics several more times, transforming herself from little girl into mole cricket and back again, then collapsing in a fit of laughter.

"How bi-i-ig?" the older boy said, moving his arms like his sister.

"How bi-i-ig?" the younger boy imitated.

"So-o big."
"So-o big."
"All right, all right," Father said when they all started doing it together. "That's enough. Let's have some quiet for a change. Please."

Even now, in the deserted schoolyard where the children had played that day, the mole crickets would be quietly burrowing their way through the sandboxes and flower beds.

14

Two stuffed toys, a tiger and a rabbit, shared the wide windowsill where the goldfish swam in its bowl. The tiger lay on its stomach, its legs thrust forward. Its head was tilted to one side so that its nose almost touched the ground, and it looked as if it were scrutinizing the movements of some industrious ant. The rabbit, wearing polka-dotted pants, faced the opposite direction. It lay on its back and stared up at the sky.

During the daytime, the two animals sat like this on the sill. Then, when night came, they were taken off to bed by the children. The younger boy always got the rabbit—there were never any quarrels about that. But the older boy and the girl had to take turns with the tiger, and many an argument broke out when one or the other of them missed a day.

One night, Father was getting ready for bed in his room at the end of the hall when he heard the children's voices rise to a fighting pitch. A moment later his wife intervened: "All right, now, who had it the day before yesterday? And yesterday? No, no, you both know the rule—forgetting doesn't count."

It was their own fault if they missed a turn, she explained, as she had so many times before. They could not demand their turn the next day. If that were allowed, neither of them would be able to count on their regular turn anymore, and there'd be no end to the fighting. If they forgot, it was just too bad. They would have to wait for their next turn.

How had this all started? Father wondered. How long had they been having these squabbles?

Sometimes several days went by without either of the children remembering to take the tiger to bed. Since neither of them could recall who had had it last or how long it had been, even their mother couldn't settle whose turn it should be. Eventually, to make sure this didn't happen again, she had begun keeping track by marking the calendar with the children's initials.

Father shook his head as he got under the covers. It was beyond him why they would want to take something like that to bed with them. *He* had slept alone when *he* was a child. And he had taken it for granted that everyone else did, too.

The children's dispute finally came to an end. That night, the tiger would sleep with the girl.

"Lucky stiff!" the boy grumbled loudly.

As Father picked up one of the books lying at the head of the bed, his thoughts drifted off to another stuffed toy they had once had—a puppy, neither so small nor so soft as the tiger the children had just been fighting over. He recalled the Christmas morning, more than ten years before, when he had found the puppy standing beside his baby daughter's bed. The tall, husky puppy had seemed so enormous next to the tiny figure of the baby.

Now what did she go and buy something like that for? he remembered thinking to himself.

Only a few minutes earlier, when he first awoke, he had been equally surprised to find a box, neatly tied with a ribbon, sitting beside his pillow. The box had contained a fedora.

Had he said he wanted one of these? He couldn't remember, but perhaps he had, sometime or other, and his wife had taken him seriously. Or perhaps he had only commented on how nice someone else's looked.

How much did hats like this cost? He really couldn't imagine. He had never considered buying one for himself, or envisioned himself wearing one to the office, so he'd never had cause to explore the hat section of the department store. His knowledge of hats was pretty much limited to the corduroy cap he got out in the summertime. But that was one of those things you could roll up and stuff in your pocket—it hardly counted as a real hat. The only other hat he had ever worn was a boater,[4] in his student days. He remembered having to hold it with one hand on top to keep it from flying off as he raced to get on the train before the doors slammed shut.

He knew he hadn't paid very much for that boater. But fedoras were in a different class altogether. It must have cost a small fortune. Why had his wife made such an extravagant purchase without consulting him? She knew they didn't have that kind of money to throw around.

Sitting up in bed, he tried on the new hat. He liked it, the way it gently pressed against his head. But he wasn't sure what position he should wear it in. If he pulled it down too far, his head would push out the crease on top and make it look like a bowler instead of a fedora. How did other people wear them? He would have to pay more attention from now on.

He returned the hat to its box and closed the lid.

Since it was a holiday, he could sleep later than usual if he wanted. But the surprise of the hat had left him wide awake. He decided to go ahead and get up.

The quiet of morning filled the house. Outside, clouds hung heavily in the sky.

It was then, when he poked his head into the next room to see if his wife and daughter were awake, that he had had his first glimpse of the toy puppy.

For several moments, all he could do was marvel at its magnificent size and beauty. In any display of stuffed toys, this puppy was bound to reign as king of beasts. Once you had seen it, all the other toys would look like mere knickknacks by comparison.

Clearly it had been made to last. It could probably hold a child on its back without collapsing.

But once again he wondered about the cost. Although he knew even

4. A stiff straw hat.

less about stuffed toys than about hats, he could guess it had been expensive. What could his wife have been thinking, spending so much money on a toy like that? With all the daily expenses they had to worry about, she should show a little more sense.

He would have to give her a little scolding, he decided. In fact, he would do it right then and there. So what if it was a holiday? It was already later than usual and time she got started on breakfast.

He called her name, but she slept on without so much as a stir. His wife was one of those people who always looked as though they hadn't had enough sleep, and at night she was lost to the world the moment her head touched the pillow. She seldom dreamed, and was never wakeful. But when the alarm went off the next morning, or when he called her, she would be up in an instant. In all the time they had been married, he couldn't remember having had to call her twice.

"Hey, wake up," he said again, reaching over to shake her shoulder. All of a sudden he noticed that what she had on was not what she normally wore to bed.

As Father lay reflecting on that Christmas morning, he thought again of the puppy. It had proved to be just as sturdy as his first impression had suggested. The girl had played with it for a long time, riding on its back, hanging on with her baby fists clutched tightly around its soft, fluffy ears. She had started doing this even before she learned to walk. When their first son came along, he had played with it, too, bouncing up and down on its back no less gleefully than his sister. But it had still held up as good as new.

Later, when they moved to their new house, the puppy had come with them. Father remembered packing it to be shipped with the other baggage.

"The fedora was a different story though," he sighed. *That* he had lost almost right away. At a movie theater. He had put it on his lap during the show, only to forget about it when he stood up to leave. He was all the way outside before he noticed, and by then it was too late. One of the ushers had kindly gone to retrieve it for him, but came back saying the theater was too crowded. He had had to give it up for lost.

15

When the boys asked for an s again one evening, Father told them another story about the old hunter.

"Next to hunting," he began, "the old man's favorite pastime is fishing. He became a hunter first, and he's been making regular trips into the mountains for more than forty years, since he was a young man. Then about thirty years ago, when he moved to the town where he lives now, he took up fishing. He liked the town so much, he's lived there ever since, and he's spent a lot of time at the nearby river ever since, too. He got started fishing, he says, because he found a good river-teacher there."

"A river-teacher?" the older boy laughed.

"That's right. Maybe you've only heard of schoolteachers, but there are river-teachers, too—and mountain-teachers, and even ocean-teachers. A long time ago, this river-teacher had worked as a raftsman for a lumber company. You see, when a lumber company cuts down trees, up in the mountains, the logs are tied together into rafts so they can be floated down the river to the lumber mill. The raftsman is the person who steers the raft down the river, through the rapids and between all the rocks and things sticking up out of the water. It's a really dangerous job. Anyway, after this river-teacher had worked as a raftsman for a while, he decided to settle down in one of the towns along the river and become a fisherman instead. He knew that river like the back of his hand. No one could match him. He could tell you exactly how many fish there were and what they were doing or which way they were swimming anywhere along the river, even in the roughest and deepest places. If you were fishing with him and he said, 'One more,' that meant there was only one fish left in that spot. And he'd be right!"

"Wow!" the older boy exclaimed.

"Wow!" the younger boy mimicked.

"That's incredible," the first added.

"The old hunter couldn't get over it either. He said he'd never heard of anyone who knew so much about rivers and fish. The river-teacher's name was Katsujiro, but since his father's name had been Katsuzo, everyone called him Little Katsu.[5] People still called him that when the hunter met him, even though he was an old man by then."

The older boy laughed when Father said "Little Katsu."

"The problem was that since Little Katsu depended on catching fish for his living, you could never believe what he told you. If you asked him where was a good spot, he would lie and send you off someplace he knew was lousy. The hunter got to be his best friend, and they would drink together almost every night, but he still couldn't get a straight answer out of him. For instance, he might ask if today was a good day, and Little Katsu would say, 'No.' Well, that would turn out to be a lie—the days he said 'No' were in fact the best days. So pretty soon the hunter tried doing the opposite of whatever Little Katsu said. If he said 'No,' the hunter would set out for the river. And sure enough, Little Katsu would be there."

"So he had to listen to him backward," the older boy said.

"That's right. With a teacher like Little Katsu, that was how you learned. Even then the hunter got tricked a lot, so he tried something new. Instead of asking Little Katsu directly, he would sneak up to his house and peek in to see if he was at home. If he found him puttering around the house or just taking a nap or something, he knew there was no sense in going to the river."

"'Cause he knew he wouldn't catch anything even if he did," the boy said.

"Uh-huh. Now, I said Little Katsu lied a lot, but actually there were some things he didn't lie about. Like how to cast a net so it would spread out the way you wanted it to. Or what's the best way to tie the hook to the line. Or how when you're fishing for dace[6] and get a nibble you have to

5. It is common practice in Japan to take the first part of a child's name, here "Katsu" from *Katsujiro*, and add the diminutive *chan* ("little").   6. Chub, a small fresh-water fish.

give the line some slack instead of pulling it in right away as most people
do.

"It was lucky for the hunter that Little Katsu told the truth about these
things. Otherwise he might never have learned how to cast the special
sweetfish[7] net that's used only on that river and nowhere else. It's about
fifteen feet long, like a huge ribbon, and getting it to spread out just right
is pretty tricky. If it goes into the water in a straight line, like this," he drew
a line with his finger, "the fish will get away. They can swim right around
it. To keep them from doing that, you have to make the net hit the water
curved like a bow. Like this." He indicated the curve with a sweep of his
arms.

"Like this?" the older boy said, making a similar arc.

"Like this?" his younger brother imitated.

"The reason it makes a difference, you see, is that sweetfish can't turn
around very well. When they bump into the net, they just wriggle a little
to one side or the other and keep trying to push ahead. That means if both
ends of the net are curved back like this, then the fish are forced to swim
toward the middle." Father cupped his left hand and poked at it with his
right index finger to show how the fish bumped against the net and kept
swimming forward until they wound up trapped in the center. The boys
paid close attention.

"But if you just leave them there," he went on, "the fish eventually get
turned around and find their way out. So, to make sure that doesn't happen, the old hunter swims down underwater to where the net is and breaks
their spines."

"What's 'spines'?" the older boy asked.

"Right about here." Father patted the back of his neck. "Then later,
after he's got quite a few, he brings them in all at once. He says he used
to catch thirty, even forty, in a single night back when he first started
fishing. On nights like that he wouldn't even notice how cold the water
was. Until he got home, that is. Then he would start shivering like crazy.
He'd take a good hot bath and jump into bed with the covers pulled all
the way up over his head, and he still couldn't stop shaking. Even in the
middle of summer. But you know what? No matter how bad the shivering
was, he'd be right back at the river again the very next night. It's hardly a
wonder he developed so many aches and pains as he got older, but he just
shrugs and says, 'That's the way it goes.'"

"Tell us about the fox," the older boy broke in again.

"Okay. That happened when he was snagging, which is another way to
catch sweetfish. Instead of a net, you use a line with a lot of hooks spaced
three or four inches apart, and you snag the fish by their gills. Sometimes
you can catch five or six all at once. With this method, too, the best fishing
is at night, especially when the river is swollen and muddy after some rain.
You can haul in dozens.

"Anyway, one night when the old hunter was snagging out in the middle of the river, a fox came along the bank and stopped to watch him. For
a long time it just stood there like a little statue, not moving a muscle."

---

7. *Ayu*, a small river fish.

Father got on all fours and made a fox's face, then continued. "Now, the hunter wouldn't have minded about the fox except that his basket of fish was sitting on the bank. You see, he had two baskets for the fish he caught—a small one that he tied around his waist, and a larger one that he left on the riverbank. Whenever the small one filled up, he would go back to shore and empty it into the larger one. The problem was the fox had stopped only a few steps away from this larger basket."

"Chase him away!" the older boy cried.

"Chase him away!" the younger boy echoed.

"You can imagine the hunter got pretty nervous about the basket. He picked up a rock from the riverbed and threw it hard at the fox, thinking that would surely send it scampering. But no, the fox just ambled a few steps to one side, stopped, and turned to eye him again. Then after a few moments it sauntered back toward the basket."

"Throw some more rocks!" the older boy said.

"That's right. He picked up another rock and yelled 'Beat it!' as he hurled it off. But the fox wasn't any more impressed this time than the first. The old hunter said he had never seen such a lackadaisical fox. Then, just as he was trying to decide what to do next, the fox grabbed the basket in its snout and trotted away."

"Too-o ba-a-ad," the older boy said sympathetically.

"Too-o ba-a-ad," the younger boy repeated.

16

"Hey Mom, Ikuko and I are going to make donuts this afternoon, okay?" the girl asked one Sunday, a little before noon.

"It's fine with me," Mother nodded.

"She said she'd bring the ingredients."

"She doesn't have to do that."

"That's what I said."

"I'm sure we have everything you need."

"I know, I told her that, but she insisted."

Ikuko arrived around two, bringing with her a bag of flour and an egg. She was a cute, cheerful girl, who never seemed to stop smiling.

"Can I help?" the older boy asked.

"There you go again," Father admonished. "Always getting into other people's projects. For girls, making donuts is like doing homework for school. You'd be bothering their studies."

"But I want to do some homework too."

"Look, there's not enough room in the kitchen for all three of you to work in there at the same time."

"Yes there is," the boy whined. He stuck out his lower lip in a pout. His eyes filled and a tear or two trickled down his cheek.

"All right, you can help," Mother agreed. "But don't get carried away now. Understand?"

"Oka-a-a-y," he promised. A smile had already spread across his face. The switch from sad to happy was just that quick.

Father looked on as his wife got the children started. Then, having nothing better to do, he decided to go lie down for a while. "Make them small," he said as he stood up to leave. "They're better that way."

In the back room he folded a cushion in half to use as a pillow and stretched out on the tatami. Even from there he could hear the voices in the kitchen.

"Stop taking so much," the girl scolded the boy. It seemed he had gotten carried away after all.

Then his wife was saying something. That was the voice of the woman he had married, he thought to himself as he listened. That was how she sounded when she did things with the kids.

For some reason he was reminded of the muffled sobs he had once heard, a long time ago. When had it been? Oh yes, it was in their old house. He was taking a nap upstairs late one Sunday afternoon—he even remembered using a folded cushion for a pillow, just like now—when all of a sudden he began to hear what sounded like a woman crying. He lifted his head to listen more closely, but the sound stopped. Then, while he was still puzzling over what to make of it, it started up again.

Was something wrong? Who could it be? Why would anyone be weeping?

Going downstairs, he found their second child fast asleep on the baby bed and his wife rinsing some spinach at the kitchen sink. Their daughter had gone out to play.

"Did you hear anything?" he asked his wife.

"No, not that I noticed," she replied, turning around with a bright face.

"That's strange. I could have sworn I heard something. That's why I came down—to see what it was."

What could it have been, then—that sound of short, broken sobs? Something being jostled by the wind, perhaps, rubbing against something else. But why had it sounded to him so much like his wife's voice?

He went back upstairs, but the sound did not return.

Father now lay on the tatami in the back room staring into space as he thought over the incident that had puzzled him so. His wife had had no cause for weeping then. And in fact she *hadn't* been weeping.

"This one's mine," the boy's voice broke through his thoughts. "I put a mark on it so I could tell."

A few moments later someone began to laugh. Then they all laughed.

Footsteps came running down the hall and the door slid open. It was the younger boy. "They're done. It's time to eat," he said, and went dashing back toward the kitchen.

Father got up and followed. He found the others at the low, round table in the front room, the donuts divided up onto several small plates. There was an extra plate for him.

"Mmm-mmm, perfect!" he said between bites. "Just as I said, the small ones are best." He finished the donut and sat back to watch as the others ate theirs.

"Have some more," his wife urged.

"No thanks. One's enough for me." He pushed his plate toward the children.

"That was fun," the girl said as she took her last bite.

"And delicious," Ikuko added, finishing hers.

The boy, too, was down to his final bite, when his sister suddenly cried out, "Wait! Save a little piece!" But it was too late. The last bit had vanished into her brother's mouth. "Ohhh well," she said, disappointed.

"What's the matter?" Mother asked.

"We forgot to save any for the goldfish."

The boy tapped his cheeks as if to prove that the donut was completely gone. Not a single crumb remained, either on the plates or on the table.

17

"We listened to the *New World* Symphony[8] in music class today," the girl said one evening near the end of dinner.

"How nice!" Mother said. "Did you like it?"

"It was beautiful."

"Yes, it really is a beautiful piece."

"But you know what? When the teacher told us he was going to play it, the boys all groaned and didn't want to listen. Only the girls wanted to hear it."

"Why? What did the boys have against it?" Father asked.

"I don't know. All they said was 'B-o-r-ing. B-o-r-ing.' I guess they didn't think it would be much fun. They must have liked it more than they expected, though, because once it started they all listened quietly."

"Do you get to choose the music you listen to?" Mother asked.

"Uh-huh. Every once in a while the teacher asks us what we'd like to hear and makes a list on the board. One time, not too long ago, a lot of people wanted the *New World* Symphony. But he didn't have it taped yet."

"Oh, so you listen to a tape," Father broke in.

"Uh-huh. He's got lots of different music on tapes."

"I see."

"Anyway, today he came in and said he'd finally had a chance to record the *New World* Symphony the other night, so let's all listen to it. But first he explained that the beginning wasn't recorded very well—he hadn't had time to adjust all the knobs before the symphony started because he forgot until the last minute that it was going to be on the radio that night; he only barely got the tape recorder set up in time. And he said there was a place in the middle where we would hear his son's voice."

"Did you?" her brother asked.

"Uh-huh."

"What did he say?"

"I couldn't tell. Something like 'Ahhh-yooo.' "

"Ahhh-yooo?"

"I couldn't really tell, it went by so fast."

Several evenings later the girl had another story.

"In Ikuko's class," she began, "they listened to *Invitation to the Dance*

---

8. By Antonin Dvorak (1841–1904), Czechoslovakian composer.

today. The teacher told them beforehand that the composer—I think his name was Weber[9]—had dedicated it to his wife, and that it was a flowery sort of piece."

"So that's what you call it," Father said.

"Then after he started the tape, he explained what was supposed to be happening at each place in the music." She had begun to speak a little faster, as she always did when she neared the best part of the story. "Well, evidently, there's a place in the middle where the music stays kind of low for a while and then gets high, and the teacher explained that the low part was where the men go up to the ladies and ask, 'May I have this dance?' Then when it came to the high part, he started to tell them that that was where the ladies turn all red and say, 'Ohhh, something-or-other.' But just as he said 'Ohhh,' his false teeth came loose, and they almost fell right out of his mouth!" Unable to hold back any longer, she burst out laughing.

Her parents stared at her in disbelief.

"His false teeth?" Father asked.

"It's really true! They almost fell out!" She laughed so hard that tears came to her eyes, and she had to hold her stomach. Before long her father began to laugh, too, and then her mother and the boys. They laughed and laughed, unable to stop.

Finally the older boy asked, "So what did the teacher do?"

"Ikuko said he turned the other way and fixed them in a real hurry," the girl answered.

18

A bagworm[1] the older boy had been keeping in a small cardboard box disappeared.

At the time, Father did not yet know about the bagworm. No one had thought to mention it to him. It was not until afterward that he heard the story.

The boy had originally found it on a tree in their neighbor's yard when he and a friend were gathering nuts to use as pellets in their toy guns. His friend told him that if he stripped the worm and put it in a box with some leaves and bits of paper, it would make itself a new nest in about three hours.

The boy brought it home and did as his friend had said. But when he peeked into the box that night, the bagworm had not moved. The next morning it still hadn't moved.

He then forgot about the worm, and three days went by before he thought to check its box again. This time it had crept into a corner and begun building a little tent-like shelter on its back. The boy poked at the half-finished canopy with his finger. To his surprise, it flipped right off.

A day or two later he found the tiny creature crawling across the floor

---

9. Carl Maria von Weber (1786–1826), German composer who did indeed write *Invitation to the Dance.*
1. A worm that produces a sticky substance with which it fastens dried leaves together into a baglike dwelling that it carries on its back.

of the study. This time, too, it had a tent on its back, about the same size as the one before. The boy carefully returned it to its box.

He neglected to check on the bagworm for several days again after that. When he finally remembered, it was no longer in the box. With his mother to help him, he scoured the floor of the study from under the sewing machine to behind the toy basket, but to no avail.

Then one evening about two weeks later, Mother went into the study and found the bagworm in a new nest on the wall, a short distance below the picture of the star children.

"Here it is!" she exclaimed in surprise.

The lost worm had made itself a new bag out of the persimmon twigs and newsprint scraps the boy had given it, plus bits of lint it had gathered on its own. Patchwork though it looked, it was a perfectly good nest.

Where could it have been hiding all that time? Father later wondered. Someplace no one would find it, that much was clear. Perhaps behind the bookshelf, where there was plenty of lint it could use to make a nest. Then, when it had finished weaving its new quarters, the worm had crawled out to a bright, sunny spot near the southern windows.

The boy was in the bath shooting his water gun at the walls and ceiling. Caught up in his game, he had stayed in much longer than he should have.

"Hurry up and dry off and come on out here. We've got a surprise for you," his mother and sister called to him.

Little imagining that the "surprise" would be his bagworm, the boy jumped out of the bath and dried himself as fast as he could.

The last one to learn about the bagworm was Father. He had gone out that evening and did not get home until late, long after the others were in bed; it was the next morning before he finally heard about the bagworm from his wife.

Out-of-doors, he had never given bagworms a second thought. But there was something rather curious about a worm that built itself a shelter when it was inside a house with a solid roof and ceiling overhead.

"I wonder what it has in mind," he said to his wife. "Does it intend to set up housekeeping there, do you think?"

"It certainly looks that way."

He noticed a tiny piece of bright red paper stuck to one side. Had his son put some bits of construction paper in the box too? Or was this something the worm had picked up in its travels around the room?

At the other end of the bay window from where the two stood inspecting the bagworm, the goldfish swam quietly in its bowl. It nibbled for a moment at some moss that had formed along the edge of the water, then lost interest and turned away.

ALAIN ROBBE-GRILLET

born 1922

More than anyone else, Alain Robbe-Grillet represents in his novels, *ciné-romans* (film-novels), and theoretical statements the rejection of the nineteenth-century realistic tradition and the exploration of a new "mental realism." Terms such as *antinovel* and *new novel*, early applied to his works, reflect both the turning away from older models (like Balzac and Flaubert), and the notion that a new experiment with form is under way. Not that it is completely new; clearly there are links to other twentieth-century works in the modernist tradition (and experiments with novel form as early as Laurence Sterne's *Tristram Shandy*, 1760–67). Robbe-Grillet himself mentions the influence of Kafka, Camus, and Faulkner (as well as *Alice in Wonderland*), and other readers will note parallel experimentation in Pirandello, Woolf, Beckett, and Joyce. Moreover, Robbe-Grillet calls on some of the same sources of fascination as his nineteenth-century predecessors. He may not use a linear plot, but he writes ambiguous, circular detective stories where erotic and violent crimes seem to have been committed. He may refuse to portray a consistently developing character, but his minute descriptions of objects and gestures impel the reader to imagine an underlying psychology and to speculate on the meaning of the observer's repetition and distortion in details.

Nonetheless, with Robbe-Grillet, we move to a particular phenomenon of mid-twentieth-century literature and a prime example of the "postmodernist" tradition. To the breakdown of conventional storytelling models familiar from literary modernism, he adds an insistence on the artificiality of all writing and representation until the reader is finally faced with total uncertainty: with a self-contained "text" in which there is no stable narrative voice or "authorized" explanation. Here is not the intellectualist puzzle of Borges but an often terrifying evocation of a sensuous reality that will not stay in place. This literature has become a "game" (as it is for Borges), but it is a deadly game. Playing with erotic and murderous images, with the treacherous undercurrents of an apparently familiar reality, Robbe-Grillet fascinates and sometimes repels his readers. At the same time that he reminds us that we cannot know what we see, and that we share the world with a host of objects different from ourselves, he entices us to figure out the meaning of events—only to reestablish, at every turn, the absolute subjectivity of our most "objective" perceptions. We cannot be disengaged from Robbe-Grillet's descriptions because they make a direct appeal to our senses; they manipulate our awareness of physical experience. Robbe-Grillet has explored the limits of representation throughout his career, with a collage-like technique that remains more true to life, he feels, than the planned coherence of a conventionally "realistic" novel.

Robbe-Grillet was born in Brittany, in northwestern France, to a family of scientists and engineers. His early training was not at all literary: in 1939 and 1941 the future writer took baccalaureate degrees in mathematics and natural science, and in 1946 (his career interrupted by forced labor in a German factory) a further degree from the National Agronomy Institute. He began work with the National Institute of Statistics and published an article on livestock possibilities before deciding to work part-time in his sister's biology laboratory and write a novel. This novel, *A Regicide*, was completed in 1949 but not published until 1978, well after Robbe-Grillet had become a successful novelist. In the meantime he took a position with an agricultural institute that sent him to Martinique, in the West Indies, to supervise banana plantations. Falling ill in 1951, Robbe-Grillet took advantage of the leisure time in the hospital and on the voyage home to write his second novel, *The Erasers*, which was immediately accepted and appeared in 1953.

The Erasers is a puzzling detective story involving confused identities, an abortive assassination carried out exactly twenty-four hours later by the muddled detective sent to investigate the original attempt, repeated allusions to the Oedipus myth, changing perspectives, and an overwhelming copiousness of detail about the most mundane natural objects. The novel became famous for its meticulous description of a tomato wedge cataloged with such scientific precision that it took on an objective existence of its own and implicitly challenged the human-centered orientation of a perspective that would see it only as part of a salad. "The flesh on the periphery, compact and uniform, of a fine chemical red, is evenly thick between a strip of shiny skin and the compartment where the seeds are lined up, yellow, well sized, held in place by a thin layer of greenish jelly alongside a swelling of the heart. This latter, of a faded and slightly grainy pink, begins, on the side of the depression below, in a cluster of white veins, one of which extends up to the seeds—in, perhaps, a somewhat uncertain manner." While minutely detailed descriptions are not new in literature, this catalog of physical properties had additional significance for its readers because it correlated so well with the notion, in contemporary phenomenological or existential philosophy, that we should recognize that things have their own existence separate from ourselves, their own "being-in-the-world."

The Erasers received the Fénéon Prize in 1954, but was not widely known; it was not until the scandal caused by *The Voyeur* (1955) that Robbe-Grillet reached a wide audience. Although *The Voyeur* was awarded the Critics' Prize in 1955, the jury was split between those who felt that it was not a "novel" at all (and was immoral and insane to boot), and those who admired its formal innovations. Mathias, the "voyeur" of the title, is a traveling watch salesman who may or may not have murdered a young girl during a sales trip on an island. The reader must piece together a version of what happened from a fragmented time span during which Mathias neglects to describe certain crucial hours, from actions and anxieties that suggest a guilty conscience, from a schizophrenic crisis when the crime is described in a café, and from obsessive erotic imaginings which may be just that—imaginings—or may be traces of the crime.

With the controversy over *The Voyeur*, Robbe-Grillet and his new mode of writing became the focus of critical debate in France. In *Objective Literature*, the influential critic Roland Barthes proposed that Robbe-Grillet had discovered a truer "neutral" writing by focusing on objects instead of repeating traditional socially inspired interpretations of reality. In 1955, Robbe-Grillet began a series of articles on modern literature, which he collected in 1963 as *For a New Novel*. The term *new novel* became popular, and although not all those described as "new novelists" wrote in the same way, they all rejected the traditional novel's assumption of a core of meaning—with a logically developing plot and psychologically consistent characters—that claimed to reflect a similar core of meaning in society. His next two novels, *Jealousy* (1957) and *In the Labyrinth* (1959), as well as the separate short pieces collected in *Snapshots* (1962), exploit the ideas developed in these articles, seeking patterns of potential meaning behind extended, "objective" description. In 1959, he temporarily abandoned novels to experiment with films, writing the script for *Last Year at Marienbad* (1961, filmed by Alain Resnais) and writing and directing *The Immortal One* (1963). Films, like novels, allowed Robbe-Grillet to manipulate visions of reality as he insistently focused on surfaces and shapes, presented different versions of the same scene, composed a sound track that contradicted or commented on photographed action and—in recent works— challenged his own imagination by including unexpected incidents that occurred on location. Robbe-Grillet published the scenarios of *Last Year at Marienbad* and

The Immortal One, and a more documentary account of *The Progressing Slippages of Pleasure* (1974) as *ciné-romans*, which represent his pluralistic, decentered view of reality in audiovisual as well as verbal form.

Novels up to and including *In the Labyrinth* could still be interpreted as the subterranean story of a single protagonist. Later novels eliminated that anchoring center to display the presence of many centers—each a competing version of reality. Here emphasis is on the writer's freedom to create different and even mutually contradictory worlds, and on the readers' freedom to choose and arrange their own version of events. Some passages do not really fit into any of the story lines; the action progresses according to the suggestions of wordplay or verbal echoes; the same narrative persona may appear grammatically as "he" or "she"; or books are composed in collage fashion. Robbe-Grillet has been taught in the classroom for many years as a master of formal experimentation and only recently challenged on the quarantined atmosphere and obsessive sadism of his work. Women, for example, are repeatedly victimized, and terror and death are constant themes. Uncomfortable, perhaps, at this change in critical perspective, he has justified sadistic fantasies in his work partly as reflecting popular themes in a correspondingly sadistic and dehumanized world, and partly as the therapeutic expression of his own obsessions (therapeutic for Robbe-Grillet because they are brought to a conscious level and thereby subject to change).

Therapeutic or not, there is no mistaking the basic images of Robbe-Grillet's world, or the disturbing angles from which they are presented. *The Secret Room*, reprinted here from *Snapshots*, arranges in an artistic homage to the Symbolist painter Gustave Moreau (1826–98) many of Robbe-Grillet's most obsessive images: the spreading bloodstain; the young woman stretched out erotically in chains and stabbed under the left breast; the ascending staircase; the different points of view directed down upon the victim; the mysterious, anonymous criminal; and even the figure eight of smoke coiling upward from the incense burner. The scene is bound to shock for its overt sadism, for the artistic savoring of human sacrifice, and for the erotic pleasure it suggests in female victimization. It would not be appropriate to ignore or repress this response, for the subject matter is not neutral or intended as such. Robbe-Grillet has presented an additional challenge, however, by insisting on the stylized *unreality* of the scene and by displacing the reader's attention to the technical triumph in which verbal art emulates a painterly style. The text imitates the Oriental luxury and morbid eroticism of a famous painter so convincingly that one could almost name the artist even without the dedication. Yet this verbal art goes beyond its painterly model when Robbe-Grillet adds to it the passage of time, thus bringing a strange life to the subject seen paradoxically both as a finished canvas and as recreated stages of the same murderous event. It is a bizarre and disturbing scene, made to unsettle readers who try to reconcile its various aspects: its manipulation of stereotypes of the victimized woman, the horror of the helpless sacrifice, and an alienated perspective that is attributed to art but at the same time suggests sadistic impersonality.

Ilona Leki, *Alain Robbe-Grillet* (1983), is a good biography and survey of Robbe-Grillet's work in historical context, discussing each work, with a last chapter on the films. Bruce Morrissette, *The Novels of Robbe-Grillet* (1975), provides a valuable critical study that takes the works and films in chronological order. Morrissette, *Novel and Film: Essays in Two Genres* (1985), makes Robbe-Grillet the chief example in a discussion of modern cinematic vision. Ben Stoltzfus, *Alain Robbe-Grillet and the New French Novel* (1964), is an earlier introduction to Robbe-Grillet in the context of the emerging new novel form. Raylene L. Ramsay, *Robbe-Grillet and Modernity: Science, Sexuality, and Subversion* (1992), interrogates contemporary culture and the thematics of sexual violence.

PRONOUNCING GLOSSARY

The following list uses common English syllables and stress accents to provide rough equivalents of selected words whose pronunciation may be unfamiliar to the general reader.

Alain Robbe-Grillet: *ah-lanh' rob–gree-yay'*
Gustave Moreau: *gyoo-stahv' mor-oh'*

The Secret Room[1]

To Gustave Moreau[2]

The first thing to be seen is a red stain, of a deep, dark, shiny red, with
almost black shadows. It is in the form of an irregular rosette, sharply
outlined, extending in several directions in wide outflows of unequal
length, dividing and dwindling afterward into single sinuous streaks. The
whole stands out against a smooth, pale surface, round in shape, at once
dull and pearly, a hemisphere joined by gentle curves to an expanse of the
same pale color—white darkened by the shadowy quality of the place: a
dungeon, a sunken room, or a cathedral—glowing with a diffused brilliance in the semidarkness.

Farther back, the space is filled with the cylindrical trunks of columns,
repeated with progressive vagueness in their retreat toward the beginning
of a vast stone stairway, turning slightly as it rises, growing narrower and
narrower as it approaches the high vaults where it disappears.

The whole setting is empty, stairway and colonnades. Alone, in the foreground, the stretched-out body gleams feebly, marked with the red stain—
a white body whose full, supple flesh can be sensed, fragile, no doubt,
and vulnerable. Alongside the bloody hemisphere another identical round
form, this one intact, is seen at almost the same angle of view; but the
haloed point at its summit, of darker tint, is in this case quite recognizable,
whereas the other one is entirely destroyed, or at least covered by the
wound.

In the background, near the top of the stairway, a black silhouette is
seen fleeing, a man wrapped in a long, floating cape, ascending the last
steps without turning around, his deed accomplished. A thin smoke rises
in twisting scrolls from a sort of incense burner placed on a high stand of
ironwork with a silvery glint. Nearby lies the milkwhite body, with wide
streaks of blood running from the left breast, along the flank and on the
hip.

It is a fully rounded woman's body, but not heavy, completely nude,
lying on its back, the bust raised up somewhat by thick cushions thrown
down on the floor, which is covered with Oriental rugs. The waist is very
narrow, the neck long and thin, curved to one side, the head thrown back
into a darker area where, even so, the facial features may be discerned, the
partly opened mouth, the wide-staring eyes, shining with a fixed brilliance,
and the mass of long, black hair spread out in a complicated wavy disorder

---

1. Translated by Bruce Morrissette.   2. French Symbolist painter (1826–1898) known for exotic, luminous scenes with subtly erotic and morbid overtones, such as *The Death of Darius* and *Dance of Salome.*

over a heavily folded cloth, of velvet perhaps, on which also rest the arm and shoulder.

It is a uniformly colored velvet of dark purple, or which seems so in this lighting. But purple, brown, blue also seem to dominate in the colors of the cushions—only a small portion of which is hidden beneath the velvet cloth, and which protrude noticeably, lower down, beneath the bust and waist—as well as in the Oriental patterns of the rugs on the floor. Farther on, these same colors are picked up again in the stone of the paving and the columns, and vaulted archways, the stairs, and the less discernible surfaces that disappear into the farthest reaches of the room.

The dimensions of this room are difficult to determine exactly; the body of the young sacrificial victim seems at first glance to occupy a substantial portion of it, but the vast size of the stairway leading down to it would imply rather that this is not the whole room, whose considerable space must in reality extend all around, right and left, as it does toward the faraway browns and blues among the columns standing in line, in every direction, perhaps toward other sofas, thick carpets, piles of cushions and fabrics, other tortured bodies, other incense burners.

It is also difficult to say where the light comes from. No clue, on the columns or on the floor, suggests the direction of the rays. Nor is any window or torch visible. The milkwhite body itself seems to light the scene, with its full breasts, the curve of its thighs, the rounded belly, the full buttocks, the stretched-out legs, widely spread, and the black tuft of the exposed sex, provocative, proffered, useless now.

The man has already moved several steps back. He is now on the first steps of the stairs, ready to go up. The bottom steps are wide and deep, like the steps leading up to some great building, a temple or theater; they grow smaller as they ascend, and at the same time describe a wide, helical curve, so gradually that the stairway has not yet made a half-turn by the time it disappears near the top of the vaults, reduced then to a steep, narrow flight of steps without handrail, vaguely outlined, moreover, in the thickening darkness beyond.

But the man does not look in this direction, where his movement nonetheless carries him; his left foot on the second step and his right foot already touching the third, with his knee bent, he has turned around to look at the spectacle for one last time. The long, floating cape thrown hastily over his shoulders, clasped in one hand at his waist, has been whirled around by the rapid circular motion that has just caused his head and chest to turn in the opposite direction, and a corner of the cloth remains suspended in the air as if blown by a gust of wind; this corner, twisting around upon itself in the form of a loose S, reveals the red silk lining with its gold embroidery.

The man's features are impassive, but tense, as if in expectation—or perhaps fear—of some sudden event, or surveying with one last glance the total immobility of the scene. Though he is looking backward, his whole body is turned slightly forward, as if he were continuing up the stairs. His right arm—not the one holding the edge of the cape—is bent sharply toward the left, toward a point in space where the balustrade should be, if this stairway had one, an interrupted gesture, almost incomprehensible, unless it arose from an instinctive movement to grasp the absent support.

As to the direction of his glance, it is certainly aimed at the body of the victim lying on the cushions, its extended members stretched out in the form of a cross, its bust raised up, its head thrown back. But the face is perhaps hidden from the man's eyes by one of the columns, standing at the foot of the stairs. The young woman's right hand touches the floor just at the foot of this column. The fragile wrist is encircled by an iron bracelet. The arm is almost in darkness, only the hand receiving enough light to make the thin, outspread fingers clearly visible against the circular protrusion at the base of the stone column. A black metal chain running around the column passes through a ring affixed to the bracelet, binding the wrist tightly to the column.

At the top of the arm a rounded shoulder, raised up by the cushions, also stands out well lighted, as well as the neck, the throat, and the other shoulder, the armpit with its soft hair, the left arm likewise pulled back with its wrist bound in the same manner to the base of another column, in the extreme foreground; here the iron bracelet and the chain are fully displayed, represented with perfect clarity down to the slightest details.

The same is true, still in the foreground but at the other side, for a similar chain, but not quite as thick, wound directly around the ankle, running twice around the column and terminating in a heavy iron embedded in the floor. About a yard farther back, or perhaps slightly farther, the right foot is identically chained. But it is the left foot, and its chain, that are the most minutely depicted.

The foot is small, delicate, finely modeled. In several places the chain has broken the skin, causing noticeable if not extensive depressions in the flesh. The chain links are oval, thick, the size of an eye. The ring in the floor resembles those used to attach horses; it lies almost touching the stone pavement to which it is riveted by a massive iron peg. A few inches away is the edge of a rug; it is grossly wrinkled at this point, doubtless as a result of the convulsive, but necessarily very restricted, movements of the victim attempting to struggle.

The man is still standing about a yard away, half leaning over her. He looks at her face, seen upside down, her dark eyes made larger by their surrounding eyeshadow, her mouth wide open as if screaming. The man's posture allows his face to be seen only in a vague profile, but one senses in it a violent exaltation, despite the rigid attitude, the silence, the immobility. His back is slightly arched. His left hand, the only one visible, holds up at some distance from the body a piece of cloth, some dark-colored piece of clothing, which drags on the carpet, and which must be the long cape with its gold-embroidered lining.

This immense silhouette hides most of the bare flesh over which the red stain, spreading from the globe of the breast, runs in long rivulets that branch out, growing narrower, upon the pale background of the bust and the flank. One thread has reached the armpit and runs in an almost straight, thin line along the arm; others have run down toward the waist and traced out, along one side of the belly, the hip, the top of the thigh, a more random network already starting to congeal. Three or four tiny veins have reached the hollow between the legs, meeting in a sinuous line, touching the point of the V formed by the outspread legs, and disappearing into the black tuft.

Look, now the flesh is still intact: the black tuft and the white belly, the soft curve of the hips, the narrow waist, and, higher up, the pearly breasts rising and falling in time with the rapid breathing, whose rhythm grows more accelerated. The man, close to her, one knee on the floor, leans farther over. The head, with its long, curly hair, which alone is free to move somewhat, turns from side to side, struggling; finally the woman's mouth twists open, while the flesh is torn open, the blood spurts out over the tender skin, stretched tight, the carefully shadowed eyes grow abnormally large, the mouth opens wider, the head twists violently, one last time, from right to left, then more gently, to fall back finally and become still, amid the mass of black hair spread out on the velvet.

Afterward, the whole setting is empty, the enormous room with its purple shadows and its stone columns proliferating in all directions, the monumental staircase with no handrail that twists upward, growing narrower and vaguer as it rises into the darkness, toward the top of the vaults where it disappears.

Near the body, whose wound has stiffened, whose brilliance is already growing dim, the thin smoke from the incense burner traces complicated scrolls in the still air: first a coil turned horizontally to the left, which then straightens out and rises slightly, then returns to the axis of its point of origin, which it crosses as it moves to the right, then turns back in the first direction, only to wind back again, thus forming an irregular sinusoidal[3] curve, more and more flattened out, and rising, vertically, toward the top of the canvas.

3. S-shaped.

NADINE GORDIMER
born 1923

In the introduction to her *Selected Stories* (1983), Nadine Gordimer observes that "a writer is selected by his subject—his subject being the *consciousness* of his own era." The emphasis is Gordimer's, her way of insisting that the writer's vision is bounded by time and place, thus fundamentally conditioned by historical context. Gordimer's observation reflects a universal truth of literary creation, but it has a more immediate bearing on her own situation in her native South Africa, until recently under the apartheid system. It speaks to the public aspect of literature as testimony, and illuminates her conception of the social responsibility of the writer, a responsibility that, in her case, derives its force from the steady moral consciousness she has brought to her vocation in the racially divided society created by apartheid. Gordimer's work is a response to the institutional racism that was for decades the distinguishing feature of the political, economic, and social life of her country; it is an expression of her refusal to accommodate herself to the system, despite her status as a member of the dominant white minority. She has summed up the active sense of commitment that informs her writings in a terse remark in

The Essential Gesture (1988): "The tension between standing apart and being fully involved—that is what makes a writer. That is where we begin."

But although Gordimer has acknowledged the moral imperative of imaginative expression in her circumstances, she has had to contend with two major problems in her development as a writer. The first has to do with the limitations imposed on her personal experience by the racial divide in her society. For if her moral consciousness sets her apart from the majority of her white compatriots, her very status seems to preclude her from a direct grasp of the experience of the nonwhite population, whose depressed condition provides the framework of her fictional universe. She has had, therefore, to risk an inadequate representation of this population in her depiction of their lives. She has also had to consider the weight of conviction her own work could assume for the disadvantaged majority of her country, even as she took on their cause, a problem she has examined with clarity in her essay *Where Do Whites Fit In?* Nonetheless, her imaginative entry into these other domains of life in South Africa has been nothing less than authoritative, carried by the powerful flow of her sympathy and facilitated by her keen observations and precise formulations.

The second problem arises from the inevitable tensions between high moral purpose and the muddy complexities of actual human lives. Gordimer's reflection in essay after essay on the pressures exerted on her art by the lived situation that forms the background to her work provides evidence, beyond her fiction, of her acute consciousness of this problem. The sensitiveness of her portrayals and the technical scruple she displays bear witness to her attention to the pitfalls of a political moralism that reduces the human condition to the single dimension of an ideological viewpoint, however generous or well meaning. Thus, even as the focus of her work remains the world of apartheid, this world takes shape as a social and moral universe within which the drama of human existence is played out. The political and social reference endows with solidity and heightened meaning such perennial themes as love and sexuality, the need for heroic sacrifice, and ultimately, the consciousness of mortality. These and other themes are developed within the symbolic framework of the South African landscape itself, which is evoked as a force in human life. Gordimer has shaped her perceptions into a personal statement that is sustained by a formal organization expressive of a mature vision of the world. While the fictional works proceed from a deep moral impulse, they also represent a mode of negotiation between the apparently conflicting demands of aesthetics and politics. It is Gordimer's constant attention to this tension that confers on her fictional works an integrity all their own.

Gordimer was born in 1923, in Springs, a small town near Johannesburg, in the Transvaal, the principal gold mining region of South Africa. She was the younger of two sisters born to a Jewish jeweler who had emigrated as a child from Lithuania and an Englishwoman. Though the family was associated with the liberal tradition of English-speaking South Africans, little in Gordimer's background suggests the radical direction her work was to take, for her early life was spent in the comfortable environment of the white minority in South Africa, the setting from which many of her novels move out to connect with events and situations in the world beyond. She has indicated that, although her formal education was by no means spotty, she was an indifferent student, describing herself as a "bolter" who in her early teens preferred the open spaces of the South African veld or the corridors of the local library to the classrooms at the Convent of Our Lady of Mercy. Her early passion for reading can be attributed to her secluded childhood, from which literature provided the most agreeable diversion, taking her out of the mundane reality of her provincial town not only into the world of children's books but also into the agitated world of adult experience. She has cited Maupassant, Chekov, Maugham, and Lawrence among the early stimulators of her imagination. Writing seems to have come to her naturally. Her first published work, a short story titled *The Quest for Seen Gold*, appeared in the children's section of the Johannesburg *Sunday Express* when she was only fourteen. She entered the University of the Witwatersrand in Johannesburg in 1945, but found it stifling and left after only a year. She thereafter devoted herself entirely to writing, producing at this stage of her career a series of short stories published in local journals, later collected as *Face to Face* (1949). Her second collection, *The Soft Voice of the Serpent*, was published in England in 1952 and quickly established her international reputation as an accomplished short story writer.

When Gordimer turned to a more extended form with her first novel, *The Lying Days* (1953), she drew on her own experience in Springs to portray the restless emotional state of Helen, her adolescent heroine, as she seeks an anchor in the world. The first-person narrative records Helen's growing disaffection toward the complacent and narrow-minded white community and her emerging dissidence, provoked in part by political developments in South Africa immediately following World War II, when the first measures were being taken by the Afrikaner government to disenfranchise Africans and the Africans themselves were displaying early resistance. Gordimer's novel registers the impact of these developments, but they remain subordinated to its primary psychological concern, in which the influence of Virginia Woolf is discernible. Still, the narrative retains a strong connection with realism in its incidental depiction of the harsh social realities of South Africa. This aspect of the work relates in particular to the situation of the Africans, who hover on the margins of the heroine's consciousness but whose plight and struggle are the prime factors in the awakening of her social awareness. Recognizable here already is what was to become an increasing preoccupation with the relationship between private experience and public events.

Gordimer confronts the problem of race relations more directly in her second novel, *A World of Strangers* (1958), which dwells on the obstacles apartheid presents to normal self-expression. The frustrating attempts of a group of black and white intellectuals and artists to establish human relations across racial lines are narrated by a young Englishman, Toby Hood, an outsider whose detached attitude to the problems of life in an atmosphere of political repression seems intended as an indictment of the shallow liberalism of many of her white compatriots. *Occasion for Loving* (1963) brings a further complication to the racial theme in its story of an uneasy love affair between a black artist and a married white woman. Here, Gordimer employs a female narrator who shares the social conventions of the white minority but is progressively drawn into the drama of the main characters. Her involvement affords a vantage point for exposing the complacency and hypocrisy of the white middle class.

Gordimer's first three novels show her evolving a personal style in which rhetorical eloquence serves a tough intelligence. In their different ways, these novels are innovative, but they appear as tentative moves toward the involved narrative strategies of her subsequent work, beginning with *The Late Bourgeois World* (1966). The overtly political plot of this novella is constructed around its protagonist's recollections of her relations with her previous husband, a white revolutionary who turns out to have betrayed his African friends and whose death is announced at the beginning of the story. The retrospective nature of her reflections, fit into a single day, sets the tone for a meditation on the possibilities of human solidarity in the face of adverse social forces. The ironic title conveys the work's critique of traditional liberalism as a response to the authoritarian posture of the apartheid regime. A certain utopianism haunts the radicalism that emerges at the end of the novella, but it is dissipated by the change of setting for Gordimer's next novel, *A Guest of Honour* (1971). Within the broad sweep of its action, which is centered on a newly independent African country, the novel explores through the psychology and fortunes of its characters, white and black, the ambiguities of political options as they flow from the personal dispositions of actors on the public stage.

The Conservationist (1974) is a parable of South Africa that offers an interpretation of the country's racial divide in cultural terms, opposing the confident materialism of its protagonist, Mehring, a white industrialist, to the mythical imagination of the Africans who work the farm he has acquired on the outskirts of Johannesburg. The novel's powerful evocation of the South African landscape establishes the symbolic context for a development in which the submerged consciousness of the Africans is reasserted over the white man's domineering and insensitive attitude to the world. The element of parable is also felt in the reversal of situations projected by Gordimer in *July's People* (1981), whose contrived plot involves a white family driven by an uprising to seek refuge with their African servant in his village. The family's painful adjustments to its displacement affords a view into the antagonisms by which South African society is riven and suggests at the same time the prospects for their resolution.

Gordimer's struggle to express formally her thematic concerns is amply demonstrated in *Burger's Daughter* (1979), a novel about the intersection between private experience and public events. Its action progresses through the long argument Rosa Burger conducts with herself on the competing claims of the ordinary life around her and pious affection for her father, a martyr of the antiapartheid movement. Gordimer's subtle delineation of Burger's mind alternates with a meticulous reconstruction of her character's social background. The density of the prose imparts to Burger's introspection a note of high seriousness: "But the change from life to death—what had all the certainties I had from my father to do with that?" Burger is finally granted the insight that these certainties—"Justice, equality, the brotherhood of man, human dignity"—are not mere abstract concepts but terms denoting universal values without whose active manifestation in the public realm private life itself may well be compromised. The procession of female characters in Gordimer's novels is given a remarkable turn in *A Sport of Nature* (1987), in the figure of Hillela, a white girl whose disrupted childhood in South Africa leads her to the personal odyssey she undertakes across Africa as she seeks to establish a total relationship, sensual and emotional, with the continent of her birth. Gordimer's latest novel, *My Son's Story* (1990), reassembles the themes of her previous work in its double perspective on the ordeals of Sonny, a "coloured" schoolteacher turned political activist whose extramarital affair with a white woman devoted to the liberal cause provokes a crisis in his family, a crisis that Gordimer places in the wider context of public experience and political commitment.

Though Gordimer is best known for her novels, she is widely acknowledged as one of the greatest contemporary practitioners of the genre of the short story. *Oral History*, from *A Soldier's Embrace* (1980) demonstrates her skilled handling of the form. The parallel between the intrusion of Christianity into the lives of the backwoods Africans (*seek, and ye shall find*) and their historical burden of colonial domination (*seek and destroy*) provides the historical and cultural background for the story's focus on the psychology of the informer. The village chief, alienated from his people by his ambiguous situation as the despised representative of a foreign power, is in the grip of a moral confusion. The wholeness of Gordimer's depiction of his community, fashioned from carefully positioned details, lends its full weight to the irony of the title, with its suggestion of the discrepancy between the status of the chief as the trusted repository of tradition and his act of betrayal, which appears less as a sign of loyalty to the colonial government than as his response to his solitude.

The story's tragic outcome is not merely a realistic report on the methods of colonial repression; it is also a measure of Gordimer's sympathy for its victims. Her identification finds symbolic expression in the numerous references to the mopane tree, whose various roles and changing features become integral to the development and meaning of the story. As the "blood and rust" of its vegetation during the spring foreshadows the calamity to come, so the mopane tree at the end of the story represents the clan's stubborn resilience. The tree thus functions as the symbolic center of the story, its suggestion of the continuity of the clan expanding the narrative scope beyond its immediate theme of the informer, to touch on that of the bond between individual and community. Thus the story does not merely record a tragic incident in modern African experience but captures a dramatic moment in the turns and paradoxes of African history.

The high esteem in which Gordimer is held stems in part from her principled stand against apartheid; no other creative writer has informed the international perception of South Africa as fully and effectively as she has done. This esteem also stems from the recognition of her accomplishment as a writer, for her work does not merely reflect events and situations in the real world but also achieves a formal distinction that is the product of a deeply considered aesthetics. The fine balance she maintains between the factual and the imaginative puts her in the company of the great political writers of our time, such as Milan Kundera and Gabriel García Márquez, while the convergence in her work of moral earnestness and technical range recalls Conrad. Her status as one of the major writers of the century has been confirmed by the many prizes and honors that have come her way, culminating in the award of the Nobel Prize for literature in 1991.

Robert F. Haugh, *Nadine Gordimer: The Meticulous Vision* (1974), is a valuable early study. Stephen Clingman, *The Novels of Nadine Gordimer: History from the Inside* (1986), and Andrew Vogel Ettin, *Betrayals of the Body Politic: The Literary Commitments of Nadine Gordimer* (1993), offer comprehensive assessments of Gordimer's fiction, while Dominic Head, *Nadine Gordimer* (1994), focuses on the relationship between Gordimer's political themes and her formal preoccupations. Rowland Smith, ed., *Critical Essays on Nadine Gordimer* (1990), contains chapters by various writers on individual works and aspects of her work. *The Essential Gesture: Writing, Politics and Places* (1988) is an important collection of Gordimer's essays; its value is enhanced by the excellent introduction and commentaries on the items by the editor, Stephen Clingman. Nancy Topping Bazin and Marilyn Dallman Seymour, eds., *Conversations with Nadine Gordimer* (1990), bring together Gordimer's interviews, dating back to 1958, thus providing a historical perspective on the evolution of her ideas in relation to her work.

PRONOUNCING GLOSSARY

The following list uses common English syllables to provide rough equivalents of selected words whose pronunciation may be unfamiliar to the general reader.

assegai: *ah-see-guy*

Empangeni: *em-pang-gay-nee*

mopane: *mo-pah-nay*

Oral History

There's always been one house like a white man's house in the village of Dilolo.[1] Built of brick with a roof that bounced signals from the sun. You

---

1. From the context, a village in Zimbabwe, formerly Southern Rhodesia, where the war of independence (ca. 1966–80) was based on guerrilla tactics.

could see it through the mopane[2] trees as you did the flash of paraffin tins the women carried on their heads, bringing water from the river. The rest of the village was built of river mud, grey, shaped by the hollows of hands, with reed thatch and poles of mopane from which the leaves had been ripped like fish-scales.

It was the chief's house. Some chiefs have a car as well but this was not an important chief, the clan is too small for that, and he had the usual stipend from the government.[3] If they had given him a car he would have had no use for it. There is no road: the army patrol Land Rovers come upon the people's cattle, startled as buck, in the mopane scrub. The village has been there a long time. The chief's grandfather was the clan's grandfathers' chief, and his name is the same as that of the chief who waved his warriors to down assegais[4] and took the first bible from a Scottish Mission Board white man.[5] *Seek and ye shall find*, the missionaries said.

The villagers in those parts don't look up, any more, when the sting-shaped army planes fly over twice a day. Only fish-eagles are disturbed, take off, screaming, keen swerving heads lifting into their invaded domain of sky. The men who have been away to work on the mines can read, but there are no newspapers. The people hear over the radio the government's count of how many army trucks have been blown up, how many white soldiers are going to be buried with *full military honours*—something that is apparently white people's way with their dead.

The chief had a radio, and he could read. He read to the headmen the letter from the government saying that anyone hiding or giving food and water to those who were fighting against the government's army would be put in prison. He read another letter from the government saying that to protect the village from these men who went over the border[6] and came back with guns to kill people and burn huts, anybody who walked in the bush after dark would be shot. Some of the young men who, going courting or drinking to the next village, might have been in danger, were no longer at home in their fathers' care, anyway. The young go away: once it was to the mines, now—the radio said—it was over the border to learn how to fight. Sons walked out of the clearing of mud huts; past the chief's house; past the children playing with the models of police patrol Land Rovers made out of twisted wire. The children called out, Where are you going? The young men didn't answer and they hadn't come back.

There was a church of mopane and mud with a mopane flagpole to fly a white flag when somebody died; the funeral service was more or less the same protestant one the missionaries brought from Scotland and it was combined with older rituals to entrust the newly-dead to the ancestors. Ululating[7] women with whitened faces sent them on their way to the missionaries' last judgment. The children were baptized with names chosen by portent in consultation between the mother and an old man who read immutable fate in the fall of small bones cast like dice from a horn cup.

---

2. A shrublike tree.   3. Under the British system of "indirect rule," African chiefs were paid a small salary for their services to the colonial government.   4. A short spear perfected by Chaka, the Zulu conqueror, for use in close combat.   5. Christian missionary activity became intense in the 1880s and 1890s in southern Africa.   6. Most likely a reference to Zambia, a neighboring country that provided a safe haven for the freedom fighters.   7. Wailing.

On all occasions and most Saturday nights there was a beer-drink, which the chief attended. An upright chair from his house was brought out for him although everyone else squatted comfortably on the sand, and he was offered the first taste from an old decorated gourd dipper (other people drank from baked-bean or pilchard tins[8]) — it is the way of people of the village.

It is also the way of the tribe to which the clan belongs and the subcontinent to which the tribe belongs, from Matadi in the west to Mombasa in the east, from Entebbe in the north to Empangeni[9] in the south, that everyone is welcome at a beer-drink. No traveller or passer-by, poling down the river in his pirogue,[1] leaving the snake-skin trail of his bicycle wheels through the sand, betraying his approach — if the dogs are sleeping by the cooking fires and the children have left their home-made highways — only by the brittle fragmentation of the dead leaves as he comes unseen through miles of mopane, is a presence to be questioned. Everyone for a long way round on both sides of the border near Dilolo has a black skin, speaks the same language and shares the custom of hospitality. Before the government started to shoot people at night to stop more young men leaving when no one was awake to ask, "Where are you going?" people thought nothing of walking ten miles from one village to another for a beer-drink.

But unfamiliar faces have become unusual. If the firelight caught such a face, it backed into darkness. No one remarked the face. Not even the smallest child who never took its eyes off it, crouching down among the knees of men with soft, little boy's lips held in wonderingly over teeth as if an invisible grown-up hand were clamped there. The young girls giggled and flirted from the background, as usual. The older men didn't ask for news of relatives or friends outside the village. The chief seemed not to see one face or faces in distinction from any other. His eyes came to rest instead on some of the older men. He gazed and they felt it.

Coming out of the back door of his brick house with its polished concrete steps, early in the morning, he hailed one of them. The man was passing with his hobbling cows and steadily bleating goats; stopped, with the turn of one who will continue on his way in a moment almost without breaking step. But the summons was for him. The chief wore a frayed collarless shirt and old trousers, like the man, but he was never barefoot. In the hand with a big steel watch on the wrist, he carried his thick-framed spectacles, and drew down his nose between the fingers of the other hand; he had the authoritative body of a man who still has his sexual powers but his eyes flickered against the light of the sun and secreted flecks of matter like cold cream at the corners. After the greetings usual between a chief and one of his headmen together with whom, from the retreat in the mopane forest where they lay together in the same age-group recovering from circumcision,[2] he had long ago emerged a man, the chief said, "When is your son coming back?"

---

8. Tins that originally contained canned fish; they were recycled for drinking.   9. A royal village in Zululand. Matadi is a port in Zaire on the Atlantic Ocean. Mombasa is a coastal town in Kenya, on the Indian Ocean. Entebbe is the principal city in Uganda.   1. Canoe.   2. The central element in the rites of initiation.

"I have no news."

"Did he sign for the mines?"[3]

"No."

"He's gone to the tobacco farms?"

"He didn't tell us."

"Gone away to find work and doesn't tell his mother? What sort of child is that? Didn't you teach him?"

The goats were tongue-ing three hunchback bushes that were all that was left of a hedge round the chief's house. The man took out a round tin dented with child's tooth-marks and taking care not to spill any snuff, dosed himself. He gestured at the beasts, for permission: "They're eating up your house . . ." He made a move towards the necessity to drive them on.

"There is nothing left there to eat." The chief ignored his hedge, planted by his oldest wife who had been to school at the mission up the river. He stood among the goats as if he would ask more questions. Then he turned and went back to his yard, dismissing himself. The other man watched. It seemed he might call after; but instead drove his animals with the familiar cries, this time unnecessarily loud and frequent.

Often an army patrol Land Rover came to the village. No one could predict when this would be because it was not possible to count the days in between and be sure that so many would elapse before it returned, as could be done in the case of a tax-collector or cattle-dipping officer.[4] But it could be heard minutes away, crashing through the mopane like a frightened animal, and dust hung marking the direction from which it was coming. The children ran to tell. The women went from hut to hut. One of the chief's wives would enjoy the importance of bearing the news: "The government is coming to see you." He would be out of his house when the Land Rover stopped and a black soldier (murmuring towards the chief the required respectful greeting in their own language) jumped out and opened the door for the white soldier. The white soldier had learned the names of all the local chiefs. He gave greetings with white men's brusqueness: "Everything all right?" And the chief repeated to him: "Everything is all right." "No one been bothering you in this village?" "No one is troubling us." But the white soldier signalled to his black men and they went through every hut busy as wives when they are cleaning, turning over bedding, thrusting gun-butts into the pile of ash and rubbish where the chickens searched, even looking in, their eyes dazzled by darkness, to the hut where one of the old women who had gone crazy had to be kept most of the time. The white soldier stood beside the Land Rover waiting for them. He told the chief of things that were happening not far from the village; not far at all. The road that passed five kilometres away had been blown up. "Someone plants land-mines in the road and as soon as we repair it they put them there again. Those people come from across the river[5] and they pass this way. They wreck our vehicles and kill people."

The heads gathered round weaved as if at the sight of bodies laid there horrifyingly before them.

---

3. That is, become a migrant worker in the gold mines in the Republic of South Africa.   4. The veterinary officer who supervised the forced wading of cattle into a shallow pool of water mixed with disinfectant, to rid them of ticks and other parasites.   5. The Zambesi.

"They will kill you, too—burn your huts, all of you—if you let them stay with you."

A woman turned her face away: "Aïe-aïe-aïe-aïe."

His forefinger half-circled his audience. "I'm telling you. You'll see what they do."

The chief's latest wife, taken only the year before and of the age-group of his elder grandchildren, had not come out to listen to the white man. But she heard from others what he had said, and fiercely smoothing her legs with grease, demanded of the chief, "Why does he want us to die, that white man!"

Her husband, who had just been a passionately shuddering lover, became at once one of the important old with whom she did not count and could not argue. "You talk about things you don't know. Don't speak for the sake of making a noise."

To punish him, she picked up the strong, young girl's baby she had borne him and went out of the room where she slept with him on the big bed that had come down the river by barge, before the army's machine guns were pointing at the other bank.

He appeared at his mother's hut. There, the middle-aged man on whom the villagers depended, to whom the government looked when it wanted taxes paid and culling orders[6] carried out, became a son—the ageless category, no matter from which age-group to another he passed in the progression of her life and his. The old woman was at her toilet.[7] The great weight of her body settled around her where she sat on a reed mat outside the door. He pushed a stool under himself. Set out was a small mirror with a pink plastic frame and stand, in which he caught sight of his face, screwed up. A large black comb; a little carved box inlaid with red lucky beans she had always had, he used to beg to be allowed to play with it fifty years ago. He waited, not so much out of respect as in the bond of indifference to all outside their mutual contact that reasserts itself when lions and their kin lie against one another.

She cocked a glance, swinging the empty loops of her stretched earlobes. He did not say what he had come for.

She had chosen a tiny bone spoon from the box and was poking with trembling care up each round hole of distended nostril. She cleaned the crust of dried snot and dust from her delicate instrument and flicked the dirt in the direction away from him.

She said: "Do you know where your sons are?"

"Yes, I know where my sons are. You have seen three of them here today. Two are in school at the mission. The baby—he's with the mother." A slight smile, to which the old woman did not respond. Her preferences among the sons had no connection with sexual pride.

"Good. You can be glad of all that. But don't ask other people about theirs."

As often when people who share the same blood share the same thought, for a moment mother and son looked exactly alike, he old-womanish, she mannish.

---

6. A regulation designed to control the cattle population.   7. That is, cleaning herself.

"If the ones we know are missing, there are not always empty places," he said.

She stirred consideringly in her bulk. Leaned back to regard him: "It used to be that all children were our own children. All sons our sons. *Old-fashion*, these people here"—the hard English word rolled out of their language like a pebble, and came to rest where aimed, at his feet.

It was spring: the mopane leaves turn, drying up and dying, spattering the sand with blood and rust—a battlefield, it must have looked, from the patrol planes. In August there is no rain to come for two months yet. Nothing grows but the flies hatch. The heat rises daily and the nights hold it, without a stir, till morning. On these nights the radio voice carried so clearly it could be heard from the chief's house all through the village. Many were being captured in the bush and killed by the army—*seek and destroy* was what the white men said now—and many in the army were being set upon in the bush or blown up in their trucks and buried with full military honours. This was expected to continue until October because the men in the bush knew that it was their last chance before the rains came and chained their feet in mud.

On these hot nights when people cannot sleep anyway, beer-drinks last until very late. People drink more; the women know this, and brew more. There is a fire but no one sits close round it.

Without a moon the dark is thick with heat; when the moon is full the dark shimmers thinly in a hot mirage off the river. Black faces are blue, there are watermarks along noses and biceps. The chief sat on his chair and wore shoes and socks in spite of the heat; those drinking nearest him could smell the suffering of his feet. The planes of jaw and lips he noticed in moonlight molten over them, moonlight pouring moths broken from white cases on the mopane and mosquitoes rising from the river, pouring glory like the light in the religious pictures people got at the mission—he had seen those faces about lately in the audacity of day, as well. An ox had been killed and there was the scent of meat sizzling in the village (just look at the behaviour of the dogs, they knew) although there was no marriage or other festival that called for someone to slaughter one of his beasts. When the chief allowed himself, at least, to meet the eyes of a stranger, the whites that had been showing at an oblique angle disappeared and he took rather than saw the full gaze of the seeing eye: the pupils with their defiance, their belief, their claim, hold, on him. He let it happen only once. For the rest, he saw their arrogant lifted jaws to each other and warrior smiles to the girls, as they drank. The children were drawn to them, fighting one another silently for places close up. Towards midnight—his watch had its own glowing galaxy—he left his chair and did not come back from the shadows where men went to urinate. Often at beer-drinks the chief would go home while others were still drinking.

He went to his brick house whose roof shone almost bright as day. He did not go to the room where his new wife and sixth son would be sleeping in the big bed, but simply took from the kitchen, where it was kept when not in use, a bicycle belonging to one of his hangers-on, relative or retainer. He wheeled it away from the huts in the clearing, his village and grandfather's village that disappeared so quickly behind him in the mopane, and began to ride through the sand. He was not afraid he would meet a patrol and be shot; alone at night in the sand forest, the forested desert he had known before and would know beyond his span of life, he didn't believe in the power of a roving band of government men to end that life. The going was heavy but he had mastered when young the art of riding on this, the only terrain he knew, and the ability came back. In an hour he arrived at the army post, called out who he was to the sentry with a machine gun, and had to wait, like a beggar rather than a chief, to be allowed to approach and be searched. There were black soldiers on duty but they woke the white man. It was the one who knew his name, his clan, his village, the way these modern white men were taught. He seemed to know at once why the chief had come; frowning in concentration to grasp details, his mouth was open in a smile and the point of his tongue curled touching at back teeth the way a man will verify facts one by one on his fingers. "How many?"

"Six or ten or—but sometimes it's only, say, three or one . . . I don't know. One is here, he's gone; they come again."

"They take food, they sleep, and off. Yes. They make the people give them what they want, that's it, eh? And you know who it is who hides them—who shows them where to sleep—of course you know."

The chief sat on one of the chairs in that place, the army's place, and the white soldier was standing. "Who is it—" the chief was having difficulty in saying what he wanted in English, he had the feeling it was not coming out as he had meant nor being understood as he had expected. "I can't know who is it"—a hand moved restlessly, he held a breath and released it—"in the village there's many, plenty people. If it's this one or this one—" He stopped, shaking his head with a reminder to the white man of his authority, which the white soldier was quick to placate. "Of course. Never mind. They frighten the people; the people can't say no. They kill people who say no, eh; cut their ears off, you know that? Tear away their lips. Don't you see the pictures in the papers?"

"We never saw it. I heard the government say on the radio."

"They're still drinking . . . How long—an hour ago?"

The white soldier checked with a look the other men, whose stance had changed to that of bodies ready to break into movement: grab weapons, run, fling themselves at the Land Rovers guarded in the dark outside. He picked up the telephone receiver but blocked the mouth-piece as if it were someone about to make an objection. "Chief, I'll be with you in a moment. —Take him to the duty room and make coffee. Just wait—" he leaned his full reach towards a drawer in a cabinet on the left of the desk and, scrabbling to get it open, took out a half-full bottle of brandy. Behind the chief's back he gestured the bottle towards the chief, and a black soldier jumped obediently to take it.

The chief went to a cousin's house in a village the other side of the army post later that night. He said he had been to a beer-drink and could not ride home because of the white men's curfew.

The white soldier had instructed that he should not be in his own village when the arrests were made so that he could not be connected with these and would not be in danger of having his ears cut off for taking heed of what the government wanted of him, or having his lips mutilated for what he had told.

His cousin gave him blankets. He slept in a hut with her father. The deaf old man was aware neither that he had come nor was leaving so early that last night's moon, the size of the bicycle's reflector, was still shiny in the sky. The bicycle rode up on spring-hares without disturbing them, in the forest; there was a stink of jackal-fouling still sharp on the dew. Smoke already marked his village; early cooking fires were lit. Then he saw that the smoke, the black particles spindling at his face, were not from cooking fires. Instead of going faster as he pumped his feet against the weight of sand the bicycle seemed to slow along with his mind, to find in each revolution of its wheels the countersurge: to stop; not go on. But there was no way not to reach what he found. The planes only children bothered to look up at any longer had come in the night and dropped something terrible and alive that no one could have read or heard about enough to be sufficiently afraid of. He saw first a bloody kaross,[8] a dog caught on the roots of an upturned tree. The earth under the village seemed to have burst open and flung away what it carried: the huts, pots, gourds, blankets, the tin trunks, alarm-clocks, curtain-booth photographs, bicycles, radios and shoes brought back from the mines, the bright cloths young wives wound on their heads, the pretty pictures of white lambs and pink children at the knees of the golden-haired Christ the Scottish Mission Board first brought long ago—all five generations of the clan's life that had been chronicled by each succeeding generation in episodes told to the next. The huts had staved in like broken anthills. Within earth walls baked and streaked by fire the thatch and roof-poles were ash. He bellowed and stumbled from hut to hut, nothing answered frenzy, not even a chicken rose from under his feet. The walls of his house still stood. It was gutted and the roof had buckled. A black stiff creature lay roasted on its chain in the yard. In one of the huts he saw a human shape transformed the same way, a thing of stiff tar daubed on a recognizable framework. It was the hut where the mad woman lived; when those who had survived fled, they had forgotten her.

The chief's mother and his youngest wife were not among them. But the baby boy lived, and will grow up in the care of the older wives. No one can say what it was the white soldier said over the telephone to his commanding officer, and if the commanding officer had told him what was going to be done, or whether the white soldier knew, as a matter of procedure laid down in his military training for this kind of war, what would be done. The chief hanged himself in the mopane. The police or the army (much the same these days, people confuse them) found the bicycle beneath his dangling shoes. So the family hanger-on still rides it; it would have been lost if it had been safe in the kitchen when the raid

8. A cloak made of animal skin.

came. No one knows where the chief found a rope, in the ruins of his village.

The people are beginning to go back. The dead are properly buried in ancestral places in the mopane forest. The women are to be seen carrying tins and grain panniers of mud[9] up from the river. In talkative bands they squat and smear, raising the huts again. They bring sheaves of reeds exceeding their own height, balanced like the cross-stroke of a majuscular[1] T on their heads. The men's voices sound through the mopane as they choose and fell trees for the roof supports.

A white flag on a mopane pole hangs outside the house whose white walls, built like a white man's, stand from before this time.

9. For rebuilding homes. *Panniers:* large baskets, usually slung over the backs of animals.   1. Capital.

YEHUDA AMICHAI
born 1924

Yehuda Amichai belongs to the first generation of Israeli poets to be fully naturalized into both the language and the landscape of modern Israel. This generation, which came of age with the establishment of the state in 1948, includes such remarkable poets as Nathan Zach, Dalia Ravikovitch, T. Carmi, and Dan Pagis. As a very diverse group, they brought to fruition the dream of preceding generations of Israeli poets, including H. N. Bialik and Saul Tchernikovsky, to create a poetic idiom that was completely at home with the colloquial rhythms and idiomatic expressions of modern Hebrew. The challenge of this task is a function of the unique history of that language. Hebrew was a spoken language only up to the close of the biblical period in the sixth century. For the next two thousand years, beginning with the exile of the Jews to Babylonia and their long dispersion from the land of Israel and continuing to the present day—a period known as the Diaspora—Hebrew ceased to be a spoken language. During the Diaspora, Hebrew was principally a vehicle for the sacred and the liturgical writings, for biblical and Talmudic discourse, and for official communication, while local Jewish dialects like Yiddish and Ladino served the more immediate function of the vernacular. The movement to modernize medieval Hebrew began in the eighteenth century, and by the late nineteenth century modern Hebrew had established itself as a vigorous literary language. But it was not revived as a spoken language and adapted to the daily needs of ordinary secular life until the early twentieth century, when European Jews emigrated to Palestine with the intention of ending the Diaspora. As an essential element of reestablishing a Jewish state in Palestine, they set about reviving Hebrew as a modern, spoken language.

The long separation of biblical Hebrew from daily life meant that it had not undergone the changes in pronunciation, grammar, syntax, and vocabulary that gradually change living languages over the years. As a result, modern Hebrew is just one step away from the biblical and preserves archaic forms of the language far more fully and immediately than modern Greek and Italian, for instance, preserve classical Greek and Latin. The poets who emerged out of Israel's war for independence in 1948, known collectively as the "Palmach generation," and those who followed them have faced the challenge of reconciling the highly charged spiritual resonance of the biblical language with the worldly concerns of contemporary Israeli society. Amichai, perhaps more than any other contemporary poet, has contributed not only to liberating the language of modern Israeli poetry from the great burden of its history but, by juxtaposing the monumental and the ordinary, to appropriating the language of the epic struggles of Israel for the mundane realities of the twentieth century.

At times there is a deceptive simplicity about Amichai's lyrics. They seem to address such ordinary moments, such casual encounters. And yet in their simplicity they capture the many, resonating layers of the language and the insistent and contradictory realities of contemporary Israeli life. His language is despairing, gently ironic, playful and passionate by turns, moving easily between a child's artlessness and the brusque directness of a war-hardened veteran. The scope of his poetry is enormous, but what he brings to each poem is a freshness of vision and metaphors that are rich in unexpected and illuminating juxtapositions—Rachel's tomb and Herzl's tomb, drying laundry and entrenched enmities, stones and undelivered messages, a lost child and a lost kid, the weariness of the poet who sees soldiers carried home from the hills like so much small change. These metaphors that thrust the deeply historical into the arms of the grittily immediate have inspired critics to compare Amichai not with his contemporaries but with Donne and Shakespeare.

Amichai's form of choice is the short lyric, but he has composed at least one memorable narrative poem, *The Travels of the Last Benjamin of Tudela*, and he often links a number of shorter poems into cycles on a single theme, as in the wrenching *Seven Laments for the War Dead* or the romantic *Six Poems for Tamar*. Many of his best poems are love poems, addressed to a woman or to Jerusalem — not as alternatives but as embedded in each others' essence. His poetry evokes with stunning immediacy that ancient city that other peoples and religions besides the Jews know as sacred and claim as home. Jerusalem is "an eternal heart, burning red," the place that must be remembered when all else is forgotten. Until 1967, it was a city divided only by a wall, across which intimate but hostile neighbors could watch each others' laundry drying.

This comfortableness with the language and landscape of Israel may appear surprising in light of the fact that Amichai was born in Würzberg, Germany, and only came to Israel with his family in 1936, when he was twelve. He had grown up in an Orthodox Jewish home and studied Hebrew since early childhood, however, and like so many other immigrants, he made the transition to modern Hebrew with relative ease. Despite the enforced move from Germany, in his poetry he speaks of his childhood as a time of happiness and peace now lost. His adult life began during the turbulent struggle to establish the Jewish state. He served with the Jewish Brigade in World War II and saw active duty as an infantryman with the Palmach during the Israeli War of Independence and with the Israeli army in 1956 and 1973.

After completing his studies at Hebrew University, Amichai became a secondary school teacher of Hebrew literature and the Bible, but his career as a teacher soon took second place to his career as a poet. He had begun writing poetry in 1949 and published his first collection of poems, *Now and in Other Days*, in 1955. With his second collection, *Two Hopes Away* (1958), he established himself as a major poet. Since then Amichai has published nine more volumes of poetry as well as novels — including the one translated as *Not of This Time, Not of This Place* (1968) — short stories, and plays.

Each volume of Amichai's poetry has sold nearly fifteen thousand copies, and that in a country with a population of only three million. His poems are included in school anthologies and recited on public occasions. In the introduction to *The*

Selected Poetry of Yehuda Amichai, Chana Bloch relates an anecdote that gives a more telling sense of the widespread popularity his works enjoy: "Some Israeli students were called up in the 1973 Yom Kippur War. As soon as they were notified, they went back to their rooms at the university, and each packed his gear, a rifle, and a book of Yehuda Amichai's poems." And this, as she points out, despite the fact that his work "isn't patriotic in the ordinary sense of the word, it doesn't cry death to the enemy, and it offers no simple consolation for killing and dying." Amichai was first brought to the attention of British and American readers by Ted Hughes, who published his work first in the journal *Modern Poetry in Translation* and collaborated with Amichai in translating a volume of selections from his early poetry, *Amen* (1977). Eight volumes of his poetry have appeared in English translation, and there are numerous translations into other languages as well.

Glenda Abramson, *The Writing of Yehuda Amichai: A Thematic Approach* (1989), provides a comprehensive overview of Amichai's work. A good sampling of his reviews can be found in *Contemporary Literary Criticism* (vols. 9, 22, and 57) and *Contemporary Authors* (vols. 85–88). Joseph Cohen, *Voices of Israel* (1990), includes a long essay on Amichai as well as an extended interview. Articles by Glenda Abramson, Naomi B. Sokoloff, and Nili Scharf Gold appear in "Amichai at Sixty" (1984), a special issue of *Prooftexts*.

PRONOUNCING GLOSSARY

The following list uses common English syllables and stress accents to provide rough equivalents of selected words whose pronunciation may be unfamiliar to the general reader.

Herzl: *hertz'-ul*

Ladino: *luh-dee'-no*

Palmach: *pall'-muhk*

Tudela: *too-del'uh*

Yehuda Amichai: *yuh-hoo'-duh a'-mi-kai*

If I Forget Thee, Jerusalem[1]

If I forget thee, Jerusalem,
Then let my right be forgotten.[2]
Let my right be forgotten, and my left remember.
Let my left remember, and your right close
And your mouth open near the gate.   5

I shall remember Jerusalem
And forget the forest—my love will remember,
Will open her hair, will close my window,
Will forget my right,
Will forget my left.   10

If the west wind does not come
I'll never forgive the walls,
Or the sea, or myself.

---

1. Translated by Assia Gutmann. The title is from Psalm 137:5.   2. Compare Psalm 137:5: "If I forget thee, O Jerusalem, let my right hand forget its cunning."

Should my right forget,
My left shall forgive,   15
I shall forget all water,
I shall forget my mother.

If I forget thee, Jerusalem,
Let my blood be forgotten.
I shall touch your forehead,   20
Forget my own,
My voice change
For the second and last time
To the most terrible of voices —
Or silence.   25

Of Three or Four in a Room[1]

Of three or four in a room
there is always one who stands beside the window.
He must see the evil among thorns
and the fires on the hill.
And how people who went out of their houses whole   5
are given back in the evening like small change.

Of three or four in a room
there is always one who stands beside the window,
his dark hair above his thoughts.
Behind him, words.   10
And in front of him, voices wandering without a knapsack,
hearts without provisions, prophecies without water,
large stones that have been returned
and stay sealed, like letters that have no
address and no one to receive them.   15

Sleep in Jerusalem[1]

While a chosen people[2]
become a nation like all the nations,
building its houses, paving its highways,
breaking open its earth for pipes and water,
we lie inside, in the low house,   5
late offspring of this old landscape.
The ceiling is vaulted above us with love
and the breath of our mouth
is as it was given us
and as we shall give it back.   10

Sleep is where there are stones.
In Jerusalem there is sleep. The radio
brings day-tunes from a land

---

1. Translated by Stephen Mitchell.   1. Translated by Harold Schimmel.   2. According to the Old Testament, God chose Abraham's descendants, the Jews, as the people through whom he would reveal himself.

where there is day.
And words that here are bitter,   15
like last year's almond on a tree,
are sung in a far country, and sweet.

And like a fire
in the hollowed trunk of an olive tree
an eternal heart is burning red   20
not far from the two sleepers.

God Has Pity on Kindergarten Children[1]

God has pity on kindergarten children.
He has less pity on school children.
And on grownups he has no pity at all,
he leaves them alone,
and sometimes they must crawl on all fours   5
in the burning sand
to reach the first-aid station
covered with blood.

But perhaps he will watch over true lovers
and have mercy on them and shelter them   10
like a tree over the old man
sleeping on a public bench.

Perhaps we too will give them
the last rare coins of compassion
that Mother handed down to us,   15
so that their happiness will protect us
now and in other days.

Jerusalem[1]

On a roof in the Old City[2]
laundry hanging in the late afternoon sunlight:
the white sheet of a woman who is my enemy,
the towel of a man who is my enemy,
to wipe off the sweat of his brow.   5

In the sky of the Old City
a kite.
At the other end of the string,
a child
I can't see   10
because of the wall.

We have put up many flags,
they have put up many flags.
To make us think that they're happy.
To make them think that we're happy.   15

---

1. Translated by Stephen Mitchell.   1. Translated by Stephen Mitchell.   2. The oldest, walled portion of Jerusalem, around which the new city has been built.

Tourists[1]

1

So condolence visits is what they're here for,
sitting around at the Holocaust Memorial, putting on a serious face
at the Wailing Wall,[2]
laughing behind heavy curtains in hotel rooms.

They get themselves photographed with the important dead   5
at Rachel's Tomb and Herzl's Tomb, and up on Ammunition Hill.[3]
They weep at the beautiful prowess of our boys,
lust after our tough girls
and hang up their underwear
to dry quickly   10
in cool blue bathrooms.

2

Once I was sitting on the steps near the gate at David's[4] Citadel and
I put down my two heavy baskets beside me. A group of tourists stood
there around their guide, and I became their point of reference. "You
see that man over there with the baskets? A little to the right of his
head there's an arch from the Roman period. A little to the right   5
of his head." "But he's moving, he's moving!" I said to myself:
Redemption will come only when they are told, "Do you see that arch
over there from the Roman period? It doesn't matter, but near it, a
little to the left and then down a bit, there's a man who has just bought
fruit and vegetables for his family."   10

An Arab Shepherd Is Searching for His Goat on Mount Zion[1]

An Arab shepherd is searching for his goat on Mount Zion
and on the opposite mountain I am searching
for my little boy.
An Arab shepherd and a Jewish father
both in their temporary failure.   5
Our voices meet above the Sultan's Pool[2]
in the valley between us. Neither of us wants
the child or the goat to get caught in the wheels
of the terrible *Had Gadya*[3] machine.

Afterward we found them among the bushes   10
and our voices came back inside us, laughing and crying.

1. Translated by Chana Bloch.   2. A remnant of the western wall of the second temple in Jerusalem;
a site of pilgrimage, lamentation, and prayer for Jews.   3. The site of a major battle in Israel's War of
Independence. Rachel was the second wife of Jacob and mother of Joseph and Benjamin. Theodor Herzl
(1860–1904), Hungarian-born founder of Zionism.   4. King David (died ca. 962 B.C.), who slew Goli-
ath and became the second king of Judah and Israel (after Saul); reputed author of many psalms.   1. Translated by Chana Bloch. The fortress of Jerusalem is built on Mt. Zion.   2. Translation of the Hebrew
name for a pool located in the valley just outside the walls of the Old City of Jerusalem.   3. One kid
(Hebrew); alludes to a Passover song in which "the goat that Daddy brought is eaten by a cat that is bitten
by a dog," and so on.

Searching for a goat or a son
has always been the beginning
of a new religion in these mountains.

North of San Francisco[1]

Here the soft hills touch the ocean
like one eternity touching another
and the cows grazing on them
ignore us, like angels.
Even the scent of ripe melon in the cellar   5
is a prophecy of peace.

The darkness doesn't war against the light,
it carries us forward
to another light, and the only pain
is the pain of not staying.   10

In my land, called holy,
they won't let eternity be:
they've divided it into little religions,
zoned it for God-zones,
broken it into fragments of history,   15
sharp and wounding unto death.
And they've turned the tranquil distances
into a nearness twitching with the pain of the present.

On the beach at Bolinas,[2] at the foot of the wooden steps,
I saw some girls lying face-down in the sand   20
naked and unashamed, drunk
on the kingdom everlasting,
their souls like doors
closing and opening,
closing and opening inside them   25
to the rhythm of the surf.

I Passed a House[1]

I passed a house where I once lived:
A man and a woman are still together in the whispers.
Many years have passed with the silent buzz
of staircase bulbs—on, off, on.

The keyholes are like small delicate wounds   5
through which all the blood has oozed out
and inside people are pale as death.

I want to stand once more as in my
first love, leaning on the doorpost
embracing you all night long, standing.   10

1. Translated by Chana Bloch.   2. A small town north of San Francisco.   1. Translated by Yehuda Amichai and Ted Hughes.

When we left at early dusk the house
started to crumble and collapse
and since then the town
and since then the whole world.

I want once more to have this longing   15
until dark-red burn marks show on the skin.

I want once more to be written
in the book of life, to be written
anew every day
until the writing hand hurts.   20

INGEBORG BACHMANN
1926–1973

Ingeborg Bachmann's reputation as one of the most significant postwar writers in
the German language is almost overshadowed by her image as an interpreter of
women's experience and a critic of Fascism. Winning early fame as a brilliant
young poet whose vivid yet philosophical lyrics brought her prize after prize, she
abandoned poetry in mid-career to write fiction that would say what "needed to be
said" and speak for those who could not speak for themselves. Women in particular
became the protagonists of her later work. Bachmann described the complex and
frequently unrecognized forces that shape women's social experience and constitute "ways of death" as often as ways of life. Her powerful intellect and gift for
precise description fused with a lyric tendency and strong ethical concerns to create a remarkable body of work that has been translated into twenty-two languages
and continues to influence contemporary writers.

Bachmann was born on June 25, 1926, in Klagenfurt, a city in southern Austria
close to the Italian and Yugoslavian borders. She was the oldest of three children;
her father was a teacher and later school principal, and her mother's family operated a knitwear firm. Although she lived outside Austria for most of her adult life,
moving permanently to Rome in 1963, much of her work is dominated by the
image of a spiritual "Austria" whose fluctuating borders and multiethnic heritage
create a unique view of the world. Several languages are spoken in her home
province of Carinthia, and the valley in which she lived had two names, German
and Slovene. Austria itself, although politically powerless, was the former center
of the multinational Hapsburg Empire and still participated in many cultures. The
notion of physical and psychological boundaries permeates all levels of her writing,
along with glimpses of an ideal freedom to move beyond artificial frontiers. Bachmann's own experience of political borders was sharpened when the Nazis
marched into Klagenfurt in 1938. She was twelve years old, and that moment, she
said, marked the end of her childhood. Attending schools in Klagenfurt throughout the war, she graduated in 1944 and studied briefly in Innsbruck and Graz
before entering the University of Vienna in 1946.

Bachmann's first story, *The Ferryboat*, was published in 1946, and other stories
as well as her first poems appeared over the next few years. While earning recognition as a creative writer, she also pursued a degree in philosophy with minors in
psychology and German literature. She prized the analytical philosophy of the
Vienna School (proscribed under Hitler) and rejected the "German irrationalism"
represented by existential philosopher Martin Heidegger (1889–1976). Her doc-

toral dissertation in 1950 was openly critical in analyzing the reception of Heidegger's philosophy. Three years later she published a major appreciative essay on the Viennese linguistic philosopher Ludwig Wittgenstein (1889–1951). What fascinated her about Wittgenstein was *"his despairing attempt to chart the limits of linguistic expression"* (emphasis in original), an attempt that is paralleled in her own poetry and fiction.

In the years following her doctorate, Bachmann traveled to Paris and London, gave poetry readings, held a series of jobs ranging from scriptwriter to newspaper correspondent, and began to write in different genres. She worked briefly in the office of the American occupation authorities in Vienna and was a member of the broadcasting group Red/White/Red between 1951 and 1953. For Red/White/Red she wrote a number of radio plays, including adaptations of works by Thomas Wolfe and Louis MacNeice. Her translation of MacNeice's radio script *The Dark Tower* was produced with music by British composer Benjamin Britten, and Bachmann's interest in mixed genres continued after she left Red/White/Red. Her second radio play, *The Cicadas*, was produced in 1954 with music by composer Hans Werner Henze, who later set several of her poems to music. Bachmann collaborated with Henze on other occasions and wrote the libretti for two of his operas as well as a ballet scenario. During the 1950s, she also wrote a novel, *City without a Name*, only to have it rejected by five publishers. Her early reputation was clearly based on the poetry, and recognition came quickly for her extraordinary combination of striking natural images and abstract argument. Addressing the constellation Ursa Major, she began "Great Bear, come down, shaggy night, / cloud-coated beast with the old eyes, star eyes. / Through the thickets your paws break / shimmering with their claws, / star claws." Her first volume, *Mortgaged Time*, appeared in 1953, and in the same year she received the prestigious annual prize awarded by Group 47 (a group of Austrian writers who banded together in 1947 in an effort to establish new directions for German literature). A second collection, *Invocation of the Great Bear*, was published in 1956, by which time she had moved to Rome, published poems in the international poetry journal *Botteghe oscure*, received a second prize, and been the subject of a cover story in the popular German magazine *Der Spiegel*.

Bachmann's work took a sharp turn in the 1960s, so that critics have often spoken of the "two Bachmanns," the first a more hermetic writer aiming at formal beauty, and the second a socially engaged writer of prose who once proclaimed: "I no longer try to make each sentence a work of art. The only thing that matters is what needs to be said." While there is a visible change in emphasis from poetry to prose (her last poem, *No More Delicacies*, was written in 1964 as she began the novel sequence *Ways of Death*), Bachmann's later fiction makes great use of lyrical elements. Unlike Alexander Solzhenitsyn or Naguib Mahfouz, she never attempted to emulate the linear style of the nineteenth-century realist novel. The prose writers who interest her are those who take a modernist perspective on problems of identity, communication, and narrative discourse: Marcel Proust, Italo Svevo (1861–1928), James Joyce, Franz Kafka, Robert Musil (1880–1942), William Faulkner, and Samuel Beckett, all of whom she discusses at length in her 1959–60 lectures "Questions of Contemporary Poetry" at the University of Frankfurt. She related their exploratory style to the problem of the self in modern society, a focus that she adapted to her own circumstances in later work.

Even during the 1950s, Bachmann had been concerned with political issues. As "R. K." in Rome, she wrote political articles for a West German newspaper from 1954 to 1955, and she later joined a committee that opposed equipping the German army with atomic weapons. In the 1960s, she wrote a public letter to Simon Wiesenthal that protested reducing the statute of limitations for Nazi war crimes, and she later marched and signed declarations against the Vietnam War. She used her influence with a major publisher to block a translation of Anna Akhmatova's poems by a former leader of the Hitler Youth (she had met Akhmatova in Rome). The change in her writing was not a sudden affirmation of social responsibility, therefore, but a new way of understanding how her writing could be an instrument of social change. Stories such as *Youth in an Austrian Town* and *Among Murderers and Madmen*, from her prize-winning collection, *The Thirtieth Year* (1961), already depicted the historical context of German fascism. Their style, however, is relatively picturesque, their conflicts inner and individual, and their situations symbolic or extraordinary. One story in the collection is narrated by a water nymph; in another, a trial judge breaks down when attempting to ascertain the truth about a defendant who has the same name.

Shifting to broader social themes, Bachmann concentrated on women's experience (compare Mariama Bâ's *So Long a Letter*, p. 2440). Instead of choosing unusual situations, she lingered over the implications of everyday scenes, describing the daily life of Austrian women who were, individually and collectively, victims of a patriarchal society. Readers accustomed to Bachmann's elegantly precise poetry were disconcerted by the presence, in the story collection *Three Paths to the Lake* (1972), of a prosaic "women's literature" that presented not only mundane topics but also rambling narrators and a diffuse awareness. Yet Bachmann's skill was still evident in the way she orchestrated inner references into a structure of cumulative significance, or employed an apparently undisciplined stream of consciousness to reveal repressed thoughts and thought patterns in women who had never been allowed to develop their own voice and identity.

There is a strong link between the writer's earlier preoccupation with Fascism and her later studies of women. Fascism must begin somewhere, she said, before it becomes a political movement and an agent of mass destruction. She located the principles of Fascism—the oppression of the weak and a sadistic desire for dominance and control—uncomfortably close to home, in the subordination of women by men. "Fascism is the first thing in the relationship between a man and a woman," she declared in an interview. Such repression permeates society in many forms. Bachmann's character Franziska Jordan (the victimized wife of her unfinished novel, *The Franza Case*) compares her situation to that of aborigines or preindustrial cultures in modern society: "I am a Papuan woman." In this view, the social structures of a patriarchal society gather all control into a central point dominated by white men, who in turn reinforce their power by pushing to the margins any other cultural or psychological identity. These newly marginalized figures, moreover, are kept in their place by being defined as childlike and primitive. Discouraged from developing a voice of their own, unable to put their experience into words, they lose control of their identity. Like modern philosophers of language and psychoanalysts, Bachmann realized that language is crucial to a sense of self. Experience that cannot be expressed is unrecognizable and soon *unspeakable*. The moral task of a writer, she felt, was to find the right words for that experience. By bringing the unspeakable into the light of consciousness, Bachmann hoped to operate a change in social consciousness itself.

She envisaged a novel cycle, *Ways of Death*, that would illuminate women's experience through the linked stories of individual figures appearing and reappearing in major or minor roles. Two projected novels, *The Franza Case* and *Requiem for Fanny Goldmann*, remained unfinished and have been published only as posthumous fragments. In 1966, however, Bachmann gave readings from a novel that would be published as *Malina* (1971), a challenging modernist work that includes a variety of forms and techniques: fairy tale, letters, dream sequences, dramatic dialogue, and finally the inexplicable disappearance of the narrator from a story that previously depended on her. The violent dreams in the second chapter, including a vision of Malira's father as a Nazi murderer, and a "cemetery of murdered daughters," give symbolic expression to Bachmann's horror of fascism as a consistent pattern of violence directed first against individual women and leading to mass destruction.

The Franza Case presents similar themes even more directly. Franziska Jordan (who also appears in The Barking) is married to the respected Viennese psychiatrist Leo Jordan, a man with sadistic tendencies and a fascination with Nazism. Franziska ("Franza") is his third wife, and he is systematically driving her mad as he did the others. He destroys her sanity by leaving notes on her "case" around the house for her to find, and in a desperate attempt to save herself she flees the clinic in which she had been placed and travels to Egypt with her brother. In the purity of a desert setting remote from the Viennese society where Dr. Jordan rules, she hopes to understand "who I am, where I come from, what is wrong with me, and what I am looking for in this waste"—in short, to reconstruct her violated identity. She never has a chance to recover from the damage inflicted by Dr. Jordan's psychological torture, for violence catches up with her again when she is attacked and raped. After Franziska's death, her brother Martin returns home alive but unable to explain what has happened. The cumulative effect is of a series of little murders, different in scale from the genocide of World War II but remarkably similar in the exercise of power to control, to suppress, and to kill.

Bachmann was still working on Ways of Death when she herself died in Rome on October 17, 1973, three weeks after the night her apartment caught fire and she was badly burned. Her second collection of stories, Three Paths to the Lake, had appeared the previous year with characters and themes growing directly out of Ways of Death. In the spring of 1973 she had traveled to Poland to give a series of readings, during which time she also visited the concentration camps at Auschwitz and Birkenau. The camps were a reminder of the destructive arrogance of power, and of a fascist mentality whose presence and cost she made it her task to describe.

The Barking, taken from Three Paths to the Lake, chronicles another aspect of The Franza Case. The major figure is Leo Jordan's mother, now old and in failing health, who is befriended by her daughter-in-law Franziska. In a series of conversations whose topic is invariably the brilliant Leo, the two women inadvertently bring to light his real selfishness and cruelty. Old Frau Jordan is unable to admit her fear and dislike of Leo and has lived a devoted lie all her life. Rather than recognize the truth emerging from these conversations, she escapes into hallucinations of barking dogs. The barking that barricades her from her son and removes "the fear of an entire lifetime" merely suggests rebellion, and yet it does recall the resentment voiced earlier by her pet dog, Nuri, who was given away because he barked at Dr. Jordan.

Franziska, in contrast, becomes more critical of Leo's behavior even though she also cannot bring herself to blame him openly. Her relationship with Leo disintegrates during the course of the story, although we are never told exactly why. There is no indication here of the systematic attempt to drive Franziska mad that governs The Franza Case, but certainly the picture of a homophobic, control-obsessed psychiatrist who belittles human relationships and specializes in concentration camp psychoses implies, for Bachmann, an essentially Nazi mentality. Much of the story's strength lies in its subtly indirect depiction of this mentality, and its simultaneous analysis of the roots of power. Leo Jordan is described obliquely, through the eyes of his dependent mother and wife. He instills fear in them and controls their lives, but this control also depends on their willingness to obliterate their own personalities to appease him. Bachmann leaves open the possibility of other modes of being: Frau Jordan's truly maternal relationship with another child, Kiki, Franziska's care for her mother-in-law, and Franziska's brother's generosity in paying the taxi bills his dead sister had incurred for Frau Jordan. The fate of the story's two main characters, however, bleakly illustrates Bachmann's conviction that the oppressive power relationships of fascism begin at an insidiously personal level, in the relationships of men and women, and in a systematic disrespect for human individuality.

Introductions by Mark Anderson to Bachmann's *In the Storm of Roses: Selected Poems* (1986) and *Three Paths to the Lake: Stories* (1989) provide an excellent overview of the writer's poetry and prose. Juliet Wigmore , "Ingeborg Bachmann" in Keith Bullivant, ed., *The Modern German Novel* (1987), is a valuable discussion of *Malina* and the *Ways of Death* cycle. Inta Ezergailis, *Women Writers—The Divided Self* (1982), has chapters on Bachmann and Doris Lessing, among others. A special issue of *Modern Austrian Literature* (1979) devoted to Austrian women writers contains several essays on Bachmann.

PRONOUNCING GLOSSARY

The following list uses common English syllables and stress accents to provide rough equivalents of selected words whose pronunciation may be unfamiliar to the general reader.

Franziska: *frahn-tsiss'-kah*

Frau: *frow*

Bachmann: *bakh'-mahn*

Johannes: *yoh-hah'-nes*

The Barking[1]

Old Frau[2] Jordan had been called "old Frau Jordan" for the past three decades because there had been first one and now another young Frau Jordan, and although she did live in Hietzing,[3] she had only a one-room apartment in a dilapidated villa, with a tiny kitchen and no more than half a tub in the bathroom. From her distinguished son Leo, the professor, she received 1,000 schillings[4] per month, and somehow she managed to make do, although those 1,000 schillings had depreciated so much over the last twenty years that she was just barely able to pay an older woman, a certain Frau Agnes, who "looked in" on her twice a week, to tidy up a little, just "the bare minimum." She even saved some of the money for birthday and Christmas presents for her son and grandson from her son's first marriage, whom the first young wife sent over punctually every Christmas to pick up his present. Leo on the other hand was too busy to notice, and since he had become famous and his local prestige had blossomed into international renown, he was busier than ever. Things only changed when the latest young Frau Jordan began to visit the old woman as often as she could, a really nice, likable girl, as the old woman soon admitted to herself, but at each visit she said only: But Franziska, it's not right, you shouldn't come so often, it's such a waste. You two surely have enough expenses as it is, but Leo is just such a good son!

Franziska always brought something with her, delicacies and sherry,

---

1. Translated by Mary Fran Gilbert.   2. Mrs. (German).   3. A suburb west of Vienna, Austria.
4. The basic Austrian unit of currency.

some pastries, because she had guessed that the old woman liked to take a sip now and then and, moreover, attached great importance to having something in the house "for the company." After all, Leo might drop by, and he mustn't notice how much she was missing and that all day long she wondered how to allocate her money and how much she could put aside for presents. Her apartment was meticulously clean, but gave off a faint "old-woman" smell which she was not aware of and which put Leo Jordan to flight, apart from the fact that he had no time to lose and no idea what to talk about with his eighty-five-year-old mother. Sometimes, seldom, he had been amused—that much Franziska knew—namely, when he was having a relationship with a married woman, because then old Frau Jordan had gone without sleep and made strange, convoluted allusions, trembling for his safety: she believed that the married men whose wives Leo Jordan was living with were dangerous and jealous and bloodthirsty, and she wasn't able to calm down until he married Franziska, who did not have a jealous husband lurking in the bushes but was young and cheerful, an orphan, admittedly not from an educated family, but at least with a brother who had gone to college. Families of the educated classes and educated men in general carried great weight with Frau Jordan, although she didn't do much socializing; she only heard about things. But her son had the right to marry into an educated family. The old woman and Franziska talked almost exclusively about Leo, because he was the only productive topic the two of them had, and Franziska was shown the photo album over and over again, Leo in a stroller, Leo at the beach, and Leo through the years, taking hikes, pasting stamps in his collection, and so on until his military service.

The Leo she came to know through the old woman was a completely different Leo from the man she had married, and when the two women sat drinking their sherry the old woman would say: He was a complicated child, a strange boy, actually you could tell all along that he was destined for great things.

For a while Franziska was happy to hear these assertions, that Leo was so good to his mother and had always done everything conceivable to help her, but then she noticed that something was wrong, and with dismay she realized—the old woman was afraid of her son. It began with the old woman saying, sometimes hastily and parenthetically (she believed it to be a clever tactic that Franziska would never see through because she was blinded by admiration for her husband): But please don't mention a word of it to Leo, you know how concerned he is, it might upset him, whatever you do, please don't tell him that something is wrong with my knee, it's such a little thing, he might get upset about it.

Although Franziska had since learned that Leo never got upset at all, certainly not because of his mother, and only listened to her reports with half an ear, she suppressed this first realization. Unfortunately she had already told him about the knee but swore to the old woman she wouldn't say a word. Leo had reacted with annoyance and then, to placate her, had explained that he really couldn't drive out to Hietzing because of such a trifle. Just tell her—he rattled off some medical terminology—she should buy this and that and do and walk as little as possible. Franziska bought the medication without further comment and claimed in Hietzing that she had secretly spoken with one of her husband's assistants without mentioning any names and that he had given her this advice, although she was at a loss as to how to keep the old woman in bed without the help of a nurse. But she no longer had enough courage to approach Leo about it, because a nurse cost money, and now she was caught in the middle. On the one hand Frau Jordan didn't want anything to do with it, and on the other Leo Jordan—albeit for completely different reasons—simply didn't want to hear about it. When Frau Jordan's knee was swollen, Franziska lied to her husband several times; she drove quickly to Hietzing, allegedly to the hairdresser's, and straightened up the little apartment, bringing all sorts of things with her. She purchased a radio but was uneasy afterward: Leo was bound to notice the expenditure, so she quickly transferred the money back and broke into the meager savings she had set aside for some sort of emergency which would hopefully never arise and could only be a minor emergency at any rate. She and her brother had divided what little remained after the death of their entire family, with the exception of a cottage in southern Carinthia[5] which was slowly falling into disrepair. In the end she called a general practitioner in the neighborhood and asked him to treat the old woman for a while, paying him out of her own savings. More importantly, she didn't dare reveal to the doctor who she was and who the old woman was, because that would only have hurt Leo's reputation, and protecting Leo's reputation was also in Franziska's best interest. But the old woman thought much more selflessly: there was no way she could ask her famous son to go so far as to come and take a look at her knee. She had used a cane before on occasion, but after this knee problem she really needed it, so Franziska sometimes drove her to town. Shopping with the old woman was a somewhat laborious undertaking: once she had only needed a comb, but there were no combs like the ones "in her day," and although the old woman was polite, standing in the store with erect dignity, she annoyed the little saleswoman by eyeing the price tags suspiciously, unable to refrain from telling Franziska in a clearly audible whisper that the prices here were outrageous, they'd better go somewhere else. The saleswoman, who was in no position to judge how important buying this comb was to the old woman, replied rudely that they wouldn't find this comb cheaper anywhere in town. Franziska launched into embarrassed negotiations with the mother, took the comb the old woman wanted but looked on as costing a fortune and quickly paid for it, saying: Just consider it a Christmas present from us, a present in advance. Prices have really gone up horrendously everywhere. The old woman didn't say a word, she sensed her defeat, but still, if prices really were so outrageous— a comb like this used to cost two schillings and nowadays it cost sixty— well then there wasn't much left for her to understand in this world.

After a while the topic "the good son" had been exhausted and Franziska repeatedly steered the conversation to the old woman herself, because the only thing she knew was that Leo's father had died young of a heart attack or stroke, quite suddenly, on a staircase, and that must have

---

5. A southwestern province of Austria.

been a long time ago, because if you stopped to figure it out this woman had been a widow for almost half a century. First she had worked for years to raise her only child, and then she was suddenly an old woman nobody cared about anymore. She never spoke about her marriage, only in connection with Leo who had had a very difficult life, without a father, and she was so preoccupied with Leo that she failed to see the parallel to Franziska, who had lost both her parents when she was young. Her son was the only one who could have had a difficult time, and then it turned out that it hadn't been so bad after all, because a distant cousin had paid for his education, a certain Johannes about whom Franziska had heard very little, merely a few derogatory, critical references to some eternal—now aging—loafer who was swimming in money and supposedly led a life of idleness with all its ridiculous affectations. He dabbled a little in art, collected Chinese lacquerware, and was just another one of those freeloaders found in every family. Franziska knew also that he was homosexual, but she was really amazed how someone like Leo, whose very profession obliged him to uphold a neutral and scientific attitude toward homosexuality and phenomena of a quite different magnitude, could go on and on about this cousin as though he had somehow, through his own negligence, fallen prey to works of art, homosexuality, and an inheritance to boot, but at that time Franziska still admired her husband too much to be more than irritated and hurt. With relief she heard from the old woman, in discussing those hard times, that Leo was infinitely grateful and had been a big help to this Johannes, who was then in the throes of a number of personal crises—which were better left untold. The old woman hesitated and then added, because she was, after all, sitting opposite the wife of a psychiatrist: I think you should know that Johannes is sexual.

Franziska controlled herself and suppressed a laugh, it was surely the most daring revelation the old woman had roused herself to in years, but with Franziska she was opening up more and more. She told her how Leo had often given Johannes advice, naturally free of charge, but Johannes was a hopeless case, and if a person didn't have the willpower to change it was understandable that he would be at his wits' end, and from what she heard, Johannes just kept on with it, the same as always. Franziska carefully translated this naive story into reality and understood even less why Leo talked about this cousin in such a disparaging and malicious way. At that time the obvious reason escaped her, namely, that Leo was reluctant to be reminded of his mother and his former wives and lovers who were nothing to him but a conspiracy of creditors from whom he could escape only by belittling them to himself and others. His tirades about his first wife were similar: she had been the epitome of everything diabolical, unappreciative and spiteful, traits that had not been revealed in depth until the divorce when her aristocratic father had hired a lawyer for her to secure some of the money for the child, money she'd given him when he was a young doctor and hard times had struck again. it was an alarmingly large sum to Franziska but, as she was told, one could expect nothing less from the "baroness," as Leo ironically called her, because the family had always treated him like an upstart, without having the slightest idea who was dwelling in their midst. It amused him to note that the "baroness" had never remarried and lived in total seclusion. After him she hadn't been able to find another fool—young and gullible and poor, as he had been—who would have married such a deserving Fräulein. She had understood nothing about his work, absolutely nothing, and although she behaved fairly in respect to the agreement about their son, sending him for regular visits and teaching him to respect his father, she obviously did it for no other reason than to prove to the world how generous she was.

The brilliant doctor's rise to fame along the thorny path of suffering had already become Franziska's religion at that time, and again and again she reproached herself with the image of him making his way, against indescribable odds and despite the obstacle that dreadful marriage posed, all the way to the top. And the cross he was forced to bear because of his mother, the financial and moral burden, was no light one for him, but that at least Franziska could take off his shoulders. Although it otherwise might not have occurred to her to spend her free hours with an old woman the time became something special when she thought of Leo: a helping hand, evidence of her love for him, allowing him to devote his undivided attention to his work.

Leo was just too good to her, he told her that she was overdoing it, the way she took care of his mother, a telephone call now and again would have sufficed. For the past few years the old woman had had a telephone which she feared more than loved: she didn't like to talk on the phone and always shouted into the mouthpiece and couldn't hear what the other party said, and besides that, the phone was too expensive, but of course Franziska wasn't to mention that to Leo. Once the old woman—prompted by Franziska and a second glass of sherry—did in fact begin to talk about the old days, the very old days, and it turned out that she wasn't from an educated family, her father had knit gloves and socks in a small factory in Lower Austria and she had been the oldest of eight children, but then she'd had a wonderful time when she took up employment with a Greek family, immensely rich people with a little boy, the most beautiful child she had ever laid eyes on, and she was his nursemaid. Being a nursemaid was a really good job, nothing degrading about it, and the Greek's young wife had had servants aplenty, oh yes, she'd had a real stroke of luck, such a good position had been hard to find back then. The child's name was Kiki, at least everyone had called him Kiki. When the old woman began talking about Kiki more and more frequently, remembering every detail—what Kiki had said, how cute and affectionate he was, the walks they'd taken together—her eyes lit up as they never did when she spoke of her own child. Kiki had simply been a little angel, never naughty, she stressed, never naughty at all, and the separation must have been terrible, they hadn't told Kiki that the Fräulein was leaving, and she had cried all night long, and once, years later, she had tried to find out what had become of the family. First she'd heard that they were traveling, then that they were back in Greece, and now she had no idea whatsoever what had happened to Kiki, who must be over sixty by now, yes, over sixty she said pensively, and she had been forced to leave because the Greek family had planned their first major trip and couldn't take her along, and when they left the young wife had given her a wonderful present. The old woman stood up and rummaged in a jewelry box, then showed her the brooch from Kiki's mother, it was the real thing, with diamonds, but she still asked herself today if they hadn't let her go because the wife had noticed that Kiki was more attached to her than to his own mother, she could understand that all right, but it had been the hardest blow of all, and she had never completely recovered from it. Franziska regarded the brooch thoughtfully; perhaps it really was quite valuable, she didn't know much about jewelry, but she was beginning to realize something else: this Kiki must have meant more to the old woman than Leo. She often hesitated to talk about Leo's childhood, or she began only to break off in fright saying abruptly: It was just childish nonsense, you know boys are so hard to raise, he didn't do it on purpose, he was just having such a bad time and it was all I could do to make ends meet. But you get everything back a hundredfold when a child has grown up and made his own way and become so famous, he takes after his father more than me, you know.

Franziska carefully handed back the brooch, and once again the old woman started in fear. Please Franziska, don't mention a word of this to Leo, it could annoy him. I have my plans, you know, if I get sick I could sell it so that I won't become even more of a burden to him. Franziska embraced the old woman with a hug that was both timid and fierce. Don't ever do that, promise me you'll never sell this brooch. You're not a burden to us at all!

On the way home she made one detour after the other, in a state of inner turmoil, this poor woman shouldn't sell her brooch while she and Leo spent money freely, went on trips, entertained. She kept debating what she should say to Leo, but a first, faint alarm sounded inside her, because even though the old woman had her quirks and exaggerated things, she must be right about something, and so in the end she didn't say a word about it at home and only reported cheerfully that his mother was doing very well. But before they left for a conference in London she arranged a contract with a garage which ran a private taxi service, made a downpayment, and said to the old woman: An idea has occurred to us, because you shouldn't walk too far by yourself. Just call a taxi when you want to go out, it hardly costs a thing, it's just a favor from an old patient, but don't say anything about it, especially not to Leo, you know how he is, he doesn't like it when you thank him and everything, and you just ride to town when you need something, and have the taxi wait, but always have Herr Pineider take you, the young one. He doesn't know that his father was one of Leo's patients though, that comes under professional secrecy, you know, I was, just there and talked to him, and you have to promise me, for Leo's sake, that you'll take the taxi, it would ease our minds. In the beginning, the old woman made little use of the taxi, and Franziska scolded her for it when she returned from England; her leg had worsened and the old woman had naturally done all her shopping on foot, once even going so far as to take the streetcar into town because one could hardly get anything in Hietzing, and Franziska said firmly, as if to a stubborn child: This is definitely not to happen again.

They exhausted one topic after another: Kiki, the life of a young nursemaid in Vienna before the First World War and before her marriage, and sometimes it was only Franziska who talked, especially when she had just returned from a trip with Leo, a brilliant talk he'd delivered at the conference, and that he had given her this offprint for his mother. The old woman labored through the title with an effort: "The Significance of Endogenous and Exogenous Factors in Connection with the Occurrence of Paranoid and Depressive Psychoses in Former Concentration Camp Inmates and Refugees." Franziska assured her it was merely the groundwork for a much larger study he was working on, and he was even letting her help him with it. It would probably become the most significant and the first really important book in the field. A work of incalculable impact.

The old woman was strangely mute, surely she didn't understand the implications of these studies, maybe nothing at all of what her son was doing. Then she said, surprisingly: I hope he won't make too many enemies with it, here in Vienna, and then there's that other thing . . .

Franziska grew agitated: But that's exactly the point, that would be a very good thing, it's a provocation, too, and Leo isn't afraid of anyone, for him it's the only thing that counts, that has a purpose far beyond its scientific significance.

Yes, of course, the old woman said quickly, and he knows how to defend himself, and if you're famous you always have enemies. I was just thinking about Johannes, but that's so long ago now. Did you know that he was in a concentration camp for a year and a half before the war ended? Franziska was surprised, she hadn't known, but she failed to see the connection. The old woman didn't want to say any more but then continued: It meant a certain amount of danger for Leo, having a relative who, well, you know what I mean. Yes, of course, said Franziska, still somewhat confused; sometimes the old woman had such a roundabout way of saying things without really saying them, and she couldn't make head or tail of it, although suddenly she was bursting with pride that a member of Leo's family had been through something so terrible and that Leo, in his tactful, modest way, had never said anything about it to her, not even about the danger he must have faced as a young doctor. That afternoon the old woman didn't want to go on talking; she merely asked disjointedly: Do you hear it, too?

What?

The dogs, the old woman said. There were never so many dogs in Hietzing, I've heard them barking again, and they bark at night, too. Frau Schönthal next door has a poodle now. It doesn't bark much though, it's such a nice dog, I see her almost every day when I go shopping, but we only say hello, her husband doesn't have much of an education.

Franziska drove home as quickly as she could; this time she wanted to ask Leo if there was anything to the fact that his mother had suddenly begun talking about dogs, if it was an alarming symptom, maybe it had something to do with her age. She had also noticed that the old woman had been upset once about ten schillings which had been lying on the table and then disappeared when Frau Agnes left, all this excitement about ten missing schillings, certainly she had only imagined it anyway, weren't those all signs of the process of aging? It couldn't possibly have been the cleaning woman, she was what people in certain circles—that is, in better circles—called a "God-fearing" woman who came more out of pity than for the money, which she didn't need anyway—she did it as a favor and nothing more. And old Frau Jordan's pitiful presents—an ancient, threadbare purse or some other useless paraphernalia—would hardly have induced Frau Agnes to come; she had realized long ago that she had nothing to expect from the old woman or from her son, and she knew nothing of Franziska's enthusiastic plans for improving the situation; Franziska had chided the old woman as though she were a child, because she didn't want to lose this valuable help over a bout of senile obstinacy and an unfounded suspicion.

More and more often she found the old woman at the window when she arrived, and they no longer sat together when Franziska came to drink sherry and nibble on pastries. The business with the dogs continued, although at the same time her hearing problem grew worse, and Franziska was at a loss. Something had to be done, and Leo, whom she bothered with none of this, was not going to avoid devoting some attention to his mother one of these days. Only then things started becoming complicated between Leo and herself, and she discovered that he had so intimidated her that she was afraid of him. But at least once, in a fit of her old courage, she overcame her inexplicable fear and suggested at dinner: Why don't we invite your mother to come and stay with us, we have enough room, and then our Rosi could always be with her and you would never have to worry, besides, she's so quiet and undemanding, she would never disturb you, and certainly not me, I'm suggesting it for your sake because I know how much you worry. Leo was in a good mood that evening and secretly happy about something. She didn't realize what it was but had decided to make use of the opportunity, and he answered, laughing: What an idea, you have no feel for the situation, my dear, you can't uproot an elderly person after a while, it would only depress her and she needs her freedom, she's a strong woman who has lived alone for decades. You don't know her the way I do, she would die of fright here, just from the kind of people who come over. She'd probably debate for hours on end whether to use the bathroom, out of fear that one of us just might want to use it. Come on, my little Franziska, please don't make such a face, I think your impulse is touching and admirable, but that wonderful idea of yours would be the death of her. Believe me, it's just that I happen to know more about these things.

But this business with the dogs. . . ? Franziska began to stutter, she hadn't wanted to talk about it and would gladly have immediately taken back what she'd said. She was no longer capable of putting her apprehension into words.

What, her husband asked in a completely different tone of voice, she doesn't still want a mutt, does she? I don't understand, Franziska answered. Why should she—you don't mean she wants to have a dog, do you?

Of course I do, and I'm more than glad that this childish interlude has blown over so quickly, at her age she just couldn't handle a dog, she should take care of herself, that's more important to me, a dog is such a nuisance, she has no idea what they would mean, with her advancing senility. She never said anything about it, Franziska replied half-heartedly, I don't think she wants a dog. I wanted to say something entirely different, but it's not important, sorry. Would you like a cognac, are you going to work later, should I type anything for you?

At her next visit Franziska didn't know how to persuade the old woman, who was always on the alert, to give her answers she needed to know. She approached the subject in a roundabout way, remarking casually: Incidentally, I saw Frau Schönthal's dog today, really a cute dog, I like poodles a lot, actually all animals, because I grew up in the country, you know, we always had dogs, I mean my grandparents and everyone in the village, and cats, too, of course. Wouldn't it be good for you to have a dog or a cat, now that you have trouble reading. I mean, certainly that kind of thing passes, but I for one would absolutely love to have a dog. But you know, in the city it's just a bother and not really fair to the dog, but here in Hietzing, where it can frisk around in the yard and you can go for walks. . .

The old woman exclaimed in agitation: A dog, no, no, I don't want a dog! Franziska realized she had done something wrong, but felt at the same time that she hadn't offended the old woman as she might have had she suggested a parrot or canaries: it must have been something else entirely that had put her in such a state of agitation. After a while the old woman said very quietly: Nuri was a really nice dog, and I got along well with him, that was, let me think, it must have been five years ago, but then I had to give him away, to a home or a place where they resell them. Leo doesn't like dogs. No, what am I saying, it was different, there was something in that dog I can't really understand, he couldn't stand Leo, he always jumped at him and barked madly whenever Leo made the slightest move toward the door, and then once he almost bit him, and Leo was so indignant, of course that's understandable, when a dog is that wild, but he was never like that otherwise, not even with strangers, and then naturally I gave him away. I couldn't let Leo be barked at and bitten by Nuri, no, that would have been too much, Leo should be able to feel at home when he visits me and not have to get angry about some poorly trained dog.

Franziska thought that, although there was no longer a dog who jumped at him and disliked him, Leo came seldom enough as it was, and even less often since Franziska came instead. How long had it been anyway since his last visit? Once the three of them had gone for a short ride along the Weinstrasse and into the Helenenthal and lunched at an inn with his mother; otherwise Franziska always came alone.

Be sure not to say anything to Leo, though, that business with Nuri really hurt his feelings, he's very sensitive, you know, and to this day I can't forgive myself for being so selfish as to want to have Nuri, but old people are very selfish, dear Franziska, you can't understand that yet, you're still so young and good, but when you're very old you get all these selfish desires, and you can't just let yourself give in to them. What would have become of me if Leo hadn't taken care of me, his father died all of a sudden like that and there was no time to make any arrangements, and there wasn't any money, either, my husband was a little careless, no, not a spendthrift, but he had a hard time of it and didn't have much of a knack with money, Leo doesn't take after him in that respect. In those days I could still work, the boy was a reason to keep going, and I was still young, but what would I do nowadays? My one fear has always been having to go to an old people's home, but Leo would never stand for that, and if I didn't have this apartment I'd have to go to some home, and I guess a dog isn't worth all that. Franziska listened to her, clenched up inside, and she said to herself: So that's it, that's it, she gave her dog away for his sake. And she asked herself: What kind of people are we?—because she was incapable of thinking: What kind of a man is my husband!—we're just so cruel, and she thinks she's selfish, and all the time we have everything we want! In order to hide her tears she quickly unpacked a small package from Meinl, little things, and acted as though she hadn't understood. Oh, by the way, I'm so scatterbrained today, I've only brought you the tea and coffee and a little smoked salmon and Russian salad. Actually it doesn't go together all that well, but I was really flustered at the store because Leo is leaving and one of the manuscripts isn't finished yet. But he'll give you a call tonight, and he'll be back in a week anyway.

He needs a break, the old woman said, see to it that he gets one if you can, you two haven't had any vacation at all yet this year. Franziska said brightly: That's a good idea, I'll convince him some way or another, I just need to think of a strategy, but thanks a lot, that's really a good piece of advice, he's constantly overworked, you know, and at some point I have to make him slow down.

What Franziska did not know was that this was her last visit to the old woman and she no longer needed the strategy, because other things came to pass, events of such hurricane force that she almost forgot the old woman and a great many other things as well.

In her fear, the old woman didn't ask her son on the phone why Franziska had stopped coming. She was worried, but her son sounded cheerful and unconcerned, and once he even came over and stayed for twenty minutes. He didn't touch the pastries, he didn't finish the sherry and he didn't talk about Franziska, but he did talk quite a bit about himself, and that made her ecstatic because it had been such a long time since he had spoken about himself. So he was leaving on vacation now, he needed a break, but the word "Mexico" gave the old woman a mild shock, wasn't that the place where they had scorpions and revolutions and savages and earthquakes, but he laughed reassuringly, kissed her and promised to write. He sent a few postcards, which she read religiously. Franziska hadn't added her regards. Once Franziska called her from Carinthia. Really, the money these young people throw out the window! Franziska had only called to ask if everything was okay. Then they talked about Leo, but the old woman kept shouting at the most inappropriate times: It's getting too expensive, child, but Franziska kept talking, yes, she had finally suc-ceeded, he was finally taking a break, and she had had to go to her broth-er's, there was something to settle here, that was why she hadn't been able to accompany Leo. Family matters in Carinthia. Because of the house. Then the old woman received a strange envelope with a few lines from Franziska. She didn't say anything, just sent her regards and wrote that she would like her to have this photo she had taken herself, the photograph was of Leo, apparently on the Semmering Pass,[6] laughing in a snowy landscape in front of a large hotel. The old woman decided not to say anything to Leo; he wouldn't have asked her anyway. She hid the photograph under the brooch in her jewelry box.

She could no longer read books and was bored by the radio; newspapers were all she wanted, and Frau Agnes got them for her. It took her hours to decipher them, she read the obituaries and always felt a certain satisfaction when someone younger than herself had passed away. Well, look at that, Professor Haderer too, he could hardly have been more than seventy. Frau Schönthal's mother had died, too, of cancer, she wasn't even sixty-five. The old woman stiffly offered her condolences in the grocery store and didn't even look at the poodle, and then she went home and stood at the window. She slept more than old people are said to sleep, but she often awoke, only to hear the dogs again. She was startled whenever the cleaning woman came: since Franziska's visits had ended, it bothered her when anyone came over, and she had the impression that she was changing. Now she actually was frightened of suddenly collapsing in the street or losing control of herself when she had to go to town for something, and so she obediently called young Herr Pineider, who drove her around. And she became accustomed to this small precaution for her own safety. She completely lost her sense of time, and when Leo once came by to see her, deeply tanned, she no longer knew if he was returning from Mexico or when he had been there at all. But she was careful not to ask, and gathered from something he said that he had just arrived from Ischia,[7] back from a trip to Italy. Confused, she said: Good, good. That was good for you. And while he was telling her something the dogs began to bark, several of them, all at once, very near, and she was so completely encircled by the barking and a very gentle, gentle terror that she was no longer afraid of her son. The fear of an entire lifetime suddenly left her.

When he said on his way out: Next time I'll bring Elfi over, you have to meet her one of these days! she had no idea what he was talking about. Wasn't he married to Franziska anymore, how long had it been, how many wives was that now anyway, she could no longer remember how long he had lived with Franziska and when, and she said: Go ahead and bring her over. Fine. Whatever is best for you. The barking was so close now that for an instant she was certain that Nuri was with her again and would jump at him and bark. She wished he would finally leave, she wanted to be alone. She thanked him out of habit, just in case, and he asked in astonishment: Whatever for? Now I really did go and forget to bring you my book after all. A phenomenal success. I'll have it sent.

Well then, thank you so much my child. Send it over, but unfortunately your dumb old mother can hardly read anymore and doesn't understand much anyway.

She let him embrace her and found herself alone again surrounded by the barking. It came from every garden and house in Hietzing, an invasion

---

6. In the Alps in southern Austria, known as a tourist resort and center for winter sports.   7. An island vacation spot north of the Bay of Naples.

of the beasts had begun, the dogs came closer, barking to her, and she stood erect, as always, no longer dreaming of the time with Kiki and the Greeks, no longer thinking of the day when the last ten schillings had disappeared and Leo had lied to her. Instead she redoubled her efforts to hide things better, wishing she could throw them away, especially the brooch and the photograph, so that Leo wouldn't find anything after she died. But she couldn't think of a good hiding place, maybe the bucket with the scraps, but she trusted Frau Agnes less and less, too, because she would have had to give her the rubbish, and she suspected that the woman would rummage through it and find the brooch. Once she said, a little too harshly: At least you could give the bones and the leftovers to the dogs.

The cleaning woman looked at her in amazement and asked: What dogs? To the dogs, of course, insisted the old woman in an imperious tone, I want the dogs to have them!

She was a suspicious looking creature, a thief. She probably took the bones home with her.

To the dogs, I said. Can't you understand me, are you deaf or something? No wonder, at your age.

Then the barking diminished, and she thought: someone has chased the dogs off or given them away, because now it was no longer that same powerful, recurrent, barking. The fainter the barking, the more adamant she became: she was only biding her time until the louder barking resumed. One had to be able to wait, and she could wait. All at once it was no longer a barking sound, although there was no doubt it came from the dogs in the neighborhood. It wasn't a growling either, just now and again the great, wild, triumphant howling of a single dog, then a whimpering, the faint barking of all the others fading into the distance.

One day nearly two years after the death of his sister Franziska, Dr. Martin Ranner received a bill from a company by the name of Pineider for taxi services listed separately by date, for which Frau Franziska Jordan had made a downpayment and signed a contract. But because only very few trips had been made while Franziska was alive and the majority after her death he called the company for an explanation of this mysterious bill. Although the explanation actually explained very little, he had no desire to call his former brother-in-law or ever see him again, so he paid the fares, in installments, for a woman he had never known and never had anything to do with. He came to the conclusion that the old Frau Jordan must have passed away some time ago; the company had let several months go by since her last trip, perhaps out of reverence, before asserting its claims.

MAHASWETA DEVI
born 1926

Author of more than a hundred books, including novels, plays, and collections of short stories, Mahasweta Devi is the leading contemporary writer in Bengali, the language of the state of West Bengal in eastern India, and of neighboring Bangladesh as well. Translations of her work into other Indian languages and into English have brought her national and international recognition. One of several modern Bengali writers committed to social and political critique from a leftist perspective, Mahasweta (the *Devi* in her name is a term of respect attached to a woman's name in Bengali) writes about peasants, outcastes, women, tribal peoples who live in the forest regions of India, and other marginalized groups struggling to survive and resisting their exploitation by dominant groups. Her fiction and plays are distinguished by a powerful, direct, unsentimental style and by the subtlety and sensitivity with which she approaches the themes of struggle, resistance, and empowerment.

Bengali fiction from the 1930s onward reflects the growing radicalization of various segments of Bengali society, including the rapidly growing middle class and the urban poor. Since the 1920s, when sharecroppers revolted against landlords and the British colonial government, Bengal has been the arena of a series of peasant uprisings and unrest among the masses. The region was devastated by a man-made famine in 1943. When India was partitioned in 1947 the eastern portion of Bengal (the former East Bengal) became East Pakistan, a part of the newly formed nation of Pakistan, which had been conceived as a homeland for the Muslim populations of the Indian subcontinent. As a result, the whole of Bengal was torn apart by Hindu-Muslim communal riots and the massive displacement of populations. Exploited as much in independent India as in the colonial era, the Munda and other tribal peoples in Bengal and the neighboring state of Bihar rose in revolt, and in the 1960s urban students participated in peasant and tribal struggles in a movement known as the Naxalbari movement (after the village where it began), only to be brutally suppressed by the Bengal state government. Yet another upheaval was caused by East Pakistan's proclamation of independence from Pakistan as the new nation of Bangladesh in 1970. Mahasweta and other major Bengali writers, such as Manik Bandyopadhyay (1908–1956), and Hasan Azizul Huq (born 1938), have responded to these events with fiction that shifted the focus of modern Bengali literature from the lives of the educated, urban middle class to the politics of the exploitation of the underclasses.

Mahasweta Devi was born into a family of distinguished and politically engaged artists and intellectuals in Dhaka (Dacca) in the former East Bengal (now Bangladesh). After graduating in 1946 from Santiniketan, the famous alternative school established by Rabindranath Tagore (p. 1448), she devoted several years to political activism in rural Bengal, in collaboration with her first husband. During this time she held a variety of jobs, including teaching. Throughout, Mahasweta wrote mainly fiction but also columns and articles for journals. In 1963, after receiving a Master's degree in English literature at Calcutta University, she became a professor of English at a Calcutta college.

Although Mahasweta's early work was motivated by a concern for social justice, it was not until the Naxalbari student-peasant uprisings of the 1960s that the lives of tribal peoples and peasants became the primary focus of her fiction. At this time she adopted a pattern of activism that she still maintains, participating in, observing, and recording the struggles of oppressed groups in Bengal. Her experience with the Naxalbari movement resulted in *Hajar Churasir Ma* (Number 1084's mother, 1973), a nationally acclaimed novel indicting organized violence on the part of the state. In *Aranyer Adhikar* (Rights over the forest, 1977), perhaps the most famous of her novels, she turned to the history of the Munda tribal revolt in Bengal and Bihar in the nineteenth century. Since 1984, when she gave up her academic position, she has devoted her time entirely to grassroots work among tribals and outcastes in rural Bengal and Bihar and also edits a quarterly journal, the main contributors to which are people from these marginalized communities.

In *Breast-Giver* (*Stanadayini*, 1980) Mahasweta focuses not so much on the resistance of the oppressed as on the dynamics of oppression itself. Theoretically a member of the highest of the Hindu castes, the brahmin Kangalicharan is a helpless victim of the rich patriarch Haldarbabu's clan. Forced to become the wage earner of the household, Kangalicharan's wife, Jashoda, becomes a wet-nurse for the Haldar family, who retain her services until she becomes useless to them. Mahasweta's narrative is aimed at exposing the relentless collusion of patriarchal and capitalist ideologies in the exploitation of the disadvantaged. Themselves victims, the women of the Haldar household are Jashoda's chief exploiters. The status of wage earner not only fails to release Jashoda from the expectations of wifehood and motherhood but saddles her with the ultimately self-destructive task of being "mother of the world." Nevertheless, neither victimization nor its awareness fully robs Jashoda and Kangalicharan of their sense of agency and power.

Like the funeral wailer and the medicine woman in Mahasweta's short story *Dhowli* or the landless tribal laborer in *Draupadi*, Jashoda, the principal character in *Breast-Giver*, is a working woman or, as the narrator puts it, *"professional mother."* As translator Gayatri Spivak has pointed out, in the story's title the author deliberately foregrounds the centrality of the female body in Jashoda's transactions with her clients—she is not just a "wet-nurse," a provider of milk, but a "breast-giver," a distinction further underscored by the grim ironies that unfold in the narrative of her career. The story offers new avenues for examining the points at which gender and class oppression intersect.

Breast-Giver is representative of Mahasweta's fiction, in which the deceptive surface of linear, seemingly realistic narrative is constantly undercut by mythic and satirical inflections. Not only is Jashoda the breast-giver named for Yashoda, the mother of the beloved cowherd-child-god Krishna, but in the course of the narrative the professional mother merges with other Indian icons of motherhood— sacred cows, the Lion-seated goddess, "mother India" herself. The story is open to competing, yet not mutually exclusive, analyses, in terms of Marxist and feminist economic and social theory, myth, or political allegory. While the many layers of meaning in *Breast-Giver* are accessible even in translation, we must note that much of the power of the original derives from Mahasweta's distinctive style and voice. In this story, as in the author's other works, classical Hindu myths connect with quotations from Shakespeare and Marx, and slang, dialect, literary Bengali, and English blend together. The result is a powerful language that in many respects resembles modern Bengali usage, yet remains a unique creation of the author.

In addition to her excellent translations of *Breast-Giver* and *Draupadi*, Gayatri Chakravorty Spivak, *In Other Worlds: Essays in Cultural Politics* (1988), offers an analysis of Mahasweta Devi's short stories from theoretical perspectives in gender and Third World studies. Compare Spivak's translation with that of Ella Dutta, *The Wet Nurse*, in Kali for Women, ed., *Truth Tales: Contemporary Stories Written by Women Writers of India* (1986). Several of Mahasweta's stories can be found in Kalpana Bardhan, *Of Women, Outcastes, Peasants, and Rebels* (1990), an anthology of translations of short fiction by the major modern Bengali writers on the themes of oppression and resistance, with reference to issues of gender and class.

PRONOUNCING GLOSSARY

The following list uses common English syllables and stress accents to provide rough equivalents of selected words whose pronunciation may be unfamiliar to the general reader.

Arun: *o-roon'* Basanti: *bah'-shon-tee*

Basini: *bah'-shee-nee* Beleghata: *bay'-lay-gah'-tah*

Dakshineswar: *dok'-khi-naysh'-wuhr*

Haldarkartha: *huhl'-duhr-kuhr-tah*

Harisal: *ho-ree'-shahl*

Jagaddhatri: *jo-god-dah'-tree*

Jashoda: *jo'-shoh-dah*

Kangalicharan Patitundo: *kahn-gah'-lee-chuh-ruhn po'-tee-toon'-do*

Kayastha: *kah-yuhs'-tuh*

Mahasweta Devi: *muh-hah'-shway-tah day'-vee*

Maniktala-Bagmari: *mah-neek'-to-lah–bahg'-mah-ree*

Nabin: *no'-been*

Naxalbari: *nuhk'-shuhl-bah'-ree*

Neno: *nay'-noh*

Padmarani: *puhd'-mah-rah-nee*

Sarala: *suh'-ro-lah*

Saratchandra: *shuh-ruht-chuhnd'-ruh*

Savitri: *shah-beet'-ree*

stanadayini: *sto'-no-dah'-ye-nee*

Tarakeswar: *tah'-ruh-kaysh-shor*

Breast-Giver[1]

1

My aunties they lived in the woods, in the forest their home
they did make.
Never did Aunt say here's a sweet dear, eat, sweetie,
here's a piece of cake.

Jashoda doesn't remember if her aunt was kind or unkind. It is as if she were Kangalicharan's wife from birth, the mother of twenty children, living or dead, counted on her fingers. Jashoda doesn't remember at all when there was no child in her womb, when she didn't feel faint in the morning, when Kangali's body didn't *drill* her body like a geologist in a darkness lit only by an oil-lamp. She never had the time to calculate if she could or could not bear motherhood. Motherhood was always her way of living and keeping alive her world of countless beings. Jashoda was a mother by profession, *professional mother*. Jashoda was not an *amateur* mama like the daughters and wives of the master's house. The world belongs to the professional. In this city, this kingdom, the amateur beggar-pickpocket-hooker has no place. Even the mongrel on the path or sidewalk, the greedy crow at the garbage don't make room for the upstart *amateur*. Jashoda had taken motherhood as her profession.

The responsibility was Mr. Haldar's new son-in-law's Studebaker and the sudden desire of the youngest son of the Haldar-house to be a driver. When the boy suddenly got a whim in mind or body, he could not rest unless he had satisfied it instantly. These sudden whims reared up in the loneliness of the afternoon and kept him at slave labor like the khalifa of Bagdad.[2] What he had done so far on that account did not oblige Jashoda to choose motherhood as a profession.

One afternoon the boy, driven by lust, attacked the cook and the cook,

---

1. Translated by Gayatri Chakravorty Spivak. Spivak has italicized English words that appeared in the original Bengali text.   2. Or caliph ("ruler") of Baghdad; according to legend, he kept a djinn ("spirit") who would do his bidding.

since her body was heavy with rice, stolen fishheads, and turnip greens, and her body languid with sloth, lay back, saying, "Yah, do what you like." Thus did the incubus of Bagdad get off the boy's shoulders and he wept repentant tears, mumbling, "Auntie, don't tell." The cook—saying, "What's there to tell?"—went quickly to sleep. She never told anything. She was sufficiently proud that her body had attracted the boy. But the thief thinks of the loot. The boy got worried at the improper supply of fish and fries in his dish. He considered that he'd be fucked if the cook gave him away. Therefore on another afternoon, driven by the Bagdad djinn, he stole his mother's ring, slipped it into the cook's pillowcase, raised a hue and cry, and got the cook kicked out. Another afternoon he lifted the radio set from his father's room and sold it. It was difficult for his parents to find the connection between the hour of the afternoon and the boy's behavior, since his father had created him in the deepest night by the astrological calendar[3] and the tradition of the Haldars of Harisal. In fact you enter the sixteenth century as you enter the gates of this house. To this day you take your wife by the astrological almanac. But these matters are mere blind alleys. Motherhood did not become Jashoda's profession for these afternoon-whims.

One afternoon, leaving the owner of the shop, Kangalicharan was returning home with a handful of stolen samosas and sweets under his dhoti.[4] Thus he returns daily. He and Jashoda eat rice. Their three offspring return before dark and eat stale samosas and sweets. Kangalicharan stirs the seething vat of milk in the sweet shop and cooks and feeds "food cooked by a good Brahmin"[5] to those pilgrims at the Lionseated goddess's[5] temple who are proud that they are not themselves "fake Brahmins by sleight of hand." Daily he lifts a bit of flour and such and makes life easier. When he puts food in his belly in the afternoon he feels a filial inclination toward Jashoda, and he goes to sleep after handling her capacious bosom. Coming home in the afternoon, Kangalicharan was thinking of his imminent pleasure and tasting paradise at the thought of his wife's large round breasts. He was picturing himself as a farsighted son of man as he thought that marrying a fresh young thing, not working her overmuch, and feeding her well led to pleasure in the afternoon. At such a moment the Haldar son, complete with Studebaker, swerving by Kangalicharan, ran over his feet and shins.

Instantly a crowd gathered. It was an accident in front of the house after all, "otherwise I'd have drawn blood," screamed Nabin, the pilgrim-guide. He guides the pilgrims to the Mother goddess of Shakti-power,[6] his temper is hot in the afternoon sun. Hearing him roar, all the Haldars who were at home came out. The Haldar chief started thrashing his son, roaring, "You'll kill a Brahmin,[7] you bastard, you unthinking bull?" The youngest

---

3. In traditional Indian belief, the position of the stars and planets at the time of conception and birth is one of the forces that shape the individual's personality and life.   4. Untailored cloth worn as a garment for the lower body by Indian men. *Samosas*: savory, hot snacks.   5. Durga, a martial goddess who rides a lion; her worship is popular throughout Bengal. In Hindu communities, food cooked by brahmins, who are highest in the caste hierarchy because of their ritually pure status, is considered to be beneficial. 6. The goddess, worshiped as the mother of the universe, is said to be a personification of Shakti, the energy of the cosmos.   7. A member of the priestly elite castes. Killing a brahmin is the worst offence a Hindu can commit.

son-in-law breathed relief as he saw that his Studebaker was not much damaged and, to prove that he was better human material than the money-rich, *culture*-poor in-laws, he said in a voice as fine as the finest muslin, "Shall we let the man die? Shouldn't we take him to the hospital?" — Kangali's boss was also in the crowd at the temple and, seeing the samosas and sweets flung on the roadway was about to say, "Eh Brahmin!! Stealing food?" Now he held his tongue and said, "Do that *sir*." The youngest son-in-law and the Haldar-chief took Kangalicharan quickly to the hospital. The master felt deeply grieved. During the Second War, when he helped the anti-Fascist struggle of the Allies by buying and selling scrap iron — then Kangali was a mere lad. Reverence for Brahmins crawled in Mr. Haldar's veins. If he couldn't get chatterjeebabu in the morning he would touch the feet of Kangali, young enough to be his son, and put a pinch of dust from his chapped feet on his own tongue.[8] Kangali and Jashoda came to his house on feast days and Jashoda was sent a gift of cloth and vermil-lion when his daughters-in-law were pregnant.[9] Now he said to Kangali — "Kangali! don't worry son. You won't suffer as long as I'm around." Now it was that he thought that Kangali's feet, being turned to ground meat, he would not be able to taste their dust. He was most unhappy at the thought and he started weeping as he said, "What has the son of a bitch done." He said to the doctor at the hospital, "Do what you can! Don't worry about cash."

But the doctors could not bring the feet back. Kangali returned as a lame Brahmin. Haldarbabu had a pair of crutches made. The very day Kangali returned home on crutches, he learned that food had come to Jashoda from the Haldar house every day. Nabin was third in rank among the pilgrim-guides. He could only claim thirteen percent of the goddess's food[1] and so had an inferiority complex. Inspired by seeing Rama-Krishna[2] in the movies a couple of times, he called the goddess "my crazy one" and by the book of the Kali-worshippers kept his consciousness immersed in local spirits. He said to Kangali, "I put flowers on the crazy one's feet in your name. She said I have a share in Kangali's house, he will get out of the hospital by that fact." Speaking of this to Jashoda, Kangali said, "What? When I wasn't there, you were getting it off with Nabin?" Jashoda then grabbed Kangali's suspicious head between the two hemispheres of the globe and said, "Two maid servants from the big house slept here every day to guard me. Would I look at Nabin? Am I not your faithful wife?"

In fact Kangali heard of his wife's flaming devotion at the big house as well. Jashoda had fasted at the mother's temple, had gone through a female ritual, and had travelled to the outskirts to pray at the feet of the

8. Younger men and women show respect to older persons and to those of higher social rank by touching their feet and (symbolically) placing dust from the feet on their own heads or lips. *Chatterjeebabu:* "Chat-terjee" is a brahmin family name; "babu" is a term of respect used for men of high castes or rank. 9. Married brahmin women are given gifts of cloth and vermilion (red cosmetic) powder, symbols of good luck, in return for the blessings that they are thought to be capable of giving pregnant women. 1. Temple priests divide up the food offerings pilgrims and devotees bring to the temple.   2. A renowned Bengali mystic and spiritual teacher (1836–1886), who was a priest and worshiper of the fierce and enigmatic goddess Kali, to whom goats are sacrificed. Some Kali worshipers engage in esoteric ritual practices, including breaking the Hindu ritual taboo against consuming alcohol.

local guru.[3] Finally the Lionseated came to her in a dream as a midwife carrying a *bag* and said, "Don't worry. Your man will return." Kangali was most overwhelmed by this. Haldarbabu said, "See, Kangali? The bastard unbelievers say, the Mother gives a dream, why togged as a midwife? I say, she creates as mother, and preserves as midwife."

Then Kangali said, "Sir! How shall I work at the sweetshop any longer. I can't stir the vat with my kerutches.[4] You are god. You are feeding so many people in so many ways. I am not begging. Find me a job."

Haldarbabu said, "Yes Kangali! I've kept you a spot. I'll make you a shop in the corner of my porch. The Lionseated is across the way! Pilgrims come and go. Put up a shop of dry sweets.[5] Now there's a wedding in the house. It's my bastard seventh son's wedding. As long as there's no shop, I'll send you food."

Hearing this, Kangali's mind took wing like a rainbug in the rainy season. He came home and told Jashoda, "Remember Kalidasa's pome? You eat because there isn't, wouldn't have got if there was? That's my lot, chuck. Master says he'll put up a shop after his son's wedding. Until then he'll send us food. Would this have happened if I had legs? All is Mother's will, dear!"[6]

Everyone is properly amazed that in this fallen age[7] the wishes and wills of the Lionseated, herself found by a dream-command a hundred and fifty years ago, are circulating around Kangalicharan Patitundo. Haldarbabu's change of heart is also Mother's will. He lives in independent India, the India that makes no distinctions among people, kingdoms, languages, varieties of Brahmins, varieties of Kayasthas[8] and so on. But he made his cash in the British era, when *Divide and Rule*[9] was the policy. Haldarbabu's mentality was constructed then. Therefore he doesn't trust anyone—not a Panjabi-Oriya-Bihari-Gujarati-Marathi-Muslim.[1] At the sight of an unfortunate Bihari child or a starvation-ridden Oriya beggar his flab-protected heart, located under a forty-two inch Gopal brand vest, does not itch with the rash of kindness. He is a successful son of Harisal. When he sees a West Bengali fly he says, "Tchah! at home even the flies were fat—in the bloody West[2] everything is pinched-skinny." All the temple people are struck that such a man is filling with the milk of humankindness toward the West Bengali Kangalicharan. For some time this news is the general talk. Haldarbabu is such a patriot that, if his nephews or grandsons read the lives of the nation's leaders in their schoolbook, he says to his employ-

3. Chaste women are thought to be capable of saving their husband's lives by the power they accumulate by fasting and performing other rituals of austerity and devotion.   4. Crutches.   5. That is, not dipped in syrup, used as offerings for the goddess.   6. Kangali misquotes a Sanskrit verse attributed to Kālidāsa (ca. A.D. 4th century), the eminent classical poet of the Gupta era.   7. Hindus believe that the current era is one of deterioration, the fourth and last phase in the pattern of fourfold cosmic era cycles (*yuga*), by means of which time is measured in the Hindu tradition.   8. A high-ranking north Indian caste of administrators and educators.   9. Refers to the British colonial government's policy of dealing with Hindu and Muslim communities as separate constituencies. Mahasweta satirizes the rhetoric of politicians who claim that the independent nation of India has achieved equality for all its members, regardless of differences in language, regional affiliation, economic class, or caste.   1. Parody of a line in the Indian national anthem (written by the Bengali author Rabindranath Tagore), in which various regions of (preindependence) India are named: "Punjab-Sindh-Gujarat-Maratha-Dravida-Utkala-Vanga."   2. Harisal is in the eastern part of Bengal, in what was formerly East Bengal, later East Pakistan, and now Bangladesh. The British colonial government partitioned the older state of Bengal into a western and an eastern section in 1905.

ees, "Nonsense! why do they make 'em read the lives of characters from Dhaka, Mymansingh, Jashore?[3] Harisal is made of the bone of the martyr god. One day it will emerge that the *Vedas* and the *Upanishads* were also written in Harisal."[4] Now his employees tell him, "You have had a *change of heart*, so much kindness for a West Bengali, you'll see there is divine *purpose* behind this." The Boss is delighted. He laughs loudly and says, "There's no East or West for a Brahmin. If there's a sacred thread[5] around his neck you have to give him respect even when he's taking a shit."

Thus all around blow the sweet winds of sympathy-compassion-kindness. For a few days, whenever Nabin tries to think of the Lionseated, the heavy-breasted, languid-hipped body of Jashoda floats in his mind's eye. A slow rise spreads in his body at the thought that perhaps she is appearing in his dream as Jashoda just as she appeared in Jashoda's as a midwife. The fifty percent pilgrim-guide says to him, "Male and female both get this disease. Bind the root of a white forget-me-not in your ear when you take a piss."

Nabin doesn't agree. One day he tells Kangali, "As the Mother's[6] son I won't make a racket with Shakti-power. But I've thought of a plan. There's no problem with making a Hare Krishna racket.[7] I tell you, get a Gopal in your dream. My Aunt brought a stony Gopal from Puri.[8] I give it to you. You announce that you got it in a dream. You'll see there'll be a to-do in no time, money will roll in. Start for money, later you'll get devoted to Gopal."

Kangali says, "Shame, brother! Should one joke with gods?"

"Ah get lost," Nabin scolds. Later it appears that Kangali would have done well to listen to Nabin. For Haldarbabu suddenly dies of heart failure. Shakespeare's *welkin*[9] breaks on Kangali and Jashoda's head.

2

Haldarbabu truly left Kangali in the lurch. Those wishes of the Lionseated that were manifesting themselves around Kangali *via-media* Haldarbabu disappeared into the blue like the burning promises given by a political party before the elections and became magically invisible like the heroine of a fantasy. A European witch's *bodkin* pricks the colored balloon of Kangali and Jashoda's dreams and the pair falls in deep trouble. At home, Gopal, Nepal, and Radharani whine interminably for food and abuse their mother. It is very natural for children to cry so for grub. Ever since Kangalicharan's loss of feet they'd eaten the fancy food of the Haldar household. Kangali also longs for food and is shouted at for trying to put his head in Jashoda's chest in the way of Gopal, the Divine Son.[1] Jashoda is fully an Indian woman, whose unreasonable, unreasoning, and unintel-

3. In eastern Bengal.   4. Haldar asserts the superiority of Harisal, revealing the extent of his provincialism in the claim that the Vedas and the Upanisads, the oldest Sanskrit sacred texts of the Hindus, were probably written in Harisal (contrary to the scholarly opinion that the Vedas were composed by the Indo-Aryans who lived in northwestern India).   5. A symbol of brahmin caste identity, received at the time of religious initiation.   6. That is, the mother goddess.   7. A reference to the worldwide Hare Krishna cult, an offshoot of the traditional worship of the Hindu god Krishna in India.   8. A pilgrimage center and the site of the great temple of Jagannath, a form of Krishna. *Stony Gopal:* an image of Krishna made of stone.   9. Sky (archaic).   1. In the manner of the infant Krishna sucking at his mother Jashoda's breast.

ligent devotion to her husband and love for her children, whose unnatural
renunciation and forgiveness have been kept alive in the popular consciousness by all Indian women from Sati-Savitri-Sita[2] through Nirupa
Roy and Chand Osmani.[3] The creeps of the world understand by seeing
such women that the old Indian tradition is still flowing free—they understand that it was with such women in mind that the following aphorisms
have been composed—"a female's life hangs on like a turtle's"—"her heart
breaks but no word is uttered"—"the woman will burn, her ashes will fly[4] /
Only then will we sing her / praise on high." Frankly, Jashoda never once
wants to blame her husband for the present misfortune. Her mother-love
wells up for Kangali as much as for the children. She wants to become
the earth and feed her crippled husband and helpless children with a
fulsome harvest. Sages did not write of this motherly feeling of Jashoda's
for her husband. They explained female and male as Nature and the
Human Principle.[5] But this they did in the days of yore—when they
entered this *peninsula* from another land.[6] Such is the power of the Indian
soil that all women turn into mothers here and all men remain immersed
in the spirit of holy childhood. Each man the Holy Child and each
woman the Divine Mother. Even those who deny this and wish to slap
current posters to the effect of the *"eternal she"*—"Mona Lisa"—"La pas-
sionaria"—"Simone de Beauvoir," et cetera, over the old ones and look at
women that way are, after all, Indian cubs. It is notable that the educated
Babus desire all this from women outside the home. When they cross the
threshold they want the Divine Mother in the words and conduct of the
revolutionary ladies. The *process* is most complicated. Because he understood this the heroines of Saratchandra[7] always fed the hero an extra
mouthful of rice. The apparent simplicity of Saratchandra's and other similar writers' writings is actually very complex and to be thought of in the
evening, peacefully after a glass of wood-apple[8] juice. There is too much
influence of fun and games in the lives of the people who traffic in studies
and intellectualism in West Bengal and therefore they should stress the
wood-apple correspondingly. We have no idea of the loss we are sustaining
because we do not stress the wood-apple-type-herbal remedies correspondingly.

　　However, it's incorrect to cultivate the habit of repeated incursions into
byelanes as we tell Jashoda's life story. The reader's patience, unlike the
cracks in Calcutta[9] streets, will not widen by the decade. The real thing is
that Jashoda was in a cleft stick. Of course they ate their fill during the

2. Or Sati ("the chaste wife"), the goddess Parvati, who sacrificed her life for the sake of her husband
Siva's honor; thus her name is a word denoting all chaste wives. In the *Mahābhārata* epic, the devoted
effort of Savitri saves her husband, Satyavan, from death. Sita is the devoted, self-sacrificing wife of Rama,
the hero of the *Rāmāyaṇa* epic.   3. Actresses in popular Hindi films made in Bombay in the 1940s and
1950s.   4. A reference to the custom of Sati (see also n. 2, above), in which virtuous widows were
encouraged to burn themselves on the funeral pyres of their husbands (Hindus cremate their dead). Sati
was officially banned in 1829 under British rule.   5. In several major schools of Indian philosophy
Nature and the Human Principle are conceived as female and male in sexual relationship.   6. Reference to the coming of the Indo-Aryan tribes into India from west and central Asia, a theory advanced by
Western scholars in the 19th and 20th centuries.   7. Saratchandra Chatterjee (1876–1938), the master
of the sentimental middle-class novel in Bengali fiction.   8. A fruit that is used for its medicinal properties, especially as a laxative.   9. Established by the British East India Company in the 17th century, it
was the capital of British India. It is now the capital of the state of West Bengal and the center of Bengali
culture.

Master's funeral days, but after everything was over Jashoda clasped Rad-harani to her bosom and went over to the big house. Her aim was to speak to the Mistress and ask for the cook's job in the vegetarian kitchen.[1]

The Mistress really grieved for the Master. But the lawyer let her know that the Master had left her the proprietorship of this house and the right to the rice warehouse. Girding herself with those assurances, she has once again taken the rudder of the family empire. She had really felt the loss of fish and fish-head.[2] Now she sees that the best butter, the best milk sweets from the best shops, heavy cream, and the best variety of bananas can also keep the body going somehow. The Mistress lights up her easychair. A six-months' babe in her lap, her grandson. So far six sons have married. Since the almanac approves of the taking of a wife almost every month of the year, the birth rooms in a row on the ground floor of the Mistress's house are hardly ever empty. The *lady doctor* and Sarala the midwife never leave the house. The Mistress has six daughters. They too breed every year and a half. So there is a constant *epidemic* of blanket-quilt-feeding spoon-bottle-oilcloth-*Johnson's baby powder*-bathing basin.

The Mistress was out of her mind trying to feed the boy. As if relieved to see Jashoda she said, "You come like a god! Give her some milk, dear, I beg you. His mother's sick—such a brat, he won't touch a bottle." Jashoda immediately suckled the boy and pacified him. At the Mistress's special request Jashoda stayed in the house until nine p.m. and suckled the Mis-tress's grandson again and again. The Cook filled a big bowl with rice and curry for her own household. Jashoda said as she suckled the boy, "Mother! The Master said many things. He is gone, so I don't think of them. But Mother! Your Brahmin-son does not have his two feet. I don't think for myself. But thinking of my husband and sons I say, give me any kind of job. Perhaps you'll let me cook in your household?"

"Let me see dear! Let me think and see." The Mistress is not as sold on Brahmins as the Master was. She does not accept fully that Kangali lost his feet because of her son's afternoon whims. It was written for Kangali as well, otherwise why was he walking down the road in the blazing sun grinning from ear to ear? She looks in charmed envy at Jashoda's *mammal projections* and says, "The good lord sent you down as the legendary Cow of Fulfillment.[3] Pull the teat and milk flows! The ones I've brought to my house, haven't a quarter of this milk in their nipples!"

Jashoda says, "How true Mother! Gopal was weaned when he was three. This one hadn't come to my belly yet. Still it was like a flood of milk. Where does it come from, Mother? I have no good food, no pampering!"

This produced a lot of talk among the women at night and the menfolk got to hear it too at night. The second son, whose wife was sick and whose son drank Jashoda's milk, was particularly uxorious. The difference between him and his brothers was that the brothers created progeny as soon as the almanac gave a good day, with love or lack of love, with irrita-tion or thinking of the accounts at the works. The second son impregnates

1. In Bengal, traditional Hindu women become strict vegetarians after the death of their husbands as a sign of austerity.   2. Fish is an important part of the Bengali diet.   3. The magical cow of Hindu legend, said to be able to fulfill all wishes.

his wife at the same *frequency*, but behind it lies deep love. The wife is often pregnant, that is an act of God. But the second son is also interested in that the wife remains beautiful at the same time. He thinks a lot about how to *combine* multiple pregnancies and beauty, but he cannot fathom it. But today, hearing from his wife about Jashoda's surplus milk, the second son said all of a sudden, "Way found."

"Way to what?"

"Uh, the way to save you pain."

"How? I'll be out of pain when you burn me. Can a year-breeder's[4] health mend?"

"It will, it will, I've got a divine engine in my hands! You'll breed yearly *and* keep your body."

The couple discussed. The husband entered his Mother's room in the morning and spoke in heavy whispers. At first the Mistress hemmed and hawed, but then she thought to herself and realized that the proposal was worth a million rupees. Daughters-in-law *will* be mothers. When they are mothers, they will suckle their children. Since they will be mothers as long as it's possible—progressive suckling will ruin their shape. Then if the sons look outside, or harass the maidservants, she won't have a voice to object. Going out because they can't get it at home—this is just. If Jashoda becomes the infants' suckling-mother, her daily meals, clothes on feast days, and some monthly pay will be enough. The Mistress is constantly occupied with women's rituals. There Jashoda can act as the fruitful Brahmin wife.[5] Since Jashoda's misfortune is due to her son, that sin too will be lightened.

Jashoda received a portfolio when she heard her proposal. She thought of her breasts as most precious objects. At night when Kangalicharan started to give her a feel she said, "Look. I'm going to pull our weight with these. Take good care how you use them." Kangalicharan hemmed and hawed that night, of course, but his Gopal frame of mind disappeared instantly when he saw the amount of grains—oil—vegetables coming from the big house. He was illuminated by the spirit of Brahma the Creator[6] and explained to Jashoda, "You'll have milk in your breasts only if you have a child in your belly. Now you'll have to think of that and suffer. You are a faithful wife, a goddess. You will yourself be pregnant, be filled with a child, rear it at your breast, isn't this why Mother came to you as a midwife?"

Jashoda realized the justice of these words and said, with tears in her eyes, "You are husband, you are guru. If I forget and say no, correct me. Where after all is the pain? Didn't Mistress-Mother breed thirteen? Does it hurt a tree to bear fruit?"

So this rule held. Kangalicharan became a professional father. Jashoda was by *profession* Mother. In fact to look at Jashoda now even the skeptic is convinced of the profundity of that song of the path of devotion.[7] The song is as follows:

---

4. A woman who gets pregnant every year.   5. Brahmin women are important participants in Hindu women's rites of fertility and auspiciousness (see n. 9, p. 2408).   6. In the Hindu triad of gods.   7. Songs of devotion (*bhakti*) to particular gods are popular at all levels of Hindu society.

Is a Mother so cheaply made?
Not just by dropping a babe!

Around the paved courtyard on the ground floor of the Haldar house over a dozen auspicious milch cows live in some state in large rooms. Two Biharis look after them as Mother Cows.[8] There are mountains of rind-bran-hay-grass-molasses. Mrs. Haldar believes that the more the cow eats, the more milk she gives. Jashoda's place in the house is now above the Mother Cows. The Mistress's sons become incarnate Brahma and create progeny. Jashoda preserves the progeny.

Mrs. Haldar kept a strict watch on the free flow of her supply of milk. She called Kangalicharan to her presence and said, "Now then, my Brahmin son? You used to stir the vat at the shop, now take up the cooking at home and give her a rest. Two of her own, three here, how can she cook at day's end after suckling five?"

Kangalicharan's intellectual eye was thus opened. Downstairs the two Biharis gave him a bit of chewing tobacco and said, "Mistress Mother said right. We serve the Cow Mother as well—your woman is the Mother of the World."

From now on Kangalicharan took charge of the cooking at home. Made the children his assistants. Gradually he became an expert in cooking plantain curry, lentil soup, and pickled fish, and by constantly feeding Nabin a head-curry with the head of the goat dedicated to the Lionseated he tamed that ferocious cannabis-artist and drunkard.[9] As a result Nabin inserted Kangali into the temple of Shiva the King.[1] Jashoda, eating well-prepared rice and curry every day, became as inflated as the *bank account* of a Public Works Department *officer*. In addition, Mistress-Mother gave her milk gratis. When Jashoda became pregnant, she would send her preserves, conserves, hot and sweet balls.

Thus even the skeptics were persuaded that the Lionseated had appeared to Jashoda as a midwife for this very reason. Otherwise who has ever heard or seen such things as constant pregnancies, giving birth, giving milk like a cow, without a thought, to others' children? Nabin too lost his bad thoughts. Devotional feelings came to him by themselves. Whenever he saw Jashoda he called out "Mother! Mother! Dear Mother!" Faith in the greatness of the Lionseated was rekindled in the area and in the air of the neighborhood blew the *electrifying* influence of goddess-glory.

Everyone's devotion to Jashoda became so strong that at weddings, showers, namings, and sacred-threadings they invited her and gave her the position of chief fruitful woman. They looked with a comparable eye on Nepal-Gopal-Neno-Boncha-Patal etc. because they were Jashoda's children, and as each grew up, he got a sacred thread and started catching pilgrims for the temple. Kangali did not have to find husbands for Radharani, Altarani, Padmarani and such daughters. Nabin found them husbands with exemplary dispatch and the faithful mother's faithful daughters

---

8. Cows that were tended but allowed to roam freely as sacred milch (milk) cows. *Biharis:* people of the state of Bihar, which borders West Bengal.   9. That is, he tamed Nabin with the power of the goddess inherent in the flesh of the goat that was ritually sacrificed to her. Nabin's consumption of alcohol and cannabis (marijuana) is part of his esoteric regimen of Kali worship.   1. One of the three great gods of the Hindu pantheon; he is also said to be the spouse of Kali.

went off each to run the household of her own Shiva! Jashoda's worth went up in the Haldar house. The husbands are pleased because the wives' knees no longer knock when they riffle the almanac. Since their children are being reared on Jashoda's milk, they can be the Holy Child in bed at will. The wives no longer have an excuse to say "no." The wives are happy. They can keep their figures. They can wear blouses and bras of "European cut." After keeping the fast of Shiva's night by watching all-night picture shows they are no longer obliged to breast-feed their babies. All this was possible because of Jashoda. As a result Jashoda become vocal and, constantly suckling the infants, she opined as she sat in the Mistress's room, "A woman breeds, so here medicine, there bloodpeshur,[2] here doctor's visits. Showoffs! Look at me! I've become a year-breeder! So is my body failing, or is my milk drying? Makes your skin crawl? I hear they are drying their milk with injishuns.[3] Never heard of such things!"

The fathers and uncles of the current young men of the Haldar house used to whistle at the maidservants as soon as hair grew on their upper lips. The young ones were reared by the Milk-Mother's milk, so they looked upon the maid and the cook, their Milk-Mother's friends, as mothers too and started walking around the girls' school. The maids said, "Joshi! You came as The Goddess! You made the air of this house change!" So one day as the youngest son was squatting to watch Jashoda's milking, she said, "There dear, my Lucky! All this because you swiped him in the leg! Whose wish was it then?" "The Lionseated's," said Haldar junior.

He wanted to know how Kangalicharan could be Brahma without feet?[4] This encroached on divine area, and he forgot the question.

All is the Lionseated's will!

3

Kangali's shins were cut in the fifties, and our narrative has reached the present. In twenty-five years, sorry in thirty, Jashoda has been confined twenty times. The maternities toward the end were profitless, for a new wind entered the Haldar house somehow. Let's finish the business of the twenty-five or thirty years. At the beginning of the narrative Jashoda was the mother of three sons. Then she became gravid[5] seventeen times. Mrs. Haldar died. She dearly wished that one of her daughters-in-law should have the same good fortune as her mother-in-law. In the family the custom was to have a second wedding if a couple could produce twenty children. But the daughters-in-law called a halt at twelve-thirteen-fourteen. By evil counsel they were able to explain to their husbands and make arrangements at the hospital. All this was the bad result of the new wind. Wise men have never allowed a new wind to enter the house. I've heard from my grandmother that a certain gentleman would come to her house to read the liberal journal *Saturday Letter*. He would never let the tome enter his home. "The moment wife, or mother, or sister reads that paper," he would say, "she'll say 'I'm a woman! Not a mother, not a sister, not a wife.'" If asked what the result would be, he'd say, "They would wear

---

2. Blood pressure. 3. Injections. 4. Haldar junior's curiosity is in regard to Kangali's sexual and procreative capabilities. 5. Pregnant.

shoes while they cooked." It is a perennial rule that the power of the new wind disturbs the peace of the women's quarter.

It was always the sixteenth century in the Haldar household. But at the sudden significant rise in the *membership* of the house the sons started building new houses and splitting. The most objectionable thing was that in the matter of motherhood, the old lady's granddaughters-in-law had breathed a completely different air before they crossed her threshold. In vain did the Mistress say that there was plenty of money, plenty to eat. The old man had dreamed of filling half Calcutta with Haldars. The granddaughters-in-law were unwilling. Defying the old lady's tongue, they took off to their husbands' places of work. At about this time, the pilgrim-guides of the Lionseated had a tremendous fight and some unknown person or persons turned the image of the goddess around. The Mistress's heart broke at the thought that the Mother had turned her back. In pain she ate an unreasonable quantity of jackfruit in full summer and died shitting and vomiting.

4

Death liberated the Mistress, but the sting of staying alive is worse than death. Jashoda was genuinely sorry at the Mistress's death. When an elderly person dies in the neighborhood, it's Basini who can weep most elaborately. She is an old maidservant of the house. But Jashoda's meal ticket was offered up with the Mistress. She astounded everyone by weeping even more elaborately.

"Oh blessed Mother!," Basini wept. "Widowed, when you lost your crown, you became the Master and protected everyone! Whose sins sent you away Mother! Ma, when I said, don't eat so much jackfruit, you didn't listen to me at all Mother!"

Jashoda let Basini get her breath and lamented in that pause, "Why should you stay, Mother! You are blessed, why should you stay in this sinful world! The daughters-in-law have moved the throne! When the tree says I won't bear, alas it's a sin! Could you bear so much sin, Mother! Then did the Lionseated turn her back, Mother! You knew the abode of good works had become the abode of sin, it was not for you Mother! Your heart left when the Master left Mother! You held your body only because you thought of the family. O mistresses, o daughters-in-law! take a vermillion print of her footstep! Fortune will be tied to the door if you keep that print! If you touch your forehead to it every morning, pain and disease will stay out!"[6]

Jashoda walked weeping behind the corpse to the burning ghat[7] and said on return, "I saw with my own eyes a chariot descend from heaven, take Mistress-Mother from the pyre, and go on up."

After the funeral days were over, the eldest daughter-in-law said to Jashoda, "Brahmin sister! the family is breaking up. Second and Third are moving to the house in Beleghata. Fourth and Fifth are departing to Maniktala-Bagmari. Youngest will depart to our Dakshineswar house."[8]

---

6. Jashoda invokes the power of a Sati (see n. 2, p. 2411).   7. The cremation ground, usually situated near a river or other body of water.   8. Areas in the city of Calcutta.

"Who stays here?"

"I will. But I'll let the downstairs. Now must the family be folded up. You reared everyone on your milk, food was sent every day. The last child was weaned, still Mother sent you food for eight years. She did what pleased her. Her children said nothing. But it's no longer possible."

"What'll happen to me, elder daughter-in-law-sister?"

"If you cook for my household, your board is taken care of. But what'll you do with yours?"

"What?"

"It's for you to say. You are the mother of twelve living children! The daughters are married. I hear the sons call pilgrims, eat temple food, stretch out in the courtyard. Your Brahmin-husband has set himself up in the Shiva temple, I hear. What do you need?"

Jashoda wiped her eyes. "Well! Let me speak to the Brahmin."

Kangalicharan's temple had really caught on. "What will you do in my temple?" he asked.

"What does Naren's niece do?"

"She looks after the temple household and cooks. You haven't been cooking at home for a long time. Will you be able to push the temple traffic?"

"No meals from the big house. Did that enter your thieving head? What'll you eat?"

"You don't have to worry," said Nabin.

"Why did I have to worry for so long? You're bringing it in at the temple, aren't you? You've saved everything and eaten the food that sucked my body."

"Who sat and cooked?"

"The man brings, the woman cooks and serves. My lot is inside out. Then you ate my food, now you'll give me food. Fair's fair."

Kangali said on the beat, "Where did you bring in the food? Could you have gotten the Haldar house? Their door opened for *you* because *my* legs were cut off. The Master had wanted to set *me* up in business. Forgotten everything, you cunt?"

"Who's the cunt, you or me? Living off a wife's carcass, you call that a man?"

The two fought tooth and nail and cursed each other to the death. Finally Kangali said, "I don't want to see your face again. Buzz off!"

"All right."

Jashoda too left angry. In the meantime the various pilgrim-guide factions conspired to turn the image's face forward, otherwise disaster was imminent. As a result, penance rituals were being celebrated with great ceremony at the temple. Jashoda went to throw herself at the goddess's feet. Her aging, milkless, capacious breasts are breaking in pain. Let the Lionseated understand her pain and tell her the way.

Jashoda lay three days in the courtyard. Perhaps the Lionseated has also breathed the new wind. She did not appear in a dream. Moreover, when, after her three days' fast, Jashoda went back shaking to her place, her youngest came by. "Dad will stay at the temple. He's told Naba and I to ring the bells. We'll get money and holy food every day."

"I see! Where's dad?"

"Lying down. Golapi-auntie is scratching the prickly heat on his back. Asked us to buy candy with some money. So we came to tell you."

Jashoda understood that her usefulness had ended not only in the Haldar house but also for Kangali. She broke her fast in name and went to Nabin to complain. It was Nabin who had dragged the Lionseated's image the other way. After he had settled the dispute with the other pilgrim-guides re the overhead income from the goddess Basanti ritual, the goddess Jagaddhatri ritual, and the autumn Durgapuja,[9] it was he who had once again pushed and pulled the image the right way. He'd poured some liquor into his aching throat, had smoked a bit of cannabis, and was now addressing the local electoral candidate: "No offerings for the Mother from you! Her glory is back. Now we'll see how you win!"

Nabin is the proof of all the miracles that can happen if, even in this decade, one stays under the temple's power. He had turned the goddess's head himself and had himself believed that the Mother was averse because the pilgrim-guides were not organizing like all the want-votes groups. Now, after he had turned the goddess's head he had the idea that the Mother had turned on her own.

Jashoda said, "What are you babbling?"

Nabin said, "I'm speaking of Mother's glory."

Jashoda said, "You think I don't know that you turned the image's head yourself?"

Nabin said, "Shut up, Joshi. God gave me ability, and intelligence, and only then could the thing be done through me."

"Mother's glory has disappeared when you put your hands on her."

"Glory disappeared! If so, how come, the fan is turning, and you are sitting under the fan? Was there ever an elettiri[1] fan on the porch ceiling?"

"I accept. But tell me, why did you burn my luck? What did I ever do to you?"

"Why? Kangali isn't dead."

"Why wait for death? He's more than dead to me."

"What's up?"

Jashoda wiped her eyes and said in a heavy voice, "I've carried so many, I was the regular milk-mother at the Master's house. You know everything. I've never left the straight and narrow."

"But of course. You are a portion of the Mother."

"But Mother remains in divine fulfillment. Her 'portion' is about to die for want of food. Haldar-house has lifted its hand from me."

"Why did you have to fight with Kangali? Can a man bear to be insulted on grounds of being supported?"

"Why did you have to plant your niece there?"

"That was divine play. Golapi used to throw herself in the temple. Little by little Kangali came to understand that he was the god's companion-incarnate and she *his* companion."

"Companion indeed! I can get my husband from her clutches with one blow of a broom!"

9. Goddesses, who are also seen as aspects or forms of the great mother goddess.   1. Electric.

Nabin said, "No! that can't be any more. Kangali is a man in his prime, how can he be pleased with you any more? Besides, Golapi's brother is a real hoodlum, and he is guarding her. Asked *me* to *get out.* If I smoke ten pipes, he smokes twenty. Kicked me in the midriff. I went to speak for you. Kangali said, don't talk to me about her. Doesn't know her man, knows her master's house. The master's house is her household god, let her go there."

"I will."

Then Jashoda returned home, half-crazed by the injustice of the world. But her heart couldn't abide the empty room. Whether it suckled or not, it's hard to sleep without a child at the breast. Motherhood is a great addiction. The addiction doesn't break even when the milk is dry. Forlorn Jashoda went to the Haldaress. She said, "I'll cook and serve, if you want to pay me, if not, not. You must let me stay here. That sonofabitch is living at the temple. What disloyal sons! They are stuck there too. For whom shall I hold my room?"

"So stay. You suckled the children, *and* you're a Brahmin. So stay. But sister, it'll be hard for you. You'll stay in Basini's room with the others. You mustn't fight with anyone. The master is not in a good mood. His temper is rotten because his third son went to Bombay and married a local girl. He'll be angry if there's noise."

Jashoda's good fortune was her ability to bear children. All this misfortune happened to her as soon as that vanished. Now is the downward time for Jashoda, the milk-filled faithful wife who was the object of the reverence of the local houses devoted to the Holy Mother. It is human nature to feel an inappropriate vanity as one rises, yet not to feel the *surrender* of "let me learn to bite the dust since I'm down" as one falls. As a result one makes demands for worthless things in the old way and gets kicked by the weak.

The same thing happened to Jashoda. Basini's crowd used to wash her feet and drink the water. Now Basini said easily, "You'll wash your own dishes. Are you my master, that I'll wash your dishes. You are the master's servant as much as I am."

As Jashoda roared, "Do you know who I am?" she heard the eldest daughter-in-law scold, "This is what I feared. Mother gave her a swelled head. Look here, Brahmin sister! I didn't call you, you begged to stay, don't break the peace."

Jashoda understood that now no one would attend to a word she said. She cooked and served in silence and in the late afternoon she went to the temple porch and started to weep. She couldn't even have a good cry. She heard the music for the evening worship at the temple of Shiva. She wiped her eyes and got up. She said to herself, "Now save me, Mother! Must I finally sit by the roadside with a tin cup? Is that what you want?"

The days would have passed in cooking at the Haldar-house and complaining to the Mother. But that was not enough for Jashoda. Jashoda's body seemed to keel over. Jashoda doesn't understand why nothing pleases her. Everything seems confused inside her head. When she sits down to cook she thinks she's the milk-mother of this house. She is going home in a showy sari with a free meal in her hand. Her breasts feel empty, as if wasted. She had never thought she wouldn't have a child's mouth at her nipple.

Joshi became bemused. She serves nearly all the rice and curry, but forgets to eat. Sometimes she speaks to Shiva the King, "If Mother can't do it, you take me away. I can't pull any more."

Finally it was the sons of the eldest daughter-in-law who said, "Mother! Is the milk-mother sick? She acts strange."

The eldest daughter-in-law said, "Let's see."

The eldest son said, "Look here? She's a Brahmin's daughter, if anything happens to her, it'll be a sin for us."

The eldest daughter-in-law went to ask. Jashoda had started the rice and then lain down in the kitchen on the spread edge of her sari.[2] The eldest daughter-in-law, looking at her bare body, said, "Brahmin sister! Why does the top of your left tit look so red? God! flaming red!"

"Who knows? It's like a stone pushing inside. Very hard, like a rock."

"What is it?"

"Who knows? I suckled so many, perhaps that's why?"

"Nonsense! One gets breast-stones or pus-in-the-tit if there's milk. Your youngest is ten."

"That one is gone. The one before survived. That one died at birth. Just as well. This sinful world!"

"Well the doctor comes tomorrow to look at my grandson. I'll ask. Doesn't look good to me."

Jashoda said with her eyes closed, "Like a stone tit, with a stone inside. At first the hard ball moved about, now it doesn't move, doesn't budge."

"Let's show the doctor."

"No, sister daughter-in-law, I can't show my body to a male doctor."

At night when the doctor came the eldest daughter-in-law asked him in her son's presence. She said, "No pain, no burning, but she is keeling over."

The doctor said, "Go ask if the *nipple* has shrunk, if the armpit is swollen like a seed."

Hearing "swollen like a seed," the eldest daughter-in-law thought, "How crude!" Then she did her field investigations and said, "She says all that you've said has been happening for some time."

"How old?"

"If you take the eldest son's age she'll be about about fifty-five."

The doctor said, "I'll give medicine."

Going out, he said to the eldest son, "I hear your *Cook* has a problem with her *breast*. I think you should take her to the *cancer hospital*. I didn't see her. But from what I heard it could be *cancer* of the *mammary gland*."

Only the other day the eldest son lived in the sixteenth century. He has arrived at the twentieth century very recently. Of his thirteen offspring he has arranged the marriages of the daughters, and the sons have grown up and are growing up at their own speed and in their own way. But even now his grey cells are covered in the darkness of the eighteenth- and the

---

2. Indian woman's garment made of a long unconstructed length of fabric. It is draped around the body, with one end hanging free over the shoulder.

pre-Bengal-Renaissance[3] nineteenth centuries. He still does not take smallpox vaccination and says, "Only the lower classes get smallpox. I don't need to be vaccinated. An upper-caste family, respectful of gods and Brahmins, does not contract that disease."

He pooh-poohed the idea of cancer and said, "Yah! Cancer indeed! That easy! You misheard, all she needs is an ointment. I can't send a Brahmin's daughter to a hospital just on your word."

Jashoda herself also said, "I can't go to hospital. Ask me to croak instead. I didn't go to hospital to breed, and I'll go now? That corpse-burning devil returned a cripple because he went to hospital!"

The elder daughter-in-law said, "I'll get you a herbal ointment. This ointment will surely soothe. The hidden boil will show its tip and burst."

The herbal ointment was a complete failure. Slowly Jashoda gave up eating and lost her strength. She couldn't keep her sari on the left side. Sometimes she felt burning, sometimes pain. Finally the skin broke in many places and sores appeared. Jashoda took to her bed.

Seeing the hang of it, the eldest son was afraid, if at his house a Brahmin died! He called Jashoda's sons and spoke to them harshly, "It's your mother, she fed you so long, and now she is about to die! Take her with you! She has everyone and she should die in a Kayastha[4] household?"

Kangali cried a lot when he heard this story. He came to Jashoda's almost-dark room and said, "Wife! You are a blessed auspicious faithful woman! After I spurned you, within two years the temple dishes were stolen, I suffered from boils in my back, and that snake Golapi tricked Napla, broke the safe, stole everything and opened a shop in Tarakeswar. Come, I'll keep you in state."

Jashoda said, "Light the lamp."

Kangali lit the lamp.

Jashoda showed him her bare left breast, thick with running sores and said, "See these sores? Do you know how these sores smell? What will you do with me now? Why did you come to take me?"

"The Master called."

"Then the Master doesn't want to keep me."—Jashoda sighed and said, "There is no solution about me. What can you do with me?"

"Whatever, I'll take you tomorrow. Today I clean the room. Tomorrow for sure."

"Are the boys well? Noblay and Gaur used to come, they too have stopped."

"All the bastards are selfish. Sons of my spunk after all. As inhuman as I."

"You'll come tomorrow?"

"Yes—yes—yes."

Jashoda smiled suddenly. A heart-splitting nostalgia-provoking smile. Jashoda said, "Dear, remember?"

"What, wife?"

"How you played with these tits? You couldn't sleep otherwise? My lap

---

3. The great flowering of cultural activity in Bengal (late 18th and the 19th centuries).   4. An elite caste, second only to brahmins.

was never empty, if this one left my nipple, there was that one, and then the boys of the Master's house. How I could, I wonder now!"

"I remember everything, wife!"

In this instant Kangali's words are true. Seeing Jashoda's broken, thin, suffering form even Kangali's selfish body and instincts and belly-centered consciousness remembered the past and suffered some empathy. He held Jashoda's hand and said, "You have fever?"

"I get feverish all the time. I think by the strength of the sores."

"Where does this rotten stink come from?"

"From these sores."

Jashoda spoke with her eyes closed. Then she said, "Bring the holy doctor. He cured Gopal's *typhoid* with *homeopathy*."

"I'll call him. I'll take you tomorrow."

Kangali left. That he went out, the tapping of his crutches, Jashoda couldn't hear. With her eyes shut, with the idea that Kangali was in the room, she said spiritlessly, "If you suckle you're a mother, all lies! Nepal and Gopal don't look at me, and the Master's boys don't spare a peek to ask how I'm doing." The sores on her breast kept mocking her with a hundred mouths, a hundred eyes. Jashoda opened her eyes and said, "Do you hear?"

Then she realized that Kangali had left.

In the night she sent Basini for *Lifebuoy* soap[5] and at dawn she went to take a bath with the soap. Stink, what a stink! If the body of a dead cat or dog rots in the garbage can you get a smell like this. Jashoda had forever scrubbed her breasts carefully with soap and oil, for the master's sons had put the nipples in their mouth. Why did those breasts betray her in the end? Her skin burns with the sting of soap. Still Jashoda washed herself with soap. Her head was ringing, everything seemed dark. There was fire in Jashoda's body, in her head. The black floor was very cool. Jashoda spread her sari and lay down. She could not bear the weight of her breast standing up.

As Jashoda lay down, she lost sense and consciousness with fever. Kangali came at the proper time: but seeing Jashoda he lost his grip. Finally Nabin came and rasped, "Are these people human? She reared all the boys with her milk and they don't call a doctor? I'll call Hari the doctor."

Haribabu took one look at her and said, "Hospital."

Hospitals don't admit people who are so sick. At the efforts and recommendations of the eldest son, Jashoda was admitted.

"What's the matter? O Doctorbabu, what's the problem?"—Kangali asked, weeping like a boy.

"Cancer."

"You can get cancer in a tit?"

"Otherwise how did she get it?"

"Her own twenty, thirty boys at the Master's house—she had a lot of milk—"

"What did you say? How many did she *feed*?"

"About fifty for sure."

"Fif-ty!"

---

5. A brand of antibacterial soap.

"Yes sir."

"She had twenty children?"

"Yes sir."

"God!"

"Sir!"

"What?"

"Is it because she suckled so many—?"

"One can't say why someone gets cancer, one can't say. But when people breast-feed too much—didn't you realize earlier? It didn't get to this in a day?"

"She wasn't with me, sir. We quarreled—"

"I see."

"How do you see her? Will she get well?"

"Get well! See how long she lasts. You've brought her in the last stages. No one survives this stage."

Kangali left weeping. In the late afternoon, harassed by Kangali's lamentations, the eldest son's second son went to the doctor. He was minimally anxious about Jashoda—but his father nagged him and he was financially dependent on his father.

The doctor explained everything to him. It happened not in a day, but over a long time. Why? No one could tell. How does one perceive breast cancer? A hard lump inside the breast toward the top can be removed. Then gradually the lump inside becomes large, hard, and like a congealed pressure. The skin is expected to turn orange, as is expected a shrinking of the nipple. The gland in the armpit can be inflamed. When there is *ulceration*, that is to say sores, one can call it the final stages. Fever? From the point of view of seriousness it falls in the second or third category. If there is something like a sore in the body, there can be fever. That is *secondary*.

The second son was confused with all this specialist talk. He said, "Will she live?"

"No."

"How long will she suffer?"

"I don't think too long."

"When there's nothing to be done, how will you treat her?"

"*Painkiller, sedative, antibiotic* for the fever. Her body is very, very down."

"She stopped eating."

"You didn't take her to a doctor?"

"Yes."

"Didn't he tell you?"

"Yes."

"What did he say?"

"That it might be cancer. Asked us to take her to the hospital. She didn't agree."

"Why would she? She'd die!"

The second son came home and said, "When Arun-doctor said she had *cancer*, she might have survived if treated then."

His mother said, "If you know that much then why didn't you take her? Did I stop you?"

Somewhere in the minds of the second son and his mother an unknown sense of guilt and remorse came up like bubbles in dirty and stagnant water and vanished instantly.

Guilt said—she lived with us, we never took a look at her, when did the disease catch her, we didn't take it seriously at all. She was a silly person, reared so many of us, we didn't look after her. Now, with everyone around her she's dying in hospital, so many children, husband living, when she clung to us, then we had ———! What an alive body she had, milk leaped out of her, we never thought she would have this disease.

The disappearance of guilt said—who can undo Fate? It was written that she'd die of *cancer*—who'd stop it? It would have been wrong if she had died here—her husband and sons would have asked, how did she die? We have been saved from that wrongdoing. No one can say anything.

The eldest son assured them, "Now Arun-doctor says no one survives *cancer*. The cancer that Brahmin-sister has can lead to cutting of the tit, removing the uterus, even after that people die of *cancer*. See, Father gave us a lot of reverence toward Brahmins—we are alive by father's grace. If Brahmin-sister had died in our house, we would have had to perform the penance-ritual."

Patients much less sick than Jashoda die much sooner. Jashoda astonished the doctors by hanging on for about a month in hospital. At first Kangali, Nabin, and the boys did indeed come and go, but Jashoda remained the same, comatose, cooking with fever, spellbound. The sores on her breast gaped more and more and the breast now looks like an open wound. It is covered by a piece of thin *gauze* soaked in *antiseptic lotion*, but the sharp smell of putrefying flesh is circulating silently in the room's air like incense-smoke. This brought an ebb in the enthusiasm of Kangali and the other visitors. The doctor said as well, "Is she not responding? All for the better. It's hard to bear without consciousness, can anyone bear such death-throes consciously?"

"Does she know that we come and go?"

"Hard to say."

"Does she eat."

"Through tubes."

"Do people live this way?"

"Now you're very ———"

The doctor understood that he was unreasonably angry because Jashoda was in this condition. He was angry with Jashoda, with Kangali, with women who don't take the signs of breast-cancer *seriously* enough and finally die in this dreadful and hellish pain. Cancer constantly defeats patient and doctor. One patient's cancer means the patient's death and the defeat of science, and of course of the doctor. One can medicate against the secondary symptom, if eating stops one can *drip glucose* and feed the body, if the lungs become incapable of breathing there is *oxygen*—but the advance of *cancer*, its expansion, spread, and killing, remain unchecked. The word *cancer* is a general signifier, by which in the different parts of the body is meant different *malignant growths*. Its characteristic properties are to destroy the infected area of the body, to spread by *metastasis*, to return after *removal*, to create *toximeia*.

Kangali came out without a proper answer to his question. Returning to the temple, he said to Nabin and his sons, "There's no use going any more. She doesn't know us, doesn't open her eyes, doesn't realize anything. The doctor is doing what he can."

Nabin said, "If she dies?"

"They have the *telephone number* of the old Master's eldest son, they'll call."

"Suppose she wants to see you. Kangali, your wife is a blessed auspicious faithful woman! Who would say the mother of so many. To see her body— but she didn't bend, didn't look elsewhere."

Talking thus, Nabin became gloomily silent. In fact, since he'd seen Jashoda's infested breasts, many a philosophic thought and sexological argument have been slowly circling Nabin's drug-and-booze-addled dim head like great rutting snakes emptied of venom. For example, I lusted after her? This is the end of that intoxicating bosom? Ho! Man's body's a zero. To be crazy for that is to be crazy.

Kangali didn't like all this talk. His mind had already *rejected* Jashoda. When he saw Jashoda in the Haldar-house he was truly affected and even after her admission into hospital he was passionately anxious. But now that feeling is growing cold. The moment the doctor said Jashoda wouldn't last, he put her out of mind almost painlessly. His sons are his sons. Their mother had become a distant person for a long time. Mother meant hair in a huge topknot, blindingly white clothes, a strong personality. The person lying in the hospital is someone else, not Mother.

Breast *cancer* makes the *brain comatose*, this was a solution for Jashoda.

Jashoda understood that she had come to hospital, she was in the hospital, and that this desensitizing sleep was a medicated sleep. In her weak, infected, dazed brain she thought, has some son of the Haldar-house become a doctor? No doubt he sucked her milk and is now repaying the milk-debt? But those boys entered the family business as soon as they left high school! However, why don't the people who are helping her so much free her from the stinking presence of her chest? What a smell, what treachery? Knowing these breasts to be the rice-winner, she had constantly conceived to keep them filled with milk. The breast's job is to hold milk. She kept her breast clean with perfumed soap, she never wore a top, even in youth, because her breasts were so heavy.

When the *sedation* lessens, Jashoda screams, "Ah! Ah! Ah!"—and looks for the *nurse* and the doctor with passionate bloodshot eyes. When the doctor comes, she mutters with hurt feelings, "You grew so big on my milk, and now you're hurting me so?"

The doctor says, "She sees her milk-sons all over the world."

Again injection and sleepy numbness. Pain, tremendous pain, the cancer is spreading *at the expense of the human host*. Gradually Jashoda's left breast bursts and becomes like the *crater* of a volcano. The smell of putrefaction makes approach difficult.

Finally one night, Jashoda understood that her feet and hands were getting cold. She understood that death was coming. Jashoda couldn't open her eyes, but she understood that some people were looking at her hand. A needle pricked her arm. Painful breathing inside. Has to be. Who is looking? Are these her own people? The people whom she suckled because she carried them, or those she suckled for a living? Jashoda thought, after all, she had suckled the world, could she then die alone? The doctor who sees her every day, the person who will cover her face with a sheet, will put her on a cart, will lower her at the burning ghat, the untouchable[6] who will put her in the furnace, are all her milk-sons. One must become Jashoda[7] if one suckles the world. One has to die friendless, with no one left to put a bit of water in the mouth. Yet someone was supposed to be there at the end. Who was it? It was who? Who was it?

Jashoda died at 11 p.m.

The Halder-house was called on the phone. The phone didn't ring. The Haldars *disconnected* their phone at night.

Jashoda Devi, Hindu female, lay in the hospital morgue in the usual way, went to the burning ghat in a van, and was burnt. She was cremated by an untouchable.

Jashoda was God manifest, others do and did whatever she thought. Jashoda's death was also the death of God. When a mortal masquerades as God here below, she is forsaken by all and she must always die alone.

6. Outcastes who handle corpses at the cremation ground. They are considered untouchable because of their contact with ritually polluting objects and substances.   7. Here mother of the divine child Krishna and hence mother of the world.

GABRIEL GARCÍA MÁRQUEZ
born 1928

One of the great novelists and prose stylists of the twentieth century, Gabriel García Márquez possesses both the technical virtuosity of the French "new novel- ists" and the breadth and historical scope of the traditional realistic writer. His most famous work, *One Hundred Years of Solitude* (1967), is also the best-known novel from the amazing literary explosion of the 1960s and 1970s called the Latin American "Boom," and embodies the mixture of fantasy and realism called "magi- cal realism." In this novel and related stories, he follows the rise and fall of the Buendía family fortunes in a mythical town called Macondo, and sketches at the same time an echoing, intricate pattern of social, cultural, and psychological themes that become a symbolic picture of Latin American society. Not all of García Márquez's works are about Macondo, but the same themes and images reappear throughout: the contrast of dreamlike and everyday reality and the "magi- cal" aspect of fictional creation, mythic overtones often rooted in local folklore, the representation of broader social and psychological conflicts through regional tales, the essential solitude of individuals facing love and death in a society of which they never quite seem a part. García Márquez is a political novelist in that many of his fictional situations are openly drawn from conditions in Latin Ameri- can history, so that local readers will recognize current history in the change from prosperity to misery in Macondo that accompanies the presence and withdrawal of the banana company, the massacre of striking banana workers by government forces in 1928, the extreme separation of rich and poor, and the grotesquely oppressive power of political dictators pictured most recently in *The Autumn of the Patriarch* (1975). Yet his fiction achieves its impact not because of its base in real events but because these events are transformed and interpreted inside an artistic vision and language which—experimenting with many forms—creates a fictional universe all its own.

García Márquez was born in the small town of Aracataca in the "banana zone" of Colombia on March 6, 1928, to Gabriel Eligio García and Maria Márquez Iguarán. The first of twelve children, he was raised by his maternal grandparents until his grandfather died in 1936. He attributes his love of fantasy to his grand-mother, who would tell him fantastic tales whenever she did not want to answer his questions. The recurring image of an old military man battered by circum-stances (the grandfather of *Leaf Storm*, 1955; the protagonist of *No One Writes to the Colonel*, 1958; and in his younger days, Colonel Aureliano Buendía of *One Hundred Years of Solitude*) likewise recalls his grandfather, a retired colonel who had served on the Liberal side of a civil war at the beginning of the century. A scholarship student at the National Colegio in Zipaquirá, García Márquez received his bachelor's degree in 1946 and studied law at universities in Bogotá and Cartagena from 1947 to 1950. In 1947 he published his first story, *The Third Resignation*, a Kafkaesque tale of a dead man who continued to grow and retain consciousness in his coffin for seventeen years after his death. García Márquez had worked as a journalist while studying law, and in 1950 he abandoned his legal studies for journalism in order to have more time as a writer. His first novel, *Leaf Storm*, was published in 1955, and—in its use of interior monologue and juxtaposi-tion of different perspectives—shows the strong influence of Faulkner. He would soon abandon the more subjective Faulknerian style for an objective manner derived both from his experience in journalism and from Ernest Hemingway. In *Leaf Storm*, we may perceive reality through the mind of a ten-year-old boy: "The heat won't let you breathe in the closed room. You can hear the sun buzzing in the streets, but that's all. The air is stagnant, like concrete; you get the feeling that it could get all twisted like a sheet of steel." In his next novel, *No One Writes to the Colonel*, an impersonal narrator catalogues the actions of the colonel about to make coffee: "He removed the pot from the fire, poured half the water onto the earthen floor, and scraped the inside of the can with a knife until the last scrapings of the ground coffee, mixed with bits of rust, fell into the pot."

In 1954 García Márquez had joined the newspaper *El Espectador* (The specta-tor) in Bogotá; a report he wrote in 1955 that indirectly revealed corruption in the navy irritated the Rojas Pinilla dictatorship and the paper was shut down. Working in Paris as *El Espectador*'s foreign correspondent when he learned that his job had been abolished, he lived in extreme poverty for the next year while beginning *The Evil Hour* (1962) and *No One Writes to the Colonel*. In 1957, after traveling in Eastern Europe, he returned to Latin America. Here he worked for several differ-ent newspapers in Venezuela, and later for the international press agency, Prensa Latina, in Cuba and New York, and for the Mexican periodicals *La Familia* and *Sucesos* (a sensationalist magazine) before beginning to write film scripts in 1963. A collection of short stories, *Big Mama's Funeral*, was published in 1962, along with the first edition of *The Evil Hour*, which, printed in Spain, was later repudi-ated by the author because of tampering by proofreaders. In 1965 the various themes and characters he had been developing throughout his earlier novels and short stories came together as the fully developed concept of a new book, and García Márquez shut himself up in his study for a year and a half to write *One Hundred Years of Solitude*. Published in 1967, the novel was a best-seller, immedi-ately translated into numerous (now twenty-five) languages; it received prizes in Italy and France in 1969, and—when published in English in 1970—was chosen by American critics as one of the twelve best books of the year.

Layers of meaning accumulate around a core story in *One Hundred Years*, as the history of the doomed Buendía family takes on different and intertwined shades of significance. The family is cursed from the moment that its founder, José Arcadio

Buendía, kills a friend who had insulted him and consummates an incestuous marriage; he then sets out in search of the sea and stops to settle in Macondo. Throughout a hundred years of family history in the nineteenth and twentieth centuries, the Buendías are soldiers, scholars, merchants, explorers, revolutionaries, inventors, lovers, ascetics, labor organizers, and above all stubborn individuals. Yet these individuals are caught up in, and defined by, a larger family history of which they sometimes appear only interrelated, component parts: names echo one another, and parallel situations evoke a feeling of half-recognition inside a mirror-like pattern of structural oppositions. The Buendía story is set in history but also exists on a mythic level: Remedios the Beauty is lifted up into heaven clutching her sheets when she dies, and when José Arcadio is killed, blood runs from his ear down the street all the way to his mother in her kitchen. The last Buendía is born with the sign of the curse—a pig's tail—and dies eaten by ants at the end. Yet this is not really the end, for in the very last pages, after his son's death and as a whirlwind gathers to destroy Macondo, Aureliano Babilonia reads the manuscript left by the dead magician Melquíades. At last able to decipher a text that could not be read until one hundred years had passed, Aureliano Babilonia finds that this text is the story of his own family; thus he is learning about his own existence, predicted and described a century ago. "It was the history of the family, written by Melquíades, down to the most trivial details, one hundred years ahead of time. He had written it in Sanskrit, which was his mother tongue, and he had encoded the even lines in the private cipher of the Emperor Augustus and the odd ones in a Lacedemonian military code." Behind García Márquez there is yet another author—Melquíades—who has written *One Hundred Years of Solitude,* a novel whose complexity and self-contained referentiality recall the circular fictions of Borges.

The magical realism of *One Hundred Years of Solitude* depends on the juxtaposition of real and fantastic worlds, and it elicits a series of interpretations whose variety can be only emulated by interpretations of Kafka. For some readers, the novel is an allegory of the human condition and its fall from innocence; for others, it recounts the destructive, alienating influence on Latin American society of the aggressive individualism in Western culture; for others, it depicts essential human loneliness and the failure to communicate—even in love; for still others, it is a "total fiction" peculiarly valid for intricate repetitive patterns that refer to folklore and real life but finally create only a fictional universe. Each interpretation draws on the novel's blurring of real and unreal worlds, so that historical facts become the basis for fiction and fictional manipulation liberates our perspective on reality—a typically modernist method of using the imagination to encourage historical change.

After *One Hundred Years of Solitude,* García Márquez found new ways to combine magical-realist techniques and social commentary. In 1972, he published a collection of seven stories, *The Incredible and Sad Story of Innocent Eréndira and Her Heartless Grandmother,* which contains the story printed here, *Death Constant Beyond Love.* From the title story, in which Eréndira's monstrously fat, tattooed, green-blooded grandmother is finally murdered after prostituting her grandchild to the entire countryside to repay a debt, to symbolic fantasies such as *A Very Old Man with Enormous Wings* (in which a castaway Angel is exhibited in a chicken coop until his feathers grow back and he can fly away), the author presents tales in which the substance is incredible but the details themselves are highly realistic. The winged man smells bad and his wings are infested with parasites; the farm truck in which Eréndira tries to escape with her lover has an old motor and can't outrun the military patrol summoned by her grandmother. The mixture of fantasy and realism is not easily interpretable in a single symbolic sense: Eréndira's prostitution may be political and cultural as well as personal, and larger social relationships may be symbolized in the town's attitude toward the Angel. Throughout, the narrative line can easily be followed but also interpreted in several ways.

Increasingly preoccupied with contemporary political events, he next published *The Autumn of the Patriarch*, an intricate study of the idea of dictatorship embodied in reactions to a first, false death of the patriarch (his double was assassinated instead), and a second, apparently real death on which new authorities are already gathering to divide up the power. García Márquez is aiming at more than a specific political situation: he points to a habit of mind, a social lethargy in which there is no apparent connection between the passive acceptance of life as it always has been and the manipulation of society by a succession of dictators. In his next novel, *Chronicle of a Death Foretold* (1981), he describes the same inertia in a small town where everyday life continues its ordinary gossipy routine around two life-shattering events: the rejection of Angela Vicario by her new husband when he finds she is not a virgin, and her brothers' murder of the local dandy whom she names (probably falsely) as her seducer. Against the background of a whole society's passive complicity in a murder that everyone knows will happen, it is death and love that are the two overriding realities.

In recent years—questioning the effectiveness of literature to remedy the social ills he so often describes—García Márquez has been more and more active politically, speaking out for revolutionary governments in Latin America and organizing assistance for political prisoners. Living in Mexico City, he nonetheless continues to write, including a number of stories that are still unpublished and an account of Cuba under the U.S. blockade. He received the Nobel Prize for literature in 1982.

The story printed here, *Death Constant Beyond Love* (1970), also has a political background although its protagonist, Senator Onésimo Sánchez, is seen chiefly as he struggles with his elemental problem of death. He is no hero: in *Innocent Eréndira* he writes a letter vouching for the grandmother's morality, and in this story he is clearly a corrupt politician who accepts bribes and stays in power by helping the local property owners avoid reform. His electoral train is a traveling circus with carnival wagons, fireworks, a readymade audience of hired Indians, and a cardboard village with imitation brick houses and a painted ocean liner to offer the illusion of future prosperity; he uses carefully placed gifts to encourage support and a feeling of dependence.

Yet the background of poverty and corruption, the entertaining spectacle of the senator's "fictional world," and the political campaign itself fade into insignificance before broader themes of life and death. Forty-two, happily married, in full control of his own and others' lives as a successful politician in midcareer, he is made to feel suddenly helpless, vulnerable, and alone when told that all this will stop and he will be dead "forever" by next Christmas. Theoretically, he knows that death is inevitable and nature cannot be defeated. He has read the Stoic philosopher Marcus Aurelius (A.D. 121–180) and even refers to the *Meditations*, which recommends the cheerful acceptance of natural order (including death and oblivion), criticizes the delusions of those "who have tenaciously stuck to life," and stresses both the tranquil "ordering of the mind" and the idea that human beings are all "fellow-citizens" of a shared "political community." The example of the philosopher is not mere chance: Marcus Aurelius was also a political figure, a Roman emperor who wrote his *Meditations* as personal guidelines in a time of plague and political unrest.

The senator does gain some Stoic insight into the illusions of his career: he notices how similar are the dusty village and the worn cardboard facade that represents its hopes, and he is fed up with what he recognizes to be background maneuverings that keep him in power by prolonging the exploitation of the poor. But he also loses sympathy for the barefoot Indians standing in the square, and his newly alienated perspective is not accompanied by the Stoic injunction to maintain a just and ordered mind, and to accept everything that happens as necessary and good. In this crisis, the senator is reduced to a basic and instinctual existence, expressed in García Márquez's recurrent themes of solitude, love, and death. The beautiful Laura provides an opportunity for him to sublimate his fear of death in erotic passion (inextricably intertwined, according to Freud). His choice means scandal and the destruction of his political career, but by now Onésimo Sánchez has felt the emptiness of his earlier activities and is engaged in a struggle to cheat death.

He does not succeed, of course, and dies weeping with rage that death separates him from Laura Farina. *Death Constant Beyond Love* has reversed the ambitious claim of a famous sonnet by the Spanish Golden Age writer Quevedo (1580–1645), according to which there is "Love Constant Beyond Death." Such love is an illusion, for it is death that awaits us beyond everything else. García Márquez repeatedly plays on these oppositions and inversions when he describes the real village and the cardboard version created by false political promises, the paper birds that magically take on life and fly out to sea, the paper butterfly that seems to fly and lands on the wall, the bribery money that flaps around like butterflies, the grotesquely padlocked chastity belt that Laura Farina wears, and even the initial opposition between the senator's living rose (symbol of womanhood and love) and the roseless town (named "The Viceroy's Rosebush") where he encounters his destiny. His destiny is to be liberated from some illusions but not all: his final delusion is to try to hide from death in erotic love. The senator's defeat at the end, which is clearly emphasized as a defeat, suggests that his response was a futile retreat, and—at the same time that it evokes pity for his loneliness, terror, and rage—puts in question what that response should be.

Regina Janes, *Gabriel García Márquez, Revolutions in Wonderland* (1981), is an excellent general study on García Márquez in a Latin American context. An introduction to the writer and his work is found in George P. McMurray, *Gabriel García Márquez* (1977). The Summer 1972 issue of *Books Abroad* is dedicated to García Márquez. Harley D. Oberhelman, ed., *Gabriel Garcia Marquez: A Study of the Short Fiction* (1991), includes a bibliography.

Death Constant Beyond Love[1]

Senator Onésimo Sánchez had six months and eleven days to go before his death when he found the woman of his life. He met her in Rosal del Virrey,[2] an illusory village which by night was the furtive wharf for smugglers' ships, and on the other hand, in broad daylight looked like the most useless inlet on the desert, facing a sea that was arid and without direction and so far from everything no one would have suspected that someone capable of changing the destiny of anyone lived there. Even its name was a kind of joke, because the only rose in that village was being worn by Senator Onésimo Sánchez himself on the same afternoon when he met Laura Farina.

It was an unavoidable stop in the electoral campaign he made every four years. The carnival wagons had arrived in the morning. Then came

---

1. Translated by Gregory Rabassa.   2. The Rosebush of the Viceroy (governor).

the trucks with the rented Indians[3] who were carried into the towns in order to enlarge the crowds at public ceremonies. A short time before eleven o'clock, along with the music and rockets and jeeps of the retinue, the ministerial automobile, the color of strawberry soda, arrived. Senator Onésimo Sánchez was placid and weatherless inside the air-conditioned car, but as soon as he opened the door he was shaken by a gust of fire and his shirt of pure silk was soaked in a kind of light-colored soup and he felt many years older and more alone than ever. In real life he had just turned forty-two, had been graduated from Göttingen[4] with honors as a metallurgical engineer, and was an avid reader, although without much reward, of badly translated Latin classics. He was married to a radiant German woman who had given him five children and they were all happy in their home, he the happiest of all until they told him, three months before, that he would be dead forever by next Christmas.

While the preparations for the public rally were being completed, the senator managed to have an hour alone in the house they had set aside for him to rest in. Before he lay down he put in a glass of drinking water the rose he had kept alive all across the desert, lunched on the diet cereals that he took with him so as to avoid the repeated portions of fried goat that were waiting for him during the rest of the day, and he took several analgesic pills before the time prescribed so that he would have the remedy ahead of the pain. Then he put the electric fan close to the hammock and stretched out naked for fifteen minutes in the shadow of the rose, making a great effort at mental distraction so as not to think about death while he dozed. Except for the doctors, no one knew that he had been sentenced to a fixed term, for he had decided to endure his secret all alone, with no change in his life, not because of pride but out of shame.[5]

He felt in full control of his will when he appeared in public again at three in the afternoon, rested and clean, wearing a pair of coarse linen slacks and a floral shirt, and with his soul sustained by the anti-pain pills. Nevertheless, the erosion of death was much more pernicious than he had supposed, for as he went up onto the platform he felt a strange disdain for those who were fighting for the good luck to shake his hand, and he didn't feel sorry as he had at other times for the groups of barefoot Indians who could scarcely bear the hot saltpeter coals of the sterile little square. He silenced the applause with a wave of his hand, almost with rage, and he began to speak without gestures, his eyes fixed on the sea, which was sighing with heat. His measured, deep voice had the quality of calm water, but the speech that had been memorized and ground out so many times had not occurred to him in the nature of telling the truth, but, rather, as the opposite of a fatalistic pronouncement by Marcus Aurelius in the fourth book of his *Meditations*.

"We are here for the purpose of defeating nature," he began, against all his convictions. "We will no longer be foundlings in our own country, orphans of God in a realm of thirst and bad climate, exiles in our own

---

3. People descended from the original inhabitants of the continent; generally poorer and less privileged than those descended from Spanish or Portuguese colonists.   4. A well-known German university.
5. "Death is such as generation is, a mystery of nature . . . altogether not a thing of which any man should be ashamed" (Marcus Aurelius, *Meditations* 4.5).

land. We will be different people, ladies and gentlemen, we will be a great
and happy people."

There was a pattern to his circus. As he spoke his aides threw clusters
of paper birds into the air and the artificial creatures took on life, flew
about the platform of planks, and went out to sea. At the same time, other
men took some prop trees with felt leaves out of the wagons and planted
them in the saltpeter soil behind the crowd. They finished by setting up a
cardboard façade with make-believe houses of red brick that had glass
windows, and with it they covered the miserable real-life shacks.

The senator prolonged his speech with two quotations in Latin in order
to give the farce more time. He promised rainmaking machines, portable
breeders for table animals, the oils of happiness which would make vegetables grow in the saltpeter and clumps of pansies in the window boxes.
When he saw that his fictional world was all set up, he pointed to it.
"That's the way it will be for us, ladies and gentlemen," he shouted. "Look!
That's the way it will be for us."

The audience turned around. An ocean liner made of painted paper
was passing behind the houses and it was taller than the tallest houses in
the artificial city. Only the senator himself noticed that since it had been
set up and taken down and carried from one place to another the superimposed cardboard town had been eaten away by the terrible climate and
that it was almost as poor and dusty as Rosal del Virrey.

For the first time in twelve years, Nelson Farina didn't go to greet the
senator. He listened to the speech from his hammock amidst the remains
of his siesta, under the cool bower of a house of unplaned boards which
he had built with the same pharmacist's hands with which he had drawn
and quartered his first wife. He had escaped from Devil's Island[6] and
appeared in Rosal del Virrey on a ship loaded with innocent macaws, with
a beautiful and blasphemous black woman he had found in Paramaribo[7]
and by whom he had a daughter. The woman died of natural causes a
short while later and she didn't suffer the fate of the other, whose pieces
had fertilized her own cauliflower patch, but was buried whole and with
her Dutch name in the local cemetery. The daughter had inherited her
color and her figure along with her father's yellow and astonished eyes,
and he had good reason to imagine that he was rearing the most beautiful
woman in the world.

Ever since he had met Senator Onésimo Sánchez during his first electoral campaign, Nelson Farina had begged for his help in getting a false
identity card which would place him beyond the reach of the law. The
senator, in a friendly but firm way, had refused. Nelson Farina never gave
up, and for several years, every time he found the chance, he would repeat
his request with a different recourse. But this time he stayed in his hammock, condemned to rot alive in that burning den of buccaneers. When
he heard the final applause, he lifted his head, and looking over the boards
of the fence, he saw the back side of the farce: the props for the buildings,

---

6. A former French penal colony off the coast of French Guiana in northern South America.   7. Capital of Surinam (formerly Dutch Guiana) and a large port.

the framework of the trees, the hidden illusionists who were pushing the ocean liner along. He spat without rancor.

"*Merde*," he said. "*C'est le Blacamán de la politique.*"[8]

After the speech, as was customary, the senator took a walk through the streets of the town in the midst of the music and the rockets and was besieged by the townspeople, who told him their troubles. The senator listened to them good-naturedly and he always found some way to console everybody without having to do them any difficult favors. A woman up on the roof of a house with her six youngest children managed to make herself heard over the uproar and the fireworks.

"I'm not asking for much, Senator," she said. "Just a donkey to haul water from Hanged Man's Well."

The senator noticed the six thin children. "What became of your husband?" he asked.

"He went to find his fortune on the island of Aruba,"[9] the woman answered good-humoredly, "and what he found was a foreign woman, the kind that put diamonds on their teeth."

The answer brought on a roar of laughter.

"All right," the senator decided, "you'll get your donkey."

A short while later an aide of his brought a good pack donkey to the woman's house and on the rump it had a campaign slogan written in indelible paint so that no one would ever forget that it was a gift from the senator.

Along the short stretch of street he made other, smaller gestures, and he even gave a spoonful of medicine to a sick man who had had his bed brought to the door of his house so he could see him pass. At the last corner, through the boards of the fence, he saw Nelson Farina in his hammock, looking ashen and gloomy, but nonetheless the senator greeted him, with no show of affection.

"Hello, how are you?"

Nelson Farina turned in his hammock and soaked him in the sad amber of his look.

"*Moi, vous savez,*"[1] he said.

His daughter came out into the yard when she heard the greeting. She was wearing a cheap, faded Guajiro Indian[2] robe, her head was decorated with colored bows, and her face was painted as protection against the sun, but even in that state of disrepair it was possible to imagine that there had never been another so beautiful in the whole world. The senator was left breathless. "I'll be damned!" he breathed in surprise. "The Lord does the craziest things!"

That night Nelson Farina dressed his daughter up in her best clothes and sent her to the senator. Two guards armed with rifles who were nodding from the heat in the borrowed house ordered her to wait on the only chair in the vestibule.

---

8. Shit. He's the Blacamán of politics (French). Blacamán is a charlatan and huckster who appears in several stories, including *Blacamán the Good, Vendor of Miracles.*   **9.** Off the coast of Venezuela, famous as a tourist resort.   **1.** Oh well, as for me, you know (French).   **2.** Inhabitant of the rural Guajira Peninsula of northern Colombia. The figure of Laura Farina is thus connected with the rustic poor, with earthy reality (*farina* means "flour") and with erotic inspiration. (*Laura* was the beloved celebrated by the Italian Renaissance poet Francesco Petrarch, 1304–1374.)

The senator was in the next room meeting with the important people of Rosal del Virrey, whom he had gathered together in order to sing for them the truths he had left out of his speeches. They looked so much like all the ones he always met in all the towns in the desert that even the senator himself was sick and tired of that perpetual nightly session. His shirt was soaked with sweat and he was trying to dry it on his body with the hot breeze from an electric fan that was buzzing like a horse fly in the heavy heat of the room.

"We, of course, can't eat paper birds," he said. "You and I know that the day there are trees and flowers in this heap of goat dung, the day there are shad instead of worms in the water holes, that day neither you nor I will have anything to do here, do I make myself clear?"

No one answered. While he was speaking, the senator had torn a sheet off the calendar and fashioned a paper butterfly out of it with his hands. He tossed it with no particular aim into the air current coming from the fan and the butterfly flew about the room and then went out through the half-open door. The senator went on speaking with a control aided by the complicity of death.

"Therefore," he said, "I don't have to repeat to you what you already know too well: that my reelection is a better piece of business for you than it is for me, because I'm fed up with stagnant water and Indian sweat, while you people, on the other hand, make your living from it."

Laura Farina saw the paper butterfly come out. Only she saw it because the guards in the vestibule had fallen asleep on the steps, hugging their rifles. After a few turns, the large lithographed butterfly unfolded completely, flattened against the wall, and remained stuck there. Laura Farina tried to pull it off with her nails. One of the guards, who woke up with the applause from the next room, noticed her vain attempt.

"It won't come off," he said sleepily. "It's painted on the wall."

Laura Farina sat down again when the men began to come out of the meeting. The senator stood in the doorway of the room with his hand on the latch, and he only noticed Laura Farina when the vestibule was empty.

"What are you doing here?"

"C'est de la part de mon père,"[3] she said.

The senator understood. He scrutinized the sleeping guards, then he scrutinized Laura Farina, whose unusual beauty was even more demanding than his pain, and he resolved then that death had made his decision for him.

"Come in," he told her.

Laura Farina was struck dumb standing in the doorway to the room: thousands of bank notes were floating in the air, flapping like the butterfly. But the senator turned off the fan and the bills were left without air and alighted on the objects in the room.

"You see," he said, smiling, "even shit can fly."

Laura Farina sat down on a schoolboy's stool. Her skin was smooth and firm, with the same color and the same solar density as crude oil, her hair

3. My father sent me (French).

was the mane of a young mare, and her huge eyes were brighter than the light. The senator followed the thread of her look and finally found the rose, which had been tarnished by the saltpeter.

"It's a rose," he said.

"Yes," she said with a trace of perplexity. "I learned what they were in Riohacha."[4]

The senator sat down on an army cot, talking about roses as he unbuttoned his shirt. On the side where he imagined his heart to be inside his chest he had a corsair's tattoo of a heart pierced by an arrow. He threw the soaked shirt to the floor and asked Laura Farina to help him off with his boots.

She knelt down facing the cot. The senator continued to scrutinize her, thoughtfully, and while he was untying the laces he wondered which one of them would end up with the bad luck of that encounter.

"You're just a child," he said.

"Don't you believe it," she said. "I'll be nineteen in April."

The senator became interested.

"What day?"

"The eleventh," she said.

The senator felt better. "We're both Aries,"[5] he said. And smiling, he added:

"It's the sign of solitude."

Laura Farina wasn't paying attention because she didn't know what to do with the boots. The senator, for his part, didn't know what to do with Laura Farina, because he wasn't used to sudden love affairs and, besides, he knew that the one at hand had its origins in indignity. Just to have some time to think, he held Laura Farina tightly between his knees, embraced her about the waist, and lay down on his back on the cot. Then he realized that she was naked under her dress, for her body gave off the dark fragrance of an animal of the woods, but her heart was frightened and her skin disturbed by a glacial sweat.

"No one loves us," he sighed.

Laura Farina tried to say something, but there was only enough air for her to breathe. He laid her down beside him to help her, he put out the light and the room was in the shadow of the rose. She abandoned herself to the mercies of her fate. The senator caressed her slowly, seeking her with his hand, barely touching her, but where he expected to find her, he came across something iron that was in the way.

"What have you got there?"

"A padlock,"[6] she said.

"What in hell!" the senator said furiously and asked what he knew only too well. "Where's the key?"

Laura Farina gave a breath of relief.

"My papa has it," she answered. "He told me to tell you to send one of your people to get it and to send along with him a written promise that you'll straighten out his situation."

4. A port on the Guajira Peninsula.   5. The first sign in the zodiac; people born between March 21 and April 19 are said to be under the sign of Aries.   6. She is wearing a chastity belt, a medieval device worn by women to prevent sexual intercourse.

The senator grew tense. "Frog[7] bastard," he murmured indignantly. Then he closed his eyes in order to relax and he met himself in the darkness. *Remember,* he remembered, *that whether it's you or someone else, it won't be long before you'll be dead and it won't be long before your name won't even be left.*[8]

He waited for the shudder to pass.

"Tell me one thing," he asked then. "What have you heard about me?"

"Do you want the honest-to-God truth?"

"The honest-to-God truth."

"Well," Laura Farina ventured, "they say you're worse than the rest because you're different."

The senator didn't get upset. He remained silent for a long time with his eyes closed, and when he opened them again he seemed to have returned from his most hidden instincts.

"Oh, what the hell," he decided. "Tell your son of a bitch of a father that I'll straighten out his situation."

"If you want, I can go get the key myself," Laura Farina said.

The senator held her back.

"Forget about the key," he said, "and sleep awhile with me. It's good to be with someone when you're so alone."

Then she laid his head on her shoulder with her eyes fixed on the rose. The senator held her about the waist, sank his face into woods-animal armpit, and gave in to terror. Six months and eleven days later he would die in that same position, debased and repudiated because of the public scandal with Laura Farina and weeping with rage at dying without her.

7. Epithet for "French."   8. A direct translation of a sentence from Marcus Aurelius's *Meditations* (4.6).

MARIAMA BÂ

1929–1981

The emergence of the "female imagination" has been a striking development in African literature since the 1970s. Women's literature in Africa draws its inspiration from the feminist challenge to male dominance and the drive toward female emancipation manifest everywhere in the modern world. The rise of women's literature in Africa is one of the pointers to the transition in modern African literature from the theme of the colonial encounter to the theme of the internal contradictions of African society. The special prominence accorded the social and psychological burdens of the African woman in the novels of Ama Ata Aidoo of Ghana; Aminata Sow of Senegal; Flora Nwapa and Buchi Emecheta, both of Nigeria; Tsitsi Dangaremba of Tanzania; and Bessie Head of South Africa, among others, reflects a decisive trend in African literature: these writers not only have brought a feminine point of view to the imaginative presentation of the continent after independence but also have given this presentation the distinctive tone of a feminine sensibility.

No work exemplifies this trend better than Mariama Bâ's *So Long a Letter,* which was first published in French in 1979 under the title *Une si longue lettre* and won the Noma Award for publishing in Africa the following year. The wide international attention the novel has received—it has been translated into more than a dozen languages—may be explained in part by the prize. But the topical significance of its theme, centered on polygamy—a social institution and a personal problem for an increasing number of African women—has aroused intense controversy. There is no question, however, that beyond these factors Bâ's novel has an intrinsic appeal that derives from its affecting style, for it both offers a moving testimony of the feminine condition in contemporary Africa and gives that testimony imaginative depth.

Bâ was born in Dakar, Senegal, where she grew up and received her early education in French, while at the same time attending koranic school. After winning first prize in the entrance examination, she entered the École Normale de Rufisque, a teacher training college near Dakar, and on graduation became a schoolteacher. Her life thereafter was largely uneventful. She married and had nine children. She also became active in the women's movement in Senegal, for which she wrote articles in local newspapers, an activity that clearly influenced her decision to write a novel on the condition of women in her society; the result was *So Long a Letter*. She died of cancer in 1981, barely six months after winning the award that propelled her into the limelight. Her second novel, *Un chant écarlate* (The scarlet song), was published posthumously in 1982. Although focused on polygamy and its effect on the African woman, *So Long a Letter* is essentially a novel of social and cultural change. The larger perspective of the narrative is that of the conflict of cultures, a determining theme of modern African literature during the colonial period. Bâ's novel derives its theme directly from this conflict, and presents its inner drama as lived, in its concrete implications, by the modern Senegalese and, by extension, the modern African woman. But Bâ brings to this theme a new dimension, for the interest of her novel resides not only in the perspective it offers on a pressing social question but also in its exploration of the conflict of cultures as a necessary prelude to the emergence of new structures of life and sensibility in contemporary Africa. The displacement of the old ways and values by the new and the adjustments in attitudes and mentalities dictated by the emerging social order constitute the background to the novel. The inevitable stresses of this process provide the context from which the novel draws its sustaining impulse. The immediate theme is thus encompassed within a global view of a continent undergoing rapid and profound social and cultural change. The central issue the novel addresses is that of the dilemma of modernity as an immediate factor of contemporary experience in Africa.

It is against this background that the drama of the main characters needs to be seen. As members of the new elite, they represent the generation caught between the liberating effect of Western education, to which they largely owe their social promotion, and the institutional force of established social conventions, associated both with the indigenous traditional order and with the Islamic way of life. The novel depicts the way the male characters are able to negotiate the conflicting demands of their situation through compromising the ideals of their Western education and the impact their solution has on the lives of the women, who still have to confront the problems of polygamy. Despite their accession to modernity, and especially their achievement of literacy, the denial of a social personality to women in both the indigenous and the Islamic spheres continues to be an obstacle to their fulfilment, so that the conflict of cultures for the modern educated woman is especially acute.

The letter by the heroine, Ramatoulaye, to her friend Aissatou, recounting her ordeal, forms the substance of the narrative. Both have been profoundly marked by a whole generation of articulate women, whose education and self-conception put them at odds with the social conventions of their milieu. The very form of the letter as a mode of private expression becomes emblematic of the condition of the class of newly educated women in Senegal: its limited scope defines the narrow margin of choice they can claim in voicing their predicament. In this way, it reflects the novelist's consciousness of the constraints imposed on her by the context in which, as a woman, she was obliged to write; her use of the epistolary novel can be seen as a textual strategy, employed to give maximum resonance to her writing. It is significant that the novel combines the different forms of the experience of the two women into a single narrative and even integrates that of a third, the Ivorian Jacqueline, into its structure. Bâ takes us into the emotional turmoil of her female characters, so that we feel the problems she touches on, not as abstract social issues but rather as lived experience. At no time does her rendering of the female condition become an analysis, offered with false objectivity; rather, it is invested with the full passion of personal involvement, and the female perspective is central to the narrative development as well as to the overall social vision of the novel.

The epistolary form and the first-person narrative technique account for the intimate tone of the novel and establish the heroine's point of view. The formal expression of this point of view is, however, complicated by the fact that her long letter incorporates two other letters, one by her friend Aissatou to her husband, Mawdo, at the point when she decides to leave him. This letter within the letter enables the reader to enter directly into the feelings of Aissatou and confirms the common disposition of the two women, despite their very different actions. If the device seems contrived—as it may when taken with other events that the heroine cannot have witnessed firsthand, such as Aunty Nabou's journey to the interior— it does effectively expand the narrative beyond a single point of view.

Still, the central interest of the narrative remains Ramatoulaye's account of her own experience. As she remarks at the outset, the letter is her diary, in which she records the events that have marked her life. Her bereavement serves as a point of departure for a retrospective view of a whole existence. The epistolary form also determines the novel's character as an outpouring of the self, one intended for a close friend, but with a message for all women. The bond of understanding between the narrator and her addressee extends to other women. However, beyond the community of women whose interests it expresses, So Long a Letter appeals to every reader, male or female, who is drawn into the confidence of a distressed soul. In this respect, the novel presents itself to a large extent as a monologue in which the heroine examines her life. Although colored by a certain bitterness, the introspection never degenerates into self-pity. Despite the heroine's consciousness of the burden the Islamic religion places on women, especially with respect to polygamy, her attachment to the faith remains unshaken. By the same token, she can express an admiration for those aspects of the traditional way of life that she finds valuable. But if her reflections do not lead to a total disaffection toward her background, they do lead to a questioning of the norms on which her identity is predicated. Seen in this light, her apparent resignation reveals itself as the obverse of a heroic struggle with the self. There is a contemplative tone to the narrative: her recent widowhood sets into motion her reflections on herself and her ambiguous situation.

It is in many ways an ordinary life that Ramatoulaye recounts. Her recollections are often made up of the petty details of the bourgeois existence that she has in common with her friends and family. We share her delights in the amenities offered by her privileged status, which she takes for granted, and her distress at being later deprived of them; indeed, her material difficulties after her desertion by her husband play no small part in her account of this distress. There is a sense in which, in another time and place, this life would have been unremarkable. But the even tenor of this life has been heightened both by her personal drama and by the larger social and political context within which this drama unfolds. In its recreation of the heady atmosphere that attended Senegal's evolution toward political independence from France, which it achieved in 1960, and of the transformations set in train by that historic event, the novel takes on a documentary character. Although the continued dominance of the male in the new society is emphasized in the heroine's account, what is ultimately at issue for Ramatoulaye is the role of women in society.

In its exploration of the female condition in Senegal, *So Long a Letter* places it at the center of national life and consciousness. It also comments on many other issues of concern to contemporary Senegalese and African society. The survival of the caste system, even in a weakened form, represents the novel's major secondary theme, but other social questions are also examined, including the problems of economic development, the conflict of generations, and the role of education in the formation of the new elite as well as the responsibility of this elite to the rest of the population. Here, the novel offers an insight into the formation of a new middle class in the African setting. The novel's treatment of all these issues is perhaps self-conscious; we feel the authorial intrusions, especially in the later chapters. But for most of the novel, Bâ is able to work her commentary into the narrative. Indeed, one distinguishing feature of the novel is its narrative style, which maintains throughout an emotional tone at once composed and intense. The occasional stiffness of language and use of a formal register—a sign of writing in a nonnative language—contribute to the gravity of Bâ's style; however, it is more often the tone of intimate conversation that predominates, marked by repetitions, homely images, and in keeping with its African setting, the recourse to traditional proverbs. The language sometimes takes on a dramatic quality associated with the oral narrative, as in the account of Aunty Nabou's journey to the ancestral homeland. It also often draws on the vernacular—in this instance, Wolof, the national language of Senegal—for some of its vocabulary and turns of phrase. These departures from the novel's European medium give it a local color, an aspect further reinforced by the descriptions of landscape and local customs. These features lend a lyrical quality to the novel, especially in the pages devoted to widowhood. But it is a lyricism devoid of sentimentality, turned as it is to an exploration of the complex feelings of her female characters.

So Long a Letter has been compared to Alice Walker's *The Color Purple* in terms of theme and form—both are epistolary novels dealing with the problems of male-female relations. The comparison underscores the parallel between the emergence of women's literature in Africa and the recent predominance of gender issues in African-American literature. Bâ's novel is considered the classic statement of the female condition in Africa. But if the novel presents a social interest directly related to African life, its appeal lies especially in its character as a human document.

The most extensive discussion of Mariama Bâ's work is to be found in Mildred Mortimer, *Journeys Through the French African Novel* (1990). Several articles have also been devoted to her first novel, notably Irène Assiba d'Alméida, *The Concept of Choice in Mariama Bâ's Fiction,* in Carol Boyce Davis and Anne Adams, eds., *Ngambika: Studies of Women in African Literature* (1986).

PRONOUNCING GLOSSARY

The following list uses common English syllables to provide rough equivalents of selected words whose pronunciation may be unfamiliar to the general reader.

Aissatou: *aye-sah-too*

Alioune: *ah-lee-woon*

Binetou: *been-too*

Bissimilai: *bee-see-mee-lie*

Casamance: *kah-zah-mans*

Daouda Dieng: *dah-oo-dah jeng*

Diack: *jak*

Diakhaw: *jah-how*

Diamniadio: *jahm-nya-joh*

Dieynaba: *jay-nah-bah*

Diola: *joh-lah*

djou-djoungs: *joo-joong*

Farba Diouf: *fahr-bah joof*

Guelewar: *gale-wahr*

gnac: *nyahk*

Linguere: *leeng-en-ger*

Madiodio: *mah-joh-joh*

Mawdo Bâ: *maoo-doh bah*

Medinatou-Minaouara: *may-dee-nah-too mee-nah-wah-rah*

Mbour: *em-boo*

Ngor: *en-gore*

Ouakham: *wah-kahm*

Ousmane: *oos-mahn*

Popenguine: *popa-en-geen*

Ramatoulaye: *rah-mah-too-lie*

Sebikotane: *say-bee-koh-tahn*

siguil ndigale: *see-geel en-dee-gahl*

thiakry: *chah-kree*

Thiaroye: *cha-roy*

Thies: *ches*

Tivaouane: *tee-vah-wahn*

So Long a Letter[1]

1

Dear Aissatou,

I have received your letter. By way of reply, I am beginning this diary, my prop in my distress. Our long association has taught me that confiding in others allays pain.

Your presence in my life is by no means fortuitous. Our grandmothers in their compounds were separated by a fence and would exchange messages daily. Our mothers used to argue over who would look after our uncles and aunts. As for us, we wore out wrappers and sandals on the same stony road to the koranic school;[2] we buried our milk teeth in the same holes and begged our fairy godmothers to restore them to us, more splendid than before.

If over the years, and passing through the realities of life, dreams die, I still keep intact my memories, the salt of remembrance.

I conjure you up. The past is reborn, along with its procession of emotions. I close my eyes. Ebb and tide of feeling: heat and dazzlement, the woodfires, the sharp green mango, bitten into in turns, a delicacy in our greedy mouths. I close my eyes. Ebb and tide of images: drops of sweat beading your mother's ochre-coloured face as she emerges from the

---

1. Translated by Modupé Bodé-Thomas.   2. Where children learn verses of the Koran by heart.

kitchen, the procession of young wet girls chattering on their way back from the springs.

We walked the same paths from adolescence to maturity, where the past begets the present.

My friend, my friend, my friend. I call on you three times.[3]

Yesterday you were divorced. Today I am a widow.

Modou is dead. How am I to tell you? One does not fix appointments with fate. Fate grasps whom it wants, when it wants. When it moves in the direction of your desires, it brings you plenitude. But more often than not, it unsettles, crosses you. Then one has to endure. I endured the telephone call which disrupted my life.

A taxi quickly hailed! Fast! Fast! Faster still! My throat is dry. There is a rigid lump in my chest. Fast: faster still. At last, the hospital: the mixed smell of suppurations[4] and ether. The hospital—distorted faces, a train of tearful people, known and unknown, witnesses to this awful tragedy. A long corridor, which seems to stretch out endlessly. At the end, a room. In the room, a bed. On the bed, Modou stretched out, cut off from the world of the living by a white sheet in which he is completely enveloped. A trembling hand moves forward and slowly uncovers the body. His hairy chest, at rest forever, is visible through his crumpled blue shirt with thin stripes. This face, set in pain and surprise, is indeed his, the bald forehead, the half-open mouth are indeed his. I want to grasp his hand. But someone pulls me away. I can hear Mawdo, his doctor friend, explaining to me: a heart attack came on suddenly in his office while he was dictating a letter. The secretary had the presence of mind to call me. Mawdo recounts how he arrived too late with the ambulance. I think: the doctor after death. He mimes the massaging of the heart that was undertaken, as well as the futile effort at mouth-to-mouth resuscitation. Again, I think: heart massage, mouth-to-mouth resuscitation, ridiculous weapons against the divine will.

I listen to the words that create around me a new atmosphere in which I move, a stranger and tormented. Death, the tenuous passage between two opposite worlds, one tumultuous, the other still.

Where to lie down? Middle age demands dignity. I hold tightly on to my prayer beads.[5] I tell the beads ardently, remaining standing on legs of jelly. My loins beat as to the rhythm of childbirth.

Cross-sections of my life spring involuntarily from my memory, grandiose verses from the Koran, noble words of consolation fight for my attention.

Joyous miracle of birth, dark miracle of death. Between the two, a life, a destiny, says Mawdo Bâ.

I look intently at Mawdo. He seems to be taller than usual in his white overall. He seems to me thin. His reddened eyes express forty years of friendship. I admire his noble hands, hands of an absolute delicacy, supple hands used to tracking down illness. Those hands, moved by friendship and a rigorous science, could not save his friend.

---

3. A convention to stress the seriousness of the subject at hand.   4. Literally, gatherings of pus in boils; here, a sickly atmosphere.   5. Strung beads, similar to the Catholic rosary.

2

Modou Fall is indeed dead, Aissatou. The uninterrupted procession of men and women who have "learned" of it, the wails and tears all around me, confirm his death. This condition of extreme tension sharpens my suffering and continues till the following day, the day of interment.[6]

What a seething crowd of human beings come from all parts of the country, where the radio has relayed the news.

Women, close relatives, are busy. They must take incense, eau-de-cologne, cotton-wool to the hospital for the washing of the dead one. The seven metres of white muslin, the only clothing Islam allows for the dead, are carefully placed in a new basket. The *Zem-Zem*, the miracle water from the holy places of Islam religiously kept by each family, is not forgotten. Rich, dark wrappers are chosen to cover Modou.

My back propped up by cushions, legs outstretched, my head covered with a black wrapper, I follow the comings and goings of people. Across from me, a new winnowing fan bought for the occasion receives the first alms. The presence of my co-wife[7] beside me irritates me. She has been installed in my house for the funeral, in accordance with tradition. With each passing hour her cheeks become more deeply hollowed, acquire ever more rings, those big and beautiful eyes which open and close on their secrets, perhaps their regrets. At the age of love and freedom from care, this child is dogged by sadness.

While the men, in a long, irregular file of official and private cars, public buses, lorries and mopeds, accompany Modou to his last rest (people were for a long time to talk of the crowd which followed the funeral procession), our sisters-in-law undo our hair. My co-wife and myself are put inside a rough and ready tent made of a wrapper pulled taut above our heads and set up for the occasion. While our sisters-in-law are constructing it, the women present, informed of the work in hand, get up and throw some coins on to the fluttering canopy so as to ward off evil spirits.

This is the moment dreaded by every Senegalese woman, the moment when she sacrifices her possessions as gifts to her family-in-law; and, worse still, beyond her possessions she gives up her personality, her dignity, becoming a thing in the service of the man who has married her, his grandfather, his grandmother, his father, his mother, his brother, his sister, his uncle, his aunt, his male and female cousins, his friends. Her behaviour is conditioned: no sister-in-law will touch the head of any wife who has been stingy, unfaithful or inhospitable.

As for ourselves, we have been deserving, and our sisters-in-law sing a chorus of praises chanted at the top of their voices. Our patience before all trials, the frequency of our gifts find their justification and reward today. Our sisters-in-law give equal consideration to thirty years and five years of married life. With the same ease and the same words, they celebrate twelve maternities and three. I note with outrage this desire to level out, in which Modou's new mother-in-law rejoices.

Having washed their hands in a bowl of water placed at the entrance to

---

6. In the Muslim religion, burial occurs within twenty-four hours of death and is followed by prayer sessions and recitation of the Koran.   7. Her husband's other wife.

the house, the men, back from the cemetery, file past the family grouped around us, the widows. They offer their condolences punctuated with praises of the deceased.

"Modou, friend of the young as of the old. . . ."

"Modou, the lion-hearted, champion of the oppressed. . . ."

"Modou, at ease as much in a suit as in a caftan. . . ."

"Modou, good brother, good husband, good Muslim. . . ."

"May God forgive him. . . ."

"May he regret his earthly stay in his heavenly bliss. . . ."

"May the earth rest lightly on him!"

They are there, his childhood playmates on the football ground, or during bird hunts, when they used catapults. They are there, his classmates. They are there, his companions in the trade union struggles.

The *Siguil ndigale* come one after the other, poignant, while skilled hands distribute to the crowd biscuits, sweets, cola[8] nuts, judiciously mixed, the first offerings to heaven for the peaceful repose of the deceased's soul.

3

On the third day, the same comings and goings of friends, relatives, the poor, the unknown. The name of the deceased, who was popular, has mobilized a buzzing crowd, welcomed in my house that has been stripped of all that could be stolen, all that could be spoilt. Mats of all sorts are spread out everywhere there is space. Metal chairs hired for the occasion take on a blue hue in the sun.

Comforting words from the Koran fill the air; divine words, divine instructions, impressive promises of punishment or joy, exhortations to virtue, warnings against evil, exaltation of humility, of faith. Shivers run through me. My tears flow and my voice joins weakly in the fervent "Amen" which inspires the crowd's ardour at the end of each verse.

The smell of the *lakh* cooling in the calabashes[9] pervades the air, exciting.

Also passed around are large bowls of red or white rice, cooked here or in neighbouring houses. Iced fruit juices, water and curds are served in plastic cups. The men's group eats in silence. Perhaps they remember the stiff body, tied up and lowered by their hands into a gaping hole, quickly covered up again.

In the women's corner, nothing but noise, resonant laughter, loud talk, hand slaps, strident exclamations. Friends who have not seen each other for a long time hug each other noisily. Some discuss the latest material on the market. Others indicate where they got their woven wrappers from. The latest bits of gossip are exchanged. They laugh heartily and roll their eyes and admire the next person's *boubou*, her original way of using henna[1] to blacken hands and feet by drawing geometrical figures on them.

---

8. Or kola; a bitter fruit chewed as a stimulant. It is used in West Africa as a token of hospitality and for divination. *Siguil ndigale:* the formal presentation of condolences to the bereaved; a Wolof term.
9. Gourds. *Lakh:* porridge made out of millet flour and eaten with curds, usually served at birth ceremonies and funerals.   1. A dark-hued powder used by Senegalese women to make designs on their hands and feet.

From time to time an exasperated manly voice rings out a warning, recalls the purpose of the gathering: a ceremony for the redemption of a soul. The voice is quickly forgotten and the brouhaha begins all over again, increasing in volume.

In the evening comes the most disconcerting part of this third day's ceremony. More people, more jostling in order to hear and see better. Groups are formed according to relationships, according to blood ties, areas, corporations. Each group displays its own contribution to the costs. In former times this contribution was made in kind: millet, livestock, rice, flour, oil, sugar, milk. Today it is made conspicuously in banknotes, and no one wants to give less than the other. A disturbing display of inner feeling that cannot be evaluated now measured in francs! And again I think how many of the dead would have survived if, before organizing these festive funeral ceremonies, the relative or friend had bought the life-saving prescription or paid for hospitalization.

The takings are carefully recorded. It is a debt to be repaid in similar circumstances. Modou's relatives open an exercise book. Lady Mother-in-Law (Modou's) and her daughter have a notebook. Fatimi, my younger sister, carefully records my takings in a note-pad.

As I come from a large family in this town, with acquaintances at all levels of society, as I am a schoolteacher on friendly terms with the pupils' parents, and as I have been Modou's companion for thirty years, I receive the greater share of money and many envelopes. The regard shown me raises me in the eyes of the others and it is Lady Mother-in-Law's turn to be annoyed. Newly admitted into the city's bourgeoisie by her daughter's marriage, she too reaps banknotes. As for her silent, haggard child, she remains a stranger in these circles.

The sudden calls from our sisters-in-law bring her out of her stupor. They reappear after their deliberation. They have contributed the large sum of two hundred thousand francs to "dress" us.[2] Yesterday, they offered us some excellent *thiakry*[3] to quench our thirst. The Fall family's *griot*[4] is proud of her role as go-between, a role handed down from mother to daughter.

"One hundred thousand francs from the father's side."

"One hundred thousand francs from the mother's side."

She counts the notes, blue and pink, one by one, shows them round and concludes: "I have much to say about you Falls, grandchildren of Damel Madiodio,[5] who have inherited royal blood. But one of you is no more. Today is not a happy day. I weep with you for Modou, whom I used to call 'bag of rice,' for he would frequently give me a sack of rice. Therefore accept this money, you worthy widows of a worthy man."

The share of each widow must be doubled, as must the gifts of Modou's grandchildren, represented by the offspring of all his male and female cousins.

Thus our family-in-law take away with them a wad of notes, painstak-

---

2. It is the duty of the husband's sisters to buy mourning clothes for his widows.   3. A drink prepared by mixing sugared curds with well-kneaded millet flour cooked in steam [Bâ's note].   4. Family bard.
5. King Madiodio of the Cayor kingdom in western Senegal.

ingly topped, and leave us utterly destitute, we who will need material support.

Afterwards comes the procession of old relatives, old acquaintances, *griots*, goldsmiths, *laobés*[6] with their honeyed language. The "goodbyes" following one after the other at an infernal rate are irritating because they are neither simple nor free: they require, depending on the person leaving, sometimes a coin, sometimes a banknote.

Gradually the house empties. The smell of stale sweat and food blend as trails in the air, unpleasant and nauseating. Cola nuts spat out here and there have left red stains: my tiles, kept with such painstaking care, are blackened. Oil stains on the walls, balls of crumpled paper. What a balance sheet for a day!

My horizon lightened, I see an old woman. Who is she? Where is she from? Bent over, the ends of her *boubou* tied behind her, she empties into a plastic bag the left-overs of red rice. Her smiling face tells of the pleasant day she has just had. She wants to take back proof of this to her family, living perhaps in Ouakam, Thiaroye or Pikine.[7]

Standing upright, her eyes meeting my disapproving look, she mutters between teeth reddened by cola nuts: "Lady, death is just as beautiful as life has been."

Alas, it's the same story on the eighth and fortieth days, when those who have "learned" belatedly make up for lost time. Light attire showing off slim waistlines, prominent backsides, the new brassière or the one bought at the second-hand market, chewing sticks wedged between teeth, white or flowered shawls, heavy smell of incense and of *gongo*,[8] loud voices, strident laughter. And yet we are told in the Koran that on the third day the dead body swells and fills its tomb; we are told that on the eighth it bursts; and we are also told that on the fortieth day it is stripped. What then is the significance of these joyous, institutionalized festivities that accompany our prayers for God's mercy? Who has come out of self-interest? Who has come to quench his own thirst? Who has come for the sake of mercy? Who has come so that he may remember?

Tonight Binetou, my co-wife, will return to her SICAP[9] villa. At last! Phew!

The visits of condolence continue: the sick, those who have journeyed or have merely arrived late, as well as the lazy, come to fulfil what they consider to be a sacred duty. Child-naming ceremonies may be missed but never a funeral. Coins and notes continue to pour on the beckoning fan.

Alone, I live in a monotony broken only by purifying baths, the changing of my mourning clothes every Monday and Friday.

I hope to carry out my duties fully. My heart concurs with the demands of religion. Reared since childhood on their strict precepts, I expect not to

6. Members of a caste of weavers, who also entertain during ceremonies.   7. Densely populated suburbs of Dakar, capital of Senegal.   8. Sweet-smelling and stimulating powder. *Chewing sticks:* bits of wood used to clean the teeth. The type of wood is chosen for its fragrance.   9. Société Immobilière du Cap-Vert, a building group that was set up, shortly after independence, by the Senegalese government to develop modern residential communities where houses were built for sale or rent.

fail. The walls that limit my horizon for four months and ten days do not bother me. I have enough memories in me to ruminate upon. And these are what I am afraid of, for they smack of bitterness.

May their evocation not soil the state of purity in which I must live.

Till tomorrow.

4

Aissatou, my friend, perhaps I am boring you by relating what you already know.

I have never observed so much, because I have never been so concerned.

The family meeting held this morning in my sitting-room is at last over. You can easily guess those who were present: Lady Mother-in-Law, her brother and her daughter, Binetou, who is even thinner; old Tamsir, Modou's brother, and the *Imam*[1] from the mosque in his area; Mawdo Bâ; my daughter and her husband Abdou.

The *mirasse*[2] commanded by the Koran requires that a dead person be stripped of his most intimate secrets; thus is exposed to others what was carefully concealed. These exposures crudely explain a man's life. With consternation, I measure the extent of Modou's betrayal. His abandonment of his first family (myself and my children) was the outcome of the choice of a new life. He rejected us. He mapped out his future without taking our existence into account.

His promotion to the rank of technical adviser in the Ministry of Public Works, in exchange for which, according to the spiteful, he checked the trade union revolt, could not control the mire of expenses by which he was engulfed. Dead without a penny saved. Acknowledgement of debts? A pile of them: cloth and gold traders, home-delivery grocers and butchers, car-purchase instalments.

Hold on. The star attraction of this "stripping": the origins of the elegant SICAP villa, four bedrooms, two bathrooms, pink and blue, large sitting-room, a three-room flat, built at his own expense at the bottom of the second courtyard for Lady Mother-in-Law. And furniture from France for his new wife and furniture constructed by local carpenters for Lady Mother-in-Law.

This house and its chic contents were acquired by a bank loan granted on the mortgage of "Villa Fallene," where I live. Although the title deeds of this house bear his name, it is nonetheless our common property, acquired by our joint savings. Insult upon injury!

Moreover, he continued the monthly payments of seventy-five thousand francs to the SICAP. These payments were to go on for about ten years before the house would become his.

Four million francs borrowed with ease because of his privileged position, which had enabled him to pay for Lady Mother-in-Law and her husband to visit Mecca to acquire the titles of *Alhaja* and *Alhaji*;[3] which

---

1. Muslim religious leader.   2. The distribution to his or her family of the belongings of the dead.
3. A man and woman, respectively, who have made the pilgrimage to Mecca, Saudi Arabia. Muslims are required to make this trip at least once during their lifetime. Because of the considerable distance of West Africa from Saudi Arabia, the pilgrimage involves great expense and thus brings great prestige to those who return.

equally enabled Binetou to exchange her Alfa Romeos at the slightest dent.

Now I understand the terrible significance of Modou's abandonment of our joint bank account. He wanted to be financially independent so as to have enough elbow room.

And then, having withdrawn Binetou from school, he paid her a monthly allowance of fifty thousand francs, just like a salary due to her. The young girl, who was very gifted, wanted to continue her studies, to sit for her *baccalauréat*.[4] So as to establish his rule, Modou, wickedly, determined to remove her from the critical and unsparing world of the young. He therefore gave in to all the conditions of the grasping Lady Mother-in-Law and even signed a paper committing himself to paying the said amount. Lady Mother-in-Law brandished the paper, for she firmly believed that the payments would continue, even after Modou's death, out of the estate.

As for my daughter, Daba, she waved about a bailiff's affidavit, dated the very day of her father's death, that listed all the contents of the SICAP Villa. The list supplied by Lady Mother-in-Law and Binetou made no mention of certain objects and items of furniture, which had mysteriously disappeared or had been fraudulently removed.

You know that I am excessively sentimental. I was not at all pleased by this display on either side.

5

When I stopped yesterday, I probably left you astonished by my disclosures.

Was it madness, weakness, irresistible love? What inner confusion led Modou Fall to marry Binetou?

To overcome my bitterness, I think of human destiny. Each life has its share of heroism, an obscure heroism, born of abdication, of renunciation and acceptance under the merciless whip of fate.

I think of all the blind people the world over, moving in darkness. I think of all the paralysed the world over, dragging themselves about. I think of all the lepers the world over, wasted by their disease.

Victims of a sad fate which you did not choose, compared with your lamentations, what is my quarrel, cruelly motivated, with a dead man who no longer has any hold over my destiny? Combining your despair, you could have been avengers and made them tremble, all those who are drunk on their wealth; tremble, those upon whom fate has bestowed favours. A horde powerful in its repugnance and revolt, you could have snatched the bread that your hunger craves.

Your stoicism has made you not violent or subversive but true heroes, unknown in the mainstream of history, never upsetting established order, despite your miserable condition.

I repeat, beside your visible deformities, what are moral infirmities from

4. That is, take the two examinations required to complete secondary school in the French educational system. The first tests the general curriculum, and the second, taken a year later, tests philosophy for students in the humanities.

which in any case you are not immune? Thinking of you, I thank God for my eyes which daily embrace heaven and earth. If today moral fatigue makes my limbs stiff, tomorrow it will leave my body. Then, relieved, my legs will carry me slowly and I shall again have around me the iodine and the blue of the sea. The star and white cloud will be mine. The breath of wind will again refresh my face. I will stretch out, turn around, I will vibrate. Oh, health, live in me. Oh, health. . . .

My efforts cannot for long take my mind off my disappointment. I think of the suckling baby, no sooner born than orphaned. I think of the blind man who will never see his child's smile. I think of the cross the one-armed man has to bear. I think. . . . But my despair persists, but my rancour remains, but the waves of an immense sadness break in me!

Madness or weakness? Heartlessness or irresistible love? What inner torment led Modou Fall to marry Binetou?

And to think that I loved this man passionately, to think that I gave him thirty years of my life, to think that twelve times over I carried his child. The addition of a rival to my life was not enough for him. In loving someone else, he burned his past, both morally and materially. He dared to commit such an act of disavowal.

And yet, what didn't he do to make me his wife!

6

Do you remember the morning train that took us for the first time to Ponty-Ville, the teachers' training college in Sebikotane?[5] Ponty-Ville is the countryside still green from the last rains, a celebration of youth right in the middle of nature, banjo music in dormitories transformed into dance floors, conversations held along the rows of geraniums or under the thick mango trees.

Modou Fall, the very moment you bowed before me, asking me to dance, I knew you were the one I was waiting for. Tall and athletically built, of course. Olive-coloured skin due to your distant Moorish blood, no question. Virility and fineness of features harmoniously blended, once again, no question. But, above all, you knew how to be tender. You could fathom every thought, every desire. You knew many undefinable things, which glorified you and sealed our relationship.

As we danced, your forehead, hairline already receding, bent over my own. The same happy smile lit up our faces. The pressure of your hand became more tender, more possessive. Everything in me gave in and our relationship endured over the school years and during the holidays, strengthened in me by the discovery of your subtle intelligence, of your embracing sensitivity, of your readiness to help, of your ambition, which suffered no mediocrity. It was this ambition which led you, on leaving school, to prepare on your own for the two examinations of the *bacca-lauréat*. Then you left for France and, according to your letters, you lived there as a recluse, attaching little importance to the glitter that met your

---

5. A village between Dakar and the railway junction at Thies, to the north. Ponty-Ville is a women's college, named after William Ponty, a noted French educator during the colonial period.

regard; but you grasped the deep sense of a history that has worked so many wonders and of a great culture that overwhelmed you. The milky complexion of the women had no hold on you. Again, quoting from your letters: "On the strictly physical plane, the white woman's advantage over the black woman lies in the variety of her colour, the abundance, length and softness of her hair. There are also the eyes which can be blue, green, often the colour of new honey." You also used to complain of the sombreness of the skies, under which no coconut trees waved their tops. You missed the swinging hips of black women walking along the pavements, this gracious deliberate slowness characteristic of Africa, which charmed your eyes. You were sick at heart at the dogged rhythm of the life of the people and the numbing effect of the cold. You would finish by saying that your studies were your staff, your buttress. You would end with a string of endearments and conclude by reassuring me: "It's you whom I carry within me. You are my protecting black angel. Would I could quickly find you, if only to hold your hand tightly so that I may forget hunger and thirst and loneliness."

And you returned in triumph. With a degree in law! In spite of your voice and your gift of oratory, you preferred obscure work, less well paid but constructive for your country, to the showiness of the lawyer.

Your achievement did not stop there. Your introduction of your friend Mawdo Bâ into our circle was to change the life of my best friend, Aissatou.

I no longer scorn my mother's reserve concerning you, for a mother can instinctively feel where her child's happiness lies. I no longer laugh when I think that she found you too handsome, too polished, too perfect for a man. She often spoke of the wide gap between your two upper incisors: the sign of the primacy of sensuality in the individual. What didn't she do, from then on, to separate us? She could see in you only the eternal khaki suit, the uniform of your school. All she remembered of you were your visits, considered too long. You were idle, she said, therefore with plenty of time to waste. And you would use that time to "stuff" my head, to the disadvantage of more interesting young people.

Because, being the first pioneers of the promotion of African women, there were very few of us. Men would call us scatter-brained. Others labelled us devils. But many wanted to possess us. How many dreams did we nourish hopelessly that could have been fulfilled as lasting happiness and that we abandoned to embrace others, those that have burst miserably like soap bubbles, leaving us empty-handed?

7

Aissatou, I will never forget the white woman who was the first to desire for us an "uncommon" destiny. Together, let us recall our school, green, pink, blue, yellow, a veritable rainbow: green, blue and yellow, the colours of the flowers everywhere in the compound; pink the colour of the dormitories, with the beds impeccably made. Let us hear the walls of our school come to life with the intensity of our study. Let us relive its intoxicating atmosphere at night, while the evening song, our joint prayer, rang out, full of hope. The admission policy, which was based on an entrance examination for the whole of former French West Africa, now broken up into autonomous republics, made possible a fruitful blend of different intellects, characters, manners and customs. Nothing differentiated us, apart from specific racial features, the Fon girl from Dahomey and the Malinke[6] one from Guinea. Friendships were made that have endured the test of time and distance. We were true sisters, destined for the same mission of emancipation.

To lift us out of the bog of tradition, superstition and custom, to make us appreciate a multitude of civilizations without renouncing our own, to raise our vision of the world, cultivate our personalities, strengthen our qualities, to make up for our inadequacies, to develop universal moral values in us: these were the aims of our admirable headmistress. The word "love" had a particular resonance in her. She loved us without patronizing us, with our plaits either standing on end or bent down, with our loose blouses, our wrappers. She knew how to discover and appreciate our qualities.

How I think of her! If the memory of her has triumphed over the ingratitude of time, now that flowers no longer smell as sweetly or as strongly as before, now that age and mature reflection have stripped our dreams of their poetic virtue, it is because the path chosen for our training and our blossoming has not been at all fortuitous. It has accorded with the profound choices made by New Africa for the promotion of the black woman.

Thus, free from frustrating taboos and capable now of discernment, why should I follow my mother's finger pointing at Daouda Dieng, still a bachelor but too mature for my eighteen years. Working as an African doctor at the Polyclinique,[7] he was well-to-do and knew how to use his position to advantage. His villa, perched on a rock on the Corniche[8] facing the sea, was the meeting place for the young elite. Nothing was missing, from the refrigerator, containing its pleasant drinks, to the record player, which exuded sometimes langorous, sometimes frenzied music.

Daouda Dieng also knew how to win hearts. Useful presents for my mother, ranging from a sack of rice, appreciated in that period of war penury, to the frivolous gift for me, daintily wrapped in paper and tied with ribbons. But I preferred the man in the eternal khaki suit. Our marriage was celebrated without dowry, without pomp, under the disapproving looks of my father, before the painful indignation of my frustrated mother, under the sarcasm of my surprised sisters, in our town struck dumb with astonishment.

8

Then came your marriage with Mawdo Bâ, recently graduated from the African School of Medicine and Pharmacy. A controversial marriage. I can still hear the angry rumours in town:

"What, a Toucouleur marrying a goldsmith's daughter?[9] He will never 'make money.' "

6. The dominant ethnic group in Mali. The Fon ethnic group is in the Benin Republic.   7. A general clinic.   8. The Dakar coastline.   9. In the rigid caste system of traditional Senegalese society, the goldsmith had an inferior status, just above that of the *griot*.

"Mawdo's mother is a Dioufene, a *Guelewar*[1] from the Sine. What an insult to her, before her former co-wives." (Mawdo's father was dead.)

"In the desire to marry a 'short skirt' come what may, this is what one gets."

"School turns our girls into devils who lure our men away from the right path."

And I haven't recounted all. But Mawdo remained firm. "Marriage is a personal thing," he retorted to anyone who cared to hear.

He emphasized his total commitment to his choice of life partner by visiting your father, not at home but at his place of work. He would return from his outings illuminated, happy to have "moved in the right direction," he would say triumphantly. He would speak of your father as a "creative artist." He admired the man, weakened as he was by the daily dose of carbon dioxide he inhaled working in the acrid atmosphere of the dusty fumes. Gold is his medium, which he melts, pours, twists, flattens, refines, chases. "You should see him," Mawdo would add. "You should see him breathe over the flame." His cheeks would swell with the life from his lungs. This life would animate the flame, sometimes red, sometimes blue, which would rise or curve, wax or wane at his command, depending on what the work demanded. And the gold specks in the showers of red sparks, and the untutored songs of the apprentices[2] punctuating the strokes of the hammer here, and the pressure of hands on the bellows there would make passers-by turn round.

Aissatou, your father knew all the rites that protect the working of gold, the metal of the djinns.[3] Each profession has its code, known only to the initiated and transmitted from father to son. As soon as your elder brothers left the huts of the circumcised, they moved into this particular world, the whole compound's source of nourishment.

But what about your younger brothers? Their steps were directed towards the white man's school. Hard is the climb up the steep hill of knowledge to the white man's school: kindergarten remains a luxury that only those who are financially sound can offer their young ones. Yet it is necessary, for this is what sharpens and channels the young ones' attention and sensibilities.

Even though the primary schools are rapidly increasing, access to them has not become any easier. They leave out in the streets an impressive number of children because of the lack of places.

Entrance into secondary school is no panacea for the child at an age fraught with the problems of consolidating his personality, with the explosion of puberty, with the discovery of the various pitfalls: drugs, vagrancy, sensuality.

The university has its own large number of despairing rejects.

What will the unsuccessful do? Apprenticeship to traditional crafts seems degrading to whoever has the slightest book-learning. The dream is to become a clerk. The trowel is spurned.

The horde of the jobless swells the flood of delinquency.

Should we have been happy at the desertion of the forges, the work-

---

1. A warrior in both Serer and Wolof. *Dioufène*: of the family of Diouf, aristocrats of the Serer ethnic group in the Sine-Saloum basin of western Senegal.   **2.** Work songs, traditionally sung to the rhythm of the bellows or anvil.   **3.** Invisible spirits.

shops, the shoemaker's shops? Should we have rejoiced so wholeheart-edly? Were we not beginning to witness the disappearance of an elite of traditional manual workers?

Eternal questions of our eternal debates. We all agreed that much dis-mantling was needed to introduce modernity within our traditions. Torn between the past and the present, we deplored the "hard sweat" that would be inevitable. We counted the possible losses. But we knew that nothing would be as before. We were full of nostalgia but were resolutely progres-sive.

9

Mawdo raised you up to his own level, he the son of a princess and you a child from the forges. His mother's rejection did not frighten him.

Our lives developed in parallel. We experienced the tiffs and reconcilia-tions of married life. In our different ways, we suffered the social con-straints and heavy burden of custom. I loved Modou. I compromised with his people. I tolerated his sisters, who too often would desert their own homes to encumber my own. They allowed themselves to be fed and pet-ted. They would look on, without reacting, as their children romped around on my chairs. I tolerated their spitting, the phlegm expertly secreted under my carpets.

His mother would stop by again and again while on her outings, always flanked by different friends, just to show off her son's social success but particularly so that they might see, at close quarters, her supremacy in this beautiful house in which she did not live. I would receive her with all the respect due to a queen, and she would leave satisfied, especially if her hand closed over the banknote I had carefully placed there. But hardly would she be out than she would think of the new band of friends she would soon be dazzling.

Modou's father was more understanding. More often than not, he would visit us without sitting down. He would accept a glass of cold water and would leave, after repeating his prayers for the protection of the house.

I knew how to smile at them all, and consented to wasting useful time in futile chatter. My sisters-in-law believed me to be spared the drudgery of housework.

"With your two housemaids!" they would say with emphasis.

Try explaining to them that a working woman is no less responsible for her home. Try explaining to them that nothing is done if you do not step in, that you have to see to everything, do everything all over again: clean-ing up, cooking, ironing. There are the children to be washed, the hus-band to be looked after. The working woman has a dual task, of which both halves, equally arduous, must be reconciled. How does one go about this? Therein lies the skill that makes all the difference to a home.

Some of my sisters-in-law did not envy my way of living at all. They saw me dashing around the house after a hard day at school. They appreciated their comfort, their peace of mind, their moments of leisure and allowed themselves to be looked after by their husbands, who were crushed under their duties.

Others, limited in their way of thinking, envied my comfort and purchasing power. They would go into raptures over the many "gadgets" in my house: gas cooker, vegetable grater, sugar tongs. They forgot the source of this easy life; first up in the morning, last to go to bed, always working.

You, Aissatou, you forsook your family-in-law, tightly shut in with their hurt dignity. You would lament to me: "Your family-in-law respects you. You must treat them well. As for me, they look down on me from the height of their lost nobility. What can I do?"

While Mawdo's mother planned her revenge, we lived: Christmas Eve parties organized by several couples, with the costs shared equally, and held in turns in the different homes. Without self-consciousness, we would revive the dances of yester-year: the lively beguine, frenzied rumbas, languid tangos.[4] We rediscovered the old beatings of the heart that strengthened our feelings.

We would also leave the stifling city to breathe in the healthy air of seaside suburbs.

We would walk along the Dakar Corniche, one of the most beautiful in West Africa, a sheer work of art wrought by nature. Rounded or pointed rocks, black or ochre-coloured, overlooking the ocean. Greenery, sometimes a veritable hanging garden spread out under the clear sky. We would go on to the road to Ouakam, which also leads to Ngor[5] and further on to Yoff airport. We would recognize on the way the narrow road leading farther on to Almadies[6] beach.

Our favourite spot was Ngor beach, situated near the village of the same name, where old bearded fishermen repaired their nets under the silk-cotton trees. Naked and snotty children played in complete freedom when they were not frolicking about in the sea.

On the fine sand, washed by the waves and swollen with water, naively painted canoes awaited their turn to be launched into the waters. In their hollows small pools of blue water would glisten, full of light from the sky and sun.

What a crowd on public holidays! Numerous families would stroll about, thirsty for space and fresh air. People would undress, without embarrassment, tempted by the benevolent caress of the iodized breeze[7] and the warmth from the sun's rays. The idle would sleep under spread parasols. A few children, spade and bucket in hand, would build and demolish the castles of their imagination.

In the evening the fishermen would return from their laborious outings. Once more, they had escaped the moving snare of the sea. At first simple points on the horizon, the boats would become more distinct from one another as they drew nearer. They would dance in the hollows of the waves, then would lazily let themselves be dragged along. Fishermen would gaily furl their sails and draw in their tackle. While some of them would gather together the wriggling catch, others would wring out their soaked clothes and mop their faces.

Under the wondering gaze of the kids, the live fish would flip up as the

---

4. Dances originating in the Caribbean and Latin America that were popular in the early decades of this century.   5. On the outskirts of Dakar.   6. The western extremity of the cape on which Dakar is built.   7. Sea air contains iodine, which is considered to be beneficial to the health.

long sea snakes would curve themselves inwards. There is nothing more beautiful than a fish just out of water, its eye clear and fresh, with golden or silvery scales and beautiful blueish glints!

Hands would sort out, group, divide. We would buy a good selection at bargain prices for the house.

The sea air would put us in good humour. The pleasure we indulged in and in which all our senses rejoiced would intoxicate both rich and poor with health. Our communion with deep, bottomless and unlimited nature refreshed our souls. Depression and sadness would disappear, suddenly to be replaced by feelings of plenitude and expansiveness.

Reinvigorated, we would set out for home. How jealously we guarded the secret of simple pleasures, health-giving remedy for the daily tensions of life.

Do you remember the picnics we organized at Sangalkam,[8] in the farm Mawdo Bâ inherited from his father? Sangalkam remains the refuge of people from Dakar, those who want a break from the frenzy of the city. The younger set, in particular, has bought land there and built country residences: these green, open spaces are conducive to rest, meditation and the letting off of steam by children. This oasis lies on the road to Rufisque.[9]

Mawdo's mother had looked after the farm before her son's marriage. The memory of her husband had made her attached to this plot of land, where their joint and patient hands had disciplined the vegetation that filled our eyes with admiration.

Yourself, you added the small building at the far end: three small, simple bedrooms, a bathroom, a kitchen. You grew many flowers in a few corners. You had a hen run built, then a closed pen for sheep.

Coconut trees, with their interlacing leaves, gave protection from the sun. Succulent sapodilla[1] stood next to sweet-smelling pomegranates. Heavy mangoes weighed down the branches. Pawpaws resembling breasts of different shapes hung tempting and inaccessible from the tops of elongated trunks.

Green leaves and browned leaves, new grass and withered grass were strewn all over the ground. Under our feet the ants untiringly built and rebuilt their homes.

How warm the shades over the camp beds! Teams for games were formed one after the other amid cries of victory or lamentations of defeat.

And we stuffed ourselves with fruits within easy reach. And we drank the milk from coconuts. And we told "juicy stories"! And we danced about, roused by the strident notes of a gramophone. And the lamb, seasoned with white pepper, garlic, butter, hot pepper, would be roasting over the wood fire.

And we lived. When we stood in front of our over-crowded classes, we represented a force in the enormous effort to be accomplished in order to overcome ignorance.

Each profession, intellectual or manual, deserves consideration,

---

8. A suburb of Dakar, noted for its lush vegetation.   9. A small town just south of Dakar, important as a railway junction.   1. A tropical fruit that looks like the kiwifruit.

whether it requires painful physical effort or manual dexterity, wide knowledge or the patience of an ant. Ours, like that of the doctor, does not allow
for any mistake. You don't joke with life, and life is both body and mind.
To warp a soul is as much a sacrilege as murder. Teachers—at kindergarten level, as at university level—form a noble army accomplishing daily
feats, never praised, never decorated. An army forever on the move, forever
vigilant. An army without drums, without gleaming uniforms. This army,
thwarting traps and snares, everywhere plants the flag of knowledge and
morality.

How we loved this priesthood, humble teachers in humble local
schools. How faithfully we served our profession, and how we spent ourselves in order to do it honour. Like all apprentices, we had learned how
to practise it well at the demonstration school, a few steps away from our
own, where experienced teachers taught the novices that we were how to
apply, in the lessons we gave, our knowledge of psychology and method.
. . . In those children we set in motion waves that, breaking, carried away
in their furl a bit of ourselves.

10

Modou rose steadily to the top rank in the trade union organizations.
His understanding of people and things endeared him to both employers
and workers. He focused his efforts on points that were easily satisfied, that
made work lighter and life more pleasant. He sought practical improvements in the workers' conditions. His slogan was: what's the use of taunting with the impossible? Obtaining the "possible" is already a victory.

His point of view was not unanimously accepted, but people relied on
his practical realism.

Mawdo could take part in neither trade unionism nor politics, for he
hadn't the time. His reputation as a good doctor was growing; he remained
the prisoner of his mission in a hospital filled to capacity with the sick, for
people were going less and less to the native doctor who specialized in
brewing the same concoctions of leaves for different illnesses.

Everybody was reading newspapers and magazines. There was unrest in
North Africa.[2]

Did these interminable discussions, during which points of view con-
curred or clashed, complemented each other or were vanquished, determine the aspect of the New Africa?

The assimilationist dream of the colonist drew into its crucible our
mode of thought and way of life. The sun helmet worn over the natural
protection of our kinky hair, smoke-filled pipe in the mouth, white shorts
just above the calves, very short dresses displaying shapely legs: a whole
generation suddenly became aware of the ridiculous situation festering in
our midst.

History marched on, inexorably. The debate over the right path to take
shook West Africa. Brave men went to prison; others, following in their
footsteps, continued the work begun.

2. A reference to the anticolonial agitation that culminated in the Algerian war of independence in the
late 1950s and early 1960s.

It was the privilege of our generation to be the link between two periods in our history, one of domination, the other of independence. We remained young and efficient, for we were the messengers of a new design. With independence achieved, we witnessed the birth of a republic, the birth of an anthem and the implantation of a flag.

I heard people repeat that all the active forces in the country should be mobilized. And we said that over and above the unavoidable opting for such-and-such a party, such-and-such a model of society, what was needed was national unity. Many of us rallied around the dominant party, infusing it with new blood. To be productive in the crowd was better than crossing one's arms and hiding behind imported ideologies.

Modou, a practical man, led his unions into collaboration with the government, demanding for his troops only what was possible. But he cursed the hasty establishment of too many embassies, which he judged to be too costly for our under-developed country. This bleeding of the country for reasons of pure vanity, among other things, such as the frequent invitation of foreigners, was just a waste of money. And, with his wage-earners in mind, he would repeatedly growl, "So many schools, or so much hospital equipment lost! So many monthly wage increases! So many tarred roads!"

You and Mawdo would listen to him. We were scaling the heights, but your mother-in-law, who saw you resplendent beside her son, who saw her son going more and more frequently to your father's workshop, who saw your mother fill out and dress better, your mother-in-law thought more and more of her revenge.

11

I know that I am shaking you, that I am twisting a knife in a wound hardly healed; but what can I do? I cannot help remembering in my forced solitude and reclusion.

Mawdo's mother is Aunty Nabou to us and Seynabou to others. She bore a glorious name in the Sine: Diouf. She is a descendant of Bour[3]-Sine. She lived in the past, unaware of the changing world. She clung to old beliefs. Being strongly attached to her privileged origins, she believed firmly that blood carried with it virtues, and, nodding her head, she would repeat that humble birth would always show in a person's bearing. And life had not been kind to Mawdo's mother. Very early, she lost her dear husband; bravely, she brought up her eldest son Mawdo and two other daughters, now married . . . and well married. She devoted herself with the affection of a tigress to her "one and only man," Mawdo Bâ. When she swore by her only son's nose, the symbol of life, she had said everything. Now, her "only man" was moving away from her, through the fault of this cursed daughter of a goldsmith, worse than a *griot* woman. The *griot* brings happiness. But a goldsmith's daughter! . . . she burns everything in her path, like the fire in a forge.

So while we lived without concern, considering your marriage a prob-

3. King.

lem of the past, Mawdo's mother thought day and night of a way to get her revenge on you, the goldsmith's daughter.

One fine day she decided to pay a visit to her younger brother, Farba Diouf, a customary chief in Diakhao.[4] She packed a few well chosen clothes into a suitcase that she borrowed from me, stuffed a basket full of various purchases: provisions and foodstuffs that are dear or rare in the Sine (fruits from France, cheese, preserves), toys for nephews, lengths of material for her brother and his four wives.

She asked Modou for some money, which she carefully folded and put away in her purse. She had her hair done, painted her feet and hands with henna. Thus dressed, adorned, she left.

These days, the road to Rufisque forks at the Diamniadio crossroads:[5] the National 1, to the right, leads, after Mbour, to the Sine-Saloum, while the National 2 goes through Thies and Tivaouane, cradle of Tidjanism,[6] towards Saint-Louis, former capital of Senegal. Aunty Nabou did not enjoy the benefit of these pleasant roads. Jostled in the bus on the bumpy road, she sought refuge in her memories. The dizzying speed of the vehicle, carrying her towards the place of her childhood, did not prevent her from recognizing the familiar countryside. Here, Sindia, and to the left, Popenguine,[7] where the Catholics celebrate Whitsun.[8]

How many generations has this same unchanging countryside seen glide past! Aunty Nabou acknowledged man's vulnerability in the face of the eternity of nature. By its very duration, nature defies time and takes its revenge on man.

The baobab trees[9] held out the giant knots of their branches towards the skies; slowly, the cows moved across the road, their mournful stare defying the vehicles; shepherds in baggy trousers, their sticks on their shoulders or in their hands, guided the animals. Men and animals blended, as in a picture risen from the depths of time.

Aunty Nabou closed her eyes every time the bus passed another vehicle. She was especially frightened of the big lorries with their huge loads.

The beautiful Medinatou-Minaouara mosque[1] had not yet been built to the glory of Islam, but in the same pious spirit, men and women prayed by the side of the road. "You have to come away from Dakar to be convinced of the survival of traditions," murmured Aunty Nabou.

On the left, prickly shrubs bordered the Ndiassane forest; monkeys darted out to enjoy the light.

Thiadiaye, Tataguine, Diouroupe, then Ndioudiouf, and finally Fatick,[2] capital of the Sine. Puffing and steaming, the bus branched off to the left. Jolts and still more jolts. Finally Diakhao, the royal Diakhao, Diakhao, cradle and tomb of the Bour-Sine, Diakhao of her ancestors, beloved Diakhao, with the vast compound of its old palace.

The same heaviness tortured her heart on each visit paid to the family domain.

---

4. A Serer village in central Senegal.   **5.** North of Dakar.   **6.** Beliefs and practices of the Tidjanis, a Muslim sect in Senegal.   **7.** Serer villages, near the coastal town of Mbour. The majority of Serer are Catholic.   **8.** The seventh Sunday after Easter, celebrated to commemorate Pentecost, the descent of the Spirit on Christ's apostles.   **9.** Large gaunt-looking trees, typical of the West African savannah. **1.** In central Senegal, named after the holy city in Saudi Arabia where the Prophet Muhammad once lived.   **2.** Villages located in the Fatick region, east of Dakar.

First of all, water for ablutions and a mat on which to pray and to meditate before the tomb of the ancestor. And then she let her gaze, marked
with sadness and filled with history, roam over the other tombs. Here, the
dead and the living lived together in the family compound: each king,
returned from his coronation, planted two trees in the yard that marked
out his last resting place. Fervently, Aunty Nabou intoned the religious
verses, directing them at the tombs of the dead. Her face wore a tragic
mask in this place of grandeur, which sang of the past to the sound of the
djou-djoungs, the royal drums.

She swore that your existence, Aissatou, would never tarnish her noble
descent.

Associating in her thoughts antiquated rites and religion, she remembered the milk to be poured into the Sine[3] to appease the invisible spirits.
Tomorrow, in the river, she would make her offerings to protect herself
from the evil eye, while at the same time attracting the benevolence of the
tours.[4]

Royally received, she immediately resumed her position as the elder
sister of the master of the house. Nobody addressed her without kneeling
down. She took her meals alone, having been served with the choicest bits
from the pots.

Visitors came from everywhere to honour her, thus reminding her of
the truth of the law of blood. For her, they revived the exploits of the
ancestor Bour-Sine, the dust of combats and the ardour of thoroughbred
horses. . . . And, heady with the heavy scent of burnt incense, she drew
force and vigour from the ancestral ashes stirred to the eclectic sound of
the *koras.*[5] She summoned her brother.

"I need a child beside me," she said, "to fill my heart. I want this child
to be both my legs and my right arm. I am growing old. I will make of this
child another me. Since the marriage of my own children, the house has
been empty."

She was thinking of you, working out her vengeance, but was very careful not to speak of you, of her hatred for you.

"Let your wish be fulfilled," replied Farba Diouf. "I have never asked
you to educate any of my daughters, not wanting to tire you. Yet today's
children are difficult to keep in check. Take young Nabou, your namesake. She is yours. I ask only for her bones."

Satisfied, Aunty Nabou packed her suitcase again, filled her basket with
all that could be found in the village and is dear in town: dried couscous,[6]
roasted groundnut paste, millet, eggs, milk, chicken. Holding young
Nabou's hand firmly in her right hand, she took the road back to town.

12

As she handed me back my suitcase, Aunty Nabou introduced young
Nabou to me; she also introduced her at the homes of all her friends.

With my help, young Nabou was admitted into the French school.

---

3. As a libation, instead of the habitual alcohol, which Muslims are forbidden to use.　4. Invisible
spirits.　5. Stringed instruments similar in tone to the harp, which accompany songs and poems in
praise of kings and heroes.　6. Here, a cereal meal, similar in texture to the North African couscous.

Maturing in her aunt's protective shade, she learned the secret of making delicious sauces, of using an iron and wielding a pestle. Her aunt never missed an opportunity to remind her of her royal origin, and taught her that the first quality in a woman is docility.

After obtaining her primary school certificate, and after a few years in secondary school, the older Nabou advised her niece to sit the entrance examination for the State School of Midwifery: "This school is good. You receive an education there. No garlands for heads. Young, sober girls without earrings, dressed in white, which is the colour of purity. The profession you will learn there is a beautiful one; you will earn your living and you will acquire grace for your entry into paradise by helping at the birth of new followers of Mohammed, the prophet. To tell the truth, a woman does not need too much education. In fact, I wonder how a woman can earn her living by talking from morning to night."

Thus, young Nabou became a midwife. One fine day, Aunty Nabou called Mawdo and said to him: "My brother Farba has given you young Nabou to be your wife, to thank me for the worthy way in which I have brought her up. I will never get over it if you don't take her as your wife. Shame kills faster than disease."

I knew about it. Modou knew about it. The whole town knew about it. You, Aissatou, suspected nothing and continued to be radiant.

And because his mother had fixed a date for the wedding night, Mawdo finally had the courage to tell you what every woman was whispering: you had a co-wife. "My mother is old. The knocks and disappointments of life have weakened her heart. If I spurn this child, she will die. This is the doctor speaking and not the son. Think of it, her brother's daughter, brought up by her, rejected by her son. What shame before society!"

It was "so as not to see his mother die of shame and chagrin" that Mawdo agreed to go to the rendezvous of the wedding night. Faced with this rigid mother moulded by the old morality, burning with the fierce ardour of antiquated laws, what could Mawdo Bâ do? He was getting on in years, worn out by his arduous work. And then, did he really want to fight, to make a gesture of resistance? Young Nabou was so tempting. . . .

From then on, you no longer counted. What of the time and the love you had invested in your home? Only trifles, quickly forgotten. Your sons? They counted for very little in this reconciliation between a mother and her "one and only man"; you no longer counted, any more than did your four sons: they could never be equal to young Nabou's sons.

The griots spoke of young Nabou's sons, exalting them: "Blood has returned to its source."

Your sons did not count. Mawdo's mother, a princess, could not recognize herself in the sons of a goldsmith's daughter.

In any case, could a goldsmith's daughter have any dignity, any honour? This was tantamount to asking whether you had a heart and flesh. Ah! for some people the honour and chagrin of a goldsmith's daughter count for less, much less, than the honour and chagrin of a Guelewar.[7]

Mawdo did not drive you away. He did his duty and wished that you

___

7. Nobleman.

would stay on. Young Nabou would continue to live with his mother; it was you he loved. Every other night he would go to his mother's place to see his other wife, so that his mother "would not die," to "fulfil a duty."

How much greater you proved to be than those who sapped your happiness!

You were advised to compromise: "You don't burn the tree which bears the fruit."

You were threatened through your flesh: "Boys cannot succeed without their father."

You took no notice.

These commonplace truths, which before had lowered the heads of many wives as they raised them in revolt, did not produce the desired miracle; they did not divert you from your decision. You chose to make a break, a one-way journey with your four sons, leaving this letter for Mawdo, in clear view, on the bed that used to be yours. I remember the exact words:

> Mawdo,
>   Princes master their feelings to fulfil their duties. "Others" bend their heads and, in silence, accept a destiny that oppresses them.
>   That, briefly put, is the internal ordering of our society, with its absurd divisions. I will not yield to it. I cannot accept what you are offering me today in place of the happiness we once had. You want to draw a line between heartfelt love and physical love. I say that there can be no union of bodies without the heart's acceptance, however little that may be.
>   If you can procreate without loving, merely to satisfy the pride of your declining mother, then I find you despicable. At that moment you tumbled from the highest rung of respect on which I have always placed you. Your reasoning, which makes a distinction, is unacceptable to me: on one side, me, "your life, your love, your choice," on the other, "young Nabou, to be tolerated for reasons of duty."
>   Mawdo, man is one: greatness and animal fused together. None of his acts is pure charity. None is pure bestiality.
>   I am stripping myself of your love, your name. Clothed in my dignity, the only worthy garment, I go my way.
>
> Goodbye,
Aissatou

And you left. You had the surprising courage to take your life into your own hands. You rented a house and set up home there. And instead of looking backwards, you looked resolutely to the future. You set yourself a difficult task; and more than just my presence and my encouragements, books saved you. Having become your refuge, they sustained you.

The power of books, this marvellous invention of astute human intelligence. Various signs associated with sound: different sounds that form the word. Juxtaposition of words from which springs the idea, Thought, History, Science, Life. Sole instrument of interrelationships and of culture, unparalleled means of giving and receiving. Books knit generations together in the same continuing effort that leads to progress. They enabled you to better yourself. What society refused you, they granted: examinations sat and passed took you also to France. The School of Interpreters, from which you graduated, led to your appointment into the Senegalese

Embassy in the United States. You make a very good living. You are developing in peace, as your letters tell me, your back resolutely turned on those seeking light enjoyment and easy relationships.

And Mawdo? He renewed his relationship with his family. Those from Diakhao invaded his house: those from Diakhao sustained young Nabou. But—and Mawdo knew it—there was no possible comparison between yourself and young Nabou; you, so beautiful and so gentle, you, whose tenderness for him was so deep and disinterested, you, who knew how to mop your husband's brow, you, who could always find the right words with which to make him relax.

And Mawdo? What didn't he say? "I am completely disoriented. You can't change the habits of a grown man. I look for shirts and trousers in the old places and I touch only emptiness."

I had no pity for Mawdo.

"My house is a suburb of Diakhao. I find it impossible to get any rest there. Everything there is dirty. Young Nabou gives my food and my clothes away to visitors."

I did not listen to Mawdo.

"Somebody told me he'd seen you with Aissatou yesterday. Is it true? Is she around? How is she? What about my sons?"

I did not answer Mawdo.

For Mawdo, and through him all men, remained an enigma to me. Your departure had truly shaken him. His sadness was clearly evident. When he spoke of you, the inflexions in his voice hardened. But his disillusioned air, the bitter criticisms of his home, his wit, which railed at everything, did not in the least prevent the periodic swelling of young Nabou's belly. Two boys had already been born.

When faced with this visible fact, proof of his intimate relations with young Nabou, Mawdo would twist with anger. His look was like a whip: "Look here, don't be an idiot. How can you expect a man to remain a stone when he is constantly in contact with the woman who runs his house?" He added as illustration: "I saw a film in which the survivors of an air crash survived by eating the flesh of the corpses. This fact demonstrates the force of the instincts in man, instincts that dominate him, regardless of his level of intelligence. Slough off this surfeit of dreamy sentimentality. Accept reality in its crude ugliness."

"You can't resist the imperious laws that demand food and clothing for man. These same laws compel the 'male' in other respects. I say 'male' to emphasize the bestiality of instincts. . . . You understand. . . . A wife must understand, once and for all, and must forgive; she must not worry herself about 'betrayals of the flesh.' The important thing is what there is in the heart; that's what unites two beings inside." (He struck his chest; at the point where the heart lies.)

"Driven to the limits of my resistance, I satisfy myself with what is within reach. It's a terrible thing to say. Truth is ugly when one analyses it."

Thus, to justify himself, he reduced young Nabou to a "plate of food." Thus, for the sake of "variety," men are unfaithful to their wives.

I was irritated. He was asking me to understand. But to understand

what? The supremacy of instinct? The right to betray? The justification of
the desire for variety? I could not be an ally to polygamic instincts. What,
then, was I to understand?

How I envied your calmness during your last visit! There you were, rid
of the mask of suffering. Your sons were growing up well, contrary to all
predictions. You did not care about Mawdo. Yes, indeed, there you were,
the past crushed beneath your heel. There you were, an innocent victim
of an unjust cause and the courageous pioneer of a new life.

13

My own crisis came three years after your own. But unlike in your own
case, the source was not my family-in-law. The problem was rooted in
Modou himself, my husband.

My daughter Daba, who was preparing for her *baccalauréat,* often
brought some of her classmates home with her. Most of the time it was
the same young girl, a bit shy, frail, made noticeably uncomfortable by
our style of life. But she was really beautiful in this her adolescent period,
in her faded but clean clothes! Her beauty shone, pure. Her shapely contours could not but be noticed.

I sometimes noticed that Modou was interested in the pair. Neither was
I worried when I heard him suggest that he should take Binetou home in
the car—"because it was getting late," he would say.

Binetou was going through a metamorphosis, however. She was now
wearing very expensive off-the-peg dresses. Smilingly, she would explain
to my daughter: "Oh, I have a sugar-daddy who pays for them."

Then one day, on her return from school, Daba confided to me that
Binetou had a serious problem: "The sugar-daddy of the boutique dresses
wants to marry Binetou. Just imagine. Her parents want to withdraw her
from school, with only a few months to go before the *bac,* to marry her off
to the sugar-daddy."

"Advise her to refuse," I said.

"And if the man in question offers her a villa, Mecca for her parents, a
car, a monthly allowance, jewels?"

"None of that is worth the capital of youth."

"I agree with you, mum. I'll tell Binetou not to give in; but her mother
is a woman who wants so much to escape from mediocrity and who regrets
so much her past beauty, faded in the smoke from the wood fires, that she
looks enviously at everything I wear; she complains all day long."

"What is important is Binetou herself. She must not give in."

And then, a few days afterwards, Daba renewed the conversation, with
its surprising conclusion.

"Mum! Binetou is heartbroken. She is going to marry her sugar-daddy.
Her mother cried so much. She begged her daughter to give her life a
happy end, in a proper house, as the man has promised them. So she
accepted."

"When is the wedding?"

"This coming Sunday, but there'll be no reception. Binetou cannot
bear the mockery of her friends."

And in the evening of this same Sunday on which Binetou was being married off I saw come into my house, all dressed up and solemn, Tamsir, Modou's brother, with Mawdo Bâ and his local *Imam*. Where had they come from, looking so awkward in their starched *boubous*? Doubtless, they had come looking for Modou to carry out an important task that one of them had been charged with. I told them that Modou had been out since morning. They entered laughing, deliberately sniffing the fragrant odour of incense that was floating on the air. I sat in front of them, laughing with them. The *Imam* attacked:

"There is nothing one can do when Allah the almighty puts two people side by side."

"True, true," said the other two in support.

A pause. He took a breath and continued: "There is nothing new in this world."

"True, true," Tamsir and Mawdo chimed in again.

"Some things we may find to be sad are much less so than others. . . ."

I followed the movement of the haughty lips that let fall these axioms, which can precede the announcement of either a happy event or an unhappy one. What was he leading up to with these preliminaries that rather announced a storm? So their visit was obviously planned.

Does one announce bad news dressed up like that in one's Sunday best? Or did they want to inspire confidence with their impeccable dress?

I thought of the absent one. I asked with the cry of a hunted beast: "Modou?"

And the *Imam*, who had finally got hold of a leading thread, held tightly on to it. He went on quickly, as if the words were glowing embers in his mouth: "Yes, Modou Fall, but, happily, he is alive for you, for all of us, thanks be to God. All he has done is to marry a second wife today. We have just come from the mosque in Grand Dakar where the marriage took place."

The thorns thus removed from the way, Tamsir ventured: "Modou sends his thanks. He says it is fate that decides men and things: God intended him to have a second wife, there is nothing he can do about it. He praises you for the quarter of a century of marriage in which you gave him all the happiness a wife owes her husband. His family, especially myself, his elder brother, thank you. You have always held us in respect. You know that we are Modou's blood."

Afterwards there were the same old words, which were intended to relieve the situation: "You are the only one in your house, no matter how big it is, no matter how dear life is. You are the first wife, a mother for Modou, a friend for Modou."

Tamsir's Adam's apple danced about in his throat. He shook his left leg, crossed over his folded right leg. His shoes, white Turkish slippers, were covered with a thin layer of red dust, the colour of the earth in which they had walked. The same dust covered Mawdo's and the Imam's shoes.

Mawdo said nothing. He was reliving his own experience. He was thinking of your letter, your reaction, and you and I were so alike. He was being wary. He kept his head lowered, in the attitude of those who accept defeat before the battle.

I acquiesced under the drops of poison that were burning me: "A quarter of a century of marriage," "a wife unparalleled." I counted backwards to determine where the break in the thread had occurred from which everything had unwound. My mother's words came back to me: "too perfect. . . ." I completed at last my mother's thought with the end of the dictum: ". . . to be honest." I thought of the first two incisors with a wide gap between them, the sign of the primacy of love in the individual. I thought of his absence, all day long. He had simply said: "Don't expect me for lunch." I thought of other absences, quite frequent these days, crudely clarified today yet well hidden yesterday under the guise of trade union meetings. He was also on a strict diet, "to break the stomach's egg," he would say laughingly, this egg that announced old age.

Every night when he went out he would unfold and try on several of his suits before settling on one. The others, impatiently rejected, would slip to the floor. I would have to fold them again and put them back in their places; and this extra work, I discovered, I was doing only to help him in his effort to be elegant in his seduction of another woman.

I forced myself to check my inner agitation. Above all, I must not give my visitors the pleasure of relating my distress. Smile, take the matter lightly, just as they announced it. Thank them for the humane way in which they have accomplished their mission. Send thanks to Modou, "a good father and a good husband," "a husband become a friend." Thank my family-in-law, the *Imam*, Mawdo. Smile. Give them something to drink. See them out, under the swirls of incense that they were sniffing once again. Shake their hands.

How pleased they were, all except Mawdo, who correctly judged the import of the event.

14

Alone at last, able to give free rein to my surprise and to gauge my distress. Ah! yes, I forgot to ask for my rival's name so that I might give a human form to my pain.

My question was soon answered. Acquaintances from Grand Dakar came rushing to my house, bringing the various details of the ceremony. Some of them did so out of true friendship for me; others were spiteful and jealous of the promotion Binetou's mother would gain from the marriage.

"I don't understand." They did not understand either the entrance of Modou, a "personality," into this extremely poor family.

Binetou, a child the same age as my daughter Daba, promoted to the rank of my co-wife, whom I must face up to. Shy Binetou! The old man who bought her the new off-the-peg dresses to replace the old faded ones was none other than Modou. She had innocently confided her secrets to her rival's daughter because she thought that this dream, sprung from a brain growing old, would never become reality. She had told everything: the villa, the monthly allowance, the offer of a future trip to Mecca for her parents. She thought she was stronger than the man she was dealing with. She did not know Modou's strong will, his tenacity before an obstacle, the pride he invests in winning, the resistance that inspires new attempts at each failure.

Daba was furious, her pride wounded. She repeated all the nicknames Binetou had given her father: old man, pot-belly, sugar-daddy! . . . the person who gave her life had been daily ridiculed and he accepted it. An overwhelming anger raged inside Daba. She knew that her best friend was sincere in what she said. But what can a child do, faced with a furious mother shouting about her hunger and her thirst to live?

Binetou, like many others, was a lamb slaughtered on the altar of affluence. Daba's anger increased as she analysed the situation: "Break with him, mother! Send this man away. He has respected neither you nor me. Do what Aunty Aissatou did; break with him. Tell me you'll break with him. I can't see you fighting over a man with a girl my age."

I told myself what every betrayed woman says: if Modou was milk, it was I who had had all the cream. The rest, well, nothing but water with a vague smell of milk.

But the final decision lay with me. With Modou absent all night (was he already consummating his marriage?), the solitude that lends counsel enabled me to grasp the problem.

Leave? Start again at zero, after living twenty-five years with one man, after having borne twelve children? Did I have enough energy to bear alone the weight of this responsibility, which was both moral and material?

Leave! Draw a clean line through the past. Turn over a page on which not everything was bright, certainly, but at least all was clear. What would now be recorded there would hold no love, confidence, grandeur or hope. I had never known the sordid side of marriage. Don't get to know it! Run from it! When one begins to forgive, there is an avalanche of faults that comes crashing down, and the only thing that remains is to forgive again, to keep on forgiving. Leave, escape from betrayal! Sleep without asking myself any questions, without straining my ear at the slightest noise, waiting for a husband I share.

I counted the abandoned or divorced women of my generation whom I knew.

I knew a few whose remaining beauty had been able to capture a worthy man, a man who added fine bearing to a good situation and who was considered "better, a hundred times better than his predecessor." The misery that was the lot of these women was rolled back with the invasion of the new happiness that changed their lives, filled out their cheeks, brightened their eyes. I knew others who had lost all hope of renewal and whom loneliness had very quickly laid underground.

The play of destiny remains impenetrable. The cowries[8] that a female neighbour throws on a fan in front of me do not fill me with optimism, neither when they remain face upwards, showing the black hollow that signifies laughter, nor when the grouping of their white backs seems to say that "the man in the double trousers"[9] is coming towards me, the promise of wealth. "The only thing that separates you from them, man and wealth,

---

8. Seashells used for divination.   9. A reference to the large size of men's pants in the local costume.

is the alms of two white and red cola nuts,"[1] adds Farmata, my neighbour.

She insists: "There is a saying that discord here may be luck elsewhere. Why are you afraid to make the break? A woman is like a ball; once a ball is thrown, no one can predict where it will bounce. You have no control over where it rolls, and even less over who gets it. Often it is grabbed by an unexpected hand. . . ."

Instead of listening to the reasoning of my neighbour, a *griot* woman who dreams of the generous tips due to the go-between,[2] I looked at myself in the mirror. My eyes took in the mirror's eloquence. I had lost my slim figure, as well as ease and quickness of movement. My stomach protruded from beneath the wrapper that hid the calves developed by the impressive number of kilometres walked since the beginning of my existence. Suckling had robbed my breasts of their round firmness. I could not delude myself: youth was deserting my body.

Whereas a woman draws from the passing years the force of her devotion, despite the ageing of her companion, a man, on the other hand, restricts his field of tenderness. His egoistic eye looks over his partner's shoulder. He compares what he had with what he no longer has, what he has with what he could have.

I had heard of too many misfortunes not to understand my own. There was your own case, Aissatou, the cases of many other women, despised, relegated or exchanged, who were abandoned like a worn-out or out-dated *boubou*.

To overcome distress when it sits upon you demands strong will. When one thinks that with each passing second one's life is shortened, one must profit intensely from this second; it is the sum of all the lost or harvested seconds that makes for a wasted or a successful life. Brace oneself to check despair and get it into proportion! A nervous breakdown waits around the corner for anyone who lets himself wallow in bitterness. Little by little, it takes over your whole being.

Oh, nervous breakdown! Doctors speak of it in a detached, ironical way, emphasizing that the vital organs are in no way disturbed. You are lucky if they don't tell you that you are wasting their time with the ever-growing list of your illnesses—your head, throat, chest, heart, liver—that no X-ray can confirm. And yet what atrocious suffering is caused by nervous breakdowns!

And I think of Jacqueline, who suffered from one. Jacqueline, the Ivorian,[3] had disobeyed her Protestant parents and had married Samba Diack, a contemporary of Mawdo Bâ's, a doctor like him, who, on leaving the African School of Medicine and Pharmacy, was posted to Abidjan.[4] Jacqueline often came round to see us, since her husband often visited our household. Coming to Senegal, she found herself in a new world, a world with different reactions, temperament and mentality from that in which she had grown up. In addition, her husband's relatives—always the relatives—were cool towards her because she refused to adopt the Muslim religion and went instead to the Protestant church every Sunday.

---

1. The cola nut, which comes in these two colors, is often used in sacrifices and other religious ceremonies.   2. The person who traditionally arranges marriages.   3. A citizen of Ivory Coast.   4. The capital of Ivory Coast.

A black African, she should have been able to fit without difficulty into a black African society, Senegal and the Ivory Coast both having experienced the same colonial power. But Africa is diverse, divided. The same country can change its character and outlook several times over, from north to south or from east to west.

Jacqueline truly wanted to become Senegalese, but the mockery checked all desire in her to co-operate. People called her *gnac*,[5] and she finally understood the meaning of this nickname that revolted her so.

Her husband, making up for lost time, spent his time chasing slender Senegalese women, as he would say with appreciation, and did not bother to hide his adventures, respecting neither his wife nor his children. His lack of precautions brought to Jacqueline's knowledge the irrefutable proof of his misconduct: love notes, check stubs bearing the names of the payees, bills from restaurants and for hotel rooms. Jacqueline cried; Samba Diack "lived it up." Jacqueline lost weight: Samba Diack was still living fast. Jacqueline complained of a disturbing lump in her chest, under her left breast; she said she had the impression that a sharp point had pierced her there and was cutting through her flesh right to her very bones. She fretted. Mawdo listened to her heart: nothing wrong there, he would say. He prescribed some tranquillizers. Eagerly, Jacqueline took the tablets, tortured by the insidious pain. The bottle empty, she noticed that the lump remained in the same place; she continued to feel the pain just as acutely as ever.

She consulted a doctor from her own country, who ordered an electrocardiogram and various blood tests. Nothing to be learned from the electric reading of the heart, nothing abnormal found in the blood. He too prescribed tranquillizers, big, effervescent tablets that could not allay poor Jacqueline's distress.

She thought of her parents, of their refusal to consent to her marriage. She wrote them a pathetic letter, in which she begged for their forgiveness. They sent their sincere blessing but could do nothing to lighten the strange weight in her chest.

Jacqueline was taken to Fann Hospital on the road to Ouakam, near the university, where medical students do their internship, as they do at the Aristide Le Dantec Hospital. This hospital did not exist at the time Mawdo Bâ and Samba Diack studied at the School of Medicine and Pharmacy. It has many departments, housed either in separate buildings or in adjoining ones to facilitate communication. These buildings, despite their number and size, do not manage to fill up the hospital's vast grounds. On entering it, Jacqueline thought of those gone mad, confined inside. It was necessary to explain to her that the mad ones were in psychiatric care and that here they were called the mentally sick and in any case, were not violent, the violent ones being confined in the psychiatric hospital at Thiaroye. Jacqueline was in a neurology ward, and those of us who went to visit her learned that the hospital also had departments for treating tuberculosis and infectious diseases.

5. A derogatory term for people from the hinterland and for foreigners, who are considered uncivilized.

Jacqueline lay prostrate in her bed. Her beautiful but neglected black hair, through which no comb had been run ever since she began consulting doctor after doctor, formed shaggy tufts on her head. When the scarf protecting it slipped out of place, it would uncover the coating of a mixture of roots that we poured on her, for we tried everything to draw this sister out of her private hell. And it was your mother, Aissatou, who went to consult the native medicine men for us and brought back *safara*[6] from her visits and directions for the sacrifices you quickly carried out.

Jacqueline's thoughts turned to death. She waited for it, frightened and tormented, her hand on her chest, where the tenacious, invisible lump foiled all the ruses, scoffed maliciously at all the tranquillizers. Jacqueline's room-mate was a French Technical Co-operation teacher of literature, posted to the Lycée Faidherbe in Saint-Louis. The only thing she knew of Saint-Louis, she said, was the bridge that spanned the river. A sore throat, an affliction as sudden as it was violent, had prevented her from taking up her duties and had brought her here, where she was waiting to be repatriated.

I observed her often. Old, for her unmarried status. Thin, angular even, without any charm. Her studies must have been her only form of recreation during her youth. Sour-tempered, she must have put off any passionate advances. It was perhaps her loneliness that had made her seek for a change. A teaching post in Senegal must have corresponded to her dreams of escape. She had come therefore, but all her frustrated dreams, all her disappointed hopes, all her crushed revolt connived to attack her throat, protected by a navy-blue scarf with white dots, which contrasted with the paleness of her chest. The medication with which her throat was painted gave a blueish tint to her thin lips, pinched over their misery. She had big, luminous, blue eyes, the only light, the only point of beauty, the only heavenly grace in her ungracious face. She tapped against her throat; Jacqueline tapped against her chest. We would laugh at their ways, especially when the patient from the next room came to "chat," as she said, and would uncover her back for the refreshing caress of the air-conditioner. She suffered from sudden flushes, which burned her terribly at this spot.

Strange and varied manifestations of neuro-vegetative dystonia.[7] Doctors, beware, especially if you are neurologists or psychiatrists. Often, the pains you are told of have their roots in moral torment. Vexations suffered and constant frustrations: these are what accumulate somewhere in the body and choke it.

Jacqueline, who enjoyed life, bravely endured blood test after blood test. Another electrocardiogram, another X-ray of the lungs. An electro-encephalogram was carried out, which revealed traces of her suffering. It then became necessary to do a gaseous electro-encephalography. This is extremely painful, always entailing a lumbar puncture.[8] That day, Jacqueline remained confined to bed, looking more pitiful and haggard than ever before.

---

6. Holy water.   7. Clinical depression.   8. An operation performed on the nervous system in the small of the back.

Samba Diack was kind and touched by his wife's breakdown.

One fine day, after a month of treatment (intravenous injections and tranquillizers), after a month of investigations, during which her French neighbour had returned to her country, the doctor who was head of the Neurology Department asked to see Jacqueline. She found in front of her a man whom maturity and the nobility of his job had made even more attractive, a man who had not been hardened by constant dealing with the most deplorable of miseries, that of mental alienation. With his sharp eyes, accustomed to judging, he looked into those of Jacqueline in order to discover in her soul the source of the distress disrupting her organism. In a soft, reassuring voice, which in itself was balm to this overstrung being, he explained: "Madame Diack, I assure you that there is nothing at all wrong with your head. The X-rays have shown nothing, and neither have the blood tests. The problem is that you are depressed, that is . . . not happy. You wish the conditions of life were different from what they are in reality, and this is what is torturing you. Moreover, you had your babies too soon after each other; the body loses its vital juices, which haven't had the time to be replaced. In short, there is nothing endangering your life.

"You must react, go out, give yourself a reason for living. Take courage. Slowly, you will overcome. We will give you a series of shock treatments with curare[9] to relax you. You can leave afterwards."

The doctor punctuated his words by nodding his head and smiling convincingly, giving Jacqueline much hope. Re-animated, she related the discussion to us and confided that she had left the interview already half-cured. She knew the heart of her illness and would fight against it. She was morally uplifted. She had come a long way, had Jacqueline!

Why did I recall this friend's ordeal? Was it because of its happy ending? Or merely to delay the formulation of the choice I had made, a choice that my reason rejected but that accorded with the immense tenderness I felt towards Modou Fall?

Yes, I was well aware of where the right solution lay, the dignified solution. And, to my family's great surprise, unanimously disapproved of by my children, who were under Daba's influence, I chose to remain. Modou and Mawdo were surprised, could not understand. . . .

Forewarned, you, my friend, did not try to dissuade me, respectful of my new choice of life.

I cried every day.

From then on, my life changed. I had prepared myself for equal sharing, according to the precepts of Islam concerning polygamic life. I was left with empty hands.

My children, who disagreed with my decision, sulked. In opposition to me, they represented a majority I had to respect.

"You have not finished suffering," predicted Daba.

I lived in a vacuum. And Modou avoided me. Attempts by friends and family to bring him back to the fold proved futile. One of the new couple's neighbours explained to me that the "child" would go "all a-quiver" each

9. A sedative.

time Modou said my name or showed any desire to see his children. He never came again; his new found happiness gradually swallowed up his memory of us. He forgot about us.

15

Aissatou, my dear friend, I've told you that there can be no possible comparison between you and young Nabou. But I also realize that there can be no possible comparison between young Nabou and Binetou. Young Nabou grew up beside her aunt, who had earmarked her as the spouse of her son Mawdo. Used to seeing him, she let herself be drawn towards him, naturally, without any shock. His greying hair did not offend her; she found his thickening features reassuring. And then she loved and still loves Mawdo, even if their interests are not always the same. School had not left a strong mark on young Nabou, preceded and dominated as it was by the strength of character of Aunty Nabou, who, in her rage for vengeance, had left nothing to chance in the education she gave her niece. It was especially while telling folk tales, late at night under the starlit sky, that Aunty Nabou wielded her power over young Nabou's soul: her expressive voice glorified the retributive violence of the warrior; her expressive voice lamented the anxiety of the Loved One, all submissive. She saluted the courage of the reckless; she stigmatized trickery, laziness, calumny; she demanded care of the orphan and respect for old age. Tales with animal characters, nostalgic songs kept young Nabou breathless. And slowly but surely, through the sheer force of repetition, the virtues and greatness of a race took root in this child.

This kind of oral education, easily assimilated, full of charm, has the power to bring out the best in the adult mind, developed in its contact with it. Softness and generosity, docility and politeness, poise and tact, all these qualities made young Nabou pleasant. Mawdo used to call her "finicky," with a shrug of his shoulders.

And then, young Nabou had a profession. She had no time to worry about her "state of mind." In charge of frequent shifts at the "Repos Mandel" Maternity Home, on the outskirts of the crowded and badly serviced suburban areas, all day and several times over she would go through the same gestures engendering life. Babies passed again and again between her expert hands.

She would come back from work railing at the lack of beds that led to the discharge, too early in her opinion, of the new mothers; worried about the lack of staff, inadequate instruments, medicines. She would say, with deep concern: "The fragile baby is let loose too quickly into a hygienically unsound social environment."

She thought of the great rate of infant mortality, which nights of care and devotion cannot decrease. She thought: What a thrilling adventure it is to turn a baby into a healthy man. But how many mothers are able to accomplish that feat?

In the midst of life, in the midst of poverty, in the midst of ugliness, young Nabou would often triumph with her knowledge and experience;

but she sometimes knew heartrending failure; she remained powerless, faced with the force of death.

Young Nabou, responsible and aware, like you, like me! Even though she is not my friend, we often shared the same problems.

She found life hard and, being a fighter, had not the least inclination for frivolities.

As for Binetou, she had grown up in complete liberty in an environment where survival was of the essence. Her mother was more concerned with putting the pot on the boil than with education. Beautiful, lively, kind-hearted, intelligent, Binetou had access to many of her friends' well-off families and was sharply aware of what she was sacrificing by her marriage. A victim, she wanted to be the oppressor. Exiled in the world of adults, which was not her own, she wanted her prison gilded. Demanding, she tormented. Sold, she raised her price daily. What she renounced, those things which before used to be the sap of her life and which she would bitterly enumerate, called for exorbitant compensations, which Modou exhausted himself trying to provide. Echoes of her life would reach me, amplified or muted according to the visitor. The seductive power of mature age, of silvery temples, was unknown to Binetou. And Modou would dye his hair every month. His waistline painfully restrained by old-fashioned trousers, Binetou would never miss a chance of laughing wickedly at him. Modou would leave himself winded trying to imprison youth in its decline, which abandoned him on all sides: the graceless sag of a double chin, the gait hesitant and heavy at the slightest cool breeze. Gracefulness and beauty surrounded him. He was afraid of disappointing, and so that there would be no time for close scrutiny of him, he would create daily celebrations during which the bright young thing would move, an elf with slender arms who with a laugh could make life beautiful or with a pout bring sadness.

People talked of bewitchment. With determination, friends begged me to react: "You are letting someone else pluck the fruits of your labour."

Vehemently, they recommended *marabouts*,[1] sure in their science, who had proved themselves by bringing husbands back to the fold, by separating them from evil women. These charlatans lived far away. Casamance was mentioned, where the Diola and Madjago excel in magic philtres.[2] They suggested Linguere,[3] the country of the Fulba, quick in vengeance through charms as through arms. They also talked of Mali, the country of the Bambara,[4] with faces deeply scarred with tribal marks.

To act as I was urged would have been to call myself into question. I was already reproaching myself for a weakness that had not prevented the degradation of my home. Was I to deny myself because Modou had chosen another path? No, I would not give in to the pressure. My mind and my faith rejected supernatural power. They rejected this easy attraction, which kills any will to fight. I looked reality in the face.

Reality had the face of Lady Mother-in-Law, swallowing up double

---

1. Muslim religious leaders, but also men who claim occult powers.   2. Potions. Casamance is in the southern part of Senegal, separated from the north by the Gambia. Diola and Madjago are ethnic groups. 3. In northern Senegal.   4. An ethnic group.

mouthfuls from the trough offered her. Her hunch about a gilded way of
life was being proved right. Her unsteady hut, with zinc walls covered with
magazine pages where pin-ups and advertisements were placed side by
side, had grown dim in her memory. One motion of her hand in her
bathroom and delicious jets of hot water would massage her back. Another
in the kitchen and ice cubes would cool the water in her glass. One more
and a flame would spring from the gas cooker and she would prepare
herself a delicious omelette.

The senior wife hitherto neglected, Lady Mother-in-Law emerged from
the shadows and took her unfaithful husband back in tow. She held valuable trump cards: grilled meats, roasted chicken and (why not?) banknotes
slipped into the pockets of the *boubou* hanging in the bedroom. She no
longer counted the cost of water bought from the Tukulor[5] hawker of the
vital liquid drawn from public springs. Having known poverty, she
rejoiced in her new-found happiness. Modou fulfilled her expectations.
He would thoughtfully send her wads of notes to spend and would offer
her, after his trips abroad, jewellery and rich *boubous*. From then on, she
joined the category of women "with heavy bracelets" lauded by the *griots*.
Thrilled, she would listen to the radio transmitting songs dedicated to
her.[6]

Her family reserved the best place for her during ceremonies and listened to her advice. When Modou's large car dropped her and she
emerged, there would be a rush of outstretched hands into which she
placed banknotes.

Reality was also Binetou, who went from night club to night club. She
would arrive draped in a long, costly garment, a gold belt, a present from
Modou on the birth of their first child, shining round her waist. Her shoes
tapped on the ground, announcing her presence. The waiters would move
aside and bow respectfully in the hope of a royal tip. With a contemptuous
look, she would eye those already seated. With a pout like that of a spoilt
child, she would indicate to Modou the table she had chosen. With a
wave of her hand, like a magician, she would have various bottles lined
up. She was showing off to the young people and wanted to impress them
with her form of success. Binetou, incontestably beautiful and desirable!
"Bewitching," people admitted. But when the moment of admiration
passed, she was the one who lowered her head at the sight of couples
graced with nothing but their youth and rich in their happiness alone.

The couples held each other or danced apart depending on the music,
sometimes slow and coaxing, sometimes vigorous and wild. When the
trumpet blared out, backed by the frenzy of the drums, the young dancers,
excited and untiring, would stamp, jump and caper about, shouting their
joy. Modou would try to follow suit. The harsh lights betrayed him to the
unpitying sarcasm of some of them, who called him a "cradle-snatcher."
What did it matter! He had Binetou in his arms. He was happy.

Worn out, Binetou would watch with a disillusioned eye the progress

---

5. An ethnic group related to the Fulani.   6. The praises of prominent people, sung by traditional
musicians, are often heard on the national radio.

of her friends. The image of her life, which she had murdered, broke her heart.

Sometimes also, despite my disapproval, Daba would go to the night clubs. Dressed simply, she would appear on her fiancé's arm; she would arrive late on purpose so as to sit in full view of her father. It was a grotesque confrontation: on one side, an ill-assorted couple, on the other two well-matched people.

And the evening created an extreme tension that opposed two former friends, a father and his daughter, a son-in-law and his father-in-law.

16

I was surviving. In addition to my former duties, I took over Modou's as well.

The purchase of basic foodstuffs kept me occupied at the end of every month; I made sure that I was never short of tomatoes or of oil, potatoes or onions during those periods when they became rare in the markets; I stored bags of "Siam" rice,[7] much loved by the Senegalese. My brain was taxed by new financial gymnastics.

The last date for payment of electricity bills and of water rates demanded my attention. I was often the only woman in the queue.[8]

Replacing the locks and latches of broken doors, replacing broken windows was a bother, as well as looking for a plumber to deal with blocked sinks. My son Mawdo Fall complained about burnt-out bulbs that needed replacement.

I survived. I overcame my shyness at going alone to cinemas; I would take a seat with less and less embarrassment as the months went by. People stared at the middle-aged lady without a partner. I would feign indifference, while anger hammered against my nerves and the tears I held back welled up behind my eyes.

From the surprised looks, I gauged the slender liberty granted to women.

The early shows at the cinema filled me with delight. They gave me the courage to meet the curious gaze of various people. They did not keep me away for long from my children.

What a great distraction from distress is the cinema! Intellectual films, those with a message, sentimental films, detective films, comedies, thrillers, all these were my companions. I learned from them lessons of greatness, courage and perseverance. They deepened and widened my vision of the world, thanks to their cultural value. The cinema, an inexpensive means of recreation, can thus give healthy pleasure.

I survived. The more I thought about it, the more grateful I became to Modou for having cut off all contact. I had the solution my children wanted—the break without having taken the initiative. The lie had not taken root. Modou was excising me from his life and was proving it by his unequivocal attitude.

---

7. A short-grained and broken rice used in the national dish.   8. Line.

What do other husbands do? They wallow in indecision; they force themselves to be present where neither their feelings nor their interests continue to reside. Nothing impresses them in their home: the wife all dressed up, the son full of tenderness, the meal tastefully served. They remain stolid, like marble. They wish only that the hours may pass rapidly. At night, feigning fatigue or illness, they snore deeply. How quick they are to greet the liberating daybreak, which puts an end to their torment!

I was not deceived, therefore. I no longer interested Modou, and I knew it. I was abandoned: a fluttering leaf that no hand dares to pick up, as my grandmother would have said.

I faced up to the situation bravely. I carried out my duties; they filled the time and channelled my thoughts. But my loneliness would emerge at night, burdensome. One does not easily undo the tenuous ties that bind two people together during a journey fraught with hardship. I lived the proof of it, bringing back to life past scenes, past conversations. Our common habits sprang up at their usual times. I missed dreadfully our nightly conversation; I missed our bursts of refreshing or understanding laughter. Like opium, I missed our daily consultations. I pitted myself against shadows. The wanderings of my thoughts chased away all sleep. I side-stepped my pain in a refusal to fight it.

The continuity of radio broadcasts was a great relief. I gave the radio the role of comforter. At night the music lulled my anxiety. I heard the message of old and new songs, which awakened hope. My sadness dissolved.

With all the force I had, I called eagerly to "another man" to replace Modou.

Distressing awakenings succeeded the nights. My love for my children sustained me. They were a pillar; I owed them help and affection.

Did Modou appreciate, in its full measure, the void created by his absence in this house? Did Modou attribute to me more energy than I had to shoulder the responsibility of my children?

I adopted a sprightly tone to rouse my battalion. The coffee warmed the atmosphere, exuding its sweet fragrance. Foaming baths, mutual teasing and laughter. A new day and increased efforts! A new day, and waiting. . . .

Waiting for what? It would not be easy to get my children to accept a new masculine presence. Having condemned their father, could they be tolerant towards another man? Besides, what man would have the courage to face twelve pairs of hostile eyes, which openly tear you apart?

Waiting! But waiting for what? I was not divorced . . . I was abandoned: a fluttering leaf that no hand dares to pick up, as my grandmother would have said.

I survived. I experienced the inadequacy of public transport. My children laughed at themselves in making this harsh discovery. One day, I heard Daba advise them: "Above all, don't let mum know that it is stifling in those buses during the rush hours."

I shed tears of joy and sadness together: joy in being loved by my children, the sadness of a mother who does not have the means to change the course of events.

I told you then, without any ulterior motive, of this painful aspect of our life, while Modou's car drove Lady Mother-in-Law to the four corners of town and while Binetou streaked along the roads in an Alfa Romeo, sometimes white, sometimes red.

I shall never forget your response, you, my sister, nor my joy and my surprise when I was called to the Fiat agency and was told to choose a car which you had paid for, in full. My children gave cries of joy when they learned of the approaching end of their tribulations, which remain the daily lot of a good many other students.

Friendship has splendours that love knows not. It grows stronger when crossed, whereas obstacles kill love. Friendship resists time, which wearies and severs couples. It has heights unknown to love.

You, the goldsmith's daughter, gave me your help while depriving yourself.

And I learned to drive, stifling my fear. The narrow space between the wheel and the seat was mine. The flattened clutch glided in the gears. The brake reduced the forward thrust and, to speed along, I had to step on the accelerator. I did not trust the accelerator. At the slightest pressure from my feet, the car lurched forward. My feet learned to dance over the pedals. Whenever I was discouraged, I would say: Why should Binetou sit behind a wheel and not I? I would tell myself: Don't disappoint Aissatou. I won this battle of nerves and *sang-froid*.[9] I obtained my driving licence and told you about it.

I told you: and now—my children on the backseat of the cream-coloured Fiat 125; thanks to you, my children can look the affluent mother-in-law and the fragile child in the eye in the streets of the town.

Modou surprised, unbelieving, inquired into the source of the car. He never accepted the true story. Like Mawdo's mother, he too believed that a goldsmith's daughter had no heart.

17

I take a deep breath.

I've related at one go your story as well as mine. I've said the essential, for pain, even when it's past, leaves the same marks on the individual when recalled. Your disappointment was mine, as my rejection was yours. Forgive me once again if I have re-opened your wound. Mine continues to bleed.

You may tell me: the path of life is not smooth; one is bruised by its sharp edges. I also know that marriage is never smooth. It reflects differences in character and capacity for feeling. In one couple the man may be the victim of a fickle woman or of a woman shut up in her own preoccupations who rejects all dialogue and quashes all moves towards tenderness. In another couple alcoholism is the leprosy that gnaws away at health, wealth and peace. It shows up an individual's disordered state through grotesque spectacles by which his dignity is undermined, in situations where physical blows become solid arguments and the menacing blade of a knife an irresistible call for silence.

9. Calm demeanor.

With others it is the lure of easy gain that dominates: incorrigible players at the gaming table or seated in the shade of a tree. The heated atmosphere of rooms full of fiendish odours, the distorted faces of tense players.
The giddy whirl of playing cards swallows up time, wealth, conscience,
and stops only with the last breath of the person accustomed to shuffling
them.

I try to spot my faults in the failure of my marriage. I gave freely, gave
more than I received. I am one of those who can realize themselves fully
and bloom only when they form part of a couple. Even though I understand your stand, even though I respect the choice of liberated women, I
have never conceived of happiness outside marriage.

I loved my house. You can testify to the fact that I made it a haven of
peace where everything had its place, that I created a harmonious symphony of colours. You know how soft-hearted I am, how much I loved
Modou. You can testify to the fact that, mobilized day and night in his
service, I anticipated his slightest desire.

I made peace with his family. Despite his desertion of our home, his
father and mother and Tamsir, his brother, still continued to visit me
often, as did his sisters. My children too grew up without much ado. Their
success at school was my pride, just like laurels thrown at the feet of my
lord and master.

And Modou was no prisoner. He spent his time as he wished. I well
understood his desire to let off steam. He fulfilled himself outside as he
wished in his trade union activities.

I am trying to pinpoint any weakness in the way I conducted myself.
My social life may have been stormy and perhaps injured Modou's trade
union career. Can a man, deceived and flouted by his family, impose
himself on others? Can a man whose wife does not do her job well honestly demand a fair reward for labour? Aggression and condescension in a
woman arouse contempt and hatred for her husband. If she is gracious,
even without appealing to any ideology, she can summon support for any
action. In a word, a man's success depends on feminine support.

And I ask myself. I ask myself, why? Why did Modou detach himself?
Why did he put Binetou between us?

You, very logically, may reply: "Affections spring from nothing; sometimes a grimace, the carriage of a head can seduce a heart and keep it."

I ask myself questions. The truth is that, despite everything, I remain
faithful to the love of my youth. Aissatou, I cry for Modou, and I can do
nothing about it.

18

Yesterday I celebrated, as is the custom, the fortieth day of Modou's
death. I have forgiven him. May God hear the prayer I say for him every
day. I celebrated the fortieth day in meditation. The initiated read the
Koran. Their fervent voices rose towards heaven. Modou Fall, may God
accept you among his chosen few.

After going through the motions of piety, Tamsir came and sat in my bedroom in the blue armchair that used to be your favourite. Sticking his head outside, he signalled to Mawdo; he also signalled to the *Imam* from the mosque in his area. The *Imam* and Mawdo joined him. This time, Tamsir speaks. There is a striking resemblance between Modou and Tamsir, the same tics donated by the inexplicable law of heredity. Tamsir speaks with great assurance; he touches, once again, on my years of marriage, then he concludes: "When you have 'come out' (that is to say, of mourning), I shall marry you.[1] You suit me as a wife, and further, you will continue to live here, just as if Modou were not dead. Usually it is the younger brother who inherits his elder brother's wife. In this case, it is the opposite. You are my good luck. I shall marry you. I prefer you to the other one, too frivolous, too young. I advised Modou against that marriage."

What a declaration of love, full of conceit, in a house still in mourning. What assurance and calm aplomb! I look Tamsir straight in the eye. I look at Mawdo. I look at the *Imam*. I draw my black shawl closer. I tell my beads. This time I shall speak out.

My voice has known thirty years of silence, thirty years of harassment. It bursts out, violent, sometimes sarcastic, sometimes contemptuous.

"Did you ever have any affection for your brother? Already you want to build a new home for yourself, over a body that is still warm. While we are praying for Modou, you are thinking of future wedding festivities.

"Ah, yes! Your strategy is to get in before any other suitor, to get in before Mawdo, the faithful friend, who has more qualities than you and who also, according to custom, can inherit the wife. You forget that I have a heart, a mind, that I am not an object to be passed from hand to hand. You don't know what marriage means to me: it is an act of faith and of love, the total surrender of oneself to the person one has chosen and who has chosen you." (I emphasized the word "chosen".)

"What of your wives, Tamsir? Your income can meet neither their needs nor those of your numerous children. To help you out with your financial obligations, one of your wives dyes, another sells fruit, the third untiringly turns the handle of her sewing machine. You, the revered lord, you take it easy, obeyed at the crook of a finger. I shall never be the one to complete your collection. My house shall never be for you the coveted oasis: no extra burden; my 'turn' every day;[2] cleanliness and luxury, abundance and calm! No Tamsir!

"And then there are Daba and her husband, who have demonstrated their financial acumen by buying up all your brother's properties. What promotion for you! Your friends are going to look at you with envy in their eyes."

Mawdo signalled with his hand for me to stop. "Shut up! Shut up! Stop! Stop!"

But you can't stop once you've let your anger loose. I concluded, more violent than ever: "Tamsir, purge yourself of your dreams of conquest. They have lasted forty days. I shall never be your wife."

---

1. According to traditional custom (the levirate), a man could marry his brother's widow.   2. The man must spend an equal number of nights with each of his wives in turn.

The *Imam* prayed God to be his witness.

"Such profane words and still in mourning!" Tamsir got up without a word. He understood fully that he'd been defeated.

Thus I took my revenge for that other day when all three of them had airily informed me of the marriage of Modou Fall and Binetou.

19

Aissatou, even in my mourning clothes I have no peace of mind.

After Tamsir, Daouda Dieng. . . . You remember Daouda Dieng, my former suitor. To his maturity I had preferred inexperience, to his generosity, poverty, to his gravity, spontaneity, to his stability, adventure.

He came to Modou's funeral. In the envelope that he gave Fatim there was a large sum of money. And his look was insistent, saying a great deal— of course.

Where he is concerned, I believe to be true what he used to tell us jokingly, whenever by chance we met again: one never forgets a first love.

After Tamsir, eliminated that memorable day when I quelled his lust for conquest; after Tamsir, then, Daouda Dieng, a candidate for my hand! Daouda Dieng was my mother's favourite. I can still hear her persuasive voice advise me: a woman must marry the man who loves her but never the one she loves; that is the secret of lasting happiness.

Daouda Dieng had kept himself well, compared with Mawdo and Modou. Just on the threshold of old age, he had resisted the repeated attacks of time and exertion. He was elegantly dressed in a suit of embroidered brocade; he remained the same well-groomed man, meticulous and close-shaved. He wore his social success boldly but without condescension.

Although a deputy at the National Assembly,[3] he remained accessible, with gestures that lent weight to his opinions. His lightly silvered hair gave him unquestionable charm.

For the last three years he had commanded attention in the political race through the sobriety of his actions and the precision of his words. His car, with its distinctive cockade[4] in the national colours, was parked on the opposite pavement.

How much I preferred his emotion to Tamsir's confident arrogance! His trembling lips betrayed him. His look swept over my face. I took refuge in banalities: "How is Aminata (his wife)? And the children? And your clinic? What's it like at the National Assembly?"

My questions came uninterrupted, as much to put him at ease as to renew the dialogue that had for so long been cut off. He replied briefly. But my last question provoked a shrug of the shoulders, to signify "It's all right," said challengingly.

I went on: "It must be all right, that male Assembly!"

I said it teasingly, rolling my eyes round. Eternal woman: even in mourning, you want to make a strike, you want to seduce, you want to arouse interest!

---

3. The legislative body. *Deputy:* an elected position. 4. Here, a ribbon tied to a part of the car.

Daouda was no fool. He knew very well that I wanted to relieve him of his embarrassment and to draw back the curtain of silence and constraint that separated us, created by the long years and my former refusal to marry him.

"Still very critical, Ramatoulaye! Why this ironical statement and this provocative epithet when there are women in the Assembly?"

"Four women, Daouda, four out of a hundred deputies. What a ridiculous ratio! Not even one for each province."

Daouda laughed, an open, communicative laugh, which I found stimulating.

We laughed noisily together. I saw again his beautiful set of teeth, capped with the circumflex accent of a black moustache, combed and very sleek. Ah! those teeth, set close together, had won my mother's confidence!

"But you women, you are like mortar shells. You demolish. You destroy. Imagine a large number of women in the Assembly. Why, everything would explode, go up in flames."

And we laughed again.

Wrinkling my brow, I commented: "But we are not incendiaries; rather, we are stimulants!" And I pressed on: "In many fields, and without skirmishes, we have taken advantage of the notable achievements that have reached us from elsewhere, the gains wrested from the lessons of history. We have a right, just as you have, to education, which we ought to be able to pursue to the furthest limits of our intellectual capacities. We have a right to equal well-paid employment, to equal opportunities. The right to vote is an important weapon. And now the Family Code[5] has been passed, restoring to the most humble of women the dignity that has so often been trampled upon.

"But Daouda, the constraints remain; but Daouda, old beliefs are revived; but Daouda, egoism emerges, scepticism rears its head in the political field. You want to make it a closed shop and you huff and puff about it.

"Nearly twenty years of independence! When will we have the first female minister involved in the decisions concerning the development of our country? And yet the militancy and ability of our women, their disinterested commitment, have already been demonstrated. Women have raised more than one man to power."

Daouda listened to me. But I had the impression that more than my ideas, it was my voice that captivated him.

And I continued: "When will education be decided for children on the basis not of sex but of talent?"

Daouda Dieng was savouring the warmth of the inner dream he was spinning around me. As for me, I was bolting like a horse that has long been tethered and is now free and revelling in space. Ah, the joy of having an interlocutor before you, especially an admirer!

I had remained the same Ramatoulaye . . . a bit of a rebel.

I drew Daouda Dieng along with my ardour. He was an upright man,

5. A law passed in the 1970s, which gives legal protection to women in the event of divorce.

and each time the situation demanded, he would fight for social justice. It was not love of show or money that had driven him towards politics, but his true love for his fellow man, the urge to redress wrongs and injustice.

"Whom are you addressing, Ramatoulaye? You are echoing my speeches at the National Assembly, where I have been called a 'feminist.' I am not, in fact, the only one to insist on changing the rules of the game and injecting new life into it. Women should no longer be decorative accessories, objects to be moved about, companions to be flattered or calmed with promises. Women are the nation's primary, fundamental root, from which all else grows and blossoms. Women must be encouraged to take a keener interest in the destiny of the country. Even you who are protesting; you preferred your husband, your class, your children to public life. If men alone are active in the parties, why should they think of the women? It is only human to give yourself the larger portion of the cake when you are sharing it out.

"Don't be self-centred in your reaction. Consider the situation of every one of the country's citizens. No one is well-off, not even those of us who are considered to be secure and financially sound, when in fact all our savings go towards the maintenance of an avid electoral clientele which believes itself to be our promoters. Developing a country is not easy. The more responsibility one has, the more one feels it; poverty breaks your heart, but you have no control over it. I am speaking of the whole range of material and moral poverty. Better living requires roads, decent houses, wells, clinics, medicines, seeds. I am one of those who advocated that independence celebrations should be rotated annually among the regions. Any initiative that enables regional investments and transformations is welcome.

"We need money, a mountain of money, which we must get from others by winning their confidence. With just one rainy season and our single crop,[6] Senegal will not go far despite all our determination."

Night fell quickly from the skies, in a hurry to darken men and things. It came through the venetian blinds in the sitting-room. The *muezzin's* invitation to the *Timiss* prayer[7] was persuasive; Ousmane stood on tiptoe and flicked on the switch. There was a sudden flood of light.

Daouda, well aware of the constraints of my situation, got up. He lifted Ousmane up towards the lamp, and Ousmane chuckled, arms stretched. He let him down. "Till tomorrow," he said. "I came to discuss something else. You led me into a political discussion. Every discussion is profitable. Till tomorrow," he repeated.

He smiled: neat rows of good teeth. He smiled and opened the door. I heard his footsteps recede. A moment later the humming of his powerful car carried him homewards.

What will he say to Aminata, his wife and cousin, to justify his lateness? . . .

Daouda Dieng did indeed come back the next day. But unfortunately for him, and fortunately for me, my maternal aunts were visiting me and

---

6. Peanuts. 7. One of the required daily prayers in Muslim life, said around 7:00 P.M. *Muezzin:* the one who calls the faithful to prayer in Muslim countries.

he was prevented from expressing himself freely. He did not dare to stay too long.

20

Today is Friday. I've taken a refreshing bath. I can feel its revitalizing effect, which, through my open pores, soothes me.

The smell of soap surrounds me. Clean clothes replace my crumpled ones. The cleanliness of my body pleases me. I think that as she is the object of attraction for so many eyes, cleanliness is one of the essential qualities of a woman. The most humble of huts is pleasing when it is clean; the most luxurious setting offers no attraction if it is right in dust.

Those women we call "house"-wives deserve praise. The domestic work they carry out, and which is not paid in hard cash, is essential to the home. Their compensation remains the pile of well ironed, sweet-smelling washing, the shining tiled floor on which the foot glides, the gay kitchen filled with the smell of stews. Their silent action is felt in the least useful detail: over there, a flower in bloom placed in a vase, elsewhere a painting with appropriate colours, hung up in the right place.

The management of the home is an art. We have learned the hard way, and it is still not over. Even deciding on the menus is not easy if one thinks of the number of days there are in a year and of the fact that there are three meals in one day. Managing the family budget requires flexibility, vigilance and prudence in performing the financial gymnastics that send you from one more or less dangerous leap to another, from the first to the last day of the month.

To be a woman! To live the life of a woman!

Ah, Aissatou!

Tonight I am restless. The flavour of life is love. The salt of life is also love.

Daouda came back. An outfit of blue brocade had replaced the grey outfit of the first visit and the chocolate-coloured one of the second.

He began right at the doorway, in the same tone of voice as I had used at our first meeting, without stopping for breath: "How are you? And the children, and your Assembly? And what about Ousmane?" Hearing his name, Ousmane appeared, his mouth and cheeks covered with the chocolate he munched all day long.

Daouda grabbed hold of this little slip of a man, who struggled and kicked his legs about. He let him go with a friendly tap on his buttocks and a picture book in his hands. Ousmane, shouting with joy, ran to show his present to the household. "No visitors? I shall lead the discussion today ... I from the male Assembly." He laughed maliciously. "Don't think that I criticize just for the fun of it. Our incipient democracy, which is changing the situation of the citizen and for which your party may take much credit, appeals to me. Socialism, which is the heart of your action, is the expression of my deepest aspirations if it is adapted to the realities of our life, as your political secretary claims. The openings it has created are considerable, and Senegal offers a new prospect of liberty regained. I appreciate all that, especially when all around us, to our right and to our left, one-party systems have been imposed. A single party never expresses the unanimous view of the citizens. If all individuals were made in the same mould, it would lead to an appalling collectivism. Differences produce conflicts, which may be beneficial to the development of a country if they occur among true patriots, whose only ambition is the happiness of the citizen.

"But enough of politics, Ramatoulaye. I refuse to go along with you, like the other day. I have had my fill of 'democracy,' 'struggle,' 'freedom' and what have you, all those expressions that float about me daily. Enough, Ramatoulaye. Listen to me, rather. The bush radio[8] has informed me of your refusal to marry Tamsir. Is it true?"

"Yes."

"I, in turn, and for the second time in my life, have come to ask for your hand . . . after you are out of mourning, of course. I have the same feeling for you as I had before. Separation, your marriage, my own, none of these has been able to sap my love for you. Indeed, separation has made it keener; time has consolidated it; my advance in years has purified it. I love you dearly, but with my head. You are a widow with young children. I am head of a family. Each of us has the weight of the 'past' to help us in understanding each other. I open my arms to you for new-found happiness; will you accept?"

I opened my eyes wide, not in astonishment—a woman can always predict a declaration of this kind—but in a kind of stupor. Ah yes, Aissatou, those well-worn words, which have for long been used and are still being used, had taken root in me. Their sweetness, of which I had been deprived for years, intoxicated me: I feel no shame in admitting it to you.

Very reasonably, the deputy concluded: "Don't give me an answer immediately. Think about my proposal. I shall come back tomorrow at the same time."

And, as if embarrassed by his own revelations, Daouda went away, after flashing a smile at me.

My neighbour, Farmata, the *griot* woman, dashed in after him, excited. She was always trying to see into the future with her cowries, and the least agreement of her predictions with reality thrilled her.

"I met the strong, rich man with the 'double trousers' seen in the cowries. He gave me five thousand francs."

She blinked her deep, piercing eyes that were always trying to probe into mysteries.

"I have given the recommended alms of two white and red cola nuts," she confessed to me. "Our destinies are linked. Your shade protects me. You don't fell the tree whose shade protects you. You water it. You watch over it."

Dear Farmata, how far from my thoughts you were! The restlessness with which I was struggling and which you had foreseen did not in the least signify the anguish of love.

8. The grapevine, rumor.

21

Tomorrow? What a short time for reflection, for the decisive commit-ment of a life, especially when that life has known, in the recent past, the bitter tears of disappointment! I still have a vision of the intelligent eye of Daouda Dieng, the pout of the stubborn lips, which contrasted with the gentleness emanating from his profoundly charitable person, who saw only the best in people and ignored the rest. I could read him like an open book in which each sign was a symbol, but an easily interpreted symbol.

My heart no longer beats wildly in the whirl of the spoken words. I am touched by the sincerity of words, but I am not carried away by it; my euphoria, born of the hunger and thirst for tenderness, fades away as the hours dance past.

I cannot put out any flags. The proposed celebration does not tempt me. My heart does not love Daouda Dieng. My mind appreciates the man. But heart and mind often disagree.

How I should have liked to be galvanized in favour of this man, to be able to say yes! It is not that the memory of the deceased lies heavy within me. The dead have only the weight conceded to them or the weight of the good they have done. It is not that the presence of my young children poses a problem; he could have filled the role of the father who had aban-doned them. Thirty years later, my own personal refusal is the only thing that conditions me. I have no definable reason. Our currents are opposed. Daouda Dieng's reputation for seriousness has already been established.

A good husband? Yes. Public rumour, so wicked and thirsty for gossip where personalities are concerned, has never mentioned any goings-on of his. His wife and cousin, whom he married five years after my marriage out of his duty as a citizen and not out of love (another male expression to explain a natural action), has borne his children. Wife and children, placed by this dutiful man on a pedestal of respectability, offered him an enviable refuge, the outcome of his own effort.

He never accepted any honour without associating his wife with it. He involved her in his political actions, his numerous travels, the various sponsorships for which he was canvassed and which increased his electoral constituency.

Before leaving, Farmata, the *griot* woman of the cowries, had said: "Your mother was right. Daouda is wonderful. What *guer*[9] gives five thou-sand francs today! Daouda has neither exchanged his wife nor abandoned his children; if he has come back looking for you, you, an old woman burdened with a family, it is because he loves you; he can look after you and your family. Think about it. Accept."

All the trump cards! But what do these count for in the uncontrollable law of attraction! So as not to hurt him under my roof, I sent Farmata, the *griot* woman of the cowries, with a sealed envelope for him, with the fol-lowing instructions. "This letter must be given to him personally, away from his wife and children."

9. Nobleman.

For the first time, I was turning to Farmata for help, and this embarrassed me. She was happy, having dreamed of this role right from our youth. But I always acted alone; she was never a participant in my problems, only informed—just like any "vulgar acquaintance," she would complain. She was thrilled, ignorant of the cruel message she was bearing.

Daouda's clinic was not far from the Villa Fallene. There was a stop for the *cars rapides*[1] just a few metres from his doorstep.

This clinic, set up with a bank loan granted by the state to those doctors and pharmacists who expressed the desire for it, enabled Daouda Dieng to continue practising his profession. He had understood that a doctor could not abandon his call: "A doctor's training is slow, long, taxing, and they are not two a penny either; they are more useful in their profession than anywhere else; if they can combine their job with other activities, so much the better; but what insensitivity, to give up looking after others for something else!" Thus would Daouda explain himself to our mutual friends, such as Mawdo Bâ and Samba Diack, his colleagues.

Farmata, therefore, patiently waited her turn and, once in front of Daouda in the consulting room, she handed the envelope over to him. Daouda read:

> Daouda,
> You are chasing after a woman who has remained the same, Daouda, despite the intense ravages of suffering.
> You who have loved me, who love me still—I don't doubt it—try to understand me. My conscience is not accommodating enough to enable me to marry you, when only esteem, justified by your many qualities, pulls me towards you. I can offer you nothing else, even though you deserve everything. Esteem is not enough for marriage, whose snares I know from experience. And then the existence of your wife and children further complicates the situation. Abandoned yesterday because of a woman, I cannot lightly bring myself between you and your family.
> You think the problem of polygamy is a simple one. Those who are involved in it know the constraints, the lies, the injustices that weigh down their consciences in return for the ephemeral joys of change. I am sure you are motivated by love, a love that existed well before your marriage and that fate has not been able to satisfy. It is with infinite sadness and tear-filled eyes that I offer you my friendship. Dear Daouda, please accept it. It is with great pleasure that I shall continue to welcome you to my house.
> Shall I hope to see you again?
>   Ramatoulaye

Farmata, who had smiled in handing over her letter, told me how her smile soured on her face as Daouda read. Then instinct and observation brought a look of sadness to her face, for Daouda wrinkled his eyebrows, creased his forehead, bit his lips and sighed.

Daouda put down my letter. Calmly, he stuffed an envelope with a wad of blue notes. He scrawled on a piece of paper the terrible words that had separated us before and that he had acquired during his medical course: "All or nothing. Adieu."

Aissatou, Daouda Dieng never came back again.

---

1. Vans used for public transport in Senegal. Villa Fallene is the compound of the Falls, her husband's family; this is Ramatoulaye's residence.

"Bissimilai! Bissimilai![2] What was it you dared to write and make me messenger of? You have killed a man. His crestfallen face cried it out to me. You have rejected the messenger sent to you by God to reward you for your sufferings. God will punish you for not having followed the path towards peace. You have refused greatness! You shall live in mud. I wish you another Modou to make you shed tears of blood.

"Who do you take yourself for? At fifty, you have dared to break the *wolere*.[3] You trample upon your luck: Daouda Dieng, a rich man, a deputy, a doctor, of your own age group, with just one wife. He offers you security, love, and you refuse! Many women, of Daba's age even, would wish to be in your place.

"You boast of reasons. You speak of love instead of bread. Madame wants her heart to miss a beat. Why not flowers, just like in the films?

"Bissimilai! Bissimilai! You so withered, you want to choose a husband like an eighteen-year-old girl. Life will spring a surprise on you and then, Ramatoulaye, you will bite your fingers. I don't know what Daouda has written. But there is money in the envelope. He is a true *samba linguere*[4] from the olden days. May God satisfy, gratify Daouda Dieng. My heart is with him."

Such was Farmata's tirade on her return from her mission. She thoroughly upset me. The truth of this woman, a childhood companion through the long association of our families, could not hold good for me, even in its logic of concern. . . . Once more, I was refusing the easy way because of my ideal. I went back to my loneliness, which a momentary flash had brightened briefly. I wore it again, as one wears a familiar garment. Its cut suited me well. I moved easily in it, despite Farmata. I wanted "something else". And this "something else" was impossible without the full agreement of my heart.

Tamsir and Daouda having been rejected, there were no more barriers between the suitors and me. I then watched filing past and besieging me old men in search of easy revenue, young men in search of adventure to occupy their leisure. My successive refusals gave me in town the reputation of a "lioness" or "mad woman."

Who let loose this greedy pack of hounds after me? For my charms had faded with the many maternities, with time, with the tears. Ah! the inheritance, the fat share acquired by my daughter Daba and her husband and put at my disposal.

They had led the fight for the distribution of Modou's estate. My son-in-law laid down on the table the advance for the SICAP villa and five years' rent.

The SICAP villa went to my daughter, who, with the bailiff's affidavit in hand, listed the contents and bought it.

The story of the Villa Fallene was easy to relate: the land and building represented a bank loan granted ten years ago on the security of our joint salaries. The contents, renewed two years ago, belonged to me, and to

---

2. An exclamation of surprise (Arabic).   3. A moral obligation.   4. Gentleman.

support this claim, I produced the receipts. There remained Modou's clothes: those that I recognized because I had chosen and cared for them; and the others . . . from the second part of his life. I found it difficult to imagine him in this get-up of a young wolf. . . . They were distributed to his family.

The jewels and presents given to Lady Mother-in-Law and her daughter were theirs by right.

Lady Mother-in-Law hiccoughed, cried. She was being stripped, and she asked for mercy. She did not want to move out. . . .

But Daba is like all the young, without pity.

"Remember, I was your daughter's best friend. You made her my mother's rival. Remember. For five years you deprived my mother and her twelve children of their breadwinner. Remember. My mother has suffered a great deal. How can a woman sap the happiness of another? You deserve no pity. Pack up. As for Binetou, she is a victim, your victim. I feel sorry for her."

Lady Mother-in-Law sobbed. Binetou? Indifference itself. What did it matter to her what was being said? She was already dead inside . . . ever since her marriage to Modou.

22

I feel an immense fatigue. It begins in my soul and weighs down my body.

Ousmane, my last born, holds out your letter to me. Ousmane is six years old. "It's Aunty Aissatou."

He has the privilege of bringing me all your letters. How does he recognize them? By their stamp? By their envelope? By the careful writing, characteristic of you? By the scent of lavender emanating from them? Children have clues different from our own. Ousmane enjoys his find. He exults in it.

These caressing words, which relax me, are indeed from you. And you tell me of the "end." I calculate. Tomorrow is indeed the end of my seclusion. And you will be there within reach of my hand, my voice, my eyes.

"End or new beginning?" My eyes will discover the slightest change in you. I have already totalled up my own; my seclusion has withered me. Worries have given me wrinkles; my fat has melted away. I often tap against bone where before there was rounded flesh.

When we meet, the signs on our bodies will not be important. The essential thing is the content of our hearts, which animates us; the essential thing is the quality of the sap that flows through us. You have often proved to me the superiority of friendship over love. Time, distance, as well as mutual memories have consolidated our ties and made our children brothers and sisters. Reunited, will we draw up a detailed account of our faded bloom, or will we sow new seeds for new harvests?

I hear Daba's footsteps. She is back from the Blaise Diagne[5] secondary

---

5. The first elected African deputy in the French parliament (he served from 1914 to 1934).

school, where she has been representing me in answer to a summons. A
conflict between my son, Mawdo Fall, and his philosophy teacher. They
clash frequently when the time comes to return corrected essays.

As you know, there is a substantial age gap between Daba and Mawdo
Fall, the result of two miscarriages.

This clash, which Daba is trying to resolve, is the third within six
months in this form. Mawdo Fall has a remarkable gift for literary work.
Right from Form One, he has been top of his class in this subject; but this
year for every capital letter forgotten, for a few commas omitted, for a
misspelt word, his teacher knocks off one or two marks. Because of this,
Jean-Claude, a white boy who has always come second, has moved up to
first position. The teacher cannot tolerate a black coming first in philosophy. And Mawdo Fall complains.

This always ends in a quarrel and a summons.

Daba was ready to tell the teacher off, and no nonsense. But I calmed
her down. Life is an eternal compromise. What is important is the examination paper. . . . This, too, will be at the mercy of the marker. No one
will have any say over him. So why fight a teacher for one or two marks
that can never change the destiny of a student?

I always tell my children: you are students maintained by your parents.
Work hard so as to merit their sacrifices. Cultivate yourselves instead of
protesting. When you are adults, if your opinions are to carry weight, they
must be based on knowledge backed by diplomas. A diploma is not
a myth. It is not everything, true. But it crowns knowledge, work. Tomorrow, you will be able to elect to power anyone of your choice, anyone
you find suitable. It is your choice, and not ours, that will direct the
country.

Now our society is shaken to its very foundations, torn between the
attraction of imported vices and the fierce resistance of old virtues.

The dream of a rapid social climb prompts parents to give their children
more knowledge than education. Pollution seeps in through hearts as well
as into the air.

"Phased out" or "outdated," perhaps even "old fogies," we belong to the
past. But all four of us were made of stern stuff, with upright minds full of
intense questionings that stuck within our inner selves, not without pain.
Aissatou, no matter how unhappy the outcome of our unions, our husbands were great men. They led the struggle of their lives, even if success
eluded their grasp; one does not easily overcome the burdens of a thousand years.

I observe the young. Where are those bright eyes, prompt to react when
scorned honour demands redress? Where is the vigorous pride that guides
a whole community towards its duty? The appetite to live kills the dignity
of living.

You can see that I digress from the problem of Mawdo Fall.

The headmaster of the school certainly understands the Mawdo Fall-
teacher conflict. But you try to side with a student against his teacher!

Daba is here beside me, lighthearted, smiling with all her teeth at a
mission successfully accomplished.

Daba does not find household work a burden. Her husband cooks rice as well as she does; her husband who claims, when I tell him he "spoils" his wife: "Daba is my wife. She is not my slave, nor my servant."

I sense the tenderness growing between this young couple, an ideal couple, just as I have always imagined. They identify with each other, discuss everything so as to find a compromise.

All the same, I fear for Daba. Life holds many surprises. When I discuss it with her, she shrugs her shoulders: "Marriage is no chain. It is mutual agreement over a life's programme. So if one of the partners is no longer satisfied with the union, why should he remain? It may be Abou (her husband); it may be me. Why not? The wife can take the initiative to make the break."

She reasons everything out, that child. . . . She often tells me: "I don't want to go into politics; it's not that I am not interested in the fate of my country and, most especially, that of women. But when I look at the fruit-less wranglings even within the ranks of the same party, when I see men's greed for power, I prefer not to participate. No, I am not afraid of ideological struggle, but in a political party it is rare for a woman to make an easy break-through. For a long time men will continue to have the power of decision, whereas everyone knows that polity should be the affair of women. No: I prefer my own association, where there is neither rivalry nor schism, neither malice nor jostling for position; there are no posts to be shared, nor positions to be secured. The headship changes every year. Each of us has equal opportunity to advance her ideas. We are given tasks according to our abilities in our activities and organizations that work towards the progress of women. Our funds go towards humanitarian work; we are mobilized by a militancy as useful as any other, but it is a healthy militancy, whose only reward is inner satisfaction."

She reasoned everything out, that child . . . She had her own opinions about everything.

I look at her, Daba, my eldest child, who has helped me so admirably with her brothers and sisters. It is Aissatou, your namesake, who has taken over from her the running of the house.

Aissatou washes the youngest ones: Omar, eight years old, and Ous-mane, your friend. The others can manage well enough on their own. Aissatou is helped in her task by Amy and her twin sister Awa, whom she is training.

My twins are so similar that I sometimes confuse them. They are mis-chievous and play tricks on everybody. Aminata works better than Awa. Physically so similar, why are they so different in character?

The upkeep and education of young children do not pose serious prob-lems; washed, fed, cared for, supervised, my own are growing well—with, of course, the nearly daily battle against sores, colds, headaches, in which I excel, simply from having had to struggle.

It is Mawdo Bâ who comes to my aid during the serious illnesses. Even though I criticize him for his weakness, which broke up your relationship, I praise him very sincerely for the help he gives me. Despite his friend Modou's desertion of our home, I can still wake him up, at no matter what hour.

23

My grown children are causing me a great deal of concern. My worries pale when I recall my grandmother, who found in popular wisdom an appropriate dictum for each event. She liked to repeat: "The mother of a family has no time to travel. But she has time to die." She would lament when, despite her sleepiness, she still had to carry out her share of the duties: "Ah, if only I had a bed on which to lie down."

Mischievously, I would point to the three beds in her room. In irritation, she would say: "You have your life before and not behind you. May God grant that you experience what I have gone through." And here I am today, "going through" just that experience.

I thought a child was born and grew up without any problem. I thought one mapped out a straight path and that he would step lightly down it. I now saw, at first hand, the truth of my grandmother's prophecies: "The fact that children are born of the same parents does not necessarily mean that they will resemble each other."

"Being born of the same parents is just like spending the night in the same bedroom."

To allay the fear of the future that her words might possibly have aroused, my grandmother would offer some solutions: "Different personalities require different forms of discipline. Strictness here, comprehension there. Smacking, which is successful with the very young ones, annoys the older ones. The nerves daily undergo severe trials! But that is the mother's lot."

Courageous grandmother, I drew from your teaching and example the courage that galvanizes one at the times when difficult choices have to be made.

The other night I surprised the trio (as they are popularly known), Arame, Yacine and Dieynaba, smoking in their bedroom. Everything about their manner showed that they were used to it: their way of holding the cigarette between their fingers or raising it gracefully to their lips, of inhaling like connoisseurs. Their nostrils quivered and let out the smoke. And these young ladies inhaled and exhaled while doing their lessons and their homework. They savoured their pleasure greedily, behind the closed door, for I try, as much as possible, to respect their privacy.

People say that Dieynaba, Arame and Yacine take after me. They are bound by their friendship and willingness to help, as well as by a multitude of similarities; they form a block, with the same defensive or distrustful reactions, before my other children; they swop dresses, trousers, tops, being nearly the same size. I have never had to intervene in their conflicts. The trio has a reputation for hard work at school.

But to grant themselves the right to smoke! They were dumbfounded before my anger. The unexpectedness of it gave me a shock. A woman's mouth exhaling the acrid smell of tobacco instead of being fragrant. A woman's teeth blackened with tobacco instead of sparkling with whiteness! Yet their teeth were white. How did they manage the feat?

I considered the wearing of trousers dreadful in view of our build, which is not that of slim Western women. Trousers accentuate the ample figure of the black woman and further emphasize the curve of the small of the back. But I gave in to the rush towards this fashion, which constricted and hampered instead of liberating. Since my daughters wanted to be "with it," I accepted the addition of trousers to their wardrobes.

Suddenly I became afraid of the flow of progress. Did they also drink? Who knows, one vice leads to another. Does it mean that one can't have modernism without a lowering of moral standards?

Was I to blame for having given my daughters a bit of liberty? My grandfather did not allow young people in his house. At ten o'clock at night, with a bell in his hand, he would warn visitors of the closure of the entrance gate. He punctuated the ringing of the bell with the same instruction: "Whoever does not live here should scram."

As for myself, I let my daughters go out from time to time. They went to the cinema without me. They received male and female friends. There were arguments to justify my behaviour. Unquestionably, at a certain age, a boy or girl opens up to love. I wanted my daughters to discover it in a healthy way, without feelings of guilt, secretiveness or degradation. I tried to penetrate their relationships: I created a favourable atmosphere for sensible behaviour and for confidence.

And the result is that under the influence of their circle they have acquired the habit of smoking. And I was left in the dark, I who wanted to control everything. My grandmother's wise words came to mind: "You can feed your stomach as well as you please; it will still provide for itself without your knowing."

I had to do some thinking. There was a need for some reorganization to stop the rot. My grandmother would perhaps have suggested, "For a new generation, a new method."

I did not mind being a "stick-in-the-mud." I was aware of the harmful effects of tobacco, and I could not agree to its use. My conscience rejected it, as it rejected alcohol.

From then on, relentlessly, I was on the lookout for its odour. It played hide-and-seek with my watchfulness. Sly and ironic, it would tease my nostrils and then disappear. Its favourite hiding place was the toilet, especially at night. But it no longer dared to expose itself openly, with jaunty shamelessness.

24

Today I was not able to finish my evening prayer as I wanted to: cries from the street made me jump up from the mat on which I was seated.

Standing on the veranda, I see my sons Alioune and Malick arriving in tears. They are in a pitiable state: torn clothes, bodies covered in dust from a fall, knees bleeding beneath the shorts. There is a large hole in the right sleeve of Malick's sweater; the arm on the same side hangs down limply. One of the boys supporting him explains to me: "A motorcyclist knocked down Malick and Alioune. We were playing football."[6]

A young man with long hair, white glasses, amulets round the neck, moves forward. The grey dust from the road covers his denim outfit.

6. That is, soccer.

Mauled by the children for whom he has become the target, a red wound on his leg, he is visibly taken aback by so much hostility. In a polite tone and manner, which contrast with his slovenly appearance, he offers his excuses: "I saw the children too late while making a left turn. I thought I would have a clear road, since it is a one-way street. I did not imagine that the children had set up a playing field. In vain, I tried to brake. I hit the stones marking the goal post. When I fell, your two sons also fell, along with three other small boys. I am sorry."

I am pleasantly surprised by the young motorcyclist. I railed, but not against him. I know from experience the difficulty of driving in town, especially in the Medina.[7] The tarred surface is a favourite area for children. Once they have taken possession, nothing else counts. They will dance around the ball like devils. Sometimes the object of their passion is a thick rag ball, all tied up. It doesn't matter! The driver's only recourse is his brakes, his horn, his composure; a small, disorderly opening is made for him, quickly closed up again in the hustle. Behind him the shouts begin again, even louder.

"It's not your fault, young man. My sons are to blame. They slipped away as I was praying. Off you go, young man—or rather, wait a moment while I get you some spirit and cotton-wool for your wound."

Aissatou, your namesake, brings methylated iodine and cotton. She takes care of the stranger and then of Alioune. The little boys of the area disapprove of my reaction. They want the man "at fault" to be punished; I give them a ticking-off. Ah, children! They cause an accident and, in addition, they want to punish.

Malick's hanging arm looks to me as if it is broken. It droops unnaturally. "Quick, Aissatou! Take him to hospital. If you can't find Mawdo, go to Casualty.[8] Quick, go, child." Aissatou dresses quickly and speedily helps Malick to clean up and change.

The dried blood from the wounds leaves dark and repulsive stains on the ground. Cleaning them up, I think of the identical nature of men: the same red blood irrigating the same organs. These organs, situated in the same places, carry out the same functions. The same remedies cure the same illnesses everywhere under the sun, whether the individual be white or black. Everything unites men. Why, then, do they kill each other in ignoble wars for causes that are futile when compared with the massacre of human lives? So many devastating wars! And yet man takes himself to be a superior being. In what way is his intelligence useful to him? His intelligence begets both good and ill, more often ill than good.

I go back to my place on the mat decorated with a picture of a mosque in green, reserved for my use only, just as is the kettle for my ablutions.[9] Alioune, still sniffing, pushes Ousmane aside so as to take his place beside me, looking for consolation, which I refuse him. On the contrary, I seize the opportunity to tell him off: "The road is not a playing field. You got off lightly today. But tomorrow, watch out! You will have some bone broken, like your brother."

---

7. A popular quarter, in the heart of Dakar.   8. The emergency room.   9. Muslims often carry a kettle of water for ritual cleansing.

Alioune complains: "But there is no playing field in the area. Mothers won't let us play football in the compounds. So what do we do?"

His comment is valid. Officers in charge of town planning must make provision for playing fields when they are developing open spaces.

Some hours later Aissatou and Malick return from the hospital where, once again, Mawdo has taken good care of them. Malick's plastered arm tells me that the drooping arm had indeed been broken. Ah, how dearly children make one pay for the joy of bringing them into the world!

Just as I thought, my friend: it never rains but it pours. This is my luck: once misfortune has me in its grip, it never lets go of me again.

Aissatou, your namesake, is three months pregnant. Farmata, the *griot* woman of the cowries, very cleverly led me to this discovery. Public rumour had spurred her on perhaps, or her keen powers of observation had simply served her well.

Each time she cast her cowries to cut short our discussions (we had diverging points of view on everything), she would breathe a "Hm" of discontent. With heavy sighs, she would point out in the jumble of cowries a young pregnant girl.

I had certainly noticed your namesake's sudden loss of weight, her lack of appetite, the swelling of her breasts: all indications of the child she was carrying. But puberty also transforms adolescents; they grow fatter or thinner, taller. And then, shortly after her father's death, Aissatou had had a violent attack of malaria, checked by Mawdo Bâ. The disappearance of her plumpness dates from this period.

Aissatou refused to regain weight, in order to keep her slender figure. I naturally ascribed her light intake of food and her distaste for certain food-stuffs to this new mania. Now thin, she swam in her trousers and, to my great joy, wore only dresses.

Little Oumar did tell me one day that Aissatou used to vomit in their bathroom every morning while bathing him. But Aissatou, when questioned, denied it, said it was the water mixed with toothpaste that she spat out. Oumar no longer spoke of vomiting. My mind focused on something else.

How could I guess that my daughter, who had calmed my anger during the cigarette affair, was now indulging in an even more dangerous game? Merciless fate had surprised me again—as usual, without any weapons with which to defend myself.

Every day Farmata would insist a bit more on the "young pregnant girl" of her cowries. She would show her to me. The girl's condition was making the woman suffer. She was eloquent: "Look, I say, look! This separate cowry, hollow side turned upwards. Look at this one, adjusting itself to the other, white side up, like a cooking pot and its cover lid. The child is in the belly. It forms one body with its mother. The two groups of cowries are separated: This indicates an unattached woman. But as the cowries are small, they indicate a young girl."

And her hand threw down, again and again, the gossipy cowries. They fell away from each other, collided, overlapped. Their tell-tale chink filled the winnowing fan, and the same group of two cowries always remained separate, to reveal distress. I followed their language dispassionately.

And then, one evening, annoyed by my naiveté, Farmata said boldly: "Question your daughters, Ramatoulaye. A mother must be pessimistic."

Worried by the relentless repetition, anxious, I accepted the proposition. Moving like a gazelle with delicate limbs, she swept into Aissatou's bedroom, afraid that I would change my mind. She came out, a triumphant gleam in her eye. Aissatou followed her, in tears. Farmata sent away Ousmane, who was nestled within my *boubou*, locked the door and declared: "The cowries cannot always be wrong. If they have insisted for so long, it means there is something there. Water and sand have been mixed; they have become mud. Gather up your mud. Aissatou does not deny her condition. I have saved her by exposing the matter. You guessed nothing. She did not dare confide in you. You would never have got out of this situation."

I was dumbfounded. I, so prone to chide, was silent. I was flushed and breathless. I closed my eyes, opened them again. I gnawed at my tongue.

The first question that comes to mind on discovering such a condition is: who? Who is behind this theft, for there has been a theft? Who is behind this injury, for injury it is. Who has dared? Who? Who? Aissatou mentioned a certain Ibrahima Sall who, as she talked, very soon became simply Iba.

Bewildered, I look at my daughter, so well brought up, so tender with me, so ready to help in the house, so efficient in every way, so many fine qualities allied with such behaviour!

Iba is a law student at the university. They met at a friend's birthday celebration. Iba sometimes went to meet her at school when she did not "come down"[1] at lunch time. He had invited her on two occasions to his room in the university halls of residence. She confessed her liking for him! No, Iba had not demanded anything, had not forced her. Everything had happened naturally between them. Iba knew of her condition. He had refused the services of one of his mates who wanted to "help" him.[2] He loved her. Though he was on a scholarship, he had decided to deprive himself for the maintenance of his child.

I learned everything at one go, from a broken voice accompanied by much sniffing but without any regret! Aissatou bent her head. I recognized the unvarnished truth of her story. I recognized her in her whole-hearted gift of herself to this lover who had succeeded in uniting in this heart my image and his own. Aissatou lowered her eyes, conscious of the pain crushing me; I remained silent. My hand supported my tired head. Aissatou lowered her eyes. She heard my inner self give way. She was fully aware of the seriousness of her action, considering my recent widow-hood, following upon my abandonment. After Daba, she was the oldest of the succession of daughters. The oldest should set an example. . . . My teeth gnashed in anger. . . .

Remembering, like a lifebuoy, the tender and consoling attitude of my daughter during my distress, my long years of loneliness, I overcame my emotion. I sought refuge in God, as at every moment of crisis in my life. Who decides death and life? God, the Almighty!

1. Go home from school.   2. That is, to procure an abortion, which is illegal in Senegal.

And also, one is a mother in order to understand the inexplicable. One is a mother to lighten the darkness. One is a mother to shield when lightning streaks the night, when thunder shakes the earth, when mud bogs one down. One is a mother in order to love without beginning or end.

To make my being a defensive barrier between my daughter and any obstacle. At this moment of confrontation, I realized how close I was to my child. The umbilical cord took on new life, the indestructible bond beneath the avalanche of storms and the duration of time. I saw her once more, newly sprung from me, kicking about, her tongue pink, her tiny face creased under her silky hair. I could not abandon her, as pride would have me do. Her life and her future were at stake, and these were powerful considerations, overriding all taboos and assuming greater importance in my heart and in my mind. The life that fluttered in her was questioning me. It was eager to blossom. It vibrated, demanding protection.

I was the one who had not been equal to the situation. Glutted with optimism, I had not suspected the crisis of her conscience, the passion of her being, the torment of her thoughts, the miracle she was carrying.

One is a mother so as to face the flood. Was I to threaten, in the face of my daughter's shame, her sincere repentance, her pain, her anguish? Was I?

I took my daughter in my arms. Painfully, I held her tightly, with a force multiplied tenfold by pagan revolt and primitive tenderness. She cried. She choked on sobs.

How could she have lived alone with her secret? I was traumatized by the effort and skill employed by this child to escape my anger whenever she felt faint or whenever she took over from me beside my troublesome youngsters. I felt sick. I felt terribly sick.

I took myself in hand with superhuman effort. The shadows faded away. Courage! The rays of light united to form an appeasing brightness. My decision to help and protect emerged from the tumult. It gained strength as I wiped the tears, as I caressed the burning brow.

Young Aissatou shall have an appointment with the doctor, not later than tomorrow.

Farmata was astonished. She expected wailing: I smiled. She wanted strong reprimands: I consoled. She wished for threats: I forgave.

No doubt about it: she will never know what to expect from me. To give a sinner so much attention was beyond her. She had dreams of sumptuous marriage celebrations for Aissatou, which would compensate her for my own meagre nuptials when she was a young girl, already tied to my steps like a shadow. She used to sing your praises, Aissatou, you who would give her a lot of money at the future wedding of your namesake. The story of the Fiat whetted her appetite and credited you with fabulous wealth. She dreamed of festivities, and here was this girl who had given herself to a penniless student, who would never be grateful to her. She reproached me for my calm: "You have mainly daughters. Adopt an attitude that you can keep up. You will see. If Aissatou can do 'this,' I wonder what your trio of smokers will do. Smother your daughter with caresses, Ramatoulaye. You will see."

I will indeed see when I ask to meet Ibrahima Sall tomorrow. . . .

25

Ibrahima Sall entered my room at the appointed time. His punctuality pleased me.

Tall, simply dressed. Pleasant features, on the whole. But with remarkably beautiful eyes, velvety, tender in the casement of his long eyelashes. One would like to see them in a woman's face .... the smile as well. I let my gaze rest on the set of his teeth. No treacherous gaps. Without being self-conscious about it, Ibrahima Sall was indeed the embodiment of the romantic young lover. He pleased me, and I noticed his cleanliness with relief: short hair combed, nails cut, shoes polished. He must be an orderly man and therefore without deceit.

It was I who had summoned him, but it was he who started the conversation: "How many times I have wanted to arrange this discussion, to let you know. I know what a daughter means to her mother, and Aissatou has told me so much about you, your closeness to her, that I think I know you already. I am not just looking for excitement. Your daughter is my first love. I want her to be the only one. I regret what has happened. If you agree, I will marry Aissatou. My mother will look after her child. We will continue with our studies."

Here then, concise and well said, was all I wanted to hear. How to reply? Should I agree readily to his propositions? Farmata, who was present during the discussion, was looking out for squalls.

She asked: "You were really the first?"

"Yes," confirmed Iba Sall.

"Then, warn your mother. We or I shall go to see her tomorrow to announce your crime. She had better save a lot of money to compensate my niece. Anyway, couldn't you have waited until you had a good job before running after girls?"

Ibrahima Sall heard the *griot* woman's remarks without showing any irritation. Perhaps he already knew her well enough by name and character to remain politely silent.

My own preoccupations were very different from those of Farmata. We were right in the middle of the school year. What was to be done to prevent my daughter's expulsion from school?

I told Iba Sall of my fears. He too had given some thought to the problem. The child would be born during the holidays. The essential thing was not to panic, just to let the months go past, and for Aissatou to dress in loose clothes. At the beginning of the following school year the baby would be two months old. Aissatou would then join the final-year class. After this final year, marriage.

My daughter's boyfriend had worked it out logically and reminded me of Daba's clearness of mind.

Ibrahima Sall himself ran no risk of being expelled from the university. And even had he still been at school, who would inform the school of his position as father-to-be? There would be no change in him. He would remain "flat" ... while my daughter's swollen belly would point an accusing finger.

When will there be a lenient law to help erring schoolgirls whose condition is not camouflaged by long holidays?

I added nothing to all this careful planning. At that moment, I felt that my child was being detached from my being, as if I were again bringing her into the world. She was no longer under my protection. She belonged more to her boyfriend. A new family was being born before my very eyes.

I accepted my subordinate role. The ripe fruit must drop away from the tree.

May God smooth the new path of this child's life.

Yet what a path!

26

Aissatou, reassuring habits regain ascendancy.

My heart beats monotonously under my black wrappers. How I like to listen to this slow rhythm! A new substance is trying to graft itself on to the household.

Ibrahima Sall comes every day and gives each of us what he can. He offers Mawdo Fall his logic and clarity in discussions of the topics of his essays. He provides chocolate regularly for Oumar and Ousmane. He is not too proud to play with Malick and Alioune, who have given up the street for my compound.

Malick's arm is still in plaster. Just as long as his leg, which cannot keep away from the ball, does not break in its turn!

But the trio (Arame, Yacine and Dieynaba) refuse to accept this "intrusion." The trio greet him correctly but without enthusiasm. The trio are hostile to his invitations. They begrudge him for having. . . .

Ibrahima Sall urges Aissatou on in her lessons and homework. He has his girlfriend's success at heart. He does not want to be responsible for any regression whatsoever. Aissatou's marks improve: there's a silver lining in every cloud!

Farmata finds it difficult to accept Ibrahima Sall, whom she describes as "cocksure," "shameless." She never misses an opportunity of hitting out at him: "Has one ever seen a stranger untie a goat in the house?"[3]

Unperturbed, Ibrahima Sall tries to adapt. He seeks out my company, discusses current events with me, sometimes brings me magazines and fruit. His parents, informed some time ago by the vigilant Farmata, also come round to see us and are anxious about Aissatou's health. And reassuring habits regain ascendancy. . . .

I envy you for having had only boys! You don't know the terrors I face in dealing with the problems of my daughters.

I have finally decided to broach the problem of sexual education. Aissatou, your namesake, caught me unawares. From now on, I will take precautions. I address myself to the trio, the twins being still too young.

How I had hesitated earlier! I did not want to give my daughters a free hand by offering them immunity in pleasure. The world is upside-down. Mothers of yore taught chastity. Their voice of authority condemned all extra-marital "wanderings."

Modern mothers favour "forbidden games." They help to limit the damage and, better still, prevent it. They remove any thorn or pebble that

---

3. An act of unwarranted boldness, an outrage.

might hinder the progress of their children towards the conquest of all forms of liberty! I apply myself painfully to this necessity.

All the same, I insist that my daughters be aware of the value of their bodies. I emphasize the sublime significance of the sexual act, an expression of love. The existence of means of contraception must not lead to an unhindered release of desires and instincts. It is through his self-control, his ability to reason, to choose, his power of attachment, that the individual distinguishes himself from the animal.

Each woman makes of her life what she wants. A profligate life for a woman is incompatible with morality. What does one gain from pleasures? Early ageing, debasement, no doubt about it, I further stressed.

My words fell uneasily on my female audience. Of us all, I was the most vulnerable. For the trio's faces registered no surprise. My chopped sentences aroused no special interest. I had the impression that I was saying the obvious.

Perhaps the trio knew already. . . . A long silence. . . . And the trio disappeared. I let out a sigh of relief. I felt that I had emerged into the light after a long journey through a dark, narrow tunnel.

27

Till tomorrow, my friend.

We will then have time to ourselves, especially as I have obtained an extension of my widow's leave.

I reflect. My new turn of mind is hardly surprising to you. I cannot help unburdening myself to you. I might as well sum up now.

I am not indifferent to the irreversible currents of women's liberation that are lashing the world. This commotion that is shaking up every aspect of our lives reveals and illustrates our abilities.

My heart rejoices each time a woman emerges from the shadows. I know that the field of our gains is unstable, the retention of conquests difficult: social constraints are ever-present, and male egoism resists.

Instruments for some, baits for others, respected or despised, often muzzled, all women have almost the same fate, which religions or unjust legislation have sealed.

My reflections determine my attitude to the problems of life. I analyse the decisions that decide our future. I widen my scope by taking an interest in current world affairs.

I remain persuaded of the inevitable and necessary complementarity of man and woman.

Love, imperfect as it may be in its content and expression, remains the natural link between these two beings.

To love one another! If only each partner could move sincerely towards the other! If each could only melt into the other! If each would only accept the other's successes and failures! If each would only praise the other's qualities instead of listing his faults! If each could only correct bad habits without harping on about them! If each could penetrate the other's most secret haunts to forestall failure and be a support while tending to the evils that are repressed!

The success of the family is born of a couple's harmony, as the harmony of multiple instruments creates a pleasant symphony.

The nation is made up of all the families, rich or poor, united or separated, aware or unaware. The success of a nation therefore depends inevitably on the family.

Why aren't your sons coming with you? Ah, their studies. . . .

So, then, will I see you tomorrow in a tailored suit or a long dress? I've taken a bet with Daba: tailored suit. Used to living far away, you will want—again, I have taken a bet with Daba—table, plate, chair, fork.

More convenient, you will say. But I will not let you have your way. I will spread out a mat. On it there will be the big, steaming bowl into which you will have to accept that other hands dip.

Beneath the shell that has hardened you over the years, beneath your sceptical pout, your easy carriage, perhaps I will feel you vibrate. I would so much like to hear you check or encourage my eagerness, just as before, and, as before, to see you take part in the search for a new way.

I warn you already, I have not given up wanting to refashion my life. Despite everything—disappointments and humiliations—hope still lives on within me. It is from the dirty and nauseating humus that the green plant sprouts into life, and I can feel new buds springing up in me.

The word "happiness" does indeed have meaning, doesn't it? I shall go out in search of it. Too bad for me if once again I have to write you so long a letter. . . .

Ramatoulaye

CHINUA ACHEBE
born 1930

The best-known African writer today is the Nigerian Chinua Achebe, whose first novel, *Things Fall Apart*, exploded the colonialist image of Africans as childlike people living in a primitive society. Achebe's novels, stories, poetry, and essays have made him a respected and prophetic figure in Africa. In Western countries, where he has traveled, taught, and lectured widely, he is admired as a major writer who has given an entirely new direction to the English-language novel. Achebe has created not only the African postcolonial novel with its new themes and characters, but also a complex narrative point of view that questions cultural images— including its own—with a subtle irony and compassion born from bicultural experience. His vantage point is different from that of Doris Lessing or Albert Camus, two authors whose work is also concerned with African experience: Achebe writes, as he says, "from the inside." For him as for many other writers in this volume, literature is important because it liberates the human imagination; it "begins as an adventure in self-discovery and ends in wisdom and human conscience."

Chinua Achebe was born in the town of Ogidi, an Igbo-speaking town of Eastern Nigeria, on November 16, 1930. He was the fifth of six children in the family of Isaiah Okafor Achebe, a teacher for the Church Missionary Society, and his wife, Janet. Achebe's parents christened him Albert after Prince Albert, husband of Queen Victoria. When he entered the university the author rejected his British name in favor of his indigenous name Chinua, which abbreviates Chinualumogu, or "My spirit come fight for me." Achebe's novels offer a picture of Igbo society with its fierce egalitarianism and "town meeting" debates. Two cultures co-existed in Ogidi: on the one hand, African social customs and traditional religion, and on the other, British colonial authority and Christianity. Instead of being torn between the two, Achebe found himself curious about both ways of life and fascinated with the dual perspective that came from living "at the crossroads of cultures."

He attended Church schools in Ogidi where instruction was carried out in English after the first two years. Achebe read the various books in his father's library, most of them primers or Church related, but he also listened eagerly to his mother and sister when they told traditional Igbo stories. Entering a prestigious government college (secondary school) in Umuahia, he immediately took advantage of its well-stocked library. Achebe later commented on the crucial importance of books in creating writers and committed readers, noting that private secondary schools had few if any books and that almost all the first generation of Nigerian writers—including himself and Wole Soyinka (born 1934)—had gone to a government college.

After graduating in 1948, Achebe entered University College, Ibadan, on a scholarship to study medicine. In the following year he changed to a program in liberal arts that combined English, history, and religious studies. Research in the last two fields deepened his knowledge of Nigerian history and culture; the assigned literary texts, however, brought into sharp focus the distorted image of African culture offered by British colonial literature. Reading Joyce Cary's *Mister Johnson* (1939), a novel recommended for its depiction of life in Nigeria, he was shocked to find Nigerians described as violent savages with passionate instincts and simple minds: "and so I thought if this was famous, then perhaps someone ought to try and look at this from the inside." He began writing while at the university, contributing articles and sketches to several campus papers, and publishing four stories in the *University Herald*, a magazine whose editor he became in his third year.

Upon receiving his B.A. in 1953, Achebe joined the Nigerian Broadcasting Service, working in the Talks Section and traveling to London in 1956 to attend the British Broadcasting Corporation Staff School. Promotions came quickly; he was named head of the Talks Section in 1957, controller of the Eastern Region Stations in 1959, and in 1961 director of External Services in charge of the Voice of Nigeria. The radio position was more than a merely administrative post, for Achebe and his colleagues were working to create a sense of shared national identity through broadcasting national news and information about Nigerian culture. Ever since the end of World War II, Nigeria had been torn by intellectual and political rivalries that overlaid the common struggle for independence (achieved in 1960). The three major ethnolinguistic groups—Yoruba, Hausa-Fulani, and Igbo (once spelled Ibo)—were increasingly locked in economic and political rivalry at the same time they were fighting to erase the vestiges of British colonial rule. These problems eventually boiled over in the Nigerian Civil War (1967–1970). The persistence of political corruption is depicted in A *Man of the People* (1966) and *Anthills of the Savannah* (1987).

Achebe is convinced of the writer's social responsibility, and he draws frequent contrasts between the European "art for art's sake" tradition and an African belief in the indivisibility of art and society. His favorite example is the Owerri Igbo custom of *mbari*, a communal art project in which villagers selected by the priest of the earth goddess Ala live in a forest clearing for a year or more, working under the direction of master artists to prepare a temple of images in the goddess's honor. This creative communal enterprise and its culminating festival are diametrically opposed, he says, to the European custom of secluding art objects in museums or private collections. Instead, *mbari* celebrates art as a cultural process, affirming that "art belongs to all and is a 'function' of society." Achebe's own practice as novelist, poet, essayist, founder and editor of two journals, lecturer, and active representative of African letters exemplifies this commitment to the community.

His first novel, *Things Fall Apart* (1958), was a conscious attempt to counteract the distortions of Cary's *Mister Johnson* by describing the richness and complexity of traditional African society before the colonial and missionary invasion. It was important, Achebe said, to "teach my readers that their past—with all its imperfections—was not one long night of savagery from which the first Europeans acting on God's behalf delivered them." The novel was recognized immediately as an extraordinary work of literature in English. It also became the first classic work of modern African fiction, translated into nine languages, and Achebe became for many readers and writers the teacher of a whole generation. In 1959 he received the Margaret Wrong Memorial prize, and in 1960—after the publication of a sequel, *No Longer at Ease*—he received the Nigerian National Trophy for literature. His later novels continue to examine the individual and cultural dilemmas of Nigerian society, although their background varies from the traditional religious society of *Arrow of God* (1964) to thinly disguised accounts of contemporary political strife.

Achebe's reputation as the "father of the African novel in English" does not depend solely on his accounts of Nigerian society. In contrast with writers such as Ngugi wa Thiong'o (born 1938), who insist that the contemporary African writer has a moral obligation to write in one of the tribal languages, Achebe maintains his right to compose in the English he has used since his school days. His literary language is an English skillfully blended with Igbo vocabulary, proverbs, images, and speech patterns to create a new voice embodying the linguistic pluralism of modern African experience. By including standard English, Igbo, and pidgin in different contexts, Achebe demonstrates the existence of a diverse society that is otherwise concealed behind language barriers—a culture, he suggests, that escaped colonial officials who wrote about African character without ever understanding the language. He also thereby acknowledges that his primary African audience is composed of younger, schooled readers who are relatively fluent in English.

It is hard to overestimate the influence of Nigerian politics on Achebe's life after 1966. In January, a military coup d'état led by young Igbo officers overthrew the government; six months later, a second coup led by non-Igbo officers took power. Ethnic rivalries intensified: thousands of Igbos were killed and driven out of the north. Achebe and his family fled the capital of Lagos when soldiers were sent to find him, and the novelist became a senior research fellow at the University of Nigeria, Nsukka (in Eastern Nigeria). In May 1967 the eastern region, mainly populated by Igbo-speakers, seceded as the new nation of Biafra. From then on until the defeat of Biafra in January 1970, a bloody civil war was waged with high civilian casualties and widespread starvation. Achebe traveled in Europe, North America, and Africa to win support for Biafra, proclaiming that "no government, black or white, has the right to stigmatize and destroy groups of its own citizens without undermining the basis of its own existence." A group of his poems about the war won the Commonwealth Poetry Prize in 1972, the same year that he published a volume of short stories, *Girls at War*, and left Nigeria to take up a three-year position at the University of Massachusetts at Amherst. Returning to Nsukka as professor of literature in 1976, Achebe continued to participate in his country's political life. He published an attack on the corrupt leadership in *The Trouble with Nigeria* (1983) and—drawing on circumstances surrounding a fifth military coup in 1985—produced his fifth novel, *Anthills of the Savannah*, in

1987. Although it reiterates Achebe's familiar indictment of ruthless politicians, alienated intellectuals, and those who accept dictatorship as a route to reform, this novel offers hope for the future through a return to the people and a symbolic child born at the end: a girl child with a boy's name, "May the Path Never Close." Badly hurt in a car accident the year after *Anthills* was published, Achebe slowly recovered and returned to his writing. He currently teaches at Bard College.

A predominant theme in Achebe's novels and essays is the notion of balance or interdependence: balance between earth and sky, individual and community, man and woman, or different perspectives on the same situation. Igbo thought is fundamentally dualistic, the novelist explains: "Wherever Something stands, Something Else will stand beside it. Nothing is absolute." Extremes carry the seeds of destruction. Indeed, destruction follows in Achebe's novels whenever balance is disturbed: when Okonkwo in *Things Fall Apart* represses any signs of "female" softness; when the priest Ezeulu in *Arrow of God* is imprisoned and refuses to authorize the feast of the New Yam, without which his people cannot plant their crops; and when, in later books, the lust for power and possessions blinds Nigerian leaders to the needs of the people.

The fundamental image of this balance is contained in the Igbo concept of *chi*, which recurs throughout Achebe's work. *Chi* is a personal deity, a fragment of the supreme being unique for each individual. A person's *chi*, says Achebe, may be visualized "as his other identity in spirit-land—his *spirit being* complementing his terrestrial *human being*." It is both all-powerful and subject to persuasion: "When a man says yes his *chi* says yes also" but at the same time "a man does not challenge his *chi* to a wrestling match." *Chi* is simultaneously destiny and an internal commitment that cannot be denied, a religious concept and also a picture of psychic harmony. Both aspects are linked throughout Achebe's novels, beginning with *Things Fall Apart*. In killing Ikemefuna, whom he loves and who calls him father, Okonkwo sins not only against the earth goddess, protector of family relations, but also against his inmost feelings and thus against his *chi*. If Okonkwo's destiny (*chi*) is marked by bad luck, one reason may be that—driven by fear of resembling his father—he struggles to repress part of his personality (*chi*), with predictably ill results. In the final assessment, no one can fully explain *chi*: it is mysteriously uncertain, the element of fate over which we have no real control.

Things Fall Apart is both Okonkwo's tragedy and that of his society. The title (taken from William Butler Yeats's *The Second Coming*) introduces a narrative in which a complex and dignified traditional society disintegrates before foreign invaders who assault its political, economic, and religious institutions. The setting is eastern Nigeria around the turn of the century in the clan of Umuofia, which is composed of nine interrelated villages. One of these villages, Iguedo, is the home of the protagonist Okonkwo, an ambitious and powerful man who is driven by the memory of his father's failure and weakness.

During the first two-thirds of the book, Achebe paints the picture of a rich and coherent society, establishing an image of traditional African culture into which the final chapters' missionaries, court messengers, and district commissioner intrude as alien and disruptive elements. In sharp contrast to the simplified vision of African life given by European novelists Joyce Cary, Joseph Conrad, or Graham Greene, he explores the complex feelings and interpersonal relationships of diverse villagers seen as men, women, parents, children, friends, neighbors, or priests of the local deities. The intricate patterns of Umuofia's economic and social customs also emerge, belying European images of African "primitive" simplicity. No one who has read about Obierika's intricate marriage negotiations, the etiquette of *kola* hospitality, the religious "week of peace," Ezeudu's elaborate funeral rites, the domestic arbitration conducted by the *egwugwu* court, the female kinship customs linking families and villages, or indeed Umuofia's entire set of taboos and punishments, will find this a simple society. The title system itself, which plays such a large part in the novel, is an ingenious social strategy for redistributing wealth throughout the community. The four honorific ozo titles (*Ozo, Idemili, Omalo,* and *Erulu*), through which a man enters the spiritual community of his ancestors and achieves increasing levels of prestige, are acquired in festivities during which the candidate divests himself of excess material wealth. There is a dignity and purpose to this society despite inner tensions that—as Achebe shows—create pain as well as vulnerability to attack from outside. The moderate Obierika disapproves of killing Ikemefuna and begins to question the practice of throwing away twins; one of the first converts to Christianity is a woman who gave birth to several sets of twins, all of whom were exposed (left in the wild) at birth. The general subordination of women is another source of tensions which have taken longer to surface. Whatever its cultural differences from European society, however, this is a highly organized and complex society that offers a great deal of continuity and coherence to its members.

Igbo names, like names throughout black Africa, consist of whole phrases or sentences. Some names are dictated by circumstance (referring to the day of birth, for example) and some (the "given" name selected by the child's father, for example) reflect the family situation or a child's expected destiny. Adults may earn additional titles of honor. Achebe uses the connotations of personal names to reinforce important themes in *Things Fall Apart*. Okonkwo's father's character as a lazy, artistic, and improvident man is suggested by the name Unoka, signifying "the home is supreme." Okonkwo's son Nwoye, who has inherited his grandfather's peace-loving nature and artistic qualities, is named after the second day of the Igbo week (*Oye*); unlike Okonkwo, Nwoye lacks a prefix specifying adulthood or even gender, for *Nwa* means "child." Ikemefuna, who is condemned to death by the Oracle and will be killed by his adoptive father, is named "My strength should not be dissipated." Although all names have significance, only those with some relevance to the story will be annotated in this edition.

Okonkwo's character and career suggest epic dimensions. He is on the one hand a hero of enormous energy and determination, "one of the greatest men in Umuofia" as his friend Obierika says, but his particular mode of greatness also causes his downfall. Like Achilles in Homer's *Iliad*, Okonkwo clings to traditionally respected values of pride and warlike aggression, and he will die to preserve those values. His unwillingness to change sets him apart from the community and eventually isolates him from the clan with its emphasis on group decisions. Okonkwo is a passionate man who counts on physical strength, hard work, and courage to make his way. Humiliated by his father's laziness, shameful death, and lack of title, compelled early to support the entire family, he struggles desperately to root out any sign of inherited "feminine" weakness in himself or his son Nwoye. By cultivating strength and valor, he finds a way to surpass his father and become one of the village leaders. Okonkwo is not without tender feelings: he loves his wife Ekwefi; his daughter, Ezinma; and the youth Ikemefuna who is given to him to foster. When he cuts down Ikemefuna so as not to appear weak, he is shattered for days thereafter. Nonetheless, his obsession with fierce masculinity, and his open disrespect for "womanly" qualities of gentleness, compassion and peace, separate him not only from other members of his clan such as the more balanced Obierika but also from the earth goddess herself. This imbalance leads to disaster.

C. L. Innes, *Chinua Achebe* (1990), is a comprehensive study of Achebe's work through 1988; it emphasizes his literary techniques and Africanization of the novel. Simon Gikandi, *Reading Chinua Achebe: Language and Ideology in Fiction* (1991), is also recommended. Robert M. Wren, *Achebe's World: The Historical and Cultural Context of the Novels of Chinua Achebe* (1980), provides historical background and cultural context for Achebe's novels and includes glossary and bibliography. Studies of *Things Fall Apart* include Kate Turkington, *Chinua Achebe: Things Fall Apart* (1977), a concise introductory study, and the multiple perspectives in Bernth Lindfors, ed., *Approaches to Teaching Achebe's Things Fall Apart* (1991). C. L. Innes and Bernth Lindfors, eds., *Critical Perspectives on Chinua Achebe*, (1978), collect twenty-one essays on Achebe's work (almost exclusively the novels) through 1973. G. D. Killam, *The Writings of Chinua Achebe* (1977), is a commentary on Achebe's work through the mid-1970s, concentrating on the first four novels.

PRONOUNCING GLOSSARY

The following list uses common English syllables and stress accents to provide rough equivalents of selected words whose pronunciation may be unfamiliar to the general reader. Most of the names in *Things Fall Apart* are pronounced basically as they would be in English (for example, Okonkwo as *oh-kon'-kwo*), except that Igbo (like other African languages and Chinese) is a tonal language and also uses high or low tones for individual syllables.

Chielo: *chee'-ay-loh*

Chinua Achebe: *chin'-oo-ah ah-chay'-bay*

egwugwu: *eg-woog'-woo*

Erulu: *air-oo'-loo*

Ezeani: *ez-ah'-nee*

Ezeugo: *e'-zoo-goh*

Idemili: *ee-day-mee'-lee*

Igbo: *ee'-boh*

Ikemefuna: *ee-kay-may'-foo-na*

mbari: *mbah'-ree*

Ndulue: *in'-doo-loo'-eh*

Nwakibie: *nwa'-kee-ee'-bee-yay*

Nwayieke: *nwah'-ee-eh'-kay*

Umuofia: *oo'-moo-off'-yah*

Things Fall Apart

Turning and turning in the widening gyre
The falcon cannot hear the falconer;
Things fall apart; the centre cannot hold;
Mere anarchy is loosed upon the world . . .
    —W. B. Yeats, "The Second Coming"

Part One

1

Okonkwo[1] was well known throughout the nine villages and even beyond. His fame rested on solid personal achievements. As a young man of eighteen he had brought honor to his village by throwing Amalinze the Cat. Amalinze was the great wrestler who for seven years was unbeaten, from Umuofia to Mbaino.[2] He was called the Cat because his back would never touch the earth. It was this man that Okonkwo threw in a fight which the old men agreed was one of the fiercest since the founder of their town engaged a spirit of the wild for seven days and seven nights.

---

1. "Four Settlements." Umuofia means "Man [*oko*] Born on Nkwo Day"; the name also suggests stubborn male pride.   2. Literally, "Children of the Forest" but *ofia*, "forest," also means "bush" or land untouched by European influence.

The drums beat and the flutes sang and the spectators held their breath. Amalinze was a wily craftsman, but Okonkwo was as slippery as a fish in water. Every nerve and every muscle stood out on their arms, on their backs and their thighs, and one almost heard them stretching to breaking point. In the end Okonkwo threw the Cat.

That was many years ago, twenty years or more, and during this time Okonkwo's fame had grown like a bush-fire in the harmattan.[3] He was tall and huge, and his bushy eyebrows and wide nose gave him a very severe look. He breathed heavily, and it was said that, when he slept, his wives and children in their houses could hear him breathe. When he walked, his heels hardly touched the ground and he seemed to walk on springs, as if he was going to pounce on somebody. And he did pounce on people quite often. He had a slight stammer and whenever he was angry and could not get his words out quickly enough, he would use his fists. He had no patience with unsuccessful men. He had had no patience with his father.

Unoka,[4] for that was his father's name, had died ten years ago. In his day he was lazy and improvident and was quite incapable of thinking about tomorrow. If any money came his way, and it seldom did, he immediately bought gourds of palm-wine, called round his neighbors and made merry. He always said that whenever he saw a dead man's mouth he saw the folly of not eating what one had in one's lifetime. Unoka was, of course, a debtor, and he owed every neighbor some money, from a few cowries[5] to quite substantial amounts.

He was tall but very thin and had a slight stoop. He wore a haggard and mournful look except when he was drinking or playing on his flute. He was very good on his flute, and his happiest moments were the two or three moons after the harvest when the village musicians brought down their instruments, hung above the fireplace. Unoka would play with them, his face beaming with blessedness and peace. Sometimes another village would ask Unoka's band and their dancing egwugwu[6] to come and stay with them and teach them their tunes. They would go to such hosts for as long as three or four markets,[7] making music and feasting. Unoka loved the good fare and the good fellowship, and he loved this season of the year, when the rains had stopped and the sun rose every morning with dazzling beauty. And it was not too hot either, because the cold and dry harmattan wind was blowing down from the north. Some years the harmattan was very severe and a dense haze hung on the atmosphere. Old men and children would then sit round log fires, warming their bodies. Unoka loved it all, and he loved the first kites[8] that returned with the dry season, and the children who sang songs of welcome to them. He would remember his own childhood, how he had often wandered around looking for a kite sailing leisurely against the blue sky. As soon as he found one he

---

3. A dusty wind from the Sahara. 4. "Home Is Supreme." 5. Glossy half-inch-long tan-and-white shells, collected in strings and used as money. A bag of twenty-four thousand cowries weighed about sixty pounds and, at the time of the story, was worth approximately one British pound. 6. Here, masked performers as part of musical entertainment. 7. Counting one important market day a week, roughly two English weeks. The Igbo week has four days: Eke, Oye, Afo, and Nkwo. Eke is a rest day and the main market day; Afo, a half day on the farm; and Oye and Nkwo, full work days. 8. A kind of hawk.

would sing with his whole being, welcoming it back from its long, long journey, and asking it if it had brought home any lengths of cloth.

That was years ago, when he was young. Unoka, the grown-up, was a failure. He was poor and his wife and children had barely enough to eat. People laughed at him because he was a loafer, and they swore never to lend him any more money because he never paid back. But Unoka was such a man that he always succeeded in borrowing more, and piling up his debts.

One day a neighbor called Okoye[9] came in to see him. He was reclining on a mud bed in his hut playing on the flute. He immediately rose and shook hands with Okoye, who then unrolled the goatskin which he carried under his arm, and sat down. Unoka went into an inner room and soon returned with a small wooden disc containing a kola nut, some alligator pepper and a lump of white chalk.[1]

"I have kola," he announced when he sat down, and passed the disc over to his guest.

"Thank you. He who brings kola brings life. But I think you ought to break it," replied Okoye, passing back the disc.

"No, it is for you, I think," and they argued like this for a few moments before Unoka accepted the honor of breaking the kola. Okoye, meanwhile, took the lump of chalk, drew some lines on the floor, and then painted his big toe.[2]

As he broke the kola, Unoka prayed to their ancestors for life and health, and for protection against their enemies. When they had eaten they talked about many things: about the heavy rains which were drowning the yams, about the next ancestral feast and about the impending war with the village of Mbaino. Unoka was never happy when it came to wars. He was in fact a coward and could not bear the sight of blood. And so he changed the subject and talked about music, and his face beamed. He could hear in his mind's ear the blood-stirring and intricate rhythms of the *ekwe* and the *udu* and the *ogene*,[3] and he could hear his own flute weaving in and out of them, decorating them with a colorful and plaintive tune. The total effect was gay and brisk, but if one picked out the flute as it went up and down and then broke up into short snatches, one saw that there was sorrow and grief there.

Okoye was also a musician. He played on the *ogene*. But he was not a failure like Unoka. He had a large barn full of yams and he had three wives. And now he was going to take the Idemili title,[4] the third highest in the land. It was a very expensive ceremony and he was gathering all his

---

9. "Man Born on Oye Day"; a generic "Everyman" name.   1. Signifies coolness and peace and is offered in rituals of hospitality so that the guest may draw his personal emblem on the floor. *Kola nut*: a bitter, caffeine-rich nut that is broken and eaten ceremonially; it indicates life or vitality. *Alligator pepper*: black pepper, known as the "pepper for kola" to distinguish it from cooking pepper, or chilies.   2. If the guest has taken the first title, he marks his big toe. Higher titles require different facial markings. 3. A bell-shaped gong made from two pieces of sheet iron. *Ekwe*: a wooden drum, about three feet long; it produces high and low tones (as does the Igbo language). *Udu*: a clay pot with a hole to one side of the neck opening; various resonant tones are produced when the hole is struck with one hand while the other hand covers or uncovers the top.   4. A title of honor named after the river god Idemili, to whom the python is sacred. *Barn*: not a building, but a walled enclosure for the yam stacks (frames on which individual yams are tied, shaded with palm leaves, and exposed to circulating air).

resources together. That was in fact the reason why he had come to see Unoka. He cleared his throat and began:

"Thank you for the kola. You may have heard of the title I intend to take shortly."

Having spoken plainly so far, Okoye said the next half a dozen sentences in proverbs. Among the Ibo the art of conversation is regarded very highly, and proverbs are the palm-oil with which words are eaten. Okoye was a great talker and he spoke for a long time, skirting round the subject and then hitting it finally. In short, he was asking Unoka to return the two hundred cowries he had borrowed from him more than two years before. As soon as Unoka understood what his friend was driving at, he burst out laughing. He laughed loud and long and his voice rang out clear as the *ogene*, and tears stood in his eyes. His visitor was amazed, and sat speechless. At the end, Unoka was able to give an answer between fresh outbursts of mirth.

"Look at that wall," he said, pointing at the far wall of his hut, which was rubbed with red earth so that it shone. "Look at those lines of chalk;" and Okoye saw groups of short perpendicular lines drawn in chalk. There were five groups, and the smallest group had ten lines. Unoka had a sense of the dramatic and so he allowed a pause, in which he took a pinch of snuff and sneezed noisily, and then he continued: "Each group there represents a debt to someone, and each stroke is one hundred cowries. You see, I owe that man a thousand cowries. But he has not come to wake me up in the morning for it. I shall pay you, but not today. Our elders say that the sun will shine on those who stand before it shines on those who kneel under them. I shall pay my big debts first." And he took another pinch of snuff, as if that was paying the big debts first. Okoye rolled his goatskin and departed.

When Unoka died he had taken no title at all and he was heavily in debt. Any wonder then that his son Okonkwo was ashamed of him? Fortunately, among these people a man was judged according to his worth and not according to the worth of his father. Okonkwo was clearly cut out for great things. He was still young but he had won fame as the greatest wrestler in the nine villages. He was a wealthy farmer and had two barns full of yams, and had just married his third wife. To crown it all he had taken two titles and had shown incredible prowess in two inter-tribal wars. And so although Okonkwo was still young, he was already one of the greatest men of his time. Age was respected among his people, but achievement was revered. As the elders said, if a child washed his hands he could eat with kings. Okonkwo had clearly washed his hands and so he ate with kings and elders. And that was how he came to look after the doomed lad who was sacrificed to the village of Umuofia by their neighbors to avoid war and bloodshed. The ill-fated lad was called Ikemefuna.[5]

2

Okonkwo had just blown out the palm-oil lamp and stretched himself on his bamboo bed when he heard the *ogene* of the town crier piercing

5. "My strength should not be dissipated."

the still night air. *Gome, gome, gome, gome,* boomed the hollow metal. Then the crier gave his message, and at the end of it beat his instrument again. And this was the message. Every man of Umuofia was asked to gather at the market place tomorrow morning. Okonkwo wondered what was amiss, for he knew certainly that something was amiss. He had discerned a clear overtone of tragedy in the crier's voice, and even now he could still hear it as it grew dimmer and dimmer in the distance.

The night was very quiet. It was always quiet except on moonlight nights. Darkness held a vague terror for these people, even the bravest among them. Children were warned not to whistle at night for fear of evil spirits. Dangerous animals became even more sinister and uncanny in the dark. A snake was never called by its name at night, because it would hear. It was called a string. And so on this particular night as the crier's voice was gradually swallowed up in the distance, silence returned to the world, a vibrant silence made more intense by the universal trill of a million million forest insects.

On a moonlight night it would be different. The happy voices of children playing in open fields would then be heard. And perhaps those not so young would be playing in pairs in less open places, and old men and women would remember their youth. As the Ibo say: "When the moon is shining the cripple becomes hungry for a walk."

But this particular night was dark and silent. And in all the nine villages of Umuofia a town crier with his *ogene* asked every man to be present tomorrow morning. Okonkwo on his bamboo bed tried to figure out the nature of the emergency—war with a neighboring clan? That seemed the most likely reason, and he was not afraid of war. He was a man of action, a man of war. Unlike his father he could stand the look of blood. In Umuofia's latest war he was the first to bring home a human head. That was his fifth head; and he was not an old man yet. On great occasions such as the funeral of a village celebrity he drank his palm-wine from his first human head.

In the morning the market place was full. There must have been about ten thousand men there, all talking in low voices. At last Ogbuefi Ezeugo stood up in the midst of them and bellowed four times, *"Umuofia kwenu,"*[6] and on each occasion he faced a different direction and seemed to push the air with a clenched fist. And ten thousand men answered *"Yaa!"* each time. Then there was perfect silence. Ogbuefi Ezeugo was a powerful orator and was always chosen to speak on such occasions. He moved his hand over his white head and stroked his white beard. He then adjusted his cloth, which was passed under his right armpit and tied above his left shoulder.

"Umuofia kwenu," he bellowed a fifth time, and the crowd yelled in answer. And then suddenly like one possessed he shot out his left hand and pointed in the direction of Mbaino, and said through gleaming white teeth firmly clenched: "Those sons of wild animals have dared to murder

6. "United Umuofia!" An orator's call on the audience to respond as a group. *Ogbuefi:* "Cow Killer" (literal trans.); indicates someone who has taken a high title (for example, the Idemili title) for which the celebration ceremony requires the slaughter of a cow. *Ezeugo:* a name denoting a priest or high initiate, someone who wears the eagle feather.

a daughter of Umuofia." He threw his head down and gnashed his teeth, and allowed a murmur of suppressed anger to sweep the crowd. When he began again, the anger on his face was gone and in its place a sort of smile hovered, more terrible and more sinister than the anger. And in a clear unemotional voice he told Umuofia how their daughter had gone to market at Mbaino and had been killed. That woman, said Ezeugo, was the wife of Ogbuefi Udo,[7] and he pointed to a man who sat near him with a bowed head. The crowd then shouted with anger and thirst for blood.

Many others spoke, and at the end it was decided to follow the normal course of action. An ultimatum was immediately dispatched to Mbaino asking them to choose between war on the one hand, and on the other the offer of a young man and a virgin as compensation.

Umuofia was feared by all its neighbors. It was powerful in war and in magic, and its priests and medicine men were feared in all the surrounding country. Its most potent war-medicine was as old as the clan itself. Nobody knew how old. But on one point there was general agreement—the active principle in that medicine had been an old woman with one leg. In fact, the medicine itself was called *agadi-nwayi*, or old woman. It had its shrine in the center of Umuofia, in a cleared spot. And if anybody was so foolhardy as to pass by the shrine after dusk he was sure to see the old woman hopping about.

And so the neighboring clans who naturally knew of these things feared Umuofia, and would not go to war against it without first trying a peaceful settlement. And in fairness to Umuofia it should be recorded that it never went to war unless its case was clear and just and was accepted as such by its Oracle—the Oracle of the Hills and the Caves. And there were indeed occasions when the Oracle had forbidden Umuofia to wage a war. If the clan had disobeyed the Oracle they would surely have been beaten, because their dreaded *agadi-nwayi* would never fight what the Ibo call *a fight of blame.*

But the war that now threatened was a just war. Even the enemy clan knew that. And so when Okonkwo of Umuofia arrived at Mbaino as the proud and imperious emissary of war, he was treated with great honor and respect, and two days later he returned home with a lad of fifteen and a young virgin. The lad's name was Ikemefuna, whose sad story is still told in Umuofia unto this day.

The elders, or *ndichie*, met to hear a report of Okonkwo's mission. At the end they decided, as everybody knew they would, that the girl should go to Ogbuefi Udo to replace his murdered wife. As for the boy, he belonged to the clan as a whole, and there was no hurry to decide his fate. Okonkwo was, therefore, asked on behalf of the clan to look after him in the interim. And so for three years Ikemefuna lived in Okonkwo's household.

Okonkwo ruled his household with a heavy hand. His wives, especially the youngest, lived in perpetual fear of his fiery temper, and so did his little children. Perhaps down in his heart Okonkwo was not a cruel man.

7. "Peace."

But his whole life was dominated by fear, the fear of failure and of weakness. It was deeper and more intimate than the fear of evil and capricious gods and of magic, the fear of the forest, and of the forces of nature, malevolent, red in tooth and claw. Okonkwo's fear was greater than these. It was not external but lay deep within himself. It was the fear of himself, lest he should be found to resemble his father. Even as a little boy he had resented his father's failure and weakness, and even now he still remembered how he had suffered when a playmate had told him that his father was *agbala*. That was how Okonkwo first came to know that *agbala* was not only another name for a woman, it could also mean a man who had taken no title. And so Okonkwo was ruled by one passion—to hate everything that his father Unoka had loved. One of those things was gentleness and another was idleness.

During the planting season Okonkwo worked daily on his farms from cock-crow until the chickens went to roost. He was a very strong man and rarely felt fatigue. But his wives and young children were not as strong, and so they suffered. But they dared not complain openly. Okonkwo's first son, Nwoye,[8] was then twelve years old but was already causing his father great anxiety for his incipient laziness. At any rate, that was how it looked to his father, and he sought to correct him by constant nagging and beating. And so Nwoye was developing into a sad-faced youth.

Okonkwo's prosperity was visible in his household. He had a large compound enclosed by a thick wall of red earth. His own hut, or *obi*, stood immediately behind the only gate in the red walls. Each of his three wives had her own hut, which together formed a half moon behind the *obi*. The barn was built against one end of the red walls, and long stacks of yam stood out prosperously in it. At the opposite end of the compound was a shed for the goats, and each wife built a small attachment to her hut for the hens. Near the barn was a small house, the "medicine house" or shrine where Okonkwo kept the wooden symbols of his personal god and of his ancestral spirits. He worshiped them with sacrifices of kola nut, food and palm-wine, and offered prayers to them on behalf of himself, his three wives and eight children.

So when the daughter of Umuofia was killed in Mbaino, Ikemefuna came into Okonkwo's household. When Okonkwo brought him home that day he called his most senior wife and handed him over to her.

"He belongs to the clan," he told her. "So look after him."

"Is he staying long with us?" she asked.

"Do what you are told, woman," Okonkwo thundered, and stammered. "When did you become one of the *ndichie* of Umuofia?"

And so Nwoye's mother took Ikemefuna to her hut and asked no more questions.

As for the boy himself, he was terribly afraid. He could not understand what was happening to him or what he had done. How could he know that his father had taken a hand in killing a daughter of Umuofia? All he knew was that a few men had arrived at their house, conversing with his

8. "Child Born on Oye Day."

father in low tones, and at the end he had been taken out and handed over to a stranger. His mother had wept bitterly, but he had been too surprised to weep. And so the stranger had brought him, and a girl, a long, long way from home, through lonely forest paths. He did not know who the girl was, and he never saw her again.

3

Okonkwo did not have the start in life which many young men usually had. He did not inherit a barn from his father. There was no barn to inherit. The story was told in Umuofia, of how his father, Unoka, had gone to consult the Oracle of the Hills and the Caves to find out why he always had a miserable harvest.

The Oracle was called Agbala,[9] and people came from far and near to consult it. They came when misfortune dogged their steps or when they had a dispute with their neighbors. They came to discover what the future held for them or to consult the spirits of their departed fathers.

The way into the shrine was a round hole at the side of a hill, just a little bigger than the round opening into a henhouse. Worshipers and those who came to seek knowledge from the god crawled on their belly through the hole and found themselves in a dark, endless space in the presence of Agbala. No one had ever beheld Agbala, except his priestess. But no one who had ever crawled into his awful shrine had come out without the fear of his power. His priestess stood by the sacred fire which she built in the heart of the cave and proclaimed the will of the god. The fire did not burn with a flame. The glowing logs only served to light up vaguely the dark figure of the priestess.

Sometimes a man came to consult the spirit of his dead father or relative. It was said that when such a spirit appeared, the man saw it vaguely in the darkness, but never heard its voice. Some people even said that they had heard the spirits flying and flapping their wings against the roof of the cave.

Many years ago when Okonkwo was still a boy his father, Unoka, had gone to consult Agbala. The priestess in those days was a woman called Chika.[1] She was full of the power of her god, and she was greatly feared. Unoka stood before her and began his story.

"Every year," he said sadly, "before I put any crop in the earth, I sacrifice a cock to Ani, the owner of all land. It is the law of our fathers. I also kill a cock at the shrine of Ifejioku, the god of yams. I clear the bush and set fire to it when it is dry. I sow the yams when the first rain has fallen, and stake them when the young tendrils appear. I weed—"

"Hold your peace!" screamed the priestess, her voice terrible as it echoed through the dark void. "You have offended neither the gods nor your fathers. And when a man is at peace with his gods and his ancestors, his harvest will be good or bad according to the strength of his arm. You, Unoka, are known in all the clan for the weakness of your machete and your hoe. When your neighbors go out with their ax to cut down virgin forests, you sow your yams on exhausted farms that take no labor to clear.

9. The Oracle is masculine, but his priestess, or Voice, is feminine.　　1. "Sky Is Supreme."

They cross seven rivers to make their farms; you stay at home and offer sacrifices to a reluctant soil. Go home and work like a man."

Unoka was an ill-fated man. He had a bad *chi* or personal god, and evil fortune followed him to the grave, or rather to his death, for he had no grave. He died of the swelling which was an abomination to the earth goddess. When a man was afflicted with swelling in the stomach and the limbs he was not allowed to die in the house. He was carried to the Evil Forest and left there to die. There was the story of a very stubborn man who staggered back to his house and had to be carried again to the forest and tied to a tree. The sickness was an abomination to the earth, and so the victim could not be buried in her bowels. He died and rotted away above the earth, and was not given the first or the second burial. Such was Unoka's fate. When they carried him away, he took with him his flute.

With a father like Unoka, Okonkwo did not have the start in life which many young men had. He neither inherited a barn nor a title, nor even a young wife. But in spite of these disadvantages, he had begun even in his father's lifetime to lay the foundations of a prosperous future. It was slow and painful. But he threw himself into it like one possessed. And indeed he was possessed by the fear of his father's contemptible life and shameful death.

There was a wealthy man in Okonkwo's village who had three huge barns, nine wives and thirty children. His name was Nwakibie[2] and he had taken the highest but one title which a man could take in the clan. It was for this man that Okonkwo worked to earn his first seed yams.

He took a pot of palm-wine and a cock to Nwakibie. Two elderly neighbors were sent for, and Nwakibie's two grown-up sons were also present in his *obi*. He presented a kola nut and an alligator pepper, which were passed round for all to see and then returned to him. He broke the nut saying: "We shall all live. We pray for life, children, a good harvest and happiness. You will have what is good for you and I will have what is good for me. Let the kite perch and let the eagle perch too. If one says no to the other, let his wing break."

After the kola nut had been eaten Okonkwo brought his palm-wine from the corner of the hut where it had been placed and stood it in the center of the group. He addressed Nwakibie, calling him "Our father."

"*Nna ayi*," he said. "I have brought you this little kola. As our people say, a man who pays respect to the great paves the way for his own greatness. I have come to pay you my respects and also to ask a favor. But let us drink the wine first."

Everybody thanked Okonkwo and the neighbors brought out their drinking horns from the goatskin bags they carried. Nwakibie brought down his own horn, which was fastened to the rafters. The younger of his sons, who was also the youngest man in the group, moved to the center, raised the pot on his left knee and began to pour out the wine. The first cup went to Okonkwo, who must taste his wine before anyone else.[3] Then the group drank, beginning with the eldest man. When everyone had

---

2. "The Child Surpasses His Neighbors."   3. A ceremonial gesture; one who gives wine tastes it first to show that it is not poisoned.

drunk two or three horns, Nwakibie sent for his wives. Some of them were not at home and only four came in.

"Is Anasi not in?" he asked them. They said she was coming. Anasi was the first[4] wife and the others could not drink before her, and so they stood waiting.

Anasi was a middle-aged woman, tall and strongly built. There was authority in her bearing and she looked every inch the ruler of the women-folk in a large and prosperous family. She wore the anklet of her husband's titles, which the first wife alone could wear.

She walked up to her husband and accepted the horn from him. She then went down on one knee, drank a little and handed back the horn. She rose, called him by his name and went back to her hut. The other wives drank in the same way, in their proper order, and went away.

The men then continued their drinking and talking. Ogbuefi Idigo was talking about the palm-wine tapper, Obiako, who suddenly gave up his trade.

"There must be something behind it," he said, wiping the foam of wine from his mustache with the back of his left hand. "There must be a reason for it. A toad does not run in the daytime for nothing."

"Some people say the Oracle warned him that he would fall off a palm tree and kill himself," said Akukalia.

"Obiako has always been a strange one," said Nwakibie. "I have heard that many years ago, when his father had not been dead very long, he had gone to consult the Oracle. The Oracle said to him, 'Your dead father wants you to sacrifice a goat to him.' Do you know what he told the Oracle? He said, 'Ask my dead father if he ever had a fowl when he was alive.' " Everybody laughed heartily except Okonkwo, who laughed uneasily because, as the saying goes, an old woman is always uneasy when dry bones are mentioned in a proverb. Okonkwo remembered his own father.

At last the young man who was pouring out the wine held up half a horn of the thick, white dregs and said, "What we are eating is finished." "We have seen it," the others replied. "Who will drink the dregs?" he asked. "Whoever has a job in hand," said Idigo, looking at Nwakibie's elder son Igwelo with a malicious twinkle in his eye.

Everyone agreed that Igwelo should drink the dregs. He accepted the half-full horn from his brother and drank it. As Idigo had said, Igwelo had a job in hand because he had married his first wife a month or two before. The thick dregs of palm-wine were supposed to be good for men who were going in to their wives.

After the wine had been drunk Okonkwo laid his difficulties before Nwakibie.

"I have come to you for help," he said. "Perhaps you can already guess what it is. I have cleared a farm but have no yams to sow. I know what it is to ask a man to trust another with his yams, especially these days when young men are afraid of hard work. I am not afraid of work. The lizard that jumped from the high iroko tree to the ground said he would praise

4. "First" or "favorite" wife—not always the same.

himself if no one else did. I began to fend for myself at an age when most people still suck at their mothers' breasts. If you give me some yam seeds I shall not fail you."

Nwakibie cleared his throat. "It pleases me to see a young man like you these days when our youth has gone so soft. Many young men have come to me to ask for yams but I have refused because I knew they would just dump them in the earth and leave them to be choked by weeds. When I say no to them they think I am hard-hearted. But it is not so. Eneke the bird[5] says that since men have learned to shoot without missing, he has learned to fly without perching. I have learned to be stingy with my yams. But I can trust you. I know it as I look at you. As our fathers said, you can tell a ripe corn by its look. I shall give you twice four hundred yams. Go ahead and prepare your farm."

Okonkwo thanked him again and again and went home feeling happy. He knew that Nwakibie would not refuse him, but he had not expected he would be so generous. He had not hoped to get more than four hundred seeds. He would now have to make a bigger farm. He hoped to get another four hundred yams from one of his father's friends at Isiuzo.[6]

Sharecropping was a very slow way of building up a barn of one's own. After all the toil one only got a third of the harvest. But for a young man whose father had no yams, there was no other way. And what made it worse in Okonkwo's case was that he had to support his mother and two sisters from his meager harvest. And supporting his mother also meant supporting his father. She could not be expected to cook and eat while her husband starved. And so at a very early age when he was striving desperately to build a barn through sharecropping Okonkwo was also fending for his father's house. It was like pouring grains of corn into a bag full of holes. His mother and sisters worked hard enough, but they grew women's crops, like coco-yams, beans and cassava. Yam, the king of crops, was a man's crop.[7]

The year that Okonkwo took eight hundred seed-yams from Nwakibie was the worst year in living memory. Nothing happened at its proper time; it was either too early or too late. It seemed as if the world had gone mad. The first rains were late, and, when they came, lasted only a brief moment. The blazing sun returned, more fierce than it had ever been known, and scorched all the green that had appeared with the rains. The earth burned like hot coals and roasted all the yams that had been sown. Like all good farmers, Okonkwo had begun to sow with the first rains. He had sown four hundred seeds when the rains dried up and the heat returned. He watched the sky all day for signs of rain clouds and lay awake all night. In the morning he went back to his farm and saw the withering tendrils. He had tried to protect them from the smoldering earth by making rings of thick sisal leaves around them. But by the end of the day the sisal rings were burned dry and gray. He changed them every day, and prayed that the

5. Proverbial.   6. "Head of the Road," a small town.   7. Yams, a staple food in Western Africa, were a sacred crop generally cultivated only by men and eaten either roasted or boiled. *Coco-yams* (a brown root also called taro) and *cassava* (or manioc, which is fermented to remove natural arsenic) were low-status root vegetables, prepared for eating by boiling and pounding.

rain might fall in the night. But the drought continued for eight market weeks and the yams were killed.

Some farmers had not planted their yams yet. They were the lazy easy-going ones who always put off clearing their farms as long as they could. This year they were the wise ones. They sympathized with their neighbors with much shaking of the head, but inwardly they were happy for what they took to be their own foresight.

Okonkwo planted what was left of his seed-yams when the rains finally returned. He had one consolation. The yams he had sown before the drought were his own, the harvest of the previous year. He still had the eight hundred from Nwakibie and the four hundred from his father's friend. So he would make a fresh start.

But the year had gone mad. Rain fell as it had never fallen before. For days and nights together it poured down in violent torrents, and washed away the yam heaps. Trees were uprooted and deep gorges appeared everywhere. Then the rain became less violent. But it went from day to day without a pause. The spell of sunshine which always came in the middle of the wet season did not appear. The yams put on luxuriant green leaves, but every farmer knew that without sunshine the tubers would not grow.

That year the harvest was sad, like a funeral, and many farmers wept as they dug up the miserable and rotting yams. One man tied his cloth to a tree branch and hanged himself.

Okonkwo remembered that tragic year with a cold shiver throughout the rest of his life. It always surprised him when he thought of it later that he did not sink under the load of despair. He knew that he was a fierce fighter, but that year had been enough to break the heart of a lion.

"Since I survived that year," he always said, "I shall survive anything." He put it down to his inflexible will.

His father, Unoka, who was then an ailing man, had said to him during that terrible harvest month: "Do not despair. I know you will not despair. You have a manly and a proud heart. A proud heart can survive a general failure because such a failure does not prick its pride. It is more difficult and more bitter when a man fails *alone*."

Unoka was like that in his last days. His love of talk had grown with age and sickness. It tried Okonkwo's patience beyond words.

4

"Looking at a king's mouth," said an old man, "one would think he never sucked at his mother's breast." He was talking about Okonkwo, who had risen so suddenly from great poverty and misfortune to be one of the lords of the clan. The old man bore no ill will towards Okonkwo. Indeed he respected him for his industry and success. But he was struck, as most people were, by Okonkwo's brusqueness in dealing with less successful men. Only a week ago a man had contradicted him at a kindred meeting which they held to discuss the next ancestral feast. Without looking at the man Okonkwo had said: "This meeting is for men." The man who had contradicted him had no titles. That was why he had called him a woman. Okonkwo knew how to kill a man's spirit.

Everybody at the kindred meeting took sides with Osugo[8] when Okonkwo called him a woman. The oldest man present said sternly that those
whose palm-kernels were cracked for them by a benevolent spirit should
not forget to be humble. Okonkwo said he was sorry for what he had said,
and the meeting continued.

But it was really not true that Okonkwo's palm-kernels had been
cracked for him by a benevolent spirit. He had cracked them himself.
Anyone who knew his grim struggle against poverty and misfortune could
not say he had been lucky. If ever a man deserved his success, that man
was Okonkwo. An an early age he had achieved fame as the greatest wrestler in all the land. That was not luck. At the most one could say that his
chi or personal god was good. But the Ibo people have a proverb that when
a man says yes his *chi* says yes also. Okonkwo said yes very strongly; so his
chi agreed. And not only his *chi* but his clan too, because it judged a man
by the work of his hands. That was why Okonkwo had been chosen by the
nine villages to carry a message of war to their enemies unless they agreed
to give up a young man and a virgin to atone for the murder of Udo's wife.
And such was the deep fear that their enemies had for Umuofia that they
treated Okonkwo like a king and brought him a virgin who was given to
Udo as wife, and the lad Ikemefuna.

The elders of the clan had decided that Ikemefuna should be in Okonkwo's care for a while. But no one thought it would be as long as three
years. They seemed to forget all about him as soon as they had taken the
decision.

At first Ikemefuna was very much afraid. Once or twice he tried to run
away, but he did not know where to begin. He thought of his mother and
his three-year-old sister and wept bitterly. Nwoye's mother was very kind
to him and treated him as one of her own children. But all he said was:
"When shall I go home?" When Okonkwo heard that he would not eat
any food he came into the hut with a big stick in his hand and stood over
him while he swallowed his yams, trembling. A few moments later he
went behind the hut and began to vomit painfully. Nwoye's mother went
to him and placed her hands on his chest and on his back. He was ill for
three market weeks, and when he recovered he seemed to have overcome
his great fear and sadness.

He was by nature a very lively boy and he gradually became popular in
Okonkwo's household, especially with the children. Okonkwo's son,
Nwoye, who was two years younger, became quite inseparable from him
because he seemed to know everything. He could fashion out flutes from
bamboo stems and even from the elephant grass. He knew the names of
all the birds and could set clever traps for the little bush rodents. And he
knew which trees made the strongest bows.

Even Okonkwo himself became very fond of the boy—inwardly of
course. Okonkwo never showed any emotion openly, unless it be the emotion of anger. To show affection was a sign of weakness; the only thing
worth demonstrating was strength. He therefore treated Ikemefuna as he
treated everybody else—with a heavy hand. But there was no doubt that

8. "Low-Status [*osu*] Person."

he liked the boy. Sometimes when he went to big village meetings or communal ancestral feasts he allowed Ikemefuna to accompany him, like a son, carrying his stool and his goatskin bag. And, indeed, Ikemefuna called him father.

Ikemefuna came to Umuofia at the end of the carefree season between harvest and planting. In fact he recovered from his illness only a few days before the Week of Peace began. And that was also the year Okonkwo broke the peace, and was punished, as was the custom, by Ezeani, the priest of the earth goddess.

Okonkwo was provoked to justifiable anger by his youngest wife, who went to plait her hair at her friend's house and did not return early enough to cook the afternoon meal. Okonkwo did not know at first that she was not at home. After waiting in vain for her dish he went to her hut to see what she was doing. There was nobody in the hut and the fireplace was cold.

"Where is Ojiugo?" he asked his second wife, who came out of her hut to draw water from a gigantic pot in the shade of a small tree in the middle of the compound.

"She has gone to plait her hair."

Okonkwo bit his lips as anger welled up within him.

"Where are her children? Did she take them?" he asked with unusual coolness and restraint.

"They are here," answered his first wife, Nwoye's mother. Okonkwo bent down and looked into her hut. Ojiugo's children were eating with the children of his first wife.

"Did she ask you to feed them before she went?"

"Yes," lied Nwoye's mother, trying to minimize Ojiugo's thoughtlessness.

Okonkwo knew she was not speaking the truth. He walked back to his *obi* to await Ojiugo's return. And when she returned he beat her very heavily. In his anger he had forgotten that it was the Week of Peace. His first two wives ran out in great alarm pleading with him that it was the sacred week. But Okonkwo was not the man to stop beating somebody half-way through, not even for fear of a goddess.

Okonkwo's neighbors heard his wife crying and sent their voices over the compound walls to ask what was the matter. Some of them came over to see for themselves. It was unheard of to beat somebody during the sacred week.

Before it was dusk Ezeani, who was the priest of the earth goddess, Ani, called on Okonkwo in his *obi*. Okonkwo brought out kola nut and placed it before the priest.

"Take away your kola nut. I shall not eat in the house of a man who has no respect for our gods and ancestors."

Okonkwo tried to explain to him what his wife had done, but Ezeani seemed to pay no attention. He held a short staff in his hand which he brought down on the floor to emphasize his points.

"Listen to me," he said when Okonkwo had spoken. "You are not a stranger in Umuofia. You know as well as I do that our forefathers

ordained that before we plant any crops in the earth we should observe a
week in which a man does not say a harsh word to his neighbor. We live
in peace with our fellows to honor our great goddess of the earth without
whose blessing our crops will not grow. You have committed a great evil."
He brought down his staff heavily on the floor. "Your wife was at fault, but
even if you came into your *obi* and found her lover on top of her, you
would still have committed a great evil to beat her." His staff came down
again. "The evil you have done can ruin the whole clan. The earth goddess whom you have insulted may refuse to give us her increase, and we
shall all perish." His tone now changed from anger to command. "You
will bring to the shrine of Ani tomorrow one she-goat, one hen, a length
of cloth and a hundred cowries." He rose and left the hut.

Okonkwo did as the priest said. He also took with him a pot of palm-
wine. Inwardly, he was repentant. But he was not the man to go about
telling his neighbors that he was in error. And so people said he had no
respect for the gods of the clan. His enemies said his good fortune had
gone to his head. They called him the little bird *nza* who so far forgot
himself after a heavy meal that he challenged his *chi*.[9]

No work was done during the Week of Peace. People called on their
neighbors and drank palm-wine. This year they talked of nothing else but
the *nso-ani*[1] which Okonkwo had committed. It was the first time for many
years that a man had broken the sacred peace. Even the oldest men could
only remember one or two other occasions somewhere in the dim past.

Ogbuefi Ezeudu, who was the oldest man in the village, was telling two
other men who came to visit him that the punishment for breaking the
Peace of Ani had become very mild in their clan.

"It has not always been so," he said. "My father told me that he had
been told that in the past a man who broke the peace was dragged on the
ground through the village until he died. But after a while this custom
was stopped because it spoiled the peace which it was meant to preserve."

"Somebody told me yesterday," said one of the younger men, "that in
some clans it is an abomination for a man to die during the Week of
Peace."

"It is indeed true," said Ogbuefi Ezeudu. "They have that custom in
Obodoani.[2] If a man dies at this time he is not buried but cast into the
Evil Forest. It is a bad custom which these people observe because they
lack understanding. They throw away large numbers of men and women
without burial. And what is the result? Their clan is full of the evil spirits
of these unburied dead, hungry to do harm to the living."

After the Week of Peace every man and his family began to clear the bush
to make new farms. The cut bush was left to dry and fire was then set to
it. As the smoke rose into the sky kites appeared from different directions
and hovered over the burning field in silent valediction. The rainy season
was approaching when they would go away until the dry season returned.

9. Personal god. *Nza*: "the one that talks back" (literal trans.); a small aggressive bird. In the story, it is
easily defeated (alternatively, caught by a hawk) when it becomes foolish enough to challenge its personal
god.   1. Sin, abomination against the earth goddess Ani.   2. "The Town of the Land" (literal trans);
that is, Anytown, Nigeria.

Okonkwo spent the next few days preparing his seed-yams. He looked at each yam carefully to see whether it was good for sowing. Sometimes he decided that a yam was too big to be sown as one seed and he split it deftly along its length with his sharp knife. His eldest son, Nwoye, and Ikemefuna helped him by fetching the yams in long baskets from the barn and in counting the prepared seeds in groups of four hundred. Sometimes Okonkwo gave them a few yams each to prepare. But he always found fault with their effort, and he said so with much threatening.

"Do you think you are cutting up yams for cooking?" he asked Nwoye. "If you split another yam of this size, I shall break your jaw. You think you are still a child. I began to own a farm at your age. And you," he said to Ikemefuna, "do you not grow yams where you come from?"

Inwardly Okonkwo knew that the boys were still too young to understand fully the difficult art of preparing seed-yams. But he thought that one could not begin too early. Yam stood for manliness, and he who could feed his family on yams from one harvest to another was a very great man indeed. Okonkwo wanted his son to be a great farmer and a great man. He would stamp out the disquieting signs of laziness which he thought he already saw in him.

"I will not have a son who cannot hold up his head in the gathering of the clan. I would sooner strangle him with my own hands. And if you stand staring at me like that," he swore, "Amadiora[3] will break your head for you!"

Some days later, when the land had been moistened by two or three heavy rains, Okonkwo and his family went to the farm with baskets of seed-yams, their hoes and machetes, and the planting began. They made single mounds of earth in straight lines all over the field and sowed the yams in them.

Yam, the king of crops, was a very exacting king. For three or four moons it demanded hard work and constant attention from cock-crow till the chickens went back to roost. The young tendrils were protected from earth-heat with rings of sisal leaves. As the rains became heavier the women planted maize, melons and beans between the yam mounds. The yams were then staked, first with little sticks and later with tall and big tree branches. The women weeded the farm three times at definite periods in the life of the yams, neither early nor late.

And now the rains had really come, so heavy and persistent that even the village rain-maker no longer claimed to be able to intervene. He could not stop the rain now, just as he would not attempt to start it in the heart of the dry season, without serious danger to his own health. The personal dynamism required to counter the forces of these extremes of weather would be far too great for the human frame.

And so nature was not interfered with in the middle of the rainy season. Sometimes it poured down in such thick sheets of water that earth and sky seemed merged in one gray wetness. It was then uncertain whether the low rumbling of Amadiora's thunder came from above or below. At such times, in each of the countless thatched huts of Umuofia, children sat

3. God of thunder and lightning.

around their mother's cooking fire telling stories, or with their father in his *obi* warming themselves from a log fire, roasting and eating maize. It was a brief resting period between the exacting and arduous planting season and the equally exacting but light-hearted month of harvests.

Ikemefuna had begun to feel like a member of Okonkwo's family. He still thought about his mother and his three-year-old sister, and he had moments of sadness and depression. But he and Nwoye had become so deeply attached to each other that such moments became less frequent and less poignant. Ikemefuna had an endless stock of folk tales. Even those which Nwoye knew already were told with a new freshness and the local flavor of a different clan. Nwoye remembered this period very vividly till the end of his life. He even remembered how he had laughed when Ikemefuna told him that the proper name for a corn cob with only a few scattered grains was *eze-agadi-nwayi*, or the teeth of an old woman. Nwoye's mind had gone immediately to Nwayieke,[4] who lived near the udala tree. She had about three teeth and was always smoking her pipe.

Gradually the rains became lighter and less frequent, and earth and sky once again became separate. The rain fell in thin, slanting showers through sunshine and quiet breeze. Children no longer stayed indoors but ran about singing:

> The rain is falling, the sun is shining,
> Alone Nnadi[5] is cooking and eating.

Nwoye always wondered who Nnadi was and why he should live all by himself, cooking and eating. In the end he decided that Nnadi must live in that land of Ikemefuna's favorite story where the ant holds his court in splendor and the sands dance forever.

5

The Feast of the New Yam was approaching and Umuofia was in a festival mood. It was an occasion for giving thanks to Ani, the earth goddess and the source of all fertility. Ani played a greater part in the life of the people than any other deity. She was the ultimate judge of morality and conduct. And what was more, she was in close communion with the departed fathers of the clan whose bodies had been committed to earth.

The Feast of the New Yam was held every year before the harvest began, to honor the earth goddess and the ancestral spirits of the clan. New yams could not be eaten until some had first been offered to these powers. Men and women, young and old, looked forward to the New Yam Festival because it began the season of plenty—the new year. On the last night before the festival, yams of the old year were all disposed of by those who still had them. The new year must begin with tasty, fresh yams and not the shriveled and fibrous crops of the previous year. All cooking pots, calabashes and wooden bowls were thoroughly washed, especially the wooden

4. "Woman Born on Eke Day." *Udala*: the African star apple tree.   5. "Father Is There" or "Father Exists."

mortar in which yam was pounded. Yam foo-foo[6] and vegetable soup was the chief food in the celebration. So much of it was cooked that, no matter how heavily the family ate or how many friends and relatives they invited from neighboring villages, there was always a large quantity of food left over at the end of the day. The story was always told of a wealthy man who set before his guests a mound of foo-foo so high that those who sat on one side could not see what was happening on the other, and it was not until late in the evening that one of them saw for the first time his in-law who had arrived during the course of the meal and had fallen to on the opposite side. It was only then that they exchanged greetings and shook hands over what was left of the food.

The New Yam Festival was thus an occasion for joy throughout Umuofia. And every man whose arm was strong, as the Ibo people say, was expected to invite large numbers of guests from far and wide. Okonkwo always asked his wives' relations, and since he now had three wives his guests would make a fairly big crowd.

But somehow Okonkwo could never become as enthusiastic over feasts as most people. He was a good eater and he could drink one or two fairly big gourds of palm-wine. But he was always uncomfortable sitting around for days waiting for a feast or getting over it. He would be very much happier working on his farm.

The festival was now only three days away. Okonkwo's wives had scrubbed the walls and the huts with red earth until they reflected light. They had then drawn patterns on them in white, yellow and dark green. They then set about painting themselves with cam wood and drawing beautiful black patterns on their stomachs and on their backs. The children were also decorated, especially their hair, which was shaved in beautiful patterns. The three women talked excitedly about the relations who had been invited, and the children reveled in the thought of being spoiled by these visitors from the motherland. Ikemefuna was equally excited. The New Yam Festival seemed to him to be a much bigger event here than in his own village, a place which was already becoming remote and vague in his imagination.

And then the storm burst. Okonkwo, who had been walking about aimlessly in his compound in suppressed anger, suddenly found an outlet.

"Who killed this banana tree?" he asked.

A hush fell on the compound immediately.

"Who killed this tree? Or are you all deaf and dumb?"

As a matter of fact the tree was very much alive. Okonkwo's second wife had merely cut a few leaves off it to wrap some food, and she said so. Without further argument Okonkwo gave her a sound beating and left her and her only daughter weeping. Neither of the other wives dared to interfere beyond an occasional and tentative, "It is enough, Okonkwo," pleaded from a reasonable distance.

His anger thus satisfied, Okonkwo decided to go out hunting. He had an old rusty gun made by a clever blacksmith who had come to live in

---

6. A mashed, edible base that is shaped into balls with the fingers and then indented for cupping and eating soup.

Umuofia long ago. But although Okonkwo was a great man whose prowess was universally acknowledged, he was not a hunter. In fact he had not killed a rat with his gun. And so when he called Ikemefuna to fetch his gun, the wife who had just been beaten murmured something about guns that never shot. Unfortunately for her, Okonkwo heard it and ran madly into his room for the loaded gun, ran out again and aimed at her as she clambered over the dwarf wall of the barn. He pressed the trigger and there was a loud report accompanied by the wail of his wives and children. He threw down the gun and jumped into the barn, and there lay the woman, very much shaken and frightened but quite unhurt. He heaved a heavy sigh and went away with the gun.

In spite of this incident the New Yam Festival was celebrated with great joy in Okonkwo's household. Early that morning as he offered a sacrifice of new yam and palm-oil to his ancestors he asked them to protect him, his children and their mothers in the new year.

As the day wore on his in-laws arrived from three surrounding villages, and each party brought with them a huge pot of palm-wine. And there was eating and drinking till night, when Okonkwo's in-laws began to leave for their homes.

The second day of the new year was the day of the great wrestling match between Okonkwo's village and their neighbors. It was difficult to say which the people enjoyed more—the feasting and fellowship of the first day or the wrestling contest of the second. But there was one woman who had no doubt whatever in her mind. She was Okonkwo's second wife, Ekwefi, whom he nearly shot. There was no festival in all the seasons of the year which gave her as much pleasure as the wrestling match. Many years ago when she was the village beauty Okonkwo had won her heart by throwing the Cat in the greatest contest within living memory. She did not marry him then because he was too poor to pay her bride-price. But a few years later she ran away from her husband and came to live with Okonkwo. All this happened many years ago. Now Ekwefi[7] was a woman of forty-five who had suffered a great deal in her time. But her love of wrestling contests was still as strong as it was thirty years ago.

It was not yet noon on the second day of the New Yam Festival. Ekwefi and her only daughter, Ezinma,[8] sat near the fireplace waiting for the water in the pot to boil. The fowl Ekwefi had just killed was in the wooden mortar. The water began to boil, and in one deft movement she lifted the pot from the fire and poured the boiling water over the fowl. She put back the empty pot on the circular pad in the corner, and looked at her palms, which were black with soot. Ezinma was always surprised that her mother could lift a pot from the fire with her bare hands.

"Ekwefi," she said, "is it true that when people are grown up, fire does not burn them?" Ezinma, unlike most children, called her mother by her name.

"Yes," replied Ekwefi, too busy to argue. Her daughter was only ten years old but she was wiser than her years.

---

7. An abbreviation of "Do you have a cow?"; the cow being a symbol of wealth. Okonkwo would presumably have repaid Ekwefi's bride-price to her first husband.   8. "True Beauty" or goodness.

"But Nwoye's mother dropped her pot of hot soup the other day and it broke on the floor."

Ekwefi turned the hen over in the mortar and began to pluck the feathers.

"Ekwefi," said Ezinma, who had joined in plucking the feathers, "my eyelid is twitching."

"It means you are going to cry," said her mother.

"No," Ezinma said, "it is this eyelid, the top one."

"That means you will see something."

"What will I see?" she asked.

"How can I know?" Ekwefi wanted her to work it out herself.

"Oho," said Ezinma at last. "I know what it is—the wrestling match."

At last the hen was plucked clean. Ekwefi tried to pull out the horny beak but it was too hard. She turned round on her low stool and put the beak in the fire for a few moments. She pulled again and it came off.

"Ekwefi!" a voice called from one of the other huts. It was Nwoye's mother, Okonkwo's first wife.

"Is that me?" Ekwefi called back. That was the way people answered calls from outside. They never answered yes for fear it might be an evil spirit calling.

"Will you give Ezinma some fire to bring to me?" Her own children and Ikemefuna had gone to the stream.

Ekwefi put a few live coals into a piece of broken pot and Ezinma carried it across the clean swept compound to Nwoye's mother.

"Thank you, Nma," she said. She was peeling new yams, and in a basket beside her were green vegetables and beans.

"Let me make the fire for you," Ezinma offered.

"Thank you, Ezigbo," she said. She often called her Ezigbo, which means "the good one."

Ezinma went outside and brought some sticks from a huge bundle of firewood. She broke them into little pieces across the sole of her foot and began to build a fire, blowing it with her breath.

"You will blow your eyes out," said Nwoye's mother, looking up from the yams she was peeling. "Use the fan." She stood up and pulled out the fan which was fastened into one of the rafters. As soon as she got up, the troublesome nanny goat, which had been dutifully eating yam peelings, dug her teeth into the real thing, scooped out two mouthfuls and fled from the hut to chew the cud in the goats' shed. Nwoye's mother swore at her and settled down again to her peeling. Ezinma's fire was now sending up thick clouds of smoke. She went on fanning it until it burst into flames. Nwoye's mother thanked her and she went back to her mother's hut.

Just then the distant beating of drums began to reach them. It came from the direction of the *ilo*, the village playground. Every village had its own *ilo* which was as old as the village itself and where all the great ceremonies and dances took place. The drums beat the unmistakable wrestling dance—quick, light and gay, and it came floating on the wind.

Okonkwo cleared his throat and moved his feet to the beat of the drums.

It filled him with fire as it had always done from his youth. He trembled with the desire to conquer and subdue. It was like the desire for a woman.

"We shall be late for the wrestling," said Ezinma to her mother.

"They will not begin until the sun goes down."

"But they are beating the drums."

"Yes. The drums begin at noon but the wrestling waits until the sun begins to sink. Go and see if your father has brought out yams for the afternoon."

"He has. Nwoye's mother is already cooking."

"Go and bring our own, then. We must cook quickly or we shall be late for the wrestling."

Ezinma ran in the direction of the barn and brought back two yams from the dwarf wall.

Ekwefi peeled the yams quickly. The troublesome nanny goat sniffed about, eating the peelings. She cut the yams into small pieces and began to prepare a pottage, using some of the chicken.

At that moment they heard someone crying just outside their compound. It was very much like Obiageli,[9] Nwoye's sister.

"Is that not Obiageli weeping?" Ekwefi called across the yard to Nwoye's mother.

"Yes," she replied. "She must have broken her waterpot."

The weeping was now quite close and soon the children filed in, carrying on their heads various sizes of pots suitable to their years. Ikemefuna came first with the biggest pot, closely followed by Nwoye and his two younger brothers. Obiageli brought up the rear, her face streaming with tears. In her hand was the cloth pad on which the pot should have rested on her head.

"What happened?" her mother asked, and Obiageli told her mournful story. Her mother consoled her and promised to buy her another pot.

Nwoye's younger brothers were about to tell their mother the true story of the accident when Ikemefuna looked at them sternly and they held their peace. The fact was that Obiageli had been making *inyanga*[1] with her pot. She had balanced it on her head, folded her arms in front of her and began to sway her waist like a grown-up young lady. When the pot fell down and broke she burst out laughing. She only began to weep when they got near the iroko tree outside their compound.

The drums were still beating, persistent and unchanging. Their sound was no longer a separate thing from the living village. It was like the pulsation of its heart. It throbbed in the air, in the sunshine, and even in the trees, and filled the village with excitement.

Ekwefi ladled her husband's share of the pottage into a bowl and covered it. Ezinma took it to him in his *obi*.

Okonkwo was sitting on a goatskin already eating his first wife's meal. Obiageli, who had brought it from her mother's hut, sat on the floor waiting for him to finish. Ezinma placed her mother's dish before him and sat with Obiageli.

9. "Born to Eat" (born into prosperity).   1. Showing off.

"Sit like a woman!" Okonkwo shouted at her. Ezinma brought her two legs together and stretched them in front of her.

"Father, will you go to see the wrestling?" Ezinma asked after a suitable interval.

"Yes," he answered. "Will you go?"

"Yes." And after a pause she said: "Can I bring your chair for you?"

"No, that is a boy's job." Okonkwo was specially fond of Ezinma. She looked very much like her mother, who was once the village beauty. But his fondness only showed on very rare occasions.

"Obiageli broke her pot today," Ezinma said.

"Yes, she has told me about it," Okonkwo said between mouthfuls.

"Father," said Obiageli, "people should not talk when they are eating or pepper may go down the wrong way."

"That is very true. Do you hear that, Ezinma? You are older than Obiageli but she has more sense."

He uncovered his second wife's dish and began to eat from it. Obiageli took the first dish and returned to her mother's hut. And then Nkechi came in, bringing the third dish. Nkechi was the daughter of Okonkwo's third wife.

In the distance the drums continued to beat.

6

The whole village turned out on the *ilo*, men, women and children. They stood round in a huge circle leaving the center of the playground free. The elders and grandees of the village sat on their own stools brought there by their young sons or slaves. Okonkwo was among them. All others stood except those who came early enough to secure places on the few stands which had been built by placing smooth logs on forked pillars.

The wrestlers were not there yet and the drummers held the field. They too sat just in front of the huge circle of spectators, facing the elders. Behind them was the big and ancient silk-cotton tree which was sacred. Spirits of good children lived in that tree waiting to be born. On ordinary days young women who desired children came to sit under its shade.

There were seven drums and they were arranged according to their sizes in a long wooden basket. Three men beat them with sticks, working feverishly from one drum to another. They were possessed by the spirit of the drums.

The young men who kept order on these occasions dashed about, consulting among themselves and with the leaders of the two wrestling teams, who were still outside the circle, behind the crowd. Once in a while two young men carrying palm fronds ran round the circle and kept the crowd back by beating the ground in front of them or, if they were stubborn, their legs and feet.

At last the two teams danced into the circle and the crowd roared and clapped. The drums rose to a frenzy. The people surged forward. The young men who kept order flew around, waving their palm fronds. Old men nodded to the beat of the drums and remembered the days when they wrestled to its intoxicating rhythm.

The contest began with boys of fifteen or sixteen. There were only three such boys in each team. They were not the real wrestlers; they merely set the scene. Within a short time the first two bouts were over. But the third created a big sensation even among the elders who did not usually show their excitement so openly. It was as quick as the other two, perhaps even quicker. But very few people had ever seen that kind of wrestling before. As soon as the two boys closed in, one of them did something which no one could describe because it had been as quick as a flash. And the other boy was flat on his back. The crowd roared and clapped and for a while drowned the frenzied drums. Okonkwo sprang to his feet and quickly sat down again. Three young men from the victorious boy's team ran forward, carried him shoulder high and danced through the cheering crowd. Everybody soon knew who the boy was. His name was Maduka, the son of Obierika.[2]

The drummers stopped for a brief rest before the real matches. Their bodies shone with sweat, and they took up fans and began to fan themselves. They also drank water from small pots and ate kola nuts. They became ordinary human beings again, talking and laughing among themselves and with others who stood near them. The air, which had been stretched taut with excitement, relaxed again. It was as if water had been poured on the tightened skin of a drum. Many people looked around, perhaps for the first time, and saw those who stood or sat next to them.

"I did not know it was you," Ekwefi said to the woman who had stood shoulder to shoulder with her since the beginning of the matches.

"I do not blame you," said the woman. "I have never seen such a large crowd of people. Is it true that Okonkwo nearly killed you with his gun?"

"It is true indeed, my dear friend. I cannot yet find a mouth with which to tell the story."

"Your *chi* is very much awake, my friend. And how is my daughter, Ezinma?"

"She has been very well for some time now. Perhaps she has come to stay."

"I think she has. How old is she now?"

"She is about ten years old."

"I think she will stay. They usually stay if they do not die before the age of six."

"I pray she stays," said Ekwefi with a heavy sigh.

The woman with whom she talked was called Chielo.[3] She was the priestess of Agbala, the Oracle of the Hills and the Caves. In ordinary life Chielo was a widow with two children. She was very friendly with Ekwefi and they shared a common shed in the market. She was particularly fond of Ekwefi's only daughter, Ezinma, whom she called "my daughter." Quite often she bought beancakes and gave Ekwefi some to take home to Ezinma. Anyone seeing Chielo in ordinary life would hardly believe she was the same person who prophesied when the spirit of Agbala was upon her.

2. "The Heart Eats [enjoys] more."   3. "Chi Who Plants."

The drummers took up their sticks and the air shivered and grew tense like a tightened bow.

The two teams were ranged facing each other across the clear space. A young man from one team danced across the center to the other side and pointed at whomever he wanted to fight. They danced back to the center together and then closed in.

There were twelve men on each side and the challenge went from one side to the other. Two judges walked around the wrestlers and when they thought they were equally matched, stopped them. Five matches ended in this way. But the really exciting moments were when a man was thrown. The huge voice of the crowd then rose to the sky and in every direction. It was even heard in the surrounding villages.

The last match was between the leaders of the teams. They were among the best wrestlers in all the nine villages. The crowd wondered who would throw the other this year. Some said Okafo was the better man; others said he was not the equal of Ikezue.[4] Last year neither of them had thrown the other even though the judges had allowed the contest to go on longer than was the custom. They had the same style and one saw the other's plans beforehand. It might happen again this year.

Dusk was already approaching when their contest began. The drums went mad and the crowds also. They surged forward as the two young men danced into the circle. The palm fronds were helpless in keeping them back.

Ikezue held out his right hand. Okafo seized it, and they closed in. It was a fierce contest. Ikezue strove to dig in his right heel behind Okafo so as to pitch him backwards in the clever *ege* style. But the one knew what the other was thinking. The crowd had surrounded and swallowed up the drummers, whose frantic rhythm was no longer a mere disembodied sound but the very heartbeat of the people.

The wrestlers were now almost still in each other's grip. The muscles on their arms and their thighs and on their backs stood out and twitched. It looked like an equal match. The two judges were already moving forward to separate them when Ikezue, now desperate, went down quickly on one knee in an attempt to fling his man backwards over his head. It was a sad miscalculation. Quick as the lightning of Amadiora, Okafo raised his right leg and swung it over his rival's head. The crowd burst into a thunderous roar. Okafo was swept off his feet by his supporters and carried home shoulder high. They sang his praise and the young women clapped their hands:

> Who will wrestle for our village?
> Okafo will wrestle for our village.
> Has he thrown a hundred men?
> He has thrown four hundred men.
> Has he thrown a hundred Cats?
> He has thrown four hundred Cats.
> Then send him word to fight for us.

4. "Strength Is Complete" (a boastful name).

7

For three years Ikemefuna lived in Okonkwo's household and the elders of Umuofia seemed to have forgotten about him. He grew rapidly like a yam tendril in the rainy season, and was full of the sap of life. He had become wholly absorbed into his new family. He was like an elder brother to Nwoye, and from the very first seemed to have kindled a new fire in the younger boy. He made him feel grown-up; and they no longer spent the evenings in mother's hut while she cooked, but now sat with Okonkwo in his *obi*, or watched him as he tapped his palm tree for the evening wine. Nothing pleased Nwoye now more than to be sent for by his mother or another of his father's wives to do one of those difficult and masculine tasks in the home, like splitting wood, or pounding food. On receiving such a message through a younger brother or sister, Nwoye would feign annoyance and grumble aloud about women and their troubles.

Okonkwo was inwardly pleased at his son's development, and he knew it was due to Ikemefuna. He wanted Nwoye to grow into a tough young man capable of ruling his father's household when he was dead and gone to join the ancestors. He wanted him to be a prosperous man, having enough in his barn to feed the ancestors with regular sacrifices. And so he was always happy when he heard him grumbling about women. That showed that in time he would be able to control his women-folk. No matter how prosperous a man was, if he was unable to rule his women and his children (and especially his women) he was not really a man. He was like the man in the song who had ten and one wives and not enough soup for his foo-foo.

So Okonkwo encouraged the boys to sit with him in his *obi*, and he told them stories of the land—masculine stories of violence and bloodshed. Nwoye knew that it was right to be masculine and to be violent, but somehow he still preferred the stories that his mother used to tell, and which she no doubt still told to her younger children—stories of the tortoise and his wily ways, and of the bird *eneke-nti-oba*[5] who challenged the whole world to a wrestling contest and was finally thrown by the cat. He remembered the story she often told of the quarrel between Earth and Sky long ago, and how Sky withheld rain for seven years, until crops withered and the dead could not be buried because the hoes broke on the stony Earth. At last Vulture was sent to plead with Sky, and to soften his heart with a song of the suffering of the sons of men. Whenever Nwoye's mother sang this song he felt carried away to the distant scene in the sky where Vulture, Earth's emissary, sang for mercy. At last Sky was moved to pity, and he gave to Vulture rain wrapped in leaves of coco-yam. But as he flew home his long talon pierced the leaves and the rain fell as it had never fallen before. And so heavily did it rain on Vulture that he did not return to deliver his message but flew to a distant land, from where he had espied a fire. And when he got there he found it was a man making a sacrifice. He warmed himself in the fire and ate the entrails.

5. "The swallow with the ear of a crocodile [who is deaf]"(literal trans.); a bird who proverbially flies without perching.

That was the kind of story that Nwoye loved. But he now knew that they were for foolish women and children, and he knew that his father wanted him to be a man. And so he feigned that he no longer cared for women's stories. And when he did this he saw that his father was pleased, and no longer rebuked him or beat him. So Nwoye and Ikemefuna would listen to Okonkwo's stories about tribal wars, or how, years ago, he had stalked his victim, overpowered him and obtained his first human head. And as he told them of the past they sat in darkness or the dim glow of logs, waiting for the women to finish their cooking. When they finished, each brought her bowl of foo-foo and bowl of soup to her husband. An oil lamp was lit and Okonkwo tasted from each bowl, and then passed two shares to Nwoye and Ikemefuna.

In this way the moons and the seasons passed. And then the locusts came. It had not happened for many a long year. The elders said locusts came once in a generation, reappeared every year for seven years and then disappeared for another lifetime. They went back to their caves in a distant land, where they were guarded by a race of stunted men. And then after another lifetime these men opened the caves again and the locusts came to Umuofia.

They came in the cold harmattan season after the harvests had been gathered, and ate up all the wild grass in the fields.

Okonkwo and the two boys were working on the red outer walls of the compound. This was one of the lighter tasks of the after-harvest season. A new cover of thick palm branches and palm leaves was set on the walls to protect them from the next rainy season. Okonkwo worked on the outside of the wall and the boys worked from within. There were little holes from one side to the other in the upper levels of the wall, and through these Okonkwo passed the rope, or *tie-tie*,[6] to the boys and they passed it round the wooden stays and then back to him; and in this way the cover was strengthened on the wall.

The women had gone to the bush to collect firewood, and the little children to visit their playmates in the neighboring compounds. The harmattan was in the air and seemed to distill a hazy feeling of sleep on the world. Okonkwo and the boys worked in complete silence, which was only broken when a new palm frond was lifted on to the wall or when a busy hen moved dry leaves about in her ceaseless search for food.

And then quite suddenly a shadow fell on the world, and the sun seemed hidden behind a thick cloud. Okonkwo looked up from his work and wondered if it was going to rain at such an unlikely time of the year. But almost immediately a shout of joy broke out in all directions, and Umuofia, which had dozed in the noon-day haze, broke into life and activity.

"Locusts are descending," was joyfully chanted everywhere, and men, women and children left their work or their play and ran into the open to see the unfamiliar sight. The locusts had not come for many, many years, and only the old people had seen them before.

6. A creeper used as a rope to lash sections in building (pidgin English from "to tie").

At first, a fairly small swarm came. They were the harbingers sent to survey the land. And then appeared on the horizon a slowly moving mass like a boundless sheet of black cloud drifting towards Umuofia. Soon it covered half the sky, and the solid mass was now broken by tiny eyes of light like shining star dust. It was a tremendous sight, full of power and beauty.

Everyone was now about, talking excitedly and praying that the locusts should camp in Umuofia for the night. For although locusts had not visited Umuofia for many years, everybody knew by instinct that they were very good to eat. And at last the locusts did descend. They settled on every tree and on every blade of grass; they settled on the roofs and covered the bare ground. Mighty tree branches broke away under them, and the whole country became the brown-earth color of the vast, hungry swarm.

Many people went out with baskets trying to catch them, but the elders counseled patience till nightfall. And they were right. The locusts settled in the bushes for the night and their wings became wet with dew. Then all Umuofia turned out in spite of the cold harmattan, and everyone filled his bags and pots with locusts. The next morning they were roasted in clay pots and then spread in the sun until they became dry and brittle. And for many days this rare food was eaten with solid palm-oil.

Okonkwo sat in his *obi* crunching happily with Ikemefuna and Nwoye, and drinking palm-wine copiously, when Ogbuefi Ezeudu came in. Ezeudu was the oldest man in this quarter of Umuofia. He had been a great and fearless warrior in his time, and was now accorded great respect in all the clan. He refused to join in the meal, and asked Okonkwo to have a word with him outside. And so they walked out together, the old man supporting himself with his stick. When they were out of earshot, he said to Okonkwo:

"That boy calls you father. Do not bear a hand in his death." Okonkwo was surprised, and was about to say something when the old man continued:

"Yes, Umuofia has decided to kill him. The Oracle of the Hills and the Caves has pronounced it. They will take him outside Umuofia as is the custom, and kill him there. But I want you to have nothing to do with it. He calls you his father."

The next day a group of elders from all the nine villages of Umuofia came to Okonkwo's house early in the morning, and before they began to speak in low tones Nwoye and Ikemefuna were sent out. They did not stay very long, but when they went away Okonkwo sat still for a very long time supporting his chin in his palms. Later in the day he called Ikemefuna and told him that he was to be taken home the next day. Nwoye overheard it and burst into tears, whereupon his father beat him heavily. As for Ikemefuna, he was at a loss. His own home had gradually become very faint and distant. He still missed his mother and his sister and would be very glad to see them. But somehow he knew he was not going to see them. He remembered once when men had talked in low tones with his father; and it seemed now as if it was happening all over again.

Later, Nwoye went to his mother's hut and told her that Ikemefuna was going home. She immediately dropped her pestle with which she was grinding pepper, folded her arms across her breast and sighed, "Poor child."

The next day, the men returned with a pot of wine. They were all fully dressed as if they were going to a big clan meeting or to pay a visit to a neighboring village. They passed their cloths under the right arm-pit, and hung their goatskin bags and sheathed machetes over their left shoulders. Okonkwo got ready quickly and the party set out with Ikemefuna carrying the pot of wine. A deathly silence descended on Okonkwo's compound. Even the very little children seemed to know. Throughout that day Nwoye sat in his mother's hut and tears stood in his eyes.

At the beginning of their journey the men of Umuofia talked and laughed about the locusts, about their women, and about some effeminate men who had refused to come with them. But as they drew near to the outskirts of Umuofia silence fell upon them too.

The sun rose slowly to the center of the sky, and the dry, sandy footway began to throw up the heat that lay buried in it. Some birds chirruped in the forests around. The men trod dry leaves on the sand. All else was silent. Then from the distance came the faint beating of the *ekwe*. It rose and faded with the wind—a peaceful dance from a distant clan.

"It is an *ozo* dance,"[7] the men said among themselves. But no one was sure where it was coming from. Some said Ezimili, others Abame or Aninta. They argued for a short while and fell into silence again, and the elusive dance rose and fell with the wind. Somewhere a man was taking one of the titles of his clan, with music and dancing and a great feast.

The footway had now become a narrow line in the heart of the forest. The short trees and sparse undergrowth which surrounded the men's village began to give way to giant trees and climbers which perhaps had stood from the beginning of things, untouched by the ax and the bush-fire. The sun breaking through their leaves and branches threw a pattern of light and shade on the sandy footway.

Ikemefuna heard a whisper close behind him and turned round sharply. The man who had whispered now called out aloud, urging the others to hurry up.

"We still have a long way to go," he said. Then he and another man went before Ikemefuna and set a faster pace.

Thus the men of Umuofia pursued their way, armed with sheathed machetes, and Ikemefuna, carrying a pot of palm-wine on his head, walked in their midst. Although he had felt uneasy at first, he was not afraid now. Okonkwo walked behind him. He could hardly imagine that Okonkwo was not his real father. He had never been fond of his real father, and at the end of three years he had become very distant indeed. But his mother and his three-year-old sister . . . of course she would not be three now, but six. Would he recognize her now? She must have grown quite big. How his mother would weep for joy, and thank Okonkwo for having looked after him so well and for bringing him back. She would want to hear everything that had happened to him in all these years. Could

---

7. Part of the *ozo* rituals, the spiritual ceremonies that accompanied the taking of titles.

he remember them all? He would tell her about Nwoye and his mother, and about the locusts. . . . Then quite suddenly a thought came upon him. His mother might be dead. He tried in vain to force the thought out of his mind. Then he tried to settle the matter the way he used to settle such matters when he was a little boy. He still remembered the song:

> *Eze elina, elina!*
> > *Sala*
> *Eze ilikwa ya*
> *Ikwaba akwa oligholi*
> *Ebe Danda nechi eze*
> *Ebe Uzuzu nete egwu*
> > *Sala*[8]

He sang it in his mind, and walked to its beat. If the song ended on his right foot, his mother was alive. If it ended on his left, she was dead. No, not dead, but ill. It ended on the right. She was alive and well. He sang the song again, and it ended on the left. But the second time did not count. The first voice gets to Chukwu, or God's house. That was a favorite saying of children. Ikemefuna felt like a child once more. It must be the thought of going home to his mother.

One of the men behind him cleared his throat. Ikemefuna looked back, and the man growled at him to go on and not stand looking back. The way he said it sent cold fear down Ikemefuna's back. His hands trembled vaguely on the black pot he carried. Why had Okonkwo withdrawn to the rear? Ikemefuna felt his legs melting under him. And he was afraid to look back.

As the man who had cleared his throat drew up and raised his machete, Okonkwo looked away. He heard the blow. The pot fell and broke in the sand. He heard Ikemefuna cry, "My father, they have killed me!" as he ran towards him. Dazed with fear, Okonkwo drew his machete and cut him down. He was afraid of being thought weak.

As soon as his father walked in, that night, Nwoye knew that Ikemefuna had been killed, and something seemed to give way inside him, like the snapping of a tightened bow. He did not cry. He just hung limp. He had had the same kind of feeling not long ago, during the last harvest season. Every child loved the harvest season. Those who were big enough to carry even a few yams in a tiny basket went with grown-ups to the farm. And if they could not help in digging up the yams, they could gather firewood together for roasting the ones that would be eaten there on the farm. This roasted yam soaked in red palm-oil and eaten in the open farm was sweeter than any meal at home. It was after such a day at the farm during the last harvest that Nwoye had felt for the first time a snapping inside him like the one he now felt. They were returning home with baskets of yams from a distant farm across the stream when they heard the voice of an infant crying in the thick forest. A sudden hush had fallen on the women, who

---

8. "King don't eat, don't eat / Sala / King if you eat it / You will weep for the abomination / Where Danda installs a king / Where Uzuzu dances / Sala." *Sala:* meaningless refrain. *Danda:* the ant. *Uzuzu:* sand. Ikemefuna reassures himself by singing his favorite song about the country where the "sands dance forever" (see p. 2519).

had been talking, and they had quickened their steps. Nwoye had heard that twins were put in earthenware pots and thrown away in the forest, but he had never yet come across them. A vague chill had descended on him and his head had seemed to swell, like a solitary walker at night who passes an evil spirit on the way. Then something had given way inside him. It descended on him again, this feeling, when his father walked in, that night after killing Ikemefuna.

8

Okonkwo did not taste any food for two days after the death of Ikemefuna. He drank palm-wine from morning till night, and his eyes were red and fierce like the eyes of a rat when it was caught by the tail and dashed against the floor. He called his son, Nwoye, to sit with him in his *obi*. But the boy was afraid of him and slipped out of the hut as soon as he noticed him dozing.

He did not sleep at night. He tried not to think about Ikemefuna, but the more he tried the more he thought about him. Once he got up from bed and walked about his compound. But he was so weak that his legs could hardly carry him. He felt like a drunken giant walking with the limbs of a mosquito. Now and then a cold shiver descended on his head and spread down his body.

On the third day he asked his second wife, Ekwefi, to roast plantains for him. She prepared it the way he liked—with slices of oil-bean and fish.

"You have not eaten for two days," said his daughter Ezinma when she brought the food to him. "So you must finish this." She sat down and stretched her legs in front of her. Okonkwo ate the food absent-mindedly. 'She should have been a boy,' he thought as he looked at his ten-year-old daughter. He passed her a piece of fish.

"Go and bring me some cold water," he said. Ezinma rushed out of the hut, chewing the fish, and soon returned with a bowl of cool water from the earthen pot in her mother's hut.

Okonkwo took the bowl from her and gulped the water down. He ate a few more pieces of plantain and pushed the dish aside.

"Bring me my bag," he asked, and Ezinma brought his goatskin bag from the far end of the hut. He searched in it for his snuff-bottle. It was a deep bag and took almost the whole length of his arm. It contained other things apart from his snuff-bottle. There was a drinking horn in it, and also a drinking gourd, and they knocked against each other as he searched. When he brought out the snuff-bottle he tapped it a few times against his knee-cap before taking out some snuff on the palm of his left hand. Then he remembered that he had not taken out his snuff-spoon. He searched his bag again and brought out a small, flat, ivory spoon, with which he carried the brown snuff to his nostrils.

Ezinma took the dish in one hand and the empty water bowl in the other and went back to her mother's hut. "She should have been a boy," Okonkwo said to himself again. His mind went back to Ikemefuna and he shivered. If only he could find some work to do he would be able to forget. But it was the season of rest between the harvest and the next planting season. The only work that men did at this time was covering the walls of their compound with new palm fronds. And Okonkwo had already done that. He had finished it on the very day the locusts came, when he had worked on one side of the wall and Ikemefuna and Nwoye on the other.

"When did you become a shivering old woman," Okonkwo asked himself, "you, who are known in all the nine villages for your valor in war? How can a man who has killed five men in battle fall to pieces because he has added a boy to their number? Okonkwo, you have become a woman indeed."

He sprang to his feet, hung his goatskin bag on his shoulder and went to visit his friend, Obierika.

Obierika was sitting outside under the shade of an orange tree making thatches from leaves of the raffia-palm. He exchanged greetings with Okonkwo and led the way into his *obi*.

"I was coming over to see you as soon as I finished that thatch," he said, rubbing off the grains of sand that clung to his thighs.

"Is it well?" Okonkwo asked.

"Yes," replied Obierika. "My daughter's suitor is coming today and I hope we will clinch the matter of the bride-price. I want you to be there."

Just then Obierika's son, Maduka, came into the *obi* from outside, greeted Okonkwo and turned towards the compound.

"Come and shake hands with me," Okonkwo said to the lad. "Your wrestling the other day gave me much happiness." The boy smiled, shook hands with Okonkwo and went into the compound.

"He will do great things," Okonkwo said. "If I had a son like him I should be happy. I am worried about Nwoye. A bowl of pounded yams can throw him in a wrestling match. His two younger brothers are more promising. But I can tell you, Obierika, that my children do not resemble me. Where are the young suckers that will grow when the old banana tree dies? If Ezinma had been a boy I would have been happier. She has the right spirit."

"You worry yourself for nothing," said Obierika. "The children are still very young."

"Nwoye is old enough to impregnate a woman. At his age I was already fending for myself. No, my friend, he is not too young. A chick that will grow into a cock can be spotted the very day it hatches. I have done my best to make Nwoye grow into a man, but there is too much of his mother in him."

"Too much of his grandfather," Obierika thought, but he did not say it. The same thought also came to Okonkwo's mind. But he had long learned how to lay that ghost. Whenever the thought of his father's weakness and failure troubled him he expelled it by thinking about his own strength and success. And so he did now. His mind went to his latest show of manliness.

"I cannot understand why you refused to come with us to kill that boy," he asked Obierika.

"Because I did not want to," Obierika replied sharply. "I had something better to do."

"You sound as if you question the authority and the decision of the Oracle, who said he should die."

"I do not. Why should I? But the Oracle did not ask me to carry out its decision."

"But someone had to do it. If we were all afraid of blood, it would not be done. And what do you think the Oracle would do then?"

"You know very well, Okonkwo, that I am not afraid of blood; and if anyone tells you that I am, he is telling a lie. And let me tell you one thing, my friend. If I were you I would have stayed at home. What you have done will not please the Earth. It is the kind of action for which the goddess wipes out whole families."

"The Earth cannot punish me for obeying her messenger," Okonkwo said. "A child's fingers are not scalded by a piece of hot yam which its mother puts into its palm."

"That is true," Obierika agreed. "But if the Oracle said that my son should be killed I would neither dispute it nor be the one to do it."

They would have gone on arguing had Ofoedu[9] not come in just then. It was clear from his twinkling eyes that he had important news. But it would be impolite to rush him. Obierika offered him a lobe of the kola nut he had broken with Okonkwo. Ofoedu ate slowly and talked about the locusts. When he finished his kola nut he said:

"The things that happen these days are very strange."

"What has happened?" asked Okonkwo.

"Do you know Ogbuefi Ndulue?"[1] Ofoedu asked.

"Ogbuefi Ndulue of Ire village," Okonkwo and Obierika said together.

"He died this morning," said Ofoedu.

"That is not strange. He was the oldest man in Ire," said Obierika.

"You are right," Ofoedu agreed. "But you ought to ask why the drum has not beaten to tell Umuofia of his death."

"Why?" asked Obierika and Okonkwo together.

"That is the strange part of it. You know his first wife who walks with a stick?"

"Yes. She is called Ozoemena."[2]

"That is so," said Ofoedu. "Ozoemena was, as you know, too old to attend Ndulue during his illness. His younger wives did that. When he died this morning, one of these women went to Ozoemena's hut and told her. She rose from her mat, took her stick and walked over to the *obi*. She knelt on her knees and hands at the threshold and called her husband, who was laid on a mat. 'Ogbuefi Ndulue,' she called, three times, and went back to her hut. When the youngest wife went to call her again to be present at the washing of the body, she found her lying on the mat, dead."

"That is very strange, indeed," said Okonkwo. "They will put off Ndulue's funeral until his wife has been buried."[3]

"That is why the drum has not been beaten to tell Umuofia."

"It was always said that Ndulue and Ozoemena had one mind," said Obierika. "I remember when I was a young boy there was a song about them. He could not do anything without telling her."

9. "The Ancestors Are Our Guide."   1. "Life Has Arrived."   2. "Another Bad Thing Will Not Happen."   3. A wife dying shortly after her husband was sometimes considered guilty of his death, so the village preserves appearances by burying Ozoemena before announcing Ogbuefi Ndulue's death.

"I did not know that," said Okonkwo. "I thought he was a strong man in his youth."

"He was indeed," said Ofoedu.

Okonkwo shook his head doubtfully.

"He led Umuofia to war in those days," said Obierika.

Okonkwo was beginning to feel like his old self again. All that he required was something to occupy his mind. If he had killed Ikemefuna during the busy planting season or harvesting it would not have been so bad; his mind would have been centered on his work. Okonkwo was not a man of thought but of action. But in absence of work, talking was the next best.

Soon after Ofoedu left, Okonkwo took up his goatskin bag to go.

"I must go home to tap my palm trees for the afternoon," he said.

"Who taps your tall trees for you?" asked Obierika.

"Umezulike," replied Okonkwo.

"Sometimes I wish I had not taken the *ozo* title," said Obierika. "It wounds my heart to see these young men killing palm trees in the name of tapping."

"It is so indeed," Okonkwo agreed. "But the law of the land must be obeyed."

"I don't know how we got that law," said Obierika. "In many other clans a man of title is not forbidden to climb the palm tree. Here we say he cannot climb the tall tree but he can tap the short ones standing on the ground. It is like Dimaragana, who would not lend his knife for cutting up dogmeat because the dog was taboo to him, but offered to use his teeth."

"I think it is good that our clan holds the *ozo* title in high esteem," said Okonkwo. "In those other clans you speak of, *ozo* is so low that every beggar takes it."

"I was only speaking in jest," said Obierika. "In Abame and Aninta the title is worth less than two cowries. Every man wears the thread of title on his ankle, and does not lose it even if he steals."

"They have indeed soiled the name of *ozo*," said Okonkwo as he rose to go.

"It will not be very long now before my in-laws come," said Obierika.

"I shall return very soon," said Okonkwo, looking at the position of the sun.

There were seven men in Obierika's hut when Okonkwo returned. The suitor was a young man of about twenty-five, and with him were his father and uncle. On Obierika's side were his two elder brothers and Maduka, his sixteen-year-old son.

"Ask Akueke's mother to send us some kola nuts," said Obierika to his son. Maduka vanished into the compound like lightning. The conversation at once centered on him, and everybody agreed that he was as sharp as a razor.

"I sometimes think he is too sharp," said Obierika, somewhat indulgently. "He hardly ever walks. He is always in a hurry. If you are sending him on an errand he flies away before he has heard half of the message."

"You were very much like that yourself," said his eldest brother. "As our people say, 'When mother-cow is chewing grass its young ones watch its mouth.' Maduka has been watching your mouth."

As he was speaking the boy returned, followed by Akueke,[4] his half-sister, carrying a wooden dish with three kola nuts and alligator pepper. She gave the dish to her father's eldest brother and then shook hands, very shyly, with her suitor and his relatives. She was about sixteen and just ripe for marriage. Her suitor and his relatives surveyed her young body with expert eyes as if to assure themselves that she was beautiful and ripe.

She wore a coiffure which was done up into a crest in the middle of the head. Cam wood was rubbed lightly into her skin, and all over her body were black patterns drawn with *uli*.[5] She wore a black necklace which hung down in three coils just above her full, succulent breasts. On her arms were red and yellow bangles, and on her waist four or five rows of *jigida*, or waist beads.

When she had shaken hands, or rather held out her hand to be shaken, she returned to her mother's hut to help with the cooking.

"Remove your *jigida* first," her mother warned as she moved near the fireplace to bring the pestle resting against the wall. "Every day I tell you that *jigida* and fire are not friends. But you will never hear. You grew your ears for decoration, not for hearing. One of these days your *jigida* will catch fire on your waist, and then you will know."

Akueke moved to the other end of the hut and began to remove the waist-beads. It had to be done slowly and carefully, taking each string separately, else it would break and the thousand tiny rings would have to be strung together again. She rubbed each string downwards with her palms until it passed the buttocks and slipped down to the floor around her feet.

The men in the *obi* had already begun to drink the palm-wine which Akueke's suitor had brought. It was a very good wine and powerful, for in spite of the palm fruit hung across the mouth of the pot to restrain the lively liquor, white foam rose and spilled over.

"That wine is the work of a good tapper," said Okonkwo.

The young suitor, whose name was Ibe, smiled broadly and said to his father: "Do you hear that?" He then said to the others: "He will never admit that I am a good tapper."

"He tapped three of my best palm trees to death," said his father, Ukegbu.

"That was about five years ago," said Ibe, who had begun to pour out the wine, "before I learned how to tap." He filled the first horn and gave to his father. Then he poured out for the others. Okonkwo brought out his big horn from the goatskin bag, blew into it to remove any dust that might be there, and gave it to Ibe to fill.

As the men drank, they talked about everything except the thing for which they had gathered. It was only after the pot had been emptied that the suitor's father cleared his voice and announced the object of their visit.

4. "Wealth of Eke" (a divinity). Similar names built on *ako* ("wealth") connote riches and are associated with the idea of women as a form of exchangeable material wealth.   5. A liquid made from crushed seeds, which caused the skin to pucker temporarily. It was used to create black tattoolike decorations. *Cam wood*: a shrub. The powdered red heartwood of the shrub was used as a cosmetic dye.

Obierika then presented to him a small bundle of short broomsticks. Ukegbu counted them.

"They are thirty?" he asked.

Obierika nodded in agreement.

"We are at last getting somewhere," Ukegbu said, and then turning to his brother and his son he said: "Let us go out and whisper together." The three rose and went outside. When they returned Ukegbu handed the bundle of sticks back to Obierika. He counted them; instead of thirty there were now only fifteen. He passed them over to his eldest brother, Machi, who also counted them and said:

"We had not thought to go below thirty. But as the dog said, 'If I fall down for you and you fall down for me, it is play.' Marriage should be a play and not a fight; so we are falling down again." He then added ten sticks to the fifteen and gave the bundle to Ukegbu.

In this way Akuke's bride-price was finally settled at twenty bags of cowries. It was already dusk when the two parties came to this agreement.

"Go and tell Akueke's mother that we have finished," Obierika said to his son, Maduka. Almost immediately the women came in with a big bowl of foo-foo. Obierika's second wife followed with a pot of soup, and Maduka brought in a pot of palm-wine.

As the men ate and drank palm-wine they talked about the customs of their neighbors.

"It was only this morning," said Obierika, "that Okonkwo and I were talking about Abame and Aninta, where titled men climb trees and pound foo-foo for their wives."

"All their customs are upside-down. They do not decide bride-price as we do, with sticks. They haggle and bargain as if they were buying a goat or a cow in the market."

"That is very bad," said Obierika's eldest brother. "But what is good in one place is bad in another place. In Umunso they do not bargain at all, not even with broomsticks. The suitor just goes on bringing bags of cowries until his in-laws tell him to stop. It is a bad custom because it always leads to a quarrel."

"The world is large," said Okonkwo. "I have even heard that in some tribes a man's children belong to his wife and her family."

"That cannot be," said Machi. "You might as well say that the woman lies on top of the man when they are making the children."

"It is like the story of white men who, they say, are white like this piece of chalk," said Obierika. He held up a piece of chalk, which every man kept in his *obi* and with which his guests drew lines on the floor before they ate kola nuts. "And these white men, they say, have no toes."[6]

"And have you never seen them?" asked Machi.

"Have you?" asked Obierika.

"One of them passes here frequently," said Machi. "His name is Amadi."

Those who knew Amadi laughed. He was a leper, and the polite name for leprosy was "the white skin."

---

6. They wear shoes.

9

For the first time in three nights, Okonkwo slept. He woke up once in the middle of the night and his mind went back to the past three days without making him feel uneasy. He began to wonder why he had felt uneasy at all. It was like a man wondering in broad daylight why a dream had appeared so terrible to him at night. He stretched himself and scratched his thigh were a mosquito had bitten him as he slept. Another one was wailing near his right ear. He slapped the ear and hoped he had killed it. Why do they always go for one's ears? When he was a child his mother had told him a story about it. But it was as silly as all women's stories. Mosquito, she had said, had asked Ear to marry him, whereupon Ear fell on the floor in uncontrollable laughter. "How much longer do you think you will live?" she asked. "You are already a skeleton." Mosquito went away humiliated, and any time he passed her way he told Ear that he was still alive.

Okonkwo turned on his side and went back to sleep. He was roused in the morning by someone banging on his door.

"Who is that?" he growled. He knew it must be Ekwefi. Of his three wives Ekwefi was the only one who would have the audacity to bang on his door.

"Ezinma is dying," came her voice, and all the tragedy and sorrow of her life were packed in those words.

Okonkwo sprang from his bed, pushed back the bolt on his door and ran into Ekwefi's hut.

Ezinma lay shivering on a mat beside a huge fire that her mother had kept burning all night.

"It is *iba*,"[7] said Okonkwo as he took his machete and went into the bush to collect the leaves and grasses and barks of trees that went into making the medicine for *iba*.

Ekwefi knelt beside the sick child, occasionally feeling with her palm the wet, burning forehead.

Ezinma was an only child and the center of her mother's world. Very often it was Ezinma who decided what food her mother should prepare. Ekwefi even gave her such delicacies as eggs, which children were rarely allowed to eat because such food tempted them to steal. One day as Ezinma was eating an egg Okonkwo had come in unexpectedly from his hut. He was greatly shocked and swore to beat Ekwefi if she dared to give the child eggs again. But it was impossible to refuse Ezinma anything. After her father's rebuke she developed an even keener appetite for eggs. And she enjoyed above all the secrecy in which she now ate them. Her mother always took her into their bedroom and shut the door.

Ezinma did not call her mother Nne like all children. She called her by her name, Ekwefi, as her father and other grown-up people did. The relationship between them was not only that of mother and child. There was something in it like the companionship of equals, which was strengthened by such little conspiracies as eating eggs in the bedroom.

Ekwefi had suffered a good deal in her life. She had borne ten children

7. A fever accompanied by jaundice, probably caused by malaria.

and nine of them had died in infancy, usually before the age of three. As she buried one child after another her sorrow gave way to despair and then to grim resignation. The birth of her children, which should be a woman's crowning glory, became for Ekwefi mere physical agony devoid of promise. The naming ceremony after seven market weeks became an empty ritual. Her deepening despair found expression in the names she gave her children. One of them was a pathetic cry, Onwumbiko—"Death, I implore you." But Death took no notice; Onwumbiko died in his fifteenth month. The next child was a girl, Ozoemena—"May it not happen again." She died in her eleventh month, and two others after her. Ekwefi then became defiant and called her next child Onwuma—"Death may please himself." And he did.

After the death of Ekwefi's second child, Okonkwo had gone to a medicine man, who was also a diviner of the Afa Oracle,[8] to inquire what was amiss. This man told him that the child was an *ogbanje*, one of those wicked children who, when they died, entered their mothers' wombs to be born again.

"When your wife becomes pregnant again," he said, "let her not sleep in her hut. Let her go and stay with her people. In that way she will elude her wicked tormentor and break its evil cycle of birth and death."

Ekwefi did as she was asked. As soon as she became pregnant she went to live with her old mother in another village. It was there that her third child was born and circumcised on the eighth day. She did not return to Okonkwo's compound until three days before the naming ceremony. The child was called Onwumbiko.

Onwumbiko was not given proper burial when he died. Okonkwo had called on another medicine man who was famous in the clan for his great knowledge about *ogbanje* children. His name was Okagbue Uyanwa. Okagbue was a very striking figure, tall, with a full beard and a bald head. He was light in complexion and his eyes were red and fiery. He always gnashed his teeth as he listened to those who came to consult him. He asked Okonkwo a few questions about the dead child. All the neighbors and relations who had come to mourn gathered round them.

"On what market-day was it born?" he asked.

"*Oye*," replied Okonkwo.

"And it died this morning?"

Okonkwo said yes, and only then realized for the first time that the child had died on the same market-day as it had been born. The neighbors and relations also saw the coincidence and said among themselves that it was very significant.

"Where do you sleep with your wife, in your *obi* or in her own hut?" asked the medicine man.

"In her hut."

"In future call her into your *obi*."

The medicine man then ordered that there should be no mourning for the dead child. He brought out a sharp razor from the goatskin bag slung

---

8. One communicates with the clients' ancestors by reading patterns made by objects (for example, seeds, teeth, shells) thrown on a flat surface.

from his left shoulder and began to mutilate the child. Then he took it away to bury in the Evil Forest, holding it by the ankle and dragging it on the ground behind him. After such treatment it would think twice before coming again, unless it was one of the stubborn ones who returned, carrying the stamp of their mutilation—a missing finger or perhaps a dark line where the medicine man's razor had cut them.

By the time Onwumbiko died Ekwefi had become a very bitter woman. Her husband's first wife had already had three sons, all strong and healthy. When she had borne her third son in succession, Okonkwo had gathered a goat for her, as was the custom. Ekwefi had nothing but good wishes for her. But she had grown so bitter about her own *chi* that she could not rejoice with others over their good fortune. And so, on the day that Nwoye's mother celebrated the birth of her three sons with feasting and music, Ekwefi was the only person in the happy company who went about with a cloud on her brow. Her husband's wife took this for malevolence, as husbands' wives were wont to. How could she know that Ekwefi's bitterness did not flow outwards to others but inwards into her own soul; that she did not blame others for their good fortune but her own evil *chi* who denied her any?

At last Ezinma was born, and although ailing she seemed determined to live. At first Ekwefi accepted her, as she had accepted others—with listless resignation. But when she lived on to her fourth, fifth and sixth years, love returned once more to her mother, and, with love, anxiety. She determined to nurse her child to health, and she put all her being into it. She was rewarded by occasional spells of health during which Ezinma bubbled with energy like fresh palm-wine. At such times she seemed beyond danger. But all of a sudden she would go down again. Everybody knew she was an *ogbanje*. These sudden bouts of sickness and health were typical of her kind. But she had lived so long that perhaps she had decided to stay. Some of them did become tired of their evil rounds of birth and death, or took pity on their mothers, and stayed. Ekwefi believed deep inside her that Ezinma had come to stay. She believed because it was that faith alone that gave her own life any kind of meaning. And this faith had been strengthened when a year or so ago a medicine man had dug up Ezinma's *iyi-uwa*. Everyone knew then that she would live because her bond with the world of *ogbanje* had been broken. Ekwefi was reassured. But such was her anxiety for her daughter that she could not rid herself completely of her fear. And although she believed that the *iyi-uwa* which had been dug up was genuine, she could not ignore the fact that some really evil children sometimes misled people into digging up a specious one.

But Ezinma's *iyi-uwa* had looked real enough. It was a smooth pebble wrapped in a dirty rag. The man who dug it up was the same Okagbue who was famous in all the clan for his knowledge in these matters. Ezinma had not wanted to cooperate with him at first. But that was only to be expected. No *ogbanje* would yield her secrets easily, and most of them never did because they died too young—before they could be asked questions.

"Where did you bury your *iyi-uwa?*" Okagbue had asked Ezinma. She was nine then and was just recovering from a serious illness.

"What is *iyi-uwa?*" she asked in return.

"You know what it is. You buried it in the ground somewhere so that you can die and return again to torment your mother."

Ezinma looked at her mother, whose eyes, sad and pleading, were fixed on her.

"Answer the question at once," roared Okonkwo, who stood beside her. All the family were there and some of the neighbors too.

"Leave her to me," the medicine man told Okonkwo in a cool, confident voice. He turned again to Ezinma. "Where did you bury your *iyi-uwa?*"

"Where they bury children," she replied, and the quiet spectators murmured to themselves.

"Come along then and show me the spot," said the medicine man.

The crowd set out with Ezinma leading the way and Okagbue following closely behind her. Okonkwo came next and Ekwefi followed him. When she came to the main road, Ezinma turned left as if she was going to the stream.

"But you said it was where they bury children?" asked the medicine man.

"No," said Ezinma, whose feeling of importance was manifest in her sprightly walk. She sometimes broke into a run and stopped again suddenly. The crowd followed her silently. Women and children returning from the stream with pots of water on their heads wondered what was happening until they saw Okagbue and guessed that it must be something to do with *ogbanje.* And they all knew Ekwefi and her daughter very well.

When she got to the big udala tree Ezinma turned left into the bush, and the crowd followed her. Because of her size she made her way through trees and creepers more quickly then her followers. The bush was alive with the tread of feet on dry leaves and sticks and the moving aside of tree branches. Ezinma went deeper and deeper and the crowd went with her. Then she suddenly turned round and began to walk back to the road. Everybody stood to let her pass and then filed after her.

"If you bring us all this way for nothing I shall beat sense into you," Okonkwo threatened.

"I have told you to let her alone. I know how to deal with them," said Okagbue.

Ezinma led the way back to the road, looked left and right and turned right. And so they arrived home again.

"Where did you bury your *iyi-uwa?*" asked Okagbue when Ezinma finally stopped outside her father's *obi.* Okagbue's voice was unchanged. It was quiet and confident.

"It is near that orange tree," Ezinma said.

"And why did you not say so, you wicked daughter of Akalogoli?" Okonkwo swore furiously. The medicine man ignored him.

"Come and show me the exact spot," he said quietly to Ezinma.

"It is here," she said when they got to the tree.

"Point at the spot with your finger," said Okagbue.

"It is here," said Ezinma touching the ground with her finger. Okonkwo stood by, rumbling like thunder in the rainy season.

"Bring me a hoe," said Okagbue.

When Ekwefi brought the hoe, he had already put aside his goatskin bag and his big cloth and was in his underwear, a long and thin strip of cloth wound round the waist like a belt and then passed between the legs to be fastened to the belt behind. He immediately set to work digging a pit where Ezinma had indicated. The neighbors sat around watching the pit becoming deeper and deeper. The dark top soil soon gave way to the bright red earth with which women scrubbed the floors and walls of huts. Okagbue worked tirelessly and in silence, his back shining with perspiration. Okonkwo stood by the pit. He asked Okagbue to come up and rest while he took a hand. But Okagbue said he was not tired yet.

Ekwefi went into her hut to cook yams. Her husband had brought out more yams than usual because the medicine man had to be fed. Ezinma went with her and helped in preparing the vegetables.

"There is too much green vegetable," she said.

"Don't you see the pot is full of yams?" Ekwefi asked. "And you know how leaves become smaller after cooking."

"Yes," said Ezinma, "that was why the snake-lizard killed his mother."

"Very true," said Ekwefi.

"He gave his mother seven baskets of vegetables to cook and in the end there were only three. And so he killed her," said Ezinma.

"That is not the end of the story."

"Oho," said Ezinma. "I remember now. He brought another seven baskets and cooked them himself. And there were again only three. So he killed himself too."

Outside the *obi* Okagbue and Okonkwo were digging the pit to find where Ezinma had buried her *iyi-uwa*. Neighbors sat around, watching. The pit was now so deep that they no longer saw the digger. They only saw the red earth he threw up mounting higher and higher. Okonkwo's son, Nwoye, stood near the edge of the pit because he wanted to take in all that happened.

Okagbue had again taken over the digging from Okonkwo. He worked, as usual, in silence. The neighbors and Okonkwo's wives were now talking. The children had lost interest and were playing.

Suddenly Okagbue sprang to the surface with the agility of a leopard.

"It is very near now," he said. "I have felt it."

There was immediate excitement and those who were sitting jumped to their feet.

"Call your wife and child," he said to Okonkwo. But Ekwefi and Ezinma had heard the noise and run out to see what it was.

Okagbue went back into the pit, which was now surrounded by spectators. After a few more hoe-fuls of earth he struck the *iyi-uwa*. He raised it carefully with the hoe and threw it to the surface. Some women ran away in fear when it was thrown. But they soon returned and everyone was gazing at the rag from a reasonable distance. Okagbue emerged and without saying a word or even looking at the spectators he went to his goatskin bag, took out two leaves and began to chew them. When he had swallowed them, he took up the rag with his left hand and began to untie it. And then the smooth, shiny pebble fell out. He picked it up.

"Is this yours?" he asked Ezinma.

"Yes," she replied. All the women shouted with joy because Ekwefi's troubles were at last ended.

All this had happened more than a year ago and Ezinma had not been ill since. And then suddenly she had begun to shiver in the night. Ekwefi brought her to the fireplace, spread her mat on the floor and built a fire. But she had got worse and worse. As she knelt by her, feeling with her palm the wet, burning forehead, she prayed a thousand times. Although her husband's wives were saying that it was nothing more than *iba*, she did not hear them.

Okonkwo returned from the bush carrying on his left shoulder a large bundle of grasses and leaves, roots and barks of medicinal trees and shrubs. He went into Ekwefi's hut, put down his load and sat down.

"Get me a pot," he said, "and leave the child alone."

Ekwefi went to bring the pot and Okonkwo selected the best from his bundle, in their due proportions, and cut them up. He put them in the pot and Ekwefi poured in some water.

"Is that enough?" she asked when she had poured in about half of the water in the bowl.

"A little more . . . I said a *little*. Are you deaf?" Okonkwo roared at her.

She set the pot on the fire and Okonkwo took up his machete to return to his *obi*.

"You must watch the pot carefully," he said as he went, "and don't allow it to boil over. If it does its power will be gone." He went away to his hut and Ekwefi began to tend the medicine pot almost as if it was itself a sick child. Her eyes went constantly from Ezinma to the boiling pot and back to Ezinma.

Okonkwo returned when he felt the medicine had cooked long enough. He looked it over and said it was done.

"Bring me a low stool for Ezinma," he said, "and a thick mat."

He took down the pot from the fire and placed it in front of the stool. He then roused Ezinma and placed her on the stool, astride the steaming pot. The thick mat was thrown over both. Ezinma struggled to escape from the choking and overpowering steam, but she was held down. She started to cry.

When the mat was at last removed she was drenched in perspiration. Ekwefi mopped her with a piece of cloth and she lay down on a dry mat and was soon asleep.

10

Large crowds began to gather on the village *ilo* as soon as the edge had worn off the sun's heat and it was no longer painful on the body. Most communal ceremonies took place at that time of the day, so that even when it was said that a ceremony would begin "after the midday meal" everyone understood that it would begin a long time later, when the sun's heat had softened.

It was clear from the way the crowd stood or sat that the ceremony was for men. There were many women, but they looked on from the fringe like outsiders. The titled men and elders sat on their stools waiting for the trials to begin. In front of them was a row of stools on which nobody sat. There were nine of them. Two little groups of people stood at a respectable distance beyond the stools. They faced the elders. There were three men in one group and three men and one woman in the other. The woman was Mgbafo and the three men with her were her brothers. In the other group were her husband, Uzowulu, and his relatives. Mgbafo and her brothers were as still as statues into whose faces the artist has molded defiance. Uzowulu and his relatives, on the other hand, were whispering together. It looked like whispering, but they were really talking at the top of their voices. Everybody in the crowd was talking. It was like the market. From a distance the noise was a deep rumble carried by the wind.

An iron gong sounded, setting up a wave of expectation in the crowd. Everyone looked in the direction of the *egwugwu*[9] house. *Gome, gome, gome* went the gong, and a powerful flute blew a high-pitched blast. Then came the voices of the *egwugwu*, guttural and awesome. The wave struck the women and children and there was a backward stampede. But it was momentary. They were already far enough where they stood and there was room for running away if any of the *egwugwu* should go towards them.

The drum sounded again and the flute blew. The *egwugwu* house was now a pandemonium of quavering voices: *Aru oyim de de de dei!*[1] filled the air as the spirits of the ancestors, just emerged from the earth, greeted themselves in their esoteric language. The *egwugwu* house into which they emerged faced the forest, away from the crowd, who saw only its back with the many-colored patterns and drawings done by specially chosen women at regular intervals. These women never saw the inside of the hut. No woman ever did. They scrubbed and painted the outside walls under the supervision of men. If they imagined what was inside, they kept their imagination to themselves. No woman ever asked questions about the most powerful and the most secret cult in the clan.

Aru oyim de de de dei! flew around the dark, closed hut like tongues of fire. The ancestral spirits of the clan were abroad. The metal gong beat continuously now and the flute, shrill and powerful, floated on the chaos.

And then the *egwugwu* appeared. The women and children sent up a great shout and took to their heels. It was instinctive. A woman fled as soon as an *egwugwu* came in sight. And when, as on that day, nine of the greatest masked spirits in the clan came out together it was a terrifying spectacle. Even Mgbafo took to her heels and had to be restrained by her brothers.

Each of the nine *egwugwu* represented a village of the clan. Their leader was called Evil Forest. Smoke poured out of his head.

The nine villages of Umuofia had grown out of the nine sons of the first

---

9. Here the term refers to the village's highest spiritual and judicial authority, prominent men who, after putting on elaborate ceremonial costumes, embody the village's ancestral spirits. 1. "Body of my friend, greetings!"

father of the clan. Evil Forest represented the village of Umueru, or the children of Eru, who was the eldest of the nine sons.

"*Umuofia kwenu!*" shouted the leading *egwugwu*, pushing the air with his raffia arms. The elders of the clan replied, "*Yaa!*"

"*Umuofia kwenu!*"

"*Yaa!*"

"*Umuofia kwenu!*"

"*Yaa!*"

Evil Forest then thrust the pointed end of his rattling staff into the earth. And it began to shake and rattle, like something agitating with a metallic life. He took the first of the empty stools and the eight other *egwugwu* began to sit in order of seniority after him.

Okonkwo's wives, and perhaps other women as well, might have noticed that the second *egwugwu* had the springy walk of Okonkwo. And they might also have noticed that Okonkwo was not among the titled men and elders who sat behind the row of *egwugwu*. But if they thought these things they kept them within themselves. The *egwugwu* with the springy walk was one of the dead fathers of the clan. He looked terrible with the smoked raffia body, a huge wooden face painted white except for the round hollow eyes and the charred teeth that were as big as a man's fingers. On his head were two powerful horns.

When all the *egwugwu* had sat down and the sound of the many tiny bells and rattles on their bodies had subsided, Evil Forest addressed the two groups of people facing them.

"Uzowulu's body, I salute you," he said. Spirits always addressed humans as "bodies." Uzowulu bent down and touched the earth with his right hand as a sign of submission.

"Our father, my hand has touched the ground," he said.

"Uzowulu's body, do you know me?" asked the spirit.

"How can I know you, father? You are beyond our knowledge."

Evil Forest then turned to the other group and addressed the eldest of the three brothers.

"The body of Odukwe, I greet you," he said, and Odukwe bent down and touched the earth. The hearing then began.

Uzowulu stepped forward and presented his case.

"That woman standing there is my wife, Mgbafo. I married her with my money and my yams. I do not owe my in-laws anything. I owe them no yams. I owe them no coco-yams. One morning three of them came to my house, beat me up and took my wife and children away. This happened in the rainy season. I have waited in vain for my wife to return. At last I went to my in-laws and said to them, 'You have taken back your sister. I did not send her away. You yourselves took her. The law of the clan is that you should return her bride-price.' But my wife's brothers said they had nothing to tell me. So I have brought the matter to the fathers of the clan. My case is finished. I salute you."

"Your words are good," said the leader of the *egwugwu*. "Let us hear Odukwe. His words may also be good."

Odukwe was short and thickset. He stepped forward, saluted the spirits and began his story.

"My in-law has told you that we went to his house, beat him up and took our sister and her children away. All that is true. He told you that he came to take back her bride-price and we refused to give it him. That also is true. My in-law, Uzowulu, is a beast. My sister lived with him for nine years. During those years no single day passed in the sky without his beating the woman. We have tried to settle their quarrels time without number and on each occasion Uzowulu was guilty—"

"It is a lie!" Uzowulu shouted.

"Two years ago," continued Odukwe, "when she was pregnant, he beat her until she miscarried."

"It is a lie. She miscarried after she had gone to sleep with her lover."

"Uzowulu's body, I salute you," said Evil Forest, silencing him. "What kind of lover sleeps with a pregnant woman?" There was a loud murmur of approbation from the crowd. Odukwe continued:

"Last year when my sister was recovering from an illness, he beat her again so that if the neighbors had not gone in to save her she would have been killed. We heard of it, and did as you have been told. The law of Umuofia is that if a woman runs away from her husband her bride-price is returned. But in this case she ran away to save her life. Her two children belong to Uzowulu. We do not dispute it, but they are too young to leave their mother. If, in the other hand, Uzowulu should recover from his madness and come in the proper way to beg his wife to return she will do so on the understanding that if he ever beats her again we shall cut off his genitals for him."

The crowd roared with laughter. Evil Forest rose to his feet and order was immediately restored. A steady cloud of smoke rose from his head. He sat down again and called two witnesses. They were both Uzowulu's neighbors, and they agreed about the beating. Evil Forest then stood up, pulled out his staff and thrust it into the earth again. He ran a few steps in the direction of the women; they all fled in terror, only to return to their places almost immediately. The nine *egwugwu* then went away to consult together in their house. They were silent for a long time. Then the metal gong sounded and the flute was blown. The *egwugwu* had emerged once again from their underground home. They saluted one another and then reappeared on the *ilo*.

"*Umuofia kwenu!*" roared Evil Forest, facing the elders and grandees of the clan.

"*Yaa!*" replied the thunderous crowd; then silence descended from the sky and swallowed the noise.

Evil Forest began to speak and all the while he spoke everyone was silent. The eight other *egwugwu* were as still as statues.

"We have heard both sides of the case," said Evil Forest. "Our duty is not to blame this man or to praise that, but to settle the dispute." He turned to Uzowulu's group and allowed a short pause.

"Uzowulu's body, I salute you," he said.

"Our father, my hand has touched the ground," replied Uzowulu, touching the earth.

"Uzowulu's body, do you know me?"

"How can I know you, father? You are beyond our knowledge," Uzo-wulu replied.

"I am Evil Forest. I kill a man on the day that his life is sweetest to him."

"That is true," replied Uzowulu.

"Go to your in-laws with a pot of wine and beg your wife to return to you. It is not bravery when a man fights with a woman." He turned to Odukwe, and allowed a brief pause.

"Odukwe's body, I greet you," he said.

"My hand is on the ground," replied Odukwe.

"Do you know me?"

"No man can know you," replied Odukwe.

"I am Evil Forest, I am Dry-meat-that-fills-the-mouth, I am Fire-that-burns-without-faggots. If your in-law brings wine to you, let your sister go with him. I salute you." He pulled his staff from the hard earth and thrust it back.

"Umuofia kwenu!" he roared, and the crowd answered.

"I don't know why such a trifle should come before the egwugwu," said one elder to another.

"Don't you know what kind of man Uzowulu is? He will not listen to any other decision," replied the other.

As they spoke two other groups of people had replaced the first before the egwugwu, and a great land case began.

11

The night was impenetrably dark. The moon had been rising later and later every night until now it was seen only at dawn. And whenever the moon forsook evening and rose at cock-crow the nights were as black as charcoal.

Ezinma and her mother sat on a mat on the floor after their supper of yam foo-foo and bitter-leaf soup. A palm-oil lamp gave out yellowish light. Without it, it would have been impossible to eat; one could not have known where one's mouth was in the darkness of that night. There was an oil lamp in all the four huts on Okonkwo's compound, and each hut seen from the others looked like a soft eye of yellow half-light set in the solid massiveness of night.

The world was silent except for the shrill cry of insects, which was part of the night, and the sound of wooden mortar and pestle as Nwayieke pounded her foo-foo. Nwayieke lived four compounds away, and she was notorious for her late cooking. Every woman in the neighborhood knew the sound of Nwayieke's mortar and pestle. It was also part of the night.

Okonkwo had eaten from his wives' dishes and was now reclining with his back against the wall. He searched his bag and brought out his snuff-bottle. He turned it on to his left palm, but nothing came out. He hit the bottle against his knee to shake up the tobacco. That was always the trouble with Okeke's snuff. It very quickly went damp, and there was too much saltpeter in it. Okonkwo had not bought snuff from him for a long time.

Idigo was the man who knew how to grind good snuff. But he had recently fallen ill.

Low voices, broken now and again by singing, reached Okonkwo from his wives' huts as each woman and her children told folk stories. Ekwefi and her daughter, Ezinma, sat on a mat on the floor. It was Ekwefi's turn to tell a story.

"Once upon a time," she began, "all the birds were invited to a feast in the sky. They were very happy and began to prepare themselves for the great day. They painted their bodies with red cam wood and drew beautiful patterns on them with *uli*.

"Tortoise saw all these preparations and soon discovered what it all meant. Nothing that happened in the world of the animals ever escaped his notice; he was full of cunning. As soon as he heard of the great feast in the sky his throat began to itch at the very thought. There was a famine in those days and Tortoise had not eaten a good meal for two moons. His body rattled like a piece of dry stick in his empty shell. So he began to plan how he would go to the sky."

"But he had no wings," said Ezinma.

"Be patient," replied her mother. "That is the story. Tortoise had no wings, but he went to the birds and asked to be allowed to go with them.

" 'We know you too well,' said the birds when they had heard him. 'You are full of cunning and you are ungrateful. If we allow you to come with us you will soon begin your mischief.'

" 'You do not know me,' said Tortoise. 'I am a changed man. I have learned that a man who makes trouble for others is also making it for himself.'

"Tortoise had a sweet tongue, and within a short time all the birds agreed that he was a changed man, and they each gave him a feather, with which he made two wings.

"At last the great day came and Tortoise was the first to arrive at the meeting place. When all the birds had gathered together, they set off in a body. Tortoise was very happy and voluble as he flew among the birds, and he was soon chosen as the man to speak for the party because he was a great orator.

" 'There is one important thing which we must not forget,' he said as they flew on their way. 'When people are invited to a great feast like this, they take new names for the occasion. Our hosts in the sky will expect us to honor this age-old custom.'

"None of the birds had heard of this custom but they knew that Tortoise, in spite of his failings in other directions, was a widely traveled man who knew the customs of different peoples. And so they each took a new name. When they had all taken, Tortoise also took one. He was to be called *All of you*.

"At last the party arrived in the sky and their hosts were very happy to see them. Tortoise stood up in his many-colored plumage and thanked them for their invitation. His speech was so eloquent that all the birds were glad they had brought him, and nodded their heads in approval of all he said. Their hosts took him as the king of the birds, especially as he looked somewhat different from the others.

"After kola nuts had been presented and eaten, the people of the sky set before their guests the most delectable dishes Tortoise had ever seen or dreamed of. The soup was brought out hot from the fire and in the very pot in which it had been cooked. It was full of meat and fish. Tortoise began to sniff aloud. There was pounded yam and also yam pottage cooked with palm-oil and fresh fish. There were also pots of palm-wine. When everything had been set before the guests, one of the people of the sky came forward and tasted a little from each pot. He then invited the birds to eat. But Tortoise jumped to his feet and asked: 'For whom have you prepared this feast?'

" 'For all of you,' replied the man.

"Tortoise turned to the birds and said: 'You remember that my name is *All of you*. The custom here is to serve the spokesman first and the others later. They will serve you when I have eaten.'

"He began to eat and the birds grumbled angrily. The people of the sky thought it must be their custom to leave all the food for their king. And so Tortoise ate the best part of the food and then drank two pots of palm-wine, so that he was full of food and drink and his body filled out in his shell.

"The birds gathered round to eat what was left and to peck at the bones he had thrown all about the floor. Some of them were too angry to eat. They chose to fly home on an empty stomach. But before they left each took back the feather he had lent to Tortoise. And there he stood in his hard shell full of food and wine but without any wings to fly home. He asked the birds to take a message for his wife, but they all refused. In the end Parrot, who had felt more angry than the others, suddenly changed his mind and agreed to take the message.

" 'Tell my wife,' said Tortoise, 'to bring out all the soft things in my house and cover the compound with them so that I can jump down from the sky without very great danger.'

"Parrot promised to deliver the message, and then flew away. But when he reached Tortoise's house he told his wife to bring out all the hard things in the house. And so she brought out her husband's hoes, machetes, spears, guns and even his cannon. Tortoise looked down from the sky and saw his wife bringing things out, but it was too far to see what they were. When all seemed ready he let himself go. He fell and fell and fell until he began to fear that he would never stop falling. And then like the sound of his cannon he crashed on the compound."

"Did he die?" asked Ezinma.

"No," replied Ekwefi. "His shell broke into pieces. But there was a great medicine man in the neighborhood. Tortoise's wife sent for him and he gathered all the bits of shell and stuck them together. That is why Tortoise's shell is not smooth."

"There is no song in the story," Ezinma pointed out.

"No," said Ekwefi. "I shall think of another one with a song. But it is your turn now."

"Once upon a time," Ezinma began, "Tortoise and Cat went to wrestle against Yams—no, that is not the beginning. Once upon a time there was a great famine in the land of animals. Everybody was lean except Cat, who was fat and whose body shone as if oil was rubbed on it . . ."

She broke off because at that very moment a loud and high-pitched voice broke the outer silence of the night. It was Chielo, the priestess of Agbala, prophesying. There was nothing new in that. Once in a while Chielo was possessed by the spirit of her god and she began to prophesy. But tonight she was addressing her prophecy and greetings to Okonkwo, and so everyone in his family listened. The folk stories stopped.

"*Agbala do-o-o-o! Agbala ekeneo-o-o-o,*"[2] came the voice like a sharp knife cutting through the night. "*Okonkwo! Agbala ekene gio-o-o-o! Agbala cholu ifu ada ya Ezinmao-o-o-o!*"[3]

At the mention of Ezinma's name Ekwefi jerked her head sharply like an animal that had sniffed death in the air. Her heart jumped painfully within her.

The priestess had now reached Okonkwo's compound and was talking with him outside his hut. She was saying again and again that Agbala wanted to see his daughter, Ezinma. Okonkwo pleaded with her to come back in the morning because Ezinma was now asleep. But Chielo ignored what he was trying to say and went on shouting that Agbala wanted to see his daughter. Her voice was as clear as metal, and Okonkwo's women and children heard from their huts all that she said. Okonkwo was still pleading that the girl had been ill of late and was asleep. Ekwefi quickly took her to their bedroom and placed her on their high bamboo bed.

The priestess screamed. "Beware, Okonkwo!" she warned. "Beware of exchanging words with Agbala. Does a man speak when a god speaks? Beware!"

She walked through Okonkwo's hut into the circular compound and went straight toward Ekwefi's hut. Okonkwo came after her.

"Ekwefi," she called, "Agbala greets you. Where is my daughter, Ezinma? Agbala wants to see her."

Ekwefi came out from her hut carrying her oil lamp in her left hand. There was a light wind blowing, so she cupped her right hand to shelter the flame. Nwoye's mother, also carrying an oil lamp, emerged from her hut. The children stood in the darkness outside their hut watching the strange event. Okonkwo's youngest wife also came out and joined the others.

"Where does Agbala want to see her?" Ekwefi asked.

"Where else but in his house in the hills and the caves?" replied the priestess.

"I will come with you, too," Ekwefi said firmly.

"*Tufia-a!*"[4] the priestess cursed, her voice cracking like the angry bark of thunder in the dry season. "How dare you, woman, to go before the mighty Agbala of your own accord? Beware, woman, lest he strike you in his anger. Bring me my daughter."

2. "Agbala wants something! Agbala greets . . ."   3. "Agbala greets you! Agbala wants to see his daughter Ezinma!"   4. A curse in words meaning "spitting" or "clearing out," often accompanied by spitting.

Ekwefi went into her hut and came out again with Ezinma.

"Come, my daughter," said the priestess. "I shall carry you on my back. A baby on its mother's back does not know that the way is long."

Ezinma began to cry. She was used to Chielo calling her "my daughter." But it was a different Chielo she now saw in the yellow half-light.

"Don't cry, my daughter," said the priestess, "lest Agbala be angry with you."

"Don't cry," said Ekwefi, "she will bring you back very soon. I shall give you some fish to eat." She went into the hut again and brought down the smoke-black basket in which she kept her dried fish and other ingredients for cooking soup. She broke a piece in two and gave it to Ezinma, who clung to her.

"Don't be afraid," said Ekwefi, stroking her head, which was shaved in places, leaving a regular pattern of hair. They went outside again. The priestess bent down on one knee and Ezinma climbed on her back, her left palm closed on her fish and her eyes gleaming with tears.

"Agbala do-o-o-o! Agbala ekeneo-o-o-o! . . ." Chielo began once again to chant greetings to her god. She turned round sharply and walked through Okonkwo's hut, bending very low at the eaves. Ezinma was crying loudly now, calling on her mother. The two voices disappeared into the thick darkness.

A strange and sudden weakness descended on Ekwefi as she stood gazing in the direction of the voices like a hen whose only chick has been carried away by a kite. Ezinma's voice soon faded away and only Chielo was heard moving farther and farther into the distance.

"Why do you stand there as though she had been kidnapped?" asked Okonkwo as he went back to his hut.

"She will bring her back soon," Nwoye's mother said.

But Ekwefi did not hear these consolations. She stood for a while, and then, all of a sudden, made up her mind. She hurried through Okonkwo's hut and went outside. "Where are you going?" he asked.

"I am following Chielo," she replied and disappeared in the darkness. Okonkwo cleared his throat, and brought out his snuff-bottle from the goatskin bag by his side.

The priestess's voice was already growing faint in the distance. Ekwefi hurried to the main footpath and turned left in the direction of the voice. Her eyes were useless to her in the darkness. But she picked her way easily on the sandy footpath hedged on either side by branches and damp leaves. She began to run, holding her breasts with her hands to stop them flapping noisily against her body. She hit her left foot against an outcropped root, and terror seized her. It was an ill omen. She ran faster. But Chielo's voice was still a long way away. Had she been running too? How could she go so fast with Ezinma on her back? Although the night was cool, Ekwefi was beginning to feel hot from her running. She continually ran into the luxuriant weeds and creepers that walled in the path. Once she tripped up and fell. Only then did she realize, with a start, that Chielo had stopped her chanting. Her heart beat violently and she stood still. Then Chielo's renewed outburst came from only a few paces ahead. But Ekwefi could not see her. She shut her eyes for a while and opened them again in an effort to see. But it was useless. She could not see beyond her nose.

There were no stars in the sky because there was a rain-cloud. Fireflies went about with their tiny green lamps, which only made the darkness more profound. Between Chielo's outbursts the night was alive with the shrill tremor of forest insects woven into the darkness.

"Agbala do-o-o-o! . . . Agbala ekeneo-o-o-o! . . . ." Ekwefi trudged behind, neither getting too near nor keeping too far back. She thought they must be going towards the sacred cave. Now that she walked slowly she had time to think. What would she do when they got to the cave? She would not dare to enter. She would wait at the mouth, all alone in that fearful place. She thought of all the terrors of the night. She remembered that night, long ago, when she had seen *Ogbu-agali-odu*, one of those evil essences loosed upon the world by the potent "medicines" which the tribe had made in the distant past against its enemies but had now forgotten how to control. Ekwefi had been returning from the stream with her mother on a dark night like this when they saw its glow as it flew in their direction. They had thrown down their water-pots and lain by the roadside expecting the sinister light to descend on them and kill them. That was the only time Ekwefi ever saw *Ogbu-agali-odu*. But although it had happened so long ago, her blood still ran cold whenever she remembered that night.

The priestess's voice came at longer intervals now, but its vigor was undiminished. The air was cool and damp with dew. Ezinma sneezed. Ekwefi muttered, "Life to you." At the same time the priestess also said, "Life to you, my daughter." Ezinma's voice from the darkness warmed her mother's heart. She trudged slowly along.

And then the priestess screamed. "Somebody is walking behind me!" she said. "Whether you are spirit or man, may Agbala shave your head with a blunt razor! May he twist your neck until you see your heels!"

Elkwefi stood rooted to the spot. One mind said to her: "Woman, go home before Agbala does you harm." But she could not. She stood until Chielo had increased the distance between them and she began to follow again. She had already walked so long that she began to feel a slight numbness in the limbs and in the head. Then it occurred to her that they could not have been heading for the cave. They must have by-passed it long ago; they must be going towards Umuachi, the farthest village in the clan. Chielo's voice now came after long intervals.

It seemed to Ekwefi that the night had become a little lighter. The cloud had lifted and a few stars were out. The moon must be preparing to rise, its sullenness over. When the moon rose late in the night, people said it was refusing food, as a sullen husband refuses his wife's food when they have quarrelled.

"Agbala do-o-o-o! Umuachi! Agbala ekene unuo-o-o!" It was just as Ekwefi had thought. The priestess was now saluting the village of Umuachi. It was unbelievable, the distance they had covered. As they emerged into the open village from the narrow forest track the darkness was softened and it became possible to see the vague shape of trees. Ekwefi screwed her eyes up in an effort to see her daughter and the priestess, but whenever she thought she saw their shape it immediately dissolved like a melting lump of darkness. She walked numbly along.

Chielo's voice was now rising continuously, as when she first set out. Ekwefi had a feeling of spacious openness, and she guessed they must be on the village *ilo*, or playground. And she realized too with something like a jerk that Chielo was no longer moving forward. She was, in fact, returning. Ekwefi quickly moved away from her line of retreat. Chielo passed by, and they began to go back the way they had come.

It was a long and weary journey and Ekwefi felt like a sleepwalker most of the way. The moon was definitely rising, and although it had not yet appeared on the sky its light had already melted down the darkness. Ekwefi could now discern the figure of the priestess and her burden. She slowed down her pace so as to increase the distance between them. She was afraid of what might happen if Chielo suddenly turned round and saw her.

She had prayed for the moon to rise. But now she found the half-light of the incipient moon more terrifying than darkness. The world was now peopled with vague, fantastic figures that dissolved under her steady gaze and then formed again in new shapes. At one stage Ekwefi was so afraid that she nearly called out to Chielo for companionship and human sympathy. What she had seen was the shape of a man climbing a palm tree, his head pointing to the earth and his legs skywards. But at that very moment Chielo's voice rose again in her possessed chanting, and Ekwefi recoiled, because there was no humanity there. It was not the same Chielo who sat with her in the market and sometimes bought bean-cakes for Ezinma, whom she called her daughter. It was a different woman—the priestess of Agbala, the Oracle of the Hills and Caves. Ekwefi trudged along between two fears. The sound of her benumbed steps seemed to come from some other person walking behind her. Her arms were folded across her bare breasts. Dew fell heavily and the air was cold. She could no longer think, not even about the terrors of night. She just jogged along in a half-sleep, only waking to full life when Chielo sang.

At last they took a turning and began to head for the caves. From then on, Chielo never ceased in her chanting. She greeted her god in a multitude of names—the owner of the future, the messenger of earth, the god who cut a man down when his life was sweetest to him. Ekwefi was also awakened and her benumbed fears revived.

The moon was now up and she could see Chielo and Ezinma clearly. How a woman could carry a child of that size so easily and for so long was a miracle. But Ekwefi was not thinking about that. Chielo was not a woman that night.

"*Agbala do-o-o-o! Agbala ekeneo-o-o-o! Chi negbu madu ubosi ndu ya nato ya uto daluo-o-o!* . . ."[5]

Ekwefi could already see the hills looming in the moonlight. They formed a circular ring with a break at one point through which the foot-track led to the center of the circle.

As soon as the priestess stepped into this ring of hills her voice was not

5. "Agbala wants something! Agbala greets . . . God who kills a man on the day his life is so pleasant he gives thanks!"

only doubled in strength but was thrown back on all sides. It was indeed the shrine of a great god. Ekwefi picked her way carefully and quietly. She was already beginning to doubt the wisdom of her coming. Nothing would happen to Ezinma, she thought. And if anything happened to her could she stop it? She would not dare to enter the underground caves. Her coming was quite useless, she thought.

As these things went through her mind she did not realize how close they were to the cave mouth. And so when the priestess with Ezinma on her back disappeared through a hole hardly big enough to pass a hen, Ekwefi broke into a run as though to stop them. As she stood gazing at the circular darkness which had swallowed them, tears gushed from her eyes, and she swore within her that if she heard Ezinma cry she would rush into the cave to defend her against all the gods in the world. She would die with her.

Having sworn that oath, she sat down on a stony ledge and waited. Her fear had vanished. She could hear the priestess's voice, all its metal taken out of it by the vast emptiness of the cave. She buried her face in her lap and waited.

She did not know how long she waited. It must have been a very long time. Her back was turned on the footpath that led out of the hills. She must have heard a noise behind her and turned round sharply. A man stood there with a machete in his hand. Ekwefi uttered a scream and sprang to her feet.

"Don't be foolish," said Okonkwo's voice. "I thought you were going into the shrine with Chielo," he mocked.

Ekwefi did not answer. Tears of gratitude filled her eyes. She knew her daughter was safe.

"Go home and sleep," said Okonkwo. "I shall wait here."

"I shall wait too. It is almost dawn. The first cock has crowed."

As they stood there together, Ekwefi's mind went back to the days when they were young. She had married Anene because Okonkwo was too poor then to marry. Two years after her marriage to Anene she could bear it no longer and she ran away to Okonkwo. It had been early in the morning. The moon was shining. She was going to the stream to fetch water. Okonkwo's house was on the way to the stream. She went in and knocked at his door and he came out. Even in those days he was not a man of many words. He just carried her into his bed and in the darkness began to feel around her waist for the loose end of her cloth.

12

On the following morning the entire neighborhood wore a festive air because Okonkwo's friend, Obierika, was celebrating his daughter's *uri*. It was the day on which her suitor (having already paid the greater part of her bride-price) would bring palm-wine not only to her parents and immediate relatives but to the wide and extensive group of kinsmen called *umunna*. Everybody had been invited—men, women and children. But it was really a woman's ceremony and the central figures were the bride and her mother.

As soon as day broke, breakfast was hastily eaten and women and children began to gather at Obierika's compound to help the bride's mother in her difficult but happy task of cooking for a whole village.

Okonkwo's family was astir like any other family in the neighborhood. Nwoye's mother and Okonkwo's youngest wife were ready to set out for Obierika's compound with all their children. Nwoye's mother carried a basket of coco-yams, a cake of salt and smoked fish which she would present to Obierika's wife. Okonkwo's youngest wife, Ojiugo, also had a basket of plantains and coco-yams and a small pot of palm-oil. Their children carried pots of water.

Ekwefi was tired and sleepy from the exhausting experiences of the previous night. It was not very long since they had returned. The priestess, with Ezinma sleeping on her back, had crawled out of the shrine on her belly like a snake. She had not as much as looked at Okonkwo and Ekwefi or shown any surprise at finding them at the mouth of the cave. She looked straight ahead of her and walked back to the village. Okonkwo and his wife followed at a respectful distance. They thought the priestess might be going to her house, but she went to Okonkwo's compound, passed through his *obi* and into Ekwefi's hut and walked into her bedroom. She placed Ezinma carefully on the bed and went away without saying a word to anybody.

Ezinma was still sleeping when everyone else was astir, and Ekwefi asked Nwoye's mother and Ojiugo to explain to Obierika's wife that she would be late. She had got ready her basket of coco-yams and fish, but she must wait for Ezinma to wake.

"You need some sleep yourself," said Nwoye's mother. "You look very tired."

As they spoke Ezinma emerged from the hut, rubbing her eyes and stretching her spare frame. She saw the other children with their water-pots and remembered that they were going to fetch water for Obierika's wife. She went back to the hut and brought her pot.

"Have you slept enough?" asked her mother.

"Yes," she replied, "Let us go."

"Not before you have had your breakfast," said Ekwefi. And she went into her hut to warm the vegetable soup she had cooked last night.

"We shall be going," said Nwoye's mother. "I will tell Obierika's wife that you are coming later." And so they all went to help Obierika's wife — Nwoye's mother with her four children and Ojiugo with her two.

As they trooped through Okonkwo's *obi* he asked: "Who will prepare my afternoon meal?"

"I shall return to do it," said Ojiugo.

Okonkwo was also feeling tired, and sleepy, for although nobody else knew it, he had not slept at all last night. He had felt very anxious but did not show it. When Ekwefi had followed the priestess, he had allowed what he regarded as a reasonable and manly interval to pass and then gone with his machete to the shrine, where he thought they must be. It was only when he had got there that it had occurred to him that the priestess might have chosen to go round the villages first. Okonkwo had returned home and sat waiting. When he thought he had waited long enough he again returned to the shrine. But the Hills and the Caves were as silent as death. It was only on his fourth trip that he had found Ekwefi, and by then he had become gravely worried.

Obierika's compound was as busy as an anthill. Temporary cooking tripods were erected on every available space by bringing together three blocks of sun-dried earth and making a fire in their midst. Cooking pots went up and down the tripods, and foo-foo was pounded in a hundred wooden mortars. Some of the women cooked the yams and the cassava, and others prepared vegetable soup. Young men pounded the foo-foo or split firewood. The children made endless trips to the stream.

Three young men helped Obierika to slaughter the two goats with which the soup was made. They were very fat goats, but the fattest of all was tethered to a peg near the wall of the compound. It was as big as a small cow. Obierika had sent one of his relatives all the way to Umuike to buy that goat. It was the one he would present alive to his in-laws.

"The market of Umuike is a wonderful place," said the young man who had been sent by Obierika to buy the giant goat. "There are so many people on it that if you threw up a grain of sand it would not find a way to fall to earth again."

"It is the result of a great medicine," said Obierika. "The people of Umuike wanted their market to grow and swallow up the markets of their neighbors. So they made a powerful medicine. Every market day, before the first cock-crow, this medicine stands on the market ground in the shape of an old woman with a fan. With this magic fan she beckons to the market all the neighboring clans. She beckons in front of her and behind her, to her right and to her left."

"And so everybody comes," said another man, "honest men and thieves. They can steal your cloth from off your waist in that market."

"Yes," said Obierika. "I warned Nwankwo to keep a sharp eye and a sharp ear. There was once a man who went to sell a goat. He led it on a thick rope which he tied round his wrist. But as he walked through the market he realized that people were pointing at him as they do to a madman. He could not understand it until he looked back and saw that what he led at the end of the tether was not a goat but a heavy log of wood."

"Do you think a thief can do that kind of thing single-handed?" asked Nwankwo.

"No," said Obierika. "They use medicine."

When they had cut the goats' throats and collected the blood in a bowl, they held them over an open fire to burn off the hair, and the smell of burning hair blended with the smell of cooking. Then they washed them and cut them up for the women who prepared the soup.

All this anthill activity was going smoothly when a sudden interruption came. It was a cry in the distance: *Oji odu achu ijiji-o-o! (The one that uses its tail to drive flies away!)* Every woman immediately abandoned whatever she was doing and rushed out in the direction of the cry.

"We cannot all rush out like that, leaving what we are cooking to burn in the fire," shouted Chielo, the priestess. "Three or four of us should stay behind."

"It is true," said another woman. "We will allow three or four women to stay behind."

Five women stayed behind to look after the cooking-pots, and all the rest rushed away to see the cow that had been let loose. When they saw it they drove it back to its owner, who at once paid the heavy fine which the village imposed on anyone whose cow was let loose on his neighbors' crops. When the women had exacted the penalty they checked among themselves to see if any woman had failed to come out when the cry had been raised.

"Where is Mgbogo?" asked one of them.

"She is ill in bed," said Mgbogo's next-door neighbor. "She has *iba.*"

"The only other person is Udenkwo," said another woman, "and her child is not twenty-eight days yet."

Those women whom Obierika's wife had not asked to help her with the cooking returned to their homes, and the rest went back, in a body, to Obierika's compound.

"Whose cow was it?" asked the women who had been allowed to stay behind.

"It was my husband's," said Ezelagbo. "One of the young children had opened the gate of the cowshed."

Early in the afternoon the first two pots of palm-wine arrived from Obierika's in-laws. They were duly presented to the women, who drank a cup or two each, to help them in their cooking. Some of it also went to the bride and her attendant maidens, who were putting the last delicate touches of razor to her coiffure and cam wood on her smooth skin.

When the heat of the sun began to soften, Obierika's son, Maduka, took a long broom and swept the ground in front of his father's *obi*. And as if they had been waiting for that, Obierika's relatives and friends began to arrive, every man with his goatskin bag hung on one shoulder and a rolled goatskin mat under his arm. Some of them were accompanied by their sons bearing carved wooden stools. Okonkwo was one of them. They sat in a half-circle and began to talk of many things. It would not be long before the suitors came.

Okonkwo brought out his snuff-bottle and offered it to Ogbuefi Ezenwa, who sat next to him. Ezenwa[6] took it, tapped it on his kneecap, rubbed his left palm on his body to dry it before tipping a little snuff into it. His actions were deliberate, and he spoke as he performed them:

"I hope our in-laws will bring many pots of wine. Although they come from a village that is known for being closefisted, they ought to know that Akueke is the bride for a king."

"They dare not bring fewer than thirty pots," said Okonkwo. "I shall tell them my mind if they do."

At that moment Obierika's son, Maduka, led out the giant goat from the inner compound, for his father's relatives to see. They all admired it and said that that was the way things should be done. The goat was then led back to the inner compound.

6. "King from Childhood" (strong praise).

Very soon after, the in-laws began to arrive. Young men and boys in single file, each carrying a pot of wine, came first. Obierika's relatives counted the pots as they came. Twenty, twenty-five. There was a long break, and the hosts looked at each other as if to say, "I told you." Then more pots came. Thirty, thirty-five, forty, forty-five. The hosts nodded in approval and seemed to say, "Now they are behaving like men." Altogether there were fifty pots of wine. After the pot-bearers came Ibe, the suitor, and the elders of his family. They sat in a half-moon, thus completing a circle with their hosts. The pots of wine stood in their midst. Then the bride, her mother and a half a dozen other women and girls emerged from the inner compound, and went round the circle shaking hands with all. The bride's mother led the way, followed by the bride and the other women. The married women wore their best cloths and the girls wore red and black waist-beads and anklets of brass.

When the women retired, Obierika presented kola nuts to his in-laws. His eldest brother broke the first one. "Life to all of us," he said as he broke it. "And let there be friendship between your family and ours."

The crowd answered: "Ee-e-e!"

"We are giving you our daughter today. She will be a good wife to you. She will bear you nine sons like the mother of our town."

"Ee-e-e!"

The oldest man in the camp of the visitors replied: "It will be good for you and it will be good for us."

"Ee-e-e!"

"This is not the first time my people have come to marry your daughter. My mother was one of you."

"Ee-e-e!"

"And this will not be the last, because you understand us and we understand you. You are a great family."

"Ee-e-e!"

"Prosperous men and great warriors." He looked in the direction of Okonkwo. "Your daughter will bear us sons like you."

"Ee-e-e!"

The kola was eaten and the drinking of palm-wine began. Groups of four or five men sat round with a pot in their midst. As the evening wore on, food was presented to the guests. There were huge bowls of foo-foo and steaming pots of soup. There were also pots of yam pottage. It was a great feast.

As night fell, burning torches were set on wooden tripods and the young men raised a song. The elders sat in a big circle and the singers went round singing each man's praise as they came before him. They had something to say for every man. Some were great farmers, some were orators who spoke for the clan; Okonkwo was the greatest wrestler and warrior alive. When they had gone round the circle they settled down in the center, and girls came from the inner compound to dance. At first the bride was not among them. But when she finally appeared holding a cock in her right hand, a loud cheer rose from the crowd. All the other dancers made way for her. She presented the cock to the musicians and began to dance. Her brass anklets rattled as she danced and her body gleamed with cam wood in the soft yellow light. The musicians with their wood, clay and metal instruments went from song to song. And they were all gay. They sang the latest song in the village:

> If I hold her hand
> She says, "Don't touch!"
> If I hold her foot
> She says, "Don't touch!"
> But when I hold her waist-beads
> She pretends not to know.

The night was already far spent when the guests rose to go, taking their bride home to spend seven market weeks with her suitor's family. They sang songs as they went, and on their way they paid short courtesy visits to prominent men like Okonkwo, before they finally left for their village. Okonkwo made a present of two cocks to them.

13

Go-di-di-go-go-di-go. Di-go-go-di-go. It was the *ekwe* talking to the clan. One of the things every man learned was the language of the hollowed-out wooden instrument. Diim! Diim! Diim! boomed the cannon at intervals.

The first cock had not crowed, and Umuofia was still swallowed up in sleep and silence when the *ekwe* began to talk, and the cannon shattered the silence. Men stirred on their bamboo beds and listened anxiously. Somebody was dead. The cannon seemed to rend the sky. Di-go-go-di-go-di-di-go-go floated in the message-laden night air. The faint and distant wailing of women settled like a sediment of sorrow on the earth. Now and again a full-chested lamentation rose above the wailing whenever a man came into the place of death. He raised his voice once or twice in manly sorrow and then sat down with the other men listening to the endless wailing of the women and the esoteric language of the *ekwe*. Now and again the cannon boomed. The wailing of the women would not be heard beyond the village, but the *ekwe* carried the news to all the nine villages and even beyond. It began by naming the clan: Umuofia *obodo dike*, "the land of the brave." Umuofia *obodo dike!* Umuofia *obodo dike!* It said this over and over again, and as it dwelt on it, anxiety mounted in every heart that heaved on a bamboo bed that night. Then it went nearer and named the village: Iguedo[7] *of the yellow grinding-stone!* It was Okonkwo's village. Again and again Iguedo was called and men waited breathlessly in all the nine villages. At last the man was named and people sighed "E-u-u, Ezeudu is dead." A cold shiver ran down Okonkwo's back as he remembered the last time the old man had visited him. "That boy calls you father," he had said. "Bear no hand in his death."

Ezeudu was a great man, and so all the clan was at his funeral. The ancient drums of death beat, guns and cannon were fired, and men dashed

7. "The yellow grindstone."

about in frenzy, cutting down every tree or animal they saw, jumping over walls and dancing on the roof. It was a warrior's funeral, and from morning till night warriors came and went in their age groups. They all wore smoked raffia skirts and their bodies were painted with chalk and charcoal. Now and again an ancestral spirit or *egwugwu* appeared from the underworld, speaking in a tremulous, unearthly voice and completely covered in raffia. Some of them were very violent, and there had been a mad rush for shelter earlier in the day when one appeared with a sharp machete and was only prevented from doing serious harm by two men who restrained him with the help of a strong rope tied round his waist. Sometimes he turned round and chased those men, and they ran for their lives. But they always returned to the long rope he trailed behind. He sang, in a terrifying voice, that Ekwensu, or Evil Spirit, had entered his eye.

But the most dreaded of all was yet to come. He was always alone and was shaped like a coffin. A sickly odor hung in the air wherever he went, and flies went with him. Even the greatest medicine men took shelter when he was near. Many years ago another *egwugwu* had dared to stand his ground before him and had been transfixed to the spot for two days. This one had only one hand and it carried a basket full of water.

But some of the *egwugwu* were quite harmless. One of them was so old and infirm that he leaned heavily on a stick. He walked unsteadily to the place where the corpse was laid, gazed at it a while and went away again— to the underworld.

The land of the living was not far removed from the domain of the ancestors. There was coming and going between them, especially at festivals and also when an old man died, because an old man was very close to the ancestors. A man's life from birth to death was a series of transition rites which brought him nearer and nearer to his ancestors.

Ezeudu had been the oldest man in his village, and at his death there were only three men in the whole clan who were older, and four or five others in his own age group. Whenever one of these ancient men appeared in the crowd to dance unsteadily the funeral steps of the tribe, younger men gave way and the tumult subsided.

It was a great funeral, such as befitted a noble warrior. As the evening drew near, the shouting and the firing of guns, the beating of drums and the brandishing and clanging of machetes increased.

Ezeudu had taken three titles in his life. It was a rare achievement. There were only four titles in the clan, and only one or two men in any generation ever achieved the fourth and highest. When they did, they became the lords of the land. Because he had taken titles, Ezeudu was to be buried after dark with only a glowing brand to light the sacred ceremony.

But before this quiet and final rite, the tumult increased tenfold. Drums beat violently and men leaped up and down in frenzy. Guns were fired on all sides and sparks flew out as machetes clanged together in warriors' salutes. The air was full of dust and the smell of gunpowder. It was then that the one-handed spirit came, carrying a basket full of water. People made way for him on all sides and the noise subsided. Even the smell of gunpowder was swallowed in the sickly smell that now filled the air. He danced a few steps to the funeral drums and then went to see the corpse.

"Ezeudu!" he called in his guttural voice. "If you had been poor in your last life I would have asked you to be rich when you come again. But you were rich. If you had been a coward, I would have asked you to bring courage. But you were a fearless warrior. If you had died young, I would have asked you to get life. But you lived long. So I shall ask you to come again the way you came before. If your death was the death of nature, go in peace. But if a man caused it, do not allow him a moment's rest." He danced a few more steps and went away.

The drums and the dancing began again and reached fever-heat. Darkness was around the corner, and the burial was near. Guns fired the last salute and the cannon rent the sky. And then from the center of the delirious fury came a cry of agony and shouts of horror. It was as if a spell had been cast. All was silent. In the center of the crowd a boy lay in a pool of blood. It was the dead man's sixteen-year-old son, who with his brothers and half-brothers had been dancing the traditional farewell to their father. Okonkwo's gun had exploded and a piece of iron had pierced the boy's heart.

The confusion that followed was without parallel in the tradition of Umuofia. Violent deaths were frequent, but nothing like this had ever happened.

The only course open to Okonkwo was to flee from the clan. It was a crime against the earth goddess to kill a clansman, and a man who committed it must flee from the land. The crime was of two kinds, male and female. Okonkwo had committed the female, because it had been inadvertent. He could return to the clan after seven years.

That night he collected his most valuable belongings into head-loads. His wives wept bitterly and their children wept with them without knowing why. Obierika and half a dozen other friends came to help and to console him. They each made nine or ten trips carrying Okonkwo's yams to store in Obierika's barn. And before the cock crowed Okonkwo and his family were fleeing to his motherland. It was a little village called Mbanta,[8] just beyond the borders of Mbaino.

As soon as the day broke, a large crowd of men from Ezeudu's quarter stormed Okonkwo's compound, dressed in garbs of war. They set fire to his houses, demolished his red walls, killed his animals and destroyed his barn. It was the justice of the earth goddess, and they were merely her messengers. They had no hatred in their hearts against Okonkwo. His greatest friend, Obierika, was among them. They were merely cleansing the land which Okonkwo had polluted with the blood of a clansman.

Obierika was a man who thought about things. When the will of the goddess had been done, he sat down in his *obi* and mourned his friend's calamity. Why should a man suffer so grievously for an offense he had committed inadvertently? But although he thought for a long time he

8. "Small Town."

found no answer. He was merely led into greater complexities. He remembered his wife's twin children, whom he had thrown away. What crime had they committed? The Earth had decreed that they were an offense on the land and must be destroyed. And if the clan did not exact punishment for an offense against the great goddess, her wrath was loosed on all the land and not just on the offender. As the elders said, if one finger brought oil it soiled the others.

Part Two

14

Okonkwo was well received by his mother's kinsmen in Mbanta. The old man who received him was his mother's younger brother, who was now the eldest surviving member of that family. His name was Uchendu,[9] and it was he who had received Okonkwo's mother twenty and ten years before when she had been brought home from Umuofia to be buried with her people. Okonkwo was only a boy then and Uchendu still remembered him crying the traditional farewell: "Mother, mother, mother is going."

That was many years ago. Today Okonkwo was not bringing his mother home to be buried with her people. He was taking his family of three wives and their children to seek refuge in his motherland. As soon as Uchendu saw him with his sad and weary company he guessed what had happened, and asked no questions. It was not until the following day that Okonkwo told him the full story. The old man listened silently to the end and then said with some relief: "It is a female *ochu*."[1] And he arranged the requisite rites and sacrifices.

Okonkwo was given a plot of ground on which to build his compound, and two or three pieces of land on which to farm during the coming planting season. With the help of his mother's kinsmen he built himself an *obi* and three huts for his wives. He then installed his personal god and the symbols of his departed fathers. Each of Uchendu's five sons contributed three hundred seed-yams to enable their cousin to plant a farm, for as soon as the first rain came farming would begin.

At last the rain came. It was sudden and tremendous. For two or three moons the sun had been gathering strength till it seemed to breathe a breath of fire on the earth. All the grass had long been scorched brown, and the sands felt like live coals to the feet. Evergreen trees wore a dusty coat of brown. The birds were silenced in the forests, and the world lay panting under the live, vibrating heat. And then came the clap of thunder. It was an angry, metallic and thirsty clap, unlike the deep and liquid rumbling of the rainy season. A mighty wind arose and filled the air with dust. Palm trees swayed as the wind combed their leaves into flying crests like strange and fantastic coiffure.

When the rain finally came, it was in large, solid drops of frozen water which the people called "the nuts of the water of heaven." They were hard and painful on the body as they fell, yet young people ran about happily

9. "The Thought Created by Life."　　1. Murder, manslaughter.

picking up the cold nuts and throwing them into their mouths to melt.

The earth quickly came to life and the birds in the forests fluttered around and chirped merrily. A vague scent of life and green vegetation was diffused in the air. As the rain began to fall more soberly and in smaller liquid drops, children sought for shelter, and all were happy, refreshed and thankful.

Okonkwo and his family worked very hard to plant a new farm. But it was like beginning life anew without the vigor and enthusiasm of youth, like learning to become left-handed in old age. Work no longer had for him the pleasure it used to have, and when there was no work to do he sat in a silent half-sleep.

His life had been ruled by a great passion—to become one of the lords of the clan. That had been his life-spring. And he had all but achieved it. Then everything had been broken. He had been cast out of his clan like a fish onto a dry, sandy beach, panting. Clearly his personal god or *chi* was not made for great things. A man could not rise beyond the destiny of his *chi*. The saying of the elders was not true—that if a man said yea his *chi* also affirmed. Here was a man whose *chi* said nay despite his own affirmation.

The old man, Uchendu, saw clearly that Okonkwo had yielded to despair and he was greatly troubled. He would speak to him after the *isa-ifi*[2] ceremony.

The youngest of Uchendu's five sons, Amikwu, was marrying a new wife. The bride-price had been paid and all but the last ceremony had been performed. Amikwu and his people had taken palm-wine to the bride's kinsmen about two moons before Okonkwo's arrival in Mbanta. And so it was time for the final ceremony of confession.

The daughters of the family were all there, some of them having come a long way from their homes in distant villages. Uchendu's eldest daughter had come from Obodo, nearly half a day's journey away. The daughters of Uchendu's brothers were also there. It was a full gathering of *umuada*,[3] in the same way as they would meet if a death occurred in the family. There were twenty-two of them.

They sat in a big circle on the ground and the bride sat in the center with a hen in her right hand. Uchendu sat by her, holding the ancestral staff of the family. All the other men stood outside the circle, watching. Their wives watched also. It was evening and the sun was setting.

Uchendu's eldest daughter, Njide, asked the questions.

"Remember that if you do not answer truthfully you will suffer or even die at childbirth," she began. "How many men have lain with you since my brother first expressed the desire to marry you?"

"None," she answered simply.

"Answer truthfully," urged the other women.

"None?" asked Njide.

"None," she answered.

---

2. A ceremony to ascertain that a wife (here, a promised bride) had been faithful to her husband during a separation.   3. The daughters, who, according to Igbo custom, married outside the clan, perform a special initiation upon returning home for important gatherings.

"Swear on this staff of my fathers," said Uchendu.

"I swear," said the bride.

Uchendu took the hen from her, slit its throat with a sharp knife and allowed some of the blood to fall on his ancestral staff.

From that day Amikwu took the young bride to his hut and she became his wife. The daughters of the family did not return to their homes immediately but spent two or three days with their kinsmen.

On the second day Uchendu called together his sons and daughters and his nephew, Okonkwo. The men brought their goatskin mats, with which they sat on the floor, and the women sat on a sisal mat spread on a raised bank of earth. Uchendu pulled gently at his gray beard and gnashed his teeth. Then he began to speak, quietly and deliberately, picking his words with great care:

"It is Okonkwo that I primarily wish to speak to," he began. "But I want all of you to note what I am going to say. I am an old man and you are all children. I know more about the world than any of you. If there is any one among you who thinks he knows more let him speak up." He paused, but no one spoke.

"Why is Okonkwo with us today? This is not his clan. We are only his mother's kinsmen. He does not belong here. He is an exile, condemned for seven years to live in a strange land. And so he is bowed with grief. But there is just one question I would like to ask him. Can you tell me, Okonkwo, why it is that one of the commonest names we give our children is Nneka, or "Mother is Supreme?" We all know that a man is the head of the family and his wives do his bidding. A child belongs to its father and his family and not to its mother and her family. A man belongs to his fatherland and not to his motherland. And yet we say Nneka—'Mother is Supreme.' Why is that?"

There was silence. "I want Okonkwo to answer me," said Uchendu.

"I do not know the answer," Okonkwo replied.

"You do not know the answer? So you see that you are a child. You have many wives and many children—more children than I have. You are a great man in your clan. But you are still a child, *my* child. Listen to me and I shall tell you. But there is one more question I shall ask you. Why is it that when a woman dies she is taken home to be buried with her own kinsmen? She is not buried with her husband's kinsmen. Why is that? Your mother was brought home to me and buried with my people. Why was that?"

Okonkwo shook his head.

"He does not know that either," said Uchendu, "and yet he is full of sorrow because he has come to live in his motherland for a few years." He laughed a mirthless laughter, and turned to his sons and daughters. "What about you? Can you answer my question?"

They all shook their heads.

"Then listen to me," he said and cleared his throat. "It's true that a child belongs to its father. But when a father beats his child, it seeks sympathy in its mother's hut. A man belongs to his fatherland when things are good and life is sweet. But when there is sorrow and bitterness he finds refuge in his motherland. Your mother is there to protect you. She is buried there. And that is why we say that mother is supreme. Is it right that you, Okonkwo, should bring to your mother a heavy face and refuse to be comforted? Be careful or you may displease the dead. Your duty is to comfort your wives and children and take them back to your fatherland after seven years. But if you allow sorrow to weigh you down and kill you, they will all die in exile." He paused for a long while. "These are now your kinsmen." He waved at his sons and daughters. "You think you are the greatest sufferer in the world? Do you know that men are sometimes banished for life? Do you know that men sometimes lose all their yams and even their children? I had six wives once. I have none now except that young girl who knows not her right from her left. Do you know how many children I have buried—children I begot in my youth and strength? Twenty-two. I did not hang myself, and I am still alive. If you think you are the greatest sufferer in the world ask my daughter, Akueni, how many twins she has borne and thrown away. Have you not heard the song they sing when a woman dies?

> For whom is it well, for whom is it well?
> There is no one for whom it is well.

"I have no more to say to you."

15

It was in the second year of Okonkwo's exile that his friend, Obierika, came to visit him. He brought with him two young men, each of them carrying a heavy bag on his head. Okonkwo helped them put down their loads. It was clear that the bags were full of cowries.

Okonkwo was very happy to receive his friend. His wives and children were very happy too, and so were his cousins and their wives when he sent for them and told them who his guest was.

"You must take him to salute our father," said one of the cousins.

"Yes," replied Okonkwo. "We are going directly." But before they went he whispered something to his first wife. She nodded, and soon the children were chasing one of their cocks.

Uchendu had been told by one of his grandchildren that three strangers had come to Okonkwo's house. He was therefore waiting to receive them. He held out his hands to them when they came into his *obi*, and after they had shaken hands he asked Okonkwo who they were.

"This is Obierika, my great friend. I have already spoken to you about him."

"Yes," said the old man, turning to Obierika. "My son has told me about you, and I am happy you have come to see us. I knew your father, Iweka. He was a great man. He had many friends here and came to see them quite often. Those were good days when a man had friends in distant clans. Your generation does not know that. You stay at home, afraid of your next-door neighbor. Even a man's motherland is strange to him nowadays." He looked at Okonkwo. "I am an old man and I like to talk. That is all I am good for now." He got up painfully, went into an inner room and came back with a kola nut.

"Who are the young men with you?" he asked as he sat down again on his goatskin. Okonkwo told him.

"Ah," he said. "Welcome, my sons." He presented the kola nut to them, and when they had seen it and thanked him, he broke it and they ate.

"Go into that room," he said to Okonkwo, pointing with his finger. "You will find a pot of wine there."

Okonkwo brought the wine and they began to drink. It was a day old, and very strong.

"Yes," said Uchendu after a long silence. "People traveled more in those days. There is not a single clan in these parts that I do not know very well. Aninta, Umuazu, Ikeocha, Elumelu, Abame—I know them all."

"Have you heard," asked Obierika, "that Abame is no more?"

"How is that?" asked Uchendu and Okonkwo together.

"Abame has been wiped out," said Obierika. "It is a strange and terrible story. If I had not seen the few survivors with my own eyes and heard their story with my own ears, I would not have believed. Was it not on an Eke day that they fled into Umuofia?" he asked his two companions, and they nodded their heads.

"Three moons ago," said Obierika, "on an Eke market day a little band of fugitives came into our town. Most of them were sons of our land whose mothers had been buried with us. But there were some too who came because they had friends in our town, and others who could think of nowhere else open to escape. And so they fled into Umuofia with a woeful story." He drank his palm-wine, and Okonkwo filled his horn again. He continued:

"During the last planting season a white man had appeared in their clan."

"An albino," suggested Okonkwo.

"He was not an albino. He was quite different." He sipped his wine. "And he was riding an iron horse.[4] The first people who saw him ran away, but he stood beckoning to them. In the end the fearless ones went near and even touched him. The elders consulted their Oracle and it told them that the strange man would break their clan and spread destruction among them." Obierika again drank a little of his wine. "And so they killed the white man and tied his iron horse to their sacred tree because it looked as if it would run away to call the man's friends. I forgot to tell you another thing which the Oracle said. It said that other white men were on their way. They were locusts, it said, and that first man was their harbinger sent to explore the terrain. And so they killed him."

"What did the white man say before they killed him?" asked Uchendu.

"He said nothing," answered one of Obierika's companions.

"He said something, only they did not understand him," said Obierika. "He seemed to speak through his nose."

"One of the men told me," said Obierika's other companion, "that he repeated over and over again a word that resembled Mbaino. Perhaps he had been going to Mbaino and had lost his way."

4. Bicycle.

"Anyway," resumed Obierika, "they killed him and tied up his iron horse. This was before the planting season began. For a long time nothing happened. The rains had come and yams had been sown. The iron horse was still tied to the sacred silk-cotton tree. And then one morning three white men led by a band of ordinary men like us came to the clan. They saw the iron horse and went away again. Most of the men and women of Abame had gone to their farms. Only a few of them saw these white men and their followers. For many market weeks nothing else happened. They have a big market in Abame on every other Afo day and, as you know, the whole clan gathers there. That was the day it happened. The three white men and a very large number of other men surrounded the market. They must have used a powerful medicine to make themselves invisible until the market was full. And they began to shoot. Everybody was killed, except the old and the sick who were at home and a handful of men and women whose *chi* were wide awake and brought them out of that market."[5] He paused.

"Their clan is now completely empty. Even the sacred fish in their mysterious lake have fled and the lake has turned the color of blood. A great evil has come upon their land as the Oracle had warned."

There was a long silence. Uchendu ground his teeth together audibly. Then he burst out:

"Never kill a man who says nothing. Those men of Abame were fools. What did they know about the man?" He ground his teeth again and told a story to illustrate his point. "Mother Kite once sent her daughter to bring food. She went, and brought back a duckling. 'You have done very well,' said Mother Kite to her daughter, 'but tell me, what did the mother of this duckling say when you swooped and carried its child away?' 'It said nothing,' replied the young kite. 'It just walked away.' 'You must return the duckling,' said Mother Kite. 'There is something ominous behind the silence.' And so Daughter Kite returned the duckling and took a chick instead. 'What did the mother of this chick do?' asked the old kite. 'It cried and raved and cursed me,' said the young kite. 'Then we can eat the chick,' said her mother. 'There is nothing to fear from someone who shouts.' Those men of Abame were fools."

"They were fools," said Okonkwo after a pause. "They had been warned that danger was ahead. They should have armed themselves with their guns and their machetes even when they went to market."

"They have paid for their foolishness," said Obierika. "But I am greatly afraid. We have heard stories about white men who made the powerful guns and the strong drinks and took slaves away across the seas, but no one thought the stories were true."

"There is no story that is not true," said Uchendu. "The world has no end, and what is good among one people is an abomination with others. We have albinos among us. Do you not think that they came to our clan by mistake, that they have strayed from their way to a land where everybody is like them?"

---

5. Achebe bases his account on a similar incident in 1905 when British troops massacred the town of Ahiara in reprisal for the death of a missionary.

Okonkwo's first wife soon finished her cooking and set before their guests a big meal of pounded yams and bitter-leaf soup. Okonkwo's son, Nwoye, brought in a pot of sweet wine tapped from the raffia palm.

"You are a big man now," Obierika said to Nwoye. "Your friend Anene asked me to greet you."

"Is he well?" asked Nwoye.

"We are all well," said Obierika.

Ezinma brought them a bowl of water with which to wash their hands. After that they began to eat and to drink the wine.

"When did you set out from home?" asked Okonkwo.

"We had meant to set out from my house before cock-crow," said Obierika. "But Nweke did not appear until it was quite light. Never make an early morning appointment with a man who has just married a new wife." They all laughed.

"Has Nweke married a wife?" asked Okonkwo.

"He has married Okadigbo's second daughter," said Obierika.

"That is very good," said Okonkwo. "I do not blame you for not hearing the cock crow."

When they had eaten, Obierika pointed at the two heavy bags.

"That is the money from your yams," he said. "I sold the big ones as soon as you left. Later on I sold some of the seed-yams and gave out others to sharecroppers. I shall do that every year until you return. But I thought you would need the money now and so I brought it. Who knows what may happen tomorrow? Perhaps green men will come to our clan and shoot us."

"God will not permit it," said Okonkwo. "I do not know how to thank you."

"I can tell you," said Obierika. "Kill one of your sons for me."

"That will not be enough," said Okonkwo.

"Then kill yourself," said Obierika.

"Forgive me," said Okonkwo, smiling. "I shall not talk about thanking you any more."

16

When nearly two years later Obierika paid another visit to his friend in exile the circumstances were less happy. The missionaries had come to Umuofia. They had built their church there, won a handful of converts and were already sending evangelists to the surrounding towns and villages. That was a source of great sorrow to the leaders of the clan; but many of them believed that the strange faith and the white man's god would not last. None of his converts was a man whose word was heeded in the assembly of the people. None of them was a man of title. They were mostly the kind of people that were called *efulefu*, worthless, empty men. The imagery of an *efulefu* in the language of the clan was a man who sold his machete and wore the sheath to battle. Chielo, the priestess of Agbala, called the converts the excrement of the clan, and the new faith was a mad dog that had come to eat it up.

What moved Obierika to visit Okonkwo was the sudden appearance of the latter's son, Nwoye, among the missionaries in Umuofia.

"What are you doing here?" Obierika had asked when after many difficulties the missionaries had allowed him to speak to the boy.

"I am one of them," replied Nwoye.

"How is your father?" Obierika asked, not knowing what else to say.

"I don't know. He is not my father," said Nwoye, unhappily.

And so Obierika went to Mbanta to see his friend. And he found that Okonkwo did not wish to speak about Nwoye. It was only from Nwoye's mother that he heard scraps of the story.

The arrival of the missionaries had caused a considerable stir in the village of Mbanta. There were six of them and one was a white man. Every man and woman came out to see the white man. Stories about these strange men had grown since one of them had been killed in Abame and his iron horse tied to the sacred silk-cotton tree. And so everybody came to see the white man. It was the time of the year when everybody was at home. The harvest was over.

When they had all gathered, the white man began to speak to them. He spoke through an interpreter who was an Ibo man, though his dialect was different and harsh to the ears of Mbanta. Many people laughed at his dialect and the way he used words strangely. Instead of saying "myself" he always said "my buttocks."[6] But he was a man of commanding presence and the clansmen listened to him. He said he was one of them, as they could see from his color and his language. The other four black men were also their brothers, although one of them did not speak Ibo. The white man was also their brother because they were all sons of God. And he told them about this new God, the Creator of all the world and all the men and women. He told them that they worshipped false gods, gods of wood and stone. A deep murmur went through the crowd when he said this. He told them that the true God lived on high and that all men when they died went before Him for judgment. Evil men and all the heathen who in their blindness bowed to wood and stone were thrown into a fire that burned like palm-oil. But good men who worshipped the true God lived forever in His happy kingdom. "We have been sent by this great God to ask you to leave your wicked ways and false gods and turn to Him so that you may be saved when you die," he said.

"Your buttocks understand our language," said someone light-heartedly and the crowd laughed.

"What did he say?" the white man asked his interpreter. But before he could answer, another man asked a question: "Where is the white man's horse?" he asked. The Ibo evangelists consulted among themselves and decided that the man probably meant bicycle. They told the white man and he smiled benevolently.

"Tell them," he said, "that I shall bring many iron horses when we have settled down among them. Some of them will even ride the iron horse

---

6. The Igbo language has high and low tones so that the same word may have different meanings according to its pronunciation. Here, Achebe is probably referring to a famous pair of near-homonyms: *íké* ("strength") and *íkè* ("buttocks").

themselves." This was interpreted to them but very few of them heard. They were talking excitedly among themselves because the white man had said he was going to live among them. They had not thought about that.

At this point an old man said he had a question. "Which is this god of yours," he asked, "the goddess of the earth, the god of the sky, Amadiora of the thunderbolt, or what?"

The interpreter spoke to the white man and he immediately gave his answer. "All the gods you have named are not gods at all. They are gods of deceit who tell you to kill your fellows and destroy innocent children. There is only one true God and He has the earth, the sky, you and me and all of us."

"If we leave our gods and follow your god," asked another man, "who will protect us from the anger of our neglected gods and ancestors?"

"Your gods are not alive and cannot do you any harm," replied the white man. "They are pieces of wood and stone."

When this was interpreted to the men of Mbanta they broke into derisive laughter. These men must be mad, they said to themselves. How else could they say that Ani and Amadiora were harmless? And Idemili and Ogwugwu too? And some of them began to go away.

Then the missionaries burst into song. It was one of those gay and rollicking tunes of evangelism which had the power of plucking at silent and dusty chords in the heart of an Ibo man. The interpreter explained each verse to the audience, some of whom now stood enthralled. It was a story of brothers who lived in darkness and in fear, ignorant of the love of God. It told of one sheep out on the hills, away from the gates of God and from the tender shepherd's care.

After the singing the interpreter spoke about the Son of God whose name was Jesu Kristi. Okonkwo, who only stayed in the hope that it might come to chasing the men out of the village or whipping them, now said:

"You told us with your own mouth that there was only one god. Now you talk about his son. He must have a wife, then." The crowd agreed.

"I did not say He had a wife," said the interpreter, somewhat lamely.

"Your buttocks said he had a son," said the joker. "So he must have a wife and all of them must have buttocks."

The missionary ignored him and went on to talk about the Holy Trinity. At the end of it Okonkwo was fully convinced that the man was mad. He shrugged his shoulders and went away to tap his afternoon palm-wine.

But there was a young lad who had been captivated. His name was Nwoye, Okonkwo's first son. It was not the mad logic of the Trinity that captivated him. He did not understand it. It was the poetry of the new religion, something felt in the marrow. The hymn about brothers who sat in darkness and in fear seemed to answer a vague and persistent question that haunted his young soul—the question of the twins crying in the bush and the question of Ikemefuna who was killed. He felt a relief within as the hymn poured into his parched soul. The words of the hymn were like the drops of frozen rain melting on the dry palate of the panting earth. Nwoye's callow mind was greatly puzzled.

17

The missionaries spent their first four or five nights in the marketplace, and went into the village in the morning to preach the gospel. They asked who the king of the village was, but the villagers told them that there was no king. "We have men of high title and the chief priests and the elders," they said.

It was not very easy getting the men of high title and the elders together after the excitement of the first day. But the missionaries persevered, and in the end they were received by the rulers of Mbanta. They asked for a plot of land to build their church.

Every clan and village had its "evil forest." In it were buried all those who died of the really evil diseases, like leprosy and smallpox. It was also the dumping ground for the potent fetishes of great medicine men when they died. An "evil forest" was, therefore, alive with sinister forces and powers of darkness. It was such a forest that the rulers of Mbanta gave to the missionaries. They did not really want them in their clan, and so they made them that offer which nobody in his right senses would accept.

"They want a piece of land to build their shrine," said Uchendu to his peers when they consulted among themselves. "We shall give them a piece of land." He paused, and there was a murmur of surprise and disagreement. "Let us give them a portion of the Evil Forest. They boast about victory over death. Let us give them a real battlefield in which to show their victory." They laughed and agreed, and sent for the missionaries, whom they had asked to leave them for a while so that they might "whisper together." They offered them as much of the Evil Forest as they cared to take. And to their greatest amazement the missionaries thanked them and burst into song.

"They do not understand," said some of the elders. "But they will understand when they go to their plot of land tomorrow morning." And they dispersed.

The next morning the crazy men actually began to clear a part of the forest and to build their house. The inhabitants of Mbanta expected them all to be dead within four days. The first day passed and the second and third and fourth, and none of them died. Everyone was puzzled. And then it became known that the white man's fetish had unbelievable power. It was said that he wore glasses on his eyes so that he could see and talk to evil spirits. Not long after, he won his first three converts.

Although Nwoye had been attracted to the new faith from the very first day, he kept it secret. He dared not go too near the missionaries for fear of his father. But whenever they came to preach in the open marketplace or the village playground, Nwoye was there. And he was already beginning to know some of the simple stories they told.

"We have now built a church," said Mr. Kiaga, the interpreter, who was now in charge of the infant congregation. The white man had gone back to Umuofia, where he built his headquarters and from where he paid regular visits to Mr. Kiaga's congregation at Mbanta.

"We have now built a church," said Mr. Kiaga, "and we want you all to come in every seventh day to worship the true God."

On the following Sunday, Nwoye passed and repassed the little red-earth and thatch building without summoning enough courage to enter. He heard the voice of singing and although it came from a handful of men it was loud and confident. Their church stood on a circular clearing that looked like the open mouth of the Evil Forest. Was it waiting to snap its teeth together? After passing and re-passing by the church, Nwoye returned home.

It was well known among the people of Mbanta that their gods and ancestors were sometimes long-suffering and would deliberately allow a man to go on defying them. But even in such cases they set their limit at seven market weeks or twenty-eight days. Beyond that limit no man was suffered to go. And so excitement mounted in the village as the seventh week approached since the impudent missionaries built their church in the Evil Forest. The villagers were so certain about the doom that awaited these men that one or two converts thought it wise to suspend their allegiance to the new faith.

At last the day came by which all the missionaries should have died. But they were still alive, building a new red-earth and thatch house for their teacher, Mr. Kiaga. That week they won a handful more converts. And for the first time they had a woman. Her name was Nneka, the wife of Amadi, who was a prosperous farmer. She was very heavy with child.

Nneka had had four previous pregnancies and childbirths. But each time she had borne twins, and they had been immediately thrown away. Her husband and his family were already becoming highly critical of such a woman and were not unduly perturbed when they found she had fled to join the Christians. It was a good riddance.

One morning Okonkwo's cousin, Amikwu, was passing by the church on his way from the neighboring village, when he saw Nwoye among the Christians. He was greatly surprised, and when he got home he went straight to Okonkwo's hut and told him what he had seen. The women began to talk excitedly, but Okonkwo sat unmoved.

It was late afternoon before Nwoye returned. He went into the *obi* and saluted his father, but he did not answer. Nwoye turned round to walk into the inner compound when his father, suddenly overcome with fury, sprang to his feet and gripped him by the neck.

"Where have you been?" he stammered.

Nwoye struggled to free himself from the choking grip.

"Answer me," roared Okonkwo, "before I kill you!" He seized a heavy stick that lay on the dwarf wall and hit him two or three savage blows.

"Answer me!" he roared again. Nwoye stood looking at him and did not say a word. The women were screaming outside, afraid to go in.

"Leave that boy at once!" said a voice in the outer compound. It was Okonkwo's uncle, Uchendu. "Are you mad?"

Okonkwo did not answer. But he left hold of Nwoye, who walked away and never returned.

He went back to the church and told Mr. Kiaga that he had decided to go to Umuofia where the white missionary had set up a school to teach young Christians to read and write.

Mr. Kiaga's joy was very great. "Blessed is he who forsakes his father and his mother for my sake," he intoned. "Those that hear my words are my father and my mother."

Nwoye did not fully understand. But he was happy to leave his father. He would return later to his mother and his brothers and sisters and convert them to the new faith.

As Okonkwo sat in his hut that night, gazing into a log fire, he thought over the matter. A sudden fury rose within him and he felt a strong desire to take up his machete, go to the church and wipe out the entire vile and miscreant gang. But on further thought he told himself that Nwoye was not worth fighting for. Why, he cried in his heart, should he, Okonkwo, of all people, be cursed with such a son? He saw clearly in it the finger of his personal god or *chi*. For how else could he explain his great misfortune and exile and now his despicable son's behavior? Now that he had time to think of it, his son's crime stood out in its stark enormity. To abandon the gods of one's father and go about with a lot of effeminate men clucking like old hens was the very depth of abomination. Suppose when he died all his male children decided to follow Nwoye's steps and abandon their ancestors? Okonkwo felt a cold shudder run through him at the terrible prospects, like the prospect of annihilation. He saw himself and his fathers crowding round their ancestral shrine waiting in vain for worship and sacrifice and finding nothing but ashes of bygone days, and his children the while praying to the white man's god. If such a thing were ever to happen, he, Okonkwo, would wipe them off the face of the earth.

Okonkwo was popularly called the "Roaring Flame." As he looked into the log fire he recalled the name. He was a flaming fire. How then could he have begotten a son like Nwoye, degenerate and effeminate? Perhaps he was not his son. No! he could not be. His wife had played him false. He would teach her! But Nwoye resembled his grandfather, Unoka, who was Okonkwo's father. He pushed the thought out of his mind. He, Okonkwo, was called a flaming fire. How could he have begotten a woman for a son? At Nwoye's age Okonkwo had already become famous throughout Umuofia for his wrestling and his fearlessness.

He sighed heavily, and as if in sympathy the smoldering log also sighed. And immediately Okonkwo's eyes were opened and he saw the whole matter clearly. Living fire begets cold, impotent ash. He sighed again, deeply.

18

The young church in Mbanta had a few crises early in its life. At first the clan had assumed that it would not survive. But it had gone on living and gradually becoming stronger. The clan was worried, but not overmuch. If a gang of *efulefu* decided to live in the Evil Forest it was their own affair. When one came to think of it, the Evil Forest was a fit home for such undesirable people. It was true they were rescuing twins from the bush, but they never brought them into the village. As far as the villagers were concerned, the twins still remained where they had been thrown away. Surely the earth goddess would not visit the sins of the missionaries on the innocent villagers?

But on one occasion the missionaries had tried to overstep the bounds. Three converts had gone into the village and boasted openly that all the gods were dead and impotent and that they were prepared to defy them by burning all their shrines.

"Go and burn your mothers' genitals," said one of the priests. The men were seized and beaten until they streamed with blood. After that nothing happened for a long time between the church and the clan.

But stories were already gaining ground that the white man had not only brought a religion but also a government. It was said that they had built a place of judgment in Umuofia to protect the followers of their religion. It was even said that they had hanged one man who killed a missionary.

Although such stories were now often told they looked like fairy-tales in Mbanta and did not as yet affect the relationship between the new church and the clan. There was no question of killing a missionary here, for Mr. Kiaga, despite his madness, was quite harmless. As for his converts, no one could kill them without having to flee from the clan, for in spite of their worthlessness they still belonged to the clan. And so nobody gave serious thought to the stories about the white man's government or the consequences of killing the Christians. If they became more troublesome than they already were they would simply be driven out of the clan.

And the little church was at that moment too deeply absorbed in its own troubles to annoy the clan. It all began over the question of admitting outcasts.

These outcasts, or *osu*, seeing that the new religion welcomed twins and such abominations, thought that it was possible that they would also be received. And so one Sunday two of them went into the church. There was an immediate stir; but so great was the work the new religion had done among the converts that they did not immediately leave the church when the outcasts came in. Those who found themselves nearest to them merely moved to another seat. It was a miracle. But it only lasted till the end of the service. The whole church raised a protest and was about to drive these people out, when Mr. Kiaga stopped them and began to explain.

"Before God," he said, "there is no slave or free. We are all children of God and we must receive these our brothers."

"You do not understand," said one of the converts. "What will the heathen say of us when they hear that we receive *osu* into our midst? They will laugh."

"Let them laugh," said Mr. Kiaga. "God will laugh at them on the judgment day. Why do the nations rage and the peoples imagine a vain thing? He that sitteth in the heavens shall laugh. The Lord shall have them in derision."

"You do not understand," the convert maintained. "You are our teacher, and you can teach us the things of the new faith. But this is a matter which we know." And he told him what an *osu* was.

He was a person dedicated to a god, a thing set apart—a taboo for ever, and his children after him. He could neither marry nor be married by the free-born. He was in fact an outcast, living in a special area of the village, close to the Great Shrine. Wherever he went he carried with him the mark of his forbidden caste—long, tangled and dirty hair. A razor was taboo to him. An *osu* could not attend an assembly of the free-born, and they, in turn, could not shelter under his roof. He could not take any of the four titles of the clan, and when he died he was buried by his kind in the Evil Forest. How could such a man be a follower of Christ?

"He needs Christ more than you and I," said Mr. Kiaga.

"Then I shall go back to the clan," said the convert. And he went. Mr. Kiaga stood firm, and it was his firmness that saved the young church. The wavering converts drew inspiration and confidence from his unshakable faith. He ordered the outcasts to shave off their long, tangled hair. At first they were afraid they might die.

"Unless you shave off the mark of your heathen belief I will not admit you into the church," said Mr. Kiaga. "You fear that you will die. Why should that be? How are you different from other men who shave their hair? The same God created you and them. But they have cast you out like lepers. It is against the will of God, who has promised everlasting life to all who believe in His holy name. The heathen say you will die if you do this or that, and you are afraid. They also said I would die if I built my church on this ground. Am I dead? They said I would die if I took care of twins. I am still alive. The heathen speak nothing but falsehood. Only the word of our God is true."

The two outcasts shaved off their hair, and soon they were the strongest adherents of the new faith. And what was more, nearly all the *osu* in Mbanta followed their example. It was in fact one of them who in his zeal brought the church into serious conflict with the clan a year later by killing the sacred python, the emanation of the god of water.

The royal python was the most revered animal in Mbanta and all the surrounding clans. It was addressed as "Our Father," and was allowed to go wherever it chose, even into people's beds. It ate rats in the house and sometimes swallowed hens' eggs. If a clansman killed a royal python accidentally, he made sacrifices of atonement and performed an expensive burial ceremony such as was done for a great man. No punishment was prescribed for a man who killed the python knowingly. Nobody thought that such a thing could ever happen.

Perhaps it never did happen. That was the way the clan at first looked at it. No one had actually seen the man do it. The story had arisen among the Christians themselves.

But, all the same, the rulers and elders of Mbanta assembled to decide on their action. Many of them spoke at great length and in fury. The spirit of wars was upon them. Okonkwo, who had begun to play a part in the affairs of his motherland, said that until the abominable gang was chased out of the village with whips there would be no peace.

But there were many others who saw the situation differently, and it was their counsel that prevailed in the end.

"It is not our custom to fight for our gods," said one of them. "Let us not presume to do so now. If a man kills the sacred python in the secrecy of his hut, the matter lies between him and the god. We did not see it. If we put ourselves between the god and his victim we may receive blows intended for the offender. When a man blasphemes, what do we do? Do we go and stop his mouth? No. We put our fingers into our ears to stop us hearing. That is a wise action."

"Let us not reason like cowards," said Okonkwo. "If a man comes into my hut and defecates on the floor, what do I do? Do I shut my eyes? No! I take a stick and break his head. That is what a man does. These people are daily pouring filth over us, and Okeke says we should pretend not to see." Okonkwo made a sound full of disgust. This was a womanly clan, he thought. Such a thing could never happen in his fatherland, Umuofia.

"Okonkwo has spoken the truth," said another man. "We should do something. But let us ostracize these men. We would then not be held accountable for their abominations."

Everybody in the assembly spoke, and in the end it was decided to ostracize the Christians. Okonkwo ground his teeth in disgust.

That night a bell-man went through the length and breadth of Mbanta proclaiming that the adherents of the new faith were thenceforth excluded from the life and privileges of the clan.

The Christians had grown in number and were now a small community of men, women and children, self-assured and confident. Mr. Brown, the white missionary, paid regular visits to them. "When I think that it is only eighteen months since the Seed was first sown among you," he said, "I marvel at what the Lord hath wrought."

It was Wednesday in Holy Week and Mr. Kiaga had asked the women to bring red earth and white chalk and water to scrub the church for Easter; and the women had formed themselves into three groups for this purpose. They set out early that morning, some of them with their water-pots to the stream, another group with hoes and baskets to the village red-earth pit, and the others to the chalk quarry.

Mr. Kiaga was praying in the church when he heard the women talking excitedly. He rounded off his prayer and went to see what it was all about. The women had come to the church with empty water-pots. They said that some young men had chased them away from the stream with whips. Soon after, the women who had gone for red earth returned with empty baskets. Some of them had been heavily whipped. The chalk women also returned to tell a similar story.

"What does it all mean?" asked Mr. Kiaga, who was greatly perplexed.

"The village has outlawed us," said one of the women. "The bell-man announced it last night. But it is not our custom to debar anyone from the stream or the quarry."

Another woman said, "They want to ruin us. They will not allow us into the markets. They have said so."

Mr. Kiaga was going to send into the village for his men-converts when he saw them coming on their own. Of course they had all heard the bell-man, but they had never in all their lives heard of women being debarred from the stream.

"Come along," they said to the women. "We will go with you to meet those cowards." Some of them had big sticks and some even machetes.

But Mr. Kiaga restrained them. He wanted first to know why they had been outlawed.

"They say that Okoli killed the sacred python," said one man.

"It is false," said another. "Okoli told me himself that it was false."

Okoli was not there to answer. He had fallen ill on the previous night. Before the day was over he was dead. His death showed that the gods were still able to fight their own battles. The clan saw no reason then for molesting the Christians.

19

The last big rains of the year were falling. It was the time for treading red earth with which to build walls. It was not done earlier because the rains were too heavy and would have washed away the heap of trodden earth; and it could not be done later because harvesting would soon set in, and after that the dry season.

It was going to be Okonkwo's last harvest in Mbanta. The seven wasted and weary years were at last dragging to a close. Although he had prospered in his motherland Okonkwo knew that he would have prospered even more in Umuofia, in the land of his fathers where men were bold and warlike. In these seven years he would have climbed to the utmost heights. And so he regretted every day of his exile. His mother's kinsmen had been very kind to him, and he was grateful. But that did not alter the facts. He had called the first child born to him in exile Nneka—"Mother is Supreme"—out of politeness to his mother's kinsmen. But two years later when a son was born he called him Nwofia—"Begotten in the Wilderness."

As soon as he entered his last year in exile Okonkwo sent money to Obierika to build him two huts in his old compound where he and his family would live until he built more huts and the outside wall of his compound. He could not ask another man to build his own obi for him, nor the walls of his compound. Those things a man built for himself or inherited from his father.

As the last heavy rains of the year began to fall, Obierika sent word that the two huts had been built and Okonkwo began to prepare for his return, after the rains. He would have liked to return earlier and build his compound that year before the rains stopped, but in doing so he would have taken something from the full penalty of seven years. And that could not be. So he waited impatiently for the dry season to come.

It came slowly. The rain became lighter and lighter until it fell in slanting showers. Sometimes the sun shone through the rain and a light breeze blew. It was a gay and airy kind of rain. The rainbow began to appear, and sometimes two rainbows, like a mother and her daughter, the one young and beautiful, and the other an old and faint shadow. The rainbow was called the python of the sky.

Okonkwo called his three wives and told them to get things together for a great feast. "I must thank my mother's kinsmen before I go," he said.

Ekwefi still had some cassava left on her farm from the previous year. Neither of the other wives had. It was not that they had been lazy, but that they had many children to feed. It was therefore understood that Ekwefi would provide cassava for the feast. Nwoye's mother and Ojiugo would provide the other things like smoked fish, palm-oil and pepper for the soup. Okonkwo would take care of meat and yams.

Ekwefi rose early on the following morning and went to her farm with her daughter, Ezinma, and Ojiugo's daughter, Obiageli, to harvest cassava tubers. Each of them carried a long cane basket, a machete for cutting down the soft cassava stem, and a little hoe for digging out the tuber. Fortunately, a light rain had fallen during the night and the soil would not be very hard.

"It will not take us long to harvest as much as we like," said Ekwefi.

"But the leaves will be wet," said Ezinma. Her basket was balanced on her head, and her arms folded across her breasts. She felt cold. "I dislike cold water dropping on my back. We should have waited for the sun to rise and dry the leaves."

Obiageli called her "Salt" because she said that she disliked water. "Are you afraid you may dissolve?"

The harvesting was easy, as Ekwefi had said. Ezinma shook every tree violently with a long stick before she bent down to cut the stem and dig out the tuber. Sometimes it was not necessary to dig. They just pulled the stump, and earth rose, roots snapped below, and the tuber was pulled out.

When they had harvested a sizable heap they carried it down in two trips to the stream, where every woman had a shallow well for fermenting her cassava.

"It should be ready in four days or even three," said Obiageli. "They are young tubers."

"They are not all that young," said Ekwefi. "I planted the farm nearly two years ago. It is a poor soil and that is why the tubers are so small."

Okonkwo never did things by halves. When his wife Ekwefi protested that two goats were sufficient for the feast he told her that it was not her affair.

"I am calling a feast because I have the wherewithal. I cannot live on the bank of a river and wash my hands with spittle. My mother's people have been good to me and I must show my gratitude."

And so three goats were slaughtered and a number of fowls. It was like a wedding feast. There was foo-foo and yam pottage, egusi[7] soup and bitter-leaf soup and pots and pots of palm-wine.

All the *umunna*[8] were invited to the feast, all the descendants of Okolo, who had lived about two hundred years before. The oldest member of this extensive family was Okonkwo's uncle, Uchendu. The kola nut was given him to break, and he prayed to the ancestors. He asked them for health and children. "We do not ask for wealth because he that has health and children will also have wealth. We do not pray to have more money but to have more kinsmen. We are better than animals because we have kinsmen. An animal rubs its itching flank against a tree, a man asks his kins-

---

7. Melon seed, which is roasted, ground, and cooked in soup.   8. "Children of the Father" (literal trans.); the clan (male).

man to scratch him." He prayed especially for Okonkwo and his family. He then broke the kola nut and threw one of the lobes on the ground for the ancestors.

As the broken kola nuts were passed round, Okonkwo's wives and children and those who came to help them with the cooking began to bring out the food. His sons brought out the pots of palm-wine. There was so much food and drink that many kinsmen whistled in surprise. When all was laid out, Okonkwo rose to speak.

"I beg you to accept this little kola," he said. "It is not to pay you back for all you did for me in these seven years. A child cannot pay for its mother's milk. I have only called you together because it is good for kinsmen to meet."

Yam pottage was served first because it was lighter than foo-foo and because yam always came first. Then the foo-foo was served. Some kinsmen ate it with egusi soup and others with bitter-leaf soup. The meat was then shared so that every member of the *umunna* had a portion. Every man rose in order of years and took a share. Even the few kinsmen who had not been able to come had their shares taken out for them in due term.

As the palm-wine was drunk one of the oldest members of the *umunna* rose to thank Okonkwo:

"If I say that we did not expect such a big feast I will be suggesting that we did not know how open-handed our son, Okonkwo, is. We all know him, and we expected a big feast. But it turned out to be even bigger than we expected. Thank you. May all you took out return again tenfold. It is good in these days when the younger generation consider themselves wiser than their sires to see a man doing things in the grand, old way. A man who calls his kinsmen to a feast does not do so to save them from starving. They all have food in their own homes. When we gather together in the moonlit village ground it is not because of the moon. Every man can see it in his own compound. We come together because it is good for kinsmen to do so. You may ask why I am saying all this. I say it because I fear for the younger generation, for you people." He waved his arm where most of the young men sat. "As for me, I have only a short while to live, and so have Uchendu and Unachukwu and Emefo. But I fear for you young people because you do not understand how strong is the bond of kinship. You do not know what it is to speak with one voice. And what is the result? An abominable religion has settled among you. A man can now leave his father and his brothers. He can curse the gods of his fathers and his ancestors, like a hunter's dog that suddenly goes mad and turns on his master. I fear for you; I fear for the clan." He turned again to Okonkwo and said, "Thank you for calling us together."

Part Three

20

Seven years was a long time to be away from one's clan. A man's place was not always there, waiting for him. As soon as he left, someone else rose and filled it. The clan was like a lizard; if it lost its tail it soon grew another.

Okonkwo knew these things. He knew that he had lost his place among the nine masked spirits who administered justice in the clan. He had lost the chance to lead his warlike clan against the new religion, which, he was told, had gained ground. He had lost the years in which he might have taken the highest titles in the clan. But some of these losses were not irreparable. He was determined that his return should be marked by his people. He would return with a flourish, and regain the seven wasted years.

Even in his first year in exile he had begun to plan for his return. The first thing he would do would be to rebuild his compound on a more magnificent scale. He would build a bigger barn than he had had before and he would build huts for two new wives. Then he would show his wealth by initiating his sons into the *ozo* society. Only the really great men in the clan were able to do this. Okonkwo saw clearly the high esteem in which he would be held, and he saw himself taking the highest title in the land.

As the years of exile passed one by one it seemed to him that his *chi* might now be making amends for the past disaster. His yams grew abundantly, not only in his motherland but also in Umuofia, where his friend gave them out year by year to sharecroppers.

Then the tragedy of his first son had occurred. At first it appeared as if it might prove too great for his spirit. But it was a resilient spirit, and in the end Okonkwo overcame his sorrow. He had five other sons and he would bring them up in the way of the clan.

He sent for the five sons and they came and sat in his *obi*. The youngest of them was four years old.

"You have all seen the great abomination of your brother. Now he is no longer my son or your brother. I will only have a son who is a man, who will hold his head up among my people. If any one of you prefers to be a woman, let him follow Nwoye now while I am alive so that I can curse him. If you turn against me when I am dead I will visit you and break your neck."

Okonkwo was very lucky in his daughters. He never stopped regretting that Ezinma was a girl. Of all his children she alone understood his every mood. A bond of sympathy had grown between them as the years had passed.

Ezinma grew up in her father's exile and became one of the most beautiful girls in Mbanta. She was called Crystal of Beauty, as her mother had been called in her youth. The young ailing girl who had caused her mother so much heartache had been transformed, almost overnight, into a healthy, buoyant maiden. She had, it was true, her moments of depression when she would snap at everybody like an angry dog. These moods descended on her suddenly and for no apparent reason. But they were very rare and short-lived. As long as they lasted, she could bear no other person but her father.

Many young men and prosperous middle-aged men of Mbanta came to marry her. But she refused them all, because her father had called her one evening and said to her: "There are many good and prosperous people here, but I shall be happy if you marry in Umuofia when we return home."

That was all he had said. But Ezinma had seen clearly all the thought and hidden meaning behind the few words. And she had agreed.

"Your half-sister, Obiageli, will not understand me," Okonkwo said. "But you can explain to her."

Although they were almost the same age, Ezinma wielded a strong influence over her half-sister. She explained to her why they should not marry yet, and she agreed also. And so the two of them refused every offer of marriage in Mbanta.

"I wish she were a boy," Okonkwo thought within himself. She understood things so perfectly. Who else among his children could have read his thoughts so well? With two beautiful grown-up daughters his return to Umuofia would attract considerable attention. His future sons-in-law would be men of authority in the clan. The poor and unknown would not dare to come forth.

Umuofia had indeed changed during the seven years Okonkwo had been in exile. The church had come and led many astray. Not only the low-born and the outcast but sometimes a worthy man had joined it. Such a man was Ogbuefi Ugonna,[9] who had taken two titles, and who like a madman had cut the anklet of his titles and cast it away to join the Christians. The white missionary was very proud of him and he was one of the first men in Umuofia to receive the sacrament of Holy Communion, or Holy Feast as it was called in Ibo. Ogbuefi Ugonna had thought of the Feast in terms of eating and drinking, only more holy than the village variety. He had therefore put his drinking-horn into his goatskin bag for the occasion.

But apart from the church, the white men had also brought a government. They had built a court where the District Commissioner judged cases in ignorance. He had court messengers who brought men to him for trial. Many of these messengers came from Umuru on the bank of the Great River, where the white men first came many years before and where they had built the center of their religion and trade and government. These court messengers were greatly hated in Umuofia because they were foreigners and also arrogant and high-handed. They were called *kotma*,[1] and because of their ash-colored shorts they earned the additional name of Ashy-Buttocks. They guarded the prison, which was full of men who had offended against the white man's law. Some of these prisoners had thrown away their twins and some had molested the Christians. They were beaten in the prison by the *kotma* and made to work every morning clearing the government compound and fetching wood for the white Commissioner and the court messengers. Some of these prisoners were men of title who should be above such mean occupation. They were grieved by the indignity and mourned for their neglected farms. As they cut grass in the morning the younger men sang in time with the strokes of their machetes:

9. "Father's Honor" (with the eagle feather).   1. Pidgin English for "court messenger."

> *Kotma* of the ash buttocks,
> He is fit to be a slave.
> The white man has no sense,
> He is fit to be a slave.

The court messengers did not like to be called Ashy-Buttocks, and they beat the men. But the song spread in Umuofia.

Okonkwo's head was bowed in sadness as Obierika told him these things.

"Perhaps I have been away too long," Okonkwo said, almost to himself. "But I cannot understand these things you tell me. What is it that has happened to our people? Why have they lost the power to fight?"

"Have you not heard how the white man wiped out Abame?" asked Obierika.

"I have heard," said Okonkwo. "But I have also heard that Abame people were weak and foolish. Why did they not fight back? Had they no guns and machetes? We would be cowards to compare ourselves with the men of Abame. Their fathers had never dared to stand before our ancestors. We must fight these men and drive them from the land."

"It is already too late," said Obierika sadly. "Our own men and our sons have joined the ranks of the stranger. They have joined his religion and they help to uphold his government. If we should try to drive out the white men in Umuofia we should find it easy. There are only two of them. But what of our own people who are following their way and have been given power? They would go to Umuru and bring the soldiers, and we would be like Abame." He paused for a long time and then said: "I told you on my last visit to Mbanta how they hanged Aneto."

"What has happened to that piece of land in dispute?" asked Okonkwo.

"The white man's court has decided that it should belong to Nnama's family, who had given much money to the white man's messengers and interpreter."

"Does the white man understand our custom about land?"

"How can he when he does not even speak our tongue? But he says that our customs are bad; and our own brothers who have taken up his religion also say that our customs are bad. How do you think we can fight when our own brothers have turned against us? The white man is very clever. He came quietly and peaceably with his religion. We were amused at his foolishness and allowed him to stay. Now he has won our brothers, and our clan can no longer act like one. He has put a knife on the things that held us together and we have fallen apart."

"How did they get hold of Aneto to hang him?" asked Okonkwo.

"When he killed Oduche in the fight over the land, he fled to Aninta to escape the wrath of the earth. This was about eight days after the fight, because Oduche had not died immediately from his wounds. It was on the seventh day that he died. But everybody knew that he was going to die and Aneto got his belongings together in readiness to flee. But the Christians had told the white man about the accident, and he sent his *kotma* to catch Aneto. He was imprisoned with all the leaders of his family. In the end Oduche died and Aneto was taken to Umuru and hanged. The other people were released, but even now they have not found the mouth with which to tell of their suffering."

The two men sat in silence for a long while afterwards.

21

There were many men and women in Umuofia who did not feel as strongly as Okonkwo about the new dispensation. The white man had indeed brought a lunatic religion, but he had also built a trading store and for the first time palm-oil and kernel[2] became things of great price, and much money flowed into Umuofia.

And even in the matter of religion there was a growing feeling that there might be something in it after all, something vaguely akin to method in the overwhelming madness.

This growing feeling was due to Mr. Brown, the white missionary, who was very firm in restraining his flock from provoking the wrath of the clan. One member in particular was very difficult to restrain. His name was Enoch and his father was the priest of the snake cult. The story went around that Enoch had killed and eaten the sacred python, and that his father had cursed him.

Mr. Brown preached against such excess of zeal. Everything was possible, he told his energetic flock, but everything was not expedient. And so Mr. Brown came to be respected even by the clan, because he trod softly on its faith. He made friends with some of the great men of the clan and on one of his frequent visits to the neighboring villages he had been presented with a carved elephant tusk, which was a sign of dignity and rank. One of the great men in that village was called Akunna[3] and he had given one of his sons to be taught the white man's knowledge in Mr. Brown's school.

Whenever Mr. Brown went to that village he spent long hours with Akunna in his *obi* talking through an interpreter about religion. Neither of them succeeded in converting the other but they learned more about their different beliefs.

"You say that there is one supreme God who made heaven and earth," said Akunna on one of Mr. Brown's visits. "We also believe in Him and call Him Chukwu. He made all the world and the other gods."

"There are no other gods," said Mr. Brown. "Chukwu is the only God and all others are false. You carve a piece of wood—like that one" (he pointed at the rafters from which Akunna's carved *Ikenga*[4] hung), "and you call it a god. But it is still a piece of wood."

"Yes," said Akunna. "It is indeed a piece of wood. The tree from which it came was made by Chukwu, as indeed all minor gods were. But He

---

2. The red fleshy husk of the palm nut is crushed manually to produce cooking oil, leaving a fibrous residue along with hard kernels. The Europeans bought both the red oil and the kernels, from which they could extract a very fine oil by using machines.   3. "Father's Wealth."   4. A carved wooden figure with the horns of a ram that symbolized the strength of a man's right hand. Every adult male kept an *Ikenga* in his personal shrine.

made them for His messengers so that we could approach Him through them. It is like yourself. You are the head of your church."

"No," protested Mr. Brown. "The head of my church is God Himself."

"I know," said Akunna, "but there must be a head in this world among men. Somebody like yourself must be the head here."

"The head of my church in that sense is in England."

"That is exactly what I am saying. The head of your church is in your country. He has sent you here as his messenger. And you have also appointed your own messengers and servants. Or let me take another example, the District Commissioner. He is sent by your king."

"They have a queen," said the interpreter on his own account.

"Your queen sends her messenger, the District Commissioner. He finds that he cannot do the work alone and so he appoints *kotma* to help him. It is the same with God, or Chukwu. He appoints the smaller gods to help Him because His work is too great for one person."

"You should not think of Him as a person," said Mr. Brown. "It is because you do so that you imagine He must need helpers. And the worst thing about it is that you give all the worship to the false gods you have created."

"That is not so. We make sacrifices to the little gods, but when they fail and there is no one else to turn to we go to Chukwu. It is right to do so. We approach a great man through his servants. But when his servants fail to help us, then we go to the last source of hope. We appear to pay greater attention to the little gods but that is not so. We worry them more because we are afraid to worry their Master. Our fathers knew that Chukwu was the Overlord and that is why many of them gave their children the name Chukwuka—"Chukwu is Supreme.""

"You said one interesting thing," said Mr. Brown. "You are afraid of Chukwu. In my religion Chukwu is a loving Father and need not be feared by those who do His will."

"But we must fear Him when we are not doing His will," said Akunna. "And who is to tell His will? It is too great to be known."

In this way Mr. Brown learned a good deal about the religion of the clan and he came to the conclusion that a frontal attack on it would not succeed. And so he built a school and a little hospital in Umuofia. He went from family to family begging people to send their children to his school. But at first they only sent their slaves or sometimes their lazy children. Mr. Brown begged and argued and prophesied. He said that the leaders of the land in the future would be men and women who had learned to read and write. If Umuofia failed to send her children to the school, strangers would come from other places to rule them. They could already see that happening in the Native Court, where the D.C. was surrounded by strangers who spoke his tongue. Most of these strangers came from the distant town of Umuru on the bank of the Great River where the white man first went.

In the end Mr. Brown's arguments began to have an effect. More people came to learn in his school, and he encouraged them with gifts of singlets[5]

5. Undershirts, T-shirts.

and towels. They were not all young, these people who came to learn. Some of them were thirty years old or more. They worked on their farms in the morning and went to school in the afternoon. And it was not long before the people began to say that the white man's medicine was quick in working. Mr. Brown's school produced quick results. A few months in it were enough to make one a court messenger or even a court clerk. Those who stayed longer became teachers; and from Umuofia laborers went forth into the Lord's vineyard. New churches were established in the surrounding villages and a few schools with them. From the very beginning religion and education went hand in hand.

Mr. Brown's mission grew from strength to strength, and because of its link with the new administration it earned a new social prestige. But Mr. Brown himself was breaking down in health. At first he ignored the warning signs. But in the end he had to leave his flock, sad and broken.

It was in the first rainy season after Okonkwo's return to Umuofia that Mr. Brown left for home. As soon as he had learned of Okonkwo's return five months earlier, the missionary had immediately paid him a visit. He had just sent Okonkwo's son, Nwoye, who was now called Isaac,[6] to the new training college for teachers in Umuru. And he had hoped that Okonkwo would be happy to hear of it. But Okonkwo had driven him away with the threat that if he came into his compound again, he would be carried out of it.

Okonkwo's return to his native land was not as memorable as he had wished. It was true his two beautiful daughters aroused great interest among suitors and marriage negotiations were soon in progress, but, beyond that, Umuofia did not appear to have taken any special notice of the warrior's return. The clan had undergone such profound change during his exile that it was barely recognizable. The new religion and government and the trading stores were very much in the people's eyes and minds. There were still many who saw these new institutions as evil, but even they talked and thought about little else, and certainly not about Okonkwo's return.

And it was the wrong year too. If Okonkwo had immediately initiated his two sons into the *ozo* society as he had planned he would have caused a stir. But the initiation rite was performed once in three years in Umuofia, and he had to wait for nearly two years for the next round of ceremonies.

Okonkwo was deeply grieved. And it was not just a personal grief. He mourned for the clan, which he saw breaking up and falling apart, and he mourned for the warlike men of Umuofia, who had so unaccountably become soft like women.

22

Mr. Brown's successor was the Reverend James Smith, and he was a different kind of man. He condemned openly Mr. Brown's policy of compromise and accommodation. He saw things as black and white. And

---

6. Son of Abraham, offered to God as a sacrifice (Genesis 22).

black was evil. He saw the world as a battlefield in which the children of light were locked in mortal conflict with the sons of darkness. He spoke in his sermons about sheep and goats and about wheat and tares. He believed in slaying the prophets of Baal.

Mr. Smith was greatly distressed by the ignorance which many of his flock showed even in such things as the Trinity and the Sacraments. It only showed that they were seeds sown on a rocky soil. Mr. Brown had thought of nothing but numbers. He should have known that the kingdom of God did not depend on large crowds. Our Lord Himself stressed the importance of fewness. Narrow is the way and few the number. To fill the Lord's holy temple with an idolatrous crowd clamoring for signs was a folly of everlasting consequence. Our Lord used the whip only once in His life—to drive the crowd away from His church.

Within a few weeks of his arrival in Umuofia Mr. Smith suspended a young woman from the church for pouring new wine into old bottles. This woman had allowed her heathen husband to mutilate her dead child. The child had been declared an *ogbanje*, plaguing its mother by dying and entering her womb to be born again. Four times this child had run its evil round. And so it was mutilated to discourage it from returning.

Mr. Smith was filled with wrath when he heard of this. He disbelieved the story which even some of the most faithful confirmed, the story of really evil children who were not deterred by mutilation, but came back with all the scars. He replied that such stories were spread in the world by the Devil to lead men astray. Those who believed such stories were unworthy of the Lord's table.

There was a saying in Umuofia that as a man danced so the drums were beaten for him. Mr. Smith danced a furious step and so the drums went mad. The over-zealous converts who had smarted under Mr. Brown's restraining hand now flourished in full favor. One of them was Enoch, the son of the snake-priest who was believed to have killed and eaten the sacred python. Enoch's devotion to the new faith had seemed so much greater than Mr. Brown's that the villagers called him the outsider who wept louder than the bereaved.

Enoch was short and slight of build, and always seemed in great haste. His feet were short and broad, and when he stood or walked his heels came together and his feet opened outwards as if they had quarreled and meant to go in different directions. Such was the excessive energy bottled up in Enoch's small body that it was always erupting in quarrels and fights. On Sundays he always imagined that the sermon was preached for the benefit of his enemies. And if he happened to sit near one of them he would occasionally turn to give him a meaningful look, as if to say, "I told you so." It was Enoch who touched off the great conflict between church and clan in Umuofia which had been gathering since Mr. Brown left.

It happened during the annual ceremony which was held in honor of the earth deity. At such times the ancestors of the clan who had been committed to Mother Earth at their death emerged again as *egwugwu* through tiny ant-holes.

One of the greatest crimes a man could commit was to unmask an *egwugwu* in public, or to say or do anything which might reduce its immortal prestige in the eyes of the uninitiated. And this was what Enoch did.

The annual worship of the earth goddess fell on a Sunday, and the masked spirits were abroad. The Christian women who had been to church could not therefore go home. Some of their men had gone out to beg the *egwugwu* to retire for a short while for the women to pass. They agreed and were already retiring, when Enoch boasted aloud that they would not dare to touch a Christian. Whereupon they all came back and one of them gave Enoch a good stroke of the cane, which was always carried. Enoch fell on him and tore off his mask. The other *egwugwu* immediately surrounded their desecrated companion, to shield him from the profane gaze of women and children, and led him away. Enoch had killed an ancestral spirit, and Umuofia was thrown into confusion.

That night the Mother of the Spirits walked the length and breadth of the clan, weeping for her murdered son. It was a terrible night. Not even the oldest man in Umuofia had ever heard such a strange and fearful sound, and it was never to be heard again. It seemed as if the very soul of the tribe wept for a great evil that was coming—its own death.

On the next day all the masked *egwugwu* of Umuofia assembled in the marketplace. They came from all the quarters of the clan and even from the neighboring villages. The dreaded Otakagu came from Imo, and Ekwensu, dangling a white cock, arrived from Uli. It was a terrible gathering. The eerie voices of countless spirits, the bells that clattered behind some of them, and the clash of machetes as they ran forwards and backwards and saluted one another, sent tremors of fear into every heart. For the first time in living memory the sacred bull-roarer was heard in broad daylight.

From the marketplace the furious band made for Enoch's compound. Some of the elders of the clan went with them, wearing heavy protections of charms and amulets. These were men whose arms were strong in *ogwu*, or medicine. As for the ordinary men and women, they listened from the safety of their huts.

The leaders of the Christians had met together at Mr. Smith's parsonage on the previous night. As they deliberated they could hear the Mother of Spirits wailing for her son. The chilling sound affected Mr. Smith, and for the first time he seemed to be afraid.

"What are they planning to do?" he asked. No one knew, because such a thing had never happened before. Mr. Smith would have sent for the District Commissioner and his court messengers, but they had gone on tour on the previous day.

"One thing is clear," said Mr. Smith. "We cannot offer physical resistance to them. Our strength lies in the Lord." They knelt down together and prayed to God for delivery.

"O Lord, save Thy people," cried Mr. Smith.

"And bless Thine inheritance," replied the men.

They decided that Enoch should be hidden in the parsonage for a day or two. Enoch himself was greatly disappointed when he heard this, for he had hoped that a holy war was imminent; and there were a few other Christians who thought like him. But wisdom prevailed in the camp of the faithful and many lives were thus saved.

The band of *egwugwu* moved like a furious whirlwind to Enoch's compound and with machete and fire reduced it to a desolate heap. And from there they made for the church, intoxicated with destruction.

Mr. Smith was in his church when he heard the masked spirits coming. He walked quietly to the door which commanded the approach to the church compound, and stood there. But when the first three or four *egwugwu* appeared on the church compound he nearly bolted. He overcame this impulse and instead of running away he went down the two steps that led up to the church and walked towards the approaching spirits.

They surged forward, and a long stretch of the bamboo fence with which the church compound was surrounded gave way before them. Discordant bells clanged, machetes clashed and the air was full of dust and weird sounds. Mr. Smith heard a sound of footsteps behind him. He turned round and saw Okeke, his interpreter. Okeke had not been on the best of terms with his master since he had strongly condemned Enoch's behavior at the meeting of the leaders of the church during the night. Okeke had gone as far as to say that Enoch should not be hidden in the parsonage, because he would only draw the wrath of the clan on the pastor. Mr. Smith had rebuked him in very strong language, and had not sought his advice that morning. But now, as he came up and stood by him confronting the angry spirits, Mr. Smith looked at him and smiled. It was a wan smile, but there was deep gratitude there.

For a brief moment the onrush of the *egwugwu* was checked by the unexpected composure of the two men. But it was only a momentary check, like the tense silence between blasts of thunder. The second onrush was greater than the first. It swallowed up the two men. Then an unmistakable voice rose above the tumult and there was immediate silence. Space was made around the two men, and Ajofia began to speak.

Ajofia was the leading *egwugwu* of Umuofia. He was the head and spokesman of the nine ancestors who administered justice in the clan. His voice was unmistakable and so he was able to bring immediate peace to the agitated spirits. He then addressed Mr. Smith, and as he spoke clouds of smoke rose from his head.

"The body of the white man, I salute you," he said, using the language in which immortals spoke to men.

"The body of the white man, do you know me?" he asked.

Mr. Smith looked at his interpreter, but Okeke, who was a native of distant Umuru, was also at a loss.

Ajofia laughed in his guttural voice. It was like the laugh of rusty metal. "They are strangers," he said, "and they are ignorant. But let that pass." He turned round to his comrades and saluted them, calling them the fathers of Umuofia. He dug his rattling spear into the ground and it shook with metallic life. Then he turned once more to the missionary and his interpreter.

"Tell the white man that we will not do him any harm," he said to the interpreter. "Tell him to go back to his house and leave us alone. We liked his brother who was with us before. He was foolish, but we liked him, and for his sake we shall not harm his brother. But this shrine which he built must be destroyed. We shall no longer allow it in our midst. It has bred untold abominations and we have come to put an end to it." He turned to his comrades. "Fathers of Umuofia, I salute you"; and they replied with one guttural voice. He turned again to the missionary. "You can stay with us if you like our ways. You can worship your own god. It is good that a man should worship the gods and the spirits of his fathers. Go back to your house so that you may not be hurt. Our anger is great but we have held it down so that we can talk to you."

Mr. Smith said to his interpreter: "Tell them to go away from here. This is the house of God and I will not live to see it desecrated."

Okeke interpreted wisely to the spirits and leaders of Umuofia: "The white man says he is happy you have come to him with your grievances, like friends. He will be happy if you leave the matter in his hands."

"We cannot leave the matter in his hands because he does not understand our customs, just as we do not understand his. We say he is foolish because he does not know our ways, and perhaps he says we are foolish because we do not know his. Let him go away."

Mr. Smith stood his ground. But he could not save his church. When the *egwugwu* went away the red-earth church which Mr. Brown had built was a pile of earth and ashes. And for the moment the spirit of the clan was pacified.

23

For the first time in many years Okonkwo had a feeling that was akin to happiness. The times which had altered so unaccountably during his exile seemed to be coming round again. The clan which had turned false on him appeared to be making amends.

He had spoken violently to his clansmen when they had met in the marketplace to decide on their action. And they had listened to him with respect. It was like the good old days again, when a warrior was a warrior. Although they had not agreed to kill the missionary or drive away the Christians, they had agreed to do something substantial. And they had done it. Okonkwo was almost happy again.

For two days after the destruction of the church, nothing happened. Every man in Umuofia went about armed with a gun or a machete. They would not be caught unawares, like the men of Abame.

Then the District Commissioner returned from his tour. Mr. Smith went immediately to him and they had a long discussion. The men of Umuofia did not take any notice of this, and if they did, they thought it was not important. The missionary often went to see his brother white man. There was nothing strange in that.

Three days later the District Commissioner sent his sweet-tongued messenger to the leaders of Umuofia asking them to meet him in his headquarters. That also was not strange. He often asked them to hold such palavers, as he called them. Okonkwo was among the six leaders he invited.

Okonkwo warned the others to be fully armed. "An Umuofia man does not refuse a call," he said. "He may refuse to do what he is asked; he does not refuse to be asked. But the times have changed, and we must be fully prepared."

And so the six men went to see the District Commissioner, armed with their machetes. They did not carry guns, for that would be unseemly. They were led into the courthouse where the District Commissioner sat. He received them politely. They unslung their goatskin bags and their sheathed machetes, put them on the floor, and sat down.

"I have asked you to come," began the Commissioner, "because of what happened during my absence. I have been told a few things but I cannot believe them until I have heard your own side. Let us talk about it like friends and find a way of ensuring that it does not happen again."

Ogbuefi Ekwueme[7] rose to his feet and began to tell the story.

"Wait a minute," said the Commissioner. "I want to bring in my men so that they too can hear your grievances and take warning. Many of them come from distant places and although they speak your tongue they are ignorant of your customs. James! Go and bring in the men." His interpreter left the courtroom and soon returned with twelve men. They sat together with the men of Umuofia, and Ogbuefi Ekwueme began to tell the story of how Enoch murdered an *egwugwu*.

It happened so quickly that the six men did not see it coming. There was only a brief scuffle, too brief even to allow the drawing of a sheathed machete. The six men were handcuffed and led into the guardroom.

"We shall not do you any harm," said the District Commissioner to them later, "if only you agree to cooperate with us. We have brought a peaceful administration to you and your people so that you may be happy. If any man ill-treats you we shall come to your rescue. But we will not allow you to ill-treat others. We have a court of law where we judge cases and administer justice just as it is done in my own country under a great queen. I have brought you here because you joined together to molest others, to burn people's houses and their place of worship. That must not happen in the dominion of our queen, the most powerful ruler in the world. I have decided that you will pay a fine of two hundred bags of cowries. You will be released as soon as you agree to this and undertake to collect that fine from your people. What do you say to that?"

The six men remained sullen and silent and the Commissioner left them for a while. He told the court messengers, when he left the guardroom, to treat the men with respect because they were the leaders of Umuofia. They said, "Yes, sir," and saluted.

As soon as the District Commissioner left, the head messenger, who was also the prisoners' barber, took down his razor and shaved off all the hair on the men's heads. They were still handcuffed, and they just sat and moped.

"Who is the chief among you?" the court messengers asked in jest. "We see that every pauper wears the anklet of title in Umuofia. Does it cost as much as ten cowries?"

---

7. "A Person Who Does What He Says" (a praise name).

The six men ate nothing throughout that day and the next. They were not even given any water to drink, and they could not go out to urinate or go into the bush when they were pressed. At night the messengers came in to taunt them and to knock their shaven heads together.

Even when the men were left alone they found no words to speak to one another. It was only on the third day, when they could no longer bear the hunger and the insults, that they began to talk about giving in.

"We should have killed the white man if you had listened to me," Okonkwo snarled.

"We could have been in Umuru now waiting to be hanged," someone said to him.

"Who wants to kill the white man?" asked a messenger who had just rushed in. Nobody spoke.

"You are not satisfied with your crime, but you must kill the white man on top of it." He carried a strong stick, and he hit each man a few blows on the head and back. Okonkwo was choked with hate.

As soon as the six men were locked up, court messengers went into Umuofia to tell the people that their leaders would not be released unless they paid a fine of two hundred and fifty bags of cowries.

"Unless you pay the fine immediately," said their head-man, "we will take your leaders to Umuru before the big white man, and hang them."

This story spread quickly through the villages, and was added to as it went. Some said that the men had already been taken to Umuru and would be hanged on the following day. Some said that their families would also be hanged. Others said that soldiers were already on their way to shoot the people of Umuofia as they had done in Abame.

It was the time of the full moon. But that night the voice of children was not heard. The village *ilo* where they always gathered for a moon-play was empty. The women of Iguedo did not meet in their secret enclosure to learn a new dance to be displayed later to the village. Young men who were always abroad in the moonlight kept to their huts that night. Their manly voices were not heard on the village paths as they went to visit their friends and lovers. Umuofia was like a startled animal with ears erect, sniffing the silent, ominous air and not knowing which way to run.

The silence was broken by the village crier beating his sonorous *ogene*. He called every man in Umuofia, from the Akakanma age group upwards, to a meeting in the marketplace after the morning meal. He went from one end of the village to the other and walked all its breadth. He did not leave out any of the main footpaths.

Okonkwo's compound was like a deserted homestead. It was as if cold water had been poured on it. His family was all there, but everyone spoke in whispers. His daughter Ezinma had broken her twenty-eight-day visit to the family of her future husband, and returned home when she heard that her father had been imprisoned, and was going to be hanged. As soon as she got home she went to Obierika to ask what the men of Umuofia were going to do about it. But Obierika had not been home since morning. His wives thought he had gone to a secret meeting. Ezinma was satisfied that something was being done.

On the morning after the village crier's appeal the men of Umuofia met in the marketplace and decided to collect without delay two hundred and fifty bags of cowries to appease the white man. They did not know that fifty bags would go to the court messengers, who had increased the fine for that purpose.

24

Okonkwo and his fellow prisoners were set free as soon as the fine was paid. The District Commissioner spoke to them again about the great queen, and about peace and good government. But the men did not listen. They just sat and looked at him and at his interpreter. In the end they were given back their bags and sheathed machetes and told to go home. They rose and left the courthouse. They neither spoke to anyone nor among themselves.

The courthouse, like the church, was built a little way outside the village. The footpath that linked them was a very busy one because it also led to the stream, beyond the court. It was open and sandy. Footpaths were open and sandy in the dry season. But when the rains came the bush grew thick on either side and closed in on the path. It was now dry season.

As they made their way to the village the six men met women and children going to the stream with their waterpots. But the men wore such heavy and fearsome looks that the women and children did not say "*nno*" or "welcome" to them, but edged out of the way to let them pass. In the village little groups of men joined them until they became a sizable company. They walked silently. As each of the six men got to his compound, he turned in, taking some of the crowd with him. The village was astir in a silent, suppressed way.

Ezinma had prepared some food for her father as soon as news spread that the six men would be released. She took it to him in his *obi*. He ate absent-mindedly. He had no appetite; he only ate to please her. His male relations and friends had gathered in his *obi*, and Obierika was urging him to eat. Nobody else spoke, but they noticed the long stripes on Okonkwo's back where the warder's whip had cut into his flesh.

The village crier was abroad again in the night. He beat his iron gong and announced that another meeting would be held in the morning. Everyone knew that Umuofia was at last going to speak its mind about the things that were happening.

Okonkwo slept very little that night. The bitterness in his heart was now mixed with a kind of childlike excitement. Before he had gone to bed he had brought down his war dress, which he had not touched since his return from exile. He had shaken out his smoked raffia skirt and examined his tall feather head-gear and his shield. They were all satisfactory, he had thought.

As he lay on his bamboo bed he thought about the treatment he had received in the white man's court, and he swore vengeance. If Umuofia decided on war, all would be well. But if they chose to be cowards he would go out and avenge himself. He thought about wars in the past. The noblest, he thought, was the war against Isike. In those days Okudo[8] was still alive. Okudo sang a war song in a way that no other man could. He was not a fighter, but his voice turned every man into a lion.

"Worthy men are no more," Okonkwo sighed as he remembered those days. "Isike will never forget how we slaughtered them in that war. We killed twelve of their men and they killed only two of ours. Before the end of the fourth market week they were suing for peace. Those were days when men were men."

As he thought of these things he heard the sound of the iron gong in the distance. He listened carefully, and could just hear the crier's voice. But it was very faint. He turned on his bed and his back hurt him. He ground his teeth. The crier was drawing nearer and nearer until he passed by Okonkwo's compound.

"The greatest obstacle in Umuofia," Okonkwo thought bitterly, "is that coward, Egonwanne.[9] His sweet tongue can change fire into cold ash. When he speaks he moves our men to impotence. If they had ignored his womanish wisdom five years ago, we would not have come to this." He ground his teeth. "Tomorrow he will tell them that our fathers never fought a 'war of blame.' If they listen to him I shall leave them and plan my own revenge."

The crier's voice had once more become faint, and the distance had taken the harsh edge off his iron gong. Okonkwo turned from one side to the other and derived a kind of pleasure from the pain his back gave him. "Let Egonwanne talk about a 'war of blame' tomorrow and I shall show him my back and head." He ground his teeth.

The marketplace began to fill as soon as the sun rose. Obierika was waiting in his *obi* when Okonkwo came along and called him. He hung his goat-skin bag and his sheathed machete on his shoulder and went out to join him. Obierika's hut was close to the road and he saw every man who passed to the marketplace. He had exchanged greetings with many who had already passed that morning.

When Okonkwo and Obierika got to the meeting place there were already so many people that if one threw up a grain of sand it would not find its way to the earth again. And many more people were coming from every quarter of the nine villages. It warmed Okonkwo's heart to see such strength of numbers. But he was looking for one man in particular, the man whose tongue he dreaded and despised so much.

"Can you see him?" he asked Obierika.

"Who?"

"Egonwanne," he said, his eyes roving from one corner of the huge marketplace to the other. Most of the men sat on wooden stools they had brought with them.

"No," said Obierika, casting his eyes over the crowd. "Yes, there he is, under the silk-cotton tree. Are you afraid he would convince us not to fight?"

8. "Great Eagle Feather" (a praise name).   9. "Wealth of a Sibling."

"Afraid? I do not care what he does to *you*. I despise him and those who listen to him. I shall fight alone if I choose."

They spoke at the top of their voices because everybody was talking, and it was like the sound of a great market.

"I shall wait till he has spoken," Okonkwo thought. "Then I shall speak."

"But how do you know he will speak against war?" Obierika asked after a while.

"Because I know he is a coward," said Okonkwo. Obierika did not hear the rest of what he said because at that moment somebody touched his shoulder from behind and he turned round to shake hands and exchange greetings with five or six friends. Okonkwo did not turn round even though he knew the voices. He was in no mood to exchange greetings. But one of the men touched him and asked about the people of his compound.

"They are well," he replied without interest.

The first man to speak to Umuofia that morning was Okika, one of the six who had been imprisoned. Okika was a great man and an orator. But he did not have the booming voice which a first speaker must use to establish silence in the assembly of the clan. Onyeka[1] had such a voice; and so he was asked to salute Umuofia before Okika began to speak.

"*Umuofia kwenu!*" he bellowed, raising his left arm and pushing the air with his open hand.

"*Yaa!*" roared Umuofia.

"*Umuofia kwenu!*" he bellowed again, and again and again, facing a new direction each time. And the crowd answered, "*Yaa!*"

There was immediate silence as though cold water had been poured on a roaring flame.

Okika sprang to his feet and also saluted his clansmen four times. Then he began to speak:

"You all know why we are here, when we ought to be building our barns or mending our huts, when we should be putting our compounds in order. My father used to say to me: 'Whenever you see a toad jumping in broad daylight, then know that something is after its life.' When I saw you all pouring into this meeting from all the quarters of our clan so early in the morning, I knew that something was after our life." He paused for a brief moment and then began again:

"All our gods are weeping. Idemili is weeping, Ogwugwu is weeping, Agbala is weeping, and all the others. Our dead fathers are weeping because of the shameful sacrilege they are suffering and the abomination we have all seen with our eyes." He stopped again to steady his trembling voice.

"This is a great gathering. No clan can boast of greater numbers or greater valor. But are we all here? I ask you: Are all the sons of Umuofia with us here?" A deep murmur swept through the crowd.

"They are not," he said. "They have broken the clan and gone their several ways. We who are here this morning have remained true to our fathers, but our brothers have deserted us and joined a stranger to soil their

---

1. "Who Surpasses [God]?" (a rhetorical question).

fatherland. If we fight the stranger we shall hit our brothers and perhaps shed the blood of a clansman. But we must do it. Our fathers never dreamed of such a thing, they never killed their brothers. But a white man never came to them. So we must do what our fathers would never have done. Eneke the bird was asked why he was always on the wing and he replied: 'Men have learned to shoot without missing their mark and I have learned to fly without perching on a twig.' We must root out this evil. And if our brothers take the side of evil we must root them out too. And we must do it *now*. We must bail this water now that it is only ankle-deep. . . ."

At this point there was a sudden stir in the crowd and every eye was turned in one direction. There was a sharp bend in the road that led from the marketplace to the white man's court, and to the stream beyond it. And so no one had seen the approach of the five court messengers until they had come round the bend, a few paces from the edge of the crowd. Okonkwo was sitting at the edge.

He sprang to his feet as soon as he saw who it was. He confronted the head messenger, trembling with hate, unable to utter a word. The man was fearless and stood his ground, his four men lined up behind him.

In that brief moment the world seemed to stand still, waiting. There was utter silence. The men of Umuofia were merged into the mute back-cloth of trees and giant creepers, waiting.

The spell was broken by the head messenger. "Let me pass!" he ordered.

"What do you want here?"

"The white man whose power you know too well has ordered this meeting to stop."

In a flash Okonkwo drew his machete. The messenger crouched to avoid the blow. It was useless. Okonkwo's machete descended twice and the man's head lay beside his uniformed body.

The waiting backcloth jumped into tumultuous life and the meeting was stopped. Okonkwo stood looking at the dead man. He knew that Umuofia would not go to war. He knew because they had let the other messengers escape. They had broken into tumult instead of action. He discerned fright in that tumult. He heard voices asking: "Why did he do it?"

He wiped his machete on the sand and went away.

25

When the District Commissioner arrived at Okonkwo's compound at the head of an armed band of soldiers and court messengers he found a small crowd of men sitting wearily in the *obi*. He commanded them to come outside, and they obeyed without a murmur.

"Which among you is called Okonkwo?" he asked through his interpreter.

"He is not here," replied Obierika.

"Where is he?"

"He is not here!"

The Commissioner became angry and red in the face. He warned the men that unless they produced Okonkwo forthwith he would lock them all up. The men murmured among themselves, and Obierika spoke again.

"We can take you where he is, and perhaps your men will help us."

The Commissioner did not understand what Obierika meant when he said, "Perhaps your men will help us." One of the most infuriating habits of these people was their love of superfluous words, he thought.

Obierika with five or six others led the way. The Commissioner and his men followed, their firearms held at the ready. He had warned Obierika that if he and his men played any monkey tricks they would be shot. And so they went.

There was a small bush behind Okonkwo's compound. The only opening into this bush from the compound was a little round hole in the red-earth wall through which fowls went in and out in their endless search for food. The hole would not let a man through. It was to this bush that Obierika led the Commissioner and his men. They skirted round the compound, keeping close to the wall. The only sound they made was with their feet as they crushed dry leaves.

Then they came to the tree from which Okonkwo's body was dangling, and they stopped dead.

"Perhaps your men can help us bring him down and bury him," said Obierika. "We have sent for strangers from another village to do it for us, but they may be a long time coming."

The District Commissioner changed instantaneously. The resolute administrator in him gave way to the student of primitive customs.

"Why can't you take him down yourselves?" he asked.

"It is against our custom," said one of the men. "It is an abomination for a man to take his own life. It is an offense against the Earth, and a man who commits it will not be buried by his clansmen. His body is evil, and only strangers may touch it. That is why we ask your people to bring him down, because you are strangers."

"Will you bury him like any other man?" asked the Commissioner.

"We cannot bury him. Only strangers can. We shall pay your men to do it. When he has been buried we will then do our duty by him. We shall make sacrifices to cleanse the desecrated land."

Obierika, who had been gazing steadily at his friend's dangling body, turned suddenly to the District Commissioner and said ferociously: "That man was one of the greatest men in Umuofia. You drove him to kill himself; and now he will be buried like a dog. . . ." He could not say any more. His voice trembled and choked his words.

"Shut up!" shouted one of the messengers, quite unnecessarily.

"Take down the body," the Commissioner ordered his chief messenger, "and bring it and all these people to the court."

"Yes, sah," the messenger said, saluting.

The Commissioner went away, taking three or four of the soldiers with him. In the many years in which he had toiled to bring civilization to different parts of Africa he had learned a number of things. One of them was that a District Commissioner must never attend to such undignified details as cutting a hanged man from the tree. Such attention would give the natives a poor opinion of him. In the book which he planned to write he would stress that point. As he walked back to the court he thought about that book. Every day brought him some new material. The story of this man who had killed a messenger and hanged himself would make interesting reading. One could almost write a whole chapter on him. Perhaps not a whole chapter but a reasonable paragraph, at any rate. There was so much else to include, and one must be firm in cutting out details. He had already chosen the title of the book, after much thought: *The Pacification of the Primitive Tribes of the Lower Niger.*

DEREK WALCOTT
born 1930

From the beginning of his career, Derek Walcott has situated his work firmly within the broad perspective of African-Caribbean experience. Invariably, his poetry, plays, and essays focus on the contradictory pressures of a complex racial and cultural situation. An early poem, *A Far Cry from Africa,* from *In a Green Night* (1962), alludes to events during the violent uprising in Kenya against British colonialism and expresses poignantly his conflicting allegiances:

> I who am poisoned with the blood of both
> Where shall I turn, divided to the vein?
> I who have cursed
> The drunken officer of British rule, how choose
> Between this Africa and the English tongue I love?
> Betray them both or give back what they give?
> How can I face such slaughter and be cool?
> How can I turn from Africa and live?

Despite its rhetorical excess, the passage conveys a personal anguish proceeding from Walcott's sense of a wider cultural and spiritual predicament. Beyond the personal reference the passage speaks to an unresolvable discord in values by which the West Indian has to live and to a resulting disunity in black West Indian consciousness. Walcott's entire imaginative work registers the African-Caribbean quest for an established sense of place and community, while positing, at the same time, the creative possibilities of a distinctive Caribbean mode of being.

Walcott was born, along with his twin brother, Roderick, in Castries, the capital of St. Lucia, on January 23, 1930. Shortly after their first birthday, their father, who was a government functionary and a talented artist, died, and the two boys were brought up by their mother, a schoolteacher who later became headmistress of the Methodist elementary school where they began their education. Both inherited their father's creative gift, Derek primarily in language, Roderick in the visual arts. Though their mother and others in the community nurtured their talents, Derek's feeling of being an orphan could not be fully assuaged. He acquired early a sense of his singularity from the fact that he was of mixed parentage in a predominantly black society as well as a Protestant and member of the educated middle class in a peasant and Catholic community. Moreover, although he was brought up to speak standard English, his exposure to the local French creole reinforced his sense of ambiguous relationship to the life around him. But far from unsettling Walcott, these factors become in his work a source of strength. For the special quality of his writings springs from his working through the implications of his marginality within his own society and in the wider world.

This trajectory of themes, recently expressed in his highly acclaimed epic poem *Omeros* (1990), has been implicit in his writing from the outset. While a secondary school student at St. Mary's College in Castries, he began writing poems and plays. By the time he left school, he had already published two volumes, *25 Poems* (1948) and *Epitaph for the Young* (1949), both of which drew from Frank Collymore, then "dean" of West Indian letters, an enthusiastic essay drawing attention to his promise. Walcott also wrote at this time a historical play, *Henri Christophe* (1950), devoted to the tragic career of one of the principal actors in the Haitian revolution, which was considered accomplished enough to be read on the BBC Caribbean Service. Enrolling that same year in the University College of the West Indies in Kingston, Jamaica, to study English, French, and Latin, he brought with him a reputation as a young writer destined for a brilliant future.

The years in Jamaica were crucial for Walcott's subsequent development. They enabled him to acquire an expanded view of the Caribbean as an area unified by a common experience and a common history. Equally important, his literary studies familiarized him with the great works of Western literature. His next volume, *Poems* (1953), shows some dependence on recognized literary models—the influence of T. S. Eliot is especially pronounced—but also demonstrates the efforts of a young writer undergoing a strenuous apprenticeship to his craft. After graduation in 1953, Walcott taught school in Kingston, while doing occasional work in journalism, before moving to Port of Spain, Trinidad, where he became a feature writer for a major local newspaper, *The Sunday Guardian*. In 1957, he was awarded a Rockefeller Fellowship to study theater at New York University. His encounter with the problems of race during his American sojourn further deepened his self-awareness as a West Indian and confirmed for him the inescapable connection between race and history with which black people in the New World have to contend. On his return two years later to Port of Spain, he founded the Trinidad Theatre Workshop, to the development of which he devoted his energies for nearly two decades.

The publication in England of *In a Green Night* established Walcott's reputation beyond the Caribbean region. Its poems are eloquent and rich in imagery. They center on his multiple heritage as a West Indian and show a determined wrestling with form: "I seek / As climate seeks its style to write / Verse crisp as sand, clear as sunlight / Cold as the curled wave, ordinary / As a tumbler of island water." With this volume, Walcott consciously assumes the weight of English literary tradition by translating its references and resources into a poetic language determined by his Caribbean sensibility. It is however in *The Castaway* (1969), his next volume, that Walcott attained full maturity as a poet. A cluster of poems devoted to the figure of Robinson Crusoe brings into prominence the presiding idea of the volume, which is to situate the poet as the central point of consciousness in the larger community. The theme is pursued again in *The Gulf* (1969).

This preoccupation with poetic vocation leads to extended self-scrutiny in *Another Life* (1973), a verse autobiography tracing Walcott's artistic development and the growth of his mind. The figure of Odysseus is evoked to depict this growth as a journey into an ambiguous self: "My sign was water / tears, and the sea / my sign was Janus / I saw with twin heads / and everything I say is contradicted." The ambiguity that Walcott spells out here becomes, however, an enabling factor, for it compels him, in a specific Caribbean context, to an urgent creative purpose: "we were the light of the world! / We were blest with a virginal unpainted world / with Adam's task of giving things their name." His next volume, *Sea Grapes* (1976), is devoted largely to reflections on the Caribbean poet's calling.

With *The Star Apple Kingdom* (1977), Walcott stresses the political and social themes that served in the previous volumes as a broad canvas. The opening poem, *The Schooner Flight*, uses the journey motif to chart the decline of the Caribbean archipelago through time, beginning with its violation by Columbus. It evokes the subsequent nightmare of the Middle Passage and the harsh experience of slavery, followed by the humiliations of colonial domination and the uncertainties of the islands' present freedom. The poem sets the pathetic tone of the volume, which is a long and anxious questioning of the destiny of the Caribbean, now being corrupted by tourism and commerce ("this chain store of islands"). This questioning continues in *The Fortunate Traveller* (1981), where Walcott's perception of the racial divide between the affluent North and the impoverished South dictates the ironic posture of the title.

Like these later poems, Walcott's plays focus on the public world. *The Sea at Dauphin* (1953) reworks in local terms the theme of Synge's *Riders to the Sea*, in which individuals pit themselves against a hostile nature. *Ti-Jean and His Brothers* (1958), a parable of Caribbean experience, highlights the social and moral odds against which the dehumanized slaves struggle. *Pantomine* (1978) returns to the Crusoe and Friday theme to dramatize the gulf between white master and black slave. *Malcochon* (1959) grimly profiles the dispossessed West Indian, haunted by his devalued status and by a dream of violence. And *The Joker of Seville* (1974) is a West Indian recasting of the Don Juan motif, in which the hero's sexual adventures are the defiant gesture of a liberated consciousness.

All these concerns come together in *Dream on Monkey Mountain* (1967), an expressionist representation of the conflicts and obsessions of the African-Caribbean mind, projected through allegorical characters drawn from the folk tradition. By fusing multiple levels of action and consciousness, the play encapsulates the varied responses of the black West Indian population to their condition. The stage directions for the first scene symbolically present the tense polarities of African-Caribbean consciousness around which the dramatic action revolves. The moon, representing the doomed aspiration to whiteness of the alienated colonized subject, is counterpoised to the African drum, symbolic of Caribbean ancestralism. Walcott develops this element of African-Caribbean life in the play through the figure of Baron Samedi, who features in Haitian vodun (voodoo)—where African deities are recalled—as the harbinger of death. The variety of language, running the whole gamut of West Indian speech, underscores the range of situations and emotions encompassed by the play.

The prologue and epilogue provide an outer frame of "reality" for the dream sequence that constitutes the play's dramatic movement. Makak, the principal character, spends a night in prison for disorderly behavior in a bar, and the play itself is essentially an enactment of his dream that night, presented in a succession of tableaux that evoke both his waking states of mind and their dream projections. Because Makak's thoughts and feelings relate to the conditions of his existence, the prison becomes an appropriate metaphor for his situation. The first part of the play is devoted to the apparatus of repression by which colonial domination is maintained and to a rehearsal, through the speeches of the mulatto Lestrade, of its ideology, an ideology that amounts to a vast indictment of the black race. Lestrade embodies the false consciousness of the agents of colonial oppression; at the same time, he has some insight into the ambiguous nature of his role. The parodic tone of his speeches gives them the character of tirades triggered by the historical grievance of the Caribbean people. The resulting psychological disorientation, generated by internalization of the negative image the black self encounters in Western representations of the race, is given unforgettable expression by Makak: "Is thirty years now since I have look in no mirror / Not a pool of cold water, when I must drink, / I stir my hands first, to break up my image." Makak's marginal situation, his isolation on the "racial mountain," is compounded by the loss of his identity. Imprisoned within a borrowed culture, he can only act out the grotesque imitation of this culture that is symbolized by his French creole nickname and is re-echoed in the play's theme song. In its objective as well as subjective references, then, the image of the prison sums up the black subject's loss of existential freedom.

The sociological framework of the first part of the play provides the troubled setting for Makak's fantasies and the violent turn they take in the second part. His dream of revolution, signified by his stabbing of Lestrade, feeds on his desire for a magical self-transformation and an ideal of deliverance associated with a lost African heritage. In representing this element of Makak's dream, Walcott draws on the myth of Africa as it has exercised the black imagination in the Americas, and especially its charismatic force, as exemplified in Marcus Garvey's Back to Africa movement during the 1930s. The regressive nature of this myth is clearly signaled by the white goddess, a symbolic figure who stands both for the ideal of whiteness, which fascinates the black self, and for the gratifying propositions of white apologists for black culture: "I behold this woman, the loveliest thing I see on this earth, floating towards me, just like the moon. . . . She say I should not live so any more, here in the forest, frighten of people because I think I ugly. She say I come from family of lions and kings."

The last scene of Makak's dream, reminiscent both of Eugene O'Neill's *The Emperor Jones* and Jean Genet's *The Blacks*, must be read as Walcott's warning of the danger of a certain form of black nationalism that is premised on a return to Africa, which inevitably degenerates into futility and even becomes aggressiveness. The scene shows the corruption of Makak's dream, which can only find fulfillment in a megalomania and brutality that culminate in the ritual slaying of the white goddess, now perceived as a sinister presence. The act signifies Makak's desire to purge whiteness from his consciousness so as to recover an undifferentiated blackness of being. But since Makak owes his visions of a mythical Africa to her promptings, her removal destroys the dream. Africa proves in the end a chimera, and Makak awakes to the drab reality of his lived situation. Yet the play does not end on a note of defeat. The epilogue dramatizes Makak's moment of self-recognition as he recovers his real name, Felix Hobain, and forms a new project of self-creation: "Lord, I have been washed from shore to shore, as a tree in the ocean. The branches of my fingers, the roots of my feet, could grip nothing, but now, God, they have found ground . . . but now this old hermit is going back home, to the green beginning of this world."

Omeros, Walcott's latest work, affirms this same recovery of the Caribbean soul. In an expansive recollection of his previous themes, he sums up the West Indian experience through the vision of Achille, a humble St. Lucian fisherman, whose travels take him to all points of the West Indian consciousness. The conflation of the poet's persona with Homer's Odysseus gives epic dimension and mythical significance to his quest for meaning in history. The poem illustrates Walcott's genius in its full scope, the gift of language by which he embodies that other life of the intellect and of the imagination that he intimates in his autobiographical poem. The award in 1992 of the Nobel Prize for literature came as a fitting recognition of a work as rich in its abundance and variety as in its human import.

Robert Hammer, *Derek Walcott* (1994), is a full-length study of the writer's work; Lloyd Brown, *West Indian Poetry* (1984), contains a helpful chapter on Walcott's poetry in the context of the development of West Indian poetry in English. Edward Baugh, *Derek Walcott: Memory as Vision* (1978), is an extended analysis of *Another Life*, and the last chapter of Patrick Taylor, *The Narrative of Liberation* (1989), is devoted in part to a discussion of *Dream on Monkey Mountain*. Essays in Stewart Brown, ed., *The Art of Derek Walcott* (1991), and Rei Terada, *Derek Walcott's Poetry: American Mimicry* (1992), examine Walcott's creative integration within his poetry of influences from various sources.

PRONOUNCING GLOSSARY

The following list uses common English syllables and stress accents to provide rough equivalents of selected words whose pronunciation may be unfamiliar to the general reader.

Conteur: *kon-ter'*

Lestrade: *le-strahd'*

Makak: *mah-kahk'*

Micoud: *mee-koo'*

Pamphilion: *pang-fi'-leeong*

Rivière: *ree-veer'*

Souris: *soo-ree'*

Tigre: *teegr*

Dream on Monkey Mountain

If the moon is earth's friend,
how can we leave the earth?
Noh Play

CHARACTERS[1]

TIGRE, *a felon*

SOURIS, *a felon*

CORPORAL LESTRADE, *a mulatto*

MAKAK, *a charbonnier or charcoal-burner*

APPARITION, *the moon, the muse, the white Goddess, a dancer*

MOUSTIQUE, *a cripple, friend to Makak*

BASIL, *a cabinet-maker, figure of death*

MARKET INSPECTOR PAMPHILION, *a government servant*

A DANCER, *also* NARRATOR

LITTER BEARERS

SISTERS OF THE REVELATION

MARKET WOMEN, WIVES OF MAKAK

Part One

Thus in certain psychoses the hallucinated person, tired of always being insulted by his demon, one fine day starts hearing the voice of an angel who pays him compliments; but the jeers don't stop for all that; only, from then on, they alternate with congratulations. This is a defence, but it is also the end of the story. The self is disassociated, and the patient heads for madness.
Sartre: Prologue to "The Wretched of the Earth,"
by Frantz Fanon[2]

---

1. The main characters are based on the folk tradition of animal tales, generally considered to be an African survival in the Caribbean. *Tigre:* tiger. *Souris:* mouse. *Makak:* monkey. *Moustique:* mosquito. *Pamphilion:* butterfly.   2. A Martinican psychiatrist (1925–1961), who joined the Algerians during their war of independence from the French. He became a leading theoretician of revolutionary nationalism. Jean-Paul Sartre (1905–1980), prominent French philosopher in the years after World War II.

PROLOGUE

A spotlight warms the white disc of an African drum until it glows like the round moon above it. Below the moon is the stark silhouette of a volcanic mountain. Reversed, the moon becomes the sun. A dancer enters and sits astride the drum. From the opposite side of the stage a top-hatted, frock-coated figure with white gloves, his face halved by white make-up like the figure of Baron Samedi,[3] enters and crouches behind the dancer. As the lament begins, dancer and figure wave their arms slowly, sinuously, with a spidery motion. The figure rises during the lament and touches the disc of the moon. The drummer rises, dancing as if in slow motion, indicating, as their areas grow distinct, two prison cages on either side of the stage. In one cell, TIGRE *and* SOURIS, *two half-naked felons are squabbling. The figure strides off slowly, the* CONTEUR[4] *and* CHORUS, *off-stage, increase the volume of their lament.*

CONTEUR: Mooma, mooma,
                   Your son in de jail a'ready,
                   Your son in de jail a'ready,
                   Take a towel and
                             band your belly.[5]

CHORUS: Mooma, mooma,
                   Your son in de jail a'ready,
                   Your son in de jail a'ready,
                   Take a towel and
                             band your belly.

CONTEUR: I pass by the police station,
                   Nobody to sign de bail bond.

CHORUS: Mooma, don't cry,
                   Your son in de jail a'ready,
                   I pass by de police station,
                   Nobody to sign de bail bond.

CONTEUR: Forty days before the Carnival,[6] Lord,
                   I dream I see me funeral.

CHORUS: Mooma, mooma,
                   Your son in de jail a'ready,
                   Take a towel and band your belly.

[*The* CORPORAL, *in Sunday uniform, enters with* MAKAK, *an old Negro with a jute sack, and lets him into the next cell.*]

TIGRE: Forty days before the Carnival,
                   Lord, I dream I see me funeral . . .

TIGRE *and* SOURIS: Mooma, don't cry, your son in de jail a'ready . . .

TIGRE: Take a towel and band you' belly,
    Mooma, don't cry, your son in de jail a'ready.

[MAKAK *sits on the cell cot, an old cloth around his shoulders.*]

SOURIS: Shut up! Ay, Corporal. Who is dat?

---

3. The emissary of death in Haitian vodun (voodoo). Vodun is an African-derived folk religion with a system of beliefs incorporating Christian symbolism; the rituals are accompanied by drumming and often involve trances and spirit possession.   4. Storyteller. The introduction of this character emphasizes the folk basis of the drama.   5. That is, take heart. The picture is that of the distraught mother tightening a piece of cloth around her waist for emotional relief; compare the biblical "gird your loins."   6. A popular festival in the Caribbean and Brazil that takes place just before Lent; it features dancing and general merrymaking.

TIGRE: [*Singing.*] Mooma, don't cry, your son in de jail a'ready.

CORPORAL: Dat, you mange-ridden habitual felon, is de King of Africa.

TIGRE: [*Singing.*] Your son in de jail a'ready,
Your son in de jail a'ready . . .

SOURIS: Tigre, shut your trap. It have Majesty there.

[*The* CORPORAL *elaborately removes a notebook and gold pencil.*]

CORPORAL: Now before I bring a specific charge against you, I will require certain particulars . . .

TIGRE, SOURIS and CORPORAL: You are required by law to supply me with certain data, for no man is guilty except so proven, and I must warn you that anything you say may be held against you . . .

CORPORAL: [*Turning.*] Look!

SOURIS: Don't tell him a damn thing! You have legal rights. Your lawyer! Get your lawyer.

TIGRE: [*Singing.*]   I pass by de police station,
Nobody to sign de bail bond,
Mooma, don't cry . . .

SOURIS: [*Shrilly.*] What he up for, Corporal? What you lock him up for?

CORPORAL: Drunk and disorderly! A old man like that! He was drunk and he mash up Alcindor café.

SOURIS: And you going cage him here on a first offence? Old man, get a lawyer and defend your name!

[*The* CORPORAL *bends down and removes a half-empty bottle of rum from the bag, and a white mask with long black sisal hair.*[7]]

CORPORAL: I must itemize these objects! Can you identify them?

SOURIS: O God, O God, Tigre! The king got a bottle! [SOURIS *and* TIGRE *grope through the bars, howling, groaning.*] O God, just one, Corporal. My throat on fire. One for the boys. Here, just one swallow, Corp.

TIGRE: Have mercy on two thieves fallen by the wayside. You call yourself a Catholic?

[*Inchoate, animal howling, leaping and pacing.*]

CORPORAL: Animals, beasts, savages, cannibals, niggers, stop turning this place to a stinking zoo!

SOURIS: Zoo? Just because you capture some mountain gorilla?

[*The* CORPORAL *with his baton cracks* SOURIS*'s extended wrist.*]

CORPORAL: In the beginning was the ape, and the ape had no name, so God call him man. Now there were various tribes of the ape, it had gorilla, baboon, orang-outan, chimpanzee, the blue-arsed monkey and the marmoset,[8] and God looked at his handiwork, and saw that it was good. For some of the apes had straighten their backbone, and start walking upright, but there was one tribe unfortunately that lingered behind, and that was the nigger. Now if you apes will behave like gentlemen, who knows what could happen? The bottle could go round, but first it behoves me, Corporal Lestrade, to perform my duty according to the rules of Her Majesty's Government, so don't interrupt. Please let

---

7. Leaves of the highly fibrous sisal plant that have been beaten into strands to resemble human hair.
8. Or squirrel monkey, found in South America. *Orang-outan:* or orangutan, an ape found in Southeast Asia.

me examine the Lion of Judah.[9] [*Goes towards* MAKAK.] What is your
name?

TIGRE: [*Singing softly.*]

>Oh, when the roll[1]
>Is called up yonder,
>When the roll
>Is called up yonder,
>When the roll
>Is called up yonder,
>When the roll is called up yonder,
>I ain't going!

[CHORUS: *When the roll . . .*]

[*Spoken.*] And nobody else here going, you all too black, except possibly
the Corporal. [*Pauses, points.*] Look, is the full moon.

CORPORAL: [*As moonlight fills the cell.*] Your name in full, occupation,
status, income, ambition, domicile or place of residence, age, and last
but not least, your race?

SOURIS: The man break my hand. The damn man break my hand.

TIGRE: Well, you can't t'hief again.

MAKAK: Let me go home, my Corporal.

SOURIS: Ay, wait, Tigre, the king has spoken.

TIGRE: What the king say?

SOURIS: He want to go home.

CORPORAL: Where is your home? Africa?

MAKAK: Sur Morne Macaque[2] . . .

CORPORAL: [*Infuriated.*] English, English! For we are observing the principles and precepts of Roman law, and Roman law is English law. Let me
repeat the query: Where is your home?

MAKAK: I live on Monkey Mountain, Corporal.

CORPORAL: What is your name?

MAKAK: I forget.

CORPORAL: What is your race?

MAKAK: I am tired.

CORPORAL: What is your denominational affiliation?

[*Silence.*]

SOURIS: [*Whispering.*] Ça qui religion-ous?[3]

MAKAK: [*Smiling.*] Cat'olique.

CORPORAL: I ask you, with all the patience of the law, what is or has been
your denominational affiliation?

MAKAK: Cat'olique.

CORPORAL: [*Revising notes.*] You forget your name, your race is tired, your
denominational affiliation is Catholique, therefore, as the law, the
Roman law, had pity on our Blessed Saviour, by giving him, even *in
extremis,* a draught of vinegar, what, in your own language, you would
call *vinegre,*[4] I shall give all and sunday here, including these two
thieves, a handful of rum, before I press my charge.

---

9. The title of the emperor of Ethiopia.   1. Judgment Day.   2. On Monkey Mountain (French creole). *Morne:* little hill.   3. What's your religion? (French creole).   4. Play on the word *nègre,* the
French for "Nigger." The malapropisms in this passage (for example, *all and Sunday* for "all and sundry")
create a comic parody.

[TIGRE *and* SOURIS *applaud loudly. The* CORPORAL *takes a swallow from the bottle and passes it through the bars to* TIGRE *and* SOURIS; *then, holding it in his hand, paces around* MAKAK.]

TIGRE: How a man like that can know so much law? Could know so much language? Is a born Q.C.[5] Still every man entitle to his own defence.

SOURIS: The wig and gown, Corporal. Put on the wig and gown!

TIGRE: You have a sense of justice, put on the wig and gown.

CORPORAL: I can both accuse and defend this man.

SOURIS: The wig and gown, Lestrade. Let us hear English!

[*The* CORPORAL *strides off.*]

SOURIS: [*Sings.*] Drill him, Constable, drill him,
              Drill him, Constable, drill him,
              Drill him, Constable, drill him.
              He t'ief a bag of coals yesterday!

CHORUS: [*Repeats.*] Drill him, Constable, drill him . . .

SOURIS: Drill him, Constable, drill him,
              He mash up old Alcindor café!

[*The* CORPORAL, *isolated in a spot, with counsel's wig and gown, returns with four towels, two yellow, two red.*[6]]

TIGRE: Order, order, order in de court.

[*A massive gong is sounded, and the* CORPORAL *gives the two prisoners the towels. They robe themselves like judges.*]

CORPORAL: My noble judges. When this crime has been categorically examined by due process of law, and when the motive of the hereby accused by whereas and ad hoc shall be established without dychotomy, and long after we have perambulated through the labyrinthine bewilderment of the defendant's ignorance, let us hope, that justice, whom we all serve, will not only be done, but will appear, my lords, to have itself, been done . . . [*The* JUDGES *applaud.*] Ignorance is no excuse. Ignorance of the law is no excuse. Ignorance of one's own ignorance is no excuse. This is the prisoner. I will ask the prisoner to lift up his face. *Levez la tête-ous!*

[MAKAK *lifts up his head. The* CORPORAL *jerks it back savagely.*]

CORPORAL: My lords, as you can see, this is a being without a mind, a will, a name, a tribe of its own. I shall ask the prisoner to turn out his hands. *Montrez-moi la main-ous!* [MAKAK *turns his palm outward.*] I will spare you the sound of that voice, which have come from a cave of darkness, dripping with horror. These hands are the hands of Esau,[7] the fingers are like roots, the arteries as hard as twine, and the palms are seamed with coal. But the animal, you observe, is tamed and obedient. Walk round the cage! *Marchez! Marchez!*

[MAKAK *rises and walks round the bench, as the* CHORUS *begins to sing.*]

CHORUS: I don't know what to say this monkey won't do,[8]
              I don't know what to say this monkey won't do.

---

5. Queen's counsel; a high distinction reserved for exceptional lawyers in the British legal system.   6. Yellow and red, often combined with green, are the colors of the Rastafarians.   7. In Genesis, he impersonated his brother, Jacob, to gain their blind father's favor.   8. The lyrics of a West Indian calypso song popular during the late 1950s and early 1960s; here, a reflection of the idea of mimicry as the essential attribute of the West Indian.

[*As the* CORPORAL, *like an animal tamer, cracks out his orders, the choir of* JUDGES *keeps time, clapping.*]

CORPORAL: About turn!

    [MAKAK *turns around wearily.*]

CHORUS: Cause when I turn round, monkey turn around too,
           I don't know what to say this monkey won't do.

CORPORAL: On your knees!

    [MAKAK *drops to his knees.* SOURIS *shrieks with delight, then collects his dignity.*]

        I kneel down, monkey kneel down too,
        I don't know what to say this monkey won't do.
        I praying, monkey praying too,
        I don't know what the hell this monkey won't do.

CORPORAL: Stand up! Sit down! Up on the bench! Sit down! Hands out! Hands in!

    [MAKAK *does all this. The* CHORUS *sings faster, and the* JUDGES *keep time.*]

CHORUS: Everything I say this monkey does do,
        I don't know what to say this monkey won't do.
        I sit down, monkey sit down too,
        I don't know what to say this monkey won't do.

    [MAKAK *sits wearily on the bench.*]

CORPORAL: [*Holds up a palm.*] The exercise, my lords, prove that the prisoner is capable of reflexes, of obeying orders, therefore of understanding justice. Sound body. Now the charge!

    [*Drum roll.*]

[*To the sound of martial drums.*] His rightful name is unknown, yet on Saturday evening, July 25th, to wit tonight, at exactly three hours ago, to wit at 5:30 p.m., having tried to dispose of four bags of charcoal in the market of Quatre Chemin,[9] to wit this place, my lords, in which aforesaid market your alias, to wit Makak, is well known to all and sunday, the prisoner, in a state of incomprehensible intoxication, from money or moneys accrued by the sale of self-said bags, is reputed to have entered the licenced alcoholic premises of one Felicien Alcindor, whom the prisoner described as an agent of the devil, the same Felicien Alcindor being known to all and sunday as a God-fearing, honest Catholic. [*He rests the bottle down.*] When some intervention was attempted by those present, the prisoner then began to become vile and violent; he engaged in a blasphemous, obscene debate with two other villagers, Hannibal Dolcis and Market Inspector Caiphas Joseph Pamphilion, describing in a foul, incomprehensible manner . . .

    [*The* JUDGES *posture: Hear no evil. Hands to their ears.*]

a dream which he claims to have experienced, a vile, ambitious, and obscene dream . . .

    [*The* JUDGES *mime: See no evil. Hands to their faces in horror.*]

elaborating on the aforesaid dream with vile words and with a variety of sexual obscenities both in language and posture! Further, the prisoner,

---

9. Four roads (French).

in defiance of Her Majesty's Government, urged the aforementioned villagers to join him in sedition and the defilement of the flag, and when all this was rightly received with civic laughter and pious horror . . .

[*The* JUDGES *mime: Speak no evil. Their hands to their mouths.*]

the prisoner, in desperation and shame, began to wilfully damage the premises of the proprietor Felicien Alcindor, urging destruction on Church and State, claiming that he was the direct descendant of African kings, a healer of leprosy and the Saviour of his race.

[*Pause. Silence.*]

You claimed that with the camera of your eye you had taken a photograph of God and all that you could see was blackness.

[*The* JUDGES *rise in horror.*]

Blackness, my lords. What did the prisoner imply? That God was neither white nor black but nothing? That God was not white but black, that he had lost his faith? Or . . . or . . . what . . .

MAKAK: I am an old man. Send me home, Corporal. I suffer from madness. I does see things. Spirits does talk to me. All I have is my dreams and they don't trouble your soul.

TIGRE: I can imagine your dreams. Masturbating in moonlight. Dreaming of women, cause you so damn ugly. You should walk on all fours.

MAKAK: Sirs, I does catch fits. I fall in a frenzy every full-moon night. I does be possessed. And after that, sir, I am not responsible. I responsible only to God who once speak to me in the form of a woman on Monkey Mountain. I am God's warrior.

[*The* JUDGES *laugh.*]

CORPORAL: You are charged with certain things. Now let the prisoner make his deposition.

MAKAK: [*During this speech, the cage is raised out of sight.*]
  Sirs, I am sixty years old. I have live all my life
  Like a wild beast in hiding. Without child, without wife.
  People forget me like the mist on Monkey Mountain.
  Is thirty years now I have look in no mirror,
  Not a pool of cold water, when I must drink,
  I stir my hands first, to break up my image.
  I will tell you my dream. Sirs, make a white mist
  In the mind; make that mist hang like cloth
  From the dress of a woman, on prickles, on branches,
  Make it rise from the earth, like the breath of the dead
  On resurrection morning, and I walking through it
  On my way to my charcoal pit on the mountain.
  Make the web of the spider heavy with diamonds
  And when my hand brush it, let the chain break.
  I remember, in my mind, the cigale[1] sawing,
  Sawing, sawing wood before the woodcutter,
  The drum of the bull-frog, the blackbird flute,
  And this old man walking, ugly as sin,
  In a confusion of vapour,

---

1. Grasshopper.

Till I feel I was God self, walking through cloud.
In the heaven on my mind. Then I hear this song.
Not the blackbird flute,
Not the bull-frog drum,
Not the whistling of parrots
As I brush through the branches, shaking the dew,
A man swimming through smoke,
And the bandage of fog unpeeling my eyes,
As I reach to this spot,
I see this woman singing
And my feet grow roots. I could move no more.
A million silver needles prickle my blood,
Like a rain of small fishes.
The snakes in my hair speak to one another,
The smoke mouth open, and I behold this woman,
The loveliest thing I see on this earth,
Like the moon walking along her own road.

[*During this, the apparition appears and withdraws.*]

[*Flute music.*]

MAKAK: You don't see her? Look, I see her! She standing right there.[2] [*He points at nothing.*] Like the moon had climbed down the steps of heaven, and was standing in front me.

CORPORAL: I can see nothing. [*To the* JUDGES.] What do you see?

JUDGES: Nothing. Nothing.

MAKAK: Nothing? Look, there she is!

TIGRE: Nothing at all. The old man mad.

SOURIS: [*Mocking.*] Yes, I see it. I can see it. Is the face of the moon moving over the floor. Come to me, darling. [*He rolls over the cell floor groaning.*]

CORPORAL: My lords, is this rage for whiteness that does drive niggers mad.

MAKAK: [*On his knees.*] Lady in heaven, is your old black warrior,
      The king of Ashanti, Dahomey, Guinea,[3]
      Is this old cracked face you kiss in his sleep
      Appear to my enemies, tell me what to do?
      Put on my rage, the rage of the lion?[4]

[*He rises slowly and assumes a warrior's stance. Drums build to a frenzy.*]

      Help poor crazy Makak, help Makak
      To scatter his enemies, to slaughter those
      That standing around him.
      So, thy hosts shall be scattered,
      And the hyena shall feed on their bones![5]

[*He falls.*]

      Sirs, when I hear that voice,
      Singing so sweetly,
      I feel my spine straighten,
      My hand grow strong.
      My blood was boiling

---

2. Reminiscent of the bedroom scene in Shakespeare's *Hamlet* 3:4.   3. Precolonial kingdoms in West Africa.   4. As befits his epithet, "Lion of Judah."   5. The inflated rhetoric, with its biblical tone, conveys an impression of deluded messianism.

Like a brown river in flood,
And in that frenzy,
I let out a cry,
I charged the spears about me,
Grasses and branches,
I began to dance,
With the splendour of a lion,
Faster and faster,
Faster and faster,
Then, my body sink,
My bones betray me
And I fall on the forest floor,
Dead, on sweating grass,
And there, maybe, sirs,
Two other woodmen find me,
And take me up the track.
Sirs, if you please . . .

[*The two prisoners carry him.*]
CORPORAL: Continue, continue, the virtue of the law is its infinite patience. Continue . . .
[*The cells rise, the others withdraw.* MAKAK *lies alone in the hut.*][6]

SCENE ONE

MAKAK *remains on the ground, the mask near him. We hear a cry far off, echoing.* MOUSTIQUE, *a little man with a limp, a jute bag over his shoulder, comes into the morning light around the hut, puffing with exhaustion.*

MOUSTIQUE: Makak, Makak, wake up. Is me, Moustique. You didn't hear me calling you from the throat of the gully? I bring a next crocus bag from Alcindor café. Today is market day, and time and tide wait for no man. I tie Berthilia to a gommier[7] tree by the ravine.
[MAKAK *has stirred.*]
MAKAK: Berthilia? Which Berthilia?
MOUSTIQUE: Listen to him! Which Berthilia? The donkey you and I buy from Felicien! Every Saturday is the same damn trouble to wake you! You have the coals ready, eh? Spare me a little to light this fire. [*He helps* MAKAK *into the hut.*] Ay, what? What happen? [*He stoops near him.*] Eh! Nègre?[8] [*He rests the back of his hand on* MAKAK's *forehead.*] No fever. No sweat. [*He walks around the hut, distressed.*] What we going to do? The last time this happen, I find you outside the hut, trembling with fever. What we going do? [*He throws down the bag.*]
MAKAK: Go alone.
MOUSTIQUE: Go alone? Tcha, go alone.
MAKAK: I going mad, Moustique.
MOUSTIQUE: Going mad? Go mad tomorrow, today is market day. We have three bags at three-and-six a bag, making ten shillings and sixpence[9] for the week and you going mad? You have coffee?

---

6. The flashback provides both an image of Makak's normal solitude and a rapid transition to the next scene.   7. Gum tree. *Crocus bag:* a bag made from the fibers of the crocus plant.   8. A term of comradeship, used without its usual negative connotation.   9. Old British Sterling denominations; then worth about $1.25.

MAKAK: I don't want.

MOUSTIQUE: Well, I want, I cold like hell. [MOUSTIQUE *prepares coffee and sits down pensively by the small fire, watching the water boil. He takes out a pipe and sighs.*]

MAKAK: Moustique?

MOUSTIQUE: Eh?

MAKAK: How many years I know you now?

MOUSTIQUE: [*Shrugs.*] Three, four. Why? [*He is making the coffee.*]

MAKAK: You find that long?

MOUSTIQUE: [*Turns, stares at him.*] No. [*Pause.*] Look, we going to the market?

MAKAK: Yes. We will go.

MOUSTIQUE: [*Crouched on his heels, poking the fire.*] Well, I just getting you something hot to drink. [*Leans back, puffs on his pipe.*] Four years. And I remember how you find me.

MAKAK: True?

MOUSTIQUE: True. Drunk. Soaking drunk, with this twist foot[1] God give me. Sleeping anywhere, and one morning when you come to market, you find me in the gutter, and you pick me up like a wet fly in the dust, and we establish in this charcoal business. You cut, burn and so on, and I sell, until we make enough to buy the donkey. [*Stretches for the coffee.*] Here, pass the cup. [*Pours.*] Yes. You was the only one to make me believe a breakfoot nigger could go somewhere in this life. Four years gone last August. Drink. [*He passes the cup.*] Drink. But after that is zwip! down the mountain!

MAKAK: [*Staring into the cup.*] Moustique . . .

MOUSTIQUE: [*Patiently.*] Ehhh?

MAKAK: Listen. You take the same short-cut to come up here?

MOUSTIQUE: *Oui.*

MAKAK: The one with the wood-bridge and white falling-water?

MOUSTIQUE: The one with the wood-bridge and white falling-water.

MAKAK: The one that so narrow, two men cannot pass?

MOUSTIQUE: The one that so narrow, two men . . . Drink.

[*Sound of a flute, bird noises.*]

MAKAK: [*Rising.*] This morning, early, the moon still up, I went to pack the coals in the pit down the mountain. I will tell you. Make a white mist in the mind; make that mist hang like cloth from the dress of a woman, on prickles, on branches; make it rise from the earth, like the breath of the dead on resurrection morning, and I walking through it on my way to my charcoal pit on the mountain. Make the web of the spider be heavy with diamonds and when my hand brush it, let the chain break. I remember, in my mind, the cigale sawing, sawing, sawing wood before the woodcutter, the drum of the bull-frog, the blackbird flute, and this old man walking, ugly as sin, in a confusion of vapour, till I feel I was God self, walking through cloud, in the heaven of my mind. Then I hear this song. Not the bull-frog drum, not the whistling

---

1. Club foot. This feature suggests the figure of Eshu, the West African (Yoruba) trickster god still featured in folk mythology in many parts of the Caribbean.

of parrots. As I brush through the branches, shaking the dew, a man swimming through smoke, and the bandage of fog unpeeling my eyes, as I reach to this spot, I see this woman singing, and my feet grow roots! I could move no more. A million silver needles prickle my blood, like a rain of small fishes. The snakes in my hair speak to one another, the smoke mouth open, and I behold this woman, the loveliest thing I see on this earth, floating towards me, just like the moon, like the moon walking along her own road. Then as I start to move, she call out my name, my real name. A name I do not use. Come here, she say. Come, don't be afraid. So I go up to her, one step by one step. She make me sit down and start to talk to me.

MOUSTIQUE: Makak.

MAKAK: [*Angrily.*] Listen to me, I not mad. Listen!

MOUSTIQUE: I have all day. [*Exasperated.*]

MAKAK: Well, well . . . the things she tell me, you would not believe. She did know my name, my age, where I born, and that it was charcoal I burn and selling for a living. She know how I live alone, with no wife and no friend . . .

MOUSTIQUE: No friend . . .

MAKAK: That Makak is not my name. And I tell her my life, and she say that if I want her, she will come and live with me, and I take her in my arms, and I bring her here.

MOUSTIQUE: [*Looking around.*] Here? A white woman? Or a *diablesse?*[2]

MAKAK: We spend all night here. Look, I make something for she to eat. We sit down by this same fire. And, Moustique, she say something I will never forget. She say I should not live so any more, here in the forest, frighten of people because I think I ugly. She say that I come from the family of lions and kings.

[*Drum roll.*]

MOUSTIQUE: Well, you lucky. [*Rises wearily.*] Me and Berthilia have three bags of coal to try and sell in the market this morning. We still have eighteen shillings for Alcindor for the shovel, and Johannes promise us a bag of provisions in exchange for half a sack. You had a bad dream, or you sleep outside and the dew seize you.

MAKAK: Is not a dream.

MOUSTIQUE: [*Exasperated.*] Is not a dream? Then where she? Where she gone? [*Searches mockingly.*] Upstairs? *Gadez!*[3] You had a dream, and she is here [*Touches his own head.*], so, bring her to market. Sun hot, and people making money.

MAKAK: I tell you is no dream.

MOUSTIQUE: You remember one morning I come up and from the time I break the bush, I see you by the side of the hut, trembling and talking, your eyes like you crazy, and was I had to gather bush, light a fire and make you sweat out that madness? Which white lady? You is nothing. You black, ugly, poor, so you worse than nothing. You like me. Small, ugly, with a foot like a "S." Man together two of us is minus one. Now where you going?

---

2. She-devil.   3. Look (French creole).

MAKAK: I going to get the coals [MAKAK *goes out,* MOUSTIQUE *cleans up, talking to himself.*]

MOUSTIQUE: The misery black people have to see in this life. [*Rummaging around, blowing out the fire, putting away the cups.*] Him and his damned fits. A man not only suppose to catch his arse in the daytime but he have to ride nightmares too. Now what the hell I looking for? [*He puts his hand under the bench, then withdraws it slowly in horror.*] Aiiiiiiiiiiie. [*He turns his head and shakes his hand in frenzy as* MAKAK *comes running into the hut.*]

MAKAK: Moustique!

MOUSTIQUE: [*Shaken.*] A spider. A spider was on the sack. A big white one with eggs. A mother with white eggs. I hate those things.

MAKAK: Where it?

MOUSTIQUE: Look it. Kill it, kill it. [*Grabs his hat and pounds it.*] Salop!⁴ Salop! When it pass over my hand, my blood turn into a million needles. [*He sits back panting.*] Well. What you looking at? [*Pause.*] Is a bad sign?

MAKAK: Yes, is a bad sign.

MOUSTIQUE: Well?

MAKAK: You know what it mean.

MOUSTIQUE: Yes. [*Holds out his hand, which is trembling.*] To hell with that! I don't believe that. I not no savage. Every man have to die. It have a million ways to die. But no spider with white eggs will bring it. [*Silence.*] You believe that, of course. You . . . you . . . you living like a beast, and you believe everything! [*Points at the spider.*] That! [*Stamps on it.*]

MAKAK: She say I will see signs.

MOUSTIQUE: Yes, every damned full moon.

MAKAK: I must do what she say, which is . . .

MOUSTIQUE: Which is to sell coals! Now, where the next sack? [*He searches under the bench and withdraws a white mask with long coarse hair.*] This is she? eh? This cheap stupidness black children putting on? [*He puts it on, wiggles and dances.*] Chatafunga, deux sous pour weh,⁵ Chatafunga, deux sous pour weh.

[MAKAK *steps back.*]

MAKAK: Where you get that?

MOUSTIQUE: You ain't see?

MAKAK: [*Slowly.*] I never see it before.

MOUSTIQUE: She leave her face behind. She leave the wrong thing. Ah, Mon Dieu. [*He sits by the fire, puffing his pipe angrily, pokes the fire.*] And the damned fire out.

MAKAK: I never see this before. [*Pause.*] Saddle my horse!

MOUSTIQUE: Eh?

MAKAK: Saddle my horse, if you love me, Moustique, and cut a sharp bamboo for me, and put me on that horse, for Makak will ride to the edge

---

4. A term of abuse; also used as an exclamation.   5. Chatafunga, would give a penny to be able to see you (French creole); words of a popular song.

of the world, Makak will walk like he used to in Africa, when his name was lion!

MOUSTIQUE: Saddle your horse? Berthilia the jackass? When you will put sense in that crack coal-pot you call your head? Which woman ever look at you, once, much less a white one? Saddle your horse? I could put this beat-up tin pot on your head, cut a bamboo for a spear, make a cup of my two hands and put you on that half-starve jackass you call a horse and send you out for the whole world to laugh. But where we going? Where two black, not-a-red-cent niggers going? To war?

MAKAK: *Non.* To Africa!

MOUSTIQUE: Oh-o! Africa? Why you didn't tell me? We walking? [*He stands in the doorway.* MAKAK *hurls him away.*]

MAKAK: Out of my way, insect!

MOUSTIQUE: [*On the floor.*] You mad. To God, you mad, O God, the day come, when I see you mad. [MAKAK *crouches over him.* MOUSTIQUE *is weeping.*]

MAKAK: I hurt you, little one? Listen, listen, Moustique. I am not mad. To God, I am not mad. You say once when I pick you up like a wet fly from the dust that you would do anything for me. I beg you now, come. Don't cry! You say we will be friends until we dead. Come, don't mind the spider. If we dead, little one, is not better to die, fighting like men, than to hide in this forest? Come, then, lean on Makak. Bring nothing, we will live. [MAKAK, *who has helped* MOUSTIQUE *to his feet, takes up the bamboo spear, and goes out of the hut.*]

MOUSTIQUE: Yes, yes, master. [MOUSTIQUE *puts out the fire, picks up the sacks, stool, then the mask, and looking at the squashed spider, shudders.*] What is to come, will come. Come on, down the mountain.

   [*The hut rises out of sight,* MAKAK *striding with his spear,* MOUSTIQUE *riding ahead.*]

MOUSTIQUE: Is the stupidest thing I ever see
                 Two jackasses and one donkey,
                 Makak turn lion, so let him pass,
                 Donkey gone mad on pangola grass,
                 Haw haw haw haw haw haw hee,
                 A man not a man without misery,
                 Down the mountain!

[*Sound of the jackass braying.*]

[MAKAK *and* MOUSTIQUE *set out,* MAKAK *striding ahead;* MOUSTIQUE, *to the rhythm of flute and drum, miming the donkey. The dancer doing the burroquite, or donkey dance, circles the stage and turns the disc of the sun to moonlight. The lights dim briefly, just long enough to establish a change of mood.*]

SCENE TWO

There is a sound of wailing. White-robed women, members of a sisterhood, bearing torches, swirl onto the stage, which is now a country road. Behind them, carrying a shrouded SICK MAN *in a bamboo hammock, are four bearers and a tall frock-coated man in black silk hat,*[6] BASIL, *his face halved by white make-up. The* SISTERS, *shaking their heads, dancing solemnly and singing, form a circle described by their leader. The bearers turn and rest the* SICK MAN *down. Around him, the* SISTERS *kneel and pray, swaying, trying to exorcise his sickness. A small fire is lit by the bearers. The silk-hatted man stands back quietly, watching, while the* SISTERS *clap and sing.*

SISTERS: Before this time another year
I may be gone, Lord,
In some lonesome graveyard
Oh Lord, how long?

MOUSTIQUE: [*Enters.*] Good night. God bless you, brother.

FIRST PEASANT: Shh. God bless you, stranger. Pray with us.

MOUSTIQUE: [*Crosses himself, prays swiftly, then in the same whisper.*] . . . And give us this day our daily bread . . . and is that self I want to talk to you about,[7] friend. Whether you could spare a little bread . . . and lead us not into temptation . . . because we are not thieves, stranger . . . but deliver us from evil . . . and we two trespassers but forgive us brother . . . for thine is the kingdom and the power and the glory . . . for our stomach sake, stranger.

FIRST PEASANT: [*Keeping the whisper.*] Where you come from, stranger . . . now and at the hour of our death, amen.[8]

MOUSTIQUE: [*Whispering.*] From Monkey Mountain, in Forestiere quarter . . . and forgive us our trespasses . . . amen, is me and my friend and old man . . . in the name of the father . . . and we was sleeping in a hut by the road there, when we see you all coming, with all those lights, I thought it was the devil.

FIRST PEASANT: . . . Now and at the hour of our death, amen. . . . It ain't have much to eat, stranger. We taking the sick man down to the hospital, and it have just enough for all of us here . . . forever and ever, amen.

MOUSTIQUE: [*In a fiercer whisper.*] . . . Our daily bread, and forgive us our trespasses . . . Anything, brother. Three days now we travelling on these roads. What is wrong with him, stranger?

FIRST PEASANT: A snake. He was working in the bush, and a snake . . . but deliver us from evil . . . and no medicine can cure him.

MOUSTIQUE: So what they doing him now?

FIRST PEASANT: . . . And at the hour of our death, amen . . . they putting coals under his body to make him sweat.[9] To break the heat in his body so he can sweat . . . forever and ever, amen . . . so they making a small fire to break the sweat with coals.

MOUSTIQUE: Coals?

FIRST PEASANT: Charcoal. You ent know charcoal?

MOUSTIQUE: Charcoal is my business, stranger.

FIRST PEASANT: They bring priest, doctor they still have no hope. He have a bad fever, and he cannot sweat.

MOUSTIQUE: And who is the man there, in the tall black hat. . . . Now and at the hour of our death, amen.

6. That is, Baron Samedi (see n. 3, p. 2602).   7. Just what I want to talk about. Note the parody of Christian liturgy.   8. The final phrase of *Ave Maria*, a Catholic prayer.   9. Folk remedy for snakebite.

FIRST PEASANT: He is Basil, the carpenter, and cabinet-maker.[1] He going down to hospital too, just in case . . . amen.

[*A* WOMAN *begins singing. A* SECOND PEASANT *comes over.*]

SECOND PEASANT: Who is he, what he want?

FIRST PEASANT: He say he hungry, and could we spare him some food?

[*The* WOMEN *have begun rubbing the* SICK MAN.]

SECOND PEASANT: It have only enough for us here, brother.

[*The* WIFE *lets out a cry.*]

MOUSTIQUE: Look, I know an old man, he been living in the forest, he know all the herbs, plants, bush. He have this power and glory, and if you want, and it have no harm in that, I could fetch him for you. Look, before you pick him up again, before you choke him with that stinking medicine, before Basil the cabinet-maker get another job . . . Forever and ever, amen . . . Just something to eat and I will go and fetch him. He don't want no money, but he could cure this sick man.

SECOND PEASANT: How far he is?

MOUSTIQUE: Around the next bend, brother. All we ask is a little bread, a little piece of meat . . . for thine is the kingdom, the power and the glory . . .

FIRST PEASANT: I will ask his wife. Give him some bread. [*He goes over to the* WOMAN, *whispers, then returns.*] All right. But if you . . . [*Goes for his cutlass.*]

MOUSTIQUE: . . . At the hour of our death, amen.

[MOUSTIQUE *scuttles off. The women resume wailing, and the other men are about to raise the litter when the* FIRST PEASANT *stops them. Enter* MAKAK; *behind him,* MOUSTIQUE.]

MOUSTIQUE: Here they are, Master. [*Hurriedly gesticulating, eating the bread, he removes his hat.*] Here he is, my master. I have explain everything. Go ahead, master.

[MAKAK *enters, stands by the litter.*]

MAKAK: Let all who want this man to heal, kneel down. I ask you. Kneel!

[*They kneel, after some delay, except one or two men, whom* MOUSTIQUE *gently forces down.*]

MOUSTIQUE: The man say kneel. Kneel!

MAKAK: Now I want a woman to put a coal in this hand, a living coal. A soul in my hand. [*He places one hand on the* SICK MAN's *forehead and holds out his palm. A* WOMAN *hesitantly places a coal in his palm.* MAKAK *winces, closing his eyes. We hear him groan, then silence.*] We will wait for the moon.

[*A pause, then the full moon emerges slowly out of a cloud. We hear the dying man breathing hard.*]

> Like the cedars of Lebanon,[2]
> like the plantains of Zion,[3]
> the hand of God plant me
> on Monkey Mountain.
> He calleth to the humble.
> And from that height

---

1. That is, coffin maker. Because Basil is associated with death, he represents Baron Samedi.   2. An exotic image.   3. Makak confuses "plantain" (a species of banana) with "platane" (the plane tree).

I see you all as trees,
like a twisted forest,
like trees without names,
a forest with no roots!
By this coal in my hand,
by this fire in my veins
let my tongue catch fire,
let my body, like Moses,
be a blazing bush.
Now sing in your darkness,[4]
[*The* WOMEN *sing "Medelico."*[5]]
sing out you forests,
and Josephus[6] will sweat,
the sick man will dance,
sing as you sing
in the belly of the boat.[7]
You are living coals,
you are trees under pressure,
you are brilliant diamonds
In the hand of your God.
[*They continue singing softly.*]
Sweat, Josephus will sweat.
The fever will go!
[*They wait. Nothing happens.*]
More coal. Hotter coal.
Sweat, Josephus, sweat.
[*They put more coals in his hand.*]
And believe in me.
Faith, faith!
Believe in yourselves.
[*Silence.*]

MOUSTIQUE: [*Furious at the failure, and frightened, he circulates among them, angrily.*] Faith, faith! what happen to you? You didn't hear the man? You ain't hear the master. Sing, sing. Come on, Josephus, let that forehead shine, boy. Sing . . .

[*But the singing peters out.* MAKAK, *broken, moves away from the body. He looks at his dry palm.*]

MAKAK: Let us go on, *compère.*[8] These niggers too tired to believe anything again. Remember, is you all self that is your own enemy.

[*The* WIFE *comes forward with a gift of food, bread, vegetables, etc.*]

WIFE: I want to thank you, stranger. But what God want, nobody can change.

FIRST PEASANT: Come, come, put back on the medicine.

[*A* WOMAN *goes over to the pall and lets out a loud cry. The others turn. Laughing and weeping, she holds up her hand, which is wet from the* SICK MAN's *brow.*]

---

4. The millennial tone here is based on some of the speeches of Marcus Garvey (1887–1940), as recorded in his *Philosophy and Opinions* (1923).   5. Presumably a ritual chant.   6. The "sick man's" name, but also Jewish historian who lived in the period between the death of Jesus Christ and the destruction by the Romans of the Temple of Jerusalem, the event that set off the exile of the Jews.   7. The dire predicament of blacks is expressed in this image that combines a reference to the biblical story of Jonah in the belly of the whale with that of African slaves in the holds of slave boats during the Middle Passage.   8. Brother, comrade.

WOMAN: *I'suait! I'suait! I'suait! I'suait!* Sweat! He sweat!
[MAKAK *and* MOUSTIQUE *are apart, watching. The others rush up and in turn touch the freely sweating body and hold up their hand and rub their faces and taste the sweat, laughing and crying. One or two begin to dance. The* WIFE *bends over the man's body. The drummer and* CHORUS *join in the rhythm.*]
ALL: *I'suait!* He sweat! *I'suait! Aie ya yie!*[9]
[*The* CHORUS *picks up the sibilance.*[1] *In the dancing and drumming to "Death, Oh Me Lord!"* MOUSTIQUE *takes over and, mounting a box, shouts above the celebration.* MAKAK, *dazed at his own power, is kneeling.*]
MOUSTIQUE: Ah, ah, you see, all you.
    Ain't white priest come and nothing happen?
    Ain't white doctor come and was agony still?
    Ain't you take bush medicine, and no sweat break?
    White medicine, bush medicine,
    not one of them work!
    White prayers, black prayers,
    and still no deliverance!
    And who heal the man?
    Makak! Makak!
    All your deliverance lie in this man.
    The man is God's messenger.
    So, further the cause, brothers and sisters.
[*He opens his haversack and holds it before him.*]
    Further the cause,
    drop what you have in there.
    Look! Look! Josephus walking.
    Next thing he will dance.
[*They laugh. The* WIFE *makes him do a little dance.*]
    I tell you he dancing!
    God's work must be done,
    and like Saint Peter[2] self,
    Moustique, that's me,
    is Secretary-Treasurer.
[*During all this, they bring him gifts of food, some put money in the haversack, one man gives him the shoes he had slung around his neck.*]
    Now dance out in the moonlight,
    let him breathe the fresh air,
    let him breathe resurrection,
    go forth, and rejoice . . .
[*They take the* SICK MAN *out, dancing and singing "Death, Oh Me Lord!"* BASIL *hangs behind.* MOUSTIQUE *removes the tall hat from* BASIL *as he passes.*]
MOUSTIQUE: You don't mind, friend? Only a black hat, in exchange for a life. You see, the man heal, you ain't going to need it.

---

9. An exclamation.   1. The *s* in both *sweat* and *suait*, both with the same meaning.   2. Believed to keep the keys to the gates of Heaven.

BASIL: My work never done, friend. And that hat is my business.

MOUSTIQUE: And mine, from now on.

BASIL: We go meet again, stranger.

MOUSTIQUE: Oh, I sure of that friend. But only at the sign of a spider. [*He is counting the take in the hat.*] Three coins, earrings. Ah, a dollar. In God we trust. Like you, brother, I don't believe in credit. Now, if you was a spider . . . The coat too, pardner.

BASIL: You know where you are? [BASIL *surrenders the coat.*]

MOUSTIQUE: At a crossroads[3] in the moonlight.

BASIL: You are standing in the middle. A white road. With four legs. Think what that mean, friend. I can wait for my hat. [BASIL *exits.*]

MOUSTIQUE: A white road. With four legs. A spider. With eggs. Eggs. White eggs! [*Shouting after* BASIL.] But I still here! And I still alive! [*Laughing, he counts again.* MAKAK *comes towards him, mistaking him for* BASIL; *he stiffens.*]

MAKAK: Moustique, Moustique. Oh, is you. You frighten me. What you doing there?

MOUSTIQUE: Counting. [*He continues.*] And believe me, as the politician said, this better than working. Well, which way now, boss?

MAKAK: You see? You see what I do there? This power, this power I now have . . .

MOUSTIQUE: I see a sick man with snake bite, and a set o' damn asses using old-time medicine. I see a road paved with silver. I see the ocean multiplying with shillings.[4] Thank God. That was good, that was good. [*Mimes the healing.*] By this power in my hand. By this coal in my hand. You ain't playing you good, nuh. Here, take what you want.

MAKAK: [*Striking the hat away.*] Move that from me. You don't understand, Moustique. This power I have, is not for profit.

MOUSTIQUE: [*Picking up the hat.*] So what you want me to do? Run behind them and give them back their money? Look, I tired telling you that nothing is for free. That some day, Makak, swing high, swing low, you will have to sell your dream, your soul, your power, just for bread and shelter. That the love of people not enough, not enough to pay for being born, for being buried. Well, if you don't want the cash, then let me keep it. 'Cause I tired begging. Look, look at us. So poor we had to sell the donkey. Barefooted, nasty, and what you want me to do, bow my head and say thanks?

MAKAK: You will never understand. [MAKAK *kneels again.*]

MOUSTIQUE: What you kneeling again for? Who you praying for now? [MAKAK *says nothing.*] If is for me, partner, don't bother. Pray for the world to change. Not your friend. Pray for the day when people will not need money, when faith alone will move mountains. Pray for the day when poverty done, and for when niggers everywhere could walk upright like men. You think I doubt you, you think I don't respect you and love you and grateful to you? But I look at that moon, and it like a plate that a dog lick clean, bright as a florin, but dogs does chase me out of people yard when I go round begging, "Food for my master, food." And I does have to stoop down, and pick up the odd shilling they

---

3. The usual haunt of the Devil and of evil spirits in folk belief.　4. Old English coins.

throw you. Look, turn your head, old man, look there, and that thing shining there, that is the ocean. Behind that, is Africa! How we going there? You think this . . . [*holds up mask*] this damned stupidness go take us there? Either you let me save money for us, or here, at this crossroads, the partnership divide.

MAKAK: [*Rising*] All right, all right. But don't take more than we need. All right, which way now?

MOUSTIQUE: [*Spinning around blindly, he points.*] This way, master. Quatre Chenin Market!

[*Music. Exeunt*]

SCENE THREE

[CORPORAL *in wig and gown enters the spotlight.*]

CORPORAL: [*Infuriated.*] My lords, behold! [*Arms extended.*] Behold me, flayed and dismayed by this impenetrable ignorance! This is our reward, we who have borne the high torch of justice through tortuous thickets of darkness to illuminate with vision the mind of primeval peoples, of backbiting tribes! We who have borne with us the texts of the law, the Mosaic tablets, the splendours of marble in moonlight, the affidavit and the water toilet, this stubbornness and ingratitude is our reward! But let me not sway you with displays of emotion, for the law is emotionless. Let me give facts! [*He controls himself.*] It was market Saturday and I, with Market and Sanitation Inspector Caiphas J. Pamphilion, was on duty at Quatre Chemin crossroads. I was armed because the area was on strike.

[*Sounds of the market: cries, etc., as the* MARKET SCENE, *baskets, cloth, etc., is lowered.*]

A village market, at a crossroads, before dawn. Vendors, crates, carts, wares slung from rope. The FIRST VENDOR'*s cries, flute music. In one corner, setting up their basket-stall, a* WOMAN, *her* HUSBAND, *and two other* VENDORS *in near-rags, drinking coffee.*

WIFE: He will tell you he see it, of course, but don't mind him, he wasn't there.

MAN: You was not there yourself. [*Piles the basket.*]

WIFE: It was on the high road. The old woman husband Josephus, well, snake bite him, and they had called the priest and everything. From the edge of his bed he could see hell. Then Makak arrive—praise be God— and pass his hand so, twice over the man face, tell him to walk, and he rise up and he walk. And before that, he hold a piece of coal, so [*demonstrates*], in his bare hand, open it, and the coal turn into a red bird, and fly out of his hand.[5]

MAN: Hear her. [*Sucks his teeth.*]

[*The market is waking around them, the light widening.*]

WIFE: Then, the next day, this I cannot kiss the Bible that I see it myself, there had a small boy, he have, you know, a . . . a . . . what you call it?

MAN: Abscess.

---

5. The Wife's speech illustrates the way myths are created and propagated.

WIFE: Right. A abscess. And he was in serious, serious pain, and the boy father bring him, and he rub a piece of bluestone[6] on the boy . . . on the boy . . .

MAN: Cheek. By his cheek.

WIFE: Who telling the story, me or you? By the boy cheek, and the tooth fall out of the boy mouth, and he was well again. You want some more tea? [*She turns away.*]

SECOND WOMAN: I hear that in Micoud he hold a stone in his hand and it turn into fire.

THIRD WOMAN: Not Micoud, it was by La Rivière.[7]

SECOND WOMAN: *Eh, bien.* Wherever it was then.

MAN: [*To his wife.*] *Gardez,* Agafa! is work you working or is talk you talking?

WIFE: What happen to you? You have no manners?

SECOND WOMAN: And for all that, he not asking for nothing.

THIRD WOMAN: They say it is a dream he have.

MAN: It have man so. It have men that have powers and nobody don't know where they getting it from. I did have a uncle so.

WIFE: If you did have a uncle so, you think is basket I would be selling? [*The* WOMEN *laugh.*] It have more than a week now that thing happen with the man on the high road. Then the next day, the boy with the . . . with the . . .

SECOND WOMAN: Abscess.

WIFE: Whatever you calling it, at Micoud . . .

SECOND WOMAN: At La Rivière. He going to the sea, he must pass there. [*The* CORPORAL, *wearing a pistol; and the* MARKET INSPECTOR, *issuing certificates to the* VENDORS.]

INSPECTOR: So hence, the pistol?

CORPORAL: No, Market and Sanitary Inspector Pamphilion. *Mens sana in corpore sano.*[8] The pistol is not to destroy but to protect. You will ask me, to protect who from what, or rather, what from who? And my reply would be, to protect people from themselves, or, to put it another way, to preserve order for the people. We are in a state of emergency.

INSPECTOR: Is not because of the strikes and the cane-burning taking place in the district?

CORPORAL: No, Market Inspector Pamphilion, it is to prevent more strikes and cane-burning happening in the district. You understand?

INSPECTOR: No.

CORPORAL: Well, the law is complicated and people very simple. [*To a* VENDOR.] Morning. That's a nice pawpaw, sir.

VENDOR: *Oui, mon corporal.* [*They move on.*]

CORPORAL: You see?

INSPECTOR: That was a melon.

CORPORAL: I know. But in the opinion of the pistol, and for the preservation of order, and to avoid any argument, we both was satisfied it was a pawpaw.

INSPECTOR: I am beginning to understand the law.

---

6. Sulfur rock used in folk medicine.　　7. Both are in St. Lucia.　　8. A sound mind in a sound body (Latin).

CORPORAL: And if you know how much I would like to do for these people, my people, you will understand even better. I would like to see them challenge the law, to show me they alive. But they paralyse with darkness. They paralyse with faith. They cannot do nothing, because they born slaves and they born tired. I could spit.

INSPECTOR: They must believe in something.

CORPORAL: Believe? Let me tell you what happen. I following this rumour good. And is the same as history, Pamphilion. Some ignorant, illiterate lunatic who know two or three lines from the Bible by heart, well one day he get tired of being poor and sitting on his arse so he make up his mind to see a vision, and once he make up his mind, the constipated, stupid bastard bound to see it. So he come down off his mountain, as if he is God self, and walk amongst the people, who too glad that he will think for them. He give them hope, miracle, vision, paradise on earth, and is then blood start to bleed and stone start to fly. And is at that point, to protect them from disappointment, I does reach for my pistol. History, Mr. Pamphilion, is just one series of breach of promise. [*They have reached the basket* VENDORS.] That's a nice set of cages you have there.

VENDOR: Is a basket, Corporal.

CORPORAL: Good! I like a nigger with spirit.

WIFE: They say that he on a long walk, going through every village, on his way to the sea, looking across to Africa, and that when he get there, God will tell him what to do. [*She sings a hymn. The others join her, working.*]

INSPECTOR: They know he is coming. The rumour like a cane fire. Faith is good business. I've never seen the market so full. It's like a fair. [*And indeed the market is filling with vendors, cripples, the sick.*] From all parts of the district.

CORPORAL: The crippled, crippled. It's the crippled who believe in miracles. It's the slaves who believe in freedom.

INSPECTOR: And with music too! It's so beautiful I could cry, but I'm in uniform. My wife has rheumatism. I wonder.

[*In a corner of the market, an improvised music of sticks, clapping and a tin grater begins under the cries of the* VENDORS. *Two men dance as another sings a bongo.*[9] *The men mime a healing.*]

SINGER: I'll show you how it happen: *Il dit Levez, Makak.*[1]

VENDOR: Pepper, pepperrrrr.[2]

VENDOR: Plantainnnn!

DANCER: Woy, woy, Makak.

SINGER: *Quittez charbon en sac.*[3]

DANCER: Woy, woy, Makak.

SINGER: *Negre ka weh twop misere.*[4]

VENDOR: Cassava, cassavaaah.[5]

SINGER: *Ous kai weh ou kai weh.*[6]

DANCER: Woooh, Makak.

---

9. A Trinidadian dance.   1. He said, "Rise, Makak" (French creole).   2. Women in the market are crying out their wares.   3. Leave your bags of coal (French creole).   4. Niggers see too much misery (French creole).   5. Or manioc, a tuber that is a staple of the local diet.   6. You'll see it for yourself (French creole).

SINGER: *Il dit Levez, Makak.*[7]

DANCER: Woiee, Makak.

SINGER: *Il dit Descendre, Makak.*[8]

DANCER: Woy, Makak.

SINGER: *Descendre Morne Makak. Il dit*[9] . . .

> [*He stops, suddenly, as a small boy, a fishing pole in his hand, comes screaming into the market, huddles behind the* SINGER *and points. In the distance we hear the sound of a stick beating on a kerosene tin, and a voice roaring.*]

SINGER: What happen? What happen, son?

BOY: I went down by the bridge by the river. I was looking in the water, down so, in the water, when I turn my head and . . . and I see a man alone singing and coming up the road, beating on a pan, and singing. With a long stick in his hand, and with a big white hair on his head, and . . . and a tall black hat, coming up the road so, one by one. I drop everything and I run like monson.[1]

SINGER: *C'est lui. C'est Makak.*

CROWD: *Makak. C'est Makak.*

> [*A woman screams.* MAKAK *enters leaping, whirling in black coat and tall hat and spear. This is in fact* MOUSTIQUE *impersonating* MAKAK.]

MOUSTIQUE: *Oui. C'est Makak.*

CROWD: *Makak, c'est Makak!*

MOUSTIQUE: *Oui.* It is Makak.

> [*Limping in his stride, he moves among the* CROWD.]

Let the enemies of Africa make way.

Let the Abyssinian[2] lion leap again,

For Makak walk in frenzy down Monkey Mountain,

And God send this message in lightning handwriting

That the sword of sunlight be in his right hand

And the moon his shield.

CORPORAL: You there!

MOUSTIQUE: Who it is dare to call Makak by name? Which man dare call the lion by his name?

CORPORAL: A corporal of police.

MOUSTIQUE: [*Turning to the* CROWD.] I laugh. I laugh. A corporal of police? Makak have come to Quatre Chemin Market and neither corporal nor spiritual stopping him today! [*Pointing at the* CROWD.] *Dire, Abou-ma-la-ka-jonga.*[3]

CROWD: [*Defiantly.*] *Abou-ma-la-ka-jonga.*

MOUSTIQUE: *Faire ça.*[4] [*Gestures, with a stance.*]

CROWD: Hunh. [*They gesture like him, many laughing.*]

MOUSTIQUE: Now sing monkey! All you.

> [*Sings.*]

I don't know what to say that monkey won't do . . . Sing!

> [WOMEN, *laughing, sing "monkey" as they strut around the* CORPORAL.]

---

7. He said, "Wake up, Makak" (French creole).   8. He said, "Come down, Makak" (French creole).
9. Go down Monkey Mountain. He said . . . (French creole).   1. The wind.   2. Now Ethiopia.
3. Nonsense words used to mystify.   4. Do so (French).

MOUSTIQUE: Take note, Corporal.

INSPECTOR: This is ignorance!

MOUSTIQUE: Ignorance? It seem to me I hear a voice, a voice, the colour of milk, cry ignorance. [*Cups his ear. More laughter.*] But that voice is not the whispering of God who does pour counsel in the cup of great men ears, but just the usual voice of small-time authority. What is your name?

INSPECTOR: I am Market Inspector Caiphas J. Pamphilion.

MOUSTIQUE: Market Inspector? Well then, inspect with respect, do not be suspect, or you will be wreck. [*To* CROWD.] They calling that English, but the colour of English is white. Inspector of milk! [*The* CROWD *is delirious.*] Yes, find room in your heart to laugh, find room inside you to be happy, because Makak shall not pass this road again. His dream call him to the sea, to the shore of Africa. And he hungry and tired. The dust of thirty roads is in his throat. [*A woman brings him water.*] Daughter of heaven, Makak will remember you. But I prefer cash, as I travelling hard. Zambesi, Congo, Niger, Limpopo,[5] is your brown milk I drink, is your taste I remember, is the roots of your trees that is the veins in my hand, is your flowers that falling now from my tongue. [*He takes the bowl from the woman.*] By belief, I make blessing. But even the black sheep of God cannot go hungry. And they shall be fed. So, children of darkness, bring what you can give, make harvest and make sacrifice, bring whatsoever you have, a shilling, a yam, and put here at the mouth of God, that Makak is the tongue, and then, when all is in one bag, we shall pray. You shall fast, and I shall pray. [*He lifts the bowl high above their heads as they place a few offerings at his feet.*] Kneel, and listen while I deliver the revelation of my experience. They say I can cure. Well, I cannot cure, except you want to be, except you believe that I can cure . . . Just put it down there, brother. Seven days and seven nights me and my friend, that great man, Moustique, who fall sick by the wayside, six days and six nights we leave Monkey Mountain, crossing hot pasture and dry river, like two leaves blowing in the hot wind. You will say how the divine sadness can fall on such men? A poor charcoal-seller that cannot see the light? *Eh bien,* listen, listen, Inspector of milk, and corporals of the law. One billion, trillion years of pressure bringing light, and is for that I say, Africa shall make light. And now . . . now . . . Makak shall sprinkle you with this water, for the cure is in yourself, and then, then he must go where his feet calling him. First, Makak will drink.

    [*They look to him. He lifts the bowl reverently to his mouth, then drops it with a cry. He seems shaken.*]

Is nothing. A spider. A spider over my hand. I cannot bear these things.

CORPORAL: A spider? A man who will bring you deliverance is afraid of a spider?

MOUSTIQUE: I not 'fraid of nothing. It just make me jump.

CORPORAL: Then show us. You. You, Basil, the carpenter, take it and bring it for the warrior Makak. Take it.

---

5. Rivers in Africa.

[BASIL *looks for the spider, holds it in his cupped palm and brings it towards* MAKAK *and places it on his body.* MAKAK *winces, enduring it. Shuddering.*]

BASIL: [*As he gets nearer, looks into his eyes.*] You cannot run fast enough, eh? Moustique! That is not Makak! His name is Moustique!

MOUSTIQUE: Eh?

[*A man comes nearer.* MOUSTIQUE, *for that is who it is, stares at him, sweating.* BASIL *steps forward.*]

LABOURER: Wait! Wait! It is Basil the carpenter. Let him speak.

[*A rustling stillness.*]

BASIL: I have little to say. Why should I talk? Look for yourselves. The tongue is on fire, but the eyes are dead.

[MOUSTIQUE *cowers, mumbling.* BASIL, *sometimes moving the spider around* MOUSTIQUE'*s body, circles him, talking slowly, slowly waving his arms. During this, he removes the silk hat.*]

You have seen coals put out by water. What comes from that mouth is vapour, steam, promises without meaning. The eyes are dead coals. [*The* CROWD *mutters.*] And the heart is ashes. [*He confronts* MOUS-TIQUE.] Ah, friend, when the spear of moonlight had pinned the white road till its legs were splayed like a spider [*He opens one palm.*], I tried to direct you. Everywhere you were shown signs. In the hut that first morning, in the white shrieking of the funeral procession, in the mask of the cold moon, but you would not listen.

MOUSTIQUE: Who in hell is he? What he want? What he want?

BASIL: I want nothing, pardner. And I go get it. You have one chance! If this is Makak, if this man will deliver the revelation of his experience, then let him show you your hope! Ask him to share it with you! Show them! Show them what you have learnt, *compère!*

CROWD: Yes! Show us! Show us!

CORPORAL: [*Shouting.*] What is your name? Your name not Moustique?

CROWD: Show us! Show us!

MOUSTIQUE: [*Pushing* BASIL *aside.*] You know who I am? You want to know who I am? Makak! Makak! or Moustique, is not the same nigger? What you want me to say? "I am the resurrection, I am the life"? "I am the green side of Jordan," or that "I am a prophet stoned by Jerusalem," or you all want me, as if this hand hold magic, to stretch it and like a flash of lightning to make you all white? God after god you change, promise after promise you believe, and you still covered with dirt; so why not believe me. All I have is this [*Shows the mask.*], black faces, white masks![6] I tried like you. Moustique then! Moustique! [*Spits at them.*] That is my name! Do what you want!

LABOURER: And you come here to rob your own people? What is one more mosquito? What is one more man?

MOUSTIQUE: Die in your ignorance! Live in darkness still! You don't know what you want!

[CROWD *grows angrier.*]

---

6. The title of a book by Frantz Fanon, which examines the problems arising from the split personality of blacks, especially those in the Caribbean, assimilated to Western culture.

LABOURER: Well then take that from us! [*Clouts him.* MOUSTIQUE *falls.*]

CROWD: Kill him! Break his legs! Beat him! Kill him!

[*They beat him to a noise of sticks rattling, tins banging and scream-ing women. The* CORPORAL *stands apart, then he moves towards them.*]

CORPORAL: All right, all right! *Assez, assez!* I say enough. Go home. Go home before I arrest all of you. Go home!

[*They disperse, leaving* MOUSTIQUE *crumpled among the heap of offerings.* BASIL *picks up his hat, puts it on, then waits.*]

INSPECTOR: Why you didn't stop them?

CORPORAL: All those people. Do you want me to get killed? Come on. I'll buy you a drink. You look afraid. Funny, I can't stand cockroaches myself.

INSPECTOR: It was a spider. Harmless.

CORPORAL: Well, whatever it was. Come on, let's go.

[MAKAK, *dusty and tattered, enters the market.*]

MAKAK: Moustique? Moustique? [*He looks around, among the wreckage, and then discovers* MOUSTIQUE, *sprawled on a heap.*] Moustique. What happen? What happen to you? What they do you? [*He lifts up* MOUS-TIQUE*'s head.*] Oh God, what they do you, little man?

MOUSTIQUE: Pardon, Makak. Pardon. To see that this is where I must die. Here, in the market. The spider, the spider. [*He shudders.*] Go back to Monkey Mountain. Go back, or you will die like this.

MAKAK: You will not die.

MOUSTIQUE: Yes, I will die. I take what you had, I take the dream you have and I come and try to sell it. I try to fool them, and they fall on me with sticks, everything, and they kill me.

MAKAK: How you could leave me alone, Moustique? In all the yards[7] and villages I pass, I hear people saying, Makak was here, Makak was here, and we give him so and so. If it was for the money, I didn't know.

MOUSTIQUE: No. You didn't know. You would never know. It was always me, since the first time in the road, where . . . always me who did have to beg . . . to do . . . [*He passes out.* MAKAK *shakes him.*]

MAKAK: Moustique, Moustique.

MOUSTIQUE: Go back, go back to Monkey Mountain. Go back.

MAKAK: No, she tell me what I must do.

MOUSTIQUE: Let me die, Makak, I hurting and I tired, tired . . .

MAKAK: You will not die, you must not die!

MOUSTIQUE: Every man have to die . . . [*He faints again.* MAKAK *shakes him.*]

MAKAK: Then look. Look then . . . Open your eyes, try and open your eyes, and tell me what you see. Look, look, then, if you dying, tell me what you see. Open them. Tell me and I will preach that. Tell me!

MOUSTIQUE: I see . . . I see . . . I see a black wind blowing . . . A black wind . . . [*He dies.*]

MAKAK: [*Forcing his eyes open.*] And nothing else? Nothing? Let me look in them, let me look, and I will keep the last picture of your eyes in

7. Neighborhoods.

mine, let me be brave and look in a dead man eye, Moustique . . . [*He peers into* MOUSTIQUE*'s gaze and what he sees there darkens his vision. He lets out a terrible cry of emptiness.*]

MAKAK: Aiieeeeee. Moustique!

[*In the darkness the drums begin, and shapes, demons, spirits, a cleft-footed woman, a man with a goat's head, imps, whirl out of the darkness around* MAKAK, *and the figure of a woman with a white face and long black hair of the mask, all singing. They take the body on a litter.*]

CHORUS: Death, O death, O me Lord,
             When my body lie down in the grave,
             Then me soul going shout for joy.

[*To a frenzied climax as* MAKAK *writhes on the ground in a fit, and the music dies.*]

Part Two

Let us add, for certain other carefully selected unfortunates, that other witchery of which I have already spoken: Western culture. If I were them, you may say, I'd prefer my mumbo-jumbo to their Acropolis. Very good: you've grasped the situation. But not altogether, because you aren't them—or not yet. Otherwise you would know that they can't choose; they must have both. Two worlds; that makes two bewitchings; they dance all night and at dawn they crowd into the churches to hear Mass; each day the split widens. Our enemy betrays his brothers and becomes our accomplice; his brothers do the same thing. The status of "native" is a nervous condition introduced and maintained by the settler among colonised people with their consent.

                              Sartre: Introduction to "The Wretched
                                  of the Earth," by Frantz Fanon

SCENE ONE

The cell. Night. TIGRE *and* SOURIS *in their cell.* MAKAK *in his. The* CORPORAL *enters, banging a tin plate with a cup.*

CORPORAL: All right, all right! Chow-time! Stand back. Up against the bars there! I ain't want you all chewing up my hand for three green figs and a sliver of salfish.[8] Hold this plate. [TIGRE *steps forward, accepts plate, steps back.*] You next. [SOURIS *steps forward, accepts plate and cup, then steps back.*] How is the old king?

SOURIS: He's been there moaning, muttering to himself, since he come in. Sometimes he sing, sometimes he letting out a cry, sometimes even a little dance, and half the time in gibberish. One more green fig, Corporal?

CORPORAL: No more figs. Any more you get will have to be in your mind. A figment of your imagination, so to speak.

SOURIS: Look at him. Just look at him. I feel sorry for him. Let him go, Corporal.

---

8. Saltfish (salted cod), a staple slave food that has remained the mainstay of the popular diet.

CORPORAL: I am an instrument of the law, Souris. I got the white man work to do. Besides, if he crazy he dangerous. If he is not, a night in jail will be good for his soul. [*Goes over to the old man's cell.*] Is chow time, King-Kong. Hey. Food, food, old man.

TIGRE: Bring me damn supper, Lestrade! I have me rights, you know!

CORPORAL: Your rights? Listen, nigger! according to this world you have the inalienable right to life, liberty, and three green figs. No more, maybe less. You can do what you want with your life, you can hardly call this liberty, and as for the pursuit of happiness, you never hear the expression, give a nigger an inch and he'll take a mile? Don't harass me further. I didn't make the rules. [*To* MAKAK.] Now, you. Come for this plate!

[MAKAK *gropes forward.*]

TIGRE: So what? Is against the law to be poor?

CORPORAL: Here, hold this. [*Turns to* TIGRE.] Don't tell me about the law. Once I loved the law. I thought the law was just, universal, a substitute for God, but the law is a whore, she will adjust her price. In some places the law does not allow you to be black, not even black, but tinged with black.

TIGRE: And that is what eating out your soul, Lestrade. That is why you punishing this man. You punishing your own grandfather.[9] Let him go home.

MAKAK: Let me go home. I will pay you. I have money. I have money that I hide . . . all of you.

CORPORAL: Bribery! [*Pulling the old man through the bars.*] Listen, you corrupt, obscene, insufferable ape, I am incorruptible, you understand? Incorruptible. The law is your salvation and mine, you imbecile, you understand that. This ain't the bush. This ain't Africa. This is not another easy-going nigger you talking to, but an officer! A servant and an officer of the law! Not the law of the jungle, but something the white man teach you to be thankful for.

MAKAK: It is the law that kill my friend. You let them kill my friend.

CORPORAL: I don't know what you talking about.

MAKAK: You lie . . . You lie. Right here, in the market . . . you let them kill my friend.

SOURIS: My figs, Corporal, my figs!

CORPORAL: Shut up! Shut up, nigger!

SOURIS: [*Dancing.*] O you beast! You filt'y fascist beast! I hungry!

MAKAK: I will give you all the money I have to go back home. O Moustique, you did warn me. I open my eyes and I see nothing. I see man quarrelling like animals in a pit. The spider there for all of us. I see us in this pit . . .

CORPORAL: How long he been like this?

TIGRE: Since you bring him in. After the first fit. Is like he is living over and over a bad dream he had.

SOURIS: I hungreeeeeeeeeee!

CORPORAL: All right! All right! The law says I must feed you. I will

9. Who is black; thus, by implication, Lestrade is punishing himself.

feed you. But God, remind me to ask for a transfer to civilization. [*Exit.*]

TIGRE: [*In a single spot.*] You hear what he say? Ain't I tell you old men so does have money hide away. We must help the old bitch escape, track him to Monkey Mountain, then put him out of his misery. Eat your food when it come, but dream about money, Souris. Dream hard and good. Shhhhhh.

TIGRE: Tell us about the money. About that . . . and Africa.

MAKAK: You will laugh at me.

SOURIS: Where is it?

TIGRE: We believe your dream, Makak. Tell us . . . and . . . look . . . You want to get out of here?

MAKAK: Yes, yes, but how?

TIGRE: Never mind how. You want to get out?

MAKAK: [*Wearily.*] Yes . . .

TIGRE: Listen. First we must kill the Corporal.

SOURIS: I know now you crazy.

TIGRE: You know why you must kill him? Because she tell you to, old man, remember, in the dream? Lion, she call you. And lion don't stop to think. The jaw of the lion, that is the opening and closing of the book of judgement. When the moon in quarter, you know what Africans say . . .

SOURIS: Where you get all that?

MAKAK: Tell me, my son, what?

TIGRE: That the jaw of the sun, that is the lion, has eaten the moon. The moon, that is nothing, but . . . a skull . . . a bone . . .

[MAKAK, *growling, begins to pace his cage.*]

SOURIS: Pappy! Eh?

TIGRE: How else can you prove your name is lion, unless you do one bloody, golden, dazzling thing, eh? And who stand in your way but your dear friend, Corporal Lestrade the straddler, neither one thing nor the next, neither milk, coal, neither day nor night, neither lion nor monkey, but a mulatto, a foot-licking servant of marble law? He cause Moustique to die. He turn his back on that. Believe me, like your friend saw the spider, I see it clearly. You bastard son of a black gorilla, you listening?

SOURIS: Look, look, he standing still.

TIGRE: He have something in his hand.

SOURIS: The same mask again.

TIGRE: No. No . . . friend . . . As the moon unsheathe its blade, I swear by the crucifix of the handle, the old black gentleman has unclouded . . .

SOURIS: [*In wonder.*] A knife!

TIGRE: Look how it shines, old man. Like the sea. Like silver. Think of the bright blood! Think like the lion that is dazzled by pity for only a second! Call the Corporal . . . Then, when the moon come out again, pretend you going mad . . . Yes. You are in the forest now, you are hunted, tired. Your heavy, hanging tongue is dry as sand. Your muscles thunder with exhaustion. You want to drink. Fall down, ask for water . . . a drink . . . Pretend you catch a fit. And then the keys, the keys! [*Loudly.*] Corporal! Corporal! Shhhhhh . . . Go back to sleep . . . Corporal!

[CORPORAL *enters with a red towel, wiping his hands.*]

CORPORAL: What you want, Tigre?

TIGRE: I cannot sleep . . . I . . . I thirsty . . . And the old man over there, groaning and coughing like a sick lion all night . . . Between him and the moon they keeping me up. The night hot like a forest fire. He must be thirsty too.

[*The* CORPORAL *comes to* MAKAK's *cell.*]

CORPORAL: Old man . . . you thirsty? [*He goes nearer.*]

TIGRE: For blood, perhaps. Not you who call him lion?

CORPORAL: He who? that ape? What you want to drink, old man . . .

MAKAK: [*With a cry.*] Blood! Blood! Blood! Lion . . . Lion . . . I am . . . a lion [*He has grabbed the* CORPORAL, *stabbing him. Then he hurls him to the floor.*]

TIGRE: The keys! The keys!

[MAKAK *takes the keys and opens the cells.*]

MAKAK: [*Holding* TIGRE *and* SOURIS *and near-weeping with rage.*] Drink it! Drink it! Drink! Is not that they say we are? Animals! Apes without law? O God, O gods! What am I, I who thought I was a man? What have I done? Which God? God dead, and his law there bleeding. Christian, cannibal, I will drink blood. You will drink it with me. For the lion, and the tiger, and the rat, yes, the gentle rat, have come out of their cages to breathe the air, the air heavy with forest, and if that moon go out . . . I will still find my way; the blackness will swallow me. I will wear it like a fish wears water . . . Come. You have tasted blood. Now, come!

TIGRE: Where? To Monkey Mountain?

MAKAK: [*Laughing.*] Come! [*Looks at body.*]

[*They exit.*]

CORPORAL: [*Clutching the towel to his wound, rises. Single spot.*] Did you feel pity for me or horror of them? Believe me, I am all right. Only a flesh wound. Times change, don't they? and people change. Even black people, even slaves. He made his point, you might say. [*Drawing out a knife.*] But this is only what they dream of. And before things grow clearer, nearer to their dream of revenge, I must play another part. We'll go hunting the lion. Except . . . [*Takes down a rifle.*] . . . They're not lions, just natives. There's nothing quite so exciting as putting down the natives. Especially after reason and law have failed. So I let them escape. Let them run ahead. Then I'll have good reason for shooting them down. Sharpeville?[1] Attempting to escape. Attempting to escape. Attempting to escape from the prison of their lives. That's the most dangerous crime. It brings about revolution. So, off we go, lads! [*Drums. Exit chanting.*]

SCENE TWO

The forest. Enter MAKAK, SOURIS, TIGRE.

MAKAK: Come, we will rest here. I know this forest. Smell it. Smell it, it speaks to your blood.

---

1. A reference to the 1960 massacre in South Africa of Africans protesting against the pass laws. These laws required blacks in South Africa to show identity cards when in the cities.

SOURIS: Yes, it saying, your damn foot bleeding. It saying, "You hungry?"
And the answer is yes. You know where we are, in all this damn darkness?

MAKAK: I can read the palm of every leaf. I can prophesy from one crystal
of dew.

SOURIS: Good! Then read what we having for supper.

MAKAK: I know the nature of fire and wind. I will make a small fire. Here,
look, you see this plant? Dry it, fire it, and your mind will cloud with a
sweet, sweet-smelling smoke. Then the smoke will clear. You will not
need to eat.

TIGRE: You crazy ganga[2]-eating bastard, I want meat. Flesh and blood.
Wet grass. Come on, come on, show us the way to Monkey Mountain.
The Corporal hunting us.

MAKAK: The first quality of animals is stillness. Keep still. I can hear the
crack of every leaf. I know all the signals of insects. It will be a small
fire. [*He moves off.*]

TIGRE: Come on, come on, old man. We have to reach Monkey Mountain.

MAKAK: Monkey Mountain?

TIGRE: I . . . I mean Africa.

SOURIS: We should 'a eat first, then killed the Corporal. [*Whispers.*] You
really think he have money? Look at him! Half-man, half-forest, a
shadow moving through the leaves.

TIGRE: Just do as he say. That's all. This is his forest. He could easily lose
us. You didn't see how he stabbed the Corporal? He coming back. Let's
mix ourselves in his madness. Let's dissolve in his dream. [*As* MAKAK
returns with twigs, bush, etc.] Ah, Africa! Ah, blessed Africa! Whose
earth is a starved mother waiting for the kiss of her prodigal, for the kiss
of my foot. Talk like that, you fool.

SOURIS: How you will take us to Africa? What we will do there? In the
darkness, now that I can see nothing, maybe, it is there I am. When I
was a little boy, living in darkness, I was so afraid, it was as if I was
sinking, drowning in a grave, and me and the darkness was the same,
and God was like a big white man,[3] a big white man I was afraid of.

MAKAK: Here, you are at home, my son. One of the forest creatures.

SOURIS: And in the darkness, big man as I am, I still afraid of him. You
'fraid God, Tigre?

TIGRE: I not 'fraid no white man.

SOURIS: Well, God help us. I really frighten. Like a child again. [MAKAK
lights the fire. They watch him.] And that is what they teach me since
I small. To be black like coal, and to dream of milk.[4] To love God, and
obey the white man.

TIGRE: [*Whispering.*] Enough! Enough! You going crazy too?

SOURIS: How we will go, old man? How we will go?

MAKAK: Once, when Moustique asked me that, I didn't know. But I know
now. What power can crawl on the bottom of the sea, or swim in the

2. Marijuana.   3. God is usually portrayed as an old white man with a flowing beard in Western iconography.   4. This goes to the heart of the play's theme of the alienated consciousness of the black
subject.

ocean of air above us? The mind, the mind. Now, come with me, the mind can bring the dead to life, it can go back, back, back, deep into time. It can make a man a king, it can make him a beast. Can you hear the sea now, can you hear the sound of suffering, we are moving back now . . . [*The* CHORUS *chants, "I going home."*] Back into the boat, a beautiful boat, and soon, after many moons, after many songs, we will see Africa, the golden sand, the rivers where lions come down to drink, lapping at the water with their red tongues, then the villages, the birds, the sound of flutes.

SOURIS: Yes, yes, I see it. I see it!

MAKAK: When your eyes open, you will be transformed, as if you have eaten a magic root.

[SOURIS *moves off.*]

TIGRE: We will need money to go there, uncle. To buy a boat. A big, big boat that will take everybody back, or otherwise, is back into jail. Back where we were! It's drizzling. Where Souris gone? Where that damn thief? Is drizzling and I cold. And the light of the coals making figures in the forest. The trees take one step nearer. The leaves are eyes and tongues. And there are eyes or diamonds winking in the bush. Old man, if I go with you, what will I find? If they don't hang us for killing the Corporal.

MAKAK: Look at those coals. When I look in the fire, I see visions. The fire will talk with its bright tongue. Tell me what you see?

TIGRE: [*Huddled, shivering.*] I see hell. I see people black like coals, twisting and burning in hell. And I see me too. The rain will put it out. Where Souris? I hungry. By tomorrow they will catch us, and three of us will hang. *Tiens,*[5] what is that? But you, they will let you go, because you old, ugly and crazy. Where that mouse? Where that damn Souris? What I will find in Africa?

MAKAK: Peace.

TIGRE: Peace? Piece of what? [*The squawk of an animal.*] What was that? What in hell is happening? Where Souris gone? For the first time in my life, I feeling frighten. Come, come on, you old bastard, let us move on.

MAKAK: [*Suddenly grabbing him.*] Then, when we get there, I will make you my general. General Tigre, and when my enemies come, I will say fight with him, because he is a man, a man who know how to hate, to whom the life of a man is like a mosquito, like a fly. [*Claps his hands at an insect, and drops it in the fire.* TIGRE *laughs.*] And the fire is up to God.

[SOURIS *enters, holding up a dead chicken.*]

SOURIS: Well then, God best keep the fire going, 'cause look what drop in through the garden. [*Drops chicken.*] And then, ay, what is this, what is this? [*Feels around in his large coat.*] O Blessed Saviour, a miracle. Ground provisions, look, potatoes, one yam, never take more than you need, for the Lord will provide, a hand of small onions, and a little pepper. [*Spills them onto the ground.*] So, how is the king?

5. By the way (French).

[MAKAK *has drawn apart, talking to himself.*]

TIGRE: Mad like a ant. He just make me general.

MAKAK: [*Trotting up to them.*] Good, my men. Good, my men. The Lord
on the day he dead [*opening his arms*] had two thief by him.

SOURIS: Only one went in heaven. [*Plucking the chicken.*]

TIGRE: You. Because I look in the fire, and I see myself burning there,
forever and forever, amen.

SOURIS: Amen. [MAKAK *walks away again, regally, mumbling.*] So what we
will do with him?

TIGRE: Let us eat first. I will peel the yams. [*He takes out a knife and they
watch* MAKAK *as they work.*]

SOURIS: Mad, mad, mad.

TIGRE: You see his eyes? That is the eyes of a man who will kill you in
your sleep. They looking at you, and like you not there. Once we letting
him believe what he is, is all right. Otherwise . . . [*Draws the knife
across his throat.*] Look, his blanket fall off.

SOURIS: I will fix it.

[MAKAK *has sat down on a log.* SOURIS *gingerly goes up to the fallen
blanket and places it around the old man's shoulders.*]

MAKAK: My crown.

SOURIS: [*Twisting a vine and crowning him.*] Crown. And don't bother
call me for your sword, until the damn yams boil.

MAKAK: [*In a thundering voice.*] Feed my armies!

SOURIS: Pardon?

MAKAK: Feed my armies! Look, look them there. [*Rises and gestures
beyond the fire.*] They waiting for their general, their king, Makak, to
tell them when to eat. Salute them. You see them where they are?
Salute them. Let my generals salute them. Like me.

TIGRE: Salute, *Couillon.*[6] [SOURIS *salutes.*]

MAKAK: General Tigre?

TIGRE: Look me, general. [*Rises, salutes.*]

MAKAK: Attention, and listen. I want to speak to my men. I want to tell my
armies, you can see their helmets shining like fireflies, you can see their
spears as thick as bamboo leaves. I want to tell them this. That now is
the time, the time of war. War. Fire, fire and destruction. [*He takes his
spear and dips it in the fire.*] Fire, death. [SOURIS *and* TIGRE *withdraw
in the darkness, and the sky grows red.*] Fire. The sky is on fire. Makak
will destroy.

SOURIS: [*Still saluting.*] Eh, bien. We reach Africa.

MAKAK: Shh! Somebody coming. The fire! Come. Into the bushes! Shh!
Somebody coming.

[*Enter the* CORPORAL *armed, alone.*]

CORPORAL: Ho! Ho! My beaters, ho! My head. My wound. Dusty blade.
Gangrene. Delirium! Thrash that bush there! Build a fire for my safari.
Set down the white man's burden. My back is breaking. Whisky and
soda, you smoke-black sod. And start smoking out the mosquitoes.
Bwana[7] Lestrade is tired. Once I knew this jungle like the black of my

6. Fool (French).   7. Master (Swahili).

hand. What-ho, chaps, more lights. Come dawn like thunder[8] and we'll blow their brains out. [*He kneels down beside the fire.*] Ah! Ashes! Ashes and naked footprints! Black footprints. Let me stalk and think. Aha! Oho! Over here! Over here, bring me my Mannlicher, then a gimlet. [*Looking down.*] Uh-huh. Footpad of tiger, ferrule of rat, spoor of lion,[9] and all leading up the garden path to ... [*Looking up.*] To Monkey Mountain.

[*Wild cackling laughter.*]

Gibberish! No fear, lads! Steady on! A calm blue eye acquired this Empire. Mine, a tawny yellow. English! You animals! English! English!

[*More laughter, coughs, howls.*]

Animals! Savages! [*Quietly.*] My wound! I'll pack my wound with earth! Niggers? God, the fire's gone out, lads! The light of civilization's finished. M'tbutu! Zola![1] Who's there? The moon, the moon, the pockmarked moon alone, the siphylitic crone. Who's that?

[*In the moonlight,* BASIL *comes out of the bushes.*]

Who are you? I'm going mad, goddammit. Stiff upper lip. Who're you in that ridiculous gear? Shoot! Or I'll stop! Stop or I'll run. It's Basil, is it? Time up. Twilight of Empire, eh? Night of the what's what? Who in hell are you? *Qui moune?* [BASIL *waits, his face hidden.*] You speak Swahili? Creole? Papiamento? Urdu? Ibo?[2] Who you?

BASIL: I am Basil, the carpenter, the charcoal seller. I do not exist. A figment of the imagination, a banana of the mind ...

CORPORAL: Banana of the mind, figment of the ... ho! That's pretty good. Goodbye. [*He goes.*]

BASIL: You have one minute to repent. To recant. To renounce.

CORPORAL: Repent? Renounce what?

BASIL: You know, Lestrade. You know.

[TIGRE *and* SOURIS *emerge.*]

CORPORAL: My mind, my mind. What's happened to my mind?

BASIL: It was never yours, Lestrade.

CORPORAL: Then if it's not mine, then I'm not mad.

BASIL: And if you are not mad, then all this is real.

CORPORAL: Impossible! There is Monkey Mountain. Here is the earth. Banana of the mind ... ha ... ha ... ha ...

TIGRE: What happen to him? What he looking at?

SOURIS: I don't know, but he look crazy. It must be the wound. Or ... Is the moon. Is the moon ...

BASIL: Confess your sins, Lestrade. Confess your sins. Strip yourself naked. Look at your skin and confess your sins.

CORPORAL: Which sins? What sins?

TIGRE: [*Stepping nearer.*] At the edge of death you'll remember them. Confess!

8. An echo of a defiant speech by Macbeth in Shakespeare's play (5.5).   9. Another echo of *Macbeth* (4.1), this time of the witches' formula for their brew.   1. An African name, though possibly a reference as well to the 19th-century French writer. *M'butu*: this African-sounding name is intended to emphasize his point.   2. The language of a major ethnic group in Nigeria. *Swahili*: widely spoken in East Africa. *Creole*: the French pidgin spoken in the Caribbean and used in this play. *Papiamento*: the Dutch pidgin spoken in Surinam and other former Dutch colonies in South America. *Urdu*: spoken in India.

CORPORAL: [*As the creatures circle him.*] Mooma, don't cry, your son in
the grave already. Our son in the grave already, Mooma, don't cry . . .
But he's crying, Mother. Mother India, Mother Africa, Mother Earth,
he is crying. Why? Why? [*Tries to sing.*] "By the light of the silvery
moon." [*Weeps.*] Whistle, boys, it's only death. [*Whistles weakly.*] The
earth, the earth was a black child holding a balloon, and somebody cut
it.

BASIL: Fifteen seconds.

TIGRE: Who de hell he talking to? I see nothing.

SOURIS: I see nothing too.

MAKAK: He is talking to nothing.

BASIL: Ten seconds.

CORPORAL: [*Flatly, like an accustomed prayer.*] All right. Too late have I
loved thee, Africa of my mind, *sero te amavi,* to cite Saint Augustine[3]
who they say was black. I jeered thee because I hated half of myself, my
eclipse. But now in the heart of the forest at the foot of Monkey Mountain [*The creatures withdraw.*] I kiss your foot, O Monkey Mountain.
[*He removes his clothes.*] I return to this earth, my mother. Naked,
trying very hard not to weep in the dust. I was what I am, but now I am
myself. [*Rises.*] Now I feel better. Now I see a new light. I sing the
glories of Makak! The glories of my race! What race? I have no race!
Come! Come, all you splendours of imagination. Let me sing of darkness now! My hands. My hands are heavy. My feet . . . [*He rises,
crouched.*] My feet grip like roots. The arteries are like rope. [*He
howls.*] Was that my voice? My voice. O God, I have become what I
mocked. I always was, I always was. Makak! Makak! forgive me, old
father.

MAKAK:[*Stepping forward.*] Now he is one of us.

CORPORAL: [*Looking up.*] Grandfather. Grandfather. Where am I? Where
is this? Why am I naked?

MAKAK: Because like all men you were born here. Here, put this around
you. [*He covers him with the sack.*] What is this?

CORPORAL: A gun.

MAKAK: We don't need this, do we?

　　[*TIGRE and SOURIS approach cautiously.*]
They reject half of you. We accept all. Rise. Take off your boots.
Doesn't the floor of the forest feel cool under your foot? Don't you hear
your own voice in the gibberish of the leaves? Look how the trees have
opened their arms. And in the hoarseness of the rivers, don't you hear
the advice of all our ancestors. When the moon is hidden, look how
you sink, forgotten, into the night. The forest claims us all, my son. No
one needs gloves in his grave.

TIGRE: Tie up the bastard and let him find his way back.

SOURIS: So how it feel to be a nigger, Corporal? Animals. Savages! Niggers!
Stop turning the place into a stinking zoo! [*Hops around.*] Who is the
monkey now, Lestrade? You bitch! I long had this for you. [*Jumps on
him, wrestling.*] And this! And this!

---

3. Philosopher of the Catholic Church (A.D. 354–430), a native of Hippo in North Africa. *Sero te amavi:*
Latin original of the phrase just pronounced. The passage dwells on the ambivalence of West Indians and
New World blacks generally to their African ancestry.

MAKAK: Enough! You hearing me? Enough! I came unto my own and they turned me away. Fighting, squabbling among yourselves. I have brought a dream to my people, and they rejected me. Now they must be taught, even tortured, killed. Their skulls will hang from my palaces. I will break up their tribes.

TIGRE: [*Picking up the rifle.*] All right. Up till now I been playing this game. Shadows and shapes been crossing my mind, I have felt my body altered by firelight, and I watched all three of you, like animals paralysed by the glare of a headlamp. About three miles back there is Quatre Chemin jail, remember that, Souris, is where you and I come from. Up there is the damn mountain, I don't know if you have money, uncle, but I intend to find out. [*Cocks trigger.*] Come on now, move! Souris, get the Corporal belt, and tie up his hands. Souris! You ent hear me?

SOURIS: No, Tigre.

TIGRE: What happen to you? You know who talking to you? You know what you are? Don't make me have to shoot.

SOURIS: You can't shoot us all, Tigre.

TIGRE: Whose side you on, nigger?

SOURIS: I believe this old man.

TIGRE: What the hell you talking about?

SOURIS: I believe I am better than I am. He teach me that. [*Picks up a rock.*] Now you know me, Tigre. You will have to shoot.

TIGRE: You know what you saying? You going break up our friendship for one worthless, lunatic old charcoal-burner?

SOURIS: He teach me more than you ever teach me, Tigre. His madness worth more to me than your friendship. Are you sure where you are, Tigre, are you sure who you are?

TIGRE: I'm a criminal with a gun, in the heart of the forest under Monkey Mountain. And I want his money.

MAKAK: Money . . . That is what you wanted? That is what it is all about . . . money. . . ?

TIGRE: Shut up! Africa, Monkey Mountain, whatever you want to call it. But you first, father, to where the money buried. Go on. You too, Lestrade. Walk.

MAKAK: [*Moves forward, then stops.*] I am lost. I have forgotten the way. Who are you?

TIGRE: My name is Tigre.

MAKAK: But you, like him, had your own dream of money. The tiger eats and lies down content, but tomorrow he must rise again. Think, Tigre, money is not what you want. I know now you cannot reach that rainbow weighted like scales with your bags of fool's gold, no more than I can ever reach that moon; and that is why I am lost.

SOURIS: You will bring us so far, then abandon us? You will surrender that dream?

MAKAK: [*Holding out the mask.*] I was a king among shadows. Either the shadows were real, and I was no king, or it is my own kingliness that created the shadows. Either way, I am lonely, lost, an old man again. No more. I wanted to leave this world. But if the moon is earth's friend, eh, Tigre, how can we leave the earth. And the earth, self. Look down and there is nothing at our feet. We are wrapped in black air, we are black, ourselves shadows in the firelight of the white man's mind. Soon, soon it will be morning, praise God, and the dream will rise like vapour, the shadows will be real, you will be corporal again, you will be thieves, and I an old man, drunk and disorderly, beaten down by a Bible, and tired of looking up to heaven. You believe I am lost now? Shoot, go ahead and shoot me. Death is the last shadow I have made. The Carpenter is waiting.

[BASIL *waits in the shadows.*]

SOURIS: But your dream touch everyone, sir. Even in those burnt-out coals of your eyes, there is still some fire. Dying, but fire. If a wind could catch them again, if some wind, some breath. [*He looks into his eyes.*]

MAKAK: And these tears will put them out. I have left death, failure, disappointment, despair in the wake of my dreams. [*The* CORPORAL *has picked up* MAKAK'S *spear. He faces* TIGRE.]

[*A dance begins.*]

The tribes! The tribes will wrangle among themselves, spitting, writhing, hissing, like snakes in a pit.

CORPORAL: I seen death face to face, Tigre, look! He's behind you. Turn, and he turns with you!

TIGRE: You turn savage, red nigger?[4]

SOURIS: Stop them, stop them. [*They are circling each other.*]

MAKAK: Locked in a dream, and treading their own darkness. Snarling at their shadows, snapping at their own tails, devouring their own entrails like the hyena, eaten with self-hatred. O God, O gods, why did you give me this burden?

SOURIS: For God sake, Tigre!

CORPORAL: Look, he's behind you!

TIGRE: Ha, ha, there's nothing behind me.

BASIL: Tigre! [TIGRE *turns. The* CORPORAL *leaps onto him with a cry and drives the spear through him.*]

MAKAK: [*Over* TIGRE'*s body.*] The tribes! The tribes! One by one, they will be broken. One will sink, and the other rise, like the gold and silver scales of the sun and the moon, and that is named progress.

CORPORAL: Now we must press on, old man. He is out of the way. This is jungle law. Come on, come on.

MAKAK: Yes, but where?

CORPORAL: Where? Anywhere! Onward, onward. Progress. Press on. We need that cry, and those who do not bend to our will, to your will, must die. You, help him up.

SOURIS: He doesn't know where to go.

CORPORAL: Put him in front. He's a shadow now. Let him face the moon and move towards it. Let him go forward. I'll take over. Come on. Go. Drag that thing there into the bush. [SOURIS *takes away* TIGRE'*s body and* BASIL *helps him.*] Now, where to, old father? No. We cannot go back. History is in motion. The law is in motion. Forward, forward.

SOURIS: Where? The world is a circle, Corporal. Remember that.

[*They move off, wearily. The* CORPORAL *remains behind in a single spot.*]

---

4. A mulatto.

CORPORAL: Bastard, hatchet-man, opportunist, executioner. I have the black man work to do, you know. I breathe over the shoulder of your leaders, I hang back always at a decent distance, but I am there to observe that the law is upheld, that those who break it, president or prince, will also be broken. I have no ambition of my own. I have no animal's name. I simply work. And if a niche in history opens for me, what else can I do, for the sake of the people, Vox Populi,[5] but to step into it? I don't know where we are going. But forward, progress! When you reach the precipice, simply step aside. That right, Basil? You see, he is not here. Now, let splendour, barbarism, majesty, noise, slogans, parades, drown out that truth. Plaster the walls with pictures of the leader, magnify our shadows, moon, if only for a moment. Gongs, warriors, bronzes! Statues, clap your hands you forests. Makak will be enthroned!

SCENE THREE

Apotheosis. Bronze trophies[6] are lowered. Masks of barbarous gods appear to a clamour of drums, sticks, the chant of a tribal triumph. A procession of warriors, chiefs and the wives of MAKAK *in splendid tribal costumes gather, chanting to drums.*

CHORUS: These are the conquests of Makak,
    King of Limpopo, eye of Zambezi, blazing spear.[7]
WARRIORS: Aieeee!
CHORUS: Who has bundled the tribes like broken sticks,
    Masai, Zulu, Ibo, Coromanti,[8]
    Who has scattered his enemies like grain in the wind.
WARRIORS: Aieeee!
CHORUS: Drinkers of milk from the Mountains of the Moon.
    Who has held captivity captive,
    Who has bridled the wind,
    Who has fathered the brood of the crocodile.
    Whose eye is the sun,
    Whose plate is the moon at its full,
    Whose sword is the moon in its crescent.
    Praise him!
WARRIORS: [*Chanting in antiphon.*][9] Aieeee!
CHORUS: And we are his wives
    For whom the sea knits its wool,
    Robes without seam
    Who is brother to God.
    [*The volume increases.*]
WARRIORS: Aieee!
CHORUS: Drinker of rivers,
    In whom Gods waken,
    Die, are reborn.

5. Voice of the people (Latin); from *vox populi, vox Dei* (the voice of the people is the voice of God).
6. Presumably from Benin, an African country noted for its bronze art. *Apotheosis:* literally, the process of deification; here, the full accomplishment of Makak's dream.   7. The Chorus employs here and below the style and imagery of African praise poems.   8. Ethnic groups in Africa.   9. Part singing, with one group responding to another.

WARRIORS: [*Leaping in the air.*] Aieeee!

CHORUS: Borne by the hands of the four corners of the earth on his golden
stool.[1]

> [MAKAK, *carried on a magnificent litter, enters. A golden stool is set
> down. The* CORPORAL, *also garbed magnificently in tribal robes,
> enters, with* SOURIS *some distance behind.*]

CORPORAL: [*Softly.*] He whose peace is the counsel of the sea, gentler than
cotton.

CHORUS: Whose hands are washed continually in milk,
Whose voice is the dove,
Whose eye is the cloud.

CORPORAL: Who shall do unto others as to him it was done.
Behold too, Basil, a dark ambassador,
Behold Pamphilion, apotheosised.

CHORUS: Who drew the thief to his bosom,
The murderer to his heart,
Whose blackness is a coal,
Whose soul is a fire,
Whose mind is a diamond,
Dispenser of justice,
Genderer and nourisher to a thousand wives,
Praise him!

> [*All have assembled. The* CORPORAL *steps forward, then addresses*
> MAKAK.]

CORPORAL: Inventor of history! [*Kisses* MAKAK's *foot.*]

MAKAK: I am only a shadow.

CORPORAL: Shh. Quiet, my prince.

MAKAK: A hollow God. A phantom.

CORPORAL: Wives, warriors, chieftains! The law takes no sides, it changes
the complexion of things. History is without pardon, justice hawk-swift,
but mercy everlasting. We have prisoners and traitors, and they must be
judged swiftly. The law of a country is the law of that country. Roman
law, my friends, is not tribal law. Tribal law, in conclusion, is not
Roman law. Therefore, wherever we are, let us have justice. We have
no time for patient reforms. Mindless as the hawk, impetuous as lions,
as dried of compassion as the bowels of a jackal. Elsewhere, the swiftness of justice is barbarously slow, but our progress cannot stop to think.
In a short while, the prisoners shall be summoned, so prepare them,
Basil and Pamphilion. First, the accused, and after them, the tributes.

> [*The prisoners are presented.*]

Read them, Basil! They are Noah, but not the son of Ham, Aristotle,
I'm skipping a bit, Abraham Lincoln, Alexander of Macedon, Shake-
speare, I can cite relevant texts, Plato, Copernicus, Galileo and perhaps
Ptolemy, Christopher Marlowe, Robert E. Lee, Sir John Hawkins, Sir
Francis Drake, The Phantom, Mandrake the Magician. [*The* TRIBES *are
laughing.*] It's not funny, my Lords, Tarzan, Dante, Sir Cecil Rhodes,
William Wilberforce, the unidentified author of The Song of Solomon,

---

1. The ceremonial stool, made of wood with gold leafing. It is believed to have been brought down from
Heaven by the mythical founder of the Ashanti empire and to house the soul (*sunsum*) of the nation.

Lorenzo de Medici, Florence Nightingale, Al Jolson, Horatio Nelson,[2] and, but why go on? Their crime, whatever their plea, whatever extenuation of circumstances, whether of genius or geography, is, that they are indubitably, with the possible exception of Alexandre Dumas, Sr. and Jr., and Alexis, I think it is Pushkin,[3] white. Some are dead and cannot speak for themselves, but a drop of milk is enough to condemn them, to banish them from the archives of the bo-leaf and the papyrus, from the waxen tablet and the tribal stone. For you, my Lords, are shapers of history. We wait your judgement, O tribes.

TRIBES: Hang them!

BASIL: It shall be done. The list continues *ad nauseam.*[4] [*His voice fades under a medley of screams and a drum roll of execution.*] So much for the past. Consider the present. Petitions, delegations, ambassadors, signatories, flatterers, potentates, dominions and powers, sects, ideologies, special dispensations, wait politely on him fearing revenge. [*Reads from a ledger.*] An offer to the Pope.

    [MAKAK *shakes his head.*]

TRIBES: No!

CORPORAL: Unanimous negative. [*He throws away the letter.*]

BASIL: An invitation to be President of the United States?

    [MAKAK *shakes his head.*]

TRIBES: Impossible!

    [CORPORAL *throws away the letter.*]

CORPORAL: Unanimous negative.

BASIL: An apology in full from the Republic of South Africa.

    [MAKAK *shakes his head, the pace increases.*]

CORPORAL: Unanimous negative! [*Throws away the letter.*]

BASIL: An offer to revise the origins of slavery. A floral tribute of lilies from the Ku Klux Klan. Congratulations from several Golf and Country Clubs. A gilt-edged doctorate from the Mississippi University. The Nobel Peace Prize. One thousand dollars from a secret admirer. An autograph of Pushkin. The Stalin Peace Prize. An offer from the UN. A sliver of bone from the thigh of Lumumba.[5] An offer from Hollywood.

    [*Throws all the letters away.*]

TRIBES: No!

CORPORAL: Unanimous negative! Now, the prisoners.

    [MOUSTIQUE, *bleeding and broken, is brought in.*]

MOUSTIQUE: How am I guilty?

CORPORAL: You have betrayed our dream.

MOUSTIQUE: I am talking to you, Makak. [MAKAK *looks away.*] Again, I must die, again?

CORPORAL: This is a lion. You are an insect whining in his ear.

MOUSTIQUE: Look around you, old man, and see who betray what. Is this what you wanted when you left Monkey Mountain? Power or love?

---

2. The names listed here are from Western history and culture, which were made familiar to colonized blacks through the educational system.   3. Russian writer (1799–1837), whose grandfather came from Africa. Alexandre Dumas Sr. (1802–1870) and Alexandre Dumas Jr. (1824–1895), French writers of romances, had African ancestry.   4. Excessively (Latin).   5. Patrice Lumumba (1925–1961), first prime minister of Congo (now Zaire), killed during the civil war that broke out shortly after the country's independence in 1960.

Who are all these new friends? You can turn a blind eye on them, because now you need them. But can you trust them for true? Oh, I remember you, in those days long ago, you had something there [*Touching his breast.*], but here all that gone. All this blood, all this killing, all this revenge. So go ahead, kill me. Go ahead. Is for the cause? Go ahead then.

MAKAK: I will be different.

MOUSTIQUE: No, you will be no different. Every man is the same. Now you are really mad. Mad, old man, and blind. Once you loved the moon, now a night will come when, because it white, from your deep hatred you will want it destroyed.

MAKAK: My hatred is deep, black, quiet as velvet.

MOUSTIQUE: That is not your voice, you are more of an ape now, a puppet. Which lion? [*Sings: I don't know what to say this monkey won't do . . .*]

CORPORAL: You waste time, your Majesty. We have other cases, and justice must be done. Even tribal justice. What says the tribunal?

TRIBES: Next!

MAKAK: Take him away! [*Softly.*] Moustique! Moustique!

CORPORAL: And now a pale, pathetic appeal for forgiveness.

[*The* APPARITION *is brought in.*]

MAKAK: Who are you? Who are you? Why have you caused me all this pain? Why are you silent? Why did you choose me? O God, I was happy on Monkey Mountain.

CORPORAL: She, too, will have to die. Kill her, behead her, and you can sleep in peace.

MAKAK: The moon sinks in the sea and rises again, no sea can extinguish it. I will never rest. Tell me please, who are you? I must do what my people want.

CORPORAL: Bring me a blade, Souris. This is a job for a king, and, your Majesty, you cannot escape it. [SOURIS *brings him a curved sword.* CORPORAL *puts it in* MAKAK'*s hand.*] You will displease your wives, your sons, the vision is exhausted, her silence is enough.

MAKAK: Let the rest go. Leave us alone.

CORPORAL: You don't mind, I have to record this for history. For the people. If General Souris and I remain behind. I understand, I understand. It is a private matter. Out, wait outside. We will show you her head.

[*All withdraw except* SOURIS, CORPORAL, BASIL, MAKAK *and the* WOMAN.]

MAKAK: Is she there? Do you see her now?

CORPORAL: Of course. Don't you, General?

SOURIS: Plain as the moon.

CORPORAL: Time, time, your Majesty.

[MAKAK *steps down and stands over the* WOMAN, *whose back is towards him.*]

MAKAK: I remember.

CORPORAL: We have no time. We have no time.

MAKAK: Please. [*He looks at the moon, then he lifts the back of her hair.*] I remember, one day, when I was younger, fifty years old, or so, I wake up, alone, and I do not know myself. I wake up, an old man that morning, with my clothes stinking of fifty years of sweat. My eye closing with gum, my two hands trembling, trembling when I open them, so, and I look in them, with all the marks like rivers, like a dead tree, and I ask myself, in a voice I do not know: Who you are, *nègre?* I say to the voice and to my hands, with the black coal in the cuts, I say, your name is what—an old man without a mirror. And I went in the little rain barrel behind my hut and look down in the quiet, quiet water at my face, an old, cracked, burn-up face, with the hair turning white. And it was Makak. So I say, if you dead now, if you dead now. Well what? No woman will cry for you, no child will look at your face in death, as if it was the first time. The water in the rain barrel will show the cloud changing, and, as it have no memory, will forget your face. It will show the hawk passing smaller than a fly, and it will lick a dead leaf with its tongue, but you will go under this earth and burn and change as if you were a coal yourself, *charbonnier.*[6] A big, big loneliness possess me, as if I was happy once, and strong, but could not remember where, as if, in some way, I was not no charcoal-burner, God be blessed, but a king, and I feel strongly to go down the mountain, and to reach the sea, as if the place I remember was across the sea. Before I do this thing, tell me who she is.

CORPORAL: She, she? What you beheld, my prince, was but an image of your longing. As inaccessible as snow, as fatal as leprosy. Nun, virgin, Venus, you must violate, humiliate, destroy her; otherwise, humility will infect you. You will come out in blotches, you will be what I was, neither one thing nor the other. Kill her! Kill her!

MAKAK: I cannot! I cannot!

CORPORAL: She is the wife of the devil, the white witch.[7] She is the mirror of the moon that this ape look into and find himself unbearable. She is all that is pure, all that he cannot reach. You see her statues in white stone, and you turn your face away, mixed with abhorrence and lust, with destruction and desire. She is lime, snow, marble, moonlight, lil-ies, cloud, foam and bleaching cream, the mother of civilization, and the confounder of blackness. I too have longed for her. She is the colour of the law, religion, paper, art, and if you want peace, if you want to discover the beautiful depth of your blackness, nigger, chop off her head! When you do this, you will kill Venus, the Virgin, the Sleeping Beauty. She is the white light that paralysed your mind, that led you into this confusion. It is you who created her, so kill her! kill her! The law has spoken.

MAKAK: I must, I must do it alone.

CORPORAL: All right!

[SOURIS, CORPORAL *and* BASIL *withdraw.*]

MAKAK: [*Removing his robe.*] Now, O God, now I am free.

[*He holds the curved sword in both hands and brings it down. The* WOMAN *is beheaded.*]

[BLACKOUT]

---

6. One who makes charcoal from burnt wood.   7. An allusion to a play by the English dramatist John Webster (1580?–1634).

EPILOGUE

The cell bars descend. TIGRE, SOURIS *and* MAKAK *in jail.*

MAKAK: Felix Hobain, Felix Hobain . . .

[*The* CORPORAL *returns into the spotlight, holds up the mask.*]

TIGRE: Mooma, don't cry,
                          You son in the jail a'ready
                          You son in the jail a'ready . . .

CORPORAL: What is your name?

MAKAK: Hobain . . . My name is Felix Hobain . . .

CORPORAL: I must itemise these objects. What is your race? What is or has been your denominational affiliation?

SOURIS: What he in for, Corporal?

MAKAK: My name is Felix Hobain . . . Hobain, I believe in my God. I have never killed a fly. And I cannot sleep. Where is General Tiger? Where is General Rat?

TIGRE: All night, with no sleep.

CORPORAL: Your name is Hobain. I must mark that on the charge.

MAKAK: Charge? What charge?

SOURIS: Drill him, Constable, drill him . . .

CORPORAL: Shut up! Charge? The reason why you in jail. It is only for a night, and the moon is growing thin. When the sun rises, I will let you go. You live up there? on Monkey Mountain?

MAKAK: Yes. *Oui.* Hobain. Sur Morne Macaque, *charbonnier.* I does burn and sell coals. And my friend . . . well, he is dead . . . Sixty-five years I have. And they calling me Makak, for my face, you see? Is as I so ugly.

TIGRE: Get a lawyer, old man, to fix your face.

CORPORAL: I see uglier than that already, friend.

MAKAK: Then why am I here? What happen to me?

CORPORAL: Drunk and disorderly. You break up the shop of Felicien Alcindor yesterday, Saturday, on market day. I watch you quarrelling, preaching in the market. You insulted a friend of mine, Market Inspector Caiphas J. Pamphilion. You called a poor carpenter an agent of death. Then you start drinking, and before you cause more damage, I bring you in here. You had a rough night, friend. But is a first offence. Now, what is this? [*Holds up the mask.*] Everybody round here have one. Why you must keep it, cut it, talk to it?

TIGRE: You like white woman, eh, old man? I can imagine your dreams . . .

SOURIS: Look, look, look, I see it. The face of the sun moving over the floor. Is morning . . .

CORPORAL: Niggers, cannibals, savages! Stop turning this place into a stinking zoo. Believe me, old man [*Unlocking the cell.*], it have no salvation for them, and no hope for us. [MAKAK *steps out.*] You want this? [MAKAK *looks at the mask.*]

MAKAK: And what day is this?

CORPORAL: It is market Saturday, it was, when you came. It is Sunday morning now. [*Singing can be heard.*] That noise is from the Church of Revelation. You want this?

[MAKAK *shakes his head.*]

SOURIS: Go with God, old man.[8]

TIGRE: What happen, nigger, you going soft in your old age?

CORPORAL: Go on. Go home. There, Monkey Mountain. Walk through
the quiet village. I will explain everything to Alcindor. Sometimes, there
is so much pressure . . . Go on. You are free. It is your first offence.

MAKAK: Moustique . . . There was a man called Moustique.

CORPORAL: Listen to them, listen to the sisters. All night. Well, some find
it in rum, some find it in religion.

[*A voice outside: "Corporal! Corporal!"*]

MOUSTIQUE: [*Entering with crocus bags.*] You have a man here named
Felix Hobain. They calling him Mak . . .

MAKAK: Is you? Is you, Moustique?

MOUSTIQUE: Time and tide wait for no man. What happen to you? What
he do, Corporal? You must forgive him. He live alone too long, and he
does catch fits. When the full moon come, a frenzy does take him. Ah,
Felix Hobain, poor old Felix Hobain. Since yesterday morning I looking
for you. I went up the Mountain, you wasn't at home. And you know
Alcindor promise us two bags? What happen? I hear how you mash up
Alcindor café . . . I have Berthilia outside . . . If is any damage, Corporal,
I will pay you for it. Sometimes, in life, Corporal, a man can take no
more . . . He don't know why he born, why he suffer, and that is what
happen . . .

CORPORAL: He had a fit here. I thought he was drunk. A night in jail, I
thought, would fix him.

MOUSTIQUE: He is a good man, Corporal. Let me take him where he
belong. He belong right here.

CORPORAL: Here is a prison. Our life is a prison. Look, is the sun.

TIGRE: My breakfast, Lestrade. I want my damn breakfast. And I want
blood. Meat, you understand?

SOURIS: Walk with God, grandfather. Walk with God.

MAKAK: [*Turning to them.*] God bless you both. Lord, I have been washed
from shore to shore, as a tree in the ocean. The branches of my fingers,
the roots of my feet, could grip nothing, but now, God, they have found
ground. Let me be swallowed up in mist again, and let me be forgotten,
so that when the mist open, men can look up, at some small clearing
with a hut, with a small signal of smoke, and say, "Makak lives there.
Makak lives where he has always lived, in the dream of his people."
Other men will come, other prophets will come, and they will be
stoned, and mocked, and betrayed, but now this old hermit is going
back home, back to the beginning, to the green beginning of this world.
Come, Moustique, we going home.

CHORUS: I going home, I going home,
                           I going home, I going home,
                           I going home, I going home,
                           To me father's kingdom . . .

[MAKAK *and* MOUSTIQUE *are walking back towards the Mountain.*]

[CURTAIN]

---

8. English rendering of *Vaya con Dios* (Spanish farewell).

KAMAU BRATHWAITE
born 1930

When Kamau Brathwaite's *Rights of Passage* appeared in 1967, it was hailed as a landmark in West Indian literature. Its fame derived from its powerful and original statement of African-Caribbean experience presented in its full historical stretch: from the distant African past, through the era of slavery, to the contemporary circumstances of the Caribbean population. The volume also announced a major new voice in Caribbean poetry written in English, bringing into the language a distinctive idiom marked by the inflexions and rhythms of West Indian speech and the forms of black music both in the West Indies and in North America. The connection between Brathwaite's sustained exploration of the situation of black people in the New World and the formal innovations he adopted to convey its tensions becomes evident in the alternation of lyrical passages with expressive breaks in voice and rhythm that render palpable the discontinuities within black historical experience. But although the poems are dominated by a sense of predicament arising from a troubled history, the final note of the volume is, paradoxically, affirmative:

> Sharp thorn
> against toe
> hard rock
>
> under heel
> feet stretched
> into stride
> made you a man
>
> again.

These lines sound the keynote of Brathwaite's poetry, which is at once a narrative of his people's confrontation with adversity and a formulation of their resolve to endure and prosper. For him, the history of Africans in the New World, and especially in the Caribbean, may have been one of pain and loss, but it initiated a process of self-re-creation in a new environment. That this endeavor has been animated largely by a sense of a racial and cultural connection to the ancestral homeland, whose presence in the islands is manifested in the life and spirituality of the common people, indicates for him a deep current of authentic being that runs beneath the prevailing social arrangements in the Caribbean and contradicts the claims of the official culture, reflecting Western values, to represent the ideal of African-Caribbean self-expression. For not only has the African substratum offered black West Indians strategies of survival in the past, but also it contains the promise of their revitalization in the present. Brathwaite's sentiments on this question, voiced in *Timehri* (1974), are a matter of public record:

> In the Caribbean, whether it be African or Amerindian, the recognition of an ancestral relationship with the folk or aboriginal culture involves the artist in a journey into the past and hinterland which is at the same time a movement of possession into the present and future. Through this movement of possession we become ourselves, truly our own creators, discovering word for object, image for word.

The conviction underlying this statement may be the driving force of Brathwaite's writings. It grew out of the circumstances of a singular career that has enabled him, as a West Indian separated from his African background, to recover this background and to appreciate its continued vitality in his native West Indies. Born Lawson Edward Brathwaite in 1930 in Barbados, an island whose landscape recalls the English countryside in the summer but has a predominantly black population, Brathwaite grew up in Bridgetown, the capital, where he received his primary education. He went on to Harrison College, an elite school in the secluded heart of the island, where he was put through the standard colonial curriculum, with its Western orientation. Upon passing the terminal examinations with distinction, he was awarded a scholarship to Cambridge University and left for England in 1950. Brathwaite has explained that, although his literary interests were already formed when he entered the university, he majored in history because he sought to understand the past that had shaped him as a West Indian. Though Brathwaite's studies at Cambridge could hardly provide him with ready answers to his questions, they laid the foundation for the imaginative and moral grasp of history from which the themes of his poetry would proceed. After graduation in 1953, he spent another year studying for a teacher's certificate; following a tradition of West Indians in the British colonial service, he left for the Gold Coast (now Ghana) to take up a position as education officer.

Brathwaite arrived in the Gold Coast at a turning point in modern African history. This was the era of decolonization, and the territory, which had been at the forefront of the nationalist movement in Africa, was in a state of transition from colony to independent nation. As with nationalism everywhere, the claims for political autonomy in Africa were legitimized by a cultural affirmation that sought to reverse the demoralizing effects of colonial ideology. Cultural nationalism in the Gold Coast itself had been forwarded since the early years of the century by a group of indigenous scholars. One of the most prominent among these was the historian J. B. Danquah, who recalled in his works African achievements and in particular revived the creation myths of the Akan-speaking people, who inhabit the central and southeastern parts of Ghana and the neighboring Ivory Coast. Another scholar, the jurist John Mensah-Sarbah, stressed the sacredness of customary law in traditional society and its continuing relevance to communal life. Brathwaite became acquainted with the works of these and other scholars who challenged the presuppositions of colonial rule. Of immediate interest for him as a poet was the work of Kwabena Nketia, whose researches into Akan music and oral poetry drew attention to their formal complexity and their function in the renewal of the collective consciousness around a cluster of consecrated symbols. The influence of the new scholarship gave impulse to an impressive cultural revival, of which the Ashanti Empire became the principal focus, its prestige undimmed despite its subjugation by the British, and its public rituals, centered on its famous golden stool, the object of devoted and regular observance. The revival fostered throughout the country a resurgence of spirit, encapsulated in the term *African personality*, which served as rallying cry for the recovery of the continent's dignity. Thus, at the accession to independence in 1957 under Kwame Nkrumah, the colony took the name *Ghana*, in a conscious gesture to reclaim the historical legacy associated with the West African medieval empire of that name.

During Brathwaite's eight-year sojourn in Ghana, he familiarized himself with the oral tradition and cultural practices of the Akan, with whom his postings afforded him prolonged contact. The experience revealed to him an indigenous African civilization to which he could relate, as an essential component of his own West Indian inheritance. Above all, the enlivening effect exerted by this kind of reaffirmation on a people of the black race became a determining factor in the cultural reappraisal he later offered to his West Indian compatriots. Appointed in 1960 to the textbook department of the Ministry of Education, he began to write children's books adapted to local conditions and based on indigenous lore, and

completed a play, *Odale's Choice*, which was later produced by the Trinidad Theatre Workshop. On his return to the West Indies in 1962, Brathwaite was
appointed a tutor in the Department of Extra-Mural Studies of the University of
the West Indies at its branch in St. Lucia. The following year, he moved, as lecturer in history, to the Mona campus of the university, in Kingston, Jamaica. His
poems began to appear in various journals, notably *Bim*, the venerable literary
journal that has played a signal role in the development of English-speaking West
Indian literature. These early poems were later revised and published in *Rights of
Passage*, which was soon followed by *Masks* (1968) and *Islands* (1969). The
organic unity of the three volumes compelled their republication in 1973 as a
single volume, under the general title *The Arrivants: A New World Trilogy*.

Meanwhile, Brathwaite had obtained a Ph.D. in 1968 from the University of
Sussex; his dissertation was titled *The Development of Creole Society in Jamaica,
1771–1820* and was published in 1973. His academic career had been developing
alongside his literary activities, and when he founded the cultural journal *Savacou*
in 1970, his reputation was considerable, established through not only his poetry
but also his lectures and essays, the most important of which have now been collected in *Roots* (1993). These reflect the scope and intensity of the intellectual and
cultural crusade he had embarked on to enlist what he saw as the restorative potential of folk culture, especially in its African dimension, for Caribbean self-knowledge. He was also active in promoting younger English-speaking Caribbean writers
through a series of anthologies devoted to their work. He rose to become professor
of social and cultural history at the University of the West Indies, a post he held
until retirement in 1991. After taking up a series of visiting positions in American
universities, he returned to full-time academic life in 1993 as professor of comparative literature at New York University, where his colleague the African novelist
Ngugi wa Thiongo gave him the African name by which he is now known. The
recipient of numerous awards and fellowships, including the Guggenheim, Brathwaite was named the winner in 1994 of the highly regarded Neustadt Prize.

The three volumes of *The Arrivants* owe their unity to the poet's effort to formulate responses to the issues raised by the black presence in the Americas. The
triadic structure, formed by the cycle of home, departure, and return, is already
fully contained in *Rights of Passage*. In this first volume, the motif of the journey
that governs the thematic progression of the sequence is established: the poems
compose a kaleidoscope of impressions of the black condition in America, framed
between a reenactment, in the prelude, of the epochal moments of African destiny
and the poet's meditation, in the epilogue, on their terminal phase for him and
his people in the West Indies. The succeeding volumes expand the themes
broached in the first, *Masks* with particular reference to the historical drama of
the black race in Africa, and *Islands* with respect to its implications for the Caribbean.

Rights of Passage marks the point of departure of the adventure recorded in the
sequence. The tragic sense of history that runs through the volume is articulated
in the annunciatory poem, *New World A-Coming*:

> Click lock
> you fire-
> lock fore-
> arm fire-
> arm flashed
> fire and our firm
> fleshed, flame
> warm, fly
> bitten warriors
> fell. . . . .

Fire
falls walls, fashions
these fire-
locks darker than iron,
and we filed down the path
locked in a new
clinked silence of iron.

The aftermath of this catastrophe from which black experience flows constitutes the burden of the volume. It is made up of a series of tableaux that detail the historical predicament of the black race, forced by conquest and enslavement from its original homeland into exile in the Americas. The individual portraits and vignettes of daily experience and the shifting modulations of tone exemplify the modes of accommodation of black people to their situation in America. The variations on the journey motif by which this presentation is developed become associated with jazz, which suggests a constantly improvised existence and a rootlessness:

Never seen
a man
travel more
seen more lands
than this poor
path-
less harbourless
spade.

The quest for an integrated consciousness felt in *Rights of Passage* translates for the poet into a dream of home and prompts his pilgrimage, of which *Masks* is a record, to the historical and cultural sources of the self, symbolized by Africa. Brathwaite revisits in this volume a history both collective and personal—hence the antiphonal structure of the volume, which places in thematic and expressive relation the two voices of the poet's mode of address: that of the institutional memory of African oral tradition, and that of the poet himself as he seeks entry into the stream of history the tradition commemorates.

Brathwaite brings into play in *Masks* the full force of his historical imagination. His reconstruction in *Pathfinders*, the opening section of the volume, of an Akan story of Exodus draws on the Akan myth of origin but invests the account of their tribulations with the quality of felt experience. The section retraces the forced departure of the Akan from their original abode near the Red Sea and their migration westward across the Nile Valley through the Sahara and then south to the West African forest. In the next section, *Limits* (printed here), the poet relives their struggle with nature, compounded by human perversities, to fashion a distinctive mode of life. The title of this section designates the area of Akan historical being, bounded by desert and sea, and denotes the overlapping of time and space in the unfolding of history. The sea emerges in the final poem, *White River*, as a symbol of the boundlessness of time and of the provisional nature of all human arrangements. More pointedly, as the determining element of the encounter between Africa and Europe, the sea becomes a figure of the ironies of history as they have affected the Akan. The sea thus comes to have meaning for the poet not only as the gateway to exile but also as the path of return, for it links his island abode to the ancestral homeland and offers him, after centuries of separation, the possibility of a reintegration into the ancestral culture.

Masks commemorates origins, but it does not present a mythical or sentimental vision of Africa. The particularity of its evocations indicates an understanding of the complex factors that have gone into the African experience and bind it to human experience everywhere.

The *Arrivants* was followed by *Other Exiles* (1975), a transitional volume between the first trilogy and Brathwaite's second, consisting of *Mother Poems* (1977), *Sun Poem* (1982), and *X/Self* (1987). The second trilogy, whose central reference is the poet's native Barbados, brings a new intensity to the fusion of large social and moral concerns with an ancestralism that underwrites the poet's vision of hope for his people. The vigor Brathwaite attains in these three volumes confirms the deeply rooted power of inspiration in all his poetry.

Gordon Rohlehr, *Pathfinder: Black Awakening in "The Arrivants" of Edward Kamau Brathwaite* (1981), is a detailed study of the first trilogy. Maureen Warner-Lewis, *Edward Kamau Brathwaite's "Masks": Essays and Annotations* (1992), is an indispensable guide to the cultural background and references of the second volume of the trilogy; the introductory essay provides an excellent analysis of Brathwaite's themes and of his poetic technique. Lloyd W. Brown, *West Indian Poetry* (1984), covers the poetry up to *The Arrivants*; Nathaniel Mackey, *Discrepant Engagement* (1993), and J. Edward Chamberlin, *Come Back to Me My Language* (1993), contain extensive discussions of Brathwaite's entire work to date.

PRONOUNCING GLOSSARY

The following list uses common English syllables to provide rough equivalents of selected words whose pronunciation may be unfamiliar to the general reader.

Akuapim: *ah-kwah-peem*

Akuse: *ah-koo-say*

Ananse: *ah-nahn-see*

Golokwati: *goh-loh-kwah-tee*

Kaneshie: *kah-neh-shee*

Koforidua: *koh-foh-ree-jwah*

Kpandu: *kpahn-doo*

Krachi: *krah-chee*

nkyekyere: *en-cheh-chreh*

Nsuta: *en-soo-tah*

Pong: *kpawng*

Shai: *shah-ee* (or *shy*)

Techiman: *teh-chee-mahn*

Limits

I

The Forest

1

Like walls the forest stops us.
Over the ford at Yeji[1] it was waiting:
tangled squat mahogany outriders[2] and then the dense, the
dark green tops, bright   5
shining standing trunks:
wawa, dahoma, esa and
odum;[3] the doom
of the thick stretching green.

---

1. A town, on the river Volta in eastern Ghana, marking the transition from open savannah to forest.
2. These tropical trees are described as *outriders* because they are few and scattered, merely dotting the sparse vegetation; but they announce the onset of denser vegetation.   3. Species of tropical trees.

Leaves gathered darkness; no
pathway showed the way.   10
The trunks grew tall and
taller, dark and darker; earth
now damp, fern cool, moss
soft. We hacked our way   15
through root and tendril, climber
shoot and yellow clinger. This
was the pistil[4] journey into moistened gloom. Dews
dripped, lights twink-   20
led, crickets chirped and still
the dark was silence, still
the dark was home. We
scorched, we raked, we
settled; cleared path,   25
cut clearing, burnt the dry rot
out of withered wood to make this farm.
And at night, so that no harm
would come from dark still heavy on us,
made this fire: fire-   30
flies[5] from sticks, from cinders; and we
sang:
in praise of those who journey
those who find the way

those who clear the path   35
those who go on before us

to prepare the way.

We sang of warmth and fires,
bodies touching, eyes of embers,[6] watching.

Where are the open spaces now   40
clear sky, the stars, horizons' distances?

We sang of warmth and fires,
bodies safe and touching.

                            2

But the lips remember
temples, gods and pharaohs,[7]   45

gold, silver ware; imagination
rose on wide unfolded wings.

But here in the dark,
we rest:

time to forget   50
the kings;

---

4. The straight stem in the center of the flower from which the fruit develops.   5. That is, sparks from the burning wood.   6. That is, bloodshot with lack of sleep. A reference to guards posted to watch over the village and, more broadly, to the anxieties of its inhabitants.   7. Rulers of ancient Egypt.

time to forget
the gods.

That fat man
with the fire-   55

light's grease
that dances

on his belly—
belly button

bunged[8]—is he   60
the king

or glutton?
He lives

on human
blood[9]   65

and dies
in human

blood;
our empire's

past of stone   70
and skulls

demands it.
And Ra,[1]

the sun
god's gold,   75

demanded blood
to make it

sacred.
Time to forget

these kings.   80
Time to forget

these gods.
The jewelled sun

has splintered
on these leaves.   85

The moon-
light rusts.

Only the frogs wear jewels
here; the cricket's chirp is

---

8. Closed up.   9. Literally, in the sense of human sacrifice, and metaphorically, in the sense of the
heavy burden of toil the ancient rulers imposed on the masses, exemplified by the death of the slaves who
were forced to construct the royal tombs.   1. The sun god of ancient Egyptian mythology.

emerald; the praying mantis'   90
topaz pleases; and termites'

tunnel eyes illuminate the dark.
No sphinx[2] eyes close and dream

us of our destiny; the desert
drifting certainties outside us.   95

Here leaf eyes shift, twigs
creak, buds flutter, the stick

becomes a snake;[3] uncertainties adrift
within us.

3

So praise the new eyes,   100
leaves' butterflies, flies'
sympathy; the dark trees
understand.

Raise the mantis face, my
brother; mother tree, your   105
rough bark mocks me
but we understand.

For night of leaves and leaves
of stars and stars' winked darkness
is a new world of discovered here;   110
new world of time and time's uncertainty.

4

So that with new warm arms the forest holds us.
From this womb'd heaven comes the new curled god
with goblin old man's grinning, flat face smiling,
crouched like a frog with monkey hands and   115
insect fingers. This we will carve and carry
with our cooking pots, wood mud and wattle;[4]
symbol sickness fetish for our sickness.
For man eats god,[5] eats life, eats world, eats wickedness.
This we now know, this we digest and hold;   120
this gives us bone and sinews, saliva grease and sweat;
this we can shit. And that no doubt will ever hit
us, the worm's mischance defeat us, dark roots
of time move in our way to trip us; look, we dance.

---

2. Mythical beast of ancient Egyptian and Greek mythology.   3. An aspect of African belief that expresses general fear of the forest, where apparently harmless objects can change their nature and become dangerous.   4. A reference to traditional houses, which were made of woven branches and leaves that were plastered with mud.   5. An Africanism meaning that human beings require spiritual sustenance. The same construction is employed to describe other human propensities.

II

Adowa[6]

No whirl of the flute
here;
bamboo shoots
flar-
ing the dryness;[7]   5
no high yodel steel
in the brightness;

into the shift of the darkness,
mud-flowered heel[8]
stamping the softness, dare   10
we now the fanged roots'
whisper and lisp of our fear's
darkness, tender and mute?

But slow-
ly our daring un-   15
curls the mute
fear; hands
whisper and twist
into move-
ment;[9] butt-   20
ocks shift
stones of inertia;
rhythms a-
rise in the darkness;
we dance   25

and we dance
on the firm
earth; cer-
tainties, farms,
tendrils un-   30
locking; wrong's
chirping lightning

no longer harms
us; birds echo
what the earth   35
learns; and the earth
with its mud, fat
and stones, burns
in the tun-
nelling drum[1]   40
of our hot
timeless

---

6. A ceremonial dance of the Ashantis.   7. A reference to the flute's thin sound in the desert air, as opposed to the deeper sound of drums, more appropriate to the forest, which accompany the *adowa* dance.   8. An extremely compressed image, suggesting the life-enhancing effect of the dance. (Compare the closing lines of Senghor's *Prayer to Masks*, p. 2198.)   9. The *adowa* dance involves elaborate hand gestures, each one with a different meaning.   1. In visual terms, the towering, elongated shape of the drum and, suggested by onomatopoeia, its deep affective impact.

morning,
explo-
ding dimensions   45
of song.

III

Techiman[2]

1

The path through gloom, dark
drip-

ping through star-
wet leaves' crevices,

will not soon   5
turn to light, set

like a square window; will not let
in the free sail of night's moon

that voyages the Arab's roomy
heaven.[3]   10

Here green's net sticks
wet, clings soft sweet comfort cunning[4]

like Ananse's[5] tune-
less, once Onyame's,[6] trap of doom.

2

But the way lost   15
is a way to be found
again;

the moist
stones, warm
pebbles of rain,   20

move into tossed
leaves of darkness; round
my mud hut I hear again

the cry of the lost
swallows, horizons' halloos, found-   25
ationless voices, voyages . . .

---

2. A trading center in Ashantiland, in central Ghana. The poem recounts a journey by the poet along the old slave route from the interior of the country to the coast and superimposes impressions of the present on memories of the past.   3. The clear, expansive sky over the desert, populated mainly by Arabs; also hints at Arab enslavement of Africans.   4. The anxieties of the forest.   5. The Spider, who features as a trickster figure in a cycle of Akan folktales, re-created in the Caribbean as "Nancy stories."   6. The name for the supreme deity in the Akan language.

Techiman drizzles in sun-
light; Peki[7] peeps
out of the valley; fun-
loving Nsuta[8] sleeps   30

in the misty, water-
well'd dawn. Burn
Koforidua,[9] holy tree
blasted by lightning;[1] turn

in your sleep, sleepers   35
at Krachi;[2] the almond leaves
scratching your rocks, rock
you awake for new journeys; stop-

ping at Golokwati, Kpandu and Pong[3]
for rest, salt and water;   40
then onward to Teshie,
Labadi, Kaneshie[4] . . .

Time's walking river is long.

IV

The White River[5]

1

From the Akuapim[6] ridge unrolled a new land.
Hands on the hoe
knew new grasses:

nkyekyere and lemon;[7]   5
and the bold knocking demon
of darkness was tamed on the Akropong rocks.[8]
Light rounded to flesh

at Aburi;[9] and the hills
of the Ga lands: Akuse   10
and Shai:[1] were like islands
burning to green in the water of pastures;[2]

plains drowned in the shallow
drifting of cloud. Crowds
flocked to the Volta, darker   15
at Ada;[3] and over we ferried

7. Peki Blengo, a town in eastern Ghana.   8. A town in central Ghana, known for its music.   9. An important junction that links two major roads from Accra, the capital of the modern state of Ghana, on the Atlantic coast, to Kumasi, the capital of the precolonial Ashanti Empire.   1. A reference to a histori- cal disaster.   2. Kete Krachi, a town on the Volta, a river in eastern Ghana, which divides the Akan- and Ewe-speaking areas.   3. Or Kpong. Golokwati and Kpandu are towns along the Volta.   4. Villages on the Atlantic coast that have become suburbs of Accra, capital of Ghana.   5. The White Volta, the upper (northern) arm of the Volta River.   6. A region inhabited by a subgroup of the Akan, the Akwapim- Twi, on a ridge north of the coastal plain on which Accra is situated.   7. Varieties of grass: "guinea grass" and "lemongrass."   8. In many myths, the founding of communities is ascribed to a hero who has to subdue a supernatural being or force.   9. The principal town of the Akwapims.   1. A town, at the southern edge of the Akwapim ridge, overlooking the coastal plain, inhabited by the Ga-speaking people.   2. Akuse is a town in the Shai hills, adjacent to Akwapim.   3. At the mouth of the Volta; the itinerary described in the poem, previously north to south, has now shifted eastward.

to the hard, sandy gold of Keta.[4]
Here at last was the rager,[5]
the growler, wet breather,
life giver, white curly smoker,   20

time's river, rushing forever: round pebbles, carved musical
shells; wet ropes in the tide,
tugging moon's motion;

wet sails in the salt; winds drying   25
the sand into powder; drying
fish, glittered silver;
guinea cock's[6] eyes of their scales in the dark

wood of boats: forest trees fallen and scooped
with tongue's fire;[7] canoes reaping danger;   30
sharp shark's teeth's death-whiteness ready;
at the slow sloping ledge of our village; time's water's

edge; the white river.[8]

2

This was at last the last;
this was the limit of motion;   35
voyages ended;
time stopped where its movement began;

horizons returned inaccessible.
Here at last was the limit;
the minutes of pebbles drop-   40
ping into the hourless pool.

Hands reached into water;
gods nudged us like fish;
black bottomless whales that we worshipped.
O new world of want, who will build the new ways,   45

the new ships?[9]

4. A coastal town, famous for fishing, in the Ewe-speaking area, on the eastern side of the Volta.
5. The Atlantic ocean.   6. A species of wild fowl.   7. Canoes are hollowed out of giant trees with
fire.   8. Here, the Atlantic Ocean. *Time's water's edge*: divides the New World blacks' historical experience in Africa from that in America.   9. Ships from Europe, ushering in a new dispensation and new
problems demanding new solutions; ultimately, these ships will lead to captivity and the exile of slavery
in the New World.

ALICE MUNRO
born 1931

"I don't take up a story and follow it as if it were a road, taking me somewhere,
with views and neat diversions along the way," writes Alice Munro in her essay
What Is Real? "I go into it and move back and forth and settle here and there, and

stay in it for a while." This description of Munro the reader applies equally to
Munro the writer. Munro's stories join the familiar to the enigmatic in a style that,
like Virginia Woolf's, savors the nuances and subtleties of human relationships.
Combining this writerly style with a hawkeyed attention to physical and psychological detail that places her in the realist tradition of Tolstoy and Chekhov, Munro's
short fiction is marked by its innovation and compassion. Whether writing about
fox farming, high school dances, chance sexual encounters, marriage, divorce or,
as in *The Albanian Virgin*, discovery and self-discovery, Munro's vision frequently
centers on the lives of girls and women and on their introspective responses to the
world around them, to the men in their lives, and to each other. Her writing is
less concerned with "getting somewhere" than with settling here and there to
reveal the mystery and complexity of seemingly simple day-to-day realities.

Born Alice Anne Laidlaw in the Scots-Irish community of Wingham, Ontario,
Munro began writing stories in her teens—tales of romance and adventure far
removed from her rural Canadian home. Her parents, Robert Eric Laidlaw and
Ann Chamney Laidlaw, struggled throughout their marriage to make ends meet—
fox farming during the Depression, selling wares door to door, raising turkeys—
but no venture was successful enough to lift the family out of poverty. In 1949,
Munro enrolled at the University of Western Ontario, leaving school in 1951 to
marry James Munro and moving with him to Victoria, British Columbia. While
raising three daughters and managing a bookshop there during the 1950s and
1960s, Munro simultaneously honed her story-telling skills. When, in 1968, *Dance
of the Happy Shades* introduced her to the reading public, the response was overwhelming. Praised by critics, recipient also of the Governor General's Award for
fiction, she had found a place for herself in the world of professional writers. In
1972 she published *Lives of Girls and Women*, a novel composed of a series of
linked stories, all recounting the emergence of the character Del Jordan from her
confined childhood to a career and an adult identity far transcending the borders
of her hometown of Jubilee. This was followed in 1974 by a third book of stories:
Something I've Been Meaning to Tell You. Munro's first marriage ended in divorce
in 1976, after which she remarried and moved to the central Canadian town of
Clinton, Ontario. Since then, she has published five other collections of short
fiction: *The Beggar Maid* (1979), *The Moons of Jupiter* (1982), *The Progress of
Love* (1986), *Friend of My Youth* (1990), and *Open Secrets* (1994), from which
The Albanian Virgin is taken.

The vagaries of life in rural Canada figure prominently in Munro's writing, and
because of this, some critics have labeled her a "regionalist." Her characters often
inhabit small fictional towns similar to the Wingham of her youth, but the worlds
of human relationships that they create for themselves are more expansive and
universal than any label implies. In this, she resembles William Faulkner writing
about his mythic Yoknapatawpha County or Lu Xun bringing China into contact
with the world at large. Munro's most memorable characters—Del Jordan of *Lives
of Girls and Women*, Rose of *The Beggar Maid*, and Claire and Charlotte of *The
Albanian Virgin*—though distinct in their circumstances and personalities, share
a breadth of vision and an openness to life's inconstancies that makes them seem
larger and more significant than their surroundings. Through their eyes, we see a
world not of heroic resolutions and tragic ends or of a linear progression from
"here" to "there," but rather of moments and of details, of disappointments and
small victories, and above all, of the inevitable swoop and sway between intimacy
and alienation. What we see most powerfully is the masks we all wear, "the faces
we put on to meet the faces that we meet" (in T. S. Eliot's memorable phrase).
Munro's characters disguise themselves from themselves and from others, but seek
at the same time to be unmasked, discovered, and more fully human, as Charlotte
longs to be while recounting the story of her "movie." Describing her fondness for

the short-story form, Munro says: "I like looking at people's lives over a number of years, without continuity. Like catching them in snapshots. And I like the way people relate, or don't relate, to the people they were earlier." Like Munro's other work, *The Albanian Virgin* touches on this fragmentary but cyclical nature of human life. One narrative interrupts another only to be interrupted itself; and when the two seem to be most discontinuous, they converge. Claire, the narrator, expresses the implied parallel in life. "We become distant, close—distant, close—over and over again," she says of an imagined future with a former lover. Using memory, storytelling, and introspection, Munro's characters struggle to understand and accept the vicissitudes of human relationships and, correspondingly, of life itself.

Probable Fictions: Alice Munro's Narrative Acts, edited by Louis MacKendrick (1983), is an excellent survey of critical essays and of interviews with the author herself. For more on Munro's approach to gender issues and male/female relationships, see Beverly Rasporich, *Dance of the Sexes: Art and Gender in the Fiction of Alice Munro* (1990).

The Albanian Virgin

In the mountains, in Maltsia e madhe,[1] she must have tried to tell them her name, and "Lottar" was what they made of it. She had a wound in her leg, from a fall on sharp rocks when her guide was shot. She had a fever. How long it took them to carry her through the mountains, bound up in a rug and strapped to a horse's back, she had no idea. They gave her water to drink now and then, and sometimes *raki*, which was a kind of brandy, very strong. She could smell pines. At one time they were on a boat and she woke up and saw the stars, brightening and fading and changing places—unstable clusters that made her sick. Later she understood that they must have been on the lake. Lake Scutari, or Sckhoder, or Skodra.[2] They pulled up among the reeds. The rug was full of vermin, which got under the rag tied around her leg.

At the end of her journey, though she did not know it was the end, she was lying in a small stone hut that was an outbuilding of the big house, called the *kula*. It was the hut of the sick and dying. Not of giving birth, which these women did in the cornfields, or beside the path when they were carrying a load to market.

She was lying, perhaps for weeks, on a heaped-up bed of ferns. It was comfortable, and had the advantage of being easily changed when fouled or bloodied. The old woman named Tima looked after her. She plugged up the wound with a paste made of beeswax and olive oil and pine resin. Several times a day the dressing was removed, the wound washed out with *raki*. Lottar could see black lace curtains hanging from the rafters, and she thought she was in her room at home, with her mother (who was dead) looking after her. "Why have you hung up those curtains?" she said. "They look horrible."

She was really seeing cobwebs, all thick and furry with smoke—ancient cobwebs, never disturbed from year to year.

1. The highlands of northern Albania; probably derived from *malesia*, "mountainous region," and *madhe*, "tall, lofty, high."   2. A lake in northern Albania, on the border with Montenegro.

Also, in her delirium, she had the sensation of some wide board being pushed against her face—something like a coffin plank. But when she came to her senses she learned that it was nothing but a crucifix, a wooden crucifix that a man was trying to get her to kiss. The man was a priest, a Franciscan. He was a tall, fierce-looking man with black eyebrows and mustache and a rank smell, and he carried, besides the crucifix, a gun that she learned later was a Browning revolver. He knew by the look of her that she was a giaour[3]—not a Muslim—but he did not understand that she might be a heretic. He knew a little English but pronounced it in a way that she could not make out. And she did not then know any of the language of the Ghegs.[4] But after her fever subsided, when he tried a few words of Italian on her, they were able to talk, because she had learned Italian at school and had been travelling for six months in Italy. He understood so much more than anyone else around her that she expected him, at first, to understand everything. What is the nearest city? she asked him, and he said, Skodra.[5] So go there, please, she said—go and find the British Consulate, if there is one. I belong to the British Empire. Tell them I am here. Or if there is no British Consul, go to the police.

She did not understand that under no circumstances would anybody go to the police. She didn't know that she belonged now to this tribe, this *kula*, even though taking her prisoner had not been their intention and was an embarrassing mistake.

It is shameful beyond belief to attack a woman. When they had shot and killed her guide, they had thought that she would turn her horse around and fly back down the mountain road, back to Bar.[6] But her horse took fright at the shot and stumbled among the boulders and she fell, and her leg was injured. Then they had no choice but to carry her with them, back across the border between the Crna Gora (which means Black Rock, or Montenegro) and Maltsia e madhe.

"But why rob the guide and not me?" she said, naturally thinking robbery to be the motive. She thought of how starved they looked, the man and his horse, and of the fluttering white rags of his headdress.

"Oh, they are not robbers!" said the Franciscan, shocked. "They are honest men. They shot him because they were in blood with him. With his house. It is their law."

He told her that the man who had been shot, her guide, had killed a man of this *kula*. He had done that because the man he had killed had killed a man of his *kula*. This would go on, it had been going on for a long time now, there were always more sons being born. They think they have more sons than other people in the world, and it is to serve this necessity.

"Well, it is terrible," the Franciscan concluded. "But it is for their honor, the honor of their family. They are always ready to die for their honor."

---

3. One who is not a Muslim, hence an infidel.   4. A northern Albanian ethnic group, which believes that the death, even the accidental death, of a kinsman can only be avenged by the murder of the guilty person or that person's relatives.   5. Or Shkoder or Scutari; capital of the Shkoder province in northwest Albania at the outlet of Lake Scutari.   6. A coastal city along the Adriatic Sea in Montenegro, approximately twenty-five miles from Shkoder.

She said that her guide did not seem to be so ready, if he had fled to Crna Gora.

"But it did not make any difference, did it?" said the Franciscan. "Even if he had gone to America, it would not have made any difference."

At Trieste she had boarded a steamer, to travel down the Dalmatian Coast.[7] She was with her friends Mr. and Mrs. Cozzens, whom she had met in Italy, and their friend Dr. Lamb, who had joined them from England. They put in at the little port of Bar, which the Italians call Antivari, and stayed the night at the European Hotel. After dinner they walked on the terrace, but Mrs. Cozzens was afraid of a chill, so they went indoors and played cards. There was rain in the night. She woke up and listened to the rain and was full of disappointment, which gave rise to a loathing for these middle-aged people, particularly for Dr. Lamb, whom she believed the Cozzenses had summoned from England to meet her. They probably thought she was rich. A transatlantic heiress whose accent they could almost forgive. These people ate too much and then they had to take pills. And they worried about being in strange places—what had they come for? In the morning she would have to get back on the boat with them or they would make a fuss. She would never take the road over the mountains to Cetinge, Montenegro's capital city—they had been told that it was not wise. She would never see the bell tower where the heads of Turks used to hang, or the plane tree under which the Poet-Prince[8] held audience with the people. She could not get back to sleep, so she decided to go downstairs with the first light, and, even if it was still raining, to go a little way up the road behind the town, just to see the ruins that she knew were there, among the olive trees, and the Austrian fortress on its rock and the dark face of Mount Lovchen.[9]

The weather obliged her, and so did the man at the hotel desk, producing almost at once a tattered but cheerful guide and his underfed horse. They set out—she on the horse, the man walking ahead. The road was steep and twisting and full of boulders, the sun increasingly hot and the intervening shade cold and black. She became hungry and thought she must turn back soon. She would have breakfast with her companions, who got up late.

No doubt there was some sort of search for her, after the guide's body was found. The authorities must have been notified—whoever the authorities were. The boat must have sailed on time, her friends must have gone with it. The hotel had not taken their passports. Nobody back in Canada would think of investigating. She was not writing regularly to anyone, she had had a falling-out with her brother, her parents were dead. You won't come home till all your inheritance is spent, her brother had said, and then who will look after you?

When she was being carried through the pine forest, she awoke and found herself suspended, lulled—in spite of the pain and perhaps because of the *raki*—into a disbelieving surrender. She fastened her eyes on the

7. The rugged eastern shore of the Adriatic Sea. Trieste is an Italian coastal town along the Adriatic Sea, directly north of the former Yugoslavia.   8. Nicholas I (1841–1921), prince of Montenegro from 1860 to 1910. In 1910, when Montenegro became independent, he became its first (and only) king.   9. Located on the Dalmatian Coast, about twenty-five miles north of Bar.

bundle that was hanging from the saddle of the man ahead of her and knocking against the horse's back. It was something about the size of a cabbage, wrapped in a stiff and rusty-looking cloth.

I heard this story in the old St. Joseph's Hospital in Victoria[1] from Charlotte, who was the sort of friend I had in my early days there. My friendships then seemed both intimate and uncertain. I never knew why people told me things, or what they meant me to believe.

I had come to the hospital with flowers and chocolates. Charlotte lifted her head, with its clipped and feathery white hair, toward the roses. "Bah!" she said. "They have no smell! Not to me, anyway. They are beautiful, of course.

"You must eat the chocolates yourself," she said. "Everything tastes like tar to me. I don't know how I know what tar tastes like, but this is what I think."

She was feverish. Her hand, when I held it, felt hot and puffy. Her hair had all been cut off, and this made her look as if she had actually lost flesh around her face and neck. The part of her under the hospital covers seemed as extensive and lumpy as ever.

"But you must not think I am ungrateful," she said. "Sit down. Bring that chair from over there—she doesn't need it."

There were two other women in the room. One was just a thatch of yellow-gray hair on the pillow, and the other was tied into a chair, wriggling and grunting.

"This is a terrible place," said Charlotte. "But we must just try our best to put up with it. I am so glad to see you. That one over there yells all night long," she said, nodding toward the window bed. "We must thank Christ she's asleep now. I don't get a wink of sleep, but I have been putting the time to very good use. What do you think I've been doing? I've been making up a story, for a movie! I have it all in my head and I want you to hear it. You will be able to judge if it will make a good movie. I think it will. I would like Jennifer Jones[2] to act in it. I don't know, though. She does not seem to have the same spirit anymore. She married that mogul.

"Listen," she said. "(Oh, could you haul that pillow up more, behind my head?) It takes place in Albania, in northern Albania, which is called Maltsia e madhe, in the nineteen-twenties, when things were very primitive. It is about a young woman travelling alone. Lottar is her name in the story."

I sat and listened. Charlotte would lean forward, even rock a little on her hard bed, stressing some point for me. Her puffy hands flew up and down, her blue eyes widened commandingly, and then from time to time she sank back onto the pillows, and she shut her eyes to get the story in focus again. Ah, yes, she said. Yes, yes. And she continued.

"Yes, yes," she said at last. "I know how it goes on, but that is enough for now. You will have to come back. Tomorrow. Will you come back?"

---

1. Capital of British Columbia, Canada.   2. American actress (born 1920), who won an Oscar in 1943 for her role in *The Song of Bernadette*. She married the millionaire Norton Simon in 1971.

I said, yes, tomorrow, and she appeared to have fallen asleep without hearing me.

The *kula* was a great, rough stone house with a stable below and the living quarters above. A veranda ran all the way around, and there would always be an old woman sitting there, with a bobbin contraption that flew like a bird from one hand to the other and left a trail of shiny black braid, mile after mile of black braid, which was the adornment of all the men's trousers. Other women worked at the looms or sewed together the leather sandals. Nobody sat there knitting, because nobody would think to sit down to knit. Knitting was what they did while they trotted back and forth to the spring with their water barrels strapped to their backs, or took the path to the fields or to the beech wood, where they collected the fallen branches. They knitted stockings—black and white, red and white, with zigzag patterns like lightning strokes. Women's hands must never be idle. Before dawn they pounded the bread dough in its blackened wooden trough, shaped it into loaves on the backs of shovels, and baked it on the hearth. (It was corn bread, unleavened and eaten hot, which would swell up like a puffball in your stomach.) Then they had to sweep out the *kula* and dump the dirty ferns and pile up armloads of fresh ferns for the next night's sleep. This was often one of Lottar's jobs, since she was so unskilled at everything else. Little girls stirred the yogurt so that lumps would not form as it soured. Older girls might butcher a kid and sew up its stomach, which they had stuffed with wild garlic and sage and apples. Or they would go together, girls and women, all ages, to wash the men's white head scarves in the cold little river nearby, whose waters were clear as glass. They tended the tobacco crop and hung the ripe leaves to dry in the darkened shed. They hoed the corn and cucumbers, milked the ewes.

The women looked stern but they were not so, really. They were only preoccupied, and proud of themselves, and eager for competition. Who could carry the heaviest load of wood, knit the fastest, hoe the most rows of cornstalks? Tima, who had looked after Lottar when she was sick, was the most spectacular worker of all. She would run up the slope to the *kula* with a load of wood bound to her back that looked ten times as big as herself. She would leap from rock to rock in the river and pound the scarves as if they were the bodies of enemies. "Oh, Tima, Tima!" the other women cried out in ironic admiration, and "Oh, Lottar, Lottar!" in nearly the same tones, when Lottar, at the other end of a scale of usefulness, let the clothes drift away downstream. Sometimes they whacked Lottar with a stick, as they would a donkey, but this had more exasperation in it than cruelty. Sometimes the young ones would say, "Talk your talk!" and for their entertainment she would speak English. They wrinkled up their faces and spat, at such peculiar sounds. She tried to teach them words—"hand," "nose," and so on. But these seemed to them jokes, and they would repeat them to each other and fall about laughing.

Women were with women and men were with men, except at times in the night (women teased about such times were full of shame and denial, and sometimes there would be a slapping) and at meals, when the women served the men their food. What the men did all day was none of women's business. Men made their ammunition, and gave a lot of care to their guns, which were in some cases very beautiful, decorated with engraved silver. They also dynamited rocks to clear the road, and were responsible for the horses. Wherever they were, there was a lot of laughing, and sometimes singing and firing off of blanks. While they were at home they seemed to be on holiday, and then some of them would have to ride off on an expedition of punishment, or to attend a council called to put an end to some particular bout of killing. None of the women believed it would work—they laughed and said that it would only mean twenty more shot. When a young man was going off on his first killing, the women made a great fuss over his clothes and his haircut, to encourage him. If he didn't succeed, no woman would marry him—a woman of any worth would be ashamed to marry a man who had not killed—and everyone was anxious to have new brides in the house, to help with the work.

One night, when Lottar served one man his food—a guest; there were always guests invited for meals around the low table, the *sofra*—she noticed what small hands he had, and hairless wrists. Yet he was not young, he was not a boy. A wrinkled, leathery face, without a mustache. She listened for his voice in the talk, and it seemed to her hoarse but womanish. But he smoked, he ate with the men, he carried a gun.

"Is that a man?" Lottar said to the woman serving with her. The woman shook her head, not willing to speak where the men might hear them. But the young girls who overheard the question were not so careful. "Is that a man? Is that a man?" they mimicked Lottar. "Oh, Lottar, you are so stupid! Don't you know when you see a Virgin?"

So she did not ask them anything else. But the next time she saw the Franciscan, she ran after him to ask him her question. What is a Virgin? She had to run after him, because he did not stop and talk to her now as he had when she was sick in the little hut. She was always working when he came to the *kula*, and he could not spend much time with the women anyway—he sat with the men. She ran after him when she saw him leaving, striding down the path among the sumac trees, heading for the bare wooden church and the lean-to church house, where he lived.

He said it was a woman, but a woman who had become like a man. She did not want to marry, and she took an oath in front of witnesses that she never would, and then she put on men's clothes and had her own gun, and her horse if she could afford one, and she lived as she liked. Usually she was poor, she had no woman to work for her. But nobody troubled her, and she could eat at the *sofra* with the men.

Lottar no longer spoke to the priest about going to Skodra. She understood now that it must be a long way away. Sometimes she asked if he had heard anything, if anybody was looking for her, and he would say, sternly, no one. When she thought of how she had been during those first weeks— giving orders, speaking English without embarrassment, sure that her special case merited attention—she was ashamed at how little she had understood. And the longer she stayed at the *kula*, the better she spoke the language and became accustomed to the work, the stranger was the thought of leaving. Someday she must go, but how could it be now? How could she leave in the middle of the tobacco-picking or the sumac harvest, or during the preparations for the feast of the Translation of St. Nicholas?[3]

In the tobacco fields they took off their jerkins and blouses and worked half naked in the sun, hidden between the rows of tall plants. The tobacco juice was black and sticky, like molasses, and it ran down their arms and was smeared over their breasts. At dusk they went down to the river and scrubbed themselves clean. They splashed in the cold water, girls and big, broad women together. They tried to push each other off balance, and Lottar heard her name cried then, in warning and triumph, without contempt, like any other name: "Lottar, watch out! Lottar!"

They told her things. They told her that children died here because of the *Striga*. Even grown-up people shrivel and die sometimes, when the *Striga* has put her spell on them. The *Striga* looks like a normal woman, so you do not know who she is. She sucks blood. To catch her, you must lay a cross on the threshold of the church on Easter Sunday when everybody is inside. Then the woman who is the *Striga* cannot come out. Or you can follow the woman you suspect, and you may see her vomit up the blood. If you can manage to scrape up some of this blood on a silver coin, and carry that coin with you, no *Striga* can touch you, ever.

Hair cut at the time of the full moon will turn white.

If you have pains in your limbs, cut some hair from your head and your armpits and burn it—then the pains will go away.

The *oras* are the devils that come out at night and flash false lights to bewilder travellers. You must crouch down and cover your head, else they will lead you over a cliff. Also they will catch the horses and ride them to death.

The tobacco had been harvested, the sheep brought down from the slopes, animals and humans shut up in the *kula* through the weeks of snow and cold rain, and one day, in the early warmth of the spring sun, the women brought Lottar to a chair on the veranda. There, with great ceremony and delight, they shaved off the hair above her forehead. Then they combed some black, bubbling dye through the hair that remained. The dye was greasy—the hair became so stiff that they could shape it into wings and buns as firm as blood puddings. Everybody thronged about, criticizing and admiring. They put flour on her face and dressed her up in clothes they had pulled out of one of the great carved chests. What for, she asked, as she found herself disappearing into a white blouse with gold embroidery, a red bodice with fringed epaulets, a sash of striped silk a yard wide and a dozen yards long, a black-and-red wool skirt, with chain after chain of false gold being thrown over her hair and around her neck. For beauty, they said. And they said when they had finished, "See! She is beautiful!" Those who said it seemed triumphant, challenging others who must have doubted that the transformation could be made. They squeezed the muscles in her arms, which she had got from hoeing and wood-carrying, and patted her broad, floured forehead. Then they shrieked, because they had

---

3. Probably December 6, the feast day of St. Nicholas of Myra (died 350), whose relics were carried (thus *translated*) to Barri in Italy. He is the saint on whom the figure of Santa Claus is based.

forgotten a very important thing—the black paint that joins the eyebrows in a single line over the nose.

"The priest is coming!" shouted one of the girls, who must have been placed as a lookout, and the woman who was painting the black line said, "Ha, he will not stop it!" But the others drew aside.

The Franciscan shot off a couple of blanks, as he always did to announce his arrival, and the men of the house fired off blanks also, to welcome him. But he did not stay with the men this time. He climbed at once to the veranda, calling, "Shame! Shame! Shame on you all! Shame!

"I know what you have dyed her hair for," he said to the women. "I know why you have put bride's clothes on her. All for a pig of a Muslim!

"You! You sitting there in your paint," he said to Lottar. "Don't you know what it is for? Don't you know they have sold you to a Muslim? He is coming from Vuthaj.[4] He will be here by dark!"

"So what of it?" said one of the women boldly. "All they could get for her was three napoleons. She has to marry somebody."

The Franciscan told her to hold her tongue. "Is this what you want?" he said to Lottar. "To marry an infidel and go to live with him in Vuthaj?"

Lottar said no. She felt as if she could hardly move or open her mouth, under the weight of her greased hair and her finery. Under this weight she struggled as you do to rouse yourself to a danger, out of sleep. The idea of marrying the Muslim was still too distant to be the danger—what she understood was that she would be separated from the priest, and would never be able to claim an explanation from him again.

"Did you know you were being married?" he asked her. "Is it something you want, to be married?"

No, she said. No. And the Franciscan clapped his hands. "Take off that gold trash!" he said. "Take those clothes off her! I am going to make her a Virgin!

"If you become a Virgin, it will be all right," he said to her. "The Muslim will not have to shoot anybody. But you must swear you will never go with a man. You must swear in front of witnesses. *Per quri e per kruch.* By the stone and by the Cross. Do you understand that? I am not going to let them marry you to a Muslim, but I do not want more shooting to start on this land."

It was one of the things the Franciscan tried so hard to prevent—the selling of women to Muslim men. It put him into a frenzy, that their religion could be so easily set aside. They sold girls like Lottar, who would bring no price anywhere else, and widows who had borne only girls.

Slowly and sulkily the women removed all the rich clothes. They brought out men's trousers, worn and with no braid, and a shirt and head scarf. Lottar put them on. One woman with an ugly pair of shears chopped off most of what remained of Lottar's hair, which was difficult to cut because of the dressing.

"Tomorrow you would have been a bride," they said to her. Some of

---

4. A Muslim stronghold in northern Albania.

them seemed mournful, some contemptuous. "Now you will never have
a son."

The little girls snatched up the hair that had been cut off and struck it
on their heads, arranging various knots and fringes.

Lottar swore her oath in front of twelve witnesses. They were, of course,
all men, and looked as sullen as the women about the turn things had
taken. She never saw the Muslim. The Franciscan berated the men and
said that if this sort of thing did not stop he would close up the churchyard
and make them bury their dead in unholy ground. Lottar sat at a distance
from them all, in her unaccustomed clothes. It was strange and unpleasant
to be idle. When the Franciscan had finished his harangue, he came over
and stood looking down at her. He was breathing hard because of his rage,
or the exertions of the lecture.

"Well, then," he said. "Well." He reached into some inner fold of his
clothing and brought out a cigarette and gave it to her. It smelled of his
skin.

A nurse brought in Charlotte's supper, a light meal of soup and canned
peaches. Charlotte took the cover off the soup, smelled it, and turned
her head away. "Go away, don't look at this slop," she said. "Come back
tomorrow—you know it's not finished yet."

The nurse walked with me to the door, and once we were in the corridor she said, "It's always the ones with the least at home who turn the
most critical. She's not the easiest in the world, but you can't help kind of
admiring her. You're not related, are you?"

Oh, no, I said. No.

"When she came in it was amazing. We were taking her things off and
somebody said, oh, what lovely bracelets, and right away she wanted to
sell them! Her *husband* is something else. Do you know him? They are
really quite the characters."

Charlotte's husband, Gjurdhi, had come to my bookstore by himself
one cold morning less than a week earlier. He was pulling a wagon full of
books, which he had wrapped up in a blanket. He had tried to sell me
some books once before, in their apartment, and I thought perhaps these
were the same ones. I had been confused then, but now that I was on my
own ground I was able to be more forceful. I said no, I did not handle
secondhand books, I was not interested. Gjurdhi nodded brusquely, as if I
had not needed to tell him this and it was of no importance to our conversation. He continued to pick up the books one by one, urging me to run
my hands over the bindings, insisting that I note the beauty of the illustrations and be impressed by the dates of publication. I had to repeat my
refusal over and over again, and I heard myself begin to attach some apologies to it, quite against my own will. He chose to understand each rejection as applying to an individual book and would simply fetch out another,
saying vehemently, "This, too! This is very beautiful. You will notice. And
it is very old. Look what a beautiful old book!"

They were travel books, some of them, from the turn of the century.
Not so very old, and not so beautiful, either, with their dim, grainy photo-

graphs. A *Trek Through the Black Peaks. High Albania. Secret Lands of Southern Europe.*

"You will have to go to the Antiquarian Bookstore," I said. "The one on Fort Street. It isn't far to take them."

He made a sound of disgust, maybe indicating that he knew well enough where it was, or that he had already made an unsuccessful trip there, or that most of these books had come from there, one way or another, in the first place.

"How is Charlotte?" I said warmly. I had not seen her for a while, although she used to visit the store quite often. She would bring me little presents—coffee beans coated with chocolate to give me energy; a bar of pure glycerine soap to counteract the drying effects, on the skin, of having to handle so much paper. A paperweight embedded with samples of rocks found in British Columbia, a pencil that lit up in the dark (so that I could see to write up bills if the lights should go out). She drank coffee with me, talked, and strolled about the store, discreetly occupied, when I was busy. Through the dark, blustery days of fall she wore the velvet cloak that I had first seen her in, and kept the rain off with an oversized, ancient black umbrella. She called it her tent. If she saw that I had become too involved with a customer, she would tap me on the shoulder and say, "I'll just silently steal away with my tent now. We'll talk another day."

Once, a customer said to me bluntly, "Who is that woman? I've seen her around town with her husband. I guess he's her husband. I thought they were peddlers."

Could Charlotte have heard that, I wondered. Could she have detected a coolness in the attitude of my new clerk? (Charlotte was certainly cool to her.) There might have been just too many times when I was busy. I did not actually think that the visits had stopped. I preferred to think that an interval had grown longer, for a reason that might have nothing to do with me. I was busy and tired, anyway, as Christmas loomed. The number of books I was selling was a pleasant surprise.

"I don't want to be any kind of character assassin," the clerk had said to me. "But I think you should know that that woman and her husband have been banned from a lot of stores in town. They're suspected of lifting things. I don't know. He wears that rubber coat with the big sleeves and she's got her cloak. I do know for sure that they used to go around at Christmastime and snip off holly that was growing in people's gardens. Then they took it round and tried to sell it in apartment buildings."

On that cold morning, after I had refused all the books in his wagon, I asked Gjurdhi again how Charlotte was. He said that she was sick. He spoke sullenly, as if it were none of my business.

"Take her a book," I said. I picked out a Penguin light verse. "Take her this—tell her I hope she enjoys it. Tell her I hope she'll be better very soon. Perhaps I can get around to see her."

He put the book into his bundle in the wagon. I thought that he would probably try to sell it immediately.

"Not at home," he said. "In the hospital."

I had noticed, each time he bent over the wagon, a large, wooden crucifix that swung down outside his coat and had to be tucked back inside.

Now this happened again, and I said, thoughtlessly, in my confusion and contrition, "Isn't that beautiful! What beautiful dark wood! It looks medieval."

He pulled it over his head, saying, "Very old. Very beautiful. Oak wood. Yes."

He pushed it into my hand, and as soon as I realized what was happening I pushed it back.

"*Wonderful* wood," I said. As he put it away I felt rescued, though full of irritable remorse.

"Oh, I hope Charlotte is not very sick!" I said.

He smiled disdainfully, tapping himself on the chest—perhaps to show me the source of Charlotte's trouble, perhaps only to feel for himself the skin that was newly bared there.

Then he took himself, the crucifix, the books, and the wagon out of my store. I felt that insults had been offered, humiliations suffered, on both sides.

Up past the tobacco field was a beech wood, where Lottar had often gone to get sticks for the fire. Beyond that was a grassy slope—a high meadow—and at the top of the meadow, about half an hour's climb from the *kula*, was a small stone shelter, a primitive place with no window, a low doorway and no door, a corner hearth without a chimney. Sheep took cover there; the floor was littered with their droppings.

That was where she went to live after she became a Virgin. The incident of the Muslim bridegroom had taken place in the spring, just about a year after she first came to Maltsia e madhe, and it was time for the sheep to be driven to their higher pastures. Lottar was to keep count of the flock and see that they did not fall into ravines or wander too far away. And she was to milk the ewes every evening. She was expected to shoot wolves, if any came near. But none did, no one alive now at the *kula* had ever seen a wolf. The only wild animals Lottar saw were a red fox, once, by the stream, and the rabbits, which were plentiful and unwary. She learned to shoot and skin and cook them, cleaning them out as she had seen the butcher girls do at the *kula* and stewing the meatier parts in her pot over the fire, with some bulbs of wild garlic.

She did not want to sleep inside the shelter, so she fixed up a roof of branches outside, against the wall, this roof an extension of the roof of the building. She had her heap of ferns underneath, and a felt rug she had been given, to spread on the ferns when she slept. She no longer took any notice of the bugs. There were some spikes pushed into the wall between the dry stones. She did not know why they were there, but they served her well for hanging up the milk pails and the few pots she had been provided with. She brought her water from the stream, in which she washed her own head scarf, and herself sometimes, more for relief from the heat than out of concern about her dirtiness.

Everything was changed. She no longer saw the women. She lost her habits of constant work. The little girls came up in the evenings to get the milk. This far away from the *kula* and their mothers, they became quite wild. They climbed up on the roof, often smashing through the arrangement of branches which Lottar had contrived. They jumped into the ferns and sometimes snatched an armful of them to bind into a crude ball, which they threw at one another until it fell apart. They enjoyed themselves so much that Lottar had to chase them away at dusk, reminding them of how frightened they got in the beech wood after dark. She believed that they ran all the way through it and spilled half the milk on their way.

Now and then they brought her corn flour, which she mixed with water and baked on her shovel by the fire. Once they had a treat, a sheep's head—she wondered if they had stolen it—for her to boil in her pot. She was allowed to keep some of the milk, and instead of drinking it fresh she usually let it go sour, and stirred it to make yogurt to dip her bread in. That was how she preferred it now.

The men often came up through the wood shortly after the little girls had run through it on their way down. It seemed that this was a custom of theirs, in the summer. They liked to sit on the banks of the stream and fire off blanks and drink *raki* and sing, or sometimes just smoke and talk. They were not making this expedition to see how she was getting on. But since they were coming anyway, they brought her presents of coffee and tobacco and were full of competing advice on how to fix up the roof of her shelter so it wouldn't fall down, how to keep her fire going all night, how to use her gun.

Her gun was an old Italian Martini, which had been given to her when she left the *kula*. Some of the men said that gun was unlucky, since it had belonged to a boy who had been killed before he himself had even shot anybody. Others said that Martinis in general were unlucky, hardly any use at all.

Mausers were what you needed, for accuracy and repeating power.

But Mauser bullets were too small to do enough damage. There were men walking around full of Mauser holes—you could hear them whistle as they passed by.

Nothing can really compare with a heavy flintlock that has a good packing of powder, a bullet, and nails.

When they weren't talking about guns, the men spoke of recent killings, and told jokes. One of them told a joke about a wizard. There was a wizard held in prison by a Pasha.[5] The Pasha brought him out to do tricks in front of guests. Bring a bowl of water, said the wizard. Now, this water is the sea. And what port shall I show you on the sea? Show a port on the island of Malta, they said. And there it was. Houses and churches and a steamer ready to sail. Now would you like to see me step on board that steamer? And the Pasha laughed. Go ahead! So the wizard put his foot in the bowl of water and stepped on board the steamer and went to America! What do you think of that!

"There are no wizards, anyway," said the Franciscan, who had climbed up with the men on this evening, as he often did. "If you had said a saint, you might have made some sense." He spoke severely, but Lottar thought he was happy, as they all were, as she, too, was permitted to be, in their

5. The title for military and civilian officers in the Balkan region.

presence and in his, though he paid no attention to her. The strong tobacco that they gave her to smoke made her dizzy and she had to lie down on the grass.

The time came when Lottar had to think about moving inside her house. The mornings were cold, the ferns were soaked with dew, and the grape leaves were turning yellow. She took the shovel and cleaned the sheep droppings off the floor, in preparation for making up her bed inside. She began to stuff grass and leaves and mud into the chinks between the stones.

When the men came they asked her what she was doing that for. For the winter, she said, and they laughed.

"Nobody can stay here in the winter," they said. They showed her how deep the snow was, putting hands against their breastbones. Besides, all the sheep would have been taken down.

"There will be no work for you—and what will you eat?" they said. "Do you think the women will let you have bread and yogurt for nothing?"

"How can I go back to the *kula*?" Lottar said. "I am a Virgin, where would I sleep? What kind of work would I do?"

"That is right," they said kindly, speaking to her and then to each other. "When a Virgin belongs to the *kula* she gets a bit of land, usually, where she can live on her own. But this one doesn't really belong to the *kula*, she has no father to give her anything. What will she do?"

Shortly after this—and in the middle of the day, when visitors never came—the Franciscan climbed the meadow, all alone.

"I don't trust them," he said. "I think they will try again to sell you to a Muslim. Even though you have been sworn. They will try to make some money out of you. If they could find you a Christian, it might not be so bad, but I am sure it will be an infidel."

They sat on the grass and drank coffee. The Franciscan said, "Do you have any belongings to take with you? No. Soon we will start."

"Who will milk the ewes?" said Lottar. Some of the ewes were already working their way down the slope; they would stand and wait for her.

"Leave them," said the Franciscan.

In this way she left not only the sheep but her shelter, the meadow, the wild grape and the sumac and mountain ash and juniper bushes and scrub oak she had looked at all summer, the rabbit pelt she had used as a pillow and the pan she had boiled her coffee in, the heap of wood she had gathered only that morning, the stones around her fire—each one of them known to her by its particular shape and color. She understood that she was leaving, because the Franciscan was so stern, but she did not understand it in a way that would make her look around, to see everything for the last time. That was not necessary, anyway. She would never forget any of it.

As they entered the beech wood the Franciscan said, "Now we must be very quiet. I am going to take another path, which does not go so near the *kula*. If we hear anybody on the path, we will hide."

Hours, then, of silent walking, between the beech trees with their smooth elephant bark, and the black-limbed oaks and the dry pines. Up and down, crossing the ridges, choosing paths that Lottar had not known existed. The Franciscan never hesitated and never spoke of a rest. When they came out of the trees at last, Lottar was very surprised to see that there was still so much light in the sky.

The Franciscan pulled a loaf of bread and a knife from some pocket in his garment, and they ate as they walked.

They came to a dry riverbed, paved with stones that were not flat and easily walkable but a torrent, a still torrent of stones between fields of corn and tobacco. They could hear dogs barking, and sometimes people's voices. The corn and tobacco plants, still unharvested, were higher than their heads, and they walked along the dry river in this shelter, while the daylight entirely faded. When they could not walk anymore and the darkness would conceal them, they sat down on the white stones of the riverbed.

"Where are you taking me?" Lottar finally asked. At the start she had thought they must be going in the direction of the church and the priest's house, but now she saw that this could not be so. They had come much too far.

"I am taking you to the Bishop's house," said the Franciscan. "He will know what to do with you."

"Why not to your house?" said Lottar. "I could be a servant in your house."

"It isn't allowed—to have a woman servant in my house. Or in any priest's house. This Bishop now will not allow even an old woman. And he is right, trouble comes from having a woman in the house."

After the moon rose they went on. They walked and rested, walked and rested, but never fell asleep, or even looked for a comfortable place to lie down. Their feet were tough and their sandals well worn, and they did not get blisters. Both of them were used to walking long distances—the Franciscan in his far-flung parish and Lottar when she was following the sheep.

The Franciscan became less stern—perhaps less worried—after a while and talked to her almost as he had done in the first days of their acquaintance. He spoke Italian, though she was now fairly proficient in the language of the Ghegs.

"I was born in Italy," he said. "My parents were Ghegs, but I lived in Italy when I was young, and that was where I became a priest. Once I went back for a visit, years ago, and I shaved off my mustache, I do not know why. Oh, yes, I do know—it was because they laughed at me in the village. Then when I got back I did not dare show my face in the *madhe*. A hairless man there is a disgrace. I sat in a room in Skodra until it grew again."

"It is Skodra we are going to?" said Lottar.

"Yes, that is where the Bishop is. He will send a message that it was right to take you away, even if it is an act of stealing. They are barbarians, in the *madhe*. They will come up and pull on your sleeve in the middle of Mass and ask you to write a letter for them. Have you seen what they put up on the graves? The crosses? They make the cross into a very thin man with a rifle across his arms. Haven't you seen that?" He laughed and shook his head and said, "I don't know what to do with them. But they are good people all the same—they will never betray you."

"But you thought they might sell me in spite of my oath."

"Oh, yes. But to sell a woman is a way to get some money. And they are so poor."

Lottar now realized that in Skodra she would be in an unfamiliar position—she would not be powerless. When they got there, she could run away from him. She could find someone who spoke English, she could find the British Consulate. Or, if not that, the French.

The grass was soaking wet before dawn and the night got very cold. But when the sun came up Lottar stopped shivering and within an hour she was hot. They walked on all day. They ate the rest of the bread and drank from any stream they found that had water in it. They had left the dry river and the mountains far behind. Lottar looked back and saw a wall of jagged rocks with a little green clinging around their bases. That green was the woods and meadows which she had thought so high. They followed paths through the hot fields and were never out of the sound of barking dogs. They met people on the paths.

At first the Franciscan said, "Do not speak to anybody—they will wonder who you are." But he had to answer when greetings were spoken.

"Is this the way to Skodra? We are going to Skodra to the Bishop's house. This is my servant with me, who has come from the mountains."

"It is all right, you look like a servant in these clothes," he said to Lottar. "But do not speak—they will wonder, if you speak."

I had painted the walls of my bookstore a clear, light yellow. Yellow stands for intellectual curiosity. Somebody must have told me that. I opened the store in March of 1964. This was in Victoria, in British Columbia.

I sat there at the desk, with my offerings spread out behind me. The publishers' representatives had advised me to stock books about dogs and horses, sailing and gardening, bird books and flower books—they said that was all anybody in Victoria would buy. I flew against their advice and brought in novels and poetry and books that explained about Sufism and relativity and Linear B.[6] And I had set out these books, when they came, so that Political Science could shade into Philosophy and Philosophy into Religion without a harsh break, so that compatible poets could nestle together, the arrangement of the shelves of books—I believed—reflecting a more or less natural ambling of the mind, in which treasures new and forgotten might be continually surfacing. I had taken all this care, and now what? Now I waited, and I felt like somebody who had got dramatically dressed up for a party, maybe even fetching jewels from the pawnshop or the family vault, only to discover that it was just a few neighbors playing cards. It was just meat loaf and mashed potatoes in the kitchen, and a glass of fizzy pink wine.

The store was often empty for a couple of hours at a time, and then when somebody did come in, it would be to ask about a book remembered

---

6. An early form of Greek script. *Sufism:* Islamic mysticism. *Relativity:* that is, Albert Einstein's theory of relativity.

from the Sunday-school library or a grandmother's bookcase or left behind twenty years ago in a foreign hotel. The title was usually forgotten, but the person would tell me the story. It is about this little girl who goes out to Australia with her father to mine the gold claims they have inherited. It is about the woman who had a baby all alone in Alaska. It is about a race between one of the old clipper ships and the first steamer, way back in the 1840s.

Oh, well. I just thought I'd ask.

They would leave without a glance at the riches around them.

A few people did exclaim in gratitude, said what a glorious addition to the town. They would browse for half an hour, an hour, before spending seventy-five cents.

It takes time.

I had found a one-room apartment with a kitchenette in an old building at a corner called the Dardanelles. The bed folded up into the wall. But I did not usually bother to fold it up, because I never had any company. And the hook seemed unsafe to me. I was afraid that the bed might leap out of the wall sometime when I was eating my tinned soup or baked-potato supper. It might kill me. Also, I kept the window open all the time, because I believed I could smell a whiff of escaping gas, even when the two burners and the oven were shut off. With the window open at home and the door open at the store, to entice the customers, it was necessary for me to be always bundled up in my black woolly sweater or my red corduroy dressing gown (a garment that had once left its pink tinge on all my forsaken husband's handkerchiefs and underwear). I had difficulty separating myself from these comforting articles of clothing so that they might be washed. I was sleepy much of the time, underfed and shivering.

But I was not despondent. I had made a desperate change in my life, and in spite of the regrets I suffered every day, I was proud of that. I felt as if I had finally come out into the world in a new, true skin. Sitting at the desk, I made a cup of coffee or of thin red soup last an hour, clasping my hands around the cup while there was still any warmth to be got from it. I read, but without purpose or involvement. I read stray sentences from the books that I had always meant to read. Often these sentences seemed so satisfying to me, or so elusive and lovely, that I could not help abandoning all the surrounding words and giving myself up to a peculiar state. I was alert and dreamy, closed off from all particular people but conscious all the time of the city itself—which seemed a strange place.

A small city, here at the western edge of the country. Pockets of fakery for tourists. The Tudor shop fronts and double-decker buses and flower-pots and horse-drawn rides: almost insulting. But the sea light in the street, the spare and healthy old people leaning into the wind as they took their daily walks along the broom-topped cliffs, the shabby, slightly bizarre bungalows with their monkey-puzzle trees and ornate shrubs in the gardens. Chestnut trees blossom as spring comes on, hawthorn trees along the streets bear red-and-white flowers, oily-leaved bushes put out lush pink and rose-red blooms such as you would never see in the hinterlands. Like a town in a story, I thought—like the transplanted seaside town of the story set in New Zealand, in Tasmania. But something North American persists.

So many people, after all, have come here from Winnipeg or Saskatche-wan.[7] At noon a smell of dinners cooking drifts out of poor, plain apart-ment buildings. Frying meat, boiling vegetables—farm dinners being cooked, in the middle of the day, in cramped kitchenettes.

How could I tell what I liked so much? Certainly it was not what a new merchant might be looking for—bustle and energy to raise the hope of commercial success. *Not much doing* was the message the town got across to me. And when a person who is opening a store doesn't mind hearing the message *Not much doing,* you could ask, What's going on? People open shops in order to sell things, they hope to become busy so that they will have to enlarge the shop, then to sell more things, and grow rich, and eventually not have to come into the shop at all. Isn't that true? But are there other people who open a shop with the hope of being sheltered there, among such things as they most value—the yarn or the teacups or the books—and with the idea only of making a comfortable assertion? They will become a part of the block, a part of the street, part of every-body's map of the town, and eventually of everybody's memories. They will sit and drink coffee in the middle of the morning, they will get out the familiar bits of tinsel at Christmas, they will wash the windows in spring before spreading out the new stock. Shops, to these people, are what a cabin in the woods might be to somebody else—a refuge and a justification.

Some customers are necessary, of course. The rent comes due and the stock will not pay for itself. I had inherited a little money—that was what had made it possible for me to come out here and get the shop going—but unless business picked up to some extent I could not last beyond the summer. I understood that. I was glad that more people started coming in as the weather warmed up. More books were sold, survival began to seem possible. Book prizes were due to be awarded in the schools at the end of term, and that brought the school-teachers with their lists and their praise and their unfortunate expectation of discounts. The people who came to browse were buying regularly, and some of them began to turn into friends—or the sort of friends I had here, where it seemed I would be happy to talk to people day after day and never learn their names.

When Lottar and the priest first saw the town of Skodra, it seemed to float above the mud flats, its domes and steeples shining as if they were made of mist. But when they entered it in the early evening all this tranquillity vanished. The streets were paved with big, rough stones and were full of people and donkey carts, roving dogs, pigs being driven somewhere, and smells of fires and cooking and dung and something terrible—like rotten hides. A man came along with a parrot on his shoulder. The bird seemed to be shrieking curses in an unknown language. Several times the Francis-can stopped people and asked the way to the Bishop's house, but they pushed by him without answering or laughed at him or said some words he didn't understand. A boy said that he would show the way, for money.

"We have no money," the Franciscan said. He pulled Lottar into a

---

7. A central Canadian province, directly west of Manitoba. Winnipeg is the capital city of Manitoba.

doorway and there they sat down to rest. "In Maltsia e madhe," he said, "many of these who think so well of themselves would soon sing a different tune."

Lottar's notion of running away and leaving him had vanished. For one thing, she could not manage to ask directions any better than he could. For another, she felt that they were allies who could not survive in this place out of sight of each other. She had not understood how much she depended on the smell of his skin, the aggrieved determination of his long strides, the flourish of his black mustache.

The Franciscan jumped up and said he had remembered—he had remembered now the way to the Bishop's house. He hurried ahead of her through narrow, high-walled back streets where nothing of houses or courtyards could be seen—just walls and gates. The paving stones were thrust up so that walking here was as difficult as in the dry riverbed. But he was right, he gave a shout of triumph, they had come to the gate of the Bishop's house.

A servant opened the gate and let them in, but only after some high-pitched argument. Lottar was told to sit on the ground just inside the gate, and the Franciscan was led into the house to see the Bishop. Soon some-one was sent through the streets to the British Consulate (Lottar was not told this), and he came back with the Consul's manservant. It was dark by then, and the Consul's servant carried a lantern. And Lottar was led away again. She followed the servant and his lantern to the consulate.

A tub of hot water for her to bathe in, in the courtyard. Her clothes taken away. Probably burned. Her greasy black, vermin-infested hair cut off. Kerosene poured on her scalp. She had to tell her story—the story of how she came to Maltsia e madhe—and this was difficult, because she was not used to speaking English, also because that time seemed so far away and unimportant. She had to learn to sleep on a mattress, to sit on a chair, to eat with a knife and fork.

As soon as possible they put her on a boat.

Charlotte stopped. She said, "That part is not of interest."

I had come to Victoria because it was the farthest place I could get to from London, Ontario, without going out of the country. In London, my husband, Donald, and I had rented a basement apartment in our house to a couple named Nelson and Sylvia. Nelson was an English major at the university and Sylvia was a nurse. Donald was a dermatologist, and I was doing a thesis on Mary Shelley—not very quickly. I had met Donald when I went to see him about a rash on my neck. He was eight years older than I was—a tall, freckled, blushing man, cleverer than he looked. A dermatologist sees grief and despair, though the problems that bring peo-ple to him may not be in the same class as tumors and blocked arteries. He sees sabotage from within, and truly unlucky fate. He sees how matters like love and happiness can be governed by a patch of riled-up cells. Expe-rience of this sort had made Donald kind, in a cautious, impersonal way. He said that my rash was probably due to stress, and that he could see that I was going to be a wonderful woman, once I got a few problems under control.

We invited Sylvia and Nelson upstairs for dinner, and Sylvia told us about the tiny town they both came from, in Northern Ontario. She said that Nelson had always been the smartest person in their class and in their school and possibly in the whole town. When she said this, Nelson looked at her with a perfectly flat and devastating expression, an expression that seemed to be waiting with infinite patience and the mildest curiosity for some explanation, and Sylvia laughed and said, "Just kidding, of course."

When Sylvia was working late shifts at the hospital, I sometimes asked Nelson to share a meal with us in a more informal way. We got used to his silences and his indifferent table manners and to the fact that he did not eat rice or noodles, eggplant, olives, shrimp, peppers, or avocados, and no doubt a lot of other things, because those had not been familiar foods in the town in Northern Ontario.

Nelson looked older than he was. He was short and sturdily built, sallow-skinned, unsmiling, with a suggestion of mature scorn and handy pugnaciousness laid over his features, so that it seemed he might be a hockey coach, or an intelligent, uneducated, fair-minded, and foul-mouthed foreman of a construction gang, rather than a shy, twenty-two-year-old student.

He was not shy in love. I found him resourceful and determined. The seduction was mutual, and it was a first affair for both of us. I had once heard somebody say, at a party, that one of the nice things about marriage was that you could have real affairs—an affair before marriage could always turn out to be nothing but courtship. I was disgusted by this speech, and frightened to think that life could be so bleak and trivial. But once my own affair with Nelson started, I was amazed all the time. There was no bleakness or triviality about it, only ruthlessness and clarity of desire, and sparkling deception.

Nelson was the one who first faced up to things. One afternoon he turned on his back and said hoarsely and defiantly, "We are going to have to leave."

I thought he meant that he and Sylvia would have to leave, they could not go on living in this house. But he meant himself and me. "We" meant himself and me. Of course he and I had said "we" of our arrangements, of our transgression. Now he had made it the "we" of our decision—perhaps of a life together.

My thesis was supposed to be on Mary Shelley's later novels, the ones nobody knows about. *Lodore, Perkin Warbeck, The Last Man.* But I was really more interested in Mary's life before she learned her sad lessons and buckled down to raising her son to be a baronet. I loved to read about the other women who had hated or envied or traipsed along: Harriet, Shelley's[8] first wife, and Fanny Imlay, who was Mary's half-sister and may have been in love with Shelley herself, and Mary's stepsister, Mary Jane Clairmont, who took my own name—Claire—and joined Mary and Shelley on their unwed honeymoon so that she could keep on chasing Byron.[9] I had often talked to Donald about impetuous Mary and married Shelley and their meetings at Mary's mother's grave, about the suicides of Harriet

---

8. Percy Bysshe Shelley (1792–1822), British Romantic poet.   9. George Gordon, Lord Byron (1788–1824), British Romantic poet.

and Fanny and the persistence of Claire, who had a baby by Byron. But I never mentioned any of this to Nelson, partly because we had little time for talk and partly because I did not want him to think that I drew some sort of comfort or inspiration from this mishmash of love and despair and treachery and self-dramatizing. I did not want to think so myself. And Nelson was not a fan of the nineteenth century or the Romantics. He said so. He said that he wanted to do something on the Muckrakers.[1] Perhaps he meant that as a joke.

Sylvia did not behave like Harriet. Her mind was not influenced or impeded by literature, and when she found out what had been going on, she went into a wholesome rage.

"You blithering idiot," she said to Nelson.

"You two-faced twit," she said to me.

The four of us were in our living room. Donald went on cleaning and filling his pipe, tapped it and lit it, nursed and inspected it, drew on it, lit it again—all so much the way someone would do in a movie that I was embarrassed for him. Then he put some books and the latest copy of *Macleans* into his briefcase, went to the bathroom to get his razor and to the bedroom to get his pajamas, and walked out.

He went straight to the apartment of a young widow who worked as a secretary at his clinic. In a letter he wrote to me later, he said that he had never thought of this woman except as a friend until that night, when it suddenly dawned on him what a pleasure it would be to love a kind and sensible, *unwracked-up* sort of person.

Sylvia had to be at work at eleven o'clock. Nelson usually walked her over to the hospital—they did not have a car. On this night she told him that she would rather be escorted by a skunk.

That left Nelson and me alone together. The scene had lasted a much shorter time than I had expected. Nelson seemed gloomy but relieved, and if I felt that short shrift had been given to the notion of love as a capturing tide, a glorious and harrowing event, I knew better than to show it.

We lay down on the bed to talk about our plans and ended up making love, because that was what we were used to doing. Sometime during the night Nelson woke up and thought it best to go downstairs to his own bed.

I got up in the dark, dressed, packed a suitcase, wrote a note, and walked to the phone at the corner, where I called a taxi. I took the six-o'clock train to Toronto, connecting with the train to Vancouver. It was cheaper to take the train, if you were willing to sit up for three nights, which I was.

So there I sat, in the sad, shambling morning in the day coach, coming down the steep-walled Fraser Canyon[2] into the sodden Fraser Valley, where smoke hung over the small, dripping houses, the brown vines, the thorny bushes and huddled sheep. It was in December that this earthquake in my life had arrived. Christmas was cancelled for me. Winter with its snowdrifts and icicles and invigorating blizzards was cancelled by this blurred season of muck and rain. I was constipated, I knew that I had bad

1. American journalists, novelists, and critics of the early 20th century who exposed abuses and corruption in big business and politics.   2. River valley in British Columbia.

breath, my limbs were cramped, and my spirits utterly bleak. And did I not think then, What nonsense it is to suppose one man so different from another when all that life really boils down to is getting a decent cup of coffee and room to stretch out in? Did I not think that even if Nelson were sitting here beside me, he would have turned into a gray-faced stranger whose desolation and unease merely extended my own?

No. No. Nelson would still be Nelson to me. I had not changed, with regard to his skin and his smell and his forbidding eyes. It seemed to be the outside of Nelson which came most readily to my mind, and in the case of Donald it was his inner quakes and sympathies, the labored-at kindness and those private misgivings that I had got knowledge of by wheedling and conniving. If I could have my love of these two men together, and settle it on one man, I would be a happy woman. If I could care for everybody in the world as minutely as I did for Nelson, and as calmly, as uncarnally as I now did for Donald, I would be a saint. Instead, I had dealt a twofold, a wanton-seeming, blow.

The regular customers who had changed into something like friends were: a middle-aged woman who was a chartered accountant but preferred such reading as *Six Existentialist Thinkers*, and *The Meaning of Meaning*; a provincial civil servant who ordered splendid, expensive works of pornography such as I had not known existed (their elaborate Oriental, Etruscan connections seemed to me grotesque and uninteresting, compared to the simple, effective, longed-for rituals of myself and Nelson); a Notary Public who lived behind his office at the foot of Johnson Street ("I live in the slums," he told me. "Some night I expect a big bruiser of a fellow to lurch around the corner hollering 'Ste-el-la.'"; and the woman I knew later as Charlotte—the Notary Public called her the Duchess. None of these people cared much for one another, and an early attempt that I made to bring the accountant and the Notary Public into conversation was a fizzle.

"Spare me the females with the withered, painted faces," the Notary Public said, the next time he came in. "I hope you haven't got her lurking around anywhere tonight."

It was true that the accountant painted her thin, intelligent, fifty-year-old face with a heavy hand, and drew on eyebrows that were like two strokes of India ink. But who was the Notary Public to talk, with his stumpy, nicotined teeth and pocked cheeks?

"I got the impression of a rather superficial fellow," the accountant said, as if she had guessed and bravely discounted the remarks made about herself.

So much for trying to corral people into couples, I wrote to Donald. *And who am I to try?* I wrote to Donald regularly, describing the store, and the city, and even, as well as I could, my own unaccountable feelings. He was living with Helen, the secretary. I wrote also to Nelson, who might or might not be living alone, might or might not be reunited with Sylvia. I didn't think he was. I thought she would believe in inexcusable behavior and definite endings. He had a new address. I had looked it up in the London phone book at the public library. Donald, after a grudging start, was writing back. He wrote impersonal, mildly interesting letters about people we both knew, events at the clinic. Nelson did not write at all. I started sending registered letters. Now I knew at least that he picked them up.

Charlotte and Gjurdhi must have come into the store together, but I did not understand that they were a couple until it was time for them to leave. Charlotte was a heavy, shapeless, but quick-moving woman, with a pink face, bright blue eyes, and a lot of glistening white hair, worn like a girl's, waving down over her shoulders. Though the weather was fairly warm, she was wearing a cape of dark-gray velvet with a scanty gray fur trim—a garment that looked as if it belonged, or had once belonged, on the stage. A loose shirt and a pair of plaid wool slacks showed underneath, and there were open sandals on her broad, bare, dusty feet. She clanked as if she wore hidden armor. An arm reaching up to get a book showed what caused the clanking. Bracelets—any number of them, heavy or slender, tarnished or bright. Some were set with large, square stones, the color of toffee or blood.

"Imagine this old fraud being still on the go," she said to me, as if continuing some desultory and enjoyable conversation.

She had picked up a book by Anaïs Nin.[3]

"Don't pay any attention," she said. "I say terrible things. I'm quite fond of the woman, really. It's him I can't stand."

"Henry Miller?" I said, beginning to follow this.

"That's right." She went on talking about Henry Miller, Paris, California, in a scoffing, energetic, half-affectionate way. She seemed to have been neighbors, at least, with the people she was talking about. Finally, naïvely, I asked her if this was the case.

"No, no. I just feel I know them all. Not personally. Well—personally. Yes, personally. What other way is there to know them? I mean, I haven't met them, face-to-face. But in their books? Surely that's what they intend? I know them. I know them to the point where they bore me. Just like anybody you know. Don't you find that?"

She drifted over to the table where I had laid out the New Directions[4] paperbacks.

"Here's the new bunch, then," she said. "Oh, my," she said, widening her eyes at the photographs of Ginsberg and Corso and Ferlinghetti.[5] She began reading, so attentively that I thought the next thing she said must be part of some poem.

"I've gone by and I've seen you here," she said. She put the book down and I realized she meant me. "I've seen you sitting in here, and I've thought a young woman would probably like to be outside some of the time. In the sun. I don't suppose you'd consider hiring me to sit there, so you could get out?"

"Well, I would like to—" I said.

---

3. French-born American novelist and diarist (1903–1977), who maintained a close relationship with American novelist Henry Miller (1891–1980).　4. Avant-garde American publisher renowned for publishing major modernist American poets, including Ezra Pound (1885–1972) and a number of key figures of the Beat generation.　5. Allen Ginsberg (born 1926), Gregory Corso (born 1930), and Lawrence Ferlinghetti (born 1919), American Beat poets.

"I'm not so dumb. I'm fairly knowledgeable, really. Ask me who wrote Ovid's *Metamorphoses*. It's all right, you don't have to laugh."

"I would like to, but I really can't afford to."

"Oh, well. You're probably right. I'm not very chic. And I would probably foul things up. I would argue with people if they were buying books I thought were dreadful." She did not seem disappointed. She picked up a copy of *The Dud Avocado* and said, "There! I have to buy this, for the title."

She gave a little whistle, and the man it seemed to be meant for looked up from the table of books he had been staring at, near the back of the store. I had known he was there but had not connected him with her. I thought he was just one of those men who wander in off the street, alone, and stand looking about, as if trying to figure out what sort of place this is or what the books are for. Not a drunk or a panhandler, and certainly not anybody to be worried about—just one of a number of shabby, utterly uncommunicative old men who belong to the city somewhat as the pigeons do, moving restlessly all day within a limited area, never looking at people's faces. He was wearing a coat that came down to his ankles, made of some shiny, rubberized, liver-colored material, and a brown velvet cap with a tassle. The sort of cap a doddery old scholar or a clergyman might wear in an English movie. There was, then, a similarity between them—they were both wearing things that might have been discards from a costume box. But close up he looked years older than she. A long, yellowish face, drooping tobacco-brown eyes, an unsavory, straggling mustache. Some faint remains of handsomeness, or potency. A quenched ferocity. He came at her whistle—which seemed half serious, half a joke—and stood by, mute and self-respecting as a dog or a donkey, while the woman prepared to pay.

At that time, the government of British Columbia applied a sales tax to books. In this case it was four cents.

"I can't pay that," she said. "A tax on books. I think it is immoral. I would rather go to jail. Don't you agree?"

I agreed. I did not point out—as I would have done with anybody else—that the store would not be let off the hook on that account.

"Don't I sound appalling?" she said. "See what this government can do to people? It makes them into *orators*."

She put the book in her bag without paying the four cents, and never paid the tax on any future occasion.

I described the two of them to the Notary Public. He knew at once who I meant.

"I call them the Duchess and the Algerian," he said. "I don't know what the background is. I think maybe he's a retired terrorist. They go around the town with a wagon, like scavengers."

I got a note asking me to supper on a Sunday evening. It was signed *Charlotte*, without a surname, but the wording and handwriting were quite formal.

My husband Gjurdhi and I would be delighted—

Up until then I had not wished for any invitations of this sort and would have been embarrassed and disturbed to get one. So the pleasure I felt surprised me. Charlotte held out a decided promise; she was unlike the others whom I wanted to see only in the store.

The building where they lived was on Pandora Street. It was covered with mustard stucco and had a tiny, tiled vestibule that reminded me of a public toilet. It did not smell, though, and the apartment was not really dirty, just horrendously untidy. Books were stacked against the walls, and pieces of patterned cloth were hung up droopily to hide the wallpaper. There were bamboo blinds on the window, sheets of colored paper— surely flammable—pinned over the light bulbs.

"What a darling you are to come," cried Charlotte. "We were afraid you would have tons more interesting things to do than visiting ancient old us. Where can you sit down? What about here?" She took a pile of magazines off a wicker chair. "Is that comfortable? It makes such interesting noises, wicker. Sometimes I'll be sitting here alone and that chair will start creaking and cracking exactly as if someone were shifting around in it. I could say it was a presence, but I'm no good at believing in that rubbish. I've tried."

Gjurdhi poured out a sweet yellow wine. For me a long-stemmed glass that had not been dusted, for Charlotte a glass tumbler, for himself a plastic cup. It seemed impossible that any dinner could come out of the little kitchen alcove, where foodstuffs and pots and dishes were piled helter-skelter, but there was a good smell of roasting chicken, and in a little while Gjurdhi brought out the first course—platters of sliced cucumber, dishes of yogurt. I sat in the wicker chair and Charlotte in the single armchair. Gjurdhi sat on the floor. Charlotte was wearing her slacks, and a rose-colored T-shirt which clung to her unsupported breast. She had painted her toenails to match the T-shirt. Her bracelets clanked against the plate as she picked up the slices of cucumber. (We were eating with our fingers.) Gjurdhi wore his cap and a dark-red silky dressing gown over his trousers. Stains had mingled with its pattern.

After the cucumber, we ate chicken cooked with raisins in golden spices, and sour bread, and rice. Charlotte and I were provided with forks, but Gjurdhi scooped the rice up with the bread. I would often think of this meal in the years that followed, when this kind of food, this informal way of sitting and eating, and even some version of the style and the untidiness of the room, would become familiar and fashionable. The people I knew, and I myself, would give up—for a while—on dining-room tables, matching wineglasses, to some extent on cutlery or chairs. When I was being entertained, or making a stab at entertaining people, in this way, I would think of Charlotte and Gjurdhi and the edge of true privation, the risky authenticity that marked them off from all these later imitations. At the time, it was all new to me, and I was both uneasy and delighted. I hoped to be worthy of such exoticism but not to be tried too far.

Mary Shelley came to light shortly. I recited the titles of the later novels, and Charlotte said dreamily, "Per-kin War-beck. Wasn't he the one— wasn't he the one who pretended to be a little Prince who was murdered in the Tower?"

She was the only person I had ever met—not a historian, not a *Tudor* historian—who had known this.

"That would make a movie," she said. "Don't you think? The question I always think about Pretenders like that is who do *they* think they are? Do they believe it's true, or what? But Mary Shelley's own life is the movie, isn't it? I wonder there hasn't been one made. Who would play Mary, do you think? No. No, first of all, start with Harriet. Who would play Harriet?

"Someone who would look well drowned," she said, ripping off a golden chunk of chicken. "Elizabeth Taylor? Not a big enough part. Susannah York?[6]

"Who was the father?" she wondered, referring to Harriet's unborn baby. "I don't think it was Shelley. I've never thought so. Do you?"

This was all very well, very enjoyable, but I had hoped we would get to explanations—personal revelations, if not exactly confidences. You did expect some of that, on occasions like this. Hadn't Sylvia, at my own table, told about the town in Northern Ontario and about Nelson's being the smartest person in the school? I was surprised at how eager I found myself, at last, to tell my story. Donald and Nelson—I was looking forward to telling the truth, or some of it, in all its wounding complexity, to a person who would not be surprised or outraged by it. I would have liked to puzzle over my behavior, in good company. Had I taken on Donald as a father figure—or as a parent figure, since both my parents were dead? Had I deserted him because I was angry at *them* for deserting *me?* What did Nelson's silence mean, and was it now permanent? (But I did not think, after all, that I would tell anybody about the letter that had been returned to me last week, marked "Not Known at This Address.")

This was not what Charlotte had in mind. There was no opportunity, no exchange. After the chicken, the wineglass and the tumbler and cup were taken away and filled with an extremely sweet pink sherbet that was easier to drink than to eat with a spoon. Then came small cups of desperately strong coffee. Gjurdhi lit two candles as the room grew darker, and I was given one of these to carry to the bathroom, which turned out to be a toilet with a shower. Charlotte said the lights were not working.

"Some repairs going on," she said. "Or else they have taken a whim. I really think they take whims. But fortunately we have our gas stove. As long as we have a gas stove we can laugh at their whims. My only regret is that we cannot play any music. I was going to play some old political songs—'I dreamed I saw Joe Hill last night,' "[7] she sang in a mocking baritone. "Do you know that one?"

I did know it. Donald used to sing it when he was a little drunk. Usually the people who sang "Joe Hill" had certain vague but discernible political sympathies, but with Charlotte I did not think this would be so. She would not operate from sympathies, from principles. She would be playful about what other people took seriously. I was not certain what I felt about her. It was not simple liking or respect. It was more like a wish to move in her

6. British film star (born 1941), known for her roles in *A Man for All Seasons* and *Tom Jones*.   7. From "Joe Hill," a political song of the late 1930s (words by Alfred Hayes; music by Earl Robinson), recounting the fate of a prominent unionist who was killed at the Utah State Penitentiary in 1915.

element, unsurprised. To be buoyant, self-mocking, gently malicious, unquenchable.

Gjurdhi, meanwhile, was showing me some of the books. How had this started? Probably from a comment I made—how many of them there were, something of that sort—when I stumbled over some on my way back from the toilet. He was bringing forward books with bindings of leather or imitation leather—how could I know the difference?—with marbled endpapers, watercolor frontispieces, steel engravings. At first, I believed admiration might be all that was required, and I admired everything. But close to my ear I heard the mention of money—was that the first distinct thing I had ever heard Gjurdhi say?

"I only handle new books," I said. "These are marvellous, but I don't really know anything about them. It's a completely different business, books like these."

Gjurdhi shook his head as if I had not understood and he would now try, firmly, to explain again. He repeated the price in a more insistent voice. Did he think I was trying to haggle with him? Or perhaps he was telling me what he had paid for the book? We might be having a speculative conversation about the price it might be sold for—not about whether I should buy it.

I kept saying no, and yes, trying to juggle these responses appropriately. *No,* I cannot take them for my store. *Yes,* they are very fine. *No,* truly, I'm sorry, I am not the one to judge.

"If we had been living in another country, Gjurdhi and I might have done something," Charlotte was saying. "Or even if the movies in this country had ever got off the ground. That's what I would love to have done. Got work in the movies. As extras. Or maybe we are not bland enough types to be extras, maybe they would have found bit parts for us. I believe extras have to be the sort that don't stand out in a crowd, so you can use them over and over again. Gjurdhi and I are more memorable than that. Gjurdhi in particular—you could *use* that face."

She paid no attention to the second conversation that had developed, but continued talking to me, shaking her head indulgently at Gjurdhi now and then, to suggest that he was behaving in a way she found engaging, though perhaps importunate. I had to talk to him softly, sideways, nodding all the while in response to her.

"Really you should take them to the Antiquarian Bookstore," I said. "Yes, they are quite beautiful. Books like these are out of my range."

Gjurdhi did not whine, his manner was not ingratiating. Peremptory, rather. It seemed as if he would give me orders, and would be most disgusted if I did not capitulate. In my confusion I helped myself to more of the yellow wine, pouring it into my unwashed sherbet glass. This was probably a dire offense. Gjurdhi looked horridly displeased.

"Can you imagine illustrations in modern novels?" said Charlotte, finally consenting to tie the two conversations together. "For instance, in Norman Mailer? They would have to be abstracts. Don't you think? Sort of barbed wire and blotches?"

I went home with a headache and a feeling of jangled inadequacy. I was a prude, that was all, when it came to mixing up buying and selling with hospitality. I had perhaps behaved clumsily, I had disappointed them. And they had disappointed me. Making me wonder why I had been asked.

I was homesick for Donald, because of "Joe Hill."

I also had a longing for Nelson, because of an expression on Charlotte's face as I was leaving. A savoring and contented look that I knew had to do with Gjurdhi, though I hardly wanted to believe that. It made me think that after I walked downstairs and left the building and went into the street, some hot and skinny, slithery, yellowish, indecent old beast, some mangy but urgent old tiger, was going to pounce among the books and the dirty dishes and conduct a familiar rampage.

A day or so later I got a letter from Donald. He wanted a divorce, so that he could marry Helen.

I hired a clerk, a college girl, to come in for a couple of hours in the afternoon, so I could get to the bank, and do some office work. The first time Charlotte saw her she went up to the desk and patted a stack of books sitting there, ready for quick sale.

"Is this what the office managers are telling their minions to buy?" she said. The girl smiled cautiously and didn't answer.

Charlotte was right. It was a book called *Psycho-Cybernetics*,[8] about having a positive self-image.

"You were smart to hire her instead of me," Charlotte said. "She is much niftier-looking, and she won't shoot her mouth off and scare the customers away. She won't have *opinions*."

"There's something I ought to tell you about that woman," the clerk said, after Charlotte left.

That part is not of interest.

"What do you mean?" I said. But my mind had been wandering, that third afternoon in the hospital. Just at the last part of Charlotte's story I had thought of a special-order book that hadn't come in, on Mediterranean cruises. Also I had been thinking about the Notary Public, who had been beaten about the head the night before, in his office on Johnson Street. He was not dead but he might be blinded. Robbery? Or an act of revenge, outrage, connected with a layer of his life that I hadn't guessed at?

Melodrama and confusion made this place seem more ordinary to me, but less within my grasp.

"Of course it is of interest," I said. "All of it. It's a fascinating story."

"Fascinating," repeated Charlotte in a mincing way. She made a face, so she looked like a baby vomiting out a spoonful of pap. Her eyes, still fixed on me, seemed to be losing color, losing their childish, bright, and self-important blue. Fretfulness was changing into disgust. An expression of vicious disgust, she showed, of unspeakable weariness—such as people might show to the mirror but hardly ever to one another. Perhaps because of the thoughts that were already in my head, it occurred to me that Charlotte might die. She might die at any moment. At this moment. Now.

8. A mid-1960s pop psychology best-seller by Maxwell Maltz.

She motioned at the water glass, with its crooked plastic straw. I held the glass so that she could drink, and supported her head. I could feel the heat of her scalp, a throbbing at the base of her skull. She drank thirstily, and the terrible look left her face.

She said, "Stale."

"I think it would make an excellent movie," I said, easing her back onto the pillows. She grabbed my wrist, then let it go.

"Where did you get the idea?" I said.

"From life," said Charlotte indistinctly. "Wait a moment." She turned her head away, on the pillow, as if she had to arrange something in private. Then she recovered, and she told a little more.

Charlotte did not die. At least she did not die in the hospital. When I came in rather late, the next afternoon, her bed was empty and freshly made up. The nurse who had talked to me before was trying to take the temperature of the woman tied in the chair. She laughed at the look on my face.

"Oh, no!" she said. "Not that. She checked out of here this morning. Her husband came and got her. We were transferring her to a long-term place out in Saanich,[9] and he was supposed to be taking her there. He said he had the taxi outside. Then we get this phone call that they never showed up! They were in great spirits when they left. He brought her a pile of money, and she was throwing it up in the air. I don't know—maybe it was only dollar bills. But we haven't a clue where they've got to."

I walked around to the apartment building on Pandora Street. I thought they might simply have gone home. They might have lost the instructions about how to get to the nursing home and not wanted to ask. They might have decided to stay together in their apartment no matter what. They might have turned on the gas.

At first I could not find the building and thought that I must be in the wrong block. But I remembered the corner store and some of the houses. The building had been changed—that was what had happened. The stucco had been painted pink; large, new windows and French doors had been put in; little balconies with wrought-iron railings had been attached. The fancy balconies had been painted white, the whole place had the air of an ice-cream parlor. No doubt it had been renovated inside as well, and the rents increased, so that people like Charlotte and Gjurdhi could have no hope of living there. I checked the names by the door, and of course theirs were gone. They must have moved out some time ago.

The change in the apartment building seemed to have some message for me. It was about vanishing. I knew that Charlotte and Gjurdhi had not actually vanished—they were somewhere, living or dead. But for me they had vanished. And because of this fact—not really because of any loss of them—I was tipped into dismay more menacing than any of the little eddies of regret that had caught me in the past year. I had lost my bearings. I had to get back to the store so my clerk could go home, but I felt as if I could as easily walk another way, just any way at all. My connection was in danger—that was all. Sometimes our connection is frayed, it is in danger, it seems almost lost. Views and streets deny knowledge of us, the air grows thin. Wouldn't we rather have a destiny to submit to, then, something that claims us, anything, instead of such flimsy choices, arbitrary days?

I let myself slip, then, into imagining a life with Nelson. If I had done so accurately, this is how it would have gone.

He comes to Victoria. But he does not like the idea of working in the store, serving the public. He gets a job teaching at a boys' school, a posh place where his look of lower-class toughness, his bruising manners, soon make him a favorite.

We move from the apartment at the Dardanelles to a roomy bungalow a few blocks from the sea. We marry.

But this is the beginning of a period of estrangement. I become pregnant. Nelson falls in love with the mother of a student. I fall in love with an intern I meet in the hospital during labor.

We get over all this—Nelson and I do. We have another child. We acquire friends, furniture, rituals. We go to too many parties at certain seasons of the year, and talk regularly about starting a new life, somewhere far away, where we don't know anybody.

We become distant, close—distant, close—over and over again.

As I entered the store, I was aware of a man standing near the door, half looking in the window, half looking up the street, then looking at me. He was a short man dressed in a trenchcoat and a fedora. I had the impression of someone disguised. Jokingly disguised. He moved toward me and bumped my shoulder, and I cried out as if I had received the shock of my life, and indeed it was true that I had. For this really was Nelson, come to claim me. Or at least to accost me, and see what would happen.

> We have been very happy.
> I have often felt completely alone.
> There is always in this life something to discover.
> The days and the years have gone by in some sort of blur.
> On the whole, I am satisfied.

When Lottar was leaving the Bishop's courtyard, she was wrapped in a long cloak they had given her, perhaps to conceal her ragged clothing, or to contain her smell. The Consul's servant spoke to her in English, telling her where they were going. She could understand him but could not reply. It was not quite dark. She could still see the pale shapes of roses and oranges in the Bishop's garden.

The Bishop's man was holding the gate open.

She had never seen the Bishop at all. And she had not seen the Franciscan since he had followed the Bishop's man into the house. She called out for him now, as she was leaving. She had no name to call, so she called, "Xoti! Xoti! Xoti," which means "leader" or "master" in the language of the Ghegs. But no answer came, and the Consul's servant swung his lantern impatiently, showing her the way to go. Its light fell by accident on the Franciscan standing half concealed by a tree. It was a little orange tree he stood behind. His face, pale as the oranges were in that light, looked out of the branches, all its swarthiness drained away. It was a wan face hanging in the tree, its melancholy expression quite impersonal and undemanding, like the expression you might see on the face of a devout but proud apostle in a church window. Then it was gone, taking the breath out of her body, as she knew too late.

She called him and called him, and when the boat came into the harbor at Trieste he was waiting on the dock.

WOLE SOYINKA
born 1934

The governing theme of Wole Soyinka's work is the dualism of life and consciousness in modern Africa. His entire output, now considerable, occupies itself with the conditions of the African community in transition. Transition, for Soyinka, carries more than a historical and social meaning. It is charged with a metaphysical significance that derives from his perception of humanity in general, while referring to the transformations of modes of life, sensibility, and thought which have taken place in contemporary Africa as Western modernities impinge on indigenous life. Soyinka's work can be read both as a meditation on the profound disruptions in the collective psyche produced by this process and as an imaginative effort to repair the collapse of the old order with a new founding myth, a myth derived from his Yoruba inheritance and embodying his vision of a new, distinctively African moral and spiritual awareness.

Soyinka's acute sense of African dualism owes much to his personal life and background. He was born on July 13, 1934, in Abeokuta, western Nigeria, the second child in a family that had strong ties to the traditional Yoruba ruling class as well as to the new educated elite produced by Christian missionary activity. Soyinka's remarkable reconstruction, in *Isarà* (1989), of his father's youth, education, and teaching career in the missionary school was undertaken primarily as a gesture of filial devotion but is important too in its recall of the formation of an articulate Yoruba intelligentsia, whose nationalist aspirations and modernizing zeal have been largely responsible for the making of modern Nigeria. The book thus evokes the social history that underlies his own development and provides an extended perspective on what was to become the immediate context of his own work. Soyinka has also recounted his early life in *Aké: The Years of Childhood* (1981).

Soyinka began his education in 1938, at the parsonage school at Aké, where his father was headmaster. He entered Abeokuta Grammar School in 1944 for his secondary education but after a year transferred to Government College, an elite boarding school at Ibadan, some sixty miles north of his native city. In 1952, he enrolled at University College, Ibadan, which had recently been founded and was then affiliated with the University of London. His earliest writing was done while there, for a student journal, which had been started and edited by Chinua Achebe, who had preceded him as a student at the university. After two years at Ibadan, Soyinka left for England and entered the University of Leeds to study English literature. The Shakespeare scholar G. Wilson Knight has often been cited as a major influence on Soyinka during his years at Leeds, but mention must also be made of Arnold Kettle, who taught English at Leeds and whose Marxist readings of literature as a product of the play of social forces Soyinka could hardly ignore.

Graduating in 1957, Soyinka moved to London, where he was for a while a schoolteacher before becoming attached, as a playreader, to the Royal Court Theatre in 1959. The central role played by this theater company in the great postwar revival of British drama, through its productions of the work of Samuel Beckett, John Osborne, and Arnold Wesker, exposed Soyinka to the most innovative endeavor in English theater during this period. Also influential was the work of John Synge and Sean O'Casey, whose plays disclosed the poetry of Irish speech and endowed with symbolism the communal experience of the Irish people. And so were the efforts of T. S. Eliot and, in a less serious vein, of Christopher Fry, to revive English verse drama. Their plays may well have suggested to Soyinka the dramatic potential of Yoruba, his own native tongue. The theater of ideas, as developed by George Bernard Shaw, the dominant figure in British theater at this time, and by the German playwright Bertolt Brecht, also made an impression on Soyinka. Brecht's plays in particular, by combining dialogue with mime and song, must have recalled to Soyinka the multiform character of the performance traditions of his native culture.

The convergence of these many influences is evident in Soyinka's two early plays, *The Lion and the Jewel* and *The Swamp Dwellers*, first performed in 1959 as a double bill at Ibadan University Arts Theatre by the student drama group. With these works, Soyinka inaugurated a new era in Nigerian drama, bringing a sophisticated dramaturgy to bear on issues of relevance to his audience: in a light-hearted commentary on cultural ambiguity in *The Lion and the Jewel* and in the stark atmosphere of *The Swamp Dwellers*, a brooding reflection on the degradation of spiritual symbols in the service of power.

Early in 1960, Soyinka returned to Nigeria to the department of English at Ibadan, whose chair, Molly Mahood, had arranged for him a Rockefeller grant to research traditional drama in west Africa. This was on the eve of Nigerian independence, and he responded to the country's mood of anticipation by writing *A Dance of the Forests*, performed by the "1960 Masks," a theatrical group he had put together for the occasion. This play contains Soyinka's first major statement on issues of national life. Its sardonic vision of history as an interminable procession of human stupidities is intended not merely to counter the exaggerated claims, based on a romantic vision of the past, of a triumphant nationalism, but also to serve as a moral challenge to the new nation. For Soyinka begins to define here his conception of the creative artist as one who, despite his own human contradictions, must serve as an agent of moral insight and renewal for the people. The forest setting and the active presence of spirit characters both recall and enlarge the allegorical implications of traditional Yoruba folktales.

Over the next two years, Soyinka traveled extensively in west Africa observing indigenous drama and absorbing the performance styles of the popular Yoruba traveling theater, which flourished alongside the university-based drama in English that his own work was helping to revitalize. His research became apparent in his next play, *The Strong Breed*, which draws on the conventions of traditional theater ritual in treating a theme of heroic sacrifice in the service of communal redemption. Appointed lecturer in English at the University of Ife in 1962, Soyinka formed the "Orisun Theatre," a semiprofessional company that he trained and directed in a wide range of plays. His own were already appearing in print, helping to establish his reputation beyond Nigeria. In 1965 his first novel, *The Interpreters*, was published; it portrayed, within a densely symbolic narrative framework, a group of young Nigerian intellectuals futilely trying to give purpose to their lives and to chart a moral course for their society. His next play, *The Road* (1965), provides a realistic depiction of the desperate conditions of the underprivileged class in Nigerian society, underlining at the same time a broader theme of the transience of life. In the play, Soyinka draws heavily on Yoruba religious belief and cultic practices to portray life as a series of transitional states of being, a mystical progress through the cosmic realm. The play introduces one of Soyinka's most memorable characters, "Professor," an ambiguous figure, half quack, half visionary, whose morbid engrossment with death provides its metaphysical focus; his quest for "the word" involves, ultimately, an intense engagement with the mystery of life.

In October 1965, Soyinka found himself drawn into a political storm that had been gathering in Nigeria for more than a year. Arrested for allegedly holding up a state radio station and broadcasting a seditious message, he was acquitted at his trial for lack of evidence. In January 1966, a military coup toppled the government, and the country was plunged into a national crisis. Soyinka had meanwhile moved to Lagos, where he had been appointed head of the department of English at the university. *Kongi's Harvest*, written during this period and produced at the Dakar Arts Festival in May 1966, gives a political focus to the social anxieties expressed in his earlier work. It represents his personal contribution to the debate on political and socioeconomic organization in postindependence Africa, but his dramatic handling of the issue extends beyond the ideological framework of the debate. The politics of the modern dictator Kongi is seen to be not only a violation of human decency but a poisoning of the wellsprings of communal existence. We begin to form an idea of what these values are from the poetically charged speeches of King Danlola, a traditional ruler who is Kongi's antithesis. The same values receive a more intense formulation in *Idanre and Other Poems* (1967), Soyinka's first collection of poems.

Civil war broke out in Nigeria in July 1967. Arrested a month later by the federal authorities for collaborating with the rebel regime of Biafra, Soyinka was held without trial until October 1969. His prison experience gave new urgency to his moral concerns. As he writes in *The Man Died* (1972), a moving account of his detention and a searing indictment of the military regime, "The man dies in all who keep silent in the face of tyranny." These years of crisis and war account for the somber mood that runs through the play *Madmen and Specialists* (1970), with its absurdist emphasis on evil as a force in the universe, and the novel *Season of Anomy* (1973), dominated by visions of carnage and waste. However, the poems in *A Shuttle in the Crypt* (1971), a lyrical record of Soyinka's moods and feelings while in solitary confinement, provide evidence of his effort, through writing, to shore up his mind and, through meditation, to achieve a new insight into human experience: "Thought is hallowed in the lean oil / of Solitude."

After a brief tenure as director of the School of Drama at Ibadan, Soyinka went into exile in 1971, living mostly in England. On a commission from the British National Theatre, he wrote *The Bacchae of Euripides* (1973), a highly personal and verbally exuberant adaptation of the Greek classic. The life-affirming impulses associated with the cult of Dionysus are summoned against an overbearing King Pentheus, representative of a repressive order. Soyinka spent the 1973–74 academic year as a visiting fellow at Churchill College, Cambridge; while there, he delivered a series of lectures later published as *Myth, Literature and the African World* (1976). The volume contains his celebrated essay *The Fourth Stage*, an exposition of the Yoruba concept of tragedy. For Soyinka, the forms of ritual in his culture display an anguished disconnection from the "fourth stage," a state of transition to a new and fuller state of being that completes the continuum formed by the living, the dead, and the unborn. Here Ogun, the Yoruba god of iron, becomes central. As the first to accomplish this transition on behalf of humanity, he is venerated as the first artist, and the ritual commemoration in traditional Yoruba drama of his accomplishment replicates it symbolically to bridge a metaphysical gulf in the culture.

Soyinka's essay must be considered not so much as a factual account of Yoruba myth as a statement of what he takes to be its spirit. *Death and the King's Horse-*

man, his next play, illustrates the function of myth as Soyinka sees it, a function linked to his theory of a tragic human incompleteness that seeks completeness in ritual. The play is based on an actual event—a British colonial officer's intervention to prevent the ritual suicide, following the king of Oyo's death, of his "horseman," a minor chief whose privileges were conditional on his accompanying his king to the afterworld. In deriving the theme from this historical incident, Soyinka shifts focus from its anecdotal and ethnographic interest to the response of human beings to death. It is, however, essential to consider both aspects, for they reflect the dualism played out in the play. The opening scene offers us a view of Yoruba collective ethos as Soyinka intends us to understand it. The market setting registers the fusion of economic, social, and religious life in Yoruba culture, rehearsing, on an eminently festive note, the people's belief system. The prominent role of Iyaloja in the scene affirms the centrality of the female principle in this belief system, founded as it is on the idea of a constant flow of life through the entire realm of being. In this light, the "Not I" episode becomes crucial. Elesin's apparently joyous assumption of his tragic burden prepares the psychological ground for his later failure of will. His reiterations of responsibility for the integrity of his world take on more and more the character of protests and thus betray an ambivalence toward his culture's strategy for confronting death. The opening scene displays the original coherence of the Yoruba world, together with a suggestion of its latent tensions. Essential for this effect are the resources of the Yoruba oral tradition, for much of the verbal exchange between the characters, and especially between Elesin and his praise singer, is an adaptation of consecrated forms of Yoruba oral poetry, proverbs, and lineage praise names (*oriki orile*) which situate the individual within a network of social relations and obligations.

The intensity of this opening scene contrasts with the deliberate flatness of the second, which exhibits the colonial world as an inverted image of its Yoruba counterpart. The conventions of drawing room theater appropriately frame Pilkings's insensitive attitude to Yoruba ritual, demonstrated in his choice of traditional Yoruba dress as costume for a vulgar masked ball. Amusa's announcement of Elesin's impending suicide leads to the collision of the colonial and indigenous worlds dramatized in scene 3. The massing of the women in this scene and their sexual taunting of Amusa, the emasculated colonial subject, are highlighted by the action that takes place off stage—Elesin's union with his new bride and the symbolic meaning attached to it, the creation of new life.

With the return onstage of Elesin, the play moves to its highpoint as he steps into the realm of transition, suspended between life and death. The ritual quality of this scene is registered in the language, as the praise singer's trance-inducing words allude more and more to the incantations employed by healers and diviners. The arrest of Elesin breaks the spell of the praise singer's words, and the play begins a downward course toward a tragic resolution. Olunde's conversation with Jane Pilkings in scene 4, in which he vindicates the Yoruba position on ritual suicide with a view of sacrifice as a cultural and moral imperative, anticipates his own gesture to save the family honor and reestablish the social and spiritual bonds broken by what he sees as his father's betrayal of a sacred trust. Dominant in the final scene is the figure of Iyaloja, who now assumes the role of Earth Mother. Her pronouncement at the end accords with the vision of humanity that she has all along embodied, one that subsumes the individual in the comprehensive vision of universal life that Yoruba myth enunciates.

Death and the King's Horseman is Soyinka's masterpiece; in it, the verbal resourcefulness and mastery of theatrical effects evident in his earlier plays come together to produce a work whose evocative power ensures its appeal both as a mode of reconnection to a living tradition and as an exploration of a universal human dilemma. In an obvious reference to the play, the citation for the award to

Soyinka of the Nobel Prize for literature in 1986 describes his work as depicting "the drama of existence." By the time Soyinka retired from the University of Ife in 1985, he had become an international figure, and his plays have been produced all over the world. Besides the Nobel Prize, he has been the recipient of many honors, including the French Legion of Honor, and the range and diversity of his work have ensured his reputation as one of the most versatile and accomplished of contemporary writers.

Derek White, *Wole Soyinka* (1993), is a comprehensive and up-to-date study of Soyinka's work; but Eldred Jones, *The Writing of Wole Soyinka* (1973), can be consulted with profit, as can Gerald Moore, *Wole Soyinka* (1971). For an extended discussion of *Death and the King's Horseman* in the context of Soyinka's system of ideas, see Biodun Jeyifo, *Wole Soyinka: A Voice of Africa* (1990). These studies are complemented by James Gibbs, ed., *Critical Perspectives on Wole Soyinka* (1980), and James Gibbs and Bernth Lindfors, eds., *Research on Wole Soyinka* (1993), both collections of essays on various aspects of Soyinka's work and career.

PRONOUNCING GLOSSARY

The following list uses common English syllables to provide rough equivalents of selected words whose pronunciation may be unfamiliar to the general reader.

agbada: *ah-gbah-dah*

Alafin: *ah-lah-feeng*

Apinke: *ah-kpeeng-keh*

egungun: *ay-goong-goong*

Elegbara: *eh-leh-gbah-rah*

Elesin Oba: *eh-leh-sheeng aw-bah*

Esu: *ay-shoo*

gbedu: *gbeh-doo*

Ifawomi: *ee-fah-woh-mee*

Ilesi: *ee-lay-see*

Iyaloja: *ee-yah-law-jah*

Olohun-iyo: *oh-loh-hoong—yaw*

Olunde: *oh-loong-day*

opele: *aw-kpeh-leh*

osugbo: *oh-shoo-gboh*

Oya: *aw-yah*

sanyan: *song-yong*

sigidi: *shee-gee-dee*

Wuraola: *woo-rah-aw-lah*

Death and the King's Horseman

CAST

PRAISE-SINGER

ELESIN, *Horseman of the King*

IYALOJA, *"Mother" of the market*

SIMON PILKINGS, *District Officer*

JANE PILKINGS, *his wife*

SERJEANT AMUSA

JOSEPH, *houseboy to the Pilkingses*

BRIDE

H. R. H. THE PRINCE

THE RESIDENT

AIDE-DE-CAMP

OLUNDE, *eldest son of Elesin*

DRUMMERS, WOMEN, YOUNG GIRLS, DANCERS *at the Ball*

Scene One

A passage through a market in its closing stages. The stalls are being emptied, mats folded. A few WOMEN *pass through on their way home, loaded with baskets. On a cloth-stand, bolts of cloth are taken down, display pieces folded and piled on a tray.* ELESIN OBA *enters along a passage before the market, pursued by his* DRUMMERS *and* PRAISE-SINGERS. *He is a man of enormous vitality, speaks, dances and sings with that infectious enjoyment of life which accompanies all his actions.*

PRAISE-SINGER: Elesin o! Elesin Oba! Howu![1] What tryst is this the cockerel goes to keep with such haste that he must leave his tail behind?

ELESIN: [*Slows down a bit, laughing.*] A tryst where the cockerel needs no adornment.

PRAISE-SINGER: O-oh, you hear that my companions? That's the way the world goes. Because the man approaches a brand new bride he forgets the long faithful mother of his children.

ELESIN: When the horse sniffs the stable does he not strain at the bridle? The market is the long-suffering home of my spirit and the women are packing up to go. That Esu[2]-harrassed day slipped into the stewpot while we feasted. We ate it up with the rest of the meat. I have neglected my women.

PRAISE-SINGER: We know all that. Still it's no reason for shedding your tail on this day of all days. I know the women will cover you in damask and *alari*[3] but when the wind blows cold from behind, that's when the fowl knows his true friends.

ELESIN: Olohun-iyo![4]

PRAISE-SINGER: Are you sure there will be one like me on the other side?

ELESIN: Olohun-iyo!

PRAISE-SINGER: Far be it for me to belittle the dwellers of that place but, a man is either born to his art or he isn't. And I don't know for certain that you'll meet my father, so who is going to sing these deeds in accents that will pierce the deafness of the ancient ones. I have prepared my going—just tell me: Olohun-iyo, I need you on this journey and I shall be behind you.

ELESIN: You're like a jealous wife. Stay close to me, but only on this side. My fame, my honour are legacies to the living; stay behind and let the world sip its honey from your lips.

PRAISE-SINGER: Your name will be like the sweet berry a child places under his tongue to sweeten the passage of food. The world will never spit it out.

ELESIN: Come then. This market is my roost. When I come among the women I am a chicken with a hundred mothers. I become a monarch whose palace is built with tenderness and beauty.

PRAISE-SINGER: They love to spoil you but beware. The hands of women also weaken the unwary.

ELESIN: This night I'll lay my head upon their lap and go to sleep. This night I'll touch feet with their feet in a dance that is no longer of this earth. But the smell of their flesh, their sweat, the smell of indigo[5] on their cloth, this is the last air I wish to breathe as I go to meet my great forebears.

---

1. An exclamation of surprise.   2. The god of fate in the Yoruba pantheon; also a trickster figure.
3. A rich woven cloth, brightly coloured [Author's note].   4. "Sweet voice": affectionate nickname for the praise-singer.   5. A deep blue dye.

PRAISE-SINGER: In their time the world was never tilted from its groove, it shall not be in yours.

ELESIN: The gods have said No.

PRAISE-SINGER: In their time the great wars came and went, the little wars came and went; the white slavers came and went, they took away the heart of our race, they bore away the mind and muscle of our race. The city fell and was rebuilt; the city fell and our people trudged through mountain and forest to find a new home but Elesin Oba do you year me?

ELESIN: I hear your voice Olohun-iyo.

PRAISE-SINGER: Our world was never wrenched from its true course.

ELESIN: The gods have said No.

PRAISE-SINGER: There is only one home to the life of a river-mussel; there is only one home to the life of a tortoise; there is only one shell to the soul of man; there is only one world to the spirit of our race. If that world leaves its course and smashes on boulders of the great void, whose world will give us shelter?

ELESIN: It did not in the time of my forebears, it shall not in mine.

PRAISE-SINGER: The cockerel must not be seen without his feathers.

ELESIN: Nor will the Not-I bird be much longer without his nest.

PRAISE-SINGER: [*Stopped in his lyric stride.*] The Not-I bird, Elesin?

ELESIN: I said, the Not-I bird.

PRAISE-SINGER: All respect to our elders but, is there really such a bird?

ELESIN: What! Could it be that he failed to knock on your door?

PRAISE-SINGER: [*Smiling.*] Elesin's riddles are not merely the nut in the kernel that breaks human teeth; he also buries the kernel in hot embers and dares a man's fingers to draw it out.

ELESIN: I am sure he called on you, Olohun-iyo. Did you hide in the loft and push out the servant to tell him you were out?

[ELESIN *executes a brief, half-taunting dance. The* DRUMMER *moves in and draws a rhythm out of his steps.* ELESIN *dances towards the market-place as he chants the story of the Not-I bird, his voice changing dexterously to mimic his characters. He performs like a born raconteur,[6] infecting his retinue with his humour and energy. More* WOMEN *arrive during his recital, including* IYALOJA.]

> Death came calling
> Who does not know his rasp of reeds?
> A twilight whisper in the leaves before
> The great araba[7] falls? Did you hear it?
> Not I! swears the farmer. He snaps
> His fingers round his head,[8] abandons
> A hard-worn harvest and begins
> A rapid dialogue with his legs.
>
> "Not I," shouts the fearless hunter, "but—
> It's getting dark, and this night-lamp
> Has leaked out all its oil. I think
> It's best to go home and resume my hunt

---

6. A storyteller.   7. A tall and majestic tropical tree.   8. The gesture for warding off evil.

Another day." But now he pauses, suddenly
Lets out a wail: "Oh foolish mouth, calling
Down a curse on your own head! Your lamp
Has leaked out all its oil, has it?"
Forwards or backwards now he dare not move.
To search for leaves and make etutu[9]
On that spot? Or race home to the safety
Of his hearth? Ten market-days have passed
My friends, and still he's rooted there
Rigid as the plinth of Orayan[1]

The mouth of the courtesan barely
Opened wide enough to take a ha'penny *robo*[2]
When she wailed: "Not I." All dressed she was
To call upon my friend the Chief Tax Officer.
But now she sends her go between instead:
"Tell him I'm ill: my period[3] has come suddenly
But not—I hope—my time."

Why is the pupil crying?
His hapless head was made to taste
The knuckles of my friend the Mallam:[4]
"If you were then reciting the Koran
Would you have ears for idle noises
Darkening the trees, you child of ill omen?"
He shuts down school before its time
Runs home and rings himself with amulets.
And take my good kinsman Ifawomi.[5]
His hands were like a carver's, strong
And true. I saw them
Tremble like wet wings of a fowl.
One day he cast his time-smoothed opele[6]
Across the divination board. And all because
The suppliant looked him in the eye and asked,
"Did you hear that whisper in the leaves?"
"Not I," was his reply; "perhaps I'm growing deaf—
Good-day." And Ifa spoke no more that day
The priest locked fast his doors,
Sealed up his leaking roof—but wait!
This sudden care was not for Fawomi
But for Osenyin,[7] a courier-bird of Ifa's
Heart of wisdom. I did not know a kite
Was hovering in the sky
And Ifa now a twittering chicken in
The brood of Fawomi the Mother Hen.[8]

Ah, but I must not forget my evening
Courier from the abundant palm, whose groan
Became Not I, as he constipated down

9. Rites of propitiation, often involving a sacrifice.   1. The mythical founder of Ife, the sacred city of
the Yoruba people. *Plinth:* a tall stone column planted into the earth at Ife, reputed to have been the staff
of Oranyan.   2. A delicacy made from crushed melon seeds, fried in tiny balls [Author's note].
3. That is, she is menstruating.   4. A teacher in a koranic school.   5. A name (later shortened to
Fawomi) that designates a devotee of Ifa, the god of divination, referred to further in the passage.   6. A
string of beads used in Ifa divination [Author's note].   7. The tutelary deity of Yoruba traditional healers.   8. That is, reduced in status, humiliated. Even a god as powerful as Ifa can be cowed by death.

A wayside bush. He wonders if Elegbara[9]
Has tricked his buttocks to discharge
Against a sacred grove. Hear him
Mutter spells to ward off penalties
For an abomination he did not intend.
If any here
Stumbles on a gourd of wine, fermenting
Near the road, and nearby hears a stream
Of spells issuing from a crouching form.
Brother to a *sigidi*,[1] bring home my wine,
Tell my tapper I have ejected
Fear from home and farm. Assure him,
All is well.

PRAISE-SINGER: In your time we do not doubt the peace of farmstead and
home, the peace of road and hearth, we do not doubt the peace of the
forest.

ELESIN: There was fear in the forest too.
Not-I was lately heard even in the lair
Of beasts. The hyena cackled loud. Not I,
The civet twitched his fiery tail and glared:
Not I. Not-I became the answering name
Of the restless bird,[2] that little one
Whom Death found nesting in the leaves
When whisper of his coming ran
Before him on the wind. Not-I
Has long abandoned home. This same dawn
I heard him twitter in the gods' abode.
Ah, companions of this living world
What a thing this is, that even those
We call immortal
Should fear to die.

IYALOJA: But you, husband of multitudes?

ELESIN: I, when that Not-I bird perched
Upon my roof, bade him seek his nest again.
Safe, without care or fear. I unrolled
My welcome mat for him to see. Not-I
Flew happily away, you'll hear his voice
No more in this lifetime—You all know
What I am.

PRAISE-SINGER: That rock which turns its open lodes
Into the path of lightning. A gay
Thoroughbred whose stride disdains
To falter though an adder[3] reared
Suddenly in his path.

ELESIN: My rein is loosened.
I am master of my Fate. When the hour comes
Watch me dance along the narrowing path
Glazed by the soles of my great precursors.
My soul is eager. I shall not turn aside.

WOMEN: You will not delay?

9. Another name for Esu.   1. A malevolent spirit.   2. Most likely the canary, which, when caged, is
constantly making short, rapid movements.   3. Or puff-adder, an extremely poisonous snake.

ELESIN: Where the storm pleases, and when, it directs
The giants of the forest. When friendship summons
Is when the true comrade goes.

WOMEN: Nothing will hold you back?

ELESIN: Nothing. What! Has no one told you yet
I go to keep my friend and master company.
Who says the mouth does not believe in
"No, I have chewed all that before?" I say I have.
The world is not a constant honey-pot.
Where I found little I made do with little.
Where there was plenty I gorged myself.
My master's hands and mine have always
Dipped together and, home or sacred feast,
The bowl was beaten bronze, the meats
So succulent our teeth accused us of neglect.
We shared the choicest of the season's
Harvest of yams. How my friend would read
Desire in my eyes before I knew the cause—
However rare, however precious, it was mine.

WOMEN: The town, the very land was yours.

ELESIN: The world was mine. Our joint hands
Raised housepots[4] of trust that withstood
The siege of envy and the termites of time.
But the twilight hour brings bats and rodents—
Shall I yield them cause to foul the rafters?

PRAISE-SINGER: Elesin Oba! Are you not that man who
Looked out of doors that stormy day
The god of luck[5] limped by, drenched
To the very lice that held
His rags together? You took pity upon
His sores and wished him fortune.
Fortune was footloose this dawn, he replied,
Till you trapped him in a heartfelt wish
That now returns to you. Elesin Oba!
I say you are that man who
Chanced upon the calabash of honour
You thought it was palm wine[6] and
Drained its contents to the final drop.

ELESIN: Life has an end. A life that will outlive
Fame and friendship begs another name.
What elder takes his tongue to his plate,
Licks it clean of every crumb?[7] He will encounter
Silence when he calls on children to fulfill
The smallest errand! Life is honour.
It ends when honour ends.

WOMEN: We know you for a man of honour.

ELESIN: Stop! Enough of that!

WOMEN: [*Puzzled, they whisper among themselves, turning mostly to* IYA-LOJA.] What is it? Did we say something to give offence? Have we slighted him in some way?

---

4. Used for storing the household's water.   5. Esu, who is represented as lame.   6. The sweet sap of the palm oil tree, which ferments naturally to become a potent drink. *Calabash:* container made from the fruit of a vine.   7. Elders are expected to deny themselves for the young.

ELESIN: Enough of that sound I say. Let me hear no more in that vein. I've heard enough.

IYALOJA: We must have said something wrong. [*Comes forward a little.*] Elesin Oba, we ask forgiveness before you speak.

ELESIN: I am bitterly offended.

IYALOJA: Our unworthiness has betrayed us. All we can do is ask your forgiveness. Correct us like a kind father.

ELESIN: This day of all days . . .

IYALOJA: It does not bear thinking. If we offend you now we have mortified the gods. We offend heaven itself. Father of us all, tell us where we went astray. [*She kneels, the other* WOMEN *follow.*]

ELESIN: Are you not ashamed? Even a tear-veiled
             Eye preserves its function of sight.
             Because my mind was raised to horizons
             Even the boldest man lowers his gaze
             In thinking of, must my body here
             Be taken for a vagrant's?

IYALOJA: Horseman of the King, I am more baffled than ever.

PRAISE-SINGER: The strictest father unbends his brow when the child is penitent, Elesin. When time is short, we do not spend it prolonging the riddle. Their shoulders are bowed with the weight of fear lest they have marred your day beyond repair. Speak now in plain words and let us pursue the ailment to the home of remedies.

ELESIN: Words are cheap. "We know you for
             A man of honour." Well tell me, is this how
             A man of honour should be seen?
             Are these not the same clothes in which
             I came among you a full half-hour ago?

[*He roars with laughter and the* WOMEN, *relieved, rise and rush into stalls to fetch rich clothes.*]

WOMEN: The gods are kind. A fault soon remedied is soon forgiven. Elesin Oba, even as we match our words with deed, let your heart forgive us completely.

ELESIN: You who are breath and giver of my being
             How shall I dare refuse you forgiveness
             Even if the offence was real.

IYALOJA: [*Dancing round him. Sings.*]
             He forgives us. He forgives us.
             What a fearful thing it is when
             The voyager sets forth
             But a curse remains behind.

WOMEN: For a while we truly feared
             Our hands had wrenched the world adrift
             In emptiness.

IYALOJA: Richly, richly, robe him richly
             The cloth of honour is alari
             Sanyan[8] is the band of friendship
             Boa-skin makes slippers of esteem.

WOMEN: For a while we truly feared

_____

8. Richly decorated woven cloth.

Our hands had wrenched the world adrift
In emptiness.

PRAISE-SINGER: He who must, must voyage forth
The world will not roll backwards
It is he who must, with one
Great gesture overtake the world.

WOMEN: For a while we truly feared
Our hands had wrenched the world
In emptiness.

PRAISE-SINGER: The gourd[9] you bear is not for shirking.
The gourd is not for setting down
At the first crossroad or wayside grove.
Only one river may know its contents.

WOMEN: We shall all meet at the great market
We shall all meet at the great market
He who goes early takes the best bargains
But we shall meet, and resume our banter.

[ELESIN *stands resplendent in rich clothes, cap, shawl, etc. His sash is of a bright red alari cloth. The* WOMEN *dance round him. Suddenly, his attention is caught by an object off-stage.*]

ELESIN: The world I know is good.
WOMEN: We know you'll leave it so.
ELESIN: The world I know is the bounty
Of hives after bees have swarmed.
No goodness teems with such open hands
Even in the dreams of deities.

WOMEN: And we know you'll leave it so.
ELESIN: I was born to keep it so. A hive
Is never known to wander. An anthill
Does not desert its roots. We cannot see
The still great womb of the world—
No man beholds his mother's womb—
Yet who denies it's there? Coiled
To the navel of the world is that
Endless cord that links us all
To the great origin. If I lose my way
The trailing cord will bring me to the roots.

WOMEN: The world is in your hands.

[*The earlier distraction, a beautiful young girl, comes along the passage through which* ELESIN *first made his entry.*]

ELESIN: I embrace it. And let me tell you, women—
I like this farewell that the world designed,
Unless my eyes deceive me, unless
We are already parted, the world and I,
And all that breeds desire is lodged
Among our tireless ancestors. Tell me friends,
Am I still earthed in that beloved market
Of my youth? Or could it be my will
Has outleapt the conscious act and I have come
Among the great departed?

---

9. Used for carrying water.

PRAISE-SINGER: Elesin Oba why do your eyes roll like a bush-rat who sees
his fate like his father's spirit, mirrored in the eye of a snake? And all
those questions! You're standing on the same earth you've always stood
upon. This voice you hear is mine, Oluhun-iyo, not that of an acolyte
in heaven.

ELESIN: How can that be? In all my life
As Horseman of the King, the juiciest
Fruit on every tree was mine. I saw,
I touched, I wooed, rarely was the answer No.
The honour of my place, the veneration I
Received in the eye of man or woman
Prospered my suit and
Played havoc with my sleeping hours.
And they tell me my eyes were a hawk
In perpetual hunger. Split an iroko tree[1]
In two, hide a woman's beauty in its heartwood
And seal it up again—Elesin, journeying by,
Would make his camp beside that tree
Of all the shades in the forest.

PRAISE-SINGER: Who would deny your reputation, snake-on-the-loose in
dark passages of the market! Bed-bug who wages war on the mat and
receives the thanks of the vanquished! When caught with his bride's
own sister he protested—but I was only prostrating myself to her as
becomes a grateful in-law. Hunter who carries his powder-horn on the
hips and fires crouching or standing! Warrior who never makes that
excuse of the whining coward—but how can I go to battle without my
trousers?—trouserless or shirtless it's all one to him. Oka[2]-rearing-from-
a-camouflage-of-leaves, before he strikes the victim is already prone!
Once they told me, Howu, a stallion does not feed on the grass beneath
him; he replied, true, but surely he can roll on it!

WOMEN: Ba-a-a-ba O![3]

PRAISE-SINGER: Ah, but listen yet. You know there is the leaf-knibbling
grub and there is the cola-chewing beetle; the leaf-nibbling grub lives
on the leaf, the cola-chewing beetle lives in the colanut. Don't we know
what our man feeds on when we find him cocooned in a woman's
wrapper?

ELESIN: Enough, enough, you all have cause
To know me well. But, if you say this earth
Is still the same as gave birth to those songs,
Tell me who was that goddess through whose lips
I saw the ivory pebbles of Oya's[4] river-bed.
Iyaloja, who is she? I saw her enter
Your stall; all your daughters I know well.
No, not even Ogun[5]-of-the-farm toiling
Dawn till dusk on his tuber patch
Not even Ogun with the finest hoe he ever
Forged at the anvil could have shaped
That rise of buttocks, not though he had

1. A tropical hardwood tree; it is a large tree with abundant foliage.   2. The python, a huge snake that
swallows its victims whole.   3. A form of salute to an elder male.   4. A Yoruba goddess said to live in
the river Niger.   5. The Yoruba god of iron and of war (equivalent in some ways to Mars).

The richest earth between his fingers.
Her wrapper was no disguise
For thighs whose ripples shamed the river's
Coils around the hills of Ilesi.[6] Her eyes
Were new-laid eggs glowing in the dark.
Her skin . . .

IYALOJA: Elesin Oba . . .

ELESIN: What! Where do you all say I am?

IYALOJA: Still among the living.

ELESIN: And that radiance which so suddenly
Lit up this market I could boast
I knew so well?

IYALOJA: Has one step already in her husband's home. She is betrothed.

ELESIN: [*Irritated.*] Why do you tell me that?

    [IYALOJA *falls silent. The* WOMEN *shuffle uneasily.*]

IYALOJA: Not because we dare give you offence Elesin. Today is your day
and the whole world is yours. Still, even those who leave town to make
a new dwelling elsewhere like to be remembered by what they leave
behind.

ELESIN: Who does not seek to be remembered?
Memory is Master of Death, the chink
In his armour of conceit. I shall leave
That which makes my going the sheerest
Dream of an afternoon. Should voyagers
Not travel light? Let the considerate traveller
Shed, of his excessive load, all
That may benefit the living.

WOMEN: [*Relieved.*] Ah Elesin Oba, we knew you for a man of honour.

ELESIN: Then honour me. I deserve a bed of honour to lie upon.

IYALOJA: The best is yours. We know you for a man of honour. You are not
one who eats and leaves nothing on his plate for children. Did you not
say it yourself? Not one who blights the happiness of others for a
moment's pleasure.

ELESIN: Who speaks of pleasure? O women, listen!
Pleasure palls. Our acts should have meaning.
The sap of the plantain[7] never dries.
You have seen the young shoot swelling
Even as the parent stalks begins to wither.
Women, let my going be likened to
The twilight hour of the plantain.

WOMEN: What does he mean Iyaloja? This language is the language of our
elders, we do not fully grasp it.

IYALOJA: I dare not understand you yet Elesin.

ELESIN: All you who stand before the spirit that dares
The opening of the last door of passage,
Dare to rid my going of regrets! My wish
Transcends the blotting out of thought
In one mere moment's tremor of the senses.

---

6. A town.   7. A plant related to the banana. It constantly regenerates itself from its young shoots
("suckers").

Do me credit. And do me honour.
I am girded for the route beyond
Burdens of waste and longing.
Then let me travel light. Let
Seed that will not serve the stomach
On the way remain behind. Let it take root
In the earth of my choice, in this earth
I leave behind.

IYALOJA: [*Turns to* WOMEN.] The voice I hear is already touched by the waiting fingers of our departed. I dare not refuse.

WOMAN: But Iyaloja . . .

IYALOJA: The matter is no longer in our hands.

WOMAN: But she is betrothed to your own son. Tell him.

IYALOJA: My son's wish is mine. I did the asking for him, the loss can be remedied. But who will remedy the blight of closed hands on the day when all should be openness and light? Tell him, you say! You wish that I burden him with knowledge that will sour his wish and lay regrets on the last moments of his mind. You pray to him who is your intercessor to the world—don't set this world adrift in your own time; would you rather it was my hand whose sacrilege wrenched it loose?

WOMAN: Not many men will brave the curse of a dispossessed husband.

IYALOJA: Only the curses of the departed are to be feared. The claims of one whose foot is on the threshold of their abode surpasses even the claims of blood. It is impiety even to place hindrances in their ways.

ELESIN: What do my mothers[8] say? Shall I step
               Burdened into the unknown?

IYALOJA: Not we, but the very earth says No. The sap in the plantain does not dry. Let grain that will not feed the voyager at his passage drop here and take root as he steps beyond this earth and us. Oh you who fill the home from hearth to threshold with the voices of children, you who now bestride the hidden gulf and pause to draw the right foot across and into the resting-home of the great forebears, it is good that your loins be drained into the earth we know, that your last strength be ploughed back into the womb that gave you being.

PRAISE-SINGER: Iyaloja, mother of multitudes in the teeming market of the world, how your wisdom transfigures you!

IYALOJA: [*Smiling broadly, completely reconciled.*] Elesin, even at the narrow end of the passage I know you will look back and sigh a last regret for the flesh that flashed past your spirit in flight. You always had a restless eye. Your choice has my blessing. [*To the* WOMEN.] Take the good news to our daughter and make her ready. [*Some* WOMEN *go off.*]

ELESIN: Your eyes were clouded at first.

IYALOJA: Not for long. It is those who stand at the gateway of the great change to whose cry we must pay heed. And then, think of this—it makes the mind tremble. The fruit of such a union is rare. It will be neither of this world nor of the next. Nor of the one behind us. As if the timelessness of the ancestor world and the unborn have joined spirits to wring an issue of the elusive being of passage . . . Elesin!

---

8. Here, a term of affection.

ELESIN: I am here. What is it?

IYALOJA: Did you hear all I said just now?

ELESIN: Yes.

IYALOJA: The living must eat and drink. When the moment comes, don't turn the food to rodents' droppings in their mouth. Don't let them taste the ashes of the world when they step out at dawn to breathe the morning dew.

ELESIN: This doubt is unworthy of you Iyaloja.

IYALOJA: Eating the awusa nut is not so difficult as drinking water afterwards.[9]

ELESIN: The waters of the bitter stream are honey to a man
Whose tongue has savoured all.

IYALOJA: No one knows when the ants desert their home; they leave the mound intact. The swallow is never seen to peck holes in its nest when it is time to move with the season. There are always throngs of humanity behind the leave-taker. The rain should not come through the roof for them, the wind must not blow through the walls at night.

ELESIN: I refuse to take offence.

IYALOJA: You wish to travel light. Well, the earth is yours. But be sure the seed you leave in it attracts no curse.

ELESIN: You really mistake my person Iyaloja.

IYALOJA: I said nothing. Now we must go prepare your bridal chamber. Then these same hands will lay your shrouds.

ELESIN: [*Exasperated.*] Must you be so blunt? [*Recovers.*] Well, weave your shrouds, but let the fingers of my bride seal my eyelids with earth and wash my body.

IYALOJA: Prepare yourself Elesin.

[*She gets up to leave. At that moment the* WOMEN *return, leading the* BRIDE. ELESIN's *face glows with pleasure. He flicks the sleeves of his agbada[1] with renewed confidence and steps forward to meet the group. As the girl kneels before* IYALOJA, *lights fade out on the scene.*]

Scene Two

The verandah of the District Officer's bungalow. A tango is playing from an old hand-cranked gramophone and, glimpsed through the wide windows and doors which open onto the forestage verandah are the shapes of SIMON PILKINGS *and his wife,* JANE, *tangoing in and out of shadows in the living room. They are wearing what is immediately apparent as some form of fancy-dress. The dance goes on for some moments and then the figure of a "Native Administration"* POLICEMAN *emerges and climbs up the steps onto the verandah. He peeps through and observes the dancing couple, reacting with what is obviously a long-standing bewilderment. He stiffens suddenly, his expression changes to one of disbelief and horror. In his excitement he upsets a flower-pot and attracts the attention of the couple. They stop dancing.*

---

9. The awasa nut eaten alone has a pleasant taste, but it turns bitter in the mouth if water is drunk just after.   1. A long flowing robe.

PILKINGS: Is there anyone out there?

JANE: I'll turn off the gramophone.

PILKINGS: [*Approaching the verandah.*] I'm sure I heard something fall over. [*The* CONSTABLE *retreats slowly, open-mouthed as* PILKINGS *approaches the verandah.*] Oh it's you Amusa. Why didn't you just knock instead of knocking things over?

AMUSA: [*Stammers badly and points a shaky finger at his dress.*] Mista Pirinkin . . . Mista Pirinkin . . .

PILKINGS: What is the matter with you?

JANE: [*Emerging.*] Who is it dear? Oh, Amusa . . .

PILKINGS: Yes it's Amusa, and acting most strangely.

AMUSA: [*His attention now transferred to* MRS. PILKINGS.] Mammadam² . . . you too!

PILKINGS: What the hell is the matter with you man!

JANE: Your costume darling. Our fancy dress.

PILKINGS: Oh hell, I'd forgotten all about that. (*Lifts the face mask over his head showing his face. His wife follows suit.*)

JANE: I think you've shocked his big pagan heart bless him.

PILKINGS: Nonsense, he's a Moslem. Come on Amusa, you don't believe in all that nonsense do you? I thought you were a good Moslem.

AMUSA: Mista Pirinkin, I beg you sir, what you think you do with that dress? It belong to dead cult, not for human being.

PILKINGS: Oh Amusa, what a let down you are. I swear by you at the club you know—thank God for Amusa, he doesn't believe in any mumbo-jumbo. And now look at you!

AMUSA: Mista Pirinkin, I beg you, take it off. Is not good for man like you to touch that cloth.

PILKINGS: Well, I've got it on. And what's more Jane and I have bet on it we're taking first prize at the ball. Now, if you can just pull yourself together and tell me what you wanted to see me about . . .

AMUSA: Sir, I cannot talk this matter to you in that dress. I no fit.

PILKINGS: What's that rubbish again?

JANE: He is dead earnest too Simon. I think you'll have to handle this delicately.

PILKINGS: Delicately my. . . ! Look here Amusa, I think this little joke has gone far enough hm? Let's have some sense. You seem to forget that you are a police officer in the service of His Majesty's Government. I order you to report your business at once or face disciplinary action.

AMUSA: Sir, it is a matter of death. How can man talk against death to person in uniform of death? Is like talking against government to person in uniform of police. Please sir, I go and come back.

PILKINGS: [*Roars.*] Now! [AMUSA *switches his gaze to the ceiling suddenly, remains mute.*]

JANE: Oh Amusa, what is there to be scared of in the costume? You saw it confiscated last month from those *egungun*³ men who were creating trouble in town. You helped arrest the cult leaders yourself—if the juju⁴

---

2. A confused stammer of the word *madam*.   3. Ancestral masks.   4. Charms and the occult power they possess.

didn't harm you at the time how could it possibly harm you now? And merely by looking at it?

AMUSA: [*Without looking down.*] Madam, I arrest the ringleaders who make trouble but me I no touch *egungun*. That *egungun* inself,[5] I no touch. And I no abuse 'am. I arrest ringleader but I treat *egungun* with respect.

PILKINGS: It's hopeless. We'll merely end up missing the best part of the ball. When they get this way there is nothing you can do. It's simply hammering against a brick wall. Write your report or whatever it is on that pad Amusa and take yourself out of here. Come on Jane. We only upset his delicate sensibilities by remaining here.

> [AMUSA *waits for them to leave, then writes in the notebook, somewhat laboriously. Drumming from the direction of the town wells up.* AMUSA *listens, makes a movement as if he wants to recall* PILKINGS *but changes his mind. Completes his note and goes. A few moments later* PILKINGS *emerges, picks up the pad and reads.*]

Jane!

JANE: [*From the bedroom.*] Coming darling. Nearly ready.

PILKINGS: Never mind being ready, just listen to this.

JANE: What is it?

PILKINGS: Amusa's report. Listen. "I have to report that it come to my information that one prominent chief, namely, the Elesin Oba, is to commit death tonight as a result of native custom. Because this is criminal offence I await further instruction at charge office. Sergeant Amusa."

> [JANE *comes out onto the verandah while he is reading.*]

JANE: Did I hear you say commit death?

PILKINGS: Obviously he means murder.

JANE: You mean a ritual murder?

PILKINGS: Must be. You think you've stamped it all out but it's always lurking under the surface somewhere.

JANE: Oh. Does it mean we are not getting to the ball at all?

PILKINGS: No-o. I'll have the man arrested. Everyone remotely involved. In any case there may be nothing to it. Just rumours.

JANE: Really? I thought you found Amusa's rumours generally reliable.

PILKINGS: That's true enough. But who knows what may have been giving him the scare lately. Look at his conduct tonight.

JANE: [*Laughing.*] You have to admit he had his own peculiar logic. [*Deepens her voice.*] How can man talk against death to person in uniform of death? [*Laughs.*] Anyway, you can't go into the police station dressed like that.

PILKINGS: I'll send Joseph with instructions. Damn it, what a confounded nuisance!

JANE: But don't you think you should talk first to the man, Simon?

PILKINGS: Do you want to go to the ball or not?

JANE: Darling, why are you getting rattled? I was only trying to be intelligent. It seems hardly fair just to lock up a man—and a chief at that—

---

5. Itself (pidgin English).

simply on the er . . . what is the legal word again? uncorroborated word of a sergeant.

PILKINGS: Well, that's easily decided. Joseph!

JOSEPH: [*From within.*] Yes master.

PILKINGS: You're quite right of course, I am getting rattled. Probably the effect of those bloody drums. Do you hear how they go on and on?

JANE: I wondered when you'd notice. Do you suppose it has something to do with this affair?

PILKINGS: Who knows? They always find an excuse for making a noise . . . [*Thoughtfully.*] Even so . . .

JANE: Yes Simon?

PILKINGS: It's different Jane. I don't think I've heard this particular— sound—before. Something unsettling about it.

JANE: I thought all bush drumming sounded the same.

PILKINGS: Don't tease me now Jane. This may be serious.

JANE: I'm sorry. [*Gets up and throws her arms around his neck. Kisses him. The houseboy enters, retreats and knocks.*]

PILKINGS: [*Wearily.*] Oh, come in Joseph! I don't know where you pick up all these elephantine notions of tact. Come over here.

JOSEPH: Sir?

PILKINGS: Joseph, are you a Christian or not?

JOSEPH: Yessir.

PILKINGS: Does seeing me in this outfit bother you?

JOSEPH: No sir, it has no power.

PILKINGS: Thank God for some sanity at last. Now Joseph, answer me on the honour of a Christian—what is supposed to be going on in town tonight?

JOSEPH: Tonight sir? You mean the chief who is going to kill himself?

PILKINGS: What?

JANE: What do you mean, kill himself?

PILKINGS: You do mean he is going to kill somebody don't you?

JOSEPH: No master. He will not kill anybody and no one will kill him. He will simply die.

JANE: But why Joseph?

JOSEPH: It is native law and custom. The King die last month. Tonight is his burial. But before they can bury him, the Elesin must die so as to accompany him to heaven.

PILKINGS: I seem to be fated to clash more often with that man than with any of the other chiefs.

JOSEPH: He is the King's Chief Horseman.

PILKINGS: [*In a resigned way.*] I know.

JANE: Simon, what's the matter?

PILKINGS: It would have to be him!

JANE: Who is he?

PILKINGS: Don't you remember? He's that chief with whom I had a scrap some three or four years ago. I helped his son get to a medical school in England, remember? He fought tooth and nail to prevent it.

JANE: Oh now I remember. He was that very sensitive young man. What was his name again?

PILKINGS: Olunde.[6] Haven't replied to his last letter come to think of it. The old pagan wanted him to stay and carry on some family tradition or the other. Honestly I couldn't understand the fuss he made. I literally had to help the boy escape from close confinement and load him onto the next boat. A most intelligent boy, really bright.

JANE: I rather thought he was much too sensitive you know. The kind of person you feel should be a poet munching rose petals in Bloomsbury.[7]

PILKINGS: Well, he's going to make a first-class doctor. His mind is set on that. And as long as he wants my help he is welcome to it.

JANE: [*After a pause.*] Simon.

PILKINGS: Yes?

JANE: This boy, he was the eldest son wasn't he?

PILKINGS: I'm not sure. Who could tell with that old ram?

JANE: Do you know, Joseph?

JOSEPH: Oh yes madam. He was the eldest son. That's why Elesin cursed master good and proper. The eldest son is not supposed to travel away from the land.

JANE: [*Giggling.*] Is that true Simon? Did he really curse you good and proper?

PILKINGS: By all accounts I should be dead by now.

JOSEPH: Oh no, master is white man. And good Christian. Black man juju can't touch master.

JANE: If he was his eldest, it means that he would be the Elesin to the next king. It's a family thing isn't it Joseph?

JOSEPH: Yes madam. And if this Elesin had died before the King, his eldest son must take his place.

JANE: That would explain why the old chief was so mad you took the boy away.

PILKINGS: Well it makes me all the more happy I did.

JANE: I wonder if he knew.

PILKINGS: Who? Oh, you mean Olunde?

JANE: Yes. Was that why he was so determined to get away? I wouldn't stay if I knew I was trapped in such a horrible custom.

PILKINGS: [*Thoughtfully.*] No, I don't think he knew. At least he gave no indication. But you couldn't really tell with him. He was rather close you know, quite unlike most of them. Didn't give much away, not even to me.

JANE: Aren't they all rather close, Simon?

PILKINGS: These natives here? Good gracious. They'll open their mouths and yap with you about their family secrets before you can stop them. Only the other day . . .

JANE: But Simon, do they really give anything away? I mean, anything that really counts. This affair for instance, we didn't know they still practised that custom did we?

PILKINGS: Ye-e-es, I suppose you're right there. Sly, devious bastards.

JOSEPH: [*Stiffly.*] Can I go now master? I have to clean the kitchen.

6. "My lord or deliverer has come"; a contraction of Olumide.   7. An area in central London associated with a brilliant group of writers in the years between the world wars; Virginia Woolf was the principal figure among them.

PILKINGS: What? Oh, you can go. Forgot you were still here.
  [JOSEPH *goes.*]
JANE: Simon, you really must watch your language. Bastard isn't just a
  simple swear-word in these parts, you know.
PILKINGS: Look, just when did you become a social anthropologist, that's
  what I'd like to know.
JANE: I'm not claiming to know anything. I just happen to have overheard
  quarrels among the servants. That's how I know they consider it a smear.
PILKINGS: I thought the extended family system took care of all that. Elastic
  family, no bastards.
JANE: [*Shrugs.*] Have it your own way.
  [*Awkward silence. The drumming increases in volume.* JANE *gets up
  suddenly, restless.*]
  That drumming Simon, do you think it might really be connected with
  this ritual? It's been going on all evening.
PILKINGS: Let's ask our native guide. Joseph! Just a minute Joseph. [JOSEPH
  re-enters.] What's the drumming about?
JOSEPH: I don't know master.
PILKINGS: What do you mean you don't know? It's only two years since
  your conversion. Don't tell me all that holy water nonsense also wiped
  out your tribal memory.
JOSEPH: [*Visibly shocked.*] Master!
JANE: Now you've done it.
PILKINGS: What have I done now?
JANE: Never mind. Listen Joseph, just tell me this. Is that drumming con-
  nected with dying or anything of that nature?
JOSEPH: Madam, this is what I am trying to say: I am not sure. It sounds
  like the death of a great chief and then, it sounds like the wedding of a
  great chief. It really mix me up.
PILKINGS: Oh get back to the kitchen. A fat lot of help you are.
JOSEPH: Yes master. [*Goes.*]
JANE: Simon . . .
PILKINGS: All right, all right. I'm in no mood for preaching.
JANE: It isn't my preaching you have to worry about, it's the preaching of
  the missionaries who preceded you here. When they make converts
  they really convert them. Calling holy water nonsense to our Joseph is
  really like insulting the Virgin Mary before a Roman Catholic. He's
  going to hand in his notice tomorrow you mark my word.
PILKINGS: Now you're being ridiculous.
JANE: Am I? What are you willing to bet that tomorrow we are going to be
  without a steward-boy? Did you see his face?
PILKINGS: I am more concerned about whether or not we will be one
  native chief short by tomorrow. Christ! Just listen to those drums. [*He
  strides up and down, undecided.*]
JANE: [*Getting up.*] I'll change and make up some supper.
PILKINGS: What's that?
JANE: Simon, it's obvious we have to miss this ball.
PILKINGS: Nonsense. It's the first bit of real fun the European club has

managed to organise for over a year, I'm damned if I'm going to miss it. And it is a rather special occasion. Doesn't happen every day.

JANE: You know this business has to be stopped Simon. And you are the only man who can do it.

PILKINGS: I don't have to stop anything. If they want to throw themselves off the top of a cliff or poison themselves for the sake of some barbaric custom what is that to me? If it were ritual murder or something like that I'd be duty-bound to do something. I can't keep an eye on all the potential suicides in this province. And as for that man—believe me it's good riddance.

JANE: [*Laughs.*] I know you better than that Simon. You are going to have to do something to stop it—after you've finished blustering.

PILKINGS: [*Shouts after her.*] And suppose after all it's only a wedding? I'd look a proper fool if I interrupted a chief on his honeymoon, wouldn't I? [*Resumes his angry stride, slows down.*] Ah well, who can tell what those chiefs actually do on their honeymoon anyway? [*He takes up the pad and scribbles rapidly on it.*] Joseph! Joseph! Joseph! [*Some moments later* JOSEPH *puts in a sulky appearance.*] Did you hear me call you? Why the hell didn't you answer?

JOSEPH: I didn't hear master.

PILKINGS: You didn't hear me! How come you are here then?

JOSEPH: [*Stubbornly.*] I didn't hear master.

PILKINGS: [*Controls himself with an effort.*] We'll talk about it in the morning. I want you to take this note directly to Sergeant Amusa. You'll find him at the charge office. Get on your bicycle and race there with it. I expect you back in twenty minutes exactly. Twenty minutes, is that clear?

JOSEPH: Yes master [*Going.*]

PILKINGS: Oh er . . . Joseph.

JOSEPH: Yes master?

PILKINGS: [*Between gritted teeth.*] Er . . . forget what I said just now. The holy water is not nonsense. *I* was talking nonsense.

JOSEPH: Yes master [*Goes.*]

JANE: [*Pokes her head round the door.*] Have you found him?

PILKINGS: Found who?

JANE: Joseph. Weren't you shouting for him?

PILKINGS: Oh yes, he turned up finally.

JANE: You sounded desperate. What was it all about?

PILKINGS: Oh nothing. I just wanted to apologise to him. Assure him that the holy water isn't really nonsense.

JANE: Oh? And how did he take it?

PILKINGS: Who the hell gives a damn! I had a sudden vision of our Very Reverend Macfarlane[8] drafting another letter of complaint to the Resident about my unchristian language towards his parishioners.

JANE: Oh I think he's given up on you by now.

PILKINGS: Don't be too sure. And anyway, I wanted to make sure Joseph

---

8. Irish priests were predominant in Catholic missionary activity in Nigeria.

didn't "lose" my note on the way. He looked sufficiently full of the holy crusade to do some such thing.

JANE: If you've finished exaggerating, come and have something to eat.

PILKINGS: No, put it all away. We can still get to the ball.

JANE: Simon . . .

PILKINGS: Get your costume back on. Nothing to worry about. I've instructed Amusa to arrest the man and lock him up.

JANE: But that station is hardly secure Simon. He'll soon get his friends to help him escape.

PILKINGS: A-ah, that's where I have out-thought you. I'm not having him put in the station cell. Amusa will bring him right here and lock him up in my study. And he'll stay with him till we get back. No one will dare come here to incite him to anything.

JANE: How clever of you darling. I'll get ready.

PILKINGS: Hey.

JANE: Yes darling.

PILKINGS: I have a surprise for you. I was going to keep it until we actually got to the ball.

JANE: What is it?

PILKINGS: You know the Prince is on a tour of the colonies don't you? Well, he docked in the capital only this morning but he is already at the Residency. He is going to grace the ball with his presence later tonight.

JANE: Simon! Not really.

PILKINGS: Yes he is. He's been invited to give away the prizes and he has agreed. You must admit old Engleton is the best Club Secretary we ever had. Quick off the mark that lad.

JANE: But how thrilling.

PILKINGS: The other provincials are going to be damned envious.

JANE: I wonder what he'll come as.

PILKINGS: Oh I don't know. As a coat-of-arms perhaps. Anyway it won't be anything to touch this.

JANE: Well that's lucky. If we are to be presented I won't have to start looking for a pair of gloves. It's all sewn on.[9]

PILKINGS: [Laughing.] Quite right. Trust a woman to think of that. Come on, let's get going.

JANE: [Rushing off.] Won't be a second. [Stops.] Now I see why you've been so edgy all evening. I thought you weren't handling this affair with your usual brilliance—to begin with, that is.

PILKINGS: [His mood is much improved.] Shut up woman and get your things on.

JANE: All right boss, coming.

[PILKINGS *suddenly begins to hum the tango to which they were dancing before. Starts to execute a few practice steps. Lights fade.*]

---

9. The masquerade costume is designed to cover the entire body of the wearer, to conceal his or her identity.

Scene Three

A *swelling, agitated hum of women's voices rises immediately in the background. The lights come on and we see the frontage of a converted cloth stall in the market. The floor leading up to the entrance is covered in rich velvets and woven cloth. The* WOMEN *come on stage, borne backwards by the determined progress of Sergeant* AMUSA *and his two* CONSTABLES *who already have their batons out and use them as a pressure against the* WOMEN. *At the edge of the cloth-covered floor however the* WOMEN *take a determined stand and block all further progress of the* MEN. *They begin to tease them mercilessly.*

AMUSA: I am tell you women for last time to commot my road.[1] I am here on official business.

WOMAN: Official business you white man's eunuch? Official business is taking place where you want to go and it's a business you wouldn't understand.

WOMAN: [*Makes a quick tug at the* CONSTABLE'S *baton.*] That doesn't fool anyone you know. It's the one you carry under your government knickers that counts. [*She bends low as if to peep under the baggy shorts. The embarrassed* CONSTABLE *quickly puts his knees together. The* WOMEN *roar.*]

WOMAN: You mean there is nothing there at all?

WOMAN: Oh there was something. You know that handbell which the whiteman uses to summon his servants. . . ?

AMUSA: [*He manages to preserve some dignity throughout.*] I hope you women know that interfering with officer in execution of his duty is criminal offence.

WOMAN: Interfere? He says we're interfering with him. You foolish man we're telling you there's nothing to interfere with.

AMUSA: I am order you now to clear the road.

WOMAN: What road? The one your father built?

WOMAN: You are a policeman not so? Then you know what they call trespassing in court. Or—[*pointing to the cloth-lined steps*]—do you think that kind of road is built for every kind of feet.

WOMAN: Go back and tell the white man who sent you to come himself.

AMUSA: If I go I will come back with reinforcement. And we will all return carrying weapons.

WOMAN: Oh, now I understand. Before they can put on those knickers the white man first cuts off their weapons.

WOMAN: What a cheek! You mean you come here to show power to women and you don't even have a weapon.

AMUSA: [*Shouting above the laughter.*] For the last time I warn you women to clear the road.

WOMAN: To where?

AMUSA: To that hut. I know he dey dere.

WOMAN: Who?

AMUSA: The chief who call himself Elesin Oba.

---

1. Get out of my way.

WOMAN: You ignorant man. It is not he who calls himself Elesin Oba, it is his blood that says it. As it called out to his father before him and will to his son after him. And that is in spite of everything your white man can do.

WOMAN: Is it not the same ocean that washes this land and the white man's land? Tell your white man he can hide our son away as long as he likes. When the time comes for him, the same ocean will bring him back.

AMUSA: The government say dat kin' ting[2] must stop.

WOMAN: Who will stop it? You? Tonight our husband and father will prove himself greater than the laws of strangers.

AMUSA: I tell you nobody go prove anyting tonight or anytime. Is ignorant and criminal to prove dat kin' prove.

IYALOJA: [Entering from the hut. She is accompanied by a group of young girls who have been attending the BRIDE.] What is it Amusa? Why do you come here to disturb the happiness of others.

AMUSA: Madame Iyaloja, I glad you come. You know me, I no like trouble but duty is duty. I am here to arrest Elesin for criminal intent. Tell these women to stop obstructing me in the performance of my duty.

IYALOJA: And you? What gives you the right to obstruct our leader of men in the performance of his duty.

AMUSA: What kin' duty be dat one Iyaloja.

IYALOJA: What kin' duty? What kin' duty does a man have to his new bride?

AMUSA: [Bewildered, looks at the women and at the entrance to the hut.] Iyaloja, is it wedding you call dis kin' ting?

IYALOJA: You have wives haven't you? Whatever the white man has done to you he hasn't stopped you having wives. And if he has, at least he is married. If you don't know what a marriage is, go and ask him to tell you.

AMUSA: This no to wedding.[3]

IYALOJA: And ask him at the same time what he would have done if anyone had come to disturb him on his wedding night.

AMUSA: Iyaloja, I say dis no to wedding.

IYALOJA: You want to look inside the bridal chamber? You want to see for yourself how a man cuts the virgin knot?

AMUSA: Madam . . .

WOMAN: Perhaps his wives are still waiting for him to learn.

AMUSA: Iyaloja, make you tell dese women make den no insult me again. If I hear dat kin' insult once more . . .

GIRL: [Pushing her way through.] You will do what?

GIRL: He's out of his mind. It's our mothers you're talking to, do you know that? Not to any illiterate villager you can bully and terrorise. How dare you intrude here anyway?

GIRL: What a cheek, what impertinence!

GIRL: You've treated them too gently. Now let them see what it is to tamper with the mothers of this market.

GIRL: Your betters dare not enter the market when the women say no!

GIRL: Haven't you learnt that yet, you jester in khaki and starch?

---

2. That kind of thing. 3. This is not a wedding.

IYALOJA: Daughters . . .

GIRL: No no Iyaloja, leave us to deal with him. He no longer knows his mother, we'll teach him.

[*With a sudden movement they snatch the batons of the two* CONSTA-BLES. *They begin to hem them in.*]

GIRL: What next? We have your batons? What next? What are you going to do?

[*With equally swift movements they knock off their hats.*]

GIRL: Move if you dare. We have your hats, what will you do about it? Didn't the white man teach you to take off your hats before women?

IYALOJA: It's a wedding night. It's a night of joy for us. Peace . . .

GIRL: Not for him. Who asked him here?

GIRL: Does he dare go to the Residency without an invitation?

GIRL: Not even where the servants eat the left-overs.

GIRLS: [*In turn. In an "English" accent.*] Well well it's Mister Amusa. Were you invited? [*Play acting to one another. The older* WOMEN *encourage them with their titters.*]

—Your invitation card please?

—Who are you? Have we been introduced?

—And who did you say you were?

—Sorry, I didn't quite catch your name.

—May I take your hat?

—If you insist. May I take yours? [*Exchanging the* POLICEMEN's *hats.*]

—How very kind of you.

—Not at all. Won't you sit down?

—After you.

—Oh no.

—I insist.

—You're most gracious.

—And how do you find the place?

—The natives are all right.

—Friendly?

—Tractable.

—Not a teeny-weeny bit restless?

—Well, a teeny-weeny bit restless.

—One might even say, difficult?

—Indeed one might be tempted to say, difficult.

—But you do manage to cope?

—Yes indeed I do. I have a rather faithful ox called Amusa.

—He's loyal?

—Absolutely.

—Lay down his life for you what?

—Without a moment's thought.

—Had one like that once. Trust him with my life.

—Mostly of course they are liars.

—Never known a native to tell the truth.

—Does it get rather close around here?

—It's mild for this time of the year.

—But the rains may still come.

—They are late this year aren't they?

—They are keeping African time.[4]

—Ha ha ha ha

—Ha ha ha ha

—The humidity is what gets me.

—It used to be whisky

—Ha ha ha ha

—Ha ha ha ha

—What's your handicap old chap?

—Is there racing by golly?

—Splendid golf course, you'll like it.

—I'm beginning to like it already.

—And a European club, exclusive.

—You've kept the flag flying.

—We do our best for the old country.

—It's a pleasure to serve.

—Another whisky old chap?

—You are indeed too too kind.

—Not at all sir. Where is that boy? [*With a sudden bellow.*] Sergeant!

AMUSA: [*Snaps to attention.*] Yessir!

[*The* WOMEN *collapse with laughter.*]

GIRL: Take your men out of here.

AMUSA: [*Realising the trick, he rages from loss of face.*] I'm give you warning . . .

GIRL: All right then. Off with his knickers! [*They surge slowly forward.*]

IYALOJA: Daughters, please.

AMUSA: [*Squaring himself for defence.*] The first woman wey touch me . . .

IYALOJA: My children, I beg of you . . .

GIRL: Then tell him to leave this market. This is the home of our mothers. We don't want the eater of white left-overs at the feast their hands have prepared.

IYALOJA: You heard them Amusa. You had better go.

GIRL: Now!

AMUSA: [*Commencing his retreat.*] We dey go now, but make you no say we no warn you.[5]

GIRLS: Now!

GIRL: Before we read the riot act—you should know all about that.

AMUSA: Make we go. [*They depart, more precipitately.*]

[*The* WOMEN *strike their palms across in the gesture of wonder.*]

WOMEN: Do they teach you all that at school?

WOMAN: And to think I nearly kept Apinke[6] away from the place.

WOMAN: Did you hear them? Did you see how they mimicked the white man?

WOMAN: The voices exactly. Hey, there are wonders in this world!

IYALOJA: Well, our elders have said it: Dada[7] may be weak, but he has a younger sibling who is truly fearless.

4. A standard colonial prejudice was that Africans lack a sense of time.   5. Don't say that we didn't warn you.   6. "One Who Is Equally Cherished by All"; the name of one of the girls.   7. A child born with tangled hair.

WOMAN: The next time the white man shows his face in this market I will set Wuraola[8] on his tail.

[*A* WOMAN *bursts into song and dance of euphoria—"Tani l'awa o l'ogbeja? Kayi! A l'ogbeja. Omo Kekere l'ogbeja."*[9] *The rest of the* WOMEN *join in, some placing the* GIRLS *on their back like infants, others dancing round them. The dance becomes general, mounting in excitement.* ELESIN *appears, in wrapper only. In his hands a white velvet cloth folded loosely as if it held some delicate object. He cries out.*]

ELESIN: Oh you mothers of beautiful brides! [*The dancing stops. They turn and see him, and the object in his hands.* IYALOJA *approaches and gently takes the cloth from him.*] Take it. It is no mere virgin stain, but the union of life and the seeds of passage. My vital flow, the last from this flesh is intermingled with the promise of future life. All is prepared. Listen! [*A steady drum beat from the distance.*] Yes. It is nearly time. The King's dog has been killed. The King's favourite horse is about to follow his master. My brother chiefs know their task and perform it well. [*He listens again.*]

[*The* BRIDE *emerges, stands shyly by the door. He turns to her.*] Our marriage is not yet wholly fulfilled. When earth and passage wed, the consummation is complete only when there are grains of earth on the eyelids of passage. Stay by me till then. My faithful drummers, do me your last service. This is where I have chosen to do my leave-taking, in this heart of life, this hive which contains the swarm of the world in its small compass. This is where I have known love and laughter away from the palace. Even the richest food cloys when eaten days on end; in the market, nothing ever cloys. Listen. [*They listen to the drums.*] They have begun to seek out the heart of the King's favourite horse. Soon it will ride in its bolt of raffia[1] with the dog at its feet. Together they will ride on the shoulders of the King's grooms through the pulse centres of the town. They know it is here I shall await them. I have told them. [*His eyes appear to cloud. He passes his hand over them as if to clear his sight. He gives a faint smile.*] It promises well; just then I felt my spirit's eagerness. The kite makes for wide spaces and the wind creeps up behind its tail; can the kite say less than—thank you, the quicker the better? But wait a while my spirit. Wait. Wait for the coming of the courier of the King. Do you know friends, the horse is born to this one destiny, to bear the burden that is man upon its back. Except for this night, this night alone when the spotless stallion will ride in triumph on the back of man. In the time of my father I witnessed the strange sight. Perhaps tonight also I shall see it for the last time. If they arrive before the drums beat for me, I shall tell him to let the Alafin[2] know I follow swiftly. If they come after the drums have sounded, why then, all is well for I have gone ahead. Our spirits shall fall in step along the great passage. [*He listens to the drums. He seems again to be falling*

---

8. "Dear as Gold"; a woman's name.   9. Who says we haven't a defender? Silence! We have our defenders. Little children are our champions [Author's translation].   1. The stem of this shrub is used for the decorative skirt worn in many African dances.   2. "Owner of the Palace" (literal trans.); the title of the king of Oyo.

into a state of semi-hypnosis; his eyes scan the sky but it is in a kind of daze. His voice is a little breathless.] The moon has fed, a glow from its full stomach fills the sky and air, but I cannot tell where is that gateway through which I must pass. My faithful friends, let our feet touch together this last time, lead me into the other market with sounds that cover my skin with down yet make my limbs strike earth like a thoroughbred. Dear mothers, let me dance into the passage even as I have lived beneath your roofs. [*He comes down progressively among them. They make way for him, the drummers playing. His dance is one of solemn, regal motions, each gesture of the body is made with a solemn finality. The* WOMEN *join him, their steps a somewhat more fluid version of his. Beneath the* PRAISE-SINGER's *exhortations the* WOMEN *dirge "Ale le le, awo mi lo."*]

PRAISE-SINGER: Elesin Alafin, can you hear my voice?
ELESIN: Faintly, my friend, faintly.
PRAISE-SINGER: Elesin Alafin, can you hear my call?
ELESIN: Faintly my king, faintly.
PRAISE-SINGER: Is your memory sound Elesin?
    Shall my voice be a blade of grass and
    Tickle the armpit of the past?
ELESIN: My memory needs no prodding but
    What do you wish to say to me?
PRAISE-SINGER: Only what has been spoken. Only what concerns
    The dying wish of the father of all.
ELESIN: It is buried like seed-yam in my mind
    This is the season of quick rains, the harvest
    Is this moment due for gathering.
PRAISE-SINGER: If you cannot come, I said, swear
    You'll tell my favourite horse. I shall
    Ride on through the gates alone.
ELESIN: Elesin's message will be read
    Only when his loyal heart no longer beats.
PRAISE-SINGER: If you cannot come Elesin, tell my dog.
    I cannot stay the keeper too long
    At the gate.
ELESIN: A dog does not outrun the hand
    That feeds it meat. A horse that throws its rider
    Slows down to a stop. Elesin Alafin
    Trusts no beasts with messages between
    A king and his companion.
PRAISE-SINGER: If you get lost my dog will track
    The hidden path to me.
ELESIN: The seven-way crossroads confuses
    Only the stranger. The Horseman of the King
    Was born in the recesses of the house.
PRAISE-SINGER: I know the wickedness of men. If there is
    Weight on the loose end of your sash, such weight
    As no mere man can shift; if your sash is
      earthed
    By evil minds who mean to part us at the last . . .
ELESIN: My sash is of the deep purple *alari*;

It is no tethering-rope. The elephant
Trails no tethering-rope; that king
Is not yet crowned who will peg an elephant—
Not even you my friend and King.

PRAISE-SINGER: And yet this fear will not depart from me
The darkness of this new abode is deep—
Will your human eyes suffice?

ELESIN: In a night which falls before our eyes
However deep, we do not miss our way.

PRAISE-SINGER: Shall I now not acknowledge I have stood
Where wonders met their end? The elephant deserves
Better than that we say "I have caught
A glimpse of something."[3] If we see the tamer
Of the forest let us say plainly, we have seen
An elephant.

ELESIN: [*His voice is drowsy.*]
I have freed myself of earth and now
It's getting dark. Strange voices guide my feet.

PRAISE-SINGER: The river is never so high that the eyes
Of a fish are covered. The night is not so dark
That the albino fails to find his way.[4] A child
Returning homewards craves no leading by the hand.
Gracefully does the mask[5] regain his grove at the end of
    the day . . .
Gracefully. Gracefully does the mask dance
Homeward at the end of the day, gracefully . . .

[ELESIN's *trance appears to be deepening, his steps heavier.*]

IYALOJA: It is the death of war that kills the valiant,
Death of water is how the swimmer goes
It is the death of markets that kills the trader
And death of indecision takes the idle away
The trade of the cutlass blunts its edge
And the beautiful die the death of beauty.
It takes an Elesin to die the death of death . . .
Only Elesin . . . dies the unknowable death of death . . .
Gracefully, gracefully does the horseman regain
The stables at the end of day, gracefully . . .

PRAISE-SINGER: How shall I tell what my eyes have seen? The Horseman
gallops on before the courier, how shall I tell what my eyes have seen?
He says a dog may be confused by new scents of beings he never dreamt
of, so he must precede the dog to heaven. He says a horse may stumble
on strange boulders and be lamed, so he races on before the horse to
heaven. It is best, he says, to trust no messenger who may falter at the
outer gate, oh how shall I tell what my ears have heard? But do you
hear me still Elesin, do you hear your faithful one?

[ELESIN *in his motions appears to feel for a direction of sound, subtly,
but he only sinks deeper into his trance dance.*]
Elesin Alafin, I no longer sense your flesh. The drums are changing

---

3. A Yoruba saying, meaning that an outstanding person or deed must be granted proper recognition.
4. Many albinos have poor eyesight.   5. Of the *egungun* masquerade.

now but you have gone far ahead of the world. It is not yet noon in heaven; let those who claim it is begin their own journey home. So why must you rush like an impatient bride: why do you race to desert your Olohun-iyo?

[ELESIN *is now sunk fully deep in his trance, there is no longer sign of any awareness of his surroundings.*]

Does the deep voice of *gbedu*[6] cover you then, like the passage of royal elephants? Those drums that brook no rivals, have they blocked the passage to your ears that my voice passes into wind, a mere leaf floating in the night? Is your flesh lightened Elesin, is that lump of earth I slid between your slippers to keep you longer slowly sifting from your feet? Are the drums on the other side now tuning skin to skin with ours in *osugbo?*[7] Are there sounds there I cannot hear, do footsteps surround you which pound the earth like *gbedu*, roll like thunder round the dome of the world? Is the darkness gathering in your head Elesin? Is there now a streak of light at the end of the passage, a light I dare not look upon? Does it reveal whose voices we often heard, whose touches we often felt, whose wisdoms come suddenly into the mind when the wisest have shaken their heads and murmured: It cannot be done? Elesin Alafin, don't think I do not know why your lips are heavy, why your limbs are drowsy as palm oil in the cold of harmattan.[8] I would call you back but when the elephant heads for the jungle, the tail is too small a handhold for the hunter that would pull him back. The sun that heads for the sea no longer heeds the prayers of the farmer. When the river begins to taste the salt of the ocean, we no longer know what deity to call on, the river-god or Olokun.[9] No arrow flies back to the string, the child does not return through the same passage that gave it birth. Elesin Oba, can you hear me at all? Your eyelids are glazed like a courtesan's, is it that you see the dark groom and master of life? And will you see my father? Will you tell him that I stayed with you to the last? Will my voice ring in your ears awhile, will you remember Olohun-iyo even if the music on the other side surpasses his mortal craft? But will they know you over there? Have they eyes to gauge your worth, have they the heart to love you, will they know what thoroughbred prances towards them in caparisons[1] of honour? If they do not Elesin, if any there cuts your yam with a small knife, or pours you wine in a small calabash, turn back and return to welcoming hands. If the world were not greater than the wishes of Olohun-iyo, I would not let you go . . .

[*He appears to break down.* ELESIN *dances on, completely in a trance. The dirge wells up louder and stronger.* ELESIN'*s dance does not lose its elasticity but his gestures become, if possible, even more weighty. Lights fade slowly on the scene.*]

---

6. Drums. Their deep resonance is caused by the hardwood from which they are made.   7. The secret executive cult of the Yoruba; its meeting place [Author's note].   8. A sharp, dry wind from the Sahara that blows over western Africa in December. The wind brings dust and noticeably cools the air. Palm oil congeals in cold weather and is thus said to sleep. Compare the American "slow as molasses in January."   9. Goddess of the sea.   1. Rich ceremonial cloth draped over the saddle of a horse.

Scene Four

*A Masque. The front side of the stage is part of a wide corridor around the
great hall of the Residency extending beyond vision into the rear and wings.
It is redolent of the tawdry decadence of a far-flung but key imperial frontier.
The* COUPLES *in a variety of fancy-dress are ranged around the walls, gazing
in the same direction. The guest-of-honour is about to make an appearance.
A portion of the local police brass band with its white* CONDUCTOR *is just
visible. At last, the entrance of* ROYALTY. *The band plays "Rule Britannia,"
badly, beginning long before he is visible. The couples bow and curtsey as
he passes by them. Both he and his companions are dressed in seventeenth
century European costume. Following behind are the* RESIDENT *and his*
PARTNER *similarly attired. As they gain the end of the hall where the orchestra dais begins the music comes to an end. The* PRINCE *bows to the guests.
The* BAND *strikes up a Viennese waltz and the* PRINCE *formally opens the
floor. Several bars later the* RESIDENT *and his companion follow suit. Others
follow in appropriate pecking order. The orchestra's waltz rendition is not of
the highest musical standard.*

Some time later the PRINCE *dances again into view and is settled into a
corner by the* RESIDENT *who then proceeds to select* COUPLES *as they dance
past for introduction, sometimes threading his way through the dancers to
tap the lucky* COUPLE *on the shoulder. Desperate efforts from many to ensure
that they are recognised in spite of perhaps, their costume. The ritual of
introductions soon takes in* PILKINGS *and his* WIFE. *The* PRINCE *is quite
fascinated by their costume and they demonstrate the adaptations they have
made to it, pulling down the mask to demonstrate how the* egungun *normally appears, then showing the various press-button controls they have
innovated for the face flaps, the sleeves, etc. They demonstrate the dance
steps and the guttural sounds made by the* egungun, *harrass other dancers
in the hall,* MRS. PILKINGS *playing the "restrainer"*[2] *to* PILKINGS' *manic
darts. Everyone is highly entertained, the Royal Party especially who lead
the applause.*

At this point a liveried FOOTMAN *comes in with a note on a salver and is
intercepted almost absent-mindedly by the* RESIDENT *who takes the note and
reads it. After polite coughs he succeeds in excusing the* PILKINGS *from the*
PRINCE *and takes them aside. The* PRINCE *considerately offers the* RESI-
DENT's WIFE *his hand and dancing is resumed.*

On their way out the RESIDENT *gives an order to his* AIDE-DE-CAMP.
They come into the side corridor where the RESIDENT *hands the note to*
PILKINGS.

RESIDENT: As you see it says "emergency" on the outside. I took the liberty
of opening it because His Highness was obviously enjoying the entertainment. I didn't want to interrupt unless really necessary.

PILKINGS: Yes, yes of course, sir.

RESIDENT: Is it really as bad as it says? What's it all about?

---

2. Masqueraders sometimes become possessed and go berserk; ropes are, therefore, tied to their waists
and held by *restrainers.*

PILKINGS: Some strange custom they have, sir. It seems because the King is dead some important chief has to commit suicide.

RESIDENT: The King? Isn't it the same one who died nearly a month ago?

PILKINGS: Yes, sir.

RESIDENT: Haven't they buried him yet?

PILKINGS: They take their time about these things, sir. The pre-burial ceremonies last nearly thirty days. It seems tonight is the final night.

RESIDENT: But what has it got to do with the market women? Why are they rioting? We've waived that troublesome tax haven't we?

PILKINGS: We don't quite know that they are exactly rioting yet, sir. Sergeant Amusa is sometimes prone to exaggerations.

RESIDENT: He sounds desperate enough. That comes out even in his rather quaint grammar. Where is the man anyway? I asked my aide-de-camp to bring him here.

PILKINGS: They are probably looking in the wrong verandah. I'll fetch him myself.

RESIDENT: No no you stay here. Let your wife go and look for them. Do you mind my dear. . . ?

JANE: Certainly not, your Excellency. [*Goes.*]

RESIDENT: You should have kept me informed, Pilkings. You realise how disastrous it would have been if things had erupted while His Highness was here.

PILKINGS: I wasn't aware of the whole business until tonight, sir.

RESIDENT: Nose to the ground Pilkings, nose to the ground. If we all let these little things slip past us where would the empire be eh? Tell me that. Where would we all be?

PILKINGS: [*Low voice.*] Sleeping peacefully at home I bet.

RESIDENT: What did you say, Pilkings?

PILKINGS: It won't happen again, sir.

RESIDENT: It mustn't, Pilkings. It mustn't. Where is that damned sergeant? I ought to get back to His Highness as quickly as possible and offer him some plausible explanation for my rather abrupt conduct. Can you think of one, Pilkings?

PILKINGS: You could tell him the truth, sir.

RESIDENT: I could? No no no no Pilkings, that would never do. What! Go and tell him there is a riot just two miles away from him? This is supposed to be a secure colony of His Majesty, Pilkings.

PILKINGS: Yes, sir.

RESIDENT: Ah, there they are. No, these are not our native police. Are these the ring-leaders of the riot?

PILKINGS: Sir, these are my police officers.

RESIDENT: Oh, I beg your pardon officers. You do look a little . . . I say, isn't there something missing in their uniform? I think they used to have some rather colourful sashes. If I remember rightly I recommended them myself in my young days in the service. A bit of colour always appeals to the natives, yes, I remember putting that in my report. Well well well, where are we? Make your report man.

PILKINGS: [*Moves close to* AMUSA, *between his teeth.*] And let's have no more superstitious nonsense from you Amusa or I'll throw you in the guardroom for a month and feed you pork![3]

RESIDENT: What's that? What has pork to do with it?

PILKINGS: Sir, I was just warning him to be brief. I'm sure you are most anxious to hear his report.

RESIDENT: Yes yes yes of course. Come on man, speak up. Hey, didn't we give them some colourful fez[4] hats with all those wavy things, yes, pink tassells . . .

PILKINGS: Sir, I think if he was permitted to make his report we might find that he lost his hat in the riot.

RESIDENT: Ah yes indeed. I'd better tell His Highness that. Lost his hat in the riot, ha ha. He'll probably say well, as long as he didn't lose his head. [*Chuckles to himself.*] Don't forget to send me a report first thing in the morning young Pilkings.

PILKINGS: No, sir.

RESIDENT: And whatever you do, don't let things get out of hand. Keep a cool head and—nose to the ground Pilkings. [*Wanders off in the general direction of the hall.*]

PILKINGS: Yes, sir.

AIDE-DE-CAMP: Would you be needing me, sir?

PILKINGS: No thanks, Bob. I think His Excellency's need of you is greater than ours.

AIDE-DE-CAMP: We have a detachment of soldiers from the capital, sir. They accompanied His Highness up here.

PILKINGS: I doubt if it will come to that but, thanks, I'll bear it in mind. Oh, could you send an orderly with my cloak.

AIDE-DE-CAMP: Very good, sir. [*Goes.*]

PILKINGS: Now, sergeant.

AMUSA: Sir . . . [*Makes an effort, stops dead. Eyes to the ceiling.*]

PILKINGS: Oh, not again.

AMUSA: I cannot against death to dead cult. This dress get power of dead.

PILKINGS: All right, let's go. You are relieved of all further duty Amusa. Report to me first thing in the morning.

JANE: Shall I come, Simon?

PILKINGS: No, there's no need for that. If I can get back later I will. Otherwise get Bob to bring you home.

JANE: Be careful Simon . . . I mean, be clever.

PILKINGS: Sure I will. You two, come with me. [*As he turns to go, the clock in the Residency begins to chime.* PILKINGS *looks at his watch then turns, horror-stricken, to stare at his wife. The same thought clearly occurs to her. He swallows hard. An* ORDERLY *brings his cloak.*] It's midnight. I had no idea it was that late.

JANE: But surely . . . they don't count the hours the way we do. The moon, or something . . .

PILKINGS: I am . . . not so sure.

[*He turns and breaks into a sudden run. The two* CONSTABLES *follow,*

---

3. Muslims are prohibited from eating pork.   4. Red caps worn by African officials in the colonial service.

also at a run. AMUSA, *who has kept his eyes on the ceiling throughout waits until the last of the footsteps has faded out of hearing. He salutes suddenly, but without once looking in the direction of the* WOMAN.]

AMUSA: Goodnight, madam.

JANE: Oh. [*She hesitates.*] Amusa . . . [*He goes off without seeming to have heard.*] Poor Simon . . . [*A figure emerges from the shadows, a young black* MAN *dressed in a sober western suit. He peeps into the hall, trying to make out the figures of the dancers.*]
Who is that?

OLUNDE: [*Emerges into the light.*] I didn't mean to startle you madam. I am looking for the District Officer.

JANE: Wait a minute . . . don't I know you? Yes, you are Olunde, the young man who . . .

OLUNDE: Mrs. Pilkings! How fortunate. I came here to look for your husband.

JANE: Olunde! Let's look at you. What a fine young man you've become. Grand but solemn. Good God, when did you return? Simon never said a word. But you do look well Olunde. Really!

OLUNDE: You are . . . well, you look quite well yourself Mrs. Pilkings. From what little I can see of you.

JANE: Oh, this. It's caused quite a stir I assure you, and not all of it very pleasant. You are not shocked I hope?

OLUNDE: Why should I be? But don't you find it rather hot in there? Your skin must find it difficult to breathe.

JANE: Well, it is a little hot I must confess, but it's all in a good cause.

OLUNDE: What cause Mrs. Pilkings?

JANE: All this. The ball. And His Highness being here in person and all that.

OLUNDE: [*Mildly.*] And that is the good cause for which you desecrate an ancestral mask?

JANE: Oh, so you are shocked after all. How disappointing.

OLUNDE: No I am not shocked, Mrs. Pilkings. You forget that I have now spent four years among your people. I discovered that you have no respect for what you do not understand.

JANE: Oh. So you've returned with a chip on your shoulder. That's a pity Olunde. I am sorry.
[*An uncomfortable silence follows.*]
I take it then that you did not find your stay in England altogether edifying.

OLUNDE: I don't say that. I found your people quite admirable in many ways, their conduct and courage in this war[5] for instance.

JANE: Ah yes, the war. Here of course it is all rather remote. From time to time we have a black-out drill just to remind us that there is a war on. And the rare convoy passes through on its way somewhere or on manoeuvres. Mind you there is the occasional bit of excitement like that ship that was blown up in the harbour.[6]

---

5. That is, World War II.   6. A reference to an incident that occurred in Lagos, the capital of Nigeria, in 1944.

OLUNDE: Here? Do you mean through enemy action?

JANE: Oh no, the war hasn't come that close. The captain did it himself. I don't quite understand it really. Simon tried to explain. The ship had to be blown up because it had become dangerous to the other ships, even to the city itself. Hundreds of the coastal population would have died.

OLUNDE: Maybe it was loaded with ammunition and had caught fire. Or some of those lethal gases they've been experimenting on.

JANE: Something like that. The captain blew himself up with it. Deliberately. Simon said someone had to remain on board to light the fuse.

OLUNDE: It must have been a very short fuse.

JANE: [*Shrugs.*] I don't know much about it. Only that there was no other way to save lives. No time to devise anything else. The captain took the decision and carried it out.

OLUNDE: Yes . . . I quite believe it. I met men like that in England.

JANE: Oh just look at me! Fancy welcoming you back with such morbid news. Stale too. It was at least six months ago.

OLUNDE: I don't find it morbid at all. I find it rather inspiring. It is an affirmative commentary on life.

JANE: What is?

OLUNDE: That captain's self-sacrifice.

JANE: Nonsense. Life should never be thrown deliberately away.

OLUNDE: And the innocent people around the harbour?

JANE: Oh, how does one know? The whole thing was probably exaggerated anyway.

OLUNDE: That was a risk the captain couldn't take. But please Mrs. Pilkings, do you think you could find your husband for me? I have to talk to him.

JANE: Simon? [*As she recollects for the first time the full significance of* OLUNDE'*s presence.*] Simon is . . . there is a little problem in town. He was sent for. But . . . when did you arrive? Does Simon know you're here?

OLUNDE: [*Suddenly earnest.*] I need your help Mrs. Pilkings. I've always found you somewhat more understanding than your husband. Please find him for me and when you do, you must help me talk to him.

JANE: I'm afraid I don't quite . . . follow you. Have you seen my husband already?

OLUNDE: I went to your house. Your houseboy told me you were here. [*He smiles.*] He even told me how I would recognise you and Mr. Pilkings.

JANE: Then you must know what my husband is trying to do for you.

OLUNDE: For me?

JANE: For you. For your people. And to think he didn't even know you were coming back! But how do you happen to be here? Only this evening we were talking about you. We thought you were still four thousand miles away.

OLUNDE: I was sent a cable.

JANE: A cable? Who did? Simon? The business of your father didn't begin till tonight.

OLUNDE: A relation sent it weeks ago, and it said nothing about my father.

All it said was, Our King is dead. But I knew I had to return home at once so as to bury my father. I understood that.

JANE: Well, thank God you don't have to go through that agony. Simon is going to stop it.

OLUNDE: That's why I want to see him. He's wasting his time. And since he has been so helpful to me I don't want him to incur the enmity of our people. Especially over nothing.

JANE: [*Sits down open mouthed.*] You . . . you Olunde!

OLUNDE: Mrs. Pilkings, I came home to bury my father. As soon as I heard the news I booked my passage home. In fact we were fortunate. We travelled in the same convoy as your Prince, so we had excellent protection.

JANE: But you don't think your father is also entitled to whatever protection is available to him?

OLUNDE: How can I make you understand? He *has* protection. No one can undertake what he does tonight without the deepest protection the mind can conceive. What can you offer him in place of his peace of mind, in place of the honour and veneration of his own people? What would you think of your Prince if he refused to accept the risk of losing his life on this voyage? This . . . showing the flag tour of colonial possessions.

JANE: I see. So it isn't just medicine you studied in England.

OLUNDE: Yet another error into which your people fall. You believe that everything which appears to make sense was learnt from you.

JANE: Not so fast Olunde. You have learnt to argue I can tell that, but I never said you made sense. However clearly you try to put it, it is still a barbaric custom. It is even worse—it's feudal! The king dies and a chieftan must be buried with him. How feudalistic can you get!

OLUNDE: [*Waves his hand towards the background. The* PRINCE *is dancing past again—to a different step—and all the guests are bowing and curtseying as he passes.*] And this? Even in the midst of a devastating war, look at that. What name would you give to that?

JANE: Therapy, British style. The preservation of sanity in the midst of chaos.

OLUNDE: Others would call it decadence. However, it doesn't really interest me. You white races know how to survive; I've seen proof of that. By all logical and natural laws this war should end with all the white races wiping out one another, wiping out their so-called civilisation for all time and reverting to a state of primitivism the like of which has so far only existed in your imagination when you thought of us. I thought all that at the beginning. Then I slowly realised that your greatest art is the art of survival. But at least have the humility to let others survive in their own way.

JANE: Through ritual suicide?

OLUNDE: Is that worse than mass suicide? Mrs. Pilkings, what do you call what those young men are sent to do by their generals in this war? Of course you have also mastered the art of calling things by names which don't remotely describe them.

JANE: You talk! You people with your long-winded, roundabout way of making conversation.

OLUNDE: Mrs. Pilkings, whatever we do, we never suggest that a thing is the opposite of what it really is. In your newsreels I heard defeats, thorough, murderous defeats described as strategic victories. No wait, it wasn't just on your newsreels. Don't forget I was attached to hospitals all the time. Hordes of your wounded passed through those wards. I spoke to them. I spent long evenings by their bedsides while they spoke terrible truths of the realities of that war. I know now how history is made.

JANE: But surely, in a war of this nature, for the morale of the nation you must expect . . .

OLUNDE: That a disaster beyond human reckoning be spoken of as a triumph? No. I mean, is there no mourning in the home of the bereaved that such blasphemy is permitted?

JANE: [*After a moment's pause.*] Perhaps I can understand you now. The time we picked for you was not really one for seeing us at our best.

OLUNDE: Don't think it was just the war. Before that even started I had plenty of time to study your people. I saw nothing, finally, that gave you the right to pass judgement on other peoples and their ways. Nothing at all.

JANE: [*Hesitantly.*] Was it the . . . colour thing? I know there is some discrimination.

OLUNDE: Don't make it so simple, Mrs. Pilkings. You make it sound as if when I left, I took nothing at all with me.

JANE: Yes . . . and to tell the truth, only this evening, Simon and I agreed that we never really knew what you left with.

OLUNDE: Neither did I. But I found out over there. I am grateful to your country for that. And I will never give it up.

JANE: Olunde, please . . . promise me something. Whatever you do, don't throw away what you have started to do. You want to be a doctor. My husband and I believe you will make an excellent one, sympathetic and competent. Don't let anything make you throw away your training.

OLUNDE: [*Genuinely surprised.*] Of course not. What a strange idea. I intend to return and complete my training. Once the burial of my father is over.

JANE: Oh, please. . . !

OLUNDE: Listen! Come outside. You can't hear anything against that music.

JANE: What is it?

OLUNDE: The drums. Can you hear the drums? Listen.

[*The drums come over, still distant but more distinct. There is a change of rhythm, it rises to a crescendo and then, suddenly, it is cut off. After a silence, a new beat begins, slow and resonant.*]

There it's all over.

JANE: You mean he's . . .

OLUNDE: Yes, Mrs. Pilkings, my father is dead. His will power has always been enormous; I know he is dead.

JANE: [*Screams.*] How can you be so callous! So unfeeling! You announce your father's own death like a surgeon looking down on some strange . . . stranger's body! You're just a savage like all the rest.

AIDE-DE-CAMP: [*Rushing out.*] Mrs. Pilkings. Mrs. Pilkings. [*She breaks down, sobbing.*] Are you all right, Mrs. Pilkings?

OLUNDE: She'll be all right. [*Turns to go.*]

AIDE-DE-CAMP: Who are you? And who the hell asked your opinion?

OLUNDE: You're quite right, nobody. [*Going.*]

AIDE-DE-CAMP: What the hell! Did you hear me ask you who you were?

OLUNDE: I have business to attend to.

AIDE-DE-CAMP: I'll give you business in a moment you impudent nigger. Answer my question!

OLUNDE: I have a funeral to arrange. Excuse me. [*Going.*]

AIDE-DE-CAMP: I said stop! Orderly!

JANE: No, no, don't do that. I'm all right. And for heaven's sake don't act so foolishly. He's a family friend.

AIDE-DE-CAMP: Well he'd better learn to answer civil questions when he's asked them. These natives put a suit on and they get high opinions of themselves.

OLUNDE: Can I go now?

JANE: No no don't go. I must talk to you. I'm sorry about what I said.

OLUNDE: It's nothing, Mrs. Pilkings. And I'm really anxious to go. I couldn't see my father before, it's forbidden for me, his heir and successor to set eyes on him from the moment of the king's death. But now . . . I would like to touch his body while it is still warm.

JANE: You will. I promise I shan't keep you long. Only, I couldn't possibly let you go like that. Bob, please excuse us.

AIDE-DE-CAMP: If you're sure . . .

JANE: Of course I'm sure. Something happened to upset me just then, but I'm all right now. Really.

[*The* AIDE DE CAMP *goes, somewhat reluctantly.*]

OLUNDE: I mustn't stay long.

JANE: Please, I promise not to keep you. It's just that . . . oh you saw yourself what happens to one in this place. The Resident's man thought he was being helpful, that's the way we all react. But I can't go in among that crowd just now and if I stay by myself somebody will come looking for me. Please, just say something for a few moments and then you can go. Just so I can recover myself.

OLUNDE: What do you want me to say?

JANE: Your calm acceptance for instance, can you explain that? It was so unnatural. I don't understand that at all. I feel a need to understand all I can.

OLUNDE: But you explained it yourself. My medical training perhaps. I have seen death too often. And the soldiers who returned from the front, they died on our hands all the time.

JANE: No. It has to be more than that. I feel it has to do with the many things we don't really grasp about your people. At least you can explain.

OLUNDE: All these things are part of it. And anyway, my father has been dead in my mind for nearly a month. Ever since I learnt of the King's death. I've lived with my bereavement so long now that I cannot think of him alive. On that journey on the boat, I kept my mind on my duties as the one who must perform the rites over his body. I went through it all again and again in my mind as he himself had taught me. I didn't want to do anything wrong, something which might jeopardise the welfare of my people.

JANE: But he had disowned you. When you left he swore publicly you were no longer his son.

OLUNDE: I told you, he was a man of tremendous will. Sometimes that's another way of saying stubborn. But among our people, you don't disown a child just like that. Even if I had died before him I would still be buried like his eldest son. But it's time for me to go.

JANE: Thank you. I feel calmer. Don't let me keep you from your duties.

OLUNDE: Goodnight, Mrs. Pilkings.

JANE: Welcome home.

[*She holds out her hand. As he takes it footsteps are heard approaching the drive. A short while later a woman's sobbing is also heard.*]

PILKINGS: [*Off.*] Keep them here till I get back. [*He strides into view, reacts at the sight of* OLUNDE *but turns to his wife.*] Thank goodness you're still here.

JANE: Simon, what happened?

PILKINGS: Later Jane, please. Is Bob still here?

JANE: Yes, I think so. I'm sure he must be.

PILKINGS: Try and get him out here as quickly as you can. Tell him it's urgent.

JANE: Of course. Oh Simon, you remember . . .

PILKINGS: Yes yes. I can see who it is. Get Bob out here. [*She runs off.*] At first I thought I was seeing a ghost.

OLUNDE: Mr. Pilkings, I appreciate what you tried to do. I want you to believe that. I can tell you it would have been a terrible calamity if you'd succeeded.

PILKINGS: [*Opens his mouth several times, shuts it.*] You . . . said what?

OLUNDE: A calamity for us, the entire people.

PILKINGS: [*Sighs.*] I see. Hm.

OLUNDE: And now I must go. I must see him before he turns cold.

PILKINGS: Oh ah . . . em . . . but this is a shock to see you. I mean er thinking all this while you were in England and thanking God for that.

OLUNDE: I came on the mail boat. We travelled in the Prince's convoy.

PILKINGS: Ah yes, a ah, hm . . . er well . . .

OLUNDE: Goodnight. I can see you are shocked by the whole business. But you must know by now there are things you cannot understand—or help.

PILKINGS: Yes. Just a minute. There are armed policemen that way and they have instructions to let no one pass. I suggest you wait a little. I'll er . . . give you an escort.

OLUNDE: That's very kind of you. But do you think it could be quickly arranged.

PILKINGS: Of course. In fact, yes, what I'll do is send Bob over with some men to the er . . . place. You can go with them. Here he comes now. Excuse me a minute.

AIDE-DE-CAMP: Anything wrong sir?

PILKINGS: [*Takes him to one side.*] Listen Bob, that cellar in the disused annexe of the Residency, you know, where the slaves were stored before being taken down to the coast . . .

AIDE-DE-CAMP: Oh yes, we use it as a storeroom for broken furniture.

PILKINGS: But it's still got the bars on it?

AIDE-DE-CAMP: Oh yes, they are quite intact.

PILKINGS: Get the keys please. I'll explain later. And I want a strong guard over the Residency tonight.

AIDE-DE-CAMP: We have that already. The detachment from the coast . . .

PILKINGS: No, I don't want them at the gates of the Residency. I want you to deploy them at the bottom of the hill, a long way from the main hall so they can deal with any situation long before the sound carries to the house.

AIDE-DE-CAMP: Yes of course.

PILKINGS: I don't want His Highness alarmed.

AIDE-DE-CAMP: You think the riot will spread here?

PILKINGS: It's unlikely but I don't want to take a chance. I made them believe I was going to lock the man up in my house, which was what I had planned to do in the first place. They are probably assailing it by now. I took a roundabout route here so I don't think there is any danger at all. At least not before dawn. Nobody is to leave the premises of course—the native employees I mean. They'll soon smell something is up and they can't keep their mouths shut.

AIDE-DE-CAMP: I'll give instructions at once.

PILKINGS: I'll take the prisoner down myself. Two policemen will stay with him throughout the night. Inside the cell.

AIDE-DE-CAMP: Right sir. [*Salutes and goes off at the double.*]

PILKINGS: Jane. Bob is coming back in a moment with a detachment. Until he gets back please stay with Olunde. [*He makes an extra warning gesture with his eyes.*]

OLUNDE: Please, Mr. Pilkings . . .

PILKINGS: I hate to be stuffy old son, but we have a crisis on our hands. It has to do with your father's affair if you must know. And it happens also at a time when we have His Highness here. I am responsible for security so you'll simply have to do as I say. I hope that's understood. [*Marches off quickly, in the direction from which he made his first appearance.*]

OLUNDE: What's going on? All this can't be just because he failed to stop my father killing himself.

JANE: I honestly don't know. Could it have sparked off a riot?

OLUNDE: No. If he'd succeeded that would be more likely to start the riot. Perhaps there were other factors involved. Was there a chieftancy dispute?

JANE: None that I know of.

ELESIN: [*An animal bellow from off.*] Leave me alone! Is it not enough

that you have covered me in shame! White man, take your hand from
my body!

    [OLUNDE *stands frozen to the spot.* JANE *understanding at last, tries to move him.*]

JANE: Let's go in. It's getting chilly out here.

PILKINGS: [*Off.*] Carry him.

ELESIN: Give me back the name you have taken away from me you ghost
from the land of the nameless!

PILKINGS: Carry him! I can't have a disturbance here. Quickly! stuff up his
mouth.

JANE: Oh God! Let's go in. Please Olunde.

    [OLUNDE *does not move.*]

ELESIN: Take your albino's hand from me you . . .

    [*Sounds of a struggle. His voice chokes as he is gagged.*]

OLUNDE: [*Quietly.*] That was my father's voice.

JANE: Oh you poor orphan, what have you come home to?

    [*There is a sudden explosion of rage from off-stage and powerful steps come running up the drive.*]

PILKINGS: You bloody fools, after him!

    [*Immediately* ELESIN, *in handcuffs, comes pounding in the direction of* JANE *and* OLUNDE, *followed some moments afterwards by* PILKINGS *and the* CONSTABLES. ELESIN, *confronted by the seeming statue of his son, stops dead.* OLUNDE *stares above his head into the distance. The* CONSTABLES *try to grab him.* JANE *screams at them.*]

JANE: Leave him alone! Simon, tell them to leave him alone.

PILKINGS: All right, stand aside you. [*Shrugs.*] Maybe just as well. It might
help to calm him down.

    [*For several moments they hold the same position.* ELESIN *moves a step forward, almost as if he's still in doubt.*]

ELESIN: Olunde? [*He moves his head, inspecting him from side to side.*]
Olunde! [*He collapses slowly at* OLUNDE's *feet.*] Oh son, don't let the
sight of your father turn you blind!

OLUNDE: [*He moves for the first time since he heard his voice, brings his head slowly down to look on him.*] I have no father, eater of left-overs.

    [*He walks slowly down the way his father had run. Light fades out on* ELESIN, *sobbing into the ground.*]

Scene Five

A wide iron barred gate stretches almost the whole width of the cell in which
ELESIN *is imprisoned. His wrists are encased in thick iron bracelets, chained
together; he stands against the bars, looking out. Seated on the ground to
one side on the outside is his recent* BRIDE, *her eyes bent perpetually to the
ground. Figures of the two* GUARDS *can be seen deeper inside the cell, alert
to every movement* ELESIN *makes.* PILKINGS *now in a police officer's uniform
enters noiselessly, observes him a while. Then he coughs ostentatiously and
approaches. Leans against the bars near a corner, his back to* ELESIN. *He is
obviously trying to fall in mood with him. Some moments' silence.*

PILKINGS: You seem fascinated by the moon.

ELESIN: [*After a pause.*] Yes, ghostly one. Your twin-brother up there engages my thoughts.

PILKINGS: It is a beautiful night.

ELESIN: Is that so?

PILKINGS: The light on the leaves, the peace of the night . . .

ELESIN: The night is not at peace, District Officer.

PILKINGS: No? I would have said it was. You know, quiet . .

ELESIN: And does quiet mean peace for you?

PILKINGS: Well, nearly the same thing. Naturally there is a subtle difference . . .

ELESIN: The night is not at peace, ghostly one. The world is not at peace. You have shattered the peace of the world for ever. There is no sleep in the world tonight.

PILKINGS: It is still a good bargain if the world should lose one night's sleep as the price of saving a man's life.

ELESIN: You did not save my life, District Officer. You destroyed it.

PILKINGS: Now come on . . .

ELESIN: And not merely my life but the lives of many. The end of the night's work is not over. Neither this year nor the next will see it. If I wished you well, I would pray that you do not stay long enough on our land to see the disaster you have brought upon us.

PILKINGS: Well, I did my duty as I saw it. I have no regrets.

ELESIN: No. The Regrets of life always come later.

[*Some moments' pause.*]

You are waiting for dawn, white man. I hear you saying to yourself: only so many hours until dawn and then the danger is over. All I must do is to keep him alive tonight. You don't quite understand it all but you know that tonight is when what ought to be must be brought about. I shall ease your mind even more, ghostly one. It is not an entire night but a moment of the night, and that moment is past. The moon was my messenger and guide. When it reached a certain gateway in the sky, it touched that moment for which my whole life has been spent in blessings. Even I do not know the gateway. I have stood here and scanned the sky for a glimpse of that door but, I cannot see it. Human eyes are useless for a search of this nature. But in the house of *osugbo,* those who keep watch through the spirit recognised the moment, they sent word to me through the voice of our sacred drums to prepare myself. I heard them and I shed all thoughts of earth. I began to follow the moon to the abode of the gods . . . servant of the white king, that was when you entered my chosen place of departure on feet of desecration.

PILKINGS: I'm sorry, but we all see our duty differently.

ELESIN: I no longer blame you. You stole from me my first-born, sent him to your country so you could turn him into something in your own image. Did you plan it all beforehand? There are moments when it seems part of a larger plan. He who must follow my footsteps is taken from me, sent across the ocean. Then, in my turn, I am stopped from fulfilling my destiny. Did you think it all out before, this plan to push our world from its course and sever the cord that links us to the great origin?

PILKINGS: You don't really believe that. Anyway, if that was my intention with your son, I appear to have failed.

ELESIN: You did not fail in the main, ghostly one. We know the roof covers the rafters, the cloth covers blemishes; who would have known that the white skin covered our future, preventing us from seeing the death our enemies had prepared for us. The world is set adrift and its inhabitants are lost. Around them, there is nothing but emptiness.

PILKINGS: Your son does not take so gloomy a view.

ELESIN: Are you dreaming now, white man? Were you not present at my reunion of shame? Did you not see when the world reversed itself and the father fell before his son, asking forgiveness?

PILKINGS: That was in the heat of the moment. I spoke to him and . . . if you want to know, he wishes he could cut out his tongue for uttering the words he did.

ELESIN: No. What he said must never be unsaid. The contempt of my own son rescued something of my shame at your hands. You have stopped me in my duty but I know now that I did give birth to a son. Once I mistrusted him for seeking the companionship of those my spirit knew as enemies of our race. Now I understand. One should seek to obtain the secrets of his enemies. He will avenge my shame, white one. His spirit will destroy you and yours.

PILKINGS: That kind of talk is hardly called for. If you don't want my consolation . . .

ELESIN: No white man, I do not want your consolation.

PILKINGS: As you wish. Your son anyway, sends his consolation. He asks your forgiveness. When I asked him not to despise you his reply was: I cannot judge him, and if I cannot judge him, I cannot despise him. He wants to come to you and say goodbye and to receive your blessing.

ELESIN: Goodbye? Is he returning to your land?

PILKINGS: Don't you think that's the most sensible thing for him to do? I advised him to leave at once, before dawn, and he agrees that is the right course of action.

ELESIN: Yes, it is best. And even if I did not think so, I have lost the father's place of honour. My voice is broken.

PILKINGS: Your son honours you. If he didn't he would not ask your blessing.

ELESIN: No. Even a thoroughbred is not without pity for the turf he strikes with his hoof. When is he coming?

PILKINGS: As soon as the town is a little quieter. I advised it.

ELESIN: Yes, white man, I am sure you advised it. You advise all our lives although on the authority of what gods, I do not know.

PILKINGS: [Opens his mouth to reply, then appears to change his mind. Turns to go. Hesitates and stops again.] Before I leave you, may I ask just one thing of you?

ELESIN: I am listening.

PILKINGS: I wish to ask you to search the quiet of your heart and tell me — do you not find great contradictions in the wisdom of your own race?

ELESIN: Make yourself clear, white one.

PILKINGS: I have lived among you long enough to learn a saying or two. One came to my mind tonight when I stepped into the market and saw what was going on. You were surrounded by those who egged you on with song and praises. I thought, are these not the same people who say: the elder grimly approaches heaven and you ask him to bear your greetings yonder; do you really think he makes the journey willingly? After that, I did not hesitate.

[*A pause.* ELESIN *sighs. Before he can speak a sound of running feet is heard.*]

JANE: [*Off.*] Simon! Simon!

PILKINGS: What on earth. . . ! [*Runs off.*]

[ELESIN *turns to his new wife, gazes on her for some moments.*]

ELESIN: My young bride, did you hear the ghostly one? You sit and sob in your silent heart but say nothing to all this. First I blamed the white man, then I blamed my gods for deserting me. Now I feel I want to blame you for the mystery of the sapping of my will. But blame is a strange peace offering for a man to bring a world he has deeply wronged, and to its innocent dwellers. Oh little mother, I have taken countless women in my life but you were more than a desire of the flesh. I needed you as the abyss across which my body must be drawn, I filled it with earth and dropped my seed in it at the moment of preparedness for my crossing. You were the final gift of the living to their emissary to the land of the ancestors, and perhaps your warmth and youth brought new insights of this world to me and turned my feet leaden on this side of the abyss. For I confess to you, daughter, my weakness came not merely from the abomination of the white man who came violently into my fading presence, there was also a weight of longing on my earth-held limbs. I would have shaken it off, already my foot had begun to lift but then, the white ghost entered and all was defiled.

[*Approaching voices of* PILKINGS *and his wife.*]

JANE: Oh Simon, you will let her in won't you?

PILKINGS: I really wish you'd stop interfering.

[*They come into view.* JANE *is in a dressing gown.* PILKINGS *is holding a note to which he refers from time to time.*]

JANE: Good gracious, I didn't initiate this. I was sleeping quietly, or trying to anyway, when the servant brought it. It's not my fault if one can't sleep undisturbed even in the Residency.

PILKINGS: He'd have done the same thing if we were sleeping at home so don't sidetrack the issue. He knows he can get round you or he wouldn't send you the petition in the first place.

JANE: Be fair Simon. After all he was thinking of your own interests. He is grateful you know, you seem to forget that. He feels he owes you something.

PILKINGS: I just wish they'd leave this man alone tonight, that's all.

JANE: Trust him Simon. He's pledged his word it will all go peacefully.

PILKINGS: Yes, and that's the other thing. I don't like being threatened.

JANE: Threatened? [*Takes the note.*] I didn't spot any threat.

PILKINGS: It's there. Veiled, but it's there. The only way to prevent serious rioting tomorrow—what a cheek!

JANE: I don't think he's threatening you Simon.

PILKINGS: He's picked up the idiom all right. Wouldn't surprise me if he's been mixing with commies or anarchists over there. The phrasing sounds too good to be true. Damn! If only the Prince hadn't picked this time for his visit.

JANE: Well, even so Simon, what have you got to lose? You don't want a riot on your hands, not with the Prince here.

PILKINGS: [*Going up to* ELESIN.] Let's see what he has to say. Chief Elesin, there is yet another person who wants to see you. As she is not a next-of-kin I don't really feel obliged to let her in. But your son sent a note with her, so it's up to you.

ELESIN: I know who that must be. So she found out your hiding place. Well, it was not difficult. My stench of shame is so strong, it requires no hunter's dog to follow it.

PILKINGS: If you don't want to see her, just say so and I'll send her packing.

ELESIN: Why should I not want to see her? Let her come. I have no more holes in my rag of shame. All is laid bare.

PILKINGS: I'll bring her in. [*Goes off.*]

JANE: [*Hesitates, then goes to* ELESIN.] Please, try and understand. Everything my husband did was for the best.

ELESIN: [*He gives her a long strange stare, as if he is trying to understand who she is.*] You are the wife of the District Officer?

JANE: Yes. My name, is Jane.

ELESIN: That is my wife sitting down there. You notice how still and silent she sits? My business is with your husband.

[PILKINGS *returns with* IYALOJA.]

PILKINGS: Here she is. Now first I want your word of honour that you will try nothing foolish.

ELESIN: Honour? White one, did you say you wanted my word of honour?

PILKINGS: I know you to be an honourable man. Give me your word of honour you will receive nothing from her.

ELESIN: But I am sure you have searched her clothing as you would never dare touch your own mother. And there are these two lizards[7] of yours who roll their eyes even when I scratch.

PILKINGS: And I shall be sitting on that tree trunk watching even how you blink. Just the same I want your word that you will not let her pass anything to you.

ELESIN: You have my honour already. It is locked up in that desk in which you will put away your report of this night's events. Even the honour of my people you have taken already; it is tied together with those papers of treachery[8] which make you masters in this land.

PILKINGS: All right. I am trying to make things easy but if you must bring in politics we'll have to do it the hard way. Madam, I want you to remain along this line and move no nearer to the cell door. Guards! [*They spring to attention.*] If she moves beyond this point, blow your whistle. Come on Jane. [*They go off.*]

IYALOJA: How boldly the lizard struts before the pigeon when it was the eagle itself he promised us he would confront.

---

7. That is, the guards.   8. The treaties of annexation forced by the British on African traditional rulers, who often did not understand their implications.

ELESIN: I don't ask you to take pity on me Iyaloja. You have a message for me or you would not have come. Even if it is the curses of the world, I shall listen.

IYALOJA: You made so bold with the servant of the white king who took your side against death. I must tell your brother chiefs when I return how bravely you waged war against him. Especially with words.

ELESIN: I more than deserve your scorn.

IYALOJA: [*With sudden anger.*] I warned you, if you must leave a seed behind, be sure it is not tainted with the curses of the world. Who are you to open a new life when you dared not open the door to a new existence? I say who are you to make so bold? [*The* BRIDE *sobs and* IYALOJA *notices her. Her contempt noticeably increases as she turns back to* ELESIN.] Oh you self-vaunted stem of the plantain, how hollow it all proves. The pith is gone in the parent stem, so how will it prove with the new shoot? How will it go with that earth that bears it? Who are you to bring this abomination on us!

ELESIN: My powers deserted me. My charms, my spells, even my voice lacked strength when I made to summon the powers that would lead me over the last measure of earth into the land of the fleshless. You saw it, Iyaloja. You saw me struggle to retrieve my will from the power of the stranger whose shadow fell across the doorway and left me floundering and blundering in a maze I had never before encountered. My senses were numbed when the touch of cold iron came upon my wrists. I could do nothing to save myself.

IYALOJA: You have betrayed us. We fed you sweetmeats such as we hoped awaited you on the other side. But you said No, I must eat the world's left-overs. We said you were the hunter who brought the quarry down; to you belonged the vital portions of the game. No, you said, I am the hunter's dog and I shall eat the entrails of the game and the faeces of the hunter. We said you were the hunter returning home in triumph, a slain buffalo pressing down on his neck; you said wait, I first must turn up this cricket hole with my toes. We said yours was the doorway at which we first spy the tapper when he comes down from the tree, yours was the blessing of the twilight wine, the purl[9] that brings night spirits out of doors to steal their portion before the light of day. We said yours was the body of wine whose burden shakes the tapper like a sudden gust on his perch. You said, No, I am content to lick the dregs from each calabash when the drinkers are done. We said, the dew on earth's surface was for you to wash your feet along the slopes of honour. You said No, I shall step in the vomit of cats and the droppings of mice; I shall fight them for the left-overs of the world.

ELESIN: Enough Iyaloja, enough.

IYALOJA: We called you leader and oh, how you led us on. What we have no intention of eating should not be held to the nose.[1]

ELESIN: Enough, enough. My shame is heavy enough.

IYALOJA: Wait. I came with a burden.

---

9. The frothy head of the palm wine. *Tapper:* one who climbs to the very top of the palm tree for its wine. The profession is a highly specialized one. *Cricket hole:* hunting crickets is a favorite game of Yoruba boys.   1. Considered uncouth by Yorubas.

ELESIN: You have more than discharged it.

IYALOJA: I wish I could pity you.

ELESIN: I need neither pity nor the pity of the world. I need understanding. Even I need to understand. You were present at my defeat. You were part of the beginnings. You brought about the renewal of my tie to earth, you helped in the binding of the cord.

IYALOJA: I gave you warning. The river which fills up before our eyes does not sweep us away in its flood.

ELESIN: What were warnings beside the moist contact of living earth between my fingers? What were warnings beside the renewal of famished embers lodged eternally in the heart of man. But even that, even if it overwhelmed one with a thousandfold temptations to linger a little while, a man could overcome it. It is when the alien hand pollutes the source of will, when a stranger's force of violence shatters the mind's calm resolution, this is when a man is made to commit the awful treachery of relief, commit in his thought the unspeakable blasphemy of seeing the hand of the gods in this alien rupture of his world. I know it was this thought that killed me, sapped my powers and turned me into an infant in the hands of unnamable strangers. I made to utter my spells anew but my tongue merely rattled in my mouth. I fingered hidden charms and the contact was damp; there was no spark left to sever the life-strings that should stretch from every fingertip. My will was squelched in the spittle of an alien race, and all because I had committed this blasphemy of thought—that there might be the hand of the gods in a stranger's intervention.

IYALOJA: Explain it how you will, I hope it brings you peace of mind. The bush rat fled his rightful cause, reached the market and set up a lamentation. "Please save me!"—are these fitting words to hear from an ancestral mask? "There's a wild beast at my heels" is not becoming language from a hunter.

ELESIN: May the world forgive me.

IYALOJA: I came with a burden I said. It approaches the gates which are so well guarded by those jackals whose spittle will from this day be on your food and drink. But first, tell me, you who were once Elesin Oba, tell me, you who know so well the cycle of the plantain: is it the parent shoot which withers to give sap to the younger or, does your wisdom see it running the other way?

ELESIN: I don't see your meaning Iyaloja?

IYALOJA: Did I ask you for a meaning? I asked a question. Whose trunk withers to give sap to the other? The parent shoot or the younger?

ELESIN: The parent.

IYALOJA: Ah. So you do know that. There are sights in this world which say different Elesin. There are some who choose to reverse the cycle of our being. Oh you emptied bark that the world once saluted for a pith-laden being, shall I tell you what the gods have claimed of you?

[*In her agitation she steps beyond the line indicated by* PILKINGS *and the air is rent by piercing whistles. The two* GUARDS *also leap forward and place safe-guarding hands on* ELESIN. IYALOJA *stops, astonished.* PILKINGS *comes racing in, followed by* JANE.]

PILKINGS: What is it? Did they try something?

GUARD: She stepped beyond the line.

ELESIN: [*In a broken voice.*] Let her alone. She meant no harm.

IYALOJA: Oh Elesin, see what you've become. Once you had no need to open your mouth in explanation because evil-smelling goats, itchy of hand and foot had lost their senses. And it was a brave man indeed who dared lay hands on you because Iyaloja stepped from one side of the earth onto another. Now look at the spectacle of your life. I grieve for you.

PILKINGS: I think you'd better leave. I doubt you have done him much good by coming here. I shall make sure you are not allowed to see him again. In any case we are moving him to a different place before dawn, so don't bother to come back.

IYALOJA: We foresaw that. Hence the burden I trudged here to lay beside your gates.

PILKINGS: What was that you said?

IYALOJA: Didn't our son explain? Ask that one. He knows what it is. At least we hope the man we once knew as Elesin remembers the lesser oaths he need not break.

PILKINGS: Do you know what she is talking about?

ELESIN: Go to the gates, ghostly one. Whatever you find there, bring it to me.

IYALOJA: Not yet. It drags behind me on the slow, weary feet of women. Slow as it is Elesin, it has long overtaken you. It rides ahead of your laggard will.

PILKINGS: What is she saying now? Christ! Must your people forever speak in riddles?

ELESIN: It will come white man, it will come. Tell your men at the gates to let it through.

PILKINGS: [*Dubiously.*] I'll have to see what it is.

IYALOJA: You will. [*Passionately.*] But this is one oath he cannot shirk. White one, you have a king here, a visitor from your land. We know of his presence here. Tell me, were he to die would you leave his spirit roaming restlessly on the surface of earth? Would you bury him here among those you consider less than human? In your land have you no ceremonies of the dead?

PILKINGS: Yes. But we don't make our chiefs commit suicide to keep him company.

IYALOJA: Child, I have not come to help your understanding. [*Points to* ELESIN.] This is the man whose weakened understanding holds us in bondage to you. But ask him if you wish. He knows the meaning of a king's passage; he was not born yesterday. He knows the peril to the race when our dead father, who goes as intermediary, waits and waits and knows he is betrayed. He knows when the narrow gate was opened and he knows it will not stay for laggards who drag their feet in dung and vomit, whose lips are reeking of the left-overs of lesser men. He knows he has condemned our king to wander in the void of evil with beings who are enemies of life.

PILKINGS: Yes er . . . but look here . . .

IYALOJA: What we ask is little enough. Let him release our King so he can ride on homewards alone. The messenger is on his way on the backs of women. Let him send word through the heart that is folded up within the bolt. It is the least of all his oaths, it is the easiest fulfilled.

[*The* AIDE-DE-CAMP *runs in.*]

PILKINGS: Bob?

AIDE-DE-CAMP: Sir, there's a group of women chanting up the hill.

PILKINGS: [*Rounding on* IYALOJA.] If you people want trouble . . .

JANE: Simon, I think that's what Olunde referred to in his letter.

PILKINGS: He knows damned well I can't have a crowd here! Damn it, I explained the delicacy of my position to him. I think it's about time I got him out of town. Bob, send a car and two or three soldiers to bring him in. I think the sooner he takes his leave of his father and gets out the better.

IYALOJA: Save your labour white one. If it is the father of your prisoner you want, Olunde, he who until this night we knew as Elesin's son, he comes soon himself to take his leave. He has sent the women ahead, so let them in.

[PILKINGS *remains undecided.*]

AIDE-DE-CAMP: What do we do about the invasion? We can still stop them far from here.

PILKINGS: What do they look like?

AIDE-DE-CAMP: They're not many. And they seem quite peaceful.

PILKINGS: No men?

AIDE-DE-CAMP: Mm, two or three at the most.

JANE: Honestly, Simon, I'd trust Olunde. I don't think he'll deceive you about their intentions.

PILKINGS: He'd better not. All right then, let them in Bob. Warn them to control themselves. Then hurry Olunde here. Make sure he brings his baggage because I'm not returning him into town.

AIDE-DE-CAMP: Very good, sir. [*Goes.*]

PILKINGS: [*To* IYALOJA.] I hope you understand that if anything goes wrong it will be on your head. My men have orders to shoot at the first sign of trouble.

IYALOJA: To prevent one death you will actually make other deaths? Ah, great is the wisdom of the white race. But have no fear. Your Prince will sleep peacefully. So at long last will ours. We will disturb you no further, servant of the white king. Just let Elesin fulfil his oath and we will retire home and pay homage to our King.

JANE: I believe her Simon, don't you?

PILKINGS: Maybe.

ELESIN: Have no fear ghostly one. I have a message to send my King and then you have nothing more to fear.

IYALOJA: Olunde would have done it. The chiefs asked him to speak the words but he said no, not while you lived.

ELESIN: Even from the depths to which my spirit has sunk, I find some joy that this little has been left to me.

[*The* WOMEN *enter, intoning the dirge "Ale le le" and swaying from side to side. On their shoulders is borne a longish object roughly like*

*a cylindrical bolt, covered in cloth. They set it down on the spot
where* IYALOJA *had stood earlier, and form a semi-circle round it. The*
PRAISE SINGER *and* DRUMMER *stand on the inside of the semi-circle
but the drum is not used at all. The* DRUMMER *intones under the*
PRAISE SINGER'S *invocations.*]

PILKINGS: [*As they enter.*] What is *that?*

IYALOJA: The burden you have made white one, but we bring it in peace.

PILKINGS: I said *what* is it?

ELESIN: White man, you must let me out. I have a duty to perform.

PILKINGS: I most certainly will not.

ELESIN: There lies the courier of my King. Let me out so I can perform
what is demanded of me.

PILKINGS: You'll do what you need to do from inside there or not at all.
I've gone as far as I intend to with this business.

ELESIN: The worshipper who lights a candle in your church to bear a
message to his god bows his head and speaks in a whisper to the flame.
Have I not seen it ghostly one? His voice does not ring out to the world.
Mine are no words for anyone's ears. They are not words even for the
bearers of this load. They are words I must speak secretly, even as my
father whispered them in my ears and I in the ears of my first-born. I
cannot shout them to the wind and the open night sky.

JANE: Simon . . .

PILKINGS: Don't interfere. Please!

IYALOJA: They have slain the favourite horse of the king and slain his dog.
They have borne them from pulse to pulse centre of the land receiving
prayers for their king. But the rider has chosen to stay behind. Is it too
much to ask that he speak his heart to heart of the waiting courier?
[PILKINGS *turns his back on her.*] So be it. Elesin Oba, you see how
even the mere leavings are denied you. [*She gestures to the* PRAISE
SINGER.]

PRAISE SINGER: Elesin Oba! I call you by that name only this last time.
Remember when I said, if you cannot come, tell my horse. [*Pause.*]
What? I cannot hear you? I said, if you cannot come, whisper in the
ears of my horse. Is your tongue severed from the roots? Elesin? I can
hear no response. I said, if there are boulders you cannot climb, mount
my horse's back, this spotless black stallion, he'll bring you over them.
[*Pauses.*] Elesin Oba, once you had a tongue that darted like a drummer's stick. I said, if you get lost my dog will track a path to me. My
memory fails me but I think you replied: My feet have found the path,
Alafin.

    [*The dirge rises and falls.*]

I said at the last, if evil hands hold you back, just tell my horse there is
weight on the hem of your smock. I dare not wait too long.

    [*The dirge rises and falls.*]

There lies the swiftest ever messenger of a king, so set me free with the
errand of your heart. There lie the head and heart of the favourite of
the gods, whisper in his ears. Oh my companion, if you had followed
when you should, we would not say that the horse preceded its rider. If
you had followed when it was time, we would not say the dog has raced

beyond and left his master behind. If you had raised your will to cut the thread of life at the summons of the drums, we would not say your mere shadow fell across the gateway and took its owner's place at the banquet. But the hunter, laden with slain buffalo, stayed to root in the cricket's hole with his toes. What now is left? If there is a dearth of bats, the pigeon must serve us for the offering.[2] Speak the words over your shadow which must now serve in your place.

ELESIN: I cannot approach. Take off the cloth. I shall speak my message from heart to heart of silence.

IYALOJA: [*Moves forward and removes the covering.*] Your courier Elesin, cast your eyes on the favoured companion of the King.

[*Rolled up in the mat, his head and feet showing at either end, is the body of* OLUNDE.]

There lies the honour of your household and of our race. Because he could not bear to let honour fly out of doors, he stopped it with his life. The son has proved the father Elesin, and there is nothing left in your mouth to gnash but infant gums.

PRAISE SINGER: Elesin, we placed the reins of the world in your hands yet you watched it plunge over the edge of the bitter precipice. You sat with folded arms while evil strangers tilted the world from its course and crashed it beyond the edge of emptiness—you muttered, there is little that one man can do, you left us floundering in a blind future. Your heir has taken the burden on himself. What the end will be, we are not gods to tell. But this young shoot has poured its sap into the parent stalk, and we know this is not the way of life. Our world is tumbling in the void of strangers, Elesin.

[ELESIN *has stood rock-still, his knuckles taut on the bars, his eyes glued to the body of his son. The stillness seizes and paralyses everyone, including* PILKINGS *who has turned to look. Suddenly* ELESIN *flings one arm round his neck, once, and with the loop of the chain, strangles himself in a swift, decisive pull. The* GUARDS *rush forward to stop him but they are only in time to let his body down.* PILKINGS *has leapt to the door at the same time and struggles with the lock. He rushes within, fumbles with the handcuffs and unlocks them, raises the body to a sitting position while he tries to give resuscitation. The* WOMEN *continue their dirge, unmoved by the sudden event.*]

IYALOJA: Why do you strain yourself? Why do you labour at tasks for which no one, not even the man lying there would give you thanks? He is gone at last into the passage but oh, how late it all is. His son will feast on the meat and throw him bones. The passage is clogged with droppings from the King's stallion; he will arrive all stained in dung.

PILKINGS: [*In a tired voice.*] Was this what you wanted?

IYALOJA: No child, it is what you brought to be, you who play with strangers' lives, who even usurp the vestments of our dead, yet believe that the stain of death will not cling to you. The gods demanded only the old expired plantain but you cut down the sap-laden shoot to feed your pride. There is your board, filled to overflowing. Feast on it. [*She*

---

2. Sacrifice.

screams at him suddenly, seeing that PILKINGS *is about to close* ELESIN*'s staring eyes.*] Let him alone! However sunk he was in debt he is no pauper's carrion abandoned on the road. Since when have strangers donned clothes of indigo[3] before the bereaved cries out his loss?

[*She turns to the* BRIDE *who has remained motionless throughout.*] Child.

[*The girl takes up a little earth, walks calmly into the cell and closes* ELESIN*'s eyes. She then pours some earth over each eyelid and comes out again.*]

Now forget the dead, forget even the living. Turn your mind only to the unborn.

[*She goes off, accompanied by the* BRIDE. *The dirge rises in volume and the* WOMEN *continue their sway. Lights fade to a black-out.*]

3. Worn for mourning.

A. B. YEHOSHUA
born 1936

A. B. Yehoshua is a master of symbolic narratives that move easily between the fantastic and the grittily real and that give life to questions of psychological depth and subtlety. His earliest stories have an abstract and allegorical quality, set in no particular time or place, and are peopled with vivid but stereotypical characters. But as he has matured as a writer Yehoshua has grounded his stories with increasing sureness in a specific social and political reality, and his characters have taken on a psychological depth and richness as well. Yehoshua is also a profoundly political writer, and, indeed, the clarity and force with which his narratives explore and illuminate current political realities in Israel have meant that critics are as likely to address the political and social implications of his works as their literary merits. He is best known in the West for his novels and short stories, but he has written plays as well. Yehoshua is also an outspoken advocate of peace and a vigorous advocate of reformulating the terms *Jew, Israeli,* and *Zionist* to lessen the tension between Israel and its Arab citizens. In addition to his writing, Yehoshua has pursued an active career as a professor of literature at Haifa University. He shares with Amos Oz the distinction of being one of the two most highly regarded prose writers in Israel today.

Yehoshua was born in Jerusalem in 1936 and raised and educated in the British Mandate Palestine of the 1940s, remote from the agonies of European Jewry in World War II. His parents both belonged to the Sephardic (Oriental) Jewish community. His father, Ja'acov, a noted Orientalist scholar, had also been born in Jerusalem. Ja'acov's mother belonged to a family that had lived in Jerusalem for generations, and his father, who had come to Jerusalem from Salonika in Greece as a baby, later became chief judge of the Sephardic court. Yehoshua's mother was one of the younger children of a wealthy Moroccan merchant who, after the death of his wife in 1932, chose to leave his home and business to move to Palestine for personal and spiritual reasons. Yehoshua's deep Sephardic roots recur as a central theme in his mature fiction. For him the Sephardic community's history in Palestine and Israel provides an instructive alternative to that of the Ashkenazi (European) Jewish community's, a counternarrative to the master narrative that has dominated efforts to establish and define an Israeli national identity.

The great watershed in the modern history of Israel was, of course, the 1948 War for Independence, which brought about the establishment of the Jewish state in what had formerly been Palestine. The successful conclusion of the long campaign by European Zionists to establish a permanent Jewish homeland in the land of their historical origin and the gathering in of the Jewish communities of the Diaspora ended the first cycle of modern Israeli history. The Diaspora was the period of Jewish history from the dispersal of the Jewish tribes outside of Israel in the sixth century B.C. to the foundation of Israel. Success is often followed by disenchantment, however, and these victories had been won at a terrible cost. The intractable problems inherent in building a new society in a new state had been put aside while the struggle before them now demanded attention. (How were they to integrate the many diverse communities that had been gathered into the new state? What was to be done with the hostile Arabs now living among them? Now that the fundamental goal of establishing a state had been achieved, what new goal could unite and energize the nation?)

The new generation of poets and writers that came into its own in the late 1950s abandoned the collectivist ideological sentiment of the generation of the War of Independence. They sought new topics, new characters, and an escape from ideology itself. The new hero, in Yehoshua's words, "was a marginal, perverted and somewhat estranged character." His works, perhaps, most fully embodied this new literary genre in which freeing the hero from ideology also freed him from clearly defined boundaries of place and time and blurred the borders between the realistic and the surreal.

Yehoshua had begun writing humorous and fantastic sketches in high school and continued to do so while serving in the parachute corps and attending Hebrew University, where he majored in literature. His first short story, *Death of the Old Man*, which appeared in 1957, is a first-person narrative in which a strong-willed old woman decides that a very old but exceptionally vital man who lives in her apartment house has lived too long. Since he refuses to die on his own, she decides to dispose of him by performing a funeral and burying him alive and enlists the aid of the other tenants to carry out her bizarre scheme. This story provides the title of his first collection of stories, which was published in 1962. The other stories in this collection also combine elements of the unusual, the unexpected, and the bizarre with sudden eruptions of violent and self-destructive energies, and they take place in a vague region outside of time or place. The stories in his second collection, *Facing the Forests* (1968), contain these same elements as well, but the characters begin to take on a psychological depth and they exist in real, identifiable contexts.

All the characters of the story *Facing the Forests* appear as types, not individuals, and this tells us at once that it is an allegory. However, there are jokers in this deck. The student, for example, is an anomaly, a bright student who inexplicably fails to live up to his promise. He is aimless and indifferent to the symbols that define his culture, both the concrete (the national forest with its shiny memorial plaques) and the abstract (the energetic striving that permits his contemporaries to advance while he lags behind). The Arab is also another anomaly, a non-Jew in a Jewish state, who is further excluded from membership in any sense by his ignorance of Hebrew. He can, in fact, speak no language since his tongue has been cut out.

Yehoshua has constructed the symbols and characters of his story to suit the facts of modern Israeli history, but in doing so he is drawing on a narrative that has an archetypal resonance. On the one hand there is the impotent intellectual who has grown disaffected with the values and concerns of his own culture and with his intellect itself. Words, the stock-in-trade of an intellectual, no longer have any meaning for him. On the other, there is the disenfranchised and inarticulate "native" who lives to right an old wrong done to him and his people by the master culture of which the intellectual is a part. He either lacks the words to make his grievances known or cannot compel his oppressors to hear them. The nihilism of the intellectual leads him to collude, consciously or unconsciously, in the violence of the disenfranchised native.

What sets Yehoshua's story apart from more conventional treatments of this basic narrative is his refusal to celebrate this alliance. The plight of the Arab is presented with sympathy but not advocacy, and the intellectual who colludes with him and betrays his own culture is an unappealing figure who has not actively espoused the Arab's cause so much as drifted under its spell out of a feeling of general malaise. The violent solution of the Arab is also no solution at all. He has destroyed the forest, but his village has not been reborn as a result. He himself will now be imprisoned, and his daughter will become a ward of the state. Finally, the student seems to have learned nothing from the experience himself.

Where the story is remarkably prescient is in its implicit warning that a failure to address these buried problems can lead to a terrible and violent despair, a despair in which even self-destructive acts become preferable to continued inaction. Israelis, Yehoshua implies, cannot afford to ignore the rights of the Arabs whom they have displaced, for the price of that neglect will be a terrible and costly conflagration.

Yehoshua's first novel, *The Lover* (1977), is written as a series of individual narratives by the principal characters, a technique that Yehoshua learned from the works of Faulkner like *As I Lay Dying* and which he has used subsequently in *A Late Divorce* (1983) and, most strikingly perhaps, in *Mr. Mani* (1992), where the monologues take the form of dialogues in which we hear the voice of only one speaker. In *The Lover*, set during the Yom Kippur War (1973), the characters have individual and distinctive personalities, they live in modern Haifa, and they tell their tales in a straightforward, realistic style. Yet it is a work built on bizarre paradoxes: a husband who seeks lovers for both his wife and his daughter with obsessive zeal, an Arab who longs to assimilate to Hebrew culture, a Sephardic Israeli soldier who first emigrates from Israel and then, on his return, both deserts from the army and takes refuge in an ultra-Orthodox Ashkenazic community. As the Israeli critic Gershon Shaked points out, these social paradoxes reflect the existential dilemmas of identity that underlie contemporary Israeli society. Moreover, in this novel Yehoshua initiates his Sephardic counternarrative in the character of Veducha, a Sephardic grandmother, whose life and character embody the principal elements of that narrative. Surely the most fully developed exploration of this theme is his latest novel, *Mr. Mani*, a work of stylistic brilliance and artistic originality that traces the evolution of one Sephardic family through five generations.

Although Yehoshua's work received substantial and favorable critical attention from the very first, with the publication of *The Lover*, which appeared in English translation only a year later, he began to receive international recognition as well. This recognition has grown with each of his subsequent works so that he is now one of the handful of Israeli writers who, like Amos Oz and Yehuda Amichai, enjoy a wide readership outside of Israel as well as within it. His works have now been translated into fourteen languages, and among other honors, he was awarded the Brenner Prize in 1983; the Alterman Prize in 1986; the Bialik Prize in 1989; and for *Mr. Mani*, the Israeli award for the best work of literature to appear in the preceding two years.

A substantial majority of Yehoshua's writings have been translated into English: *Three Days and a Child* (1970), the collection from which the story printed here was taken; *Early in the Summer of 1970* (1977), a novella; two plays, *A Night in May and Last Treatment* (1974) and *Until Winter* (1974); and a second short story collection. All his novels have been translated: *The Lover* (1978), *A Late Divorce* (1983), *Five Seasons* (1989), and *Mr. Mani* (1992). A book of political essays, *Between Right and Right* (1981), has also been published in English.

There are no book-length studies of Yehoshua in English as yet, but his works are reviewed in major American journals. Robert Alter, *Modern Hebrew Literature* (1975), an anthology with extensive introductions, contains a detailed analysis of *Facing the Forests*.

PRONOUNCING GLOSSARY

The following list uses common English syllables and stress accents to provide rough equivalents of selected words whose pronunciation may be unfamiliar to the general reader.

Ashkenazi: *ash'-kuh-nah'-zee*

Diaspora: *dee-ass'-puh-ruh*

Sephardic: *suh-far'-dik*

Veducha: *vuh-dew'-chuh*

Yehoshua: *ye-hoh-shoo'-uh*

Facing the Forests[1]

I

Another winter lost in fog. As usual he did nothing; postponed examinations, left papers unwritten. He had completed all his courses long ago, attended all the lectures, and the string of signatures on his tattered student card testified that all had performed their duty toward him, silently disappeared, and left the rest of the task in his own limp hands. But words weary him; his own, let alone the words of others. He drifts from one rented room to another, rootless, jobless. But for an occasional job tutoring backward children he would starve to death. Here he is approaching thirty and a bald spot crowns his wilting head. His defective eyesight blurs many things. His dreams at night are dull. They are uneventful; a yellow waste, where a few stunted trees may spring up in a moment of grace, and a naked woman. At student revels he is already looked at with faint ridicule. The speed with which he gets drunk is a regular part of the program. He never misses a party. They need him still. His limp figure is extremely popular and there is no one like him for bridging gaps between people. His erstwhile fellow students have graduated since and may be seen carrying bulging briefcases, on their way to work every morning of the week. Sometimes, at noon, returning from their offices, they may encounter him in the street with his just-awake eyes: a gray moth in search of its first meal. They, having heard of his dissipations, promptly pronounce the unanimous, half-pitying, half-exasperated decree: "Solitude!"

Solitude is what he needs. For he is not without talent nor does he lack brains. He needs to strengthen his willpower.

---

1. Translated by Miriam Arad.

He, as a rule, will drop his arms by his sides in a gesture of pious despair, back up against the nearest available wall, languidly cross his legs and plead in a whisper:

"But where? Go on, tell me, where?"

For look, he himself craves solitude. He plainly needs to renew his acquaintance with words, to try and concentrate on the material that threatens ever to wear him down. But then he would have to enter prison. He knows himself (a sickly smile): if there should be the tiniest crack of escape through, he would make it a tunnel at once. No, please, no favors. Either—or.

Some content themselves with this feeble excuse, shrug their shoulders wryly, and go their way. But his real friends, those whose wives he loves as well, two budding lecturers who remember him from days gone by, remember him favorably for the two or three amazingly original ideas that he had dropped at random during his student days—friends who are concerned for his future—these two are well aware that the coming spring is that much more dangerous to him, that his desultory affairs with women will but draw zeal from the blue skies. Is it any wonder, then, if one fine day they will catch hold of him in the street, their eyes sparkling. "Well, your lordship, we've found the solution to your lordship's problem at last." And he will be quick to show an expectant eagerness, though cunning enough to leave himself ample means of retreat.

"What?"

The function of forest scout. A fire-watcher. Yes, it's something new. A dream of a job, a plum. Utter, profound solitude. There he will be able to scrape together his crumbled existence.

Where did they get the idea?

From the papers, yes, from a casual skimming of the daily papers.

He is astonished, laughs inordinately, hysterically almost. What now? What's the idea? Forests . . . What forests? Since when do we have forests in this country? What do they mean?

But they refuse to smile. For once they are determined. Before he has time to digest their words they have burned the bridges over which he had meant to escape, as usual. "You said, either—or. Here is your solution."

He glances at his watch, pretending haste. Will not a single spark light up in him then? For he, too, loathes himself, doesn't he?

II

And so, when spring has set the windows ajar, he arrives early one morning at the Afforestation Department. A sunny office, a clerk, a typist, several typists. He enters quickly, armed with impressive recommendations, heralded by telephone calls. The man in charge of the forests, a worthy character edging his way to old age, is faintly amused (his position permits him as much), grins to himself. Much ado about nothing, about such a marginal job. Hence he is curious about the caller, even considers rising to receive him. The plain patch of barrenness atop the head of the candidate adds to his stature. The fellow inspires surely trust, is surely meant for better things.

"Are you certain that this is what you want? The observation post is a grim place. Only really primitive people can bear such solitude. What is it you wish to write? Your doctorate?"

No, sad to say, he is still at the elementary stages of his study.

Yes, he has wasted much time.

No, he has no family.

Yes, with glasses, his vision is sound.

Gently the old manager explains, that in accordance with a certain semiofficial agreement, this work is reserved for social cases only and not for how-shall-I-put-it, romantics, ha-ha, intellectuals in search of solitude . . . However, he is prepared, just this once, to make an exception and include an intellectual among the wretched assortment of his workers. Yes, he is himself getting sick of the diverse social cases, the invalids, the cripples, the cranks. A fire breaks out, and these fellows will do nothing but stand and stare panic-stricken at the flames till the fire brigade arrives. Whenever he is forced to send out one such unstable character he stays awake nights thinking what if in an obscure rage, against society or whatever, the fire-watcher should himself set the forest on fire. He feels certain that he, the man in front of him here, though occupied with affairs of the mind, will be sufficiently alert to his duty to abandon his books and fight the fire. Yes, it is a question of moral values.

Sorry, the old man has forgotten what it is his candidate wishes to write? A doctorate?

Once more he apologizes. He is still, sad to say, at the elementary stages of his study. Yes, he has wasted much time. Indeed, he has no family.

A young secretary is called in.

Then he is invited to sign an inoffensive little contract for six months: spring, summer (ah, summer is dangerous!), and half the autumn. Discipline, responsibility, vigilance, conditions of dismissal. A hush descends while he runs his eyes cursorily over the document. Manager and secretary are ready with a pen, but he prefers to sign with his own. He signs several copies. First salary due on April the fifth. Now he eases himself into his chair, unable to rise, tired still. He is not used to waking so early. Meanwhile he tries to establish some sort of contact, display an interest. He inquires about the size of the forests, the height of the trees. To tell the truth—he runs on expansively, in a sort of dangerous drowsiness—the fact is that he has never yet seen a real forest in this country. An occasional ancient grove, yes, but he hardly believes (ha-ha-ha) that the Authorities in charge of Afforestation have anything to do with that. Yes, he keeps hearing over the radio about forests being planted to honor this, that, and the other personage. Though apparently one cannot actually see them yet . . . The trees grow slowly . . . don't gain height . . . Actually he understands . . . this arid soil . . . In other countries, now . . .

At last he falters. Naturally he realizes, has realized from the start, that he has made a bad blunder, has sensed it from the laughter trembling in the girl's eyes, from the shocked fury coloring the face of the manager who is edging his way to old age. The candidate has, to use a tangible image, taken a careless step and trampled a tender spot in the heart of the man in charge of forests, who is fixing him now in a harsh stare and delivering a monologue for his benefit.

What does he mean by small trees? He has obviously failed to use his eyes. Of course there are forests. Real forests. Jungles, no; but forests, yes, indeed. If he will pardon the question: What does he know about what happens in this country anyway? For even when he travels through it on a bus he won't bother to take his head out of his book. It's laughable, really, these flat allegations. He, the old man, has come across this kind of talk from young people, but the candidate is rather past that age. If he, the manager, had the time to spare, he could show him maps. But soon he will see for himself. There are forests in the Hills of Judea, in Galilee, Samaria, and elsewhere. Perhaps the candidate's eyesight is weak, after all. Perhaps he needs a stronger pair of spectacles. The manager would like to ask the candidate to take spare spectacles with him. He would rather not have any more trouble. Good-bye.

Where are they sending him?

A few days later he is back. This time he is received not by the manager, but by an underling. He is being sent to one of the larger forests. He won't be alone there but with a laborer, an Arab. They feel certain he has no prejudices. Good-bye. Ah yes, departure is on Sunday.

III

Things happen fast. He severs connections and they appear to come loose with surprising ease. He vacates his room and his landlady is glad of it, for some reason. He spends the last nights with one of his learned friends, who sets to work at once to prepare a study schedule for him. While his zealous friend is busy in one room cramming books into a suitcase, the prospective fire-watcher fondles the beloved wife in another. He is pensive, his hands gentle, there is something of joy in his expectations of the morrow. What shall he study? His friends suggest the Crusades. Yes, that would be just right for him. Everyone specializes in a certain subject. He may yet prove to be a little researcher all in his own right, just so long as he won't fritter his time away. He ought to bring some startling scientific theory back from the forests. His friends will take care of the facts later.

But in the morning, when the lorry[2] of the Afforestation Department comes to fetch him out of his shattered sleep, he suddenly imagines that all this has been set in motion just to get rid of him; and, shivering in the cold morning air, he can but console himself with the thought that this adventure will go the way of all others and be drowned in somnolence. Is it any wonder that Jerusalem, high on its hills, Jerusalem, which is left behind now, is fading like a dream? He abandons himself to the jolts and pitches of the lorry. The laborers with their hoes and baskets sit huddled away from him in the back of the car. They sense that he belongs to another world. The bald patch and the glasses are an indication, one of many.

Traveling half a day.

The lorry leaves the highway and travels over long, alien dirt roads, among nameless immigrant settlements. Laborers alight, others take their place. Everyone receives instructions from the driver, who is the one in command around here. We are going south, are we? Wide country meet-

2. Truck.

ing a spring-blue sky. The ground is damp still and clods of earth drop off the lorry's tires. It is late in the morning when he discovers the first trees scattered among rocks. Young slender pines, tiny, light green. "Then I was right," he tells himself with a smile. But farther on the trees grow taller. Now the light bursts and splinters. Long shadows steal aboard the lorry like stowaways. People keep changing and only the driver, the passenger and his suitcases stay put. The forests grow denser, no more bare patches now. Pines, always, and only the one species, obstinately, unvaryingly. He is tired, dusty, hungry, has long ago lost all sense of direction. The sun is playing tricks, twisting around him. He does not see where he is going, only what he is leaving behind. At three o'clock the lorry is emptied of laborers and only he is left. For a long time the lorry climbs over a rugged track. He is cross, his mouth feels dry. In despair he tries to pull a book out of one suitcase, but then the lorry stops. The driver gets off, bangs the door, comes around to him and says:

"This is it. Your predecessor's already made off—yesterday. Your instructions are all up there. You at least can read, for a change."

Laboriously he hauls himself and his two suitcases down. An odd, charming, stone house stands on a hill. Pines of all sizes surround it. He is at a high altitude here, though he cannot yet see everything from where he is. Silence, a silence of trees. The driver stretches his legs, looks around, breathes the air, then suddenly he nods good-bye and climbs back into his cab and switches the engine on.

He who must stay behind is seized with regret. Despair. What now? Just a minute! He doesn't understand. He rushes at the car, beats his fists against the door, whispers furiously at the surprised driver.

"But food . . . what about food?"

It appears that the Arab takes care of everything.

IV

Alone he trudges uphill, a suitcase in each hand. Gradually the world comes into view. The front door stands open and he enters a large room, the ground floor. Semidarkness, dilapidated objects on the floor, food remnants, traces of a child. The despair mounts in him. He lets go of the suitcases and climbs absently to the second floor. The view strikes him with awe. Five hills covered with a dense green growth—pines. A silvery blue horizon with a distant sea. He is instantly excited, on fire, forgetting everything. He is even prepared to change his opinion of the Afforestation Department.

A telephone, binoculars, a sheet covered with instructions. A large desk and an armchair beside it. He settles himself into the chair and reads the instructions five times over, from beginning to end. Then he pulls out his pen and makes a few stylistic corrections. He glances fondly at the black instrument. He is in high spirits. He considers calling up one of his friends in town, to say something tender to one of his aging ladyloves. He might announce his safe arrival, describe the view perhaps. Never has he had a public telephone at his disposal yet. He lifts the receiver to his ear. An endless purring. He is not familiar with the proceedings. He tries dialing.

In vain. The purr remains steady. At last he dials zero, like a sober citizen expecting a sober reply.

The telephone breaks its silence.

The Fire Brigade comes on with a startled "What's happened?" Real alarm at the other side. (Where, where, confound it!) Before he has said a word, questions rain down on him. How large is the fire? What direction the wind? They are coming at once. He tries to put in a word, stutters, and already they are starting a car over there. Panic grips him. He jumps up, the receiver tight in his hand. He breaks out in a cold sweat. With the last remnant of words in his power he explains everything. No. There is no fire. There is nothing. Only getting acquainted. He has just arrived. Wanted to get through to town. His name is so-and-so. That is all.

A hush at the other side. The voice changes. This must be their chief now. Pleased to meet you, Sir, we've taken down your name. Have you read all the instructions? Personal calls are quite out of the question. Anyway, you've only just arrived, haven't you? Or is there some urgent need? Your wife? Your children?

No, he has no family.

Well, then, why the panic? Lonely? He'll get used to it. Please don't disturb again in the future. Good-bye.

The ring closes in on him a little. Pink streaks on the horizon. He is tired, hungry. He has risen early, and he is utterly unused to that. This high, commanding view makes him dizzy. The silence. He picks up the binoculars with a limp hand and raises them to his eyes. The world leaps close, blurred. Pines lunge at him upright. He adjusts the forest, the hills, the sea horizon to the quality of his eyes. He amuses himself a bit, then lets go of the binoculars and eases himself into the chair. He has a clear conception of his new job now. Just watching. His eyes grow heavy. He dozes, sleeps perhaps.

Suddenly he wakes—a red light is burning on his glasses. He is bewildered, scared, his senses heavy. The forest has caught fire, apparently, and he has missed it. He jumps up, his heart wildly beating, grabs the telephone, the binoculars, and then it occurs to him that it is the sun, only the sun setting beyond the trees. He is facing west. Now he knows. Slowly he drops back into the chair. His heart contracts with something like terror, like emptiness. He imagines himself deserted in this place, forgotten. His glasses mist over and he takes them off and wipes them.

When dusk falls, he hears steps.

V

An Arab and a little girl are approaching the house. Swiftly he rises to his feet. They notice him, look up and stop in their tracks—startled by the soft, scholarly figure. He bows his head. They walk on but their steps are hesitant now. He goes down to them.

The Arab turns out to be old and mute. His tongue was cut out during the war. By one of them or one of us? Does it matter? Who knows what the last words were that stuck in his throat? In the dark room, its windows ablaze with the last light, the fire-watcher shakes a heavy hand, bends to pat the child, who flinches, terrified. The ring of loneliness closes in on him. The Arab puts on lights. The fire-watcher will sleep upstairs.

The first evening, and a gnawing sadness. The weak yellow light of the bulbs is depressing. For the time being, he draws comfort only from the wide view, from the soft blue of the sea in the distance and the sun writhing in it. He sits cramped on his chair and watches the big forests entrusted to his eyes. He imagines that the fire may break out at any moment. After a long delay, the Arab brings up his supper. An odd taste, a mixture of tastes. But he devours everything, leaves not a morsel. His eyes rove hungrily between the plate and the thick woods. Suddenly, while chewing, he discovers a few faraway lights—villages. He broods a while about women, then takes off his clothes, opens the suitcase that does not hold books, and takes out his things. It seems a long time since he left town. He wraps himself in blankets, lies facing the forests. A cool breeze caresses him. What sort of sleep will come to one here? The Arab brings him a cup of coffee to help him stay awake. The fire-watcher would like to talk to him about something; perhaps about the view, or about the poor lighting perhaps. He has words left in him still from the city. But the Arab does not understand Hebrew. The fire-watcher smiles wearily in thanks. Something about his bald crown, the glint of his glasses, seems to daunt the Arab.

It is half-past nine—the beginning of night. Cicadas strike up. He struggles against sleep engulfing him. His eyes close and his conscience tortures him. The binoculars dangle from their strap around his neck, and from time to time he picks them up, lifts them to his eyes blinded with sleep, glasses clicking against glass. He opens his eyes in a stare and finds himself in the forest, among pines, hunting for flames. Darkness.

How long does it take for a forest to burn down? Perhaps he will only look every hour, every two hours. Even if the forest should start to burn, he would still manage to raise the alarm in time to save the rest. The murmur downstairs has died down. The Arab and his child are asleep. And he is up here, light-headed, tired after his journey, between three walls and a void gaping to the sea. He must not roll over onto his other side. He nods, and his sleep is pervaded by the fear of fire, fire stealing upon him unaware. At midnight he transfers himself from bed to chair; it is safer that way. His head droops heavily onto the desk, his spine aches, he is crying out for sleep, full of regret, alone against the dark empire swaying before him. Till at last the black hours of the first night pass; till out of the corner of his eye he sees the morning grow among the hills.

Only fatigue makes him stay on after the first night. The days and nights following after revolve as on a screen, a misty, dreamlike screen lit up once every twenty-four hours by the radiant glow of the setting sun. It is not himself but a stranger who wanders those first days between the two stories of the house, the binoculars slung across his chest, absently chewing on the food left him by the unseen Arab. The heavy responsibility that has suddenly fallen upon his shoulders bewilders him. Hardest of all is the silence. Even with himself he hardly manages to exchange a word. Will he be able to open a book here? The view amazes and enchants him still and he cannot have enough of it. After ten days of anguish he is himself again. In one brief glance he can embrace all the five hills now. He has learned to sleep with his eyes open. A new accomplishment; rather interesting, one must admit.

VI

At last the other suitcase, the one with the books, gets opened, with a slight delay of but a fortnight or so. The delay does not worry him in the least, for aren't the spring, the summer, and half the autumn still before him? The first day is devoted to sorting the books, spelling out titles, thumbing the pages. One can't deny that there is some pleasure in handling the fat, fragrant, annotated volumes. The texts are in English, the quotations all in Latin. Strange phrases from alien worlds. He worries a little. His subject—"The Crusades." From the human, that is to say, the ecclesiastical aspect. He has not gone into particulars yet. "Crusades," he whispers softly to himself and feels joy rising in him at the word, the sound. He feels certain that there is some dark issue buried within the subject and that it will startle him, startle other issues in him. And it will be just out of this drowsiness that envelops his mind like a permanent cloud that the matter will be revealed to him.

The following day is spent on pictures. The books are rich in illustrations. Odd, funny ones. Monks, cardinals; a few blurred kings, thin knights, tiny, villainous Jews. Curious landscapes, maps. He studies them, compares, dozes. On the hard road to the abstract he wishes to linger a while with the concrete. That night he is kept from his studies by a gnat. Next morning he tells himself: Oh, wondrous time, how fast it flies upon these lonely summits. He opens the first book on the first page, reads the author's preface, his grateful acknowledgment. He reads other prefaces, various acknowledgments, publication data. He checks a few dates. At noon his mind is distracted from the books by an imaginary flame flashing among the trees. He remains tense for hours, excited, searching with the binoculars, his hand on the telephone. At last, toward evening, he discovers that it is only the red dress of the Arab's little daughter who is skipping among the trees. The following day, when he is all set to decipher the first page, his father turns up suddenly with a suitcase in his hand.

"What's happened?" the father asks anxiously.

"Nothing . . . Nothing's happened . . ."

"But what made you become a forester then?"

"A bit of solitude . . ."

"Solitude . . ." he marvels. "You want solitude?"

The father bends over the open book, removes his heavy glasses and peers closely at the text. "The Crusades," he murmurs. "Is that what you're engaged in?"

"Yes."

"Aren't I disturbing you in your work? I haven't come to disturb you . . . I have a few days' leave."

"No, you're not disturbing me."

"Magnificent view."

"Yes, magnificent."

"You're thinner."

"Could be."

"Couldn't you study in the libraries?"

Apparently not. Silence. The father sniffs around the room like a little hedgehog. At noon he asks his son:

"Do you think it is lonely here? That you'll find solitude?"

"Yes, what's to disturb me?"

"I'm not going to disturb you."

"Of course not. What makes you think that?"

"I'll go away soon."

"No, don't go. Please stay."

The father stays a week.

In the evening the father tries to become friendly with the Arab and his child. A few words of Arabic have stuck in his memory from the days of his youth, and he will seize any occasion to fill them with meaning. But his pronunciation is unintelligible to the Arab, who only nods his head dully.

They sit together, not speaking. The son cannot read a single line with the father there, even though the father keeps muttering: "Don't bother about me. I'll keep myself in the background." At night the father sleeps on the bed and the fire-watcher stretches himself out on the floor. Sometimes the father wakes in the night to find his son awake. "Perhaps we could take turns," he says. "You go to sleep on the bed and I'll watch the forest." But the son knows that his father will see not a forest but a blurred stain. He won't notice the fire till it singes his clothes. In the daytime they change places—the son lies on the bed and the father sits by the desk and tries to read the book, which lies open still. How he would like to strike up a conversation with his son, stir up some discussion. For example, he fails to understand why his son won't deal with the Jews, the Jewish aspect of the Crusades. For isn't mass suicide a wonderful and terrible thing?[3] The son gives him a kindly grin, a noncommittal reply, and silence. During the last days of his visit the father occupies himself with the dumb Arab. A host of questions bubbles up in him. Who is the man? Where is he from? Who cut his tongue out? Why? Look, he has seen hatred in the man's eyes. A creature like that may yet set the forest on fire some day. Why not?

On his last day the father is given the binoculars to play with.

Suitcase in hand, back bent, he shakes his son's hand. Then—tears in the eyes of the little father.

"I've been disturbing you, I know I have . . ."

In vain does the son protest, in vain mumble about the oceans of time still before him—about half the spring, the whole long summer, half the distant autumn.

From his elevated seat he watches his lost, blind father fumbling for the back of the lorry. The driver is rude and impatient with him. When the lorry moves off, the father waves good-bye to the forest by mistake. He has lost his bearings.

---

3. The father's allusion may be to a dark chapter in the history of the Crusades. In the late 11th century, German crusaders attacked and slaughtered Jewish communities in Germany before continuing on to Palestine. In many instances Jews committed suicide to escape torture or forced conversion.

VII

For a week he crawls from line to line over the difficult text. After every sentence he raises his head to look at the forest. He is still awaiting a fire. The air grows hot. A haze shimmers above the sea horizon. When the Arab returns at dusk his garments are damp with sweat, the child's gestures are tired. Anyway you look at it, he himself is lucky. At such a time to be here, high above any town. Ostensibly, he is working all the time, but observing could hardly be called work, could it? The temperature rises day by day. He wonders whether it is still spring, or whether perhaps the summer has crept upon the world already. One can gather nothing from the forest, which shows no change, except thorns fading to yellow among the trees perhaps. His hearing has grown acute. The sound of trees whispers incessantly in his ears. His eyes shine with the sun's gaining strength, his senses grown keen. In a way he is becoming attached to the forest. Even his dreams are growing richer in trees. The women sprout leaves.

His text is difficult, the words distant. It has turned out to be only the preface to a preface. Yet, thorough as he is, he does not skip a single passage. He translates every word, then rewrites the translation in rhyme. Simple, easy rhymes, in order that the words should merge in his mind, should not escape into the silence.

No wonder that by Friday he can count but three pages read, out of the thousands. "Played out," he whispers to himself and trails his fingertips over the desk. Perhaps he'll take a rest? A pensive air comes over the green empire before him each Sabbath eve and makes his heart contract. Though he believes neither in God nor in all his angels, there is a sacredness that brings a lump to his throat.

He combs his beard in honor of the holy day. Yes, there is a new beard growing here along with the pines. He brings some order into the chaos of his room, picks a page off the floor. What is this? The instruction sheet. Full of interest, he reads it once more and discovers a forgotten instruction, or one added by his own hand, perhaps.

"Let the forest scout go out from time to time for a short walk among the trees, in order to sharpen his senses."

His first steps in the forest are like a baby's. He circles the observation post, hugging its walls as though afraid to leave them. Yet the trees attract him like magic. Little by little he ventures among the hills, deeper and deeper. If he should smell burning, he will run back.

But this isn't a forest yet, only the hope and promise of one. Here and there the sun appears through the foliage and a traveler among the trees is dappled with flickers of light. This isn't a rustling forest but a very small one, like a graveyard. A forest of solitudes. The pines stand erect, slim, serious; like a company of new recruits awaiting their commander. The ranging fire-watcher is pleased by the play of light and shadow. With every step he crushes dry pine needles underfoot. Softly, endlessly, the pines shed their needles; pines arrayed in a garment of mingling life and death.

The rounded human moving among trees whose yearning is so straight, so fierce. His body aches a bit, the ache of cramped limbs stretching; his legs are heavy. Suddenly he catches sight of the telephone line. A yellowish wire smelling of mold. Well, so this is his contact with the world. He starts tracing the yellow wire, searching for its origin, is charmed by its pointless twists and loops between the trees. They must have let some joker unwind the drum over the hills.

Suddenly he hears voices. He wavers, stops, then sees the little clearing in the woods. The Arab is seated on a pile of rocks, his hoe by his side. The child is talking to him excitedly, describing something with animated gestures. The scout tiptoes nearer, as lightly as his bulk will permit. They are instantly aware of him, sniff his alien being, and fall silent. The Arab jumps up, stands by his hoe as though hiding something. He faces them, wordless. It is the Sabbath eve today, isn't it, and there is a yearning in his heart. He stands and stares, for all the world like a supervisor bothered by some obscure triviality. The soft breeze caresses his eyes. If he did not fear for his status, he would hum them a little tune, perhaps. He smiles absently, his eyes stray and slowly he withdraws, with as much dignity as he can muster.

The two remain behind, petrified. The child's joy has shriveled halfway through her interrupted story, the Arab starts weeding the thorns at his feet. But the scout has retreated already, gone forth into the empire. He has been wandering in the woods for all of an hour now and is still making new discoveries. The names of donors, for example. It had never occurred to him that this wouldn't be just some anonymous forest but one with a name, and not just one name either. Many rocks bear copper plates, brilliantly burnished. He stoops, takes off his glasses, reads: Louis Schwartz of Chicago; the King of Burundi and his People. Flickers of light play over the letters. The names cling to him, like the falling pine needles that slip into his pocket. How odd! The tired memory tries to refresh itself with these faceless names. Name after name is absorbed by him as he walks, and by the time he reaches the observation post he can already hold a little rehearsal. He recites the sorted names, a vacuous smile on his face.

Friday night.

A wave of sadness wells within him. His mind happens to be perfectly lucid at the moment. We'll clear out on Sunday he whispers suddenly, and starts humming a snatch of song; inaudibly at first, the sound humming inside him, but soon trilling and rising high to the darkening sky. A hidden abyss behind him echoes in reply. The light drips, drips. Strings of light tear the sunset across and he shouts song at it, shrills recklessly, wanton with solitude. He starts one song, stops, plunges into another without change of key. His eyes fill with tears. The dark stifles his throat at last, suddenly he hears himself and falls silent.

Peace returns to the forest. Remnants of light linger. Five minutes pass and then the Arab and the girl emerge from the cover of the underbrush and hurry to the house with bent heads.

The Sabbath passes in a wonderful tranquillity. He is utterly calm. He has begun counting the trees for a change. Sunday he is on the verge of escaping but then the lorry brings him his salary, a part of the job he had forgotten. He is amazed, gushes his thanks to the mocking driver. So there's a prize in the whispering world, is there?

He returns to the books.

VIII

Hot summer. Yes, but we have forgotten the birds. Presumably the observation post stands on an ancient crossroads of bird trajectories. How else to explain the mad flocks swooping in from the forest to beat their wings against the walls, drop on the bed, dive at the books, shed gray feathers and green dung, shatter the dull air with their restlessness—and vanish on their circuitous flight to the sea. A change has come over him. Sunburned, yes, but there is more to it than that. The heat wells up in him, frightens him. A dry flow of desert wind may rouse the forest to suicide; hence he redoubles his vigilance, presses the binoculars hard against his eyes and subjects the forest in his care to a strict survey. How far has he come? Some slight twenty pages are behind him, thousands still before. What does he remember? A few words, the tail end of a theory, the atmosphere on the eve of the Crusades. The nights are peaceful. He could have studied, could have concentrated, were it not for the gnats. Night after night he extinguishes the lights and sits in darkness. The words have dropped away from him like husks. Cicadas. Choruses of jackals. A bat wings heavily across the gloom. Rustlings.

Hikers start arriving in the forest. Lone hikers some of them, but mostly they come in groups. He follows them through the binoculars. Various interesting ages. Like ants they swarm over the forest, pour in among the trees, calling out to each other, laughing; then they cast off their rucksacks all at once, unburden themselves of as many clothes as possible and hang them up on branches, and promptly come over to the house.

Water is what they want. Water!

He comes down to them, striking them with wonder. The bald head among the green pines, the heavy glasses. Indeed, everything indicates an original character.

He stands by the water tap, firm and upright, and slakes their thirst. Everyone begs permission to go upstairs for a look at the view. He consents, joyfully. They crowd into his little room and utter the stock formula of admiring exclamations. He smiles as though he had created it all. Above everything, they are surprised by the sea. They had never imagined one could see the sea from here. Yet how soon they grow bored! One glance, a cry of admiration, and they grow restless already and eager to be away. They peep at his notes, at the heavy books, and descend the staircase brimming with veneration for him and his view. The group leaders ask him to give some account of the place, but there is no account to give. Everything is still artificial here. There is nothing here, not even some archaeology for amateurs, nothing but a few donors inscribed on rocks. Would they be interested in the names? Well, for instance . . .

They laugh.

The girls look at him kindly. No, he isn't handsome. But might he not become engraved on one of their hearts?

They light campfires.

They wish to cook their food, or to warm themselves. A virtuous alarm strikes him. Tiny flames leap up in the forest, a bluish smoke starts blowing gaily about the treetops. A fire? Yes and no. He stays glued, through his binoculars, to the lively figures.

Toward evening he goes to explore his flickering, merrymaking empire. He wishes to sound a warning. Softly, soundlessly he draws near the camp-fires, the figures wreathed in flames. He approaches them unnoticed, and they are startled when they discover him beside them. Dozens of young eyes look up at him together. The leaders rise at once.

"Yes? What do you want?"

"The fire. Be careful! One spark, and the forest may burn down."

They are quick to assure him. Laying their hands on their young hearts they give him their solemn promise to watch with all the eyes shining in a row before him. They will keep within bounds, of course they will, what does he think?

He draws aside. Appeased? Yes and no. There, among the shadows, in the twilight of the fire, he lingers and lets his eyes rove. The girls and their bare, creamy legs, slender does. The flames crackle and sing, softly, gently. He clenches his fists in pain. If only he could warm his hands a little.

"Like to join us?" they ask politely. His vertical presence is faintly embarrassing.

No, thanks. He can't. He is busy. His studies. They have seen the books, haven't they? Now there is nothing for it but to withdraw with measured tread. But as soon as he has vanished from their view he flings himself behind the trees, hides among the needle branches. He looks at the fire from afar, at the girls, till everything fades, and blankets are spread for sleep. Giggles, girls' affected shrieks, leaders' rebukes. Before he can begin to think, select one out of the many figures, it will be dawn. Silence is still best. At midnight he feels his way through the trees, back to the observa-tion post. He sits in his place, waiting. One of the figures may be working its way in the darkness toward him. But no, nothing. They are tired, sleep-ing already.

And the same next day, and all the days following.

Early in the morning he will open his book and hear wild song in the distance. He does not raise his eyes from the page but his hand strays to the binoculars. A dappled silence. Flashes of light through branches. His eyes are faithful to the written page, but his thoughts have gone whoring already. From the corner of his eye he follows the procession threading through the forest—sorting, checking ages, colors, joys of youth. There is something of abandon about them from afar, like a procession of Crusad-ers; except that these women are bare. He trembles, choking suddenly. He removes his glasses and beats his head against the books. Half an hour later they arrive. Asking for water to drink and the view to look at, as usual. They have heard about the wonderful view to be seen from up here. Perhaps they have heard about the scholar as well, but they say nothing. The group leaders take them, a batch at a time, into his room turned public property. No sooner have they scattered about the forest than the campfires leap up, as though that were their prime necessity. In the eve-ning he rushes over the five hills, from fire to fire, impelled by his duty to warn them or by an obscure desire to reveal himself. He never joins any of the circles though. He prefers to hide in the thicket. Their singing throbs in his heart, and even more than that—the whisperings. Warm summer nights—something constantly seeping through the leaves.

Gradually the groups of hikers blend. One excursion leaves, another arrives. By the time he has managed to learn a few outstanding names, their owners are gone and the sounds alone survive among the branches. Languor comes over him. No longer does he trouble to caution against fire. On the contrary. He would welcome a little conflagration, a little local tumult. The hikers, however, are extremely responsible. They, themselves, take care to stamp out every dying ember. Their leaders come in advance to set his mind at rest.

The birds know how much he has neglected his studies; the birds whom he watches constantly lest they approach his desk. A month has passed since last he turned a page and he is stuck squirming between two words. He says: let the heat abate, the hikers be gone—then I shall race over the lines. If only he could skip the words and get to the essence. From time to time he scribbles in his notebook. Stray thoughts, speculations, musings, outlines of assumptions. Not much. A sentence a day. He would like to gain a hold upon it all indirectly. Yet he is doubtful whether he has gained a hold even upon the forest in front of his eyes. Look, here the Arab and the girl are disappearing among the trees and he cannot find them. Toward evening they emerge from an unforeseen direction as though the forest had conceived them even now. They tread the soil softly. They avoid people, choose roundabout ways. He smiles at them both but they recoil.

Friday. The forest is overrun, choking with people. They come on foot and by car, crowds disgorged by the faraway cities. Where is his solitude now? He sprawls on his chair like a dethroned king whose empire has slipped from his hands. Twilight lingers on the treetops. Sabbath eve. His ears alone can catch, beyond the uproar of voices, beyond the rustling, the thin cry of the weary soil ceaselessly crushed by the teeth of young roots. A hikers' delegation comes to see him. They just want to ask him a question. They have argued, laid wagers, and he shall be their arbiter. Where exactly is this Arab village that is marked on the map? It ought to be somewhere around here, an abandoned Arab village. Here, they even know its name, something like . . . actually, it must be right here, right in the forest. . . . Does he know anything about it perhaps? They're simply curious.

The fire-watcher gives them a tired look. "A village?" he repeats with a polite, indulgent smile at their folly. No, there is no village here. The map must be wrong, the surveyor's hand must have shaken.

But in the small hours of the night, somewhere between a doze and a slumber, in the face of the whispering, burgeoning forest, the name floats back into his mind of a sudden and he is seized with restlessness. He descends to the ground floor, feels his way in the dark to the bed of the Arab, who lies asleep covered with rags. Roughly he wakes him and whispers the name of the village. The Arab does not understand. His eyes are consumed with weariness. The fire-watcher's accent must be at fault. He tries again, therefore, repeats the name over and over and the Arab listens and suddenly he understands. An expression of surprise, of wonder and eagerness, suffuses all his wrinkles. He jumps up, stands there in his hairy nakedness and flings up a heavy arm in the direction of the window, pointing fervently, hopelessly, at the forest.

The fire-watcher thanks him and departs, leaving the big naked figure in the middle of the room. When he wakes tomorrow, the Arab will think he has dreamed it.

IX

Ceremonies. A season of ceremonies. The forest turns all ceremonial. The trees stand bowed, heavy with honor, they take on meaning, they belong. White ribbons are strung to delimit new domains. Luxurious buses struggle over the rocky roads, a procession of shining automobiles before and behind. Sometimes they are preceded by a motorcycle mounted by an excited policeman. Unwieldy personages alight, shambling like black bears. The women flutter around them. Little by little they assemble, crush out cigarettes with their black shoes and fall silent— paying homage to the memory of themselves. The fire-watcher, too, participates in the ceremony, from afar, he and his binoculars. A storm of obedient applause breaks out, a gleam of scissors, a flash of photographers, ribbons sag. A plaque is unveiled, a new little truth is revealed to the world. A brief tour of the conquered wood, and then the distinguished gathering dissolves into its various vehicles and sallies forth.

Where is the light gone?

In the evening, when the fire-watcher comes down to the drooping ribbons, to the grateful trees, he will find nothing but a pale inscription saying, for example: "Donated by the Sackson children in honor of Daddy Sackson of Baltimore, a fond tribute to his paternity. End of Summer Nineteen Hundred and . . ."

Sometimes the fire-watcher, observing from his heights, will notice one of the party who is darting troubled looks about him, raising his eyes at the trees as though searching for something. It takes many ceremonies before the fire-watcher's wandering mind will grasp that this is none other than the old man in charge of Afforestation, who comes and repeats himself, dressed always in the same clothes, at every ceremony.

Once he goes down to him.

The old man is walking among his distinguished foreign party, is jesting with them haltingly in their language. The fire-watcher comes out of the trees and plants himself in front of him for the inevitable encounter. The distinguished party stops, startled. An uneasy silence falls over them. The ladies shrink back.

"What do you want?" demands the old man masterfully.

The fire-watcher gives a weak smile.

"Don't you know me? I'm the watchman. That is to say, the fire-watcher . . . employee of yours . . ."

"Ah!" fist beating against aged forehead, "I didn't recognize you, was alarmed, these tatters have changed your appearance so, this heavy beard. Well, young man, and how's the solitude?"

"Solitude?" he wonders.

The old man presents him to the party.

"A scholar . . ."

They smile, troubled, meet his hand with their fingertips, move on. They do not have complete faith in his cleanliness. The old man, on the other hand, looks at him affectionately. A thought crosses his mind and he stays behind a moment.

"Well, so there *are* forests," he grins with good-natured irony.

"Yes," admits the scout honestly. "Forests, yes . . . but . . ."

"But what?"

"But fires, no."

"Fires?" the old man wonders, bending toward him.

"Yes, fires. I spend whole days here sitting and wondering. Such a quiet summer."

"Well, why not? Actually, there hasn't been a fire here for several years now. To tell you the truth, I don't think there has ever been a fire at all in this forest. Nature itself is harnessed to our great enterprise here, ha-ha."

"And I was under the impression . . ."

"That what?"

"That fires broke out here every other day. By way of illustration, at least. This whole machinery waiting on the alert, is it all for nothing? The fire engines . . . telephone lines . . . the manpower . . . for months my eyes have been strained with waiting."

"Waiting? Ha-ha, what a joke!"

The old one hurries along. The drivers are switching on their engines. That is all he needs, to be left overnight in this arboreal silence. Before he goes he would just like to know the watchman's opinion of the dumb Arab. The lorry driver has got the idea into his head that the fellow is laying in a stock of kerosene. . . .

The watchman is stirred. "Kerosene?"

"Daresay it's some fancy of that malicious driver. This Arab is a placid kind of fellow, isn't he?"

"Wonderfully placid," agrees the fire-watcher eagerly. Then he walks a few steps around the old man and whispers confidentially: "Isn't he a local?"

"A local?"

"Because our forest is growing over, well, over a ruined village. . . ."

"A village?"

"A small village."

"A small village? Ah—" (Something is coming back to him anyway.) "Yes, there used to be some sort of a farmstead here. But that is a thing of the past."

Of the past, yes, certainly. What else . . . ?

X

One day's program as an example.

Not having slept at night, he does not wake up in the morning. Light springs up between his fingers. What date is today? There is no telling. Prisoners score lines on the walls of their cell, but he is not in prison. He has come of his own free will, and so he will go. He could lift the receiver and find out the date from the firemen bent over their fire engines, waiting in some unknown beyond, but he does not want to scare them yet.

He goes down to the tap and sprinkles a few drops of water over his beard to freshen it up. Then he climbs back to his room, snatches up the binoculars and holds a pre-breakfast inspection. Excitement grips him. The forest filled with smoke? No, the binoculars are to blame. He wipes the lenses with a corner of his grimy shirt. The forest clears up at once, disappointingly. None of the trees has done any real growing overnight.

He goes down again. He picks up the dry loaf of bread and cuts himself a rough slice. He chews rapidly, his eyes roving over a torn strip of newspaper in which tomatoes are wrapped. It is not, God forbid, out of a hunger for news, but to keep his eyes in training lest they forget the shape of the printed letter. He returns to his observation post, his mouth struggling with an enormous half-rotten tomato. He sucks, swallows, gets smeared with the red, trickling sap. At last he throws a sizable remnant away. Silence. He dozes a bit, wakes, looks for a long time at the treetops. The day stretches out ahead of him. Softly he draws near the books.

Where are we? How many pages read? Better not count them or he will fall prey to despair; for the time being he is serene, and why spoil it. It isn't a question of quantity, is it? And he remembers what he has read up to now perfectly well, forward and backward. The words wave and whirl within him. For the time being, therefore, for the past few weeks, that is, he has been devoting his zeal to one single sheet of paper. A picture? Rather, a map. A map of the area. He will display it on this wall here for the benefit of his successors, that they may remember him. Look, he has signed his name already, signed it to begin with, lest he forget.

What is he drawing? Trees. But not only trees. Hills too, a blue horizon too. He is improving day by day. If he had colored crayons he could have added some birds as well; at least, say, those native to the area. What interests him in particular is the village buried beneath the trees. That is to say, it hasn't always been as silent here. His curiosity is of a strictly scientific nature. What was it the old man had said? "A scholar." He strokes the beard and his hand lingers, disentangles a few hairs matted with filth. What time is it? Early still. He reads a line about the attitude of the Pope to the German emperor and falls asleep. He wakes with a start. He lights a cigarette, tosses the burning match out into the forest, but the match goes out in mid-air. He flings the cigarette butt among the trees and it drops on a stone and burns itself out in solitude.

He gets up, paces about restlessly. What time is it? Early still.

He goes in search of the Arab, to say good morning. He must impress his own vigilant existence upon the man, lest he be murdered some morning between one nap and another. Ever since the fire-watcher has spoken the name of the vanished village in his ears, the Arab has become suspicious, as though he were being watched all the time. The fire-watcher strides rapidly between the pines. How light his footstep has grown during the long summer months. His soundless appearance startles the two.

"Shalom,"[4] he says.

They reply in two voices. The child—a voice that has sweetness in it, the Arab—a harsh grunt. The fire-watcher smiles to himself and hurries on as though he were extremely busy. Chiseled stones lie scattered among the trees, outlines of buildings, ruins and relics. He searches for marks left by humans. Every day he comes and disturbs a few stones, looking for traces.

A man and a woman are lying here entwined, like statues toppled from their base. Their terror when the bearded head bends silently over them! Smile at them and run, you! A couple slipped away from a group-hike, no doubt.

What is he looking for? Relics of thoughts that have flitted here, words that have completed their mission. But what will he find one fine day, say even the day that we have taken for a sample? Small tins filled with kerosene. How wonderful! The zeal with which someone has filled tin after tin here and covered them up with the girl's old dress. He stoops over the treasure, the still liquid on whose surface dead pine needles drift. His reflection floats back at him together with the faint smell.

Blissfully he returns to the house, opens a tin of meat and bolts its contents to the last sliver. He wipes his mouth and spits far out among the branch-filled air. He turns two pages of a book and reads the Cardinal's reply to a Jew's epistle. Funny, these twists and turns of the Latin, but what a threat is conveyed by them. He falls asleep, wakes, realizes he has nearly missed an important ceremony on the easternmost hill. From now on the binoculars stay glued to his eyes and he mingles with the distinguished crowd from afar. He can even make out the movements of the speakers' lips; he will fill in the missing sound himself. But then the flames of the sunset catch his eye and divert his attention, and with a daily returning excitement he becomes absorbed in the splendor, the terrible splendor.

Afterward he wipes the dust off the silent telephone. To give him his due—he bestows meticulous care on the equipment that belongs to the Afforestation Department, whereas his own equipment is already falling apart. The loose buttons shed among the trees, the frayed shirt, the ragged trousers.

A private outing of joyriders arrives with loud fanfare to spend the night in the forest. Wearily he chews his supper. Nightfall brings the old familiar sadness.

The Arab and his daughter go to bed. Darkness. The first giggle that emerges from the trees is a slap in his listening face. He turns over a few dark pages, swats a gnat, whistles.

Night. He does not fall asleep.

XI

Then it is the end of summer. The forest is emptying. And with the first autumn wind, who is blown to him like a withered leaf? His aging mistress, the wife of the friend who sent him here. Clad in a summer frock she comes, a wide-brimmed straw hat on her head. Then she is clicking her high heels around his room, rummaging through his drawers, bending over the books, peering through the papers. She had gone for a brief vacation by herself somewhere in this neighborhood and had remembered him. How is it when a man sits solitary, facing the forest, night after night? She had wanted to surprise him. Well, and what has he come up with? A fresh Crusade perhaps? She is awfully curious. Her husband speaks well of him too. In this solitude, among the trees, says the husband, he may yet flower into greatness.

The fire-watcher is moved. Without a word, he points at the map on the wall. She trips over to look, does not understand. Actually she is interested in texts. What has he written? She is very tired. Such a time till she found this place and she's more dead than alive. The view is pretty, yes, but the place looks awfully neglected. Who lives downstairs? The Arab? Is that so! She met him on the way, tried to ask him something and suddenly—the shock! Dumb, his severed tongue. But the Afforestation Department—hats off to them. Who would have imagined such forests growing in this country! He has changed, though. Grown fatter? This new beard of his is just awful. Why doesn't he say something?

She sinks down on the bed.

Then he rises, approaches her with that quiet which is in his blood now. He removes her hat, crouches at her feet, unbuckles her shoes. He is trembling with desire, choking.

She is shocked. She draws back her bare tired feet at once with something of terror, perhaps with relief. But he has let go already, stands holding the binoculars and looks at the forest, looks long, peering through the trees, waiting for fire. Slowly he turns to her, the binoculars at his eyes, turns the lenses upon her mischievously, sees the tiny wrinkles whittled in her face, the sweat drops, her fatigue. She smiles at him as in an old photograph. But when the moment drags, her smile turns into protest. She draws herself together crossly, holds up a hand.

"Hey, you! Stop it!"

Only toward sunset does he finally manage to undress her. The binoculars are still on his chest, pressed between their bodies. From time to time he coolly interrupts his kisses and caresses, raises the binoculars to his eyes and inspects the forest.

"Duty," he whispers apologetically, smiling oddly to the naked, embarrassed woman. Everything mingles with the glory of the crimson sun—the distant blue of the sea, the still trees, the blood on his cracked lips, the despair, the futility, the loneliness of the act. Accidentally her hand touches the bald crown and flinches.

When the Arab returns, it is all over. She is lying in the tangle of her clothes, drowsy. A beautiful night has descended on the world. He sits by his desk, what else should he do? The dark transforms her into a silhouette. The forest bewitches her. Suddenly she rouses herself. The soft voice of the little Arab girl sends a shiver through her. What is she doing here? She dresses rapidly, buttons, buckles. Her voice floats on the darkness.

Actually, she has come out of pity. No one had thought he would persist so long. When does he sleep anyway? She has been sent here to deliver him, deliver him from this solitude. His silence rouses suspicions. Her husband and his friends have suddenly begun to wonder, have become afraid, ha-ha, afraid that he may be nursing some secret, some novel idea, that he may outshine them all with some brilliant research.

A sudden dark breeze bursts into the room through the gap where there is no wall, whirls around for a little and dies out in the two corners. He is kindled. His eyes glow.

"Pity? No, unnecessary. When do I sleep? Always . . . though different from the city sleep. Leave here now, just like that? Too late. I haven't finished counting the trees yet. Novel ideas? Maybe, though not what they imagine . . . not exactly scientific . . . Rather, human . . ."

Does she wish him to accompany her on her way back through the forest, or perhaps would she go by herself?

She jumps up.

They cut diagonally across the hills. He walks in front, she drags behind, staggering over the rocks in her high heels, hurt and humiliated. Though thickset, his feet are light and he slips through the foliage swift as a snake, never turning his head. She struggles with the branches whipping back behind him. The moonlight reveals them on their silent trip. What do you say now, my autumn love? Have I gone completely out of my mind? But that was to be expected, wasn't it? Out of my round of pleasures, you have cast me into solitude. Trees have taken the place of words for me, forests the place of books. That is all. Eternal autumn, fall, needles falling endlessly on my eyes. I am still awaiting a conflagration.

Wordless they reach the black highway. Her heels click on the asphalt with a last fury. Now he looks at her. Her face is scratched, her arms bloodstained. How assertively the forest leaves its mark. She contains the thin cry rising in her. Her silence grants her dignity. After some minutes a sleek car driven by a lone gray-templed man halts at her waving hand. She joins him in the car without a parting word. She will yet crumble between his fingers on the long road.

He turns in his tracks. After a few paces, the Arab pops up in front of him. He is breathing heavily, his face is dull. And what do you have to say, mister? From where have you sprung now? The Arab holds out her forgotten hat, the straw hat. The fire-watcher smiles his thanks, spreads his arms in a gesture of nothing we can do, she's gone. But how amazing, this attention. Nothing will escape the man's eye. He takes the hat from the Arab and pitches it on top of his own head, gives him a slight bow and the other is immediately alarmed. His face is alert, watching. Together, in silence, they return to the forest, their empire, theirs alone. The fire-watcher strides ahead and the Arab tramples on his footsteps. A few clouds, a light breeze. Moonlight pours over the branches and makes them transparent. He leads the Arab over roads that are the same roads always. Barefoot he walks, the Arab, and so quietly. Round and round he is led, roundabout and to his hideout, amid chiseled stones and silence. The Arab's steps falter. His footfalls lag, die, and come alive again. A deathly cold grips the fire-watcher's heart, his hands freeze. He kneels on the rustling earth. Who will give him back all the empty hours? The forest is dark and empty. No one there. Not one campfire. Just now, when he would dip his hands in fire, warm them a little. He heaps up some brown needles, takes a match, lights it, and the match goes out at once. He takes another and cups his hands around it, strikes, and this one too flares up and dies. The air is damp and treacherous. He rises. The Arab watches him, a gleam of lunatic hope in his eyes. Softly the fire-watcher walks around the pile of stones to the sorry little hideout, picks up a tin of clear liquid and empties it over the heap of pine needles, tosses in a burning match and leaps up with the surging flame—singed, happy. At last he, too, is lit up a little. Stunned, the Arab goes down on his knees. The fire-watcher spreads his palms over the flame and the Arab does likewise. Their bodies press in on the fire, which has already reached its highest pitch. He might leave the flame now and go and bathe in the sea. Time, time wasting here among the trees, will do his work for him. He muses, his mind distracted. The fire shows signs of languishing, little by little it dies at his feet. The Arab's face takes on a look of bitter disappointment. The bonfire fades. Last sparks are stamped out meticulously. Thus far it was only a lesson. The wandering mind of the fire-watcher trembles between compromises. He rises wearily and leaves. The Arab slouches in his wake.

Who is sitting on the chair behind the book-laden desk? The child. Her eyes are wide open, drinking in the dark. The Arab has put her there to replace the roving fire-watcher. It's an idea.

XII

Strange days follow. We would say: autumn—but that means nothing yet. The needles seem to fall faster, the sun grows weaker, clouds come to stay, and a new wind. His mind is slipping, growing unhinged. The ceremonies are over. The donors have gone back to their countries, the hikers to their work, pupils to their study. His own books lie jumbled in a glow of dust. He is neglecting his duties, has left his chair, his desk, his faithful binoculars, and has begun roving endlessly about the forest, by day and by night; a broken twig in his hand, he slashes at the young tree trunks as he walks, as though marking them. Suddenly he slumps down, rests his head against a shining copper plaque, removes his glasses and peers through the blurring foliage, searches the gray sky. Something like a wail, suddenly. Foul fantasies. Then he collects himself once more, jumps up to wander through the wood, among the thistles and rocks. The idea has taken hold in his dim consciousness that he is being called insistently to an encounter at the edge of the forest, at its other end. But when he plunges out of the forest and arrives there, whether it be at night or at noon or in the early dawn, he finds nothing but a yellow waste, a strange valley, a kind of cursed dream. And he will stand there for a long time, facing the empty, treeless silence and feeling that the encounter is taking place, is being successful even though it happens wordlessly. He has spent a whole spring and a long summer never once properly sleeping, and what wonder is it if these last days should be like a trance.

He has lost all hope of fire. Fire has no hold over this forest. He can therefore afford to stay among the trees, not facing them. In order to soothe his conscience he sits the girl in his chair. It has taken less than a minute to teach her the Hebrew word for "fire." How she has grown during his stay here! She is like a noble mare now with marvelous eyes. Unexpectedly her limbs have ripened, her filth become a woman's smell. At first her old father had been forced to chain her to the chair, or she would have escaped. Yes, the old Arab has grown very attached to the negligent fire-watcher, follows him wherever he goes. Ever since the night when the two of them hugged the little bonfire the Arab, too, has grown languid. He has abandoned his eternal hoe. The grass is turning yellow under his feet, the thistles multiply. The fire-watcher will be lying on the ground and see the dusky face thrusting at him through the branches. As a rule he ignores the Arab, continues lying with his eyes on the sky. But sometimes he calls him and the man comes and kneels by his side, his heavy eyes wild with terror and hope. Perhaps, he, too, will fail to convey anything and it will all remain dark.

The fire-watcher talks to him therefore, quietly, reasonably, in a positively didactic manner. He tells him about the Crusades, and the other bends his head and absorbs the hard, alien words as one absorbing a melody. He tells him about the fervor, about the cruelty, about Jews committing suicide, about the Children's Crusade; things he has picked up from the books, the unfounded theories he has framed himself. His voice is warm, alive with imagination. The Arab listens with mounting tension and is filled with hate. When they return at twilight, lit by a soft autumnal glow, the fire-watcher will lead the Arab to the tree-engulfed house and will linger a moment. Then the Arab explains something with hurried, confused gestures, wiggling his severed tongue, tossing his head. He wishes to say that this is his house and that there used to be a village here as well and that they have simply hidden it all, buried it in the big forest.

The fire-watcher looks on at this pantomime and his heart fills with joy. What is it that rouses such passion in the Arab? Apparently his wives have been murdered here as well. A dark affair, no doubt. Gradually he moves away, pretending not to understand. Did there used to be a village here? He sees nothing but trees.

More and more the Arab clings to him. They sit there, the three of them like a family, in the room on the second floor. The fire-watcher sprawling on the bed, the child chained to the chair, the Arab crouching on the floor. Together they wait for the fire that does not come. The forest is dark and strong, a slow-growing world. These are his last days. His contract is drawing to an end. From time to time he gets up and throws one of the books back into the suitcase, startling the old Arab.

The nights are growing longer. Hot desert winds and raindrops mingle, soft shimmers of lightning flash over the sea. The last day is come. Tomorrow he will leave this place. He has discharged his duty faithfully. It isn't his fault that no fires have broken out. All the books are packed in the suitcase, scraps of paper litter the floor. The Arab has disappeared, has been missing since yesterday. The child is miserable. From time to time she raises her voice in a thin, ancient lament. The fire-watcher is growing worried. At noon the Arab turns up suddenly. The child runs toward him but he takes no notice of her. He turns to the abdicating fire-watcher instead, grabs him between two powerful hands and—feeble and soft as he is and suffering from a slight cold—impels him toward the edge of the observation post and explains whatever he can explain to him with no tongue. Perhaps he wishes to throw the abdicating fire-watcher down two stories and into the forest. Perhaps he believes that only he, the fire-watcher, can understand him. His eyes are burning. But the fire-watcher is serene, unresponsive; he shades his eyes with his palm, shrugs his shoulders, gives a meaningless little smile. What else is left him?

He collects his clothes and bundles them into the other suitcase.

Toward evening the Arab disappears again. The child has gone to look for him and has come back empty-handed. Gently the hours drift by. A single drop of rain. The fire-watcher prepares supper and sets it before the child, but she cannot bring herself to eat. Like a little animal she scurries off once more into the forest to hunt for her father and returns in despair, by herself. Toward midnight she falls asleep at last. He undresses her and carries the shabby figure to the bed, covers it with the torn blanket. What a lonely woman she will grow up to be. He muses. Something is flowing between his fingers, something like compassion. He lingers awhile. Then he returns to his observation post, sits on his chair, sleepy. Where will he be tomorrow? How about saying good-bye to the Fire Brigade? He picks up the receiver. Silence. The line is dead. Not a purr, not a gurgle. The sacred hush has invaded the wire as well.

He smiles contentedly. In the dark forest spread out before him, the Arab is moving about like a silent dagger. He sits watching the world as one may watch a great play before the rising of the curtain. A little excitement, a little drowsing in one's seat. Midnight performance.

Then, suddenly—fire. Fire, unforeseen, leaping out of the corner. A long graceful flame. One tree is burning, a tree wrapped in prayer. For a long moment one tree is going through its hour of judgment and surrendering its spirit. He lifts the receiver. Yes, the line is dead. He is leaving here tomorrow.

The loneliness of a single flame in a big forest. He is beginning to worry whether the ground may not be too wet and the thistles too few, and the show be over after one flame. His eyes are closing. His drowsiness is greatest now, at this most wonderful of moments. He rises and starts pacing nervously through the room in order to walk off his fatigue. A short while passes and then a smile spreads over his face. He starts counting the flames. The Arab is setting the forest on fire at its four corners, then takes a firebrand and rushes through the trees like an evil spirit, setting fire to the rest. The thoroughness with which he goes about his task amazes the fire-watcher. He goes down to look at the child. She is asleep. Back to the observation post—the forest is burning. He ought to run and raise the alarm, call for help. But his movements are so tranquil, his limbs leaden. Downstairs again. He adjusts the blanket over the child, pushes a lock of hair out of her eyes, goes back up, and a blast of hot air blows in his face. A great light out there. Five whole hills ablaze. Flames surge as in a frenzy high over the trees, roar at the lighted sky. Pines split and crash. Wild excitement sweeps him, rapture. He is happy. Where is the Arab now? The Arab speaks to him out of the fire, wishes to say everything, everything and at once. Will he understand?

Suddenly he is aware of another presence in the room. Swiftly he turns his head and sees the girl, half-naked, eyes staring, the light of the fire playing over her face. He smiles and she weeps.

Intense heat wells up from the leisurely burning forest. The first excitement has passed. The fire is turning from a vision into a fact. Flames are mobilizing from all the four winds to come and visit the observation post. He ought to take his two suitcases and disappear. But he only takes the child. The lights of the neighboring settlements have become so pitiful, so plain. They are no doubt sure, over there, that the fight against the fire is in full swing here already. Who would imagine that the fire is still being nourished here, brooded over? Hours will go by before the village watchmen come to wake the sleepers. The nights are cold already and people not disposed to throw off their blankets. He seizes the trembling child by the hand, goes down and begins his retreat. The road is lit up far into the distance. Behind his back the fire, and in his face—a red, mad, burning moon that floats in the sky as though it wished to see the blaze as well. His head feels heavy, the road stretches ahead. They drag along, dipping in light and in darkness. In the lanes the trees whisper, agitated, waiting. A fearful rumor has reached them.

The observation post can be seen from afar, entirely lit up. The earth is casting off its shackles. After a long walk the trees start thinning out at last, they grow smaller, then disappear. He arrives at the yellow waste, the valley, his dream. A few dry, twisted trees, desert trees, alien and salty; trees that have sprung up parched, over which the fire has no hold. He sits the barefoot girl on the ground, slumps beside her. His exhaustion erupts within him and covers them both.

With sleeping eyes he sees the shining fire engines arrive at last, summoned by another. They, too, know that all is lost. In a dream the Arab appears—tired, disheveled, black with soot, his face ravaged—takes the child and vanishes. The fire-watcher falls asleep, really asleep.

XIII

At dawn, shivering and damp, he emerges from the cover of the rocks, polishes his glasses and once more he is the little scholar who has some kind of future before him. Five, bare, black hills, and slender wisps of blue-gray smoke rising from them. The observation post juts out over the bare landscape like a great demon grinning with white windows. For a moment it seems as though the forest had never burned down but had simply pulled up its roots and gone off on a journey, far off on a journey, far off to the sea, for instance, which has suddenly come into view. The air is chilly. He adjusts his rumpled clothes, does up the last surviving button, rubs his hands to warm them, then treads softly among the smoking embers, light of foot. The first rays of the sun hit his bald patch. There is a sadness in this sudden nudity, the sadness of wars lost, blood shed in vain. Stately clouds sail in the cold sky. Soon the first rain will fall. He hears sounds of people everywhere. Utter destruction. Soot, a tangle of charred timber, its wounds still smoldering, and a residue of living branches unvisited by fire. Wherever he sets foot a thousand sparks fly. The commemorative plaques alone have survived; more than that, they have gained luster after their baptism of fire. There they lie, golden in the sun: Louis Schwartz of Chicago, the King of Burundi and his People.

He enters the burned building, climbs the singed stairs. Everything is still glowing hot. it is as though he were making his way through hell. He arrives at his room. The fire has visited it in his absence and held its riot of horror and glee. Shall we start with the books burned to ashes? Or the contorted telephone? Or perhaps the binoculars fused to a lump? The map of the area has miraculously survived, is only blackened a bit at the edges. Gay fire kittens are still frolicking in the pillow and blankets. He turns his gaze to the fire-smoking hills, frowns—there, out of the smoke and haze, the ruined village appears before his eyes; born anew in its basic outlines as an abstract drawing, as all things past and buried. He smiles to himself, a thin smile. Then abruptly it dies on his face. Directly under him, in the bluish abyss at the foot of the building, he sees the one in charge of forests who is edging his way to old age, wrapped in an old windbreaker, his face blue with cold. How has this one sprung up here, all of a sudden?

The old one throws his gray head back and sends up a look full of hatred. Looking down upon the man from his high post, his own eyes would be faintly contemptuous in any case. For a few seconds they stay thus, their eyes fixed on each other; at last the fire-watcher gives his employer a fatuous smile of recognition and slowly starts coming down to him. The old man approaches him with quick, mad steps. He would tear him to pieces if he could. He is near collapse with fury and pain. In a choking voice he demands the whole story, at once.

But there is no story, is there? There just isn't anything to tell. All there is, is: Suddenly the fire sprang up. I lifted the receiver—the line was dead. That's it. The child had to be saved.

The rest is obvious. Yes, the fire-watcher feels for the forest too. He has grown extremely attached to it during the spring, the summer, and half the autumn. So attached, in fact, that (to tell the truth, for once) he hasn't managed to learn a single line, actually.

He feels that the old man would like to sink to the ground and beat his head against some rock, would tear out the last of his white hair. The late fire-watcher is surprised. Because the forests are insured, aren't they (at least they ought to be, in his humble and practical opinion), and the fire won't be deducted from the budget of the old man's department, will it? Right now (this morning has found him amazingly clearheaded), he would very much like to be told about other forest fires. He is willing to bet that they were quite puny ones.

Except that now, ghostlike through the smoke, the firemen appear, accompanied by some fat and perspiring policemen. Soon he is surrounded by uniforms. Some of the men drop to the ground with exhaustion. Though the fire has not been completely tracked down as yet, they have already unearthed a startling piece of intelligence.

It has been arson.

Yes, arson. The smell of morning dew comes mingled with a smell of kerosene.

The old man is shattered.

"Arson?" he turns to the fire-watcher.

But the other smiles gently.

The investigation is launched at once. First the firemen, who are supposed to write a report. They draw the fire-watcher aside, take out large
sheets of paper, ornate ballpoints, and then it appears that they have difficulty with the language, with phrasing and spelling. They are embarrassed. Tactfully he helps them, spells out words, formulates their
sentences for them. They are very grateful.

"What have *you* lost in the fire?" they inquire sympathetically.

"Oh, nothing of importance. Some clothes and a few textbooks. Nothing to worry about."

By the time they are through, it is far into the morning. The Arab and
the child appear from nowhere, led by two policemen. If he will be careful
not to let his glance encounter those burning eyes, he may possibly sleep
in peace in the nights to come. Two tough-looking sergeants improvise a
kind of emergency interrogation cell among the rocks, place him on a
stone and start cross-examining him. For hours they persist, and that surprises him—the plodding tenacity, the diligence, page upon written page.
A veritable research is being compiled before his eyes. The sun climbs to
its zenith. He is hungry, thirsty. His interrogators chew enormous sandwiches and do not offer him a crumb. His glasses mist with sweat. A queer
autumn day. Inside the building, they are conducting a simultaneous
interrogation of the Arab, in Arabic, eked out with gestures. Only the questions are audible.

The old forest manager dodges back and forth between the two interro-
gations, adding questions of his own, noting down replies. The interrogators have their subject with his back against the rock, they repeat the same
questions over and over. A foul stench rises from the burned forest, as
though a huge carcass were rotting away all around them. The interrogation gains momentum. A big bore. What did he see? What did he hear?
What did he do? It's insulting, this insistence upon the tangible—as
though that were the main point, as though there weren't some idea
involved here.

About noon his questioners change, two new ones appear and start the
whole process over again. The subject is dripping with sweat. How humiliating, to be interrogated thus baldly on scorched earth, on rocks, after a
sleepless night. The tedium of it. The fire-watcher spits, grows angry, loses
his temper. He removes his glasses and his senses go numb. He starts
contradicting himself. At three o'clock he breaks in their hands, is prepared to suggest the Arab as a possible clue.

This, of course, is what they have been waiting for. They suspected the
Arab all along. Promptly they handcuff him, and then all at once everything is rapidly wound up. The police drivers start their cars. The Arab is
bundled into one of them and there is a gratified expression in his eyes
now, a sense of achievement. The child clings to him desperately. Autumn
clouds, autumn sadness, everything is flat. Stupid. Suddenly he walks over
to the forest manager and boldly demands that something be done for the
child. The other makes no reply. His old eyes wander over the lost forest
as though in parting. This old one is going mad as well, his senses are
growing confused. He stares at the fire-watcher with vacant eyes as though

he, too, had lost the words, as though he understood nothing. The fire-watcher repeats his demand in a loud voice. The old man steps nearer.

"What?" he mumbles in a feeble voice, his eyes watery. Suddenly he throws himself at the fire-watcher, attacks him with shriveled fists, hits out at him. With difficulty, the firemen pull him back. To be sure, he blames only this one here. Yes, this one with the books, with the dim glasses, with that smug cynicism of his.

The policemen extricate the fire-watcher and whisk him into one of their cars. They treat him roughly, something of the old man's hostility has stuck to them. Before he has time to say good-bye to the place where he has spent nearly six months he is being borne away at a mad pace toward town. They dump him on one of the side streets. He enters the first restaurant he comes to and gorges himself to bursting point. Afterward he paces the streets, bearded, dirty, sunburned—a savage. The first dusty rain has already smirched the pavements.

At night, in some shabby hotel room, he is free to have a proper sleep, to sleep free from obligations for the first time, just sleep without any further dimensions. Except that he will not fall asleep, will only go on drowsing. Green forests will spring up before his troubled eyes. He may yet smart with sorrow and yearning, may feel constricted because he is shut in by four walls, not three.

And so it will be the day after, and perhaps all the days to come. The solitude has proved a success. True, his notes have been burned along with the books, but if anyone thinks that he does not remember—he does.

Yet he has become a stranger now in his so-familiar town. He seems to have forgotten already. A new generation is breaking into the circles. His waggish friends meet him, slap him on the back, and with ugly grins say, "We hear your forest burned down!" As we said, he is still young. But his real friends have given him up in despair. He drops in on them, winter nights, shivering with cold—wet dog begging for fire and light—and they scowl and ask:

"Well, what now?"

ANITA DESAI
born 1937

Author of eight novels and a collection of short stories, Anita Desai is a distinguished novelist, a leading figure among a number of Indian writers who write mainly or exclusively in English. Born of a Bengali father and German mother in Mussoorie in north India, Desai was educated in Delhi and started writing English fiction at the age of ten. Her first novel, *Cry, the Peacock*, was published in 1963. *Fire on the Mountain* (1977) won India's National Academy of Letters Award as well as Britain's Royal Society of Literature's Winifred Holtby Memorial Prize. *Clear Light of Day* (1980) and *In Custody* (1984) were nominated for the Booker Prize in Britain, and James Ivory and Ismail Merchant have recently made a film version of *In Custody*. Desai has lived in Bombay and Delhi and has taught at

Amherst College, Smith College, and Mount Holyoke College in the United States. She currently teaches at the Massachusetts Institute of Technology.

Like many other modern Indian writers in Indian languages as well in English, Desai focuses on the interaction of men and women within the institutions of marriage and the family. But her novels are distinguished by her overwhelming preoccupation with the inner lives of her characters. Without abandoning realistic narrative, Desai subordinates it to an interior perspective, represented chiefly through the discourses of memory and stream of consciousness, in a technique reminiscent of that of Virginia Woolf. The events that shaped Indian consciousness in the twentieth century figure importantly in Desai's novels, which are rich with the flavor of particular times and places—Delhi in 1947, the year in which British India was divided into the independent nations of India and Pakistan (*Clear Light of Day*); the city of Calcutta (*Voices in the City*, 1965); Kasauli, a small resort town in the hills of Himachal Pradesh in north India (*Fire on the Mountain*). And yet, her characters represent not so much individuals trying to define themselves in relation to changing social and political realities but deeply sensitive people trying to come to terms with a world that seems incapable of understanding them.

The British colonial government's decision in the mid-nineteenth century to introduce Western education in the English language in India had a profound impact on Indian literature. Literary works in English and the European languages became available to the English-educated elite, and Indian writers began to adapt Western genres, such as the novel and short story, in the modern Indian languages. The few who wrote in English came from Bengal, where cultural contact between Indians and the British had been most extensive in the eighteenth and nineteenth centuries, and their preferred medium was poetry. The 1920s and 1930s, however, saw the nationwide emergence of several Indian writers of stature and originality in English-language fiction. R. K. Narayan (born 1907), the best known of the so-called Indo-Anglian novelists, continues to be active. Desai represents a later generation, and since the 1980s yet another group of original young writers has appeared on the landscape of Indian English fiction, among them Amitav Ghosh (*The Circle of Reason*, 1986) and I. Allan Sealy (*The Trotter-Nama*, 1988).

A major difference between Indian writing in the modern Indian languages and that in English is audience, the former being accessible mainly to readers in the regions in which a particular language is spoken, and the latter both to the small number of Indians who are educated in English and to readers of English literature abroad. The two types of literature also tend to be divided along thematic lines. Social issues, including those raised by the problems of modernization, have been the major preoccupation of writers in the regional languages. The English-language writers have been more concerned with the lives of the more Westernized, English-educated segment of modern Indian society, in cosmopolitan milieux in India and abroad. But it would be wrong to insist on the differences between the two literatures, for the division is by no means clear-cut or represents a separation along East-West lines. Among the older English-language writers, Mulk Raj Anand (born 1905) began his career by writing novels with a leftist perspective, focusing on social justice and the underclasses. Narayan's fictional town of Malgudi is a microcosm of the modern south Indian world. And all the modern writers, regardless of the language of their choice, have responded deeply to events in recent history, especially India's freedom struggle, which, in the years between 1915 and 1947, brought English-educated Indians in greater contact with the less Westernized segments of the population and bound them together in a common cause. Nevertheless, political engagement and social realism are secondary issues in Desai's novels, whose principal focus is the inner life of the characters.

Women are the central characters in the majority of Desai's novels. Maya, the protagonist of *Cry, the Peacock*, is a young woman trying to cope with the pressures of emotional obsession and a difficult marriage. The events in *Where Shall We Go This Summer* (1975) are seen from the perspective of Sita, as she tries to take stock of her life in the context of an unexpected pregnancy, and *Fire on the Mountain* is the narrative of the widowed Nanda Kaul, who lives alone, and her great-grand-daughter Raka, who is sent to live with Nanda against her own and Nanda's wishes. The fragile sensibilities of these women (and girls) are strained not by the burden imposed by social institutions (the customary target of progressive Indian intellectuals and critics) but by the psychological oppression stemming from the denial of self-expression and the failure of those closest to them—especially men—to respond to their emotional selves. Tracing her protagonists' responses to their intolerable situations (death and insanity often wait in the wings in these novels), Desai meticulously documents the subtle yet devastating power of emotional violence in the setting of the family. Whether rich or impoverished, living alone or with their husbands, her female characters react most deeply to what they perceive to be the inherent, stifling violence and meaninglessness of routinized domesticity and externally imposed roles for women. In her two most recent novels, *In Custody* (1984) and *Baumgartner's Bombay* (1988), Desai has ventured in new directions, focusing on male protagonists and exploring the tragicomic (*In Custody*) and tragic (*Baumgartner*) responses of sensitive men to the world in which they find themselves.

Although Desai continues to grow in depth and range as a writer, *Clear Light of Day*, her sixth novel, is in many ways her most fully realized work. Its narrative centers on the process by which, during a summer visit from her sister Tara, Bim (short for Bimla) Das, a history professor in a Delhi college, comes to terms with her complex relationship with her siblings and their shared past. That past is intertwined with the lives of two very different families—the Hyder Alis and the Misras—and with events on the larger canvas of history, the tragic events surrounding the Partition of India, as well as older, more shadowy ones in the history of the city of Old Delhi, represented especially by the Moghal period, in which Bim specializes. The novel is pervaded with the atmosphere of Old Delhi, the walled older section of the city of Delhi, which had been the seat of several Muslim dynasties from the twelfth century onward and which was supplanted as the administrative center by New Delhi, the city completed in 1931 to serve as the capital of British India.

Neither family history nor great historical events are presented in a linear narrative in the novel. Instead, the reader is guided through an intricately woven tapestry of events, those of the "present" alternating with the momentous events of the summer of 1947, refracted mainly through the consciousness of Bim and Tara. For Bim and her siblings the summer of 1947 brings the division not only of the nation but of their own family. Old Delhi, city of elegant poetry and ancient monuments, endures, albeit in symbolic decay, but Hindus and Muslims, once co-sharers of a rich civilization, are violently torn apart by Partition. Bim's brother Raja's break with her (Bim) is nearly as brutal, and the fire of his tubercular fever in that summer blends with the cremation fires of dead relatives and the conflagration of the Hindu-Muslim riots that sends the city up in flames.

The structure of *Clear Light of Day* images the structure of memory itself. Through Tara's and Bim's recollections we are presented with the same events from divergent perspectives. We see how memory distorts, plays tricks, but we also see how, though suppressed with effort, it comes back to haunt the two women like the whining mosquitoes of summer evenings in an Old Delhi garden. Each in her own way, the sisters must confront the pain of the past.

And yet memory and the past are not omnipotent, even as the family and the crumbling house in Old Delhi are not simply the arenas for illness, emotional oppression, and separation. In contrast to the nostalgic Tara, the mentally retarded brother Baba (who lives in an eternal present), and the absent brother Raja, with his romantic obsession with an aristocratic pre-British past embodied in Urdu poetry, Bim is a robust, dynamic person. A historian by profession, she savors the past but has no patience with those who wish to live in it. At once sensitive and strong, Bim is an attractive and uplifting character. If, at the end of the novel, she is able to draw on her familial past and her love for her siblings as a source of inner strength, it is because, unlike other women in Desai's novels, including the other women in *Clear Light of Day*, she learns how to be nurturing without denying herself, to give and love without being destroyed in the process.

Much of the power of Desai's novels derives from their richly conceived atmosphere and mood. Desai works with the English language like an Indian ivory carver, creating finely wrought, textured sentences and images. In *Clear Light of Day* her evocative style captures with precision the atmosphere of the gardens of Shah Jahan's city, the dusty banks of the Jumna, and the endless summers of childhood. The delicate yet intense colors of Desai's descriptions and their intricate design invite comparison with Moghal miniature paintings, while the novel's structure suggests the complex patterning of Indian *raga* music. These stylistic achievements, coupled with the quietly compelling voice that emerges in all her fiction, make Desai one of the major novelists of our time.

William Walsh, *Indian Literature in English* (1990), Meenakshi Mukherjee, *The Twice-born Fiction* (1971), and M. K. Naik, *A History of Indian English Literature* (1982), are good introductions to Indian literature in English. Feroza Jussawalla, *Family Quarrels: Towards a Criticism of Indian Writing in English* (1985), offers a critical approach to Indian English fiction at a more advanced level. Two recent studies of Anita Desai's fiction, both published in India, are Jasbir Jain, *Stairs to the Attic: The Novels of Anita Desai* (1987), and Ramesh K. Srivastava, *Perspectives on Anita Desai* (1984).

PRONOUNCING GLOSSARY

The following list uses common English syllables and stress accents to provide rough equivalents of selected words whose pronunciation may be unfamiliar to the general reader.

Bakul: *buh'-kool*

Bardol Thodol: *bahr'-dohl toh'-dohl*

Bare-mia: *buh-ray'—mee-yah'*

Bhagavad-Gita: *buh'-guh-vuhd–gee'tah*

bhai: *bah'-yee*

Biswas: *bee'-shas*

chameli: *chuh-may'-lee*

Daulatabad: *dow'-luh-tah-bad'*

farishtha: *fuh-reesh'-tah*

Indraprastha: *een'-druh-pruhs'-thuh*

Jamia Millia: *jah'-mee-yah mee'-lee-yah*

Janaki: *jahn'-kee*

Khilji: *kheel'-jee*

koel: *koh'-yuhl*

Lala Ram Narain: *lah'-lah rahm nah-rah'-yuhn*

mithai: *mee'-tah-yee*

mubarak: *moo-bah'-ruhk*

Mulk: *moolk*

nawab: *nuh-vahb'*

Nur-jehan: *noor'–juh-han'*

pan: *pahn*

Panipat: *pah'-nee-puht*

pipal: *pee-puhl*

Rakhibandhan: *rah'-kee-buhn-duhn*

rossogolla: *ro'-sho-gol-lah*

salwar-kameez: *suhl-vahr'–kuh-meez'*

Sardar-ji: *suhr-dahr'–jee*

shehnai: *sheh-nah'-yee*

shikakai: *shee'-kah-kai*

suar ka baccha: *soo'-vuhr kah buhc'-*
    chah

Tughlaq: *toog'-luhk*

vilayat: *vee-lah'-yuht*

Zauq: *zowk*

zindagi: *zeen'-duh-gee*

Clear Light of Day

Memory is a strange bell—
Jubilee and knell—
    Emily Dickinson[1]

See, now they vanish,
The faces and places, with the self which, as it could, loved them,
To become renewed, transfigured, in another pattern.
    T. S. Eliot[2]

I

    The koels[3] began to call before daylight. Their voices rang out from the dark trees like an arrangement of bells, calling and echoing each others' calls, mocking and enticing each other into ever higher and shriller calls. More and more joined in as the sun rose and when Tara could no longer bear the querulous demand in their voices, she got up and went out onto the veranda to find the blank white glare of the summer sun thrusting in between the round pillars and the purple bougainvillea. Wincing, she shielded her eyes as she searched for the birds that had clamoured for her appearance, but saw nothing. The cane chairs on the veranda stood empty. A silent line of ants filed past her feet and down the steps into the garden. Then she saw her sister's figure in white, slowly meandering along what as children they had called "the rose walk."

    Dropping her hands to pick up the hem of her long nightdress, Tara ran down the steps, bowing her head to the morning sun that came slicing down like a blade of steel onto the back of her neck, and crossed the dry crackling grass of the lawn to join her sister who stood watching, smiling.

    The rose walk was a strip of grass, still streaked green and grey, between two long beds of roses at the far end of the lawn where a line of trees fringed the garden—fig and silver oak, mulberry and eucalyptus. Here there was still shade and, it seemed to Tara, the only bit of cultivation left; everything else, even the papaya and lemon trees, the bushes of hibiscus and oleander, the beds of canna lilies, seemed abandoned to dust and neglect, to struggle as they could against the heat and sun of summer.

    But the rose walk had been maintained almost as it was. Or was it? It seemed to Tara that there had been far more roses in it when she was a child—luscious shaggy pink ones, small crisp white ones tinged with green, silky yellow ones that smelt of tea—and not just these small negligible crimson heads that lolled weakly on their thin stems. Tara had grown to know them on those mornings when she had trailed up and down after

---

1. American lyric poet (1830–1886).   2. From *Little Gidding*, lines 163–65.   3. Common Indian songbirds.

her mother who was expecting her youngest child and had been advised by her doctor to take some exercise. Her mother had not liked exercise, perhaps not the new baby either, and had paced up and down with her arms folded and her head sunk in thought while the koels mocked and screamed and dive-bombed the trees. Tara had danced and skipped after her, chattering, till she spied something flashing from under a pile of fallen rose petals—a pearl, or a silver ring?—and swooped upon it with a cry that broke into her mother's reverie and made her stop and frown. Tara had excitedly swept aside the petals and uncovered—a small, blanched snail. Her face wrinkling with disgust, her mother turned and paced on without a word, leaving Tara on her knees to contemplate the quality of disillusion.

But here was Bim. Bim, grey and heavy now and not so unlike their mother in appearance, only awake, watchful, gazing at her with her fullest attention and appraisal. Bim laughed when she saw Tara panting slightly in her eagerness.

Tara laughed back. "Bim, the old rose walk is still here."

"Of course," said Bim, "only the roses grow smaller and sicker every year," and she bent to shake a long spindly branch from which a fully bloomed rose dangled. It came apart instantly, revealing a small naked centre and a few pathetic stamens clinging to the bald head while the petals fell in a bunch to the chocolate earth below.

Tara's mouth opened in dismay at the destruction of a rose in full bloom—she would never have done what Bim did—and then she saw the petals that had clung together in a bunch in their fall part and scatter themselves. As she stared, a petal rose and tumbled onto its back and she saw uncovered the gleam of a—a pearl? a silver ring? Something that gleamed, something that flashed, then flowed—and she saw it was her childhood snail slowly, resignedly making its way from under the flower up a clod of earth only to tumble off the top onto its side—an eternal, miniature Sisyphus.[4] She brought her hands together in a clap and cried, "Look, a snail!"

Bim watched her sister in surprise and amusement. Was Tara, grown woman, mother of grown daughters, still child enough to play with a snail? Would she go down on her knees to scoop it up on a leaf and watch it draw its albuminous trail, lift its tiny antennae, gaze about it with protruding eyes and then, the instant before the leaf dipped and it slid downwards, draw itself into its pale pod?

As Tara performed the rites of childhood over the handy creature, Bim stood with lowered head, tugging at the hair that hung loosely about her face as she had done when she had sat beside her brother's bed that summer that he was ill, with her forehead lowered to the wooden edge of the bed, a book of poetry open on her lap, reading aloud the lines:

Now sleeps the crimson petal, now the white;
Nor waves the cypress in the palace walk;

---

4. In Greek mythology, king of Corinth; condemned by Zeus to push a rock up a hill eternally.

Nor winks the gold fin in the porphyry font:
The firefly wakens[5] . . .

Her lips moved to the lines she had forgotten she remembered till she saw the crimson petals fall in a heap on the snail in the mud, but she would not say them aloud to Tara. She had no wish to use the lines as an incantation to revive that year, that summer when he had been ill and she had nursed him and so much had happened in a rush. To bury it all again, she put out her toe and scattered the petals evenly over the damp soil.

Now Tara's hand trembled, the leaf she held dipped and the doomed creature slid soundlessly back to earth.

They both stood staring as it lay there, shocked and still.

Tara murmured "You looked so like Mama from a distance, Bim—I mean, it's so—the sun—" for she realised at once that Bim would not like the comparison.

But Bim did not seem to hear, or care. "Did you sleep at all?" she asked instead, for last night on arriving from the airport Tara had laughed and chattered and claimed to be too excited to sleep.

"How could I?" cried Tara, laughing, and talked of the koels in the morning, and the dog barking in the night, and the mosquitoes singing and stinging in the dark, as they walked together up the grassy path, Tara in her elegant pale blue nylon nightgown and elegant silver slippers and Bim in a curious shapeless hand-made garment that Tara could see she had fashioned out of an old cotton sari[6] by sewing it up at both sides, leaving enough room for her arms to come through and cutting out a wide scoop for her neck. At the feet a border of blue and green peacocks redeemed the dress from total shabbiness and was—Tara laughed lightly—original. "How he barks," she repeated. "Don't the neighbours complain?"

"I think they've grown used to him at last, or else they've realised it does no good to complain—I never will chain him up and, as I tell them when they do protest, he has such a beautiful voice, it's a pleasure to hear him. Not like the yipping and yapping of other people's little lap dogs," she said with a toss of her grey head.

Although they spoke softly, no louder than a pair of birds to each other, the dog must have heard his name or realised he was being discussed. When Tara had come out onto the veranda he had been asleep under the wooden divan, hidden from her by the striped cotton rug with which it was covered, and he had only twitched his whiskers when he heard her pass by. Now he was suddenly out there on the grass walk with them, standing with his four legs very wide apart, his nose diving down into the clods of earth where the snail still lay futilely struggling to upright itself. As it finally flipped onto its edge, he gave a thunderous sneeze.

"Badshah!"[7] cried Bim, delighted with his theatrical performance, and his one eye gleamed at the approval in her voice while the other followed

5. From Alfred, Lord Tennyson's *Now Sleeps the Crimson Petal*, a song in his narrative poem *The Princess*.   6. Indian woman's garment, a long sheet of cloth that is pleated and draped around the body.   7. Emperor (Urdu, of Persian origin).

the snail. But it disappeared under the rose petals once more and he came lolloping towards them, stubbed his moist nose into their legs, scuffed his dirty claws into their heels, salivated over their feet and then rushed past them in a show of leadership.

"He does like to be first always," Bim explained.

"Is he nine now, Bim, or ten?"

"Twelve," exclaimed Bim. "See his old whiskers all white," she said, diving forwards at his head and catching him by the ears, making him stand still with his head against her thigh. He closed his eyes and smiled a foolish smile of pleasure at her attention, then drew away with a long line of saliva dribbling from his jaws onto the grass, more copious and irregular than the fluent snail's. "He is Begum's[8] son, you know, and she lived to be—fourteen?"

Tara lifted her hair from the back of her neck and let it fall again, luxuriantly, with a sigh. "How everything goes on and on here, and never changes," she said. "I used to think about it all," and she waved her arm in a circular swoop to encompass the dripping tap at the end of the grass walk, the trees that quivered and shook with birds, the loping dog, the roses—"and it is all exactly the same, whenever we come home."

"Does that disappoint you?" Bim asked drily, giving her a quick side-ways look. "Would you like to come back and find it changed?"

Tara's face was suddenly wound up tightly in a frown as if such a thought had never struck her before and she found it confusing. "Changed? How? You mean the house newly painted, the garden newly planted, new people coming and going? Oh no, how could I, Bim?" and she seemed truly shocked by the possibility.

"But you wouldn't want to return to life as it used to be, would you?" Bim continued to tease her in that dry voice. "All that dullness, boredom, waiting. Would you care to live that over again? Of course not. Do you know anyone who would—secretly, sincerely, in his innermost self—*really* prefer to return to childhood?"

Still frowning, Tara murmured meaninglessly "Prefer to what?"

"Oh, to going on—to growing up—leaving—going away—into the world—something wider, freer—brighter," Bim laughed. "Brighter! Brighter!" she called, shading her eyes against the brightness.

Tara's head sank low, her frown deepened. She could not trust Bim to be quite serious: in her experience, the elder sister did not take the younger seriously—and so all she said was a murmured "But you didn't, Bim."

"I?" said Bim flatly, with her eyes still shaded against the light that streamed across the parched lawn and pressed against the trees at the fringe. "Oh, I never go anywhere. It must seem strange to you and Bakul who have travelled so much—to come back and find people like Baba and me who have never travelled at all. And if we still had Mira-*masi*[9] with us, wouldn't that complete the picture? This faded old picture in its petrified frame?" She stopped to pluck the dead heads off a rose bush dusted grey with disease. "Mira-*masi* swigging secretly from her brandy

8. Princess, lady (Urdu/Persian).   9. Aunt (Hindi), specifically, mother's younger sister.

bottle. Baba winding up his gramophone. And Raja, if Raja were here, playing Lord Byron[1] on his death-bed. I, reading to him. That is what you might have come back to, Tara. How would you have liked that?"

Tara stood staring at her silver toes, at the clods of upturned earth in the beds and the scattered dead heads, and felt a prickle of distrust in Bim. Was Bim being cruel again? There could be no other motive. There could be no reply. She made none and Bim swung away and marched on, striding beside Badshah.

"That is the risk of coming home to Old Delhi,"[2] she announced in the hard voice that had started up the prickle of distrust that ran over the tips of the hairs on Tara's arms, rippling them. "Old Delhi does not change. It only decays. My students tell me it is a great cemetery, every house a tomb. Nothing but sleeping graves. Now *New* Delhi, they say is different. That is where things happen. The way they describe it, it sounds like a nest of fleas. So much happens there, it must be a jumping place. I never go. Baba never goes. And here, here nothing happens at all. Whatever happened, happened long ago—in the time of the Tughlaqs, the Khiljis, the Sultanate, the Moghuls[3]—that lot." She snapped her fingers in time to her words, smartly. "And then the British built New Delhi and moved everything out. Here we are left rocking on the backwaters, getting duller and greyer, I suppose. Anyone who isn't dull and grey goes away—to New Delhi, to England, to Canada, the Middle East. They don't come back."

"I must be peculiar then," Tara's voice rose bravely. "I keep coming back. And Bakul."

"They pay your fare, don't they?" her sister said.

"But we *like* to come, Bim. We *must* come—if we are not to lose touch, I with all of you, with home, and he with the country. He's been planning this trip for months. When the girls arrive, and we go to Hyderabad[4] for the wedding, Bakul wants to go on from there and do a tour of the whole country. He did it ten years ago and he says it is time to do it again, to make sure—"

"Of what?"

The question was sarcastic but Tara gave her head a toss of assurance and pride. Her voice too had taken on the strength and sureness that Bim noticed it usually did when she spoke of her husband. She told Bim evenly "That he hasn't forgotten, or lost touch with the way things are here. If you lose touch, then you can't represent your country, can you?" she ended, on an artificial note.

Bim of course detected that. She grunted "Hmph. I don't know. If that is what they tell you in the diplomatic service then that is what you must say."

"But it's true," Tara exclaimed, immediately dropping artificiality and sounding earnest. "One has to come back, every few years, to find out and

1. English Romantic poet (1788–1824), who died working for Greek independence.　2. One of the two major sections of Delhi, the capital of India. Old Delhi denotes the portion of the city that had been built and ruled by several Muslim dynasties from the 13th century onward and greatly enlarged and beautified by the Moghal emperor Shah Jahan (ruled 1627–58). The British government moved its capital from Calcutta to Delhi in 1912 and then built New Delhi between 1920 and 1930.　3. The names of various Muslim dynasties who ruled Delhi from the 12th century onward.　4. South Indian city, center of Muslim culture.

make sure again. I'd like to travel with him really. But there's the wedding in Raja's house, I suppose that will be enough to keep us busy. Are you coming, Bim? You and Baba? Couldn't we all go together? Then it will be a proper family reunion. Say you'll come! You have your summer vacation now. What will you do alone in Delhi, in the heat? Say you'll come!"

Bim said nothing. In the small silence a flock of mynahs suddenly burst out of the green domes of the trees and, in a loud commotion of yellow beaks and brown wings, disappeared into the sun. While their shrieks and cackles still rang in the air, they heard another sound, one that made Bim stop and stare and the dog lift his head, prick up his ears and then charge madly across to the eucalyptus trees that grew in a cluster by the wall. Rearing up on his hind legs, he tore long strips of blue and mauve bark off the silken pink tree-trunks and, throwing back his head, bellowed in that magnificent voice that Bim admired so much and that soured—or spiced—her relations with the neighbours.

"What is it?" called Tara as Bim ran forwards, lifting the peacock-edged nightie in order to hurry.

It was her cat, crouched in the fork of the blue and pink tree, black and bitter at being stranded where she could not make her way down. Discovered first by the mynahs and then by Badshah, she felt disgraced.

Bim stood below her, stretching out her arms and calling, imploring her to jump. Badshah warned her not to do anything of the sort in a series of excited barks and whines. Tara waited, laughing, while the cat turned her angry face from one to the other, wondering whom to trust. At last Bim coaxed her down and she came slithering along the satiny bark, growling and grumbling with petulance and complaint at her undignified descent. Then she was in Bim's arms, safely cradled and shielded from Badshah's boisterous bumps and jumps, cuddled and cushioned and petted with such an extravagance of affection that Tara could not help raising her eyebrows in embarrassment and wonder.

Although Bim was rubbing her chin on the cat's flat-topped head and kissing the cold tips of her ears, she seemed to notice Tara's expression. "I know what you're thinking," she said. "You're thinking how old spinsters go ga-ga over their pets because they haven't children. Children are the *real* thing, you think."

Tara's look of surprise changed to guilt. "What makes you say that? Actually, I was thinking about the girls. I was wondering—"

"Exactly. That's what I said. You think animals take the place of babies for us love-starved spinsters," Bim said with a certain satisfaction and lowered the rumpled cat to the gravel walk as they came up to the house. "But you're wrong," she said, striding across the sun-slashed drive. "You can't possibly feel for them what I do about these wretched animals of mine."

"Oh Bim," protested Tara, recognising the moment when Bim went too far with which all their encounters had ended throughout their childhood, but she was prevented from explaining herself by the approach of a monstrous body of noise that seemed to be pushing its way out through a tight tunnel, rustily grinding through, and then emerged into full brassy volume, making the pigeons that lived on the ledge under the veranda

ceiling throw up their wings and depart as if at a shot. It was not Bakul who
was responsible for the cacophony. He was sitting—flabbily, flaccidly—in
one of the cane chairs on the veranda with the tea tray in front of him,
waiting for someone to come and pour. The noise beat and thrummed in
one of the curtained rooms behind him. "Sm-o-oke gets in your eyes,"
moaned an agonised voice, and Tara sighed, and her shoulders drooped
by a visible inch or two.

"Baba still plays the same old records?" she asked as they went slowly
up the wide stairs between the massed pots of spider lilies and asparagus
fern to the veranda.

"He never stops," said Bim, smiling. "Not for a day."

"Don't you mind the noise?"

"Not any more," said Bim, the lightness of her tone carefully contrived.
"I don't hear it any more."

"It's loud," complained Tara in a distressed voice. "I used to look for
records to send Baba—I thought he'd like some new ones—but they don't
make 78s any more."

"Oh he doesn't want any new records," said Bim. "He wouldn't play
them. He loves his old ones."

"Isn't it strange," said Tara, wincing at the unmodulated roar that swept
across the still, shady veranda in an almost visible onslaught of destruction.

"We *are* strange, I *told* you," laughed Bim, striding across the tiled floor
to the cane chairs and the tea tray. "Oh, Bakul-*bhai*,[5] you're up. Did you
sleep?" she asked carelessly, sitting down in front of the tray. But instead
of pouring out the tea she only lifted the milk jug and, bending down,
filled a saucer for the cat who crouched before it and began to lap even
before Bim had finished pouring so that some drops fell on her ears and
on her whiskers, a sight that made Bim laugh as she held the jug, waiting
for the cat to finish the milk. Then she bent and refilled the saucer. Tara,
who had poured out a cup of tea for Bakul, waited for her to surrender the
milk jug. When she did, there was very little left in it for Bakul's tea. Tara
shook it to bring out a few reluctant drops.

"Is that enough?" she asked uneasily, even guiltily, handing the cup to
Bakul.

He shrugged, making no reply, his lower lip thrust out in the beginning
of a sulk. It may not have been the lack of milk, though, it might have
been the din that stood about them like sheets of corrugated iron, making
conversation impossible. As he stirred his tea thoughtfully with a little
spoon, the song rose to its raucous crescendo as though the singer had a
dagger plunged into his breast and were letting fly the heartfelt notes of
his last plaint on earth. Then at last the rusty needle ground to a halt
in the felt-embedded groove of the antique record and they all sighed,
simultaneously, and sank back in their chairs, exhausted.

The pigeons that had retreated to the roof came fluttering back to their
nests and settled down with small complaining sounds, guttural and com-

5. "Brother," a common form of address. Here Bim addresses her brother-in-law in the customary
manner.

fortable. The bamboo screen in the doorway lifted and Baba came out for his tea.

He did not look as if he could be held responsible for any degree of noise whatsoever. Coming out into the veranda, he blinked as if the sun surprised him. He was in his pyjamas—an old pair with frayed ends, over which he wore a grey bush-shirt[6] worn and washed almost to translucency. His face, too, was blanched, like a plant grown underground or in deepest shade, and his hair was quite white, giving his young, fine face a ghostly look that made people start whenever he appeared.

But no one on the veranda started. Instead, they turned on him their most careful smiles, trying to make their smiles express feelings that were comforting, reassuring, not startling.

Then Bim began to bustle. Now she called out for more milk and a freshly refilled jug appeared from the pantry, full to the brim, before Bakul's widened eyes. Baba's cup was filled not with tea at all but with milk that had seemed so short a moment ago. Then, to top it, a spoonful of sugar was poured in as well and all stirred up with a tremendous clatter and handed, generously slopping, to Baba who took it without any expression of distaste or embarrassment and sat down on his little cane stool to sip it. Even the cat was transfixed by the spectacle and sat back on her haunches, staring at him with eyes that were circles of sharp green glass.

Only Bim seemed to notice nothing odd. Nor did she seem to think it necessary to speak to or be spoken to by Baba. She said, "Look at her. You'd think I had given her enough but no, if we take any ourselves, she feels it's come out of her share."

After a minute Tara realised she was speaking of the cat. Tara had lost the childhood habit of including animals in the family once she had married and begun the perpetual travels and moves that precluded the keeping of pets. It was with a small effort that she tore her eyes away from her brother and regarded the reproachful cat.

"She's too fat," she said, thinking pet-owners generally liked such remarks. It was not a truthful one: the cat was thin as a string.

Bim put out her toe and scratched the creature under her ear but the cat turned angrily away, refusing such advances, and kept her eyes riveted on Baba till he had sipped the last drop of milk and put the cup back on the saucer with an unmistakably empty ring. Then she dropped sulkily onto the tiles and lay there noisily tearing at her fur with a sandpapered tongue of an angry red.

While the two women sat upright and tense and seethed with unspoken speech, the two men seemed dehydrated, emptied out, with not a word to say about anything. Only the pigeons cooed on and on, too lazy even to open their beaks, content to mutter in their throats rather than sing or call. The dog, stretched out at Bim's feet, writhed and coiled, now catching his tail between his teeth, now scrabbling with his paws, then bit at fleas and chewed his hair, weaving a thick mat of sound together with the cat who was busy with herself.

Bakul could bear it no longer. When his expression had grown so thin

---

6. Man's shirt, made without tails and worn over pants.

and so sour that it was about to split, he said, in a voice meant to be sonorous, "Our first morning in Delhi." To Bim's wonder and astonishment, Tara smiled at this radiantly as though he had made a profound remark on which he was to be congratulated. He gave her a small, confidential smile in return. "What shall we do with it?"

Bim suddenly scratched her head as if the dog had started up something there. "I don't know about you," she said, "but I have some of my students coming over this morning."

"Students? But Bim, I thought your summer vacation had begun."

"Yes, yes, but I wanted to give them some reading lists so they don't waste all their time walking up and down the Mall in Simla[7] or going to the pictures. Then they reminded me I had missed a tutorial and had to see some of their papers. You see, it isn't just I who make them work— they make me work, too. So I asked them to come down here—they love to come, I don't know why. I'll go and get ready—I'm late. And you? You two? What will you do?"

Tara gazed at her husband for answer till he finally lowered his eyes by careful inches from the plaster moulding under the ceiling where the pigeons strutted and squatted and puffed themselves, and said "Perhaps I could ask my uncle to send us a car. Then we could go and call on some of my relations in New Delhi. They will be expecting us."

"I'll get ready," said Tara, instantly getting to her feet as if in relief.

Bim, who remembered her as a languid little girl, listless, a dawdler, noted her quick movements, her efficient briskness, with some surprise, but said nothing. Instead, she turned to Baba and drawled, slowly, "And Baba," as she bent forward and started stacking the cups onto the wooden tray. The others got up and stretched and walked about the veranda except for Baba who sat calmly with his long white hands dangling loosely on either side of him. When Bim said "Baba" again, he smiled gently at the floor. "Baba," she said again in a very low voice so that Bakul, standing on the steps and scrutinizing the bougainvilleas at the pillars, would not hear her, "do you think you might go to the office today?"

Tara, who was at the door at the end of the veranda, about to lift the bamboo curtain and go in, paused. Somehow she had heard. Even in her rush to get dressed and be ready for anything her husband might suggest, she paused in shock to find that Bim still made attempts to send Baba to the office. Considering their futility, she thought they must have been given up long ago. She could not help stopping and turning round to see Bim piling up the tea tray and Baba seated on his small child's stool, smiling, his hands helplessly dangling, the busy dog licking, scratching, while the morning took another stride forward and stood with its feet planted on the tiled floor.

"Won't you go today, Baba?" Bim asked softly, not looking at him, looking at the tea cups. "Do go. You could catch a bus. It'll make a change. We'll all be busy. Then come home to lunch. Or stay if you find it interesting."

7. A hill resort town to which the British colonial government and much of the British expatriate population retired during the hottest summer months. It continues to be a popular vacation spot.

Baba smiled at the bare tiles. His hands swung as if loose in their sockets, as if in a light breeze. But there was no breeze: the heat dropped out of the sky and stood before them like a sheet of foil.

Then Bim got up and lifted the tray and went barefoot down the other end of the veranda to the pantry. Tara could hear her talking to the cook in her normal speaking voice. She turned and went into the room herself, unable to face the sight of Baba alone and hopeless on the veranda. But Baba did not stay either. He must have gone back to his room, too, for in another minute or two she heard that ominous roar pushing its way through the tunnel and emerging as the maudlin clamour of "Lilli Marlene."

"Now this is precisely what I told you," Bakul said, bustling into the bedroom after making his phone call. "I pointed out to you how much more convenient it would be to stay with my uncle and aunt, right in the centre of town, on Aurangzeb[8] Road, how it would save us all the trouble of finding a car to travel up and down in . . ."

Tara, who was bending over the bed, laying out his clothes, straightened and said in a strained voice "But I had not meant to go anywhere. I only wanted to stay at home."

He flicked his silk dressing gown open and said impatiently "You know you can't do that when there's so much to do—relations to visit, colleagues to look up, all that shopping you had planned to do—"

"I'll wait till the girls come. I'll go shopping with them," said Tara with an unaccustomed stubbornness. She held up a cluster of ties and waited, a bit sullenly, for him to choose one.

He put out his hand and picked one of broadly striped raw silk and said "You surely don't mean that. You can't just sit about with your brother and sister all day, doing nothing."

"But it's what I want—just to be at home again, with them. And of course there are the neighbours—I'll see them. But I don't want to go anywhere today, and I don't want to go to New Delhi at all."

"Of course you will come," Bakul said quite sharply, going towards the bathroom with an immense towel he had picked up. "There's no question about that."

When the bathroom door had shut, Tara went out onto the veranda again. The veranda ran all around the house and every room opened out onto it. This room had been hers and Bim's when they were girls. It opened onto the dense grove of guava trees that separated the back of the house from the row of servants' quarters. Bright morning sounds of activity came from them—a water tap running, a child crying, a cock crowing, a bicycle bell ringing—but the house was separated from them by the thick screen of low, dusty guava trees in which invisible parrots screamed and quarrelled over the fruit. Now and then one fell to the ground with a soft thud. Tara could see some lying in the dust with chunks bitten out by the parrots. If she had been younger—no, if she had been sure Bakul would

8. The last of the eminent Moghal emperors; he ruled from 1658 to 1707.

not look out and see—she would have run down the veranda steps and searched for one that was whole. Her mouth tingled with longing to bite into that hard astringent flesh under the green rind. She wondered if her girls would do it when they arrived to spend their holidays here. No, they would not. Much travelled, brought up in embassies, fluent in several languages, they were far too sophisticated for such rustic pleasures, she knew, and felt guilty over her own lack of that desirable quality. She had fooled Bakul into believing that she had acquired it, that he had shown her how to acquire it. But it was all just dust thrown into his eyes, dust.

Further up the veranda was Baba's room and from behind the light bamboo curtain that hung in the doorway came the guttural rattling of "Don't Fence Me In." For a while Tara leant her head against a pillar, listening. It was not unfamiliar, yet it disturbed.

A part of her was sinking languidly down into the passive pleasure of having returned to the familiar—like a pebble, she had been picked up and hurled back into the pond, and sunk down through the layer of green scum, through the secret cool depths to the soft rich mud at the bottom, sending up a line of bubbles of relief and joy. A part of her twitched, stirred like a fin in resentment: why was the pond so muddy and stagnant? Why had nothing changed? She had changed—why did it not keep up with her?

Why did Bim allow nothing to change? Surely Baba ought to begin to grow and develop at last, to unfold and reach out and stretch. But whenever she saw them, at intervals of three or five years, all was exactly as before.

Drawing away from the pillar, she moved towards his room, propelled by her disturbance, by her resentment at this petrified state in which her family lived. Bakul was right to criticise it, disapprove of it. Yes, he was right, she told herself and, lifting the dusty bamboo curtain, slipped into Baba's room.

He was sitting on his bed, a string cot spread with a cotton rug and an old sheet, that stood in the centre of the room under the slowly revolving electric fan. He was crouched low, listening raptly to the last of "Don't Fence Me In" unwinding itself on the old HMV[9] gramophone on a small bamboo table beside his bed. The records, not so very many of them— there must have been breakages after all—were stacked on a shelf beneath the table in their tattered yellow sleeves. The string cot, the table, the HMV gramophone, a canvas chair and a wardrobe—nothing else. It was a large room and looked bare. Once it had been Aunt Mira's room, and crowded. Baba looked up at her.

Tara stood staring, made speechless by his fine, serene face, the shapeliness of his long fingers, his hands that either moved lightly as if in a breeze or rested calmly at his sides. He was an angel, she told herself, catching her lip between her teeth—an angel descended to earth, unsoiled by any of it.

But then why did he spend his days and years listening to this appalling noise? Her daughters could not live through a day without their record-

---

9. An acronym for His Master's Voice, a major manufacturer of early phonographs and records.

player either; they, too, kept it heaped with records that slipped down onto the turntable in a regular sequence, keeping them supplied with an almost uninterrupted flow of music to which they worked and danced with equal ease. But, she wanted to explain to him, theirs was an ever-growing, ever-changing collection, their interest in it was lively, fresh, developing all the time. Also, she knew they would outgrow their need of it. Already Maya had friends who took her to concerts from which she returned with a sheen of uplifting pleasure spread across her face and talked of learning to play the flute. Soon it would be behind her—this need for an elemental, primitive rhythm automatically supplied. But Baba would never leave his behind, he would never move on.

Her anguish and impatience made her say, very quickly and loudly, as the record ground to a halt and before Baba could turn it over, "Are you going out this morning, Baba? We've sent for a car—can we give you a lift?"

Baba lifted the smoothly curving metal arm off the record and sat with his hand resting on it, protectively. It was clear he would have liked to turn over the record but he hesitated, politely, his eyes cast down, flickering slightly as if with fear or guilt.

Tara too began to squirm with guilt at having caused him this panic. "Are you, Baba?"

He glanced at her very quickly, with a kind of pleading, and then looked away and shook his head very slightly.

This made her cry out "But don't you go to the office in the mornings?" He kept his head lowered, smiling slightly, sadly.

"Never?"

The room rang with her voice, then with silence. In the shaded darkness, silence had the quality of a looming dragon. It seemed to roar and the roar to reverberate, to dominate. To escape from it would require a burst of recklessness, even cruelty. Was it to keep it at bay that Baba played those records so endlessly, so obsessively? But it was not right. She herself had been taught, by her husband and by her daughters, to answer questions, to make statements, to be frank and to be precise. They would have none of these silences and shadows. Here things were left unsaid and undone. It was what they called "Old Delhi decadence." She knotted her fingers together in an effort to break it.

"Do you think you will go to the office today?" she persisted, beads of perspiration welling out of her upper lip.

Now Baba took his hand off the gramophone arm, relinquishing it sadly, and his hands hung loosely at his sides, as helplessly as a dead man's. His head, too, sank lower and lower.

Tara was furious with herself for causing him this shame, this distress. She hated her probing, her questioning with which she was punishing him. Punishing him for what? For his birth—and for that he was not responsible. Yet it was wrong to leave things as they were—she knew Bakul would say so, and her girls, too. It was all quite lunatic. Yet there was no alternative, no solution. Surely they would see there was none. Sighing, she said in a tone of defeat "I'll ask Bim."

She had said the right thing at last. Quite inadvertently, even out of cowardice. It made Baba raise his head and smile, sweetly and gently as he used to do. He even nodded, faintly, in agreement. Yes, Bim, he seemed to say, Bim will decide. Bim can, Bim will. Go to Bim. Tara could not help smiling back at his look of relief, his happy dependence. She turned to leave the room and heard him lift the record and turn it over. As she escaped down the veranda she heard Bing Crosby's voice bloating luxuriantly out into "Ah-h'm dream-in' of a wha-ite Christmas . . ."

But now something had gone wrong. The needle stuck in a groove. "Dream-in', dream-in', dream-in' " hacked the singer, his voice growing more and more officious. Shocked, Baba's long hands moved with speed to release it from the imprisoning groove. Then he found the needle grown so blunt and rusty that, as he peered at it from every angle and turned it over and over with a melancholy finger, he accepted it would do no longer. He sighed and dropped it into the little compartment that slid out of the green leather side of the gramophone and the sight of all the other obsolete needles that lay in that concealed grave seemed to place a weight on his heart. He felt defeated and infinitely depressed. Too depressed to open the little one-inch square tin with the picture of the dog on it, and pick out a clean needle to insert in the metal head. It remained empty, toothless. The music had come to a halt. Out in the garden a koel called its wild, brazen call. It was not answered so it repeated the call, more demandingly.

For a while Baba paced about the room, his head hanging so low that one would have thought it unnatural, physically impossible. Now and then he lifted his hands to his head and ran his long bony fingers nervously through his white hair so that it was grooved and furrowed like the lines of an aged face. The silence of the room, usually so loud with the rollicking music of the '40s, seemed to admit those other sounds that did not soothe or protect him but, on the contrary, startled him and drove him into a panic—the koel calling, calling out in the tall trees, a child crying in the servants' quarters, a bicycle dashing past, its bell jangling. Baba began to pace up and down faster and faster as if he were running away from it. Then, when he could bear it no longer, he went to the cupboard and pulled open its door, searched frantically for clothes to wear, pulled out whatever seemed to him appropriate, and began to dress hurriedly, dropping his pyjamas onto the floor, flinging others onto the sagging canvas chair by the bed, hurriedly buttoning and lacing and pulling on and off till he felt sufficiently clothed.

Without a glance into the mirror on the cupboard door or an attempt to tidy the room, he fled from it.

Tara, still sitting on the steps with an arm around the veranda pillar, waiting for Bakul to emerge so that she could go in and dress, saw a pale elongated shape lurching and blundering down the veranda and onto the drive, bent almost double as if in pain or in fear—or perhaps because of the sun beating down with white-hot blows. She stood up in fright and it took her a minute to realize it was Baba.

By then he was already at the gate and had turned out of it into the road. Tara hurried down the steps onto the drive, shading her eyes, her mouth open to call him, but she stopped herself. How old was Baba now? If he wanted to go out, ought he at his age to be called back and asked to explain?

If she had, Baba would have been grateful. If anything, anyone had stopped him now, he would have collapsed with relief and come crawling home like a thirsty dog to its water bowl. Once, when he had ventured out, a bicycle had dashed against him as he stood hesitating at the edge of the road, wondering whether to cross. The bicyclist had fallen and cursed him, his voice rising to a shrill peak and then breaking on Baba's head like eggs, or slivers of glass. Another time, he had walked as far as the bus stop but when the bus had arrived there was such a scuffle between those trying to get off and those trying to get on that people were pushed and bumped and shoved and when one man was somehow expelled from the knotted mob, Baba saw his sleeve torn off his shirt, hanging limply as if he had no arm, were an amputee. Baba thought of the man's face, of the ruined shirt. He heard all those shouts again, the shouts that had been flung at his head, knocking into him till he was giddy with blows.

He was small. He was standing on the dunes. There was nothing here but the silver sand and the grey river and the white sky. But out of that lunar stillness a man loomed up, military in a khaki uniform and towering scarlet turban, and roughly pushed past him shouting "*Hato! Hato!*"[1] to make way for a white horse that plunged up out of the dunes and galloped past Baba, crouching on his knees in the sand, the terror of the horse hooves beating through his head, the sand flying back into his face and the voice still commanding "*Hato! Hato!*"

His knees trembled in anticipation, knowing he would be forced down, or flung down if he continued down the road. But it was as if Tara had given him a push down a steep incline. She had said he was to go. Bim had said he was to go. Bim and Tara, both of them, wanted him to go. He was going.

His feet in their unfastened sandals scuffed through the dust of Bela Road. Sharp gravel kept slipping into them, prodding him. His arms swung wildly, propelling him along. His head bobbed, his white hair flopped. His eyes strained and saw black instead of white. Was he going to faint? Would he fall? Should he stop? Could he? Or would they drive him on? "*Hato! Hato!*"

Then he heard the crash he knew would come. Instantly he flinched and flung up his arm to protect his face. But it was not he who had crashed. It was a cart carrying a load of planks that had tipped forwards as the horse that drew it fell first onto its knees, then onto its nose and lay squirming in the middle of the road. Baba shrank back, against the wall, and held his arm before his eyes but still he saw what happened: the driver, a dark man with a red rag tied about his head, leapt down from the mound of planks and raised his arm, and a switch or a whip, and brought it down with all his force on the horse's back. The horse gave a neighing scream, reared up its head with the wet, wringing mane streaming from it, and then stretched out on the stones, a shiver running up and down its

---

1. Get out of the way! (Hindi).

legs so that it twitched and shook. Again the man raised the whip, again it came down on the horse's back, neck, head, legs—again and again. Baba heard screams but it was the man who screamed as he whipped and slashed and beat, screamed abuse at the animal who did not move but seemed to sink lower and lower into the dust. "Swine! Son of a swine!" the man panted, red eyes straining out of the dark face. "*Suar! Sala! Suar ka bachcha!*"[2] All the time his arm rose up in the air and came down, cutting and slashing the horse's flesh till black stuff oozed onto the white dust and ran and spread, black and thick, out of the horse.

Baba raised both his arms, wrapped them about his head, his ears and eyes, tightly, and, blind, turned and stumbled, almost fell but ran on back up the road to the house, to the gate. His shoulder hit the white gate-post so that he lurched and fell to his knees, then he rose and stumbled, his arms still doubled over his eyes so that he should not see and about his ears so that he should not hear.

Tara saw him as he came climbing up the steps on his knees and ran forwards to help him to his feet. Tugging at his arms to drag them away from his face, she cried "Are you hurt? Baba, Baba, say—are you hurt? Has someone hurt you?" Pulling his arms away, she uncovered his face and saw his eyes rolling in their sockets like a wild horse's, his lips drawn back from his teeth as if he were racing, and the blue-black shadows that always lay under his eyes spreading over his face like a bruise, wet with his tears. Then she stopped demanding that he should speak, and helped him to his room, onto his bed, rushed out and down the veranda in search of Bim, in search of water. There was no one on the veranda or in the kitchen. The cook had gone out to market. She tilted the earthen water jar to fill a tumbler and hurried back with it, her legs cutting into her nightgown and the water spilling in splashes onto the tiles as she hurried, thinking of Baba's face. She lifted his head to help him drink but most of it ran down his chin into his shirt. When she lowered his head, he shrank into a heap, shivering, and she stayed a while, smoothing his hair and patting his cheek till she thought he was quieter, nearly asleep, then went to find Bim.

But Bakul stepped out of their room, his tie in one hand and his shoes in another, to ask "Aren't you getting ready, Tara? We'll be late. The car will be here any minute and you know Uncle is very punctual. We mustn't keep him waiting." He went back to finish dressing without having seen Tara's face or anything there to stop him.

He noticed nothing—a missing shoe-horn and frayed laces having presented him with a problem meanwhile—till she came in, her shoulders sloping, her hair hanging, and sat down on the foot of the bed instead of going in to dress. Then he spoke more sharply. "Why aren't you getting ready?"

"I don't think I'll come after all," she mumbled. She always mumbled when she was afraid, as if she hoped not to be heard.

She expected him to explode of course. But even for Bakul it was too

2. Swine! Bastard! Son of a swine! (Hindi).

hot, the atmosphere of the old house too turgid and heavy to push or manipulate. Bending down to tie two perfect bows, he merely sighed "So, I only have to bring you home for a day, Tara, and you go back to being the hopeless person you were before I married you."

"Yes," she muttered, "hopeless." Like Baba's, her face looked bruised.

"And you won't let me help you. I thought I had taught you a different life, a different way of living. Taught you to execute your will. Be strong. Face challenges. Be decisive. But no, the day you enter your old home, you are as weak-willed and helpless and defeatist as ever." He stood up and looked down to see if his shoes were bright enough to reflect his face. Nothing less would do. Yes, yes. He shrugged his shoulders inside his shirtsleeves. "What should I do with you? I ought to take you away imme-diately. Let us go and stay with my uncle in New Delhi."

"No." She shook her head. "Leave me here."

"You're not happy here," he said, and the unexpectedness of these words made her look up at him, questioning. "Look at your face—so sad, so worried." He even came close to her and touched her cheek, very lightly, as if he could hardly bear the unpleasant contact but forced him-self to do it out of compassion. "If only you would come with me, I would show you how to be happy. How to be active and busy—and then you would be happy. If you came."

But she shook her head. She felt she had followed him enough, it had been such an enormous strain, always pushing against her grain, it had drained her of too much strength, now she could only collapse, inevitably collapse.

Bakul had married her when she was eighteen. He knew her. He left her, saying "Then I'll tell Uncle you are busy with your own family and will come another time," and went out to wait for the car.

He passed Bim as he went through the drawing room. Bim was holding court there—seated on the divan with her legs drawn up under her—like Tara, she had not dressed yet and was still in her nightdress—and on the carpet below sat the students, a brightly coloured bunch of young girls in jeans and in *salwar-kameez*,[3] laughing and eyeing each other and him as he went through. He raised his eyebrows at Bim and gave her a significant look as if to say "*This*—your history lesson?"

Bim nodded and laughed and wriggled her toes and waggled her pencil, completely at ease and without the least sense of guilt. "No, no, you won't," he heard her say as he went out onto the veranda, "you won't get me started on the empress Razia—nor on the empress Nur Jehan. I refuse. We must be serious. We are going to discuss the war between Shivaji[4] and Aurangzeb—no empresses."

The girls groaned exaggeratedly. "Please, miss," he heard them beg as he sat down on a creaking cane chair to wait, "please let's talk about some-thing interesting, miss. You will enjoy it too, miss."

3. Tunic and gathered trousers traditionally worn by women in northwestern India, now a popular style of dress for young women in most Indian cities.   **4.** The most famous of the Maratha warrior-chiefs of western India, who resisted Moghal and British power in the 17th and 18th centuries; he ruled from 1627 to 1680. Queen (Sultana) Tazia ruled Delhi from 1236 to 1240. Nur Jehan, consort of the Moghal emperor Jehangir (ruled 1605–27), was the most illustrious of the Moghal queens.

"Enjoy? You rascals, I haven't asked you here to enjoy yourselves. Come on, Keya, please begin—I'm listening—" and then there was some semblance of order and of a tutorial going on that Bakul could almost recognise and approve. He wondered, placing one leg over the other reflectively, as he had sometimes wondered when he had first started coming to this house, as a young man who had just entered the foreign service and was in a position to look around for a suitable wife, if Bim were not, for all her plainness and brusqueness, the superior of the two sisters, if she had not those qualities—decision, firmness, resolve—that he admired and tried to instil in his wife who lacked them so deplorably. If only Bim had not that rather coarse laugh and way of sitting with her legs up . . . now Tara would never . . . and if her nose were not so large unlike Tara's which was small . . . and Tara was gentler, more tender . . . He sighed a bit, shifting his bottom on the broken rattan seat of the chair. Things were as they were and had to be made the most of, he always said. At least in this country, he sighed, and just then his uncle's car appeared at the gate, slowly turned in, its windshield flooded by the sun, and came up the drive to park beneath the bougainvilleas.

Bim did get Tara to smile before the morning was over, however. Tara was leaning against the veranda pillar, watching the parrots quarrel in the guava trees, listening for a sound from Baba's room, hoping to hear a record played, when Bim came out with her band of girls and suddenly shouted "Ice-cream! Caryhom Ice-cream-wallah!"[5] and, before Tara's startled eyes, a bicycle with a small painted van attached to it that had been rolling down the empty, blazing road, stopped and turned in at the gate with its Sikh[6] driver beaming broadly at the laughing girls and their professor.

Seeing Tara, Bim called out "Look at these babies, Tara. When they hear the Caryhom ice-cream man going by they just stop paying any attention to my lecture. I can't do anything till I've handed each of them a cone. I suppose strawberry cones are what you all want, you babies? Strawberry cones for all of them, *Sardar-ji*,"[7] she ordered and stood laughing on the steps as she watched him fill the cones with large helpings of pink icecream and hand them to the girls who were giggling, Tara realised, as much at their professor as at this childish diversion.

Bim noticed nothing. Swinging her arms about, she saw to it that each girl got her cone and then had one of them, a pretty child dressed in *salwar-kameez* patterned with pink and green parrots, carry a dripping cone down the veranda to Tara. "Tara," she called, "that's for you. *Sardar-ji* made it specially for you," she laughed, smiling at the ice-cream man who had a slightly embarrassed look, Tara thought. Embarrassed herself, she took the slopping cone from the girl and licked it to please Bim, her tongue recoiling at the synthetic sweetness. "Oh Bim, if my daughters were to see me now—or Bakul," she murmured, as Bim walked past holding like a cornucopia a specially heaped and specially pink ice-cream cone

---

5. Seller, vendor. *Caryhom:* a brand name of ice cream.   6. One who follows the Sikh religion, founded in Punjab by Guru Nanak, ca. 1500.   7. Term of address for a male member of the Sikh religious community. *Ji:* a suffix denoting respect for the person addressed.

into Baba's room. Tara stopped licking, stared, trying to probe the bamboo screen into the room where there had been silence and shadows all morning. She heard Bim's voice, loud and gay, and although Baba made no audible answer, she saw Bim come out without the cone and knew Baba was eating it, perhaps quite happily. There was something magnetic about the icy pink sweetness, the synthetic sweet pinkness, she reflected, licking.

Now Bim let out a shout and began to scold. One of the girls had tipped the remains of her cone onto the veranda steps for the dog to lick—she had seen him standing by, watching, his tongue lolling and leaking. "You silly, don't you know dogs shouldn't eat anything sweet? His hair will fall out—he'll get worms—it'll be your fault—he'll be spoilt—he won't eat his bread and soup now."

"Let him enjoy himself, miss," said the girl, smirking at the others because they all knew perfectly well how pleased Bim was to see them spoil her dog.

Tara narrowed her eyes at the spectacle of Bim scolding her students and smiling with pleasure because of the attention they had paid her dog, who had now licked up all the ice-cream and was continuing to lick and lick the floor as if it might have absorbed some of the delicious stuff. Remembering how Bim used to scold her for not disciplining her little daughters and making them eat up everything on their plates or go to bed on time, she shook her head slightly.

But the ice-cream did have, she had to admit, a beneficial effect all round: in a little while, as the students began to leave the house, prettily covering their heads against the sun with coloured veils and squealing as the heat of the earth burnt through their slippers, the gramophone in Baba's room stirred and rumbled into life again. Tara was grateful for it. She wished Bakul could see them now—her family.

When Bakul did come, late in the afternoon, almost comatose from the heat and the heavy lunch he had eaten, to fall onto his bed and sleep, this passage of lightness was over, or overcome again by the spirit of the house.

Tara, upright in a chair, tried first to write a letter to her daughters, then decided it was too soon, she would wait till she had more to say to them, and put the letter away in her case and tried to read instead, a book from the drawing room bookshelf that had been there even when she was a child—Jawaharlal Nehru's *Letters To A Daughter*[8] in a green cloth binding—and sitting on the stuffed chair, spongy and clammy to touch, she felt that heavy spirit come and weigh down her eyelids and the back of her neck so that she was pinned down under it, motionless.

It seemed to her that the dullness and the boredom of her childhood, her youth, were stored here in the room under the worn dusty red rugs, in the bloated brassware, amongst the dried grasses in the swollen vases, behind the yellowed photographs in the oval frames—everything, every-

8. A collection of letters written by Jawaharlal Nehru (1899–1964)—one of the chief leaders of India's independence struggle and the first prime minister of independent India—to his daughter Indira. The letters were written from jail, where he served several sentences for political activities against the British colonial government. His daughter Indira Gandhi (1917–1984) herself became prime minister of India in 1966.

thing that she had so hated as a child and that was still preserved here as if this were the storeroom of some dull, uninviting provincial museum.

She stared sullenly, without lifting her head, at a water-colour above the plaster mantelpiece—red cannas painted with some watery fluid that had trickled weakly down the brown paper: who could have painted that? Why was it hung here? How could Bim bear to look at it for all of her life? Had she developed no taste of her own, no likings that made her wish to sweep the old house of all its rubbish and place in it things of her own choice? Tara thought with longing of the neat, china-white flat in Washington, its cleanliness, its floweriness. She wished she had the will to get to her feet and escape from this room—where to? Even the veranda would be better, with the pigeons cooing soothingly, expressing their individual genius for combining complaint and contentment in one tone, and the spiky bougainvilleas scraping the outer walls and scattering their papery magenta flowers in the hot, sulphur-yellow wind. She actually got up and went to the door and lifted the bamboo screen that hung there, but the blank white glare of afternoon slanted in and slashed at her with its flashing knives so that she quickly dropped the screen. It creaked into place, releasing a noseful of dust. On the wall a gecko[9] clucked loudly and disapprovingly at this untoward disturbance. She went back to the chair. If she could sleep, she might forget where she was, but it was not possible to sleep with the sweat trickling down one's face in rivulets and the heat enclosing one in its ring of fire.

Bakul said one could rise above the climate, that one could ignore it if one filled one's mind with so many thoughts and activities that there was no room for it. "Look at me," he had said the winter that they froze in Moscow. "I don't let the cold immobilize me, do I?" and she and the girls, swaddled in all their warm clothing and the quilts and blankets off their beds, had had to agree that he did not. And gradually he had trained her and made her into an active, organised woman who looked up her engagement book every morning, made plans and programmes for the day ahead and then walked her way through them to retire to her room at night, tired with the triumphant tiredness of the virtuous and the dutiful. Now the engagement book lay at the bottom of her trunk. Bim had said nothing of engagements and, really, she could not bear to have any in this heat. The day stretched out like a sheet of glass that reflected the sun— too bare, too exposed to be faced.

Out in the garden only the coppersmiths were awake, clinging to the tree-trunks, beating out their mechanical call—tonk-tonk-tonk. Tonk-tonk-tonk.

Here in the house it was not just the empty, hopeless atmosphere of childhood, but the very spirits of her parents that brooded on—here they still sat, crouched about the little green baize folding table that was now shoved into a corner with a pile of old *Illustrated Weeklies*[1] and a brass pot full of red and yellow spotted canna lilies on it as if to hold it firmly down, keep it from opening up with a snap and spilling out those stacks of cards, those long note-books and thin pencils with which her parents had sat,

9. Small lizard.   1. A leading popular English-language periodical of the 1950s through 1970s.

day after day and year after year till their deaths, playing bridge with friends like themselves, mostly silent, heads bent so that the knobs in their necks protruded, soft stained hands shuffling the cards, now and then speaking those names and numbers that remained a mystery to the children who were not allowed within the room while a game was in progress, who had sometimes folded themselves into the dusty curtains and stood peeping out, wondering at this strange, all-absorbing occupation that kept their parents sucked down into the silent centre of a deep, shadowy vortex while they floated on the surface, staring down into the underworld, their eyes popping with incomprehension.

Raja used to swear that one day he would leap up onto the table in a lion-mask, brandishing a torch, and set fire to this paper-world of theirs, while Bim flashed her sewing scissors in the sunlight and declared she would creep in secretly at night and snip all the cards into bits. But Tara simply sucked her finger and retreated down the veranda to Aunt Mira's room where she could always tuck herself up in the plum-coloured quilt that smelt so comfortingly of the aged relation and her ginger cat, lay her head down beside that purring creature and feel such a warmth, such a softness of comfort and protection as not to feel the need to wreck her parents' occupation or divert their attention. It would have frightened her a bit if they had come away, followed her and tried to communicate with her.

And now she stirred uneasily in her chair although it held her damply as if with suckers, almost afraid that they would rise from their seats, drop their cards on the table and come towards her with papery faces, softly shuffling fingers, smoky breath, and welcome her back, welcome her home.

Once her father had risen, padded quietly to her mother's bedroom behind that closed door, and Tara had slipped in behind him, folded herself silently into the faded curtain and watched. She had seen him lean over her mother's bed and quickly, smoothly press a little shining syringe into her mother's arm that lay crookedly on the blue cover, press it in very hard so that she tilted her head back with a quick gasp of shock, or pain— Tara saw her chin rising up into the air and the grey head sinking back into the pillow and heard a long, whimpering sigh like an air-bag minutely punctured so that Tara had fled, trembling, because she was sure she had seen her father kill her mother.

All her life Tara had experienced that fear—her father had killed her mother. Even after Aunt Mira and Bim and Raja had explained to her what it was he did, what he kept on doing daily, Tara could not rid herself of the feel of that original stab of suspicion. Sometimes, edging up close to her mother, she would study the flabby, floury skin punctured with a hundred minute needle-holes, and catch her breath in an effort not to cry out. Surely these were the signs of death, she felt, not of healing?

Now she stared fixedly at the door in the wall, varnished a bright hideous brown with the varnish swelling into blisters or cracking into spidery patterns in the heat, and felt the same morbid, uncontrollable fear of it opening and death stalking out in the form of a pair of dreadfully familiar ghosts that gave out a sound of paper and filled her nostrils with white insidious dust.

In the sleeping garden the coppersmiths beat on and on monotonously like mechanics at work on a metal sheet—tonk-tonk-tonk. Tonk-tonk-tonk.

To look at Bim one would not think she had lived through the same childhood, the same experiences as Tara. She led the way so briskly up the stairs on the outside of the house to the flat rooftop where, as children, they had flown kites and hidden secrets, that it was clear she feared no ghosts to meet her there. Now they leant upon the stucco balustrade and looked down at the garden patterned with the light and shade of early evening. The heat of the day and the heavy dust were being sluiced and washed away by the garden hose as the gardener trained it now on the jasmines, now on the palms, bringing out the green scent of watered earth and refreshed plants. Flocks of parrots came winging in, a lurid, shrieking green, to settle on the sunflowers and rip their black-seeded centres to bits, while mynahs hopped up and down on the lawn, quarrelling over insects. Bim's cat, jet-black, picked her way carefully between the puddles left by the gardener's generously splashing, spraying hose, and twitched her whiskers and went "meh-meh-meh" with annoyance when the mynahs shrieked at the sight of her and came to swoop over and divebomb her till she retreated under the hedge. A pair of hoopoes[2] promenaded sedately up and down the lawn, furling and unfurling the striped fans on their heads. A scent of spider lilies rose from the flowerpots massed on the veranda steps as soon as they were watered, like ladies newly bathed, powdered and scented for the evening.

On either side of their garden were more gardens, neighbours' houses, as still and faded and shabby as theirs, the gardens as overgrown and neglected and teeming with wild, uncontrolled life. From the roof-top they could see the pink and yellow and grey stucco walls, peeling and spotted, or an occasional *gol mohur* tree scarlet with summer blossom.

Outside the sagging garden gate the road led down to the Jumna river.[3] It had shrunk now to a mere rivulet of mud that Tara could barely make out in the huge flat expanse of sand that stretched out to the furry yellow horizon like some sleeping lion, shabby and old. There were no boats on the river except for a flat-bottomed ferry boat that idled slowly back and forth. There was no sign of life beyond an occasional washerman picking his washing off the sand dunes and loading it onto his donkey, and a few hairless *pai*[4] dogs that slunk about the mud flats, nosing about for a dead fish or a frog to devour. A fisherman strode out into the river, flung out his net with a wave of his wrists and then drew in an empty net.

Tara could tell it was empty because he did not bend to pick up anything. There was nothing. "Imagine," she said, with wonder, for she could not believe the long-remembered, always-remembered childhood had had a backdrop as drab as this, "we used to *like* playing there—in that dust and mud. What could we have seen in it—in that muddy little trickle? Why, it's hardly a river—it's nothing, just nothing."

"Now Tara, your travels have made you very snobbish," Bim protested, but lazily, good-naturedly. She was leaning heavily on her elbows, letting her grey-streaked hair tumble in whatever bit of breeze came off the river

2. Birds.   3. One of the two major rivers of north India. Delhi is on the Jumna.   4. Stray.

up to them, and now she turned to lean back against the balustrade and look up at the sky that was no longer flat and white-hot but patterned and wrinkled with pale brush-strokes of blue and grey and mauve. A flock of white egrets rose from the river bed and stitched their way slowly and evenly across this faded cloth. "Nothing?" she repeated Tara's judgement. "The holy river Jumna?[5] On whose banks Krishna played his flute and Radha danced?"

"Oh Bim, it is nothing of the sort," Tara dared to say, sure she was being teased. "It's a little trickle of mud with banks of dust on either side."

"It's where my ashes will be thrown after I am dead and burnt,"[6] Bim said unexpectedly and abruptly. "It is where Mira-*masi*'s ashes were thrown. Then they go down into the sea." Seeing Tara start and quiver, she added more lightly "It's where we played as children—ran races on the dunes and dug holes to bury ourselves in and bullied the ferryman into giving us free rides to the melon fields. Don't you remember the melons baking in the hot sand and splitting them open and eating them all warm and red and pouring with pink juice?"

"That was you and Raja," Tara reminded her. "I never dared get into that boat, and of course Baba stayed at home. It was you and Raja who used to play there, Bim."

"I and Raja," Bim mused, continuing to look up at the sky till the egrets pierced through the soft cloth of it and disappeared into the dusk like so many needles lost. "I and Raja," she said, "I and Raja." Then "And the white horse and Hyder Ali Sahib[7] going for his evening ride?" she asked Tara almost roughly, trying to shake out of her some corroboration as if she were unsure if this image were real or only imagined. It had the making of a legend, with the merest seed of truth. "Can you remember playing on the sand late in the evening and the white horse riding by, Hyder Ali Sahib up on it, high above us, and his peon[8] running in front of him, shouting, and his dog behind him, barking?" She laughed quite excitedly, seeing it again, this half-remembered picture. "We stood up to watch them go past and he wouldn't even look at us. The peon shouted to us to get out of the way. I think Hyder Ali Sahib used to think of himself as some kind of prince, a nawab.[9] And Raja *loved* that." Her eyes gleamed as much with malice as with remembrance. "Raja stood up straight and stared and stared and I'm sure he longed to ride on a white horse with a dog to run behind him just as old Hyder Ali did. Hyder Ali Sahib was always Raja's ideal, wasn't he?" she ended up.

Her words had cut a deep furrow through Tara's forehead. She too pressed down on her elbows, feeling the balustrade cut into her flesh as she tried to remember. Did she really remember or was it only Bim's picture that she saw, in shades of white and black and scarlet, out there on the shadowy sand-bank? To cover up a confusion she failed to resolve, she said "Yes, and d'you remember Raja marching up and down here on

5. The Jumma is sacred to Hindus, especially because of its association with the lovemaking of the flute-playing cowherd god Krishna and the herdswoman Radha.   6. Hindus cremate their dead and often strew the ashes in the waters of holy rivers such as the Ganges and Jumna.   7. Lord, master (Urdu), a term of respect, often indicating aristocratic status.   8. Attendant, errand boy.   9. A prince in the Moghal aristocracy.

the roof, swinging his arms and reciting his poems to us while we sat here on the balustrade, swinging our legs and listening? I used to feel like crying, it was so beautiful—those poems about death, and love, and wine, and flames."

"They weren't. They were terrible," Bim said icily, tossing her head with a stubborn air, like a bad-tempered mare's. "*Terrible* verses he wrote."

"Oh Bim," Tara exclaimed in dismay, widening her eyes in horror at such sacrilege. It was a family dictum that Raja was a poet and wrote great poetry. Now Bim, his favourite sister, was denying this doctrine. What had happened?

"Of course it was, Tara—terrible, terrible," Bim insisted. "We're not fifteen and ten years old any more—you and I. Have you tried reading it recently? It's *nauseating*. Can you remember any two lines of it that wouldn't make you sick with embarrassment now?"

Tara was too astounded, and too stricken to speak. Throughout her childhood, she had always stood on the outside of that enclosed world of love and admiration in which Bim and Raja moved, watching them, sucking her finger, excluded. Now here was Bim, cruelly and wilfully smashing up that charmed world with her cynicism, her criticism. She stood dismayed.

Bim was fierce. She no longer leant on the balustrade, drooping with reminiscences. She walked up and down agitatedly, swinging her arms in agitation, as Raja had done when quoting poetry in those days when he was a poet, at least to them. "If you'll just come to my room," she said, suddenly stopping, "I'll show you some of those poems—I think they must be still lying around although I don't know why I haven't torn them all up."

"Of course you wouldn't!" Tara exclaimed.

"Why not?" Bim flung at her. "Come and see, tell me if you think it worth keeping," and she swept down the stairs with a martial step, looking back once to shout at Tara "*And*, apart from poetry recitals, Tara, this terrace is where I cut your hair for you and made you cry. What an uproar there was." She gave her head a quick, jerky toss. "And here you are, with your hair grown long again, and it's mine that's cut short. Only no one cared when I cut *mine*."

Tara hung back. She had been perfectly content to pace the terrace in the faint breeze, watch the evening darken, wait for the stars to come out and talk about the old days. Even if it was about the haircut, painful as that had been. But Bim was clattering down the stone stairs, the bells of the pink-spired temple at the bend of the river were suddenly clanging loudly and discordantly, the sky had turned a deep green with a wide purple channel through it for the night to come flowing in, and there was nothing for it but to follow Bim down the stairs, into the house, now unbearably warm and stuffy after the freshness and cool of the terrace, and then into Bim's cluttered, untidy room.

It had been their father's office room and the furniture in it was still office furniture—steel cupboards to hold safes and files, metal slotted shelves piled with registers and books, and the roll-top desk towards which Bim marched as Tara hesitated unwillingly by the door. Throwing down the lid, Bim started pulling out papers from the pigeon-holes and opening drawers and rifling through files and tutorial papers and college registers. Out of this mass of paper she separated some sheets and held them out to Tara with an absent-minded air.

Tara, glancing down at them, saw that they were in Urdu,[1] a language she had not learnt. It was quite useless her holding these sheets in her hand and pretending to read the verses that Raja had once recited to them and that had thrilled her then with their Persian glamour. But Bim did not notice her predicament, she was still occupied with the contents of the rifled desk. Finally she found what she was looking for and handed that, too, to Tara with a grim set of her mouth that made Tara quake.

"What is this, Bim?" she asked, looking down and seeing it was in Raja's English handwriting.

"A letter Raja wrote—read it. Read it," she repeated as Tara hesitated, and walked across to the window and stood there staring out silently, compelling Tara to read while she tensely waited.

Tara read—unwillingly, unbelievingly.

Raja had written it years ago, she saw, and tried to link the written date with some event in their family history that might provide it with a context.

> You will have got our wire with the news of Hyder Ali Sahib's death. I know you will have been as saddened by it as we are. Perhaps you are also a bit worried about the future. But you must remember that when I left you, I promised I would always look after you, Bim. When Hyder Ali Sahib was ill and making out his will, Benazir herself spoke to him about the house and asked him to allow you to keep it at the same rent we used to pay him when father and mother were alive. He agreed—you know he never cared for money, only for friendship—and I want to assure you that now that he is dead and has left all his property to us, you may continue to have it at the same rent, I shall never think of raising it or of selling the house as long as you and Baba need it. If you have any worries, Bim, you have only to tell—Raja.

It took Tara some minutes to think out all the implications of this letter. To begin with, she studied the date and tried to recall when Hyder Ali had died. Instead a series of pictures of the Hyder Ali family flickered in the half-dark of the room. There was Hyder Ali, once their neighbour and their landlord, as handsome and stately as a commissioned oil painting hung over a mantelpiece, all in silver and grey and scarlet as he had been on the white horse on which he rode along the river bank in the evenings while the children stood and watched. He had cultivated the best roses in Old Delhi and given parties to which poets and musicians came. Their parents were not amongst his friends. Then there was his daughter Benazir, a very young girl, plump and pretty, a veil thrown over her head as she hurried into the closed carriage that took her to school, and the Begum whom they seldom saw, she lived in the closed quarters of the house, but at Id[2] sent them, and their other tenant-neighbours, rich sweets

---

1. A hybrid language that evolved during the reign of various Muslim dynasties in India, from the combination of north Indian Hindi dialects with Persian and Arabic vocabulary. Urdu poetry, which has its origins in Persian poetry, was cultivated in the courts of India from the 17th century onward. Urdu is written in the Persian script, and modern Urdu is primarily associated with Muslim culture in India.
2. An important Muslim religious festival.

covered with fine silver foil on a tray decked with embroidered napkins. They had lived in the tall stucco house across the road, distinguished from all the others by its wealth of decorative touches like the coloured fanlight above the front door, the china tiles along the veranda walls and the coloured glass chandeliers and lamps. They had owned half the houses on that road. When they left Delhi during the partition riots of 1947,[3] they sold most of these houses to their Hindu tenants for a song—all except for Bim's house which she did not try to buy and which he continued to let to her at the same rent as before. It was to this that Raja, his only son-in-law and inheritor of his considerable property, referred in his letter. It was a very old letter.

Still confused, she said slowly "But, Bim, it's a very old letter—years old."

"But I still have it," Bim said sharply, staring out of the window as if she too saw pictures in the dark. "I still keep it in my desk—to remind me. Whenever I begin to wish to see Raja again or wish he would come and see us, then I take out that letter and read it again. Oh, I can tell you, I could write him such an answer, he wouldn't forget it for many years either!" She gave a short laugh and ended it with a kind of a choke, saying "You say I should come to Hyderabad with you for his daughter's wedding. How can I? How can I enter his house—my landlord's house? I, such a poor tenant? Because of me, he can't raise the rent or sell the house and make a profit—imagine that. The sacrifice!"

"Oh Bim," Tara said helplessly. Whenever she saw a tangle, an emotional tangle of this kind, rise up before her, she wanted only to turn and flee into that neat, sanitary, disinfected land in which she lived with Bakul, with its set of rules and regulations, its neatness and orderliness. And seemliness too—seemliness. She sat down weakly on the edge of Bim's bed, putting the letter down on the bedside table beside a pile of history books. She turned the pages of Sir Mortimer Wheeler's *Early India and Pakistan*[4] and thought how relevant such a title was to the situation in their family, their brother's marriage to Hyder Ali's daughter. She wished she dared lighten the atmosphere by suggesting this to Bim, but Bim stood with her back arched, martial and defiant. "Why let this go on and on?" she sighed instead. "Why not end it now by going to Moyna's wedding, and then forget it all?"

"I have ended it already," Bim said stubbornly, "by not going to see them and not having them here either. It is ended. But I don't forget, no."

"I wouldn't ever have believed—no one would ever have believed that you and Raja who were so close—so close—could be against each other ever. It's just unbelievable, Bim, and so—unnecessary, too," she ended in a wail.

"Yes?" said Bim with scorn, turning around to stare at her sister. "I don't

---

3. The British colonial government relinquished India after partitioning the country into the two nations of India and Pakistan, on August 15, 1947. The process of partition was violent and tumultuous. Hindu and Muslim communities rioted against each other, and millions of people fled each country to take refuge in the other.   4. A book about the Indus Valley civilization (ca. 3000–1600 B.C.), the oldest civilization in India. The ancient cities of Mohenjo-daro, Harappa, and others were discovered through archaeological excavations conducted in the 1920s. These major cities of the Indus Valley civilization ended up in Pakistan, after the partition of India in 1947.

think so. I don't think it is unnecessary to take offence when you are insulted. What was he trying to say to me? Was he trying to make me thank him—go down on my knees and thank him for this house in which we all grew up? Was he trying to threaten me with eviction and warn me what might happen if I ever stopped praising him and admiring him?"

"Of course not, Bim. How silly. He simply didn't know quite what he was writing. I suppose he was in a state—his father-in-law having just died, and you know how he always felt about him—and then having to take over Benazir's family business and all that. He just didn't know what he was writing."

"A poet—not knowing what he was writing?" Bim laughed sarcastically as she came and picked up the letter and put it back in the desk. It seemed to have a pigeon-hole all to itself as if it were a holy relic like fingernails or a crooked yellow tooth.

"Do tear it up," cried Tara, jumping up. "Don't put it back there to take out and look at and hold against Raja. Tear it up, Bim, throw it away," she urged.

Bim put the lid up with a harsh set to her mouth. "I will keep it. I must look at it and remind myself every now and then. Whenever you come here and ask why I don't go to Hyderabad and visit him and see my little nieces and nephews—well then, I feel I have to explain to you, prove to you . . ." She stammered a bit and faltered to a stop.

"Why, Bim?"

But Bim would not tell her why she needed this bitterness and insult and anger. She picked up an old grey hairbrush that had lost half its bristles and was so matted with tangles of hair that Tara shuddered at the sight of it, and began to brush her hair with short, hard strokes. "Come, let's go and visit the Misras. They've been asking about you, they want to see you. Ask Bakul to come, too—he must be getting bored. And he knows the Misras. You *met* him at their house—I'd nearly forgotten," she laughed, a bit distractedly.

Tara followed her out, relieved to be in the open again, out of the dense musty web of Bim's room, Bim's entanglements, and to see the evening light and the garden. A bush of green flowers beside the veranda shook out its night scent as they came out and covered them with its powdery billows. Badshah rushed up, whining with expectation.

The sound of a 1940s foxtrot on Baba's gramophone followed them down the drive to the gate as if a mechanical bird had replaced the koels and pigeons of daylight. Here Bim stopped and told Badshah firmly to sit. They stood watching, waiting for him to obey. He made protesting sounds, turned around in circles, pawed Bim's feet with his claws, even whined a bit under his breath. Finally he yawned in resignation and sank onto his haunches. Then they turned out of the gate and ceased to hear the tinny rattle of the wartime foxtrot.

Walking up the Misras' driveway, they could hear instead the sounds of the music and dance lessons that the Misra sisters gave in the evenings after their little nursery school had closed for the day, for it seemed that they never ceased to toil and the pursuit of a living was unending. Out on the dusty lawn cane chairs were set in a circle and here the Misra brothers sat taking their rest—which they also never ceased to do—dressed in summer clothes of fine muslin, drinking iced drinks and discussing the day which meant very little since the day for them had been as blank and unblemished as an empty glass.

They immediately rose to welcome their neighbours but Bim stood apart, feeling a half-malicious desire to go into the house and watch the two grey-haired, spectacled, middle-aged women—once married but both rejected by their husbands soon after their marriage—giving themselves up to demonstrations of ecstatic song and dance, the songs always Radha's in praise of Krishna, the dance always of Radha pining for Krishna.[5] She hadn't the heart after all and instead of joining the men on the lawn, she went up the steps to the veranda where the old father half-sat, half-reclined against the bolsters on a wooden divan, a glass of soda water in his hand, looking out and listening to his sons and occasionally shouting a command at them that went unheard, then sadly, meditatively burping. Tara and Bakul sat down with the brothers on the lawn and talked and listened to the voices of pupils and teachers mournfully rising and falling down the scales played on a lugubrious harmonium[6] and tried, while talking of Delhi and Washington, politics and travel, to imagine the improbable scene indoors. Eventually the little pupils came out, drooping and perspiring, and rushed off down the drive to the gate where their ayahs waited for them, chatting and chewing betel leaves.[7] After a while, the teachers, too, emerged onto the veranda. They too drooped and perspired and were grey with fatigue. There was nothing remotely amusing about them.

"Bim, Bim, why must you sit here with Papa? Come into the garden and have a drink," they cried at once, together.

But Bim would not listen. She tucked up her feet under her to make it plain she was not getting up. "No, no, I want to listen to Uncle," she said, not wishing to add that she had no liking for his sons' company. "Uncle is telling me how he was sent to England to study law but somehow landed up in Burma and made a fortune instead. I want to hear the whole story. And you must go and meet Tara and Bakul. They've come."

"Tara and Bakul?" cried the two sisters and, straightening their spectacles and smoothing down their hair and their saris, they rushed down into the garden while Bim stayed by the sick old man.

"But Uncle, is it a true story?" she teased him. "I never know with you."

"Can't you see the proof?" he asked, waving his glass of soda water so that it spilt and frothed and sizzled down his arm. "Now if I had gone north and had to work in a cold climate, learnt to wear a tie and button a jacket and keep my shoes laced and polished, I would have returned a proper person, a disciplined man. Instead, as you see, I went east, in order to fulfil a *swami's*[8] prophecy, and there I could make money without working, and had to undress to keep cool, and sleep all afternoon, and drink

5. The myth of the love of Radha and the god Krishna provides the subject matter for a large portion of lyric poetry and song in the Indian languages as well as in Kathak, a major classical dance tradition of north India. 6. A keyboard instrument used for accompanying north Indian vocal music. 7. Eaten with spices and condiments as a digestive after meals. *Ayahs*: female caretakers of children, who played a central role in the life of Europeans in India. 8. Holy man, teacher of mystical doctrines.

all evening—and so I came back with money and no discipline and no degree," he laughed, deliberately spilling some more soda water as if in a gesture of fatalism.

"What, all to satisfy a *swami?*"

"Yes, yes, it is true, Bimla. My father used to go to this *swami-ji*, no great man, just one of those common little *swamis* who sit outside the railway station and catch those people who come from the village to make their fortunes in the city. "*Swami-ji, swami-ji,* will I have luck?" they ask, and he puts his hand on their heads in blessing and says "Yes, son, if you first put five rupees[9] in my pocket." That sort of man. My father went to him to buy a blessing for me—I was leaving for England next day. My trunk was packed, my passage booked, my mother was already weeping. But perhaps my father didn't give the *swami-ji* enough money. He said "Your son go to England? To Vilayat?[1] Certainly not. He will never go north. He will go east." "No, no," said my father, "his passage is already booked on a P & O[2] boat, he is leaving for Bombay tomorrow to catch it, he is going to study law in a great college in England." But *swami-ji* only shook his head and refused to say another word. So, as my father was walking home, very slowly and thoughtfully, who should bump into him, outside the Kashmere Gate post office, but an old friend of his who had been in school with him and then gone to Burma to set up in the teak business. And this man, this scoundrel, may he perish—oh, I forgot! He perished long ago, Bimla, leaving me all his money—he clasped my father in his arms and said "You are like a brother to me. Your son is my son. Send him to me, let him work for me and I will make a man of him." And so my passage was cancelled, I gave up my studies and went east, to Burma. "He gulped down half a glass of soda water suddenly, thirstily. "That *swami-ji,*" he burped.

"And do you think if the *swami-ji* had not made that prophecy, your father would not have accepted his friend's offer?" asked Bim, filled with curiosity.

"Who can tell?" groaned the old man, shifting about in search of a more comfortable position. "Fate—they talk about Fate. What is it?" He struck his head dramatically. "This fate?"

"What is it, uncle? Does it pain?" Bim asked because his face, normally as smooth and bland as butter, was furrowed and gleaming with sweat.

He sank back, sighing "Nothing, nothing, Bimla, my daughter, it is only old age. Just fate and old age and none of us escapes from either. You won't. You don't know, you don't think—and then suddenly it is there, it has come. When it comes, you too will know."

Bim laughed, helping herself to some of the betel leaves in the silver box at his side. As she smeared them with lime and sprinkled them with aniseed and cardamoms, she said "You think one doesn't know pain when one is young, uncle? You should sit down some day with ninety examination papers to correct and try and make out ninety different kinds of handwriting, all illegible, and see that your class has presented you with ninety

---

9. The currency of India.   1. Abroad, foreign country (Urdu/Persian).   2. The Peninsular and Orient Steamship Company.

different versions of what you taught them—all wrong!" She laughed and rolled up the betel leaf and packed it into her mouth. "That is what I have been doing all day and it has given me a fine pain, too." She grasped her head theatrically and the old man laughed. Bim had always made him laugh, even when she was a little girl and did tricks on her bicycle going round the drive while his two daughters screamed "Bim, you'll fall!"

"You work too hard," he said. "You don't know how to enjoy life. You and my two girls—you are too alike—you work and let the brothers enjoy. Look at my sons there—" he waved his arm at them, the muslin sleeve of his shirt falling back to reveal an amulet tied to his arm with a black thread running through the thick growth of white hair. "Look at them—fat, lazy slobs, drinking whisky. Drinking whisky all day that their sisters have to pay for—did you ever hear of such a thing? In my day, our sisters used to tie coloured threads on our wrists on Rakhibandhan[3] day, begging for our protection, and we gave them gifts and promised to protect them and take care of them, and even if it was only a custom, an annual festival, we at least meant it. When my sister's husband died, I brought her to live here with us. She has lived here for years, she and her children. Perhaps she is still here, I don't know, I haven't seen her," he trailed off vaguely, then ended up with a forceful "But *they*—they let their sisters do the same ceremony, and they just don't care what it means as long as they can get their whisky and have the time to sit on their backsides, drinking it. Useless rubbish, my sons. Everything they ever did has failed . . ."

"What, not the new business as well? The real estate business that Brij started? Has that failed already?"

"Of course," cried the old man, almost with delight. "Of course it has. Can it succeed when Brij, the manager, cannot go to the office because he thinks it is degrading and refuses to speak to his clients because they are Punjabis, from Pakistan,[4] and don't belong to the old families of Delhi? What is one to do with a fool like that? Am I to kick him out of the house and flog him down the road to the office? And look at Mulk— our great musician—all he does is wave his hand in the air and look at the stars in the daytime sky, and sing. Sing! He only wants to sing. Why? For whom? Who asked him to sing? Nobody. He just wants to, that is all. He doesn't think anyone should ask him to work or earn money—they should only ask him to sing."

Out on the lawn there was a burst of laughter.

"And what about the old business they ran—the ice factory and soda water business? They had a good manager to run that."

"Good manager—ho, yes! Very good manager. Had them eating out of his hand. They thought he was an angel on earth—a *farishtha*[5]—slaving for their sakes, to fill their coffers with gold—till one day they went to the office to open the coffer for some gold—they must have needed it for

---

3. Tying the amulet (literal trans.); a festival in which women tie string amulets or bracelets on the wrists of their own brothers or of men whom they wish to claim as brothers. The brothers promise to protect them.   4. Refugees from the portion of the Punjab region that became Pakistan when India was partitioned.   5. A Persian word.

those Grant Road[6] women they go to, those song-and-dance women—and they found it empty, and the money gone."

"And the manager?"

"Gone! He took care of money—the money went—he went with it." The old man roared, slapping his thigh so that a fold of his *dhoti*[7] fell aside, revealing the grey-haired stretch of old, slack flesh. Straightening it casually, he added "What did they think? Someone else will work so that they can eat?"

"I didn't know about that," said Bim, concerned. She had thought the Misras had at least one secure business behind them, as her own family still had their father's insurance business that still existed quietly and unspectacularly without their aid and kept them housed and fed. If the manager made more money than he ought to, Bim did not grudge him that. She earned her own living to supplement that unearned income, and it was really only Baba who needed to be supported. But the Misra boys— fat, hairy brutes—why should others look after them? The poor Misra girls, so grey and bony and needle-faced, still prancing through their Radha-Krishna dances and impersonating lovelorn maidens in order to earn their living . . . Bim shook her head.

"Fools," the old man was still muttering as he fumbled about, looking for something under the pillows and bolsters and not finding it. Bim knew it was the hookah[8] he was no longer allowed to smoke. "Ugh," he cried, the corners of his mouth turned down as though he were about to cry, like a baby. "Not even my hookah any more. The doctor has said no, and the girls listen to the doctor, not to their father. What it is to be a father, to live without a smoke, or drink . . ."

Out on the lawn they were laughing again, their laughter spiralling up, up in the dark, as light as smoke.

"Laugh, laugh," said the old man. "Yes, laugh now—before it is all up with you and you are like me—washed up. But never mind, never mind," he said to Bim, straightening his head and folding his arms so that he looked composed again, like a piece of stone sculpture. "When I was young, when I was their age—do you think I was any better?" He winked suddenly at the surprised Bim. "Was *I* a saint?" he laughed. "I can tell you, I was just as fat, as greedy, as stupid, as wicked as *any* of them," he suddenly roared, flinging out an arm as if to push them out of his way in contempt. "A boozer, a womaniser, a bankrupt—running after drink, women, money—that was all I did, just like them, *worse* than them, any of them . . ." he chuckled and now his head wobbled on his neck as if something had come loose. "*Much* worse than any of them," he repeated with desperate pride.

Bim, red-faced in the dark shadows, let down her feet cautiously and searched for her slippers.

And here was Jaya coming up the steps to fetch her. "Bim, come and join us," she called. "Tara is telling us about Washington—it is such fun—and

6. In Bombay, notorious as a prostitute's quarter. A reference to courtesans or dancers.   7. Man's lower garment; a length of cotton cloth draped around the waist and legs.   8. A clay waterpipe, smoked all over north India.

Papa should eat his dinner and go to sleep. Papa, I'm sending the cook with your dinner—" and she rushed off towards the kitchen while Bim went down the steps into the garden. The old man had sunk back against the bolsters and shut his eyes. She even thought he might have fallen asleep, he was so still, but a little later she heard him call "The pickle, Jaya—don't forget the black lemon pickle—let me have a little of it, will you?"

Out on the lawn the talk was more sober, more predictable in spite of the whisky that accompanied it. Someone brought Bim a tall glass that chattered with ice. Could it be from their factory, Bim wondered, sipping, stretching her bare feet in the grass and feeling its dry tickle.

"Bakul-*bhai*, tell me," said the older brother, rolling the ice cubes around in his glass, "as a diplomat in an Indian embassy, how do you explain the situation to foreigners? Now when the foreign press asks you, perhaps you just say 'No comment,' but when you meet friends at a party, and they ask you what is going on here—how can a Prime Minister behave as ours does—how can ministers get away with all they do here—what is being done about the problems of this country—who is going to solve them—how, why is it like this?—then what do you say to them, Bakul-*bhai*?"

Bim, who was lighting herself a cigarette, stopped to watch her brother-in-law cope with this interrogation. It was quite dark on the lawn and although a light had been switched on in the veranda so that the old father could see to eat his dinner, it only threw a pale rectangle of light across the beds of cannas close to the house, and did not illuminate Bakul's face. He kept them all waiting in silence as he considered and then began his measured and diplomatic reply.

Elegantly holding his cigarette in its holder at arm's length, Bakul told them in his ripest, roundest tones, "What I feel is my duty, my vocation, when I am abroad, is to be my country's ambassador. All of us abroad are, in varying degrees, ambassadors. I refuse to talk about famine or drought or caste wars or—or political disputes. I refuse—I *refuse* to discuss such things. "No comment" is the answer if I am asked. I can discuss such things here, with you, but not with foreigners, not in a foreign land. There I am an ambassador and I choose to show them and inform them only of the best, the finest."

"The Taj Mahal?"[9] asked Bim, blowing out a spume of smoke that wavered in the darkness, and avoiding Tara's eye, watchful and wary.

"Yes, exactly," said Bakul promptly. "The Taj Mahal—the Bhagavad Gita[1]—Indian philosophy—music—art—the great, immortal values of ancient India. But why talk of local politics, party disputes, election mal-practices, Nehru, his daughter, his grandson[2]—such matters as will soon pass into oblivion? *These* aren't important when compared with India, eternal India—"

"Yes, it does help to live abroad if you feel that way," mused Bim, while her foot played with the hem of her sari and she looked carefully away

---

9. The renowned marble tomb monument built by the Moghal emperor Shah Jahan (ruled 1627–58) for his beloved wife Mumtaz Mahal.   1. Important Hindu sacred text.   2. Most likely Sanjay Gandhi (1947–1980), who was active in Indian politics in the 1970s. See also n. 8, p. 2788.

from Tara who watched. "If you lived here, and particularly if you served
the Government here, I think you would be obliged to notice such things:
you would see their importance. I'm not sure if you could ignore bribery
and corruption, red-tapism, famine, caste warfare and all that. In fact, living here, working here, you might easily forget the Taj Mahal and the
message of the Gita—"

"Never," interrupted Bakul firmly, ripely. "A part of me lives here, the
deepest part of me, always—"

"Ah," Bim in turn interrupted him. "Then it is definitely important to
live abroad. In all the comfort and luxury of the embassy, it must be much
easier, *very* easy to concentrate on the Taj, or the Emperor Akbar.[3] Over
here I'm afraid you would be too busy queueing up for your rations and
juggling with your budget, making ends meet—"

"Oh Bim," Tara burst out in protest, "you *do* exaggerate. I don't see you
queueing up for your rations—or even for a *bus!*"

Bim burst out laughing, delighted at having provoked Tara, and agreed
there was some exaggeration in what she said. This annoyed Bakul who
had taken it all so perfectly seriously, and he tapped his cigarette holder
on the arm of his chair with the air of a judge tapping a gavel at a meeting
grown unruly.

Tara cast her eyes around, looking for an escape. But Bim had thrown
back her head in laughter, all the men beside her were laughing. Then
she leant forward, a cigarette in her mouth, and Bakul leant towards her
to light it. Seeing the match flare, the cigarette catch fire with a little
throb, Tara was pricked with the realisation that although it was she who
was the pretty sister, had always been, so that in their youth the young
men had come flocking about her like inquisitive, hopeful, sanguine bees
in search of some nectar that they sniffed on the air, it was Bim who was
attractive. Bim who, when young, had been too tall and square-shouldered
to be thought pretty, now that she was grey—and a good deal grey,
observed Tara—had arrived at an age when she could be called handsome. All the men seemed to acknowledge this and to respond. There was
that little sensual quiver in the air as they laughed at what she said, and a
kind of quiet triumph in the way in which she drew in her cheeks to make
the cigarette catch fire and then threw herself back into her chair, giving
her head a toss and holding the cigarette away so that a curl of smoke
circled languidly about her hand. Tara thought how attractive a woman
who smokes is: there is some link formed between the man who leans
forward with a match and the woman who bends her head towards that
light, as Bakul and Bim did.

Tara did not smoke and no one offered her a light. Or was it just that
Tara, having married, had rescinded the right to flirt, while Bim, who had
not married, had not rescinded? No, it was not, for Bim could not be said
to flirt. Slapping hard at a mosquito that had lighted on her arm, she was
saying to Manu who had offered to fetch a Flit-gun,[4] "That's too much of
a bother—don't." Bim never bothered.

---

3. Jalaluddin Akbar (ruled 1565–1605), eminent, eccentric Moghal emperor, known for his eclectic policies in religion, culture, and politics.   4. Insect repellent. *Flit:* a brand name.

The Misra brothers and sisters were not interested in the subtleties underlying such exchanges. One brother wanted to know "What is the price of good whisky in Washington? Not that terrible thing called bourbon but scotch—can you get scotch?" and the sisters asked Tara where she had bought her chiffon sari and her leather bag, and for how much. Bim listened to Tara giving them shoppers' information glibly but a little too fast, making her sound unreliable. It amused Bim to see, through a haze of cigarette smoke, Tara's not quite assimilated cosmopolitanism that sat on her oddly, as if a child had dressed up in its mother's high-heeled shoes—taller, certainly, but wobbling. Then the sisters' heads drew closer still to Tara, their voices dropped an octave, and they murmured, one from the left and one from the right, "But how much longer can you keep your girls abroad? Mustn't they come home to marry now?"

Tara cowered back in her basket chair. "They are only sixteen and seventeen," she said plaintively.

"Time to marry—better to marry—time, time," they cried, and Tara rubbed her mosquito-bitten toe in the grass in pained embarrassment, and Bim, overhearing them, lifted her eyebrows in horror and turned to Mulk, the younger brother who was silent, for sympathy.

Mulk had already drunk more glasses of whisky than anyone could count and sat ignoring the company, beating one hand on his knee, singing in little snatches in his hoarse, cracked voice, swaying his head joyfully to music that was audible only to him. Even since she had last seen him, he seemed to have deteriorated—his jaws prickled with several days' growth of beard, he wore a shirt with several buttons missing and a sleeve irremediably stained with betel juice, the slippers on his unwashed feet needed mending. He rolled his eyes in their sockets like a dog howling at the moon and hummed to himself. "*Zindagi,*[5] *O Zindagi,*" he sang, tunelessly, and refreshed himself with another gulp of whisky.

Then suddenly the scene split, with a tearing sound. It was only whisky pouring out of an overturned glass and Mulk struggling to get out of the canvas chair, too tight for his heavy frame. As they all stopped talking to stare at him, he gestured widely and shouted dramatically, "Where is my *tabla*[6]-player? My harmonium player? My accompanists? Where are they? *Chotu-mia!*[7] *Bare-mia!*" Standing, swaying on his thick legs, he roared at the lighted house and the scurrying figures on the veranda.

"Shh, Mulk-*bhai,*" cried Jaya and Sarla, their faces shrinking into small dark knots. "You will wake Papa. Why are you shouting? You know they aren't there."

"Yes, I know they aren't there" he blasted them, turning around and staggering towards them so that Bim and Tara had to hastily draw up their feet or he would have tripped over them. "I know who turned them out—you two—you two turned them out—"

"Mulk, Mulk," murmured his brothers.

Suddenly Mulk was clutching his hands to his chest like two puffy little

---

5. Life, existence (Urdu/Persian). 6. A pair of single-headed drums used as principal percussion accompaniment for north Indian (Hindustani) classical vocal and instrumental music. 7. *Mia* is an Urdu term of respect.

birds and his voice rose in shrill, grotesque mimicry. " 'It is a waste of money. How can we afford to keep them? We have to feed ourselves. Tell them to go, they must go—go—go—' " and he pushed out the two birds so that they fluttered away and fell at his sides. "That is all I hear from them—these two—"

"Mulk, Mulk," rose the pacifying croon from the pigeons in the chairs.

Mulk swung around to face Bim and Tara and Bakul now. "They have got rid of my musicians," he nearly wept. "Sent them away. How am I to sing without accompaniment?"

"Mulk-*bhai*, we only pointed out that we haven't the money to pay them and we could not keep feeding them on kebabs and pilaos and kormas[8] as you expected us to. Is it our fault if they went away once we stopped serving such food?"

"Food! It wasn't food they wanted. You are insulting them. You are insulting my *guru*.[9] He does not want food, or money. He wants respect. Regard. That is what we must pay to a *guru*. But you have no respect, no regard. You think only of money—money—money. That is what you think about, you two—"

"Mulk, Mul-lk."

"They have minds full of money, *dirty* minds. They don't understand the artist, how the artist lives for his art. They don't know how it is only music—" here he clasped his chest with a moist, sweating paw—"only music that keeps me alive. Not food. Not money. Music: what can it mean to those who only think of money? If I say 'I must have accompaniment for my singing,' they say 'Oh there is no money!' If I say, 'I want my friends to come tonight so I can sing for them, cook dinner for them please,' they cry 'Oh we have no money!' Do you need money to make music?" he roared, lifting his arm so that the torn sleeve showed his armpit and the bush of grey hair in it. He stood, swaying, with the arm uplifted, the torn sleeve drooping, as he faced his visitors. "Do you?" he roared, and they could see spit flying from his mouth and spraying them where they sat, helpless. "Tell me—do you?"

The visitors were frozen. The family seethed. Then the sisters cracked like old dry pods from which the black seeds of protest and indignation spilt, infertile. Money, they were both saying, where were they to find money to pay for concerts and dinners?

"Don't I give you money?" shouted Mulk, lowering his head and swaying it from side to side threateningly. "Where is all the money I give you—hey? Tell me. Tell me. Where is that five hundred rupee note I gave you—hey? Where is it? Show it to me. I want to see it. I want it."

He began to plunge his legs up and down in the grass like a beast going methodically out of control. One of the small bamboo tables was knocked down, a glass spilt. Now at last Bakul acted. Rising to his feet casually, elegantly, he took Mulk by the arm, murmured to him in his most discreet voice, began to lead him away towards the house. They heard Mulk crying something about "My *guru*—his birthday—I want to give—they won't let

8. Various dishes introduced into Indian cuisine via the Persian-based culture brought by the Moghals and other Muslim rulers of India. 9. Teacher, whom the pupil must revere.

me—for my *guru*—" and then some sobbing intakes of breath, gasps for reason and control, and then only the flow of Bakul's voice, slipping and spreading as smoothly and evenly as oil, and then silence in which they became aware of Badshah barking fiercely out on the road.

Bim rose at last, brushing her sari as if there were crumbs, saying "Listen to Badshah—he's saying we must get back. Come, Tara, if we don't go home at once, the cook will fall asleep and we'll have no dinner and Baba will go to bed without any."

Now the Misra sisters too were released from their shell-shocked postures and rose gratefully, chattering once more. "But why don't you stay to dinner, Bim?" "Tara, have pot luck with us. We can't throw a dinner party as we would have in the old days—but pot luck . . ." and the brothers shouted "Let's call Baba. Tell him we'll have music that will make him forget that rubbish he listens to—we'll get Mulk to sing!" Strangely enough, and much to Bim's and Tara's astonishment, Brij and Manu began to laugh, thumping each other like schoolboys. One even wiped his eyes of tears as he repeated "Get Mulk to sing—Mulk to sing for us—" as if it were a family joke that only needed to be mentioned to set them off uncontrollably.

The sisters, a little more circumspect, edged closer to Tara, saying "Mulk gets that way when he has had too much to drink. He doesn't mean it—he will forget about it—we'll give him his dinner—and, oh stay for pot luck, Tara!"

But Bim would not listen. The last time she had accepted an invitation to "pot luck" she had been distressed to see the two Misra sisters halving and sharing a *chapati*[1] between them, and jars of pickles had had to be opened to make up for the lack of meat and vegetables. It would not do. "No, that won't do," she said firmly. "Can you hear Badshah calling? Listen to that bark—he'll have all the neighbours up, and your father, too," and she swept up the veranda to say good night to the old man who lay supine on the divan, his two white, knobbed feet sticking out at the end of the sheet that covered him, saw that he was asleep and then went down to herd Tara and Bakul down the drive.

The sisters came to the gate with them, lingering by the jasmine bush to pick some for Tara. Giving her a handful, Jaya said "Oh, Tara, these flowers make me think of that picnic—so many years ago now—do you remember, too? It was springtime—the flowers in Lodi Gardens[2]—"

"And bees!" cried Sarla suddenly, catching Tara by the wrist so that a few of the jasmines fell. "How those bees attacked Bim—oh don't you remember?"

But Tara withdrew her hand, dropping the remaining jasmines as she did so. She shook her head, refusing to remember any more. Bim, smiling faintly, covered up her ears with her hands and said "How that dog barks— he has a voice like a trumpet," and led Tara and Bakul across the road to their own gate where Badshah waited.

As they crossed the dusty road, Bakul cast a look at the tall dark house

---

1. Flat, unleavened bread; a staple of north Indian cuisine.   2. Gardens with tomb monuments built by rulers of the Lodhi Dynasty (1451–1526); a popular picnic spot.

behind the hedge and asked "What has happened to the Hyder Alis'
house? Doesn't anyone live there?"

"No. I mean, only a poor relation of theirs. He must have been a nuisance to Raja in Hyderabad so they sent him here as caretaker. He takes
opium—he just lies around—and the house is falling down about his ears.
No one's replaced a brick or painted a wall there for years."

"Oh what a shame—it was a lovely house, you know, Bakul," said Tara.

Badshah's barks grew so urgent they could not speak to each other any
more.

Baba was already asleep on his bed in the veranda when the sisters slipped
quietly past, only glancing to see him lying on his side, one leg stretched
out and the other slightly bent at the knee as if he were running, half-
flying through the sky, one hand folded under his chin and the other
uncurled beside it, palm upwards and fingers curved in—a finely composed piece of sculpture in white. Marble. Or milk. Or less: a spider's
web, faint and shadowy, or just some moonlight spilt across the bed. There
was something unsubstantial about his long slimness in the light white
clothes, such a total absence of being, of character, of clamouring traits
and characteristics. He was no more and no less than a white flower or
harmless garden spider, the sisters thought, as if, when he was born, his
parents, late in their lives, had no vitality and no personality left to hand
down to him, having given it away in thoughtless handfuls to the children
born earlier. Lying there in the dark, dressed in white, breathing quite
imperceptibly, he might have been a creature without blood in his veins,
without flesh on his bones, the sisters thought as they tiptoed past him,
down the steps to the lawn to stroll.

The whole neighbourhood was silent now, asleep. The sound of traffic
on the highway was distant, smothered by dust and darkness. At last one
became aware of the presence of stars, the scent of night-flowering plants.
The sisters, sleepless, rustled through the grass, up and down beside the
long hedge. The black cat, pacing sedately beside them to begin with,
suddenly leapt up into the air, darted sideways and disappeared.

Hands behind her back as she paced, Bim murmured "Do you know,
for a long time after Mira-*masi* died—for a long, long time—I used to
keep seeing her, just here by the hedge—"

"Bim," Tara cried incredulously.

"Yes, yes, I used to *feel* I was seeing her—just out of the corner of my
eye, never directly before me, you know—just slipping past this hedge
here—" she put out her hand and touched the white-flowering
chandni[3]—"quite white and naked, as she was when she—when she—"

"Then—at that time," Tara helped, pained.

"—small, like a thin little dog, a white one, just slipping along quietly—
I felt as if towards the well at the back—that well—"

"That the cow drowned in?"

"And she used to say she would drown herself in but because she didn't,
because she died, after all, in bed, I felt she was still trying to get there. A

---

3. Moonlight (Hindi).

person needs to choose his death. But if I turned my head very quickly—then she would vanish—just disappear into the hedge—" and Bim touched it again, to remember, and had the back of her hand scratched by a thorn and heard some small creature skitter away into the leaves. "I felt like one of those Antarctic explorers T. S. Eliot wrote about in his notes to *The Waste Land*, to that verse, do you know it, Tara?

> Who is the third who walks always beside you?
> When I count, there are only you and I together
> But when I look ahead up the white road
> There is always another one walking beside you
> Gliding wrapt in a brown mantle, hooded
> I do not know whether a man or a woman
> —But who is that on the other side of you?"[4]

They were silent as they scraped through the catching grasses at their feet, and had their heads bowed, not looking. Tara gave a small sigh that she disguised as a yawn: she had listened so often to Bim and Raja quoting poetry—the two of them had always had so much poetry that they carried in their heads. As a little girl, tongue-tied and shy, too diffident to attempt reciting or even memorising a poem—there had been that wretched episode in school when she was made to stand up and recite "The Boy Stood On the Burning Deck" and it was found she could not proceed beyond the title—Tara was always struck dumb with wonder at their ability to memorise and quote. It was another of those games they shared and she did not. She felt herself shrink into that small miserable wretch of twenty years ago, both admiring and resenting her tall, striding sister who was acquainted with Byron, with Iqbal,[5] even with T. S. Eliot.

Bim was calmly unaware of any of her sister's agonies, past or present. "Only I was not at any extremity like those explorers in the icy wastes who used to see ghost figures," she continued. "I was not frozen or hungry or mad. Or even quite alone. I had Baba. After you married, and Raja went to Hyderabad, and Mira-*masi* died, I still had Baba. And that summer I got my job at the college and felt so pleased to be earning my living—"

She stopped abruptly as though there were a stone in the grass that she had stumbled on. Tara walked on, distracted, till she noticed Bim was not with her, then stopped to look back, fearfully. But Bim did not revive her tirade against Raja although Tara had feared they were beginning to slip into it again.

"Really, I was not mad in the least," said Bim, strolling on. "So then I thought there might be something in what the Tibetans say about the dead—how their souls linger on on earth and don't really leave till the forty-ninth day when a big feast is given and the last prayers are said and a final farewell given to the departed. It takes forty-nine days, they say in their Bardol Thodol,[6] to travel through the three Bardos of death and all

4. Eliot's note, to line 360, reads: "The following lines were stimulated by the account of one of the Antarctic expeditions (I forget which, but I think one of Shackleton's): it was related that the party of the explorers, at the extremity of their strength, had the constant delusion that there was *one more member* than could actually be counted" (emphasis in the original).   5. Muhammad Iqbal (1873–1938), poet-philosopher from Punjab, who contributed greatly to the idea of a separate Muslim civilization in India and the need for the state of Pakistan.   6. The Tibetan Book of the Dead.

their stages. I felt Mira-*masi* was lingering on, in the garden, not able to leave because she hadn't been seen through all the stages with the relevant prayers and ceremonies. But then, who is?" Bim said more loudly, tossing her head, "except for the Buddhist monks and nuns who die peacefully in their monasteries in the Himalayas? We were anything but peaceful that summer."

"Yes, *what* a summer," Tara murmured.

"Isn't it strange how life won't *flow*, like a river, but moves in jumps, as if it were held back by locks that are opened now and then to let it jump forwards in a kind of flood? There are these long still stretches—nothing happens—each day is exactly like the other—plodding, uneventful—and then suddenly there is a crash—mighty deeds take place—momentous events—even if one doesn't know it at the time—and then life subsides again into the backwaters till the next push, the next flood? That summer was certainly one of them—the summer of '47—"

"For everyone in India," Tara reminded primly. "For every Hindu and Muslim. In India and in Pakistan."

Bim laughed. "Sometimes you sound exactly like Bakul."

Tara stopped, hurt. Bim had always had this faculty of cutting her short, hurting her, and not even knowing.

But this time, it seemed, she did know. She touched Tara's elbow lightly. "Of course you must—occasionally—when you've been married so long," she explained good-humouredly and even apologetically.

"But wouldn't you agree?" Tara said coldly.

"Yes, yes, you are perfectly right, Tara—it was so for all of us—for the whole family, and for everyone we knew, here in this neighbourhood. Nineteen forty-seven. That summer. We could see the fires burning in the city every night—"

Tara shuddered. "I hate to think about it."

"Why? It was the great event of our lives—of our youth. What would our youth have been without it to round it off in such a definite and dramatic way?"

"I was glad when it was over," Tara's voice trembled with the passion she was always obliged to conceal. "I'm so glad it is over and we can never be young again."

"Young?" said Bim wonderingly, and as they were now near the veranda, she sank down on the steps where the quisqualis creeper threw its bunches of inky shadow on the white-washed steps, and sat there hugging her knees. Tara leaned against the pillar beside her, staring out and up at the stars that seemed to be swinging lower and lower as the night grew stiller. They made her deeply uneasy—they seemed so many milestones to mark the long distances, the dark distances that stretched and stretched beyond human knowledge and beyond human imagination. She huddled against the pillar, hugging it with one arm, like a child.

"Youth?" said Bim, her head sinking as if with sleep, or sorrow. "Yes, I am glad, too, it is over—I never wish it back. Terrible, what it does to one—what it did to us—and one is too young to know how to cope, how to deal with that first terrible flood of life. One just goes under—it sweeps one along—and how many years and years it is before one can stand up to it, make a stand against it—" she shook her head sleepily. "I never wish it back. I would never be young again for anything."

An invisible cricket by her feet at that moment began to weep inconsolably.

II

The city was in flames that summer. Every night fires lit up the horizon beyond the city walls so that the sky was luridly tinted with festive flames of orange and pink, and now and then a column of white smoke would rise and stand solid as an obelisk in the dark. Bim, pacing up and down on the rooftop, would imagine she could hear the sound of shots and of cries and screams, but they lived so far outside the city, out in the Civil Lines where the gardens and bungalows[7] were quiet and sheltered behind their hedges, that it was really rather improbable and she told herself she only imagined it. All she really heard was the ceaseless rattling of frogs in the mud of the Jumna and occasionally a tonga[8] horse nervously dashing down the road.

Raja, who had been ill all that year and could not climb the stairs to the terrace with her, groaned with impatience till she came down to tell him what she had seen.

Finding him soaked with perspiration from tossing on his bed in that small airless room on a close summer night, she hurried to bring a wet sponge and wipe his face.

"What do you think is happening?" he moaned. "Can't you ask the Misras to go and find out? Did you see a light in Hyder Ali's house? Where do you think Hyder Ali Sahib could have gone? How could he have gone without sending a message to anyone? Not even to me?"

"How could he, Raja? You know it is far too dangerous."

"He could have trusted *me*," Raja cried.

Bim wanted to remind him he was only a boy, still in college, and that their neighbour, the old and venerable and wealthy Hyder Ali, could hardly be expected to take him into his confidence, but she knew better than to upset him. The slightest upset made his temperature rise. She dipped the sponge in the enamel bowl in which blocks of ice clinked, and dabbed at his head again. Lifting his dark, wavy hair, she trailed the sponge across his white forehead and saw how waxen and sick his white face was, with a physical pang that made her twinge. His face had been heavy once, his lips pouting and self-indulgent: now all was bloodless, fine and drawn. He moved his head aside angrily and the cold drops fell on the pillow, soaking it.

"Go to his house and find out, Bim," he begged.

"I told you—I've just been up on the roof to see. One can see right into the garden from there. There's no one there, not even a gardener. The house is dark, all the doors are shut. There's no one there. They must have planned it in advance, Raja—it all looks quite orderly, as if they had

---

7. A type of low-roofed house built by European colonial settlers in tropical countries. *Civil Lines:* located immediately outside and to the north of the walled city of Old Delhi. The older European quarters in British colonial cities were usually divided into civil and military sections.   8. A cart, drawn by a single horse, which was used for carrying passengers.

planned and organised it all in advance just as if they were going up to Simla for the summer."

"They could have been taken away—dragged out and taken away—"

"Of course not" Bim snapped. "In that case, we would all have come to know, all the neighbours would have heard. We would have seen the mob arriving, seen the lights and heard all the noise. The Hyder Alis could have called for help, we would all have gone to help. There was no sound. No one came. They've just gone."

"How is it you didn't hear them go then?" Raja snapped, equally angry.

"Raja, they must have done it *quietly* so as not to let anyone know," Bim said in exasperation. "Now you must just wait till you hear from them— they are sure to send word as soon as it is safe."

"Safe? For Muslims? Here in India? It will be safe after every Muslim has had his throat slit," Raja said with great viciousness. He half-lifted himself from the bed and then threw himself violently back again. "And here I am—too ill to even get up and help. And the only time in my life that I've ever been ill," he added bitterly.

Bim was quiet, floating the sponge back and forth in the bowl with wrinkled, frozen fingertips. She felt her exasperation blotted out by won-der at Raja's ways of thinking and feeling, so different from anyone else's at that time or day. She could not help admiring what she saw as his heroism, his independent thinking and courage. Raja was truly the stuff of which heroes are made, she was convinced, and yet here he lay, ironi-cally, too ill to play the hero he longed to and, she half-believed, was meant to be. She lifted her eyes to see his chest rising and falling far too fast and excitedly and the twitching of his hands on the bedsheet.

"If you're not quiet, Raja, I shall have to call the doctor," she said mournfully, and got up from the cane stool beside his bed. "Let me read to you—it will take your mind off—"

"No, it won't," he said explosively. "Nothing can take my mind off— but read anyway, read if you like," he mumbled.

She went to the bookshelves that lined one wall of the room, straight to a volume of Byron's poems that she knew, by experience, were what capti-vated him soonest, most easily swept him away into a mood of pleasure and appreciation. She brought it to his bed and, sitting down on the cane stool again, opened it at random and began to read aloud:

> "The Assyrian came down like a wolf on the fold,
> And his cohorts were gleaming in purple and gold . . ."

and Raja lay quiet, his hands gathered together on his chest, stilled by the splendour of this vision, transported by the strength and rhythm of the lines, and Bim gloated that she could lead him so simply into a world out of this sickness and anxiety and chaos that burnt around them and across the country that summer.

All summer she nursed him and read to him. Sitting on the stool by his bed, her hair falling straight and lank on either side of her dark face, her eyes lowered to the book on her lap, she murmured aloud the poems of Tennyson and Byron and Swinburne that she and Raja both loved.

"Now sleeps the crimson petal, now the white;
Nor waves the cypress in the palace walk;
Nor winks the gold fin in the porphyry font;
The firefly wakens: waken thou with me.

Now droops the milkwhite peacock like a ghost,
And like a ghost she glimmers on to me.

Now lies the earth all Danaë to the stars
And all thy heart lies open unto me[9] . . ."

Silent for a while, looking up to see if Raja's eyes were open and staring
up at the flies crawling across the ceiling, or closed as he listened, half in
sleep, she turned to another book and read:

From too much love of living,
From hope and fear set free,
We thank with brief thanksgiving
Whatever gods may be
That no man lives forever,
That dead men rise up never;
That even the weariest river
Winds somewhere safe to sea.[1]

That was one of Raja's favourite poems, one he used to recite to her when
they were up on the terrace together, reluctant to come down into the
house at twilight, trying to prolong the evening and the sense of freedom
they had up there under the unlimited sky. But now he would not express
his enthusiasm quite so frankly. Now he would sometimes grunt "Hmm,
very lovely to hear, but—too many words, all words, just words. Now any
Urdu poet could put all that into one couplet, Bim, just one couplet,"[2]
and she would pause for him to quote from his beloved Urdu poetry, all
of which sounded exactly alike to her only she would rather have cut out
her tongue than said so to him. It was always, as far as she could make
out, the cup, the wine, the star, the lamp, ashes and roses—always the
same. But to him each couplet was a new-cut gem.

"We have passed every day from morning to night in pain,
We have forever drunk tears of blood,"

he would quote in an expiring voice and with a roll of his eyes that she
found excessively romantic and embarrassing so that she simply nodded
in agreement in order to keep from bursting out in protest.

"But you don't understand," Raja groaned, clasping his hands on his
chest. "You don't know any Urdu, you can't understand."

Raja had studied Urdu in school in those days before the Partition when
students had a choice between Hindi and Urdu.[3] It was a natural enough

9. From Alfred, Lord Tennyson's *The Princess*.   1. From Algernon Charles Swinburne's *The Garden
of Proserpine.*   2. The standard unit of the Urdu *ghazal* poetic genre.   3. Basically variants of one
and the same language, differing in script and vocabulary. Modern Hindi uses a vocabulary derived largely
from classical Sanskrit and is written in the Sanskrit Devanagari script, whereas Urdu (especially in poetry)
tends to have a predominantly Persian vocabulary and is written in the Persian script.

choice to make for the son of a Delhi family: Urdu had been the court language in the days of the Muslim and Moghul rulers and had persisted as the language of the learned and the cultivated. Hindi was not then considered a language of great pedigree; it had little to show for itself in its modern, clipped, workaday form, and its literature was all in ancient, extinct dialects. Raja, who read much and had a good ear, was aware of such differences.

"See," he told his sisters when he came upon them, bent over their homework at the veranda table, laboriously writing out Hindi composi- tions on My Village or The Cow, "you can't call this a language." He made a scornful sound in his nose, holding up one of their Hindi copy- books as if it were an old sock. "Look, its angles are all wrong. And this having to go back and cross every word as you finish writing it, it is an— an impediment. How can you think fluently when you have to keep going back and crossing? It impedes the flow of the—the composition," he told them and they were thunderstruck by such intellectual revelations. "Look," he said again and wrote out a few lines in the Urdu script with a flourish that made them quiver with admiration.

Their neighbour and landlord, Hyder Ali, came to hear of the boy's interests. He himself had a substantial library housed in a curious tower- like protuberance built at one corner of his bungalow. Seeing Raja swing- ing on the garden gate as he was coming back from his evening ride along the banks of the Jumna, he stopped to invite him to visit his library. Raja, appalled at having been caught at the childish pastime of hanging on the creaking, swaying garden gate, dazzled by the impressive figure of the old gentleman with silvery hair, dressed in white riding clothes and seated upon the white horse that Raja had for years envied him, often climbing up the garden wall to watch it being fed and groomed in the stable at the back, quite overcome at being given an invitation that he had only dreamt of in secret, nodded his acceptance in dumbfounded silence at which the old landlord smiled.

He presented himself at the Hyder Alis' next day, was shown in by a suspicious servant, waved into the library by a preoccupied Hyder Ali in his office room, and let loose amongst the books and manuscripts that were to him as the treasures of Haroun al Raschid.[4] He would sit there for hours, daily, turning over the more valuable of Hyder Ali's manuscripts under the watchful eye of an old clerk employed by the landlord to keep his books, an aged priest with the face of a white goat who glared, slit-eyed, through his wire-rimmed spectacles at this son of the heathen allowed by some dangerous whim of the rich landlord's to touch holy manuscripts he should not have come near. The air was so sharp, so pungent with the old man's distaste and suspicion that finally Raja would become physically uncomfortable and go home, often with several volumes of poetry lent him by the amused and generous Hyder Ali.

Aunt Mira seemed as perturbed as the old clerk by this strange friend- ship. Sitting on the veranda with her mending, she saw Raja come out of

4. Legendary caliph of Baghdad, a central character in the *Arabian Nights*.

his room with an armful of books to return to Hyder Ali and warned him in an awkward mumble "Raja, don't you think you go there a little too often? Are you sure you are not in their way?"

"But Hyder Ali Sahib invited me—he told me I could take all the books I wanted, as often as I liked."

"That was generous of him. But perhaps he didn't mean *quite* so often, *quite* so many."

"Why?" asked Raja stubbornly. He stood on the steps a minute, waiting for Aunt Mira to reply. When she did not, he went off with a disgusted look.

If Hyder Ali found his visits too frequent and the hours spent in his library too long, he neither said so nor even implied it by a look. He himself was either out on business or in his office room adjoining the library, going through his letters and files with a pair of clerks, for he was the owner of much property in Old Delhi and this seemed to entail an endless amount of paper work. Raja would hear him dictating to his clerks and the scratching of their pens while he himself sat cross-legged on a rug in the "tower" or on a curly sofa upholstered in velvet and backed with painted tiles set in the ornately carved rosewood, reading and glorying in the beauty of the manuscripts and the poetry and in the extraordinary fact of his being here at all.

As he grew older and more sure of himself, he began to take part in Hyder Ali's family life, for they all grew accustomed to him so that the sharp watchfulness softened into baffled acceptance. Coming out of the library, he would see Hyder Ali's wife and daughter sitting on a divan on the veranda, cutting up vegetables for pickles or embroidering their coloured veils, and accept a slice of guava held out by the Begum or stop to tell them of his parents' health or some gossip about the servants demanded of him. In the evenings, tired of his own noisy sisters and peculiar old aunt and still more peculiar little brother, he would wander across to the Hyder Ali's garden where there was always a gathering of friends at that hour, chairs and divans and bolsters arranged in a circle on the lawn, drinks and ice and betel leaves served on silver trays, and gentlemen discussing politics and quoting poetry. It was an almost shocking contrast to the shabbiness of their own house, its peculiarities that hurt Raja by embarrassing him as he grew up and began to compare them with other homes, other families. Raja naturally inclined towards society, company, applause; towards colour, song, charm. It amazed and enchanted him that in the Hyder Ali household such elements were a part of their lives, of their background. In his own home they were totally alien. He felt there could be no house as dismal as his own, as dusty and grimy and uncharming. Surely no other family could have as much illness contained in it as his, or so much oddity, so many things that could not be mentioned and had to be camouflaged or ignored. The restraints placed on him by such demands made him chafe—he was naturally one to burst out and overflow with enthusiasm or praise or excitement. These possibilities were enticingly held out to him at the Hyder Alis'.

Once he had outgrown his khaki school shorts and taken to fine white muslin shirts and pyjamas,[5] he acquired sufficient self-confidence to join the circle of much older men on the lawn, and wisely sat listening rather than talking, saving up the talk for later when he would return home and tell Bim every detail, however casual or trivial, that glowed in his eyes with a special radiance related to everything that was Hyder Ali's.

Having angered everyone in his own family by coming home very late one night, long after their dinner time, he lay awake on his cot in the garden and gave Bim a whispered account of the glories of a party at the Hyder Alis'.

"There was a poet there tonight," he whispered, too tense with excitement to sleep. "A real poet, from Hyderabad, who is visiting them. He read out his poetry to us—it was wonderful—and Hyder Ali Sahib gave him a ring with a ruby in it."

"Was it that good?" Bim murmured sleepily, exhausted by having waited up so late for Raja to come home and by Aunt Mira's tearful laments about his bad ways.

"Good—but I think I could write as good verse. And, you know, Hyder Ali Sahib asked me to recite, too."

"Did you?"

"Yes, but not my own," he said regretfully. "They asked me to recite my favourite verses so I read them Iqbal's,"[6] and he quoted to the uncomprehending Bim in proud, triumphant tones:

"Thou didst create night but I made the lamp.
Thou didst create clay but I made the cup.
Thou didst create the deserts, mountains and forests,
I produced the orchards, gardens and groves.
It is I who made the glass out of stone
And it is I who turn a poison into an antidote."

The words were absorbed by the dusty night garden so brimful of sleep and quiet as to seem crowded and to press upon them with its weight. Then Bim asked ironically "And did Hyder Ali Sahib give you a ring with a ruby in it too?"

Raja might have been offended if he had caught the irony in the low voice but all he heard were the voices of Hyder Ali's guests as they praised his excellent diction, his perfect pronunciation. The poet from Hyderabad had fondled his shoulder, saying "He will go far, Hyder Ali Sahib. A mind that can appreciate Iqbal at such a tender age will surely go far." Entirely missing the sycophancy behind the words, the gesture, Raja had glowed almost as if he had written the verses himself. Even Bim and the dark garden could not dampen his glow.

But he was affronted when, seeing him write frenziedly all one afternoon that they were locked into the house because of a dust-storm raging outside, she had asked "Are you going to be an Urdu poet when you grow up, Raja?"

He felt that she ought to know that he was one already. But of course

5. Loose pants worn by many north Indian men under muslin or cotton tunic shirts (kurta).   6. See n. 5, p. 2807.

an ignorant younger sister could not see that. He gave her a bitter look through a haze of cigarette smoke. He had taken to smoking.

The summer his final school examination results came out, his parents were obliged to pay some attention to him. Raja would stand in their way as they went down the veranda steps to the car waiting to take them to the Roshonara Club for their daily game of bridge, or he would wait up for them in the veranda till they returned, late at night when the others were asleep.

"Why are you still awake?" his mother sighed disapprovingly as she drifted towards her bedroom, fatigued as always.

"Father, I have to give in my application form for college. You have to sign."

"Give it to me," his father grunted through the disintegrating flakes of a moist cigar. Then, peering at the form in the dim light that came through the open front door, he frowned "But this is no college for you. It is a Jamia Millia[7] form."

"That is where I want to study. I went there to get a form."

"You can't study there," his father said, taking the cigar out of his mouth and spitting out a shred of tobacco. "It is a college for Muslim boys."

"No, anyone can go there who wants to specialise in Islamic studies."

It was a phrase Raja liked to use. He had picked it up from Hyder Ali. It had impressed his sisters and his aunt. He gazed into his father's face in the hope of similarly impressing him.

But his father's face darkened by several shades and he stuttered in his curiously insipid and uninflected voice, "Specialise in Islamic studies? What are you talking about, you dunce?"

"That is what I am going in for, father," Raja said steadily, somehow managing to imply his pride in his unusual choice, and his steadfastness, and his scorn for this vague old man who could not understand.

"Rubbish," said his father flatly. "Bunkum," he said, using one of his favourite phrases, and tore the form in two before marching off to his room.

It was a stormy summer. Bim and Tara would chew their lips and exchange puzzled looks as they stood listening behind the curtains while father and son argued hotly whenever they met which was only occasionally and briefly so that all the arguments they built up inside themselves in silence burst out with great explosiveness on those few occasions. In the meantime, Raja grew more and more sullen and unpredictable in his temper while their father appeared to retreat deeper into the shadows off-stage where he existed unseen by his children. Finally, late one night when Raja forced him to sit down after his return from the club, not brush him aside as he walked past quickly, his father explained. Perhaps he had

---

7. Jamia Millia Ismailia, a university founded in 1921 by a group of nationalist Muslims (under the leadership of freedom fighter Muhammad Ali, 1978–1931) to provide Islamic education in the context of a diverse and secular society. Fostering Hindu-Muslim coexistence and harmony is an important educational goal of the university.

played a good game at the club. Perhaps he had enjoyed his dinner there. He was puffing at his cigar with an air of calm self-confidence as he talked.

"If you had asked me a few years ago, I would have said yes at once: yes, all right."

"How could I ask a few years ago? I've only finished school this year, in April."

"I know, I know. I am not talking about you, about your school record." He waved his cigar so that the thick odour of tobacco swept through the closed room like a damp rag. "I'm talking about the political situation. Don't you know anything about it? Don't you know what a struggle is going on for Pakistan? How the Muslims are pressing the British to divide the country and give them half? There is going to be trouble, Raja—there are going to be riots and slaughter," he said, dropping his voice cautiously. "If you, a Hindu boy, are caught in Jamia Millia, the centre of Islamic studies—as you call it—you will be torn to bits, you will be burnt alive—"

"*Who* will do that to me?" asked Raja in astonishment, somewhat feigned for he knew of the political situation well enough from the evening gatherings in the Hyder Alis' garden. The men there talked freely, forgetting the young boy's presence, or his religion, and he listened, he was aware. Only he had never related such talk to his own plans or life. At that time he was still childish enough to consider it a kind of adults' game in which he was not allowed to take part. He was somewhat flattered that his father, of all people, appeared to consider him adult enough now. He was flattered enough to listen attentively.

"*Who* will do that to you? Muslims, for trying to join them when they don't want you and don't trust you, and Hindus, for deserting them and going over to the enemy. Hindus and Muslims alike will be out for your blood. It isn't safe, Raja, it isn't safe, son."

Raja was thrilled by the idea and looked as bright-eyed as a child presented with a bright sword, but a thin, irritated voice whined from the bedroom "What is it you are telling the boy?"

"Some facts," shouted the father, suddenly determined, suddenly decisive, "that he should know." He had seen Raja's steadfastness waver and he jumped to take advantage: he was a practised bridge player.

Seeing this triumph, Raja shrunk visibly on the stool and became sullen again. He had not expected either quickness of response or reasoned opposition from the man who appeared to deal with both family and business by following a policy of neglect. Raja had known him only as someone leaving for the office or for the club, returning late and too tired for anything. He was startled by this unexpected aspect of his father, startled and put out.

His father saw his advantage with the shrewd, watchful eye of the card-player, and went on expounding his theme to the boy—superfluously, no more was really needed. When his wife called again, he went in to pacify her but took up the matter with Raja again the next day and the next. Now it was Raja who retreated, who avoided him and tried to wriggle out of these confrontations by staying close to Aunt Mira and his sisters. They were all astonished by the way the father began to turn up in their midst while they were having a quietly domestic tea, or bickering over their homework, and began to address Raja as though he were not one of them but one of the adults, a person with whom adult affairs could be discussed. Raja was silent now. He had not expected this. He had certainly expected his father to oppose him, but ineffectually and non-verbally, merely with arrogance and silence. Raja was not really prepared to reason or debate with his father. He was carried away by ideas, on wings of imagination, not by reason or analysis. Recognising his father's superior forces, he dispiritedly gave in and ceased to argue.

Their father's visits to their part of the house ceased, too. Once again he went through the day without addressing a word to them on his way out of it or into it. They knew him only as the master of the entrance and the exit.

And then their mother, for the first time in twenty years, missed an evening at the club, said she did not feel well and would stay in bed. That night she passed quietly into a coma so that when her husband returned from the club after an unsatisfactory game with an unaccustomed partner, he found her lying still and flaccid on her bed, quite beyond questioning him on his game.

The ambulance came. The children stumbled out of their beds to watch her being carried out like a parcel containing some dangerous material that had to be carefully handled.

Next day, Tara, possessed by a childish memory of trailing after her mother along the rose walk on a summer morning, clamoured to be taken to see her, but a trembling Aunt Mira held her in her arms as if to protect her from something so unsuitable, and their father told them bluntly that she was unconscious and there was no point in their visiting her.

Instead of going to the club, he went to the hospital every evening now. The children sat on the veranda steps waiting for him to come home with some news. While they waited, they told stories, read, played games, and forgot. Only the whiff of hospital disinfectants and anaesthetics that clung to his clothes when he returned, reminded them that he had been to the hospital and not to the club. His face looked even gloomier than when he had played a bad game at the bridge table and, looking at it, they did not want to question him after all. Instead they turned instinctively to Aunt Mira who smiled with grotesque unnaturalness into their troubled faces and made them laugh by dropping things, forgetting others and stumbling about the house like a sad comedian.

Their mother died without seeing any of them again. If she ever, for a minute, regained consciousness, it was only to murmur the names of familiar cards that seemed to drift through her mind with a dying rustle.

Since they were not taken to her funeral, it was a little difficult for the children to remember always that she was not at the club, playing cards, but dead. The difference was not as large as friends and neighbours supposed it to be and the children, exchanging looks of mutual guilt when the neighbours came and wept a few tears required by custom and commiserated and tried to console, tacitly agreed to keep their guilt a secret. The secret replaced their mother's presence in the house, a kind of ghostly surrogate which they never quite acknowledged and quite often forgot.

Raja went dispiritedly to Hindu College one day with one of the Misra
boys summoned by his father to take him, since he was already a student
of this college in Kashmere Gate picked by his father as suitable since he
had studied there himself. When he came back, admission forms filled,
subscriptions paid, a student enrolled in the English Literature course, he
flung himself onto his bed and sulked for a week, refusing even to get up
and go across to the Hyder Alis' in the evenings although the Begum
herself, hearing of their mother's death, sent across a personal invitation.

"Father's gone to the club—get up, Raja. Come on. We're playing
Seven Tiles[8] in the garden—won't you play?" coaxed Bim from the doorway. She was afraid that he was not only brooding over his defeat in the
matter of the Jamia Millia but over their mother's death, and could not
bear the thought of his silent feelings.

He only snarled a reply and flung a book at her to drive her away. It was
a little volume of Urdu poetry. Shocked, she bent to pick it up and dust it
before quietly placing it on his bookshelf.

Raja started cycling to college with the Misra boys. This activity seemed
to rouse him out of his sulks and, in spite of himself, he did begin to grow
interested in college life and in his studies. He brought home volumes of
Tennyson and Swinburne and lent them to Bim to read. No one in their
family had studied literature before. Now she and Raja fell upon it with a
kind of hunger, as if it were the missing element in their lives at last made
available, and devoured it with an appetite, reading aloud to each other
and memorising verses to quote aloud till Tara squirmed in misery and
Aunt Mira's jaw swung from its hinges in admiration.

But English literature, newly come upon and radiant in its freshness,
was not the only gate opened to Raja now. His father had been a student
of the college long ago; it had been very different in his time, and he had
no idea how politically aware the students now were, what a hotbed it was
for political fanaticism, and how many politicians and fanatics from outside had successfully infiltrated it. The quickly-aroused and enthusiastic
Raja was drawn into this feverish atmosphere by curiosity and by an adolescent need for a cause. The boys there saw an easy recruit but had no
inkling that Raja's true and considered reaction to their fanatical Hindu
beliefs would be one of outrage and opposition. They had not known, after
all, about his admiration for Hyder Ali, for Urdu poetry, for the evening
gatherings of poets and politicians in the garden. There was an immediate
clash between them that roused each of them to greater, wilder enthusiasm for his particular cause. The atmosphere was so explosive, the air
vibrated with threats and rumours of violence and enemity. Raja withdrew,
began to be a bit cautious in what he said, assumed a cool air, watched,
listened. He read mostly Lord Byron. Reading, he seemed to form a picture of himself, an image, that Bim, not his college acquaintances, was
the first to recognise.

Bim remembered how, as small children, Raja had announced, so
grandly, "When I grow up, I shall be a hero," making her instantly, with
shining eyes, respond "And I will be a heroine," which had made Tara
feel so miserable and excluded that she ran to Aunt Mira, whimpering

8. An Indian game.

"Bim and Raja say they will be a hero and heroine. They laugh when I say I will be a mother," and made Aunt Mira call the two of them for a scolding.

Bim remembered that when she heard Raja read aloud to her from Byron:

> "Place me on Sunium's marbled steep,
> Where nothing, save the waves and I,
> May hear our mutual murmurs sweep:
> There, swan-like, let me sing and die:
> A land of slaves shall ne'er be mine:
> Dash down yon cup of Samian wine."

and tell her the story of Byron's fight for Greek independence and his death in Greece as a hero and poet.[9] "Like you," Bim murmured, making Raja stare hard at her to see if she were mocking. She gazed back at him innocently. Then he gave a slight curl of his lip as if he were pleased, and she was both perturbed and annoyed at herself. She did not like it and she later wondered if it had put ideas into his head—dangerous, heady ones about his heroism, his poetry. He must have let the boys in college know this somehow because Bim overheard the Misra boys call him "Lord Byron" and, at times, simply "Lord." It made her hot with anger and remorse at her own part in it.

Raja started going to the Hyder Alis' for those evening gatherings again. Aunt Mira was perturbed. She had heard their father talk, she had heard talk amongst the servants and the neighbours, that worried her. Her lips closed about a thread she was sucking to a fineness so that it would enter a needle's eye, she frowned and shook her head at him as he went leaping down the veranda steps and raced down the drive.

"Why, Mira-*masi?*" Bim asked, putting one hand on her knee, moved by her aunt's expression.

Her aunt sat helplessly sucking the thread that dangled from her lips like a fine tail. As she put up her hand to remove it, her hand trembled. "He should not," she said in a kind of whimper. "It isn't safe."

"They are our neighbours, Mira-*masi,*" Bim exclaimed in surprise.

"But Muslims—it isn't safe," her aunt whispered, trembling. "Oh, Bim," she said distractedly, "won't you get me your father's brandy bottle from the sideboard? A drop—just a drop in my tea—I do need it—it might help—it isn't safe . . ." And Bim, astonished and also tickled by the idea, rushed to fetch the bottle from the dark and richly odoriferous recesses of the great gloomy sideboard in the dining room and tipped it over her aunt's tumbler of tea. "More, Mira-*masi*, more?" she asked as the drops trickled in and Aunt Mira, pressing her fingers to her trembling lips, nodded: more, more, till the tumbler was full and then she seized it and drank it, watched open-mouthedly by her nieces. They heard the tumbler chatter against her false teeth and laughed. But "No, it isn't safe," she repeated with a hiccup, lowering the tumbler to the tea tray with a nervous clatter. "Run and put the bottle back, Bim—it's not safe."

9. See p. 2775, n. 1.

Raja didn't care. He climbed over the gate and jumped into the road rather than laboriously open and shut it, then strolled into the Hyder Alis' garden, past the bushes of flowering jasmine and oleander, the rose beds and the fountain, slightly surprised to find the gathering much shrunk since he had last visited it. Many of the Hyder Alis' friends seemed to have vanished. Had they already gone to the Pakistan that was to be? Raja wondered. He was slightly stalled, too, when he felt the welcome at the Hyder Alis' not quite so warm, as gracious and effusive as before. He wondered if it could be because he had joined Hindu College and was studying English Literature instead of Urdu at Jamia Millia as Hyder Ali had advised him to do. But it was not Hyder Ali who was cool to him—in fact there was something gently loving in his gesture of placing his arm across the boy's shoulders as he came up, somehow making Raja think that Hyder Ali had no son, only a daughter—a curious thought, never spoken of, yet clearly felt. It was his friends who seemed to fall silent when he came and to ostentatiously change the subject of discussion. The awkwardness did not last. Glasses of whisky were passed around, some poetry quoted, and soon they forgot Raja, or Raja's Hindu presence, and picked up the subject they had dropped on seeing him—Pakistan, as ever Pakistan. Raja listened silently as they spoke of Jinnah, of Gandhi and Nehru, of Mountbatten and Attlee and Churchill,[1] because he knew this was not a matter in which he should express an opinion, but he listened and he began to see Pakistan as they did—as a possibility, very close to them, palpable and real.

When the boys at Hindu College found that Raja was one Hindu who actually accepted the idea of Pakistan as feasible, they changed from charmed friends into dangerous enemies. Raja, whose home and family gave him an exceptionally closed and sheltered background, was slow to realise this. The boys had taken him to tea-shops and given him cigarettes and samosas,[2] he had gone to cinema shows with them, sung songs with them as they cycled back at night. Now they were strangely and abruptly altered. When he spoke to them of Pakistan as something he quite accepted, they turned on him openly, called him a traitor, drowned out his piping efforts at reasonableness with the powerful arguments of fanatics. Some of them, his two or three closest friends, disclosed to him that they were members of terrorist societies; they told him they were not giving in cravenly to the partitioning of the country no matter what Gandhi said or Nehru did—they were going to fight to defend their country, their society, their religion.[3] As they declaimed, they watched Raja carefully for signs of wavering, of weakening. They so much wanted him to join them.

1. Louis Mountbatten of Burma (1900–1979), British Prime Minister Clement Richard Attlee (1883–1967) and Winston Churchill (1874–1965) each played a role in the negotiations between Indian leaders and the British colonial government. Mountbatten oversaw the partition of India and the transfer of power in 1947. Muhammad Ali Hinnah (1876–1949), chief leader of the Muslim League Party, contributed the most toward the goal of achieving a separate state for Indian Muslims. Mahatma Gandhi (1869–1948), the preeminent leader of India's freedom struggle, opposed the partition of India as best he could but was ultimately assassinated by a Hindu supremacist. For Nehru see n. 8, p. 2788.   2. Savory snacks. 3. Perhaps a reference to the Rashtriya Swayamsevak Sangh (RSS), a Hindu nationalist organization with a paramilitary branch whose young members were trained in weapons and attack techniques and indoctrinated with Hindu supremacist and anti-Muslim propaganda. Mahatma Gandhi's assassin, Nathuram Godse, was associated with this organization.

He was so desirable as a member of their cause in his idealistic enthusiasm, his graceful carriage, his incipient heroism. They wanted him. They pursued him. When he did not come to college, they came to see him at his house, after dark.

For Raja had fallen ill. His father and his aunt were convinced it was something to do with the atmosphere of that spring, the threatening, advancing violence in the air at one with the dust storms that gathered and broke, the koels that called frantically in the trees all day, the terrific heat that was already rising out of the parched, cracked yellow earth, and all the rumours that drifted in from the city like sand, or smoke. The doctor felt him over with the stethoscope, then ordered various tests to be carried out, saw the reports and said it was nothing so mental or emotional—the boy had become infected with tuberculosis.

"Tuberculosis?" Aunt Mira screamed, her voice slicing through Bim like a cold knife. "How can it be? The boy lives a healthy life—he drinks milk, eats eggs, eats meat . . ." she stammered, beginning to shred the end of her sari with her hands.

"No, no, it isn't always malnutrition that brings it on," the doctor broke in irritably. "He could have picked up a germ while drinking tea from a dirty cup, from using a soiled towel somewhere. Anywhere. But it is t.b.," he insisted in the face of her incredulity.

Raja, too, was incredulous. He felt ill. He felt he couldn't get to his feet at all. To raise his head for a sip of water required a great effort and made a sharp pain leap and throb at his temples. But he was sure it was merely fatigue, anxiety, something to do with—what? He couldn't quite say—so much whirled through his head: Lord Byron, heroism, Pakistan, Jinnah, Gandhi, the boys at college, hissing at him from behind the gate-post, Hyder Ali sipping his whisky so slowly and reflectively in that group of poets and politicians in the garden across the road. It made him quite giddy, as if he were being whirled about in a dust-storm.

The whole family found it unacceptable that Raja was seriously ill. For a while they allowed the college boys to visit him, to sit about his bed, giving him news of refugee camps and killings, of looting and burning in the city, and pleading with him, in conspirators' voices, to join their society. They would not let him go.

"T.b?" they scoffed. "The doctor's mad. A little heat fever. You'll soon be up. Then you can come with us. We'll show you where we hide our guns, and daggers, and where we meet to exercise and practise—"

They were sure Raja—so impetuous, so bold and dashing—would be fired by such talk. They cajoled him, they flattered. Aunt Mira even sent in lemonade for them to drink.

But they met with blazing opposition from Raja. He was too weak to say much, too weak and dizzy, but when he thought of Hyder Ali, of Hyder Ali's library, of Hyder Ali's Begum and daughter quietly humming and chattering as they embroidered their veils together, and all those cool, calm evenings in their garden that had made his spirit rejoice by offering it all he craved, he felt giddy with rage at these boys and what they stood for.

Very near to tears in his weakness and frustration, he told them "I'll tell the police that—I have only to phone the police to stop you—"

"You would never do that," they gasped, taken aback. Then, more harshly, "We'll see to it that you don't do that. We'll inform the police about *you*. You are more dangerous to India than we are—you're a traitor."

That was what they must have done for soon a plainclothes policeman began to hover about their gate, from six in the evening to six in the morning, too punctually to be anything but a plainclothes policeman. Bim peered out through the bamboo screen at the door at him. At first she thought it might be someone planning a burglary. She watched while Raja dozed. When he woke, she told him. He realised at once that his terrorist friends had warned the police that he was a Muslim sympathiser. Perhaps they had made him out to be a Pakistani spy.

For a moment, he thrilled at the idea of his importance, his dangerousness. He saw himself as fighting for the Hyder Alis, brandishing a sword, keeping the mob at bay. The very thought made him break into a sweat. His clothes, his bed were soaked. Left weak and trembling, he confessed to Bim that he was afraid.

"What will they do if their house is attacked?" he muttered. "Who will protect them? The police won't do it—they're afraid of the mob."

Bim tried to reassure him but he wanted to talk, not listen to her. He talked of Hyder Ali, of the Begum, of their daughter, the young girl Benazir. He asked Bim questions about her but Bim hardly knew her at all—she was a good deal younger, still at school, a pretty child with a round porcelain face, always clinging close to her mother like a young pigeon that still needs to be nourished.

"She doesn't come to school any more," Bim said, trying to find something to say. "None of the Muslim girls come any more."

"Her parents must be afraid to send her out of the house. I *wish* I could go and see her."

"Go and see her?" Bim repeated, puzzled. "Why?"

"I know I can't—the doctor says everyone is to keep away from me. Damn this t.b. Damn it—why must I have t.b. *now?*"

"The doctor says it could have been a tea-cup or a dirty towel—"

"A dirty towel? A tea-cup?" Raja cried, lifting his head from the pillow to glare at her. "When I ought to be out in the streets—fighting the mobs—saving Hyder Ali and Benazir—"

"Oh God, Raja," moaned Bim, running for the thermometer. "Be quiet or your temperature will go up. It is all this worry—all this nonsense—"

"Nonsense!" he gasped at her, white and damp with rage. He wanted to roar at her, he was so outraged and so frustrated, but all he could manage was a gasp.

"It's making you worse," Bim cried angrily, mopping his face with a sponge and going to get a change of nightshirt for him. "How will you get better if you keep worrying about fighting in the streets? *What* fighting in the streets?"

"Don't you *see*—there is going to be fighting in the streets, people like Hyder Ali Sahib are going to be driven out, their property will be burnt and looted, the government is helpless, they're not preventing—preventing—" but now tears of weakness rose in his throat, flooding it, and he closed his mouth and turned his head from side to side like a dog tied to a tight leash.

His situation was Romantic in the extreme, Bim could see as she sponged his face and helped him struggle out of one muslin shirt and into another—his heavy, limp body as she lifted it as spent and sapped as a bled fish, and the city of Delhi burning down about them. He hoped, like Byron, to go to the rescue of those in peril. Instead, like Byron, he lay ill, dying. Bim was sure he was dying. Her eyes streamed with tears as she buttoned up his shirt. "Shall I read to you, Raja?" she asked with a brave gulp.

"Shall I read to you, Raja?"

Sometimes he nodded yes, sometimes he shook his head no.

"No. Won't you go up on the roof again, Bim, and see what's happening?"

"Here, on Bela Road?" Bim asked in surprise, letting the book fall from her lap in surprise.

"At the Hyder Alis' of course," Raja explained with an irritated twitch. "Go up and see."

Sometimes Bim grumbled but went, dragging her feet because she was tired and knew nothing was happening either on Bela Road or in the Hyder Alis' garden, or in the Misras' compound, or anywhere closer than the horizon where the city walls smouldered and smoked by day and blazed by night.

Sometimes she was glad to leave the stuffy, airless sickroom with its stale, disinfected odours and Raja's low spirits and her own headache, to stroll on the terrace for a while and see the river birds descending from the sky to settle on the sand dunes for the night with harsh, alarmed cries, or hang over the balustrade and search the quiet leafy gardens and walled compounds for some sign of life, or action, that she could report to Raja. A bicycle wobbled drunkenly out of the servants' quarters at the back of the house and past the guava trees. A washerman was going in at the Misras' gate with a neatly tied bundle of white washing on his head. A dog barked in the Hyder Alis' garden. That was all. It was nothing.

One day, less than nothing.

"The house seems empty," she told Raja bluntly as she came down. "I think they've gone."

"Who?"

"The Hyder Alis, of course," she said irritably, going straight to the dressing table where the medicines were lined up, for his evening dose.

"Gone where?"

"I don't know, Raja, I only went up on the terrace to see. The house is dark, and everything seems shut."

"But then—but then—go and find out," he cried in a kind of muffled scream. "Go and find out!"

Bim gave him a dark look from over the brimming medicine spoon. "I will if you swallow this and stop screaming."

"I'm not screaming—I'm shouting!" He gulped down the medicine and the hysteria in his voice with an effort. "But go. Go."

"I *wish* there was someone else who would go," Bim could not keep from saying as she swept out. "There is never anybody except me."

There was no one except Bim. Everything was left to her. Aunt Mira was strangely absent. To begin with, she used to come stumbling into Raja's room and try ineffectually to tidy his books and medicines with shaking hands and ask tentatively about his meals, his temperature. Or she would huddle up in a cane chair on the veranda, just outside his door, saying to Bim "Call me when you need me. I'll wait here for Tara."

Tara was always out now. Since their mother's death, and Raja's illness, she had taken to going to the Misras' every evening and often they would take her to the cinema, to Connaught Place to shop, or to the Roshonara Club to play badminton and drink lemonade. They would bring her back in the family car quite punctually at whatever hour Aunt Mira had stipulated. Only now Aunt Mira seldom managed to stay up so long. For a while she would sit hunched on the cane chair, inspecting with narrowed eyes her cheesy, blue-nailed hands through which thick veins twisted like green worms, then begin to shiver and to mutter to herself as Bim watched her out of the corner of her eye from Raja's bedside, and then she would be seen—and heard—to go stumbling down the veranda to her own room and vanish into her bed. Bim was perturbed but far too busy with Raja to think much about Aunt Mira. Sometimes, when she went into the dining room for dinner and found neither Tara nor her aunt at the table, their plates turned upside down and waiting on the tablecloth, she frowned and went down to Aunt Mira's room to implore her to come and eat a little. The meals on the table did not look appealing but they had to be eaten all the same, Bim thought. But Aunt Mira, huddling under her blanket— why a blanket in the middle of summer? It was crazy—shook her head and smiled with her lower lip hanging loosely and gleaming wet in the dark. There was a strange smell in the closed, stuffy room. Bim wrinkled up her nose. She went and sat on the veranda, waiting up for Tara in place of her aunt.

Baba sat there, on the veranda steps, beside a pot of petunias that flowered now in the dark with a kind of lunar luminosity, giving out a maidenly white scent that made one soon feel cooler, calmer. Baba's presence, too, was so much less than a presence, that it could not intrude or chafe. He did not turn to Bim or speak. He had his handful of pebbles that Aunt Mira had given him years ago and with which he played perpetually so that they were quite smooth and round from use. Everyone in the household knew the sound they made as he scattered them across the tiles with a little, quiet unfolding gesture of his hand, then gathered them up again with that curiously remote and peaceful smile on his thin face. It was the sound of the house, as much as the contented muttering of the pigeons in the veranda. It gave time a continuity and regularity that the ticking of a clock in the hall might convey in other homes. Bim was at times grateful for it and at times irritated beyond endurance by it, just as one might be by the perpetual sameness of clock hands.

"Tara's late," Bim said to him, to herself, sighing.

Baba smiled vaguely but not quite in her direction and jiggled the pebbles in his fist for a moment before he let them fall again. Bim had to set her jaw firmly to keep from rebuking him for the clatter. Leaning back in her broken basket chair, she kept her eyes on the gate at the end of the drive, worriedly. The street lamp shone on it without illuminating it, it was so dim and the air so dusty. She knew Tara could come to no harm—harm was beyond Tara's childish capacity. Yet she was uneasy for unease was in the air like a swarm of germs, an incipient disease. The empty house across the road breathed it at them. Its emptiness and darkness was a warning, a threat perhaps.

Bim wondered at Tara going again and again to visit the Misra sisters. All through their school years they had chafed at this too close relationship with girls they considered dull and conservative. But they were neighbours and so had had to cycle to school together—it was considered safer for four girls to bicycle together than for two groups of two girls—and sometimes do their homework together in the evenings or crawl through the hedge between the two gardens to borrow a book or get some sewing done by the many and useful aunts in the Misra household. Yet they had always regarded—or at least Bim had—the Misra girls as too boring to be cultivated. They had also been more than a little nervous of the Misra boys who had been merely rough and loud-mouthed as children but, when they grew older, with bristly jaws and swelling thighs and bellies, ran their eyes over the girls in a smiling, appraising way that made them shiver as horses do when flies settle. When Bim finished with school and went to college, she was relieved that the Misra girls did not follow; they stayed home to help their mother and aunts with the housekeeping and await marriages to be arranged for them. Then Tara took to visiting them on her own, almost every evening. "D'you think I could have mother's bracelet to wear, Bim?" she would ask before leaving, or "Can I have your white Lucknow[4] sari just for today, Bim? They're taking me to the club."

When Tara did appear in the pool of green, insect-fretted light at the gate, she was not alone. Bim had known, in those bones that jarred every time Baba threw his pebbles across the tiles, that she would have someone with her when she came. Here he was.

"This is Bakul," Tara told her in an almost inaudible murmur, turning their mother's bracelet about her wrist, round and round and round. "The Misras—the Misras—" she stammered, "took us to the Roshonara Club. There was a dance."

While she stammered and Bakul tried gallantly to help with some more polished and assured phrases that he slipped in with a self-assurance that filled in the gaps left by Tara and even propped up the little that she managed to say, coolly and powerfully, Aunt Mira came out of her room to stare. "This is my aunt," whispered Tara, dropping her eyes so as not to have to see the way Aunt Mira's mouth twitched and a nerve jumped in her cheek, making her left eye flicker, and Bakul said at once "I came to ask if Tara may come to a party at my house tomorrow. My sisters are

---

4. A north Indian city famous for a special type of embroidery on fine cotton cloth.

giving a party and the Misra girls are coming. They could bring Tara with them—with your permission." He actually made a little bow when he said this, and aunt and sister regarded him with astonishment that made the aunt's face twitch and flicker and jerk and the sister's face solidify into stone. They might have stared in this fashion if a young prince had ridden up on horseback to sweep Tara up onto the saddle and away. This wonderfully good-looking, well-groomed, well-spoken young man who had arrived on their doorstep with Tara was just such an apparition to them— unexpected, unsought, and yet exactly what they would have sought for Tara, expected for Tara if they had sought, or expected. Suddenly they did.

"Yes, she may go," Bim said slowly. "Can't she, Mira-*masi?*" she demanded of her aunt.

Aunt Mira, nodding frantically, looked for a moment or two as if she would come sweeping across the veranda and fall upon Bakul, hold him fast for her niece before he had time to flee. Instead, to Tara's relief, she teetered upon her toes, swung around and dived back into her room, leaving Bim to give Bakul sober directions about when to send Tara home. After Bakul had promised and left, she went in to see Aunt Mira for a moment and was so engrossed in this new prospect with which Tara had presented them that she didn't notice, or remark on, her aunt hastily pouring a drink into her tumbler from a familiar looking bottle on her cupboard shelf, and only said "Mira-*masi,* do you think he will want to marry Tara?"

"Yes," said Aunt Mira with a loud hiccup. "Yes, yes, I do," and she dipped her face into the tumbler and drank, agitatedly, as if to hide from the intolerable prospect.

The prospect was entirely Bim's to survey.

Their father had died suddenly. On his way back from the club one night, the car had bumped slightly against the curb of a traffic roundabout on a deserted street on the Ridge. The slight bump had caused the door to fly open and the father to be flung out. He was dead, of a broken neck, when the driver stopped the car and ran out to him. There was no damage to the car at all. It could scarcely be called an accident, so minor was it in appearance, and harmless, but of course that was the only label that fitted, and it was fatal. Dressed in his usual dark suit for the club, with a white handkerchief and a cigar in his breast pocket, he seemed prepared for death as if it were an evening at the club.

Few of the people, mostly club members and bridge players, who came to condole, realised how little difference his death made to the household—they were so accustomed to his absence that it was but a small transition from the temporary to the permanent.

Also, he left so little behind. A wardrobe full of very dark and sombre suits and very white and crisp shirts, a shelf ranged with shoes—all old but polished to the glow of wood, walnut, mahogany or black lacquer—and a desk piled with office files: that was all. He had even just come to the end of his stock of cigars, as if he had prepared for his accidental end. There was not one left for his son to try if he wanted, or to give his room a familiar whiff that might linger.

For a while all that disturbed the children was the continuous presence of the car in the garage—it made them uneasy. They were simply not used to seeing it so much at home. When would it leave—for the club? for the office? Why did it not go? The driver, a surly man who seldom spoke a word, sat on his haunches by the garage door, sometimes smoking and staring over the caps of his knees, and sometimes just staring. Made nervous by their perpetual presence in the back yard, Bim told Raja they must decide on what to do about it. Raja simply telephoned a garage owner, whose son he knew at college, and sold him the car at the very first price he offered. It was taken off to the garage the very next day, leaving the driver still sitting on his haunches by the garage door, looking more surly and more vacant than before.

For a while Bim dreaded seeing the car on the road, passing her by on her way to college. She knew she would strain to see the familiar figures in it, and knew it would be a blow to find unfamiliar ones instead. But she did not. The car was too old and too large to be in demand any more, and it simply rotted in the junk yard behind the garage—Bim often saw it from the No. 9 bus window—till only a rusted skeleton was left.

The driver, after waiting a while as if in expectation of the car being returned to him, finally got to his feet and began to help the gardener by mending his hose pipe and oiling his shears while Bim wondered what to do. Then this problem, too, was resolved quite simply and accidentally: the gardener was called home to his village since his elder brother had died and he was required to work on the farm, and the driver moved in to take his place. That was all.

The garage door remained shut on the cobwebs, the oil stains and the empty tin cans.

The effect of this death in the family then, was pecuniary only, for the father had been, if nothing else, a provider.

When his junior partner at the insurance firm came to call on the family after the cremation—attended largely by the office staff and bridge players distinguished by their age, apparel and complexion—even Raja got himself out of bed and came to the drawing room in his pyjamas. The drawing room was as still and petrified as in their parents' lifetime—the card table ready in the corner, the brass pot filled with spotted cannas from the garden, the thick red curtains and red carpets and red rexine[5] sofas all emitting a faint pall of dust that seemed to stifle anyone who entered as if it were a vault containing the mortal remains of the departed.

Raja was feverish—he had been to the cremation at the height of the afternoon to light his father's funeral pyre: it was what he had to do[6]—and he spoke rapidly, gesturing with his hands which had grown very long and thin and artistic after so many months of fever.

---

5. A sturdy plastic.   6. In the Hindu tradition it is the duty of the eldest son to light the pyre at his parents' cremations.

"No, I don't care what my father has written in his will—I don't want to be a partner. I won't have anything to do with it—I'm not a business-man—I'm—"

"Raja," Bim burst out in agitation, "do *think*—"

"Bim, I know what I'm saying," he snapped at her, tossing back the hair that had grown so long and lanky from his moist forehead. "I know what I'm doing. Baba can take whatever position father meant for me—"

"Baba? What are you talking about? You know Baba," Bim cried out in disbelief. "You are making fun of him, very cruelly, Raja, if you want to send him to the office—"

"No, no, no, that is not necessary at all," the young man from the office soothed her, perching on the edge of the sofa like a teetering pigeon and making not dissimilar sounds of solace. "Not necessary at all. You know, your father himself was not at all concerned with the day-to-day adminis-tration—he left it all to me and to the staff. We can manage all that. All we need is the name, the signature—the name must remain, for the firm, that is all."

"Oh, is that all?" said Bim, and Raja looked at her in triumph.

"You see," he told her, "that is all. Don't you think Baba can manage that much? Just signing papers?"

"No, he can't," Bim said more sharply. "But *you* can."

"Nonsense. I'll speak to Baba—I'll explain to him. He can go to the office for an hour or two—and then—Mr. Sharma will help him. Don't baby him, Bim, you treat him like a baby—"

"What else can I do?" she flared up, furious with Raja for talking so carelessly, with such cynical thoughtlessness, and furious with Mr. Sharma for listening.

"Let him grow up, let him take a little responsibility. Give him a simple task or two to perform. See if he can't manage."

"And if he can't—what then?"

"Then," said Mr. Sharma, giving a little bounce on the sofa to attract their attention and distract them from their quarrel, "then I shall manage. I can bring the files here to the house for you to see—"

"You do that, Mr. Sharma," Raja said hurriedly. "Yes, you do that. What a good idea. And Baba and I will sign whatever you ask us to—"

"Raja," Bim warned him again; her face looked thin and elderly with warning.

Mr. Sharma smiled at her reassuringly. "It is what your father did also in these last years. It is all he did. The work was left to the clerks and myself. We will manage—you will have no worries."

"Then that's all right," Raja said with relief and stood up to go back to bed while Mr. Sharma hurried away, explaining he had to get back before the curfew.

When Bim went in to take Raja's temperature and see that he was quiet again, he said "It's nothing to worry about, see, Bim. These aren't the things to worry about in life."

"No?" she said shortly as she shook down the thermometer with a pro-fessional air. "What do *you* worry about then?"

"Oh Bim, Bim," he said, dramatically gesturing towards the door that opened out into the thick, dusty twilight. "Look there—look," he said, "the city's burning down. Delhi is being destroyed. The whole country is split up and everyone's become a refugee. Our friends have been driven away, perhaps killed. And you ask me to worry about a few cheques and files in father's office."

"No, that's only for me to worry about," said Bim, as dour as her father, as their house, popping the thermometer into his mouth. "That, and the rent to be paid on the house, and five, six, seven people to be fed every day, and Tara to be married off, and Baba to be taken care of for the rest of his life, and you to be got well again—and I don't know what else."

Raja sputtered a bit and the thermometer wobbled between his lips so that she had to snap "Don't talk."

That day Bim was so disturbed, so little reassured by Raja's argument, that when the doctor came to visit him in the evening, she did not simply shove the temperature chart at him and ask for a new prescription but actually invited him to sit down with her on the veranda before he left.

"How much longer do you think it will be before he begins to get better?" she asked him.

The doctor, a soft-spoken and awkward young Bengali sent them by their father's partner and not unlike him—they both went to the Ramakrishna Mission[7] for the lectures and the hymn singing—was so taken aback by her unusual invitation to sit down and talk that his knees gave way and he collapsed onto the creaking cane sofa weakly, then took a few minutes to understand what she had asked him and to notice that her face was drawn and colourless and that her lank, untidy hair had a distinct streak of grey in it, just over her left ear. It seemed to him at least twenty years too early for such an occurrence, and he was shocked. In his family the women washed their hair with *shikakai*[8] solution and oiled it with coconut oil every morning so that at forty, at fifty even, their hair was black and glossy as a newly-opened tin of shoe polish. His mouth was a little open as he stared.

Then, in a concerned voice, he urged, "You mustn't worry so much, Miss Das. It is a very mild attack of t.b. These days we can control t.b. with drugs, quite effectively, yes. The drugs, combined with good nursing and good diet, will cure him, yes. Only it will take time, yes. One has to have patience also—"

"How much time?" Bim persisted. "You know, my father—" she began, then stopped short, wondering how she had let herself go to such an extent. The young doctor's face, his posture—clutching the bag set on his knees neatly placed together but every now and then giving an uncontrollable twitch or jerk—were the face and the posture of all nonentities, people seen in a bus queue, bending over a table in a tea-shop, huddled in a suburban train, at desks in cluttered offices or at counters in crowded shops: anxious, fretting, conscious of failing, of not managing, and trying only not to let it show. He had nothing to give her. Why did she ask?

7. A social service and religious organization founded in 1897 by Hindu social reformer and spiritual leader Swami Vivekananda (1863–1902) to honor and propagate the teachings of his teacher, the mystic Ramakrishna (1836–1886).   8. A nut. A shampoo is made from the powdered nut.

"I know, I know," the young doctor stammered urgently, shyly. "He has passed away. I am so—so sorry. I came to the—the ceremony. You did not see me. I was with Mr. Sharma—"

"I know," Bim broke in abruptly, untruthfully. "Will you have a cup of tea?"

"Yes," gasped the young man, as much to his own surprise as to Bim's.

Bim went down the veranda and called "Mira-*masi*, send some tea for the doctor, will you? Tell Janaki to make tea for the doctor." Aunt Mira gave an agitated cry in her room and Bim came back to the circle of cane chairs and sat down.

"I see, I see it all," Dr. Biswas hurried on, staring hard at his shoes, making the most of this unusual burst of courage while it lasted. "There are great problems. Your father—the house—the family—Raja's illness— it is all too much for a young lady. Raja must recover, he must take his father's place—"

Bim gave a laugh, or a snort. An ugly sound that stopped him short. In the sudden silence they heard a handful of pebbles fall with a clatter on the veranda steps, making them aware, too, of Baba's presence. The doctor had not mentioned Baba. Now they both breathed heavily, adding Baba to his list.

"Father's place?" Bim mocked, and then stopped: she would not reveal more. The hedges round the garden grew high—to hide, to conceal. She would not cut them short, or reveal. She got up impatiently, restlessly, and went down to the kitchen to call Janaki herself, knowing that Aunt Mira had done nothing about the tea. Janaki gave her a surly look from the yellow smoke she was stirring up out of the coal fire. Bim glared back. Eventually the tea appeared on a brass tray that had not been polished for years.

The doctor's bag fell down as he rose with a jerk to accept the cup of tea. He held the cup in one hand, picked up the bag with the other, spilling tea as he did so. Then there was the need to keep his knees together. To be positive and reassuring. To calm himself, he stirred and stirred the tea with a loud spoon. Then he looked up at Bim with timid respect. "I see how it is," he said, wanting her also to see that he saw. "I see what a difficult position—I mean, for you—the problems—"

"No, no, what problems," blustered Bim, wanting to clear him out now, be on her own again. "Baba," she shouted, "d'you want tea? Sugar?"

"I think I may reassure you on one point at least—Raja *will* get well."

Bim gave him a quick look to see if he was being honest, or only kind. He had a very honest face, she decided, painfully honest, like a peeled vegetable. But it was also kind, dreadfully kind. She sighed "Are you sure? You don't think we will have to send him to hospital, or to a sanatorium?"

Dr. Biswas stirred and stirred his tea with a crazy clatter, frowning with concentration, making the spoon spin round and round the cup like some mechanism gone out of control. Then he stopped it with his little finger very abruptly so that the tea sloshed over the rim into the saucer. "Let us say," he said, staring at the puddle of spilt tea, "that it is not necessary *now* because there has been no deterioration. If the position remains stable, then once the cool weather starts, I feel his health will begin to pick up, he will regain his strength. He should show improvement in the winter. If *not*—if *not*," he repeated, with renewed agitation making the teaspoon tremble, the cup wobble, the puddle slop, "then, at the end of the winter, when it is no longer cold, we might send him to a sanatorium—in Kasauli, or Dagshai.[9] *But*," he added desperately, tearing his mind away from such a possibility and looking up at her with remorse, "I have no doubt, *no* doubt, it will *not* be necessary, he will improve—"

But Bim, although she nodded, looked doubtful again, and unsure. Having failed in his effort to reassure her, Dr. Biswas raised the cup to his mouth at last and drank the cold tea in one gulp while the cup dripped down onto his knees, and then rose to leave, realising he had not given her what she needed, had not been up to it. As usual, he had not been up to it. The look of failure overcame the look of anxiety.

When Tara came home with Bakul, she found Bim alone in the veranda, her face so grey and old that the glow went out of Tara's and she, too, became subdued.

Bakul did not notice and sat down to chat with the sisters with that bland oil of self-confidence smoothing his voice and giving it a kind of calculated ease that made Tara gaze at him with maidenly admiration and made Bim look away into the shadowy garden in boredom. It was the opposite of poor Dr. Biswas's tone: then why did they equally bore her, she wondered as she watched Aunt Mira's cat stealing past the flowerpots, stalking something in the tall grass that edged the ill-kept lawn. A cloud of mosquitoes followed her, hovering over her flattened head and the two pointed ears, like a filmy parasol. Bim watched her, her chin cupped in her hand. She was the only thing that moved in the stiff, desiccated garden which, at that time, lay between two gardeners, in transition.

Bakul had just said something that she had failed to hear—the cat had at that instance pounced on a stalk of grass and a purple moth had fluttered up out of reach, exquisitely in time.

"Bim," Tara said, perturbed by such absent-mindedness, "Bakul's posting has just come through."

Was that what he had said? Bim turned to look at them, smiling at each other.

"Tell her, Bakul," Tara urged, now that Bim's attention was drawn to them even if her look were tired and not interested enough to really do Bakul justice.

"I have been told to proceed to Ceylon," Bakul told her, somewhat smugly, she thought. "Of course it isn't the country of my choice, but it's to be only while I am in training. After a year, I expect to be sent to the West since I specialised in European languages and asked for a posting in Western Europe. That was my first preference—not Ceylon."

"Ceylon?" Bim responded at last, slowly and quite dreamily, Tara thought, as if it aroused romantic, scented pictures in her mind as it did in Tara's. But all she said was "That will be interesting."

"Exactly. That is what I told Tara," he said gaily, still not noticing Bim's

9. Hill resort towns near Simla in north India.

abstraction, her preoccupation. He smiled at Tara sitting beside her sister and tensely watching her, watching him, and Tara smiled back. Bim gazed at them, at their happiness, as if she were seeing it through a gauze screen, vaguely, not clearly.

"Bakul," she said with sudden crispness, "what is happening?"

"Happening?" he asked, turning his handsome profile to look directly at her. "But I was expecting it any day—it is the foreign service after all— I had told Tara—"

"No, no, no. I mean, in New Delhi."

"In New Delhi?"

"Yes, yes," she said impatiently. "I mean—about Independence—about Pakistan—"

"Oh," he said. "Well, we are all waiting—for the date to be set—for partition, for independence. It will come any day now."

"And then?"

"And then there will be trouble," he said simply, not liking to dramatize a situation that he himself feared. "But you needn't worry. All steps are being taken to carry out partition smoothly, we hope safely. Refugee camps are being formed. Special trains are being arranged. The police, the army—all are alerted. Anyway, you will be quite safe here, outside the city walls. There won't be riots here, and the Muslims who live here—"

"Yes, exactly—I'm worried about them. So is Raja. Our neighbours, you know, the Hyder Alis, they have disappeared."

"Most of them have already left. They have acted quickly, wisely. The Hyder Alis must have done that."

"But they must still be in the country, somewhere. What will happen to them?"

"They will have police protection. They can go to the refugee camps. It is all arranged."

Bim shook her head and was silent while Bakul went on about measures taken by the government, about Mountbatten's goodwill and integrity, about Nehru's idealism and integrity, about Jinnah and Pakistan—but Bim felt she was listening to banal newspaper articles being read aloud and she brushed her hand across her forehead and got up. "I'll go and tell Raja what you say," she said. "He keeps asking for news—he's anxious about the Hyder Alis."

Bakul instantly got up. "You must tell him there is no need," he said. "Please tell him I will go back and make enquiries about them and will see to it personally that they are not harmed."

"We don't even know where they are," Bim said, giving him an ironical look as she walked away, and Bakul looked puzzled for a moment. He wondered if he had been snubbed—Bim did have such discouraging ways. He was a very junior servant in the foreign service, it was true. In fact, he was still in training. He did not really know what was to be done. Still, he did like everyone to think he did.

So he sat down again beside Tara and picked up her hand and squeezed it lightly. To Tara he could speak in a different tone. From Tara he got a different response. He smiled at her fondly, like an indulgent father. She smiled back gratefully—she had not had an indulgent father, after all. She wore a white *chameli*[1] flower in her hair. She was very like it herself. He told her so.

"I must take you with me, Tara," he said softly. "This place is bad for you—so much sickness, so many worries. You are too young for all this. I must take you away."

There was rioting all through the country and slaughter on both sides of the new border when a letter came from Hyder Ali. Bim ran into the room when Raja called, loudly and excitedly. "Raja, don't roar," she panted, "it's bad for you. Dr. Biswas said—"

"Bim," he shouted, sitting up in bed, with his hair grown long and wild about his flushed face. "Look, a letter from Hyder Ali Sahib!"

She gave a shiver as at a touch of ice. Raja's anxiety had transferred itself to her, kept her awake nights: both had wondered if the Hyder Alis were not dead, murdered while trying to escape to Pakistan.

"Where are they, Raja?"

"In Hyderabad—quite safe. In Hyder Ali Sahib's home—his mother lives there, and his sister. They're all safe. He says there is no trouble in Hyderabad. They are in hiding, but they are safe and well, and they even found a friend to post this letter to me. Bim," he said joyfully, "wasn't it good of Hyder Ali Sahib to write to me? To *me?* He even says Benazir sends her best wishes." He handed Bim the letter to share the joy of it with her. She sat on the edge of his bed, reading, and laughing with relief, relief as much for his sake as for theirs.

It seemed the evening light that came in that day was softer, milder, not so lurid. They listened to the mynahs chattering on the lawn, to Baba playing with his pebbles on the steps, and looked at each other in relief and joy. Raja, sitting upright in bed, looked as if he were going to get well.

"I wonder how they did the journey—he doesn't say."

"Of course not—he can't—it's not safe to. Only I wish he had told me— he could have trusted me—"

"How could he, Raja? With a plainclothes policeman posted at our gate? And the sort of friends you picked up at college?"

"They weren't my friends—they were traitors. And he should have known I was never one of them."

"He knew—that's why he has written to you."

"Look, Bim, he has asked me to look up the house—see what has happened to it. Will you do that for me?"

"Of course," said Bim, springing up. "Has he left anything there? Does he want me to see if they're safe?" and when Raja said there were no instructions, nothing specific, she went instantly, calling to Baba to put his pebbles away and come with her. They crossed the road together, her hand on his elbow, to the house that had stood silent and dark across from them for weeks now.

Lifting the catch of the gate and letting it down again as they entered the garden, Baba turned as if to go back, then drew closer to Bim and although

---

1. A variety of jasmine with a delicate scent.

she gave him a little encouraging push, she was affected by his unwilling-ness nevertheless. It was as if they had walked into a cobweb—they could feel it on their faces, a clinging, slightly moist net which they brushed at with ineffectual fingers.

The house was so strangely unlit and deserted as it had never been for as long as they had known it—like a body whose life and warmth they were accustomed to and took for granted, now grown cold and stiff and faded. It looked accusing, too, as if it held them responsible. The envied roses still bloomed in the formal beds of precise geometrical shapes but their petals lay scattered and unswept: even the gardeners had gone. Ripe fruit had fallen to the ground beneath the trees along the drive, ripe man-goes and guavas, and lay there rotting, touched by a few birds and then left, mutilated. A long-tailed hornbill swooped out of the tall jacaranda tree by the porch and gave a harsh, croaking cry as it rattled through the air into the trees by the drive, making Baba raise his arm to protect his face, and duck. But Bim held his hand and led him on.

The fanlight above the door, glowing in the orange evening light, deceived them for an instant into thinking there was a light on in the hall. But when they pushed open the door by its painted porcelain handle and went in, the bulb inside the pendulous glass globe was unlit and there was nothing there but a hatstand with its many extended hooks, empty, and a wilting potted plant.

All the rooms were unnaturally enlarged by emptiness for all the small objects of ornament and comfort had been taken away and only the large pieces of furniture left, ornate and heavily carved sofas and marble-topped tables that, stripped of cushions and vases and silver boxes and coloured glassware, sulked and looked as accusing as abandoned husbands in the gloom. The squares and oblongs on the walls from which pictures had been removed were marked by brown rims of grime.

They walked down the tiled passages, opening frosted glass-paned doors to the left and right, peering in, half-expecting to find someone left behind—perhaps an old sick aunt with embroidery spools heaped on her lap and fluttering a ghostly fan, or the kittens Benazir used to play with and cuddle. But there was no one there. A mirror on the wall flashed a blank, empty glare at them—the heathen, unwanted. At the library door Bim hesitated with her hand on the glass knob, wanting intensely to go in and see this room that Raja had for years regarded as his own retreat, his spiritual home, and somehow not daring to violate what he had kept scrupulously private. Would the books still be there? she wondered. She walked past without looking to see—some day Raja could come here about them.

Only in Benazir's room there was still a childish, girlish debris strewn across the heavy, carved bed—bits of ribbon and lace, pictures cut out of illustrated magazines, a little velvet bag with gold tassels. Bim curled her lip: Benazir was untidy, she noted, a spoilt only child. "Can't I take them with me?" she seemed to hear the pouting voice. "Oh why can't I?" Con-temptuously, Bim tried to sweep everything into a heap, tidy up.

Baba had been silent all through this ghostly tour, keeping close to her except when she made some small, nervous comment, when he gave a start and jumped away from her. Now he pointed his finger and made a little desperate sound like a bell that won't ring when pressed. Bim looked. "What?" she asked, "that?" Baba nodded, and she went with him to a corner where an old-fashioned His Master's Voice gramophone stood on a small three-legged table, on the lower shelf of which were stacked the records Benazir and her friends had listened to, in the afternoons when her father was out and her mother asleep and not likely to hear the profane sounds so unlike the music the family enjoyed under the drawing room chandelier or in the flowering summer garden. Bim shuffled through them out of curiosity—it amused her to think of a scholar poet's daughter listening to these American foxtrots and quicksteps that the World War and the American GIs and British Tommies had brought to India. What would Raja think of her taste?

"Come, let's go," said Bim, turning away. "Let's go and look in the servants' quarters—there may be someone there." But Baba would not go. He stood there fingering the smooth shining metal gadgetry in the green box, his long fingers closing about the curved silver horn, admiringly, lovingly. "Come, Baba, come," Bim said several times, more and more impatiently, but he was smiling to himself, quite deaf and unresponsive in the enclosed bubble of his dream, till she said angrily "Then I'm going alone," whereupon he reluctantly let down the lid, closing the box with a gentle creak, and followed her, dragging his foot and looking whipped so that she said in exasperation "If you want it, I suppose there's nothing to stop you taking it. But first let's go and see if there's anyone outside, at the back, whom we can ask." He raised his chin and gave her a shy, fearful look of hope then and followed her more willingly.

As they entered the dark, cavernous kitchen at the back, packed full of the smell of coal and smoke, and stained and blotched with the signs of many feasts and much drudgery, they heard a whine. They opened cupboards and looked into coal holes but could find nothing. Then they opened the door onto the back veranda and there, behind the woodbox, found the dog that whined so pathetically, in such a shrunken, faded voice. It was Hyder Ali's dog, they had not been able to take her with them. Exceptionally sweet and gentle of face, with long, drooping ears and hopeful, tearful eyes that gazed at the visitors in fear, she thumped her long tail in tentative greeting.

"It's Begum," cried Bim in an outburst of relief at seeing something alive in this deserted house. She patted the overcome creature in pity and reassurance while Baba knelt on the ground, fondling her, clasping her dribbling mouth to his chest in gentle protectiveness. "We'll have to take her back with us or she'll starve," Bim said, and Baba lowered his face to the dog's brow and kissed it in gratitude.

Their voices and the ecstatic whining of the half-starved creature did flush someone out of the servants' quarters. At first they were only aware of someone peeping out from the cracks of a heavily barred wooden door but obviously their features and their behaviour were not intimidating to the owner of the eyes for after a moment the door creaked open and one of Hyder Ali's old servants, the groom who had looked after Hyder Ali's white mare, came sidling out. He salaamed[2] extravagantly as Bim cried out in surprise, then whispered "Please don't speak so loudly. People may come. They may call the police. I will be taken to jail—"

"Why?" asked Bim, puzzled. She hated the way the man cringed although the cringing of the dog had only aroused compassion. "What have you done?" she asked coldly. "You haven't murdered the Hyder Ali family, have you?"

The poor man nearly screamed in terror and his eyes flashed to the left and to the right as if he expected the police to fall out of the guava trees or bound out of the well. "They will take me to jail and question me," he hissed. "They will torture me till I speak. That is what they do—I have heard."

"But why? What information have you got?"

"None, none at all," whined the man, striking his head. "Hyder Ali Sahib packed and left so quietly—his friends came to help, sent them cars to take them to the station, and armed guards too. But they did not tell me where they were going. The police will want to know. They will ask. They will think I helped them to escape—"

"Escape?" Bim said scornfully. "What do you mean, escape? They have every right to leave their house in Delhi and go and live in their house in Hyderabad. If they took their belongings with them, well, they were *their* belongings, it's not theft."

"Ah, but they were Muslims," wailed the old man, doubling up in front of her and swaying nearly to the ground. "We should not have allowed them to go."

"You had better go away," Bim told him in disgust. "You had better go to your village. Did Hyder Ali Sahib leave you any money?"

"Yes, yes, Hyder Ali Sahib was always good to me—Muslim though he was. May God keep him—his God and ours. But how can I travel? These are bad times, murderers and thugs are everywhere, and if I meet anyone who knew I worked for Muslims, I will be—" he drew his finger across his throat and rolled his eyes.

"Then you had better come to our house. Janaki will give you a bed—you can stay till it is safe for you to go home." Then, when he looked as if he would really grovel at her feet, she said sharply "And where is Hyder Ali Sahib's horse?"

He straightened up then and babbled quickly "Oh, Hyder Ali Sahib gave her away to Lala Ram Narain who helped them to pack and leave. He tried to send Begum also, but Begum would not leave the compound—she lay on the ground and would not let anyone touch her. She tried to bite me—see." He began to roll up his sleeve to show them.

"Then Begum must come with us," said Bim and whistled to the dog who crawled after them on bent legs as they walked round to the front of the house, the old man hobbling after them, his sleeve rolled back and his arm still extended as if to show them the bite, or to beg. When Bim went up the steps to the front door to make sure it was shut, Baba suddenly

---

2. Made a gesture of respect in the traditional Muslim style.

darted past her and disappeared into the house. She stopped to wait for him, wondering at the unusual decisiveness of his movements, and in a little while he came out, staggering under the weight of the gramophone that he carried in his arms, carefully balancing the stack of records on top of it.

"Oh Baba," she grumbled, helping him by taking the records off and carrying them for him. "Do you have to have this stupid old thing? I don't suppose it matters," she added as she saw Baba's face fall. "Benazir can always write and ask for it when she wants it. Come, Begum, come," she called encouragingly to the dog who hung back at the gate, not quite knowing how to act, equally reluctant to abandon her home and to give up these newly-found protectors. Finally she followed them across the road and into their own garden, growing more animated and more upright as she realised she was welcome here.

Raja was waiting for them on the veranda. Bim ran forward, crying "Raja, why didn't you wait in bed? Go to bed at once. I'll come and tell you all about it as soon as I've found a quarter for Bhakta here and some food for Begum—they're all we found in the house. It's quite empty. And oh, this gramophone."

"Benazir's gramophone," Raja said in astonishment at the sight of Baba so carefully and proudly carrying in his treasure. "And records—she used to play those records when her friends came. I used to see them dancing together in her room on my way to the library."

"She won't mind Baba having it, will she? You can write and tell her about it. But go to bed now, and I'll go and ask Mira-*masi* what to do about Bhakta, and the poor dog—"

"That's what I wanted to tell you, Bim," Raja said, soberly. "You'd better go and see Mira-*masi*, she doesn't seem very well."

"No?" said Bim in surprise, stopping short on her way to the kitchen, and then turned and flew down the veranda to her aunt's room, fear thudding hard at her side.

Raja had bolted the door on the outside. Drawing back the bolt, Bim threw open the door, then quickly shut it behind her so that no one should come in, for Aunt Mira was in a disgraceful state, a state no one should see her in. She had clawed off her clothes from her body so that her blouse hung in strips from the little shrivelled flaps of her blue-veined breasts and her sari trailed behind her on the floor as she lurched about the room in a kind of halting dance, her feet getting tangled in the torn muslin that lay everywhere, her one hand jerking at her side while the other held onto a glass of what smelt unmistakably like raw, undiluted liquor. Yes, there was the brandy bottle, nearly empty, on the floor by her bed. Bim rushed towards her aunt with her arms outstretched to catch her and enclose her and hold her, but Aunt Mira stepped aside as lightly as a nimble old goat and, making a comical face at Bim's dismay, sang out in a quavering trill:

"Said the night-in-gale to the ro-o-ose,"

when her feet caught in a loop of trailing muslin, she stumbled and knocked over the bottle that fell with a clatter and spilt out its reeking liquid. Seeing it leak and spread about her feet, soaking the shed clothes, Aunt Mira stopped in mid-song, clutched her throat, gave a little choked cry and sank onto her bed, whimpering soggily. Her cat, sitting on the edge with her paws tucked neatly together as if into a white muff, watched her with huge eyes of amber slit with black—shocked and disdainful.

Next door, in Baba's room, a strange rasping roar started out of the stillness, grew louder like a train approaching through a tunnel, and emerged, not in a whistle, but in a woman's voice smokily wailing:

"Underneath the lamp-post . . ."

Life spread in a pool around her, low and bright, lapping at her feet, but then quickly, treacherously rising to her ankles, to her knees. She had to get out of it. She had to lift herself out before it rose to her waist, to her armpits. If only they had not wrapped her in those long swaddlings as if she was a baby, or a mummy—these long strips that went round and round her, slipping over her eyes, crossing over her nose, making her breath stop so that she had to gasp and clutch and tear—

Not to panic, not to panic, she whispered to herself. It is a pool, it must not spread. Gather it, contain it. Here, in this bottle. A tall, fine bottle. She had it by its neck, her fingers went round it—almost around it, not quite—but she could, could grasp it—just. She would contain it. Pour it into a glass. See, how it trickled in, colourless, but she could feel it, smell it: it was real, she had not imagined it. When she lowered her mouth to the rim, it leapt up to meet her, went scorching up her nostrils and burning down her throat, leaving it raw and bleeding. She drew back in fright, her eyes leapt quickly in and out of their red sockets.

That was the way life was: it lay so quiet, so still that you put your fingers out to touch it, stroke it. Then it leapt up and struck you full in the face so that you spun about and spun about, gasping. The flames leapt up all around, rising by inches every minute, rising in rings.

At first they had been only little flames, so pretty in the dark. So many candles at a celebration, a festival. She would hear their voices ringing, as pure as glass, or flame. Raja and Bim, tall and straight and true, their voices ringing out: "I will be a hero," one had called out from the pure white peak of a candle flame, and the other had echoed back, as in a song, "And I will be a heroine." But then they had shot up into such tall, towering flames, crackling and spitting, making her shut her eyes and cower. Down at her knees the little Tara whimpered "*Masi*, they say I'm silly. *Masi*, they called me a fool." The child's fingers stuck to her, waxy and white, and the flames crackled up above them, taller and fiercer every minute. When she put out her hands to stop them, the flames pricked her like pins, drawing out beads of blood so that she dropped her hands with a cry and backed away from them. This made them jump higher. They grew taller and taller.

They cast huge shadows on the walls around her. White walls, livid shadows, lurching from side to side. "Bim and Raja," she called desperately, "stop it, stop it!" But the shadows did not listen. The shadows lurched towards her, and the flames leapt higher to meet them. Flames and shadows of flames, they advanced on each other, they merged with each other and she was caught between them, helpless as a splinter, a scrap of paper.

She could not manage them, she could not cope—they were too big for her, too hot and fierce and frightening. It was no good petting, consoling—they did not listen. They made such harsh, piercing sounds in her ears. She wished they would stop, it hurt so, it was torture. She pulled her white hair about her face, shielding herself. And some soft cloth to stop up her ears, her nose, shut herself up, hide from them. They prowled about, searching her out, menacing her. She moaned in fright. She needed protection. She wanted help. She reached out for the hand that would help her, protect her . . .

. . . Here it was. Here, in this tall, slim coolness just by her hand, at the tips of her fingers. If she got her fingers around it, its slender pale glassiness, and then drew it closer, close to her mouth, she could close her lips about it and suck, suck little, little sips, with little, little juicy sounds, and it would be so sweet, so sweet again, just as when they were little babies, little babies for her to feed, herself a little baby sucking, sucking at the little trickle of juice that came hurrying in, sliding in . . .

And she sucked and laughed and sucked and cried.

There was much for Dr. Biswas to do in their house. That summer he was summoned almost every day, if not to subdue Aunt Mira and put her somehow to sleep so that she could not get at the bottle or scream and fight for it, then for Raja whose temperature remained obstinately at the same point, giving him a flushed, unnatural colour and at times raising his spirits to dangerous heights, then plunging them into the deepest gloom, neither of them governable by Bim who rushed from one room to the other in an effort to cope, always to the sound of Baba's records grinding out on the gramophone one cabaret tune after the other, relentlessly gay, unquenchably merry.

"How can you bear it?" Dr. Biswas once asked her as she stood leaning briefly against a veranda pillar, waiting for him to come out of Aunt Mira's room while trombones shrieked and saxophones howled in Baba's room, making poor Begum, who lay at Bim's feet on the top step, raise her head and gaze into Bim's face like a sick child pleading for comfort.

Bim shrugged, too tired to explain how her mind was occupied with far worse problems so that it barely registered the sounds that had become so essential to the calm rhythm and silent contentment of Baba's existence.

"You do care for music, don't you?" persisted Dr. Biswas who was always very reluctant to leave although he got no encouragement and hardly any attention from her.

"Do I?" wondered Bim. "I don't know—I seldom hear any—apart from that—" she jerked her chin slightly.

"But Miss Das, you should, you must," he pleaded seriously. "Music is one of the greatest joys we can have on earth. If one has that pleasure, then one can bear almost anything in life."

Bim at last paid him the little attention that he craved. "Yes?" she asked in slow surprise. "Does it mean that much to you?"

His eyes shone as he stood there, dark and awkward, his bag in one hand, smelling like a pharmacy. "It is almost the only pleasure I have," he assured her. "Without it, life would be too drab—it would be only drudgery. Miss Das," he added quickly, clutching his bag to him, "will you come with me to a concert on Sunday, by the Delhi Music Society in the Freemasons' Hall? They are giving a performance of Brahms and Schubert, and they really play quite well, they are not professionals, they are amateurs, but not bad—and for two hours one hears these beautiful sounds," he rushed on, sweating, "and one forgets everything—everything."

Bim studied him as if he were a curiosity in a museum. But all she said was "Sunday? No, quite impossible, doctor. I can't leave the house—" she waved her hand in a sweeping gesture, taking in one, two, three bedrooms all opening out onto the veranda where they stood, and containing their one, two, three patients. Suddenly she was struck by the humour of it—it seemed so immensely funny: her standing here with the doctor, guarding these three doors with the three patients behind them, and the doctor inviting her to a concert of eighteenth-century European music in the middle of the riot-torn city—so that she began to laugh and laugh. Collapsing against the pillar, she hung her head and rang like a bell with laughter, quite uncontrollably, making the doctor smile uneasily and then murmur good-bye and slide off sideways in a hurry.

She was still grinning to herself when Bakul brought Tara home. Tara smiled at her with the same small apprehensive smile the doctor's face had had, and then slipped up the steps and went towards her room, almost guiltily. Bakul stopped beside Bim on the steps, lighting himself a cigarette. "You find life amusing, Bim, do you?" he asked.

She placed her elbows on the balustrade, her chin on her hands, and looked down on him with her usual sardonic look. "Amusing isn't exactly the word, but interesting—interesting enough."

He sucked at his cigarette, regarding her, his eyes openly admiring her. Suddenly he took the cigarette from his lips and exclaimed "Bim, why do you have grey hair already? You're much too young for that!"

"Grey hair? Where? I don't!" She stood up straight, feeling her hair, tugging out bits to stare at down her nose. "You're making fun of me."

"No, I'm not. Look, here," he said, and touched the hair at her temple with his fingers, drawing it softly down her brow to her ear. She took the strand from him, brought it before her eyes and frowned at it.

"Yes," she said flatly, even a little proudly, perhaps. "It is grey. I didn't know."

"You have too many worries," he said.

Bim did not reply. She had already had that kind of conversation a few minutes ago and was bored with it. Bakul did always bore her: it was his smoothness of manner; there was no roughness that could catch the interest, snag it.

But he would not bore her today. "Bim," he said again with unusual suddenness, "would it add to your worries or would it lessen them if Tara married me?"

"What?" She was startled. She had still been regarding the grey hair between her fingers. Now she let it go so that it hung by her ear like a bit of pale ribbon. "Oh. Oh, I see. You want to marry Tara. Yes, I thought you did. I think she wants to marry you too."

"Yes, she says she does but wanted me to speak to you first."

"Oh, did she?" laughed Bim. "I'm head of the family now, am I? You think so, so I must be." She shrugged, looking plain again. "I don't think you need to ask anyone—except Tara. Modern times. Modern India. Independent India."

Bakul turned aside. He never liked Bim when she spoke in this manner. He liked nothing abrupt, staccato. He held out the cigarette at a slight angle from him and looked down at the dog stretched out on the step by his foot, studying a flea that crawled past her nose and his toe. "I can speak to Raja, of course, if you think I should."

"No, don't worry him," she said sharply.

"I don't like you having all the worries of the family."

"You are lessening them, aren't you, by taking Tara off my hands?"

"Will I? Or is she a help to you? In that case, I won't press her now— not till later when Raja is well and Baba settled and your aunt—"

"You'll be grey-haired yourself if you wait that long," Bim interrupted, flatly. "There's no need to wait. Do marry—quickly. But what about your parents?"

"They know Tara. They love her. And since I am to go to Ceylon shortly, they will agree to an early marriage."

"An early marriage—that is exactly what I'd like for Tara," Bim said. "It will suit her. And she will suit you. Blessings, blessings," she called lightly, and began to laugh again as she saw Tara, half-hidden behind the bamboo screen at her door, listening, waiting.

Bakul was happier now that she laughed. He waved his cigarette in the air gaily, looking lighthearted and absurdly debonair. "I'll have to buy you a bottle of Blacko for your hair, Bim," he teased. "I won't have you coming grey-haired to my wedding. Can't have such an elderly sister-in-law, I can't. You'll have to dye your hair for the wedding, Bim," and they laughed together, she tugging at the grey strand in her hair and he drawing elegant designs in the air with his cigarette.

The dog suddenly pounced upon the flea.

With Tara married and gone, Aunt Mira more and more confined to her room and secret access to the bottle and less and less sober or controlled, Baba happily watching the records turn on Benazir's old green gramophone, Bim and Raja were thrown together for company and comfort even more than at any time of their lives.

Raja was calmer now that he had regular news of the Hyder Ali family and was left alone by the college terrorists who were too occupied in arson, looting and murder in the city to come out to the quiet suburbs and persuade an erstwhile comrade made useless by illness and poetic ideas of heroism and loyalty. He spent more time in reading aloud to Bim as she sat by his bed or, when he felt well enough to be propped up, in writing Urdu verse of his own. This caused him much mental anguish and he would read out every line to Bim as he wrote it, easily grow discouraged and crumple up the papers and fling them on the floor for her to clear away. She was made shy by these verses—something in her cringed at a kind of heavy sentimentality of expression that was alien to her and also, she felt, to him, except when he chose to express himself in Urdu so that she regretted its effect on him while at the same time her admiration for him was too great to allow her to even admit it to herself. Instead, she suggested in a low voice "Why not take up a more original subject for your new poem? You know—just for the sake of—originality," and that was enough to make him tug at his hair and roar with despair.

Bim began to wish Raja would not discuss his poetry with her. Why did he not read it to Dr. Biswas, she suggested suddenly, quite surprised by the idea herself. Surely Biswas' soul was a sensitive one and would be more responsive than her own unpoetic one. "He plays the violin, you know," she informed Raja. "He told me."

"Ugh. I can imagine what it must sound like—the kind of thing that makes Begum raise her face to the sky and howl," laughed Raja, fondling the dog's muzzle that she liked to lay on Bim's foot or on the edge of his bed when she sat with them. "Can't you just imagine?" Raja pretended to sweep a bow across some violin strings. "O wine and ro-oses, O mo-on and sta-ars" he wailed, and Bim laughed.

"He plays Mozart, Raja, and Brahms, so he couldn't be so hopeless!"

"Have you ever heard him? No? Then what makes you think he could ever be a musician? He just hasn't the guts."

"He has soul, Raja—soul."

"Soul!" Raja exclaimed. "Who hasn't soul? It's guts you need—like Iqbal had. Now Iqbal said:

"O painter divine, Thy painting is still imperfect
Lying in ambush for mankind are the vagabond, the exploiter and
the monk.
In Thy universe the old order still continueth."

Nevertheless Bim suggested to Dr. Biswas that he bring his violin with him one day and play for them but this embarrassed him so much that he became quite agitated. Dropping his bag, spilling his stethoscope, he fumbled about on the floor, picked them up, mumbling "Oh no. Impossible. You won't—I can't—you don't really—it won't—no, no, no. I can't play. Miss Das, instead—I will be so honoured—will you come—can you—a concert—you will hear—it will be—I would like—"

She was so exasperated by his spinsterish nerves that she swooped down on the stethoscope that had fallen again and shoved it at him, saying angrily "All right, I'll come," which made him snap his mouth shut in astonishment so that he looked like a fish that had snapped up a hook by accident.

Raja lay back against his pillows and laughed and laughed. "That did for him," he laughed as Dr. Biswas hurried away down the drive. "Oh you really put the lid on him this time, Bim. That was great. Like seeing a man knocked down in the first round. You should have been a lady wrestler, Bim—you're great. Terrific. But poor Biswas. Poor Mozart. *Ach, so*

Mozart!" he wailed in tremolo, clasping his hands under his chin, and Bim, shamefaced, laughed.

"Mozart," said Dr. Biswas with great earnestness, leaning forwards with his elbows on the table on either side of a glass of beer, "when I first heard Mozart, Miss Das, I closed my eyes, and it was as if my whole past vanished, just rolled away from me—the country of my birth, my ancestors, my family, everything—and I arrived in a new world. It was a new world, a shining new world. I felt that when I heard Mozart for the first time— not when I stepped off the boat at Hamburg, or saw strange white faces and heard the strange language, or drank my first glass of beer—no. These experiences were nothing by comparison. After that there was nothing in my life—only Mozart."

"Only Mozart, hmm?" repeated Bim, thoughtfully smoking her first cigarette. It was a more complicated process than she had guessed and required more than a little attention. Also, Dr. Biswas perplexed her. She could hardly believe her ears heard right.

"That was the beginning. Then the whole world of music unfolded for me. It was lucky I went to Germany, you know, Miss Das. It is what makes the German nation great—that love, no, not just love, but a belief that music is essential, a part of one's daily life, like bread or water. Or wine. In every small village you could hear music of the highest standard, and in Berlin—ah, it was magnificent!" His eyes flashed behind his spectacles, quite electrically.

"I wonder you still had time for medicine once you were so taken up with music," said Bim, rolling the taste of tobacco on her tongue, finding it familiar, like something she had tasted before. When? And what?

"Oh, I never slept at all, in those years. No, no—there was medicine, there was music, there was the German language to be learnt, there was no time for sleep. I think I was delirious in those years. I used to walk down the broad avenues, and look at the cherry trees in bloom, and smell the lime blossom, and hear music at every street café, in every park—and, really, I was delirious. I was floating in the air in those days—floating!" He laughed and his hand trembled as he poured himself some more beer and drank. He had already had a great deal, Bim felt.

Bim stirred restlessly on the faded velvet sofa. The velvet curtains hanging beside her were so dusty, she felt she would sneeze. She felt they had been sitting here in this almost empty hall of velvet and gilt and blank-faced waiters for a very long time.

"You don't believe me," he said, his eyes fading. "I can hardly believe it myself any more. When I came back to India—to my mother and my sister and my practice here—it vanished so completely, nothing was left. It was—gone."

"But you do still play the violin, you said."

"Yes. Yes, I do. That is only an attempt to keep something of what I had in Germany in my student years—I had so much there, I was so *rich* then! Now I feel very poor, useless. I touch my violin and try to make sounds to remind me of that time. I take lessons from the first violinist of the Delhi

Music Society orchestra, and I play to myself and inflict my playing on my mother who is an old-fashioned Bengali lady and likes only Tagore's[3] songs and suffers in silence because she loves me. I am her only son."

"She lives with you?"

"Yes, we have a flat in Darya Ganj. My sister married and went to live in Calcutta[4] so not I am an only child. It is a great responsibility, being an only child of a loving mother," he sighed, his face darkening visibly.

"I wouldn't know," said Bim, stubbing out her cigarette in the square white ashtray and immediately reaching for another one from the pack Dr. Biswas had placed on the table. "I didn't have one."

Dr. Biswas looked at her vaguely, as if he had not heard, his thoughts were on another continent and moved to a different tune. Just then the band returned from the retiring room, tiredly mounted the small stage at the far end of the hall, picked up their instruments and then, turning on professional smiles as if at the lift of a puppeteer's strings, began to play a medley of Strauss waltzes. The waltzes spun and staggered from table to table like exhausted bees. Dr. Biswas's head drooped.

"Yes," he sighed, "that is what we have here—the band in Davico's playing 'medleys' as we drink tea."

"I have finished," said Bim, having quite lost interest in Dr. Biswas' story which was not quite as interesting as it might have been, and also in the unaccustomed setting of Davico's restaurant which had entertained her for a while in the beginning—the arched doorways with the red velvet curtains, the thick pile carpet smeared with icecream and smelling of cigarette ash, the plates of meringues and cups of vanilla ice cream balanced by graceful waiters, the long windows that looked out onto the leafy trees in the centre of Connaught Place,[5] the red buses that trundled loudly by in the dust, the violet dusk falling out of the murky sky onto the home-going crowds from shops and offices all around, and the sweet treacle of music that the band spread over it all, slowing everything down till it seemed stuck. "Now we *must* go," she urged, "I've never left Raja alone for so long, or Mira-*masi*." They had been to the concert at Freemasons' Hall before coming to Davico's.

He stood up at once, apologetically saying "But that is why I brought you out—oh yes, for the pleasure of taking you to hear this little orchestra, but also to give you a change. You can't always be at home, nursing your family—you will fall ill yourself."

Bim laughed with more scorn than humour. She had no patience with weakness, she thought, none. "I could have been a nurse—or a matron—in a plague hospital. I can handle it all."

"Have you really thought of nursing?" Dr. Biswas asked, hurrying after her down the mirror-lined passage and the marble stairs to the dusty, crowded street below.

"It is all I do," she snapped at him.

"Of course, of course," he stammered, flushing. "I meant—but we must

3. Rabindranath Tagore (1861–1941), Nobel laureate author and educationist, who wrote the words and music for more than two thousand Bengali songs, which have become a central part of modern Bengali culture (see p. 1448).   4. The capital of the state of West Bengal and center of Bengali culture. Darya Ganj is an area of Old Delhi.   5. The center of New Delhi, until the expansion of the city in the 1960s.

go round this corner to the No. 9 bus stop. I must get you home before the curfew. I meant—have you considered it as a profession? You do it so—so excellently."

"No," she assured him. "What I think I shall do—I mean when Raja is well again and I have the time—I think I'll go back to college and finish my history course that I dropped when my aunt too fell ill, and when I get my degree—I might teach," she ended up in a rush, the idea having just come to her as in a natural sequence of affairs.

He was all admiration. In the bus going home, while Bim gazed out of the window at the violet globes of the street lamps casting their harsh light on the passers-by below, at the shops being lighted up and filled with after-office crowds, at the pavement stalls with their paper and plastic and tin goods, and the beggars and their individual and flamboyant ways of attracting attention and small change, he talked again of his student days, of his professors who had invited him home for fruit wine and biscuits, and his landlady who had brought up seven children on her own, her husband being a cripple, and how inspiring it had all been and how much he owed them all, how they had made him what he was.

"Yes," said Bim turning to him briefly, "You are lucky, Dr. Biswas."

"Lucky?" He stopped short in his patter of reminiscence. "How am I lucky, do you think?"

"You have known such glories—such joys."

"Ah," he said, and folded his arms across his chest and looked gloomy. "Yes."

He did not speak again, only shook his head stubbornly when she asked him not to bother to see her home. The bus lumbered on past the city walls and the massed jungle of rag-and-tin huts that had grown beneath them, housing the millions of refugees who were struggling in across the new border. Here there was no light except for the dull glow of small cooking fires, blotted out by smoke and dust and twilight. They swarmed and crawled with a kind of crippled, subterranean life that made Bim feel that the city would never recover from this horror, that it would be changed irremediably, that it was already changed, no longer the city she had been born in. She set her jaw and stared into its shadowy thickness, wretched with its wretchedness.

Dr. Biswas' lips, too, were pinched together, although his silence had a different reason, she felt. Silently, he accompanied her all the way to her bus stop and then walked down Bela Road to her gate. There he stood, with the insects frizzling in the green light cast by the street lamp onto the gate and the bougainvillea, while Begum barked hysterically from the veranda. "Miss Das," he said, clasping the catch of the gate, "Miss Das, I want to tell you—thank you for having given me such—such pleasure. It was the most beautiful evening I have had since coming back to India. I wish that you—"

"Now," laughed Bim, uncomfortably, "you are prompting me to say the things I should be saying to you. I am the one to say thank you, surely."

"No," he cried in anguish, gripping the catch so that Begum, thwarted, howled more piteously. "You don't know—you can't possibly know what it has meant to me. Only, please do come with me again—"

"Oh, I don't know," cried Bim in a panic, and pushed at the gate so that he had to let go of the catch to save his fingers. Hurrying through, she shut the gate between them. "It's really not right for me to have been out for so long—with Raja ill—and my aunt—you know my aunt—"

"Yes, yes, but you can't be a slave to them. I can't be a slave to my mother. We must be ourselves. We must go out, have a little rest, some refreshment. Miss Das," he gulped, "come and meet my mother, please."

This was worse than anything she had feared. Growing darkly red, she said hastily "Yes, but I must run—I must see if Raja—and my aunt—you know my aunt—and Begum is barking. Begum, stop!"

Dashing up the drive to the veranda, she quietened Begum with a quick pat on the head and then flew up the steps to where Raja was sitting in the dark, watching. She sank down on a basket chair beside him, put her face into her hands and grimaced as hideously as she knew how while Raja laughed.

"Did he play you the vi-oh-lin, Bim?" Raja demanded. "Diddly-dum, diddly-dum? No? Then did he sing you a Tagore song?" When she raised her face and shook her head, smiling, he placed one hand on his heart and quavered "O mango flower, fall into my lap! O lamp, flicker in the dark!" which made her laugh and protest "Oh Raja, you don't know a word of Bengali. You've never read Tagore."

"I don't have to know Bengali—all you do is pronounce 's' as 'sh' and roll the vowels like round, sweet *rossogollas*[6] in your mouth," he said airily. "O mango flower . . . Has he asked you to meet his mother? Has his mother sent you her home-made *rossogollas*, Bim?"

But now Bim stopped laughing. Crossly, she got up to go to her room. As she went, followed by Begum, she heard Raja sigh dramatically "*Ach, so Mozart!*"

It was a long time before Dr. Biswas could persuade her to come out again. It was true that Raja improved steadily now that the cold weather had come, with dew on the lawn early in the mornings and beds of coloured flowers blooming in the sunshine, and he could sit out in the garden, wrapped in Bim's *pashmina*[7] shawl, eating oranges and nuts and alternating between reading letters from the Hyder Ali family and composing Urdu verses for them. He looked unusually bulky and compact, and when he removed the shawl or his thick pullover, both brother and sister were startled to find that the bulk adhered to him, not to the woollen garments. They stared at each other in disbelief. It was all the rest, and the milk and the butter, they saw, and shook their heads in amazement.

Still, Bim had her hands full with Aunt Mira. She had made good her promise to herself and gone back to college to complete the course in history, and she had also picked up a hint dropped by Dr. Biswas and gone to help in a clinic for women in the Kingsway Camp for refugees. It was close to the University and she could go there after the lectures and help hand out vitamin drops to pregnant women and mix powdered milk for

6. A dessert made of milk solids and sugar, rolled into balls, and soaked in syrup.   7. The wool of the *pashmina* goat.

the babies, but it took up all afternoon and she came home after dusk and regretted it for when she was out of the house there was no one to keep an eye on Aunt Mira who grew rapidly more difficult.

To begin with, Raja and Bim had told each other Aunt Mira was going through the bottles left in the sideboard by their father. But as time went on and Aunt Mira spent fewer hours in sobriety and slipped off to her room more frequently—guiltily and desperately—coming out only rarely and then stumbling and brushing her hands constantly over her face as if she felt a cobweb growing across it, her tongue slipping thickly from one bit of nonsense to another as if from one cup of drink to another, they had to admit those few bottles could not still be providing her. She was getting her supply of liquor from somewhere. Bim had taken over the household accounts from her a long time ago and old Janaki did not appear to be charging more than usual. It could not be her connivance that kept Aunt Mira floating and splashing in drink. Who was it then?

"I suspect that old Bhakta I brought across from the Hyder Alis, Raja," Bim said, striking her head in dismay as they heard Aunt Mira drop a glass in her room and shriek as it shattered. "He gives me such an insolent look when I glare at him for sitting idle outside the kitchen all day, just waiting for Janaki to bring him his meals—as if he had a secret that made him superior to me. I'm sure it's him."

"How can you say that when you have no proof?" Raja answered. He could bear no criticism of anything or anyone who had to do with the Hyder Ali family.

"No proof—just instinct," said Bim, and rushing off to clean the mess in Aunt Mira's room, found that she had cut her hands and was crying and bleeding all over the bed, more over the spilt drink and the splintered glass than over the strips of blood that hung from her spidery grey fingers in scarlet webs and which she barely noticed in her lament. It was Bim who cried over them.

Dr. Biswas came and handled Aunt Mira with such gentleness and compassion that, watching him from the foot of the bed, Bim softened to see him wrap bandages around Aunt Mira's childish wrists and hear him give her such kindly, good-humoured advice that Aunt Mira lay back on her pillows and weakly glowed with pleasure and gratitude like a very small dim bulb with a fine, weak filament. Bim realised with a pang that she had not seen such a happy look on the old lady's face since before the troubles of last summer began. Holding onto her aunt's small-boned and cold feet, she saw now what her aunt had suffered through their parents' deaths, through Raja's illness, Tara's going away and the perpetual sorrow over Baba. It was all scored over her face, about her quivering mouth and watery eyes, and Bim had not cared to see it. Now she was lying back calmly on her pillows, smiling at the young doctor, smiling guilelessly and purely as a baby relieved from discomfort. Clasping those knuckled ankles, Bim wished she could remain such a baby in a cot, innocent and malleable.

Seeing out Dr. Biswas, she said, quite humbly, yes, she would come to tea with his mother next week.

She was soaked, clammy wet cloths bound her. They had bound her. She had thought they were bandaging her wounds, stemming the blood, but actually they had bound her so that she could not get free, could not get her hands free and reach out. Swaddled and bound, she was suffocating in this mass of cloth. If she could only tear it off, or tear herself out—then she could reach out and touch, trembling, and grab. But they would not let her. They would come and stand over her and press her down into this soft, cottony mass, deep down. Sleep baby, sleep, they sang to her. She had sung to them in their cots, rocking them gently. But they were not gentle to her—sleep baby sleep, they roared at her, and kicked the side of her cot. They had grown so loud, so big. They were bigger than her, they loomed over her and threatened her if they saw her wriggle one finger out of the cotton bandaging towards the tall shining bottle in the dark. She had held out the bottle to them, held it to their lips and chuckled to see them drink. But they threatened her and pushed her back into the grey suffocating cell and denied her.

A drudge in her cell, sealed into her chamber. A grey chamber, woven shut. Here she lived, here she crawled, dragging her heavy wings behind her. Crawled from cell to cell, feeding the fat white larvae that lived in the cells and swelled on the nourishment she brought them. The cells swarmed with them, with their little tight white glistening lives. And she slaved and toiled, her long wings dragging. The air was filled with the angry buzzing of the queen bee. It bored through her ears and zoomed through the greyness like a lurid meteor, making her shut her eyes and burrow down into her cell, into her cotton swaddling, hiding. When it receded, she peeped out with flickering eyes. Where was the bottle? Where was its laughing, sparkling gleam in the dark, winking at her, beckoning to her? They had hidden it.

If she could only reach out and fetch it, then draw it close to her mouth—she whimpered with want. Just a sip, she whimpered, it was time for a drop. Time for milk. The children must have their milk—and leave a little for me, please, just a drop.

But there was no milk, the cow had died, drowned in the well. In that well, deep and stony and still, in which all must drown to die. The navel of the world it was, secret and hidden in thick folds of grass, from which they all emerged and to which they must return, crawling on their hands and knees.

She crawled towards it, dragging the cotton wings. When she reached the edge, she would peer in, then lower her head and go tumbling down, and at some point, at some time, strike the shining surface and break through to the dark and secret drink. She opened her mouth to drink. She whimpered for that drink.

The tea party was of course a mistake and Bim scowled and cursed herself for having softened and let herself in for what was a humiliation and a disaster for everyone concerned.

Had Mrs. Biswas dressed for it? Bim had never seen anyone so dressed. So bathed, so powdered. She seemed to be dusted all over with flour. Perhaps she had fallen into a flour bin, like a large bun. But she smelt so powerfully of synthetic flowers, it must be powder after all. And her white sari crackled with starch, like a biscuit. And her hair gleamed with coconut oil, and flecks of gold glinted at the lobes of her ears and in the ringed folds of her neck. Altogether a piece of confectionery, thought Bim.

She was given a platter with all the goodies already heaped on it—neatly counted out, so many biscuits, so many pieces of *mithai*,[8] so many fritters and a spoonful of chutney. Similar plates with exactly the same number of goodies were handed to Dr. Biswas, one kept by her. They ate.

A china cabinet against the wall watched them. It stood on four legs and housed little plaster figures from Germany—a miniature beer mug, Hansel and Gretel skipping in a meadow, a squirrel dressed in a daisy chain. There were Indian dolls, less travelled but more worn, tinsel garlands flaking off onto red organdie saris and gold turbans. There were clay toys in cane baskets—yellow bananas, green chillies. A parrot. A cow. A plastic baby. And they all stared at Bim munching her way through the goodies. Dr. Biswas stared at his brown shoes, so highly polished. He ate nothing.

His mother sighed. "Eat a little, Shona,"[9] she coaxed in a discontented mutter like a pigeon's. He did not and she took the plate away from him with a sigh, limped to the table to put it down. Earlier she had not limped: it was his not eating that brought on her limp. Now she cast a suspicious look at Bim who still ate, who ate on and on, blaming her.

Why blame me? thought Bim, her mouth full of syrup.

But then the old lady sat down, sighing, to complain. It was not her son and his poor appetite she complained of: she began with her husband who was dead, and went on to her arthritis which was painful and for which there was no cure—*he* said there was no cure—and ended up with the servant boy who had run away that very morning on being told there was a visitor coming to tea. Lazy, that was the trouble. Too lazy. And you? she questioned, her small eyes like raisins in the large soft bun of her face. How many servants? What do they do? What do you pay them?

"Ma," Dr. Biswas gasped, pressing down with all his weight on his toes so that the new shoes shrieked.

The little raisin eyes gave him a quick sharp look. Then the puffy white hand waved him away. "He—he is the only one who knows what work is," she went on. Work, work, nothing but work. Did any man ever work so hard? He was killing himself.

Sitting back on the sofa with the pink-flowered cushion behind her, she talked and talked—quite often in Bengali which gave Bim time to glance at Dr. Biswas with some curiosity, wondering how she could have overlooked so many virtues, such glorious and unique qualities. His mother made it seem he was Apollo in disguise. His degrees in medicine—his dedication to his profession—the love his patients felt for him. And his music, too. Here the mother clasped her hands together, wrung them almost as if in despair. "Play your violin," she even said, "for Miss Das. I don't understand all this Western music he plays, but perhaps you can. You are a college girl? What degree?"

---

8. Sweets (Hindi).   9. "Golden one" or "dear" (Bengali); term of endearment.

Bim's mouth was full of crumbs. They were even more difficult to get through than the syrup. While she coughed and choked, the mother went on, about the violin, the music. What was it all about—could the college girl explain? "I don't understand. He wants someone who understands—"

"Ma," Dr. Biswas broke in hastily, perspiring even. "Perhaps Miss Das would like to hear you sing. Mother sings Tagore's songs, Miss Das—she has a trained voice. Would you like to hear?"

Now Bim began to feel annoyed. Let them play and sing to each other as much as they liked, she felt, why must I listen to them too? I listen to enough as it is, from everyone. Putting down her plate with several of the goodies still untouched—unfortunately they were the very ones Mrs. Biswas had spent all morning cooking, but how was Bim to know that?—she listened to mother and son arguing more and more heatedly, the old lady on the brink of tears, determined to sacrifice herself for his sake, he somewhat maliciously as if to punish her for this embarrassing scene. Then Bim decided it was enough, and rose to her feet, saying brusquely "I must get home before dark."

Unfortunately, just as she stood up and said that, Mrs. Biswas had relented and agreed, in Bengali, to fetch her harmonium and sing. Bim had of course not understood. Now here was Bim saying she would not stay, she would go. It was very unfortunate. Very rude and impolite and intolerable.

Setting her lips together, Mrs. Biswas said, after a moment of silence, "Of course you must go. It is getting dark."

Dr. Biswas, on his feet, swaying a bit as if struck with disaster, had no alternative now that she had been dismissed but to see her out. Then, casting a look over his shoulder at his mother as she shuffled about the small, drab room, collecting the scattered cups and plates and looking over all the uneaten goodies, he hurried down the stairs after Bim.

"I'll go back alone," she said, her voice rising too high. "Really, I *want* to, I'd *like* to."

"You don't know what you are saying. It's not safe, these days, after dark, for a woman, alone."

"Of course it's safe," she said scornfully. "Anyway, quite safe for a woman like *me*."

He hunched his shoulders, taking the blow in silence, but would not give up and came clattering down the many flights of stairs after her onto the street. "I would feel ashamed of myself," he mumbled, as he caught up with her by the park railing across the road from his block of flats. "I would never forgive myself," he went on, hurrying past a cripple who sat propped up against the railings, holding out a begging bowl silently, and walked at her side.

She gave her shoulders an impatient twitch and walked on very fast past a drycleaner's shop, a tea-shop and a stationery shop to the main street and the bus stop. How much his mother's son he was, she said to herself: he had inherited her gift for loading the weight of his self-sacrifices onto others.

The main street of Darya Ganj did look strangely empty and rather menacing in the early winter dusk, she had to admit. The few people they passed hurried by, unnaturally engrossed, and some shopkeepers were pulling down their shutters although it was surely still too early to be closing. Only around one tea-shop was there a group of people and the sound of a news broadcast on the radio turned up above the babble.

"What do you think . . ." she began to ask when she nearly stumbled over a cobbler who had chosen to sit in a dark corner with his tool box and broken sandals spread before him. The man was saying almost as if to himself: "Gandhi-*ji* is dead. Murdered,[1] they say. Who would murder a good man, a saint?" He was shaking his head and swaying as he repeated the words in a monotone and Bim and Dr. Biswas walked past him, barely taking note of his mutter when the words struck them and they stopped short to stare at each other and then at the cobbler.

"What—" cried Dr. Biswas, "what did you say?"

His voice was so high-pitched, so hysterical, that the cobbler stopped mumbling to himself and looked up at them. Then he waved his hand towards the group of people around the tea-shop, listening to the radio. "Go and hear for yourself," he said. "Gandhi-*ji* is dead. Murdered, they say . . ." and he began to sway from side to side in ritual mourning again.

Dr. Biswas tore away towards the tea-shop, Bim flying along behind him when she saw her bus come lumbering up and in a panic veered away from Dr. Biswas and leapt onto the bus instead.

Hearing the bus screech to a halt by the curb, Dr. Biswas too stopped and looked around wildly. "Bimla," he shouted, "Bimla," and waved to her to stop. She leant out from the crowd on the step, waving back, and saw him abandoned, scraps of paper blowing about his feet, the lamplight striking onto and ricocheting off the bald spot on his head. Then she disappeared into the bus and forgot him completely: she thought only of rushing to Raja with the news.

She heard him coughing as she rushed into his room. He was lying in bed under his thick winter quilt with Begum at his feet as limp as a rug. Both stiffened to hear her race in.

"Raja," she shouted, "Mahatma Gandhi's been killed. Murdered. He's dead."

Raja gave a violent jerk and shot out of bed, the heavy quilt sliding to one side and falling to the floor, rolled up like a corpse. Raja's hair stood on end. Begum's began to bristle, too. "You must be mad," he shouted at her. "You're crazy."

"I tell you—everyone in the city knows—everybody in the bus was talking—where's the radio? Turn it on—let's listen."

Raja hurried to the radio on his bookshelf and fiddled with the knobs in a kind of desperation. "Bim," he said, almost sobbing, "there'll be more riots—killing—they'll slaughter every Muslim they can find—anywhere."

"God no, not again, not again," whispered Bim, but then the crackling of the radio sorted itself out and resolved into formal music, wailing miserably. A woman's voice was singing the *Ram Dhun*[2] mournfully. Raja and

1. Mahatma Gandhi was assassinated by a Hindu nationalist at a prayer meeting in Delhi on January 30, 1948.   2. Musical repetition of the name *Ram*, the Hindi word for God, often specifically used for Ram, an incarnation of the hero of the Hindu epic *The Ramayana* (in Volume 1).

Bim stood by, cracking their knuckles, waiting for a news announcement. When it came, they sank onto Raja's bed with relief to hear it was not a Muslim but a Hindu who had killed the Mahatma.

"Thank God," Raja cried out, pulling up the quilt off the floor and hugging it to him almost violently. "Thank God. I thought of the Hyder Alis—what they would have to go through—"

Bim glanced at him and his expression made her look away in embarrassment. It was as if the skin had been drawn off his face, leaving it peeled and bare. "What do you think will happen now?" she murmured, turning to pat Begum who was calmed by her low voice and came to lay her muzzle on her lap, looking for reassurance.

"I think now perhaps Indians will forget Pakistan for a bit. Perhaps they will turn to their own problems at last. I don't know—at a time like this—it must be all chaos, Bim, chaos."

They spent the evening listening to the news broadcasts, heard Nehru weep, were reduced to silence and shivering, then to irritation by the mournful dirges that were being sung continuously, sat together worried and relieved, shocked and thoughtful.

At last Raja said "And your tea-party, Bim? How was it? Has Mrs. Biswas approved of you as her daughter-in-law?"

That made Bim leap to her feet, switch on the light and start bustling about as if electrified. "Daughter-in-law?" she spluttered. "Dr. Biswas's mother—just don't talk to me about her—about them—I hope I never have to see Dr. Biswas again—he gives me the creeps—he's—he's just—"

"Oh Bim, don't be so hard on him—poor violinist, poor musician. So Mozart—ach so Mozart," sang Raja, laughing, clasping his hands under his chin and making a sad clown face to make Bim laugh. And Bim laughed.

She always told herself that was the last time she saw him, the day that Mahatma Gandhi was shot. But it was not true—there was one more time, one that she never admitted and tried never to remember.

It had been at the end of spring. Raja had not needed the doctor since the winter—he was so much better, his temperature down to normal, getting stronger, puffing out with a thick padding of fat, as he sat in the sun, nibbling at nuts, tossing the shells to the squirrels that stole out of the trees and crept across the lawn to his feet to pick them up and scuttle back amongst the leaves. But as the weather grew warmer, the air seemed swollen with heat again, the garden was filled with drying, flying leaves, sand sprang out of the dunes by the river and blew all day long through the house and the garden, covering every leaf and every table and book and paper with grey grit, and Raja grew restless. He put away his verses, his books of poetry that he had found sufficient all winter, and paced up and down the long veranda, complaining about the heat and the dust, and "Why isn't the drive ever swept up? Look at the leaves and the papers flying about. Can't you do something about this house, Bim? It grows dirtier and shabbier every day—like the house of the dead. Are we all dead? Don't you care any more? Don't you care about anything?" and he paced up and down, glowering, and Bim refused to pay attention to such petty complaints. But she knew it was not the dust or the untidiness of the place that was upsetting Raja, she knew he had begun to think beyond his illness, beyond his body, to the outer world and was restless to set out into it.

On a day late in spring, the koel began to call in the trees and went on and on ringing its obstreperous bell through that day of flying leaves and dust and summer heat that thrummed and vibrated like an electric line coiled around them. Bim was preparing for an exam—she sat before her books with her elbows glued to the sticky desk-top, trying to ignore Raja who paced up and down, interrupting and annoying her by mocking at the absurdity of her ambitions and putting forth ridiculous schemes for his own future that she could not bring herself to take seriously or encourage. She knew he was on the boil with impatience, longing to burst out, reach out to life and friends and movement, and that was at the bottom of all his grousing and grumbling, his unfair attacks on her and baiting of her, like a fire smouldering under a pot. Still, it was hard to tolerate.

"Oh Raja," she sighed finally, bitterly, "go back to bed, will you?"

This made him furious. His face bloated with temper as with angry gas and he stopped to lean on a chair-back with such pressure that the wood flinched and squeaked. "I will not go to bed," he hissed, spit flying. "I will go—go to—to Hyderabad. Hyder Ali Sahib has asked me to come. He has plenty of work—I will work for him. I—I will—go today—today I will catch the train—I won't stop here, with you, another day. It's enough—enough—" and he let go of the chair and spread out his arms as if to push everything out of his way.

Bim tried to stay calm. She merely tapped her pencil against her teeth and found it better not to look at his face—she had not suspected it capable of such ugliness. She looked critically at the sand accumulating on the desk, on her books, flying in and settling in grey, gritty flecks on the white surfaces.

Raja left the room but was not quiet. He could be heard striding about in his room, dragging out boxes and trunks, throwing things into them with all his strength so that there was a rumbling and shaking of danger. Danger. That roused Bim and made her go to his door and try to pacify him and bring him back to normalcy. Hearing them, a distraught Aunt Mira crawled out of her room and watched Raja pack with appalled eyes, pressing her trembling fingers to her lips. Bim tried to persuade her to go back to her room. She wept. In exasperation, Raja gave up packing and flung himself down onto his bed. To tell the truth, he was exhausted and could feel his temperature rising. It was heavy as lead but it rose, as inexorably as the mercury in a thermometer. The heat enclosed the house and all of them in it, sulphur-yellow in colour and tinged, like an egg-yolk, with blood. Aunt Mira locked herself into her room. Raja slept—or smouldered, and Bim watched, watched.

At three o'clock when the heat of the day had risen to its violent, brick-red peak above the house, threatening it, a door slid open—audaciously, dangerously—and out darted a naked white figure, screeching and prancing, streaked through the room, out onto the veranda and then fled pell-mell down the steps into the sun.

Bim, who had spent the afternoon stretched out on a sofa in the hall in between her brother's and her aunt's room, not quite certain what to expect from either, gave a violent start when she saw what she took to be a noontime ghost slipping through the room, then sprang to her feet and rushed after her.

Aunt Mira was naked, whipping herself around and around in the driveway, screeching as she whipped and spun till she fell into the gravel and rolled there in agony, crying "Oh God—the rats, the rats! Rats, lizards, snakes—they are eating me—oh, they are eating me—" and her frantic hands tore the creatures from her throat, dragged them out of her hair. Then she doubled up and rolled and howled. When Bim flung herself at her and held her down with her arm, weeping and crying for Raja and Baba and Janaki to come, it was old Bhakta who heard and came running with knees bent. The aunt raged and bit their wrists and thrashed her legs, crying "They're eating—eating—eating my *hands*," and tried to fling off her fingers. Finally someone fetched a blanket and threw it on top of her and Bim rolled her up in it, picking up the shreds and soft blobs of grey flesh that leaked from the spindly body, the little empty balloons of skin and flesh, smelling and mouldy with age, from off the gravel and sand, that clung on in bits and shards, rolled them up into the blanket and carried her in like a corpse.

Then Dr. Biswas came: that was all that Raja had been able to do from his bed—he had telephoned the doctor. Just one injection and the old woman lay still, slipping neatly as a little tube into heavy, sad sleep, not stirring when Bim lifted and turned and dressed her. The doctor helped. Together they tucked her out of sight—the little sad wisp of grey pubic hair like a bedraggled rat's tail, the empty slack pouches of her ancient breasts, the bits and scraps of her—then sat on either side of her bed, each holding one bird-boned wrist, the doctor to confirm the pulse, Bim to plead for forgiveness for the indignity of it all and for a return to her old, comforting self. Finally he spoke. "I'll give you a bottle, Bimla, of brandy. When she wakes up, give her this much," and he got up stiffly, brought out a bottle from his bag and poured some into a tumbler. Bim gasped at the amount and began to protest but he said "She must have it. Or she'll go mad. Every three hours, give her some. After some time, you can water it. Water it more and more. Make it a long, watery drink that she can sip slowly by the hour. You will have to do this yourself—keep the bottle with you—or you will have to put her into hospital for some very drastic treatment that will kill her." Bim hung her head and would not speak. So he got up to pack his bag and leave, saying "I'll just go and see Raja for a few minutes." At the door he paused for a moment, looked back at Bim mournfully. "Now I understand everything," he said with a deep sigh.

"What?" asked Bim, not very interested. She was more conscious of her aunt's pulse beating like a bird's under her finger—less than a bird, beating like the pulse of an embryo in a fine-shelled egg—only the merest flutter that she had to strain to feel and keep between her thumb and finger, safe.

"Now I understand why you do not wish to marry. You have dedicated your life to others—to your sick brother and your aged aunt and your little brother who will be dependent on you all his life. You have sacrificed your own life for them."

Bim's mouth fell open with astonishment at this horrendous speech so solemnly, so leadenly spoken as if engraved on steel for posterity. Then, to her relief, Dr. Biswas left and she was alone with her aunt. Looking down, she found she had dropped the thin wrist from her hand in shock, and now she pressed her hands together as if she wished to break, to wreck something. She even hissed slightly in her rage and frustration—at being so misunderstood, so totally misread, then gulped a little with laughter at such grotesque misunderstanding, and her tangled emotions twisted her face and shook her, shook the thought of Biswas out of her. Later, she never acknowledged, even to herself, that this ridiculous scene had ever taken place.

That was the beginning of the aunt's death for no one really expected her to recover. It was the long slow journey begun in earnest, and Bim sat reading, reading. She read the *Thodol Bardol* which she found, to her surprise, amongst her aunt's few books, and she read Lawrence's[3] *Ship of Death*, moving her lips to silent words, wishing she dared speak them aloud:

> Now launch the small ship, now as the body dies
> and life departs, launch out, the fragile soul
> in the fragile ship of courage, the ark of faith
> with its store of food and little cooking pans
> and change of clothes,
> upon the flood's black waste
> upon the waters of the end
> upon the sea of death, where still we sail
> darkly, for we cannot steer, and have no port.

and wished, almost, that she could herself lower herself into that dark tunnel and slip along behind the passage made for her by the older, the dying woman.

> Have you built your ship of death, O have you?
> O build your ship of death, for you will need it,

she murmured, almost aloud, but Aunt Mira did not hear. She lay quite still now, shrinking and shrivelling, till she almost ceased to be human, became bird instead, an old bird with its feathers plucked, its bones jutting out from under the blue-tinged skin, too antique, too crushed to move. Now Bim kept the brandy bottle in the cupboard and measured out the drink for her. She became a baby, crying and whimpering for the bottle if it was not there, her lips making little sucking sounds in hungry anticipation. Sometimes she trembled so much she could not drink from the glass, only spilt it all, and then Bim had to spoon it into her mouth and she would suck and suck the spoon as if it were a teat, blissfully, her little buried eyes shining with joy. She began to foul the bed. Bim engaged the gardener's wife to help her clean and wash. The woman was strong and lifted and washed and turned with vigour, but liked to talk. She would

3. D. H. Lawrence (1885–1930), British writer.

even try to force the aunt to eat a little of the rice and *dal*[4] Janaki sent for her, but it seemed to hurt her to eat. She did it so unwillingly and pathetically that Bim, out of pity, sent the woman away with the dishes and gave her to drink instead.

Only on one night did she rouse herself out of the stupor that Bim had thought permanent, and then she tore at her clothes as if they were a net, tore at invisible things that seemed attached to her throat and fingers and hair, even screamed "Let me go—let me jump into the well—*let* me!" She screamed that intermittently all through the night, like an owl, or a nightjar starting out of the silence, waking Bim. She seemed obsessed by the idea of the well—the hidden, scummy pool in which the bride-like cow they had once had, had drowned, and to which she seemed drawn. Bim held her wrists all night, wondering why of all things in this house and garden it was the well she wanted, to drown in that green scum that had never shown a ripple in its blackened crust since the cow's death. Even as children they had not gone very close to it ever: they had dared each other to throw pebbles in it but only Raja had accepted the dare, even Bim had lied and pretended but not actually gone. Now it seemed to encroach on the aunt's enclosing darkness like a dark flood and she seemed helpless to resist it—on the contrary, hopelessly attracted by it.

Trying to distract her, quieten her, Bim brought her a glassful of drink and helped her to sip it. While drinking, her head slipped to one side, the glass spilt across her chin, dribbled down her neck into her nightie, and she died, not hideously by drowning, but quietly in her bed, pleasantly overcome by fumes of alcohol. Yet it was as if she had drowned for Bim dreamt night after night of her bloated white body floating naked on the surface of the well. Even when drinking her morning tea, she had only to look into the tea-cup to see her aunt's drowned face in it, her fine-spun silver hair spread out like Ophelia's, floating in the tea. She would turn very pale and leave the tea cold in the white cup. Aunt Mira had not drowned, she told herself over and over again—not drowned, just died.

Bim and Janaki and the gardener's wife washed her clean and Bim fetched her only silk sari out of her trunk, the white silk that had a broad border of crimson and gold and that Aunt Mira had never worn while she lived, and they dressed her in it like a doll at a wedding, an idol on an altar. Janaki even lit some sticks of incense because of the smell in the room that shamed the family. Then the neighbours came and lifted the string cot[5] on which she lay and carried it out of the house: it was as light as a leaf or a piece of paper.

Raja rose from his bed and accompanied Bim to the cremation ground. He lit the pyre with a torch and they stood watching, with perspiration streaming in sheets from their faces, the heat tremble and vibrate in the brilliant light of the summer afternoon like wings, or theosophical[6] phantoms, till it was reduced to a mound of white ash on the silver sand beside

---

4. Lentil stew or soup eaten as an accompaniment to rice or unleavened bread.   5. Made of string woven on a frame, commonly used in north India.   6. The Theosophical Society, founded in 1875 by Madame Blavatsky and Colonel Olcott, advocated a mystical religion called Theosophy, compounded of occult beliefs and aspects of Eastern religions, including the belief in reincarnation. The Irish political activist Annie Besant (1847–1933) and others popularized Theosophy in India in the 1900s.

the river. The earthen pot containing the ash was handed to Bim still warm, and she walked with Raja to the river's edge to lower it into the water and watch it bob for a while, a wreath of red roses around it, till the grey current caught it and swirled it away and it sank. A washerman, knee-deep in water, straightened up and watched, too. A donkey brayed. A lapwing cried. The river ran. They went home.

Yet for a long time Bim continued to see her, was certain that she saw her: the shrunken little body naked, trailing a torn shred of a nightie, a wisp of pubic hair, as she slipped surreptitiously along the hedge, head bent low as if she hoped no one would notice her as she hurried towards the well. Bim would catch her breath and shut her eyes before opening them again to stare wildly at the hedge and find only the tassels of the malaviscus dangling there, like leering red tongues, and nothing else. She thought of what she had read in Raja's copy of *The Waste Land*:

> "Who is the third who walks always beside you?
> When I count there are only you and I together
> But when I look ahead up the white road
> There is always another one walking beside you
> Gliding wrapt in a brown mantle, hooded
> I do not know whether a man or a woman
> —But who is that on the other side of you?"[7]

At the end, she found a note to say that these lines were suggested by an account of an Antarctic expedition: "The explorers at the extremity of their strength, had the constant delusion that there was one more member than could actually be counted."

Bim caught her lip in her teeth in understanding when she read that, although she could not see the connection between explorers of the Antarctic and her little drunken aunt, but she was sure now that she was that extra person, that small shadow thrown by a subliminal ghost that existed in the corner of the eye. She wondered if she were losing her mind but then she ceased to see this vision, it receded gradually and then went altogether. Perhaps, as the Tibetans believed, the soul had lingered on earth for a while till it was finally fetched away on its long journey. The ship of death, O ship of death, Bim chanted to keep herself calm, calm.

She kept calm while Raja packed his bags, put away all his things, telling her that now he would go to Hyderabad. Looking up at her as she watched silently, he shouted "I have to go. Now I can go. I have to begin my life some time, don't I? You don't want me to spend all my life down in this hole, do you? You don't think I can go on living just to keep my brother and sister company, do you?"

"I never said a word," said Bim coldly.

"You don't have to. It's written all over your face. Just go, go, take your face away. Don't sit there staring. Don't stop me."

"I won't stop you."

"I'm going."

"Go," said Bim.

7. See n. 4, p. 2807.

When the tonga arrived to take his things to the station and Bhakta was loading his bags onto it, each bag making the tonga dip down so that the horse had to spread its legs to steady itself, he spoke to Bim again. "Bim, I'll come back," he said. "I'm leaving all my books and papers with you. Look after them till I come back."

"Why should you come back?" Bim asked stonily.

"Bim, don't be so *hard*. You know I must come back—to look after you and Baba. I can't leave you alone."

She started to say something but then only shrugged slightly and bent to hold Begum back as Raja swung himself onto the tonga, when Bhakta suddenly jumped onto the tonga step, clung to it, pleaded with Raja to take him, too, to Hyderabad, back to Hyder Ali Sahib, and then crouched down at Raja's feet, and went with him. Begum whined and quivered as the tonga driver raised his whip over his head and got the ribbed yellow nag started with a lurch. Bim stood petting her, quieting her, and when the tonga had lumbered out of the gate, she became aware of Baba coming out of his room as the gramophone ceased to rattle out the jolly rattle of Nelson Eddy singing "The Donkey Serenade," and quietly settling down to play with his pebbles on the veranda tiles.

Bim sank down onto the steps beside him, sat there in a slumped way, both tired and relieved, her arms hanging limply over her knees and her head drooping. She watched Baba's pebbles scatter and fall, then his long fingers reach out to gather them together again, and began to talk, more to herself than to him.

"So now there are just you and I left, Baba," she muttered. "Does the house seem empty to you? Everyone's gone, except you and I. They won't come back. We'll be alone now. But we don't have to worry about anyone now—Tara or Raja or Mira-*masi*. We needn't worry now that they're all gone. We're just by ourselves and there's nothing to worry about. You're not afraid, are you? There's no need to be afraid. It's as if we were children again—sitting on the veranda, waiting for father and mother, when it's growing dark and it's bedtime. Really, it'll be just the way it was when we were children." She yawned hugely, her eyes starting out of her head and her cheek bones straining at her stretched skin. "It wasn't so bad then," she mumbled, shaking her head sleepily, "was it? No. When we were children—"

But she didn't say any more. She laid her head on her lap and seemed nearly asleep.

III

Every morning, when the dew still lay fresh on the grass, the mother followed the doctor's orders and strolled up and down the rose walk at the far end of the garden. To Tara it was a long grassy tunnel between two beds of roses. Her father was supposed to have planted them. The gardener was ordered to take care of them. But neither the father nor the gardener knew roses: they put in cuttings and watched them come up, either small, weakly crimson ones or shaggy sick-pink ones, nothing else. Tara sighed, thinking of the sight that met her eyes whenever she peered through the wrought iron gate at their neighbour Hyder Ali Sahib's house, at the round, square, rectangular, triangular and star-shaped beds filled with roses like scoops of vanilla ice cream, pink ones like the flounced skirts of English dolls, silky yellow ones that had the same smell as the tea her mother drank, and crimson ones that others called "black" and which she always studied with narrowed eyes, wondering why she could not see the blackness but only the rich velvety crimson of their waxen petals . . . Why could they not have such roses, too? Still, this early in the morning, even these negligible pink and crimson buttons gave off a cool, fresh scent. They should have pleased the mother and Tara cried continually "Look, Mama, look," but she seemed to notice nothing, to be absorbed in other worlds, as invisible to Tara as the black of the red roses.

Usually the mother did not take exercise. She either sat up at the card table, playing, or lay very still on her bed, with a suffering face tilted upwards in warning so that Tara did not dare approach. Even now she kept her distance. She paced slowly, obediently, her arms folded, her chin sunk into her neck, as if considering a hand of cards, while Tara, in her nightie, skipped and danced after her, her bare feet making tracks through the misty dew on the grass.

Suddenly she stopped with a shout: she had spied something under the rose bushes—a gleam of pearly white. Perhaps a jewel, a ring: Tara was always expecting to find treasure, to make her fortune, discover herself a princess. She stooped to part the leaves that hid it and saw the pale, whorled orb of a stopped snail. For a while she stayed on her knees, crushed with disappointment, then lifted it onto a leaf and immediately delight gushed up as in a newly mined well at seeing the small creature unfold, tentatively protrude its antennae and begin to slide forward on a stream of slime. "Look, Mama, look what I've found," she cried, darting forwards, and of course it tumbled off the leaf and when the mother turned to look, there was Tara staring at the slimy leaf, then searching for the lost creature in the mud. Wrinkling her nose, the mother walked on, brooding. She had not chosen to walk here: the doctor had told her to; it was good for her, he had said. If one became pregnant so late in life—and yes, there were strands of grey thickening and spreading in her hair above her ears—and that, too, when one was so severely diabetic, one would have to be careful. She would have to take walks. Sullenly, she walked, frowning to hear the chattering of the mynah birds in the mulberry trees, wincing at Tara's sudden scream of delight and discovery followed by wails of distress and disappointment. Tara was still the baby of the family. She did not know her days were numbered, that she was soon to lose all her privileges and be removed to a distance, disregarded, as another made its appearance into their lives. That was life—a snail found, a pearl lost. Always, life was that.

The new baby was the prettiest of all, everyone declared, when they came to see him lying in his crib, so delicately pink, so divinely quiet. Even Tara, ordered to keep away, edged closer to where he lay sleeping and hung over the edge of the cot, wide-eyed and breathing heavily at the miracle of this tiny live thing, whole and complete and alive and yet able to fit, like a child's toy, into the crook of an arm, or onto a knee, folded into his shawl, so quietly content as if he did not wish to emerge any more than the snail from its shell.

No one could help noticing how slow he was to learn such baby skills as turning over, sitting up, smiling in response, talking, standing or walking. It all seemed to take an age with him. He seemed to have no desire to reach out and take anything. It was as if his parents, too aged, had given birth to a child without vitality or will—all that had gone into the other, earlier children and there had been none left for this last, late one. He would lie on his back, gazing at the light that rippled the ceiling, or propped up on someone's lap, and stare at the ants that crawled industriously by, not even reaching out a finger to them. His mother soon tired of carrying him about, feeding him milky foods with a silver spoon, washing and powdering him. She became restless, spoke of her bridge four; "My bridge is suffering," she complained. There was the ayah of course, Tara's ayah made nurse again, but she could only be made to work twelve hours a day, or sixteen, or eighteen, not more. She could not stay awake for twenty-four. For some time the mother tried to train her to but it was impossible—she was a stupid woman and would not learn. She would fall asleep with the child in her arms and the mother never knew how often he rolled off her lap onto the floor because he protested so gently, his cries did not disturb her as she sat playing cards with her friends in the drawing room. But the ayah spoke to her, told her it was time the child sat up, and stood, and talked. She said she could not bear the burden single-handed any more: he had grown too large and too heavy.

Then Aunt Mira was sent for. Aunt Mira was not exactly an aunt, she was a cousin of the mother's, a poor relation who had been widowed at the age of fifteen and had lived with her husband's family ever since as maid of all work, growing shabbier and skinnier and seedier with the years. By then there were more daughters-in-law in the house, younger, stronger and abler, and she was no longer indispensable. So when the mother wrote, asking her to come and stay with them, she was allowed to leave their house and come. Good riddance, they had even said. Aunt Mira had been frequently ill, had aged young, was growing dotty and bald. Useless, but another household might find some use for her, as the worn article, thrown away by one, is picked up and employed by another.

"She is coming to look after you children," their mother told them. "You have become too much for me—you are all so noisy and naughty. She will discipline you. And look after your brother. I don't know what is wrong with him—he should be walking by now and doing things for himself. She will keep him in her room and look after him. And you will have to learn to be quiet."

Led to expect some fierce disciplinarian, a kind of female general equipped with tools of punishment, they stood hiding behind the veranda pillars and peeping to see her when she arrived, and were both relieved and disappointed by her appearance. She was a poor relation, they could see that by the way she was greeted by their mother and the way in which she returned the greeting—tremulously, gratefully. Her luggage was all in bits and pieces, bedding rolls and tin trunks, like the servants', no better.

Yet, when she was shown into her room—"Show Mira-*masi* her room, children"—and opened the green-painted tin trunk, they found it was crammed with presents for them. As they stood around in a ring, sucking their fingers or scratching their necks, she drew out the things she had been making for them ever since she had received their mother's summons—there were paper hats trimmed with parrot feathers, little slippers of felt and velvet for Tara's dolls, a scrapbook of wedding and birthday cards for Bim, lions and giraffes made out of sticks and straw for Raja. She took more and more stuff out of that battered trunk and they came closer, kneeling beside her, sitting cross-legged by her trunk, quickly growing accustomed to the scarecrow-like appearance that had caused them both disgust and reassurance at first appearance, growing accustomed to the unfortunately protruding teeth and collar-bones, the thin wispy hair drawn over the white scalp into an untidy blob, the myopic eyes that seemed to blink and twitch perpetually with nervousness, and were quite enthralled—no one had ever *made* them things before, no one had ever had the time. "I'm just going to the club, I'm waiting for the car," the mother had said irritably when approached, and the ayah would lift her arms out of the wash-tub, dripping, to threaten them as she shouted "If you bother me, I'll thrash you," while no one had even considered approaching anyone so unapproachable as the father.

Now they had an aunt, handed to them like a discarded household appliance they might find of use. They exchanged deep, understanding looks with each other: they had understood their power over her, they had seen she was buying, or begging for their tolerance and patronage. They were not beyond, even at that age, feeling the superiority of their position and of extending their gratitude from that elevated position of power. Perhaps Aunt Mira felt all this, too. But it did not seem to matter to her. She said "I saw green mangoes on those trees outside. Can you make mango sherbet?" They shook their heads, dumbly, wondering if she had been ordered to teach them cooking. But she only said, gleefully sucking in her breath, "I'll make it for you if you fetch me a basket of mangoes from your garden," and with a yell they streamed out as in wild celebration at this new season in their lives, a season of presents and green mangoes and companionship. She went to the kitchen with all of them dancing behind her, to watch while she cut and sliced and chopped and stirred, and let them taste in little sips from a spoon. The cook watched stonily for a while, then grudgingly gave up the cooking spoon and even began to help.

When they left the kitchen, Tara clasped her aunt's knees, not caring if the shabby sari smelt somewhat of onions and cooking fat, and asked "Have you come to look after us? Or are you to look after Baba only?"

"I am to look after Baba," Aunt Mira agreed, "but I would like to play with *you.*" It was not said ingratiatingly. It seemed to Tara that her aunt's darting eyes and trembling fingers were searching for friends and she was happy to have them. Hope and trust instantly springing up like grass inside her, Tara squeezed the creaking knees and said "*I'll* play with you."

Aunt Mira even played with Baba, teaching him games no one else had tried to play with him, thinking him too hopelessly backward. To begin with, she stopped feeding him those milky sops from the tip of a silver spoon. Instead, she cut up small pieces of bread and let him pick them up and put them in his mouth himself. His sisters and his brother, who had not seen him perform this skill before, stood by, entranced, applauding him. Then she showed him how to slip a button into a buttonhole. They got a great deal of amusement out of that, too. Eventually he could do up his buttons himself and then would stand basking in their congratulations like a duck in a shower of rain. Visitors could hardly believe their eyes when they saw him sitting on the veranda and playing a game of marbles with Aunt Mira—how his fingers got round the rolling globes of glass, how he manipulated them and rolled them back to her: it was a miracle. Baba would lift his head timidly—pale, shining—then drop it in shy triumph. On winter evenings Aunt Mira would place him on her bed, tucked up in her plum-coloured quilt, and play a game of bagatelle[8] with him on Raja's old board with its row of heavy lead balls and small baton with which to strike them and send them rambling down a long chute to wander about the board, amidst the nailed enclosures and the lead pits, till they rolled into one or the other or, as mostly happened in Aunt Mira's case, returned to the bottom of the board without running up any marks at all. Then they were gathered up and rolled back into the chute for the next player. Bim and Tara would keep the score and hug their knees with delight when Baba won.

Only their efforts to make him talk failed. He would say one word at a time, if pressed, but seemed happier not to and could not be made to repeat a whole line. Gradually, as his family learnt how to anticipate his few needs and how to respond, they ceased to notice his silence—his manner of communication seemed full and rich enough to them: he no more needed to converse than Aunt Mira's cat did.

Not only Baba but animals, too, followed in her wake as she scurried busily through the household. One day a small kitten took to mewing desperately under the veranda. A saucer of milk was set out for it, surreptitiously, a watch kept on the parents's door to make sure they did not suddenly emerge and catch them at it. The kitten had no such qualms and in no time was slipping up the steps and rolling about the veranda, catching its tail or scampering after a wasp, and soon it was wrapped up in Aunt Mira's quilt where it grew larger and larger and eyed them commandingly with its yellow eyes, more mistress than Aunt Mira.

Then Aunt Mira summoned courage to speak out on a matter that had been bothering her. Slipping into their mother's room, she described how she had often watched the milkman fill up the milk can at the garden tap before coming up the drive to the kitchen door to ladle out the watered milk into the saucepan held out by the cook. "It is more blue than white," Aunt Mira's voice cracked into splinters with indignation, "and there's no cream at all. It is as if the children were drinking water. They get no nourishment. It can't go on."

---

8. A board game in which marbles or balls are shot through a labyrinth into a goal.

The mother seemed as displeased with Aunt Mira as with the milkman, or possibly more. "Then what do you suggest?" she asked sourly as if to put a stop to the distasteful conversation and get on with the inserting of ear-rings into the waiting ear-lobes.

"It would be best to have a cow," Aunt Mira said excitedly, and the children at the door jumped in surprise and joy at the unexpected boldness of her imagination. "The gardener could look after it. He could bring it to the door and I could watch it being milked myself every morning. We would have pure milk for the children."

The mother looked at her as if she were mad. A cow? A cow to give them milk? She shook her head in amazement, but now the ayah came up and loudly supported the aunt, and then the cook. It seemed the milkman was a rogue, had swindled them all, they did not wish to have anything to do with him. Faced with a rebellion of this size, the mother capitulated and the cow arrived, led in by the gardener on a rope to be examined and admired like a new bride even if she had her calf with her.

There was something bride-like about her white face, her placid eyes and somewhat sullen expression. The children fondled her pink, opaque ears that let in the light and glowed shell-pink in the sun. Tara laid her face against the folds of her neck, milky white and warm. She smelt sweetly of straw, and cud. She was housed in a shed. For a week, she was treated like a bride, fed on the tenderest of grass and newest of shoots. Her milk was the subject of ecstatic admiration: how it frothed into the pan, how thick the cream that rose on it. She stood in the garden, under the jacaranda tree, the lilac flowers showering down on her as at a wedding.[9]

It was spring. The nights grew warmer. The gardener left her out instead of putting her in the shed at night. In the dark, while everyone slept, she broke the rope that tethered her and wandered through the garden like a white ghost, her hooves silent in the grass. She blundered her way through the carvanda hedge at the back of the house, and tumbled into the well and drowned in a welter of sounds that no one heard.

The well then contained death as it once had contained merely water, frogs and harmless floating things. The horror of that death by drowning lived in the area behind the carvanda hedge like a mad relation, a family scandal or a hereditary illness waiting to re-emerge. It was a blot, a black and stinking blot.

The parents were furious at this disastrous expenditure, the gardener guilty and therefore sulky, and the children shocked. Most horrifying of all, the calf pined and died. It kept Aunt Mira awake in the night and nightly she saw the white cow die in the black well.

Aunt Mira was younger than their mother although she looked so much older. She had been twelve years old when she married and was a virgin when she was widowed—her young student husband, having left to study in England immediately after their wedding, caught a cold in the rain one winter night, and died. She was left stranded with his family and they

---

9. At Indian weddings, guests shower the bride and groom with flower petals.

blamed her bitterly for his death: it was her unfortunate horoscope that had brought it about, they said.[1] She should be made to pay for her guilt. Guiltily, she scrubbed and washed and cooked for them. At night she massaged her mother-in-law's legs and nursed wakeful babies and stitched trousseaux for her sisters-in-law. Of course she aged. Not only was her hair white but she was nearly bald. At least that saved her from being used by her brothers-in-law who would have put the widow to a different use had she been more appetising. Since she was not, they eyed her unpleasing person sullenly and made jokes loudly enough for her to overhear. There was laughter, till they grew bored. She stayed with them so long that she became boring. They suspected her of being a parasite. It was time she was turned out. She was turned out. Another household could find some use for her: cracked pot, torn rag, picked bone.

The children wondered why she always wore white. The mother explained, smoothing down her own ripe, flushed silks, that white was the widow's colour. "But now she is not a widow, now she lives with *us*," said Raja, and the girls asked if she had not had any wedding finery. Oh yes, she said without resentment, she had had some but had given it all away to her sisters-in-law when they married, to fill out their dowries. She added, with regret, that she wished she had been allowed to keep some for her nieces. The girls, too, regretted this and looked through the green tin trunk once again for some remnant of her wedding, of her improbable married life. And there was one: a stripe of crimson and gold edging an untouched Benares[2] silk sari. Since it was white, she had been allowed to retain it, and now it was yellowed like old ivory. The strip of crimson and gold made it impossible for her to wear: taboo. It was wrapped carefully in tissue and laid away like some precious relic. The girls would try and persuade her to wear it once when her Theosophist friends took her out to a meeting or arranged a tea for a visiting Friend, but she always shook her head nervously and refused, superstitiously afraid. The girls fondled it, buried their faces in it, sniffed at its old, musky scent that they preferred to their mother's French perfumes: it seemed more human. After all, it contained Aunt Mira's past, and the might-have-been future, as floating and elusive as the musk itself. But she would not touch it. When they became insistent, she said, laughing, "All right, when I die, you may dress me in it for the funeral pyre," then immediately looked guilty and repentant at the shock that swept across their faces.

Aunt Mira, though widowed, could not be said to be abandoned. She was searched out, even, by those whom misery attracted just as it nauseated others. As she was such a useful slave, she might be a useful convert, these thought, and burrowing into the suspicious family like persistent wood-borers, they found her out and carried her off to the Theosophy Lodge for meetings, lectures and teas. Aunt Mira shook at the possibilities, at the stormy wastes she glimpsed there, and the cyclones and avalanches and apparitions that swept through it. While she shivered and dithered, the

---

1. It was common for young Hindu girls to be married before puberty. Hindu marriages are arranged by the family, and horoscopes are consulted in the matchmaking process. Widows were considered inauspicious, and high-caste widows could not remarry.   2. A north Indian city famous for silk weaving.

dead man's family disapproved, disapproved. Removed from them, she dithered again—should she? could she now? Raja and Bim urged her on, excited, giggling—it was as good as opening up a cupboard full of ghosts, they felt, shivering in delighted anticipation. They fully expected polter-geists to arrive by air, three-legged tables to rise to the ceiling, strange messages to be imparted. But Aunt Mira was too weak. She had to be dragged to meetings, she was so afraid of them, and soon found excuses for not going. So they sent her books. She had little time for reading. Yet she seemed to imbibe something from their uncut pages and closed cov-ers, and grew more vague, absent-minded—"ectoplasmic,"[3] Raja said.

To Tara, she was nothing of the sort: she was solid as a bed, she smelt of cooking and was made of knitting. Tara could wrap herself up in her as in an old soft shawl. This Tara needed for she had lost most at Baba's birth and the turning of the entire family from her to the new baby. Wrapped in the folds of Aunt Mira's white cotton sari, or into her loosely knitted grey shawl, or the plump billows of the plum-coloured quilt in winter, she became baby again, breathing in her aunt's smell, finding in it a deep, musty comfort. On summer nights she lay on the pallet closest to her aunt's string bed out on the lawn where they slept in a row of cots under the stars. Then Aunt Mira would tell them stories: "Once there was a king and a queen. The queen said to her pet parrot, Go to the king and tell him I want the red ruby that the king cobra keeps hidden under its hood . . ." and Tara, who believed ardently in jewels, gave a wriggle of pleasure. Aunt Mira's voice murmured on and on, following all the loops and turns of the story as skilfully as water flowing down its necessary channel, till the car's headlights lit up the gate-posts with its green flood of phosphores-cence and came sliding up the drive, bringing their parents home from the club. Then they would hastily lie down flat and stiff as a row of corpses, pretending to be fast asleep. When the parents had gone in to change and to sleep on their own veranda at the other end of the house, Tara would whisper urgently, "And then, Mira-*masi*? And then?" and the voice would continue, in an even lower register, "And the cobra said, I will give you my ruby if the Queen sends me the princess dressed in a gold wedding sari and holding the Queen's pet parrot on her finger . . ." and the stars blurred and the jasmines shook out the powdery frills and flounces of their night scent till sleep came out of the dark hedges to devour them.

Sunny winter mornings had the same quality of perfection. Then the quilts would all be carried out and laid onto a string cot in the sun to air and Tara and Baba would roll themselves into them till they went pink from the heat of the cotton stuffing and the sun. Aunt Mira would sit on her cane stool, the knitting needles going clack-clack while she knitted their school sweaters, and now and then turned the brown and white pot-tery jars filled with pickles that lined the veranda so that each side of the jars got the sun in turn. When she was not looking, they would lift the lids off the jars and fish out bits with their fingers to eat, but it always made them sneeze and their eyes water so that Aunt Mira would know what they had been up to and scold, in a low voice so as not to be heard by their

3. Continually changing shape.

mother who sat playing cards with her friends on the veranda amongst the massed pots of chrysanthemums, pink and egg-yellow and bronze, fretted and shaggy and spicy. The cat stalked the butterflies that fluttered two by two over the flower-beds, as packed and coloured as a paint-box, but Aunt Mira was quick and never let her catch them.

Quick, nervy and jumpy—yet to the children she was as constant as a staff, a tree that can be counted on not to pull up its roots and shift in the night. She was the tree that grew in the centre of their lives and in whose shade they lived. Strange, when she was not their mother and did not rule the household. She really had not the qualities required by a mother or a wife. Even the children did not believe she had. Looking at her, they could not blame the husband for going away to England and dying. Aunt Mira would not have made a wife. What does make a wife? Why, they felt, a wife is someone like their mother who raised her eyes when the father rose from the table and dropped them when he sat down; who spent long hours at a dressing-table before a mirror, amongst jars and bottles that smelt sweet and into which she dipped questing fingers and drew out the ingredients of a wife—sweet-smelling but soon rancid; who commanded servants and chastised children and was obeyed like a queen. Aunt Mira had none of these attributes. Stick-like, she whipped her sari about her, jammed a few long steel pins into the little knot of hair on her head, and was dressed in an instant, ready to fly. She neither commanded nor chastised, and was certainly never obeyed. She was not soft or scented or sensual. She was bony and angular, wrinkled and desiccated—like a stick, or an ancient tree to which they adhered.

They grew around her knees, stubby and strong, some as high as her waist, some rising to her shoulders. She felt their limbs, brown and knobby with muscle, hot with the life force. They crowded about her so that they formed a ring, a protective railing about her. Now no one could approach, no threat, no menace. Their arms were tight around her, keeping her for themselves. They owned her and yes, she wanted to be owned. She owned them too, and they needed to be owned. Their opposing needs seemed to mingle and meet at the very roots, inside the soil in which they grew.

Touching them, dressing them, lifting them, drawing them to her, she felt how their life streams met and flowed into each other. They drew from her and she gave readily—she could not have not given. Would it weaken her? Would she be stronger if she put them away and stood by herself, alone? No, that was not her way any more than it was the way of nature. She fed them with her own nutrients, she reared them in her own shade, she was the support on which they leaned as they grew.

Soon they grew tall, soon they grew strong. They wrapped themselves around her, smothering her in leaves and flowers. She laughed at the profusion, the beauty of this little grove that was the whole forest to her, the whole world. If they choked her, if they sucked her dry of substance, she would give in without any sacrifice of will—it seemed in keeping with nature to do so. In the end they would swarm over her, reach up above her, tower into the sky, and she would be just the old log, the dried mass of roots on which they grew. She was the tree, she was the soil, she was the earth.

Touching them, watching them, she saw them as the leaves and flowers and fruit of the earth. So beautiful, she murmured, touching, watching— so beautiful and strong and living.

The first summer that Aunt Mira was with them, Bim and Raja caught typhoid. They were fortunate to have her in the house since she nursed them alone. They were so ill they were often unconscious, drifting about without any moorings in the luminous world of fever and then returning to the edge of consciousness in a kind of daze, not really aware who it was that lifted their heads and spooned barley water into their mouths or held cold sponges to their foreheads so that the water trickled into their eyes and ran down their cheeks onto their pillows. The doctor would come but he had no medicine for them: nursing was all, he said, and nursing was what Aunt Mira did best.

Tara hovered at the door, not allowed in, or played quietly on the veranda, now and then lifting the bamboo screen at their door to peep in, and Aunt Mira would make a great effort and rouse herself from her anxiety and exhaustion and go out and play a game of cat's cradle with her, or give her a poem to memorize, or thread a string of leaves to tie round her waist for a dance or, if she could not leave Bim's and Raja's bedsides when they were delirious, wave gaily to Tara at the door and point out a squirrel on a tree to her. This became the basis of their special relationship—an affectionate, demonstrative one, always assuring each other of their love, while the one that grew up between Aunt Mira and the two older children was silent and instinctive, seldom demonstrated, often quite sarcastic, but organic, a part of their sinews and their blood.

The difference showed when they played their favourite game of questioning each other: "What will you be when you grow up?"

Raja said promptly and proudly: "A hero."

Tara said you could not be a hero, you could only be a heroic soldier, a heroic explorer, a heroic something, but he insisted he would be, simply and purely, a hero.

Then Bim declared, with glistening eyes, that she would be a heroine, although she would secretly have preferred to be a gipsy or a trapeze artist in a circus.

Tara looked from one to the other in incomprehension. "I am going to be a mother and knit for my babies," she said complacently, but the older two laughed at her so uproariously, so scornfully, that she burst into tears and ran to bury her head in her aunt's lap and complain that they made fun of her.

Aunt Mira smiled faintly when she heard of Bim's and Raja's ambitions and was really in complete sympathy with them, but she stroked Tara's head and consoled her. "There, there, you'll see you grow up to be exactly what you want to be, and I very much doubt if Bim and Raja will be what *they* say they will be." This consoled Tara entirely and turned out to be true as well.

They had other games to play on summer afternoons, lying on bamboo matting on the floor under the slowly revolving electric fan, watching the geckoes crawl across the ceiling after the flies, wiping the perspiration from their faces and feeling swollen and flushed by the heat.

"What is the hottest thing you can think of?"

"Melting lead over the kitchen fire and going out in the sun to pour it into a groove in the clay," said Bim because that was what they had done that morning and she felt sure she had got heat-stroke.

"Holding a magnifying glass over a sheet of paper in the sun and burning a hole into it," said Raja.

"White chicken feathers lying in the ash heap by the kitchen door," said Tara unexpectedly, and then instantly mumbled "No, no, not really," because she had just remembered what it had felt like to roll off Aunt Mira's bed and crawl under it to visit the cat's newest litter, all lined up against her panting flesh like leeches. The dust under her bed, the cats' fur, matted and grey and marmalade, immobilized by the heat except for their panting breath and little pointed pink tongues hanging out of their open mouths—that was the warmest thing she knew.

"And the coolest thing you can find in summer?" the game continued.

"A long drink of water from the earthen jar on the veranda."

"Watering the rush matting at the door with a hose-pipe, seeing it trickle down and smelling the wet *khus*."[4]

"A water-melon cut open and sliced, all red and juicy."

In search of such balm, they would steal out of the house although forbidden to do so under pain of sun-stroke. They could hear the grass frizzling in the sun, the dust seething in the air, nothing else—even the pigeons were dumb, and the coppersmiths. They made a dash across the scorching earth to the water tap at the end of the rose walk, quietly trickling into the green mud around it. They squirted each other with the water but it was tepid and lifeless. The gardener's family lay on a string cot under the mulberry trees, and their smallest baby cried and cried, its skin angry and sore with prickly heat.

They wandered down to the long row of servants' quarters behind the guava trees. There Tara's old ayah sat like a bag of rags, chewing her betel nut and stirring up a fire of smouldering sticks to boil some tea. The acrid smoke billowed out into their eyes and made them cry. This made her laugh: "If the smoke follows you like this, it means you will have faithful husbands." They snorted at her scornfully and went into her room, odorous of cowdung fires and mustard oil, to look through her bags and baskets filled with old rubbish gleaned from their house over the years—bent forks, scraps of lace, curling yellow photographs and empty tins. The sooty walls were papered with bright pictures from the illustrated papers but it was too dark and smoky to make them out, and they soon grew bored and drifted out, stopped to whistle at the bedraggled parrot she kept in a cage,

---

4. Aromatic rushes woven into mats and screens, which when watered give off a cool, scented breeze.

feed it a chilli or two that it only stared at beadily and refused to touch, then went back to the house to collapse onto the bamboo matting spread on the floor for them, pinioned to it like leaves drying and fading into mere brown tissue held together by bleached skeletons.

"What is the most frightening thing you can think of?"

"Finding a centipede inside your slipper just as you are putting it on."

"The well the cow drowned in."

"A cholera injection," said Tara, but immediately followed that by a small gasp for it had led her to think of something far more frightening and disquieting, something she feared to speak of at all. It gave her face a baffled, secretive look as she grappled with a memory that heaved out of her mind like a shape emerging from the surface of dark water, at first grey and indistinguishable, then gradually coming closer and growing larger as she backed away in fright.

She had followed her father into her mother's bedroom on a day when her mother had not emerged at all, very quietly so as not to disturb her and therefore not noticed by her father. Then what she saw made her back into the dusty crimson curtain that hung at the door and hide in its folds, watching something she did not wish to see: her father, with his mouth folded up very primly, his eyes pinpointed with concentration behind the lens of his spectacles, bending over the bed, pressing a syringe into the thick, flabby arm that lay there. As the needle went in, the mother's head tilted back and sank deeper and deeper into the pillow, the trembling chin rose into the air and a little sigh issued through her dry lips as if the needle had punctured an air-bag and it was the very life of her that was being released, withdrawn from her. Then Tara knew she had witnessed a murder—her father had killed her mother. She stumbled out of the room and was sick on the drawing room carpet.

"What is the matter, Tara?"

Tara had crawled into Aunt Mira's bed in the garden that night and lay in a ball, pressing against her aunt's feet as she sat cross-legged, telling them a story that began "Once upon a time there was a king and he had three sons . . ."

"When will they come home?" Tara whispered. To her baffled wonder, that evening the car had driven up to the veranda steps and her mother had come out of the house and stepped into the car with the father and driven off to the club as usual, dressed in green silk and several pearls, palpably alive. They had not returned yet and the square of light that was the dining-room door kept Tara awake as a tyrant does its prisoner.

"Soon," her aunt comforted her.

"Poor Abu, still waiting up with the dinner," Bim grumbled. "It's so late, why don't they come home to dinner?"

"When people play cards, they don't notice the time."

"*Why* do they play cards?"

There seemed to be only one answer, too obvious to make, but that night Aunt Mira gently hinted at another as if she knew what kept Tara so miserably awake and tortured. "It helps your mother to forget her pain," she suggested.

Tara stiffened immediately. Bim and Raja were startled. What pains had she? they clamoured to know. Then Tara heard the word: diabetes. Now they understood why the doctor came so often to the house. Injections, said Aunt Mira, it was the daily injections that kept her alive.

"Alive?" wondered Tara, the morning scene unreeling through her mind like a film cut loose in the projector and wildly flying backwards.

Bim and Raja argued "If she is ill, she should stay in bed. Then she would get better. She should not go to the club," they said censoriously.

"She is trying to lead a normal life, for your father's sake," Aunt Mira explained, but such adult clichés could satisfy no child. Unappeased, they continued to question Aunt Mira. Insulin, they wanted to know more about insulin. Their aunt could tell them nothing beyond the need for the daily injection of insulin that their father gave her.

"Oh," sighed Tara, "is *that* why she has those little blue marks in her arm?" and she laid her head against her aunt's shoulder, weak with relief and gratitude at having been given an explanation that would cover up the livid, throbbing scene in her mind as a scab covers a cut.

Raja of course outgrew the efficacy of his aunt's answers to his questions and her stories spun shining through their nights like a spider's silver webs. He would make scornful remarks, point out the illogic of her fairy tales. Impatient, he would leave his sisters to his aunt and go off to the servants' quarters or hail the soda-man, a jaunty young Sikh who came to the house driving a cart in which blocks of ice and crates of soda bottles slithered on the wet sacking and smelt pleasantly of damp straw. While the cook exchanged empty bottles for full ones and had a block of ice put in his ice-box, Raja drank a bottle of ginger beer, tingling to its spiciness, and then leapt up onto the cart and, waving the whip over the yellow nag's ears, set off at a rumble down the drive, making the soda-man rush out and abuse him and the girls jump up and down with delight and cheer him. He would drive it at a furious rattle up to the gate and then stop and jump off, surrendering the whip to the angry driver, and smile smugly at the admiring girls. Or he would go and call Hamid,[5] the driver's son who worked in a cinema house in Kashmere Gate and was already a wage-earner although not much older than Raja. Hamid used to take him for rides on his bicycle when he was small, then taught him how to cycle. He also taught him wrestling. The two of them dug a shallow pit behind the garage, beat and crumbled the earth till it was smooth and even and then they would wrestle, grunting and groaning and pushing at each other in mock combat that always ended in being serious. Raja was always beaten and emerged bleary-eyed and dusty but panting with pride at having partaken of this manly sport. For a while he went in for a daily oil massage and for eating blanched almonds with his morning milk, absolutely serious in his pursuit of excellence, but after a while Hamid's own dilettantism infected him. Cutting short a half-hearted wrestling bout, they would get onto their bicycles and set off for the cinema in Kashmere Gate and Hamid would smuggle Raja in without a ticket to see the latest Charlie

5. A Muslim name.

Chaplin or Douglas Fairbanks or any Bombay film for which Sehgal[6] had sung the songs. Raja had no ear for music but the Urdu lyrics that were sung appealed to him powerfully and he would recite them emotionally and dramatically as they cycled slowly home at night, passing from lamplight to shadow along the pipal-tree lined street, quite sure that the parents would not be back from the club and that the girls would be asleep.

But Bim, a light sleeper, would lift her head when she heard him steal up across the inky lawn and murmur a muffled reprimand at which he would stick out his tongue.

As he grew long-legged and lanky, he became more difficult to catch. Tara, who had always felt at a disadvantage when competing for Raja's attention since she was the smaller and weaker one, born to trail behind the others, while Bim and Raja were not only closer in age but a match for each other in many other ways, began to realize that she and Bim were actually comrades-in-arms for they pursued Raja together now and Raja eluded them both.

In games of hide-and-seek in the garden, on summer evenings when the long, flattened-out afternoon could at last be ripped away so that their refreshed evening selves could spring up and come into being, it was always Raja who was the leader, who did the counting-out, who ran and hid, and it was always the two girls who were left to run about in frenzied pursuit, tearing their dresses and bruising their knees, quite unmindful of stains and scratches and beads of blood while their eyes gleamed and their faces flushed with lust to find and capture him and call him captive.

There was one glorious moment when they cornered him, up against the impenetrable carvanda hedge, and leapt upon him, from east and west, all nails and teeth and banshee screams. But, ducking beneath their arms, he turned and dashed his head madly into that thick, solid hedge behind him and broke his way through it with one desperate, inspired thrust of his body. And they, too, were sucked into the tunnel he had so surprisingly made in that wall of thorns and twigs and leaves, fell into it and blew through it, then streamed after him, made limitless by surprise, into the forbidden area of the back garden. This was the still, uninhabited no-man's land into which the gardener hurled branches of thorn and broken flower pots. Here he built his steaming, fetid compost heaps. Here was the well in which the cow had drowned, the deep stone well that held green scum and black deeds.

Here the girls stopped, halted in their mad stampede by the sad realization that Raja had escaped them again, fled past these barriers and probably found shelter in the servants' quarters where Hamid would help to hide him from them. Out of breath, heated, glaring, they looked down at the thorns they stood in that had scratched long strings of blood-beads out of their brown legs, and at the convolvulus and the castor oil plants that grew thickly about the well.

For a while they panted noisily, unnecessarily noisily, trying to recapture the glory of that moment when they had caught Raja, nearly caught

6. K. L. Sehgal, one of the most popular singers in Hindi films made in the 1930s and 1940s.

him, up against the hedge. Then they bent to wipe the blood from their legs and straightened to slap at the mosquitoes that rose humming from out of the moist compost heap and hovered about their heads in dark nets.

Then Tara breathed "Bim, we're right next to the well," and instinctively they moved closer to each other in order to face together what was such a source of horror to them all and definitely out of bounds as well. But Bim, left flat and emptied out by disappointment at Raja's escape, gave Tara a sudden little push, saying "Let's look." When Tara hung back, she took her firmly by the elbow and made her kneel beside her, then bent forward to peer through the weeds into the depths of the well.

The water at the bottom was black, with an oily, green sheen. It was very still except when a small frog plopped in from a crack between the stones, making the girls start slightly. They narrowed their eyes and searched but no white and milky bone lifted out of it. The cow had never been hauled out. Although men had come with ropes and pulleys to help the gardener, it had proved impossible. She had been left to rot: that was what made the horror of it so dense and intolerable. The girls stared, scarcely breathing, till their eyes started out of their heads, but no ghostly ship of bones rode the still water. It must have sunk to the bottom and rooted itself in the mud, like a tree. There was nothing to see—neither hoof nor horn nor one staring, glittering eye. The water had stagnated and blackened, closing over the bones like a new skin. But even the new skin was black now and although it stank, it gave away nothing.

Nothing in their hands, the girls backed away on their knees till it was safe to stand, then turned and hurried away, through the grey thorns and over the midden heap,[7] and finally butted their way through the hedge back into the garden, the familiar and permitted and legitimate part of the garden where they found Raja coolly sitting on a cane stool beside Aunt Mira, eating the slices of guava that she cut and peeled for him.

Rushing forward with renewed fury, they screamed and jeered and raged at him. He stuck out his tongue at them for he had no idea that they were not screaming with rage at his escape from their clutching fingers and pinching nails but at the horror behind the hedge, the well that waited for them at the bottom of the garden, bottomless and black and stinking.

When Bim realized, although incredulously, that Raja was withdrawing, that his maleness and his years were forcing him to withdraw from the cocoon-cosiness spun by his aunt and his sisters out of their femaleness and lack—or surfeit—of years, she grew resentful. She still sat listening to Aunt Mira's fairy tales but with a brooding air, resenting being left there, bored and inactive, by Raja. Her resentment led her at times to be cruel to Tara.

She knew how Tara longed for curls. Tara's hair was as lank and black as Bim's, hanging limp to her shoulders, so that she yearned for a little wave to it, some soft curls. To ask for the golden locks of fairy-tale heroines was too much, Tara knew, but at least she might ask for a slight wave, a bit of a curl. Bim overheard her confiding in her aunt: "*Masi*, I wish God

7. Refuse pile.

would give me curls. If I pray to him, will he give me curls, *masi?*" Bim
went immediately to the sewing box and fetched a pair of scissors. Flashing
them at Tara, she whispered "Come, I'll cut your hair for you. Then it
will curl by itself. Long hair never curls—it has to be cut very, very short."
Tara was enticed by this promise and at once slipped out of Aunt Mira's
bed and followed her sister.

But when she saw Bim leading her out of the house and up the outer
staircase to the rooftop, she grew apprehensive and hung back, putting her
hands round her long bunches of hair, protectively. "Come on, come on,"
Bim hurried her roughly, snipping the air with the big heavy sewing scissors and, making Tara crouch down behind the cast-iron water-tank on
the roof, she cut through her hair at the ears with great sure crunches of
the steel blades. Thick inky swathes lay about their feet, peppered Tara's
neck and back with snippets and drifted with the evening breeze to the
edge of the terrace, then lifted up and floated over the balustrade and into
the garden.

Tara began to whimper as she felt the unaccustomed touch of cool air
on her neck, bared and naked, then raised her hands to feel the bristles
about her ears, as sharp and rough as stubble, and let out a loud wail of
distress. When Bim marched off with the scissors, looking undeniably
smug, Tara stayed back and refused to go down.

After a while the strands of hair floating down from the terrace were
noticed by those in the garden and in the veranda. They came out to stand
in the driveway and gaze with shaded eyes to see where it was coming
from. The white sky stared blankly back. A circling kite whistled thinly—
and Tara sobbed and whined. They could hear her now.

Bim was asked to go up and fetch her but would not—she was doing
her homework, she importantly said. Then Raja and Hamid went and
shouted with laughter at the sight that met their eyes—they said Tara
looked like a baby pigeon fallen out of its nest, blue-skinned and bristly,
crouching behind the water-tank and crying for her lost hair. As the boys
roared with laughter, her crying grew wilder. Finally Bim stomped up and
grabbed her by the arm. "Stop howling, you booby," she said roughly.
"You wanted curls, now you've got curls. You *said* I could cut your hair
and I *did*. How was I to know you didn't mean it?" and she pulled the
wailing sister down the stairs and scornfully turned her over to Aunt Mira's
tender ministrations.

Tara was sure she would never forgive Bim her cruelty. Bim's big-sister-
liness would always be linked with that ruthless and cynical chopping of
her long hair, Tara felt. It grew again, as Aunt Mira assured her it would,
but as straight and lank as it had been before.

These were the dramas that seemed not so much to make cracks in the
dull metal bands that held them all down into a world, an age, of unbearable, total inactivity, eventlessness and apathy, as to emphasize them by
hitting them with a hammer so that they clanged and the clangs
resounded and echoed. As they grew into adolescence it seemed to Raja,
Bim and Tara that they were suffocating in some great grey mass through
which they tried to thrust as Raja had thrust through the thorny hedge,
and emerge into a different atmosphere. How was it to be different? Oh,

they thought, it should have colour and event and company, be rich and vibrant with possibilities. Only they could not—the greyness was so massed as to baffle them and defeat their attempts to fight through. Only Raja sometimes did. On his bicycle, cycling off to the cinema in Kashmere Gate, or in the wrestling pit with Hamid, or rattling down the drive in the soda-man's cart, hallooing and waving a whip over the startled nag's head, or flying kites on the terrace in the evenings, he seemed to come alive and glow, even if briefly, to be followed by a long trough of brooding sullenness and irritability.

Raja also had the faculty of coming alive to ideas, to images picked up in the books he read. The usual boyhood adventure stories, *Robin Hood* and *Beau Geste,* set him on fire till he almost blazed with enthusiasm as he showed Hamid how to fashion swords out of bamboo poles and battle with him, or pictured himself in the desert, in the Foreign Legion, playing some outsize, heroic role in a splendid battle. He cycled to Connaught Place and bought cheap paperbacks printed specially for the American Army[8] and sold on the pavements, and took them home to share with his sisters. "Book worms, book worms," Aunt Mira called them, rather proudly and indulgently, as they lay stretched on their beds under the stickily revolving fans, reading with almost audible concentration.

The sisters, however, read themselves not into a blaze but a stupor, sinking lower and lower under the dreadful weight of *Gone With the Wind* and *Lorna Doone,* their eyes growing glazed so that they seemed to read through an opaque film and the stories and characters never quite emerged into the bright light of day and only made vague, blurred impressions on their drowsy, drugged minds, rather than vivid and clear-cut ones. They hadn't the vitality that Raja had, to participate in what they read— they were passive receivers, bulging with all they read, sinking with its weight like water-logged rafts.

While Tara would be dragged helplessly into the underworld of semi-consciousness by the romances she read, Bim was often irritated and would toss them aside in dissatisfaction. She began to realize they were not what she wanted. What did she want? Oh, she jerked her shoulders in irritation, something different—facts, history, chronology, preferably. She was bored by the books Raja brought her and tried not to disappoint him by showing her boredom but of course Raja saw and was hurt. Bim began to read, laboriously, sitting up at a table with her elbows placed on either side of the book, Gibbon's *Decline and Fall* that she had found on the drawing-room bookshelf. Raja secretly admired her for it as he could not have tackled a study of such length himself, but would not show it and said only that she did not know what she was missing, that she had no imagination: to him, the saddest sin. That hurt and puzzled Bim: what need of imagination when one could have knowledge instead? That created a gap between them, a trough or a channel that the books they shared did not bridge.

Yet when they came together it was with a pure and elemental joy that shot up and stood straight and bright above the surrounding dreariness.

8. U.S. Army troops were stationed in India during World War II.

There were still those shining summer evenings on the banks of the Jumna when they went together, Bim and Raja, barefoot over the sand to wade across the river, at that time of the year no more than a sluggish trickle, to the melon fields on the other bank to pick a ripe, round one and cut it open with Raja's pen-knife and bite into the juice-suffused slices while the sun sank into the saffron west and the cannon boomed in the city to announce the end of the day's fast in the month of Ramzaan and the start of prayers in the great mosque.[9] At this hour the dome of the sky would soften from white-hot metal to a soft mauve tapestry streaked with pink. The washermen would fold the dried washing spread out on the sand and load it onto their donkeys and ride away. Smoke would rise from small fires in the hovels at the bend of the river and from under the thatch of the melon-growers' huts, turning the evening air furry and soft. A lapwing would start out of the dark with a cry and a star wink into life simultaneously, it seemed.

Tara was sent to fetch them home. She came, holding Baba by the hand. Now and then she bent to pick up a small, insignificant river shell and press it confidingly into his hand. Seeing Raja and Bim wading slowly back through the river, muddy and tired, she waved. They shouted. The two pairs of children trudged slowly towards each other over the dry silver of the sand. When they met, they became a blur in the dark, wavering homewards.

As they turned to make their way back to the house, a kind of low drumbeat started up in the pits of their stomachs, reverberated through them, making them stop and clutch each other by the hand.

"*Hato! Hato!*" shouted a man in a khaki uniform and a scarlet turban, and pounded past them on urgent heels, making way for a white horse that loomed up out of the dunes and floated by with a dimmed roar of hoofbeats on the sand, followed by a slim golden dog with a happy plume of a tail waving in the purple air. The pampas grass bent and parted for this procession and then rustled silkily upright into place again.

When the three figures had vanished into a dip in the dunes and then reappeared in the white dust of the road ahead, at a distance, Raja breathed out in awe "It is Hyder Ali Sahib on his horse. He looks like a general! Like a king!"

"Perhaps he likes to imagine he is one," said Bim tartly, drawing Baba forward by the hand. Some of the sand had been flung into their eyes. They were all rubbing at the grains.

Tara jumped up and down on her toes, watching them still. "And his dog," she cried. "See the lovely dog running after the horse."

"I wish he were a friend of Papa's," Raja said wistfully as they shuffled up the road, sand filling the spaces between their toes. "Then he might let me ride his horse sometimes."

"You don't know how to," Bim said.

Ahead of them, the magical procession turned in at the Hyder Alis' tall wrought-iron gate and a light came on in the porch and, a moment later, another one in their own house behind the trees.

---

9. The Jama Masjid, or "Friday Mosque," built by the Moghal emperor Shah Jahan.

After that the sense of dullness and hopelessness that reigned over their house took on the intense aspect of waiting. They were always waiting now—superficially, for their parents to come home from the club, or Aunt Mira to put Baba to bed and come and tell them a story. Yet when the parents were back and Aunt Mira free, they were still unfulfilled, still waiting. Perhaps for the white horse to appear again on the dunes, followed by the golden dog. Or for some greater event, some more drastic change, a complete reversal of their present lives and the beginning of a new, wondrous phase. They would wander about the garden, peering intently into the phosphorescent green tunnel of a furled banana leaf, or opening a canna lily pod and gazing at its inner compartments and the embedded pearly seeds, or following the path of a silent snail, searching for a track that might lead somewhere, they had no idea where.

Bim felt she knew the answer for at least some of the daylight hours on six days of the week—the hours she spent in school. At school Bim became a different person—active, involved, purposeful. A born organiser, she was patrol leader of the Bluebirds[1] when still a small pig-tailed junior, later of the Girl Guides, then captain of the netball team, class prefect, even— gloriously, in her final year at school—Head Girl. A bright, slapdash student, she spent little time at her studies but did almost as well as those dim, bespectacled daughters of frustrated failures who drove their children frantically, bitterly, to beat everyone else in the exams and to spend all their waking hours poring myopically over their schoolbooks. Bim had an easy, teasing manner with the teachers who liked her for it even if they sometimes scolded her. They were always admonishing Tara in reproachful tones: "Look at your sister Bimla. You should try to be more like your sister Bimla. *She* plays games, *she* takes part in all activities, *she* is a monitor, the head girl. And you . . ."

Tara hung her head lower and lower, dragging her foot as she walked, irritating them still further. Physically smaller and weaker than Bim, she lacked her vigour, her stamina. The noise, the dense populace, the hustle and jostle of school made her shrink into a still smaller, paler creature who could not rouse herself out of a dismal apathy that made the lessons as irrelevant and meaningless as the buzzing of a fly against the windowpane, and friendship with the loud, vulgar, vigorous young girls in the class, so full of unpleasant secrets and revelations and so quick to betray and mock, an impossibility, vaguely wished for but quite beyond her capacity to undertake.

Whereas school brought out Bim's natural energy and vivacity that was kept damped down at home because of the peculiar atmosphere of their house, school to Tara was a terror, a blight, a gathering of large, loud, malicious forces that threatened and mocked her fragility. When confined within its high stone boundary walls, she thought of home with tearful yearning, almost unable to bear the separation from Aunt Mira, from Baba, from the comfortable, old, accustomed ayah, the rose walk, the somnolent mutter of the pigeons in the sunny veranda eaves, all of which took on an aura of paradise for her when she was separated from it.

---

1. An organization for young girls.

To Bim, school and its teachers and lessons were a challenge to her natural intelligence and mental curiosity that she was glad to meet. Tara, on the other hand, wilted when confronted by a challenge, shrank back into a knot of horrified stupor and tended to gaze dully at the teachers when asked a question, making them wonder if she were not somewhat retarded (in the staff room, over tea, they said "There is a brother, I've heard, who is . . ." and tapped their heads significantly). Tara was capable of spending a whole lesson seemingly hypnotised by a fly exploring a windowpane beside her desk or sticking the broken nib of her pen into a scrap of blotting paper and watching the ink ooze and spread. She did this quite without any curiosity in the scene that might have made her preoccupation excusable. Her teachers did not know that she had only to enter a classroom for the mucous membrane in her nostrils to swell and block her breathing apparatus. She was too polite to sniff but it gave her face a set, congested look that they took to be stubbornness, even insolence. She made them all bridle, teachers and students alike. She made no friends. When the others clustered together, sharing a delicious secret like a lollipop passed from one to the other for an unhygienic lick, Tara was left out. If they were choosing teams for a game, Tara was always left to the last, standing forgotten and wretched, and then one of the leaders would reluctantly agree to include her. She was no good at any game while Bim had a natural affinity with the bat and ball, and had the most splendid coordination, trained in sports as she was by Raja and Hamid who had often made use of her as a fielder when they got up a cricket game between them.

If only Tara had made up by showing some talent in the field of arts, as it was called by the staff, it might have given them cause to excuse her lassitude, her "insolence." But her fingers were so stiff, she could neither draw nor paint or even knit or weave paper baskets in the crafts class. She tended to reduce things to the smallest possible circumference as if in the hope they might then vanish altogether—a large brass jug and great pestle and mortar set up on a table in the arts class would appear on her sheet of drawing paper as a series of knobs and buttons, rubbed and rubbed at with her eraser till smudged to a shaky blur; a scrap of weaving or knitting in her hands became a tight knot that had to be cut away from the loom or knitting needles when it could be worked no tighter.

The missionary ladies who ran the grey, austere mission school, found this lack of ability, this lack of will too deplorable. They were all elderly spinsters—had, in fact, taken the vow of celibacy although not the nun's habit—awesomely brisk, cheerful and resourceful. Having left the meadows and hedgerows, the parsonages and village greens of their homes behind in their confident and quixotic youth, they had gone through experiences of a kind others might have buckled under but that they had borne and survived and overcome like boats riding the waves—wars and blitzes, riots and mutinies, famines and droughts, floods, fires and native customs—and they had then retired, not to the parsonages and village greens, but to the running of a sober, disciplined mission school with all their confidence, their cheerfulness and their faith impeccably intact. Tara could not suppress a baleful look as she observed them bustling about the classrooms, cracking open the registers or working out algebraic problems across the blackboards, blowing whistles and rushing across the netball fields, organising sports days and annual school concerts, leading the girls in singing hymns and, every so often, dropping suddenly to their knees, burying their faces in worn and naked hands, and praying with most distinguished intensity. Tara wondered uneasily if hers were one of the lost souls they prayed for.

Yet she preferred them to the Christian converts who made up the rest of the staff. She deplored their taste in clothes and definitely preferred the missionary ladies' grey tunics to the fancifully patterned and embroidered saris of pink and purple georgette that the converts favoured. She was offended by their names which were usually Rose and Lily or even, in one case, Pansy. Many of them were spinsters but even in those who were married and were met at the gate after school by husbands on bicycles or even had some of their children in the school, unnaturally clean and with charity clearly stamped on their subdued faces and shabby clothes, Tara sensed a bank of frustration — surely that was what made them so frighteningly spiteful, bitter and ill-tempered. They had such very sarcastic tongues and always seemed to single out Tara, as if sensing her distaste and disapproval, for their sharpest tongue-lashings. The other girls, instead of siding with her against the enemy, tittered and smirked to see her scolded and have her homework flung at her in rage. The truth was that they all considered Tara unbearably snobbish and conceited. The very fact that she wandered about the playground by herself during the lunch-break, morose and aloof, watching the kites that circled in the white sky waiting to swoop down on an unprotected lunch-box in a flash of claws and beaks, or picking up the neem pods under the scattering, yellowed trees, simply out of an embarrassed need to have something to do with herself, led them to conclude she was too conceited to join them in their songs and their gossip and chatter.

Bim, observing her out of the corner of her eye while she played a wild impromptu game of basketball with the bigger girls, carefully avoided having anything to do with her anti-social misery: it was contagious.

The dreariness of school intensified and reached its intolerable acme, for Tara, on Thursdays when the girls were sent, two by two, with a teacher at the head, to the mission hospital on the other side of the thick stone wall, to distribute fruit and blankets to the nonpaying patients. These blankets were made up of squares of red wool that the girls knitted during craft class on thick, blunt wooden needles. White chalk dust became thickly embedded in the coarse wool. Tara suffered genuine physical agonies working the rough wool with her perspiring fingers, getting it knotted tighter and tighter on the thick needles till they couldn't move any more and she had to appeal for help and be soundly castigated by the very cross crafts teacher, a Miss Jacob who had a wart on the side of her nose and whom Tara saw as a medieval witch. When enough squares had accumulated, they were sewn together and these thick, scratchy, hot blankets were borne in triumph to the hospital wards along with baskets of blackened, oozing bananas and green, sour oranges. The girls would form a crocodile and be marched through the hospital wards, stopping at the iron bedsteads to unload their bounty upon women who had just given birth and were obliged to wrap their fragile new babies in these coarse, itching blankets, others who had open, running sores or wore green eye patches or lay groaning and calling upon God to deliver them—nightmare figures emanating an odour as thick as chloroform, compounded of poverty and charity, disease and cure. Sometimes they would meet the hospital kitchen squad dishing out the patients' meals and once when Tara saw the rice and *dal* being ladled out of pails onto aluminum platters in slopping piles, she was obliged to run out behind a hedge to be sick. After that, charity always had, for her, the sour reek of vomit. The next Thursday she pretended to be ill. Other weeks, she made the most preposterous excuses, trying anything to be let off going to school on charity Thursdays. But Bim realized what was going on and told Aunt Mira. Aunt Mira was puzzled and concerned, Bim outraged.

"You could do just that little bit without complaining," she said severely. "It's not too much to ask of anyone—just to save up their breakfast fruit and give it to someone who needs it."

"I don't mind giving them my breakfast fruit," cried Tara passionately, tearful and red-faced now that she had been found out. "They can have *all* my fruit, every bit. Only *I* don't want to go and give it to them!"

"Why not?" said Bim. "Too fine a lady to step into the hospital ward? The smells upset you, do they? The sights keep you awake at night, do they? Oh, you poor little thing, you'd better get a bit tougher, hadn't you—auntie's baby? Otherwise what good will you ever be? If you can't even do this little bit for the poor, what will you ever be able to do when you grow up?"

Bim of course worshipped Florence Nightingale along with Joan of Arc in her private pantheon of saints and goddesses, and Tara did not tell her that she hoped never to have to do anything in the world, that she wanted only to hide under Aunt Mira's quilt or behind the shrubs in the garden and never be asked to come out and do anything, prove herself to be anything. When challenged to name her own particular heroine, she looked vague, tried to shift away, saying she would think about it. Seeing Bim's eyes flash so righteously, her mouth fixed so censoriously, Tara lacked the boldness to make an answer even if she could think of one.

Forced to go back to school, she accepted with a weak abandonment of hope that these grey, wretched days would stretch on forever, blighting her life with their creeping mildew. When she came home in the afternoon, she would embrace her aunt with such fervid passion, with such excellent intentions of helping her more, being patient and sisterly to her little brother, that her family wondered at her intensity, saying "You're only a day girl, Tara, you haven't been sent to boarding school, after all," quite failing to gauge the depth of her despondency. She would sit on a stool on the veranda, winding woollen balls for her aunt, or read nursery rhymes to Baba, trying to make him say "Ba-ba, Black Sheep" after her, till the wool was all in tight knotted balls and Baba failed to make any response beyond the faintest smile, not in her direction but the cat's, and then she would walk off to trail amongst the rose bushes or climb up to the terrace and watch Bim and Raja fly paper kites.

Two episodes cut through the grey chalk dust of school life with stripes of shocking colour.

In the first case, it was the colour of blood itself, perhaps not seen but sensed in all its scandalous outrage. It happened when Tara was still in the primary section. Their class was at the end of the building, and just outside, across a dusty strip of playing field, stood a row of tin-roofed, tin-walled latrines. There was something sinister about them that kept Tara away from them even when desperate to go. She would come home quite frantic with the need to urinate or even with her knickers stained damp and yellow rather than go into them in schooltime.

One day, glancing up from her slate, she saw some unusual activity outside the tin doors: the principal was there, gesticulating excitedly in a way novel to that calm lady, along with a man in a strange costume of khaki shorts, khaki shirt, a large khaki *topee* balanced on his prominent ears, and a rifle over his shoulder, just like a figure in a cartoon from Kipling's[2] days. Tara gave a gasp of alarm that made the other children look too and they all began to scream—Tara had for once not been alone in finding a sight sinister. The teacher was torn between her duty to silence them and her curiosity to see what was going on.

What had happened was that a mad dog had found its way into the school compound and crawled into one of the tin latrines. No one knew who had alerted the municipal dog shooter—nevertheless he was there, with his gun, obviously for the purpose of shooting the dog.

Hearing the alarm spread through the primary school, the principal left him to his abominable duty and came hurrying to herd them indoors, shut the doors and windows and command them not to see. They did not see but could hardly help hearing the shot followed by the squealing of the dog that seemed to spurt and squelch out of its body like blood till it was silenced by a second shot. Some of the children, made wild by the sounds, ran to see the dog dragged by its legs across the playing field by the comic hunter in khaki, and squeaked "Ooh, look, blood—bl-ood all over." Tara did not see, kept her fingers pressed into her eyes till blue and red stars burst out of them, but she was aware that blood had been spilt and washed over her feet, warm and thick and living.

Unlike Bim and Raja, she never pestered her parents for a dog. She knew what her father meant when he spoke darkly of the danger of rabies.

The other episode of colour was the more glamorous one of an adolescent crush of a pupil on her teacher. In this case, an unusually young and somehow appealing woman with strange grey cat's eyes set in her narrow face, who was soon seen to be a neurotic by everyone, even Tara, but who nevertheless exercised a fascination over the young girls who longed for

2. Rudyard Kipling (1865–1936), important British author and poet on British India. *Topee*: a pith helmet. Europeans living in India wore them as protection from the sun.

an element of colour in a life so singularly monochrome. By being different, by being quite obviously unsuitable, the new teacher made people talk. Very soon after she arrived, while Tara was still making tentative introductory gestures of bringing her a bunch of sweetpeas and offering to carry her load of books, there was a murmur, a susurration of scandal. The teacher had been called out of the classroom. She had been summoned by the principal. The principal had accused her of a misdemeanour. No one knew exactly what, but the girls gossiped. A foreigner, a blonde young man with an ascetic face and the saffron robes of a monk, had been seen loitering at the school gates. Miss Singh had been seen rushing out after school. She would come to class in the mornings, her pale eyes glittering, too bright, and laughingly confess she had not had the time to correct their books or prepare the new lesson: should they read some poetry instead? Tara was charmed. The girls said she had a "boyfriend." What had the principal caught her at? Had she tried to elope? With the blonde Buddhist monk? The gossip grew wilder. Miss Singh came out of the principal's office in tears. In class, she broke down completely in front of the appalled girls who did not know whether to rush up with their sympathy and handkerchiefs or drop their heads and pretend decorously not to notice. Miss Singh took a few days off. The principal took her classes. She found the girls in an unruly mood, defiant and excited and strangely rebellious. Five hundred lines were given them to write.

Miss Singh had not been sent away. They found out by standing in the flower bed under her window, trampling the flowers as they lifted each other up to peep in. They saw her lying fully-dressed on her bed, a wet cloth covering her eyes. Her thin wrist dangling helplessly out of the bed aroused their pity. They had read *Lorna Doone*, they had read *Camille*. They tiptoed away, awe-struck. They shot accusing looks at the principal whenever she strode past their classroom, swinging the spectacles that hung on a black ribbon round her neck.

Tara collected a bunch of velvet brown and purple pansies in the garden to take to school next day. But next day Miss Singh was gone. She had left, with her bags, without a word, without a goodbye to a single girl, not even to Tara who stood at the open door of her room, holding the bunch of pansies with their wide-eyed step-child faces. Tara was hurt, offended. She had thought up a plan to help Miss Singh: she was going to offer to carry messages for her, deliver notes to the blonde Buddhist monk or whoever it was who had caused Miss Singh this trouble. Now she could not. One of the big girls swooped down on her, snatched the pansies out of her hand and went laughing away. At home, Bim teased her for moping over Miss Singh so that she burst into tears and ran to Aunt Mira to complain. Bim was scolded for her tactlessness but only stuck out her tongue, unrepentant.

A great cloud of accusation settled over the principal's head: the girls refused to excuse her role in this painful affair. Often the resentment verged on near-rebellion. Some of the more lawless played practical tricks on the old lady. There was even a plan to secretly open the bird-cages that lined the length and breadth of her small private veranda and set all her pet budgerigars free. But Bim appeared on the scene of the conspiracy like a wrathful thunderbolt, her eyes angrily flashing, and stopped them (Tara was one of the guilty band). "Do you know," she hissed at them, "do you know that Miss Stephen is *dying*—dying of *cancer?*" The guilty ones shrank back into the hedge, horrified, disbelieving. "What do you mean, Bim?" the boldest stuttered. "You're making up stories. How could you know?" "I know," Bim hissed, "I know because she goes to see Dr. Cherian at the hospital and Dr. Cherian told my aunt when they met at a tea party. Miss Stephen is *ill*. She has cancer. And she will die. And it's very, very painful. But she's brave enough to carry on working and running the school," she said through her teeth, glaring at each one so ferociously that they turned and fled.

Miss Stephen faced a strangely subdued assembly the next day. There were no stink bombs, no water balloons, no rude sounds. Instead, the girls bent their heads dutifully over their hymn books and sang Nearer My God To Thee most soulfully. Some had tears in their eyes. Some blew their noses.

Tara was not one of them. She stood silently, stonily, mourning not the slow death that was settling about Miss Stephen but the abrupt death of romance brought about so effectively by her sister Bim. Back in the classroom, stooped over her needlework, she continued to brood over the figure of Miss Singh lying on the bed, the thin wrist dangling, the blonde Buddhist lingering near the gate—the figures of her first real-life romance—and continued to nurse a grudge against Miss Stephen and Bim till, with time, they faded from her memory, the same dull grey mildew settling upon them as on everything else within the stone walls of the mission school.

As schooldays with their somehow supernatural elasticity stretched and stretched over the years, the girls became infected with something of Raja's restlessness. It made Bim more ambitious at school, working consciously and deliberately at coming first in the examinations and winning honours. She was not quite sure where this would lead but she seemed to realize it was a way out. A way out of what? They still could not say, could not define the unsatisfactory atmosphere of their home. They did not realize now that this unsatisfactoriness was not based only on their parents' continual absence, their seemingly total disinterest in their children, their absorption in each other. The secret, hopeless suffering of their mother was somehow at the root of this subdued greyness, this silent desperation that pervaded the house. Also the disappointment that Baba's very life and existence were to them, his hopeless future, their anxiety over him. The children could only sense all this, they did not share it, except unwillingly. To them Baba was the perpetual baby who would never grow up—that was his charm, they felt, and never thought of his actual age.

When Bim became head girl of her school the principal came to congratulate the parents on her honour. They were not at home, and she had tea with Aunt Mira instead, and Aunt Mira so awkward with joy and pride that she poured the milk into the sugar pot and offered the tea strainer instead of the biscuits, much to her own anguish and the girls'. Then Raja won a poetry prize offered by his school magazine. His poem about the

Battle of Panipat[3] was a fine, ringing one with plenty of rhyme and rhythm and nothing to be ashamed of at all—it was recited by his friends and chanted at football games and on bicycle rides. When a teacher referred to "the young Lord Byron in our midst," Raja's fate seemed sealed, the future was clear. A little crack seemed to open in the stony shell that enclosed them at home, letting in a little tantalising light. The future . . .

Lying on the bamboo matting on yet another summer afternoon, the game they played seemed quite without savour.

"What would you most like to eat?"

"A watermelon."

"A piece of ice."

"What would you most like to drink?"

"Ginger beer."

"Vimto.[4] No. Aa—agh."

They rolled over onto their stomachs in revolt against the flatness, the insipidity of it all. Then, rolling off the matting, they stole barefoot into Raja's room—he was not back from school. Everyone else in the house was asleep. They could do anything they liked. What should they do that was daring enough, wild and unlawful enough for such a splendid opportunity? They searched. They sniffed and hunted.

There was Raja's copy of Iqbal—stained, much-thumbed, marked and annotated—his scattered papers covered with the beautiful script they could not read and which therefore had an added cachet in their admiring eyes. But today they would have preferred to see an unexpected photograph, a stranger's handkerchief . . . What made the two sisters expect such shocking revelations? Somehow they felt that today such secrets should be revealed, would be in keeping. Squatting, they searched along his bookshelves where Urdu verse lay cheek by jowl with American paperbacks—those long thick flapping American army editions that he picked up second-hand on Connaught Circus pavements: Louis Bromfield's *Night in Bombay*, Saroyan's *The Human Comedy*, *Huckleberry Finn*, *Moby Dick*, *The Postman Always Rings Twice*; also the enormous green volumes containing Keats and Shelley, Blake and Donne; the verses of Zauq and Ghalib, Dagh and Hali[5] in cheap tattered yellow copies—that odd ragbag of reading that went to make up their romantic and inaccessible and wonderful brother.

But they had sat there, cross-legged, beside the long low book-shelf on countless afternoons, reading while Raja lay on his bed, asleep or half-awake and humming the songs that seemed to be always vibrating inside him like a taut, shining, invisible wire. Today they wanted something more from Raja, of Raja. Finally they opened the cupboard into which he threw his clothes. Here they rummaged, shaking out his shirts and rolling them up again, shoving his socks and handkerchiefs into corners as they searched.

"Look, Tara, I'm nearly as tall as he is now," said Bim, holding up a pair of his trousers at her waist.

---

3. Fought in 1526, in which the Central Asian conqueror Babar defeated Ibrahim Lodhi and established the Moghal Empire in India.   4. A popular soft drink.   5. Eminent Urdu poets of the 18th and 19th centuries, patronized by the Moghal court in Delhi (see p. 1051).

"No, you're not," Tara giggled. "They're much, much too long."

"They are not," protested Bim and suddenly stepped into them. She pulled them up high above her waist, up to her chest, tucked the bunches of her frock into them, then drew them close about her waist. Reaching into the cupboard again, she found a belt with which to fasten it around her. Tara was doubled over with laughter, stuffing her hands into her mouth, and crying tears of laughter to see the preposterous figure of her sister in the bunched up old khaki trousers over her flowered frock, with her black hair tumbling about her hot, excited face. Then Bim found another pair of trousers, the white ones Raja wore for tennis, and handed them to Tara. Tara had even more trouble than Bim in putting them on over her frock and tightening them about her smaller, slighter figure, yet she managed it more neatly and emerged looking like one of those slight, elegant young boys who play girls' roles on stage, pressing her hair close to her head to make her face more boyish. They pranced about the room in their trousers, feeling grotesquely changed by them, not only in appearance but in their movements, their abilities. Great possibilities unexpectedly opened up now they had their legs covered so sensibly and practically and no longer needed to worry about what lay bare beneath ballooning frocks and what was so imperfectly concealed by them. Why did girls have to wear frocks? Suddenly they saw why they were so different from their brother, so inferior and negligible in comparison: it was because they did not wear trousers. Now they thrust their hands into their pockets and felt even more superior—what a sense of possession, of confidence it gave one to have pockets, to shove ones fists into them, as if in simply owning pockets one owned riches, owned independence.

Carried away by the splendour of their trousered selves, Bim suddenly dashed across to the desk and pulled out the small top drawer in which Raja kept cigarettes. She found an opened packet with a few cheap, foul smelling, loosely packed cigarettes spilling out of it. She pushed it into her pocket, along with a box of matches. She strutted about the room, feeling the cigarettes and matches in her pocket, realizing now why Raja walked with that fine, careless swagger. If she had pockets, if she had cigarettes, then it was only natural to swagger, to feel rich and superior and powerful. Crowing with delight, she flashed a look at Tara to see if she shared her exhilaration and whispered "Let's go out for a walk, Tara."

"Oh Bim, no!" squeaked Tara, squeezing into a corner by the desk in alarm at the very suggestion. "No, no, Bim!"

"Come on, Tara, no one will see—everyone's asleep."

"The gardener might be outside," warned Tara as Bim cautiously opened the door to the veranda and peeped out.

"He's half-blind. He'll think we're Raja's friends," said Bim, tossing her mane of hair to show how confident she felt, and slipped out onto the veranda, slightly unnerved by the brilliant glare of the afternoon light. "Come *on*," she hissed sharply at Tara who then came scurrying and squealing after her. They tumbled down the stairs into the garden together, then the blank white glare and the brazen heat made them blink and falter. "Come *on*," hissed Bim again, and dived into a great bush of magenta bougainvillea that bloomed beside the stairs.

Here they crept in, rustling, sat down on the upraised roots and mounds of dry leaves, giggling at their own nervousness. To make up for this lapse of confidence—Bim had thought momentarily of going up to the garage, taking out their bicycles and going for a ride, in their trousers—Bim drew out the cigarettes and matches from her pocket. "Let's try," she whispered, bending very low because a thorny branch was scraping at the back of her head, plucking at her hair.

"Oh, Bim, no—o!" cried Tara in fright. Her sister was driving her, forcing her through fear again, as usual. She tried to resist, hopelessly. This was why she distrusted Bim so: Bim never knew when to stop. Discontented with mere fantasy, she insisted on turning their games into reality, usually disastrously. There was always the one sickening moment when she overstepped and began to hurtle downwards into disaster, trying always to drag her sister along with her. "Oh no," protested Tara, weakly.

"But why *not?*" demanded Bim, impatiently. "Raja smokes. Father *knows* he smokes. Mother knows too. We must at least do it once," and sticking the cigarette between her lips, she struck a match and lit it in a cloud of stinging yellow smoke, puffing hard so that her eyes stood out and watered. Then she passed it to Tara and lit herself another. But Tara threw hers away wildly after one puff, spluttering with disgust.

"Tara!" screamed Bim, seeing the cigarette fall on a heap of dry leaves and grass, and scrambled up to stamp it out before it turned into a blaze. Her hair caught in the bougainvillea, her legs felt suddenly hampered by the trousers that did not fit. She heard Tara struggling to get out of the bush and then someone's voice raised and the garage door swinging open. So there was nothing for it but to fling the cigarette out into the open driveway and race after Tara, up the steps and into Raja's room. Someone was coming up the veranda. It was—was it?—it *was* Raja. Back so early from school—why? Screaming at each other to hurry, they ran into Raja's bathroom to tear off their trousers. By then Raja was already in his room. They heard the crash of an armful of books as they landed on his desk and scattered. He had heard—or seen?—them! He was at the bathroom door, shouting "Who's in there? Open!" But they had bolted it. Trousers off and flung into a corner, their legs feeling naked and exposed, they opened the outer door and fled, leaving him to rattle at the inner door and shout "I know it's you—you rascals! Come out at once, you horrors!"

It was not spite or retaliation that made Tara abandon Bim—it was the spider fear that lurked at the centre of the web-world for Tara. Yet she did abandon Bim, it was true that she did.

The Misra family had taken the girls with them to the Lodi Gardens one day in early spring when the *bignonia venustra* was in bloom, enfolding the dark walls of the Lodi tombs in long cloaks of flamboyant orange. The picnickers lay on the grass in the honey-gold sun, eating peanuts out of paper cones and peeling oranges and urging each other to sing songs. Two young men had been invited as well, possible suitors[6] for Jaya and Sarla, and the picnic had been arranged to give their first meeting

---

6. The picnic is an occasion for matchmaking in the context of arranged marriage.

an air of informality. Yet everyone's eyes were on each other so sharply, sharpening on each other like blades, snip-snip-snip, that they made Bim and Tara feel anything but informal. On the contrary, they were deeply uneasy. The Misra girls had become strangely artificial in their speech and manners—Bim and Tara could scarcely recognise them. The two chosen young men were sullen and mostly silent, their dark heads sunk between their shoulders as they gloomily picked at grass and avoided looking at each other. Only the Misra brothers remained themselves, as jocular and loud and coarse as usual, making foul jokes and managing to suggest vulgarities even when they did not state them. Bim and Tara, infected both by the Misra girls' self-conscious artificiality of manner and the young swains' deep gloom, did not know how to deal with them or with the Misra brothers—how to defend themselves against their jokes or deflect them by repartee as Jaya and Sarla could do, being more practised. So when the others were fussing over the unpacking of the picnic baskets, they wandered away together, saying they would look at the tombs.

They walked in silence up a knoll to one of the smaller tombs and stood uncertainly gazing at its blackened walls and thought of sitting down on the grass outside by themselves, but a boy in striped pyjamas and a cricket cap hung about the small porch, leaning against a pillar, watching them while he tossed a pebble from one hand to the other. After a moment's hesitation, they chose the uninviting dark inside and the dizzying stench of bats that it contained.

The boy must have flung the pebble after them. They heard a small dull thwack as it hit something soft but it was followed by a sinister crepitation that began to stir in the corners of that octagon of pitch darkness, began to swirl invisibly about them, the humming growing louder and more menacing, at the same time descending towards them till they realized what it meant and, with yelps, pushing into each other in their hurry, ran out together.

Tara catapulted out and went hurtling down the grassy slope, her head bent and her hands pressed over her ears, screaming like a whistle as she went. At the foot of the knoll she turned to look for Bim and saw that she was still at the top—she had not got away, the swarm had got her. They had settled about her head and shoulders till they had wrapped her about in a helmet of chainmail that glittered, gun-metal blue, and shivered and crept over her skin, close-fitting, adhesive. Bim, too, had her head bent and her arms crossed over her face but she was not screaming—she seemed locked into the hive, as if she were the chosen queen, made prisoner. The whole hillside, the brilliant cobalt sky, the honey air, the grassy slope and flowering creepers were covered with the pall of bees, shrouded by them as by a thundercloud. It was a bees' festival, a celebration, Bim their appointed victim, the sacrificial victim on whom they had draped the ceremonial shawl, drawing it close about her neck as she stood drooping, shivering under the weight of their gauzy wings, their blue-black humming.

What was Tara to do? Helplessly, she ran back up the hill a little, but instantly the bees rose, hummed a warning, swayed towards her, and she screamed to see them approach so that Bim, spying her out of her swollen eyes, cried in a thick, congested voice "Get away, go—run, run!" and Tara ran, ran down the knoll back to the Misras, screaming for help.

They heard her at last—or, rather, at last connected the frenzied screams they had heard with Tara's running, maddened figure—and leapt to their feet, left the paper cones and radios and songs behind, and came at a gallop to see what it was all about. Tara was conscious, as she half-stood, half-crouched, shivering, of Jaya and Sarla flying up the knoll and flinging Jaya's pink veil over Bim's head, the men tearing off branches and beating them in the air, someone lighting a rolled newspaper and sending its smoke coiling through the air like a whip, and the young boy who had thrown the stone being dragged across the grass to be thrashed.

Then they were all bustling out of the park and into the waiting cars, and Sarla was dabbing at the bee stings with some lemonade out of a bottle and Bim was sitting with her head in her lap, growling "Don't *touch* me, don't *touch* me!" She was swollen to a great size, and tinted a strange shade of plum-blue, quite unrecognisable. Tara, squeezed into a corner of the overcrowded car, very small and meek, whimpered to herself. She had one bite to nurse, on her knuckles, but although the sting was still embedded in it like a needle in a pocket, she dared not ask for any attention or sympathy—she knew Bim deserved it all.

That whole episode was an accident that ought to have been followed by a thorough investigation, a cure, each sting withdrawn, put away. But in the uproar that followed, it was all somehow bundled out of sight, hurriedly. Tara had not the opportunity, nor found the courage, to go to Bim and say "Bim, I'm sorry I ran away—I wasn't brave—I didn't come to help you. I am ashamed—I shall never forgive myself. Forgive me." Nor did Bim ever care to explain what she meant when she growled at her sister "You couldn't help it—if you'd stayed, you'd have been stung, like me—you had to run." Only Raja raged openly "You nitwit. Why didn't you stay and help Bim to beat them off?" Aunt Mira said instantly "Tara's just a baby—what could she have done?" and there was the powerful ammoniac stench of vinegar to bring tears to their eyes as she poured out a bottleful onto a napkin and doused Bim with it. The old ayah shook her head over such inefficacious treatment and fetched her betel-nut box and dipped her finger into the jar of lime paste and smeared it on Bim's stings till she looked as if she had dabs of cotton wool stuck to her, or a strange, erratic growth of feathers. Whenever Tara smelt vinegar or tasted lime paste in a betel leaf, her flesh crept, she shivered, she recalled the zig-zag advance of threatening bees emerging from that dark, stinking tomb to capture Bim and leave her bloated and blue like a plum. Aunt Mira and the ayah between them treated Bim and drew out all her stings, but Tara kept hers hidden.

Tara began to avoid both Bim and Raja. Aunt Mira did not provide sufficient defence—so thin, so scrawny, she could no more hide Tara from them than a thin reed. She began to shut herself away in her room, or slip out by herself, quote often to the Misras' house next door.

The Misras had been their neighbours for as long as they could remember (theirs was not a neighbourhood from which people moved—they were born and married and even died in the same houses, no one ever gave one up) and yet the friendship between the two families was only a token one, formal and never close. Bim and Raja, especially, were so scornful of the Misra children that Tara dared not admit openly that she herself did not judge them or find them lacking. Now she found neither Bim nor Raja holding her back—studying hard for their examinations, they hardly noticed Tara any more and had no intention of pursuing her or bullying her—Tara found herself free to edge closer to the warmth she felt emanating from them, from their large, full, bustling household. The two Misra girls who had been to the same school as Bim and Tara, although they were a few years older, responded to her touchingly hesitant advances in a kindly, patronising way that almost developed into a friendship, the closest certainly to friendship in Tara's forlorn experience.

What attracted Tara was the contrast their home provided to hers. Even externally there were such obvious differences—at the Misras' no attempt was made, as at Tara's house, to "keep up appearances." They were so sure of their solid, middle-class bourgeois position that it never occurred to them to prove it or substantiate it by curtains at the windows, carpets on the floors, solid pieces of furniture placed at regular intervals, plates that matched each other on the table, white uniforms for the house servants and other such appurtenances considered indispensable by Tara's parents. At the Misras' string beds might be carried into the drawing room for visiting relations, or else mats spread on the veranda floor when an influx of visitors grew so large that it overflowed. Meals were ordered in a haphazard way and when the family smelt something good cooking, they dipped impatiently into the cooking pots as soon as it was ready instead of waiting for the clock hands to move to the appointed hour. The chauffeur might be set to minding a fractious baby, driving it up to the gate and back for its amusement or dandling it on his lap and letting it spin the steering wheel, while the cook might be called out of the kitchen and set to massaging the grandmother's legs. Elaborate arrangements might be made for a prayer meeting on the lawns to please an elderly relative and then suddenly set aside so that the whole clan could go and see the latest film at the Regal. Theirs was a large family of many generations spread through the city, and there was constant coming and going, friends and relations perpetually under one's feet. The Misra girls complained to Tara how difficult it was to study and prepare for exams in such circumstances, and sometimes brought their books across to work in Tara's room, but never for very long since their interest in academic work was weak and wavering at best, and often they would abandon it and set out shopping for clothes and bangles or to attend a family festivity like a wedding or naming ceremony, leaving school-work undone and Tara abandoned and envious.

But now they noticed Tara standing on the edge, watching, with kindly eyes, and often swept her along. Although she was consumed with shyness and embarrassment at finding herself in a society to which she realized she did not belong, she enjoyed the break in routine, the change of scene, and came back flushed and excited, too excited to sleep even if the outing had been no more than a visit to a tailor or a jeweller in the city.

Once she wandered across on a bleak winter day with an old woollen coat drawn over her school uniform that she had not changed out of through laziness, to find the whole family on the lawn, posing for a photographer who kept darting out from behind his black cloth and cyclopean instrument to marshal them into straight rows, some on chairs and some on their feet, little ones in front, big ones at the back. Tara backed away, hoping to disappear through the hedge, but the Misra girls spied her, broke rank and darted at her, dragged her along to stand beside them and be photographed. That was their kindliness, their easy, careless hospitality, and the result was the incongruous appearance of Tara, bundled into her grey woollen coat and looking like a mouse with a bad cold, standing along with the ranks of Misras in their silk and brocade finery, posing for a family photograph. Whenever she saw it, silver-framed, up on the cabinet in their hall, she looked away in embarrassment. Had she been a little younger, she might have attempted stealing it and cutting it out, but she was too big for such adventures now, she was quite big enough for adventures of another kind.

The Misra girls realized that, in their prosaic, accepting way, and often invited her to come to cinema shows with them, or to the Roshonara club where she sat on the lawn, sipping lemonade, listening to the band, stiff as a puppet in her consciousness of being looked at by young men returning from the tennis courts or the cricket field or standing around the bar. It was a novel experience for Tara whose own parents sat playing bridge in the green-lit, soundless aquarium of the card-room, unaware of their daughter's presence outside, and to whom it had never occurred that the child was now a young girl and might like to be taken out with them. The Misra girls themselves found the Roshonara club too boring—they did not play tennis, they did not dance, they knew all the Old Delhi families spread over the verandas and lawns in clusters of cane chairs, had known them all their lives and knew they could not offer them any novelty, any excitement.

Besides, they were already engaged to be married—the picnic at Lodi Gardens, so disastrous for Bim and Tara, had reaped a different harvest for Jaya and Sarla—and life did not hold out the shadowy promises and expectations that it still did to Tara. They enjoyed seeing Tara perch, trembling, on the edge of her chair, casting her eyes quickly around the prospect, then dropping them, half-frightened by what she saw. They gave her Vimto to drink, lent her bits of jewellery to wear, introduced her to the families they had known all their lives but who had been screened away from Tara by the particular circumstances of her home and family. They were touched to see Tara blinking as she looked about her—it made them feel matronly and condescending, experienced and wise.

It was to their engagement party that Tara wore her first silk sari—a pale shell-pink edged with silver that Aunt Mira had thought suitable for her youngest niece. There were two parties thrown on the same day—an afternoon affair for all the women of the family and the two sisters' girl friends, to be followed by a formal evening affair. Bim and Tara were invited to the first, their parents to the second. Bim was forced to accompany Tara and sat glumly on the carpet at the far end of the room, bored and irritated by it all—the musicians who had been invited to play and sat grouped decoratively on a white sheet spread over the carpet with their instruments before them, the songs sung by the ladies and the young girls, invariably mournful ones of heart-break and romantic yearning—till she could stand no more and, beckoning sternly to Tara, got up and slipped out into the garden where gardeners and electricians were at work on strings of lights and pyramids of potted plants in preparation for the evening party. A group of workmen, staggering under the weight of a long table, shouted to them to keep out of the way and as they turned they bumped into a servant hurrying up with white tablecloths and silver vases stuffed with papery zinnias and gomphrenias.

"Let's go up on the roof, it'll be quieter there," said Bim, and Tara was forced to follow her up the stairs to the terrace. Tara felt they might as well have stayed at home if this was all they were going to do at the party, and Bim leant on the balustrade and looked across the hedge at their own silent, already darkening house as if that were exactly what she wished she had done.

They watched the workmen scurrying about the lawn, dropping a ladder, setting up a branched tree of electric lights over the porch and draping tangled strips of fairy lights on the domed trees along the drive with the maximum possible amount of argument and contradiction and muddle. The Misra boys were standing about on straddled legs, shouting orders and abuse in their lordly, uncivilised way that made Bim direct dark looks at them.

"I don't know how those two girls are going to study and pass their finals with all this going on," she said.

"I don't think it matters to them," said Tara, picking at flakes of blackened lichen on the balustrade sulkily. "They're getting married afterwards anyway."

The Misra boy standing below shouted "Donkey! Fool! Look, you've smashed another bulb. D'you think they belong to your father that you can go smashing them up as you like?"

Bim gave a snort of disgust. "I don't know why they're in such a hurry to get married," she said. "Why don't they go to college instead?"

"Their mother wanted them to be married soon. She said she married when she was twelve and Jaya and Sarla are already sixteen and seventeen years old."

"But they're not educated yet," Bim said sharply. "They haven't any degrees. They should go to college," she insisted.

"Why?" said Tara, suddenly rebellious, impatient to go back down the stairs, get away from Bim and join the women who were now streaming out of the house, laughing, calling to each other, flocking to the long tables on which platters of sweetmeats, pink and yellow and topped with silver, had been placed between the silver vases with the zinnias and gomphrenias, while a waiter in a white coat with something embroidered in red across the pocket, frenziedly uncapped bottles of lemonade and stuck straws into them and handed them out with automatic efficiency.

The hired band arrived just then in an open lorry and began jumping out of it with huge instruments of shining brass clutched in their arms. The Misra brothers rushed up and began to bawl at them for being late. They hurried off into a brightly striped pavilion that had been set up at the far end of the garden. The Hyder Alis' dog was barking as though in pain at all this noise and confusion.

"Why?" repeated Bim indignantly. "Why, because they might find marriage isn't enough to last them the whole of their lives," she said darkly, mysteriously.

"What else could there be?" countered Tara. "I mean," she fumbled, "for them."

"What *else?*" asked Bim. "Can't you think? I can think of hundreds of things to do instead. *I* won't marry," she added, very firmly.

Tara glanced at her sideways with a slightly sceptical smile.

"I won't," repeated Bim, adding "I shall never leave Baba and Raja and Mira-*masi*," making Tara look away before her face could betray her admission that she, closely attached as she was to home and family, would leave them instantly if the opportunity arose. Bim did not notice her. She was looking down, across the lighted, bustling garden to her own house, dark and smouldering with a few dim lights behind the trees, and raised her hands to her hair, lifting it up and letting it fall with a luxuriant, abundant motion. "I shall work—I shall *do* things," she went on, "I shall earn my own living—and look after Mira-*masi* and Baba and—and be independent. There'll be so many things to do—when we are grown up—when all this is over—" and she swept an arm out over the garden party, dismissing it. "When we are grown up at last—then—then—" but she couldn't finish for emotion, and her eyes shone in the dusk.

In the garden below, the little blue buds of lights in the trees bloomed suddenly to the sound of excited twittering from the guests.

IV

Bim was correcting papers at the dining table, her own desk being insufficient for their size and number. All the doors were shut against the dust storm raging outside so that they could only hear the sand and gravel scraping past the walls and window-panes but not see it. It seeped in through every crack and opening, however, so that every surface of wood or stone or paper in the room was coated with it, yellow and gritty. It coloured the light too, made the daylight so pallid that they had to have the electric light on and that was turned to a lurid shade of orange which, far from being festive, was actually sinister.

Tara, trying to pen a letter to her daughters, one last hurried one before they arrived in India, felt she was being roasted like a chicken under the burning orange bulb. She wished she could switch it off and she and Bim could put their papers aside and sit in a companionable dusk, but Bim's concentration on her work was so intense, it crackled a warning through the air. So she huddled inside her kimono and tore at her hair, trying to get on with the letter. It would not go. She laid down the pen. Suddenly coming to a decision that pinched her nostrils and made her look almost severe, she said "Bim, you *must* come. With Baba. It will be so good for you."

"What do you mean?" Bim asked, pushing her spectacles up onto the bridge of her nose. They reflected the orange light that was swaying in the breeze that had somehow got into the closed room, a ghostly reflection of the storm outside. The lenses reflected the darting light, swinging from left to right crazily, dangerously.

"I mean," said Tara, looking away, "I mean—you need a change."

"What makes you think that?" asked Bim in wonder, and her sister's expression which was rather as if a tooth were being extracted from her mouth very slowly, made her take off her spectacles and hold them in her hand so that they could face each other directly.

"I mean—I've been watching you, Bim. Do—d'you know you talk to yourself? I've heard you—muttering—as you walk along—when you think you're alone—"

"I didn't know I was being watched," Bim broke in, flushing with anger.

"I—I couldn't help overhearing. And then—your hands. You keep gesturing with them, you know. I don't think you know, Bim."

"I don't—and I didn't know I was supposed to keep my hands still when I talked. The girls in college did a skit once—one of them acted me, waving her hands while she talked. It was quite funny."

"No, Bim, you do it even when you're not talking. I mean, you must be talking to yourself."

"Don't we all?" Bim enquired, her voice and her eyebrows rising simultaneously.

It was a look that would have made Tara quail as a child. But now she insisted "Not *aloud*, Bim."

"I must be getting old then," Bim said, with a careless sniff. "I *am* getting old, of course."

"You're not. You're worrying."

"Worrying? I have no more worries," cried Bim, laying down her spectacles and slapping the tabletop with one hand. "No worries at all." She lifted her hand and touched the white lock of hair over her ear.

"About Raja," insisted Tara, grimly determined to have it all out and be done.

"Oh, you want to talk about Raja *again*," Bim groaned disgustedly. She picked up her spectacles and made to put them on, bending over the stack of papers on the table with an exaggerated air of interest. But she gave it up in an instant, laying the spectacles down on top of the papers. "I'm *bored* with Raja. Utterly bored," she said evenly. "He is too rich to be interesting any more, too fat and too successful. Rich, fat and successful people are *boring*. I'm not interested, Tara."

Tara threw herself forward on her arms, her hair in its long curls—yes, at last she had achieved the curls she had prayed for as a little girl; now they were as luxuriant as vines, thanks to the best hairdressers of the international capitals—sweeping over her ears and across her cheeks, casting purple shadows. Between them, her eyes and her mouth agonised. "*Why* do you imagine such things about Raja? You haven't even seen him—in how many years, Bim? You live in the same country and never visit each other. I come, from abroad, every three years, to see you, to see Baba and Raja. I know more about Raja's home and family than you do, Bim. You don't know anything about his life, about his family or his work."

"Yes, I *do* know," Bim replied loudly. "He is invited to weddings, engagement parties, anniversaries—they spread out carpets and cushions for him to recline on, like a pasha[7]—and he recites his poems." She made a clownish face, ridiculing such pomp, such show, such empty vanity. "I can imagine the scene—all those perfumed verses about wine, the empty goblet, the flame, and ash . . ." she laughed derisively.

"You haven't read any of it in years—how do you know?"

"I know Raja. I know his poems."

"Why can't it have changed? Grown better?"

"How can it—when he lives in that style? Living in his father-in-law's house, making money on his father-in-law's property, fathering one baby after another—"

"Five. And they're quite grown up now—the girls are anyway."

"And the little boy is so spoilt, he's impossible."

"You've never even seen him, Bim!"

"I couldn't bear to—I can imagine it all—after four daughters, much lamented, at last the little boy, the little prince arrives. What a dumpling he must be, what a rice-ball—with all the feeding that goes on in that house, Benazir cooking and tasting and eating all day, and in between meals little snacks arriving to help them on their way. Imagine what he must look like, and Raja! Imagine eating so much!"

"Why do you imagine they eat all day?" cried Tara in distress.

"I *know*. They *did* visit me once. Have you forgotten? After their marriage, after their first baby was born, they did come to visit us. And Benazir was already so plump, and Raja—Raja looked like a pasha, he was so fat. They were visiting too, as if they were pashas, with presents to dazzle us with. He brought me a string of pearls—imagine, pearls!—and told me how Hyderabad was known for them. And I just told him 'But Raja, you know I don't wear jewellery!' Then he brought a hi-fi set for Baba—'the latest model,' he told us," she went on, laughing. "And Baba just smiled and never touched it. He only loves his old HMV gramophone, he loves to wind it up and sit by it, watching the record turn. All through their visit he was so afraid Benazir might ask for it back—it was hers, you know. Then Raja sulked and sulked. 'Tara would have worn the pearls,' he said, 'and Bakul would have known what a fine hi-fi set that is—you two know nothing.'" Bim laughed again and repeated, mockingly, "No, we know nothing, we two—nothing."

They sat in silence together, listening to the storm blow itself out, so that the roar of the trees bending and the creepers dashing against the walls and the gravel flying gradually lessened, seemed to recede, leaving them in a kind of grey cave that still echoed with the tides.

"And now that baby is to be married," Bim mused, drumming her fingers on the table. "Moyna. I wonder if she's as plump as Benazir used to

7. A Turkish potentate.

be? Benazir must be huge. She never liked to get up or move if she could get someone to fetch and carry for her. And she fed that baby all day long. Little silver dishes of milk puddings would arrive—she'd brought along a woman to cook for them, she didn't trust Janaki or me—and she would spoon it into her mouth, fattening her up. And Raja—how he'd grown to *enjoy* Benazir's food—"

"It's very good," Tara said earnestly. "It really is."

"Yes, I know, but it's disgusting to enjoy it so much, and eat so much of it. Such rich foods. They must be bad for him, I kept telling him that, but of course he wouldn't listen." She shook her head, a bit saddened now. Then she sat up straight. "It's unhappy people who eat like that," she said suddenly, authoritatively. "I read that somewhere. They compensate themselves with the food they eat for the things they missed."

"*What* things has Raja missed, Bim? He has a wife, children, his own house, his business, his hobby—"

"But that's just it," Bim exploded. "All—all that nonsense. That's not what Raja had wanted from life. He doesn't need a hobby, he needs a vocation. He knows he has given his up, just given up what used to be his vocation, turned it into a silly, laughable little hobby . . . That is why he needs to console himself with food and more food. Don't you *see?*"

Tara's mouth was open, she was full of protest. She felt it was wrong to allow Bim to follow the path of such misunderstanding. But she only wrung her hands in a distressed way, wondering how to persuade someone so headstrong, so habitually headstrong, as her sister. Finally she said "You should go and visit them, Bim, and see for yourself how it is. There's the wedding. They want you there. Here's a letter. Let me read it to you . . ."

"No, it's for you," said Bim, waving it away as Tara started to draw it out of its envelope.

But Tara pretended not to notice. She opened out the sheets of blue paper and began to read. " 'It's time you met your young nephew. We have just bought him a pony, a plump young white one that the girls say looks like a pearl so they call her Moti. Benazir has made him a velvet suit and when he sits on her back he looks like a prince in a Persian miniature . . .' "

Bim slapped the tabletop with her hand, loudly. "You see," she said, in triumph, "what did I tell you? He may be a grown man, respectable citizen, father of a family and all that—but what is he still trying to do, to be? Remember Hyder Ali Sahib's white horse and how we would see him riding by while we played in the sand by the Jumna?"

"Of course," Tara nodded, with a sentimental list to her head.

"That's what Raja was thinking of when he bought the white pony. Raja always admired Hyder Ali Sahib—probably envied him cutting such a fine figure on the white horse, a servant running ahead of him to clear the way of rabble like us and a dog to bring up the rear. Impressive, I suppose— and wasn't Raja impressed! See, this late in life, he's still trying to be Hyder Ali Sahib," she laughed. "Hyder Ali Sahib was his ideal in life and it's the ideal he's still pursuing, poor Raja. To gratify his own boyhood desire, he now forces his poor little boy to ride. Terrible, isn't it, how parents drive their children to fulfil their own ungratified desires?" Her face shone with vindication as if it were oily.

Tara drew back, affronted. "I don't think little Riyaz is at all aware of his father's ungratified desires," she said, primly.

"No, but he will be. When that pony throws him and he howls and no longer wants to ride and his father insists he get back on, *then* he will know what it's all for."

"Why do you foresee such terrible things?" Tara protested, wincing, her maternal instinct touched as if with a knife-point. "The pony won't throw little Riyaz. What a terrible thing to imagine, Bim."

Bim was holding her head in both her hands, shaking it slowly from side to side. "That's my trouble," she mumbled. "I do foresee all these terrible things. I see them all," she said, closing her eyes, as if tired, or in pain.

Tara, afraid of that expression, said gently "Well, when one grows old, one is said to have all kinds of fears, become very apprehensive," and then looked down at the letter in her hands and read on, details of the arrangements for Moyna's wedding that were going on in Raja's household, elaborate and expensive arrangements, for she was the first of his daughters to marry and it was to be a grand affair. There were to be lighted torches along the driveway, a *shehnai* player from Benares[8] to play at the wedding, ice carved into swans on the tables . . .

But Bim did not make any response. Although she opened her eyes and stared at all the books and papers and letters scattered over the dusty table, she did not seem to be seeing anything. If she was listening to anything, it was to the sounds of returning normality outside, the usual summer morning sounds of mynahs quarrelling and shrieking on the lawn, the pigeons beginning to mutter comfortably to each other in the veranda, dry leaves and scraps of paper swirling down the drive and blowing into hedges and corners. Leaving Tara to read on, she stood up and picked up a plate of orange peels that had been lying on the table since breakfast.

Roughly interrupting Tara's low, monotonous recital, she said sharply "Why do you peel oranges and then leave them uneaten, Tara? It's such a waste." Tara, startled, put down the letter but did not say it was Bakul who had left the orange on the plate.

"It's half-rotten, Bim," she said. "I only left the rotten bits."

"It's not rotten," Bim retorted. "It's perfectly all right. I do hate waste," she added and went out of the room with an oddly uncertain step. Tara was disconcerted by it but would have been far more upset if she had seen how Bim's lip was trembling and how her hand shook so that the orange peels slipped off the plate and littered the way to the kitchen. Something about Raja's letter, Tara's comments, the world of luxury and extravagance created by them and approved by both of them, excluding her, her standards, too rough and too austere for them, made anger flower in her like some wild red tropical bloom, and a kind of resentment mixed with fear

8. The sacred center of Hinduism and home of the major styles of north Indian classical music. *Shehnai:* an oboelike reed instrument played at weddings and festive occasions.

made her stutter, half-aloud, "I mean—I mean she's only five years younger than I am and she thinks I'm *old.* And she spies on me—she's been spying. She is cruel, Tara, and cold. And Raja selfish, too selfish to care. And what about the letter he wrote *me?* Oh yes, he writes beautiful letters to Tara—all wedding, all gold—but what about the letter he wrote *me? My* letter? Has Tara forgotten it—in my desk? And I—"

She pottered about the kitchen for a while—Janaki must have gone out to roll herself a betel leaf and chew it quietly out by the servants' quarters—washing the plate, putting it away, seeing if there were any more oranges left in spite of her sister's and brother-in-law's wasteful ways, and then went out on the veranda to find that the dust-storm had left the whole garden shrouded in grey. Each leaf, each bush drooped with the weight of dust. Even the sun appeared to be swathed in grey cobwebs. Everything seemed ancient and bent. Everything seemed to have gone into eclipse. The house would need a thorough cleaning. She stood on the steps and shouted "Janaki! Janaki!" both angrily and desperately.

Tara began to keep an eye on Bim as she moved about the house, watchful and wary. She wondered why she had not noticed before how very queerly Bim ran the house—or was this queerness something new, something that had happened just now under pressure? She could not help noticing Bim's excessive meanness—the way she would scrape all left-overs onto saucers and keep them for the next meal so that some of the meals that arrived on the table were just a long procession of little saucers with little portions smudged onto them, like meals for a family of kittens. Tara felt ashamed of them, knowing how Bakul's fastidious nostrils would crinkle at the sight. She noticed that he tried to have luncheon and dinner engagements in the city as often as possible, telephoning old colleagues and cronies, finding something he had to discuss with them over a meal, at the club, almost every day. She was glad. She was more relaxed sitting at the meagre table with just Bim and Baba. At the same time she worried that they didn't eat properly. Then she noticed a pound of the best, the most expensive tea turning to dust on the kitchen shelf. Bim had bought it long ago, in a moment of largesse, then obviously suffered pangs of remorse and not been able to bring herself to use it. And yet packets of books kept arriving—expensive volumes of history and art. They must cost a great deal. When she hinted at the expense, Bim said of course, but she needed them for her work. Were they not available at the library? ventured Tara, and Bim gave her a withering look.

Then, while perambulating the garden early in the morning when it was still fresh although the day's heat was beginning to rise at the fringes and form shimmering banks like cumulus clouds, she found a great mound of manure lying behind the garage. When she asked the gardener who was squatting by the garage door, mending some broken tool, she learnt Bim had ordered a cartload of manure one day and then claimed to have no money left for seeds. The gardener began to wheeze self-pityingly to Tara, "What am I to do? Times are bad. I have to grow vegetables, I have to grow food—but how? When there is no fertilizer, no seed, and whenever I turn on the tap, Bim—missahib[9] comes and tells me not to waste water?" Tara, embarrassed, gathered her kimono about her and walked on, confused.

She had always thought Bim so competent, so capable. Everyone had thought that—Aunt Mira, the teachers at school, even Raja. But Bim seemed to stampede through the house like a dishevelled storm, creating more havoc than order. Tara would be ashamed to run a house like this. Bakul would have been horrified if she did. Then how had Bim acquired her fine reputation? Or had her old capability, her old competence begun to crumble now and go to seed? Tara saw how little she had really observed—either as a child or as a grown woman. She had seen Bim through the lenses of her own self, as she had wanted to see her. And now, when she tried to be objective, when she was old enough, grown enough and removed enough to study her objectively, she found she could not— her vision was strewn, obscured and screened by too much of the past.

"What did we really *see?*" she wondered aloud in the evening when the dark laid a comfortingly protective blanket on her and no one could make out too much in the dark or the dust as they sat idly flapping palm-leaf fans against the turgid heat and the swarming mosquitoes that rose from the lawn or dropped from the trees, making walls about them: a form of torture that was well-known to them; it was simply summer. "I think it's simply amazing—how very little one sees or understands even about one's own home or family," she felt obliged to explain when the silence grew too strained.

"What have you seen now that you had not known before?" Bakul asked in a slow, amused tone. He was smoking a cigar. It made his voice riper than ever. Juice might run, through the cracks, purple.

"Only that I had noticed nothing before," Tara said, thrown into confusion by his measured tone. She would have preferred simply to ramble.

"What else do children ever do?" Bakul asked. He had been out all day, he had eaten and drunk well, he was in a mood to be indulgent this evening. "Do you think our own daughters notice anything about us? Of course not—they are too occupied with themselves. Children may see— but they don't comprehend."

"No one," said Bim, slowly and precisely, "comprehends better than children do. No one feels the atmosphere more keenly—or catches all the nuances, all the insinuations in the air—or notes those details that escape elders because their senses have atrophied, or calcified."

Bakul gave an uncomfortable laugh. "Only if they stop to think, surely, and children don't. They are too busy playing, or chattering, or—"

"Or dreaming," mused Tara, dreamily.

"No." Bim rejected that. "We were not busy—*we* hardly ever chattered. Most of the time we simply sat there on the veranda steps, staring at the gate. Didn't we, Tara?"

Tara nodded silently. She felt Bim's hold on her again—that rough,

9. Abbreviation for *memsahib* ("master," feminine form).

strong, sure grasp—dragging her down, down into a well of oppression, of lethargy, of ennui. She felt the waters of her childhood closing over her head again—black and scummy as in the well at the back.

"Or we lay on our backs at night, and stared up at the stars," Bim went on, more easily now. "Thinking. Wondering. Oh, we thought and we felt all right. Yes, Bakul, in our family at least we had the time. We felt every-thing in the air—Mira-*masi's* insignificance and her need to apologise for it, mother's illness and father's preoccupation—only we did nothing about it. Nothing."

Tara gave a sudden small moan and dipped her face into her hands so that her long curls fell about her head. "Oh Bim," she moaned through her fingers. "I didn't come and help—help chase those bees away—"

"What can you be talking about?" Bakul asked in amazement.

"Bim knows," moaned Tara. "Bim knows what I'm talking about."

Bim flapped her palm-leaf fan with a brisk clatter as if to call Tara to attention, remind her of the need to be sensible. Bakul said, when a little light dawned, "You've always had this thing about bees, Tara."

"So would you," she cried, "if you'd seen that swarm that attacked Bim—that *huge* black swarm."

"Oh," said Bim, seeing at last what Tara saw. She laughed and flapped her fan airily. "You mean in the Lodi Gardens. That awful picnic when the Misra girls were being looked over by those boys. And we felt so awk-ward, we walked away to that tomb. And a boy threw a stone, I think, and that was how the bees were disturbed and attacked us."

"And I ran away," moaned Tara, rocking back and forth. "I just turned and *fled*."

"What else could you do?" asked Bim, genuinely surprised that Tara should find in it any matter for debate.

"They would have attacked you too if you had stayed," Bakul agreed.

"You ran for help," said Bim in the voice of a sensible nurse applying medicine to a wound. "I *sent* you to fetch help."

Tara raised her face and gave her a quick look to see if she were aware she was telling a lie, if she were deliberately doing it to salve Tara's con-science. It was too dark that moonless night to make out an expression on any face, and Tara had to calm her agitation by accepting that Bim had genuinely forgotten the details, not blurred or distorted them for Tara's sake. She felt a certain relief that time had blurred the events of that bizarre day, even if only in others' minds and not hers.

"You still remember that?" Bim asked. "I had quite forgotten."

Tara opened her mouth to say something more—now that she had brought it out in the open, even if only under cover of darkness, she wanted to pursue it to its end. She wanted to ask for forgiveness and understanding, not simply forgetfulness and incomprehension. But neither Bim nor Bakul was interested. They were talking about the Misra family.

"It is very strange," said Bakul, "meeting them at intervals of several years." He drew on his cigar. "One imagines they too have spent the time in travelling, working, having all kinds of experiences—and then one comes back and finds them exactly as they were, exactly where they were."

"Only more so," said Bim, laughing.

"Yes, that is true—more so," he said and gave her an approving look. He had always admired Bim, even if she infuriated him often, and Tara sensed this admiration in the murky air. She sensed it with a small prick of jealousy—a minute prick that simply reminded her how very close she was to Bakul, how entirely dependent on him for her own calm and happiness. She felt very vulnerable that evening. Perhaps it was the prickly heat spreading over her skin like a red map.

"The boys never were any good," he was saying, "and now they are grown men they are even more silly and idle and obese. Where are their wives, by the way? The last time we came to Delhi, I think we saw a wife or two."

"The wives come sometimes but soon go back to their families in disgust. Women like change, you know," said Bim. "The wives wanted the new life, they wanted to be modern women. I think they wanted to move into their own separate homes, in New Delhi, and cut their hair short and give card parties, or open boutiques or learn modelling. They can't stand our sort of Old Delhi life—the way the Misras vegetate here in the bosom of the family. So they spend as much time as they can away."

"And Jaya and Sarla," Tara said sympathetically, almost tearfully, feeling for them as well as for herself, feeling for all women, helpless and abandoned. "Poor things."

"Yes, abandoned by their husbands. Isn't it odd how they were married together and abandoned together?"

"Abandoned? Are they actually divorced?"

"I think they are—but it's not a word that's used in their family, you know. In their case, it was the husbands who were too modern, too smart. They played golf and they danced and gave cocktail parties. Imagine, poor Jaya and Sarla who only ever wanted to knit them sweaters and make them pickles. They soon came home to Papa and Mama—were *sent* home, actually. For years they used to talk of going back to their husbands and make up reasons for not joining them where they were—they were in the army and the navy, I think, which was convenient. Now I notice they no longer do. Now all they talk about is their school."

"At least they have that."

"Least is the right word—the very least," said Bim with asperity. "I think they hate it really—they hate children, they hate teaching."

"Do they?" said Tara, shocked. Hate was a word that always shocked her. The image of a dead dog immediately rose before her, bleeding. "Then they shouldn't teach."

"Oh they don't say they do—perhaps they don't even know they do— but you can see it by the way they look, so haggard and eaten up." Having said that, she fell silent quite abruptly and would say nothing more. Tara wondered if she were drawing a parallel between her own life and those of the Misra girls. There had been that doctor once, she recalled. The memory came whining out of the dark like a mosquito, dangling its long legs and hovering just out of reach. Tara could not remember his name.

How stupid, when he had been in and out of their house all that year that Raja had been ill. And Aunt Mira. Tara recalled his narrow, underprivileged face, his cautious way of holding his bag close to him as he came up the drive as if afraid that Bim would bark at him or even bite.

Amused in spite of herself, she uncharacteristically interrupted some tediously long-drawn platitude of Bakul's to say "Oh, and Bim, do you ever see Dr. — Dr. — what was his name?"

Bim sat very still, very rigid, a shape in grey wedged into a canvas chair. She turned her face slightly towards Tara like an elderly bird inclining its beak. "Who do you mean?" she asked, and her voice was like a bird's, a little hoarse, cracked.

"Oh, the doctor who used to look after Raja," said Tara, striking her forehead with her hand. But she sensed Bim's disapproval—or was it distress?—and wished now to withdraw. "I've forgotten. It doesn't matter."

"Dr. Biswas," Bim told her flatly. "No, I haven't seen him since Mira-masi died," she added.

Then they were all three silent. All three were annoyed—Bakul at not being listened to, Tara at her own obtuseness, and Bim at having to listen to her and Bakul and not be left alone. She gathered her feet under the hem of her sari and looked straight ahead of her, into the screen of shrubs, absolutely remote from them.

And Tara, who had thought of redeeming herself tonight from years of sticky guilt, felt she had thoughtlessly plunged into greater depths—murkier, blacker depths—and was coated with the scum of an even greater guilt. She looked despairingly towards Bakul to help her out. But Bakul was glaring. Bakul was wagging his foot in disapproval and distaste at this unsatisfactory audience.

They all sat together as if at the bottom of a well, caught by its stone walls, trapped in its gelatinous waters. Till Bim gave her arm one loud thwack with her palm-leaf fan and exclaimed "Mosquitoes! They are *impossible.*"

Badshah started up out of his sleep at the whack which had resounded like a shot in the night. Ready to charge, he looked wildly about him. It made Bim laugh. "Lie down, lie down," she placated him, pushing at him with her bare foot and he lay down again with a sigh, edging a little closer to her.

The mosquitoes that night were like the thoughts of the day embodied in monster form, invisible in the dark but present everywhere, most of all in and around the ears, piercingly audible. Bim could hear Tara's voice repeating all the cruel things she had so gently said—"Do you ever see Dr. — Dr. — what was his name?" and "When one is old, one has all kinds of fears, apprehensions"—and Tara reading aloud a letter from Raja, a letter Raja had written to her, not to Bim. Her own name was not mentioned in that letter. Raja had not written to her or referred to her. Had there not been a quiet, primly folded-up pride in Tara's tone as she read that letter addressed to her? At last the adored, the admired elder brother was paying attention to her, whom he had always ignored, for now he had turned his back on Bim.

Bim saw all their backs, turned on her, a row of backs, turned. She folded her arms across her face—she did not want to see the ugly sight. She wanted them to go away and leave her.

They had come like mosquitoes—Tara and Bakul, and behind them the Misras, and somewhere in the distance Raja and Benazir—only to torment her and, mosquito-like, sip her blood. All of them fed on her blood, at some time or the other had fed—it must have been good blood, sweet and nourishing. Now, when they were full, they rose in swarms, humming away, turning their backs on her.

All these years she had felt herself to be the centre—she had watched them all circling in the air, then returning, landing like birds, folding up their wings and letting down their legs till they touched solid ground. Solid ground. That was what the house had been—the lawn, the rose walk, the guava trees, the veranda: Bim's domain. The sound of Baba's gramophone and the pigeons. Summer days and nights. In winter, flower-beds and nuts and cotton quilts. Aunt Mira and the dog, roses and the cat—and Bim. Bim, who had stayed, and become part of the pattern, inseparable. They had needed her as much as they had needed the sound of the pigeons in the veranda and the ritual of the family gathering on the lawn in the evening.

But the pattern was now very old. Tara called it old. It had all faded. The childhood colours, blood-red and pigeon-blue, were all faded and sunk into the muddy greys and browns of the Jumna river itself. Bim, too, grey-haired, mud-faced, was only a brown fleck in the faded pattern. If you struck her, dust would fly. If you sniffed, she'd make you sneeze. An heir-loom, that was all—not valuable, not beautiful, but precious on account of age. Precious—to whom?

Turning on her side, her cheek glued with sweat to the thick fold of her elbow, she stared at Baba lying stretched out so peacefully, so passively on the cot next to hers on the dark veranda. Was she precious to him? But he was unaware of her, as unaware in waking as in sleep. He never raised his eyes from the gramophone turntable, never noticed if she were gay or sad, grey or young. If she were to vanish, if a loop of the Jumna river were to catch her round the waist and swirl her away like an earthen pot, or urn of ashes, then Baba would not know. He would not see. He would beautifully continue to sleep.

And that was for the best, that was how it should be, she told herself. But a mosquito came circling round her head, inserted its drill into her ear and began to whine. She flapped at it in fury.

When a letter arrived from their father's office in the familiar long brown envelope, she marched straight into Baba's room with it and said, abruptly, "Baba, here's another letter from Sharma. He wants one of us to come to the office to attend a meeting. He doesn't say what it's about but he says it is important for one of us to come. Will you go?"

Baba, who had given a start when she bounded in, her hair streaming, with such decision and determination, shrank against the pillow on his bed, shrivelled up as at some too great blaze of heat, while the gramophone wailed on. He compressed his white lips, inclined his head towards the record with the most acute attention, as though it might supply him with an answer.

Bim paced up and down quickly, making abrupt turns. "Or would you like me to go? Hmm, yes, I suppose I should. But Sharma hates that—I embarrass him. He hates having to talk to me, so he doesn't. Shall I send Bakul? Ask Bakul?" She looked at Baba so fiercely that his head began to wag as if she had tapped it. "Yes? You think so? I could ask him—but I won't," she immediately added, grimly. "He'll go, and he'll be so patronising, and he'll come back full of advice. I have to make up my own mind. And yours," she said, with a small, vicious stab. Then seeing him helplessly wagging his head, she clutched her head and burst out "Oh, if only Raja would take care of these things."

Baba's head wagged in agreement and, when she had stalked out of the room, continued to wag as if he could not stop. Then the record ran down and he put out his hand to wind it up again. As he wound, he became intent on the winding, and it calmed him. His head steadied itself. He forgot Bim. Music unfurled itself. On and on like a long scroll that he held in his hands.

"You see," she pounded on Tara next when she saw Bakul leaving the house, freshly redolent of shaving cream, lotions and colognes, in his uncle's chauffeur-driven car, and found Tara folding clothes and packing them into suitcases opened out on her bed, with a happy air of preoccupation and of imagining the busy days ahead with her daughters, at the wedding, in Raja's house. Bim's sudden interruption made her drop a bag of shoes onto her toes and start.

"*This* is what I mean," Bim was almost shouting, waving a letter in her face. "It's all very well for Raja to write sentimental letters and say how he cares, and how he will never, and how he will ever—but who is to deal with Sharma? He writes letter upon letter to say we must attend an important meeting, he wants to discuss—then who is to go down to Chandni Chowk[1] and do it? Where is Raja then? Then Raja isn't there— ever, never."

"But he hasn't been here for years, Bim," Tara said in amazement. "He's been in Hyderabad all his adult life. Sharma knows that. He must be used to dealing with you."

"He may be—but I am not. I don't understand the insurance business. Father never bothered to teach me. For all father cared, I could have grown up illiterate and—and *cooked* for my living, or *swept*. So I had to teach myself history, and teach myself to teach. But father never realized—and Raja doesn't realize—that that doesn't prepare you for running an insurance business. Sometimes I think we should just sell our shares in it—sell out to Sharma. What do you think?"

Tara sat down on the edge of the bed and frowned to show she was considering the matter although she was too alarmed by Bim's wild appearance and wild speech to think. "Why not speak to Bakul first?" she

1. The principal market area in Old Delhi.

said at last, with great relief at this piece of inspiration. "Let me discuss it with Bakul—he may be able to advise you."

But although this had been Bim's own initial idea, now she pulled a sour face at it and went on with her tirade as if Tara's suggestion were not worth considering. "Because one's parents never considered the future, never made provisions for it, one is left to feel a fool—to make a fool of oneself," she stormed on. "Why must I appeal to Bakul, to Raja, for help? Yet that is what I am doing, going down on my knees to them—"

"Oh Bim, just asking for a bit of advice," Tara clucked, a little afraid of her tone.

"How my students would laugh at me. I'm always trying to teach them, *train* them to be different from what we were at their age—to be a new kind of woman from you or me—and if they knew how badly handicapped I still am, how I myself haven't been able to manage on my own—they'd laugh, wouldn't they? They'd *despise* me."

"I don't see why, Bim," Tara said as consolingly as she could. She was so frightened by this revelation of Bim's fears and anxieties that she was too unnerved to be tactful. "Don't see it as a man's business or a woman's business—that is silly nowadays. Just see it as a—a family business. Yes, a family business," she repeated, happy to have come upon such a felicitous expression. "The whole family should be consulted—Raja and Bakul and everyone—before you do anything. Yes, we should have a family consultation," she said excitedly, seeing a way at last to bring about the family gathering she pined for.

"And will Raja come?" said Bim bitterly, in a quieter tone, as she settled down on the windowsill and leaned against the netting that covered it. It sagged beneath her weight, holding her back like a hammock.

"If you asked him to—I think he'd be *thrilled*," Tara assured her at once.

"Oh yes, *thrilled*," Bim made a sour face. "Who would be thrilled to return to this—this dead old house?" She thwacked the wire screen with her fist so that the dust flew out of it. "Anyone would be horrified to return to it. Weren't you horrified?" she demanded. "To see it so dead and stale—just as it's always been?"

"But it's not," Tara assured her earnestly. "I mean—only superficially, Bim. Yes, when we arrived, I did notice the house hadn't been painted and the garden is neglected—that sort of thing. But I think the *atmosphere* has changed—ever since you took over, Bim. The kind of atmosphere that used to fill it when father and mother were alive, always ill or playing cards or at the club, always *away*, always leaving us out, leaving us behind—and then Mira-*masi* becoming so—so strange, and Raja so ill—till it seemed that the house was ill, illness passing from one generation to the other so that anyone who lived in it was bound to become ill and the only thing to do was to get away from it, *escape* . . ." she stuttered to a halt, quite pale with the passion she had allowed into her words, and aghast at it.

Bim's eyes narrowed as she sat listening to her sister's outburst. "Did you feel that way?" she asked, coolly curious. "I didn't know. I think I was so occupied with Raja and Mira-*masi* that I didn't notice what effect it had

on you. Why didn't I?" she mused, swinging her leg casually. "And that is
why you married Bakul instead of going to college?"

"Oh Bim, I couldn't have stood college—not Indraprastha College, just
down the road, no further. And the high walls, and the gate, and the
hedges—it would have been like school all over again. I couldn't have
borne that—I *had* to escape."

"But was that why you married Bakul?" Bim pursued, hardly able to
credit her little sister with such cool calculation.

Yet Tara did not deny it altogether. "I didn't think of it that way then,"
she said seriously. "At that time I was just—just swept off my feet," she
giggled a bit. "Bakul was so much older, and so impressive, wasn't he?
And then, he picked *me*, paid *me* attention—it seemed too wonderful, and
I was overwhelmed."

They sat together in the dusty, darkened room, running their fingers
through their hair with a twin gesture of distracted contemplation, and
listened to Baba's record "The Donkey Serenade" trotting in endless circles and the parrots quarrelling over the ripe guavas in the garden.

"Of course now I do see," Tara went on at last, "that I must have used
him as an instrument of escape. The completest escape I could have
made—right out of the country." She laughed a small artificial laugh.

Bim gave her a curious look. She thought of Tara as a child—moody,
touchy, passionately affectionate, with the high-pitched voice of a much
smaller child, an irritating habit of clinging to Aunt Mira long after she
ought to have outgrown cuddling and caresses, a love of lying in bed,
clutching a pillow and sucking her thumb—and she shook her head in
disbelief. She could not believe that these feelings that the adult Tara laid
claim to had actually sprung up in her as a child. "Did you think that all
out? Did you think like that?"

"No," Tara readily admitted. "I only felt it. The thoughts—the words—
came later. Have only come now!" she exclaimed in surprise.

Bim nodded, accepting that. "You used to be happiest at home—never
even wanted to go to school," she reminded her.

"And *you* were the rebel—*you* used to want the world outside," Tara
agreed. "Can you remember how we used to ask each other 'What will
you be when you grow up?' and I only said 'A mother' and you and Raja
said 'Hero and heroine.'" She began to laugh. After all these years, she
found she could laugh at that.

But Bim did not. Her head sank low, her chin settled into her neck.
There was a dark shadow across her face from which her eyes glinted with
a kind of anger.

"Oh Bim," said Tara, in fear.

Bim raised her chin, looked up at her with a little crooked smile—a
horrible smile, thought Tara. "And how have we ended?" she asked, mockingly. "The hero and heroine—where are they? Down at the bottom of
the well—gone, disappeared."

"What well?" asked Tara with dry lips, afraid.

"The well at the back—the well the cow drowned in," Bim waved at
the darkness outside the window. "I always did feel that—that I shall end
up in that well myself one day."

"Oh, Bim, don't."

Bim laughed. She got to her feet and made for the door leaving Tara to wonder, in a panic, if she were serious or if she were only acting a melodramatic scene to impress Tara. Either was possible.

"I feel afraid for her," Tara said, in a low voice, holding her kimono close about her neck as she sat at the foot of her bed that had been made for the night at the end of the moonlit veranda. "I don't know what has happened to her. When we first came, she seemed so normal and everyday and—contented, I felt, as if Bim had found everything she wanted in life. It seemed so incredible that she hadn't had to go anywhere to find it, that she had stayed on here in the old house, taught in the old college, and yet it had given her everything she wanted. Isn't that strange, Bakul?"

Bakul, in his white pyjamas, was pacing up and down the veranda, smoking a last cigar before lying down to sleep. He was going over all the arrangements he had made for his tour of India after the week-long family reunion in Hyderabad was over. He was mentally checking all the bookings he had made, the tickets he had bought. He felt vaguely uneasy— somehow he no longer trusted the Indian railway system or the Indian travel agencies. He was wondering if it would not have been better to spend the entire vacation in his uncle's house in New Delhi. And Tara's rambling, disconnected chatter interrupted his line of thought like the chirping of a single sparrow that would not quieten down at night. Tara was repeating her question.

"She did not find it—she made it," he replied sagely, knocking off half an inch of cigar ash into a flowerpot that contained a spider lily. Its heavy, luxuriant scent, feminine and glamorous, combined with the smell of the cigar in a heady, stifling way, stopping just short of the fetid. "She *made* what she wanted."

"Yes," Tara agreed, quite thrilled. "And she seemed contented, too, didn't she?"

"Contented?" he asked. "Contented enough," he answered. "No more and no less than most of us."

Now Tara was not satisfied. She wanted the question, the problem of Bim solved and resolved tonight. The light of the full moon was so clear, surely it could illuminate everything tonight. Like snow, or whitewash, it fell upon the house and the veranda and the garden, covering everything with its white drifts except where the shadows lay or the trees reared up, black as carbon. Like snow, its touch was cold, marmoreal, and made Tara shiver. "And now she's simply lost all control," she complained to Bakul. "So angry and unhappy and upset."

"I hadn't noticed," he confessed. Perhaps another travel agency—not the small new one just started by his nephew on the wrong side of Connaught Circus. He would have felt more confident about Thomas Cook. Or he could have taken his wife and children to Kashmir and they could have had a houseboat holiday[2] together. But then Tara would have

2. Vacations on houseboats on the many lakes and canals of the Himalayan valley of Kashmir are popular with tourists. *Thomas Cook:* a British travel agency.

insisted on Bim and Baba coming with her. She could not free herself of them, of this shabby old house that looked like a tomb in the moonlight, a whitewashed tomb rising in the midst of the inky shadows of trees and hedges, so silent—everyone asleep, or stunned by moonlight.

"Haven't you?" cried Tara in that voice of the anguished sparrow, chirping. "Haven't you noticed how angry she seems all the time—how she snaps even at Baba and walks about the house all day, doing nothing?"

"What is the matter with her?" asked Bakul, realizing Tara had to talk. He had his own suspicions about Bim but thought better of telling them to Tara. "Is it that business with Sharma you told me about? Surely it can't be—she's been dealing with him for years."

"It can't be that then," Tara agreed. "It seems to be Raja again, as far as I can see."

"What, haven't they made up that quarrel yet?" Bakul asked in a bored voice. Really, the house had an atmosphere—a chilling one, like a cemetery. "I can't even remember what it was about—it was so long ago."

"It wasn't really a quarrel—it was a letter—it's just that Bim can't forget old grudges. They make her so miserable—I wish I could end them for her."

Bakul paid her some attention now. He could always find a solution to any problem, he liked to think. He rather relished problems. He relished solving them for anyone as easily impressed as Tara. He thought how nice it would be to have Tara stop looking so preoccupied and concerned and be impressed by him instead. Really, it was a night of Persian glamour and beauty. They should be sitting together in the moonlight, looking together at the moon that hung over the garden like some great priceless pearl, flawed and blemished with grey shadowy ridges as only a very great beauty can risk being. Why were they worrying instead about Bim, and Raja? He came and stood close to Tara, his large solid thighs in their white pyjamas just before her eyes like two solid pillars, and his cigar glowing between two fingers. "You must arrange for them to meet and speak," he said in a thick, rich voice.

But Tara made no response to his presence. She seemed to fly apart in rejection and agitation, the bird that would not be stilled. "But that's what I've been trying to do all the time that we've been here!" she cried. She did not sound satisfied or grateful at all.

"Oh, have you?" he muttered, moving away towards his own bed. "I didn't know, I've had so much on my own mind. Must check the girls' flight arrival time tomorrow. Remind me, Tara." He yawned, flung the cigar stub out into the drive and sank, creaking, onto his bed. "Another night on this damn uncomfortable bed," he grumbled. "All the strings loose. Need tightening." He creaked and groaned and sighed till he found a comfortable position and then lay there like a bolster.

Tara remained stiffly upright on the foot of her bed, staring miserably into the brilliant, pierrot-shaded garden. The moon had struck everything in it speechless, even the crickets were silenced by its white incandescence. They sat in the shadows, intimidated. Only Badshah was not intimidated. Excited by the great flat mask hanging over the trees, looking down and mocking him as he sat, shivering slightly, on the whitewashed steps, he bounded up and raced down the drive to sit by the gate and bellow at it as if it were an intruder he had to guard his property against, warning the sleeping household of its unearthly presence. His barks rang out in the night like notes on a bugle.

On his way to the airlines office next morning, Bakul stopped at Bim's door and, seeing her sitting at her desk with her papers, said "Tara spoke to me about Sharma's letter to you. Would you like me to stop at the office and find out what it's about?"

She answered immediately, brusquely, "No, it doesn't matter. I have decided to sell out."

"Decided?" Bakul exclaimed. His face was already wet with the sheen of perspiration. The light was brassy and remorseless as the heat. "Now Bim, slow down. Why don't we sit down, all of us, around a table, and discuss it thoroughly before deciding what to do?"

"Discuss it with whom? Baba?" Bim laughed in that coarse way that always offended him. "He and I are the only ones concerned any more. I have to decide for him."

"Hmm," said Bakul, perplexed, and wiped his face carefully with the clean linen handkerchief Tara had handed him that morning. Remembering all Tara had said to him, he went on "But why not consult Raja first? He has had a great deal of experience in business, in property—he will know how to get the best deal from Sharma. His advice will be worth listening to, Bim."

Bim shook her head positively. "No, not Raja," she said. "He wouldn't care." She gave her hand a small wave, dismissing him.

Tara was ready to appeal to anyone now. When Jaya's little visit one morning was over, she insisted on accompanying her down to the gate although the sun was already white-hot and they had to cover their heads with the ends of their saris and keep their eyes on the ground. It had burnt everything into a landscape of black and white, of coal and ash. Tara felt giddy under its blaze.

"What strange ideas Bim does have," Jaya said.

"Yes," Tara agreed, happy to have this opportunity to ask for Jaya's advice. But Jaya was only referring to their conversation over glasses of fresh lemonade under the cantankerously complaining and squeaking fan of the drawing room. Jaya had herself come for advice. "The school is shut for the summer now so Sarla and I thought we'd renovate everything, paint the furniture. What colour do you think we should paint the children's tables and chairs?" While Tara pretended to consider the question seriously, Bim answered at once: "Red." "Oh no." Jaya was appalled. "Not *red*. Pink or blue—it must be pink or blue." "Why?" demanded Bim argumentatively. Jaya had not been able to say, but "It must be pink or blue," she had insisted.

Now she appealed to Tara. "It can't be red," she complained. "Red would be *awful*. It must be something soft, like pink or blue."

"What?" said Tara, not having realized this was what had brought Jaya to visit them.

"The furniture," said Jaya, hurt at her lack of interest. "The school tables and chairs."

"Oh," said Tara. "Bim is—is in a strange mood these days," she explained, trying to bring in her own anxieties for Jaya's attention. "I'm worried about her, Jaya."

"About Bim?" Jaya was scornful. Indignation still burnt in her. How burnt and blackened her skin was, Tara noted, staring at their feet in slippers, making their way through the heavy white dust of the driveway. Jaya's feet were like the claws of an old rook, twisted and charred. Her voice, too, sounded like a burnt twig breaking, brittle and dry. "No need to worry about Bim—she's always looked after herself. She can take care of herself."

"For how long?" worried Tara, holding her white cotton sari like a veil across her face against the blinding light. "Bim's not young. And Baba's not young either. And here they are, just the two of them, while we are all away."

"There are two of them—they have each other," Jaya's voice angrily smouldered. "Bim has Baba to look after—she has always liked to rule others—and he needs her. Bim's all right."

There seemed no way of conveying her anxiety to Jaya. Tara paused by the gate. Here a mulberry tree cast its shade over them and they stood adjusting their eyes to the shade that seemed pitch-black in comparison with the white heat shimmering outside its dusky circle. Ripe mulberries lay in the dust, blackening. Some had been squashed underfoot, their juice soaked into the earth like blood. Their resemblance to worms made Tara squirm. She tried to keep her feet off them but they were everywhere.

"We'll be going away to the wedding, Jaya, as soon as the girls arrive," Tara said.

"Is Bim going with you?"

"No," Tara shook her head mournfully. "That's the trouble—she won't come. She refuses to come."

Jaya gave a horsey snort. "Bim has her own mind," she said. "Bim always did. You were always so different, you two sisters." She gave Tara an almost maternal look, both approving and preening.

But Tara would not accept that. "We're not really," she said. "We may seem to be—but we have everything in common. That makes us one. No one else knows all we share, Bim and I."

"Of course," said Jaya carelessly. "That is only natural. But Bim is so stubborn. Not like you. You were never stubborn. I hope you enjoy the wedding, Tara. Give our love to Raja, to Benazir. Thank them for the invitation—we got such a grand one," and she went off into the sun's blaze again and Tara stood amongst the fallen, mutilated mulberries and their smeared juice in the shade of the tree, watching her till her eyes smarted and her head reeled. She would have to go back to the house if she were not to faint from the heat.

Tara's concern quivering in the air, like the moist nose of a dog that is restless and won't lie down, made Bim want to stamp on it and stamp it out, rudely and roughly, just as she would have done when they were children. "Must you wear those jingle-bells at your waist, Tara?" she asked irritably as Tara came in, veiled, from outdoors. "All those gold bangles on your wrists—and then all those silver bells at your waist, too. I never thought you'd be the kind of woman that carries a bunch of keys at the waist."

"Our suitcases," Tara explained apologetically, startled into feeling guilty. "Our trunks. Bakul gives me the keys to keep."

"Yes, but how can you bear them jingling so?" Bim asked querulously, pressing her hand to her head. The electric fan creaked and complained over their heads for want of an oiling. A gecko on the wall let loose a series of clucked warnings. Its tail flicked at the tip, spitefully. Tara edged past it and past Bim at the table, keeping a safe distance from both, her hand pressed against the key chain to silence it.

But Bim was not appeased. Her anger was as raw as a rash of prickly heat that she compulsively scratched and made worse. At lunch there was a hot curry that Tara could not bear to eat and tried to pass down the table unobtrusively. Bim pounced on her. "What's the matter? Don't you like Janaki's curry? It isn't very good—Janaki can't cook—but one mustn't *fuss*. Take some, Tara." When Tara shook her head, she insisted till Tara nearly cried and finally took a spoonful, splashing the red gravy onto the plate and onto the tablecloth which made Bim go pale with anger.

When she swung down the veranda for a baleful afternoon rest, she nearly stepped on a smashed pigeon's egg and the unsightly corpse of a baby bird that had plunged to its death at birth from its disastrously inadequate nest. The scattered bits of shell, the shapeless smudge of yellow-tipped feathers and bluish-red flesh and outsize beak made Bim draw back for a moment, then plunge on with a gasp of anger, as if the pigeon had made its nest so crudely, so insecurely, simply to lose its egg and anger her and give her the trouble of clearing it. It was a piece of filth—Bim nearly sobbed—not sad, not pathetic, just filthy.

All afternoon her anger swelled and spread, acquiring demonic proportions. It was like the summer itself, rising to its peak, or like the mercury in the barometer that hung on the veranda wall, swelling and bulging and glinting.

Then Baba, shaded and sequestered in his own room, played "Don't Fence Me In" once too often. It was what Bim needed to break her in two, decapitate her with anger. Clutching at her throat, she strode into his room and jerked the needle-head off the record and twisted back the arm. In the silence that gaped like a wound left by a tooth that has been pulled, she said in a loud, loose voice, "I want to have a talk with you, Baba. You'll have to leave that off and listen to me," and sitting down in a canvas chair by his bed, she rattled down a straight line aimed at Baba, shocked and confused before her, like a train racing down a line, driven by a mad driver. She would not look at Baba's widening eyes, more white than black, as she rattled on, straight at him, for he was the target she had chosen to hit—and hit and hit. She was telling him of her idea of selling their shares of the firm to Sharma, using that as a line on which to run. "If I sell, it'll mean the end of that part of our income. It was too small to count anyway, but it did cover some of the expenses. With my salary, I'll be able to pay the rent, keep on the house, I'll manage—but I might have to send you to live with Raja. I came to ask you—what would you think of that?" She was hitting the target now—hitting and hitting it. "Are you willing to go and live with Raja in Hyderabad?"

She had not known she was going to say that till she had said it. She had only walked in to talk to Baba—cut down his defence and demand some kind of a response from him, some kind of justification from him for herself, her own life, her ways and attitudes, like a blessing from Baba. She had not known she would be led into making such a threat, or blackmailing Baba. She was still hardly aware of what she had said, only something seemed to slam inside her head, painfully, when she looked at Baba.

He did not say anything. He only sat on the edge of his bed as he always did, his long hands dangling loosely over his knees, but he seemed to draw back from her, as far as he could, and his mouth was drawn awry as if he had been slapped, hard.

"I mean," she cried, leaning out of her chair towards him, "I mean—it's just an idea—I've been wondering—I wanted to ask you, Baba—what you thought."

But Baba never told what he thought. No one knew if he thought.

"I didn't mean," she said hoarsely, "Baba, I didn't mean—"

Then Bim's rage was spent at last. It had reached its peak, its acme, like a great glittering wave that had hovered over everyone and that now collapsed, fell on the sand and seeped away, leaving nothing but a soggy shadow in the shape of Baba's silence.

No afternoon in all that summer had been so quiet, so empty as the one Bim spent that day, lying as still as a bone left on the sand by the river.

Silence roared around the house and thundered through it, making her press her hands against her ears. She would have relished the sound of the gramophone if it could have drowned out the sound of silence.

Now she pressed her hands across her eyes but the resulting flashes and pin-pricks of light darting and dashing across her eyelids did not amount to an answer. Only the questions thundered and thundered, one dark wave succeeding another. Why had she chosen Baba to vent her hurt and pain and frustration on? Why had she not written a letter to Raja, pouring out all she had to say to him over the years? Or attacked Tara instead since she could never be driven quite away, but always came back crawling to cling out of the habit of affection and her own insecurity? Or Bakul, smashing his complacence into satisfying smithereens with one judicious blow for he would only pretend nothing had happened, remain certain no one could do this to him?

She knew why of course: she could so easily have drawn an answer out of them—she already knew the answers they would have yielded up. Their answers were all so open, so strident, so blatant, she knew every line and nuance of them.

It was Baba's silence and reserve and otherworldliness that she had wanted to break open and ransack and rob, like the hunter who, moved by the white bird's grace as it hovers in the air above him, raises his crossbow and shoots to claim it for his own—his treasure, his loot—and brings it hurtling down to his feet—no white spirit or symbol of grace but only a dead albatross, a cold package of death.

Like the smashed egg and the bird with a broken neck outside. Filth to be cleaned up.

Her eyes opened at this sight against her will and she looked around the room almost in fear. But it was dark and shadowy, shaded by the bamboo screen at the door, the damp rush mats at the windows, the old heavy curtains and the spotted, peeling walls, and in their shade she saw how she loved him, loved Raja and Tara and all of them who had lived in this house with her. There could be no love more deep and full and wide than this one, she knew. No other love had started so far back in time and had had so much time in which to grow and spread. They were really all parts of her, inseparable, so many aspects of her as she was of them, so that the anger or the disappointment she felt in them was only the anger and disappointment she felt at herself. Whatever hurt they felt, she felt. Whatever diminished them, diminished her. What attacked them, attacked her. Nor was there anyone else on earth whom she was willing to forgive more readily or completely, or defend more instinctively and instantly. She could hardly believe, at that moment, that she would live on after they did or they would continue after she had ended. If such an unimaginable phenomenon could take place, then surely they would remain flawed, damaged for life. The wholeness of the pattern, its perfection, would be gone.

She lay absolutely still, almost ceasing to breathe, afraid to diminish by even a breath the wholeness of that love.

Although it was shadowy and dark, Bim could see as well as by the clear light of day that she felt only love and yearning for them all, and if there were hurts, these gashes and wounds in her side that bled, then it was only because her love was imperfect and did not encompass them thoroughly enough, and because it had flaws and inadequacies and did not extend to all equally. She did not feel enough for her dead parents, her understanding of them was incomplete and she would have to work and labour to acquire it. Her love for Raja had had too much of a battering, she had felt herself so humiliated by his going away and leaving her, by his reversal of role from brother to landlord, that it had never recovered and become the tall, shining thing it had been once. Her love for Baba was too inarticulate, too unthinking: she had not given him enough thought, her concern had not been keen, acute enough. All these would have to be mended, these rents and tears, she would have to mend and make her net whole so that it would suffice her in her passage through the ocean.

Somehow she would have to forgive Raja that unforgivable letter. Somehow she would have to wrest forgiveness from Baba for herself. These were great rents torn in the net that the knife of love had made. Stains of blood that the arrow of love had left. Stains that darkened the light that afternoon. She laid her hands across her eyes again.

When she took Baba's tea in to him later that afternoon, she found him asleep. That was why the gramophone had been silent in the afternoon—

not because he was sulking, or wished to punish her, but simply because he was asleep. She ought to have known—Baba knew neither grudge nor punishment. She touched him on the cheek with one finger—its whiteness seemed to be like a saint's that suffers itself to be kissed. He woke at once and, seeing her, smiled.

"Your tea, Baba," she murmured. "I brought you your tea." She felt an immense, almost irresistible yearning to lie down beside him on the bed, stretch out limb to limb, silent and immobile together. She felt that they must be the same length, that his slightness would fit in beside her size, that his concavities would mould together with her convexities. Together they would form a whole that would be perfect and pure. She needed only to lie down and stretch out beside him to become whole and perfect.

Instead, she went out. In the garden, a koel lifted itself out of the heavy torpor of the afternoon and called tentatively, as if enquiring into the existence of the evening.

In the evening, the sisters paced the terrace, waiting for a bit of breeze to come and lighten the air. Tara tried to talk—there were not many evenings left to them—but Bim was silent and seemed tired. After a while they stopped and leaned on the balustrade together, looking out over the stretch of sand to the still-standing river and above it the gauzy screen of dust into which the sun was sinking—a serene glass bubble filled with a pale liquid that did not quiver or ripple but was absolutely calm, weighting it down and forcing it to fall. The scene beneath reflected its lack of colour and its stillness. The river did not seem to run, the ferry boat was static and the egrets stood stock-still in the shallows.

"I'm going to bed early tonight," said Tara and Bim nodded, her eyelids drooping with tiredness. She, too, wanted to sleep. She was exhausted—by Tara, by Baba, by all of them. Loving them and not loving them. Accepting them and not accepting them. Understanding them and not understanding them. The conflicts that rose inside her with every word they spoke and every gesture they made had been an enormous strain, she now felt, leaving her worn out. In spite of her exhaustion, she feared the night and the long hours and the dark when she would have to face herself. How would she swim through that ocean and come out again? she wondered.

In the event, she decided not to go to bed. She ignored the bed laid out for her at the end of the veranda, next to Baba's. She dreaded seeing his sleeping shape, unresponsive as a god, guilt-arousing as a saint. She dreaded the unreal light of the moon and Badshah's crazed barking. She dreaded hearing Tara's and Bakul's voices murmuring at their end of the veranda, forcing her to imagine their conversations and tones. No, she would stay in her stifling, dust-choked room, propped up by cushions on her hard wooden divan, the lamp with the brown paper shade lit and her books beside her to help her through the night. While she listened to the others switch off their lights and settle into bed, she rustled through page after page, the leaves of her mind falling one on top of the other as thick as cards, the cards her mother's, her father's hands had so expertly shuffled.

They still shuffled and the cards, the leaves, fell upon each other with a dry, dusty crepitation, as meaningless and endless as their games.

To try and halt this crazy paper-dance, she reached out towards her bookshelf for a book that would draw the tattered shreds of her mind together and plait them into a composed and concentrated whole after a day of fraying and unravelling. It was the *Life of Aurangzeb* that lay at the top of the stack and came away from it between her fingers. Bim gave a little sigh and sank down on her cushions with relief at finding some history, a table of dates and facts with which to steady her mind. But, as if by instinct, she opened it to an account of the emperor's death:

> Alone he had lived and alone he made ready to die . . . he wrote to Prince A'zam: . . . "Many were around me when I was born. but now I am going alone. I know not why I am or wherefore I came into the world . . . Life is transient and the lost moment never comes back . . . When I have lost hope in myself, how can I hope in others? Come what will, I have launched my bark upon the waters . . ."
>
> To his favourite Kam-Baksh he wrote: "Soul of my soul . . . Now I am going alone. I grieve for your helplessness, but what is the use? Every torment I have inflicted, every sin I have committed, every wrong I have done, I carry the consequences with me. Strange that I came with nothing into the world, and now go away with this stupendous caravan of sin!"
>
> . . . In accordance with his command "Carry this creature of dust to the nearest burial-place, and lay him in the earth with no useless coffin," he was buried simply near Daulatabad beside the tombs of Muslim saints.

Then Bim's mind seemed stilled at last. A silence settled upon it as a shroud that is drawn up over the dead. Laying her open book across her chest, she lay with her eyes closed, repeating the emperor's last words to herself like a prayer. She felt tears seep from under her eyelids involuntarily: they were warm as they ran down the sides of her face into the wells of her ears. They left a map of river-beds in the dust, trickling a little and then drying.

When she moved, it was to go to her desk and carefully draw out the entire lower drawer and carry it, heavily loaded with papers, to the divan where she could kneel beside it as she took out the papers in bundles and read them intently by the dim brown-papered light for the first time in many years.

They were not her papers, they were the translations she had made once of Raja's poems. They would be difficult to read, she feared, and her face was white as if with fear, or pain. Then it proved easy. The years had made them impersonal. Nowhere in them could she find Raja, not the Raja now and not the young Raja, the child Raja. For the poems were really very derivative. On each of them she could clearly see the influence of the poets he loved and copied. There was no image, no metaphor, no turn of phrase that was original. Each was a meticulous imitation of what he had read, memorised and recited. He had made no effort to break the iron rings of clichés, he had seemed content to link them, ring to ring, so that they clinked and jingled down the lengths of his verses. He had not, it seemed, really set out to startle by originality, to burst upon the literary world as a new star, fresh and vivid. One could see in them only a wish to emulate and to step where his heroes had stepped before him.

Touched, Bim laid them carefully in a heap beside her knees, one sheet on the other, like so many cards in a game. She had not realized that Raja's ambitions were so modest and unassertive. Far from playing the hero, he had only worshipped the heroes of his youth. Since he had set about imitating them and deriving from them so meticulously and pain-stakingly, they were not quite so bad as they might have been if he had trusted only in his own worth. Bim had to admit that he had learnt his craft well. He had acquired a surprising command over the craft of writing Urdu verse. He had learnt his lessons in metre, rhyme and rhythm and acquitted himself well.

But would he like her still to keep them? Would he want to be shown them again? Would they embarrass him, pain him, dismay him? She sat half the night wondering. She had thought of tearing them to bits, empty-ing her desk of them so that no trace should be left of those "heroic" days of theirs. Now she was not certain. Her eyelids flickered with tiredness as her fingers shuffled through them again and again, and even her sand-coloured lips moved silently as she debated with herself what to do.

"Strange that I came with nothing into the world and now go away with this stupendous caravan of sin!"

Why load the bark with this accumulation made through a thoughtless life? Would it not sink? Would it not be better to jettison everything, to lighten the bark and go free, with ease?

"Many were around me when I was born but now I am going alone."

But they were Raja's papers, not hers. It was not for her to decide whether he would take them with him or disown them and discard them, the litter and rubble left by the human picnic.

In the end, the only paper she tore that night was the letter he had written her and she had never answered. It was too late to answer it now. The only course left was to pretend it had never been written.

Having torn it, she felt she had begun the clearing of her own decks, the lightening of her own bark. After that, she spent the rest of the night in tearing and throwing away great piles of her own papers—old, dry, impersonal things, examination papers she had set her students, notes she had made in her own student days, tutorial papers she had forgotten to hand back, trivial letters that did not bear re-reading, pamphlets and cata-logues sent by bookshops and academic journals, empty cheque books and full pass books, files dating back to her father's lifetime . . . Why had she kept them all these years? Now she flung them in a heap in the centre of the floor, and her shelves and desk were bare except for dust.

While she worked, she felt a sharp, fiery pining for college to re-open and her ordinary working life to be resumed. Then she would be able to end all this storm of emotion in which she had been dragged back and forth all summer as in a vast, warm ocean, and return to what she did best, most efficiently, with least expense of spirit—the keeping to a schedule, the following of a time-table, the application of the mind to facts, figures, rules and analyses. Once again, she felt with a certain bitterness, what a strain Tara's visit had been, what it had cost her by constantly dragging her apart into love and hostility, resentment and acceptance, forgiveness and hate. Worn out by it, she threw away the last paper, lifted the empty drawer off the divan and then lay down and slept. Even Badshah had fallen silent by then.

When Bim woke in the morning, she found her nieces sitting on the edge of the divan, looking into her confused face and laughing. They leaned forward to kiss her, and Tara came in, laughing too, to kiss them. Tara and Bakul had been, early that morning, in the dark, to fetch them. "Here they are," she was saying with such pride, such triumph, that they might have been fruit she had raised, or prizes she had secured. "Look, Bim, here are your nieces again," she laughed and Bim, struggling to free herself from the night and reach them, reached out to touch their faces and draw them to hers to be kissed.

She had not held anyone so close for years. Their young faces loomed, their brightness and pinkness filled her vision, and the scent of their fresh skin and fine hair and the soap and water with which they had just washed wafted down to her, making her draw back into her cushions, overwhelmed.

"Are you tired, Bim-*masi?*" they laughed at her. "Aren't you awake yet? What have you been doing all night? Your room looks like a storm's been through it."

"Tired? Not awake?" She sat up then, as straight as she could, feeling a dreadful pain in her back from the hard wooden divan on which she had spent the night. "You just wait—you just see—I'll be up and have your tea ready and we'll be out on the veranda, all of us, in five minutes, and then Tara will have her family gathering at last," and she plunged past them and stood over them, tall and refreshed.

"What *are* you wearing, *masi?*" they teased. "The very latest fashion—a caftan! Ma, you never told us how fashionable Bim-*masi* has grown." No one mentioned that her face seemed made of clay—old dried clay that had cracked. Only Bim felt it, with the tips of trembling fingers.

"You're making fun of me now," said Bim, finding her way back to her aunt-self, her aunt-persona. "Come along, come out to the veranda—I want some light—I want my tea. Have you seen Badshah? Have you seen my jet black cat?"

It was with Baba that the nieces chiefly spent their time. They would slip into his room and sit cross-legged on his bed, listening to the old records that they had listened to on all their previous visits to the house, playing with his gramophone as if it were the most novel toy of the year. They squabbled so much for turns at winding it up that Bim and Tara would have to go in and see that they were fair about taking turns. Baba, sitting in the canvas chair by the bed with his knees looming up under his chin, watched them, chuckling.

Then they found the old bagatelle board and insisted he play with them, noisy games that led them all to shriek and roar with laughter and howl with rage as they watched the metal balls roll inexorably into the traps and channels set for them. Once Bim and Tara even heard Baba calling out excitedly on winning five hundred points and turned to each other in disbelief.

When Bakul enquired "When will you take them shopping? You said they needed saris for the wedding. Shall I send for the car?" Tara shook her head fiercely, refusing to break up Baba's party.

They were to leave early in the morning. There was just time for Bim to give them tea out on the veranda. Still sleepy, they were all subdued. The girls sat side by side on the divan, petting the cat that lay stretched out like a black string between them and drawing it out longer and longer with their caressing fingers till Bim begged them to stop.

The pigeons strutted up and down on their spidery pink claws, dipping their beaks into their breasts and drawing out from them those chiding, gossiping sounds as if they were long thick worms.

Out on the lawn Badshah was following a suspicious scent laid invisibly in the night. His paws made saucers of colour on the pale dew drawn across the grass like a gauzy sheen.

Teacups clinked on the saucers, tinnily.

The sunlight spread like warm oil, slowly oozing and staining the tiles.

Of course it was Bakul who spoke then, as Bim knew he would. Placing his empty cup in the centre of an empty saucer, he said, blowing his words through his lips like bubbles through a pipe, "Our last day in Delhi. The last day of this family gathering. Tomorrow, another one in Hyderabad." The bubbles sailed over their heads, bloated and slow, then sank to earth with their weight.

"Oh it will be more than just a family gathering," said Tara, worriedly tightening the belt around her kimono. "A wedding always means such crowds—Benazir has relations coming all the way from Pakistan—there'll be such confusion—we won't have time to sit about our tea like this."

One of the girls let out a little shriek as the cat suddenly swatted at her with its quick paw. Laughing, they both began to tickle her belly, making her kick.

"But, Bim, we'll soon be back," said Tara, lifting her voice above their giggles. "You'll have me and the girls back after the wedding. That's what I'm really looking forward to—a few quiet weeks while Bakul does all the travelling. The girls will love it."

The cat sprang up in protest and fled. The girls rocked with laughter.

"Do they love quiet times?" Bim asked, whacking one of them on her knee.

"They *will*," Tara was certain. "But perhaps not all that quiet—they do have fun with Baba, don't they? Did you hear them playing bagatelle? The way they squabble over his gramophone! Did you hear Baba laughing?"

Bim nodded. She kept her hand on Mala's knee. It seemed to her its round shape was the size and consistency of a ripe apple.

"They must do something besides sit and listen to Baba's records," Bakul said fussily, getting up and pacing up and down the veranda. "D'you hear, you two? You are to visit all the relatives. They want to meet you. They want to introduce you to young people in New Delhi . . ."

"And marry you off as soon as they can arrange it," Bim interrupted, giving the little knee a shake.

The girls went pink and looked and winked at each other, but Tara protested, "No, no. What makes you think so? They're still studying, Bim."

"That won't stand in your way," said Bim. "If you can find two eligible young men—*you* wouldn't insist on their going back to college."

"No," Tara agreed, "but *they* might," and the girls gazed into her face, a bit warily. "Mightn't you?" Tara asked them gently. They seemed not quite out of their cocoons yet, they were somehow still fuzzy and moist, their eyes half-open, like kittens'.

"Now *that*" said Bim, standing up to collect the tea-tray, "is good news. You must give me a little time with my nieces and give me a licence to influence them—an aunt has that prerogative, surely."

"You can have all the time you want with them," Tara said graciously, helping to hand over the empty cups, "and influence them as much as you like. In our family, aunts have that prerogative. Like Mira-*masi* had."

Bim gave a little start, scattering sugar, and her hand jerked to one side. The others looked at her. She was staring at the ranks of flowerpots on the steps and the dusty shrubbery outside as if she saw something there. Then "Hmm," she said, settling her chin into her neck, and lifted the tray and went off down the veranda and heard Tara say "Mala! Maya! Why don't you get up? Why don't you help your aunt? You *should*, girls."

"They must go and dress," Bakul boomed. "Why is everyone sitting around here? Hurry!"

When they had all disappeared into their rooms, Bim came out of the kitchen slowly and went down the steps into the garden. She was tired, had not slept well, there was a mist before her eyes that bothered her. The bright light of day cut into her temples, leaving a wake of pain. She wanted shade, quiet. She went down to the rose walk to be by herself for a bit.

As summer advanced, any pretence the garden made during milder seasons shrivelled up and disappeared. The stretches of arid yellow dust extended and the strips of green shrank. Now there was really nothing left but these two long beds of roses, the grey-green domes of the mulberry and eucalyptus trees at the far end, and the water tap that trickled into a puddle of green mud. A party of parched mynahs stood around it, drinking and bathing. As they saw Bim and Badshah shuffling up the path, they rose and twittered with loud indignation from the tree tops. Drops of water flew, bright and sharp as nails, from their agitated wings.

Bim trailed up the path, looking at her toes, not at the hedges where white things might slip ghost-like in the blaze of day, or even at the crimson roses, all edged with black now in this scorching heat. She thought how Aunt Mira would have trembled if told to influence her nieces, how her hands would have shaken when she lifted the tumbler that concealed her brandy, how it would have rattled against her nervous teeth as she drank, and then the long hands would have shaken even more . . .

"Bim!" called Tara, quickly crossing the frizzling lawn to the shade of the rose walk, her hand shielding her eyes from the sun.

Bim watched her come with tired resignation. She would have liked to wave Tara away, to be alone to mutter to herself, make gestures, groan aloud and behave like the solitary old woman she was, not as a sister or an aunt. "Haven't you to pack?" she asked, a bit coldly. Perhaps that was what

Aunt Mira had needed, she felt, and missed—they had never allowed her to be alone, never stopped pursuing her and surrounding her for a minute. They had not realized and she had not told. Nor could she tell Tara.

"All done," Tara called back. "Bakul and the girls are getting ready."

"And you?"

Tara came up to her and for a fleeting moment Bim thought she was going to take her by the arm. They had never held hands, not even as children. How would she do it? She stood with her arms hanging stiffly by her sides. But Tara only brushed against her faintly and then, side by side, they strolled up the path, the dog leading the way, his tail rising into the air like a plume as he pranced to annoy the mynahs, giving them just a glint of his eye as a warning.

Then when Bim thought the danger over and relaxed, Tara's hand did suddenly creep up and her fingers closed on Bim's arm with sudden urgency. She pulled at Bim's elbow, urging her to stop, to listen. They stumbled on the hems of their long dresses and came to a stop, clumsily. Hurriedly, Tara said in a rush that made Bim realize that she had kept these words bottled up till they burst: "Bim, I always wanted to say—I can't go away without saying—*I'm sorry*—I can never forgive myself—or forget—"

"Oh Tara," Bim groaned. "Not those bloody bees again!"

"No, no, Bim, much worse, Bim," Tara hurried on, clutching her kimono at the knees, "much worse. When I married—and left—and didn't even come back and help you nurse Mira-*masi*, Bim—whenever I think of that—how *could* I?"

"What! You'd only just married and gone. You couldn't have come back here immediately after you'd gone. It wasn't as if you were in New Delhi— you had gone all the way to Ceylon."

"I could have come—I *should* have come," Tara cried, and bit her lip. She tried to tell Bim what was even worse, still worse—that, taken up with her husband, her new home and her new life, she had not even thought of Aunt Mira, had not once worried about her. Not till after her death. And of that she heard only after the funeral. "I didn't even come to the funeral," she wailed.

Bim's feet kicked impatiently into the hem of her nightdress. She must stop this. She must bring all this to a stop. To Tara's visit, to this summer, all those summers before. Looking desperately about her, she shaded her eyes against the sun, and said "There's Bakul—on the veranda—calling you."

"Tara! Tara!" Bakul called, and Bim felt well-disposed to him for the first time that summer. "Go, Tara," she said.

But Tara clung to her arm, her face puffy and angry. She wanted some-thing of Bim—a punishment or at least a reprimand with which she could finally plaster the episode, medicate it. "I never even came to the funeral," she repeated, as if Bim might not have heard.

"I didn't ask you to it," Bim said roughly. "You didn't need to. Don't be so *silly*, Tara—it was all so long ago."

"Yes, but" cried Tara desperately, turning towards the house now, and Bakul, as if against her will "but it's never over. Nothing's *over*, ever."

"No," Bim agreed, growing gentler. She saw in Tara's desperation a reflection of her own despairs. They were not so unalike. They were more alike than any other two people could be. They had to be, their hands were so deep in the same water, their faces reflected it together. "Nothing's over," she agreed. "Ever," she accepted.

Tara seemed comforted to have Bim's corroboration. When Bim repeated "Go, Tara," she went. At least they had agreed to a continuation.

Bim's agitation rose humming out of her depths as the family got ready to depart. Bakul's uncle's car had arrived to take them to the station. It was standing in the drive. The gardener had come to help the driver load it with their smart American suitcases. The girls, in their travelling jeans and T-shirts, hopped about, crying with alarm every time a suitcase tilted or bulged or threatened to fall. Bakul was handing out tips to the servants who had gathered on the veranda steps as if posing for an old-fashioned photograph of family retainers: they even smirked uncharacteristically ingratiating smirks as they stretched out their palms and salaamed. Bakul looked in his element, his lower lip moistly pouting with fulfilment. Tara darted back into the house, remembering something. Baba's gramophone was churning out "The Donkey Serenade" like a jolly concrete-mixer. The gardener and driver were lashing a rope around the bags, strapping them to the carrier. Bakul shouted orders to them. Then he turned to Bim and shouted, having forgotten to lower his voice in turning from one to the other, "Where's that sister of yours gone now?"

"Tara, Tara," Bim shouted, as tense and impatient as Bakul. She stood staring at the shuttered door in fear that Tara might bring Baba out with her, or that Baba might follow Tara and get into the car with her to go to Hyderabad. Had she not ordered him to go, asked him to go? At any moment, at any second, Baba might come out and leave with them. "You'll be late," she fretted aloud, shifting from one foot to the other as if it were she who was to travel.

"I know," he fumed. "Tara!"

Then Tara darted out. Alone. Bim felt herself go limp, her tension recede. "Hurry, hurry," she said, brushing aside Tara's last affectionate squeeze and trying to propel her towards the open door of the car. But Tara put out her hand to block the door and would not go in. She stood stiffly, stubbornly, beside the car, refusing to let everyone's impatience budge her. She was frowning with the distress of unfulfilment.

"Baba won't come out," she murmured to Bim who still tried to bundle her physically into the car.

"Let him be," Bim said, relief blowing her words into large light bubbles that rolled off her tongue and floated effervescently into the orange air. "He feels frightened by all this—this coming and going. You know he's not used to it."

Tara nodded sadly. But this was not all that was on her mind. There was another block, halting her. She tried to force her voice past that block. "Shall I tell Raja—?"

"Yes," Bim urged, her voice flying, buoyant. "Tell him how we're not used to it—Baba and I. Tell him we never travel any more. Tell him we couldn't come—but *he* should come. Bring him back with you, Tara—or tell him to come in the winter. All of them. And he can see Sharma about the firm—and settle things. And see to Hyder Ali's old house—and repair it. Tell him I'm—I'm waiting for him—I want him to come—I want to see him."

As if frightened by this breakdown in Bim's innermost self, this crumbling of a great block of stone and concrete, a dam, to release a flood of roaring water, Tara unexpectedly let go Bim's hand and fell forwards into the car. At once, the driver, who had been waiting with his foot on the accelerator, released the brake so that the car gave a sudden jolt, then stalled, throwing them all backwards. The girls laughed, Tara squealed. The driver started the engine again. Bakul sank back with a groan of relief. The suitcases on the carrier wobbled. Tara and the girls began to wave their hands at Bim and the servants lined on the steps, as the car glided forwards, at first slowly in first gear, then accelerating with a spurt, making the gravel fly from under the wheels and Tara sink back so that her face was wiped out from the window with a brisk suddenness. It reappeared at the rear window now, and again her hand rose, to wave. Bim waved back, laughing, doubled over as if she were gasping for breath, heaving with laughter helplessly. Badshah sprang after the car, barking. It turned out of the gate. The bougainvillea closed upon it.

It had grown too long, it needed trimming.

"Chandu," Bim said, straightening up and turning soberly towards the servants who were watching with her, "that bougainvillea needs to be trimmed."

But now they had all lost their ingratiating smiles. They looked sullen again. The tips had been moderate ones, nothing lavish. Chandu nodded noncommittally and sidled off. When they had all gone, Bim went up the steps and sank down into one of the cane chairs with the slow movements of an old woman who feels she is no longer watched and need no longer make a pretence. Her black cat came to her and climbed into her lap.

Then the terribly familiar rattling and churning of Baba's record slowed down and came to a stop. The bamboo screen lifted and Baba came out. For a moment he stood blinking as if he could not quite believe that the veranda was so empty, so quiet.

"They've left," Bim assured him.

He came and sat down beside her. It was very still. Lifting her black cat's chin on one finger, Bim said, staring directly into her green glass eyes, "Would you have liked to go with them, Baba—to the wedding, I mean?" With the cat's chin still balanced on her finger, she looked at his face from under heavy, tired lids.

Baba, gazing at the cat, too, shook his head quietly. Then the cat grew irritated and jumped off Bim's lap and twitched the tip of her tail angrily.

They sat in silence then, the three of them, for now there seemed no need to say another word. Everything had been said at last, cleared out of the way finally. There was nothing left in the way of a barrier or a shadow, only the clear light pouring down from the sun. They might be floating in the light—it was as vast as the ocean, but clear, without colour or substance or form. It was the lightest and most pervasive of all elements and they floated in it. They found the courage, after all, to float in it and bathe in it and allow it to pour onto them, illuminating them wholly, without allowing them a single shadow to shelter in.

They were sitting—wordlessly and expressionlessly—inside this great bubble of light when a black smudge beetle-like entered it at its circumference and came crawling up the drive, in the shade of a white cotton sari, for it was only Jaya. They waited, almost without breathing, for her to come within screeching distance.

"What, just sitting about?" she screeched. "Oh, and I'm so busy—so busy—but I had to come myself to tell you. Of course, Tara's left, hasn't she? Is that why you are sitting like that?" She came up the steps, her slippers striking each one emphatically. "But I have so much to do. You know, Mulk is going to sing. It is Mulk's guru's birthday and Papa has given him permission to celebrate it. He is to come on a visit and sing for us, and Mulk will sing, too." She sat down on a creaking chair and began to fan herself with the end of her sari. "So many people are to come—Mulk has invited everybody—and you must come too—it will be a big affair—out in the garden—just like old times again—Sarla and I are to make all the arrangements—I'm so busy—so little time left—will you help, Bim? And you must come, with Baba—"

"It's Moyna's wedding day," Bim told Jaya and Sarla as they met her in the porch, and at once they clasped her to their plain cotton bosoms, crying excitedly "Mubarak![3] Mubarak! And it's Mulk's guru's birthday, too, you know," and then rushing away because it wasn't the wedding that excited them—they tended now to brush aside weddings as so much fluff, rather unsightly and not at all necessary—it was really the unaccustomed noise and bustle in the old house, the return to old times and the hectic effect of music that made them fly and flap about, screaming at the servants to bring out more trays, more cushions and rugs, and greeting the guests who were pouring in at this late hour, all having dined fully and at leisure and now come out of the steamy city to the cool dark lawn in Old Delhi to listen to a little music under the dusty stars.

Bim and Baba lowered themselves onto a cotton rug spread over the prickly dry grass, close to the edge of the lawn where cannas, hibiscus and oleanders grappled together in a green combat for life. "Can you see, Baba?" Bim murmured, tucking her feet under her sari, and he inclined his head a little and blinked worriedly. They could just make out, between the shoulders and over the heads in front of them, the wooden divan that had been carried out and placed in front of the dry fountain, spread with a white cloth, a Persian carpet and some coloured bolsters, and on which the musicians were already seated, having first been fed by the sisters, and were tuning their instruments with the absorption of grasshoppers or bees. The sounds, too, were insect-like and buzzed and chirruped and zoomed in the spotty dark of the lamplit garden, and the atmosphere was as busy and complicated as sitar[4] strings.

The tanpura[5] player had the rapt, wall-eyed stare of a madman or a

---

3. Congratulations (Urdu).   4. String instrument in north Indian (Hindustani) classical music.
5. Instrument used as a background accompaniment in Indian classical music.

fanatic. Tall and thin as a charred pole, his face was completely disfigured by pockmarks, huge black pits that seemed to carve up the whole of his face into grossly uneven surfaces, and one eye was quite blinded by small-pox. He did not need his eyes, however, and strummed the *tanpura* strings as if in a mesmerised state, his eyes gazing sightlessly into the dark. The *tabla* player, on the other hand, was as round and fat as a marrow, a little plump man who bounced on his buttocks with excitement, rolled his eyes at the audience as if to say "Just wait! See what's coming—hold on!" and then threw back his head and chortled in anticipation of their applause.

Mulk, who was one of the two star performers of the evening, sat cross-legged, jovial and at ease in the centre of the fiddling, drumming, wag-gling musicians, dressed in fresh white pyjamas and a sky-blue embroi-dered Lucknow shirt, passing round betel leaves on a silver tray to his accompanists and laughing at jokes flung at him from the audience with exaggerated enjoyment.

His brothers were sitting in the front row, relaxing against large, thick bolsters, with somewhat self-conscious looks of scepticism and indulgence on their faces as if they weren't quite sure they could digest the huge and festive dinner they had just had. "Mulk-*bhai*, begin with a lullaby," one of them shouted loud enough for Bim and Baba at the back to hear. "First put us to sleep—then you can do what you like," and Mulk threw back his head and opened a mouth crimson with betel-juice to make a raucous pretence at laughter and good humour. An instrument loudly whined, then was stilled.

All the instruments were stilled. The drums ceased to tap, the *tanpura* to strum. Fingers steadied, held them still. Mulk, letting his chin sink down into the folds of his neck, appeared to be plunged in deep thought. Then he lifted one hand, the one with the opal ring that gleamed in a shaft of light from the lamp in the porch, raised his heavy triple chin, looked vaguely upwards at the dim stars, and then sang a tentative phrase in his rich, dark voice. He roved from note to note, searching for harmony, experimenting with sequences, till at last he found the right combination, the sequence that pleased him by its harmony.[6] He sang it in a voice that resounded with the pride of discovery, rang out in triumph. Now all the instruments joined in, made confident by his success. The *tabla* rollicked with delight at the rhythm he had found for it, the *tanpura* skipped and hurried to keep up with him. Swaying their heads with approval, the musi-cians followed Mulk with perfect accord. He had launched their boat, now they were all in motion. Now they rose upon a crest, now they moved forward upon a wave of sound.

Bim, swaying slightly too with the melody that swelled about them, let her eyes rove over the audience that was scattered over the lawn, partly lit by the light that fell through the pillars of the veranda and partly shadowed by the nervous dancing shadows of the foliage so that they were like pierrot figures in a theatre. There were people only just coming up the drive, others milling restlessly about, settling on the cotton rugs only to rise again and move closer to friends, form new groups and then break up and shift

6. Solo improvisation on varied sequences of notes in particular scales (called *raga*) forms an important part of Indian classical vocal and instrumental music.

again. Some fanned themselves with the palm-leaf fans they had brought along, either languidly or frenziedly as they forgot or recalled the heat. Others opened up their silver *pan*[7] boxes and rolled themselves betel leaves or shared them with their families or friends. The quieter ones merely smoked cigarettes, each no more than a small pinpoint of flame in the darkness. Bim had just lit herself one when she had to draw in her feet and make room for a young couple who came and settled down before her with their small daughter in a crackling violet dress trimmed with silver and little gold rings in her ears. She peeped at Bim over a shoulder with great, kohl-rimmed eyes, then clutched her mother's soft, powdered neck and hissed "Look, Ma, a woman is smoking!" making Bim remove the cigarette from her mouth and smile. The child stared and stared till a packet of biscuits was opened for her and then she concentrated mouse-like on them till she was patted to sleep on her mother's lap by hands that jingled in time to the music with their load of glass bangles.

All this commotion, confusion and uproar might have drowned out Mulk's song and yet it did not. It simply formed a part of the scene, like the lamps and the dark and the scent of night-flowering plants, a kind of crepitating tapestry through which Mulk's song wound purposefully, never losing the thread but following a kind of clear, infallible instinct with his musicians to accompany him, and the purpose and the harmony and the melody of his song were a part of the tapestry too, the gold thread that traced a picture on the shimmering background, and no one minded if it was haphazard or arbitrary.

Mulk's brothers were no longer lolling against the bolsters. They were sitting cross-legged and bolt upright, beating out the rhythm on their knees and swaying their heads to the melody and crying "Vah! Vah!"[8] loudly with pleasure and congratulation at every pleasant or unexpected piece of inspiration on Mulk's part, or of intuitive accord and foresight on that of the accompanists. No one would ever have thought that they disapproved of their brother's singing or grudged him what he spent on his musicians, for their delight and sympathy was obvious in every wag of their heads and slap of their hand on their knees. They were also a part of the tapestry, as much as the singer and the musicians forming that composed, absorbed group before them. Mulk's song sung in that pleasant, resonant voice, bound them all together in a pattern, a picture as perfectly composed as a Moghul miniature of a garden scene by night, peopled with lovers, princes and musicians at play.

And there was still another element to this composition. Now the sisters were hurrying down the veranda steps, followed by men with great kettles and small, smoking braziers, and others with trays loaded with cups. As they busily set up a kind of open-air tea shop beside the cannas and the oleanders, Mulk's song rose to a joyful climax, his voice swelling to its fullest strength and the *tanpura* and the *tabla* rising and expanding with it, so that they all arrived together at the peak from which they could do nothing but come rolling down, hilariously, into laughter, congratulation and joviality.

"Tea, tea—come get your tea," Sarla and Jaya were calling, and the

7. Betel leaves.   8. Fine, excellent (Persian).

servants were bustling to pass the cups up and down the rows seated on the rugs. Bim chose to rise, stretching her cramped limbs, to go and fetch two cups. "Wonderful music, Jaya," she said as she bent to pick up the cups held beneath the spout of a great black kettle by a little grubby servant boy. "What a voice Mulk still has—it's wonderful," she said, but Jaya and Sarla, with sweat pouring down their faces and glittering on their foreheads, pumping their arms up and down at the elbows, only smiled worriedly and hardly seemed to hear. The time for them to hear and to think had not come yet. The tea was only a break for refreshment, for the chief part of the programme was still to follow and Mulk's singing was not the star performance as Bim had imagined.

There was a shuffle taking place on the divan. While the accompanists were drinking their tea with loud, appreciative smacks and slurps, an aged little man in a crumpled *dhoti* and faded shirt, wearing a small black cap on his head, was being helped up onto the divan by the Misra brothers and settled onto the centre of it while the others shifted aside and made room for him with an air of both affection and respect.

"Mulk's guru," Sarla explained quickly as Bim moved away with two cups of tea in her hands. "Mulk has asked his guru to sing tonight."

"Ah," said Bim and all round her people were saying "Ahh" with the same note of awe and expectation for the guru, once a famous singer, now lived in retirement and hardly ever appeared in public.

"Mulk's guru is going to sing now," Bim told Baba as she handed down a tea cup to him, slopping, and then carefully settled down beside him to stir and sip the scalding, sweet, milky tea. All round them there was a babble, a hubbub, as the audience prepared for the chief treat of the evening. On the divan too, there was a continuing stir and an atmosphere of both relaxation and mounting anticipation as the musicians exchanged jokes and compliments, sipped tea, chewed betel leaves, flexed their muscles, cleared their throats, tuned their instruments and prepared themselves.

Pleasure and confidence and well-being exuded from all of them, as if music were food and drink to them, a rich nourishment that they had imbibed and gave away generously to all—all except for the elderly guru whose face and little, wizened figure were so dried and aged, so brown and faded and wrinkled, that they could exude nothing at all except a kind of weary acquiescence. Mulk was chaffing him now, teasing him, but the old man, resting the palms of his hands on his knees and leaning forwards, did not smile or in any way respond. He seemed to be having trouble with his teeth which were false and did not fit.

Then he turned one palm upwards on his knee, and immediately Mulk and the accompanists fell silent. Out of that silence his ancient voice crept out and began to circle in the dark, a skeletal bird making its swoops and darts hesitantly, enquiringly. The accompanist followed at a little distance, discreetly, as if not to disturb him. Mulk sank into a listening pose, rapt, swaying his large head very, very gently.

Up on the veranda, on a large white bed, the old father had been lying, listening, quite mute. Now his heavy bulk seemed to stir for a shadow loomed up against the whitewashed wall and swayed like a monument that is crumbling.

Watching that pyramidal shadow that had risen in the night on hearing the old singer's voice, Bim listened to the small, ancient voice, too, rough-edged and raw as if in pain. There was about that voice a tinge of snuff, of crimson betel spittle, of phlegm. Also of conflict, failure and disappointment. The contrast between Mulk's voice and his was great: whereas Mulk's voice had been almost like a child's, so sweet and clear, or a young man's full and ripe and with a touch of sweetness to it, the old man's was sharp, even a little cracked, inclined to break, although not merely with age but with the bitterness of his experiences, the sadness and passion and frustration. All the storms and rages and pains of his life were in that voice, impinging on every song he chose to sing, giving the verses of love and romance a harsh edge that was mocking and disturbing. He sang like a man who had come, at the end of his journey, within sighting distance of death so that he already stood in its looming presence and measured the earth and his life on it by that great shadow. One day perhaps Mulk would also sing like this, if Mulk were to take the same journey his guru had. After all, they belonged to the same school and had the same style of singing and there was this similarity despite the gulf between them.

Listening to him, Bim was suddenly overcome with the memory of reading, in Raja's well-thumbed copy of Eliot's *Four Quartets*, the line:

"Time the destroyer is time the preserver."

Its meaning seemed to fall out of the dark sky and settle upon her like a cloak, or like a great pair of feathered wings. She huddled in its comfort, its solace. She saw before her eyes how one ancient school of music contained both Mulk, still an immature disciple, and his aged, exhausted guru with all the disillusionments and defeats of his long experience. With her inner eye she saw how her own house and its particular history linked and contained her as well as her whole family with all their separate histories and experiences—not binding them within some dead and airless cell but giving them the soil in which to send down their roots, and food to make them grow and spread, reach out to new experiences and new lives, but always drawing from the same soil, the same secret darkness. That soil contained all time, past and future, in it. It was dark with time, rich with time. It was where her deepest self lived, and the deepest selves of her sister and brothers and all those who shared that time with her.

Now the guru sang:

"Your world is the world of fish and fowl. My world is the cry at dawn."

Bim's hand flew up to brush aside the grey hair at her face, and she leant excitedly towards Baba. "Iqbal's," she whispered. "Raja's favourite."

Baba gave a single nod. His face was grave, like an image carved in stone, listening.

The old singer's voice rose higher, in an upward spiral of passion and pain:

"In your world I am subjected and constrained, but over my world You have dominion."

"Vah! Vah!" someone called out in rapture—it might have been the old man listening alone on the veranda—and the singer lifted a shaking hand in acknowledgment.

LORNA GOODISON
born 1947

Lorna Goodison's work belongs to a hitherto neglected but impressive tradition of feminine endeavor and expression in the Caribbean, a tradition that is only now receiving attention in the historical accounts and literary representations of the region. The note of intense engagement that Goodison brings to her interpretation of Caribbean life provides a reminder that women have been not merely bearers of the race—the role in which they are often cast in the largely male-oriented literature—but also closely involved in the making of Caribbean history. The heroic legacy of Caribbean women has come to be exemplified by the slave rebel "Maroon Nanny," who has been accorded the status of national hero in Jamaica and whom Goodison celebrates in a dramatic monologue that concludes with this vibrant, prophetic statement:

> I was sent, tell that to history
>
> When your sorrow obscures the skies
> other women like me will rise.

But apart from the involvement of exceptional female figures in Caribbean history, women have functioned even more fundamentally as the principal repositories of the collective memory. The tales and legends in the oral tradition, transmitted from generation to generation since the time of slavery, compose a comprehensive narrative of collective survival distinctive to the Caribbean people. The compulsion to uncover the unbroken continuity of this experience has led to a reappraisal of the formative role of women in Caribbean life. Thus writers, in particular women writers, have begun to bring into new prominence this essential component of Caribbean history. Perhaps the most striking example of this orientation is the central role played by the character Telumée Miracle in the novel by the Guadeloupean author Simone Schwartz-Bart, *The Bridge of Beyond*. The trend can be observed even earlier in the English-speaking Caribbean, notably in the poetry of Louise Bennet, written in the Jamaican dialect, or patois; more recently, it can be seen in the work of Caribbean writers such as Olive Senior, Pamela Mordecai, Maryse Condé, Merle Hodge, and Jamaica Kincaid.

Goodison's work represents a significant contribution to this movement. In two of her best-known poems, she assumes the legacy bequeathed to the present generation by the long line of Caribbean women whose devotion and tenacity have nurtured the Caribbean people in body and spirit. *For My Mother* is a poem of filial devotion and appreciation, but its wider relevance as homage to the resourcefulness displayed by her mother and other women like her is unmistakable from its tone. Goodison's homage in that poem assumes a symbolic resonance in the final lines of the title poem of her second volume, *I Am Becoming My Mother* (1986):

> My mother raises rare blooms
> and waters them with tea
> her birth waters sang like rivers
> my mother is now me

The movement here toward a defining moment of personal identification shows Goodison situating herself within the historical procession of indomitable Caribbean women. "Guinea Woman," the archetype of the Caribbean grandmother celebrated in Goodison's poem of that title, becomes emblematic of the matriarchal culture, with origins in Africa, which her poetry seeks to endow with imaginative significance. Goodison thus places her individual voice in what she calls in another poem "a singing chain of ancient names."

Goodison was born on August 1, 1947, in Kingston, Jamaica, to a family of modest means. After her primary and secondary education, she entered the Jamaica School of Art to study painting and sculpture, continuing to the Arts Students' League in New York for further training. This beginning as artist has left a mark on her poetry, which often alludes directly to the visual arts and incorporates a strong visual element in its imagery. Goodison has continued to paint, and her art works have been exhibited in the West Indies, Britain, and the United States; she has also illustrated many books, including all her own volumes. She was for a while a teacher and has also held visiting positions at several American universities. Now resident in Jamaica, she is frequently in demand for her powerful readings of her own poetry.

Goodison's first volume, *Tamarind Seasons* (1980), published in Jamaica, revolves around the daily realities of the common people's depressed condition. This theme underlies much of her work and is further developed in her second volume, *I Am Becoming My Mother*, which won the Commonwealth Prize for poetry for the Caribbean region and brought her international attention. *Heartease* (1988) expands considerably the scope of her two previous volumes not only in its greater emphasis on social issues but also in its more developed lyrical register and mystical orientation. Goodison has also published a collection of short stories, *Baby Mother and the King of Swords* (1990), which explores the social geography of feminine experience in Jamaica.

Although Goodison has turned increasingly to social themes, her work conveys a wholehearted acceptance of the gift of life. This accounts for the vigor of her expression, a feature of her work that is deliberately cultivated in the self-portraits she offers in several poems, most notably in *Songs of Release*: "I stand with palms open, salute the sun / the old ways over. / I new born one." The open disposition to experience these lines bespeak is evident in *New York Is a Subway Stop*, where she revels in the spectacle that the city offers. The youthful exuberance displayed in this poem translates her "layered love of simplest ways," which is transposed into a heroic key in *To Us, All Flowers Are Roses*, a poem of remembrance in which the geographical features of Jamaica function both as signposts of history and as metaphors of the national consciousness.

Goodison's imaginative investment in her world provides the framework for the celebration in her poetry of everyday existence in the Caribbean. From vignettes charged with social meaning, such as *Kenscoff*, to the more extended "reportage" of social mores in such poems as *Wedding in Hanover* and *Bridge Views*, she is attentive to the varied texture of lived experience. Her vision ranges from the centers of power in her male-dominated society, which she regards with an ironic interest, to the margins inhabited by the dispossessed, in whom she discerns the true pulse of the communal sensibility. Goodison's confident embrace of life is most apparent in her handling of the theme of love. The discreet eroticism of *Letter to My Love* illustrates her vision of sexual love as natural self-expression and as a gift of the self. Her profound reverence for the integrity of personal relationships is expressed in *Love Song of Cane in Three Parts*: "Something happens when we love. In some ways it is outside telling."

The theme of maternity links her love poetry, with its emphasis on individual fulfillment, to her representations of the communal experience. *Songs for My Son* demonstrates her conception of a maternity that goes beyond the conventional view of woman as perpetuator of the race ("her life's work begun") to a more personal valuation of her offspring, who not only represents an extension of her self but connects her with another individual ("the connection three way") and, beyond him, with an organic community of blood and values. At the same, the child's existence puts the mother's private history in immediate touch with social fact, a connection clarified in *My Will*, in which the poet bequeathes to her son "the gift of song" and in a telling colloquial turn continues:

> eat each day's salt and bread
> with praise
> and may you never know hungry.

Goodison's attention to her world attests to the deep sincerity of her social commitment. However, her critical consciousness, sharply focused on the female condition, is sustained at the price of a tension between her vital enthusiasms and her moral response to the harsh realities of the real world. This tension is evident in such poems as *This Is a Hymn* and *My Last Poem*; in both, her documentation of material and moral discomfort yields to an optimism that seems contrived. Nonetheless her characterization of the plight of Caribbean women remains sharp, even in the unstressed pathos of this portrait in *Tamarind Season*

> The soft welcome within
> needs protecting
> so she grows wasp-waited.
> again
> wasp-waited
>
> The welcome turns sour
> she finds a woman's tongue
> and clacks curses at the wind
> for taking advantage
>
> box her about this way
> and that is the reason
>
> wait is the reason
>
> Tamarind Season.

In this and other poems centered on the female condition, Goodison displays an understanding of her subjects' anxieties and sympathy for their daily miseries. This generous impulse does not imply ambivalence, for she is capable of sounding the occasional note of revolt, as in the conclusion of *Judges*: "I'm lining up these words / holding them behind the barrier of my teeth / biding my time as only a woman can / I have a poem for you, judge man." Perhaps the poem that best sums up the tension in her work is *We Are the Women*, a vindication of the stoicism that enables the Caribbean woman to wrest some form of triumph over an immemorial adversity: "We've made peace / with want / if it doesnt kill us / we'll live with it." At the same time, she perceives the disabling effect of a self-sacrifice that impedes change:

> We've buried our hope
> too long
> as the anchor to our navel strings
> we are rooting at
> the burying sport
> we are uncovering our hope.

Ultimately, Goodison's poetry proposes a redeeming vision of art. Her acute sense of her vocation informs the lyricism of *I Shall Light a Candle of Understanding*, a poem that is both a powerful expression of spiritual commitment and, in its measured simplicity, a triumph of form. Her achievement both in this poem and in her work as a whole points to the moral purpose she ascribes to her artistic mission: "this voice is to heal / to speak of possibility."

The most comprehensive discussion of Goodison's work is contained in Edward Baugh's two essays, "Lorna Goodison in the Context of Feminist Criticism" and "Goodison on the Road to Heartease," both in the *Journal of West Indian Literature*, 1986 and 1990 respectively. J. Edward Chamberlin, *Come Back to Me, My Language* (1993), also contains a lengthy and enthusiastic appraisal of Goodison's poetry. Carole Boyce Davis and Elaine Savory Fido, eds., *Out of the Kumbla: Caribbean Women and Literature* (1990), offers an essential general introduction to Caribbean women's literature; in her chapter "Textures of Third World Reality in the Poetry of Four Caribbean Women," Elaine Savory Fido considers the relationship between Goodison's poetry and its social reference. The volume also contains Rhonda Cobham's survey, "Women in Jamaican Literature: 1900–1950." Carolyn Cooper, *Noises in the Blood* (1993), is a rewarding study of Jamaican popular culture in its social context and is thus useful as background to Goodison's poetry.

PRONOUNCING GLOSSARY

The following list uses common English syllables to provide rough equivalents of selected words whose pronunciation may be unfamiliar to the general reader.

Accompong: *ah-cawm-pong*

Ashanti: *ah-shan-tee*

Catadupa: *kah-tah-doo-pah*

Kumina: *koo-mee-nah*

Nyamekopon: *en-yah-me-caw-pong*

To Us, All Flowers Are Roses

Accompong is Ashanti, root, Nyamekopon[1]
appropriate name Accompong, meaning
warrior or lone one. Accompong,
home to bushmasters, bushmasters being
maroons,[2] maroons dwell in dense places   5
deep mountainous well sealed
strangers unwelcome. Me No Send You No Come.[3]

I love so the names of this place
how they spring brilliant like "roses"
(to us all flowers are roses) engage you   10
in flirtation. What is their meaning? pronunciation?
a strong young breeze that just takes
these names like blossoms and waltzes
them around, turn and wheel them on the tongue.

---

1. The Supreme Being (Ashanti). Accompong is a town in the hilly region of western Jamaica, founded by escaped slaves. Most of the proper nouns in this poem are places in Jamaica. *Ashanti:* an ethnic group in the central region of present-day Ghana; also their language. 2. Escaped slaves. Because of their long isolation, maroon communities preserved intact their genetic stock and way of life inherited from their African ancestors. 3. Jamaican English for "strangers unwelcome."

There are angels in St. Catherine somewhere.   15
Arawak[4] is a post office in St. Ann.
And if the Spaniards hear of this
will they come again in Caravelles[5]
to a post office (in suits of mail)
to enquire after any remaining Arawaks?   20
Nice people, so gentle, peaceful, and hospitable.

There is everywhere here.[6]
There is Alps and Lapland and Berlin.
Armagh, Carrick Fergus, Malvern[7]
Rhine and Calabar,[8] Askenish   25
where freed slaves went to claim
what was left of the Africa within,
staging secret woodland ceremonies.

Such ceremonies! such dancing, ai Kumina![9]
drum sound at Barking Lodge where we hear   30
a cargo of slaves landed free, because
somebody signed a paper[1] even as they
rode as cargo shackled on the high seas.
So they landed here, were unchained, went free.
So in some places there is almost pure Africa.   35

Some of it is lost, though, swept away forever,
maybe at Lethe[2] in Hanover, Lethe springs
from the Greek, a river which is the river
of Oblivion. There is Mount Peace here
and Tranquility and Content. May Pen   40
Dundee Pen, Bamboo Pen and for me,
Faith's Pen, therefore will I write.

There is Blackness here which is sugar land
and they say is named for the ebony[3] of the soil.
At a wedding there once the groom wore cobalt blue   45
and young bride, cloud white, at Blackness.
But there is blood, red blood in the fields
of our lives, blood the bright banner flowing
over the order of cane and our history.

The Hope River in hot times goes under   50
but pulses underground strong enough to rise
again and swell to new deep, when the May rains
fall for certain. There was a surfeit once
of Swine in Fat Hog quarter and somehow
Chateau Vert slipped on the Twi[4] of our tongue   55
and fell to rise up again as "Shotover."

They hung Paul Bogle's[5] body at sea
so there is blood too in the sea, especially

---

4. Named after the native Carib inhabitants of Jamaica.   5. Spanish sailing ships.   6. A reference to
the extraordinary genetic mixture of different peoples in the Caribbean.   7. Towns in Ireland, from
which part of the Jamaican population emigrated.   8. A coastal town in eastern Nigeria, which served
as a slave depot.   9. An African-derived ritual and the dance form associated with it.   1. The Abolition Decree of August 1, 1934.   2. Note the play on the classical connotation of this place name—that
is, the river of forgetfulness in the underworld of Greek mythology (lines 38–39).   3. Darkness or richness.   4. Another name for the Ashanti language.   5. In October 1865 he led the Morant Bay Rebellion, a weeklong uprising against British authorities in Jamaica. Within the week he was captured and
executed.

at Bloody Bay where they punctured balloons
of great grey whales. There is Egypt here   60
at Catadupa, a name they spoke first softly
to the white falling cataracts of the Nile.
There is Amity and Friendship and Harmony Hall

Stonehenge, . . . Sevens, Duppy Gate, Wait a Bit,
Wild Horses, Tan and See, Time and Patience,   65
Unity. It is Holy here, Mount Moses
dew falls upon Mount Nebo, south of Jordan,
Mount Nebo, rises here too hola Mount Zion high.
Paradise is found here, from Pisgah we look out
and Wait a Bit Wild Horses, Tan and See Time and Patience.   70

Unity, for the wounded a Doctor's Cave
and at Phoenix Park from Burnt Ground new rising.
Good Hope, the mornings dawn crystalline
at Cape Clear. It is good for brethren
and sistren to dwell together in Unity   75
on Mount Pleasant. Doctor Breezes issue from the side
of the sea across parishes[6] named for saints.

Rivers can be tied together in eights.
Mountains are Lapis Lazuli or Sapphire[7]
impossibly blue and rivers wag their waters   80
or flow Black or White or of Milk.
And the waters of the Fish River do contain
and will yield up good eating fish. O heart
when some night you cannot sleep

for wondering why you have been charged   85
to keep some things of which you cannot speak,
think what release will mean, when your name
is changed to Tranquility. I was born at Lineen—
Jubilee!—on the anniversary of Emancipation Day.[8]
I recite these names in a rosary, speak them   90
when I pray, for Heartease, my Mecca, aye Jamaica.

Guinea[1] Woman

Great grandmother
was a guinea woman
wide eyes turning
the corners of her face
could see behind her,   5
her cheeks dusted with
a fine rash of jet-bead warts
that itched when the rain set up.

Great grandmother's waistline
the span of a headman's hand,   10
slender and tall like a cane stalk
with a guinea woman's antelope-quick walk

6. Administration areas, similar to counties.   7. Blue gemstones; a reference to the Blue Mountains of
Jamaica.   8. See n. 1, p. 2930.   1. A general term for the West African coast.

and when she paused,
her gaze would look to sea[2]
her profile fine like some obverse impression   15
on a guinea coin from royal memory.[3]

It seems her fate was anchored
in the unfathomable sea
for great grandmother caught the eye of a sailor
whose ship sailed without him from Lucea harbor.   20
Great grandmother's royal scent of
cinnamon and scallions
drew the sailor up the straits of Africa,
the evidence my blue-eyed grandmother
the first Mulatta,[4]   25
taken into backra's[5] household
and covered with his name.
They forbade great grandmother's
guinea woman presence.
They washed away her scent of   30
cinnamon and scallions,
controlled the child's antelope walk,
and called her uprisings rebellions.

But, great grandmother,
I see your features blood dark   35
appearing
in the children of each new
breeding.
The high yellow brown
is darkening down.   40
Listen, children,
it's great grandmother's turn.

"I Shall Light a Candle of Understanding in Thine Heart Which Shall Not Be Put Out"

—Esdras[1]

I shall light.
First debts to pay and fences to mend,
lay to rest the wounded past, foes disguised as friends.

I shall light a candle of understanding

Cease the training of impossible hedges round this life   5
for as fast as you sow them, serendipity's thickets will appear
and outgrow them.

I shall light a candle of understanding in thine heart.

---

2. That is, to Africa. In Caribbean folk belief, the souls of slaves who died went back to Africa.   3. A
reference to both the idea of the great-grandmother's noble ancestry and the coin struck for the British
royal family from pure gold obtained from mines in West Africa.   4. Person of mixed blood (Spanish,
feminine form).   5. White man, master (Jamaican).   1. The title is taken from Esdras II, 14:25—an
apocryphal book in the Bible.

All things in their place then, in this many-chambered heart.
For each thing a place and for HIM a place apart.   10

I shall light a candle of understanding in thine heart
which shall not be put out.

By the hand that lit the candle.
By the never to be extinguished flame.
By the candle-wax which wind-worried drips   15
into candle wings luminous and rare.
By the illumination of that candle
exit, death and fear and doubt,
here love and possibility
within a lit heart, shining out.   20

Heartease II[1]

In what looked like the blackout[2] last week
a meteorite burst from the breast of the sky
smoking like a censer, it spelled out in
incandescent calligraphy
a message for all who had deep eyes.   5

If you did not see it I'll tell you what
it said:
Cultivate the search-mi-heart[3] and
acres of sincerity grass and turn your
face towards Heartease.   10

Set out a wash pan and catch mercy rain[4]
forget bout drought, catch the mercy rain,
bathe and catch a light from this meteoric flame
and sit down cleansed, to tell a rosary of your
ancestor's names,   15
a singing chain of ancient names to bind them tight
all who work evil downward through the night.

    And toward morning the sun come and tell you
    "sleep, I'll mark your place with this azure / rose ribbon
    taken from the hidden locks of the dawn   20
    sleep in the day and you will dream when you sleep
    the second surah[5] of this message."

And who hear, do all that and sleep in the darkened day and
dream as them sleep, how the one whose hand draw the veil,
(for it was not a blackout) the one who fling the meteor   25
was in a celestial vexation
saying, Imagine, how I put you here so in this most favored place
and look how you take it and less count it.[6]
Look how you root up my rarest blooms,

---

1. Heartease is a Jamaican place name.   2. A reference to the frequent power outages, common in developing countries.   3. Introspection.   4. In homes without plumbing, rainwater is collected for storage and later use.   5. A chapter in the Koran, the Muslim holy book.   6. That is, do not appreciate it.

look how you take my flower bed dem turn tombs,   30
look how you eye red from looking over a next one yard
from envying everything him have.
Like him concrete-stressed-cast-iron-lawn
and him man-made-robot-made-by-man-to-replace-man,
you want to know how far this thing gone?   35
Some calling Siberia a nice open land.
At this point it look like him was too grieved to go on
him had to drink some dew water from the throat
of a glass-petaled flower.
And when his wrath was dampened he spoke again: 40

I have many names and one is merciful . . .
So in that name I have decided that the veil I draw
will be lifted, when you look to the condition of
your part of this yard.[7]
When you stop draw blood cross the promise line in the   45
young people's palms.
When the scribes cleanse their hands and rise to write
new psalms.
When you sight up why outta the whole human race
is you of all people I choose to dwell in this place.   50
So who hear send me here to tell you say
we do not know bout the intentions of a next one
but we catching mercy rain in zinc and tub pan
and in addition
to the search-mi-heart   55
the sincerity seeds
and the pilgrimage to Heartease
we planting some one-love
undivided ever-living healing trees
and next week if you want to come, welcome   60
for we going to set up again
to extend the singing rosary of our ancestors' names
till the veil is rent from the eyes of the sky
of everyone
forever and ever   65
illumination.

The Pictures of My New Day

The pictures of my new day
will now be colored, drawn,
by the tempera of first light
stored for me by a thoughtful dawn
who knew of my love for late sleeping.   5

Now, more than love on earth,
the untamed imaginings rooted under
my hair,
more than the sanded varnished scars

---

7. A neighborhood composed of adjoining households.

jeweled now I wear,   10
more than the silver life sign of survival
and the paid penance of poems,
this light.
It flared up one evening, a Sunday
towards seven.   15
I swear it descended a living shaft
of brightest light
lit from within by light.
And as if sighting the woman's love
of show   20
not content with the perfection of itself
perfect pole running floor to ceiling
to floor[1]
it spawned and spiraled from itself
ribbons and banners of light, more light.   25
I have seen it.

Heartease New England 1987

I see a bird trapped
under the iron girders of the Ashmont station[1] overpass.
It is trying to measure the distance between columns
with its given wing span, and it fails
for being alone and not having a wing span wide enough.   5
I am told that birds travel faster over greater distances
when they move in chevron formation[2]
a group of birds could measure the width of the Ashmont
station overpass . . . I know how the bird feels.
I have come to see the backyards of the richest lands   10
on earth, their basements, their backrooms,
I have seen the poor asleep in carcasses of rooms.
Those who sleep together are fortunate
not to be one of the ultimate dispossessed
the truly homeless are usually alone   15
and tend to wakefulness.
In the fall I search for signs
a pattern in the New England flaming trees
"What is my mission? Speak, leaves"
(for all journeys have hidden missions).   20
The trees before dying, only flame brighter
maybe that is the answer, live glowing while you can.

That is the only answer, except one evening in November
I see an African in Harvard Square.
He is telling himself a story as he walks   25
in telling it, he takes all the parts
and I see that he has taken himself home.
And I have stories too, until I tell them

---

1. Possible reference to the central pole (*poteau mitan*) in Haitian cult houses, around which vodun (voodoo) rituals are celebrated.   1. In Boston.   2. That is, in a V-formation, which apparently facilitates communication within the group.

I will not find release, that is my mission.
Some nights though, anxiety assails me   30
a shroud spinning in the snow.
They say it's the affliction of this age,
it appears unasked, an unwelcome companion
who always wants you
to sit down and die with him   35
when for your own good you should keep going.
I know how the bird trying to measure the overpass
feels.
I too can never quite get the measure of this world's structure
somewhere I belong to community, there   40
I am part of a grouping of many souls and galaxies
I am part of something ever evolving, familiar, and most mighty
I reaffirm this knowing one evening, a Wednesday
as I go up Shephard Street.[3] Someone is playing
Bob Marley[4] and the notes are levitating   45
across the Garden Street end of the street.
They appear first as notes and then feather into birds
pointing their wings, arranging themselves for traveling
long distances.
And birds are the soul's symbol, so I see   50
that I am only a sojourner here but I came as friend
came to record and sing and then, depart.
For my mission this last life is certainly this
to be the sojourner poet caroling for peace
calling lost souls to the way of Heartease.   55

Mother the Great Stones Got to Move

Mother, one stone is wedged across the hole in our history
and sealed with blood wax.
In this hole is our side of the story, exact figures,
headcounts, burial artifacts, documents, lists, maps
showing our way up through the stars; lockets of brass   5
containing all textures of hair clippings.
It is the half that has never been told, some of us
must tell it.

Mother, there is the stone on the hearts of some women and men
something like an onyx, cabochon-cut[1]   10
which hung on the wearer seeds bad dreams. Speaking for the small
dreamers of this earth, plagued with nightmares, yearning
for healing dreams
we want that stone to move.

Upon an evening like this, mother, when one year is making way 15
for another, in a ceremony attended by a show of silver stars,[2]
mothers see the moon, milk-fed, herself a nursing mother

---

3. In Cambridge, Massachusetts, where Harvard University is located.   4. Popular Jamaican musician
(1945–1981), who helped to make reggae music world famous.   1. That is, cut in a round, convex
shape. *Onyx:* a translucent quartz stone, usually black or red.   2. Fireworks to celebrate the new year.

and we think of our children and the stones upon their future
and we want these stones to move.

For the year going out came in fat at first   20
but towards the harvest it grew lean.
And many mouth corners gathered white[3]
and another kind of poison, powdered white
was brought in to replace what was green.
And death sells it with one hand   25
and with the other death palms a gun
then death gets death's picture
in the papers asking,
"where does all this death come from?"
Mother, stones are pillows   30
for the homeless sleep on concrete sheets.
Stone flavors soap, stone is now meat,
the hard-hearted giving our children
stones to eat.

Mother, the great stones over mankind got to move.   35
It's been ten thousand years we've been watching them now
from various points in the universe.
From the time of our birth as points of light
in the eternal coiled workings of the cosmos.
Roll away stone of poisoned powders come   40
to blot out the hope of our young.
Move stone of sacrificial lives we breed
to feed to tribalistic economic machines.
From across the pathway to mount morning
site of the rose quartz fountain   45
brimming anise[4] and star water
bright fragrant for our children's future.
Mother these great stones got to move.

3. From undernourishment and hunger.   4. A licorice-tasting herb used in drinks and medicines.

LESLIE MARMON SILKO
born 1948

Novelist, poet, memoirist, and writer of short fiction, Leslie Silko, within the confines of a single work, can comfortably alternate between prose and poetry in a
manner reminiscent of the traditional native American narrators from whom she
descends. Among her primary concerns as an artist are the continuity of native
tradition and the power of ancient forces to govern modern life. The people of
whom she writes draw vitality from the mysterious personifications that represent
the land; and reciprocally, the land maintains, or regains, its freshness through
prescribed contact with its human tenants. Conflict, illness, and despair are traced
to a disharmony between people and nature, sometimes recognizable in the form
of witchcraft, or witchery. Such trouble is as old as time itself and perhaps ineradi-
cable. For healing to take place, at least temporarily, the disharmony and its perpe-

trators must be removed. It follows that modern evils are neither caused nor cured by Western civilization. The West simply does not have that power. Control, then, rests in the hands of those who harness the energies of native thought. The techniques involve ritual and, especially, storytelling. Since the latter implies a mixture of humor and detachment, it is understandable that Silko's work, for all its seriousness and its lyricism, is marked by a touch of irreverence. She is well acquainted with the proverbial trickster, Coyote, and has demonstrated that she herself is an accomplished live teller of Coyote tales. But storytelling holds more than amusement. "I will tell you something about stories," protests an unnamed voice in one of her novels. "They aren't just entertainment. Don't be fooled."

Storytelling has deep roots. But if a story is to be viable it must be constantly reshaped; and Silko is an unabashed reshaper. Her view of tradition as an ever-shifting body of knowledge, responsive to new influences even if deeply planted, is objectively correct, yet it may also be said to emerge from her personal background. She has written:

> My family are the Marmons at Old Laguna on the Laguna Pueblo Reservation where I grew up. We are mixed bloods—Laguna, Mexican, white—but the way we live is like Marmons, and if you are from Laguna Pueblo you will understand what I mean. All those languages, all those ways of living are combined, and we live somewhere on the fringes of all three. But I don't apologize for this any more—not to whites, not to full bloods—our origin is unlike any other. My poetry, my storytelling rise out this source.

She has also written: "I grew up at Laguna Pueblo. I am of mixed-breed ancestry, but what I know is Laguna. This place I am from is everything I am as a writer and human being."

Situated on a knoll above the San José River, forty miles west of the Rio Grande, Laguna Pueblo, like its near neighbor Acoma, is one of the Keresan-speaking communities of northern New Mexico. In existence at its present site since the 1400s, it has absorbed migrants from other Keresan towns and from among the Zuni, Hopi, and Navajo. In the 1860s and 1870s, two surveyors from Ohio, first Walter Marmon and, a little later, his brother, Robert, both government employees, settled in Laguna and married Laguna women. The Marmons wrote a constitution for Laguna modeled after the United States Constitution, and each served a term as governor of the pueblo, an office never before held by a nonnative. The second of the two Marmons to arrive in Laguna, Robert Gunn Marmon, was the great-grandfather of Leslie Marmon Silko.

Born in Albuquerque on March 5, 1948, Silko spent her early years at Laguna, attending Laguna Day School until fifth grade, when she was transferred to Manzano Day School, a small private school in Albuquerque. Between 1964 and 1969 she attended the University of New Mexico (where she earned a B.A. in English), married, and gave birth to the first of her two sons, Cazimir Silko. During these years she published her first story, *Tony's Story*, a provocative tale of witchery and renewal that foreshadowed her masterwork, *Ceremony*, which would not appear for another decade.

Following graduation, she stayed on at the university and taught courses in creative writing and oral literature. After giving birth to her second son, Robert William Chapman, she studied for three semesters in the university's American Indian Law Program, with the intention of filing native land claims. In 1971 a National Endowment for the Arts Discovery grant changed her mind about law school, and she quit to devote herself to writing. Seven of her stories, including *Yellow Woman*, were published in 1974 in a collection edited by Kenneth Rosen—*The Man to Send Rain Clouds: Contemporary Stories by American Indians*. It was from this that her reputation began to build.

The novel *Ceremony*, her first large-scale work, appeared in 1977. Widely hailed, it propelled her into the front rank of a growing legion of indigenous writers in the United States whose combined activity would now be recognized as a native American renaissance. This group's success in winning critical attention and a broad audience would be comparable to the earlier "boom" in Latin American letters that had brought acclaim to such writers as Jorge Luis Borges and Gabriel García Márquez. The Kiowa novelist N. Scott Momaday, whose *House Made of Dawn* had won the Pulitzer Prize in 1969, was already being viewed as the father of the new movement; and the prolific, talented Louise Erdrich, of Chippewa descent, would eventually be accorded its greatest commercial success. But it was Silko—and *Ceremony*—that enabled the movement to come of age.

Though of average length, *Ceremony* is a complex novel; it has two casts of characters, one predominantly male and human, the other female-dominated and intimately connected to the landscape. It is a story of illness and healing, witchery and exorcism, drought and revivification, with political overtones that acknowledge the influence of nonnative society without permitting this to overwhelm or even direct the inner core of native experience. *Ceremony* is a love story but of a special native American kind that connects the human and nonhuman worlds, transferring power from nature to culture. With a sure grasp of its material, the novel rolls to its conclusion, sweeping up smaller, parable-like stories along the way, creating a many-chambered vehicle that energizes subplots as well as the larger story.

On the strength of *Ceremony*, Silko in 1981 was awarded a MacArthur Fellowship. That same year she brought out a second large work, *Storyteller*, combining previously published poems and short stories (including *Yellow Woman*) with new material in an arrangement one critic has called an autobiography. It is at least partly that, partly a tribute to Laguna, and partly a showcase in which her earlier work, contextualized, takes on a deeper significance.

Another result of *Ceremony* had been the opportunity to teach at the University of Arizona in Tucson. But with the MacArthur grant Silko was able to withdraw from teaching and (while continuing to live in Tucson) concentrate on an ambitious new writing project. Virtually silent for ten years, as rumors of a major new novel kept building, Silko in due course brought forth *The Almanac of the Dead* (1991). An ocean of story, spreading far beyond Laguna Pueblo to embrace all of North America, including Mexico, Silko's largest work documents the imagined history of an American apocalypse. Inspired by prophetic texts ranging from the Maya Books of Chilam Balam to the songs of the Plains Ghost Dance, native people in league with the spirits of their ancestors conspire to heal the American land and rid it of alien influence. As the various stories converge and the millennium draws near, an irresistible army led by twin heroes, newly emerged from ancient native American tradition, marches northward out of Mexico to reclaim the continent. In the words of one critic the novel is a "wild, jarring, graphic, mordant, prodigious book" with "genius in the sheer, tireless variousness of its interconnecting tales."

Over the years, as Silko's work has expanded and deepened, one of her shortest and earliest pieces, *Yellow Woman*, has continued to grow in esteem. Often reprinted, it became the subject of a volume of critical essays published in 1993. In traditional Laguna lore Yellow Woman is either the heroine or a minor character in a wide range of tales. Occasionally Yellow Woman is mentioned together with her three sisters, Blue Woman, Red Woman, and White Woman, thus completing the four colors of corn. But although she may originally have been a corn spirit, she eventually became a kind of Everywoman. In fact, a traditional Laguna prayer-song, recited at the naming ceremony for a newborn daughter, begins, "Yellow Woman is born, Yellow Woman is born." In narrative lore, however, Yellow

Woman most frequently appears in tales of abduction, where she is said to have been captured by a strange man at a stream while she is fetching water. Her captor, who carries her off to another world, is sometimes a kachina, or ancestral spirit; and when at last she returns to her home she is imbued with new power that proves of value for her people. In Silko's version, these traditional elements are constantly in the foreground. Or are they merely in the background? The story's ambiguity, frequently commented on by critics, is the source of its fascination.

Melody Graulich, ed., "Yellow Woman": Leslie Marmon Silko (1993), is the collection of critical essays mentioned above. The story itself is profitably read, or reread, in Silko's Storyteller (1981), where it appears in context with several of her other short pieces on the Yellow Woman theme. For traditional texts on Yellow Woman and other figures in Laguna mythology, the best source is Franz Boas, Keresan Texts (1928); the stories in Boas's volume were obtained in 1919 to 1921 from several Laguna informants, including Leslie Silko's great-grandfather, Robert Marmon.

PRONOUNCING GLOSSARY

The following list uses common English syllables and stress accents to provide rough equivalents of selected words whose pronunciation may be unfamiliar to the general reader.

ka'tsina: *kuht-see'-nuh*

kachina: *kuh-chee'-nuh*

Keres: *kay'-ruhs*

Yellow Woman

My thigh clung to his with dampness, and I watched the sun rising up through the tamaracks and willows. The small brown water birds came to the river and hopped across the mud, leaving brown scratches in the alkali-white crust. They bathed in the river silently. I could hear the water, almost at our feet where the narrow fast channel bubbled and washed green ragged moss and fern leaves. I looked at him beside me, rolled in the red blanket on the white river sand. I cleaned the sand out of the cracks between my toes, squinting because the sun was above the willow trees. I looked at him for the last time, sleeping on the white river sand.

I felt hungry and followed the river south the way we had come the afternoon before, following our footprints that were already blurred by lizard tracks and bug trails. The horses were still lying down, and the black one whinnied when he saw me but he did not get up—maybe it was because the corral was made out of thick cedar branches and the horses had not yet felt the sun like I had. I tried to look beyond the pale red mesas to the pueblo. I knew it was there, even if I could not see it, on the sandrock hill above the river, the same river that moved past me now and had reflected the moon last night.

The horse felt warm underneath me. He shook his head and pawed the sand. The bay whinnied and leaned against the gate trying to follow, and I remembered him asleep in the red blanket beside the river. I slid off the horse and tied him close to the other horse, I walked north with the river again, and the white sand broke loose in footprints over footprints.

"Wake up."

He moved in the blanket and turned his face to me with his eyes still closed. I knelt down to touch him.

"I'm leaving."

He smiled now, eyes still closed. "You are coming with me, remember?" He sat up now with his bare dark chest and belly in the sun.

"Where?"

"To my place."

"And will I come back?"

He pulled his pants on. I walked away from him, feeling him behind me and smelling the willows.

"Yellow Woman," he said.

I turned to face him. "Who are you?" I asked.

He laughed and knelt on the low, sandy bank, washing his face in the river. "Last night you guessed my name, and you knew why I had come."

I stared past him at the shallow moving water and tried to remember the night, but I could only see the moon in the water and remember his warmth around me.

"But I only said that you were him and that I was Yellow Woman—I'm not really her—I have my own name and I come from the pueblo on the other side of the mesa. Your name is Silva and you are a stranger I met by the river yesterday afternoon."

He laughed softly. "What happened yesterday has nothing to do with what you will do today, Yellow Woman."

"I know—that's what I'm saying—the old stories about the ka'tsina[1] spirit and Yellow Woman can't mean us."

My old grandpa liked to tell those stories best. There is one about Badger and Coyote who went hunting and were gone all day, and when the sun was going down they found a house. There was a girl living there alone, and she had light hair and eyes and she told them that they could sleep with her. Coyote wanted to be with her all night so he sent Badger into a prairie-dog hole, telling him he thought he saw something in it. As soon as Badger crawled in, Coyote blocked up the entrance with rocks and hurried back to Yellow Woman.

"Come here," he said gently.

He touched my neck and I moved close to him to feel his breathing and to hear his heart. I was wondering if Yellow Woman had known who she was—if she knew that she would become part of the stories. Maybe she'd had another name that her husband and relatives called her so that only the ka'tsina from the north and the storytellers would know her as Yellow Woman. But I didn't go on; I felt him all around me, pushing me down into the white river sand.

Yellow Woman went away with the spirit from the north and lived with him and his relatives. She was gone for a long time, but then one day she came back and she brought twin boys.

---

1. Kachina, an ancestral spirit.

"Do you know the story?"

"What story?" He smiled and pulled me close to him as he said this. I was afraid lying there on the red blanket. All I could know was the way he felt, warm, damp, his body beside me. This is the way it happens in the stories, I was thinking, with no thought beyond the moment she meets the ka'tsina spirit and they go.

"I don't have to go. What they tell in stories was real only then, back in time immemorial, like they say."

He stood up and pointed at my clothes tangled in the blanket. "Let's go," he said.

I walked beside him, breathing hard because he walked fast, his hand around my wrist. I had stopped trying to pull away from him, because his hand felt cool and the sun was high, drying the river bed into alkali. I will see someone, eventually I will see someone, and then I will be certain that he is only a man—some man from nearby—and I will be sure that I am not Yellow Woman. Because she is from out of time past and I live now and I've been to school and there are highways and pickup trucks that Yellow Woman never saw.

It was an easy ride north on horseback. I watched the change from the cottonwood trees along the river to the junipers that brushed past us in the foothills, and finally there were only piñons, and when I looked up at the rim of the mountain plateau I could see pine trees growing on the edge. Once I stopped to look down, but the pale sandstone had disappeared and the river was gone and the dark lava hills were all around. He touched my hand, not speaking, but always singing softly a mountain song and looking into my eyes.

I felt hungry and wondered what they were doing at home now—my mother, my grandmother, my husband, and the baby. Cooking breakfast, saying, "Where did she go?—maybe kidnapped." And Al going to the tribal police with the details: "She went walking along the river."

The house was made with black lava rock and red mud. It was high above the spreading miles of arroyos and long mesas. I smelled a mountain smell of pitch and buck brush. I stood there beside the black horse, looking down on the small, dim country we had passed, and I shivered.

"Yellow Woman, come inside where it's warm."

He lit a fire in the stove. It was an old stove with a round belly and an enamel coffeepot on top. There was only the stove, some faded Navajo blankets, and a bedroll and cardboard box. The floor was made of smooth adobe plaster, and there was one small window facing east. He pointed at the box.

"There's some potatoes and the frying pan." He sat on the floor with his arms around his knees pulling them close to his chest and he watched me fry the potatoes. I didn't mind him watching me because he was always watching me—he had been watching me since I came upon him sitting on the river bank trimming leaves from a willow twig with his knife. We ate from the pan and he wiped the grease from his fingers on his Levi's.

"Have you brought women here before?" He smiled and kept chewing, so I said, "Do you always use the same tricks?"

"What tricks?" He looked at me like he didn't understand.

"The story about being a ka'tsina from the mountains. The story about Yellow Woman."

Silva was silent; his face was calm.

"I don't believe it. Those stories couldn't happen now," I said.

He shook his head and said softly, "But someday they will talk about us, and they will say, 'Those two lived long ago when things like that happened.'"

He stood up and went out. I ate the rest of the potatoes and thought about things—about the noise the stove was making and the sound of the mountain wind outside. I remembered yesterday and the day before, and then I went outside.

I walked past the corral to the edge where the narrow trail cut through the black rim rock. I was standing in the sky with nothing around me but the wind that came down from the blue mountain peak behind me. I could see faint mountain images in the distance miles across the vast spread of mesas and valleys and plains. I wondered who was over there to feel the mountain wind on those sheer blue edges—who walks on the pine needles in those blue mountains.

"Can you see the pueblo?" Silva was standing behind me.

I shook my head. "We're too far away."

"From here I can see the world." He stepped out on the edge. "The Navajo reservation begins over there." He pointed to the east. "The Pueblo boundaries are over here." He looked below us to the south, where the narrow trail seemed to come from. "The Texans have their ranches over there, starting with that valley, the Concho Valley. The Mexicans run some cattle over there too."

"Do you ever work for them?"

"I steal from them," Silva answered. The sun was dropping behind us and the shadows were filling the land below. I turned away from the edge that dropped forever into the valleys below.

"I'm cold," I said, "I'm going inside." I started wondering about this man who could speak the Pueblo language so well but who lived on a mountain and rustled cattle. I decided that this man Silva must be Navajo, because Pueblo men didn't do things like that.

"You must be a Navajo."

Silva shook his head gently. "Little Yellow Woman," he said, "you never give up, do you? I have told you who I am. The Navajo people know me, too." He knelt down and unrolled the bedroll and spread the extra blankets out on a piece of canvas. The sun was down, and the only light in the house came from outside—the dim orange light from sundown.

I stood there and waited for him to crawl under the blankets.

"What are you waiting for?" he said, and I lay down beside him. He undressed me slowly like the night before beside the river—kissing my face gently and running his hands up and down my belly and legs. He took off my pants and then he laughed.

"Why are you laughing?"

"You are breathing so hard."

I pulled away from him and turned my back to him.

He pulled me around and pinned me down with his arms and chest. "You don't understand, do you, little Yellow Woman? You will do what I want."

And again he was all around me with his skin slippery against mine, and I was afraid because I understood that his strength could hurt me. I lay underneath him and I knew that he could destroy me. But later, while he slept beside me, I touched his face and I had a feeling—the kind of feeling for him that overcame me that morning along the river. I kissed him on the forehead and he reached out for me.

When I woke up in the morning he was gone. It gave me a strange feeling because for a long time I sat there on the blankets and looked around the little house for some object of his—some proof that he had been there or maybe that he was coming back. Only the blankets and the cardboard box remained. The .30-30 that had been leaning in the corner was gone, and so was the knife I had used the night before. He was gone, and I had my chance to go now. But first I had to eat, because I knew it would be a long walk home.

I found some dried apricots in the cardboard box, and I sat down on a rock at the edge of the plateau rim. There was no wind and the sun warmed me. I was surrounded by silence. I drowsed with apricots in my mouth, and I didn't believe that there were highways or railroads or cattle to steal.

When I woke up, I stared down at my feet in the black mountain dirt. Little black ants were swarming over the pine needles around my foot. They must have smelled the apricots. I thought about my family far below me. They would be wondering about me, because this had never happened to me before. The tribal police would file a report. But if old Grandpa weren't dead he would tell them what happened—he would laugh and say, "Stolen by a ka'tsina, a mountain spirit. She'll come home—they usually do." There are enough of them to handle things. My mother and grandmother will raise the baby like they raised me. Al will find someone else, and they will go on like before, except that there will be a story about the day I disappeared while I was walking along the river. Silva had come for me; he said he had. I did not decide to go. I just went. Moonflowers blossom in the sand hills before dawn, just as I followed him. That's what I was thinking as I wandered along the trail through the pine trees.

It was noon when I got back. When I saw the stone house I remembered that I had meant to go home. But that didn't seem important any more, maybe because there were little blue flowers growing in the meadow behind the stone house and the gray squirrels were playing in the pines next to the house. The horses were standing in the corral, and there was a beef carcass hanging on the shady side of a big pine in front of the house. Flies buzzed around the clotted blood that hung from the carcass. Silva was washing his hands in a bucket full of water. He must have heard me coming because he spoke to me without turning to face me.

"I've been waiting for you."

"I went walking in the big pine trees."

I looked into the bucket full of bloody water with brown-and-white animal hairs floating in it. Silva stood there letting his hand drip, examining me intently.

"Are you coming with me?"

"Where?" I asked him.

"To sell the meat in Marquez."

"If you're sure it's O.K."

"I wouldn't ask you if it wasn't," he answered.

He sloshed the water around in the bucket before he dumped it out and set the bucket upside down near the door. I followed him to the corral and watched him saddle the horses. Even beside the horses he looked tall, and I asked him again if he wasn't Navajo. He didn't say anything; he just shook his head and kept cinching up the saddle.

"But Navajos are tall."

"Get on the horse," he said, "and let's go."

The last thing he did before we started down the steep trail was to grab the .30-30 from the corner. He slid the rifle into the scabbard that hung from his saddle.

"Do they ever try to catch you?" I asked.

"They don't know who I am."

"Then why did you bring the rifle?"

"Because we are going to Marquez where the Mexicans live."

The trail leveled out on a narrow ridge that was steep on both sides like an animal spine. On one side I could see where the trail went around the rocky gray hills and disappeared into the southeast where the pale sand-rock mesas stood in the distance near my home. On the other side was a trail that went west, and as I looked far into the distance I thought I saw the little town. But Silva said no, that I was looking in the wrong place, that I just thought I saw houses. After that I quit looking off into the distance; it was hot and the wildflowers were closing up their deep-yellow petals. Only the waxy cactus flowers bloomed in the bright sun, and I saw every color that a cactus blossom can be; the white ones and the red ones were still buds, but the purple and the yellow were blossoms, open full and the most beautiful of all.

Silva saw him before I did. The white man was riding a big gray horse, coming up the trail towards us. He was traveling fast and the gray horse's feet sent rocks rolling off the trail into the dry tumbleweeds. Silva motioned for me to stop and we watched the white man. He didn't see us right away, but finally his horse whinnied at our horses and he stopped. He looked at us briefly before he lapped the gray horse across the three hundred yards that separated us. He stopped his horse in front of Silva, and his young fat face was shadowed by the brim of his hat. He didn't look mad, but his small, pale eyes moved from the blood-soaked gunny sacks hanging from my saddle to Silva's face and then back to my face.

"Where did you get the fresh meat?" the white man asked.

"I've been hunting," Silva said, and when he shifted his weight in the saddle the leather creaked.

"The hell you have, Indian. You've been rustling cattle. We've been looking for the thief for a long time."

The rancher was fat, and sweat began to soak through his white cowboy shirt and the wet cloth stuck to the thick rolls of belly fat. He almost seemed to be panting from the exertion of talking, and he smelled rancid, maybe because Silva scared him.

Silva turned to me and smiled. "Go back up the mountain, Yellow Woman."

The white man got angry when he heard Silva speak in a language he couldn't understand. "Don't try anything, Indian. Just keep riding to Marquez. We'll call the state police from there."

The rancher must have been unarmed because he was very frightened and if he had a gun he would have pulled it out then. I turned my horse around and the rancher yelled, "Stop!" I looked at Silva for an instant and there was something ancient and dark—something I could feel in my stomach—in his eyes, and when I glanced at his hand I saw his finger on the trigger of the .30-30 that was still in the saddle scabbard. I slapped my horse across the flank and the sacks of raw meat swung against my knees as the horse leaped up the trail. It was hard to keep my balance, and once I thought I felt the saddle slipping backward; it was because of this that I could not look back.

I didn't stop until I reached the ridge where the trail forked. The horse was breathing deep gasps and there was a dark film of sweat on its neck. I looked down in the direction I had come from, but I couldn't see the place. I waited. The wind came up and pushed warm air past me. I looked up at the sky, pale blue and full of thin clouds and fading vapor trails left by jets.

I think four shots were fired—I remember hearing four hollow explosions that reminded me of deer hunting. There could have been more shots after that, but I couldn't have heard them because my horse was running again and the loose rocks were making too much noise as they scattered around his feet.

Horses have a hard time running downhill, but I went that way instead of uphill to the mountain because I thought it was safer. I felt better with the horse running southeast past the round gray hills that were covered with cedar trees and black lava rock. When I got to the plain in the distance I could see the dark green patches of tamaracks that grew along the river; and beyond the river I could see the beginning of the pale sandrock mesas. I stopped the horse and looked back to see if anyone was coming; then I got off the horse and turned the horse around, wondering if it would go back to its corral under the pines on the mountain. It looked back at me for a moment and then plucked a mouthful of green tumbleweeds before it trotted back up the trail with its ears pointed forward, carrying its head daintily to one side to avoid stepping on the dragging reins. When the horse disappeared over the last hill, the gunny sacks full of meat were still swinging and bouncing.

I walked toward the river on a wood-hauler's road that I knew would eventually lead to the paved road. I was thinking about waiting beside the road for someone to drive by, but by the time I got to the pavement I had decided it wasn't very far to walk if I followed the river back the way Silva and I had come.

The river water tasted good, and I sat in the shade under a cluster of silvery willows. I thought about Silva, and I felt sad at leaving him; still, there was something strange about him, and I tried to figure it out all the way back home.

I came back to the place on the river bank where he had been sitting the first time I saw him. The green willow leaves that he had trimmed from the branch were still lying there, wilted in the sand. I saw the leaves and I wanted to go back to him—to kiss him and to touch him—but the mountains were too far away now. And I told myself, because I believe it, he will come back sometime and be waiting again by the river.

I followed the path up from the river into the village. The sun was getting low, and I could smell supper cooking when I got to the screen door of my house. I could hear their voices inside—my mother was telling my grandmother how to fix the Jell-O and my husband, Al, was playing with the baby. I decided to tell them that some Navajo had kidnaped me, but I was sorry that old Grandpa wasn't alive to hear my story because it was the Yellow Woman stories he liked to tell best.

MURAKAMI HARUKI
born 1949

Although he was born in 1949 and is thus a generation older than most of his audience, Murakami Haruki is undisputedly the current writer of choice for college students, newly graduated professionals, and others under the age of thirty in Japan. Young urban Japanese readers lavishly admire Murakami's creation of what might be called a computer-age fictional hybrid, in which screwball comedy, science fiction, magical realism, and detective story in the *film noir* mode have all somehow strangely mutated. As a result, Murakami's books generate the kind of sales figures (two million copies of *Norwegian Wood* in 1987) that in the United States would be associated with the recordings of a rock star. Commercial success of this magnitude has cost Murakami, perhaps predictably, the respect of Japanese literary critics. They charge his deadpan, slightly surreal stories of nameless, rootless loners—"nowhere men," to use a locution of the Beatles, of whom Murakami is so fond—with being export-model fiction, stripped of anything meaningful that is culture-specific to Japan and, therefore, conspiring in "an erasure of history."

One might ask, however, who is really doing the erasing, Murakami or the society he records? A postwar baby who grew up in a country trying to get back on its feet after the ravages of World War II and the humiliation of foreign occupation, Murakami matured with the Japanese economy. Along the way, he saw customs jettisoned and compromises made for the sake of development. Some changes were sudden and drastic (the demotion of the emperor from divinity to earthling), others incremental (the diffusion of popular American culture). By the time he began writing in 1979, 25 percent of the Japanese population was crowded into the urban sprawl of Tokyo, thirty million people trying to live on less than 5 percent of the total land, paying the equivalent of two hundred thousand dollars for six-hundred-square-foot apartments and commuting up to six hours a day. As the dissonance between the gross national product and standard of living has continued to increase, so has the malaise beneath the surface of the "Japanese miracle." It is not uncommon to hear people now question the government's long-standing postwar policy of promoting industry at the expense of consumer benefits or to hear them assert that their country is a nation adrift. "There is something wrong with Japanese society," begins a typical newspaper editorial. "Children study too much; university students play too much; wage-earners work too much, and retired persons have too much leisure. Everything is in excess. . . . There is definitely a lack of balance. Japanese people want change. However, no one seems to know in which direction to turn; all we know is that we are dissatisfied."*

After the war, in starting over with a clean slate, writers like Murakami seem to be saying, all Japan has accomplished is to create a blank slate. The country that cornered the market on tape recorders and VCRs has put its own culture into partial erasure. The static void can be filled only with software from abroad. Just as Sony bought Columbia Pictures, the Murakami protagonist—nondescript and disillusioned—spends his days ricocheting from one American artifact to another: banana daiquiris and aloha shirts; Woody Allen, Meryl Streep, Jodie Foster; *Penthouse* and kidney-shaped sofas; Ralph Lauren and American Express; *Star Trek* and *Casablanca*; McDonald's Quarter Pounders, Filofax, and Jell-O; Cyndi Lauper, Santana, "I Heard It Through the Grapevine"; Gillette Lemon-Lime Foamy.

Murakami was born and raised in Ashiya, a suburb of Kobe, one of Japan's largest commercial ports, southwest of Kyoto. From an early age he took to the city's cosmopolitan atmosphere. Keeping a distance that would later characterize his voice as a writer, the young Murakami liked to ride around the harbor in a sight-seeing boat. He studied the freighters and the large tankers, the seamen and the tourists, and he saw his native place from a different perspective. He frequented the secondhand shops for books left behind by Americans. "Kobe is a big port city with many used-book shops, and I could find American paperbacks very cheaply and very easily. It was like opening a treasure chest. I read mostly hard-boiled detective stories or science fiction—Raymond Chandler or Ed McBain or Mickey Spillane. Later I found Scott Fitzgerald and Truman Capote. They were all so different from Japanese writers. They provided a small window in the wall of my room through which I could look out onto a foreign landscape, a fantasy world."**

This fantasy world was preferable to the mundane and overly familiar world around him. Both his parents taught Japanese literature, and as a teenager he rejected it. He claims that he never read a Japanese novel with interest until he began his own writing at the age of twenty-nine. "American culture was so vibrant back then, and I was very influenced by its music, television shows, cars, clothes, everything. . . . It was so shiny and bright that it seemed like a fantasy world. We loved that fantasy world."†

One of the things that Murakami came to feel from his reading of American novels was the need for a new kind of Japanese fiction and a new language with which to write it, "tools," he says, "to create a new story." The essential tool was what might be called "Japanese lite," a language from which the weight of traditional cadence, circuitous syntax, and literary rhetoric has been burned off. Ready

*Hironaka Wakako, "Through Rosy Glasses, Darkly," reprinted in *The New York Times*, June 5, 1993, section A, p. 21.   **Quoted in "Roll Over Basho: Who Japan Is Reading, and Why," *The New York Times Book Review*, September 27, 1992, p. 28.   †Ibid.

access to computer technology; the escalating speed of production and consumption (including literary); the spread of a beeper culture, where it is hard not to be electronically engaged; the rise of the visual image in the age of video; the proliferation of adult comics as a new form of simplified narrative; and the omnipresence of advertising copy with its streamlined style and short, staccato sentences are all currents feeding into the new linguistic minimalism.

As a teenager, Murakami dreamed of writing novels in English, a far less oblique language than Japanese, he felt, and one that would, therefore, allow him to express his emotions and perceptions more directly. It would take more than ten years before he was ready to attempt a novel in Japanese. In the interim, the experience of translating American fiction by writers like Raymond Carver helped him reshape Japanese syntax into a terse, even blunt medium peppered with American idioms. When he tried his hand at fiction, it is not totally surprising that he resorted to a foreign language, writing the first part of his maiden work in English and then translating it into Japanese. He has said that he wanted to see to what extent the two very different languages might be interchangeable. "I wasn't really setting out with the idea that I would write a novel in English. It's just that by using English I wanted to try coming up with a different way of writing in Japanese. Unfortunately, I am neither a Conrad nor a Nabokov [who both wrote fluently in English, although it was not their native language], so I could only write using the simplest vocabulary and grammatical structures." In the process, he realized that literature could be crafted using nothing but simple language, a discovery he says felt like having a heavy burden lifted from his shoulders. "The writer *can* get across weighty truths through the careful building up of insubstantial words."

If Murakami's particular combination of simple, "insubstantial" words coined a style that has become a common language for the new generation of Japanese writers (not to mention the house style for a spate of magazines attempting to track the latest trends among the twenty-something segment of the Japanese market), "tools" are only the beginning. The stresses and absurdities of contemporary Japanese life form the thematic concerns of Murakami's fiction. His novels and short stories seem to function as a reality check for readers who have spent their lives going to cram school to get into the right high school to get into the right university to get into the right company to work fourteen-hour days to buy a car they can use only on Sundays to drive to the world's largest indoor ski slope because there isn't time to travel to the mountains, or to swim at "the beach," a chlorinated, salt-free simulation fitted with plastic palms and an artificial volcano and safe under its steel dome from the nasty pollution of the real thing. Small wonder that so many of Murakami's characters are lethargic. They're worn out from the rat race before they're much more than thirty, benumbed by all the ways that daily life turns out to be surreal, and made skeptical as unwitting pawns of the system.

Dance, Dance, Dance (1988) is the fitting title of one of Murakami's most recent novels. It derives from advice offered to the protagonist by the Sheep Man, an elusive figure who may be a wise elder or an extraterrestrial or even the hero's conscience: "You gotta dance. As long as the music plays. You gotta dance. Don't even think why. Start to think, your feet stop. Your feet stop, we get stuck. We get stuck, you're stuck. . . . You gotta limber up. You gotta loosen what you bolted down. You gotta use all you got. We know you're tired, tired and scared. Happens to everyone, okay? Just don't let your feet stop."

Murakami's novels tend to describe a disjointed quest bereft of logic. His usual protagonist, a downwardly mobile young man with no name and no discernible family ties, except possibly an ex-wife, leaves his stalled career on the fringes of a fashionable profession (copywriter, perhaps, or food critic, or free-lance journalist) to embark on a search with as many layers to it as an onion. In *Dance, Dance,*

Dance he takes it into his head to find an "ear model," that is, a call girl he once knew whose ears are so seductive that exposing them makes "the white plaster walls seem to ripple"—an attribute she trades on to earn extra money posing for television commercials. The hero's quest takes him in search of the seedy hotel where they slept together, in far northern Japan, but it too has disappeared, replaced by a luxury high-rise with a pretentious French name. From there he returns to Tokyo before flying back and forth to Hawaii. He follows the Sheep Man's advice to keep his feet moving, but the more ground he covers, the more he seems to be running in place. The novel is actually a sequel to Murakami's first big success, *A Wild Sheep Chase* (1982), where the object of the quest is a mysterious mutant sheep with a star-shaped pattern on its fleece and the chase pulls the hero through an underworld full of people who can pass before mirrors without leaving a reflection and kindly chauffeurs who offer to provide God's telephone number.

Part of the appeal of Murakami's shaggy-dog stories is the whirling verve of his ingenious plots; he is undeniably a writer of popular fiction. Part of his appeal lies in the agility of his pared-down style. Murakami's audience clearly also appreciates his playful sense of humor, slightly off-center as it oscillates between an innocent, almost romantic whimsy and a cool postmodern cynicism.

But perhaps the main reason he seems to have become the voice of young Japan has more to do with an identification, or vicarious envy, on the part of his readers toward characters who are not caught in the web of familial and corporate ties that bind the ordinary Japanese citizen so oppressively. The Murakami hero is neither a salaried robot moving slowly toward retirement nor, despite the brand names, a mere shopper whose sole identity is consumption. He has not completely sacrificed his ability to view himself objectively or to stand to one side of his society and so observe its incongruities.

Here, where daily life degenerates into the absurd, where the most harmless act can drag one through the looking glass, Murakami captures the prevalent sense in Japan today (and, for that matter, in much of the rest of the world) that things are badly askew. *TV People* (1989), printed here, is an appropriate example. While it lacks the thrill of the chase of Murakami's fabulist-detective novels, this epigram on television static articulates a perfect vision of the void. It calls to mind the warning of Nietzsche—one of the few Western writers, curiously, whom Murakami doesn't mention—that if we look too long into the abyss it may look back into us.

Several works by Murakami are available in English. *TV People* is contained in the collection of short stories *The Elephant Vanishes* (1993), translated by Alfred Birnbaum and Jay Rubin. See also three translations by Alfred Birnbaum: *A Wild Sheep Chase* (1989), *Hard-Boiled Wonderland and the End of the World* (1991); and *Dance, Dance, Dance* (1994). A variety of contemporary Japanese literature has begun to appear in translation. The following is a representative sampling: Alfred Birnbaum, ed., *Monkey Brain Sushi: New Tastes in Japanese Fiction* (1991); Helen Mitsios, ed., *New Japanese Voices: The Best Contemporary Fiction from Japan* (1991); Shimada Masahiko, *Dream Messenger* (1992); and Maruya Saiichi, *Singular Rebellion* (1986). Tsushima Yūko, *Child of Fortune* (1983), *The Shooting Gallery* (1988), and *Woman Running in the Mountains* (1991); Murakami Ryū, *Almost Transparent Blue* (1977) and *Sixty-Nine* (1993); and Yoshimoto Banana, *Kitchen* (1993) and *N.P.* (1994), are also available in English.

PRONOUNCING GLOSSARY

The following list uses common English syllables to provide rough equivalents of selected words whose pronunciation may be unfamiliar to the general reader.

Murakami Haruki: *moo-rah-kah-mee hah-roo-kee*

shiitake: *shee-ee-tah-ke*

tamago-yaki: *tah-mah-goh–yah-kee*

zōsui: *zoh-soo-ee*

TV People[1]

It was Sunday evening when the TV People showed up.

The season, spring. At least, I think it was spring. In any case, it wasn't particularly hot as seasons go, not particularly chilly.

To be honest, the season's not so important. What matters is that it's a Sunday evening.

I don't like Sunday evenings. Or, rather, I don't like everything that goes with them—that Sunday-evening state of affairs. Without fail, come Sunday evening my head starts to ache. In varying intensity each time. Maybe a third to a half of an inch into my temples, the soft flesh throbs— as if invisible threads lead out and someone far off is yanking at the other ends. Not that it hurts so much. It ought to hurt, but strangely, it doesn't— it's like long needles probing anesthetized areas.

And I hear things. Not sounds, but thick slabs of silence being dragged through the dark. *KRZSHAAAL KKRZSHAAAAAL KKKKRMMMS*. Those are the initial indications. First, the aching. Then, a slight distortion of my vision. Tides of confusion wash through, premonitions tugging at memories, memories tugging at premonitions. A finely honed razor moon floats white in the sky, roots of doubt burrow into the earth. People walk extra loud down the hall just to get me. *KRRSPUMK DUWB KRRSPUMK DUWB KRRSPUMK DUWB*.

All the more reason for the TV People to single out Sunday evening as the time to come around. Like melancholy moods, or the secretive, quiet fall of rain, they steal into the gloom of that appointed time.

Let me explain how the TV People look.

The TV People are slightly smaller than you or me. Not obviously smaller—*slightly* smaller. About, say, 20 or 30%. Every part of their bodies is uniformly smaller. So rather than "small," the more terminologically correct expression might be "reduced."

In fact, if you see TV People somewhere, you might not notice at first that they're small. But even if you don't, they'll probably strike you as somehow strange. Unsettling, maybe. You're sure to think something's odd, and then you'll take another look. There's nothing unnatural about them at first glance, but that's what's so unnatural. Their smallness is completely different from that of children and dwarfs. When we see children,

---

1. Translated by Alfred Birnbaum.

we *feel* they're small, but this sense of recognition comes mostly from the misproportioned awkwardness of their bodies. They are small, granted, but not uniformly so. The hands are small, but the head is big. Typically, that is. No, the smallness of TV People is something else entirely. TV People look as if they were reduced by photocopy, everything mechanically calibrated. Say their height has been reduced by a factor of 0.7, then their shoulder width is also in 0.7 reduction; ditto (0.7 reduction) for the feet, head, ears, and fingers. Like plastic models, only a little smaller than the real thing.

Or like perspective demos.[2] Figures that look far away even close up. Something out of a trompe-l'oeil[3] painting where the surface warps and buckles. An illusion where the hand fails to touch objects close by, yet brushes what is out of reach.

That's TV People.

That's TV People.

That's TV People.

There were three of them altogether.

They don't knock or ring the doorbell. Don't say hello. They just sneak right in. I don't even hear a footstep. One opens the door, the other two carry in a TV. Not a very big TV. Your ordinary Sony color TV. The door was locked, I think, but I can't be certain. Maybe I forgot to lock it. It really wasn't foremost in my thoughts at the time, so who knows? Still, I think the door was locked.

When they come in, I'm lying on the sofa, gazing up at the ceiling. Nobody at home but me. That afternoon, the wife has gone out with the girls—some close friends from her high-school days—getting together to talk, then eating dinner out. "Can you grab your own supper?" the wife said before leaving. "There's vegetables in the fridge and all sorts of frozen foods. That much you can handle for yourself, can't you? And before the sun goes down, remember to take in the laundry, okay?"

"Sure thing," I said. Doesn't faze me a bit. Rice, right? Laundry, right? Nothing to it. Take care of it, simple as *SLUPPP KRRRTZ!*

"Did you say something, dear?" she asked.

"No, nothing," I said.

All afternoon I take it easy and loll around on the sofa. I have nothing better to do. I read a bit—that new novel by García Márquez[4]—and listen to some music. I have myself a beer. Still, I'm unable to give my mind to any of this. I consider going back to bed, but I can't even pull myself together enough to do that. So I wind up lying on the sofa, staring at the ceiling.

The way my Sunday afternoons go, I end up doing a little bit of various things, none very well. It's a struggle to concentrate on any one thing. This particular day, everything seems to be going right. I think, Today I'll read this book, listen to these records, answer these letters. Today, for sure, I'll

2. Mock-ups, or models, employing perspective, the technique in art that gives a sense of the relative sizes of various objects.   3. A type of painting that employs illusionist devices like perspective and foreshortening to persuade the viewer that what he or she sees is real.   4. Gabriel García Márquez (born 1928), Colombian author (see p. 2426).

clean out my desk drawers, run errands, wash the car for once. But two
o'clock rolls around, three o'clock rolls around, gradually dusk comes on,
and all my plans are blown. I haven't done a thing; I've been lying around
on the sofa the whole day, same as always. The clock ticks in my ears.
TRPP Q SCHAOUS TRPP Q SCHAOUS. The sound erodes everything
around me, little by little, like dripping rain. *TRPP Q SCHAOUS TRPP
Q SCHAOUS*. Little by little, Sunday afternoon wears down, shrinking in
scale. Just like the TV People themselves.

The TV People ignore me from the very outset. All three of them have
this look that says the likes of me don't exist. They open the door and carry
in their TV. The two put the set on the sideboard, the other one plugs it
in. There's a mantel clock and a stack of magazines on the sideboard. The
clock was a wedding gift, big and heavy—big and heavy as time itself—
with a loud sound, too. *TRPP Q SCHAOUS TRPP Q SCHAOUS*. All
through the house you can hear it. The TV People move it off the sideboard, down onto the floor. The wife's going to raise hell, I think. She
hates it when things get randomly shifted about. If everything isn't in its
proper place, she gets really sore. What's worse, with the clock there on
the floor, I'm bound to trip over it in the middle of the night. I'm forever
getting up to go to the toilet at two in the morning, bleary-eyed and stumbling over something.
     Next, the TV People move the magazines to the table. All of them
women's magazines. (I hardly ever read magazines; I read books—personally, I wouldn't mind if every last magazine in the world went out of business.) *Elle* and *Marie Claire* and *Home Ideas*, magazines of that ilk. Neatly
stacked on the sideboard. The wife doesn't like me touching her magazines—change the order of the stack, and I never hear the end of it—so I
don't go near them. Never once flipped through them. But the TV People
couldn't care less: They move them right out of the way, they show no
concern, they sweep the whole lot off the sideboard, they mix up the order.
Marie Claire is on top of *Croissant*; *Home Ideas* is underneath *An-An*.[5]
Unforgivable. And worse, they're scattering the bookmarks onto the floor.
They've lost her place, pages with important information. I have no idea
what information or how important—might have been for work, might
have been personal—but whatever, it was important to the wife, and she'll
let me know about it. "What's the meaning of this? I go out for a nice time
with friends, and when I come back, the house is a shambles!" I can just
hear it, line for line. Oh, great, I think, shaking my head.

Everything gets removed from the sideboard to make room for the television. The TV People plug it into a wall socket, then switch it on. Then
there is a tinkling noise, and the screen lights up. A moment later, the
picture floats into view. They change the channels by remote control.
But all the channels are blank—probably, I think, because they haven't
connected the set to an antenna. There has to be an antenna outlet somewhere in the apartment. I seem to remember the superintendent telling

5. All are popular women's magazines.

us where it was when we moved into this condominium. All you had to do was connect it. But I can't remember where it is. We don't own a television, so I've completely forgotten.

Yet somehow the TV People don't seem bothered that they aren't picking up any broadcast. They give no sign of looking for the antenna outlet. Blank screen, no image—makes no difference to them. Having pushed the button and had the power come on, they've completed what they came to do.

The TV is brand-new. It's not in its box, but one look tells you it's new. The instruction manual and guarantee are in a plastic bag taped to the side; the power cable shines, sleek as a freshly caught fish.

All three TV People look at the blank screen from here and there around the room. One of them comes over next to me and verifies that you can see the TV screen from where I'm sitting. The TV is facing straight toward me, at an optimum viewing distance. They seem satisfied. One operation down, says their air of accomplishment. One of the TV People (the one who'd come over next to me) places the remote control on the table.

The TV People speak not a word. Their movements come off in perfect order, hence they don't need to speak. Each of the three executes his prescribed function with maximum efficiency. A professional job. Neat and clean. Their work is done in no time. As an afterthought, one of the TV People picks the clock up from the floor and casts a quick glance around the room to see if there isn't a more appropriate place to put it, but he doesn't find any and sets it back down. *TRPP Q SCHAOUS TRPP Q SCHAOUS*. It goes on ticking weightily on the floor. Our apartment is rather small, and a lot of floor space tends to be taken up with my books and the wife's reference materials. I am bound to trip on that clock. I heave a sigh. No mistake, stub my toes for sure. You can bet on it.

All three TV People wear dark-blue jackets. Of who-knows-what fabric, but slick. Under them, they wear jeans and tennis shoes. Clothes and shoes all proportionately reduced in size. I watch their activities for the longest time, until I start to think maybe it's *my* proportions that are off. Almost as if I were riding backward on a roller coaster, wearing strong prescription glasses. The view is dizzying, the scale all screwed up. I'm thrown off balance, my customary world is no longer absolute. That's the way the TV People make you feel.

Up to the very last, the TV People don't say a word. The three of them check the screen one more time, confirm that there are no problems, then switch it off by remote control. The glow contracts to a point and flickers off with a tinkling noise. The screen returns to its expressionless, gray, natural state. The world outside is getting dark. I hear someone calling out to someone else. Anonymous footsteps pass by down the hall, intentionally loud as ever. *KRRSPUMK DUWB KRRSPUMK DUWB*. A Sunday evening.

The TV People give the room another whirlwind inspection, open the door, and leave. Once again, they pay no attention to me whatsoever. They act as if I don't exist.

From the time the TV People come into the apartment to the moment they leave, I don't budge. Don't say a word. I remain motionless, stretched out on the sofa, surveying the whole operation. I know what you're going to say: That's unnatural. Total strangers—not one but three—walk unannounced right into your apartment, plunk down a TV set, and you just sit there staring at them, dumbfounded. Kind of odd, don't you think?

I know, I know. But for whatever reason, I don't speak up, I simply observe the proceedings. Because they ignore me so totally. And if you were in my position, I imagine you'd do the same. Not to excuse myself, but *you* have people right in front of you denying your very presence like that, then see if you don't doubt whether you actually exist. I look at my hands half expecting to see clear through them. I'm devastated, powerless, in a trance. My body, my mind are vanishing fast. I can't bring myself to move. It's all I can do to watch the three TV People deposit their television in my apartment and leave. I can't open my mouth for fear of what my voice might sound like.

The TV People exit and leave me alone. My sense of reality comes back to me. These hands are once again my hands. It's only then I notice that the dusk has been swallowed by darkness. I turn on the light. Then I close my eyes. Yes, that's a TV set sitting there. Meanwhile, the clock keeps ticking away the minutes. *TRPP Q SCHAOUS TRPP Q SCHAOUS.*

Curiously, the wife makes no mention of the appearance of the television set in the apartment. No reaction at all. Zero. It's as if she doesn't even see it. Creepy. Because, as I said before, she's extremely fussy about the order and arrangement of furniture and other things. If someone dares to move anything in the apartment, even by a hair, she'll jump on it in an instant. That's her ascendancy. She knits her brows, then gets things back the way they were.

Not me. If an issue of *Home Ideas* gets put under an *An-An*, or a ballpoint pen finds its way into the pencil stand, you don't see me go to pieces. I don't even notice. This is her problem; I'd wear myself out living like her. Sometimes she flies into a rage. She tells me she can't abide my carelessness. Yes, I say, and sometimes I can't stand carelessness about universal gravitation and π and $E = mc^2$,[6] either. I mean it. But when I say things like this, she clams up, taking them as a personal insult. I never mean it that way; I just say what I feel.

That night, when she comes home, first thing she does is look around the apartment. I've readied a full explanation—how the TV People came and mixed everything up. It'll be difficult to convince her, but I intend to tell her the whole truth.

She doesn't say a thing, just gives the place the once-over. There's a TV on the sideboard, the magazines are out of order on the table, the mantel clock is on the floor, and the wife doesn't even comment. There's nothing for me to explain.

"You get your own supper okay?" she asks me, undressing.

6. Einstein's theory of relativity. *Universal gravitation*: the theory that all objects in the universe have a gravitational attraction for each other. π: pi = 3.14, the ratio of the circumference to the diameter of a circle.

"No, I didn't eat," I tell her.

"Why not?"

"I wasn't really hungry," I say.

The wife pauses, half-undressed, and thinks this over. She gives me a long look. Should she press the subject or not? The clock breaks up the protracted, ponderous silence. *TRPP Q SCHAOUS TRPP Q SCHAOUS.* I pretend not to hear; I won't let it in my ears. But the sound is simply too heavy, too loud to shut out. She, too, seems to be listening to it. Then she shakes her head and says, "Shall I whip up something quick?"

"Well, maybe," I say. I don't really feel much like eating, but I won't turn down the offer.

The wife changes into around-the-house wear and goes to the kitchen to fix zosui and tamago-yaki[7] while filling me in on her friends. Who'd done what, who'd said what, who'd changed her hairstyle and looked so much younger, who'd broken up with her boyfriend. I know most of her friends, so I pour myself a beer and follow along, inserting attentive uh-huhs at proper intervals. Though, in fact, I hardly hear a thing she says. I'm thinking about the TV People. That, and why she didn't remark on the sudden appearance of the television. No way she couldn't have noticed. Very odd. Weird, even. Something is wrong here. But what to do about it?

The food is ready, so I sit at the dining-room table and eat. Rice, egg, salt plum.[8] When I've finished, the wife clears away the dishes. I have another beer, and she has a beer, too. I glance at the sideboard, and there's the TV set, with the power off, the remote-control unit sitting on the table. I get up from the table, reach for the remote control, and switch it on. The screen glows and I hear it tinkling. Still no picture. Only the same blank tube. I press the button to raise the volume, but all that does is increase the white-noise roar. I watch the snowstorm for twenty, thirty seconds, then switch it off. Light and sound vanish in an instant. Meanwhile, the wife has seated herself on the carpet and is flipping through *Elle*, oblivious of the fact that the TV has just been turned on and off.

I replace the remote control on the table and sit down on the sofa again, thinking I'll go on reading that long García Márquez novel. I always read after dinner. I might set the book down after thirty minutes, or I might read for two hours, but the thing is to read every day. Today, though, I can't get myself to read more than a page and a half. I can't concentrate; my thoughts keep returning to the TV set. I look up and see it, right in front of me.

I wake at half past two in the morning to find the TV still there. I get out of bed half hoping the thing has disappeared. No such luck. I go to the toilet, then plop down on the sofa and put my feet up on the table. I take the remote control in hand and try turning on the TV. No new developments in that department, either; only a rerun of the same glow and noise. Nothing else. I look at it awhile, then switch it off.

7. A dish of beaten eggs and condiments cooked in a frying pan, resembling an omelet. *Zosui:* a porridge of rice and vegetables.   8. Small pickled plums, a traditional side dish in Japanese cuisine.

I go back to bed and try to sleep. I'm dead tired, but sleep isn't coming. I shut my eyes and I see them. The TV People carrying the TV set, the TV People moving the clock out of the way, the TV People transferring magazines to the table, the TV People plugging the power cable into the wall socket, the TV People checking the screen, the TV People opening the door and silently exiting. They've stayed on in my head. They're in there walking around. I get back out of bed, go to the kitchen, and pour a double brandy into a coffee cup. I down the brandy and head over to the sofa for another session with Márquez. I open the pages, yet somehow the words won't sink in. The writing is opaque.

Very well, then, I throw García Márquez aside and pick up *Elle*. Reading *Elle* from time to time can't hurt anyone. But there isn't anything in *Elle* that catches my fancy. New hairstyles and elegant white silk blouses and eateries that serve good beef stew and what to wear to the opera, articles like that. Do I care? I throw *Elle* aside. Which leaves me the television on the sideboard to look at.

I end up staying awake until dawn, not doing a thing. At six o'clock, I make myself some coffee. I don't have anything else to do, so I go ahead and fix ham sandwiches before the wife gets up.

"You're up awful early," she says drowsily.

"Mmm," I mumble.

After a nearly wordless breakfast, we leave home together and go our separate ways to our respective offices. The wife works at a small publishing house. Edits a natural-food and lifestyle magazine. "Shiitake Mushrooms Prevent Gout," "The Future of Organic Farming," you know the kind of magazine. Never sells very well, but hardly costs anything to produce; kept afloat by a handful of zealots. Me, I work in the advertising department of an electrical-appliance manufacturer. I dream up ads for toasters and washing machines and microwave ovens.

In my office building, I pass one of the TV People on the stairs. If I'm not mistaken, it's one of the three who brought the TV the day before—probably the one who first opened the door, who didn't actually carry the set. Their singular lack of distinguishing features makes it next to impossible to tell them apart, so I can't swear to it, but I'd say I'm eight to nine out of ten on the mark. He's wearing the same blue jacket he had on the previous day, and he's not carrying anything in his hands. He's merely walking down the stairs. I'm walking up. I dislike elevators, so I generally take the stairs. My office is on the ninth floor, so this is no mean feat. When I'm in a rush, I get all sweaty by the time I reach the top. Even so, getting sweaty has got to be better than taking the elevator, as far as I'm concerned. Everyone jokes about it: doesn't own a TV or a VCR, doesn't take elevators, must be a modern-day Luddite.[9] Maybe a childhood trauma leading to arrested development. Let them think what they like. They're the ones who are screwed up, if you ask me.

In any case, there I am, climbing the stairs as always; I'm the only one

9. A member of a group of 19th-century English workmen who protested the use of labor-saving machinery by destroying it.

on the stairs—almost nobody else uses them—when between the fourth and fifth floors I pass one of the TV People coming down. It happens so suddenly I don't know what to do. Maybe I should say something?

But I don't say anything. I don't know what to say, and he's unapproachable. He leaves no opening; he descends the stairs so functionally, at one set tempo, with such regulated precision. Plus, he utterly ignores my presence, same as the day before. I don't even enter his field of vision. He slips by before I can think what to do. In that instant, the field of gravity warps.

At work, the day is solid with meetings from the morning on. Important meetings on sales campaigns for a new product line. Several employees read reports. Blackboards fill with figures, bar graphs proliferate on computer screens. Heated discussions. I participate, although my contribution to the meetings is not that critical because I'm not directly involved with the project. So between meetings I keep puzzling things over. I voice an opinion only once. Isn't much of an opinion, either—something perfectly obvious to any observer—but I couldn't very well go without saying anything, after all. I may not be terribly ambitious when it comes to work, but so long as I'm receiving a salary I have to demonstrate responsibility. I summarize the various opinions up to that point and even make a joke to lighten the atmosphere. Half covering for my daydreaming about the TV People. Several people laugh. After that one utterance, however, I only pretend to review the materials; I'm thinking about the TV People. If they talk up a name for the new microwave oven, I certainly am not aware of it. My mind is all TV People. What the hell was the meaning of that TV set? And why haul the TV all the way to my apartment in the first place? Why hasn't the wife remarked on its appearance? Why have the TV People made inroads into my company?

The meetings are endless. At noon, there's a short break for lunch. Too short to go out and eat. Instead, everyone gets sandwiches and coffee. The conference room is a haze of cigarette smoke, so I eat at my own desk. While I'm eating, the section chief comes around. To be perfectly frank, I don't like the guy. For no reason I can put my finger on: There's nothing you can fault him on, no single target for attack. He has an air of breeding. Moreover, he's not stupid. He has good taste in neckties, he doesn't wave his own flag or lord it over his inferiors. He even looks out for me, invites me out for the occasional meal. But there's just something about the guy that doesn't sit well with me. Maybe it's his habit of coming into body contact with people he's talking to. Men or women, at some point in the course of the conversation he'll reach out a hand and touch. Not in any suggestive way, mind you. No, his manner is brisk, his bearing perfectly casual. I wouldn't be surprised if some people don't even notice, it's so natural. Still—I don't know why—it does bother me. So whenever I see him, almost instinctively I brace myself. Call it petty, it gets to me.

He leans over, placing a hand on my shoulder. "About your statement at the meeting just now. Very nice," says the section chief warmly. "Very simply put, very pivotal. I was impressed. Points well taken. The whole room buzzed at that statement of yours. The timing was perfect, too. Yessir, you keep 'em coming like that."

And he glides off. Probably to lunch. I thank him straight out, but the honest truth is I'm taken aback. I mean, I don't remember a thing of what I said at the meeting. Why does the section chief have to come all the way over to my desk to praise me for *that?* There have to be more brilliant examples of *Homo loquens*[1] around here. Strange. I go on eating my lunch, uncomprehending. Then I think about the wife. Wonder what she's up to right now. Out to lunch? Maybe I ought to give her a call, exchange a few words, anything. I dial the first three digits, have second thoughts, hang up. I have no reason to be calling her. My world may be crumbling, out of balance, but is that a reason to ring up her office? What can I say about all this, anyway? Besides, I hate calling her at work. I set down the receiver, let out a sigh, and finish off my coffee. Then I toss the Styrofoam cup into the wastebasket.

At one of the afternoon meetings, I see TV People again. This time, their number has increased by two. Just as on the previous day, they come traipsing across the conference room, carrying a Sony color TV. A model one size bigger. Uh-oh. Sony's the rival camp. If, for whatever reason, any competitor's product gets brought into our offices, there's hell to pay, barring when other manufacturers' products are brought in for test comparisons, of course. But then we take pains to remove the company logo — just to make sure no outside eyes happen upon it. Little do the TV People care: The Sony mark is emblazoned for all to see. They open the door and march right into the conference room, flashing it in our direction. Then they parade the thing around the room, scanning the place for somewhere to set it down, until at last, not finding any location, they carry it backward out the door. The others in the room show no reaction to the TV People. And they can't have missed them. No, they've definitely seen them. And the proof is they even got out of the way, clearing a path for the TV People to carry their television through. Still, that's as far as it went: a reaction no more alarmed than when the nearby coffee shop delivered. They'd made it a ground rule not to acknowledge the presence of the TV People. The others all knew they were there; they just acted as if they weren't.

None of it makes any sense. Does everybody know about the TV People? Am I alone in the dark? Maybe the wife knew about the TV People all along, too. Probably. I'll bet that's why she wasn't surprised by the television and why she didn't mention it. That's the only possible explanation. Yet this confuses me even more. Who or what, then, are the TV People? And why are they always carrying around TV sets?

One colleague leaves his seat to go to the toilet, and I get up to follow. This is a guy who entered the company around the same time I did. We're on good terms. Sometimes we go out for a drink together after work. I don't do that with most people. I'm standing next to him at the urinals. He's the first to complain. "Oh, joy! Looks like we're in for more of the same, straight through to evening. I swear! Meetings, meetings, meetings, going to drag on forever."

---

1. Human speech (Latin).

"You can say that again," I say. We wash our hands. He compliments me on the morning meeting's statement. I thank him.

"Oh, by the way, those guys who came in with the TV just now . . ." I launch forth, then cut off.

He doesn't say anything. He turns off the faucet, pulls two paper towels from the dispenser, and wipes his hands. He doesn't even shoot a glance in my direction. How long can he keep drying his hands? Eventually, he crumples up his towels and throws them away. Maybe he didn't hear me. Or maybe he's pretending not to hear. I can't tell. But from the sudden strain in the atmosphere, I know enough not to ask. I shut up, wipe my hands, and walk down the corridor to the conference room. The rest of the afternoon's meetings, he avoids my eyes.

When I get home from work, the apartment is dark. Outside, dark clouds have swept in. It's beginning to rain. The apartment smells like rain. Night is coming on. No sign of the wife. I loosen my tie, smooth out the wrinkles, and hang it up. I brush off my suit. I toss my shirt into the washing machine. My hair smells like cigarette smoke, so I take a shower and shave. Story of my life: I go to endless meetings, get smoked to death, then the wife gets on my case about it. The very first thing she did after we were married was make me stop smoking. Four years ago, that was.

Out of the shower, I sit on the sofa with a beer, drying my hair with a towel. The TV People's television is still sitting on the sideboard. I pick up the remote control from the table and push the "on" switch. Again and again I press, but nothing happens. The screen stays dark. I check the plug; it's in the socket, all right. I unplug it, then plug it back in. Still no go. No matter how often I press the "on" switch, the screen does not glow. Just to be sure, I pry open the back cover of the remote-control unit, remove the batteries, and check them with my handy electrical-contact tester. The batteries are fine. At this point, I give up, throw the remote control aside, and slosh down more beer.

Why should it upset me? Supposing the TV did come on, what then? It would glow and crackle with white noise. Who cares, if that's all that'd come on?

I care. Last night it worked. And I haven't laid a finger on it since. Doesn't make sense.

I try the remote control one more time. I press slowly with my finger. But the result is the same. No response whatsoever. The screen is dead. Cold.

Dead cold.

I pull another beer out of the fridge and eat some potato salad from a plastic tub. It's past six o'clock. I read the whole evening paper. If anything, it's more boring than usual. Almost no article worth reading, nothing but inconsequential news items. But I keep reading, for lack of anything better to do. Until I finish the paper. What next? To avoid pursuing that thought any further, I dally over the newspaper. Hmm, how about answering letters? A cousin of mine has sent us a wedding invitation, which I have to turn down. The day of the wedding, the wife and I are going to be off on a trip. To Okinawa.[2] We've been planning it for ages; we're both taking time off from work. We can't very well go changing our plans now. God only knows when we'll get the next chance to spend a long holiday together. And to clinch it all, I'm not even that close to my cousin; haven't seen her in almost ten years. Still, I can't leave replying to the last minute. She has to know how many people are coming, how many settings to plan for the banquet. Oh, forget it. I can't bring myself to write, not now. My heart isn't in it.

I pick up the newspaper again and read the same articles over again. Maybe I ought to start preparing dinner. But the wife might be working late and could come home having eaten. Which would mean wasting one portion. And if I am going to eat alone, I can make do with leftovers; no reason to make something up special. If she hasn't eaten, we can go out and eat together.

Odd, though. Whenever either of us knows he or she is going to be later than six, we always call in. That's the rule. Leave a message on the answering machine if necessary. That way, the other can coordinate: go ahead and eat alone, or set something out for the late arriver, or hit the sack. The nature of my work sometimes keeps me out late, and she often has meetings, or proofs to dispatch, before coming home. Neither of us has a regular nine-to-five job. When both of us are busy, we can go three days without a word to each other. Those are the breaks—just one of those things that nobody planned. Hence we always keep certain rules, so as not to place unrealistic burdens on each other. If it looks as though we're going to be late, we call in and let the other one know. I sometimes forget, but she, never once.

Still, there's no message on the answering machine.

I toss the newspaper, stretch out on the sofa, and shut my eyes.

I dream about a meeting. I'm standing up, delivering a statement I myself don't understand. I open my mouth and talk. If I don't, I'm a dead man. I have to keep talking. Have to keep coming out with endless blah-blah-blah. Everyone around me is dead. Dead and turned to stone. A roomful of stone statues. A wind is blowing. The windows are all broken; gusts of air are coming in. And the TV People are here. Three of them. Like the first time. They're carrying a Sony color TV. And on the screen are the TV People. I'm running out of words; little by little I can feel my fingertips growing stiffer. Gradually turning to stone.

I open my eyes to find the room aglow. The color of corridors at the Aquarium. The television is on. Outside, everything is dark. The TV screen is flickering in the gloom, static crackling. I sit up on the sofa, and press my temples with my fingertips. The flesh of my fingers is still soft; my mouth tastes like beer. I swallow. I'm dried out; the saliva catches in my throat. As always, the waking world pales after an all-too-real dream. But no, this is real. Nobody's turned to stone. What time is it getting to

2. The largest of several islands that constitute Okinawa Prefecture, all part of the Ryūkyū archipelago, which are the southern-most islands of Japan; they are located between the Pacific Ocean and the China Sea.

be? I look for the clock on the floor. *TRPP Q SCHAOUS TRPP Q SCHAOUS.* A little before eight.

Yet, just as in the dream, one of the TV People is on the television screen. The same guy I passed on the stairs to the office. No mistake. The one who first opened the door to the apartment. I'm 100% sure. He stands there—against a bright, fluorescent white background, the tail end of a dream infiltrating my conscious reality—staring at me. I shut, then reopen my eyes, hoping he'll have slipped back to never-never land. But he doesn't disappear. Far from it. He gets bigger. His face fills the whole screen, getting closer and closer.

The next thing I know, he's stepping through the screen. Hands gripping the frame, lifting himself up and over, one foot after the other, like climbing out of a window, leaving a white TV screen glowing behind him.

He rubs his left hand in the palm of his right, slowly acclimating himself to the world outside the television. On and on, reduced right-hand fingers rubbing reduced left-hand fingers, no hurry. He has that all-the-time-in-the-world nonchalance. Like a veteran TV-show host. Then he looks me in the face.

"We're making an airplane," says my TV People visitant. His voice has no perspective to it. A curious, paper-thin voice.

He speaks, and the screen is all machinery. Very professional fade-in. Just like on the news. First, there's an opening shot of a large factory interior, then it cuts to a close-up of the work space, camera center. Two TV People are hard at work on some machine, tightening bolts with wrenches, adjusting gauges. The picture of concentration. The machine, however, is unlike anything I've ever seen: an upright cylinder except that it narrows toward the top, with streamlined protrusions along its surface. Looks more like some kind of gigantic orange juicer than an airplane. No wings, no seats.

"Doesn't look like an airplane," I say. Doesn't sound like my voice, either. Strangely brittle, as if the nutrients had been strained out through a thick filter. Have I grown so old all of a sudden?

"That's probably because we haven't painted it yet," he says. "Tomorrow we'll have it the right color. Then you'll see it's an airplane."

"The color's not the problem. It's the shape. That's not an airplane."

"Well, if it's not an airplane, what is it?" he asks me. If he doesn't know, and I don't know, then what *is* it? "So, that's why it's got to be the color." The TV People rep puts it to me gently. "Paint it the right color, and it'll be an airplane."

I don't feel like arguing. What difference does it make? Orange juicer or airplane—flying orange juicer?—what do I care? Still, where's the wife while all this is happening? Why doesn't she come home? I massage my temples again. The clock ticks on. *TRPP Q SCHAOUS TRPP Q SCHAOUS.* The remote control lies on the table, and next to it the stack of women's magazines. The telephone is silent, the room illuminated by the dim glow of the television.

The two TV People on the screen keep working away. The image is much clearer than before. You can read the numbers on the dials, hear the faint rumble of machinery. *TAABZHRAYBGG TAABZHRAYBGG ARP*

ARRP TAABZHRAYBGG. This bass line is punctuated periodically by a sharp, metallic grating. *AREEEENBT AREEEENBT.* And various other noises are interspersed through the remaining aural space;[3] I can't hear anything clearly over them. Still, the two TV People labor on for all they're worth. That, apparently, is the subject of this program. I go on watching the two of them as they work on and on. Their colleague outside the TV set also looks on in silence. At them. At that *thing*—for the life of me, it does not look like an airplane—that insane machine all black and grimy, floating in a field of white light.

The TV People rep speaks up. "Shame about your wife."

I look him in the face. Maybe I didn't hear him right. Staring at him is like peering into the glowing tube itself.

"Shame about your wife," the TV People rep repeats in exactly the same absent tone.

"How's that?" I ask.

"How's that? It's gone too far," says the TV People rep in a voice like a plastic-card hotel key. Flat, uninflected, it slices into me as if it were sliding through a thin slit. "It's gone too far: She's out there."

"It's gone too far: She's out there," I repeat in my head. Very plain, and without reality. I can't grasp the context. Cause has effect by the tail and is about to swallow it whole. I get up and go to the kitchen. I open the refrigerator, take a deep breath, reach for a can of beer, and go back to the sofa. The TV People rep stands in place in front of the television, right elbow resting on the set, and watches me extract the pull-tab. I don't really want to drink beer at this moment; I just need to do something. I drink one sip, but the beer doesn't taste good. I hold the can in my hand dumbly until it becomes so heavy I have to set it down on the table.

Then I think about the TV People rep's revelation, about the wife's failure to materialize. He's saying she's gone. That she isn't coming home. I can't bring myself to believe it's over. Sure, we're not the perfect couple. In four years, we've had our spats; we have our little problems. But we always talk them out. There are things we've resolved and things we haven't. Most of what we couldn't resolve we let ride. Okay, so we have our ups and downs as a couple. I admit it. But is this cause for despair? C'mon, show me a couple who don't have problems. Besides, it's only a little past eight. There must be some reason she can't get to a phone. Any number of possible reasons. For instance . . . I can't think of a single one. I'm hopelessly confused.

I fall back deep into the sofa.

How on earth is that airplane—if it is an airplane—supposed to fly? What propels it? Where are the windows? Which is the front, which is the back?

I'm dead tired. Exhausted. I still have to write that letter, though, to beg off from my cousin's invitation. My work schedule does not afford me the pleasure of attending. Regrettable. Congratulations, all the same.

The two TV People in the television continue building their airplane, oblivious of me. They toil away; they don't stop for anything. They have

---

3. That is, the range of sound that can be heard by the human ear.

an infinite amount of work to get through before the machine is complete. No sooner have they finished one operation than they're busy with another. They have no assembly instructions, no plans, but they know precisely what to do and what comes next. The camera ably follows their deft motions. Clear-cut, easy-to-follow camera work. Highly credible, convincing images. No doubt other TV People (Nos. 4 and 5?) are manning the camera and control panel.

Strange as it may sound, the more I watch the flawless form of the TV People as they go about their work, the more the thing starts to look like an airplane. At least, it'd no longer surprise me if it actually flew. What does it matter which is front or back? With all the exacting detail work they're putting in, it *has* to be an airplane. Even if it doesn't appear so— to them, it's an airplane. Just as the little guy said, "If it's not an airplane, then what is it?"

The TV People rep hasn't so much as twitched in all this time. Right elbow still propped up on the TV set, he's watching me. I'm being watched. The TV People factory crew keeps working. Busy, busy, busy. The clock ticks on. *TRPP Q SCHAOUS TRPP Q SCHAOUS.* The room has grown dark, stifling. Someone's footsteps echo down the hall.

Well, it suddenly occurs to me, maybe so. Maybe the wife *is* out there. She's gone somewhere far away. By whatever means of transport, she's gone somewhere far out of my reach. Maybe our relationship has suffered irreversible damage. Maybe it's a total loss. Only I haven't noticed. All sorts of thoughts unravel inside me, then the frayed ends come together again. "Maybe so," I say out loud. My voice echoes, hollow.

"Tomorrow, when we paint it, you'll see better," he resumes. "All it needs is a touch of color to make it an airplane."

I look at the palms of my hands. They have shrunk slightly. Ever so slightly. Power of suggestion? Maybe the light's playing tricks on me. Maybe my sense of perspective has been thrown off. Yet, my palms really do look shriveled. Hey now, wait just a minute! Let me speak. There's something I should say. I must say. I'll dry up and turn to stone if I don't. Like the others.

"The phone will ring soon," the TV People rep says. Then, after a measured pause, he adds, "In another five minutes."

I look at the telephone; I think about the telephone cord. Endless lengths of phone cable linking one telephone to another. Maybe somewhere, at some terminal of that awesome megacircuit, is my wife. Far, far away, out of my reach. I can feel her pulse. Another five minutes, I tell myself. *Which way is front, which way is back?* I stand up and try to say something, but no sooner have I got to my feet than the words slip away.

A Note on Translation

Reading literature in translation is a pleasure on which it is fruitless to frown. The purist may insist that we ought always read in the original languages, and we know ideally that this is true. But it is a counsel of perfection, quite impractical even for the purist, since no one in a lifetime can master all the languages whose literatures it would be a joy to explore. Master languages as fast as we may, we shall always have to read to some extent in translation, and this means we must be alert to what we are about: if in reading a work of literature in translation we are not reading the "original," what precisely are we reading? This is a question of great complexity, to which justice cannot be done in a brief note, but the following sketch of some of the considerations may be helpful.

One of the memorable scenes of ancient literature is the meeting of Hector and Andromache in Book VI of Homer's *Iliad*. Hector, leader and mainstay of the armies defending Troy, is implored by his wife Andromache to withdraw within the city walls and carry on the defense from there, where his life will not be constantly at hazard. In Homer's text her opening words to him are these: δαιμόνιε, φθίσει σε τὸ σὸν μένος (daimonie, phthisei se to son menos). How should they be translated into English?

Here is how they have actually been translated into English by capable translators, at various periods, in verse and prose:

1. George Chapman, 1598:

> O noblest in desire,
> Thy mind, inflamed with others' good, will set thy self on fire.

2. John Dryden, 1693:

> Thy dauntless heart (which I foresee too late),
> Too daring man, will urge thee to thy fate.

3. Alexander Pope, 1715:

> Too daring Prince! . . .
> For sure such courage length of life denies,
> And thou must fall, thy virtue's sacrifice.

4. William Cowper, 1791:

> Thy own great courage will cut short thy days,
> My noble Hector. . .

5. Lang, Leaf, and Myers, 1883 (prose):

> Dear my lord, this thy hardihood will undo thee. . . .

6. A. T. Murray, 1924 (prose):

> Ah, my husband, this prowess of thine will be thy doom. . . .

7. E. V. Rieu, 1950 (prose):

> "Hector," she said, "you are possessed. This bravery of yours will be your end."

8. I. A. Richards, 1950 (prose):

> "Strange man," she said, "your courage will be your destruction."

9. Richmond Lattimore, 1951:

> Dearest,
> Your own great strength will be your death. . . .

10. Robert Fitzgerald, 1979:

> O my wild one, your bravery will be
> Your own undoing!

11. Robert Fagles, 1990:

> reckless one,
> Your own fiery courage will destroy you!

From these strikingly different renderings of the same six words, certain facts about the nature of translation begin to emerge. We notice, for one thing, that Homer's word μένος (menos) is diversified by the translators into "mind," "dauntless heart," "such courage," "great courage," "hardihood," "prowess," "bravery," "courage," "great strength," "bravery," and "fiery courage." The word has in fact all these possibilities. Used of things, it normally means "force"; of animals, "fierceness" or "brute strength" or (in the case of horses) "mettle"; of men and women, "passion" or "spirit" or even "purpose." Homer's application of it in the present case points our attention equally—whatever particular sense we may imagine Andromache to have uppermost—to Hector's force, strength, fierceness in battle, spirited heart and mind. But since English has no matching term of like inclusiveness, the passage as the translators give it to us reflects this lack and we find one attribute singled out to the exclusion of the rest.

Here then is the first and most crucial fact about any work of literature read in translation. It cannot escape the linguistic characteristics of the language into which it is turned: the grammatical, syntactical, lexical, and phonetic boundaries that constitute collectively the individuality or "genius" of that language. A Greek play or a Russian novel in English will be governed first of all by the resources of the English language, resources that are certain to be in every instance very different, as the efforts with μένος show, from those of the original.

Turning from μένος to δαιμόνιε (daimonie) in Homer's clause, we encounter a second crucial fact about translations. Nobody knows exactly what shade of meaning δαιμόνιε had for Homer. In later writers the word normally suggests divinity, something miraculous, wondrous; but in Homer it appears as a vocative of address for both chieftain and commoner, man and wife. The coloring one gives it must therefore be determined either by the way one thinks a Greek wife of Homer's era might actually address her husband (a subject on which we have no information whatever) or in the way one thinks it suitable for a hero's wife to address her husband in an epic poem, that is to say, a highly stylized and formal work. In general, the translators of our century will be seen to have abandoned formality to stress the intimacy; the wifeliness; and, especially in Lattimore's case, a certain chiding tenderness, in Andromache's appeal: (6) "Ah, my husband," (7) "Hector" (with perhaps a hint, in "you are possessed," of the alarmed distaste with which wives have so often viewed their husbands' bellicose moods), (8) "Strange man," (9) "Dearest," (10) "O my wild one" (mixing an almost motherly admiration with reproach and concern), and (11) "reckless one." On the other hand, the older translators have obviously removed Andromache to an epic or heroic distance from her beloved, whence she sees and kindles to his selfless courage, acknowledging, even in the moment of pleading with him to be otherwise, his moral grandeur and the tragic destiny this too certainly implies: (1) "O noblest in desire, . . . inflamed by others' good"; (2) "Thy dauntless heart (which I foresee too late), / Too daring man"; (3) "Too daring Prince! . . . / And thou must fall, thy virtue's sacrifice"; (4) "My noble Hector." Even the less specific "Dear my lord" of Lang, Leaf, and Myers looks in the same direction because of its echo of the speech of countless Shakespearean men and women who have shared this powerful moral sense: "Dear my lord, make me acquainted with your cause of grief"; "Perseverance, dear my lord, keeps honor bright"; etc.

The fact about translation that emerges from all this is that just as the translated work reflects the individuality of the language it is turned into, so it reflects the individuality of the age in which it is made, and the age will permeate it everywhere like yeast in dough. We think of one kind of permeation when we think of the governing verse forms and attitudes toward verse at a given epoch. In Chapman's time, experiments seeking an "heroic" verse form for English were widespread, and accordingly he tries a "fourteener" couplet (two rhymed lines of seven stresses each) in his *Iliad* and a pentameter couplet in his *Odyssey*. When Dryden and Pope wrote, a closed pentameter couplet had become established as the heroic form par excellence. By Cowper's day, thanks largely to the prestige of *Paradise Lost*, the couplet had gone out of fashion for narrative poetry in favor of blank verse. Our age, inclining to prose and in verse to proselike informalities and relaxations, has, predictably, produced half a dozen excellent prose translations of the *Iliad* but only three in verse (by Fagles, Lattimore, and Fitzgerald), all relying on rhythms that are much of the time closer to the verse of William Carlos Williams and some of the prose of novelists like Faulkner than to the swift firm tread of Homer's Greek. For if it is true that what we translate from a given work is what, wearing the spectacles of our time, we see in it, it is also true that we see in it what we have the power to translate.

Of course, there are other effects of the translator's epoch on a translation besides those exercised by contemporary taste in verse and verse forms. Chapman writes in a great age of poetic metaphor and, therefore, almost instinctively translates his understanding of Homer's verb φθίσει (phthisei, "to cause to wane, consume, waste, pine") into metaphorical terms of flame, presenting his Hector to us as a man of burning generosity who will be consumed by his very ardor. This is a conception rooted in large part in the psychology of the Elizabethans, who had the habit of speaking of the soul as "fire," of one of the four temperaments as "fiery," of even the more material bodily processes, like digestion, as if they were carried on by the heat of fire ("concoction," "decoction"). It is rooted too in that characteristic Renaissance élan so unforgettably expressed in characters such as Tamburlaine and Dr. Faustus, the former of whom exclaims to the stars above:

> . . . I, the chiefest lamp of all the earth,
> First rising in the East with mild aspect,
> But fixèd now in the meridian line,
> Will send up fire to your turning spheres,
> And cause the sun to borrow light of you. . . .

Pope and Dryden, by contrast, write to audiences for whom strong metaphor has become suspect. They therefore reject the fire image (which we must recall is not present in the Greek) in favor of a form of speech more congenial to their age, the *sententia* or aphorism, and give it extra vitality by making it the scene of a miniature drama: in Dryden's case, the hero's dauntless heart "urges" him (in the double sense of physical as well as moral pressure) to his fate; in Pope's, the hero's courage, like a judge, "denies" continuance of life, with the consequence that he "falls"—and here Pope's second line suggests analogy to the sacrificial animal— the victim of his own essential nature, of what he is.

To pose even more graphically the pressures that a translator's period brings, consider the following lines from Hector's reply to Andromache's appeal that he withdraw, first in Chapman's Elizabethan version, then in Lattimore's twentieth-century one:

Chapman, 1598:

> The spirit I did first breathe
> Did never teach me that—much less since the contempt of death
> Was settled in me, and my mind knew what a Worthy was,
> Whose office is to lead in fight and give no danger pass
> Without improvement. In this fire must Hector's trial shine.
> Here must his country, father, friends be in him made divine.

Lattimore, 1951:

> and the spirit will not let me, since I have learned to be valiant
> and to fight always among the foremost ranks of the Trojans,
> winning for my own self great glory, and for my father.

If one may exaggerate to make a necessary point, the world of Henry V and Othello suddenly gives way here to our own, a world whose discomfort with any form of heroic self-assertion is remarkably mirrored in the burial of Homer's key terms (*spirit, valiant, fight, foremost, glory*)—five out of twenty-two words in the original, five out of thirty-six in the translation—in a cushioning huddle of harmless sounds.

Besides the two factors so far mentioned (language and period) as affecting the character of a translation, there is inevitably a third—the translator, with a particular degree of talent; a personal way of regarding the work to be translated; a special hierarchy of values, moral, aesthetic, metaphysical (which may or may not be summed up in a "worldview"); and a unique style or lack of it. But this influence all readers are likely to bear in mind, and it needs no laboring here. That, for example, two translators of Hamlet, one a Freudian, the other a Jungian, will produce impressively different translations is obvious from the fact that when Freudian and Jungian argue about the play in English they often seem to have different plays in mind.

We can now return to the question from which we started. After all allowances have been made for language, age, and individual translator, is anything of the original left? What, in short, does the reader of translations read? Let it be said at once that in utility prose—prose whose function is mainly referential—the reader who reads a translation reads everything that matters. "Nicht Rauchen," "Défense de Fumer," and "No Smoking," posted in a railway car, make their point, and the differences between them in sound and form have no significance for us in that context. Since the prose of a treatise and of most fiction is preponderantly referential, we rightly feel, when we have paid close attention to Cervantes or Montaigne or Machiavelli or Tolstoy in a good English translation, that we have had roughly the same experience as a native Spaniard, Frenchman, Italian, or Russian. But *roughly* is the correct word; for good prose points iconically *to* itself as well as referentially beyond itself, and everything that it points to in itself in the original (rhythms, sounds, idioms, wordplay, etc.) must alter radically in being translated. The best analogy is to imagine a Van Gogh painting reproduced in the medium of tempera, etching, or engraving: the "picture" remains, but the intricate interanimation of volumes with colorings with brushstrokes has disappeared.

When we move on to poetry, even in its longer narrative and dramatic forms—plays like *Oedipus*, poems like the *Iliad* or the *Divine Comedy*—our situation as English readers worsens appreciably, as the many unlike versions of Andromache's appeal to Hector make very clear. But, again, only appreciably. True, this is the point at which the fact that a translation is *always* an interpretation explodes irresistibly on our attention; but if it is the best translation of its time, like John Ciardi's translation of the *Divine Comedy* for our time, the result will be not only a sensitive interpretation but also a work with intrinsic interest in its own right—at very best, a true work of art, a new poem. In these longer works, moreover, even if the translation is uninspired, many distinctive structural features—plot, setting, characters, meetings, partings, confrontations, and specific episodes generally—survive virtually unchanged. Hence even in translation it remains both possible and instructive to compare, say, concepts of the heroic or attitudes toward women or uses of religious ritual among civilizations as various as those reflected in the *Iliad*, the *Mahābhārata, Beowulf,* and the epic of *Son-Jara.* It is only when the shorter, primarily lyrical forms of poetry are presented that the reader of translations faces insuperable disadvantage. In these forms, the referential aspect of language has a tendency to disappear into, or, more often, draw its real meaning and accreditation from, the iconic aspect. Let us look for just a moment at a brief poem by Federico García Lorca and its English translation (by Stephen Spender and J. L. Gili):

> ¡Alto pinar!
> Cuatro palomas por el aire van.
>
> Cuatro palomas
> vuelan y tornan.
> Llevan heridas
> sus cuatro sombras.
>
> ¡Bajo pinar!
> Cuatro palomas en la tierra están.

> Above the pine trees:
> Four pigeons go through the air.
>
> Four pigeons
> fly and turn round.
> They carry wounded
> their four shadows.
>
> Below the pine trees:
> Four pigeons lie on the earth.

In this translation the referential sense of the English words follows with remarkable exactness the referential sense of the Spanish words they replace. But the life of Lorca's poem does not lie in that sense. It lies in such matters as the abruptness, like an intake of breath at a sudden revelation, of the two exclamatory lines (1 and 7), which then exhale musically in images of flight and death; or as the echoings of *palomas* in *heridas* and *sombras,* bringing together (as in fact the hunter's gun has done) these unrelated nouns and the unrelated experiences they stand for in a sequence that seems, momentarily, to have all the logic of a tragic action, in which *doves* become *wounds* become *shadows,* or as the external and internal rhyming among the five verbs, as though all motion must (as in fact it must) end with *están.*

Since none of this can be brought over into another tongue (least of all Lorca's rhythms), the translator must decide between leaving a reader to wonder why Lorca is a poet to be bothered about at all and making a new but true poem, whose merit will almost certainly be in inverse ratio to its likeness to the original. Samuel Johnson made such a poem in translating Horace's famous *Diffugere nives,* and so did A. E. Housman. If we juxtapose the last two stanzas of each translation, and the corresponding Latin, we can see at a glance that each has the consistency and inner life of a genuine poem and that neither of them (even if we consider only what is obvious to the eye, the line-lengths) is very close to Horace:

> Cum semel occideris, et de te splendida Minos
>   fecerit arbitria,
> non, Torquate, genus, non te facundia, non te
>   restituet pietas.

> Infernis neque enim tenebris Diana pudicum
>   liberat Hippolytum
> nec Lethaea valet Theseus abrumpere caro
>   vincula Pirithoo.

Johnson:

> Not you, Torquatus, boast of Rome,
> When Minos once has fixed your doom,
> Or eloquence, or splendid birth,
> Or virtue, shall restore to earth.
> Hippolytus, unjustly slain,
> Diana calls to life in vain;
> Nor can the might of Theseus rend
> The chains of hell that hold his friend.

Housman:

> When thou descendest once the shades among,
>   The stern assize and equal judgment o'er,
> Not thy long lineage nor thy golden tongue,
>   No, nor thy righteousness, shall friend thee more.

> Night holds Hippolytus the pure of stain,
>   Diana steads him nothing, he must stay;
> And Theseus leaves Pirithous in the chain
>   The love of comrades cannot take away.

The truth of the matter is that when the translator of short poems chooses to be literal, most or all of the poetry is lost; and when the translator succeeds in forging a new poetry, most or all of the original author is lost. Since there is no way out of this dilemma, we have always been sparing, in this anthology, in our use of short poems in translation.

In this Expanded Edition, we have adjusted our policy to take account of the two great non-Western literatures in which the short lyric or "song" has been the principal and by far most cherished expression of the national genius. During much of its history from earliest times, the Japanese imagination has cheerfully exercised itself, with all the delicacy and grace of an Olympic figure skater, inside a rigorous verse pattern of five lines and thirty-one syllables: the *tanka*. Chinese poetry, while somewhat more liberal to itself in line length, has been equally fertile in the fine art of compression and has only occasionally, even in its earliest, most experimental phase, indulged in verse lines of more than seven characters, often just four, or in poems of more than fifty lines, usually fewer than twenty. What makes the Chinese and Japanese lyric more difficult than most other lyrics to translate satisfactorily into English is that these compressions combine with a flexibility of syntax (Japanese) or a degree of freedom from it (Chinese) not available in our language. They also combine with a poetic sensibility that shrinks from exposition in favor of sequences and juxtapositions of images: images grasped and recorded in, or *as if in*, a moment of pure perception unencumbered by the explanatory linkages, background scenarios, and other forms of contextualization that the Western mind is instinctively driven to establish.

Whole books, almost whole libraries, have been written recently on the contrast of East and West in worldviews and value systems as well as on the need of each for the other if there is ever to be a community of understanding adequate to the realities both face. Put baldly, much too simply, and without the many exceptions and qualifications that rightly spring to mind, it may be said that a central and characteristic Western impulse, from the Greeks on down, has been to see the world around us as something to be *acted on:* weighed, measured, managed, used, even (when economic interests prevail over all others) fouled. Likewise, put oversimply, it may be said that a central and characteristic Eastern counterpart to this over many centuries (witness Taoism, Buddhism, and Hinduism, among others) has been to see that same world as something to be *received:* contemplated, touched, tasted, smelled, heard, and most especially, immersed in until observer and observed are one. To paint a bamboo, a stone, a butterfly, a person—so runs a classical Chinese admonition for painters—you must *become* that bamboo, that stone, that butterfly, that person, then paint from the inside. No one need be ashamed of being poor, says Confucius, putting a similar emphasis on *receiving* experience, "only of not being cultivated in the perception of beauty."

The problem that these differences in linguistic freedom and philosophical outlook pose for the English translator of classical Chinese and Japanese poetry may be glimpsed, even if not fully grasped, by considering for a moment in some detail a typical Japanese *tanka* (*Kokinshu,* 9) and a typical Chinese "song" (*Book of Songs,* 23). In its own language but transliterated in the Latin alphabet of the West, the *tanka* looks like this:

> kasumi tachi
> ko no me mo haru no
> yuki fureba
> hana naki sato mo
> hana zo chirikeru

In a literal word-by-word translation (so far as this is possible in Japanese, since the language uses many particles without English equivalents and without dictionary meaning in modifying and qualifying functions—for example, *no, mo,* and *no* in line 2), the poem looks like this:

> haze rises
> tree-buds swell
> when snow falls
> village(s) without flower(s)
> flower(s) fall(s)

The three best-known English renderings of this *tanka* look like this:

1. Helen Craig McCullough:

> When snow comes in spring—
> fair season of layered haze
> and burgeoning buds—
> flowers fall in villages
> where flowers have yet to bloom.

2. Laurel Rasplica Rodd and Mary Catherine Henkenius:

> When the warm mists veil
> all the buds swell while yet the

> spring snows drift downward
> even in the hibernal
> village crystal blossoms fall.

3. Robert H. Brower and Earl Miner:

> With the spreading mists
> The tree buds swell in early spring
> And wet snow petals fall—
> So even my flowerless country village
> Already lies beneath its fallen flowers.

The reader will notice at once how much the three translators have felt it desirable or necessary to add, alter, rearrange, and explain. In McCullough's version the time of year is affirmed twice, both as "spring" and as "fair season of . . . haze"; the haze is now "layered"; the five coordinate perceptions of the original (haze, swelling buds, a snowfall, villages without flowers, flowers drifting down) have been structured into a single sentence with one main verb and two subordinate clauses spelling out "when" and "where"; and the original poem's climax, in a scene of drifting petallike snowflakes, has been shifted to a bleak scenery of absence: "flowers have yet to bloom." The final stress, in other words, is not on the fulfilled moment in which snow flowers replace the cherry blossoms, but on the cherry blossoms not yet arrived.

Similar additions and explanations occur in Rodd and Henkenius's version. This time the mist is "warm" and "veil[s] all" to clarify its connection with "buds." Though implicit already in "warm" and "burgeoning," spring is invoked again in "spring snows," and the snows are given confirmation in the following line by the insistently Latinate "hibernal," chosen, we may reasonably guess, along with "veil," "all," "swell," "while," "crystal," and "fall" to replace some of the chiming internal rhyme in the Japanese: *ko, no, mo, no, sato, mo, zo.* To leave no *i* undotted, "crystal" is imported to assure us that the falling "blossoms" of line 5 are really snowflakes, and the scene of flowerlessness that in the original (line 4) accounts for a special joy in the "flowering" of the snowflakes (line 5) vanishes without trace.

Brower and Miner's also fills in the causative links between "spreading mists" and swelling buds; makes sure that we do not fail to see the falling snow in flower terms ("wet snow petals"), thus losing, alas, the element of surprise, even magic, in the transformation of snowflakes into flowers that the original poem holds in store in its last two lines; and tells us (somewhat redundantly) that villages are a "country" phenomenon and (somewhat surprisingly) that this one is the speaker's home. In this version, as in the original and Rodd and Henkenius's, the poem closes with the snow scene, but here it is a one-time affair and "already" complete (lines 4 and 5), not a recurrent phenomenon that may appear under certain conditions anywhere at any time.

Some of the differences in these translations arise inevitably from different trade-offs, as in the first version, where the final vision of falling snow blossoms is let go presumably to achieve the lovely lilting echo and rhetorical turn of "flowers fall in villages / where flowers have yet to bloom." Or as in Rodd and Henkenius's version, where preoccupations with internal rhyme have obviously influenced word choices, not always for the better. Or as in all three versions, where different efforts to remind the reader of the wordplay on *haru* (in the Japanese poem both a noun meaning "spring" and a verb meaning "swell") have had dissimilar but perhaps equally indifferent results. Meantime, the immense force compacted into that small word in the original as both noun and verb, season of springtime and principal of growth, cause and effect (and thus in a sense the whole mighty process of earth's renewal, in which an interruption by snow only foretells a greater loveliness to come) fizzles away unfelt. A few differences do seem to arise from insufficient command of the nerves and sinews of English poetry, but most spring from the staggering difficulties of responding in any uniform way to the minimal clues proffered by the original text. The five perceptions—haze, buds, snowfall, flowerless villages, flowers falling—do not as they stand in the Japanese or any literal translation quite compose for readers accustomed to Western poetic traditions an adequate poetic whole. This is plainly seen in the irresistible urge each of the translators has felt to catch up the individual perceptions, as English tends to require, in a tighter overall grammatical and syntactical structure than the original insists on. In this way they provide a clarifying network of principal and subordinate, time when, place where, and cause why. Yet the inevitable result is a disassembling, a spinning out, spelling out, thinning out of what in the Japanese is an as yet unraveled imagistic excitement, creating (or memorializing) in the poet's mind, and then in the mind of the Japanese readers, the original thrill of consciousness when these images, complete with the magical transformation of snow into the longed-for cherry blossoms, first flashed on the inward eye.

What is comforting for us who must read this and other Japanese poems in translation is that each of the versions given here retains in some form or other all or most of the five images intact. What is less comforting is that the simplicity and suddenness, the explosion in the mind, have been diffused and defused.

When we turn to the Chinese song, we find similarly contesting forces at work. In one respect, the Chinese language comes over into English more readily than Japanese, being like English comparatively uninflected and heavily dependent on word order for its meanings. But in other respects, since Chinese like Japanese lacks distinctions of gender, of singular and plural, of *a* and *the*, and in the classical mode in which the poems in this anthology are composed, also of tenses, the pressure of the English translator to rearrange, straighten out, and fill in to "make sense" for his or her readers remains strong.

Let us examine song no. 23 of the *Shijing*. In its own Chinese characters, it looks like this:

野有死麕，白茅包之。
有女懷春，吉士誘之。
林有樸樕，野有死鹿。
白茅純束，有女如玉。
舒而脫脫兮，無感我帨兮，
無使尨也吠。

Eleven lines in all, each line having four characters as its norm, the poem seemingly takes shape around an implicit parallel between a doe in the forest, possibly killed by stealth and hidden under long grass or rushes (though on this point as on all others the poem refuses to take us wholly into confidence), and a young girl possibly "ruined" (as she certainly would have been in the post-Confucian society in which the *Shijing* was prized and circulated, though here again the poem keeps its own counsel) by loss of her virginity before marriage.

In its bare bones, with each character given an approximate English equivalent, a translation might look like this:

wild(s)	is	dead	deer
white	grass(es)	wrap/cover	(it).
is	girl	feel	spring.
fine	man	tempt	(her).
woods	is(are)	bush(es),	underbrush.
wild(s)	is	dead	deer.
white	grass(es)	bind	bundle.
is	girl	like	jade.
slow	___	slow	slow.
not	move	my	sash.
not	cause	dog	bark.

(line 5 marked at "underbrush."; line 10 marked at "sash.")

Lines 1 to 4, it seems plain, propose the parallel of slain doe and girl, whatever that parallel may be intended to mean. Lines 5 to 8 restate the parallel, adding that the girl is as beautiful as jade and (apparently) that the doe lies where the "wild" gives way to smaller growth. If we allow ourselves to account for the repetition (here again is a Western mind-set in search of explanatory clues) by supposing that lines 1 to 4 signal at some subliminal level the initiation of the seduction and lines 5 to 8, again subliminally, its progress or possibly its completion, lines 9 to 11 fall easily into place as a miniature drama enacting in direct speech the man's advances and the girl's gradually crumbling resistance. They also imply, it seems, that the seduction takes place not in the forest, as we might have been led to suppose by lines 1 to 8, but in a dwelling with a vigilant guard dog.

Interpreted just far enough to accommodate English syntax, the poem reads as follows:

1. Wai-lim Yip:

> In the wilds, a dead doe.
> White reeds to wrap it.
> A girl, spring-touched.
> A fine man to seduce her.
> In the woods, bushes.   5
> In the wilds, a dead deer.
> White reeds in bundles.
> A girl like jade.
> Slowly. Take it easy.
> Don't feel my sash!   10
> Don't make the dog bark!

Interpreted a stage further in a format some have thought better suited to English poetic traditions, the poem reads:

2. Arthur Waley:

> In the wilds there is a dead doe,
> With white rushes we cover her.
> There was a lady longing for spring,
> A fair knight seduced her.
>
> In the woods there is a clump of oaks,   5
> And in the wilds a dead deer
> With white rushes well bound.
> There was a lady fair as jade.
>
> "Heigh, not so hasty, not so rough.
> "Heigh, do not touch my handkerchief.   10
> "Take care or the dog will bark."

Like the original and the literal translation, this version leaves the relationship between the doe's death and the girl's seduction unspecified and problematic. It holds the doe story in present tenses, assigning the girl story to the past. Still, much has been changed to give the English poem an explanatory scenario. The particular past assigned to the girl story, indeterminate in the Chinese original, is here fixed as the age of knights and ladies; and the seduction itself, which in the Chinese hovers as an eternal possibility within the timeless situation of man and maid ("A fine man *to* seduce her"), is established as completed long ago: "A fair knight seduced her." A teasing oddity in this version is the mysterious "we" who "cover" the slain doe, never to be heard from again.

Take interpretation toward its outer limits and we reach what is perhaps best called a "variation" on this theme:

3. Ezra Pound:

Lies a dead doe on yonder plain
whom white grass covers,
A melancholy maid in spring
is luck
for
lovers.
Where the scrub elm skirts the wood
be it not in white mat bound,
As a jewel flawless found
dead as a doe is maidenhood.
Hark!
Unhand my girdle knot.
Stay, stay, stay
or the dog
may
bark.

Here too the present is pushed back to a past by the language the translator uses: not a specific past, as with the era of knights and ladies, but any past in which contemporary speech still features such (to us) archaic formalisms as "Unhand" or "Hark," and in which the term "maid" still signifies a virgin and in which virginity is prized to an extent that equates its loss with the doe's loss of life. But these evocations of time past are so effectively countered by the obtrusively present tense throughout (lines 1, 2, 4, 7, 8, 10, 11, 12, 13, and 15) that the freewheeling "variation" remains in this important respect closer to the spirit of the original than Waley's translation. On the other hand, it departs from the original and the two other versions by brushing aside the reticence that they carefully preserve as to the precise implications of the girl-deer parallel, choosing instead to place the seduction in the explanatory framework of the oldest story in the world: the way of a man with a maid in the springtime of life.

What both these examples make plain is that the Chinese and Japanese lyric, however contrasting in some ways, have in common at their center a complex of highly charged images generating something very like a magnetic field of potential meanings that cannot be got at in English without bleeding away much of the voltage. In view of this, the best practical advice for those of us who must read these marvelous poems in English translations is to focus intently on these images and ask ourselves what there is in them or in their effect on each other that produces the electricity. To that extent, we can compensate for a part of our losses, learn something positive about the immense explosive powers of imagery, and rest easy in the secure knowledge that translation even in the mode of the short poem brings us (despite losses) closer to the work itself than not reading it at all. "To a thousand cavils," said Samuel Johnson, "one answer is sufficient; the purpose of a writer is to be read, and the criticism which would destroy the power of pleasing must be blown aside." Johnson was defending Pope's Homer for those marks of its own time and place that make it the great interpretation it is, but Johnson's exhilarating common sense applies equally to the problem we are considering here. Literature is to be read, and the criticism that would destroy the reader's power to make some form of contact with much of the world's great writing must indeed be blown aside.

Maynard Mack

Sources

Brower, Robert H., and Earl Miner. *Japanese Court Poetry*. Stanford: Stanford University Press, 1961.

The Classic Anthology Defined by Confucius. Tr. Ezra Pound. New Directions, 1954.

Kokinshū: A Collection of Poems Ancient and Modern. Tr. Laurel Rasplica Rodd and Mary Catherine Henkenius. Princeton: Princeton University Press, 1984.

Kokin Wakashū: The First Imperial Anthology of Japanese Poetry. Tr. and ed. Helen Craig McCullough. Stanford: Stanford University Press, 1985.

Legge, James. *The Chinese Classics*. Hong Kong: Hong Kong University Press, 1960.

Waley, Arthur. *170 Chinese Poems*. New York, 1919.

Shall Not Be Put Out, The Pictures of My New Day, Heartease II, Heartease New England 1987, and *Mother the Great Stones Got to Move* from HEARTEASE. Copyright © 1988 by New Beacon Books Ltd. Reprinted by permission of New Beacon Books, Ltd. *To Us All Flowers Are Roses* from LORNA GOODISON: SELECTED POEMS. Copyright © Lorna Goodison. Reprinted by permission of the author.

Nadine Gordimer: *Oral History* from A SOLDIER'S EMBRACE. Copyright © 1975, 1977, 1980 by Nadine Gordimer. Reprinted by permission of Viking Penguin, a division of Penguin Books, USA.

Tawfik al-Hakim: *The Sultan's Dilemma* from FATE OF A COCKROACH, translated by Denys Johnson-Davies. Published by Three Continents Press, Colorado Springs, Colorado. Reprinted by permission of Three Continents Press and Denys Johnson-Davies.

Heinrich Heine: *Babylonian Sorrows, The Rose, The Lily, the Sun, and the Dove,* and *The Silesian Weavers* from THE POETRY OF HEINRICH HEINE, edited by Frederick Ewen, translated by P. L. G. Webb and Aaron Kramer. Copyright © 1969 by the Citadel Press. Reprinted by permission of Caroll Publishing Group. *At Parting* from AN ANTHOLOGY OF GERMAN POETRY FROM HOLDERLIN TO RILKE: ENGLISH TRANSLATIONS WITH GERMAN ORIGINALS, translated by Dwight Durling, edited by Angel Flores. Reprinted by permission of Estate of Angel Flores. *A Spruce Is Standing Lonely* from SELECTED WORKS by Heinrich Heine, translated by Max Knight and Joseph Fabry. Copyright © 1973 by Random House, Inc. Reprinted by permission of Random House, Inc. *My Beauty, My Love, You Have Bound Me,* translated by Meno Spano. Reprinted by permission of Random Century Group and Bodley Head as publisher. *A Young Man Loves a Maiden, Loreley, The Asra, How Slowly Time the Loathsome Snail, The Migratory Rats,* and *Morphine* from HEINRICH HEINE: LYRIC POEMS AND BALLADS, translated by Ernst Feise. Copyright © 1961, 1989 by University of Pittsburgh Press. Reprinted by permission of University of Pittsburgh Press from HEINRICH HEINE: LYRIC POEMS AND BALLADS, Ernst Feise translator.

Victor Hugo: *Reverie, Tomorrow at Daybreak, Memory of the Night of the Fourth, Et Nox Facta Est, Sowing Season Evening,* translated by Mary Ann Caws. Copyright © 1990 by Mary Ann Caws. Reprinted by permission of the translator.

Henrik Ibsen: *Hedda Gabler* from HEDDA GABLER AND THREE OTHER PLAYS, translated by Michael Meyer. Copyright © 1962 and 1974 by Michael Meyer. Copyright © renewed 1989 by Michael Meyer. Reprinted by permission of Harold Ober Associates.

Higuichi Ichiyō: *Child's Play* from IN THE SHADE OF SPRING LEAVES, translated by Robert Lyons Danly. Copyright © Robert Lyons Danly. Reprinted by permission of the translator.

James Joyce: *Part I* from A PORTRAIT OF THE ARTIST AS A YOUNG MAN. Copyright © 1916 by B. W. Huebsch. Copyright © 1964 by Nora Joyce. Copyright © 1964 by the Estate of James Joyce. Reprinted by permission of Viking Penguin, a division of Penguin Books USA, Inc.

Franz Kafka: THE METAMORPHOSIS, translated by Stanley Corngold. Translation copyright © 1972 by Stanley Corngold. Reprinted by permission of the translator.

Kawabata Yasunari: SNOW COUNTRY, translated by Edward G. Seidensticker. Copyright © 1956 by Alfred A. Knopf, Inc. Reprinted by permission of G. P. Putnam's Sons.

Kojima Nobuo: *The American School* from CONTEMPORARY JAPANESE LITERATURE, translated by William F. Sibley, edited by Howard Hibbett. Copyright © 1977 by Alfred A. Knopf, Inc. Reprinted by permission of Alfred A Knopf, Inc.

K'ung Shang-jen: THE PEACH BLOSSOM FAN, translated by Chen Shih-hsiang and Harold Acton with the collaboration of Cyril Birch. Copyright © 1976 by The Regents of the University of California. Reprinted by permission of the University of California.

D. H. Lawrence: *Odor of Chrysanthemums* from THE COMPLETE STORIES OF D. H. LAWRENCE. Copyright © 1933 by the Estate of D. H. Lawrence. Copyright renewed © 1961 by Angelo Ravagli and C. M. Weekley. Reprinted by permission of Viking Penguin, a division of Penguin Books USA, Inc.

Giacomo Leopardi: *The Broom* from LEOPARDI: POEMS AND PROSE, edited by Angel Flores, translated by Edwin Morgan. Copyright © by the Estate of Angel Flores. Reprinted by permission of the editor.

Lu Xun: *Diary of A Madman* and *Upstairs in a Wine Shop* from DIARY OF A MADMAN AND OTHER STORIES, translated by William A. Lyell. Copyright © by University of Hawaii Press. Reprinted by permission of University of Hawaii Press.

Naguib Mahfouz: *Zaabalawi* from MODERN ARABIC SHORT STORIES, translated by Denys Johnson-Davies. Translation copyright © 1967 by Denys Johnson-Davies. Reprinted by permission of the translator.

Thomas Mann: DEATH IN VENICE, translated by Dr. David Luke. Copyright © 1988 by Dr. David Luke. Reprinted by permission of Bantam Books, a division of Bantam Doubleday Dell, Inc., and Martin Secker and Warburg.

Herman Melville: BILLY BUDD, SAILOR. Copyright © 1962 by the University of Chicago Press. Reprinted by permission of the University of Chicago Press.

Jean-Baptiste Moliere: TARTUFFE, translated by Richard Wilbur. Copyright © 1963 by Richard Wilbur. Copyright renewed © 1991. Reprinted by permission of Harcourt Brace & Company. CAUTION: Professionals and amateurs are hereby warned that this translation being fully protected under the copyright laws of the United States of America, the British Commonwealth, including Canada, and all other countries which are subject to royalty. All rights, including professio

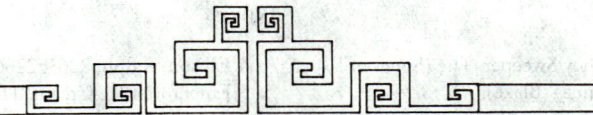

Index